COLLINS

BRITAIN ATLAS AND GAZETTEER

CONTENTS

HarperCollinsPublishers

Key to Road Maps

108 - 109 Lerwick

106 - 107 Kirkwall

100 - 101 Stornoway

102 - 103 Lochinver

104 - 105 Thurso

Atlantic Ocean

92 - 93 Portree

94 - 95 Ullapool

96 - 97 Inverness

98 - 99 Peterhead

84 - 85

86 - 87 Fort William

88 - 89 Braemar

90 - 91 Aberdeen

North Sea

SCOTLAND

78 - 79 Oban

80 - 81 Inveraray

82 - 83 Perth / Dundee

72 - 73 Greenock

74 - 75 Glasgow

Edinburgh 76 - 77

66 - 67 Ayr

68 - 69 Dumfries

70 - 71 Newcastle upon Tyne

64 - 65 Stranraer

NORTHERN IRELAND

60 - 61 Carlisle

62 - 63 Middlesbrough

REPUBLIC OF IRELAND

Isle of Man

54 - 55 Blackpool

56 - 57 Leeds

58 - 59 York

Irish Sea

46 - 47 Caernarfon / Liverpool

48 - 49 Manchester

50 - 51

52 - 53 Lincoln

ENGLAND

36 - 37 Aberystwyth

38 - 39 Stoke-on-Trent / Birmingham

40 - 41 Derby / Leicester

42 - 43 Peterborough

44 - 45 Norwich

26 - 27 Llandrindod Wells

28 - 29 Worcester

30 - 31 Cheltenham

32 - 33 Cambridge / Luton

34 - 35 Ipswich

WALES

16 - 17 Swansea

Cardiff 18 - 19 / Bristol

20 - 21 Oxford / Reading

London 22 - 23

24 - 25 Maidstone

6 - 7 Taunton / Exeter

8 - 9 Weymouth

10 - 11 Southampton

12 - 13 Brighton

14 - 15 Folkestone

2 - 3 Penzance

4 - 5 Plymouth

Isles of Scilly

English Channel

FRANCE

i

ROAD INFORMATION

M4	Motorway
30 — 29	Motorway junction with full / limited access
Maidstone • Sarn / Birch	Motorway service areas (off road, full & limited access)
	Projected or under construction motorway
A48	Primary route number
	Primary route dual carriageway
	Primary route single carriageway
	Primary route with passing places
A30	'A' Road number
	'A' Road dual carriageway
	'A' Road single carriageway
	'A' Road with passing places
	Projected or under construction 'A' Road
B1403	'B' Road number
	'B' Road dual carriageway
	'B' Road single carriageway
	'B' Road with passing places
	Projected or under construction 'B' Road
	Minor road
	Restricted access due to road condition or private ownership
⊗	Multi-level junction
	Roundabout
10	Road distances in miles
	Road tunnel
→	Steep hill (arrows point downhill)
××	Level crossing
Toll	Toll

OTHER TRANSPORT INFORMATION

Poole 2¹/₃ hrs (3 hrs)	Car ferry route with journey times; daytime and (night-time)
○	Railway line and station
←	Railway tunnel
✈	Airport with scheduled services
Ⓗ	Heliport

CITIES, TOWNS & VILLAGES

	Built up area
□ □ ▫	Towns, villages and other settlements
CROYDON	Primary route destination

TOURIST INFORMATION

A selection of tourist detail is shown. It is advisable to check with the local tourist information office regarding opening times and facilities available. The classification of tourist features specific to the Gazetteer is given, where appropriate, in italics.

ℹ ℹ	Tourist information office (all year / seasonal)
🚂 ⊢•─•─⊣	Preserved railway (other feature of interest)
⚔ 1738	Battle site
�	Ancient monument (historic / prehistoric site)
✝	Ecclesiastical building
🏰	Castle
🏛	Historic house (with or without garden)
✳	Garden
🏛	Museum / Art gallery (leisure / recreation)
⛩	Theme park (leisure / recreation)
⚲	Major sports venue (leisure / recreation)
🏁	Motor racing circuit
🏇	Racecourse
🌳	Country park (leisure / recreation)
🦅	Nature reserve
🐘	Wildlife park or Zoo (leisure / recreation)
★	Other feature of interest
★ 🐘	Proposed millennium site; (relevant symbol shown)
⚑	Golf course
(NT) (NTS) (MNT)	National Trust property; Great Britain, Scotland & Isle of Man

OTHER FEATURES

	National boundary
	County / Unitary Authority boundary
	National / Regional park boundary
	Forest park boundary
Danger Zone	Military range
	Woodland
468 ▲941	Spot height / Summit height in metres
	Beach
	Lake, dam and river
	Canal / Dry canal / Canal tunnel
▲92	Adjoining page indicator

water	land below	0	165	490	985	1640	2295	2950	ft
	sea level	0	50	150	300	500	700	900	m

Scale 1 : 259,403 (4.15 miles to 1 inch)

0	4	8	12 miles
0	5	10	15	20 km

Introduction

This is a brand new version of the original Bartholomew Gazetteer of Places in Britain last published in 1986, now called The Collins Britain Atlas and Gazetteer, it has been expanded to include over 55,000 separate, fully updated entries and has been completely redesigned to take it into the 21st Century.

Each entry has a brief description of what type of feature it is, a reference for its location, a population figure where appropriate and many other interesting facts. The entries have been written in a structured and concise style. The name of the feature comes first and is in purple type, then the administrative area in *italics*, followed by the population figure if applicable. The entries have been categorized into broad feature types, such as village, hamlet, mountain etc, these are shown in ***bold italics***. A full list and explanation of all the different feature types can be found on page 120. Following this is a description of the place, then the height if applicable, the map reference and the National Grid Reference. For example:

Ben Cleuch *Clack.* ***Mountain***, summit of Ochil Hills, 3m/4km NW of Tillicoultry. Height 2362 feet or 720 metres. **81 K7** NN9000.

The Collins Britain Atlas and Gazetteer also includes a full-colour map section based on the best-selling Collins Road Atlas Britain. Most of the gazetteer entries are clearly referenced in **bold** to the appropriate grid square on the map. For entries depicted by a point symbol, such as man-made settlements, named summits and tourist detail, the reference indicates the grid square in which the symbol falls. Entries which relate to either a linear or area feature, such as rivers, sea features and mountain ranges, are referenced to the grid square in which the name begins. Where no such grid reference is given, then that feature, although it exists, is not shown on the map.

For example:

Tadpole Bridge *Oxon.* ***Settlement***, on River Thames, 2m/3km SE of Bampton. SP3300.

The above entry is not named on the map.

Tadworth *Surr.* Population: 18,622. ***Locality***, residential locality 3m/4km SW of Banstead. **23 F6** TQ2356.

This entry is named on the road maps on page 23 in square F6.

The Gazetteer is listed alphabetically on a word by word basis whereby Fair Oak will come before Fairbourne. Places such as Upper Norwood and East Grinstead have been listed under U and E, and places such as The Needles and Isle of Lewis have been listed under T and I respectively. All place names incorporating the word 'Saint' have been abbreviated to 'St.' but are listed as if they were given in full.

All distances are measured 'as the crow flies' and are shown in both miles and kilometres. Cardinal directions are abbreviated and include the eight compass points: N, NE, E, SE, S, SW, W and NW. In most cases heights are shown in feet as well as metres.

Human settlements are described as cities, towns, suburbs, villages, hamlets, settlements, or localities. The criteria dividing these are not definitive, with one category tending to merge into another, but a description has been included in the feature type listing, on page 120 which is as accurate as possible.

All places are given with the administrative area in which they fall. Exceptions to this are large or linear features such as mountain ranges or rivers which fall on, or cross boundaries. The administrative areas are shown in the maps on pages (v) to (x) and include all the latest changes. In the main gazetteer listing, these have been abbreviated and are shown in *italics*. Full names and descriptions can be found in the administrative area lists which start on page 121.

To facilitate the use of the gazetteer in the London area, maps at a scale of 1 mile to 1 inch have been included, and can be found on pages 111 to 119.

The National Grid System

All main entries have a national grid reference: the reference given for rivers is that of its mouth or confluence with a river of a different name; mountains are referenced to their summits; and large features generally to a notional centre point.

The National Grid System was devised by the Ordnance Survey and consists of a series of letters and numbers, each representing progressively smaller squares. The first letter H, N, S or T represent 500km squares. These are then broken down into twenty-five 100km squares designated by the second letter in the reference. Within the 100km squares each smaller grid of 10km, 1km or 100m is numbered, firstly by the distance of its lower left-hand corner eastwards (eastings) and secondly northwards (northings). In the gazetteer the references are taken down to the 1km level with a four-figure reference, for example TQ2356.

Alternative Names and Cross References

Where possible, the most commonly used name has been used as the main entry. Where there are alternative names these have been added in brackets after the main entry name. A separate entry is also included for the alternative name which cross-references the main entry, and is shown in *italics*, for example:

Caernarfon (Caernarvon). *Gwyn.* Population: 9695. ***Small town***, port near SW end of Menai Strait at mouth of River Seiont, 8m/13km SW of Bangor. Medieval castle built by Edward I and remains of town walls (Cadw). Site of Roman fort of Segontium (Cadw) in SE part of town. **46 C6** SH4762.

The above is the main entry.

Caernarvon *Gwyn. English form of Caernarfon, qv.*

This is the cross reference entry.

Some entries may also refer specifically to another, related, main entry at the end of their descriptive text, for example:

Dartford Tunnel ***Other feature of interest***, conveys road traffic under River Thames northbound from Dartford on S bank to Purfleet on N bank. See also Queen Elizabeth II Bridge. **23 J4** TQ5676.

Population figures

Population figures for large towns in England and Wales have been derived from '1991 Census: Urban Centres in England and Wales' produced by the Office of Population Censuses and Surveys. An 'urban area' is essentially defined as a continuous area of urban land extending for 20 hectares or more, which includes most built-up areas of over 1000 population.

For Scotland, figures have been derived from '1991 Census: Key Statistics for Localities in Scotland', HMSO, 1995. Localities are generally defined as continuous built-up areas with a population of over 500.

Throughout this book, great care has been taken to be accurate, but if you have any suggestions or comments that you feel might help us to improve it still further, please contact us at:

Collins Gazetteer Check
HarperCollinsPublishers
4 Manchester Park
Tewkesbury Road
Cheltenham
GL51 9EJ

email: gazcheck@harpercollins.co.uk

Squares U, X, W do not exist.

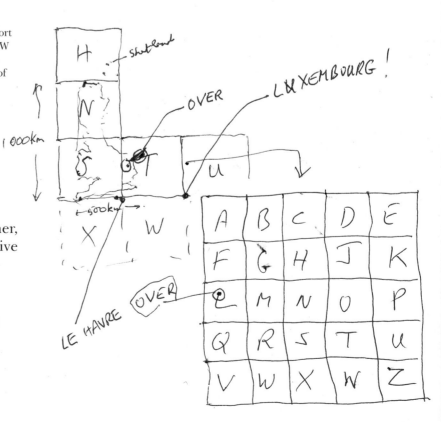

WALES Counties

BLAENAU GWENT
BRIDGEND
CAERPHILLY
CARDIFF
CARMARTHENSHIRE
CEREDIGION
CONWY
DENBIGHSHIRE
FLINTSHIRE
GWYNEDD
ISLE OF ANGLESEY
MERTHYR TYDFIL
MONMOUTHSHIRE
NEATH PORT TALBOT
NEWPORT
PEMBROKESHIRE
POWYS
RHONDDA CYNON TAFF
SWANSEA
TORFAEN
VALE OF GLAMORGAN
WREXHAM

**ENGLAND
Counties & Districts**

**BATH AND NORTH
EAST SOMERSET**

BEDFORDSHIRE
1 North Bedfordshire
2 Mid Bedfordshire
3 South Bedfordshire

BOURNEMOUTH

BRACKNELL FOREST

BRIGHTON & HOVE

BRISTOL

BUCKINGHAMSHIRE
1 Aylesbury Vale
2 Wycombe
3 Chiltern
4 South Buckinghamshire

CAMBRIDGESHIRE
1 Fenland
2 Huntingdonshire
3 East Cambridgeshire
4 South Cambridgeshire
5 Cambridge

CORNWALL
1 North Cornwall
2 Caradon
3 Restormel
4 Carrick
5 Kerrier
6 Penwith

DEVON
1 North Devon
2 Torridge
3 Mid Devon
4 East Devon

5 Exeter
6 Teignbridge
7 West Devon
8 South Hams

DORSET
1 North Dorset
2 East Dorset
3 Christchurch
4 Purbeck
5 West Dorset
6 Weymouth & Portland

EAST SUSSEX
1 Lewes
2 Wealden
3 Eastbourne
4 Rother
5 Hastings

Scale 1:1,250,000

0   10   20   30   40 kilometres
0   10   20   30 miles

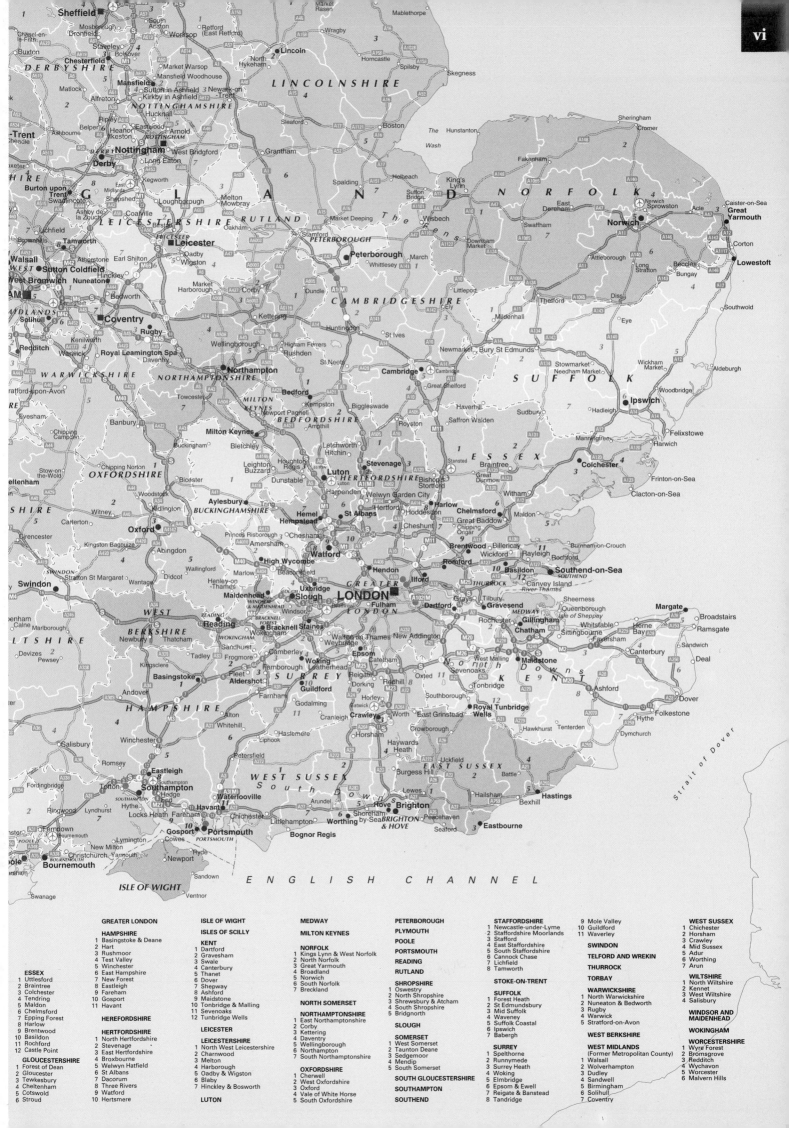

AND
BUTE

FIFE
Gleneagles
Crail
Glenrothes
Pittenweem
Anstruther
Callander
Dunblane
Bridge of Allan
CLACKMANNAN-SHIRE
Dollar
Buckhaven
Elie
Colonsay
Scalasaig
Firth
Lochgoilhead
Aberfoyle
Stirling
Alloa
Tillicoultry
Clackmannan
North Berwick
Kincardine
Cowdenbeath
Lochgelly
Kirkcaldy
Burntisland
Dunfermline
Garelochhead
Denny
M80
Falkirk
Bo'ness
Grangemouth
FALKIRK
Linlithgow
EDINBURGH
Gullane
Haddington
EAST LOTHIAN
Jura
Lochgilphead
Loch Fyne
Helensburgh
WEST DUNBARTON-SHIRE
Kilsyth
Cumbernauld
Broxburn
WEST LOTHIAN
Bathgate
Livingston
Edinburgh
Musselburgh
Dalkeith
Bonnyrigg
Port Askaig
Alexandria
Greenock
Dumbarton
Milngavie
EAST DUNBARTON-SHIRE
Kirkintilloch
NORTH LANARKSHIRE
Whitburn
MIDLOTHIAN
Dunoon
Port Glasgow
Wemyss Bay
INVERCLYDE
Bearsden
GLASGOW
Airdrie
Whitburn
Penicuik
Islay
Clydebank
GLASGOW
Coatbridge
Bowmore
Largs
RENFREW-SHIRE
Johnstone
Paisley
Barrhead
Hamilton
Motherwell
Wishaw
Lauder
Stow
Tarbert
Newton Mearns
EAST RENFREW-SHIRE
East Kilbride
Carluke
Carnwath
Peebles
SCOTTI
Portnahaven
Beith
Dunlop
SOUTH LANARKSHIRE
Lanark
Biggar
Galashiels
Earlston
Port Ellen
Dalry
Kilwinning
Stewarton
Strathaven
Innerleithen
Melrose
NORTH AYRSHIRE
Ardrossan
Saltcoats
Stevenston
Kilmarnock
Galston
Douglas
BORDER
Carradale
Brodick
Irvine
Abington
Hawick
Arran
Troon
Prestwick
EAST AYRSHIRE
Mauchline
Muirkirk
Selkirk
Newto St Bosw
Campbeltown
Prestwick
Ayr
Cumnock
Sanquhar
Moffat
SOUTHERN UPLANDS
New Cumnock
Maybole
Dalmellington
SOUTH AYRSHIRE
Ailsa Craig
Girvan
Moniaive
Thornhill
DUMFRIES & GALLOWAY
Langholm
Ballantrae
New Galloway
Lochmaben
Lockerbie
Cairnryan
Dumfries
Newton Stewart
Annan
Gretna
Stranraer
Glenluce
Wigtown
Kirkcudbright
Solway Firth
Carlisle
Portpatrick
Sandhead
Port William
Whithorn
Wigton
Aspatria
A595
M6
Drummore
Maryport
CUMBRIA
Penrith
Cockermouth
Workington
Keswick
Patterdale
Shap
Whitehaven
Egremont
Grasmere
Ambleside
Coniston
Windermere
Kendal
ISLE OF MAN
Andreas
Broughton in Furness
Ramsey
Milnthorpe
Kirk Michael
Ulverston
Peel
Laxey
Foxdale
Onchan
Douglas
Barrow-in-Furness
Morecambe
Morecambe Bay
Lancaster
Dalby
Port Erin
Isle of Man
Castletown
Port St Mary
Fleetwood
LANCA
Cleveleys
Thornton
Poulton-le-Fylde
BLACKPOOL
Blackpool
Preston
IRISH
Lytham St Anne's
Leyland
SEA
Southport
Chorley
Formby
Ormskirk
Skelmersdale
MERSEYSIDE
Crosby
Kirkby
Bootle
St Helens
Amlwch
Wallasey
Birkenhead
LIVERPOOL
ISLE OF ANGLESEY
Bebington
Widnes
Llandudno
Prestatyn
West Kirby
Heswall
Holyhead
Anglesey
Holy Island
Colwyn Bay
Abergele
Rhyl
Holywell
Ellesmere Port
Llangefni
St Asaph (Llanelwy)
Flint
Connah's Quay
FLINTSHIRE
Hawarden
Buckley
Bretton
Chester
Menai Bridge
Bangor
Denbigh
Mold
Caernarfon
CONWY
Ruthin
CHE
Caernarfon Bay
DENBIGHSHIRE
Rhosllanerchrugog
Wrexham
WREXHAM
Nefyn
Trefriw
Tremadog
Criccieth
Corwen
Ellesmere
Pwllheli
Dolgellau
Oswestry
Aberdaron
Abersoch
GWYNEDD

Firth of Jura
Sound of Jura
Kilbrannan Sound
Firth of Clyde
Firth of Forth
Morecambe Bay

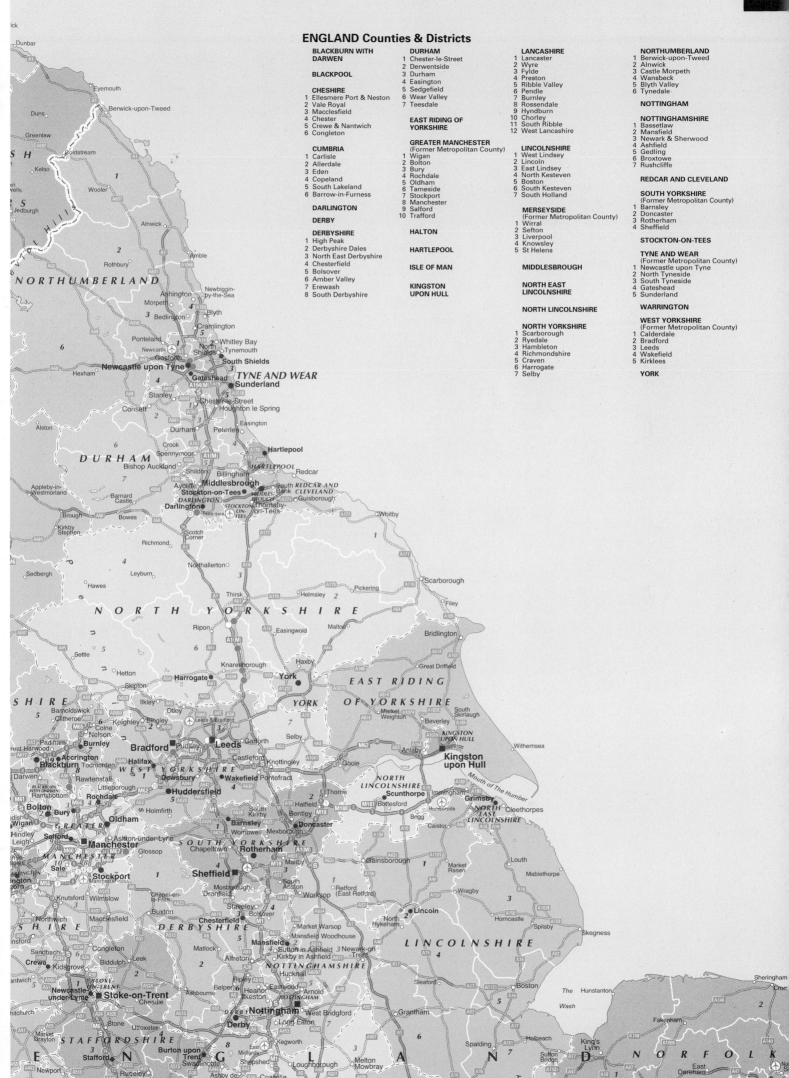

ENGLAND Counties & Districts

BLACKBURN WITH DARWEN

BLACKPOOL

CHESHIRE
1 Ellesmere Port & Neston
2 Vale Royal
3 Macclesfield
4 Chester
5 Crewe & Nantwich
6 Congleton

CUMBRIA
1 Carlisle
2 Allerdale
3 Eden
4 Copeland
5 South Lakeland
6 Barrow-in-Furness

DARLINGTON

DERBY

DERBYSHIRE
1 High Peak
2 Derbyshire Dales
3 North East Derbyshire
4 Chesterfield
5 Bolsover
6 Amber Valley
7 Erewash
8 South Derbyshire

DURHAM
1 Chester-le-Street
2 Derwentside
3 Durham
4 Easington
5 Sedgefield
6 Wear Valley
7 Teesdale

EAST RIDING OF YORKSHIRE

GREATER MANCHESTER
(Former Metropolitan County)
1 Wigan
2 Bolton
3 Bury
4 Rochdale
5 Oldham
6 Tameside
7 Stockport
8 Manchester
9 Salford
10 Trafford

HALTON

HARTLEPOOL

ISLE OF MAN

KINGSTON UPON HULL

LANCASHIRE
1 Lancaster
2 Wyre
3 Fylde
4 Preston
5 Ribble Valley
6 Pendle
7 Burnley
8 Rossendale
9 Hyndburn
10 Chorley
11 South Ribble
12 West Lancashire

LINCOLNSHIRE
1 West Lindsey
2 Lincoln
3 East Lindsey
4 North Kesteven
5 Boston
6 South Kesteven
7 South Holland

MERSEYSIDE
(Former Metropolitan County)
1 Wirral
2 Sefton
3 Liverpool
4 Knowsley
5 St Helens

MIDDLESBROUGH

NORTH EAST LINCOLNSHIRE

NORTH LINCOLNSHIRE

NORTH YORKSHIRE
1 Scarborough
2 Ryedale
3 Hambleton
4 Richmondshire
5 Craven
6 Harrogate
7 Selby

NORTHUMBERLAND
1 Berwick-upon-Tweed
2 Alnwick
3 Castle Morpeth
4 Wansbeck
5 Blyth Valley
6 Tynedale

NOTTINGHAM

NOTTINGHAMSHIRE
1 Bassetlaw
2 Mansfield
3 Newark & Sherwood
4 Ashfield
5 Gedling
6 Broxtowe
7 Rushcliffe

REDCAR AND CLEVELAND

SOUTH YORKSHIRE
(Former Metropolitan County)
1 Barnsley
2 Doncaster
3 Rotherham
4 Sheffield

STOCKTON-ON-TEES

TYNE AND WEAR
(Former Metropolitan County)
1 Newcastle upon Tyne
2 North Tyneside
3 South Tyneside
4 Gateshead
5 Sunderland

WARRINGTON

WEST YORKSHIRE
(Former Metropolitan County)
1 Calderdale
2 Bradford
3 Leeds
4 Wakefield
5 Kirklees

YORK

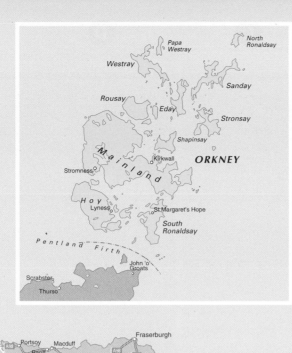

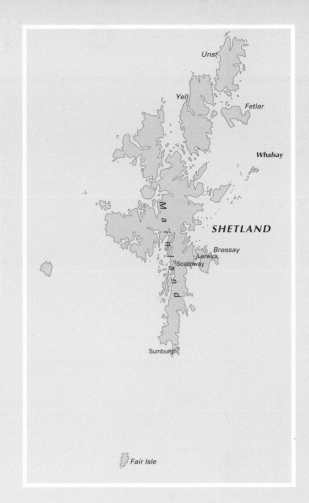

ORKNEY

North Ronaldsay
Papa Westray
Westray
Sanday
Rousay
Eday
Stronsay
Shapinsay
Kirkwall
Mainland
Stromness
Hoy
Lyness
St Margaret's Hope
South Ronaldsay
Pentland Firth
Scrabster
Thurso
John o' Groats

SHETLAND

Unst
Yell
Fetlar
Whalsay
Mainland
Bressay
Lerwick
Scalloway
Sumburgh
Fair Isle

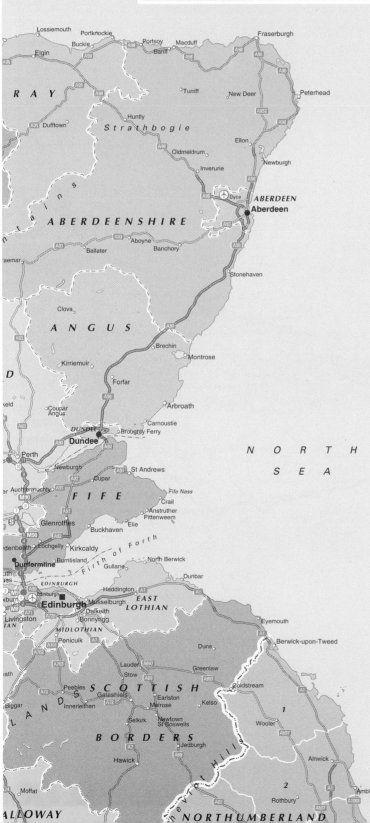

Lossiemouth
Portknockie
Buckie
Portsoy
Macduff
Fraserburgh
Elgin
Banff
RAY
Turriff
New Deer
Peterhead
Huntly
Dufftown
Strathbogie
Ellon
Oldmeldrum
Newburgh
Inverurie
Dyce
ABERDEEN
Aberdeen
ABERDEENSHIRE
Aboyne
Banchory
Ballater
Stonehaven
Clova
ANGUS
Kirriemuir
Brechin
Montrose
Forfar
Coupar Angus
Arbroath
DUNDEE
Carnoustie
Dundee
Broughty Ferry
NORTH SEA
Perth
Newburgh
St Andrews
Cupar
Fife Ness
Auchtermuchty
FIFE
Crail
Anstruther
Pittenweem
Glenrothes
Elie
Buckhaven
Kirkcaldy
Dunfermline
Burntisland
North Berwick
Lochgelly
Firth of Forth
Gullane
Dunbar
EDINBURGH
Haddington
Edinburgh
Musselburgh
EAST LOTHIAN
Livingston
Dalkeith
Bonnyrigg
Eyemouth
MIDLOTHIAN
Penicuik
Duns
Berwick-upon-Tweed
Lauder
Greenlaw
Stow
Coldstream
Peebles
SCOTTISH
Galashiels
Earlston
Melrose
Kelso
Innerleithen
Biggar
Selkirk
Newtown St Boswells
Wooler
BORDERS
Jedburgh
Hawick
Alnwick
Moffat
Amble
GALLOWAY
Rothbury
NORTHUMBERLAND

SCOTLAND Councils

- ABERDEEN
- ABERDEENSHIRE
- ANGUS
- ARGYLL AND BUTE
- CLACKMANNANSHIRE
- DUMFRIES AND GALLOWAY
- DUNDEE
- EAST AYRSHIRE
- EAST DUNBARTONSHIRE
- EAST LOTHIAN
- EAST RENFREWSHIRE
- EDINBURGH
- FALKIRK
- FIFE
- GLASGOW
- HIGHLAND
- INVERCLYDE
- MIDLOTHIAN
- MORAY
- NORTH AYRSHIRE
- NORTH LANARKSHIRE
- ORKNEY
- PERTH AND KINROSS
- RENFREWSHIRE
- SCOTTISH BORDERS
- SHETLAND
- SOUTH AYRSHIRE
- SOUTH LANARKSHIRE
- STIRLING
- WEST DUNBARTONSHIRE
- WEST LOTHIAN
- WESTERN ISLES (NA H-EILEANAN AN IAR)

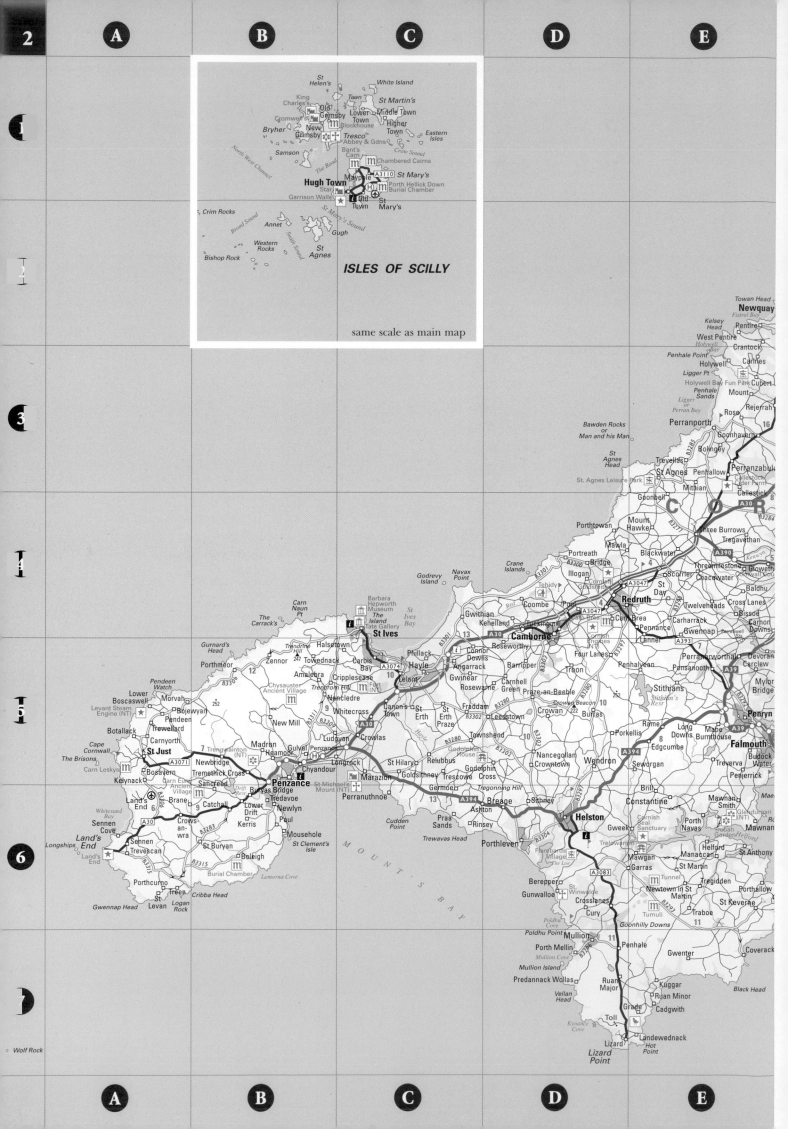

ISLES OF SCILLY

same scale as main map

Isles of Scilly inset labels:

St Helen's
White Island
Teän
King Charles's
St Martin's
Old Grimsby
Lower Town
Middle Town
Cromwell's
Blockhouse
Higher Town
New Grimsby
Bryher
Tresco
Abbey & Gdns
Eastern Isles
Samson
Bant's Carn
Chambered Cairns
Crow Sound
North West Channel
The Road
Maypole
A3110
St Mary's
Porth Hellick Down Burial Chamber
Hugh Town
Star
Old Town
St Mary's
Garrison Walls
St Mary's Sound
Crim Rocks
Brood Sound
Annet
Gugh
Western Rocks
Smith Sound
St Agnes
Bishop Rock

Main map labels (Cornwall):

Newquay
Towan Head
Fistral Bay
Kelsey Head
West Pentire
Pentire
Holywell Bay
Crantock
Penhale Point
Holywell
Carnes
Ligger Pt
Cubert
Holywell Bay Fun Park
Penhale Sands
Mount
Ligger or Perran Bay
Rejerrah
Rose
Perranporth
Bawden Rocks or Man and his Man
Goonhavern
St Agnes Head
Trevellas
St Agnes
Penhallow
Perranzabuloe
Callestick Cider Farm
St. Agnes Leisure Park
Mithian
Callestick
Goonbell
C O R
Porthtowan
Mount Hawke
Three Burrows
Tregavethan
Crane Islands
Portreath
Mawla
Blackwater
Scorrier
Threemilestone
Gloweth
Bridge
Illogan
Tehidy
Pool
St Day
Chacewater
Baldhu
Cross Lanes
Godrevy Island
Navax Point
Coombe
Redruth
Twelveheads
Bissoe
Gwithian
Kehelland
Tuckingmill
Carn Brea
Pennance
Carharrack
Carnon Downs
Barbara Hepworth Museum
The Island
Tate Gallery
St Ives Bay
Camborne
Cornish Engines (NT)
Lanner
Gwennap
Perrran-ar-worthal
Devoran
Carclew
The Carrack's
St Ives
Roseworthy
Four Lanes
Penhalvean
Ponsanooth
Mylor Bridge
Gurnard's Head
Phillack
Connor Downs
Barripper
Treon
Stithians
Porthmeor
Carbis Bay
Hayle
Angarrack
Carnell Green
Praze-an-Beeble
Stithian's Resr
Penryn
Zennor
Cripplesease
Lelant
Gwinear
Rosewarne
Crowan Beacon
Rame
Mabe Burnthouse
Falmouth
Trendrine Hill
Towednack
Treojrom Hill
Fort (NT)
Fraddam
Crowan
Long Downs
Burnthouse
Budock Water
Amalebra
Nancledre
Canon's Town
St Erth
St Erth Praze
Leedstown
Burras
Edgcumbe
Treverva
Pendeen Watch
Chysauster Ancient Village
Whitecross
Townshend
Porkellis
Sewargan
Penjerrick
Lower Boscaswell
Morvah
Bojewyan
New Mill
Ludgvan
Crowlas
Godolphin House
Nancegollan
Wendron
Constantine
Mawnan Smith
Levant Steam Engine (NT)
Pendeen
Madron
Gulval
Longrock
St Hilary
Relubbus
Godolphin Cross
Crowntown
Glendurgan (NT)
Mawnan
Botallack
Carnyorth
Heamoor
Chyandour
Marazion
Goldsithney
Trescowe
Sithney
Cornish Seal Sanctuary
Porth Navas
Helford
St Just
Trewellard
Trengwainton (NT)
Penzance
St Michael's Mount (NT)
Germoe
Tregonning Hill
Helston
Gweek
Trelowarren
Trebah Garden
Manaccan
St Anthony
Cape Cornwall
Newbridge
Tremethick Cross
Perranuthnoe
Breage
Ashton
Brill
Constantine
Helford
The Brisons
Bosavern
Carn Euny Ancient Village
Buryas Bridge
St Michael's Penzance
Praa Sands
Rinsey
Flambards Village
The Loe
Garras
Mawgan
St Martin
Tregidden
Porthallow
Carn Leskys
Kelynack
Sancreed
Drift Resr
Tredavoe
Newlyn
Cudden Point
Porthleven
Berepper
Cury
Newtown in St Martin
St Keverne
Land's End
Brane
Catchall
Lower Drift
Paul
St Clement's Isle
Trewavas Head
A3083
Gunwalloe
St Winwalde
Tumuli
Traboe
Sennen Cove
Crows-an-wra
Kerris
Mousehole
Mount's Bay
Crosslanes
Whitesand Bay
Sennen
St Buryan
Boleigh
Poldhu Cove
Goonhilly Downs
Gwenter
Coverack
Land's End
Trevescan
Burial Chamber
Lumorna Cove
Poldhu Point
Mullion
Penhale
Longships
Porthcurno
Treen
Cribba Head
Mullion Cove
Mullion Island
Porth Mellin
Gwennap Head
St Levan
Logan Rock
Predannack Wollas
Ruan Major
Küggar
Black Head
Wolf Rock
Vellan Head
Ruan Minor
Cadgwith
Kynance Cove
Toll
Grade
Lizard
Hot Point
Landewednack
Lizard Point

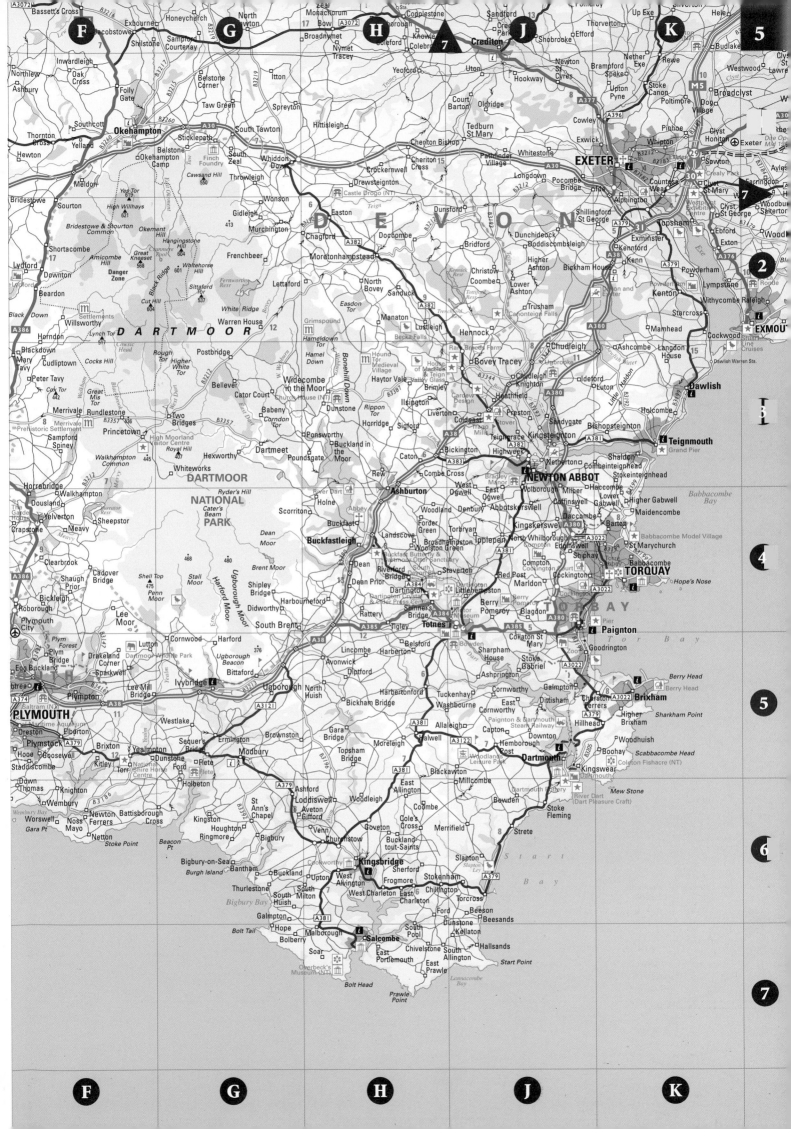

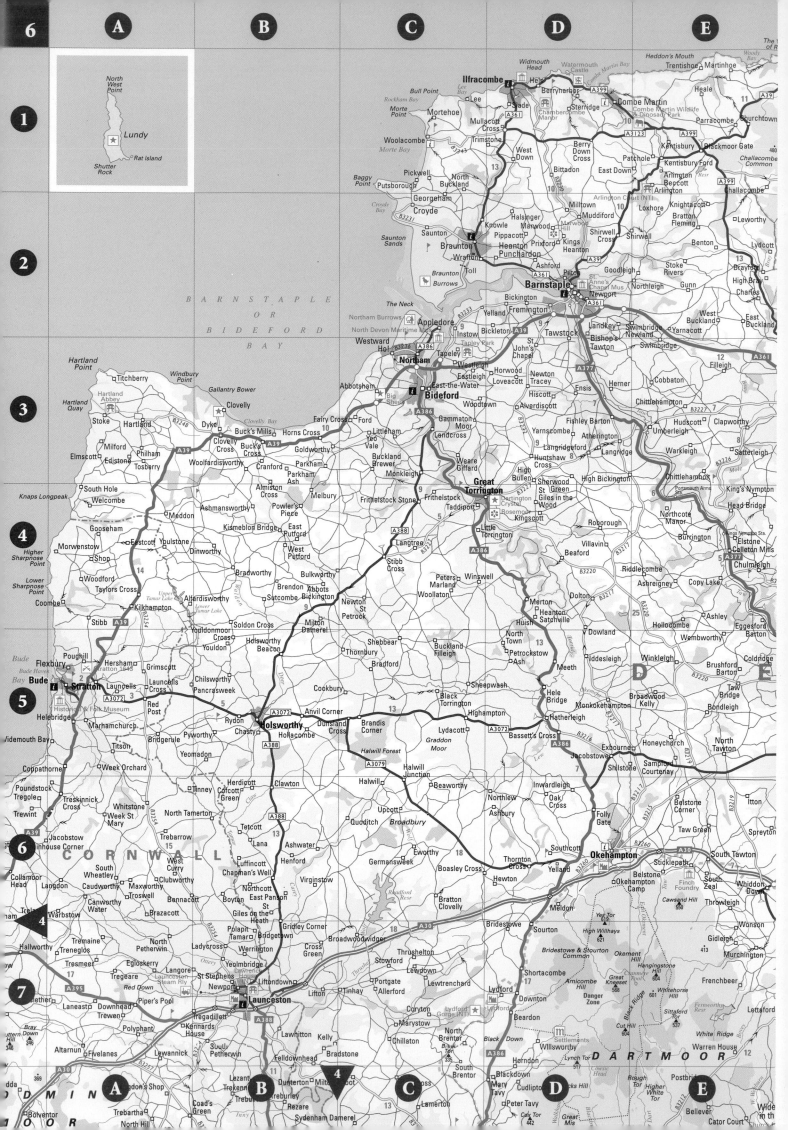

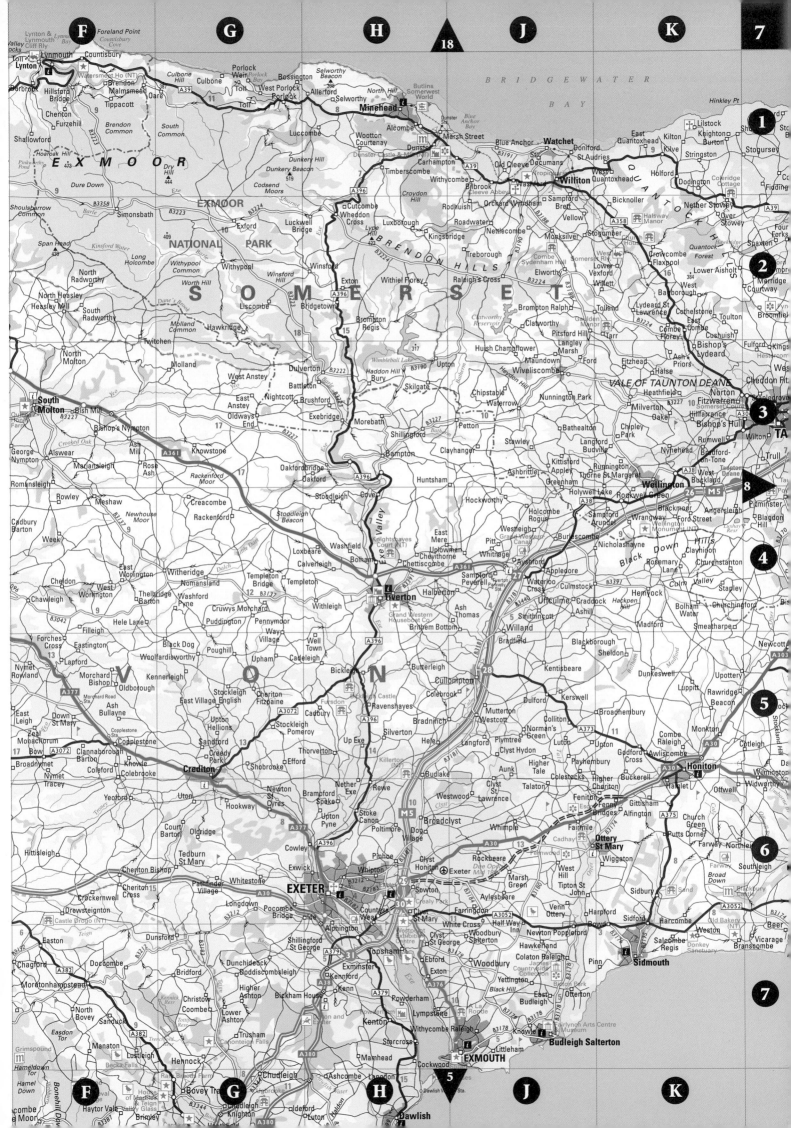

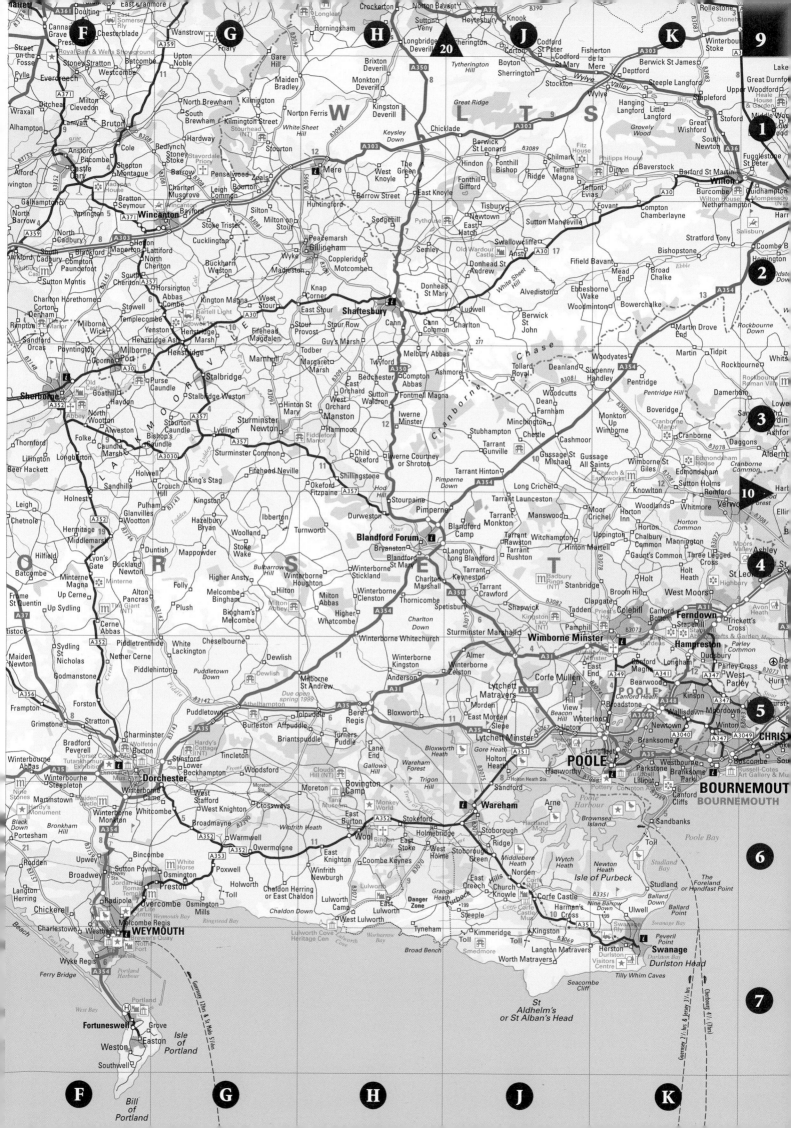

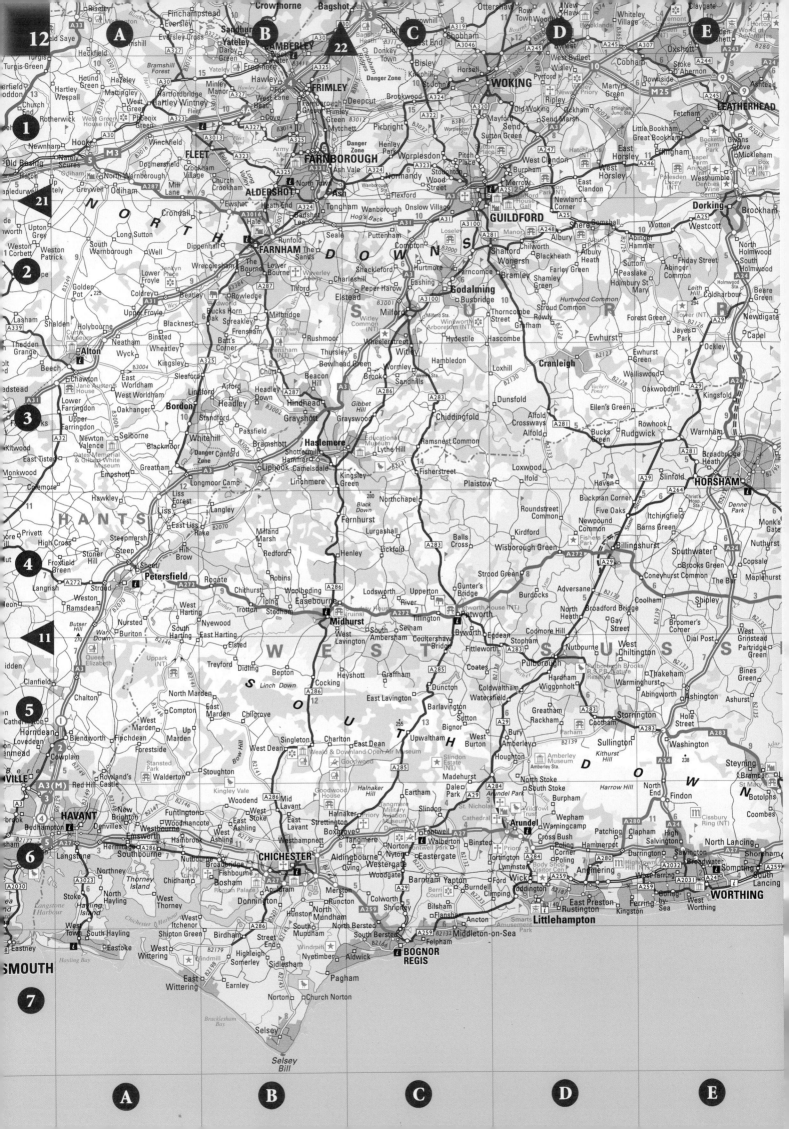

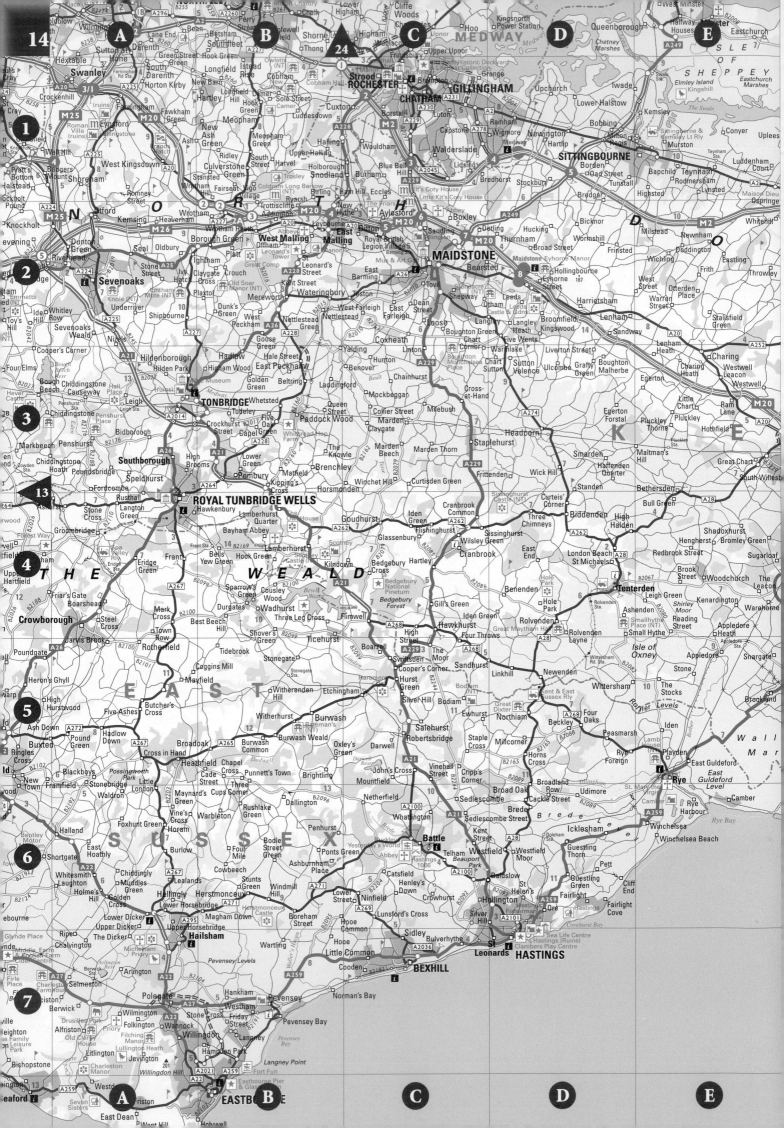

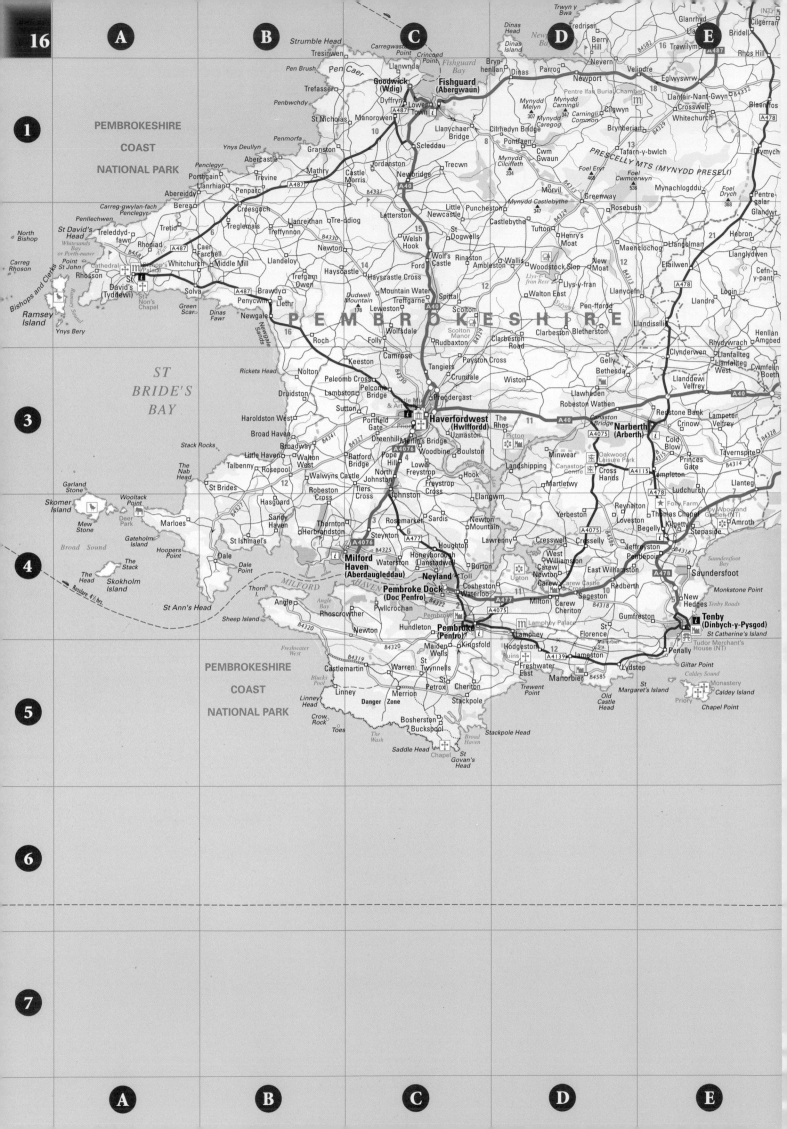

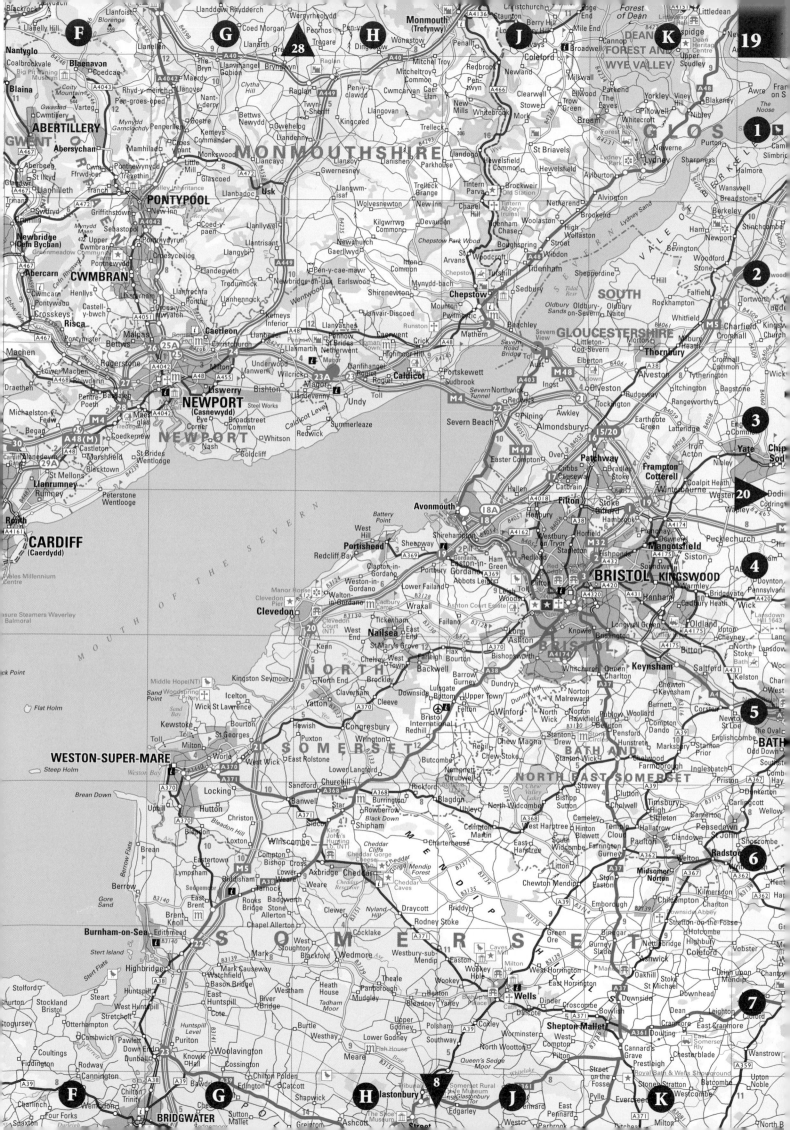

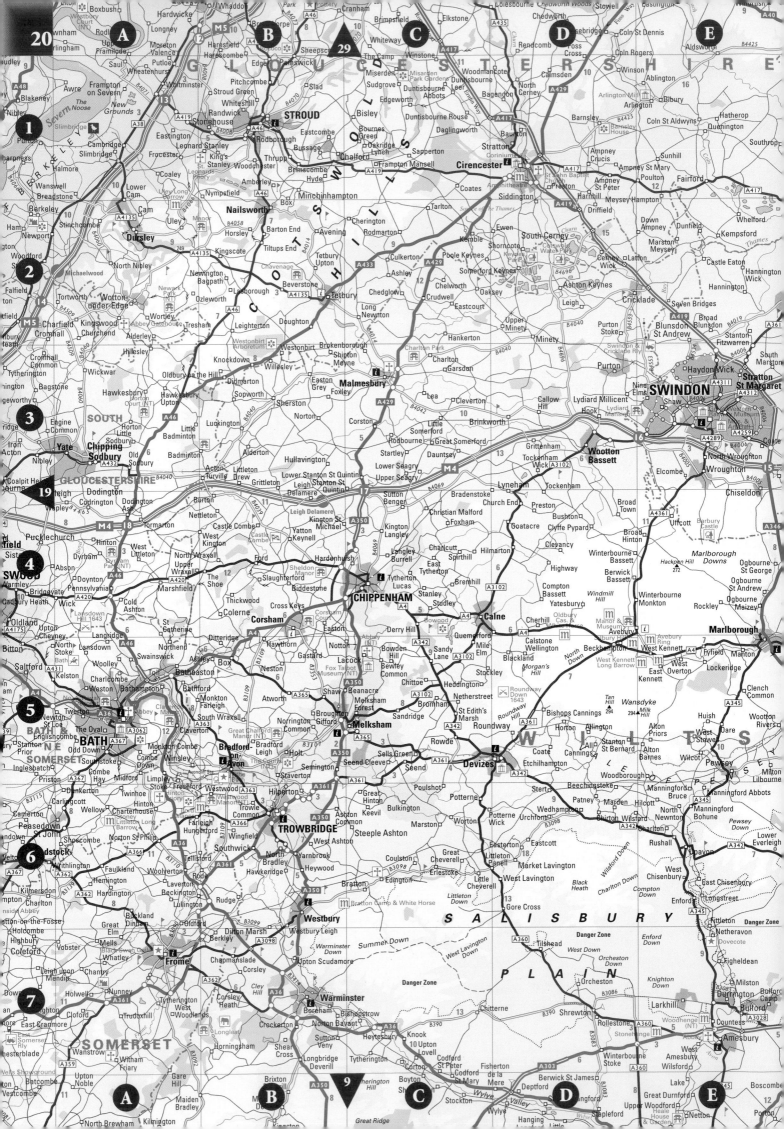

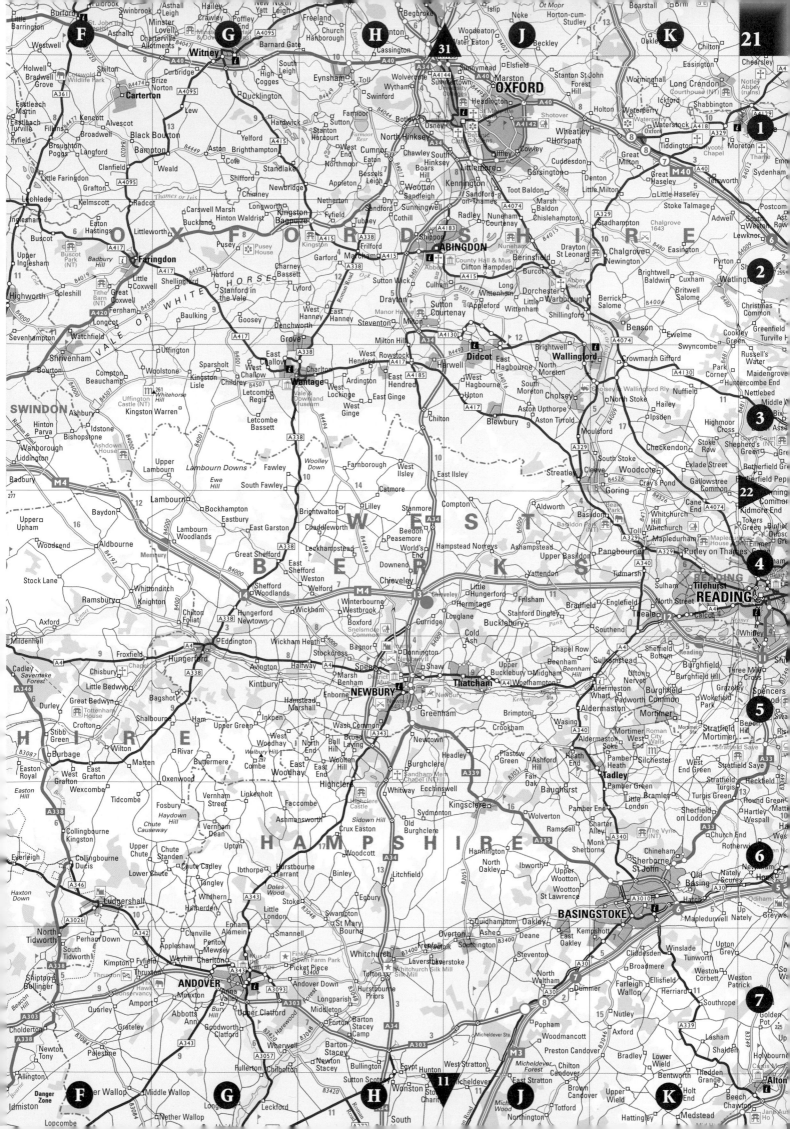

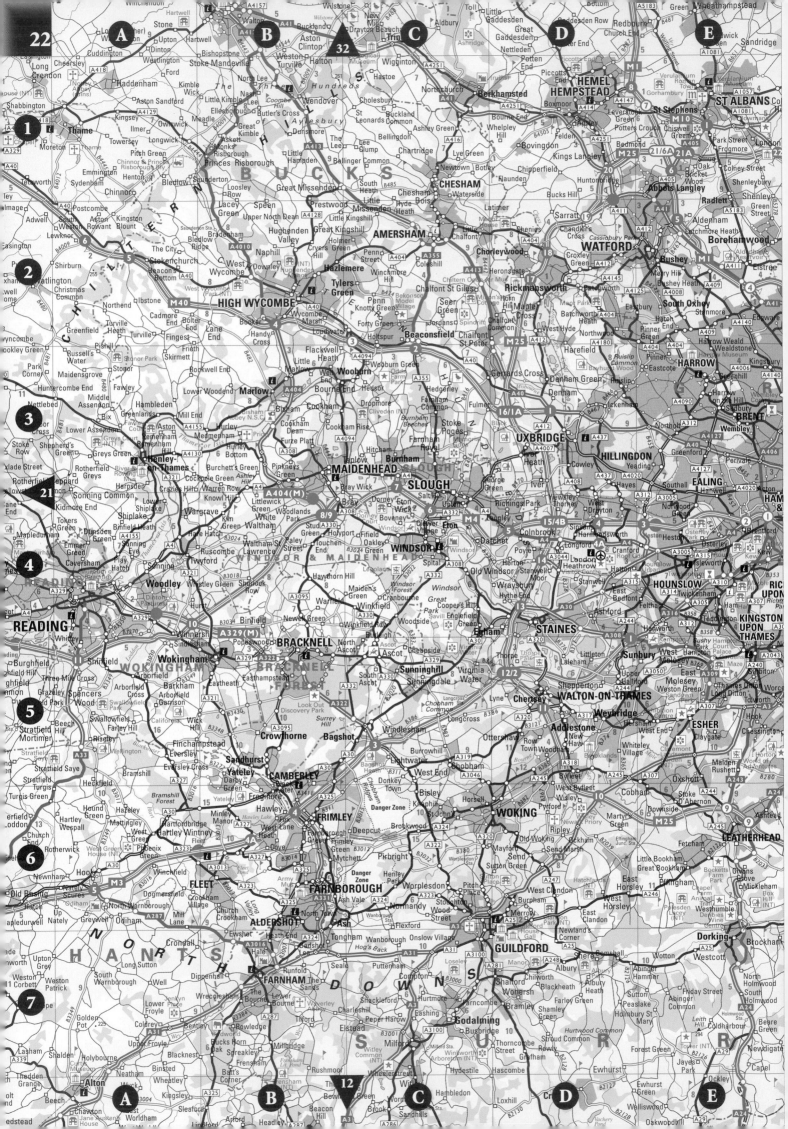

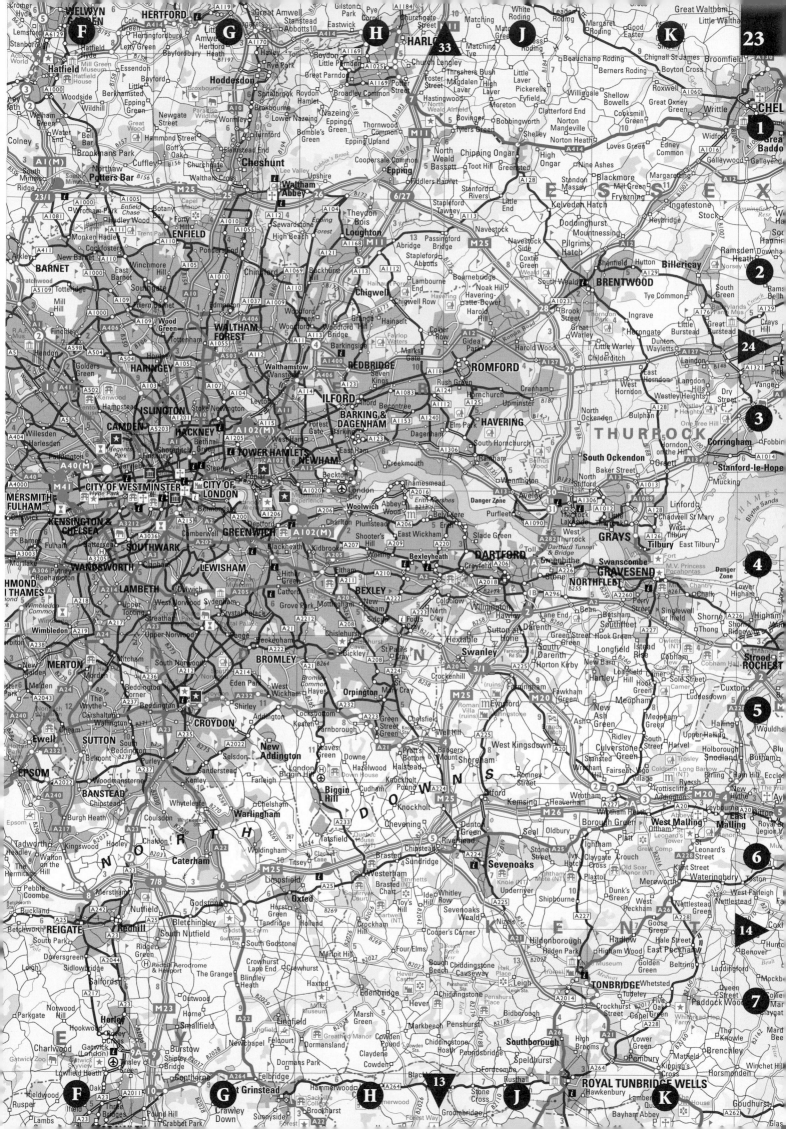

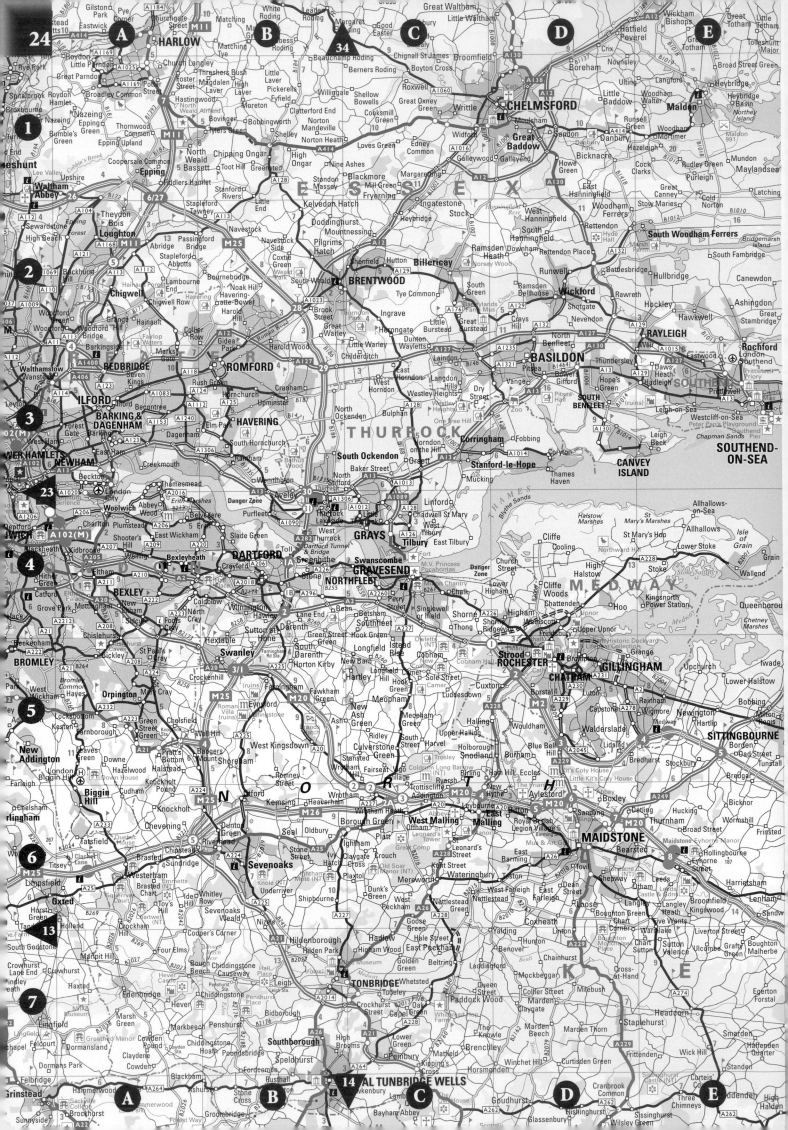

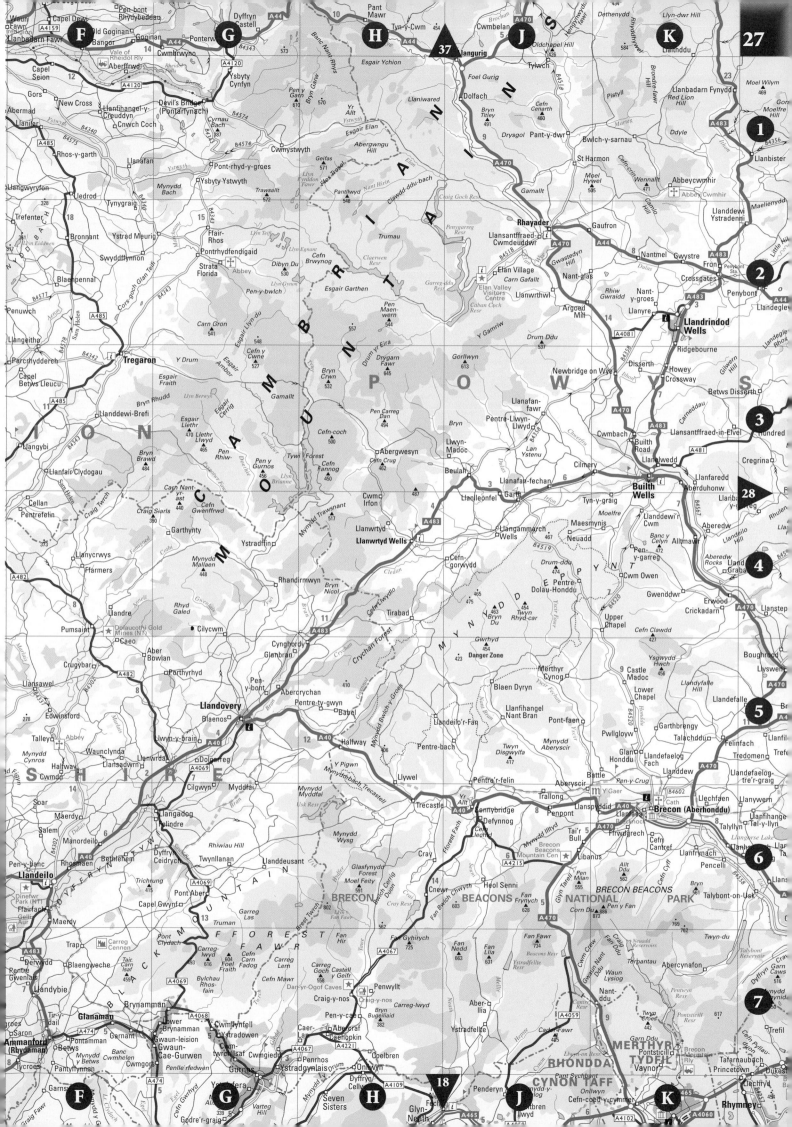

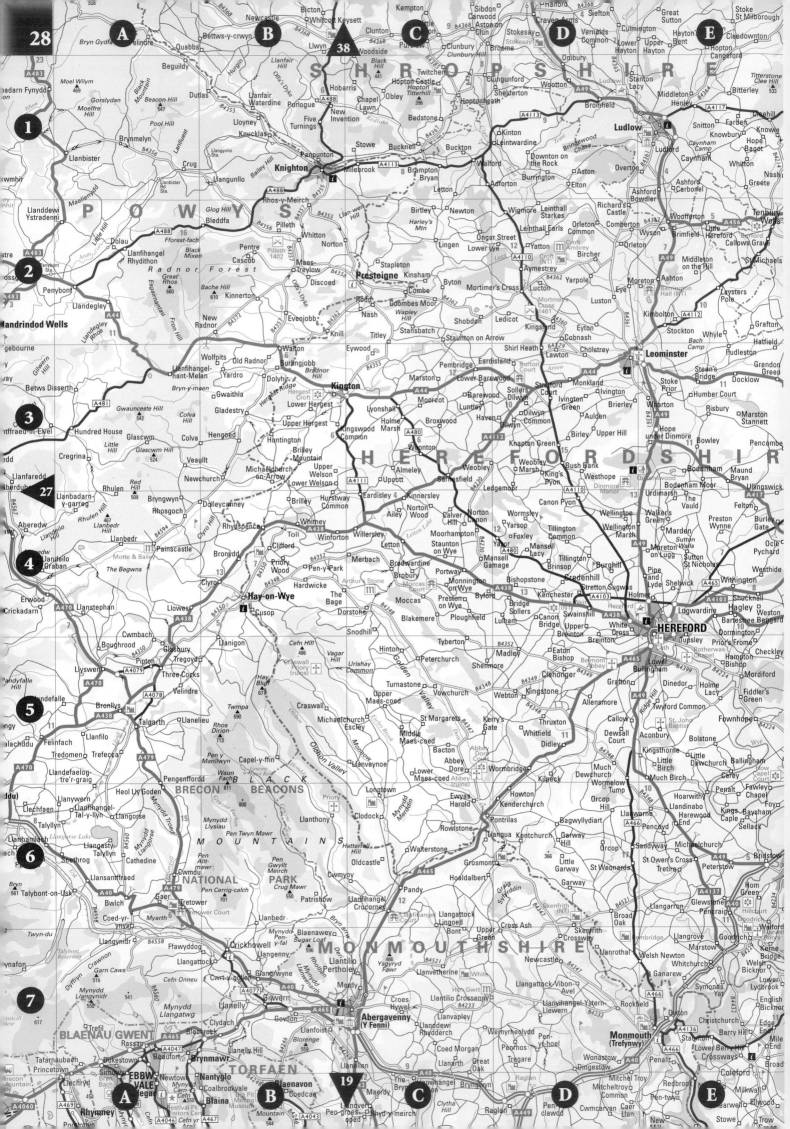

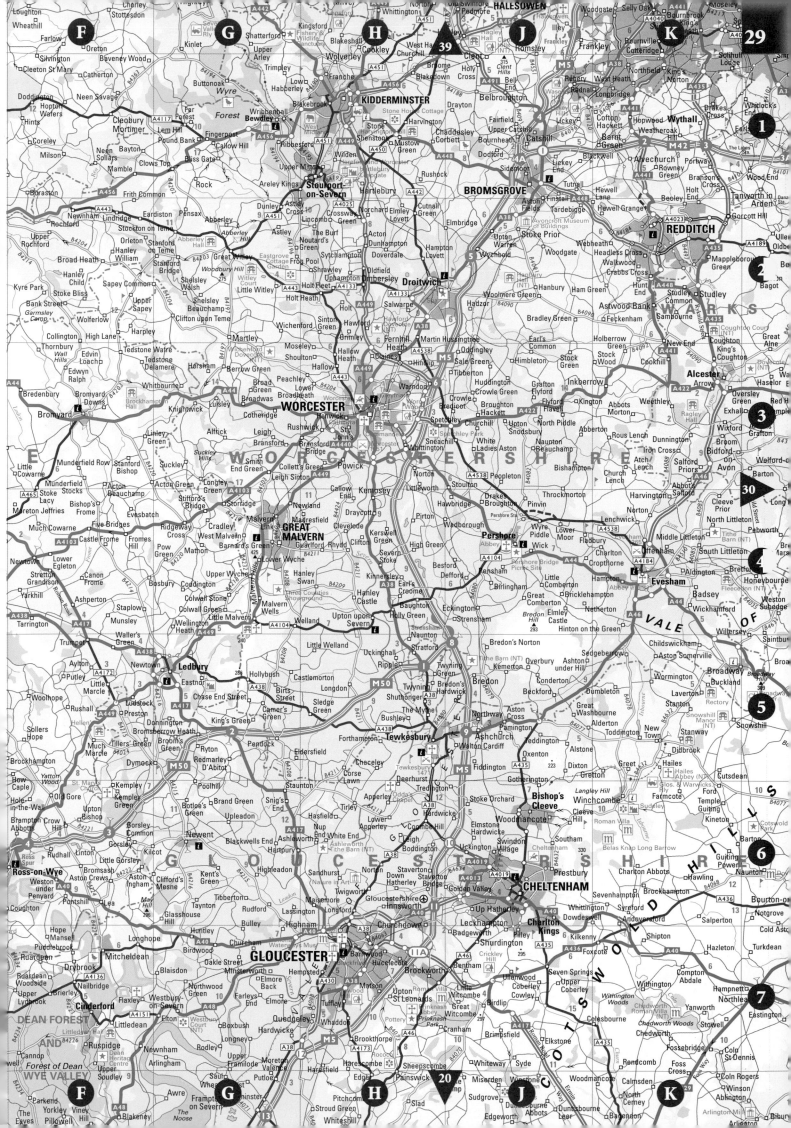

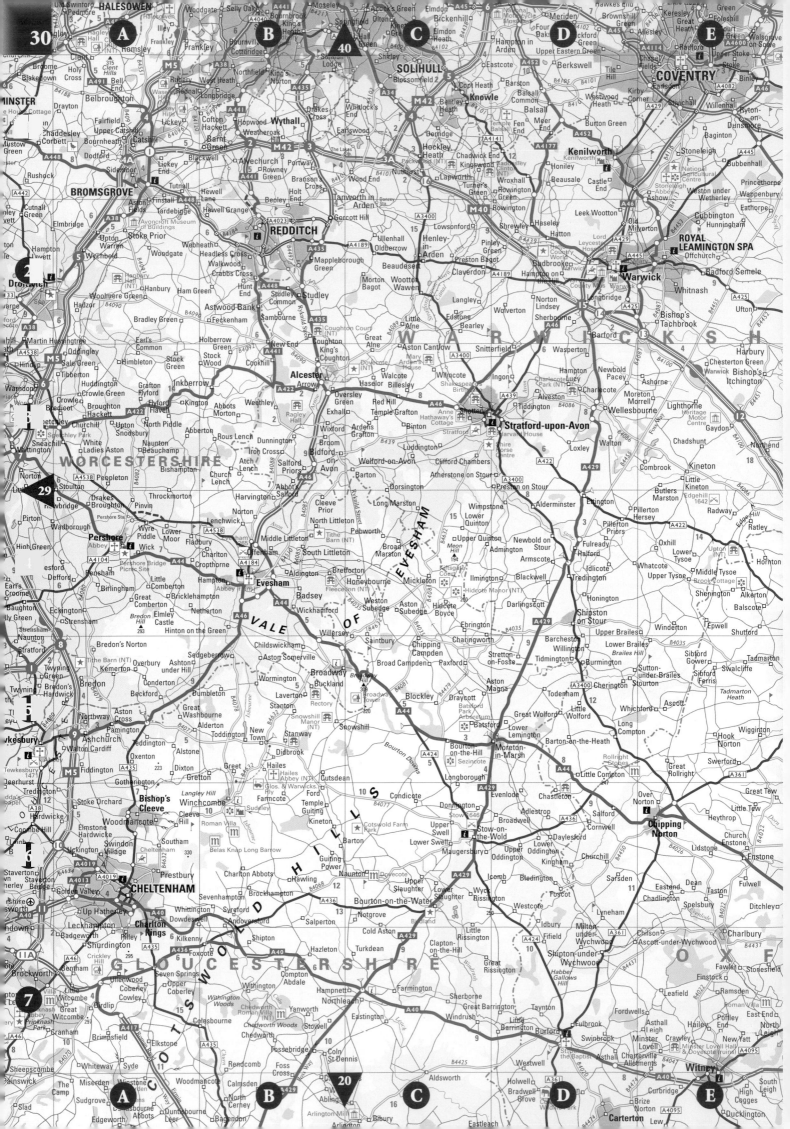

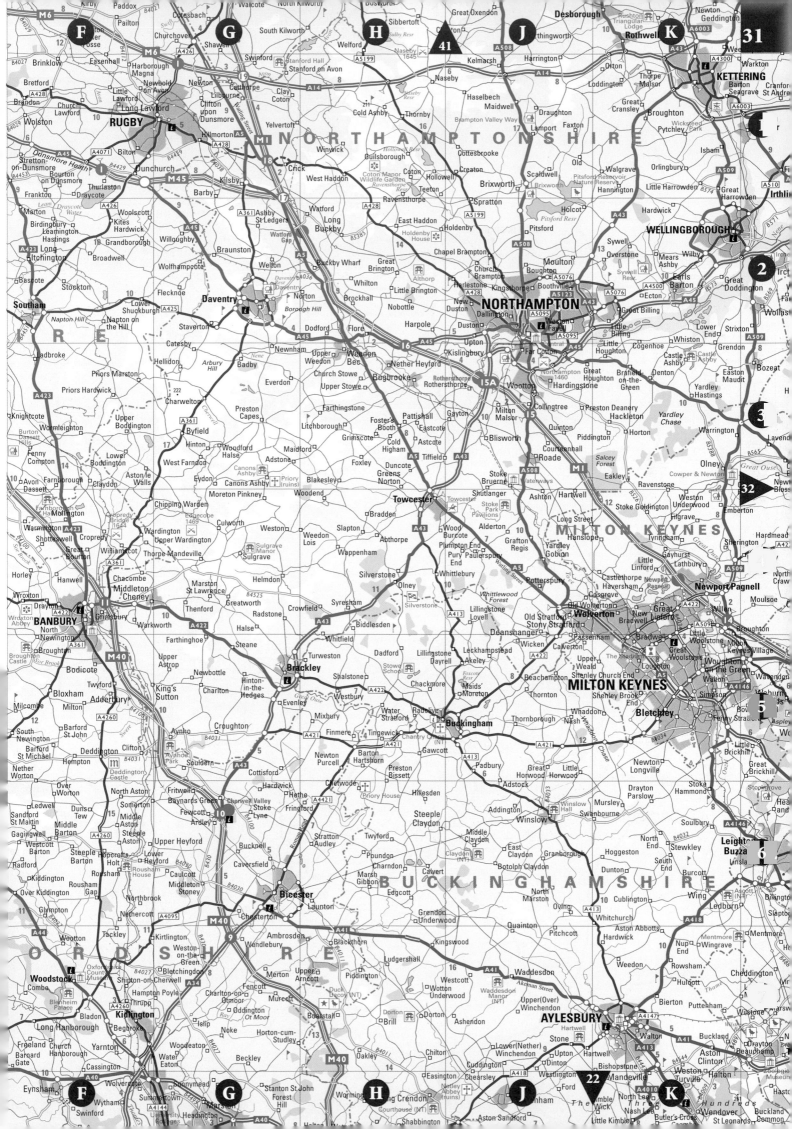

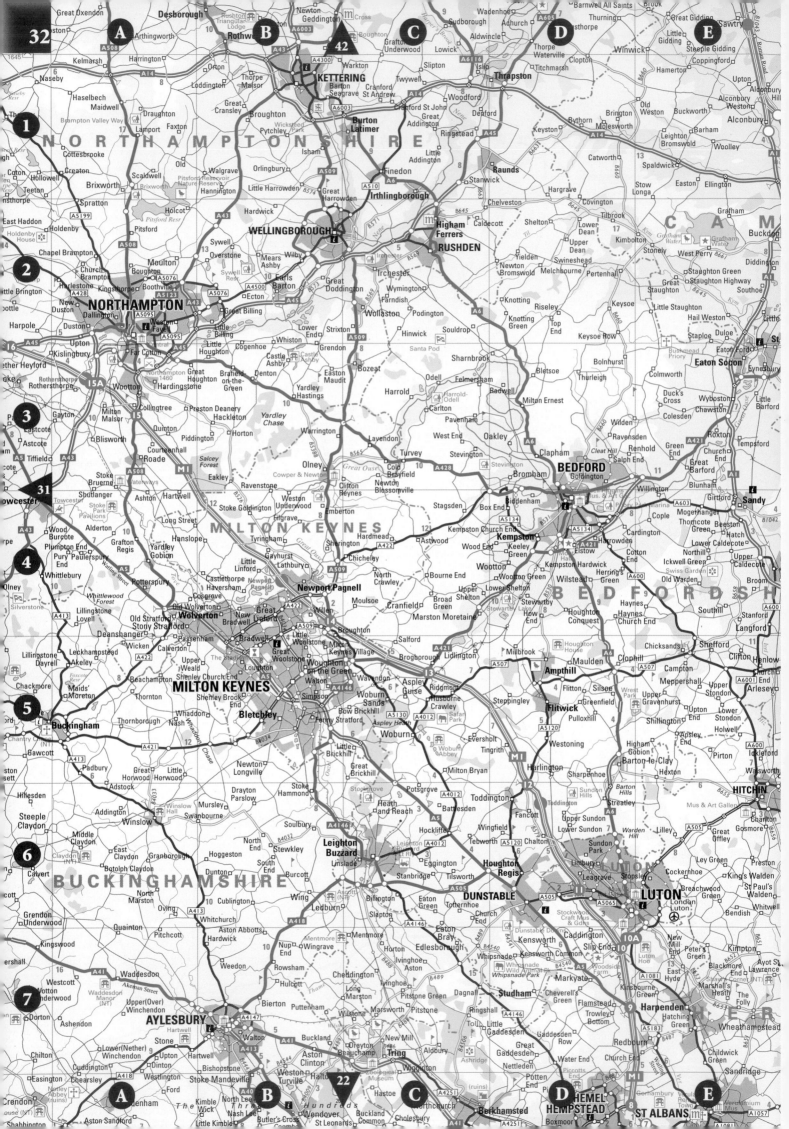

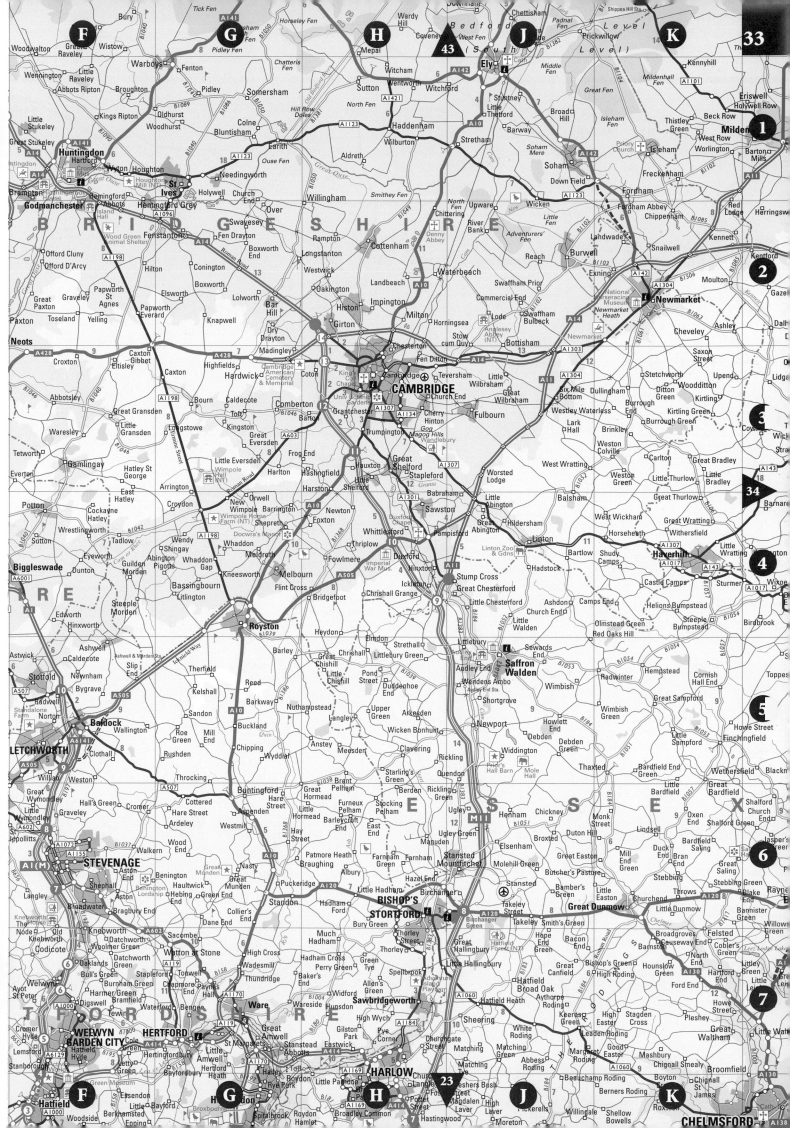

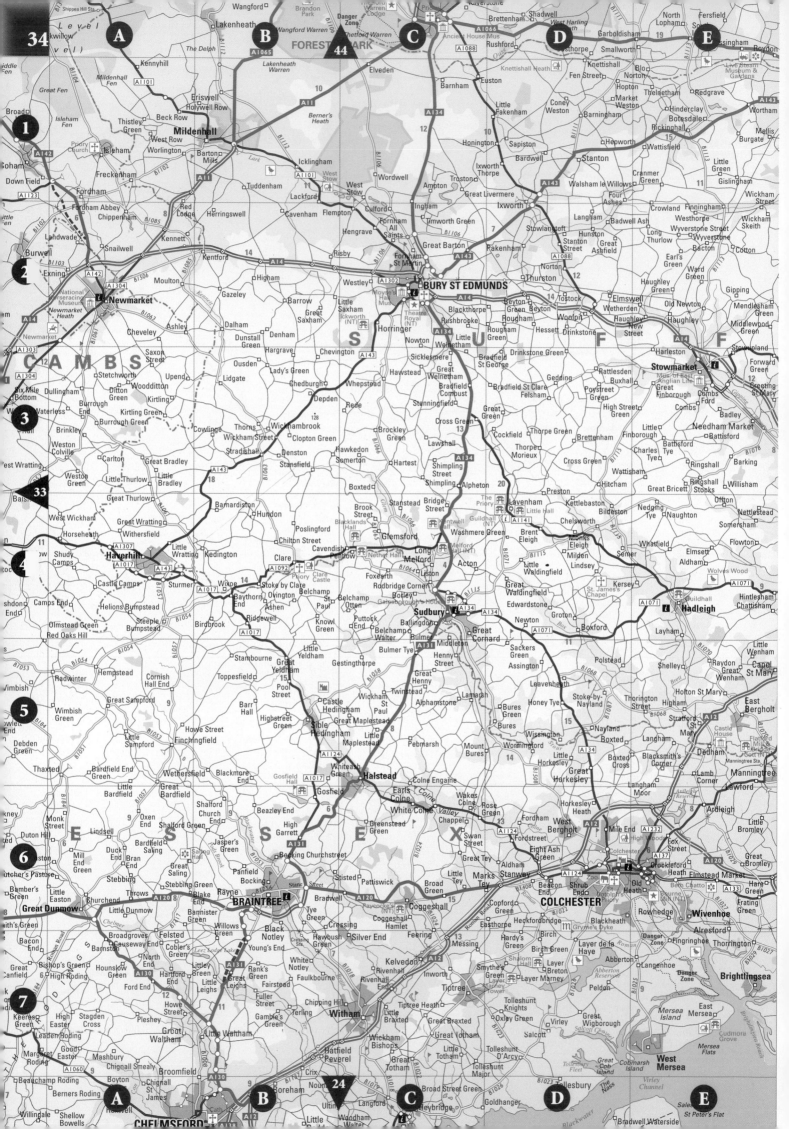

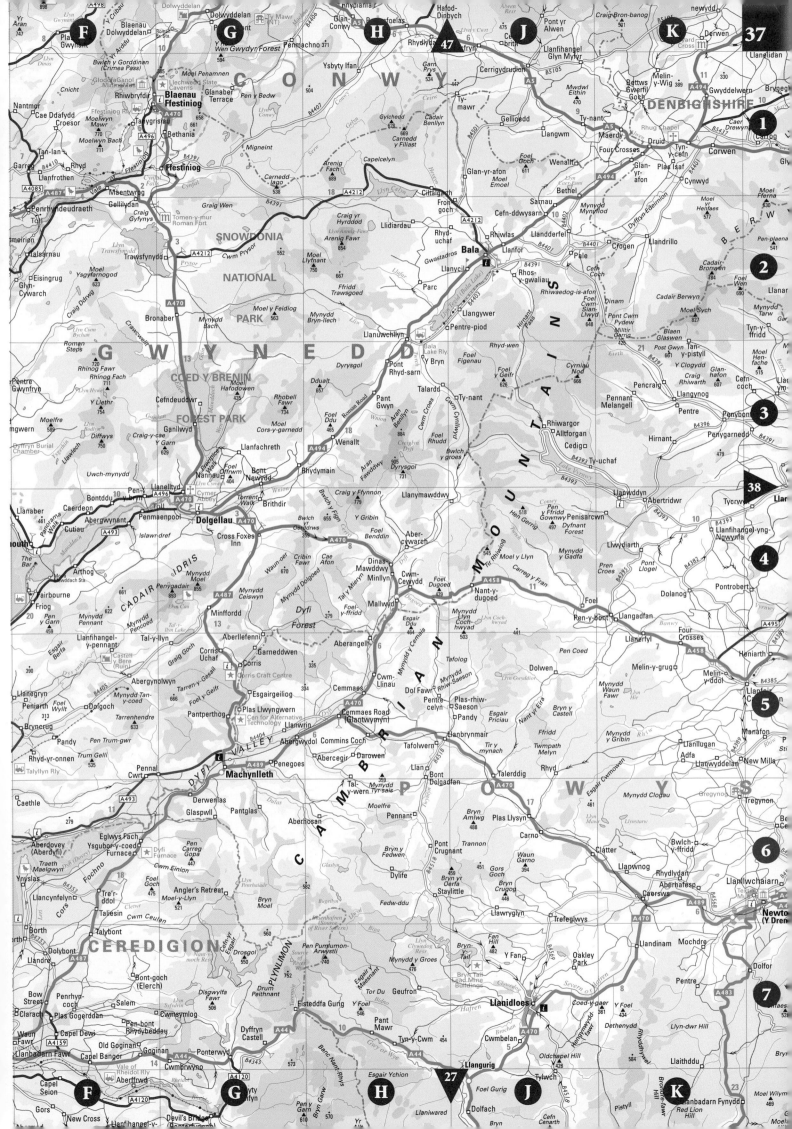

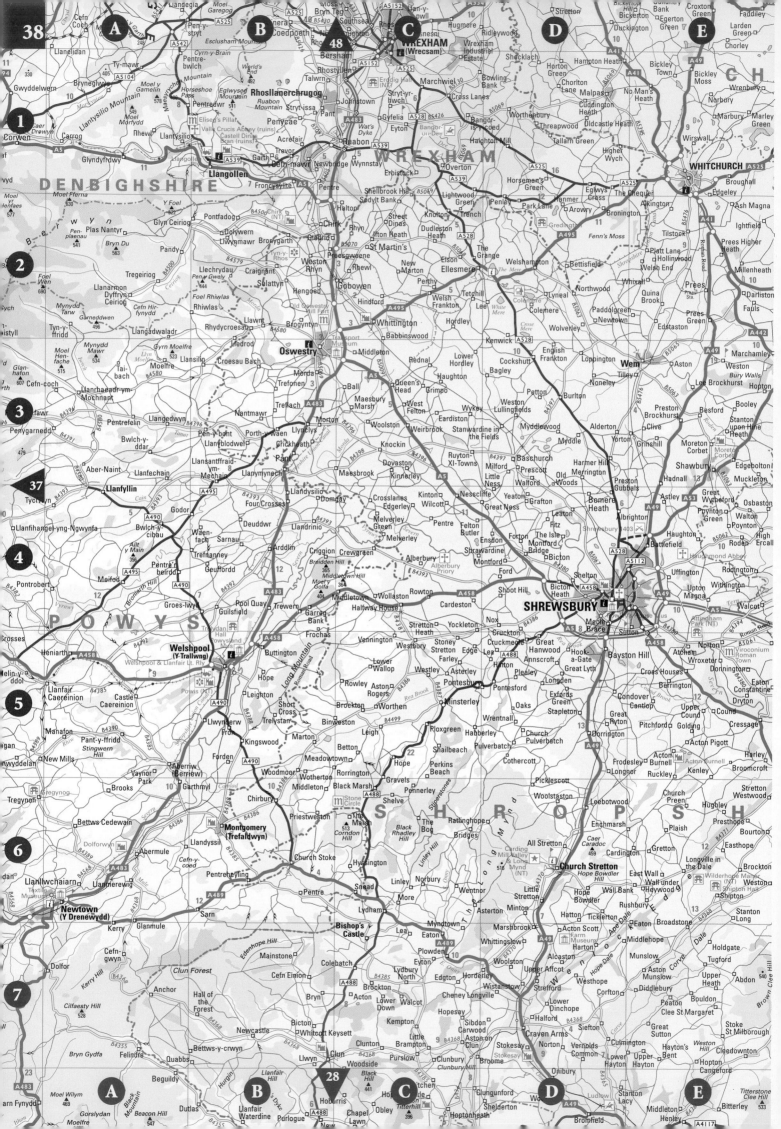

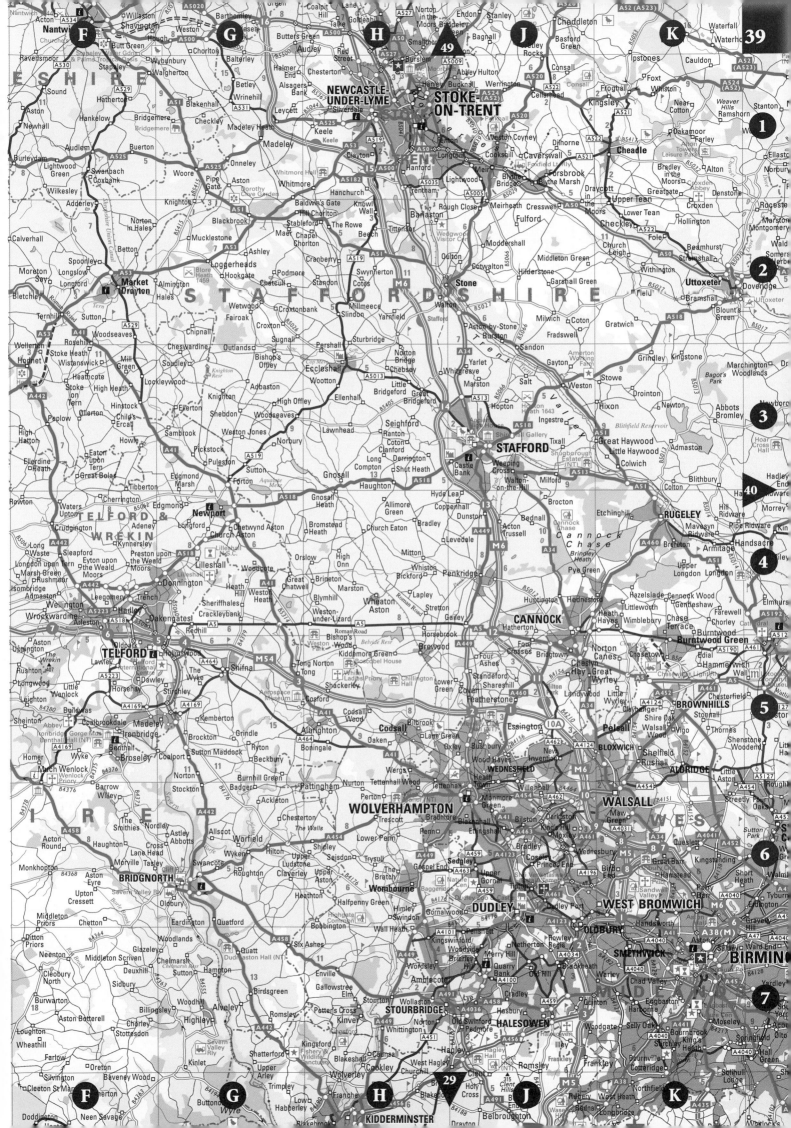

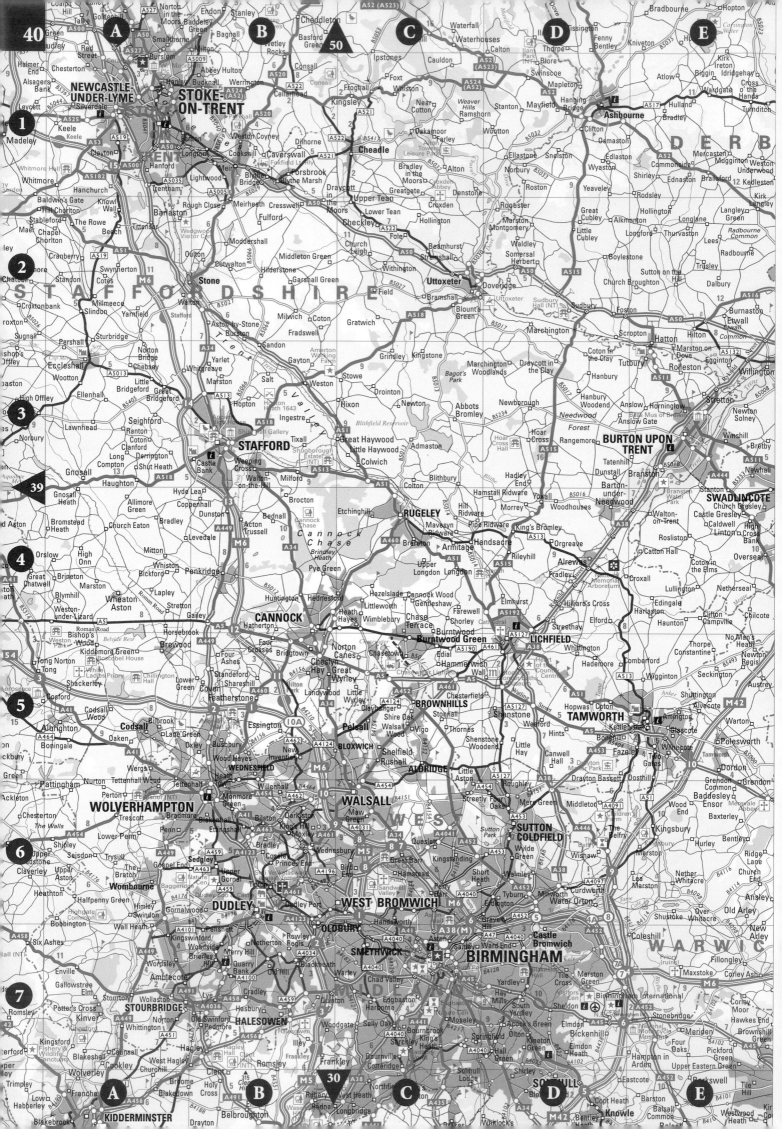

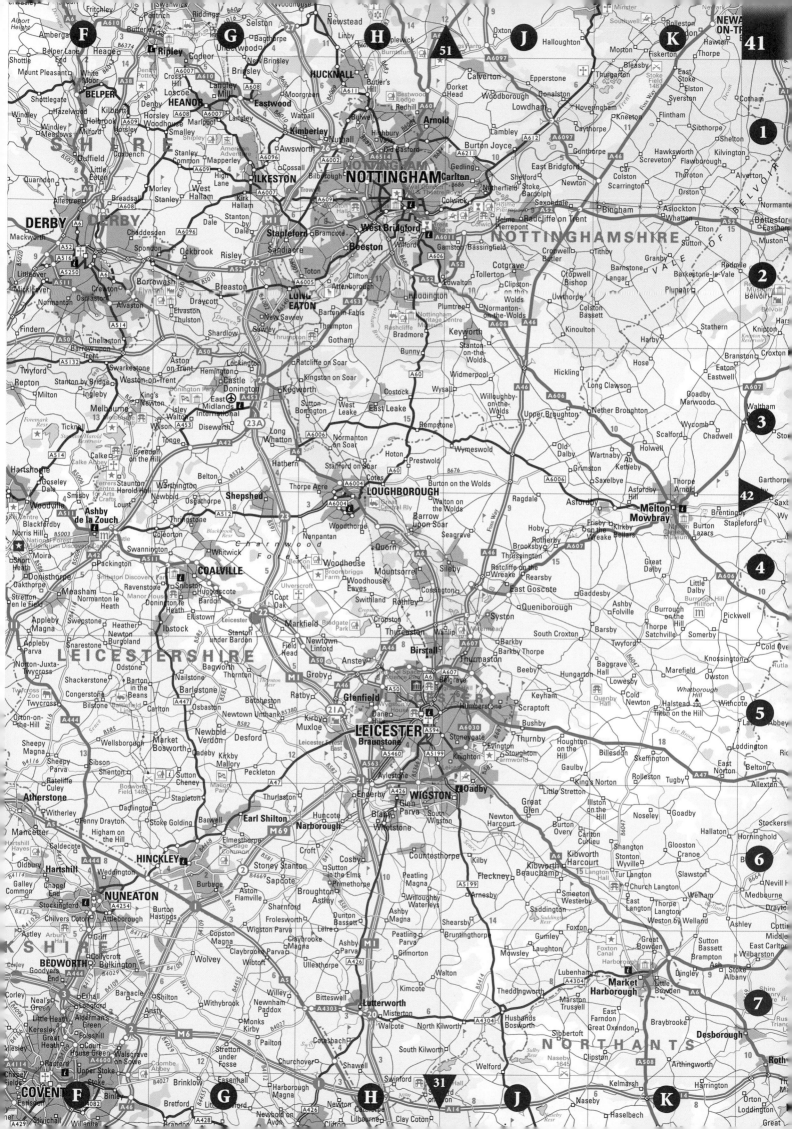

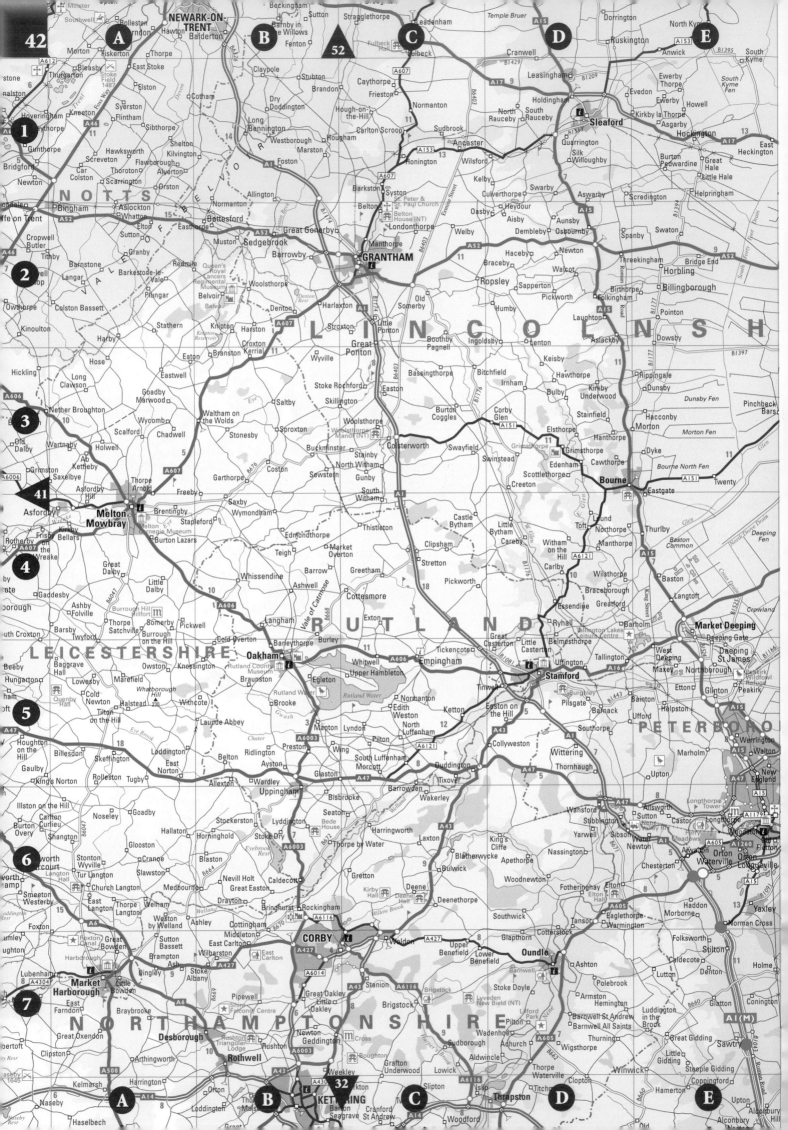

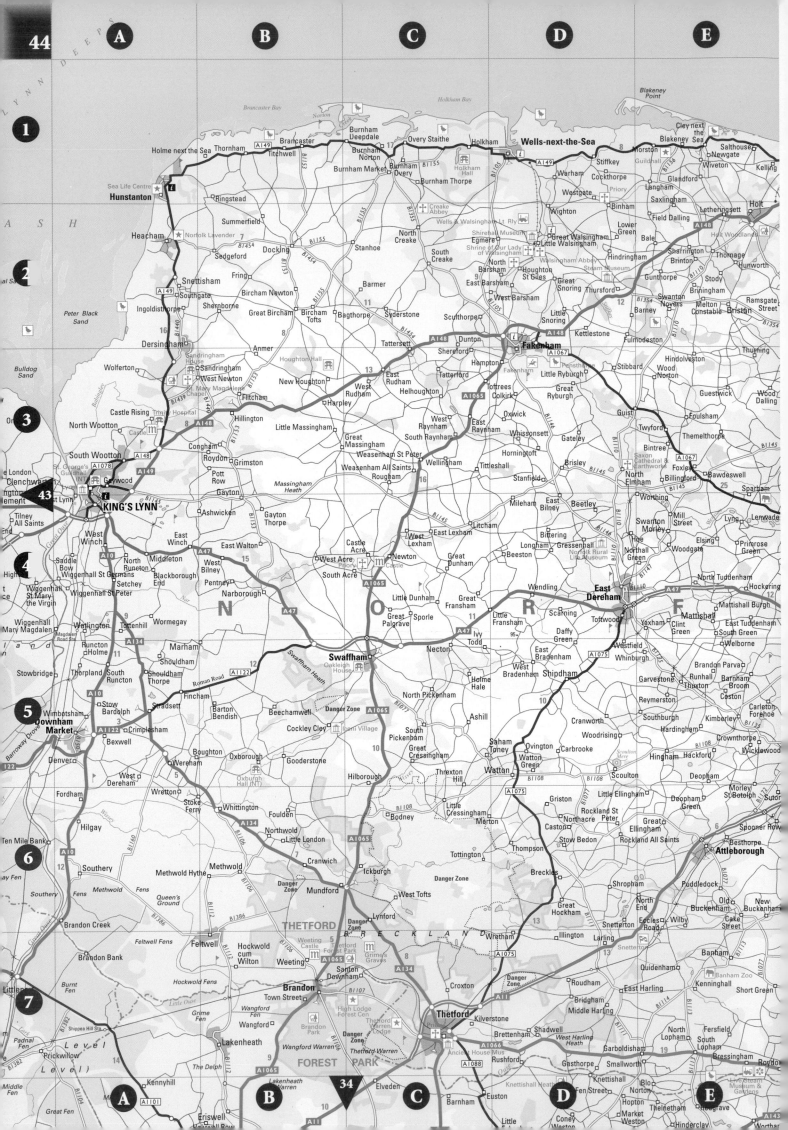

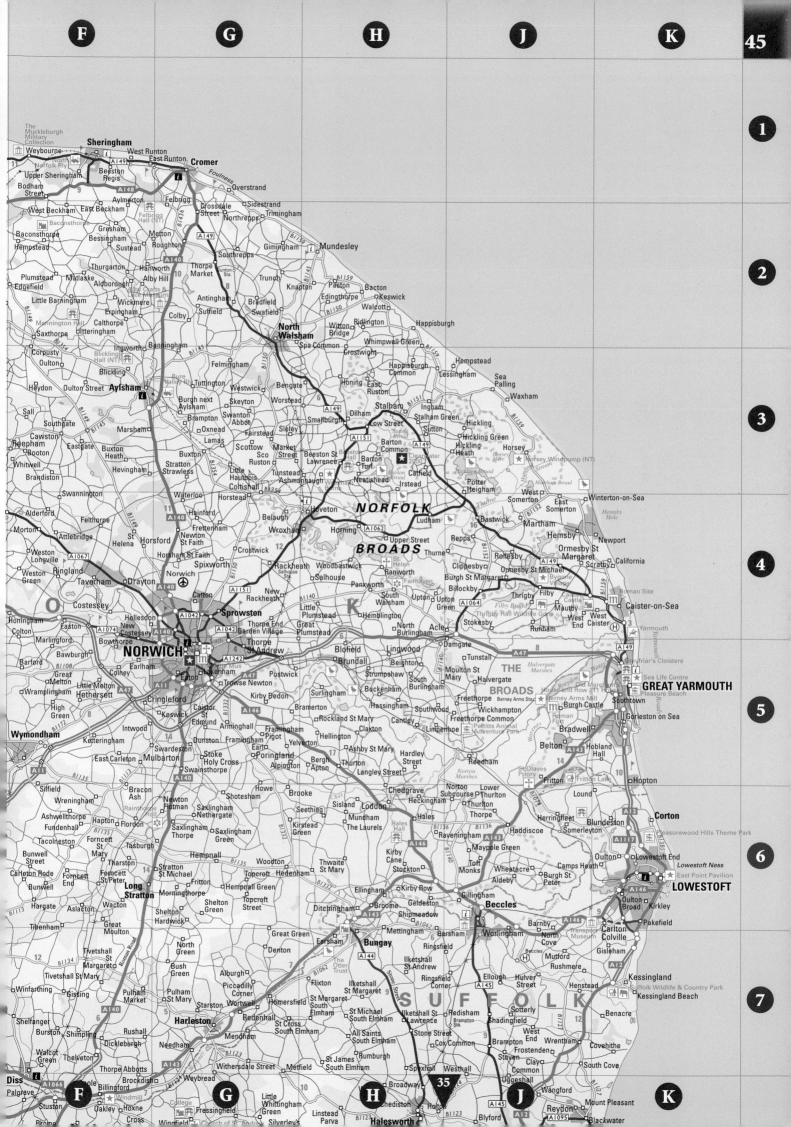

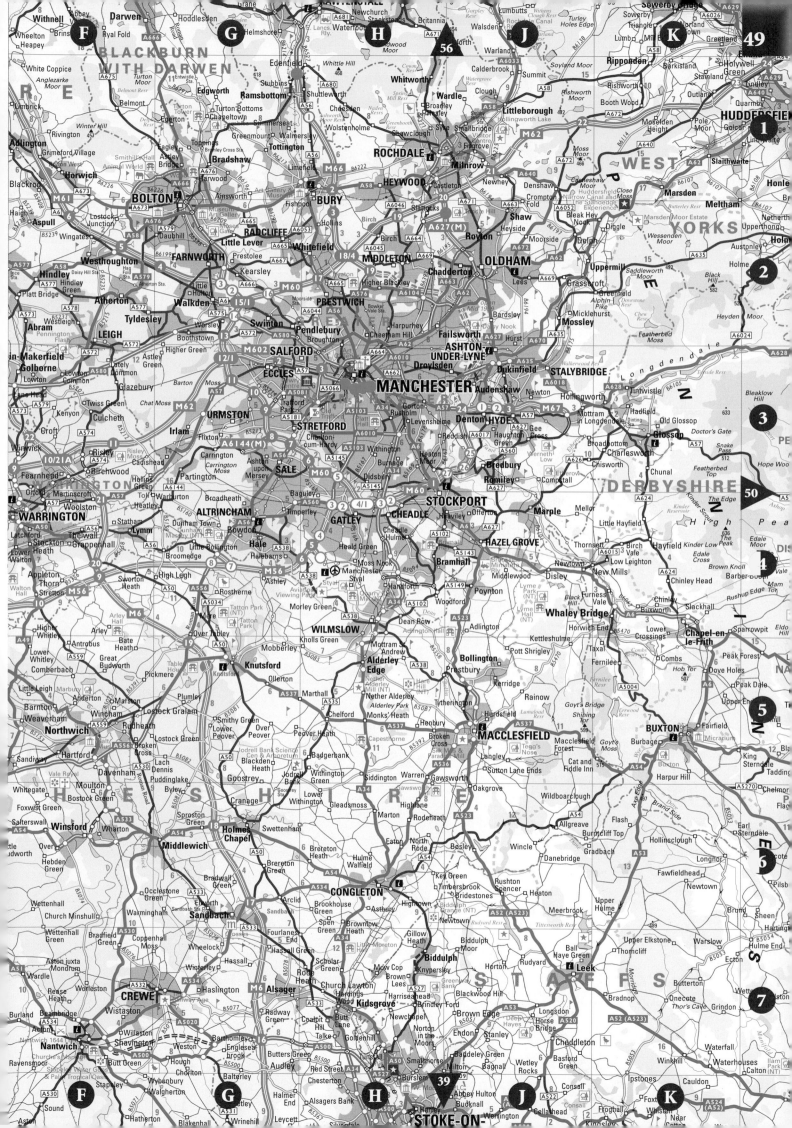

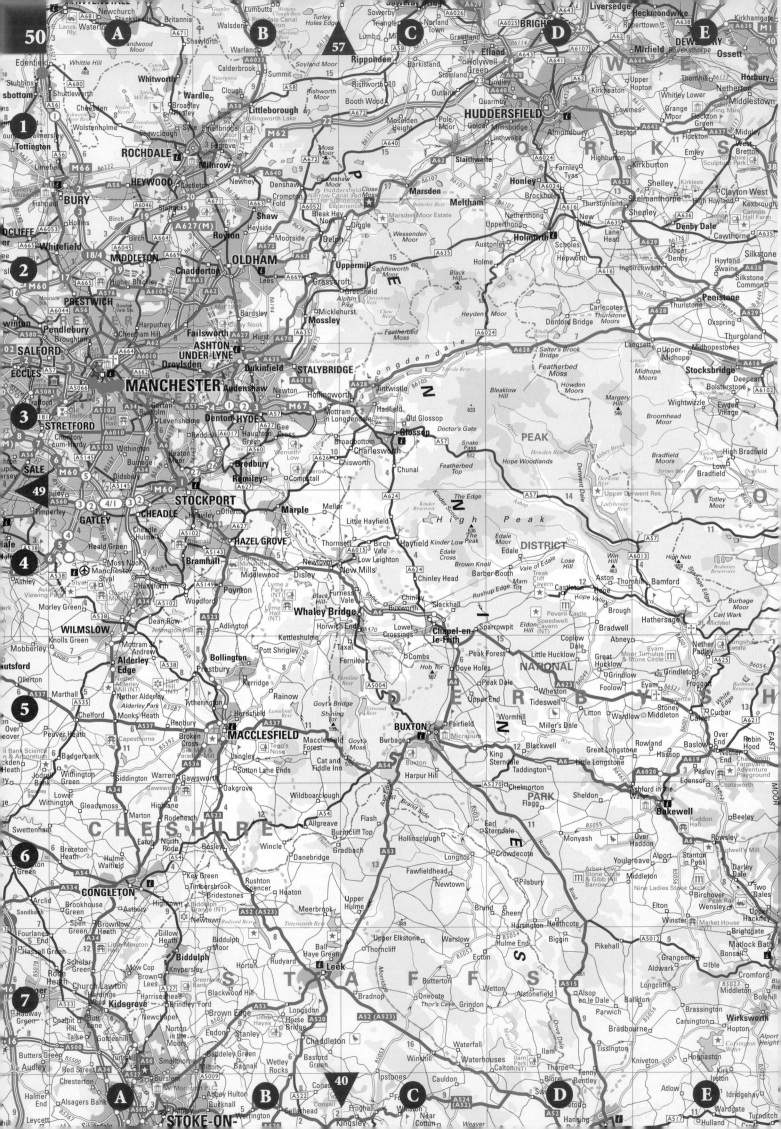

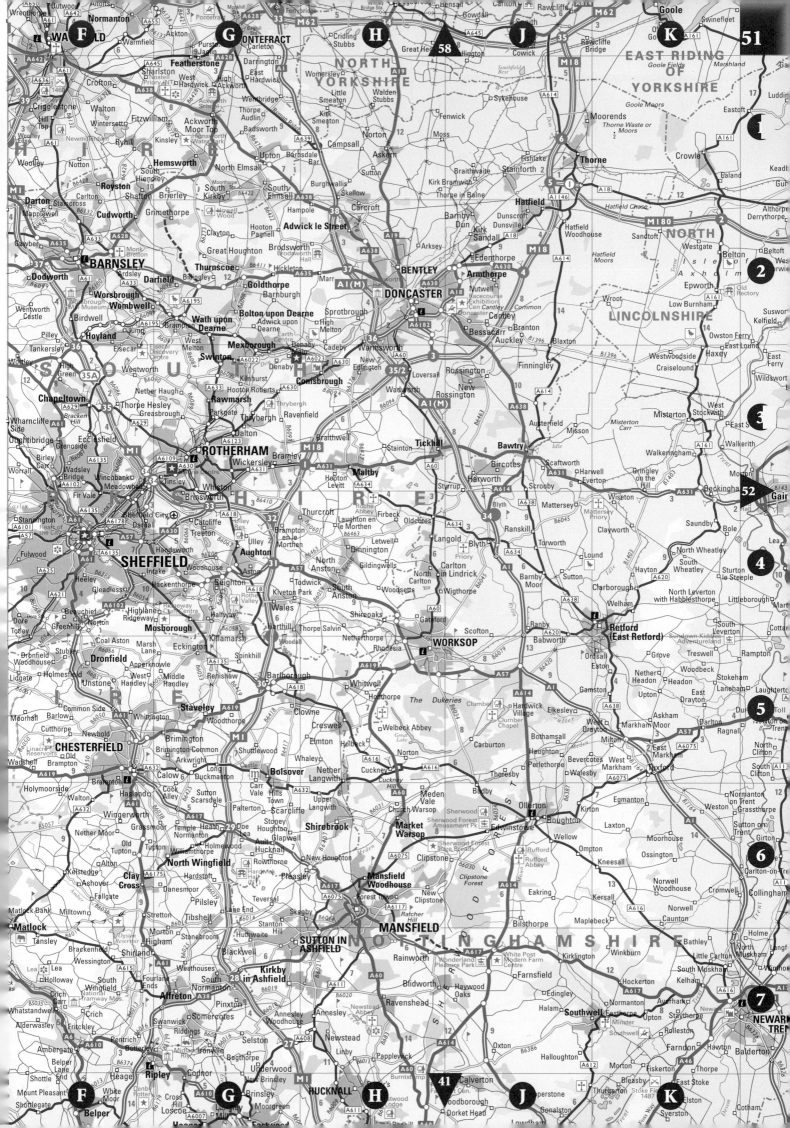

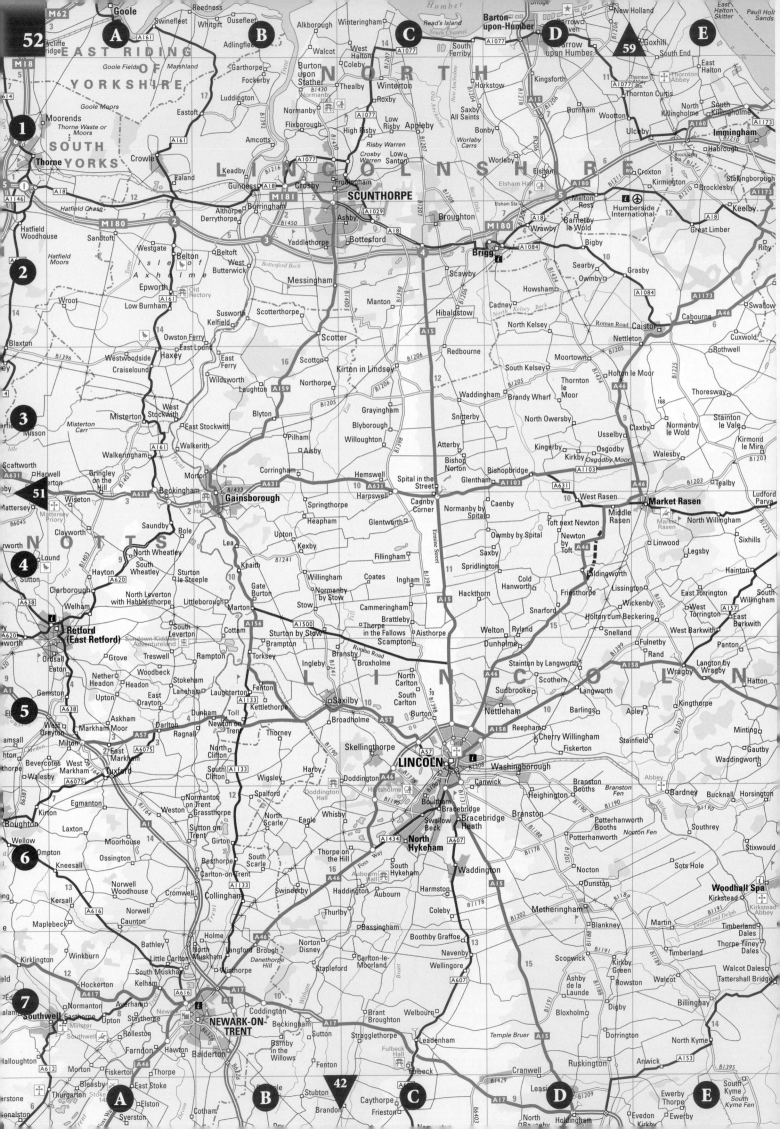

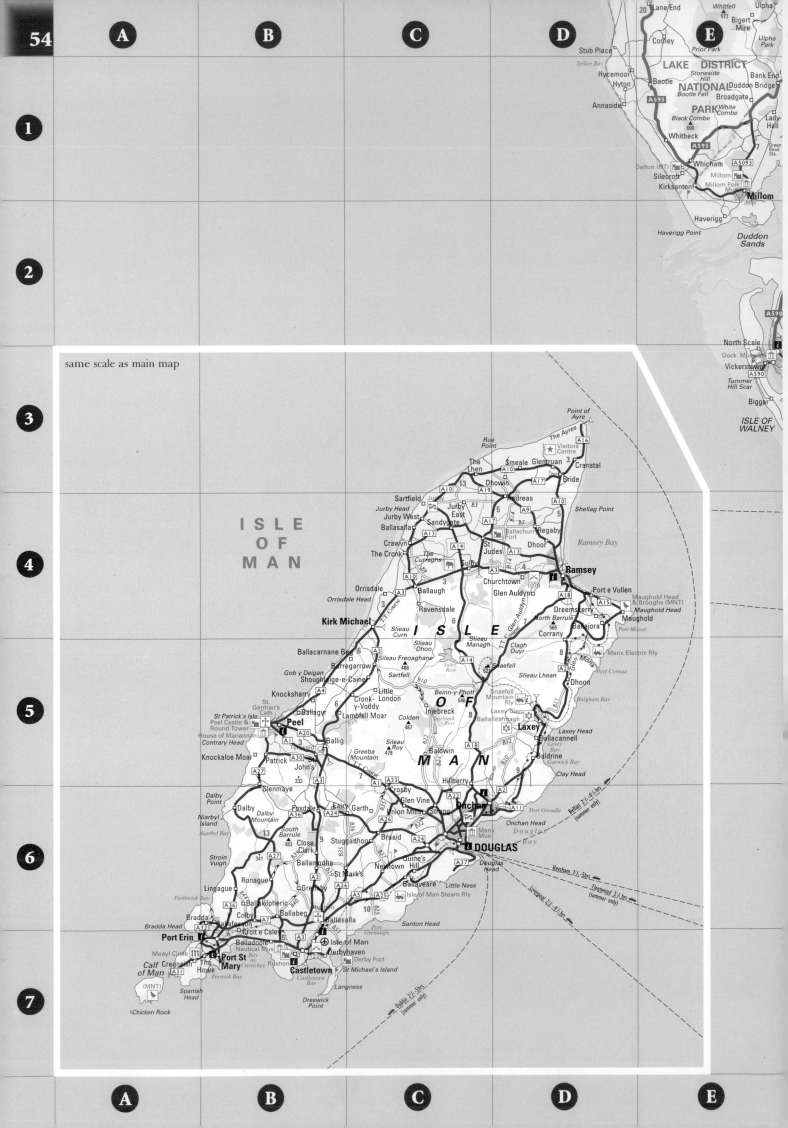

same scale as main map

ISLE
OF
MAN

ISLE OF WALNEY

LAKE DISTRICT NATIONAL PARK

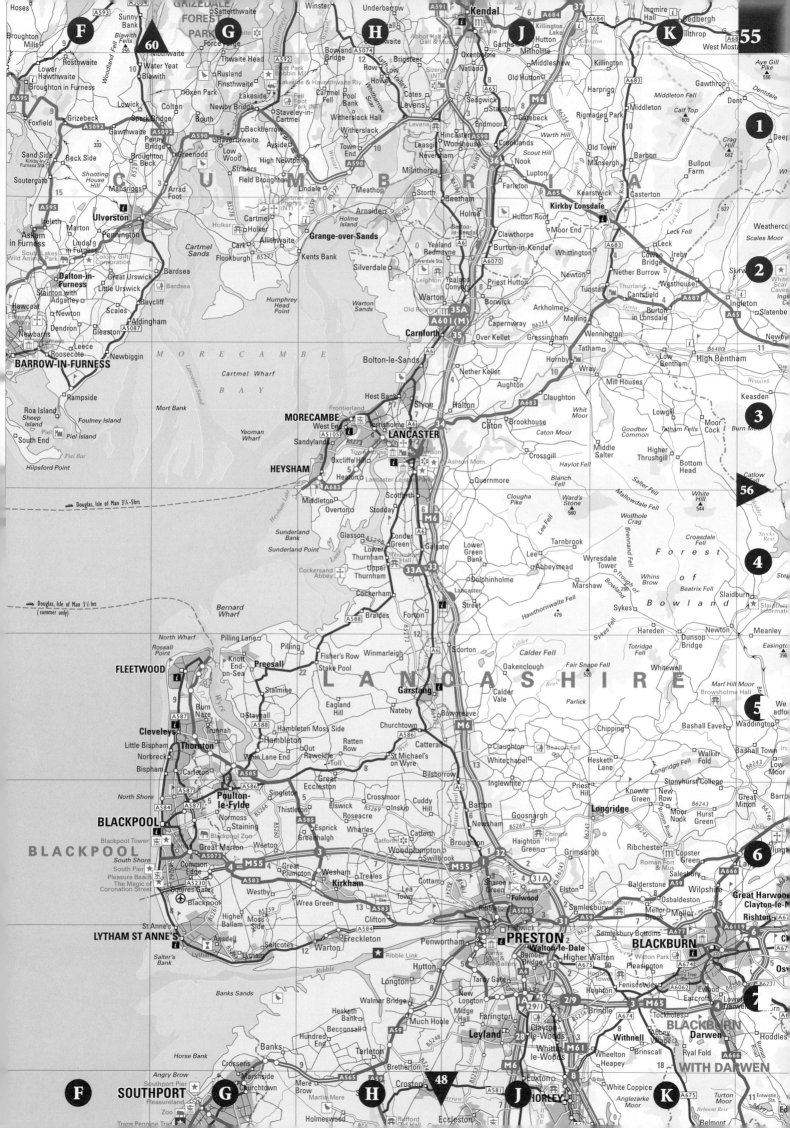

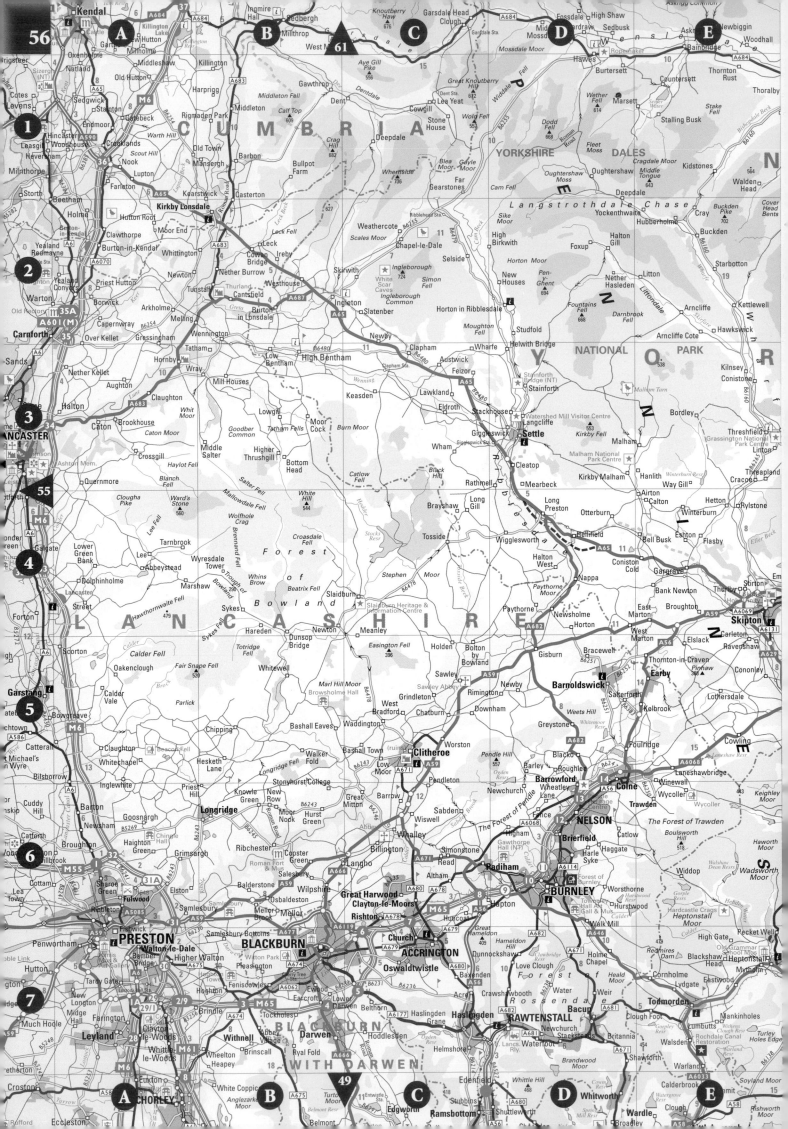

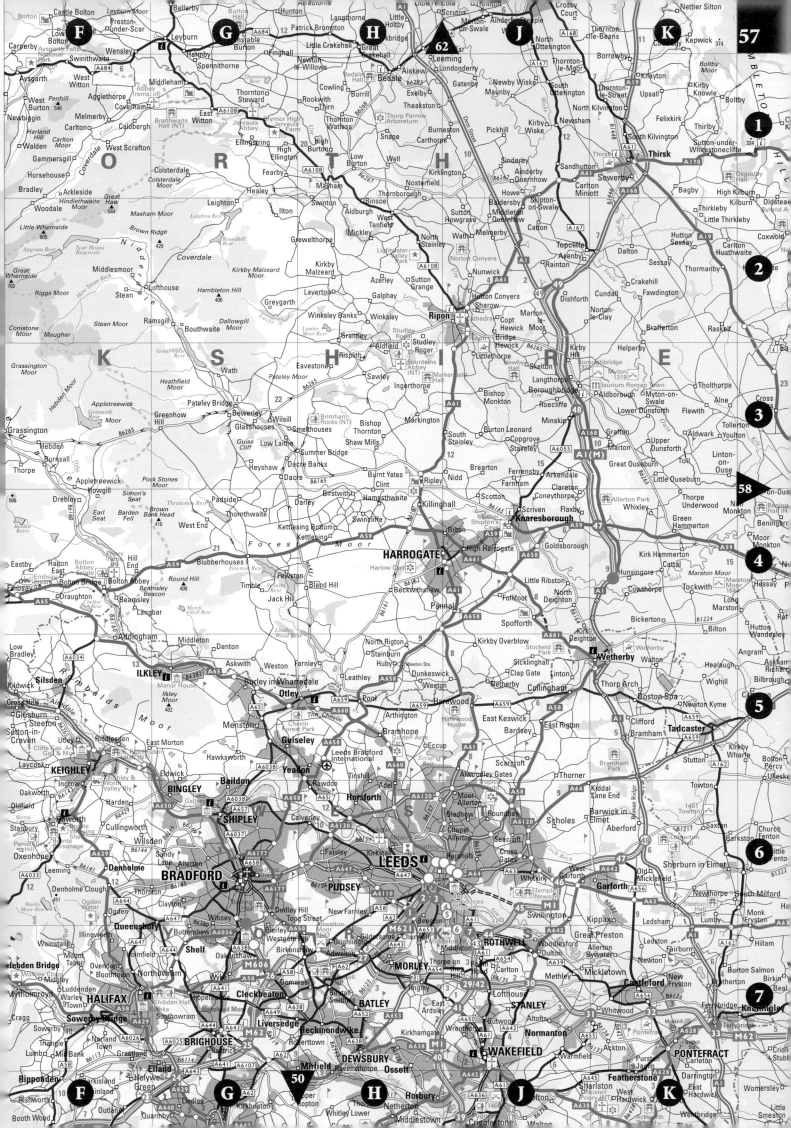

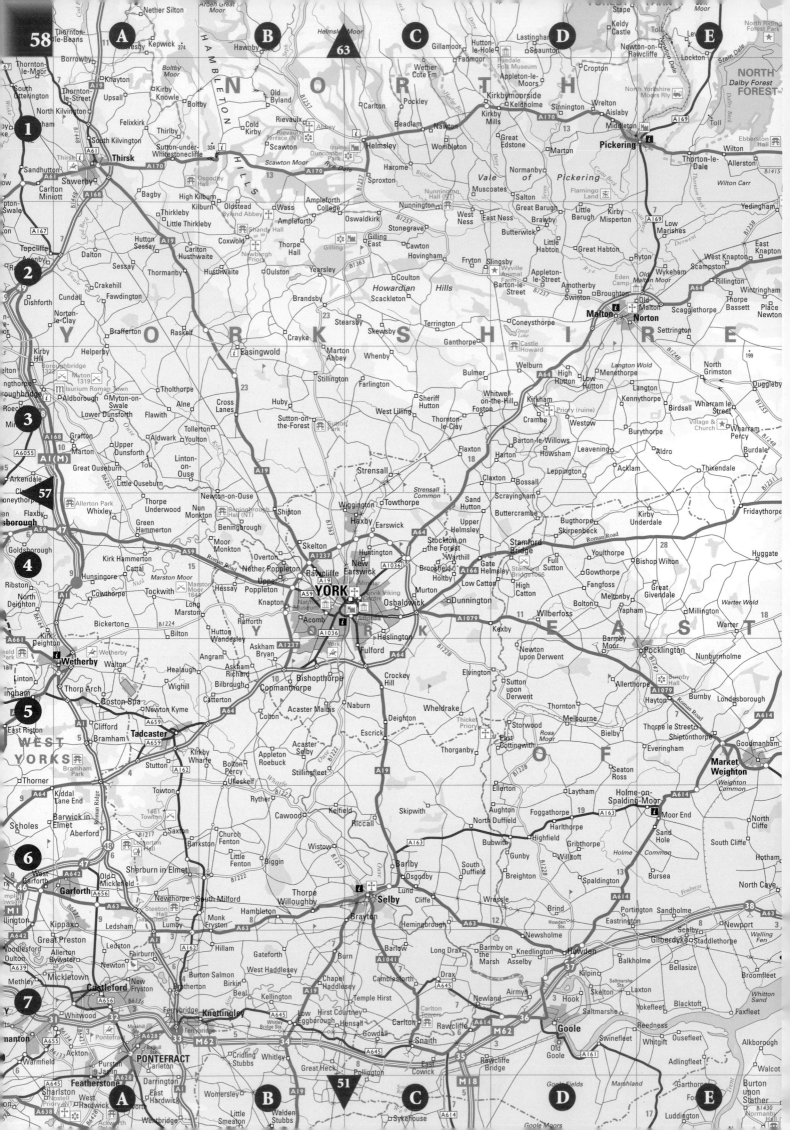

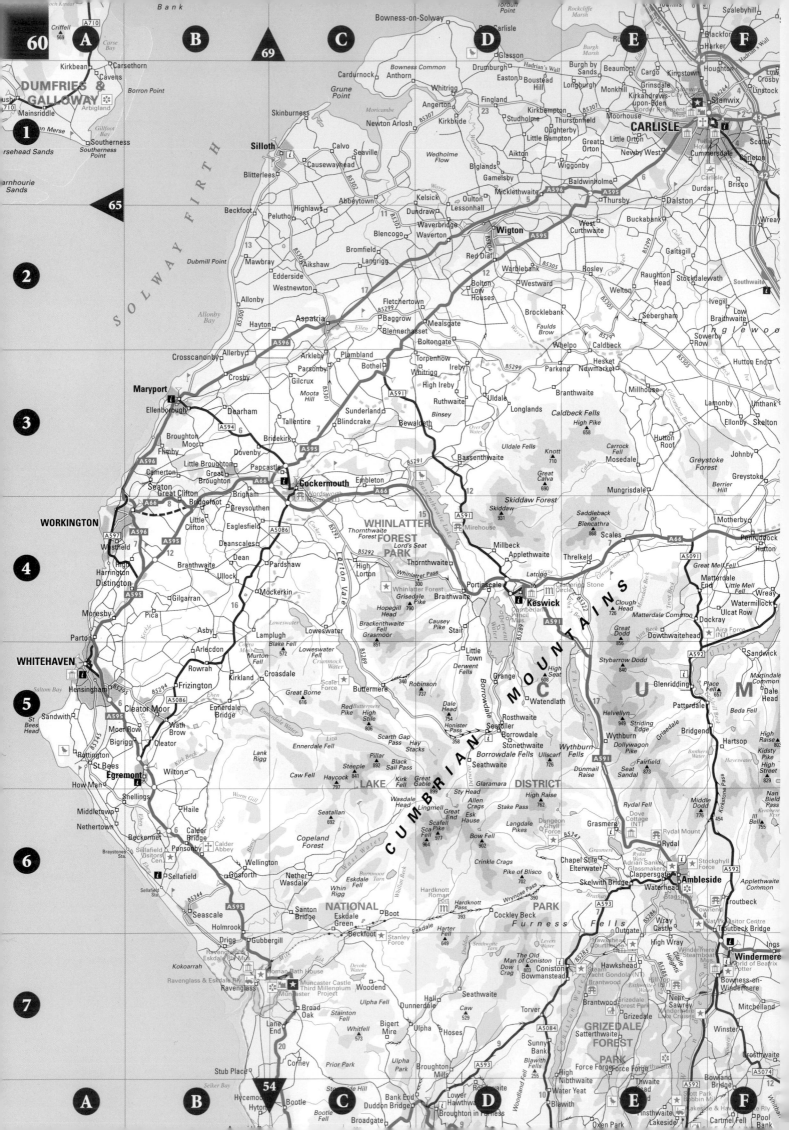

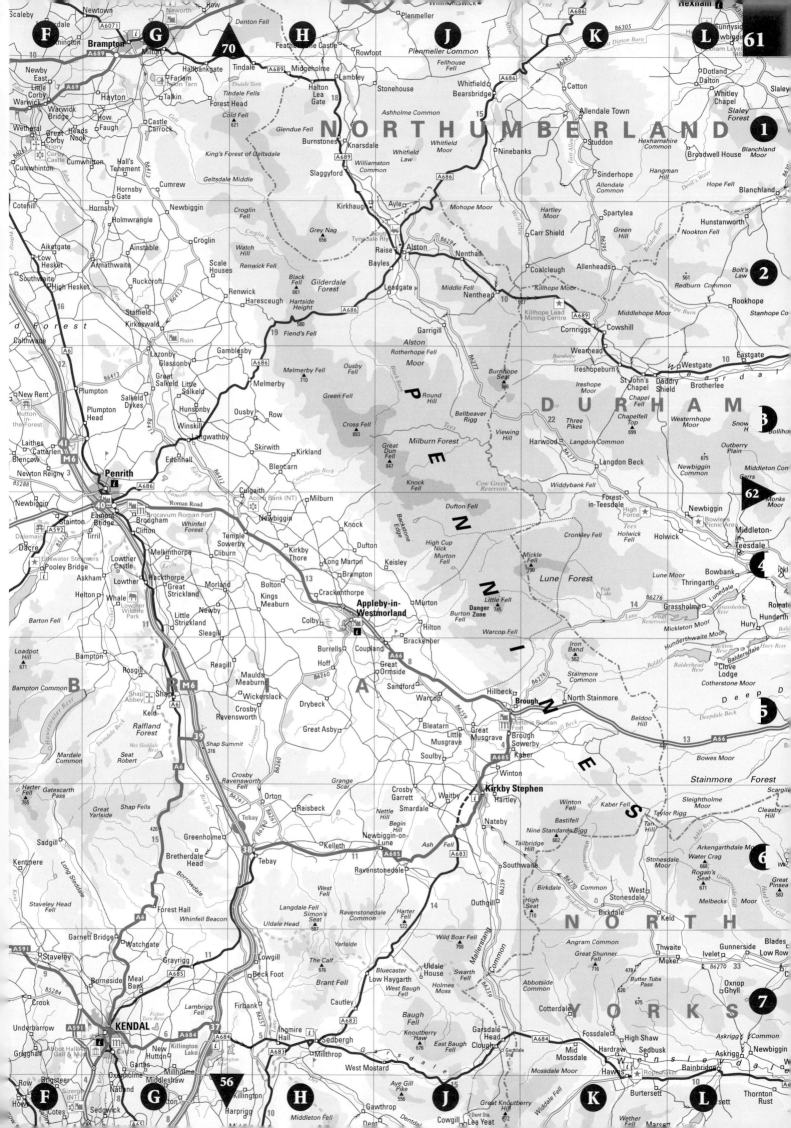

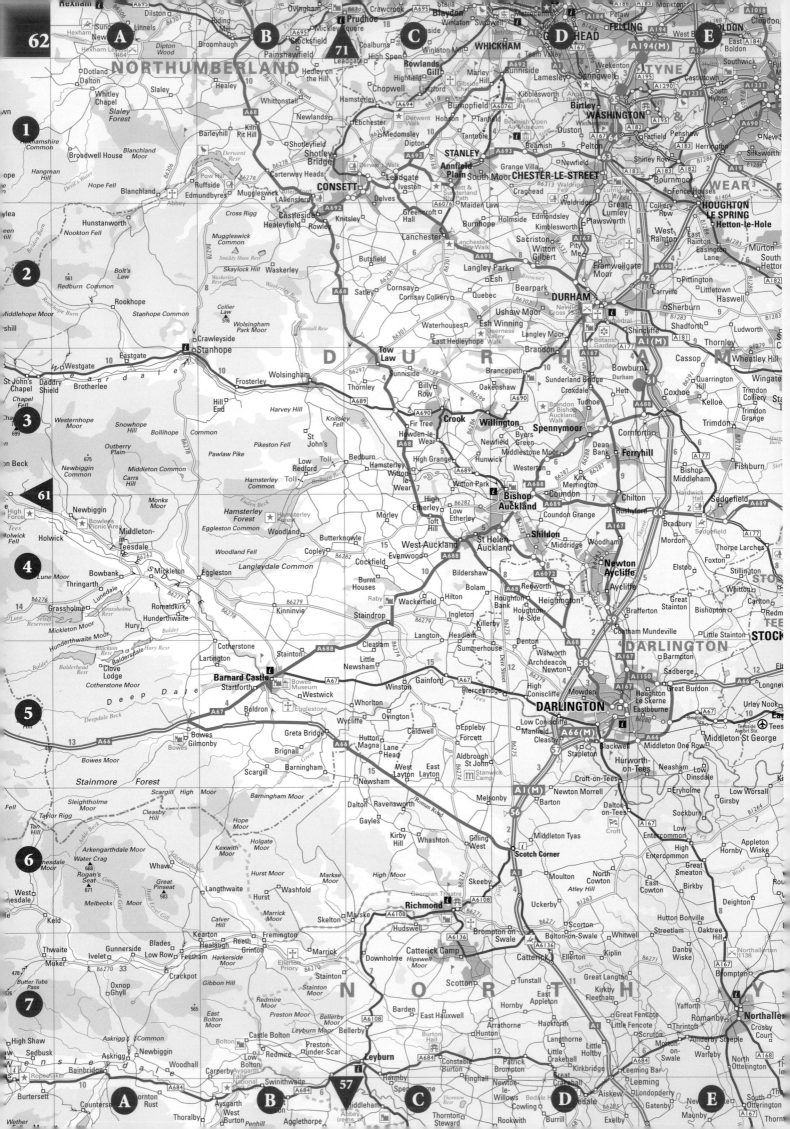

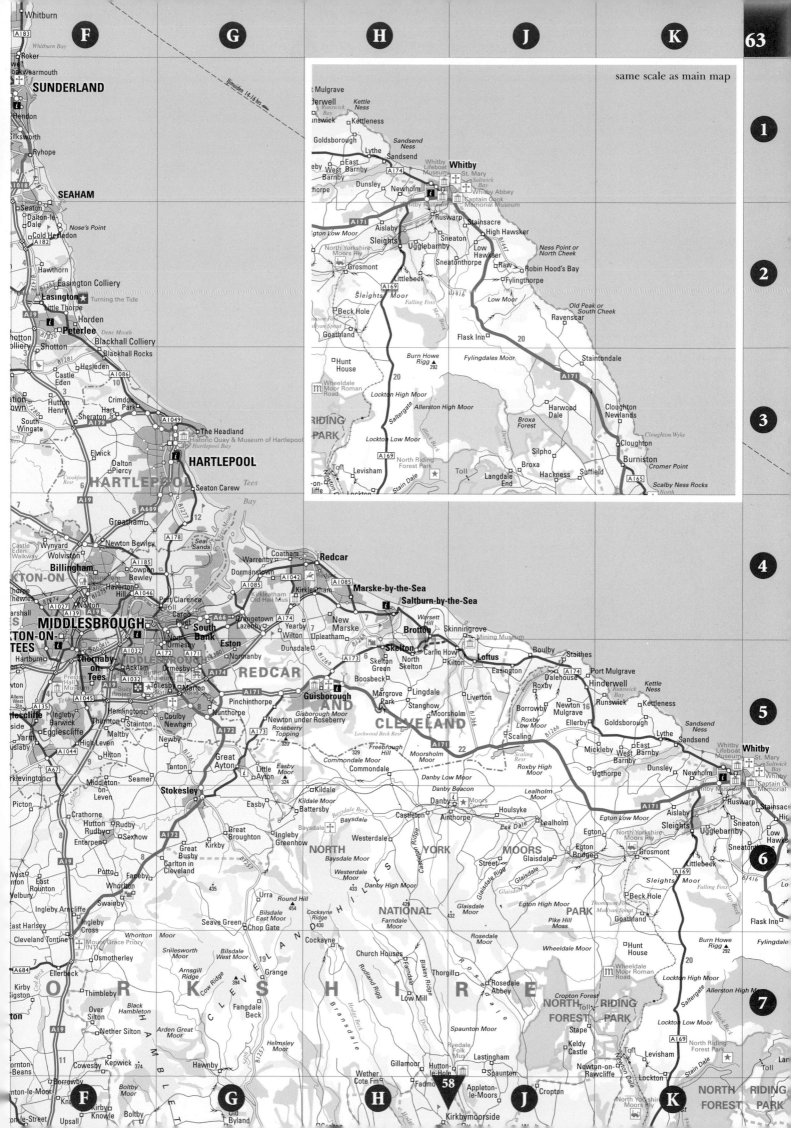

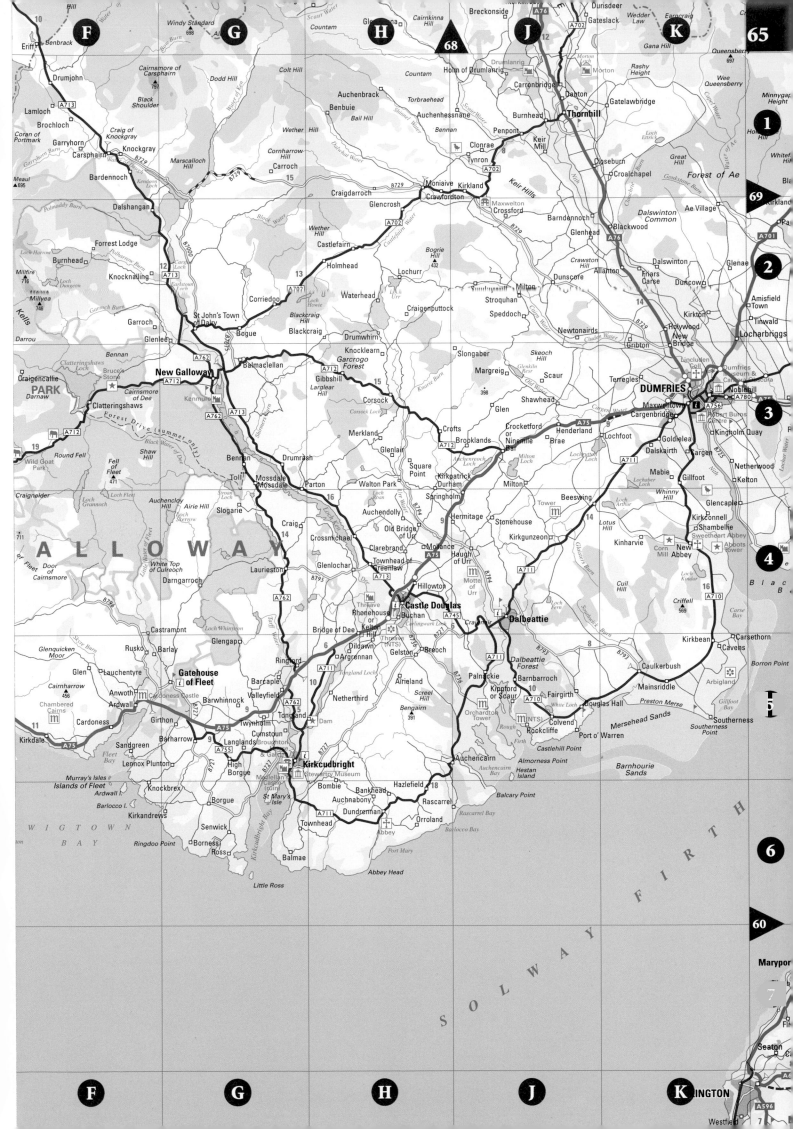

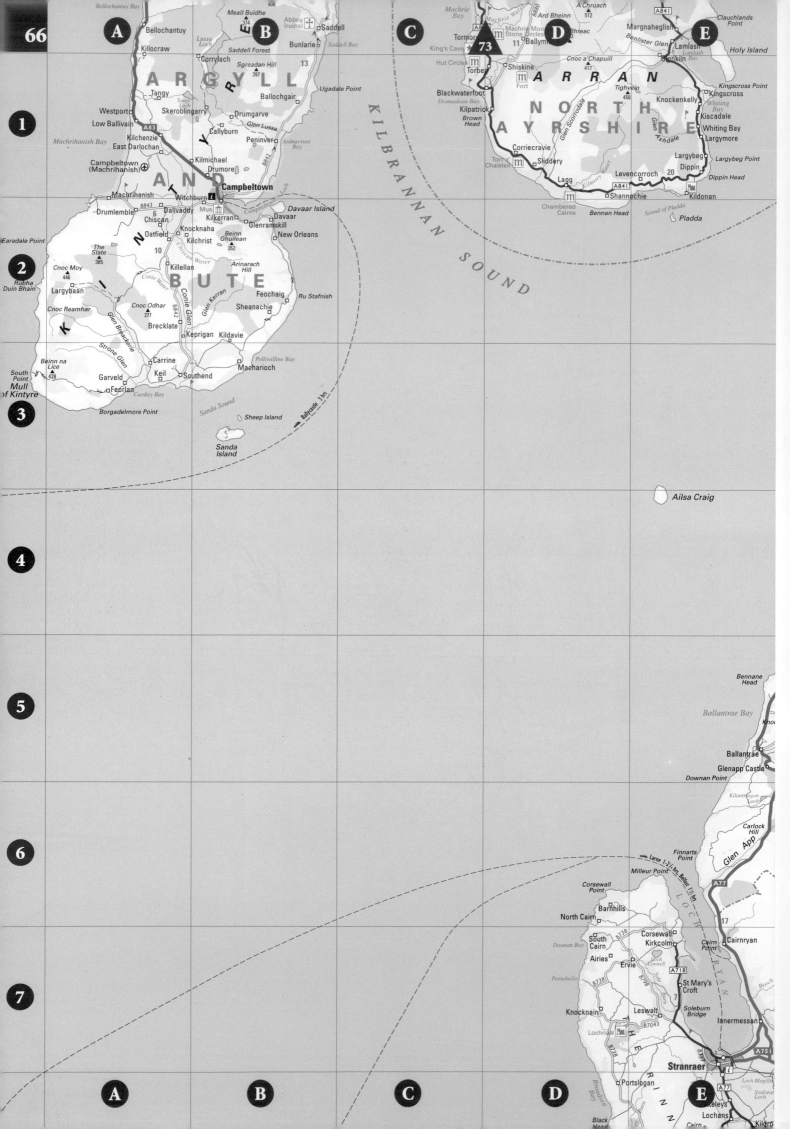

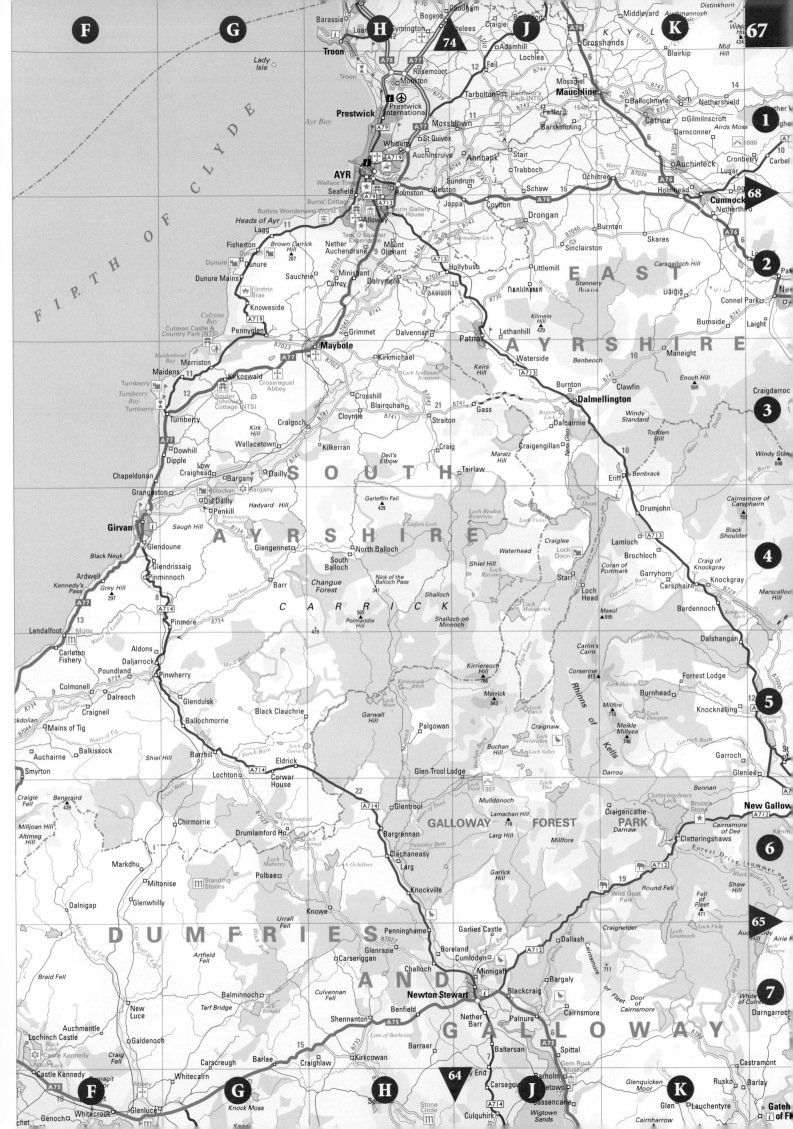

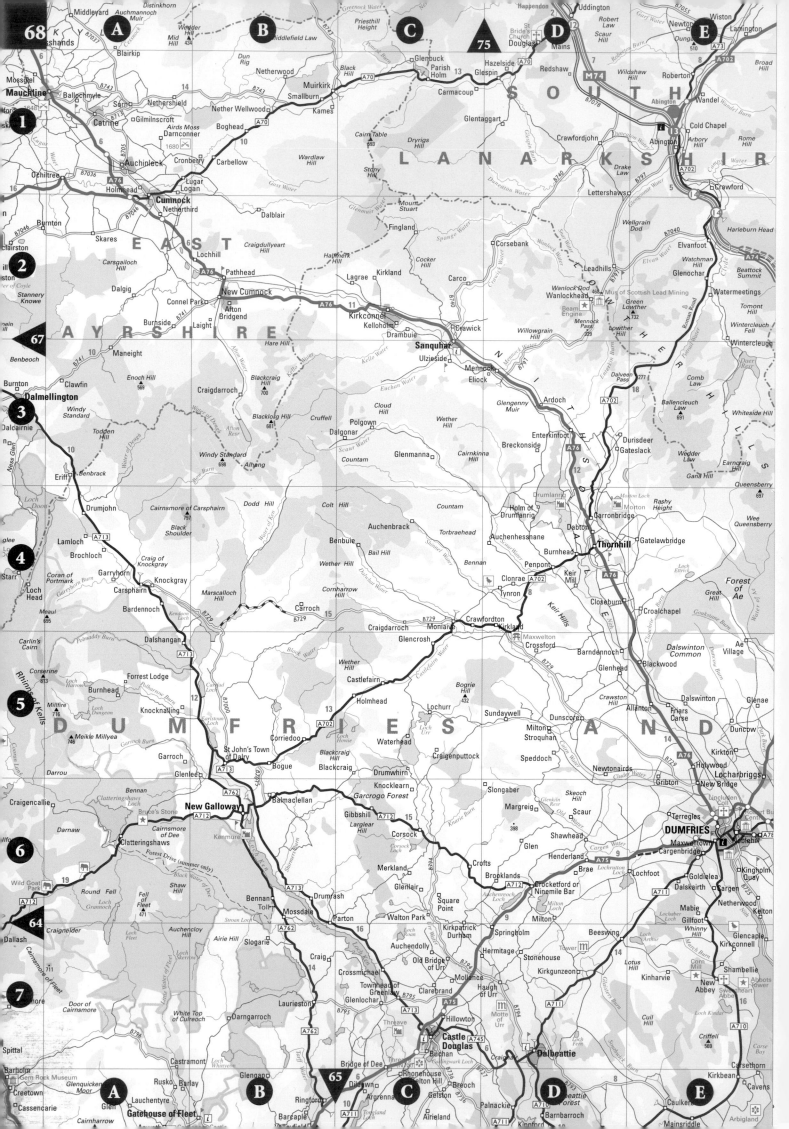

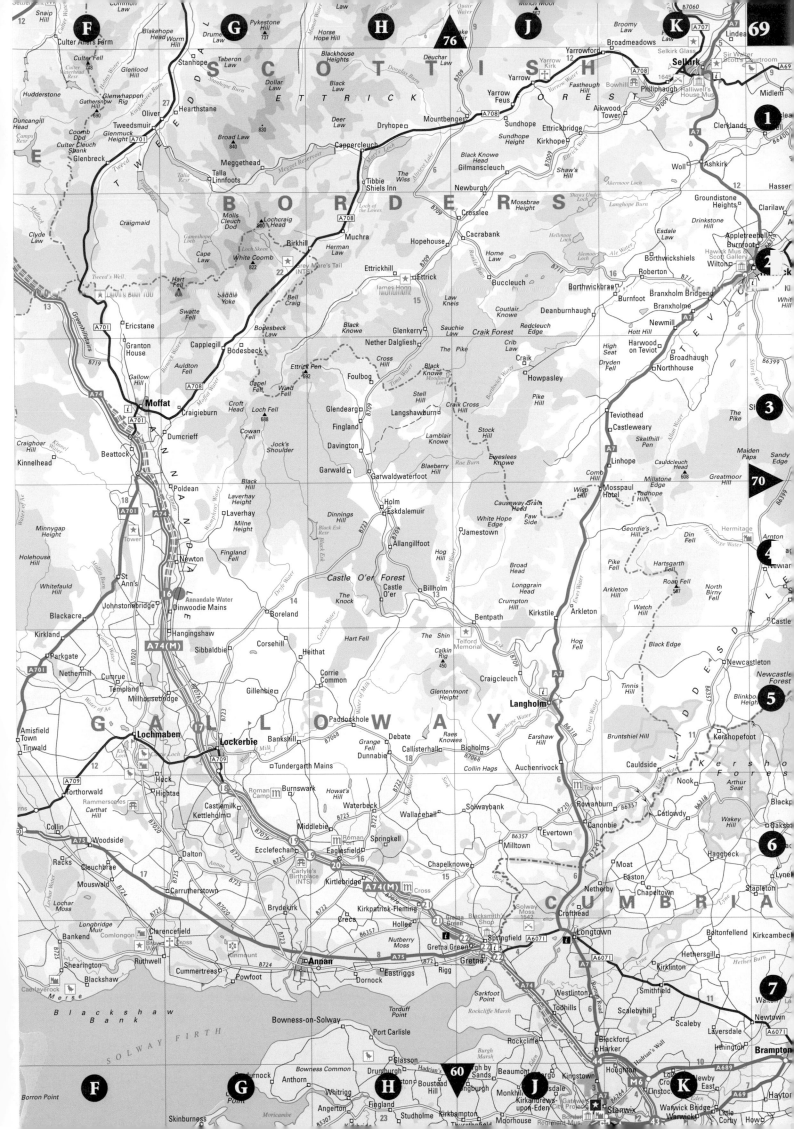

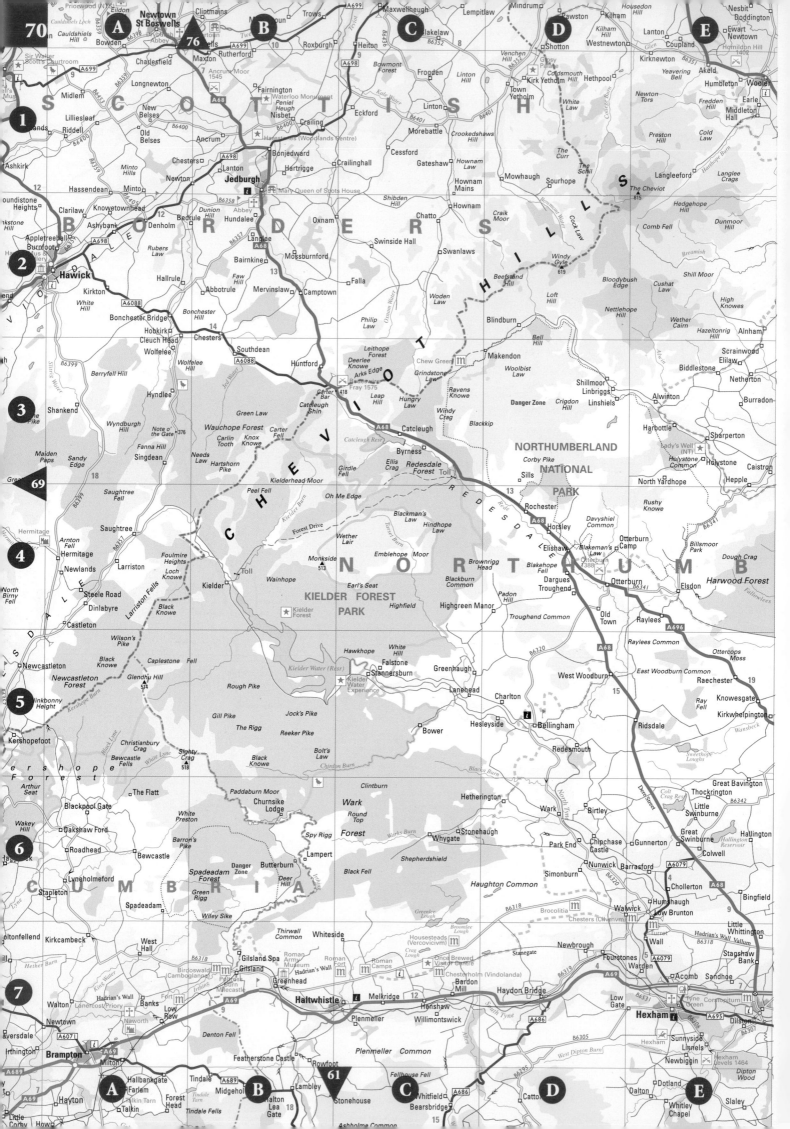

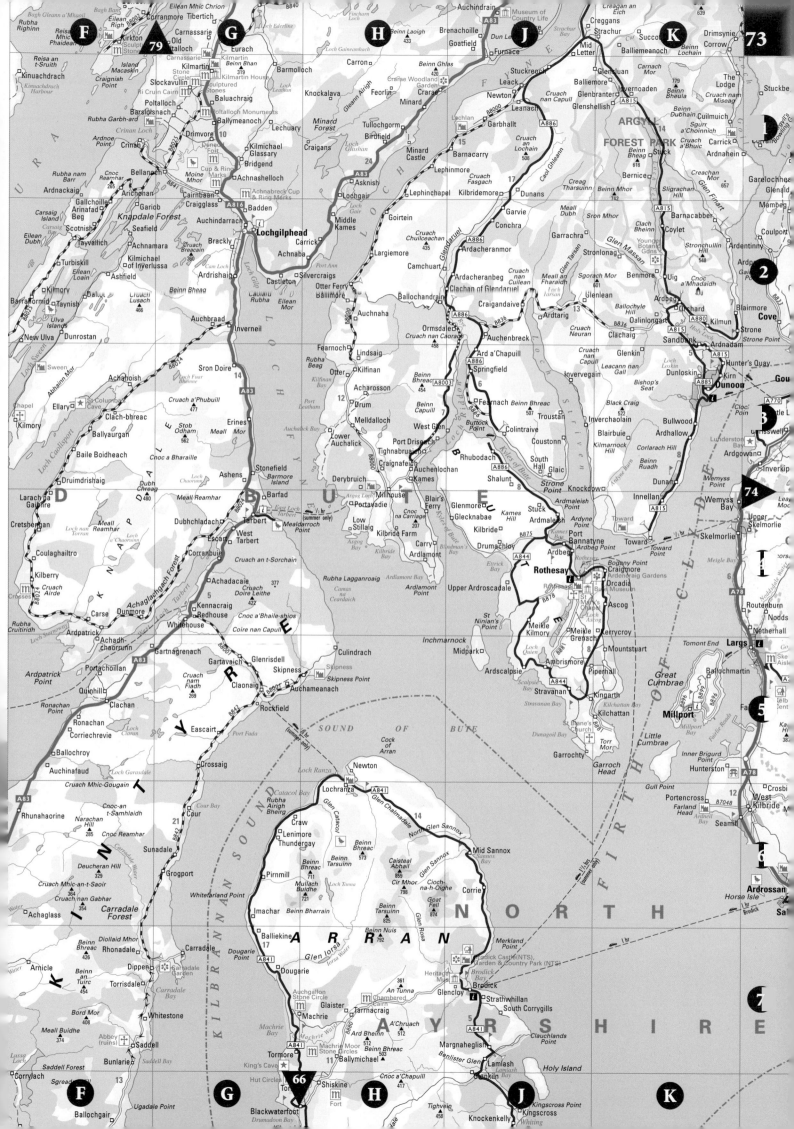

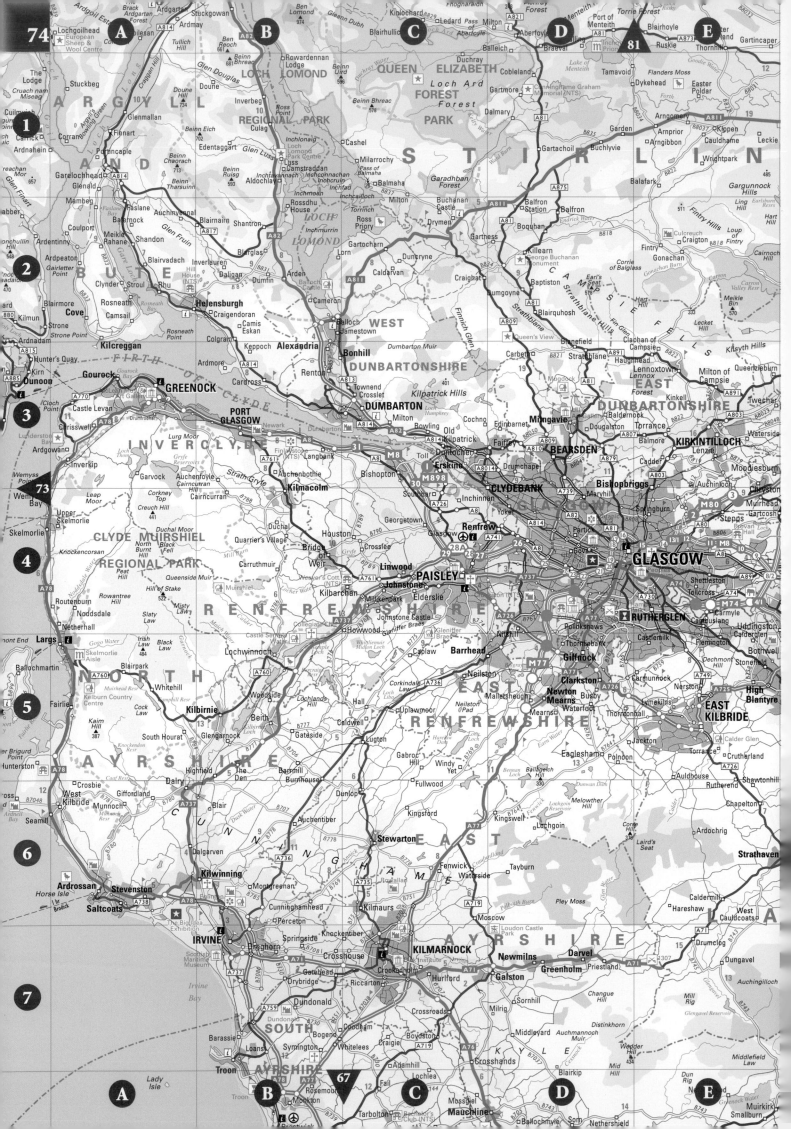

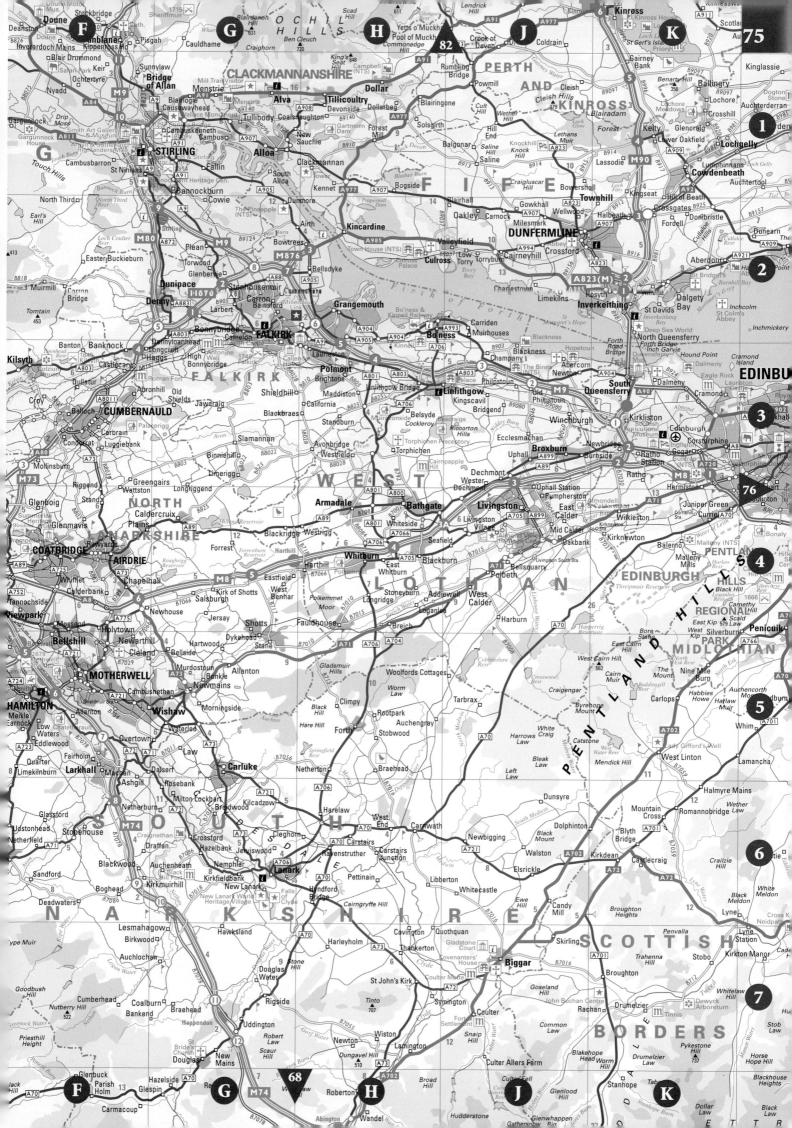

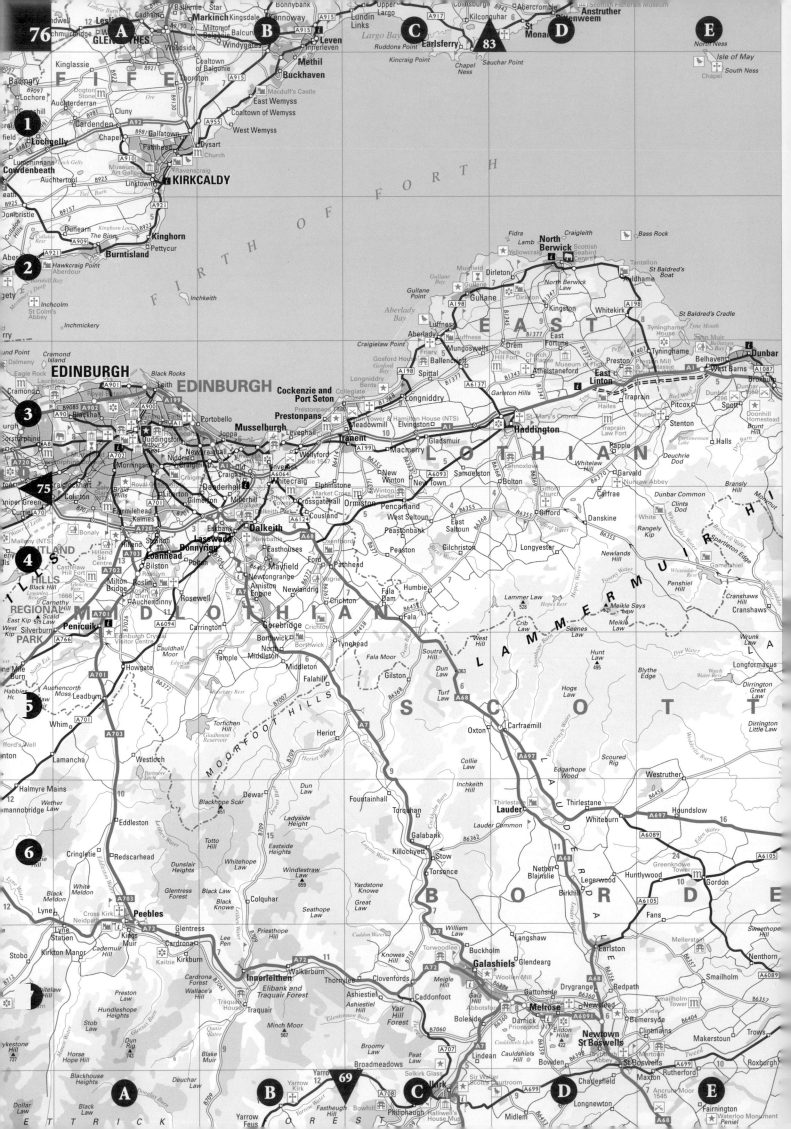

A B C D E

85

SEA OF THE HEBRIDES

1

INNER HEBRIDES

Eag na
Maoile
Eilean
Mor
Rubha
Mor
Bousd
Rubha Sgor-
Innis
Sorisdale
Rubh'
a'Bhinnein
Torastan
Loch
Fada
Bagh
na Coille

Cliad
Bay
Arnabost
Grishipoll Bay
Clabhach
Grishipoll
Ballyhaugh
Ben
Hogh
104
73
Hogh Bay
Totamore
Arinagour
Loch
Etharna

2

2½ hrs–3½ hrs

Caliach
Point
Port
na Ba
Sunipol
Langamull

Totronald
COLL
Arileod
Acha
5
Eilean
Ornsay
Mornish
Cruach
Sleibhe
Fachadil
166

Port Mine
Uig
Gorton

Calgary
Point
Crossapol
Friesland
Bay
Loch
Breachacha
Rubha
Fasachd

Calgary

Gunna
Crossapool
Bay
Rubha
nan Oirean

Urvaig
Port a'Mhurain
Soa

1 hr

Treshnish
Point
Treshnish
Ensay

Sgeir
Bharrach
Miodar
Rubha Dubh

Treshnish
Isles
Beinn
Duill
191
Cruachan
Odhar
256

The Green
Balephetrish
Bay
Vaul
Caolas
Port Ban

3

Balephetrish
Hill
Brock
Ruaig
Rubha
Liath
Soa
Rubh'
a'Chaoil
Rubh' an
t-Suibhein
Port
Burg
Tostarie

Hough
Bay
TIREE
Tiree
Scarinish
Gott
Bay
Loch Tuath

Kilkenneth
Crossapoll
Baugh
Heanish
Cairn na Burgh More
Cairn na
Burgh Beg
Rubha
Chulinish

Moss
Cairn na Burgh More
Fladda
Eilean
Dioghlum
Gometra
Ho.

Saundaig
Heylipoll
Sgeir a
Chaisteil
Gometra
Beinn
Eolasary

Barrapoll
Hynish Bay
Lunga
Rubha
Maol na Mine
Maisgeir

Balemartine
Treshnish Isles

Mannel
Balephuil
Skerryvore
Museum
Bac Mor or
Dutchman's Cap
Little
Colonsay

Rinn Thorbhais
Hynish
Bac Beag

Staffa
Eilean Dubh

4

Fingal's
Cave
Staffa
(NTS)

A
Erisgeir

Aird na h
Iolaire

Reidh
Eilean
Eilean Chalbha
Rubha
nan
Cearc

5

Port
an
Duine Mhairbh
Dun I
Iona
Abbey
Maclean's
Cross
Kintra
Beinn Chladan

Stac
an
Aoineidh
Ruanaich
Iona (NTS)
Aridhglas
A849
Eorabus
Ardtun

Iona
Fionnphort
Bunessan

Rubha
na
Carraig-geire
Fidden
Ross of Mull

Soa Island
Knockvologan
Ardalanish
Uisken

Erraid
Torr Fada

Eilean
Dubh
Aird Mor
Ardchiavaig
Port Mor

Eilean
a'Chalmain
Eilean
Mor
Rubh' Ardalanish

Torran Rocks
Dearg
Sgeir

6

Na Torrain
Ruadh Sgeir

West
Reef
McPhail's Anvil
Torran
Sgoilte

Sgeir
Ghobhlach

Otter Rock

7

A B C D E

Kiloran
Bay
Kiloran
Kiloran Gardens
Loch an Sgoltaire
COLONSAY

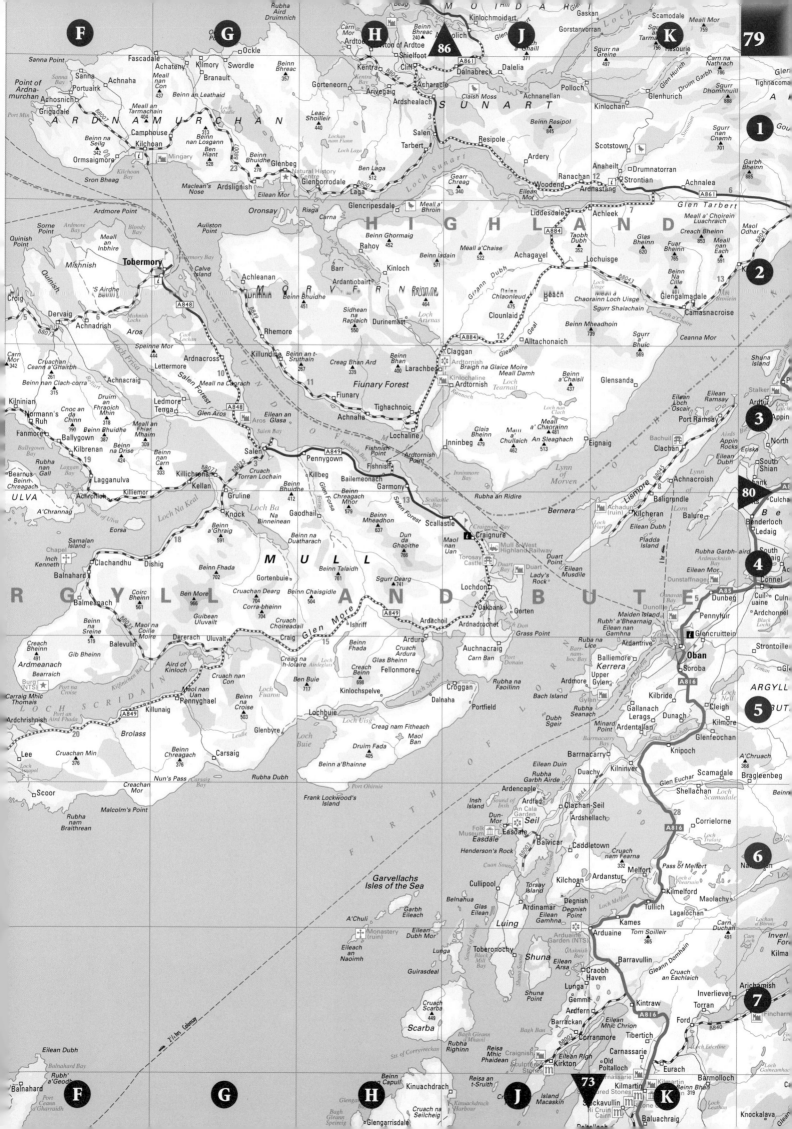

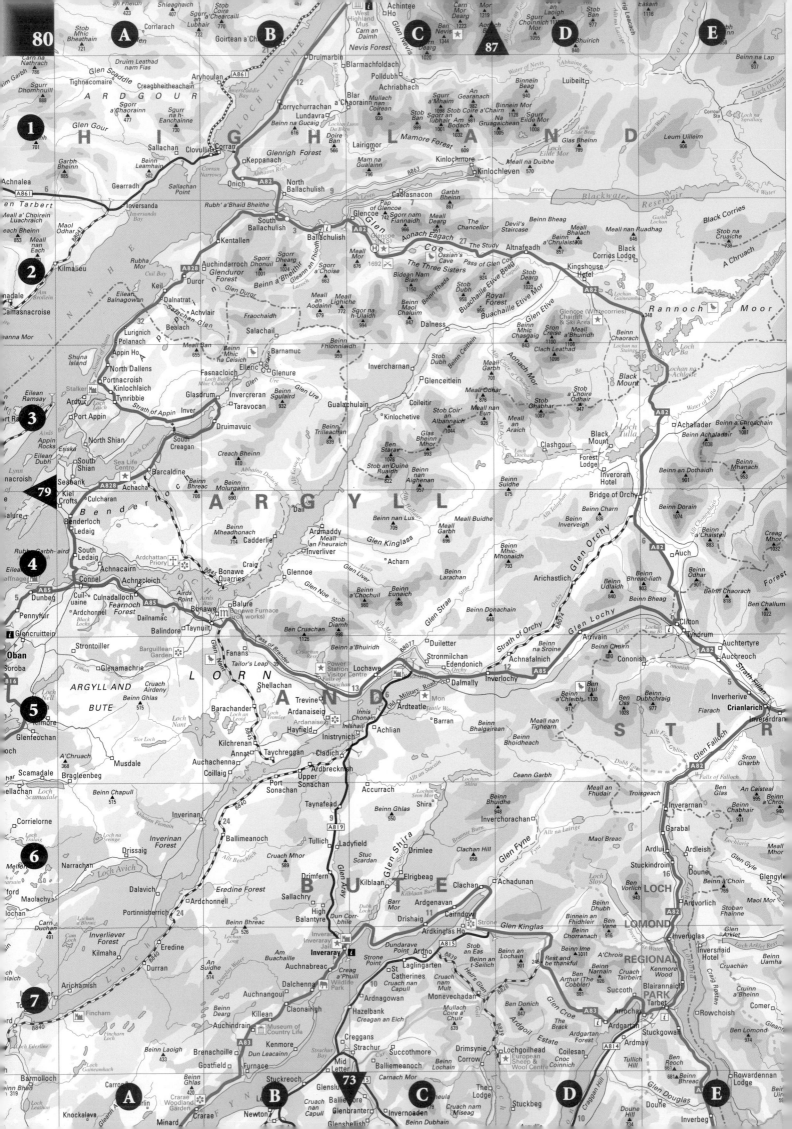

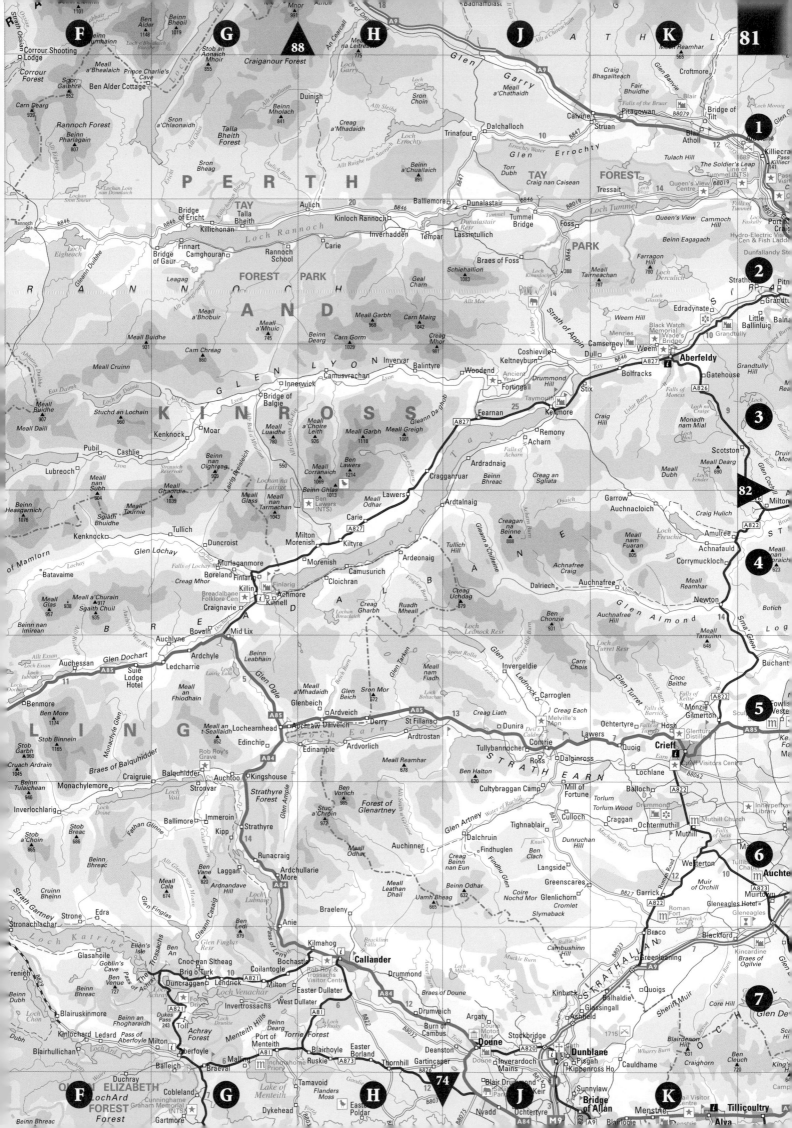

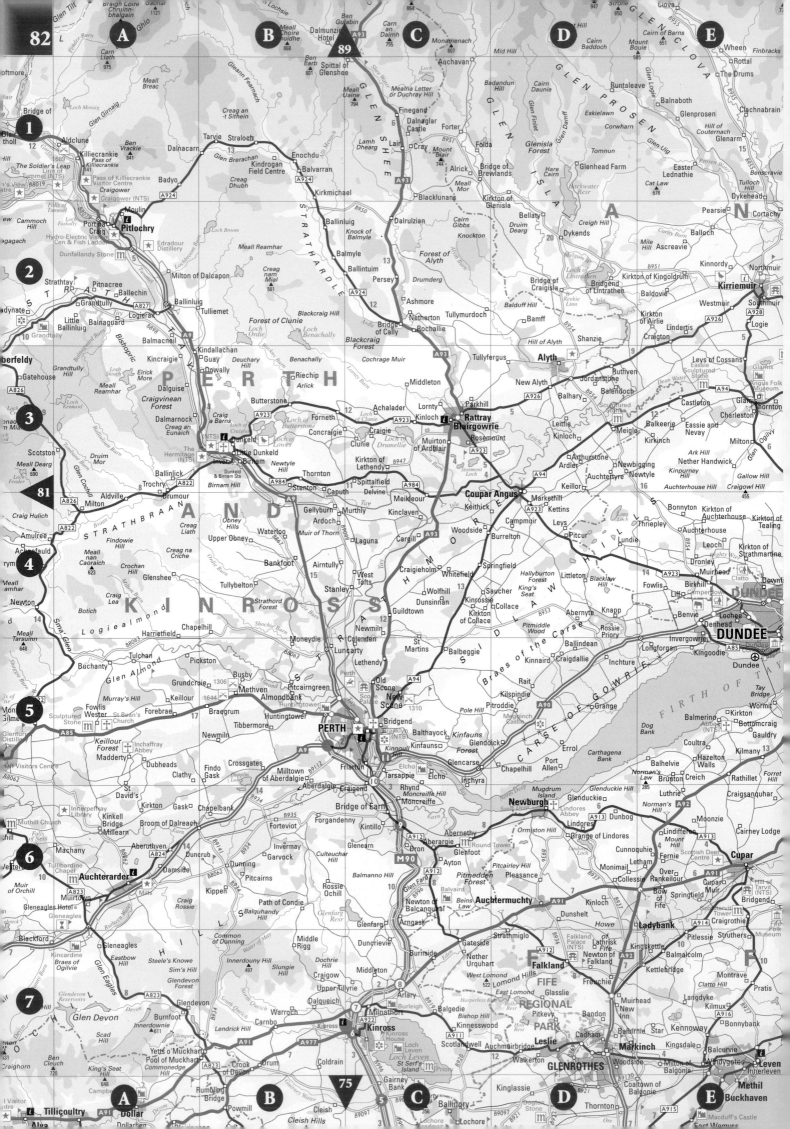

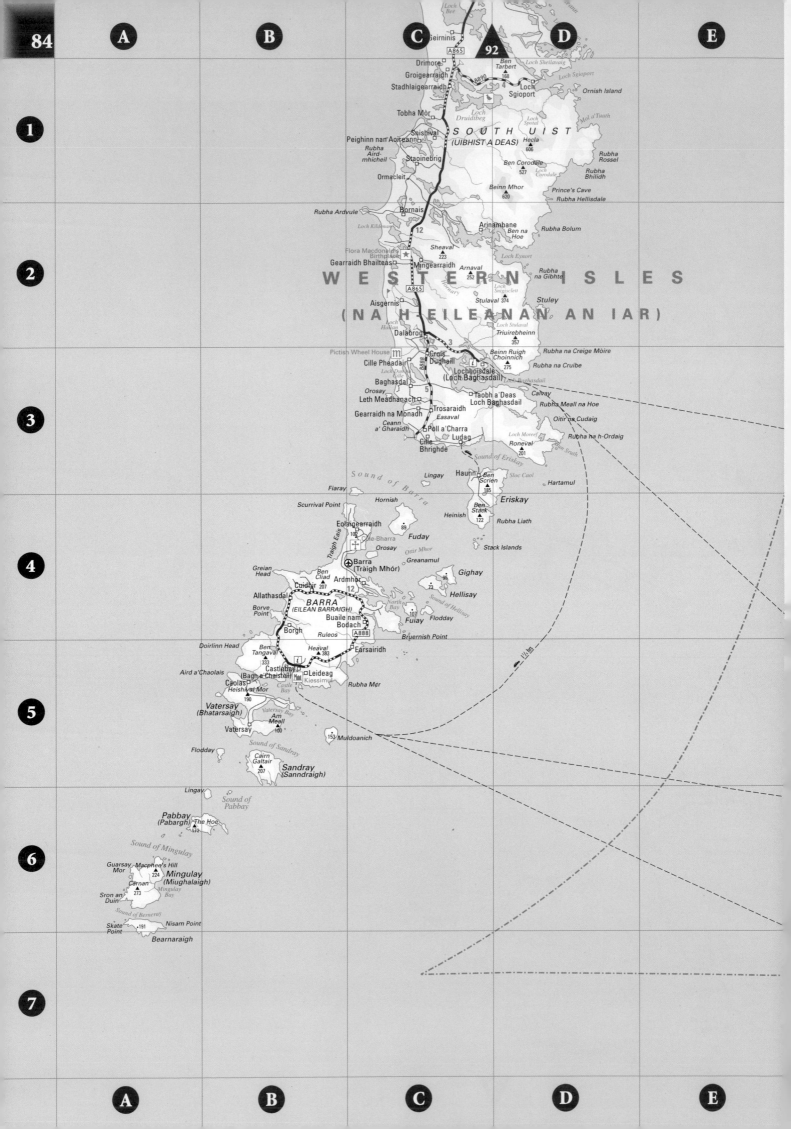

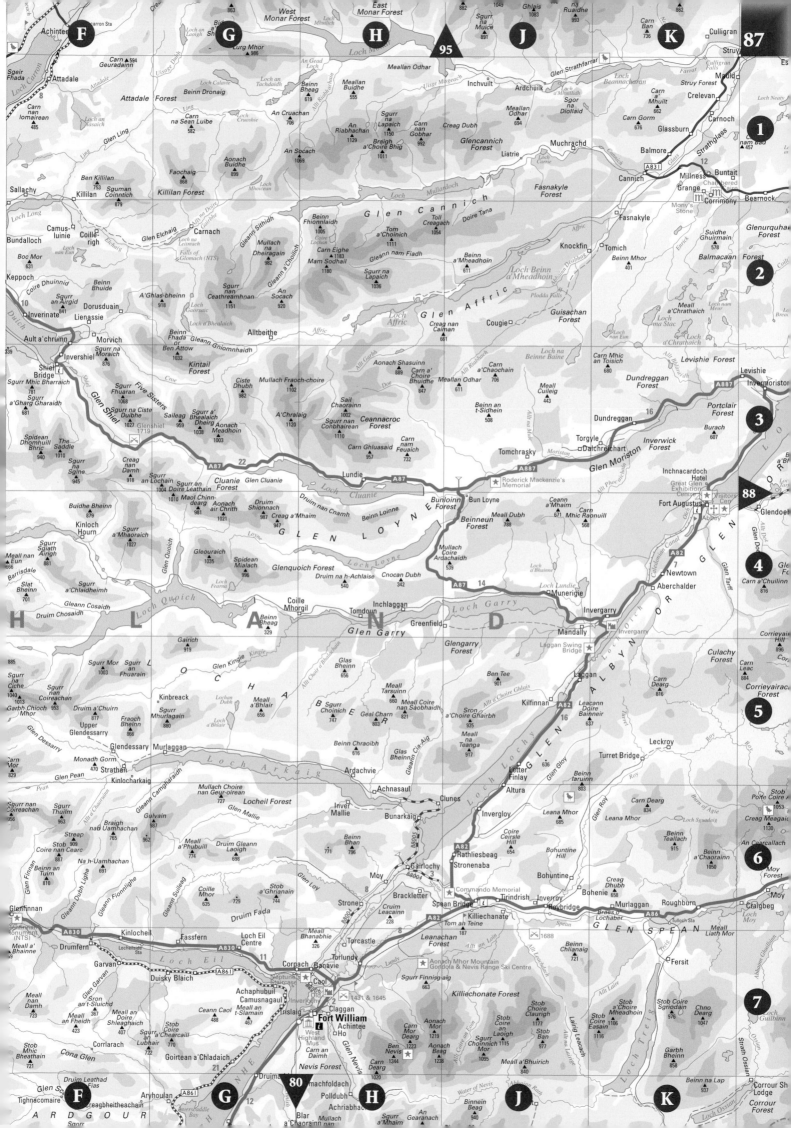

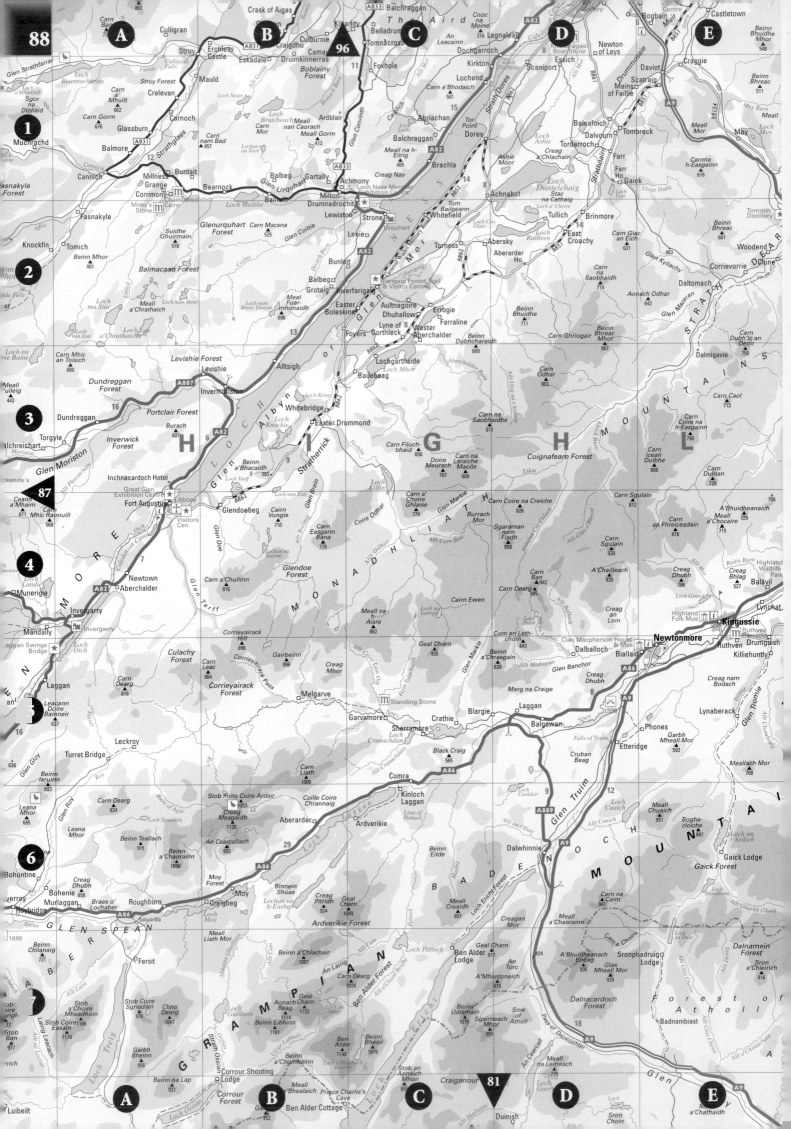

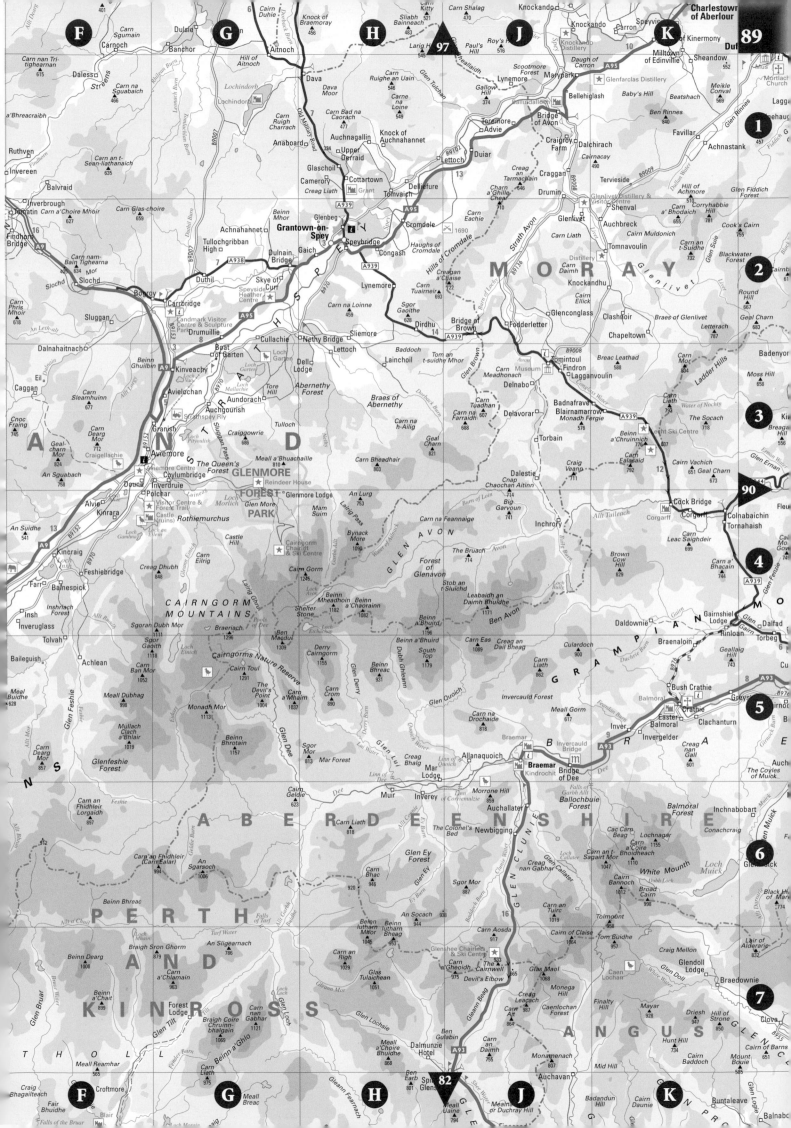

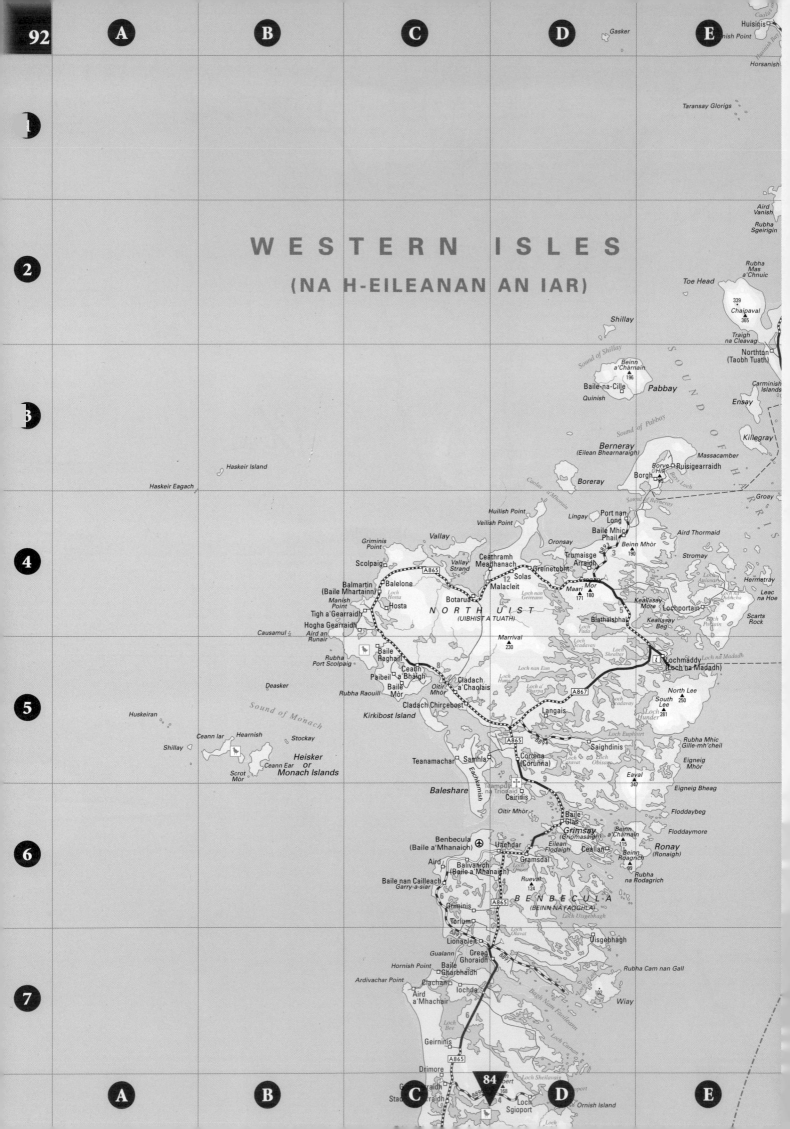

WESTERN ISLES
(NA H-EILEANAN AN IAR)

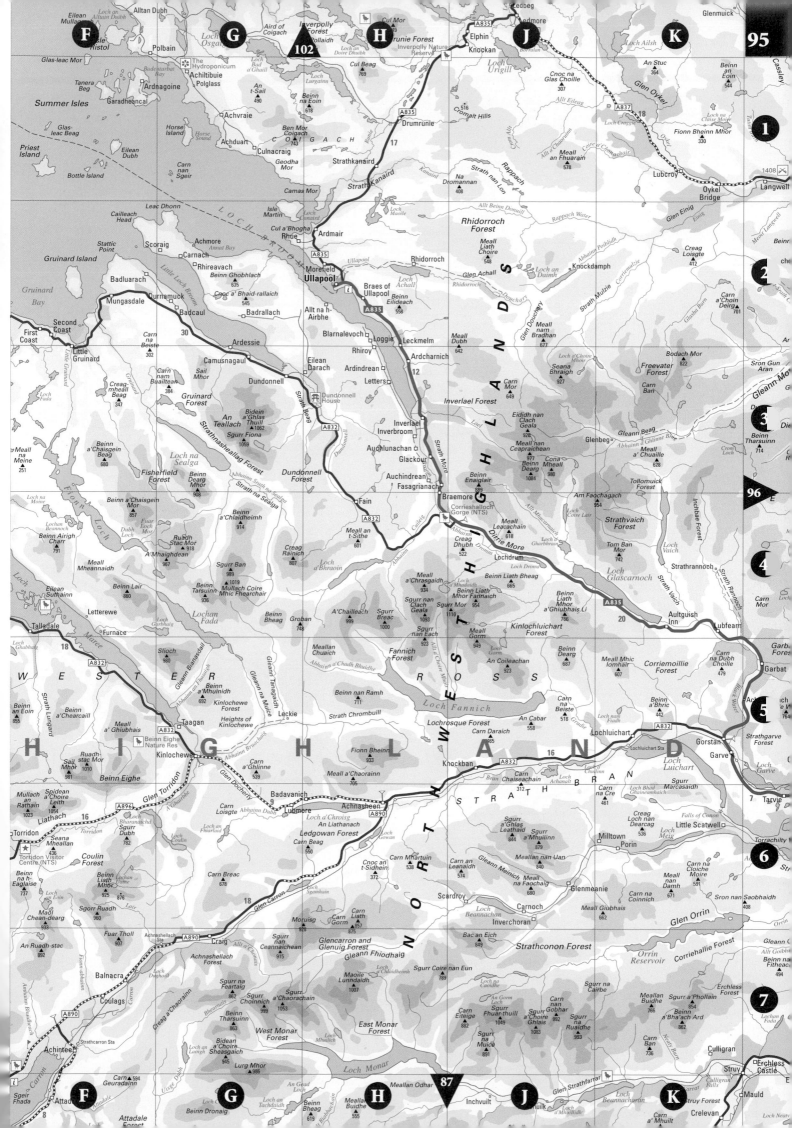

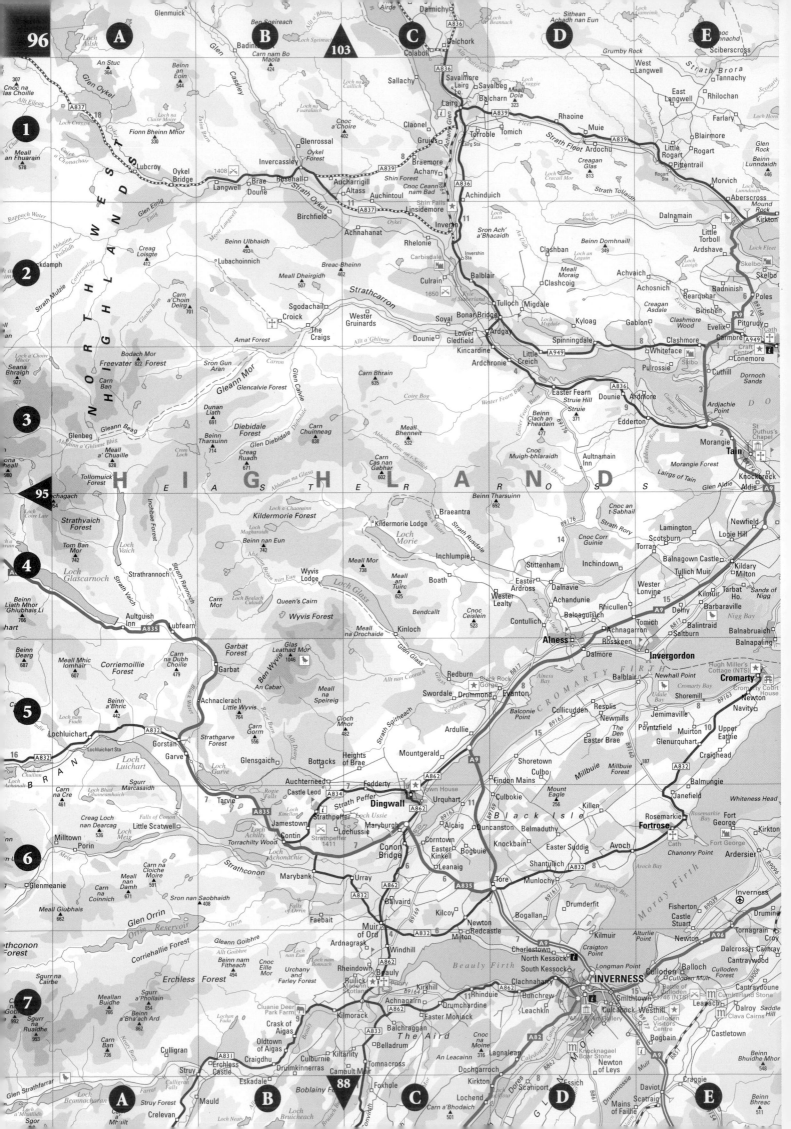

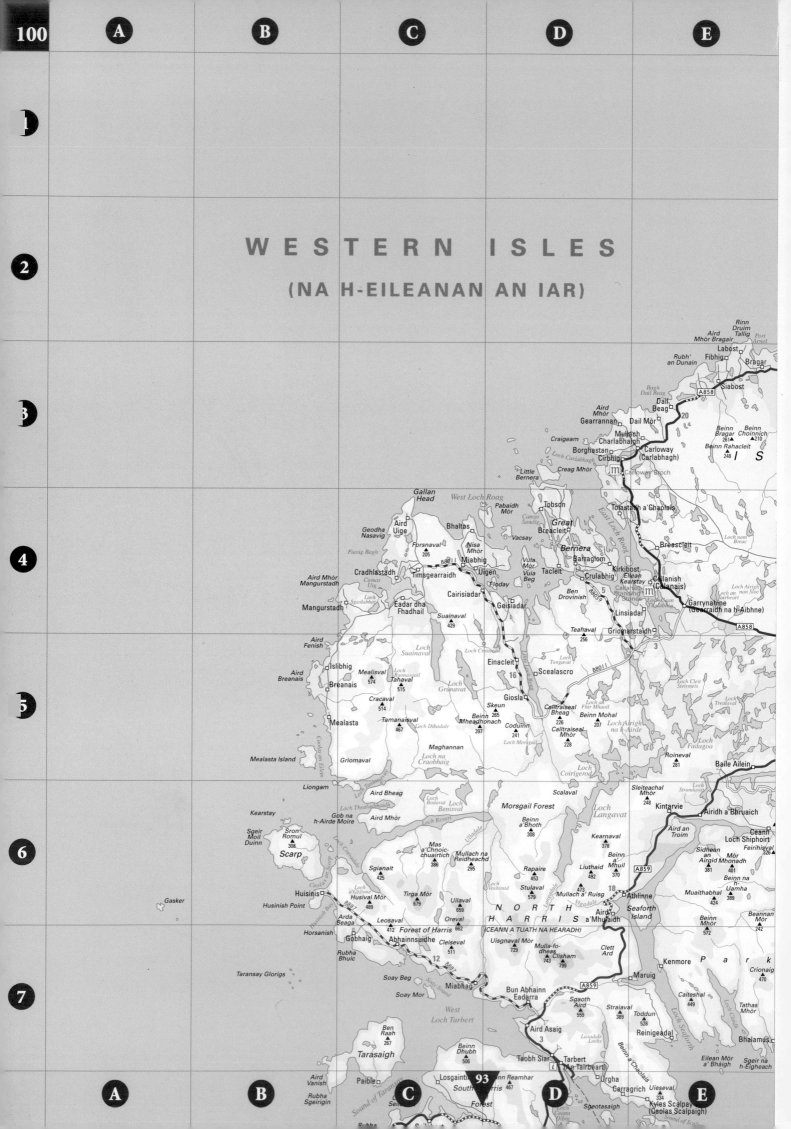

A   B   C   D   E

WESTERN ISLES
(NA H-EILEANAN AN IAR)

Rinn
Druim
Tallig
Port
Arnol
Aird
Mhòr Bragair
Labost
Rubh'
an Dunain
Fibhig
Bragar
Bàgh
Dail Beag
A858
Siabost
Aird
Mhòr
Gearrannan
Dail
Beag
20
Craigeam
Dail Mòr
Mullach
Charlabhaigh
Beinn
Bragar
261
Beinn
Choinnich
210
Borghastan
Carloway
(Carlabhagh)
Beinn Rahacleit
248
IS
Loch Carlabhagh
Cirbhig
Creag Mhòr
m
Little
Bernera
Carloway Broch

Gallan
Head
West Loch Roag
Pabaidh
Mòr
Tolastadh a'Chaolais
Aird
Uige
Bhaltos
Tobson
Great
Breacleit
Camas
Sandig
Breascleit
Loch nam
Breac
Geodha
Nasavig
Forsnaval
205
Nisa
Mhòr
Vacsay
Bernera
Fiavig Bagh
B8011
Miabhig
Vuia
Mòr
Barraglom
Kirkibost
Callanish
(Calanais)
Cradhlastadh
Timsgearraidh
Uigen
Vuia
Beg
Taclet
Crulabhig
Ellean
Kearstay
Aird Mhòr
Mangurstadh
Camas
Uig
Floday
Cairisiadar
Callanish
Standing
Stones
Loch an
Tairbeart
Loch
Sgaslabhal
Eadar dha
Fhadhail
Ben
Drovinish
m
Loch Ceann
T'Hulabhig
Garrynahine
(Gearraidh na h'Aibhne)
Mangurstadh
Geisiadar
Linsiadar
A858
Aird
Fenish
Suainaval
429
Teahaval
256
Griomarstaidh
B8052
Loch
Suainaval
Loch Croistean
Loch
Tungavat
Aird
Breanais
Islibhig
Mealisval
574
Tahaval
515
Einacleit
Scealascro
B8011
Loch Cleit
Steirmeis
Breanais
Loch
Ruonasgail
Loch
Grunavat
16
Loch
Trealaval
Cracaval
514
Giosla
Calltraiseal
Bheag
226
Loch an
Fhir Mhaoil
Mealasta
Tamanaisval
467
Skeun
Beinn
Mheadhonach
397
Coduinn
241
Beinn Mohal
207
Loch Airigh
na h-Airde
Loch
Fadagoa
Loch Dibadale
265
Calltraiseal
Mhòr
228
Mealasta Island
Griomaval
Maghannan
Loch na
Craobhaig
Loch Morsgail
Roineval
281
Baile Ailein
Loch
Coirigerod
Liongam
Aird Bheag
Scalaval
Loch
Strandavat
Kearstay
Loch
Bodavat
Loch
Benisval
Morsgail Forest
Sleiteachal
Mhòr
248
Kintarvie
Airidh a'Bhruaich
Sgeir
Moil
Duinn
Gob na
h-Airde Moire
Aird Mhòr
Loch Reiseil
Beinn
a'Bhoth
308
Loch
Langavat
Aird an
Troim
Ceann
Loch Shiphoirt
Sron
Romul
308
Ulladale
Kearnaval
378
Sidhean
an
Airgid
381
Mòr
Mhonadh
401
Feirihisval
326
Scarp
Mas
a'Chnoic-
chuairtich
386
Mullach na
Reidheachd
295
Rapaire
453
Beinn
a'
Mhuil
370
A859
Beinn na
h-
Uamha
424
389
Sgianait
425
Loch
Voshimid
Liuthaid
492
18
Muaithabhal
Gasker
Tirga Mòr
679
Stulaval
579
Mullach a' Ruisg
473
Athlinne
Huisinis
Loch
a'Ghinne
Husival Mòr
489
Ullaval
659
Aird
a'Mhuraidh
Seaforth
Island
Beinn
Mhòr
572
Beannan
Mòr
242
Husinish Point
Leosaval
Oreval
662
NORTH
Arda
Beaga
412
Forest of Harris
HARRIS
Horsanish
Gobhaig
Cleiseval
511
(CEANN A TUATH NA HEARADH)
Clett
Ard
Kenmore
Park
Rubha
Bhuic
Abhainnsuidhe
Uisgnaval Mòr
729
Mulla-fo-
dheas
743
Clisham
799
Crionaig
470
12
B887
Maruig
Taransay Glorigs
Soay Beg
Miabhag
Bun Abhainn
Eadarra
A859
Caiteshal
449
Tathas
Mhòr
Soay Mor
Sgaoth
Aird
559
Straiaval
389
Toddun
528
West
Loch Tarbert
Aird Asaig
Reinigeadal
Bhalamus
Ben
Raah
267
Beinn
Dhubh
506
Laxadale
Lochs
3
Eilean Mòr
a' Bhàigh
Sgeir na
h-Eigheach
Tarasaigh
Taobh Siar
Tarbert
(An Tairbeart)
Urgha
Aird
Vanish
Paible
Losgaintir
93
Inn Reamhar
467
Carragrich
Uieseval
334
Rubha
Sgeirigin
South Harris
Forest
Kyles Scalpay
(Caolas Scalpaigh)
Sound of Taransay
Sgeotasaigh
Sound of Scalpay

A   B   C   D   E

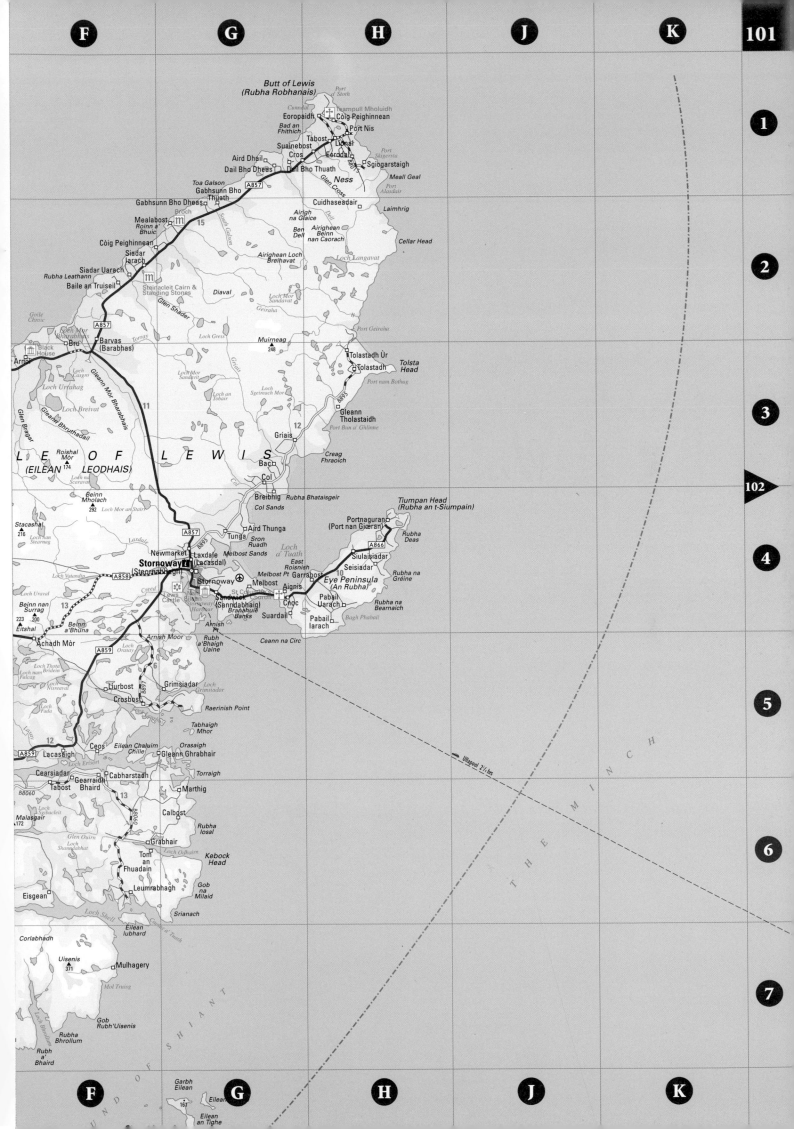

Butt of Lewis
(Rubha Robhanais)
Port a' Stoth

Cunndal

Teampull Mholuidh

Eoropaidh Còig Peighinnean
Bad an
Fhithich Port Nis
Tàbost Lìonal
Suainebost Eòrodal
Aird Dhail Cros Sgiogarstaigh
Dail Bho Dheas Dail Bho Thuath Port Skigersta
 Ness Meall Geal
Toa Galson Port Alasdair
Gabhsunn Bho Glen Cross
Gabhsunn Bho Dheas Thuath
 Cuidhaseadair
 A857 Laimhrig
Mealabost Broch Airigh
Roinn a' na Glaice
Bhuic 15 Airighean Cellar Head
Còig Peighinnean Ben Beinn
Siadar South Galson Dell nan Caorach
Rubha Leathann Iarach Airighean Loch
Siadar Uarach Breihavat Loch Langavat
Baile an Truiseil Steinacleit Cairn &
 Standing Stones Diaval
Goile Loch Mòr
Chroic Glen Shader Sandavat Geiraha Port Geiraha

Loch Mòr Black Bru Torray Loch Gress
Bharabhais House Barvas Graip Muirneag Tolastadh Ùr
Arnol (Barabhas) 248 Tolastadh Tolsta
 Loch A857 Loch Mòr Head
 Casgro Sanduvit Port nam Bothag
Loch Urrahag Gleann Mòr Bharabhais Loch an
 Tobair Gleann
Glen Bragar 11 Loch Sgeireach Mòr Tholastaidh
Roishal Mòr Loch Breivat 12 Griais Port Bun a' Ghlinne
LE O F L E W I S 174 Bac Creag
(EILEAN LEODHAIS) Col Fhraoich
Loch nc Scaravat
Beinn Breibhig Rubha Bhataisgeir Tiumpan Head
Mholach Col Sands (Rubha an t-Siumpain)
292 Loch Mòr an Stairr Portnaguran
Stacashal Aird Thunga (Port nan Giòran)
216 Loch nan Tunga Sron A866 Rubha
 Stearnag Ruadh Deas
 A857 Melbost Sands Siulaisiadar
Newmarket Laxdale East Seisiadar
 Stornoway (Lacasdal) Roisnish Rubha na
 (Steòrnabhagh) B895 10 Garrabost Gréine
Loch Vatandip A858 Melbost Pt **Eye Peninsula**
Loch Uraval Stornoway Melbost (An Rubha) Rubha na
Beinn nan Creed St Columba's Aignis Bearnaich
Surrag Lewis 13 Sandwick Cnoc Pabail
223 200 Castle (Sanndabhaig) Uarach
Eitshal Branahuie Suardail Rubha na
Achadh Mòr Banks Bearnaich
 A859 Arnish Pabail Bagh Phabail
 Arnish Moor Rubh Iarach
 a'Bhaigh
 Loch Uaine
 Orasay Ceann na Circ
 6
Loch Thota Liurbost Grimsiadar Loch
Bridein B897 Grimsiadar
Loch nam Crosbost
Falcag Loch Raerinish Point
Loch Nisreaval Fada
 Tabhaigh
 Mhor
 12 Orasaigh
 Ceos Eilean Chaluim Gleann Ghrabhair
A859 Lacasaigh Chille
 Loch Erisort
Cearsiadar Cabharstadh Torraigh
 Gearraidh
Tabost Bhaird Marthig
B8060 13
Malasgair B8060 Calbost
172 Rubha
 Iosal
Glen Ouirn Grabhair
Loch Loch
Shanndabhat Odhairn Kebock
Tom Head
an
Fhuadain
 Leumrabhagh Gob
 na
Eisgean Milaid
 Srianach
Loch Shell
 Clyde a' Tuath
Corlabhadh Eilean
 Iubhard
Uisenis T H E M I N C H
371 Mulhagery
 Mol Truisg

Ullapool 2½ hrs

S O U N D O F S H I A N T
Gob Rubh'Uisenis
Rubha
Bhrollum
Rubh Garbh
a' Eilean
Bhaird 161 Eilean
 Eilean
 an Tighe

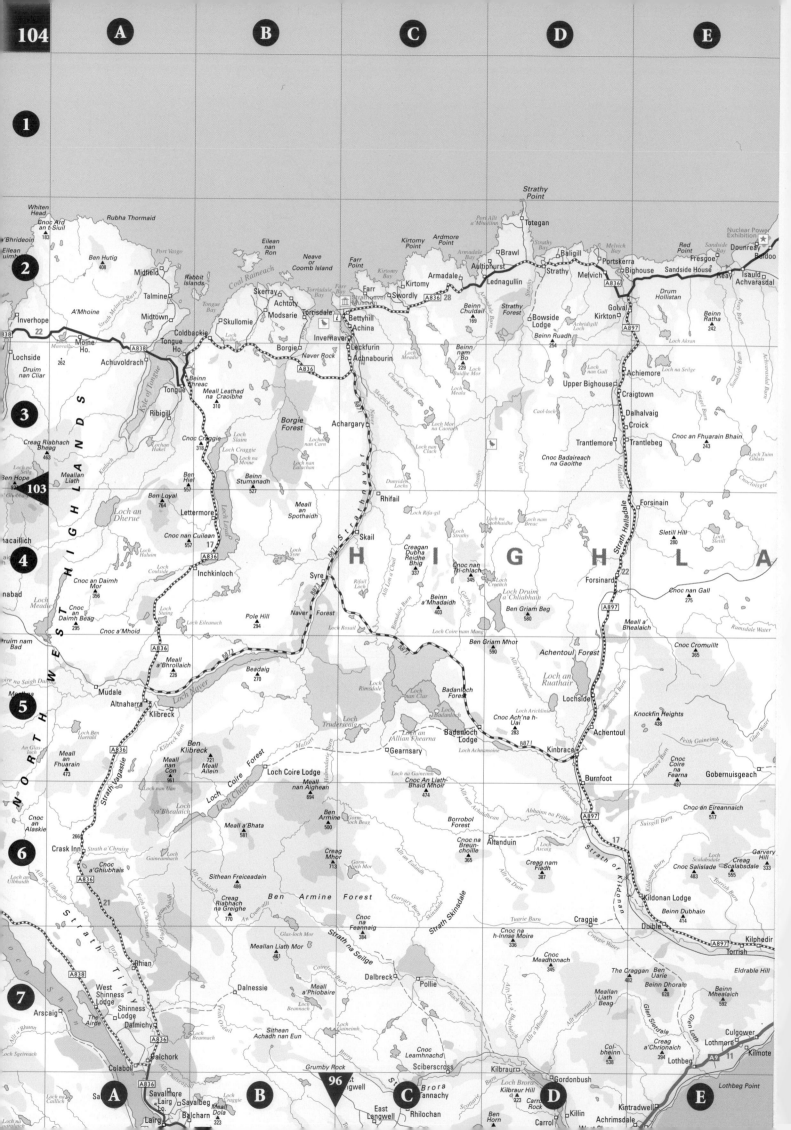

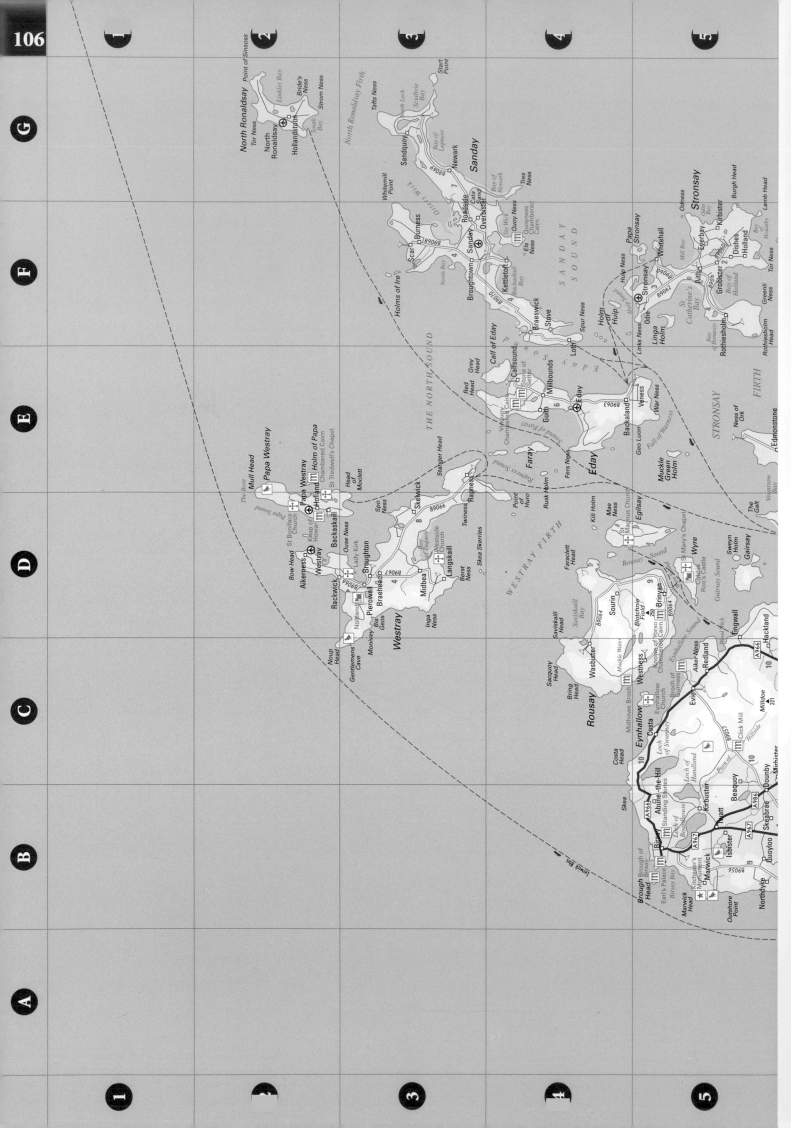

North Ronaldsay
Point of Sinsoss
Tor Ness
Linklet Bay
Bride's Ness
North
Ronaldsay
Hollandstoun
Strom Ness
South Bay

Start Point

North Ronaldsay Firth

Tafts Ness
North Loch
Scuthvie Bay

Sandquoy
Bay of Lopness
Newark
B9069
Sanday

Whitemill Point

Scar
Burness
B9069
Otters Wick
Roadside
Cata Sand
Tres Ness
Bay of Newark

Holms of Ire

Broughtown
Sanday
Kettletoft
Backaskaill Bay
Sty Quoy
Ness

Quoy Ness
Quoyness Chambered Cairn
Overbister
Stronsay
Burgh Head

North Bay
Els Ness
SANDAY SOUND
Lamb Head

Holland
Holm of Papa
Chambered Cairn
St Tredwell's Chapel
Head of Moclett
Braeswick
Stove
Spur Ness
Odin Bay

Mull Head
The Bore
Papa Westray
Papa Westray
Odness
Kirbister
Papa Stronsay
Stronsay
Airth
B9060
Grobister

Bow Head
St Boniface Church
Aikerness
Westray
Klap of Howar
Backaskaill
Lady Kirk
Ouse Ness
Broughton
Spo Ness
Skelwick
Stanger Head
B9066
Rapness

Rackwick
Pierowall
Braehead
B9067
Midbea
Westside Church
Twiness
Langskaill
Berst Ness
Skea Skerries
Point of Huro
Rusk Holm
Calf of Eday
Stone of Setter
Gunn
Eday
B9063
Veness
War Ness
Backaland
Geo Luon
Fall of Warness
Ness of Ork
Edmonstone

Noltland
Bis Geos
Monivey
Gentlemens' Cave
Westray
Inga Ness
Noup Head

Rousay Sound
St Mary's Chapel
Wyre
Cobbie Roo's Castle
Gairsay
Sweyn Holm
Gairsay Sound

Saviskaill Head
Saviskaill Bay
B9064
Sourin
Blotchnie Fiold
250
Knowe of Yorso
Chambered Cairn
Brinyan
B9064
Egilsay
St Magnus Church
Faraclett Head

Sacquoy Head
Bring Head
Rousay
Wasbister
Westness
Midhowe Broch
Westray Firth
Muckle Water
Knowe of Yorso

Costa Head
Eynhallow
Costa
Eynhallow Church
Broch of Gurness
Evie
Aiker Ness
Redland
Tingwall
Hackland
A966

Skea
A966
Abune-the-Hill
Standing Stones
Loch of Swannay
Click Mill
Hillside
Milldoe
221
Mirbister

Brough of Birsay
Kitchener's Monument
Earl's Palace
Marwick Head
Birsay
Loch of Boardhouse
Twatt
Marwick
Kirbuster
Beaquoy
A986
Dounby
Loch of Harray
B9057
Loch of Hundland

Outshore Point
Northdyke
Quoyloo
Isbister
A967
Skeabrae
Loch of Swannay

Kili Holm
Mae Ness

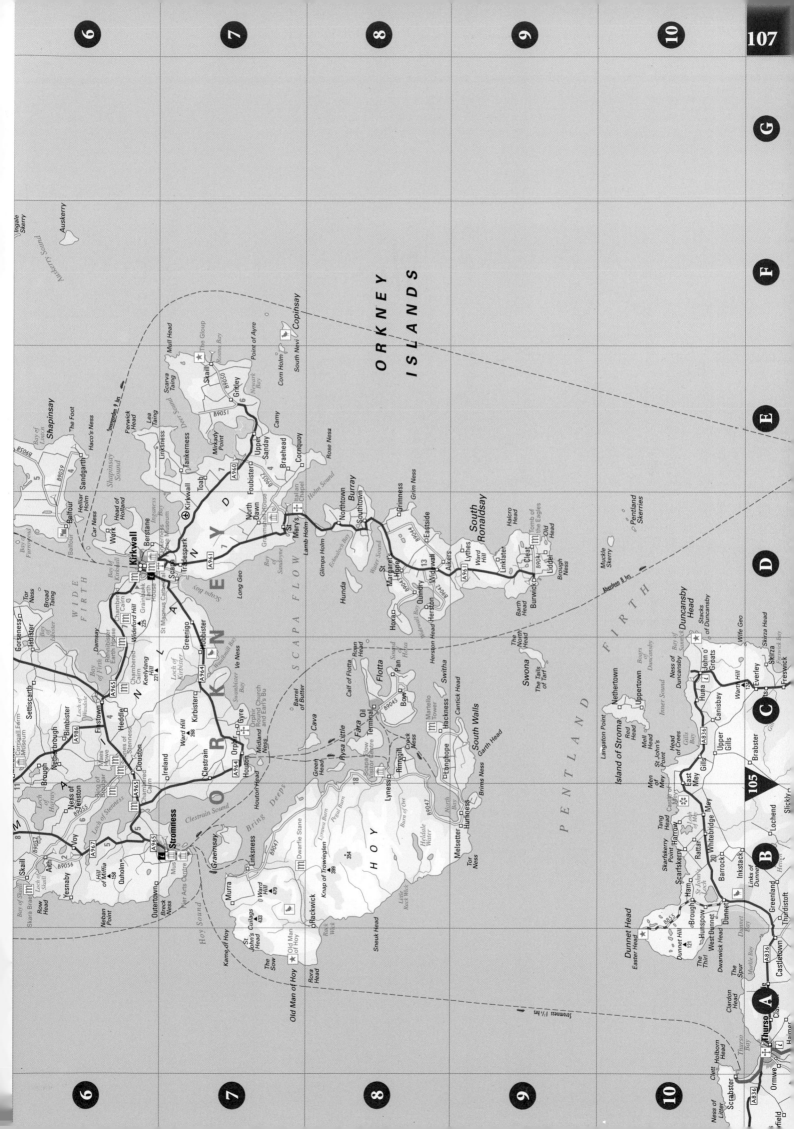

ORKNEY ISLANDS

ORKNEY

SCAPA FLOW

PENTLAND FIRTH

Shapinsay

South Ronaldsay

HOY

Kirkwall

Stromness

Thurso

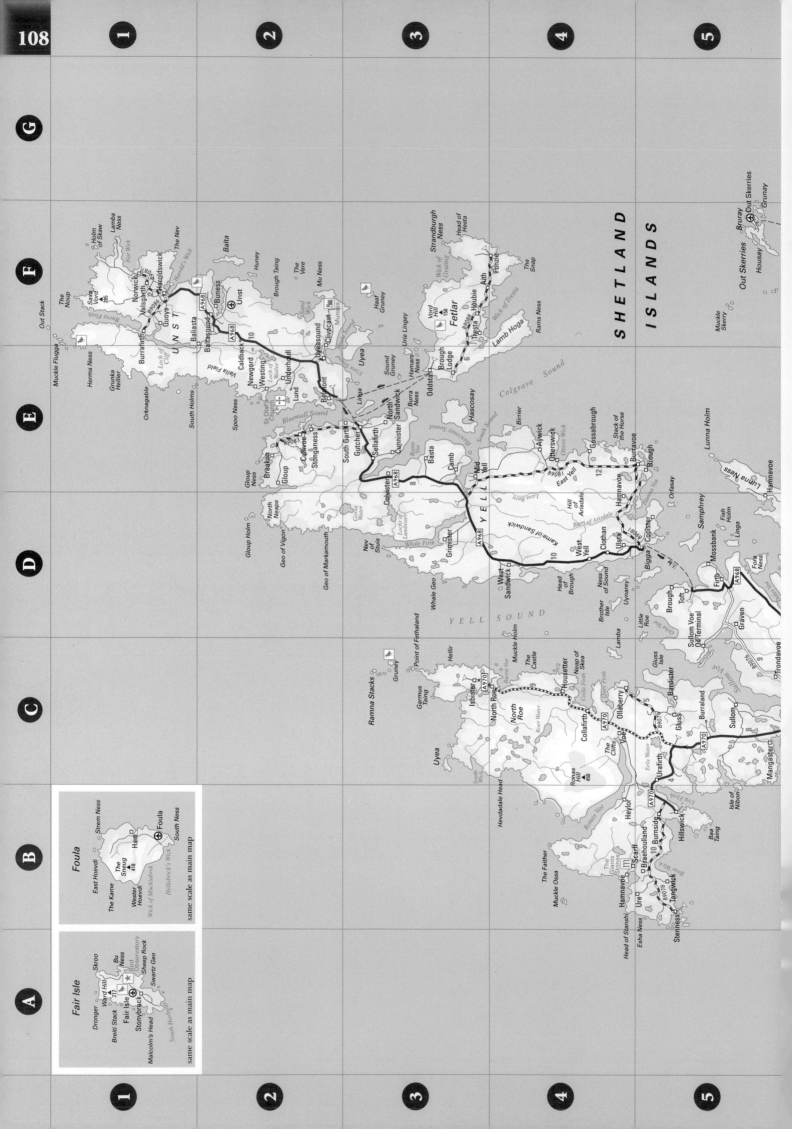

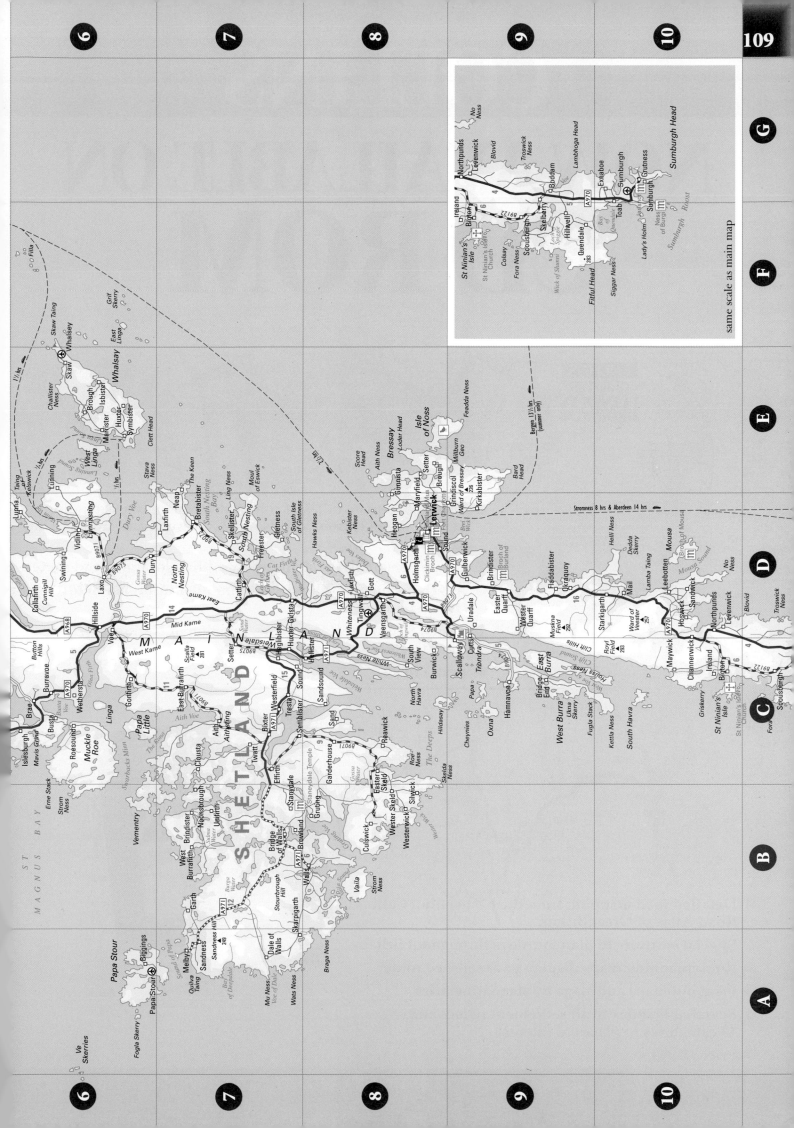

same scale as main map

MAINLAND

SHETLAND

ST MAGNUS BAY

Papa Stour

Ve Skerries

Fogla Skerry

Biggings
Papa Stour

Melby
Sandness
Sandness Hill 249
Quixa Taing
Mu Ness
Wats Ness
Ben of Deepdale
Sound of Papa

Dale of Walls
Voe of Dale

Skarpigarth
Walls
A971 6
Browland
Bridge of Walls
Stourbrough Hill
Burga Water
Vaila
Strom Ness
Braga Ness

Garth
West Burrafirth
Brindister
Noonsbrough
Clousta
Unifirth
Aith
Airthsting
Bixter
A971
Westerfield
Sound
Tresta
Semblister
Twatt
Effirth
Stanydale
Stanydale Temple
Gruting
Garderhouse
Sand
Sandsound
B9071 9
Reawick
Easter Skeld
Wester Skeld
Silwick
Culswick
Westerwick
Gruting Voe
Gossa Voe
Skelda Ness
Roe Ness

The Deeps
Hildasay
Papa
North Havra
South Havra
Cheynies
Oxna
Kettla Ness
Fugla Stack
Griskerry
St Ninian's Isle
St Ninian's Isle Church
Ford
Scousburgh

Muckle Roe
Papa Little
Linga
Roesound
Wetherста
Gonfirth
Voe
A970
West Kame
Scalla Field 281
Setter
Houlland
Highliston
Whiteness
A971
Weisdale
Mid Kame
14
East Kame
Sand Water
Strand
Veensgarth
Tingwall
Gott

Isbister
Busta
Busta Voe
Brae
A970
Burravoe
Hillside
A970
Gossa Water
A968
Button Hills
5
Mavis Grind
Mangaster Voe
Olna Firth
The Houb
Aith Voe
East Burrafirth
B9071
Swarbacks Minn
Vementry
Aith

Collafirth
Cunnigill Hill
Swining
Laxo
Vidlin
Lunna Ness
Lunning
Lunna
Laxo Voe
B9071
B9075
Dury Voe
Dury
North Nesting
Cattfirth
Stava Ness
Ling Ness
Neap
Laxfirth
Brettabister
South Nesting Bay
Skellister
South Nesting
Froster
Gletness
South Isle of Gletness
Hawks Ness
Kebister Ness
19
The Keen
Moul of Eswick

Collister Ness
Challister Ness
Clett Head
Mossbank
Marister
Isbister
Brough
Huxter
Symbister
West Linga
East Linga
Whalsay
Skaw
1½ hrs
Linga
Lunning Sound
½ hrs
Skaw Taing
Grif Skerry

Filla
8
Mainland

North Havra
Burwick
South View
White Ness
Weisdale Voe
Strand
Wadbister
Wadbister Voe
Catfirth
Cat Firth
Lax Firth
Dale Voe

Heogan
Bressay
Maryfield
Gunnista
Setter
 Giundiscol
Ward of Bressay
Brough
Kirkabister
Millburn
Score Head
Aith Ness
Isle of Noss
Loder Head
Bard Head
Feadda Ness
Gardie House
Bressay Sound
Noss Head

Lerwick
Holmsgarth
A970
Clickimin Broch
Sound
Fort Charlotte
Gulberwick
A970
Brindister
Broch of Burland
Easter Quarff
Wester Quarff
Fladdabister
Okraquoy
Cliff Hills
Musina Field 292
Ward of Veester 257
16
Mail
Starkigarth
Royl Field 293
Lamba Taing

Scalloway
Cutts
Tiondra
Hamnavoe
Bridge End
East Burra
West Burra
Ukna Skerry
Houss Ness

Maywick
Ireland
Bigton
St Ninian's Isle
Channerwick
Levenwick
Hoswick
Sandwick
Northpunds
Blovid
Troswick Ness
B9122
4
A970

Helli Ness
Dadda Skerry
Leebotten
Lamba Taing
No Ness
Mousa
Broch of Mousa
Mousa Sound

Stromness 8 hrs & Aberdeen 14 hrs
Bergen 13½ hrs (summer only)

Uradale
Easter Quarff

B9074
A970
4
B9073
B9073

Bay of Ocraquoy

Inset (same scale as main map):

Northpunds
Levenwick
Blovid
Troswick Ness
Boddam
Lambhoga Head
Ireland
Bigton
6
4
B9122
Scousburgh
Skelberry
Hillwell
Quendale
283
Colsay
Fora Ness
Wick of Shunni
Fitful Head
Siggar Ness
Loch of Spiggie
Bay of Quendale
Lady's Holm
St Ninian's Isle
St Ninian's Isle Church
No Ness
Exnaboe
Sumburgh
Toab
A970
5
Grutness
Sumburgh
Ness of Burgi
Sumburgh Head
Sumburgh Roost

COLLINS

NOW AVAILABLE ON
CD ROM

- Over 1660 square miles of colour street mapping, extending beyond the M25 from Windsor to Gravesend and from Harlow to Gatwick

- Create personalised databases by adding locations and routes

- Attach documents, photographs or other information to chosen location

- Search 80,000 streets by name, junction or National Grid co-ordinates

- Price £29.99

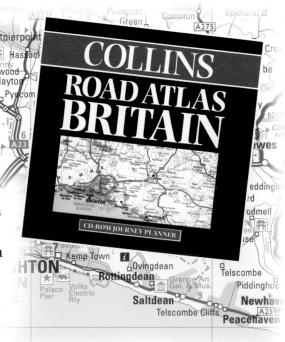

- Detailed road mapping from the best-selling Collins Road Atlas of Great Britain

- Special software to plan journeys throughout Britain

- Routeplanning maps display your selected route

- Print out maps and stage by stage itineraries

- Searchable index to all settlement names and 15 categories of places of interest

- Price £24.99

ORDER NOW ON THE 24 HOUR TELEPHONE ORDERING SERVICE 0141 306 3296
(QUOTE DEPT NUMBER 942J). POSTAGE AND PACKING FREE.

Key to London Map Pages

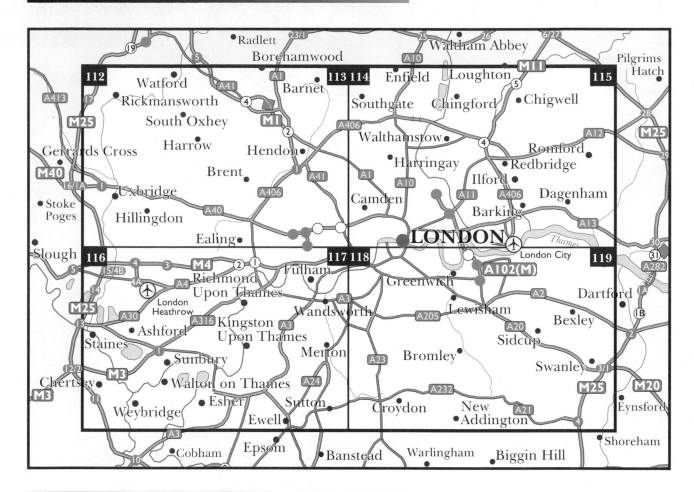

Key to London Map Symbols

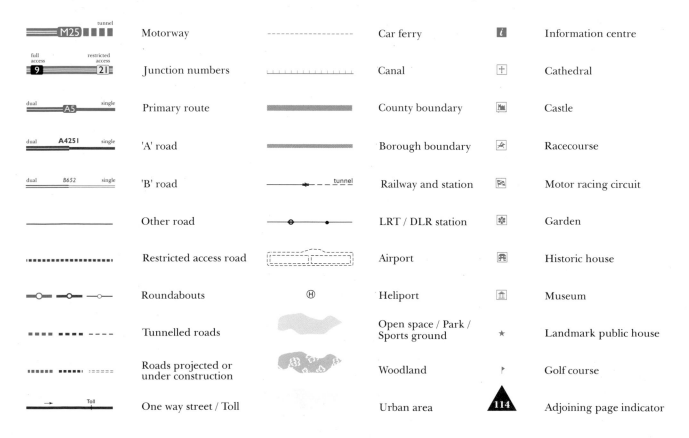

	Motorway		Car ferry		Information centre
	Junction numbers		Canal		Cathedral
	Primary route		County boundary		Castle
	'A' road		Borough boundary		Racecourse
	'B' road		Railway and station		Motor racing circuit
	Other road		LRT / DLR station		Garden
	Restricted access road		Airport		Historic house
	Roundabouts		Heliport		Museum
	Tunnelled roads		Open space / Park / Sports ground		Landmark public house
	Roads projected or under construction		Woodland		Golf course
	One way street / Toll		Urban area		Adjoining page indicator

Scale 1: 63360 (1 inch to 1 mile)

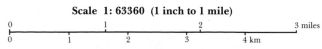

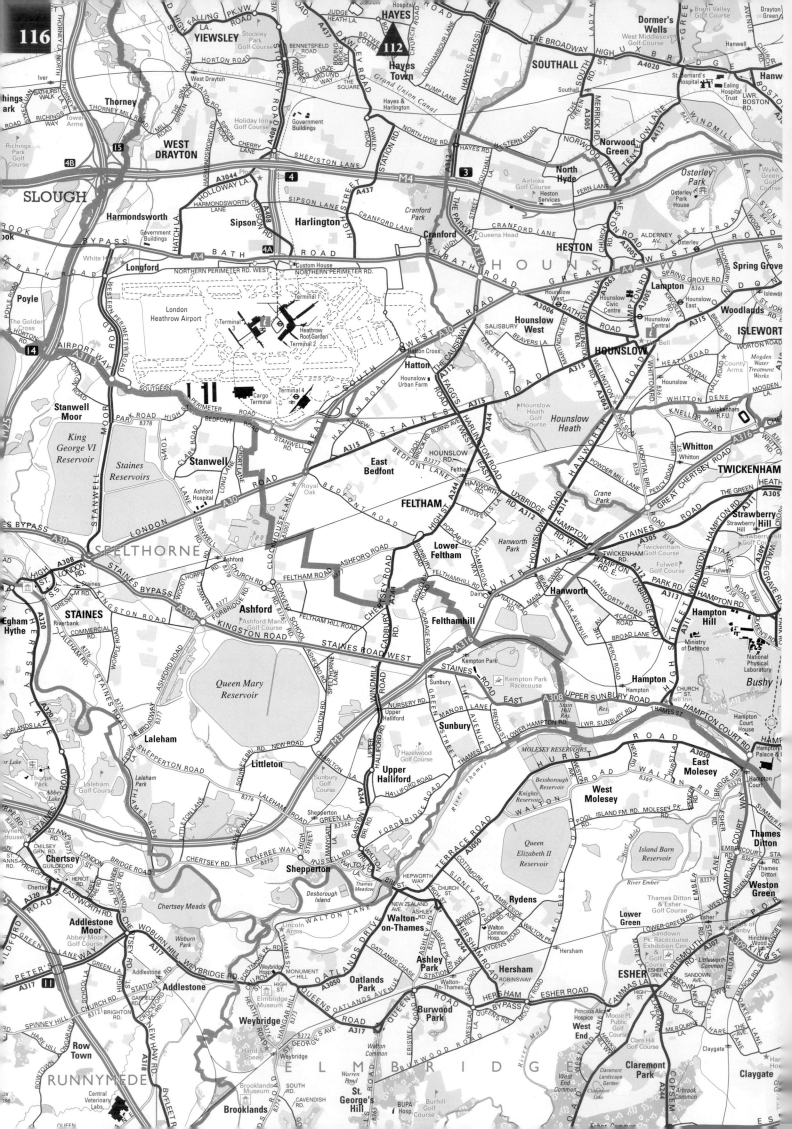

113
118

Feature Types

All the entries in the Gazetteer have been classified into broad feature types and are shown in **bold italics** in the listings. In many cases there is a degree of overlap, but an attempt has been made to use the one most appropriate. For example, a cave on the coast would be classified as a cave rather than a coastal feature as this is a more specific description. The feature types used are broken down into three main areas as follows:

Settlements and Localities
These categories are primarily man-made and have been divided into the following feature types:

City
Designated as a city by Royal Charter, they generally have a cathedral and are often large in size.

Town
Settlements with a definite central business district and urban character. They are administered as towns.

Small town
Administered as towns but are small and often have the character of a village.

Suburb
Primarily a residential locality linked to, or within a town or city.

Village
Settlements with a definite nucleus, possibly with a small number of facilities such as a post office, public house and village green.

Hamlet
Small collection of residential buildings, generally clustered together.

Settlement
Scattered buildings with no definite nucleus, or possibly, consisting of only one or two buildings.

Locality
This is a "catch all" category. It includes settlements that do not fall easily into any of the other categories. It may include industrial estates, areas within villages or several settlements with a collective name. It may also be a geographic region.

Physical Features
These feature types are essentially natural rather than man-made. The dividing lines between them are not always clear cut, but a best attempt has been made to choose the most applicable category.

Bay
These are water features and range from small coves to large bays such as Cardigan Bay.

Cave
These include coastal and inland caves, and although this is generally a physical feature may also include caves modified and enlarged by man.

Coastal feature
These include only 'land' features such as headlands and cliffs and do not include 'sea' features such as straits, sounds and bays.

Forest/woodland
This is an area which is predominantly afforested.

Hill
For the purposes of the gazetteer these have been classified as being under 1000 feet or 305 metres in height.

Mountain
These are taken as being 1000 feet or 305 metres and over. A subdivision of this feature type is Munro, these are a purely Scottish feature, are over 3000 feet or 914 metres and have been designated by the Scottish Mountaineering Club.

Inland physical feature
These include features which do not fit comfortably into any of the more specific categories and may include corries, ridges, swallow holes etc.

Island
Includes island rocks and groups of offshore rocks as well as the more traditional islands. Stacks adjacent to the shore are not included as these would be categorised as coastal features.

Lake/loch
These include all natural lakes, lochs, tarns and lochans but exclude sea lochs which would be considered to be sea features.

Large natural feature
Includes mountain ranges, plains and National Parks.

Marsh/bog
This an open space, with marshes generally considered to be coastal and bogs taken as being inland features.

Open space
Includes moorlands, hillslopes and areas with no specific defining features.

River
These range from small streams to large rivers.

Sea feature
These are 'water' features such as sea lochs, inlets, estuaries and straits.

Valley
These are commonly called vales, straths and glens and may be created by river or glacier.

Waterfall
This category also includes rapids as well as waterfalls.

Other Features
In many cases, the remaining feature types are self explanatory, or are clarified in the description that follows in the gazetteer listing.

The balance of the feature type categories are listed below:

Airport/airfield, Battle site, Bridge, Canal, Castle, Ecclesiastical building, Educational establishment, Garden, Historic house, Historic/prehistoric site, Leisure/recreation, Military establishment, Motor racing circuit, Nature reserve, Other building, Other feature of interest, Other water feature, Racecourse and Reservoir.

Notes: Listed below are the administrative areas for Great Britain and Isle of Man used in this Gazetteer. Where an area is dual language, the English form is given first, followed by the alternative in parenthesis. Each entry includes its standard abbreviation in *italics* which will appear in the main listings. Population figures are derived from 1991 Census information, or mid Census estimates, with modifications to allow for the newly created unitary authorities. A brief description of the area then follows, which includes: adjoining administrative areas; main centres (based on descending order of population); historical, physical and economic characteristics. For English counties or former Metropolitan counties, each district, city or borough authority is listed under the heading, **Districts**. A selection of the most visited tourist attractions then follows under the heading, **Places of interest**.

Aberdeen *Aberdeen* Population: 219,120.
Unitary authority surrounding Aberdeen, Scotland's third largest city, on the NE coast and neighbouring Aberdeenshire. Aberdeen is the major commercial and administrative centre for N Scotland. It is the second largest fishing port in Scotland, with docks at the mouth of the River Dee, and is the oil and gas capital of Europe.
Places of interest: Aberdeen Art Gallery; Aberdeen Exhibition and Conference Centre; Duthie Park & Winter Gardens; Provost Skene's House.

Aberdeenshire *Aber.* Population: 226,530.
Unitary authority on the NE coast of Scotland neighbouring Aberdeen, Angus, Highland, Moray and Perth & Kinross. Main centres are Peterhead, Fraserburgh, Inverurie, Stonehaven, Ellon, Banchory, Portlethan and Huntly. Aberdeenshire is split geographically into two main areas. The W is dominated by the Grampian Mountains and is largely unpopulated. The undulating lowlands of the E are mainly rural and are populated by farming and fishing communities. The major rivers are the Dee, which flows through Royal Deeside, and the Don.
Places of interest: Aden Country Park, Mintlaw; Balmedie Country Park; Balmoral Castle, Crathie; Crathes Castle (NTS); Haddo House Country Park (NTS); Storybook Glen, Maryculter.

Angus *Angus* Population: 111,329.
Unitary authority on the E coast of Scotland neighbouring Aberdeenshire, Dundee and Perth & Kinross. The chief centres are Arbroath, Forfar, Montrose, Carnoustie, the ancient cathedral city of Brechin, Kirriemuir and Monifieth. Angus occupies an area of 2200 square km and is an important agricultural area. It combines ancient relics and castles with highland terrain and market towns. Rivers include the North Esk, Isla and Prosen Water.
Places of interest: Glamis Castle; Monikie Country Park.

Argyll & Bute *Arg. & B.* Population: 90,550.
Unitary authority on the W coast of Scotland combining mainland and island life and neighbouring Highland, Inverclyde, North Ayrshire, Perth & Kinross, Stirling, and West Dunbartonshire. The main towns are Helensburgh, Dunoon, Oban, Campbeltown, Rothesay and Lochgilphead. It includes the former districts of Argyll and Bute as well as the islands of Islay, Jura, Colonsay and Mull. The main industries are fishing, agriculture, whisky production and tourism.
Places of interest: Inveraray Castle; Inveraray Jail; Iona Abbey; Loch Lomond Park Centre, Luss.

Bath & North East Somerset *B. & N.E.Som.* Population: 158,692.
Unitary authority in SW England neighbouring Bristol, North Somerset, Somerset, South Gloucestershire and Wiltshire. It surrounds the city of Bath, and includes the towns of Keynsham, Radstock and Midsomer Norton. The Georgian spa of Bath is considered to be one of the most beautiful cities in Britain, and is an important commercial and ecclesiastical centre popular with tourists. The River Avon flows through the area.
Places of interest: Bath Abbey; Museum of Costume, Bath; Roman Baths & Pump Room, Bath.

Bedfordshire *Beds.* Population: 352,434.
S midland county of England bounded by Buckinghamshire, Cambridgeshire, Hertfordshire, Luton, Milton Keynes and Northamptonshire. Main centres are the county town of Bedford, Dunstable, Leighton Buzzard, Kempston and Biggleswade. The N end of the Chiltern Hills runs through the S and SE of the county, which is otherwise mostly flat. Most of Bedfordshire is rural, and includes many stately homes. Industries include light engineering, brick manufacture, mineral extraction and vegetable growing. Chief river is the Great Ouse.
Districts: Bedford; Mid Bedfordshire; South Bedfordshire.
Places of interest: Dunstable Downs; Harrold-Odell Country Park; Stockgrove Country Park, Leighton Buzzard; Sundon Hills Country Park, Upper Sundon; Whipsnade Wild Animal Park, Dunstable; Woburn Safari Park.

Blackburn with Darwen *B'burn.* Population: 136,612.
Unitary authority in NW England surrounding Blackburn and Darwen and neighbouring Greater Manchester and Lancashire. Blackburn is a market and retail centre with a wide spread of industry including textiles, brewing and electronic engineering.
Places of interest: Blackburn Museum; Witton Country Park Visitor Centre, Blackburn.

Blackpool *B'pool* Population: 146,069.
Unitary authority on the NW coast of England surrounding Blackpool and neighbouring Lancashire. Blackpool receives around 7.2 million visitors each year, making it the most popular seaside resort in Europe. Attractions including the Tower, Pleasure Beach, Winter Gardens and Illuminations.
Places of interest: Blackpool Pleasure Beach; Blackpool Tower; Blackpool Zoo; Louis Tussaud's Waxworks; Sea Life Centre; South Pier; The Magic of Coronation Street; Winter Gardens.

Blaenau Gwent *B.Gwent* Population: 73,000.
Unitary authority in S Wales bounded by Caerphilly, Monmouthshire, Powys, and Torfaen. The chief towns are Ebbw Vale, Tredegar, Bryn-mawr and Abertillery. The area was previously dependent upon coal, iron and steel industries but has since developed a broader industrial base. Part of the Brecon Beacons are in the N of the area.
Places of interest: Bryn Bach Country Park, Tredgar; Festival Park Visitor Centre, Ebbw Vale.

Bournemouth *Bourne.* Population: 151,302.
Unitary authority on the S coast of England surrounding Bournemouth and neighbouring Dorset and Poole. Bournemouth is a major resort, conference and commercial centre.
Places of interest: Bournemouth International Centre & Pavilion; Russell-Cotes Art Gallery & Museum.

Bracknell Forest *Brack.F.* Population: 95,949.
Unitary authority to the W of Greater London and bounded by Hampshire, Surrey, Windsor & Maidenhead and Wokingham. Bracknell is the chief town, while to the N of the area there are the villages of Winkfield and Binfield. To the S lies forest and heathland, and the towns of Crowthorne and Sandhurst. Bracknell has many hi-tech industries, and is a shopping and leisure centre.
Places of interest: Look Out Discovery Park & Visitor Centre, Bracknell.

Bridgend (Pen-y-Bont ar Ogwr). *Bridgend* Population: 128,340.
Unitary authority in S Wales bounded by Neath Port Talbot, Rhondda Cynon Taff, Vale of Glamorgan and the sea. Main centres are Bridgend, Maesteg and Porthcawl. The area is mountainous to the N, having ribbon development along river valleys; there is greater urbanisation in the S.
Places of interest: Bryngarw Country Park; Coity Castle.

Brighton & Hove *B. & H.* Population: 155,000.
Unitary authority on the S coast of England neighbouring East Sussex and West Sussex. It encompasses the seaside resort of Brighton, which is a major commercial and conference centre, and the surrounding area which includes Hove, Portslade-by-Sea, Portslade, Rottingdean, Saltdean and part of the South Downs.
Places of interest: Brighton Centre; Brighton Museum & Art Gallery; Royal Pavilion, Brighton; Sea Life Centre, Brighton; The Palace Pier, Brighton.

Bristol *Bristol* Population: 374,000.
Unitary authority in SW England neighbouring Bath & North East Somerset, North Somerset, South Gloucestershire and the Bristol Channel. The area includes the city of Bristol and surrounding urban area, including Avonmouth. Bristol is an important industrial and commercial centre of W England. A former major port, its character varies from docks and a busy city centre, to parks and gardens and Georgian terracing. The city hosts the Balloon Fiesta and Harbour Regatta. River Avon forms part of the W border of the area.
Places of interest: Arnolfini Gallery; Ashton Court Estate; Bristol Cathedral; Bristol City Museum & Art Gallery; Bristol Zoo; Colston Hall; Maritime Heritage Centre; S.S. Great Britain; The Exploratory.

Buckinghamshire *Bucks.* Population: 432,487.
S midland county of England bounded by Bedfordshire, Greater London, Hertfordshire, Northamptonshire, Oxfordshire, Surrey, Windsor & Maidenhead and Wokingham. Chief towns are High Wycombe, the county town of Aylesbury, Amersham, Chesham, Marlow and Beaconsfield, around which, and other smaller towns, is a variety of light industry, as well as extensive residential areas. The chalk downs of the Chiltern Hills traverse the S part of the county, which is otherwise mostly flat. The River Thames flows along its S border.
Districts: Aylesbury Vale; Chiltern; South Bucks; Wycombe.
Places of interest: Bekonscot Model Village, Beaconsfield; Black Park, Wexham; Cliveden (NT); Langley Park; Odd Farm Park, Woburn Common; Waddesdon Manor (NT), Aylesbury.

Caerphilly (Caerffili). *Caerp.* Population: 172,000.
Unitary authority in S Wales bordered by Blaenau Gwent, Cardiff, Merthyr Tydfil, Rhondda Cynon Taff and Torfaen. The chief centres are Caerphilly, Gelligaer, Risca, Bargoed, Blackwood and Bedwas. The geography of the area varies from open moorland to busy market towns. The former mining industry has been replaced by electronics and automotive companies, with tourism also being important to the local economy. Rivers include the Rhymney and Sirhowy.
Places of interest: Caerphilly Castle; Sirhowy Valley Country Park, Cross Keys.

Cambridgeshire *Cambs.* Population: 491,959.
County of E England bounded by Bedfordshire, Essex, Hertfordshire, Lincolnshire, Norfolk, Northamptonshire, Peterborough and Suffolk. Cambridgeshire is mostly flat, with fenland to N and E, although there are low chalk hills in the S and SE. Chief centres are the city and county town of Cambridge, Wisbech, St. Ives, March, Huntingdon, St. Neots and the cathedral city of Ely. Agriculture is a major industry with sugar beet, potatoes and corn all important crops; soft fruit and vegetable cultivation and canning are also significant rural industries. There has been recent growth of medical, pharmaceutical and hi-tech industries around Cambridge. Rivers include the Cam, Nene, and Great Ouse.
Districts: Cambridge; East Cambridgeshire; Fenland; Huntingdonshire; South Cambridgeshire.
Places of interest: Anglesey Abbey (NT), Lode; Corn Exchange, Cambridge; Ely Cathedral; Fitzwilliam Museum, Cambridge; Grafham Water, Huntingdon; Great St. Mary, Cambridge; Holy Sepulchre, Cambridge; Imperial War Museum, Duxford; King's College Chapel, Cambridge; Linton Zoo & Gardens; Wandlebury Country Park, Cambridge; Wimpole Home Farm (NT), Arrington; Wood Green Animal Shelter, Godmanchester.

Cardiff (Caerdydd). *Cardiff* Population: 315,000.
Unitary authority in S Wales surrounding the city of Cardiff and bordered by Caerphilly, Newport, Rhondda Cynon Taff, Vale of Glamorgan and the Bristol Channel. Cardiff, the capital of Wales, is a major administrative, commercial, cultural and tourism centre. It contains the Welsh Office, Welsh National Stadium, remains of medieval castle, cathedral at Llandarff and university. Cardiff docks, which were formerly used to export Welsh coal, are part of an ongoing major redevelopment. The city has excellent shopping facilities, notably at the St. David's Centre. There are associations with Roald Dahl.
Places of interest: Cardiff Bay Visitor Centre; Cardiff Castle; Museum of Welsh Life; National Museum of Wales; St. David's Hall; Techniquest.

Carmarthenshire (Sir Gaerfyrddin). *Carmar.* Population: 68,900.
Unitary authority in S Wales bounded by Ceredigion, Neath Port Talbot, Pembrokeshire, Powys, Swansea and the sea. The chief towns are Llanelli, Carmarthen and Ammanford. The geography varies from the Brecon Beacons in the E, to the river valleys in the N, and the fishing villages, beaches and coastal towns in the S. The 50m coastline runs along the S of the area. Rivers include the Tywi, Cothi, Gwendaeth Fach and Gwendaeth Fawr.
Places of interest: Pembrey Country Park.

Ceredigion *Cere.* Population: 68,900.
Unitary authority in W Wales bounded by Carmarthenshire, Gwynedd, Pembrokeshire, Powys and the sea at Cardigan Bay. The main towns are Aberystwyth, Cardigan, Aberaeron, Lampeter, Tregaron and Llandysul. Part of the Cambrian Mountains lie in the E of the area and the 50m coast has many sandy beaches. Tourism and agriculture are the most important industries. The main river is the Teifi.
Places of interest: Ceredigion Museum, Aberystwyth; Vale of Rheidol Railway, Aberystwyth.

Cheshire *Ches.* Population: 639,900.
County of NW England bounded by Derbyshire, Greater Manchester, Halton, Merseyside, Staffordshire, Shropshire, Warrington and the Welsh authorities of Flintshire and Wrexham. Chief centres are the cathedral city of Chester and the towns of Ellesmere Port, Crewe, Macclesfield, Northwich, Wilmslow, Winsford and Congleton. The country is mainly flat, except in the NE, where the foothills of The Pennines enter the county. The rural areas, which are mostly in the S and W, are noted for dairy products. Much of the county is industrialised; there are large salt mines with an associated chemicals industry in the N, silk and cotton mills, and engineering. Chief rivers are the Dane, Dee, and Weaver. In the NW the county reaches the estuaries of the River Dee and River Mersey.
Districts: Chester; Congleton; Crewe & Nantwich; Ellesmere Port & Neston; Macclesfield; Vale Royal.
Places of interest: Blakemere Craft Centre, Northwich; Brookside Miniature Railway, Poynton; Cheshire Candle Workshops Ltd., Burwardsley; Cheshire Ice Cream Farm, Tattenhall; Chester Cathedral; Chester Visitor Centre; Chester Zoo; Grosvenor Museum, Chester; Jodrell Bank Science Centre & Arboretum, Macclesfield; Lyme Hall (NT); Lyme Park (NT); Marbury Country Park; Ness Gardens, Neston; Palms Tropical Oasis (Stapeley Water Gardens), Stapeley; Quarry Bank Mill (NT), Styal; Styal Country Park, Wilmslow; Tatton Park (NT); Tatton Park, Knutsford; Tegg's Nose Country Park.

Clackmannanshire *Clack.* Population: 47,679.
Unitary authority in central Scotland neighbouring Fife, Perth & Kinross and Stirling. The N includes the Ochil Hills, while the lowland surrounding the Forth estuary contains the chief towns which are Alloa, Tullibody, Tillicoultry and Alva. Clackmannanshire has over 50 sites of nature conservation and five historic castles and towers. The main rivers are the Devon and the Forth.
Places of interest: Gartmorn Dam Country Park, Coalsnaughton; Mill Trail Visitor Centre, Alva.

Conwy *Conwy* Population: 113,000.
Unitary authority in N Wales bordered by Denbighshire, Gwynedd and the sea. The chief towns are Colwyn Bay, Llandudno, Abergele, Rhôs-on-Sea and Conwy. Around 40 per cent of Conwy is within Snowdonia National Park and there are 29m of coastline. The coastal resorts attract tourism which is a key industry, but agriculture and light manufacturing are also important to the local economy. The main river is the Conwy.
Places of interest: Bodnant Gardens (NT), Tal-y-Cafn; Conwy Castle; Great Orme Tramway; North Wales Theatre, Llandudno; Swallow Falls, Betws-y-Coed.

Cornwall *Cornw.* Population: 468,425.
South-westernmost county of England bounded by Devon and the sea. Chief centres are St. Austell, Falmouth, Penzance, the cathedral city and administrative centre of Truro, Redruth, Camborne and Newquay. The coastline is wild and rocky; headlands and cliffs are interspersed with large sandy beaches in the N, and deeply indented with river estuaries in the S. The interior is dominated by areas of moorland, notably the granite mass of Bodmin Moor in the NE. There are also farmlands

providing rich cattle-grazing, and deep river valleys. The climate is mild, and flower cultivation is carried on extensively. The many derelict tin mines are witness to the former importance of this industry; there has recently been a partial revival. The chief industry is tourism. China clay is produced in large quantities in the St. Austell area, and there is some fishing. Rivers include the Tamar, forming the boundary with Devon; Fowey, East and West Looe, Fal, Camel, and Lynher.

Districts: Caradon; Carrick; Kerrier; North Cornwall; Penwith; Restormel.

Places of interest: Boscastle Pottery; Callestock Cider Farm, Truro; Camel Trail, Bodmin; Cornish Goldsmiths, Portreath; Cornish Seal Sanctuary, Gweek; Dobwalls Family Adventure Park; Flambards Village Theme Park, Helston; Holywell Bay Fun Park, Newquay; Land's End; Lanhydrock (NT), Bodmin; Lost Gardens of Heligan, St. Austell; Mount Edgcumbe Country Park, Torpoint; Newquay Pearl; Newquay Zoo; St. Just in Roseland; St. Michael's Mount (NT), Marazion; St. Winwaloe, Gunwalloe; Sea Life Centre, Newquay; Tate Gallery, St. Ives; Tehidy Country Park, Coombe; Tintagel Castle; Trebah Garden, Mawnan Smith; Trelissick (NT), Feock; Truro Cathedral.

Cumbria *Cumb.* Population: 483,163.

County of NW England bounded by Durham, Lancashire, Northumberland and North Yorkshire; the Scottish authorities of Dumfries & Galloway and Scottish Borders; and the Solway Firth and Irish Sea. Chief centres are the city of Carlisle and the towns of Barrow-in-Furness, Whitehaven, Workington, Kendal, Penrith and Ulverston. A narrow strip of flat country along the coast widens to a plain in the N and around Carlisle. Otherwise the county is composed of mountains, moorland and lakes, and includes the scenically famous Lake District. Cumbria is mostly rural and uncultivated, with industry centred on Carlisle and the urban centres. Whitehaven, Workington, and Maryport all once relied on coal, while Barrow-in-Furness developed due to shipbuilding and heavy industry. There are links with nuclear technology: Calder Hall, N of Seascale, was Britain's first atomic power station, Sellafield is the site of a nuclear reprocessing plant and Trident submarines were built at Barrow-in-Furness. Tourism in the Lake District and sheep farming are also important industries. The area is noted for its radial drainage, with Windermere and Ullswater being the largest of the lakes and the River Eden being the chief of many rivers.

Districts: Allerdale; Barrow-in-Furness; Carlisle; Copeland; Eden; South Lakeland.

Places of interest: Adrian Sankey Glass Makers, Ambleside; Carlisle Cathedral; Colony Gift Corporation, Lindal-in-Furness; Cumberland Pencil Museum, Keswick; Dock Museum, Barrow-in-Furness; Fell Foot Park (NT), Staveley-in-Cartmel; Grizedale Forest Park; Lakeside & Haverthwaite Railway, Lakeside; National Park Visitor Centre, Brockhole; Ravenglass & Eskdale Railway, Ravenglass; Sellafield Visitors Centre; South Lakes Wild Animal Park, Dalton-in-Furness; Talkin Tarn Country Park, Farlam; Tullie House, Carlisle; Ullswater Steamers, Kendal; Whinlatter Forest; Windermere Lake Cruises; World of Beatrix Potter Exhibition, Bowness-on-Windermere.

Darlington *Darl.* Population: 98,906.

Unitary authority in NE England surrounding Darlington and neighbouring Durham, North Yorkshire and Stockton-on-Tees. Darlington has a variety of industries, including iron, steel and textiles. The River Tees forms the S border.

Denbighshire (Sir Ddinbych). *Denb.* Population: 91,000.

Unitary authority in N Wales neighbouring Conwy, Flintshire, Gwynedd, Powys, Wrexham and the sea. The chief towns are Rhyl, Prestatyn, Denbigh, Ruthin, the ancient city of St. Asaph, and Llangollen. Main industries are tourism, centred on the coastal resorts of Rhyl and Prestatyn, and agriculture. Rivers include the Morwynion.

Places of interest: Llangollen Railway; Llyn Brenig Visitor Centre, near Corwen; Loggerheads Country Park; Moel Famau Country Park; Ocean Beach Amusement Park, Rhyl; Ruthin Craft Centre; Sea Life Centre, Rhyl; Sky Tower, Rhyl.

Derby *Derby* Population: 218,802.

Unitary authority in central England surrounding the city of Derby and bordered by Derbyshire. Derby has a history dating back to Roman times and is now important in the rail industry; other key industries are manufacturing and aerospace engineering. The River Derwent passes through the area.

Places of interest: Derby Industrial Museum; Pickfords House Museum.

Derbyshire *Derbys.* Population: 709,834.

Midland county of England bounded by Cheshire, Derby, Greater Manchester, Leicestershire, Nottinghamshire, South Yorkshire, Staffordshire and West Yorkshire. Chief towns are Chesterfield, Long Eaton, Swadlincote, Ilkeston, Staveley, Dronfield, Alfreton, Heanor and Buxton. The high steep hills in the N, which include the dramatic scenery of The Peak, are the S extremity of The Pennines, and provide grazing for sheep and cattle. There is some textile industry in the towns of the N and W, while the S of the county is dominated by heavy industry, mining, and quarrying. Tourism is based on the scenic Peak District National Park, most of which falls in the county. Principal rivers are the Dove, forming much of the boundary with Staffordshire and noted for its scenery and fishing, and the Derwent; the Trent flows through the S corner of the county.

Districts: Amber Valley; Bolsover; Chesterfield; Derbyshire Dales; Erewash; High Peak; North East Derbyshire; South Derbyshire.

Places of interest: Calke Abbey (NT), Ticknall; Carsington Water, Ashbourne; Caudwell's Mill, Matlock; Chatsworth Farmyard & Adventure Playground, Edensor; Chatsworth House, Bakewell; Denby Pottery; Elvaston Castle Country Park; Ferrers Centre for Arts & Crafts, Staunton Harold; Foremark Reservoir, Milton; Haddon Hall, Bakewell; Linacre Reservoirs, Cutthorpe; Midland Railway, Butterley; National Tramway Museum, Matlock; Ogston Reservoir, Clay Cross; St. Lawrence, Eyam; St. Michael, Hathersage; Shipley Country Park, Heanor; Staunton Harold Reservoir, Melbourne; The American Adventure Theme Park, Shipley; Upper Derwent Reservoirs, Bamford.

Devon *Devon* Population: 646,903.

Large county in SW peninsula of England bounded by Cornwall, Dorset, Plymouth, Somerset, Torbay and the Bristol and English Channels. The chief centres are the city of Exeter, Exmouth, Barnstaple, Newton Abbot, Tiverton, Bideford and Teignmouth. The county includes the W end of Exmoor and the whole of the granite mass of Dartmoor, whose summit, High Willhays, is the highest point in S England. Moorland areas apart, the county is largely given over to agriculture, and on the coast, to fishing and tourism. On Dartmoor there are quarries and a military training area; there are china clay workings in the S. Daffodils are grown commercially in River Tamar valley. Chief rivers are Exe, Teign, Dart, Avon, Erme, Tamar and Tavy in the S; and Taw and Torridge in the N. The granite island of Lundy is included in the county for administrative purposes.

Districts: East Devon; Exeter; Mid Devon; North Devon; South Hams; Teignbridge; Torridge; West Devon.

Places of interest: Bicton Park Gardens, East Budleigh; Big Sheep, Bideford; Buckfast Abbey; Canonteign Falls, Exeter; Cardew Design, Bovey Tracey; Castle Drogo (NT), Chagford; Clovelly Village, Clovelly; Combe Martin Wildlife & Dinosaur Park; Crealy Park, Exeter; Dartington Crystal and Cider Press Centre; Dartington Crystal Ltd., Great Torrington; Donkey Sanctuary, Sidmouth; Exeter Cathedral; Grand Western Canal Country Park, Tiverton; High Moorland Visitor Centre, Princetown; Killerton (NT); Lynton & Lynmouth Cliff Railway; Morwellham Quay Museum; National Shire Horse Centre; Northam Burrows Country Park, Bideford; Paignton & Dartmouth Steam Railway, Paignton; Quince Honey Farm, South Molton; River Dart (Dart Pleasure Craft), Dartmouth; Rosemoor, Torrington; Royal Albert Memorial Museum, Exeter; South Devon Railway, Buckfastleigh; Stuart Line Cruises, Exmouth; The Grand Pier, Teignmouth; Trago Mills, Newton Abbot; Watermouth Castle, Ilfracombe; Westpoint Exhibition Centre, Exeter; Woodlands Leisure Park, Totnes.

Dorset *Dorset* Population: 360,814.

County in SW England bounded by Bournemouth, Devon, Hampshire, Poole, Somerset, Wiltshire and the English Channel. The chief towns are Weymouth, Christchurch, Wimborne Minster, the county town of Dorchester, Bridport, Swanage and Blandford Forum. The county is hilly, with chalk downs and impressive geological formations along the coastline. Sand, gravel, stone and oil extraction takes place around the Isle of Portland and the Isle of Purbeck. Dorset is also noted for its agricultural and dairy produce. Tourism is an important industry due to the beautiful scenery, the proliferation of prehistoric and Roman remains, and the connection with Thomas Hardy's Wessex. Among numerous minor rivers are the Stour, Frome, and Piddle or Trent.

Districts: Christchurch; East Dorset; North Dorset; Purbeck; West Dorset; Weymouth & Portland.

Places of interest: Abbotsbury Swannery & Sub-Tropical Gardens, Weymouth; Avon Heath Country Park, St. Leonards; Brownsea Island; Christchurch Priory; Corfe Castle (NT); Corfe Castle Museum; Dinosaur Museum, Dorchester; Durlston Country Park Visitor Centre, Swanage; Durlston Country Park, Swanage; Kingston Lacy (NT), Wimborne Minster;

Monkey World, Wareham; Moors Valley Country Park, Ringwood; Sea Life Centre, Weymouth; Stapehill Abbey Crafts & Garden, Wimborne Minster; Swanage Railway; Tank Museum, Bovington Camp; The Tutankhamun Exhibition, Dorchester; Wimborne Minster.

Dumfries & Galloway *D. & G.* Population: 147,900.

Unitary authority in SW Scotland neighbouring East Ayrshire, Scottish Borders, South Ayrshire, South Lanarkshire, the English county of Cumbria and the sea. It comprises the former counties of Dumfries, Kirkcudbright, and Wigtown. Chief towns are Dumfries, Stranraer, Annan, Dalbeattie, Lockerbie, Castle Douglas, Newton Stewart and Kirkcudbright. The hilly area to the N is largely given over to sheep-grazing and afforestation, while farther S there is some good-quality arable farmland. At the extreme W of the area is the peninsula known as the Rinns of Galloway, and the port of Stranraer, which provides passenger and car ferry services to Larne in Northern Ireland. Main rivers are the Esk, Annan, Nith, Dee and Cree which descend S to the Solway Firth from the Tweedsmuir Hills, Lowther Hills and the Rhinns of Kells in the N.
Places of interest: Blacksmith's Shop, Gretna Green; Threave Gardens (NTS), Castle Douglas.

Dundee *Dundee* Population: 155,000.

Unitary authority on the E coast of Scotland surrounding the city of Dundee and neighbouring Angus and Perth & Kinross. Dundee is Scotland's fourth largest city and is a centre of excellence in a variety of areas from telecommunications to medical research. The Firth of Tay borders Dundee to the S.
Places of interest: Discovery Point & R.R.S. Discovery; McManus Galleries.

Durham *Dur.* Population: 494,524.

County in NE England bounded by Cumbria, Darlington, Hartlepool, Northumberland, North Yorkshire, Stockton-on-Tees, Tyne & Wear and the North Sea. Chief centres are the cathedral city and county town of Durham; and the towns of Chester-le-Street, Peterlee, Newton Aycliffe, Bishop Auckland, Seaham and Consett. The W part of the county includes The Peninnes and consists mostly of open moorlands which provide rough sheep-grazing and water for the urban areas from a number of large reservoirs. Economic activity is concentrated on the lowland in the E which is more heavily populated, and was formerly a centre for coal-mining and heavy industry. Diversification has since provided a broad industrial base. The principal rivers are the Tees and the Wear.
Districts: Chester-le-Street; Derwentside; Durham; Easington; Sedgefield; Teesdale; Wear Valley.
Places of interest: Allensford Country Park; Beamish Open Air Museum; Bowlees Picnic Area, Middleton-in-Teesdale; Brandon/Bishop Auckland Walk; Consett & Sunderland Railway Path, Stanley; Deerness Valley Walk; Derwent Walk Country Park, Consett; Derwent Walk; Durham Cathedral; Hamsterley Forest; Hardwick Hall Country Park, Sedgefield; Lanchester Valley Walk; Pow Hill Country Park, Edmundbyres.

East Ayrshire *E.Ayr.* Population: 124,000.

Unitary authority in SW Scotland bounded by Dumfries & Galloway, East Renfrewshire, North Ayrshire, South Ayrshire and South Lanarkshire. The principal towns are Kilmarnock, Cumnock, Stewarton, Galston and Auchinleck. Traditional industries centred on textiles and lace in the Irvine valley, coal mining and engineering. Dairy farming is also an important industry, particularly beef and sheep production. The area is a popular tourist destination, with several castles, battle sites and associations with Robert Burns and Keir Hardie. Rivers include the Irvine, Annick and Cessnock.
Places of interest: Blackshaw Farm Park Ltd., Kilmarnock; Loudon Castle Park, Galston.

East Dunbartonshire *E.Dun.* Population: 110,220.

Unitary authority in central Scotland bounded by Glasgow, North Lanarkshire, Stirling and West Dunbartonshire. The chief centres are Bearsden, Bishopbriggs, Kirkintilloch and Milngavie. Much of the urban and industrial development occurs on the N periphery of Greater Glasgow. The Campsie Fells lie in the N of the area.
Places of interest: Lillie Art Gallery.

East Lothian *E.Loth.* Population: 85,500.

Unitary authority in central Scotland neighbouring Edinburgh, Midlothian, Scottish Borders and the North Sea. The main towns are Musselburgh, Haddington, Tranent, Prestonpans, Dunbar, North Berwick and Cockenzie and Port Seton. There are 43m of varied coastline and the topography includes the Lammermuir Hills in the S, and the ancient volcanoes at North Berwick and Traprain. Much of the urban and industrial development is in the NW and N of the area. Rivers include Whitehead Water, the Tyne, Peffer Burn and Gifford Water.
Places of interest: Gullane Bents; John Muir Country Park; Longniddry Bents; Yellowcraig, Dirleton.

East Renfrewshire *E.Renf.* Population: 86,780.

Unitary authority in SW Scotland bounded by East Ayrshire, Glasgow, Inverclyde, North Ayrshire, Renfrewshire and South Lanarkshire. The principal centres are Newton Mearns, Clarkston, Barrhead and Giffnock, which lie on the S periphery of Greater Glasgow. Over two-thirds of East Renfrewshire is farmland; the rest being mostly residential, with some light industry.

East Riding of Yorkshire *E.Riding* Population: 310,000.

Unitary authority on the E coast of England neighbouring Kingston upon Hull, North Lincolnshire, North Yorkshire, South Yorkshire and York. The chief centres are Bridlington, Beverley, Goole, Great Driffield, Hornsea, Brough, Hedon and Withernsea. The area is mostly low-lying, except for the central ridge which forms part of The Wolds. The coastline is subject to much erosion, with material being moved from Flamborough Head to the large spit of Spurn Head, at the mouth of the River Humber. Key industries in the area include agriculture, aerospace, gas and oil industries.
Places of interest: Beverley Minster; Hornsea Freeport; Park Rose Pottery & Leisure Park, Bridlington; Sewerby Hall; Wolds Village, Great Driffield.

East Sussex *E.Suss.* Population: 535,447.

County of SE England bounded by Brighton & Hove, Kent, Surrey, West Sussex and the English Channel. Main towns are Eastbourne, Hastings, Bexhill, Seaford, Crowborough, Hailsham, Peacehaven and the county town of Lewes; Rye is a small historic town in the E of the county. In the W, the coast is backed by the chalk ridge of the South Downs, ending with the white cliffs of the Seven Sisters and Beachy Head, just W of Eastbourne. E of this point, there are extensive areas of reclaimed marshland, which provide good sheep-grazing. Inland is the heavily wooded Weald, a former centre of the iron industry, interspersed with hill ridges, the largest being the open heathland of Ashdown Forest. Rivers, none large, include the Cuckmere, Ouse, Rother, and upper reaches of the Medway.
Districts: Eastbourne; Hastings; Lewes; Rother; Wealden.
Places of interest: Battle Abbey; Bewl Water, Lamberhurst; Bodiam Castle (NT); Buckleys Yesterday's World, Battle; Clambers Play Centre, Hastings; Drusillas Park, Alfriston; Eastbourne Pier; Filching Manor, Polegate; Fort Fun, Eastbourne; Glass Studio, Eastbourne; Hastings Castle (Ruins); Hastings Fishermen's Museum; Middle Farm & English Farm Cider Centre, West Firle; Paradise Family Leisure Park, Newhaven; St. Mary the Virgin, Rye; Sea Life Centre, Hastings; Sheffield Park (NT), Uckfield; Smugglers Adventure, Hastings; Volks Electric Railway.

Edinburgh *Edin.* Population: 447,550.

Unitary authority on the E coast of central Scotland surrounding the city of Edinburgh and neighbouring East Lothian, Midlothian, West Lothian and the sea at the Firth of Forth. Edinburgh as the capital of Scotland, is a major administrative, cultural, commercial and tourist centre. It contains most of Scotland's national and cultural institutions. Its historic core is centred around Edinburgh Castle and the Royal Mile, attracting much tourism. The city is also a centre for education and scientific research; other important industries are electronics and food and drink production. The river Water of Leith runs through the city to the docks at Leith.
Places of interest: City Art Centre; Edinburgh Castle; Edinburgh Zoo; Gorgie City Farm; Museum of Antiquities; Museum of Childhood; National Gallery of Scotland; Palace of Holyroodhouse; People's Story Museum; Queen's Hall; Royal Botanic Garden; Royal Highland Centre; Royal Museum of Scotland; St. Giles Cathedral; Scotch Whisky Heritage Centre; Scottish National Gallery of Modern Art; Scottish National Portrait Gallery; Scottish United Services Museum, Edinburgh Castle; The Royal Scots Regimental Museum; Tron Kirk; Usher Hall.

Essex *Essex* Population: 1,228,209.
County of SE England bounded by Cambridgeshire, Greater London, Hertfordshire, Southend, Thurrock and the sea at the Thames estuary and North Sea. Chief towns are Basildon, the county town of Chelmsford, Colchester, Harlow, Brentwood, Clacton-on-Sea, Loughton, Canvey Island, Billericay, and Braintree. The landscape is mostly flat or gently undulating, and the low-lying coast is deeply indented with river estuaries. Along the county's S and W sides, there is a concentration of urban development, with a mixture of light engineering and service industries. In the N and central parts are farmlands, orchards, market and nursery gardens. The NE coast has the busy passenger and container port of Harwich, and the popular seaside resort of Clacton-on-Sea. Rivers include the Stour, forming part of the boundary with Suffolk, the Lea, forming part of the boundary with Hertfordshire, and the Blackwater.
Districts: Basildon; Braintree; Brentwood; Castle Point; Chelmsford; Colchester; Epping Forest; Harlow; Maldon; Rochford; Tendring; Uttlesford.
Places of interest: Audley End, Saffron Walden; Clacton Pier; Colchester Castle; Colchester Zoo; Hainault Forest Country Park; High Woods Country Park, Colchester; Lee Valley Country Park, Waltham Abbey; Marsh Farm Country Park, Chelmsford; New Walton Pier, Walton on the Naze; North Weald Airfield, Epping; Pitsea Hall Country Park.

Falkirk *Falk.* Population: 142,530.
Unitary authority in central Scotland surrounding Falkirk and neighbouring Clackmannanshire, Fife, North Lanarkshire, Stirling and West Lothian. Main towns are Falkirk, Grangemouth, Polmont, Stenhousemuir and Bo'ness. Petrochemical and chemical industries are important to the local economy, as well as bus manufacturing, toffees and paper-making. The Firth of Forth borders Falkirk to the N. Other rivers include the Carron and Pow Burn.
Places of interest: Blackness Castle, Linlithgow; Bo'ness & Kinneil Railway.

Fife *Fife* Population: 351,200.
Unitary authority in E Scotland neighbouring Clackmannanshire and Perth & Kinross, and lying between the Firth of Tay and Firth of Forth. Main towns are Dunfermline, Kirkcaldy, Glenrothes, Buckhaven, Cowdenbeath and St. Andrews. Fife comprises the former county of the same name, known since ancient times as the Kingdom of Fife, and is noted for its fine coastline with many distinctive small towns and fishing ports. The historic town of St. Andrews, on the coast between the two firths, is a university town, and the home of the world's premier golf club. Inland, the area is outstandingly fertile, with agriculture being an important industry. The SW of the area is a former coal-mining area.
Places of interest: Craigtoun Country Park, near St. Andrews; Deep Sea World, North Queensferry; Lochore Meadows Country Park, Crosshill; Sea Life Centre, St. Andrews.

Flintshire (Sir y Fflint). *Flints.* Population: 144,000.
Unitary authority in N Wales neighbouring Conwy, Denbighshire, Wrexham, the English county of Cheshire and the mouth of the River Dee. Main towns are Buckley, Connah's Quay, Flint, Hawarden, Shotton, Queensferry, Mold and Holywell. Known as the Gateway to N Wales, the landscape varies from the mountains which form the Clwydian Range, to small villages and woodlands.
Places of interest: Wepre Country Park, Connah's Quay.

Glasgow *Glas.* Population: 618,430.
Unitary authority in SW Scotland surrounding Glasgow and bounded by East Dunbartonshire, East Renfrewshire, North Lanarkshire, Renfrewshire, South Lanarkshire and West Dunbartonshire. Glasgow is Scotland's largest city and its principal industrial and shopping centre. The city developed significantly due to heavy industry, notably shipbuilding, being centred on the Clyde. While such industry has declined, Glasgow has emerged as a major cultural centre of Europe, due to its impressive arts and cultural scene. The River Clyde runs through the city.
Places of interest: Burrell Collection; Gallery of Modern Art; Glasgow Botanic Garden; Glasgow Cathedral; Hunterian Museum & Art Gallery; Kelvingrove Art Gallery & Museum; McLellan Galleries; Museum of Transport, Kelvin Hall; People's Palace Museum; Royal Concert Hall; St. Mungo's Museum; Scottish Exhibition & Conference Centre (S.E.C.C.).

Gloucestershire *Glos.* Population: 528,370.
County of W England bounded by Herefordshire, Oxfordshire, South Gloucestershire, Swindon, Warwickshire, Wiltshire, Worcestershire and the Welsh authority of Monmouthshire. Main centres are the cathedral city and county town of Gloucester and the towns of Cheltenham, Stroud, Cirencester and Dursley. The limestone mass of the Cotswold Hills dominates the centre of the county, and provides the characteristic pale golden stone of many of its buildings. The River Severn forms a wide valley to the W, ending in a long tidal estuary, beyond which are the hills of the Forest of Dean. Industry is centred on the fertile Severn Vale, with aerospace, light engineering, food production, and service industries in and around the towns; in rural areas market gardening and orchards dominate. The River Thames rises in the county, and forms part of its S boundary in the vicinity of Lechlade. Apart from the Severn and the Thames, there is the River Wye, which forms part of the boundary with Monmouthshire, and many smaller rivers, among them the Chelt, Coln, Evenlode, Leach, Leadon, and Windrush.
Districts: Cheltenham; Cotswold; Forest of Dean; Gloucester; Stroud; Tewkesbury.
Places of interest: Birdland, Bourton on the Water; Crickley Hill Country Park, Birdlip; Gloucester Cathedral; Gloucestershire & Warwickshire Railway, Toddington; Hidcote Manor (NT), Chipping Campden; Historic Gloucester Docks; Prinknash Abbey Pottery, Gloucester; St. John Baptist, Cirencester; Slimbridge Wildfowl & Wetlands Trust; Snowshill Manor (NT); Sudeley Castle, Winchcombe; Tewkesbury Abbey; Westonbirt Arboretum, Tetbury.

Greater London *Gt.Lon.* Population: 6,675,557.
Former metropolitan county of 32 boroughs and the City of London which together form the conurbation of London, the capital of the UK. Greater London is the largest financial, commercial, cultural, distribution and communications centre in the country, including all but primary industrial sectors. London developed from the City of London, a walled Roman settlement on the Thames, and Westminster, which was a Saxon religious settlement and later a Norman seat of government. The Great Fire of 1666 destroyed most of the medieval city, and was followed by a period of rebuilding and rapid, unplanned expansion. Industrialisation and improved public transport over the last two centuries have caused major suburban growth, and the absorption of most of the surrounding settlements and countryside. Tourism is a major industry, with most attractions situated in and around the historic core, and along the Thames bankside. Other notable tourist areas include Greenwich, Hampstead, Kew and Richmond. Industrial activity is widespread, with major concentrations in the E along the Thames. Leisure facilities include national and major sports stadiums, and many big parks and gardens. Airports at Heathrow and docklands. The main river is the Thames.
Districts: Barking & Dagenham; Barnet; Bexley; Brent; Bromley; Camden; City of London; City of Westminster; Croydon; Ealing; Enfield; Greenwich; Hackney; Hammersmith & Fulham; Haringey; Harrow; Havering; Hillingdon; Hounslow; Islington; Kensington & Chelsea; Kingston upon Thames; Lambeth; Lewisham; Merton; Newham; Redbridge; Richmond upon Thames; Southwark; Sutton; Tower Hamlets; Waltham Forest; Wandsworth.
Places of interest: Albert Memorial Visitor Centre; Alexandra Palace Exhibition Centre; Baden-Powell House; Bank of England Museum; Barbican Art Gallery; Barbican Centre; Battersea Park Children's Zoo; Bethnal Green Museum of Childhood; Brass Rubbing Centre (Westminster Abbey); British Museum; Buckingham Palace; Business Design Centre; Cabaret Mechanical Theatre (Covent Garden); Cabinet War Rooms; Central Criminal Court (Old Bailey); Chapter House (Westminster Abbey); Chessington World of Adventure; Commonwealth Institute; Courtauld Institute Gallery; Crystal Palace Park Farmyard; Cutty Sark; Design Museum; Earl's Court; Fairfield Halls, Croydon; Funland & Laserbowl, Trocadero; H.M.S. Belfast; Hampton Court Garden and Maze; Hampton Court Palace; Harrow Museum, Harrow; Hayward Gallery; Heathrow Roof Garden; Heathrow Visitor Centre; Horniman Museum; Hounslow Urban Farm; Imperial War Museum; Kensington Palace; Kenwood House; Kew Gardens; Labatt's Apollo; London Arena; London Docklands Visitor Centre; London Dungeon; London Transport Museum; London Zoo; Lord's Cricket Ground; Madame Tussaud's; Morden Hall Park, Morden; Museum of London; Museum of the Moving Image; National Army Museum; National Gallery; National Maritime Museum; National Portrait Gallery; Natural History Museum; Old Royal Observatory; Olympia; Osterley Park (NT), Isleworth; Queen Elizabeth Hall; Queen Elizabeth II Conference Centre; Queen's Gallery; Rock Circus; Royal Academy of Arts; Royal Air Force Museum; Royal Albert Hall; Royal Festival Hall Complex; Royal Horticultural Halls; Royal Opera House; St. Martin in-the-Fields; St. Paul's

Cathedral; Science Museum; Serpentine Gallery; Sir John Soane's Museum; Southwark Cathedral; Tate Gallery; The Photographer's Gallery; Theatre Museum; Tower Bridge; Tower Hill Pageant; Tower of London; Twickenham Rugby Football Ground; Victoria & Albert Museum; Wallace Collection; Wembley Stadium Complex; Westminster Abbey; Westminster Cathedral; Whitechapel Art Gallery; Wimbledon Lawn Tennis Club; Winston Churchill's Britain At War Experience.

Greater Manchester *Gt.Man.* Population: 2,499,441.

Former metropolitan county of NW England neighbouring Blackburn with Darwen, Cheshire, Derbyshire, Lancashire, Merseyside, Warrington and West Yorkshire. It comprises the near-continuous urban complex which includes the adjoining cities of Manchester and Salford; and towns including Bolton, Stockport, Oldham, Rochdale, Wigan, Bury and Sale. The conurbation is framed by the wild moorland of The Pennines to the N and the Peak District and Cheshire Plain to the S. Development occurred during the 18c and 19c, creating a series of cotton producing textile towns, while Manchester established itself as the commercial and trading hub, later becoming an inland port linked to Liverpool via the canal network. As textile production declined, the industrial base of the area broadened to include brewing, food production, electronics, plastics, printing, light engineering, financial, leisure and service sectors. Retail is based on town shopping centres and malls such as the Arndale and Trafford Centres. There are many major sporting venues in the area, and cultural facilities include the G-MEX centre, numerous universities, museums and galleries and a diverse nightlife. The area is served by Manchester Airport. Main rivers are Irwell and Mersey.
Districts: Bolton; Bury; Manchester; Oldham; Rochdale; Salford; Stockport; Tameside; Trafford; Wigan.
Places of interest: Animal World, Bolton; Aviation Viewing Park, Manchester; Bolton Museum & Art Gallery; Dunham Massey Country Park, Altrincham; Etherow Country Park, Compstall; G-MEX Centre, Manchester; Granada Studios Tour, Salford; Haigh Hall Country Park, Wigan; Heaton Park, Manchester; Hollingworth Lake Country Park Visitor Centre, Rochdale; Hollingworth Lake Country Park, Littleborough; Labatt's Apollo, Manchester; Manchester City Art Galleries; Manchester Museum; Manchester United Museum & Tour Centre; Museum of Science & Industry, Manchester; Pennington Flash Country Park, Leigh; Whitworth Art Gallery, Manchester; Wigan Pier.

Gwynedd *Gwyn.* Population: 116,000.

Unitary authority in NW Wales bounded by Ceredigion, Conwy, Denbighshire, Isle of Anglesey, Powys and the sea. Main centres are the cathedral city of Bangor, Caernarfon, Ffestiniog, Blaenau Ffestiniog, Llanddeiniolen, Pwllheli, Llanllynfi, Bethesda and Porthmadog. The whole mainland area, except the Lleyn Peninsula in the NW, is extremely mountainous and contains the scenically famous Snowdonia National Park. There is slate-quarrying in the Ffestiniog valley, otherwise sheep-farming and tourism are the principal occupations; the coastline has been much developed for the holiday trade. The area contains many lakes and reservoirs, among them are Llyn Trawsfynedd, Llyn Celyn and Llyn Tegid. Of the many rivers, the Wnion and the Dyfi, which flows through part of the area, are most significant.
Places of interest: Butlin's Starcoast World, Pwllheli; Caernarfon Castle; Ffestiniog Railway, Porthmadog; Llechwedd Slate Caverns, Blaenau Ffestiniog; Padarn Country Park; Penrhyn Castle (NT), Bangor; Portmeirion Village, Penrhyndeudraeth; Royal Welch Fusiliers Regiment Museum, Caernarfon; Snowdon Mountain Railway.

Halton *Halton* Population: 123,716.

Unitary authority in NW England neighbouring Cheshire, Merseyside and Warrington. The principal towns are Runcorn and Widnes, separated by the River Mersey. The area is industrialised, being dominated by petro-chemicals and chemicals industries due to the nearby salt mines and port facilities.
Places of interest: Catalyst Museum, Widnes; Norton Priory & Museum, Runcorn.

Hampshire *Hants.* Population: 1,169,986.

County of S England bounded by Bracknell Forest, Dorset, Portsmouth, Southampton, Surrey, West Berkshire, West Sussex, Wiltshire, Wokingham and the English Channel. Main towns are Basingstoke, Gosport, Waterlooville, Farnborough, Aldershot, Eastleigh, Havant, the ancient city and county town of Winchester, Andover and Fleet. The centre of the county consists largely of chalk downs interspersed with fertile valleys. In the SW is the New Forest, while in the NE is the military area centred on Aldershot. The much indented coastline borders The Solent and looks across to the Isle of Wight. Main industries are in the service sector, with chemicals and pharmaceuticals also important. The chief rivers are the Itchen and Test, both chalk streams flowing into Southampton Water, and the Meon flowing into The Solent.
Districts: Basingstoke & Deane; East Hampshire; Eastleigh; Fareham; Gosport; Hart; Havant; New Forest; Rushmoor; Test Valley; Winchester.
Places of interest: Beaulieu Abbey; Beaulieu House; Birdworld, Holt Pound; Buckler's Hard Maritime Museum, Beaulieu; Eling Tide Mill, Totton; Exbury Gardens, Exbury; Finkley Down Farm Park, Andover; Manor Farm Country Park, Bursledon; Marwell Zoo, Colden Common; Mottisfont Abbey Gardens (NT); National Motor Museum, Beaulieu; Paulton's Park, Ower; Queen Elizabeth Country Park, Horndean; The Great Hall, Winchester; Winchester Cathedral.

Hartlepool *Hart.* Population: 90,409.

Unitary authority on the NE coast of England surrounding Hartlepool and bordering Darlington, Durham, Stockton-on-Tees and the North Sea. Fishing is a major industry and a marina has been created from part of the old docks. The mouth of the River Tees forms part of the E border.
Places of interest: Hartlepool Power Station Visitor Centre; Museum of Hartlepool.

Herefordshire *Here.* Population: 164,700.

Unitary authority in W England bounded by Gloucestershire, Shropshire, Worcestershire and the Welsh authorities of Monmouthshire and Powys. Main centres are the cathedral city of Hereford and the towns of Ross-on-Wye, Leominster and Ledbury. Herefordshire lies between the Malvern Hills to the E and the Black Mountains to the W. It is mainly rural, with dairy farming, orchards and market gardening in evidence. The main river is the Wye, which provides excellent fishing.
Places of interest: Hereford Cathedral; Queenswood Country Park, Leominster.

Hertfordshire *Herts.* Population: 975,829.

S midland county of England bounded by Bedfordshire, Buckinghamshire, Cambridgeshire, Essex, Greater London and Luton. Chief centres are Watford, the cathedral city of St. Albans, Hemel Hempstead, Stevenage, Cheshunt, Welwyn Garden City, Hoddesdon, Hitchin, Letchworth and Hatfield; the county town is Hertford. The Chilterns rise along the W border, and there are chalk hills in the N around Royston; otherwise the landscape is mostly flat or gently undulating. There is a mixture of rural and urban life, with agricultural and hi-tech industries represented. While the urban centres in the S lie on the N periphery of the Greater London conurbation, there are many villages with the traditional large green or common. The more urban S part of the county includes a dense network of major roads bypassing, and leading N from London. Rivers include the Colne, Ivel, and Lee.
Districts: Broxbourne; Dacorum; East Herts; Hertsmere; North Hertfordshire; St. Albans; Stevenage; Three Rivers; Watford; Welwyn Hatfield.
Places of interest: Adventure Island Playbarn, Sawbridgeworth; Aldenham Reservoir Country Park, Elstree; Bowmans Farm, London Colney; Hatfield House; Knebworth House; Paradise Wildlife Park, Broxbourne; St. Albans Cathedral; Standalone Farm, Letchworth.

Highland *High.* Population: 207,500.

Unitary authority covering a large part of N Scotland and neighbouring Aberdeenshire, Argyll & Bute, Moray and Perth & Kinross. It contains a mixture of mainland and island life, comprising the former districts of Badenoch and Strathspey, Caithness, Inverness, Lochaber, Nairn, Ross and Cromarty, Skye and Lochalsh, and Sutherland. Main towns are Inverness, Fort William, Thurso, Nairn, Wick, Alness and Dingwall. Overall, Highland is very sparsely inhabited, being wild and remote in character. It is scenically outstanding, containing as it does part of the Cairngorm Mountains, Ben Nevis, and the North West Highlands. Many of the finest sea and inland lochs in Scotland are also here, such as Loch Ness, Loch Linnhe, Loch Torridon and Loch Broom. The discovery of North Sea oil has made an impact on the towns and villages around the Moray Firth. Elsewhere, tourism, crofting, fishing and skiing are important locally.

Places of interest: Aonach Mhor Mountain Gondola Lift & Nevis Range Ski Centre, Fort William; Ben Nevis, Fort William; Bught Floral Hall and Visitor Centre, Inverness; Culloden Visitor Centre, near Inverness; Dunvegan Castle; Fort Augustus Abbey Visitor Centre; Glencoe Visitor Centre (NTS); Inverewe Gardens (NTS), Londubh; Loch Ness Monster Exhibition Centre, Drumnadrochit; Rothiemurchus Visitor Centre & Forest Trail; Shin Falls; Speyside Heather Centre, Dulnain Bridge; Urquhart Castle, Drumnadrochit.

Inverclyde *Inclyde* Population: 89,990.
Unitary authority on the W coast of central Scotland, on the S bank of the River Clyde. It is bordered by North Ayrshire, Renfrewshire and the Firth of Clyde. The chief towns are Greenock, Port Glasgow, Gourock, and Kilmacolm.
Places of interest: Lunderston Bay, Gourock; McLean Museum & Art Gallery, Greenock.

Isle of Anglesey (Sir Ynys Môn). *I.o.A.* Population: 71,000.
Unitary authority island of NW Wales divided from Gwynedd and the mainland by the Menai Strait, and with Holy Island lying to the W. Main towns are Holyhead, Llangefni, Amlwch and Menai Bridge. Anglesey has 125m of coastline and 16 beaches. Agriculture is an important industry to the island, with other industries including aluminium smelting and food processing. Holyhead is an important port terminus for the Republic of Ireland. Rivers include the Braint and Cefni.
Places of interest: Anglesey Sea Zoo, Brynsiencyn; Beaumaris Castle.

Isle of Man *I.o.M.* Population: 69,788.
Self-governing island in the Irish Sea, situated in the centre of the British Isles. The chief towns are Douglas, Ramsey, Peel, Castletown, Port St. Mary, Port Erin and Laxey. Apart from the N tip, the topography is generally mountainous, rising to a peak at Snaefell. The main industries are agriculture, fishing and tourism as well as financial services and manufacturing. The island is synonymous with motorsport, being the home of the internationally renowned Tourist Trophy Circuit. Rivers include the Glen Auldyn and Neb.
Places of interest: Ballachurry Fort; Ballaheannagh.

Isle of Wight *I.o.W.* Population: 130,000.
County and island with an area of 147 square miles or 381 square km, separated from the S coast of England by The Solent. Chief towns are the capital, Newport, Ryde, Cowes, Shanklin, Sandown, Ventnor, and Yarmouth. The island is geologically diverse, composed of sedimentary rocks and contains many important fossil remains. Tourism flourishes owing to the mild climate and the natural beauty of the island. There are Royal associations as Queen Victoria lived and died at Osborne House in the N of the island. There is a strong naval tradition, with the island historically acting as a defence for Portsmouth. Cowes is internationally famous for yachting. There are ferry and hovercraft connections at Cowes, Ryde, and Yarmouth (ferry to Lymington). Chief river is the Medina.
Places of interest: All Saints, Godshill; Blackgang Chine; Brickfields Horse Country, Binstead; Carisbrooke Castle & Museum; Flamingo Park; Isle of Wight Pearl, Brighstone; Isle of Wight Zoo, Sandown; Museum of Isle of Wight Geology, Sandown; Needles Pleasure Park; Osborne House; St. Mildred, Whippingham; Shanklin Chine; Ventnor Botanic Gardens.

Isles of Scilly *I.o.S.* Population: 1964.
Group of some 140 islands 48m/45km SW of Land's End, Cornwall, of which five are inhabited: Bryher, St. Agnes, St. Martin's, St. Mary's and Tresco. Chief industries are fishing, and the growing of early flowers and vegetables due to the exceptionally mild climate.
Places of interest: Isles of Scilly Museum, St. Mary's; Tresco Abbey Gardens.

Kent *Kent* Population: 1,268,052.
South-easternmost county of England bounded by East Sussex, Greater London, Medway, Surrey, and the sea at the Thames estuary and the Strait of Dover. Chief centres are the county town of Maidstone, Royal Tunbridge Wells, Dartford, Margate, Ashford, Gravesend, Folkestone, Sittingbourne, Ramsgate, the cathedral city of Canterbury, Tonbridge and Dover. The chalk ridge of the North Downs runs along the N side, then SE to Folkestone and Dover. The River Medway cuts through the chalk in the vicinity of Maidstone, and there are low lying areas to the E of Canterbury and of Tonbridge, on Romney Marsh in the S, and bordering the Thames estuary in the N. Chief industrial areas are around Maidstone, Ashford and Tonbridge; Dover and Folkestone are major ports, with the Channel Tunnel terminus to the N of Folkestone; Sheerness is a port of growing importance and Ramsgate is a hovercraft terminal. Industrial activity includes mineral extraction, cement manufacture and papermaking. On the highly productive agricultural land, Kent's reputation as the Garden of England is earned, with market gardening, fruit and hop production. Romney Marsh is used for extensive sheep-grazing. Rivers include the Medway, Stour, and Beult.
Districts: Ashford; Canterbury; Dartford; Dover; Gravesham; Maidstone; Sevenoaks; Shepway; Swale; Thanet; Tonbridge & Malling; Tunbridge Wells.
Places of interest: Brogdale Horticultural Trust, Faversham; Canterbury Cathedral; Chartwell (NT), Westerham; Dover Castle; Dover Museum; Dreamland Theme Park, Margate; Eastbridge Hospital, Canterbury; Hever Castle Gardens; Hever Castle; Howletts Wildlife Park; Ightham Mote (NT), Sevenoaks; Kent & East Sussex Railway; Knole (NT), Sevenoaks; Leeds Castle Gardens; Leeds Castle; M.V. Princess Pocahontas, Northfleet; Port Lympne Zoo Park; R.A.F. Manston Spitfire & Hurricane Memorial Building, Manston; Romney, Hythe & Dymchurch Railway, Romney; Rotunda Amusement Park, Folkestone; St. Mary in Castro, Dover; Scotney Castle Garden (NT), Lamberhurst; Sissinghurst Castle (NT), Cranbrook; The Canterbury Tales, Canterbury; The Friars; Whitbread Hop Farm, Beltring; White Cliffs Experience, Dover.

Kingston upon Hull *Hull* Population: 265,000.
Unitary authority on the E coast of England surrounding the city of Kingston upon Hull and bounded by East Riding of Yorkshire and the mouth of the River Humber. Kingston upon Hull is a major sea port and a great industrial city, with key industries including chemicals, food processing, pharmaceuticals and engineering. The River Hull passes through the area, and the River Humber forms the S border.
Places of interest: Ferens Art Gallery; Humber Bridge Country Park.

Lancashire *Lancs.* Population: 1,101,317.
County of NW England bounded by Blackburn with Darwen, Cumbria, Greater Manchester, Merseyside, North Yorkshire, West Yorkshire and the Irish Sea. Chief towns are the administrative centre of Preston, Burnley, Morecambe, the historic county town of Lancaster, Skelmersdale, Lytham St. Anne's, Leyland, Accrington and Chorley; Fleetwood and Heysham are ports. The inland side of the county is hilly and includes the wild and impressive Forest of Bowland. The W side contains the coastal plain, where vegetables are extensively cultivated. The S is largely urban; industries include cotton spinning and weaving, chemicals, glass, rubber, electrical goods, and motor vehicles. The principal rivers are the Lune and the Ribble.
Districts: Burnley; Chorley; Fylde; Hyndburn; Lancaster; Pendle; Preston; Ribble Valley; Rossendale; South Ribble; West Lancashire; Wyre.
Places of interest: Beacon Fell Country Park, White Chapel; Beacon Park, Upholland; Camelot Theme Park; East Lancashire Railway, Waterfoot; Frontierland, Morecambe; Harris Museum & Art Gallery, Preston; Lancaster Leisure Park; Leighton Moss, Carnforth; Martin Mere; St. Mary, Lancaster; Towneley Hall Art Gallery & Museum, Burnley; Williamson Park, Lancaster; Wycoller Country Park.

Leicester *Leic.* Population: 270,493.
Unitary authority in central England surrounding Leicester and bounded by Leicestershire. It is one of the leading shopping regions in the Midlands. Traditional industries such as hosiery and footwear, as well as hi-tech industries, are important to the local economy. Leicester is aiming to be one of the most environmentally-friendly cities in Europe. It is involved in pioneering electronic toll road schemes in order to encourage the use of public transport. The Rivers Sence and Soar run through the area.
Places of interest: Gorse Hill City Farm; Leicester Guildhall.

Leicestershire *Leics.* Population: 565,539.
Midland county of England bounded by Derbyshire, Leicester, Lincolnshire, Northamptonshire, Nottinghamshire, Rutland, Staffordshire and Warwickshire. Chief towns are Loughborough, Hinckley, Wigston, Coalville, Melton Mowbray, Oadby, Market Harborough, Shepshed and Ashby de la Zouch. The landscape is mostly of low, rolling hills. E and W of Leicester are areas of higher ground, notably Charnwood Forest. The W is largely industrial; industries include light engineering, hosiery, and

footwear. The E is rural, with large fields and scattered woods, and is noted for field sports and food production. Part of the legacy left by the Roman occupation of Leicestershire are the Great North Road, Watling Street and Fosse Way which dissect the county. River Soar traverses the county from S to N, while River Welland forms part of the boundary with Northamptonshire to the S.

Districts: Blaby; Charnwood; Harborough; Hinckley & Bosworth; Melton; North West Leicestershire; Oadby & Wigston.

Places of interest: Beacon Hill Country Park; Bosworth Battlefield Country Park; Bradgate Park, Newtown Linford; Broombriggs Farm, Loughborough; Burbage Common, Hinckley; Farmworld, Oadby; Foxton Canal, Market Harborough; Queen's Royal Lancers Regiment Museum, Belvoir; Snibston Discovery Park, Coalville; Twycross Zoo, Atherstone.

Lincolnshire *Lincs.* Population: 584,534.
County of E England bounded by Cambridgeshire, Leicestershire, Norfolk, Northamptonshire, North East Lincolnshire, North Lincolnshire, Nottinghamshire, Peterborough, Rutland and the North Sea. Main towns are the cathedral city and county town of Lincoln and the towns of Boston, Grantham, Gainsborough, Spalding, Stamford, Skegness and Louth. Much of the county is flat and includes a large area of The Fens in the S. This reclaimed marshland is richly fertile, producing large crops of peas (for canning), sugar beet, potatoes, corn, and around Spalding, flower bulbs. Two ranges of hills traverse the county N and S: the narrow limestone ridge, a continuation of the Cotswold Hills, running from Grantham to Scunthorpe, and the chalk Wolds, about 12m/20km wide, running N from Spilsby and Horncastle. Apart from agriculture, industries include manufacture of agricultural machinery and tourism, which is centred on historic Lincoln, and the coastal resorts of Skegness and Mablethorpe. The rivers, of which the chief are the Witham and Welland, are largely incorporated into the extensive land-drainage system, and scarcely distinguishable from man-made channels.

Districts: Boston; East Lindsey; Lincoln; North Kesteven; South Holland; South Kesteven; West Lindsey.

Places of interest: Belton House (NT); Gibraltar Point, Skegness; Grimsthorpe Castle; Hartsholme Country Park, Lincoln; Lincoln Castle; Lincoln Cathedral; St. Botolph, Boston; Skegness Natureland Seal Sanctuary; The Lawn, Lincoln.

Luton *Luton* Population: 171,671.
Unitary authority in SE England surrounding Luton and bounded by Bedfordshire and Hertfordshire. Luton is one of the major centres of employment and manufacturing in SE England, with automotive, electrical and retail industries among the most important. The production and export of high fashion and straw hats remains a feature of the local economy. London Luton Airport is situated in the SE of the area, and the River Lea rises nearby.

Places of interest: Stockwood Craft Museum & Gardens; Woodside Farm.

Medway *Med.* Population: 240,821.
Unitary authority on SE coast of England S of the River Thames estuary and neighbouring Kent. The chief centres are Gillingham, the naval base of Chatham, Strood and the cathedral city of Rochester. The S part of the area, surrounding the River Medway, is largely urban and industrialised. The marshland to the N includes Kingsnorth Power Station and the Isle of Grain, but is mostly rural, and contains Northward Hill Nature Reserve which is a haven for birds.

Places of interest: Chatham Historic Dockyard & Lifeboat Collection; Guildhall Museum, Rochester; Rochester Castle; Rochester Cathedral.

Merseyside *Mersey.* Population: 1,403,642.
Former metropolitan county of NW England. It neighbours Cheshire, Greater Manchester, Halton, Lancashire, Warrington and the sea. It comprises the near-continuous urban complex which includes the city of Liverpool and the towns of St. Helens, Birkenhead, Southport, Bootle, Wallasey, Bebington, Huyton and Crosby. The county straddles the long, wide estuary of the River Mersey, which accounts for the development of the area. During the 18c, growing Imperial trade of goods and slaves, led to the explosion of urban development surrounding the docks at Liverpool, Birkenhead and Bootle. Liverpool went on to become Britain's premier transatlantic port and a significant terminus during the migration flows of the 19c, leading to an ethnically diverse city culture. Over the last century the docks have declined, leaving behind an impressive waterfront and cityscape as testament to a mercantile and maritime heritage. Inland, the urban spread has reached the industrial town of St. Helens which is famed for glass production. To the N are the residential areas of Crosby, Formby and the coastal resort of Southport. The area includes race courses at Aintree and Haydock, and a local airport at Speke.

Districts: Knowsley; Liverpool; St. Helens; Sefton; Wirral.

Places of interest: Albert Dock Village, Liverpool; Cavern Club, Liverpool; Croxteth Hall Country Park, Liverpool; Croxteth Hall, Liverpool; H.M. Customs National Museum, Liverpool; Knowsley Safari Park, Prescot; Liverpool Cathedral; Liverpool Metropolitan Cathedral (RC); Liverpool Museum, Liverpool; Maritime Museum, Liverpool; Mersey Ferries, Liverpool; Museum of Liverpool Life; Natural History Centre, Liverpool; New Palace and Adventureland, New Brighton; Philharmonic Hall, Liverpool; Pleasureland Amusement Park, Southport; St. George's Hall, Liverpool; Southport Pier; Tate Gallery, Liverpool; Voirrey Embroidery, Wirral; Walker Art Gallery, Liverpool.

Merthyr Tydfil *M.Tyd.* Population: 60,000.
Unitary authority in S Wales bounded by Caerphilly, Powys and Rhondda Cynon Taff. Main centres are the town of Merthyr Tydfil and the villages of Treharris, Abercanaid and Troedyrhiw. The area stretches from the Brecon Beacons, along the Taff Valley, to the centre of the former Welsh coal mining district. The local economy has diversified from primary industry, with Merthyr Tydfil being an important centre for public administration, shopping and employment for the region. The River Taff flows through the area.

Places of interest: Brecon Mountain Railway; Cyfarthfa Museum.

Middlesbrough *Middbro.* Population: 146,000.
Unitary authority in NE England surrounding Middlesbrough and bounded by North Yorkshire, Redcar & Cleveland and Stockton-on-Tees. Middlesbrough is an industrial town, with chemical and petro-chemical industries in evidence. It is also an important sub-regional shopping and entertainment centre between Leeds and Newcastle upon Tyne.

Places of interest: Albert Park; Captain Cook Birthplace Museum; Stewart Park, Marton.

Midlothian *Midloth.* Population: 79,901.
Unitary authority in central Scotland neighbouring East Lothian, Edinburgh and Scottish Borders. Main towns are Penicuik, Bonnyrigg, Dalkeith, Gorebridge and Loanhead. The area is mostly rural, including the rolling moorland of the Pentland Hills and Moorfoot Hills in the S. To the N, the urban area is comprised of satellite towns to the SE of Edinburgh. Rivers include Tyne Water and South Esk.

Places of interest: Edinburgh Crystal Visitor Centre, Penicuik; Vogrie Country Park, near Ford.

Milton Keynes *M.K.* Population: 200,000.
S midland unitary authority of England bounded by Bedfordshire, Buckinghamshire and Northamptonshire. The area includes the city of Milton Keynes, Bletchley, Newport Pagnell, Great Linford, Stony Stratford and Wolverton. Over the past 30 years, the area has undergone the fastest rate of growth in the country, attracting numerous industries. The Great Ouse and Ouzel rivers pass through the area.

Places of interest: Cowper & Newton Museum, Olney; Emberton Park.

Monmouthshire (Sir Fynwy). *Mon.* Population: 80,400.
Unitary authority in SE Wales bounded by Blaenau Gwent, Newport, Powys, Torfaen, the English areas of Gloucestershire, Herefordshire and the Bristol Channel. The main towns are Abergavenny, Caldicot, Chepstow and Monmouth. Part of the Brecon Beacons are found in NW Monmouthshire, whereas the SW area is mainly flat. Agriculture, mineral extraction and the service sector are important to the local economy. Rivers include the Wye, which forms part of E border, and the Usk, Trothy and Monnow.

Places of interest: Tintern Abbey (Ruin); The Old Station, Tintern.

Moray *Moray* Population: 85,000.
Unitary authority in N Scotland neighboured by Aberdeenshire, Highland and the sea. Main towns are Elgin, Forres, Buckie,

Lossiemouth and Keith. The area is mainly mountainous, including part of the Cairngorm Mountains in the S. It is dissected by many deep river valleys, most notably that of the River Spey. Along with the local grain and peat, the abundant waters provide the raw materials for half of Scotland's malt whisky distilleries, leading to the Whisky Trail and much tourism through Speyside.
Places of interest: Baxters Visitor Centre, Fochabers; Glenfiddich Distillery, Dufftown; Johnstons Cashmere Visitor Centre, Elgin.

Neath Port Talbot (Castell-nedd Port Talbot). *N.P.T.*
Population: 139,650.
Unitary authority in S Wales neighbouring Bridgend, Powys, Rhondda Cynon Taff, Swansea and the sea. The chief centres are Neath, Port Talbot, Pontardawe, Baglan, Glyncorrwg and Briton Ferry. The area is mostly mountainous, divided up by the river valleys of the Tawe, Neath, Afan and Dulais, which all flow out to sea at Swansea Bay. The lower valley of the River Neath is heavily industrialised.
Places of interest: Afan Argoed Country Park, Cynonville; Margam Country Park; Penscynor Wildlife Park, Cilfrew.

Newport (Casnewydd). *Newport* Population: 137,700.
Unitary authority on the S coast of Wales, N of the mouth of the River Severn, and bounded by Caerphilly, Cardiff, Monmouthshire and Torfaen. Main centres are Newport, Liswerry, Malpas and Caerleon. Steel manufacturing and hi-tech industries are important to the local economy. The rivers Ebbw and Usk run through the area.
Places of interest: Caerleon Roman Fortress, Baths & Amphitheatre; Newport Museum & Art Gallery.

Norfolk *Norf.* Population: 745,613.
County of E England bounded by Cambridgeshire, Lincolnshire, Suffolk and the North Sea. Chief centres are the cathedral city and county town of Norwich, Great Yarmouth on the E coast, the expanding port of King's Lynn near the mouth of the Great Ouse and The Wash, Thetford, which is known as the Breckland 'capital', East Dereham and Wymondham. Norfolk is mainly flat or gently undulating, with fenland in the W characterised by large drainage channels emptying into The Wash. In the SW is Breckland, an expanse of heath and conifer forest used for military training; other afforested areas are near King's Lynn and North Walsham. NE of Norwich are The Broads, an area of meres and rivers popular for boating; reeds for thatching are grown here. The N Norfolk coastline is an Area of Outstanding Natural Beauty and Heritage Coast, and includes the popular resorts of Cromer and Sheringham. Otherwise the county is almost entirely agricultural, with farming an important activity; service and manufacturing industries are also significant. Rivers include the Great Ouse, Bure, Nar, Wensum, Wissey, and Yare; the Little Ouse and Waveney both enter the county briefly, but mainly form the boundary with Suffolk.
Districts: Breckland; Broadland; Great Yarmouth; King's Lynn & West Norfolk; North Norfolk; Norwich; South Norfolk.
Places of interest: Banham Zoo; Blickling Hall (NT); Bressingham Live Steam Museum; Mustard Shop, Norwich; Norfolk Lavender, Heacham; North Norfolk Railway, Sheringham; Norwich Castle Museum; Norwich Cathedral; Pettitts Animal Adventure Park, Reedham; Pleasure Beach, Great Yarmouth; St. Andrew's Hall, Norwich; St. Mary Magdalene Chapel, Sandringham; Sea Life Centre, Great Yarmouth; Sea Life Centre, Hunstanton; Shrine of Our Lady of Walsingham, Little Walsingham; The Thursford Collection Steam Museum, Fakenham; Thetford Forest Park; Wroxham Barns, Hoveton.

North Ayrshire *N.Ayr.* Population: 139,175.
Unitary authority in central Scotland including the islands of Arran, Great Cumbrae and Little Cumbrae. It is bounded by East Ayrshire, East Renfrewshire, Inverclyde, Renfrewshire, South Ayrshire and the sea. The principal towns are Irvine, Kilwinning, Saltcoats, Largs, Ardrossan, Stevenston, and Kirbirnie. The area includes mountains and part of Clyde Muirshiel Regional Park in the N, and the lower lands of Cunninghame in the S. There is a maritime heritage to the area; ferry routes operate from Largs and Ardrossan. Rivers include the Garnock, Dusk Water and Noddsdale Water.
Places of interest: Brodick Castle (NTS); Kelburn Country Centre, near Largs.

North East Lincolnshire *N.E.Lincs.* Population: 164,000.
Unitary authority in NE England, S of the mouth of the River Humber and bounded by Lincolnshire, North Lincolnshire and the North Sea. Chief towns are Grimsby, Cleethorpes and Immingham. Grimsby and Cleethorpes together are the shopping and commercial centres of the area. Fishing, food, tourism, chemical and port industries are all important to the local economy. The main rivers are the Humber and Freshney.
Places of interest: Cleethorpes Discovery Centre; National Fishing Heritage Centre, Grimsby; Pleasure Island Theme Park, Cleethorpes.

North Lanarkshire *N.Lan.* Population: 326,750.
Unitary authority in central Scotland neighbouring East Dunbartonshire, Falkirk, Glasgow, South Lanarkshire, Stirling and West Lothian. The chief centres are Cumbernauld, Coatbridge, Airdrie, Motherwell, Wishaw and Bellshill. North Lanarkshire contains a mixture of urban and rural areas, and formerly depended heavily upon the coal, engineering and steel industries. Regeneration and diversification have occurred in recent years.
Places of interest: Drumpellier Country Park, Coatbridge; Palacerigg Country Park, Cumbernauld; Strathclyde Country Park, Motherwell; Summerlee Heritage Trust, Coatbridge.

North Lincolnshire *N.Lincs.* Population: 153,000.
Unitary authority in NE England neighbouring East Riding of Yorkshire, Leicestershire, Norfolk, North East Lincolnshire, Nottinghamshire, Peterborough, Rutland, South Yorkshire and the River Humber. The main centres are Scunthorpe, Bottesford, Barton-upon-Humber and Brigg. The area is mainly rural, but does include oil refineries, steel and manufacturing industries; the River Humber provides pool and wharf facilities. Rivers include the Humber, Trent and the Old Ancholme.
Places of interest: Barton Clay Pits Project, Barton-upon-Humber; Normanby Hall Country Park.

North Somerset *N.Som.* Population: 177,000.
Unitary authority in W England, S of the mouth of the River Severn, and neighbouring Bath & North East Somerset, Bristol, Somerset and the Bristol Channel. Chief towns are Weston-super-Mare, Clevedon, Nailsea and Portishead. The area is largely rural with tourism, centred on the coastal resort of Weston-super-Mare, being a major industry. Bristol International Airport is located in the E of the area.
Places of interest: Clevedon Pier; Winter Gardens, Weston-super-Mare.

North Yorkshire *N.Yorks.* Population: 556,200.
Large county of N England bounded by Cumbria, Darlington, Durham, East Riding of Yorkshire, Lancashire, Middlesbrough, Redcar & Cleveland, South Yorkshire, Stockton-on-Tees, West Yorkshire, York and the North Sea. Main centres are Harrogate, Scarborough, Hetton, Selby, the cathedral city of Ripon, the county town of Northallerton, Whitby, Skipton and Knaresborough. Apart from the wide plain around York, through which flow River Ouse and its tributaries, and the smaller Vale of Pickering, watered by the Derwent and its tributary the Rye, the county is dominated by two ranges of hills; The Pennines in the W and the Cleveland Hills in the NE. The plains are pastoral and agricultural, while the hills provide rough sheep-grazing. The county includes the popular resorts of Scarborough and Whitby, and the majority of the North York Moors and Yorkshire Dales National Parks which promote tourism. Other economic activities include light engineering, service and hi-tech industries. Principal rivers are the Ouse and its tributaries the Derwent, Swale, Ure, Nidd and Wharfe, all draining into the Humber; the Esk, flowing into the North Sea at Whitby; and in the W, the Ribble, passing out into Lancashire and the Irish Sea.
Districts: Craven; Hambleton; Harrogate; Richmondshire; Ryedale; Scarborough; Selby.
Places of interest: Beningbrough Hall (NT); Bolton Abbey Estate, Skipton; Bolton Priory (Ruins); Brymor, High Jervaulx Farm, Masham; Castle Howard, Coneysthorpe; Eden Camp, Malton; Embsay Steam Railway, Skipton; Flamingo Land Theme Park, Malton; Fountains Abbey (NT), Ripon; Grassington National Park Centre; Harlow Carr, Harrogate; Harrogate International Centre; Holy Trinity, Skipton; Kinderland, Scarborough; Malham National Park Centre; Moors Centre, Danby; Mother Shipton's Cave, Knaresborough; Newby Hall, Skelton; North Riding Forest Park, Pickering; North York Moors Railway, Pickering; Ripon Cathedral; St. Mary, Whitby; Sea Life Centre, Scarborough; Skipton Castle; Spa Complex, Scarborough; W.R. Outhwaite & Son Ropemakers, Hawes; Watershed Mill

Visitor Centre, Settle; Whitby Abbey; Whitby Lifeboat Museum; Wyville Animal Farm, Slingsby.

Northamptonshire *Northants.* Population: 578,807.

Midland county of England bounded by Bedfordshire, Buckinghamshire, Cambridgeshire, Leicestershire, Lincolnshire, Milton Keynes, Oxfordshire, Peterborough, Rutland and Warwickshire. Chief towns are Northampton, Corby, Kettering, Wellingborough, Rushden and Daventry. The county consists largely of undulating agricultural country rising locally to low hills, especially along the W border. Large fields and scattered woods provide terrain for field sports. Northamptonshire still retains its rural and agricultural charm, despite undergoing rapid population growth recently. There are many villages of architectural, scenic and historic interest. Industrial development is modest, concentrating on the traditional footwear manufacture. Corby is undergoing regeneration following the decline of its steel industry. Tourism is set to increase due to the county's natural Middle England ambience, and the seasonal opening of the Althorp Estate, the family home and resting place of Diana, Princess of Wales. The principal rivers are the Nene and Welland.
Districts: Corby; Daventry; East Northamptonshire; Kettering; Northampton; South Northamptonshire; Wellingborough.
Places of interest: Barnwell Country Park, Oundle; Brampton Valley Way Country Park, Lamport; Brigstock Country Park, Kettering; Brixworth Country Park; Daventry Country Park; Irchester Country Park; Sywell Reservoir Country Park, Ecton; Wicksteed Park.

Northumberland *Northumb.* Population: 307,709.

Northernmost county of England bounded by Cumbria, Durham and Tyne & Wear, the Scottish authority of Scottish Borders and the North Sea. The principal towns are Blyth, Ashington, Cramlington, Bedlington, Morpeth, Berwick-upon-Tweed, Prudhoe and Hexham. There is some industry in the SE coastal area, otherwise the county is almost entirely rural, the greater part being high moorland, culminating in the Cheviot Hills along the Scottish border. The most spectacular stretches of Hadrian's Wall traverse the county to the N of Haltwhistle and Hexham. There is extensive afforestation, including Kielder Forest Park and part of the Northumberland National Park in the NW; parts of these forests are used for military training. The large reservoir, Kielder Water, also occurs in the NW of the area. Rivers include the Aln, Blyth, Breamish, Coquet, East and West Allen, North and South Tyne, Till, and Wansbeck. The Tweed forms part of the Scottish border and flows out to sea at Berwick-upon-Tweed.
Districts: Alnwick; Berwick-upon-Tweed; Blyth Valley; Castle Morpeth; Tynedale; Wansbeck.
Places of interest: Bamburgh Castle; Bedlington Country Park; Belsay Hall and Gardens; Bolam Lake Country Park; Cragside (NT), Rothbury; Cragside Country Park, Rothbury; Druridge Bay Country Park, Morpeth; Hexham Abbey; Housesteads (Vercovicivm), Bardon Mill; Kielder Forest; Kielder Water, Hexham; Morpeth Chantry; Northumbria Craft Centre, Morpeth; Once Brewed Visitor Centre, Bardon Mill; Plessey Woods Country Park, Bedlington; Queen Elizabeth II Country Park, Ashington; St. Mary, Holy Island; Tyne Green Country Park, Hexham; Wallington (NT), near Cambo; Wansbeck Country Park, near Stakeford.

Nottingham *Nott.* Population: 263,522.

Unitary authority in central England surrounding the city of Nottingham and bounded by Nottinghamshire. The city of Nottingham has a long history, having been granted many Royal Charters; Nottingham Castle and Wollaton Hall are among its many historical buildings. It is also an industrial and engineering centre, and a university city. Its main industries include the manufacture of chemicals, tobacco, cycles, lace and hosiery. The River Trent flows through the city.
Places of interest: Lace Centre; Nottingham Castle Museum; Royal Centre; Royal Concert Hall and Theatre Royal; Tales of Robin Hood; Wollaton Hall Natural History Museum.

Nottinghamshire *Notts.* Population: 730,260.

Midland county of England bounded by Derbyshire, Leicestershire, Lincolnshire, North Lincolnshire, Nottingham and South Yorkshire. Principal towns are Mansfield, Carlton, Sutton in Ashfield, Arnold, Worksop, Newark-on-Trent, West Bridgford, Beeston, Stapleford, Hucknall and Kirkby in Ashfield. Much of the county is rural, with extensive woodlands in the central area of The Dukeries, part of the larger Sherwood Forest. Cattle-grazing is the chief farming activity. Around the large towns there is much industry, including iron and steel, engineering, knitwear, pharmaceuticals, and coal-mining. The county has associations with Robin Hood, at Sherwood Forest, and D.H. Lawrence, at Eastwood. The most important river is the Trent.
Districts: Ashfield; Bassetlaw; Broxtowe; Gedling; Mansfield; Newark & Sherwood; Rushcliffe.
Places of interest: Bestwood Lodge Country Park, Bestwood Village; Clumber Country Park (NT), Hardwick Village; Newark Castle; Newstead Abbey Gardens, Linby; Patchings Farm Art Centre, Calverton; Rufford Country Park; Sherwood Country Park, Edwinstowe; Sherwood Forest Amusement Park, Edwinstowe; Sherwood Pines Forest Park, Edwinstowe; Southwell Minster; Sundown Kiddies Adventureland, Rampton; Watermead Country Park, Syston; White Post Modern Farm Centre, Farnsfield.

Orkney *Ork.* Population: 19,900.

Group of some fifteen main islands and numerous smaller islands, islets and rocks. Designated an Islands Area for administrative purposes, and lying N of the NE end of the Scottish mainland across the Pentland Firth. Kirkwall is the capital, situated on the island Mainland, 24m/38km N of Duncansby Head. Stromness is the only other town. About twenty of the islands are inhabited. In general the islands are low-lying but have steep, high cliffs on W side. The climate is generally mild for the latitude but storms are frequent. Fishing and farming (mainly cattle-rearing) are the chief industries. The oil industry is also represented, with an oil terminal on the island of Flotta, and oil service bases at Car Ness and Stromness, Mainland and at Lyness, Hoy. Lesser industries include whisky distilling, knitwear and tourism. The islands are noted for their unique prehistoric and archaeological remains. The main airport is at Grimsetter, near Kirkwall, with most of the populated islands being served by airstrips. Ferries also operate from the Scottish mainland, and between islands in the group.
Places of interest: Italian Chapel, Lambholm; Skara Brae.

Oxfordshire *Oxon.* Population: 547,584.

S midland county of England bounded by Buckinghamshire, Gloucestershire, Northamptonshire, Reading, Swindon, Warwickshire, West Berkshire, Wiltshire and Wokingham. Chief centres are the county town, cathedral and university city of Oxford and towns of Banbury, Abingdon, Bicester, Witney, Didcot, Thame and Henley-on-Thames. Burford and Chipping Norton are small Cotswold towns in the W and NW respectively. The landscape is predominantly flat or gently undulating, forming part of the Thames Valley. High ground occurs where the Chiltern Hills enter the county in the SE and the Cotswold Hills in the NW. The county is largely agricultural, with industries centred on the towns. Scientific, medical and research establishments are attracted by the proximity of Oxford's universities. Printing and publishing industries have their greatest concentration outside London. The motor industry is well represented with car manufacture at Cowley, Oxford, and the county has the world's largest concentration of performance car development and manufacturing. Tourism, attracted to stately homes, notably Blenheim Palace, and Oxford city centre, is also important. Chief rivers are the Thames (or Isis), Cherwell, Ock, Thame, and Windrush.
Districts: Cherwell; Oxford; South Oxfordshire; Vale of White Horse; West Oxfordshire.
Places of interest: Ashmolean Museum, Oxford; Blenheim Palace, Woodstock; Christ Church College, Oxford; Cotswold Wildlife Park, Burford; Museum of Modern Art, Oxford; Oxford Cathedral; Oxford Story; Oxford University Museum; Pitt Rivers Museum, Oxford; St. John the Baptist, Burford; St. Mary the Virgin, Oxford; Salter Bros. Passenger Boats, Oxford; University of Oxford Botanical Garden.

Pembrokeshire (Sir Benfro). *Pembs.* Population: 117,000.

Unitary authority in the SW corner of Wales neighbouring Carmarthenshire, Ceredigion and the sea. The chief centres are Haverfordwest, Pembroke Dock, Pembroke, Tenby, Saundersfoot, Neyland, Fishguard and the ancient cathedral city of St. David's. Key industries are tourism, agriculture and oil refining. The deep estuarial waters of Milford Haven provide a berth for oil tankers. A large part of Pembrokeshire's coastline forms Britain's only coastal National Park. Ferries from Fishguard and Pembroke Dock sail to Rosslare in the Republic of Ireland.
Places of interest: Canaston Centre, Narberth; Folly Farm, Kilgetty; Llys-y-Fran Reservoir Country Park; Oakwood Leisure Park, near Narberth; Pembroke Castle.

Perth & Kinross *P. & K.* Population: 131,780.
Unitary authority in Scotland bounded by Aberdeenshire, Angus, Argyll & Bute, Clackmannanshire, Fife, Highland and Stirling. Chief centres are the city of Perth, Blairgowrie, Crieff, Kinross, Auchterader and Pitlochry. The area is mountainous, containing large areas of remote open moorland, especially in the N and W; the vast upland expanses of Breadalbane, Rannoch and Atholl, form the S edge of the Grampian Mountains. The lower land of the S and E is more heavily populated and is dominated by the ancient city of Perth. The area is rich in history as it links the Highlands to the N with the central belt and lowlands to the S via important mountain passes, most notably the Pass of Dromochter. The area has many castles, and Scottish Kings were traditionally enthroned at Scone Abbey, to the N of Perth. There are many lochs, including Loch Rannoch and Loch Tay. Main industries are tourism and whisky production. The world famous Gleneagles golf course is in the S of the area. Rivers include the Tay, Almond and Earn.
Places of interest: Blair Castle, Blair Atholl; Crieff Visitor Centre; Edradour Distillery, Pitlochry; Glenturret Distillery, Hosh; Hydro-Electrical Visitor Centre & Fish Ladder, Pitlochry; Queen's View Centre, Loch Tummel; Scone Palace, Perth.

Peterborough *Peter.* Population: 153,166.
Unitary authority in E England neighbouring Cambridgeshire, Lincolnshire, Northamptonshire and Rutland. The area includes the city of Peterborough, which lies at the heart of an important agricultural area. Developing as a railway hub, it has become a major industrial, distribution and shopping centre. The River Nene passes through Peterborough.
Places of interest: Peakirk Wildfowl Refuge; Peterborough Cathedral.

Plymouth *Plym.* Population: 243,373.
Unitary authority on the SW coast of England surrounding the city of Plymouth and neighbouring Cornwall and Devon. Plymouth stands at the mouth of the River Tamar and is the largest city on the S coast of England. It has strong mercantile and naval traditions; it is closely linked with Sir Francis Drake, and has maintained a Royal Naval Dockyard for 300 years. Plymouth is a regional shopping centre and a popular resort.
Places of interest: Plymouth City Museum & Art Gallery; Plymouth Dome; Plymouth Pavilions.

Poole *Poole* Population: 133,050.
Unitary authority on S coast of England surrounding Poole and bordered by Bournemouth and Dorset. Poole Harbour is the second largest natural harbour in the world, which enabled Poole to prosper through trading, especially with Newfoundland. Poole has now attracted a variety of industries including boat-building, fishing, pottery, engineering and electronics. It is also the ferry terminus for the Channel Islands and Cherbourg.
Places of interest: Poole Pottery; Upton Park Country Park.

Portsmouth *Ports.* Population: 174,697.
Unitary authority on the S coast of England surrounding the city of Portsmouth and bordered by Hampshire. Portsmouth developed as a strategic port around Portsmouth Harbour, and it is still the home of the Royal Navy. It has become a culturally diverse centre, attracting a wide range of industries which include leisure, tourism, financial services, distribution, manufacturing and hi-tech industries.
Places of interest: H.M.S. Victory; H.M.S. Warrior; Mary Rose Exhibition; Mary Rose; Portsmouth Guildhall; Portsmouth Historic Dockyard; Royal Naval Museum; Sea Life Centre.

Powys *Powys* Population: 123,600.
Large unitary authority in central Wales bordering Blaenau Gwent, Caerphilly, Carmarthenshire, Ceredigion, Denbighshire, Gwynedd, Merthyr Tydfil, Monmouthshire, Neath Port Talbot, Rhondda Cynon Taff, Wrexham, and the English areas of Herefordshire and Shropshire. Main centres are Newtown, Gurnos, Brecon, Welshpool, Ystradgynlais, Llanllwchaiarn, Llandrindod Wells, Knighton, Llanidloes, Builth Wells and Machynlleth. Powys is almost entirely rural, with mountainous terrain; most of the Brecon Beacons National Park falls within the S part of the area, while the Cambrian Mountains are in the W. There is considerable afforestation, and a number of large reservoirs, including Lake Vyrnwy. To the N of Brecon, on

Mynydd Eppynt, is an extensive military training area. Main economic activities are agriculture, which is predominantly based around hill farming. Tourism is significant, owing to the natural beauty of the area, and innovative attractions such as the Centre for Alternative Technology. Industrial development is gradually increasing. Among the many rivers, the largest are the Severn, Usk, and Wye.
Places of interest: Brecon Beacons Mountain Centre, Libanus; Centre For Alternative Technology, Machynlleth; Elan Valley Visitor Centre, Rhayader; Powis Castle (NT), Welshpool.

Reading *Read.* Population: 128,877.
Unitary authority in S England to W of Greater London, surrounding Reading and bordered by Oxfordshire, West Berkshire, Windsor & Maidenhead and Wokingham. Reading developed as a crossing point of the River Thames and River Kennet. Traditional industries include brewing and food production, notably biscuits. These are accompanied by an increasing sector of hi-tech and computer-based companies, attracted by Reading's location in the M4 corridor. Reading has also established itself as a major entertainments centre.
Places of interest: Blake's Lock Museum; Museum of Reading.

Redcar & Cleveland *R. & C.* Population: 144,000.
Unitary authority on the NE coast of England neighbouring Hartlepool, Middlesbrough and North Yorkshire. The main centres are Redcar, South Bank, Eston, Guisborough, Marske-by-the-Sea, Saltburn-by-the-Sea, Loftus and Skelton. The area is one of great contrasts. It combines rural villages, market towns and coastal resorts, along with heavily populated urban areas and industrialised port facilities. Industries include steel-making, due to the local ironstone, and chemicals, based around the River Tees to the NW of the area. The coastal towns attract some tourism. The River Tees forms part of the border to the W.
Places of interest: Flatts Lane Woodland Country Park, Eston; Kirkleatham Old Hall Museum.

Renfrewshire *Renf.* Population: 176,970.
Unitary authority in central Scotland bordering East Renfrewshire, Glasgow, Inverclyde, North Ayrshire, West Dunbartonshire and the Firth of Clyde. Main centres are Paisley, Renfrew, Johnstone, Erskine and Linwood. The area emerges W from the Greater Glasgow periphery into a contrasting countryside of highlands, lochs and glens. Industry is centred on the urban area and includes electronics, engineering, food and drink production and service sectors; in rural areas to the W, agriculture is still important. The W part of the area includes some of Clyde Muirshiels Regional Park; Glasgow Airport is in the E.
Places of interest: Castle Semple Country Park; Gleniffer Braes Country Park, Paisley.

Rhondda Cynon Taff (Rhondda Cynon Taf). *R.C.T.*
Population: 232,581.
Unitary authority in S Wales bounded by Bridgend, Caerphilly, Cardiff, Merthyr Tydfil, Neath Port Talbot, Powys and Vale of Glamorgan. The principal towns are Treorchy, Aberdare, Pontypridd, Ferndale and Mountain Ash. Rhondda Cynon Taff is a mountainous area, dissected by deep narrow valleys, with urbanisation typified by ribbon development. The area was the former heart of the Welsh coal mining industry, and has experienced a sharp economic decline as pits closed. Diversification into light engineering and service sectors are gradually improving the industrial base. Main rivers are the Rhondda and Cynon.
Places of interest: Dare Valley Country Park, Aberdare;

Rutland *Rut.* Population: 31,489.
Unitary authority in E England neighbouring Leicestershire, Lincolnshire, Northamptonshire and Peterborough. The main town is Oakham. Agriculture is the main industry; other important industries are engineering, cement-making, plastics, clothing and tourism. The area includes the large reservoir, Rutland Water, which is an important feature for leisure, tourism and wildlife.
Places of interest: East Carlton Countryside Park; Rutland Water, Empingham.

Scottish Borders *Sc.Bord.* Population: 105,300.
Administrative region of SE Scotland bordering Dumfries &
Galloway, East Lothian, Midlothian, South Lanarkshire, West
Lothian, the English counties of Cumbria and Northumberland,
and the North Sea. It comprises the former counties of Berwick,
Peebles, Roxburgh and Selkirk. Main towns are Hawick,
Galashiels, Peebles, Kelso, Selkirk and Jedburgh. It extends from
the Tweedsmuir Hills in the W to the North Sea on either side of
St. Abb's Head in the E, and from the Pentland, Moorfoot and
Lammermuir Hills in the N to the Cheviot Hills and the English
border in the S. The fertile area of rich farmland between the
hills to N and S is known as The Merse. The area around Peebles
and Galashiels is noted for woollen manufacture. Elsewhere, the
electronics industry is of growing importance. The River Tweed
rises in the extreme W and flows between Kelso and Coldstream,
finally passing into England, 4m/6km W of Berwick-upon-Tweed.
Places of interest: Abbotsford House, Melrose; St. Abb's Head.

Shetland *Shet.* Population: 22,522.
Group of over 100 islands, lying beyond Orkney to the NE of the
Scottish mainland; Sumburgh Head being about 100m/160km
from Duncansby Head. Designated an Islands Area for
administrative purposes, the chief islands are Mainland, on which
the capital and chief port of Lerwick is situated, Unst, and Yell.
Some twenty of the islands are inhabited. The islands are mainly
low-lying, the highest point being Ronas Hill, on Mainland. The
oil industry has made an impact on Shetland, with oil service bases
at Lerwick and Sandwick, and a large terminal at Sullom Voe.
Other industries include cattle and sheep-rearing, knitwear and
fishing. The climate is mild, considering the latitude, but severe
storms are frequent. The islands are famous for the small
Shetland breed of pony, which is renowned for its strength and
hardiness. There is an airport at Sumburgh, on S part of
Mainland.
Places of interest: Jarlshof, Sumburgh; Shetland Museum, Lerwick.

Shropshire *Shrop.* Population: 262,957.
W midland county of England bounded by Cheshire,
Herefordshire, Staffordshire, Telford & Wrekin, Worcestershire
and the Welsh authorities of Powys and Wrexham. Main towns
are the county town of Shrewsbury, Oswestry, Bridgnorth, Market
Drayton, Ludlow and Whitchurch. The S and W borders are hilly,
with large areas of open moorland, including The Long Mynd and
Wenlock Edge, which provide good sheep-grazing. Elsewhere the
county undulates towards the Severn Valley, which provides fertile
agricultural land served by prosperous market towns. Agricultural
output includes dairy, poultry and pig farming, along with corn
crops. As the former heart of the Marches of Wales, Shropshire
contains the remains of numerous border defences. There are
also the remains of several monasteries, for instance, at Much
Wenlock and Buildwas. The most important river is the Severn,
which flows across the county from W to SE; others include the
Clun, Corve, Perry, Rea Brook, and Teme.
Districts: Bridgnorth; North Shropshire; Oswestry; Shrewsbury &
Atcham; South Shropshire.
Places of interest: Aerospace Museum, Cosford; Bridgnorth Cliff Railway,
Bridgnorth; Severn Valley Railway.

Slough *Slo.* Population: 107,000.
Unitary authority in SE England to the W of London,
surrounding Slough and bordering Buckinghamshire, Greater
London, Surrey and Windsor & Maidenhead. Slough has grown
significantly over the past 30 years, and is a major regional
shopping centre. Industry is centred on the large Slough Trading
Estate, which was planned after World War I. Numerous sectors
are represented in Slough, among them is confectionery.

Somerset *Som.* Population: 460,368.
County in SW England bounded by Bath & North East Somerset,
Devon, Dorset, North Somerset, Wiltshire and the Bristol
Channel. The chief centres are the county town of Taunton;
Yeovil, Bridgwater, Frome, Chard, Street, Burnham-on-Sea,
Highbridge, the small cathedral city of Wells, Wellington and
Minehead. Somerset consists of several hill ranges, including the
Mendip, Polden, Quantock, Brendon Hills, along with most of
Exmoor. These uplands are separated by valleys, or, on either side
of the River Parrett, by the extensive marshy flats of Sedgemoor.

Economic activity is mainly based on agriculture in the fertile
vales, with manufacturing, distribution and service industries
centred on the urban areas. Tourism is important with attractions
including Exmoor National Park, a holiday complex at Minehead
and the county's natural rural charm. Somerset also holds one of
Europe's largest music festivals at Glastonbury. The chief rivers
are Axe, Brue, Parrett, and Tone, draining into the Bristol
Channel; and Barle and Exe, rising on Exmoor and flowing into
Devon and the English Channel.
Districts: Mendip; Sedgemoor; South Somerset; Taunton Deane; West
Somerset.
Places of interest: Black Swan Guild, Frome; Butlin's Somerwest World,
Minehead; Cheddar Caves; Cheddar Gorge Cheese Co.; Crinkley Bottom,
Cricket St. Thomas; Dunster Castle (NT); Fleet Air Arm Museum, Yeovilton;
Glastonbury Abbey; Montacute House (NT); Royal Bath & Wells
Showground, Shepton Mallet; Wells Cathedral; West Somerset Railway,
Minehead; Wookey Hole Caves & Paper Mill, Wells.

South Ayrshire *S.Ayr.* Population: 114,000.
Unitary authority in SW Scotland bounded by Dumfries &
Galloway, East Ayrshire, North Ayrshire and the sea. The chief
towns are Ayr, Troon, Prestwick, Girvan and Maybole. The area
consists of a long coastline, with lowlands surrounding Ayr Bay
and higher ground to the S. Agriculture is a major economic
activity on the uplands. To the N, aerospace and hi-tech industries
are located near Prestwick International Airport and Ayr, the main
retail centre. Notable sporting venues include a race course at Ayr
and open championship golf courses at Troon and Turnberry.
Tourism is a major feature of the local economy. The area was the
birthplace of Robert the Bruce and Robert Burns; it contains
Scotland's first country park at Culzean Castle; and it has a holiday
camp on the coast near Ayr. Rivers include the Ayr, Water of
Girvan and Stinchar.
Places of interest: Butlin's Wonderwest World, Ayr; Culzean Castle (NTS);
Culzean Country Park (NTS); Tam o'Shanter Experience, Alloway.

South Gloucestershire *S.Glos.* Population: 235,000.
Unitary authority in SW England neighbouring Bath & North East
Somerset, Bristol, Gloucestershire and Wiltshire. The chief
centres are Kingswood, Chipping Sodbury, Mangotsfield,
Frampton Cotterell, Yate, Thornbury, Patchway and Filton. The S
part of the area lies on the N and E fringes of Bristol. The
Cotswold hills are in the E, and the Severn Vale in the W. Main
industries are in the S, and include aerospace engineering; the N
is mainly agricultural. South Gloucestershire includes the English
side of both Severn road bridges. Badminton Park in the E of the
area, is the location for the Badminton Horse Trials. The River
Severn borders the area to the NW.
Places of interest: Dyrham Park (NT); Oldown, Thornbury.

South Lanarkshire *S.Lan.* Population: 307,400.
Unitary authority in central Scotland bordering Dumfries &
Galloway, East Ayrshire, East Renfrewshire, Glasgow, North
Lanarkshire, Scottish Borders and West Lothian. The main towns
are East Kilbride, Hamilton, Blantyre, Larkhall, Carluke, Lanark
and Bothwell. Urban development is mainly in the N, merging
with the SE periphery of Greater Glasgow. The S part is mostly
farmland and not highly populated. Tourism is mainly centred on
the picturesque valley of the upper Clyde; there is a race course at
Hamilton. The area has associations with the industrial
philanthropist, Robert Owen, who built a model village at New
Lanark. Rivers include the Clyde, Avon and Dippool Water.
Places of interest: Calder Glen Country Park, East Kilbride; Chatelherault
Country Park, Hamilton; New Lanark World Heritage Village.

South Yorkshire *S.Yorks.* Population: 1,262,630.
Former metropolitan county of N England bordered by
Derbyshire, East Riding of Yorkshire, North Lincolnshire, North
Yorkshire, Nottinghamshire and West Yorkshire. It comprises the
industrial and urban area around the city of Sheffield and the
towns of Rotherham, Barnsley and Doncaster. Located at the
heart of a major coalfield, South Yorkshire prospered through the
development of heavy industry. Barnsley and Rotherham were
coal mining towns, with steel and fine cutlery centred on Sheffield.
The decline of these industries has led to the area redefining itself.
Sheffield has become a centre of learning, tourism and
conferences, aided by its environmental improvements. Barnsley,
Rotherham and Doncaster have increased their industrial base,

especially via light industries. Leisure and recreation are an important feature of the area, with venues including Barnsley's Metrodome, Doncaster's race course and Dome, and Sheffield's Arena and Don Valley Stadium. Retail has increased with city and town centre redevelopment, and the Meadowhall complex. The surrounding countryside includes country parks at Rother Valley and Thrybergh, with part of the Peak District National Park W and NW of Sheffield. The chief river is the Don.

Districts: Barnsley; Doncaster; Rotherham; Sheffield.
Places of interest: Cannon Hall Country Park, Cawthorne; Cannon Hall Farm, Barnsley; Doncaster Racecourse Exhibition Centre; Elsecar Discovery Centre, Barnsley; Graves Art Gallery, Sheffield; Heeley City Farm, Sheffield; Rother Valley Country Park, Beighton; Sheffield City Museum & Mappin Art Gallery; Thrybergh Country Park; Ulley Reservoir Country Park; Worsbrough Mill Country Park.

Southampton *S'ham.* Population: 196,864.

Unitary authority on the S coast of England surrounding the city of Southampton, and bordered by Hampshire. Southampton owes much to the deep waters of Southampton Water, which have enabled the development of Europe's busiest cruise port. Water and the waterfront remain very important to the local economy, with marine technology, oceanography, boat shows and yacht races all prominent. The city is also a leading media, recreational, entertainment and retail centre. The chief river is the Itchen.

Places of interest: Itchen Valley Country Park; Royal Victoria Country Park.

Southend *S'end* Population: 169,000.

Unitary authority in SE England, N of the mouth of the River Thames, surrounding Southend-on-Sea and bordering Essex. Southend is a commerical, residential, shopping and holiday centre, with tourism among its main industries. It includes a 7m shoreline from Leigh-on-Sea to Shoeburyness, a famous pier and a sea life centre.

Places of interest: Sea Life Centre; Southend Pier.

Staffordshire *Staffs.* Population: 786,498.

Midland county of England bounded by Cheshire, Derbyshire, Leicestershire, Shropshire, Stoke-on-Trent, Telford & Wrekin, Warwickshire, West Midlands and Worcestershire. Chief centres are Newcastle-under-Lyme, Tamworth, the county town of Stafford, Burton upon Trent, Cannock, Burntwood, the cathedral city of Lichfield, Kidsgrove, Rugeley and Leek. The urban development occurs around the West Midlands conurbation in the S, where main industries include engineering, iron and steel, rubber goods and leather production, while to the N, there is an urban concentration around Stoke-on-Trent. Burton upon Trent is noted for brewing. The ancient hunting forest and former mining district of Cannock Chase is in the centre of the county and contains preserved tracts of moorland. In the NE lies part of the Peak District National Park. The rest of the county is predominantly agricultural, with milk, wheat and sugar beet produced. To the E of Leek, moorland broken up by limestone walls extends across the Manifold valley to the Derbyshire border. In additon to the Trent, which dominates much of the county, rivers include the Blithe, Manifold, Sow and Tame. River Dove forms the boundary with Derbyshire.

Districts: Cannock Chase; East Staffordshire; Lichfield; Newcastle-under-Lyme; South Staffordshire; Stafford; Staffordshire Moorlands; Tamworth.
Places of interest: Alton Towers Leisure Park; Amerton Working Farm, Stowe-by-Chartley; Bass Museum of Brewing, Burton upon Trent; Branston Water Park, Burton upon Trent; Drayton Manor Park, Tamworth; Heart of the Country Centre, Lichfield; Lichfield Cathedral; Rudyard Lake, Leek; Shire Hall Gallery, Stafford; Shugborough Estate (NT), Milford; The Children's Farm, Middleton; Tittesworth Reservoir, Leek; Wedgwood Visitor Centre, Barlaston; Weston Park.

Stirling *Stir.* Population: 82,000.

Unitary authority in central Scotland neighbouring Argyll & Bute, Clackmannanshire, East Dunbartonshire, Falkirk, North Lanarkshire, Perth & Kinross and West Dunbartonshire. The chief centres are Stirling, the ancient cathedral city of Dunblane, Bannockburn, Bridge of Allan and Callander. The fertile agricultural lands of the Forth valley are in the centre of the area, bounded by mountains: The Trossachs and the mountain peaks of Ben Lomond, Ben More and Ben Lui in the N, while in the S are the Campsie Fells. Tourism is an important industry with Stirling including many sites of historical significance to Scotland,

particularly during the struggle to retain independence. There are associations with Rob Roy, and the battle site of Bannockburn. Other features include The Trossachs, part of the Loch Lomond Regional Park and the Queen Elizabeth Forest Park. There are several lochs, including Loch Lomond, which forms part of the W border, and Loch Katrine. Scotland's only lake named as such, Lake of Menteith, is also in Stirling. The main river is the Forth.

Places of interest: Argyll & Sutherland Highlanders Museum; Bannockburn Heritage Centre; Blair Drummond Safari Park; Breadalbane Folklore Centre, Killin; Mugdock Country Park, Milngavie; Queen Elizabeth Forest Park, Aberfoyle; Rob Roy & Trossachs Visitor Centre, Callander; Royal Burgh of Stirling Visitor Centre; Stirling Castle; Wallace Monument, Causewayhead.

Stockton-on-Tees *Stock.* Population: 178,000.

Unitary authority in NE England neighbouring Darlington, Durham, Hartlepool, Middlesbrough, North Yorkshire and Redcar & Cleveland. The main centres are Stockton-on-Tees, Billingham, Thornaby-on-Tees, Eaglescliffe, Egglescliffe and Yarm. The area has a diverse mix of picturesque villages, large-scale urbanisation and heavy industry. The area has recently undergone major renewal and regeneration, with industries now including electronics, food technology and chemical production. Stockton is the main shopping centre for the area, and includes the Teesside Retail Park. The main river is the Tees, which is controlled by the Tees Barrage. This has created Britain's largest purpose-built whitewater canoeing course.

Places of interest: Billingham Beck Valley Country Park; Castle Eden Walkway Country Park; Preston Hall Museum, Eaglescliffe.

Stoke-on-Trent *Stoke* Population: 244,637.

Unitary authority in England surrounding the city of Stoke-on-Trent and neighbouring Staffordshire. The city has six town centres: Burslem, Fenton, Hanley, Longton, Stoke-upon-Trent and Tunstall. Hanley is where most current city centre activities are located. The area forms The Potteries, and is the largest claywear producer in the world, although now it is largely a finishing centre for imported pottery. There are a wide variety of other industries, including steel, engineering, paper, glass and furniture. Stoke-on-Trent is a centre of employment, leisure and shopping for the surrounding areas. It is noted for its environmental approach, particularly with land reclamation which accounts for around 10 per cent of the city area; sites include Festival Park, Central Forest Park and Westport Lake. The River Trent flows through the area.

Places of interest: Stoke-on-Trent Museum & Art Gallery, Hanley; W. Moorcroft plc, Burslem.

Suffolk *Suff.* Population: 636,266.

Easternmost county of England bounded by Cambridgeshire, Essex, Norfolk and the North Sea. Main towns are the county town of Ipswich, Lowestoft, Bury St. Edmunds, Felixstowe, Sudbury, Haverhill, Newmarket, Stowmarket and Woodbridge. The county is low-lying and gently undulating. It is almost entirely agricultural, with cereal crops and oil seed rape in abundance. The low coastline, behind which are areas of heath and marsh, afforested in places, is subject to much erosion; it is deeply indented with long river estuaries which provide good sailing. The NW corner of the county forms part of Breckland. The central region includes many notable historic Wool Towns, for instance, Lavenham. Apart from agriculture, industries include electronics, telecommunications, printing and port facilities. Lowestoft is a prominent fishing port and Felixstowe is a container port of growing importance. River Stour forms the S boundary with Essex, and the Little Ouse and Waveney form most of the N boundary with Norfolk. The many other small rivers include the Alde with its estuary the Ore, Deben, and Gipping with its estuary the Orwell, in the E and Lark in the W.

Districts: Babergh; Forest Heath; Ipswich; Mid Suffolk; St. Edmundsbury; Suffolk Coastal; Waveney.
Places of interest: Alton Water, Ipswich; Clare Castle Country Park; East Point Pavilion, Lowestoft; Fritton Lake & Gardens Country Park; High Lodge Forest Centre, Brandon; Ickworth (NT), Bury St. Edmunds; Knettishall Heath Country Park; Manning's Amusement Park, Felixstowe; Pleasurewood Hills Theme Park; Stonham Barns Craft Centre, Stowmarket; Suffolk Country Park; Suffolk Wildlife Park, Kessingland; West Stow Country Park.

Surrey *Surr.* Population: 1,018,003.
County of SE England bounded by Bracknell Forest, East Sussex, Greater London, Hampshire, Kent, Slough, West Sussex and Windsor & Maidenhead. The prinicpal towns are Woking, the cathedral and university town of Guildford, Staines, Leatherhead, Farnham, Epsom, Ewell, Sunbury, Walton-on-Thames, Weybridge, Egham, Redhill, Reigate, Esher, Camberley, Frimley and Godalming. The chalk ridge of the North Downs, gently sloping on the N side but forming a steep escarpment on the S, traverses the county from E to W. Extensive sandy heaths in the W are much used for military training. The county is heavily wooded, and contains many traces of the former iron industry in the predominantly rural S. Much of the urbanised E and N areas include commuter or dormitory towns which form the residential outskirts of the Greater London conurbation. Industries include the agricultural activites of dairy farming and horticulture. Tourism and recreation are also important, with Surrey including numerous stately homes, Wentworth golf course, four race courses, and a theme park at Thorpe Park. The chief river is the Thames, into which flow the Wey and the Mole.
Districts: Elmbridge; Epsom & Ewell; Guildford; Mole Valley; Reigate & Banstead; Runnymede; Spelthorne; Surrey Heath; Tandridge; Waverley; Woking.
Places of interest: Bocketts Farm Park, Fetcham; Chapel Farm Animal Trail, West Humble; Claremont Landscape Garden (NT), Esher; Denbies Wine Centre, Dorking; Godstone Farm; Guildford House Gallery; Horton Park Farm, Epsom; Loseley House; Polesden Lacey (NT), Dorking; Sandown Exhibition Centre, Esher; Thorpe Park, Chertsey; Wisley R.H.S. Gardens, Woking.

Swansea (Abertawe). *Swan.* Population: 232,000.
Unitary authority in S Wales bordering Carmarthenshire, Neath Port Talbot and the sea. Main centres are the city of Swansea, Gorseinon, The Mumbles, Sketty, Cockett and Clydach. The area includes mountains in the N, the urban centre surrounding Swansea, and the Gower peninsula in the S. Swansea originally developed as a port serving the W coalfield of S Wales. The area gained an international reputation for tin-plating and copper and nickel production. Swansea is now a regional shopping and commercial centre, including a university and marina development. The Gower peninsula attracts many tourists with its fine beaches and cliff scenery; hang-gliding is popular at Rhossili Down, and there are associations with Dylan Thomas. The Mumbles is a popular resort, formerly connected to Swansea via a tramway. The chief river is the Tawe.
Places of interest: Glynn Vivian Art Gallery & Museum; Swansea Maritime & Industrial Museum.

Swindon *Swin.* Population: 177,271.
Unitary authority in SW England neighbouring Gloucestershire, Oxfordshire and Wiltshire. Main centres are Swindon, Stratton St. Margaret, Highworth and Wroughton. The area is located between the Cotswold Hills and Wiltshire Downs, on the fringes of the Thames Valley. Originally a railway town, Swindon has experienced rapid recent growth and is now a centre for car manufacture and central commercial operations. The town is a regional shopping centre with a redeveloped town centre and the Designer Outlet Village. The River Thames borders the area to the N and the River Cole to the E.
Places of interest: Great Western Railway Museum; Swindon Museum & Art Gallery.

Telford & Wrekin *Tel. & W.* Population: 143,430.
Unitary authority in W England bordered by Shropshire and Staffordshire. Main centres are Telford, Wellington, Madeley, Donnington, Oakengates, Hadley and Newport. The area was the cradle of the Industrial Revolution, with notable firsts including Darby's discovery of the iron smelting process at Coalbrookdale, the casting and construction of the first cold blast iron bridge at Ironbridge, and the construction of the first iron ship. The new town of Telford, named after the famous engineer, surveyor and road builder, Thomas Telford, is the major commercial centre. The River Severn runs S through the area.
Places of interest: Ironbridge Gorge Museum; Telford International Centre.

Thurrock *Thur.* Population: 131,368.
Unitary authority in SE England, N of the mouth of the River Thames. It is bounded by Essex and Greater London. The main centres are Grays, South Ockendon, Stanford-le-Hope, Corringham and Tilbury. The area is a mix of old and modern, rural and urban. In the N there are historic villages set in agricultural land, while in the S, there are the modern urban developments, and industrial activities surrounding oil refining and the container port of Tilbury. Grays is the commercial centre of Thurrock, with the major retail centre being Thurrock Lakeside. The area includes the N stretch of the Dartford Tunnel and Queen Elizabeth II Bridge, both of which cross the River Thames.
Places of interest: Tilbury Fort; Westley Heights Country Park.

Torbay *Torbay* Population: 119,674.
Unitary authority located on the SW coast of England neighbouring Devon. The major towns are Torquay, Paignton and Brixham. The area, situated on Tor Bay, is among Britain's main holiday resorts, and is widely regarded as the English Riviera. Tourism is the main industry, with Torbay receiving over 1.5 million visitors per year. Excellent leisure, recreation and conference facilities are added attractions.
Places of interest: Babbacombe Model Village; Cockington Court, Torquay; English Riviera Centre, Torquay; Paignton Pier; Paignton Zoo.

Torfaen (Tor-faen). *Torfaen* Population: 90,700.
Unitary authority in S Wales bounded by Blaenau Gwent, Caerphilly, Monmouthshire and Newport. The principal towns are Cwmbran, Pontypool and Blaenavon. Torfaen contains rugged mountains with a 12-mile-long valley running N to S from Blaenavon to Cwmbran. The area is a manufacturing centre which includes electronics, engineering and automotive companies. The industrial past of the area has led to the growth of tourist attractions, with notable sites including The Valley Inheritance at Pontypool, and Big Pit Mining Museum and 19c ironworks at Blaenavon. The river Afon Llwyd runs through the area.
Places of interest: Big Pit Mining Museum, Blaenafon; Greenmeadow Community Farm, Cwmbran.

Tyne & Wear *T. & W.* Population: 1,095,152.
Maritime county of NE England bordered by Durham and Northumberland. It comprises the urban complex around the cities of Newcastle upon Tyne and Sunderland, South Shields, Gateshead, Washington and Wallsend. Named after its two important rivers, the area developed largely through the coal mining and ship-building industries. As these industries declined, the area has undergone urban and industrial regeneration. Newcastle upon Tyne is now a commercial, university and cultural centre, with a historic heart including a cathedral, 12c castle and the Tyne Bridge; the historic Quayside has recently been developed. Sunderland gained city status in 1992, and is now a centre for car manufacture, with recreational facilities including the Crowtree Leisure Complex and the National Glass Centre. Elsewhere, Wallsend has hi-tech and off-shore industries; South Tyneside has electronics industries, and tourism, via its Catherine Cookson links. Gateshead has an international athletics stadium, Europe's largest undercover shopping centre, the Metrocentre, and the modern symbol of renewal, the Angel of the North. The area is served by the Port of Tyne and Newcastle International Airport.
Districts: Gateshead; Newcastle upon Tyne; North Tyneside; South Tyneside; Sunderland.
Places of interest: Hancock Museum, Newcastle upon Tyne; Laing Art Gallery, Newcastle upon Tyne; Metroland, Gateshead; Newcastle Discovery; People's Museum of Memorabilia, Newcastle upon Tyne; Saltwell Park, Gateshead; Sea Life Centre, Tynemouth; South Shields Museum & Art Gallery; Spanish City, Whitley Bay; Sunderland Museum & Art Gallery.

Vale of Glamorgan (Bro Morgannwg). *V. of Glam.*
Population: 119,500.
Unitary authority on the S coast of Wales neighbouring Bridgend, Cardiff and Rhondda Cynon Taff. The chief towns are Barry, Penarth and Llantwit Major. Vale of Glamorgan is a lowland area between Cardiff and Bridgend, with some agricultural activities, and tourism at the resorts of Barry and Penarth. Cardiff International Airport is situated in the SE near Rhoose. Main river is the Ely, which passes through the area.
Places of interest: Barry Island Pleasure Park; Cosmeston Country Park;

Pleasure Steamers Waverley and Balmoral, Penarth; Porthkerry Country Park, Barry.

Warrington *Warr.* Population: 193,000.
Unitary authority in NW England surrounding Warrington and bounded by Cheshire, Greater Manchester, Halton and Merseyside. The area developed as a main crossing point of the River Mersey and latterly the Manchester Ship Canal. During industrialisation it became an important strategic trading centre for the NW region. In 1968, Warrington was granted New Town status, leading to traditional industries such as chemicals, brewing and food processing being joined by hi-tech industries and research and development facilities. Warrington retains its importance as a regional shopping, leisure and commercial centre. The River Mersey flows through the area.
Places of interest: Mount Pleasant Farm Craft Centre; Walton Hall Gardens.

Warwickshire *Warks.* Population: 484,247.
Midland county of England bounded by Gloucestershire, Leicestershire, Northamptonshire, Oxfordshire, Staffordshire, West Midlands and Worcestershire. Chief towns are Nuneaton, Rugby, Royal Leamington Spa, Bedworth, the county town of Warwick, Stratford-upon-Avon and Kenilworth. Warwickshire consists of mostly flat or undulating farmland, although the foothills of the Cotswold Hills spill over the SW border. Main manufacturing activites occur in an industrial belt extending NW from Rugby to the boundary with Staffordshire. They include motor and component industries, service sectors, electrical and general engineering. Tourism is centred on the historic town of Warwick with its medieval castle, and Stratford-upon-Avon with its Shakespeare associations. The principal river is the Avon.
Districts: North Warwickshire; Nuneaton & Bedworth; Rugby; Stratford-on-Avon; Warwick.
Places of interest: Anne Hathaway's Cottage; Baddesley Clinton (NT), Lapworth; Charlecote Park (NT), Wellesbourne; Hall's Croft, Stratford-upon-Avon; Hatton Country World, Warwick; Holy Trinity, Stratford-upon-Avon; Kenilworth Castle; Mary Arden's House; National Agricultural Centre, Stoneleigh; New Place Museum, Stratford-upon-Avon; St. Mary, Warwick; Shakespeare's Birthplace, Stratford-upon-Avon; Stratford-upon-Avon Shire Horse Centre; Warwick Castle; Warwickshire County Museum, Warwick.

West Berkshire *W.Berks.* Population: 136,700.
Unitary authority in S England bordered by Hampshire, Oxfordshire, Reading, Wiltshire and Wokingham. The chief centres are Newbury, Thatcham and Hungerford. West Berkshire is a mixture of old market towns, historic buildings and waterways, and includes the famous Newbury racecourse. Rivers include the Kennet and the Pang.
Places of interest: Beale Park; Newbury Conference & Exhibition Centre.

West Dunbartonshire *W.Dun.* Population: 97,790.
Unitary authority in central Scotland bordered by Argyll & Bute, East Dunbartonshire, Glasgow, Inverclyde, Renfrewshire and Stirling. The chief towns are Clydebank, Dumbarton, Alexandria and Bonhill. The area is mountainous, containing the Kilpatrick Hills, and is bounded by Loch Lomond in the N and the Firth of Clyde in the S. The urban SE area of West Dunbartonshire forms part of the NW periphery of Greater Glasgow. There is a broad base of light manufacturing and service sector industries. Tourism and leisure are a feature, with the SE tip of Loch Lomond Regional Park and the whole of Balloch Castle Country Park falling within the area. West Dunbartonshire includes the Erskine Bridge which spans the River Clyde, other rivers include the Leven.
Places of interest: Balloch Castle Country Park; Dumbarton Castle.

West Lothian *W.Loth.* Population: 147,870.
Unitary authority in central Scotland neighbouring Edinburgh, Falkirk, Midlothian, North Lanarkshire, Scottish Borders and South Lanarkshire. The chief towns are Livingston, Bathgate, Linlithgow, Broxburn, Whitburn and Armadale. The area undulates to the S of the Firth of Forth, and rises to moorland at the foot of the Pentland Hills in the S. The main urban areas are situated along commuter corridors between Glasgow, Edinburgh and Falkirk; elsewhere the area is mostly rural. Hi-tech and computing industries are in evidence.

Places of interest: Almondell & Calderwood Country Park, East Calder; Beecraigs Country Park, Linlithgow; Muiravonside Country Park, Linlithgow; Polkemmet Country Park, Whitburn.

West Midlands *W.Mid.* Population: 2,552,205.
Former metropolitan county of central England bordered by Staffordshire, Warwickshire and Worcestershire. It comprises the urban complex around the cities of Birmingham and Coventry, and the towns of Wolverhampton, Dudley, Walsall, West Bromwich, Sutton Coldfield and Solihull. The West Midlands developed as a manufacturing and engineering centre which specialised in the metalworking and motor trades. The area around Dudley, Walsall and Wolverhampton became known as the Black Country, with heavy industry centred on the local deposits of coal, iron ore and limestone. Other local trades included glassware, saddlery and lock-making. Birmingham became Britain's second city by specialising in 1001 trades from confectionery to cars, and has developed into the major business, industrial, commercial and cultural centre for the area. As the traditional industries have declined, there has been a shift towards service, leisure and recreation sectors of the economy; several significant corporate service centres and venues, such as the National Exhibition Centre and the Indoor Arena, are in the West Midlands. The area is served by Birmingham International Airport. Rivers include the Tame and the Cole.
Districts: Birmingham; Coventry; Dudley; Sandwell; Solihull; Walsall; Wolverhampton.
Places of interest: Birmingham Botanical Gardens; Birmingham City Museum & Art Gallery; Birmingham International Airport Visitor Centre; Birmingham Museum of Science & Technology; Birmingham Nature Centre; Black Country Museum, Dudley; Cadbury World, Birmingham; Cannon Hill Park, Birmingham; Coombe Abbey Country Park; Cotwall End Nature Centre, Sedgley; Coventry Cathedral; Dudley Canal Tunnel & Singing Cavern; Dudley Zoo & Castle; Himley Country Park, Dudley; National Exhibition Centre, Birmingham; National Indoor Arena, Birmingham; National Motorcycle Museum, Solihull; National Sea Life Centre, Birmingham; Ryton Gardens, Coventry; Sandwell Park Farm, West Bromwich; Sandwell Priory, West Bromwich; Sandwell Valley Country Park, West Bromwich; Walsall Arboretum Illuminations; Wolverhampton Art Gallery.

West Sussex *W.Suss.* Population: 702,290.
County of S England bounded by Brighton & Hove, East Sussex, Hampshire, Surrey and the English Channel. Main towns are Worthing, Crawley, Bognor Regis, Littlehampton, Horsham, Haywards Heath, East Grinstead, the cathedral city and county town of Chichester, Burgess Hill and Shoreham-by-Sea. N of a level coastal strip run the South Downs, a steep-sided chalk ridge which is thickly wooded in parts. The remaining inland area, The Weald, is largely well-wooded farmland, although there is industrial development around Crawley, Gatwick (London) Airport, Horsham, and Haywards Heath, as well as among the predominantly residential towns on the coast. Tourism is a major activity throughout the county. There are many castles and stately homes, such as Arundel Castle and Goodwood House, the popular seaside resorts of Bognor Regis and Worthing, race courses at Goodwood and Fontwell, Chichester Harbour, which is a centre for yachtsmen and wildfowl, historic Chichester itself, and numerous picturesque villages. The N of the county includes Gatwick (London) Airport. The rivers, none large, include the Adur and Arun, with its tributary the Rother; the Medway rises in the E of the county.
Districts: Adur; Arun; Chichester; Crawley; Horsham; Mid Sussex; Worthing.
Places of interest: Arundel Castle; Arundel Cathedral (RC); Arundel Wildfowl & Wetlands Trust; Bluebell Railway; Body Shop Visitor Centre, Littlehampton; Chichester Cathedral; Fishbourne Roman Palace; Gatwick Skyview; Nymans (NT), Handcross; Petworth House (NT); Pulborough Brooks R.S.P.B. Nature Reserve; Smarts Amusement Park, Littlehampton; Tilgate Forest Country Park, Crawley; Wakehurst Place (NT), Ardingley; Weald & Downland Open Air Museum, Chichester.

West Yorkshire *W.Yorks.* Population: 2,013,693.
Former metropolitan county of N England bordering Derbyshire, Greater Manchester, Lancashire, North Yorkshire and South Yorkshire. It comprises the area around the cities of Leeds, Bradford and Wakefield, and the towns of Huddersfield, Halifax, Dewsbury, Keighley, Batley, Morley, Castleford, Brighouse, Pudsey, Pontefract and Shipley. West Yorkshire developed as a centre for wool and textiles, manufacturing and engineering, creating an

industrial urban landscape set against rural moorland. As the traditional industries have declined, the area has undergone regeneration and diversification, moving towards tertiary economic sectors. Leeds is the industrial, administrative, commercial and cultural centre of the area, containing regional government offices and many corporate service centres and head offices. Emerging economic activities across West Yorkshire have included printing, distribution, chemicals, food and drink production, hi-tech industries and financial services. Haworth with its Brontë associations, Holmfirth and the moorlands are the centres of tourism. The area includes Leeds Bradford International Airport. The chief rivers are the Aire and the Calder, while the Wharfe forms its N boundary below Addingham.
Districts: Bradford; Calderdale; Kirklees; Leeds; Wakefield.
Places of interest: 1853 Gallery, Saltaire; Bradford Cathedral; Brontë Parsonage, Haworth; Brontë Weaving Shed, Haworth; Cartwright Hall Art Gallery, Bradford; Cliffe Castle Art Gallery & Museum, Keighley; Dean Clough Galleries, Halifax; Eureka, The Museum for Children, Halifax; Golden Acre Park, Leeds; Harewood House; Hemsworth Water Park, Pontefract; Keighley & Worth Valley Railway, Keighley; Leeds City Art Gallery and Museum; Lotherton Hall Country Park, Old Mickleford; National Museum of Photography, Bradford; Newmillerdam Country Park; Oakwell Hall Country Park, Batley; Ogden Water, Illingworth; Piece Hall, Halifax; Pugneys Country Park, Wakefield; Royal Armouries Museum, Leeds; Temple Newsam Country Park, Whitkirk; Transperience Centre, Bradford; Tropical World, Leeds; Walkley Clogs, Hebden Bridge; Yorkshire Sculpture Park, Bretton.

Western Isles (Na h-Eileanan an Iar. Also known as Outer Hebrides.) *W.Isles* Population: 27,815.
String of islands off the W coast of Scotland and separated from Skye and the mainland by The Minch. They extend for some 130m/209km from Butt of Lewis in the N, to Barra Head in the S. Stornoway, situated on the Isle of Lewis, is the main town; elsewhere, there are mainly scattered coastal villages and settlements. The chief islands are Isle of Lewis, North Uist, Benbecula, South Uist and Barra. North Harris and South Harris form significant areas in the S part of the Isle of Lewis. The topography of the islands consists of undulating moorland, mountains and lochs. The main industries are fishing, grazing and, on the Isle of Lewis, tweed manufacture. There are airfields with scheduled passenger flights on the Isle of Lewis, Benbecula and Barra.
Places of interest: An Lanntair Gallery, Stornoway; Calanais Standing Stones.

Wiltshire *Wilts.* Population: 387,200.
County of S England bounded by Bath & North East Somerset, Dorset, Gloucestershire, Hampshire, Oxfordshire, Somerset, South Gloucestershire, Swindon and West Berkshire. Main centres are the cathedral city of Salisbury, the county town of Trowbridge, Chippenham, Warminster, Devizes and Melksham. Wiltshire consists of extensive chalk uplands scattered with prehistoric remains, notably at Avebury and Stonehenge, and interspersed with wide, well-watered valleys. The N of the county is dominated by the Marlborough Downs which are much used for racehorse training, while in the S, the chalk plateau of Salisbury Plain is an important military training area. Between these two upland areas lies the fertile Vale of Pewsey where dairy production and bacon-curing are important agricultural activities. Other industries include electronics, computing, pharmaceuticals, plastics, telecommunications and service sector activities. Wiltshire attracts tourism with its prehistoric remains, stately houses and picturesque market towns and villages. Rivers include the so-called Bristol and Wiltshire Avons, Ebble, Kennet, Nadder, Wylye, and the upper reaches of the Thames.
Districts: Kennet; North Wiltshire; Salisbury; West Wiltshire.
Places of interest: Bowood, Calne; Keynes Park; Longleat House; Longleat Safari Park; Salisbury Cathedral; Stonehenge; Stourhead (NT), Stourton; Wilton House.

Windsor & Maidenhead *W. & M.* Population: 132,465.
Unitary authority in SE England to the W of Greater London, and bounded by Bracknell Forest, Buckinghamshire, Slough, Surrey and Wokingham. The towns of Maidenhead and Windsor are the main centres for industry, leisure and recreation. The area is particularly noted for its strong Royal connections as it includes Windsor Castle and the former Royal hunting estate of Windsor Great Park. Other popular tourist attractions include Ascot race course, Windsor Legoland and Eton College. The River Thames forms the N boundary.
Places of interest: Legoland, Windsor; Queen Mary's Dolls' House, Windsor; Windsor Castle.

Wokingham *W'ham* Population: 139,189.
Unitary authority in SE England, to the W of Greater London. The area encompasses Wokingham and is bordered by Bracknell Forest, Buckinghamshire, Hampshire, Oxfordshire, Reading, West Berkshire and Windsor & Maidenhead. The area includes riverside villages in the N, with undulating ridges covered by woodlands and commons in the S. Wokingham is a growing centre for hi-tech and computer industries. The River Thames forms the N border, and the River Blackwater forms the border to the S.
Places of interest: California Country Park; Dinton Pastures Country Park.

Worcestershire *Worcs.* Population: 534,285.
S midland county of England neighbouring Gloucestershire, Herefordshire, Shropshire, Warwickshire and West Midlands. Main centres are the cathedral city and the county town of Worcester, and the towns of Redditch, Kidderminster, Great Malvern, Bromsgrove, Droitwich Spa, Stourport-on-Severn and Evesham. The urban areas in the N of the county form part of the periphery and commuter belt of the West Midlands conurbation, and attract much of the industrial development. The central and S sections of the county are largely rural, containing the fertile Severn Valley and Vale of Evesham, with market gardening and orchard-growing being the main agricultural activities. Tourism is an important industry, much of it being centred on historic Worcester, with its cathedral, the triennial Three Choirs Festival, Worcester Sauce and china factories. Other popular attractions include boating on the River Severn and visiting the Vale of Evesham whilst the flowers are in full bloom. The main river is the Severn.
Districts: Bromsgrove; Malvern Hills; Redditch; Worcester; Wychavon; Wyre Forest.
Places of interest: Clent Hills Country Park; Kingsford Country Park; Leapgate Country Park, Stourport; Lickey Hills Country Park, Rednal; Pershore Bridge Picnic Site; Ragley Hall, Alcester; Royal Worcester; Shatterford Fishery & Wildlife Sanctuary; Three Counties Showground, Great Malvern; Waseley Hills Country Park, Rubery; Worcester Cathedral; Worcester Woods Country Park, Worcester.

Wrexham (Wrecsam). *Wrex.* Population: 123,500.
Unitary authority in NE Wales bordering Denbighshire, Flintshire, Powys and the English counties of Cheshire and Shropshire. Main centres are Wrexham, Rhosllanerchrugog, Gwersyllt, Cefn-mawr and Coedpoeth. The area is mountainous in the SW, containing part of the Berwyn range; the Dee valley lies in the NE. The area was formerly dominated by the iron, coal and limestone industries. Food manufacture, brewing, plastics and hi-tech industries are now important to the local economy. Wrexham is the largest commercial and shopping centre in N Wales. The River Dee flows through the area.
Places of interest: Chirk Castle (NT); Erddig Hall.

York *York* Population: 174,760.
Unitary authority in N England surrounding the historic cathedral city of York and bordered by East Riding of Yorkshire and North Yorkshire. York is a major archaeological, episcopal, industrial, commercial and cultural centre, situated at the confluence of the River Foss and the River Ouse. The city has a unique history dating from the original Roman military camp, which has led to it becoming one of the main museum and tourist centres in the country. The historic core, situated around the centrepiece of the medieval Minster, is well preserved. Other major attractions include the Jorvik Viking Centre, the medieval city walls and the National Railway Museum. Economic sectors include the confectionery industry, company head offices, Government departmental offices, and research and development establishments. The main river is the Ouse.
Places of interest: Castle Museum; Clifford's Tower; Impressions Gallery; Jorvik Viking Centre; Museum of Automata; National Railway Museum; York City Art Gallery; York Dungeon; York Minster; Yorkshire Museum.

A' Bheinn Bhan *High.* ***Mountain***, 4m/7km NW of Sallachan Point, Lochaber district. Height 1565 feet or 477 metres. **80 A1** NM9466.

A' Bhrideanach *High.* ***Coastal feature***, headland on westernmost point of Rum. **85 H5** NM2999.

A' Bhuidheanach Bheag ***Mountain***, on border of Highland and Perth & Kinross, 1m/2km S of A' Bhuidheanach. Munro: height 3070 feet or 936 metres. **88 D7** NN6677.

A' Bhuidheanaich *High.* ***Mountain***, in Badenoch and Strathspey district, 5m/8km NE of Kingussie. Height 2391 feet or 729 metres. **88 E4** NH7708.

A' Chailleach *High.* ***Mountain***, in Ross and Cromarty district 2m/3km S of Loch a' Bhraoin. Munro: height 3277 feet or 999 metres. **95 H4** NH1371.

A' Chailleach *High.* ***Mountain***, in Monadhliath range, in Badenoch and Strathspey district, 5m/8km NW of Kingussie. Munro: height 3050 feet or 930 metres. **88 D4** NH6804.

A' Chearc *W.Isles Gaelic form of Chicken Rock, qv.*

A' Chill *High.* ***Settlement***, on S coast of Canna, to W of Canna harbour opposite Sanday. **85 H4** NG2605.

A' Chleit *High.* ***Island***, rocky islet 2m/3km off Kirkaig Point on W coast of Sutherland district near Lochinver. **102 C6** NC0320.

A' Chràlaig (Anglicised form: Cralic. Also known as Garbh Leac). *High.* ***Mountain***, on border of Inverness and Skye and Lochalsh districts, 3m/5km NE of head of Loch Cluanie. Munro: height 3674 feet or 1120 metres. **87 G3** NH0914.

A' Chrannag *Arg. & B.* ***Hill***, on Ulva, 1m/2km W of easternmost point of island. Height 387 feet or 118 metres. **79 F4** NM4338.

A' Chrois *Arg. & B.* ***Mountain***, in Argyll 2m/3km N of head of Loch Long. Height 2785 feet or 849 metres. **80 D7** NN2807.

A' Chruach ***Inland physical feature***, ridge on border of Perth & Kinross and Highland between Blackwater Reservoir and Loch Laidon. Summit is Stob na Cruaiche, 2420 feet or 738 metres. **80 E2** NN3657.

A' Chruach *Arg. & B.* ***Mountain***, 5m/8km E of Kilninver. Height 1207 feet or 368 metres. **80 A5** NM9021.

A' Chruach *High.* ***Mountain***, 1m/2km S of Inverie, Lochaber district. Height 1296 feet or 395 metres. **86 D5** NM7797.

A' Chruach *N.Ayr.* ***Mountain***, on Arran, 3m/5km SW of Brodick. Height 1679 feet or 512 metres. **73 H7** NR9633.

A' Chùli *Arg. & B.* ***Island***, one of the Garvellachs group of islands in Firth of Lorn. Lies between Eileach an Naoimh and Garbh Eileach. **79 H6** NM6511.

A' Ghairbhe *High.* ***River***, flowing NE out of Loch Clair through Kinlochewe, just N of which it joins Abhainn Bruachaig to form Kinlochewe River. **95 G6** NH0362.

A' Ghlas-bheinn *High.* ***Mountain***, 4m/7km E of head of Loch Duich in Skye and Lochalsh district. Munro: height 3011 feet or 918 metres. **87 G2** NH0023.

A' Ghoil *High.* ***Island***, on W side of mouth of Kyle of Durness. **103 F1** NC3472.

A La Ronde *Devon* ***Historic house***, 16-sided 18c house, 2m/3km N of Exmouth, of curious construction and content. Includes feather frieze and shell-encrusted gallery. **7 J7** SY0083.

A' Mhaighdean (Anglicised form: The Maiden.) *High.* ***Mountain***, summit in S part of Fisherfield Forest, Ross and Cromarty district. Munro: height 3172 feet or 967 metres. **95 G4** NH0074.

A' Mharconaich *High.* ***Mountain***, in Dalnaspidal Forest, 5m/8km SW of Dalwhinnie. Munro: height 3198 feet or 975 metres. **88 D7** NN6076.

A' Mhòine *High.* ***Locality***, on borders of Caithness and Sutherland districts, between Kyle of Tongue and Loch Eriboll, consisting of upland tract. **103 H2** NC5361.

Ab Kettleby *Leics.* ***Village***, 3m/5km NW of Melton Mowbray. **42 A3** SK7223.

Ab Lench *Worcs.* ***Settlement***, 5m/8km NW of Evesham. SP0151.

Abaty Cwmhir *Powys Welsh form of Abbeycwmhir, qv.*

Abbas Combe *Som.* ***Village***, 4m/6km S of Wincanton. **9 G2** ST7022.

Abberley *Worcs.* ***Village***, 5m/7km SW of Stourport-on-Severn. Victorian Gothic clocktower on Abberley Hill to S. **29 G2** SO7567.

Abberley Common *Worcs.* ***Village***, 5m/8km SW of Stourport-on-Severn. SO7467.

Abberley Hall *Worcs.* ***Historic house***, 1km W of Great Witley and 12m/19km NW of Worcester. Features Victorian decor. Now a boarding school. **29 G2** SO7466.

Abberley Hill *Worcs.* ***Hill***, to SW of Abberley, 4m/7km SW of Stourport-on-Severn. **29 G2** SO7566.

Abberton *Essex* ***Village***, 4m/6km S of Colchester. **34 E7** TM0019.

Abberton *Worcs.* ***Village***, 6m/9km NE of Pershore. **29 J3** SO9953.

Abberton Reservoir *Essex* ***Reservoir***, large reservoir to W of Abberton. **34 D7** TM0019.

Abberwick *Northumb.* ***Settlement***, 4m/6km W of Alnwick. **71 G2** NU1213.

Abbess End *Essex* ***Settlement***, just SW of Abbess Roding, 2m/4km SW of Leaden Roding. TL5610.

Abbess Roding *Essex* ***Village***, 2m/3km SW of Leaden Roding. **33 J7** TL5711.

Abbey *Devon* ***Hamlet***, 6m/10km N of Honiton. Site of ruined 13c Dunkeswell Abbey. ST1410.

Abbey Brook *S.Yorks.* ***River***, stream rising on Howden Moors in The Pennines, and flowing E to Derwent Reservoir. **50 D3** SK1792.

Abbey Cwmhir *Powys* ***Ecclesiastical building***, in village of Abbeycwmhir, 6m/9km N of Llandrindod Wells. Scant remains of abbey founded in 1143 for Cistercian monks. **27 K1** SO0571.

Abbey Dore *Here.* ***Ecclesiastical building***, beautiful 12c-13c church, 1m/2km N of Ewyas Harold and 9m/15km SW of Hereford. Originally part of a Cistercian abbey, restored in 1634. **28 C5** SO3830.

Abbey Dore *Here.* ***Village***, 2m/3km N of Pontrilas. **28 C5** SO3830.

Abbey Dore Court Garden *Here.* ***Garden***, 9m/14km SW of Hereford. Five acres of gardens on River Dore, including shrubs, rock garden and ponds. **28 C5** SO3830.

Abbey Gate *Kent* ***Settlement***, 2m/3km N of Maidstone. Remains of medieval Boxley Abbey on E side. TQ7558.

Abbey Green *S.Lan. Alternative name for Lesmahagow, qv.*

Abbey Head *D. & G.* ***Coastal feature***, headland 3m/4km S of Dundrennan. **65 H6** NX7343.

Abbey House Museum *W.Yorks.* ***Other feature of interest***, in gatehouse of 12c church at Kirkstall. Includes 18c and 19c cottages and shops with period furnishings. **57 H6** SE2536.

Abbey Hulton *Stoke* ***Suburb***, 3m/5km NE of Stoke-on-Trent city centre. **40 B1** SJ9148.

Abbey St. Bathans *Sc.Bord.* ***Village***, on River Whiteadder, 5m/8km N of Duns. Church incorporates fragments of 13c nunnery. **77 F4** NT7562.

Abbey Trading Estate *Worcs.* ***Locality***, N of Redditch town centre. SP0468.

Abbey Village *Lancs.* ***Village***, 1km E of Withnell. **56 B7** SD6422.

Abbey Wood *Gt.Lon.* ***Suburb***, in borough of Greenwich, 2m/3km E of Woolwich and 10m/17km E of Charing Cross. **23 H4** TQ4678.

Abbeycwmhir (Abaty Cwmhir). *Powys* ***Hamlet***, in valley of Clywedog Brook, 6m/10km N of Llandrindod Wells. Slight remains of 12c abbey. **27 K1** SO0571.

Abbeydale *S.Yorks.* ***Suburb***, 4m/6km SW of Sheffield city centre. SK3282.

Abbeydale *Worcs.* ***Suburb***, to E of Redditch town centre. SP0467.

Abbeyhill *Edin.* ***Suburb***, 1m/2km E of Edinburgh city centre. NT2774.

Abbeylands *I.o.M.* ***Locality***, 3m/4km N of Douglas. SC3779.

Abbeystead *Lancs.* ***Hamlet***, in River Wyre valley, 7m/11km SE of Lancaster. **55 J4** SD5654.

Abbeytown *Cumb.* ***Village***, 4m/7km SE of Silloth. Church comprises most of the nave of Holme Cultram Abbey, 12c. **60 C1** NY1750.

Abbot Hall Art Gallery and Museum *Cumb.* ***Other feature of interest***, Georgian house on W bank of River Kent in Kendal. Includes art gallery with works by Ruskin, Constable and Romney, and Museum of Lakeland Life and Industry, showing social history of Lake District, including a Victorian street and farm scene. **61 G7** SD5192.

Abbotrule *Sc.Bord.* ***Hamlet***, 2m/3km NE of Bonchester Bridge. **70 B2** NT6012.

Abbots Bickington *Devon* ***Village***, 7m/11km NE of Holsworthy. **6 B4** SS3813.

Abbots Bromley *Staffs.* Population: 1356. ***Village***, 6m/9km W of Uttoxeter. **40 C3** SK0824.

Abbot's Fish House *Som.* ***Historic/prehistoric site***, well-preserved 14c fish house (English Heritage) at Meare, 4m/6km NW of Glastonbury. Used to preserve and store fish caught at Meare Pool, now drained, for monks at Glastonbury Abbey. **19 H7** ST4541.

Abbots Langley *Herts.* ***Suburb***, 3m/5km N of Watford. **22 E1** TL0902.

Abbots Leigh *N.Som.* ***Village***, 3m/4km W of Bristol. **19 J4** ST5473.

Abbots Morton *Worcs.* ***Village***, 7m/11km N of Evesham. **30 B3** SP0355.

Abbots Ripton *Cambs.* ***Village***, 4m/6km N of Huntingdon. **33 F1** TL2378.

Abbot's Salford *Warks.* ***Hamlet***, 5m/7km NE of Evesham. **30 B3** SP0650.

Abbots Worthy *Hants.* ***Hamlet***, on River Itchen, 2m/4km N of Winchester. SU4932.

Abbotsbury *Dorset* ***Village***, 8m/13km NW of Weymouth. Ruined abbey (English Heritage). 15c tithe barn. Swannery. **8 E6** SY5785.

Abbotsbury Abbey *Dorset* ***Ecclesiastical building***, founded by Benedictines in 11c to S of Abbotsbury, but destroyed during Dissolution. Scant remains (English Heritage) consist mainly of part of N wall. **8 E6** SY5785.

Abbotsbury Sub-tropical Gardens *Dorset* ***Garden***, 1km W of Abbotsbury, overlooking Chesil Beach. Shelter provided by surrounding hills creates climate suitable for delicate species. **8 E6** SY5685.

Abbotsbury Swannery *Dorset* ***Other feature of interest***, medieval reserve for mute swans, 1km S of Abbotsbury. **8 E6** SY5784.

Abbotsfield *Mersey.* ***Settlement***, 3m/5km SE of St. Helens. SJ5492.

Abbotsford House *Sc.Bord.* ***Historic house***, mansion erected by Sir Walter Scott on S bank of River Tweed, 2m/4km W of Melrose. Scott lived and died here. **76 D7** NT5034.

Abbotsham *Devon* ***Village***, 2m/3km W of Bideford. **6 C3** SS4226.

Abbotside Common *N.Yorks.* ***Open space***, moorland to SE of Mallerstang Common, highest point of which is 2184 feet or 666 metres, 6m/9km NW of Hawes. **61 K7** SD8096.

Abbotsinch Airport *Renf. Former name of Glasgow Airport, qv.*

Abbotskerswell *Devon* ***Village***, 2m/3km S of Newton Abbot. **5 J4** SX8568.

Abbotsleigh *Devon* ***Locality***, 5m/8km SW of Dartmouth. SX8048.

Abbotsley *Cambs.* ***Village***, 4m/6km SE of St. Neots. **33 F3** TL2256.

Abbotstone *Hants.* ***Settlement***, 2m/3km NW of New Alresford. SU5634.

Abbotswood *Surr.* ***Suburb***, 1m/2km NE of Guildford town centre. TQ0151.

Abbotts Ann *Hants.* Population: 1459. ***Village***, 3m/4km SW of Andover. **21 G7** SU3243.

Abbott's Barton *Hants.* ***Suburb***, in N part of Winchester. SU4830.

Abbottswood *Hants.* ***Settlement***, 1m/2km N of Romsey. **10 E2** SU3623.

Abdon *Shrop.* ***Village***, 8m/13km NE of Ludlow. **38 E7** SO5786.

Abdy *S.Yorks.* ***Settlement***, 4m/6km N of Rotherham. SK4398.

Abenhall *Glos.* ***Hamlet***, 2m/3km NE of Cinderford. SO6717.

Aber *Gwyn. Former name of Abergwyngregyn, qv.*

Aber *Gwyn.* ***Settlement***, to NW of Llaniestyn, 1m/2km S of Dinas. **36 B2** SH2634.

Aber-banc *Cere.* ***Settlement***, 3m/5km E of Newcastle Emlyn. **26 C4** SN3541.

Aber Bowlan *Carmar.* ***Settlement***, 3m/4km SE of Pumsaint. **17 K1** SN6938.

Aber-Cywarch *Gwyn.* ***Settlement***, 1m/2km NE of Dinas-Mawddwy. **37 H4** SH8615.

Aber Dysynni *Gwyn.* ***Bay***, at mouth of River Dysynni, 2m/3km NW of Tywyn. **36 E5** SH5503.

Aber Falls (Rhaeadr Fawr). *Gwyn.* ***Waterfall***, high vertical waterfall 2m/3km S of Abergwyngregyn, in course of River Goch which rises on NW slopes of Foel-Fras. **46 E5** SH6670.

Aber-llia *Powys* ***Settlement***, 1km N of Ystradfellte. **27 J7** SN9314.

Aber-Naint *Powys* ***Settlement***, 2m/3km NW of Llanfyllin. **38 A3** SJ1221.

Aber-nant *R.C.T.* ***Locality***, adjoining to NE of Aberdare. **18 D1** SO0103.

Aber-pergwm *N.P.T.* ***Settlement***, 1m/2km W of Glyn-neath. **18 B1** SN8606.

Aber Village *Powys* ***Hamlet***, 1m/2km S of Talybont-on-Usk. SO1021.

Aberaeron *Cere.* ***Small town***, former port on Cardigan Bay, 14m/23km SW of Aberystwyth. Previously a ship-building town, now a centre for sailing enthusiasts. Home of the late Sir Geraint Evans. **26 D2** SN4562.

Aberafan *N.P.T. Welsh form of Aberavon, qv.*

Aberaman *R.C.T.* ***Locality***, adjoining to SE of Aberdare. **18 D1** SO0101.

Aberangell *Gwyn.* ***Village***, at confluence of Rivers Angell and Dyfi, 2m/3km SW of Mallwyd. **37 H5** SH8410.

Aberarad *Carmar.* ***Hamlet***, 1km SE of Newcastle Emlyn. **17 G1** SN3140.

Aberarder *High.* ***Settlement***, on NW side of Loch Laggan, 4m/6km W of Kinloch Laggan. **88 B6** NN4787.

Aberarder House *High.* ***Settlement***, 6m/9km SE of Dores. **88 D2** NH6225.

Aberargie *P. & K.* ***Village***, 2m/3km W of Abernethy. **82 C6** NO1615.

Aberarth *Cere.* ***Village***, on Cardigan Bay, 1m/2km NE of Aberaeron. **26 D2** SN4763.

Aberavon (Aberafan). *N.P.T.* ***Suburb***, of Port Talbot, on W side of River Afan. **18 A3** SS7590.

Aberbargod *Caerp. Welsh form of Aberbargoed, qv.*

Aberbargoed (Aberbargod). *Caerp.* ***Village***, on E side of Bargoed. **18 E1** ST1599.

Aberbechan *Powys* ***Settlement***, at confluence of Bechan Brook and River Severn, 3m/4km NE of Newtown. SO1493.

Aberbeeg (Aberbig). *B.Gwent* ***Locality***, 1m/2km S of Abertillery. **19 F1** SO2002.

Aberbig *B.Gwent Welsh form of Aberbeeg, qv.*

Aberbran *Powys* ***Settlement***, 4m/6km W of Brecon. SN9829.

Abercanaid *M.Tyd.* Population: 5285. ***Village***, 2m/3km S of Merthyr Tydfil. **18 D1** SO0503.

Abercarn *Caerp.* Population: 7034. ***Small town***, on Ebbw River, 7m/11km NW of Newport. **19 F2** ST2195.

Abercastell *Pembs. Welsh form of Abercastle, qv.*

Abercastle (Abercastell). *Pembs.* ***Hamlet***, on coast 2m/3km NW of Mathry. **16 B1** SM8533.

Abercegin *Gwyn.* ***Locality***, 1m/2km E of Bangor. SH5972.

Abercegir *Powys* ***Hamlet***, 2m/3km SW of Cemmaes Road. **37 H5** SH8001.

Aberchalder *High.* ***Settlement***, at NE end of Loch Oich, 5m/7km SW of Fort Augustus. **87 K4** NH3403.

Aberchalder Burn *High.* ***River***, formed by tributaries on slopes of Carn na Saobhaidhe and flowing NW into Loch Mhòr at Wester Aberchalder. **88 C3** NH5420.

Aberchirder *Aber.* Population: 1097. ***Village***, 8m/13km SW of Banff. **98 E5** NJ6252.

Aberconwy House *Conwy* ***Historic house***, in Conwy. 14c timber and stone merchant's house (National Trust) with local history exhibitions. **47 F5** SH7678.

Abercorn *W.Loth.* ***Settlement***, on S side of Firth of Forth, 3m/5km W of Forth Road Bridge. **75 J3** NT0878.

Abercraf *Powys* ***Village***, 4m/6km NE of Ystalyfera. **27 H7** SN8112.

Abercregan *N.P.T.* ***Village***, 3m/5km N of Maesteg. SS8496.

Abercrombie *Fife* ***Settlement***, 1m/2km NW of St. Monans. **83 G7** NO5102.

Abercrychan *Carmar.* ***Settlement***, 2m/3km NE of Llandovery. **27 G5** SN7936.

Abercwmboi *R.C.T.* ***Village***, 2m/3km SE of Aberdare. **18 D1** ST0299.

Abercych *Pembs.* ***Village***, 4m/6km W of Newcastle Emlyn. **26 B4** SN2440.

Abercynafon *Powys* ***Settlement***, 8m/12km NE of Merthyr Tydfil. **27 K7** SO0817.

Abercynffig *Bridgend Welsh form of Aberkenfig, qv.*

Abercynon *R.C.T.* Population: 10,650. ***Village***, at confluence of Rivers Cynon and Taff, 3m/5km N of Pontypridd. **18 D2** ST0894.

Aberdalgie *P. & K.* ***Settlement***, 3m/5km SW of Perth. **82 B5** NO0720.

Aberdâr *R.C.T. Welsh form of Aberdare, qv.*

Aberdare (Aberdâr). *R.C.T.* Population: 29,040. ***Town***, on River Cynon, 20m/32km NW of Cardiff. **18 C1** SO0002.

Aberdaron *Gwyn.* ***Village***, on Aberdaron Bay near tip of Lleyn Peninsula. **36 A3** SH1726.

Aberdaron Bay *Gwyn.* ***Bay***, extends from Pen y Cil NE to Trwyn y Penrhyn. **36 A3** SH1726.

Aberdaugleddau *Pembs. Welsh form of Milford Haven, qv.*

Aberdeen *Aberdeen* Population: 189,707. ***City***, cathedral and university city and commercial centre on E coast 57m/92km NE of Dundee. Known as 'The Granite City', local stone having been used in many of its buildings. By 13c, Aberdeen had become an important centre for trade and fishing and remains a major port and commercial base. In 19c ship building brought great prosperity to the city. These industries had receded by mid 20c but the city's prospects were transformed when North Sea oil was discovered in 1970, turning it into a city of great wealth. Many museums and art galleries. Extensive flower gardens. Airport at Dyce, 6m/9km NW of Aberdeen. **91 H4** NJ9406.

Aberdeen Airport (Formerly known as Dyce Airport.) *Aberdeen* ***Airport/airfield***, international airport on S side of River Don, 6m/9km NW of Aberdeen. **91 G3** NJ8712.

Aberdeen Art Gallery *Aberdeen* ***Other feature of interest***, art gallery in Schoolhill, Aberdeen, with English and French paintings and a Henry Moore sculpture. British artists represented include Spencer, Nash and Bacon. **91 H4** NJ9307.

Aberdeen Maritime Museum *Aberdeen* ***Other feature of interest***, museum in Shiprow, Aberdeen, commemorating sea-faring history of Aberdeen, from harbour and port to offshore oil industry base. Exhibition features 8.5 metre high model of oil platform. Building includes Provost Ross's House. **91 H4** NJ9306.

Aberdesach *Gwyn.* ***Settlement***, on Caernarfon Bay, at mouth of River Desach, 8m/12km SW of Caernarfon. **46 C7** SH4251.

Aberdour *Fife* Population: 1524. ***Small town***, resort on N shore of Firth of Forth, 3m/4km W of Burntisland. Remains of 14c castle (Historic Scotland). 12c St. Colomba's Abbey is sited on Inchcolm Island, just off shore. **75 K2** NT1985.

Aberdour Bay *Aber.* ***Bay***, on N coast of Buchan district, N of New Aberdour. **99 G4** NJ8965.

Aberdour Castle *Fife* ***Castle***, 14c castle (Historic Scotland) with 16c-17c additions in Aberdour, on N shore of Firth of Forth. Former home of Earl of Moray, then Douglas family. Circular dovecote. **75 K2** NT1985.

Aberdovey *Gwyn. English form of Aberdyfi, qv.*

Aberdovey Bar *Gwyn. English form of Aberdyfi Bar, qv.*

Aberduhonw *Powys* ***Settlement***, 1m/2km E of Builth Wells. **27 K3** SO0650.

Aberdulais *N.P.T.* ***Village***, 2m/3km NE of Neath. **18 A2** SS7799.

Aberdulais Falls *N.P.T.* ***Other feature of interest***, National Trust property, 2m/3km NE of Neath. Waterfall has powered successive smelting works since 16c and now drives an unusual hydro-electric scheme via Europe's largest electricity-generating waterwheel. **18 A2** SS7799.

Aberdyfi (Aberdovey). *Gwyn.* ***Small town***, resort on N shore of River Dyfi estuary near mouth, 9m/14km W of Machynlleth. **37 F6** SN6196.

Aberdyfi Bar (Aberdovey Bar). *Gwyn.* ***Coastal feature***, sandbank opposite mouth of River Dyfi about 1m/2km W of Aberdyfi. **36 E6** SN6196.

Aberedw *Powys* ***Village***, 3m/5km SE of Builth Wells across River Wye. Limited remains of baronial castle to W. **27 K4** SO0747.

Aberedw Rocks *Powys* ***Inland physical feature***, terraced outcrop of Silurian rock above River Wye, to S of Aberedw. **27 K4** SO0747.

Abereiddi *Pembs. Welsh form of Abereiddy, qv.*

Abereiddy (Abereiddi). *Pembs.* ***Hamlet***, on Abereiddi Bay, 5m/7km NE of St. David's. **16 B1** SM7931.

Abererch *Gwyn.* ***Village***, on River Erch, 2m/3km NE of Pwllheli. **36 D2** SH3936.

Aberfan *M.Tyd.* ***Village***, on River Taff, 4m/6km S of Merthyr Tydfil. **18 D1** SO0700.

Aberfeldy *P. & K.* Population: 1748. ***Small town***, astride Urlar Burn near its confluence with River Tay, 8m/13km SW of Pitlochry. Distillery. **81 K3** NN8549.

Aberffraw *I.o.A.* ***Village***, on Anglesey at head of River Ffraw estuary, 12m/20km W of Menai Bridge. Barclodiad y Gawres Chambered Cairn (Cadw) on coast 2m/3km NW, Din Dryfol Burial Chamber (Cadw) 3m/5km NE. **46 B6** SH3568.

Aberffraw Bay *I.o.A.* ***Bay***, at mouth of River Ffraw, on SW coast of Anglesey. **46 B6** SH3567.

Aberffrwd *Cere.* ***Locality***, 4m/6km W of Devil's Bridge. **27 F1** SN6878.

Aberford *W.Yorks.* ***Village***, 3m/5km NE of Garforth. **57 K6** SE4337.

Aberfoyle *Stir.* ***Village***, 8m/13km SW of Callander. Situated on River Forth between Achray and Loch Ard Forests and below SW end of Menteith Hills. **81 G7** NN5201.

Abergarw *Bridgend* ***Locality***, 3m/5km N of Bridgend. **18 C3** SS9184.

Abergarwed *N.P.T.* ***Settlement***, 1m/2km W of Resolven across River Neath. SN8102.

Abergavenny (Y Fenni). *Mon.* Population: 14,092. ***Town***, market town at S end of Black Mountains, at confluence of Rivers Gavenny and Usk, 9m/14km N of Pontypool. Contains Roman Gobannium and slight remains of medieval castle. **28 C7** SO2914.

Abergavenny and District Museum *Mon.* ***Other feature of interest***, local exhibits, crafts and tools can be seen along with remains of castle at Abergavenny. **28 C7** SO2913.

Abergavenny Castle *Mon.* ***Castle***, originally a 12c motte and bailey castle, then stone additions. Owned by William de Broose. Ruins situated to S of Abergavenny at junction of Rivers Usk and Gwenny. **28 B7** SO2913.

Abergele *Conwy* Population: 7373. ***Small town***, resort near North Wales coast, 5m/7km SW of Rhyl. Castell Cawr is ancient British hill camp 1m/2km SW. Gwrych Castle, 19c house in Gothic style, 1m/2km W. **47 H5** SH9477.

Abergele Roads *Conwy* ***Bay***, shallow bay N of Abergele. **47 H5** SH9379.

Abergiar *Carmar.* ***Settlement***, 2m/4km SW of Llanybydder. **26 E4** SN5041.

Abergorlech *Carmar.* ***Hamlet***, 3m/4km SW of Llansawel. **17 J1** SN5833.

Abergwaun *Pembs. Welsh form of Fishguard, qv.*

Abergwesyn *Powys* ***Hamlet***, 4m/7km N of Llanwrtyd Wells. **27 H3** SN8552.

Abergwili *Carmar.* ***Village***, 2m/3km E of Carmarthen. Palace of Bishop of St. David's is here. **17 H2** SN4321.

Abergwngu Hill *Cere.* ***Mountain***, rising to over 390 metres, 3m/5km NW of head of Craig Goch Reservoir. **27 H1** SN8674.

Abergwydol *Powys* ***Locality***, 3m/5km E of Machynlleth. **37 G5** SH7902.

Abergwynant *Gwyn.* ***Settlement***, 3m/5km W of Dolgellau. **37 F4** SH6717.

Abergwynfi *N.P.T.* ***Village***, 5m/8km W of Rhondda. **18 B2** SS8996.

Abergwyngregyn (Formerly known as Aber.) *Gwyn.* ***Village***, 2m/3km SW of Llanfairfechan. Mound marks site of motte and bailey castle. **46 E5** SH6572.

Abergynolwyn *Gwyn.* ***Village***, at confluence of Rivers Dysynni and Gwernol, 7m/11km NE of Tywyn. **37 F5** SH6707.

Aberhafesp *Powys* ***Hamlet***, 3m/4km W of Newtown. **37 K6** SO0792.

Aberhonddu *Powys Welsh form of Brecon, qv.*

Aberhosan *Powys* ***Hamlet***, 5m/7km SE of Machynlleth. **37 H6** SN8197.

Aberkenfig (Abercynffig). *Bridgend* Population: 4706. ***Village***, 3m/4km N of Bridgend. **18 B3** SS8983.

Aberlady *E.Loth.* ***Village***, on Aberlady Bay, 6m/10km SW of North Berwick. **76 C2** NT4679.

Aberlemno *Angus* ***Village***, 5m/8km NE of Forfar. Aberlemno Sculptured Stones (Historic Scotland) in churchyard. **83 G2** NO5255.

Aberlemno Sculptured Stones *Angus* ***Historic/prehistoric site***, upright cross slab (Historic Scotland) with Pictish symbols and combat relief in churchyard at Aberlemno, 2m/3km SE of Finavon. Three other stones by B9134 road nearby. **83 G2** NO5255.

Aberllefenni *Gwyn.* ***Village***, 6m/9km N of Machynlleth. **37 G5** SH7709.

Aberllynfi *Powys Welsh form of Three Cocks, qv.*

Aberlour *Moray Alternative name for Charlestown of Aberlour, qv.*

Abermad *Cere.* ***Settlement***, 1m/2km SE of Llanfarian. **26 E1** SN5976.

Abermaw *Gwyn. Welsh form of Barmouth, qv.*

Abermenai Point *I.o.A.* ***Coastal feature***, headland on Anglesey at SW end of Menai Strait. **46 C6** SH4461.

Abermeurig *Cere.* ***Settlement***, 5m/8km N of Lampeter. **26 E3** SN5656.

Abermiwl *Powys Welsh form of Abermule, qv.*

Abermorddu *Flints.* ***Settlement***, 1km S of Caergwrle. SJ3056.

Abermule (Abermiwl). *Powys* ***Hamlet***, on River Severn, 4m/6km NE of Newtown. **38 A6** SO1694.

Abernant *Carmar.* ***Hamlet***, 5m/8km W of Carmarthen. **17 G2** SN3323.

Abernethy *P. & K.* ***Village***, 3m/5km W of Newburgh. Round tower (Historic Scotland). Remains of Roman fortress and naval base to NE in grounds of Carpow, near S bank of River Tay. **82 C6** NO1916.

Abernethy Forest *High.* ***Forest/woodland***, coniferous forest 6m/10km S of Grantown-on-Spey in Badenoch and Strathspey district. **89 H3** NJ9917.

Abernethy Round Tower *P. & K.* ***Historic/prehistoric site***, tower (Historic Scotland) with lower part dating from 9c and upper part from late 11c, at SE side of Abernethy; height 74 feet or nearly 23 metres. **82 C6** NO1916.

Abernyte *P. & K.* ***Village***, 9m/14km W of Dundee. **82 D4** NO2531.

Aberogwr *V. of Glam. Welsh form of Ogmore-by-Sea, qv.*

Aberpennar *R.C.T. Welsh form of Mountain Ash, qv.*

Aberporth *Cere.* Population: 1431. ***Village***, 6m/10km NE of Cardigan. **26 B3** SN2651.

Aberriw (Berriew). *Powys* ***Village***, 5m/8km SW of Welshpool. **38 A5** SJ1800.

Aberscross *High.* ***Locality***, 1m/2km NW of head of Loch Fleet. **96 E1** NC7600.

Abersky *High.* ***Settlement***, 5m/8km S of Dores. **88 C2** NH5926.

Abersoch *Gwyn.* ***Small town***, small resort and former fishing village, on St. Tudwal's Road at mouth of River Soch, 6m/9km SW of Pwllheli across bay. Popular as a yachting centre. **36 C3** SH3128.

Abersychan *Torfaen* ***Town***, 2m/3km NW of Pontypool. **19 F1** SO2603.

Abertawe *Swan. Welsh form of Swansea, qv.*

Aberteifi *Cere. Welsh form of Cardigan, qv.*

Aberthin *V. of Glam.* ***Village***, 1m/2km NE of Cowbridge. **18 D4** ST0075.

Abertillery (Abertyleri). *B.Gwent* Population: 11,680. ***Town***, 12m/19km NW of Newport. **19 F1** SO2104.

Abertridwr *Caerp.* Population: 6358. ***Village***, 3m/5km NW of Caerphilly. **18 E3** ST1289.

Abertridwr *Powys* ***Village***, 1m/2km E of Lake Vyrnwy dam. **37 K4** SJ0319.

Abertyleri *B.Gwent Welsh form of Abertillery, qv.*

Abertysswg *Caerp.* ***Village***, 1m/2km SE of Rhymney. **18 E1** SO1305.

Aberuthven *P. & K.* ***Village***, on Ruthven Water, 3m/4km NE of Auchterader. **82 A6** NN9715.

Aberyscir *Powys* ***Settlement***, 3m/5km W of Brecon. Remains of Roman fort of Bannium (Cadw) across River Yscir. **27 J6** SO0029.

Aberystwyth *Cere.* Population: 11,154. ***Town***, resort, small port and university town at mouth of Rivers Rheidol and Ystwyth on Cardigan Bay, 82m/132km NW of Cardiff. Commercial capital of Mid-Wales. Remains of 13c castle on sea front. Location of National Library of Wales and Ceredigion Museum. Camera Obscura with 14 inch lens, on Constitution Hill, accessible by Electric Cliff Railway. Terminus of Vale of Rheidol Railway. Development of pier and large marina. **36 E7** SN5881.

Aberystwyth Castle *Cere.* ***Castle***, on rocky coastal prominence 2m/3km S of Aberystwyth town centre. Built in early 12c by Gilbert de Clare, rebuilt by Edward I in 13c to subdue Welsh. Captured by Owain Glyndŵr in 1404. A royal mint was established between 1637 and 1646 using locally mined silver. Castle was blown up in 1649 during Civil War and subsequently looted, leaving it in ruins. Gorsedd stone circle within grounds. **36 E7** SN5781.

Aberystwyth Electric Cliff Railway *Cere.* ***Leisure/recreation***, Britain's longest cliff railway, built in 1896. It runs from Grand Terminus building up S slope of Constitution Hill, Aberystwyth. **36 E7** SN5882.

Abhainn a' Chadh' Bhuidhe *High.* ***River***, rising between Meallan Chuaich and Groban, flowing S, then E into NW part of Loch Fannich. **95 H5** NH1567.

Abhainn a' Choire *High.* ***River***, rising below Meallan a' Chuail, flowing through Loch Dubh a' Chuail, then flowing SE into Loch Shin. **103 F6** NC3625.

Abhainn a' Ghiubhais Li *High.* ***River***, flowing E from N slopes of Meall Gorm to confluence with Allt an Loch Sgeirich, forming Abhainn an Torrain Duibh. NH2672.

Abhainn a' Ghlinne Bhig *High.* ***River***, forming border between Ross and Cromarty and Sutherland districts. Formed from streams flowing down N slopes of Beinn Dearg massif and running E into Abhainn a' Ghlinne Mhòir just N of Meall a' Chaorainn. **95 K3** NH3684.

Abhainn a' Ghlinne Ghil *High.* ***River***, in Lochaber district, running W to River Aline 4m/6km N of Lochaline. NM6950.

Abhainn a' Ghlinne Mhòir *High.* ***River***, fed by Abhainn a' Ghlinne Bhig and flowing NE along Gleann Mòr to confluence with Alladale River, 3m/4km SW of The Craigs, Sutherland district. NH4489.

Abhainn an Fhasaigh *High.* ***River***, flowing SW from SE end of Lochan Fada, down Gleann Bianasdail, and into SE end of Loch Maree. **95 G5** NH0165.

Abhainn an Lòin *High.* ***River***, flowing W into Loch Stack, Sutherland district. **103 F4** NC3042.

Abhainn an t-Srath Chuileannaich *High.* ***River***, in Sutherland district, running SE along Strath Cuileannaich before becoming Black Water, S of Croick and flowing into Strathcarron 8m/13km W of Bonar Bridge. NH4393.

Abhainn an t-Srathain *High.* ***River***, in Sutherland district running NW to confluence with Lón Mòr at head of Strath Shinary. **102 E2** NC2363.

Abhainn an t-Stratha Charnaig *High.* ***River***, issuing from Loch Buidhe in Sutherland district, and flowing E along Srath Carnaig, passing over Torboll Falls, to confluence with River Fleet, 1m/2km NW of head of Loch Fleet. **96 D2** NH7598.

Abhainn Beinn nan Eun *High.* ***River***, rising in Kildermorie Forest, Ross and Cromarty district, and flowing S, then E, to enter W end of Loch Glass. **96 B4** NH4873.

Abhainn Bhearnais *High.* ***River***, flowing SW into Loch an Laoigh and forming boundary between Ross and Cromarty and Skye and Lochalsh districts. **95 G7** NH0343.

Abhainn Bhuidheach *High.* ***River***, flowing S into head of Loch Carron. **95 F7** NG9242.

Abhainn Bruachaig *High.* ***River***, in Ross and Cromarty district, flowing from Heights of Kinlochewe SW to Kinlochewe, where it joins with A' Ghairbhe to form Kinlochewe River. **95 G5** NH0362.

Abhainn Chuaig *High.* ***River***, flowing NW to W coast of Ross and Cromarty district, 2m/3km SW of Rubha na Fearn and entrance to Loch Torridon. **94 D6** NG7058.

Abhainn Crò Chlach *High.* ***River***, running NE from N slopes of Carn Bàn into River Findhorn, 9m/15km NW of Kingussie. **88 D4** NH6512.

Abhainn Cuileig *High.* ***River***, flowing NE from Loch a' Bhraoin into River Broom, 1km NW of Corrieshalloch Gorge. **95 H4** NH1979.

Abhainn Dalach ***River***, running SE into Loch Etive, Argyll, 5m/8km NE of narrows at Bonawe. **80 B3** NN0538.

Abhainn Deabhag *High.* ***River***, formed at confluence of Féith na Leitreach and Allt Riabhach, and flowing NE to confluence with River Affric to form River Glass. **87 J2** NH3022.

Abhainn Dearg *High.* ***River***, flowing into S end of Loch Damh, Ross and Cromarty district. **94 E7** NG8647.

Abhainn Droma *High.* ***River***, rising in Loch Droma and flowing NW through Dirrie More to its confluence with Abhainn Cuileig to form River Broom. **95 J4** NH1979.

Abhainn Dubh *High.* ***River***, rising on mountains S of Loch Lundie and flowing N through loch into Loch Shieldaig, 7m/11km W of Torridon, Ross and Cromarty district. **94 D6** NG7854.

Abhainn Dubh *High.* ***River***, flowing E from Loch an Fhiarlaid into W end of Loch a' Chroisg, 4m/6km W of Achnasheen. **95 G6** NH0957.

Abhainn Duibhe ***River***, running NE down Gleann Duibhe to River Gaur below Loch Eigheach. **81 F3** NN4656.

Abhainn Fionain *Arg. & B.* ***River***, flowing E into Loch Awe, 3m/5km NE of Dalavich. **80 A6** NN0017.

Abhainn Gaoire *P. & K. Gaelic form of (River) Gaur, qv.*

Abhainn Ghuilbinn *High.* ***River***, running from Loch Ghuilbinn and flowing into Loch Laggan Reservoir 5m/8km E of Tulloch Station. **88 B7** NN4282.

Abhainn Glac an t-Seilich *High.* ***River***, rising N of Garbhan Mòr and flowing SW into Black Water at head of Strath Rusdale. **96 C3** NH5678.

Abhainn Inbhir Ghuiserein *High. See Gleann na Guiserein.*

Abhainn Mòr *Arg. & B.* ***River***, in Knapdale, flowing SW into Loch Caolisport 1m/2km NE of Knapdale Head. **73 F3** NR7275.

Abhainn na Frithe *High.* ***River***, in Sutherland district, flowing E and joining River Helmsdale 2m/3km S of Burnfoot. **104 D6** NC8726.

Abhainn na Glasa *High.* ***River***, rising on E slopes of Beinn a' Chaisteil and flowing circuitously, but generally E then SE through Gleann Mhuire and into Loch Morie. **96 B3** NH5177.

Abhainn Poiblidh *High.* ***River***, flowing NE from Loch an Daimh into Rappach Water. **95 J2** NH3197.

Abhainn Rath *High.* ***River***, in Lochaber district running E to head of Loch Treig. **80 D1** NN3168.

Abhainn Righ *High.* ***River***, in Lochaber district running W down Glen Righ to Loch Linnhe, 1m/2km NW of Onich. Series of waterfalls nearly 1m/2km above mouth. **80 B1** NN0162.

Abhainn Sgeamhaidh *High.* ***River***, flowing SW to join River Tirry SW of Rhian, Sutherland district. **103 H7** NC5516.

Abhainn Srath na Sealga *High.* ***River***, running NW down Strath na Sealga into head of Loch na Sealga in W part of Ross and Cromarty district. **95 G3** NH0680.

Abhainnsuidhe (Also known as Amhuinnsuidhe.) *W.Isles* ***Locality***, on coast of North Harris, on N side of West Loch Tarbert, 2m/3km E of Gobhaig. **100 C7** NB0408.

Abingdon *Oxon.* Population: 35,234. ***Town***, historic market town on River Thames, 6m/9km S of Oxford. Notable buildings in a range of styles, including 15c and 18c almshouses and 17c county hall (English Heritage). **21 H2** SU4997.

Abingdon Abbey *Oxon.* ***Ecclesiastical building***, scant remains of Benedictine Abbey, founded in 10c on site of original Saxon abbey to E of Abingdon's main square. Entrance is via impressive 15c gatehouse adjacent to medieval church. **21 H2** SU4995.

Abingdon Museum and County Hall *Oxon.* ***Other feature of interest***, 17c hall (English Heritage) in market place in Abingdon, built to house Assize Courts. **21 J2** SU4997.

Abinger Common *Surr.* ***Hamlet***, 4m/6km SW of Dorking. **22 E7** TQ1145.

Abinger Hammer *Surr.* ***Village***, 5m/7km W of Dorking. Site of Roman building 1 km E. **22 D7** TQ0947.

Abington *Northants.* ***Suburb***, 2m/3km NE of Northampton town centre. SP7762.

Abington *S.Lan.* ***Village***, on River Clyde, 11m/18km SW of Biggar. **68 E1** NS9323.

Abington Pigotts *Cambs.* ***Village***, 4m/6km NW of Royston. **33 G4** TL3044.

Abington Vale *Northants.* ***Suburb***, 2m NE of Northampton town centre. SP7861.

Abingworth *W.Suss.* ***Hamlet***, 1m/2km NE of Storrington. **12 E5** TQ1016.

Ablington *Glos.* ***Village***, 1m/2km NW of Bibury. **20 E1** SP1007.

Ablington *Wilts.* ***Settlement***, just SE of Figheldean, 4m/6km N of Amesbury. SU1546.

Abney *Derbys.* ***Hamlet***, 2m/4km SW of Hathersage. **50 E5** SK1979.

Above Church *Staffs.* ***Hamlet***, adjoins to NW of Ipstones. SK0150.

Aboyne *Aber.* Population: 2067. ***Village***, on N bank of River Dee, 10m/16km E of Ballater, with Loch of Aboyne 1m/2km to NE. **90 D5** NO5298.

Abram *Gt.Man.* Population: 11,482. ***Town***, 3m/5km SE of Wigan. **49 F2** SD6001.

Abriachan *High.* ***Settlement***, on W side of Loch Ness, Inverness district, 3m/5km from NE end of loch. **88 C1** NH5535.

Abridge *Essex* ***Village***, 3m/5km S of Epping. Site of Roman settlement 1m/2km W. **23 H2** TQ4696.

Abronhill *N.Lan.* ***Suburb***, 1m/2km NE of Cumbernauld town centre. **75 F3** NS7875.

Abson *S.Glos.* ***Hamlet***, 5m/8km S of Chipping Sodbury. **19 K4** ST7074.

Abthorpe *Northants.* ***Village***, 3m/5km SW of Towcester. **31 H4** SP6546.

Abune-the-Hill *Ork.* ***Settlement***, 1km S of N coast of Mainland. **106 B5** HY2828.

Aby *Lincs.* ***Village***, 3m/5km NW of Alford. **53 H5** TF4178.

Acaster Malbis *York* ***Village***, on W bank of River Ouse, 4m/7km S of York. **58 B5** SE5845.

Acaster Selby *N.Yorks.* ***Village***, on W bank of River Ouse, 6m/9km E of Tadcaster. **58 B5** SE5741.

Accrington *Lancs.* Population: 36,466. ***Town***, 5m/8km E of Blackburn. **56 C7** SD7528.

Accurrach *Arg. & B.* ***Settlement***, 8m/12km N of Inveraray. **80 C6** NN1120.

Acha *Arg. & B.* ***Settlement***, on Coll, 3m/5km SW of Arinagour. **78 C2** NM1854.

Achacha *Arg. & B.* ***Settlement***, 1km SW of Barcaldine. **80 A3** NM9440.

Achadacaie *Arg. & B.* ***Settlement***, on SE side of West Loch Tarbert, 4m/6km SW of Tarbert. **73 G4** NR8363.

Achadh-chaorrunn *Arg. & B.* ***Settlement***, on NW side of West Loch Tarbert, 9m/14km SW of Tarbert. **73 F5** NR7559.

Achadh Mòr (Anglicised form: Achmore.) *W.Isles* ***Village***, on Isle of Lewis, 8m/12km W of Stornoway. **101 F5** NB3029.

Achadophris *High.* ***Locality***, on E side of Loch Shin in Sutherland district, 4m/6km N of Lairg. NC5611.

Achadun Castle *Arg. & B.* ***Castle***, remains of castle on N coast of Lismore in Loch Linnhe, 3m/5km W of Achnacroish. **79 K4** NM8039.

Achadunan *Arg. & B.* ***Settlement***, at SW end of Glen Fyne, 2m/3km NE of Cairndow. **80 C6** NN1913.

Achagavel *High.* ***Settlement***, near head of Gleann Dubh, 3m/4km SW of Liddesdale, Lochaber district. **79 J2** NM7656.

Achaglachgach Forest *Arg. & B.* ***Forest/woodland***, on Knapdale, on NW side of West Loch Tarbert. **73 F4** NR7861.

Achaglass *Arg. & B.* ***Settlement***, on Kintyre, 3m/5km S of Tayinloan. **73 F6** NR7041.

Achahoish *Arg. & B.* ***Village***, in Knapdale, Argyll, at head of Loch Caolisport and 7m/11km SW of Ardrishaig. **73 F3** NR7877.

Achairn Burn *High.* ***River***, in Caithness district, rising on Hill of Toftgun and flowing N, then E, briefly disappearing underground before flowing N to join Wick River, 3m/4km W of Wick. **105 H4** ND3252.

Achalader *P. & K.* ***Settlement***, 3m/5km W of Blairgowrie. **82 C3** NO1245.

Achaleven *Arg. & B.* ***Settlement***, on S shore of Loch Etive, Argyll, 1km E of Connel. NM9234.

Achallader *Arg. & B.* ***Settlement***, 3m/5km NE of Bridge of Orchy. **80 E3** NN3244.

Achamore *Arg. & B.* ***Locality***, on E coast of Jura, 3m/5km NE of Ardfernal. **72 D3** NR5876.

Achamore Gardens *Arg. & B.* ***Garden***, on Gigha Island, developed over last 40 years, containing rhododendrons, camellias and many subtropical plants. **72 E6** NR6447.

Achanalt *High.* ***Locality***, in Ross and Cromarty district, 4m/6km W of head of Loch Luichart. NH2561.

Achandunie *High.* ***Settlement***, 1m/2km N of Alness. **96 D4** NH6472.

Achany *High.* ***Settlement***, to W of River Shin, 3m/5km S of Lairg. **96 C1** NC5601.

Achany Glen *High.* ***Valley***, carrying River Shin S from Loch Shin into Kyle of Sutherland. **96 C1** NC5703.

Achaphubuil *High.* ***Settlement***, 2m/3km NW of Fort William across head of Loch Awe. **87 G7** NN0876.

Acharacle *High.* ***Village***, in Lochaber district, 2m/4km N of Salen. **79 H1** NM6767.

Achargary *High.* ***Settlement***, on River Naver, 4m/7km S of Bettyhill, Caithness district. **104 C3** NC7154.

Acharn *Arg. & B.* ***Settlement***, in Glen Kinglass, 6m/10km NW of Dalmally. **80 C4** NN1235.

Acharn *P. & K.* ***Village***, on S shore of Loch Tay at foot of Acharn Burn, 2m/3km SW of Kenmore. **81 J3** NN7543.

Acharn Burn *P. & K.* ***River***, flowing into Loch Tay 2m/3km SW of Kenmore. Falls of Acharn, cascade nearly 1km S. **81 J4** NN7543.

Acharosson *Arg. & B.* ***Settlement***, 4m/6km NW of Tighnabruaich. **73 H3** NR9377.

Achateny *High.* ***Locality***, near N coast of Ardnamurchan peninsula, in Lochaber district, 7m/12km E of Point of Ardnamurchan. **79 G1** NM5270.

Achath *Aber.* ***Settlement***, 2m/3km NW of Dunecht. **91 F3** NJ7310.

Achavanich *High.* ***Locality***, in Caithness district, 6m/10km NW of Lybster. **105 G4** ND1742.

Achdalieu Lodge *High. See Loch Eil Centre.*

Achddu *Carmar.* ***Suburb***, in N part of Burry Port. SN4401.

Achduart *High.* ***Settlement***, 1km E of Rubha Dubh Ard, Ross and Cromarty district. **95 G1** NC0403.

Achentoul *High.* ***Settlement***, in Sutherland district, 1m/2km N of Kinbrace. **104 D5** NC8733.

Achentoul Forest *High.* ***Forest/woodland***, tract in Sutherland district to N of Kinbrace. **104 D5** NC8638.

Achfary *High.* ***Settlement***, in Sutherland district, at lower end of Loch More. **102 E4** NC2939.

Achgarve *High.* ***Settlement***, 1m/2km NW of Laide, Ross and Cromarty district. **94 E2** NG8893.

Achiemore *High.* ***Settlement***, on W side of Kyle of Durness where it opens out to include Balnakeil Bay. **103 F2** NC3567.

Achiemore *High.* ***Settlement***, on E bank of Halladale River, 4m/6km S of Melvich. **104 D3** NC8958.

Achies *High.* ***Settlement***, 3m/4km S of Halkirk. **105 G3** ND1355.

Achiltibuie *High.* ***Village***, on NW coast of Ross and Cromarty district, 10m/16km NW of Ullapool. Location of The Hydroponicum. **95 G1** NC0208.

Achina *High.* ***Settlement***, near N coast of Caithness district, 1km S of Bettyhill. **104 C2** NC7060.

Achindown *High.* ***Settlement***, 1m/2km S of Cawdor. **97 F7** NH8348.

Achinduich *High.* ***Settlement***, 4m/6km S of Lairg, on E side of Achany Glen. **96 C1** NC5800.

Achingills *High.* ***Locality***, 3m/4km NE of Halkirk. Includes a number of scattered dwellings. **105 G2** ND1663.

Achintee *High.* ***Settlement***, in Ross and Cromarty district, at head of Loch Carron. **95 F7** NG9441.

Achintee House *High.* ***Settlement***, in valley of River Nevis, 1m/2km SE of Fort William. **87 H7** NN1272.

Achintraid *High.* ***Locality***, at head of Loch Kishorn, Ross and Cromarty district. **86 E1** NG8438.

Achlean *High.* ***Settlement***, 6m/10km SE of Kingussie. **89 F5** NN8597.

Achleanan *High.* ***Settlement***, in Lochaber district, 1km SE of Drimnin. **79 G2** NM5654.

Achleek *High.* ***Settlement***, on S shore of Loch Sunart, 2m/3km SW of Strontian across loch. **79 J2** NM7959.

Achlian *Arg. & B.* ***Settlement***, near N end of Loch Awe, 3m/5km SW of Dalmally. **80 C5** NN1224.

Achluachrach *High.* ***Locality***, in Glen Spean, Lochaber district, 2m/4km E of Roybridge. NN3081.

Achlyness *High.* ***Settlement***, 1km NW of Rhiconich, at head of Loch Inchard, W coast of Sutherland district. **102 E3** NC2452.

Achmelvich *High.* ***Locality***, on W coast of Sutherland district, 2m/4km NW of Lochinver. **102 C6** NC0624.

Achmelvich Bay *High.* ***Bay***, NW of Achmelvich, 3m/5km NW of Lochinver. **102 C6** NC0525.

Achmony *High.* ***Settlement***, 1km NW of Drumnadrochit. **88 B1** NH5030.

Achmore *High.* ***Hamlet***, in Skye and Lochalsh district, 1m/2km SW of Stromeferry. **86 E1** NG8533.

Achmore *High.* ***Settlement***, on SW side of Annat Bay, 6m/10km NW of Ullapool. Access via ferry from Badluarach on S shore of Little Loch Broom, followed by overland tracks. **95 G2** NH0296.

Achmore *Stir.* ***Settlement***, 1km E of Killin across River Dochart. **81 G4** NN5832.

Achmore *W.Isles Anglicised form of Achadh Mòr, qv.*

Achnaba *Arg. & B.* ***Settlement***, on NW shore of Loch Fyne, 3m/4km SE of Lochgilphead. **73 H2** NR9085.

Achnabat *High.* ***Settlement***, 3m/5km S of Dores. **88 C1** NH5930.

Achnabourin *High.* ***Settlement***, 2m/3km S of Bettyhill, Caithness district. **104 C3** NC7058.

Achnabreck Cup and Ring Marks *Arg. & B.* ***Historic/prehistoric site***, Britain's largest site for rock carvings with 135 well-preserved Bronze Age cup and ring marks (Historic Scotland), 1m/2km N of Lochgilphead. Great range of techniques from rudimentary to skilled work. **73 G1** NR8590.

Achnacairn *Arg. & B.* ***Settlement***, on N shore of Loch Etive, 1m/2km NE of North Connel. **80 A4** NM9235.

Achnacarnin *High.* ***Settlement***, 3m/4km SE of Point of Stoer, W coast of Sutherland district. **102 C5** NC0431.

Achnacarry *High.* ***Settlement***, in Lochaber district, between Loch Lochy and foot of Loch Arkaig. Home of Camerons of Lochiel. NN1787.

Achnaclerach *High.* ***Settlement***, in valley of Black Water, 3m/4km N of Garve. **96 B5** NH4065.

Achnacloich *Arg. & B.* ***Settlement***, 3m/4km E of Connel. **80 A4** NM9533.

Achnacloich *High.* ***Settlement***, near W coast of Sleat peninsula, Skye, 1km S of Tarskavaig. **86 B4** NG5908.

Achnaclyth *High.* ***Settlement***, to N of Dunbeath Water, 5m/8km NW of Dunbeath. **105 F5** ND0933.

Achnacraig *Arg. & B.* ***Settlement***, on NE bank of River Bellart, 4m/6km NE of Fanmore, Mull. **79 F3** NM4747.

Achnacroish *Arg. & B.* ***Village***, with landing stage, halfway along E coast of Lismore in Loch Linnhe. **79 K3** NM8540.

Achnadrish *Arg. & B.* ***Settlement***, on Mull, 1m/2km E of Dervaig. **79 F2** NM4551.

Achnafalnich *Arg. & B.* ***Settlement***, in Glen Orchy, 4m/6km NE of Dalmally. **80 D5** NN2129.

Achnafauld *P. & K.* ***Settlement***, 9m/14km N of Crieff. **81 K4** NN8736.

Achnafree Craig *P. & K.* ***Mountain***, rising to over 720 metres, 9m/14km NE of Comrie. **81 J4** NN8034.

Achnagairn *High.* ***Settlement***, 2m/3km SE of Beauly. **96 C7** NH5544.

Achnagarron *High.* ***Locality***, in Ross and Cromarty district, 2m/3km NW of Invergordon. **96 D4** NH6870.

Achnaha *High.* ***Settlement***, on Ardnamurchan peninsula, 3m/5km NW of Kilchoan. **79 F1** NM4668.

Achnaha *High.* ***Settlement***, 2m/3km W of Lochaline, Lochaber district. **79 H3** NM6445.

Achnahanat *High.* ***Settlement***, in Sutherland district, 7m/12km NW of Bonar Bridge. **96 C2** NH5198.

Achnahannet *High.* ***Settlement***, 2m/3km NW of Dulnain Bridge. **89 G2** NH9727.

Achnairn *High.* ***Settlement***, on E side of Loch Shin in Sutherland district, 4m/7km N of Lairg. NC5512.

Achnalea *High.* ***Settlement***, 2m/3km E of Strontian, Lochaber district. **79 K1** NM8586.

Achnamara *Arg. & B.* ***Settlement***, on inlet on E side of Loch Sween in Knapdale, Argyll, 5m/7km S of Crinan. **73 F2** NR7787.

Achnanellan *High.* ***Settlement***, on S shore of Loch Shiel, 4m/7km NE of Salen. **79 J1** NM7467.

Achnasaul *High.* ***Settlement***, on N side of E end of Loch Arkaig, 1m/2km NW of Achnacarry across loch. **87 H6** NN1589.

Achnasheen *High.* ***Village***, at head of Strath Bran in Ross and Cromarty district. **95 H6** NH1658.

Achnashellach *High.* ***Settlement***, with lodge and railway station, in Glen Carron, Ross and Cromarty district, at NE end of Loch Dùghaill. **95 G7** NH0048.

Achnashellach Forest *High.* ***Open space***, deer forest astride Glen Carron. **95 G7** NH0048.

Achnashelloch *Arg. & B.* ***Settlement***, 3m/4km NW of Lochgilphead. **73 G1** NR8591.

Achnastank *Moray* ***Settlement***, 5m/8km SW of Dufftown. **89 K1** NJ2733.

Achorn *High.* ***Settlement***, 2m/3km W of Dunbeath. **105 G5** ND1330.

Achosnich *High.* ***Settlement***, 5m/8km NW of Dornoch. **96 E2** NH7293.

Achosnich *High.* ***Settlement***, on Ardnamurchan peninsula, 3m/5km NW of Kilchoan. **79 F1** NM4467.

Achranich *High.* ***Locality***, in Lochaber district, near mouth of Rannoch River at head of Loch Aline. NM7047.

Achray Forest *Stir.* ***Forest/woodland***, surrounding Loch Achray, W of Loch Venachar. Forms part of Queen Elizabeth Forest Park. **81 G7** NN5104.

Achreamie *High.* ***Settlement***, near N coast of Caithness district, 2m/3km E of Dounreay Atomic Energy Establishment. **105 F2** ND0166.

Achriabhach *High.* ***Settlement***, in Glen Nevis, 5m/8km NW of Kinlochleven. **80 C1** NN1468.

Achridigill Loch *High.* ***Lake/loch***, small loch 3m/4km SW of Melvich, Caithness district. **104 D2** NC8561.

Achriesgill *High.* ***Settlement***, 1m/2km N of Rhiconich, at head of Loch Inchard, W coast of Sutherland district. **102 E3** NC2554.

Achrimsdale *High.* ***Settlement***, 2m/3km N of Brora, Sutherland district. **97 G1** NC9006.

Achronich *Arg. & B.* ***Settlement***, on Mull, 5m/8km W of Gruline. **79 F4** NM4639.

Achterneed *High.* ***Locality***, in Ross and Cromarty district, 1m/2km N of Strathpeffer. NH4859.

Achtoty *High.* ***Settlement***, near N coast of Caithness district, 2m/4km W of Bettyhill across Torrisdale Bay. **103 J2** NC6762.

Achurch *Northants.* ***Village***, 4m/6km S of Oundle. **42 D7** TL0283.
Achuvoldrach *High.* ***Settlement***, near causeway on W side of Kyle of Tongue. **103 H3** NC5658.
Achvaich *High.* ***Settlement***, in valley of River Evelix, 6m/10km NW of Dornoch. **96 E2** NH7194.
Achvarasdal *High.* ***Settlement***, in Caithness district, 1m/2km E of Reay. **104 E2** NC9864.
Achvarasdal Burn *High.* ***River***, flowing into E side of Sandside Bay, on N coast of Caithness district. **104 E3** NC9665.
Achvlair *High.* ***Settlement***, in Salachan Glen, 2m/3km S of Duror. **80 A2** NM9952.
Achvraie *High.* ***Settlement***, on Allt Ach' a' Bhraighe, 1km from W coast, Ross and Cromarty district. **95 G1** NC0406.
Ackenthwaite *Cumb.* ***Settlement***, 1km E of Milnthorpe. SD5081.
Ackergill *High.* ***Settlement***, in Caithness district, 1m/2km N of Wick. Airport to E. **105 J3** ND3553.
Ackergill Tower *High.* ***Historic/prehistoric site***, dates from 14c-15c, on S side of Sinclair's Bay. **105 J3** ND3554.
Acklam *Middbro.* ***Suburb***, 2m/3km S of Middlesbrough town centre. **63 F5** NZ4817.
Acklam *N.Yorks.* ***Village***, 6m/10km NE of Stamford Bridge. **58 D3** SE7861.
Ackleton *Shrop.* ***Village***, 5m/8km NE of Bridgnorth. **39 G6** SO7798.
Acklington *Northumb.* ***Village***, 3m/4km SW of Amble. **71 H3** NU2201.
Ackton *W.Yorks.* ***Hamlet***, 1km W of Featherstone. **57 K7** SE4121.
Ackworth *W.Yorks.* ***Locality***, parish and group of villages: High Ackworth, Low Ackworth, and Ackworth Moor Top, 4m/6km S of Pontefract. SE4417.
Ackworth Moor Top *W.Yorks.* Population: 5851. ***Village***, 3m/5km to 4m/6km S of Pontefract. Forms part of Ackworth parish. **51 G1** SE4417.
Acle *Norf.* Population: 2208. ***Small town***, attractive market town, 8m/13km W of Great Yarmouth. Church of St. Edmund King and Martyr, with round tower, dates from 11c. **45 J4** TG4010.
Acock's Green *W.Mid.* ***Suburb***, 4m/7km SE of Birmingham city centre. **40 D7** SP1283.
Acol *Kent* ***Village***, on Isle of Thanet, 4m/6km SW of Margate. **25 J5** TR3067.
Acomb *Northumb.* ***Village***, 1m/2km N of Hexham across River Tyne. **70 E7** NY9266.
Acomb *York* ***Suburb***, 2m/3km W of York city centre. **58 B4** SE5751.
Acombe *Som.* ***Locality***, 5m/8km SE of Wellington. ST1913.
Aconbury *Here.* ***Village***, 4m/7km S of Hereford. **28 E5** SO5133.
Acorn Bank *Cumb.* ***Historic house***, partly 16c, but mainly 18c (National Trust), on Crowdundle Beck, 1km NE of Temple Sowerby. **61 H4** NY6128.
Acre *Lancs.* ***Settlement***, 1m/2km N of Haslingden. **56 C7** SD7824.
Acrefair *Wrex.* ***Hamlet***, 2m/3km W of Ruabon. **38 B1** SJ2743.
Acrise *Kent* ***Settlement***, 4m/7km N of Folkestone. TR1942.
Acrise Place *Kent* ***Settlement***, 1m/2km NW of Densole. **15 G3** TR1942.
Acton *Ches.* ***Village***, 1m/2km W of Nantwich. **49 F7** SJ6353.
Acton *Dorset* ***Hamlet***, 3m/4km W of Swanage. SY9878.
Acton *Gt.Lon.* ***Suburb***, in borough of Ealing, 6m/10km W of Charing Cross. **22 E4** TQ2080.
Acton *Shrop.* ***Settlement***, 3m/4km S of Bishop's Castle. **38 C7** SO3184.
Acton *Staffs.* ***Hamlet***, 1m/2km NE of Whitmore. SJ8241.
Acton *Suff.* ***Village***, 3m/4km NE of Sudbury. Church contains brass of Sir Robert de Bures, 1302. **34 C4** TL8944.
Acton *Worcs.* ***Hamlet***, 3m/5km SE of Stourport-on-Severn. **29 H2** SO8467.
Acton *Wrex.* ***Suburb***, N district of Wrexham. SJ3451.
Acton Beauchamp *Here.* ***Village***, 3m/5km SE of Bromyard. **29 F3** SO6750.
Acton Bridge *Ches.* ***Village***, 4m/6km W of Northwich. **48 E5** SJ5975.
Acton Burnell *Shrop.* ***Village***, 7m/11km S of Shrewsbury. Remains of 13c fortified manor house (English Heritage). 16c Langley Chapel (English Heritage) 1m/2km S, contains 17c fittings and furniture. **38 E5** SJ5302.
Acton Burnell Castle *Shrop.* ***Castle***, ruin of fortified red sandstone 13c manor house (English Heritage), 8m/13km S of Shrewsbury. **38 E5** SJ5301.
Acton Green *Gt.Lon.* ***Suburb***, in borough of Ealing, to S of Acton. TQ2079.
Acton Green *Here.* ***Hamlet***, 4m/7km SE of Bromyard. **29 F3** SO6950.
Acton Pigott *Shrop.* ***Settlement***, 1m/2km NE of Acton Burnell. **38 E5** SJ5402.
Acton Round *Shrop.* ***Village***, 3m/5km S of Much Wenlock. **39 F6** SO6395.
Acton Scott *Shrop.* ***Village***, 3m/4km S of Church Stretton. Site of Roman villa. **38 D7** SO4589.
Acton Trussell *Staffs.* ***Village***, 3m/5km S of Stafford. **40 B4** SJ9318.
Acton Turville *S.Glos.* ***Village***, 5m/8km E of Chipping Sodbury. **20 B3** ST8080.
Ad Fines *Northumb.* *See Chew Green.*
Adabrock *W.Isles* ***Settlement***, near N end of Isle of Lewis, 1m/2km S of Port Nis. NB5362.
Adamhill *S.Ayr.* ***Settlement***, 2m/3km N of Tarbolton. **74 C7** NS4330.
Adbaston *Staffs.* ***Village***, 6m/9km N of Newport. **39 G3** SJ7627.
Adber *Dorset* ***Hamlet***, 4m/6km NE of Yeovil. **8 E2** ST5920.
Add *Arg. & B.* ***River***, in Argyll rising 4m/7km NW of Furnace on W shore of Loch Fyne and flowing SW to Crinan Loch, Sound of Jura. **73 G1** NR7994.
Adderbury *Oxon.* Population: 2348. ***Village***, comprising East Adderbury and West Adderbury, separated by Sor Brook, 3m/5km S of Banbury. **31 F5** SP4735.
Adderley *Shrop.* ***Village***, 4m/6km N of Market Drayton. **39 F2** SJ6639.
Adderley Green *Stoke* ***Suburb***, 3m/5km E of Stoke-on-Trent city centre. SJ9144.
Adderstone *Northumb.* ***Settlement***, 3m/5km SE of Belford. **77 K7** NU1330.
Addie Hill *Moray* ***Hill***, 4m/6km SE of Buckie. Height 892 feet or 272 metres. **98 C5** NJ4459.
Addiewell *W.Loth.* Population: 1338. ***Village***, 4m/7km S of Bathgate. **75 H4** NS9862.
Addingham *W.Yorks.* Population: 2769. ***Village***, 3m/5km NW of Ilkley. **57 F5** SE0749.
Addington *Bucks.* ***Village***, 2m/3km W of Winslow. **31 J6** SP7428.
Addington *Cornw.* ***Suburb***, NE district of Liskeard. SX2565.
Addington *Gt.Lon.* ***Suburb***, in borough of Croydon, 3m/5km E of Croydon town centre. **23 G5** TQ3764.
Addington *Kent* ***Village***, 2m/3km E of Wrotham Heath. Prehistoric burial chambers to NW. **23 K6** TQ6559.
Addiscombe *Gt.Lon.* ***Suburb***, 1m/2km E of Croydon town centre. TQ3466.
Addlestone *Surr.* Population: 14,637. ***Suburb***, 2m/3km W of Weybridge. **22 D5** TQ0464.
Addlethorpe *Lincs.* ***Hamlet***, 4m/6km N of Skegness. **53 J6** TF5468.
Adel *W.Yorks.* ***Suburb***, 4m/7km N of Leeds city centre. **57 H6** SE2740.
Aden Country Park *Aber.* ***Leisure/recreation***, country park covering 230 acres on estate dating from 18c, 1km NE of Old Deer. Ruined mansion, farm museum and woodland walks. **99 H6** NJ9848.
Adeney *Tel. & W.* ***Settlement***, 3m/5km W of Newport. **39 F4** SJ7018.
Adeyfield *Herts.* ***Suburb***, to E of Hemel Hempstead town centre. TL0707.
Adfa *Powys* ***Hamlet***, 1m/2km W of Llanwyddelan. **37 K5** SJ0601.
Adforton *Here.* ***Village***, 7m/12km E of Knighton. **28 C1** SO4071.
Adgestone *I.o.W.* ***Hamlet***, 1m/2km SW of Brading. SZ5986.
Adisham *Kent* ***Village***, 3m/4km SW of Wingham. **15 H2** TR2253.
Adlestrop *Glos.* ***Village***, 4m/6km E of Stow-on-the-Wold. **30 D6** SP2427.
Adlingfleet *E.Riding* ***Village***, 7m/11km E of Goole. **58 E7** SE8420.
Adlington *Ches.* ***Hamlet***, 2m/4km NW of Bollington. **49 J4** SJ9180.
Adlington *Lancs.* Population: 8556. ***Small town***, 7m/12km NW of Bolton. **49 F1** SD6013.
Adlington Hall *Ches.* ***Historic house***, 15c-18c house to W of Adlington. **49 J4** SJ9180.
Admaston *Staffs.* ***Hamlet***, on W side of Blithfield Reservoir, 4m/6km N of Rugeley. **40 C3** SK0523.
Admaston *Tel. & W.* ***Village***, 2m/3km NW of Wellington. **39 F4** SJ6313.
Admington *Warks.* ***Village***, 5m/8km NW of Shipston on Stour. **30 C4** SP2046.
Admiral Blake Museum *Som.* ***Other feature of interest***, in Bridgwater, with Battle of Sedgemoor artefacts and a John Chubb gallery. **8 C1** ST3036.
Admiralty Arch *Gt.Lon.* ***Other feature of interest***, massive Edwardian triple arch by Sir Aston Webb, 1910, straddling The Mall, in City of Westminster to W of Charing Cross. Constructed as a memorial to Queen Victoria. TQ2980.
Adsborough *Som.* ***Hamlet***, 4m/7km NE of Taunton. **8 B2** ST2729.
Adscombe *Som.* ***Hamlet***, on Quantock Hills, 1m/2km SW of Nether Stowey. ST1837.
Adstock *Bucks.* ***Village***, 3m/4km NW of Winslow. **31 J5** SP7330.
Adstone *Northants.* ***Village***, 6m/10km W of Towcester. **31 G3** SP5951.
Adswood *Gt.Man.* ***Suburb***, 1m/2km E of Cheadle. SJ8887.
Adur ***River***, rising W of Horsham in West Sussex and flowing S into English Channel at Shoreham-by-Sea. Another branch rises near Burgess Hill and joins former branch 1m/2km W of Henfield. **12 E5** TQ2304.
Advent *Cornw.* ***Locality***, to SE of Camelford. SX1081.
Adventurers' Fen *Cambs.* ***Open space***, fenland 3m/4km NW of Burwell. **33 J2** TL5468.
Adventurers' Land *Cambs.* ***Open space***, reclaimed land on N side of River Nene, 5m/8km NW of March. **43 G5** TF3502.
Adversane *W.Suss.* ***Hamlet***, 2m/3km SW of Billingshurst. **12 D4** TQ0723.
Advie *High.* ***Settlement***, in Badenoch and Strathspey district, 7m/12km NE of Grantown-on-Spey. **89 J1** NJ1234.
Adwalton *W.Yorks.* ***Locality***, 2m/3km W of Morley. To W is site of Battle of Adwalton Moor, Royalist victory in Civil War, 1643. **57 H7** SE2328.
Adwell *Oxon.* ***Locality***, 3m/5km N of Watlington. **21 K2** SU6999.
Adwick le Street *S.Yorks.* Population: 10,288. ***Town***, 4m/6km NW of Doncaster. **51 H2** SE5307.
Adwick upon Dearne *S.Yorks.* ***Village***, 1m/2km N of Mexborough. **51 G2** SE4701.
Adziel *Aber.* ***Settlement***, 1m/2km S of Strichen. NJ9453.
Ae Village (Village of Ae). *D. & G.* ***Village***, 8m/13km N of Dumfries, on S side of Forest of Ae. **68 E5** NX9889.
Aeron *Cere.* ***River***, rising W of Blaenpennal and flowing, in a wide loop to S, into Cardigan Bay at Aberaeron. **26 E3** SN4563.
Aesica *Northumb.* *See Great Chesters Roman Fort.*
Afan *N.P.T.* ***River***, rising E of Blaengwynfi and flowing SW through Afan Forest Park to Swansea Bay at Port Talbot. **18 A2** SS7488.
Afan Argoed Country Park *N.P.T.* ***Leisure/recreation***, country park and countryside centre in River Afan valley within Afan Forest Park, 5m/8km NE of Port Talbot. Facilities for walking, cycling and orienteering. Welsh Miners' Museum. Countryside centre has geology, forestry and natural history displays. **18 B2** SS8195.
Afan Forest Park *N.P.T.* ***Leisure/recreation***, designated forest park on upland to E of Neath. River Afan flows through in a SW direction. Afan Argoed Country Park located in River Afan valley. **18 B2** SS8296.
Affetside *Gt.Man.* ***Settlement***, on site of Roman road, 3m/5km SW of Ramsbottom. SD7513.
Affleck *Aber.* ***Settlement***, 1km E of Whiterashes. **91 G2** NJ8623.
Affleck *Angus* ***Settlement***, adjoining Monikie, 5m/8km NW of Carnoustie. **83 F4** NO4838.
Affleck Castle *Angus* ***Castle***, well-preserved 15c tower house (Historic Scotland), 7m/12km NE of Dundee. **83 F4** NO4938.
Affpuddle *Dorset* ***Village***, on River Piddle or Trent, 3m/5km E of Puddletown. **9 H5** SY8093.
Affric *High.* ***River***, formed in Inverness district by streams of Allt Cam-bàn and Allt a Chòmhlain at their confluence just N of Ciste Dhubh. From there it flows NE through Glenaffric Forest, then E via Loch Affric and Loch Beinn a' Mheadhoin to River Glass at Fasnakyle. **87 J2** NH3028.
Afon Eitha *Wrex.* ***Hamlet***, 1m/2km NW of Ruabon. Named after stream on which it is situated. SJ2945.
Afon-wen *Flints.* ***Settlement***, nearly 1m/2km S of Caerwys. **47 K5** SJ1371.
Afon Wen *Gwyn.* ***Settlement***, at mouth of river of same name, 4m/6km W of Criccieth. SH4437.
Afton *I.o.W.* ***Hamlet***, 1m/2km S of Freshwater. SZ3586.
Afton Bridgend *E.Ayr.* ***Locality***, opposite New Cumnock, near mouth of Afton Water. **68 B2** NS6213.
Afton Reservoir *E.Ayr.* ***Reservoir***, in course of Afton Water, 6m/10km S of New Cumnock. **68 B3** NS6304.
Afton Water ***River***, rising on NW slopes of Alhang, 1m/2km S of Afton Reservoir and flowing N through reservoir to River Nith at New Cumnock. **68 B3** NS6214.
Agden Reservoir *S.Yorks.* ***Reservoir***, on W side of High Bradfield. **50 E3** SK2692.
Aggborough *Worcs.* ***Suburb***, S district of Kidderminster. SO8375.
Agglethorpe *N.Yorks.* ***Hamlet***, 2m/3km S of Wensley. **57 F1** SE0886.
Aglionby *Cumb.* ***Locality***, 3m/5km E of Carlisle. NY4456.
Agneash *I.o.M.* ***Locality***, 1m/2km N of Laxey. SC4386.
Aigburth *Mersey.* ***Suburb***, 4m/6km SE of Liverpool city centre. **48 C4** SJ3886.
Aignis (Anglicised form: Aignish.) *W.Isles* ***Hamlet***, on Eye Peninsula, Isle of Lewis, 2m/3km W of Garrabost. **101 G4** NB4832.
Aignish *W.Isles Anglicised form of Aignis, qv.*
Aike *E.Riding* ***Hamlet***, 4m/7km N of Beverley. **59 G5** TA0445.
Aiker Ness *Ork.* ***Coastal feature***, headland on NE coast of Mainland, 2m/3km N of Woodwick. Site of Broch of Gurness (Historic Scotland). **106 C5** HY3826.
Aikerness *Ork.* ***Locality***, on N peninsula of Westray, running out to Bow Head. **106 D2** HY4552.
Aikers *Ork.* ***Settlement***, 2m/3km S of St. Margaret's Hope, South Ronaldsay. **107 D8** ND4590.
Aiketgate *Cumb.* ***Hamlet***, 1m/2km E of Low Hesket. **61 F2** NY4846.
Aikhead *Cumb.* ***Locality***, 1m/2km NW of Wigton. NY2349.
Aikrigg End *Cumb.* ***Suburb***, in N part of Kendal. SD5193.
Aikshaw *Cumb.* ***Settlement***, 3m/5km NW of Aspatria. **60 C2** NY1246.
Aikton *Cumb.* ***Hamlet***, 4m/6km SE of Kirkbride. **60 D1** NY2753.
Aikwood Tower *Sc.Bord.* ***Historic house***, 3m/5km SW of Selkirk. 16c tower house restored in 1990s by Steel family. Exhibition of life and work of James Hogg, the 'Ettrick Shepherd' (1770-1835). **69 K1** NT4126.
Ailby *Lincs.* ***Settlement***, 1m/2km NW of Alford. TF4376.
Ailey *Here.* ***Settlement***, 8m/12km NE of Hay-on-Wye. **28 C4** SO3348.
Ailnack Water *See Water of Ailnack.*
Ailsa Craig *S.Ayr.* ***Island***, bleak granite island and prominent seamark in the Firth of Clyde, some 2m/3km in circumference, lying 10m/17km W of Girvan. 1114 feet or 340 metres high. Haunt of sea birds. Lighthouse on E side. Rock itself was used to make some of the finest curling stones. **66 E4** NX0199.
Ailstone *Warks.* ***Settlement***, 3m/4km S of Stratford-upon-Avon. SP2051.
Ailsworth *Peter.* ***Village***, 5m/8km W of Peterborough city centre. **42 E6** TL1199.
Aimes Green *Essex* ***Settlement***, 2m/3km NE of Waltham Abbey. TL3902.
Aimster *High.* ***Settlement***, 1km E of Buckies and 3m/4km S of Thurso. **105 G2** ND1163.
Ainderby Quernhow *N.Yorks.* ***Village***, 5m/8km W of Thirsk across River Swale. **57 J1** SE3480.
Ainderby Steeple *N.Yorks.* ***Village***, 2m/4km SW of Northallerton. **62 E7** SE3392.
Aingers Green *Essex* ***Hamlet***, 5m/8km NW of Clacton-on-Sea. **35 F7** TM1120.
Ainleys *W.Yorks.* ***Locality***, 3m/4km NW of Huddersfield. SE1119.
Ainsdale *Mersey.* ***Suburb***, 4m/6km SW of Southport town centre. **48 C1** SD3112.
Ainsdale-on-Sea *Mersey.* ***Settlement***, with holiday village and nature reserve, 1m/2km W of Ainsdale. SD2912.
Ainshval *High.* ***Mountain***, 2m/3km N of Rubha nam Meirleach, Rum. Height 2562 feet or 781 metres. **85 J5** NM3794.
Ainstable *Cumb.* ***Village***, 10m/16km SE of Carlisle. **61 G2** NY5346.

Ainsworth *Gt.Man.* ***Village***, 3m/4km W of Bury. **49 G1** SD7610.

Ainthorpe *N.Yorks.* ***Village***, on S bank of River Esk opposite Danby. **63 J6** NZ7008.

Aintree *Mersey.* ***Suburb***, 6m/9km NE of Liverpool. Racecourses. **48 C3** SJ3798.

Aintree Racecourse *Mersey. Familiar form of Liverpool (Aintree) Racecourse.*

Aira Beck *Cumb.* ***River***, rising to S of Matterdale Common and flowing E to Dockray, then S to Ullswater 1m/2km S of Dockray. **60 E4** NY4019.

Aira Force *Cumb.* ***Waterfall***, in Aira Beck 1m/2km SE of Dockray. **60 F4** NY4020.

Aird *W.Isles* ***Settlement***, on NW coast of Benbecula. **92 C6** NF7654.

Aird *W.Isles* ***Village***, on Eye Peninsula, Isle of Lewis, 1m/2km SW of Tiumpan Head. NB5536.

Aird a' Chaolais *W.Isles* ***Coastal feature***, headland on NW coast of Vatersay. **84 A5** NL6197.

Aird a' Mhachair (Anglicised form: Ardivachar.) *W.Isles* ***Settlement***, S of Ardivachar Point, at NW corner of South Uist. **92 C7** NF7445.

Aird a' Mhulaidh (Anglicised form: Ardvourlie.) *W.Isles* ***Settlement***, on W shore of Loch Seaforth, North Harris, opposite Seaforth Island. **100 D6** NB1810.

Aird an Rùnair *W.Isles* ***Coastal feature***, headland at westernmost point of North Uist. **92 B4** NF6870.

Aird an Troim *W.Isles* ***Locality***, 4m/6km SE of Baile Ailein on W shore of Loch Seaforth, Isle of Lewis. **100 E6** NB2206.

Aird Asaig (Anglicised form: Ardhasaig.) *W.Isles* ***Settlement***, on North Harris, 2m/4km NW of Tarbert. **100 D7** NB1202.

Aird Bheag *W.Isles* ***Coastal feature***, peninsula on W coast of Isle of Lewis to S of Loch Tamanavay. **100 C6** NB0219.

Aird Breanais (Anglicised form: Aird Brenish.) *W.Isles* ***Coastal feature***, headland on W coast of Isle of Lewis, 1m/2km NW of Breanais. **100 B5** NA9226.

Aird Brenish *W.Isles Anglicised form of Aird Breanais, qv.*

Aird Castle *Arg. & B. See Carradale.*

Aird Dell *W.Isles Anglicised form of Aird Dhail, qv.*

Aird Dhail (Anglicised form: Aird Dell.) *W.Isles* ***Settlement***, near NW coast of Isle of Lewis, 4m/6km SW of Butt of Lewis. **101 G1** NB4761.

Aird Fenish *W.Isles* ***Coastal feature***, headland on W coast of Isle of Lewis, 7m/12km SW of Gallan Head. **100 B5** NA9929.

Aird Leimhe (Anglicised form: Ardslave.) *W.Isles* ***Settlement***, on SE coast of South Harris, 3m/5km SW of Greosabhagh. **93 G3** NG1189.

Aird Mhànais *W.Isles Gaelic form of Ard Manish, qv.*

Aird Mhige (Anglicised form: Ardvey.) *W.Isles* ***Settlement***, at head of Loch Stockinish, on E coast of South Harris. **93 G2** NG1292.

Aird Mhighe (Anglicised form: Ardvey.) *W.Isles* ***Settlement***, on S coast of South Harris, 3m/5km NE of Rodel. **93 F3** NG0787.

Aird Mhòr *W.Isles* ***Coastal feature***, peninsula on W coast of Isle of Lewis to N of entrance to Loch Resort. **100 C6** NB0217.

Aird Mhòr *W.Isles* ***Coastal feature***, promontory on NW coast of Isle of Lewis, 2m/3km NW of Carloway. **100 D3** NB1945.

Aird Mhòr Bragair *W.Isles* ***Coastal feature***, headland on NW coast of Isle of Lewis, 1m/2km N of Bragar. **100 E2** NB2850.

Aird Mhòr Mangurstadh (Anglicised form: Ard More Mangersta.) *W.Isles* ***Coastal feature***, headland on W coast of Isle of Lewis, 4m/6km W of Timsgearraidh. **100 C4** NA9932.

Aird Mòr *Arg. & B.* ***Hill***, on SW coast of Ross of Mull, 3m/4km NW of Rubh' Ardalanish. Height 292 feet or 89 metres. **78 E6** NM3217.

Aird na h-Iolaire *Arg. & B.* ***Coastal feature***, headland on W coast of Ardmeanach, Mull. **79 F5** NM4028.

Aird of Coigach *High.* ***Locality***, with notable viewpoint, to N of Loch Bad a' Ghaill. **102 C7** NC0611.

Aird of Kinloch *Arg. & B.* ***Coastal feature***, low-lying promontory almost enclosing Loch Beg, at head of Loch Scridain, Mull. **79 G5** NM5228.

Aird of Sleat *High.* ***Village***, at S end of Sleat peninsula, Skye, 2m/4km E of Point of Sleat. **86 B4** NG5900.

Aird Thormaid *W.Isles* ***Coastal feature***, headland on NE coast of North Uist, 2m/3km E of Beinn Mhòr. **92 E4** NF9276.

Aird Thunga *W.Isles* ***Coastal feature***, headland on E coast of Isle of Lewis, 4m/6km NE of Stornoway across Melbost Sands. **101 G4** NB4636.

Aird Uige *W.Isles* ***Settlement***, 1km S of Gallan Head, Isle of Lewis. **100 C4** NB0437.

Aird Vanish *W.Isles* ***Coastal feature***, headland to W of Taransay. **92 E2** NF9999.

Airdrie *Fife* ***Settlement***, 3m/5km W of Crail. **83 G7** NO5608.

Airdrie *N.Lan.* Population: 36,998. ***Town***, 11m/17km E of Glasgow. **75 F4** NS7665.

Airdriehead *N.Lan.* ***Settlement***, 1m/2km NW of Cumbernauld town centre. NS7475.

Airds Bay *Arg. & B.* ***Bay***, on N side of entrance to Loch Creran, Argyll, just SW of Port Appin. **79 K3** NM9044.

Airds Bay *Arg. & B.* ***Bay***, 1m/2km SE of Airds Point in Loch Etive and 1km N of Taynuilt. **80 B4** NM9834.

Airds Moss *E.Ayr.* ***Open space***, desolate moorland area NE of Cumnock. Scene of skirmish in 1680 between Royalists and Covenanters. **67 K1** NS5924.

Airds Point *Arg. & B.* ***Coastal feature***, headland on S side of Loch Etive, Argyll, 2m/4km NW of Taynuilt. **80 A4** NM9834.

Aire ***River***, whose source lies underground in limestone country in vicinity of Malham Tarn, and which issues above ground at foot of Malham Cove. River then flows SE by Skipton, Keighley, Bingley, Shipley and Leeds to Knottingley. SE7226.

Aire View *N.Yorks.* ***Hamlet***, adjoining to SE of Cononley, 3m/5km S of Skipton. SD9946.

Airedale *W.Yorks.* ***Valley***, carrying upper reaches of River Aire from Malham Cove, where river emerges at foot of cliff, to Bingley. **57 F5** SE0345.

Airidh a' Bhruaich (Anglicised form: Aribruach.) *W.Isles* ***Village***, on Isle of Lewis at N end of Loch Seaforth, 4m/6km SW of Baile Ailein. **100 E6** NB2417.

Airie Hill *D. & G.* ***Hill***, 6m/9km S of New Galloway. Height 954 feet or 291 metres. **65 G4** NX6268.

Airieland *D. & G.* ***Settlement***, 3m/5km S of Castle Douglas. **65 H5** NX7557.

Airies *D. & G.* ***Locality***, comprising Mains of Airies and Little Airies, 7m/11km NW of Stranraer. **66 D7** NW9767.

Airigh-drishaig *High.* ***Settlement***, on coast of Ross and Cromarty district, 3m/5km NW of Plockton across entrance to Loch Carron. **86 D1** NG7636.

Airigh na Glaice *W.Isles* ***Locality***, 1km N of Ben Dell, Isle of Lewis. **101 G2** NB4957.

Airighean Beinn nan Caorach *W.Isles* ***Locality***, 3m/5km W of Cellar Head, Isle of Lewis. **101 H2** NB5156.

Airighean Loch Breihavat *W.Isles* ***Locality***, 5m/8km W of Cellar Head, Isle of Lewis. **101 G2** NB4854.

Airmyn *E.Riding* ***Village***, on right bank of River Aire near its confluence with River Ouse and 2m/3km NW of Goole. **58 D7** SE7225.

Airntully *P. & K.* ***Village***, 2m/3km N of Stanley. **82 B4** NO0935.

Airor *High.* ***Locality***, with jetty, on coast of Knoydart, Lochaber district, 4m/7km E of Kilbeg, Skye across Sound of Sleat. **86 D4** NG7105.

Airor Island *High.* ***Island***, in Sound of Sleat off coast of Knoydart. NG7105.

Airth *Falk.* ***Village***, 5m/7km N of Falkirk. **75 G2** NS8987.

Airton *N.Yorks.* ***Village***, on River Aire, 4m/6km NW of Gargrave. **56 E4** SD9059.

Airyhassen *D. & G.* ***Settlement***, 4m/6km N of Monreith. **64 D6** NX3746.

Aisby *Lincs.* ***Hamlet***, 1m/2km N of Corringham. **52 B3** SK8792.

Aisby *Lincs.* ***Hamlet***, 6m/9km SW of Sleaford. **42 D2** TF0138.

Aisgernis *W.Isles* ***Locality***, near W coast of South Uist, 4m/6km S of Rubha Ardvule. **84 C2** NF7424.

Aisgill *Cumb.* ***Settlement***, 7m/11km S of Kirkby Stephen. SD7797.

Aish *Devon* ***Hamlet***, just NW of South Brent. SX6960.

Aish *Devon* ***Hamlet***, 3m/4km SE of Totnes. SX8458.

Aisholt *Som.* ***Hamlet***, on E slopes of Quantock Hills, 3m/4km S of Nether Stowey. ST1935.

Aiskew *N.Yorks.* ***Village***, adjoining to NE of Bedale. **57 H1** SE2788.

Aislaby *N.Yorks.* ***Hamlet***, 2m/3km NW of Pickering. **58 D1** SE7785.

Aislaby *N.Yorks.* ***Village***, 3m/5km SW of Whitby. **63 K6** NZ8508.

Aislaby *Stock.* ***Hamlet***, 1m/2km W of Yarm across River Tees. **63 F5** NZ4012.

Aisthorpe *Lincs.* ***Village***, between Brattleby and Scampton, 6m/9km N of Lincoln. **52 C4** SK9480.

Aith *Ork.* ***Locality***, at centre of Stronsay. **106 F5** HY6425.

Aith *Ork.* ***Settlement***, on SE shore of Loch of Skaill, Mainland. **107 B6** HY2417.

Aith *Shet.* ***Settlement***, near S coast of Fetlar. **108 F3** HU6390.

Aith *Shet.* ***Village***, on Mainland at head of Aith Voe. **109 C7** HU3455.

Aith Ness *Shet.* ***Coastal feature***, headland at N end of Bressay, S of Score Head. **109 E8** HU5144.

Aith Voe *Shet.* ***Sea feature***, large inlet S of Papa Little. **109 C7** HU3455.

Aithsetter *Shet.* ***Settlement***, on Mainland, 1m/2km S of Fladdabister. HU4430.

Aithsting *Shet.* ***Locality***, SW of Aith Voe, Mainland. **109 C7** HU3355.

Aithsting and Sandsting *Shet.* ***Locality***, district of Mainland lying between Aith Voe and Bixter Voe. HU3254.

Aitnoch *Moray* ***Settlement***, 4m/6km SE of Ferness. **89 G1** NH9839.

Akebar *N.Yorks.* ***Locality***, 1m/2km S of Hunton, 2m/3km W of Patrick Brompton. SE1990.

Akeld *Northumb.* ***Hamlet***, 2m/4km W of Wooler. **70 E1** NT9529.

Akeley *Bucks.* ***Village***, 3m/4km N of Buckingham. **31 J5** SP7037.

Akeman Street *Bucks.* ***Other feature of interest***, Roman road from Tring to Cirencester, via Aylesbury and Bicester. Route followed by present course of A41 road from Tring to Bicester, and by minor roads and Oxfordshire Way from Bicester to Cirencester. **31 J7** SP7614.

Akenham *Suff.* ***Village***, 3m/5km N of Ipswich. **35 F4** TM1448.

Akermoor Loch *Sc.Bord.* ***Lake/loch***, small loch 4m/7km W of Ashkirk. **69 K1** NT4021.

Aketon *N.Yorks.* ***Settlement***, 1m/2km NW of Spofforth. SE3552.

Alaw Reservoir *I.o.A. Alternative name for Llyn Alaw, qv.*

Albany *T. & W.* ***Suburb***, to N of Washington town centre. NZ2957.

Albaston *Cornw.* ***Hamlet***, 1m/2km NW of Calstock. **4 E3** SX4270.

Alberbury *Shrop.* ***Village***, 8m/13km W of Shrewsbury. Remains of castle beside church. Remains of medieval priory 1m/2km NE, incorporated in farmhouse. **38 C4** SJ3514.

Alberbury Priory *Shrop.* ***Ecclesiastical building***, 8m/12km W of Shrewsbury, noted for medieval saddleback tower. **38 C4** SJ3514.

Albert Town *Pembs.* ***Suburb***, adjoining to W of Haverfordwest. SM9415.

Albourne *W.Suss.* ***Village***, 1m/2km W of Hurstpierpoint. **13 F5** TQ2616.

Albourne Green *W.Suss.* ***Settlement***, at N end of Albourne. TQ2616.

Albrighton *Shrop.* ***Village***, 4m/6km N of Shrewsbury. **38 D4** SJ4918.

Albrighton *Shrop.* Population: 6135. ***Village***, 7m/11km NW of Wolverhampton. **40 A5** SJ8104.

Albro Castle *Pembs.* ***Settlement***, adjoining to N of St. Dogmaels. SN1646.

Alburgh *Norf.* ***Village***, 3m/5km NE of Harleston. **45 G7** TM2786.

Alburgh Street *Norf.* ***Village***, adjoins to NW of Alburgh. TM2786.

Albury *Herts.* ***Village***, 3m/5km E of Puckeridge. **33 H6** TL4324.

Albury *Oxon.* ***Settlement***, 4m/6km W of Thame. SP6505.

Albury *Surr.* ***Village***, 4m/6km E of Guildford. **22 D7** TQ0447.

Albury End *Herts.* ***Settlement***, 1km SW of Albury. TL4323.

Albury Heath *Surr.* ***Settlement***, 1m/2km SW of Shere. **22 D7** TQ0646.

Albury Park *Surr.* ***Historic house***, originally a Tudor house re-modelled several times, most notably by Pugin in mid-19c, 1m/2km E of Albury; garden designed by John Evelyn in 1667. **22 D7** TQ0647.

Alby Hill *Norf.* ***Settlement***, 1km E of Aldborough. **45 F2** TG1934.

Albyfield *Cumb.* ***Settlement***, 2m/3km S of Castle Carrock, on W side of Cardunneth Pike. NY5452.

Alcaig *High.* ***Village***, in Ross and Cromarty district, 1m/2km SE of Dingwall across head of Cromarty Firth. **96 C6** NH5657.

Alcaston *Shrop.* ***Hamlet***, 3m/5km NE of Craven Arms. **38 D7** SO4587.

Alcester *Warks.* Population: 6282. ***Small town***, on site of Roman settlement at confluence of River Alne and River Arrow, 7m/11km W of Stratford-upon-Avon. Ragley Hall 2m/3km to SW. **30 B3** SP0857.

Alcester Lane's End *W.Mid.* ***Suburb***, 4m/7km S of Birmingham city centre. SP0780.

Alciston *E.Suss.* ***Village***, below South Downs, 2m/3km N of Alfriston. **13 J6** TQ5005.

Alcombe *Som.* ***Locality***, adjoining to SE of Minehead. **7 H1** SS9745.

Alconbury *Cambs.* Population: 2419. ***Village***, 4m/7km NW of Huntingdon. **32 E1** TL1875.

Alconbury Hill *Cambs.* ***Settlement***, 3m/5km S of Sawtry. **32 E1** TL1878.

Alconbury Weston *Cambs.* ***Village***, 5m/8km NW of Huntingdon. **32 E1** TL1776.

Aldborough *Norf.* ***Village***, 5m/8km N of Aylsham. **45 F2** TG1834.

Aldborough *N.Yorks.* ***Village***, 1km SE of Boroughbridge on site of Isurium Roman Town (English Heritage). **57 K3** SE4066.

Aldborough Hatch *Gt.Lon.* ***Suburb***, in borough of Redbridge, 2m/3km NE of Ilford. TQ4589.

Aldbourne *Wilts.* Population: 1682. ***Village***, 6m/10km NE of Marlborough. **21 F4** SU2675.

Aldbrough *E.Riding* ***Village***, 6m/10km SE of Hornsea. **59 J6** TA2438.

Aldbrough St. John *N.Yorks.* ***Village***, 4m/6km N of Scotch Corner. **62 C5** NZ2011.

Aldburgh *N.Yorks.* ***Settlement***, on E bank of River Ure, 1m/2km SE of Masham. **57 H2** SE2379.

Aldbury *Herts.* ***Village***, 3m/5km NW of Berkhamsted. **32 C7** SP9612.

Aldcliffe *Lancs.* ***Suburb***, SW district of Lancaster. SD4660.

Aldclune *P. & K.* ***Settlement***, 2m/3km SE of Blair Atholl. **82 A1** NN9063.

Alde ***River***, rising in parish of Tannington and flowing SE past Swefling and Stratford St. Andrew to Snape Maltings. It then forms estuary which runs to Slaughden, S of Aldeburgh, before turning SW parallel to coast, and becoming River Ore below Blackstakes Reach. River Ore continues SW, inland from Orford Ness, before flowing into North Sea, 1m/2km E of Hollesley. **35 G2** TM4249.

Aldeburgh *Suff.* Population: 2654. ***Small town***, on E coast, 6m/10km SE of Saxmundham. Sea encroachment; medieval Moot Hall now on beach. Annual music festival at Snape Maltings at head of River Alde estuary to W. **35 J3** TM4656.

Aldeburgh Bay *Suff.* ***Bay***, on E coast, including Aldeburgh and Thorpeness. **35 J3** TM4654.

Aldeby *Norf.* ***Village***, 2m/4km S of Headdiscoe. **45 J6** TM4493.

Aldenham *Herts.* ***Village***, 2m/4km NE of Watford. **22 E2** TQ1398.

Aldenham Reservoir *Herts.* ***Reservoir***, surrounded by country park, 3m/4km SE of Aldenham and 1km W of Elstree. **22 E2** TQ1695.

Alder Forest *Gt.Man.* ***Suburb***, 1m/2km N of Eccles. SJ7599.

Alder Moor *Staffs.* ***Settlement***, 3m/4km NW of Burton upon Trent. SK2227.

Alderbury *Wilts.* Population: 1859. ***Village***, 3m/5km SE of Salisbury. **10 C2** SU1827.

Aldercar *Derbys.* ***Suburb***, 1m/2km NE of Heanor. SK4447.

Aldercarr Green *Norf.* ***Locality***, 2m/3km NW of Bungay across River Waveney. TM3191.

Alderford *Norf.* ***Village***, 9m/15km NW of Norwich. **45 F4** TG1218.

Alderholt *Dorset* Population: 2880. ***Village***, 2m/3km SW of Fordingbridge. **10 C3** SU1212.

Alderley *Glos.* ***Village***, 2m/3km S of Wotton-under-Edge. **20 A2** ST7690.

Alderley Edge *Ches.* Population: 5280. ***Small town***, residential town, 2m/3km S of Wilmslow. Wooded sandstone escarpment (NT) of same name to E, commanding wide views. **49 H5** SJ8478.

Alderley Park *Ches.* ***Open space***, 1m/2km S of Nether Alderley. **49 H5** SJ8475.

Alderman's Green *W.Mid.* ***Suburb***, 3m/5km NE of Coventry city centre. **41 F7** SP3583.

Aldermaston *W.Berks.* ***Village***, 8m/12km E of Newbury. Atomic Energy Research Establishment to S. **21 J5** SU5965.

Aldermaston Soke *Hants.* ***Settlement***, 1km NW of Silchester. **21 K5** SU6163.

Aldermaston Wharf *W.Berks.* ***Village***, on Kennet and Avon Canal, 1m/2km N of Aldermaston. **21 K5** SU5965.

Alderminster *Warks.* ***Village***, 4m/7km SE of Stratford-upon-Avon. **30 D4** SP2348.

Alder's End *Here.* ***Settlement***, 7m/11km E of Hereford. SO6239.

Aldersbrook *Gt.Lon.* ***Suburb***, 1m/2km S of Wanstead, in borough of Redbridge. Site of Roman building in Wanstead Park to N. TQ4186.

Aldersey Green *Ches.* ***Settlement***, 7m/11km SE of Chester. **48 D7** SJ4656.

Aldershot *Hants.* Population: 51,356. ***Town***, garrison town 8m/13km W of Guildford. Both military and civilian parts redeveloped in 1960s and 1970s. Several military museums. **22 B6** SU8650.

Aldershot Military Museum *Hants.* ***Other feature of interest***, 1m/2km N of Aldershot town centre, covering the last 140 years of history of the Army. **22 B6** SU8652.

Aldersyde *York* ***Suburb***, 2m/4km SW of York city centre. SE5849.

Alderton *Glos.* ***Village***, 4m/6km NW of Winchcombe. **29 J5** SP0033.

Alderton *Northants.* ***Village***, 3m/5km E of Towcester. **31 J4** SP7446.

Alderton *Shrop.* ***Settlement***, 7m/11km N of Shrewsbury. **38 D3** SJ4923.

Alderton *Suff.* ***Village***, 7m/11km SE of Woodbridge. **35 H4** TM3441.

Alderton *Wilts.* ***Village***, 7m/11km W of Malmesbury. **20 B3** ST8482.

Alderwasley *Derbys.* ***Village***, 2m/3km E of Wirksworth. **51 F7** SK3153.

Aldfield *N.Yorks.* ***Village***, 3m/5km W of Ripon. **57 H3** SE2669.

Aldford *Ches.* ***Village***, 5m/7km S of Chester. **48 D7** SJ4159.

Aldham *Essex* ***Village***, 5m/8km W of Colchester. **34 D6** TL9125.

Aldham *Suff.* ***Hamlet***, 1m/2km NE of Hadleigh. **34 E4** TM0444.

Aldham Street *Suff.* ***Hamlet***, 1km NE of Aldham. TM0444.

Aldie *Aber.* ***Settlement***, 3m/4km NW of Cruden Bay. **91 J1** NK0639.

Aldie *High.* ***Settlement***, 1km SE of Tain. **96 E3** NH7880.

Aldin Grange *Dur.* ***Settlement***, 2m/3km W of Durham. NZ2442.

Aldingbourne *W.Suss.* ***Village***, 4m/7km E of Chichester. **12 C6** SU9205.

Aldingham *Cumb.* ***Hamlet***, on Morecambe Bay, 4m/6km SE of Dalton-in-Furness. **55 F2** SD2871.

Aldington *Kent* ***Village***, 6m/9km W of Hythe. **15 F4** TR0736.

Aldington *Worcs.* ***Village***, 2m/3km E of Evesham. **30 B4** SP0644.

Aldington Corner *Kent* ***Hamlet***, 1m/2km W of Aldington. TR0736.

Aldington Frith *Kent* ***Hamlet***, 2m/4km to W of Aldington. TR0436.

Aldivalloch *Moray* ***Settlement***, 2m/3km W of Cabrach. **90 B2** NJ3626.

Aldochlay *Arg. & B.* ***Settlement***, on W shore of Loch Lomond, 1m/2km S of Luss. **74 B1** NS3591.

Aldon *Shrop.* ***Locality***, 2m/3km S of Craven Arms. SO4379.

Aldons *S.Ayr.* ***Settlement***, in Stinchar valley, 5m/8km S of Girvan. **67 F5** NX1989.

Aldoth *Cumb.* ***Locality***, 2m/4km SW of Abbeytown. NY1448.

Aldous's Corner *Suff.* ***Settlement***, 3m/5km NW of Halesworth. TM3681.

Aldreth *Cambs.* ***Village***, 7m/11km SW of Ely. **33 H1** TL4473.

Aldridge *W.Mid.* Population: 16,862. ***Town***, former mining town, 3m/5km NE of Walsall. **40 C5** SK0500.

Aldringham *Suff.* ***Village***, 1m/2km S of Leiston. **35 J2** TM4461.

Aldrington *B. & H.* ***Suburb***, W district of Hove. TQ2705.

Aldro *N.Yorks.* ***Settlement***, 1m/2km E of Leavening, 5m/8km S of Norton. **58 E3** SE8163.

Aldsworth *Glos.* ***Village***, 6m/10km W of Burford. **30 C7** SP1510.

Aldsworth *W.Suss.* ***Settlement***, 2m/3km NE of Emsworth. SU7608.

Aldunie *Moray* ***Settlement***, 1m/2km W of Cabrach. **90 B2** NJ3626.

Aldville *P. & K.* ***Settlement***, 6m/10km SW of Dunkeld. **82 A4** NN9439.

Aldwark *Derbys.* ***Hamlet***, 4m/7km NW of Wirksworth. **50 E7** SK2257.

Aldwark *N.Yorks.* ***Village***, on River Ouse, 6m/9km SW of Easingwold. 1m/2km S is Aldwark Bridge, over River Ouse. **57 K3** SE4663.

Aldwarke *S.Yorks.* ***Locality***, 2m/3km NE of Rotherham. SK4494.

Aldwick *W.Suss.* ***Suburb***, W district of Bognor Regis. **12 C7** SZ9198.

Aldwincle *Northants.* ***Village***, 4m/7km SW of Oundle. **42 D7** TL0081.

Aldworth *W.Berks.* ***Village***, 3m/4km W of Streatley. **21 J4** SU5579.

Ale Water *Sc.Bord.* ***River***, running NE through Alemoor Loch to Ashkirk and Lilliesleaf. River then flows E to Ancrum, where it turns briefly S to run into River Teviot. **69 K2** NT6223.

Aled *Conwy* ***River***, rising in Llyn Aled and flowing N through Aled Isaf Reservoir and Llansannan to River Elwy, 2m/3km E of Llanfair Talhaiarn. **47 H6** SH9571.

Aled Isaf Reservoir *Conwy* ***Reservoir***, in course of River Aled 4m/7km S of Llansannan. **47 H7** SH9159.

Alemoor Loch *Sc.Bord.* ***Lake/loch***, and reservoir 7m/11km W of Hawick. **69 J2** NT3914.

Alexandria *W.Dun.* Population: 14,150. ***Town***, on River Leven, 3m/5km N of Dumbarton. **74 B3** NS3979.

Aley *Som.* ***Hamlet***, on lower slopes of Quantock Hills, 1m/2km S of Nether Stowey. ST1838.

Aley Green *Beds.* ***Hamlet***, 1km S of Caddington, 3m/4km SW of Luton. TL0618.

Alfardisworthy *Devon* ***Hamlet***, 6m/9km NW of Holsworthy. **6 A4** SS2911.

Alfington *Devon* ***Village***, 2m/3km NE of Ottery St. Mary. **7 K6** SY1197.

Alfold *Surr.* ***Village***, 4m/6km SW of Cranleigh. **12 D3** TQ0334.

Alfold Bars *W.Suss.* ***Hamlet***, 6m/9km NW of Billingshurst. TQ0333.

Alfold Crossways *Surr.* ***Hamlet***, 3m/4km SW of Cranleigh. **12 D3** TQ0435.

Alford *Aber.* Population: 1394. ***Small town***, 23m/37km W of Aberdeen. Site of defeat of Covenanters by Montrose in 1645. Grampian Transport Museum. **90 D3** NJ5715.

Alford *Lincs.* Population: 2989. ***Small town***, market town, 11m/17km SE of Louth. 19c windmill with five sails. **53 H5** TF4575.

Alford *Som.* ***Village***, 2m/4km W of Castle Cary. **9 F1** ST6032.

Alfreton *Derbys.* Population: 22,822. ***Town***, market town, 10m/15km S of Chesterfield. **51 G7** SK4155.

Alfrick *Worcs.* ***Village***, 7m/11km W of Worcester. **29 G3** SO7453.

Alfrick Pound *Worcs.* ***Hamlet***, 7m/11km W of Worcester. SO7452.

Alfriston *E.Suss.* ***Village***, South Downs village on Cuckmere River, 4m/6km NE of Newhaven. **13 J6** TQ5103.

Alfriston Clergy House *E.Suss.* ***Historic house***, 14c house 6m/10km NW of Eastbourne. First building acquired by The National Trust, in 1896 for £10. **13 J6** TQ5202.

Algarkirk *Lincs.* ***Village***, 6m/10km SW of Boston. **43 F2** TF2935.

Alhampton *Som.* ***Village***, 2m/3km NW of Castle Cary. **9 F1** ST6234.

Alhang ***Mountain***, rising to over 640 metres, on border of Dumfries & Galloway and East Ayrshire, 8m/13km S of New Cumnock. Source of Afton Water on NW slopes. **68 B3** NS6401.

Alkborough *N.Lincs.* ***Village***, 7m/11km N of Scunthorpe. **58 E7** SE8821.

Alkerton *Oxon.* ***Village***, 5m/8km W of Banbury. **30 E4** SP3742.

Alkham *Kent* ***Village***, 4m/6km W of Dover. **15 H3** TR2542.

Alkington *Shrop.* ***Settlement***, 2m/3km SW of Whitchurch. **38 E2** SJ5238.

Alkmonton *Derbys.* ***Hamlet***, 4m/7km NE of Sudbury. **40 D2** SK1838.

All Cannings *Wilts.* ***Village***, 4m/7km E of Devizes. **20 D5** SU0761.

All Saints South Elmham *Suff.* ***Hamlet***, 4m/7km NW of Halesworth. **45 H7** TM3482.

All Stretton *Shrop.* ***Village***, 1m/2km NE of Church Stretton. **38 D6** SO4695.

Alladale *High.* ***River***, rising on N slope of An Socach, flowing E then NE, via confluence with Water of Glencalvie, into River Carron. NH4791.

Allaleigh *Devon* ***Hamlet***, 5m/8km W of Dartmouth. **5 J5** SX8053.

Allan Water ***River***, rising near Blackford and running SW down Strathallan to Dunblane, then continuing S to River Forth 2m/3km N of Stirling. **81 J7** NS7896.

Allan Water *Sc.Bord.* ***River***, running N to River Teviot at Newmill, 4m/7km SW of Hawick. **69 K3** NT4510.

Allanaquoich *Aber.* ***Settlement***, on N bank of Quoich Water, 2m/3km W of Braemar. **89 J5** NO1191.

Allancreich *Aber.* ***Settlement***, 1km NW of Marywell. **90 D5** NO5796.

Allandale *Falk.* ***Hamlet***, on SW side of Bonnybridge. NS7978.

Allanfearn *High.* ***Settlement***, in Inverness district, 4m/6km E of Inverness. NH7147.

Allangillfoot *D. & G.* ***Settlement***, on E bank of White Esk River, 5m/8km NW of Bentpath. **69 H4** NY2595.

Allanton *D. & G.* ***Settlement***, 3m/5km E of Dunscore. **68 E5** NX9184.

Allanton *E.Ayr.* ***Settlement***, 3m/4km E of Darvel. Site of Roman fort. NS6037.

Allanton *N.Lan.* Population: 1186. ***Village***, 4m/6km NE of Wishaw. **75 G5** NS8557.

Allanton *Sc.Bord.* ***Village***, 1m/2km S of Chirnside, at confluence of Blackadder Water and Whiteadder Water. **77 G5** NT8654.

Allanton *S.Lan.* ***Hamlet***, 2m/4km SE of Hamilton. **75 F5** NS7454.

Allardice *Aber.* ***Locality***, comprises Mains of Allardice, Mill of Allardice and Castle of Allardice, 1m/2km NW of Inverbervie. **91 G7** NO8174.

Allasdale *W.Isles* *Anglicised form of Allathasdal, qv.*

Allaston *Glos.* ***Locality***, adjoining to N of Lydney. SO6304.

Allathasdal (Anglicised form: Allasdale.) *W.Isles* ***Settlement***, on W coast of Barra, 3m/5km N of Castlebay. **84 B4** NF6603.

Allbrook *Hants.* ***Suburb***, N district of Eastleigh. SU4521.

Allen *Cornw.* ***River***, rising to S of Newlyn Downs and flowing S through Truro to join River Kenwyn and form Truro River. SW8244.

Allen *Cornw.* ***River***, rising S of Delabole and flowing SW into River Camel 1m/2km SE of Wadebridge. **4 A3** SX0071.

Allen *Northumb.* ***River***, formed by confluence of Rivers East Allen and West Allen, 3m/5km NW of Allendale Town, and flowing N through deep wooded valley into River South Tyne, 1m/2km E of Bardon Bridge. **70 C7** NY8064.

Allen Crags *Cumb.* ***Mountain***, 1m/2km NW of Bow Fell. Height 2575 feet or 785 metres. **60 D6** NY2308.

Allendale Common *Northumb.* ***Open space***, heathland to SW of Hexhamshire Common, 3m/5km S of Allendale Town. **61 K1** NY8551.

Allendale Cottages *Dur.* ***Locality***, 1m/2km E of Ebchester. NZ1155.

Allendale Town *Northumb.* ***Small town***, market town on River East Allen, 5m/9km S of Haydon Bridge. **61 K1** NY8355.

Allenheads *Northumb.* ***Village***, 4m/6km N of Wearhead. **61 K2** NY8545.

Allen's Green *Herts.* ***Hamlet***, 4m/6km SW of Bishop's Stortford. **33 H7** TL4516.

Allensford ***Settlement***, on River Derwent, straddling border of Durham and Northumberland, 2m/3km W of Consett. **62 B1** NZ0750.

Allensford Country Park *Dur.* ***Leisure/recreation***, in River Derwent valley, 2m/3km SW of Consett. **62 B1** NZ0850.

Allensmore *Here.* ***Village***, 4m/6km SW of Hereford. **28 D5** SO4635.

Allenton *Derby* ***Suburb***, 3m/4km SE of Derby city centre. SK3732.

Aller *Devon* ***Hamlet***, 3m/5km E of South Molton. SS7625.

Aller *Som.* ***Village***, 2m/3km NW of Langport. **8 C2** ST4029.

Allerby *Cumb.* ***Hamlet***, 4m/6km NE of Maryport. **60 B3** NY0839.

Allercombe *Devon* ***Hamlet***, 3m/5km W of Ottery St. Mary. SY0494.

Allerdeanmill Burn *Northumb.* ***River***, small stream which rises 3m/4km SW of Berwick-upon-Tweed and flows SE to join with other streams before flowing to North Sea, 2m/3km NW of Haggerston. **77 H6** NT9747.

Allerford *Devon* ***Settlement***, 2m/3km E of Lifton. **6 C7** SX4285.

Allerford *Som.* ***Village***, 1m/2km E of Porlock. **7 H1** SS9046.

Allerston *N.Yorks.* ***Village***, 5m/8km E of Pickering. **58 E1** SE8782.

Allerston High Moor *N.Yorks.* ***Forest/woodland***, afforestation to W of Langdale Forest, adjacent to Lockton High Moor, 5m/8km SE of Goathland. **63 K7** SE8795.

Allerthorpe *E.Riding* ***Village***, 2m/3km SW of Pocklington. **58 D5** SE7847.

Allerthorpe *N.Yorks.* ***Locality***, 3m/5km SE of Leeming. SE3386.

Allerton *Mersey.* ***Suburb***, 5m/8km SE of Liverpool city centre. **48 D4** SJ4086.

Allerton *W.Yorks.* ***Suburb***, 3m/5km W of Bradford city centre. **57 G6** SE1234.

Allerton Bywater *W.Yorks.* ***Village***, on River Aire, 2m/3km NW of Castleford. **57 K7** SE4127.

Allerton Mauleverer *N.Yorks.* ***Settlement***, on E side of Allerton Park, 6m/9km S of Boroughbridge. SE4158.

Allerton Park *N.Yorks.* ***Historic house***, 19c mansion in large park with lakes, 4m/6km NE of Knaresborough. **57 K4** SE4158.

Allesley *W.Mid.* ***Suburb***, 3m/5km W of Coventry city centre. Also parish adjoining Coventry to NW. **40 E7** SP2980.

Allestree *Derby* ***Suburb***, N of Derby. **41 F2** SK3539.

Allet Common *Cornw.* ***Settlement***, 3m/5km NW of Truro. SW7948.

Allexton *Leics.* ***Village***, 3m/5km W of Uppingham. **42 B5** SK8100.

Allgreave *Ches.* ***Hamlet***, in Peak District National Park, 6m/9km SE of Macclesfield. **49 J6** SJ9766.

Allhallows *Med.* ***Village***, 8m/13km NE of Rochester. **24 E4** TQ8377.

Allhallows-on-Sea *Med.* ***Settlement***, 1km N of Allhallows. **24 E4** TQ8378.

Alligin *High.* *See Inveralligin.*

Alligin Shuas *High.* ***Settlement***, on N shore of Upper Loch Torridon, 4m/7km W of Torridon, Ross and Cromarty district. **94 E6** NG8358.

Allimore Green *Staffs.* ***Settlement***, 1m/2km SW of Haughton. **40 A4** SJ8519.

Allington *Dorset* ***Suburb***, N district of Bridport. SY4693.

Allington *Kent* ***Suburb***, in N part of Maidstone, beside River Medway, with a restored medieval castle (Allington Castle). TQ7457.

Allington *Lincs.* ***Village***, 5m/7km NW of Grantham. **42 B1** SK8540.

Allington *Wilts.* ***Hamlet***, 2m/3km NW of Chippenham. ST8975.

Allington *Wilts.* ***Village***, 4m/7km E of Devizes. **20 D5** SU0663.

Allington *Wilts.* ***Village***, on River Bourne, 7m/11km NE of Salisbury. **10 D1** SU2039.

Allington Castle *Kent* ***Castle***, on N side of Maidstone, dating from 1281. Many alterations and repairs were carried out by Sir Henry Wyatt in early 16c. Currently home of Order of Carmelites who use it as a retreat and conference centre. **14 C2** TQ7557.

Allison Lane End *E.Riding* ***Locality***, just NE of Lissett. TA1458.

Allithwaite *Cumb.* ***Village***, 1m/2km S of Cartmel. **55 G2** SD3876.

Allnabad *High.* ***Settlement***, 2m/3km NE of Loch Meadie. **103 G4** NC4641.

Alloa *Clack.* Population: 18,842. ***Town***, former coal port on N side of River Forth, 6m/9km E of Stirling. Small harbour. **75 G1** NS8892.

Allonby *Cumb.* ***Village***, on Solway Firth, 5m/8km NE of Maryport. **60 B2** NY0842.

Allonby Bay *Cumb.* ***Bay***, extends N from Maryport to Dubmill Point. **60 B2** NY0842.

Allostock *Ches.* ***Village***, 5m/7km S of Knutsford. SJ7471.

Alloway *S.Ayr.* ***Village***, 2m/4km S of Ayr. Birthplace of Robert Burns, 1759; cottage is Burns museum. Auld Brig o'Doon, with Burns associations, spans River Doon to S. **67 H2** NS3318.

Allowenshay *Som.* ***Hamlet***, 2m/4km SE of Ilminster. ST3913.

Allscot *Shrop.* ***Settlement***, 2m/3km NE of Bridgnorth. **39 G6** SO7396.

Allscott *Tel. & W.* ***Settlement***, 3m/4km NW of Wellington. SJ6113.

Allt a' Bhunn *High.* ***River***, rising from Loch Sgeireach and flowing E into Loch Shin. **103 G7** NC5112.

Allt a' Chaoil Reidhe *High.* ***River***, in Ben Alder Forest, flowing NE into Loch Pattack, 8m/12km SW of Dalwhinnie. **88 C7** NN5378.

Allt a' Chaoruinn *High.* ***River***, rising on NE slopes of Meall a' Bhùirich Rapaig and flowing N to join Allt nan Clach Aoil to form Allt Eilean. **95 J1** NC2806.

Allt a' Chaoruinn *High.* ***River***, in Lochaber district, flowing NE into River Pean 1m/2km W of head of Loch Arkaig. **87 F6** NM9690.

Allt a' Chireachain *P. & K.* ***River***, flowing SW into River Garry, 4m/6km NE of Trinafour. **88 E7** NN7569.

Allt a' Choire *High.* ***River***, flowing W into Loch Beoraid, Lochaber district. **86 E6** NM8584.

Allt a' Choire Ghlais *High.* ***River***, flowing NE from Sròn a' Choire Ghiarbh into Kilfinnan Burn, 1m/2km W of Laggan. **87 J5** NN2796.

Allt a' Choire Mhòir *High.* ***River***, flowing S from slopes of Sgurr nan Clach Geala into Loch Fannich. **95 H5** NH2066.

Allt a' Chonais *High.* ***River***, flowing N from slopes of Sgurr Choinnich, then NW to join River Carron, 3m/5km E of Achnashellach Station. **95 G7** NH0449.

Allt a' Chuil *P. & K.* ***River***, flowing W into Bruar Water, 9m/14km N of Calvine. **89 F6** NN8180.

Allt a' Ghlinne *High.* ***River***, rising on N slopes of Cnoc nan Sac and flowing NE into River Carron, 4m/6km W of Bonar Bridge. **96 C2** NH5491.

Allt a' Mhuilinn *High.* ***River***, flowing S and joining Allt Ach' a' Bhàthàich 1km N of confluence with River Brora, 2m/3km NW of Gordonbush. **104 D7** NC8211.

Allt Ach' a' Bhàthàich *High.* ***River***, flowing S and joining Allt a' Mhuilinn 1km N of confluence with River Brora, 2m/3km NW of Gordonbush. **104 D7** NC8211.

Allt Airigh-dhamh *High.* ***River***, in Sutherland district, flowing SE and joining Eileag Burn before flowing into Loch Arichlinie. **104 D5** NC8237.

Allt an Dùin *High.* ***River***, in Sutherland district, flowing N and joining Abhainn na Frithe at Altanduin. **104 D6** NC8126.

Allt an Ealaidh *High.* ***River***, in Sutherland district rising to N of Ben Armine and flowing SE to become River Skinsdale. **104 C6** NC7426.

Allt an Lochan Dhuibh *High.* ***River***, flowing out of Loch Dubh into River Calder, 3m/5km W of Newtonmore. **88 D4** NN6598.

Allt an Loin *High.* ***River***, flowing E through Leanachan Forest to its confluence with Allt Coire an Eòin, 2m/3km SE of Spean Bridge. **87 J7** NN2379.

Allt an Stacain *Arg. & B.* ***River***, flowing generally W into Cladich River, 1m/2km SE of Cladich. **80 C5** NN1120.

Allt an Tiaghaich *High.* ***River***, rising in Loch a' Ghlinnein and flowing NW into Lochan an Iasgaich. NC1524.

Allt an t'Sluic *High.* ***River***, flowing SE into River Truim, just N of Dalwhinnie. **88 D6** NN6485.

Allt an Ulbhaidh *High.* ***River***, rising SW of Meall an Fhuarain and flowing S through Loch an Ulbhaidh, to join River Tirry. **103 H6** NC5120.

Allt Arder *Moray* ***River***, rising on Carn Shalag and flowing E into River Spey 1km S of Upper Knockando. **97 J7** NJ1841.

Allt Bail a' Mhuilinn *P. & K.* ***River***, stream running N into River Lyon at Milton Eonan. **81 G3** NN5746.

Allt Ballach *High.* ***River***, rising on slopes of Carn Bàn and flowing S into River Calder, 3m/5km W of Newtonmore. **88 D4** NN6598.

Allt Beinn Donuill *High.* ***River***, small stream in Rhidorroch Forest, flowing E and, with other tributaries, forming Rappach Water. **95 J2** NH2399.

Allt Beithe *High.* ***River***, in Sutherland district, rising from Lochan a' Bhealaich between Carn Dearg and Carn an Tionail, and flowing S through Loch Ulbhach Coire before joining Allt na Glaise and Allt Coir' a' Chruiteir to form Allt nan Albannach. **103 F5** NC3833.

Allt Beochlich *Arg. & B.* ***River***, running W into Loch Awe, 3m/4km NE of Dalavich across loch. **80 B6** NN0115.

Allt Bhlàraidh *High.* ***River***, rising in Loch Liath and flowing SE into River Moriston 3m/4km W of Invermoriston. **87 K3** NH3816.

Allt Bhran *High.* ***River***, running NE into River Tromie, 6m/10km S of Kingussie. **89 F6** NN7590.

Allt Breinag *High.* ***River***, in Inverness district rising on Glendoe Forest and running N down Glen Brein to River Feehlin at Whitebridge, 3m/5km S of Foyers. **88 B4** NH4815.

Allt Cam *High.* ***River***, flowing N, then E into Abhainn Ghuilbinn, 3m/4km SW of Loch Laggan. **88 B7** NN4279.

Allt Cam *High.* ***River***, running NE by An Lairing, then ultimately SE into Loch Pattack, 7m/11km SW of Dalwhinnie. **88 C7** NN5379.

Allt Cam Ban *High.* ***River***, rising on W slopes of Sgaraman nam Fiadh and flowing W into Glen Markie, 10m/17km E of Fort Augustus. **88 C4** NH5407.

Allt Camghouran *P. & K.* ***River***, running NE into Loch Rannoch, 7m/11km W of Kinloch Rannoch. **81 G2** NN5456.

Allt Car *High.* ***River***, rising on E slopes of Cnoc Glas na Crionaiche and flowing E along Strath an Lòin into Loch Shin. **103 G7** NC4716.

Allt Chaiseagail *High.* ***River***, flowing W into River Tirry, 2m/4km N of Lairg. **103 H7** NC5710.

Allt Choir a' Bhalachain *High.* ***River***, running NE from source, 2m/3km N of Loch Arkaig, into River Garry, 2m/3km W of head of Loch Garry. **87 H5** NH1301.

Allt Chomhraig *High.* ***River***, rising near Meallach Mhòr and flowing NE down Gleann Chomhraig, into River Feshie, 6m/9km E of Kingussie. **88 E5** NH8400.

Allt Chonoghlais *Arg. & B.* ***River***, in Argyll rising on S side of Beinn a' Dothaidh and running in a wide loop round Beinn Dòrain to River Orchy, 1km S of Bridge of Orchy. **80 E4** NN2938.

Allt Coire a' Chaolain *High.* ***River***, rising on N slopes of Stob Gabhar, and flowing NE into River Etive 8m/12km SE of Glencoe village. **80 D3** NN1951.

Allt Coire an Eòin *High.* ***River***, flowing N through Killiechonate Forest to its confluence with Allt na Loin, 2m/3km SE of Spean Bridge. **87 J7** NN2379.

Allt Coire Lain Oig *High.* ***River***, running S through Sherramore Forest and entering River Spey 6m/9km W of Laggan. **88 C5** NN5294.

Allt Coire na Saighe Duibhe *High.* ***River***, rising from Loch Coire na Saighe Duibhe and flowing E, where it joins Allt an t-Strath a Dhuibh to form River Mudale. **103 G5** NC5135.

Allt Con *P. & K.* ***River***, flowing SE from Loch Con into Loch Errochty, 2m/3km NW of Trinafour. NN7066.

Allt Conait *P. & K.* ***River***, flowing generally SE from Loch an Daimh into River Lyon, 3m/5km SW of Bridge of Balgie. **81 G3** NN5344.

Allt Connie *Aber.* ***River***, stream running NE, which joins with other streams to flow into River Dee at Inverey. **89 H6** NO0786.

Allt Crunachdain *High.* ***River***, running NE down Glen Shirra, entering Loch Crunachdan 4m/7km SW of Laggan. **88 C5** NN5492.

Allt Cuaich *High.* ***River***, flowing W then NW into River Truim, 2m/3km NE of Dalwhinnie. **88 D6** NN6587.

Allt Darrarie *Aber.* ***River***, stream running N to River Muick nearly 1km N of Spittal of Glenmuick. **90 B6** NO3085.

Allt Ddu *Powys* ***Mountain***, on NE side of Brecon Beacons, 3m/4km SW of Brecon. Height 1843 feet or 562 metres. **27 K6** SO0224.

Allt Dearg *High.* ***River***, rising on slopes of Cnoc nan Each Mòr and flowing into River Peffery just E of Strathpeffer. **96 B5** NH4958.

Allt Dearg *High.* ***River***, rising on NE slopes of Meall a' Bhreacain and flowing SE, then S into Loch Sheilah and into Balnagown River, 5m/8km NE of Alness. **96 D3** NH6777.

Allt Dearg *High.* ***River***, rising on N slopes of Carn nan Tri-tighearnan and flowing N to Dalcharn, then NE through Cawdor into River Nairn, 4m/6km SW of Nairn. Waterfalls in upper course. **97 F7** NH8451.

Allt Dearg *P. & K.* ***River***, stream in Dalnamein Forest, flowing S into Allt Glas Choire, 9m/15km SE of Dalwhinnie. **88 E7** NN7474.

Allt Dearg Mòr *High.* ***River***, rising on Cuillin Hills, Skye, and running NE to join River Sligachan about 1km above head of Loch Sligachan. **85 K2** NG4829.

Allt Dochard *Arg. & B.* ***River***, flowing S into Loch Dochard, 6m/9km NW of Bridge of Orchy. **80 D3** NN2142.

Allt Doe *High.* ***River***, rising in Glendoe Forest and flowing N through steep-sided Glen Doe into SE side of Loch Ness, 1m/2km E of Fort Augustus. NH4010.

Allt Easach ***River***, running S into Loch Etive, Argyll, 5m/7km from head of loch. **80 B3** NN0639.

Allt Eigheach ***River***, running S into Loch Eigheach. **81 F2** NN4457.

Allt Eileag *High.* ***River***, formed by confluence of Allt nan Clach Aoil and Allt a' Chaoruinn, flowing E to form River Oykel. **95 J1** NC3207.

Allt Essan *Stir.* ***River***, flowing E from Loch Essan, then S into River Dochart, 4m/6km NE of Crianlarich. **81 F5** NN4428.

Allt Fearnach *P. & K.* ***River***, running S down Gleann Fearnach to join Brerachan Water and form River Ardle, 3m/5km NW of Kirkmichael. NO0463.

Allt Fionn Ghlinne *Stir.* ***River***, running SE into River Falloch, 3m/5km NE of Ardlui, at head of Loch Lomond. **80 E5** NN3320.

Allt Garbh *High.* ***River***, rising on N slopes of Carn a' Choire Gairbh and flowing NE through Loch an Sgùid into E end of Loch Affric at Affric Lodge. **87 H3** NH1822.

Allt Garbh *High.* ***River***, rising on Eskdale Moor and flowing NE into River Beauly, 3m/4km E of Erchless Castle. **88 B1** NH4540.

Allt Garbh Buidhe *P. & K.* ***River***, flowing SW into River Tilt, 11m/18km NE of Blair Atholl. **89 G6** NN9879.

Allt Gharbh Ghaig *High.* ***River***, stream in Gaick Forest, flowing NW into Loch an t-Seilich, 9m/12km E of Dalwhinnie. **88 E6** NN7585.

Allt Ghlas *P. & K.* ***River***, flowing SW from Talla Bheith Forest into River Ericht at S end of Loch Ericht. **81 G1** NN5365.

Allt Glas a' Bheoil *High.* ***River***, rising on N slopes of Meall a' Bhothian and flowing NE into Elrick Burn, 8m/12km N of Newtonmore. **88 D4** NH6811.

Allt Glas Choire *P. & K.* ***River***, flowing S into River Garry, 12m/19km SE of Dalwhinnie. **88 E7** NN7569.

Allt Gleann Da-Eig *P. & K.* ***River***, running N into River Lyon 2m/4km E of Bridge of Balgie. Waterfalls 1km from mouth. **81 G3** NN6147.

Allt Gleann nam Meann *Stir.* ***River***, running S into Glen Finglas Reservoir, 6m/10km N of Aberfoyle. **81 G6** NN5210.

Allt Gobhlach *High.* ***River***, flowing S and joining An Crom-allt, 5m/8km S of W end of Loch Choire, to form River Brora. **103 J6** NC6218.

Allt Laire *High.* ***River***, in Lochaber district, flowing NE into River Spean, 5m/7km E of Roybridge. **87 K7** NN3479.

Allt Leachdach *High.* ***River***, flowing N into River Spean, 2m/3km SE of Spean Bridge. **87 J7** NN2580.

Allt Lon a' Chuil *High.* ***River***, rises on W slopes of Creagan Dubha Réidhe Bhig and flowing S into Loch Rimsdale, Caithness district. **104 C4** NC7339.

Allt Lorgy *High.* ***River***, rising on N slopes of Carn Dearg Mòr, and flowing NE into River Dulnain at Ellan. **89 F3** NH8922.

Allt Madagain *High.* ***River***, flowing E into River Calder, 3m/5km W of Newtonmore. **88 D5** NN6598.

Allt Menach *P. & K.* ***River***, stream rising in mountains to W of Glen Shee and flowing S to River Ardle, 1m/2km S of Kirkmichael. **82 B1** NO0858.

Allt Mhoille *Arg. & B.* ***River***, rising to NE of Ben Cruachan and flowing SE into River Strae, 2m/3km NW of Dalmally. **80 C4** NN1328.

Allt Mhucarnaich *High.* ***River***, rising between Beinn Dearg and Beinn Enaiglair, and flowing SE into Allt a' Gharbhrain. **95 J4** NH2678.

Allt Mòr *High.* ***River***, flowing SW into Loch Beag, near Bracadale, Skye. **85 J1** NG3638.

Allt Mòr *High.* ***River***, flowing NE through locality of Caiplich into Moniack Burn, 3m/5km SE of Beauly. **88 C1** NH5538.

Allt Mòr *High.* ***River***, formed from tributaries rising on N slopes of Carn Ghriogair and flowing NW into River Nairn, 6m/10km SE of Dores. **88 D2** NH6224.

Allt Mòr *High.* ***River***, flowing N from Loch Ashie into Big Burn, 3m/5km S of Inverness. **88 D1** NH6538.

Allt Mòr *High.* ***River***, rising on slopes of Meall na Gearra and flowing SE, then S, through Kingussie and into River Spey, 1km S of town. **88 E4** NH7500.

Allt Mòr *High.* ***River***, flowing NE into Allt Chomhraig, 4m/7km SE of Kingussie. **89 F5** NN8298.

Allt Mòr *P. & K.* ***River***, flowing E, below S slopes of Schiehallion, into Keltney Burn 5m/8km S of Tummel Bridge. **81 J2** NN7652.

Allt na Caim *High.* ***River***, flowing S into E end of Blackwater Reservoir. **80 E1** NN3761.

Allt na Doire Gairbhe *High.* ***River***, stream rising in Loch Mhoicean and flowing SW into Loch na Leitreach at Carnach, 6m/10km NE of head of Loch Duich. **87 G2** NH0228.

Allt na h-Airbhe *High.* ***Locality***, on W shore of Loch Broom, Ross and Cromarty district, opposite Ullapool. Ferry for pedestrians. **95 H2** NH1193.

Allt na h-Eirigh *High.* ***River***, flowing NW to W coast of Ross and Cromarty district, 1m/2km S of Rubha Chuaig. **94 D6** NG6956.

Allt na Lairige *Arg. & B.* ***River***, flowing W into River Fyne, 4m/6km NE of head of Loch Fyne. **80 D6** NN2316.

Allt na Lairige *High.* ***River***, in Lochaber district running S to head of Loch Treig. **87 J7** NN3069.

Allt na Lùibe *High.* ***River***, flowing SE and becoming Lettie River before joining River Fleet 7m/11km E of Lairg. NC6706.

Allt na Muic *High.* ***River***, flowing S from E slopes of Carn a' Chaochain into Glen Moriston, 1m/2km W of Dalchreichart. **87 J3** NH2613.

Allt-na-subh *High.* ***Settlement***, on N shore of Loch Long, 3m/4km NE of Dornie, Skye and Lochalsh district. **87 F2** NG9029.

Allt nan Achaidhean *High.* ***River***, rising on E slope of Cnoc an Liath-bhaid Mhòir, and flowing SE to join Abhainn na Frithe, 1m/2km NE of Altanduin. **104 C6** NC8127.

Allt nan Caorach *High.* ***River***, rising on Ben Wyvis, and flowing E into River Glass, 3m/4km NW of Evanton. **96 C5** NH5667.

Allt nan Ramh *High.* ***River***, rising in Reay Forest and flowing SW into Loch Allt nan Ramh. **102 E5** NC2036.

Allt Odhar *High.* ***River***, formed from tributaries on slopes of Meall Caca, and flowing NE into River Killin. **88 C4** NH5307.

Allt Phocaichain *High.* ***River***, formed from tributaries on slopes of Carn Mhic Raonuill and flowing N into River Moriston opposite Dundreggan. **87 K3** NH3214.

Allt Riabhach *High.* ***River***, flowing NE along NW slope of Meallan Odhar to form Abhainn Deabhag at Coudie. **87 J3** NH2421.

Allt Riabhachain *High.* ***River***, flowing N down slopes between Beinn Bheag and An Riabhachan into Loch Monar. **87 H1** NH1239.

Allt Riobain *Stir.* ***River***, flowing S into River Dochart, 9m/13km SW of Killin. **81 F5** NN4527.

Allt Ruadh *High.* ***River***, rising on NW slopes of Carn Bàn Mòr and flowing NW into River Feshie, 5m/9km E of Kingussie. **89 F4** NH8401.

Allt Ruighe nan Saorach *P. & K.* ***River***, flowing NE into Loch Errochty, 3m/5km N of Kinloch Rannoch. **81 H1** NN6664.

Allt Saigh *High.* ***River***, rising on E slopes of Carn a' Mheallain Odhair and flowing E to enter Loch Ness at Alltsigh, 3m/4km NE of Invermoriston. NH4519.

Allt Shallainn *P. & K.* ***River***, flowing E into S end of Loch Garry, 6m/10km NW of Kinloch Rannoch. **81 G1** NN5867.

Allt Sleibh *P. & K.* ***River***, flowing E into NW side of Loch Errochty, 4m/7km N of Kinloch Rannoch. **81 H1** NN6665.

Allt Srath a' Ghlinne *P. & K.* ***River***, flowing SE in Glen Artney and joining Water of Ruchill 8m/10km NE of Callander. **81 H6** NN6915.

Allt Tolaghan *Arg. & B.* ***River***, in Argyll running NE to join Linne nam Beathach at W end of Loch Tulla. **80 D4** NN2742.

Allt Uisg an t-Sìthein *High.* ***River***, rising on slopes of Carn Mhic Iamhair and flowing N into River Farigaig, 3m/4km E of Errogie. **88 D3** NH6019.

Allt Wen *Cere.* ***Coastal feature***, cliff 1m/2km S of Aberystwyth. **26 E1** SN5779.
Allt y Main *Powys* ***Mountain***, 3m/4km NE of Meifod. Height 1168 feet or 356 metres. **38 A4** SJ1615.
Allt-yr-yn *Newport* ***Suburb***, to NW of Newport town centre. ST3088.
Alltachonaich *High.* ***Settlement***, 7m/11km N of Rubha an Ridire, Lochaber district. **79 J2** NM7450.
Alltami *Flints.* ***Hamlet***, 2m/3km NE of Mold. SJ2665.
Alltan Dubh *High.* ***Settlement***, on NW coast of Ross and Cromarty district, 4m/6km S of Rubha Coigeach. **102 B7** NB9812.
Alltbeithe *High.* ***Settlement***, with youth hostel, 4m/6km W of W end of Glen Affric. Not accessible by road. **87 G2** NH0820.
Alltcailleach Forest *Aber.* ***Forest/woodland***, 3m/5km SW of Ballater. NO3392.
Alltforgan *Powys* ***Settlement***, at N end of Lake Vyrnwy, 5m/8km NW of Llanwddyn. **37 J3** SH9624.
Alltmawr *Powys* ***Hamlet***, on River Wye, 3m/5km SE of Builth Wells. **27 K4** SO0746.
Alltnacaillich *High.* ***Settlement***, on E side of Strath More, 3m/5km S of Loch Hope. **103 G4** NC4545.
Alltsigh *High.* ***Settlement***, on NW shore of Loch Ness, 3m/4km NE of Invermoriston. **88 B3** NH4519.
Alltwalis *Carmar.* ***Hamlet***, 8m/12km N of Carmarthen. **17 H1** SN4431.
Alltwen *N.P.T.* ***Village***, 1km SE of Pontardawe. **18 A1** SN7203.
Alltyblaca *Cere.* ***Village***, 1m/2km N of Llanybydder. **26 E4** SN5245.
Allweston *Dorset* ***Village***, 2m/4km SE of Sherborne. **9 F3** ST6614.
Allwood Green *Suff.* ***Settlement***, 2m/3km W of Gislingham. TM0472.
Almeley *Here.* ***Village***, 4m/6km SE of Kington. **28 C3** SO3351.
Almeley Wooton *Here.* ***Hamlet***, 1km N of Almeley. SO3352.
Almer *Dorset* ***Hamlet***, 5m/8km S of Blandford Forum. **9 J5** SY9198.
Almholme *S.Yorks.* ***Hamlet***, 3m/5km NE of Doncaster. SE5908.
Almington *Staffs.* ***Hamlet***, 2m/3km E of Market Drayton. **39 F2** SJ7034.
Almiston Cross *Devon* ***Hamlet***, 8m/12km SW of Bideford. **6 B3** SS3420.
Almodington *W.Suss.* ***Locality***, 3m/5km NW of Selsey. SZ8297.
Almond *Edin.* ***River***, rising W of Whitburn and flowing NE to enter Firth of Forth, 1m/2km NE of Cramond Bridge. **75 K3** NT1877.
Almond *P. & K.* ***River***, rising 1km E of Loch Tay, and flows E through Glen Almond to join River Tay on N side of Perth. **82 B5** NO1026.
Almond Valley Heritage Centre (Also known as Livingston Mill Farm.) *W.Loth.* ***Other feature of interest***, museum of history and environment of West Lothian, on S bank of River Almond to W of Livingston Village. 20 acre site includes shale oil museum, activity centre and farmyard animals. **75 J4** NT0366.
Almondbank *P. & K.* Population: 1198. ***Village***, on River Almond, 4m/6km NW of Perth. **82 B5** NO0626.
Almondbury *W.Yorks.* Population: 1626. ***Suburb***, 2m/3km SE of Huddersfield town centre. **50 D1** SE1615.
Almondell and Calderwood Country Park *W.Loth.* ***Leisure/recreation***, in wooded River Almond valley, 1km N of East Calder. Over 200 acres of woods and riverside walks. Visitor centre holds local and natural history exhibitions and contains an aquarium. **75 J4** NT0868.
Almondsbury *S.Glos.* ***Village***, 7m/12km N of Bristol. Four-level motorway interchange 1m/2km E. **19 J3** ST6084.
Almorness Point *D. & G.* ***Coastal feature***, headland at S end of peninsula, 6m/9km S of Dalbeattie. **65 J5** NX8451.
Aln *Northumb.* ***River***, rising at Alnham, and flowing E by Alnwick into North Sea at Alnmouth. **71 G2** NU2410.
Alne ***River***, rising E of Redditch, and flowing in a loop, E then S then SW, into River Arrow at Alcester. **30 C2** SP0957.
Alne *N.Yorks.* ***Village***, 3m/5km SW of Easingwold. **57 K3** SE4965.
Alness *High.* *Alternative name for (River) Averon, qv.*
Alness *High.* Population: 5696. ***Small town***, on N side of Cromarty Firth, Ross and Cromarty district, 3m/5km W of Invergordon. Expansion in connection with North Sea oil developments. **96 D5** NH6569.
Alness Bay *High.* ***Bay***, on Cromarty Firth, 2m/3km SW of Alness. **96 D5** NH6367.
Alney Island *Glos.* ***Locality***, between branches of River Severn, in W part of Gloucester. SO8219.
Alnham *Northumb.* ***Hamlet***, 5m/8km W of Whittingham. **70 E2** NT9910.
Alnmouth *Northumb.* ***Small town***, resort with wide sands, at mouth of River Aln, 4m/7km SE of Alnwick. **71 H2** NU2410.
Alnmouth Bay *Northumb.* ***Coastal feature***, extending from Seaton Point in N to Amble in S. **71 H3** NU2410.
Alnwick *Northumb.* Population: 7419. ***Small town***, on River Aln, 17m/28km N of Morpeth. Norman castle, stronghold of Percys, much enlarged and restored. **71 G2** NU1813.
Alnwick Abbey *Northumb.* ***Ecclesiastical building***, 1m/2km NW of Alnwick, founded in 1147 for Premonstratensian canons. Only 14c gatehouse remains. **71 G2** NU1714.
Alnwick Castle *Northumb.* ***Castle***, 11c castle just N of Alnwick town centre, on S bank of River Aln. Home of Duke of Northumberland and second largest lived-in castle in England. Features dungeons, collection of Meissen Porcelain, gardens including restoration of 19c Italian gardens. **71 G2** NU1813.
Alnwick Moor *Northumb.* ***Open space***, moorland 3m/5km SW of Alnwick. **71 G2** NU1410.
Alperton *Gt.Lon.* ***Suburb***, in borough of Brent, 8m/12km W of Charing Cross. TQ1883.
Alphamstone *Essex* ***Village***, 4m/6km S of Sudbury. **34 C5** TL8735.
Alpheton *Suff.* ***Village***, 3m/5km N of Long Melford. **34 C3** TL8851.
Alphin Pike *Gt.Man.* ***Mountain***, 1m/2km S of Tunstead and 1km SW of Dovestone Reservoir. Height 1538 feet or 469 metres. **49 J2** SE0002.
Alphington *Devon* ***Suburb***, 2m/3km S of Exeter city centre. Parish of same name lies to W and S of city. **7 H6** SX9190.
Alpington *Norf.* ***Settlement***, 6m/10km SW of Norwich. **45 G5** TG2901.
Alport *Derbys.* ***River***, rising on Bleaklow Hill, 5m/8km E of Glossop, and flowing SE through Hope Forest into River Ashop, 4m/6km N of Castleton. **50 D3** SK1489.
Alport *Derbys.* ***Village***, on River Lathkill, in former lead-mining area, 3m/4km S of Bakewell. **50 E6** SK2264.
Alport Height *Derbys.* ***Mountain***, 4m/6km NW of Belper. Masts at summit. Height 1030 feet or 314 metres. **50 E7** SK3051.
Alpraham *Ches.* ***Village***, 3m/5km SE of Tarporley. **48 E7** SJ5859.
Alresford *Essex* Population: 2141. ***Village***, 2m/3km E of Wivenhoe. **34 E6** TM0621.
Alrewas *Staffs.* Population: 2907. ***Village***, 5m/8km NE of Lichfield. **40 D4** SK1715.
Alrick *Angus* ***Settlement***, 1km NW of Brewlands Bridge. **82 C1** NO1961.
Alsager *Ches.* Population: 13,435. ***Town***, pottery town, 6m/10km E of Crewe. **49 G7** SJ7955.
Alsager Heath *Ches.* ***Locality***, 1m/2km NW of Alsager. SJ7955.
Alsagers Bank *Staffs.* ***Hamlet***, 3m/5km NW of Newcastle-under-Lyme. **40 A1** SJ8048.
Alsop en le Dale *Derbys.* ***Hamlet***, 6m/9km N of Ashbourne. **50 D7** SK1655.
Alston *Cumb.* ***Small town***, market town, situated above River South Tyne, 16m/26km NE of Penrith. Now busy service and tourist centre. **61 J2** NY7146.
Alston *Devon* ***Hamlet***, 1m/2km S of Chardstock. **8 C4** ST3002.
Alston Moor *Cumb.* ***Open space***, moorland 4m/6km S of Alston. **61 J2** NY7240.
Alston Sutton *Som.* ***Hamlet***, 3m/4km NW of Wedmore. ST4151.
Alstone *Glos.* ***Suburb***, W district of Cheltenham. SO9322.
Alstone *Glos.* ***Village***, 4m/6km NW of Winchcombe. **29 J5** SO9832.
Alstone *Som.* ***Village***, 1km SW of Highbridge. ST3146.
Alstone *Staffs.* ***Settlement***, 1m/2km NW of Bradley. SJ8518.
Alstonefield *Staffs.* ***Village***, 6m/10km NW of Ashbourne. **50 D7** SK1355.
Alswear *Devon* ***Village***, 3m/4km S of South Molton. **7 F3** SS7222.
Alt ***River***, rising at Roby and flowing NW into Crosby Channel, 3m/4km S of Formby. **48 C2** SD2903.
Alt *Gt.Man.* ***Suburb***, 2m/3km SE of Oldham town centre. SD9403.
Alt Hill *Gt.Man.* ***Settlement***, 2m/3km SE of Oldham. SD9402.
Altanduin *High.* ***Settlement***, in Sutherland district, 4m/6km S of Loch Achnamoine. **104 D6** NC8026.
Altarnun *Cornw.* ***Village***, attractive village below NE side of Bodmin Moor, 7m/11km W of Launceston. Parish church known as 'Cathedral of the Moors'. 15c packhorse bridge. **4 C2** SX2281.
Altass *High.* ***Settlement***, in Sutherland district on edge of Oykel Forest, 7m/11km SW of Lairg. **96 C1** NC4900.
Altens *Aberdeen* ***Locality***, industrial area on coast, 2m/3km S of Aberdeen harbour. **91 H4** NJ9402.
Alterwall *High.* ***Settlement***, 1m/2km NE of Lyth. **105 H2** ND2865.
Altgaltraig *Arg. & B.* ***Locality***, comprising Upper Altgaltraig and Lower Altgaltraig in Argyll on E shore of Kyles of Bute, 1m/2km SE of Colintraive. NS0473.
Altham *Lancs.* ***Village***, 2m/3km W of Padiham. **56 C6** SD7732.
Althorne *Essex* ***Village***, 3m/5km NW of Burnham-on-Crouch. **25 F2** TQ9199.
Althorp *Northants.* ***Historic house***, seat of Spencer family, 5m/9km NW of Northampton. 16c mansion with notable gardens, set in extensive parkland. Houses splendid collection of pictures and furniture. Diana, Princess of Wales is buried on an island within grounds. **31 H2** SP6865.
Althorpe *N.Lincs.* ***Village***, on W bank of River Trent, 4m/6km W of Scunthorpe. **52 B2** SE8309.
Alticry *D. & G.* ***Settlement***, 7m/11km SE of Glenluce. **64 C5** NX2849.
Altimeg Hill *S.Ayr.* ***Open space***, hillslope rising to 340 metres on W side of Deer's How, 4m/7km SE of Ballantrae. **64 B3** NX1076.
Altnabreac *High.* ***Locality***, with railway station, in Caithness district, 12m/19km SW of Halkirk. **105 F4** ND0045.
Altnafeadh *High.* ***Settlement***, on approach to Pass of Glencoe, 4m/6km SE of Kinlochleven. **80 D2** NN2256.
Altnaharra *High.* ***Village***, in Caithness district at W end of Loch Naver, 13m/22km S of Tongue. **103 H5** NC5635.
Altofts *W.Yorks.* ***Locality***, 1m/2km NW of Normanton. **57 J7** SE3723.
Alton *Derbys.* ***Village***, 2m/3km W of Clay Cross. **51 F6** SK3664.
Alton *Hants.* Population: 16,005. ***Town***, market town 10m/16km SE of Basingstoke. Civil War battle in 1764 when Royalist Colonel Boles was killed in the church. **11 J1** SU7139.
Alton *Staffs.* ***Village***, 4m/7km E of Cheadle. Remains of Norman castle beside River Churnet. **40 C1** SK0742.
Alton Barnes *Wilts.* ***Village***, adjoining to W of Alton Priors and 4m/6km NW of Pewsey. **20 E5** SU1062.
Alton Pancras *Dorset* ***Village***, 2m/3km N of Piddletrenthide. **9 F4** ST6902.
Alton Priors *Wilts.* ***Village***, adjoining to E of Alton Barnes and 4m/6km NW of Pewsey. **20 E5** SU1162.
Alton Towers *Staffs.* ***Leisure/recreation***, leisure park built in 500 acre grounds of a ruined 19c house, designed largely by Pugin in Gothic style. Ruins and amusement park are to N of Alton across River Churnet. **40 C1** SK0743.
Alton Water Reservoir *Suff.* ***Reservoir***, 1km W of Holbrook. Includes nature reserve. **35 F5** TM1535.
Altonhill *E.Ayr.* ***Suburb***, N district of Kilmarnock. NS4239.
Altonside *Moray* ***Settlement***, on Red Burn, 5m/8km N of Rothes. **97 K6** NJ2957.
Altrincham *Gt.Man.* Population: 40,042. ***Town***, old market town, 8m/13km SW of Manchester. **49 G4** SJ7687.
Altura *High.* ***Settlement***, on SE side of Loch Lochy, 5m/8km NE of Spean Bridge. **87 J6** NN2489.
Alturlie Point *High.* ***Coastal feature***, headland in Inverness district on S side of Inner Moray Firth or Inverness Firth, 4m/7km NE of Inverness. **96 E7** NH7149.
Altyre Woods *Moray* ***Forest/woodland***, on E side of River Findhorn, 4m/6km S of Forres. **97 H6** NJ0253.
Alum Bay *I.o.W.* ***Bay***, to NE of The Needles, noted for its sand of many different colours, caused by varying mineral deposits in the vertical bands of clay and sands. **10 E6** SZ3085.
Alum Rock *W.Mid.* ***Suburb***, 4m/6km E of Birmingham city centre. SP1287.
Alun ***River***, rising on N slopes of Maesyrychen Mountain, N of Llangollen. It flows N to Rhydymwyn, then SE past Mold to Bradley, N of Wrexham, then NE by Gresford to Rossett, and finally into River Dee 2m/4km E of Rossett. **48 A6** SJ3956.
Alun *Pembs.* ***River***, rising 4m/6km NE of St. David's and flowing SW by St. David's into St. Brides Bay. **16 A2** SM7423.
Alva *Clack.* Population: 5201. ***Small town***, 3m/4km N of Alloa. **75 G1** NS8896.
Alvanley *Ches.* ***Village***, 1m/2km S of Helsby. **48 D5** SJ4974.
Alvaston *Derby* ***Suburb***, 3m/4km SE of Derby. **41 F2** SK3833.
Alvechurch *Worcs.* Population: 3317. ***Village***, 3m/5km N of Redditch. **30 B1** SP0272.
Alvecote *Warks.* ***Hamlet***, 3m/4km E of Tamworth. **40 E5** SK2404.
Alvediston *Wilts.* ***Village***, 4m/7km W of Broad Chalke. **9 J2** ST9723.
Alveley *Shrop.* Population: 2051. ***Village***, 6m/10km SE of Bridgnorth. **39 G7** SO7684.
Alverdiscott *Devon* ***Hamlet***, 4m/7km E of Bideford. **6 D3** SS5225.
Alverstoke *Hants.* ***Suburb***, S district of Gosport. **11 H5** SZ6098.
Alverstone *I.o.W.* ***Village***, 2m/3km NW of Sandown. **11 G6** SZ5785.
Alverthorpe *W.Yorks.* ***Suburb***, 2m/3km NW of Wakefield city centre. SE3121.
Alverton *Notts.* ***Hamlet***, 7m/12km S of Newark-on-Trent. **42 A1** SK7942.
Alves *Moray* ***Settlement***, 5m/9km W of Elgin. **97 J5** NJ1362.
Alvescot *Oxon.* ***Village***, 5m/8km NE of Lechlade. **21 F1** SP2704.
Alveston *S.Glos.* Population: 2525. ***Village***, 1m/2km S of Thornbury. **19 K3** ST6388.
Alveston *Warks.* ***Village***, 2m/4km E of Stratford-upon-Avon. **30 D3** SP2356.
Alvie *High.* ***Settlement***, in Badenoch and Strathspey district, on shore of Loch Alvie, 3m/4km SW of Aviemore. **89 F4** NH8609.
Alvingham *Lincs.* ***Village***, 3m/5km NE of Louth. **53 G3** TF3691.
Alvington *Glos.* ***Village***, 2m/4km SW of Lydney. **19 K1** SO6000.
Alwalton *Cambs.* ***Village***, 4m/7km SW of Peterborough. Manor house of c. 1700. East of England Showground to E. **42 E6** TL1395.
Alway *Newport* ***Suburb***, 2m/3km E of Newport town centre. ST3488.
Alwen ***River***, rising in Llyn Alwen and running E into Alwen Reservoir, then SE into River Dee, 1m/2km SW of Corwen. SJ0642.
Alwen Reservoir *Conwy* ***Reservoir***, large reservoir 3m/4km N of Cerrigydrudion. **47 H7** SH9552.
Alwin ***River***, rising near Cushat Law in Cheviot Hills and flowing S into River Coquet at Low Alwinton, near Alwinton. **70 E3** NT9205.
Alwington *Devon* ***Hamlet***, 4m/6km SW of Bideford. SS4023.
Alwinton *Northumb.* ***Village***, in Upper Coquetdale, 9m/14km W of Rothbury. **70 E3** NT9206.
Alwoodley *W.Yorks.* ***Suburb***, residential district 4m/6km N of Leeds city centre. SE3040.
Alwoodley Gates *W.Yorks.* ***Locality***, 1m/2km E of Alwoodley. **57 J5** SE3140.
Alyth *P. & K.* Population: 2383. ***Small town***, market town, 5m/8km NE of Blairgowrie. Former cloth-manufacturing town. **82 D3** NO2448.
Alyth Burn *P. & K.* ***River***, rising in Forest of Alyth and flowing SE, by Alyth, to join River Isla 2m/3km E of Alyth. **82 C2** NO2749.
Am Balg *High.* ***Island***, group of islets 1m/2km NW of Rubh' a Bhuachaille headland, on NW coast of Sutherland district. **102 D2** NC1866.
Am Basteir *High.* ***Mountain***, in Cuillin Hills, Skye, 3m/4km N of head of Loch Coruisk. Munro: height 3067 feet or 935 metres. **85 K2** NG4625.

Am Bodach *High.* ***Mountain***, on Mamore Forest in Lochaber district, 2m/3km N of Kinlochleven. Munro: height 3392 feet or 1034 metres. **80 C1** NN1765.

Am Broilein *High.* ***Bay***, small bay on NW shore of Loch Linnhe, 1m/2km NE of Rubha na h-Airde Uinnsinn. **79 K2** NM8853.

Am Buachaille *Arg. & B.* ***Mountain***, in Argyll, 3m/4km W of Inveraray. Height 1059 feet or 323 metres. **80 B7** NN0507.

Am Buachaille *High.* ***Coastal feature***, headland 7m/11km SW of Cape Wrath, Sutherland district. **102 D2** NC2065.

Am Faochagach *High.* ***Mountain***, in Ross and Cromarty district 3m/5km W of head of Loch Vaich. Munro: height 3129 feet or 954 metres. **95 K4** NH3079.

Am Fraoch Eilean *Arg. & B.* ***Island***, at S end of Jura, at entrance to Sound of Islay. **72 C4** NR4662.

Am Maol *High.* ***Hill***, 1m/2km N of Loch Duagrich, Skye. Height 695 feet or 212 metres. **93 K7** NG4041.

Am Meall *W.Isles* ***Hill***, at SE corner of Vatersay. Height 328 feet or 100 metres. **84 B5** NL6594.

Am Plastair *W.Isles* ***Island***, islet (National Trust for Scotland) off N coast of Soay and 1m/2km NW of St. Kilda. NA0502.

Amalebra *Cornw.* ***Settlement***, 3m/5km SW of St. Ives. **2 B5** SW4936.

Aman *Carmar. Welsh form of Amman (river), qv.*

Amat Forest *High.* ***Open space***, deer forest at head of Strathcarron 8m/13km W of Bonar Bridge Woods on left bank of River Carron above its confluence with Abhainn an t-Srath Chuileannaich. **96 B2** NH4690.

Ambaston *Derbys.* ***Hamlet***, 1m/2km E of Elvaston, in River Derwent valley. SK4232.

Amber *Derbys.* ***River***, rising 4m/6km NE of Darley Bridge and flowing SE through Ogston Reservoir, then S, and finally W to join River Derwent at Ambergate 3m/4km N of Belper. **51 F6** SK3451.

Amber Hill *Lincs.* ***Settlement***, 6m/10km W of Boston. **43 F1** TF2346.

Amber Row *Derbys.* ***Settlement***, 1km NE of South Wingfield. SK3856.

Ambergate *Derbys.* Population: 1836. ***Hamlet***, 3m/4km N of Belper. **51 F7** SK3451.

Amberley *Glos.* ***Village***, 1m/2km N of Nailsworth. Museum exhibiting industrial history of region. **20 B1** SO8501.

Amberley *W.Suss.* ***Village***, 4m/6km N of Arundel. **12 D5** TQ0313.

Amberley Museum *W.Suss.* ***Other feature of interest***, working museum of industrial archaeology, 1km S of Amberley. Houses Milne electrical collection with displays on technical developments in South East. **12 D5** TQ0212.

Amberstone *E.Suss.* ***Locality***, adjoining to N of Hailsham. TQ5911.

Amble *Northumb.* Population: 5639. ***Small town***, popular centre for fishing and sailing, on S side of River Coquet estuary, 7m/12km SE of Alnwick. **71 H3** NU2604.

Amblecote *W.Mid.* ***Suburb***, N district of Stourbridge. **40 A7** SO8985.

Ambler Thorn *W.Yorks.* ***Locality***, S district of Queensbury, 3m/4km N of Halifax. SE0929.

Ambleside *Cumb.* Population: 2905. ***Small town***, resort in Lake District, 4m/7km NW of Windermere. Remains of 1c-2c Roman fort of Galava, 1km SW. **60 E6** NY3704.

Ambleston (Treamlod). *Pembs.* ***Village***, 7m/11km NE of Haverfordwest. **16 D2** SN0025.

Ambrismore *Arg. & B.* ***Settlement***, on Bute, 1km NE of Scalpsie Bay. **73 J5** NS0658.

Ambrosden *Oxon.* Population: 1693. ***Village***, 2m/4km SE of Bicester. **31 H7** SP6019.

Amcotts *N.Lincs.* ***Village***, on W bank of River Trent, 5m/8km E of Crowle. **52 B1** SE8514.

Amen Corner *Brack.F.* ***Settlement***, 2m/3km E of Wokingham. SU8469.

America *Shrop.* ***Settlement***, 2m/3km NW of Shrawardine. SJ3716.

American Adventure Theme Park *Derbys.* ***Leisure/recreation***, 2m/3km NW of Ilkeston. History of an entire continent transformed into a variety of fairground rides. **41 G1** SK4544.

Amersham *Bucks.* Population: 21,711. ***Town***, old market town, 3m/4km S of Chesham. Brick pillars support 17c market hall. **22 C2** SU9597.

Amersham on the Hill *Bucks.* ***Suburb***, to N of Amersham. SU9698.

Amerton *Staffs.* ***Settlement***, 6m/9km NE of Stafford. SJ9927.

Amesbury *Wilts.* Population: 6333. ***Small town***, on River Avon at SE corner of Salisbury Plain, 7m/11km N of Salisbury. 1m/2km W, locality of West Amesbury. 2m/3km W, Stonehenge, Neolithic-Bronze Age earthwork and stone circle (English Heritage). **20 E7** SU1541.

Amesbury Abbey *Wilts.* ***Ecclesiastical building***, to NW of Amesbury. Only monastic church remains. **20 E7** SU1541.

Ameysford *Dorset* ***Settlement***, 1m/2km SW of West Moors. SU0702.

Amhuinnsuidhe *W.Isles Alternative name for Abhainnsuidhe, qv.*

Amicombe Hill *Devon* ***Mountain***, above Amicombe Brook, 4m/6km NE of Lydford, in Dartmoor National Park. Height 1919 feet or 585 metres. **6 D7** SX5586.

Amington *Staffs.* ***Locality***, 2m/3km E of Tamworth. **40 E5** SK2304.

Amisfield Town *D. & G.* ***Village***, 5m/7km NE of Dumfries. **69 F5** NY0082.

Amlwch *I.o.A.* Population: 3519. ***Small town***, former copper-producing town on N coast of Anglesey, 15m/24km NW of Menai Bridge. **46 C3** SH4492.

Amlwch Port *I.o.A.* ***Locality***, E of Amlwch town centre. **46 C3** SH4593.

Amman (Aman). *Carmar.* ***River***, rising on Black Mountain as two streams, Aman Fawr and Aman Fach, which join 1m/2km NE of Rhosaman and then flow W into River Loughor on S side of Ammanford. SN6210.

Ammanford (Rhydaman). *Carmar.* Population: 12,106. ***Town***, former mining town on SW side of Black Mountain, 12m/20km N of Swansea. **17 K3** SN6212.

Amotherby *N.Yorks.* ***Village***, 3m/4km NW of Malton. **58 D2** SE7473.

Ampfield *Hants.* ***Village***, 3m/5km E of Romsey. **10 E2** SU4023.

Ampleforth *N.Yorks.* ***Village***, 10m/16km E of Thirsk. Ampleforth Abbey and College 1m/2km E. **58 B2** SE5878.

Ampney Crucis *Glos.* ***Village***, 3m/4km E of Cirencester. **20 D1** SP0601.

Ampney St. Mary *Glos.* ***Village***, 4m/7km E of Cirencester. **20 D1** SP0802.

Ampney St. Peter *Glos.* ***Village***, 4m/6km E of Cirencester. **20 D1** SP0801.

Amport *Hants.* ***Village***, 4m/7km W of Andover. **21 G7** SU2944.

Ampthill *Beds.* Population: 6230. ***Small town***, old coaching town, 8m/12km S of Bedford. Houghton House, ruined 16c house (English Heritage) 1m/2km N. Cooper's Hill Nature Reserve. **32 D5** TL0338.

Ampton *Suff.* ***Village***, 4m/7km N of Bury St. Edmunds. **34 C1** TL8671.

Amroth *Pembs.* ***Village***, on Saundersfoot Bay, 2m/4km NE of Saundersfoot. Submerged forest visible at low tide. **16 E4** SN1607.

Amulree *P. & K.* ***Village***, on River Quaich, 9m/14km SW of Dunkeld. **81 K4** NN9036.

An Cabar *High.* ***Mountain***, in Ross and Cromarty district on SE side of Loch Fannich, 7m/11km NE of Achnasheen. Height 1830 feet or 558 metres. **95 J5** NH2564.

An Cabar *High.* ***Mountain***, summit to SW of Ben Wyvis, 5m/7km NE of Garve. Height 3116 feet or 950 metres. **96 B5** NH4566.

An Caisteal *Stir.* ***Mountain***, 4m/6km S of Crianlarich. Munro: height 3264 feet or 995 metres. **80 E6** NN3719.

An Cala Garden *Arg. & B.* ***Garden***, S of Seil, 1km E of Easdale and 6m/10km SW of Oban. Notable plants include rhododendron, rhabdotum, acer, hydrangea and camellia. **79 J6** NM7517.

An Cearcall *P. & K.* ***Open space***, steep slope to NE of Loch Garry, 9m/14km S of Dalwhinnie. **88 D7** NN6169.

An Cearcallach *High.* ***Mountain***, in Moy Forest, 2m/3km NW of SW end of Loch Laggan. Height 3257 feet or 993 metres. **88 B6** NN4285.

An Coileach *W.Isles* ***Mountain***, 1km E of Heileasbhal Mòr, South Harris. Height 1266 feet or 386 metres. **93 F2** NG0892.

An Coileachan *High.* ***Mountain***, in Ross and Cromarty district, 2m/3km NW of lower end of Loch Fannich. Munro: height 3027 feet or 923 metres. **95 J5** NH2468.

An Crom-allt *High.* ***River***, flowing SW and joining Allt Gobhlach, 5m/8km S of W end of Loch Craggie to form River Brora. **103 J6** NC6318.

An Cruachan *High.* ***Hill***, 1km SE of Cleadale, Eigg. Height 981 feet or 299 metres. **85 K6** NM4887.

An Cruachan *High.* ***Mountain***, 2m/3km NW of head of Loch Brittle, Skye. Height 1427 feet or 435 metres. **85 J2** NG3822.

An Cruachan *High.* ***Mountain***, in Skye and Lochalsh district, 4m/6km N of W end of Loch Mullardoch. Height 2316 feet or 706 metres. **87 G1** NH0935.

An Cuaidh *High.* ***Hill***, 1m/2km SE of Rubha Réidh, in Ross and Cromarty district. Radio mast. Height 971 feet or 296 metres. **94 D3** NG7689.

An Dornabac *High.* ***Hill***, 3m/4km N of Rubha Sgorr an t-Snidhe, Rum. Height 863 feet or 263 metres. **85 J5** NM3597.

An Dubh-sgeir *Arg. & B.* ***Island***, group of rocks nearly 1km N of Gigha. NR6655.

An Dubh-sgeir *High.* ***Island***, rock island on E side of Eilean Hoan at mouth of Loch Eriboll, N coast of Sutherland district. NC4568.

An Dubh Sgeir *High.* ***Island***, islet 4m/6km W of Idrigill Point, Skye. **85 G1** NG1936.

An Dubh-sgeir *High.* ***Island***, rock island nearly 1km off SW coast of Skye at S side of entrance to Loch Eynort. NG3422.

An Dùnan *Arg. & B.* ***Historic/prehistoric site***, fort on small headland on E coast of Jura, 1m/2km NE of Ardfernal across Lowlandman's Bay. **72 D3** NR5773.

An Fùr *High.* ***Mountain***, in Ross and Cromarty district, 6m/10km SW of Torridon. Height 1269 feet or 387 metres. **94 E6** NG8051.

An Garbh-eilean (Anglicised form: Garve Island.) *High.* ***Island***, islet lying off Cléit Dhubh headland on N coast of Sutherland district, 4m/7km E of Cape Wrath. **103 F1** NC3373.

An Garbh-mheall *High.* ***Mountain***, 5m/8km S of Rubha na Fearn, Ross and Cromarty district. Height 1617 feet or 493 metres. **94 D6** NG7252.

An Gead Loch *High.* ***Lake/loch***, 2m/3km S of W end of Loch Monar. **87 H1** NH1038.

An Gearanach *High.* ***Mountain***, in Lochaber district, on Mamore Forest 3m/5km N of Kinlochleven. Munro: height 3231 feet or 985 metres. **80 C1** NN1866.

An Glas-loch *High.* ***Lake/loch***, small loch 3m/5km NE of Loch Fiag, Sutherland district. **103 G5** NC4931.

An Gorm-loch *High.* ***Lake/loch***, in East Monar Forest, Ross and Cromarty district. **95 J7** NH2244.

An Grianan *High.* ***Mountain***, 5m/8km NE of Kinlochbervie, Sutherland district. Height 1532 feet or 467 metres. **102 E2** NC2662.

An Lairig *High.* ***Open space***, valley side comprising N slopes of Carn Dearg and Aonach Beag. **88 B7** NN4876.

An Leacainn *High.* ***Mountain***, in Inverness district, 5m/8km W of Inverness. Height 1358 feet or 414 metres. **96 C7** NH5741.

An Lean-charn *High.* ***Mountain***, situated between S ends of Loch Eriboll and Loch Hope. Height 1709 feet or 521 metres. **103 G3** NC4152.

An Leth-allt *High.* ***River***, rising on slopes below Carn Coire na Caorach and flowing E into River Dulnain, 4m/6km W of Carrbridge. **89 F2** NH8621.

An Liathanach *High.* ***Mountain***, in Ross and Cromarty district, consisting of twin peaks at 1666 feet or 508 metres and 1588 feet or 484 metres in height, on S shore of Loch a' Chroisg 2m/3km SW of Achnasheen. **95 H6** NH1057.

An Lurg *High.* ***Mountain***, 4m/7km E of Loch Morlich. Height 2470 feet or 753 metres. **89 H4** NJ0409.

An Riabhachan *High.* ***Mountain***, in Skye and Lochalsh district rising to N of Loch Mullardoch. Munro: height 3703 feet or 1129 metres. **87 H1** NH1334.

An Ruadh-mheallan *High.* ***Mountain***, 2m/3km W of Beinn Alligin, Ross and Cromarty district. Height 2204 feet or 672 metres. **94 E5** NG8361.

An Ruadh-stac *High.* ***Mountain***, peak on Ben-damph forest, Ross and Cromarty district, 4m/6km N of head of Loch Carron. Height 2926 feet or 892 metres. **95 F7** NG9248.

An Rubha *W.Isles Gaelic form of Eye Peninsula, qv.*

An Sgarsoch ***Mountain***, 12m/19km N of Blair Atholl, on border of Aberdeenshire and Perth & Kinross. Munro: height 3300 feet or 1006 metres. **89 G6** NN9383.

An Sguabach *High.* ***Mountain***, in Badenoch and Strathspey district, 4m/6km SW of Aviemore. Height 2486 feet or 758 metres. **89 F3** NH8310.

An Sgurr *High.* ***Mountain***, 3m/4km W of Lochcarron, Ross and Cromarty district. Height 1286 feet or 392 metres. **86 E1** NG8538.

An Sgurr (Also known as Scuir of Eigg or Sgurr of Eigg.) *High.* ***Mountain***, basaltic peak on Eigg, highest point on island. Height 1289 feet or 393 metres. **85 K6** NM4684.

An Sleaghach *High.* ***Mountain***, 3m/5km NE of Rubha an Ridire, Lochaber district. Height 1683 feet or 513 metres. **79 J3** NM7643.

An Sligearnach *P. & K.* ***Mountain***, on NW side of Glen Tilt, 9m/15km NE of Blair Atholl. Height 2578 feet or 786 metres. **89 G7** NN9578.

An Socach *Aber.* ***Inland physical feature***, mountain ridge, 6m/9km S of Inverey. W summit is a Munro at height of 3097 feet or 944 metres. **89 H6** NO0879.

An Socach *High.* ***Mountain***, 3m/4km NE of Kinlochbervie, Sutherland district. Height 1174 feet or 358 metres. **102 E3** NC2658.

An Socach *High.* ***Mountain***, on border between Inverness and Skye and Lochalsh districts, 4m/6km S of W end of Loch Mullardoch. Munro: height 3018 feet or 920 metres. **87 G2** NH0822.

An Socach *High.* ***Mountain***, in Skye and Lochalsh district, 2m/3km N of W end of Loch Mullardoch. Munro: height 3506 feet or 1069 metres. **87 G1** NH0933.

An Stac *High.* ***Mountain***, 2m/3km S of Lochailort, Lochaber district. Height 2670 feet or 814 metres. **86 D7** NM7679.

An Stac *High.* ***Mountain***, peak in Lochaber district 1km S of head of Loch Morar. Height 2355 feet or 718 metres. **86 E6** NM8688.

An Staonach *High.* ***Mountain***, in Ross and Cromarty district, 4m/6km N of head of Loch Kishorn. Height 1683 feet or 513 metres. **94 E7** NG8348.

An Stuc *High.* ***Mountain***, rising above Glen Oykel, 3m/4km SE of Loch Ailsh. Height 1194 feet or 364 metres. **95 K1** NC3409.

An Stuc *P. & K.* ***Mountain***, in Ben Lawers group, 1m/2km N of Ben Lawers and 7m/12km NE of Killin. Munro: height 3667 feet or 1118 metres. NN6343.

An Suidhe *Arg. & B.* ***Mountain***, in Eredine Forest, 5m/9km W of Inveraray. Height 1686 feet or 514 metres. **80 B7** NN0007.

An Suidhe *High.* ***Mountain***, in Badenoch and Strathspey district, 5m/8km NE of Kingussie. Height 1774 feet or 541 metres. **89 F4** NH8107.

An t-Eilean Meadhoin *High.* ***Island***, wooded islet in Loch Morar, Lochaber district, 1m/2km E of dam at W end of loch. NM7092.

An T-òb *W.Isles Gaelic form of Leverburgh, qv.*

An t-Sàil *High.* ***Mountain***, midway between Loch Lurgainn and W coast of Ross and Cromarty district. Height 1607 feet or 490 metres. **95 G1** NC0607.

An Tairbeart *W.Isles Gaelic form of Tarbert, qv.*

An Teallach *High.* ***Mountain***, in W part of Ross and Cromarty district 3m/4km SW of Little Loch Broom. Summit is Bidein a' Ghlas Thuill, a Munro at height of 3483 feet or 1062 metres. **95 G3** NH0684.

An Torc (Also known as Boar of Badenoch.) ***Mountain***, on border of Perth & Kinross and Highland, on W side of Pass of Drumochter and 6m/9km S of Dalwhinnie. Height 2424 feet or 739 metres. **88 D7** NN6276.

An Tunna *N.Ayr.* ***Mountain***, on Arran, 3m/5km W of Brodick. Height 1184 feet or 361 metres. **73 H7** NR9736.

An Uidh *High.* ***River***, rising on slopes of Sròn Ach' a' Bhacaidh and flowing SE into Loch an Lagain, 3m/5km NE of Bonar Bridge. **96 D2** NH6297.

Anaboard *High.* ***Settlement***, 3m/4km E of S end of Lochindorb, and 3m/5km S of Dava. **89 H1** NJ0033.

Anafon *Gwyn.* ***River***, rising S of Llyn Anafon, running through tarn, then NW into River Rhaeadr-fawr, 2m/3km SW of Llanfairfechan. **46 E5** SH6671.

Anaheilt *High.* ***Settlement***, adjoining to N of Strontian, Lochaber district. **79 K1** NM8162.

Ancaster *Lincs.* ***Village***, 5m/9km W of Sleaford, on site of Roman town of Causennae. Airfield on Barkston Heath to SW. **42 C1** SK9843.

Ancholme ***River***, rising near Spridlington and flowing N into River Humber at Ferriby Sluice. From Bishopbridge, New River Ancholme has been artificially created and follows a straight course, almost entirely separate from mostly circuitous course of Old River Ancholme. See also Old Ancholme and New Ancholme. SE9721.

Anchor *Shrop.* ***Hamlet***, 6m/10km SE of Newcastle. **38 A7** SO1785.

Anchor Corner *Norf.* ***Settlement***, 3m/5km NW of Attleborough. TM0098.
Anchor Street *Norf.* ***Locality***, 4m/7km SE of North Walsham. TG3124.
Anchorsholme *B'pool* ***Suburb***, of Blackpool, 1m/2km W of Thornton. SD3241.
Ancient House Museum *Norf.* ***Other feature of interest***, in Tudor house in Thetford, with displays of local history. **44 C7** TL8683.
Ancient Yew Tree (Also known as Fortingall Yew.) *P. & K.* ***Other feature of interest***, yew tree in Fortingall churchyard, reputedly more than 3000 years old and possibly the oldest tree in Europe. **81 J3** NN7347.
Ancoats *Gt.Man.* ***Suburb***, 1m/2km E of Manchester city centre. SJ8598.
Ancroft *Northumb.* ***Hamlet***, 5m/8km S of Berwick-upon-Tweed. **77 H6** NU0045.
Ancrum *Sc.Bord.* ***Village***, 3m/5km NW of Jedburgh. **70 B1** NT6224.
Ancton *W.Suss.* ***Suburb***, in Middleton-on-Sea, 3m/5km E of Bognor Regis. **12 C6** SU9800.
Anderby *Lincs.* ***Village***, 4m/7km E of Alford. **53 J5** TF5275.
Anderby Creek *Lincs.* ***Hamlet***, on coast, at outfall of stream known as Main Drain, 3m/4km N of Chapel St. Leonards. TF5476.
Anderida *E.Suss.* *See Pevensey.*
Andersea *Som.* ***Hamlet***, 3m/5km SE of Bridgwater. ST3333.
Andersfield *Som.* ***Hamlet***, 1km W of Goathurst and 4m/6km SW of Bridgwater. ST2434.
Anderson *Dorset* ***Hamlet***, 3m/4km NE of Bere Regis. **9 H5** SY8897.
Anderton *Ches.* ***Locality***, 1m/2km NW of Northwich. Boat lift forms junction between River Weaver and Trent and Mersey Canal. **49 F5** SJ6475.
Andover *Hants.* Population: 34,647. ***Town***, medieval market town on River Anton, 13m/21km NW of Winchester. New town development. Museum of Iron Age sited here. **21 G7** SU3645.
Andover Down *Hants.* ***Settlement***, 2m/3km E of Andover. **21 G7** SU3946.
Andoversford *Glos.* ***Village***, 5m/8km E of Cheltenham. **30 B6** SP0219.
Andreas *I.o.M.* ***Village***, 4m/7km NW of Ramsey. **54 D4** SC4199.
Anelog *Gwyn.* ***Settlement***, on SW tip of Lleyn Peninsula, 1m/2km NW of Aberdaron. **36 A3** SH1527.
Anerley *Gt.Lon.* ***Suburb***, in borough of Bromley, 1m/2km S of Crystal Palace. TQ3469.
Anfield *Mersey.* ***Suburb***, 3m/4km NE of Liverpool city centre. SJ3793.
Angarrack *Cornw.* ***Village***, 2m/3km E of Hayle. **2 C5** SW5838.
Angarrick *Cornw.* ***Settlement***, 2m/3km N of Penryn. SW7937.
Angel Corner *Suff.* *See Bury St. Edmunds.*
Angelbank *Shrop.* ***Hamlet***, 4m/6km E of Ludlow. SO5776.
Angell Town *Gt.Lon.* ***Suburb***, in borough of Lambeth, 3m/4km S of Charing Cross. TQ3176.
Angersleigh *Som.* ***Hamlet***, 4m/6km SE of Wellington. **7 K4** ST1919.
Angerton *Cumb.* ***Locality***, adjoining to N of Kirkbride. **60 D1** NY2257.
Angle *Pembs.* ***Village***, fishing village at W end of Angle Bay on S side of Milford Haven channel. **16 B4** SM8602.
Angle Bay *Pembs.* ***Bay***, on S side of Milford Haven channel. **16 B4** SM8602.
Angler's Retreat *Cere.* ***Settlement***, 5m/8km S of Machynlleth on N shore of New Pool. **37 G6** SN7492.
Anglesey *Hants.* ***Suburb***, S district of Gosport. SZ6098.
Anglesey (Ynys Môn). *I.o.A.* ***Island***, known to the Romans as Mona, measuring 26m/42km E to W and 21m/33km N to S, separated from NW coast of Welsh mainland by Menai Strait. To W of main island lies Holy Island on which Holyhead, the principal town, is situated. Anglesey is connected to Welsh mainland, and Holy Island to main island, by road and railway bridges. **46 B4** SH4080.
Anglesey Abbey *Cambs.* ***Historic house***, National Trust property built c. 1600 on site of medieval Augustinian monastery, at Lode. Includes 100 acre garden and arboretum. **33 J2** TL5262.
Anglezarke *Lancs.* ***Locality***, moorland parish, to N of Horwich. SD6217.
Anglezarke Moor ***Open space***, moorland on border of Lancashire and Blackburn with Darwen, 4m/7km SW of Darwen with Anglezarke Reservoir on SW side. **49 F1** SD6318.
Angmering *W.Suss.* ***Suburb***, 3m/5km NE of Littlehampton. **12 D6** TQ0604.
Angmering-on-Sea *W.Suss.* ***Suburb***, part of coastal resort development, 2m/3km S of Angmering. TQ0601.
Angram *N.Yorks.* ***Hamlet***, 4m/6km NE of Tadcaster. **58 B5** SE5148.
Angram *N.Yorks.* ***Settlement***, 2m/3km NW of Muker. SD8899.
Angram Common *N.Yorks.* ***Open space***, remote moorland at head of Swaledale, 4m/7km W of Muker. **61 K7** SD8499.
Angram Grange *N.Yorks.* ***Settlement***, 1m/2km N of Husthwaite. SE5176.
Angram Reservoir *N.Yorks.* ***Reservoir***, near source of River Nidd 10m/16km NW of Pateley Bridge. **57 F2** SE0476.
Angry Brow *Mersey.* ***Coastal feature***, sandbank on N side of small channel on Southport Sands, 3m/4km W of Southport. **48 C1** SD3019.
Angus Folk Museum *Angus* ***Other feature of interest***, National Trust for Scotland property in Glamis, 4m/7km S of Kirriemuir; collection of 19c domestic memorabilia and furniture. **82 E3** NO3846.
Anick *Northumb.* ***Locality***, 1m/2km NE of Hexham. NY9565.
Anie *Stir.* ***Settlement***, 3m/5km NW of Callander. **81 G6** NN5810.
Anker ***River***, rising near Wolvey and flowing NW into River Tame at Tamworth. SK2003.
Ankerville *High.* ***Settlement***, in Ross and Cromarty district, 3m/5km W of Balintore on E coast. **97 F4** NH8174.
Ankerville Corner *High.* ***Locality***, adjoins to NE of Ankerville. NH8174.
Ankle Hill *Leics.* ***Suburb***, to S of Melton Mowbray town centre. SK7518.
Anlaby *E.Riding* ***Village***, 4m/7km W of Kingston upon Hull city centre. **59 G7** TA0328.
Anmer *Norf.* ***Village***, 10m/15km NE of King's Lynn. **44 B3** TF7429.
Anmore *Hants.* ***Hamlet***, 1km E of Denmead and 3m/4km W of Horndean. SU6711.
Anna Valley *Hants.* ***Village***, 2m/3km SW of Andover. **21 G7** SU3443.
Annan *D. & G.* ***River***, rising on Devil's Beeftub, N of Moffat, and flowing S past Moffat, Lochmaben and Annan to Solway Firth 1m/2km S of Annan. **69 G6** NY1963.
Annan *D. & G.* Population: 8930. ***Small town***, near mouth of River Annan, 15m/24km E of Dumfries and same distance NW of Carlisle across Solway Firth. Market. **69 G7** NY1966.
Annandale *D. & G.* ***Valley***, carrying River Annan from Ericstane in N to Moffat in S. **69 F3** NT0903.
Annaside *Cumb.* ***Settlement***, 1m/2km SW of Bootle. **54 D1** SD0986.
Annat *Arg. & B.* ***Settlement***, on N side of Loch Awe, 1km S of Kilchrenan. **80 B5** NN0322.
Annat *High.* ***Locality***, at head of Loch Linnhe, 2m/4km NW of Fort William across head of loch. NN0877.
Annat *High.* ***Settlement***, at head of Upper Loch Torridon, Ross and Cromarty district, 1m/2km S of Torridon. **94 E6** NG8954.
Annat Bay *High.* ***Bay***, gently curving bay on SW side of entrance to Loch Broom, on W coast of Ross and Cromarty district. **95 G2** NH0496.
Annathill *N.Lan.* ***Settlement***, 3m/5km N of Coatbridge. NS7271.
Annbank *S.Ayr.* ***Village***, 5m/7km E of Ayr. **67 J1** NS4023.
Anne Hathaway's Cottage *Warks.* ***Historic house***, with garden, in Shottery, W part of Stratford-upon-Avon. Traditional birthplace of Shakespeare's wife. **30 C3** SP1854.
Annell ***River***, rising at NE corner of Dolaucothi Estate, NE of Pumsaint and flowing SW into River Cothi 1m/2km E of Llansawel. **27 F4** SN6435.
Annesley *Notts.* ***Hamlet***, adjoining to E of Annesley Woodhouse, 5m/8km SW of Mansfield. **51 H7** SK5053.
Annesley Woodhouse *Notts.* ***Locality***, 2m/3km S of Kirkby in Ashfield. **51 H7** SK4953.
Annet *I.o.S.* ***Island***, second largest of uninhabited islands of Isles of Scilly, lying W of St. Agnes. **2 B2** SV8608.
Annet Burn *Stir.* ***River***, flowing S into River Teith, 5m/8km SE of Callander. **81 H7** NN7002.
Annfield Plain *Dur.* Population: 10,522. ***Town***, 2m/3km SW of Stanley. Previously a sheep-farming town, then 19c mining community. **62 C1** NZ1751.
Annick Water ***River***, running SW past Stewarton to join River Irvine on S side of town of Irvine. **74 B6** NS3237.
Anniesland *Glas.* ***Suburb***, 4m/6km NW of Glasgow city centre. NS5468.
Annitsford *T. & W.* ***Locality***, 2m/3km S of Cramlington. NZ2674.
Annscroft *Shrop.* ***Settlement***, 4m/6km SW of Shrewsbury. **38 D5** SJ4507.
Ansdell *Lancs.* ***Suburb***, to N of Lytham St. Anne's town centre. **55 G7** SD3428.
Ansford *Som.* ***Village***, adjoining to N of Castle Cary. **9 F1** ST6333.
Ansley *Warks.* ***Village***, 4m/6km W of Nuneaton. **40 E6** SP2991.
Anslow *Staffs.* ***Village***, 2m/3km NW of Burton upon Trent. **40 E3** SK2125.
Anslow Gate *Staffs.* ***Hamlet***, 1m/2km W of Anslow. **40 D3** SK2125.
Anslow Leys *Staffs.* ***Hamlet***, 1km SW of Anslow. SK2024.
Ansteadbrook *Surr.* ***Settlement***, 2m/3km E of Haslemere. SU9332.
Anstey *Herts.* ***Village***, 4m/6km NE of Buntingford. **33 H5** TL4033.
Anstey *Leics.* Population: 6192. ***Village***, 4m/6km NW of Leicester. **41 H5** SK5408.
Anstruther *Fife* Population: 3154. ***Small town***, resort and fishing port on Firth of Forth, 9m/14km SE of St. Andrews. Formerly port for herring fishing industry. Scottish Fisheries museum. **83 G7** NO5603.
Anstruther Easter *Fife* ***Locality***, adjoins to E of Anstruther, on N coast of Firth of Forth. NO5703.
Anstruther Wester *Fife* ***Locality***, adjoins to W of Anstruther, on N coast of Firth of Forth. NO5603.
Ansty *Dorset* ***Locality***, in parish of Hilton, 6m/10km N of Puddletown. Comprises hamlets of Higher Ansty and Lower Ansty, with settlements of Ansty Cross and Little Ansty. ST7603.
Ansty *Warks.* ***Village***, 5m/8km NE of Coventry. **41 F7** SP3983.
Ansty *W.Suss.* ***Village***, 1m/2km SW of Cuckfield. **13 F4** TQ2923.
Ansty *Wilts.* ***Village***, 2m/3km S of Tisbury. **9 J2** ST9526.
Ansty Coombe *Wilts.* ***Hamlet***, adjoining to W of Ansty, 2m/3km S of Tisbury. ST9526.
Ansty Cross *Dorset* ***Settlement***, forms part of Ansty locality in parish of Hilton, 6m/10km N of Puddletown. ST7603.
Ant ***River***, rising at Antingham and flowing S, past North Walsham, through marshland and Barton Broad to River Bure, 2m/3km E of Horning. TG3715.
Anthill Common *Hants.* ***Hamlet***, 1m/2km S of Hambledon. **11 H3** SU6412.
Anthorn *Cumb.* ***Hamlet***, on N shore of River Wampool estuary, 3m/4km W of Kirkbride across river. **60 C1** NY1958.
Antingham *Norf.* ***Village***, 3m/4km NW of North Walsham. **45 G2** TG2532.
Antonine Wall ***Historic/prehistoric site***, Roman fortification (Historic Scotland) dating from 1c, now only intermittently visible, extending 37m/60km from Old Kilpatrick on N bank of River Clyde to Carriden, E of Bo'ness on S bank of River Forth. **75 G3** NS7677.
Anton's Gowt *Lincs.* ***Hamlet***, at confluence of River Witham and Newham Drain, 3m/5km NW of Boston. **43 F1** TF2947.
Antony *Cornw.* ***Village***, 3m/4km W of Torpoint. Antony House (National Trust) to NE. **4 D5** SX3954.
Antony House *Cornw.* ***Historic house***, 18c mansion (National Trust), to NE of Antony and NW of Torpoint. Grounds run down to St. Germans River, and include a woodland garden. **4 E5** SX4156.
Antrobus *Ches.* ***Hamlet***, 2m/3km NW of Great Budworth. **49 F5** SJ6479.
Anvil Corner *Devon* ***Hamlet***, 2m/3km E of Holsworthy. **6 B5** SS3704.
Anvil Green *Kent* ***Settlement***, 6m/9km SW of Canterbury. TR1049.
Anwick *Lincs.* ***Village***, 4m/7km NE of Sleaford. **52 E7** TF1150.
Anwoth *D. & G.* ***Village***, 1m/2km W of Gatehouse of Fleet. 8c cross in churchyard of former, ruined, church. **65 F5** NX5856.
Aonach air Chrith *High.* ***Mountain***, peak to E of Maol Chinn-dearg and summit of ridge on border of Lochaber and Skye and Lochalsh districts. Munro: height 3349 feet or 1021 metres. **87 G4** NH0508.
Aonach Beag *High.* ***Mountain***, in Lochaber district 2m/3km E of Ben Nevis. Munro: height 4054 feet or 1236 metres. **87 H7** NN1971.
Aonach Beag *High.* ***Mountain***, in Badenoch and Strathspey district 2m/3km W of Loch an Sgòir. Munro: height 3654 feet or 1114 metres. **88 B7** NN4574.
Aonach Buidhe *High.* ***Mountain***, on Killilan Forest, Skye and Lochalsh district. Height 2949 feet or 899 metres. **87 G1** NH0532.
Aonach Dubh *High.* *See The Three Sisters.*
Aonach Eagach *High.* ***Inland physical feature***, mountain ridge on N side of Glen Coe. Summit is Sgorr nam Fiannaidh at W end of ridge; Munro at height 3172 feet or 967 metres. **80 C2** NN1458.
Aonach Meadhoin *High.* ***Mountain***, in Lochaber district on N side of Glen Shiel, 2m/4km W of Loch Cluanie. Munro: height 3290 feet or 1003 metres. **87 G3** NH0413.
Aonach Mòr *High.* ***Inland physical feature***, mountain ridge rising to summit of 2837 feet or 865 metres in Lochaber district, to W of Clach Leathad. **80 D3** NN2247.
Aonach Mòr *High.* ***Mountain***, E of Ben Nevis, 1m/2km along ridge to N of Aonach Beag. Munro: height 3998 feet or 1219 metres. **87 H7** NN1972.
Aonach Odhar *High.* ***Mountain***, in Inverness district, 15m/24km N of Newtonmore. Height 2106 feet or 642 metres. **88 E2** NH7022.
Aonach Sgoilte *High.* ***Inland physical feature***, mountain ridge in Knoydart, 1m/2km NE of Loch an Dubh-Lochain. **86 E4** NG8302.
Aonach Shasuinn *High.* ***Mountain***, in Inverness district 5m/8km N of dam of Loch Cluanie. Height 2916 feet or 889 metres. **87 H3** NH1718.
Aoradh *Arg. & B.* ***Settlement***, on Islay, 5m/8km NW of Bridgend. **72 A4** NR2767.
Ape Dale *Shrop.* ***Valley***, carrying Byne Brook, on W side of Wenlock Edge to NE of Craven Arms. **38 D7** SO4889.
Apes Dale *Worcs.* ***Locality***, 3m/4km NE of Bromsgrove. SO9972.
Apes Hall *Cambs.* ***Settlement***, 2m/3km NW of Littleport. **43 J7** TL5590.
Apethorpe *Northants.* ***Village***, 4m/6km SW of Wansford. Site of Roman villa in park of mainly 16c and 17c hall. **42 D6** TL0295.
Apeton *Staffs.* ***Settlement***, 1km NE of Church Eaton. SJ8518.
Apley *Lincs.* ***Village***, 2m/4km SW of Wragby. **52 E5** TF1075.
Apperknowle *Derbys.* ***Village***, 2m/3km E of Dronfield. **51 F5** SK3878.
Apperley *Glos.* ***Village***, 7m/11km NW of Cheltenham. **29 H6** SO8628.
Apperley Bridge *W.Yorks.* ***Suburb***, on River Aire, in NE part of Bradford, 1m/2km NW of Calverley. SE1937.
Apperley Dene *Northumb.* ***Locality***, 4m/6km NW of Ebchester. Site of small Roman fort to S. NZ0558.
Appersett *N.Yorks.* ***Settlement***, at confluence of Widdale Beck and River Ure, 1m/2km NW of Hawes. SD8590.
Appin ***Large natural feature***, mountainous area bounded by E shore of Loch Linnhe, Glen Creran and Glen Coe. Strath of Appin runs across SW part, forming a natural pass between Loch Linnhe and Loch Creran. NN0051.
Appin House *Arg. & B.* ***Settlement***, 3m/5km NE of Port Appin. **80 A3** NM9349.
Appin of Dull *P. & K.* *Alternative name for Strath of Appin, qv.*
Appin Rocks *Arg. & B.* ***Coastal feature***, 1km SW of Port Appin at NW entrance to Airds Bay. **79 K3** NM8944.
Appleby *N.Lincs.* Population: 2570. ***Village***, 5m/8km NE of Scunthorpe. **52 C1** SE9514.
Appleby-in-Westmorland *Cumb.* ***Small town***, on River Eden, 12m/19km SE of Penrith. Castle with 12c keep. Famous for its Horse Fair, which attracts many gypsies. **61 H4** NY6820.
Appleby-in-Westmorland Castle *Cumb.* ***Castle***, 12c castle with original keep, on W side of River Eden, on S side of Appleby-in-Westmorland; restored in 17c. **61 H4** NY6819.
Appleby Magna *Leics.* ***Village***, 5m/8km SW of Ashby de la Zouch. **41 F4** SK3109.

Appleby Parva *Leics.* ***Village***, 1km SW of Appleby Magna. **41 F5** SK3109.
Appleby Street *Herts.* ***Locality***, 2m/4km NW of Cheshunt. TL3304.
Applecross *High.* ***River***, runs SW into Applecross Bay on W coast of Ross and Cromarty district. **94 D7** NG7144.
Applecross *High.* ***Village***, at S end of Applecross Bay on W coast of Ross and Cromarty district, opposite Raasay across Inner Sound. **94 D7** NG7144.
Applecross Bay *High.* ***Bay***, on W coast of Ross and Cromarty district, N of Applecross, opposite Raasay across Inner Sound. NG7145.
Applecross Forest *High.* ***Open space***, deer forest to E of Applecross. **94 D7** NG7144.
Appledore *Devon* ***Hamlet***, 7m/11km SW of West Wellington. **7 J4** ST0614.
Appledore *Devon* Population: 2187. ***Village***, on W side of River Torridge estuary, at its confluence with River Taw, 3m/4km N of Bideford. **6 C2** SS4630.
Appledore *Kent* ***Village***, on W side of Romney Marsh, 5m/8km SE of Tenterden. **14 E5** TQ9529.
Appledore Heath *Kent* ***Hamlet***, adjoins to N of Appledore. 14c Horne's Place Chapel (English Heritage) to NE. **14 E4** TQ9530.
Appledram *W.Suss.* *Alternative spelling of Apuldram, qv.*
Appleford *Oxon.* ***Village***, 2m/4km N of Didcot. **21 J2** SU5293.
Applegarth Town *D. & G.* ***Locality***, 3m/4km NW of Lockerbie. NY1084.
Appleshaw *Hants.* ***Village***, 4m/7km NW of Andover. **21 G7** SU3048.
Applethwaite *Cumb.* ***Hamlet***, 1m/2km N of Keswick. **60 D4** NY2625.
Applethwaite Common *Cumb.* ***Open space***, heathland 3m/5km E of Ambleside. **60 F6** NY4202.
Appleton *Ches.* ***Suburb***, 1m/2km N of Widnes town centre. SJ5186.
Appleton *Norf.* ***Locality***, 1m/2km SE of Sandringham. Site of Roman villa 1km E. TF7027.
Appleton *Oxon.* ***Village***, 4m/7km NW of Abingdon. **21 H1** SP4401.
Appleton-le-Moors *N.Yorks.* ***Village***, 5m/7km NW of Pickering. **58 D1** SE7387.
Appleton-le-Street *N.Yorks.* ***Village***, 4m/6km W of Malton. **58 D2** SE7373.
Appleton Roebuck *N.Yorks.* ***Village***, 4m/7km E of Tadcaster. **58 B5** SE5542.
Appleton Thorn *Warr.* ***Village***, in SE part of Warrington. **49 F4** SJ6383.
Appleton Wiske *N.Yorks.* ***Village***, 6m/9km SW of Yarm. **62 E6** NZ3904.
Appletreehall *Sc.Bord.* ***Settlement***, 2m/4km NE of Hawick. **70 A2** NT5117.
Appletreewick *N.Yorks.* ***Village***, in Wharfedale, 2m/3km SE of Burnsall. **57 F3** SE0560.
Appletreewick Moor *N.Yorks.* ***Open space***, moorland on N side of Grimwith Reservoir, 6m/9km W of Pateley Bridge. **57 F3** SE0665.
Appley *I.o.W.* ***Suburb***, to NE of Ryde and to S of Ryde East Sands. SZ6092.
Appley *Som.* ***Hamlet***, 4m/7km W of Wellington. **7 J3** ST0721.
Appley Bridge *Lancs.* Population: 5618. ***Village***, 1m/2km NW of Shevington. **48 E1** SD5209.
Appuldurcombe House *I.o.W.* ***Historic house***, ruined early 18c home (English Heritage) of Worsley family, 1km W of Wroxhall. **11 G7** SZ5480.
Apse Heath *I.o.W.* ***Village***, 2m/3km W of Sandown. **11 G6** SZ5683.
Apsey Green *Suff.* ***Settlement***, 1km W of Framlingham. TM2763.
Apsley *Herts.* ***Suburb***, to S of Hemel Hempstead. **22 D1** TL0605.
Apsley End *Beds.* ***Hamlet***, 5m/8km NW of Hitchin. **32 E5** TL1233.
Apuldram (Name of village sometimes spelled Appledram.) *W.Suss.* ***Village***, 1m/2km SW of Chichester. Medieval manor house. **12 B6** SU8403.
Aquae Arnemetiae *Derbys.* *See Buxton.*
Aquae Sulis *B. & N.E.Som.* *See Bath.*
Aqualate Mere *Staffs.* ***Lake/loch***, large lake in park 2m/3km NE of Newport. **39 G3** SJ7720.
Aquhythie *Aber.* ***Locality***, 2m/3km N of Kemnay. NJ7418.
Arabella *High.* ***Locality***, in Ross and Cromarty district, 4m/7km S of Tain. NH8075.
Aran *Powys* ***River***, rising about 4m/6km NE of Llanbister and flowing S into River Ithon, 1m/2km N of Penybont. **28 A2** SO1165.
Aran Benllyn *Gwyn.* ***Inland physical feature***, mountain ridge rising to 2900 feet or 884 metres, 4m/6km S of Llanuwchllyn. **37 H3** SH8624.
Aran Fawddwy *Gwyn.* ***Mountain***, 5m/7km N of Dinas-Mawddwy. Height 2975 feet or 907 metres. **37 H3** SH8622.
Arbeadie *Aber.* ***Suburb***, NE district of Banchory. NO7096.
Arberth *Pembs.* *Welsh form of Narberth, qv.*
Arbigland *D. & G.* ***Garden***, on Solway Firth, 1m/2km SE of Kirkbean, which includes water gardens, woodland and a bay. Birthplace of John Paul, later known as Paul Jones, 1747-92, founder of the American navy, whose father was gardener here. **65 K5** NX9857.
Arbirlot *Angus* ***Village***, 3m/4km W of Arbroath. To SE is Kellie Castle, 16c and earlier, former seat of the Auchterlonies. **83 G3** NO6040.
Arbor Low *Derbys.* ***Historic/prehistoric site***, ancient stone circle (English Heritage), 3m/5km W of Youlgreave. Gib Hill Barrow (English Heritage) to W. **50 D6** SK1663.
Arborfield *W'ham* Population: 1825. ***Village***, 5m/7km SE of Reading. **22 A5** SU7567.
Arborfield Cross *W'ham* ***Village***, 1km SE of Arborfield. **22 A5** SU7567.
Arborfield Garrison *W'ham* ***Military establishment***, garrison of Royal Electrical Mechanical Engineers, 3m/5km SW of Wokingham. Includes REME Museum of Technology. **22 A5** SU7665.
Arbory Hill *S.Lan.* ***Mountain***, with hillfort at summit, 1m/2km E of Abington. Height 1407 feet or 429 metres. **68 E1** NS9423.
Arbourthorne *S.Yorks.* ***Suburb***, 2m/3km SE of Sheffield city centre. SK3785.
Arbroath *Angus* Population: 23,474. ***Town***, industrial town, port with small harbour, and resort, 15m/25km NE of Dundee. Substantial remains of Arbroath Abbey (Historic Scotland). Famed for local delicacy of traditionally smoked haddock, or smokies. **83 H3** NO6440.
Arbroath Abbey *Angus* ***Ecclesiastical building***, substantial remains of Tironensian monastery (Historic Scotland) in centre of Arbroath. Founded in 1178 by William the Lion, King of Scots, it is linked with Scottish nationalism. Declaration of Arbroath, asserting Scotland's independence from England was signed here in 1320, and Stone of Destiny was found here in 1951, having been taken from Westminster Abbey. Notable remains include good example of an abbot's residence. **83 H3** NO6441.
Arbury *Warr.* ***Settlement***, 1km E of Winwick. SJ6192.
Arbury *Warks.* ***Historic house***, 17c-18c Gothic Revival mansion in park, 2m/4km SW of Nuneaton. **41 F7** SP3389.
Arbury Hill *Northants.* ***Hill***, 3m/4km SW of Daventry. Height 735 feet or 224 metres. **31 G3** SP5458.
Arbuthnot Museum *Aber.* ***Other feature of interest***, museum of local fishing industry history and art gallery in St. Peter Street, Peterhead. Includes large coin collection. **99 K6** NK1247.
Arbuthnott *Aber.* ***Village***, 2m/4km NW of Inverbervie. **91 G7** NO8074.
Arbuthnott House *Aber.* ***Historic house***, on N side of Bervie Water, 3m/4km NE of Inverbervie. 13c home of Arbuthnott family, featuring 17c walled garden. **91 F7** NO7975.
Arcadia *Kent* ***Locality***, 2m/3km N of Tenterden. TQ8736.
Archdeacon Newton *Darl.* ***Hamlet***, on site of former village, 3m/4km NW of Darlington. **62 D5** NZ2517.
Archiestown *Moray* ***Village***, 4m/6km W of Craigellachie. **97 K7** NJ2344.
Arclid *Ches.* ***Village***, 2m/3km NE of Sandbach. **49 G6** SJ7862.
Arcuil *High.* *Gaelic form of Arkle, qv.*
Ard a' Chapuill (Anglicised form: Ardachuple). *Arg. & B.* ***Settlement***, lodge and farm dwellings, 1m/2km S of Auchenbreck. **73 J3** NS0279.
Ard Bheinn *N.Ayr.* ***Mountain***, on Arran, 4m/6km NE of Blackwaterfoot. Height 1679 feet or 512 metres. **73 H7** NR9432.
Ard Manish (Gaelic form: Aird Mhànais.) *W.Isles* ***Island***, small island off SE coast of South Harris, 1km S of Aird Leimhe. **93 G3** NG1188.
Ard More Mangersta. *W.Isles* *Anglicised form of Aird Mhòr Mangurstadh, qv.*
Ard Thurinish *High.* ***Coastal feature***, headland at S end of Sleat peninsula, Skye, 2m/4km E of Point of Sleat. **86 C5** NM5999.
Arda Beaga *W.Isles* ***Coastal feature***, promontory on W coast of North Harris, 1m/2km SE of Huisinis. **100 C6** NA9909.
Ardachadail *High.* ***Locality***, on NE shore of Loch Broom, 3m/5km NW of Ullapool. NH0997.
Ardacheranbeg *Arg. & B.* ***Settlement***, 1m/2km N of Clachan of Glendaruel. Standing stone to NE. **73 J2** NS0085.
Ardacheranmor *Arg. & B.* ***Settlement***, 3m/4km NE of Clachan of Glendaruel. **73 J2** NS0087.
Ardachoil *Arg. & B.* ***Settlement***, 3m/4km W of Grass Point, to N of Loch Spelve, Mull. **79 J4** NM7030.
Ardachuple *Arg. & B.* *Anglicised form of Ard a' Chapuill, qv.*
Ardachvie *High.* ***Settlement***, on NE side of Loch Arkaig, 4m/7km NW of Gairlochy. **87 H5** NN1390.
Ardailly *Arg. & B.* ***Settlement***, on N part of Gigha, just N of Mill Loch. **72 E5** NR6450.
Ardalanish *Arg. & B.* ***Settlement***, on Ross of Mull, 2m/3km S of Bunessan, a short distance inland from Ardalanish Bay on S coast. **78 E6** NM3719.
Ardalanish Point *Arg. & B.* *Anglicised form of Rubh' Ardalanish, qv.*
Ardallie *Aber.* ***Settlement***, 3m/5km NW of Hatton. **91 J1** NK0039.
Ardanaiseig *Arg. & B.* ***Settlement***, 3m/4km SW of Lochawe across NW arm of Loch Awe. **80 B5** NN0824.
Ardanaiseig Gardens *Arg. & B.* ***Garden***, mainly woodland gardens with a variety of trees, rhododendrons and flowering shrubs. Magnificent views across Loch Awe. 3m/4km SW of Lochawe across NW arm of Loch Awe. **80 B5** NN0824.
Ardaneaskan *High.* ***Settlement***, in Ross and Cromarty district, on N shore of Loch Carron, 2m/3km NE of Plockton across loch. **86 E1** NG8335.
Ardanstur *Arg. & B.* ***Settlement***, on N shore of Loch Melfort, on W side of Fearnach Bay. **79 K6** NM8213.
Ardantiobairt *High.* ***Settlement***, at head of Loch Teacuis, Lochaber district. **79 H2** NM6454.
Ardantrive *Arg. & B.* ***Settlement***, on Kerrera, 1km S of Rubh' a' Bhearnaig. **79 K5** NM8429.
Ardarroch *High.* ***Settlement***, in Ross and Cromarty district, at head of Loch Kishorn. **86 E1** NG8339.
Ardbeg *Arg. & B.* ***Hamlet***, S of Ardbeg Point, forming part of Port Bannatyne, large village and resort extending along coast on both sides of headland. **73 J4** NS0867.
Ardbeg *Arg. & B.* ***Settlement***, in Argyll, at head of Holy Loch. **73 K2** NS1583.
Ardbeg *Arg. & B.* ***Village***, small fishing village on S coast of Islay, 3m/5km E of Port Ellen. **72 C6** NR4146.
Ardbeg Point *Arg. & B.* ***Coastal feature***, headland on E coast of Bute between Kames Bay to N and Rothesay Bay to S. **73 J4** NS0867.
Ardblair *High.* ***Settlement***, 5m/7km N of Drumnadrochit. **88 B1** NH5036.
Ardbrecknish *Arg. & B.* ***Settlement***, on S side of Loch Awe, 1m/2km E of Portsonachan. **80 B5** NN0721.
Ardcharnich *High.* ***Settlement***, in Ross and Cromarty district, on E side of Loch Broom, 5m/7km SE of Ullapool. **95 H3** NH1788.
Ardchattan Gardens *Arg. & B.* ***Garden***, 4m/6km E of North Connel, to N of Loch Etive. 3 acres of wild and formal gardens, with good varieties of shrubs and roses. **80 A4** NM9734.
Ardchattan Priory *Arg. & B.* ***Ecclesiastical building***, 13c ruin (Historic Scotland) of Valliscaulian Priory on N side of Loch Etive, Argyll, opposite Airds Point. Meeting place of one of Robert the Bruce's parliaments in 1308; burned by English in 1654. **80 A4** NM9835.
Ardchiavaig *Arg. & B.* ***Settlement***, on S coast of Ross of Mull, 2m/3km S of Bunessan. **78 E6** NM3918.
Ardchonnel *Arg. & B.* ***Settlement***, 1m/2km S of Connel. **80 A4** NM9031.
Ardchonnell *Arg. & B.* ***Settlement***, on SE shore of Loch Awe, 1km E of Dalavich across loch. **80 A6** NM9812.
Ardchonnell Castle *Arg. & B.* *See Innis Chonnell.*
Ardchrishnish *Arg. & B.* ***Settlement***, near N coast of Ross of Mull, 3m/4km NE of Bunessan. **79 F5** NM4224.
Ardchronie *High.* ***Settlement***, on shore at NW end of Dornoch Firth, 2m/3km S of Bonar Bridge. **96 D3** NH6188.
Ardchuilk *High.* ***Settlement***, in Glen Strathfarrar, 11m/18km NW of Cannich. **87 J1** NH2638.
Ardchullarie More *Stir.* ***Settlement***, on E side of Loch Lubnaig, 4m/7km NW of Callander. **81 G6** NN5813.
Ardchyle *Stir.* ***Locality***, in Glen Dochart, 4m/7km SW of Killin. **81 G5** NN5229.
Ardclach Bell Tower *High.* ***Historic/prehistoric site***, fortified 17c belfry (Historic Scotland) above River Findhorn, 8m/13km SE of Nairn. **97 G7** NH9545.
Arddleen (Arddlin). *Powys* ***Hamlet***, 6m/9km NE of Welshpool. **38 B4** SJ2515.
Arddlin *Powys* *Alternative spelling of Arddleen, qv.*
Ardeer *N.Ayr.* ***Settlement***, adjoining to SE of Stevenston. NS2740.
Ardeley *Herts.* ***Village***, 5m/8km E of Stevenage. **33 G6** TL3027.
Ardelve *High.* ***Settlement***, on N side of Loch Alsh, Skye and Lochalsh district, 1km W of Dornie across entrance to Loch Long. **86 E2** NG8726.
Arden *Arg. & B.* ***Hamlet***, on SW shore of Loch Lomond, 3m/4km NW of Balloch. **74 B2** NS3684.
Arden Great Moor *N.Yorks.* ***Open space***, moorland 2m/4km NE of Cowesby and 8m/13km E of Northallerton. **63 G7** SE5092.
Ardencaple *Arg. & B.* ***Settlement***, on Seil, 1m/2km W of Clachan Bridge. **79 J6** NM7619.
Ardencraig Gardens *Arg. & B.* ***Garden***, on Bute, 1km E of Rothesay. Rare plants, ornamental ponds and aviaries. **73 K4** NS1064.
Ardens Grafton *Warks.* ***Village***, 5m/9km W of Stratford-upon-Avon. **30 C3** SP1154.
Ardentallan *Arg. & B.* ***Settlement***, on N shore of Loch Feochan, 1m/2km NE of Kilninver across loch. **79 K5** NM8323.
Ardentinny *Arg. & B.* ***Village***, on W shore of Loch Long, 4m/7km N of Strone Point. **73 K2** NS1887.
Ardeonaig *Stir.* ***Village***, on S side of Loch Tay, 6m/10km NE of Killin. **81 H4** NN6635.
Ardersier (Formerly known as Campbelltown.) *High.* Population: 1055. ***Village***, in Inverness district, on E shore of Inner Moray Firth or Inverness Firth, 2m/3km SE of Fort George. **96 E6** NH7855.
Ardery *High.* ***Settlement***, in Sunart, Lochaber district, 4m/6km W of Strontian. **79 J1** NM7562.
Ardessie *High.* ***Settlement***, in Ross and Cromarty district, on S shore of Little Loch Broom, 5m/8km SE of Badluchrach. **95 G3** NH0589.
Ardestie *Angus* ***Locality***, 1m/2km N of Monifieth, including ancient souterrain or earth-house (Historic Scotland). NO5034.
Ardfad *Arg. & B.* ***Settlement***, on Seil, 1m/2km N of Balvicar. **79 J6** NM7619.
Ardfern *Arg. & B.* ***Settlement***, on W side of Loch Craignish, in Argyll, 1m/2km SW of head of loch. **79 K7** NM8004.
Ardfin *Arg. & B.* ***Locality***, on Jura, 4m/6km SW of Craighouse. **72 C4** NR4863.
Ardgartan *Arg. & B.* ***Locality***, on W shore of Loch Long, at foot of Glen Croe, in Argyll. **80 D7** NN2702.
Ardgartan Forest *Arg. & B.* ***Forest/woodland***, to N and S along side of Loch Long, forming part of Argyll Forest Park. **80 D7** NN2702.
Ardgay *High.* ***Village***, in Sutherland district, 1m/2km SW of Bonar Bridge. Location of Bonar Bridge railway station. **96 C2** NH5990.
Ardgenavan *Arg. & B.* ***Settlement***, on N shore of NE arm of Loch Fyne, 5m/8km NE of Inveraray. **80 C6** NN1711.
Ardgoil Estate *Arg. & B.* ***Open space***, mountainous area between Loch Long and Loch Goil, forming part of Argyll Forest Park. **80 D7** NN2200.
Ardgour *High.* ***Locality***, mountainous area of Lochaber district, to E of Sunart and bounded by Lochs Shiel, Eil and Linnhe. Mountains are noted for craggy rock faces and signs of glacial weathering. They rise above deeply incised valleys of Glen Cona, Glen Scaddle and Glen Gour which all run E to Loch Linnhe. **80 A1** NM9570.
Ardgowan *Inclyde* ***Settlement***, 1km N of Inverkip. Includes ancient tower. **74 A3** NS2172.
Ardgowse *Aber.* ***Settlement***, on NW side of Corrennie Moor, 3m/5km SE of Alford. **90 E3** NJ6011.
Ardgye *Moray* ***Settlement***, 4m/6km W of Elgin. **97 J5** NJ1563.
Ardhallow *Arg. & B.* ***Settlement***, on Firth of Clyde, 3m/4km SW of Dunoon. **73 K3** NS1673.

Ardhasaig *W.Isles Anglicised form of Aird Asaig, qv.*
Ardheslaig *High.* ***Locality***, on SW side of Loch Torridon, Ross and Cromarty district, 3m/4km NW of Shieldaig. **94 D6** NG7856.
Ardiecow *Moray* ***Settlement***, on N side of Hill of Summertown, 1m/2km E of Kirktown of Deskford. **98 D4** NJ5361.
Ardinamar *Arg. & B.* ***Settlement***, on E coast of Luing, opposite Torsa. **79 J6** NM7511.
Ardindrean *High.* ***Settlement***, on W shore of Loch Broom, Ross and Cromarty district, 2m/4km from head of loch. **95 H3** NH1588.
Ardingly *W.Suss.* Population: 1594. ***Village***, 4m/6km N of Haywards Heath. Agricultural showground to N. **13 G4** TQ3429.
Ardingly Reservoir *W.Suss.* ***Reservoir***, 2m/3km to NW of Ardingly. **13 G4** TQ3429.
Ardington *Oxon.* ***Village***, 2m/4km E of Wantage. **21 H3** SU4388.
Ardington Wick *Oxon.* ***Settlement***, 3m/4km NE of Wantage. SU4389.
Ardintoul *High.* ***Settlement***, on S shore of Loch Alsh, 2m/3km SE of Balmacara across loch. **86 E2** NG8324.
Ardintoul Point *High.* ***Coastal feature***, promontory on S shore of Loch Alsh, Skye and Lochalsh district, 2m/3km E of entrance to Kyle Rhea. **86 E2** NG8324.
Ardivachar *W.Isles Anglicised form of Aird a' Mhachair, qv.*
Ardivachar Point *W.Isles* ***Coastal feature***, headland at NW corner of South Uist. **92 C7** NF7445.
Ardjachie Point *High.* ***Coastal feature***, promontory on S shore of Dornoch Firth, 2m/4km NW of Tain. **96 E3** NH7585.
Ardkinglas Woodland Garden *Arg. & B.* ***Garden***, surrounding Strone House in valley of Kinglas Water, 6m/9km N of Lochgoilhead. Woodland section dominated by collection of giant conifers, with formal gardens containing rhododendrons and azaleas. **80 C6** NN1810.
Ardlair *Aber.* ***Settlement***, 1m/2km SE of Kennethmont and 2m/3km S of Knockandy Hill. **90 D2** NJ5528.
Ardlamont *Arg. & B.* ***Settlement***, on SE tip of Cowal peninsula, 4m/7km S of Tighnabruaich. **73 H4** NR9865.
Ardlamont Bay *Arg. & B.* ***Bay***, 1m/2km NW of Ardlamont Point, 6m/10km W of Rothesay across Kyles of Bute. **73 H4** NR9663.
Ardlamont Point *Arg. & B.* ***Coastal feature***, headland in Argyll on N side of Sound of Bute, at junction of Kyles of Bute and Loch Fyne. **73 H4** NR9963.
Ardle *P. & K.* ***River***, running SE down Strathardle to join Black Water below Bridge of Cally and form River Ericht. **82 C2** NO1451.
Ardleigh *Essex* ***Village***, 5m/7km NE of Colchester. **34 E6** TM0529.
Ardleigh Green *Gt.Lon.* ***Suburb***, in borough of Havering, 1m/2km E of Romford. TQ5389.
Ardleigh Heath *Essex* ***Settlement***, 1km N of Ardleigh. TM0530.
Ardleigh Reservoir *Essex* ***Reservoir***, 3m/5km NE of Colchester town centre. **34 E6** TM0328.
Ardleish *Arg. & B.* ***Settlement***, at N end of Loch Lomond, 1km E of Ardlui across loch. **80 E6** NN3215.
Ardler *P. & K.* ***Village***, 3m/5km E of Coupar Angus. **82 D3** NO2641.
Ardley *Oxon.* ***Village***, 4m/7km NW of Bicester. **31 G6** SP5427.
Ardley End *Essex* ***Settlement***, 3m/5km E of Sawbridgeworth. TL5214.
Ardlui *Arg. & B.* ***Settlement***, at head of Loch Lomond, on W shore. **80 E6** NN3115.
Ardlussa *Arg. & B.* ***Settlement***, on E coast of Jura, nearly 1m/2km NE of Inverlussa, at mouth of Lussa River. Small bay and landing stage. **72 E2** NR6487.
Ardmaddy *Arg. & B.* ***Locality***, consisting of settlement and bay on E side of Loch Etive, Argyll, 5m/9km from head of loch. **80 B4** NN0737.
Ardmair *High.* ***Locality***, on W coast of Ross and Cromarty district, 3m/5km NW of Ullapool. **95 H2** NH1198.
Ardmaleish *Arg. & B.* ***Settlement***, on E coast of Bute, 1km S of Ardmaleish Point. **73 J4** NS0768.
Ardmaleish Point *Arg. & B.* ***Coastal feature***, headland on Bute at entrance to E arm of Kyles of Bute. **73 J4** NS0769.
Ardmay *Arg. & B.* ***Settlement***, on NE shore of Loch Long, at its N end, 1m/2km SW of Arrochar. **80 D7** NN2802.
Ardmeanach *Arg. & B.* ***Locality***, district on W coast of Mull, N of Loch Scridain. At its SW corner lies Burg, an area of National Trust for Scotland property. **79 F5** NM4428.
Ardmenish *Arg. & B.* ***Settlement***, 2m/3km NE of Ardfernal across Lowlandman's Bay, Jura. **72 D3** NR5774.
Ardmhòr *W.Isles* ***Settlement***, on peninsula of Àrd Mhòr, NE coast of Barra. **84 C4** NF7103.
Ardminish *Arg. & B.* ***Village***, with jetty on Ardminish bay on E side of Gigha. **72 E6** NR6448.
Ardminish Bay *Arg. & B.* ***Bay***, on E side of Gigha. **72 E6** NR6448.
Ardmolich *High.* ***Settlement***, at head of Loch Moidart. **86 D7** NM7172.
Ardmore *Arg. & B.* ***Settlement***, on Kerrera, 1km E of Rubha na Feundain. **79 J5** NM7927.
Ardmore *Arg. & B.* ***Settlement***, 7m/11km NE of Port Ellen, Islay. **72 C6** NR4650.
Ardmore *Arg. & B.* ***Settlement***, on peninsula, 2m/3km NW of Cardross. **74 B3** NS3178.
Ardmore *High.* ***Settlement***, on S shore of Dornoch Firth, 6m/9km NW of Tain, Ross and Cromarty district. **96 E3** NH7086.
Ardmore Bay *Arg. & B.* ***Bay***, on N coast of Mull, 3m/5km NW of Tobermory. **79 F2** NM4759.
Ardmore Bay *High.* ***Bay***, small bay on Skye, 4m/7km S of Vaternish Point. **93 H5** NG2260.
Ardmore Point *Arg. & B.* ***Coastal feature***, headland at E end of Ardmore Bay on N coast of Mull, 3m/5km NW of Tobermory. **79 F2** NM4759.
Ardmore Point *Arg. & B.* ***Coastal feature***, headland on SE coast of Islay, 5m/8km NE of Ardbeg. **72 C5** NR4750.
Ardmore Point *High.* ***Coastal feature***, headland on W coast of Sutherland district on E side of entrance to Loch Laxford. **102 D3** NC1851.
Ardmore Point *High.* ***Coastal feature***, headland on N coast of Caithness district, 2m/3km NW of Armadale. **104 C2** NC7666.
Ardmore Point *High.* ***Coastal feature***, headland on NW coast of Skye, 5m/8km S of Vaternish Point. **93 H6** NG2159.
Ardmucknish Bay *Arg. & B.* ***Bay***, on S side of Benderloch, between Rubha Garbh-àird and Ledaig Point, Argyll. **79 K4** NM8937.
Ardnackaig *Arg. & B.* ***Settlement***, 2m/3km N of Tayvallich. **73 F1** NR7490.
Ardnacross *Arg. & B.* ***Settlement***, on Mull, 4m/7km SE of Tobermory. **79 G3** NM5449.
Ardnacross Bay *Arg. & B.* ***Bay***, on E coast of Kintyre, 4m/7km NE of Campbeltown. **66 B1** NR7625.
Ardnadam *Arg. & B.* ***Village***, on S side of Holy Loch in Argyll, 2m/4km N of Dunoon. **73 K3** NS1780.
Ardnadrochet *Arg. & B.* ***Settlement***, on Mull, 1m/2km NW of Grass Point. **79 J4** NM7331.
Ardnagoine *High.* ***Settlement***, on Tanera Mòr, largest of Summer Isles group, off W coast of Ross and Cromarty district. **95 F1** NB9908.
Ardnagowan *Arg. & B.* ***Settlement***, on E shore of Loch Fyne, 3m/4km S of Inveraray across loch. **80 C7** NN1005.
Ardnagrask *High.* ***Settlement***, in Ross and Cromarty district, 1m/2km SW of Muir of Ord. **96 C7** NH5149.
Ardnahein *Arg. & B.* ***Settlement***, on W shore of Loch Goil, 1m/2km SE of Carrick. **74 A1** NS1993.
Ardnahoe *Arg. & B.* ***Settlement***, on shore of Ardnahoe Loch, on E coast of Islay, 1m/2km N of Port Askaig. **72 C3** NR4271.
Ardnameacan *High.* ***Coastal feature***, headland on SE coast of Skye on E side of entrance to Loch na Dal. **86 D3** NG7114.
Ardnamurchan *High.* ***Locality***, large upland peninsula on W coast in Lochaber district, running W from Salen to Point of Ardnamurchan. **79 F1** NM5766.
Ardnandave Hill *Stir.* ***Mountain***, on W side of Loch Lubnaig, 5m/8km NW of Callander. Height 2345 feet or 715 metres. **81 G6** NN5612.
Ardnarff *High.* ***Locality***, on SE shore of Loch Carron, Skye and Lochalsh district. **86 E1** NG8935.
Ardnastang *High.* ***Settlement***, on N side of Loch Sunart, in Lochaber district, 1m/2km of W of Strontian. **79 K1** NM8161.
Ardnave *Arg. & B.* ***Settlement***, on N of Islay, 1m/2km SW of Ardnave Point. **72 A3** NR2873.
Ardnave Loch *Arg. & B.* ***Lake/loch***, on N coast of Islay, 1m/2km S of Ardnave Point. **72 A3** NR2872.
Ardnave Point *Arg. & B.* ***Coastal feature***, headland on N coast of Islay, on W side of entrance to Loch Gruinart. **72 A3** NR2975.
Ardneil Bay *N.Ayr.* ***Bay***, on Firth of Clyde, on E side of Farland Head, 1m/2km W of West Kilbride. **73 K6** NS1848.
Ardnish *High.* ***Coastal feature***, peninsula on coast of Lochaber district between Loch Ailort and Loch nan Uamh, the S and N arms respectively of Sound of Arisaig. **86 D6** NM7281.
Ardno *Arg. & B.* ***Settlement***, on S shore of NE arm of Loch Fyne, 3m/5km E of Inveraray across loch. **80 C7** NN1408.
Ardnoe Point *Arg. & B.* ***Coastal feature***, S side of mouth of Loch Crinan, 1m/2km W of Crinan. **73 F1** NR7794.
Ardo *Aber.* ***Locality***, comprises many dispersed settlements, 1m/2km N of Methlick and 4m/7km SW of New Deer. **91 G1** NJ8539.
Ardoch *D. & G.* ***Settlement***, above River Nith, 4m/7km SE of Sanquhar. **68 D3** NS8305.
Ardoch *Moray* ***Settlement***, 1km S of Dallas. **97 J6** NJ1251.
Ardoch *P. & K.* ***Settlement***, 1km S of Murthly. **82 B4** NO0937.
Ardoch Burn *Stir.* ***River***, running SE then S from Loch Mahaick to River Teith on S side of Doune. **81 J7** NN7300.
Ardoch Roman Camp *P. & K.* ***Historic/prehistoric site***, 4m/7km SW of Muthill. Well preserved site, but lacking visible stonework. Permanent camp for legions, dating from 1c-3c. **81 K6** NN8309.
Ardochrig *S.Lan.* ***Settlement***, 4m/7km NW of Strathaven. **74 E6** NS6346.
Ardochu *High.* ***Settlement***, in Sutherland district, 6m/10km E of Lairg. **96 D1** NC6703.
Ardoyne *Aber.* ***Settlement***, 1m/2km NW of Oyne. **90 E2** NJ6527.
Ardpatrick *Arg. & B.* ***Settlement***, on NW coast of Kintyre, at seaward end of West Loch Tarbert, 9m/15km SW of Tarbert. **73 F4** NR7559.
Ardpatrick Point *Arg. & B.* ***Coastal feature***, headland at S end of Knapdale, Argyll, at entrance to West Loch Tarbert. **73 F5** NR7357.
Ardpeaton *Arg. & B.* ***Hamlet***, on E shore of Loch Long, 2m/3km N of Cove. **74 A2** NS2285.
Ardradnaig *P. & K.* ***Settlement***, on SE side of Loch Tay, 4m/7km SW of Kenmore. **81 J3** NN7142.
Ardrishaig *Arg. & B.* Population: 1315. ***Small town***, in Argyll on W shore of Loch Gilp, 2m/3km S of Lochgilphead. Television and radio transmitting station. SE terminus of Crinan Canal. **73 G2** NR8585.
Ardroe *High.* ***Settlement***, 2m/3km NW of Lochinver, Sutherland district. **102 C6** NC0623.
Ardroil *W.Isles Anglicised form of Eadar dha Fhadhail, qv.*
Ardross *High.* ***Settlement***, in Ross and Cromarty district, 4m/6km NW of Alness. NH6174.
Ardrossan *N.Ayr.* Population: 10,750. ***Town***, port on Firth of Clyde, 12m/20km W of Kilmarnock. Passenger boat services to Arran. **74 A6** NS2342.
Ardrossan Castle *N.Ayr.* ***Castle***, of mid 12c, situated on a hill overlooking Ardrossan Bay. Was destroyed by Cromwell and only the north tower and two arched cellars remain. **74 A6** NS2244.
Ardscalpsie *Arg. & B.* ***Settlement***, on Bute, above W side of Scalpsie Bay. **73 J5** NS0558.
Ardshave *High.* ***Settlement***, 4m/7km NW of Dornoch. **96 E2** NH7695.
Ardshealach *High.* ***Settlement***, 1km SE of Acharacle. **79 H1** NM6867.
Ardshellach *Arg. & B.* ***Settlement***, 3m/5km SW of Kilninver. **79 J6** NM7818.
Ardslave *W.Isles Anglicised form of Aird Leimhe, qv.*
Ardsley *S.Yorks.* ***Suburb***, 3m/4km E of Barnsley town centre. **51 F2** SE3805.
Ardslignish *High.* ***Locality***, on S side of Ardnamurchan peninsula, in Lochaber district, 8m/13km W of Salen. **79 G1** NM5661.
Ardtalla *Arg. & B.* ***Settlement***, on E coast of Islay, 9m/14km NE of Port Ellen. **72 C5** NR4654.
Ardtalnaig *P. & K.* ***Village***, on S side of Loch Tay, 6m/10km SW of Kenmore. Old copper and lead mines in vicinity. **81 H4** NN7039.
Ardtarig *Arg. & B.* ***Settlement***, 1km S of head of Loch Striven on E shore, 8m/12km NW of Dunoon. **73 J2** NS0582.
Ardteatle *Arg. & B.* ***Locality***, 2m/3km SW of Dalmally. **80 C5** NN1325.
Ardtoe *High.* ***Settlement***, in Lochaber district, on N side of entrance to Kentra Bay, 3m/5km NW of Acharacle. **86 C7** NM6270.
Ardtornish *High.* ***Garden***, 24 acres of gardens surrounding Ardtornish House, at head of Loch Aline, Lochaber district. **79 J3** NM7047.
Ardtornish *High.* ***Settlement***, at head of Loch Aline, 3m/4km NE of Lochaline, Lochaber district. **79 J3** NM7047.
Ardtornish Point *High.* ***Coastal feature***, headland on Sound of Mull 1m/2km SE of entrance to Loch Aline, Lochaber district. Ruins of 14c castle, stronghold of the Lords of the Isles. **79 H3** NM6942.
Ardtreck Point *High.* ***Coastal feature***, headland in Loch Bracadale, Skye, at entrance to Loch Harport. **85 J1** NG3336.
Ardtrostan *P. & K.* ***Settlement***, on S side of Loch Earn, 1m/2km SW of St. Fillans. **81 H5** NN6723.
Ardtun *Arg. & B.* ***Settlement***, scattered locality on Ross of Mull, to NE of Bunessan. **78 E5** NM3923.
Ardtur *Arg. & B.* ***Settlement***, 1km NE of Port Appin. **80 A3** NM9146.
Arduaine *Arg. & B.* ***Locality***, on Asknish Bay, on coast of Argyll, 4m/6km SW of Kilmelford. **79 K7** NM8010.
Arduaine Garden *Arg. & B.* ***Garden***, to W of Arduaine, and inland from Arduaine Point. Woodland and gardens with coastal viewpoint, including rhododendrons, azaleas and perennial borders. **79 J6** NM7910.
Ardullie *High.* ***Settlement***, 2m/3km SW of Evanton. **96 C5** NH5863.
Ardura *Arg. & B.* ***Settlement***, to S of Lussa River, near head of Loch Spelve, 4m/6km W of Grass Point, Mull. **79 H4** NM6830.
Ardvar *High.* ***Settlement***, on W side of Loch Ardvar, Sutherland district. **102 D5** NC1734.
Ardvasar *High.* ***Village***, on E coast of Sleat peninsula, Skye, 5m/8km NE of Point of Sleat. **86 C4** NG6303.
Ardveenish *W.Isles* ***Settlement***, on peninsula of Ard Veenish, at head of North Bay, Barra. NF7103.
Ardveich *Stir.* ***Settlement***, on N side of Loch Earn, 1m/2km E of Lochearnhead. **81 H5** NN6224.
Ardverikie *High.* ***Settlement***, on S shore of Loch Laggan, 3m/4km SW of Kinloch Laggan. **88 C6** NN5087.
Ardverikie Forest *High.* ***Open space***, deer forest in Badenoch and Strathspey district, S of Lochan na h-Earba. **88 B6** NN5081.
Ardvey *W.Isles Anglicised form of Aird Mhighe, qv.*
Ardvey *W.Isles Anglicised form of Aird Mhige, qv.*
Ardvorlich *Arg. & B.* ***Settlement***, on W side of N end of Loch Lomond, 2m/3km S of Ardlui. **80 E6** NN3211.
Ardvorlich *P. & K.* ***Settlement***, on S side of Loch Earn, 3m/4km SE of Lochearnhead. **81 H5** NN6322.
Ardvourlie *W.Isles Anglicised form of Aird a' Mhulaidh, qv.*
Ardvreck Castle *High.* ***Castle***, situated on promontory on N side of Loch Assynt. Ruined 16c tower where Montrose was handed over to Parliament in 1650. **102 E6** NC2323.
Ardwall *D. & G.* ***Settlement***, on N shore of Fleet Bay, 1m/2km SW of Gatehouse of Fleet. **65 F5** NX5854.
Ardwall Island *D. & G.* ***Island***, one of the Islands of Fleet, off E shore of Wigtown Bay. Foundations of several early Christian churches have been uncovered. **65 F6** NX5749.
Ardwell *D. & G.* ***Village***, on E coast of Rinns of Galloway, 3m/5km S of Sandhead. **64 B6** NX1045.
Ardwell *Moray* ***Settlement***, near confluence of Black Water and River Deveron, 2m/3km N of Cabrach. **90 B1** NJ3730.
Ardwell *S.Ayr.* ***Settlement***, on coast, 3m/4km S of Girvan. **67 F4** NX1694.
Ardwell Bay *D. & G.* ***Bay***, on W coast of Rinns of Galloway, 2m/4km W of Ardwell. **64 A6** NX1045.
Ardwell House *D. & G.* ***Garden***, woodland garden and pond walk with sea views, 1km from Ardwell on W side of Luce Bay. Displays of daffodils and rhododendrons. **64 A6** NX1045.
Ardwick *Gt.Man.* ***Suburb***, 1m/2km E of Manchester city centre. SJ8597.
Ardyne Burn *Arg. & B.* ***River***, running S down Glen Fyne to Firth of Clyde 2m/4km W of Toward Point. **73 K3** NS1068.
Ardyne Point *Arg. & B.* ***Coastal feature***, headland in Argyll, 3m/4km W of Toward Point. **73 J4** NS0968.
Areley Kings *Worcs.* ***Locality***, 1km SW of Stourport-on-Severn across River Severn. **29 G1** SO8070.

Arenig Fach *Gwyn.* ***Mountain***, 1m/2km W of Llyn Celyn. Height 2260 feet or 689 metres. **37 H1** SH8241.
Arenig Fawr *Gwyn.* ***Mountain***, 6m/10km E of Trawsfynydd. Height 2801 feet or 854 metres. **37 H2** SH8236.
Arford *Hants.* ***Village***, 4m/6km W of Hindhead. **12 B3** SU8236.
Argaty *Stir.* ***Settlement***, 1m/2km NE of Doune. **81 J7** NN7303.
Argill Beck *Cumb.* ***River***, rising on S side of Stainmore Common and flowing SW into River Belah, 2m/3km SE of Brough. **61 K5** NY8213.
Argoed *Caerp.* ***Hamlet***, 2m/3km N of Blackwood. **18 E2** SO1700.
Argoed *Shrop.* ***Settlement***, 1km W of Kinnerley. SJ3220.
Argoed Mill *Powys* ***Settlement***, on River Wye, 4m/6km S of Rhayader. **27 J2** SN9962.
Argos Hill *E.Suss.* ***Settlement***, 1m/2km SE of Rotherfield. Windmill at top of hill. TQ5728.
Argrennan House *D. & G.* ***Settlement***, in Dee Valley, 4m/7km N of Kirkcudbright. **65 H5** NX7158.
Argyll and Sutherland Highlanders Museum *Stir.* ***Other feature of interest***, in Stirling Castle, with displays on regiment and a medal collection. **75 F1** NS7893.
Argyll Forest Park *Arg. & B.* ***Forest/woodland***, forest and mountain area in Argyll between Loch Long and Loch Fyne, occupying much of N part of Cowal peninsula. **73 K1** NS1396.
Argyll Wildlife Park *Arg. & B.* ***Leisure/recreation***, large collection of indigenous wildlife, waterfowl and owls, 2m/3km SW of Inveraray. **80 B7** NN0805.
Argyll's Bowling Green *Arg. & B.* ***Large natural feature***, mountainous area in Argyll between Loch Goil and Loch Long. **74 A1** NS2298.
Aribruach *W.Isles Anglicised form of Airidh a' Bhruaich, qv.*
Arichamish *Arg. & B.* ***Settlement***, on N shore of Loch Awe, 3m/4km NE of Ford. **80 A7** NM9005.
Arichastlich *Arg. & B.* ***Settlement***, in Glen Orchy, 5m/8km NW of Tyndrum. **80 D4** NN2534.
Arichonan *Arg. & B.* ***Settlement***, in Knapdale, 5m/7km W of Cairnbaan. **73 F1** NR7790.
Aridhglas *Arg. & B.* ***Settlement***, on Mull, 1m/2km S of Rubha nan Cearc. **78 E5** NM3123.
Arienskill *High.* ***Settlement***, 1m/2km E of Lochailort, Lochaber district. **86 D6** NM7883.
Arileod *Arg. & B.* ***Settlement***, on Coll, 4m/7km SW of Arinagour. **78 C2** NM1654.
Arinacrinachd *High.* ***Locality***, in Ross and Cromarty district, on SW coast of Loch Torridon, 6m/9km NW of Shieldaig. **94 D6** NG7458.
Arinafad Beg *Arg. & B.* ***Settlement***, on NW coast of Caol Scotnish, 3m/5km SW of Crinan. **73 F2** NR7689.
Arinagour *Arg. & B.* ***Village***, sole village and port of Coll, situated on SE coast 5m/8km from NE end, at head of Loch Eatharna. **78 D2** NM2256.
Arinambane *W.Isles* ***Settlement***, on South Uist, 3m/5km NE of Mingearraidh. **84 C2** NF7928.
Arinarach Hill *Arg. & B.* ***Mountain***, on Kintyre, 3m/4km SE of Campeltown. Height 1030 feet or 314 metres. **66 B2** NR7316.
Arisaig *High.* ***Locality***, area in Lochaber district surrounding hinterland of village of Arisaig. It rises from coastal flats to mountains between South Morar and Moidart. **86 C6** NM6687.
Arisaig *High.* ***Village***, within surrounding area of Arisaig on W coast of Lochaber district. Village is 7m/11km S of Mallaig, at head of Loch nan Ceall. **86 C6** NM6586.
Arivegaig *High.* ***Settlement***, 1m/2km W of Acharacle, Lochaber district. **79 H1** NM6568.
Ark Hill *Angus* ***Mountain***, 3m/5km SW of Glamis. Height 1115 feet or 340 metres. **82 E3** NO3542.
Arkendale *N.Yorks.* ***Village***, 4m/6km S of Boroughbridge. **57 J3** SE3860.
Arkengarthdale *N.Yorks.* ***Valley***, carrying Arkle Beck SE to Reeth in Swaledale. **62 A6** NZ0102.
Arkengarthdale Moor *N.Yorks.* ***Open space***, moorland on W side of Arkle Beck, 4m/7km NE of Keld. **62 A6** NY9305.
Arkesden *Essex* ***Village***, 5m/7km SW of Saffron Walden. **33 H5** TL4834.
Arkholme *Lancs.* ***Village***, 4m/7km SW of Kirkby Lonsdale. **55 J2** SD5872.
Arkle (Gaelic form: Arcuil.) *High.* ***Mountain***, rising to ridge along summit in Sutherland district, 5m/8km SE of Rhiconich. Height 2581 feet or 787 metres. **103 F4** NC3046.
Arkle Beck *N.Yorks.* ***River***, rising on Arkengarthdale Moor and flowing first NE, then SE through Langthwaite into River Swale at Grinton, 1km SE of Reeth. Valley of Arkle Beck is known as Arkengarthdale. **62 A6** SE0498.
Arkle Town *N.Yorks.* ***Hamlet***, in Arkengarthdale, 3m/4km NW of Reeth. NZ0002.
Arkleby *Cumb.* ***Settlement***, 2m/3km S of Aspatria. **60 C3** NY1439.
Arkleside *N.Yorks.* ***Settlement***, 7m/11km SW of Middleham. **57 F1** SE0480.
Arkleton *D. & G.* ***Settlement***, in valley of Ewes Water, 4m/7km N of Langholm. **69 J4** NY3791.
Arkleton Hill *D. & G.* ***Mountain***, steep-sided mountain, with rounded summit, 6m/9km NE of Langholm. Height 1709 feet or 521 metres. **69 K4** NY4092.
Arkley *Gt.Lon.* ***Settlement***, in borough of Barnet, 11m/17km NW of Charing Cross and 2m/3km SE of Borehamwood. **23 F2** TQ2295.
Arks Edge *Sc.Bord.* ***Inland physical feature***, mountain ridge E of Carter Bar in Cheviot Hills, 447 metres at highest point. **70 C3** NT7107.
Arksey *S.Yorks.* ***Suburb***, 2m/4km N of Doncaster. **51 H2** SE5706.
Arkwright Town *Derbys.* ***Village***, 3m/5km E of Chesterfield. **51 G5** SK4270.
Arlary *P. & K.* ***Settlement***, 1m/2km NE of Milnathort. **82 C7** NO1305.
Arle *Glos.* ***Suburb***, in NW part of Cheltenham. SO9223.
Arle Court *Glos.* ***Locality***, W district of Cheltenham. SO9121.
Arlecdon *Cumb.* ***Village***, 5m/8km E of Whitehaven. **60 B5** NY0419.
Arlesey *Beds.* Population: 4374. ***Village***, elongated village, 5m/7km N of Hitchin. **32 E5** TL1936.
Arleston *Tel. & W.* ***Suburb***, SE suburb of Wellington. **39 F4** SJ6610.
Arley *Ches.* ***Hamlet***, 4m/7km N of Northwich. **49 F4** SJ6780.
Arley Hall *Ches.* ***Historic house***, 19c home of Viscount Ashbrook, representing an excellent example of Victorian Jacobean architecture, located in Arley, 3m/4km SE of Appleton Thorn and 5m/8km NW of Northwich. 12 acres of award-winning gardens include 19c double herbaceous border, herb and walled garden, exotic trees, shrubs and rhododendrons. **49 F4** SJ6780.
Arlick *P. & K.* ***Mountain***, 1m/2km NW of Butterstone. Height 1046 feet or 319 metres. **82 B3** NO0746.
Arlingham *Glos.* ***Village***, in loop of River Severn, 9m/15km NW of Stroud. St. Augustine's Farm is working farm open to public. **29 G7** SO7010.
Arlington *Devon* ***Hamlet***, 6m/9km NE of Barnstaple. **6 E1** SS6140.
Arlington *E.Suss.* ***Village***, in valley of Cuckmere River below South Downs, 3m/5km W of Hailsham. **13 J6** TQ5407.
Arlington *Glos.* ***Locality***, adjoining to W of Bibury. **20 E1** SP1106.
Arlington Beccott *Devon* ***Village***, to NE of Arlington. **6 E1** SS6140.
Arlington Court *Devon* ***Historic house***, and grounds (National Trust), to W of Arlington church. Houses several collections, including horse-drawn carriages. **6 E1** SS6140.
Arlington Reservoir *E.Suss.* ***Reservoir***, 4m/6km NW of Polegate. **13 J6** TQ5307.
Armadale *High.* ***Locality***, 1km NE of Ardvasar, on E coast of Sleat peninsula on Skye. Includes Armadale Bay and pier, and Armadale Castle. **86 C4** NG6304.
Armadale *High.* ***Village***, near N coast of Caithness district, 6m/10km W of Melvich. **104 C2** NC7864.
Armadale *W.Loth.* Population: 8958. ***Small town***, 7m/11km SW of Linlithgow. **75 H4** NS9368.
Armadale Bay *High.* ***Bay***, to E of Armadale, on N coast of Caithness district. **104 C2** NC7965.
Armadale Bay *High.* ***Bay***, with pier, 1km NE of Ardvasar, on E coast of Sleat peninsula on Skye. **86 C4** NG6303.
Armadale Burn *High.* ***River***, stream running N into Armadale Bay. **104 C2** NC7864.
Armathwaite *Cumb.* ***Village***, on River Eden, 6m/9km SE of Wetheral and 9m/15km SE of Carlisle. **61 G2** NY5046.
Arminghall *Norf.* ***Village***, 3m/5km SE of Norwich. **45 G5** TG2504.
Armitage *Staffs.* Population: 4049. ***Village***, 3m/4km SE of Rugeley. **40 C4** SK0716.
Armitage Bridge *W.Yorks.* ***Suburb***, 2m/3km S of Huddersfield town centre, on W side of River Holme. SE1213.
Armley *W.Yorks.* ***Suburb***, 2m/3km W of Leeds city centre. SE2733.
Armscote *Warks.* ***Village***, 3m/4km N of Shipston on Stour. **30 D4** SP2444.
Armshead *Staffs.* ***Settlement***, 1km N of Werrington. SJ9348.
Armston *Northants.* ***Hamlet***, 2m/3km SE of Oundle. **42 D7** TL0685.
Armstrong *T. & W.* ***Locality***, industrial estate in NW part of Washington. NZ2957.
Armthorpe *S.Yorks.* Population: 12,499. ***Suburb***, 3m/5km E of Doncaster. **51 J2** SE6205.
Arnabost *Arg. & B.* ***Settlement***, 2m/3km NW of Arinagour, Coll. **78 D2** NM2060.
Arnaby *Cumb.* ***Settlement***, just E of The Green, 3m/5km N of Millom. SD1884.
Arnaval *High.* ***Mountain***, 3m/5km N of Beinn Bhreac, Skye. Height 1210 feet or 369 metres. **85 J1** NG3431.
Arnaval *W.Isles* ***Hill***, 5m/8km SE of Rubha Ardvule, South Uist. Height 827 feet or 252 metres. **84 C2** NF7825.
Arncliffe *N.Yorks.* ***Village***, in Littondale, 7m/11km NW of Grassington. **56 E2** SD9371.
Arncliffe Cote *N.Yorks.* ***Locality***, 1m/2km SE of Arncliffe. **56 E2** SD9470.
Arncroach *Fife* ***Village***, 2m/4km N of St. Monans. **83 G7** NO5105.
Arne *Dorset* ***Hamlet***, 3m/5km E of Wareham, in area of heath and marsh at W end of Poole Harbour. **9 J6** SY9788.
Arnesby *Leics.* ***Village***, 5m/8km N of Husbands Bosworth. **41 J6** SP6192.
Arnfield *Derbys.* ***Settlement***, 1km NW of Tintwistle. SK0198.
Arngask *P. & K.* ***Hamlet***, to E of Glenfarg, 5m/8km N of Kinross. **82 C6** NO1310.
Arngibbon *Stir.* ***Settlement***, 2m/3km E of Buchlyvie. Ancient earthworks in wooded glen to W. **74 E1** NS6094.
Arngomery *Stir.* ***Settlement***, 1m/2km W of Kippen. **74 E1** NS6394.
Arnhall *Aber.* ***Hamlet***, 1km E of Edzell across River North Esk. **83 H1** NO6169.
Arnicle *Arg. & B.* ***Settlement***, on Kintyre, 3m/4km NE of Glenbarr. **73 F7** NR7138.
Arnipol *High.* ***Settlement***, 2m/3km NW of Lochailort, Lochaber district. **86 D6** NM7483.
Arnisdale *High.* ***Village***, in Lochaber district on N shore of Loch Hourn, some 5m/8km E of entrance to loch from Sound of Sleat. Also river running W down Glen Arnisdale to Loch Hourn, 1m/2km SE of village. **86 E3** NG8410.
Arnish *High.* ***Settlement***, on Raasay, 3m/5km from N end of island. **94 C7** NG5948.
Arnish Moor *W.Isles* ***Open space***, 3m/4km SE of Stornoway, Isle of Lewis, consisting of numerous small lochs and rocky outcrops. **101 G5** NB3929.
Arnish Point *W.Isles* ***Coastal feature***, headland with lighthouse on W side of entrance to Stornoway Harbour, Isle of Lewis. **101 G4** NB4330.
Arniston Engine *Midloth.* ***Suburb***, NW district of Gorebridge, 3m/5km S of Dalkeith. **76 B4** NT3462.
Arnol *W.Isles* ***Village***, near NW coast of Isle of Lewis, 3m/5km W of Barvas. Black House (Historic Scotland) to N. **101 F3** NB3148.
Arnold *E.Riding* ***Village***, adjoining to S of Long Riston. TA1241.
Arnold *Notts.* Population: 37,646. ***Town***, 4m/6km NE of Nottingham city centre. **41 H1** SK5845.
Arno's Vale *Bristol* ***Suburb***, 2m/3km SE of Bristol city centre. ST6071.
Arnprior *Stir.* ***Village***, 12m/19km W of Stirling. **74 E1** NS6194.
Arnsgill Ridge *N.Yorks.* ***Open space***, ridge on Snilesworth Moor, 4m/7km E of Osmotherley. **63 G7** SE5196.
Arnside *Cumb.* Population: 1627. ***Small town***, on E bank of River Kent estuary, 6m/9km N of Carnforth. **55 H2** SD4578.
Arnton Fell *Sc.Bord.* ***Mountain***, wooded on E side, 5m/8km NE of Castleton. Height 1328 feet or 405 metres. **70 A4** NY5294.
Aros *Arg. & B.* ***Locality***, on Mull, to S of Tobermory. **79 F2** NM5150.
Aros Bay *High.* ***Bay***, small bay on E coast of Vaternish peninsula, 5m/8km SE of Vaternish Point, Skye. **93 H5** NG2760.
Aros Castle *Arg. & B.* ***Castle***, formerly stronghold of the Lords of the Isles, at mouth of Aros River. **79 G3** NM5051.
Arowry *Wrex.* ***Settlement***, 5m/8km W of Whitchurch. **38 D2** SJ4539.
Arrad Foot *Cumb.* ***Hamlet***, 1m/2km S of Penny Bridge. **55 G1** SD3080.
Arradoul *Moray* ***Locality***, 1m/2km S of Buckie. **98 C4** NJ4263.
Arram *E.Riding* ***Village***, 3m/5km N of Beverley, with New Arram adjoining to NW. **59 G5** TA0344.
Arran *N.Ayr.* ***Island***, mountainous island, with mild though wet climate and fertile valleys, on W side of Firth of Clyde and separated from Kintyre by Kilbrannan Sound. Measures 20m/32km N to S and about 9m/15km E to W; area 166 square miles or 430 square km. Industries are tourism, sheep and cattle grazing and fishing. Highest point is Goat Fell, 2866 feet or 874 metres. Brodick, on E coast, is chief town. **73 G7** NR9536.
Arras *E.Riding* ***Settlement***, 3m/5km E of Market Weighton. SE9241.
Arrat *Angus* ***Settlement***, 2m/3km SE of Brechin. **83 H2** NO6358.
Arrathorne *N.Yorks.* ***Hamlet***, 5m/8km NW of Bedale. **62 C7** SE2093.
Arreton *I.o.W.* ***Village***, 3m/5km SE of Newport. **11 G6** SZ5486.
Arrington *Cambs.* ***Village***, 6m/10km N of Royston. **33 G3** TL3250.
Arrivain *Arg. & B.* ***Settlement***, in Glen Lochy, 4m/6km W of Tyndrum. **80 D4** NN2630.
Arrochar *Arg. & B.* ***Village***, at head of Loch Long on E side of loch, 1m/2km W of Tarbet on Loch Lomond and 13m/21km N of Helensburgh. **80 E7** NN2904.
Arrow ***River***, rising near Glascwm and flowing E through Kington into River Lugg, 2m/3km SE of Leominster. **28 D3** SO5156.
Arrow ***River***, rising 8m/13km SW of Birmingham and flowing S into River Avon, 5m/8km NE of Evesham. **30 B2** SP0850.
Arrow *Warks.* ***Village***, on River Arrow 1m/2km SW of Alcester. **30 B3** SP0856.
Arrowe Hill *Mersey.* ***Suburb***, 3m/5km SW of Birkenhead town centre. SJ2787.
Arrowfield Top *Worcs.* ***Settlement***, 4m/7km N of Redditch. SP0274.
Arscaig *High.* ***Settlement***, on W side of Loch Shin, 6m/10km NW of Lairg. **103 H7** NC5014.
Arscott *Shrop.* ***Hamlet***, 1m/2km NE of Longden. SJ4307.
Artfield Fell *D. & G.* ***Large natural feature***, 6m/10km N of Glenluce. Rising to height of 800 feet or 244 metres at Green Top. **64 C4** NX2267.
Arth *Cere.* ***River***, rising 3m/5km W of Llangeitho and flowing W into Cardigan Bay at Aberarth. **26 D2** SN4764.
Arthington *W.Yorks.* ***Village***, 5m/7km E of Otley. **57 H5** SE2744.
Arthingworth *Northants.* ***Village***, 4m/6km S of Market Harborough. **42 A7** SP7581.
Arthog *Gwyn.* ***Hamlet***, 5m/7km NE of Llwyngwril. **37 F4** SH6414.
Arthrath *Aber.* ***Settlement***, 4m/6km N of Ellon. **91 H1** NJ9636.
Arthur Seat *Cumb.* ***Open space***, wooded uplands on S side of Kershope Forest, 3m/5km SE of Kershopefoot. **69 K6** NY4978.
Arthuret *Cumb.* ***Locality***, on River Esk, adjoining Longtown, 8m/13km N of Carlisle. NY3869.
Arthur's Round Table *Cumb. See Eamont Bridge.*
Arthur's Seat *Edin.* ***Hill***, of volcanic origin, 1m/2km SE of Edinburgh city centre. Height 823 feet or 251 metres. **76 A3** NT2772.
Arthur's Stone *Here.* ***Historic/prehistoric site***, burial chamber (English Heritage), 1km N of Dorstone. Chambered long barrow of which chamber and ruined passageway survive. **28 C4** SO3143.
Arthursdale *W.Yorks.* ***Locality***, adjoining to N of Scholes. SE3737.
Arthurstone *P. & K.* ***Settlement***, 1km N of Ardler. **82 D3** NO2542.

Artrochie *Aber.* ***Settlement***, 3m/4km NE of Ellon. **91 J1** NK0031.
Aruadh *Arg. & B.* ***Settlement***, 4m/6km NE of Kilchiaran. **72 A4** NR2464.
Arun *W.Suss.* ***River***, rising in St. Leonard's Forest to E of Horsham, flowing W and then S via Pulborough and Arundel into English Channel at Littlehampton. **12 D6** TQ0201.
Arundel *W.Suss.* Population: 3033. ***Small town***, on hill above River Arun, 3m/5km N of Littlehampton. Castle originally Norman but mainly Victorian, in spacious Arundel Park, which contains site of Romano-British settlement N of Swanbourne Lake. 19c Roman Catholic cathedral. **12 D6** TQ0107.
Arundel Castle *W.Suss.* ***Castle***, in Arundel. Although castle rests on 12c foundations it was extensively restored and rebuilt by 11th and 15th Dukes of Norfolk between 1787 and 1890. **12 D6** TQ0107.
Arundel Cathedral *W.Suss.* ***Ecclesiastical building***, Roman Catholic cathedral built in centre of Arundel, 3m/5km N of Littlehampton, by 15th Duke of Norfolk between 1868 and 1873; designed by Joseph Hansom. **12 D6** TQ0107.
Arundel Park *W.Suss.* ***Open space***, to N of Arundel Castle. **12 D6** TQ0108.
Arundel Priory *W.Suss.* ***Ecclesiastical building***, remains of priory, 1m/2km SW of Arundel. **12 D6** TQ0005.
Arundel Wildfowl and Wetlands Trust *W.Suss.* ***Nature reserve***, open water, wet grassland and reedbed viewed from observation hides, 1km NE of Arundel. **12 D6** TQ0208.
Aryhoulan *High.* ***Settlement***, in valley of River Scaddle, 5m/8km SW of Fort William across Loch Linnhe. **80 B1** NN0168.
Asby *Cumb.* ***Hamlet***, 1m/2km NE of Arlecdon. **60 B4** NY0620.
Ascog *Arg. & B.* ***Village***, on E coast of Bute, 1m/2km SE of Rothesay, extending N and S of Ascog Point. **73 K4** NS1063.
Ascot *W. & M.* Population: 7880. ***Locality***, residential locality 6m/10km SW of Windsor across Windsor Great Park. Famous racecourse. **22 C5** SU9268.
Ascot Racecourse *W. & M.* ***Racecourse***, at NW side of Ascot, 3m/5km E of Bracknell. Thirteen flat and ten National Hunt race days each year, including the four-day flat racing Royal Meeting in June, which is a prestigious social event. **22 C5** SU9169.
Ascott *Bucks.* ***Historic house***, 17c farmhouse converted to Tudor style house in 19c by Leopold de Rothschild, 2m/4km SW of Leighton Buzzard. Surrounding estate includes formal and informal gardens (National Trust), with unique topiary sundial. **31 K6** SP8922.
Ascott *Warks.* ***Hamlet***, 5m/8km N of Chipping Norton. **30 E5** SP3234.
Ascott d'Oyley *Oxon.* ***Settlement***, adjoining to E of Ascott-under-Wychwood. SP3018.
Ascott Earl *Oxon.* ***Settlement***, adjoining to SW of Ascott-under-Wychwood. SP2918.
Ascott-under-Wychwood *Oxon.* ***Village***, 4m/6km W of Charlbury. **30 D7** SP3018.
Ascreavie *Angus* ***Settlement***, 4m/6km NW of Kirriemuir. **82 E2** NO3357.
Ascrib Islands *High.* ***Island***, group of small uninhabited islands at entrance to Loch Snizort, Skye. Named islands, from N to S, are Eilean Iosal, Eilean Creagach, Sgeir na Capaill, Eilean Garave and South Ascrib. **93 J5** NG3064.
Asenby *N.Yorks.* ***Village***, 5m/8km SW of Thirsk on W bank of River Swale. **57 J2** SE3975.
Asfordby *Leics.* Population: 2221. ***Village***, 3m/5km W of Melton Mowbray. **42 A4** SK7018.
Asfordby Hill *Leics.* ***Hamlet***, 1m/2km E of Asfordby. **42 A4** SK7219.
Asgarby *Lincs.* ***Hamlet***, 3m/5km E of Sleaford. **42 E1** TF1145.
Asgarby *Lincs.* ***Hamlet***, 4m/7km W of Spilsby. **53 G6** TF3366.
Asgog Bay *Arg. & B.* ***Bay***, on E side of Loch Fyne, Argyll, 4m/6km NW of Ardlamont Point. **73 H4** NR9367.
Asgog Loch *Arg. & B.* ***Lake/loch***, small loch 2m/3km N of Asgog Bay. **73 H4** NR9367.
Asgog Loch Castle *Arg. & B.* ***Castle***, on shore of Loch Asgog, 3m/4km SW of Tighnabruaich. **73 H3** NR9470.
Ash *Devon* ***Settlement***, 3m/5km NW of Hatherleigh. **6 D5** SS5108.
Ash *Dorset* ***Hamlet***, at SW end of Cranborne Chase, 3m/4km NW of Blandford Forum. ST8610.
Ash *Herts.* ***River***, rising about 3m/5km E of Buntingford and flowing S into River Lea, 1m/2km SE of Ware. **33 G7** TL3713.
Ash *Kent* ***Village***, 3m/5km S of Longfield. **24 C5** TQ6064.
Ash *Kent* Population: 2024. ***Village***, 3m/5km W of Sandwich. **15 H2** TR2858.
Ash *Som.* ***Village***, 1m/2km NE of Martock. **8 D2** ST4720.
Ash *Surr.* ***Suburb***, 2m/3km E of Aldershot. **22 B6** SU8950.
Ash Bullayne *Devon* ***Settlement***, 5m/8km NW of Crediton. **7 F5** SS7704.
Ash Fell *Cumb.* ***Open space***, moorland 1km E of Ravenstonedale. **61 J6** NY7305.
Ash Green *Surr.* ***Hamlet***, 1km SE of Ash. SU9049.
Ash Green *Warks.* ***Suburb***, 2m/3km SW of Bedworth. SP3384.
Ash Magna *Shrop.* ***Village***, 2m/4km SE of Whitchurch. **38 E2** SJ5739.
Ash Mill *Devon* ***Village***, 5m/8km SE of South Molton. **7 F3** SS7823.
Ash Parva *Shrop.* ***Hamlet***, adjoins to SE of Ash Magna. SJ5739.
Ash Priors *Som.* ***Village***, 3m/5km NE of Milverton. **7 K3** ST1529.
Ash Street *Suff.* ***Hamlet***, 3m/5km N of Hadleigh. TM0146.
Ash Thomas *Devon* ***Hamlet***, 3m/5km SE of Tiverton. **7 J4** ST0010.
Ash Vale *Surr.* ***Suburb***, 2m/3km NE of Aldershot. **22 B6** SU8952.
Ash Wharf *Surr.* ***Locality***, beside Basingstoke Canal, 2m/3km NE of Aldershot. SU8951.
Ashampstead *W.Berks.* ***Village***, 3m/5km SW of Streatley. **21 J4** SU5676.
Ashampstead Green *W.Berks.* ***Settlement***, adjoining to N of Ashampstead. SU5677.
Ashbocking *Suff.* ***Hamlet***, 6m/10km N of Ipswich. **35 F3** TM1754.
Ashbocking Green *Suff.* ***Village***, 1m/2km E of Ashbocking. TM1754.
Ashbourne *Derbys.* Population: 6300. ***Small town***, on Henmore Brook, near its junction with River Dove, 13m/20 km NW of Derby. **40 D1** SK1846.
Ashbrittle *Som.* ***Village***, 6m/9km W of Wellington. **7 J3** ST0521.
Ashburnham Place *E.Suss.* ***Settlement***, 4m/6km W of Battle. Ashburnham Forge is settlement 1m/2km N. **13 K5** TQ6914.
Ashburton *Devon* Population: 3660. ***Small town***, market town close to E side of Dartmoor, 7m/11km W of Newton Abbot. **5 H4** SX7569.
Ashbury *Devon* ***Hamlet***, 5m/9km NW of Okehampton. **6 D6** SX5098.
Ashbury *Oxon.* ***Village***, 7m/11km E of Swindon. **21 F3** SU2685.
Ashby *N.Lincs.* ***Suburb***, 2m/3km SE of Scunthorpe town centre. **52 C2** SE9008.
Ashby *Suff.* ***Settlement***, 5m/9km NW of Lowestoft. TM4899.
Ashby by Partney *Lincs.* ***Village***, 2m/3km E of Spilsby. **53 H6** TF4266.
Ashby cum Fenby *N.E.Lincs.* ***Village***, 5m/9km S of Grimsby. Wray Almshouses, 1641. **53 F2** TA2500.
Ashby de la Launde *Lincs.* ***Village***, 6m/9km N of Sleaford. Site of Roman building to E of Ashby de la Launde Hall. **52 D7** TF0555.
Ashby de la Zouch *Leics.* Population: 10,595. ***Town***, market town and former spa, 16m/26km NW of Leicester. Remains of castle (English Heritage). Fine 15c church. **41 F4** SK3516.
Ashby de la Zouch Castle *Leics.* ***Castle***, ruins of Norman castle (English Heritage) to E of Ashby de la Zouch. Castle fell into disrepair after Civil War, although Hastings Tower is intact, affording panoramic view. Associations with Sir Walter Scott's novel, Ivanhoe. **41 F4** SK3616.
Ashby Dell *Suff.* ***Settlement***, 5m/9km NW of Lowestoft. TM4899.
Ashby Folville *Leics.* ***Village***, 5m/8km SW of Melton Mowbray. **42 A4** SK7012.
Ashby Hill *N.E.Lincs.* ***Settlement***, 1m/2km SW of Brigsley, TA2400.
Ashby Magna *Leics.* ***Village***, 4m/7km N of Lutterworth. **41 H6** SP5690.
Ashby Parva *Leics.* ***Village***, 3m/4km N of Lutterworth. **41 H7** SP5288.
Ashby Puerorum *Lincs.* ***Village***, 5m/7km E of Horncastle. **53 G5** TF3271.
Ashby St. Ledgers *Northants.* ***Village***, 4m/6km N of Daventry. Ancient manor house was seat of the Catesbys. **31 G2** SP5768.
Ashby St. Mary *Norf.* ***Village***, 3m/5km NW of Loddon. **45 H5** TG3202.
Ashchurch *Glos.* Population: 5043. ***Village***, 2m/3km E of Tewkesbury. **29 J5** SO9233.
Ashclyst Forest *Devon* *See Broadclyst.*
Ashcombe *Devon* ***Village***, 3m/5km E of Chudleigh. **5 K3** SX9179.
Ashcombe *N.Som.* ***Suburb***, E district of Weston-super-Mare. ST3361.
Ashcott *Som.* ***Village***, 3m/5km W of Street. **8 D1** ST4337.
Ashdon *Essex* ***Village***, 4m/6km NE of Saffron Walden. Site of Roman building 1m/2km NW. **33 J4** TL5842.
Ashdown Forest *E.Suss.* ***Forest/woodland***, ancient forest now mainly heath, extending from Coleman's Hatch in N to Fairwarp in S, and from Crowborough in E to Chelwood Gate in W. A.A. Milne's Winnie the Pooh stories are set here. **13 H3** TQ4530.
Ashdown House *Oxon.* ***Historic house***, 17c house (National Trust) in park 4m/7km N of Aldbourne. **21 F3** SU2881.
Ashe *Hants.* ***Hamlet***, 1m/2km E of Overton, at source of River Test. **21 J7** SU5349.
Asheldham *Essex* ***Village***, 4m/6km NE of Burnham-on-Crouch. **25 F1** TL9701.
Ashen *Essex* ***Village***, 5m/8km SE of Haverhill. **34 B4** TL7442.
Ashenden *Kent* ***Settlement***, 1m/2km S of Tenterden. **14 D4** TQ8931.
Ashendon *Bucks.* ***Village***, 5m/8km N of Thame. **31 J7** SP7014.
Ashens *Arg. & B.* ***Settlement***, in Knapdale, 2m/3km N of Tarbert. **73 G3** NR8571.
Ashfield *Arg. & B.* ***Settlement***, in Knapdale, 5m/8km W of Ardrishaig. **73 F2** NR7685.
Ashfield *Hants.* ***Locality***, 1m/2km SE of Romsey. SU3619.
Ashfield *Here.* ***Suburb***, in S part of Ross-on-Wye. SO5923.
Ashfield *Stir.* ***Hamlet***, 2m/3km N of Dunblane. **81 J7** NN7803.
Ashfield *Suff.* ***Village***, 2m/4km E of Debenham. **35 G2** TM2162.
Ashfield Green *Suff.* ***Hamlet***, 2m/3km E of Stradbroke. **35 G1** TM2673.
Ashfield Green *Suff.* ***Settlement***, to N of Wickhambrook, 8m/12km SW of Bury St. Edmunds. TL7655.
Ashfields *Shrop.* ***Settlement***, 1km E of Hinstock. SJ7026.
Ashfold Crossways *W.Suss.* ***Hamlet***, 1m/2km SW of Handcross. **13 F4** TQ2328.
Ashford *Devon* ***Hamlet***, 1km N of Aveton Gifford and 3m/5km SE of Modbury. **5 G6** SX6848.
Ashford *Devon* ***Village***, 2m/3km NW of Barnstaple. **6 D2** SS5335.
Ashford *Hants.* ***Village***, 1km W of Fordingbridge. **10 C3** SU1314.
Ashford *Kent* Population: 52,002. ***Town***, market, industrial and dormitory town on Great Stour River, 13m/21km SW of Canterbury. Large medieval church. **15 F3** TR0142.
Ashford *Surr.* ***Locality***, urban locality, 2m/3km E of Staines. **22 D4** TQ0671.
Ashford Bowdler *Shrop.* ***Village***, on W side of River Teme, 3m/4km S of Ludlow. **28 E1** SO5170.
Ashford Carbonel *Shrop.* ***Village***, on E side of River Teme, 3m/4km S of Ludlow. **28 E1** SO5270.
Ashford Hill *Hants.* ***Village***, 3m/5km NE of Kingsclere. **21 J5** SU5562.
Ashford in the Water *Derbys.* ***Village***, 2m/3km NW of Bakewell. **50 E6** SK1969.
Ashgill *S.Lan.* Population: 1067. ***Village***, 2m/3km SE of Larkhall. **75 F5** NS7850.
Ashgrove *Moray* ***Suburb***, SE district of Elgin. NJ2262.
Ashholme Common *Northumb.* ***Open space***, heathland, with many streams flowing N, 3m/4km SE of Lambley. **61 J1** NY7055.
Ashie Moor *High.* ***Open space***, moorland 2m/3km S of Dores. **88 D1** NH6032.
Ashiestiel *Sc.Bord.* ***Settlement***, in River Tweed valley, 1m/2km W of Caddonfoot. **76 C7** NT4234.
Ashiestiel Hill *Sc.Bord.* ***Mountain***, 3m/4km SW of Clovenfords. Height 1315 feet or 401 metres. **76 C7** NT4134.
Ashill *Devon* ***Village***, 5m/8km NE of Cullompton. **7 J4** ST0811.
Ashill *Norf.* ***Village***, 5m/8km SE of Swaffham. Site of Roman building 2m/3km NE. **44 C5** TF8804.
Ashill *Som.* ***Village***, 3m/5km NW of Ilminster. **8 C3** ST3217.
Ashingdon *Essex* ***Suburb***, 2m/3km N of Rochford. **24 E2** TQ8693.
Ashington *Northumb.* Population: 27,962. ***Town***, 5m/8km E of Morpeth. Restored Saxon church contains Woodhorn Church Museum. **71 H5** NZ2787.
Ashington *Som.* ***Hamlet***, 4m/6km N of Yeovil. **8 E2** ST5621.
Ashington *W.Suss.* ***Village***, 4m/7km NW of Steyning. Site of Roman building to W. **12 E5** TQ1316.
Ashkirk *Sc.Bord.* ***Village***, on Ale Water, 4m/6km S of Selkirk. **69 K1** NT4722.
Ashlett *Hants.* ***Settlement***, on W shore of Southampton Water, adjoining to E of Fawley. SU4603.
Ashleworth *Glos.* ***Village***, 5m/7km N of Gloucester. **29 H6** SO8125.
Ashleworth Quay *Glos.* ***Hamlet***, on W bank of River Severn, 4m/7km N of Gloucester. 15c tithe barn (National Trust). **29 H6** SO8125.
Ashley *Cambs.* ***Village***, 4m/6km E of Newmarket. **33 K2** TL6961.
Ashley *Ches.* ***Village***, 2m/4km S of Altrincham. **49 G4** SJ7784.
Ashley *Devon* ***Hamlet***, 3m/5km SW of Chulmleigh. **6 E4** SS6411.
Ashley *Glos.* ***Hamlet***, 3m/4km NE of Tetbury. **20 C2** ST9394.
Ashley *Hants.* ***Suburb***, adjoining to E of New Milton. **10 D5** SZ2595.
Ashley *Hants.* ***Village***, 3m/5km SE of Stockbridge. Remains of old castle. **10 E1** SU3831.
Ashley *Kent* ***Village***, 5m/7km N of Dover. **15 H3** TR3048.
Ashley *Northants.* ***Village***, 5m/7km NE of Market Harborough. **42 A6** SP7990.
Ashley *Staffs.* ***Village***, 6m/10km NW of Eccleshall. **39 G2** SJ7636.
Ashley *Wilts.* ***Locality***, consisting of Great and Little Ashley, about 1m/2km NW of Bradford-on-Avon. ST8162.
Ashley *Wilts.* ***Village***, 5m/8km NE of Bath. **20 B5** ST8168.
Ashley Dale *Staffs.* ***Settlement***, 1km SW of Ashley. SJ7636.
Ashley Down *Bristol* ***Suburb***, 2m/3km NE of Bristol city centre. ST5975.
Ashley Green *Bucks.* ***Village***, 2m/3km SW of Berkhamsted. **22 C1** SP9705.
Ashley Heath *Dorset* Population: 2852. ***Village***, 2m/3km W of Ringwood. **10 C4** SU1104.
Ashley Heath *Staffs.* ***Hamlet***, 1m/2km W of Ashley. SJ7436.
Ashley Hill *W. & M.* ***Hill***, afforested hill 3m/5km NE of Wargrave. Height 472 feet or 144 metres. **22 B3** SU8281.
Ashley Park *Surr.* ***Suburb***, adjoining to S of Walton-on-Thames. TQ1065.
Ashmanhaugh *Norf.* ***Hamlet***, 3m/4km NE of Wroxham. **45 H3** TG3121.
Ashmansworth *Hants.* ***Village***, 4m/7km NE of Hurstbourne Tarrant. **21 H6** SU4157.
Ashmansworthy *Devon* ***Hamlet***, 9m/14km SW of Bideford. **6 B4** SS3318.
Ashmill *Devon* ***Settlement***, 6m/10km SE of Holsworthy. SX3995.
Ashmore *Dorset* ***Village***, on Cranborne Chase, 5m/8km SE of Shaftesbury. **9 J3** ST9117.
Ashmore *P. & K.* ***Settlement***, 1m/2km N of Bridge of Cally. **82 C2** NO1453.
Ashmore Green *W.Berks.* ***Village***, 3m/4km NE of Newbury. SU5069.
Ashop *Derbys.* ***River***, rising 3m/5km SE of Glossop and flowing E into Ladybower Reservoir. **50 D4** SK1489.
Ashorne *Warks.* ***Village***, 5m/8km S of Royal Leamington Spa. **30 E3** SP3057.
Ashover *Derbys.* ***Village***, 3m/5km W of Clay Cross. **51 F6** SK3463.
Ashover Hay *Derbys.* ***Hamlet***, 3m/4km SW of Clay Cross. SK3560.
Ashow *Warks.* ***Village***, on River Avon, 2m/3km SE of Kenilworth. **30 E1** SP3170.

Ashperton *Here.* ***Village***, 5m/8km NW of Ledbury. **29 F4** SO6441.
Ashprington *Devon* ***Village***, 2m/4km SE of Totnes. **5 J5** SX8157.
Ashreigney *Devon* ***Village***, 4m/6km W of Chulmleigh. **6 E4** SS6213.
Ashridge Estate ***Open space***, partly National Trust estate on border of Hertfordshire and Buckinghamshire, 3m/4km N of Berkhamsted. Consists of woodlands, commons and chalk downland running along main ridge of Chiltern Hills from Berkhamsted to Ivinghoe Beacon. **32 C7** SP9912.
Ashtead *Surr.* ***Suburb***, 2m/3km NE of Leatherhead. Site of Roman villa beyond Ashtead Common to N. **22 E6** TQ1858.
Ashton *Ches.* ***Village***, 1m/2km SW of Tarvin. **48 E6** SJ5069.
Ashton *Cornw.* ***Settlement***, 2m/3km SE of Callington. **4 D4** SX3868.
Ashton *Cornw.* ***Village***, 4m/6km W of Helston. **2 C6** SW6028.
Ashton *Devon* ***Locality***, parish 3m/5km N of Chudleigh, containing hamlets of Higher and Lower Ashton. SX8584.
Ashton *Hants.* ***Settlement***, 1m/2km N of Bishop's Waltham. SU5419.
Ashton *Here.* ***Hamlet***, 4m/6km N of Leominster. **28 E2** SO5164.
Ashton *Inclyde* ***Suburb***, SW district of Gourock. NS2377.
Ashton *Lancs.* ***Locality***, to E of River Lune estuary, 3m/5km SW of Lancaster. Hall dates partly from 14c. SD4657.
Ashton *Northants.* ***Village***, 5m/8km E of Towcester. **31 J4** SP7649.
Ashton *Northants.* ***Village***, 1m/2km E of Oundle. **42 D7** TL0588.
Ashton *Peter.* ***Hamlet***, 1m/2km W of Helpston, 5m/8km E of Stamford. TF1005.
Ashton Common *Wilts.* ***Hamlet***, 3m/4km E of Trowbridge. **20 B6** ST8958.
Ashton-in-Makerfield *Gt.Man.* Population: 28,105. ***Town***, 4m/6km S of Wigan. **48 E3** SJ5799.
Ashton Keynes *Wilts.* ***Village***, 4m/6km W of Cricklade. **20 D2** SU0494.
Ashton on Ribble *Lancs.* ***Suburb***, 2m/4km W of Preston town centre. SD5030.
Ashton under Hill *Worcs.* ***Village***, 4m/7km SW of Evesham. **29 J5** SO9938.
Ashton-under-Lyne *Gt.Man.* Population: 43,906. ***Town***, mill town, 6m/10km E of Manchester. Church has magnificent 15c stained glass window. **49 J3** SJ9399.
Ashton upon Mersey *Gt.Man.* ***Suburb***, 1m/2km NW of Sale town centre. **49 G3** SJ7792.
Ashton Watering *N.Som.* ***Locality***, 5m/7km W of Bristol. ST5269.
Ashurst *Hants.* Population: 1270. ***Locality***, residential locality 3m/5km NE of Lyndhurst. **10 E3** SU3310.
Ashurst *Kent* ***Village***, 5m/8km W of Royal Tunbridge Wells. **13 J3** TQ5138.
Ashurst *Lancs.* ***Suburb***, N district of Skelmersdale. SD4807.
Ashurst *W.Suss.* ***Village***, 3m/5km N of Steyning. **12 E5** TQ1716.
Ashurst Bridge *Hants.* ***Settlement***, 1m/2km SW of Totton. SU3312.
Ashurstwood *W.Suss.* ***Village***, 2m/3km SE of East Grinstead. **13 H3** TQ4236.
Ashwater *Devon* ***Village***, 6m/10km SE of Holsworthy. **6 B6** SX3895.
Ashwell *Herts.* Population: 1629. ***Village***, 4m/6km NE of Baldock. **33 F5** TL2639.
Ashwell *Rut.* ***Village***, 3m/5km N of Oakham. **42 B4** SK8613.
Ashwell End *Herts.* ***Settlement***, 1m/2km NW of Ashwell and 4m/7km N of Baldock. TL2540.
Ashwellthorpe *Norf.* ***Village***, 3m/5km SE of Wymondham. **45 F6** TM1497.
Ashwick *Som.* ***Village***, 3m/5km N of Shepton Mallet. **19 K7** ST6348.
Ashwicken *Norf.* ***Hamlet***, 5m/8km E of King's Lynn. **44 B4** TF7018.
Ashworth Moor Reservoir *Gt.Man.* ***Reservoir***, 4m/7km NW of Rochdale. **49 H1** SD8315.
Ashybank *Sc.Bord.* ***Settlement***, 3m/5km NE of Hawick. **70 A2** NT5417.
Askam in Furness *Cumb.* Population: 2212. ***Village***, 3m/4km N of Dalton-in-Furness. **55 F2** SD2177.
Askern *S.Yorks.* Population: 5862. ***Small town***, 7m/11km N of Doncaster. **51 H1** SE5613.
Askerswell *Dorset* ***Village***, 4m/7km E of Bridport. **8 E5** SY5292.
Askett *Bucks.* ***Village***, 1m/2km NE of Princes Risborough. **22 B1** SP8105.
Askham *Cumb.* ***Village***, 4m/7km S of Penrith. **61 G4** NY5123.
Askham *Notts.* ***Village***, 3m/4km N of Tuxford. **51 K5** SK7474.
Askham Bryan *York* ***Village***, 4m/6km SW of York. **58 B5** SE5548.
Askham Richard *York* ***Village***, 5m/8km SW of York. HM prison (Askham Grange). **58 B5** SE5347.
Askival *High.* ***Mountain***, highest point on Rum, 3m/5km S of Kinloch. Height 2663 feet or 812 metres. **85 J5** NM3995.
Asknish Bay *Arg. & B.* ***Bay***, small bay on coast of Argyll, 4m/6km SW of Kilmelford. **79 J7** NM7910.
Askrigg *N.Yorks.* ***Village***, in Wensleydale, 4m/6km NW of Aysgarth. **62 A7** SD9491.
Askrigg Common *N.Yorks.* ***Open space***, moorland between Swaledale and Wensleydale, 2m/3km N of Askrigg. **62 A7** SD9493.
Askwith *N.Yorks.* ***Village***, in Wharfedale, 3m/4km NW of Otley across River Wharfe. **57 G5** SE1648.
Aslackby *Lincs.* ***Village***, 7m/11km N of Bourne. **42 D2** TF0830.
Aslacton *Norf.* ***Village***, 7m/12km NE of Harleston. **45 F6** TM1590.
Asland *See (River) Douglas.*
Aslockton *Notts.* ***Village***, 2m/4km E of Bingham. Birthplace of Thomas Cranmer, 1489. **42 A1** SK7440.
Asloun *Aber.* ***Locality***, comprises Castleton of Asloun and Mains of Asloun surrounding Asloun Castle, 2m/3km SW of Alford. **90 D3** NJ5414.
Aspall *Suff.* ***Settlement***, 1m/2km N of Debenham. **35 F2** TM1765.
Asparagus Island *Cornw.* ***Island***, rock island lying off Kynance Cove, 1m/2km NW of Lizard. SW6813.
Aspatria *Cumb.* Population: 2219. ***Small town***, 8m/12km NE of Maryport. Church has Viking tombstone. **60 C2** NY1441.
Aspenden *Herts.* ***Village***, 1km S of Buntingford. **33 G6** TL3528.
Asperton *Lincs.* ***Hamlet***, 1m/2km N of Wigtoft and 4m/6km NE of Donington. TF2637.
Aspley *Notts.* ***Suburb***, 3m/4km NW of Nottingham city centre. SK5342.
Aspley *Staffs.* ***Settlement***, 1m/2km W of Millmeece. SJ8133.
Aspley Guise *Beds.* ***Village***, 2m/3km N of Woburn. **32 C5** SP9435.
Aspley Heath *Beds.* ***Village***, on heathland, 2m/3km NW of Woburn. **32 C5** SP9235.
Aspley Heath *Warks.* ***Settlement***, 4m/7km NW of Henley-in-Arden. SP0970.
Aspull *Gt.Man.* Population: 4765. ***Small town***, 3m/4km NE of Wigan. **49 F2** SD6108.
Aspull Common *Gt.Man.* ***Suburb***, 1m/2km SW of Leigh. SJ6498.
Asselby *E.Riding* ***Village***, 2m/3km W of Howden. **58 D7** SE7127.
Asserby *Lincs.* ***Settlement***, 3m/4km NE of Alford. TF4977.
Asserby Turn *Lincs.* ***Locality***, 2m/3km NE of Alford. TF4777.
Assich Forest *High.* ***Forest/woodland***, in Nairn district, to S and SW of Cawdor. **97 F7** NH8146.
Assington *Suff.* ***Village***, 4m/7km SE of Sudbury. **34 D5** TL9338.
Assington Green *Suff.* ***Hamlet***, 4m/6km N of Clare. TL7751.
Astbury *Ches.* ***Village***, 1m/2km SW of Congleton. **49 H6** SJ8461.
Astcote *Northants.* ***Village***, 3m/5km N of Towcester. **31 H3** SP6753.
Asterby *Lincs.* ***Hamlet***, 6m/10km N of Horncastle. **53 F5** TF2679.
Asterleigh *Oxon.* ***Settlement***, 2m/4km SE of Enstone. SP4022.
Asterley *Shrop.* ***Hamlet***, 2m/3km W of Pontesbury. **38 C5** SJ3707.
Asterton *Shrop.* ***Hamlet***, 4m/6km SW of Church Stretton across The Long Mynd. **38 C6** SO3991.
Asthall *Oxon.* ***Village***, 2m/4km E of Burford. Site of Romano-British settlement. Site of Roman villa 1m/2km E. **30 D7** SP2811.
Asthall Leigh *Oxon.* ***Village***, 4m/6km E of Burford. **30 E7** SP3012.
Astle *Ches.* ***Settlement***, 1m/2km E of Chelford. SJ8373.
Astley *Shrop.* ***Village***, 5m/8km NE of Shrewsbury. **38 E4** SJ5218.
Astley *Warks.* ***Village***, 4m/6km SW of Nuneaton. **41 F7** SP3189.
Astley *W.Yorks.* ***Locality***, 7m/11km SE of Leeds. SE3828.
Astley *Worcs.* ***Village***, 3m/5km SW of Stourport-on-Severn. **29 G2** SO7867.
Astley Abbotts *Shrop.* ***Village***, 2m/4km N of Bridgnorth. **39 G6** SO7096.
Astley Bridge *Gt.Man.* ***Suburb***, 1m/2km N of Bolton town centre. **49 G1** SD7111.
Astley Cross *Worcs.* ***Locality***, 1m/2km S of Stourport-on-Severn. **29 G2** SO8069.
Astley Green *Gt.Man.* ***Locality***, 2m/3km SE of Tyldesley. **49 G3** SJ7099.
Astley Hall *Lancs.* ***Historic house***, 16c house with later additions, 1km NW of Chorley town centre. **48 E1** SD5718.
Astley Lodge *Shrop.* ***Settlement***, 1km NW of Astley. SJ5219.
Astley Town *Worcs.* ***Locality***, 3m/4km SW of Stourport-on-Severn. SO7968.
Astmoor *Halton* ***Locality***, industrial area in NE Runcorn. SJ5383.
Aston *Ches.* ***Hamlet***, 4m/6km SE of Runcorn. **48 E5** SJ5578.
Aston *Ches.* ***Village***, 4m/7km SW of Nantwich. **39 F1** SJ6146.
Aston *Derbys.* ***Hamlet***, 1km E of Sudbury. SK1631.
Aston *Derbys.* ***Village***, 3m/5km NW of Hathersage. **50 D4** SK1883.
Aston *Flints.* ***Suburb***, to S of Shotton, 6m/10km W of Chester. **48 C6** SJ3067.
Aston *Here.* ***Hamlet***, 4m/6km SW of Ludlow. **28 D1** SO4671.
Aston *Here.* ***Settlement***, 3m/5km NW of Leominster. SO4662.
Aston *Herts.* ***Village***, 3m/4km SE of Stevenage. **33 F6** TL2722.
Aston *Oxon.* ***Village***, 4m/7km S of Witney. **21 G1** SP3403.
Aston *Shrop.* ***Hamlet***, 1m/2km E of Wem. **38 E3** SJ5228.
Aston *Shrop.* ***Settlement***, 6m/10km E of Bridgnorth. SO8093.
Aston *S.Yorks.* ***Locality***, 5m/8km SE of Rotherham. **51 G4** SK4685.
Aston *Staffs.* ***Settlement***, 2m/3km W of Stafford. SJ8923.
Aston *Staffs.* ***Village***, 7m/11km SW of Newcastle-under-Lyme. **39 G1** SJ7541.
Aston *Tel. & W.* ***Settlement***, 1m/2km E of Uppington. **39 F5** SJ6109.
Aston *W.Mid.* ***Suburb***, 2m/3km NE of Birmingham city centre. **40 C7** SP0889.
Aston *W'ham* ***Village***, 2m/3km NE of Henley-on-Thames across river. **22 A3** SU7884.
Aston Abbotts *Bucks.* ***Village***, 4m/7km NE of Aylesbury. **32 B7** SP8420.
Aston Blank *Glos. Alternative name for Cold Aston, qv.*
Aston Botterell *Shrop.* ***Hamlet***, 6m/10km NW of Cleobury Mortimer. **39 F7** SO6384.
Aston-By-Stone *Staffs.* ***Village***, 2m/3km S of Stone. **40 B2** SJ9131.
Aston Cantlow *Warks.* ***Village***, 4m/6km NE of Alcester. **30 C3** SP1359.
Aston Clinton *Bucks.* Population: 3467. ***Locality***, parish and village, 4m/6km E of Aylesbury. **32 B7** SP8712.
Aston Common *S.Yorks.* ***Locality***, adjoining to S of Aston. SK4684.
Aston Crews *Here.* ***Village***, 4m/6km SW of Newent. **29 F6** SO6723.
Aston Cross *Glos.* ***Locality***, 3m/5km E of Tewkesbury. **29 J5** SO9433.
Aston End *Herts.* ***Village***, 2m/4km E of Stevenage. **33 F6** TL2724.
Aston Eyre *Shrop.* ***Village***, 4m/7km W of Bridgnorth. **39 F6** SO6594.
Aston Fields *Worcs.* ***Suburb***, SE district of Bromsgrove. **29 J1** SO9669.
Aston Flamville *Leics.* ***Village***, 3m/4km E of Hinckley. **41 G6** SP4692.
Aston Hall *W.Mid.* ***Historic house***, large 17c house in Aston suburb of Birmingham. **40 C6** SP0889.
Aston Heath *Ches.* ***Settlement***, 1km NE of Aston. SJ5678.
Aston Ingham *Here.* ***Village***, 3m/5km SW of Newent. **29 F6** SO6823.
Aston juxta Mondrum *Ches.* ***Settlement***, 4m/6km W of Crewe. **49 F7** SJ6556.
Aston le Walls *Northants.* ***Village***, 7m/11km NE of Banbury. **31 F3** SP4950.
Aston Magna *Glos.* ***Village***, 2m/3km N of Moreton-in-Marsh. **30 C5** SP1935.
Aston Munslow *Shrop.* ***Hamlet***, 6m/9km NE of Craven Arms. **38 E7** SO5186.
Aston on Carrant *Glos.* ***Hamlet***, 4m/6km E of Tewkesbury. SO9434.
Aston on Clun *Shrop.* ***Village***, 3m/4km W of Craven Arms. **38 C7** SO3981.
Aston-on-Trent *Derbys.* Population: 1214. ***Village***, 6m/9km SE of Derby. **41 G3** SK4129.
Aston Pigott *Shrop.* ***Hamlet***, 1m/2km NE of Worthen. SJ3305.
Aston Rogers *Shrop.* ***Hamlet***, 1m/2km NE of Worthen. **38 C5** SJ3406.
Aston Rowant *Oxon.* ***Village***, 4m/6km NE of Watlington. **22 A2** SU7299.
Aston Sandford *Bucks.* ***Village***, 3m/5km E of Thame. **22 A1** SP7507.
Aston Somerville *Worcs.* ***Village***, 4m/6km S of Evesham. **30 B5** SP0438.
Aston Subedge *Glos.* ***Village***, below escarpment of Cotswold Hills, 2m/3km N of Chipping Campden. **30 C4** SP1341.
Aston Tirrold *Oxon.* ***Village***, 3m/5km SE of Didcot. **21 J3** SU5585.
Aston Upthorpe *Oxon.* ***Village***, 3m/5km SE of Didcot. **21 J3** SU5586.
Astonlane *Shrop.* ***Locality***, 4m/7km W of Bridgnorth. SO6494.
Astrop *Northants.* ***Settlement***, 4m/7km SE of Banbury. SP5036.
Astrope *Herts.* ***Settlement***, 3m/5km NW of Tring. SP8914.
Astwick *Beds.* ***Village***, 4m/6km NW of Baldock. **33 F5** TL2138.
Astwith *Derbys.* ***Hamlet***, 2m/3km S of Heath. SK4464.
Astwood *M.K.* ***Village***, 6m/10km W of Bedford. **32 C4** SP9547.
Astwood Bank *Worcs.* Population: 2235. ***Village***, 4m/6km S of Redditch. **30 B2** SP0462.
Aswarby *Lincs.* ***Hamlet***, 4m/6km S of Sleaford. **42 D1** TF0639.
Aswardby *Lincs.* ***Village***, 3m/5km NW of Spilsby. **53 G5** TF3770.
Aswick Grange *Lincs.* ***Hamlet***, on Moulton East Fen, 5m/8km NE of Crowland. **43 G4** TF3114.
Atch Lench *Worcs.* ***Hamlet***, 4m/7km N of Evesham. **30 B3** SP0350.
Atcham *Shrop.* ***Village***, on River Severn, 4m/6km SE of Shrewsbury, 18c bridge. **38 E5** SJ5409.
Athelhampton *Dorset* ***Historic house***, late 15c mansion, 1km E of Puddletown. Built on site of King Athelstone's Palace with impressive gardens containing rare plants and trees. **9 G5** SY7694.
Athelhampton *Dorset* ***Settlement***, 1m/2km E of Puddletown. SY7794.
Athelington *Suff.* ***Village***, 2m/4km SW of Stradbroke. **35 G1** TM2171.
Athelney *Som.* ***Hamlet***, 5m/8km W of Langport. Obelisk erected 1801 commemorates King Alfred's having hidden here in 878. **8 C2** ST3428.
Athelstaneford *E.Loth.* ***Village***, 3m/4km NE of Haddington. **76 D3** NT5377.
Athelstaneford Church *E.Loth. Alternative name for Church of Plaque, qv.*
Atherfield Green *I.o.W.* ***Settlement***, 2m/4km S of Shorwell. SZ4679.
Atherfield Point *I.o.W.* ***Coastal feature***, rocky headland on SW coast between Brighstone Bay and Chale Bay. **11 F7** SZ4579.
Atherington *Devon* ***Village***, 7m/11km S of Barnstaple. **6 D3** SS5923.
Atherington *W.Suss.* ***Hamlet***, on coast, 5m/8km E of Bognor Regis. TQ0000.

Athersley *S.Yorks.* ***Suburb***, 2m/3km N of Barnsley town centre. SE3509.
Athersley North *S.Yorks.* ***Suburb***, 2m/3km N of Barnsley town centre. SE3509.
Atherstone *Som.* ***Settlement***, 2m/3km NE of Ilminster. ST3816.
Atherstone *Warks.* Population: 10,677. ***Town***, old market town, 5m/8km NW of Nuneaton. Ruins of 12c Merevale Abbey nearby. **41 F6** SP3097.
Atherstone on Stour *Warks.* ***Village***, 3m/4km S of Stratford-upon-Avon. **30 D3** SP2050.
Atherton *Gt.Man.* Population: 21,696. ***Town***, former cotton town, 4m/7km SW of Bolton. **49 F2** SD6703.
Athlinne *W.Isles* ***Settlement***, on NW shore of Loch Seaforth, opposite Seaforth Island. **100 D6** NB1911.
Atholl *P. & K.* ***Locality***, area of some 450 square miles or 1200 square km at S end of Grampian Mountains, including Forest of Atholl. **88 E7** NN7671.
Atholl Sow *P. & K. Alternative name for The Sow of Atholl, qv.*
Atley Hill *N.Yorks.* ***Settlement***, 4m/7km NE of Catterick Bridge. **62 D6** NZ2802.
Atlow *Derbys.* ***Village***, 4m/6km E of Ashbourne. **40 E1** SK2348.
Attadale *High.* ***River***, flowing NW into Loch Carron at settlement of Attadale, Ross and Cromarty district. **87 F1** NG9138.
Attadale *High.* ***Settlement***, 2m/3km S of head of Loch Carron. **87 F1** NG9238.
Attadale Forest *High.* ***Open space***, deer forest on borders of Ross and Cromarty and Skye and Lochalsh districts SE of head of Loch Carron. **87 F1** NG9935.
Attenborough *Notts.* ***Locality***, adjoining to S of Beeston. **41 H2** SK5134.
Atterby *Lincs.* ***Hamlet***, 5m/8km SE of Kirton in Lindsey. **52 C3** SK9893.
Attercliffe *S.Yorks.* ***Suburb***, 2m/3km NE of Sheffield city centre. The centre of Sheffield's former heavy steel industry, it now contains Sheffield Arena and Don Valley Stadium. SK3788.
Attercliffe Hill Top *S.Yorks.* ***Locality***, to NE of Attercliffe, 2m/4km NE of Sheffield city centre. SK3889.
Atterley *Shrop.* ***Settlement***, 2m/3km SE of Much Wenlock. SO6497.
Atterton *Leics.* ***Settlement***, 3m/4km E of Atherstone. SP3598.
Attingham *Shrop.* ***Historic house***, 18c mansion (National Trust) in large park 4m/6km SE of Shrewsbury. Grounds notable for autumnal displays. **38 E4** SJ5509.
Attleborough *Norf.* Population: 6530. ***Small town***, busy Saxon market town, 14m/23km SW of Norwich. **44 E6** TM0495.
Attleborough *Warks.* ***Suburb***, SE district of Nuneaton. **41 F6** SP3790.
Attlebridge *Norf.* ***Village***, on River Wensum, 8m/13km NW of Norwich. **45 F4** TG1216.
Attleton Green *Suff.* ***Hamlet***, to W of Wickhambrook, 7m/12km NE of Haverhill. TL7354.
Atwick *E.Riding* ***Village***, near coast, 2m/3km NW of Hornsea. **59 H4** TA1950.
Atworth *Wilts.* Population: 942. ***Village***, 3m/5km NW of Melksham. Site of Roman villa 1km NW. **20 B5** ST8665.
Auberrow *Here.* ***Hamlet***, 5m/8km N of Hereford. SO4947.
Aubourn *Lincs.* ***Village***, 6m/10km SW of Lincoln. **52 C6** SK9262.
Aubourn Hall *Lincs.* ***Historic house***, 16c house with new rose garden attributed to J. Smythson (Junior), 2m/3km N of Bassingham and 7m/11km S of Lincoln. **52 C6** SK9262.
Auch *Arg. & B.* ***Settlement***, 3m/4km SE of Bridge of Orchy. **80 E4** NN3235.
Auchachenna *Arg. & B.* ***Settlement***, on NW shore of Loch Awe, 1m/2km SW of Kilchrenan. **80 B5** NN0221.
Auchagallon *N.Ayr.* ***Historic/prehistoric site***, stone circle (Historic Scotland) on W coast of Arran, 4m/7km N of Blackwaterfoot. **73 H7** NR8934.
Auchairne *S.Ayr.* ***Settlement***, 2m/3km E of Ballantrae. **67 F5** NX1081.
Auchalick Bay *Arg. & B.* ***Bay***, on E side of Loch Fyne, 3m/5km S of Kilfinan. **73 G3** NR9174.
Auchallater *Aber.* ***Settlement***, 2m/3km S of Braemar. **89 J6** NO1588.
Auchameanach *Arg. & B.* ***Settlement***, on Kintyre, 1m/2km E of Claonaig. **73 G5** NR8956.
Auchamore (Also known as South Thundergay.) *N.Ayr.* ***Settlement***, on NW coast of Arran, 1m/2km N of Pirnmill. NR8745.
Aucharnie *Aber.* ***Settlement***, 4m/6km S of Inverkeithny. **98 E6** NJ6340.
Aucharrigill *High.* ***Settlement***, 1m/2km E of Invercassley. **96 B1** NC4901.
Auchattie *Aber.* ***Hamlet***, 1km S of Banchory. **90 E5** NO6994.
Auchavan *Angus* ***Settlement***, in Glen Isla, 5m/8km E of Spittal of Glenshee. **82 C1** NO1969.
Auchbraad *Arg. & B.* ***Settlement***, 3m/4km SW of Ardrishaig. **73 G2** NR8381.
Auchbreck *Moray* ***Settlement***, at road junction, 2m/3km N of Tomnavoulin. **89 K2** NJ2028.
Auchenback *E.Renf.* ***Suburb***, in SE part of Barrhead. NS5058.
Auchenblae *Aber.* ***Village***, 8m/12km NW of Inverbervie. **91 F7** NO7278.
Auchenbothie *Inclyde* ***Settlement***, 1km NW of Kilmacolm. **74 B3** NS3571.
Auchenbrack *D. & G.* ***Settlement***, 4m/6km N of Moniaive. **68 C4** NX7696.
Auchenbreck *Arg. & B.* ***Settlement***, to E of confluence of Auchenbreck Burn and River Ruel, 3m/4km SE of Clachan of Glendaruel. **73 J2** NS0281.
Auchencairn *D. & G.* ***Village***, 7m/11km S of Dalbeattie. **65 J5** NX7951.
Auchencairn Bay *D. & G.* ***Bay***, inlet on Solway Firth, to E of Auchencairn. **65 J5** NX7951.
Auchencloy Hill *D. & G.* ***Hill***, 1km N of Loch Skerrow, 8m/13km N of Gatehouse of Fleet. Height 686 feet or 209 metres. **65 F4** NX6069.
Auchencorth Moss *Midloth.* ***Large natural feature***, upland plateau on border with Scottish Borders, about 3m/5km SW of Penicuik. **75 K5** NT2055.
Auchencrow *Sc.Bord.* ***Village***, 3m/5km N of Chirnside. **77 G4** NT8560.
Auchendinny *Midloth.* ***Village***, 2m/3km NE of Penicuik. **76 A4** NT2562.
Auchendolly *D. & G.* ***Settlement***, 4m/6km N of Castle Douglas. **65 H4** NX7668.
Auchenfoyle *Inclyde* ***Settlement***, 3m/4km W of Kilmacolm. **74 B3** NS3170.
Auchengillan *Stir.* ***Settlement***, 3m/5km W of Strathblane. NS5180.
Auchengray *S.Lan.* ***Village***, 5m/8km N of Carnwath. **75 H5** NS9954.
Auchenhalrig *Moray* ***Settlement***, near N coast, 4m/6km SW of Buckie. **98 B4** NJ3761.
Auchenheath *S.Lan.* ***Hamlet***, 1m/2km E of Blackwood across River Nethan. **75 G6** NS8043.
Auchenhessnane *D. & G.* ***Settlement***, 5m/8km W of Thornhill. **68 D4** NX8096.
Auchenlochan *Arg. & B.* ***Hamlet***, in Argyll, on W shore of Kyles of Bute, 1km S of Tighnabruaich. **73 H3** NR9772.
Auchenmalg *D. & G.* ***Settlement***, adjacent to E of Glen of Luce, 4m/6km SE of Glenluce. **64 C5** NX2352.
Auchenmalg Bay *D. & G.* ***Bay***, S facing bay on E side of Luce Bay, 4m/7km SE of Glenluce. **64 C5** NX2351.
Auchenreoch Loch *D. & G.* ***Lake/loch***, 1m/2km SW of Crocketford. **65 J3** NX8171.
Auchenrivock *D. & G.* ***Settlement***, on W side of River Esk, 3m/4km S of Langholm. **69 J5** NY3780.
Auchentiber *N.Ayr.* ***Hamlet***, 4m/6km W of Stewarton. **74 B6** NS3647.
Auchessan *Stir.* ***Settlement***, in Glen Dochart, 9m/13km SW of Killin. **81 F5** NN4427.
Auchgourish *High.* ***Settlement***, 2m/3km S of Boat of Garten. **89 G3** NH9315.
Auchinafaud *Arg. & B.* ***Settlement***, on W coast of Kintyre, 4m/6km NE of Tayinloan. **73 F5** NR7251.
Auchinairn *E.Dun.* ***Suburb***, 1km SE of Bishopbriggs. NS6169.
Auchinbee *N.Lan.* ***Settlement***, 2m/3km W of Cumbernauld town centre. NS7375.
Auchindarrach *Arg. & B.* ***Hamlet***, just NW of Lochgilphead. **73 G2** NR8688.
Auchindarroch *High.* ***Settlement***, in Appin, 4m/6km SW of South Ballachulish. **80 B2** NN0055.
Auchindoun Castle *Moray* ***Castle***, ruined 16c fortress (Historic Scotland) built over ancient earthworks, 2m/3km SE of Dufftown. **90 B1** NJ3437.
Auchindrain *Arg. & B.* ***Settlement***, 2m/3km N of Furnace. An original West Highland township which has survived much in its original form, with buildings restored and equipped to demonstrate life of Highlanders in past centuries. **80 B7** NN0203.
Auchindrain Township Open Air Museum *Arg. & B.* ***Other feature of interest***, museum of original West Highland township, 5m/8km SW of Inveraray, showing Highland life through displays and exhibitions. **80 B7** NN0303.
Auchindrean *High.* ***Settlement***, in valley of River Broom, 10m/15km SE of Ullapool. **95 H3** NH1980.
Auchingilloch *S.Lan.* ***Mountain***, 6m/9km S of Strathaven. Height 1515 feet or 462 metres. **74 E7** NS7035.
Auchininna *Aber.* ***Settlement***, above S side of River Deveron, 4m/6km SE of Aberchirder. **98 E6** NJ6446.
Auchinleck *E.Ayr.* Population: 4116. ***Small town***, 1m/2km NW of Cumnock. **67 K1** NS5521.
Auchinloch *N.Lan.* ***Hamlet***, 2m/3km S of Kirkintilloch. **74 E3** NS6670.
Auchinner *P. & K.* ***Settlement***, in Glen Artney, 6m/10km NE of Callander. **81 H6** NN6915.
Auchinroath *Moray* ***Settlement***, 1m/2km N of Rothes. **97 K6** NJ2651.
Auchintore *High.* ***Locality***, on E shore of Loch Linnhe, 1m/2km SW of Fort William. NN0972.
Auchintoul *Aber.* ***Locality***, comprises Auchintoul Moss and settlements of Newtown of Auchintoul and Home Farm Auchintoul, 1km NW of Aberchirder. **98 E5** NJ6152.
Auchintoul *Aber.* ***Settlement***, on S side of River Don, 3m/4km W of Alford. **90 D3** NJ5316.
Auchintoul *High.* ***Settlement***, in Sutherland district, 3m/4km W of Linsidemore. **96 C1** NH5299.
Auchinvennal *Arg. & B.* ***Settlement***, on N side of Glen Fruin, 4m/6km N of Helensburgh. **74 A2** NS2888.
Auchiries *Aber.* ***Settlement***, 1m/2km NW of Cruden Bay. **91 J1** NK0837.
Auchleven *Aber.* ***Village***, 3m/4km S of Insch. **90 E2** NJ6224.
Auchlochan *S.Lan.* ***Settlement***, on S bank of River Nethan, 2m/3km S of Lesmahagow. **75 G7** NS8037.
Auchlunachan *High.* ***Settlement***, in valley of River Broom, 1m/2km S of head of Loch Broom. **95 H3** NH1783.
Auchlunies *Aber.* ***Settlement***, 3m/5km NW of Portlethen. **91 G5** NO8899.
Auchlunkart *Moray* ***Settlement***, 4m/6km E of Rothes. **98 B6** NJ3449.
Auchlyne *Stir.* ***Settlement***, in Glen Dochart, 4m/7km SW of Killin. **81 G5** NN5129.
Auchlyne West Burn *Stir.* ***River***, running SE, then S into River Dochart, 5m/7km SW of Killin. **81 F4** NN5028.
Auchmacoy *Aber.* ***Locality***, and estate, 2m/4km E of Ellon. **91 H1** NJ9930.
Auchmair *Moray* ***Settlement***, on E side of River Deveron, 1km N of Cabrach. **90 B2** NJ3828.
Auchmannoch Muir *E.Ayr.* ***Open space***, moorland 2m/4km NW below Wedder Hill. **74 D7** NS5632.
Auchmantle *D. & G.* ***Settlement***, 2m/3km SW of New Luce. **64 B4** NX1562.
Auchmithie *Angus* ***Village***, with harbour, 3m/5km NE of Arbroath. **83 H3** NO6844.
Auchmuirbridge *Fife* ***Locality***, 2m/3km W of Leslie. **82 D7** NO2101.
Auchmull *Angus* ***Hamlet***, 4m/6km NW of Edzell. **90 D7** NO5874.
Auchmuty *Fife* ***Suburb***, central district of Glenrothes. NO2700.
Auchnabony *D. & G.* ***Settlement***, 4m/6km E of Kirkcudbright. **65 H6** NX7448.
Auchnabreac *Arg. & B.* ***Settlement***, on NW side of Loch Fyne, 1m/2km SW of Inveraray. **80 B7** NN0806.
Auchnacloich *P. & K.* ***Settlement***, in Glen Quaich, 10m/16km N of Crieff. **81 K4** NN8439.
Auchnacraig *Arg. & B.* ***Settlement***, on Mull, 1m/2km SW of Grass Point. **79 J5** NM7330.
Auchnacree *Angus* ***Hamlet***, 1m/2km E of Glenogil. **83 F1** NO4663.
Auchnafree *P. & K.* ***Settlement***, in Glen Almond, 8m/12km NW of Crieff. **81 K4** NN8133.
Auchnafree Hill *P. & K.* ***Mountain***, 2m/4km E of Ben Chonzie, S of Glen Almond. Height 2565 feet or 782 metres. **81 K4** NN8030.
Auchnagallin *High.* ***Settlement***, 4m/6km N of Grantown-on-Spey. **89 H1** NJ0533.
Auchnagatt *Aber.* ***Village***, 4m/6km S of Maud. **99 H6** NJ9341.
Auchnaha *Arg. & B.* ***Settlement***, on Cowal peninsula, 6m/10km NW of Tighnabruaich. **73 H2** NR9381.
Auchnangoul *Arg. & B.* ***Settlement***, 3m/5km SW of Inveraray. **80 B7** NN0505.
Aucholzie *Aber.* ***Settlement***, next to River Muick, 4m/6km SW of Ballater. **90 B5** NO3490.
Auchorrie *Aber.* ***Settlement***, 4m/7km W of Echt. **90 E4** NJ6605.
Auchrannie *Angus* ***Hamlet***, 3m/5km NE of Alyth. NO2852.
Auchraw *Stir.* ***Settlement***, to E of Lochearnhead. **81 G5** NN5923.
Auchreoch *Stir.* ***Settlement***, in Strath Fillan, 3m/4km NW of Crianlarich. **80 E5** NN3528.
Auchronie *Angus* ***Settlement***, 1m/2km E of Loch Lee. **90 C6** NO4480.
Auchtascailt *High.* ***Locality***, in Ross and Cromarty district, at head of Little Loch Broom on W coast. NH0987.
Auchter *N.Lan.* ***River***, rising on NW slopes of Black Law in Kingshill Plantation, and flowing E, then N to join South Calder Water to NE at Newmains. **75 G5** NS8356.
Auchterarder *P. & K.* Population: 3549. ***Small town***, former wool and linen-weaving town, 8m/12km SE of Crieff. Gleneagles golf courses nearby. **82 A6** NN9412.
Auchtercairn *High.* ***Settlement***, adjoining to S of Gairloch, Ross and Cromarty district. **94 E4** NG8076.
Auchterderran *Fife* ***Village***, 4m/7km NE of Cowdenbeath. **76 A1** NT2196.
Auchterhouse *Angus* ***Settlement***, nearly 1m/2km W of Kirkton of Auchterhouse. **82 E4** NO3337.
Auchterhouse Hill *Angus* ***Mountain***, with ancient fort on Sidlaw Hills, 1m/2km W of Craigowl Hill and 6m/10km NW of Dundee. Height 1397 feet or 426 metres. **82 E3** NO3539.
Auchterless *Aber. Alternative name for Kirktown of Auchterless, qv.*
Auchtermuchty *Fife* Population: 1932. ***Small town***, 4m/7km S of Newburgh. Site of Roman camp on E side of town. **82 D6** NO2311.
Auchterneed *High.* ***Settlement***, 1km N of Strathpeffer. **96 B5** NH4859.
Auchtertool *Fife* ***Village***, 4m/6km W of Kirkcaldy. **76 A1** NT2190.
Auchtertyre *Angus* ***Settlement***, 1km W of Newtyle. **82 D3** NO2841.
Auchtertyre *High.* ***Settlement***, in Skye and Lochalsh district, 3m/4km W of Dornie. NG8427.
Auchtertyre *Moray* ***Settlement***, 3m/5km SW of Elgin. **97 J6** NJ1858.
Auchtertyre *Stir.* ***Settlement***, in Strath Fillan, 3m/5km NW of Crianlarich. **80 E5** NN3529.
Auchtertyre Hill *High.* ***Mountain***, in Skye and Lochalsh district, 1m/2km NW of Auchtertyre. Height 1483 feet or 452 metres. **86 E2** NG8328.
Auchtoo *Stir.* ***Settlement***, 1m/2km E of Balquidder. **81 G5** NN5520.
Auckengill *High.* ***Settlement***, near E coast of Caithness district, 6m/9km S of John o' Groats. **105 J2** ND3664.
Auckland Castle *Dur.* ***Castle***, on NE side of Bishop Auckland. Palace of Bishops of Durham, built 17c-18c, with chapel dating from 12c banqueting hall. 18c Deer House (English Heritage) in surrounding park. **62 D3** NZ2130.
Auckland Park *Dur.* ***Locality***, 1m/2km E of Bishop Auckland. NZ2228.
Auckley *S.Yorks.* ***Village***, 5m/8km E of Doncaster. **51 J2** SE6501.
Audenshaw *Gt.Man.* Population: 13,173. ***Town***, 5m/8km E of Manchester. **49 J3** SJ9196.
Audlem *Ches.* Population: 1797. ***Village***, 6m/10km N of Market Drayton. **39 F1** SJ6643.
Audley *Staffs.* Population: 6180. ***Village***, 4m/7km NW of Newcastle-under-Lyme. **49 G7** SJ7950.
Audley End *Essex* ***Hamlet***, 1m/2km W of Saffron Walden. Audley End (English Heritage) house to N. **33 J5** TL5237.
Audley End *Essex* ***Historic house***, large 17c Jacobean house (English Heritage) set in parkland landscaped by 'Capability' Brown in 1760s. Situated to N of Audley End hamlet and adjacent to W of Saffron Walden. **33 J5** TL5238.
Audley End *Essex* ***Settlement***, to S of Gestingthorpe, 4m/7km N of Halstead. TL8137.
Audley End *Suff.* ***Hamlet***, 5m/7km N of Long Melford. TL8553.

Audley's Cross *Staffs. See Battle of Blore Heath 1459, qv.*
Audmore *Staffs.* ***Settlement***, 1km NE of Gnosall. SJ8321.
Auds *Aber.* ***Settlement***, 2m/3km W of Banff. **98 E4** NJ6564.
Aughton *E.Riding* ***Village***, 11m/18km W of Market Weighton. Earthworks of motte and bailey castle. **58 D6** SE7038.
Aughton *Lancs.* ***Hamlet***, 6m/10km NE of Lancaster. **55 J3** SD5567.
Aughton *Lancs.* ***Village***, 2m/4km SW of Ormskirk. **48 C2** SD3905.
Aughton *S.Yorks.* Population: 14,122. ***Locality***, 4m/7km S of Rotherham. **51 G4** SK4586.
Aughton *Wilts.* ***Hamlet***, just N of Collingbourne Kingston and 4m/6km N of Ludgershall. SU2356.
Aughton Park *Lancs.* ***Suburb***, S district of Ormskirk. **48 D2** SD3905.
Auld Brig o'Doon *S.Ayr. See Alloway.*
Auld Darkney *Angus* ***Mountain***, 1m/2km NE of Glenmoy. Height 1788 feet or 545 metres. **83 F1** NO4266.
Auld Kirk *S.Ayr.* ***Ecclesiastical building***, built 1654 in centre of Ayr. Robert Burns baptised here. **67 H1** NS3422.
Auldearn *High.* ***Village***, in Nairn district, 2m/4km E of Nairn. Site of battle in 1645 in which Montrose defeated Covenanters under General Hurry. **97 G6** NH9155.
Aulden *Here.* ***Hamlet***, 3m/5km SW of Leominster. **28 D3** SO4654.
Auldgirth *D. & G.* ***Village***, on E bank of River Nith, 7m/12km NW of Dumfries. NX9186.
Auldhame *E.Loth.* ***Hamlet***, 2m/3km N of Whitekirk. **76 D2** NT5984.
Auldhouse *S.Lan.* ***Settlement***, 3m/4km S of East Kilbride. **74 E5** NS6250.
Auldton Fell *D. & G.* ***Mountain***, 3m/4km NE of Moffat. Height 1643 feet or 501 metres. **69 G3** NT1108.
Aulich *P. & K.* ***Settlement***, on N shore of Loch Rannoch, 3m/5km W of Kinloch Rannoch. **81 H2** NN6059.
Aulich Burn *P. & K.* ***River***, flowing SE into Loch Rannoch, 3m/5km W of Kinloch Rannoch. **81 G1** NN6058.
Auliston Point *High.* ***Coastal feature***, headland to S of entrance into Loch Sunart, 3m/5km NE of Tobermory across Sound of Mull. **79 G2** NM5458.
Ault a' chruinn *High.* ***Settlement***, at head of Loch Duich, 1m/2km NE of Shiel Bridge. **87 F2** NG9420.
Ault Hucknall *Derbys.* ***Hamlet***, 5m/8km NW of Mansfield. **51 G6** SK4665.
Aultanrynie *High.* ***Settlement***, on N side of Loch More, Sutherland district. **103 F5** NC3436.
Aultbea *High.* ***Village***, on E shore of Loch Ewe, W coast of Ross and Cromarty district, 5m/8km N of Poolewe. **94 E3** NG8789.
Aultgrishan *High.* ***Village***, on W coast of Ross and Cromarty district, 4m/6km S of Rubha Réidh. **94 D3** NG7485.
Aultguish Inn *High.* ***Settlement***, at SE end of Loch Glascarnoch, 5m/8km NW of Gorstan. **95 K4** NH3570.
Aultibea *High.* ***Settlement***, on N bank of River Langwell Water, 5m/8km W of Berriedale. **105 F6** ND0423.
Aultiphurst *High.* ***Settlement***, 3m/5km SW of Strathy Point, Caithness district. **104 D2** NC8065.
Aultmore *Moray* ***Forest/woodland***, wooded region 6m/9km NE of Keith. **98 C5** NJ4657.
Aultmore *Moray* ***Locality***, 2m/4km NW of Keith. Also wooded tract to NE, from which Burn of Aultmore runs S to River Isla. **98 C5** NJ4053.
Aultnagoire *High.* ***Settlement***, 3m/5km NE of Foyers. **88 C2** NH5423.
Aultnamain Inn *High.* ***Settlement***, 8m/12km SE of Bonar Bridge. **96 D3** NH6681.
Aultnapaddock *Aber.* ***Settlement***, 5m/8km E of Dufftown. **98 B6** NJ3941.
Aulton *Aber.* ***Settlement***, 2m/3km W of Insch. **90 E2** NJ6028.
Aultvaich *High.* ***Settlement***, in Ross and Cromarty district, 1m/2km SW of Muir of Ord. NH5148.
Aultvoulin *High.* ***Settlement***, adjoining to W of Inverie, on Inverie Bay, Lochaber district. **86 D4** NG7600.
Aunby *Lincs.* ***Settlement***, 5m/8km N of Stamford. TF0214.
Aundorach *High.* ***Settlement***, 3m/5km SW of Nethy Bridge. **89 G3** NH9816.
Aunk *Devon* ***Hamlet***, 5m/7km NW of Ottery St. Mary. **7 J5** ST0400.
Aunsby *Lincs.* ***Village***, 5m/7km S of Sleaford. **42 D2** TF0438.
Auquhorthies *Aber.* ***Settlement***, 2m/3km NE of Oldmeldrum. **91 G2** NJ8329.
Auskerry *Ork.* ***Island***, uninhabited island 1m/2km N to S and 1km E to W, situated 2m/4km S of Stronsay across Auskerry Sound. Lighthouse at S end. **107 F6** HY6716.
Auskerry Sound *Ork.* ***Sea feature***, stretch of sea separating Auskerry and Stronsay islands. **107 F6** HY6716.
Aust *S.Glos.* ***Village***, below E end of Severn Road Bridge, 4m/7km W of Thornbury. **19 J3** ST5789.
Austcliffe *Worcs.* ***Locality***, 3m/4km NE of Kidderminster. SO8480.
Austendike *Lincs.* ***Locality***, 3m/5km E of Spalding. TF2921.
Austerfield *S.Yorks.* ***Village***, 1m/2km NE of Bawtry. **51 J3** SK6694.
Austerlands *Gt.Man.* ***Suburb***, 2m/3km E of Oldham town centre. SD9505.
Austhorpe *W.Yorks.* ***Suburb***, 4m/7km E of Leeds city centre. SE3733.
Austonley *W.Yorks.* ***Locality***, 2m/3km W of Holmfirth. **50 D2** SE1107.
Austrey *Warks.* ***Village***, 5m/9km N of Atherstone. **40 E5** SK2906.
Austwick *N.Yorks.* ***Village***, 4m/7km NW of Settle. **56 C3** SD7668.
Authorpe *Lincs.* ***Village***, 5m/8km NW of Alford. **53 H4** TF4080.
Authorpe Row *Lincs.* ***Settlement***, 1m/2km N of Hogsthorpe. **53 J5** TF5373.
Avebury *Wilts.* ***Village***, 6m/9km W of Marlborough. National Trust site partly enclosed by megalithic stone circle of Avebury Ring (National Trust). **20 D4** SU1069.
Avebury Manor and Garden *Wilts.* ***Historic house***, much altered 16c house (National Trust) featuring Queen Anne and Edwardian renovations, 6m/10km W of Marlborough. Topiary and flower gardens with medieval walls, ancient box and numerous compartments. **20 D4** SU0970.
Avebury Ring *Wilts.* ***Historic/prehistoric site***, stone circle (National Trust) encompassing part of village of Avebury, enclosed by ditch and external bank. **20 E5** SU1069.
Avebury Trusloe *Wilts.* ***Settlement***, just W of Avebury. SU0969.
Aveley *Thur.* Population: 7295. ***Small town***, 3m/5km NW of Grays. **23 J3** TQ5680.
Avening *Glos.* ***Village***, 2m/3km SE of Nailsworth. **20 B2** ST8897.
Averham *Notts.* ***Village***, 2m/4km W of Newark-on-Trent across River Trent. **51 K7** SK7654.
Averon (Also known as Alness (River)). *High.* ***River***, running from NW through Alness to Cromarty Firth. **96 D4** NH6569.
Avery Hill *Gt.Lon.* ***Suburb***, in borough of Greenwich, 1m/2km E of Eltham. TQ4474.
Aveton Gifford *Devon* ***Village***, at head of River Avon estuary, 3m/5km NW of Kingsbridge. **5 G6** SX6947.
Avich *Arg. & B.* ***River***, in Argyll running from Loch Avich to Loch Awe. NM9713.
Avielochan *High.* ***Settlement***, 2m/3km N of Aviemore. **89 G3** NH9016.
Aviemore *High.* Population: 2214. ***Village***, and skiing centre on River Spey, in Badenoch and Strathspey district, 11m/18 km NE of Kingussie. **89 F3** NH8912.
Aviemore Centre *High.* ***Other feature of interest***, leisure, sport and conference centre in Aviemore, with particular emphasis on winter sports. **89 F3** NH8911.
Avill *Som.* ***River***, rising on Exmoor and flowing past Dunster into Blue Anchor Bay. SS9945.
Avington *Hants.* ***Hamlet***, 4m/6km NE of Winchester. **11 G1** SU5332.
Avington *W.Berks.* ***Hamlet***, 2m/4km E of Hungerford. **21 G5** SU3768.
Avington Park *Hants.* ***Historic house***, 17c house in park with lake, beside River Itchen. **11 G1** SU5332.
Avoch *High.* Population: 1010. ***Village***, in Ross and Cromarty district, on W shore of Inner Moray Firth or Inverness Firth, 2m/3km SW of Fortrose. **96 D6** NH7055.
Avoch Bay *High.* ***Bay***, small bay at Avoch on Moray Firth, on S coast of Black Isle. **96 D6** NH6954.
Avon ***River***, rising on Cairngorm Mountains and running E through Loch Avon and down Glen Avon, then N to Tomintoul and down Strath Avon to River Spey just below Ballindalloch Castle, 7m/11km SW of Charlestown of Aberlour. **89 J3** NJ1737.
Avon ***River***, rising near South Kilworth and flowing generally SW by Rugby, Stratford-upon-Avon, Evesham and Pershore, and into River Severn at Tewkesbury. **30 D3** SO8833.
Avon ***River***, rising W of Sherston and flowing W to Malmesbury before meandering SW to Bath via Chippenham, Melksham and Bradford-on-Avon. At Bath river cuts a steep valley through S extension of Cotswold Hills; it also forms W end of Kennet and Avon canal. From Bath river continues NW to Bristol and flows through narrow Avon Gorge before joining River Severn estuary at Avonmouth. Navigable to Bristol for large vessels; tidal to Swineford, E of Keynsham. ST5078.
Avon ***River***, rising in Vale of Pewsey and flowing S through Amesbury, Salisbury, Fordingbridge and Ringwood, and then into Christchurch Harbour. **10 C2** SZ1692.
Avon *Devon* ***River***, rising on Dartmoor and flowing generally S into Bigbury Bay, 1m/2km NW of Thurlestone. **5 H5** SX6543.
Avon *Hants.* ***Hamlet***, on River Avon, 4m/6km N of Christchurch. **10 C5** SZ1498.
Avon Dassett *Warks.* ***Village***, 7m/11km NW of Banbury. **31 F3** SP4150.
Avon Heath Country Park *Dorset* ***Leisure/recreation***, 2m/3km SW of Ringwood. Over 1200 acres of grassland, heath and coniferous woodlands. Also nature trails, including some especially for children. **10 C4** SU1203.
Avon Valley Railway *S.Glos.* ***Other feature of interest***, steam railway running for about 1m/2km between Oldland and Bitton through the scenic River Avon valley, 5m/8km E of Bristol. **19 K4** ST6571.
Avon Water ***River***, rising 6m/10km SE of Galston and flowing NE past Strathaven to Larkhall, then N to River Clyde 1m/2km E of Hamilton. **75 F6** NS7356.
Avonbridge *Falk.* ***Village***, 5m/8km S of Falkirk. **75 H3** NS9172.
Avoncliff *Wilts.* ***Hamlet***, on S bank of River Avon, 1m/2km SW of Bradford-on-Avon, with railway station across river. **20 B5** ST8059.
Avoncroft Museum of Buildings *Worcs.* ***Other feature of interest***, collection of re-erected historic buildings, 1m/2km S of Bromsgrove town centre. Demonstrations of nail-making, chain-making, brick-making, windmilling and wood-turning. **29 J2** SO9568.
Avondale *Torfaen* ***Locality***, industrial estate in N part of Cwmbran. ST2996.
Avonmouth *Bristol* ***Town***, port of Bristol, 6m/9km NW of city centre. Large docks and industrial area. River Avon here spanned by M5 motorway. **19 J4** ST5178.
Avonwick *Devon* ***Village***, on River Avon, 2m/3km SE of South Brent. **5 H5** SX7158.
Awbridge *Hants.* ***Village***, 2m/4km NW of Romsey. **10 E2** SU3223.
Awe *Arg. & B.* ***River***, running from Loch Awe through Pass of Brander to Loch Etive at Bonawe. **80 B4** NN0132.
Awhirk *D. & G.* ***Settlement***, 3m/5km E of Portpatrick. **64 A5** NX0553.
Awkley *S.Glos.* ***Settlement***, 1m/2km NW of Almondsbury. **19 J3** ST5985.
Awliscombe *Devon* ***Village***, 2m/3km NW of Honiton. **7 K5** ST1301.
Awre *Glos.* ***Village***, on River Severn estuary, 2m/4km E of Blakeney. **20 A1** SO7008.
Awsworth *Notts.* Population: 2903. ***Village***, 6m/10km NW of Nottingham. **41 G1** SK4844.
Axbridge *Som.* ***Village***, 2m/3km W of Cheddar. **19 H6** ST4354.
Axe ***River***, rising under Mendip Hills and flowing out above ground at Wookey Hole, then NW into Bristol Channel at Weston Bay, to S of Weston-super-Mare. **19 G6** ST2959.
Axe ***River***, rising N of Beaminster and flowing W and then SW into Lyme Bay to E of Seaton. **8 B5** SY2589.
Axe Edge *Staffs.* ***Mountain***, 3m/4km SW of Buxton. Height 1807 feet or 551 metres. **50 C6** SK0268.
Axford *Hants.* ***Village***, 1m/2km N of Preston Candover. **21 K7** SU6143.
Axford *Wilts.* ***Village***, on River Kennet, 3m/5km E of Marlborough. **21 F4** SU2370.
Axminster *Devon* Population: 3472. ***Small town***, market town on River Axe, 5m/8km NW of Lyme Regis. Famous for its carpet factory. **8 B5** SY2998.
Axminster Museum *Devon* ***Other feature of interest***, in Axminster town centre, situated in old 19c police station's court room. **8 C5** SY2998.
Axmouth *Devon* ***Small town***, small resort near mouth of River Axe, 1m/2km NE of Seaton across river. **8 B5** SY2591.
Axton *Flints.* ***Hamlet***, 3m/4km SE of Prestatyn. SJ1080.
Axtown *Devon* ***Hamlet***, 1km SW of Yelverton. SX5167.
Aycliffe *Dur.* ***Village***, 5m/8km N of Darlington. Adjoins Aycliffe Industrial Estate in Newton Aycliffe. **62 D4** NZ2822.
Aycliffe Industrial Estate *Dur.* ***Locality***, large industrial estate in S part of Newton Aycliffe, adjoining Aycliffe. NZ2723.
Aydon *Northumb.* ***Hamlet***, 2m/3km NE of Corbridge. Aydon Castle (English Heritage), 1km NW. **71 F7** NZ0066.
Aye Gill Pike *Cumb.* ***Mountain***, with steep sides to N and S, 1m/2km N of Dent. Height 1824 feet or 556 metres. **56 C1** SD7288.
Aygill *N.Yorks.* ***Locality***, 1km S of Keld. NY8800.
Aylburton *Glos.* ***Village***, 1m/2km SW of Lydney. **19 K1** SO6101.
Ayle *Northumb.* ***Settlement***, 2m/3km N of Alston. **61 J2** NY7149.
Aylesbeare *Devon* ***Village***, 5m/7km SW of Ottery St. Mary. **7 J6** SY0392.
Aylesbury *Bucks.* Population: 58,058. ***Town***, on plain below N escarpment of Chiltern Hills, 36m/58km NW of London. Many old buildings and streets. The King's Head (National Trust), still an inn, dates partly from 15c. **32 B7** SP8113.
Aylesby *N.E.Lincs.* ***Village***, 4m/7km W of Grimsby. **53 F2** TA2007.
Aylesford *Kent* Population: 8028. ***Village***, on River Medway, 3m/5km NW of Maidstone. 13c Carmelite priory. 14c bridge spans river. Industrial and residential development to W. **14 C2** TQ7258.
Aylesford Bridge *Kent* ***Bridge***, 14c curved bridge built of Kentish ragstone over River Medway at Aylesford, 3m/4km NW of Maidstone. TQ7258.
Aylesford Priory (The Friars). *Kent* ***Ecclesiastical building***, Carmelite priory, built in 1242, 1m/2km N of Maidstone. Now a pilgrimage shrine. **14 C2** TQ7258.
Aylesham *Kent* Population: 4044. ***Village***, 7m/11km SE of Canterbury. **15 H2** TR2352.
Aylestone *Leic.* ***Suburb***, 2m/4km S of Leicester city centre. **41 H5** SK5700.
Aylestone Bridge *Leics.* ***Bridge***, 15c stone packhorse bridge over River Soar in Leicester. Only 4 feet wide between parapets. SK5701.
Aylestone Park *Leics.* ***Suburb***, adjoining to NE of Aylestone, 2m/3km S of Leicester city centre. SK5801.
Aylmerton *Norf.* ***Village***, 3m/4km SW of Cromer. **45 F2** TG1839.
Aylsham *Norf.* Population: 4910. ***Small town***, market town on River Bure, 12m/19km N of Norwich. **45 F3** TG1926.
Aylton *Here.* ***Hamlet***, 3m/5km W of Ledbury. **29 F5** SO6537.
Aymestrey *Here.* ***Village***, 6m/9km NW of Leominster. **28 D2** SO4265.
Aynho *Northants.* ***Village***, 6m/9km SE of Banbury. **31 G5** SP5133.
Aynhoe Park *Northants.* ***Historic house***, 17c mansion at Aynho, 6m/10km SE of Banbury. **31 G5** SP5133.
Ayot Green *Herts.* ***Hamlet***, 1m/2km NW of Welwyn Garden City. TL2114.
Ayot St. Lawrence *Herts.* ***Village***, 2m/4km W of Welwyn. Shaw's Corner (National Trust), formerly home of George Bernard Shaw. **32 E7** TL1916.
Ayot St. Peter *Herts.* ***Hamlet***, 1m/2km SW of Welwyn. **33 F7** TL2115.
Ayr *E.Ayr.* ***River***, rising E of Muirkirk and flowing W through Sorn and Catrine to Firth of Clyde. **67 H1** NS3321.
Ayr *S.Ayr.* Population: 47,962. ***Town***, resort on Firth of Clyde at mouth of River Ayr, 12m/19km SW of Kilmarnock. Commercial and administrative centre. Racecourse. **67 H1** NS3321.
Ayr Bay *S.Ayr.* ***Bay***, wide, W facing bay between Troon and Heads of Ayr. Town of Ayr is situated at centre of bay. **67 H1** NS3222.
Ayr Racecourse *S.Ayr.* ***Racecourse***, to NE of Ayr town centre across Water of Girvan. Stages Scottish Grand National. One mixed, sixteen flat and fourteen National Hunt race days each year. **67 H1** NS3522.

Ayre's Quay *T. & W.* ***Locality***, on S bank of River Wear in Sunderland, 1km NW of city centre. NZ3857.
Aysgarth *N.Yorks.* ***Village***, in Wensleydale, 7m/12km W of Leyburn. The waterfall, Aysgarth Falls, is 1m/2km downstream to E. **57 F1** SE0088.
Aysgarth Falls (Also known as Aysgarth Force.) *N.Yorks.* ***Waterfall***, two separate waterfalls in course of River Ure, just NE of Aysgarth. Cut into limestone, they descend in series of rock 'steps'. Location of Yorkshire Dales National Park Centre, with nature trails and information centre. **57 F1** SE0188.
Aysgarth Force *N.Yorks. Alternative name for Aysgarth Falls, qv.*
Ayshford *Devon* ***Hamlet***, 1m/2km NE of Sampford Peverell. **7 J4** ST0317.
Ayside *Cumb.* ***Hamlet***, 2m/4km SE of Newby Bridge. **55 G1** SD3983.
Ayston *Rut.* ***Hamlet***, 1m/2km N of Uppingham. **42 B5** SK8600.
Aythorpe Roding *Essex* ***Settlement***, with windmill, to N of Leaden Roding. **33 J7** TL5815.
Ayton *P. & K.* ***Settlement***, 1m/2km SW of Abernethy. **82 C6** NO1615.
Ayton *Sc.Bord.* ***Village***, on Eye Water, 3m/4km SW of Eyemouth. **77 H4** NT9261.
Ayton *T. & W.* ***Suburb***, to SW of Washington town centre. NZ2855.
Ayton Castle *Sc.Bord.* ***Castle***, on NW side of Ayton, 7m/11km N of Berwick-upon-Tweed. Mid 19c sandstone castle designed by James Gillespie Graham, and now fully restored. **77 H4** NT9261.
Ayton Hill *Sc.Bord.* ***Hill***, with mast, 2m/3km SE of Ayton. Height 653 feet or 199 metres. **77 H5** NT9459.
Aywick *Shet.* ***Locality***, on Yell, 1m/2km NE of Otterswick, comprising North Aywick and South Aywick. **108 E4** HU5386.
Azerley *N.Yorks.* ***Hamlet***, 4m/6km NW of Ripon. **57 H2** SE2574.

B

Bà *High.* ***River***, in Lochaber district rising S of Clach Leathad and running E through Loch Buidhe, Lochan na Stainge and Loch Bà, to head of Loch Laidon. **80 D3** NN3551.
Baa Taing *Shet.* ***Coastal feature***, headland, with lighthouse, on S coast of Ness of Hillswick, Mainland. **108 B5** HU2774.
Babbacombe *Torbay* ***Suburb***, to N of Torquay town centre and giving its name to bay stretching from Hope's Nose in S to The Parson and Clerk, between Teignmouth and Dawlish, in N. **5 K4** SX9265.
Babbacombe Bay *Devon* ***Bay***, wide bay stretching S from River Teign estuary to Hope's Ness at Torquay. **5 K4** SX9668.
Babbacombe Model Village *Torbay* ***Other feature of interest***, 1m/2km N of Torquay town centre. 400 models and a model railway, with evening illuminations. **5 K4** SX9266.
Babbet Ness *Fife* ***Coastal feature***, headland at SE end of St. Andrews Bay, 1m/2km N of Kingsbarn. **83 G6** NO5914.
Babbington *Notts.* ***Hamlet***, 1km SW of Kimberley. SK4943.
Babbinswood *Shrop.* ***Hamlet***, 1m/2km SE of Whittington. **38 C2** SJ3330.
Babb's Green *Herts.* ***Hamlet***, 3m/4km NE of Ware. TL3916.
Babcary *Som.* ***Village***, 3m/5km NW of Sparkford. **8 E2** ST5628.
Babel *Carmar.* ***Settlement***, 4m/7km E of Llandovery. **27 H5** SN8335.
Babel Green *Suff.* ***Settlement***, to W of Hundon, 4m/7km NE of Haverhill. TL7348.
Babell *Flints.* ***Settlement***, 2m/4km SW of Holywell. **47 K5** SJ1573.
Babeny *Devon* ***Settlement***, 3m/5km SW of Widecombe in the Moor. **5 G3** SX6775.
Babingley *Norf.* ***Locality***, 2m/3km SW of Sandringham. TF6726.
Babingley *Norf.* ***River***, rising E of Flitcham and flowing W then SW into River Great Ouse at its mouth, to N of King's Lynn. **44 A3** TF6023.
Bablock Hythe *Oxon.* ***Settlement***, on River Thames, 3m/5km S of Eynsham. SP4304.
Babraham *Cambs.* ***Village***, 7m/11km SE of Cambridge. **33 J4** TL5150.
Babworth *Notts.* ***Village***, 1m/2km W of Retford. **51 J4** SK6880.
Babylon *Flints.* ***Hamlet***, 2m/3km NE of Hope. SJ3260.
Baby's Hill *Moray* ***Settlement***, on N flank of Ben Rinnes, 5m/8km W of Dufftown. **89 K1** NJ2437.
Bac (Anglicised form: Back.) *W.Isles* ***Village***, near E coast of Isle of Lewis, 6m/10km NE of Stornoway. **101 G3** NB4840.
Bac an Eich *High.* ***Mountain***, on Strathconon Forest, Ross and Cromarty district. Height 2785 feet or 849 metres. **95 J7** NH2248.
Bac Beag *Arg. & B.* ***Island***, at SW end of Treshnish Isles group, with larger island of Bac Mòr to N. **78 D4** NM2337.
Bac Mòr (Also known as Dutchman's Cap.) *Arg. & B.* ***Island***, towards SW end of Treshnish Isles group. Bac Beag, its neighbour to S, is at extreme SW of group. **78 D4** NM2438.
Baca Ruadh *High.* ***Mountain***, 3m/4km NW of The Storr, Skye. Height 2089 feet or 637 metres. **93 K6** NG4757.
Bach Camp *Here.* ***Historic/prehistoric site***, small hillfort 3m/5km E of Leominster. Defensive features included steep slopes on all sides and a bank, ditch and counter-scarp bank. **28 E2** SO5460.
Bach Island *Arg. & B.* ***Island***, small island in Firth of Lorn, off Rubha na Feundain at SW end of Kerrera. **79 J5** NM7726.
Bachau *I.o.A.* ***Hamlet***, 1km E of Llanerchymedd. SH4383.
Bache Hill *Powys* ***Mountain***, in Radnor Forest, 6m/10km W of Presteigne. Height 2001 feet or 610 metres. **28 B2** SO2163.
Bachelors' Club *S.Ayr.* ***Historic house***, thatched house (National Trust for Scotland) in Tarbolton where Burns and associates formed a literary debating society in 1780. Contains period furnishings. **67 J1** NS4327.
Back *W.Isles Anglicised form of Bac, qv.*
Back of Keppoch *High.* ***Settlement***, 1km NW of Arisaig, Lochaber district. **86 C6** NM6587.
Back o'th' Brook *Staffs.* ***Hamlet***, just N of Waterfall, 1m/2km S of Grindon. SK0851.
Back Street *Suff.* ***Settlement***, 7m/11km SE of Newmarket. TL7458.
Backaland *Ork.* ***Locality***, near S end of Eday. To E is Bay of Backaland. **106 E4** HY5730.
Backaskail Bay *Ork.* ***Bay***, wide bay on S coast of Sanday, 4m/6km W of Tres Ness. **106 F4** HY6438.
Backaskaill *Ork.* ***Settlement***, on W coast of Papa Westray. **106 D2** HY4850.
Backbarrow *Cumb.* ***Hamlet***, 1m/2km SW of Newby Bridge. **55 G1** SD3584.
Backburn *Aber.* ***Settlement***, on NW side of Gartly Moor, 3m/5km S of Huntly. **90 D1** NJ5334.
Backe *Carmar.* ***Settlement***, 1m/2km E of St. Clears. SN2615.
Backfolds *Aber.* ***Settlement***, 3m/5km N of Mintlaw. **99 J5** NK0252.
Backford *Ches.* ***Village***, 3m/5km N of Chester. **48 C5** SJ3971.
Backford Cross *Ches.* ***Locality***, at S edge of Ellesmere Port, 1m/2km NW of Backford. SJ3873.
Backhill *Aberdeen* ***Suburb***, 3m/5km W of Aberdeen city centre. NJ8905.
Backhill *Aber.* ***Locality***, 2m/3km NE of Fyvie. **91 F1** NJ7939.
Backhill of Clackriach *Aber.* ***Locality***, 1m/2km S of Maud. **99 H6** NJ9246.
Backhill of Trustach *Aber.* ***Settlement***, 4m/6km W of Banchory. **90 E5** NO6397.
Backies *High.* ***Settlement***, 1m/2km N of Golspie, Sutherland district. **97 F1** NC8302.
Backies *Moray* ***Settlement***, 6m/10km SE of Buckie. **98 C5** NJ4958.
Backlass *High.* ***Settlement***, 2m/3km W of Watten. **105 H3** ND2053.
Backmoor *S.Yorks.* ***Suburb***, 3m/5km S of Sheffield city centre. SK3682.
Backmuir of New Gilston *Fife* ***Village***, 3m/5km N of Largo. **83 F7** NO4308.
Back's Green *Suff.* ***Settlement***, 1m/2km W of Redisham and 4m/7km SW of Beccles. TM3884.
Backside *Aber.* ***Settlement***, 6m/9km SE of Dufftown. **90 C1** NJ4136.
Backstone Edge *Cumb.* ***Mountain***, 4m/7km NE of Appleby-in-Westmorland, with The Pennine Way footpath on SE side. Height 2053 feet or 626 metres. **61 J4** NY7226.
Backwater Reservoir *Angus* ***Reservoir***, nearly 4m/6km long N to S, in Glenisla Forest 7m/11km N of Alyth. **82 D1** NO2559.
Backwell *N.Som.* Population: 3989. ***Village***, 6m/10km SW of Bristol. **19 H5** ST4968.
Backworth *T. & W.* ***Hamlet***, 3m/5km W of Whitley Bay. **71 H6** NZ3072.
Bacon End *Essex* ***Settlement***, 2m/4km SW of Great Dunmow. **33 J7** TL6018.
Baconend Green *Essex* ***Settlement***, 1km N of Bacon End. TL6019.
Bacon's End *W.Mid.* ***Locality***, 2m/3km SW of Coleshill. SP1787.
Baconsthorpe *Norf.* ***Village***, 3m/5km SE of Holt. Remains of 15c castle (English Heritage) and of 16c hall to NW. **45 F2** TG1237.
Baconsthorpe Castle *Norf.* ***Castle***, ruined 15c castle (English Heritage), 3m/4km E of Holt. Former home to the Heydons. **45 F2** TG1238.
Bacton *Here.* ***Village***, 4m/6km NW of Pontrilas. **28 C5** SO3732.
Bacton *Norf.* ***Village***, on coast, 5m/7km NE of North Walsham. **45 H2** TG3433.
Bacton *Suff.* ***Village***, 5m/9km N of Stowmarket. **34 E2** TM0567.
Bacton Green *Suff.* ***Settlement***, 1m/2km SW of Bacton. TM0365.
Bacup *Lancs.* Population: 13,682. ***Town***, former cotton town, near head of River Irwell valley, 6m/10km S of Burnley and N of Rochdale. **56 D7** SD8623.
Bad a' Chreamha *High.* ***Mountain***, in Ross and Cromarty district, 1m/2km N of Stromeferry across Loch Carron. Height 1296 feet or 395 metres. **86 E1** NG8536.
Bad an Fhithich *W.Isles* ***Coastal feature***, on NW coast of Isle of Lewis, 1m/2km SW of Butt of Lewis. **101 G1** NB5064.
Badachro *High.* ***Village***, on S shore of Gair Loch, W coast of Ross and Cromarty district. **94 D4** NG7873.
Badandun Hill *Angus* ***Mountain***, 4m/7km NW from N end of Backwater Reservoir. Height 2427 feet or 740 metres. **82 C1** NO2067.
Badanloch Forest *High.* ***Open space***, deer forest in Sutherland district to NW of Kinbrace. **104 C5** NC8035.
Badanloch Lodge *High.* ***Settlement***, at W end of Loch Badanloch, Sutherland district. **104 C5** NC7933.
Badavanich *High.* ***Settlement***, on N shore of Loch a' Chroisg, 3m/5km W of Achnasheen. **95 H6** NH1058.
Badbea *High.* ***Settlement***, 3m/5km SW of Berriedale. **105 F7** ND0819.
Badbury *Swin.* ***Village***, 4m/6km SE of Swindon. **20 E3** SU1980.
Badbury Hill *Oxon.* ***Hill***, National Trust property with Iron Age fort, 2m/3km W of Faringdon. Height 531 feet or 162 metres. **21 F2** SU2694.
Badbury Rings *Dorset* ***Historic/prehistoric site***, Iron Age fort enclosing a wood, 4m/6km NW of Wimborne Minster. **9 J4** ST9603.
Badbury Wick *Swin.* ***Settlement***, 1m/2km NW of Badbury. SU1881.
Badby *Northants.* ***Village***, 3m/4km SW of Daventry. **31 G3** SP5659.
Badcall *High.* ***Locality***, comprising Upper Badcall and Lower Badcall, on N side of Badcall Bay, W coast of Sutherland district, 2m/3km S of Scourie. **102 D4** NC1541.
Badcall *High.* ***Settlement***, on N side of Loch Inchard, 1m/2km E of Kinlochbervie, near W coast of Sutherland district. **102 E3** NC2455.
Badcall Bay *High.* ***Bay***, on W coast of Sutherland district, 2m/3km S of Scourie. **102 D4** NC1541.
Badcaul *High.* ***Village***, on SW side of Little Loch Broom, W coast of Ross and Cromarty district. **95 G2** NH0191.
Baddeley Edge *Stoke* ***Suburb***, 3m/5km NE of Hanley. SJ9150.
Baddeley Green *Stoke* ***Locality***, 1m/2km SW of Endon. **49 J7** SJ9151.
Badden *Arg. & B.* ***Settlement***, 1km N of Lochgilphead. **73 G2** NR8589.
Baddesley Clinton *Warks.* ***Hamlet***, 7m/11km NW of Warwick. SP2072.
Baddesley Clinton Hall *Warks.* ***Historic house***, moated medieval manor house (National Trust) dating from 14c, 1m/2km SW of Baddesley Clinton. **30 C1** SP2071.
Baddesley Ensor *Warks.* Population: 3479. ***Village***, former mining village, 2m/3km W of Atherstone. **40 E6** SP2798.
Baddidarach *High.* ***Hamlet***, on N side of Loch Inver, Sutherland district, 1km SW of Lochinver. **102 C6** NC0823.
Baddinsgill Reservoir *Sc.Bord.* ***Reservoir***, on Pentland Hills 3m/4km NW of West Linton. **75 K5** NT1255.
Baddoch *High.* ***Mountain***, with twin summits, the S one being higher, 5m/8km E of Nethy Bridge. Height 1863 feet or 568 metres. **89 H3** NJ0719.
Baddoch Burn *Aber.* ***River***, stream running NE to join Clunie Water, 5m/8km S of Braemar. **89 J6** NO1383.
Baden Bay *High. Alternative name for Badentarbat Bay, qv.*
Badenoch *High.* ***Locality***, S part of Badenoch and Strathspey district round about Kingussie, traversed by River Spey, between Monadhliath Mountains and central Grampian Mountains, S of Cairngorm Mountains. **88 C6** NN6592.
Badenscoth *Aber.* ***Settlement***, 2m/3km NW of Rothienorman. **90 E1** NJ7038.
Badentarbat Bay (Also known as Baden Bay.) *High.* ***Bay***, on NW coast of Ross and Cromarty district, between Scottish mainland and Tanera Mòr, to W of Achiltibuie. **95 F1** NC0108.
Badenyon *Aber.* ***Settlement***, to N of Ladylea Hill, 4m/6km N of Strathdon. **90 B3** NJ3419.
Badernonach Hill *Aber.* ***Mountain***, 4m/6km NW of Tarland. Height 1558 feet or 475 metres. **90 C4** NJ4308.
Badgall *Cornw.* ***Hamlet***, 6m/10km W of Launceston. SX2386.
Badgeney *Cambs.* ***Suburb***, in E part of March. TL4296.
Badger *Shrop.* ***Village***, 5m/8km NE of Bridgnorth. **39 G6** SO7699.
Badgerbank *Ches.* ***Settlement***, 3m/4km NE of Goostrey. **49 H5** SJ8071.
Badgers Mount *Kent* ***Hamlet***, and road junction, 3m/5km SE of Orpington. **23 H5** TQ4962.
Badgeworth *Glos.* ***Village***, 3m/5km SW of Cheltenham. **29 J7** SO9019.
Badgworth *Som.* ***Village***, 3m/4km SW of Axbridge. **19 G6** ST3952.
Badharlick *Cornw.* ***Hamlet***, 4m/7km W of Launceston. SX2686.
Badicaul *High.* ***Settlement***, in Skye and Lochalsh district, on coast 1m/2km N of Kyle of Lochalsh. **86 D2** NG7529.
Badingham *Suff.* ***Village***, 3m/5km NE of Framlingham. **35 H2** TM3068.
Badintagairt *High.* ***Settlement***, to E of River Cassley, 2m/3km NW of Glencassley Castle. **103 G7** NC4210.
Badlesmere *Kent* ***Village***, 5m/8km S of Faversham. **15 F2** TR0054.
Badley *Suff.* ***Locality***, and parish, 2m/3km SE of Stowmarket. **34 E3** TM0655.
Badlipster *High.* ***Settlement***, 3m/5km S of Watten. **105 H4** ND2449.
Badluarach *High.* ***Village***, on W side of Little Loch Broom, W coast of Ross and Cromarty district, nearly 2m/3km SE of Stattic Point. **95 F2** NG9994.
Badminton *S.Glos.* ***Village***, at S end of Badminton Park, 5m/8km E of Chipping Sodbury. **20 B3** ST8082.
Badminton Park *S.Glos.* ***Historic house***, seat of Dukes of Beaufort since 1608, 5m/8km E of Chipping Sodbury. House and parkland date from 17c and early 18c. Park modelled by William Kent and 'Capability' Brown. Annual Three Day Event Horse Trials held in May. **20 B3** ST8082.
Badnaban *High.* ***Hamlet***, on S side of Loch Inver, Sutherland district, 2m/3km SW of Lochinver. **102 C6** NC0721.
Badnabay *High.* ***Settlement***, 1km SW of head of Loch Laxford. **102 E4** NC2146.
Badnafrave *Moray* ***Settlement***, 3m/5km SE of Tomintoul. **89 K3** NJ2015.
Badnagie *High.* ***Settlement***, 1km NW of Dunbeath. **105 G5** ND1531.
Badnambiast *P. & K.* ***Settlement***, 8m/12km SE of Dalwhinnie. **88 E7** NN7173.
Badninish *High.* ***Settlement***, 6m/10km NW of Dornoch. **96 E2** NH7693.
Badrallach *High.* ***Settlement***, on NE side of Little Loch Broom, on W coast of Ross and Cromarty district, 3m/5km from head of loch. **95 G2** NH0691.
Badsey *Worcs.* Population: 2556. ***Village***, 2m/4km E of Evesham. **30 B4** SP0743.

Badshot Lea *Surr.* ***Village***, 2m/3km NE of Farnham. **22 B7** SU8648.
Badsworth *W.Yorks.* ***Village***, 3m/4km NE of Hemsworth. **51 G1** SE4614.
Badwell Ash *Suff.* ***Village***, 4m/6km E of Ixworth. **34 D2** TL9969.
Badwell Green *Suff.* ***Settlement***, 1m/2km E of Badwell Ash. TM0169.
Badworthy *Devon* ***Hamlet***, 2m/3km NW of South Brent. SX6861.
Badyo *P. & K.* ***Settlement***, 4m/7km NE of Pitlochry. **82 A1** NN9861.
Bae Cinmel *Conwy Welsh form of Kinmel Bay, qv.*
Bae Colwyn *Conwy Welsh form of Colwyn Bay, qv.*
Bae Penrhyn *Conwy Welsh form of Penrhyn Bay, qv.*
Baffins *Ports.* ***Suburb***, E district of Portsmouth. SU6601.
Bag Enderby *Lincs.* ***Village***, 5m/8km NW of Spilsby. **53 G5** TF3472.
Bagber *Dorset* ***Hamlet***, 1km E of Lydlinch and 2m/3km W of Sturminster Newton. ST7513.
Bagborough Hill *Som.* ***Mountain***, summit of Quantock Hills, 1m/2km N of West Bagborough. Height 1260 feet or 384 metres. ST1635.
Bagby *N.Yorks.* ***Village***, 2m/4km SE of Thirsk. **57 K1** SE4680.
Bagendon *Glos.* ***Village***, 3m/5km N of Cirencester. **20 D1** SP0106.
Baggeridge Country Park *Staffs.* ***Leisure/recreation***, bracken and heather-clad heathland 3m/5km SW of Wolverhampton. **40 A6** SO8992.
Bagginswood *Shrop.* ***Hamlet***, 4m/6km N of Cleobury Mortimer. SO6881.
Baggrave Hall *Leics.* ***Settlement***, 1m/2km NE of Hungarton. **42 A5** SK6909.
Baggrow *Cumb.* ***Hamlet***, 2m/3km E of Aspatria. **60 C2** NY1742.
Baggy Point *Devon* ***Coastal feature***, headland (National Trust) 8m/13km SW of Ilfracombe between Barnstaple (or Bideford) Bay to S and Morte Bay to N. **6 C1** SS4140.
Bagh a' Chaisteil *W.Isles Gaelic form of Castlebay, qv.*
Bagh an t-Srathaidh *High.* ***Bay***, small bay on coast of Skye and Lochalsh district, 1m/2km SW of Plockton. **86 D1** NG7832.
Bàgh Bàn *Arg. & B.* ***Bay***, small bay 3m/4km SW of Ardfern. **79 J7** NM7703.
Bagh Dail Beag (Anglicised form: Dalbeg Bay.) *W.Isles* ***Bay***, on NW coast of Isle of Lewis, 2m/4km NE of Carloway. **100 E3** NB2246.
Bàgh Gleann a' Mhaoil *Arg. & B.* ***Bay***, on SE coast of Scarba, 1km NE of Rubha Righinn. **79 J7** NM7103.
Bàgh Gleann Speireig *Arg. & B.* ***Bay***, on NW coast of Jura, 1km SW of Glengarrisdale Bay. **72 E1** NR6396.
Bàgh Hirivagh *W.Isles See Northbay.*
Bàgh Huisinis *W.Isles Gaelic form of Hushinish Bay, qv.*
Bàgh Loch an Ròin *High.* ***Bay***, on W coast of Sutherland district, 2m/3km SW of Kinlochbervie. **102 D3** NC1854.
Bagh na Coille *Arg. & B.* ***Bay***, on NE coast of Coll, 4m/7km NE of Arinagour. **78 D1** NM2762.
Bagh na h-Uamha *High.* ***Bay***, small bay on E coast of Rum, 2m/3km SE of Kinloch. **85 K5** NM4297.
Bagh nam Faoileann *W.Isles* ***Sea feature***, stretch of sea containing numerous islets between Benbecula and South Uist on E side. **92 D7** NF8444.
Bagh Phabail (Anglicised form: Bayble Bay.) *W.Isles* ***Bay***, consisting of two small bays, Bagh Phabail Uarach (Upper Bayble Bay) and Bagh Phabail Iarach (Lower Bayble Bay) to N and S respectively on SE coast of Eye Peninsula, Isle of Lewis. **101 H4** NB5230.
Bagham *Kent* ***Settlement***, 5m/9km SW of Canterbury, on N bank of Great Stour. TR0753.
Baghasdal (Anglicised form: North Boisdale.) *W.Isles* ***Village***, on South Uist, 2m/3km S of Dalabrog. **84 C3** NF7417.
Bagillt *Flints.* Population: 3073. ***Village***, on River Dee estuary, 2m/3km NW of Flint. **48 B5** SJ2275.
Bagillt Bank *Flints.* ***Coastal feature***, sandbank in estuary of River Dee, stretching from Greenfield to Flint. SJ2275.
Baginton *Warks.* ***Village***, 3m/4km S of Coventry. Coventry Civil Airport To E. **30 E1** SP3474.
Baglan *N.P.T.* ***Small town***, 2m/3km NW of Port Talbot. **18 A2** SS7592.
Bagley *Shrop.* ***Hamlet***, 5m/8km S of Ellesmere. **38 D3** SJ4027.
Bagley *Som.* ***Hamlet***, 2m/3km SE of Wedmore. ST4546.
Bagley *W.Yorks.* ***Locality***, 1m/2km N of Pudsey. Observatory. SE2235.
Bagley Green *Som.* ***Hamlet***, 1m/2km SW of Wellington. ST1219.
Bagmore *Hants.* ***Hamlet***, 5m/8km S of Basingstoke. SU6644.
Bagnall *Staffs.* ***Village***, 5m/8km NE of Stoke-on-Trent. **49 J7** SJ9250.
Bagnor *W.Berks.* ***Hamlet***, 2m/3km NW of Newbury. **21 H5** SU4569.
Bagot's Park *Staffs.* ***Open space***, heath to E of Bagot Forest, 4m/6km S of Uttoxeter. **40 C3** SK0827.
Bagpath *Glos.* ***Hamlet***, 3m/5km E of Wotton-under-Edge. ST8094.
Bagshot *Surr.* Population: 5190. ***Small town***, 4m/6km NE of Camberley. **22 C5** SU9163.
Bagshot *Wilts.* ***Settlement***, 3m/4km SW of Hungerford. **21 G5** SU3165.
Bagshot Heath *Surr.* ***Leisure/recreation***, former haunt of highwaymen, now a Country Park traversed by M3 motorway, to S of Bagshot. **22 C5** SU9161.
Bagslate Moor *Gt.Man.* ***Suburb***, 2m/3km W of Rochdale town centre. SD8613.
Bagstone *S.Glos.* ***Settlement***, 3m/5km NW of Yate. **19 K3** ST6887.
Bagthorpe *Norf.* ***Hamlet***, 4m/6km SE of Docking. **44 B2** TF7932.
Bagthorpe *Notts.* ***Hamlet***, 3m/5km N of Eastwood. **51 G7** SK4751.
Baguley *Gt.Man.* ***Locality***, 2m/4km SE of Altrincham. Includes 14c timber-framed Baguley Hall (English Heritage). **49 H4** SJ8189.
Bagworth *Leics.* ***Village***, 4m/7km S of Coalville. Originally a coal mining village. **41 G5** SK4408.
Bagwyllydiart *Here.* ***Hamlet***, 3m/5km E of Pontrilas. **28 D6** SO4426.
Bail Hill *D. & G.* ***Mountain***, 4m/7km NW of Moniaive. Height 1692 feet or 516 metres. **68 C4** NX7295.
Baildon *W.Yorks.* Population: 15,385. ***Suburb***, 4m/6km N of Bradford. **57 G6** SE1539.
Baildon Green *W.Yorks.* ***Locality***, 1km SW of Baildon. SE1438.
Baile a' Mhanaich *W.Isles Gaelic form of Balivanich, qv.*
Baile Ailein (Anglicised form: Balallan.) *W.Isles* ***Village***, on N side of Loch Erisort, E coast of Isle of Lewis, near head of loch. **100 E5** NB2920.
Baile an Truiseil (Anglicised form: Ballantrushal.) *W.Isles* ***Village***, near NW coast of Isle of Lewis, 3m/4km N of Barvas. **101 F2** NB3753.
Baile Boidheach *Arg. & B.* ***Settlement***, on SW side of Loch Caolisport, 3m/5km SW of Achahoish. **73 F3** NR7473.
Baile Gharbhaidh (Anglicised form: Balgarva.) *W.Isles* ***Settlement***, on N part of South Uist, 1m/2km E of Ardivachar Point. **92 C7** NF7646.
Baile Glas (Anglicised form: Ballaglasa.) *W.Isles* ***Settlement***, on Grimsay, between North Uist and Benbecula. **92 D6** NF8457.
Baile Mhartainn *W.Isles Gaelic form of Balmartin, qv.*
Baile Mhic Phail (Anglicised form: Newton.) *W.Isles* ***Settlement***, on North Uist, 1m/2km S of Port nan Long. **92 D4** NF8976.
Baile Mòr *Arg. & B.* ***Village***, on E coast of Iona. Site of 6c monastery; 13c remains. 15c Maclean's Cross (Historic Scotland). Cathedral to N. Ferry to Fionnphort on Mull across Sound of Iona. NM2824.
Baile Mòr (Anglicised form: Balemore.) *W.Isles* ***Settlement***, on North Uist, 4m/6km SE of Aird an Rùnair. **92 C5** NF7367.
Baile nan Cailleach (Anglicised form: Nunton.) *W.Isles* ***Locality***, on W coast of Benbecula. **92 C6** NF7653.
Baile Raghaill (Anglicised form: Balranald.) *W.Isles* ***Settlement***, on North Uist, 2m/3km E of Aird an Rùnair. Nature reserve to W. **92 C5** NF7269.
Bailebeag *High.* ***Settlement***, 2m/3km SE of Foyers. **88 C3** NH5018.
Baileguish *High.* ***Settlement***, 4m/7km SE of Kingussie. **89 F5** NN8298.
Bailemeonach *Arg. & B.* ***Settlement***, on Mull, 3m/4km S of Lochaline across Sound of Mull. **79 H3** NM6541.
Bailenacille *W.Isles* ***Settlement***, on S part of Pabbay. **92 D3** NF8886.
Bailetonach *High.* ***Settlement***, on Eilean Shona, Lochaber district. **86 C7** NM6373.
Bailey Green *Hants.* ***Settlement***, 3m/4km NE of West Meon. SU6727.
Bailey Grove *Notts.* ***Suburb***, to W of Eastwood. SK4646.
Bailey Hill *Powys* ***Mountain***, rising to over 420 metres and running NE to SW, 3m/4km W of Knighton. **28 B1** SO2472.
Bailey Mill *Cumb.* ***Settlement***, at bridge over Bailey Water, 6m/10km S of Newcastleton. NY5178.
Bailiff Bridge *W.Yorks.* ***Suburb***, on Clifton Beck, 1m/2km N of Brighouse. SE1425.
Baillieston *Glas.* ***Suburb***, 5m/9km E of Glasgow city centre. NS6763.
Bailliesward *Aber.* ***Settlement***, 3m/5km SE of Haugh of Glass. **90 C1** NJ4737.
Bailrigg *Lancs.* ***Locality***, 2m/3km S of Lancaster. Site of University of Lancaster. SD4858.
Bain *Lincs.* ***River***, rising at Ludford Parva and flowing S through Lincolnshire West Wolds, past Horncastle and into River Witham at Dogdyke. **53 F5** TF2055.
Bainbridge *N.Yorks.* ***Village***, on River Bain, near its confluence with River Ure, 4m/6km E of Hawes. Site of Roman fort to E. **62 A7** SD9390.
Bainsford *Falk.* ***Suburb***, adjoining to N of Falkirk, on S bank of River Carron. **75 G2** NS8881.
Bainshole *Aber.* ***Settlement***, on N side of Glen Water in Glens of Foudland, 6m/9km SE of Huntly. **90 E1** NJ6035.
Bainton *E.Riding* ***Village***, 5m/8km SW of Great Driffield. **59 F4** SE9652.
Bainton *Oxon.* ***Settlement***, 3m/5km N of Bicester. SP5826.
Bainton *Peter.* ***Village***, 4m/7km E of Stamford. **42 D5** TF0906.
Bairnkine *Sc.Bord.* ***Hamlet***, 2m/3km NW of Camptown. **70 B2** NT6415.
Bait Island *T. & W. Alternative name for St. Mary's Island, qv.*
Bakebare *Moray* ***Settlement***, below N slopes of Hill of Mackalea, 3m/4km E of Dufftown. **90 B1** NJ3639.
Baker Street *Thur.* ***Hamlet***, 3m/5km N of Tilbury. **24 C3** TQ6381.
Baker's Bridge *Lincs.* ***Locality***, with bridge over New Hammond Beck, 3m/5km W of Boston. TF2842.
Baker's End *Herts.* ***Settlement***, 3m/5km SE of Ware. **33 G7** TL3917.
Baker's Hill *Glos.* ***Settlement***, 1m/2km NE of Coleford. SO5811.
Baker's Island *Hants.* ***Island***, uninhabited island in Langstone Harbour off Farlington Marshes. SU6903.
Baker's Lane *Warks.* ***Locality***, 4m/7km SE of Solihull. SP1874.
Bakestone Moor *Derbys.* ***Locality***, adjoining to SW of Whitwell, 4m/7km SW of Worksop. SK5276.
Bakewell *Derbys.* Population: 3818. ***Small town***, old market town on River Wye, 7m/12km NW of Matlock. Saxon cross in churchyard. 15c bridge spans river. **50 E6** SK2168.
Bakewell Bridge *Derbys.* ***Bridge***, 15c stone bridge over River Wye in Bakewell. SK2168.
Bakewell Old House Museum *Derbys.* ***Other feature of interest***, 16c townhouse in Bakewell, once owned by Richard Arkwright. Includes exhibits on Tudor life in Bakewell and Arkwright memorabilia. **50 E6** SK2168.
Bala *Gwyn.* Population: 1922. ***Small town***, market town on River Tryweryn near its confluence with River Dee, near NE end of Llyn Tegid. **37 J2** SH9236.
Bala Lake *Gwyn. English form of Llyn Tegid, qv.*
Bala Lake Railway *Gwyn.* ***Other feature of interest***, narrow gauge railway running along SE shore of Llyn Tegid (Bala Lake) from Llanuwchllyn in SW to just S of Bala in NE. **37 H2** SH8830.
Balachuirn *High.* ***Settlement***, near W coast of Raasay, 3m/4km N of Clachan. **94 B7** NG5540.
Balado *P. & K.* ***Settlement***, 2m/3km W of Kinross. NO0802.
Balafark *Stir.* ***Settlement***, 3m/4km N of Fintry. **74 E1** NS6190.
Balaldie *High.* ***Settlement***, 3m/5km N of Balintore. **97 F4** NH8779.
Balallan *W.Isles Anglicised form of Baile Ailein, qv.*
Balavil *High.* ***Settlement***, in Badenoch and Strathspey district, 2m/4km NE of Kingussie. **88 E4** NH7802.
Balbeg *High.* ***Settlement***, 4m/6km W of Drumnadrochit. **88 B1** NH4531.
Balbeg *High.* ***Settlement***, 4m/6km SW of Drumnadrochit. **88 B2** NH4924.
Balbeggie *P. & K.* ***Village***, 5m/8km NE of Perth. **82 C5** NO1629.
Balbirnie *Fife* ***Locality***, to NW of Glenrothes, comprising Balbirnie Burns and Balburnie House. **82 D7** NO2802.
Balbithan *Aber.* ***Garden***, surrounding late 17c tower house. Attractive old-world garden, 3m/5km SE of Inverurie. **91 G3** NJ8118.
Balbithan *Aber.* ***Settlement***, on E side of River Don, 1km E of Kintore. **91 F3** NJ7917.
Balblair *High.* ***Settlement***, in Inverness district, 1m/2km SW of Beauly. NH5045.
Balblair *High.* ***Settlement***, 2m/3km NW of Bonar Bridge. **96 C2** NH5894.
Balblair *High.* ***Settlement***, on W side of Edderton, in Ross and Cromarty district. NH7084.
Balblair *High.* ***Village***, on S side of Cromarty Firth, Ross and Cromarty district, opposite Invergordon. **96 E5** NH7066.
Balby *S.Yorks.* ***Suburb***, 2m/3km SW of Doncaster town centre. SE5501.
Balcary Point *D. & G.* ***Coastal feature***, headland on SE side of Balcary Bay. **65 J6** NX8249.
Balcharn *High.* ***Settlement***, 1m/2km E of Lairg, Sutherland district. **96 C1** NC5906.
Balcherry *High.* ***Locality***, consisting of dispersed settlements, 2m/4km E of Tain. **97 F3** NH8183.
Balchers *Aber.* ***Settlement***, on SW side of Wood of Balchers, 4m/7km S of Macduff. **99 F5** NJ7158.
Balchladich *High.* ***Settlement***, on W coast of Sutherland district, 3m/5km S of Point of Stoer. **102 C5** NC0330.
Balchraggan *High.* ***Settlement***, 2m/3km SE of Beauly. **96 C7** NH5343.
Balchraggan *High.* ***Settlement***, 5m/7km NE of Drumnadrochit. **88 C1** NH5634.
Balchrick *High.* ***Village***, near W coast of Sutherland district, 3m/5km NW of Kinlochbervie. **102 D2** NC1959.
Balcombe *W.Suss.* Population: 1746. ***Locality***, residential locality, 4m/7km N of Haywards Heath. **13 G3** TQ3030.
Balcombe Lane *W.Suss.* ***Settlement***, 1m/2km N of Balcombe and 4m/6km SE of Crawley. TQ3132.
Balconie Point *High.* ***Coastal feature***, shingle point on Cromarty Firth, 1m/2km SE of Evanton. **96 D5** NH6265.
Balcurvie *Fife* ***Village***, adjoining to N of Windygates. **82 E7** NO3400.
Balder ***River***, rising as Balder Beck on Stainmore Common and flowing E through Balderhead, Blackton and Hury Reservoirs into River Tees to N of Cotherstone. **61 K5** NZ0120.
Balderhead Reservoir *Dur.* ***Reservoir***, first of three reservoirs in course of River Balder, 5m/8km NW of Bowes. **62 A5** NY9218.
Baldernock *E.Dun.* ***Settlement***, 1m/2km E of Milngavie. **74 D3** NS5775.
Baldersby *N.Yorks.* ***Village***, 5m/8km SW of Thirsk. **57 J2** SE3578.
Baldersby St. James *N.Yorks.* ***Hamlet***, 5m/8km NE of Ripon, between A1 trunk road and River Swale. SE3676.
Baldersdale *Dur.* ***Valley***, carrying River Balder and containing reservoirs of Balderhead, Blackton and Hury, 7m/11km W of Barnard Castle. **62 A5** NY9418.
Balderstone *Gt.Man.* ***Suburb***, 2m/3km SE of Rochdale town centre. SD9011.
Balderstone *Lancs.* ***Village***, 4m/7km NW of Blackburn. **56 B6** SD6332.
Balderton *Ches.* ***Settlement***, 1m/2km NE of Dodleston. SJ3762.
Balderton *Notts.* ***Suburb***, adjoining to SE of Newark-on-Trent. **52 B7** SK8151.
Baldhoon *I.o.M.* ***Locality***, 1m/2km W of Laxey. SC4184.
Baldhu *Cornw.* ***Settlement***, 4m/6km W of Truro. **2 E4** SW7742.
Baldingstone *Gt.Man.* ***Suburb***, 2m/4km N of Bury town centre. SD8014.
Baldinnie *Fife* ***Hamlet***, 4m/6km SE of Cupar. **83 F6** NO4211.
Baldock *Herts.* Population: 9232. ***Small town***, 6m/10km N of Stevenage. **33 F5** TL2433.
Baldon Row *Oxon.* ***Settlement***, to S of Toot Baldon, 5m/8km SE of Oxford. SP5600.
Baldoon Sands *D. & G.* ***Coastal feature***, area of mud and sand 2m/3km SE of Wigtown. **64 E5** NX4553.
Baldovan *Dundee* ***Suburb***, 3m/4km N of Dundee city centre. NO3834.

B

Baldovie *Angus* ***Settlement***, 1m/2km SW of Kirkton of Kingoldrum. **82 E2** NO3254.
Baldovie *Dundee* ***Settlement***, 4m/6km NE of Dundee city centre, to N of Dighty Water. **83 F4** NO4532.
Baldrine *I.o.M.* ***Village***, 2m/3km S of Laxey. **54 D5** SC4281.
Baldslow *E.Suss.* ***Settlement***, adjoining to N of Hastings. **14 C6** TQ7913.
Balduff Hill *P. & K.* ***Mountain***, 3m/5km NW of Alyth. Height 1394 feet or 425 metres. **82 D2** NO2253.
Baldwin *I.o.M.* ***Hamlet***, 4m/6km NW of Douglas. **54 C5** SC3581.
Baldwinholme *Cumb.* ***Settlement***, 2m/4km NW of Dalston. **60 E1** NY3351.
Baldwin's Gate *Staffs.* ***Settlement***, 1m/2km SW of Whitmore. **39 G1** SJ7939.
Baldwins Hill *Surr.* ***Settlement***, adjoining to N of East Grinstead. TQ3839.
Bale *Norf.* ***Village***, 4m/7km W of Holt. **44 E2** TG0136.
Balelone *W.Isles* ***Settlement***, on North Uist, 2m/3km S of Griminis Point. **92 C4** NF7273.
Balemartine *Arg. & B.* ***Village***, on Hynish Bay, Tiree, 4m/7km SW of Scarinish across the bay. **78 A3** NL9841.
Balemore *W.Isles Anglicised form of Baile Mòr, qv.*
Balendoch *P. & K.* ***Settlement***, 2m/3km N of Meigle. **82 D3** NO2847.
Balephetrish Bay *Arg. & B.* ***Bay***, wide bay on N coast of Tiree, 3m/5km NW of Scarinish. **78 A3** NM0047.
Balephetrish Hill *Arg. & B.* ***Hill***, rising to over 20 metres near N coast of Tiree, overlooking Balephetrish Bay. **78 B3** NM0147.
Balephuil *Arg. & B.* ***Settlement***, on E side of Balephuil Bay, Tiree. **78 A3** NL9540.
Balerno *Edin.* ***Village***, 7m/12km SW of Edinburgh. 17c Malleny House; garden (National Trust for Scotland). **75 K4** NT1666.
Balernock *Arg. & B.* ***Locality***, comprises High and Laigh Balernock, 2m/3km SE of Garelochhead. **74 A2** NS2588.
Baleromindubh *Arg. & B.* ***Settlement***, on S part of Colonsay, 1m/2km S of Scalasaig. **72 B1** NR3892.
Balerominmore *Arg. & B.* ***Settlement***, on S of Colonsay, 2m/3km S of Scalasaig. **72 B1** NR3891.
Baleshare *W.Isles* ***Island***, low-lying island off W coast of North Uist to W of Cairinis. **92 C5** NF7861.
Balevulin *Arg. & B.* ***Settlement***, on Mull, 4m/6km SE of Balnahard. **79 F5** NM4829.
Balfield *Angus* ***Settlement***, 1km E of Bridgend, in valley of West Water. **83 G1** NO5468.
Balfour *Aber.* ***Settlement***, 2m/3km SE of Aboyne. **90 D5** NO5596.
Balfour *Ork.* ***Hamlet***, and small harbour, on S coast of Shapinsay, near its western end. **107 D6** HY4716.
Balfour Castle *Angus See Kirkton of Kingoldrum.*
Balfour Castle *Ork.* ***Historic house***, baronial-style Victorian mansion to W of Balfour on S coast of Shapinsay. **107 D6** HY4716.
Balfron *Stir.* Population: 1397. ***Village***, 6m/9km N of Strathblane. **74 D2** NS5488.
Balfron Station *Stir.* ***Settlement***, at site of former railway station, 2m/3km W of Balfron. **74 D2** NS5289.
Balgarva *W.Isles Anglicised form of Baile Gharbhaidh, qv.*
Balgavies *Angus* ***Hamlet***, 2m/3km N of Letham. **83 G2** NO5351.
Balgedie *P. & K.* ***Locality***, comprises two villages of Wester Balgedie and Easter Balgedie, to NE of Loch Leven. **82 C7** NO1604.
Balgonar *Fife* ***Settlement***, 1m/2km N of Saline. **75 J1** NT0193.
Balgove *Aber.* ***Settlement***, 1km S of Barthol Chapel and 4m/7km SE of Fyvie. **91 G1** NJ8133.
Balgowan *D. & G.* ***Settlement***, on W coast of Luce Bay, 1m/2km S of Ardwell. **64 B6** NX1143.
Balgowan *High.* ***Settlement***, in Badenoch and Strathspey district, 1m/2km E of Laggan Bridge. **88 D5** NN6394.
Balgown *High.* ***Settlement***, 4m/6km N of Uig, Skye. **93 J5** NG3868.
Balgray *Angus* ***Village***, 5m/8km N of Dundee. **83 F4** NO4038.
Balgray Reservoir *E.Renf.* ***Reservoir***, 1m/2km SE of Barrhead. **74 D5** NS5157.
Balgreen *Aber.* ***Settlement***, 4m/7km SE of Macduff. **99 F5** NJ7458.
Balgreggan *D. & G.* ***Settlement***, 1km W of Sandhead, at W end of Sands of Luce. **64 A5** NX0950.
Balgy *High.* ***Settlement***, near S shore of Upper Loch Torridon, 3m/5km SW of Torridon. **94 E6** NG8454.
Balhaldie *Stir.* ***Settlement***, in Strathallan, 3m/4km NE of Dunblane. **81 K7** NN8105.
Balhalgardy *Aber.* ***Hamlet***, 2m/3km NW of Inverurie. **91 F2** NJ7623.
Balham *Gt.Lon.* ***Suburb***, in borough of Wandsworth, 1m/2km S of Clapham Common. TQ2873.
Balhary *P. & K.* ***Settlement***, 2m/3km SE of Alyth. **82 D3** NO2646.
Balhelvie *Fife* ***Hamlet***, 5m/8km NE of Newburgh. **82 E5** NO3021.
Balhinny *Moray Alternative name for Belhinnie, qv.*
Balhousie *Fife* ***Settlement***, 3m/4km N of Lower Largo. **83 F7** NO4206.
Baliasta *Shet.* ***Settlement***, on Unst, 1m/2km W of Baltasound. **108 F2** HP6009.
Baligill *High.* ***Settlement***, on N coast of Caithness district, 3m/5km SE of Strathy Point. **104 D2** NC8566.
Baligrundle *Arg. & B.* ***Settlement***, on Lismore, 4m/6km SW of Port Ramsay. **79 K4** NM8340.
Balindore *Arg. & B.* ***Settlement***, 1m/2km W of Taynuilt. **80 A4** NM9830.
Balintore *Angus* ***Hamlet***, and castle, 7m/11km NW of Kirriemuir. NO2859.
Balintore *High.* Population: 1181. ***Village***, on E coast of Ross and Cromarty district, 7m/11km SE of Tain. **97 F4** NH8675.
Balintraid *High.* ***Settlement***, on Cromarty Firth, Ross and Cromarty district, 2m/4km NE of Invergordon. Developed due to North Sea oil industry. **96 E4** NH7370.
Balintyre *P. & K.* ***Settlement***, 3m/5km W of Fortingall. **81 H3** NN6847.
Balivanich (Gaelic form: Baile a' Mhanaich.) *W.Isles* ***Village***, on NW coast of Benbecula. Benbecula (Baile a' Mhanaich) Aerodrome on low promontory to N. **92 C6** NF7855.
Balk *N.Yorks.* ***Locality***, 3m/5km E of Thirsk. SE4780.
Balk Field *Notts.* ***Suburb***, in E part of Retford. SK7181.
Balkeerie *Angus* ***Settlement***, 3m/5km NE of Newtyle. **82 E3** NO3244.
Balkholme *E.Riding* ***Hamlet***, 2m/4km E of Howden. **58 D7** SE7828.
Balkissock *S.Ayr.* ***Settlement***, 3m/5km E of Ballantrae. **67 F5** NX1382.
Ball *Shrop.* ***Hamlet***, 2m/4km SE of Oswestry. **38 C3** SJ3026.
Ball Green *Stoke* ***Suburb***, 2m/3km NE of Tunstall. SJ8852.
Ball Haye Green *Staffs.* ***Locality***, 1km NE of Leek. **49 J7** SJ9857.
Ball Hill *Hants.* ***Village***, 4m/7km SW of Newbury. **21 H5** SU4263.
Balla *W.Isles* ***Village***, at NW end of Eriskay. NF7811.
Ballabeg *I.o.M.* ***Village***, 2m/3km NW of Castletown. **54 B6** SC2470.
Ballacannell *I.o.M.* ***Locality***, 1m/2km S of Laxey. **54 D5** SC4382.
Ballacarnane Beg *I.o.M.* ***Settlement***, 2m/3km SW of Kirk Michael. **54 C5** SC3088.
Ballachulish (Formerly known as East Laroch and West Laroch.) *High.* ***Settlement***, in Lochaber district on S shore of Loch Leven at mouth of River Laroch. Disused slate quarries. **80 B2** NN0858.
Balladoole *I.o.M.* ***Settlement***, 1m/2km NW of Castletown. **54 B7** SC2468.
Ballafesson *I.o.M.* ***Locality***, 1km NE of Port Erin. **54 B6** SC2070.
Ballageich Hill *E.Renf.* ***Mountain***, 3m/5km SW of Eaglesham. Height 1082 feet or 330 metres. **74 D5** NS5350.
Ballaglasa *W.Isles Anglicised form of Baile Glas, qv.*
Ballagyr *I.o.M.* ***Settlement***, 1m/2km NE of Peel. **54 B5** SC2684.
Ballajora *I.o.M.* ***Settlement***, 3m/5km SE of Ramsey. **54 D4** SC4790.
Ballakilpheric *I.o.M.* ***Hamlet***, nearly 1m/2km NW of Colby. **54 B6** SC2271.
Ballalheannagh Gardens *I.o.M.* ***Garden***, large natural woodland garden with streams and waterfalls, 2m/3km W of Laxey. Specializes in woodland bulbs. **54 D5** SC4083.
Ballamodha *I.o.M.* ***Settlement***, 3m/4km N of Ballasalla. **54 B6** SC2773.
Ballantrae *S.Ayr.* ***Small town***, small fishing port on Ballantrae Bay 12m/19km SW of Girvan. Not scene of Robert Louis Stevenson's Master of Ballantrae (for reference to this, see Borgue). **66 E5** NX0882.
Ballantrae Bay *S.Ayr.* ***Bay***, 12m/19km SW of Girvan. **66 E5** NX0882.
Ballantrushal *W.Isles Anglicised form of Baile an Truiseil, qv.*
Ballaragh *I.o.M.* ***Locality***, 1m/2km NE of Laxey. SC4485.
Ballard Down *Dorset* ***Open space***, downland 1km S of Studland, adjoining Ballard Cliffs on SW coast. **10 B6** SZ0381.
Ballard Point *Dorset* ***Coastal feature***, headland at E end of Purbeck Hills and at N end of Swanage Bay. **10 B6** SZ0481.
Ballards Gore *Essex* ***Hamlet***, 4m/6km E of Hockley. **25 F2** TQ9092.
Ballasalla *I.o.M.* ***Settlement***, 3m/4km N of Ballaugh. **54 C4** SC3497.
Ballasalla *I.o.M.* ***Village***, 2m/3km NE of Castletown. **54 B6** SC2870.
Ballater *Aber.* Population: 1362. ***Village***, resort on River Dee, 14m/22km E of Braemar and 17m/28km W of Aberdeen. **90 B5** NO3695.
Ballaterach *Aber.* ***Settlement***, 3m/5km E of Ballater. **90 C5** NO4196.
Ballathona *I.o.M. Alternative name for The Lhen, qv.*
Ballaugh *I.o.M.* ***Village***, 7m/11km W of Ramsey. **54 C4** SC3493.
Ballaveare *I.o.M.* ***Settlement***, 3m/4km SW of Douglas. **54 C6** SC3473.
Ballchraggan *High.* ***Village***, in Ross and Cromarty district, 5m/7km S of Tain. NH7675.
Ballechin *P. & K.* ***Settlement***, 3m/5km S of Pitlochry across River Tummel. **82 A2** NN9353.
Balleich *Stir.* ***Settlement***, on N edge of Loch Ard Forest, 1km SW of Aberfoyle. **81 G7** NN5100.
Ballencleuch Law *S.Lan.* ***Mountain***, in Lowther Hills, 8m/12km S of Elvanfoot. Height 2266 feet or 691 metres. **68 E3** NS9304.
Ballencrieff *E.Loth.* ***Village***, 3m/5km NW of Haddington. **76 C3** NT4878.
Ballharn Hill *High.* ***Hill***, 2m/3km N of Cnoc an Earrannaiche. Height 476 feet or 145 metres. **105 H4** ND2444.
Ballidon *Derbys.* ***Hamlet***, 5m/8km N of Ashbourne. **50 E7** SK2054.
Balliekine *N.Ayr.* ***Settlement***, on NW coast of Arran, 3m/4km S of Pirnmill. **73 G7** NR8739.
Balliemeanoch *Arg. & B.* ***Settlement***, on N side of Glenbranter Forest, 1km SE of Strachur. **80 C7** NN1000.
Balliemore *Arg. & B.* ***Settlement***, on Kerrera, 2m/3km SW of Rubh' a' Bhearnaig. **79 K5** NM8228.
Balliemore *Arg. & B.* ***Settlement***, 2m/3km S of Strachur. **73 K1** NS1099.
Balliemore *P. & K.* ***Settlement***, on N side of Dunalastair Water, 3m/4km E of Kinloch Rannoch. **81 J2** NN7059.
Ballig *I.o.M.* ***Settlement***, 1km NE of St. John's. **54 B5** SC2882.
Ballimeanoch *Arg. & B.* ***Settlement***, on E shore of Loch Awe, 4m/6km NE of Dalavich. **80 B6** NN0116.
Ballimore *Arg. & B.* ***Settlement***, on Cowal peninsula, 5m/8km SE of Lochgilphead across Loch Fyne. **73 H2** NR9283.
Ballimore *Stir.* ***Settlement***, on W side of Glen Buckie, 2m/3km S of Balquhidder. **81 G6** NN5317.
Ballinaby *Arg. & B.* ***Settlement***, on NW of Islay, 1km NW of Loch Gorm. **72 A4** NR2267.
Ballindalloch Castle *Moray* ***Castle***, baronial castle, with modern additions and alterations, on E bank of River Avon near its confluence with River Spey 7m/11km SW of Charlestown of Aberlour. **89 J1** NJ1736.
Ballindean *P. & K.* ***Hamlet***, at foot of Braes of the Carse, 3m/5km W of Longforgan. **82 D5** NO2529.
Ballingdon *Suff.* ***Suburb***, adjoining to SW of Sudbury across River Stour. **34 C4** TL8640.
Ballinger Common *Bucks.* ***Village***, 3m/5km W of Chesham. **22 C1** SP9103.
Ballingham *Here.* ***Village***, in loop of River Wye, 7m/11km SE of Hereford. **28 E5** SO5731.
Ballingry *Fife* Population: 6393. ***Small town***, 3m/4km N of Cowdenbeath. **75 K1** NT1797.
Ballinlick *P. & K.* ***Settlement***, in Strathbraan, 3m/5km SW of Dunkeld. **82 A3** NN9840.
Ballinloan Burn *P. & K.* ***River***, flowing SE into River Braan, 3m/5km SW of Dunkeld. **82 A3** NN9740.
Ballinluig *P. & K.* ***Settlement***, in Strathardle, 1m/2km S of Kirkmichael. **82 B2** NO0957.
Ballinluig *P. & K.* ***Village***, on River Tummel, 4m/7km SE of Pitlochry. **82 A2** NN9752.
Ballintuim *P. & K.* ***Village***, in Strathardle, 3m/5km NW of Bridge of Cally. **82 C2** NO1054.
Ballo Reservoir *Fife* ***Reservoir***, largest of a series of four small reservoirs in Lomond Hills, 2m/3km NW of Leslie. **82 D7** NO2106.
Balloch *Angus* ***Hamlet***, 3m/5km NW of Kirriemuir. **82 E2** NO3557.
Balloch *High.* Population: 1121. ***Hamlet***, in Inverness district, 4m/7km E of Inverness. **96 E7** NH7347.
Balloch *N.Lan.* ***Suburb***, 1m/2km W of Cumbernauld town centre. **75 F3** NS7374.
Balloch *P. & K.* ***Settlement***, 2m/3km SW of Crieff. **81 K6** NN8419.
Balloch *W.Dun.* ***Locality***, at S end of Loch Lomond, adjoining Alexandria to N. **74 B2** NS3981.
Balloch Castle Country Park *W.Dun.* ***Leisure/recreation***, 200 acre country park 1m/2km N of Balloch on S shore of Loch Lomond. Early 19c mansion of Balloch Castle is now visitor centre for park. Site of old castle is marked by a moated mound. **74 B2** NS3882.
Balloch Wood ***Forest/woodland***, on border of Aberdeenshire and Moray, 3m/5km E of Keith. **98 C6** NJ4748.
Ballochan *Aber.* ***Settlement***, in Forest of Birse, near head of Water of Feugh, 5m/8km S of Aboyne. **90 D5** NO5290.
Ballochandrain *Arg. & B.* ***Settlement***, 6m/9km N of Tighnabruaich. **73 H2** NR9983.
Ballochbuie Forest *Aber.* ***Forest/woodland***, forest on S side of River Dee 3m/5km E of Braemar. **89 J6** NO1990.
Ballochford *Moray* ***Settlement***, on W slopes of Garbet Hill, 4m/7km SE of Dufftown. **90 B1** NJ3633.
Ballochgair *Arg. & B.* ***Settlement***, on E coast of Kintyre, 2m/3km NW of Peninver. **66 B1** NR7727.
Ballochmartin *N.Ayr.* ***Settlement***, on Great Cumbrae, 2m/3km NE of Millport. **73 K5** NS1757.
Ballochmorrie *S.Ayr.* ***Settlement***, on W bank of Duisk River, 2m/3km NW of Barrhill. **67 G5** NX2184.
Ballochmyle House *E.Ayr. See Catrine.*
Ballochroy *Arg. & B.* ***Settlement***, on NW coast of Kintyre, 4m/7km NE of Tayinloan. **73 F5** NR7252.
Ballochyle Hill *Arg. & B.* ***Mountain***, above W bank of River Eachaig, 1m/2km W of Orchard. Height 1253 feet or 382 metres. **73 K2** NS1382.
Ballogie *Aber.* ***Locality***, and estate, 4m/6km SE of Aboyne. **90 D5** NO5795.
Balls Cross *W.Suss.* ***Hamlet***, 3m/5km N of Petworth. **12 C4** SU9826.
Ball's Green *E.Suss.* ***Hamlet***, 1km NE of Withyham and 6m/9km W of Royal Tunbridge Wells. TQ4936.
Balls Green *Essex* ***Hamlet***, 6m/10km E of Colchester. TM0924.
Ball's Green *Glos.* ***Hamlet***, 1m/2km E of Nailsworth. ST8699.
Balls Green *W.Suss.* ***Settlement***, 2m/3km SE of Billingshurst. TQ1023.
Balls Hill *W.Mid.* ***Suburb***, 2m/3km N of West Bromwich town centre. SO9993.
Ballyaurgan *Arg. & B.* ***Settlement***, on SE side of Loch Caolisport, 1m/2km SW of Clachbreck. **73 F3** NR7574.
Ballygown *Arg. & B.* ***Settlement***, on Ballygown Bay, on N side of Loch Tuath, Mull. Ruined broch. **79 F3** NM4343.
Ballygown Bay *Arg. & B.* ***Bay***, on N side of Loch Tuath, Mull. **79 F3** NM4343.
Ballygrant *Arg. & B.* ***Village***, on Islay, 3m/5km SW of Port Askaig. Loch Ballygrant, is small loch to E. **72 B4** NR3966.
Ballyhaugh *Arg. & B.* ***Settlement***, 3m/5km W of Arinagour, Coll. **78 C2** NM1757.
Ballymeanoch *Arg. & B.* ***Settlement***, 5m/8km N of Lochgilphead. **73 G1** NR8396.
Ballymichael *N.Ayr.* ***Settlement***, on Arran, 3m/4km NE of Blackwaterfoot. **73 H7** NR9231.
Balm Hill *Lancs.* ***Suburb***, 1m/2km SE of Morecambe town centre. SD4463.
Balmacaan Forest *High.* ***Open space***, deer forest in Inverness district SW of Drumnadrochit. **87 K2** NH4125.
Balmacara *High.* ***Locality***, in Skye and Lochalsh district, 3m/5km E of Kyle of Lochalsh. Balmacara Estate (National Trust for Scotland) to N. **86 E2** NG8127.

Balmacara Estate *High.* ***Open space***, National Trust for Scotland property to N of Balmacara on N shore of Loch Alsh, 4m/6km E of Kyle of Lochalsh. **86 E2** NG7828.
Balmaclellan *D. & G.* ***Village***, 1m/2km NE of New Galloway. **65 G3** NX6579.
Balmacneil *P. & K.* ***Settlement***, on W side of Strath Tay, 5m/8km SE of Pitlochry. **82 A2** NN9750.
Balmadies *Angus* ***Hamlet***, 1m/2km NE of Letham. **83 G3** NO5549.
Balmae *D. & G.* ***Settlement***, 4m/6km S of Kirkcudbright. **65 G6** NX6845.
Balmaha *Stir.* ***Village***, on E shore of Loch Lomond, 3m/5km W of Drymen. **74 C1** NS4290.
Balmalcolm *Fife* ***Hamlet***, 3m/4km NE of Freuchie. **82 E7** NO3108.
Balmanno Hill *P. & K.* ***Hill***, on N edge of Ochil Hills, 3m/4km N of Glenfarg. Height 751 feet or 229 metres. **82 C6** NO1414.
Balmaqueen *High.* ***Settlement***, near N end of Skye, 1m/2km S of Rubha na h-Aiseig. NG4474.
Balmartin (Gaelic form: Baile Mhartainn.) *W.Isles* ***Settlement***, near NW coast of North Uist, 2m/3km S of Griminis Point. **92 C4** NF7273.
Balmeanach *Arg. & B.* ***Settlement***, 1km S of Balnahard, Mull. **79 F4** NM4433.
Balmedie *Aber.* Population: 1260. ***Village***, 7m/12km N of Aberdeen. **91 H3** NJ9617.
Balmedie Country Park *Aber.* ***Leisure/recreation***, country park with over 150 acres of grassland and beach situated between Balmedie and Balmedie Beach. Attracts variety of seabirds. **91 H3** NJ9717.
Balmer Heath *Shrop.* ***Settlement***, 3m/5km E of Ellesmere. SJ4434.
Balmerino *Fife* ***Village***, on Firth of Tay, 5m/7km SW of Newport-on-Tay. Ruins of 13c abbey (National Trust for Scotland). **82 E5** NO3524.
Balmerino Abbey *Fife* ***Ecclesiastical building***, Cistercian abbey (National Trust for Scotland) in Balmerino, 5m/8km SW of Newport-on-Tay. Founded in 1229 and ruined during Reformation. **82 E5** NO3524.
Balmerlawn *Hants.* ***Hamlet***, 1km NE of Brockenhurst. **10 E4** SU3003.
Balminnoch *D. & G.* ***Settlement***, 1km W of Black Loch, 7m/11km NE of Glenluce. **64 C4** NX2765.
Balmoral Castle *Aber.* ***Historic house***, royal residence since 1852. New castle on site of earlier castle was completed in 1855 and was designed by Prince Albert and William Smith. Situated on S bank of River Dee, 7m/11km E of Braemar. **89 K5** NO2595.
Balmoral Forest *Aber.* ***Open space***, deer forest to S of Balmoral Castle. **89 K6** NO2595.
Balmore *E.Dun.* ***Village***, 3m/5km E of Milngavie. **74 E3** NS6073.
Balmore *High.* ***Settlement***, on Skye, 1m/2km NE of Harlosh Point. **93 H7** NG2941.
Balmore *High.* ***Settlement***, in Strathglass, 2m/3km NE of Cannich. **87 K1** NH3533.
Balmore *High.* ***Settlement***, 7m/11km S of Nairn. **97 F7** NH8845.
Balmullo *Fife* Population: 1108. ***Village***, 2m/3km W of Leuchars. **83 F5** NO4220.
Balmungie *High.* ***Settlement***, 1m/2km N of Rosemarkie. **96 E6** NH7459.
Balmyle *P. & K.* ***Hamlet***, 4m/6km NW of Bridge of Cally. **82 B2** NO1055.
Balnabodach *W.Isles Anglicised form of Buaile nam Bodach, qv.*
Balnaboth *Angus* ***Settlement***, 9m/15km NW of Kirriemuir. **82 E1** NO3166.
Balnabruaich *High.* ***Settlement***, 1m/2km N of Cromarty across mouth of Cromarty Firth. **96 E4** NH7969.
Balnacra *High.* ***Settlement***, in Glen Carron, Ross and Cromarty district, at SW end of Loch Dùghaill or Doule. **95 F7** NG9746.
Balnafoich *High.* ***Settlement***, in Inverness district, 7m/11km S of Inverness. **88 D1** NH6835.
Balnagall *High.* ***Settlement***, 3m/5km E of Tain. **97 F3** NH8381.
Balnagown Castle *High.* ***Castle***, 15c tower castle with modifications, 2m/3km NW of Invergordon, on S bank of River Balnagown. **96 E4** NH7575.
Balnaguard *P. & K.* ***Village***, in Strath Tay, 2m/3km W of confluence of Rivers Tay and Tummel. **82 A2** NN9451.
Balnaguard Burn *P. & K.* ***River***, rising on Grandtully Hill and flowing NE to Balnaguard and then into River Tay. Course includes Falls of Balnaguard, 1km upstream of Balnaguard. **82 A3** NN9551.
Balnaguisich *High.* ***Settlement***, 1m/2km NE of Alness. **96 D4** NH6771.
Balnahard *Arg. & B.* ***Locality***, on W coast of Mull, 1m/2km S of entrance to Loch na Keal. **79 F4** NM4534.
Balnahard *Arg. & B.* ***Settlement***, on NE corner of Colonsay, 4m/6km NE of Scalasaig. **72 C1** NR4199.
Balnahard Bay *Arg. & B.* ***Bay***, small E facing bay to N of Rubh' a' Geodha at NE tip of Colonsay. **79 F7** NM4300.
Balnain *High.* ***Settlement***, in Glen Urquhart, 4m/6km W of Drumnadrochit. **88 B1** NH4430.
Balnakeil *High.* ***Settlement***, on Balnakeil Bay, on N coast of Sutherland district, 1m/2km NW of Durness. **103 F2** NC3968.
Balnakeil Bay *High.* ***Bay***, on N coast of Sutherland district, 1m/2km NW of Durness. **103 F1** NC3968.
Balnaknock *High.* ***Settlement***, 1m/2km E of Uig, Skye. **93 K5** NG4162.
Balnamoon *Angus* ***Hamlet***, 4m/6km NW of Brechin. **83 G1** NO5563.
Balnapaling *High.* ***Settlement***, N of Cromarty, 1m/2km across mouth of Cromarty Firth. **96 E5** NH7969.
Balnespick *High.* ***Settlement***, 5m/8km E of Kingussie. **89 F4** NH8303.
Balornock *Glas.* ***Suburb***, 2m/3km NE of Glasgow city centre. NS6168.
Balquhandy Hill *P. & K.* ***Mountain***, 2m/3km S of Dunning. Height 1168 feet or 356 metres. **82 B6** NO0311.
Balquhidder *Stir.* ***Village***, at foot of Loch Voil, 4m/6km SW of Lochearnhead. Burial place of outlaw Rob Roy, d. 1734. **81 G5** NN5320.
Balranald *W.Isles Anglicised form of Baile Raghaill, qv.*
Balsall *W.Mid.* Population: 6953. ***Village***, 5m/7km NW of Kenilworth. **30 D1** SP2476.
Balsall Common *W.Mid.* ***Village***, 6m/10km W of Coventry. **30 D1** SP2377.
Balsall Heath *W.Mid.* ***Suburb***, 2m/3km S of Birmingham city centre. SP0784.
Balsall Street *W.Mid.* ***Hamlet***, to W of Balsall Common. SP2276.
Balscote *Oxon.* ***Village***, 4m/7km W of Banbury. **30 E4** SP3941.
Balsham *Cambs.* ***Village***, 6m/10km NW of Haverhill. **33 J3** TL5850.
Balstonia *Thur.* ***Suburb***, 1m/2km NE of Stanford-le-Hope. TQ6983.
Balta *Shet.* ***Island***, uninhabited island 1m/2km N to S at entrance to Balta Sound, E coast of Unst. **108 F2** HP6608.
Baltasound *Shet.* ***Village***, at head of inlet of Balta Sound on E coast of Unst. To S lies Baltasound airstrip. **108 F2** HP6208.
Balterley *Staffs.* ***Hamlet***, 2m/4km W of Audley. **49 G7** SJ7650.
Balterley Green *Staffs.* ***Settlement***, to N of Balterley. SJ7650.
Balterley Heath *Staffs.* ***Settlement***, to W of Balterley. SJ7450.
Baltersan *D. & G.* ***Settlement***, 3m/4km S of Newton Stewart. **64 E4** NX4261.
Balthangie *Aber.* ***Settlement***, 2m/4km NE of Cuminestown. **99 G5** NJ8351.
Balthayock *P. & K.* ***Locality***, 4m/6km E of Perth. **82 C5** NO1723.
Baltonsborough *Som.* ***Village***, 4m/6km SE of Glastonbury. **8 E1** ST5434.
Baluachraig *Arg. & B.* ***Settlement***, 6m/9km N of Lochgilphead. **73 G1** NR8397.
Balulive *Arg. & B.* ***Settlement***, 1m/2km W of Port Askaig, on NE of Islay. **72 C4** NR4069.
Balure *Arg. & B.* ***Settlement***, 2m/3km W of Benderloch across Ardmucknish Bay. **79 K4** NM8738.
Balure *Arg. & B.* ***Settlement***, on S coast of Loch Etive, 1km NE of Taynuilt. **80 B4** NN0132.
Balvaird *High.* ***Settlement***, scattered settlement, 1km NE of Muir of Ord. **96 C6** NH5351.
Balvaird Castle *P. & K.* ***Castle***, remains of late 15c tower on an L-plan, 2m/4km E of Glenfarg. Extended in 1581 by addition of walled courtyard and gatehouse. **82 C6** NO1611.
Balvarran *P. & K.* ***Settlement***, 1m/2km N of Kirkmichael. **82 B1** NO0762.
Balvenie *Moray* ***Locality***, 1m/2km N of Dufftown. Includes remains of 13c moated Balvenie Castle (Historic Scotland). NJ3242.
Balvenie Castle *Moray* ***Castle***, ruin of 13c castle (Historic Scotland) on N side of Dufftown, with 15c-16c additions, dry moat and high stone walls. Visited by Mary, Queen of Scots in 1562. Jacobite troops stayed here after Battle of Killiecrankie in 1689. **98 B6** NJ3240.
Balvicar *Arg. & B.* ***Village***, on Balvicar Bay, E coast of Seil, 2m/4km S of Clachan Bridge. **79 J6** NM7616.
Balvraid *High.* ***Settlement***, in Gleann Beag, Skye and Lochalsh district, 3m/4km SE of Glenelg. **86 E3** NG8416.
Balvraid *High.* ***Settlement***, 5m/7km SE of Moy. **89 F1** NH8231.
Balwest *Cornw.* ***Hamlet***, 4m/7km W of Helston. SW5929.
Bamber Bridge *Lancs.* ***Locality***, 3m/5km SE of Preston. **55 J7** SD5625.
Bamber's Green *Essex* ***Hamlet***, 3m/5km W of Great Dunmow. **33 J6** TL5723.
Bamburgh *Northumb.* ***Village***, on North Sea coast, opposite Farne Islands and 5m/7km E of Belford. Large castle, Norman but much restored. St. Aidan died here, AD 651. Grace Darling Museum; Grace Darling buried in churchyard. **77 K7** NU1834.
Bamburgh Castle *Northumb.* ***Castle***, on E coast just E of Bamburgh, built on site of Iron Age, Roman and Anglo-Saxon forts. Medieval ruins now remain. **77 K7** NU1835.
Bamff *P. & K.* ***Settlement***, 3m/4km NW of Alyth. **82 D2** NO2251.
Bamford *Derbys.* ***Village***, 2m/3km NW of Hathersage. **50 E4** SK2083.
Bamford *Gt.Man.* ***Suburb***, 2m/3km W of Rochdale town centre. SD8613.
Bamfurlong *Glos.* ***Settlement***, 3m/5km W of Cheltenham. SO8921.
Bamfurlong *Gt.Man.* ***Locality***, 2m/4km NE of Ashton-in-Makerfield. SD5901.
Bampton *Cumb.* ***Hamlet***, 3m/5km NW of Shap. **61 G5** NY5118.
Bampton *Devon* ***Small town***, market town on River Batherm, 6m/10km N of Tiverton. Annual pony fair in October. **7 H3** SS9522.
Bampton *Oxon.* Population: 2459. ***Village***, 5m/8km SW of Witney. **21 G1** SP3103.
Bampton Common *Cumb.* ***Open space***, high moorland on N side of Haweswater Reservoir, 6m/9km W of Shap. **61 F5** NY4716.
Bampton Grange *Cumb.* ***Hamlet***, just E of Bampton, on River Lowther. NY5218.
Banavie *High.* ***Hamlet***, adjacent to Lower Banavie, in Lochaber district, beside Caledonian Canal, 2m/3km N of Fort William. Series of locks on canal. **87 H7** NN1177.
Banbury *Oxon.* Population: 39,906. ***Town***, on River Cherwell, 22m/35km N of Oxford. Former cake and cloth-making town. **31 F4** SP4540.
Banbury Museum *Oxon.* ***Other feature of interest***, in Banbury town centre, situated in boardroom of Poor Law Guardians. Consists of changing exhibitions and displays. **31 F4** SP4540.
Banc Cwmhelen *Carmar.* ***Mountain***, rising to over 320 metres, 1m/2km SE of Glanaman. **17 K3** SN6811.
Banc Nant-Rhys *Cere.* ***Mountain***, 4m/6km NE of Cwmystwyth. Height 1791 feet or 546 metres. **37 H7** SN8180.
Banc y Celyn *Powys* ***Mountain***, 3m/5km S of Builth Wells. Height 1548 feet or 472 metres. **27 K4** SO0446.
Banc-y-ffordd *Carmar.* ***Hamlet***, 2m/3km S of Llandysul. **17 H1** SN4037.
Bancffosfelen *Carmar.* ***Village***, 1m/2km NW of Pontyberem. **17 H3** SN4811.
Banchor *High.* ***Settlement***, 5m/7km SW of Ferness. **97 G7** NH9140.
Banchory *Aber.* Population: 6230. ***Small town***, on River Dee at its confluence with Water of Feugh, 11m/18km NW of Stonehaven. 1m/2km S is Bridge of Feugh, with salmon leap observation platform. **91 F5** NO6995.
Banchory-Devenick *Aber.* ***Locality***, 3m/5km SW of Aberdeen city centre across River Dee. **91 H4** NJ9102.
Bancycapel *Carmar.* ***Hamlet***, 3m/5km S of Carmarthen. SN4315.
Bancyfelin *Carmar.* ***Village***, 3m/5km NE of St. Clears. **17 G3** SN3218.
Bandley Hill *Herts.* ***Suburb***, E district of Stevenage. TL2623.
Bandon *Fife* ***Settlement***, 2m/3km N of Glenrothes. **82 D7** NO2704.
Bandrake Head *Cumb.* ***Settlement***, 3m/4km N of Penny Bridge. SD3187.
Banff *Aber.* Population: 4110. ***Small town***, on N coast, on W side of Banff Bay. Industrial estate adjoining town centre. To S is Duff House (Historic Scotland), in Georgian baroque style by William Adam. **98 E4** NJ6863.
Banff Bay *Aber.* ***Bay***, on N coast of Banff and Buchan district, between Banff and Macduff. **98 E4** NJ6863.
Bangor *Gwyn.* Population: 12,330. ***City***, ancient cathedral city (Royal Charter granted 1883) and resort on Menai Strait 51m/82km W of Chester. University College of North Wales, constituent college of University of Wales. **46 D5** SH5771.
Bangor Cathedral *Gwyn.* ***Ecclesiastical building***, in Bangor city centre. Founded c. AD 525 by St. Deiniol. Boasts longest continuous use of any cathedral in Britain, but present spacious building dates mainly from 13c to 15c, and was heavily restored by Gilbert Scott in 1866. **46 D5** SH5872.
Bangor-is-y-coed (Also known as Bangor-on-Dee.) *Wrex.* ***Village***, on River Dee, 5m/7km SE of Wrexham. **38 C1** SJ3845.
Bangor-on-Dee *Wrex. Alternative name for Bangor-is-y-coed, qv.*
Bangor Teifi *Cere.* ***Settlement***, 3m/4km W of Llandysul. **26 C4** SN3740.
Bangor's Green *Lancs.* ***Settlement***, 1km SE of Halsall and 2m/4km W of Ormskirk. SD3709.
Bangrove *Suff.* ***Locality***, adjoining to S of Bardwell. TL9472.
Banham *Norf.* ***Village***, 6m/10km NW of Diss. **44 E7** TM0688.
Bank *Hants.* ***Hamlet***, 1m/2km SW of Lyndhurst. **10 D4** SU2807.
Bank End *Cumb.* ***Locality***, 1m/2km NW of Broughton in Furness. **54 E1** SD1988.
Bank Newton *N.Yorks.* ***Settlement***, on Leeds and Liverpool Canal, 2m/3km SW of Gargrave. **56 E4** SD9053.
Bank of England *Gt.Lon.* ***Other feature of interest***, in City of London, 2m/3km NE of Charing Cross. Bank vaults hold national gold reserves. Outer walls are still original design by Sir John Soane, architect to the Bank 1788-1833. Rebuilt by Sir Herbert Baker 1925-39. Museum recreates history of the 'Old Lady of Threadneedle Street', along with history of the banknote and real gold bars. TQ3281.
Bank Side *S.Yorks.* ***Settlement***, on E side of River Don, 3m/4km N of Thorne. SE6716.
Bank Street *Worcs.* ***Settlement***, 5m/7km SE of Tenbury Wells. **29 F2** SO6362.
Bank Top *Lancs.* ***Hamlet***, 3m/4km NE of Skelmersdale. SD5207.
Bank Top *Stoke* ***Suburb***, 1m/2km E of Tunstall town centre. SJ8751.
Bank Top *W.Yorks.* ***Suburb***, 1m/2km SE of Halifax town centre. SE1024.
Bank Top *W.Yorks.* ***Suburb***, 2m/4km NE of Bradford city centre. SE1836.
Bankend *D. & G.* ***Village***, on Lochar Water, 6m/10km SE of Dumfries. **69 F7** NY0268.
Bankend *S.Lan.* ***Locality***, comprises South and North Bankend, 2m/3km SW and 2m/3km W of Coalburn respectively. **75 G7** NS8033.
Bankfoot *P. & K.* Population: 1009. ***Village***, 5m/8km SE of Dunkeld. **82 B4** NO0635.
Bankglen *E.Ayr.* ***Hamlet***, 1m/2km SW of New Cumnock. NS5912.
Bankhead *Aberdeen* ***Suburb***, to NW of Aberdeen city centre. **91 G4** NJ8910.
Bankhead *Aber.* ***Settlement***, on E bank of River Don, 3m/5km NE of Alford. **90 E3** NJ6117.
Bankhead *Aber.* ***Settlement***, 3m/5km SW of Sauchen. **90 E4** NJ6507.
Bankhead *D. & G.* ***Settlement***, 1km NE of Dundreddan. **65 H6** NX7648.
Bankland *Som.* ***Hamlet***, 3m/4km NW of Stoke St. Gregory. ST3129.
Banknock *Falk.* Population: 2675. ***Village***, 4m/6km E of Kilsyth. **75 F3** NS7779.
Banks *Cumb.* ***Settlement***, 3m/5km NE of Brampton. Section of Hadrian's Wall to E contains turrets of Banks East, Leahill and Piper Sike (all English Heritage). **70 A7** NY5664.

Banks *Lancs.* Population: 3245. ***Village***, 4m/7km NE of Southport. **55 G7** SD3920.
Banks Sands *Lancs.* ***Coastal feature***, sandbank on S side of River Ribble estuary, 1m/2km S of Lytham jetty across River Ribble channel. **55 G7** SD3624.
Bankshill *D. & G.* ***Settlement***, 4m/6km E of Lockerbie. **69 G5** NY1981.
Bannau Brycheiniog *Powys Welsh form of Brecon Beacons, qv.*
Bannaventa *Northants. See Norton.*
Banners Gate *W.Mid.* ***Suburb***, 3m/4km W of Sutton Coldfield. SP0895.
Banningham *Norf.* ***Village***, 2m/4km NE of Aylsham. **45 G3** TG2129.
Bannister Green *Essex* ***Village***, 4m/7km W of Braintree. **33 K6** TL6921.
Bannium *Powys See Aberyscir.*
Bannock Burn *High.* ***River***, in Sutherland district, running S from Loch an Ruathair to River Helmsdale 1m/2km SW of Kinbrace. **104 D5** NC8530.
Bannock Burn *Stir.* ***River***, rising on E slopes of Earl's Hill, 6m/9km SW of Stirling, passing through North Third Reservoir and running E to Bannockburn, then NE to River Forth 2m/4km E of Stirling. **75 F1** NS8393.
Bannockburn *Stir.* Population: 5799. ***Small town***, 2m/4km SE of Stirling. Nearby is site of battle of 1314 in which Scots under Robert the Bruce routed English under Edward II. **75 G1** NS8393.
Bannockburn Monument and Heritage Centre *Stir.* ***Other feature of interest***, monument (National Trust for Scotland) and heritage centre at Borestone Brae, 1m/2km S of Stirling, commemorating Battle of Bannockburn 1314. Includes rotunda and equestrian statue of Robert the Bruce. **75 F1** NS7990.
Banovallum *Lincs. See Horncastle.*
Banstead *Surr.* Population: 18,623. ***Town***, 3m/5km S of Sutton. Former wool and mutton village. **23 F6** TQ2559.
Bantam Grove *W.Yorks.* ***Suburb***, 1m/2km E of Morley town centre. SE2727.
Bantham *Devon* ***Hamlet***, on S side of River Avon estuary near its mouth, 4m/7km W of Kingsbridge. **5 G6** SX6643.
Banton *N.Lan.* ***Village***, 2m/4km E of Kilsyth. **75 F3** NS7479.
Bant's Carn *I.o.S.* ***Historic/prehistoric site***, Bronze Age round chambered tomb (English Heritage) roofed by four large stones, on hill overlooking Halangy Point, 1m/2km N of Hugh Town on St. Mary's. Iron Age village of Halangy Down (English Heritage) below hill. **2 C1** SV9012.
Banwell *N.Som.* Population: 1850. ***Village***, 5m/8km E of Weston-super-Mare. **19 G6** ST3959.
Banwen Pyrddin *N.P.T.* ***Settlement***, 3m/4km NW of Glyn-neath. SN8509.
Banwy *Powys* ***River***, rising 5m/9km W of Llangadfan and flowing E to join River Einion, 2m/3km NW of Llanfair Caereinion. Combined stream, known indifferently as Banwy or Einion, then continues SE to Llanfair Caereinion, then NE into River Vyrnwy 1m/2km SW of Meifod. SJ1411.
Banyard's Green *Suff.* ***Settlement***, 1km NE of Laxfield. TM3072.
Baosbheinn *High.* ***Mountain***, in W part of Ross and Cromarty district 5m/8km N of Upper Loch Torridon. Height 2870 feet or 875 metres. **94 E5** NG8665.
Bapchild *Kent* ***Village***, 2m/3km E of Sittingbourne. **25 F5** TQ9262.
Baptist End *W.Mid.* ***Suburb***, 1m/2km S of Dudley town centre. SO9488.
Baptiston *Stir.* ***Settlement***, 4m/6km NW of Strathblane. **74 D2** NS5283.
Bapton *Wilts.* ***Hamlet***, 1m/2km NW of Wylye, in Wylye valley. ST9938.
Bar End *Hants.* ***Suburb***, SE district of Winchester. SU4828.
Bar Hill *Cambs.* Population: 4397. ***Village***, with industrial estate, 5m/8km NW of Cambridge. **33 G2** TL3863.
Bar Moor *T. & W.* ***Suburb***, adjoining to W of Ryton. NZ1464.
Barabhas *W.Isles Gaelic form of Barvas, qv.*
Barachander *Arg. & B.* ***Settlement***, 4m/6km SE of Taynuilt. **80 B5** NN0325.
Barassie *S.Ayr.* ***Locality***, on Firth of Clyde, adjoining to N of Troon. **74 B7** NS3232.
Baravaig *High.* ***Locality***, on Camas Baravaig, bay on E coast of Sleat peninsula, Skye, 2m/3km S of Eilean Iarmain. Loch Baravaig is small loch to W. NG6909.
Barbara Hepworth Museum *Cornw.* ***Other feature of interest***, at St. Ives in home of the artist, displaying workshop and 47 pieces of her work. **2 C4** SW5240.
Barbaraville *High.* ***Village***, on Nigg Bay, Cromarty Firth, 4m/6km NE of Invergordon, Ross and Cromarty district. **96 E4** NH7472.
Barber Booth *Derbys.* ***Settlement***, 4m/7km NE of Chapel-en-le-Frith. **50 D4** SK1184.
Barber Green *Cumb.* ***Hamlet***, 1km W of High Newton, and 3m/4km SE of Newby Bridge. SD3982.
Barber's Moor *Lancs.* ***Settlement***, 1km E of Croston, 6m/9km W of Chorley. SD4919.
Barbican *Plym.* ***Locality***, central district of Plymouth near harbour and Plymouth Hoe. SX4854.
Barbican Arts and Conference Centre *Gt.Lon.* ***Leisure/recreation***, complex in City of London, 2m/3km NE of Charing Cross. Includes a concert hall, two theatres, three cinemas, a public library, an art gallery and sculpture court. Home of London Symphony Orchestra. TQ3281.
Barbon *Cumb.* ***Village***, 3m/4km N of Kirkby Lonsdale. **56 B1** SD6282.
Barbourne *Worcs.* ***Suburb***, N district of Worcester. SO8457.
Barbridge *Ches.* ***Hamlet***, 4m/6km NW of Nantwich. SJ6156.
Barbrook *Devon* ***Village***, on West Lyn River 1m/2km S of Lynton. **7 F1** SS7147.
Barbrook Reservoir *Derbys.* ***Reservoir***, 4m/6km NE of Baslow. **50 E5** SK2777.
Barbury Castle *Swin.* ***Historic/prehistoric site***, ancient hillfort on N edge of Marlborough Downs, 5m/8km S of Swindon, with surrounding country park. Probable site of medieval village to S. **20 E4** SU1476.
Barby *Northants.* ***Village***, 4m/6km SE of Rugby. **31 G1** SP5470.
Barcaldine *Arg. & B.* ***Settlement***, on Dearg Abhainn, on S side of Loch Creran, Argyll. **80 A3** NM9641.
Barcaple *D. & G.* ***Settlement***, 4m/6km N of Kirkcudbright. **65 G5** NX6757.
Barcheston *Warks.* ***Village***, 1km SE of Shipston on Stour. **30 D4** SP2639.
Barclodiad y Gawres Chambered Cairn *I.o.A.* ***Historic/prehistoric site***, reconstructed remains of burial chamber (Cadw) on SW coast of Anglesey, 2m/3km SE of Rhosneigr and 2m/3km NW of Aberffraw. Formerly of stone, now grass-covered, with rare carved stones dating from 3000 BC and protected by concrete dome. **46 B5** SH3270.
Barclose *Cumb.* ***Hamlet***, just SW of Scaleby, 5m/8km NE of Carlisle. NY4462.
Barco Hill *Cumb.* ***Suburb***, E district of Penrith. NY5230.
Barcombe *E.Suss.* ***Village***, in River Ouse valley, 3m/4km N of Lewes. **13 H5** TQ4114.
Barcombe Cross *E.Suss.* ***Village***, 4m/6km N of Lewes. **13 H5** TQ4215.
Barcraigs Reservoir *N.Ayr.* ***Reservoir***, western part of reservoir 2m/3km S of Howwood. Eastern part known as Rowbank Reservoir. **74 B5** NS3857.
Bard Head *Shet.* ***Coastal feature***, southernmost point of Bressay. **109 E9** HU5135.
Barden *N.Yorks.* ***Hamlet***, 3m/5km NE of Leyburn. **62 C7** SE1493.
Barden Fell *N.Yorks.* ***Open space***, moorland area S of Burnsall, to W of River Wharfe. **57 F4** SE0858.
Barden Park *Kent* ***Suburb***, in W part of Tonbridge. TQ5746.
Bardennoch *D. & G.* ***Settlement***, 1m/2km SE of Carsphairn. **67 K4** NX5791.
Bardfield End Green *Essex* ***Hamlet***, 1m/2km E of Thaxted. **33 K5** TL6230.
Bardfield Saling *Essex* ***Hamlet***, 5m/8km NE of Great Dunmow. **33 K6** TL6826.
Bardister *Shet.* ***Settlement***, on Mainland, at head of Gluss Voe, 2m/3km S of Ollaberry. **108 C5** HU3577.
Bardney *Lincs.* ***Village***, 9m/14km W of Horncastle. Slight remains of Saxon abbey to N. **52 E6** TF1169.
Bardney Abbey *Lincs.* ***Ecclesiastical building***, remains of Benedictine abbey where St. Oswald was buried (d. AD 642), 1km N of Bardney. **52 E6** TF1170.
Bardon *Leics.* ***Village***, 2m/3km SE of Coalville. **41 G4** SK4412.
Bardon *Moray* ***Settlement***, 1m/2km NE of Glenlatterach Reservoir, 6m/9km S of Elgin. **97 K6** NJ2054.
Bardon Mill *Northumb.* ***Village***, on River South Tyne, 4m/6km W of Haydon Bridge. Housesteads Roman Fort (National Trust and English Heritage) 3m/4km N. **70 C7** NY7764.
Bardowie *E.Dun.* ***Hamlet***, 2m/3km SE of Milngavie, on E side of Bardowie Loch. NS5873.
Bardrainney *Inclyde* ***Suburb***, 1m/2km SE of Port Glasgow. NS3372.
Bardsea *Cumb.* ***Village***, on W bank of River Leven estuary, 3m/4km S of Ulverston. **55 G2** SD3074.
Bardsea Country Park *Cumb.* ***Leisure/recreation***, country park 1km SW of Bardsea, 4m/6km S of Ulverston. Coastal strip offering views across Morecambe Bay. Good ornithological location. **55 G2** SD2974.
Bardsea Green *Cumb.* ***Settlement***, adjoining to W of Bardsea, 2m/3km S of Ulverston. SD2974.
Bardsey *W.Yorks.* Population: 1530. ***Village***, 7m/11km NE of Leeds. **57 J5** SE3643.
Bardsey Island (Ynys Enlli). *Gwyn.* ***Island***, sparsely inhabited island lying 2m/3km off SW tip of Lleyn Peninsula across Bardsey Sound. It is about 2m/3km long N to S and 1km wide E to W. Remains of abbey near N end. Lighthouse near S end. **36 A3** SH1221.
Bardsey Sound *Gwyn.* ***Sea feature***, sea passage with dangerous currents, between Bardsey Island and SW extremity of Lleyn Peninsula. **36 A3** SH1323.
Bardsley *Gt.Man.* ***Suburb***, 2m/3km S of Oldham town centre. **49 J2** SD9201.
Bardwell *Suff.* ***Village***, 2m/4km N of Ixworth. **34 D1** TL9473.
Bare *Lancs.* ***Suburb***, NE district of Morecambe. SD4564.
Barewood *Here.* ***Hamlet***, 5m/9km E of Kington. **28 C3** SO3856.
Barfad *Arg. & B.* ***Settlement***, in Knapdale, 1km N of Tarbert. **73 G4** NR8669.
Barford *Norf.* ***Village***, 8m/12km W of Norwich. **45 F5** TG1107.
Barford *Warks.* ***Village***, 3m/5km S of Warwick. **30 D2** SP2760.
Barford Park *Som.* ***Historic house***, Queen Anne house, 4m/7km W of Bridgwater. Includes contemporary furniture and walled garden with water garden and archery glade. **8 B1** ST2335.
Barford St. John *Oxon.* ***Village***, 2m/4km NW of Deddington. **31 F5** SP4333.
Barford St. Martin *Wilts.* ***Village***, on River Nadder, 3m/4km W of Wilton. **10 B1** SU0531.
Barford St. Michael *Oxon.* ***Village***, 2m/4km W of Deddington. **31 F5** SP4332.
Barforth *Dur.* ***Settlement***, 1km W of Gainford across River Tees. NZ1616.
Barfreston *Kent* ***Hamlet***, with Norman church, 6m/10km NW of Dover. **15 H2** TR2650.
Bargaly *D. & G.* ***Settlement***, in Bargaly Glen, 3m/5km E of Newton Stewart. **64 E4** NX4666.
Bargany *S.Ayr.* ***Settlement***, 2m/3km W of Dailly. Bargany House and estate to S across Water of Girvan. **67 G3** NS2400.
Bargany Gardens *S.Ayr.* ***Garden***, 4m/6km E of Girvan. Woodland walks with spring flowers and display of rhododendrons around lily pond in May and June. **67 G4** NX2400.
Bargate *Derbys.* ***Hamlet***, 1m/2km SE of Belper. SK3646.
Bargeddie *N.Lan.* ***Small town***, 2m/3km W of Coatbridge. NS7064.
Bargod *Caerp. Welsh form of Bargoed, qv.*
Bargoed (Bargod). *Caerp.* Population: 14,979. ***Town***, in former coal-mining valley 8m/12km N of Caerphilly. **18 E2** ST1599.
Bargrennan *D. & G.* ***Locality***, on river Cree, 8m/12km NW of Newton Stewart. **64 D3** NX3576.
Barguillean Garden *Arg. & B.* ***Garden***, natural garden with bulbs, azaleas and rhododendrons, 3m/4km SW of Taynuilt. **80 A5** NM9828.
Barham *Cambs.* ***Village***, 7m/11km NW of Huntingdon. **32 E1** TL1375.
Barham *Kent* ***Village***, 6m/10km SE of Canterbury. **15 G2** TR2050.
Barham *Suff.* ***Village***, scattered village, 5m/7km N of Ipswich. **35 F3** TM1451.
Barharrow *D. & G.* ***Settlement***, 3m/4km S of Gatehouse of Fleet. **65 G5** NX6152.
Barholm *D. & G.* ***Settlement***, adjoining to NW of Creetown, 6m/9km SE of Newton Stewart. **64 E5** NX4759.
Barholm *Lincs.* ***Village***, 5m/7km NE of Stamford. **42 D4** TF0910.
Barkby *Leics.* ***Village***, 5m/7km NE of Leicester. **41 J5** SK6309.
Barkby Thorpe *Leics.* ***Hamlet***, 1km S of Barkby. **41 J5** SK6309.
Barkers Green *Shrop.* ***Hamlet***, 1m/2km SE of Wem. SJ5228.
Barkestone-le-Vale *Leics.* ***Village***, 8m/13km W of Grantham. **42 A2** SK7834.
Barkeval *High.* ***Mountain***, 2m/3km SW of Kinloch, Rum. Height 1938 feet or 591 metres. **85 J5** NM3797.
Barkham *W'ham* ***Village***, 3m/4km SW of Wokingham. **22 A5** SU7866.
Barkin Isles *W.Isles* ***Island***, group of islets at entrance to Loch Leurbost, E coast of Isle of Lewis. NB3923.
Barking *Gt.Lon.* ***Town***, in borough of Barking and Dagenham, on N side of River Thames, 8m/12km E of London Bridge. **23 H3** TQ4483.
Barking *Suff.* ***Village***, 4m/6km S of Stowmarket. **34 E3** TM0753.
Barking Tye *Suff.* ***Village***, 4m/7km S of Stowmarket. TM0652.
Barkingside *Gt.Lon.* ***Suburb***, in borough of Redbridge, 2m/3km N of Ilford. **23 H3** TQ4489.
Barkisland *W.Yorks.* ***Village***, 1m/2km E of Ripponden. **50 C1** SE0519.
Barkla Shop *Cornw.* ***Hamlet***, 1m/2km E of St. Agnes. SW7350.
Barkston *Lincs.* ***Village***, 4m/6km N of Grantham. **42 C1** SK9341.
Barkston *N.Yorks.* ***Village***, 4m/7km S of Tadcaster. **57 K6** SE4936.
Barkston Ash *N.Yorks.* ***Village***, adjoining to W of Barkston, 4m/7km S of Tadcaster. SE4936.
Barkway *Herts.* ***Village***, 4m/6km SE of Royston. **33 G5** TL3835.
Barlae *D. & G.* ***Settlement***, 3m/5km W of Kirkcowan. **64 C4** NX2760.
Barland *Powys* ***Settlement***, 3m/4km SW of Presteigne. Motte and bailey castle. SO2862.
Barlaston *Staffs.* Population: 2119. ***Village***, 3m/5km N of Stone. Wedgwood pottery was produced here. **40 A2** SJ8938.
Barlavington *W.Suss.* ***Hamlet***, 4m/6km S of Petworth. **12 C5** SU9716.
Barlay *D. & G.* ***Settlement***, on E bank of Water of Fleet, 1m/2km N of Gatehouse of Fleet. **65 F5** NX5958.
Barlborough *Derbys.* ***Village***, 7m/11km W of Worksop. Barlborough Hall is Elizabethan. **51 G5** SK4777.
Barlby *N.Yorks.* Population: 2432. ***Village***, 1m/2km NE of Selby. **58 C6** SE6334.
Barle *Som.* ***River***, rising on Exmoor at Pinkworthy Pond and flowing SE through Withypool and Dulverton to join River Exe 1km NE of Exebridge. **7 H3** SS9325.
Barlestone *Leics.* Population: 2547. ***Village***, 2m/3km NE of Market Bosworth. **41 G5** SK4205.
Barley *Herts.* ***Village***, 3m/5km SE of Royston. **33 G5** TL3938.
Barley *Lancs.* ***Village***, 3m/5km NW of Nelson. **56 D5** SD8240.
Barley Green *Suff.* ***Settlement***, 1km E of Stradbroke. TM2473.
Barley Hole *S.Yorks.* ***Settlement***, 1m/2km SW of Wentworth. SK3797.
Barley Mow *T. & W.* ***Village***, 1m/2km S of Birtley. NZ2754.
Barleycroft End *Herts.* ***Village***, E end of Furneux Pelham, 4m/7km NE of Puckeridge. **33 H6** TL4327.
Barleyhill *Northumb.* ***Settlement***, 1m/2km N of Derwent Reservoir. **62 B1** NZ0254.
Barleythorpe *Rut.* ***Village***, 1m/2km NW of Oakham. **42 B5** SK8409.
Barling *Essex* ***Village***, 3m/5km N of Shoeburyness. **25 F3** TQ9389.
Barlings *Lincs.* ***Hamlet***, 7m/11km E of Lincoln. **52 D5** TF0774.
Barlocco Bay *D. & G.* ***Bay***, small bay 3m/4km E of Dundrennan. **65 H6** NX7946.
Barlocco Isle *D. & G.* ***Island***, southernmost of the Islands of Fleet, group of small islands near E side of Wigtown Bay. **65 F6** NX5748.

Barlow *Derbys.* ***Village***, 3m/5km NW of Chesterfield. **51 F5** SK3474.
Barlow *N.Yorks.* ***Village***, 3m/5km SE of Selby. **58 C7** SE6428.
Barlow *T. & W.* ***Village***, 2m/4km SW of Blaydon. **71 G7** NZ1560.
Barlow Moor *Gt.Man.* ***Suburb***, on River Mersey, 4m/6km SW of Manchester city centre. SJ8292.
Barmby Moor *E.Riding* ***Village***, 2m/3km W of Pocklington. **58 D5** SE7748.
Barmby on the Marsh *E.Riding* ***Village***, 4m/6km W of Howden. **58 C7** SE6928.
Barmekin Hill *Aber.* ***Hill***, 1m/2km NW of Echt. Height 899 feet or 274 metres. **91 F4** NJ7207.
Barmer *Norf.* ***Hamlet***, 4m/6km SE of Docking. **44 C2** TF8133.
Barming Heath *Kent* ***Suburb***, of Maidstone, adjoining to N of East Barming. TQ7255.
Barmolloch *Arg. & B.* ***Settlement***, 8m/12km N of Lochgilphead. **73 G1** NR8799.
Barmoor Lane End *Northumb.* ***Hamlet***, 1m/2km W of Lowick. **77 J6** NU0039.
Barmore Island *Arg. & B.* ***Coastal feature***, peninsula on W side of Loch Fyne, Argyll, 2m/3km N of Tarbert. **73 G3** NR8771.
Barmouth (Abermaw). *Gwyn.* Population: 2306. ***Small town***, resort on Barmouth Bay, on N side of mouth of River Mawddach, 8m/12km W of Dolgellau. **37 F4** SH6115.
Barmouth Bay *Gwyn.* ***Bay***, on W coast of Wales, 8m/12km W of Dolgellau. The bay, which forms part of much larger Cardigan Bay, extends from Morfa Dyffryn (N) to Llwyngwril (S). **36 E4** SH6115.
Barmpton *Darl.* ***Hamlet***, 3m/5km NE of Darlington. **62 E5** NZ3118.
Barmston *E.Riding* ***Village***, near coast, 5m/8km S of Bridlington. **59 H4** TA1659.
Barmston *T. & W.* ***Suburb***, E district of Washington. NZ3156.
Barnaby Green *Suff.* ***Settlement***, 1km NE of Wangford. TM4779.
Barnacabber *Arg. & B.* ***Settlement***, 1m/2km NW of Ardentinny. **73 K2** NS1788.
Barnacarry *Arg. & B.* ***Settlement***, on S shore Loch Fyne, 2m/3km SW of Garbhallt. **73 J1** NS0094.
Barnack *Peter.* ***Village***, 3m/4km SE of Stamford. Remains of limestone quarries known as 'Hills and Holes'. **42 D5** TF0705.
Barnacle *Warks.* ***Village***, 5m/8km NE of Coventry. **41 F7** SP3884.
Barnamuc *Arg. & B.* ***Settlement***, in Glen Creran, 4m/7km NE of head of Loch Creran. **80 B3** NN0449.
Barnard Castle *Dur.* ***Castle***, remains of 11c-12c castle (English Heritage) on E side of River Tees in Barnard Castle town. Built on rocky crag which guarded crossing point on River Tees. Originally belonged to Balliol family. **62 B5** NZ0516.
Barnard Castle *Dur.* Population: 6084. ***Small town***, on River Tees, 15m/24km W of Darlington. Remains of 12c castle (English Heritage). Bowes Museum has large collection of art treasures. **62 B5** NZ0516.
Barnard Gate *Oxon.* ***Hamlet***, 3m/5km E of Witney. **31 F7** SP4010.
Barnardiston *Suff.* ***Hamlet***, 3m/5km NE of Haverhill. **34 B4** TL7148.
Barnard's Green *Worcs.* ***Suburb***, in E part of Great Malvern. **29 G4** SO7945.
Barnbarroch *D. & G.* ***Settlement***, 3m/5km SW of Wigtown. **64 D5** NX3951.
Barnbarroch *D. & G.* ***Settlement***, 3m/4km S of Dalbeattie. **65 J5** NX8456.
Barnburgh *S.Yorks.* Population: 2000. ***Village***, 2m/4km N of Mexborough. **51 G2** SE4803.
Barnby *Suff.* ***Village***, 4m/6km E of Beccles. **45 J6** TM4789.
Barnby Dun *S.Yorks.* ***Village***, 5m/8km NE of Doncaster. **51 J2** SE6109.
Barnby in the Willows *Notts.* ***Village***, 4m/7km E of Newark-on-Trent. **52 B7** SK8652.
Barnby Moor *Notts.* ***Village***, on former Great North Road, 4m/6km NW of Retford. **51 J4** SK6684.
Barndennoch *D. & G.* ***Settlement***, 3m/5km NE of Dunscore. **68 D5** NX8988.
Barne Barton *Plym.* ***Suburb***, 3m/5km NW of Plymouth city centre. SX4457.
Barnehurst *Gt.Lon.* ***Suburb***, in borough of Bexley, 1m/2km N of Crayford and 12m/21km E of Charing Cross. TQ5075.
Barnes *Gt.Lon.* ***Suburb***, in loop of River Thames, in borough of Richmond upon Thames, to S of Hammersmith Bridge. Barnes Common to S. **23 F4** TQ2276.
Barnes Street *Kent* ***Hamlet***, 4m/6km E of Tonbridge. TQ6448.
Barnet Gate *Gt.Lon.* ***Settlement***, in borough of Barnet, 11m/17km NW of Charing Cross and 2m/3km SE of Borehamwood. TQ2195.
Barnetby le Wold *N.Lincs.* ***Village***, 4m/6km E of Brigg. **52 D2** TA0509.
Barnettbrook *Worcs.* ***Locality***, 4m/6km E of Kidderminster. SO8876.
Barney *Norf.* ***Village***, 5m/8km E of Fakenham. **44 D2** TF9932.
Barnham *Suff.* ***Village***, 3m/4km S of Thetford. **34 C1** TL8779.
Barnham *W.Suss.* Population: 3566. ***Village***, 4m/6km NE of Bognor Regis. **12 C6** SU9604.
Barnham Broom *Norf.* ***Village***, 4m/7km N of Wymondham. **44 E5** TG0807.
Barnhead *Angus* ***Settlement***, 3m/5km W of Montrose across Montrose Basin. **83 H2** NO6657.
Barnhill *Ches.* ***Settlement***, 2m/3km E of Clutton. SJ4854.
Barnhill *Dundee* ***Suburb***, 1m/2km E of Broughty Ferry. NO4831.
Barnhill *Moray* ***Settlement***, 6m/9km SW of Elgin. 13c Pluscarden Priory to NE. **97 J6** NJ1457.
Barnhill Bay *Fife* ***Bay***, small shingle bay on N side of Firth of Forth, 1km SW of Aberdour. **75 K2** NT1884.
Barnhills *D. & G.* ***Settlement***, 1km SE of Corsewall Point. **64 A3** NW9871.
Barnhourie Sands *D. & G.* ***Coastal feature***, sandbank in Solway Firth, 1km S of Mersehead Sands. **65 K5** NX9150.
Barningham *Dur.* ***Village***, 4m/7km SE of Barnard Castle. **62 B5** NZ0810.
Barningham *Suff.* ***Village***, 5m/8km NE of Ixworth. **34 D1** TL9676.
Barningham Green *Norf.* ***Settlement***, 1m/2km W of Little Barningham. TG1233.
Barningham Moor *Dur.* ***Open space***, moorland 2m/3km SW of Barningham. **62 B6** NZ0309.
Barnoldby le Beck *N.E.Lincs.* ***Village***, 4m/7km SW of Grimsby. **53 F2** TA2303.
Barnoldswick *Lancs.* Population: 10,038. ***Town***, industrial town, 4m/7km N of Colne. Preserved mill engine in Bancroft Mill Engine Museum. **56 D5** SD8746.
Barns Green *W.Suss.* ***Hamlet***, 3m/4km E of Billingshurst. **12 E4** TQ1227.
Barns Ness *E.Loth.* ***Coastal feature***, headland with lighthouse, 3m/5km E of Dunbar. **77 F3** NT7277.
Barnsbury *Gt.Lon.* ***Suburb***, in borough of Islington, 2m/4km N of Charing Cross. TQ3084.
Barnsdale Bar ***Locality***, with road junction, on border of North Yorkshire and South Yorkshire, 2m/4km W of Campsall. **51 H1** SE5113.
Barnsley *Glos.* ***Village***, 4m/6km NW of Cirencester. Contains Barnsley House with the beautiful garden created by Rosemary Verey. **20 D1** SP0705.
Barnsley *Shrop.* ***Locality***, 3m/4km E of Bridgnorth. SO7592.
Barnsley *S.Yorks.* Population: 75,120. ***Town***, industrial town on River Dearne, 12m/19km N of Sheffield. **51 F2** SE3406.
Barnsley House Garden *Glos.* ***Garden***, in Barnsley, 4m/6km NE of Cirencester. 18c gardens, re-planned in 1960, with Laburnum avenue, Lime walk and knot garden. Features include 18c Gothic summerhouse and temple. **20 D1** SP0704.
Barnsole *Kent* ***Settlement***, 2m/4km SE of Wingham. TR2856.
Barnstaple *Devon* Population: 27,691. ***Town***, old market town at head of River Taw estuary, 34m/55km NW of Exeter. Former woollen garment producing town which traded with America. Several interesting buildings. **6 D2** SS5533.
Barnstaple Bay (Also known as Bideford Bay.) *Devon* ***Bay***, extends W from Baggy Point to Hartland Point. **6 A2** SS4033.
Barnstaple Bridge *Devon* ***Bridge***, 13c stone bridge consisting of 16 arches, over River Taw at Barnstaple. SS5532.
Barnston *Essex* ***Village***, 2m/3km SE of Great Dunmow. **33 K7** TL6419.
Barnston *Mersey.* ***Village***, 1m/2km NE of Heswall. **48 B4** SJ2883.
Barnstone *Notts.* ***Village***, 3m/5km SE of Bingham. **42 A2** SK7335.
Barnt Green *Worcs.* Population: 4784. ***Village***, 4m/7km NW of Redditch. **30 B1** SP0073.
Barnton *Ches.* ***Suburb***, 1m/2km NW of Northwich. **49 F5** SJ6573.
Barnton *Edin.* ***Suburb***, 4m/7km NW of Edinburgh city centre. NT1975.
Barnwell *Cambs.* ***Suburb***, E district of Cambridge. TL4658.
Barnwell *Northants.* ***Locality***, parish containing adjoining villages of Barnwell St. Andrew and Barnwell All Saints, 2m/4km S of Oundle. TL0484.
Barnwell All Saints *Northants.* ***Village***, forms parish of Barnwell, along with Barnwell St. Andrew, 2m/4km S of Oundle. **42 D7** TL0484.
Barnwell Country Park *Northants.* ***Leisure/recreation***, small country park with an emphasis on lakes and wildlife, 1km S of Oundle. **42 D7** TL0387.
Barnwell St. Andrew *Northants.* ***Village***, forms parish of Barnwell, along with Barnwell All Saints, 2m/4km S of Oundle. **42 D7** TL0484.
Barnwood *Glos.* ***Suburb***, E district of Gloucester. **29 H7** SO8518.
Barons' Cross *Here.* ***Suburb***, to W of Leominster. SO4758.
Barr *Arg. & B.* ***Settlement***, on Islay, 4m/7km E of Bowmore. **72 B4** NR3960.
Barr *High.* ***Settlement***, in Morvern, Lochaber district, 4m/7km W of Drimnin. **79 H2** NM6155.
Barr *Som.* ***Hamlet***, 2m/3km W of Taunton. ST1925.
Barr *S.Ayr.* ***Village***, on River Stinchar 6m/10km SE of Girvan. **67 G4** NX2794.
Barr Common *W.Mid.* ***Suburb***, to S of Aldridge. SP0599.
Barr Hall *Essex* ***Settlement***, 3m/4km NW of Sible Hedingham. **34 B5** TL7435.
Barr Mòr *Arg. & B.* ***Hill***, on E side of Glen Shira, 3m/5km NE of Inveraray. Height 836 feet or 255 metres. **80 C6** NN1312.
Barr-nam-boc Bay *Arg. & B.* ***Bay***, on W coast of Kerrera, 4m/7km W of Oban across Sound of Kerrera. **79 J5** NM7928.
Barr Point *D. & G.* ***Coastal feature***, headland 2m/3km NW of Port William. **64 D6** NX3145.
Barr Water *Arg. & B.* ***River***, in Kintyre, running SW to Glenbarr and into Atlantic Ocean 1km SW of village. **72 E7** NR6635.
Barra (Gaelic form: Eilean Barraigh.) *W.Isles* ***Island***, about 20 square miles or 52 square km lying S of South Uist across Sound of Barra, shortest distance being 5m/7km (Scurrival Point to Cille Bhrighde). Island is hilly, rising to 1260 feet or 384 metres at Heaval. Silver sands on much indented coastline. Airfield (Northbay) on Tràigh Mhòr. Fishing and crofting are important. **84 B4** NF6801.
Barra (Tràigh Mhòr) Airport *W.Isles* ***Airport/airfield***, on Barra, located on Tràigh Mhòr strand 1m/2km SW of Eoligarry. **84 C4** NF7005.
Barrachan *D. & G.* ***Hamlet***, 4m/6km NE of Port William. NX3649.
Barrack Hill *Newport* ***Suburb***, to N of Newport town centre. ST3089.
Barrackan *Arg. & B.* ***Settlement***, 2m/3km SW of Ardfern. **79 J7** NM7803.
Barraer *D. & G.* ***Settlement***, 3m/4km SW of Newton Stewart. **64 D4** NX3861.
Barraglom *W.Isles* ***Locality***, at S end of Great Bernera, W coast of Isle of Lewis, just E of road bridge connecting Great Bernera to main island. **100 D4** NB1634.
Barrahormid *Arg. & B.* ***Settlement***, 3m/4km SW of Tayvallich. **73 F2** NR7183.
Barran *Arg. & B.* ***Settlement***, 1m/2km S of Dalmally. No access by road. **80 C5** NN1624.
Barrapol *Arg. & B.* ***Settlement***, near W end of Tiree, 3m/4km SE of Rubha Chràiginis. **78 A3** NL9542.
Barrasford *Northumb.* ***Village***, 6m/10km N of Hexham. **70 E6** NY9173.
Barravullin *Arg. & B.* ***Settlement***, 1m/2km N of head of Loch Craignish. **79 K7** NM8107.
Barregarrow *I.o.M.* ***Settlement***, 2m/3km S of Kirk Michael. **54 C5** SC3188.
Barrel of Butter *Ork.* ***Island***, rock with beacon in Scapa Flow, 2m/3km E of lighthouse at N end of Cava. **107 C7** HY3500.
Barrets Green *Ches.* ***Settlement***, 3m/5km SE of Tarporley. SJ5959.
Barrhead *E.Renf.* Population: 17,251. ***Town***, former textile town, 4m/6km S of Paisley. **74 D5** NS4958.
Barrhill *S.Ayr.* ***Village***, on Duisk River 10m/16km S of Girvan. **67 G5** NX2382.
Barrie's House *Angus* ***Historic house***, Kirriemuir birthplace of Sir J.M. Barrie (National Trust for Scotland), famous as creator of Peter Pan. Includes exhibition. **82 E2** NO3854.
Barrington *Cambs.* ***Village***, 6m/10km NE of Royston. **33 G4** TL3949.
Barrington *Glos.* ***Locality***, parish containing villages of Great and Little Barrington, to W of Burford. SP2013.
Barrington *Som.* ***Village***, 3m/5km NE of Ilminster. Barrington Court (National Trust) at E end of village. **8 C3** ST3818.
Barrington Court *Som.* ***Historic house***, restored early 16c house (National Trust) with notable gardens, at E end of Barrington. **8 C3** ST3918.
Barripper *Cornw.* ***Village***, 1m/2km SW of Camborne. **2 D5** SW6338.
Barrisdale *High.* ***Locality***, in Lochaber district, at head of Barrisdale Bay, on S side of Loch Hourn. **86 E4** NG8704.
Barrisdale Bay *High.* ***Bay***, on S side of Loch Hourn. **86 E4** NG8704.
Barrmill *N.Ayr.* ***Village***, 2m/3km SE of Beith. **74 B5** NS3651.
Barrnacarry *Arg. & B.* ***Settlement***, 1m/2km NW of Kilninver. **79 K5** NM8122.
Barrnacarry Bay *Arg. & B.* ***Bay***, N facing bay on S side of entrance to Loch Feochan, in Argyll, 1m/2km NW of Kilninver. **79 K5** NM8122.
Barrock *High.* ***Settlement***, near N coast of Caithness district, 2m/4km E of Dunnet. **105 H1** ND2571.
Barron's Pike *Cumb.* ***Mountain***, on W side of Spadeadam Forest, 2m/3km E of Bewcastle. Height 1164 feet or 355 metres. **70 A6** NY5975.
Barrow *Glos.* ***Hamlet***, 4m/7km NW of Cheltenham. SO8824.
Barrow *Lancs.* ***Village***, 1m/2km N of Whalley. **56 C6** SD7338.
Barrow *Rut.* ***Hamlet***, 4m/7km NE of Oakham. **42 B4** SK8915.
Barrow *Shrop.* ***Settlement***, 2m/4km E of Much Wenlock. **39 F5** SJ6500.
Barrow *Som.* ***Settlement***, 3m/4km S of Wells. ST5541.
Barrow *Som.* ***Village***, 4m/6km SE of Bruton. **9 G1** ST7231.
Barrow *Suff.* ***Village***, 6m/9km W of Bury St. Edmunds. **34 B2** TL7663.
Barrow Bridge *Gt.Man.* ***Suburb***, 2m/4km NW of Bolton town centre. SD6811.
Barrow Green *Kent* ***Settlement***, adjoining to N of Teynham. TQ9563.
Barrow Gurney *N.Som.* ***Village***, 5m/7km SW of Bristol. Reservoirs to SE. **19 J5** ST5367.
Barrow Hann *N.Lincs.* ***Settlement***, 1m/2km NE of Barrow upon Humber. TA0822.
Barrow Haven *N.Lincs.* ***Village***, on S bank of River Humber, 1m/2km W of New Holland. Site of motte and bailey castle to S. **59 G7** TA0622.
Barrow Hill *Derbys.* ***Locality***, 4m/6km NE of Chesterfield. SK4175.
Barrow Hill *Hants.* ***Hamlet***, 2m/3km NE of Cadnam. SU3114.
Barrow-in-Furness *Cumb.* Population: 48,947. ***Town***, port on Irish Sea, 18m/29km NW of Lancaster across Morecambe Bay. Former steel and shipbuilding town. Ruins of 12c Furness Abbey. Dock Museum. **55 F3** SD1969.
Barrow-in-Furness Dock Museum *Cumb.* ***Other feature of interest***, museum in Barrow-in-Furness charting town's maritime history and industrial development through iron and steel, then shipbuilding. **54 E3** SD1869.
Barrow Mere *N.Lincs.* ***Settlement***, 1m/2km NW of Barrow upon Humber. Windmill to E. TA0521.

Barrow Nook *Lancs.* ***Settlement***, 6m/10km NW of St. Helens. **48 D2** SD4402.

Barrow Street *Wilts.* ***Hamlet***, 2m/3km SE of Mere. **9 H1** ST8330.

Barrow upon Humber *N.Lincs.* Population: 2161. ***Village***, 3m/4km E of Barton-upon-Humber. **59 G7** TA0721.

Barrow upon Soar *Leics.* Population: 4773. ***Village***, 3m/5km SE of Loughborough. **41 H4** SK5717.

Barrow upon Trent *Derbys.* ***Village***, 5m/8km S of Derby. **41 F3** SK3528.

Barroway Drove *Norf.* ***Locality***, 3m/4km W of Downham Market. **43 J5** TF5703.

Barrowby *Lincs.* Population: 2084. ***Village***, 2m/4km W of Grantham. **42 B2** SK8836.

Barrowcliff *N.Yorks.* ***Suburb***, 1m/2km NW of Scarborough town centre. TA0289.

Barrowden *Rut.* ***Village***, 5m/8km E of Uppingham. **42 C5** SK9400.

Barrowford *Lancs.* Population: 5212. ***Small town***, 1m/2km N of Nelson. **56 D6** SD8539.

Barrows Green *Ches.* ***Suburb***, 2m/3km NW of Crewe. SJ6958.

Barrows Green *Cumb.* ***Hamlet***, 3m/5km S of Kendal. SD5288.

Barrow's Green *Halton* ***Suburb***, 2m/3km NE of Widnes. SJ5287.

Barry *Angus* ***Village***, 2m/3km W of Carnoustie. **83 G4** NO5334.

Barry (Y Barri). *V. of Glam.* Population: 49,887. ***Town***, port and resort 7m/11km SW of Cardiff. Gateway of ruined 13c castle to W. **18 E5** ST1168.

Barry Buddon Camp *Angus* ***Military establishment***, 1m/2km E of Monifieth. **83 G4** NO5132.

Barry Island *V. of Glam.* ***Coastal feature***, peninsula to S of Barry with bathing and a holiday camp. **18 E5** ST1168.

Barry Links *Angus* ***Coastal feature***, large area of flat land forming headland between N bank of Firth of Tay and North Sea coast to S of Carnoustie. Buddon Ness is at S tip. **83 G4** NO5332.

Barry Mill *Angus* ***Other feature of interest***, 18c mill (National Trust for Scotland), 2m/3km W of Carnoustie. Displays and demonstrations. **83 G4** NO5335.

Barsalloch Fort *D. & G.* ***Historic/prehistoric site***, Iron Age fort (Historic Scotland), on Barsalloch Point headland, 1m/2km S of Port William. **64 D6** NX3441.

Barsalloch Point *D. & G.* ***Coastal feature***, headland on E side of Luce Bay, 2m/3km S of Port William. **64 D6** NX3441.

Barsby *Leics.* ***Hamlet***, 6m/9km SW of Melton Mowbray. **42 A4** SK6911.

Barsham *Suff.* ***Village***, 2m/3km W of Beccles. **45 H6** TM3989.

Barsham Hill *Suff.* ***Settlement***, 1m/2km E of Barsham. TM4089.

Barskimming *E.Ayr.* ***Settlement***, on N bank of River Ayr, 2m/3km SW of Mauchline. Old Barskimming to S of river across bridge. **67 J1** NS4825.

Barsloisnach *Arg. & B.* ***Settlement***, 2m/3km NE of Crinan across Loch Crinan. **73 G1** NR8195.

Barstable *Essex* ***Suburb***, to E of Basildon town centre. TQ7288.

Barston *W.Mid.* ***Village***, 4m/6km E of Solihull. **30 D1** SP2078.

Bartestree *Here.* ***Village***, 4m/6km E of Hereford. **28 E4** SO5640.

Barth Head *Ork.* ***Coastal feature***, headland on W coast of S part of South Ronaldsay. **107 D9** ND4285.

Barthol Chapel *Aber.* ***Village***, 4m/6km SE of Fyvie. **91 G1** NJ8134.

Bartholomew Green *Essex* ***Hamlet***, 3m/4km SW of Braintree. TL7221.

Barthomley *Ches.* ***Village***, 4m/7km SE of Crewe. **49 G7** SJ7652.

Bartley *Hants.* ***Village***, 1m/2km E of Cadnam. **10 E3** SU3013.

Bartley Green *W.Mid.* ***Suburb***, 5m/8km SW of Birmingham city centre. SP0081.

Bartlow *Cambs.* ***Village***, 5m/9km W of Haverhill. **33 J4** TL5845.

Barton *Cambs.* ***Village***, 3m/5km SW of Cambridge. **33 H3** TL4055.

Barton *Ches.* ***Village***, 2m/4km E of Holt. **48 D7** SJ4454.

Barton *Cumb.* ***Hamlet***, 3m/5km SW of Penrith. NY4826.

Barton *Glos.* ***Settlement***, 6m/9km W of Stow-on-the-Wold. **30 B6** SP1025.

Barton *I.o.W.* ***Suburb***, to E of Newport town centre across River Medina. SZ5089.

Barton *Lancs.* ***Hamlet***, 4m/7km W of Ormskirk. **48 C2** SD3509.

Barton *Lancs.* ***Village***, 5m/8km N of Preston. **55 J6** SD5139.

Barton *N.Yorks.* ***Village***, 2m/4km NE of Scotch Corner. **62 D6** NZ2308.

Barton *Oxon.* ***Suburb***, 3m/4km NE of Oxford city centre. SP5507.

Barton *Suff.* ***Settlement***, 1m/2km SE of Great Barton. TL9065.

Barton *Torbay* ***Suburb***, 2m/3km N of Torquay town centre. **5 K4** SX9067.

Barton *Warks.* ***Hamlet***, on River Avon, 6m/10km NE of Evesham. **30 C3** SP1051.

Barton Bendish *Norf.* ***Village***, 4m/6km N of Stoke Ferry. **44 B5** TF7105.

Barton Broad *Norf.* ***Lake/loch***, broad or lake on course of River Ant 5m/8km NE of Wroxham. **45 H3** TG3621.

Barton Common *Norf.* ***Village***, 5m/8km NE of Wroxham. **45 H3** TG3522.

Barton End *Glos.* ***Hamlet***, 1m/2km S of Nailsworth. **20 B2** ST8497.

Barton Fell *Cumb.* ***Open space***, moorland on E side of Ullswater, 2m/4km S of Pooley Bridge. **61 F4** NY4621.

Barton Gate *Devon* ***Settlement***, 1km NE of Barton Town and 5m/8km SE of Lynton. SS6840.

Barton Gate *Staffs.* ***Hamlet***, 1km NW of Barton-under-Needwood. SK1719.

Barton Green *Staffs.* ***Hamlet***, adjoining to SW of Barton-under-Needwood. SK1818.

Barton Hartshorn *Bucks.* ***Hamlet***, 4m/7km SW of Buckingham. **31 H5** SP6430.

Barton Hill *N.Yorks.* ***Hamlet***, on A64, 7m/11km SW of Malton. SE7064.

Barton Hills *Beds.* ***Hill***, small range of hills, 1km SE of Barton-le-Clay. Ravensburgh Castle (hillfort) to SE. **32 D6** TL0929.

Barton in Fabis *Notts.* ***Village***, 5m/8km SW of West Bridgford. Site of Roman villa 1km S. **41 H2** SK5232.

Barton in the Beans *Leics.* ***Village***, 7m/11km SE of Ashby de la Zouch. **41 F5** SK3906.

Barton in the Clay *Beds.* *Former name of Barton-le-Clay, qv.*

Barton-le-Clay (Formerly called Barton in the Clay.) *Beds.* Population: 3488. ***Village***, 6m/10km N of Luton. **32 D5** TL0832.

Barton-le-Street *N.Yorks.* ***Village***, 4m/7km W of Malton. **58 D2** SE7274.

Barton-le-Willows *N.Yorks.* ***Village***, 5m/8km N of Stamford Bridge. **58 D3** SE7163.

Barton Manor Gardens *I.o.W.* ***Garden***, water garden and grounds surrounding Barton Manor, to NE of Whippingham, 1m/2km SE of East Cowes. **11 G5** SZ5294.

Barton Mills *Suff.* ***Village***, on S bank of River Lark, 8m/13km NE of Newmarket. **34 B1** TL7273.

Barton Moss *Gt.Man.* ***Settlement***, and moorland 2m/4km NE of Irlam. **49 G3** SJ7397.

Barton on Sea *Hants.* ***Suburb***, W district of Lymington, on Christchurch Bay. **10 D5** SZ2393.

Barton-on-the-Heath *Warks.* ***Village***, 3m/5km E of Moreton-in-Marsh. **30 D5** SP2532.

Barton St. David *Som.* ***Village***, 1m/2km NW of Keinton Mandeville. **8 E1** ST5431.

Barton Seagrave *Northants.* ***Suburb***, in SE part of Kettering. **32 B1** SP8877.

Barton Stacey *Hants.* ***Village***, 5m/8km SW of Whitchurch. **21 H7** SU4341.

Barton Stacey Camp *Hants.* ***Military establishment***, army camp 1m/2km N of Barton Stacey. **21 H7** SU4342.

Barton Town *Devon* ***Hamlet***, on W edge of Exmoor, 6m/9km W of Simonsbath. SS6840.

Barton Turf *Norf.* ***Hamlet***, 4m/7km NE of Wroxham. **45 H3** TG3522.

Barton Turn *Staffs.* ***Village***, 1km E of Barton-under-Needwood. SK2018.

Barton-under-Needwood *Staffs.* Population: 4327. ***Village***, 5m/8km SW of Burton upon Trent. **40 D4** SK1818.

Barton-upon-Humber *N.Lincs.* Population: 9422. ***Small town***, on S bank of River Humber, 6m/9km SW of Kingston upon Hull across river. 15c former parish church (English Heritage) with Anglo-Saxon tower. **59 G7** TA0321.

Barton upon Irwell *Gt.Man.* ***Suburb***, to SW of Eccles town centre. SJ7697.

Barton Waterside *N.Lincs.* ***Locality***, on S bank of River Humber, adjoining to N of Barton-upon-Humber. TA0323.

Bartongate *Oxon.* ***Settlement***, 4m/6km SW of Deddington. SP4425.

Barugh *S.Yorks.* ***Locality***, 2m/4km NW of Barnsley. SE3108.

Barugh Green *S.Yorks.* ***Locality***, 1km S of Barugh, 3m/4km NW of Barnsley. SE3107.

Barvas (Gaelic form: Barabhas.) *W.Isles* ***Village***, near NW coast of Isle of Lewis, 11m/18km NW of Stornoway. **101 F2** NB3649.

Barvick Burn *P. & K.* ***River***, flowing SE into Turret Burn, 1m/2km NW of Crieff. **81 K5** NN8524.

Barway *Cambs.* ***Hamlet***, 3m/5km S of Ely. **33 J1** TL5475.

Barwell *Leics.* ***Village***, large village, 2m/4km NE of Hinckley. **41 G6** SP4496.

Barwhinnock *D. & G.* ***Settlement***, 1km NW of Twynholm, 3m/5km NW of Kirkcudbright. **65 G5** NX6554.

Barwick *Herts.* ***Settlement***, 4m/6km NE of Ware. TL3819.

Barwick *Norf.* ***Locality***, just S of Stanhoe, 3m/4km E of Docking. Includes Barwick House, in parkland. TF8035.

Barwick *Som.* ***Village***, 2m/3km S of Yeovil. **8 E3** ST5613.

Barwick in Elmet *W.Yorks.* Population: 2368. ***Village***, 7m/11km E of Leeds. **57 J6** SE3937.

Barwinnock *D. & G.* ***Settlement***, 2m/4km NE of Monreith. **64 D6** NX3843.

Basaleg *Newport* *Welsh form of Bassaleg, qv.*

Baschurch *Shrop.* ***Village***, 7m/11km NW of Shrewsbury. **38 D3** SJ4221.

Bascote *Warks.* ***Settlement***, 1m/2km NW of Southam. **31 F2** SP4063.

Base Green *Suff.* ***Settlement***, 1km NE of Wetherden. TM0163.

Basford *Ches.* ***Settlement***, 2m/3km S of Crewe. SJ7152.

Basford *Notts.* ***Suburb***, 2m/3km NW of Nottingham city centre. SK5543.

Basford *Staffs.* ***Suburb***, 1m/2km NE of Newcastle-under-Lyme town centre. SJ8646.

Basford Green *Staffs.* ***Settlement***, 1m/2km SE of Cheddleton. **49 J7** SJ9951.

Bashall Eaves *Lancs.* ***Hamlet***, 4m/6km W of Clitheroe. **56 B5** SD6943.

Bashall Town *Lancs.* ***Settlement***, 2m/3km W of Clitheroe. **56 C5** SD7142.

Bashley *Hants.* ***Hamlet***, 5m/8km SW of Brockenhurst. **10 D5** SZ2497.

Basildon *Essex* Population: 100,924. ***Town***, New Town designated 1949, 26m/42km E of London. Business, shopping, sports and leisure centre. Basildon has grown rapidly since early 1900s, when it was made up of several independent villages. Market. 11c church. National Motorboat Museum. Zoo. **24 D3** TQ7088.

Basildon *W.Berks.* ***Village***, 2m/4km NW of Pangbourne. Site of Roman building beside River Thames to N. **21 K4** SU6178.

Basildon Park *W.Berks.* ***Historic house***, to S of Lower Basildon, 7m/11km NW of Reading. Palladian mansion built 1776-83 (National Trust), with an octagonal room. **21 K4** SU6178.

Basingstoke *Hants.* Population: 77,837. ***Town***, market town 17m/27km NE of Winchester. Re-developed in 1960s to house London overspill. **21 K6** SU6351.

Basingwerk Abbey *Flints.* ***Ecclesiastical building***, remains of abbey founded 1131 (Cadw), at Greenfield, 4m/6km NW of Flint. **47 K5** SJ1977.

Baslow *Derbys.* Population: 1184. ***Village***, 3m/5km NE of Bakewell. **50 E5** SK2572.

Bason Bridge *Som.* ***Village***, on River Brue 2m/3km SE of Highbridge. **19 G7** ST3445.

Bass Rock *E.Loth.* ***Island***, small island of basalt rock in Firth of Forth 1m/2km N of Tantallon Castle. Height 350 feet or 107 metres. Haunt of sea birds, especially gannets. Lighthouse. **76 E2** NT6087.

Bassaleg (Basaleg). *Newport* ***Village***, 2m/4km W of Newport across Ebbw River. **19 F3** ST2787.

Bassenthwaite *Cumb.* ***Village***, 2m/3km E of N end of Bassenthwaite Lake and 6m/10km N of Keswick. **60 D3** NY2332.

Bassenthwaite Lake *Cumb.* ***Lake/loch***, northernmost lake of the Lake District, runs roughly N to S. Length 4m/6km. Formed by River Derwent. **60 D3** NY2332.

Bassett *S'ham.* ***Suburb***, N district of Southampton. **11 F3** SU4116.

Bassett's Cross *Devon* ***Settlement***, 1km SE of Hatherleigh. **6 D5** SS5503.

Bassingbourn *Cambs.* Population: 3400. ***Village***, 3m/4km NW of Royston. Airfield to N. **33 G4** TL3343.

Bassingfield *Notts.* ***Hamlet***, 2m/3km SW of Radcliffe on Trent. **41 J2** SK6137.

Bassingham *Lincs.* ***Village***, 8m/13km SW of Lincoln. **52 C6** SK9159.

Bassingthorpe *Lincs.* ***Hamlet***, 6m/9km SE of Grantham. Small 16c manor house. **42 C3** SK9628.

Basta *Shet.* ***Settlement***, on Yell, on W side of Basta Voe. **108 E3** HU5294.

Basta Voe *Shet.* ***Sea feature***, long inlet on E coast of Yell, running up to Dalsetter. **108 E3** HU5296.

Bastifell *Cumb.* ***Mountain***, highest point of Winton Fell, 3m/5km E of Kirkby Stephen. Height 2024 feet or 617 metres. **61 K6** NY8207.

Baston *Lincs.* ***Village***, 4m/7km S of Bourne. **42 E4** TF1113.

Baston Common *Lincs.* ***Open space***, lowland 4m/6km SE of Bourne. **42 E4** TF1316.

Bastonford *Worcs.* ***Hamlet***, 4m/6km SW of Worcester. SO8150.

Bastwick *Norf.* ***Village***, 2m/3km W of Martham. **45 J4** TG4217.

Baswich *Staffs.* ***Suburb***, 2m/3km SE of Stafford town centre. SJ9422.

Batavaime *Stir.* ***Settlement***, at W end of Glen Lochy, 6m/10km NE of Crianlarich. **81 F4** NN4234.

Batch *Som.* ***Hamlet***, just S of River Axe, 3m/4km N of Brent Knoll. ST3255.

Batchley *Worcs.* ***Suburb***, 1m/2km W of Redditch town centre. SP0267.

Batchworth *Herts.* ***Locality***, on River Colne, adjoining to SE of Rickmansworth. **22 D2** TQ0694.

Batchworth Heath *Herts.* ***Hamlet***, 1m/2km SE of Batchworth. **22 D2** TQ0792.

Batcombe *Dorset* ***Village***, below the steep Batcombe Hill, 4m/6km NW of Cerne Abbas. **9 F4** ST6104.

Batcombe *Som.* ***Village***, 3m/4km N of Bruton. **9 F1** ST6939.

Bate Heath *Ches.* ***Settlement***, 4m/7km W of Knutsford. **49 F5** SJ6879.

Bateman's *E.Suss.* ***Historic house***, 17c ironmaster's house (National Trust) with garden, home of Rudyard Kipling from 1902 to 1936, 1km S of Burwash. **13 K4** TQ6623.

Batesmoor *Norf.* ***Settlement***, 1m/2km NE of Foulsham. TG0425.

Batford *Herts.* ***Suburb***, to NE of Harpenden town centre. TL1415.

Bath *B. & N.E.Som.* Population: 85,202. ***City***, spa on River Avon, 11m/18km SE of Bristol. Abbey church rebuilt 1501. Roman baths. Natural hot springs unique in Britain drew Romans to Bath, which they named 'Aquae Sulis'. Roman baths still exist and are open to visitors. In 18c, it was most fashionable resort in country. Many 18c buildings. University to E above Claverton. Tourism is an important industry. Holds annual summer music festival. **20 A5** ST7564.

Bath Abbey *B. & N.E.Som.* ***Ecclesiastical building***, pre-Reformation church built in late Perpendicular style, in centre of Bath. Known as Lantern of the West due to size and number of windows. **20 A5** ST7464.

Bathampton *B. & N.E.Som.* ***Village***, 2m/3km NE of Bath. **20 A5** ST7766.

Bathealton *Som.* ***Village***, 4m/7km NW of Wellington. **7 J3** ST0724.

Batheaston *B. & N.E.Som.* ***Suburb***, 3m/4km NE of Bath. Iron Age fort (National Trust) at Little Solsbury Hill, 1km W. **20 A5** ST7767.

Batherm ***River***, rising 1km SW of Clatworthy Reservoir and flowing SW into River Exe, 1m/2km S of Bampton. **7 J3** SS9520.

Bathford *B. & N.E.Som.* ***Village***, 3m/5km NE of Bath. **20 A5** ST7866.

Bathgate *W.Loth.* Population: 13,819. ***Town***, 5m/9km S of Linlithgow. Industrial town, previously important to weaving and coalmining. **75 H4** NS9768.

Bathley *Notts.* ***Village***, 4m/6km N of Newark-on-Trent. **51 K7** SK7759.

Bathpool *Cornw.* ***Village***, 6m/9km NW of Callington. **4 C3** SX2874.

Bathpool *Som.* ***Village***, 2m/3km E of Taunton. **8 B2** ST2525.

Bathway *Som.* ***Hamlet***, 1km SW of Chewton Mendip. ST5952.

Batlers Green *Herts.* ***Settlement***, adjoining to S of Radlett. TQ1598.

Batley *W.Yorks.* Population: 48,030. ***Town***, 7m/11km SW of Leeds. Butterfly Conservation Centre. **57 H7** SE2424.

Batley Carr *W.Yorks.* ***Suburb***, adjoining to S of Batley, 1km NW of Dewsbury town centre. SE2422.

Batsford *Glos.* ***Village***, 1m/2km NW of Moreton-in-Marsh. Batsford Park to W includes arboretum and Cotswold Falconry Centre. **30 C5** SP1833.

Batsford Park Arboretum *Glos.* ***Garden***, 2m/3km NW of Moreton-in-Marsh. 50 acres, originally planned as wild, now containing over 1500 different trees and shrubs. **30 C5** SP1833.

Batson *Devon* ***Hamlet***, at head of creek, 1km N of Salcombe. SX7339.

Battersby *N.Yorks.* ***Village***, 3m/5km SE of Great Ayton. **63 G6** NZ5907.

Battersby Junction *N.Yorks.* ***Locality***, at former railway junction, 1km SW of Battersby. NZ5907.

Battersea *Gt.Lon.* ***Suburb***, on S side of River Thames in borough of Wandsworth. Battersea Park between Albert and Chelsea Bridges. Battersea Power Station at Nine Elms. Heliport beside river on Battersea Reach. **23 F4** TQ2876.

Battery Point *N.Som.* ***Coastal feature***, point on River Severn estuary, at N end of Woodhill Bay, N of Portishead. Lighthouse. **19 H4** ST4677.

Battisborough Cross *Devon* ***Hamlet***, near S coast, 3m/5km SE of Yealmpton. **5 G6** SX5948.

Battisford *Suff.* ***Settlement***, 3m/5km S of Stowmarket. **34 E3** TM0554.

Battisford Tye *Suff.* ***Village***, 3m/5km SW of Stowmarket. **34 E3** TM0254.

Battle *E.Suss.* Population: 5235. ***Small town***, 6m/9km NW of Hastings. Remains of abbey (English Heritage), including 14c Great Gatehouse, overlook site of Battle of Hastings, 1066. **14 C6** TQ7415.

Battle (Y Batel). *Powys* ***Hamlet***, 3m/4km NW of Brecon. **27 K5** SO0031.

Battle Abbey *E.Suss.* ***Ecclesiastical building***, abbey (English Heritage) founded by William the Conqueror and begun in 1067, on site of Battle of Hastings. Impressive 14c Great Gatehouse overlooking town square. Other buildings either ruined or now incorporated into a girls' school, on S side of Battle. **14 C6** TQ7415.

Battle of Adwalton Moor 1643 *W.Yorks.* ***Battle site***, significant Civil War battle site in Drighlington, where Royalists defeated Parliamentarians and gained control of N of England for a year. **57 H7** SE2228.

Battle of Airds Moss 1680 *E.Ayr.* ***Battle site***, scene of skirmish in 1680 between Royalists and Covenanters on Airds Moss, 3m/4km NE of Cumnock. **67 K1** NS5923.

Battle of Alford 1645 *Aber.* ***Battle site***, 1m/2km W of Alford. Site of battle where Montrose defeated Covenanters. **90 D3** NJ5616.

Battle of Alnwick 1093 *Northumb.* ***Battle site***, 1m/2km N of Alnwick, where Malcolm III of Scotland invaded England and was slain; marked by Malcolm's Cross. **71 G2** NU1914.

Battle of Ancrum Moor 1545 *Sc.Bord.* ***Battle site***, to N of Ancrum, 5m/8km NW of Jedburgh. Site of battle of 1545 in which Scots repelled English raiders after a dispute following death of James V over betrothal of infant Mary, Queen of Scots to Henry VIII's son, Edward. **70 B1** NT6127.

Battle of Auldearn 1645 *High.* ***Battle site***, to S of Auldearn, where Earl of Montrose defeated Covenanters. **97 G6** NH9155.

Battle of Bannockburn 1314 *Stir.* ***Battle site***, 2m/3km SE of Stirling and 1m/2km N of Bannockburn, where Scots under Robert the Bruce defeated English under Edward II, gaining independence and national identity. Battle is commemorated at Bannockburn Heritage Centre, 1m/2km SW. **75 G1** NS8191.

Battle of Barnet 1471 *Gt.Lon.* ***Battle site***, 1m/2km NW of New Barnet, where Earl of Warwick was defeated and slain by Edward IV, who thus recovered crown. **23 F2** TQ2497.

Battle of Barra Hill 1308 *Aber.* ***Battle site***, 1m/2km S of Oldmeldrum on Barra Hill. Battle where Robert the Bruce decisively defeated John Comyn on Christmas Eve. **91 F2** NJ8025.

Battle of Blore Heath 1459 *Staffs.* ***Battle site***, at Audley's Cross, 3m/4km E of Market Drayton. Cross marks spot where James Tuchet, Lord Audley, who led Lancastrian army, met his death during Wars of the Roses. **39 G2** SJ7135.

Battle of Boroughbridge 1322 *N.Yorks.* ***Battle site***, on N side of Boroughbridge across River Ure, where rebellious Earl of Lancaster was defeated and executed by his cousin, Edward II, after hostilities broke out. **57 K3** SE3967.

Battle of Bosworth Field 1485 *Leics.* ***Battle site***, 2m/3km S of Market Bosworth. Battle of great significance, where Henry Tudor defeated and killed Richard III, proclaiming himself as Henry VII, and putting an end to Plantagenet dynasty and Wars of the Roses. **41 F5** SK3800.

Battle of Bothwell Bridge 1679 *S.Lan.* ***Battle site***, to SE of Bothwell, where Covenanters were heavily defeated by Monmouth and Claverhouse. **75 F5** NS7157.

Battle of Carbisdale 1650 *High.* ***Battle site***, 3m/5km NW of Bonar Bridge. Site of final stand by Montrose. **96 C2** NH5694.

Battle of Carham 1018 *Northumb.* ***Battle site***, 2m/4km E of Carham and 2m/4km W of Cornhill-on-Tweed, where Scots defeated English and established River Tweed as border between England and Scotland. NT8338.

Battle of Chalgrove Field 1643 *Oxon.* ***Battle site***, to NE of Chalgrove, where Royalists, led by Prince Rupert, defeated Parliamentarians, securing their headquarters at Oxford. **21 K2** SU6497.

Battle of Cheriton 1644 *Hants.* ***Battle site***, 1m/2km NE of Cheriton, where Civil War battle took place in which Sir Ralph Hopton retreated with Royalists in face of Sir William Waller's Parliamentarians. **11 G2** SU5929.

Battle of Chevy Chase 1388 *Northumb. See Otterburn.*

Battle of Corrichie 1562 *Aber.* ***Battle site***, 3m/5km N of Banchorry, where Earl of Huntly was defeated by followers of Mary, Queen of Scots, led by Moray. **90 E4** NJ6902.

Battle of Cropredy Bridge 1644 *Oxon.* ***Battle site***, to E of Cropredy, where Parliamentarians were defeated by Royalists whilst trying to capture King's capital, Oxford. This defeat led to formation of New Model Army as Parliament's permanent full-time army. **31 F4** SP4746.

Battle of Culloden 1746 *High.* ***Battle site***, on Culloden Muir, 5m/8km E of Inverness, where Jacobean cause led by Prince Charles Edward Stuart was finally defeated by Duke of Cumberland on 16th April 1746. Visitor Centre on battlefield site. **96 E7** NH7445.

Battle of Dunbar 1296 *E.Loth.* ***Battle site***, 2m/3km S of Dunbar, site of defeat of John Balliol by Edward I. **76 E3** NT6776.

Battle of Dunbar 1650 *E.Loth.* ***Battle site***, 2m/3km SE of Dunbar, where Cromwell defeated Charles, Prince of Wales, and his Scottish army under Leslie, hampering Royalists' campaign in N. **76 E3** NT6976.

Battle of Edgcote 1469 *Northants.* ***Battle site***, 1m/2km E of Edgcote and 6m/9km NE of Banbury, where Earl of Pembroke, leading a Lancastrian army, was defeated and executed by the Yorkists. **31 G4** SP5247.

Battle of Edgehill 1642 *Warks.* ***Battle site***, 4m/6km NW of Edgehill, where Royalists defeated Parliamentarians and took Oxford, which became their capital for remainder of Civil War. Edgehill Battle Museum is situated at Farnborough Hall (National Trust). **30 E4** SP3549.

Battle of Evesham 1265 *Worcs.* ***Battle site***, 1m/2km N of Evesham, where a baronial faction led by Simon de Montfort was eventually defeated by Prince Edward's army in 1267. Battle was decisive element in struggle of de Montfort and Barons against absolute monarchy, leading to 1275 Statute of Westminster which enshrined role of Parliament as adviser to King. **30 B4** SP0345.

Battle of Falkirk 1746 *Falk.* ***Battle site***, 1m/2km SW of Falkirk across Union Canal, where a Jacobite army of Highlanders defeated a Hanoverian army. **75 G3** NS8779.

Battle of Flodden 1513 *Northumb.* ***Battle site***, to SW of Branxton, 4m/6km SE of Coldstream. Where James IV led Scots against English as a diversionary tactic to help French. Led by Earl of Surrey, English defeated Scots and James IV was killed. **77 G7** NT8937.

Battle of Glen Trool 1307 *D. & G.* ***Battle site***, at E end of Glen Trool. Bruce's Stone marks the site of rout of English by Robert the Bruce's men in 1307. **64 E3** NX4279.

Battle of Glenshiel 1719 *High.* ***Battle site***, in Glen Shiel, 4m/7km SE of Shiel Bridge where Jacobites, backed by Spain, were defeated by George I's army. **87 F3** NG9913.

Battle of Halidon Hill 1333 *Northumb.* ***Battle site***, 2m/4km NW of Berwick-upon-Tweed, where Edward III defeated Scots after expulsion of Edward Balliol from Scottish throne. **77 H5** NT9654.

Battle of Harlaw 1411 *Aber.* ***Battle site***, 2m/4km NW of Inverurie, where Donald, Lord of the Isles, tried to claim Earldom of Ross and was defeated by Earl of Mar. **91 F2** NJ7524.

Battle of Hastings 1066 *E.Suss.* ***Battle site***, 6m/9km NW of Hastings, on outskirts of town of Battle. Site of last battle which led to conquest of England, when on 14th October 1066, William, Duke of Normandy, defeated and killed King Harold II, thus becoming known as William the Conqueror, King of England. English Heritage property. **14 C6** TQ7415.

Battle of Haughs of Cromdale 1690 *High.* ***Battle site***, in Haughs of Cromdale, 4m/7km E of Grantown-on-Spey, where government forces defeated Jacobites in 1690. **89 J2** NJ1027.

Battle of Hedgeley Moor 1464 *Northumb.* ***Battle site***, site of battle in Wars of the Roses, in which Yorkists defeated Lancastrians, 1km SE of Wooperton. Percy's Cross monument marks spot where Lancastrian leader was killed. **71 F2** NU0419.

Battle of Hexham Levels 1464 *Northumb.* ***Battle site***, on E bank of Devil's Water, 2m/3km SE of Hexham, where Lancastrians attempted a rising against Edward IV but were defeated by Yorkist Lord Montagu. **70 E7** NY9561.

Battle of Homildon Hill 1402 *Northumb.* ***Battle site***, to NW of Humbleton, 2m/3km NW of Wooler. Site of battle in 1402, result of border raids and antagonism between Scots and English. Last expedition ever led by an English King in person to Scotland, and was a victory for Henry IV's army. Hill now known as Humbleton Hill. **70 E1** NT9629.

Battle of Hopton Heath 1643 *Staffs.* ***Battle site***, 3m/5km NE of Stafford, where Royalists defeated Parliamentarians and secured Stafford, although their leader, Earl of Northampton, was killed. **40 B3** SJ9526.

Battle of Inveresk 1547 *E.Loth. Alternative name for Battle of Pinkie 1547, qv.*

Battle of Inverlochy 1429, 1431 and 1645 *High.* ***Battle site***, at Inverlochy Castle, built in 13c and scene of battles in 1429, 1431 and 1645. In last and most important battle, Covenanters led by Argyll were defeated by Montrose. This led to Charles I breaking off negotiations with Parliament and ultimately to his defeat. **87 H7** NN1375.

Battle of Keppoch 1688 *High.* ***Battle site***, at Keppoch, to SW of Roybridge across River Roy. Site of Scotland's last real clan battle, caused by territorial dispute between MacDonalds and Mackintoshes. **87 J7** NN2679.

Battle of Killiecrankie 1689 *P. & K.* ***Battle site***, where Government troops were defeated by Jacobites in 1689, 4m/6km N of Pitlochry. **82 A1** NN9162.

Battle of Kilsyth 1645 *N.Lan.* ***Battle site***, 1m/2km to E of Kilsyth. Battle site, now covered by Townhead Reservoir, where Montrose defeated Covenanters, killing some 6000 of enemy with loss of only ten men. **75 F3** NS7478.

Battle of Langport 1645 *Som.* ***Battle site***, to NE of Langport, 4m/6km SW of Somerton, on bank of River Yeo. Parliamentarians' New Model Army defeated Royalists, enabling them to advance on Royalists supporters in SW. **8 D2** ST4327.

Battle of Langside 1568 *Glas.* ***Battle site***, 3m/4km S of Glasgow city centre. Site where Mary, Queen of Scots' forces were defeated by Moray after her escape from Loch Leven. **74 D4** NS5861.

Battle of Lansdown Hill 1643 *S.Glos.* ***Battle site***, 4m/6km NW of Bath. Battle in which Royalists tried to break Parliamentarians' hold on Bath, their rallying point. Battle was a stalemate. Sir Bevil Grenville's Monument (English Heritage) commemorates heroism of Royalist commander. **20 A4** ST7270.

Battle of Lewes 1264 *E.Suss.* ***Battle site***, 1m/2km NW of Lewes, where Simon de Montfort led a baronial army against King Henry III, resulting in negotiations and increased power for Barons. **13 G5** TQ3911.

Battle of Loudoun Hill 1307 *E.Ayr.* ***Battle site***, to S of Loudoun Hill, 3m/5km E of Darvel, where Robert the Bruce defeated Earl of Pembroke. **74 E7** NS6037.

Battle of Maldon 991 *Essex* ***Battle site***, 1km SE of Maldon, where an East Saxon force was defeated trying to stop Viking raiders. This was inspiration for Anglo-Saxon poem, The Battle of Maldon. **24 E1** TL8605.

Battle of Marston Moor 1644 *N.Yorks.* ***Battle site***, 1m/2km E of Tockwith, and scene of largest battle of Civil Wars. Royalists, led by Prince Rupert, were defeated by Parliamentarians and lost control of North. **57 K4** SE4952.

Battle of Methven 1306 *P. & K.* ***Battle site***, to N of Methven, where Robert the Bruce was defeated by Earl of Pembroke. **82 B5** NO0226.

Battle of Mortimer's Cross 1461 *Here.* ***Battle site***, 4m/7km NW of Leominster, where Edward, Earl of March, defeated Lancastrians and took English crown, becoming Edward IV. **28 D2** SO4262.

Battle of Musselburgh 1547 *E.Loth. Alternative name for Battle of Pinkie 1547, qv.*

Battle of Myton 1319 *N.Yorks.* ***Battle site***, 3m/4km E of Boroughbridge, just NE of Myton-on-Swale across River Swale. Here Edward II was defeated by Scots during Scottish Wars of Independence. Rare documentation from the time shows military tactics used in this period. **57 K3** SE4366.

Battle of Nantwich 1644 *Ches.* ***Battle site***, at Acton 1m/2km W of Nantwich, where Parliamentarians under Fairfax defeated Royalists, ending their chance of controlling NW of England. **49 F7** SJ6352.

Battle of Naseby 1645 *Northants.* ***Battle site***, 1m/2km N of Naseby, where Parliament's New Model Army defeated Royalists and killed many of their experienced soldiers. **41 J7** SP6880.

Battle of Nechtanesmere 685 *Angus* ***Battle site***, 1km W of Letham, on Dunnichen Hill, where Egfrith of Northumbria was killed by Picts, ending Anglian incursions into this area. **83 G3** NO5148.

Battle of Neville's Cross 1346 *Dur.* ***Battle site***, 1km W of Durham, at Neville's Cross, where Scots, led by David II, were crushingly defeated by Edward III's army while trying to create a diversion for French. It took them a century to recover all the land they lost. **62 D2** NZ2642.

Battle of Newburn Ford 1640 *T. & W.* ***Battle site***, next to River Tyne, 1km N of Ryton. Site where Scots defeated English and went on to occupy Newcastle after Charles I tried to impose a new prayer book. **71 G7** NZ1565.

Battle of Newbury 1643 *W.Berks.* ***Battle site***, 1m/2km SW of Newbury town centre, where Charles I and his army were defeated by Parliamentarians during Civil War. **21 H5** SU4565.

Battle of Newbury 1644 *W.Berks.* ***Battle site***, 1m/2km N of Newbury town centre, where neither Parliamentarians nor Royalists achieved their aims, both sides having retreated during night, thinking they had lost. **21 H5** SU4668.

Battle of Northallerton 1138 *N.Yorks. See Battle of The Standard 1138.*

Battle of Northampton 1460 *Northants.* ***Battle site***, 1m/2km SE of Northampton, where Yorkists defeated Henry VI's army, and submitted a claim for English throne to Parliament. **31 J3** SP7658.

Battle of Otterburn 1388 *Northumb.* ***Battle site***, 1km NW of Otterburn, where Scots defeated English and captured Sir Henry Percy, and where Scottish leader James, Earl of Douglas, was killed. **70 D4** NY8894.

Battle of Philiphaugh 1645 *Sc.Bord.* ***Battle site***, on private land in grounds of Philiphaugh House, 1m/2km SW of Selkirk across Ettrick Water. Here, after defeating English, Scottish leader Sir David Leslie took prisoners to Newark Castle and murdered them in cold blood. **69 K1** NT4528.

Battle of Pilleth 1402 *Powys* ***Battle site***, at Pilleth, 4m/7km NW of Presteigne. Important battle where Owain Glyndŵr defeated and captured Sir Edmund Mortimer and established his claim as leader of Welsh. **28 B2** SO2567.

Battle of Pinkie 1547 (Also known as Battle of Inveresk or Musselburgh.) *E.Loth.* ***Battle site***, 1km S of Pinkie Braes and 1m/2km SE of Musselburgh. Duke of Somerset, regent to Edward VI, sought to impose betrothal treaty between English and Scottish monarchs, leading to battle in 1547. Although English were victorious, they failed in their objective as Mary, Queen of Scots was sent to France to marry the Dauphin. **76 B3** NT3671.

Battle of Preston 1648 *Lancs.* ***Battle site***, at Fulwood, 2m/3km NE of Preston town centre, where Royalists were defeated by a Parliamentarian army led by Oliver Cromwell during Second Civil War. **55 J6** SD5532.
Battle of Prestonpans 1745 *E.Loth.* ***Battle site***, 1m/2km W of Prestonpans, where English defeated Jacobites. **76 C3** NT4074.
Battle of Ramsey 1079 *I.o.M.* ***Battle site***, 1m/2km W of Ramsey. Final Viking and Manx battle in which a victory by Godred Crovan united Isle of Man with Hebrides. **54 D4** SC4394.
Battle of Redeswire Fray 1575 *Sc.Bord.* ***Battle site***, just NE of Carter Bar summit. Site of last significant Borders skirmish between English and Scots, marked by stone. **70 C3** NT7007.
Battle of Ronaldsway 1275 *I.o.M.* ***Battle site***, on coast to N of Derby Haven, 2m/3km NE of Castletown. Battle in which Edward I regained control of island from Scots. **54 B7** SC2868.
Battle of Roundway Down 1643 *Wilts.* ***Battle site***, 1m/2km SE of Heddington, where Parliamentarians were defeated by heavily outnumbered Royalists. **20 D5** SU0165.
Battle of Rowton Heath 1645 *Ches.* ***Battle site***, to N of Rowton, where Civil War battle in 1645 was fought, in which Royalists were defeated by Parliamentarian force. **48 D6** SJ4464.
Battle of Sedgemoor 1685 *Som.* ***Battle site***, to NW of Westonzoyland, 3m/5km SE of Bridgwater. Last pitched battle fought in England, where rebel Duke of Monmouth was defeated by James II's army. Monmouth was later executed. **8 C1** ST3535.
Battle of Sherrifmuir 1715 *Stir.* ***Battle site***, on Sherrif Muir, 3m/4km S of Greenloaning, where a Jacobite army fought army of George I. **81 K7** NN8202.
Battle of Shrewsbury 1403 *Shrop.* ***Battle site***, 3m/5km NE of Shrewsbury town centre, where rebel Henry Percy, or Hotspur, was defeated and killed by Henry IV. This was first major battle in which English archers fought each other on their own soil. **38 E4** SJ5117.
Battle of Solway Moss 1542 *Cumb.* ***Battle site***, marshy tract to W of Longtown and scene of battle in 1542 where Henry VIII's army defeated Scots, so shocking James V that he died soon after. **69 J7** NY3469.
Battle of Stamford Bridge 1066 *E.Riding* ***Battle site***, 1km E of Stamford Bridge, where Harold II defeated and killed his brother, Tostig, and Norwegian claimant to English throne, Harald Hardrada. **58 D4** SE7255.
Battle of Stamford Hill 1643 *Cornw. Alternative name for Battle of Stratton 1643, qv.*
Battle of Stirling Bridge 1297 *Stir.* ***Battle site***, to NE of Stirling, at site of former bridge over River Forth, where Scots under Wallace routed English under Warenne. **75 G1** NS8094.
Battle of Stoke Field 1487 *Notts.* ***Battle site***, to SW of East Stoke, 4m/6km SW of Newark-on-Trent. Here last pitched battle of Wars of the Roses took place, in which a royal victory established Tudor dynasty and Henry VII as king. **42 A1** SK7549.
Battle of Stow 1646 *Glos.* ***Battle site***, 1m/2km N of Stow-on-the-Wold. Last battle of first Civil War in which Royalists, led by Lord Astley, were defeated by Parliamentarians. **30 C6** SP1827.
Battle of Strathpeffer 1411 *High.* ***Battle site***, on edge of Strathpeffer. Site of affray between Munros and Macdonalds and commemorated by Eagle Stone. **96 B6** NH4856.
Battle of Stratton 1643 (Also known as Battle of Stamford Hill 1643.) *Cornw.* ***Battle site***, to N of Stratton, where Sir Ralph Hopton led Royalists to victory against Parliamentarian army led by Earl of Stamford. **6 A5** SS2207.
Battle of Tewkesbury 1471 *Glos.* ***Battle site***, adjoining to SW of Tewkesbury. Scene of battle in which Yorkists, commanded by Edward IV, defeated Lancastrians. Queen Margaret was imprisoned shortly afterwards and King Henry VI was executed. **29 H5** SO8831.
Battle of The Standard 1138 (Battle of Northallerton 1138). *N.Yorks.* ***Battle site***, 3m/4km N of Northallerton, where David I of Scotland was defeated by an English army led by King Stephen. The standard was a ship's mast mounted on a wagon, from which sacred banners were flown. **62 E7** SE3698.
Battle of Tibbermore 1644 *P. & K.* ***Battle site***, 1m/2km E of Tibbermore and 2m/3km SE of Methven. Site of first battle between Montrose and Covenanters, in which Montrose was victorious, gaining control of Perth. **82 B5** NO0623.
Battle of Towton 1461 *N.Yorks.* ***Battle site***, 1km N of Saxton and 3m/5km S of Tadcaster, where reputedly largest and bloodiest battle ever fought on English soil took place. Yorkists, led by Edward, Earl of March, defeated Lancastrians, leaving 28,000 dead. **57 K6** SE4737.
Battle of Turiff 1639 *Aber.* ***Battle site***, adjacent to NE of Turriff. Site of first skirmish in Civil War, known as 'Trot of Turriff', where Royalist Gordons defeated the Covenanters. **99 F5** NJ7350.
Battle of Wakefield 1460 *W.Yorks.* ***Battle site***, on N side of Pugneys Country Park lake, 2m/3km S of Wakefield, where Richard, Duke of York, was killed by Lancastrians. **51 F1** SE3318.
Battle of Winceby 1643 *Lincs.* ***Battle site***, 1km to NW of Winceby. Site of 1643 Civil War battle where Parliamentarians, led by Cromwell, defeated Royalist army. **53 G6** TF3168.
Battle of Worcester 1651 *Worcs.* ***Battle site***, on S side of Worcester, to W of River Severn. Final battle of Civil War took place here, when Charles Stuart (later Charles II) was defeated by Parliamentary troops, and fled to France. **29 H3** SO8452.
Battledown *Glos.* ***Suburb***, 1m/2km E of Cheltenham. SO9621.
Battlefield *Glas.* ***Suburb***, 3m/5km S of Glasgow city centre. NS5861.
Battlefield *Shrop.* ***Hamlet***, on site of Battle of Shrewsbury, 1403, 3m/5km N of Shrewsbury. **38 E4** SJ5116.
Battlefield Line *Leics.* ***Other feature of interest***, tourist railway which runs for 9m/14km from Shackerstone to Shenton via Market Bosworth. It passes site of Battle of Bosworth Field. Includes museum of railway memorabilia. **41 F5** SK3706.
Battlesbridge *Essex* ***Village***, near head of River Crouch estuary, 2m/4km E of Wickford. **24 D2** TQ7794.
Battlesden *Beds.* ***Settlement***, 3m/5km SE of Woburn. M1 motorway service area 1m/2km E. **32 C6** SP9628.
Battlesea Green *Suff.* ***Hamlet***, 1m/2km NW of Stradbroke. TM2275.
Battleton *Som.* ***Hamlet***, on River Barle, just S of Dulverton. **7 H3** SS9127.
Battlies Green *Suff.* ***Settlement***, 3m/5km E of Bury St. Edmunds. TL8964.
Battramsley *Hants.* ***Settlement***, 2m/3km S of Brockenhurst. **10 E5** SZ3099.
Batt's Corner *Surr.* ***Hamlet***, 4m/6km SW of Farnham. **22 B7** SU8141.
Battye Ford *W.Yorks.* ***Locality***, NW district of Mirfield. SE1920.
Bauds of Cullen *Moray* ***Locality***, between Bin of Cullen and Portnockie, 3m/5km E of Buckie. **98 C4** NJ4767.
Baugh *Arg. & B.* ***Settlement***, on S coast of Tiree, 1m/2km SW of Scarinish. **78 B3** NM0243.
Baugh Fell *Cumb.* ***Open space***, extensive moorland 4m/7km E of Sedbergh, with Knoutberry Haw (676 metres) as highest point. Small lakes of East Tarns lie 1km E of this. **61 J7** SD7393.
Baughton *Worcs.* ***Hamlet***, 6m/9km N of Tewkesbury. **29 H4** SO8742.
Baughurst *Hants.* ***Village***, 4m/6km NE of Kingsclere. **21 J6** SU5861.
Baulds *Aber.* ***Settlement***, 6m/9km SW of Banchory. **90 E5** NO6093.
Baulking *Oxon.* ***Village***, 4m/6km SE of Faringdon. **21 G2** SU3190.
Baumber *Lincs.* ***Village***, 4m/6km NW of Horncastle. **53 F5** TF2274.
Baunton *Glos.* ***Village***, 2m/3km N of Cirencester. **20 D1** SP0204.
Baveney Wood *Shrop.* ***Locality***, 3m/4km NE of Cleobury Mortimer. Roman fort 1km SW. **29 F1** SO6979.
Baverstock *Wilts.* ***Village***, 4m/7km W of Wilton. **10 B1** SU0232.
Bawburgh *Norf.* ***Village***, on River Yare 5m/7km W of Norwich. **45 F5** TG1508.
Bawden Rocks (Also known as Man and his man.) *Cornw.* ***Island***, two island rocks, 1m/2km N of St. Agnes Head. **2 D3** SW7053.
Bawdeswell *Norf.* ***Village***, 6m/9km NE of East Dereham. **44 E3** TG0420.
Bawdrip *Som.* ***Village***, 3m/5km NE of Bridgwater. **8 C1** ST3439.
Bawdsey *Suff.* ***Village***, near coast, 7m/12km SE of Woodbridge. **35 H4** TM3440.
Bawdsey Manor *Suff.* ***Settlement***, on coast, 1m/2km SW of Bawdsey. TM3337.
Bawn *W.Yorks.* ***Suburb***, 3m/5km W of Leeds city centre. SE2532.
Bawtry *S.Yorks.* Population: 2696. ***Small town***, 8m/13km SE of Doncaster. Site of small Roman fort 1km E across River Idle. **51 J3** SK6593.
Baxenden *Lancs.* ***Village***, 2m/3km SE of Accrington. **56 C7** SD7726.
Baxterley *Warks.* ***Village***, 2m/3km SW of Atherstone. **40 E6** SP2797.
Baxter's Green *Suff.* ***Settlement***, 2m/4km W of Chedburgh. TL7558.
Bay *Dorset* ***Hamlet***, on NE side of Gillingham. ST8127.
Bay ny Carrickey *I.o.M.* ***Bay***, between Port St. Mary and Castletown, extending from Kallow Point eastwards to Scarlett Point. **54 B7** SC2268.
Bay of Bomasty *Ork.* ***Bay***, on W coast of Rothiesholm, Stronsay. **106 F5** HY6123.
Bay of Cruden *Aber.* ***Bay***, extends S from Cruden Bay to headland opposite The Skares. Firm sands backed by sand dunes. **91 J1** NK0935.
Bay of Deepdale *Shet.* ***Bay***, on W coast of Mainland. Caves to N of bay. **109 A7** HU1754.
Bay of Firth *Ork.* ***Bay***, on coast of Mainland, facing NE towards Shapinsay. Village of Finstown at head of bay. **107 C6** HY3814.
Bay of Furrowend *Ork.* ***Bay***, large wide bay on W coast of Shapinsay. **107 D6** HY4718.
Bay of Holland *Ork.* ***Bay***, large bay on S coast of Stronsay, between Greenli Ness and Tor Ness. **106 F5** HY6422.
Bay of Houseby *Ork.* ***Bay***, on S coast of Stronsay. **106 F5** HY6721.
Bay of Isbister *Ork.* ***Bay***, an inlet of Wide Firth, 5m/8km NW of Kirkwall across firth. **107 D6** HY3918.
Bay of Keisgaig *High.* ***Bay***, small bay on NW coast of Sutherland district, 4m/6km S of Cape Wrath. **102 E2** NC2469.
Bay of Kirkwall *Ork.* ***Bay***, on N side of Kirkwall. Contains harbour and opens out into Wide Firth. **107 D6** HY4411.
Bay of Laig *High.* ***Bay***, on W coast of Eigg. **85 K6** NM4688.
Bay of Linton *Ork.* ***Bay***, small bay on E coast of Shapinsay. **107 E6** HY5318.
Bay of Lopness *Ork.* ***Bay***, on Sanday, extending W from headland of Lop Ness to Long Taing of Newark. **106 G3** HY7443.
Bay of Meil *Ork.* ***Bay***, on coast of Mainland, between Head of Work and Head of Holland, 2m/3km E of Kirkwall. HY4812.
Bay of Newark *Ork.* ***Bay***, on SE coast of Sanday, to S of Newark. **106 G4** HY7242.
Bay of Pierowall *Ork.* ***Bay***, on E coast of Westray. HY4348.
Bay of Quendale *Shet.* ***Bay***, wide bay on S coast of Mainland, 4m/6km NW of Sumburgh Head. **109 F10** HU3713.
Bay of Sandoyne *Ork.* ***Bay***, on SW coast of Mainland, 1km NW of St. Mary's. **107 D7** HY4601.
Bay of Sannick *High.* ***Bay***, to W of Duncansby Head, 1km NE of John o' Groats. **105 J1** ND3973.
Bay of Skaill *Ork.* ***Bay***, small bay on W coast of Mainland, 4m/6km W of Dounby. On S side is Skara Brae, remains of Neolithic settlement. **107 B6** HY2319.
Bay of Stoer *High.* ***Bay***, small bay on W coast of Sutherland district, 4m/7km S of Point of Stoer and 5m/8km NW of Lochinver. **102 C6** NC0328.
Bay of Tuquoy *Ork.* ***Bay***, large bay on S coast of Westray. **106 D3** HY4644.
Bayble Bay *W.Isles Anglicised form of Bagh Phabail, qv.*
Baybridge *Northumb.* ***Hamlet***, 1km W of Blanchland. NY9550.
Baycliff *Cumb.* ***Village***, 4m/6km S of Ulverston. **55 F2** SD2872.
Baydon *Wilts.* ***Village***, 3m/5km W of Lambourn. **21 F4** SU2878.
Bayford *Herts.* ***Village***, 3m/4km S of Hertford. **23 G1** TL3108.
Bayford *Som.* ***Village***, 1m/2km E of Wincanton. **9 G2** ST7229.
Bayfordbury *Herts.* ***Locality***, 2m/3km SW of Hertford. **33 G7** TL3010.
Bayham Abbey *E.Suss.* ***Ecclesiastical building***, ruined medieval abbey (English Heritage), by River Teise on Kent border, 2m/3km W of Lamberhurst. Also 19c mansion in Jacobean style in park on Kent side of river. **13 K3** TQ6536.
Bayham Abbey *Kent* ***Historic house***, 19c mansion in Jacobean style, N of River Teise, 3m/5km N of Wadhurst. Ruined medieval abbey (English Heritage) to SE across river, in East Sussex. **13 K3** TQ6436.
Bayhead *W.Isles Anglicised form of Ceann a' Bhàigh, qv.*
Bayherivagh *W.Isles Alternative name for Northbay, qv.*
Bayhurst Wood Country Park *Gt.Lon.* ***Leisure/recreation***, 2m/3km SW of Northwood. Hilly woodland in NW London which is significant wildlife habitat. **22 D3** TQ0688.
Bayles *Cumb.* ***Settlement***, 1m/2km SW of Alston. **61 J2** NY7045.
Baylham *Suff.* ***Village***, 6m/9km NW of Ipswich. **35 F3** TM1051.
Baylis Green *Worcs.* ***Settlement***, 3m/5km NE of Redditch. SP0870.
Baynard's Green *Oxon.* ***Settlement***, 5m/8km NW of Bicester. **31 G6** SP5429.
Bays Loch *W.Isles* ***Bay***, on SE coast of Berneray, 1km NE of Borve. **92 E3** NF9281.
Baysdale *N.Yorks.* ***Valley***, narrow valley through which Baysdale Beck flows, to W of Castleton. **63 H6** NZ6207.
Baysdale Abbey *N.Yorks.* ***Ecclesiastical building***, Cistercian monastery founded 1163 situated on Baysdale Beck, 4m/7km W of Castleton. **63 H6** NZ6206.
Baysdale Moor *N.Yorks.* ***Open space***, moorland on Cleveland Hills, 4m/7km SW of Castleton. **63 H6** NZ6204.
Baysham *Here.* ***Hamlet***, 3m/5km NW of Ross-on-Wye across loop of river. **28 E6** SO5727.
Bayston Hill *Shrop.* Population: 5462. ***Village***, 3m/4km S of Shrewsbury. **38 D5** SJ4808.
Bayswater *Gt.Lon.* ***Suburb***, in City of Westminster, on N side of Hyde Park. TQ2580.
Baythorn End *Essex* ***Hamlet***, 4m/6km SE of Haverhill. **34 B4** TL7242.
Baythorpe *Lincs.* ***Locality***, 1m/2km NE of Swineshead. TF2441.
Bayton *Worcs.* ***Village***, 2m/3km SE of Cleobury Mortimer. **29 F1** SO6973.
Bayton Common *Worcs.* ***Hamlet***, 3m/5km SE of Cleobury Mortimer. SO7172.
Bayworth *Oxon.* ***Hamlet***, 3m/4km N of Abingdon. SP5001.
Beach *High.* ***Settlement***, 6m/9km NE of Ardtornish, Lochaber district. **79 J2** NM7653.
Beach *S.Glos.* ***Hamlet***, 5m/8km NW of Bath. ST7070.
Beachampton *Bucks.* ***Village***, 2m/4km SW of Stony Stratford. **31 J5** SP7736.
Beachamwell *Norf.* ***Village***, 5m/8km SW of Swaffham. **44 B5** TF7505.
Beacharr *Arg. & B.* ***Settlement***, on W coast of Kintyre, 2m/3km S of Tayinloan. **72 E6** NR6943.
Beachborough *Kent* ***Settlement***, 2m/3km N of Hythe. **15 G4** TR1638.
Beachley *Glos.* ***Village***, below W end of Severn Road Bridge. **19 J2** ST5491.
Beachy Head *E.Suss.* ***Coastal feature***, chalk headland on coast, 3m/5km SW of Eastbourne. Lighthouse at foot. **13 J7** TV5895.
Beacon *Devon* ***Hamlet***, 3m/5km N of Honiton. **7 K5** ST1805.
Beacon *Devon* ***Hamlet***, 1km NW of Yarcombe. ST2308.
Beacon End *Essex* ***Suburb***, 3m/4km W of Colchester. **34 D6** TL9524.
Beacon Fell Country Park *Lancs.* ***Leisure/recreation***, on small hill, 5m/8km SE of Garstang. Views of Lakeland hills and Welsh mountains. Nature trails and scenic drive. **55 J5** SD5642.
Beacon Hill *Bucks.* ***Settlement***, 3m/4km E of High Wycombe. SU9093.
Beacon Hill *Dorset* ***Locality***, hill with village of same name to W, 4m/6km NW of Poole town centre. **9 J5** SY9794.
Beacon Hill *E.Suss.* ***Suburb***, on W side of Crowborough. TQ5030.
Beacon Hill *Essex* ***Hamlet***, 3m/4km SE of Witham. TL8512.

Beacon Hill *Powys* ***Mountain***, 5m/8km NE of Llanbister. Height 1794 feet or 547 metres. **28 A1** SO1776.
Beacon Hill *Surr.* ***Village***, 1m/2km NW of Hindhead. **12 B3** SU8736.
Beacon Hill *Wilts.* ***Hill***, rising to over 180 metres, to E of Bulford Camp. **21 F7** SU2044.
Beacon Hill Country Park *Leics.* ***Leisure/recreation***, country park in Charnwood Forest area to NW of Woodhouse Eaves, 3m/5km SW of Loughborough. Includes remnants of Bronze Age occupants. Claims have been made that one-fifth of England is visible from summit. **41 H4** SK5114.
Beacon Point *Devon* ***Coastal feature***, 2m/3km NW of Bigbury-on-Sea. **5 G6** SX6145.
Beacon Point *Northumb.* ***Coastal feature***, headland on North Sea coast, 1m/2km N of Newbiggin-by-the-Sea. **71 J5** NZ3189.
Beacon's Bottom *Bucks.* ***Village***, 5m/8km W of High Wycombe. **22 A2** SU7895.
Beacons Reservoir *Powys* ***Lake/loch***, small reservoir in course of River Taf Fawr, 5m/8km NE of Ystradfellte. **27 J7** SN9818.
Beaconsfield *Bucks.* Population: 12,292. ***Town***, former coaching town, 5m/8km SE of High Wycombe. Enid Blyton lived here. Bekonscot Model Village with miniature railway. **22 C2** SU9490.
Beacravik *W.Isles* ***Settlement***, on SE coast of South Harris, 1m/2km NE of Manais. NG1190.
Beadaig *High.* ***Hill***, S of Loch Naver and 5m/8km E of Altnaharra. Height 886 feet or 270 metres. **103 J5** NC6437.
Beadlam *N.Yorks.* ***Hamlet***, adjoining to W of Nawton, 3m/4km E of Helmsley. **58 C1** SE6584.
Beadlow *Beds.* ***Settlement***, 1m/2km E of Clophill. TL1038.
Beadnell *Northumb.* ***Village***, fishing village and resort on North Sea coast, 2m/3km S of Seahouses. 18c lime kilns (National Trust) by harbour. **71 H1** NU2329.
Beadnell Bay *Northumb.* ***Bay***, to S of Beadnell; foreshore partly owned by National Trust. **71 H1** NU2329.
Beaford *Devon* ***Village***, 5m/7km SE of Great Torrington. **6 D4** SS5515.
Beal *N.Yorks.* ***Village***, on S bank of River Aire, 2m/4km NE of Knottingley. **58 B7** SE5325.
Beal *Northumb.* ***Hamlet***, 6m/10km NW of Belford. Access to Holy Island along road to E leading to causeway across Beal Sands. **77 J6** NU0642.
Beal Sands *Northumb.* ***Coastal feature***, sandy foreshore, with causeway giving access from mainland to Holy Island, passable at low tide. NU0842.
Bealach *High.* ***Settlement***, in Salachan Glen, 1m/2km SE of Dalnatrat. **80 A2** NM9851.
Bealach na Bà *High.* ***Other feature of interest***, mountain pass between Meall Gorm and Sgurr a' Chaorachain in Ross and Cromarty district. Rises to 2053 feet or 626 metres, carrying highest road in Scotland, with steep gradients and sharp hairpin bends. Viewpoints across Loch Kishorn at S end, and to Raasay and Skye at N end. **94 D7** NG7742.
Beale Park *W.Berks.* ***Leisure/recreation***, wildlife park with river and railway trips, unusually focused around a mausoleum 2m/3km SE of Goring. **21 K4** SU6178.
Bealsmill *Cornw.* ***Hamlet***, on River Inny, 5m/7km N of Callington. SX3576.
Beam Hill *Staffs.* ***Hamlet***, 2m/3km NW of Burton upon Trent. SK2326.
Beambridge *Ches.* ***Hamlet***, 1m/2km N of Nantwich. **49 F7** SJ6453.
Beamhurst *Staffs.* ***Settlement***, 3m/5km NW of Uttoxeter. **40 C2** SK0636.
Beaminster *Dorset* Population: 2769. ***Small town***, 5m/9km N of Bridport. **8 D4** ST4801.
Beamish *Dur.* ***Village***, 2m/3km E of Stanley. Beamish North of England Open Air Museum to W. **62 D1** NZ2253.
Beamish Burn *Dur.* ***Settlement***, situated on stream of same name, 1m/2km N of Stanley. NZ2054.
Beamish North of England Open Air Museum *Dur.* ***Other feature of interest***, museum recreating life in early 20c Northern mining village, to N of Beamish and 2m/3km NE of Stanley. **62 D1** NZ2154.
Beamond End *Bucks.* ***Hamlet***, 3m/4km W of Amersham. SU9196.
Beamsley *N.Yorks.* ***Village***, 4m/6km NW of Ilkley. **57 F4** SE0752.
Beamsley Beacon (Also known as Howber Hill.) *N.Yorks.* ***Mountain***, to E of Beamsley, topped by cairn and forming notable landmark. Height 1289 feet or 393 metres. **57 G4** SE0952.
Bean *Kent* ***Hamlet***, 1m/2km SW of Swanscombe. **23 J4** TQ5872.
Beanacre *Wilts.* ***Village***, 1m/2km N of Melksham. **20 B5** ST9066.
Beanfield *Northants.* ***Suburb***, W district of Corby. SP8688.
Beanley *Northumb.* ***Hamlet***, 2m/3km W of Eglingham. **71 F2** NU0818.
Beannan Mòr *W.Isles* ***Hill***, 1km SW of head of Loch Shell, Isle of Lewis. Height 794 feet or 242 metres. **100 E6** NB2810.
Beansburn *E.Ayr.* ***Suburb***, to N of Kilmarnock. NS4339.
Beaquoy *Ork.* ***Settlement***, to E of Loch of Sabiston, Mainland. **106 C5** HY3022.
Bear Cross *Bourne.* ***Suburb***, 4m/6km NW of Bournemouth town centre. SZ0596.
Bearasay *W.Isles* ***Island***, small uninhabited island off W coast of Isle of Lewis, 2m/3km NW of Great Bernera. NB1242.
Beardon *Devon* ***Settlement***, 1km SE of Lydford. **6 D7** SX5184.
Beardwood *B'burn.* ***Suburb***, 1m/2km NW of Blackburn town centre. SD6629.
Beare *Devon* ***Hamlet***, on River Culm, 4m/7km SW of Cullompton. SS9801.
Beare Green *Surr.* ***Hamlet***, 4m/7km S of Dorking. **22 E7** TQ1743.
Bearfield *Wilts.* ***Suburb***, N district of Bradford-on-Avon. ST8261.
Bearley *Warks.* ***Village***, 4m/6km N of Stratford-upon-Avon. **30 C2** SP1760.
Bearley Cross *Warks.* ***Settlement***, 1km NW of Bearley. SP1760.
Bearnaraigh (Anglicised form: Berneray.) *W.Isles* ***Island***, of about 450 acres or 180 hectares nearly 1km S of Mingulay. High cliffs, with lighthouse, at W end of island. Grazing for sheep. The most southerly island of Western Isles or Outer Hebrides. **84 A7** NL5580.
Bearnie *Aber.* ***Settlement***, 3m/4km N of Ellon. **91 H1** NJ9634.
Bearnock *High.* ***Settlement***, in Glen Urquhart, 6m/9km W of Drumnadrochit. **88 B1** NH4130.
Bearnus *Arg. & B.* ***Settlement***, on Ulva, 1m/2km NW of Beinn Chreagach. **79 F3** NM3941.
Bearpark *Dur.* ***Village***, 2m/4km W of Durham. **62 D2** NZ2343.
Bearraich *Arg. & B.* ***Mountain***, near SW coast of Ardmeanach, Mull. Height 1417 feet or 432 metres. **79 F5** NM4127.
Bearreraig Bay *High.* ***Bay***, small bay on E coast of Skye, 1m/2km E of The Storr. **94 B6** NG5153.
Bearsbridge *Northumb.* ***Hamlet***, 6m/9km SW of Haydon Bridge. **61 J1** NY7857.
Bearsden *E.Dun.* Population: 27,806. ***Town***, largely residential town on line of Antonine Wall 5m/8km NW of Glasgow. **74 D3** NS5472.
Bearsted *Kent* ***Suburb***, to E of Maidstone. **14 C2** TQ8055.
Bearstone *Shrop.* ***Hamlet***, 1m/2km NE of Norton in Hales. SJ7038.
Bearwardcote *Derbys.* ***Settlement***, 5m/8km SW of Derby. SK2833.
Bearwood *Poole* ***Suburb***, 4m/6km NE of Poole town centre. **10 B5** SZ0496.
Bearwood *W.Mid.* ***Suburb***, 3m/4km W of Birmingham city centre. SP0286.
Beath Bleachfield *Fife* ***Suburb***, SW district of Cowdenbeath. NT1590.
Beatrix Fell *Lancs.* ***Open space***, moorland, partly wooded, on Forest of Bowland, 2m/3km N of Dunsop Bridge. **56 B4** SD6653.
Beatshach *Moray* ***Open space***, lower NE slopes of Ben Rinnes, 4m/6km S of Charlestown of Aberlour. **89 K1** NJ2537.
Beattock *D. & G.* ***Village***, 2m/3km S of Moffat. Site of Roman camp 1m/2km SE. **69 F3** NT0702.
Beattock Summit *S.Lan.* ***Other feature of interest***, highest point on London to Glasgow main railway line, 10m/16km NW of Beattock; height 1029 feet or 314 metres. **68 E2** NT0702.
Beauchamp Roding *Essex* ***Hamlet***, 2m/4km S of Leaden Roding. **23 J1** TL5810.
Beauchief *S.Yorks.* ***Settlement***, 4m/7km S of Sheffield. **51 F4** SK3381.
Beauclerc *Northumb.* ***Settlement***, 1km W of Riding Mill. NZ0061.
Beaudesert *Warks.* ***Locality***, adjoining to E of Henley-in-Arden. Traces of motte and bailey castle. **30 C2** SP1566.
Beaufort (Cendl). *B.Gwent* ***Town***, 2m/3km N of Ebbw Vale. **28 A7** SO1611.
Beaulieu *Hants.* ***Village***, at head of Beaulieu River estuary, 6m/9km NE of Lymington. Yachting. Remains of 13c abbey, of which Palace House is restored 14c gatehouse; motor museum in grounds. **10 E4** SU3802.
Beaulieu Abbey *Hants.* ***Ecclesiastical building***, Cistercian abbey founded by King John at Beaulieu, 6m/9km E of Brockenhurst. Now mainly ruins apart from Early English refectory which serves as parish church. **10 E4** SU3902.
Beaulieu Hall *Northants.* *See Hemington.*
Beaulieu Heath *Hants.* ***Open space***, heath 2m/3km SW of Beaulieu. **10 E4** SU3500.
Beaulieu Heath *Hants.* ***Open space***, heath 2m/3km N of Beaulieu. **10 E4** SU3905.
Beaulieu Palace House *Hants.* ***Historic house***, Lord Montagu's family home at Beaulieu, 4m/6km NE of Lymington. Abbey founded in 1204 and has exhibition of medieval monastic life. Also houses National Motor Museum. **10 E4** SU3802.
Beauly *High.* ***River***, formed by confluence of Rivers Farrar and Glass, flowing NE past town of Beauly and into head of Beauly Firth. **96 B7** NH5246.
Beauly *High.* Population: 1354. ***Small town***, on River Beauly in Inverness district. Ruins of 13c priory (Historic Scotland). **96 C7** NH5246.
Beauly Firth *High.* ***Sea feature***, wide inlet at mouth of River Beauly, extends out to Inner Moray Firth or Inverness Firth. **96 C7** NH5246.
Beauly Priory *High.* ***Ecclesiastical building***, ruins of Valliscaulian Priory founded in 13c, in Beauly on banks of River Beauly. **96 C7** NH5246.
Beaumaris (Biwmaris). *I.o.A.* Population: 1561. ***Small town***, resort on Anglesey on W side of Conwy Bay. Remains of castle (Cadw), dating in part from late 13c. **46 E5** SH6076.
Beaumaris Castle *I.o.A.* ***Castle***, remains of castle (Cadw), dating in part from late 13c, on SE coast of Anglesey at entrance to Menai Strait. World Heritage listed site, built by Edward I; an excellent example of medieval military architecture. **46 E5** SH6077.
Beaumont *Cumb.* ***Village***, on River Eden, 4m/6km NW of Carlisle. **60 E1** NY3459.
Beaumont *Essex* ***Village***, 6m/10km N of Clacton-on-Sea. **35 F6** TM1725.
Beaumont Hill *Darl.* ***Hamlet***, 3m/4km N of Darlington. NZ2918.
Beaumont Leys *Leic.* ***Locality***, 3m/4km NW of Leicester city centre. SK5608.
Beauport Park *E.Suss.* ***Open space***, 4m/6km NW of Hastings. Golf course. **14 C6** TQ7714.
Beausale *Warks.* ***Village***, 5m/7km NW of Warwick. **30 D1** SP2470.
Beauty Hill *Aber.* ***Hill***, 2m/3km NE of Newmachar. Height 548 feet or 167 metres. **91 G2** NJ9020.
Beauvale *Notts.* ***Suburb***, E district of Eastwood. SK4846.
Beauworth *Hants.* ***Hamlet***, 4m/7km S of New Alresford. **11 G2** SU5726.
Beaver Green *Kent* ***Suburb***, SW district of Ashford. TQ9941.
Beaworthy *Devon* ***Village***, 8m/13km NW of Okehampton. **6 C6** SX4699.
Beazley End *Essex* ***Hamlet***, 4m/6km N of Braintree. **34 B6** TL7429.
Bebington *Mersey.* Population: 60,148. ***Town***, 3m/5km S of Birkenhead. Ancient church. **48 C4** SJ3384.
Bebside *Northumb.* ***Locality***, 2m/4km W of Blyth. **71 H5** NZ2881.
Beccles *Suff.* Population: 10,337. ***Town***, on River Waveney, 8m/13km W of Lowestoft. Perpendicular church has detached tower. Many elegant Georgian buildings. **45 J6** TM4290.
Beccles Museum *Suff.* ***Other feature of interest***, in Beccles, includes printing, domestic and natural history artefacts. **45 J6** TM4290.
Becconsall *Lancs.* ***Village***, 2m/3km N of Tarleton. **55 H7** SD4423.
Beck Bottom *W.Yorks.* ***Locality***, adjoining to E of Kirkhamgate, 2m/4km NW of Wakefield. SE3023.
Beck Foot *Cumb.* ***Settlement***, 4m/6km NW of Sedbergh. **61 H7** SD6196.
Beck Foot *W.Yorks.* ***Settlement***, at confluence of Harden Beck and River Aire, on S side of Bingley, 1m/2km E of Harden. SE1038.
Beck Hole *N.Yorks.* ***Settlement***, 2m/3km S of Grosmont. **63 K6** NZ8202.
Beck Row *Suff.* ***Village***, 2m/4km NW of Mildenhall. **33 K1** TL6977.
Beck Side *Cumb.* ***Hamlet***, 4m/6km SE of Broughton in Furness. **55 F1** SD2382.
Beck Side *Cumb.* ***Settlement***, 1m/2km N of Cartmel. SD3780.
Becka Falls *Devon* ***Waterfall***, in wooded valley of Becka Brook, tributary of River Bovey, 4m/6km S of Moretonhampstead. **5 H3** SX7580.
Beckbury *Shrop.* ***Village***, 4m/7km S of Shifnal. **39 G5** SJ7601.
Beckenham *Gt.Lon.* ***Suburb***, in borough of Bromley, 8m/13km SE of Charing Cross. **23 G5** TQ3769.
Beckering *Lincs.* ***Settlement***, 2m/3km NW of Wragby. TF1280.
Beckermet *Cumb.* ***Village***, 3m/4km S of Egremont. **60 B6** NY0106.
Beckermonds *N.Yorks.* ***Settlement***, in Langstrothdale, on upper reaches of River Wharfe, 5m/8km NW of Buckden. SD8780.
Becker's Green *Essex* ***Locality***, adjoining to SE of Braintree. TL7722.
Beckery *Som.* ***Locality***, on SW side of Glastonbury. ST4838.
Beckett End *Norf.* ***Settlement***, 1km E of Foulden. TL7798.
Beckfoot *Cumb.* ***Settlement***, 4m/6km SE of Nether Wasdale. **60 C6** NY1600.
Beckfoot *Cumb.* ***Village***, on Solway Firth, 3m/5km S of Silloth. **60 B2** NY0949.
Beckford *Worcs.* ***Village***, 6m/9km E of Tewkesbury. **29 J5** SO9735.
Beckhampton *Wilts.* ***Hamlet***, and road junction, 1m/2km SW of Avebury. **20 D5** SU0868.
Beckhithe *Norf.* ***Settlement***, 1m/2km N of Hethersett. TG1506.
Beckingham *Lincs.* ***Village***, 5m/8km E of Newark-on-Trent. **52 B7** SK8753.
Beckingham *Notts.* ***Village***, 3m/4km W of Gainsborough. **51 K4** SK7790.
Beckington *Som.* ***Village***, 3m/5km NE of Frome. **20 A6** ST8051.
Beckley *E.Suss.* ***Village***, 5m/8km NW of Rye. **14 D5** TQ8523.
Beckley *Oxon.* ***Village***, 5m/7km NE of Oxford. Site of Roman building to E. **31 G7** SP5611.
Beckside *Cumb.* ***Hamlet***, 4m/6km SW of Sedbergh. SD6188.
Beckton *Gt.Lon.* ***Suburb***, in borough of Newham, 1m/2km S of East Ham. **23 H3** TQ4381.
Beckwith *N.Yorks.* ***Settlement***, 2m/3km SW of Harrogate. SE2852.
Beckwithshaw *N.Yorks.* ***Village***, 3m/4km SW of Harrogate. **57 H4** SE2653.
Becontree *Gt.Lon.* ***Suburb***, in borough of Barking and Dagenham, 3m/5km E of Barking town centre. **23 H3** TQ4885.
Beda Fell *Cumb.* ***Open space***, on Martindale Common, 2m/3km NE of Patterdale. Highest point is Beda Head (1670 feet or 509 metres). **60 F5** NY4216.
Bedale *N.Yorks.* Population: 2828. ***Small town***, old market town, 7m/11km SW of Northallerton. Weekly market has been held since 1251. Thorpe Perrow Arboretum contains many species of trees and shrubs. **57 H1** SE2688.
Bedale Hall *N.Yorks.* ***Historic house***, Georgian mansion with huge ballroom, 11m/18km NW of Thirsk. Now contains museum and tourist centre. Surrounding park includes 18c Ice House. **57 H1** SE2688.
Bedburn *Dur.* ***Settlement***, on Bedburn Beck, 3m/5km W of Witton-le-Wear. **62 C3** NZ1031.
Bedburn Beck *Dur.* ***River***, rising on Eggleston Common, flowing E through Hamsterley Forest then past Bedburn to confluence with River Wear 1m/2km NW of Witton-le-Wear. **62 B3** NZ1232.

Bedchester *Dorset* ***Hamlet***, 3m/5km S of Shaftesbury. **9 H3** ST8317.
Beddau *R.C.T.* Population: 7105. ***Village***, 3m/5km S of Pontypridd. **18 D3** ST0585.
Beddgelert *Gwyn.* ***Village***, at confluence of Rivers Colwyn and Glaslyn, 12m/19km SE of Caernarfon and 4m/7km S of Snowdon. **36 E1** SH5948.
Beddgelert Forest *Gwyn.* ***Forest/woodland***, 2m/3km NW of Beddgelert. **46 D7** SH5650.
Beddingham *E.Suss.* ***Village***, 2m/4km SE of Lewes. **13 H6** TQ4407.
Beddington *Gt.Lon.* ***Suburb***, in borough of Sutton, 2m/3km W of Croydon. Beddington Park 1km NW. Site of Roman bath house 1m/2km N. **23 G5** TQ2964.
Beddington Corner *Gt.Lon.* ***Locality***, 1m/2km NW of Beddington. **23 F5** TQ2866.
Bede's World *T. & W.* ***Other feature of interest***, museum at Jarrow dedicated to life of the Venerable Bede (7c) and early local medieval history. **71 J7** NZ3365.
Bedfield *Suff.* ***Village***, 4m/6km NE of Debenham. **35 G2** TM2266.
Bedfield Little Green *Suff.* ***Settlement***, 1m/2km SE of Bedfield. TM2365.
Bedfield Long Green *Suff.* ***Hamlet***, adjoins to N of Bedfield. TM2266.
Bedford *Beds.* Population: 73,917. ***Town***, county town on River Great Ouse, 46m/74km N of London. While in prison here John Bunyon wrote Pilgrims Progress. Cecil Higgins Art Gallery exhibits include local glass and ceramics. Site of De Montfort University. **32 D4** TL0449.
Bedford Level ***Large natural feature***, large drainage area of the Fens consisting of North Level between Rivers Welland and Nene; Middle Level, between River Nene and New Bedford River; and South Level, between New Bedford River and Brandon. TL3590.
Bedford Park *Gt.Lon.* ***Suburb***, on borders of Ealing and Hounslow boroughs, 6m/9km W of Charing Cross. TQ2079.
Bedgebury Cross *Kent* ***Settlement***, 1m/2km E of Kilndown. **14 C4** TQ7134.
Bedgebury Forest *Kent* ***Forest/woodland***, large wooded area some 3m/5km S of Goudhurst. **14 C4** TQ7233.
Bedgebury Pinetum *Kent* ***Forest/woodland***, S of Bedgebury Park and W of Bedgebury Forest, it contains many varieties of trees and shrubs. **14 C4** TQ7233.
Bedgrove *Bucks.* ***Suburb***, SE district of Aylesbury. SP8412.
Bedham *W.Suss.* ***Hamlet***, 3m/4km E of Petworth. TQ0121.
Bedhampton *Hants.* ***Suburb***, W district of Havant. **11 J4** SU6906.
Bedingfield *Suff.* ***Village***, 4m/6km N of Debenham. **35 F2** TM1868.
Bedingfield Green *Suff.* ***Settlement***, 1m/2km S of Bedingfield. TM1866.
Bedingfield Street *Suff.* ***Hamlet***, 1km S of Bedingfield. TM1868.
Bedingham Green *Norf.* ***Hamlet***, 3m/5km W of Ditchingham. TM2892.
Bedlam *Lancs.* ***Hamlet***, 1m/2km S of Accrington. SD7526.
Bedlam *N.Yorks.* ***Hamlet***, 1m/2km NW of Ripley. SE2661.
Bedlam *Som.* ***Settlement***, 2m/3km NW of Frome. ST7549.
Bedlar's Green *Essex* ***Hamlet***, 3m/4km E of Bishop's Stortford. TL5220.
Bedlington *Northumb.* Population: 15,430. ***Town***, market town, 4m/7km SE of Morpeth. Birthplace of Sir Daniel Gooch, founder of the Great Western Railway. **71 H5** NZ2581.
Bedlington Country Park *Northumb.* ***Leisure/recreation***, wooded area in River Blyth valley offering horse riding and nature trails, 1m/2km SE of Bedlington. **71 H5** NZ2680.
Bedlinog *M.Tyd.* ***Village***, 3m/4km N of Treharris. **18 D1** SO0901.
Bedminster *Bristol* ***Suburb***, 1m/2km S of Bristol city centre. ST5771.
Bedminster Down *Bristol* ***Suburb***, 2m/3km SW of Bristol city centre. ST5769.
Bedmond *Herts.* ***Village***, 4m/6km SE of Hemel Hempstead. **22 E1** TL0903.
Bednall *Staffs.* ***Village***, 4m/7km SE of Stafford. **40 B4** SJ9517.
Bedol *Flints.* ***Locality***, adjoining to SE of Bagillt, 1m/2km NW of Flint. **48 B5** SJ2274.
Bedrule *Sc.Bord.* ***Village***, on Rule Water, 4m/6km SW of Jedburgh. **70 A2** NT6018.
Bedruthan Steps *Cornw.* ***Coastal feature***, sandy beach with rocks and caves, 5m/8km NE of Newquay. Impressive rock scenery. **3 F2** SW8469.
Bedstone *Shrop.* ***Village***, 6m/9km E of Knighton. **28 C1** SO3675.
Bedwas *Caerp.* Population: 8488. ***Small town***, 2m/3km NE of Caerphilly. **18 E3** ST1788.
Bedwell *Herts.* ***Suburb***, to E of Stevenage town centre. TL2424.
Bedwellte *Caerp.* *See Bedwellty.*
Bedwellty (Bedwellte). *Caerp.* ***Hamlet***, 1m/2km E of Bargoed. **18 E1** SO1600.
Bedwellty Pits *B.Gwent* ***Locality***, 2m/3km S of Tredegar. SO1506.
Bedworth *Warks.* Population: 31,932. ***Town***, former mining and silk-weaving town, 5m/8km N of Coventry. **41 F7** SP3587.
Bedworth Heath *Warks.* ***Suburb***, 1m/2km W of Bedworth. SP3486.
Bedworth Little Heath *Warks.* ***Locality***, adjoins to S of Bedworth Heath. SP3386.
Bedworth Woodlands *Warks.* ***Settlement***, 1m/2km W of Bedworth. SP3487.
Beeby *Leics.* ***Hamlet***, 5m/9km NE of Leicester. **41 J5** SK6608.
Beech *Hants.* ***Village***, 1m/2km W of Alton. **11 H1** SU6938.
Beech *Staffs.* ***Hamlet***, 5m/8km S of Newcastle-under-Lyme. **40 A2** SJ8538.
Beech Hedge *P. & K.* *See Meikleour.*
Beech Hill *Gt.Man.* ***Suburb***, 1m/2km NW of Wigan town centre. SD5607.
Beech Hill *W.Berks.* ***Village***, 6m/9km S of Reading. **21 K5** SU6964.
Beech Lane *W.Mid.* ***Suburb***, 3m/5km W of Birmingham city centre. SP0185.
Beeches Farm *E.Suss.* ***Garden***, 1m/2km W of Uckfield; traditional and sunken garden. **13 H4** TQ4520.
Beechingstoke *Wilts.* ***Village***, 5m/8km W of Pewsey. **20 D6** SU0859.
Beechwood *Halton* ***Suburb***, S district of Runcorn. SJ5380.
Beechwood *Newport* ***Suburb***, 2m/3km E of Newport town centre. ST3388.
Beecraigs Country Park *W.Loth.* ***Leisure/recreation***, 500 acre country park 2m/3km S of Linlithgow featuring rock climbing, water sports, deer park and trout farm. **75 H3** NT0074.
Beedon *W.Berks.* ***Village***, 7m/11km N of Newbury. **21 H4** SU4878.
Beedon Hill *W.Berks.* ***Settlement***, adjoining to S of Beedon. SU4877.
Beeford *E.Riding* ***Village***, 7m/11km E of Great Driffield. **59 H4** TA1354.
Beefstand Hill *Sc.Bord.* ***Mountain***, 3m/4km NW of Blindburn. Height 1840 feet or 561 metres. **70 D2** NT8214.
Beeley *Derbys.* ***Village***, 5m/8km N of Matlock. **50 E6** SK2667.
Beelsby *N.E.Lincs.* ***Village***, 6m/10km SW of Grimsby. **53 F2** TA2001.
Beenham *W.Berks.* ***Village***, 9m/14km W of Reading. **21 J5** SU5868.
Beenham Hill *W.Berks.* ***Hill***, rising to over 90 metres, 1km E of Beenham. **21 J5** SU5968.
Beenham Stocks *W.Berks.* ***Settlement***, adjoining to E of Beenham. SU5968.
Beenham's Heath *W. & M.* ***Settlement***, 4m/6km E of Twyford. SU8475.
Beeny *Cornw.* ***Hamlet***, near coast, 2m/3km NE of Boscastle. SX1192.
Beer *Devon* ***Village***, resort on Seaton Bay, 1m/2km W of Seaton. Attractive village, with cottages built in local stone. **8 B6** SY2289.
Beer Crocombe *Som.* *Alternative spelling of Beercrocombe, qv.*
Beer Hackett *Dorset* ***Village***, 4m/6km SW of Sherborne. **8 E3** ST5911.
Beer Head *Devon* ***Coastal feature***, headland at W end of Seaton Bay, 1m/2km S of Beer. **8 B6** SY2289.
Beercrocombe (Also spelled Beer Crocombe.) *Som.* ***Village***, 4m/7km NW of Ilminster. **8 C2** ST3220.
Beesands *Devon* ***Village***, 2m/4km N of Start Point. **5 J6** SX8240.
Beesby *Lincs.* ***Village***, 3m/5km N of Alford. **53 H4** TF4680.
Beesby *N.Lincs.* ***Settlement***, 2m/3km SW of North Thoresby. Beesby Village is site of former village to SE. TF2696.
Beesdale *W.Isles* ***Valley***, hollowed-out valley near N coast of South Harris, 3m/4km W of Tarbert. NB1100.
Beeson *Devon* ***Village***, 1km from coast and 3m/4km NW of Start Point. **5 J6** SX8140.
Beeston *Beds.* ***Village***, 1km S of Sandy across River Ivel. **32 E4** TL1748.
Beeston *Ches.* ***Hamlet***, 3m/4km S of Tarporley. Remains of 13c castle (English Heritage) on hill to NW. **48 E7** SJ5458.
Beeston *Norf.* ***Village***, 5m/9km W of East Dereham. **44 D4** TF9015.
Beeston *Notts.* Population: 33,313. ***Town***, adjoining to SW of Nottingham. Home of Boots, the pharmaceutical company. **41 H2** SK5236.
Beeston *W.Yorks.* ***Suburb***, 2m/3km S of Leeds city centre. **57 H6** SE2830.
Beeston Castle *Ches.* ***Castle***, 1km NE of Beeston and 10m/16km SE of Chester. Ruins of 13c castle (English Heritage) built by Earl of Chester and enlarged by Henry III, who used it as a prison. **48 E7** SJ5359.
Beeston Hall *Norf.* ***Historic house***, 18c Gothic house 3m/4km NE of Hoveton. **45 H3** TG3321.
Beeston Park Side *W.Yorks.* ***Suburb***, adjoining to S of Beeston, 3m/4km S of Leeds city centre. SE2929.
Beeston Regis *Norf.* ***Suburb***, 1m/2km E of Sheringham. **45 F1** TG1742.
Beeston Royds *W.Yorks.* ***Settlement***, 1m/2km W of Beeston. SE2630.
Beeston St. Lawrence *Norf.* ***Locality***, 4m/6km NE of Wroxham. **45 H3** TG3222.
Beeswing *D. & G.* ***Village***, 7m/11km SW of Dumfries. **65 J4** NX8969.
Beetham *Cumb.* ***Village***, 6m/9km N of Carnforth. **55 H2** SD4979.
Beetham *Som.* ***Hamlet***, 2m/3km NW of Combe St. Nicholas. ST2712.
Beetley *Norf.* ***Village***, 4m/6km N of East Dereham. **44 D4** TF9718.
Beffcote *Staffs.* ***Settlement***, 2m/3km SW of Gnosall. SJ8019.
Began *Caerp.* ***Settlement***, 6m/9km NE of Cardiff city centre. **19 F3** ST2283.
Begbroke *Oxon.* ***Village***, 6m/9km NW of Oxford. **31 F7** SP4713.
Begdale *Cambs.* ***Hamlet***, 2m/3km S of Wisbech. TF4506.
Begeli *Pembs.* *Welsh form of Begelly, qv.*
Begelly (Begeli). *Pembs.* ***Village***, 4m/7km N of Tenby. **16 E4** SN1107.
Beggarington Hill *W.Yorks.* ***Locality***, 2m/4km SE of Morley. SE2724.
Beggar's Bush *Powys* ***Settlement***, 3m/5km W of Presteigne. SO2664.
Beggars Pound *V. of Glam.* ***Settlement***, adjoining to N of St. Athan, 3m/5km E of Llantwit Major. ST0168.
Beggearn Huish *Som.* ***Hamlet***, on edge of Exmoor National Park, 3m/4km SW of Watchet. ST0439.
Beggshill *Aber.* ***Settlement***, 4m/6km E of Huntly. **90 D1** NJ5938.
Begin Hill *Cumb.* ***Mountain***, rising to over 310 metres, 2m/3km N of Ravenstonedale. **61 J6** NY7106.
Beguildy (Bugeildy). *Powys* ***Village***, in River Teme valley, 7m/12km NW of Knighton. **28 A1** SO1979.
Beich Burn ***River***, on border of Stirling and Perth & Kinross, running S down Glen Beich to Loch Earn, 2m/3km E of Lochearnhead. **81 H5** NN6124.
Beighton *Norf.* ***Village***, 2m/3km SW of Acle. **45 H5** TG3808.
Beighton *S.Yorks.* Population: 9467. ***Suburb***, 6m/10km SE of Sheffield city centre. **51 G4** SK4483.
Beili-glas *Mon.* ***Settlement***, 3m/4km S of Abergavenny. SO3010.
Beinn a' Bha'ach Ard *High.* ***Mountain***, in Inverness district 3m/5km NW of Struy Bridge. Height 2827 feet or 862 metres. **95 K7** NH3643.
Beinn a' Bhacaidh *High.* ***Mountain***, in Inverness district, on SE shore of Loch Ness, 4m/6km NE of Fort Augustus. Height 1820 feet or 555 metres. **88 B3** NH4311.
Beinn a' Bhainne *Arg. & B.* ***Mountain***, in Laggan Deer Forest, 2m/3km SE of Lochbuie, Mull. Height 1237 feet or 377 metres. **79 H5** NM6222.
Beinn a' Bheithir (Anglicised form: Ben Vair.) *High.* ***Inland physical feature***, horseshoe shaped ridge in Lochaber district S of Ballachulish. Summit is Sgorr Dhearg, a Munro at height of 3359 feet or 1024 metres. **80 B2** NN0555.
Beinn a' Bhoth *W.Isles* ***Mountain***, 2m/3km N of Rapaire. Height 1010 feet or 308 metres. **100 D6** NB1316.
Beinn a' Bhragaidh *High.* ***Mountain***, 1m/2km NW of Golspie, Sutherland district. Height 1292 feet or 394 metres. **97 F1** NC8100.
Beinn a' Bhràghad *High.* ***Mountain***, 2m/3km E of head of Loch Eynort, Skye. Height 1512 feet or 461 metres. **85 K2** NG4125.
Beinn a' Bhric *High.* ***Mountain***, in Ross and Cromarty district, 3m/5km NW of Gorstan. Height 1450 feet or 442 metres. **95 K5** NH3465.
Beinn a' Bhùird *Aber.* ***Mountain***, fifth in height in Cairngorm Mountains, and with twin summits running N and S about 6m/10km NW of Braemar. North Top, a Munro on border with Moray, is higher at 3923 feet or 1196 metres, 5m/8km E of Loch Avon. South Top, almost 2m/3km distant, is 3861 feet or 1177 metres in height. E face of mass has many corries with craggy cliffs. **89 H5** NJ0900.
Beinn a' Bhùiridh *Arg. & B.* ***Mountain***, peak 2m/3km SE of summit of Ben Cruachan in Argyll. Height 2939 feet or 896 metres. **80 C5** NN0928.
Beinn a' Bhuna *W.Isles* ***Hill***, 2m/3km NE of Achadh Mòr, Isle of Lewis. Height 489 feet or 149 metres. **101 F4** NB3330.
Beinn a' Bhutha *High.* ***Mountain***, 2m/3km S of Loch More. Height 1794 feet or 547 metres. **102 E5** NC2934.
Beinn a' Chàisgein Beag *High.* ***Mountain***, in W part of Ross and Cromarty district, 3m/4km N of Beinn a' Chàisgein Mòr. Height 2230 feet or 680 metres. **95 F3** NG9682.
Beinn a' Chàisgein Mòr *High.* ***Mountain***, in W part of Ross and Cromarty district, 2m/3km N of head of Fionn Loch. Height 2811 feet or 857 metres. **95 F4** NG9878.
Beinn a' Chaisil *High.* ***Mountain***, 5m/8km E of Ardtornish. Height 1433 feet or 437 metres. **79 J3** NM7847.
Beinn a' Chaisteil ***Mountain***, on border of Argyll & Bute and Perth & Kinross, 4m/7km N of Tyndrum. Height 2906 feet or 886 metres. **80 E4** NN3436.
Beinn a' Chait *P. & K.* ***Mountain***, on Forest of Atholl 6m/10km N of Blair Atholl. Height 2949 feet or 899 metres. **89 F7** NN8674.
Beinn a' Chaoinich *High.* ***Mountain***, 3m/4km E of Glenelg, Skye and Lochalsh district. Height 1338 feet or 408 metres. **86 E3** NG8518.
Beinn a' Chaolais *Arg. & B.* ***Mountain***, westernmost and third in height of Paps of Jura. Height 2408 feet or 734 metres. **72 C3** NR4873.
Beinn a' Chaolais *W.Isles* ***Mountain***, 3m/5km E of Tarbert, North Harris. Height 1053 feet or 321 metres. **100 D7** NB2000.
Beinn a' Chaorainn *Aber.* ***Mountain***, in Cairngorm Mountains 4m/6km NE of Ben Macdui. Munro: height 3549 feet or 1082 metres. **89 H4** NJ0401.
Beinn a' Chaorainn *High.* ***Mountain***, in Lochaber district 3m/4km NE of W end of Loch Moy. Munro: height 3444 feet or 1050 metres. **87 K6** NN3884.
Beinn a' Chapuill *High.* ***Mountain***, in Lochaber district 3m/4km SE of Glenelg. Height 2434 feet or 742 metres. **86 E3** NG8215.
Beinn a' Charnain *W.Isles* ***Hill***, in NW Ronay; highest point of island. Height 377 feet or 115 metres. **92 D6** NF8856.
Beinn a' Charnain *W.Isles* ***Hill***, highest point on Pabbay. Height 643 feet or 196 metres. **92 D3** NF8988.
Beinn a' Chearcaill *High.* ***Mountain***, in Ross and Cromarty district, 6m/10km W of Kinlochewe. Height 2378 feet or 725 metres. **95 F5** NG9363.
Beinn a' Chlachair *High.* ***Mountain***, in Badenoch and Strathspey district, 2m/3km S of SW end of Lochan na h-Earba. Munro: height 3565 feet or 1087 metres. **88 B7** NN4778.
Beinn a' Chlaidheimh *High.* ***Mountain***, in Ross and Cromarty district, 10m/16km N of Kinlochewe. Height 3000 feet or 914 metres. **95 G4** NH0677.
Beinn a' Chleibh ***Mountain***, peak on border of Argyll & Bute and Stirling, 1m/2km SW of summit of Ben Lui. Munro: height 3008 feet or 917 metres. **80 D5** NN2525.

Beinn a' Chochuill *Arg. & B.* ***Mountain***, in Lorn, 6m/10km E of Taynuilt. Munro: height 3214 feet or 980 metres. **80 C4** NN1032.
Beinn a' Choin *Stir.* ***Mountain***, on E side of Loch Lomond, 3m/4km SE of Ardlui across the loch. Height 2522 feet or 769 metres. **80 E6** NN3513.
Beinn a' Chonnaich *P. & K. Gaelic form of Ben Chonzie, qv.*
Beinn a' Chraisg *High.* ***Hill***, 2m/3km NE of Kinlochbervie, Sutherland district. Height 843 feet or 257 metres. **102 E3** NC2359.
Beinn a' Chràsgain *High.* ***Mountain***, in Badenoch and Strathspey district, 6m/10km W of Newtonmore. Height 2716 feet or 828 metres. **88 D5** NN6098.
Beinn a' Chreachain *P. & K.* ***Mountain***, 3m/5km N of head of Loch Lyon. Munro: height 3546 feet or 1081 metres. **80 E3** NN3744.
Beinn a' Chroin *Stir.* ***Mountain***, 4m/7km S of Crianlarich. Munro: height 3083 feet or 940 metres. **80 E6** NN3918.
Beinn a' Chruinnich *Moray* ***Mountain***, 5m/9km SE of Tomintoul. Height 2545 feet or 776 metres. **89 K3** NJ2313.
Beinn a' Chrùlaiste *High.* ***Mountain***, in Lochaber district, 5m/8km SE of Kinlochleven. Height 2811 feet or 857 metres. **80 D2** NN2456.
Beinn a' Chuallaich *P. & K.* ***Mountain***, 2m/4km NE of Kinloch Rannoch. Height 2922 feet or 891 metres. **81 H1** NN6861.
Beinn a' Chuirn *High.* ***Mountain***, mass in Skye and Lochalsh district, 3m/5km NE of Glenelg. Height 1978 feet or 603 metres. **86 E2** NG8621.
Beinn a' Chumhainn ***Mountain***, on border of Highland and Perth & Kinross, 2m/3km W of Ben Alder. Height 2959 feet or 902 metres. **88 B7** NN4671.
Beinn a' Ghlinne Bhig *High.* ***Hill***, 5m/8km W of Portree, Skye. Height 682 feet or 208 metres. **93 J7** NG3945.
Beinn a' Ghlo (Also known as Ben-y-Gloe.) *P. & K.* ***Mountain***, massif 8m/12km NE of Blair Atholl. Summit is Carn nan Gabha, a Munro at height 3674 feet or 1120 metres. **89 G7** NN9773.
Beinn a' Ghràig *Arg. & B.* ***Mountain***, on Mull, 2m/3km S of Gruline. Height 1938 feet or 591 metres. **79 G4** NM5436.
Beinn a' Mhadaidh *High.* ***Mountain***, 3m/4km W of Loch Druim a' Chliabhain, Caithness district. Height 1322 feet or 403 metres. **104 C4** NC7641.
Beinn a' Mheadhoin *High.* ***Mountain***, in Inverness district, on N side of Loch Beinn a' Mheadhoin. Height 2004 feet or 611 metres. **87 J2** NH2125.
Beinn a' Mhuil *W.Isles* ***Mountain***, 3m/4km E of head of Loch Langavat. Height 1214 feet or 370 metres. **100 D6** NB1913.
Beinn a' Mhùinidh *High.* ***Mountain***, summit in W area of Kinlochewe Forest, Ross and Cromarty district, 2m/4km N of Kinlochewe. Height 2270 feet or 692 metres. **95 G5** NH0366.
Beinn a' Sgà *High.* ***Mountain***, 6m/9km SE of Uig, Skye. Height 1483 feet or 452 metres. **93 K6** NG4356.
Beinn Achaladair ***Mountain***, on border of Argyll & Bute and Perth & Kinross, 2m/4km E of Loch Tulla. Munro: height 3405 feet or 1038 metres. **80 E3** NN3443.
Beinn Airein *High.* ***Hill***, highest point on Muck, 1m/2km W of Port Mòr. Height 449 feet or 137 metres. **85 K7** NM4079.
Beinn Airigh Chàrr *High.* ***Mountain***, in Ross and Cromarty district, between Loch Maree and Fionn Loch, 4m/6km N of Talladale across Loch Maree. Height 2594 feet or 791 metres. **95 F4** NG9376.
Beinn Alligin *High.* ***Mountain***, in Ross and Cromarty district 2m/4km N of Upper Loch Torridon. The two peaks of Sgurr Mhòr, a Munro, and Tom na Gruagaich are respectively 3231 feet or 985 metres and 3018 feet or 920 metres in height. **94 E5** NG8660.
Beinn an Amair *High.* ***Hill***, to W of Kyle of Durness. Height 912 feet or 278 metres. **103 F2** NC3665.
Beinn an Armuinn *High. Gaelic form of Ben Armine, qv.*
Beinn an Dòthaidh *Arg. & B.* ***Mountain***, in Argyll, 2m/3km E of Bridge of Orchy. Munro: height 3293 feet or 1004 metres. **80 E3** NN3240.
Beinn an Eòin *High.* ***Mountain***, 1m/2km S of Loch Lurgainn. Height 2027 feet or 618 metres. **95 H1** NC1006.
Beinn an Eòin *High.* ***Mountain***, 4m/7km N of Oykel Bridge. Height 1784 feet or 544 metres. **95 K1** NC3808.
Beinn an Eòin *High.* ***Mountain***, 1m/2km W of head of Loch Brittle, Skye. Height 1046 feet or 319 metres. **85 J2** NG3820.
Beinn an Eòin *High.* ***Mountain***, in Ross and Cromarty district 5m/8km N of head of Upper Loch Torridon. Height 2804 feet or 855 metres. **95 F5** NG9064.
Beinn an Fhogharaidh *Stir.* ***Mountain***, on N side of Loch Ard, 4m/6km NW of Aberfoyle. Height 2020 feet or 616 metres. **81 F7** NN4703.
Beinn an Leathaid *High.* ***Mountain***, on Ardnamurchan peninsula, 3m/5km NE of Kilchoan. Height 1315 feet or 401 metres. **79 G1** NM5167.
Beinn an Lochain *Arg. & B.* ***Mountain***, in Argyll 4m/7km N of Lochgoilhead. Height 2955 feet or 901 metres. **80 D7** NN2107.
Beinn an Oir *Arg. & B.* ***Mountain***, highest of Paps of Jura. Height 2575 feet or 785 metres. **72 D3** NR4975.
Beinn an t-Seilich *Arg. & B.* ***Mountain***, in Argyll 4m/7km N of Lochgoilhead. Height 2358 feet or 719 metres. **80 C7** NN2007.
Beinn an t-Sìdhein *High.* ***Mountain***, rounded summit in Inverness district, 4m/7km NW of Dalchreichart. Height 1666 feet or 508 metres. **87 J3** NH2315.
Beinn an t-Sruthain *High.* ***Hill***, 5m/8km NW of Lochaline, Lochaber district. Height 876 feet or 267 metres. **79 H3** NM6048.
Beinn an Tuim *High.* ***Mountain***, 3m/4km NE of Glenfinnan, Lochaber district. Height 2657 feet or 810 metres. **87 F6** NM9283.
Beinn an Tuirc *Arg. & B.* ***Mountain***, on Kintyre, 4m/6km SW of Carradale. Height 1489 feet or 454 metres. **73 F7** NR7536.
Beinn Aoidhdailean *High.* ***Mountain***, 1m/2km NE of Beinn nan Caorach. Height 2076 feet or 633 metres. **86 E3** NG8813.
Beinn Bhalgairean *Arg. & B.* ***Mountain***, 3m/5km SE of Dalmally. Height 2086 feet or 636 metres. **80 C5** NN2024.
Beinn Bhàn *Arg. & B.* ***Mountain***, on Islay, 8m/11km NE of Port Ellen. Height 1545 feet or 471 metres. **72 C5** NR3956.
Beinn Bhan *Arg. & B.* ***Mountain***, 8m/12km N of Lochgilphead. Height 1046 feet or 319 metres. **73 G1** NR8599.
Beinn Bhàn *High.* ***Mountain***, mass in Ross and Cromarty district 6m/9km S of Shieldaig. Height 2939 feet or 896 metres. **94 E7** NG8045.
Beinn Bhàn *High.* ***Mountain***, rising to over 400 metres in Morvern, Lochaber district, 3m/4km N of Lochaline. **79 H3** NM6648.
Beinn Bhàn *High.* ***Mountain***, in Lochaber district 3m/4km W of SW end of Loch Lochy. Height 2611 feet or 796 metres. **87 H6** NN1385.
Beinn Bharrain (Anglicised form: Ben Varren.) *N.Ayr.* ***Mountain***, on Arran 2m/3km SE of Pirnmill. Height 2365 feet or 721 metres. **73 G6** NR9042.
Beinn Bheag ***Mountain***, on border of Argyll & Bute and Stirling, 2m/3km NW of Tyndrum. Height 2148 feet or 655 metres. **80 E4** NN3132.
Beinn Bheag *Arg. & B.* ***Mountain***, on Knapdale, 3m/4km SW of Ardrishaig. Height 1086 feet or 331 metres. **73 G2** NR8184.
Beinn Bheag *Arg. & B.* ***Mountain***, with craggy E face in Argyll Forest Park, rising above W shore of Loch Eck. Height 2027 feet or 618 metres. **73 K1** NS1293.
Beinn Bheag *High.* ***Mountain***, in Lochaber district, at E end of Loch Quoich. Height 1115 feet or 340 metres. **87 G4** NH0700.
Beinn Bheag *High.* ***Mountain***, with twin summits at 2191 feet or 668 metres and 2017 feet or 615 metres in height, in Ross and Cromarty district, 7m/11km NE of Kinlochewe. **95 G4** NH0771.
Beinn Bheag *High.* ***Mountain***, rounded summit in Skye and Lochalsh district, 2m/4km S of W end of Loch Monar. Height 2030 feet or 619 metres. **87 H1** NH1037.
Beinn Bheag *High.* ***Mountain***, 3m/5km SE of Kinlochleven. Height 2001 feet or 610 metres. **80 D2** NN2257.
Beinn Bheigeir *Arg. & B.* ***Mountain***, highest point on Islay, 3m/5km SW of McArthur's Head. Height 1610 feet or 491 metres. **72 C5** NR4256.
Beinn Bheòil *High.* ***Mountain***, in Badenoch and Strathspey district between Loch Ericht and Loch a' Bhealaich Bheithe. Munro: height 3342 feet or 1019 metres. **88 C7** NN5171.
Beinn Bheula *Arg. & B.* ***Mountain***, in Argyll, 4m/6km SW of Lochgoilhead. Height 2555 feet or 779 metres. **73 K1** NS1598.
Beinn Bhòidheach *Arg. & B.* ***Mountain***, in Argyll, 3m/5km SE of Dalmally. Height 1932 feet or 589 metres. **80 D5** NN1922.
Beinn Bhreac *Aber.* ***Mountain***, in Grampian Mountains, 5m/8km NW of Inverey. Munro: height 3054 feet or 931 metres. **89 H5** NO0597.
Beinn Bhreac *Arg. & B.* ***Hill***, on N part of Islay, 4m/7km NW of Ballygrant. Height 938 feet or 286 metres. **72 B3** NR3571.
Beinn Bhreac *Arg. & B.* ***Mountain***, 2m/3km SE of Barcaldine. Height 2322 feet or 708 metres. **80 A4** NM9940.
Beinn Bhreac *Arg. & B.* ***Mountain***, in Argyll, 4m/6km SE of Dalavich across Loch Awe. Height 1725 feet or 526 metres. **80 B6** NN0210.
Beinn Bhreac *Arg. & B.* ***Mountain***, 3m/5km S of Tarbet on W shore of Loch Lomond. Height 2234 feet or 681 metres. **74 B1** NN3200.
Beinn Bhreac *Arg. & B.* ***Mountain***, on Jura in N part of Jura Forest, 7m/11km N of Craighouse. Height 1440 feet or 439 metres. **72 D3** NR5377.
Beinn Bhreac *Arg. & B.* ***Mountain***, in N part of Jura, 4m/6km NW of Lussagiven. Height 1532 feet or 467 metres. **72 D1** NR5990.
Beinn Bhreac *Arg. & B.* ***Mountain***, on Kintyre, 4m/6km W of Carradale. Height 1397 feet or 426 metres. **73 F7** NR7538.
Beinn Bhreac *Arg. & B.* ***Mountain***, on Cowal peninsula, 3m/4km N of Tighnabruaich. Height 1489 feet or 454 metres. **73 H3** NR9877.
Beinn Bhreac *Arg. & B.* ***Mountain***, on tongue of land between Loch Riddon and Loch Striver. Height 1663 feet or 507 metres. **73 J3** NS0576.
Beinn Bhreac *High.* ***Hill***, highest point on Soay, off S coast of Skye. Height 462 feet or 141 metres. **85 K3** NG4615.
Beinn Bhreac *High.* ***Hill***, 3m/4km N of Acharacle, Lochaber district. Height 787 feet or 240 metres. **86 C7** NM6871.
Beinn Bhreac *High.* ***Mountain***, rising to over 310 metres, 1m/2km E of Tongue, Caithness district. **103 J3** NC6056.
Beinn Bhreac *High.* ***Mountain***, 3m/5km N of Dunvegan, Skye. Height 1073 feet or 327 metres. **93 H6** NG2553.
Beinn Bhreac *High.* ***Mountain***, 3m/4km W of head of Loch Eynort, Skye. Height 1460 feet or 445 metres. **85 J2** NG3426.
Beinn Bhreac *High.* ***Mountain***, 3m/4km SE of head of Loch Harport, Skye. Height 1214 feet or 370 metres. **85 K2** NG4328.
Beinn Bhreac *High.* ***Mountain***, on Skye, 3m/5km E of head of Loch Eishort. Height 1430 feet or 436 metres. **86 D3** NG7116.
Beinn Bhreac *High.* ***Mountain***, 3m/4km NW of Beinn Alligin, Ross and Cromarty district. Height 2047 feet or 624 metres. **94 E5** NG8363.
Beinn Bhreac *High.* ***Mountain***, in Inverness district, 3m/5km W of Tomatin. Height 1971 feet or 601 metres. **88 E2** NH7527.
Beinn Bhreac *High.* ***Mountain***, in Inverness district, 4m/6km E of Daviot. Height 1676 feet or 511 metres. **88 E1** NH7837.
Beinn Bhreac *High.* ***Mountain***, on Ardnamurchan peninsula, 3m/4km S of Rubha Aird Druimnich. Height 1171 feet or 357 metres. **79 G1** NM5968.
Beinn Bhreac (Anglicised form: Ben Vrackie.) *N.Ayr.* ***Mountain***, on Arran 2m/4km E of Pirnmill. Height 2332 feet or 711 metres. **73 H6** NR9044.
Beinn Bhreac *N.Ayr.* ***Mountain***, on N part of Arran, 3m/5km S of Lochranza. Height 1879 feet or 573 metres. **73 H6** NR9445.
Beinn Bhreac *N.Ayr.* ***Mountain***, on Arran, 5m/7km NE of Blackwaterfoot. Height 1650 feet or 503 metres. **73 H7** NR9531.
Beinn Bhreac *P. & K. Gaelic form of Ben Vrackie, qv.*
Beinn Bhreac *P. & K.* ***Mountain***, 2m/3km E of Ardtalnaig. Height 2348 feet or 716 metres. **81 J3** NN7340.
Beinn Bhreac *P. & K.* ***Mountain***, 10m/17km N of Blair Atholl. Height 2991 feet or 912 metres. **89 F6** NN8682.
Beinn Bhreac *Stir.* ***Inland physical feature***, mountain ridge rising to 2253 feet or 687 metres, 6m/9km SW of Strathyre. **81 F6** NN4714.
Beinn Bhreac *Stir.* ***Mountain***, 6m/9km NW of Aberfoyle. Height 2296 feet or 700 metres. **81 F7** NN4505.
Beinn Bhreac *Stir.* ***Mountain***, rising above E shore of Loch Lomond, 4m/6km N of Balmaha. Height 1893 feet or 577 metres. **74 C1** NS4296.
Beinn Bhreac-liath *Arg. & B.* ***Mountain***, in Argyll 3m/5km NW of Tyndrum. Height 2634 feet or 803 metres. **80 E4** NN3033.
Beinn Bhreac Mhòr *High.* ***Mountain***, in Inverness district 5m/8km S of East Croachy. Height 2647 feet or 807 metres. **88 D2** NH6719.
Beinn Bhrotain (Anglicised form: Ben Vrottan.) *Aber.* ***Mountain***, at S end of Cairngorm Mountains. Munro: height 3795 feet or 1157 metres. **89 G5** NN9592.
Beinn Bhuide *High.* ***Mountain***, in Skye and Lochalsh district, 3m/5km NE of Shiel Bridge. Height 2303 feet or 702 metres. **87 F2** NG9523.
Beinn Bhuidhe *Arg. & B.* ***Mountain***, 3m/4km E of Fanmore, Mull. Height 1269 feet or 387 metres. **79 F3** NM4644.
Beinn Bhuidhe *Arg. & B.* ***Mountain***, 3m/4km SE of Salen, Mull. Height 1351 feet or 412 metres. **79 G4** NM5939.
Beinn Bhuidhe *Arg. & B.* ***Mountain***, in Argyll 4m/7km N of head of Loch Fyne. Munro: height 3109 feet or 948 metres. **80 D6** NN2018.
Beinn Bhuidhe *High.* ***Hill***, 2m/3km NE of Rubha Suisnish, Skye. Height 909 feet or 277 metres. **86 C3** NG6017.
Beinn Bhuidhe *High.* ***Hill***, on Ardnamurchan peninsula, 1m/2km N of Rubha Aird Shlignich. Height 912 feet or 278 metres. **79 G1** NM5662.
Beinn Bhuidhe *High.* ***Mountain***, in Inverness district, 8m/13km E of Foyers. Height 2332 feet or 711 metres. **88 D2** NH6221.
Beinn Bhuidhe *High.* ***Mountain***, in Morvern, Lochaber district, 3m/5km E of Drimnin. Height 1479 feet or 451 metres. **79 H2** NM6052.
Beinn Bhuidhe *High.* ***Mountain***, in Knoydart, in Lochaber district, 2m/3km NE of Kylesknoydart on Loch Nevis. Height 2804 feet or 855 metres. **86 E5** NM8296.
Beinn Bhuidhe Mhòr *High.* ***Mountain***, in Inverness district, 4m/7km E of Daviot. Height 1797 feet or 548 metres. **96 E7** NH7840.
Beinn Bragar *W.Isles* ***Hill***, 3m/5km E of Carloway, Isle of Lewis. Height 856 feet or 261 metres. **100 E3** NB2643.
Beinn Capuill *Arg. & B.* ***Mountain***, on E side of Cowal peninsula, 1m/2km N of Tighnabruaich. Height 1437 feet or 438 metres. **73 H3** NR9775.
Beinn Ceannabeinne *High.* ***Mountain***, 3m/4km SE of Durness, Sutherland district. Height 1256 feet or 383 metres. **103 G2** NC4264.
Beinn Ceitlein *High.* ***Mountain***, in Argyll to E of Glen Etive, 5m/8km NE of head of Loch Etive. Height 2729 feet or 832 metres. **80 C3** NN1749.
Beinn Chabhair *Stir.* ***Mountain***, 5m/8km S of Crianlarich. Munro: height 3054 feet or 931 metres. **80 E6** NN3617.
Beinn Chàisgidle *Arg. & B.* ***Mountain***, 5m/8km N of Lochbuie, Mull. Height 1653 feet or 504 metres. **79 H4** NM6033.
Beinn Chaorach *Arg. & B.* ***Mountain***, 3m/5km E of Garelochhead. Height 2339 feet or 713 metres. **74 A1** NS2892.
Beinn Chaorach *High.* ***Mountain***, 1m/2km W of Loch Bà and 7m/11km SE of Kinlochleven. Height 1558 feet or 475 metres. **80 D2** NN2950.
Beinn Chaorach *Stir.* ***Mountain***, 2m/4km NE of Tyndrum. Height 2683 feet or 818 metres. **80 E4** NN3532.
Beinn Chapull *Arg. & B.* ***Mountain***, 2m/3km E of head of Loch Scammadale. Height 1689 feet or 515 metres. **80 A6** NM9319.
Beinn Chladan *Arg. & B.* ***Hill***, 1km E of Aridhglas, Mull. Height 266 feet or 81 metres. **78 E5** NM3223.
Beinn Chlaonleud *High.* ***Mountain***, in Morvern, Lochaber district, 5m/8km NE of Ardtornish. Height 1568 feet or 478 metres. **79 J2** NM7452.
Beinn Chlianaig *High.* ***Mountain***, in Lochaber district, on S side of Glen Spean, 2m/3km SE of Roybridge. Height 2365 feet or 721 metres. **87 J7** NN2978.
Beinn Choinnich *W.Isles* ***Hill***, 4m/7km E of Carloway, Isle of Lewis. Height 689 feet or 210 metres. **100 E3** NB2843.
Beinn Chorranach *Arg. & B.* ***Mountain***, in Argyll 4m/7km NW of Arrochar. Height 2903 feet or 885 metres. **80 D7** NN2509.
Beinn Chraoibh *High.* ***Mountain***, in Lochaber district, on N side of Loch Arkaig, 6m/9km NW of Gairlochy. Height 2020 feet or 616 metres. **87 H5** NN1492.

Beinn Chreagach *Arg. & B.* ***Mountain***, highest point on Ulva, 1m/2km S of northernmost point of island. Height 1027 feet or 313 metres. **79 F3** NM4040.
Beinn Chreagach *Arg. & B.* ***Mountain***, 3m/5km S of Pennyghael, Mull. Height 1233 feet or 376 metres. **79 G5** NM5121.
Beinn Chreagach *High.* ***Mountain***, 4m/6km NE of Dunvegan, Skye. Height 1069 feet or 326 metres. **93 H6** NG2853.
Beinn Chreagach Mhòr *Arg. & B.* ***Mountain***, 4m/7km SE of Salen, Mull. Height 1899 feet or 579 metres. **79 H4** NM6339.
Beinn Chuirn ***Mountain***, on border of Argyll & Bute and Stirling, 3m/5km W of Tyndrum. Height 2886 feet or 880 metres. **80 D5** NN2829.
Beinn Chuldail *High.* ***Hill***, 1m/2km S of Armadale, near N coast of Caithness district. Height 554 feet or 169 metres. **104 C2** NC7961.
Beinn Clach an Fheadain *High.* ***Mountain***, in Ross and Cromarty district, 6m/9km SE of Bonar Bridge. Height 1565 feet or 477 metres. **96 D3** NH6383.
Beinn Clachach *High.* ***Mountain***, 2m/3km E of Arnisdale. Height 2027 feet or 618 metres. **86 E3** NG8710.
Beinn Cleith Bric *High. Gaelic form of Ben Klibreck, qv.*
Beinn Damh (Anglicised form: Ben Damph.) *High.* ***Mountain***, in Ross and Cromarty district 2km E of Loch Damh and 3m/5km S of head of Upper Loch Torridon. Height 2959 feet or 902 metres. **94 E6** NG8950.
Beinn Dearg *Arg. & B.* ***Mountain***, in Argyll, 3m/5km N of Furnace. Height 1581 feet or 482 metres. **80 B7** NN0204.
Beinn Dearg *High.* ***Inland physical feature***, mountain ridge on Skye, 2m/3km W of head of Loch Ainort. **86 B2** NG5027.
Beinn Dearg *High.* ***Mountain***, 6m/9km S of Cape Wrath. Height 1387 feet or 423 metres. **102 E2** NC2765.
Beinn Dearg *High.* ***Mountain***, in Ross and Cromarty district, 3m/5km N of head of Upper Loch Torridon. Height 2998 feet or 914 metres. **94 E5** NG8960.
Beinn Dearg *High.* ***Mountain***, in Ross and Cromarty district, 6m/9km SE of head of Loch Broom. Munro: height 3556 feet or 1084 metres. **95 J3** NH2581.
Beinn Dearg *High.* ***Mountain***, in Kinlochluichart Forest, Ross and Cromarty, 8m/13km NW of Garve. Height 2253 feet or 687 metres. **95 J5** NH2868.
Beinn Dearg *P. & K.* ***Mountain***, 2m/3km NE of Innerwick in Glen Lyon. Height 2703 feet or 824 metres. **81 H2** NN6049.
Beinn Dearg *P. & K.* ***Mountain***, on Forest of Atholl, 8m/12km N of Blair Atholl. Munro: height 3306 feet or 1008 metres. **89 F7** NN8577.
Beinn Dearg *Stir.* ***Mountain***, 4m/6km SW of Callander. Height 1397 feet or 426 metres. **81 G7** NN5803.
Beinn Dearg Mhòr *High.* ***Mountain***, 3m/5km W of Broadford, Skye. Height 2326 feet or 709 metres. **86 B2** NG5822.
Beinn Dearg Mòr *High.* ***Mountain***, in Fisherfield Forest, Ross and Cromarty district, 4m/6km SW of An Teallach. Height 2978 feet or 908 metres. **95 G3** NH0379.
Beinn Dhorain *High.* ***Mountain***, in Sutherland district, 3m/5km N of Lothbeg. Height 2060 feet or 628 metres. **104 E7** NC9215.
Beinn Dhubh *W.Isles* ***Mountain***, near N coast of South Harris. Height 1660 feet or 506 metres. **100 C7** NB0800.
Beinn Domhnaill *High.* ***Mountain***, in Sutherland district, 5m/8km NE of Bonar Bridge. Height 1145 feet or 349 metres. **96 D2** NH6796.
Beinn Donachain *Arg. & B.* ***Mountain***, in Lorn, 4m/6km NE of Dalmally. Height 2125 feet or 648 metres. **80 C4** NN1931.
Beinn Dòrain (Anglicised form: Ben Douran.) *Arg. & B.* ***Mountain***, in Argyll, 2m/3km SE of Bridge of Orchy. Munro: height 3523 feet or 1074 metres. **80 E4** NN3237.
Beinn Dronaig *High.* ***Mountain***, in Skye and Lochalsh district on SW side of Loch Calavie. Height 2611 feet or 796 metres. **87 G1** NH0338.
Beinn Dubh *Arg. & B.* ***Hill***, on E coast of Islay, 3m/5km S of Port Askaig. Height 876 feet or 267 metres. **72 C4** NR4263.
Beinn Dubh *Arg. & B.* ***Mountain***, on W side of Loch Sloy, 3m/5km NW of Inveruglas on W shore of Loch Lomond. Height 2535 feet or 773 metres. **80 D6** NN2711.
Beinn Dubh *Stir.* ***Mountain***, on NE side of Gleann Dubh, 3m/5km S of Stronachlachar. Height 1666 feet or 508 metres. **81 F7** NN4004.
Beinn Dubhain *Arg. & B.* ***Mountain***, rising above E shore of Loch Eck, 2m/3km E of Glenbranter. Height 2129 feet or 649 metres. **73 K1** NS1497.
Beinn Dubhain *High.* ***Mountain***, in Sutherland district, 2m/3km SE of Kildonan Lodge. Height 1358 feet or 414 metres. **104 E6** NC9320.
Beinn Dubhcharaidh *High.* ***Mountain***, rising above S side of Loch Conagleann, 6m/10km E of Foyers. Height 2260 feet or 689 metres. **88 C3** NH5819.
Beinn Dubhchraig *Stir.* ***Mountain***, 5m/8km W of Crianlarich. Munro: height 3205 feet or 977 metres. **80 E5** NN3025.
Beinn Duill *Arg. & B.* ***Hill***, on NW Mull, 4m/6km W of Kilninian. Height 626 feet or 191 metres. **78 E3** NM3447.
Beinn Eagagach *P. & K.* ***Mountain***, 5m/8km W of Pitlochry. Height 2260 feet or 689 metres. **81 K2** NN8556.
Beinn Edra *High.* ***Mountain***, 4m/7km W of Rubha nam Brathairean, Skye. Height 2004 feet or 611 metres. **93 K5** NG4562.
Beinn Eibhinn *High.* ***Mountain***, on border of Lochaber and Badenoch and Strathspey districts 2m/3km E of Loch Ghuilbinn. Munro: height 3611 feet or 1101 metres. **88 B7** NN4473.
Beinn Eich *Arg. & B.* ***Mountain***, 4m/6km W of Luss. Height 2303 feet or 702 metres. **74 B1** NS3094.
Beinn Eighe (Anglicised form: Ben Eay.) *High.* ***Mountain***, mass and national nature reserve in Ross and Cromarty district to W of Kinlochewe. Highest peak is Ruadh-stac Mòr, a Munro at 3312 feet or 1010 metres. Nature reserve is good example of old pine forest. **95 F5** NG9561.
Beinn Eilde *High.* ***Mountain***, in Badenoch and Strathspey district, 4m/7km W of Dalwhinnie. Height 2211 feet or 674 metres. **88 C6** NN5685.
Beinn Eilideach *High.* ***Mountain***, in Ross and Cromarty district, on N slope of Loch Broom, 3m/5km SE of Ullapool. Height 1830 feet or 558 metres. **95 H2** NH1692.
Beinn Enaiglair *High.* ***Mountain***, in Ross and Cromarty district, 2m/3km NE of Corrieshalloch Gorge. Height 2916 feet or 889 metres. **95 J3** NH2280.
Beinn Eolasary *Arg. & B.* ***Mountain***, 1m/2km E of W point of Ulva. Height 1004 feet or 306 metres. **78 E4** NM3840.
Beinn Eunaich *Arg. & B.* ***Mountain***, in Argyll 4m/6km NW of Dalmally. Munro: height 3241 feet or 988 metres. **80 C4** NN1332.
Beinn Fhada *Arg. & B.* ***Inland physical feature***, mountain ridge rising to 2303 feet or 702 metres in SE, 1m/2km N of Ben More, Mull. **79 G4** NM5335.
Beinn Fhada *Arg. & B.* ***Mountain***, 3m/5km NW of Lochbuie, Mull. Height 1643 feet or 501 metres. **79 H5** NM6329.
Beinn Fhada *High. See The Three Sisters.*
Beinn Fhada *High.* ***Inland physical feature***, mountain ridge rising to 3041 feet or 927 metres and running NE to SW on S side of Glen Coe, 5m/8km SE of Glencoe village. **80 C2** NN1553.
Beinn Fhada (Also known as Ben Attow.) *High.* ***Mountain***, on Kintail Forest (National Trust for Scotland), in Skye and Lochalsh district, 5m/8km E of Shiel Bridge. Munro: height 3385 feet or 1032 metres. **87 G3** NH0119.
Beinn Fhionnlaidh *Arg. & B.* ***Mountain***, in Argyll, 3m/5km N of head of Loch Etive. Munro: height 3146 feet or 959 metres. **80 B3** NN0949.
Beinn Fhionnlaidh *High.* ***Mountain***, on S side of Loch Mullardoch, Skye and Lochalsh district. Munro: height 3296 feet or 1005 metres. **87 H2** NH1128.
Beinn Gàire *High.* ***Mountain***, 5m/8km NE of Ardmolich, Lochaber district. Height 2184 feet or 666 metres. **86 D7** NM7874.
Beinn Gharbh *High.* ***Mountain***, with summit 1km S of Loch Assynt. Height 1771 feet or 540 metres. **102 E6** NC2122.
Beinn Ghlas *Arg. & B.* ***Mountain***, 5m/8km E of Kilmore. Height 1689 feet or 515 metres. **80 A5** NM9525.
Beinn Ghlas *Arg. & B.* ***Mountain***, in Argyll, 6m/10km NE of Inveraray. Height 1804 feet or 550 metres. **80 C6** NN1318.
Beinn Ghlas *Arg. & B.* ***Mountain***, 10m/16km NE of Lochgilphead. Height 1378 feet or 420 metres. **73 H1** NR9899.
Beinn Ghlas *P. & K.* ***Mountain***, SW shoulder (National Trust for Scotland) of Ben Lawers. Slopes noted for alpine plants. Munro: height 3618 feet or 1103 metres. **81 H3** NN6240.
Beinn Ghobhlach *High.* ***Mountain***, in Ross and Cromarty district, 5m/8km W of Ullapool across Loch Broom. Height 2083 feet or 635 metres. **95 G2** NH0594.
Beinn Ghormaig *High.* ***Mountain***, 2m/3km E of entrance to Loch Teacuis. Height 1483 feet or 452 metres. **79 H2** NM6557.
Beinn Ghuilbin *High.* ***Mountain***, in Badenoch and Strathspey district, 3m/4km N of Aviemore. Height 1896 feet or 578 metres. **89 F3** NH8917.
Beinn Ghuilean *Arg. & B.* ***Mountain***, on Kintyre, 2m/3km SE of Campbeltown. Height 1155 feet or 352 metres. **66 B2** NR7217.
Beinn Heasgarnich *P. & K.* ***Mountain***, 2m/3km S of Loch Lyon. Munro: height 3529 feet or 1076 metres. **81 F4** NN4138.
Beinn Iaruinn *High.* ***Mountain***, in Lochaber district 4m/7km S of head of Loch Lochy. Height 2634 feet or 803 metres. **87 J5** NN2990.
Beinn Ime (Anglicised form: Ben Ime.) *Arg. & B.* ***Mountain***, in Argyll 4m/6km NW of Arrochar. Munro: height 3316 feet or 1011 metres. **80 D7** NN2508.
Beinn Inverveigh *Arg. & B.* ***Mountain***, 2m/3km SE of Bridge of Orchy. Height 2096 feet or 639 metres. **80 D4** NN2738.
Beinn Iutharn Bheag ***Mountain***, on border of Aberdeenshire and Perth & Kinross, 1m/2km E of Beinn Iutharn Mhòr. Height 3126 feet or 953 metres. **89 H7** NO0679.
Beinn Iutharn Mhòr ***Mountain***, on border of Aberdeenshire and Perth & Kinross, 10m/16km SW of Braemar. Munro: height 3428 feet or 1045 metres. **89 H7** NO0479.
Beinn ladain *High.* ***Mountain***, 7m/11km N of Lochaline, Lochaber district. Height 1873 feet or 571 metres. **79 H2** NM6955.
Beinn Làir *High.* ***Mountain***, in Letterewe Forest, Ross and Cromarty district, 1m/2km W of head of Lochan Fada. Height 2821 feet or 860 metres. **95 F4** NG9873.
Beinn Laoghal *High. Gaelic form of Ben Loyal, qv.*
Beinn Laoigh *Arg. & B.* ***Mountain***, 3m/5km N of Minard. Height 1420 feet or 433 metres. **80 A7** NM9601.
Beinn Laoigh *Stir. Gaelic form of Ben Lui, qv.*
Beinn Larachan *Arg. & B.* ***Mountain***, in Lorn, 5m/7km N of Dalmally. Height 2345 feet or 715 metres. **80 C4** NN1633.
Beinn Leabhain *Stir.* ***Mountain***, on NE side of Glen Ogle, 3m/4km S of Killin. Height 2312 feet or 705 metres. **81 G5** NN5728.
Beinn Leamhain *High.* ***Mountain***, 2m/3km W of Sallachan Point, Lochaber district. Height 1647 feet or 502 metres. **80 A1** NM9662.
Beinn Leòid (Also spelled Ben Leoid.) *High.* ***Mountain***, in Sutherland district 6m/10km NE of Inchnadamph. Height 2598 feet or 792 metres. **103 F6** NC3229.
Beinn Liath Bheag *High.* ***Mountain***, in Ross and Cromarty district, 4m/6km SE of Corrieshalloch Gorge. Height 2181 feet or 665 metres. **95 J4** NH2473.
Beinn Liath Mhòr *High.* ***Mountain***, in Ross and Cromarty district, 3m/5km NW of Achnashellach Lodge. Munro: height 3034 feet or 925 metres. **95 F6** NG9651.
Beinn Liath Mhòr a' Ghiubhais Li *High.* ***Mountain***, in Ross and Cromarty district, to SW of Loch Glascarnoch, 9m/15km NW of Garve. Height 2512 feet or 766 metres. **95 J4** NH2871.
Beinn Liath Mhòr Fannaich *High.* ***Mountain***, in Ross and Cromarty district, 4m/6km S of Corrieshalloch Gorge. Munro: height 3129 feet or 954 metres. **95 J4** NH2172.
Beinn Lice *High.* ***Mountain***, 1km S of Loch More. Height 1542 feet or 470 metres. **103 F5** NC3335.
Beinn Lochain *Arg. & B.* ***Mountain***, in Argyll 3m/4km W of Lochgoilhead. Height 2306 feet or 703 metres. **80 C7** NN1600.
Beinn Loinne *High.* ***Mountain***, in Inverness district on S side of Loch Cluanie. Height 2542 feet or 775 metres. **87 H4** NH1507.
Beinn Lunndaidh *High.* ***Mountain***, 1km N of Loch Lunndaith, Sutherland district. Height 1463 feet or 446 metres. **96 E1** NC7902.
Beinn Maol Chaluim *High.* ***Inland physical feature***, mountain ridge rising to 2778 feet or 847 metres, above Glen Coe and Glen Etive, 5m/8km SE of Glencoe village. **80 C2** NN1451.
Beinn Mhanach (Anglicised form: Ben Vannoch.) *P. & K.* ***Mountain***, 1m/2km N of head of Loch Lyon. Munro: height 3126 feet or 953 metres. **80 E3** NN3741.
Beinn Mheadhoin *High.* ***Mountain***, 6m/10km S of Strontian, Lochaber district. Height 2424 feet or 739 metres. **79 J2** NM7951.
Beinn Mheadhoin *Moray* ***Mountain***, in Cairngorm Mountains, 3m/5km NE of Ben Macdui. Munro: height 3877 feet or 1182 metres. **89 H4** NJ0201.
Beinn Mheadhon *Arg. & B.* ***Mountain***, 4m/7km W of Craignure, Mull. Height 2089 feet or 637 metres. **79 H4** NM6537.
Beinn Mheadhonach *Arg. & B.* ***Mountain***, 4m/6km N of Taynuilt. Height 2342 feet or 714 metres. **80 B4** NN0136.
Beinn Mheadhonach *W.Isles* ***Mountain***, 4m/6km N of head of Loch Resort and 1m/2km S of Loch Grunavat, Isle of Lewis. Height 1302 feet or 397 metres. **100 C5** NB0923.
Beinn Mhealaich *High.* ***Mountain***, 4m/7km W of Helmsdale, Sutherland district. Height 1942 feet or 592 metres. **104 E7** NC9614.
Beinn Mhialairigh *High.* ***Mountain***, in Skye and Lochalsh district, 4m/6km S of Glenelg. Height 1797 feet or 548 metres. **86 E3** NG8012.
Beinn Mhic Chasgaig *High.* ***Mountain***, on E side of Glen Etive in Lochaber district, 1m/2km W of Clach Leathad. Height 2827 feet or 862 metres. **80 D2** NN2250.
Beinn Mhic-Mhonaidh *Arg. & B.* ***Mountain***, in Argyll 6m/10km NE of Dalmally. Height 2601 feet or 793 metres. **80 D4** NN2035.
Beinn Mhic na Ceisich *Arg. & B.* ***Mountain***, in Argyll, 15m/25km NE of Oban. Height 2093 feet or 638 metres. **80 B3** NN0149.
Beinn Mholach *P. & K.* ***Mountain***, 3m/5km SW of S end of Loch Garry. Height 2758 feet or 841 metres. **81 G1** NN5865.
Beinn Mholach *W.Isles* ***Hill***, 5m/8km NW of Stornoway, Isle of Lewis. Height 958 feet or 292 metres. **101 F4** NB3538.
Beinn Mhòr *Arg. & B.* ***Mountain***, in Argyll, 2m/3km W of Loch Eck. Height 2430 feet or 741 metres. **73 K1** NS1090.
Beinn Mhòr *High.* ***Mountain***, rounded summit, 4m/6km S of Cannich. Height 1315 feet or 401 metres. **87 K2** NH3225.
Beinn Mhòr *High.* ***Mountain***, in Badenoch and Strathspey district, 2m/3km N of Dulnain Bridge. Height 1545 feet or 471 metres. **89 G2** NH9828.
Beinn Mhòr *W.Isles* ***Hill***, on North Uist, 3m/5km NE of Maari. Height 623 feet or 190 metres. **92 D4** NF8976.
Beinn Mhòr *W.Isles* ***Mountain***, on Isle of Lewis, 2m/3km N of head of Loch Claidh. Height 1876 feet or 572 metres. **100 E7** NB2509.
Beinn Mhòr *W.Isles* ***Mountain***, on South Uist, 2m/4km N of Loch Eynort. Height 2034 feet or 620 metres. **84 D1** NF8031.
Beinn Mohal (Anglicised form: Ben Mohal.) *W.Isles* ***Hill***, 3m/4km E of head of Little Loch Roag, Isle of Lewis. Height 679 feet or 207 metres. **100 D5** NB1723.
Beinn Molurgainn *Arg. & B.* ***Mountain***, 5m/9km N of Taynuilt. Height 2263 feet or 690 metres. **80 B4** NN0140.
Beinn Muic Duibhe *Moray Gaelic form of Ben Macdui, qv.*
Beinn na Boineid *High.* ***Mountain***, 1km N of Ben Idrigill, Skye. Height 1217 feet or 371 metres. **85 H1** NG2339.
Beinn na Caillich *Arg. & B.* ***Mountain***, near E coast of Islay, 10m/16km NE of Port Ellen. Height 1105 feet or 337 metres. **72 C5** NR4559.
Beinn na Caillich *High.* ***Mountain***, 3m/4km W of Broadford, Skye. Height 2401 feet or 732 metres. **86 C2** NG6023.
Beinn na Caillich *High.* ***Mountain***, 2m/4km SE of Kyleakin near E end of Skye. Height 2394 feet or 730 metres. **86 D2** NG7722.
Beinn na Caillich *High.* ***Mountain***, in Knoydart, in Lochaber district, 3m/4km NW of Ladhar Bheinn. Height 2575 feet or 785 metres. **86 D4** NG7906.
Beinn na Cille *High.* ***Mountain***, in Lochaber district, 1m/2km N of Loch a' Choire. Height 2135 feet or 651 metres. **79 K2** NM8554.
Beinn na Cloiche *High.* ***Hill***, 2m/3km N of Bracadale, Skye. Height 761 feet or 232 metres. **93 J7** NG3641.
Beinn na Creiche *High.* ***Hill***, 3m/5km W of Dunvegan, Skye. Height 859 feet or 262 metres. **93 H7** NG2048.

Beinn na Croise *Arg. & B.* ***Mountain***, on Mull 3m/4km NE of Carsaig. Source of Leidle River. Height 1650 feet or 503 metres. **79 G5** NM5625.
Beinn na Drise *Arg. & B.* ***Mountain***, 6m/10km W of Salen, Mull. Height 1391 feet or 424 metres. **79 F3** NM4742.
Beinn na Duatharach *Arg. & B.* ***Mountain***, 1m/2km E of head of Loch Bà, Mull. Height 1492 feet or 455 metres. **79 H4** NM6036.
Beinn na Faoghla *W.Isles Gaelic form of Benbecula, qv.*
Beinn na Greine *High.* ***Mountain***, 1m/2km SW of Portree, Skye. Height 1368 feet or 417 metres. **93 K7** NG4541.
Beinn na Gucaig *High.* ***Mountain***, in Lochaber district, 6m/9km SW of Fort William. Height 2020 feet or 616 metres. **80 B1** NN0665.
Beinn na h-Eaglaise *High.* ***Mountain***, on Ben-damph Forest, Ross and Cromarty district, 2m/3km S of head of Loch Torridon. Height 2417 feet or 737 metres. **95 F6** NG9052.
Beinn na h-Iolaire *High.* ***Hill***, 1km N of Torran, Raasay. Height 833 feet or 254 metres. **94 C6** NG6050.
Beinn na h-Uamha *High.* ***Mountain***, 6m/9km N of Lochaline, Lochaber district. Height 1522 feet or 464 metres. **79 H2** NM6853.
Beinn na h-Uamha *W.Isles* ***Mountain***, on North Harris, 1km NE of Muaithabhal. Height 1276 feet or 389 metres. **100 E6** NB2611.
Beinn na Lap *High.* ***Mountain***, in Lochaber district, 1m/2km N of Loch Ossian. Munro: height 3073 feet or 937 metres. **80 E1** NN3769.
Beinn na' Leac *High.* ***Mountain***, near E coast of Raasay, 2m/3km N of Eyre Point. Height 1046 feet or 319 metres. **86 B1** NG5937.
Beinn na Lice *Arg. & B.* ***Mountain***, at S end of Kintyre, 5m/8km W of Southend. Height 1404 feet or 428 metres. **66 A3** NR6008.
Beinn na Seamraig *High.* ***Mountain***, on Skye, 3m/4km S of Glen Arroch. Height 1840 feet or 561 metres. **86 D3** NG7217.
Beinn na Seilg *High.* ***Mountain***, 2m/3km W of Kilchoan. Height 1122 feet or 342 metres. **79 F1** NM4564.
Beinn na Sreine *Arg. & B.* ***Mountain***, 3m/4km S of Balnahard, Mull. Height 1702 feet or 519 metres. **79 F5** NM4530.
Beinn na Sroine *Arg. & B.* ***Mountain***, 4m/7km E of Dalmally. Height 2086 feet or 636 metres. **80 D5** NN2328.
Beinn nam Bad Mòr *High.* ***Hill***, rising above Loch Scye. Height 951 feet or 290 metres. **105 F3** NC9955.
Beinn nam Bò *High.* ***Hill***, 1m/2km W of Strathy Forest, Caithness district. Height 751 feet or 229 metres. **104 C3** NC7858.
Beinn nam Fitheach *High.* ***Mountain***, rounded summit in Inverness district, 7m/11km W of Beauly. Height 1620 feet or 494 metres. **96 B7** NH4146.
Beinn nan Aighenan *Arg. & B.* ***Mountain***, in Argyll 4m/6km SE of head of Loch Etive. Munro: height 3139 feet or 957 metres. **80 C3** NN1440.
Beinn nan Cabar *High.* ***Mountain***, in South Morar, Lochaber district, 3m/4km N of Lochailort. Height 1883 feet or 574 metres. **86 D6** NM7686.
Beinn nan Caorach *High.* ***Mountain***, in Lochaber district 2m/3km NE of Arnisdale on Loch Hourn. Height 2535 feet or 773 metres. **86 E3** NG8712.
Beinn nan Capull *Arg. & B.* ***Hill***, on N coast of Jura, 8m/12km N of Ardlussa. Height 827 feet or 252 metres. **72 E1** NR6899.
Beinn nan Carn *Arg. & B.* ***Mountain***, 3m/5km NW of Gruline, Mull. Height 1092 feet or 333 metres. **79 G3** NM5042.
Beinn nan Càrn *High.* ***Hill***, 1km NW of Heast, Skye. Height 987 feet or 301 metres. **86 C3** NG6318.
Beinn nan Clach-corra *Arg. & B.* ***Mountain***, on Mull, 2m/3km N of Fanmore. Height 1033 feet or 315 metres. **79 F3** NM4247.
Beinn nan Eun *High.* ***Mountain***, in Ross and Cromarty district, 10m/15km NE of Gorstan. Height 2434 feet or 742 metres. **96 B4** NH4476.
Beinn nan Imirean *Stir.* ***Mountain***, 4m/7km NE of Crianlarich. Height 2768 feet or 844 metres. **81 F4** NN4130.
Beinn nan Losgann *High.* ***Mountain***, 1km W of head of Loch Mudle. Height 1027 feet or 313 metres. **79 G1** NM5364.
Beinn nan Lus *Arg. & B.* ***Mountain***, in Argyll on N side of Glen Kinglass. Height 2326 feet or 709 metres. **80 C4** NN1337.
Beinn nan Oighreag ***Mountain***, on border of Perth & Kinross and Stirling, 6m/10km W of Ben Lawers. Height 2982 feet or 909 metres. **81 G3** NN5441.
Beinn nan Ramh *High.* ***Mountain***, in Ross and Cromarty district, 8m/12km NE of Kinlochewe. Height 2332 feet or 711 metres. **95 H5** NH1366.
Beinn nan Surrag *W.Isles* ***Hill***, 4m/7km NW of Liurbost, Isle of Lewis. Height 656 feet or 200 metres. **101 F4** NB3131.
Beinn Narnain *Arg. & B.* ***Mountain***, in Argyll 2m/3km NW of head of Loch Long. Munro: height 3037 feet or 926 metres. **80 D7** NN2706.
Beinn Nuis *N.Ayr.* ***Mountain***, on Arran 2m/4km SW of Goat Fell. Height 2598 feet or 792 metres. **73 H7** NR9539.
Beinn Odhar ***Mountain***, on border of Argyll & Bute and Stirling, 2m/4km N of Tyndrum. Height 2955 feet or 901 metres. **80 E4** NN3333.
Beinn Odhar ***Mountain***, on border of Perth & Kinross and Stirling, 6m/10km NE of Callander. Height 2073 feet or 632 metres. **81 J6** NN7112.
Beinn Odhar Bheag *High.* ***Mountain***, nearly 1m/2km S of Beinn Odhar Mhòr. Height 2893 feet or 882 metres. **86 E7** NM8579.
Beinn Odhar Mhòr *High.* ***Mountain***, in Moidart, Lochaber district, 4m/6km W of Glenfinnan. Height 2854 feet or 870 metres. **86 E7** NM8579.
Beinn Pharlagain *P. & K.* ***Mountain***, on Rannoch Forest, 4m/6km N of Loch Eigheach. Height 2647 feet or 807 metres. **81 F1** NN4464.
Beinn Rahacleit *W.Isles* ***Hill***, 3m/5km E of Carloway, Isle of Lewis. Height 813 feet or 248 metres. **100 E3** NB2642.
Beinn Raimh *High.* ***Mountain***, in Skye and Lochalsh district, 3m/4km SW of Stromeferry. Height 1466 feet or 447 metres. **86 E1** NG8430.
Beinn Ràtha *High.* ***Hill***, in Caithness district, 2m/3km S of Reay. Height 794 feet or 242 metres. **104 E2** NC9561.
Beinn Resipol *High.* ***Mountain***, in Sunart, Lochaber district, 4m/6km W of Scotstown. Height 2772 feet or 845 metres. **79 J1** NM7665.
Beinn Rodagrich *W.Isles* ***Hill***, in S part of Ronay. Height 325 feet or 99 metres. **92 D6** NF8954.
Beinn Ruadh *Arg. & B.* ***Mountain***, 4m/6km SW of Dunoon. Height 1059 feet or 323 metres. **73 K3** NS1371.
Beinn Ruadh *High.* ***Hill***, 4m/6km S of Strathy, Caithness district. Height 833 feet or 254 metres. **104 D2** NC8459.
Beinn Ruigh Choinnich *W.Isles* ***Hill***, on South Uist, 1m/2km E of Lochboisdale. Height 902 feet or 275 metres. **84 D3** NF8019.
Beinn Ruisg *Arg. & B.* ***Mountain***, overlooking Loch Lomond, 2m/4km SW of Luss. Height 1945 feet or 593 metres. **74 B1** NS3291.
Beinn Sgaillinish *Arg. & B.* ***Hill***, on E coast of Jura, 2m/3km SW of Lussagiven. Height 623 feet or 190 metres. **72 E2** NR6184.
Beinn Sgreamhaidh *High.* ***Mountain***, 1m/2km S of Strath an Lòin. Height 1427 feet or 435 metres. **103 G7** NC4415.
Beinn Sgritheall (Also known as Ben Screel.) *High.* ***Mountain***, on Loch Hourn in Lochaber district, 1m/2km N of Arnisdale. Munro: height 3195 feet or 974 metres. **86 E3** NG8312.
Beinn Sgulaird *Arg. & B.* ***Mountain***, 3m/5km E of head of Loch Creran, Argyll. Munro: height 3073 feet or 937 metres. **80 B3** NN0546.
Beinn Shiantaidh *Arg. & B.* ***Mountain***, easternmost and second highest of Paps of Jura. Height 2476 feet or 755 metres. **72 D3** NR5174.
Beinn Sholum *Arg. & B.* ***Mountain***, on Islay, 4m/6km NE of Port Ellen. Height 1138 feet or 347 metres. **72 C6** NR3949.
Beinn Spionnaidh *High.* ***Mountain***, in Sutherland district 3m/4km NW of head of Loch Eriboll. Height 2532 feet or 772 metres. **103 F3** NC3657.
Beinn Staic *High.* ***Mountain***, 1m/2km NE of An Cruachan, Skye. Height 1348 feet or 411 metres. **85 J2** NG3923.
Beinn Stumanadh *High.* ***Mountain***, 1m/2km E of Loch Loyal. Height 1729 feet or 527 metres. **103 J3** NC6449.
Beinn Suidhe *Arg. & B.* ***Mountain***, in Argyll 6m/9km W of Bridge of Orchy. Height 2214 feet or 675 metres. **80 D3** NN2140.
Beinn Talaidh *Arg. & B.* ***Mountain***, 6m/10km N of Lochbuie, Mull. Height 2496 feet or 761 metres. **79 H4** NM6234.
Beinn Tarsuinn *Arg. & B.* ***Mountain***, with craggy slopes, 6m/10km N of Craighouse on Jura. Height 1364 feet or 416 metres. **72 D3** NR5476.
Beinn Tarsuinn *High.* ***Mountain***, in Ross and Cromarty district, 7m/11km N of Kinlochewe, on N side of Lochan Fada. Munro: height 3070 feet or 936 metres. **95 G4** NH0372.
Beinn Tarsuinn *N.Ayr.* ***Mountain***, on Arran, 4m/6km S of Lochranza. Comprises two distinct peaks at 1817 feet or 554 metres and 1715 feet or 523 metres. **73 H6** NR9244.
Beinn Tarsuinn *N.Ayr.* ***Mountain***, on Arran, 5m/8km NW of Brodick. Height 2706 feet or 825 metres. **73 H6** NR9540.
Beinn Tart a' Mhill *Arg. & B.* ***Hill***, on Rinns of Islay, 4m/6km NE of Portnahaven. Height 761 feet or 232 metres. **72 A5** NR2156.
Beinn Teallach *High.* ***Mountain***, in Lochaber district 3m/5km N of W end of Loch Moy. Munro: height 3001 feet or 915 metres. **87 K6** NN3685.
Beinn Tharsuinn *Arg. & B.* ***Mountain***, 3m/5km E of Garelochhead. Height 2152 feet or 656 metres. **74 A1** NS2891.
Beinn Tharsuinn *High.* ***Mountain***, on West Monar Forest on border of Ross and Cromarty and Skye and Lochalsh districts. Height 2831 feet or 863 metres. **95 G7** NH0543.
Beinn Tharsuinn *High.* ***Mountain***, in Sutherland district, 13m/22km N of Garve. Height 2342 feet or 714 metres. **96 B3** NH4183.
Beinn Tharsuinn *High.* ***Mountain***, in Ross and Cromarty district, 8m/12km S of Bonar Bridge. Height 2270 feet or 692 metres. **96 D4** NH6079.
Beinn Tighe *High.* ***Mountain***, 1km SE of Rubha an Fhasaidh, Eigg. Height 1033 feet or 315 metres. **85 K6** NM4486.
Beinn Totaig *High.* ***Mountain***, rising to over 340 metres, 4m/6km SE of Bracadale, Skye. **85 K1** NG4036.
Beinn Trilleachan *Arg. & B.* ***Mountain***, 2m/3km SW of head of Loch Etive, on border with Highland. Height 2752 feet or 839 metres. **80 B3** NN0843.
Beinn Tulaichean *Stir.* ***Mountain***, 4m/6km SE of Crianlarich. Munro: height 3100 feet or 945 metres. **81 F6** NN4119.
Beinn Uamha *Stir.* ***Mountain***, 1m/2km S of Loch Arklet and 4m/7km NE of Tarbet across Loch Lomond. Height 1961 feet or 598 metres. **80 E7** NN3806.
Beinn Udlaidh *Arg. & B.* ***Mountain***, in Argyll 4m/6km NW of Tyndrum. Height 2755 feet or 840 metres. **80 D4** NN2833.
Beinn Udlamain *P. & K.* ***Mountain***, in Dalnaspidal Forest to E of Loch Ericht. Munro: height 3313 feet or 1010 metres. **88 C7** NN5773.
Beinn Uidhe *High.* ***Mountain***, 3m/4km NE of S end of Loch Assynt. Height 2427 feet or 740 metres. **102 E6** NC2825.
Beinn Uird *Stir.* ***Mountain***, overlooking E shore of Loch Lomond, 3m/4km E of Rowardennan Lodge. Height 1955 feet or 596 metres. **74 B1** NS3998.
Beinn Ulbhaidh *High.* ***Mountain***, rounded mountain with three summits, in Sutherland district, 4m/6km SW of Invercassley. Height 1617 feet or 493 metres. **96 B2** NH4396.
Beinn Uraraidh *Arg. & B.* ***Mountain***, rocky summit on Islay, 6m/10km NE of Port Ellen. Height 1489 feet or 454 metres. **72 C5** NR4153.
Beinn-y-Phott *I.o.M.* ***Mountain***, 6m/9km N of Douglas. Height 1784 feet or 544 metres. **54 C5** SC3886.
Beinneun Forest *High.* ***Open space***, deer forest on border of Inverness and Lochaber districts E of Loch Loyne. **87 J4** NH2208.
Beins Law *P. & K.* ***Hill***, in Ochil Hills, 3m/4km S of Abernethy. Height 879 feet or 268 metres. **82 C6** NO1812.
Beith *N.Ayr.* Population: 6358. ***Small town***, 10m/16km SW of Paisley. **74 B5** NS3453.
Bekesbourne *Kent* ***Village***, 3m/5km SE of Canterbury. **15 G2** TR1955.
Bekesbourne Hill *Kent* ***Settlement***, 1km N of Bekesbourne. TR1856.
Belah *Cumb.* ***River***, rising on Kaber Fell, E of Kirkby Stephen, and flowing generally NW into River Eden 2m/3km SW of Brough. **61 K6** NY7712.
Belah *Cumb.* ***Suburb***, 1m/2km N of Carlisle city centre. NY3957.
Belas Knap Long Barrow *Glos.* ***Historic/prehistoric site***, impressive chambered long barrow (English Heritage) over 150 feet or 46 metres long and 12 feet or 4 metres high, 2m/3km S of Winchcombe. **30 B6** SP0125.
Belaugh *Norf.* ***Village***, 1m/2km NW of Wroxham across River Bure. **45 G4** TG2818.
Belaugh Green *Norf.* ***Settlement***, 1m/2km N of Wroxham. TG2919.
Belbroughton *Worcs.* ***Village***, 5m/8km S of Stourbridge. **29 J1** SO9176.
Belchalwell *Dorset* ***Hamlet***, 3m/5km S of Sturminster Newton. ST7909.
Belchalwell Street *Dorset* ***Hamlet***, 1km SE of Belchalwell, 3m/5km S of Sturminster Newton. ST7909.
Belchamp Otten *Essex* ***Village***, 5m/7km W of Sudbury. **34 C4** TL8041.
Belchamp St. Paul *Essex* ***Village***, 5m/8km W of Sudbury. **34 B4** TL7942.
Belchamp Walter *Essex* ***Village***, 3m/5km W of Sudbury. **34 C4** TL8140.
Belchford *Lincs.* ***Village***, 4m/7km NE of Horncastle. **53 F5** TF2975.
Beldon Burn ***River***, rising on Byerhope Moss and flowing E though steep-sided valley to Blanchland, and then into Derwent Reservoir. Forms border of Northumberland and County Durham for much of its length. **61 K2** NY9851.
Beldoo Hill ***Mountain***, on border of Cumbria and Northumberland, 6m/10km E of Brough. Height 1565 feet or 477 metres. **61 K5** NY8913.
Beldorney Castle *Aber.* ***Castle***, 16c Z-plan tower on W side of River Deveron, 6m/10km E of Dufftown. **90 C1** NJ4137.
Belfield *Gt.Man.* ***Suburb***, on Rochdale Canal, 1m/2km E of Rochdale town centre. SD9113.
Belford *Northumb.* ***Village***, 14m/23km SE of Berwick-upon-Tweed. **77 K7** NU1033.
Belgrano *Conwy* ***Locality***, 1m/2km NE of Abergele. SH9578.
Belgrave *Leic.* ***Suburb***, 2m/3km N of Leicester city centre. **41 H5** SK5906.
Belgrave *Staffs.* ***Suburb***, 1m/2km SE of Tamworth town centre. SK2202.
Belgrave Hall *Leic.* ***Historic house***, Queen Anne house with gardens, 2m/3km N of Leicester. **41 H5** SK5907.
Belgravia *Gt.Lon.* ***Suburb***, fashionable residential locality of City of Westminster, W of Victoria Station and S of Knightsbridge. TQ2879.
Belhaven *E.Loth.* ***Suburb***, W area of Dunbar. **76 E3** NT6678.
Belhaven Bay *E.Loth.* ***Bay***, on W side of Dunbar. **76 E3** NT6578.
Belhelvie *Aber.* ***Hamlet***, 7m/12km N of Aberdeen. **91 H3** NJ9417.
Belhinnie (Also known as Balhinny.) *Moray* ***Settlement***, 2m/4km W of Rhynie. **90 C2** NJ4627.
Belig *High.* ***Mountain***, on Skye, 1km NE of Garbh-bheinn. Height 2303 feet or 702 metres. **86 B2** NG5424.
Bell Bar *Herts.* ***Hamlet***, 3m/4km SE of Hatfield. **23 F1** TL2505.
Bell Busk *N.Yorks.* ***Village***, 3m/4km NW of Gargrave. **56 E4** SD9056.
Bell Craig *D. & G.* ***Mountain***, 3m/5km NW of Bodesbeck. Height 2047 feet or 624 metres. **69 G2** NT1812.
Bell End *Worcs.* ***Hamlet***, 4m/7km N of Bromsgrove. **29 J1** SO9377.
Bell Green *Gt.Lon.* ***Suburb***, in borough of Lewisham, 2m/3km S of Lewisham and 7m/11km SE of Charing Cross. TQ3672.
Bell Green *Suff.* ***Locality***, N part of Cratfield. TM3175.
Bell Green *W.Mid.* ***Suburb***, 2m/4km NE of Coventry city centre. SP3681.
Bell Hall *York See Naburn.*
Bell Heath *Worcs.* ***Settlement***, 4m/7km N of Bromsgrove. SO9577.
Bell Hill *Hants.* ***Settlement***, adjoining to NW of Petersfield. SU7424.
Bell Hill *Northumb.* ***Mountain***, in Cheviot Hills, 1m/2km SE of Blindburn. Height 1610 feet or 491 metres. **70 D2** NT8410.
Bell o' th' Hill *Ches.* ***Settlement***, 3m/5km NW of Whitchurch. SJ5245.

Bell Rock *Angus* *Alternative name for Inchcape Rock, qv.*
Bellabeg *Aber.* ***Settlement***, near bridge over River Don, at NE side of Strathdon. **90 B3** NJ3513.
Belladrum *High.* ***Settlement***, 3m/5km S of Beauly. **96 C7** NH5241.
Bellahouston *Glas.* ***Suburb***, 2m/4km SW of Glasgow city centre. NS5564.
Bellanoch *Arg. & B.* ***Hamlet***, in Argyll, on SW side of Crinan Canal, 2m/3km from Crinan village. Road bridge across canal and River Add. **73 G1** NR8092.
Bellart *Arg. & B.* ***River***, on Mull running NW to Loch na Cuilce, 5m/8km W of Tobermory. **79 F3** NM4351.
Bellasize *E.Riding* ***Settlement***, 5m/8km E of Howden. **58 E7** SE8227.
Bellaty *Angus* ***Settlement***, in valley of River Isla, 3m/5km N of Bridge of Craigisla. **82 D2** NO2359.
Bellbeaver Rigg *Cumb.* ***Mountain***, flat-topped moorland rising to over 610 metres on Tynehead Fell, 4m/6km NW of Cow Green Reservoir. **61 J3** NY7635.
Belle Isle *Cumb.* ***Island***, about 1km long, on Windermere, opposite Bowness-on-Windermere. SD3996.
Belle Isle *W.Yorks.* ***Suburb***, 3m/5km S of Leeds city centre. SE3129.
Belle Vale *W.Mid.* ***Suburb***, 1m/2km NW of Halesowen town centre. SO9584.
Belle Vue *Cumb.* ***Locality***, 1m/2km NW of Cockermouth across River Derwent. NY1131.
Belle Vue *Cumb.* ***Suburb***, 2m/3km W of Carlisle city centre. NY3755.
Belle Vue *Shrop.* ***Suburb***, to S of Shrewsbury town centre across River Severn. SJ4911.
Belle Vue *W.Yorks.* ***Suburb***, 1m/2km SE of Wakefield city centre across River Calder. SE3419.
Belleau *Lincs.* ***Village***, 4m/6km NW of Alford. **53 H5** TF4078.
Bellehiglash *Moray* ***Settlement***, 4m/6km S of Upper Knockando. **89 J1** NJ1837.
Bellerby *N.Yorks.* ***Village***, 1m/2km N of Leyburn. **62 C7** SE1192.
Bellerby Moor *N.Yorks.* ***Open space***, moorland 2m/3km NW of Leyburn. **62 B7** SE0893.
Bellever *Devon* ***Hamlet***, on Dartmoor, 1m/2km S of Postbridge. Clapper bridge over East Dart River. **5 G3** SX6577.
Bellfields *Surr.* ***Suburb***, to N of Guildford. SU9951.
Belliehill *Angus* ***Settlement***, 3m/5km NW of Brechin. **83 G1** NO5663.
Bellingdon *Bucks.* ***Village***, 3m/4km N of Chesham. **22 C1** SP9405.
Bellinge *Northants.* ***Suburb***, to E of Northampton, comprising suburbs of Great and Little Billing. SP8062.
Bellingham *Gt.Lon.* ***Suburb***, in borough of Lewisham, 2m/3km S of Lewisham and 7m/11km SE of Charing Cross. TQ3772.
Bellingham *Northumb.* ***Small town***, on River North Tyne, 14m/23km NW of Hexham. **70 D5** NY8383.
Bellister *Shet.* ***Hamlet***, on S side of Dury Voe on Mainland, 1km NE of Laxfirth. HU4860.
Belloch *Arg. & B.* ***Settlement***, on W side of Kintyre, 1m/2km N of Glenbarr. **72 E7** NR6737.
Bellochantuy *Arg. & B.* ***Village***, on Bellochantuy Bay, on W coast of Kintyre. **72 E7** NR6632.
Bellochantuy Bay *Arg. & B.* ***Bay***, on W coast of Kintyre, 9m/15km NW of Campbeltown. **72 E7** NR6532.
Bell's Close *T. & W.* ***Suburb***, on N side of River Tyne, 4m/6km W of Newcastle upon Tyne. NZ1964.
Bells Creek *Kent* *See Isle of Harty.*
Bell's Cross *Suff.* ***Settlement***, 5m/8km N of Ipswich. TM1552.
Bells Yew Green *E.Suss.* ***Hamlet***, 3m/4km SE of Royal Tunbridge Wells. **13 K3** TQ6036.
Bellsdyke *Falk.* ***Settlement***, 3m/5km N of Falkirk. **75 H2** NS9085.
Bellshill *N.Lan.* Population: 21,624. ***Suburb***, 3m/4km NW of Motherwell. **75 F5** NS7360.
Bellshill *Northumb.* ***Hamlet***, 2m/4km SE of Belford. **77 K7** NU1230.
Bellside *N.Lan.* ***Hamlet***, 2m/3km NW of Newmains. **75 G5** NS8158.
Bellsquarry *W.Loth.* ***Suburb***, 2m/3km SW of Livingston town centre. **75 J4** NT0465.
Belluton *B. & N.E.Som.* ***Hamlet***, 3m/4km E of Chew Magna. **19 K5** ST6164.
Belmaduthy *High.* ***Settlement***, on Black Isle, 1m/2km N of Munlochy. **96 D6** NH6456.
Belmesthorpe *Rut.* ***Village***, 2m/4km NE of Stamford. **42 D4** TF0410.
Belmont *B'burn.* ***Village***, 5m/8km NW of Bolton. **49 F1** SD6716.
Belmont *Gt.Lon.* ***Suburb***, in borough of Harrow, 11m/17km NW of Charing Cross. TQ1690.
Belmont *Gt.Lon.* ***Suburb***, in borough of Sutton, 1m/2km S of Sutton town centre. **23 F5** TQ2562.
Belmont *Shet.* ***Settlement***, at SW end of Unst near Wick of Belmont. **108 E2** HP5601.
Belmont *S.Ayr.* ***Suburb***, to S of Ayr. NS3420.
Belmont Abbey *Here.* ***Ecclesiastical building***, Benedictine abbey, originally built as parish church, on SW side of Hereford. **28 D5** SO4838.
Belmont Reservoir *B'burn.* ***Reservoir***, to N of Belmont. **49 F1** SD6716.
Belmont Television Transmitter *Lincs.* *See Benniworth.*
Belnahua *Arg. & B.* ***Island***, 1m/2km W of NW coast of Luing. **79 J6** NM7112.
Belnie *Lincs.* ***Settlement***, 1m/2km SE of Gosberton. TF2530.
Belowda *Cornw.* ***Hamlet***, 4m/6km E of St. Columb Major. **3 G2** SW9661.
Belper *Derbys.* Population: 18,213. ***Town***, 7m/11km N of Derby. **41 F1** SK3447.
Belper Lane End *Derbys.* ***Hamlet***, 1m/2km NW of Belper. **41 F1** SK3447.
Belph *Derbys.* ***Settlement***, 1m/2km SE of Whitwell, 3m/5km SW of Worksop. SK5475.
Belsar's Hill *Cambs.* *See Willingham.*
Belsay *Northumb.* ***Village***, 5m/9km NW of Ponteland. 14c Belsay Castle, 17c Belsay Hall and gardens (all English Heritage) 1m/2km W. **71 G6** NZ1078.
Belsay Hall and Gardens *Northumb.* ***Garden***, 30 acre gardens surrounding ruined 14c Belsay Castle and 19c Belsay Hall (all English Heritage), 1km W of Belsay. Includes rare and exotic trees, rhododendrons and heather garden. Notable for autumn colours. **71 F6** NZ0878.
Belsford *Devon* ***Hamlet***, 2m/4km W of Totnes. **5 H5** SX7659.
Belsize *Herts.* ***Hamlet***, 3m/4km SW of Kings Langley. TL0300.
Belstead *Suff.* ***Village***, 3m/5km SW of Ipswich. **35 F4** TM1341.
Belston *S.Ayr.* ***Settlement***, 3m/4km E of Ayr. **67 H1** NS3820.
Belstone *Devon* ***Village***, on N edge of Dartmoor, 2m/4km SE of Okehampton. **6 E6** SX6193.
Belstone Corner *Devon* ***Hamlet***, 3m/5km NE of Okehampton. **6 E6** SX6298.
Belsyde *W.Loth.* ***Settlement***, 2m/3km SW of Linlithgow. **75 H3** NS9775.
Belthorn *B'burn.* ***Village***, 4m/6km SE of Blackburn. **56 C7** SD7224.
Beltie Burn *Aber.* ***River***, rising on Corrennie Moor and flowing S, then SE, to Torphins and Glassel, where it becomes Burn of Canny and eventually joins River Dee, 2m/3km W of Banchory. **90 E4** NO6599.
Beltinge *Kent* ***Suburb***, to E of Herne Bay. **25 H5** TR1967.
Beltingham *Northumb.* ***Hamlet***, on S bank of River South Tyne, 3m/5km W of Haydon Bridge. NY7863.
Beltoft *N.Lincs.* ***Village***, 3m/4km NE of Epworth. **52 B2** SE8006.
Belton *Leics.* ***Village***, 6m/9km W of Loughborough. **41 G3** SK4420.
Belton *Lincs.* ***Village***, 3m/4km NE of Grantham. **42 C2** SK9339.
Belton *Norf.* Population: 4625. ***Village***, 4m/7km SW of Great Yarmouth. **45 J5** TG4802.
Belton *N.Lincs.* Population: 2300. ***Village***, 2m/3km N of Epworth. **51 K2** SE7806.
Belton *Rut.* ***Village***, 3m/5km W of Uppingham. **42 B5** SK8101.
Belton House *Lincs.* ***Historic house***, late 17c house (National Trust), 3m/5km N of Grantham. Arranged in an H shape, with large park laid out in 18c by William Eames. **42 C2** SK9239.
Beltring *Kent* ***Hamlet***, 2m/3km N of Paddock Wood. Large group of oasthouses. **23 K7** TQ6747.
Belvedere *Gt.Lon.* ***Suburb***, in borough of Bexley, comprising Lower and Upper Belvedere. **23 H4** TQ4978.
Belvide Reservoir *Staffs.* ***Reservoir***, 1m/2km NW of Brewood. **40 A4** SJ8610.
Belvoir *Leics.* ***Hamlet***, 6m/10km W of Grantham. **42 B2** SK8233.
Belvoir Castle *Leics.* ***Castle***, 6m/10km SW of Grantham. Early 19c edifice on hilltop site of Norman castle which suffered severe damage during Wars of the Roses. Now home of Duke and Duchess of Rutland, and houses Queen's Royal Lancers Museum. Statue Gardens in grounds. **42 B2** SK8133.
Bembridge *I.o.W.* Population: 3397. ***Small town***, resort and yachting centre, 4m/7km SE of Ryde. Airport to W. To SW, Bembridge and Culver Downs (National Trust). **11 H6** SZ6488.
Bembridge Down *I.o.W.* *See Bembridge.*
Bembridge Point *I.o.W.* ***Coastal feature***, point 1km NW of Bembridge. **11 H6** SZ6488.
Bembridge Windmill *I.o.W.* ***Other feature of interest***, island's sole surviving windmill (National Trust), built c. 1700, 1m/2km SW of Bembridge. Most of original wooden machinery intact. Impressive views from top. **11 H6** SZ6387.
Bemersley Green *Stoke* ***Settlement***, 3m/4km NE of Tunstall. SJ8854.
Bemersyde *Sc.Bord.* ***Hamlet***, 4m/6km S of Earlston. **76 D7** NT5933.
Bemerton *Wilts.* ***Suburb***, in W part of Salisbury, beside River Nadder. SU1230.
Bempton *E.Riding* ***Village***, 3m/5km N of Bridlington. **59 H2** TA1972.
Ben-a-chielt *High.* ***Hill***, 3m/4km N of Latheron. Height 941 feet or 287 metres. **105 G5** ND1937.
Ben A'an *Stir.* *Alternative name for Stob Binnein, qv.*
Ben Aden *High.* ***Mountain***, peak in Lochaber district 2m/3km W of head of Loch Quoich. Height 2903 feet or 885 metres. **87 F5** NM8998.
Ben Aigan *Moray* ***Mountain***, 2m/3km E of Rothes. Height 1545 feet or 471 metres. **98 B6** NJ3148.
Ben Aird da Loch *High.* ***Mountain***, 1km N of Loch Glencoul. Height 1738 feet or 530 metres. **102 E5** NC2831.
Ben Aketil *High.* ***Hill***, 4m/7km E of Dunvegan, Skye. Height 872 feet or 266 metres. **93 J7** NG3246.
Ben Alder *High.* ***Mountain***, in Badenoch and Strathspey district to W of Loch a' Bhealaich Bheithe. Munro: height 3765 feet or 1148 metres. **88 B7** NN4971.
Ben Alder Cottage *P. & K.* ***Settlement***, on E side of Loch Ericht, 8m/12km N of Bridge of Gaur. **81 F1** NN4968.
Ben Alder Forest *High.* ***Large natural feature***, mountain area extending NE of Ben Alder, on NW side of Loch Ericht. **88 C7** NN5275.
Ben Alder Lodge *High.* ***Settlement***, on NW shore of Loch Ericht, 5m/8km SW of Dalwhinnie. **88 C7** NN5778.
Ben Alisky *High.* ***Mountain***, 4m/6km SW of Loch More. Height 1141 feet or 348 metres. **105 F5** ND0438.
Ben An *Stir.* ***Mountain***, in The Trossachs, 4m/7km N of Aberfoyle. Height 1512 feet or 461 metres. **81 G7** NN5008.
Ben Armine (Gaelic form: Beinn an Armuinn.) *High.* ***Mountain***, in Sutherland district, 5m/8km SE of Loch Choire. Height 2309 feet or 704 metres. **103 J6** NC6924.
Ben Armine Forest *High.* ***Open space***, deer forest surrounding Ben Armine in Sutherland district. **103 J6** NC6621.
Ben Arnaboll *High.* ***Hill***, situated between Loch Eriboll and Loch Hope. Height 754 feet or 230 metres. **103 G3** NC4559.
Ben Arthur (Also known as The Cobbler.) *Arg. & B.* ***Mountain***, in Argyll 3m/4km W of Arrochar. Height 2890 feet or 881 metres. **80 D7** NN2505.
Ben Aslak *High.* ***Mountain***, on Skye, 4m/7km S of Kyleakin. Height 2001 feet or 610 metres. **86 D3** NG7518.
Ben Attow *High.* *Alternative name for Beinn Fhada, qv.*
Ben Auskaird *High.* ***Mountain***, 4m/7km SE of Scourie, Sutherland district. Height 1266 feet or 386 metres. **102 E4** NC2040.
Ben Avon *Aber.* ***Large natural feature***, massif 7m/11km N of Braemar. For individual peaks see Mullach Lochan nan Gabhar, Stob Bac an Fhurain, and the summit and Munro, Leabaidh an Daimh Bhuidhe. **89 J4** NJ1301.
Ben Buie *Arg. & B.* ***Mountain***, on Mull 1m/2km N of Lochbuie. Height 2352 feet or 717 metres. **79 H5** NM6027.
Ben Challum *Stir.* ***Mountain***, 4m/6km E of Tyndrum. Munro: height 3352 feet or 1022 metres. **80 E4** NN3832.
Ben Chonzie (Gaelic form: Beinn a' Chonnaich.) *P. & K.* ***Mountain***, 6m/9km N of Comrie. Munro: height 3054 feet or 931 metres. **81 J4** NN7730.
Ben Clach *P. & K.* ***Mountain***, 4m/7km SW of Comrie. Height 1748 feet or 533 metres. **81 J6** NN7515.
Ben Cleuch *Clack.* ***Mountain***, summit of Ochil Hills, 3m/4km NW of Tillicoultry. Height 2362 feet or 720 metres. **81 K7** NN9000.
Ben Cliad *W.Isles* ***Hill***, on Barra, 2m/3km W of Ardmhòr. Height 679 feet or 207 metres. **84 B4** NF6704.
Ben Connan *High.* ***Hill***, 4m/6km NW of Idrigill Point, Skye. Height 800 feet or 244 metres. **93 G7** NG1940.
Ben Corkeval *High.* ***Mountain***, rising to over 350 metres on Skye, 1m/2km E of Ramasaig. **93 G7** NG1844.
Ben Corodale *W.Isles* ***Mountain***, 1m/2km NE of Beinn Mhòr, South Uist. Height 1729 feet or 527 metres. **84 D1** NF8225.
Ben Creach *Arg. & B.* *Anglicised form of Creach Beinn, qv.*
Ben Cruachan *Arg. & B.* ***Mountain***, in Argyll 4m/6km E of Bonawe. Munro: height 3693 feet or 1126 metres. Hydro-electricity generating station within mountain pumps water from Loch Awe to Cruachan Reservoir. **80 B4** NN0630.
Ben Damph *High.* *Anglicised form of Beinn Damh, qv.*
Ben-damph Forest *High.* ***Open space***, deer forest in Ross and Cromarty district to S of Upper Loch Torridon. **94 E6** NG8852.
Ben Dearg *High.* ***Mountain***, 4m/6km N of Portree, Skye. Height 1811 feet or 552 metres. **93 K6** NG4750.
Ben Dell *W.Isles* ***Locality***, 4m/7km W of Cellar Head, Isle of Lewis. **101 G2** NB4956.
Ben Diubaig *High.* ***Hill***, 3m/5km NW of head of Loch Greshornish, Skye. Height 708 feet or 216 metres. **93 J6** NG3155.
Ben Donich *Arg. & B.* ***Mountain***, in Argyll 2m/4km N of Lochgoilhead. Height 2778 feet or 847 metres. **80 D7** NN2104.
Ben Dorrery *High.* ***Hill***, summit lies 1km to E of Loch Shurrery. Height 800 feet or 244 metres. **105 F3** ND0655.
Ben Douran *Arg. & B.* *Anglicised form of Beinn Dorain, qv.*
Ben Drovinish *W.Isles* ***Hill***, 3m/4km SW of Earshader, Isle of Lewis. Height 607 feet or 185 metres. **100 D4** NB1531.
Ben Duagrich *High.* ***Hill***, to S of Loch Duagrich, Skye. Height 997 feet or 304 metres. **85 K1** NG3938.
Ben Earb *P. & K.* ***Mountain***, 2m/3km SW of Spittal of Glenshee. Height 2627 feet or 801 metres. **82 B1** NO0769.
Ben Eay *High.* *Anglicised form of Beinn Eighe, qv.*
Ben Garrisdale *Arg. & B.* ***Mountain***, in N part of Jura, 5m/7km NW of Ardlussa. Height 1197 feet or 365 metres. **72 E1** NR6394.
Ben Geary *High.* ***Hill***, 4m/6km S of Vaternish Point, Skye. Height 932 feet or 284 metres. **93 H5** NG2561.
Ben Glas *Stir.* ***Mountain***, craggy area rising to over 610 metres, 3m/4km NE of Ardlui. **80 E6** NN3418.
Ben Gorm *High.* ***Mountain***, 3m/4km E of Uig, Skye. Height 1053 feet or 321 metres. **93 K5** NG4364.
Ben Griam Beg *High.* ***Mountain***, 1m/2km E of Loch Druim a' Chliabhain, Caithness district. Height 1902 feet or 580 metres. **104 D4** NC8341.
Ben Griam Mhòr *High.* ***Mountain***, 1km S of Loch Druim a' Chliabhain and 3m/5km NE of Loch nan Clàr, Sutherland district. Height 1935 feet or 590 metres. **104 D5** NC8038.
Ben Gulabin *P. & K.* ***Mountain***, 1m/2km N of Spittal of Glenshee. Height 2644 feet or 806 metres. **89 J7** NO1072.
Ben Halton *P. & K.* ***Mountain***, to N of Glen Artney, 4m/6km W of Dalginross. Height 2034 feet or 620 metres. **81 J5** NN7220.
Ben Hee *High.* ***Mountain***, in Sutherland district 9m/14km W of Altnaharra. Height 2863 feet or 873 metres. **103 G5** NC4233.
Ben Hiant *High.* ***Mountain***, near S coast of Ardnamurchan peninsula in Lochaber district 3m/5km E of Kilchoan. Height 1732 feet or 528 metres. **79 G1** NM5363.
Ben Hiel *High.* ***Mountain***, 2m/3km NW of Lettermore, Caithness district. Height 1752 feet or 534 metres. **103 H3** NC5950.

Ben Hogh *Arg. & B.* ***Hill***, 3m/4km NW of Arinagour, Coll. Height 341 feet or 104 metres. **78 C2** NM1858.
Ben Hope *High.* ***Mountain***, in Sutherland district 1m/2km E of head of Loch Hope. Munro: height 3041 feet or 927 metres. **103 G3** NC4750.
Ben Horn *High.* ***Mountain***, 1km E of Loch Horn, 4m/7km NW of Golspie. Height 1709 feet or 521 metres. **97 F1** NC8006.
Ben Horneval *High.* ***Hill***, 2m/4km NE of Dunvegan, Skye. Height 866 feet or 264 metres. **93 H7** NG2849.
Ben Hutig *High.* ***Mountain***, 3m/5km NW of Talmine, Caithness district. Height 1338 feet or 408 metres. **103 H2** NC5365.
Ben Idrigill *High.* ***Mountain***, rising to over 340 metres on Skye, 1m/2km NW of Idrigill Point. **85 H1** NG2338.
Ben Ime *Arg. & B. Anglicised form of Beinn Ime, qv.*
Ben Killilan *High.* ***Mountain***, in Skye and Lochalsh district 2km NE of Killilan and 2m/3km NE of head of Loch Long. Height 2470 feet or 753 metres. **87 F1** NG9631.
Ben Klibreck (Gaelic form: Beinn Cleith Bric.) *High.* ***Mountain***, in Caithness district 4m/6km S of Altnaharra. Summit of Meall nan Con is a Munro. Height 3152 feet or 961 metres. **103 J5** NC5829.
Ben Laga *High.* ***Mountain***, 3m/4km E of Glenborrodale, Lochaber district. Height 1679 feet or 512 metres. **79 H1** NM6462.
Ben Lawers *P. & K.* ***Mountain***, 3m/5km NW of Lawers on Loch Tay. The peak and S slopes are National Trust for Scotland property. It commands views extending from Atlantic Ocean to North Sea. Munro: height 3982 feet or 1214 metres. Known as 'the echoing mountain'. **81 H3** NN6341.
Ben Ledi *Stir.* ***Mountain***, 4m/7km NW of Callander. Height 2883 feet or 879 metres. **81 G7** NN5609.
Ben Lee *High.* ***Mountain***, 1m/2km W of Peinchorran, Skye. Height 1460 feet or 445 metres. **86 B1** NG5033.
Ben Leoid *High. Alternative spelling of Beinn Leòid, qv.*
Ben Lomond *Stir.* ***Mountain***, 3m/5km N of Rowardennan on E shore of Loch Lomond. Munro: height 3195 feet or 974 metres. **80 E7** NN3602.
Ben Loyal (Gaelic form: Beinn Laoghal.) *High.* ***Mountain***, in Caithness district 5m/8km S of Tongue. Height 2506 feet or 764 metres. **103 H4** NC5748.
Ben Lui (Gaelic form: Beinn Laoigh.) *Stir.* ***Mountain***, 7m/11km E of Dalmally. Munro: height 3706 feet or 1130 metres. **80 D5** NN2626.
Ben Macdui (Gaelic form: Beinn Muic Duibhe.) *Moray* ***Mountain***, in Cairngorm Mountains 9m/15km SE of Aviemore. Highest mountain in Britain after Ben Nevis. Munro: height 4294 feet or 1309 metres. **89 G5** NN9898.
Ben Meabost *High.* ***Mountain***, 2m/3km NE of Elgol, Skye. Height 1135 feet or 346 metres. **86 B3** NG5315.
Ben Mohal *W.Isles Anglicised form of Beinn Mohal, qv.*
Ben Mòr Coigach *High.* ***Mountain***, 2m/3km E of Culnacraig. Height 2437 feet or 743 metres. **95 G1** NC0904.
Ben More *Arg. & B.* ***Mountain***, highest point on Mull, 3m/4km NW of head of Loch Scridain. Munro: height 3168 feet or 966 metres. **79 G4** NM5233.
Ben More *Stir.* ***Mountain***, 3m/5km E of Crianlarich. Munro: height 3851 feet or 1174 metres. **81 F5** NN4324.
Ben More Assynt *High.* ***Mountain***, in Sutherland district 5m/7km E of Inchnadamph at head of Loch Assynt. Munro: height 3273 feet or 998 metres. **103 F6** NC3120.
Ben na Hoe *W.Isles* ***Hill***, 7m/11km E of Rubha Ardvule, on South Uist. Height 843 feet or 257 metres. **84 D2** NF8128.
Ben Nevis *High.* ***Mountain***, in Lochaber district 4m/7km E of Fort William. Highest mountain in Britain. Munro: height 4408 feet or 1344 metres. **87 H7** NN1671.
Ben Oss *Stir.* ***Mountain***, 4m/7km SW of Tyndrum. Munro: height 3372 feet or 1028 metres. **80 D5** NN2825.
Ben Raah *W.Isles* ***Hill***, highest point on Tarasaigh, off the coast of South Harris. Height 876 feet or 267 metres. **100 C7** NB0301.
Ben Reoch *Arg. & B.* ***Mountain***, on W side of Loch Lomond, 2m/3km SW of Tarbet. Height 2168 feet or 661 metres. **80 E7** NN3002.
Ben Rhydding (Formerly known as Wheatley.) *W.Yorks.* ***Suburb***, E district of Ilkley. SE1347.
Ben Rinnes *Moray* ***Mountain***, 5m/8km SW of Dufftown. Height 2755 feet or 840 metres. Distillery to N at foot of mountain. **89 K1** NJ2535.
Ben Sca *High.* ***Hill***, 1km NE of Ben Aketil, Skye. Height 938 feet or 286 metres. **93 J7** NG3347.
Ben Scoravick *W.Isles* ***Hill***, highest point of Scalpay, 1km NE of Kennavay. Height 341 feet or 104 metres. **93 H2** NG2395.
Ben Screavie *High.* ***Mountain***, at N end of Loch More. Height 1089 feet or 332 metres. **103 F5** NC3039.
Ben Screel *High. Alternative name for Beinn Sgritheall, qv.*
Ben Scrien *W.Isles* ***Hill***, highest point on Eriskay, 1km SE of Haunn. Height 607 feet or 185 metres. **84 C3** NF7911.
Ben Sgeireach *High.* ***Mountain***, 2m/3km NE of Badintagairt, Glen Cassley. Height 1561 feet or 476 metres. **103 G7** NC4511.
Ben Shieldaig *High.* ***Inland physical feature***, mountain ridge in Ross and Cromarty district, rising to 516 metres, 1m/2km SE of Shieldaig and 5m/8km SW of Torridon. **94 E6** NG8353.
Ben Skriaig *High.* ***Mountain***, on Skye, 2m/3km S of Dunvegan Head. Height 1007 feet or 307 metres. **93 G6** NG1653.
Ben Stack *High.* ***Mountain***, rising steeply from SW shore of Loch Stack, Sutherland district. Height 2365 feet or 721 metres. **102 E4** NC2642.
Ben Stack *W.Isles* ***Hill***, on Eriskay, 2m/3km S of Haunn. Height 400 feet or 122 metres. **84 C4** NF7909.
Ben Starav *High.* ***Mountain***, 2m/3km S of foot of Glen Etive, on border of Argyll and Lochaber districts. Munro: height 3536 feet or 1078 metres. **80 C3** NN1242.
Ben Strome *High.* ***Mountain***, with summit 1m/2km NE of Kylestrome. Height 1397 feet or 426 metres. **102 E5** NC2436.
Ben Suardal *High.* ***Hill***, 2m/3km S of Broadford, Skye. Height 928 feet or 283 metres. **86 C2** NG6320.
Ben Tangaval *W.Isles* ***Mountain***, in SW part of Barra 2m/3km W of Castlebay. Height 1092 feet or 333 metres. **84 B5** NL6399.
Ben Tarbert *W.Isles* ***Hill***, 5m/9km SE of Hornish Point, South Uist. Height 551 feet or 168 metres. **84 D1** NF8039.
Ben Tee *High.* ***Mountain***, on Glengarry Forest, Lochaber district, 5m/8km SW of Invergarry. Height 2955 feet or 901 metres. **87 J5** NN2497.
Ben Tianavaig *High.* ***Mountain***, 3m/4km SE of Portree, Skye. Height 1355 feet or 413 metres. **94 B7** NG5140.
Ben Tirran *Angus* ***Mountain***, 3m/5km E of Clova. Height 2939 feet or 896 metres. **90 B7** NO3774.
Ben Uarie *High.* ***Mountain***, in Sutherland district, 4m/6km N of Lothbeg. Height 2043 feet or 623 metres. **104 E7** NC9216.
Ben Uigshader *High.* ***Hill***, 5m/8km S of Lyndale Point, Skye. Height 807 feet or 246 metres. **93 J7** NG3649.
Ben Vair *High. Anglicised form of Beinn a' Bheithir, qv.*
Ben Vane *Arg. & B.* ***Mountain***, 4m/6km NW of Arrochar. Munro: height 3004 feet or 916 metres. **80 D7** NN2709.
Ben Vannoch *P. & K. Anglicised form of Beinn Mhanach, qv.*
Ben Varren *N.Ayr. Anglicised form of Beinn Bharrain, qv.*
Ben Venue *Stir.* ***Mountain***, 4m/7km NW of Aberfoyle. Height 2385 feet or 727 metres. **81 F7** NN4706.
Ben Vorlich *Arg. & B.* ***Mountain***, 3m/4km SW of Ardlui at head of Loch Lomond. Munro: height 3093 feet or 943 metres. **80 D6** NN2912.
Ben Vorlich *P. & K.* ***Mountain***, 4m/6km SE of Lochearnhead. Munro: height 3231 feet or 985 metres. **81 H6** NN6218.
Ben Vrackie *N.Ayr. Anglicised form of Beinn Bhreac, qv.*
Ben Vrackie (Gaelic form: Beinn Bhreac.) *P. & K.* ***Mountain***, 3m/5km N of Pitlochry. Height 2758 feet or 841 metres. **82 A1** NN9563.
Ben Vrottan *Aber. Anglicised form of Beinn Bhrotain, qv.*
Ben Vuirich *P. & K.* ***Mountain***, 8m/13km NE of Blair Atholl. Height 2959 feet or 902 metres. NN9970.
Ben Wyvis *High.* ***Mountain***, in Ross and Cromarty district 8m/13km NW of Dingwall. Summit is Glas Leathad Mòr. Height 3431 feet or 1046 metres. **96 B5** NH4668.
Ben-y-Gloe *P. & K. Alternative name for Beinn a' Ghlo, qv.*
Benachally *P. & K.* ***Mountain***, to SW of Loch Benachally, in Forest of Clunie. Height 1594 feet or 486 metres. **82 B3** NO0648.
Benacre *Suff.* ***Hamlet***, 5m/8km N of Southwold. **45 K7** TM5184.
Benanchie *Aber. See Bennachie.*
Benaquhallie *Aber.* ***Mountain***, on Corrennie Moor, 3m/5km NE of Lumphanan. Height 1620 feet or 494 metres. **90 E4** NJ6008.
Benarty Hill *Fife* ***Mountain***, to S of Loch Leven, 1m/2km W of Benarty. Height 1168 feet or 356 metres. **75 K1** NT1597.
Benbecula (Gaelic form: Beinn na Faoghla.) *W.Isles* ***Island***, low-lying island, 6m/10km by 5m/8km in size, between North and South Uist, containing innumerable lochs. Sand dunes on W coast; many islets off E coast. Airfield to N of Balivanich at NW corner of island. Road causeways to both North and South Uist. **92 D6** NF8050.
Benbecula (Baile a' Mhanaich) Aerodrome *W.Isles* ***Airport/airfield***, local airport NE of Balivanich, at N end of Benbecula. **92 C6** NF7956.
Benbeoch *E.Ayr.* ***Mountain***, 2m/3km NW of Dalmellington. Height 1522 feet or 464 metres. **67 J3** NS4908.
Benbrack *E.Ayr.* ***Mountain***, 4m/7km SE of Dalmellington to E of Carsphain Forest. Height 1469 feet or 448 metres. **67 K3** NS5201.
Benbuie *D. & G.* ***Settlement***, 6m/9km NW of Moniaive. **68 C4** NX7196.
Benchill *Gt.Man.* ***Suburb***, of Manchester, 1m/2km W of Gatley. SJ8288.
Bendcallt *High.* ***Mountain***, in Ross and Cromarty district, 5m/7km NW of Evanton. Height 1850 feet or 564 metres. **96 C4** NH5570.
Benderloch *Arg. & B.* ***Locality***, in Argyll, lying between Loch Creran and Loch Etive. **80 A4** NM9338.
Benderloch *Arg. & B.* ***Village***, on Ardmucknish Bay, Benderloch peninsula, 3m/4km N of Connel, Argyll. **80 A4** NM9038.
Bendish *Herts.* ***Hamlet***, 5m/8km E of Luton. **32 E6** TL1621.
Benenden *Kent* ***Village***, 3m/5km SE of Cranbrook. Girls' boarding school. Roman ford to S. **14 D4** TQ8032.
Beneraird ***Mountain***, to W of Arecleoch Forest, on border of Ayrshire and Dumfries & Galloway, 4m/6km SE of Ballantrae. Height 1440 feet or 439 metres. **64 B3** NX1378.
Benfield *D. & G.* ***Settlement***, 2m/4km SW of Newton Stewart. **64 D4** NX3763.
Benfieldside *Dur.* ***Suburb***, to NW of Consett. NZ0952.
Bengairn *D. & G.* ***Mountain***, 5m/8km S of Castle Douglas. Height 1282 feet or 391 metres. **65 H5** NX7754.
Bengate *Norf.* ***Settlement***, 1m/2km N of Worstead. **45 H3** TG3027.
Bengeo *Herts.* ***Suburb***, N district of Hertford. **33 G7** TL3213.
Bengeworth *Worcs.* ***Suburb***, E district of Evesham. SP0443.
Benhall *Glos.* ***Suburb***, W district of Cheltenham. SO9221.
Benhall *Suff.* ***Settlement***, 1m/2km SW of Saxmundham. TM3761.
Benhall Green *Suff.* ***Village***, 1m/2km S of Saxmundham. TM3861.
Benhall Street *Suff.* ***Hamlet***, 1km N of Stratford St. Andrew. TM3561.
Benhilton *Gt.Lon.* ***Suburb***, in borough of Sutton, to N of Sutton town centre. TQ2565.
Benholm *Aber.* ***Hamlet***, near E coast, 3m/4km SE of Inverbervie. **83 K1** NO8069.
Beningbrough *N.Yorks.* ***Hamlet***, 6m/9km NW of York. **58 B4** SE5257.
Beningbrough Hall *N.Yorks.* ***Historic house***, built by John Bourchier in 1716 and set in large park to NW of Beningbrough, 8m/13km NW of York. Owned by National Trust. **58 B4** SE5257.
Benington *Herts.* ***Village***, 4m/6km E of Stevenage. **33 F6** TL2923.
Benington *Lincs.* ***Village***, 5m/8km E of Boston. **43 G1** TF3946.
Benington Lordship *Herts.* ***Garden***, hilltop garden to W of Benington, including ruins, Queen Anne manor and medieval barns. **33 F6** TL2923.
Benington Sea End *Lincs.* ***Hamlet***, 1km SE of Benington. **43 H1** TF4046.
Benlister Glen *N.Ayr.* ***Valley***, on Arran, carrying Benlister Burn. **73 H7** NS0230.
Benllech *I.o.A.* Population: 1858. ***Small town***, coastal resort on E side of Anglesey, 8m/13km SE of Amlwch. **46 D4** SH5182.
Benmore *Arg. & B.* ***Settlement***, at confluence of Rivers Massan and Eachaig, 2m/3km NW of Orchard. **73 K2** NS1385.
Benmore *Stir.* ***Settlement***, on W side of Ben More, 2m/3km E of Crianlarich. **81 F5** NN4125.
Benmore Forest *High.* ***Open space***, deer forest in Sutherland district to S of Ben More Assynt. **103 F7** NC3115.
Bennachie (Benanchie). *Aber.* ***Large natural feature***, upland area surrounded by Bennachie Forest, 7m/11km W of Inverurie. **90 E2** NJ6622.
Bennacott *Cornw.* ***Hamlet***, 5m/8km NW of Launceston. **4 C1** SX2992.
Bennan *D. & G.* ***Mountain***, 1m/2km NE of Clatteringshaws Loch and 4m/7km W of New Galloway. Height 1250 feet or 381 metres. **65 F3** NX5679.
Bennan *D. & G.* ***Mountain***, rising to over 350 metres, 3m/4km N of Moniaive. **68 C4** NX7994.
Bennan *D. & G.* ***Settlement***, on W side of Loch Ken, 4m/6km SE of New Galloway. **65 G3** NX6571.
Bennan Head *N.Ayr.* ***Coastal feature***, headland on S coast of Arran, 7m/11km S of Lamlash. **66 D2** NR9920.
Bennan Loch *E.Renf.* ***Lake/loch***, and reservoir 4m/6km W of Eaglesham. **74 D5** NS5250.
Bennane Head *S.Ayr.* ***Coastal feature***, headland at N end of Ballantrae Bay. **66 E5** NX0986.
Bennetland *E.Riding* ***Settlement***, adjoining to SW of Gilberdyke. SE8228.
Bennett End *Bucks.* ***Hamlet***, to S of Radnage, 2m/3km NE of Stokenchurch. SU7897.
Bennett Head *Cumb.* ***Settlement***, 2m/3km W of Pooley Bridge. NY4423.
Bennetts End *Herts.* ***Suburb***, to SE of Hemel Hempstead town centre. TL0605.
Benniworth *Lincs.* ***Village***, 5m/9km NE of Wragby. Belmont Television Transmitter to NE. **53 F4** TF2081.
Benover *Kent* ***Village***, 1m/2km S of Yalding. **14 C3** TQ7048.
Benscravie *Angus* ***Mountain***, 2m/3km NE of Dykehead. Height 1404 feet or 428 metres. **82 E1** NO4062.
Benson *Oxon.* Population: 4796. ***Village***, 2m/3km N of Wallingford across River Thames. Airfield to E. **21 K2** SU6191.
Benston *Shet.* ***Hamlet***, in South Nesting, Mainland, 2m/3km W of Moul of Eswick. HU4653.
Bent Gate *Lancs.* ***Suburb***, 1m/2km S of Haslingden. SD7921.
Bent Lanes *Gt.Man.* ***Locality***, 1m/2km NW of Urmston. SJ7596.
Bentfield Bury *Essex* ***Settlement***, adjacent to Bentfield Green. TL4925.
Bentfield Green *Essex* ***Locality***, to NW of Stansted Mountfitchet, 3m/5km N of Bishop's Stortford. TL5025.
Benthall *Northumb.* ***Settlement***, at N end of Beadnell Bay, 1km SE of Beadnell. **71 H1** NU2328.
Benthall *Shrop.* ***Hamlet***, 1m/2km SW of Ironbridge. **39 F5** SJ6602.
Benthall Hall *Shrop.* ***Historic house***, built in 16c (National Trust) 1km NW of Benthall. **39 F5** SJ6502.
Bentham *Glos.* ***Hamlet***, 4m/7km SW of Cheltenham. **29 J7** SO9116.
Benthoul *Aberdeen* ***Settlement***, 3m/5km NW of Peterculter. **91 G4** NJ8003.
Bentilee *Stoke* ***Suburb***, 3m/4km E of Stoke-on-Trent city centre. SJ9146.
Bentlawn *Shrop.* ***Hamlet***, 1km SW of Hope. SJ3301.
Bentley *E.Riding* ***Hamlet***, 3m/4km S of Beverley. **59 G6** TA0235.
Bentley *Essex* ***Village***, 3m/4km NW of Brentwood. TQ5696.
Bentley *Hants.* ***Village***, 4m/6km SW of Farnham. Site of Roman building 1m/2km NW. **22 A7** SU7844.
Bentley *S.Yorks.* Population: 32,675. ***Suburb***, adjoining to N of Doncaster. **51 H2** SE5605.
Bentley *Suff.* ***Village***, 5m/8km SW of Ipswich. **35 F5** TM1138.
Bentley *Warks.* ***Hamlet***, 2m/4km SW of Atherstone. **40 E6** SP2895.
Bentley *W.Mid.* ***Suburb***, W district of Walsall. SO9898.
Bentley *W.Yorks.* ***Suburb***, 2m/3km N of Leeds city centre. SE2836.
Bentley Heath *Herts.* ***Hamlet***, 1m/2km S of Potters Bar. TQ2499.
Bentley Heath *W.Mid.* ***Suburb***, 2m/4km S of Solihull town centre. **30 C1** SP1676.

Bentley Rise *S.Yorks.* ***Suburb***, 1m/2km NW of Doncaster town centre. SE5604.

Bentley Wildfowl Park and Motor Museum *E.Suss.* ***Other feature of interest***, 3m/5km S of Uckfield, including a variety of birds, vintage vehicles, a house and an educational centre. **13 H5** TQ4815.

Benton *Devon* ***Hamlet***, 1m/2km SE of Bratton Fleming. **6 E2** SS6536.

Benton Square *T. & W.* ***Locality***, 2m/3km NE of Longbenton. **71 J6** NZ2970.

Bentpath *D. & G.* ***Village***, on River Esk, 5m/8km NW of Langholm. **69 J4** NY3190.

Bents Green *S.Yorks.* ***Suburb***, 3m/5km SW of Sheffield city centre. SK3183.

Bentwaters Airfield *Suff. See Wantisden.*

Bentworth *Hants.* ***Village***, 3m/5km W of Alton. **21 K7** SU6640.

Benvane *Stir.* ***Mountain***, 4m/7km S of Balquhidder. Height 2690 feet or 820 metres. **81 G6** NN5313.

Benvie *Dundee* ***Hamlet***, 2m/3km NE of Longforgan. **82 E4** NO3231.

Benville Lane *Dorset* ***Hamlet***, 2m/4km W of Evershot. **8 E4** ST5403.

Benwell *T. & W.* ***Suburb***, 2m/3km W of Newcastle upon Tyne city centre. Roman remains include cavalry fort of Condercum, with visible Temple of Atenciticus and stone-built causeway (both English Heritage). NZ2164.

Benwell Roman Fort (Condercum) *T. & W.* ***Historic/prehistoric site***, 2m/3km W of Newcastle upon Tyne city centre. Cavalry fort, now mainly covered by houses. Two notable extant features include Temple of Atenciticus and stone-built causeway or Vallum Crossing (both English Heritage), providing access to fort. **71 H7** NZ2164.

Benwick *Cambs.* ***Village***, on River Nene (old course), 4m/7km NW of Chatteris. **43 G7** TL3490.

Beoch Burn *D. & G.* ***River***, rising on E slopes of Beoch Hill and running SW into Loch Ryan near Leffnoll Point, 3m/4km NE of Stranraer. **64 A4** NX0764.

Beoley *Worcs.* ***Village***, 2m/3km NE of Redditch. **30 B2** SP0669.

Beoraidbeg *High.* ***Hamlet***, in Lochaber district, 2m/3km S of Mallaig. NM6793.

Bepton *W.Suss.* ***Village***, at foot of South Downs, 3m/4km SW of Midhurst. **12 B5** SU8618.

Berden *Essex* ***Village***, 5m/9km N of Bishop's Stortford. **33 H6** TL4629.

Bere Alston *Devon* Population: 2362. ***Small town***, in market-gardening area between Rivers Tamar and Tavy, 5m/8km SW of Tavistock. **4 E4** SX4466.

Bere Ferrers *Devon* ***Village***, beside River Tavy, 7m/11km S of Tavistock. Abandoned silver mines towards River Tamar. **4 E4** SX4563.

Bere Regis *Dorset* Population: 1767. ***Village***, 7m/11km NW of Wareham. **9 H5** SY8494.

Berea *Pembs.* ***Settlement***, 4m/6km NE of St. David's. **16 A2** SM7929.

Berepper *Cornw.* ***Hamlet***, 3m/5km S of Helston. **2 D6** SW6522.

Bergh Apton *Norf.* ***Village***, 7m/11km SE of Norwich. **45 H5** TG3001.

Berhill *Som.* ***Hamlet***, 3m/4km W of Street. ST4436.

Berinsfield *Oxon.* Population: 2933. ***Village***, 5m/8km NW of Wallingford. **21 J2** SU5796.

Berkeley *Glos.* ***Village***, 5m/8km W of Dursley. Nuclear power station beside River Severn estuary to W. **19 K2** ST6899.

Berkeley Castle *Glos.* ***Castle***, 12c castle, home of Berkeleys, 5m/8km W of Dursley. Contains rare paintings and is surrounded by Elizabethan gardens with lily ponds, lawns and bowling green. Scene of Edward II's murder in 1327. **19 K2** ST6899.

Berkhamsted *Herts.* Population: 18,044. ***Town***, in narrow gap of Chiltern Hills, 25m/40km NW of London. Remains of motte and bailey castle (English Heritage), with keep of later date. **22 C1** SP9907.

Berkhamsted Castle *Herts.* ***Castle***, on N bank of River Bulbourne in NE Berkhamsted. Ruins of 11c motte and bailey castle (English Heritage). **22 C1** SP9908.

Berkley *Som.* ***Village***, 3m/4km E of Frome. **20 B7** ST8149.

Berkley Marsh *Som.* ***Hamlet***, to W of Berkley, 2m/3km NE of Frome. ST8049.

Berkswell *W.Mid.* ***Village***, 6m/9km W of Coventry. **30 D1** SP2479.

Bermondsey *Gt.Lon.* ***Suburb***, S of River Thames, in vicinity of Tower Bridge, and in borough of Southwark. **23 G4** TQ3379.

Bernard Wharf *Lancs.* ***Coastal feature***, sandbank 3m/4km N of Fleetwood on E side of River Wyre channel. **55 G4** SD3451.

Bernard's Heath *Herts.* ***Suburb***, to NE of St. Albans city centre. TL1508.

Bernera *Arg. & B.* ***Island***, off W coast of Lismore, in Loch Linnhe. **79 J4** NM7939.

Bernera *High.* ***Settlement***, in Skye and Lochalsh district, 1km N of Glenelg. **86 E2** NG8020.

Bernera Barracks *High.* ***Other feature of interest***, ruins of 18c English garrison to N of Glenelg. **86 E3** NG8119.

Berneray *W.Isles Anglicised form of Bearnaraigh, qv.*

Berneray (Gaelic form: Eilean Bhearnaraigh.) *W.Isles* ***Island***, on W side of Sound of Harris, lying off N end of North Uist. Nearly 4m/6km NE to SW and 2m/3km across at widest point. **92 E3** NF9181.

Berner's Heath *Suff.* ***Open space***, heath, 6m/10km SW of Thetford. **34 B1** TL7976.

Berners Roding *Essex* ***Hamlet***, 2m/4km S of Leaden Roding. **24 C1** TL6009.

Berney Arms Mill *Norf.* ***Other feature of interest***, 19c marsh windmill (English Heritage), still in working order and tallest in this area at 70 feet or 21 metres high, 3m/5km NE of Reedham across Reedham Marshes. **45 J5** TG4604.

Bernice *Arg. & B.* ***Settlement***, at foot of Bernice Glen on W shore of Loch Eck, 4m/6km S of Invernoaden. **73 K1** NS1391.

Bernisdale *High.* ***Village***, on W side of head of Loch Snizort Beag, Skye, 7m/11km NW of Portree. **93 K6** NG4050.

Berri Court *W.Suss.* ***Garden***, eleven linked small gardens surrounding Queen Anne house, 5m/8km SW of Arundel. **12 C6** SU9702.

Berrick Prior *Oxon.* ***Hamlet***, 3m/5km N of Wallingford. SU6294.

Berrick Salome *Oxon.* ***Village***, 3m/5km N of Wallingford. **21 K2** SU6293.

Berriedale *High.* ***Village***, near E coast of Caithness district, 8m/12km NE of Helmsdale. Situated at confluence of Langwell Water and Berriedale Water. **105 G6** ND1122.

Berriedale Water *High.* ***River***, rising on Knockfin Heights and flowing E, S, then SE to join Langwell Water at Berriedale before combined river flows out to North Sea. **105 F6** ND1122.

Berrier *Cumb.* ***Locality***, 2m/3km NW of Penruddock. NY4029.

Berrier Hill *Cumb.* ***Mountain***, at S end of Greystoke Forest, 3m/4km W of Greystoke. Height 1171 feet or 357 metres. **60 F3** NY4030.

Berriew *Powys Alternative name for Aberriw, qv.*

Berrington *Northumb.* ***Settlement***, 2m/4km N of Lowick. **77 J6** NU0043.

Berrington *Shrop.* ***Hamlet***, 4m/7km SE of Shrewsbury. Cantlop Bridge (English Heritage), single-span cast-iron road bridge designed by Thomas Telford, 1m/2km SW. **38 E5** SJ5206.

Berrington *Worcs.* ***Hamlet***, 1m/2km W of Tenbury Wells. SO5767.

Berrington Green *Worcs.* ***Hamlet***, 1km SE of Berrington. SO5766.

Berrington Hall *Here.* ***Historic house***, late 18c neo-classical house designed by Henry Holland (National Trust) in grounds laid out by 'Capability' Brown, 3m/5km N of Leominster. **28 E2** SO5063.

Berriowbridge *Cornw.* ***Hamlet***, on River Lynher, 7m/11km SW of Launceston. SX2775.

Berrow *Som.* ***Village***, 1m/2km N of Burnham-on-Sea. **19 F6** ST2952.

Berrow *Worcs.* ***Hamlet***, 6m/10km W of Tewkesbury. SO7934.

Berrow Flats *Som.* ***Coastal feature***, mudflats along coast from Brean Down, S to Berrow. **19 F6** ST2853.

Berrow Green *Worcs.* ***Hamlet***, 7m/11km W of Worcester. **29 G3** SO7458.

Berry Brow *W.Yorks.* ***Suburb***, 1m/2km SW of Huddersfield town centre, on E side of River Holme. SE1313.

Berry Cross *Devon* ***Hamlet***, 3m/5km SW of Great Torrington. SS4714.

Berry Down Cross *Devon* ***Hamlet***, 4m/7km SE of Ilfracombe. **6 D1** SS5743.

Berry Head *Torbay* ***Coastal feature***, headland at S end of Tor Bay to E of Brixham. **5 K5** SX9456.

Berry Head Country Park *Torbay* ***Leisure/recreation***, on headland to NE of Brixham offering scenic views, a coastal path and examples of rare flora and fauna. **5 K5** SX9456.

Berry Hill *Bucks.* ***Hamlet***, 1m/2km E of Maidenhead. SU9081.

Berry Hill *Glos.* ***Village***, 1m/2km N of Coleford. **28 E7** SO5712.

Berry Hill *Pembs.* ***Hamlet***, 1m/2km NE of Newport. **26 A4** SN0640.

Berry Pomeroy *Devon* ***Village***, 2m/3km E of Totnes. 12c Berry Pomeroy Castle (English Heritage). **5 J4** SX8261.

Berry Pomeroy Castle *Devon* ***Castle***, fortified 12c house (English Heritage) with 16c Tudor mansion built inside it by Edward VI, 3m/4km NE of Totnes. **5 J4** SX8362.

Berry Top *Aber.* ***Hill***, 4m/6km W of Portlethen. Height 558 feet or 170 metres. **91 G5** NO8696.

Berryfell Hill *Sc.Bord.* ***Mountain***, 5m/8km SE of Hawick. Height 1289 feet or 393 metres. **70 A3** NT5307.

Berryhillock *Moray* ***Hamlet***, near N coast, 4m/6km S of Cullen. **98 D4** NJ5060.

Berrylands *Gt.Lon.* ***Suburb***, in borough of Kingston upon Thames, to E of Surbiton. TQ1967.

Berryl's Point *Cornw.* ***Coastal feature***, headland at N end of Beacon Cove, 1km SW of Trenance. **3 F2** SW8467.

Berrynarbor *Devon* ***Village***, 3m/5km E of Ilfracombe. **6 D1** SS5646.

Berry's Green *Gt.Lon.* ***Settlement***, in borough of Bromley, 1m/2km E of Biggin Hill. TQ4359.

Bers *Wrex. Welsh form of Bersham, qv.*

Bersham (Bers). *Wrex.* ***Village***, 2m/3km W of Wrexham. **38 C1** SJ3049.

Berst Ness *Ork.* ***Coastal feature***, headland on S coast of Westray. **106 D3** HY4441.

Berstane *Ork.* ***Settlement***, on Mainland, SE of Kirkwall and close to Bay of Berstane. **107 D6** HY4610.

Berth-ddu *Flints.* ***Settlement***, 3m/4km W of Northop. SJ2069.

Berthengam *Flints.* ***Hamlet***, 4m/6km SE of Prestatyn. SJ1179.

Berthlŵyd *Swan.* ***Settlement***, 1m/2km W of Gowerton. SS5696.

Bervie Bay *Aber.* ***Bay***, on E side of Inverbervie. **91 G7** NO8372.

Bervie Water *Aber.* ***River***, rising in Drumtochty Forest and running SE to E coast at Bervie Bay, on E side of Inverbervie. **91 F7** NO8372.

Berwick *E.Suss.* ***Village***, below South Downs, 1m/2km N of Alfriston. **13 J6** TQ5105.

Berwick Bassett *Wilts.* ***Village***, 2m/3km N of Avebury. **20 D4** SU0973.

Berwick Hill *Northumb.* ***Settlement***, 2m/3km NE of Ponteland. **71 G6** NZ1775.

Berwick Hills *Middbro.* ***Suburb***, 2m/3km SE of Middlesbrough town centre. NZ5118.

Berwick St. James *Wilts.* ***Village***, on River Till, 5m/8km N of Wilton. **10 B1** SU0739.

Berwick St. John *Wilts.* ***Village***, 6m/10km E of Shaftesbury. **9 J2** ST9422.

Berwick St. Leonard *Wilts.* ***Village***, 8m/12km NE of Shaftesbury. **9 J1** ST9233.

Berwick-upon-Tweed *Northumb.* Population: 13,544. ***Town***, border town at mouth of River Tweed, 58m/93km NW of Newcastle upon Tyne and 47m/76km SE of Edinburgh. Medieval town walls (English Heritage); remains of Norman castle (English Heritage); 18c Ravensdowne Barracks and Georgian Guard House (both English Heritage) and town hall. **77 H5** NT9953.

Berwick-upon-Tweed Castle *Northumb.* ***Castle***, remains of 12c castle (English Heritage) to W of Berwick-upon-Tweed on N bank of River Tweed. **77 H5** NU0244.

Berwyn (Y Berwyn). ***Large natural feature***, mountain range running SW from Llangollen. Highest peak is Moel Sych. Its twin peak Cadair Berwyn is fractionally lower. **37 K2** SJ0734.

Bescar *Lancs.* ***Village***, 1km E of Scarisbrick. **48 C1** SD3913.

Bescot *W.Mid.* ***Suburb***, in S part of Walsall. SP0096.

Besford *Shrop.* ***Settlement***, 2m/3km N of Shawbury. **38 E3** SJ5524.

Besford *Worcs.* ***Village***, 2m/4km W of Pershore. **29 J4** SO9144.

Besom Hill *Gt.Man.* ***Locality***, 1km NE of Sholver. SD9508.

Bessacarr *S.Yorks.* Population: 19,907. ***Suburb***, 3m/4km SE of Doncaster town centre. **51 J2** SE6001.

Bessels Green *Kent* ***Locality***, to W of Sevenoaks. TQ5055.

Bessels Leigh *Oxon.* ***Hamlet***, 4m/6km NW of Abingdon. **21 H1** SP4501.

Besses o' th' Barn *Gt.Man.* ***Suburb***, 1m/2km SE of Whitefield. SD8105.

Bessingby *E.Riding* ***Village***, 1m/2km SW of Bridlington town centre. **59 H3** TA1565.

Bessingham *Norf.* ***Village***, 4m/7km S of Sheringham. **45 F2** TG1636.

Best Beech Hill *E.Suss.* ***Hamlet***, 2m/3km W of Wadhurst. **13 K3** TQ6131.

Besthorpe *Norf.* ***Village***, 1m/2km E of Attleborough. **44 E6** TM0695.

Besthorpe *Notts.* ***Village***, 7m/12km N of Newark-on-Trent. **52 B6** SK8264.

Bestwood *Notts.* ***Suburb***, 3m/5km N of Nottingham. SK5645.

Bestwood *Notts.* ***Village***, 5m/8km N of Nottingham. SK5547.

Bestwood Lodge Country Park *Notts.* ***Leisure/recreation***, country park within Sherwood Forest to SW of Bestwood, 5m/8km N of Nottingham. Once hunting park of Duke of St. Albans. Woodland, grassland and adventure playground. **41 H1** SK5647.

Beswick *E.Riding* ***Village***, 5m/9km N of Beverley. **59 G5** TA0148.

Beswick *Gt.Man.* ***Suburb***, 1m/2km E of Manchester city centre. SJ8697.

Betchton Heath *Ches.* ***Locality***, 1m/2km E of Sandbach. SJ7760.

Betchworth *Surr.* ***Village***, 3m/5km E of Dorking. **23 F6** TQ2149.

Bethania *Cere.* ***Hamlet***, 2m/3km E of Cross Inn. **26 E2** SN5763.

Bethania *Gwyn.* ***Locality***, adjoining to S of Blaenau Ffestiniog. **37 G1** SH7045.

Bethel *Gwyn.* ***Hamlet***, at road junction, 4m/7km NE of Bala. **37 J1** SH9839.

Bethel *Gwyn.* ***Village***, 3m/5km NE of Caernarfon. **46 D6** SH5265.

Bethel *I.o.A.* ***Hamlet***, on Anglesey, 5m/8km SW of Llangefni. **46 B5** SH3970.

Bethersden *Kent* ***Village***, 6m/9km W of Ashford. **14 E3** TQ9240.

Bethesda *Gwyn.* Population: 3558. ***Small town***, 5m/7km SE of Bangor. Development of town based on Penrhyn Slate Quarry, formerly world's largest. **46 E6** SH6266.

Bethesda *Pembs.* ***Hamlet***, 2m/4km NW of Narberth. **16 D3** SN0917.

Bethlehem *Carmar.* ***Hamlet***, 3m/4km SW of Llangadog. **17 K2** SN6825.

Bethnal Green *Gt.Lon.* ***Suburb***, in borough of Tower Hamlets, 2m/3km NE of London Bridge. **23 G3** TQ3482.

Bethnal Green Museum of Childhood *Gt.Lon.* ***Other feature of interest***, toy museum in borough of Tower Hamlets, administered by Victoria and Albert Museum, includes a fine display of dolls houses. TQ3582.

Betley *Staffs.* ***Village***, 6m/10km W of Newcastle-under-Lyme. **39 G1** SJ7548.

Betley Common *Staffs.* ***Hamlet***, to W of Betley. SJ7448.

Betsham *Kent* ***Village***, 2m/3km S of Swanscombe. **24 C4** TQ6071.

Betteshanger *Kent* ***Hamlet***, 4m/7km W of Deal. **15 J2** TR3152.

Bettiscombe *Dorset* ***Village***, 4m/6km SW of Broadwindsor. **8 C5** ST3800.

Bettisfield *Wrex.* ***Village***, on Shropshire Union Canal, 4m/6km E of Ellesmere. **38 D2** SJ4535.

Betton *Shrop.* ***Hamlet***, 2m/3km NE of Market Drayton. **39 F2** SJ6936.

Betton *Shrop.* ***Settlement***, 4m/6km SW of Minsterley. **38 C5** SJ3102.

Betton Abbots *Shrop.* ***Settlement***, 3m/5km SE of Shrewsbury. SJ5107.

Betton Alkmere *Shrop.* ***Settlement***, 2m/4km SE of Shrewsbury. SJ5009.

Betton Strange *Shrop.* ***Hamlet***, 2m/4km SE of Shrewsbury. SJ5009.

Bettws (Betws). *Newport* Population: 2860. ***Village***, 2m/3km N of Newport. **19 F2** ST2990.

Bettws Bledrws (Betws Bledrws). *Cere.* ***Hamlet***, 3m/4km NE of Lampeter. **26 E3** SN5952.

Bettws Cedewain *Powys* ***Village***, on Bechan Brook, 4m/6km N of Newtown. Ruins of Dolforwyn Castle (Cadw) 2m/3km SE. **38 A6** SO1296.
Bettws Evan *Cere. English form of Betws Ifan, qv.*
Bettws Gwerfil Goch *Denb.* ***Hamlet***, 4m/6km NW of Corwen. **37 K1** SJ0346.
Bettws Newydd *Mon.* ***Hamlet***, 3m/5km W of Raglan. **19 G1** SO3605.
Bettws-y-crwyn *Shrop.* ***Hamlet***, 6m/10km W of Clun. **38 B7** SO2081.
Bettyhill *High.* ***Village***, near N coast of Caithness district, 9m/15km SW of Strathy Point. **104 C2** NC7061.
Betws *Bridgend* ***Village***, 4m/7km N of Bridgend. **18 C3** SS8986.
Betws *Carmar.* ***Locality***, 1km SE of Ammanford. **17 K3** SN6311.
Betws *Newport Welsh form of Bettws, qv.*
Betws Bledrws *Cere. Welsh form of Bettws Bledrws, qv.*
Betws Disserth *Powys* ***Settlement***, 2m/3km N of Hundred House. **28 A3** SO1156.
Betws Garmon *Gwyn.* ***Hamlet***, 5m/8km SE of Caernarfon. **46 D7** SH5456.
Betws Ifan (Bettws Evan). *Cere.* ***Hamlet***, 4m/7km N of Newcastle Emlyn. **26 C4** SN3047.
Betws-y-coed *Conwy* ***Village***, and tourist centre among woods and streams, 14m/23km S of Colwyn Bay. **47 F7** SH7956.
Betws-yn-Rhos *Conwy* ***Village***, 4m/6km SW of Abergele. **47 H5** SH9073.
Beul an Toim *W.Isles* ***Sea feature***, channel between Baleshare and N coast of Benbecula. NF7857.
Beulah *Cere.* ***Hamlet***, 4m/6km N of Newcastle Emlyn. **26 B4** SN2846.
Beulah *Powys* ***Village***, 4m/6km NE of Llanwrtyd Wells. **27 J3** SN9251.
Beult *Kent* ***River***, rising SW of Ashford and flowing W into River Medway at Yalding. **14 C3** TQ6850.
Bevendean *B. & H.* ***Suburb***, 2m/3km NE of Brighton town centre. **13 G6** TQ3406.
Bevercotes *Notts.* ***Hamlet***, 3m/4km NW of Tuxford. **51 K5** SK6972.
Beverley *E.Riding* Population: 23,632. ***Town***, attractive market town, 8m/12km N of Kingston upon Hull. Minster, Early English to Perpendicular. **59 G6** TA0339.
Beverley Minster *E.Riding* ***Ecclesiastical building***, 7m/11km NW of Kingston upon Hull, in Beverley town centre. Equal in size and architecture to a cathedral, and particularly noted for its Perpendicular West Front, built c. 1400. Was place of pilgrimage for many years for believers in miracles of St. John of Beverley. **59 G6** TA0437.
Beverstone *Glos.* ***Village***, 2m/3km W of Tetbury. **20 B2** ST8693.
Bevington *Glos.* ***Settlement***, 3m/4km SW of Berkeley. **19 K2** ST6597.
Bewaldeth *Cumb.* ***Hamlet***, 3m/5km SE of Bothel. Site of Roman fort 1m/2km N. **60 D3** NY2034.
Bewbush *W.Suss.* ***Suburb***, SW district of Crawley. TQ2535.
Bewcastle *Cumb.* ***Hamlet***, 9m/14km N of Brampton, on site of Roman fort. Saxon cross, headless, in churchyard. Remains of medieval castle. **70 A6** NY5674.
Bewcastle Fells *Cumb.* ***Forest/woodland***, on E side of Kershope Forest, 6m/10km SE of Newcastleton. **70 A5** NY5681.
Bewdley *Worcs.* Population: 9009. ***Small town***, mainly 17c and 18c, on River Severn, 3m/5km W of Kidderminster. Fine Georgian buildings. Birthplace of Stanley Baldwin. **29 G1** SO7875.
Bewdley Museum *Worcs.* ***Other feature of interest***, in centre of Bewdley, 3m/4km W of Kidderminster across River Severn. Local history museum with exhibits and demonstrations of crafts and industry. **29 G1** SO7875.
Bewell Head *Worcs.* ***Suburb***, in N part of Bromsgrove. SO9571.
Bewerley *N.Yorks.* ***Village***, on SW side of Pateley Bridge across River Nidd. **57 G3** SE1565.
Bewholme *E.Riding* ***Village***, 3m/5km NW of Hornsea. **59 H5** TA1650.
Bewick *Northumb.* ***Locality***, parish SE of Wooler, containing hamlets of Old and New Bewick. NU0621.
Bewick Moor *Northumb.* ***Open space***, moorland 2m/3km NE of New Bewick. **71 F1** NU0922.
Bewl Water ***Reservoir***, on border of East Sussex and Kent, 2m/3km S of Lamberhurst. **13 K3** TQ6833.
Bewley Common *Wilts.* ***Village***, 3m/5km S of Chippenham, at foot of Bowden Hill. Surrounding land is partly National Trust property. **20 C5** ST9268.
Bexhill *E.Suss.* Population: 38,905. ***Town***, seaside resort, 5m/8km W of Hastings. **14 C7** TQ7407.
Bexleyheath *Gt.Lon.* ***Suburb***, in borough of Bexley, 2m/3km SW of Erith and 12m/19km E of Charing Cross. **23 H4** TQ4875.
Bexleyhill *W.Suss.* ***Settlement***, 3m/5km NE of Midhurst. SU9125.
Bexton *Ches.* ***Locality***, 1m/2km S of Knutsford. Bexton Hall located here. SJ7476.
Bexwell *Norf.* ***Village***, 1m/2km E of Downham Market. **44 A5** TF6303.
Beyton *Suff.* ***Village***, 5m/8km E of Bury St. Edmunds. **34 D2** TL9362.
Beyton Green *Suff.* ***Village***, adjoins to N of Beyton. **34 D2** TL9363.
Bhalamus *W.Isles* ***Settlement***, on S coast of Isle of Lewis, 6m/9km S of head of Loch Shell. **100 E7** NB2901.
Bhaltos (Anglicised form: Valtos.) *W.Isles* ***Village***, on W shore of West Loch Roag, 3m/5km SE of Gallan Head. **100 C4** NB0936.
Bhatarsaidh *W.Isles Gaelic form of Vatarsay, qv.*
Bhatarsaigh *W.Isles Gaelic form of Vatersay (island), qv.*
Bhatarsaigh *W.Isles Gaelic form of Vatersay (settlement), qv.*
Bhatarsaigh Bay *W.Isles Gaelic form of Vatersay Bay, qv.*
Bhatasgeir *W.Isles Gaelic form of Vatisker, qv.*
Biallaid *High.* ***Settlement***, adjoining to W of Newtonmore across River Calder. **88 E5** NN7098.
Bibra *Cumb. See Newtown.*
Bibury *Glos.* ***Village***, on River Coln, 7m/11km NE of Cirencester. Well-known for its picturesque 17c cottages, Arlington Row. **20 E1** SP1106.
Bicester *Oxon.* Population: 22,128. ***Town***, old market town, 11m/18km NE of Oxford. **31 G6** SP5822.
Bickenhall *Som.* ***Village***, 5m/9km SE of Taunton. **8 B3** ST2818.
Bickenhill *W.Mid.* ***Village***, 3m/5km NE of Solihull. National Exhibition Centre, opened 1976. **40 D7** SP1882.
Bicker *Lincs.* ***Village***, 2m/3km NE of Donington. **43 F2** TF2237.
Bicker Bar *Lincs.* ***Settlement***, 1m/2km NE of Bicker. TF2338.
Bicker Friest *Lincs.* ***Settlement***, 1km SW of Bicker. TF2137.
Bicker Gauntlet *Lincs.* ***Hamlet***, 1m/2km NW of Bicker. TF2139.
Bicker Haven *Lincs.* ***Open space***, lowland containing small lake, between Sutterton to NE, and Gosberton to SW. **43 F2** TF2433.
Bickershaw *Gt.Man.* ***Village***, 3m/5km SE of Wigan town centre. SD6202.
Bickerstaffe *Lancs.* ***Village***, 2m/3km SW of Skelmersdale. **48 D2** SD4404.
Bickerton *Ches.* ***Hamlet***, 4m/6km NE of Malpas, on SE side of Bickerton Hill. **48 E7** SJ5052.
Bickerton *Devon* ***Hamlet***, 2m/3km NW of Start Point. SX8138.
Bickerton *N.Yorks.* ***Village***, 3m/5km NE of Wetherby. **57 K4** SE4550.
Bickerton *Northumb.* ***Settlement***, 4m/6km W of Rothbury. NT9900.
Bickerton Hill *Ches.* ***Hill***, rising to over 180 metres, adjacent to NW of Bickerton. Iron Age fort, Maiden Castle on hill. **48 D7** SJ5053.
Bickford *Staffs.* ***Hamlet***, 2m/4km W of Penkridge. **40 A4** SJ8814.
Bickham *Som.* ***Hamlet***, 3m/4km SW of Dunster. SS9541.
Bickham Bridge *Devon* ***Settlement***, on River Avon, 4m/6km SE of South Brent. **5 H5** SX7255.
Bickham House *Devon* ***Settlement***, 1m/2km S of Kennford. **7 H7** SX9184.
Bickington *Devon* ***Village***, 2m/3km W of Barnstaple. **6 D2** SS5332.
Bickington *Devon* ***Village***, 3m/5km NE of Ashburton. **5 H3** SX7972.
Bickleigh *Devon* ***Village***, with thatched cottages and bridge over River Exe, 4m/6km S of Tiverton. **7 H5** SS9407.
Bickleigh *Devon* ***Village***, 6m/9km NE of Plymouth. **5 F4** SX5262.
Bickleigh Bridge *Devon* ***Bridge***, rubble stone bridge, probably 14c, spanning River Exe at Bickleigh. SS9307.
Bickleigh Castle *Devon* ***Historic house***, to W of Bickleigh over River Exe. Dates from 11c, later famous as Royalist stronghold during Civil War. Includes moated garden. **7 H5** SS9306.
Bickleigh Vale *Devon* ***Valley***, to E of Bickleigh, wooded stretch of River Plym valley running down to Plym Forest. SX5261.
Bickleton *Devon* ***Hamlet***, 4m/6km SW of Barnstaple. **6 D2** SS5031.
Bickley *Gt.Lon.* ***Suburb***, in borough of Bromley, 1m/2km E of Bromley town centre. **23 H5** TQ4269.
Bickley *N.Yorks.* ***Locality***, 6m/10km W of Scalby. SE9191.
Bickley Moss *Ches.* ***Village***, 5m/8km N of Whitchurch. **38 E1** SJ5449.
Bickley Town *Ches.* ***Settlement***, 4m/7km N of Whitchurch. **38 E1** SJ5348.
Bickmarsh *Worcs.* ***Hamlet***, 6m/9km NE of Evesham. SP1049.
Bicknacre *Essex* Population: 2452. ***Village***, 5m/8km SW of Maldon. **24 D1** TL7802.
Bicknoller *Som.* ***Village***, at foot of Quantock Hills, 4m/6km SE of Watchet. **7 K2** ST1139.
Bicknor *Kent* ***Hamlet***, 4m/7km SW of Sittingbourne. **14 D2** TQ8658.
Bickton *Hants.* ***Village***, on River Avon, 1m/2km S of Fordingbridge. **10 C3** SU1412.
Bicton *Devon* ***Locality***, comprising Bicton House (now an agricultural college) and Bicton Park, 3m/5km N of Budleigh Salterton. SY0686.
Bicton *Here.* ***Settlement***, 4m/6km NW of Leominster. SO4663.
Bicton *Shrop.* ***Hamlet***, 1m/2km NW of Clun. **38 B7** SO2882.
Bicton *Shrop.* ***Village***, 3m/5km NW of Shrewsbury. **38 D4** SJ4415.
Bicton Heath *Shrop.* ***Suburb***, 3m/4km W of Shrewsbury town centre. **38 D4** SJ4513.
Bicton Park *Devon* ***Garden***, 60 acres of parkland surrounding 18c Bicton House, now agricultural institute, to N of Bicton. Includes James Countryside Collection, American and Italian gardens and Palm House. **7 J7** SY0785.
Bidborough *Kent* ***Village***, 3m/5km SW of Tonbridge. **23 J7** TQ5643.
Biddenden *Kent* ***Village***, 4m/6km S of Headcorn. **14 D4** TQ8538.
Biddenden Green *Kent* ***Settlement***, 4m/6km E of Headcorn. TQ8843.
Biddenham *Beds.* ***Suburb***, in loop of River Great Ouse, to W of Bedford. **32 D4** TL0250.
Biddestone *Wilts.* ***Village***, 4m/6km W of Chippenham. **20 B4** ST8673.
Biddick *T. & W.* ***Suburb***, to SE of Washington town centre. NZ3055.
Biddisham *Som.* ***Village***, 3m/5km W of Axbridge. **19 G6** ST3853.
Biddlesden *Bucks.* ***Hamlet***, 4m/6km NE of Brackley. **31 H4** SP6340.
Biddlestone *Northumb.* ***Settlement***, 3m/4km NE of Alwinton. **70 E3** NT9608.
Biddulph *Staffs.* Population: 16,725. ***Town***, 7m/12km N of Stoke-on-Trent. Biddulph Grange Garden (National Trust) to N. **49 H7** SJ8856.
Biddulph Grange Garden *Staffs.* ***Garden***, to N of Biddulph, Stoke-on-Trent. Unusual compartmentalised 19c garden (National Trust) designed by James Bateman. Features mini Great Wall of China, pinetum and fernery. **49 H6** SJ8959.
Biddulph Moor *Staffs.* ***Village***, 2m/3km E of Biddulph. **49 J7** SJ9058.
Bidean nam Bian *High.* ***Mountain***, in Lochaber district, S of Glen Coe. Munro: height 3772 feet or 1150 metres. **80 C2** NN1454.
Bideford *Devon* Population: 14,326. ***Town***, 36m/58km NW of Exeter. Small port with quay on River Torridge crossed by 15c bridge. **6 C3** SS4526.
Bideford Bay *Devon Alternative name for Barnstaple Bay, qv.*
Bidein a' Choire Sheasgaich *High.* ***Mountain***, peak on West Monar Forest on border of Ross and Cromarty and Skye and Lochalsh districts, 2m/3km W of W end of Loch Monar. Munro: height 3100 feet or 945 metres. **95 G7** NH0441.
Bidein a' Ghlas Thuill *High.* ***Mountain***, summit of An Teallach in Ross and Cromarty district, 7m/11km SW of Ullapool across Loch Broom. Munro: height 3483 feet or 1062 metres. **95 G3** NH0684.
Bidford-on-Avon *Warks.* Population: 3842. ***Village***, 7m/11km W of Stratford-upon-Avon. **30 B3** SP1051.
Bidhein Bad na h-Iolaire *High.* ***Mountain***, rising to over 520 metres, 2m/3km SE of Fort William. **87 H7** NN1070.
Bidlake *Devon* ***Hamlet***, 7m/11km SW of Okehampton. SX4988.
Bidno *Powys* ***River***, running SE through S part of Hafren Forest and into River Wye, 1m/2km W of Llangurig. **37 H7** SN8980.
Bidston *Mersey.* ***Suburb***, in NW corner of Birkenhead. **48 B3** SJ2890.
Bidwell *Beds.* ***Settlement***, 2m/3km N of Dunstable. TL0124.
Biel Water *E.Loth.* ***River***, rising in Lammermuir Hills and flowing NW to North Sea at Belhaven Bay, 1m/2km W of Dunbar. **76 E3** NT6578.
Bielby *E.Riding* ***Village***, 5m/9km W of Market Weighton. **58 D5** SE7843.
Bieldside *Aberdeen* ***Suburb***, 4m/7km SW of Aberdeen city centre. **91 G4** NJ8802.
Bierley *I.o.W.* ***Hamlet***, 1m/2km N of Niton. **11 G7** SZ5178.
Bierley *W.Yorks.* ***Suburb***, 2m/3km SE of Bradford city centre. **57 G6** SE1730.
Bierton *Bucks.* ***Village***, 2m/3km NE of Aylesbury. **32 B7** SP8415.
Big Garvoun *Moray* ***Mountain***, 6m/10km S of Tomintoul. Height 2430 feet or 741 metres. **89 J4** NJ1408.
Big Mancot *Flints.* ***Suburb***, between Harwarden and Queensferry. SJ3167.
Big Pit Mining Museum *Torfaen* ***Other feature of interest***, on W side of Blaenavon. Situated in 100-year-old coal mine, which closed in 1980. Includes tour of underground pit, showing old and new methods of coal mining; many of the guides are ex-miners themselves. **19 F1** SO2408.
Big Sand *High.* ***Settlement***, on W coast of Ross and Cromarty district, 3m/5km NW of Gairloch. **94 D4** NG7578.
Biga *Powys* ***River***, running E through Hafren Forest into Llyn Clywedog Reservoir. **37 H7** SN8789.
Bigbury *Devon* ***Village***, on high ground, to W of River Avon estuary, 3m/5km S of Modbury. **5 G6** SX6646.
Bigbury Bay *Devon* ***Bay***, on SW coast of Devon, extending from Bolt Tail to Stoke Point. **5 G6** SX6443.
Bigbury-on-Sea *Devon* ***Small town***, resort with extensive sands, situated on Bigbury Bay, 5m/8km S of Modbury. **5 G6** SX6544.
Bigby *Lincs.* ***Village***, 4m/6km E of Brigg. **52 D2** TA0507.
Bigert Mire *Cumb.* ***Settlement***, on E side of Whitfell, 4m/6km NW of Broughton in Furness. **60 C7** SD1792.
Bigga *Shet.* ***Island***, uninhabited island of about 235 acres or 95 hectares midway between Mainland and Yell at SE end of Yell Sound. **108 D5** HU4479.
Biggar *Cumb.* ***Hamlet***, on Isle of Walney, 2m/3km S of causeway to Barrow-in-Furness. **54 E3** SD1966.
Biggar *S.Lan.* Population: 1994. ***Small town***, 13m/21km W of Peebles. Slight remains of Boghall Castle on S side. **75 J7** NT0437.
Biggar Road *N.Lan.* ***Suburb***, adjoining to NE of Newarthill, 3m/5km NE of Hamilton. NS7860.
Bigges' Pillar *Northumb.* ***Hill***, rising to over 260 metres, 2m/3km SE of Edlingham. **71 G3** NU1207.
Biggin *Derbys.* ***Hamlet***, 5m/8km E of Ashbourne. **40 E1** SK2648.
Biggin *Derbys.* ***Village***, 8m/13km N of Ashbourne. **50 D7** SK1559.
Biggin *N.Yorks.* ***Hamlet***, 2m/4km SE of Church Fenton. **58 B6** SE5434.
Biggin Hill *Gt.Lon.* Population: 14,107. ***Town***, in borough of Bromley, 4m/6km E of Warlingham. Airfield. **23 H6** TQ4159.
Biggings *Shet.* ***Settlement***, on Papa Stour, off Mainland. **109 A6** HU1760.
Biggleswade *Beds.* Population: 12,350. ***Town***, former coaching stop on River Ivel, in market-gardening area, 9m/15km SE of Bedford. Biggleswade (Old Warden) Aerodrome, 3m/4km W, houses Shuttleworth Collection of historic aircraft and motor vehicles. **32 E4** TL1844.
Bigholms *D. & G.* ***Settlement***, 4m/6km SW of Langholm. **69 J5** NY3181.
Bighouse *High.* ***Settlement***, at mouth of Halladale River, 1km E of Melvich. **104 D2** NC8964.
Bighton *Hants.* ***Village***, 2m/3km NE of New Alresford. **11 H1** SU6134.

Biglands *Cumb.* ***Hamlet***, 3m/4km SE of Kirkbride. **60 D1** NY2553.
Bignall End *Staffs.* ***Suburb***, adjoining to E of Audley. SJ8051.
Bignell's Corner *Herts.* ***Settlement***, 2m/3km W of Potters Bar. TL2200.
Bignor *W.Suss.* ***Village***, below South Downs, 5m/7km S of Petworth. Roman villa to E. **12 C5** SU9814.
Bigod's Hill *Norf.* ***Settlement***, 2m/3km NW of Beccles. TM3992.
Bigrigg *Cumb.* ***Village***, 2m/3km N of Egremont. **60 B5** NY0013.
Bigton *Shet.* ***Village***, on bay of Bigton Wick, on W coast of Mainland, 9m/14km N of Sumburgh Head. **109 C10** HU3722.
Bilberry *Cornw.* ***Settlement***, 1km N of Bugle. **4 A4** SX0160.
Bilborough *Nott.* ***Suburb***, 3m/5km NW of Nottingham city centre. **41 H1** SK5241.
Bilbrook *Som.* ***Hamlet***, 3m/5km SE of Dunster. **7 J1** ST0341.
Bilbrook *Staffs.* ***Locality***, adjoining to E of Codsall. **40 A5** SJ8803.
Bilbrough *N.Yorks.* ***Village***, 4m/6km NE of Tadcaster. **58 B5** SE5346.
Bilbster *High.* ***Settlement***, 3m/4km SE of Watten. **105 H3** ND2852.
Bilby *Notts.* ***Settlement***, 4m/6km NE of Worksop. SK6383.
Bildershaw *Dur.* ***Hamlet***, 3m/5km S of Bishop Auckland. **62 C4** NZ2024.
Bildeston *Suff.* ***Village***, with many half-timbered houses, 5m/7km N of Hadleigh. **34 D4** TL9949.
Bill of Portland (Portland Bill). *Dorset* ***Coastal feature***, S tip of peninsula of Isle of Portland marking E extremity of Lyme Bay. **9 F7** SY6771.
Bill Quay *T. & W.* ***Suburb***, E district of Felling, on S bank of River Tyne. NZ2962.
Bill Street *Med.* ***Suburb***, adjoining to N of Rochester. TQ7470.
Billericay *Essex* Population: 33,377. ***Town***, 5m/8km E of Brentwood. Pilgrim Fathers met in 16c Chantry House. **24 C2** TQ6794.
Billesdon *Leics.* ***Village***, 8m/13km E of Leicester. **42 A5** SK7102.
Billesley *Warks.* ***Hamlet***, 4m/6km W of Stratford-upon-Avon. **30 C3** SP1456.
Billesley *W.Mid.* ***Suburb***, 4m/7km SE of Birmingham city centre. SP0980.
Billholm *D. & G.* ***Settlement***, in loop of River Esk, 3m/4km NW of Bentpath. **69 H4** NY2792.
Billingborough *Lincs.* ***Village***, 9m/14km N of Bourne. **42 E2** TF1134.
Billinge *Mersey.* Population: 6943. ***Small town***, 3m/5km NE of St. Helens. **48 E2** SD5300.
Billingford *Norf.* ***Hamlet***, 3m/5km E of Diss. **35 F1** TM1678.
Billingford *Norf.* ***Village***, 5m/8km NE of East Dereham. **44 E3** TG0120.
Billingham *Stock.* Population: 36,869. ***Town***, industrial town, 2m/4km NE of Stockton-on-Tees. **63 F4** NZ4522.
Billinghay *Lincs.* ***Village***, 8m/13km NE of Sleaford. **52 E7** TF1554.
Billingley *S.Yorks.* ***Village***, 2m/3km W of Goldthorpe. **51 G2** SE4304.
Billingley Green *S.Yorks.* ***Settlement***, to S of Billingley, 1m/2km W of Goldthorpe. SE4404.
Billingshurst *W.Suss.* Population: 4980. ***Small town***, 6m/10km SW of Horsham. **12 D4** TQ0825.
Billingsley *Shrop.* ***Village***, 5m/8km S of Bridgnorth. **39 G7** SO7085.
Billington *Beds.* ***Village***, 2m/3km SE of Leighton Buzzard. **32 C6** SP9422.
Billington *Lancs.* ***Small town***, just SW of Whalley across River Calder. **56 C6** SD7235.
Billington *Staffs.* ***Hamlet***, 3m/4km SW of Stafford. SJ8820.
Billockby *Norf.* ***Hamlet***, 2m/4km NE of Acle. **45 J4** TG4213.
Billsmoor Park *Northumb.* ***Open space***, wooded hillsides on Park Burn, 2m/3km N of Elsdon. **70 E4** NY9496.
Billy Mill *T. & W.* ***Suburb***, 1m/2km W of North Shields. NZ3369.
Billy Row *Dur.* Population: 1393. ***Village***, 1m/2km N of Crook. **62 C3** NZ1637.
Bilsborrow *Lancs.* ***Village***, 2m/3km N of Barton. **55 J5** SD5139.
Bilsby *Lincs.* ***Village***, 1m/2km E of Alford. **53 H5** TF4676.
Bilsby Field *Lincs.* ***Settlement***, adjoining to SE of Alford. TF4675.
Bilsdale East Moor *N.Yorks.* ***Open space***, moorland 1m/2km SE of Urra. **63 G6** NZ5700.
Bilsdale West Moor *N.Yorks.* ***Open space***, moorland in Cleveland Hills on W side of Bilsdale, 8m/13km NW of Helmsley. **63 G7** SE5596.
Bilsdean *E.Loth.* ***Hamlet***, near coast, 6m/10km SE of Dunbar. **77 F3** NT7672.
Bilsham *W.Suss.* ***Hamlet***, 3m/5km NE of Bognor Regis. **12 C6** SU9702.
Bilsington *Kent* ***Village***, 6m/9km S of Ashford. **15 F4** TR0434.
Bilson Green *Glos.* ***Suburb***, adjoining to W of Cinderford. SO6514.
Bilsthorpe *Notts.* Population: 3283. ***Village***, 4m/7km S of Ollerton. **51 J6** SK6460.
Bilsthorpe Moor *Notts.* ***Village***, 1km S of Bilsthorpe. SK6559.
Bilston *Midloth.* Population: 1648. ***Village***, 1m/2km SW of Loanhead. **76 A4** NT2664.
Bilston *W.Mid.* ***Suburb***, SE district of Wolverhampton. **40 B6** SO9596.
Bilston Glen *Midloth.* ***Locality***, to E of Bilston. NT2764.
Bilstone *Leics.* ***Hamlet***, 7m/11km S of Ashby de la Zouch. **41 F5** SK3605.
Bilting *Kent* ***Hamlet***, 5m/8km NE of Ashford. **15 F3** TR0549.
Bilton *E.Riding* ***Village***, 5m/8km NE of Kingston upon Hull. **59 H6** TA1632.
Bilton *N.Yorks.* ***Suburb***, N district of Harrogate. **57 J4** SE3057.
Bilton *N.Yorks.* ***Village***, 5m/8km E of Wetherby. **57 K4** SE4750.
Bilton *Northumb.* ***Hamlet***, 1m/2km W of Alnmouth. **71 H2** NU2210.
Bilton *Warks.* ***Suburb***, SW district of Rugby. **31 F1** SP4873.
Bilton Barns *Northumb.* ***Settlement***, 1km SW of Bilton. NU2210.
Bilton Dene *N.Yorks.* ***Hamlet***, 1km E of Bilton, 2m/3km W of Knaresborough. SE3157.
Bimbister *Ork.* ***Settlement***, on Mainland, 3m/4km NW of Finstown. **107 C6** HY3216.
Bin of Cullen *Moray* ***Mountain***, 3m/5km SW of Cullen, commanding wide views. Height 1050 feet or 320 metres. **98 C4** NJ4764.
Binbrook *Lincs.* ***Village***, 7m/11km NE of Market Rasen. Binbrook Airfield to NW. **53 F3** TF2193.
Binchester *Dur.* ***Settlement***, 1m/2km N of Bishop Auckland across loop of River Wear, near site of Roman fort of Vinovia. NZ2031.
Binchester Blocks *Dur.* ***Settlement***, 2m/3km SW of Spennymoor. NZ2232.
Bincombe *Dorset* ***Village***, 4m/6km S of Dorchester and N of Weymouth. **9 F6** SY6884.
Bindal *High.* ***Settlement***, 1km E of Portmahomack. **97 G3** NH9284.
Bindalein Island *W.Isles* ***Island***, rock on S side of entrance to Loch Carlabhagh on W coast of Isle of Lewis, 2m/3km W of Carloway village. NB1741.
Bindon *Som.* ***Hamlet***, 1m/2km SW of Milverton. ST1024.
Bindon Abbey *Dorset* ***Ecclesiastical building***, remains of medieval Cistercian abbey, 1km E of Wool, on S bank of River Frome. **9 H6** SY8586.
Binegar *Som.* ***Village***, 4m/6km N of Shepton Mallet. **19 K7** ST6149.
Bines Green *W.Suss.* ***Settlement***, beside River Adur, 4m/6km N of Steyning. **12 E5** TQ1817.
Binfield *Brack.F.* ***Village***, 2m/3km NW of Bracknell. **22 B4** SU8471.
Binfield Heath *Oxon.* ***Village***, 3m/4km S of Henley-on-Thames. **22 A4** SU7478.
Bingfield *Northumb.* ***Hamlet***, 5m/8km N of Corbridge. **70 E6** NY9772.
Bingham *Notts.* Population: 7057. ***Village***, 8m/13km E of Nottingham. 1m/2km N is site of Roman town of Margidunum. **42 A2** SK7039.
Bingham's Melcombe *Dorset* ***Hamlet***, 5m/8km N of Puddletown. **9 G4** ST7702.
Bingley *W.Yorks.* Population: 19,585. ***Town***, market town on River Aire and on Leeds and Liverpool Canal, 5m/8km NW of Bradford. 18c Five Rise Locks nearby. **57 G6** SE1039.
Bings Heath *Shrop.* ***Hamlet***, 5m/8km NE of Shrewsbury. SJ5418.
Binham *Norf.* ***Village***, 5m/8km SE of Wells-next-the-Sea. Remains of 13c priory with adjacent medieval cross (both English Heritage). **44 D2** TF9839.
Binham Priory *Norf.* ***Ecclesiastical building***, extensive remains of 13c Benedictine priory (English Heritage) on NE side of Binham, 4m/7km SE of Wells-next-the-Sea. Nave now used as parish church. Medieval Wayside Cross (English Heritage) on village green adjacent to priory. **44 D1** TF9839.
Binley *Hants.* ***Village***, 3m/4km E of Hurstbourne Tarrant. **21 H6** SU4253.
Binley *W.Mid.* ***Suburb***, E district of Coventry. **30 E1** SP3778.
Binnegar *Dorset* ***Hamlet***, 3m/4km E of Wool. SY8887.
Binnein an Fhidhleir *Arg. & B.* ***Mountain***, on N side of Glen Kinglas, 8m/12km E of Inveraray. Height 2660 feet or 811 metres. **80 D6** NN2110.
Binnein Beag *High.* ***Mountain***, peak 1m/2km NE of Binnein Mòr. Munro: height 3083 feet or 940 metres. **80 D1** NN2267.
Binnein Mòr *High.* ***Mountain***, on Mamore Forest in Lochaber district 3m/5km NE of Kinlochleven. Munro: height 3700 feet or 1128 metres. **80 D1** NN2166.
Binnein Shuas *High.* ***Mountain***, between Loch Laggan and Lochan na h-Earba, 6m/10km SW of Kinloch Laggan. Height 2447 feet or 746 metres. **88 B6** NN4682.
Binniehill *Falk.* ***Settlement***, 1km S of Slamannan. **75 G3** NS8572.
Binnimoor Fen *Cambs.* ***Open space***, lowland 1km E of March. **43 H6** TL4397.
Binscombe *Surr.* ***Locality***, residential area to N of Godalming. SU9646.
Binsey *Cumb.* ***Mountain***, 3m/4km NE of N end of Bassenthwaite Lake. Height 1466 feet or 447 metres. **60 D3** NY2235.
Binsoe *N.Yorks.* ***Hamlet***, 1m/2km NW of West Tanfield. **57 H2** SE2579.
Binstead *I.o.W.* ***Suburb***, 1m/2km W of Ryde. **11 G5** SZ5792.
Binsted *Hants.* ***Village***, 4m/6km NE of Alton. **22 A7** SU7741.
Binsted *W.Suss.* ***Hamlet***, 2m/4km W of Arundel. **12 C6** SU9806.
Binton *Warks.* ***Village***, 4m/6km W of Stratford-upon-Avon. **30 C3** SP1454.
Bintree *Norf.* ***Village***, 7m/12km SE of Fakenham. **44 E3** TG0123.
Binweston *Shrop.* ***Hamlet***, 2m/3km W of Worthen. **38 B5** SJ3004.
Biod Mòr *High.* ***Mountain***, 1km NW of head of Loch Eynort, Skye. Height 1256 feet or 383 metres. **85 J2** NG3727.
Biod nan Laogh *High.* ***Coastal feature***, headland on E coast of Vaternish peninsula, 7m/11km SE of Vaternish Point, Skye. **93 J6** NG2958.
Bioda Buidhe *High.* ***Mountain***, 3m/5km NE of Uig, Skye. Height 1528 feet or 466 metres. **93 K5** NG4366.
Birch *Essex* ***Village***, 5m/8km SW of Colchester. **34 D7** TL9419.
Birch *Gt.Man.* ***Hamlet***, 1m/2km NW of Middleton. **49 H2** SD8507.
Birch Cross *Staffs.* ***Hamlet***, 1km W of Marchington. SK1230.
Birch Green *Essex* ***Village***, 5m/8km SW of Colchester. **34 D7** TL9418.
Birch Green *Herts.* ***Hamlet***, 2m/4km W of Hertford. TL2911.
Birch Green *Lancs.* ***Suburb***, to N of Skelmersdale town centre. SD4906.
Birch Grove *W.Suss.* ***Hamlet***, 2m/3km NE of Horsted Keynes. TQ4029.
Birch Heath *Ches.* ***Hamlet***, 1km SW of Tarporley. **48 E6** SJ5461.
Birch Hill *Brack.F.* ***Suburb***, S district of Bracknell. SU8766.
Birch Vale *Derbys.* ***Village***, 1m/2km W of Hayfield. **50 C4** SK0286.
Birch Wood *Som.* ***Hamlet***, 2m/3km NW of Buckland St. Mary. ST2414.
Bircham Newton *Norf.* ***Village***, 1km N of Great Bircham. **44 B2** TF7633.
Bircham Tofts *Norf.* ***Village***, 1km E of Great Bircham. **44 B2** TF7732.
Birchanger *Essex* ***Village***, 2m/3km NE of Bishop's Stortford. **33 J6** TL5022.
Birchencliffe *W.Yorks.* ***Suburb***, 3m/4km NW of Huddersfield town centre. SE1118.
Bircher *Here.* ***Hamlet***, 4m/7km N of Leominster. **28 D2** SO4765.
Bircher Common *Here.* ***Settlement***, partly National Trust, 5m/8km NW of Leominster. SO4666.
Birches *Staffs.* ***Suburb***, SW district of Rugeley. SK0316.
Birches Green *W.Mid.* ***Suburb***, 4m/7km NE of Birmingham city centre. SP1190.
Birches Head *Stoke* ***Suburb***, 1m/2km NE of Hanley. SJ8948.
Birchett's Green *E.Suss.* ***Settlement***, 2m/3km NW of Ticehurst. TQ6631.
Birchfield *High.* ***Settlement***, 7m/11km SW of Lairg. **96 B2** NH4999.
Birchfield *W.Mid.* ***Suburb***, 3m/4km N of Birmingham city centre. SP0790.
Birchgrove *Cardiff* ***Suburb***, 3m/4km N of Cardiff city centre. **18 E3** ST1680.
Birchgrove *Swan.* ***Village***, 3m/5km W of Neath. **18 A2** SS7098.
Birchington *Kent* ***Town***, N coast resort, 3m/5km W of Margate. Burial site of poet and artist Dante Gabriel Rossetti. **25 J5** TR3069.
Birchley Heath *Warks.* ***Settlement***, 3m/4km SW of Atherstone. SP2894.
Birchmoor *Warks.* ***Hamlet***, 1m/2km SW of Polesworth. SK2501.
Birchover *Derbys.* ***Village***, 4m/6km W of Matlock. **50 E6** SK2362.
Birchwood *Herts.* ***Suburb***, N district of Hatfield. TL2209.
Birchwood *Warr.* ***Suburb***, 4m/6km NE of Warrington town centre. **49 F3** SJ6591.
Bircotes *Notts.* Population: 3906. ***Locality***, 2m/3km SW of Bawtry. **51 J3** SK6291.
Bird Dyke *Cumb.* ***Settlement***, just N of Lamplugh. NY0921.
Bird End *W.Mid.* ***Locality***, 2m/3km NE of West Bromwich town centre. **40 C6** SP0193.
Bird Street *Suff.* ***Settlement***, 4m/7km SW of Stowmarket. TM0052.
Birdbrook *Essex* ***Village***, 4m/6km SE of Haverhill. **34 B4** TL7041.
Birdbush *Wilts.* ***Hamlet***, 4m/6km E of Shaftesbury. ST9123.
Birdfield *Arg. & B.* ***Settlement***, on NW side of Loch Fyne, 2m/3km SE of Minard. **73 H1** NR9694.
Birdforth *N.Yorks.* ***Hamlet***, 1km NW of Thormanby. SE4875.
Birdham *W.Suss.* ***Village***, 4m/6km SW of Chichester and 1km N of Chichester Yacht Basin. **12 B7** SU8200.
Birdingbury *Warks.* ***Village***, 4m/7km N of Southam. **31 F2** SP4368.
Birdland *Glos.* ***Other feature of interest***, in centre of Bourton-on-the-Water, including 7 acres of gardens and a penguin colony. **30 C6** SP1620.
Birdlip *Glos.* ***Village***, at top of steep hill, on escarpment of Cotswold Hills, 6m/10km SE of Gloucester and 5m/8km SW of Cheltenham. **29 J7** SO9214.
Birdoswald *Cumb.* ***Settlement***, 1m/2km W of Gilsland, on site of Roman fort of Camboglanna (English Heritage). One thousand yards of Wall with turrets and bridge (English Heritage) at Willowford, 1km E. NY6166.
Birdoswald Roman Fort (Camboglanna) *Cumb.* ***Historic/prehistoric site***, site of 5-acre Roman fort (English Heritage) which guarded bridge over River Irthing, 3m/4km W of Greenhead and 6m/10km NE of Brampton. Parts of walls, gateway and towers remain. Linked to Harrow's Scar Milecastle (English Heritage) by section of wall. To W is Pike Hill Signal Tower (English Heritage), joined to wall at angle of 45 degrees. **70 B7** NY6166.
Birds Green *Essex* ***Hamlet***, 3m/5km S of Leaden Roding. TL5808.
Birdsall *N.Yorks.* ***Village***, 4m/7km SE of Malton. **58 E3** SE8165.
Birdsgreen *Shrop.* ***Hamlet***, 6m/10km SE of Bridgnorth. **39 G7** SO7684.
Birdsmoor Gate *Dorset* ***Hamlet***, 3m/5km W of Broadwindsor. **8 C4** ST3900.

Birdston *E.Dun.* ***Hamlet***, 1m/2km N of Kirkintilloch. NS6575.
Birdwell *S.Yorks.* Population: 2832. ***Village***, 3m/5km S of Barnsley. **51 F2** SE3401.
Birdwood *Glos.* ***Hamlet***, 6m/9km W of Gloucester. **29 G7** SO7418.
Birgham *Sc.Bord.* ***Village***, 3m/5km W of Coldstream. **77 F7** NT7939.
Birichen *High.* ***Settlement***, in Sutherland district, 3m/5km NW of Dornoch. **96 E2** NH7592.
Birk Beck *Cumb.* ***River***, rising on Shap Fells and flowing SE into River Lune on W side of Old Tebay. **61 G6** NY6105.
Birkacre *Lancs.* ***Settlement***, on River Yarrow, 2m/3km SW of Chorley. SD5714.
Birkby *Cumb.* ***Hamlet***, 2m/3km NE of Maryport. NY0537.
Birkby *N.Yorks.* ***Hamlet***, 6m/9km N of Northallerton. **62 E6** NZ3302.
Birkdale *Mersey.* ***Suburb***, SW district of Southport. Golf course, venue for The Open Championship. **48 C1** SD3214.
Birkdale *N.Yorks.* ***Settlement***, on N side of Birkdale Beck, 3m/4km W of Keld. **61 K6** NY8501.
Birkdale Beck *N.Yorks.* ***River***, rising from many streams on Birkdale Common and flowing E to meet Great Sleddale Beck and Whitsundale Beck, forming River Swale. **61 K6** NY8701.
Birkdale Common *N.Yorks.* ***Open space***, moorland straddling Birkdale Beck, 6m/9km SE of Kirkby Stephen. **61 K6** NY8102.
Birkenhead *Mersey.* Population: 93,087. ***Town***, former ship-building town and port on Wirral peninsula, near mouth of River Mersey, 1m/2km SW of Liverpool across river. Connected with Liverpool by two road tunnels and one railway tunnel. Two museums in former warships. **48 C4** SJ3288.
Birkenhills *Aber.* ***Settlement***, 3m/5km SE of Turriff. **99 F6** NJ7445.
Birkenshaw *W.Yorks.* ***Village***, 4m/6km SE of Bradford. **57 H7** SE2028.
Birkenshaw Bottoms *W.Yorks.* ***Locality***, adjoining to SE of Birkenshaw, 3m/4km NW of Batley. SE2127.
Birkhall *Aber.* ***Settlement***, 2m/3km SW of Ballater. **90 B5** NO3493.
Birkhill *Angus* Population: 920. ***Hamlet***, 4m/6km NW of Dundee. **82 E4** NO3534.
Birkhill *D. & G.* ***Settlement***, 4m/6km SW of St. Mary's Loch. **69 H2** NT2015.
Birkhill *Sc.Bord.* ***Settlement***, 4m/6km SE of Lauder. **76 D6** NT5642.
Birkholme *Lincs.* ***Settlement***, 3m/4km E of Colsterworth. SK9623.
Birkin *N.Yorks.* ***Village***, 3m/4km NE of Knottingley across River Aire. **58 B7** SE5326.
Birks *W.Yorks.* ***Suburb***, 2m/3km W of Bradford city centre. SE1332.
Birks *W.Yorks.* ***Suburb***, adjoining to S of Morley. SE2626.
Birkshaw *Northumb.* ***Hamlet***, 1m/2km NW of Bardon Mill. NY7765.
Birkwood *S.Lan.* ***Settlement***, adjoining to S of Lesmahagow. **75 G7** NS8039.
Birley *Here.* ***Village***, 4m/7km SW of Leominster. **28 D3** SO4553.
Birley *S.Yorks.* ***Suburb***, 4m/6km SE of Sheffield city centre. SK3983.
Birley Carr *S.Yorks.* ***Suburb***, 4m/6km NW of Sheffield city centre. **51 F3** SK3392.
Birley Edge *S.Yorks.* ***Suburb***, 4m/6km NW of Sheffield city centre, to S of Grenoside. SK3392.
Birling *Kent* ***Village***, 2m/3km N of West Malling. **24 C5** TQ6860.
Birling *Northumb.* ***Hamlet***, 1km N of Warkworth. **71 H3** NU2406.
Birling Gap *E.Suss.* ***Locality***, on coast, 2m/3km W of Beachy Head, at E end of Seven Sisters cliffs. **13 J7** TV5596.
Birlingham *Worcs.* ***Village***, 2m/3km SW of Pershore across loop of River Avon. **29 J4** SO9343.
Birmingham *W.Mid.* Population: 965,928. ***City***, England's second city and manufacturing, commercial and communications centre, 100m/160km NW of London. Birmingham was home to many pioneers of industrial revolution and to every kind of manufacturing during this period. Consequently the population trebled between 1780 and 1830. Current economic trend is towards post-industrial activities, concentrating on convention and exhibition trades and tourism. To S of city is planned village of Bournville, established by Quaker chocolate magnates George and Richard Cadbury in 1879, influenced by utopian ideas of William Morris. City has many galleries and museums, particularly around 19c Victoria and Chamberlain Squares. Anglican and Catholic cathedrals. Universities. Birmingham International Airport 7m/11km E of city centre. **40 C7** SP0686.
Birmingham Cathedral *W.Mid.* ***Ecclesiastical building***, in Birmingham city centre. Originally built, in classical style, in early 18c as a parish church for an expanding town. Elevated to cathedral status in 1905. **40 C7** SP0687.
Birmingham International Airport *W.Mid.* ***Airport/airfield***, 7m/11km E of Birmingham city centre, adjacent to W of National Exhibition Centre, and with motorway access from M42. Viewing gallery and visitors centre. **40 D7** SP1784.
Birmingham Nature Centre *W.Mid.* ***Other feature of interest***, in Cannon Hill Park, 2m/3km S of Birmingham city centre, including European animals in grounds designed to attract wild animals and birds. **40 C7** SP0683.
Birnam *P. & K.* ***Village***, on S side of River Tay, 1km SE of Dunkeld. **82 B3** NO0341.
Birnam Hill *P. & K.* ***Mountain***, partly wooded summit of King's Seat, 1m/2km S of Dunkeld. Height 1312 feet or 400 metres. **82 B3** NO0340.
Birnam Wood *P. & K.* ***Forest/woodland***, famous from Shakespeare's Macbeth, 2m/3km SE of Birnam. NO0439.
Birnbeck Island *N.Som.* ***Island***, rock at N end of Weston Bay connected to mainland by a pier. ST3062.
Birnie *Moray* ***Locality***, comprising settlement of Nether Birnie and 12c church, 3m/4km S of Elgin. NJ2058.
Birnock Water *D. & G.* ***River***, rising on Swatte Fell and flowing SW to join River Annan at Moffat. **69 G3** NT0804.
Birns Water *E.Loth.* ***River***, rising on Lammermuir Hills and flowing NW, then N into River Tyne 4m/6km SE of Tranent. **76 C4** NT4568.
Birrenswark *D. & G.* *Alternative name for Burnswark, qv.*
Birrier *Shet.* ***Coastal feature***, small rocky promontory on E coast of Yell, 1m/2km NE of Aywick. **108 E4** HU5488.
Birsay *Ork.* ***Locality***, near NW end of Mainland, 1m/2km E of Brough Head. Earl's Palace, ruined 16c palace of Earls of Orkney. **106 B5** HY2825.
Birsay Bay *Ork.* ***Bay***, in NW Mainland, bounded by Brough Head to N. **106 B5** HY2427.
Birse *Aber.* ***Hamlet***, on N edge of Forest of Birse, 2m/3km SE of Aboyne. **90 D5** NO5597.
Birsemore *Aber.* ***Hamlet***, 1km S of Aboyne across River Dee. **90 D5** NO5297.
Birstall *Leics.* Population: 11,770. ***Suburb***, 3m/5km N of Leicester. **41 H5** SK5909.
Birstall *W.Yorks.* ***Locality***, 2m/3km NW of Batley. SE2226.
Birstall Smithies *W.Yorks.* ***Settlement***, adjoining to S of Birstall. **57 H7** SE2125.
Birstwith *N.Yorks.* ***Village***, 5m/8km NW of Harrogate. **57 H4** SE2359.
Birthorpe *Lincs.* ***Hamlet***, 1m/2km W of Billingborough. **42 E2** TF1134.
Birtle *Gt.Man.* ***Hamlet***, 3m/4km NE of Bury. SD8313.
Birtley *Here.* ***Settlement***, 4m/7km NE of Presteigne. **28 C2** SO3669.
Birtley *Northumb.* ***Village***, 4m/7km SE of Bellingham. **70 D6** NY8778.
Birtley *T. & W.* ***Town***, 5m/8km S of Gateshead. Former coalmining and iron-making town. **62 D1** NZ2755.
Birts Street *Worcs.* ***Village***, 5m/8km E of Ledbury. **29 G5** SO7836.
Birtsmorton *Worcs.* ***Hamlet***, 6m/10km W of Tewkesbury. SO8035.
Biruaslum *W.Isles* ***Island***, uninhabited island off W coast of Vatersay. NL6096.
Bis Geos *Ork.* ***Coastal feature***, small indentations of W coast of Westray. **106 D3** HY4147.
Bisbrooke *Rut.* ***Village***, 1m/2km E of Uppingham. **42 B6** SP8899.
Biscathorpe *Lincs.* ***Hamlet***, 1m/2km N of Donington on Bain. TF2284.
Biscot *Luton* ***Suburb***, to NW of Luton town centre. TL0722.
Bish Mill *Devon* ***Hamlet***, 2m/3km E of South Molton. **7 F3** SS7425.
Bisham *W. & M.* ***Village***, 1km S of Marlow across River Thames. **22 B3** SU8585.
Bishampton *Worcs.* ***Village***, 5m/7km NE of Pershore. **29 J3** SO9851.
Bishop Auckland *Dur.* Population: 23,154. ***Town***, old market town on W bank of River Wear, 9m/15km SW of Durham. Castle, of various dates, is residence of Bishops of Durham. **62 D3** NZ2029.
Bishop Burn *D. & G.* ***River***, rising to SW of Newton Stewart and flowing SE, then NE into River Cree, opposite Creetown. NX4558.
Bishop Burton *E.Riding* ***Village***, 3m/5km W of Beverley. **59 F6** SE9839.
Bishop Burton Wold *E.Riding* ***Open space***, partly wooded lowland 4m/6km W of Barnsley. **59 F6** SE9638.
Bishop Hill *P. & K.* ***Mountain***, rising to over 460 metres, 4m/7km E of Milnathort. Noted for gliding. **82 C7** NO1804.
Bishop Loch *Glas.* ***Lake/loch***, small loch 6m/10km E of Glasgow city centre. **74 E4** NS6866.
Bishop Middleham *Dur.* ***Village***, 2m/4km NW of Sedgefield. **62 E3** NZ3231.
Bishop Monkton *N.Yorks.* ***Village***, 3m/5km S of Ripon. **57 J3** SE3266.
Bishop Norton *Lincs.* ***Village***, 5m/8km SE of Kirton in Lindsey. **52 C3** SK9892.
Bishop Rock *I.o.S.* ***Island***, rock with lighthouse at W extremity of Isles of Scilly, 5m/7km W of St. Agnes. **2 B2** SV8006.
Bishop Sutton *B. & N.E.Som.* ***Village***, 2m/4km S of Chew Magna. **19 J6** ST5859.
Bishop Thornton *N.Yorks.* ***Village***, 2m/4km NW of Ripley. **57 H3** SE2663.
Bishop Wilton *E.Riding* ***Village***, 5m/8km E of Stamford Bridge. **58 D4** SE7955.
Bishopbridge *Lincs.* ***Hamlet***, at road crossing of River Ancholme, 5m/8km W of Market Rasen. **52 D3** TF0391.
Bishopbriggs *E.Dun.* Population: 23,825. ***Suburb***, 3m/5km N of Glasgow. **74 E4** NS6070.
Bishopdale Beck *N.Yorks.* ***River***, rising N of Buckden Pike and flowing NE into River Ure, 2m/3km E of Aysgarth. **56 E1** SE0289.
Bishopdown *Wilts.* ***Suburb***, 1m/2km NE of Salisbury city centre. SU1531.
Bishopmill *Moray* ***Suburb***, N district of Elgin. **97 K5** NJ2665.
Bishopric *P. & K.* ***Open space***, upland area on W side of Tay valley, 5m/8km NW of Dunkeld. **82 A2** NN9548.
Bishops and Clerks *Pembs.* ***Island***, group of over twenty small rocky islands lying off St. David's Head, the largest being North Bishop, Carreg Rhoson, Daufraich and South Bishop, the latter having a lighthouse. **16 A2** SM6723.
Bishop's and Earl's Palaces *Ork.* ***Historic/prehistoric site***, at Kirkwall, on Mainland. Earl Patrick's palace, built in 1607, is excellent example of Renaissance architecture. Nearby 13c Bishop's Palace has 16c round tower. **107 D6** HY4410.
Bishops Bridge *Norf.* ***Bridge***, 13c brick and sandstone bridge with flint facings, over River Wensum in Norwich. TG2308.
Bishops Cannings *Wilts.* ***Village***, 3m/4km NE of Devizes. **20 D5** SU0364.
Bishop's Castle *Shrop.* ***Small town***, market town in hills on Welsh border, 8m/12km NW of Craven Arms. Scant remains of castle. **38 C7** SO3288.
Bishop's Caundle *Dorset* ***Village***, in Blackmoor Vale, 4m/7km SE of Sherborne. **9 F3** ST6913.
Bishop's Cleeve *Glos.* Population: 10,098. ***Village***, 4m/6km N of Cheltenham. **29 J6** SO9527.
Bishop's Clyst *Devon* ***Locality***, adjacent to Clyst St. Mary, 4m/6km E of Exeter. SX9791.
Bishop's Fonthill *Wilts.* *Alternative name for Fonthill Bishop, qv.*
Bishop's Frome *Here.* ***Village***, 4m/7km S of Bromyard. **29 F4** SO6648.
Bishops Gate *Surr.* ***Settlement***, in Windsor Great Park, 4m/6km W of Staines. SU9871.
Bishop's Green *Essex* ***Hamlet***, 3m/4km S of Great Dunmow. **33 K7** TL6317.
Bishop's Green *Hants.* ***Hamlet***, 3m/5km SE of Newbury. SU5063.
Bishop's Hull *Som.* ***Suburb***, W district of Taunton. **8 B2** ST2024.
Bishop's Itchington *Warks.* Population: 2052. ***Village***, 3m/5km SW of Southam. **30 E3** SP3857.
Bishop's Lydeard *Som.* Population: 2270. ***Village***, 5m/8km NW of Taunton. **7 K3** ST1629.
Bishop's Norton *Glos.* ***Hamlet***, 4m/6km N of Gloucester. SO8424.
Bishop's Nympton *Devon* ***Village***, 3m/5km SE of South Molton. **7 F3** SS7523.
Bishop's Offley *Staffs.* ***Hamlet***, 3m/5km W of Eccleshall. **39 G3** SJ7829.
Bishop's Palace *Pembs.* ***Historic/prehistoric site***, in St. David's. Built between 1280 and 1350, now a ruin. **16 A2** SM7525.
Bishop's Palace *Som.* ***Historic house***, fortified early 13c palace in Wells, with moat and Great Hall remaining. 15c wing now lived in by Bishop of Bath and Wells. **19 J7** ST5545.
Bishop's Seat *Arg. & B.* ***Mountain***, rising from upland plateau, 3m/4km W of Dunoon. Height 1653 feet or 504 metres. **73 K3** NS1377.
Bishop's Stortford *Herts.* Population: 28,403. ***Town***, former coaching town on River Stort, 8m/13km N of Harlow. Birthplace of Cecil Rhodes. **33 H6** TL4821.
Bishop's Sutton *Hants.* ***Village***, 2m/3km SE of New Alresford. **11 H1** SU6031.
Bishop's Tachbrook *Warks.* Population: 2002. ***Village***, 3m/5km S of Royal Leamington Spa. **30 E2** SP3161.
Bishop's Tawton *Devon* ***Village***, 2m/3km S of Barnstaple. **6 D2** SS5630.
Bishop's Waltham *Hants.* Population: 5423. ***Small town***, 7m/11km N of Fareham. Remains of 12c-14c Bishop's Palace (English Heritage). **11 G3** SU5517.
Bishop's Waltham Palace *Hants.* ***Historic/prehistoric site***, ruins of moated palace (English Heritage) in Bishop's Waltham. Medieval seat of Bishops of Winchester, built c. 1135, with 14c additions. Mainly destroyed by Parliamentarians during Battle of Cheriton 1644, although Great Hall, tower and moat are among remains. **11 G3** SU5517.
Bishops Wood *Som.* *Alternative spelling of Bishopswood, qv.*
Bishop's Wood *Staffs.* ***Village***, 8m/13km NW of Wolverhampton. **40 A5** SJ8309.
Bishopsbourne *Kent* ***Village***, 4m/7km SE of Canterbury. **15 G2** TR1852.
Bishopsdale *Kent* ***Locality***, 3m/5km W of Tenterden. TQ8434.
Bishopsteignton *Devon* Population: 1969. ***Village***, on N side of River Teign estuary, 2m/3km W of Teignmouth. Remains of medieval Bishop's Palace to NE. **5 K3** SX9173.
Bishopstoke *Hants.* Population: 16,680. ***Suburb***, to E of Eastleigh. **11 F3** SU4619.
Bishopston *Bristol* ***Suburb***, 2m/3km N of Bristol city centre. ST5875.
Bishopston (Llandeilo Ferwallt). *Swan.* Population: 4165. ***Village***, 5m/9km SW of Swansea. **17 J6** SS5789.
Bishopstone *Bucks.* ***Village***, 3m/4km S of Aylesbury. **32 B7** SP8010.
Bishopstone *E.Suss.* ***Village***, 1m/2km N of Seaford. **13 H6** TQ4701.
Bishopstone *Here.* ***Village***, 7m/11km W of Hereford. **28 D4** SO4143.
Bishopstone *Kent* ***Suburb***, 2m/3km E of Herne Bay town centre. TR2068.
Bishopstone *Swin.* ***Village***, 6m/10km E of Swindon. Site of Roman building to SE. **21 F3** SU2483.
Bishopstone *Wilts.* ***Village***, on River Ebble, 4m/6km SW of Wilton. **10 B2** SU0725.
Bishopstrow *Wilts.* ***Village***, 2m/3km SE of Warminster. **20 B7** ST8943.
Bishopswood (Bishops Wood). *Som.* ***Village***, 5m/8km NW of Chard. **8 B3** ST2512.
Bishopsworth *Bristol* ***Suburb***, SW district of Bristol. **19 J5** ST5668.
Bishopthorpe *York* Population: 3148. ***Village***, 3m/4km S of York. Archbishop's palace on E side on banks of River Ouse. **58 B5** SE5947.
Bishopton *Darl.* ***Village***, 5m/8km W of Stockton-on-Tees. **62 E4** NZ3621.
Bishopton *N.Yorks.* ***Suburb***, adjoining to W of Ripon. SE2971.
Bishopton *Renf.* Population: 5394. ***Village***, 6m/9km NW of Paisley. **74 C3** NS4371.
Bishopton *Warks.* ***Suburb***, adjoining to NW of Stratford-upon-Avon. SP1856.

Bishpool *Newport* ***Suburb***, 3m/4km E of Newport town centre. ST3488.
Bishton (Trefesgob). *Newport* ***Village***, 5m/8km E of Newport. **19 G3** ST3987.
Bishton *Staffs.* ***Hamlet***, SE of Colwich, on River Trent, 3m/4km NW of Rugeley. SK0120.
Bisley *Glos.* ***Village***, 4m/6km E of Stroud. **20 C1** SO9006.
Bisley *Surr.* ***Village***, 4m/6km W of Woking. Bisley Camp and rifle ranges to SW. **22 C6** SU9559.
Bispham *B'pool* ***Locality***, on coast, 3m/4km N of Blackpool town centre. **55 G5** SD3140.
Bispham Green *Lancs.* ***Hamlet***, 2m/3km N of Parbold. SD4813.
Bissoe *Cornw.* ***Village***, 4m/6km SW of Truro. **2 E4** SW7741.
Bisterne *Hants.* ***Hamlet***, 3m/4km S of Ringwood. **10 C4** SU1401.
Bisterne Close *Hants.* ***Settlement***, 1m/2km E of Burley and 6m/9km E of Ringwood. **10 D4** SU2202.
Bitchet Green *Kent* ***Hamlet***, 3m/4km E of Sevenoaks. TQ5654.
Bitchfield *Lincs.* ***Village***, 6m/10km SE of Grantham. **42 C3** SK9828.
Bittadon *Devon* ***Hamlet***, 4m/7km SE of Ilfracombe. **6 D1** SS5441.
Bittaford *Devon* ***Village***, on S edge of Dartmoor, 2m/3km E of Ivybridge. **5 G5** SX6657.
Bittering *Norf.* ***Hamlet***, 4m/7km NW of East Dereham. **44 D4** TF9317.
Bittering Street *Norf.* ***Hamlet***, 1m/2km E of Bittering. TF9317.
Bitterley *Shrop.* ***Village***, 4m/6km NE of Ludlow. **28 E1** SO5677.
Bitterne *S'ham.* ***Suburb***, E of Southampton to E of River Itchen. Includes Roman riverside settlement of Clausentum. **11 F3** SU4413.
Bitterne Park *S'ham.* ***Suburb***, 2m/3km NE of Southampton city centre across River Itchen. SU4414.
Bitterscote *Staffs.* ***Suburb***, 1km SW of Tamworth town centre across River Tame. SK2003.
Bittesby *Leics.* ***Locality***, 3m/4km W of Lutterworth. SP5085.
Bitteswell *Leics.* ***Village***, 1m/2km N of Lutterworth. Airfield to W. **41 H7** SP5385.
Bitton *S.Glos.* ***Village***, 2m/3km E of Keynsham. **19 K5** ST6869.
Biwmaris *I.o.A.* *Welsh form of Beaumaris, qv.*
Bix *Oxon.* ***Village***, 3m/4km NW of Henley-on-Thames. Site of Roman building to E. **22 A3** SU7285.
Bixter *Shet.* ***Settlement***, on Mainland, on E side of Bixter Voe, 6m/10km E of Walls. **109 C7** HU3352.
Bla Bheinn (Also known as Blaven.) *High.* ***Mountain***, 2m/4km W of head of Loch Slapin, Skye. Munro: height 3044 feet or 928 metres. **86 B2** NG5221.
Blaby *Leics.* Population: 6538. ***Suburb***, 5m/7km S of Leicester. **41 H6** SP5697.
Black Bank *Warks.* ***Suburb***, in S part of Bedworth. SP3586.
Black Beck *N.Yorks.* ***River***, lower reaches of Crosscliff Beck before it joins River Derwent just S of Langdale End, 4m/7km W of Scalby. **63 H3** SE9490.
Black Bourton *Oxon.* ***Village***, 6m/9km SW of Witney. **21 F1** SP2804.
Black Bridge *Pembs.* ***Settlement***, 1km E of Milford Haven. SM9106.
Black Buoy Sand *Lincs.* ***Coastal feature***, area of mud and sand on W side of The Wash, 1m/2km E of mouth of The Haven. **43 H1** TF4138.
Black Burn (Also known as Shield Water.) *Cumb.* ***River***, rising on N slopes of Cross Fell and flowing N into River South Tyne, 2m/3km S of Alston. **61 J3** NY7143.
Black Burn *D. & G.* ***River***, rising S of Barrhill near Eldrig Loch and running W into River Bladnoch, 3m/5km N of Kirkcowan. **64 C4** NX3365.
Black Burn *Moray* ***River***, rising on Romach Hill and flowing NE through Miltonduff to join River Lossie, 1m/2km W of Elgin. **97 J6** NJ1862.
Black Callerton *T. & W.* ***Hamlet***, 6m/9km NW of Newcastle upon Tyne. **71 G7** NZ1769.
Black Carr *Norf.* ***Hamlet***, 3m/5km E of Attleborough. TM0995.
Black Carr *W.Yorks.* ***Locality***, 2m/3km NW of Queensbury. SE0831.
Black Clauchrie *S.Ayr.* ***Settlement***, 4m/7km E of Barrhill. **67 G5** NX2984.
Black Combe *Cumb.* ***Mountain***, steep-sided mountain with cliffs on E side of summit ridge, 4m/7km W of Broughton in Furness. Height 1968 feet or 600 metres. **54 E1** SD1385.
Black Corries *High.* ***Inland physical feature***, corries on N slopes of A' Chruach, 2m/3km S of E end of Blackwater Reservoir. **80 E2** NN3757.
Black Corries Lodge *High.* ***Settlement***, on NW side of Rannoch Moor, 10m/16km N of Bridge of Orchy. **80 D2** NN2956.
Black Craig *Aber.* ***Mountain***, 3m/5km SW of Oldhall. Height 1735 feet or 529 metres. **90 C5** NO4394.
Black Craig *Arg. & B.* ***Mountain***, between Inverchaolain Glen and Glen Fyne. Height 1712 feet or 522 metres. **73 K3** NS1176.
Black Craig *High.* ***Mountain***, on NE side of Strath Mashie, 10m/15km SW of Newtonmore. Height 1853 feet or 565 metres. **88 C5** NN5791.
Black Crofts *Arg. & B.* ***Hamlet***, on N shore of Loch Etive, Argyll, 1m/2km E of Ledaig Point. NM9234.
Black Cross *Cornw.* ***Hamlet***, 2m/3km S of St. Columb Major. **3 G2** SW9060.
Black Devon ***River***, rising as Nettly Burn, Saline Burn and Roughcleugh Burn and running W to Clackmannan, then SW into River Forth at Clackmannan Pow, 1m/2km below Alloa. **75 H1** NS8990.
Black Dog *Devon* ***Hamlet***, 6m/10km NW of Crediton. **7 G5** SS8009.
Black Down *Devon* ***Open space***, hillslope 2m/3km S of Lydford. **6 D7** SX5082.
Black Down *Dorset* ***Hill***, 1m/2km N of Portesham, with Hardy Monument, tumuli and viewpoint at summit. Height 777 feet or 237 metres. **9 F6** SY6087.
Black Down *Som.* ***Open space***, hillslope at N of Mendip Hills, 3m/5km E of Winscombe. **19 H6** ST4757.
Black Down *W.Suss.* ***Viewpoint***, National Trust land surrounded by sandy heaths and woods. Highest point in Sussex at 919 feet or 280 metres. **12 C4** SU9129.
Black Down Hills ***Large natural feature***, ridge running E to W on border of Devon and Somerset, 6m/10km SW of Taunton. Wellington Monument (National Trust) is prominent landmark. **7 K4** ST1121.
Black Edge ***Open space***, on border of Dumfries & Galloway and Scottish Borders, on S side of Cooms Fell, 5m/8km NE of Langholm. **69 K5** NY4388.
Black Esk *D. & G.* ***River***, running S through Black Esk Reservoir and Castle O'er Forest to join River White Esk and form River Esk, 8m/13km NW of Langholm. **69 H4** NY2590.
Black Esk Reservoir *D. & G.* ***Reservoir***, 9m/14km to SE of Moffat, in Castle O'er Forest. **69 H4** NY2096.
Black Fell *Cumb.* ***Mountain***, 3m/5km E of Renwick. Height 2178 feet or 664 metres. **61 H2** NY6444.
Black Fell *N.Ayr.* ***Open space***, hillslope on E edge of North Burnt Hill, 6m/10km S of Greenock. **74 A4** NS2666.
Black Fell *Northumb.* ***Forest/woodland***, wooded area in Wark Forest, 6m/9km N of Haltwhistle. **70 C6** NY7073.
Black Halls *Dur.* ***Settlement***, near coast, 3m/5km SE of Peterlee. NZ4738.
Black Hambleton *N.Yorks.* ***Mountain***, flat-topped mountain on NW side of Arden Great Moor, across which runs Cleveland Way long distance footpath, 3m/4km SE of Osmotherley. Height 1309 feet or 399 metres. **63 F7** SE4894.
Black Head *Cornw.* ***Coastal feature***, headland on E coast of Lizard peninsula, 6m/9km NE of Lizard Point across bay. **2 E7** SW7716.
Black Head *Cornw.* ***Coastal feature***, headland at W end of St. Austell Bay and N end of Mevagissey Bay. **4 A6** SX0447.
Black Head *D. & G.* ***Coastal feature***, headland with lighthouse at S end of small Killantringan Bay on coast of Rinns of Galloway, 2m/3km NW of Portpatrick. Lighthouse is known as Killantringan Lighthouse. **64 A5** NW9856.
Black Heath *Wilts.* ***Open space***, area of downland on Salisbury Plain within area used by military, 4m/6km SE of Market Lavington. Numerous prehistoric remains in vicinity. **20 D6** SU0651.
Black Heddon *Northumb.* ***Hamlet***, 2m/4km SW of Belsay. **71 F6** NZ0776.
Black Hill ***Mountain***, on border of Aberdeenshire and Moray, 3m/4km E of Bridgend. Height 1656 feet or 505 metres. **90 C1** NJ4030.
Black Hill ***Mountain***, on border of Derbyshire and West Yorkshire, 5m/8km SW of Holmfirth. Height 1909 feet or 582 metres. **50 C2** SE0704.
Black Hill *Aber.* ***Hill***, 2m/3km S of Monymusk. Height 607 feet or 185 metres. **90 E3** NJ6711.
Black Hill *Aber.* ***Mountain***, on N side of River Don, 4m/6km S of Insch. Height 1410 feet or 430 metres. **90 E2** NJ6321.
Black Hill *Ches.* ***Mountain***, 1m/2km E of Lyme Park. Height 1338 feet or 408 metres. **49 J4** SJ9882.
Black Hill *Devon* ***Hill***, 1m/2km SE of Woodbury. Height 548 feet or 167 metres. **7 J7** SY0285.
Black Hill *D. & G.* ***Mountain***, 4m/6km NW of Black Esk Reservoir. Height 1555 feet or 474 metres. **69 G3** NT1500.
Black Hill *E.Ayr.* ***Mountain***, 1m/2km N of Muirkirk. Height 1161 feet or 354 metres. **68 C1** NS7029.
Black Hill *Midloth.* ***Mountain***, in Pentland Hills Regional Park, 3m/4km SE of Balerno. Height 1637 feet or 499 metres. **75 K4** NT1863.
Black Hill *Moray* ***Hill***, 4m/6km SE of Buckie. Height 836 feet or 255 metres. **98 C4** NJ4660.
Black Hill *Moray* ***Hill***, with wooded summit, 5m/8km NE of Keith. Height 859 feet or 262 metres. **98 C5** NJ4757.
Black Hill *N.Yorks.* ***Hill***, rising to over 300 metres, 1km to E of Gisburn Forest and 4m/6km SW of Settle. **56 C3** SD7660.
Black Hill *Shrop.* ***Mountain***, 4m/7km NE of Knighton. Height 1446 feet or 441 metres. **28 C1** SO3279.
Black Hill *S.Lan.* ***Hill***, on border with West Lothian, rising to over 280 metres, 2m/3km NW of Forth. **75 H5** NS9155.
Black Hill *T. & W.* ***Suburb***, 3m/5km SE of Gateshead town centre. NZ2859.
Black Hill *Warks.* ***Settlement***, 3m/5km NE of Stratford-upon-Avon. SP2359.
Black Hill of Mark ***Mountain***, 3m/4km S of Spittal of Glenmuick. Summit on border of Aberdeenshire and Angus. Height 2539 feet or 774 metres. **90 B6** NO3281.
Black Hillfort *S.Lan.* ***Historic/prehistoric site***, Iron Age hillfort (National Trust for Scotland) and settlement on Black Hill, 2m/4km E of Blackwood, with outlook point over River Clyde valley. **75 G6** NS8343.
Black Holm *Ork.* ***Island***, small islet 1km NW of Copinsay and 1m/2km S of Point of Ayre at E end of Mainland. HY5902.
Black House *W.Isles* ***Other feature of interest***, former dwelling house (Historic Scotland), now museum and national monument, to N of Arnol, near NW coast of Isle of Lewis. **101 F3** NB3149.
Black Isle *High.* ***Large natural feature***, peninsula in Ross and Cromarty district, between Cromarty Firth and Moray Firth, running out to Cromarty and South Sutor. **96 D6** NH6557.
Black Knowe ***Mountain***, on border of Dumfries & Galloway and Scottish Borders, 4m/7km S of Ettrick. Height 1479 feet or 451 metres. **69 H3** NT2807.
Black Knowe *Northumb.* ***Mountain***, in wooded area, 1m/2km E of Larriston Fells, and 6m/10km W of Kielder. Height 1496 feet or 456 metres. **70 A4** NY5891.
Black Knowe *Northumb.* ***Mountain***, with rocky outcrop on E side, 6m/10km SW of Falstone. Height 1614 feet or 492 metres. **70 B5** NY6481.
Black Knowe *Sc.Bord.* ***Mountain***, 4m/6km SW of Ettrick. Height 1771 feet or 540 metres. **69 H2** NT2210.
Black Knowe *Sc.Bord.* ***Mountain***, 4m/7km E of Peebles. Height 1709 feet or 521 metres. **76 B6** NT3140.
Black Knowe *Sc.Bord.* ***Mountain***, in Newcastleton Forest, 4m/6km E of Newcastleton. Height 1240 feet or 378 metres. **70 A5** NY5484.
Black Knowe Head *Sc.Bord.* ***Mountain***, 1m/2km NW of Gilmanscleuch. Height 1804 feet or 550 metres. **69 J1** NT3122.
Black Lake *W.Mid.* ***Suburb***, 1m/2km N of West Bromwich town centre. SO9992.
Black Lane *Gt.Man.* ***Locality***, adjoining to N of Radcliffe. SD7708.
Black Law *N.Ayr.* ***Mountain***, 4m/7km E of Largs. Height 1528 feet or 466 metres. **74 A5** NS2759.
Black Law *Sc.Bord.* ***Mountain***, on Ettrick Forest, 3m/5km NW of St. Mary's Loch. Height 2283 feet or 696 metres. **69 H1** NT2127.
Black Law *Sc.Bord.* ***Mountain***, 4m/6km NE of Peebles. Height 1765 feet or 538 metres. **76 B6** NT3042.
Black Loch *D. & G.* ***Lake/loch***, within Lochinch Castle grounds, to E of White Loch and 4m/6km E of Stranraer. **64 B4** NX1161.
Black Lochs *Arg. & B.* ***Lake/loch***, series of lochs, 2m/3km SE of Connel. **80 A4** NM9231.
Black Lyne *Cumb.* ***River***, rising on Kershope Forest and flowing SW to join River White Lyne and form River Lyne, 5m/7km W of Bewcastle. **70 A5** NY4973.
Black Marsh *Shrop.* ***Settlement***, 5m/8km NE of Church Stoke. **38 C6** SO3299.
Black Meldon *Sc.Bord.* ***Mountain***, 3m/5km NW of Peebles. Hillfort near summit. Height 1335 feet or 407 metres. **75 K6** NT2042.
Black Mill Bay *Arg. & B.* ***Bay***, on W coast of Luing, 1m/2km W of Toberonochy. **79 J7** NM7308.
Black Mixen *Powys* ***Mountain***, on Radnor Forest, 2m/4km N of New Radnor. Mast at summit. Height 2132 feet or 650 metres. **28 A2** SO1964.
Black Moor *Lancs.* ***Locality***, on E side of River Douglas, 1m/2km W of Mawdesley. SD4814.
Black Moor *W.Yorks.* ***Suburb***, 4m/6km N of Leeds city centre. SE2939.
Black Mount *Arg. & B.* ***Settlement***, on N side of Loch Tulla, 2m/3km NW of Bridge of Orchy. **80 D3** NN2842.
Black Mount *High.* ***Large natural feature***, moorland area on border of Lochaber district with Argyll, containing several small lochs and traversed by road running N from Bridge of Orchy towards Glen Coe. River Bà flows through centre of area from W to E. **80 D3** NN2747.
Black Mount *S.Lan.* ***Mountain***, above South Medwin valley, 1m/2km S of Dunsyre. Height 1692 feet or 516 metres. **75 J6** NT0746.
Black Mountain (Y Mynydd Du). ***Large natural feature***, range running 14m/22km from Trecastle in NE to Brynamman in SW. Culminating in Carmarthen Van at height of 2631 feet or 802 metres. **17 K3** SN7518.
Black Mountain *Powys* ***Mountain***, 4m/6km NE of Llanbister. Height 1584 feet or 483 metres. **28 A1** SO1677.
Black Mountains ***Large natural feature***, range of Old Red Sandstone hills, intersected by deep valleys, mainly in Wales but partly in England, extending from Hay-on-Wye (N) to Abergavenny (S) and from Longtown (E) to Llangorse Lake (W). **28 B6** SO2223.
Black Neuk *S.Ayr.* ***Coastal feature***, headland 2m/3km SW of Girvan. **67 F4** NX1695.
Black Notley *Essex* ***Village***, 2m/3km S of Braintree. **34 B6** TL7620.
Black Park *Bucks.* ***Leisure/recreation***, country park with lake, 2m/3km E of Stoke Poges. Pinewood Film Studios to NE. **22 D3** TQ0083.
Black Pill *Swan.* ***Suburb***, 3m/4km SW of Swansea city centre. **17 K5** SS6190.
Black Pole *Lancs.* ***Settlement***, 1m/2km NW of Woodplumpton, 5m/8km NW of Preston. SD4836.
Black Rhadley Hill *Shrop.* ***Mountain***, 4m/7km N of Bishop's Castle. Height 1319 feet or 402 metres. **38 C6** SO3495.
Black Ridge *Devon* ***Inland physical feature***, mountain slope, rising to 1880 feet or 570 metres, on SE side of Great Kneeset on Dartmoor, 5m/8km W of Lydford. **6 D7** SX5985.
Black Rock Gorge *High.* ***Inland physical feature***, rocky gorge in course of River Glass, 1m/2km long and 1m/2km W of Evanton. **96 C5** NH5866.
Black Rock Sands *Gwyn.* ***Coastal feature***, beach on NW side of River Glaslyn estuary, 3m/4km SW of Porthmadog. **36 E2** SH5337.
Black Rocks *Derbys.* ***Inland physical feature***, rock outcrop on wooded hillside, 1km S of Cromford. **50 E7** SK2955.
Black Rocks *Edin.* ***Coastal feature***, series of rocks on Firth of Forth coast, 1km NW of Leith. **76 A3** NT2777.
Black Rocks *N.Yorks.* ***Coastal feature***, rocks to S of Scarborough. **59 G1** TA0586.
Black Sail Pass *Cumb.* ***Other feature of interest***, steep mountain path from Ennerdale to Wasdale, passing between Pillar and Kirk Fell. **60 C5** NY1811.
Black Scar *Pembs.* ***Island***, rocky islet on W side of Green Scar, 1m/2km W of Dinas Fawr. SM7922.
Black Shoulder *D. & G.* ***Mountain***, 4m/6km NE of Carsphairn. Height 2257 feet or 688 metres. **67 K4** NX5996.

Black Street *Suff.* ***Hamlet***, 1m/2km W of Kessingland. TM5186.

Black Tar *Pembs.* ***Locality***, on W bank of Daugleddau estuary above Blacktar Point, to E of Llangwm. SM9909.

Black Torrington *Devon* ***Village***, 5m/8km W of Hatherleigh. **6 C5** SS4605.

Black Vein *Caerp.* ***Hamlet***, on S side of Crosskeys across Ebbw River. ST2291.

Black Ven *Dorset* *See Golden Cap.*

Black Water *D. & G.* ***River***, issuing from Troston Loch and flowing W into Water of Ken, 5m/8km N of St. John's Town of Dalry. **68 B5** NX6188.

Black Water *High.* *Anglicised form of Uisge Dubh, qv.*

Black Water *High.* ***River***, in Sutherland district, running SE from Ben Armine Forest to River Brora 8m/12km NW of Brora village. **104 C7** NC8011.

Black Water *High.* ***River***, in Ross and Cromarty district running S down Strath Garve to Loch Garve, then SE through Contin to River Conon, 2m/3km S of Strathpeffer. **95 K5** NH4754.

Black Water *High.* ***River***, flowing from confluence of two tributaries at head of Strath Rusdale into River Averon, 5m/7km NW of Alness. **96 C4** NH5974.

Black Water *High.* ***River***, in Lochaber district running W to head of Blackwater Reservoir. **80 E1** NN3760.

Black Water *Moray* ***River***, rising 5m/7km SW of Cabrach and running NE to River Deveron, 3m/4km N of village. **90 B2** NJ3830.

Black Water *P. & K.* ***River***, originating in Shee Water and running S down Glen Shee to join River Ardle, forming River Ericht nearly 1km E of Bridge of Cally. NO1451.

Black Water of Dee *D. & G.* ***River***, issuing from Loch Dee and flowing through Clatteringshaws Loch, then W into Loch Ken. Stretch below Loch Ken is known as River Dee. **65 F3** NX6870.

Blacka Burn *Northumb.* ***River***, rising in Wark Forest and flowing E, then NE to join March Burn and Swineshaw Burn to form Houxty Burn. **70 C5** NY8279.

Blackaburn *Northumb.* ***Settlement***, on Blacka Burn, Wark Forest, 4m/7km W of Wark. NY7977.

Blackacre *D. & G.* ***Settlement***, 3m/4km NE of Parkgate. **69 F4** NY0490.

Blackadder *Sc.Bord.* ***Hamlet***, 4m/6km SE of Duns. **77 G5** NT8452.

Blackadder Water *Sc.Bord.* ***River***, rising on Lammermuir and running SE to Greenlaw, then NE to Whiteadder Water at Allanton. **77 F6** NT8654.

Blackawton *Devon* ***Village***, 5m/7km W of Dartmouth. **5 J5** SX8050.

Blackbeck *Cumb.* ***Hamlet***, 1km E of Beckermet. NY0206.

Blackborough *Devon* ***Village***, 5m/8km E of Cullompton. **7 J5** ST0909.

Blackborough *Norf.* ***Settlement***, 1km SE of Blackborough End, 5m/8km SE of King's Lynn. Faint remains of 12c priory. TF6714.

Blackborough End *Norf.* ***Village***, 4m/7km SE of King's Lynn. **44 A4** TF6614.

Blackboys *E.Suss.* ***Village***, 3m/5km E of Uckfield. **13 J4** TQ5220.

Blackbraes *Aber.* ***Settlement***, 1km SE of Newmachar. **91 G3** NJ8918.

Blackbraes *Falk.* ***Settlement***, 1m/2km SE of Shieldhill. **75 H3** NS9075.

Blackbrook *Derbys.* ***Hamlet***, 1m/2km W of Belper. SK3347.

Blackbrook *Devon* ***River***, rising at Blackbrook Head on Dartmoor and flowing S past Princetown prison then E into West Dart River, 1m/2km SE of Two Bridges. **5 F3** SX6174.

Blackbrook *Leics.* ***Settlement***, 5m/8km W of Loughborough. SK4618.

Blackbrook *Mersey.* ***Suburb***, 2m/3km E of St. Helens. SJ5496.

Blackbrook *Staffs.* ***Hamlet***, 6m/10km NE of Market Drayton. **39 G2** SJ7639.

Blackbrook Reservoir *Leics.* ***Reservoir***, to S of Blackbrook. **41 G4** SK4617.

Blackburn *Aber.* Population: 1130. ***Village***, 8m/13km NW of Aberdeen. **91 G3** NJ8212.

Blackburn *B'burn.* Population: 105,994. ***Town***, on River Darwen and on Leeds and Liverpool Canal, 21m/34km NW of Manchester. Modern cathedral is former parish church. Industrial, market and retail centre. Previously dependent upon cotton industry and brewing, it now has a far wider variety of industries. Lewis Textile Museum. **56 B7** SD6828.

Blackburn *S.Yorks.* ***Locality***, adjoining to NE of Sheffield, 3m/4km W of Rotherham town centre. SK3992.

Blackburn *W.Loth.* Population: 5014. ***Small town***, 2m/3km S of Bathgate. Former coalmining town. **75 H4** NS9865.

Blackburn Common *Northumb.* ***Open space***, heathland 6m/10km NW of Bellingham. **70 C4** NY7992.

Blackburn Rig *Sc.Bord.* ***Open space***, steep NE facing hill, 1m/2km NW of Grantshouse. **77 F4** NT7966.

Blackbury Camp *Devon* ***Historic/prehistoric site***, oval hillfort (English Heritage) near S coast, with single rampart and ditch, 2m/3km SW of Southleigh. **7 K6** SY1892.

Blackcastle *High.* ***Settlement***, 4m/5km SW of Nairn. **97 F6** NH8254.

Blackchambers *Aber.* ***Settlement***, 3m/5km NW of Westhill. **91 F3** NJ7911.

Blackcraig *D. & G.* ***Locality***, 3m/4km E of Newton Stewart. **64 E4** NX4464.

Blackcraig *D. & G.* ***Settlement***, 6m/9km E of St. John's Town of Dalry. **68 C5** NX7180.

Blackcraig Forest *P. & K.* ***Forest/woodland***, on W side of Strathardle and Bridge of Cally. **82 C2** NO1051.

Blackcraig Hill *D. & G.* ***Mountain***, 5m/8km E of St. John's Town of Dalry. Height 1332 feet or 406 metres. **68 B5** NX7082.

Blackcraig Hill *E.Ayr.* ***Mountain***, 5m/8km S of New Cumnock. Height 2296 feet or 700 metres. **68 B3** NS6406.

Blackcraig Hill *P. & K.* ***Mountain***, in Blackcraig Forest, 3m/5km NW of Bridge of Cally. Height 1571 feet or 479 metres. **82 B2** NO0952.

Blackden Heath *Ches.* ***Hamlet***, 3m/4km NE of Holmes Chapel. **49 G5** SJ7871.

Blackdog *Aber.* ***Settlement***, 1km inland from coast and 3m/4km S of Balmedie. **91 H3** NJ9514.

Blackdog Rock *Aber.* ***Coastal feature***, small rock on sands, 3m/4km S of Balmedie. **91 H3** NJ9613.

Blackdown *Devon* ***Settlement***, to E of Mary Tavy, 4m/6km NE of Tavistock. **5 F3** SX5079.

Blackdown *Dorset* ***Hamlet***, 3m/4km W of Broadwindsor. **8 C4** ST3903.

Blackdown Hill *Warks.* ***Settlement***, 2m/3km N of Royal Leamington Spa. SP3168.

Blackdyke *Cumb.* ***Locality***, 2m/4km E of Silloth. NY1452.

Blacker *S.Yorks.* ***Locality***, adjoining to SE of Staincross, 2m/3km N of Barnsley town centre. SE3309.

Blacker Hill *S.Yorks.* ***Village***, 1m/2km N of Hoyland. SE3602.

Blackfell *T. & W.* ***Suburb***, W district of Washington. NZ2956.

Blackfen *Gt.Lon.* ***Suburb***, in borough of Bexley, 1m/2km N of Sidcup and 11m/17km SE of Charing Cross. TQ4674.

Blackfield *Hants.* ***Village***, 1m/2km SW of Fawley. **11 F4** SU4402.

Blackford *Aber.* ***Settlement***, 1m/2km W of Rothienorman. **90 E1** NJ7035.

Blackford *Cumb.* ***Hamlet***, 4m/6km N of Carlisle. **69 J7** NY3962.

Blackford *P. & K.* ***Village***, 4m/6km SW of Auchterarder. **81 K7** NN8909.

Blackford *Som.* ***Village***, 2m/3km W of Wedmore. **19 H7** ST4147.

Blackford *Som.* ***Village***, 4m/6km W of Wincanton. **9 F2** ST6526.

Blackford Bridge *Gt.Man.* ***Suburb***, 2m/3km S of Bury town centre. SD8007.

Blackford Hill *Edin.* ***Hill***, 2m/3km S of Edinburgh city centre. Royal Observatory. Fort at summit. Height 538 feet or 164 metres. NT2570.

Blackfordby *Leics.* ***Village***, 2m/3km NW of Ashby de la Zouch. **41 F4** SK3217.

Blackfriars *Glos.* ***Ecclesiastical building***, Dominican friary (English Heritage) founded in 1217 by St. Dominic, to W of Gloucester city centre. **29 H7** SO8218.

Blackgang *I.o.W.* ***Village***, above coast and Blackgang Chine, 1km SE of Chale. **11 F7** SZ4876.

Blackgang Chine *I.o.W.* ***Leisure/recreation***, 2m/3km W of Niton. Fantasy theme park surrounding ravine, with gardens set on cliff top 400 feet or 120 metres above sea. Opened in 1843. **11 F7** SZ4876.

Blackgate *Lancs.* ***Village***, 1m/2km E of Mere Brow. SD4319.

Blackhall *Edin.* ***Suburb***, 2m/4km W of Edinburgh city centre. **76 A3** NT2174.

Blackhall *Renf.* ***Suburb***, SE district of Paisley. NS4963.

Blackhall Colliery *Dur.* Population: 5307. ***Village***, 1m/2km SE of Peterlee. **63 F3** NZ4539.

Blackhall Forest *Aber.* ***Forest/woodland***, afforested estate to W of Banchory across River Dee. **90 E5** NO6795.

Blackhall Mill *T. & W.* ***Village***, on River Derwent, 4m/6km N of Consett. NZ1256.

Blackhall Rocks *Dur.* ***Village***, adjacent to coast, to NE of Black Halls. **63 F3** NZ4738.

Blackhall Wood *Cumb.* ***Settlement***, 1m/2km NE of Dalston. NY3851.

Blackham *E.Suss.* ***Hamlet***, 6m/9km W of Royal Tunbridge Wells. **13 J3** TQ4939.

Blackhaugh *Sc.Bord.* ***Settlement***, on Caddon Water, 2m/3km NW of Clovenfords. NT4238.

Blackheath *Essex* ***Suburb***, in S part of Colchester. **34 D6** TM0021.

Blackheath *Gt.Lon.* ***Suburb***, in borough of Lewisham, 1m/2km NE of Lewisham and 7m/11km SE of Charing Cross. The heath itself is a large open space, although traversed by roads. **23 G4** TQ3976.

Blackheath *Suff.* ***Hamlet***, 1km S of Wenhaston. **35 J1** TM4274.

Blackheath *Surr.* ***Village***, 3m/5km SE of Guildford. **22 D7** TQ0346.

Blackheath *W.Mid.* ***Suburb***, 2m/3km W of Warley town centre. **40 B7** SO9786.

Blackheddon Burn *Northumb.* ***River***, rising on Ingoe Moor and flowing E to converge with Pont River. **71 F6** NZ0576.

Blackhill *Aber.* ***Locality***, 2m/3km E of Crimond and 2m/3km S of Loch of Strathbeg. **99 J5** NK0755.

Blackhill *Aber.* ***Settlement***, 3m/5km W of Boddam. **99 J6** NK0843.

Blackhill *Dur.* ***Suburb***, to W of Consett town centre. NZ0951.

Blackhill *Glas.* ***Suburb***, 2m/4km E of Glasgow city centre. NS6266.

Blackhill *High.* ***Settlement***, on S part of Skye, 2m/4km SW of Luib. **86 B2** NG5326.

Blackhillock *Moray* ***Locality***, 5m/8km W of Keith. NJ3550.

Blackhillock *Moray* ***Locality***, 2m/3km S of Keith. **98 C6** NJ4348.

Blackhills *Aber.* ***Locality***, near E coast, 1km W of Murdoch Head and 3m/4km NE of Cruden Bay. NK1139.

Blackhills *Moray* ***Locality***, 4m/7km SE of Elgin. **97 K6** NJ2758.

Blackhills *Swan.* ***Hamlet***, 1km E of Swansea Airport. SS5891.

Blackhope Scar *Sc.Bord.* ***Mountain***, highest in Moorfoot range, 6m/10km NE of Peebles. Height 2135 feet or 651 metres. **76 B6** NT3148.

Blackhorse *Devon* ***Hamlet***, 4m/6km E of Exeter. SX9793.

Blackhouse Heights *Sc.Bord.* ***Mountain***, 4m/7km NW of St. Mary's Loch. Height 2214 feet or 675 metres. **69 H1** NT2229.

Blackjack *Lincs.* ***Settlement***, 2m/3km E of Swineshead. TF2639.

Blackkip *Northumb.* ***Mountain***, in Cheviot Hills, 3m/4km NE of Byrness. Height 1469 feet or 448 metres. **70 C3** NT7904.

Blackland *Wilts.* ***Settlement***, 2m/3km SE of Calne. **20 D5** SU0168.

Blacklands *Som.* ***Hamlet***, 1m/2km NW of Withypool on Exmoor. SS8336.

Blacklaw Hill *Dundee* ***Hill***, in Sidlaw Hills, 3m/5km NW of Longforgan. Height 932 feet or 284 metres. **82 D4** NO2834.

Blackleach *Lancs.* ***Settlement***, 1km W of Swillbrook, 5m/8km NW of Preston. SD4734.

Blackley *Gt.Man.* ***Suburb***, on SW side of Boggart Hole Clough, 3m/5km NE of Manchester city centre. SD8502.

Blackley *W.Yorks.* ***Settlement***, 3m/5km NW of Huddersfield, near junction 24 of M62 motorway. SE1019.

Blacklorg Hill *E.Ayr.* ***Mountain***, on border with Dumfries & Galloway, 6m/10km SE of New Cumnock. Height 2234 feet or 681 metres. **68 B3** NS6504.

Blacklunans *P. & K.* ***Village***, on Black Water, 9m/15km N of Blairgowrie. **82 C1** NO1460.

Blackman's Law *Northumb.* ***Mountain***, on S edge of Redesdale Forest, 3m/5km SW of Byrness. Height 1502 feet or 458 metres. **70 C4** NY7498.

Blackmill (Melin Ifan Ddu). *Bridgend* ***Hamlet***, 5m/8km N of Bridgend. **18 C3** SS9386.

Blackmoor *Gt.Man.* ***Locality***, 1m/2km S of Tyldesley. SD6900.

Blackmoor *Hants.* ***Village***, 4m/6km W of Liphook. **11 J1** SU7833.

Blackmoor *Som.* ***Settlement***, 2m/3km SE of Wellington, on N slope of Black Down Hills. **7 K4** ST1618.

Blackmoor Gate *Devon* ***Hamlet***, on NW edge of Exmoor National Park, 5m/8km SE of Combe Martin. **6 E1** SS6443.

Blackmoor Vale ***Valley***, fertile stretch of country extending roughly from Wincanton, S to Haselbury Bryan (or Hazelbury Bryan) and then W to Yetminster. **9 F3** ST7315.

Blackmoorfoot *W.Yorks.* ***Hamlet***, on N side of Blackmoorfoot Reservoir, 1m/2km SE of Slaithwaite. SE0913.

Blackmore *Essex* ***Village***, 3m/5km NW of Ingatestone. **24 C1** TL6001.

Blackmore *Shrop.* ***Settlement***, 3m/4km W of Westbury. SJ3109.

Blackmore End *Essex* ***Village***, 5m/8km N of Braintree. **34 B5** TL7430.

Blackmore End *Herts.* ***Village***, 3m/5km NE of Harpenden. **32 E7** TL1616.

Blackness *Aber.* ***Settlement***, 2m/3km S of Banchory. **90 E5** NO6992.

Blackness *Dundee* ***Suburb***, 2m/3km W of Dundee city centre. NO3730.

Blackness *Falk.* ***Village***, on Blackness Bay, on S side of Firth of Forth, 4m/6km E of Bo'ness. **75 J3** NT0579.

Blackness *High.* ***Settlement***, 1km SE of Mid Clyth. **105 H5** ND2937.

Blackness Castle *Falk.* ***Castle***, 3m/4km NE of Linlithgow. 14c-16c artillery fortress (Historic Scotland) with barracks added in 18c. Restored in 1920s. **75 J2** NT0580.

Blacknest *Hants.* ***Hamlet***, 4m/7km SW of Farnham. **22 A7** SU7941.

Blacknest *W. & M.* ***Hamlet***, at W end of lake of Virginia Water, 1km NE of Sunningdale. SU9568.

Blackney *Dorset* ***Settlement***, 3m/5km SW of Beaminster. SY4399.

Blacko *Lancs.* ***Village***, 2m/4km N of Nelson. **56 D5** SD8541.

Blackpole *Worcs.* ***Suburb***, in NE part of Worcester. SO8657.

Blackpool *B'pool* Population: 146,262. ***Town***, large coastal resort and conference centre on Irish Sea, 15m/24km W of Preston. 19c fashionable resort, still very popular today. Blackpool Pleasure Beach, annual Illuminations, Tower, Zoo Park, Sandcastle and Winter Gardens. Airport 3m/5km S. **55 G6** SD3035.

Blackpool *Devon* ***Hamlet***, on S coast, 3m/4km SW of Dartmouth. SX8547.

Blackpool *Pembs.* ***Hamlet***, 1km SW of Canaston Bridge. SN0614.

Blackpool Airport ***Airport/airfield***, close to coast, 3m/4km S of Blackpool town centre, on border of Blackpool and Lancashire. **55 G6** SD3231.

Blackpool Corner *Devon* ***Hamlet***, on Dorset border, 3m/4km E of Axminster. SY3398.

Blackpool Gate *Cumb.* ***Settlement***, 2m/3km NE of Oakshaw Ford, to S of Kershope Forest and S of Black Lyne river. **70 A6** NY5377.

Blackpool Pleasure Beach *B'pool* ***Leisure/recreation***, large amusement park at Blackpool's South Shore containing both modern and vintage roller-coasters. **55 G6** SD3033.

Blackpool Tower *B'pool* ***Other feature of interest***, notable landmark, built between 1891 and 1894 in style of Eiffel Tower. It is 518 feet or 158 metres in height. **55 G6** SD3036.

Blackridge *W.Loth.* Population: 1560. ***Village***, 3m/5km W of Armadale. **75 G4** NS8967.

Blackrock *Arg. & B.* ***Settlement***, at head of Loch Indaal, 2m/3km W of Bridgend, Islay. **72 B4** NR3064.

Blackrock *Cornw.* ***Settlement***, 3m/5km S of Camborne. SW6634.

Blackrock *Mon.* ***Settlement***, 2m/3km E of Bryn-mawr. **28 B7** SO2112.

Blackrod *Gt.Man.* Population: 5681. ***Small town***, 7m/11km W of Bolton. **49 F1** SD6110.

Blackshaw *D. & G.* ***Settlement***, near shore of Solway Firth, 8m/13km SE of Dumfries. **69 F7** NY0465.
Blackshaw Bank *D. & G.* ***Coastal feature***, sandbank to S of Blackshaw. **69 F7** NY0462.
Blackshaw Head *W.Yorks.* ***Village***, 2m/4km W of Hebden Bridge. **56 E7** SD9527.
Blacksmith's Corner *Essex* ***Settlement***, 4m/7km N of Colchester. **34 E5** TM0231.
Blacksmith's Green *Suff.* ***Settlement***, 1m/2km SE of Wetheringsett. TM1465.
Blacksmith's Shop *D. & G.* ***Other feature of interest***, at Gretna Green, one of first places in Scotland where young runaway lovers could be married without parental consent, 1km N of Gretna. **69 J7** NY3268.
Blacksnape *B'burn.* ***Settlement***, 1m/2km E of Darwen. SD7121.
Blackstone *W.Suss.* ***Hamlet***, 2m/3km E of Henfield. **13 F5** TQ2416.
Blacktar Point *Pembs.* ***Coastal feature***, headland on W side of Daugleddau estuary to E of Llangwm. SM9909.
Blackthorn *Oxon.* ***Village***, 3m/5km SE of Bicester. **31 H7** SP6219.
Blackthorpe *Suff.* ***Village***, 3m/5km E of Bury St. Edmunds. **34 D2** TL9063.
Blacktoft *E.Riding* ***Village***, on N bank of River Ouse, 3m/5km S of Gilberdyke. **58 E7** SE8329.
Blackton Reservoir *Dur.* ***Reservoir***, middle of three, in Baldersdale, 7m/11km W of Barnard Castle. **62 A5** NY9418.
Blacktop *Aberdeen* ***Hamlet***, 5m/8km W of Aberdeen. **91 G4** NJ8604.
Blacktown *Newport* ***Village***, 5m/8km SW of Newport. **19 F3** ST2581.
Blackwall *Gt.Lon.* ***Suburb***, in borough of Tower Hamlets, 4m/6km E of London Bridge. Location of road tunnel under River Thames. TQ3880.
Blackwater ***River***, rising at Aldershot and flowing N to Sandhurst then W into River Loddon at Swallowfield, to S of Reading. SU7265.
Blackwater *Cornw.* ***Village***, 4m/6km NE of Redruth. **2 E4** SW7346.
Blackwater *Dorset* ***Locality***, on River Stour 3m/4km NW of Christchurch. SZ1396.
Blackwater *Essex* ***River***, rising N of Braintree and flowing via Coggeshall, Kelvedon and Witham to Maldon, then E into North Sea to S of Mersea Island. **25 F1** TM0010.
Blackwater *Hants.* ***Suburb***, 1m/2km W of Camberley. **22 B6** SU8559.
Blackwater *I.o.W.* ***Village***, 2m/3km S of Newport. **11 G6** SZ5086.
Blackwater *Norf.* ***Settlement***, 2m/3km S of Reepham. TG0820.
Blackwater *Som.* ***Hamlet***, 1m/2km N of Buckland St. Mary and 6m/9km NW of Chard. ST2615.
Blackwater *Suff.* ***Suburb***, to N of Southwold across Buss Creek. **35 J1** TM5077.
Blackwater Forest *Moray* ***Forest/woodland***, astride upper reaches of Black Water, 8m/13km S of Dufftown. Contains deer. **89 K2** NJ3126.
Blackwater Reservoir *High.* ***Reservoir***, in Lochaber district, 8m/12km long E to W. Dam is 4m/6km E of Kinlochleven. **80 D1** NN3059.
Blackwaterfoot *N.Ayr.* ***Village***, on Drumadoon Bay, W coast of Arran, at mouth of Black Water, 9m/14km SW of Brodick. **66 D1** NR8928.
Blackwaters *Staffs.* ***Settlement***, 4m/6km NW of Eccleshall. SJ7732.
Blackwell *Darl.* ***Suburb***, 1m/2km SW of Darlington town centre. **62 D5** NZ2712.
Blackwell *Derbys.* ***Hamlet***, 4m/7km E of Buxton. **50 D5** SK1272.
Blackwell *Derbys.* Population: 3179. ***Village***, 3m/4km NE of Alfreton. **51 G7** SK4458.
Blackwell *Warks.* ***Village***, 2m/3km NW of Shipston on Stour. **30 D4** SP2443.
Blackwell *W.Suss.* ***Suburb***, to N of East Grinstead. TQ3939.
Blackwell *Worcs.* ***Village***, 2m/3km NE of Bromsgrove. **29 J1** SO9872.
Blackwells End Green *Glos.* ***Hamlet***, 5m/9km NW of Gloucester. **29 G6** SO7825.
Blackwood (Coed-duon). *Caerp.* Population: 14,466. ***Town***, 7m/11km N of Caerphilly. **18 E2** ST1797.
Blackwood *D. & G.* ***Settlement***, 1km NW of Auldgirth, 3m/5km NE of Dunscore. **68 E5** NX9087.
Blackwood *S.Lan.* Population: 1900. ***Village***, 6m/9km W of Lanark and adjoining to N of Kirkmuirhill. **75 F6** NS7943.
Blackwood Hill *Staffs.* ***Hamlet***, 4m/6km W of Leek. **49 J7** SJ9255.
Blacon *Ches.* ***Suburb***, NW district of Chester. **48 C6** SJ3868.
Bladbean *Kent* ***Settlement***, 3m/4km E of Stelling Minnis. **15 G3** TR1746.
Blades *N.Yorks.* ***Settlement***, adjoining to W of Feetham, in Swaledale, 4m/6km W of Reeth. **62 A7** SD9898.
Bladnoch *D. & G.* ***River***, issuing from Loch Maberry and flowing generally SE to Glassoch, then S past Kirkcowan, and finally E through Bladnoch and into Wigtown Bay. **64 D5** NX4655.
Bladnoch *D. & G.* ***Village***, on N bank of River Bladnoch, 1m/2km SW of Wigtown. River issues from Loch Maberry and flows SE to Wigtown Bay on S side of Wigtown. **64 E5** NX4254.
Bladon *Oxon.* ***Village***, 1m/2km S of Woodstock across park of Blenheim Palace. Sir Winston Churchill buried in churchyard. **31 F7** SP4414.
Blaeberry Hill *D. & G.* ***Mountain***, on Eskdalemuir Forest, 3m/5km NE of Eskdalemuir. Height 1374 feet or 419 metres. **69 H3** NT2801.
Blaen Celyn *Cere.* ***Hamlet***, 3m/4km E of Llangranog. SN3554.
Blaen Clydach *R.C.T.* ***Village***, 1km NW of Tonypandy. SS9893.
Blaen-geuffordd *Cere.* ***Settlement***, 1km W of Capel Bangor. SN6480.
Blaen Glaswen *Powys* ***Valley***, carrying River Disgynfa E towards River Rhaeadr, 3m/4km N of Llangynog. **37 K2** SJ0430.
Blaen-y-coed *Carmar.* ***Hamlet***, 6m/9km NW of Carmarthen. **17 G2** SN3527.
Blaenafon *Torfaen* *Welsh form of Blaenavon, qv.*
Blaenannerch *Cere.* ***Hamlet***, 2m/3km SW of Aberporth. **26 B4** SN2449.
Blaenau *B.Gwent* *Welsh form of Blaina, qv.*
Blaenau Dolwyddelan *Conwy* ***Settlement***, dispersed settlement 4m/6km N of Blaenau Ffestiniog. **46 E7** SH6951.
Blaenau Ffestiniog *Gwyn.* Population: 4546. ***Small town***, 3m/4km N of Ffestiniog and 17m/27km SE of Caernarfon. Llechwedd Slate Caverns, with underground shafts, 1km N. Terminus of Ffestiniog Railway. **37 F1** SH7045.
Blaenau-Gwent *B.Gwent* ***Locality***, adjoining to NW of Abertillery. SO2104.
Blaenavon (Blaenafon). *Torfaen* Population: 6066. ***Small town***, 5m/8km N of Pontypool. Blaenavon Ironworks (Cadw) to NW, dating from 1788, are well-preserved ruins showing blast furnaces, casting houses and workers' cottages. **19 F1** SO2508.
Blaenawey *Mon.* ***Hamlet***, 3m/5km N of Abergavenny. **28 B7** SO2919.
Blaencwm *R.C.T.* ***Hamlet***, 1m/2km NW of Treherbert. **18 C1** SS9298.
Blaendulais *N.P.T.* *Welsh form of Seven Sisters, qv.*
Blaendyryn *Powys* ***Hamlet***, 2m/3km N of Llanfihangel Nant Bran. **27 J5** SN9336.
Blaenffos *Pembs.* ***Hamlet***, 6m/9km S of Cardigan. **16 E1** SN1937.
Blaengarw *Bridgend* ***Village***, 8m/13km N of Bridgend. **18 C2** SS9092.
Blaengwawr *R.C.T.* ***Locality***, adjoining to SE of Aberdare. SO0001.
Blaengweche *Carmar.* ***Settlement***, 3m/5km NE of Ammanford. **17 K3** SN6417.
Blaengwrach *N.P.T.* ***Village***, 2m/3km SW of Glyn-neath. **18 B1** SN8605.
Blaengwynfi *N.P.T.* Population: 1741. ***Village***, 5m/8km W of Rhondda. **18 B2** SS8996.
Blaenhafren *Powys* ***River***, source of River Severn on NE slopes of Plynlimon. **37 H7** SN8289.
Blaenllechau *R.C.T.* ***Hamlet***, in Rhondda Fach valley, 1km N of Ferndale. ST0097.
Blaenos *Carmar.* ***Settlement***, 1km W of Llandovery. **27 G5** SN7534.
Blaenpennal *Cere.* ***Hamlet***, 4m/7km NW of Tregaron. **27 F2** SN6364.
Blaenplwyf *Cere.* ***Hamlet***, 4m/6km S of Aberystwyth. **26 E1** SN5775.
Blaenporth *Cere.* ***Village***, 2m/3km S of Aberporth. **26 B4** SN2648.
Blaenrhondda *R.C.T.* ***Village***, at head of Rhondda Fawr valley, 1m/2km NW of Treherbert. **18 C1** SS9299.
Blaenwaun *Carmar.* ***Hamlet***, 7m/11km N of Whitland. **17 F2** SN2327.
Blagdon *Devon* ***Locality***, 5m/7km SE of Holsworthy. SX3697.
Blagdon *N.Som.* ***Village***, below N slopes of Mendip Hills, 5m/8km SE of Congresbury. **19 H6** ST5058.
Blagdon *Torbay* ***Settlement***, 2m/4km W of Paignton. **5 J4** SX8561.
Blagdon Hill *Som.* ***Hamlet***, 4m/7km S of Taunton. **8 B3** ST2118.
Blagdon Lake (Yeo Reservoir). *N.Som.* ***Reservoir***, on border with Bath & North East Somerset, to NE of Blagdon in valley of River Yeo or Congresbury Yeo. **19 J6** ST5159.
Blaguegate *Lancs.* ***Settlement***, adjoining to W of Skelmersdale. SD4506.
Blaich *High.* ***Village***, in Lochaber district on S side of Loch Eil. **87 G7** NN0376.
Blaina (Blaenau). *B.Gwent* ***Village***, 2m/4km S of Bryn-mawr. **19 F1** SO1908.
Blainslie *Sc.Bord.* ***Locality***, 3m/4km S of Lauder. NT5443.
Blair Atholl *P. & K.* ***Village***, at confluence of River Tilt and River Garry, 6m/10km NW of Pitlochry. **81 K1** NN8765.
Blair Castle *N.Ayr.* ***Castle***, mainly of 17c, with later additions, 1m/2km SE of Dalry. **74 B6** NS3048.
Blair Castle *P. & K.* ***Castle***, to NW of Blair Atholl. White turreted in Scottish baronial style dating in part from 13c, seat of Dukes and Earls of Atholl. The present Duke maintains the only private army in Europe, The Atholl Highlanders. **81 K1** NN8765.
Blair Drummond *Stir.* ***Leisure/recreation***, estate with safari and leisure park on S bank of River Teith, 5m/8km NW of Stirling. **75 F1** NS7398.
Blairadam Forest *Fife* ***Forest/woodland***, partly in Perth & Kinross on W side of Kelty. **75 K1** NT1195.
Blairannaich *Arg. & B.* ***Settlement***, on W side of Loch Lomond, 1m/2km NE of Tarbet. **80 E7** NN3206.
Blairbuie *Arg. & B.* ***Settlement***, in Glen Fyne, 3m/4km NE of Knockdow. **73 K3** NS1174.
Blairdenon Hill *Clack.* ***Mountain***, 4m/7km SW of Blackford. Height 2070 feet or 631 metres. **81 K7** NN8601.
Blairgowrie *P. & K.* Population: 8001. ***Small town***, on River Ericht, 17m/27km NW of Dundee. **82 C3** NO1745.
Blairhall *Fife* ***Village***, 6m/9km W of Dunfermline. **75 J2** NT0089.
Blairhoyle *Stir.* ***Settlement***, 2m/3km E of Port of Menteith. **81 H7** NN6101.
Blairhullichan *Stir.* ***Settlement***, on W shore of Loch Ard, 1km SW of Kinlochard. **81 F7** NN4401.
Blairingone *P. & K.* ***Village***, 4m/6km NW of Saline. **75 H1** NS9896.
Blairkip *E.Ayr.* ***Settlement***, 2m/4km NW of Sorn. **74 D7** NS5430.
Blairlinn *N.Lan.* ***Locality***, industrial area 1m/2km S of Cumbernauld town centre. NS7572.
Blairlogie *Stir.* ***Village***, 3m/5km NE of Stirling. **75 G1** NS8296.
Blairmore *Arg. & B.* ***Village***, resort in Argyll 1m/2km N of Strone Point at entrance to Loch Long. **73 K2** NS1981.
Blairmore *High.* ***Settlement***, near W coast of Sutherland district, 3m/4km NW of Kinlochbervie. **102 D2** NC1959.
Blairmore *High.* ***Settlement***, 1km E of Little Rogart, Sutherland district. **96 E1** NC7404.
Blairnairn *Arg. & B.* ***Settlement***, in Glen Fruin, 4m/6km N of Helensburgh. **74 B2** NS2988.
Blairnamarrow *Moray* ***Settlement***, 3m/5km SE of Tomintoul. **89 K3** NJ2115.
Blairpark *N.Ayr.* ***Settlement***, 3m/5km SE of Largs. **74 A5** NS2457.
Blairquhan *S.Ayr.* ***Settlement***, 1m/2km NW of Straiton. **67 H3** NS3605.
Blairquhosh *Stir.* ***Settlement***, 3m/4km NW of Strathblane. **74 D2** NS5282.
Blair's Ferry *Arg. & B.* ***Settlement***, on W shore of Kyles of Bute, 2m/3km S of Tighnabruaich. **73 H4** NR9869.
Blairshinnoch *Aber.* ***Settlement***, 3m/5km SW of Banff. **98 E4** NJ6462.
Blairuskinmore *Stir.* ***Settlement***, at S end of Loch Chon, 6m/10km W of Aberfoyle. **81 F7** NN4303.
Blairvadach *Arg. & B.* ***Settlement***, above E shore of Gare Loch, 1m/2km NW of Rhu. **74 A2** NS2685.
Blairydryne *Aber.* ***Hamlet***, 4m/6km SE of Banchory. **91 F5** NO7492.
Blairythan *Aber.* ***Settlement***, 4m/6km N of Balmedie. **91 H2** NJ9723.
Blaisdon *Glos.* ***Village***, 4m/6km NE of Cinderford. **29 G7** SO7016.
Blake End *Essex* ***Hamlet***, 4m/6km W of Braintree. **33 K6** TL7022.
Blake Fell *Cumb.* ***Mountain***, on Loweswater Fell, 4m/6km NE of Ennerdale Bridge. Height 1879 feet or 573 metres. **60 C5** NY1119.
Blake Muir *Sc.Bord.* ***Mountain***, on Southern Upland Way, 4m/7km SW of Innerleithen. Height 1532 feet or 467 metres. **76 B7** NT3030.
Blakebrook *Worcs.* ***Suburb***, to W of Kidderminster. **29 H1** SO8176.
Blakedown *Worcs.* ***Village***, 3m/5km E of Kidderminster. **29 H1** SO8878.
Blakehope Fell *Northumb.* ***Open space***, hillside to E of Brownrigg Head, 2m/4km S of Rochester. **70 D4** NY8394.
Blakehope Head *Sc.Bord.* ***Mountain***, 4m/6km N of Tweedsmuir. Height 1781 feet or 543 metres. **75 J7** NT1030.
Blakelaw *Sc.Bord.* ***Settlement***, 4m/6km SE of Kelso. **77 F7** NT7630.
Blakelaw *T. & W.* ***Suburb***, 2m/4km NW of Newcastle upon Tyne city centre. **71 H7** NZ2166.
Blakeley *Staffs.* ***Suburb***, adjoining to SW of Wombourne, 5m/8km SW of Wolverhampton. SO8692.
Blakeley Lane *Staffs.* ***Settlement***, 2m/3km E of Werrington. SJ9747.
Blakelow *Ches.* ***Settlement***, 2m/3km E of Nantwich. SJ6851.
Blakeman's Law *Northumb.* ***Hill***, 2m/3km NW of Otterburn. Height 899 feet or 274 metres. **70 D4** NY8795.
Blakemere *Ches.* ***Hamlet***, 7m/11km W of Northwich. SJ5571.
Blakemere *Here.* ***Village***, 9m/15km W of Hereford. **28 C4** SO3641.
Blakenall Heath *W.Mid.* ***Suburb***, 2m/3km N of Walsall town centre. SK0001.
Blakeney *Glos.* ***Village***, near River Severn estuary, 4m/6km NE of Lydney. **19 K1** SO6707.
Blakeney *Norf.* ***Village***, near coast, 5m/7km NW of Holt. Yachting centre. Remains of 14c guildhall (English Heritage). **44 E1** TG0343.
Blakeney Guildhall *Norf.* ***Other feature of interest***, remains of 14c guildhall (English Heritage) in Blakeney, 1m/2km W of Cley next the Sea. Only basement has survived. **44 E1** TG0243.
Blakeney Point *Norf.* ***Nature reserve***, National Trust property on spit of land to N of Blakeney. Shingle, salt marsh and dunes. Noted for seal colonies. **44 E1** TG0047.
Blakenhall *Ches.* ***Hamlet***, 6m/9km SE of Nantwich. **39 G1** SJ7247.
Blakenhall *W.Mid.* ***Suburb***, to S of Wolverhampton. **40 B6** SO9297.
Blakenham Woodland Garden *Suff.* ***Garden***, 1km SW of Great Blakenham. 5 acres of woodland garden with daffodils, bluebells and camellias in spring. **35 F4** TM1149.
Blakeshall *Worcs.* ***Hamlet***, 3m/5km N of Kidderminster. **40 A7** SO8381.
Blakesley *Northants.* ***Village***, 4m/7km W of Towcester. **31 H3** SP6250.
Blakesley Hall *W.Mid.* ***Historic house***, late 16c yeoman farmhouse, 4m/6km E of Birmingham city centre. Contains period rooms and preserved 16c wall paintings. **40 D7** SP1286.
Blakey Ridge *N.Yorks.* ***Open space***, moorland ridge on S side of North York Moors, running N to S and crossed by narrow road, 6m/10km N of Kirkbymoorside. **63 H7** SE6897.
Blanch Fell *Lancs.* ***Open space***, N facing hillside on moors, 6m/9km E of Lancaster. **55 J3** SD5760.
Blanchland *Northumb.* ***Village***, with large square in upper valley of River Derwent, 9m/14km S of Hexham. Built on remains of medieval monastery, Blanchland Abbey, in 18c by Bishop of Durham for local lead-mining industry. Post Office and shop was former abbey gatehouse, Lord Crewe Arms was abbey guesthouse, and its garden the cloister. **62 A1** NY9650.

Blanchland Abbey *Dur.* ***Ecclesiastical building***, remains of 12c monastery founded by Walter de Bolbec, now site of Blanchland village. Parish church of St. Mary was former north transept. **62 A1** NY9650.

Blanchland Moor *Northumb.* ***Open space***, moorland to W of Derwent Reservoir, 2m/3km N of Blanchland. **62 A1** NY9553.

Bland Hill *N.Yorks.* ***Hamlet***, 5m/8km N of Otley. **57 H4** SE2053.

Blandford *Dorset Familiar form of Blandford Forum, qv.*

Blandford Forum (Commonly known as Blandford.) *Dorset* Population: 8880. ***Small town***, on River Stour, 16m/26km NW of Bournemouth. Some fine Georgian buildings. **9 H4** ST8806.

Blandford St. Mary *Dorset* ***Village***, 1km S of Blandford Forum across River Stour. **9 H4** ST8905.

Blanefield *Stir.* ***Village***, 1km NW of Strathblane. **74 D3** NS5579.

Blanerne *Sc.Bord.* ***Settlement***, on Whiteadder Water, 4m/6km NE of Duns. NT8356.

Blankney *Lincs.* ***Village***, 9m/15km SE of Lincoln. **52 D6** TF0660.

Blantyre *S.Lan.* ***Town***, former cotton town, adjoining to NW of Hamilton. Birthplace of David Livingstone, 19c explorer. NS6857.

Blar a' Chaorainn *High.* ***Settlement***, 5m/8km NW of North Ballachulish. **80 C1** NN1066.

Blàr a' Ghille Dhomhnaich *High.* ***Mountain***, 7m/11km W of Berriedale. Height 1082 feet or 330 metres. **105 F6** ND0022.

Blargie *High.* ***Settlement***, in valley of River Spey, 8m/12km SW of Newtonmore. **88 D5** NN6094.

Blarglas *Arg. & B.* ***Settlement***, 4m/6km NE of Helensburgh. **74 B2** NS3486.

Blarmachfoldach *High.* ***Hamlet***, in Lochaber district, 3m/5km S of Fort William. **80 B1** NN0969.

Blarnalevoch *High.* ***Settlement***, 1m/2km W of Leckmelm across Loch Broom. **95 H2** NH1490.

Blasford Hill *Essex* ***Settlement***, 3m/4km N of Chelmsford town centre. TL7011.

Blashaval *W.Isles Anglicised form of Blathaisbhal, qv.*

Blashford *Hants.* ***Hamlet***, 1m/2km N of Ringwood. **10 C4** SU1506.

Blaston *Leics.* ***Village***, 5m/8km SW of Uppingham. **42 B6** SP8095.

Blathaisbhal (Anglicised form: Blashaval.) *W.Isles* ***Settlement***, on E coast North Uist, 2m/3km NW of Lochmaddy. **92 D4** NF8970.

Blatherwycke *Northants.* ***Village***, 6m/10km NW of Oundle. **42 C6** SP9795.

Blatobulgium Roman Fort *D. & G.* ***Historic/prehistoric site***, 2m/3km E of Ecclefechan. Roman station occupied from AD 80 to AD 180. Visible remains date from AD 152, following construction of Antonine Wall. **69 H6** NY2175.

Blaven *High. Alternative name for Bla Bheinn, qv.*

Blawith *Cumb.* ***Hamlet***, 6m/10km N of Ulverston. **55 F1** SD2888.

Blawith Fells *Cumb.* ***Open space***, on W side of S end of Coniston Water and containing Beacon Tarn, 4m/7km S of Coniston. **60 D7** SD2790.

Blawith Point *Cumb.* ***Locality***, adjoining to NE of Grange-over-Sands. SD4178.

Blaxhall *Suff.* ***Village***, at N end of Tunstall Forest, 4m/7km S of Saxmundham. **35 H3** TM3657.

Blaxton *S.Yorks.* ***Village***, 5m/8km N of Bawtry. **51 J2** SE6700.

Blaydon *T. & W.* Population: 15,510. ***Town***, on S side of River Tyne, 5m/7km W of Gateshead. **71 G7** NZ1863.

Blaydon Burn *T. & W.* ***Locality***, 1m/2km SW of Blaydon. NZ1662.

Blea Moor ***Open space***, moorland on border of Cumbria and North Yorkshire, highest point of which is Crag of Blea Moor (1755 feet or 535 metres), to E of Whernside, 6m/10km NW of Horton in Ribblesdale. **56 C1** SD7681.

Bleadney *Som.* ***Hamlet***, 4m/7km W of Wells. **19 H7** ST4845.

Bleadon *N.Som.* ***Village***, 3m/5km SE of Weston-super-Mare, and below S slope of Bleadon Hill. **19 G6** ST3456.

Bleadon Hill *N.Som.* ***Hill***, 3m/5km SE of Weston-super-Mare. Panoramic viewpoint. Height 574 feet or 175 metres. **19 G6** ST3557.

Bleak Hey Nook *Gt.Man.* ***Settlement***, 6m/10km NE of Oldham. **50 C2** SE0009.

Bleak House *Kent* ***Historic house***, small Regency house in Broadstairs town centre, where Dickens wrote novel of same name and also David Copperfield. Now Dickens and Maritime Museum, housing collection of Dickensiana. **25 K5** TR3967.

Bleak Law *S.Lan.* ***Mountain***, in Pentland Hills, 2m/3km N of Dunsyre. Height 1460 feet or 445 metres. **75 J5** NT0651.

Bleaklow Hill *Derbys.* ***Inland physical feature***, mountain ridge on High Peak extending from Bleaklow Head to Bleaklow Stones (each 2060 feet or 628 metres above sea level) that forms the watershed for the head waters of Rivers Derwent, Westend, Alport and Ashop, as well as several streams feeding River Etherow to N and W. **50 D3** SK1096.

Blean *Kent* Population: 3270. ***Village***, 3m/4km NW of Canterbury. **25 H5** TR1260.

Bleasby *Lincs.* ***Settlement***, 3m/5km SE of Market Rasen. TF1384.

Bleasby *Notts.* ***Village***, 3m/5km S of Southwell. **42 A1** SK7149.

Bleasby Moor *Lincs.* ***Hamlet***, 3m/4km NW of East Barkwith. TF1283.

Bleatarn *Cumb.* ***Settlement***, 2m/3km SW of Warcop. **61 J5** NY7313.

Bleathwood Common *Here.* ***Settlement***, 3m/5km NW of Tenbury Wells. SO5570.

Bleaval *W.Isles* ***Mountain***, on South Harris, 3m/5km N of Leverburgh. Height 1305 feet or 398 metres. **93 F2** NG0391.

Blebocraigs *Fife* ***Village***, 5m/8km W of St. Andrews. **83 F6** NO4315.

Bleddfa *Powys* ***Village***, 6m/9km SW of Knighton. Earthworks mark site of former castle. **28 B2** SO2068.

Bledington *Glos.* ***Village***, 4m/6km SE of Stow-on-the-Wold. **30 D6** SP2422.

Bledlow *Bucks.* ***Village***, 2m/3km SW of Princes Risborough. Site of Roman building 1km SW. **22 A1** SP7702.

Bledlow Ridge *Bucks.* ***Village***, 5m/8km NW of High Wycombe. **22 A2** SU7997.

Bleet *Wilts.* ***Hamlet***, 3m/4km E of Trowbridge. ST8958.

Blencarn *Cumb.* ***Village***, 2m/3km NW of Milburn. **61 H3** NY6331.

Blencathra *Cumb. Alternative name for Saddleback, qv.*

Blencogo *Cumb.* ***Village***, 4m/6km W of Wigton. **60 C2** NY1948.

Blendworth *Hants.* ***Village***, 1km NE of Horndean. **11 J3** SU7113.

Bleng *Cumb.* ***River***, rising in Cumbrian Mountains, 2m/4km S of head of Ennerdale Water, flowing SW to Wellington, near Gosforth, then E into River Irt, 1m/2km NW of Santon Bridge. **60 B6** NY1003.

Blenheim *Oxon.* ***Locality***, parish to S and W of Woodstock, containing Blenheim Palace. SP4416.

Blenheim Palace *Oxon.* ***Historic house***, in large park with lake, to S of Woodstock, 8m/13km NW of Oxford. Built in early 18c by Vanbrugh and Hawksmoor as a gift from Queen Anne to Duke of Marlborough, rewarding him for his military services. It is named after one of his victories. Sir Winston Churchill born here in 1874. **31 F7** SP4416.

Blennerhasset *Cumb.* ***Hamlet***, 2m/3km E of Aspatria. **60 C2** NY1741.

Blervie Castle *Moray* ***Settlement***, 3m/4km SE of Forres. Standing stones and castle ruins nearby. **97 H6** NJ0757.

Blestium *Mon. See Monmouth.*

Bletchingdon *Oxon.* ***Village***, 7m/11km N of Oxford. **31 G7** SP5017.

Bletchingley *Surr.* Population: 2558. ***Village***, 3m/5km E of Redhill. Site of Roman building 1m/2km N. **23 G6** TQ3250.

Bletchley *M.K.* Population: 41,435. ***Town***, at S end of Milton Keynes, 43m/70km NW of London. **32 B5** SP8733.

Bletchley *Shrop.* ***Hamlet***, 4m/6km W of Market Drayton. **39 F2** SJ6233.

Bletherston (Trefelen). *Pembs.* ***Hamlet***, 5m/8km NW of Narberth. **16 D2** SN0621.

Bletsoe *Beds.* ***Village***, 6m/9km N of Bedford. Site of Roman building to W. Remains of original castle moat E of church. **32 D3** TL0258.

Blewbury *Oxon.* Population: 1479. ***Village***, 3m/5km S of Didcot. Prehistoric fort to E. **21 J3** SU5385.

Blickling *Norf.* ***Village***, 1m/2km NW of Aylsham. **45 F3** TG1728.

Blickling Hall *Norf.* ***Historic house***, National Trust property 1m/2km NW of Aylsham. Mainly 17c house in large grounds. **45 F3** TG1728.

Blidworth *Notts.* Population: 4215. ***Village***, 5m/7km SE of Mansfield. **51 H7** SK5956.

Blidworth Bottoms *Notts.* ***Hamlet***, 1km S of Blidworth. SK5954.

Blindburn *Aber.* ***Settlement***, 4m/6km N of Ellon. **91 H1** NJ9435.

Blindburn *Northumb.* ***Settlement***, on upper reaches of River Coquet, in Cheviot Hills, 4m/6km NW of Shillmoor. **70 D2** NT8210.

Blindcrake *Cumb.* ***Village***, 3m/5km NE of Cockermouth. **60 C3** NY1434.

Blindley Heath *Surr.* ***Village***, 5m/8km N of East Grinstead. **23 G7** TQ3645.

Blindman's Bay *Arg. & B.* ***Bay***, on W side of Kyles of Bute, 1m/2km N of Ardlamont Point, Argyll. **73 H4** NR9965.

Blinkbonny Height *Sc.Bord.* ***Hill***, on NE side of Kershope Forest, 2m/3km SE of Newcastleton. Height 866 feet or 264 metres. **69 K5** NY4984.

Blisland *Cornw.* ***Village***, typical moorland village 4m/7km NE of Bodmin. Parish church is part Norman. **4 B3** SX1073.

Bliss Gate *Worcs.* ***Hamlet***, 3m/5km SW of Bewdley. **29 G1** SO7472.

Blissford *Hants.* ***Hamlet***, on edge of New Forest, 2m/3km E of Fordingbridge. **10 C3** SU1713.

Blisworth *Northants.* Population: 1658. ***Village***, at N end of long tunnel on Grand Union Canal, 4m/6km NE of Towcester. **31 J3** SP7253.

Blithbury *Staffs.* ***Hamlet***, 3m/4km NE of Rugeley. **40 C3** SK0820.

Blithe ***River***, rising E of Stoke-on-Trent and flowing SE through Blithfield Reservoir and into River Trent 1km NW of King's Bromley. **40 C3** SK1117.

Blithfield *Staffs.* ***Locality***, W of Blithfield Reservoir, 4m/6km N of Rugeley. SK0424.

Blithfield Reservoir *Staffs.* ***Reservoir***, large reservoir to E of Blithfield. **40 C3** SK0524.

Blitterlees *Cumb.* ***Settlement***, adjoining to S of Silloth. **60 C1** NY1052.

Blo' Norton *Norf.* ***Village***, 7m/11km W of Diss. **34 E1** TM0179.

Blockley *Glos.* ***Village***, 3m/5km NW of Moreton-in-Marsh. Sleepy Hollow Farm Park includes collection of farmlife and wild animals. **30 C5** SP1635.

Blofield *Norf.* ***Village***, 7m/11km E of Norwich. **45 H5** TG3309.

Bloodstone Hill *High.* ***Mountain***, near NW coast of Rum, 1m/2km NE of A' Bhrìdeanach, westernmost point of island. Height 1273 feet or 388 metres. **85 J4** NG3100.

Bloody Bay *Arg. & B.* ***Bay***, on N coast of Mull, 2m/3km NW of Tobermory. **79 F2** NM4857.

Bloody Moss *High.* ***Open space***, moorland 1m/2km SW of Halkirk, to W of River Thurso. **105 G3** ND1157.

Bloodybush Edge *Northumb.* ***Mountain***, in Cheviot Hills, 5m/8km NE of Blindburn. Height 2001 feet or 610 metres. **70 D2** NT9014.

Bloomfield *W.Mid.* ***Suburb***, in Tipton, to W of West Bromwich. SO9593.

Bloomsbury *Gt.Lon.* ***Locality***, district of central London in borough of Camden, about 1m/2km N of Charing Cross. Contains London University buildings and British Museum. TQ2982.

Blore *Staffs.* ***Hamlet***, 3m/5km NW of Ashbourne. **40 D1** SK1349.

Blorenge *Mon.* ***Mountain***, 3m/4km SW of Abergavenny. Height 1834 feet or 559 metres. **28 B7** SO2611.

Blossomfield *W.Mid.* ***Suburb***, 2m/3km SW of Solihull. **30 C1** SP1378.

Blotchnie Fiold *Ork.* ***Hill***, situated to SE of Muckle Water. Height 820 feet or 250 metres. **106 D5** HY4128.

Blount's Green *Staffs.* ***Hamlet***, 1m/2km SW of Uttoxeter. **40 C2** SK0832.

Blovid *Shet.* ***Coastal feature***, promontory on E coast of Mainland, 1m/2km SE of Levenwick. **109 G9** HU4119.

Blowick *Mersey.* ***Suburb***, 2m/3km E of Southport town centre. SD3516.

Blowing Sands *B'pool* ***Suburb***, 2m/4km SE of Blackpool town centre. SD3232.

Bloxham *Oxon.* Population: 2356. ***Village***, 4m/6km SW of Banbury. **31 F5** SP4235.

Bloxholm *Lincs.* ***Hamlet***, 5m/8km N of Sleaford. **52 D7** TF0653.

Bloxwich *W.Mid.* ***Suburb***, 3m/4km NW of Walsall town centre. **40 B5** SJ9902.

Bloxworth *Dorset* ***Village***, 2m/4km E of Bere Regis. **9 H5** SY8894.

Bloxworth Heath *Dorset* ***Open space***, wooded heath E of Wareham Forest, 1m/2km S of Bloxworth. **9 H5** SY8892.

Blubberhouses *N.Yorks.* ***Hamlet***, 7m/11km N of Otley. **57 G4** SE1655.

Blucks Pool *Pembs.* ***Sea feature***, inlet between The Pole and Berry Slade, 2m/3km SW of Castlemartin. **16 B5** SR8897.

Blue Anchor *Cornw.* ***Hamlet***, 1km S of Indian Queens. **3 G3** SW9157.

Blue Anchor *Som.* ***Hamlet***, on coast (Blue Anchor Bay), 2m/4km W of Watchet. **7 J1** ST0343.

Blue Anchor *Swan.* ***Village***, to S of Pen-clawdd, on Gower peninsula, 7m/11km W of Swansea. SS5495.

Blue Anchor Bay *Som.* ***Bay***, 2m/4km W of Watchet, on N coast of Somerset. **7 J1** ST0046.

Blue Bell Hill *Kent* ***Village***, 4m/6km S of Rochester. **24 D5** TQ7462.

Blue Head *High.* ***Coastal feature***, headland on Black Isle, 1m/2km E of Cromarty. **97 F5** NH8166.

Bluebell Railway *W.Suss.* ***Other feature of interest***, preserved tourist railway, with headquarters at Sheffield Park Station, 1m/2km NW of Newick. Important collection of steam locomotives and rolling stock. **13 G4** TQ4023.

Bluecaster *Cumb.* ***Mountain***, rising to over 340 metres on NW side of Baugh Fell, 4m/7km NE of Sedbergh. **61 J7** SD7196.

Bluemull Sound *Shet.* ***Sea feature***, strait separating Unst and Yell. **108 E2** HP5503.

Blundellsands *Mersey.* ***Suburb***, to NW of Crosby. SJ3099.

Blundeston *Suff.* ***Village***, 4m/6km NW of Lowestoft. **45 K6** TM5197.

Blunham *Beds.* ***Village***, 2m/3km NW of Sandy. **32 E3** TL1551.

Blunsdon St. Andrew *Swin.* ***Village***, 4m/6km N of Swindon. **20 E2** SU1389.

Bluntington *Worcs.* ***Village***, 4m/7km E of Kidderminster. SO8974.

Bluntisham *Cambs.* Population: 1202. ***Village***, 7m/12km S of Chatteris. **33 G1** TL3674.

Blunts *Cornw.* ***Hamlet***, 6m/10km E of Liskeard. **4 D4** SX3462.

Blurton *Stoke* ***Suburb***, to SW of Longton. SJ8941.

Bluther Burn ***River***, stream rising near Craigluscar Hill, flowing W before turning SE into Torry Bay on N side of Firth of Forth, to W of Torryburn. **75 H1** NT0186.

Blyborough *Lincs.* ***Hamlet***, 3m/5km S of Kirton in Lindsey. **52 C3** SK9394.

Blyford *Suff.* ***Hamlet***, 3m/4km E of Halesworth. **35 J1** TM4276.

Blymhill *Staffs.* ***Village***, 6m/10km SE of Newport. **40 A4** SJ8012.

Blymhill Common *Staffs.* ***Settlement***, 1m/2km W of Blymhill. SJ7812.

Blymhill Lawn *Staffs.* ***Settlement***, 1m/2km SE of Blymhill. SJ8111.

Blyth *Northumb.* ***River***, rising W of Kirkheaton and flowing E across open country to Bedlington and into North Sea at Blyth. **71 G6** NZ3280.

Blyth *Northumb.* Population: 35,327. ***Town***, port and resort on North Sea coast at mouth of River Blyth, 8m/13km N of Tynemouth. **71 J5** NZ3181.

Blyth *Notts.* ***Village***, in loop of River Ryton, 6m/10km NW of Retford. Church, mainly Norman, incorporates remains of former priory. **51 J4** SK6287.

Blyth *Suff.* ***River***, rising near Laxfield and flowing E through Blythburgh into North Sea between Southwold and Walberswick. Tidal to a point 1km below Blyford. **35 J1** TM5074.

Blyth Bridge *Sc.Bord.* ***Village***, 6m/10km N of Broughton. **75 K6** NT1345.

Blyth End *Warks.* ***Settlement***, 2m/3km NE of Coleshill. SP2190.

Blythburgh *Suff.* ***Village***, on River Blyth, 4m/6km W of Southwold. **35 J1** TM4575.

Blythe *River*, rising at Shirley Heath, Solihull and flowing into *River* Cole at Blyth End, 1m/2km NE of Coleshill. **40 E7** SP2191.

Blythe Bridge *Staffs.* ***Locality***, 5m/9km SE of Stoke-on-Trent. **40 B1** SJ9541.
Blythe Edge *Sc.Bord.* ***Inland physical feature***, mountain escarpment 1476 feet or 450 metres high and facing SW, 3m/5km W of Watch Water Reservoir. **76 E5** NT6056.
Blythe Marsh *Staffs.* ***Locality***, 4m/8km SW of Cheadle. **40 B1** SJ9641.
Blythe Sands *Med.* ***Coastal feature***, sandbank in River Thames estuary, 2m/3km N of Cliffe. **24 D4** TQ7579.
Blyton *Lincs.* ***Village***, 4m/7km NE of Gainsborough. **52 B3** SK8594.
Boar of Badenoch *High. Alternative name for An Torc, qv.*
Boarhills *Fife* ***Village***, 4m/7km SE of St. Andrews. **83 G6** NO5714.
Boarhunt *Hants.* ***Hamlet***, 2m/3km NE of Fareham. **11 H4** SU6008.
Boar's Head *Gt.Man.* ***Locality***, residential locality, 2m/3km N of Wigan. SD5708.
Boar's Head Rock *Moray* ***Island***, islet in Spey Bay, 4m/6km SE of Lossiemouth. **97 K5** NJ2867.
Boars Hill *Oxon.* ***Hamlet***, 3m/5km SW of Oxford. **21 H1** SP4802.
Boars of Duncansby *High.* ***Sea feature***, sea passage between Island of Stroma and Ness of Duncansby on N coast of Caithness district. **105 J1** ND3775.
Boarsgreave *Lancs.* ***Hamlet***, 2m/3km SE of Rawtenstall. SD8320.
Boarshead *E.Suss.* ***Hamlet***, 2m/3km NE of Crowborough. **13 J3** TQ5332.
Boarstall *Bucks.* ***Hamlet***, 6m/9km SE of Bicester. Boarstall Tower (National Trust), moated 14c gatehouse with 16c-17c additions. **31 H7** SP6214.
Boarzell *E.Suss.* ***Settlement***, 2m/3km N of Etchingham. **14 C5** TQ7229.
Boasley Cross *Devon* ***Hamlet***, 6m/9km W of Okehampton. **6 D6** SX5093.
Boat o' Brig *Moray* ***Settlement***, in River Spey valley, where road and railway cross river, 3m/5km NE of Rothes. **98 B5** NJ3151.
Boat of Garten *High.* ***Village***, on River Spey in Badenoch and Strathspey district, 5m/8km NE of Aviemore. **89 G3** NH9418.
Boath *High.* ***Locality***, 5m/8km NW of Alness. **96 C4** NH5774.
Boath Doocot *High. Alternative spelling of Boath Dovecot, qv.*
Boath Dovecot (Boath Doocot). *High.* ***Other feature of interest***, 17c dovecot, 2m/3km SE of Nairn, built on site of castle where Earl of Montrose raised standard of Charles I after defeating Covenanters in 1645. **97 G6** NH9155.
Boath of Toft *Shet. Alternative name for Toft, qv.*
Bobbing *Kent* ***Village***, 1m/2km NW of Sittingbourne. **24 E5** TQ8865.
Bobbington *Staffs.* ***Village***, 6m/10km E of Bridgnorth. **40 A6** SO8090.
Bobbingworth *Essex* ***Hamlet***, 2m/3km NW of Chipping Ongar. **23 J1** TL5305.
Bobby Hill *Suff.* ***Settlement***, adjoining to N of Wattisfield. TM0074.
Boblainy Forest *High.* ***Forest/woodland***, in Inverness district 6m/10km S of Beauly. Includes deer. **88 B1** NH4837.
Boc Mòr *High.* ***Mountain***, in Skye and Lochalsh district, 2m/3km E of Dornie. Height 2070 feet or 631 metres. **87 F2** NG9125.
Bocaddon *Cornw.* ***Settlement***, 6m/9km NW of Looe. **4 B5** SX1758.
Bochastle *Stir.* ***Settlement***, 1m/2km W of Callander. **81 H7** NN6007.
Bochrwyd *Powys Welsh form of Boughrood, qv.*
Bockhampton *Dorset* ***Locality***, contains settlements of Middle, North, and South Bockhampton, about 3m/4km NE of Christchurch town centre. SZ1796.
Bockhampton *W.Berks.* ***Settlement***, just SE of Lambourn. **21 G4** SU3378.
Bocking *Essex* ***Suburb***, NW part of Braintree. For adminstrative purposes the two places are treated as one place, referred to as Braintree and Bocking. **34 B6** TL7523.
Bocking Churchstreet *Essex* ***Suburb***, adjoining to N of Braintree. **34 B6** TL7525.
Bockleton *Worcs.* ***Hamlet***, 4m/7km S of Tenbury Wells. SO5961.
Bockmer End *Bucks.* ***Settlement***, 3m/4km W of Marlow. SU8186.
Boconnoc *Cornw.* ***Settlement***, 3m/4km E of Lostwithiel. **4 B4** SX1460.
Bodach Mòr *High.* ***Mountain***, in Freevater Forest, Sutherland district, 7m/11km W of head of Strathcarron. Height 2696 feet or 822 metres. **95 K3** NH3689.
Boddam *Aber.* Population: 1435. ***Village***, fishing village on E coast, 2m/4km S of Peterhead. **99 K6** NK1342.
Boddam *Shet.* ***Settlement***, at head of inlet on E coast of Mainland, 5m/8km N of Sumburgh Head. **109 G9** HU3915.
Bodden *Som.* ***Hamlet***, 1m/2km E of Shepton Mallet. ST6344.
Boddin Point *Angus* ***Coastal feature***, headland on E coast at N end of Lunan Bay, 3m/5km S of Montrose. **83 J2** NO7153.
Boddington *Glos.* ***Village***, 4m/6km NW of Cheltenham. **29 H6** SO8925.
Bodedern *I.o.A.* ***Village***, on Anglesey, 3m/4km E of Valley. **46 B4** SH3380.
Bodelwyddan *Denb.* ***Village***, 2m/4km W of St. Asaph. 19c church has arcades of marble. **47 J5** SJ0075.
Bodenham *Here.* ***Village***, 7m/11km N of Hereford. **28 E3** SO5351.
Bodenham *Wilts.* ***Village***, on River Avon, 3m/5km SE of Salisbury. **10 C2** SU1626.
Bodenham Moor *Here.* ***Village***, 1m/2km SE of Bodenham. **28 E3** SO5450.
Bodesbeck *D. & G.* ***Settlement***, in Moffat Water valley, 6m/9km NW of Moffat. **69 G3** NT1509.
Bodesbeck Law *D. & G.* ***Mountain***, 1m/2km NE of Bodesbeck. Height 2171 feet or 662 metres. **69 G2** NT1610.
Bodewryd *I.o.A.* ***Hamlet***, on Anglesey, 3m/4km SE of Cemaes. **46 B3** SH3990.
Bodfari *Denb.* ***Village***, 4m/6km NE of Denbigh. **47 J5** SJ0970.
Bodffordd *I.o.A.* ***Village***, at W end of Cefni Reservoir, Anglesey, and 2m/4km W of Llangefni. **46 C5** SH4276.
Bodfuan *Gwyn.* ***Hamlet***, 4m/6km NW of Pwllheli. **36 C2** SH3237.
Bodham Street *Norf.* ***Village***, 3m/5km E of Holt. **45 F1** TG1240.
Bodiam *E.Suss.* ***Village***, 2m/3km SW of Sandhurst. Bodiam Castle (National Trust) to E. **14 C5** TQ7825.
Bodiam Castle *E.Suss.* ***Castle***, 14c moated castle (National Trust) on rising ground above River Rother valley to E of Bodiam. **14 C5** TQ7825.
Bodicote *Oxon.* ***Village***, 2m/3km S of Banbury. **31 F5** SP4637.
Bodieve *Cornw.* ***Hamlet***, 1km N of Wadebridge. **3 G1** SW9973.
Bodinnick *Cornw.* ***Village***, on River Fowey connected with town of Fowey by car ferry. **4 B5** SX1352.
Bodior *I.o.A.* ***Settlement***, in S part of Holy Island, 4m/6km SE of Holyhead. **46 A5** SH2876.
Bodle Street Green *E.Suss.* ***Village***, 5m/8km NE of Hailsham. **13 K5** TQ6514.
Bodmin *Cornw.* Population: 12,553. ***Town***, old county town below SW edge of Bodmin Moor, 26m/42km W of Plymouth. 15c parish church of St. Petroc is largest in county. Tudor Guildhall. 17c Lanhydrock House (National Trust) nearby. **4 A4** SX0767.
Bodmin and Wenford Railway *Cornw.* ***Other feature of interest***, tourist railway which runs NW from Bodmin Parkway Station, along S edge of Bodmin, to N of Nanstallon. **4 A4** SX0665.
Bodmin Moor *Cornw.* ***Large natural feature***, large expanse of granite moorland between Launceston in NE, Liskeard in S, Bodmin in SE and Wadebridge in W. Attains height of 1375 feet or 419 metres at Brown Willy. Bronze Age and Neolithic remains. **4 B3** SX0767.
Bodnant Garden *Conwy* ***Garden***, on E bank of River Conwy, 3m/5km S of Llandudno Junction. World-famous 19c garden (National Trust) overlooking Snowdonia, with Italianate terrace, lawns, woodland valley and wild garden. Features 36 metre tunnel of laburnum which flowers in May. **47 G5** SH8072.
Bodney *Norf.* ***Hamlet***, 4m/6km NE of Mundford. **44 C6** TL8398.
Bodorgan *I.o.A.* ***Settlement***, on Anglesey, on W side of River Cefni estuary, 1m/2km S of Llangadwaladr. Bodorgan railway station lies 1km NE of Llangadwaladr. **46 B6** SH3867.
Bodowyr Burial Chamber *I.o.A.* ***Historic/prehistoric site***, Neolithic tomb on S part of Anglesey, 1m/2km NW of Brynsiencyn. Constructed from substantial stones supporting an 8 foot by 6 foot capstone which is almost pyramidal in shape. **46 C6** SH4668.
Bodrane *Cornw.* ***Hamlet***, 3m/5km SW of Liskeard. SX2061.
Bodrhyddan Hall *Denb.* ***Garden***, 3 acre gardens surrounding 17c manor house, 1km SW of Dyserth. Includes formal parterre on S front of manor surrounded by lawns, clipped yews and old oak trees. **47 J5** SJ0478.
Bodsham Green *Kent* ***Hamlet***, 6m/10km E of Ashford. **15 G3** TR1045.
Bodwen *Cornw.* ***Hamlet***, 5m/8km N of St. Austell. **4 A4** SX0360.
Bodymoor Heath *Warks.* ***Hamlet***, 4m/7km N of Coleshill. SP2095.
Bogallan *High.* ***Settlement***, on Black Isle, 2m/3km SW of Munlochy. **96 D6** NH6350.
Bogany Point *Arg. & B.* ***Coastal feature***, headland on E coast of Bute, at E end of Rothesay Bay. **73 K4** NS1065.
Bogbain *High.* ***Settlement***, 2m/3km NW of Daviot. **96 E7** NH7041.
Bogbrae *Aber.* ***Settlement***, 2m/3km SW of Hatton. **91 J1** NK0334.
Bogbuie *High.* ***Settlement***, 3m/4km E of Conon Bridge. **96 C6** NH5855.
Bogend *S.Ayr.* ***Settlement***, 1m/2km NE of Symington. **74 B7** NS3932.
Bogfern *Aber.* ***Settlement***, 3m/5km NE of Tarland. **90 D4** NJ5207.
Bogfields *Aber.* ***Settlement***, 4m/6km NE of Tarland. **90 D4** NJ5208.
Bogfold *Aber.* ***Settlement***, on E side of Bracklamore Hill, 3m/4km NW of New Pitsligo. **99 G5** NJ8558.
Bogha-cloiche *High.* ***Mountain***, on Gaick Forest, in Badenoch and Strathspey district, 7m/11km E of Dalwhinnie. Height 2942 feet or 897 metres. **88 E6** NN7486.
Boghall *W.Loth.* ***Village***, 1m/2km E of Bathgate. NS9968.
Boghall Castle *S.Lan. See Biggar.*
Boghead *Aber.* ***Settlement***, 3m/4km E of Aberchirder. **98 E5** NJ6553.
Boghead *E.Ayr.* ***Settlement***, 5m/8km NE of Cumnock. **68 B1** NS6324.
Boghead *S.Lan.* ***Village***, 1m/2km SW of Kirkmuirhill. **75 F6** NS7741.
Boghole Farm *High.* ***Settlement***, 5m/8km E of Nairn. **97 G6** NH9655.
Bogie *Aber.* ***River***, rising on E side of The Buck and running NE to Rhynie, then N to River Deveron 1m/2km NE of Huntly. Upper course is known as Water of Bogie. **90 D1** NJ5341.
Bogmoor *Moray* ***Settlement***, 3m/5km N of Fochabers. **98 B4** NJ3562.
Bogniebrae *Aber.* ***Settlement***, on E side of Fourman Hill, 4m/7km S of Aberchirder. **98 D6** NJ5945.
Bognor Regis *W.Suss.* Population: 56,744. ***Town***, seaside resort and former fishing hamlet, 6m/10km SE of Chichester. Royal suffix obtained after George V convalesced here. **12 C7** SZ9399.
Bograxie *Aber.* ***Settlement***, 3m/4km NW of Kemnay. **91 F3** NJ7019.
Bogrie Hill *D. & G.* ***Mountain***, 3m/5km S of Moniaive. Height 1417 feet or 432 metres. **68 C5** NX7885.
Bogroy *High.* ***Settlement***, adjoining to N of Carrbridge. **89 G2** NH9023.
Bogside *Fife* ***Settlement***, 4m/6km SE of Clackmannan. **75 H1** NS9690.
Bogston *Aber.* ***Settlement***, 4m/6km SE of Strathdon. **90 B4** NJ3909.
Bogthorn *W.Yorks.* ***Locality***, 2m/3km SW of Keighley. SE0439.
Bogton *Aber.* ***Settlement***, 3m/5km W of Turriff. **98 E5** NJ6751.
Bogton Loch *E.Ayr.* ***Lake/loch***, in course of River Doon, 1m/2km W of Dalmellington. **67 J3** NS4605.
Bogue *D. & G.* ***Settlement***, 2m/3km E of St. John's Town of Dalry. **68 B5** NX6481.
Bohemia *Wilts.* ***Hamlet***, 5m/9km NE of Fordingbridge. SU2019.
Bohenie *High.* ***Settlement***, at S end of Glen Roy, 2m/3km NE of Roybridge. **87 J6** NN2982.
Bohetherick *Cornw.* ***Hamlet***, above River Tamar, 4m/6km SE of Callington. SX4167.
Bohortha *Cornw.* ***Hamlet***, 2m/4km SW of Portscatho. **3 F5** SW8632.
Bohuntine *High.* ***Settlement***, in Lochaber district, 2m/3km NE of Roybridge. **87 J6** NN2883.
Bohuntine Hill *High.* ***Mountain***, in Lochaber district, on W side of Glen Roy, 3m/4km NE of Roybridge. Summit is Beinn a' Mhonicag. Height 1860 feet or 567 metres. **87 J6** NN2885.
Boirseam (Anglicised form: Borsham.) *W.Isles* ***Settlement***, on S coast of South Harris, 3m/4km NE of Rodel. **93 F3** NG0785.
Bojewyan *Cornw.* ***Settlement***, 2m/4km NE of St. Just. **2 A5** SW3934.
Bokiddick *Cornw.* ***Hamlet***, 3m/5km S of Bodmin. SX0562.
Bolam *Dur.* ***Village***, 4m/7km S of Bishop Auckland. **62 C4** NZ1922.
Bolam *Northumb.* ***Hamlet***, 3m/4km N of Belsay. NZ0982.
Bolam Lake *Northumb.* ***Lake/loch***, with adjoining country park, 1m/2km SW of Bolam. **71 F5** NZ0881.
Bolberry *Devon* ***Hamlet***, 3m/5km W of Salcombe. **5 G7** SX6939.
Bold Heath *Mersey.* ***Hamlet***, 3m/5km NE of Widnes. **48 E4** SJ5389.
Bolderwood *Hants.* ***Locality***, including Bolderwood Farm, Bolderwood Cottage and Bolderwood Grounds, 6m/10km NE of Ringwood. **10 D4** SU2409.
Boldmere *W.Mid.* ***Suburb***, 1m/2km S of Sutton Coldfield town centre. SP1194.
Boldon *T. & W.* Population: 12,420. ***Town***, between South Shields and Sunderland, consisting of East and West Boldon. **71 J7** NZ3561.
Boldon Colliery *T. & W.* ***Village***, to W of Boldon. NZ3462.
Boldre *Hants.* ***Village***, 2m/3km N of Lymington. **10 E5** SZ3298.
Boldron *Dur.* ***Hamlet***, 2m/3km SW of Barnard Castle. **62 B5** NZ0314.
Bole *Notts.* ***Village***, 2m/3km S of Beckingham. **51 K4** SK7987.
Bolehall *Staffs.* ***Suburb***, to E of Tamworth town centre. SK2103.
Bolehill *Derbys.* ***Village***, 1km NE of Wirksworth. **50 E7** SK2955.
Bolehill *S.Yorks.* ***Suburb***, in Norton Woodseats district of Sheffield, 3m/5km S of city centre. SK3582.
Boleigh *Cornw.* ***Hamlet***, 3m/5km SW of Newlyn. **2 B6** SW4324.
Bolenowe *Cornw.* ***Hamlet***, 2m/3km SE of Camborne. SW6737.
Boleside *Sc.Bord.* ***Settlement***, in Tweed valley, 2m/3km S of Galashiels. **76 C7** NT4933.
Bolfracks *P. & K.* ***Settlement***, 2m/3km W of Aberfeldy. **81 K3** NN8248.
Bolgoed *Swan.* ***Settlement***, 1m/2km SE of Pontarddulais. **17 K4** SN6002.
Bolham *Devon* ***Hamlet***, 2m/3km N of Tiverton. **7 H4** SS9514.
Bolham *Devon* ***River***, rising 2m/3km SW of Dunkeswell and flowing N, then NW to join River Culm just NE of Uffculme. **7 K5** ST0813.
Bolham *Notts.* ***Settlement***, on E bank of River Idle, 1km N of Retford. SK7082.
Bolham Water *Devon* ***Hamlet***, 6m/10km SE of Wellington. **7 K4** ST1612.
Bolingbroke Castle *Lincs. See Old Bolingbroke.*
Bolingey *Cornw.* ***Village***, on SE side of Perranporth. **2 E3** SW7653.
Bollihope Common *Dur.* ***Open space***, heathland 3m/5km S of Stanhope. **62 A3** NY9734.
Bollin ***River***, rising 3m/5km SE of Macclesfield and flowing NW through Macclesfield and Wilmslow into River Mersey, 5m/8km E of Warrington. **49 J5** SJ6888.
Bolling Hall *W.Yorks.* ***Historic house***, 15c manor house near Bowling Park, 1m/2km SE of Bradford city centre. Now a museum featuring some pieces by Chippendale. **57 G6** SE1731.
Bollington *Ches.* Population: 6767. ***Small town***, 3m/4km NE of Macclesfield. **49 J5** SJ9377.
Bollington Cross *Ches.* ***Locality***, adjoining to SW of Bollington. SJ9277.
Bolney *W.Suss.* ***Village***, 3m/5km W of Cuckfield. **13 F4** TQ2622.

Bolnhurst *Beds.* ***Village***, 7m/11km NE of Bedford. **32 D3** TL0859.
Bolshan *Angus* ***Settlement***, 2m/3km NE of Friockheim. **83 H2** NO6152.
Bolsover *Derbys.* Population: 11,743. ***Town***, market town, 6m/9km E of Chesterfield. Norman castle (English Heritage) rebuilt in 17c. 17c Riding School. **51 G5** SK4770.
Bolsover Castle *Derbys.* ***Castle***, 11c Norman castle (English Heritage) built by William Peveril in Bolsover, later enlarged in 17c. Noted for elaborate fireplaces, panelling and wall paintings. **51 G5** SK4670.
Bolsover Woodhouse *Derbys.* ***Suburb***, 1m/2km NW of Bolsover. SK4671.
Bolster Moor *W.Yorks.* ***Hamlet***, 1m/2km N of Slaithwaite. SE0815.
Bolsterstone *S.Yorks.* ***Village***, 1m/2km S of Stocksbridge. **50 E3** SK2796.
Bolstone *Here.* ***Hamlet***, 5m/8km SE of Hereford. **28 E5** SO5532.
Bolt Head *Devon* ***Coastal feature***, headland at mouth of Kingsbridge Estuary, 2m/3km S of Salcombe. Cliffs from here to Bolt Tail are National Trust property. **5 H7** SX7235.
Bolt Tail *Devon* ***Coastal feature***, headland at SE end of Bigbury Bay, 5m/7km W of Salcombe. Cliffs from here to Bolt Head are National Trust property. **5 G7** SX6639.
Boltby *N.Yorks.* ***Village***, 5m/8km NE of Thirsk. **57 K1** SE4986.
Boltby Moor *N.Yorks.* ***Open space***, moorland, partly afforested and rising to over 250 metres, 4m/6km N of Sutton-under-Whitestonecliffe. **57 K1** SE4788.
Bolter End *Bucks.* ***Hamlet***, 4m/7km W of High Wycombe. **22 A2** SU7992.
Bolton *Cumb.* ***Village***, 4m/6km NW of Appleby-in-Westmorland. **61 H4** NY6323.
Bolton *E.Loth.* ***Village***, 3m/4km S of Haddington. **76 D3** NT5070.
Bolton *E.Riding* ***Hamlet***, 4m/7km SE of Stamford Bridge. **58 D4** SE7752.
Bolton *Gt.Man.* Population: 139,020. ***Town***, on River Croal, 10m/17km NW of Manchester. Important commercial and industrial centre. Formerly major textile industry town. Samuel Crompton invented the spinning mule here and is buried in churchyard of Bolton parish church. **49 G2** SD7109.
Bolton *Northumb.* ***Hamlet***, 5m/8km W of Alnwick. **71 G2** NU1013.
Bolton *W.Yorks.* ***Suburb***, 1m/2km N of Bradford city centre. SE1735.
Bolton Abbey *N.Yorks.* ***Village***, 5m/8km NW of Ilkley. 17c tithe barn. **57 F4** SE0753.
Bolton Abbey Estate Country Park *N.Yorks.* ***Leisure/recreation***, estate of Duke and Duchess of Devonshire in Wharfedale, stretching S along River Wharfe for 7m/11km from Burnsall to Bolton Bridge. Includes village of Bolton Abbey, remains of 12c Bolton Priory, The Strid, Strid Wood, 19c Cavendish Pavilion and ruined Tudor house, Barden Tower. Nature trails and walks in Strid Wood and Valley of Desolation. **57 F4** SE0654.
Bolton Bridge *N.Yorks.* ***Settlement***, at road crossing of River Wharfe, 2m/3km N of Addingham. **57 F4** SE0653.
Bolton by Bowland *Lancs.* ***Village***, 3m/5km W of Gisburn. **56 C5** SD7849.
Bolton Castle *N.Yorks.* ***Castle***, ruins of 14c castle built by John Lewyn at Castle Bolton, 2m/4km S of Leyburn. Mary, Queen of Scots was imprisoned here for six months. **62 B7** SE0391.
Bolton Green *Lancs.* ***Settlement***, 2m/3km W of Chorley. SD5517.
Bolton Houses *Lancs.* ***Settlement***, 1m/2km NE of Kirkham. SD4433.
Bolton-le-Sands *Lancs.* Population: 6772. ***Small town***, 4m/7km N of Lancaster. **55 H3** SD4867.
Bolton Low Houses *Cumb.* ***Hamlet***, 3m/5km SW of Wigton. **60 D2** NY2344.
Bolton Museum and Art Gallery *Gt.Man.* ***Other feature of interest***, to SE of Bolton town centre, with displays and exhibitions, including natural history, zoology and archaeology. **49 G2** SD7308.
Bolton New Houses *Cumb.* ***Locality***, on S side of River Waver, 3m/4km S of Wigton. NY2444.
Bolton-on-Swale *N.Yorks.* ***Village***, 5m/8km E of Richmond. **62 D7** SE2599.
Bolton Percy *N.Yorks.* ***Village***, 3m/5km SE of Tadcaster. **58 B5** SE5341.
Bolton Priory *N.Yorks.* ***Ecclesiastical building***, remains of 12c Augustinian priory beside River Wharfe at Bolton Abbey, 5m/8km NW of Ilkley. Reputed to have been founded by Alice de Romilly after her son drowned at The Strid. Restored nave is parish church. **57 F4** SE0754.
Bolton Town End *Lancs.* ***Locality***, adjoining to S of Bolton-le-Sands, on E side of Morecambe Bay. SD4867.
Bolton upon Dearne *S.Yorks.* ***Town***, 2m/4km NW of Mexborough. **51 G2** SE4502.
Bolton Woods *W.Yorks.* ***Suburb***, 1m/2km SE of Shipley. SE1536.
Boltonfellend *Cumb.* ***Hamlet***, 6m/9km NW of Brampton. **69 K7** NY4768.
Boltongate *Cumb.* ***Hamlet***, 5m/8km S of Wigton. **60 D2** NY2240.
Boltonwood Lane *Cumb.* ***Village***, 3m/4km S of Wigton. NY2544.
Bolt's Law *Dur.* ***Mountain***, 2m/3km N of Rookhope. Height 1771 feet or 540 metres. **62 A2** NY9445.
Bolt's Law *Northumb.* ***Mountain***, 4m/7km SW of Falstone. Mast at summit. Height 1296 feet or 395 metres. **70 B5** NY6982.
Bolventor *Cornw.* ***Village***, on Bodmin Moor, 9m/15km NE of Bodmin. Site of Daphne du Maurier's 'Jamaica Inn'. **4 B3** SX1876.
Bomarsund *Northumb.* ***Hamlet***, 2m/3km S of Ashington. NZ2784.
Bombie *D. & G.* ***Settlement***, 2m/3km E of Kirkcudbright. **65 H5** NX7150.
Bomby *Cumb.* ***Locality***, 1km SE of Bampton, between Haweswater Beck and River Lowther. NY5217.
Bomere Heath *Shrop.* ***Village***, 5m/7km N of Shrewsbury. **38 D4** SJ4719.
Bon-y-maen *Swan.* ***Suburb***, 2m/3km NE of Swansea city centre across River Tawe. **17 K5** SS6795.
Bonahaven *Arg. & B.* *Anglicised form of Bunnahabhainn, qv.*
Bonar Bridge *High.* ***Village***, in Sutherland district at head of Dornoch Firth, 14m/23km W of Dornoch. Railway station at Ardgay, 1m/2km SW. **96 D2** NH6191.
Bonawe *Arg. & B.* ***Locality***, in Argyll, on N side of Loch Etive, 1m/2km N of Taynuilt. **80 B4** NN0033.
Bonawe Furnace *Arg. & B.* ***Historic/prehistoric site***, restored charcoal-fuelled iron works (Historic Scotland) on S side of Loch Etive, 1km NE of Taynuilt. Furnace operated from 1753 to 1874, producing canon and shot for navy. **80 B4** NN0131.
Bonawe Quarries *Arg. & B.* ***Settlement***, on N coast of Loch Etive, 1m/2km N of Taynuilt across loch. **80 B4** NN0133.
Bonbusk *Notts.* ***Settlement***, 1km SE of Creswell. SK5373.
Bonby *N.Lincs.* ***Village***, 5m/7km SW of Barton-upon-Humber. **52 D1** TA0015.
Boncath *Pembs.* ***Hamlet***, 5m/8km S of Cardigan. **17 F1** SN2038.
Bonchester Bridge *Sc.Bord.* ***Village***, on Rule Water, 6m/9km E of Hawick. **70 A2** NT5812.
Bonchester Hill *Sc.Bord.* ***Mountain***, rising to over 320 metres, to E of Bonchester. Surmounted by ancient earthworks. **70 A2** NT5911.
Bonchurch *I.o.W.* ***Suburb***, 1m/2km NE of Ventnor. **11 G7** SZ5778.
Bond End *Staffs.* ***Locality***, adjoining to S of Yoxall. SK1418.
Bondend *Glos.* ***Locality***, 3m/5km SE of Gloucester. SO8615.
Bondgate *N.Yorks.* ***Locality***, adjoining to NW of Selby. SE6033.
Bondleigh *Devon* ***Village***, 3m/4km SE of Winkleigh. **6 E5** SS6504.
Bonds *Lancs.* ***Hamlet***, adjoining to SE of Garstang. SD4944.
Bond's Green *Here.* ***Locality***, 4m/7km SE of Kington. SO3554.
Bonehill *Staffs.* ***Settlement***, 1m/2km SW of Tamworth. **40 D5** SK1902.
Bonehill Down *Devon* ***Inland physical feature***, hill ridge 1m/2km E of Widecombe in the Moor, running from Honeybag Tor in N to Top Tor in S. **5 H3** SX7377.
Bo'ness (Name contracted from Borrowstounness.) *Falk.* Population: 14,595. ***Town***, industrial town on S side of Firth of Forth, 17m/27km W of Edinburgh. Kinneil House, 1m/2km SW, is 16c-17c mansion. Vintage train centre. **75 H2** NS9981.
Bo'ness and Kinneil Railway *Falk.* ***Other feature of interest***, tourist steam railway running from Bo'ness docks to Birkhill Clay Mine, 3m/4km SW of Bo'ness, crossing line of Antonine Wall. Examples of locomotives, carriages and wagons, some over 100 years old. Exhibition telling story of movement of goods and people before motorway travel. **75 H2** NS9781.
Boney Hay *Staffs.* ***Suburb***, N district of Burntwood. SK0510.
Bonfire Hill *Dorset* ***Settlement***, adjoining to NE of Alderholt, 2m/3km SW of Fordingbridge. SU1213.
Bonhill *W.Dun.* Population: 10,094. ***Town***, on E bank of River Leven 3m/5km N of Dumbarton. **74 B3** NS3979.
Boningale *Shrop.* ***Village***, 5m/8km SE of Shifnal. **40 A5** SJ8102.
Bonjedward *Sc.Bord.* ***Hamlet***, 2m/3km N of Jedburgh. **70 B1** NT6523.
Bonkle *N.Lan.* ***Village***, 3m/5km NE of Wishaw. **75 G5** NS8356.
Bonner's Cottage *Norf.* *See East Dereham.*
Bonning Gate *Cumb.* ***Settlement***, 3m/4km NW of Kendal. SD4795.
Bonnington *Angus* ***Settlement***, 3m/5km N of Carnoustie. **83 G4** NO5739.
Bonnington *Edin.* ***Hamlet***, 1m/2km SW of Ratho. NT1269.
Bonnington *Kent* ***Village***, 5m/8km SE of Ashford. **15 F4** TR0535.
Bonnington Linn *S.Lan.* ***Waterfall***, on River Clyde 2m/3km S of Lanark. **75 G6** NS8840.
Bonnybank *Fife* ***Settlement***, 1m/2km NE of Kennoway. **82 E7** NO3503.
Bonnybridge *Falk.* Population: 6017. ***Village***, on Bonny Water, 4m/6km W of Falkirk. To E is well-preserved section of Antonine Wall, with Roman fort of Rough Castle (National Trust for Scotland). **75 G2** NS8280.
Bonnykelly *Aber.* ***Locality***, 2m/3km SW of New Pitsligo. **99 G5** NJ8553.
Bonnyrigg *Midloth.* Population: 13,696. ***Town***, 2m/3km SW of Dalkeith. **76 B4** NT3065.
Bonnyton *Aber.* ***Settlement***, 3m/4km SE of Kirkton of Culsalmond. **90 E1** NJ6730.
Bonnyton *Angus* ***Hamlet***, 3m/5km SE of Newtyle. **82 E4** NO3338.
Bonnyton *Angus* ***Hamlet***, 4m/6km SW of Montrose. **83 H2** NO6655.
Bonnyton *E.Ayr.* ***Suburb***, to W of Kilmarnock. NS4138.
Bonsall *Derbys.* ***Village***, 2m/3km SW of Matlock. **50 E7** SK2758.
Bont *Mon.* ***Hamlet***, 6m/9km NE of Abergavenny. **28 C7** SO3819.
Bont Dolgadfan *Powys* ***Hamlet***, on River Twymyn, 5m/8km N of head of Llyn Clywedog Reservoir. **37 H5** SH8800.
Bont-goch (Also known as Elerch.) *Cere.* ***Village***, 3m/4km SE of Talybont. **37 F7** SN6886.
Bont-newydd *Conwy* ***Settlement***, at road bridge across River Elwy, 2m/3km E of Llannefydd. SJ0170.
Bont Newydd *Gwyn.* ***Settlement***, in valley of River Wnion, 3m/5km NE of Dolgellau. **37 G3** SH7720.
Bontddu *Gwyn.* ***Hamlet***, 4m/6km NE of Barmouth. **37 F4** SH6718.
Bonthorpe *Lincs.* ***Settlement***, 1m/2km NE of Willoughby. TF4872.
Bontnewydd *Cere.* ***Hamlet***, 4m/6km S of Llangwyryfon and 1m/2km SE of Llyn Eiddwen. SN6165.
Bontnewydd *Gwyn.* ***Village***, on River Gwyrfai, 2m/3km S of Caernarfon. **46 C6** SH4859.
Bontuchel *Denb.* ***Hamlet***, on River Clywedog, 3m/4km W of Ruthin. **47 J7** SJ0857.
Bonvilston (Tresimwn). *V. of Glam.* ***Village***, 4m/7km E of Cowbridge. **18 D4** ST0674.
Boode *Devon* ***Hamlet***, 5m/7km NW of Barnstaple. SS5038.
Boohay *Devon* ***Settlement***, 1m/2km NE of Kingswear. **5 K5** SX8952.
Booker *Bucks.* ***Suburb***, to SW of High Wycombe. **22 B2** SU8391.
Booley *Shrop.* ***Settlement***, 2m/3km SE of Lee Brockhurst. **38 E3** SJ5725.
Boon Hill *Staffs.* ***Settlement***, 1km E of Audley. SJ8150.
Boondreigh Water *Sc.Bord.* ***River***, formed by confluence of Blyth Water and Brunta Burn, 3m/5km E of Lauder, and flowing SW to join Leader Water, 2m/3km SE of Lauder. NT5545.
Boor *High.* ***Settlement***, near head of Loch Ewe, 1km NW of Poolewe. **94 E3** NG8481.
Boorley Green *Hants.* ***Settlement***, 1km N of Botley. SU5014.
Boosbeck *R. & C.* ***Village***, 3m/5km S of Saltburn. **63 H5** NZ6516.
Boose's Green *Essex* ***Hamlet***, 2m/3km E of Halstead. TL8430.
Boot *Cumb.* ***Hamlet***, 6m/10km NE of Ravenglass. **60 C6** NY1701.
Boot Street *Suff.* ***Hamlet***, adjoining to W of Great Bealings, 3m/5km W of Woodbridge. TM2248.
Booth *E.Riding* ***Hamlet***, on N bank of River Ouse, 2m/3km N of Goole. SE7326.
Booth *W.Yorks.* ***Hamlet***, 2m/3km NE of Mytholmroyd. SE0427.
Booth Bank *W.Yorks.* ***Settlement***, 1m/2km SW of Slaithwaite. SE0613.
Booth Green *Ches.* ***Settlement***, 1m/2km S of Poynton. SJ9281.
Booth Wood *W.Yorks.* ***Hamlet***, 2m/3km S of Ripponden. **50 C1** SE0316.
Boothby Graffoe *Lincs.* ***Village***, 8m/12km S of Lincoln. **52 C7** SK9859.
Boothby Pagnell *Lincs.* ***Village***, 5m/7km SE of Grantham. Moated Norman manor house in grounds of hall. **42 C2** SK9730.
Boothen *Stoke* ***Suburb***, to S of Stoke-on-Trent city centre. SJ8744.
Boothgate *Derbys.* ***Locality***, 1km S of Heage, 2m/3km NE of Belper. SK3749.
Boothorpe *Leics.* ***Settlement***, 2m/4km W of Ashby de la Zouch. SK3117.
Boothroyd *W.Yorks.* ***Suburb***, to W of Dewsbury town centre. SE2321.
Boothstown *Gt.Man.* ***Settlement***, 2m/3km SE of Tyldesley. **49 G2** SD7100.
Boothtown *W.Yorks.* ***Suburb***, 1m/2km N of Halifax town centre. **57 F7** SE0826.
Boothville (Also known as Buttock's Booth.) *Northants.* ***Suburb***, in NE part of Northampton. Site of Roman building. **31 J2** SP7864.
Bootle *Cumb.* ***Village***, 7m/11km NW of Millom. **54 E1** SD1088.
Bootle *Mersey.* Population: 65,454. ***Town***, on River Mersey estuary, adjoining to N of Liverpool. Former resort destroyed when docks were built. **48 C3** SJ3494.
Bootle Fell *Cumb.* ***Open space***, moorland to N of Black Combe, 5m/8km W of Broughton in Furness. **54 E1** SD1488.
Booton *Norf.* ***Hamlet***, 1m/2km E of Reepham. Booton Street locality 1km W. **45 F3** TG1222.
Boots Green *Ches.* ***Settlement***, 3m/5km N of Holmes Chapel. SJ7572.
Booze *N.Yorks.* ***Hamlet***, 1km E of Langthwaite. NZ0102.
Boquhan *Stir.* ***Settlement***, 1m/2km SW of Balfron. **74 D2** NS5387.
Boraston *Shrop.* ***Village***, 2m/3km NE of Tenbury Wells. **29 F1** SO6170.
Bord Mòr *Arg. & B.* ***Mountain***, on Kintyre, 5m/8km SW of Carradale. Height 1338 feet or 408 metres. **73 F7** NR7533.
Borde Hill Garden *W.Suss.* ***Garden***, over 200 acres of parkland with woodland and lakeside walks, 1m/2km NW of Haywards Heath. **13 G4** TQ3226.
Borden *Kent* ***Village***, 2m/3km W of Sittingbourne. **24 E5** TQ8862.
Borden *W.Suss.* ***Settlement***, 4m/7km NW of Midhurst. SU8224.
Border *Cumb.* ***Locality***, 4m/6km E of Silloth. NY1654.
Border Forest Park ***Leisure/recreation***, large area of hills and conifer forests crossing border of England and Scotland, running from Wooler in NE to Bewcastle Fells in SW. NY7090.
Bordesley *Worcs.* ***Suburb***, to N of Redditch. SP0469.
Bordesley Green *W.Mid.* ***Suburb***, 3m/4km E of Birmingham city centre. SP1086.
Bordley *N.Yorks.* ***Settlement***, 3m/5km W of Threshfield. **56 E3** SD9464.
Bordon *Hants.* Population: 15,230. ***Village***, adjoining to SE of Bordon Camp, 5m/9km W of Hindhead. **11 J1** SU8035.

B

Boreham *Essex* Population: 3170. ***Village***, 4m/6km NE of Chelmsford. **24 D1** TL7509.
Boreham *Wilts.* ***Village***, 1m/2km SE of Warminster. **20 B7** ST8844.
Boreham Street *E.Suss.* ***Village***, 5m/8km NW of Bexhill. **13 K5** TQ6611.
Borehamwood *Herts.* Population: 29,837. ***Town***, 3m/4km N of Edgware. **22 E2** TQ1996.
Boreland *D. & G.* ***Settlement***, 2m/3km N of Newton Stewart. **64 D4** NX3967.
Boreland *D. & G.* ***Village***, 6m/10km N of Lockerbie. **69 G4** NY1791.
Boreland *Stir.* ***Settlement***, 1m/2km NW of Killin. **81 G4** NN5534.
Boreley *Worcs.* ***Settlement***, 4m/7km S of Stourport-on-Severn. SO8265.
Boreraig *High.* ***Locality***, on N shore of Loch Eishort, Skye, 2m/3km E of Rubha Suisnish. NG6116.
Boreraig *High.* ***Settlement***, on W shore of Loch Dunvegan, Skye, 2m/3km S of Dunvegan Head. **93 G6** NG1853.
Boreray *W.Isles* ***Island***, rocky island (National Trust for Scotland) with steep cliffs, in St. Kilda group about 52m/83km W of North Harris. Area about 190 acres or 77 hectares. Haunt of sea birds. NA1505.
Boreray *W.Isles* ***Island***, uninhabited island off N coast of North Uist, measuring 1m/2km by 1km. **92 D3** NF8581.
Borgadelmore Point *Arg. & B.* ***Coastal feature***, headland on S coast of Kintyre, 2m/3km E of Mull of Kintyre. **66 A3** NR6305.
Borgh (Anglicised form: Borve.) *W.Isles* ***Village***, on Barra, 2m/3km N of Castlebay. Ancient burial ground between village and Borve Point. Chambered cairn 1m/2km E. **84 B4** NF6501.
Borgh (Anglicised form: Borve.) *W.Isles* ***Village***, on SE coast of Berneray, in Sound of Harris. **92 E3** NF9281.
Borghastan (Anglicised form: Borrowston.) *W.Isles* ***Settlement***, on N shore of Loch Carlabhagh, Isle of Lewis. **100 D3** NB1942.
Borgie *High.* ***River***, in Caithness district, running NE through Lochs Loyal and Craggie to Torrisdale Bay on N coast. **103 J2** NC6862.
Borgie *High.* ***Settlement***, 2m/4km SW of Bettyhill. **103 J3** NC6759.
Borgie Forest *High.* ***Forest/woodland***, afforested area astride River Borgie 3m/5km S of Torrisdale Bay, N coast of Caithness district. **103 J3** NC6653.
Borgue *D. & G.* ***Village***, 4m/6km SW of Kirkcudbright. Scene of Robert Louis Stevenson's Master of Ballantrae. **65 G6** NX6348.
Borgue *High.* ***Settlement***, near E coast of Caithness district, 3m/5km SW of Dunbeath. **105 G6** ND1325.
Borle Brook *Shrop.* ***River***, rising 4m/7km W of Bridgnorth and flowing SE into River Severn, 6m/10km NW of Kidderminster. **39 F6** SO7581.
Borley *Essex* ***Hamlet***, 2m/3km NW of Sudbury. Site of the former Borley Rectory, which was once the most haunted place in Britain. **34 C4** TL8442.
Borley Green *Essex* ***Settlement***, 1km W of Borley. TL8442.
Borley Green *Suff.* ***Hamlet***, 4m/6km NW of Stowmarket. TL9960.
Bornais (Anglicised form: Bornish.) *W.Isles* ***Settlement***, on South Uist, on N side of Loch Bornish, 1m/2km E of Rubha Ardvule. **84 C2** NF7329.
Bornaskitaig *High.* ***Settlement***, on N coast of Skye, inland from Ru Bornaskitaig and 5m/8km N of Uig. NG3771.
Borness *D. & G.* ***Settlement***, 5m/8km SW of Kirkcudbright. **65 G6** NX6145.
Bornish *W.Isles Anglicised form of Bornais, qv.*
Borough *Gt.Lon.* ***Suburb***, in borough of Southwark, on S side of River Thames between Southwark and London Bridges. On E side of High Street, George Inn (National Trust), only remaining galleried inn in London, built in 1677. TQ3279.
Borough Fen *Peter.* ***Open space***, lowland 3m/4km SW of Crowland. **43 F5** TF2107.
Borough Green *Kent* Population: 4373. ***Village***, 5m/8km E of Sevenoaks. **23 K6** TQ6057.
Borough Head *Pembs.* ***Coastal feature***, headland on S side of St. Brides Bay, 1km N of Talbenny. SM8312.
Borough Hill *Northants.* ***Hill***, embanked hill rising to over 200 metres, 1m/2km E of Daventry. Remains of fort on summit. Suburb of Borough Hill to W. **31 G2** SP5862.
Boroughbridge *N.Yorks.* Population: 1903. ***Small town***, on S bank of River Ure, 6m/10km SE of Ripon. On W side of town are Devil's Arrows, three monoliths, probably Neolithic. **57 J3** SE3966.
Borras Head *Wrex.* ***Settlement***, 3m/4km NE of Wrexham. **48 C7** SJ3653.
Borrobol Forest *High.* ***Open space***, deer forest in Sutherland district to SW of Kinbrace. **104 C6** NC7726.
Borrodale Burn *High.* ***River***, flowing SW and joining Beasdale Burn at Druimindarroch, Lochaber district. NM6984.
Borron Point *D. & G.* ***Coastal feature***, headland on Solway Firth, 3m/4km NE of Southerness. **65 K5** NX9958.
Borrow Beck *Cumb.* ***River***, rising on Borrowdale Moss, 7m/11km W of Tebay, and flowing SE into River Lune at Low Borrowbridge, 2m/3km S of Tebay. NY6101.
Borrowash *Derbys.* Population: 7092. ***Suburb***, 4m/7km E of Derby. **41 G2** SK4134.
Borrowby *N.Yorks.* ***Settlement***, 2m/3km S of Staithes. **63 J5** NZ7715.
Borrowby *N.Yorks.* ***Village***, 5m/7km N of Thirsk. **57 K1** SE4289.
Borrowdale *Cumb.* ***Locality***, towards upper end of Borrowdale valley, below Borrowdale Fells, 6m/9km S of Keswick. **60 D5** NY2514.
Borrowdale *Cumb.* ***Valley***, carrying River Derwent, to S of Derwent Water. Locality of same name towards upper end of valley. **60 D5** NY2515.
Borrowdale *Cumb.* ***Valley***, carrying Borrow Beck SE from High House Fell to Low Borrowbridge. **61 G6** NY5603.
Borrowdale Fells *Cumb.* ***Open space***, hillslopes, rising steeply to S, at upper end of Borrowdale valley. **60 D5** NY2313.
Borrowfield *Aber.* ***Settlement***, 1m/2km W of Netherley. **91 G5** NO8393.
Borrowston *W.Isles Anglicised form of Borghastan, qv.*
Borrowstounness *Falk. Full name of Bo'ness, qv.*
Borsham *W.Isles Anglicised form of Boirseam, qv.*
Borstal *Med.* ***Suburb***, S of Rochester. **24 D5** TQ7366.
Borth *Cere.* Population: 1289. ***Small town***, resort on Cardigan Bay, 5m/8km N of Aberystwyth. **37 F7** SN6089.
Borth-y-Gest *Gwyn.* ***Village***, resort on River Glaslyn estuary, 1m/2km S of Porthmadog. **36 E2** SH5637.
Borthwick *Midloth.* ***Hamlet***, 2m/3km SE of Gorebridge. **76 B5** NT3659.
Borthwick Castle *Midloth.* ***Castle***, massive 15c tower house 12m/20km SE of Edinburgh. **76 B5** NT3759.
Borthwick Water *Sc.Bord.* ***River***, running NE along SE side of Craik Forest to Roberton, then E to River Teviot 2m/3km SW of Hawick. **69 J3** NT4713.
Borthwickbrae *Sc.Bord.* ***Settlement***, with adjacent pastureland, to NE of Burnfoot. **69 K2** NT4113.
Borthwickshiels *Sc.Bord.* ***Settlement***, 4m/7km W of Hawick. **69 K2** NT4315.
Borve *High.* ***Village***, 4m/6km W of Portree, Skye. **93 K7** NG4448.
Borve *W.Isles Anglicised form of Borgh (Barra), qv.*
Borve *W.Isles Anglicised form of Borgh (Berneray), qv.*
Borve Hill *W.Isles* ***Hill***, to NW of Borve on Berneray. Height 279 feet or 85 metres. **92 E3** NF9181.
Borve Point *W.Isles* ***Coastal feature***, headland 1m/2km W of Borgh. Ancient burial ground between headland and Borgh. **84 B4** NF6402.
Borvemore *W.Isles Anglicised form of Buirgh, qv.*
Borwick *Lancs.* ***Village***, 2m/4km NE of Carnforth. Hall has 14c peel tower. **55 J2** SD5273.
Borwick Rails *Cumb.* ***Settlement***, adjoining to SE of Millom. SD1879.
Bosavern *Cornw.* ***Hamlet***, 1km S of St. Just. **2 A5** SW3630.
Bosbury *Here.* ***Village***, 4m/6km N of Ledbury. **29 F4** SO6943.
Boscarne *Cornw.* ***Hamlet***, 3m/4km W of Bodmin. SX0367.
Boscastle *Cornw.* ***Village***, 5m/7km N of Camelford. 14c cottages on hillside overlook 16c quay. Coast to N is National Trust. **4 B1** SX0990.
Boscobel House *Shrop.* ***Historic house***, early 17c timber-framed house (English Heritage), 8m/12km NW of Wolverhampton. Charles II sought refuge in house and nearby Royal Oak following Battle of Worcester 1651. **40 A5** SJ8308.
Boscombe *Bourne.* ***Suburb***, seaside district of Bournemouth, with pier, 2m/3km E of town centre. **10 C5** SZ1191.
Boscombe *Wilts.* ***Village***, on River Bourne just S of Allington and 7m/11km NE of Salisbury. **10 D1** SU2038.
Boscoppa *Cornw.* ***Locality***, on NE outskirts of St. Austell. **4 A5** SX0353.
Bosham *W.Suss.* Population: 2270. ***Village***, at head of Chichester Harbour (Bosham Channel), 4m/6km W of Chichester. Yachting centre. **12 B6** SU8004.
Bosham Channel *See Chichester Harbour.*
Bosham Hoe *W.Suss.* ***Hamlet***, on N side of Chichester Channel, 2m/3km S of Bosham. SU8101.
Bosherston *Pembs.* ***Village***, 4m/7km S of Pembroke. **16 C5** SR9694.
Bosleake *Cornw.* ***Settlement***, 2m/3km E of Camborne. SW6740.
Bosley *Ches.* ***Village***, 5m/8km S of Macclesfield. **49 J6** SJ9165.
Bossall *N.Yorks.* ***Hamlet***, 3m/5km N of Stamford Bridge. **58 D3** SE7160.
Bossiney *Cornw.* ***Village***, near N coast, 4m/7km NW of Camelford. **4 A2** SX0688.
Bossingham *Kent* ***Village***, 6m/9km S of Canterbury. **15 G3** TR1549.
Bossington *Hants.* ***Settlement***, 3m/5km S of Stockbridge. **10 E1** SU3330.
Bossington *Som.* ***Village***, near coast, 1m/2km NE of Porlock, below Bossington Hill. **7 G1** SS8947.
Bostock Green *Ches.* ***Hamlet***, 3m/5km NW of Middlewich. **49 F6** SJ6769.
Boston *Lincs.* Population: 34,606. ***Town***, ancient port on River Witham near mouth, 28m/45km SE of Lincoln. Pilgrim Fathers sailed from here, 1620. Medieval church has tower known as The Stump, 272 feet or 83 metres high. **43 G1** TF3244.
Boston Deeps ***Sea feature***, sea channel on W side of The Wash off Lincolnshire coast, separated from mainland by mud and sand flats. **43 J1** TF5047.
Boston Guildhall *Lincs.* ***Other feature of interest***, museum in medieval Guildhall in Boston. Pilgrim Fathers were imprisoned here in 1607 for attempting to emigrate illegally. **43 G1** TF3343.
Boston Spa *W.Yorks.* Population: 5627. ***Village***, 4m/6km W of Tadcaster. **57 K5** SE4245.
Boswarthan *Cornw.* ***Settlement***, 3m/4km NW of Penzance. SW4433.
Boswinger *Cornw.* ***Village***, above Veryan Bay, 3m/5km SW of Mevagissey. **3 G4** SW9941.
Bosworth Field *Leics. See Market Bosworth.*
Botallack *Cornw.* ***Village***, to N of St. Just. Location of Nampara, home of Ross Poldark in TV series. Geevor Tin Mine and Heritage Centre has exhibits and demonstrations of tin mining, with a museum displays mining artefacts. **2 A5** SW3632.
Botany Bay *Bristol* ***Suburb***, to N of Bristol. ST5679.
Botany Bay *Gt.Lon.* ***Village***, in borough of Enfield, 3m/4km NW of Enfield. **23 F2** TQ2999.
Botarua *W.Isles* ***Settlement***, on N coast of North Uist, at S end of Vallay Strand. **92 C4** NF7873.
Botcherby *Cumb.* ***Suburb***, 1m/2km E of Carlisle city centre. NY4255.
Botcheston *Leics.* ***Hamlet***, to W of Leicester, 1m/2km N of Desford. **41 G5** SK4804.
Botesdale *Suff.* Population: 1300. ***Village***, adjoining to NE of Rickinghall, 5m/8km SW of Diss. **34 E1** TM0475.
Bothal *Northumb.* ***Village***, 3m/4km E of Morpeth. **71 H5** NZ2386.
Bothamsall *Notts.* ***Village***, 4m/7km NE of Ollerton. Earthwork marks site of former castle. **51 J5** SK6773.
Bothel *Cumb.* ***Village***, 3m/5km SE of Aspatria. **60 C3** NY1838.
Bothenhampton *Dorset* ***Village***, 1m/2km SE of Bridport. **8 D5** SY4791.
Bothwell *S.Lan.* Population: 6542. ***Small town***, 2m/3km NW of Hamilton across River Clyde. Developed around coal, iron and steel industries. To SE, site of Battle of Bothwell Bridge 1679. **75 F5** NS7058.
Bothwell Castle *S.Lan.* ***Castle***, ruined 13c castle (Historic Scotland) standing in woods above River Clyde, 1m/2km NW of Bothwell. **74 E5** NS6859.
Bothwell Water *Sc.Bord.* ***River***, rising in Lammermuir Hills and flowing S to join Whiteadder Water, 1km NW of Cranshaws. **76 E4** NT6863.
Botich *P. & K.* ***Mountain***, 7m/11km NW of Crieff. Height 1758 feet or 536 metres. **82 A4** NN9231.
Botley *Bucks.* ***Village***, 1m/2km E of Chesham. **22 C1** SP9802.
Botley *Hants.* Population: 2297. ***Small town***, on River Hamble 6m/10km E of Southampton. To S, Steeple Court, 17c house. **11 G3** SU5113.
Botley *Oxon.* ***Suburb***, 2m/3km W of Oxford. **21 H1** SP4806.
Botley Pound *Oxon.* ***Locality***, adjoins to W of Botley. SP4806.
Botloe's Green *Glos.* ***Hamlet***, 2m/3km N of Newent. **29 G6** SO7228.
Botolph Claydon *Bucks.* ***Village***, 3m/5km SW of Winslow. **31 J6** SP7324.
Botolphs *W.Suss.* ***Settlement***, on W bank of River Adur, 3m/5km N of Lancing. **12 E6** TQ1909.
Botolph's Bridge *Kent* ***Settlement***, 3m/4km W of Hythe. TR1233.
Bottacks *High.* ***Settlement***, 1m/2km N of Strathpeffer. **96 B5** NH4860.
Bottesford *Leics.* Population: 2619. ***Village***, 7m/11km W of Grantham. **42 B2** SK8038.
Bottesford *N.Lincs.* ***Village***, 2m/4km S of Scunthorpe. **52 C2** SE8907.
Bottesford Beck *N.Lincs.* ***River***, rising to E of Scunthorpe and flowing W to enter River Trent at East Butterwick, 4m/6km SW of Scunthorpe. **52 B2** SE8406.
Bottisham *Cambs.* Population: 1784. ***Village***, 6m/10km E of Cambridge. **33 J2** TL5460.
Bottle Island *High.* ***Island***, small island in Summer Isles group. Lies 1m/2km SW of Eilean Dubh. **95 F1** NB9501.
Bottlesford *Wilts.* ***Hamlet***, just S of Woodborough, 3m/5km W of Pewsey. SU1159.
Bottom Boat *W.Yorks.* ***Village***, 3m/4km SE of Rothwell, on W side of River Calder. SE3524.
Bottom Head *Lancs.* ***Settlement***, at end of road on W side of Lythe Fell, 4m/7km S of High Bentham. **56 B3** SD6662.
Bottom of Hutton *Lancs.* ***Settlement***, 1m/2km W of Hutton, 4m/6km SW of Preston. SD4827.
Bottom o'th'Moor *Gt.Man.* ***Settlement***, on S side of Smithills Moor, 1m/2km E of Horwich. SD6511.
Bottomcraig *Fife* ***Hamlet***, 1km NW of Gauldry. **82 E5** NO3624.
Bottoms *W.Yorks.* ***Hamlet***, 2m/3km S of Todmorden. SD9321.
Botts Green *Warks.* ***Settlement***, 4m/6km NE of Coleshill. SP2492.
Botusfleming *Cornw.* ***Village***, 2m/3km NW of Saltash. **4 E4** SX4061.
Botwnnog *Gwyn.* ***Village***, 4m/6km NW of Abersoch. Elizabethan grammar school (restored). **36 B2** SH2631.
Bough Beech *Kent* ***Village***, 3m/5km E of Edenbridge. **23 H7** TQ4846.
Bough Beech Reservoir *Kent* ***Reservoir***, to N of Bough Beech. **23 J7** TQ4846.
Boughrood (Bochrwyd). *Powys* ***Hamlet***, 4m/6km NW of Talgarth across River Wye. **28 A5** SO1239.
Boughrood Brest *Powys* ***Hamlet***, 1m/2km E of Boughrood. SO1438.
Boughspring *Glos.* ***Hamlet***, 3m/4km NE of Chepstow. Site of Roman building. **19 J2** ST5597.
Boughton *Norf.* ***Village***, 1m/2km N of Stoke Ferry. **44 A5** TF6902.
Boughton *Northants.* ***Historic house***, 16c home of Duke of Buccleuch and Queensberry KT, 3m/5km NE of Kettering town centre. Monastic in origins, it has French-style additions and an excellent collection of 16c-18c furnishings and art. Set in parkland which includes a garden centre. **42 C7** SP9081.
Boughton *Northants.* ***Village***, 4m/6km N of Northampton. **31 J2** SP7565.
Boughton *Notts.* Population: 5221. ***Village***, 2m/3km E of Ollerton. **51 J6** SK6768.
Boughton Aluph *Kent* ***Settlement***, 4m/6km NE of Ashford. **15 F3** TR0348.
Boughton Green *Kent* ***Village***, in parish of Boughton Monchelsea, 3m/5km S of Maidstone. Site of Roman building to E. **14 C2** TQ7651.
Boughton Heath *Ches.* ***Suburb***, adjoining to E of Chester. SJ4265.
Boughton Lees *Kent* ***Village***, 3m/5km N of Ashford. **15 F3** TR0247.
Boughton Malherbe *Kent* ***Hamlet***, 2m/3km SW of Lenham. **14 D3** TQ8849.
Boughton Monchelsea *Kent See Boughton Green.*
Boughton Monchelsea Place *Kent* ***Historic house***, battlemented manor house built of Kentish ragstone in 1567 and set in deer park, 1km S of Boughton Monchelsea and 4m/6km S of Maidstone. **14 C3** TQ7749.

Boughton Street *Kent* ***Village***, 3m/5km E of Faversham. **15 F2** TR0559.
Boulby *R. & C.* ***Settlement***, at E end of steep, high cliffs on North Sea coast, 1m/2km W of Staithes. **63 J5** NZ7518.
Boulder Clough *W.Yorks.* ***Locality***, 2m/3km W of Sowerby Bridge. SE0323.
Bouldnor *I.o.W.* ***Hamlet***, 1m/2km E of Yarmouth. SZ3789.
Bouldon *Shrop.* ***Hamlet***, 7m/11km N of Ludlow. **38 E7** SO5485.
Boulge *Suff.* ***Hamlet***, 2m/4km N of Woodbridge. TM2552.
Boulmer *Northumb.* ***Village***, on North Sea coast, 3m/4km NE of Alnmouth. **71 H2** NU2614.
Boulmer Haven *Northumb.* ***Bay***, to S of Boulmer, 4m/7km E of Alnwick. **71 H2** NU2613.
Boulston *Pembs.* ***Settlement***, 2m/4km SE of Haverfordwest. **16 C3** SM9712.
Boulsworth Hill *Lancs.* ***Open space***, moorland rising to 1696 feet or 517 metres at Lad Law, to S of Forest of Trawden, 4m/7km E of Nelson. **56 E6** SD9335.
Boultenstone *Aber.* ***Settlement***, with hotel, at bridge over Deskry Water, 4m/6km E of Strathdon. **90 C3** NJ4110.
Boultham *Lincs.* ***Suburb***, 2m/3km SW of Lincoln city centre. **52 C6** SK9569.
Boulton *Derby* ***Suburb***, 3m/5km SE of Derby city centre. SK3832.
Bound Skerry *Shet.* *See Out Skerries.*
Boundary *Derbys.* ***Hamlet***, 3m/4km E of Swadlincote. SK3318.
Boundary *Staffs.* ***Hamlet***, 2m/3km W of Cheadle. SJ9842.
Bourn *Cambs.* ***Village***, 8m/13km W of Cambridge. Hall stands within earthworks of 11c castle. **33 G3** TL3256.
Bournbrook *W.Mid.* ***Suburb***, 3m/5km SW of Birmingham city centre. **40 C7** SP0482.
Bourne ***River***, rising in parish of Burbage to E of Pewsey and flowing S through North Tidworth into River Avon on SE side of Salisbury. SU1529.
Bourne *Lincs.* Population: 8777. ***Small town***, market town 10m/15km W of Spalding. **42 D3** TF0920.
Bourne *Surr.* ***River***, rising on Westend Common and flowing E to N of Woking, then NE into River Thames 1km N of Weybridge. **22 D5** TQ0765.
Bourne End *Beds.* ***Hamlet***, 6m/10km SW of Bedford. **32 C4** SP9644.
Bourne End *Beds.* ***Settlement***, 2m/3km E of Sharnbrook. TL0160.
Bourne End *Bucks.* Population: 6781. ***Locality***, residential locality on River Thames, 3m/5km E of Marlow. **22 B3** SU8987.
Bourne End *Herts.* ***Village***, on W edge of Hemel Hempstead. **22 D1** TL0206.
Bourne North Fen *Lincs.* ***Open space***, lowland, containing drainage ditches, on E side of Bourne. **42 E3** TF1221.
Bournebridge *Essex* ***Village***, 4m/6km N of Romford. **23 J2** TQ5094.
Bournemouth *Bourne.* Population: 155,488. ***Town***, large seaside resort with mild climate, 24m/39km SW of Southampton. Town developed from a few cottages in 1810 to present conurbation. University. Conference, business and shopping centre. Bournemouth International Airport, 5m/8km NE of town centre. **10 B5** SZ0891.
Bournemouth International Airport *Dorset* ***Airport/airfield***, international airport, 5m/8km NE of Bournemouth town centre. **10 C5** SZ1198.
Bournes Green *Glos.* ***Hamlet***, 4m/6km E of Stroud. Site of Roman villa. **20 C1** SO9004.
Bournes Green *S'end* ***Suburb***, to E of Southend-on-Sea. TQ9186.
Bournes Green *Worcs.* ***Locality***, 4m/7km NW of Bromsgrove. SO9174.
Bournheath *Worcs.* ***Village***, 2m/4km N of Bromsgrove. **29 J1** SO9473.
Bournmoor *Dur.* ***Hamlet***, 2m/4km E of Chester-le-Street. **62 E1** NZ3151.
Bournville *W.Mid.* ***Suburb***, 4m/6km SW of Birmingham city centre. Originated as estate developed in late 19c for housing people employed in chocolate factory. **40 C7** SP0481.
Bourton *Bucks.* ***Settlement***, to E of Buckingham. SP7033.
Bourton *Dorset* ***Village***, 4m/6km E of Wincanton. **9 G1** ST7730.
Bourton *N.Som.* ***Settlement***, 5m/7km NE of Weston-super-Mare. **19 G5** ST3864.
Bourton *Oxon.* ***Village***, 5m/8km E of Swindon. **21 F3** SU2387.
Bourton *Shrop.* ***Village***, 3m/5km SW of Much Wenlock. **38 E6** SO5996.
Bourton *Wilts.* ***Hamlet***, 3m/5km NE of Devizes. SU0464.
Bourton Downs *Glos.* ***Open space***, hilly area 2m/4km SW of Blockley. **30 C5** SP1231.
Bourton on Dunsmore *Warks.* ***Village***, 5m/9km SW of Rugby. **31 F1** SP4370.
Bourton-on-the-Hill *Glos.* ***Village***, 2m/3km W of Moreton-in-Marsh. **30 C5** SP1732.
Bourton-on-the-Water *Glos.* Population: 2239. ***Small town***, attractive town on River Windrush, 4m/6km SW of Stow-on-the-Wold. Many tourist attractions including Birdland, model village, model railway, perfumery exhibition and Cotswold Motor Museum and Toy Collection. **30 C6** SP1620.
Bourtonville *Bucks.* ***Suburb***, in E part of Buckingham. SP7033.
Bousd *Arg. & B.* ***Settlement***, in N part of Coll, 4m/7km NE of Arinagour. **78 D1** NM2563.
Boustead Hill *Cumb.* ***Hamlet***, 2m/3km W of Burgh by Sands. **60 D1** NY2959.
Bouth *Cumb.* ***Village***, 2m/3km NE of Greenodd. **55 G1** SD3285.
Bouthwaite *N.Yorks.* ***Hamlet***, 4m/7km NW of Pateley Bridge. **57 G2** SE1271.
Bovain *Stir.* ***Settlement***, at NE end of Glen Dochart, 3m/4km SW of Killin. **81 G4** NN5430.
Bovehill *Swan.* ***Hamlet***, on Gower peninsula, 1m/2km E of Llanmadoc. SS4693.
Boveney *Bucks.* ***Settlement***, 3m/4km SW of Slough. **22 C4** SU9377.
Boveridge *Dorset* ***Hamlet***, 1m/2km NE of Cranborne. **10 B3** SU0614.
Boverton (Trebefered). *V. of Glam.* ***Locality***, on E side of Llantwit Major. **18 C5** SS9868.
Bovey *Devon* ***River***, rising on North Dartmoor and flowing first NE, then SE past Bovey Tracey and into River Teign 1m/2km S of Chudleigh Knighton. **6 E7** SX8475.
Bovey Tracey *Devon* Population: 3492. ***Small town***, on River Bovey 5m/9km NW of Newton Abbot. Church of St. Thomas is 15c. **5 J3** SX8178.
Bovingdon *Herts.* Population: 3464. ***Village***, 3m/5km SW of Hemel Hempstead. Airfield to W. **22 D1** TL0103.
Bovingdon Green *Bucks.* ***Locality***, adjoining to W of Marlow. SU8387.
Bovinger *Essex* ***Settlement***, 3m/4km SW of Chipping Ongar. **23 J1** TL5205.
Bow *Cumb.* ***Settlement***, 4m/6km W of Carlisle. NY3356.
Bow *Devon* ***Hamlet***, 3m/4km S of Totnes at head of Bow Creek, running into River Dart estuary. SX8156.
Bow *Devon* ***Village***, 7m/12km W of Crediton. **7 F5** SS7201.
Bow *Gt.Lon.* ***Suburb***, in borough of Tower Hamlets, 3m/5km NE of London Bridge. TQ3783.
Bow *Ork.* ***Settlement***, on Flotta, 1km SW of Pan. **107 C8** ND3693.
Bow Brickhill *M.K.* ***Village***, 2m/3km E of Bletchely. **32 C5** SP9034.
Bow Burn *D. & G.* ***River***, rising to W of Moorbrock Hill and flowing NW, then SW to join Water of Deugh, 2m/4km N of Carsphairn. **68 B3** NX5597.
Bow Common *Gt.Lon.* ***Suburb***, 1m/2km S of Bow. TQ3781.
Bow Fell *Cumb.* ***Mountain***, in Lake District, 5m/8km W of Chapel Stile. Height 2959 feet or 902 metres. **60 D6** NY2406.
Bow Head *Ork.* ***Coastal feature***, headland at N end of Westray. **106 D2** HY4553.
Bow Hill *W.Suss.* ***Hill***, 6m/9km E of Rowland's Castle. Viewpoint. Height 676 feet or 206 metres. **12 B5** SU8211.
Bow of Fife *Fife* ***Locality***, 4m/6km W of Cupar. **82 E6** NO3213.
Bow Street *Cere.* ***Village***, 3m/5km NE of Aberystwyth. **37 F7** SN6284.
Bow Street *Norf.* ***Settlement***, 3m/5km NW of Attleborough. TM0197.
Bowbank *Dur.* ***Settlement***, 1m/2km S of Middleton-in-Teesdale. **62 A4** NY9423.
Bowburn *Dur.* Population: 3296. ***Village***, 4m/6km SE of Durham. **62 E3** NZ3038.
Bowcombe *I.o.W.* ***Hamlet***, 3m/4km SW of Newport. **11 F6** SZ4686.
Bowd *Devon* ***Settlement***, 2m/3km NW of Sidmouth. **7 K7** SY1090.
Bowden *Devon* ***Settlement***, 3m/4km SW of Dartmouth. **5 J6** SX8449.
Bowden *Sc.Bord.* ***Village***, 2m/4km S of Melrose beyond Eildon Hills. **76 D7** NT5530.
Bowden Close *Dur.* ***Locality***, 1m/2km W of Willington. NZ1835.
Bowden Hill *Wilts.* ***Village***, 4m/6km S of Chippenham. Bewley Common to NW is partly National Trust property. **20 C5** ST9367.
Bowdon *Gt.Man.* Population: 5141. ***Small town***, 1m/2km SW of Altrincham. **49 G4** SJ7586.
Bower *Northumb.* ***Settlement***, on W side of Chirdon Burn, 3m/5km SE of Falstone. **70 C5** NY7583.
Bower Ashton *Bristol* ***Suburb***, 2m/3km SW of Bristol city centre. ST5671.
Bower Fold *Gt.Man.* ***Locality***, 1m/2km SE of Stalybridge. SJ9797.
Bower Hinton *Som.* ***Locality***, at S end of Martock. **8 D3** ST4518.
Bower House Tye *Suff.* ***Settlement***, 1m/2km E of Boxford, 3m/4km SW of Hadleigh. TL9840.
Bowerchalke *Wilts.* ***Village***, 2m/3km SW of Broad Chalke. **10 B2** SU0123.
Bowerhill *Wilts.* ***Suburb***, 2m/3km SE of Melksham. ST9162.
Bowermadden *High.* ***Settlement***, in Caithness district, 4m/6km SE of Castletown. **105 H2** ND2364.
Bowers *Staffs.* ***Hamlet***, 4m/7km N of Eccleshall. SJ8135.
Bowers Gifford *Essex* ***Village***, 3m/4km E of Basildon. **24 D3** TQ7588.
Bowershall *Fife* ***Hamlet***, 2m/3km N of Dunfermline. **75 J1** NT0991.
Bowertower *High.* ***Settlement***, 4m/6km SE of Castletown. **105 H2** ND2362.
Bowes *Dur.* ***Small town***, on site of Roman town of Lavatrae, 4m/6km SW of Barnard Castle. Remains of Norman keep of castle (English Heritage). The Otter Trust's North Pennines Reserve is 230 acre wildlife reserve, 3m/5km W. **62 A5** NY9913.
Bowes Castle *Dur.* ***Castle***, remains of 12c keep (English Heritage) standing on site of Roman fort, in Bowes, 14m/22km NE of Kirkby Stephen. **62 A5** NY9813.
Bowes Moor *Dur.* ***Open space***, moorland on edge of Stainmore Forest, 4m/6km W of Bowes. **62 A5** NY9913.
Bowes Museum *Dur.* ***Other feature of interest***, large collection of art treasures in museum, on S side of Barnard Castle. **62 B5** NZ0516.
Bowes Park *Gt.Lon.* ***Suburb***, on borders of Enfield and Haringey boroughs, 7m/11km N of Charing Cross. TQ3091.
Bowgreave *Lancs.* ***Village***, 1km S of Garstang. **55 H5** SD4944.
Bowgreen *Gt.Man.* ***Suburb***, adjoining to S of Bowdon, 1m/2km S of Altrincham. SJ7586.
Bowhill *Devon* *See Exeter.*
Bowhill *Sc.Bord.* ***Historic house***, house and estate 3m/5km W of Selkirk. Excellent collections of art and French furniture. Home of Dukes of Buccleuch. **69 K1** NT4227.
Bowhousebog (Also known as Liquo.) *N.Lan.* ***Settlement***, 2m/3km SW of Shotts, on banks of South Calder Water. NS8558.
Bowithick *Cornw.* ***Hamlet***, 5m/8km E of Camelford. SX1882.
Bowker's Green *Lancs.* ***Hamlet***, 3m/4km S of Ormskirk. SD4004.
Bowland *Sc.Bord.* ***Settlement***, on Gala Water, 3m/5km NW of Galashiels. NT4540.
Bowland Bridge *Cumb.* ***Settlement***, at crossing of River Winster, 4m/6km NE of Newby Bridge. **55 H1** SD4189.
Bowlee *Gt.Man.* ***Settlement***, 2m/3km W of Middleton. SD8406.
Bowley *Here.* ***Hamlet***, 5m/8km SE of Leominster. **28 E3** SO5452.
Bowley Town *Here.* ***Settlement***, to N of Bowley. SO5353.
Bowlhead Green *Surr.* ***Hamlet***, 3m/4km NE of Hindhead. **12 C3** SU9138.
Bowling *W.Dun.* ***Village***, on N bank of River Clyde, 3m/5km E of Dumbarton. Developed via shipbuilding and distilling industries. W terminus of Forth and Clyde Canal (disused). **74 C3** NS4474.
Bowling *W.Yorks.* ***Suburb***, 1m/2km SE of Bradford city centre. (Bradford annual holiday is known as Bowling Tide). SE1731.
Bowling Bank *Wrex.* ***Settlement***, 4m/7km E of Wrexham. **38 C1** SJ3948.
Bowling Green *Worcs.* ***Locality***, 3m/5km SW of Worcester. SO8151.
Bowlish *Som.* ***Suburb***, NW district of Shepton Mallet. **19 K7** ST6144.
Bowmanstead *Cumb.* ***Hamlet***, 1km S of Coniston. **60 E7** SD2996.
Bowmont Forest *Sc.Bord.* ***Forest/woodland***, 3m/5km S of Kelso. **70 C1** NT7328.
Bowmont Water ***River***, rising in Cheviot Hills, on slopes of Cock Law, and flowing N across border of Scotland and England via Mowhaugh, Town Yetholm and Pawston, then W to join with College Burn to become River Glen, NE of Westnewton. **70 D2** NT9030.
Bowmore *Arg. & B.* ***Village***, fishing port on E side of Loch Indaal, Islay, 4m/6km NE of Laggan Point. **72 B5** NR3159.
Bowness Common *Cumb.* ***Open space***, coastal plain on S side of Solway Firth to N of Anthorn, 6m/10km NE of Silloth. **60 C1** NY2059.
Bowness-on-Solway *Cumb.* ***Village***, on Solway Firth, 4m/6km N of Kirkbride. Roman sites in vicinity, at W end of Hadrian's Wall. **69 H7** NY2262.
Bowness-on-Windermere *Cumb.* ***Locality***, on E shore of Windermere, adjoining Windermere town to S. **60 F7** SD4096.
Bowood *Wilts.* ***Historic house***, 18c home of Earl of Shelburne, 4m/6km SE of Chippenham, partly demolished in 1950s. Includes Diocletian wing by Robert Adam, and laboratory where Joseph Priestley discovered oxygen gas in 1774. 2000 acres of beautiful gardens, landscaped by 'Capability' Brown, feature Doric temple and pinetum. **20 C4** ST9769.
Bowscale *Cumb.* ***Settlement***, 1m/2km N of Mungrisdale. NY3531.
Bowsden *Northumb.* ***Hamlet***, 2m/3km NW of Lowick. **77 H6** NT9941.
Bowside Lodge *High.* ***Settlement***, on E side of River Strathy, 3m/5km S of Strathy Bay. **104 D2** NC8261.
Bowston *Cumb.* ***Hamlet***, on W bank of River Kent, 3m/5km N of Kendal. SD4996.
Bowthorpe *Norf.* ***Suburb***, 3m/5km W of Norwich city centre. **45 F5** TG1709.
Bowtrees *Falk.* ***Settlement***, 1m/2km S of Airth. **75 H2** NS9086.
Box *Glos.* ***Village***, 1m/2km NE of Nailsworth. **20 B1** SO8500.
Box *Suff.* ***River***, rising 2m/3km S of Lavenham and flowing SE into River Stour, 1m/2km SW of Higham. **34 D4** TM0234.
Box *Wilts.* ***Village***, 5m/8km NE of Bath. Site of Roman villa. **20 B5** ST8268.
Box End *Beds.* ***Hamlet***, 3m/4km W of Bedford across River Great Ouse. **32 D4** TL0049.
Box Hill *Surr.* ***Hill***, steep chalk hill (National Trust), with country park and viewpoint, forming part of North Downs, 1m/2km NE of Dorking. Height 564 feet or 172 metres. Settlement of same name 1m/2km E. **22 E6** TQ1751.
Boxbush *Glos.* ***Settlement***, 4m/7km SW of Newent. SO6720.
Boxbush *Glos.* ***Settlement***, on W bank of River Severn, 2m/3km E of Westbury-on-Severn. **29 G7** SO7413.
Boxford *Suff.* ***Village***, 4m/7km W of Hadleigh. **34 D4** TL9640.
Boxford *W.Berks.* ***Village***, 4m/6km NW of Newbury. Site of Roman building 1m/2km E. **21 H4** SU4271.
Boxgrove *W.Suss.* Population: 1090. ***Village***, 3m/5km NE of Chichester. Benedictine priory church, with fragments of monastic buildings (English Heritage). **12 C6** SU9007.
Boxgrove Priory *W.Suss.* ***Ecclesiastical building***, site of Benedictine priory founded c. 1117 at Boxgrove, 3m/5km NE of Chichester. Remains (English Heritage) include Guest House, Chapter House and church, now parish church. **12 C6** SU9007.
Boxley *Kent* ***Village***, 2m/4km N of Maidstone, in conservation area on edge of North Downs. **14 C2** TQ7759.
Boxley Abbey *Kent* ***Ecclesiastical building***, remains of medieval abbey to W of Boxley. **14 C2** TQ7759.
Boxmoor *Herts.* ***Suburb***, SW district of Hemel Hempstead. **22 D1** TL0406.

Box's Shop *Cornw.* ***Settlement***, 3m/5km S of Bude. SS2101.

Boxted *Essex* ***Hamlet***, 5m/8km N of Colchester. **34 D5** TL9933.

Boxted *Suff.* ***Village***, 4m/6km NW of Long Melford. **34 C3** TL8250.

Boxted Cross *Essex* ***Hamlet***, 1km SE of Boxted. **34 E5** TL9933.

Boxted Heath *Essex* ***Hamlet***, 1m/2km S of Boxted. TM0031.

Boxwell *Glos.* ***Settlement***, 5m/8km W of Tetbury. ST8192.

Boxworth *Cambs.* ***Village***, 7m/11km NW of Cambridge. **33 G2** TL3464.

Boxworth End *Cambs.* ***Locality***, S end of Swavesey. **33 G2** TL3667.

Boyd *S.Glos.* ***River***, rising S of Chipping Sodbury and flowing into River Avon 2m/3km above Keynsham. **20 A4** ST6868.

Boyden Gate *Kent* ***Village***, 3m/5km SE of Herne Bay. **25 J5** TR2265.

Boydston *S.Ayr.* ***Settlement***, 1m/2km S of Crossroads. **74 C7** NS4632.

Boylestone *Derbys.* ***Village***, 3m/4km NE of Sudbury. **40 D2** SK1835.

Boyndie *Aber.* ***Village***, 3m/5km W of Banff. **98 E4** NJ6463.

Boyndie Bay *Aber.* ***Bay***, sandy bay extending W from Banff to Knock Head, on N coast of Banff and Buchan district. **98 E4** NJ6463.

Boyndlie *Aber.* ***Locality***, comprising Upper and Nether Boyndlie near N coast, 5m/9km SW of Fraserburgh. NJ9062.

Boyne Bay *Aber.* ***Bay***, on N coast of Banff and Buchan district, 2m/3km E of Portsoy. Burn of Boyne runs N into bay. **98 E4** NJ6166.

Boyne Castle *Aber.* ***Castle***, remains located on Burn of Boyne nearly 1km from Boyne Bay. **98 E4** NJ6166.

Boynton *E.Riding* ***Village***, 3m/5km W of Bridlington. Hall dates from 16c. **59 H3** TA1368.

Boys Hill *Dorset* ***Settlement***, in Blackmoor Vale, 5m/7km SE of Sherborne. ST6710.

Boys Village *V. of Glam.* ***Settlement***, 1km E of Gileston. ST0267.

Boysack *Angus* ***Hamlet***, 2m/3km E of Friockheim, on S bank of Lunan Water. **83 H3** NO6249.

Boythorpe *Derbys.* ***Suburb***, 1m/2km SW of Chesterfield town centre. SK3770.

Boyton *Cornw.* ***Village***, 5m/8km N of Launceston. **6 B6** SX3292.

Boyton *Suff.* ***Village***, 7m/11km E of Woodbridge. **35 H4** TM3747.

Boyton *Wilts.* ***Village***, on River Wylye, 3m/4km SE of Heytesbury. **9 J1** ST9539.

Boyton Cross *Essex* ***Hamlet***, 4m/6km NW of Chelmsford. **24 C1** TL6409.

Boyton End *Suff.* ***Hamlet***, 3m/5km E of Haverhill. TL7144.

Bozeat *Northants.* Population: 1864. ***Village***, 6m/9km S of Wellingborough. **32 C3** SP9059.

Braaid *I.o.M.* ***Hamlet***, 4m/6km W of Douglas. **54 C6** SC3276.

Braal Castle (Also spelled Brawl Castle.) *High.* ***Castle***, ancient castle on W bank of River Thurso on NE side of Halkirk, Caithness district. **105 G2** ND1360.

Braan *P. & K.* ***River***, running NE down Strath Braan to River Tay at Dunkeld. **82 A4** NO0242.

Brabling Green *Suff.* ***Settlement***, 1m/2km NE of Framlingham. **35 G2** TM2964.

Brabourne *Kent* ***Village***, 6m/9km E of Ashford. **15 F3** TR1041.

Brabourne Lees *Kent* Population: 1925. ***Village***, 5m/8km SE of Ashford. **15 F3** TR0740.

Brabster *High.* ***Locality***, in Caithness district, 4m/6km S of St. John's Point on Pentland Firth. **105 J2** ND3269.

Bracadale *High.* ***Village***, near SW coast of Skye, 10m/16km NW of Sligachan. Loch Bracadale is large inlet to W. **85 J1** NG3438.

Braceborough *Lincs.* ***Village***, 5m/8km NE of Stamford. **42 D4** TF0813.

Bracebridge *Lincs.* ***Suburb***, 2m/3km S of Lincoln city centre. **52 C6** SK9668.

Bracebridge Heath *Lincs.* Population: 2758. ***Suburb***, 3m/4km S of Lincoln. **52 C6** SK9867.

Bracebridge Low Fields *Lincs.* ***Suburb***, 3m/4km S of Lincoln city centre. SK9667.

Braceby *Lincs.* ***Hamlet***, 6m/10km E of Grantham. **42 D2** TF0135.

Bracewell *Lancs.* ***Hamlet***, 1m/2km NW of Barnoldswick. **56 D5** SD8746.

Brachla *High.* ***Settlement***, on W shore of Loch Ness, 4m/7km NE of Drumnadrochit. **88 C1** NH5633.

Bracken Bank *W.Yorks.* ***Suburb***, 2m/3km SW of Keighley town centre. SE0439.

Bracken Hill *S.Yorks.* ***Locality***, 1m/2km N of Grenoside. **51 F3** SK3396.

Bracken Hill *W.Yorks.* ***Village***, on River Calder, 1m/2km NW of Mirfield. SE1821.

Brackenber *Cumb.* ***Settlement***, 1km S of Shap. NY5614.

Brackenber *Cumb.* ***Settlement***, 3m/4km E of Appleby-in-Westmorland. **61 J4** NY7219.

Brackenborough *Lincs.* ***Locality***, 2m/3km N of Louth. TF3290.

Brackenbottom *N.Yorks.* ***Settlement***, just E of Horton in Ribblesdale. SD8172.

Brackenfield *Derbys.* ***Hamlet***, 5m/8km E of Matlock. **51 F7** SK3759.

Brackenfield Green *Derbys.* ***Settlement***, to SW of Brackenfield. SK3759.

Brackenhall *W.Yorks.* ***Suburb***, 2m/3km N of Huddersfield town centre. SE1519.

Brackenhill *W.Yorks.* ***Locality***, adjoining to W of Ackworth Moor Top. SE4216.

Brackens *Aber.* ***Settlement***, on W side of Hill of Brackans, 3m/5km NE of Fyvie. **99 F5** NJ7553.

Brackenthwaite *Cumb.* ***Locality***, 1m/2km NE of Loweswater hamlet. NY1522.

Brackenthwaite *Cumb.* ***Locality***, 3m/4km SE of Wigton. NY2946.

Brackenthwaite *N.Yorks.* ***Settlement***, 3m/5km SW of Harrogate. SE2851.

Brackenthwaite Fell *Cumb.* ***Open space***, steep hillside to N of Grasmoor, 1m/2km E of N end of Crummock Water. **60 C4** NY1621.

Brackla *High.* ***Locality***, in Nairn district, 4m/6km SW of Nairn. Includes distillery which produces Royal Brackla whisky. NH8651.

Bracklach *Moray* ***Settlement***, 1m/2km S of Cabrach. **90 B2** NJ3824.

Bracklamore *Aber.* ***Settlement***, on SE side of Bracklamore Hill, 3m/4km NW of New Pitsligo. **99 G5** NJ8458.

Bracklamore Hill *Aber.* ***Hill***, 4m/7km SE of Gardenstown. Height 722 feet or 220 metres. **99 G5** NJ8358.

Bracklesham *W.Suss.* ***Village***, on coast, adjoining to SE of East Wittering. SZ8096.

Bracklesham Bay *W.Suss.* ***Bay***, formed by gently curving coast extending from Chichester Harbour to Selsey Bill. **12 B7** SZ8096.

Brackletter *High.* ***Settlement***, 3m/4km NW of Spean Bridge. **87 H6** NN1882.

Brackley *High.* ***Settlement***, 3m/4km SE of Ardersier. **97 F6** NH8052.

Brackley *Northants.* Population: 9113. ***Small town***, 8m/13km E of Banbury. **31 G5** SP5837.

Brackley Gate *Derbys.* ***Settlement***, 5m/7km NE of Derby. SK3842.

Brackley Hatch *Northants.* ***Settlement***, 5m/8km NE of Brackley. SP6441.

Bracklinn Falls (Falls of Bracklinn). *Stir.* ***Waterfall***, in course of Keltie Water 1m/2km E of Callander. **81 H7** NN6408.

Brackly *Arg. & B.* ***Settlement***, 1m/2km SW of Lochgilphead across Crinan Canal. **73 G2** NR8587.

Brackmills *Northants.* ***Locality***, with industrial estate, 2m/3km SE of Northampton town centre. SP7758.

Bracknell *Brack.F.* Population: 60,895. ***Town***, New Town designated 1949, 4m/6km E of Wokingham. Home of Meteorological Office. **22 B5** SU8769.

Braco *P. & K.* ***Village***, on River Knaik, 6m/10km NE of Dunblane. In grounds of Ardoch House to N is well-preserved site of Roman fort; site of Roman camp 1km N of fort. **81 K7** NN8309.

Bracobrae *Moray* ***Locality***, on W side of Sillyearn Wood, 4m/6km NW of Milltown of Rothiemay. **98 D5** NJ5053.

Bracon *N.Lincs.* ***Locality***, adjoining to NE of Belton, 2m/3km N of Epworth. SE7807.

Bracon Ash *Norf.* ***Village***, 6m/10km SW of Norwich. **45 F6** TM1899.

Bracora *High.* ***Settlement***, on N shore of Loch Morar, in Lochaber district, 4m/6km SE of Mallaig. **86 D5** NM7192.

Bracorina *High.* ***Settlement***, in Lochaber district, 1km E of Bracora. **86 D5** NM7292.

Bradbourne *Derbys.* ***Village***, 4m/7km NE of Ashbourne. **50 E7** SK2052.

Bradbury *Dur.* ***Village***, 3m/4km W of Sedgefield. **62 E4** NZ3128.

Bradda *I.o.M.* ***Locality***, consisting of Bradda East and Bradda West, 1km N of Port Erin. **54 B6** SC1970.

Bradda East *I.o.M.* ***Locality***, with Bradda West, forms locality of Bradda, 1km N of Port Erin. SC1970.

Bradda Head *I.o.M.* ***Coastal feature***, headland 1km W of Bradda West. **54 A6** SC1970.

Bradda West *I.o.M.* ***Locality***, with Bradda East, forms locality of Bradda, 1km N of Port Erin. SC1969.

Bradden *Northants.* ***Village***, 3m/5km W of Towcester. **31 H4** SP6448.

Braddock (Also known as Broadoak.) *Cornw.* ***Settlement***, 4m/6km NE of Lostwithieland. Site of Civil War Battle of Braddock Down in 1643 in which Ralph Hopton, leading a Royalist army, defeated Parliamentarians, putting Cornwall into hands of Royalists. **4 B4** SX1662.

Braddocks Hay *Staffs.* ***Suburb***, adjoining to E of Biddulph. SJ8857.

Bradeley *Stoke* ***Suburb***, 1m/2km NE of Burslem. SJ8851.

Braden Heath *Shrop.* ***Hamlet***, 3m/5km E of Ellesmere. SJ4436.

Bradenham *Bucks.* ***Village***, 4m/6km NW of High Wycombe. **22 B2** SU8297.

Bradenstoke *Wilts.* ***Village***, 5m/7km W of Wootton Bassett. **20 D3** SU0079.

Brades Village *W.Mid.* ***Locality***, 1km NW of Oldbury. SO9790.

Bradfield *Devon* ***Hamlet***, 3m/4km NE of Cullompton. **7 J5** ST0509.

Bradfield *Essex* ***Village***, 3m/4km E of Manningtree. **35 F5** TM1430.

Bradfield *Norf.* ***Hamlet***, 1m/2km E of Antingham. **45 G2** TG2633.

Bradfield *W.Berks.* ***Village***, 3m/5km SW of Pangbourne. Boys' public school. **21 K4** SU6072.

Bradfield Combust *Suff.* ***Village***, 5m/8km SE of Bury St. Edmunds. Name recalls burning of hall during 14c riots. **34 C3** TL8957.

Bradfield Green *Ches.* ***Hamlet***, 3m/5km NW of Crewe. **49 F7** SJ6859.

Bradfield Grove *Oxon.* ***Locality***, 3m/4km N of Wantage. SU4091.

Bradfield Heath *Essex* ***Village***, 2m/4km SE of Manningtree. **35 F6** TM1329.

Bradfield Moors *S.Yorks.* ***Open space***, moorland at E side of The Pennines, 3m/4km W of High Bradfield, with continuation to S of Dale Dike Reservoir. **50 E3** SK2292.

Bradfield St. Clare *Suff.* ***Village***, 1m/2km E of Bradfield Combust. **34 D3** TL9057.

Bradfield St. George *Suff.* ***Village***, 4m/7km SE of Bury St. Edmunds. **34 D3** TL9160.

Bradford *Cornw.* ***Hamlet***, 6m/10km NE of Bodmin. SX1175.

Bradford *Derbys.* ***Hamlet***, adjoining to E of Youlgreave, 3m/4km S of Bakewell. SK2164.

Bradford *Devon* ***Hamlet***, 5m/9km NE of Holsworthy. **6 C5** SS4207.

Bradford *Gt.Man.* ***Suburb***, 2m/3km E of Manchester city centre. SJ8698.

Bradford *Northumb.* ***Hamlet***, 2m/4km W of Belsay. NZ0679.

Bradford *Northumb.* ***Settlement***, 3m/4km SW of Bamburgh. **77 K7** NU1532.

Bradford *W.Yorks.* Population: 289,376. ***City***, industrial city, 8m/13km W of Leeds. Cathedral is former parish church. Leeds Bradford International Airport at Yeadon, 6m/10km NE. Previously known as wool capital of the world, Bradford is now less dependent upon the textile industry; nowadays, other industries such as tourism are important to local economy. University. Home to National Museum of Photography, Film and Television. **57 G6** SE1633.

Bradford Abbas *Dorset* ***Village***, on River Yeo, 3m/4km SE of Yeovil. **8 E3** ST5814.

Bradford Cathedral *W.Yorks.* ***Ecclesiastical building***, former parish church located just N of Bradford city centre. Largely a 14c-15c rebuilding of early church. Attained cathedral status in 1919. **57 G6** SE1633.

Bradford Leigh *Wilts.* ***Hamlet***, 1m/2km NE of Bradford-on-Avon. **20 B5** ST8362.

Bradford-on-Avon *Wilts.* Population: 8815. ***Small town***, hillside town of Bath stone, 3m/5km NW of Trowbridge. Church of St. Laurence is considered to be finest Saxon church in country, dating from c. AD 705. Medieval tithe barn (English Heritage). **20 B5** ST8260.

Bradford-on-Avon Tithe Barn *Wilts.* ***Other feature of interest***, 17c threshing barn (English Heritage), 1km SW of Bradford-on-Avon across River Avon. Includes displays on local rural domestic life. **20 B5** ST8260.

Bradford-on-Tone *Som.* ***Village***, 3m/4km NE of Wellington. **7 K3** ST1722.

Bradford Peverell *Dorset* ***Village***, on River Frome, 3m/4km NW of Dorchester. **9 F5** SY6593.

Bradgate *Leics.* ***Historic house***, ruins of 15c-16c brick mansion in deer park and surrounded by Bradgate Park, 5m/8km NW of Leicester. Birthplace of Lady Jane Grey, 1537. **41 H4** SK5310.

Bradgate *S.Yorks.* ***Suburb***, 1m/2km W of Rotherham town centre. SK4193.

Bradiford *Devon* ***Suburb***, on NW outskirts of Barnstaple. SS5434.

Brading *I.o.W.* Population: 2077. ***Village***, 2m/3km N of Sandown. To SW, remains of Roman villa. **11 H6** SZ6087.

Brading Roman Villa *I.o.W.* ***Historic/prehistoric site***, built c. AD 300, with notable mosaic floor, 1km NW of Brading. **11 H6** SZ5986.

Bradley *Ches.* ***Settlement***, 1m/2km SE of Frodsham. SJ5377.

Bradley *Cumb.* ***Locality***, adjoining to NW of Ousby, 1m/2km N of Skirwith. NY6135.

Bradley *Derbys.* ***Village***, 3m/5km E of Ashbourne. **40 E1** SK2245.

Bradley *Hants.* ***Village***, 5m/9km NW of Alton. **21 K7** SU6341.

Bradley *N.E.Lincs.* ***Village***, 3m/4km SW of Grimsby. **53 F2** TA2406.

Bradley *N.Yorks.* ***Settlement***, 6m/10km NE of Kettlewell. **57 F1** SE0380.

Bradley *Staffs.* ***Village***, 4m/7km SW of Stafford. **40 A4** SJ8717.

Bradley *W.Mid.* ***Suburb***, SE district of Wolverhampton. **40 B6** SO9595.

Bradley *W.Yorks.* ***Locality***, 3m/5km NE of Huddersfield. To E, junction of Huddersfield Canal and Calder and Hebble Navigation. SE1720.

Bradley *Worcs.* ***Village***, 6m/10km E of Droitwich Spa. SO9860.

Bradley *Wrex.* ***Suburb***, 2m/4km N of Wrexham. SJ3253.

Bradley Common *Ches.* ***Locality***, 2m/3km SE of Malpas. SJ5145.

Bradley Fold *Gt.Man.* ***Suburb***, 2m/4km E of Bolton. SD7508.

Bradley Green *Warks.* ***Settlement***, on Coventry Canal, 2m/3km NW of Atherstone. SK2800.

Bradley Green *Worcs.* ***Hamlet***, 5m/9km E of Droitwich Spa. **29 J2** SO9861.

Bradley Hill *Som.* ***Hill***, 1m/2km NW of Somerton. Height 194 feet or 59 metres. **8 D2** ST4730.

Bradley in the Moors *Staffs.* ***Village***, 4m/6km E of Cheadle. **40 C1** SK0641.

Bradley Manor *Devon* ***Historic house***, well-preserved 15c manor house to SW of Newton Abbot. **5 J3** SX8470.

Bradley Mills *W.Yorks.* ***Suburb***, to NE of Huddersfield town centre. SE1517.

Bradley Mount *Ches.* ***Suburb***, to E of Prestbury. SJ9177.

Bradley Stoke *S.Glos.* ***Locality***, 6m/9km N of Bristol. **19 K3** ST6281.

Bradmore *Notts.* ***Village***, 6m/9km S of Nottingham. **41 H2** SK5831.

Bradmore *W.Mid.* ***Suburb***, W district of Wolverhampton. **40 A6** SO8997.

Bradney *Som.* ***Hamlet***, 3m/4km NE of Bridgwater. ST3338.

Bradninch *Devon* Population: 1763. ***Small town***, former wool and lace town, 8m/12km NE of Exeter. **7 J5** SS9903.

Bradnop *Staffs.* ***Village***, 2m/3km SE of Leek. **50 C7** SK0155.

Bradnor Green *Here.* ***Hamlet***, 1km NW of Kington. Adjacent to Bradnor Hill. SO2957.

Bradnor Hill *Here.* ***Mountain***, National Trust land near Bradnor Green, 2m/3km NW of Kington. Height 1282 feet or 391 metres. **28 B3** SO2858.

Bradpole *Dorset* ***Village***, adjoining to NE of Bridport. **8 D5** SY4894.
Bradshaw *Gt.Man.* ***Locality***, 2m/4km N of Bolton. **49 G1** SD7312.
Bradshaw *W.Yorks.* ***Settlement***, 2m/3km N of Marsden. SE0514.
Bradshaw *W.Yorks.* ***Village***, 1m/2km W of Queensbury, 3m/5km N of Halifax. SE0730.
Bradstone *Devon* ***Hamlet***, 4m/6km SE of Launceston. **6 B7** SX3880.
Bradwall Green *Ches.* ***Hamlet***, 2m/3km N of Sandbach. **49 G6** SJ7563.
Bradway *S.Yorks.* ***Suburb***, 5m/7km SW of Sheffield city centre, comprising Upper Bradway and Lower Bradway. SK3380.
Bradwell *Derbys.* ***Village***, 4m/6km W of Hathersage. **50 D4** SK1781.
Bradwell *Devon* ***Settlement***, 3m/5km SW of Ilfracombe. SS4942.
Bradwell *Essex* ***Village***, 3m/5km E of Braintree. **34 C6** TL8023.
Bradwell (Also known as Old Bradwell.) *M.K.* ***Village***, in Milton Keynes, 1m/2km SE of Wolverton. Remains of medieval priory to W across railway. **32 B5** SP8339.
Bradwell *Norf.* ***Suburb***, 1m/2km W of Gorleston-on-Sea. **45 K5** TG5003.
Bradwell *Staffs.* ***Suburb***, 2m/3km N of Newcastle-under-Lyme town centre. SJ8449.
Bradwell Grove *Oxon.* ***Settlement***, 3m/5km NW of Carterton. **21 F1** SP2308.
Bradwell-on-Sea *Essex* ***Village***, 2m/3km from E coast and 7m/12km NE of Burnham-on-Crouch. On coast to E is Othona, remains of Roman fort of the Saxon shore. **25 F1** TM0006.
Bradwell Waterside *Essex* ***Village***, near right bank of River Blackwater estuary, 8m/12km NE of Burnham-on-Crouch. Marina. **25 F1** TL9907.
Bradworthy *Devon* ***Village***, 7m/11km N of Holsworthy. **6 B4** SS3214.
Brae *D. & G.* ***Settlement***, 7m/11km NE of Dumfries. **65 J3** NX8674.
Brae *High.* ***Settlement***, on S side of River Oykel, at confluence with Meoir Langwell, 1km NW of Doune. **96 B1** NC4301.
Brae *Shet.* ***Village***, on Mainland at head of Busta Voe. To W is the narrow neck of land separating Busta Voe from Sullom Voe. **109 C6** HU3567.
Brae of Achnahaird *High.* ***Settlement***, near NW coast of Ross and Cromarty district, 3m/5km SE of Rubha Coigeach. NC0013.
Brae of Glenbervie *Aber.* ***Inland physical feature***, hillside to S of Feteresso Forest, 2m/4km N of Glenbervie. **91 F6** NO7684.
Brae Wick *Shet.* ***Bay***, on N shore of St. Magnus Bay, 1m/2km E of Esha Ness, Mainland. Locality of Braewick at head of bay. **108 B5** HU2478.
Braeantra *High.* ***Settlement***, at head of Strath Rusdale, 8m/12km NW of Alness. **96 C4** NH5678.
Braedownie *Angus* ***Settlement***, at head of Glen Clova, 3m/5km NW of Clova. **89 K7** NO2875.
Braefoot *Aber.* ***Settlement***, 3m/4km SW of Turriff. **99 F6** NJ7146.
Braegrum *P. & K.* ***Settlement***, 1m/2km SW of Methven. **82 B5** NO0025.
Braehead *Angus* ***Settlement***, 3m/5km SW of Montrose. **83 H2** NO6853.
Braehead *D. & G.* ***Hamlet***, 1km N of Kirkinner, to S of Wigtown. NX4252.
Braehead *Moray* ***Settlement***, 4m/7km NE of Dufftown. **98 B6** NJ3843.
Braehead *Ork.* ***Hamlet***, on Westray, 1km SE of Pierowall. **106 D3** HY4447.
Braehead *Ork.* ***Settlement***, in S part of Mainland, 1km N of Cornquoy. **107 E7** HY5101.
Braehead *S.Ayr.* ***Suburb***, N district of Ayr. NS3422.
Braehead *S.Lan.* ***Hamlet***, adjoining to E of Coalburn. **75 G7** NS8134.
Braehead *S.Lan.* ***Village***, 3m/5km NW of Carnwath. **75 H5** NS9550.
Braehoulland *Shet.* ***Settlement***, S of Hamna Voe, on neck of Esha Ness, Mainland. **108 B5** HU2479.
Braeleny *Stir.* ***Settlement***, 2m/3km N of Callander. **81 H6** NN6310.
Braemar *Aber.* ***Village***, in district of same name, on Clunie Water near its confluence with River Dee. Tourist centre. Braemar Gathering (Highland Games) held in September. Castle dates from 17c. **89 J5** NO1591.
Braemar Castle *Aber.* ***Castle***, 1km NE of Braemar, in River Dee valley. 17c stronghold of Earl of Mar. Rebuilt in 18c and lived in today. **89 J5** NO1592.
Braemore *High.* ***Settlement***, 3m/4km SW of Lairg. **96 C1** NC5503.
Braemore *High.* ***Settlement***, in Caithness district, 5m/8km W of Dunbeath. **105 F5** ND0730.
Braemore *High.* ***Settlement***, in valley of River Broom, 1m/2km NW of Corrieshalloch Gorge. **95 H4** NH1979.
Braenaloin *Aber.* ***Settlement***, 3m/5km NE of Bush Crathie. **89 K5** NO2799.
Braeriach (Gaelic form: Braigh Riabhach.) ***Mountain***, in Cairngorm Mountains on border of Aberdeenshire and Highland, 4m/7km SW of Cairn Gorm and 18m/28km SE of Aviemore. Munro: height 4251 feet or 1296 metres. **89 G4** NN9599.
Braes o' Lochaber *High.* ***Large natural feature***, part of Glen Spean, in Lochaber district, between Roybridge and confluence of Rivers Spean and Treig. **87 K6** NN3280.
Braes of Abernethy *High.* ***Open space***, upland area E of Abernethy Forest in Badenoch and Strathspey district. **89 H3** NJ0615.
Braes of Balquhidder *Stir.* ***Large natural feature***, upland area W of Balquhidder and N of Loch Doine and Loch Voil. **81 F5** NN4921.
Braes of Doune *Stir.* ***Large natural feature***, upland area, 3m/5km NW of Doune. **81 H7** NN6905.
Braes of Enzie *Moray* ***Settlement***, 3m/4km S of Portgordon. **98 B5** NJ3959.
Braes of Foss *P. & K.* ***Settlement***, 3m/4km SW of Tummel Bridge. **81 J2** NN7555.
Braes of Glenlivet *Moray* ***Large natural feature***, upland area, S of Glenlivet, 5m/8km E of Tomintoul. **89 K2** NJ2421.
Braes of Ogilvie *P. & K.* ***Locality***, in Strathallan, 1km S of Blackford. **82 A7** NN8907.
Braes of the Carse *P. & K.* ***Large natural feature***, foothills of Sidlaw Hills, above Carse of Gowrie, between Perth and Dundee. **82 C5** NO2530.
Braes of Ullapool *High.* ***Settlement***, on E shore of Loch Broom, Ross and Cromarty district, 1m/2km SE of Ullapool. **95 H2** NH1493.
Braeside *Inclyde* ***Suburb***, 1m/2km S of Gourock. NS2375.
Braeswick *Ork.* ***Settlement***, on small bay of Braes Wick, on W coast of Sanday, 2m/4km N of Spur Ness. **106 F4** HY6137.
Braeval *Stir.* ***Settlement***, 1km SE of Aberfoyle. **81 G7** NN5300.
Braewick *Shet.* ***Settlement***, at head of Brae Wick bay, on Mainland. HU2478.
Brafferton *Darl.* ***Village***, 4m/7km N of Darlington. **62 D4** NZ2921.
Brafferton *N.Yorks.* ***Village***, on River Swale, 6m/9km W of Easingwold. **57 K2** SE4370.
Brafield-on-the-Green *Northants.* ***Village***, 4m/7km E of Northampton. **32 B3** SP8258.
Braga Ness *Shet.* ***Coastal feature***, headland on W coast of Mainland, 2m/3km SE of Wats Ness. **109 A8** HU1948.
Bragar *W.Isles* ***Village***, near NW coast of Isle of Lewis, 5m/7km W of Barvas. **100 E3** NB2947.
Bragbury End *Herts.* ***Hamlet***, 3m/4km SE of Luton. **33 F6** TL2621.
Bragenham *Bucks.* ***Settlement***, 3m/4km NW of Leighton Buzzard. SP9028.
Bragleenbeg *Arg. & B.* ***Settlement***, 1km E of Loch Scammadale. **80 A5** NM9020.
Braich Anelog *Gwyn.* ***Coastal feature***, headland on SW tip of Lleyn Peninsula 2m/3km NW of Aberdaron. **36 A3** SH1427.
Braich y Pwll *Gwyn.* ***Coastal feature***, W extremity (National Trust) of Lleyn Peninsula, where Celtic pilgrims once embarked for Bardsey Island. Holy well and site of St. Mary's Chapel. **36 A3** SH1325.
Braichmelyn *Gwyn.* ***Hamlet***, 1km S of Bethesda. **46 E6** SH6265.
Braid *Edin.* ***Suburb***, 2m/4km S of Edinburgh city centre. NT2470.
Braid Cairn ***Mountain***, on border of Aberdeenshire and Angus, 6m/10km SE of Ballater. Height 2909 feet or 887 metres. **90 C6** NO4287.
Braid Fell *D. & G.* ***Hill***, 3m/5km SE of Cairnryan, on E side of Loch Ryan. Height 771 feet or 235 metres. **64 B4** NX1166.
Braid Hills *Edin.* ***Hill***, rising to over 210 metres, to SE of Braid. **76 A4** NT2569.
Braides *Lancs.* ***Settlement***, to E of Cockerham Marsh, 4m/7km NW of Garstang. **55 H4** SD4451.
Braidford *Glas.* ***Suburb***, 3m/5km SE of Glasgow city centre. NS6363.
Braidon Bay *Aber.* ***Bay***, small bay, 4m/6km NE of Inverbervie. **91 G7** NO8677.
Braidwood *S.Lan.* ***Village***, 2m/3km S of Carluke. **75 G6** NS8447.
Bràigh a' Choire Bhig *High.* ***Inland physical feature***, mountain ridge in Ross and Cromarty district, 1m/2km S of summit of Sgurr na Lapaich. **87 H1** NH1533.
Bràigh Coire Chruinn-bhalgain *P. & K.* ***Mountain***, to W of Beinn a' Ghlo massif, 6m/10km NE of Blair Atholl. Munro: height 3510 feet or 1070 metres. **89 G7** NN9472.
Bràigh Mòr *W.Isles* ***Sea feature***, stretch of sea separating South Harris from Scalpay. NG1994.
Bràigh na Glaice Mòire *High.* ***Open space***, upland moor 1m/2km NE of Ardtornish, Lochaber district. **79 J3** NM7248.
Braigh na h-Eaglaise *High.* ***Mountain***, 4m/6km W of Berriedale. Height 1384 feet or 422 metres. **105 F6** ND0622.
Bràigh-nam-bàgh *W.Isles* ***Locality***, on South Harris to W of Loch Langavat, comprising numerous small lochs. **93 F3** NG0789.
Bràigh nan Uamhachan *High.* ***Mountain***, 6m/9km NE of Glenfinnan. Height 2509 feet or 765 metres. **87 F6** NM9786.
Braigh Riabhach *Gaelic form of Braeriach, qv.*
Bràigh Sròn Ghorm *P. & K.* ***Mountain***, 3m/5km E of Beinn Dearg, N of Blair Atholl. Height 2883 feet or 879 metres. **89 G7** NN9078.
Braigo *Arg. & B.* ***Settlement***, on NW of Islay, 8m/12km NW of Bridgend. **72 A4** NR2369.
Brailes Hill *Warks.* ***Hill***, 1m/2km SW of Lower Brailes. Height 761 feet or 232 metres. **30 D5** SP2938.
Brailsford *Derbys.* ***Village***, 7m/11km NW of Derby. **40 E1** SK2541.
Brailsford Green *Derbys.* ***Hamlet***, adjoining to W of Brailsford. SK2541.
Brain *Essex* ***River***, rising near Braintree and flowing SE into River Blackwater 1m/2km SE of Witham. **34 C7** TL8313.
Brain's Green *Glos.* ***Settlement***, 1km NW of Blakeney. SO6608.
Braint *I.o.A.* ***River***, rising E of Pentraeth and flowing SW into Menai Strait on E side of Newborough Warren. **46 D5** SH4363.
Braintree *Essex* Population: 33,229. ***Town***, 11m/17km NE of Chelmsford. Cloth-weaving was previously an important industry; also silk-making, which is recalled in Working Silk Museum. **34 B6** TL7523.
Braiseworth *Suff.* ***Hamlet***, 2m/3km SW of Eye. **35 F1** TM1371.
Braishfield *Hants.* ***Village***, 3m/5km NE of Romsey. **10 E2** SU3725.
Braithwaite *Cumb.* ***Village***, 2m/4km W of Keswick. **60 D4** NY2323.
Braithwaite *S.Yorks.* ***Village***, 3m/5km NW of Hatfield. **51 J1** SE6112.
Braithwaite *W.Yorks.* ***Suburb***, on W side of Keighley. SE0441.
Braithwaite Hall *N.Yorks.* ***Historic house***, 17c house, now a farmhouse (National Trust), 1m/2km SW of Middleham, with Braithwaite Moor to S. **57 G1** SE1185.
Braithwell *S.Yorks.* ***Village***, 2m/3km N of Maltby. **51 H3** SK5292.
Brakefield Green *Norf.* ***Settlement***, 4m/6km SE of East Dereham. TG0309.
Bramall Hall *Gt.Man.* ***Historic house***, well-preserved black and white 16c house with chapel with wall painting dating back even earlier, 1m/2km N of Bramall and 3m/5km S of Stockport. **49 H4** SJ8986.
Bramber *W.Suss.* ***Village***, in River Adur valley, 4m/6km NW of Shoreham-by-Sea. Ruins of Norman castle (National Trust). **12 E5** TQ1810.
Bramber Castle *W.Suss.* ***Castle***, 1km SE of Steyning. Built between 1070 and 1073 and destroyed by Cromwell's troops in 1644; only gaunt ruins remain (English Heritage). **12 E5** TQ1810.
Brambletye *E.Suss.* ***Settlement***, 2m/3km NW of Forest Row. **13 H3** TQ4136.
Brambridge *Hants.* ***Hamlet***, 2m/3km NE of Eastleigh. SU4721.
Bramcote *Notts.* ***Locality***, 1m/2km NW of Beeston. **41 H2** SK5037.
Bramcote Mains *Warks.* ***Settlement***, 4m/6km SE of Nuneaton. SP4087.
Bramdean *Hants.* ***Village***, 3m/5km SE of New Alresford. 1m/2km E, site of Roman villa. **11 H2** SU6128.
Bramerton *Norf.* ***Village***, 5m/8km SE of Norwich. **45 G5** TG2904.
Bramfield *Herts.* ***Village***, 3m/5km NW of Hertford. **33 F7** TL2915.
Bramfield *Suff.* ***Village***, 3m/4km S of Halesworth. **35 H1** TM3973.
Bramford *Suff.* Population: 1994. ***Village***, 3m/4km NW of Ipswich. **35 F4** TM1246.
Bramhall *Gt.Man.* Population: 19,865. ***Town***, 4m/6km S of Stockport. **49 H4** SJ8984.
Bramham *W.Yorks.* ***Village***, 4m/6km S of Wetherby. Site of Battle of Bramham Moor 1408, 1m/2km SE. **57 K5** SE4242.
Bramham Park *W.Yorks.* ***Historic house***, to SW of Bramham, 18c classical mansion in grounds modelled on those of Versailles. **57 K5** SE4242.
Bramhope *W.Yorks.* Population: 3363. ***Village***, 7m/11km NW of Leeds. **57 H5** SE2543.
Bramley *Derbys.* ***Hamlet***, 1m/2km W of Eckington. SK4079.
Bramley *Hants.* ***Village***, 5m/7km N of Basingstoke. **21 K6** SU6458.
Bramley *S.Yorks.* ***Suburb***, 4m/6km E of Rotherham. **51 G3** SK4992.
Bramley *Surr.* Population: 2278. ***Village***, long village, 3m/5km S of Guildford. **22 D7** TQ0044.
Bramley *W.Yorks.* ***Suburb***, 3m/5km W of Leeds city centre. SE2434.
Bramley Corner *Hants.* ***Hamlet***, 5m/7km N of Basingstoke. SU6359.
Bramley Green *Hants.* ***Settlement***, 5m/8km NE of Basingstoke. SU6658.
Bramley Head *N.Yorks.* ***Settlement***, on Whit Moor, 3m/5km NW of Blubberhouses. SE1258.
Bramley Meade *Lancs.* ***Locality***, 1km NE of Whalley. SD7336.
Bramley Vale *Derbys.* ***Hamlet***, 6m/9km NW of Mansfield. SK4666.
Bramling *Kent* ***Settlement***, 5m/8km E of Canterbury city centre. **15 H2** TR2256.
Brampford Speke *Devon* ***Village***, on River Exe, 4m/6km N of Exeter. **7 H6** SX9298.
Brampton *Cambs.* Population: 4673. ***Village***, 2m/3km W of Huntingdon. **33 F1** TL2170.
Brampton *Cumb.* Population: 3957. ***Small town***, 9m/14km NE of Carlisle. Village destroyed by Robert the Bruce. 14c church. **70 A7** NY5361.
Brampton *Cumb.* ***Village***, 2m/3km N of Appleby-in-Westmorland. **61 H4** NY6823.
Brampton *Derbys.* ***Suburb***, W district of Chesterfield. **51 F5** SK3671.
Brampton *Lincs.* ***Hamlet***, 7m/11km S of Gainsborough. **52 B5** SK8479.
Brampton *Norf.* ***Village***, 3m/4km SE of Aylsham. **45 G3** TG2224.
Brampton *S.Yorks.* ***Village***, 1m/2km SE of Wombwell. **51 G2** SE4101.
Brampton *Suff.* ***Hamlet***, 4m/6km NE of Halesworth. **45 J7** TM4381.
Brampton Abbotts *Here.* ***Village***, 2m/3km N of Ross-on-Wye. **29 F6** SO6027.
Brampton Ash *Northants.* ***Village***, 4m/6km E of Market Harborough. **42 A7** SP7987.
Brampton Bryan *Here.* ***Village***, 5m/8km E of Knighton. **28 C1** SO3772.
Brampton en le Morthen *S.Yorks.* ***Village***, 5m/9km SE of Rotherham. **51 G4** SK4888.
Brampton Street *Suff.* ***Settlement***, 1km W of Brampton. TM4281.

Bramshall *Staffs.* ***Village***, 2m/3km W of Uttoxeter. **40 C2** SK0633.

Bramshaw *Hants.* ***Village***, in New Forest, 2m/3km NW of Cadnam. **10 D3** SU2715.

Bramshill *Hants.* ***Settlement***, 2m/3km SE of Riseley. 1m/2km SE, Bramshill House, Jacobean house, now police college. **22 A5** SU7461.

Bramshott *Hants.* ***Village***, 1m/2km N of Liphook. **12 B3** SU8432.

Bramwell *Som.* ***Hamlet***, 2m/3km N of Langport. **8 D2** ST4329.

Brân *Carmar.* ***River***, rising 2m/3km SE of Myddfai, and flowing W into River Tywi 1km W of Llangadog. **27 G6** SN6928.

Brân *Carmar.* ***River***, rising E of Llyn Brianne Reservoir and flowing S into River Tywi 1m/2km SW of Llandovery. **27 H4** SN7532.

Bran *High.* ***River***, in Ross and Cromarty district, running E from Achnasheen down Strath Bran to Loch Luichart. NH3162.

Bran End *Essex* ***Village***, 3m/4km NE of Great Dunmow. **33 K6** TL6525.

Branahuie *W.Isles* ***Settlement***, adjoining Melbost, 2m/4km E of Stornoway, Isle of Lewis. NB4632.

Branahuie Banks *W.Isles* ***Bay***, to S of Branahuie, Isle of Lewis. **101 G4** NB4632.

Branault *High.* ***Settlement***, on Ardnamurchan peninsula, 4m/7km NE of Kilchoan. **79 G1** NM5269.

Brancaster *Norf.* ***Village***, near coast, 4m/6km W of Burnham Market. Slight remains of Roman fort of Branodunum to E. **44 B1** TF7743.

Brancaster Bay *Norf.* ***Bay***, to N of Brancaster, on N coast of Norfolk. **44 B1** TF7743.

Brancaster Staithe *Norf.* ***Village***, to S of Brancaster Harbour, 1m/2km E of Brancaster. TF7944.

Brancepeth *Dur.* ***Village***, 4m/7km SW of Durham. Castle dates partly from 14c though mainly 19c. **62 D3** NZ2237.

Brancepeth Castle *Dur.* ***Castle***, on S side of Brancepeth village, 3m/5km NW of Spennymoor. 14c castle, restored in 19c, belonging to Neville family. **62 D3** NZ2237.

Branch End *Northumb.* ***Locality***, 2m/4km SW of Prudhoe. NZ0661.

Branchill *Moray* ***Settlement***, 5m/8km SE of Forres. **97 H6** NJ0852.

Brand End *Lincs.* ***Locality***, adjoining to W of Butterwick, 4m/6km E of Boston. TF3745.

Brand Green *Glos.* ***Locality***, 2m/3km NE of Newent. **29 G6** SO7428.

Brand Side *Derbys.* ***Inland physical feature***, steep mountainside rising to 1411 feet or 430 metres above upper reaches of River Dove, 3m/5km S of Buxton. **50 C6** SK0368.

Brandelhow (Also known as Old Brandelhow.) *Cumb.* ***Hamlet***, on W shore of Derwent Water, 2m/3km S of Keswick. NY2420.

Branderburgh *Moray* ***Town***, on N coast adjoining, and forming, N part of, Lossiemouth. **97 K4** NJ2371.

Brandesburton *E.Riding* ***Village***, 6m/9km W or Hornsea. **59 H5** TA1147.

Brandeston *Suff.* ***Village***, 5m/7km NW of Wickham Market. **35 G2** TM2460.

Brandhill *Shrop.* ***Locality***, 3m/4km S of Craven Arms. SO4278.

Brandis Corner *Devon* ***Hamlet***, 4m/7km E of Holsworthy. **6 C5** SS4103.

Brandish Street *Som.* ***Hamlet***, 1m/2km E of Porlock. SS9046.

Brandiston *Norf.* ***Village***, 3m/5km SE of Reepham. **45 F3** TG1421.

Brandon *Dur.* Population: 9162. ***Small town***, 3m/4km SW of Durham. **62 D3** NZ2440.

Brandon *Lincs.* ***Village***, 8m/12km N of Grantham. **42 C1** SK9048.

Brandon *Northumb.* ***Settlement***, on River Breamish, 2m/4km NW of Glanton. **71 F2** NU0417.

Brandon *Suff.* Population: 7804. ***Small town***, on Little Ouse River, 5m/8km NW of Thetford. Former centre of flint-knapping industry. **44 B7** TL7886.

Brandon *Warks.* ***Village***, 5m/8km E of Coventry. Faint traces of 13c castle. **31 F1** SP4076.

Brandon Bank *Norf.* ***Settlement***, on N bank of Little Ouse River, 4m/7km NE of Littleport. **44 A7** TL6288.

Brandon Creek *Norf.* ***Settlement***, at confluence of Rivers Great and Little Ouse, 4m/7km NE of Littleport. **44 A6** TL6091.

Brandon Park *Suff.* ***Leisure/recreation***, 30 acre country park 1km S of Brandon, set within larger Thetford Forest Park, comprising parkland, woodland and ornamental lake. **44 B7** TL7883.

Brandon Parva *Norf.* ***Hamlet***, 5m/8km NW of Wymondham. **44 E5** TG0708.

Brands Hatch *Kent* ***Motor racing circuit***, 3m/4km SE of Farningham. **23 J5** TQ5764.

Brands Hill *Slo.* ***Suburb***, 3m/5km SE of Slough town centre. TQ0177.

Brandsbutt *Aber.* ***Locality***, in NW part of Inverurie, 15m/23km NW of Aberdeen. NJ7622.

Brandsby *N.Yorks.* ***Village***, 4m/6km NE of Easingwold. **58 B2** SE5872.

Brandwood End *W.Mid.* ***Suburb***, 4m/7km S of Birmingham city centre. SP0779.

Brandwood Moor *Lancs.* ***Open space***, moorland 2m/3km SW of Bacup with Cowpe Reservoir on W side. **56 D7** SD8520.

Brandy Hill *Carmar.* ***Hill***, 2m/3km SE of Whitland. Height 672 feet or 205 metres. **17 F3** SN2113.

Brandy Wharf *Lincs.* ***Hamlet***, 2m/3km SW of South Kelsey. **52 D3** TF0196.

Brane *Cornw.* ***Settlement***, 3m/5km SE of St. Just. **2 A6** SW4028.

Branklyn Garden *P. & K.* ***Garden***, collection of rare plants (National Trust for Scotland), in Perth, including Himalayan blue poppy, golden Cedrus, rhododendrons and alpines. **82 C5** NO1222.

Branksome *Darl.* ***Suburb***, 2m/3km NW of Darlington town centre. NZ2616.

Branksome *Poole* ***Suburb***, to E of Poole and N of Branksome Park, across stream which runs down to Branksome Chine. **10 B5** SZ0592.

Branksome Park *Poole* ***Suburb***, 3m/4km E of Poole town centre. **10 B5** SZ0590.

Brannie Burn *Arg. & B.* ***River***, flowing generally W from slopes of Beinn Bhuidhe into River Shira, 6m/10km NE of Inveraray. **80 C6** NN1416.

Branodunum *Norf.* *See Brancaster.*

Bransbury *Hants.* ***Hamlet***, 1m/2km NW of Barton Stacey. SU4242.

Bransby *Lincs.* ***Hamlet***, 3m/4km N of Saxilby. **52 B5** SK8979.

Branscombe *Devon* ***Village***, in combe above S coast, 5m/7km E of Sidmouth. Coast is National Trust property. **7 K7** SY1988.

Bransdale *N.Yorks.* ***Locality***, 9m/15km N of Helmsley, including Bransdale Moor to NW of Bransdale Lodge and valley of Hodge Beck running S from Cockayne. SE6298.

Bransford *Worcs.* ***Village***, 4m/7km W of Worcester. Bransford Bridge carries road over River Teme 1km NE. **29 G3** SO7952.

Bransford Bridge *Worcs.* ***Settlement***, on S bank of River Teme, 3m/5km SW of Worcester. Adjacent bridge carries road over river. **29 H3** SO8053.

Bransgore *Hants.* Population: 3843. ***Village***, 4m/6km NE of Christchurch. **10 C5** SZ1897.

Bransholme *Hull* ***Suburb***, 4m/6km N of Kingston upon Hull city centre. TA1032.

Bransly Hill *E.Loth.* ***Mountain***, 4m/6km S of Spott. Height 1302 feet or 397 metres. **76 E3** NT6770.

Branson's Cross *Worcs.* ***Settlement***, 4m/6km NE of Redditch. **30 B1** SP0870.

Branston *Leics.* ***Village***, 7m/12km NE of Melton Mowbray. **42 B3** SK8129.

Branston *Lincs.* ***Village***, 4m/6km SE of Lincoln. **52 D6** TF0267.

Branston *Staffs.* Population: 3350. ***Village***, 2m/3km SW of Burton upon Trent. **40 E3** SK2221.

Branston Booths *Lincs.* ***Hamlet***, 3m/5km E of Branston. **52 D6** TF0267.

Branston Fen *Lincs.* ***Open space***, lowland 2m/4km W of Bardney. **52 D6** TF0869.

Branstone *I.o.W.* ***Hamlet***, 3m/4km W of Sandown. **11 G6** SZ5583.

Bransty *Cumb.* ***Suburb***, 1km N of Whitehaven town centre. NX9719.

Brant *Lincs.* ***River***, rising at Gelston and flowing N into River Witham 5m/8km S of Lincoln. **52 C7** SK9563.

Brant Broughton *Lincs.* ***Village***, 7m/12km E of Newark-on-Trent. **52 C7** SK9154.

Brant Fell *Cumb.* ***Open space***, moorland to S of Howgill Fells, highest point of which is The Calf (2218 feet or 676 metres), 3m/4km N of Sedbergh. **61 H7** SD6695.

Brantham *Suff.* Population: 2292. ***Village***, 7m/12km SW of Ipswich. **35 F5** TM1134.

Branthwaite *Cumb.* ***Settlement***, 2m/3km SW of Caldbeck. **60 D3** NY2937.

Branthwaite *Cumb.* ***Village***, 5m/7km SE of Workington. **60 B4** NY0524.

Brantingham *E.Riding* ***Village***, 2m/3km N of Brough. Site of Roman villa 1km SW. **59 F7** SE9429.

Branton *Northumb.* ***Hamlet***, 2m/3km NW of Glanton. **71 F2** NU0416.

Branton *S.Yorks.* Population: 1345. ***Village***, 4m/7km E of Doncaster. **51 J2** SE6401.

Branton Green *N.Yorks.* ***Hamlet***, 1km NW of Great Ouseburn. SE4462.

Brantwood *Cumb.* ***Historic house***, built in 1797, Brantwood was home of John Ruskin from 1872-1900, and some rooms are much as he left them. On E bank of Coniston Water, 1m/2km SE of Coniston across lake. **60 E7** SD3195.

Branxholm Bridgend *Sc.Bord.* ***Settlement***, 1m/2km NE of Branxholme, on River Teviot. **69 K2** NT4712.

Branxholme *Sc.Bord.* ***Settlement***, with castle, in Teviotdale, 3m/5km SW of Hawick. Old castle blown up in 1570; present house dates in part from 1571-6. **69 K2** NT4611.

Branxton *Northumb.* ***Village***, 2m/4km SE of Cornhill on Tweed. Site of Battle of Flodden Field, 1513, in which English defeated Scots. **77 G7** NT8937.

Brassey Green *Ches.* ***Settlement***, 2m/3km SW of Tarporley. SJ5260.

Brassington *Derbys.* ***Village***, 4m/6km W of Wirksworth. **50 E7** SK2354.

Brasted *Kent* ***Village***, 2m/3km E of Westerham. **23 H6** TQ4755.

Brasted Chart *Kent* ***Village***, 1m/2km S of Brasted. **23 H6** TQ4755.

Brat Bheinn *Arg. & B.* ***Mountain***, on Jura, 2m/3km W of Craighouse. Height 1122 feet or 342 metres. **72 C4** NR4966.

Brathay *Cumb.* ***River***, rising to E of Pike of Blisco, flowing E through Little Langdale Tarn, then N into Elter Water and finally E again into head of Windermere. **60 E6** NY3703.

Brathens *Aber.* ***Locality***, 2m/4km NW of Banchory. **90 E5** NO6798.

Bratoft *Lincs.* ***Village***, 6m/9km W of Skegness. **53 H6** TF4764.

Brattleby *Lincs.* ***Village***, 6m/10km N of Lincoln. **52 C4** SK9480.

Bratton *Som.* ***Hamlet***, on edge of Exmoor National Park, 1m/2km W of Minehead. SS9446.

Bratton *Tel. & W.* ***Settlement***, 2m/3km NW of Wellington. SJ6313.

Bratton *Wilts.* ***Village***, 3m/4km E of Westbury. Iron Age camp (English Heritage) on hill to W. **20 C6** ST9152.

Bratton Camp *Wilts.* ***Historic/prehistoric site***, rectangular Iron Age hillfort (English Heritage) with single bank and ditch, and containing a 220 foot New Stone Age long barrow, at NW edge of Salisbury Plain, 1m/2km SW of Bratton. **20 B6** ST8951.

Bratton Clovelly *Devon* ***Village***, 8m/13km W of Okehampton. **6 C6** SX4691.

Bratton Fleming *Devon* ***Village***, 6m/10km NE of Barnstaple. **6 E2** SS6437.

Bratton Road *Tel. & W.* ***Locality***, to S of Bratton. SJ6314.

Bratton Seymour *Som.* ***Village***, 3m/4km W of Wincanton. **9 F2** ST6729.

Braughing *Herts.* ***Village***, 1m/2km N of Puckeridge. **33 G6** TL3925.

Braughing Friars *Herts.* ***Settlement***, 1km W of Albury, 2m/4km NE of Puckeridge. TL4124.

Brauncewell *Lincs.* ***Locality***, 4m/7km N of Sleaford. TF0452.

Braunston *Northants.* Population: 1669. ***Village***, at junction of Oxford and Grand Union Canals, 3m/5km NW of Daventry. Canal basin, locks and tunnel. **31 G2** SP5366.

Braunston *Rut.* ***Village***, 2m/3km SW of Oakham. **42 B5** SK8306.

Braunstone *Leic.* ***Suburb***, 2m/4km SW of Leicester city centre. **41 H5** SK5502.

Braunton *Devon* Population: 9227. ***Small town***, near N coast, 5m/8km NW of Barnstaple. Chivenor Airfield to S of town. Braunton Burrows coastal dune system, with much interesting wildlife, lies to W of town. **6 C2** SS4836.

Braunton Burrows *Devon* ***Coastal feature***, to W of Braunton behind Saunton sands. Dune system includes nature reserve. **6 C2** SS4836.

Bravoniacum *Cumb.* *See Kirkby Thore.*

Brawby *N.Yorks.* ***Village***, 5m/8km NW of Malton. **58 D2** SE7378.

Brawdy (Breudeth). *Pembs.* ***Settlement***, 4m/6km E of Solva. Airfield to NW. **16 B2** SM8524.

Brawl *High.* ***Settlement***, 3m/4km SW of Strathy Point, Caithness district. **104 D2** NC8066.

Brawl Castle *High.* *Alternative spelling of Braal Castle, qv.*

Brawlbin *High.* ***Locality***, in Caithness district, 1m/2km S of Loch Calder. **105 F3** ND0757.

Braworth *N.Yorks.* ***Settlement***, 1m/2km SW of Stokesley. NZ5007.

Bray *Devon* ***River***, rising on Exmoor and running S into River Mole 3m/5km SW of South Molton. **6 E2** SS6722.

Bray *W. & M.* ***Village***, on River Thames, 1m/2km SE of Maidenhead. Locality of Bray Wick 1km W. **22 C4** SU9079.

Bray Down *Cornw.* ***Mountain***, 2m/3km NW of Altarnun. Cairns near summit. Height 1135 feet or 346 metres. **4 B2** SX1882.

Bray Shop *Cornw.* ***Village***, 4m/6km NW of Callington. **4 D3** SX3374.

Bray Wick *W. & M.* ***Locality***, 1km W of Bray. **22 B4** SU8979.

Braybrooke *Northants.* ***Village***, 3m/4km SE of Market Harborough. **42 A7** SP7684.

Braydon *Wilts.* ***Locality***, 4m/6km N of Wootton Bassett. SU0588.

Braydon Side *Wilts.* ***Settlement***, 5m/9km E of Malmesbury. SU0185.

Brayford *Devon* ***Village***, 6m/10km NW of South Molton below Exmoor. **6 E2** SS6834.

Brays Grove *Essex* ***Suburb***, 1m/2km SE of Harlow town centre. TL4608.

Brayshaw *N.Yorks.* ***Settlement***, 4m/6km W of Long Preston, on E side of Gisburn Forest. **56 C4** SD7758.

Braystones *Cumb.* ***Locality***, 3m/5km S of Egremont. NY0005.

Braythorn *N.Yorks.* ***Hamlet***, 4m/6km NE of Otley. SE2449.

Brayton *N.Yorks.* Population: 2404. ***Village***, 1m/2km SW of Selby. **58 C6** SE6030.

Braytown *Dorset* ***Hamlet***, adjoining to W of Wool. SY8386.

Braywoodside *W. & M.* ***Settlement***, 4m/6km S of Maidenhead. SU8775.

Brazacott *Cornw.* ***Hamlet***, 6m/9km NW of Launceston. **4 C1** SX2691.

Brea *Cornw.* ***Village***, 1m/2km E of Camborne. SW6640.

Breabag *High.* ***Mountain***, 4m/6km SE of Loch Assynt. Height 2355 feet or 718 metres. **102 E7** NC2917.

Breac-Bheinn *High.* ***Mountain***, on N side of Strathcarron, in Sutherland district, 8m/12km NW of Bonar Bridge. Height 1515 feet or 462 metres. **96 B2** NH4995.

Breac Leathad *Moray* ***Open space***, 3m/5km E of Tomintoul. **89 K3** NJ2118.

Breach *Kent* ***Hamlet***, 1m/2km NW of Newington. TQ8465.

Breach *Kent* ***Settlement***, 1m/2km S of Barham. **15 G3** TR1947.

Breach *W.Suss.* ***Locality***, N part of Southbourne, 1m/2km E of Emsworth. SU7606.

Breachwood Green *Herts.* ***Village***, 4m/6km E of Luton. **32 E6** TL1522.

Breacleit (Anglicised form: Breaclete.) *W.Isles* ***Village***, at centre of Great Bernera, off W coast of Isle of Lewis. **100 D4** NB1536.

Breaclete *W.Isles* *Anglicised form of Breacleit, qv.*

Bread Street *Glos.* ***Locality***, 1m/2km NW of Stroud. SO8306.

Breadalbane ***Large natural feature***, area of Grampian Mountains between Glen Lyon and Strathearn, and between Bridge of Orchy and Dunkeld. **81 H4** NN4735.

Breadsall *Derbys.* ***Village***, 2m/4km NE of Derby. **41 F2** SK3739.

Breadsall Hilltop *Derbys.* ***Suburb***, 1m/2km NE of Derby city centre, to S of Breadsall. SK3638.

Breadstone *Glos.* ***Hamlet***, 2m/3km NE of Berkeley. **20 A1** SO7000.
Breagach Hill *Aber.* ***Mountain***, 1m/2km NW of Strathdon. Height 1824 feet or 556 metres. **90 B3** NJ3313.
Breage *Cornw.* ***Village***, 3m/4km W of Helston. 17c Godolphin House to N. 15c wallpaintings in church. **2 D6** SW6128.
Breakish (Also known as Upper Breakish.) *High.* ***Settlement***, 2m/3km E of Broadford, Skye. **86 C2** NG6823.
Breakon *Shet.* ***Settlement***, on N coast of Yell. **108 E2** HP5204.
Breaksea Point *V. of Glam.* ***Coastal feature***, headland on Bristol Channel coast, 1m/2km S of Gileston. **18 D5** ST0265.
Bream *Glos.* Population: 2704. ***Village***, 2m/4km NW of Lydney. **19 K1** SO6005.
Breamish *Northumb.* ***River***, rising in Cheviot Hills and flowing E via Ingram, then N, to become River Till about 4m/7km SE of Wooler. **70 E2** NT0423.
Breamore *Hants.* ***Village***, 3m/4km N of Fordingbridge. **10 C3** SU1518.
Breamore House *Hants.* ***Historic house***, 16c manor house and countryside museum, 1km NW of Breamore and 6m/10km S of Salisbury. **10 C3** SU1519.
Brean *Som.* ***Village***, on Bristol Channel coast, 4m/7km N of Burnham-on-Sea. **19 F6** ST2955.
Brean Down *Som.* ***Coastal feature***, promontory (National Trust) protruding into Bristol Channel at S end of Weston Bay and SW of Weston-super-Mare. Can be reached by ferry from Uphill. **19 F6** ST2859.
Breanais (Anglicised form: Brenish.) *W.Isles* ***Village***, near W coast of Isle of Lewis, 6m/10km SW of Timsgearraidh. **100 B5** NA9926.
Brearley *W.Yorks.* ***Locality***, on River Calder, 1m/2km E of Mytholmroyd. SE0225.
Brearton *N.Yorks.* ***Village***, 2m/4km E of Ripley. **57 J3** SE3260.
Breascleit (Anglicised form: Breasclete.) *W.Isles* ***Village***, on East Loch Roag, W coast of Isle of Lewis, 13m/21km W of Stornoway. **100 E4** NB2135.
Breasclete *W.Isles Anglicised form of Breascleit, qv.*
Breast Sand *Norf.* ***Coastal feature***, area of mud and sand in S part of The Wash, between mouths of River Nene and River Great Ouse. **43 J3** TF5427.
Breaston *Derbys.* Population: 7284. ***Suburb***, 2m/3km W of Long Eaton. **41 G2** SK4633.
Breawick *Shet.* ***Settlement***, on Mainland, on W side of Aith Voe, 1m/2km N of Aith. HU3357.
Brechfa *Carmar.* ***Village***, at centre of Forest of Brechfa, 10m/15km NE of Carmarthen. **17 J1** SN5230.
Brechin *Angus* Population: 7655. ***City***, ancient cathedral city on River South Esk, 7m/12km W of Montrose. Remains of 13c cathedral with 11c round tower attached. **83 H1** NO5960.
Brechin Cathedral *Angus* ***Ecclesiastical building***, built in 13c on site of previous foundation in centre of Brechin. Brechin Round Tower is attached. **83 G2** NO5960.
Brechin Round Tower *Angus* ***Historic/prehistoric site***, Irish-type round tower dating from 11c (Historic Scotland), attached to Brechin Cathedral in centre of city. One of two such towers remaining on Scottish mainland. **83 G2** NO5960.
Breck Ness *Ork.* ***Coastal feature***, headland on W coast of Mainland, 2m/3km W of Stromness. **107 B7** HY2209.
Breckenbrough *N.Yorks.* ***Locality***, 1m/2km S of Kirby Wiske. SE3883.
Breckland ***Open space***, area of sandy heaths, much of it planted with conifers, around Thetford and Brandon. Area is archaeologically important, charting changes in settlement and farming practices from Neolithic times when original deciduous woodland was cleared. It includes Neolithic flint pits at Grime's Graves, 6m/9km NW of Thetford; Bronze Age round barrows; deserted and ruined church towers; and geometric enclosures of heathland. Much of area now used for conifer plantations or military training. Stone stripes, stone circles and crop patterning indicate former periglacial activity. **44 C7** TL8090.
Brecklate *Arg. & B.* ***Settlement***, at S end of Kintyre, 2m/3km N of Southend. **66 A2** NR6912.
Breckles *Norf.* ***Hamlet***, 5m/8km SE of Watton. **44 D6** TL9594.
Brecknock Museum *Powys* ***Other feature of interest***, in Brecon town centre, displaying 400 year collection of Welsh betrothal love spoons, local industries and agricultural artefacts, and history of Wales. **27 K6** SO0428.
Breckonside *D. & G.* ***Settlement***, 6m/9km SE of Sanquhar. **68 D3** NS8302.
Brecon (Aberhonddu). *Powys* Population: 7523. ***Small town***, market town at confluence of Rivers Honddu and Usk, 14m/22km N of Merthyr Tydfil. Cathedral is former priory church. Remains of medieval castle. Canal navigable to Pontypool. Remains of ancient British camps on Pen-y-Crug, 1m/2km NW, and Slwch Tump, 1km E. **27 K6** SO0428.
Brecon Beacons (Bannau Brycheiniog). *Powys* ***Large natural feature***, mountain range, largely National Trust, to S and SW of Brecon. The two chief peaks are Pen y Fan at 2906 feet or 886 metres and Corn Du at 2863 feet or 873 metres. **27 K6** SO0020.
Brecon Beacons Mountain Centre *Powys* ***Other feature of interest***, at Mynydd Illtyd, 4m/6km SE of Sennybridge. Includes local plants and history display and shop with hiking equipment. **27 J6** SN9726.
Brecon Beacons National Park *Powys* ***Large natural feature***, covering an area of 519 square miles or 1344 square km, National Park extends from Llandeilo in W to Abergavenny in E and from Hay-on-Wye in N to Pontypool in S. Dominated by four tilted Devonian sandstone and brownstone masses, it comprises Black Mountain, Fforest Fawr, Brecon Beacons and Black Mountains. Steep scarp slopes occur in central and W areas, while Black Mountains are topped by plateaux. Craggy ridges, faulting and extensive cave systems all occur in S where carboniferous limestone is present. River Usk flows through park from N to SE, cutting valley between Brecon Beacons and Black Mountains. Highest point in park is Pen-y-Fan (2906 feet or 886 metres). Mountain Centre at Mynydd Illtyd. **28 B6** SO0121.
Brecon Cathedral *Powys* ***Ecclesiastical building***, built originally as a priory church in centre of Brecon and elevated to cathedral status in 1923. Restored in 1860 by Sir Gilbert Scott. **27 K6** SO0428.
Brecon Mountain Railway *M.Tyd.* ***Other feature of interest***, tourist railway running 2m/3km N, from N side of Merthyr Tydfil to S end of Pontsticill Reservoir. **27 K7** SO0610.
Bredbury *Gt.Man.* Population: 14,103. ***Town***, 3m/4km E of Stockport. **49 J3** SJ9391.
Brede *E.Suss.* ***River***, rising near Battle and flowing E into River Rother at Rye. **14 C6** TQ9220.
Brede *E.Suss.* ***Village***, 6m/9km N of Hastings. **14 D6** TQ8218.
Brede Level *E.Suss.* ***Open space***, low-lying area in valley of River Brede. **14 D6** TQ8417.
Bredenbury *Here.* ***Village***, 3m/5km NW of Bromyard. **29 F3** SO6056.
Bredfield *Suff.* ***Village***, 3m/4km N of Woodbridge. **35 G3** TM2653.
Bredgar *Kent* ***Village***, 3m/4km SW of Sittingbourne. Site of Roman building 1m/2km N. **24 E5** TQ8860.
Bredhurst *Kent* ***Village***, 3m/5km S of Gillingham. **24 D5** TQ7962.
Bredicot *Worcs.* ***Settlement***, 4m/6km E of Worcester. **29 J3** SO9054.
Bredon *Worcs.* Population: 2008. ***Village***, on E bank of River Avon, 3m/5km NE of Tewkesbury. 14c barn (National Trust). **29 J5** SO9236.
Bredon Hill *Worcs.* ***Hill***, outlier of Cotswold Hills, 6m/10km NE of Tewkesbury. Iron Age hillfort and 18c tower, Parsons Folly, at summit. Height 961 feet or 293 metres. **29 J4** SO9640.
Bredon's Hardwick *Worcs.* ***Hamlet***, 2m/3km NE of Tewkesbury. **29 J5** SO9135.
Bredon's Norton *Worcs.* ***Village***, 5m/8km NE of Tewkesbury. **29 J5** SO9339.
Bredwardine *Here.* ***Village***, on River Wye, 11m/18km W of Hereford. **28 C4** SO3344.
Breedon on the Hill *Leics.* ***Village***, 5m/8km NE of Ashby de la Zouch. Church is within ramparts of Iron Age fort. **41 G3** SK4022.
Brei Wick *Shet.* ***Bay***, bounded by Lerwick, Mainland, to N and Ness of Sound to S. **109 D9** HU4740.
Breibhig (Anglicised form: Breivig.) *W.Isles* ***Settlement***, near E coast of Isle of Lewis, 1km S of Bac. **101 G4** NB4839.
Breich *W.Loth.* ***Settlement***, 3m/5km S of Whitburn. **75 H4** NS9660.
Breich Water *W.Loth.* ***River***, running NE to River Almond 5m/7km NE of Breich. **75 H4** NS9660.
Breidden Hill *Powys* ***Mountain***, northernmost peak of Breidden Hills. Largely wooded, and bears monument commemorating naval victory of 1782 (Rodney's Pillar). Height 1197 feet or 365 metres. **38 B4** SJ2914.
Breidden Hills *Powys* ***Large natural feature***, isolated group of three peaks, Breidden Hill, Middletown Hill and Moel y Golfa, above E bank of River Severn about 6m/9km NE of Welshpool. There are ancient earthworks of uncertain origin. SJ2914.
Breightmet *Gt.Man.* ***Suburb***, to E of Bolton. SD7409.
Breighton *E.Riding* ***Village***, 1m/2km S of Bubwith. **58 D6** SE7034.
Breinton *Here.* ***Village***, on N bank of River Wye, 3m/4km W of Hereford. **28 D4** SO4739.
Breinton Common *Here.* ***Hamlet***, 4m/6km W of Hereford. SO4539.
Breiti Stack *Shet.* ***Coastal feature***, stack off W coast of Fair Isle. **108 A1** HZ2072.
Breivig *W.Isles Anglicised form of Breibhig, qv.*
Brelston Green *Here.* ***Locality***, 4m/6km SW of Ross-on-Wye. SO5520.
Bremenium *Northumb. See Rochester.*
Bremetennacum *Lancs. See Ribchester.*
Bremhill *Wilts.* ***Village***, 2m/3km NW of Caine. **20 C4** ST9873.
Bremhill Wick *Wilts.* ***Hamlet***, 1km NW of Bremhill, 3m/5km E of Chippenham. ST9774.
Brenachoille *Arg. & B.* ***Settlement***, 1m/2km N of Furnace. **80 B7** NN0102.
Brenchley *Kent* ***Village***, 2m/3km S of Paddock Wood. **23 K7** TQ6741.
Brendon *Devon* ***Hamlet***, 2m/3km SE of Bradworthy. **6 B4** SS3513.
Brendon *Devon* ***Hamlet***, 3m/4km NE of Holsworthy. SS3607.
Brendon *Devon* ***Village***, on East Lyn River, 3m/5km SE of Lynton. **7 F1** SS7648.
Brendon Common *Devon* ***Open space***, moorland 2m/3km S of Brendon at N of Exmoor. **7 F1** SS7644.
Brendon Hills *Som.* ***Large natural feature***, range of hills extending E from Exmoor Forest and included in Exmoor National Park. **7 H2** SS9935.
Brenig Reservoir *Conwy English form of Llyn Brenig, qv.*
Brenish *W.Isles Anglicised form of Breanais, qv.*
Brenkley *T. & W.* ***Settlement***, 7m/11km N of Newcastle upon Tyne. **71 H6** NZ2175.
Brennand Fell *Lancs.* ***Open space***, moorland on Forest of Bowland, 3m/5km NW of Dunsop Bridge. **56 B4** SD6355.
Brent Eleigh *Suff.* ***Village***, 2m/3km SE of Lavenham. **34 D4** TL9447.
Brent Knoll *Som.* ***Village***, at W foot of hill of same name and 2m/3km NE of Burnham-on-Sea. **19 G6** ST3350.
Brent Knoll Hillfort *Som.* ***Historic/prehistoric site***, Iron Age hillfort (National Trust) at summit of Brent Knoll (449 feet or 137 metres), 2m/4km NE of Burnham-on-Sea. **19 G6** ST3350.
Brent Moor *Devon* ***Open space***, moorland in Dartmoor National Park, 3m/5km NW of South Brent. **5 G4** SX6663.
Brent Pelham *Herts.* ***Village***, 5m/7km E of Buntingford. **33 H5** TL4330.
Brent Tor *Devon* ***Mountain***, 1m/2km SW of North Brentor. Conical peak topped by medieval church. Height 1099 feet or 335 metres. **6 C7** SX4881.
Brentford *Gt.Lon.* ***Suburb***, in borough of Hounslow, 8m/13km W of Charing Cross. **22 E4** TQ1777.
Brentingby *Leics.* ***Hamlet***, 2m/3km E of Melton Mowbray. **42 A4** SK7818.
Brentwood *Essex* Population: 49,463. ***Town***, commuter town, and shopping and entertainment centre, 11m/17km SW of Chelmsford. New (1991) Roman Catholic cathedral designed by Quinlan Terry. **23 J2** TQ5993.
Brenzett *Kent* ***Village***, on Romney Marsh, 3m/5km SE of Appledore. **15 F5** TR0027.
Brenzett Green *Kent* ***Hamlet***, 1m/2km NE of Brenzett. TR0128.
Breoch *D. & G.* ***Settlement***, 2m/3km SE of Castle Douglas. **65 H5** NX7859.
Brerachan Water *P. & K.* ***River***, running E down Glen Brerachan to join Allt Fearnach and form River Ardle, 3m/5km NW of Kirkmichael. NO0463.
Brereton *Staffs.* ***Locality***, 2m/3km SE of Rugeley. **40 C4** SK0516.
Brereton Cross *Staffs.* ***Settlement***, 2m/4km SE of Rugeley. SK0615.
Brereton Green *Ches.* ***Village***, 2m/3km S of Holmes Chapel. **49 G6** SJ7764.
Brereton Heath *Ches.* ***Hamlet***, 4m/6km W of Congleton. **49 H6** SJ8064.
Breretonhill *Staffs.* ***Hamlet***, 2m/3km SE of Rugeley. SK0515.
Bressay *Shet.* ***Island***, 11 square miles or 28 square km off E coast of Mainland, from which it is separated by Bressay Sound. Island attains height of 741 feet or 226 metres, with Ward of Bressay being the highest point. **109 E8** HU4453.
Bressingham *Norf.* ***Village***, 3m/4km W of Diss. **44 E7** TM0780.
Bressingham Common *Norf.* ***Settlement***, 1km NE of Bressingham. TM0982.
Bressingham Live Steam Museum and Gardens *Norf.* ***Other feature of interest***, over 2 miles of railway through Waveney Valley designed by Alan Bloom, 1m/2km W of Roydon. Informal 6 acre garden includes the Dell Garden and Europe's largest plant nursery with collection of over 5000 herbaceous plants. Norfolk Fire Museum is also at this site. **44 E7** TM0880.
Brest Twrch *Carmar.* ***Open space***, hillslope 6m/10km N of Ystradgynlais. **27 G7** SN8020.
Bretabister (Also spelled Brettabister.) *Shet.* ***Settlement***, on South Nesting Bay, Mainland, 2m/3km NE of Skellister. **109 D7** HU4857.
Bretby *Derbys.* ***Village***, 4m/6km E of Burton upon Trent. Earthworks mark site of former castle. **40 E3** SK2923.
Bretford *Warks.* ***Village***, 5m/8km W of Rugby. **31 F1** SP4277.
Bretforton *Worcs.* ***Village***, 4m/6km E of Evesham. **30 B4** SP0943.
Bretherdale Beck *Cumb.* ***River***, rising on Bretherdale Bank and flowing SE to Bretherdale Hall, then NE into Birk Beck at Low Scales, 1m/2km NW of Tebay. NY5506.
Bretherdale Head *Cumb.* ***Settlement***, on Bretherdale Beck, 3m/4km W of Tebay. **61 G6** NY5705.
Bretherton *Lancs.* ***Village***, 5m/7km W of Leyland. **55 H7** SD4720.
Brett *Suff.* ***River***, rising 1m/2km N of Brettenham and flowing S into River Stour just S of Higham. **34 E5** TM0335.
Brettabister *Shet. Alternative spelling of Bretabister, qv.*
Brettenham *Norf.* ***Hamlet***, 4m/6km E of Thetford, on N bank of River Thet. Site of Romano-British settlement to NE. **44 D7** TL9383.
Brettenham *Suff.* ***Village***, 5m/7km NE of Lavenham. **34 D3** TL9654.
Bretton *Derbys.* ***Settlement***, and Youth Hostel, 1m/2km E of Great Hucklow. SK2077.
Bretton *Flints.* ***Hamlet***, 4m/6km SW of Chester across River Dee. **48 C6** SJ3563.
Bretton *Peter.* ***Suburb***, to NW of Peterborough. TF1601.
Breudeth *Pembs. Welsh form of Brawdy, qv.*
Brevig *W.Isles* ***Settlement***, on Brevig Bay, on Barra, 2m/3km E of Castlebay. NL6998.
Brewer Street *Surr.* ***Settlement***, 2m/3km W of Godstone. TQ3251.
Brewers Green *Norf.* ***Settlement***, to NE of Roydon. TM1080.
Brewham *Som.* ***Locality***, parish 3m/4km NE of Bruton, containing villages of North and South Brewham. ST7236.
Brewood *Staffs.* Population: 2233. ***Village***, on Shropshire Union Canal, 7m/11km N of Wolverhampton. **40 A5** SJ8808.
Breydon Water *Norf.* ***Sea feature***, wide part of River Yare estuary, to W of Great Yarmouth, 3m/5km long and about 1km wide. **45 J5** TG4907.
Briach *Moray* ***Settlement***, 4m/7km SE of Forres. **97 H6** NJ0954.
Briantspuddle *Dorset* ***Village***, on River Piddle or Trent, 2m/4km SW of Bere Regis. **9 H5** SY8193.

B

Brick End *Essex* ***Hamlet***, 4m/7km NW of Great Dunmow. TL5725.
Bricket Wood *Herts.* ***Suburb***, 4m/6km NE of Watford. **22 E1** TL1302.
Brickfields *Worcs.* ***Suburb***, NE district of Worcester. SO8656.
Brickkiln Green *Essex* ***Settlement***, 3m/5km E of Finchingfield. TL7331.
Bricklehampton *Worcs.* ***Village***, 4m/6km W of Evesham. **29 J4** SO9842.
Bride *I.o.M.* ***Village***, 4m/7km N of Ramsey. **54 D3** NX4401.
Bridekirk *Cumb.* ***Village***, 2m/3km N of Cockermouth. **60 C3** NY1133.
Bridell *Pembs.* ***Settlement***, 3m/4km S of Cardigan. **26 A4** SN1742.
Bride's Ness *Ork.* ***Coastal feature***, rocky headland on SE coast of North Ronaldsay. **106 G2** HY7752.
Bridestones *Staffs.* ***Settlement***, 3m/5km E of Biddulph. **49 J6** SJ9062.
Bridestowe *Devon* ***Village***, 6m/10km SW of Okehampton. **6 D7** SX5189.
Bridestowe and Sourton Common *Devon* ***Open space***, heath, 3m/5km NE of Lydford, on NW side of Dartmoor National Park. **6 D7** SX5488.
Brideswell *Aber.* ***Settlement***, 3m/5km E of Huntly. **90 D1** NJ5739.
Bridford *Devon* ***Village***, 4m/6km E of Moretonhampstead. **7 G7** SX8186.
Bridge *Cornw.* ***Hamlet***, 2m/3km NW of Redruth. **2 D4** SW6744.
Bridge *Kent* ***Village***, 3m/5km SE of Canterbury. **15 G2** TR1854.
Bridge End *Beds.* ***Settlement***, adjoining to S of Bromham, 2m/4km W of Bedford. TL0050.
Bridge End *Cumb.* ***Locality***, at bridge over River Cardew, 1m/2km S of Dalston. NY3748.
Bridge End *Cumb.* ***Locality***, adjoining to S of Kirkby Thore, at bridge over Trout Beck. NY6325.
Bridge End *Cumb.* ***Locality***, just SE of The Green, 3m/4km N of Millom. SD1884.
Bridge End *Cumb.* ***Settlement***, 3m/5km NE of Broughton in Furness. SD2490.
Bridge End *Devon* ***Hamlet***, on S side of River Avon, opposite Aveton Gifford, 3m/5km NW of Kingsbridge. SX6946.
Bridge End *Dur.* ***Hamlet***, just W of Frosterley across River Wear. NZ0236.
Bridge End *Essex* ***Settlement***, N end of Great Bardfield, 1m/2km SW of Finchingfield. TL6730.
Bridge End *Flints.* ***Hamlet***, at S end of Hope, 4m/7km NW of Wrexham. SJ3157.
Bridge End *Lincs.* ***Settlement***, 4m/7km W of Donington. **42 E2** TF1436.
Bridge End *Northumb.* ***Locality***, at N end of bridge over River South Tyne, 2m/3km NW of Hexham. NY9066.
Bridge End *Northumb.* ***Locality***, at Hexham, at N end of road bridge across River Tyne. NY9464.
Bridge End *Shet.* ***Hamlet***, on West Burra, at road bridge connection with East Burra. **109 C9** HU3733.
Bridge End *Surr.* ***Settlement***, adjoining to NE of Ockham, 5m/8km of Woking. TQ0757.
Bridge End *Warks.* ***Suburb***, in S part of Warwick. SP2864.
Bridge Green *Essex* ***Settlement***, 3m/5km E of Great Chishill. TL4637.
Bridge Green *Norf.* ***Settlement***, 3m/5km NE of Diss. TM1483.
Bridge Hewick *N.Yorks.* ***Hamlet***, 2m/3km E of Ripon. **57 J2** SE3370.
Bridge of Alford *Aber.* ***Hamlet***, at road bridge across River Don, 1m/2km NW of Alford. **90 D3** NJ5617.
Bridge of Allan *Stir.* Population: 4864. ***Small town***, former Victorian spa town, 3m/4km N of Stirling. **75 F1** NS7997.
Bridge of Avon *Moray* ***Bridge***, road bridge over River Avon 1km above Ballindalloch Castle, 7m/11km SW of Charlestown of Aberlour. **89 J1** NJ1835.
Bridge of Balgie *P. & K.* ***Locality***, in Glen Lyon, 10m/16km W of Fortingall. **81 G3** NN5746.
Bridge of Bogendreip *Aber.* ***Settlement***, beside Water of Dye, 4m/6km SW of Banchory. **90 E5** NO6691.
Bridge of Brewlands *Angus* ***Settlement***, with road bridge across River Isla, 2m/3km NW of Kirkton of Glenisla. **82 C1** NO1961.
Bridge of Brown *High.* ***Settlement***, on border with Moray, 3m/5km NW of Tomintoul. **89 J2** NJ1220.
Bridge of Cally *P. & K.* ***Village***, at road crossing of River Ardle, 5m/7km NW of Blairgowrie. **82 C2** NO1451.
Bridge of Canny *Aber.* ***Village***, and road bridge over Burn of Canny, 3m/5km W of Banchory. **90 E5** NO6597.
Bridge of Craigisla *Angus* ***Locality***, on River Isla, 4m/6km N of Alyth. Reekie Linn waterfall to SE. **82 D2** NO2553.
Bridge of Dee *Aberdeen* ***Bridge***, 16c bridge, with seven arches, spanning River Dee on S approach to Aberdeen. **91 H4** NJ9203.
Bridge of Dee *Aber.* ***Locality***, at S side of Banchory, next to road crossing of River Dee. **90 E5** NO6995.
Bridge of Dee *Aber.* ***Settlement***, where A93 road crosses River Dee, 3m/4km E of Braemar. **89 J5** NO1891.
Bridge of Dee *D. & G.* ***Village***, settlement and road bridge across River Dee, 3m/4km SW of Castle Douglas. **65 H4** NX7360.
Bridge of Don *Aberdeen* ***Village***, on N bank of River Don, 2m/4km N of centre of Aberdeen. Road bridge spans river. **91 H4** NJ9409.
Bridge of Dun *Angus* ***Hamlet***, with railway station on Brechin to Bridge of Dun Railway, on N side of River South Esk, 3m/5km W of Montrose. **83 H2** NO6658.
Bridge of Dye *Aber.* ***Locality***, in Glen Dye, 4m/6km S of Strachan. **90 E6** NO6586.
Bridge of Earn *P. & K.* Population: 2386. ***Village***, on River Earn, 4m/6km S of Perth. **82 C6** NO1318.
Bridge of Ericht *P. & K.* ***Settlement***, and road bridge near mouth of River Ericht, on N side of Loch Rannoch. **81 G2** NN5258.
Bridge of Ess *Aber.* ***Settlement***, 1m/2km SW of Aboyne, on Water of Tanar. **90 D5** NO5097.
Bridge of Feugh *Aber.* ***Bridge***, road bridge over Water of Feugh, 1km S of Banchory. Incorporates platform for observing salmon-leap. **90 E5** NO7095.
Bridge of Forss *High.* ***Settlement***, and bridge in Caithness district, carrying A836 road over Forss Water, 5m/8km W of Thurso. **105 F2** ND0368.
Bridge of Gairn *Aber.* ***Hamlet***, 1m/2km NW of Ballater, where A93 road crosses River Gairn. **90 B5** NO3497.
Bridge of Gaur *P. & K.* ***Settlement***, at W end of Loch Rannoch. 18c house The Barracks sited on S bank of River Gaur. **81 G2** NN5056.
Bridge of Muchalls *Aber.* ***Hamlet***, 1km SW of Muchalls. **91 G5** NO8991.
Bridge of Orchy *Arg. & B.* ***Village***, on River Orchy, 2m/3km S of Loch Tulla, Argyll. **80 E4** NN2939.
Bridge of Tilt *P. & K.* ***Settlement***, adjoining to N of Blair Atholl. **81 K1** NN8765.
Bridge of Tynet *Moray* ***Settlement***, at bridge over Burn of Tynet, 3m/5km SW of Buckie. **98 B4** NJ3861.
Bridge of Walls *Shet.* ***Settlement***, on Mainland, at head of Gruting Voe. **109 B7** HU2651.
Bridge of Weir *Renf.* Population: 5151. ***Small town***, on River Gryfe, 6m/10km W of Paisley. **74 B4** NS3865.
Bridge Reeve *Devon* ***Hamlet***, on River Taw, 2m/3km W of Chulmleigh. SS6613.
Bridge Sollers *Here.* ***Village***, on River Wye, 6m/10km W of Hereford. **28 D4** SO4142.
Bridge Street *Suff.* ***Hamlet***, 2m/4km W of Lavenham. **34 C4** TL8749.
Bridge Trafford *Ches.* ***Village***, on River Gowy, 4m/7km NE of Chester. **48 D5** SJ4471.
Bridgefoot *Cambs.* ***Settlement***, 3m/5km NE of Royston. **33 H4** TL4042.
Bridgefoot *Cumb.* ***Locality***, adjoining to N of Little Clifton. **60 B4** NY0529.
Bridgehampton *Som.* ***Hamlet***, 3m/5km E of Ilchester, beyond Yeovilton airfield. **8 E2** ST5624.
Bridgehill *Dur.* ***Suburb***, W district of Consett. NZ0851.
Bridgemarsh Island *Essex* ***Island***, marshy island in River Crouch estuary, 3m/5km W of Burnham-on-Crouch. **24 E2** TQ8996.
Bridgemary *Hants.* ***Suburb***, to NW of Gosport. **11 G4** SU5803.
Bridgemere *Ches.* ***Hamlet***, 4m/6km NW of Madeley. **39 G1** SJ7145.
Bridgend *Aber.* ***Settlement***, on N bank of Priest's Water, 3m/5km S of Huntly. **90 D1** NJ5136.
Bridgend *Aber.* ***Settlement***, on S side of Turriff across Burn of Turriff. NJ7249.
Bridgend *Aber.* ***Settlement***, 1km S of Ballater. **90 B5** NO3694.
Bridgend *Angus* ***Settlement***, on West Water, 4m/6km W of Edzell. **83 G1** NO5368.
Bridgend *Arg. & B.* ***Village***, on Islay, at NE end of Loch Indaal. **72 B4** NR3362.
Bridgend *Arg. & B.* ***Village***, 3m/4km N of Lochgilphead, in valley of River Add. **73 G1** NR8592.
Bridgend (Pen-y-Bont ar Ogwr). *Bridgend* Population: 35,841. ***Town***, industrial town on Ogmore River, 18m/28km W of Cardiff. Bryngarw Country Park has Japanese garden. **18 C4** SS9079.
Bridgend *Cere.* ***Locality***, at S end of bridge across River Teifi at Cardigan. SN1745.
Bridgend *Cornw.* ***Suburb***, of Lostwithiel, E of River Fowey. **4 B4** SX1159.
Bridgend *Cumb.* ***Settlement***, 1m/2km S of Patterdale. **60 F5** NY3914.
Bridgend *Fife* ***Village***, 2m/3km SE of Cupar. **82 E6** NO3911.
Bridgend *Glos.* ***Locality***, adjoining to S of Stonehouse, 3m/5km W of Stroud. SO8004.
Bridgend *Moray* ***Locality***, 6m/10km SE of Dufftown. **90 B1** NJ3731.
Bridgend *P. & K.* ***Suburb***, to E of Perth across River Tay. **82 C5** NO1223.
Bridgend *W.Loth.* ***Village***, 3m/5km E of Linlithgow. **75 J3** NT0475.
Bridgend of Lintrathen *Angus* ***Village***, on E side of Loch of Lintrathen. **82 D2** NO2854.
Bridgeness *Falk.* ***Suburb***, on S side of Firth of Forth, adjoining to E of Bo'ness. NT0181.
Bridgerule *Devon* ***Village***, 4m/7km W of Holsworthy. **6 A5** SS2702.
Bridges *Shrop.* ***Locality***, 6m/10km NE of Bishop's Castle. **38 C6** SO3996.
Bridgeton *Aber.* ***Settlement***, 3m/4km SW of Alford. **90 D3** NJ5512.
Bridgeton *Glas.* ***Suburb***, 1m/2km SE of Glasgow city centre. NS6164.
Bridgetown *Cornw.* ***Hamlet***, 3m/5km N of Launceston. **6 B7** SX3489.
Bridgetown *Som.* ***Village***, on River Exe just S of Exton and 3m/5km N of Dulverton. **7 H2** SS9233.
Bridgeyate *S.Glos.* ***Hamlet***, 6m/10km E of Bristol. **19 K4** ST6873.
Bridgham *Norf.* ***Village***, 6m/10km E of Thetford. **44 D7** TL9585.
Bridgnorth *Shrop.* Population: 11,229. ***Town***, with centre (High Town) on cliff top, and Low Town across River Severn; cable railway connects the two. Remains of Norman castle, with leaning keep. Half-timbered town hall of 17c. St. Mary's church designed by Thomas Telford. N terminus of Severn Valley Railway. **39 G6** SO7193.
Bridgtown *Staffs.* ***Suburb***, 1m/2km S of Cannock. **40 B5** SJ9808.
Bridgwater *Som.* Population: 34,610. ***Town***, industrial town and small port on River Parrett, 9m/15km NE of Taunton. Well-supported Bridgwater Carnival takes place each November. **8 B1** ST2937.
Bridgwater Bay *Som.* ***Bay***, wide bay in Bristol Channel extending from Brean Down, W of Weston-super-Mare, to Greenaleigh Point NW of Minehead. **18 D7** ST1852.
Bridlington *E.Riding* Population: 31,334. ***Town***, old port and fishing town, also modern North Sea coastal resort, 24m/39km N of Kingston upon Hull. **59 H3** TA1766.
Bridlington Bay *E.Riding* ***Bay***, extends from Flamborough Head to Hornsea. **59 J3** TA1766.
Bridport *Dorset* Population: 11,667. ***Town***, market town, 14m/23km W of Dorchester. Traditional rope and net-making industries still survive. **8 D5** SY4692.
Bridstow *Here.* ***Village***, 1m/2km W of Ross-on-Wye across River Wye. **28 E6** SO5824.
Briercliffe *Lancs.* ***Locality***, 3m/4km SE of Nelson. SD8834.
Brierfield *Lancs.* Population: 9567. ***Small town***, adjoining to SW of Nelson. **56 D6** SD8436.
Brierley *Glos.* ***Village***, 2m/3km NW of Cinderford. **29 F7** SO6215.
Brierley *Here.* ***Hamlet***, 2m/3km S of Leominster. **28 D3** SO4956.
Brierley *S.Yorks.* Population: 3460. ***Village***, 2m/3km SW of Hemsworth. **51 G1** SE4110.
Brierley Hill *W.Mid.* ***Suburb***, SW district of Dudley. **40 B7** SO9186.
Brierton *Hart.* ***Settlement***, 3m/4km SW of Hartlepool. **63 F4** NZ4730.
Briery *Cumb.* ***Locality***, 1m/2km E of Keswick. NY2824.
Briery Hill *B.Gwent* ***Suburb***, on W side of Ebbw Vale. SO1608.
Briestfield *W.Yorks.* ***Settlement***, 3m/5km NE of Fenay Bridge. SE2317.
Brig o'Turk *Stir.* ***Village***, 6m/10km W of Callander. **81 G7** NN5306.
Brigehaugh *Moray* ***Settlement***, at bridge over River Fiddich, 3m/4km SE of Dufftown. **90 B1** NJ3435.
Brigflatts *Cumb.* ***Settlement***, 1m/2km W of Sedbergh. SD6491.
Brigg *N.Lincs.* Population: 5768. ***Small town***, market town, 7m/12km E of Scunthorpe. Annual Horse Fair. **52 D2** TA0007.
Briggate *Norf.* ***Hamlet***, 3m/5km SE of North Walsham. TG3127.
Briggswath *N.Yorks.* ***Village***, on N bank of River Esk opposite Sleights. NZ8608.
Brigham *Cumb.* ***Village***, 2m/4km W of Cockermouth. **60 B3** NY0830.
Brigham *E.Riding* ***Hamlet***, 4m/7km SE of Great Driffield. **59 G4** TA0753.
Brighouse *W.Yorks.* Population: 32,198. ***Town***, former textile town on River Calder, 4m/7km N of Huddersfield. **57 G7** SE1423.
Brighstone *I.o.W.* ***Village***, 2m/3km W of Shorwell. **11 F6** SZ4282.
Brighstone Bay *I.o.W.* ***Bay***, to S of Brighstone, extending from Chilton Chine SE to Atherfield Point. **11 F6** SZ4282.
Brighstone Forest *I.o.W.* ***Forest/woodland***, 1m/2km N of Brighstone. **11 F6** SZ4185.
Brightgate *Derbys.* ***Settlement***, 2m/4km W of Matlock. **50 E7** SK2659.
Brighthampton *Oxon.* ***Hamlet***, 4m/7km SE of Witney. **21 G1** SP3803.
Brightholmlee *S.Yorks.* ***Hamlet***, 1km NW of Wharncliffe Side. SK2995.
Brightling *E.Suss.* ***Village***, 5m/8km NW of Battle. Obelisk and observatory to E on Brightling Down. **13 K4** TQ6821.
Brightlingsea *Essex* Population: 7441. ***Small town***, on Brightlingsea Creek near mouth of River Colne, 8m/12km SE of Colchester. **34 E7** TM0816.
Brightlingsea Reach ***Sea feature***, inlet to E of Mersea Island, forming estuary of River Colne. **34 E7** TM0714.
Brighton *B. & H.* Population: 124,851. ***Town***, seaside resort, 48m/77km S of London. Previously a fishing village known as Brighthelmstone. Sailing centre. Regency squares at Kemp Town. Pavilion built in Oriental style for Prince Regent. Annual Festival. Universities. **13 G6** TQ3104.
Brighton *Cornw.* ***Settlement***, 7m/12km SE of Newquay. **3 G3** SW9054.
Brighton le Sands *Mersey.* ***Suburb***, on coast 1m/2km NW of Crosby town centre. SJ3099.
Brightons *Falk.* ***Village***, 3m/5km SE of Falkirk. **75 H3** NS9277.
Brightside *S.Yorks.* ***Suburb***, 2m/3km NE of Sheffield city centre. SK3789.
Brightwalton *W.Berks.* ***Village***, 8m/13km N of Newbury. **21 H4** SU4279.
Brightwalton Green *W.Berks.* ***Hamlet***, 1km S of Brightwalton. SU4278.
Brightwalton Holt *W.Berks.* ***Hamlet***, 1m/2km SE of Brightwalton. SU4377.
Brightwell *Oxon.* *See Brightwell-cum-Sotwell.*
Brightwell *Suff.* ***Village***, 6m/9km E of Ipswich. **35 G4** TM2543.
Brightwell Baldwin *Oxon.* ***Village***, 2m/4km W of Watlington. **21 K2** SU6595.
Brightwell-cum-Sotwell *Oxon.* ***Village***, 2m/3km NW of Wallingford. Formed by adjoining hamlets of Brightwell and Sotwell. **21 J2** SU5790.
Brightwell Upperton *Oxon.* ***Hamlet***, 2m/3km W of Watlington. SU6594.
Brigmerston *Wilts.* ***Settlement***, adjoining to N of Milston, 3m/4km N of Amesbury. SU1645.
Brignall *Dur.* ***Village***, above Brignall Banks, beside River Greta, 3m/5km SE of Barnard Castle. **62 B5** NZ0712.
Brignall Banks *Dur.* ***Forest/woodland***, wooded N side of River Greta gorge, 3m/5km S of Barnard Castle. NZ0511.

Brigsley *N.E.Lincs.* ***Village***, 5m/8km S of Grimsby. **53 F2** TA2501.
Brigsteer *Cumb.* ***Village***, 2m/4km N of Levens. **55 H1** SD4889.
Brigstock *Northants.* ***Village***, 4m/6km SE of Corby. Manor house medieval and later. **42 C7** SP9485.
Brill *Bucks.* ***Village***, 6m/10km NW of Thame. **31 H7** SP6513.
Brill *Cornw.* ***Hamlet***, 5m/8km SW of Penryn. **2 E6** SW7229.
Brilley *Here.* ***Village***, 5m/8km NE of Hay-on-Wye. **28 B4** SO2649.
Brilley Mountain *Here.* ***Settlement***, 4m/6km SW of Kington. **28 B3** SO2651.
Brimaston (Treowman). *Pembs.* ***Hamlet***, 1m/2km E of Hayscastle Cross. SM9325.
Brimfield *Here.* ***Village***, 4m/7km W of Tenbury Wells. **28 E2** SO5267.
Brimfieldcross *Here.* ***Hamlet***, 3m/5km W of Tenbury Wells. SO5368.
Brimham Rocks *N.Yorks.* ***Inland physical feature***, large group of rocks (National Trust) fantastically shaped by erosion, 3m/5km E of Pateley Bridge. **57 H3** SE2064.
Brimington *Derbys.* ***Locality***, 2m/3km NE of Chesterfield. **51 G5** SK4073.
Brimington Common *Derbys.* ***Locality***, 1m/2km S of Brimington. **51 G5** SK4072.
Brimley *Devon* ***Hamlet***, 5m/8km NE of Ashburton. **5 J3** SX7977.
Brimmond Hill *Aberdeen* ***Hill***, with panoramic viewpoint, 5m/8km W of Aberdeen. Height 869 feet or 265 metres. **91 G4** NJ8509.
Brimpsfield *Glos.* ***Village***, 6m/9km S of Cheltenham. **29 J7** SO9312.
Brimpton *W.Berks.* ***Village***, 4m/7km NE of Kingsclere. **21 J5** SU5564.
Brims *Ork.* ***Settlement***, at S end of Hoy, 1m/2km SE of Melsetter. ND2888.
Brims Ness *High.* ***Coastal feature***, headland on N coast of Caithness district, 5m/8km W of Thurso. **105 F1** ND0471.
Brims Ness *Ork.* ***Coastal feature***, headland on Hoy to E of Brims. **107 B9** ND2888.
Brimscombe *Glos.* ***Village***, 2m/3km SE of Stroud. **20 B1** SO8602.
Brimsdown *Gt.Lon.* ***Suburb***, in River Lea valley, 3m/4km E of Enfield, in borough of Enfield. TQ3697.
Brimstage *Mersey.* ***Hamlet***, 4m/7km SW of Birkenhead. Oratory of 14c-15c. **48 C4** SJ3082.
Brinacory *High.* ***Settlement***, on N shore of Loch Morar, in Lochaber district, 4m/7km E of foot of loch. NM7591.
Brinacory Island *High.* ***Island***, islet in Loch Morar, to S of Brinacory. NM7590.
Brincliffe *S.Yorks.* ***Suburb***, 2m/3km SW of Sheffield city centre. SK3385.
Brind *E.Riding* ***Hamlet***, 2m/3km N of Howden. **58 D6** SE7430.
Brindham *Som.* ***Settlement***, 1m/2km NE of Glastonbury. ST5140.
Brindister *Shet.* ***Settlement***, on Mainland, on W shore of Brindister Voe. **109 B7** HU2857.
Brindister *Shet.* ***Settlement***, on Mainland, 1m/2km N of Easter Quarff. **109 D9** HU4336.
Brindle *Lancs.* ***Village***, 6m/9km SW of Blackburn. **55 J7** SD5924.
Brindle Heath *Gt.Man.* ***Suburb***, 2m/3km NW of Salford city centre. SD8000.
Brindley Ford *Stoke* ***Hamlet***, 2m/4km NE of Tunstall. **49 H7** SJ8754.
Brindley Heath *Staffs.* ***Open space***, heath to SE of Cannock Chase Forest. **40 B4** SJ9914.
Brineton *Staffs.* ***Hamlet***, 5m/9km SE of Newport. **40 A4** SJ8013.
Bring Deeps *Ork.* ***Sea feature***, sea passage between Bring Head on Hoy and Houton Head on Mainland. **107 B7** HY2902.
Bring Head *Ork.* ***Coastal feature***, headland on NW coast of Rousay. **106 C4** HY3633.
Bringewood Chase ***Inland physical feature***, largely wooded ridge rising to 1191 feet or 363 metres, on border of Herefordshire and Shropshire, 3m/5km W of Ludlow. **28 D1** SO4473.
Bringhurst *Leics.* ***Village***, 4m/7km NW of Corby. **42 B6** SP8492.
Brington *Cambs.* ***Village***, 6m/9km E of Thrapston. **32 D1** TL0875.
Brington *Northants.* ***Locality***, parish containing villages of Great and Little Brington, 6m/10km NW of Northampton. SP6664.
Briningham *Norf.* ***Village***, 4m/6km SW of Holt. **44 E2** TG0334.
Brinkburn Priory *Northumb.* ***Ecclesiastical building***, priory of c. 1200 (English Heritage) restored 1858, in loop of River Coquet, 4m/7km SE of Rothbury. **71 G4** NZ1198.
Brinkhill *Lincs.* ***Village***, 5m/8km N of Spilsby. **53 G5** TF3773.
Brinkley *Cambs.* ***Village***, 6m/9km S of Newmarket. **33 K3** TL6254.
Brinkley *Notts.* ***Settlement***, 1m/2km SE of Southwell. SK7152.
Brinklow *Warks.* ***Village***, 6m/10km E of Coventry. Remains of motte and bailey castle. **31 F1** SP4379.
Brinkworth *Wilts.* ***Village***, 5m/9km E of Malmesbury. **20 D3** SU0184.
Brinmore *High.* ***Settlement***, 10m/16km S of Inverness. **88 D2** NH6628.
Brinnington *Gt.Man.* ***Suburb***, 2m/3km NE of Stockport town centre. SJ9192.
Brinscall *Lancs.* ***Village***, 6m/9km SW of Blackburn. **56 B7** SD6221.
Brinscombe *Som.* ***Settlement***, at foot of Brinscombe Hill, 3m/5km N of Wedmore. ST4252.
Brinsea *N.Som.* ***Hamlet***, 1m/2km S of Congresbury. ST4462.
Brinsford *Staffs.* ***Settlement***, 1m/2km SE of Coven. SJ9105.
Brinsley *Notts.* Population: 3917. ***Village***, 1m/2km N of Eastwood. **41 G1** SK4648.
Brinsop *Here.* ***Settlement***, 5m/9km NW of Hereford. **28 D4** SO4444.
Brinsworth *S.Yorks.* ***Village***, 2m/3km S of Rotherham. **51 G4** SK4189.
Brinton *Norf.* ***Village***, 3m/5km SW of Holt. **44 E2** TG0335.
Brinyan *Ork.* ***Locality***, with pier or landing stage, at SE end of Rousay. **106 D5** HY4327.
Brisco *Cumb.* ***Hamlet***, 3m/5km SE of Carlisle. **60 F1** NY4251.
Brisley *Norf.* ***Village***, 6m/9km NW of East Dereham. **44 D3** TF9521.
Brislington *Bristol* ***Suburb***, 3m/4km SE of Bristol city centre. **19 K4** ST6270.
Brissenden Green *Kent* ***Hamlet***, 1m/2km SE of Bethersden. TQ9339.
Bristnall Fields *W.Mid.* ***Suburb***, 1m/2km SE of Oldbury town centre. SO9986.
Bristol *Bristol* Population: 407,992. ***City***, 106m/171km W of London. Port on River Avon dates from medieval times, with docks in the city itself and at Avonmouth and Portishead. Bristol grew from transatlantic trade in rum, tobacco and slaves. In Georgian times, Bristol's population was second only to London and many Georgian buildings still stand, including the Theatre Royal, the oldest working theatre in the country, along with Victorian buildings. Bristol is now a commercial and industrial centre. Cathedral dates from 12c and was originally an abbey. 15c Temple Church tower and walls (English Heritage). Universities. Bristol International Airport at Lulsgate 7m/11km SW. **19 J4** ST5872.
Bristol (Lulsgate) Airport *N.Som.* *Former name of Bristol International Airport, qv.*
Bristol Cathedral *Bristol* ***Ecclesiastical building***, originally an abbey church founded for Augustinian canons in 1140 to W of Bristol city centre and a rare example of a hall church. Granted cathedral status in 1542. **19 J4** ST5872.
Bristol Channel ***Sea feature***, extension of mouth of River Severn separating South Wales from SW Peninsula of England. **18 C6** SS7060.
Bristol International Airport (Formerly known as Bristol (Lulsgate) Airport.) *N.Som.* ***Airport/airfield***, 7m/11km SW of Bristol city centre. **19 H5** ST5065.
Briston *Norf.* Population: 2184. ***Village***, 4m/6km S of Holt. **44 E2** TG0632.
Brit *Dorset* ***River***, rising N of Beaminster and flowing S through Bridport into Lyme Bay at West Bay. **8 D5** SY4690.
Britannia *Lancs.* ***Hamlet***, 1m/2km SE of Bacup. **56 D7** SD8821.
Britford *Wilts.* ***Village***, in River Avon valley, 1m/2km SE of Salisbury. **10 C2** SU1628.
Brithdir *Caerp.* ***Village***, 1m/2km N of Bargoed. SO1502.
Brithdir *Gwyn.* ***Hamlet***, 3m/4km E of Dolgellau. **37 G4** SH7618.
Brithem Bottom *Devon* ***Hamlet***, 2m/3km NW of Cullompton. **7 J4** ST0110.
British Golf Museum *Fife* ***Other feature of interest***, at N side of St. Andrews. Displays on championships and famous players, as well as history of golf. Exhibitions of evolution of golf equipment and fun features of game. **83 G6** NO5017.
British Library *Gt.Lon.* ***Other feature of interest***, in borough of Camden, 2m/3km N of Charing Cross. National copyright library which holds one copy of every printed book published in UK. Also a wide-ranging reference library with an incomparable collection of books, periodicals and manuscripts in English and foreign languages. Admission to Bloomsbury Reading Rooms is restricted to academics and professional researchers. Incorporates extensive Map Library, Official Publications and Social Sciences Service, Literature Library, Music Library, and Humanities and Social Sciences Library. TQ2982.
British Museum *Gt.Lon.* ***Leisure/recreation***, one of world's largest and greatest museums, in borough of Camden, 1m/2km N of Charing Cross. Built by Sir Robert Smirke, 1823-47, with domed reading room, 1857, by Sidney Smirke. Egyptian artefacts include sarcophagi, mummies, Rosetta Stone, tomb paintings and papyri, including editions of Book of the Dead. Extensive Greek and Roman collections. Basement houses Wolfson galleries, with large collection of sculpture and notable exhibits in Assyrian Transept and Babylonian Room. Europe 1500-1800 collection brings together artefacts from Renaissance to Neo-classical period. Many other notable collections. TQ3081.
Briton Ferry (Llansawel). *N.P.T.* ***Small town***, on E bank of mouth of River Neath, 2m/3km S of Neath. **18 A2** SS7494.
Brittle *High.* ***River***, in S part of Skye, rising in Cuillin Hills and running down to head of Loch Brittle. **85 K2** NG4020.
Britwell *Oxon.* *See Britwell Salome.*
Britwell *Slo.* ***Suburb***, 2m/3km N of Slough. SU9582.
Britwell Salome (Britwell). *Oxon.* ***Village***, 1m/2km SW of Watlington. **21 K2** SU6393.
Brixham *Torbay* Population: 15,865. ***Town***, fishing town on coast, 5m/8km S of Torquay across Tor Bay. Busy and attractive harbour with replica of the Golden Hind. William of Orange landed here in 1688. **5 K5** SX9256.
Brixton *Devon* ***Village***, 5m/8km E of Plymouth. **5 F5** SX5552.
Brixton *Gt.Lon.* ***Suburb***, in borough of Lambeth, 3m/5km S of Charing Cross. TQ3175.
Brixton Deverill *Wilts.* ***Village***, 4m/7km S of Warminster and 5m/8km NE of Mere. **9 H1** ST8638.
Brixworth *Northants.* Population: 3789. ***Village***, 7m/11km N of Northampton. **31 J1** SP7470.
Brize Norton *Oxon.* ***Village***, 4m/6km W of Witney. Airfield to SW. **21 F1** SP3007.
Broad Alley *Worcs.* ***Hamlet***, 3m/5km N of Droitwich Spa. SO8867.
Broad Bay *W.Isles* *Alternative name for Loch a' Tuath, qv.*
Broad Bench *Dorset* ***Coastal feature***, headland between Hobarrow Bay and Kimmeridge Bay, 4m/7km NW of St. Alban's Head. **9 H7** SY8978.
Broad Blunsdon *Swin.* ***Village***, 4m/6km N of Swindon. **20 E2** SU1590.
Broad Cairn ***Mountain***, on border of Aberdeenshire and Angus, 2m/3km W of head of Loch Muick. Munro: height 3273 feet or 998 metres. **89 K6** NO2481.
Broad Campden *Glos.* ***Village***, 1m/2km SE of Chipping Campden. **30 C5** SP1537.
Broad Carr *W.Yorks.* ***Hamlet***, adjoining to E of Holywell Green, 4m/6km NW of Huddersfield town centre. SE0919.
Broad Chalke *Wilts.* ***Village***, on River Ebble, 5m/8km SW of Wilton. **10 B2** SU0325.
Broad Clough *Lancs.* ***Locality***, 1km N of Bacup. SD8624.
Broad Colney *Herts.* ***Settlement***, adjoining to S of London Colney. TL1703.
Broad Down *Devon* ***Hill***, with tumuli on summit, 4m/7km NE of Sidmouth. Height 768 feet or 234 metres. **7 K6** SY1793.
Broad Ford *Kent* ***Settlement***, 1m/2km SE of Horsmonden. TQ7139.
Broad Green *Beds.* ***Hamlet***, adjoining to N of Cranfield, 7m/11km SW of Bedford. **32 C4** SP9543.
Broad Green *Cambs.* ***Hamlet***, 4m/6km SE of Newmarket. TL6859.
Broad Green *Essex* ***Hamlet***, 2m/3km E of Coggeshall. **34 C6** TL8723.
Broad Green *Essex* ***Settlement***, adjoining to W of Chrishall, 5m/9km E of Royston. TL4439.
Broad Green *Gt.Lon.* ***Suburb***, in borough of Croydon, 1m/2km N of Croydon town centre. TQ3166.
Broad Green *Mersey.* ***Suburb***, 4m/7km E of Liverpool city centre. SJ4090.
Broad Green *Suff.* ***Settlement***, 1km SW of Chevington. TL7859.
Broad Green *Suff.* ***Settlement***, 1km W of Forward Green. TM0859.
Broad Green *Suff.* ***Settlement***, 2m/3km NW of Debenham. TM1464.
Broad Green *Worcs.* ***Hamlet***, 5m/8km W of Worcester. **29 G3** SO7655.
Broad Green *Worcs.* ***Settlement***, 2m/4km E of Bromsgrove. SO9970.
Broad Haven *Pembs.* ***Bay***, small sandy bay on S Pembrokeshire coast, 1km NE of St. Govan's Head. **16 C5** SR9794.
Broad Haven *Pembs.* ***Village***, on St. Brides Bay, 6m/9km W of Haverfordwest. **16 B3** SM8613.
Broad Head *D. & G.* ***Mountain***, on uplands to S of Craik Forest, 6m/10km N of Langholm. Height 1614 feet or 492 metres. **69 J4** NY3494.
Broad Heath *Worcs.* ***Hamlet***, 6m/10km N of Bromyard. **29 F2** SO6665.
Broad Hill *Cambs.* ***Settlement***, 2m/4km N of Soham. **33 J1** TL5976.
Broad Hill *S.Lan.* ***Mountain***, 2m/3km SE of Lamington. Height 1522 feet or 464 metres. **68 E1** NT0029.
Broad Hinton *Wilts.* ***Village***, 4m/7km N of Avebury. **20 E4** SU1076.
Broad Lanes *Shrop.* ***Settlement***, 5m/8km SE of Bridgnorth. SO7788.
Broad Law *Sc.Bord.* ***Mountain***, 3m/5km E of Tweedsmuir. Height 2755 feet or 840 metres. **69 G1** NT1423.
Broad Laying *Hants.* ***Village***, 4m/6km SW of Newbury. **21 H5** SU4362.
Broad Marston *Worcs.* ***Hamlet***, 5m/7km N of Chipping Campden. **30 C4** SP1446.
Broad Meadow *Staffs.* ***Suburb***, 2m/3km N of Newcastle-under-Lyme town centre. SJ8348.
Broad Oak (Derwen-fawr). *Carmar.* ***Hamlet***, 3m/5km W of Llandeilo. **17 J2** SN5722.
Broad Oak *Cumb.* ***Settlement***, 4m/7km N of Bootle. **60 C7** SD1194.
Broad Oak *Devon* ***Village***, adjoining S end of West Hill. SY0693.
Broad Oak *E.Suss.* Population: 1764. ***Village***, 6m/10km W of Rye. **14 D6** TQ8219.
Broad Oak *Here.* ***Village***, 6m/9km N of Monmouth. **28 D6** SO4821.
Broad Oak *Mersey.* ***Suburb***, 1m/2km E of St. Helens town centre. SJ5395.
Broad Piece *Cambs.* ***Locality***, 1km NW of Soham. TL5874.
Broad Road *Suff.* ***Settlement***, 1km SE of Fressingfield. TM2776.
Broad Sound *I.o.S.* ***Sea feature***, sea channel from N of Western Rocks to W of Annet, 5m/8km SW of St. Mary's. **2 B2** SV8207.
Broad Sound *Pembs.* ***Sea feature***, sea channel between islands of Skomer and Skokholm off SW coast of Wales. **16 A4** SM7206.
Broad Street *E.Suss.* ***Hamlet***, adjoining to W of Icklesham. TQ8616.
Broad Street *Essex* ***Village***, NE end of Hatfield Broad Oak, 5m/8km SE of Bishop's Stortford. TL5516.
Broad Street *Kent* ***Settlement***, 5m/7km NW of Hythe. TR1140.
Broad Street *Kent* ***Village***, 5m/7km E of Maidstone. **14 D2** TQ8256.
Broad Street *Wilts.* ***Settlement***, 4m/6km W of Pewsey. SU1059.
Broad Street Green *Essex* ***Settlement***, 2m/3km N of Maldon. **24 E1** TL8609.
Broad Taing *Ork.* ***Coastal feature***, headland to E of Bay of Isbister, Mainland. **107 D6** HY4117.

Broad Town *Wilts.* ***Village***, 3m/5km SE of Wootton Bassett. **20 D4** SU0977.
Broadbottom *Gt.Man.* ***Locality***, 3m/5km E of Hyde. **49 J3** SJ9993.
Broadbridge *W.Suss.* ***Village***, 3m/5km W of Chichester. Site of Roman building. **12 B6** SU8105.
Broadbridge Heath *W.Suss.* ***Suburb***, 2m/3km W of Horsham. Field Place to N is birthplace of Shelley. **12 E3** TQ1431.
Broadbury *Devon* ***Forest/woodland***, upland area 8m/13km W of Okehampton. **6 C6** SX4596.
Broadclyst *Devon* ***Village***, 5m/8km NE of Exeter. Most of village is National Trust property, as are Killerton House and Park, Danes Wood and Ashclyst Forest, all within parish. **7 H6** SX9897.
Broadfield *Gt.Man.* ***Suburb***, 1m/2km W of Heywood town centre. SD8410.
Broadfield *Inclyde* ***Suburb***, 1m/2km SE of Port Glasgow. NS3473.
Broadfield *Lancs.* ***Suburb***, to W of Leyland. SD5222.
Broadfield *Lancs.* ***Suburb***, 1m/2km S of Accrington town centre. SD7427.
Broadfield *Pembs.* ***Settlement***, 2m/3km N of Tenby. SN1303.
Broadfield *W.Suss.* ***Suburb***, to SW of Crawley. TQ2534.
Broadford *High.* ***Village***, on Broadford Bay, Skye, 7m/11km SW of Kyleakin. **86 C2** NG6423.
Broadford Airport *High.* ***Airport/airfield***, 3m/5km E of Broadford, Skye. **86 C2** NG6924.
Broadford Bay *High.* ***Bay***, on Skye, 7m/11km SW of Kyleakin. **86 C2** NG6423.
Broadford Bridge *W.Suss.* ***Hamlet***, 3m/5km S of Billingshurst. **12 D4** TQ0921.
Broadgate *Cumb.* ***Settlement***, 3m/4km W of Broughton in Furness across River Duddon. **54 E1** SD1786.
Broadgate *Lincs.* ***Locality***, 2m/4km S of Sutton St. Edmund. TF3609.
Broadgrass Green *Suff.* ***Settlement***, 1km NW of Woolpit. TL9663.
Broadgroves *Essex* ***Settlement***, adjoining to N of Barnston, 1km SE of Great Dunmow. **33 K7** TL6419.
Broadhaigh *Gt.Man.* ***Suburb***, 1m/2km W of Rochdale town centre. SD8713.
Broadhaugh *Sc.Bord.* ***Settlement***, 2m/3km SW of Branxholme. **69 K3** NT4409.
Broadhaven *High.* ***Settlement***, to E of Wick, on small bay of Broad Haven, on E coast of Caithness district. ND3751.
Broadheath *Gt.Man.* ***Suburb***, 1m/2km N of Altrincham town centre. **49 G4** SJ7689.
Broadheath *Here.* ***Hamlet***, 5m/8km SE of Tenbury Wells. SO6665.
Broadhembury *Devon* ***Village***, 5m/7km NW of Honiton. **7 K5** ST1004.
Broadhempston *Devon* ***Village***, 4m/6km SE of Ashburton. **5 J4** SX8066.
Broadholme *Lincs.* ***Settlement***, 1km S of Saxilby and 6m/9km NW of Lincoln. **52 B5** SK8974.
Broadland Row *E.Suss.* ***Hamlet***, 1m/2km NE of Brede. **14 D6** TQ8319.
Broadlands *Devon* ***Suburb***, W district of Newton Abbot. SX8571.
Broadlands *Hants.* ***Historic house***, 18c mansion 1km S of Romsey. Former home of Lord Palmerston and later of Lord Mountbatten. **10 E2** SU3520.
Broadlay *Carmar.* ***Settlement***, 1km SE of Ferryside. **17 G4** SN3709.
Broadley *Lancs.* ***Hamlet***, adjoining to S of Whitworth, 3m/4km NW of Rochdale town centre. **49 H1** SD8816.
Broadley *Moray* ***Settlement***, near N coast, 3m/5km SW of Buckie. **98 B4** NJ3961.
Broadley Common *Essex* ***Hamlet***, 2m/3km SW of Harlow. **23 H1** TL4207.
Broadmayne *Dorset* ***Village***, 4m/6km SE of Dorchester. **9 G6** SY7386.
Broadmeadows *Sc.Bord.* ***Hamlet***, 4m/6km NW of Selkirk. **69 K1** NT4130.
Broadmere *Hants.* ***Settlement***, 1km NW of Farleigh Wallop and 3m/5km SW of Basingstoke. **21 K7** SU6611.
Broadmoor *Glos.* ***Locality***, 1m/2km NW of Cinderford. SO6415.
Broadmoor *Pembs.* ***Hamlet***, 4m/6km NW of Tenby. SN0905.
Broadmoor Hospital *Brack.F. See Crowthorne.*
Broadmore Green *Worcs.* ***Settlement***, 3m/4km W of Worcester. SO8153.
Broadnymett *Devon* ***Hamlet***, 2m/4km E of North Tawton. **7 F5** SS7000.
Broadoak *Cornw. Alternative name for Braddock, qv.*
Broadoak *Dorset* ***Hamlet***, 3m/5km NW of Bridport. **8 D5** SY4396.
Broadoak *E.Suss.* ***Village***, 1m/2km E of Heathfield. **13 K4** TQ6022.
Broadoak *Glos.* ***Locality***, on N bank of River Severn, 3m/4km E of Cinderford. SO6912.
Broadoak *Hants.* ***Settlement***, 1km W of Botley. SU5013.
Broadoak *Kent* ***Village***, 1m/2km NW of Sturry. **25 H5** TR1661.
Broadoak *Wrex.* ***Settlement***, 1m/2km N of Rossett. SJ3658.
Broadoak End *Herts.* ***Suburb***, in W part of Hertford. TL3013.
Broadrashes *Moray* ***Settlement***, 3m/4km N of Keith. **98 C5** NJ4354.
Broad's Green *Essex* ***Hamlet***, 4m/6km N of Chelmsford town centre. TL6912.
Broadsea *Aber.* ***Suburb***, to NW of Fraserburgh. **99 H4** NJ9967.
Broadsea Bay *D. & G.* ***Bay***, 4m/6km N of Portpatrick. **64 A5** NW9759.
Broadshard *Som.* ***Suburb***, N district of Crewkerne. ST4410.
Broadstairs *Kent* Population: 22,116. ***Town***, resort on E coast of Isle of Thanet, 2m/3km N of Ramsgate. Dickens Festival and Folk Festival held each year. **25 K5** TR3967.
Broadstone *Poole* ***Suburb***, 3m/5km N of Poole. **10 B5** SZ0095.
Broadstone *Shrop.* ***Hamlet***, 8m/13km NE of Craven Arms. **38 E7** SO5489.
Broadstreet Common *Newport* ***Hamlet***, 4m/6km SE of Newport. **19 G3** ST3584.
Broadwas *Worcs.* ***Village***, 6m/9km W of Worcester. **29 G3** SO7555.
Broadwater *Herts.* ***Suburb***, S district of Stevenage. **33 F6** TL2422.
Broadwater *Lincs.* ***Locality***, 2m/4km SW of Sleaford. TF0344.
Broadwater *W.Suss.* ***Suburb***, 1m/2km N of Worthing town centre. **12 E6** TQ1404.
Broadwater Down *Kent* ***Suburb***, SW district of Royal Tunbridge Wells. TQ5737.
Broadwaters *Worcs.* ***Suburb***, in NE part of Kidderminster. SO8478.
Broadwath *Cumb.* ***Locality***, 1m/2km E of Wetheral. NY4854.
Broadway *Carmar.* ***Locality***, adjoining to SW of Laugharne. **17 F3** SN2910.
Broadway *Carmar.* ***Settlement***, 2m/3km NW of Kidwelly. **17 G4** SN3808.
Broadway *Pembs.* ***Settlement***, 5m/8km W of Haverfordwest. **16 B3** SM8713.
Broadway *Som.* ***Locality***, adjoining to S of Chilcompton, 3m/4km SW of Midsomer Norton. ST6451.
Broadway *Som.* ***Village***, 3m/4km W of Ilminster. **8 C3** ST3215.
Broadway *Suff.* ***Settlement***, 1m/2km N of Halesworth. **35 H1** TM3978.
Broadway *Worcs.* Population: 2328. ***Small town***, built of Cotswold stone, below escarpment of Cotswold Hills, 5m/9km SE of Evesham, attracting many tourists. **30 B5** SP0937.
Broadway Hill *Worcs.* ***Mountain***, with viewpoint, N of Broadway Tower Country Park, 1m/2km SE of Broadway. Height 1014 feet or 309 metres. **30 C5** SP1136.
Broadway Tower Country Park *Worcs.* ***Leisure/recreation***, 1m/2km SE of Broadway. Tower offers views over 12 counties while grounds hold adventure playground, red deer and giant chess boards. **30 C5** SP1035.
Broadwell *Glos.* ***Settlement***, 1km E of Coleford. **28 E7** SO5811.
Broadwell *Glos.* ***Village***, 1m/2km NE of Stow-on-the-Wold. Site of Roman building to NW. **30 D6** SP2027.
Broadwell *Oxon.* ***Village***, 4m/6km NE of Lechlade. **21 F1** SP2503.
Broadwell *Warks.* ***Village***, 4m/6km NE of Southam. **31 F2** SP4565.
Broadwell House *Northumb.* ***Settlement***, 3m/4km S of Whitley Chapel and 7m/11km S of Hexham. **62 A1** NY9153.
Broadwell Lane End *Glos.* ***Locality***, 1m/2km E of Coleford. SO5811.
Broadwey *Dorset* ***Locality***, 3m/5km N of Weymouth. **9 F6** SY6683.
Broadwindsor *Dorset* ***Village***, 3m/5km W of Beaminster. 1m/2km S, Lewesdon Hill (National Trust), wooded summit commanding wide views. **8 D4** ST4302.
Broadwood Kelly *Devon* ***Village***, 2m/3km SW of Winkleigh. **6 E5** SS6105.
Broadwoodwidger *Devon* ***Village***, 6m/9km NE of Launceston. **6 C7** SX4189.
Brobury *Here.* ***Settlement***, 11m/17km W of Hereford. **28 C4** SO3444.
Broc-bheinn *High.* ***Mountain***, rising to over 1083 feet or 330 metres, 3m/4km NE of head of Loch Harport, Skye. **85 K1** NG4333.
Brocair *W.Isles Gaelic form of Broker, qv.*
Brocastle *V. of Glam.* ***Hamlet***, 3m/4km SE of Bridgend. SS9377.
Brocavum Roman Fort (Brougham Fort). *Cumb.* ***Historic/prehistoric site***, Roman station, 1m/2km SE of Penrith. Fort located on Carlisle road. 12c castle stands on site; some Roman work survives on grassy banks. Inscribed Roman stones in castle keep. **61 G4** NY5328.
Broch of Burland *Shet.* ***Historic/prehistoric site***, fortified Iron Age homestead situated on headland, 1m/2km NE of Easter Quarff, Mainland. **109 D9** HU4436.
Broch of Gurness *Ork.* ***Historic/prehistoric site***, prehistoric castle and domestic settlement (Historic Scotland) on headland of Aiker Ness, Mainland. **106 C5** HY3826.
Broch of Mousa *Shet.* ***Historic/prehistoric site***, Pictish broch or castle (Historic Scotland) on W coast of Mousa. It is 45 feet or 14 metres high, and thought to be nearly 2000 years old. **109 D10** HU4523.
Brochan *Powys* ***River***, running NE into River Dulas on SW side of Llanidloes. **37 J7** SN9483.
Brochel *High.* ***Locality***, near E coast of Raasay, 5m/7km from N end of Skye. Ruined castle of Macleods of Raasay. **94 B7** NG5846.
Brochloch *D. & G.* ***Settlement***, 2m/4km NW of Carsphairn. **67 K4** NX5395.
Brock *Arg. & B.* ***Settlement***, on E shore of Gott Bay, Tiree, immediately S of Ruaig. **78 B3** NM0647.
Brock *Lancs.* ***River***, rising on Holme House Fell on Forest of Bowland and flowing W into River Wyre just E of St. Michael's on Wyre, 3m/5km SW of Garstang. **55 J5** SD4641.
Brock *Lancs.* ***Settlement***, on river of same name, adjoining to N of Bilsborrow, 3m/5km S of Garstang. SD5140.
Brock Hill *Essex* ***Hamlet***, 2m/3km N of Wickford. TQ7396.
Brockamin *Worcs.* ***Hamlet***, 5m/8km W of Worcester. SO7753.
Brockbridge *Hants.* ***Hamlet***, just E of Droxford across River Meon. **11 H3** SU6118.
Brockdish *Norf.* ***Village***, 3m/5km SW of Harleston. **35 G1** TM2179.
Brockencote *Worcs.* ***Settlement***, adjoining to W of Chaddesley Corbett, 4m/6km SE of Kidderminster. SO8873.
Brockenhurst *Hants.* Population: 3048. ***Village***, on S edge of New Forest, 4m/6km S of Lyndhurst. **10 E4** SU3002.
Brockfield *N.Yorks.* ***Settlement***, 1km W of Warthill, 5m/8km NE of York. **58 C4** SE6655.
Brockford Green *Suff.* ***Settlement***, 1m/2km S of Wetheringsett. TM1265.
Brockford Street *Suff.* ***Hamlet***, 4m/7km NW of Debenham. **35 F2** TM1166.
Brockhall *Northants.* ***Village***, 4m/6km E of Daventry. **31 H2** SP6362.
Brockham *Surr.* Population: 2669. ***Village***, 2m/3km E of Dorking. **22 E7** TQ1949.
Brockhampton *Glos.* ***Hamlet***, 3m/4km N of Cheltenham. SO9426.
Brockhampton *Glos.* ***Village***, 4m/6km S of Winchcombe. **30 B6** SP0322.
Brockhampton *Hants.* ***Suburb***, SW district of Havant. SU7106.
Brockhampton *Here.* ***Hamlet***, 2m/3km E of Bromyard. Parish contains area of farmland and woods (National Trust) which includes Brockhampton, and Lower Brockhampton. SO6855.
Brockhampton *Here.* ***Historic house***, modernised early Georgian house, 2m/3km E of Bromyard. **29 F3** SO6855.
Brockhampton *Here.* ***Village***, 5m/8km N of Ross-on-Wye across loop of river. **28 E5** SO5931.
Brockhampton Green *Dorset* ***Hamlet***, 1m/2km W of Mappowder and 7m/11km SW of Sturminster Newton. ST7106.
Brockhole National Park Visitor Centre *Cumb.* ***Other feature of interest***, on W bank of Windermere lake, 3m/4km S of Ambleside. Visitor centre for Lake District, with gardens, exhibitions and activities relating to area. **60 E6** NY3900.
Brockholes *W.Yorks.* ***Village***, 4m/6km S of Huddersfield. **50 D1** SE1511.
Brockhurst *Hants.* ***Suburb***, 1m/2km NW of Gosport town centre. SU6001.
Brockhurst *W.Suss.* ***Settlement***, 1km SE of East Grinstead. **13 H3** TQ4037.
Brocklebank *Cumb.* ***Locality***, 5m/7km SE of Wigton. **60 E2** NY3043.
Brocklesby *Lincs.* ***Village***, 9m/14km W of Grimsby. **52 E1** TA1411.
Brocklesby Park *Lincs.* ***Locality***, park, with estate village at park gates, in Brocklesby. TA1411.
Brockley *Gt.Lon.* ***Suburb***, in borough of Lewisham, 5m/8km SE of Charing Cross. TQ3675.
Brockley *N.Som.* ***Village***, 3m/5km NE of Congresbury. **19 H5** ST4767.
Brockley *Suff.* ***Locality***, 6m/9km S of Bury St. Edmunds. TL8255.
Brockley *Suff.* ***Settlement***, 1km N of Culford. TL8371.
Brockley Green *Suff.* ***Settlement***, 3m/5km NE of Haverhill. TL7247.
Brockley Green *Suff.* ***Village***, 6m/9km NW of Long Melford. **34 C3** TL8254.
Brockleymoor *Cumb.* ***Locality***, adjoining to W of Plumpton. NY4936.
Brockmoor *W.Mid.* ***Suburb***, 3m/5km SW of Dudley town centre. SO9087.
Brock's Green *Hants.* ***Settlement***, 2m/4km NW of Kingsclere. SU5061.
Brockton *Shrop.* ***Hamlet***, 6m/10km E of Welshpool. **38 C5** SJ3104.
Brockton *Shrop.* ***Hamlet***, 1m/2km SW of Kemberton. **39 G5** SJ7203.
Brockton *Shrop.* ***Village***, 2m/3km S of Bishop's Castle. **38 C7** SO3285.
Brockton *Shrop.* ***Village***, 5m/8km SW of Much Wenlock. **38 E6** SO5793.
Brockton *Staffs.* ***Settlement***, 2m/3km N of Eccleshall. SJ8131.
Brockton *Tel. & W.* ***Hamlet***, 2m/3km SW of Newport. SJ7216.
Brockweir *Glos.* ***Village***, on River Wye, 5m/8km N of Chepstow. **19 J1** SO5301.
Brockwood Park *Hants.* ***Other building***, 1m/2km SE of Bramdean. Includes Brockwood Park School, The Krishnamurti Centre and The Krishnamurti Foundation Trust. **11 H2** SU6226.
Brockworth *Glos.* ***Suburb***, 4m/6km SE of Gloucester city centre. **29 H7** SO8916.
Brocolitia *Northumb.* ***Historic/prehistoric site***, remains of Roman fort on Hadrian's Wall, by bank of River North Tyne, 4m/6km W of Humshaugh. Site of Mithraic temple (English Heritage) at Carrawbrough to E. **70 D6** NY8571.
Brocton *Staffs.* ***Village***, 4m/6km SE of Stafford. **40 B4** SJ9619.
Brodick (Formerly known as Invercloy.) *N.Ayr.* ***Small town***, port and resort on Brodick Bay on E coast of Arran. Passenger ferry to Ardrossan on mainland. **73 J7** NS0136.
Brodick Bay *N.Ayr.* ***Bay***, on E coast of Arran. **73 J7** NS0136.
Brodick Castle *N.Ayr.* ***Castle***, on Arran, with country park (National Trust for Scotland) 2m/3km N of Brodick. Mainly Victorian but original parts date from 13c. Famous rhododendron collection and one of Europe's best woodland gardens. **73 J7** NS0136.
Brodie Castle *Moray* ***Castle***, seat of Brodie of Brodie, 4m/6km W of Forres. Oldest parts date from 16c, with 17 and 19c additions. Park contains notable Pictish stone and impressive daffodil collection. **97 G6** NH9757.
Brodsworth *S.Yorks.* ***Village***, 5m/8km NW of Doncaster. **51 H2** SE5007.
Brodsworth Hall *S.Yorks.* ***Historic house***, unchanged and intact Victorian country house (English Heritage) of Charles Thellusson, 2m/3km W of Adwick le Street. **51 H2** SE5107.

Brogborough *Beds.* ***Hamlet***, 5m/7km W of Ampthill. **32 C5** SP9638.
Brogden *Lancs.* ***Settlement***, on site of Roman road, 1m/2km W of Barnoldswick. SD8547.
Brogyntyn *Shrop.* ***Settlement***, 2m/3km NW of Oswestry. **38 B2** SJ2731.
Broken Cross *Ches.* ***Locality***, 2m/3km W of Macclesfield. **49 H5** SJ8973.
Broken Cross *Ches.* ***Settlement***, 2m/3km E of Northwich. **49 F5** SJ6872.
Brokenborough *Wilts.* ***Village***, 2m/3km NW of Malmesbury. **20 C3** ST9189.
Broker (Gaelic form: Brocair.) *W.Isles* ***Settlement***, on Eye Peninsula, Isle of Lewis, 1m/2km SW of Tiumpan Head. NB5536.
Brokerswood *Wilts.* ***Hamlet***, 3m/4km NW of Westbury. ST8352.
Brokes *N.Yorks.* ***Settlement***, 1m/2km SW of Richmond. SE1599.
Brolass *Arg. & B.* ***Forest/woodland***, tract on Ross of Mull between Pennyghael to N and Malcolm's Point to S. **79 F5** NM5022.
Bromborough *Mersey.* ***Suburb***, 2m/3km SE of Bebington town centre. **48 C4** SJ3482.
Brome *Suff.* ***Village***, 2m/3km N of Eye. **35 F1** TM1376.
Brome Street *Suff.* ***Hamlet***, 1m/2km E of Brome. **35 F1** TM1376.
Bromeswell *Suff.* ***Village***, 2m/3km NE of Woodbridge across River Deben. **35 G3** TM3050.
Bromfield *Cumb.* ***Village***, 4m/6km NE of Aspatria. **60 C2** NY1746.
Bromfield *Shrop.* ***Village***, at confluence of River Onny and River Teme, 3m/4km NW of Ludlow. Site of Roman camp to N. **28 D1** SO4876.
Bromford *W.Mid.* ***Suburb***, 4m/7km NE of Birmingham city centre. SP1290.
Bromham *Beds.* Population: 3909. ***Village***, 3m/4km W of Bedford. Site of Roman building 1km S. **32 D3** TL0051.
Bromham *Wilts.* ***Village***, 4m/6km NW of Devizes. **20 C5** ST9665.
Bromley *S.Yorks.* ***Hamlet***, 1m/2km E of Wortley. SK3298.
Bromley *W.Mid.* ***Suburb***, 3m/4km SW of Dudley town centre. SO9088.
Bromley-by-Bow *Gt.Lon.* ***Suburb***, in borough of Tower Hamlets, 3m/5km NE of London Bridge. TQ3782.
Bromley Common *Gt.Lon.* ***Suburb***, and open space in borough of Bromley, 2m/3km SE of Bromley town centre. **23 H5** TQ4266.
Bromley Cross *Gt.Man.* ***Suburb***, 3m/5km N of Bolton, just S of Jumbles Reservoir. SD7313.
Bromley Green *Kent* ***Hamlet***, 4m/6km S of Ashford. **14 E4** TQ9936.
Bromley Hurst *Staffs.* ***Locality***, 1m/2km S of Abbots Bromley. SK0922.
Brompton *Med.* ***Suburb***, N district of Gillingham. **24 D5** TQ7768.
Brompton *N.Yorks.* Population: 1841. ***Suburb***, 1m/2km N of Northallerton. 1m/2km NW is site of Battle of the Standard, 1138. **62 E7** SE3796.
Brompton *N.Yorks.* ***Village***, 7m/11km SW of Scarborough. **59 F1** SE9482.
Brompton *Shrop.* ***Settlement***, 1km NE of Cross Houses and 5m/7km SE of Shrewsbury. SJ5508.
Brompton-on-Swale *N.Yorks.* ***Village***, 3m/5km E of Richmond. **62 D6** SE2199.
Brompton Ralph *Som.* ***Village***, 3m/5km N of Wiveliscombe. **7 J2** ST0832.
Brompton Regis *Som.* ***Village***, on Exmoor, 3m/5km NE of Dulverton. **7 H2** SS9531.
Bromsash *Here.* ***Village***, 3m/5km E of Ross-on-Wye. **29 F6** SO6424.
Bromsberrow *Glos.* ***Hamlet***, 3m/5km SE of Ledbury. SO7434.
Bromsberrow Heath *Glos.* ***Village***, 3m/5km SE of Ledbury. **29 G5** SO7333.
Bromsgrove *Worcs.* Population: 26,366. ***Town***, market town 12m/20km SW of Birmingham. Medieval woollen trade; nail-making in 17c and 18c. Avoncroft Museum of Buildings. Poet A.E. Housman born here in 1859. **29 J1** SO9570.
Bromstead Heath *Staffs.* ***Village***, 4m/6km SE of Newport. **40 A4** SJ7917.
Bromyard *Here.* Population: 3117. ***Small town***, old market town, 12m/19km W of Worcester. **29 F3** SO6554.
Bromyard Downs *Here.* ***Settlement***, 1km NE of Bromyard. **29 F3** SO6655.
Bron-y-Gaer *Carmar.* ***Settlement***, 5m/8km N of Laugharne. **17 G3** SN3019.
Bronaber *Gwyn.* ***Locality***, 3m/4km S of Trawsfynydd. **37 G2** SH7131.
Brondesbury *Gt.Lon.* ***Suburb***, in borough of Brent, 4m/7km NW of Charing Cross. TQ2484.
Brondesbury Park *Gt.Lon.* ***Suburb***, to SW of Brondesbury. TQ2383.
Brondre-fawr Hill *Powys* ***Inland physical feature***, mountain ridge rising to 1667 feet or 508 metres, 4m/6km W of Llanbadarn Fynydd. **27 K1** SO0478.
Brongest *Cere.* ***Hamlet***, 3m/5km N of Newcastle Emlyn. **26 C4** SN3245.
Broniarth Hill *Powys* ***Hill***, on S side of, and running parallel to Dyffryn Meifod, 5m/8km NW of Welshpool. Height 449 feet or 137 metres. **38 A4** SJ1612.
Bronie Burn *Aber.* ***River***, rising on Burreldale Moss and flowing NE, past Pitmedden, to merge with Yowlie Burn before joining River Ythan 2m/3km W of Ellon. **91 H2** NJ9230.
Bronington *Wrex.* ***Village***, 4m/6km SW of Whitchurch. **38 D2** SJ4839.
Bronkham Hill *Dorset* ***Hill***, 2m/3km SW of Martinstown, with line of tumuli along ridge. Height 672 feet or 205 metres. **9 F6** SY6287.
Bronllys *Powys* ***Village***, 1m/2km NW of Talgarth. Remains of 12c-13c castle (Cadw) to SE. **28 A5** SO1434.
Bronllys Castle *Powys* ***Castle***, 12c motte and bailey castle in valley of River Llynfi, 1km NW of Talgarth. **28 A5** SO1434.
Bronnant *Cere.* ***Hamlet***, 2m/3km S of Lledrod. **27 F2** SN6467.
Brontë Parsonage *W.Yorks.* ***Historic house***, former home of Brontë family, adjacent to church in Haworth, 3m/5km SW of Keighley. Now a museum, furnished as the Brontë sisters knew it. **57 F6** SE0237.
Bronwydd Arms *Carmar.* ***Village***, 2m/4km N of Carmarthen. SN4123.
Bronydd *Powys* ***Settlement***, 1m/2km NE of Clyro. **28 B4** SO2245.
Bronygarth *Shrop.* ***Hamlet***, 2m/3km W of Chirk. **38 B2** SJ2637.
Brook *Carmar.* ***Settlement***, 2m/3km W of Laugharne. **17 F4** SN2609.
Brook *Hants.* ***Hamlet***, in New Forest, 2m/3km NW of Cadnam. **10 D3** SU2714.
Brook *Hants.* ***Settlement***, 4m/7km N of Romsey. **10 E2** SU3428.
Brook *I.o.W.* ***Village***, near S coast, 4m/7km W of Shorwell. **10 E6** SZ3983.
Brook *Kent* ***Village***, 4m/6km E of Ashford. **15 F3** TR0644.
Brook *Surr.* ***Hamlet***, 4m/7km SE of Guildford. TQ0646.
Brook *Surr.* ***Village***, 3m/5km SW of Milford. **12 C3** SU9238.
Brook *Wilts.* ***Locality***, 1m/2km W of Westbury. ST8551.
Brook Bottom *Gt.Man.* ***Suburb***, to NW of Mossley. SD9602.
Brook Cottage Gardens *Oxon.* ***Garden***, in Alkerton, 6m/10km NW of Banbury. Four-acre garden set on hill, with herbaceous plants, shrubs, trees and a water garden, as well as over 200 climbing roses and shrubs. **30 E4** SP3742.
Brook Down *I.o.W.* ***Open space***, downland (National Trust) 3m/5km NW of Brighstone. **10 E6** SZ3885.
Brook End *Beds.* ***Hamlet***, N end of Keysoe, 3m/5km SE of Kimbolton. TL0763.
Brook End *Beds.* ***Locality***, W end of Stotfold, 3m/5km NW of Baldock. TL2136.
Brook End *Beds.* ***Settlement***, 1m/2km SW of Sandy. TL1647.
Brook End *Cambs.* ***Settlement***, just W of Catworth. TL0873.
Brook End *Herts.* ***Settlement***, 3m/4km W of Buntingford. TL3229.
Brook End *M.K.* ***Settlement***, 3m/4km E of Newport Pagnell. SP9144.
Brook End *Staffs.* ***Locality***, adjoining to N of Longdon, 3m/5km SE of Rugeley. SK0814.
Brook End *Worcs.* ***Settlement***, 3m/5km S of Worcester. SO8649.
Brook Green *Gt.Lon.* ***Suburb***, in borough of Hammersmith and Fulham, 4m/7km W of Charing Cross. TQ2379.
Brook Hill *Hants.* ***Hamlet***, to N of Brook, 7m/12km E of Fordingbridge. SU2714.
Brook House *Denb.* ***Suburb***, 1m/2km E of Denbigh. SJ0765.
Brook Houses *Derbys.* ***Hamlet***, 2m/3km SW of Chapel-en-le-Frith. SK0478.
Brook Street *Essex* ***Suburb***, to W of Brentwood. **23 J2** TQ5792.
Brook Street *Kent* ***Hamlet***, 3m/5km E of Tenterden. **14 E4** TQ9233.
Brook Street *Suff.* ***Locality***, adjoining to N of Glemsford, 2m/4km NE of Cavendish. **34 C4** TL8248.
Brook Street *W.Suss.* ***Hamlet***, 1m/2km N of Cuckfield. **13 G4** TQ3026.
Brooke *Norf.* ***Village***, 7m/11km SE of Norwich. **45 G6** TM2999.
Brooke *Rut.* ***Hamlet***, 2m/3km S of Oakham. **42 B5** SK8405.
Brookend *Essex* ***Locality***, 2m/3km E of Chelmsford. TL7307.
Brookend *Glos.* ***Hamlet***, 2m/3km N of Berkeley. SO6802.
Brookend *Glos.* ***Hamlet***, 3m/5km SW of Lydney. Site of Roman villa 1km S beside River Severn estuary. **19 J2** ST5999.
Brookend *Oxon.* ***Settlement***, 3m/4km NW of Charlbury. SP3221.
Brookfield *Derbys.* ***Suburb***, 2m/3km NW of Glossop. SK0195.
Brookfield *Glos.* ***Locality***, 4m/6km E of Gloucester. SO8920.
Brookfield *Renf.* ***Hamlet***, 1m/2km NW of Johnstone. NS4164.
Brookfoot *W.Yorks.* ***Locality***, 1km W of Brighouse. SE1323.
Brookgreen *I.o.W.* ***Locality***, just S of Brook, 3m/4km W of Brighstone. SZ3883.
Brookhampton *Oxon.* ***Settlement***, adjoining to S of Stadhampton, 6m/9km N of Wallingford. SU6098.
Brookhouse *Ches.* ***Settlement***, 3m/4km NE of Macclesfield. SJ9475.
Brookhouse *Lancs.* ***Village***, 5m/7km NE of Lancaster. **55 J3** SD5464.
Brookhouse *S.Yorks.* ***Village***, 1m/2km E of Thurcroft. SK5189.
Brookhouse Green *Ches.* ***Hamlet***, 3m/5km W of Congleton. **49 H6** SJ8161.
Brookhouses *Staffs.* ***Hamlet***, 1m/2km W of Cheadle. SJ9943.
Brookland *Kent* ***Village***, 5m/8km W of New Romney. **14 E5** TQ9825.
Brooklands *D. & G.* ***Settlement***, 4m/6km SE of Corsock. **65 J3** NX8173.
Brooklands *Gt.Man.* ***Suburb***, to S of Sale town centre. SJ7890.
Brooklands *Gt.Man.* ***Suburb***, 2m/3km NE of Altrincham. SJ7990.
Brooklands *Shrop.* ***Settlement***, 1m/2km NW of Whitchurch. SJ5342.
Brooklands *Surr.* ***Locality***, former motor-racing circuit, now an industrial site on N side of Byfleet. Brooklands Museum to N. TQ0662.
Brooklands Museum *Surr.* ***Other feature of interest***, 1m/2km N of Byfleet, on 1907 motor racing circuit, with steepest section of old banked track and 1-in-4 Test Hill. Also has bomber aircraft on display. **22 D5** TQ0762.
Brookmans Park *Herts.* Population: 3315. ***Suburb***, 2m/3km N of Potters Bar. **23 F1** TL2404.
Brooks *Powys* ***Settlement***, 3m/5km W of Aberriw. **38 A6** SO1499.
Brooks Green *W.Suss.* ***Settlement***, 3m/4km E of Billingshurst. **12 E4** TQ1224.
Brooksby *Leics.* ***Locality***, 5m/8km W of Melton Mowbray. **41 J4** SK6716.
Brookside *Tel. & W.* ***Suburb***, of Telford, to SE of Dawley. SJ7005.
Brookthorpe *Glos.* ***Village***, 4m/7km S of Gloucester. **29 H7** SO8312.
Brookvale *Halton* ***Suburb***, to SE of Runcorn. SJ5580.
Brookville *Norf.* ***Hamlet***, 1m/2km N of Methwold. Site of Roman building to SW. TL7396.
Brookwood *Surr.* ***Village***, beside Basingstoke Canal, 4m/6km W of Woking. Brookwood Cemetery to SE. **22 C6** SU9457.
Broom *Beds.* ***Village***, 2m/3km SW of Biggleswade. **32 E4** TL1742.
Broom *Dur.* ***Village***, 2m/3km W of Durham. NZ2441.
Broom *Fife* ***Suburb***, to NW of Leven. NO3701.
Broom *High.* ***River***, running N down Strath More to head of Loch Broom, Ross and Cromarty district. **95 H3** NH1785.
Broom *Pembs.* ***Settlement***, 1km NW of Begelly. SN1108.
Broom *S.Yorks.* ***Suburb***, 1m/2km SE of Rotherham town centre. SK4491.
Broom *Warks.* ***Village***, 7m/11km W of Stratford-upon-Avon. **30 B3** SP0953.
Broom Green *Norf.* ***Hamlet***, 1m/2km SW of Guist, on W side of River Wensum. TF9824.
Broom Hill *Aber.* ***Mountain***, 3m/5km N of Tarland. Height 1883 feet or 574 metres. **90 C4** NJ4609.
Broom Hill *Dorset* ***Hamlet***, 3m/4km NE of Wimborne Minster. **10 B4** SU0302.
Broom Hill *Dur.* ***Hamlet***, 1km SE of Ebchester. NZ1054.
Broom Hill *Gt.Lon.* ***Suburb***, in borough of Bromley, between Petts Wood and Orpington. TQ4566.
Broom Hill *Gt.Man.* ***Locality***, 2m/3km SW of Heywood. SD8408.
Broom Hill *S.Yorks.* ***Hamlet***, 1m/2km E of Wombwell. SE4102.
Broom Hill *Worcs.* ***Hamlet***, 4m/7km NW of Bromsgrove. SO9175.
Broom of Dalreach *P. & K.* ***Hamlet***, 2m/3km NW of Dunning. **82 B6** NO0017.
Broomcroft *Shrop.* ***Settlement***, 3m/4km SW of Cressage. **38 E5** SJ5601.
Broome *Norf.* ***Village***, 1m/2km NE of Bungay. **45 H6** TM3591.
Broome *Shrop.* ***Hamlet***, 2m/4km SW of Craven Arms. **38 C7** SO4080.
Broome *Worcs.* ***Village***, 4m/6km S of Stourbridge. **29 J1** SO9078.
Broome Street *Norf.* ***Hamlet***, 1km N of Broome. TM3591.
Broome Wood *Northumb.* ***Settlement***, 4m/6km SW of Alnwick. **71 G2** NU1312.
Broomedge *Warr.* ***Village***, 2m/3km E of Lymm. **49 G4** SJ7085.
Broomer's Corner *W.Suss.* ***Hamlet***, 1m/2km S of Coolham. **12 E4** TQ1221.
Broomfield *Aber.* ***Settlement***, 1m/2km N of Ellon. **91 H1** NJ9532.
Broomfield *Essex* ***Suburb***, 2m/4km N of Chelmsford. **34 B7** TL7010.
Broomfield *Kent* ***Suburb***, SE district of Herne Bay. **25 H5** TR1966.
Broomfield *Kent* ***Village***, 5m/9km E of Maidstone. **14 D2** TQ8352.
Broomfield *Som.* ***Hamlet***, on E slopes of Quantock Hills, 4m/7km W of North Petherton. **8 B1** ST2232.
Broomfields *W.Yorks.* ***Suburb***, 1m/2km NW of Leeds city centre. SE2735.
Broomfleet *E.Riding* ***Village***, 4m/6km SW of South Cave. **58 E7** SE8827.
Broomhall *Surr.* ***Locality***, residential locality on N edge of Chobham Common, 1km S of Sunningdale. SU9566.
Broomhall Green *Ches.* ***Settlement***, 3m/5km NW of Audlem. SJ6247.
Broomhaugh *Northumb.* ***Village***, adjoining to SE of Riding Mill. **71 F7** NZ0161.
Broomhaugh Island *Northumb.* ***Island***, in River Tyne, below bridge across river at Hexham. NY9464.
Broomhead *Aber.* ***Settlement***, 2m/3km S of Fraserburgh. **99 H4** NJ9863.
Broomhead Moor *S.Yorks.* ***Open space***, moorland at E side of The Pennines, 4m/6km SW of Stocksbridge. **50 E3** SK2095.
Broomhead Reservoir *S.Yorks.* ***Reservoir***, below Broomhead Moor, 2m/3km S of Stocksbridge. **50 E3** SK2695.
Broomhill *Bristol* ***Suburb***, 3m/5km NE of Bristol city centre. ST6276.
Broomhill *Glas.* ***Suburb***, 3m/4km NW of Glasgow city centre in Partick district. NS5467.
Broomhill *Norf.* ***Locality***, adjoining to NE of Downham Market. TF6104.
Broomhill *Northumb.* ***Village***, 2m/3km SW of Amble. **71 H3** NU2500.
Broomholm *Norf.* ***Hamlet***, adjoining to SW of Bacton, 4m/7km NE of North Walsham. TG3433.

Broomhouse *Edin.* ***Suburb***, 4m/6km SW of Edinburgh city centre. NT2071.

Broomielaw *Dur.* ***Settlement***, 2m/4km E of Barnard Castle. NZ0818.

Broomlee Lough *Northumb.* ***Lake/loch***, to E of Greenlee Lough, 3m/5km N of Bardon Mill. **70 C7** NY7969.

Broomley *Northumb.* ***Hamlet***, 4m/7km SE of Corbridge. NZ0360.

Broom's Green *Glos.* ***Hamlet***, 3m/5km S of Ledbury. **29 G5** SO7132.

Broomside *Dur.* ***Suburb***, adjoining to E of Carville, 2m/3km E of Durham. NZ3043.

Broomsthorpe *Norf.* ***Settlement***, 1m/2km E of East Rudham. TF8428.

Broomy Law *Sc.Bord.* ***Mountain***, 2m/3km N of Broadmeadows. Height 1519 feet or 463 metres. **76 C7** NT4131.

Brora *High.* ***River***, rising on Ben Armine Forest and flowing SE down Strath Brora, through Loch Brora to E coast at Brora. **97 F1** NC9103.

Brora *High.* Population: 1687. ***Village***, on E coast of Sutherland district at mouth of River Brora, 10m/17km SW of Helmsdale. **97 G1** NC9004.

Brosdale Island *Arg. & B.* ***Island***, off S coast of Jura, 4m/6km SW of Craighouse. **72 D4** NR4962.

Broseley *Shrop.* Population: 5089. ***Village***, 1m/2km S of Ironbridge. **39 F5** SJ6701.

Broseley Wood *Shrop.* ***Locality***, to N of Broseley. SJ6702.

Brother Isle *Shet.* ***Island***, uninhabited island off Mainland in Yell Sound, 1m/2km N of Mio Ness. **108 D4** HU4281.

Brotherhouse Bar *Lincs.* ***Settlement***, on E side of New River, 2m/3km S of Cowbit. TF2614.

Brotheridge Green *Worcs.* ***Locality***, 3m/5km E of Malvern Wells. SO8241.

Brotherlee *Dur.* ***Hamlet***, 3m/4km E of St. John's Chapel. **62 A3** NY9237.

Brothers Water *Cumb.* ***Lake/loch***, small lake 2m/3km S of Patterdale. **60 E5** NY4012.

Brothertoft *Lincs.* ***Hamlet***, 4m/6km W of Boston. **43 F1** TF2746.

Brotherton *N.Yorks.* ***Village***, on River Aire, 1km N of Ferrybridge across river. **57 K7** SE4825.

Brotherton *W.Loth.* ***Locality***, 3m/4km SW of Livingston. NT0365.

Brothybeck *Cumb.* ***Settlement***, 2m/3km NW of Sebergham. NY3343.

Brotton *R. & C.* Population: 4735. ***Small town***, 2m/3km SE of Saltburn. Former centre for ironstone mining. **63 H4** NZ6819.

Broubster *High.* ***Settlement***, 3m/4km N of Loch Shurrery. **105 F2** ND0360.

Brough *Cumb.* ***Village***, 4m/6km N of Kirkby Stephen. Remains of medieval castle (English Heritage), restored in 17c, on site of Roman town. **61 J5** NY7914.

Brough *Derbys.* ***Hamlet***, 3m/5km W of Hathersage. Site of Roman fort of Navio beside River Noe. **50 D4** SK1882.

Brough *E.Riding* Population: 6818. ***Locality***, on N bank on River Humber, on site of Roman Petuaria, 10m/16km W of Kingston upon Hull. Airfield to SE. **59 F7** SE9326.

Brough *High.* ***Hamlet***, 2m/4km SE of Easter Head, N coast of Caithness district. **105 H1** ND2273.

Brough *Notts.* ***Hamlet***, on site of Roman settlement of Crococalana on Foss Way, 4m/7km NE of Newark-on-Trent. **52 B7** SK8358.

Brough *Ork.* ***Settlement***, on Mainland, 2m/3km SE of Dounby. **107 C6** HY3118.

Brough *Shet.* ***Settlement***, on NE coast of Mainland, opposite SW end of Yell. **108 D5** HU4377.

Brough *Shet.* ***Settlement***, near E coast of Mainland, 2m/3km W of Moul of Eswick. HU4754.

Brough *Shet.* ***Settlement***, 1km SE of Setter, Bressay. **109 E8** HU5141.

Brough *Shet.* ***Settlement***, on W side of Burravoe, Yell. **108 E5** HU5179.

Brough *Shet.* ***Village***, near N coast of Whalsay. **109 E6** HU5565.

Brough Castle *Cumb.* ***Castle***, remains of castle (English Heritage) built by William II on site of Roman fort to S of Brough. Restored by Lady Anne Clifford in 17c. **61 J5** NY7914.

Brough Head *High.* ***Coastal feature***, headland on E coast of Caithness district, 6m/10km S of John o' Groats. **105 J2** ND3763.

Brough Head *Ork.* ***Coastal feature***, headland with beacon at W end of islet of Brough of Birsay, off NW coast of Mainland, accessible on foot at low tide. St. Peter's Chapel (Historic Scotland), at other end of islet. **106 B5** HY2328.

Brough Lodge *Shet.* ***Settlement***, near to W coast of Fetlar, 3m/5km NW of Harbie. **108 E3** HU5892.

Brough Ness *Ork.* ***Coastal feature***, headland to S of Brough at S end of South Ronaldsay. **107 D9** ND4482.

Brough of Birsay *Ork.* ***Historic/prehistoric site***, remains of Norse settlement on Brough of Birsay islet, off NW coast of Mainland. **106 B5** HY2328.

Brough Sowerby *Cumb.* ***Hamlet***, 1m/2km S of Brough. **61 J5** NY7912.

Brough Taing *Shet.* ***Coastal feature***, rocky headland on E coast of Unst. **108 F2** HP6304.

Broughall *Shrop.* ***Village***, 2m/3km E of Whitchurch. **38 E1** SJ5641.

Brougham *Cumb.* ***Settlement***, 2m/3km SE of Penrith. Castle (English Heritage) dates from 12c. To SE of castle is site of Roman fort of Erocavum. **61 G4** NY5328.

Brougham Castle *Cumb.* ***Castle***, 12c castle (English Heritage) on River Eamont, 1m/2km SE of Penrith. Late 12c-13c keep restored by Lady Anne Clifford in 17c. **61 G4** NY5329.

Broughton *Bucks.* ***Settlement***, 2m/3km E of Aylesbury town centre. SP8413.

Broughton *Cambs.* ***Village***, 5m/7km NE of Huntingdon. **33 F1** TL2877.

Broughton *Flints.* Population: 5375. ***Village***, 2m/3km SE of Hawarden. **48 C6** SJ3363.

Broughton *Gt.Man.* ***Suburb***, 1m/2km NW of Manchester city centre. **49 H3** SJ8299.

Broughton *Hants.* ***Village***, 3m/5km SW of Stockbridge. **10 E1** SU3032.

Broughton *Lancs.* Population: 1310. ***Village***, 4m/6km N of Preston. **55 J6** SD5235.

Broughton *M.K.* ***Village***, 3m/4km SE of Newport Pagnell. **32 B4** SP8940.

Broughton *N.Lincs.* Population: 4448. ***Village***, 3m/5km NW of Brigg. **52 C2** SE9608.

Broughton *N.Yorks.* ***Hamlet***, 3m/5km W of Skipton. Hall dates from mid-18c. **56 E4** SD9451.

Broughton *N.Yorks.* ***Village***, 2m/3km NW of Malton. **58 D2** SE7673.

Broughton *Northants.* Population: 2005. ***Village***, 3m/4km SW of Kettering. **32 B1** SP8375.

Broughton *Ork.* ***Settlement***, on clifftop to S of Bay of Pierowall, Westray. **106 D3** HY4448.

Broughton *Oxon.* ***Village***, 3m/5km SW of Banbury. **31 F5** SP4238.

Broughton *Sc.Bord.* ***Village***, 4m/7km E of Biggar. **75 K7** NT1136.

Broughton *V. of Glam.* ***Hamlet***, 6m/9km S of Bridgend. **18 C4** SS9270.

Broughton Astley *Leics.* Population: 6487. ***Village***, 5m/8km N of Lutterworth. **41 H6** SP5292.

Broughton Bay *Swan.* ***Bay***, 1m/2km W of Llanmadoc. **17 H5** SS4293.

Broughton Beck *Cumb.* ***Hamlet***, 3m/4km N of Ulverston. **55 F1** SD2882.

Broughton Castle *Oxon.* ***Historic house***, in Broughton, 2m/3km SW of Banbury Cross. 14c family home of Lord Saye and Sele, built by John de Broughton, and used as secret meeting place for Parliamentarians during Civil War. Moated, with 3 acres of mixed bordered gardens. **31 F5** SP4138.

Broughton Common (The Common). *Wilts.* ***Hamlet***, 2m/3km W of Melksham. ST8764.

Broughton Cross *Cumb.* ***Locality***, 3m/5km W of Cockermouth, adjoining to W of Brigham. NY0730.

Broughton Gifford *Wilts.* ***Village***, 2m/3km W of Melksham. **20 B5** ST8763.

Broughton Green *Worcs.* ***Hamlet***, 4m/6km SE of Droitwich Spa. SO9560.

Broughton Hackett *Worcs.* ***Village***, 5m/8km E of Worcester. **29 J3** SO9254.

Broughton Heights *Sc.Bord.* ***Mountain***, 3m/5km NE of Skirling. Height 1873 feet or 571 metres. **75 K6** NT1141.

Broughton House *D. & G.* ***Historic house***, Georgian mansion on River Dee, in Kirkcudbright, containing museum and art gallery. Gardens. **65 G5** NX6851.

Broughton in Furness *Cumb.* ***Village***, 8m/12km NW of Ulverston. **55 F1** SD2187.

Broughton Mills *Cumb.* ***Hamlet***, 2m/3km N of Broughton in Furness. **60 D7** SD2290.

Broughton Moor *Cumb.* ***Village***, 2m/3km SE of Maryport. **60 B3** NY0533.

Broughton Park *Gt.Man.* ***Suburb***, with small lake, 2m/3km N of Salford city centre. SD8302.

Broughton Poggs *Oxon.* ***Village***, 3m/5km NE of Lechlade. **21 F1** SP2303.

Broughtown *Ork.* ***Settlement***, on Sanday, 1km SW of head of Otters Wick bay. **106 F3** HY6641.

Broughty Castle *Dundee* ***Castle***, 15c castle (Historic Scotland), located at Broughty Ferry. **83 F4** NO4630.

Broughty Ferry *Dundee* ***Suburb***, 4m/6km E of Dundee city centre. **83 F4** NO4631.

Brow of the Hill *Norf.* ***Locality***, 4m/7km E of King's Lynn. TF6819.

Brow Well *D. & G.* ***Other feature of interest***, 3m/5km S of Carrutherstown. Ancient mineral well, visited by Robert Burns. **69 F7** NY0867.

Browland *Shet.* ***Settlement***, on Mainland, on E side of Voe of Browland. **109 B7** HU2651.

Brown Bank Head *N.Yorks.* ***Mountain***, moorland summit on Rocking Moor, 4m/7km NW of Blubberhouses. Height 1345 feet or 410 metres. **57 G4** SE1058.

Brown Candover *Hants.* ***Village***, 4m/7km N of New Alresford. **11 G1** SU5739.

Brown Carrick Hill *S.Ayr.* ***Hill***, commanding wide views, 2m/3km E of Dunure. Height 941 feet or 287 metres. **67 G2** NS2815.

Brown Caterthun *Angus* ***Historic/prehistoric site***, Iron Age fort with four concentric entrenchments, 5m/8km NW of Brechin. **83 G1** NO5566.

Brown Clee Hill *Shrop.* ***Mountain***, prominent mountain and landmark, 9m/15km NE of Ludlow. Height 1771 feet or 540 metres. **38 E7** SO5986.

Brown Cow Hill *Aber.* ***Mountain***, 3m/4km E of Loch Builg and 9m/15km SE of Tomintoul. Height 2699 feet or 823 metres. **89 K4** NJ2204.

Brown Edge *Lancs.* ***Hamlet***, 2m/4km SE of Southport. **48 C1** SD3614.

Brown Edge *Mersey.* ***Suburb***, 2m/3km SW of St. Helens town centre. SJ4993.

Brown Edge *Staffs.* ***Village***, 3m/5km SE of Biddulph. **49 J7** SJ9053.

Brown Gelly *Cornw.* ***Mountain***, on Browngelly Downs, 3m/5km N of St. Neot. Height 1122 feet or 342 metres. **4 B3** SX1972.

Brown Head *N.Ayr.* ***Coastal feature***, headland on SW coast of Arran, 2m/3km S of Blackwaterfoot. **66 C1** NR9025.

Brown Heath *Ches.* ***Hamlet***, 4m/6km E of Chester. SJ4564.

Brown Heath *Hants.* ***Settlement***, 2m/3km NE of Botley. SU5216.

Brown Knoll *Derbys.* ***Mountain***, in High Peak 3m/4km W of Edale. Height 1866 feet or 569 metres. **50 C4** SK0885.

Brown Lees *Staffs.* ***Suburb***, to SW of Biddulph. **49 H7** SJ8756.

Brown Ridge *N.Yorks.* ***Open space***, moorland between Nidderdale and Masham Moor, 3m/5km N of Lofthouse and 8m/12km W of Masham. **57 F2** SE0977.

Brown Street *Suff.* ***Settlement***, 3m/5km N of Stowmarket. TM0663.

Brown Willy *Cornw.* ***Mountain***, granite tor on Bodmin Moor, 4m/7km SE of Camelford. Highest point in Cornwall. Height 1378 feet or 420 metres. **4 B3** SX1579.

Brownber *Cumb.* ***Hamlet***, 1km N of Newbiggin-on-Lune and 6m/9km E of Tebay. NY7005.

Brownbread Street *E.Suss.* ***Settlement***, 5m/7km W of Battle. TQ6715.

Browndown *Hants.* ***Suburb***, 3m/4km W of Gosport town centre. Rifle ranges. SZ5899.

Brownedge *Lancs.* ***Locality***, 2m/4km SE of Preston. SD5526.

Browney *Dur.* ***River***, rising S of Consett and flowing E into River Wear 3m/4km S of Durham. **62 D2** NZ2738.

Brownheath *Shrop.* ***Hamlet***, 3m/5km W of Wem. SJ4629.

Brownhill *Aber.* ***Settlement***, 2m/3km N of Methlick. **99 G6** NJ8640.

Brownhill *B'burn.* ***Suburb***, 2m/3km N of Blackburn town centre. SD6830.

Brownhills *Fife* ***Hamlet***, 1m/2km SE of St. Andrews. **83 G6** NO5315.

Brownhills *W.Mid.* Population: 18,159. ***Town***, former mining town, 5m/8km NE of Walsall. **40 C5** SK0405.

Brownieside *Northumb.* ***Hamlet***, 1km NW of North Charlton. **71 G1** NU1623.

Browninghill Green *Hants.* ***Hamlet***, 4m/6km E of Kingsclere. SU5859.

Brownlow *Ches.* ***Settlement***, 2m/4km SW of Congleton. SJ8361.

Brownlow Heath *Ches.* ***Locality***, 1km S of Brownlow. **49 H6** SJ8260.

Brownrigg Head *Northumb.* ***Mountain***, to W of Blakehope Fell, 3m/4km S of Rochester. Height 1197 feet or 365 metres. **70 C4** NY8194.

Brown's Bank *Ches.* ***Settlement***, 1m/2km SW of Audlem. SJ6443.

Brown's Green *W.Mid.* ***Suburb***, 3m/5km NW of Birmingham city centre. SP0491.

Brownsea Island *Dorset* ***Island***, largest island in Poole Harbour, about 1m/2km by 1km. Nature reserve. Remains of Tudor castle at E end. The Scout movement was started here in 1907. Island is National Trust property. **10 A6** SZ0288.

Brownshill *Glos.* ***Village***, 3m/5km SE of Stroud. SO8802.

Brownshill Green *W.Mid.* ***Suburb***, 3m/5km NW of Coventry city centre. **41 F7** SP3082.

Brownside *Lancs.* ***Suburb***, 2m/3km E of Burnley, on E side of River Brun. SD8632.

Brownsover *Warks.* ***Suburb***, on N edge of Rugby. SP5177.

Brownston *Devon* ***Village***, 3m/4km E of Modbury. **5 G5** SX6952.

Brownstone *Devon* ***Locality***, 2m/3km SE of Dartmouth across River Dart estuary. SX9050.

Browsholme Hall *Lancs.* ***Historic house***, 4m/7km NW of Clitheroe, property of Parker family, whose ancestors built house in 1507. Has stained glass from Whalley Abbey. **56 B5** SD6845.

Browston Green *Norf.* ***Hamlet***, 4m/6km SW of Great Yarmouth town centre. TG4901.

Broxa *N.Yorks.* ***Hamlet***, 6m/10km W of Scarborough. **63 J3** SE9491.

Broxa Forest *N.Yorks.* ***Forest/woodland***, afforested area on E side of Derwent valley, 6m/10km NW of Scarborough. **63 J3** SE9493.

Broxbourne *Herts.* ***Suburb***, 1m/2km S of Hoddesdon. **23 G1** TL3707.

Broxbourne Nature Reserve *Herts.* ***Forest/woodland***, 3m/5km S of Hertford. **23 G1** TL3207.

Broxburn *E.Loth.* ***Hamlet***, 1m/2km SE of Dunbar. **76 E3** NT6977.

Broxburn *W.Loth.* Population: 11,607. ***Town***, 11m/18km W of Edinburgh. **75 J3** NT0872.

Broxholme *Lincs.* ***Settlement***, 6m/9km NW of Lincoln. **52 C5** SK9177.

Broxted *Essex* ***Village***, 3m/5km SW of Thaxted. **33 J6** TL5727.

Broxton *Ches.* ***Hamlet***, 8m/13km N of Whitchurch. **48 D7** SJ4754.

Broxwood *Here.* ***Village***, 5m/7km E of Kington. **28 C3** SO3654.

Broyle Side *E.Suss.* ***Village***, 1m/2km NE of Ringmer and 4m/6km NE of Lewes. TQ4613.

Bru (Anglicised form: Brue.) *W.Isles* ***Village***, near NW coast of Isle of Lewis, 1m/2km W of Barvas across River Barvas. **101 F2** NB3449.

Bruach na Frithe *High.* ***Mountain***, peak of Cuillin Hills, Skye. Munro: height 3142 feet or 958 metres. **85 K2** NG4625.

Bruachmary *High.* ***Settlement***, 6m/10km S of Nairn. **97 F7** NH8846.

Bruan *High.* ***Settlement***, on E coast of Caithness district, 5m/8km NE of Lybster. **105 J5** ND3039.

Bruar Water *P. & K.* ***River***, running S down Glen Bruar to River Garry, 3m/5km W of Blair Atholl. Falls of the Bruar 1m/2km NE of Calvine. **89 F7** NN8265.

Brucefield *W.Loth.* ***Village***, 3m/4km SW of Livingston. NT0464.

Brucehill *W.Dun.* ***Suburb***, to W of Dumbarton town centre. NS3875.

Bruce's Stone (The King's Stone). *D. & G.* ***Other feature of interest***, granite boulder on E shore of Clatteringshaws Loch, 5m/8km W of New Galloway. Marks site of battle of 1307 in which Robert the Bruce defeated English. **65 F3** NX5576.

Brucklay *Aber.* ***Locality***, comprising Brucklay Castle and Brucklay House, 3m/5km S of Strichen. NJ9150.

Brue *Som.* ***River***, rising about 5m/8km E of Bruton and flowing W into River Parrett estuary, 1m/2km S of Burnham-on-Sea. **19 H7** ST3047.

Brue *W.Isles Anglicised form of Bru, qv.*

Bruera *Ches.* ***Settlement***, 4m/7km SE of Chester town centre. **48 D6** SJ4360.

Bruern *Oxon.* ***Settlement***, 5m/8km N of Burford. SP2620.

Bruernish *W.Isles* ***Settlement***, on NE coast of Barra, 1km SE of Northbay. NF7202.

Bruernish Point *W.Isles* ***Coastal feature***, 1m/2km SE of Bruernish. **84 C4** NF7300.

Bruiach Burn *High.* ***River***, flowing E from Loch Bruicheach, then NE through Boblainy Forest and into River Beauly, 1m/2km N of Kiltarlity. **88 B1** NH5043.

Bruichladdich *Arg. & B.* ***Village***, on W side of Loch Indaal, Islay, 2m/3km N of Port Charlotte. **72 A4** NR2661.

Bruisyard *Suff.* ***Village***, 3m/5km NE of Framlingham. **35 H2** TM3266.

Bruisyard Street *Suff.* ***Village***, 1m/2km E of Bruisyard. **35 H2** TM3266.

Brumby *N.Lincs.* ***Suburb***, 1m/2km S of Scunthorpe town centre. SE8909.

Brumstead *Norf.* ***Locality***, 1m/2km NE of Stalham. TG3626.

Brund *Staffs.* ***Settlement***, 2m/3km NW of Hartington. **50 D6** SK1061.

Brundall *Norf.* Population: 6076. ***Village***, 6m/10km E of Norwich. **45 H5** TG3208.

Brundish *Norf.* ***Settlement***, 1km S of Raveningham. TM3995.

Brundish *Suff.* ***Village***, 4m/6km N of Framlingham. **35 G2** TM2769.

Brundish Street *Suff.* ***Hamlet***, 1m/2km NW of Brundish. **35 G1** TM2670.

Brunery Hill *High.* ***Mountain***, 2m/3km NE of Ardmolich, Lochaber district. Height 1548 feet or 472 metres. **86 D7** NM7373.

Brunshaw *Lancs.* ***Suburb***, 1m/2km E of Burnley town centre. SD8532.

Brunstock *Cumb.* ***Hamlet***, 2m/3km NE of Carlisle. NY4159.

Brunswick Village *T. & W.* ***Village***, 5m/8km N of Newcastle upon Tyne. NZ2372.

Brunt Hill *E.Loth.* ***Hill***, 3m/4km S of Dunbar. Height 738 feet or 225 metres. **76 E3** NT6774.

Bruntcliffe *W.Yorks.* ***Locality***, 1m/2km W of Morley. SE2427.

Bruntingthorpe *Leics.* ***Village***, 4m/7km NW of Husbands Bosworth. Airfield to S. **41 J7** SP6089.

Bruntland *Aber.* ***Settlement***, 3m/4km W of Rhynie. **90 C2** NJ4528.

Brunton *Fife* ***Village***, 5m/8km NW of Cupar. **82 E5** NO3220.

Brunton *Northumb.* ***Hamlet***, 2m/3km NW of Embleton. **71 H1** NU2024.

Brunton *Northumb.* ***Hamlet***, on line of Hadrian's Wall, 1km NE of Wall. NY9269.

Brunton *T. & W.* ***Locality***, adjoining to N of Gosforth. NZ2370.

Brunton *Wilts.* ***Hamlet***, 1km NE of Collingbourne Kingston and 4m/6km N of Ludgershall. SU2456.

Brunton Turret *Northumb.* ***Historic/prehistoric site***, remains of turret (English Heritage) on Hadrian's Wall, 1m/2km W of Walwick and 5m/8km NE of Fourstones. **70 E7** NY9269.

Bruntsfield *Edin.* ***Suburb***, 1m/2km SW of Edinburgh city centre. NT2472.

Bruntshiel Hill *D. & G.* ***Hill***, rising to over 250 metres in Tinnisburn Forest, 3m/5km E of Langholm. **69 K5** NY4182.

Bruray *Shet.* ***Island***, second largest of Out Skerries group of islands, NE of Whalsay. Island is connected to Housay by a road bridge. **108 F5** HU6972.

Brushes *Gt.Man.* ***Suburb***, 1m/2km E of Stalybridge. SJ9799.

Brushfield *Derbys.* ***Settlement***, 1m/2km E of Taddington. SK1571.

Brushford *Devon* ***Hamlet***, 3m/4km E of Winkleigh. SS6707.

Brushford *Som.* ***Village***, 2m/3km SE of Dulverton. **7 H3** SS9225.

Brushford Barton *Devon* ***Hamlet***, location of Brushford parish church. **6 E5** SS6707.

Bruton *Som.* Population: 2111. ***Small town***, 7m/11km SE of Shepton Mallet. Many buildings made of Doulting stone. **9 F1** ST6834.

Brux Hill *Aber.* ***Mountain***, 4m/6km S of Rhynie. Height 1558 feet or 475 metres. **90 D2** NJ5021.

Bruxie Hill *Aber.* ***Hill***, 3m/5km E of Glenbervie. Mast at summit. Height 708 feet or 216 metres. **91 G6** NO8280.

Bryan's Green *Worcs.* ***Hamlet***, 3m/5km N of Droitwich Spa. SO8868.

Bryanston *Dorset* ***Village***, 1m/2km W of Blandford Forum across River Stour. Boys' school in landscaped park. **9 H4** ST8607.

Bryant's Bottom *Bucks.* ***Hamlet***, 4m/7km N of High Wycombe. SU8599.

Brydekirk *D. & G.* ***Village***, 3m/4km N of Annan. **69 G6** NY1870.

Bryher *I.o.S.* ***Island***, smallest of five inhabited islands of Isles of Scilly. **2 B1** SV8714.

Brylach Hill *Moray* ***Mountain***, 3m/5km NW of Rothes. Height 1066 feet or 325 metres. **97 K6** NJ2352.

Brymbo *Wrex.* Population: 4930. ***Small town***, 3m/5km NW of Wrexham. Former steel working centre. **48 B7** SJ2953.

Brympton *Som.* ***Hamlet***, 2m/4km W of Yeovil. ST5115.

Bryn *Caerp.* ***Suburb***, S district of Pontllanfraith, 1m/2km S of Blackwood. ST1795.

Bryn *Carmar.* ***Village***, 3m/4km E of Llanelli. **17 J4** SN5400.

Bryn *Ches.* ***Hamlet***, 4m/6km W of Northwich. SJ6072.

Bryn *Gt.Man.* ***Suburb***, adjoining to N of Ashton-in-Makerfield. **48 E2** SD5700.

Bryn *N.P.T.* ***Village***, 4m/6km NE of Port Talbot. **18 B2** SS8192.

Bryn *Powys* ***Mountain***, 3m/4km N of Beulah. Height 1571 feet or 479 metres. **27 J3** SN9055.

Bryn *Powys* ***Mountain***, 4m/6km SE of Brecon. Height 1840 feet or 561 metres. **27 K6** SO0722.

Bryn *Shrop.* ***Hamlet***, 3m/5km N of Clun. **38 B7** SO2985.

Bryn Amlwg *Powys* ***Mountain***, 2m/3km S of Talerddig. Height 1601 feet or 488 metres. **37 J6** SN9297.

Bryn arrw *Mon.* ***Mountain***, 3m/4km N of Abergavenny. Height 1250 feet or 381 metres. **28 B6** SO3019.

Bryn Bras Castle *Gwyn.* ***Historic house***, 3m/4km NW of Llanberis. 19c neo-Norman mansion, with fine views of Snowdon and Anglesey. Attractive gardens, with walled knot garden being particularly notable. **46 D6** SH5462.

Bryn Brawd *Cere.* ***Mountain***, 3m/5km SE of Llanddewi-Brefi. Height 1588 feet or 484 metres. **27 F3** SN6951.

Bryn Bugeiliaid *Powys* ***Mountain***, 3m/4km E of Abercraf. Height 1253 feet or 382 metres. **27 H7** SN8513.

Bryn-bwbach *Gwyn.* ***Hamlet***, 3m/5km SW of Maentwrog. SH6237.

Bryn Celin *Flints.* ***Suburb***, toN of Holywell. SJ1876.

Bryn Celli Ddu *I.o.A.* ***Historic/prehistoric site***, ancient stone circles and restored Neolithic passage grave (Cadw) on Anglesey, 3m/5km W of Menai Bridge. **46 D5** SH5170.

Bryn-côch *N.P.T.* ***Village***, 2m/3km NW of Neath. **18 A2** SS7499.

Bryn Crugog *Powys* ***Mountain***, 4m/6km E of Staylittle. Height 1463 feet or 446 metres. **37 J6** SN9492.

Bryn Crwn *Powys* ***Mountain***, 3m/5km N of Cefn Coch. Height 1745 feet or 532 metres. **27 H3** SN8257.

Bryn Du *Powys* ***Mountain***, 3m/5km S of Llangammarch Wells. Height 1519 feet or 463 metres. **27 J4** SN9342.

Bryn Du *Wrex.* ***Open space***, hillslope 2m/3km N of Llanarmon Dyffryn Ceiriog. **38 A2** SJ1535.

Bryn Eden *Gwyn.* ***Settlement***, 4m/6km S of Trawsfynydd. SH7129.

Bryn Eglwys *Gwyn.* ***Village***, 1m/2km W of Bethesda. SH6066.

Bryn Garw *Cere.* ***Mountain***, rising to over 560 metres, 3m/4km NE of Cwmystwyth. **27 H1** SN8076.

Bryn Gates *Gt.Man.* ***Village***, 2m/3km NE of Ashton-in-Makerfield. **48 E2** SD5901.

Bryn Golau *R.C.T.* ***Village***, adjoining to W of Tonyrefail. ST0088.

Bryn Gydfa *Powys* ***Mountain***, 3m/4km NE of Llanbadarn. Height 1571 feet or 479 metres. **38 A7** SO1280.

Bryn-henllan *Pembs.* ***Village***, 1m/2km S of Dinas Head. **16 D1** SN0039.

Bryn Llyndŵr *Powys Welsh form of Bryn-dŵr Hill, qv.*

Bryn-mawr *B.Gwent* Population: 14,581. ***Town***, on N edge of South Wales valleys, 7m/11km W of Abergavenny. **28 A7** SO1911.

Bryn-mawr *Gwyn.* ***Hamlet***, 2m/3km S of Tudweiliog. SH2433.

Bryn Meurig *I.o.A.* ***Settlement***, 2m/3km NE of Menai Bridge. SH5874.

Bryn Moel *Powys* ***Mountain***, 3m/5km N of Plynlimon. Height 1610 feet or 491 metres. **37 G6** SN7791.

Bryn Nicol *Carmar.* ***Mountain***, rising to over 460 metres, 6m/10km SW of Llanwrtyd Wells. **27 H4** SN8244.

Bryn Pen-y-lan *Wrex.* ***Hamlet***, 2m/3km E of Ruabon. SJ3342.

Bryn-penarth *Powys* ***Settlement***, 1m/2km S of Llanfair Caereinion. SJ1004.

Bryn Rhudd *Cere.* ***Mountain***, rising to over 470 metres, 2m/3km E of Llanddewi-Brefi. **27 F3** SN6955.

Bryn Tail Lead Mine Buildings *Powys* ***Other feature of interest***, preserved 19c lead mine near foot of Llyn Clywedog Reservoir, 3m/4km NW of Llandiloes. Now an open-air museum. **37 J7** SN9186.

Bryn Teg *Wrex.* ***Suburb***, 3m/4km NW of Wrexham town centre. **48 C7** SJ3052.

Bryn Titley *Powys* ***Mountain***, 3m/5km SE of Llangurig. Height 1610 feet or 491 metres. **27 J1** SN9375.

Bryn Trillyn *Conwy* ***Mountain***, 6m/10km N of Cerrigydrudion. Height 1627 feet or 496 metres. **47 H7** SH9459.

Bryn y Castell *Powys See Knighton.*

Bryn y Castell *Powys* ***Mountain***, 5m/8km N of Carno. Height 1204 feet or 367 metres. **37 J5** SH9704.

Bryn-y-cochin *Shrop.* ***Hamlet***, 2m/4km W of Ellesmere. SJ3635.

Bryn y Fedwen *Powys* ***Mountain***, rising to over 540 metres, 3m/5km NW of Staylittle. **37 H6** SN8495.

Bryn-y-maen *Conwy* ***Hamlet***, 2m/3km S of Colwyn Bay. **47 G5** SH8376.

Bryn-y-maen *Powys* ***Mountain***, 9m/14km W of Kington. Height 1578 feet or 481 metres. **28 A3** SO1657.

Bryn-y-mor *Gwyn.* ***Locality***, on coast on W side of Tywyn. SH5700.

Bryn-y-Tail *Powys* ***Mountain***, rising from SE shore of Llyn Clywedog. Height 1322 feet or 403 metres. **37 J7** SN9187.

Bryn-yr-Eos *Wrex.* ***Hamlet***, 2m/3km N of Chirk. SJ2840.

Brynamman *Carmar.* Population: 2956. ***Locality***, 6m/9km E of Ammanford. **27 G7** SN7114.

Brynawel *Caerp.* ***Hamlet***, 2m/4km W of Risca. ST2091.

Brynberian *Pembs.* ***Hamlet***, 4m/6km SE of Newport. **16 E1** SN1035.

Brynbryddan *N.P.T.* ***Suburb***, adjoining to W of Cwmafan, 2m/3km N of Port Talbot. SS7792.

Brynbuga *Mon. Welsh form of Usk, qv.*

Bryncae *R.C.T.* ***Village***, 1km W of Llanharan. **18 C3** SS9982.

Bryncethin *Bridgend* ***Village***, 3m/5km N of Bridgend. **18 C3** SS9184.

Bryncir *Gwyn.* ***Hamlet***, 4m/7km N of Criccieth. **36 D1** SH4884.

Bryncoch *Bridgend* ***Village***, adjoining to NE of Sarn, 3m/4km N of Bridgend. SS9183.

Bryncroes *Gwyn.* ***Hamlet***, 5m/7km NE of Aberdaron. **36 B2** SH2231.

Bryncrug *Gwyn.* ***Village***, 2m/4km NE of Tywyn. **37 F5** SH6003.

Bryneglwys *Denb.* ***Village***, 5m/8km NE of Corwen. **38 A1** SJ1447.

Brynfields *Wrex.* ***Suburb***, on E side of Ruabon. SJ3044.

Brynford *Flints.* ***Village***, 1m/2km SW of Holywell. **47 K5** SJ1774.

Bryngarw Country Park *Bridgend* ***Leisure/recreation***, 3m/5km N of Bridgend in beautiful and largely unspoiled Garw valley. House contains restaurant and conference facilities, while gardens are notable for flower collections and woodlands. **18 C3** SS9085.

Bryngias *Newport* ***Suburb***, 1m/2km N of Newport town centre. ST3089.

Bryngwran *I.o.A.* ***Village***, on Anglesey, 4m/6km E of Valley. **46 B5** SH3577.

Bryngwyn *Mon.* ***Hamlet***, 2m/3km NW of Raglan. **19 G1** SO3909.

Bryngwyn *Powys* ***Hamlet***, 5m/8km NW of Hay-on-Wye. **28 A4** SO1849.

Brynhoffnant *Cere.* ***Hamlet***, 2m/3km SE of Llangranog. **26 C3** SN3351.

Brynhyfryd *Swan.* ***Suburb***, 2m/3km N of Swansea city centre. SS6596.

Bryning *Lancs.* ***Settlement***, 2m/3km SW of Kirkham. SD4029.

Brynithel *B.Gwent* ***Village***, 2m/3km SW of Abertillery. SO2101.

Brynmelyn *Powys* ***Settlement***, 3m/4km E of Llanbister. **28 A1** SO1473.

Brynmenyn *Bridgend* ***Hamlet***, 3m/5km N of Bridgend. **18 C3** SS9084.

Brynmill *Swan.* ***Suburb***, 1m/2km W of Swansea city centre. University College of Swansea to W. SS6392.

Brynna *R.C.T.* ***Village***, 5m/8km E of Bridgend. **18 C3** SS9883.

Brynnau Gwynion *R.C.T.* ***Village***, 1m/2km NE of Pencoed. SS9782.

Brynog *Cere.* ***Settlement***, on N bank of River Aeron, 6m/9km SE of Aberaeron. **26 E3** SN5357.

Brynowen *Cere.* ***Settlement***, 1m/2km S of Borth. SN6088.

Brynrefail *Gwyn.* ***Village***, 2m/3km NW of Llanberis at N end of Llyn Padarn. **46 D6** SH5562.

Brynrefail *I.o.A.* ***Hamlet***, on Anglesey, 5m/7km SE of Amlwch. **46 C4** SH4886.

Brynrodyn *Cere.* ***Settlement***, 1m/2km S of Borth. SN6088.

Brynsadler *R.C.T.* ***Village***, 2m/3km SW of Llantrisant. **18 D3** ST0280.

Brynsaithmarchog *Denb.* ***Hamlet***, 4m/7km N of Corwen. SJ0750.

Brynsiencyn *I.o.A.* ***Village***, on Anglesey, 6m/9km SW of Menai Bridge. **46 C6** SH4867.

Brynteg *I.o.A.* ***Hamlet***, on Anglesey, 5m/8km NE of Llangefni. **46 C4** SH4982.

Brynteg *R.C.T.* ***Hamlet***, 1km NE of Llantrisant. ST0683.

Brynteg *Wrex.* ***Village***, 2m/4km NW of Wrexham. SJ3052.

Brynygwenin *Mon.* ***Hamlet***, 2m/4km NE of Abergavenny. SO3316.

Bu Ness *Shet.* ***Coastal feature***, promontory on E coast of Fair Isle, approximately 1km from N to S, connected to Mainland by narrow neck of land. **108 A1** HZ2272.

Buachaille Etive Beag *High.* ***Large natural feature***, ridge in Lochaber district, to S of Glen Coe and W of Buachaille Etive Mòr. Summit is Stob Dubh at SW end of ridge; Munro at height of 3142 feet or 958 metres. **80 C2** NN1753.

Buachaille Etive Mòr *High.* ***Large natural feature***, mountain mass (National Trust for Scotland) on Royal Forest, on N side of Glen Etive, Lochaber district. Summit is Stob Dearg, at NE end; Munro at height of 3352 feet or 1022 metres. **80 D2** NN2254.

Buaile an Ochd *W.Isles* ***Settlement***, on E coast of Isle of Lewis, on S side of Bac. NB4839.

Buaile nam Bodach (Anglicised form: Balnabodach.) *W.Isles* ***Settlement***, on E part of Barra, 4m/6km NE of Castlebay. **84 C4** NF7101.

Bualadubh *W.Isles* ***Settlement***, at N end of South Uist, 3m/5km E of Ardivachar Point. NF7846.

Bualintur *High.* ***Settlement***, in SW part of Skye, at head of Loch Brittle. **85 K2** NG4020.

Bualnaluib *High.* ***Settlement***, on E shore of Loch Ewe, Ross and Cromarty district, 1m/2km NW of Aultbea. **94 E3** NG8690.

Bubbenhall *Warks.* ***Village***, 5m/8km NE of Royal Leamington Spa. **30 E1** SP3672.

Bubbleton *Pembs.* ***Locality***, 2m/4km SW of Tenby. SS0999.

Bubnell *Derbys.* ***Settlement***, on River Derwent, 1km NW of Baslow. SK2472.

Bubwith *E.Riding* ***Village***, on E bank of River Derwent, 5m/9km NW of Howden. **58 D6** SE7136.

Buccleuch *Sc.Bord.* ***Hamlet***, on Rankle Burn, 11m/18km W of Hawick. **69 J2** NT3214.

Buchan *Aber.* ***Locality***, stretch of country lying roughly NE of a line drawn from Banff, on N coast, to Newburgh, on E. **99 G5** NJ9549.

Buchan *D. & G.* ***Settlement***, on W bank of Carlingwark Loch, 1km S of Castle Douglas. **65 H4** NX7561.

Buchan Burn *D. & G.* ***River***, rising on S side of Mewick and flowing S, with waterfalls, to Loch Troon, 5m/8km NE of Bargrennan. **67 J5** NX4181.

Buchan Country Park *W.Suss.* ***Leisure/recreation***, country park with visitor centre, 2m/3km SW of Crawley centre. Two ponds are focal point of this country park which is otherwise predominantly woodland. **13 F3** TQ2434.

Buchan Hill *D. & G.* ***Mountain***, 1m/2km N of Loch Trool, 6m/9km NE of Bangrennan. Height 1617 feet or 493 metres. **67 J5** NX4281.

Buchan Ness *Aber.* ***Coastal feature***, headland with lighthouse on E coast, 3m/4km S of Peterhead. **99 K6** NK1342.
Buchanan Castle *Stir.* ***Castle***, remains of former seat of Duke of Montrose, 1km W of Drymen. **74 C2** NS4688.
Buchanhaven *Aber.* ***Suburb***, N district of Peterhead. **99 K6** NK1247.
Buchanty *P. & K.* ***Settlement***, in Glen Almond, 6m/9km NE of Crieff. **82 A5** NN9328.
Buchlyvie *Stir.* ***Village***, 14m/22km W of Stirling. **74 D1** NS5793.
Bucinch *Stir.* ***Island***, wooded islet (National Trust for Scotland) in Loch Lomond, 2m/4km W of Balmaha. NS3891.
Buckabank *Cumb.* ***Hamlet***, 1m/2km S of Dalston. **60 E2** NY3749.
Buckby Wharf *Northants.* ***Locality***, on Grand Union Canal, 3m/5km NE of Daventry. **31 H2** SP6165.
Buckden *Cambs.* Population: 2534. ***Village***, 4m/6km SW of Huntingdon. **32 E2** TL1967.
Buckden *N.Yorks.* ***Village***, in Upper Wharfedale, 4m/6km N of Kettlewell. **56 E2** SD9477.
Buckden Pike *N.Yorks.* ***Mountain***, to NE of Buckden. Height 2303 feet or 702 metres. **56 E2** SD9678.
Buckenham *Norf.* ***Hamlet***, 4m/6km SW of Acle. **45 H5** TG3506.
Buckenhill *Here.* ***Locality***, 1m/2km N of Bromyard. SO6556.
Buckerell *Devon* ***Locality***, 3m/4km W of Honiton. **7 K5** ST1200.
Buckfast *Devon* ***Village***, 1m/2km N of Buckfastleigh, 20c abbey. **5 H4** SX7467.
Buckfast Abbey *Devon* ***Ecclesiastical building***, 1km N of Buckfastleigh. Founded by King Canute in 1018, then refounded by King Stephen for Cistercian monks in 1147. Abandoned after Dissolution until taken over by French Benedictine monks in 1882, and subsequently rebuilt. Little remains of original building. **5 H4** SX7467.
Buckfastleigh *Devon* Population: 2786. ***Small town***, market town, once famous for woollens, 5m/8km NW of Totnes. **5 H4** SX7366.
Buckhaven *Fife* Population: 17,069. ***Town***, and former fishing port on N coast of Firth of Forth, 7m/11km NE of Kirkcaldy. Formerly a joint burgh with Methil. **76 B1** NT3698.
Buckholm *Sc.Bord.* ***Hamlet***, 2m/3km NW of Galashiels. **76 C7** NT4838.
Buckholt *Mon.* ***Settlement***, on border with England, 2m/3km N of Monmouth. SO5016.
Buckhorn Weston *Dorset* ***Village***, 4m/6km W of Gillingham. **9 G2** ST7524.
Buckhurst Hill *Essex* ***Locality***, large residential area to S of Epping Forest, 11m/17km NE of London. **23 H2** TQ4193.
Buckie *Moray* Population: 8425. ***Small town***, fishing port and resort on Spey Bay, 13m/21km E of Elgin. **98 C4** NJ4265.
Buckies *High.* ***Hamlet***, 3m/4km NW of Halkirk. **105 G2** ND1063.
Buckingham *Bucks.* Population: 10,168. ***Town***, market town on River Great Ouse, 11m/18km W of Bletchley. Chantry chapel with Norman doorway (National Trust) on Market Hill. University of Buckingham. **31 H5** SP6933.
Buckingham Palace *Gt.Lon.* ***Historic house***, in central London, 1km W of Westminster Abbey. Principal royal residence since early 18c, remodelled by Nash 1825 and Edward Blore 1830-47; refaced 1913 by Sir Aston Webb. Royal standard flies from roof when Queen is in residence. Changing of the Guard takes place daily inside palace railings. **23 F4** TQ2979.
Buckinghamshire County Museum *Bucks.* ***Other feature of interest***, in Aylesbury town centre. Includes hands-on displays on a range of different topics, as well as a Roald Dahl exhibition. **32 B7** SP8113.
Buckland *Bucks.* ***Village***, 2m/4km W of Tring. **32 B7** SP8812.
Buckland *Devon* ***Hamlet***, just N of Thurlestone, 4m/6km W of Kingsbridge. **5 G6** SX6743.
Buckland *Devon* ***Suburb***, to E of Newton Abbot. SX8771.
Buckland *Glos.* ***Village***, 1m/2km SW of Broadway. **30 B5** SP0836.
Buckland *Hants.* ***Settlement***, 1km NW of Lymington. SZ3196.
Buckland *Here.* ***Settlement***, 4m/7km E of Leominster. SO5556.
Buckland *Herts.* ***Village***, 3m/5km N of Buntingford. **33 G5** TL3533.
Buckland *Kent* ***Suburb***, 1m/2km NW of Dover town centre. **15 H3** TR3042.
Buckland *Oxon.* ***Village***, 4m/6km NE of Faringdon. **21 G2** SU3498.
Buckland *Surr.* ***Village***, 2m/3km W of Reigate. **23 F6** TQ2250.
Buckland Abbey *Devon* ***Historic house***, 1m/2km S of Buckland Monachorum. Former home of Drake family (National Trust). **4 E4** SX4866.
Buckland Brewer *Devon* ***Village***, 4m/7km SW of Bideford. **6 C3** SS4120.
Buckland Common *Bucks.* ***Village***, 4m/7km NW of Chesham. **22 C1** SP9206.
Buckland Dinham *Som.* ***Village***, 3m/4km NW of Frome. **20 A6** ST7551.
Buckland End *W.Mid.* ***Suburb***, 5m/8km E of Birmingham city centre. SP1488.
Buckland Filleigh *Devon* ***Hamlet***, 6m/9km NW of Hatherleigh. **6 C5** SS4609.
Buckland in the Moor *Devon* ***Hamlet***, on E edge of Dartmoor, 3m/5km NW of Ashburton. **5 H3** SX7273.
Buckland Monachorum *Devon* ***Village***, 4m/6km S of Tavistock. **4 E4** SX4968.
Buckland Newton *Dorset* ***Village***, 8m/13km NW of Puddletown. **9 F4** ST6905.
Buckland Rectory *Glos.* ***Historic house***, in Buckland, 1m/2km SW of Broadway. England's oldest rectory, including 15c great hall. **30 B5** SP0836.
Buckland Ripers *Dorset* ***Hamlet***, 3m/4km NW of Weymouth. SY6482.
Buckland St. Mary *Som.* ***Village***, 5m/7km NW of Chard. **8 B3** ST2713.
Buckland-tout-Saints *Devon* ***Hamlet***, 2m/3km NE of Kingsbridge. **5 H6** SX7546.
Buckland Valley *Kent* ***Suburb***, 1m/2km N of Dover town centre. TR3043.
Bucklandwharf *Bucks.* ***Hamlet***, on section of Old Grand Union Canal, 2m/3km W of Tring. SP8911.
Bucklebury *W.Berks.* ***Village***, 6m/9km NE of Newbury. **21 J4** SU5570.
Bucklegate *Lincs.* ***Settlement***, 3m/4km SE of Kirton. TF3335.
Bucklerheads *Angus* ***Hamlet***, 1km N of Kellas. **83 F4** NO4636.
Bucklers Hard *Hants.* ***Village***, with quay on Beaulieu River, 2m/3km SE of Beaulieu. Maritime museum. **11 F4** SU4000.
Bucklesham *Suff.* ***Village***, 5m/9km E of Ipswich. **35 G4** TM2441.
Buckley (Bwcle). *Flints.* Population: 17,753. ***Town***, 9m/15km N of Wrexham. **48 B6** SJ2864.
Buckley *Gt.Man.* ***Suburb***, 1m/2km NE of Rochdale town centre. SD9015.
Buckley Green *Warks.* ***Hamlet***, 1m/2km NE of Henley-in-Arden. SP1567.
Buckley Hill *Mersey.* ***Suburb***, 2m/3km N of Bootle town centre. SJ3499.
Buckley Mountain *Flints.* ***Suburb***, to N of Buckley. SJ2764.
Bucklow Hill *Ches.* ***Village***, 3m/5km NW of Knutsford. SJ7383.
Buckman Corner *W.Suss.* ***Settlement***, 2m/3km N of Billingshurst. **12 D4** TQ0929.
Buckminster *Leics.* ***Village***, 3m/5km W of Colsterworth. **42 B3** SK8722.
Bucknall *Lincs.* ***Village***, 3m/5km E of Bardney. **52 E6** TF1668.
Bucknall *Stoke* ***Suburb***, 1m/2km E of Hanley. **40 B1** SJ9047.
Bucknell *Oxon.* ***Village***, 3m/4km NW of Bicester. **31 G6** SP5525.
Bucknell *Shrop.* ***Village***, 4m/7km E of Knighton. **28 C1** SO3573.
Buckny Burn *P. & K.* ***River***, stream rising in mountains of Forest of Clunie, and flowing SE to join Lunan Burn, 4m/7km NE of Dunkeld. **82 B3** NO0845.
Buckpool *Moray* ***Suburb***, to W of Buckie, on N coast. NJ4165.
Buckpool *W.Mid.* ***Suburb***, 4m/6km SW of Dudley town centre. SO8986.
Buckridge *Worcs.* ***Hamlet***, 4m/7km W of Bewdley. SO7274.
Buck's Cross *Devon* ***Hamlet***, 2m/4km SE of Clovelly. **6 B3** SS3422.
Bucks Green *W.Suss.* ***Hamlet***, 3m/5km SE of Alfold Crossways. **12 D3** TQ0832.
Bucks Hill *Herts.* ***Hamlet***, 4m/6km NW of Watford. **22 D1** TL0500.
Bucks Horn Oak *Hants.* ***Hamlet***, in Alice Holt Forest, 4m/6km SW of Farnham. **22 B7** SU8041.
Buck's Mills *Devon* ***Hamlet***, in steeply descending coombe above Barnstaple (or Bideford) Bay, 3m/4km SE of Clovelly. **6 B3** SS3523.
Bucksburn *Aberdeen* ***Suburb***, to NW of Aberdeen. **91 G4** NJ8909.
Buckskin *Hants.* ***Suburb***, W district of Basingstoke. SU6051.
Buckspool *Pembs.* ***Hamlet***, to S of Bosherston, 1m/2km NW of St. Govan's Head. **16 C5** SR9694.
Buckton *E.Riding* ***Hamlet***, 4m/6km N of Bridlington. **59 H2** TA1872.
Buckton *Here.* ***Hamlet***, 6m/10km E of Knighton. **28 C1** SO3873.
Buckton *Northumb.* ***Hamlet***, 3m/5km NW of Belford. **77 J7** NU0838.
Buckton Vale *Gt.Man.* ***Village***, 2m/3km NE of Stalybridge. SD9800.
Buckworth *Cambs.* ***Village***, 6m/10km NW of Huntingdon. **32 E1** TL1476.
Budbrooke *Warks.* Population: 1969. ***Village***, 2m/3km W of Warwick. **30 D2** SP2565.
Budby *Notts.* ***Hamlet***, 3m/5km NW of Ollerton. **51 J6** SK6170.
Buddo Ness *Fife* ***Coastal feature***, rocky headland on North Sea coast, 3m/5km SE of St. Andrews. **83 G6** NO5515.
Buddon Ness *Angus* ***Coastal feature***, low headland on N side of entrance to Firth of Tay, 3m/5km S of Carnoustie. **83 G5** NO5430.
Budd's Titson *Cornw.* *Alternative name for Titson, qv.*
Bude (Bude-Stratton). *Cornw.* Population: 3681. ***Small town***, resort with good sandy beaches, on N coast 15m/24km NW of Launceston. Centre for surfing. **6 A5** SS2006.
Bude Bay *Cornw.* ***Bay***, on N coast of Cornwall, extending 4m/7km S from Lower Sharpnose Point to Dizzard Point. Town of Bude is situated centrally on bay. **6 A5** SS1406.
Bude Haven *Cornw.* ***Bay***, sandy bay at Bude, where River Bude enters sea. **6 A5** SS2006.
Bude-Stratton *Cornw.* *See Bude.*
Budge's Shop *Cornw.* ***Hamlet***, 6m/9km SE of Liskeard. SX3259.
Budlake *Devon* ***Hamlet***, 5m/8km SW of Cullompton. **7 H5** SS9800.
Budle *Northumb.* ***Settlement***, on S side of Budle Bay, 1m/2km W of Bamburgh. **77 K7** NU1535.
Budle Bay *Northumb.* ***Bay***, on North Sea coast, 2m/3km NW of Bamburgh. **77 K7** NU1536.
Budle Point *Northumb.* ***Coastal feature***, headland on North Sea coast on E side of mouth of Budle Bay. **77 K7** NU1636.
Budleigh Salterton *Devon* Population: 3759. ***Small town***, resort on S coast, 4m/7km E of Exmouth. **7 J7** SY0682.
Budlett's Common *E.Suss.* ***Hamlet***, 1km SE of Maresfield. TQ4723.
Budock Water *Cornw.* ***Village***, 2m/3km W of Falmouth. **2 E5** SW7832.
Budworth Heath *Ches.* ***Settlement***, 1km N of Great Budworth. SJ6678.
Buersil *Gt.Man.* ***Suburb***, 1m/2km S of Rochdale town centre. SD8911.
Buersil Head *Gt.Man.* ***Locality***, 2m/3km SE of Rochdale town centre. SD9010.
Buerton *Ches.* ***Village***, 2m/3km E of Audlem. **39 F1** SJ6843.
Buerton Moss *Ches.* ***Settlement***, 1km N of Buerton. SJ6844.
Buffler's Holt *Bucks.* ***Settlement***, 2m/3km NW of Buckingham. SP6635.
Bugbrooke *Northants.* Population: 2711. ***Village***, 5m/9km SW of Northampton. **31 H3** SP6757.
Bugeildy *Powys* *Welsh form of Beguildy, qv.*
Bugeilyn *Powys* ***Lake/loch***, 4m/7km W of head of Llyn Clywedog Reservoir. **37 H6** SN8292.
Buglawton *Ches.* ***Suburb***, to NE of Congleton town centre. SJ8763.
Bugle *Cornw.* Population: 1348. ***Village***, in china clay district, 4m/7km N of St. Austell. **4 A5** SX0158.
Bugthorpe *E.Riding* ***Village***, 4m/7km E of Stamford Bridge. **58 D4** SE7757.
Buidhe Bheinn *High.* ***Mountain***, in Lochaber district 1m/2km N of Kinloch Hourn. Height 2883 feet or 879 metres. **87 F4** NG9508.
Building End *Essex* ***Hamlet***, 6m/9km SE of Royston. TL4337.
Buildwas *Shrop.* ***Village***, 3m/5km NE of Much Wenlock. Remains of 12c abbey (English Heritage) across River Severn to SE. **39 F5** SJ6304.
Buildwas Abbey *Shrop.* ***Ecclesiastical building***, ruins of Cistercian abbey (English Heritage) founded in 1135, 2m/3km N of Much Wenlock. Mainly Norman in style, much of church survives intact, though without a roof. **39 F5** SJ6404.
Builg Burn *Moray* ***River***, issuing from Loch Builg and flowing N to join River Avon, 7m/11km S of Tomintoul. **89 J4** NJ1707.
Builth Road *Powys* ***Settlement***, and railway station, 2m/3km NW of Builth Wells. **27 K3** SO0253.
Builth Wells (Llanfair-ym-Muallt). *Powys* Population: 2474. ***Small town***, former spa town on River Wye, 14m/23km N of Brecon. Remains of castle consist almost entirely of Norman motte and bailey. **27 K3** SO0451.
Buirgh (Anglicised form: Borvemore.) *W.Isles* ***Locality***, on W coast of South Harris, 5m/7km N of Leverburgh. **93 F2** NG0294.
Bulabhall *W.Isles* ***Mountain***, 1m/2km N of Loch Langavat, South Harris. Height 1161 feet or 354 metres. **93 F2** NG0593.
Bulbarrow Hill *Dorset* ***Hill***, 3m/4km SE of Hazelbury Bryan. Height 820 feet or 250 metres. **9 G4** ST7604.
Bulbourne *Herts.* ***Hamlet***, 1m/2km N of Tring. SP9313.
Bulby *Lincs.* ***Hamlet***, 5m/8km NW of Bourne. **42 D3** TF0526.
Bulcote *Notts.* ***Village***, adjoining to NE of Burton Joyce, 6m/10km NE of Nottingham. SK6544.
Buldoo *High.* ***Settlement***, 2m/4km NE of Reay, Caithness district. Airfield to N. **104 E2** NC9966.
Bulford *Wilts.* Population: 4739. ***Village***, and large military barracks, 2m/3km NE of Amesbury. **20 E7** SU1643.
Bulford Camp *Wilts.* ***Military establishment***, artillery camp to E of Bulford, 2m/3km NE of Amesbury. **20 E7** SU1843.
Bulg *Angus* ***Mountain***, 1m/2km S of Fernybank. Height 1991 feet or 607 metres. **90 D7** NO5476.
Bulgham Bay *I.o.M.* ***Bay***, 2m/3km NE of Laxey. **54 D5** SC4585.
Bulkeley *Ches.* ***Village***, 8m/12km W of Nantwich. **48 E7** SJ5354.
Bulkington *Warks.* Population: 6708. ***Village***, 2m/3km E of Bedworth. **41 F7** SP3986.
Bulkington *Wilts.* ***Village***, 4m/7km SE of Melksham. **20 C6** ST9458.
Bulkworthy *Devon* ***Village***, 7m/11km SW of Great Torrington. **6 B4** SS3914.
Bull Bay (Porthllechog). *I.o.A.* ***Village***, small resort on N coast of Anglesey to NW of Amlwch. Name also applies to bay to E (Welsh form: Porth Llechog). **46 C3** SH4393.
Bull Green *Kent* ***Settlement***, to SW of Bethersden, 6m/9km SW of Ashford. **14 E4** TQ9239.
Bull Green *Suff.* ***Settlement***, 3m/5km S of Bury St. Edmunds town centre. TL8459.
Bull Hill *Hants.* ***Hamlet***, 2m/3km NE of Lymington. SZ3498.
Bull Point *Devon* ***Coastal feature***, headland on N coast 4m/6km W of Ilfracombe. **6 C1** SS4646.
Bullamoor *N.Yorks.* ***Hamlet***, 2m/3km E of Northallerton. SE3994.
Bullbridge *Derbys.* ***Village***, 3m/5km N of Belper. SK3552.
Bullbrook *Brack.F.* ***Suburb***, E district of Bracknell. SU8869.
Bulldog Sand *Norf.* ***Coastal feature***, area of mud and sand off N Norfolk coast to E side of mouth of River Great Ouse, 5m/8km NW of King's Lynn. **43 J3** TF5727.
Bullen's Green *Herts.* ***Hamlet***, 2m/3km SW of Hatfield. TL2106.
Bullers of Buchan *Aber.* ***Coastal feature***, huge circular cavern on E coast, 2m/3km NE of Cruden Bay. Sea enters cavern at its base, top being open to sky. In stormy weather sea climbs to top of vertical walls of rock. **91 K1** NK1138.

Bulley *Glos.* ***Settlement***, 4m/7km W of Gloucester. **29 G7** SO7619.
Bullgill *Cumb.* ***Hamlet***, 4m/6km E of Maryport. NY0938.
Bullie Burn *P. & K.* ***River***, flowing E, then S through Braco and into River Allan at Greenloaning. **81 J7** NN8307.
Bullinghope *Here.* ***Hamlet***, 2m/3km S of Hereford. SO5137.
Bullington *Hants.* ***Hamlet***, 4m/7km S of Whitchurch. **21 H7** SU4541.
Bullington *Lincs.* ***Hamlet***, 3m/4km W of Wragby. TF0977.
Bullpot Farm *Cumb.* ***Settlement***, on SW side of Barbon High Fell, 4m/6km NE of Kirkby Lonsdale. Numerous potholes and caves on moor to E. **56 B1** SD6681.
Bulls Cross *Herts.* ***Settlement***, 1m/2km SW of Waltham Cross. TQ3499.
Bull's Green *Herts.* ***Hamlet***, 3m/4km E of Welwyn. **33 F7** TL2717.
Bull's Green *Norf.* ***Settlement***, 3m/4km N of Beccles. TM4194.
Bullwood *Arg. & B.* ***Settlement***, on Firth of Clyde, 1m/2km SW of Dunoon. **73 K3** NS1674.
Bulmer *Essex* ***Village***, 2m/3km W of Sudbury. **34 C4** TL8440.
Bulmer *N.Yorks.* ***Village***, 6m/10km W of Malton. **58 C3** SE6967.
Bulmer Tye *Essex* ***Village***, 2m/4km SW of Sudbury. **34 C5** TL8438.
Bulphan *Thur.* ***Village***, 5m/8km SW of Basildon. **24 C3** TQ6385.
Bulstone *Devon* ***Hamlet***, 4m/6km NE of Sidmouth. SY1789.
Bulverhythe *E.Suss.* ***Locality***, on coast, 3m/4km W of Hastings town centre. **14 C7** TQ7708.
Bulwark *Aber.* ***Locality***, 1m/2km S of Maud. **99 H6** NJ9345.
Bulwark Fort *Mon.* ***Historic/prehistoric site***, Iron Age fort (Cadw) to SE of Chepstow on W bank of River Wye. **19 J2** ST5392.
Bulwell *Nott.* ***Suburb***, 4m/6km NW of Nottingham city centre. **41 H1** SK5344.
Bulwick *Northants.* ***Village***, 6m/10km NW of Oundle. **42 C6** SP9693.
Bumble Hole *W.Mid.* ***Suburb***, 1m/2km S of Dudley town centre. SO9488.
Bumble's Green *Essex* ***Village***, 4m/6km SW of Harlow. **23 H1** TL4005.
Bun Abhainn Eadarra (Anglicised form: Bunavoneader.) *W.Isles* ***Hamlet***, on North Harris at head of Loch Bun Abhainn-eadar, inlet of West Loch Tarbert. **100 D7** NB1304.
Bun Loyne *High.* ***Settlement***, 2m/3km E of E end of Loch Cluanie. **87 J4** NH2109.
Bun Sruth *W.Isles* ***Sea feature***, inlet near SE extremity of South Uist, 4m/7km E of Ludag. **84 D3** NF8414.
Bunacaimb *High.* ***Settlement***, on W coast of Lochaber district, 1m/2km N of Arisaig. NM6588.
Bunarkaig *High.* ***Settlement***, in Lochaber district, on NW shore of Loch Lochy, 2m/3km N of S end of loch. **87 H6** NN1887.
Bunavoneader *W.Isles Anglicised form of Bun Abhainn Eadarra, qv.*
Bunbury *Ches.* ***Village***, 3m/5km S of Tarporley. **48 E7** SJ5658.
Bunbury Heath *Ches.* ***Settlement***, to W of Bunbury. SJ5557.
Bunchrew *High.* ***Locality***, in Inverness district, to S of Beauly Firth, 3m/5km W of Inverness. **96 D7** NH6145.
Buncton *W.Suss.* ***Locality***, below South Downs, 2m/3km E of Washington. Site of Roman building to S. TQ1413.
Bundalloch *High.* ***Settlement***, on shore of Loch Long, Skye and Lochalsh district, 1m/2km NE of Dornie. **86 E2** NG8927.
Buness *Shet.* ***Settlement***, with small jetty, to E of Baltasound, Unst. **108 F2** HP6208.
Bunessan *Arg. & B.* ***Village***, on Ross of Mull, at SE corner of Loch na Lathaich. **78 E5** NM3821.
Bungay *Suff.* Population: 3393. ***Small town***, above River Waveney valley, 14m/21km SE of Norwich. Remains of 12c castle of the Bigods. 17c market cross. **45 H7** TM3389.
Bungay Castle *Suff.* ***Castle***, in centre of Bungay. Ruins dating from early 12c. Originally a motte, with house built on site in 18c. **45 H6** TM3390.
Bunkers Hill *Lancs.* ***Locality***, 1m/2km W of Colne. SD8739.
Bunker's Hill *Lincs.* ***Settlement***, 1m/2km SE of New York and 4m/6km SE of Coningsby. TF2653.
Bunker's Hill *Norf.* ***Suburb***, 3m/4km W of Norwich city centre. TG1809.
Bunkers Hill *Norf.* ***Suburb***, 3m/5km NW of Norwich city centre. TG1810.
Bunker's Hill *Torfaen* ***Locality***, on N side of Blaenavon. SO2509.
Bunkers Hill *W.Mid.* ***Suburb***, to E of Wolverhampton. SO9597.
Bunlarie *Arg. & B.* ***Settlement***, on Kintyre, 8m/12km NE of Campbeltown. **73 F7** NR7830.
Bunloinn Forest *High.* ***Open space***, deer forest in Inverness district between Lochs Cluanie and Loyne. **87 H4** NH1608.
Bunloit *High.* ***Settlement***, on NW side of Loch Ness, 3m/5km S of Drumnadrochit, Inverness district. **88 C2** NH5025.
Bunmhullin *W.Isles* ***Settlement***, on N coast of Eriskay. NF7912.
Bunnahabhainn (Anglicised form: Bonahaven.) *Arg. & B.* ***Village***, on bay of same name on NE coast of Islay, 3m/4km N of Port Askaig. **72 C3** NR4273.
Bunnahabhainn Bay *Arg. & B.* ***Bay***, small bay on E coast of Islay, to N of Bunnahabhain. **72 C3** NR4273.
Bunny *Notts.* ***Village***, 7m/11km S of Nottingham. **41 H3** SK5829.
Buntait *High.* ***Locality***, scattered settlement 4m/6km E of Cannich. **87 K1** NH3930.
Buntingford *Herts.* Population: 4376. ***Small town***, 10m/15km N of Ware. **33 G6** TL3629.
Bunting's Green *Essex* ***Hamlet***, 2m/3km E of Halstead. TL8330.
Bunwell *Norf.* ***Hamlet***, 6m/9km S of Wymondham. **45 F6** TM1193.
Bunwell Hill *Norf.* ***Settlement***, 1km S of Bunwell. TM1291.
Bunwell Street *Norf.* ***Village***, 1m/2km NW of Bunwell. **45 F6** TM1292.
Burach *High.* ***Mountain***, in Inverness district, 3m/4km SW of Invermoriston. Height 1991 feet or 607 metres. **87 K3** NH3814.
Burbage *Derbys.* ***Suburb***, 1m/2km W of Buxton town centre. **50 C5** SK0472.
Burbage *Leics.* ***Suburb***, to SE of Hinckley. **41 G6** SP4492.
Burbage *Wilts.* Population: 1246. ***Village***, 4m/7km E of Pewsey. **21 F5** SU2361.
Burbage Common *Leics.* ***Leisure/recreation***, country park with over 150 acres of woodland, grassland and ponds, 1m/2km E of Hinckley town centre. **41 G6** SP4495.
Burbage Moor *S.Yorks.* ***Open space***, moorland at E side of The Pennines, 2m/4km NE of Hathersage. **50 E4** SK2782.
Burchett's Green *W. & M.* ***Village***, 3m/5km W of Maidenhead. **22 B3** SU8481.
Burcombe *Wilts.* ***Village***, on River Nadder, 2m/3km W of Wilton. **10 B1** SU0730.
Burcot *Oxon.* ***Village***, 4m/7km E of Abingdon. **21 J2** SU5696.
Burcot *Worcs.* ***Village***, 2m/3km E of Bromsgrove. SO9871.
Burcote *Shrop.* ***Settlement***, 2m/4km NE of Bridgnorth. SO7494.
Burcott *Bucks.* ***Hamlet***, 3m/5km W of Leighton Buzzard. **32 B6** SP8723.
Burdale *N.Yorks.* ***Locality***, 2m/3km N of Fridaythorpe. **58 E3** SE8762.
Burdiehouse *Edin.* ***Suburb***, 4m/7km S of Edinburgh city centre. NT2767.
Burdocks *W.Suss.* ***Settlement***, 4m/6km SW of Billingshurst. **12 D4** TQ0323.
Burdon *T. & W.* ***Hamlet***, 2m/3km SW of Ryhope. NZ3851.
Burdrop *Oxon.* ***Hamlet***, adjoining to E of Sibford Gower, 6m/10km W of Banbury. SP3537.
Bure *Norf.* ***River***, rising near Melton Constable and flowing SE into River Yare at Great Yarmouth. **45 G3** TG5107.
Bure Valley Railway *Norf.* ***Other feature of interest***, tourist railway running for 9m/15km alongside River Bure, from Aylsham to Wroxham, on trackbed of old Great Eastern Railway. **45 G3** TG2026.
Bures *Suff.* ***Village***, comprised of two villages, Bures St. Mary and Bures Hamlet, astride River Stour 5m/8km SE of Sudbury. St. Edmund was crowned here in 855. **34 D5** TL9034.
Bures Green *Suff.* ***Settlement***, 1km NE of Bures. **34 D5** TL9135.
Burfa *Powys* ***Settlement***, 3m/5km SW of Presteigne. Ancient British camp in woods to SE. SO2761.
Burford *Oxon.* Population: 1171. ***Small town***, attractive Cotswold town on River Windrush, 7m/11km W of Witney. Former medieval wool town. **30 D7** SP2512.
Burford *Shrop.* ***Village***, 1km W of Tenbury Wells across River Teme. SO5868.
Burford *Som.* ***Hamlet***, 2m/3km SW of Shepton Mallet. ST5941.
Burford House Gardens *Shrop.* ***Garden***, 1m/2km W of Tenbury Wells, houses National Clematis Collection and 2000 varieties of plants; particularly noted for hardy perennials. **28 E2** SO5868.
Burg *Arg. & B.* ***Locality***, area on Mull (National Trust for Scotland), at SW end of Ardmeanach, rising steeply from Loch Scridain and culminating in mountain of Bearraich, 1416 feet or 432 metres. **79 F5** NM4226.
Burg *Arg. & B.* ***Settlement***, near W coast of Mull, 3m/5km E of Rubh' a' Chaoil. Dùn Bàn is 1c galleried fort to SE on coast. NM3845.
Burga Water *Shet.* ***Lake/loch***, on Mainland, L-shaped and 1km by 1km at its widest points. **109 B7** HU2353.
Burgate *Suff.* ***Hamlet***, 4m/6km SW of Diss. **34 E1** TM0875.
Burgate Great Green *Suff.* ***Settlement***, 1m/2km N of Burgate. TM0776.
Burgate Little Green *Suff.* ***Settlement***, 1km SW of Burgate. TM0774.
Burgates *Hants.* ***Hamlet***, adjoining to N of Liss, 5m/8km SW of Liphook. SU7728.
Burge End *Herts.* ***Settlement***, at N end of Pirton, 3m/5km NW of Hitchin. TL1432.
Burgess Hill *W.Suss.* Population: 26,077. ***Town***, 9m/15km N of Brighton. **13 G5** TQ3119.
Burgh *Suff.* ***Village***, 3m/5km NW of Woodbridge. Site of Roman building near church. **35 G3** TM2351.
Burgh by Sands *Cumb.* ***Village***, on line of Hadrian's Wall, 5m/9km NW of Carlisle. **60 E1** NY3259.
Burgh Castle *Norf.* ***Village***, 3m/5km SW of Great Yarmouth. Remains of 3c Roman fort of Gariannonum (English Heritage) on River Waveney. **45 J5** TG4805.
Burgh Castle Roman Fort *Norf.* ***Historic/prehistoric site***, intermediate fort of Saxon Shore system, dating to AD 275, to N of Burgh Castle and 4m/6km SW of Great Yarmouth. Some walls still standing; an excellent example of Roman masonry, some parts up to 15 feet high and 10 feet thick at base. **45 J5** TG4704.
Burgh Head *Ork.* ***Coastal feature***, headland on E coast of Stronsay. **106 G5** HY6923.
Burgh Heath *Surr.* ***Locality***, residential locality 1m/2km SW of Banstead. **23 F6** TQ2457.
Burgh Island *Devon* ***Island***, in Bigbury Bay opposite Bigbury-on-Sea, from which it is accessible on foot at low tide. **5 G6** SX6443.
Burgh le Marsh *Lincs.* Population: 1701. ***Village***, 5m/7km W of Skegness. **53 H6** TF5065.
Burgh Marsh *Cumb.* ***Marsh/bog***, marshland on S side of Solway Firth, 1km NW of Burgh by Sands. **69 J7** NY3060.
Burgh Marsh *Lincs.* ***Open space***, lowland between Burgh le Marsh and Skegness. **53 J6** TF5264.
Burgh next Aylsham *Norf.* ***Village***, on River Bure, 2m/3km SE of Aylsham. **45 G3** TG2125.
Burgh on Bain *Lincs.* ***Village***, 7m/11km W of Louth. **53 F4** TF2286.
Burgh St. Margaret *Norf.* ***Village***, 4m/6km NE of Acle. **45 J4** TG4414.
Burgh St. Peter *Norf.* ***Village***, 3m/4km SE of Haddiscoe. **45 J6** TM4693.
Burghclere *Hants.* ***Village***, 4m/6km NW of Kingsclere. **21 H5** SU4761.
Burghead *Moray* Population: 1495. ***Village***, large fishing village, 8m/12km NW of Elgin. Radio transmitting station. Well, or early Christian baptistry (Historic Scotland), within remains of Iron Age fort. **97 J5** NJ1168.
Burghead Bay *Moray* ***Bay***, extends W from Burghead to mouth of River Findhorn. **97 H5** NJ0767.
Burghead Well *Moray* ***Other feature of interest***, spring-fed pool, formerly a water source for Burghead, situated in carved rock chamber. **97 J5** NJ1169.
Burghfield *W.Berks.* ***Village***, 4m/7km SW of Reading. **21 K5** SU6668.
Burghfield Common *W.Berks.* Population: 4750. ***Village***, 6m/9km SW of Reading. **21 K5** SU6566.
Burghfield Hill *W.Berks.* ***Hamlet***, 1m/2km SW of Burghfield and 5m/8km SW of Reading. **21 K5** SU6567.
Burghill *Here.* ***Village***, 4m/6km NW of Hereford. **28 D4** SO4744.
Burghley House *Peter.* ***Historic house***, Elizabethan mansion in large park on SE side of Stamford. Built by William Cecil, Lord High Treasurer to Elizabeth I. **42 D5** TF0406.
Burghwallis *S.Yorks.* ***Village***, 6m/10km N of Doncaster. **51 H1** SE5311.
Burham *Kent* ***Village***, above River Medway valley, 4m/7km S of Rochester. Several Roman sites in vicinity. **24 D5** TQ7262.
Buriton *Hants.* ***Village***, 2m/3km S of Petersfield. **11 J2** SU7320.
Burland *Ches.* ***Village***, 2m/4km W of Nantwich. **49 F7** SJ6153.
Burlawn *Cornw.* ***Village***, 1m/2km S of Wadebridge. **3 G1** SW9970.
Burleigh *Brack.F.* ***Suburb***, 1m/2km NW of Ascot. **22 C5** SU9170.
Burleigh Castle *P. & K.* ***Castle***, ruined 15c-16c castle (Historic Scotland) on E side of Milnathort. **82 C7** NO1204.
Burlescombe *Devon* ***Hamlet***, 5m/8km SW of Wellington. **7 J4** ST0716.
Burleston *Dorset* ***Hamlet***, 1m/2km E of Puddletown. **9 G5** SY7794.
Burley *Hants.* ***Village***, 4m/7km SE of Ringwood. **10 D4** SU2103.
Burley *Rut.* ***Village***, 2m/3km NE of Oakham. **42 B4** SK8810.
Burley *W.Yorks.* ***Suburb***, 1m/2km NW of Leeds city centre. SE2734.
Burley Gate *Here.* ***Hamlet***, 7m/11km NE of Hereford. **28 E4** SO5947.
Burley in Wharfedale *W.Yorks.* Population: 5528. ***Village***, 3m/5km E of Ilkley. **57 G5** SE1646.
Burley Lawn *Hants.* ***Settlement***, 1km NE of Burley and 5m/8km E of Ringwood. SU2103.
Burley Street *Hants.* ***Village***, 4m/6km E of Ringwood. **10 D4** SU2004.
Burley Woodhead *W.Yorks.* ***Village***, 1m/2km SW of Burley in Wharfedale. SE1544.
Burleydam *Ches.* ***Village***, 4m/6km W of Audlem. **39 F1** SJ6042.
Burlingham Green *Norf.* ***Hamlet***, 1km N of North Burlingham and 3m/4km W of Acle. TG3610.
Burlingjobb *Powys* ***Settlement***, 3m/5km SE of New Radnor. **28 B3** SO2558.
Burlow *E.Suss.* ***Hamlet***, 1km S of Horam. **13 J5** TQ5716.
Burlton *Shrop.* ***Hamlet***, 4m/6km SW of Wem. **38 D3** SJ4526.
Burmantofts *W.Yorks.* ***Suburb***, 1m/2km E of Leeds city centre. SE3134.
Burmarsh *Kent* ***Village***, at E corner of Romney Marsh, 4m/7km W of Hythe. **15 G4** TR1032.
Burmington *Warks.* ***Village***, 2m/3km S of Shipston on Stour. **30 D5** SP2637.
Burn *N.Yorks.* ***Village***, 3m/4km SW of Selby. **58 B7** SE5928.
Burn Howe Rigg *N.Yorks.* ***Open space***, moorland on S side of Fylingdales Moor, 3m/5km W of Harwood Dale Forest and 7m/11km NW of Burniston. **63 H3** SE9198.
Burn Moor ***Open space***, large area of moorland straddling border of Lancashire and North Yorkshire, 4m/6km SE of High Bentham. **56 C3** SD6964.
Burn Naze *Lancs.* ***Suburb***, 1m/2km E of Cleveleys. **55 G5** SD3343.
Burn of Acharole *High.* ***River***, flowing NE to join Strath Burn 1km S of Watten. **105 H3** ND2150.
Burn of Agie *High.* ***River***, flowing N through Braeroy Forest into River Roy at upper reach of Glen Roy, 2m/3km E of Turret Bridge. **87 K6** NN3692.
Burn of Arisdale *Shet.* ***River***, running S down Aris Dale valley to Hamna Voe. **108 D4** HU4882.
Burn of Aultmore *Moray* ***River***, rising on Hill of Clashmadin and flowing S to River Isla, 2m/3km E of Keith. **98 C5** NJ4551.
Burn of Boyne *Aber.* ***River***, rising on NE slopes of Knock Hill and flowing NE to enter sea at Boyne Bay, 2m/3km E of Portsoy. **98 D4** NJ6166.
Burn of Branny *Angus* ***River***, flowing S to Water of Mark, one of headwaters of River North Esk. **90 C6** NO4480.
Burn of Brown *See Glen Brown.*
Burn of Cairnie ***River***, on Aberdeenshire and Moray border, flowing E to Cairnie then NE by Ruthven to River Isla, 5m/8km N of Huntly. **98 C6** NJ5147.

Burn of Calletar *Angus* ***River***, stream flowing E of West Water, 1m/2km NW of Bridgend. **83 F1** NO5269.
Burn of Cambus *Stir.* ***Settlement***, 5m/8km SE of Callander. **81 J7** NN7003.
Burn of Canny *Aber.* ***River***, running S into River Dee 2m/3km W of Banchory. NO6796.
Burn of Cattie *Aber.* ***River***, stream rising in Forest of Birse, and flowing E to join River Dee 4m/7km W of Banchory. **90 D5** NO6295.
Burn of Corrichie *Aber.* ***River***, rising on Hill of Fare and flowing E, then S between Brown Hill and Meikle Tap, to merge with Bo Burn. **91 F4** NO7399.
Burn of Cowlatt *Moray* ***River***, issuing from Loch of the Cowlatt and flowing E to join Knockando Burn, 1m/2km N of Upper Knockando. **97 J7** NJ1744.
Burn of Craig *Aber.* ***River***, flowing E to join Burn of Glenny near Auchindoir, 2m/3km SW of Rhynie. **90 C2** NJ4724.
Burn of Durn *Aber.* ***River***, rising on W slopes of Hill of Summertown and flowing NE to sea at Links Bay, Portsoy. **98 D4** NJ5966.
Burn of Hillside *Ork.* ***River***, flowing NW into Loch of Hundland, Mainland. **106 C5** HY2925.
Burn of Houstry *High.* ***River***, flowing S to join Dunbeath Water 1km NW of Dunbeath. **105 G5** ND1530.
Burn of Kergord *Shet.* *See Weisdale.*
Burn of Lochy (Lochy Burn). ***River***, continuance of Burn of Brown running NE down Glen Lochy to River Avon, 4m/7km N of Tomintoul. **89 J2** NJ1424.
Burn of Loin *Moray* ***River***, flowing E through Glen Loin, then S to join River Avon at E end of Glen Avon. **89 J4** NJ1506.
Burn of Lyth *High.* ***River***, in Caithness district, running SE from Loch Heilen to Sinclair's Bay, N of Wick. **105 H2** ND3357.
Burn of Ore *Ork.* ***River***, on Hoy, rising on Bakingstone Hill and flowing E into Ore Bay. **107 B8** ND2693.
Burn of Pettawater *Shet.* *See Sand Water.*
Burn of Rothes *Moray* ***River***, rising in wooded area between Carn na Cailliche and Green Hill, and flowing E to join River Spey on NE side of Rothes. **97 K7** NJ2850.
Burn of Sheeoch *Aber.* ***River***, running NE to River Dee, 5m/8km E of Banchory. **91 F6** NO7796.
Burn of Tennet *Angus* ***River***, stream which flows SW to join Water of Tarf, 1m/2km N of Tarfside. **90 D6** NO4981.
Burn of Turret *Angus* ***River***, stream which flows S to join River North Esk at Millden Lodge. **90 D6** NO5478.
Burnage *Gt.Man.* ***Suburb***, 4m/6km SE of Manchester city centre. **49 H3** SJ8692.
Burnaston *Derbys.* ***Village***, 5m/8km SW of Derby. **40 E2** SK2832.
Burnbank *S.Lan.* ***Suburb***, to NW of Hamilton. NS7056.
Burnbanks *Cumb.* ***Hamlet***, 1m/2km S of Bampton, at N end of Haweswater Reservoir. NY5016.
Burnbrae *N.Lan.* ***Settlement***, 1km S of Shotts to W of Stane. NS8759.
Burnby *E.Riding* ***Village***, 3m/4km SE of Pocklington. **58 E5** SE8346.
Burnby Hall *E.Riding* ***Garden***, 13m/21km E of York. Two lakes display 80 varieties of hardy water lilies, designated a National Collection. Includes a sporting trophy museum. **58 E5** SE8147.
Burncross *S.Yorks.* ***Village***, adjoining to SW of Chapeltown. SK3496.
Burndell *W.Suss.* ***Settlement***, adjoining to E of Yapton. **12 C6** SU9802.
Burnden *Gt.Man.* ***Suburb***, 1m/2km SE of Bolton town centre. SD7207.
Burnedge *Gt.Man.* ***Hamlet***, 1m/2km N of Shaw. SD9210.
Burnend *Aber.* ***Locality***, in valley of Burn of Asleid, 5m/8km NE of Fyvie. **99 G6** NJ8441.
Burneside *Cumb.* ***Village***, 2m/3km N of Kendal. **61 G7** SD5095.
Burness *Ork.* ***Locality***, in NW part of Sanday. **106 F3** HY6644.
Burneston *N.Yorks.* ***Village***, 3m/5km SE of Bedale. **57 J1** SE3085.
Burnett *B. & N.E.Som.* ***Hamlet***, 2m/4km S of Keynsham. **19 K5** ST6665.
Burnfoot *High.* ***Settlement***, in Sutherland district, 1m/2km S of Kinbrace. **104 D5** NC8630.
Burnfoot *P. & K.* ***Settlement***, 4m/6km NE of Dollar. **82 A7** NN9804.
Burnfoot *Sc.Bord.* ***Hamlet***, 1m/2km SW of Roberton. **69 K2** NT4112.
Burnfoot *Sc.Bord.* ***Suburb***, adjoining to N of Hawick. **70 A2** NT5116.
Burnham *Bucks.* ***Village***, 3m/5km NW of Slough. **22 C3** SU9382.
Burnham *N.Lincs.* ***Hamlet***, 4m/6km SE of Barton-upon-Humber. **52 D1** TA0517.
Burnham Beeches *Bucks.* ***Forest/woodland***, 3m/5km NW of Slough. Name also applied to residential locality on E side of area. **22 C3** SU9585.
Burnham Deepdale *Norf.* ***Hamlet***, 2m/4km NW of Burnham Market. **44 C1** TF8044.
Burnham Green *Herts.* ***Suburb***, 2m/4km E of Welwyn. **33 F7** TL2616.
Burnham Market *Norf.* ***Village***, 5m/8km W of Wells-next-the-Sea. **44 C1** TF8342.
Burnham Norton *Norf.* ***Hamlet***, 1m/2km N of Burnham Market. **44 C1** TF8243.
Burnham-on-Crouch *Essex* Population: 7067. ***Small town***, on River Crouch estuary, 9m/14km SE of Maldon. Yachting centre, second largest after Cowes on Isle of Wight. Oyster fisheries. **25 F2** TQ9496.
Burnham-on-Sea *Som.* Population: 9794. ***Small town***, resort on Bristol Channel 8m/12km N of Bridgwater. Industrial development inland. **19 G7** ST3049.
Burnham Overy Staithe (Also known as Overy Staithe.) *Norf.* ***Village***, 2m/3km NE of Burnham Market. **44 C1** TF8444.
Burnham Overy Town *Norf.* ***Hamlet***, 1m/2km NE of Burnham Market across River Burn. **44 C1** TF8442.
Burnham Sutton and Ulph *Norf.* ***Locality***, adjoining to S of Burnham Market. TF8341.
Burnham Thorpe *Norf.* ***Village***, 2m/3km SE of Burnham Market. Birthplace of Nelson 1758. **44 C1** TF8541.
Burnham Westgate *Norf.* ***Locality***, W end of Burnham Market. TF8342.
Burnhaven *Aber.* ***Village***, 1m/2km S of Peterhead across Peterhead Bay. **99 K6** NK1244.
Burnhead *D. & G.* ***Settlement***, 6m/9km NW of St. John's Town of Dalry. **67 K5** NX5485.
Burnhead *D. & G.* ***Settlement***, 1km W of Thornhill. **68 D4** NX8695.
Burnhervie *Aber.* ***Hamlet***, on River Don, 3m/5km W of Inverurie. **91 F3** NJ7319.
Burnhill Green *Staffs.* ***Hamlet***, 3m/4km SW of Albrighton. **39 G5** SJ7800.
Burnhope *Dur.* Population: 1530. ***Village***, 2m/3km E of Lanchester. **62 C2** NZ1948.
Burnhope Reservoir *Dur.* ***Reservoir***, in course of Burnhope Burn 1m/2km W of Wearhead. **61 K3** NY8539.
Burnhope Seat ***Mountain***, on border of Cumbria and Durham, 5m/7km W of Wearhead. Height 2447 feet or 746 metres. **61 J3** NY7837.
Burnhouse *N.Ayr.* ***Hamlet***, 3m/5km SE of Beith. **74 B5** NS3850.
Burniston *N.Yorks.* Population: 2069. ***Village***, 3m/5km NW of Scarborough. **63 K3** TA0192.
Burnlee *W.Yorks.* ***Locality***, 1m/2km SW of Holmfirth. SE1307.
Burnley *Lancs.* Population: 74,661. ***Town***, former cotton town, 22m/36km N of Manchester. Leeds and Liverpool Canal, which runs through town centre, was largely responsible for Burnley's wealth in 19c. **56 D6** SD8332.
Burnley Lane *Lancs.* ***Suburb***, 1m/2km N of Burnley town centre. SD8434.
Burnmoor Tarn *Cumb.* ***Lake/loch***, National Trust owned, 2m/3km N of Boot. **60 C6** NY1804.
Burnmouth *Sc.Bord.* ***Village***, on coast, 2m/3km S of Eyemouth. **77 H4** NT9560.
Burnopfield *Dur.* Population: 4268. ***Village***, 3m/5km NW of Stanley. **62 C1** NZ1756.
Burnrigg *Cumb.* ***Locality***, 1km S of Warwick Bridge. NY4755.
Burns' Cottage *S.Ayr.* ***Historic house***, museum commemorating birthplace of Robert Burns in 1759. Located in Alloway, suburb to S of Ayr. **67 H2** NS3318.
Burn's Green *Herts.* ***Hamlet***, 5m/7km SE of Stevenage. TL3022.
Burnsall *N.Yorks.* ***Village***, in Wharfedale, 3m/4km SE of Grassington. **57 F3** SE0361.
Burnside *Aber.* ***Settlement***, 3m/5km SW of Kintore. **91 F3** NJ7712.
Burnside *Angus* ***Hamlet***, 3m/5km E of Forfar. **83 G2** NO5050.
Burnside *E.Ayr.* ***Hamlet***, 3m/4km SW of New Cumnock. **67 K2** NS5811.
Burnside *Fife* ***Hamlet***, 4m/6km SW of Strathmiglo. **82 C7** NO1608.
Burnside *Shet.* ***Settlement***, on Mainland, 1m/2km W of head of Ura Firth. **108 B5** HU2778.
Burnside *W.Loth.* ***Locality***, adjacent to E of Broxburn. **75 J3** NT0972.
Burnside of Duntrune *Angus* ***Hamlet***, on Fithie Burn, 4m/6km NE of Dundee. **83 F4** NO4334.
Burnstones *Northumb.* ***Settlement***, on W bank of Thinhope Burn, 3m/4km S of Lambley. **61 H1** NY6754.
Burnswark (Also known as Birrenswark.) *D. & G.* ***Hill***, 3m/4km N of Ecclefechan. Earthworks of Roman and earlier settlements. Height 630 feet or 192 metres. NY1878.
Burnswark *D. & G.* ***Settlement***, 3m/4km N of Ecclefechan, below E slopes of Burnswark hill. **69 G6** NY1978.
Burnswark Hill Roman Camp *D. & G.* ***Historic/prehistoric site***, Iron Age hillfort on Burnswark, 3m/4km N of Ecclefechan, flanked by Roman artillery range and two practice seige works below hill. **69 G6** NY1878.
Burnt Fen *Cambs.* ***Open space***, fenland 3m/4km E of Littleport. **44 A7** TL6087.
Burnt Hill *W.Berks.* ***Hamlet***, 4m/7km W of Pangbourne. SU5674.
Burnt Houses *Dur.* ***Hamlet***, 1km S of Cockfield. **62 C4** NZ1223.
Burnt Islands *Arg. & B.* ***Island***, group of small islands in Kyles of Bute on E side of Buttock Point, at N end of Bute. NS0275.
Burnt Mill *Essex* ***Suburb***, N district of Harlow. TL4410.
Burnt Mills *Essex* ***Locality***, industrial estate in NE part of Basildon. TQ7390.
Burnt Oak *E.Suss.* ***Hamlet***, 3m/4km S of Crowborough. TQ5127.
Burnt Oak *Gt.Lon.* ***Suburb***, in borough of Barnet, 2m/3km NW of Hendon and 9m/15km NW of Charing Cross. TQ2091.
Burnt Yates *N.Yorks.* ***Village***, 2m/4km W of Ripley. **57 H3** SE2561.
Burntcliff Top *Ches.* ***Settlement***, 6m/10km SE of Macclesfield. **49 J6** SJ9966.
Burntisland *Fife* Population: 5951. ***Small town***, resort on N bank of Firth of Forth, 4m/7km SW of Kirkcaldy. 17c Rossend Castle overlooks harbour. **76 A2** NT2385.
Burnton *E.Ayr.* ***Hamlet***, 1km N of Dalmellington. **67 J3** NS4706.
Burnton *E.Ayr.* ***Settlement***, 3m/5km E of Drongan. **67 J2** NS4917.
Burntstump Country Park *Notts.* ***Leisure/recreation***, country park at S end of Sherwood Forest, with walk through rhododendrons and woodland to top of Burntstump Hill, 3m/4km NE of Hucknall. **51 H7** SK5750.
Burntwick Island *Kent* ***Island***, in estuary of River Medway, S of Isle of Grain. TQ8572.
Burntwood *Staffs.* Population: 28,801. ***Village***, large village created by residential expansion of former hamlets, 3m/4km N of Brownhills. **40 C4** SK0609.
Burntwood Green *Staffs.* ***Hamlet***, adjoining to SE of Burntwood. **40 C5** SK0708.
Burnworthy *Som.* ***Hamlet***, 4m/7km SE of Wellington. ST1815.
Burpham *Surr.* ***Suburb***, NE district of Guildford. **22 D6** TQ0151.
Burpham *W.Suss.* ***Village***, on River Arun, 4m/7km N of Littlehampton. **12 D6** TQ0408.
Burra Firth *Shet.* ***Sea feature***, deep inlet on N coast of Unst. **108 F1** HP6114.
Burra Ness *Shet.* ***Coastal feature***, headland at easternmost point of Yell. **108 E3** HU5595.
Burra Voe *Shet.* ***Bay***, on NE coast of Mainland, on Yell Sound, 4m/6km S of Point of Fethaland. **108 C4** HU3689.
Burrach Mòr *High.* ***Mountain***, in Monadhliath range, 10m/16km NW of Newtonmore. Height 2716 feet or 828 metres. **88 C4** NH5808.
Burradon *Northumb.* ***Hamlet***, 6m/9km NW of Rothbury. **70 E3** NT9806.
Burradon *T. & W.* ***Locality***, 5m/8km N of Newcastle upon Tyne. **71 H6** NZ2772.
Burrafirth *Shet.* ***Locality***, at head of Burra Firth inlet. **108 F1** HP6114.
Burraland *Shet.* ***Settlement***, to N of, and overlooking, Loch of Burraland, Mainland. **108 C5** HU3475.
Burras *Cornw.* ***Hamlet***, 5m/7km S of Redruth. **2 D5** SW6734.
Burraton *Cornw.* ***Hamlet***, 4m/6km SE of Callington. SX4167.
Burraton *Cornw.* ***Suburb***, W district of Saltash. SX4159.
Burraton Coombe *Cornw.* ***Locality***, adjoining to W of Saltash. SX4058.
Burrator Reservoir *Devon* ***Reservoir***, on W side of Dartmoor 4m/6km SW of Princetown. **5 F4** SX5568.
Burravoe *Shet.* ***Hamlet***, on Mainland, on E shore of Busta Voe. **109 C6** HU3667.
Burravoe *Shet.* ***Village***, on inlet of Burra Voe, at SE end of Yell. **108 E5** HU5179.
Burray *Ork.* ***Island***, inhabited island between South Ronaldsay and Mainland and linked to both by Churchill Barrier. Measures 4m/6km E to W and 2m/4km N to S. **107 D8** ND4796.
Burray Ness *Ork.* ***Coastal feature***, headland at E end of Burray. ND5096.
Burrell Collection *Glas.* ***Other feature of interest***, art gallery set in Pollok Grounds, 3m/5km SW of Glasgow city centre. **74 D4** NS5562.
Burrells *Cumb.* ***Locality***, 1m/2km S of Appleby-in-Westmorland. **61 H5** NY6718.
Burrelton *P. & K.* ***Village***, adjoining to S of Woodside, 2m/4km SW of Coupar Angus. **82 C4** NO2037.
Burridge *Devon* ***Hamlet***, 2m/3km SW of Chard. ST3106.
Burridge *Devon* ***Settlement***, 2m/3km N of Barnstaple. SS5635.
Burridge *Hants.* ***Village***, 1m/2km N of Park Gate. **11 G3** SU5110.
Burrigill *High.* ***Settlement***, near E coast of Caithness district, 1m/2km W of Lybster. ND2234.
Burrill *N.Yorks.* ***Hamlet***, 2m/3km W of Bedale. **57 H1** SE2387.
Burringham *N.Lincs.* ***Village***, on E bank of River Trent, 4m/6km W of Scunthorpe. **52 B2** SE8309.
Burrington *Devon* ***Village***, 4m/6km NW of Chulmleigh. **6 E4** SS6316.
Burrington *Here.* ***Village***, 5m/8km W of Ludlow. **28 D1** SO4472.
Burrington *N.Som.* ***Village***, below N slopes of Mendip Hills 1m/2km W of Blagdon. **19 H6** ST4759.
Burrium *Mon.* *See Usk.*
Burrough End *Cambs.* ***Settlement***, E end of Westley Waterless. **33 K3** TL6255.
Burrough Green *Cambs.* ***Village***, 5m/8km S of Newmarket. The Hall is Elizabethan. **33 K3** TL6355.
Burrough Hill Hillfort *Leics.* ***Historic/prehistoric site***, four-sided Iron Age hillfort, 5m/8km S of Melton Mowbray. Occupied for several centuries and, though abandoned in Roman times, remained important for festivals and fairs until 18c. Grand National run here in 1873. **42 A4** SK7611.
Burrough on the Hill *Leics.* ***Village***, 5m/9km S of Melton Mowbray. **42 A4** SK7510.
Burrow *Devon* ***Hamlet***, 1km W of Newton Poppleford. SY0789.
Burrow *Som.* ***Hamlet***, on N slopes of Exmoor, 4m/6km SW of Dunster. SS9342.
Burrow *Som.* ***Hamlet***, 3m/5km W of Martock. ST4119.
Burrow Bridge *Som.* ***Village***, on River Parrett, 4m/7km NW of Langport. Panoramic views from nearby Burrow Mump. **8 C1** ST3629.
Burrow Head *D. & G.* ***Coastal feature***, headland 2m/3km SW of Isle of Whithorn, at W end of Wigtown Bay. **64 E7** NX4534.
Burrowhill *Surr.* ***Village***, adjoining to N of Chobham. **22 C5** SU9763.
Burrows Cross *Surr.* ***Settlement***, 5m/7km N of Cranleigh. TQ0846.
Burrows Hole *Northumb.* ***Sea feature***, sound off Guile Point on NE coast, 1km S of Holy Island. **77 K6** NU1340.
Burry *Swan.* ***Hamlet***, on Gower peninsula, 2m/3km W of Reynoldston. SS4590.
Burry Green *Swan.* ***Hamlet***, on Gower peninsula, 2m/3km E of Llangennith. SS4691.
Burry Holms *Swan.* ***Coastal feature***, detached headland and bird sanctuary at N end of Rhossili Bay, at W end of Gower peninsula. **17 G5** SS4092.

Burry Port (Porth Tywyn). *Carmar.* Population: 8058. ***Small town***, port on N bank of Burry Inlet, 4m/6km W of Llanelli. **17 H4** SN4400.
Burscough *Lancs.* ***Village***, 2m/3km NE of Ormskirk. **48 D1** SD4310.
Burscough Bridge *Lancs.* Population: 8201. ***Village***, on Leeds and Liverpool Canal, 1m/2km NE of Burscough. **48 D1** SD4411.
Bursea *E.Riding* ***Hamlet***, 5m/8km NE of Howden. **58 E6** SE8033.
Bursea Lane Ends *E.Riding* ***Settlement***, at crossroads, 3m/4km SW of Holme-on-Spalding-Moor. SE7935.
Burshill *E.Riding* ***Hamlet***, 7m/11km NE of Beverley. **59 G5** TA0948.
Bursledon *Hants.* Population: 6077. ***Village***, on W bank of River Hamble, 2m/3km NW of Park Gate. **11 F4** SU4809.
Burslem *Stoke* ***Town***, one of the towns that form city of Stoke-on-Trent: Burslem, Fenton, Hanley, Longton, Stoke-upon-Trent, Tunstall. Burslem lies 3m/5km N of city centre. Pottery town, with Royal Doulton as main manufacturer. Good Georgian architecture. **40 A1** SJ8745.
Burstall *Suff.* ***Village***, 4m/7km W of Ipswich. **35 F4** TM0944.
Burstock *Dorset* ***Village***, 1m/2km W of Broadwindsor. **8 D4** ST4202.
Burston *Norf.* ***Village***, 3m/4km NE of Diss. **45 F7** TM1383.
Burston *Staffs.* ***Hamlet***, 4m/6km SE of Stone. **40 B2** SJ9330.
Burstow *Surr.* ***Village***, 2m/3km SE of Horley. **23 G7** TQ3141.
Burstwick *E.Riding* ***Village***, 3m/4km E of Hedon. **59 J7** TA2227.
Burtersett *N.Yorks.* ***Hamlet***, 1m/2km E of Hawes. **56 D1** SD8989.
Burthorpe Green *Suff.* ***Hamlet***, adjoining to NE of Barrow. TL7764.
Burthwaite *Cumb.* ***Hamlet***, 4m/6km S of Carlisle. NY4149.
Burtle *Som.* ***Hamlet***, 3m/4km N of Catcott across Catcott Heath. **19 H7** ST3943.
Burtle Hill *Som.* ***Settlement***, to NW of Burtle, 8m/12km NW of Glastonbury. ST3943.
Burton *Ches.* ***Hamlet***, 3m/5km W of Tarporley. **48 E6** SJ5063.
Burton *Ches.* ***Village***, 3m/4km SE of Neston. **48 C5** SJ3174.
Burton *Dorset* ***Hamlet***, 1km N of Dorchester. **9 F5** SY6891.
Burton *Dorset* Population: 3651. ***Suburb***, 1m/2km NE of Christchurch. **10 C5** SZ1694.
Burton *Lincs.* ***Village***, 2m/4km N of Lincoln. **52 C5** SK9674.
Burton *Northumb.* ***Settlement***, 1m/2km S of Bamburgh. **77 K7** NU1733.
Burton *Pembs.* ***Village***, 3m/4km S of Llangwm. **16 C4** SM9805.
Burton *Som.* ***Hamlet***, 3m/4km N of Nether Stowey. **7 K1** ST1944.
Burton *Wilts.* ***Hamlet***, 1km E of Mere. ST8232.
Burton *Wilts.* ***Village***, 1m/2km SE of Acton Turville. **20 B4** ST8179.
Burton *Wrex.* ***Hamlet***, 1km W of Rossett. SJ3557.
Burton Agnes *E.Riding* ***Village***, 5m/8km SW of Bridlington. Hall, brick building of early 17c. Norman Manor House (English Heritage) dates from 1170. **59 H3** TA1063.
Burton Agnes Hall *E.Riding* ***Historic house***, 17c brick hall in Burton Agnes, 6m/10km SW of Bridlington. Family collections from as far back as 16c. Art collection includes Renoir, Picasso and various Impressionist paintings. Gardens include alpine plants, mature trees and re-developed walled garden with maze, jungle garden and giant games set. **59 H3** TA1062.
Burton Bradstock *Dorset* ***Village***, near coast, 3m/4km SE of Bridport. **8 D6** SY4889.
Burton Coggles *Lincs.* ***Village***, 3m/5km NE of Colsterworth. **42 C3** SK9725.
Burton Constable *E.Riding* ***Locality***, parish containing Burton Constable Hall, 7m/10km NE of Kingston upon Hull. TA1836.
Burton Constable Country Park *E.Riding* ***Leisure/recreation***, landscaped parkland and lakes designed by 'Capability' Brown, 1km NW of Sproatley. Formerly part of Burton Constable Hall estate. **59 H6** TA1836.
Burton Constable Hall *E.Riding* ***Historic house***, 16c house with 18c state rooms to NW of Sproatley, 7m/11km NE of Hull. **59 H6** TA1836.
Burton Court *Here.* ***Historic house***, 4m/7km W of Leominster. Built on 14c hall and redesigned by Sir Clough Williams-Ellis at beginning of 20c. Various exhibitions including working model fairground. **28 D3** SO4257.
Burton Dassett *Warks.* ***Hamlet***, 4m/6km E of Kineton. Burton Dassett Hills Country Park to N. **31 F3** SP3951.
Burton End *Essex* ***Hamlet***, 3m/5km NE of Bishop's Stortford, on N side of Stansted Airport. TL5323.
Burton Fell *Cumb.* ***Open space***, moorland 4m/7km N of Brough. **61 J4** NY7721.
Burton Ferry *Pembs.* ***Hamlet***, on N bank of Daugleddau estuary, to SW of Burton. SM9705.
Burton Fleming (Also known as North Burton.) *E.Riding* ***Village***, 7m/11km NW of Bridlington. **59 G2** TA0872.
Burton Green *Warks.* ***Hamlet***, on border with West Midlands, 3m/5km NW of Kenilworth. **30 D1** SP2675.
Burton Green *Wrex.* ***Hamlet***, 1m/2km NW of Rossett. **48 C7** SJ3458.
Burton Hastings *Warks.* ***Village***, 3m/5km E of Nuneaton. **41 G6** SP4189.
Burton-in-Kendal *Cumb.* ***Village***, 4m/7km NE of Carnforth. M6 motorway service area to W. **55 J2** SD5376.
Burton in Lonsdale *N.Yorks.* ***Village***, on River Greta, 3m/5km W of Ingleton. **56 B2** SD6572.
Burton Joyce *Notts.* Population: 3854. ***Suburb***, 5m/9km NE of Nottingham. **41 J1** SK6443.
Burton Latimer *Northants.* Population: 5549. ***Small town***, 3m/5km SE of Kettering. **32 C1** SP9074.
Burton Lazars *Leics.* ***Village***, 2m/3km SE of Melton Mowbray. **42 A4** SK7616.
Burton Leonard *N.Yorks.* ***Village***, 5m/8km S of Ripon. **57 J3** SE3263.
Burton on the Wolds *Leics.* ***Village***, 4m/6km of Loughborough. **41 H3** SK5921.
Burton on Trent *Staffs. Alternative name for Burton upon Trent, qv.*
Burton Overy *Leics.* ***Village***, 7m/11km SE of Leicester. **41 J6** SP6798.
Burton Pedwardine *Lincs.* ***Village***, 2m/3km SW of Heckington. **42 E1** TF1142.
Burton Pidsea *E.Riding* ***Village***, 4m/7km NE of Hedon. **59 J6** TA2431.
Burton Salmon *N.Yorks.* ***Village***, 2m/3km N of Ferrybridge. **57 K7** SE4927.
Burton Stather *N.Lincs.* ***Hamlet***, on E bank of River Trent, 1km NW of Burton upon Stather. SE8618.
Burton upon Stather *N.Lincs.* Population: 2719. ***Village***, 5m/7km N of Scunthorpe. **52 B1** SE8717.
Burton upon Trent (Also known as Burton on Trent.) *Staffs.* Population: 60,525. ***Town***, 11m/17km SW of Derby. Major brewing town; has links with William Worthington and William Bass; Bass Museum is major tourist attraction. **40 E3** SK2423.
Burton's Green *Essex* ***Hamlet***, 3m/4km S of Halstead. TL8226.
Burtonwood *Warr.* Population: 3692. ***Small town***, 4m/6km NW of Warrington. Airfield to S. **48 E3** SJ5692.
Burtree Ford *Dur.* ***Locality***, adjoining to E of Cowshill, 1km N of Wearhead. NY8540.
Burwardsley *Ches.* ***Village***, 5m/7km SW of Tarporley. **48 E7** SJ5156.
Burwarton *Shrop.* ***Village***, 8m/13km SW of Bridgnorth. **39 F7** SO6185.
Burwash *E.Suss.* ***Village***, on ridge, between valleys of Rivers Rother and Dudwell, 6m/10km E of Heathfield. Bateman's, 17c ironmaster's house (National Trust), once home of Rudyard Kipling, is 1km S. **13 K4** TQ6724.
Burwash Common *E.Suss.* ***Village***, 2m/4km W of Burwash. **13 K4** TQ6423.
Burwash Weald *E.Suss.* ***Village***, 2m/3km SW of Burwash. **13 K4** TQ6523.
Burwell *Cambs.* Population: 4628. ***Village***, 4m/7km NW of Newmarket. Site of 12c castle W of Church. **33 J2** TL5866.
Burwell *Lincs.* ***Village***, 5m/9km S of Louth. **53 G5** TF3579.
Burwen *I.o.A.* ***Hamlet***, near N coast of Anglesey, 2m/3km W of Amlwch. **46 C3** SH4193.
Burwick *Ork.* ***Settlement***, on S coast of South Ronaldsay. **107 D9** ND4384.
Burwick *Shet.* ***Settlement***, 1m/2km NW of Scalloway, Mainland. **109 C8** HU3940.
Burwick Holm *Shet.* ***Island***, tiny island at entrance to Bur Wick, Mainland. HU3840.
Bury *Cambs.* ***Village***, 1m/2km S of Ramsey. **43 F7** TL2883.
Bury *Gt.Man.* Population: 62,633. ***Town***, former cotton and paper town on River Irwell, 8m/13km N of Manchester. Birthplace of Sir Robert Peel. 15c castle ruins. **49 H1** SD8010.
Bury *Som.* ***Village***, on River Haddeo, 2m/3km E of Dulverton. **7 H3** SS9427.
Bury *W.Suss.* ***Village***, in River Arun valley, 4m/6km N of Arundel. **12 D5** TQ0113.
Bury Art Gallery and Museum *Gt.Man.* ***Other feature of interest***, in Moss Street, in SW part of Bury; contains paintings by Turner and Constable in art gallery. **49 G1** SD7810.
Bury End *Beds.* ***Settlement***, at N end of Shillington, 3m/5km SW of Shefford. TL1234.
Bury End *Bucks.* ***Locality***, at S end of Amersham. SU9697.
Bury End *Worcs.* ***Settlement***, 1km S of Broadway. SP0936.
Bury Green *Herts.* ***Hamlet***, 2m/4km W of Bishop's Stortford. **33 H6** TL4521.
Bury Green *Herts.* ***Suburb***, 1m/2km W of Cheshunt town centre. TL3401.
Bury Hill *Hants.* ***Hill***, rising to over 100 metres and surmounted by ancient hillfort, 2m/3km SW of Andover. **21 G7** SU3443.
Bury St. Edmunds *Suff.* Population: 31,237. ***Town***, on River Lark 23m/37km NW of Ipswich. Many old buildings, especially Georgian. Remains of abbey (English Heritage), St. James's church now cathedral. Moyse's Hall, 12c, East Anglian museum. Angel Corner (National Trust) 18c house, with collection of clocks and watches. Town is noted for splendid floral displays. **34 C2** TL8564.
Bury St. Edmunds Cathedral *Suff.* ***Ecclesiastical building***, parish church built in 15c in Bury St. Edmunds town centre and elevated to cathedral status in 1913. **34 C2** TL8564.
Bury St. Edmunds Theatre Royal *Suff.* ***Other feature of interest***, late Georgian playhouse (National Trust) in Bury St. Edmunds, built 1819 by William Wilkins. Theatre attracts best touring companies in country. **34 C2** TL8562.
Bury Walls *Shrop.* ***Historic/prehistoric site***, large Iron Age fort 2m/3km E of Lee Brockhurst and 10m/16km NE of Shrewsbury. **38 E3** SJ5727.
Buryas Bridge *Cornw.* ***Hamlet***, on W side of Penzance. **2 B6** SW4429.
Burythorpe *N.Yorks.* ***Village***, 4m/7km S of Malton. **58 D3** SE7964.
Busbridge *Surr.* ***Locality***, residential locality adjoining to SE of Godalming. **22 C7** SU9742.
Busby *E.Renf.* Population: 1617. ***Suburb***, 6m/9km S of Glasgow. **74 D5** NS5756.
Busby *P. & K.* ***Settlement***, 1km NE of Methven. **82 B5** NO0326.
Buscot *Oxon.* ***Village***, 2m/3km SE of Lechlade. National Trust property, together with Buscot House, 2km SE. **21 F2** SU2397.
Buscot House *Oxon.* ***Historic house***, National Trust property set in Buscot Park, 3m/4km NW of Faringdon. **21 F2** SU2496.
Buscot Wick *Oxon.* ***Hamlet***, 1m/2km W of Buscot. SU2197.
Bush *Cornw.* ***Hamlet***, 1km N of Stratton. SS2307.
Bush *Pembs.* ***Locality***, 2m/3km W of Saundersfoot. SN1005.
Bush Bank *Here.* ***Village***, 8m/13km NW of Hereford. **28 D3** SO4551.
Bush Crathie *Aber.* ***Settlement***, 1m/2km NW of Crathie. **89 K5** NO2596.
Bush Estate *Norf.* ***Locality***, on coast, adjoining to S of Eccles on Sea, 2m/3km SE of Happisburgh. TG4029.
Bush Fair *Essex* ***Suburb***, 1m/2km SE of Harlow town centre. TL4608.
Bush Green *Norf.* ***Hamlet***, 1m/2km NE of Pulham Market. **45 G7** TM2187.
Bush Green *Norf.* ***Settlement***, 2m/4km NW of Attleborough. TM0297.
Bush Green *Suff.* ***Settlement***, 1m/2km E of Bradfield Combust. TL9157.
Bush Hill *Gt.Lon.* ***Suburb***, in borough of Enfield, to S of Enfield town centre, 9m/14km N of Charing Cross. TQ3295.
Bush Hill Park *Gt.Lon.* ***Suburb***, adjoining to E of Bush Hill. TQ3395.
Bushbury *W.Mid.* ***Suburb***, 2m/4km N of Wolverhampton town centre. **40 B5** SJ9202.
Bushby *Leics.* ***Locality***, 4m/7km E of Leicester. **41 J5** SK6504.
Bushey *Herts.* Population: 16,488. ***Town***, residential town 3m/4km SE of Watford. **22 E2** TQ1395.
Bushey Heath *Herts.* ***Suburb***, adjoining to SE of Bushey. **22 E2** TQ1594.
Bushey Mead *Gt.Lon.* ***Suburb***, in borough of Merton, 1m/2km S of Wimbledon. TQ2468.
Bushley *Worcs.* ***Village***, 1m/2km NW of Tewkesbury across River Severn and River Avon. **29 H5** SO8734.
Bushley Green *Worcs.* ***Hamlet***, 2m/4km NW of Tewkesbury. SO8634.
Bushmead *Beds.* ***Settlement***, 4m/7km W of St. Neots. Remains of 12c Augustinian priory (English Heritage). **32 E2** TL1160.
Bushton *Wilts.* ***Hamlet***, 3m/5km S of Wootton Bassett. **20 D4** SU0677.
Bushy Common *Norf.* ***Settlement***, 2m/4km W of East Dereham. TF9513.
Bushy Park *Gt.Lon.* ***Open space***, large deer park in borough of Richmond upon Thames, opposite Kingston upon Thames across River Thames. Hampton Court Palace is at SW corner. **22 E5** TQ1569.
Busk *Cumb.* ***Settlement***, 1m/2km SE of Renwick. NY6042.
Busk *Gt.Man.* ***Suburb***, 1m/2km E of Oldham town centre. SD9105.
Buslingthorpe *Lincs.* ***Hamlet***, 1m/2km E of Faldingworth. TF0885.
Bussage *Glos.* ***Village***, 2m/4km SE of Stroud. **20 B1** SO8803.
Busta *Shet.* ***Settlement***, on W side of Busta Voe, Mainland, 1km N of Roesound. **109 C6** HU3466.
Busta Voe *Shet.* ***Sea feature***, inlet on W side of Mainland, E of Muckle Roe. **109 C6** HU3566.
Bustard's Green *Norf.* ***Settlement***, 1km W of Long Stratton. TM1792.
Butcher Hill *W.Yorks.* ***Locality***, 1m/2km SW of Todmorden. SD9323.
Butcher's Common *Norf.* ***Hamlet***, 3m/5km NE of Wroxham. TG3320.
Butcher's Cross *E.Suss.* ***Locality***, at N end of Five Ashes, 2m/3km W of Mayfield. **13 J4** TQ5525.
Butcher's Pasture *Essex* ***Village***, 2m/3km NW of Great Dunmow. **33 K6** TL6024.
Butcher's Row *W.Suss.* ***Settlement***, across River Adur from West Grinstead, 6m/10km S of Horsham. TQ1720.
Butcombe *N.Som.* ***Village***, 2m/3km NE of Blagdon. **19 J5** ST5161.
Bute *Arg. & B.* ***Island***, in Firth of Clyde, separated from mainland of Argyll by narrow channel, the Kyles of Bute. E coast, S of Kyles of Bute, is about 5m/8km from Argyll mainland across Firth of Clyde, and SW coast about 6m/10km from Arran. Area nearly 50 square miles or 130 square km. Chief town and port is Rothesay. Mild climate. Industries include tourism and farming, especially dairy farming. Car ferry services from Colintraive and Wemyss Bay. **73 J3** NS0563.
Bute Museum *Arg. & B.* ***Other feature of interest***, on Bute, in Rothesay. Artefacts and exhibitions concerning natural history and the Isle of Bute. **73 J4** NS0964.
Bute Town *Caerp.* ***Hamlet***, 2m/3km NW of Rhymney. SO1009.
Butetown *Cardiff* ***Locality***, dockland area of Cardiff, 1km S of city centre. ST1875.
Buthill *Moray* ***Settlement***, 3m/4km SE of Burghead. **97 J5** NJ1365.
Butleigh *Som.* ***Village***, 3m/5km SE of Street. **8 E1** ST5233.
Butleigh Wootton *Som.* ***Hamlet***, 2m/3km SE of Street. **8 E1** ST5035.
Butler Green *Gt.Man.* ***Locality***, 2m/3km SW of Oldham. SD9003.
Butler's Cross *Bucks.* ***Hamlet***, 2m/3km W of Wendover. **22 B1** SP8407.
Butler's Cross *Bucks.* ***Hamlet***, adjoining to SW of Chalfont St. Giles. SU9792.
Butler's Hill *Notts.* ***Settlement***, adjoining to SE of Hucknall. **41 H1** SK5448.
Butlers Marston *Warks.* ***Village***, 1m/2km SW of Kineton. **30 E3** SP3150.
Butlersbank *Shrop.* ***Settlement***, 2m/3km NE of Shawbury. SJ5822.

Butley *Suff.* ***Village***, 4m/6km W of Orford. **35 H3** TM3651.
Butley Abbey *Suff.* ***Settlement***, to S of Butley, with remains of priory. TM3749.
Butley Corner *Suff.* ***Locality***, 1m/2km SE of Butley and 3m/4km W of Orford across Butley River. Consisting of Butley Low Corner and Butley High Corner. TM3849.
Butley Mills *Suff.* ***Hamlet***, 1m/2km E of Butley. TM3851.
Butley Town *Ches.* ***Hamlet***, 1m/2km W of Bollington. SJ9177.
Butleylow Corner *Suff.* ***Settlement***, 1m/2km SE of Butley and 3m/4km W of Orford across Butley River. TM3849.
Butlins Somerwest World *Som.* ***Leisure/recreation***, theme park and holiday camp to E of Minehead. **7 H1** SS9845.
Butlins Wonderwest World Theme Park *S.Ayr.* ***Leisure/recreation***, holiday camp 3m/4km SW of Ayr. Includes funfair and birds of prey collection. **67 H2** NS3018.
Butlocks Heath *Hants.* ***Hamlet***, 1km NE of Netley. SU4609.
Butser Hill *Hants.* ***Hill***, highest point of South Downs, 3m/4km SW of Petersfield, with mast at summit and many prehistoric barrows, banks, and field systems. Height 886 feet or 270 metres. **11 J2** SU7120.
Butsfield *Dur.* ***Locality***, 4m/6km SW of Lanchester. **62 C2** NZ1145.
Butt Green *Ches.* ***Hamlet***, 1m/2km SE of Nantwich. **49 F7** SJ6651.
Butt Lane *Staffs.* ***Locality***, adjoining to W of Kidsgrove. **49 H7** SJ8254.
Butt of Lewis (Gaelic form: Rubha Robhanais.) *W.Isles* ***Coastal feature***, headland with lighthouse at N end of Isle of Lewis. **101 H1** NB5166.
Butter Tubs Pass *N.Yorks.* ***Other feature of interest***, pass between Hawes and Muker, with deeply eroded limestone rocks forming pillars resembling butter tubs on N slope. **61 K7** SD8796.
Butterburn *Cumb.* ***Settlement***, on W bank of Butter Burn in Spadeadam Forest, 6m/9km N of Greenhead. **70 B6** NY6774.
Buttercrambe *N.Yorks.* ***Hamlet***, on River Derwent, 2m/3km NE of Stamford Bridge. **58 D4** SE7358.
Butterknowle *Dur.* ***Village***, 4m/6km N of Staindrop. **62 C4** NZ1025.
Butterleigh *Devon* ***Village***, 3m/5km SE of Tiverton. **7 H5** SS9708.
Butterley *Derbys.* ***Locality***, 1m/2km N of Ripley. **51 G7** SK4051.
Butterley Reservoir *W.Yorks.* ***Reservoir***, 1km S of Marsden. **50 C2** SE0410.
Buttermere *Cumb.* ***Hamlet***, between Crummock Water and Buttermere lake. **60 C5** NY1716.
Buttermere *Cumb.* ***Lake/loch***, formed by River Cocker, S of Crummock Water. Hamlet of Buttermere at N end. National Trust property. **60 C5** NY1815.
Buttermere *Wilts.* ***Hamlet***, 2m/4km SE of Shalbourne. **21 G5** SU3461.
Buttern Hill *Cornw.* ***Mountain***, 3m/5km W of Altarnun. Cairns near summit. Height 1135 feet or 346 metres. **4 B2** SX1781.
Butters Green *Staffs.* ***Locality***, 4m/6km NW of Newcastle-under-Lyme. **49 H7** SJ8150.
Buttershaw *W.Yorks.* ***Suburb***, 3m/5km SW of Bradford city centre. **57 G7** SE1329.
Butterstone *P. & K.* ***Village***, 3m/5km NE of Dunkeld. Loch of Butterstone is small loch to SW. **82 B3** NO0645.
Butterton *Staffs.* ***Hamlet***, 2m/4km SW of Newcastle-under-Lyme. SJ8242.
Butterton *Staffs.* ***Village***, 6m/9km E of Leek. **50 C7** SK0756.
Butterwick *Dur.* ***Hamlet***, 2m/3km E of Sedgefield. NZ3829.
Butterwick *Lincs.* ***Village***, 4m/6km E of Boston. **43 G1** TF3845.
Butterwick *N.Yorks.* ***Hamlet***, 5m/8km NW of Malton. **58 D2** SE7377.
Butterwick *N.Yorks.* ***Village***, 9m/14km N of Great Driffield. **59 F2** SE9971.
Butterwick Low *Lincs.* ***Coastal feature***, area of mud and sand on W side of The Wash, 6m/10km E of Boston. **43 H1** TF4243.
Buttington *Powys* ***Hamlet***, 2m/3km NE of Welshpool across River Severn. **38 B5** SJ2408.
Buttock Point *Arg. & B.* ***Coastal feature***, headland on Kyles of Bute at N end of Bute. **73 J3** NS0175.
Buttock's Booth *Northants. Alternative name for Boothville, qv.*
Button Hills *Shet.* ***Large natural feature***, range of hills rising to 827 feet or 252 metres, to NE of Burravoe, Mainland. **109 C6** HU3868.
Button Street *Kent* ***Locality***, 1m/2km E of Swanley. TQ5368.
Buttonbridge *Shrop.* ***Hamlet***, 4m/7km NE of Cleobury Mortimer. SO7379.
Buttonoak *Shrop.* ***Hamlet***, 3m/5km NW of Bewdley. **29 G1** SO7577.
Buttons' Green *Suff.* ***Settlement***, 3m/4km N of Lavenham. TL9153.
Butts *Devon* ***Hamlet***, adjoining to W of Dunsford, 4m/6km NE of Moretonhampstead. SX8089.
Butt's Green *Essex* ***Hamlet***, 4m/7km SE of Chelmsford town centre. TL7603.
Butt's Green *Hants.* ***Hamlet***, 1km SE of Lockerley and 4m/7km NW of Romsey. SU3026.
Buttsash *Hants.* ***Suburb***, at S end of Hythe, 3m/4km NW of Fawley. SU4205.
Buxhall *Suff.* ***Village***, 3m/5km W of Stowmarket. **34 E3** TM0057.
Buxhall Fen Street *Suff.* ***Hamlet***, 1m/2km N of Buxhall. TM0058.
Buxted *E.Suss.* ***Village***, 2m/3km NE of Uckfield. **13 H4** TQ4923.
Buxton *Derbys.* Population: 19,854. ***Town***, elevated inland spa (the Roman Aquae Arnemetiae) and resort, 21m/34km SE of Manchester, with many interesting buildings, notably late 18c crescent designed by John Carr. Limestone quarrying in vicinity. Annual International Festival of Music and the Arts. **50 C5** SK0573.
Buxton *Norf.* ***Village***, 4m/6km SE of Aylsham. **45 G3** TG2322.
Buxton Country Park *Derbys.* ***Leisure/recreation***, 100 acres of woodland, 1m/2km SW of Buxton. Includes Pooles Cavern, a 1000 foot or 305 metre long natural cave formation containing underground source of River Wye. Guided tours available. **50 C5** SK0472.
Buxton Heath *Norf.* ***Hamlet***, 1m/2km S of Buxton. TG2321.
Buxton Heath *Norf.* ***Village***, 1m/2km W of Hevingham. **45 F3** TG1821.
Buxworth *Derbys.* ***Village***, 1m/2km NE of Whaley Bridge. **50 C4** SK0282.
Bwcle *Flints. Welsh form of Buckley, qv.*
Bwlch *Powys* ***Village***, 5m/8km NW of Crickhowell. **28 A6** SO1422.
Bwlch Cerrig Duon *Powys* ***Other feature of interest***, pass to E of Moel Feity, 4m/6km N of Glyntawe. **27 H6** SN8522.
Bwlch-clawdd *Carmar.* ***Settlement***, 4m/6km SW of Llandysul. **17 G1** SN3835.
Bwlch-derwin *Gwyn.* ***Hamlet***, 1m/2km W of Pant-glas. **36 D1** SH4646.
Bwlch-Llan *Cere.* ***Hamlet***, 6m/10km W of Tregaron. **26 E3** SN5758.
Bwlch Mawr *Gwyn.* ***Mountain***, on N side of Lleyn Peninsula, 1m/2km SE of Clynnog-fawr. Height 1670 feet or 509 metres. **36 D1** SH4247.
Bwlch-y-cibau *Powys* ***Hamlet***, 3m/4km SE of Llanfyllin. **38 A4** SJ1717.
Bwlch-y-ffridd *Powys* ***Hamlet***, 4m/6km NW of Newtown. **37 K6** SO0695.
Bwlch y Fign *Gwyn.* ***Other feature of interest***, pass, 5m/8km E of Dolgellau. **37 H4** SH8218.
Bwlch y Gorddinan (Also known as Crimea Pass.) *Gwyn.* ***Other feature of interest***, pass through mountains between Blaenau Ffestiniog and Dolwyddelan. **37 F1** SH7049.
Bwlch y groes *Gwyn.* ***Other feature of interest***, pass between Craig yr Ogof and Pennant, 3m/4km N of Llanymawddwy. **37 H3** SH9122.
Bwlch-y-groes *Pembs.* ***Hamlet***, 5m/8km SW of Newcastle Emlyn. **17 F1** SN2436.
Bwlch-y-Rhiw *Gwyn. Alternative name for Rhiw, qv.*
Bwlch-y-sarnau *Powys* ***Hamlet***, 6m/9km NE of Rhayader. **27 K1** SO0274.
Bwlch yr Oerddrws *Gwyn.* ***Other feature of interest***, mountain pass to E of Dolgellau, between Cross Foxes Inn and Pentrewern. **37 G4** SH8016.
Bwlchgwyn *Wrex.* ***Village***, 5m/8km NW of Wrexham. **48 B7** SJ2653.
Bwlchnewydd *Carmar.* ***Hamlet***, 3m/5km NW of Carmarthen. **17 G2** SN3624.
Bwlchtocyn *Gwyn.* ***Hamlet***, 1m/2km S of Abersoch. **36 C3** SH3026.
Bwlchyddar *Powys* ***Hamlet***, 3m/4km NE of Llanfyllin. **38 A3** SJ1722.
Bwlchyfadfa *Cere.* ***Hamlet***, 1m/2km SE of Talgarreg. SN4349.
Bwlchyllyn *Gwyn.* ***Settlement***, 5m/8km S of Caernarfon. SH5055.
Bwlchymynydd *Swan.* ***Suburb***, adjoining to W of Gorseinon and to N of Loughor. SS5798.
Bye Green *Bucks.* ***Settlement***, adjoining to E of Weston Turville, 3m/5km SE of Aylesbury. SP8611.
Byeastwood *Bridgend* ***Hamlet***, on E side of Coity, 2m/3km NE of Bridgend. SS9281.
Byermoor *T. & W.* ***Settlement***, 1m/2km NE of Burnopfield. NZ1857.
Byers Green *Dur.* ***Village***, 2m/3km W of Spennymoor. **62 D3** NZ2234.
Byfield *Northants.* ***Village***, 7m/11km SW of Daventry. **31 G3** SP5153.
Byfleet *Surr.* ***Village***, large village 4m/6km NE of Woking. **22 D5** TQ0661.
Byford *Here.* ***Village***, on N side of River Wye, 7m/12km W of Hereford. **28 C4** SO3942.
Bygrave *Herts.* ***Village***, 2m/3km NE of Baldock. **33 F5** TL2636.
Byker *T. & W.* ***Suburb***, 2m/3km E of Newcastle upon Tyne city centre. **71 H7** NZ2764.
Byland Abbey *N.Yorks.* ***Hamlet***, 2m/4km W of Ampleforth. Ruins of 12c monastery (English Heritage). **58 B2** SE5478.
Bylane End *Cornw.* ***Settlement***, 1m/2km NW of Widegates. **4 C5** SX2759.
Bylaugh *Norf.* ***Hamlet***, on N side of River Wensum, 4m/7km NE of East Dereham. TG0318.
Bylchau *Conwy* ***Hamlet***, 5m/8km SW of Denbigh. **47 H6** SH9763.
Bylchau Rhos-fain *Carmar.* ***Other feature of interest***, mountain pass between Garreg Lwyd and Foel Fraith, 3m/5km NE of Brynamman. **27 G7** SN7517.
Byley *Ches.* ***Hamlet***, 2m/4km NE of Middlewich. **49 G6** SJ7269.
Bynack Burn *Aber.* ***River***, running NE to Geldie Burn, 5m/8km W of Inverey. NO0086.
Bynack More (Formerly known as Caiplich.) *High.* ***Mountain***, in Cairngorm Mountains, in Badenoch and Strathspey district, 3m/4km NE of Cairn Gorm. Munro: height 3575 feet or 1090 metres. **89 H4** NJ0406.
Bynea *Carmar.* ***Hamlet***, 3m/5km E of Llanelli. **17 J5** SS5599.
Byram *N.Yorks.* ***Village***, 1km N of Ferrybridge across River Aire. SE4825.
Byrehope Mount *Sc.Bord.* ***Mountain***, in Pentland Hills, 3m/5km NW of West Linton. Height 1752 feet or 534 metres. **75 J5** NT1055.
Byrness *Northumb.* ***Hamlet***, in Upper Redesdale, 1m/2km SE of Catcleugh Reservoir. **70 C3** NT7602.
Bystock *Devon* ***Suburb***, 2m/3km NE of Exmouth town centre. SY0283.
Bythorn *Cambs.* ***Village***, 4m/7km SE of Thrapston. **32 D1** TL0575.
Byton *Here.* ***Village***, 4m/6km E of Presteigne. **28 C2** SO3764.
Bywell *Northumb.* ***Hamlet***, on N bank of River Tyne, 4m/7km SE of Corbridge. NZ0461.
Byworth *W.Suss.* ***Village***, 1m/2km SE of Petworth. **12 C4** SU9821.

C

Caaf Reservoir *N.Ayr.* ***Reservoir***, small reservoir 2m/4km W of Dalry. **74 A5** NS2550.
Cabharstadh (Anglicised form: Caversta.) *W.Isles* ***Locality***, on S side of Loch Erisort, Isle of Lewis, 2m/4km SE of Lacasaigh. **101 F5** NB3620.
Cabourne *Lincs.* ***Village***, 2m/3km E of Caistor. **52 E2** TA1401.
Cabourne Parva *Lincs.* ***Settlement***, 1m/2km NE of Cabourne. TA1503.
Cabrach *Arg. & B.* ***Settlement***, on Jura, 3m/5km SW of Craighouse. **72 C4** NR4964.
Cabrach *Moray* ***Village***, on River Deveron, 7m/11km W of Rhynie. **90 B2** NJ3826.
Cac Carn Beag *Aber.* ***Mountain***, summit of Lochnagar ridge. Munro: height 3788 feet or 1155 metres. **89 K6** NO2486.
Cac Carn Mòr *Aber. See Lochnagar.*
Cachlaidh Mhòr *Arg. & B.* ***Open space***, 3m/5km E of Bridgend, Islay. **72 B4** NR3961.
Cackle Street *E.Suss.* ***Settlement***, 1m/2km SE of Nutley. TQ4526.
Cackle Street *E.Suss.* ***Settlement***, 1m/2km SE of Brightling. TQ6919.
Cackle Street *E.Suss.* ***Settlement***, adjoining to N of Brede. **14 D6** TQ8218.
Cacrabank *Sc.Bord.* ***Settlement***, 3m/4km NE of Ettrick. **69 J2** NT3017.
Cadair Benllyn *Gwyn.* ***Mountain***, 4m/6km SW of Cerrigydrudion. Height 1335 feet or 407 metres. **37 H1** SH9045.
Cadair Berwyn *Denb.* ***Mountain***, peak of Berwyn mountains, 1km NE of Moel Sych. Height 2713 feet or 827 metres. **37 K2** SJ0732.
Cadair Bronwen *Wrex.* ***Mountain***, peak of Berwyn mountains, 3m/5km SE of Llandrillo. Height 2572 feet or 784 metres. **37 K2** SJ0734.
Cadair Fawr *Powys* ***Mountain***, 4m/7km N of Hirwaun. Height 1591 feet or 485 metres. **27 J7** SN9712.
Cadair Idris *Gwyn.* ***Inland physical feature***, precipitous ridge 3m/5km SW of Dolgellau. Central peak and summit is Penygadair; Mynydd Moel and Tyrrau Mawr are E and W peaks respectively. **37 F4** SH7113.
Cadboll *High.* ***Settlement***, 2m/3km NE of Balintore. **97 F4** NH8777.
Cadbury *Devon* ***Village***, 6m/9km NE of Crediton. **7 H5** SS9104.
Cadbury Barton *Devon* ***Settlement***, 2m/3km N of Chulmleigh. **6 E4** SS6917.
Cadbury Camp *N.Som.* ***Historic/prehistoric site***, Iron Age hillfort (National Trust) 3m/5km NE of Clevedon. **19 H4** ST4572.
Cadbury Castle *Som.* ***Historic/prehistoric site***, extensive Iron Age camp 2m/3km SE of Sparkford. Possible site of King Arthur's legendary Camelot. **9 F2** ST6225.
Cadbury Heath *S.Glos.* ***Suburb***, 5m/8km E of Bristol. **19 K4** ST6672.
Cadder *E.Dun.* ***Hamlet***, on W bank of Forth and Clyde Canal, 2m/3km N of Bishopbriggs. Roman fort to N. **74 E3** NS6172.
Cadderlie *Arg. & B.* ***Settlement***, 4m/7km NE of Taynuilt across Loch Etive. **80 B4** NN0436.
Caddington *Beds.* Population: 3679. ***Village***, 2m/3km SW of Luton. **32 D7** TL0619.
Caddletown *Arg. & B.* ***Settlement***, on Ardmaddy Bay, 4m/7km SW of Kilninver. **79 J6** NM7815.
Caddon Water *Sc.Bord.* ***River***, rising on N side of Windlestraw Law and flowing SE via Stantling Craig Reservoir to River Tweed at Caddonfoot, 3m/5km W of Galashiels. **76 C7** NT4434.
Caddonfoot *Sc.Bord.* ***Settlement***, at mouth of Caddon Water, 3m/5km W of Galashiels. **76 C7** NT4434.
Cade Street *E.Suss.* ***Hamlet***, 1m/2km E of Heathfield. **13 K4** TQ6020.
Cadeby *Leics.* ***Village***, 1m/2km SE of Market Bosworth. **41 G5** SK4202.
Cadeby *S.Yorks.* ***Village***, 3m/4km E of Mexborough. **51 H2** SE5100.
Cadeleigh *Devon* ***Village***, 4m/6km SW of Tiverton. **7 H5** SS9108.
Cademuir Hill *Sc.Bord.* ***Mountain***, two distinct summits at 1361 feet or 415 metres and 1335 feet or 407 metres, 2m/3km SW of Peebles. **76 A7** NT2237.
Cader *Denb.* ***Settlement***, 4m/7km SW of Denbigh. SJ0160.
Cadgwith *Cornw.* ***Village***, tiny fishing village on E coast of Lizard peninsula, 3m/4km NE of Lizard Point. To S, rock ring known as The Devil's Frying Pan. Surrounding cliffs are National Trust property. **2 E7** SW7214.
Cadham *Fife* ***Suburb***, NE district of Glenrothes. **82 D7** NO2702.
Cadhay *Devon* ***Historic house***, mid 16c house built by John Haydon, 1km NW of Ottery St. Mary. Includes listed gardens with medieval fishponds. **7 J6** SY0996.
Cadishead *Gt.Man.* ***Locality***, on N side of Manchester Ship Canal, 2m/3km SW of Irlam. **49 G3** SJ7092.
Cadle *Swan.* ***Suburb***, 3m/5km NW of Swansea city centre. **17 K5** SS6297.

Cadley *Lancs.* ***Suburb***, 2m/3km NW of Preston town centre. SD5231.
Cadley *Wilts.* ***Hamlet***, 2m/3km SE of Marlborough, in Savernake Forest. **21 F5** SU2066.
Cadley *Wilts.* ***Hamlet***, adjoining to NE of Collingbourne Ducis and 2m/4km NW of Ludgershall. SU2454.
Cadmore End *Bucks.* ***Village***, 3m/5km SE of Stokenchurch. **22 A2** SU7892.
Cadnam *Hants.* Population: 1866. ***Village***, on edge of New Forest, 4m/7km W of Totton. **10 E3** SU2913.
Cadnant *Conwy* ***River***, rising on Moel Seisiog and flowing S into River Conwy 1km W of Pentrefoelas. **47 G7** SH8651.
Cadney *N.Lincs.* ***Village***, 3m/4km SE of Brigg. **52 D2** TA0103.
Cadole *Flints.* ***Hamlet***, 2m/4km SW of Mold. **48 B6** SJ2062.
Cadover Bridge *Devon* ***Locality***, and bridge over River Plym, on SW edge of Dartmoor National Park, 2m/3km NW of Lee Moor. **5 F4** SX5564.
Cadoxton (Tregatwg). *V. of Glam.* ***Suburb***, NE district of Barry. **18 E5** ST1269.
Cadoxton-Juxta-Neath (Llangatwg). *N.P.T.* ***Village***, on N side of Neath across River Neath. **18 A2** SS7598.
Cadson Bury *Cornw.* ***Historic/prehistoric site***, ancient British camp (National Trust), 2m/3km SW of Callington. SX3467.
Cadwell *Herts.* ***Settlement***, 2m/3km N of Hitchin. TL1832.
Cadwell *Lincs.* ***Locality***, comprising settlements of Cadwell Park, Cadwell Highfield and Cadwell Slates, 4m/7km SW of Louth. Location of Cadwell Park motor racing circuit. TF2980.
Cadwst *Denb.* ***Settlement***, 1m/2km S of Llandrillo. SJ0335.
Cadzow *S.Lan.* ***Suburb***, S district of Hamilton. NS7153.
Cae Afon *Gwyn.* ***Mountain***, 3m/4km W of Dinas-Mawddwy. Height 2109 feet or 643 metres. **37 H4** SH8114.
Cae Ddafydd *Gwyn.* ***Settlement***, 2m/3km SE of Beddgelert. **37 F1** SH6145.
Caeathro *Gwyn.* ***Hamlet***, 2m/3km SE of Caernarfon. **46 D6** SH5061.
Caehopkin *Powys* ***Hamlet***, 4m/7km NE of Ystalyfera. **27 H7** SN8212.
Caen *High.* ***Settlement***, 2m/3km NW of Helmsdale, to N of River Helmsdale. **105 F7** ND0117.
Caenby *Lincs.* ***Village***, 7m/11km W of Market Rasen. **52 D4** TF0089.
Caenby Corner *Lincs.* ***Settlement***, and cross roads, 2m/3km W of Caenby. **52 C4** SK9689.
Caenlochan Forest *Angus* ***Open space***, deer forest to S of Glas Maol. National Nature Reserve. **89 J7** NO1775.
Caeo *Carmar.* ***Village***, 1m/2km E of Pumsaint. **17 K1** SN6739.
Caeo Forest *Carmar.* ***Forest/woodland***, area of wooded hills to E of Caeo. SN7041.
Cae'r-bont *Powys* ***Hamlet***, 3m/4km NE of Ystalyfera. SN8011.
Caer Caradoc *Shrop.* ***Mountain***, of volcanic origin, surmounted by hillfort, 1m/2km NE of Church Stretton. Height 1506 feet or 459 metres. **38 D6** SO4795.
Caer Drewyn *Denb.* ***Historic/prehistoric site***, stone rampart on hill, 1m/2km NE of Corwen across River Dee. Probably dates from about 5c. **37 K1** SJ0844.
Caer-Estyn *Flints.* ***Settlement***, 1m/2km SE of Hope. SJ3257.
Caer Gybi Roman Fort *I.o.A.* ***Historic/prehistoric site***, reconstructed walls of 4c Roman fort built at edge of harbour on W side of Holyhead, containing 13c church of St. Cybi. **46 A4** SH2482.
Cae'r-Lan *Powys* ***Hamlet***, 3m/5km NE of Ystalfera. **27 H7** SN8012.
Caer Leb *I.o.A.* *See Llanidan.*
Caer Llan *Mon.* ***Settlement***, 3m/4km SE of Monmouth. **19 H1** SO4908.
Caerau *Bridgend* ***Village***, 2m/3km N of Maesteg. **18 B2** SS8594.
Caerau *Cardiff* ***Suburb***, 3m/5km W of Cardiff city centre. **18 E4** ST1375.
Cae'rbryn *Carmar.* ***Hamlet***, 1m/2km SW of Llandybie. SN5913.
Caerdeon *Gwyn.* ***Settlement***, 3m/5km NE of Barmouth. **37 F4** SH6518.
Caerdydd *Cardiff Welsh form of Cardiff, qv.*
Caerfarchell *Pembs.* ***Hamlet***, 3m/5km NE of St. David's. **16 A2** SM7927.
Caerffili *Caerp. Welsh form of Caerphilly, qv.*
Caerfyrddin *Carmar. Welsh form of Carmarthen, qv.*
Caergeiliog *I.o.A.* ***Village***, on Anglesey, 1m/2km SE of Valley. **46 B5** SH3078.
Caergwrle *Flints.* Population: 2277. ***Village***, on River Alun, 5m/8km N of Wrexham. Once a Roman military station. Remains of medieval castle. **48 C7** SJ3057.
Caergwrle Castle *Flints.* ***Castle***, ruined castle in Caergwrle, 8m/12km SW of Chester, on site of Iron Age fort. **48 C7** SJ3057.
Caergybi *I.o.A. Welsh form of Holyhead, qv.*
Caerhun *Conwy* ***Hamlet***, 4m/7km S of Conwy. Church stands on site of Roman fort of Canovium. **47 F5** SH7770.
Caerhun *Gwyn.* ***Hamlet***, 2m/3km S of Bangor. SH5769.
Caerilion *Newport See Caerleon.*
Caeriw *Pembs. Welsh form of Carew, qv.*
Caerlaverock Castle *D. & G.* ***Castle***, ruined late 13c castle (Historic Scotland) near shore of Solway Firth, 7m/12km SE of Dumfries. **69 F7** NY0265.
Caerlaverock Wildfowl and Wetlands Trust *D. & G.* ***Nature reserve***, on E side of mouth of River Nith. One of Britain's largest unclaimed saltmarshes. Breeding ground for natterjack toad and winter feeding ground of barnacle geese. **69 F7** NY0365.
Caerleon (Caerilion). *Newport* Population: 8931. ***Small town***, on N bank of River Usk, on site of Roman town of Isca, 3m/4km NE of Newport. Remains of Roman amphitheatre and legionary fortress (Cadw). **19 G2** ST3390.
Caerleon Roman Fortress and Baths *Newport* ***Historic/prehistoric site***, 50 acre permanent fortress of Isca (Cadw) at Caerleon, 3m/4km NE of Newport. Founded in c. AD 75 and rebuilt in stone c. AD 100. Parts of wall and internal buildings remain, together with magnificent amphitheatre. **19 G2** ST3390.
Caernarfon (Caernarvon). *Gwyn.* Population: 9695. ***Town***, port near SW end of Menai Strait at mouth of River Seiont, 8m/13km SW of Bangor. Medieval castle built by Edward I and remains of town walls (Cadw). Site of Roman fort of Segontium (Cadw) in SE part of town. **46 C6** SH4762.
Caernarfon Bay (Caernarvon Bay). *Gwyn.* ***Bay***, opposite Caernarfon, extending S from Holy Island, Anglesey, to Lleyn Peninsula. **46 A7** SH3536.
Caernarfon Castle *Gwyn.* ***Castle***, medieval castle (Cadw) in Caernarfon, on E bank of River Seiont, near its mouth. Built in 13c by Edward I, as symbol of his conquest of Wales, but never actually finished. Site of investiture of Charles, Prince of Wales, in 1969. **46 C6** SH4762.
Caernarvon *Gwyn. English form of Caernarfon, qv.*
Caernarvon Bay *Gwyn. English form of Caernarfon Bay, qv.*
Caerphilly (Caerffili). *Caerp.* Population: 28,481. ***Town***, 6m/10km N of Cardiff. Remains of large 13c castle (Cadw). Known for Caerphilly cheese, which is still made here. Birthplace of Tommy Cooper. **18 E3** ST1586.
Caerphilly Castle *Caerp.* ***Castle***, 13c concentric castle (Cadw) built on site of Roman fort in Caerphilly, 7m/11km N of Cardiff, with extensive restoration in 20c. Famed for its leaning tower. **18 E3** ST1587.
Caersws *Powys* ***Village***, on River Severn, 5m/8km W of Newtown. Site of Roman military station. **37 K6** SO0391.
Caerwedros *Cere.* ***Hamlet***, 3m/4km S of New Quay. SN3755.
Caerwent *Mon.* ***Village***, 5m/8km SW of Chepstow, on site of Roman town of Venta Silurum (Cadw). Parts of the Roman walls are visible. Traces of early British fort 1m/2km N at Llanmellin. **19 H2** ST4690.
Caerwent Brook *Mon.* ***Hamlet***, 1km S of Caerwent. Limestone quarries to S. ST4789.
Caerwent Roman Town *Mon.* ***Historic/prehistoric site***, 1m/2km N of Caldicot. Known as Venta Silurum, founded in c. AD 75 after submission of Silures tribe. The only walled civilian town in Wales. **19 H2** ST4690.
Caerwys *Flints.* ***Village***, 4m/6km SW of Holywell. **47 K5** SJ1272.
Caethle *Gwyn.* ***Settlement***, 1m/2km SE of Tywyn. **37 F6** SN6099.
Cagar Feosaig *High.* ***Mountain***, 1m/2km N of Backries, Sutherland district. Height 1237 feet or 377 metres. **97 F1** NC8404.
Cage Green *Kent* ***Suburb***, to NE of Tonbridge town centre. TQ5947.
Caggan *High.* ***Settlement***, in River Dulnain valley, 5m/8km NW of Aviemore. **89 F3** NH8216.
Caggle Street *Mon.* ***Hamlet***, 1km NE of Llanvetherine, 5m/8km NE of Abergavenny. SO3617.
Cailiness Point *D. & G.* ***Coastal feature***, headland on E side of Rinns of Galloway, 3m/5km N of Mull of Galloway. **64 B7** NX1535.
Cailleach Head *High.* ***Coastal feature***, headland on NE side of entrance to Little Loch Broom, W coast of Ross and Cromarty district. **95 F2** NG9898.
Caim *I.o.A.* ***Hamlet***, on Anglesey, 1m/2km NE of Llangoed. SH6280.
Cain *Powys* ***River***, formed by confluence of Rivers Abel and Fyllon at Llanfyllin, and flowing E into River Vyrnwy on E side of Llansantffraid-ym-Mechain. SJ2220.
Caiplich *High. Former name of Bynack More, qv.*
Caiplich *High.* ***Locality***, 5m/8km NE of Drumnadrochit. **88 C1** NH5437.
Caiplich Water *See Water of Ailnack.*
Cairinis (Anglicised form: Carinish.) *W.Isles* ***Village***, at S end of North Uist, 8m/13km SW of Lochmaddy. **92 D6** NF8159.
Cairisiadar (Anglicised form: Carishader.) *W.Isles* ***Village***, on Isle of Lewis, 1m/2km SE of Miabhig. **100 C4** NB0933.
Cairminis (Anglicised form: Carminish.) *W.Isles* ***Settlement***, on SW coast of South Harris, 1km SE of Leverburgh. **93 F3** NG0284.
Cairn Baddoch *Angus* ***Mountain***, 2m/3km N of Runtaleave, on W side of Glenclova Forest. Height 1932 feet or 589 metres. **89 K7** NO2770.
Cairn Bannoch ***Mountain***, 3m/5km W of Loch Muick, with summit on border of Angus and Aberdeenshire. Munro: height 3319 feet or 1012 metres. **89 K6** NO2282.
Cairn Cattoch *Moray* ***Mountain***, 3m/5km SW of Rothes. Height 1210 feet or 369 metres. **97 K7** NJ2346.
Cairn Daunie *Angus* ***Mountain***, 3m/5km W of Runtaleave. Height 2070 feet or 631 metres. **82 D1** NO2468.
Cairn Duhie *High.* ***Mountain***, 2m/3km SE of Ferness. Height 1023 feet or 312 metres. **97 G7** NH9842.
Cairn Ellick *Moray* ***Mountain***, 3m/5km NE of Tomintoul. Height 1735 feet or 529 metres. **89 J2** NJ1823.
Cairn Ewen *High.* ***Mountain***, on border of Inverness and Badenoch and Strathspey districts, 9m/12km NW of Newtonmore. Height 2870 feet or 875 metres. **88 C4** NH5802.
Cairn Galtar *W.Isles* ***Hill***, highest point on Sandray. Height 679 feet or 207 metres. **84 B5** NL6491.
Cairn Geldie *Aber.* ***Mountain***, 6m/10km S of Ben Macdui and 10m/15km W of Braemar. Height 2043 feet or 623 metres. **89 G6** NN9988.
Cairn Gibbs *Angus* ***Mountain***, 4m/6km W of Bellaty. Height 1706 feet or 520 metres. **82 C2** NO1859.
Cairn Gorm ***Mountain***, in Cairngorm Mountains on border of Highland and Moray, 8m/13km SE of Aviemore. Range named after peak although only fourth in altitude. Munro: height 4084 feet or 1245 metres. Ski slopes and chair lifts on NW side. **89 H4** NJ0004.
Cairn Gorm of Derry *Aber. Alternative name for Derry Cairngorm, qv.*
Cairn Leuchan *Aber.* ***Mountain***, 3m/5km S of Ballater. Height 2194 feet or 669 metres. **90 B5** NO3891.
Cairn-mon-earn *Aber.* ***Mountain***, 3m/5km NW of Rickarton, in Durris Forest. Masts at summit. Height 1240 feet or 378 metres. **91 F5** NO7891.
Cairn Mona Gowan *Aber.* ***Mountain***, 4m/7km S of Strathdon. Height 2457 feet or 749 metres. **90 B4** NJ3305.
Cairn Muir *Sc.Bord.* ***Open space***, mountainous moorland area in Pentland Hills, 4m/6km NW of West Linton, traversed N to S by Old Drove Road. **75 K5** NT1156.
Cairn Muldonich *Moray* ***Mountain***, 2m/3km E of Tomnavoulin. Height 1902 feet or 580 metres. **89 K2** NJ2427.
Cairn na Burgh Beg *Arg. & B.* ***Island***, at NE end of Treshnish Isles, with remains of an old fort. **78 E3** NM3044.
Cairn na Burgh More *Arg. & B.* ***Island***, at NE end of Treshnish Isles, with ruin of an ancient castle. **78 E3** NM3044.
Cairn of Barns *Angus* ***Mountain***, 1m/2km SW of Clova. Height 2135 feet or 651 metres. **90 B7** NO3271.
Cairn of Claise ***Mountain***, on Aberdeenshire and Angus border, 7m/12km NE of Spittal of Glenshee. Munro: height 3490 feet or 1064 metres. **89 J7** NO1878.
Cairn of Get (Also known as Garrywhin.) *High.* ***Historic/prehistoric site***, prehistoric chambered tomb (Historic Scotland), 1km NW of Ulbster. **105 J4** ND3141.
Cairn o'Mount (Cairn o'Mounth). *Aber.* ***Mountain***, summit of lower Grampian Mountains, 5m/8km N of Fettercairn, along Old Military Road linking Fettercairn and Banchory. Height 1492 feet or 455 metres. **90 E6** NO6480.
Cairn o'Mounth *Aber. Alternative spelling of Cairn o'Mount, qv.*
Cairn Pat *D. & G.* ***Hill***, 3m/4km S of Stranraer. Mast and ancient fort at summit. Height 597 feet or 182 metres. **64 A5** NX0456.
Cairn Point *D. & G.* ***Coastal feature***, point with lighthouse on E side of Loch Ryan, 5m/8km N of Stranraer. **64 A4** NX0668.
Cairn Table *S.Lan.* ***Mountain***, 3m/5km SE of Muirkirk. Height 1945 feet or 593 metres. **68 C1** NS7224.
Cairn Taggart *Aber. Alternative name for Carn an t-Sagairt Mòr, qv.*
Cairn Toul *Aber.* ***Mountain***, in Cairngorm Mountains 2m/3km SW of Ben Macdui. Munro: height 4234 feet or 1291 metres. **89 G5** NN9697.
Cairn Uish *Moray* ***Mountain***, 3m/4km S of Kellas. Height 1197 feet or 365 metres. **97 J6** NJ1750.
Cairn Vachich *Aber.* ***Mountain***, 2m/3km N of Corgarff. Height 2135 feet or 651 metres. **89 K3** NJ2611.
Cairn Vungie *High.* ***Mountain***, in Inverness district, 5m/8km E of Fort Augustus. Height 2329 feet or 710 metres. **88 B4** NH4507.
Cairn Water *D. & G.* ***River***, flowing SE from near Moniaive to join Old Water and form Cluden Water, 6m/10km NW of Dumfries. **68 D5** NX8879.
Cairn William *Aber.* ***Mountain***, in Pitfichie Forest, 2m/3km NW of Monymusk. Height 1469 feet or 448 metres. **90 E3** NJ6516.
Cairnacay *Moray* ***Mountain***, 4m/7km N of Tomnavoulin. Height 1607 feet or 490 metres. **89 K1** NJ2032.
Cairnargat *Aber.* ***Settlement***, 2m/3km E of Haugh of Glass. **90 C1** NJ4539.
Cairnbaan *Arg. & B.* ***Village***, on Crinan Loch, in Argyll, 2m/4km NW of Lochgilphead. Cup and ring marked rocks (Historic Scotland); also at Achnabreck, 1m/2km E. **73 G1** NR8390.
Cairnbaan Cup and Ring Marks *Arg. & B.* ***Historic/prehistoric site***, adjacent to N of Cairnbaan, 3m/4km NW of Lochgilphead. Two cup and ring marked rocks (Historic Scotland); ringed carvings feature up to four rings. **73 G1** NR8391.
Cairnbeathie *Aber.* ***Settlement***, 1km S of Lumphanan. **90 D4** NJ5703.
Cairnbrallan *Moray* ***Mountain***, 4m/6km SW of Cabrach. Height 2027 feet or 618 metres. **90 B2** NJ3324.
Cairnbrogie *Aber.* ***Settlement***, 3m/4km E of Oldmeldrum. **91 G2** NJ8426.
Cairnbulg *Aber.* ***Locality***, on NE coast, adjoining to W of Inverallochy. **99 J4** NK0365.
Cairnbulg Castle *Aber.* ***Castle***, set in woodland 2m/3km SE of Fraserburgh. Mid-13c rectangular tower, with later additions, and home of Comyn family. Converted to a mansion late 19c. **99 J4** NK0163.
Cairnbulg Point *Aber.* ***Coastal feature***, headland to NW of Cairnbulg, at E end of Fraserburgh Bay. **99 J4** NK0366.
Cairncross *Sc.Bord.* ***Hamlet***, 2m/3km SW of Coldingham. **77 G4** NT8963.
Cairncurran *Inclyde* ***Settlement***, 3m/4km W of Kilmacolm. **74 B4** NS3169.
Cairncurran Hill *Inclyde* ***Hill***, 4m/6km W of Kilmacolm. Height 909 feet or 277 metres. **74 A3** NS2970.
Cairndoon *D. & G.* ***Settlement***, 2m/3km SE of Monreith. **64 D7** NX3838.
Cairndow *Arg. & B.* ***Village***, at mouth of Kinglas Water, on Loch Fyne in Argyll, near head of loch. **80 C6** NN1711.
Cairne *Aber.* ***Settlement***, 1m/2km SW of Westhill. **91 G4** NJ8005.
Cairness *Aber.* ***Settlement***, 5m/7km SE of Fraserburgh. **99 J4** NK0360.
Cairney Lodge *Fife* ***Hamlet***, 1m/2km N of Cupar. **82 E6** NO3717.
Cairneyhill *Fife* Population: 2092. ***Village***, 3m/5km W of Dunfermline. **75 J2** NT0486.
Cairngarroch Bay *D. & G.* ***Bay***, on coast of Rinns of Galloway, 4m/6km SE of Portpatrick. **64 A6** NX0449.
Cairngorm Chairlift and Ski Centre *High.* ***Other feature of interest***, two-stage chairlift, 9m/13km SE of Aviemore, serving Britain's most popular ski resort. Lift operates from Cairngorm Day Lodge (2150 feet or 655 metres) to Ptarmigan Café (3600 feet or 1097 metres), below summit of Cairn Gorm. **89 G4** NH9805.

Cairngorm Mountains ***Large natural feature***, granite mountain mass with rounded summits within Grampian Mountains on borders of Aberdeenshire, Highland and Moray between Aviemore and Braemar. Popular with walkers, climbers and skiers. Deep defile of Lairig Ghru divides range into E and W parts. Summit is Ben Macdui, 4296 feet or 1309 metres. **89 G4** NJ0103.
Cairngorms National Nature Reserve ***Nature reserve***, largest nature reserve in Britain, in S part of Cairngorm Mountains, about 12m/16km NW of Braemar. Notable for sub-arctic summit plateau with arctic-alpine animal and plant communities. Wildlife includes eagles, buzzards, mountain hare, wild cat and deer. **89 G5** NN9396.
Cairngryffe Hill *S.Lan.* ***Mountain***, rising to over 330 metres with quarried SE face, 4m/6km SE of Lanark. **75 H6** NS9441.
Cairnharrow *D. & G.* ***Mountain***, 4m/7km W of Gatehouse of Fleet. Height 1496 feet or 456 metres. **65 F5** NX5355.
Cairnhill *Aber.* ***Settlement***, 1m/2km E of Kirkton of Culsalmond. **90 E1** NJ6632.
Cairnhill *Aber.* ***Settlement***, 2m/3km S of Ellon. **91 H2** NJ9427.
Cairnholy *D. & G.* ***Historic/prehistoric site***, chambered cairns (Historic Scotland), 4m/6km SE of Creetown. **65 F5** NX5153.
Cairnie *Aber.* ***Hamlet***, on N side of Burn of Cairnie, 4m/7km NW of Huntly. **98 C6** NJ4844.
Cairnkinna Hill *D. & G.* ***Mountain***, 5m/8km S of Sanquhar. Height 1811 feet or 552 metres. **68 C3** NS7901.
Cairnoch Hill *Stir.* ***Mountain***, overlooking N shore of Carron Valley Reservoir, 5m/8km E of Fintry. Height 1355 feet or 413 metres. **75 F2** NS6985.
Cairnorrie *Aber.* ***Settlement***, 4m/6km S of New Deer. **99 G6** NJ8641.
Cairnpapple Hill *W.Loth.* ***Hill***, rising to over 300 metres, 1m/2km SE of Torphichen. Henge and cairn (Historic Scotland) at summit. **75 H3** NS9871.
Cairnryan *D. & G.* ***Small town***, port on E side of Loch Ryan. Car ferry service to Larne in Northern Ireland. **64 A4** NX0668.
Cairns of Coll *Arg. & B.* ***Island***, two island rocks lying nearly 2m/3km NE of Coll. NM2866.
Cairnsmore *D. & G.* ***Settlement***, 4m/6km E of Newton Stewart. **64 E4** NX4764.
Cairnsmore of Carsphairn (Also known as Cairnsmore of Deugh.) *D. & G.* ***Mountain***, 4m/6km NE of Carsphairn. Height 2614 feet or 797 metres. **67 K4** NX5998.
Cairnsmore of Dee *D. & G.* ***Mountain***, 3m/5km W of New Galloway. Height 1617 feet or 493 metres. **65 F3** NX5875.
Cairnsmore of Deugh *D. & G. Alternative name for Cairnsmore of Carsphairn, qv.*
Cairnsmore of Fleet *D. & G.* ***Mountain***, massif 6m/9km E of Newton Stewart. Height 2329 feet or 710 metres. **64 E4** NX5067.
Cairntrodlie *Aber.* ***Suburb***, W district of Peterhead. NK1246.
Cairnwell Pass *P. & K.* ***Other feature of interest***, mountain pass to E of The Cairnwell, carrying road from Braemar to Spittal of Glenshee, is highest main road pass in Britain (2199 feet or 670 metres). NO1477.
Cairnywhing *Aber.* ***Open space***, hillslope with settlement, 1m/2km NW of New Pitsligo. **99 G5** NJ8757.
Caisteal Abhail *N.Ayr.* ***Mountain***, on Arran, 6m/9km NW of Brodick. Height 2818 feet or 859 metres. **73 H6** NR9644.
Caisteal Dubh *P. & K. See Moulin.*
Caisteal Maol (Anglicised form: Castle Moil.) *High.* ***Castle***, remains of 14c keep on Skye, to E of Kyleakin. **86 D2** NG7526.
Caister Castle *Norf.* ***Castle***, ruined 15c castle with 100-foot or 31 metre tower, 1m/2km W of Caister-on-Sea. **45 J4** TG5012.
Caister-on-Sea *Norf.* Population: 8070. ***Small town***, coastal resort 3m/5km N of Great Yarmouth. Site of Roman town (English Heritage). Remains of 15c castle 1m/2km W. **45 K4** TG5212.
Caister Roman Site *Norf.* ***Historic/prehistoric site***, remains of 3c Roman town, harbour and trading centre (English Heritage) to W of Caister-on-Sea and 3m/5km N of Great Yarmouth. **45 K4** TG5112.
Caistor *Lincs.* Population: 2502. ***Small town***, on site of Roman station 8m/12km N of Market Rasen. **52 E2** TA1101.
Caistor St. Edmund *Norf.* ***Village***, 3m/5km S of Norwich. Site of Roman town of Venta Icenorum to SW. **45 G5** TG2303.
Caistron *Northumb.* ***Hamlet***, in Coquetdale, 2m/3km SW of Thropton. **70 E3** NT9901.
Caiteshal *W.Isles* ***Mountain***, rising steeply on E shore of Loch Seaforth, 2m/3km N of entrance to loch. Height 1473 feet or 449 metres. **100 E7** NB2404.
Caiy Stane *Edin.* ***Historic/prehistoric site***, ancient standing stone, National Trust for Scotland property, 4m/6km S of Edinburgh city centre. 9 feet or 3 metres high, with traces of cup marks on E side. **76 A4** NT2468.
Cake Street *Norf.* ***Locality***, 3m/5km SE of Attleborough. **44 E6** TM0790.
Cake Street *Suff.* ***Locality***, S end of Beck Row, 2m/3km NW of Mildenhall. TL6977.
Cakebole *Worcs.* ***Settlement***, 4m/6km E of Stourport-on-Severn. SO8772.
Calabrie Island (Gaelic form: Eilean Chalaibrigh.) *W.Isles* ***Island***, islet at entrance to Loch Erisort, E coast of Isle of Lewis. NB3822.
Calair Burn *Stir.* ***River***, flowing N into head of Loch Voil at Balquhidder. **81 G6** NN5320.
Calais Street *Suff.* ***Hamlet***, SE of Boxford, 4m/6km W of Hadleigh. TL9739.
Calanais *W.Isles Gaelic form of Callanish, qv.*
Calbha Beag (Anglicised form: Calva Beg). *High.* ***Island***, one of two small uninhabited islands in Eddrachillis Bay, along with Calbha Mòr, 3m/5km S of Badcall, W coast of Sutherland district. **102 D5** NC1536.
Calbha Mòr (Anglicised form: Calva Mòr.) *High.* ***Island***, one of two small uninhabited islands in Eddrachillis Bay, along with Calbha Beag, 3m/5km S of Badcall, W coast of Sutherland district. **102 D5** NC1636.
Calbost *W.Isles* ***Settlement***, on E coast of Isle of Lewis, 2m/4km N of Kebock Head across mouth of Loch Odhairn. **101 G6** NB4117.
Calbourne *I.o.W.* ***Village***, 5m/8km W of Newport. **11 F6** SZ4286.
Calcaria *N.Yorks. See Tadcaster.*
Calceby *Lincs.* ***Settlement***, 3m/5km SE of Burwell. A 'lost village' of The Wolds; limestone ruin was once parish church of village which dwindled away in 1621, and only present buildings remain. TF3975.
Calcoed *Flints.* ***Settlement***, 1m/2km SW of Holywell. SJ1774.
Calcot *W.Berks.* ***Suburb***, 3m/5km W of Reading town centre. **21 K4** SU6671.
Calcot Row *W.Berks.* ***Suburb***, 3m/5km W of Reading. SU6671.
Calcott *Kent* ***Hamlet***, 2m/3km N of Sturry. **25 H5** TR1762.
Calcott *Shrop.* ***Hamlet***, 3m/5km W of Shrewsbury. SJ4413.
Calcott Green *Glos.* ***Hamlet***, 3m/5km W of Gloucester. SO7817.
Calcutt *Wilts.* ***Settlement***, 1km E of Cricklade. SU1193.
Caldarvan *W.Dun.* ***Settlement***, 3m/5km NE of Balloch. **74 C2** NS4384.
Caldback *Shet.* ***Settlement***, situated in centre of Unst, with chambered cairn and Hill of Caldback to SE. **108 F2** HP6007.
Caldbeck *Cumb.* ***Village***, 7m/11km SE of Wigton. **60 E3** NY3239.
Caldbeck Fells *Cumb.* ***Large natural feature***, mountain group on N side of Lake District, highest point of which is High Pike (658 metres), 3m/5km S of Caldbeck. **60 E3** NY3135.
Caldbergh *N.Yorks.* ***Hamlet***, 3m/4km SW of Middleham. **57 F1** SE0985.
Caldecote *Cambs.* ***Village***, 1m/2km SW of Stilton. **42 E7** TL1488.
Caldecote *Cambs.* ***Village***, 6m/10km W of Cambridge. **33 G3** TL3456.
Caldecote *Herts.* ***Hamlet***, 3m/5km N of Baldock. **33 F5** TL2338.
Caldecote *Northants.* ***Settlement***, 2m/3km N of Towcester. SP6851.
Caldecote *Warks.* ***Hamlet***, 2m/3km NW of Nuneaton. **41 F6** SP3594.
Caldecott *Northants.* ***Village***, 2m/3km W of Higham Ferrers. **32 C2** SP9868.
Caldecott *Oxon.* ***Suburb***, to S of Abingdon. SU4996.
Caldecott *Rut.* ***Village***, in River Welland valley, 4m/6km S of Uppingham. **42 B6** SP8693.
Caldecotte *M.K.* ***Settlement***, 2m/3km NE of Bletchley. Site of former village to N. SP8935.
Calder ***River***, rising at W end of Ennerdale Fell and flowing SW past Calder Hall Atomic Power Station into Irish Sea, 1m/2km NW of Seascale. NY0102.
Calder ***River***, rising 4m/7km SE of Burnley and flowing NW through Burnley, Padiham and Whalley, to join River Ribble 2m/3km W of Whalley. SD7037.
Calder *Cumb.* ***Locality***, 2m/3km N of Seascale. Calder Hall Atomic Power Station to W. NY0303.
Calder *High.* ***River***, in Badenoch and Strathspey district, running E to River Spey 1m/2km SW of Newtonmore. NN7097.
Calder *Lancs.* ***River***, rising on Bleasdale Moors on W side of Forest of Bowland and flowing SW into River Wyre at Catterall. SD4943.
Calder *Renf.* ***River***, rising as Calder Water on slopes N of Burnt Hill and flowing E and SE before widening into River Calder below weir to W of Muirshiel Country Park. River continues SE to Castle Semple Loch, to SE of Lochwinnoch. **74 B4** NS3558.
Calder *W.Yorks.* ***River***, rising near Todmorden and flowing E by Hebden Bridge, Sowerby Bridge, Brighouse, Dewsbury and Wakefield to join River Aire at Castleford. **57 J7** SE4226.
Calder Abbey *Cumb.* ***Ecclesiastical building***, on W bank of River Calder, 1km NE of Calder Bridge. Ruined abbey, built 12c. **60 B6** NY0506.
Calder Bridge *Cumb.* ***Village***, 4m/6km SE of Egremont. **60 B6** NY0406.
Calder Burn *High.* ***River***, flowing N down Glen Buck from N slopes of Aberchalder Forest, then flowing NE to enter Loch Oich just S of Aberchalder. NH3303.
Calder Fell *Lancs.* ***Open space***, area of moorland on Bleasdale Moors, 4m/7km NE of Garstang. **55 J5** SD5548.
Calder Glen Country Park *S.Lan.* ***Leisure/recreation***, country park centred around Torrance House on Calder Water, 1m/2km E of East Kilbride town centre. 300 acres of grounds including parkland, children's zoo and several waterfalls. **74 E5** NS6552.
Calder Grove *W.Yorks.* ***Village***, 3m/5km SW of Wakefield, near junction 39 of M1 motorway. SE3016.
Calder Mains *High.* ***Hamlet***, 1km E of Loch Calder. **105 F3** ND0959.
Calder Vale *Lancs.* ***Hamlet***, 3m/4km E of Garstang. **55 J5** SD5345.
Calderbank *N.Lan.* Population: 1709. ***Village***, 2m/3km S of Airdrie. **75 F4** NS7763.
Calderbrook *Gt.Man.* ***Village***, 1m/2km N of Littleborough. **49 J1** SD9418.
Caldercruix *N.Lan.* Population: 2292. ***Village***, 4m/7km NE of Airdrie. **75 G4** NS8267.
Calderglen *S.Lan.* ***Settlement***, 3m/5km NW of Hamilton. **74 E5** NS6859.
Caldermill *S.Lan.* ***Hamlet***, on Calder Water, 3m/5km SW of Strathaven. **74 E6** NS6641.
Caldermoor *Gt.Man.* ***Locality***, adjoining to W of Littleborough. SD9316.
Calderstones *Mersey.* ***Suburb***, 4m/7km SE of Liverpool city centre. SJ4087.
Calderwood *S.Lan.* ***Suburb***, to N of East Kilbride town centre. NS6455.
Caldew *Cumb.* ***River***, rising on E slopes of Skiddaw, and flowing N past Hesket Newmarket and Dalston to join River Eden on N side of Carlisle. **60 E3** NY3956.
Caldey Island (Ynys Bŷr). *Pembs.* ***Island***, at SW end of Carmarthen Bay about 1m/2km E to W and 1km N to S, separated from mainland at Giltar Point by Caldey Sound. Old Priory, 12c-15c. Abbey, early 20c, houses community of Reformed Cistercian monks. Lighthouse at SE corner of island. **16 E5** SS1496.
Caldey Island Abbey *Pembs.* ***Ecclesiastical building***, 3m/4km S of Tenby. Celtic monks settled on Caldey Island in 6c, since then there has been a succession of foundations. The present abbey was built in 1906-11 and is occupied by a Reformed Cistercian order. **16 E5** SS1496.
Caldey Island Old Priory *Pembs.* ***Ecclesiastical building***, 3m/4km S of Tenby. Remains of 12c Benedictine priory, including St. Illtud's Church, with its 6c inscribed Ogham Cross. **16 E5** SS1496.
Caldey Sound *Pembs.* ***Sea feature***, strait about 1km wide at SW end of Carmarthen Bay, separating mainland from Caldey Island. **16 E5** SS1296.
Caldhame *Angus* ***Hamlet***, 2m/3km S of Forfar. **83 F3** NO4748.
Caldicot *Mon.* Population: 12,153. ***Town***, 5m/8km SW of Chepstow. Castle has round 13c-14c keep. **19 H3** ST4888.
Caldicot Castle *Mon.* ***Castle***, on E side of Caldicot, 10m/16km E of Newport. Originally a 12c motte castle with two baileys, becoming a stone castle in 13c. **19 H3** ST4888.
Caldicot Level *Newport* ***Open space***, artificial drainage area along River Severn estuary between Whitson and Caldicot, about 6m/9km SE of Newport. **19 G3** ST3984.
Caldwell *Derbys.* ***Hamlet***, 3m/5km SW of Swadlincote. **40 E4** SK2517.
Caldwell *E.Renf.* ***Settlement***, 1m/2km SW of Uplawmoor. **74 C5** NS4154.
Caldwell *N.Yorks.* ***Village***, 4m/6km SW of Piercebridge. **62 C5** NZ1613.
Caldy *Mersey.* ***Locality***, 1m/2km SE of West Kirby. **48 B4** SJ2285.
Caldy Hill *Mersey.* ***Hill***, National Trust property in S part of West Kirby rising to over 70 metres, affording view across River Dee estuary. SJ2285.
Cale ***River***, rising N of Wincanton and flowing S through town into River Stour to W of Marnhull. **9 G2** ST7519.
Calebrack *Cumb.* ***Settlement***, on E side of Caldbeck Fells, 2m/3km S of Hesket Newmarket. NY3435.
Caledfwlch *Carmar.* ***Hamlet***, 2m/3km NE of Llandeilo. SN6525.
Caledonian Canal *High.* ***Canal***, ship canal built by Thomas Telford, connecting Moray Firth at Inverness to Loch Linnhe, through Lochs Ness, Oich, Lochy and mouth of Loch Eil. Nowadays used by small cargo boats and pleasure craft. **96 D7** NH6446.
Caledonian Railway *Angus* ***Other feature of interest***, travelling 4m/6km from Brechin to Bridge of Dun. **83 H2** NO6658.
Caledrhydiau *Cere.* ***Settlement***, 1m/2km SE of Mydroilyn. **26 D3** SN4753.
Calf of Eday *Ork.* ***Island***, uninhabited island of about 750 acres or 300 hectares lying off NE coast of Eday, separated from it by narrow strait of Calf Sound. **106 E4** HY5839.
Calf of Flotta *Ork.* ***Island***, small uninhabited island off NE end of Flotta across narrow strait of Calf Sound. **107 C8** ND3896.
Calf of Man *I.o.M.* ***Island***, Manx National Trust property about 1m/2km across, off SW extremity of Isle of Man, separated from main island by Calf Sound. Noted for bird life. **54 A7** SC1565.
Calf Sound *Ork.* ***Sea feature***, narrow strait separating Calf of Eday from Eday. HY5638.
Calf Top *Cumb.* ***Mountain***, on W side of Barbondale, 3m/4km W of Dent. Height 1998 feet or 609 metres. **56 B1** SD6685.
Calford Green *Suff.* ***Hamlet***, 2m/3km E of Haverhill. TL6945.
Calfsound *Ork.* ***Settlement***, at NE end of Eday. Uninhabited island of Calf of Eday to N across Calf Sound. **106 E4** HY5738.
Calgary *Arg. & B.* ***Village***, near W coast of Mull, at Calgary Bay. Emigrants from here gave Calgary in Alberta its name, Canada. **78 E2** NM3751.
Calgary Bay *Arg. & B.* ***Bay***, on W coast of Mull. **78 E3** NM3751.
Calgary Point *Arg. & B.* ***Coastal feature***, headland at SW end of Coll. **78 C2** NM0152.
Caliach Point *Arg. & B.* ***Coastal feature***, headland on W coast of Mull, 10m/16km W of Tobermory. **78 E2** NM3454.
Califer *Moray* ***Settlement***, 3m/4km E of Forres. **97 H6** NJ0857.
California *Derby* ***Suburb***, 1m/2km SW of Derby city centre. SK3335.
California *Falk.* ***Village***, 3m/5km SE of Falkirk. **75 H3** NS9076.
California *Norf.* ***Town***, coastal resort 5m/7km N of Great Yarmouth. **45 K4** TG5114.
California *Suff.* ***Suburb***, 1m/2km E of Ipswich town centre. TM1844.

Calke *Derbys.* ***Village***, 4m/6km N of Ashby de la Zouch. **41 F3** SK3722.
Calke Abbey *Derbys.* ***Historic house***, in park to W of Calke, large 18c house on site of former priory. **41 F3** SK3622.
Calkin Rig (Also spelled Cauldkine Rig.) *D. & G.* ***Mountain***, 5m/8km NW of Langholm. Height 1476 feet or 450 metres. **69 H5** NY2987.
Callaly *Northumb.* ***Settlement***, 2m/3km SW of Whittingham. **71 F3** NU0509.
Callaly Castle *Northumb.* ***Historic house***, 17c-19c mansion built around a pele tower, 2m/3km SW of Whittingham. **71 F2** NU0509.
Callander *Stir.* Population: 2622. ***Small town***, 14m/22km NW of Stirling. Tourist centre on edge of Trossachs. **81 H7** NN6207.
Callanish (Gaelic form: Calanais.) *W.Isles* ***Village***, on W coast of Isle of Lewis, 13m/21km W of Stornoway and 1m/2km S of Breascleit. Callanish Standing stones (Historic Scotland). **100 E4** NB2133.
Callanish Standing Stones *W.Isles* ***Historic/prehistoric site***, thirty-nine standing stones (Historic Scotland), are ancient gravestones of uncertain date, near coast of Isle of Lewis at entrance to Loch Cean Thulabhig, 1m/2km S of Breascleit. **100 E4** NB2133.
Callater Burn *Aber.* ***River***, running N through Loch Callater and down Glen Callater to join Clunie Water 2m/3km S of Braemar. NO1588.
Callaughton *Shrop.* ***Settlement***, 2m/3km S of Much Wenlock. SO6197.
Callender House *Falk.* ***Historic house***, set in parkland to SE of Falkirk town centre. Contains a working kitchen of 1825 and an exhibition charting its 900 year history. **75 G3** NS8979.
Callerton *T. & W.* ***Hamlet***, 1m/2km E of Callerton Lane End and 5m/8km NW of Newcastle upon Tyne. NZ1768.
Callerton Lane End *T. & W.* ***Locality***, 1m/2km W of Callerton. **71 G7** NZ1669.
Callestick *Cornw.* ***Hamlet***, 3m/4km SE of Perranporth. **2 E3** SW7750.
Calleva *Hants.* *See Silchester.*
Calligarry *High.* ***Settlement***, 1km W of Ardvasar, on E side of Sleat peninsula, Skye. **86 C4** NG6203.
Callington *Cornw.* Population: 3511. ***Small town***, market town standing on high ground above River Lynher, 8m/13km NW of Saltash. 15c chapel containing Dupath Well (English Heritage) 1m/2km SE. **4 D4** SX3669.
Callingwood *Staffs.* ***Settlement***, 3m/5km W of Burton upon Trent. SK1923.
Callisterhall *D. & G.* ***Settlement***, at head of Pokeskine Sike, 4m/6km NE of Waterbeck. **69 H5** NY2881.
Callop *High.* ***River***, flowing NW into head of Loch Shiel, to E of Glenfinnan. NM9080.
Callow *Here.* ***Village***, 4m/6km S of Hereford. **28 D5** SO4934.
Callow End *Worcs.* ***Village***, 4m/6km S of Worcester. **29 H4** SO8349.
Callow Hill *Wilts.* ***Hamlet***, 3m/4km NW of Wootton Bassett. **20 D3** SU0384.
Callow Hill *Worcs.* ***Suburb***, 3m/4km SW of Redditch town centre. SP0264.
Callow Hill *Worcs.* ***Village***, 3m/4km SW of Bewdley. **29 G1** SO7473.
Callowell *Glos.* ***Suburb***, N district of Stroud. SO8406.
Callows Grave *Worcs.* ***Locality***, 1m/2km S of Tenbury Wells. **28 E2** SO5966.
Calltraiseal Bheag (Anglicised form: Caultrashal Beag.) *W.Isles* ***Hill***, 1km E of head of Little Loch Roag, Isle of Lewis. Height 741 feet or 226 metres. **100 D5** NB1424.
Calltraiseal Mhòr (Anglicised form: Caultrashal Mòr.) *W.Isles* ***Hill***, 1m/2km SE of head of Little Loch Roag, Isle of Lewis. Height 748 feet or 228 metres. **100 D5** NB1522.
Callyburn *Arg. & B.* ***Settlement***, on Kintyre, 3m/4km N of Campbeltown. **66 B1** NR7225.
Calmore *Hants.* ***Village***, 2m/3km NW of Totton. **10 E3** SU3314.
Calmsden *Glos.* ***Hamlet***, 4m/7km N of Cirencester. **20 D1** SP0408.
Calne *Wilts.* Population: 11,516. ***Town***, former wool town, 5m/8km E of Chippenham. Bacon formerly an important industry. 18c Bowood House, set in fine parkland, 2m/3km to W. **20 C4** ST9971.
Calow *Derbys.* ***Village***, 2m/3km E of Chesterfield. **51 G5** SK4071.
Calrossie *High.* ***Settlement***, 3m/4km SE of Tain. **96 E4** NH8077.
Calshot *Hants.* ***Village***, 2m/3km SW of Fawley. **11 F4** SU4701.
Calstock *Cornw.* ***Small town***, former port on River Tamar, 5m/8km E of Callington. Cotehele (National Trust) house and garden above river, 1m/2km to W. **4 E4** SX4368.
Calstone Wellington *Wilts.* ***Village***, 3m/4km SE of Calne. **20 D5** SU0268.
Calternish *W.Isles* ***Locality***, on E coast of South Uist, 4m/6km E of Geirninis. NF8341.
Calthorpe *Norf.* ***Village***, 3m/5km N of Aylsham. **45 F2** TG1831.
Calthorpe Street *Norf.* ***Hamlet***, 2m/3km E of Stalham. TG4025.
Calthwaite *Cumb.* ***Village***, 7m/11km N of Penrith. **61 F2** NY4640.
Calton *Glas.* ***Suburb***, 1m/2km SE of Glasgow city centre. NS6064.
Calton *N.Yorks.* ***Hamlet***, 7m/11km NW of Skipton. **56 E4** SD9059.
Calton *Staffs.* ***Village***, 5m/9km NW of Ashbourne. **50 D7** SK1050.
Calton Green *Staffs.* ***Settlement***, adjoining to E of Calton, 5m/8km NW of Ashbourne. SK1050.
Calton Hill *Edin.* ***Hill***, to E of Edinburgh city centre. National Monument, Nelson's Monument, City Observatory located here. Height 328 feet or 100 metres. NT2674.
Calva Beg *High.* *Anglicised form of Calbha Beag, qv.*
Calva Mòr *High.* *Anglicised form of Calbha Mòr, qv.*
Calvay *W.Isles* ***Island***, islet in Sound of Eriskay, off NE point of Eriskay. NF8112.
Calvay *W.Isles* ***Island***, small island with lighthouse on S side of entrance to Loch Baghasdail, South Uist. **84 D3** NF8218.
Calve Island *Arg. & B.* ***Island***, uninhabited island at entrance to Tobermory Bay, Mull. **79 G2** NM5254.
Calveley *Ches.* ***Hamlet***, 2m/3km NE of Bunbury. **48 E7** SJ5958.
Calver *Derbys.* ***Village***, 4m/7km N of Bakewell. **50 E5** SK2374.
Calver Hill *Here.* ***Hamlet***, 4m/6km E of Willersley. **28 C4** SO3748.
Calver Hill *N.Yorks.* ***Mountain***, W of Arkengarthdale, 1m/2km S of Langthwaite. Height 1597 feet or 487 metres. **62 B6** NZ0100.
Calver Sough *Derbys.* ***Settlement***, adjoining to N of Calver, 4m/7km N of Bakewell. SK2374.
Calverhall (Also known as Cloverley.) *Shrop.* ***Village***, 5m/8km SE of Whitchurch. **39 F2** SJ6037.
Calverleigh *Devon* ***Hamlet***, 2m/4km NW of Tiverton. **7 H4** SS9214.
Calverley *W.Yorks.* ***Village***, 4m/6km NE of Bradford. **57 H6** SE2037.
Calverley Carr *W.Yorks.* ***Locality***, adjoining to W of Calverley. SE2037.
Calvert *Bucks.* ***Hamlet***, 6m/10km S of Buckingham. **31 H6** SP6824.
Calverton *M.K.* ***Village***, 1m/2km S of Stony Stratford. **31 J5** SP7938.
Calverton *Notts.* Population: 6669. ***Village***, 7m/11km NE of Nottingham. **41 J1** SK6149.
Calveshay *Som.* ***Hamlet***, 3m/4km SW of North Petherton. ST2531.
Calvine *P. & K.* ***Village***, near confluence of Errochty Water and River Garry, 4m/7km W of Blair Atholl. **81 K1** NN8065.
Calvo *Cumb.* ***Hamlet***, 2m/4km E of Silloth. **60 C1** NY1453.
Calzeat *Sc.Bord.* ***Locality***, part of Broughton village, 4m/7km E of Biggar. NT1135.
Cam ***River***, with upper reaches in two branches: River Cam or Granta rises 3m/5km W of Thaxted; River Cam or Rhee rises at Ashwell. The two branches flow NW and NE respectively to join S of Grantchester, and flow NE as River Cam or Granta into Cambridge, becoming River Cam downstream of weir at Mill Lane. It then continues through Cambridge and into River Great Ouse, 4m/6km S of Ely. **33 J2** TL5374.
Cam *Glos.* ***Village***, 1m/2km N of Dursley. **20 A2** ST7599.
Cam Beck *N.Yorks.* ***River***, stream rising on Cam Fell, crossed by The Pennine Way and flowing S into River Ribble, 1km NE of Selside and 3m/4km NW of Horton in Ribblesdale. **56 C2** SD7976.
Cam Chreag *P. & K.* ***Mountain***, 3m/5km NW of Bridge of Balgie. Height 2821 feet or 860 metres. **81 G3** NN5949.
Cam Fell *N.Yorks.* ***Open space***, partly wooded moorland to W of Langstrothdale, 5m/8km N of Horton in Ribblesdale. **56 D1** SD8080.
Cam Loch *Arg. & B.* ***Lake/loch***, small loch in Inverliever Forest, 4m/7km SE of Kilmelford. **80 A7** NM9009.
Cam Loch *Arg. & B.* ***Lake/loch***, small loch 3m/4km SW of Lochgilphead. **73 G2** NR8287.
Cam Loch *High.* ***Lake/loch***, loch in Sutherland district 6m/9km S of Inchnadamph. **102 E7** NC2113.
Cama' Choire *P. & K.* ***Valley***, carrying Allt a' Chama' Choire, with waterfalls to W, 5m/8km SE of Dalwhinnie. **88 D7** NN6978.
Camas Baravaig *High.* *See Baravaig.*
Camas Coille *High.* ***Sea feature***, small inlet on NE coast of Rubha Mòr peninsula, Ross and Cromarty district. **102 C7** NC0016.
Camas Eilean Ghlais *High.* ***Bay***, small bay on W coast of Ross and Cromarty district, 4m/6km NW of Polbain. **102 B7** NB9615.
Camas Fhionnairigh *High.* ***Sea feature***, inlet of Loch Scavaig on S coast of Skye, 3m/5km N of Elgol. **86 B3** NG5118.
Camas Mòr *High.* ***Bay***, to N of the mouth of River Kanaird, 4m/7km NW of Ullapool. **95 H1** NC1000.
Camas Mòr *High.* ***Bay***, small bay on coast of Ross and Cromarty district, 1m/2km E of Rubha Réidh and 10m/16km NW of Poolewe. **94 D2** NG7591.
Camas Mòr *High.* ***Sea feature***, small inlet on W coast of Trotternish peninsula, Skye, 4m/7km SW of Rubha Hunish. **93 J4** NG3470.
Camas na Ceardaich *Arg. & B.* ***Bay***, small, shallow bay on NE coast of Kintyre, 5m/8km SE of Tarbert. **73 H4** NR9162.
Camas na Fisteodh *High.* ***Bay***, small bay on E coast of Scalpay, Skye and Lochalsh district. **86 C2** NG6328.
Camas nan Gall *High.* ***Bay***, on S coast of Soay, island off S coast of Skye. **85 K3** NG4514.
Camas Sandig *W.Isles* ***Bay***, small bay on W coast of Great Bernera, off W coast of Isle of Lewis. **100 D4** NB1338.
Camas Tharbernish *High.* ***Bay***, small bay on N coast of Canna, 2m/3km E of Garrisdale Point. **85 H4** NG2306.
Camas Uig *W.Isles* ***Bay***, on W coast of Isle of Lewis, 2m/3km W of Timsgearraidh. **100 C4** NB0233.
Camascross *High.* ***Settlement***, on bay of same name, on E coast of Sleat peninsula, Skye, 1km S of Eilean Iarmain. **86 D3** NG6911.
Camasnacroise *High.* ***Settlement***, in Lochaber district, 1km W of Rubha na h-Airde Uinnsinn. **79 K2** NM8652.
Camastianavaig *High.* ***Settlement***, on E coast of Skye, 3m/5km SE of Loch Portree. **86 B1** NG5039.
Camasunary *High.* ***Settlement***, on S coast of Skye, 3m/5km N of Elgol. **86 B3** NG5118.
Camault Muir *High.* ***Settlement***, in Inverness district, 4m/7km S of Beauly. **96 C7** NH5040.
Camb *Shet.* ***Hamlet***, on Yell, on N side of Mid Yell Voe. **108 E3** HU5192.
Cambeak *Cornw.* ***Coastal feature***, headland (National Trust) 4m/7km NE of Boscastle. **4 B1** SX1296.
Camber *E.Suss.* ***Town***, seaside resort on Rye Bay, 3m/5km E of Rye. **14 E6** TQ9618.
Camber Castle *E.Suss.* ***Castle***, coastal fort (English Heritage) built in 1539 by Henry VIII to protect joint harbour of Rye and Winchelsea, 1m/2km S of Rye. **14 E6** TQ9218.
Camberley *Surr.* Population: 23,060. ***Town***, 6m/9km S of Bracknell. Royal Staff College on N side. **22 B5** SU8660.
Camberwell *Gt.Lon.* ***Suburb***, in borough of Southwark, 3m/4km SE of Charing Cross. **23 G4** TQ3276.
Camblesforth *N.Yorks.* ***Village***, 3m/4km N of Snaith. **58 C7** SE6426.
Cambo *Northumb.* ***Village***, 11m/17km W of Morpeth. Village is largely an estate village of Wallington Hall, 1m/2km S. **71 F5** NZ0285.
Cambo Ness *Fife* ***Coastal feature***, rocky headland 2m/4km NW of Fife Moss. **83 H6** NO6011.
Camboglanna *Cumb.* *See Birdoswald Roman Fort.*
Cambois *Northumb.* ***Locality***, on North Sea coast, 1m/2km N of Blyth across River Blyth. Power station on N bank of estuary. **71 J5** NZ3083.
Camborne *Cornw.* Population: 17,957. ***Town***, 11m/18km W of Truro. Formerly a centre of tin-mining industry. East Pool engine house has working beam engines. **2 D4** SW6440.
Camborne Beacon *Cornw.* ***Suburb***, S district of Camborne. SW6539.
Cambrian Mountains ***Large natural feature***, mountain range of central Wales, extending from Cadair Idris in NW to Brecon Beacons in SE. Consists largely of remote, bare hills, although there is extensive afforestation in places. **37 G6** SH9022.
Cambridge *Cambs.* Population: 95,682. ***City***, university city on River Cam 49m/79km N of London. First college founded here in 1271. Historic tensions existed between students and townspeople since 14c, and came to a head during Peasants' Revolt of 1381 in which five townsfolk were hanged. Oliver Cromwell was a graduate of Sidney Sussex College and local MP at a time when the University was chiefly Royalist. 1870's saw foundation of first women's colleges, but women were not awarded degrees until after 1947. University's notable graduates include prime ministers, foreign heads of state, literary giants, philosophers and spies. Cambridge Footlights regularly provide a platform for future stars of stage, screen and television. Cambridge boasts many fine museums, art galleries and buildings of interest, including King's College Chapel and Fitzwilliam Museum. Airport at Teversham 3m/4km E. **33 H3** TL4458.
Cambridge *Glos.* ***Village***, 4m/6km N of Dursley. **20 A1** SO7403.
Cambridge American Military Cemetery *Cambs.* ***Other feature of interest***, large cemetery dedicated to American servicemen killed during World War II, at Madingley, 3m/5km W of Cambridge city centre. **33 G3** TL4059.
Cambridge Town *S'end* ***Suburb***, E district of Southend-on-Sea, to W of Shoeburyness. TQ9284.
Cambridge University Botanic Gardens *Cambs.* ***Garden***, 1m/2km S of Cambridge city centre. 40 acres with lake and glasshouses. Nine national collections. **33 H3** TL4556.
Cambrose *Cornw.* ***Hamlet***, 2m/3km E of Portreath. SW6845.
Cambus *Clack.* ***Village***, 2m/3km W of Alloa. **75 G1** NS8593.
Cambus o'May *Aber.* ***Settlement***, 3m/5km NE of Ballater, on N side of River Dee. **90 C5** NO4198.
Cambusbarron *Stir.* ***Suburb***, 1m/2km W of Stirling. **75 F1** NS7792.
Cambuscurrie Bay *High.* ***Bay***, on S side of Dornoch Firth and E side of Edderton, Ross and Cromarty district. **96 E3** NH7285.
Cambushinnie Hill *Stir.* ***Hill***, 5m/8km N of Dunblane. Height 876 feet or 267 metres. **81 J7** NN7809.
Cambuskenneth *Stir.* ***Hamlet***, with remains of medieval abbey (Historic Scotland), 1km NE of Stirling across River Forth (footbridge). **75 G1** NS8094.
Cambuskenneth Abbey *Stir.* ***Ecclesiastical building***, ruins of abbey with fine detached tower (Historic Scotland) founded in 1147 for Augustinian canons, 1km E of Stirling town centre across loop in River Forth. Location of Robert the Bruce's Parliament and burial place of James III. **75 G1** NS8094.
Cambuslang *S.Lan.* ***Town***, on S bank of River Clyde, 5m/8km SE of Glasgow. Previously known for iron and steel manufacturing. **74 E4** NS6460.
Cambusnethan *N.Lan.* ***Suburb***, adjoining to E of Wishaw. **75 G5** NS8155.
Camchuart *Arg. & B.* ***Settlement***, 7m/11km N of Tighnabruaich. **73 H2** NR9985.
Camddwr *Cere.* ***River***, rising about 6m/9km E of Tregaron and flowing SE to join River Tywi in Llyn Brianne Reservoir. SN7952.
Camden Town *Gt.Lon.* ***Suburb***, in borough of Camden, 2m/4km N of Charing Cross. TQ2984.
Camdentown *Hants.* ***Suburb***, 1m/2km NW of Gosport town centre. SU6000.
Camel *Cornw.* ***River***, rising near Davidstow and flowing S, then NW past Wadebridge and Padstow into sea at Padstow Bay. **4 A3** SW9278.
Camel Hill *Som.* ***Settlement***, 1km N of Queen Camel. ST5825.
Camel Trail *Cornw.* ***Other feature of interest***, sandy trail for walkers and cyclists along disused railway line, on S side of River Camel between Wadebridge and Padstow. **3 G1** SW9573.
Cameley *B. & N.E.Som.* ***Village***, 4m/6km NW of Midsomer Norton. **19 K6** ST6157.

C

Camelford *Cornw.* ***Small town***, 11m/17km N of Bodmin and 4m/7km E of coast at Port Isaac Bay. Slate quarries in vicinity. Bodmin Moor extends SE. **4 B2** SX1083.
Camelon *Falk.* ***Locality***, residential and industrial area to W of Falkirk. **75 G2** NS8680.
Camelot Theme Park *Lancs.* ***Leisure/recreation***, 130 acre theme park based on Arthurian legend, 1m/2km W of Charnock Richard. Includes over 100 rides, falconry displays and jousting. **48 E1** SD5315.
Camelsdale *W.Suss.* ***Village***, 1m/2km W of Haslemere. **12 B3** SU8832.
Camer *Kent* ***Settlement***, 1km NE of Meopham and 5m/7km S of Gravesend. **24 C5** TQ6567.
Camer Country Park *Kent* ***Leisure/recreation***, 1km NE of Meopham. Small area of parkland with fine collection of trees. **24 C5** TQ6566.
Cameron *W.Dun.* ***Locality***, on Loch Lomond, 1km N of foot of loch. **74 B2** NS3782.
Cameron Burn *Fife* ***River***, stream which flows E from Cameron Reservoir to join with Kinaldy Burn to form Kenly Water, 4m/6km SE of St. Andrews and 3m/5km from where Kenly Water flows into North Sea. **83 G6** NO5411.
Cameron Reservoir *Fife* ***Reservoir***, small reservoir, 4m/7km SW of St. Andrews. **83 F6** NO4611.
Camerory *High.* ***Settlement***, 3m/4km N of Grantown-on-Spey. **89 H1** NJ0231.
Camer's Green *Worcs.* ***Hamlet***, to E of S end of Malvern Hills, 8m/12km W of Tewkesbury. **29 G5** SO7735.
Camerton *B. & N.E.Som.* ***Village***, 2m/3km N of Radstock. **19 K6** ST6857.
Camerton *Cumb.* ***Village***, 3m/5km NE of Workington. **60 B3** NY0330.
Camghouran *P. & K.* ***Settlement***, on S side of Loch Rannoch, 8m/12km W of Kinloch Rannoch. **81 G2** NN5556.
Camis Eskan *Arg. & B.* ***Settlement***, 1km E of Craigendoran. **74 B2** NS3381.
Camlachie *Glas.* ***Suburb***, 2m/3km E of Glasgow city centre. NS6164.
Camlad ***River***, rising near More and flowing W to Church Stoke, then N to Hockleton Bridge, then W into River Severn 4m/7km S of Welshpool. **38 B6** SJ2000.
Camlo Hill *Powys* ***Mountain***, 5m/8km N of Llandrindod Wells. Height 1670 feet or 509 metres. **27 K1** SO0369.
Cammachmore *Aber.* ***Village***, 7m/12km S of Aberdeen. **91 H5** NO9094.
Cammeringham *Lincs.* ***Village***, 7m/11km N of Lincoln. **52 C4** SK9482.
Cammoch Hill *P. & K.* ***Mountain***, 3m/4km NW of Pitlochry. Height 1391 feet or 424 metres. **81 K2** NN8959.
Camore *High.* ***Hamlet***, in Sutherland district, 1m/2km W of Dornoch. **96 E2** NH7790.
Camp Hill *Pembs.* ***Hamlet***, 1km S of Narberth. SN1113.
Camp Hill *Warks.* ***Suburb***, 2m/3km NW of Nuneaton town centre. SP3493.
Camp Town *W.Yorks.* ***Suburb***, 3m/5km N of Leeds city centre. SE2939.
Campay *W.Isles* ***Island***, small uninhabited island off W coast of Isle of Lewis, 1m/2km N of Great Bernera. NB1442.
Campbelltown *High.* *Former name of Ardersier, qv.*
Campbeltown *Arg. & B.* Population: 5722. ***Small town***, chief town and port of Kintyre, at head of Campbeltown Loch, 30m/48km S of Tarbert. **66 B2** NR7120.
Campbeltown (Machrihanish) Airport *Arg. & B.* ***Airport/airfield***, to NE of Machrihanish beyond Machrihanish Water, on Kintyre peninsula. **66 A1** NR6320.
Campbeltown Loch *Arg. & B.* ***Sea feature***, sea-loch on Kintyre, to E of Cambeltown. **66 B2** NR7120.
Campbeltown Museum and Library *Arg. & B.* ***Other feature of interest***, in Campbeltown, on Kintyre, 12m/20km SW of Carradale, with exhibits on local history. **66 B2** NR7220.
Camperdown *T. & W.* ***Locality***, 5m/8km N of Newcastle upon Tyne. **71 H6** NZ2771.
Camperdown Country Park *Dundee* ***Leisure/recreation***, country park containing 500 acres of gardens, parkland and woodland with many rare trees, 3m/4km NW of Dundee city centre. Also includes wildlife centre with Scottish and European wildlife, Golf course, adventure playground and nature trails. **82 E4** NO3632.
Camphill Reservoir *N.Ayr.* ***Reservoir***, 3m/5km W of Kilbirnie. **74 A5** NS2755.
Camphouse *High.* ***Settlement***, on Ardnamurchan peninsula, 1m/2km E of Kilchoan. **79 G1** NM5164.
Campmuir *P. & K.* ***Hamlet***, 2m/3km S of Coupar Angus. Site of Roman camp to SE. **82 D4** NO2137.
Camps *W.Loth.* ***Village***, 1km N of Kirknewton. NT1068.
Camps End *Cambs.* ***Hamlet***, 4m/7km SW of Haverhill. **33 K4** TL6142.
Camps Heath *Suff.* ***Hamlet***, 3m/4km W of Lowestoft. **45 K6** TM5194.
Camps Reservoir *S.Lan.* ***Reservoir***, 3m/5km E of Crawford. **69 F1** NT0022.
Camps Water *S.Lan.* ***River***, issuing from Camps reservoir and flowing W to join River Clyde to N of Crawford. **68 E1** NS9521.
Campsall *S.Yorks.* Population: 2048. ***Village***, 7m/11km N of Doncaster. **51 H1** SE5413.
Campsey Ash (Sometimes spelled Campsey Ashe.) *Suff.* ***Village***, 2m/3km E of Wickham Market. **35 H3** TM3255.
Campsey Ashe *Suff.* *Occasional spelling of Campsey Ash, qv.*
Campsie *E.Dun.* *Alternative name for Clachan of Campsie, qv.*
Campsie Fells ***Large natural feature***, range of hills E of Killearn. Summit is Earl's Seat at 578m, with other notable summits: Garloch Hill at 1781 feet or 543 metres; Holehead at 1807 feet or 551 metres; Lecket Hill at 1791 feet or 546 metres and Cort-ma Law at 1742 feet or 531 metres. Source of River Carron is on slopes 3m/4km N of Lennoxtown. **74 D2** NS5783.
Campton *Beds.* ***Village***, 1m/2km SW of Shefford. **32 E5** TL1338.
Camptown *Sc.Bord.* ***Settlement***, on Jed Water, 5m/8km S of Jedburgh. **70 B2** NT6713.
Camros *Pembs.* *Welsh form of Camrose, qv.*
Camrose (Camros). *Pembs.* ***Village***, 3m/5km NW of Haverfordwest. Remains of motte and bailey castle. **16 C3** SM9220.
Camsail *Arg. & B.* ***Settlement***, 2m/3km NE of Kilcreggan. **74 A2** NS2581.
Camserney *P. & K.* ***Village***, 2m/4km W of Aberfeldy. **81 K3** NN8149.
Camster Burn *High.* ***River***, rising to NE of Upper Camster and flowing N by Lower Camster to Rowens where it becomes Rowens Burn. **105 H4** ND2248.
Camstraddan *Arg. & B.* ***Settlement***, on W shore of Loch Lomond, 1km S of Luss. **74 B1** NS3692.
Camulodunum *Essex* *See Colchester.*
Camus Castle *High.* *Alternative name for Knock Castle, qv.*
Camus Croise *High.* ***Settlement***, adjoining to S of Eilean Iarmain, Skye. **86 C3** NG6911.
Camus-luinie *High.* ***Settlement***, in Skye and Lochalsh district, 4m/6km NE of Dornie. **87 F2** NG9428.
Camusdarrach *High.* ***Locality***, on coast of Lochaber district, 3m/5km N of Arisaig. NM6691.
Camusnagaul *High.* ***Settlement***, on S shore of Little Loch Broom, Ross and Cromarty district, 2m/3km from head of loch. **95 G3** NH0689.
Camusnagaul *High.* ***Settlement***, 1km N of Fort William across Loch Linnhe. **87 G7** NN0975.
Camusrory *High.* ***Settlement***, on N shore and near head of Loch Nevis, 6m/10km SE of Inverie, Lochaber district. **86 E5** NM8595.
Camusteel *High.* ***Settlement***, on W coast of Ross and Cromarty district, 1m/2km S of Applecross. **94 D7** NG7042.
Camusterrach *High.* ***Hamlet***, on W coast of Ross and Cromarty district, 2m/3km S of Applecross. **94 D7** NG7141.
Camusurich *P. & K.* ***Settlement***, on S side of Loch Tay, 4m/6km NE of Killin. **81 H4** NN6334.
Camusvrachan *P. & K.* ***Settlement***, in Glen Lyon, 3m/5km E of Bridge of Balgie. **81 H3** NN6247.
Camy *Ork.* ***Coastal feature***, rocky foreshore 1m/2km SW of narrow isthmus joining Deerness to SE part of Mainland. **107 E7** HY5401.
Can *Essex* ***River***, rising near High Roding to S of Great Dunmow and flowing SE into River Chelmer at Chelmsford. **23 K1** TL7106.
Canada *Hants.* ***Village***, 3m/5km N of Cadnam. **10 D3** SU2818.
Canal Side *S.Yorks.* ***Locality***, on SW side of Thorne across Stainforth and Keadby Canal. SE6812.
Canary Wharf Tower *Gt.Lon.* ***Other building***, office block and notable landmark situated on Isle of Dogs in borough of Tower Hamlets, 4m/7km E of Charing Cross. Tallest building in UK at 800 feet or 244 metres, and with 50 storeys. It is clad in stainless steel and topped by a pyramid. TQ3780.
Canaston Bridge *Pembs.* ***Locality***, at crossing of Eastern Cleddau River, 3m/5km W of Narberth. **16 D3** SN0615.
Candacraig *Aber.* ***Settlement***, 3m/5km NW of Ballater. **90 B5** NO3399.
Candle Street *Suff.* ***Hamlet***, to S of Rickinghall Inferior. TM0374.
Candlesby *Lincs.* ***Village***, 4m/6km E of Spilsby. **53 H6** TF4567.
Candy Mill *S.Lan.* ***Hamlet***, on Candy Burn, 3m/5km NE of Biggar. **75 J6** NT0741.
Cane End *Oxon.* ***Hamlet***, 5m/7km NW of Reading. **21 K4** SU6779.
Canewdon *Essex* ***Village***, 3m/5km NE of Rochford. **24 E2** TQ8994.
Canfield End *Essex* ***Hamlet***, 3m/4km W of Great Dunmow. TL5821.
Canford Bottom *Dorset* ***Locality***, 2m/3km E of Wimborne Minster. **10 B4** SU0400.
Canford Cliffs *Poole* ***Suburb***, 3m/5km SE of Poole town centre. **10 B6** SZ0589.
Canford Heath *Poole* ***Open space***, large open space to S of Canford Magna and 4m/7km NW of Bournemouth town centre. **10 B5** SZ0295.
Canford Magna *Poole* ***Hamlet***, 2m/3km SE of Wimborne Minster. Canford School beside River Stour in Canford Park. **10 B5** SZ0398.
Cangate Common *Norf.* ***Settlement***, 3m/4km NE of Wroxham. TG3219.
Canham's Green *Suff.* ***Settlement***, 1m/2km S of Bacton. TM0565.
Canisbay *High.* ***Village***, near N coast of Caithness district, 4m/6km W of Duncansby Head. **105 J1** ND3472.
Canisp *High.* ***Mountain***, in Sutherland district 4m/6km SW of Inchnadamph. Height 2775 feet or 846 metres. **102 E7** NC2018.
Canklow *S.Yorks.* ***Suburb***, 1m/2km S of Rotherham town centre. SK4290.
Canley *W.Mid.* ***Suburb***, 2m/4km SW of Coventry city centre. SP3077.
Cann *Dorset* ***Hamlet***, 1m/2km S of Shaftesbury. **9 H2** ST8521.
Cann Common *Dorset* ***Hamlet***, 2m/3km SE of Shaftesbury. **9 H2** ST8820.
Canna *High.* ***Island***, in Inner Hebrides 4m/6km NW of Rum. Nearly 5m/8km E to W and up to 1m/2km N to S. Crofting, lobster fishing. Harbour at E end. **85 H4** NG2405.
Canna Harbour *High.* ***Sea feature***, inlet separating Sanday and Canna. **85 H4** NG2804.
Cannard's Grave *Som.* ***Hamlet***, 1m/2km SE of Shepton Mallet. **19 K7** ST6241.
Cannich *High.* ***River***, rising from E end of Loch Mullardoch and initially flowing NE through a series of small lochs, then E and finally SE to enter River Glass just E of Cannich. **87 K1** NH3431.
Cannich *High.* ***Village***, in Inverness district, at confluence of Rivers Cannich and Glass, 7m/11km SW of Struy Bridge. **87 K1** NH3431.
Canning Town *Gt.Lon.* ***Suburb***, in borough of Newham, 4m/7km E of London Bridge. TQ4081.
Cannington *Som.* Population: 1951. ***Village***, 3m/5km NW of Bridgwater. **8 B1** ST2539.
Cannock *Staffs.* Population: 60,106. ***Town***, market town, 8m/13km NE of Wolverhampton. **40 B4** SJ9810.
Cannock Chase *Staffs.* ***Forest/woodland***, to N of Cannock, elevated and wooded area with tracts of moorland; former hunting forest. **40 B4** SJ9715.
Cannock Chase Country Park *Staffs.* ***Leisure/recreation***, 2660 acre country park in Cannock Chase featuring forest and natural history trails, Iron Age fort and large herd of fallow deer. **40 B4** SJ9915.
Cannock Wood *Staffs.* ***Village***, 4m/7km E of Cannock. **40 C4** SK0412.
Cannon Hall *S.Yorks.* ***Historic house***, 18c house built by Carr of York and set in 70 acre country park to NW of Cawthorne, 4m/7km NW of Barnsley. Contains art gallery, including woks by Constable, and collections of furniture and glassware. Museum of 13th and 18th Royal Hussars. **50 E2** SE2708.
Cannop *Glos.* ***Locality***, in Forest of Dean, 2m/3km E of Coleford. **29 F7** SO6011.
Canon Bridge *Here.* ***Hamlet***, on S side of River Wye, 5m/8km W of Hereford. No bridge over river, despite name. **28 D4** SO4340.
Canon Frome *Here.* ***Village***, 6m/9km NW of Ledbury. **29 F4** SO6543.
Canon Pyon *Here.* ***Village***, 6m/10km NW of Hereford. **28 D4** SO4648.
Canonbie *D. & G.* ***Village***, on River Esk, 6m/9km S of Langholm. **69 J6** NY3976.
Canonbury *Gt.Lon.* ***Suburb***, in borough of Islington, 3m/5km NE of Charing Cross. TQ3284.
Canons Ashby *Northants.* ***Village***, 10m/16km NE of Banbury. **31 G3** SP5750.
Canons Ashby House *Northants.* ***Historic house***, 2m/3km S of Weedon and 3m/4km SE of Woodford Halse. 16c home of Dryden family, with Jacobean plasterwork, formal gardens and 70 acre park. **31 G3** SP5750.
Canons Ashby Priory *Northants.* ***Ecclesiastical building***, church located 7m/11km S of Daventry. Relic of Augustinian priory, founded c. 1250 (National Trust). Monuments to Dryden family. **31 G3** SP5850.
Canonstown *Cornw.* ***Village***, 2m/3km SW of Hayle. **2 C5** SW5335.
Canonteign Falls *Devon* ***Waterfall***, on stream in narrow wooded valley which runs E to River Teign, 1m/2km N of Hennock. **7 G7** SX8382.
Canovium *Conwy* *See Caerhun.*
Canterbury *Aber.* ***Settlement***, 1m/2km NW of Cornhill and 4m/7km S of Portsoy. **98 D5** NJ5659.
Canterbury *Kent* Population: 36,464. ***City***, premier cathedral city and seat of Primate of Church of England on Great Stour River, 54m/88km E of London. Site of Roman settlement Durovernum. After Romans left, Saxons renamed town Cantwarabyrig. First cathedral in England built on site of current Christ Church Cathedral in AD 602. Thomas à Becket assassinated in Canterbury in 1170, turning Cathedral into great Christian shrine and destination of many pilgrimages, such as those detailed in Geoffrey Chaucer's Canterbury Tales. Becket's tomb destroyed on orders of Henry VIII. Cathedral was backdrop for premiere of T.S. Eliot's play 'Murder in the Cathedral' in 1935. City suffered extensive damage during World War II. Many museums and galleries explaining city's rich heritage. Roman and medieval remains, including city walls. Modern shopping centre; industrial development on outskirts. University of Kent on hill to N. **15 G2** TR1457.
Canterbury Cathedral *Kent* ***Ecclesiastical building***, seat of Archibishop of Canterbury and Mother Church of Anglican Christianity, situated in Canterbury city centre. Original church founded by St. Augustine, but current building is creation of two periods: 1070-1184 and 1391-1505. **15 G2** TR1557.
Cantick Head *Ork.* ***Coastal feature***, headland on Hoy at E end of South Walls peninsula. Lighthouse on S side and beacon on N. **107 C9** ND3489.
Cantley *Norf.* ***Village***, 4m/7km SW of Acle. **45 H5** TG3804.
Cantley *S.Yorks.* ***Village***, 4m/6km E of Doncaster. **51 J2** SE6202.
Cantley Common *S.Yorks.* ***Open space***, lowland 4m/6km E of Doncaster, across which runs M18 motorway. **51 J2** SE6302.
Cantlop *Shrop.* ***Settlement***, 2m/3km E of Condover. **38 E5** SJ5205.
Canton (Cantwn). *Cardiff* ***Suburb***, 1m/2km W of Cardiff city centre. **18 E4** ST1676.
Cantray *High.* ***Locality***, 1m/2km S of Croy. **96 E7** NH7948.
Cantraydoune *High.* ***Settlement***, 2m/3km SW of Croy. **96 E7** NH7846.
Cantraywood *High.* ***Settlement***, 1m/2km SW of Croy. **96 E7** NH7848.
Cantref Reservoir *Powys* ***Reservoir***, in valley of Taf fawr River, 6m/10km N of Merthyr Tydfil. **27 J7** SN9915.
Cantsfield *Lancs.* ***Village***, 4m/6km S of Kirkby Lonsdale. **56 B2** SD6272.
Cantwarabyrig *Kent* *See Canterbury.*
Cantwn *Cardiff* *Welsh form of Canton, qv.*
Canvey Island *Essex* ***Island***, on N bank of River Thames estuary bounded by River Thames and Holehaven, East Haven and Benfleet Creeks. Island contains town of same name. TQ7883.
Canvey Island *Essex* Population: 36,406. ***Town***, resort with bungalow and industrial development on island of same name, 6m/10km SW of Southend-on-Sea. Lobster Smack Inn featured in Great Expectations. **24 D3** TQ7883.

Canwell Hall *Staffs.* ***Settlement***, 4m/7km SW of Tamworth. **40 D5** SK1400.
Canwick *Lincs.* ***Village***, 1m/2km SE of Lincoln. **52 C6** SK9869.
Canworthy Water *Cornw.* ***Village***, on River Ottery, 8m/13km NW of Launceston. **4 C1** SX2291.
Caol *High.* ***Village***, at head of Loch Linnhe in Lochaber district, 1m/2km N of Fort William. **87 H7** NN1076.
Caol Ghleann *Arg. & B.* ***Valley***, narrow steep sided valley carrying upper River Ruel, 5m/8km SW of Strachur. **73 J1** NS0693.
Caol-loch *High.* ***Lake/loch***, small narrow loch, 1m/2km E of S end of Strathy Forest. **104 D3** NC8455.
Caol Lochan *Arg. & B.* ***Lake/loch***, small loch 3m/4km S of Tobermory, Mull. **79 G2** NM5150.
Caol Mòr *High. Alternative name for Kyle More, qv.*
Caol Rona *High. Alternative name for Kyle Rona, qv.*
Caolard Rubha *Arg. & B.* ***Coastal feature***, headland on Loch Fyne, 3m/5km SE of Lochgilphead in Argyll. **73 G2** NR8783.
Caolas *Arg. & B.* ***Settlement***, near E end of Tiree, 1km W of Rubha Dubh. **78 B3** NM0848.
Caolas *W.Isles* ***Settlement***, on N coast of Vatersay. **84 B5** NL6397.
Caolas a' Mhòrain *W.Isles* ***Sea feature***, stretch of sea separating Boreray from North Uist. **92 D3** NF8480.
Caolas a' Tuath *W.Isles* ***Sea feature***, stretch of sea separating Isle of Lewis from Eilean Iubhard, 1km S of Leumrabhagh. **101 F6** NB3810.
Caolas an Eilein *Arg. & B.* ***Sea feature***, strait between S coast of Islay and Texa. **72 B6** NR3944.
Caolas an Eilein *W.Isles* ***Sea feature***, stretch of sea separating Mealasta Island from Isle of Lewis. **100 B5** NA9821.
Caolas an Scarp *W.Isles* ***Sea feature***, narrow strait between Scarp and W coast of North Harris. **100 B6** NA9913.
Caolas Bàn *Arg. & B.* ***Sea feature***, strait dividing Gunna from Coll. **78 C2** NM1052.
Caolas Mòr *Arg. & B.* ***Sea feature***, strait separating Oronsay from Eilean Ghaoideamal and rocks to SW thereof. **72 B2** NR3687.
Caolas Mòr *High.* ***Sea feature***, stretch of sea separating Crowlin Islands from Scottish mainland. **86 C1** NG7035.
Caolas Scalpaigh (Anglicised form: Kyles Scalpay.) *W.Isles* ***Settlement***, on N coast of East Loch Tarbert, opposite Scalpay. **93 H2** NG2198.
Caolas Scalpay *High.* ***Sea feature***, stretch of sea separating Scalpay from Skye. **86 C2** NG6027.
Caolasnacon *High.* ***Settlement***, on S side of Loch Leven, 3m/5km W of Kinlochleven. **80 C1** NN1360.
Cape Cornwall *Cornw.* ***Coastal feature***, headland 1m/2km W of St. Just. The Brisons, 1km offshore, pair of rocks well-known for causing shipwrecks. **2 A5** SW3431.
Cape Law *Sc.Bord.* ***Mountain***, rising to over 710 metres, 1m/2km NE of Hart Fell and 2m/3km SE of Fruid Reservoir. **69 G2** NT1315.
Cape Wrath *High.* ***Coastal feature***, headland with lighthouse at NW point of Sutherland district. **102 E1** NC2574.
Capel *Kent* ***Hamlet***, 3m/5km E of Tonbridge. **23 K7** TQ6344.
Capel *Surr.* ***Village***, 6m/9km S of Dorking. **22 E7** TQ1740.
Capel Bangor *Cere.* ***Hamlet***, 4m/7km E of Aberystwyth. **37 F7** SN6580.
Capel Betws Lleucu *Cere.* ***Hamlet***, 5m/7km W of Tregaron. **27 F3** SN6058.
Capel Carmel *Gwyn.* ***Settlement***, on SW end of Lleyn Peninsula, 1m/2km NW of Aberdaron. **36 A3** SH1628.
Capel Coch *I.o.A.* ***Hamlet***, on Anglesey, 4m/7km N of Llangefni. **46 C4** SH4582.
Capel Colman *Pembs.* ***Locality***, 1m/2km E of Boncath. SN2138.
Capel Curig *Conwy* ***Hamlet***, at confluence of Rivers Nantygwryd and Llugwy, 5m/8km W of Betws-y-coed. **47 F7** SH7258.
Capel Cynon *Cere.* ***Hamlet***, 7m/11km NE of Newcastle Emlyn. **26 C4** SN3849.
Capel Dewi *Carmar.* ***Hamlet***, 4m/6km E of Carmarthen. **17 H2** SN4720.
Capel Dewi *Cere.* ***Hamlet***, on River Clettwr, 2m/4km NE of Llandysul. **26 D4** SN4542.
Capel Dewi *Cere.* ***Hamlet***, 3m/5km E of Aberystwyth. **37 F7** SN6382.
Capel Fell ***Mountain***, on border of Dumfries & Galloway and Scottish Borders, 5m/8km E of Moffat. Height 2224 feet or 678 metres. **69 G3** NT1606.
Capel Fleet *Kent See Isle of Harty.*
Capel Garmon *Conwy* ***Village***, 4m/7km S of Llanrwst. 1km S is large Bronze Age burial-chamber (Cadw). **47 G7** SH8155.
Capel Garmon Burial Chamber *Conwy* ***Historic/prehistoric site***, 4m/6km NW of Pentrefoelas. Well preserved and renovated chambered long barrow, 140 feet long, dating from New Stone Age. **47 G7** SH8154.
Capel Gwyn *Carmar.* ***Settlement***, 4m/6km NE of Carmarthen. **17 H2** SN4622.
Capel Gwyn *I.o.A.* ***Settlement***, on Anglesey, 1m/2km S of Bryngwran. **46 B5** SH3475.
Capel Gwynfe *Carmar.* ***Hamlet***, 4m/6km S of Llangadog. **27 G6** SN7222.
Capel Hendre *Carmar.* ***Village***, 2m/4km W of Ammanford. **17 J3** SN5911.
Capel Isaac *Carmar.* ***Settlement***, 2m/3km E of Llanfynydd. **17 J2** SN5826.
Capel Iwan *Carmar.* ***Village***, 3m/5km S of Newcastle Emlyn. **17 F1** SN2936.
Capel le Ferne *Kent* Population: 1699. ***Village***, 3m/4km NE of Folkestone. **15 H4** TR2539.
Capel Llanilltern (Llanilltern). *Cardiff* ***Settlement***, 6m/9km NW of Cardiff. ST0979.
Capel Manor *Gt.Lon.* ***Garden***, 30 acres of gardens situated around 19c manor, 2m/3km NE of Enfield town centre. A specialist College of Horticulture and Countryside Studies. Includes rock and water gardens, disabled persons garden, 17c garden and demonstration gardens. **23 G2** TQ3499.
Capel Mawr *I.o.A.* ***Hamlet***, on Anglesey, 4m/6km SW of Llangefni. SH4171.
Capel Newydd *Pembs. Welsh form of Newchapel, qv.*
Capel Parc *I.o.A.* ***Hamlet***, on Anglesey, 4m/6km S of Amlwch. **46 C4** SH4486.
Capel St. Andrew *Suff.* ***Hamlet***, 7m/11km E of Woodbridge. **35 H4** TM3748.
Capel St. Mary *Suff.* Population: 3176. ***Village***, 5m/8km SE of Hadleigh. **34 E5** TM0838.
Capel St. Silin *Cere.* ***Locality***, 4m/7km NW of Lampeter. **26 E3** SN5251.
Capel Seion *Cere.* ***Hamlet***, 3m/5km SE of Aberystwyth. **27 F1** SN6379.
Capel Trisant *Cere.* ***Settlement***, 2m/3km SW of Devil's Bridge. SN7175.
Capel Tygwydd *Cere.* ***Settlement***, 3m/5km NW of Newcastle Emlyn. **26 B4** SN2743.
Capel Uchaf *Powys Welsh form of Upper Chapel, qv.*
Capel Vicar *Cere.* ***Settlement***, 1m/2km NW of Mydroilyn. SN4556.
Capel Water *D. & G.* ***River***, rising on S slopes of Earncraig Hill as Capel Burn and running S to join Water of Ae in Forest of Ae, 3m/5km N of Ae village. NX9893.
Capel-y-ffin *Powys* ***Settlement***, in Vale of Ewyas, 3m/5km NW of Llanthony. **28 B5** SO2531.
Capel-y-graig *Gwyn.* ***Hamlet***, 3m/4km SW of Bangor. SH5469.
Capeluchaf *Gwyn.* ***Settlement***, 1m/2km E of Clynnog-fawr. **36 D1** SH4349.
Capelulo *Conwy* ***Village***, 2m/4km W of Conwy. **47 F5** SH7476.
Capenhurst *Ches.* ***Village***, 5m/8km NW of Chester. Atomic energy plant to N. **48 C5** SJ3673.
Capernwray *Lancs.* ***Hamlet***, 2m/4km E of Carnforth. **55 J2** SD5371.
Capesthorne Hall *Ches.* ***Historic house***, 5m/8km W of Macclesfield town centre. 18c home of Bromley-Davenport family, with gardens which include a nature trail and aboretum. **49 H5** SJ8472.
Capheaton *Northumb.* ***Hamlet***, 4m/6km SE of Kirkwhelpington. Capheaton Hall built in 1868. Grounds, landscaped in 18c, include large lake known as Sir Edward's Lake. **71 F5** NZ0380.
Caplaw *E.Renf.* ***Settlement***, 4m/7km SW of Paisley. **74 C5** NS4458.
Caplestone Fell *Northumb.* ***Open space***, moorland, wooded on N side, with highest point of 1571 feet or 479 metres, 4m/6km SW of Kielder. **70 A5** NY5987.
Capon's Green *Suff.* ***Settlement***, 1km E of Dennington. TM2867.
Cappercleuch *Sc.Bord.* ***Locality***, on W shore of St. Mary's Loch, in Ettrick Forest. **69 H1** NT2423.
Capplegill *D. & G.* ***Hamlet***, 5m/8km NE of Moffat. **69 G3** NT1409.
Capster Hill *Gt.Man.* ***Suburb***, 1m/2km S of Oldham town centre. SD9203.
Capstone *Med.* ***Settlement***, 2m/4km SE of Chatham town centre. **24 D5** TQ7865.
Captain Cook's Monument *N.Yorks.* ***Other feature of interest***, obelisk on Easby Moor, 1m/2km NE of Easby, commemorating 18c explorer. NZ5910.
Captain Fold *Gt.Man.* ***Suburb***, 1km E of Heywood town centre. SD8610.
Capton *Devon* ***Hamlet***, 3m/4km NW of Dartmouth. **5 J5** SX8353.
Capton *Som.* ***Hamlet***, 1m/2km S of Williton. ST0839.
Caputh *P. & K.* ***Village***, 4m/7km E of Dunkeld. **82 B3** NO0840.
Car Colston *Notts.* ***Village***, 2m/4km NE of Bingham. **42 A1** SK7142.
Car Ness *Ork.* ***Coastal feature***, headland on Mainland, 2m/4km NE of Kirkwall. Oil service base. **107 D6** HY4614.
Cara Island *Arg. & B.* ***Island***, 1km S of Gigha. **72 E6** NR6344.
Caradon Hill *Cornw.* ***Mountain***, on SE side of Bodmin Moor. Mast at summit. Height 1214 feet or 370 metres. **4 C3** SX2770.
Caradon Town *Cornw.* ***Hamlet***, 4m/7km NW of Callington. SX2971.
Carbellow *E.Ayr.* ***Settlement***, 3m/5km NE of Cumnock. **68 B1** NS6122.
Carberry Tower *E.Loth.* ***Historic house***, enlarged 16c house, now a Church of Scotland training centre, 2m/4km SE of Musselburgh. **76 B3** NT3669.
Carbeth *Stir.* ***Locality***, scattered settlement 2m/4km W of Strathblane. **74 D3** NS5379.
Carbis Bay *Cornw.* ***Suburb***, with sheltered beach to SE of St. Ives; gives name also to small bay within St. Ives Bay. **2 C5** SW5238.
Carbost *High.* ***Settlement***, 5m/8km NW of Portree, Skye. **93 K7** NG4248.
Carbost *High.* ***Village***, on SW shore of Loch Harport, Skye, 10m/16km SW of Portree. **85 J1** NG3731.
Carbrain *N.Lan.* ***Suburb***, central district of Cumbernauld. **75 F3** NS7674.
Carbrook *S.Yorks.* ***Suburb***, 3m/4km NE of Sheffield city centre. SK3889.
Carbrooke *Norf.* ***Village***, 2m/4km E of Watton. **44 D5** TF9402.
Carburton *Notts.* ***Settlement***, in The Dukeries, on S side of Clumber Park. **51 J5** SK6173.
Carcary *Angus* ***Hamlet***, 4m/6km SE of Brechin. **83 H2** NO6455.
Carclew *Cornw.* ***Hamlet***, 3m/4km N of Penryn. **2 E5** SW7838.
Carco *D. & G.* ***Settlement***, 3m/4km N of Sanquhar. **68 C2** NS7813.
Carcroft *S.Yorks.* Population: 8483. ***Locality***, 5m/8km NW of Doncaster. **51 H2** SE5410.
Cardenden *Fife* Population: 5390. ***Village***, 4m/7km NE of Cowdenbeath. **76 A1** NT2195.
Cardeston *Shrop.* ***Hamlet***, 6m/10km W of Shrewsbury. **38 C4** SJ3912.
Cardew *Cumb.* ***Settlement***, 2m/3km SW of Dalston. NY3449.
Cardewlees *Cumb.* ***Locality***, 1m/2km NW of Dalston. NY3551.
Cardiff (Caerdydd). *Cardiff* Population: 272,129. ***City***, capital of Wales since 1955. Romans founded military fort and small settlement on site of present day Cardiff. Uninhabited between departure of Romans and Norman conquest centuries later. Fishing village until development of coal mining in 19c. Population rose from 1000 in 1801 to 170,000 a century later, with city becoming one of busiest ports in the world. Dock trade collapsed in 1930's. Since establishment as Welsh capital, many governmental, administrative and media organisations have moved to city. Major refurbishment and development programme still under way. Cardiff Bay area now major tourist centre and includes Techniquest, a science discovery centre, and has been selected as the location of the New Welsh Assembly building. Many museums including National Museum of Wales. Universities. **18 E4** ST1876.
Cardiff Castle *Cardiff* ***Castle***, in central Cardiff. 11c earth and timber motte replaced with present stone keep in 12c. Additions were made in 15c and in each subsequent century. **18 E4** ST1776.
Cardiff International Airport *V. of Glam.* ***Airport/airfield***, international airport at Rhoose, 10m/16km SW of Cardiff. **18 D5** ST0667.
Cardigan (Aberteifi). *Cere.* Population: 3758. ***Small town***, on River Teifi estuary, 34m/54km SW of Aberystwyth across Cardigan Bay. Remains of 12c castle. National shrine of Roman Catholic Church in Wales, Our Lady of the Taper. Aberteifi Heritage Centre. **26 A4** SN1846.
Cardigan Bay ***Bay***, large bay on W coast of Wales, stretching from Lleyn Peninsula in N to St. David's Head in S. **36 C4** SH5085.
Cardigan Island *Cere.* ***Island***, uninhabited offshore island at mouth of River Teifi, 4m/6km N of Cardigan. Area 35 acres or 14 hectares. **26 A3** SN1651.
Cardigan Wildlife Park *Pembs.* ***Leisure/recreation***, 1km S of Cardigan, presenting a variety of animals in their natural habitat. **26 A4** SN1844.
Cardinal's Green *Cambs.* ***Hamlet***, 4m/6km NW of Haverhill. TL6146.
Carding Mill Valley *Shrop.* ***Valley***, steep-sided valley (National Trust) running SE into Church Stretton, with spectacular scenery. **38 D6** SO4494.
Cardington *Beds.* ***Village***, 3m/4km SE of Bedford. **32 D4** TL0847.
Cardington *Shrop.* ***Village***, 4m/6km E of Church Stretton. **38 E6** SO5095.
Cardinham *Cornw.* ***Village***, on W slopes of Bodmin Moor, 4m/6km NE of Bodmin. **4 B4** SX1268.
Cardinham Moor *Cornw.* ***Open space***, moorland to SW of Bodmin Moor, 5m/8km NE of Bodmin. **4 B3** SX1371.
Cardno *Aber.* ***Locality***, comprises Easter Cardno, Wester Cardno, Mains of Cardno and Ord of Cardno, 2m/3km SW of Fraserburgh. **99 H4** NJ9664.
Cardonald *Glas.* ***Suburb***, on S side of River Clyde, 4m/6km W of Glasgow city centre. NS5264.
Cardoness *D. & G.* ***Settlement***, on W shore of Fleet Bay, 3m/4km SW of Gatehouse of Fleet. **65 F5** NX5653.
Cardoness Castle *D. & G.* ***Castle***, ruined 15c tower of the McCullochs (Historic Scotland), 1m/2km SW of Gatehouse of Fleet. **65 F5** NX5955.
Cardow *Moray* ***Hamlet***, 6m/10km W of Craigellachie. **97 J7** NJ1942.
Cardrona *Sc.Bord.* ***Settlement***, 3m/4km NW of Innerleithen. **76 A7** NT2938.
Cardrona Forest *Sc.Bord.* ***Forest/woodland***, 2m/3km W of Innerleithen across River Tweed. Ruined tower of Cardrona on NE edge of forest. **76 A7** NT3036.
Cardross *Arg. & B.* Population: 1958. ***Village***, on N side of Firth of Clyde, 3m/5km NW of Dumbarton. Robert the Bruce died here from leprosy in 1329. 18c novelist Tobias Smollett born here. **74 B3** NS3477.
Cardurnock *Cumb.* ***Hamlet***, near coast of Solway Firth, 4m/6km W of Kirkbride across River Wampool estuary. Sites of small Roman forts in vicinity. **60 C1** NY1758.
Careby *Lincs.* ***Village***, 6m/10km N of Stamford. **42 D4** TF0216.
Careless Green *W.Mid.* ***Suburb***, 2m/3km E of Stourbridge town centre. SO9283.
Careston *Angus* ***Settlement***, 4m/7km W of Brechin. **83 G1** NO5360.
Carew *Pembs.* ***River***, rising W of Saundersfoot and flowing W to Carew, where it forms an estuary which continues NW to join Cresswell River and flow into Daugleddau estuary at Jenkins Point. SN0106.
Carew (Caeriw). *Pembs.* ***Village***, on River Carew, 4m/7km E of Pembroke. Remains of medieval castle. **16 D4** SN0403.
Carew Castle and Cross *Pembs.* ***Castle***, situated in Carew, on the Carew River. 12c castle, altered 14c-15c, and converted to a mansion. Besieged and badly damaged during Civil War. **16 D4** SN0403.
Carew Cheriton *Pembs.* ***Hamlet***, 4m/6km E of Pembroke. **16 D4** SN0402.
Carew Newton *Pembs.* ***Hamlet***, 1km N of Carew. **16 D4** SN0404.
Carey *Devon* ***River***, rising near Halwill and flowing SW into River Tamar, 1m/2km NE of Launceston. **6 B6** SX3584.
Carey *Here.* ***Hamlet***, in River Wye valley, 6m/10km SE of Hereford. **28 E5** SO5631.

Carfin *N.Lan.* ***Village***, 2m/3km NE of Motherwell. Contains Carfin Grotto. NS7758.
Carfrae *E.Loth.* ***Hamlet***, 1m/2km N of Danskine. **76 D4** NT5769.
Carfraemill *Sc.Bord.* ***Settlement***, with hotel, 4m/6km NW of Lauder. **76 D5** NT5153.
Cargate Common *Norf.* ***Settlement***, 1m/2km S of Bunwell. TM1390.
Cargate Green *Norf.* ***Hamlet***, just NW of Upton, 2m/3km NW of Acle. TG3912.
Cargen *D. & G.* ***Settlement***, 2m/4km S of Dumfries. **65 K3** NX9672.
Cargen Water *D. & G.* ***River***, stream flowing E then SE to River Nith, 2m/4km S of Dumfries. **65 J3** NX9772.
Cargenbridge *D. & G.* ***Village***, on Cargen Water, 1m/2km SW of Dumfries. **65 K3** NX9574.
Cargill *P. & K.* ***Hamlet***, on River Tay, 5m/8km W of Coupar Angus. **82 C4** NO1536.
Cargo *Cumb.* ***Village***, 3m/5km NW of Carlisle. **60 E1** NY3659.
Cargo Fleet *Middbro.* ***Locality***, on River Tees, 1m/2km E of Middlesbrough. **63 G4** NZ5120.
Cargreen *Cornw.* ***Village***, beside River Tamar, 7m/11km SE of Callington. **4 E4** SX4362.
Carham *Northumb.* ***Hamlet***, on River Tweed, 4m/6km W of Cornhill on Tweed. Site of Battle of Carham 1018, 2m/4km E, beyond Wark. **77 F7** NT7938.
Carhampton *Som.* ***Village***, 1m/2km SE of Dunster. **7 J1** ST0142.
Carharrack *Cornw.* ***Village***, among former tin and copper mines, 2m/3km E of Redruth. **2 E4** SW7341.
Carhouse *N.Lincs.* ***Hamlet***, 1km W of Belton. SE7706.
Carie *P. & K.* ***Settlement***, on S side of Loch Rannoch, 3m/4km SW of Kinloch Rannoch. **81 H2** NN6157.
Carie *P. & K.* ***Settlement***, just N of Loch Tay, 6m/9km NE of Killin. **81 H4** NN6437.
Carines *Cornw.* ***Settlement***, 2m/3km SW of Newquay. **2 E3** SW7959.
Carinish *W.Isles* *Anglicised form of Cairinis, qv.*
Carisbrooke *I.o.W.* ***Village***, adjoining to SW of Newport. **11 F6** SZ4888.
Carisbrooke Castle *I.o.W.* ***Castle***, mainly Tudor castle (English Heritage) situated 1m/2km SW of Newport town centre. Charles I was imprisoned here. Includes a museum. **11 F6** SZ4887.
Carishader *W.Isles* *Anglicised form of Cairisiadar, qv.*
Carity Burn *Angus* ***River***, stream rising NE of Loch of Lintrathen and flowing E to River South Esk, 4m/6km NE of Kirriemuir. **82 E2** NO4257.
Cark *Cumb.* ***Village***, 2m/3km SW of Cartmel. Hall of 16c-17c on N side of village. **55 G2** SD3676.
Carkeel *Cornw.* ***Village***, 2m/3km NW of Saltash. **4 E4** SX4160.
Carl Wark *S.Yorks.* ***Mountain***, 2m/3km E of Hathersage. Height 1050 feet or 320 metres. **50 E4** SK2581.
Carlabhagh *W.Isles* *Gaelic form of Carloway, qv.*
Carland Cross *Cornw.* ***Settlement***, 5m/8km SE of Newquay. **3 F3** SW8454.
Carlatton *Cumb.* ***Settlement***, 6m/10km S of Brampton. NY5251.
Carlbury *Darl.* ***Hamlet***, adjoining to E of Piercebridge. NZ2115.
Carlby *Lincs.* ***Village***, 5m/7km N of Stamford. **42 D4** TF0513.
Carlecotes *S.Yorks.* ***Hamlet***, 4m/7km W of Penistone. **50 D2** SE1703.
Carleen *Cornw.* ***Hamlet***, 3m/5km NW of Helston. SW6130.
Carleton *Cumb.* ***Locality***, 1m/2km SE of Egremont. NY0109.
Carleton *Cumb.* ***Settlement***, 3m/5km SE of Carlisle. **60 F1** NY4252.
Carleton *Cumb.* ***Settlement***, 1m/2km SE of Drigg. SD0898.
Carleton *Cumb.* ***Suburb***, 1m/2km E of Penrith town centre. NY5329.
Carleton *Lancs.* ***Hamlet***, 3m/4km NE of Blackpool. **55 G5** SD3339.
Carleton *N.Yorks.* ***Village***, 2m/3km SW of Skipton. **56 E5** SD9749.
Carleton *W.Yorks.* ***Locality***, 1m/2km SE of Pontefract. **57 K7** SE4620.
Carleton Fishery *S.Ayr.* ***Settlement***, at end of Carleton Bay, 5m/8km NE of Ballantrae. **67 F5** NX1289.
Carleton Forehoe *Norf.* ***Village***, 3m/5km N of Wymondham. **44 E5** TG0905.
Carleton Rode *Norf.* ***Village***, 5m/7km SE of Attleborough. **45 F6** TM1192.
Carleton St. Peter *Norf.* ***Hamlet***, 3m/5km NW of Loddon. TG3402.
Carley Hill *T. & W.* ***Suburb***, 2m/3km N of Sunderland city centre. Quarries. NZ3859.
Carlidnack *Cornw.* ***Hamlet***, 3m/4km SW of Falmouth, adjoining Mawnan Smith. SW7729.
Carlin How *R. & C.* ***Locality***, 1m/2km E of Brotton. **63 J5** NZ7019.
Carlin Tooth *Sc.Bord.* ***Mountain***, in Cheviot Hills, 3m/4km E of Note o' the Gate. Height 1807 feet or 551 metres. **70 B3** NT6302.
Carlingcott *B. & N.E.Som.* ***Hamlet***, 2m/4km N of Radstock. **19 K6** ST6958.
Carlingheugh Bay *Angus* ***Bay***, small bay 2m/3km NE of Arbroath. **83 H3** NO6742.
Carlingwark Loch *D. & G.* ***Lake/loch***, loch on S side of Castle Douglas. Haunt of wildfowl. **65 H4** NX7661.
Carlin's Cairn *D. & G.* ***Mountain***, rising to over 800 metres, 9m/14km NW of St. John's Town of Dalry. **67 J5** NX4988.
Carlisle *Cumb.* Population: 72,439. ***City***, cathedral city at confluence of River Eden and River Caldew, 54m/87km W of Newcastle upon Tyne. Once a Roman military base and later fought over by Scots and English. Line of Hadrian's Wall runs through N suburbs. Remains of Norman castle (English Heritage) above River Eden. University of Northumbria. Racecourse 2m/4km S. Airport 6m/9km NE. **60 F1** NY4056.
Carlisle Castle *Cumb.* ***Castle***, remains of Norman castle (English Heritage) above River Eden, partly built by William Rufus and completed by David I of Scotland when he captured it in 12c. Sandstone keep, Queen Mary's Tower, houses museum of Carlisle Border Regiment, with displays of weapons, medals and uniforms from last 300 years. **60 E1** NY3956.
Carlisle Cathedral *Cumb.* ***Ecclesiastical building***, in centre of Carlisle, with a magnificent E window. Partly destroyed by fire in 17c, but two surviving bays of nave are 12c. **60 E1** NY4055.
Carlisle Museum and Art Gallery *Cumb.* ***Other feature of interest***, in Tullie House (1689) in central Carlisle, showing local history with details on Romans and on border troubles in 16c-17c between Scots and English. **60 E1** NY3955.
Carlock Hill *S.Ayr.* ***Mountain***, 3m/5km S of Ballantrae. Height 1046 feet or 319 metres. **64 A3** NX0877.
Carloggas *Cornw.* ***Hamlet***, 4m/7km NE of Newquay. SW8765.
Carlops *Sc.Bord.* ***Village***, on E side of Pentland Hills, 3m/5km N of West Linton. **75 K5** NT1655.
Carloway (Gaelic form: Carlabhagh.) *W.Isles* ***Village***, near W coast of Isle of Lewis at head of estuary of Carloway River, which rises among lochs to S. **100 E3** NB2042.
Carlton *Beds.* ***Village***, 7m/11km NW of Bedford, adjoining to S of Chellington. **32 C3** SP9555.
Carlton *Cambs.* ***Village***, 5m/8km N of Haverhill. **33 K3** TL6453.
Carlton *Leics.* ***Village***, 1m/2km NW of Market Bosworth. **41 F5** SK3905.
Carlton *N.Yorks.* ***Hamlet***, 2m/3km N of Helmsley. **58 C1** SE6186.
Carlton *N.Yorks.* ***Village***, 4m/6km SW of Wensley. **57 F1** SE0684.
Carlton *N.Yorks.* Population: 1640. ***Village***, 1m/2km N of Snaith. **58 C7** SE6423.
Carlton *Notts.* Population: 47,302. ***Town***, adjoining to E of Nottingham. Hosiery was an important industry. Large Victorian church. **41 J1** SK6141.
Carlton *S.Yorks.* ***Suburb***, 3m/4km NE of Barnsley town centre. **51 F2** SE3610.
Carlton *Stock.* ***Village***, 4m/6km NW of Stockton-on-Tees. **62 E4** NZ3921.
Carlton *Suff.* ***Village***, 1m/2km N of Saxmundham. **35 H2** TM3864.
Carlton *W.Yorks.* ***Village***, 4m/6km N of Wakefield. **57 J7** SE3327.
Carlton Colville *Suff.* ***Village***, 3m/5km SW of Lowestoft. **45 K6** TM5190.
Carlton Curlieu *Leics.* ***Village***, 7m/11km NW of Market Harborough. **41 J6** SP6997.
Carlton Green *Cambs.* ***Settlement***, 1m/2km S of Carlton and 4m/7km N of Haverhill. TL6451.
Carlton Husthwaite *N.Yorks.* ***Village***, 5m/8km N of Easingwold. **57 K2** SE4976.
Carlton in Cleveland *N.Yorks.* ***Village***, 3m/5km SW of Stokesley. **63 G6** NZ5004.
Carlton in Lindrick *Notts.* Population: 6376. ***Village***, 3m/4km N of Worksop. **51 H4** SK5984.
Carlton-le-Moorland *Lincs.* ***Village***, 9m/15km SW of Lincoln. **52 C7** SK9057.
Carlton Miniott *N.Yorks.* ***Village***, 2m/4km W of Thirsk. **57 J1** SE3981.
Carlton Moor *N.Yorks.* ***Open space***, moorland 2m/3km SE of West Burton, between Bishopdale and Coverdale, with Harland Hill (1758 feet or 536 metres) as its highest point. **57 F1** SE0384.
Carlton-on-Trent *Notts.* ***Village***, 6m/10km N of Newark-on-Trent. **52 B6** SK7963.
Carlton Scroop *Lincs.* ***Village***, 6m/10km NE of Grantham. **42 C1** SK9445.
Carlton Towers *N.Yorks.* ***Historic house***, on E side of Carlton, 1m/2km N of Snaith and 6m/10km W of Goole. 19c Victorian Gothic house by E. Pugin and John Frances Bentley, who designed Westminster Cathedral. Built over original Jacobean home of Stapleton family. **58 C7** SE6523.
Carluke *S.Lan.* Population: 12,921. ***Town***, 5m/8km NW of Lanark. **75 G5** NS8450.
Carlungie *Angus* ***Settlement***, 2m/4km N of Monifieth, including ancient souterrain or earth-house (Historic Scotland). NO5135.
Carlyle's Birthplace *D. & G.* ***Historic house***, at Ecclefechan. Known as The Arched House and birthplace of Thomas Carlyle, scholar and Victorian thinker, in 1795. Now a museum (National Trust for Scotland). **69 G6** NY1974.
Carlyon Bay *Cornw.* ***Town***, coastal resort 2m/4km E of St. Austell. **4 A5** SX0552.
Carmacoup *S.Lan.* ***Settlement***, 1m/2km SW of Glespin. **68 C1** NS7927.
Carmarthen (Caerfyrddin). *Carmar.* Population: 13,524. ***Town***, administrative centre on River Tywi, 22m/36km NW of Swansea, on site of Roman fort of Moridunum. Busy market. Museum in Bishop's Palace at Abergwili. **17 H3** SN4120.
Carmarthen Bay ***Bay***, off S coast of Wales, extending from Worms Head westwards to Caldy Island. Receives the waters of Rivers Loughor, Tywi and Taf, and of several lesser streams. **17 F5** SN3000.
Carmarthen Castle *Carmar.* ***Castle***, early 12c motte built by Normans at SE of Carmarthen on bluff above River Tywi. Made centre of administration for SW Wales by Edward I; now in ruins with only 14c gatehouse and section of curtain wall remaining. County Hall now occupies site. **17 H2** SN4120.
Carmarthen Van (Fan Brycheiniog). *Powys* ***Mountain***, above W side of Llyn y Fan Fawr, 4m/6km SE of Llanddeusant. Highest peak of Black Mountain. Height 2631 feet or 802 metres. SN8221.
Carmel *Carmar.* ***Village***, 4m/7km SW of Llandeilo. **17 J3** SN5816.
Carmel *Flints.* ***Village***, adjoining to NW of Holywell. **47 K5** SJ1776.
Carmel *Gwyn.* ***Village***, 5m/8km S of Caernarfon. **46 C7** SH4955.
Carmel *I.o.A.* ***Settlement***, in central Anglesey, 8m/12km SW of Amlwch. **46 B4** SH3882.
Carmel Head (Trwyn y Gader). *I.o.A.* ***Coastal feature***, headland on N coast of Anglesey, 5m/7km W of Cemaes Bay. **46 A3** SH2993.
Carmichael *S.Lan.* ***Settlement***, 3m/5km W of Thankerton. NS9339.
Carminish *W.Isles* *Anglicised form of Cairminis, qv.*
Carminish Islands *W.Isles* ***Island***, group of islets off S coast of South Harris about 3m/5km NW of Renish Point. **92 E3** NG0185.
Carmont *Aber.* ***Hamlet***, 4m/7km W of Stonehaven. **91 G6** NO8184.
Carmunnock *Glas.* ***Village***, 3m/5km NW of East Kilbride. **74 E5** NS5957.
Carmyle *Glas.* ***Suburb***, on N bank of River Clyde, 4m/7km SE of Glasgow. **74 E4** NS6561.
Carmyllie *Angus* ***Locality***, 6m/10km W of Arbroath. **83 G3** NO5442.
Carn *Arg. & B.* ***Settlement***, on SE coast of Rinns of Islay, 1m/2km SW of Port Charlotte. **72 A5** NR2457.
Carn a' Bhacain *Aber.* ***Mountain***, 7m/11km NW of Ballater. Height 2440 feet or 744 metres. **89 K4** NJ2904.
Carn a' Bhodaich *High.* ***Mountain***, in Inverness district, 6m/10km NE of Drumnadrochit. Height 1643 feet or 501 metres. **88 C1** NH5737.
Carn a' Bhodaich *Moray* ***Mountain***, 8m/13km W of Cabrach. Height 2148 feet or 655 metres. **89 K2** NJ2628.
Carn a' Chaochain *High.* ***Mountain***, in Inverness district, 5m/8km NW of Dalchreichart. Height 2316 feet or 706 metres. **87 J3** NH2318.
Carn a' Chlamain *P. & K.* ***Mountain***, in Forest of Atholl, 7m/11km NE of Blair Atholl. Munro: height 3159 feet or 963 metres. **89 G7** NN9175.
Carn a' Choin Deirg *High.* ***Mountain***, in Sutherland district, 6m/9km S of Oykel Bridge. Height 2299 feet or 701 metres. **95 K2** NH3992.
Carn a' Choire Bhuidhe *High.* ***Mountain***, in Inverness district 4m/7km N of dam of Loch Cluanie. Height 2778 feet or 847 metres. **87 H3** NH1817.
Carn a' Choire Ghlaise *High.* ***Mountain***, in Inverness district 11m/17km E of Fort Augustus. Height 2555 feet or 779 metres. **88 C4** NH5408.
Carn a' Choire Mhòir *High.* ***Mountain***, in Inverness district, 3m/4km E of Tomatin. Height 2057 feet or 627 metres. **89 F2** NH8429.
Carn a' Chrasgie *High.* ***Mountain***, in Nairn district, 5m/7km S of Cawdor. Height 1315 feet or 401 metres. **97 F7** NH8643.
Carn a' Chuilinn *High.* ***Mountain***, on Glendoe Forest, Inverness district, 4m/6km SE of Fort Augustus. Height 2676 feet or 816 metres. **88 B4** NH4103.
Carn a' Coire Bhoidheach *Aber.* ***Mountain***, peak to NW of White Mounth, 3m/5km NW of Loch Muick. Munro: height 3641 feet or 1110 metres. **89 K6** NO2284.
Carn a' Ghaill *High.* ***Hill***, highest point of Canna, 1km N of A' Chill. Height 689 feet or 210 metres. **85 H4** NG2606.
Carn a' Gheoidh ***Mountain***, on border of Aberdeenshire and Perth & Kinross, 4m/7km N of Spittal of Glenshee. Munro: height 3198 feet or 975 metres. **89 J7** NO1076.
Carn a' Ghlinne *High.* ***Mountain***, rounded summit in Ross and Cromarty district, on NE side of Glen Docherty, 2m/4km E of Kinlochewe. Height 1768 feet or 539 metres. **95 G5** NH0660.
Carn a' Mhadaidh-ruaidh *High.* ***Mountain***, 3m/5km NE of Arisaig. Height 1650 feet or 503 metres. **86 D6** NM7088.
Carn a' Mhaim *Aber.* ***Mountain***, in Cairngorm Mountains 2m/4km S of Ben Macdui. Munro: height 3401 feet or 1037 metres. **89 G5** NN9995.
Carn a' Mhuilt *High.* ***Mountain***, rounded summit on NW side of Strathglass, 3m/5km N of Cannich. Height 2171 feet or 662 metres. **87 K1** NH3436.
Carn Ait *P. & K.* ***Mountain***, 3m/5km NE of Spittal of Glenshee. Height 2834 feet or 864 metres. **89 J7** NO1473.
Carn an Daimh *P. & K.* ***Mountain***, 2m/3km NE of Spittal of Glenshee. Height 2476 feet or 755 metres. **89 J7** NO1371.
Carn an Fhidhleir (Anglicised form: Carn Ealar.) ***Mountain***, on borders of Aberdeenshire, Highland and Perth & Kinross, 12m/19km N of Blair Atholl. Munro: height 3260 feet or 994 metres. **89 G6** NN9084.
Carn an Fhidhleir Lorgaidh *High.* ***Mountain***, on Glenfeshie Forest in Badenoch and Strathspey district, 10m/16km SE of Kingussie. Height 2785 feet or 849 metres. **89 F6** NN8587.
Carn an Fhreiceadain *High.* ***Mountain***, in Monadhliath range in Badenoch and Strathspey district, 5m/7km NW of Kingussie. Height 2880 feet or 878 metres. **88 E4** NH7207.
Carn an Leanaidh *High.* ***Mountain***, in Ross and Cromarty district, 4m/6km NW of Inverchoran. Height 1883 feet or 574 metres. **95 J6** NH2154.
Carn an Leth-choin *High.* ***Mountain***, in Badenoch and Strathspey district, 5m/8km W of Newtonmore. Height 2765 feet or 843 metres. **88 D5** NN6299.
Carn an Righ *P. & K.* ***Mountain***, 7m/11km NW of Spittal of Glenshee. Munro: height 3375 feet or 1029 metres. **89 H7** NO0277.
Carn an t-Sagairt Mòr (Also known as Cairn Taggart). *Aber.* ***Mountain***, 6m/9km SE of Braemar. Munro: height 3434 feet or 1047 metres. **89 K6** NO2084.

Carn an t-Sean-liathanaich *High.* ***Mountain***, on borders of Inverness and Nairn districts, 15m/24km S of Nairn. Height 2083 feet or 635 metres. **89 F1** NH8632.
Carn an t-Suidhe *Moray* ***Mountain***, 6m/10km SE of foot of Glenlivet. Height 2401 feet or 732 metres. **89 K2** NJ2626.
Carn an Tionail *High.* ***Mountain***, 1km E of Carn Dearg. Height 2490 feet or 759 metres. **103 F5** NC3939.
Carn an Tuirc *Aber.* ***Mountain***, 7m/11km S of Braemar. Munro: height 3342 feet or 1019 metres. **89 J6** NO1780.
Carn Aosda *Aber.* ***Mountain***, 8m/12km S of Braemar. Munro: height 3008 feet or 917 metres. **89 J7** NO1379.
Carn Bad na Caorach *High.* ***Mountain***, 4m/7km N of Grantown-on-Spey. Height 1565 feet or 477 metres. **89 H1** NJ0335.
Carn Bàn *Arg. & B.* ***Hill***, 1m/2km NW of Rubha na Faoilinn, Mull. Height 813 feet or 248 metres. **79 J5** NM7228.
Carn Bàn *High.* ***Mountain***, in Inverness district, 6m/10km N of Cannich. Height 2414 feet or 736 metres. **95 K7** NH3341.
Carn Bàn *High.* ***Mountain***, in Freevater Forest in Ross and Cromarty district, 5m/8km N of Loch Vaich. Height 2772 feet or 845 metres. **95 K3** NH3387.
Carn Bàn *High.* ***Mountain***, in Monadhliath range, on border of Inverness and Badenoch and Strathspey districts, 6m/9km NW of Newtonmore. Height 3090 feet or 942 metres. **88 D4** NH6303.
Carn Bàn Mòr *High.* ***Mountain***, in Badenoch and Strathspey district in W part of Cairngorm Mountains, 7m/11km SE of Kincraig. Height 3451 feet or 1052 metres. **89 F5** NN8997.
Carn Beag *High.* ***Mountain***, in Ledgowan Forest, Ross and Cromarty district, 4m/6km SE of Achnasheen. Height 1804 feet or 550 metres. **95 H6** NH1055.
Carn Beag Dearg *High. See Carn Mòr Dearg.*
Carn Bhac ***Mountain***, on border of Aberdeenshire and Perth & Kinross, 5m/8km SW of Inverey. Munro: height 3018 feet or 920 metres. **89 H6** NO0482.
Carn Bheadhair *High.* ***Mountain***, 6m/10km SE of Nethy Bridge. Height 2634 feet or 803 metres. **89 H3** NJ0511.
Carn Bhrain *High.* ***Mountain***, in Sutherland district, 6m/9km SW of Bonar Bridge. Height 2083 feet or 635 metres. **96 C3** NH5287.
Carn Brea *Cornw.* ***Hill***, National Trust property, 3m/5km NE of Land's End, with wide sea view. Two Bronze Age barrows. Height 623 feet or 190 metres. SW3828.
Carn Brea *Cornw.* ***Hill***, granite tor to SW of Carn Brea Village, commanding wide views and topped by monument of 1836 commemorating Lord de Dunstanville. Height 738 feet or 225 metres. **2 D4** SW6840.
Carn Brea Village *Cornw.* ***Hamlet***, adjoining to W of Church Town, 1km SW of Redruth. To SW, granite tor of Carn Brea. **2 D4** SW6841.
Carn Breac *High.* ***Mountain***, in Ross and Cromarty district, 4m/6km NE of Achnashellach Station. Height 2224 feet or 678 metres. **95 G6** NH0453.
Carn Caglau *N.P.T.* ***Historic/prehistoric site***, tumulus at summit of Moel yr Hyrddod, 6m/10km N of Maesteg. **18 B1** SN8600.
Carn Caol *High.* ***Mountain***, on border of Inverness and Badenoch and Strathspey districts, 9m/15km N of Kingussie. Height 2339 feet or 713 metres. **88 E3** NH7616.
Carn Cas nan Gabhar *High.* ***Mountain***, in Ross and Cromarty district, 10m/16km NW of Alness. Height 1975 feet or 602 metres. **96 C3** NH5280.
Carn Chaiseachain *High.* ***Mountain***, low, rounded summit in Ross and Cromarty district on S side of Strath Bran, 5m/9km NE of Achnasheen. Height 1023 feet or 312 metres. **95 J5** NH2560.
Carn Chòis *P. & K.* ***Mountain***, on W side of Loch Turret Reservoir. Height 2578 feet or 786 metres. **81 J5** NN7927.
Carn Chrom *Moray* ***Mountain***, 4m/6km S of Dufftown. Height 1650 feet or 503 metres. **90 B1** NJ3333.
Carn Chuinneag *High.* ***Mountain***, in Diebidale Forest on border of Ross and Cromarty and Sutherland districts, 5m/7km NW of head of Loch Morie. Height 2749 feet or 838 metres. **96 B3** NH4883.
Carn Coire na Creiche *High.* ***Mountain***, in Inverness district, 9m/13km NW of Newtonmore. Height 2709 feet or 826 metres. **88 D4** NH6108.
Carn Coire na h-Easgainn *High.* ***Mountain***, in Monadhliath range, on border of Inverness and Badenoch and Strathspey districts, 8m/13km N of Kingussie. Height 2591 feet or 790 metres. **88 E3** NH7313.
Carn Crom *Aber.* ***Mountain***, in Grampian Mountains, 6m/9km NW of Inverey. Height 2919 feet or 890 metres. **89 H5** NO0295.
Carn Daimh *Moray* ***Mountain***, to E of Strath Avon and 2m/3km W of Tomnavoulin. Height 1837 feet or 560 metres. **89 J2** NJ1824.
Carn Daraich *High.* ***Mountain***, in Ross and Cromarty district, 5m/8km NE of Achnasheen. Height 1525 feet or 465 metres. **95 J5** NH2363.
Carn Dearg ***Mountain***, on border of Highland and Perth & Kinross, 3m/5km E of head of Loch Ossian. Munro: height 3086 feet or 941 metres. **81 F1** NN4166.
Carn Dearg *High.* ***Mountain***, 4m/6km N of Loch Merkland. Height 2611 feet or 796 metres. **103 F5** NC3738.
Carn Dearg *High.* ***Mountain***, summit of Monadhliath range, in Badenoch and Strathspey district, 8m/12km W of Kingussie. Munro: height 3100 feet or 945 metres. **88 D4** NH6302.
Carn Dearg *High.* ***Mountain***, NW and SW peaks of Ben Nevis, in Lochaber district. Height of NW peak 3975 feet or 1212 metres; height of SW peak 3347 feet or 1020 metres. **87 H7** NN1572.
Carn Dearg *High.* ***Mountain***, in Lochaber district 7m/11km NE of Roybridge. Height 2736 feet or 834 metres. **87 K6** NN3488.
Carn Dearg *High.* ***Mountain***, in Lochaber district 4m/6km E of NE end of Loch Lochy. Height 2673 feet or 815 metres. **87 K5** NN3496.
Carn Dearg *High.* ***Mountain***, in Badenoch and Strathspey district, 10m/16km SW of Dalwhinnie. Munro: height 3392 feet or 1034 metres. **88 C7** NN5076.
Carn Dearg *High.* ***Settlement***, 3m/4km W of Gairloch, in Ross and Cromarty district. **94 D4** NG7677.
Carn Dearg Mòr *High.* ***Mountain***, in Badenoch and Strathspey district, 2m/3km E of Aviemore. Height 2335 feet or 712 metres. **89 F3** NH8613.
Carn Dearg Mòr *High.* ***Mountain***, in Badenoch and Strathspey district, 7m/11km SE of Kingussie. Height 2811 feet or 857 metres. **89 F5** NN8291.
Carn Deas *High.* ***Island***, small island in Summer Isles group. Adjacent to and E of Carn Iar, Carn Deas lies less than 1km SW of Eilean Dubh. NB9602.
Carn Dubh'Ic an Deòir *High.* ***Mountain***, on border of Inverness and Badenoch and Strathspey districts, 9m/14km NW of Aviemore. Height 2460 feet or 750 metres. **88 E3** NH7719.
Carn Duchan *Arg. & B.* ***Mountain***, 3m/5km SE of Kilmelford. Height 1610 feet or 491 metres. **79 K7** NM8910.
Carn Dulnan *High.* ***Mountain***, rising to over 740 metres in Badenoch and Strathspey district, 6m/10km N of Kingussie. **88 E3** NH7510.
Carn Eachie *High.* ***Mountain***, on Hills of Cromdale, 5m/8km N of Bridge of Brown. Height 2296 feet or 700 metres. **89 J2** NJ1328.
Carn Ealar *Anglicised form of Carn an Fhidhleir, qv.*
Carn Ealasaid ***Mountain***, on border of Aberdeenshire and Moray, 6m/9km SE of Tomintoul. Height 2598 feet or 792 metres. **89 K3** NJ2211.
Carn Eas *Aber.* ***Mountain***, in Grampian Mountains, 5m/8km NW of Braemar. Height 3572 feet or 1089 metres. **89 J5** NO1299.
Carn Easgann Bàna *High.* ***Mountain***, in Inverness district, 7m/11km E of Fort Augustus. Height 2552 feet or 778 metres. **88 B4** NH4806.
Carn Eige *High.* ***Mountain***, on border of Inverness and Skye and Lochalsh districts, 3m/5km N of Loch Affric. Munro: height 3880 feet or 1183 metres. **87 H2** NH1226.
Carn Eilrig *High.* ***Mountain***, in Badenoch and Strathspey district, to S of Rothiemurchus and 5m/8km SE of Aviemore. Height 2434 feet or 742 metres. **89 G4** NH9305.
Carn Eiteige *High.* ***Mountain***, peak on East Monar Forest, Ross and Cromarty district, 2m/4km N of dam of Loch Monar. Height 2893 feet or 882 metres. **95 J7** NH2143.
Carn Euny Ancient Village *Cornw.* ***Historic/prehistoric site***, well restored Iron Age village (English Heritage), 4m/6km W of Newlyn. Notable fogou, or underground passage, in village centre. **2 B6** SW4028.
Carn Fadryn *Gwyn.* ***Mountain***, on Lleyn Peninsula, 5m/8km NW of Abersoch. Height 1217 feet or 371 metres. **36 B2** SH2735.
Carn Fliuch-bhaid *High.* ***Mountain***, in Inverness district, 12m/20km SE of Foyers. Height 2152 feet or 656 metres. **88 C3** NN5512.
Carn Gafallt *Powys* ***Mountain***, 1km SE of Elan Village. Height 1528 feet or 466 metres. **27 J2** SN9464.
Carn Geuradainn *High.* ***Mountain***, in Attadale Forest, 4m/6km E of Attadale. Height 1948 feet or 594 metres. **87 F1** NG9839.
Carn Ghiubhais *Moray* ***Mountain***, 6m/10km NE of Dava. Height 1410 feet or 430 metres. **97 H7** NJ0845.
Carn Ghluasaid *High.* ***Mountain***, peak on border of Inverness and Skye and Lochalsh districts, 3m/5km NW of dam of Loch Cluanie. Munro: height 3139 feet or 957 metres. **87 H3** NH1412.
Carn Ghriogair *High.* ***Mountain***, in Inverness district, 15m/24km NW of Newtonmore. Height 2640 feet or 805 metres. **88 D2** NH6520.
Carn Glac an Eich *High.* ***Mountain***, in Inverness district, 16m/26km N of Newtonmore. Height 2070 feet or 631 metres. **88 D2** NH6926.
Carn Glas-choire *High.* ***Mountain***, on borders of Inverness, Nairn and Badenoch and Strathspey districts, 4m/6km N of Carrbridge. Height 2162 feet or 659 metres. **89 F2** NH8928.
Carn Gorm *High.* ***Mountain***, on Glencarron and Glenuig Forest, Ross and Cromarty district, 6m/9km S of Achnasheen. Height 2870 feet or 875 metres. **95 H6** NH1350.
Carn Gorm *High.* ***Mountain***, in Inverness district, 3m/4km N of Cannich. Height 2217 feet or 676 metres. **87 K1** NH3235.
Carn Gorm *High.* ***Mountain***, in Ross and Cromarty district, 4m/6km E of Gorstan. Height 1824 feet or 556 metres. **96 B5** NH4362.
Càrn Gorm *P. & K.* ***Mountain***, 6m/9km S of Kinloch Rannoch. Munro: height 3375 feet or 1029 metres. **81 H2** NN6350.
Carn Gron *Cere.* ***Mountain***, 4m/6km E of Tregaron. Height 1774 feet or 541 metres. **27 G2** SN7461.
Carn Iar *High.* ***Island***, small island in Summer Isles group. Lies 1km SW of Eilean Dubh. NB9602.
Carn Icean Duibhe *High.* ***Mountain***, in Monadhliath range, on border of Inverness and Badenoch and Strathspey districts, 7m/12km NW of Kingussie. Height 2650 feet or 808 metres. **88 E3** NH7111.
Carn Kitty *Moray* ***Mountain***, 6m/9km NE of Dava. Height 1709 feet or 521 metres. **97 H7** NJ0842.
Carn Leac *High.* ***Mountain***, on borders of Inverness, Lochaber, and Badenoch and Strathspey districts, 7m/12km S of Fort Augustus. Height 2900 feet or 884 metres. **88 B5** NN4097.
Carn Leac Saighdeir *Aber.* ***Mountain***, 1m/2km S of Corgarff. Height 2293 feet or 699 metres. **89 K4** NJ2706.
Carn Liath *Aber.* ***Mountain***, on border of Aberdeenshire and Moray, 6m/10km W of Strathdon. Height 2598 feet or 792 metres. **89 K3** NJ2515.
Carn Liath *Aber.* ***Mountain***, 4m/6km SW of Inverey. Height 2683 feet or 818 metres. **89 H6** NO0386.
Carn Liath *Aber.* ***Mountain***, in Grampian Mountains, 4m/6km N of Braemar. Height 2827 feet or 862 metres. **89 J5** NO1697.
Carn Liath *High.* ***Historic/prehistoric site***, chambered cairn 1m/2km S of Eyre, Skye. **93 K6** NG4151.
Carn Liath *High.* ***Mountain***, in Ross and Cromarty district, forming twin summit with Carn Gorm in Glencarron and Glenuig Forest, 8m/12km W of Inverchoran. Height 2811 feet or 857 metres. **95 H6** NH1350.
Carn Liath *High.* ***Mountain***, in Badenoch and Strathspey district, 4m/6km W of head of Loch Laggan. Munro: height 3300 feet or 1006 metres. **88 B5** NN4790.
Carn Liath *Moray* ***Mountain***, to E of Strath Avon and 2m/3km W of Tomnavoulin. Height 1801 feet or 549 metres. **89 J2** NJ1726.
Carn Liath *P. & K.* ***Mountain***, SW shoulder of Beinn a' Ghlo, 7m/12km N of Pitlochry. Munro: height 3198 feet or 975 metres. **82 A1** NN9369.
Carn Loisgte *High.* ***Mountain***, rounded summit in Ross and Cromarty district, 8m/12km W of Achnasheen. Height 1463 feet or 446 metres. **95 G6** NH0357.
Carn Macsna *High.* ***Mountain***, in Inverness district, 4m/6km SW of Drumnadrochit. Height 1722 feet or 525 metres. **88 B2** NH4427.
Càrn Mairg *P. & K.* ***Mountain***, 5m/8km S of Kinloch Rannoch. Munro: height 3418 feet or 1042 metres. **81 H2** NN6851.
Carn Màiri *High.* ***Mountain***, 1km NE of mouth of River Barrisdale, near S shore of Loch Hourn. Height 1647 feet or 502 metres. **86 E4** NG8805.
Carn Meadhonach *Moray* ***Mountain***, 2m/3km W of Tomintoul. Height 1929 feet or 588 metres. **89 J3** NJ1317.
Carn Mhartuin *High.* ***Mountain***, rounded summit in Ross and Cromarty district, 5m/8km S of Achnasheen. Height 1765 feet or 538 metres. **95 H6** NH1754.
Carn Mhic an Toisich *High.* ***Mountain***, in Dundreggan Forest, Ross and Cromarty district, 3m/5km N of Dundreggan. Height 2230 feet or 680 metres. **87 K3** NH3118.
Carn Mhic Raonuill *High.* ***Mountain***, rounded summit in Inverness district, 5m/8km W of Fort Augustus. Height 1856 feet or 566 metres. **87 J4** NH2908.
Carn Mòr *Arg. & B.* ***Mountain***, on Mull, 2m/3km N of Kilninian. Height 1122 feet or 342 metres. **79 F3** NM3948.
Carn Mòr *High.* ***Hill***, 1km S of Farquhar's Point, Lochaber district. Height 400 feet or 122 metres. **86 C7** NM6271.
Carn Mòr *High.* ***Mountain***, in Ross and Cromarty district, 10m/14km SE of Ullapool. Height 2129 feet or 649 metres. **95 J3** NH2486.
Carn Mòr *High.* ***Mountain***, rounded summit in Ross and Cromarty district, 6m/10km NE of Gorstan. Height 2099 feet or 640 metres. **96 B4** NH4271.
Carn Mòr *High.* ***Mountain***, rocky summit in Inverness district, 5m/8km NW of Drumnadrochit. Height 1496 feet or 456 metres. **88 B1** NH4334.
Carn Mòr *High.* ***Mountain***, 3m/4km E of head of Loch Morar, Lochaber district. Height 2719 feet or 829 metres. **87 F5** NM9090.
Carn Mòr *Moray* ***Mountain***, highest point of Ladder Hills, 6m/10km E of Tomintoul. Height 2637 feet or 804 metres. **89 K3** NJ2618.
Carn Mòr Dearg *High.* ***Mountain***, in Lochaber district 1m/2km NE of Ben Nevis. Munro: height 4011 feet or 1223 metres. Carn Beag Dearg, 1m/2km along ridge to NW, 3264 feet or 995 metres. **87 H7** NN1772.
Carn na Béiste *High.* ***Hill***, 4m/6km S of entrance to Little Loch Broom, Ross and Cromarty district. Height 991 feet or 302 metres. **95 F3** NG9989.
Carn na Bèiste *High.* ***Mountain***, in Ross and Cromarty district, at E end of Loch Fannich and 2m/3km NE of Achanalt. Height 1699 feet or 518 metres. **95 J5** NH2864.
Carn na Cailliche *Moray* ***Mountain***, 3m/4km N of Upper Knockando. Height 1325 feet or 404 metres. **97 J7** NJ1847.
Carn na Caim ***Mountain***, on border of Highland and Perth & Kinross, 3m/5km SE of Dalwhinnie. Munro: height 3086 feet or 941 metres. **88 D6** NN6782.
Carn na Cloiche Mòire *High.* ***Mountain***, in Ross and Cromarty district, 10m/16km NW of Beauly. Height 1938 feet or 591 metres. **95 K6** NH3753.
Carn na Cóinnich *High.* ***Mountain***, in Ross and Cromarty district, 2m/3km N of W end of Orrin Reservoir. Height 2207 feet or 673 metres. **95 K6** NH3251.
Carn na Crè *High.* ***Mountain***, in Ross and Cromarty district, 2m/3km N of Milton. Height 1499 feet or 457 metres. **95 K6** NH3059.
Carn na Drochaide *Aber.* ***Mountain***, in Grampian Mountains, 3m/4km NW of Braemar. Height 2683 feet or 818 metres. **89 J5** NO1293.
Carn na Dubh Choille *High.* ***Mountain***, in Ross and Cromarty district, 3m/5km N of Gorstan. Height 1571 feet or 479 metres. **95 K5** NH3867.
Carn na Farraidh *High.* ***Mountain***, 4m/6km SW of Tomintoul. Height 2257 feet or 688 metres. **89 J3** NJ1114.
Carn na Feannaige *Moray* ***Mountain***, on N side of Glen Avon, 8m/12km SW of Tomintoul. Height 2394 feet or 730 metres. **89 H4** NJ1008.
Carn na h-Ailig *High.* ***Mountain***, 6m/9km SE of Nethy Bridge. Height 2089 feet or 637 metres. **89 H3** NJ0614.
Carn na h-Easgainn *High.* ***Mountain***, in Inverness district, 5m/8km SE of Daviot. Height 2020 feet or 616 metres. **88 E1** NH7432.

Carn na Làraiche Maoile *High.* ***Mountain***, in Monadhliath range, 9m/13km SE of Foyers. Height 2654 feet or 809 metres. **88 C3** NH5811.
Carn na Loinne *High.* ***Mountain***, 3m/4km NE of Nethy Bridge. Height 1506 feet or 459 metres. **89 H2** NJ0322.
Carn na Nathrach *High.* ***Mountain***, 4m/6km SE of Scamodale and 1m/2km SW of Lochan Dubh, Lochaber district. Height 2578 feet or 786 metres. **79 K1** NM8869.
Carn na Saobhaidh *High.* ***Mountain***, in Inverness district, 12m/20km S of Inverness. Height 2342 feet or 714 metres. **88 D2** NH6724.
Carn na Saobhaidhe *High.* ***Mountain***, in Inverness district, 9m/13km SE of Foyers. Height 2660 feet or 811 metres. **88 C3** NH5914.
Carn na Sean-lùibe *High.* ***Mountain***, in Killilan Forest, Skye and Lochalsh district. Height 1909 feet or 582 metres. **87 G1** NH0235.
Carn na Sguabaich *High.* ***Mountain***, in Nairn district, 12m/20km S of Nairn. Height 1528 feet or 466 metres. **89 F1** NH8737.
Carn nam Bad *High.* ***Mountain***, rocky summit in Inverness district, 4m/7km NE of Cannich. Height 1499 feet or 457 metres. **88 B1** NH4033.
Carn nam-Bain Tighearna *High.* ***Mountain***, on border of Inverness and Badenoch and Strathspey districts, 4m/6km SE of Tomatin. Height 2080 feet or 634 metres. **89 F2** NH8425.
Carn nam Bò Maola *High.* ***Mountain***, 1m/2km NE of Glencassley Castle, on E side of Glen Cassley. Height 1391 feet or 424 metres. **96 B1** NC4509.
Carn nam Buailtean *High.* ***Mountain***, in Ross and Cromarty district, 6m/9km W of head of Little Loch Broom. Height 1260 feet or 384 metres. **95 G3** NH0087.
Carn nam Feuaich *High.* ***Mountain***, in Inverness district, 1m/2km N of E end of Loch Cluanie. Height 2401 feet or 732 metres. **87 H3** NH1712.
Carn nan Gabhar *P. & K.* ***Mountain***, summit of Beinn a' Ghlo, 8m/12km NE of Blair Atholl. Munro: height 3677 feet or 1121 metres. **89 G7** NN9773.
Carn nan Gobhar *High.* ***Mountain***, in Inverness district 3m/5km NW of dam of Loch Mullardoch. Munro: height 3254 feet or 992 metres. **87 H1** NH1834.
Carn nan Gobhar *High.* ***Mountain***, in Inverness district, 4m/6km S of Inverchoran. Munro: height 3254 feet or 992 metres. **95 J7** NH2743.
Carn nan Iomairean *High.* ***Mountain***, 3m/5km E of Stromeferry. Height 1594 feet or 486 metres. **87 F1** NG9135.
Càrn nan Sgeir *High.* ***Island***, 1m/2km SW of Horse Island, off W coast of Ross and Cromarty district. **95 G1** NC0101.
Carn nan Tri-tighearnan *High.* ***Mountain***, on border of Inverness and Nairn districts, 5m/7km NE of Moy. Height 2017 feet or 615 metres. **89 F1** NH8239.
Carn Nant-yr-ast *Carmar.* ***Mountain***, 5m/8km SE of Llanddewi-Brefi. Height 1443 feet or 440 metres. **27 G4** SN7149.
Carn Naun Point *Cornw.* ***Coastal feature***, headland on N coast, 3m/4km W of St. Ives. **2 B4** SW4741.
Carn Odhar *High.* ***Mountain***, in Inverness district, 12m/20km NW of Newtonmore. Height 2631 feet or 802 metres. **88 D3** NH6317.
Carn Phris Mhòir *High.* ***Mountain***, on border of Inverness and Badenoch and Strathspey districts, 9m/13km NW of Aviemore. Height 2027 feet or 618 metres. **89 F2** NH8021.
Carn Ruigh Charrach *High.* ***Mountain***, 5m/8km NW of Grantown-on-Spey. Height 1588 feet or 484 metres. **89 G1** NH9834.
Carn Ruighe an Uain *High.* ***Mountain***, 4m/6km E of Dava. Height 1791 feet or 546 metres. **89 H1** NJ0637.
Carn Sgùlain *High.* ***Mountain***, in Monadhliath range on border of Inverness and Badenoch and Strathspey districts, 6m/9km NW of Kingussie. Munro: height 3018 feet or 920 metres. **88 D4** NH6805.
Carn Sgùlain *High.* ***Mountain***, on borders of Inverness and Badenoch and Strathspey districts, 6m/10km N of Newtonmore. Height 2663 feet or 812 metres. **88 D4** NH6909.
Carn Sgumain *High.* ***Mountain***, in Nairn district, 10m/16km S of Nairn. Height 1368 feet or 417 metres. **97 F7** NH8740.
Carn Shalag *Moray* ***Mountain***, with plateau 4m/7km W of Upper Knockando. Height 1542 feet or 470 metres. **97 J7** NJ1142.
Carn Sleamhuinn *High.* ***Mountain***, in Kinveachy Forest, Badenoch and Strathspey district, 3m/5km NW of Aviemore. Height 2221 feet or 677 metres. **89 F3** NH8516.
Carn Tuadhan *High.* ***Mountain***, 3m/5km S of Bridge of Brown. Height 1991 feet or 607 metres. **89 J3** NJ1215.
Carn Tuairneir *High.* ***Mountain***, on Hills of Cromdale, 2m/3km NW of Bridge of Brown. Height 2273 feet or 693 metres. **89 H2** NJ0923.
Carna *High.* ***Island***, at entrance to Loch Teacuis, Lochaber district. **79 H2** NM6158.
Carnaby *E.Riding* ***Village***, 2m/3km SW of Bridlington. **59 H3** TA1465.
Carnaby Moor *E.Riding* ***Open space***, moorland to S of Bridlington. **59 H3** TA1563.
Carnach *High.* ***Settlement***, on N shore of Little Loch Broom, near mouth of loch. Virtually inaccessible by road, with main access being by ferry from Badluarach on S side of loch. **95 G2** NH0196.
Carnach *High.* ***Settlement***, 6m/10km NE of Morvich at head of Loch Duich. Accessible only by narrow track. **87 G2** NH0228.
Carnach Mòr *Arg. & B.* ***Mountain***, 2m/3km NE of Glenbranter. Height 2080 feet or 634 metres. **73 K1** NS1499.
Carnachie *Moray* ***Mountain***, in wooded area, 5m/8km NW of Knockando. Height 1178 feet or 359 metres. **97 J7** NJ1047.
Carnan *W.Isles* ***Hill***, highest point on Mingulay. Height 895 feet or 273 metres. **84 A6** NL5582.
Carnassarie *Arg. & B.* ***Settlement***, 1m/2km N of Kilmartin. **79 K7** NM8301.
Carnassarie Castle *Arg. & B.* ***Castle***, 16c castle (Historic Scotland) in Argyll, 3m/5km S of head of Loch Craignish. **79 K7** NM8300.
Carnbee *Fife* ***Village***, 3m/5km NW of Anstruther. **83 G7** NO5306.
Carnbo *P. & K.* ***Village***, 4m/7km W of Kinross. **82 B7** NO0503.
Carndu *High.* ***Settlement***, in Skye and Lochalsh district, on shore of Loch Long, 1km NE of Dornie. NG8827.
Carnduncan *Arg. & B.* ***Settlement***, on N of Islay, 1km NE of Loch Gorm. **72 A4** NR2467.
Carne *Cornw.* ***Hamlet***, 1km S of Veryan. **3 G5** SW9138.
Carne *Cornw.* ***Settlement***, to N of St. Dennis, 6m/9km NW of St. Austell. SW9558.
Carne na Lòine *High.* ***Mountain***, 4m/7km E of Dava. Height 1801 feet or 549 metres. **89 H1** NJ0736.
Carnedd Dafydd *Conwy* ***Mountain***, 3m/5km SE of Bethesda. Height 3424 feet or 1044 metres. **46 E6** SH6663.
Carnedd Iago *Gwyn.* ***Mountain***, 5m/8km E of Ffestiniog. Height 1765 feet or 538 metres. **37 G1** SH7840.
Carnedd Llywelyn *Conwy* ***Mountain***, 5m/7km NW of Capel Curig. Height 3490 feet or 1064 metres. **46 E6** SH6864.
Carnedd y Cribau *Gwyn.* ***Mountain***, 4m/6km SW of Capel Curig. Craggy edge on E side. Height 1938 feet or 591 metres. **46 E7** SH6753.
Carnedd y Filiast *Gwyn.* ***Mountain***, 3m/4km N of Llyn Celyn dam. Height 2194 feet or 669 metres. **37 H1** SH8744.
Carneddau *Gwyn.* ***Open space***, extensive upland area (National Trust) 10m/16km across, between N Wales coast, Vale of Conwy and Nant Ffrancon. High plateau rising to 1064 metres at Carnedd Llywelyn. SH6665.
Carneddau *Powys* ***Mountain***, 3m/4km NE of Builth Wells. Height 1348 feet or 411 metres. **27 K3** SO0654.
Carnethy Hill *Midloth.* ***Mountain***, in Pentland Hills, with cairn at summit, 3m/4km NW of Penicuik. Height 1889 feet or 576 metres. **75 K4** NT2061.
Carnetown *R.C.T.* ***Village***, adjoining to S of Abercynon, 3m/5km N of Pontypridd. ST0794.
Carnferg *Aber.* ***Mountain***, 3m/5km S of Aboyne. Height 1722 feet or 525 metres. **90 D5** NO5293.
Carnforth *Lancs.* Population: 7442. ***Small town***, and railway junction, 6m/9km N of Lancaster. **55 H2** SD4970.
Carnglas *Swan.* ***Suburb***, 2m/4km W of Swansea city centre. SS6193.
Carnhedryn Uchaf *Pembs.* ***Hamlet***, 3m/5km NE of St. David's. SM8027.
Carnhell Green *Cornw.* ***Hamlet***, 2m/4km SW of Camborne. **2 D5** SW6137.
Carnichal *Aber.* ***Settlement***, 3m/4km SW of Strichen. **99 H5** NJ9351.
Carningli Common *Pembs.* ***Open space***, 4m/7km SE of Dinas Head. **16 D1** SN0536.
Carnkie *Cornw.* ***Village***, former mining village, 1m/2km SW of Redruth. SW6839.
Carnkie *Cornw.* ***Village***, 4m/7km W of Penryn. SW7134.
Carnmore *Arg. & B.* ***Settlement***, 1km NW of Port Ellen. **72 B6** NR3545.
Carno *Powys* ***Village***, 5m/8km NW of Caersws. Site of Roman fort. **37 J6** SN9696.
Carnoch *High.* ***Settlement***, in valley of River Meig, 8m/12km SE of Achnasheen. **95 J6** NH2551.
Carnoch *High.* ***Settlement***, in Strathglass, 4m/6km NE of Cannich. **87 K1** NH3836.
Carnoch *High.* ***Settlement***, 10m/16km S of Nairn. **97 F7** NH8740.
Carnock *Fife* ***Village***, 3m/5km W of Dunfermline. **75 J2** NT0489.
Carnon Downs *Cornw.* ***Village***, 3m/5km SW of Truro. **2 E4** SW7940.
Carnousie *Aber.* ***Locality***, includes Auldtown of Carnousie and Newton of Carnousie, 4m/6km W of Turriff. **98 E5** NJ6650.
Carnoustie *Angus* Population: 10,673. ***Town***, and coastal resort, 6m/10km SW of Arbroath. Golf-courses, including one of championship status. **83 G4** NO5634.
Carntyne *Glas.* ***Suburb***, 2m/4km E of Glasgow city centre. NS6365.
Carntyne Industrial Estate *Glas.* ***Locality***, to S of Carntyne, 3m/4km E of Glasgow city centre. NS6365.
Carnwadric *Glas.* ***Suburb***, 5m/7km SW of Glasgow city centre. NS5459.
Carnwath *S.Lan.* Population: 1353. ***Village***, 7m/11km E of Lanark. **75 H6** NS9846.
Carnyorth *Cornw.* ***Hamlet***, on N side of St. Just. **2 A5** SW3733.
Carol Green *W.Mid.* ***Settlement***, 5m/9km W of Coventry. SP2577.
Caroy *High.* ***River***, flowing S into Loch Caroy, 4m/7km SE of Dunvegan, Skye. **93 J7** NG3043.
Carperby *N.Yorks.* ***Village***, 1m/2km N of Aysgarth across River Ure. **62 B7** SE0089.
Carpow *P. & K.* *See Abernethy.*
Carr *Gt.Man.* ***Suburb***, adjoining to N of Ramsbottom. SD7817.
Carr *S.Yorks.* ***Hamlet***, 2m/3km SW of Maltby. SK5190.
Carr Cross *Lancs.* ***Settlement***, just N of Scarisbrick, 3m/5km SE of Southport. SD3714.
Carr Gate *W.Yorks.* ***Settlement***, 2m/4km NW of Wakefield. SE3124.
Carr Hill *Notts.* ***Settlement***, 1km NW of Everton. SK6892.
Carr Houses *Mersey.* ***Settlement***, adjoining to E of Ince Blundell, 3m/5km W of Maghull. SD3203.
Carr Mill *Mersey.* ***Suburb***, NE district of St. Helens. Lake to N. SJ5297.
Carr Shield *Northumb.* ***Village***, 5m/9km E of Alston. **61 K2** NY8047.
Carr Vale *Derbys.* ***Suburb***, adjoining to SW of Bolsover. **51 G5** SK4669.
Carradale *Arg. & B.* ***Village***, on E coast of Kintyre, 1m/2km E of Dippen. Ruins of Aird Castle on cliff to S of pier. **73 G7** NR8138.
Carradale Bay *Arg. & B.* ***Bay***, on E coast of Kintyre, 11m/18km NE of Campbeltown. **73 G7** NR8037.
Carradale Forest *Arg. & B.* ***Forest/woodland***, astride Carradale Water, Kintyre. **73 F6** NR7842.
Carradale Garden *Arg. & B.* ***Garden***, on Kintyre, 1km SW of Carradale overlooking Kilbrennan Sound, with flowering shrubs, mainly rhododendrons. **73 G7** NR8037.
Carradale Water *Arg. & B.* ***River***, running S into Carradale Bay. **73 F6** NR8037.
Carragrich *W.Isles* ***Settlement***, on N side of East Loch Tarbert, 3m/4km E of Tarbet, North Harris. **93 G2** NG1998.
Carraig Bhàn *Arg. & B.* ***Coastal feature***, rocky area on N coast of Islay, 9m/13km NW of Bridgend. **72 A3** NR2571.
Carraig Mhic Thòmais *Arg. & B.* ***Coastal feature***, rock below cliffs on SW coast of Ardmeanach, Mull. **79 F5** NM4026.
Carrawbrough *Northumb.* *See Brocolitia.*
Carrbridge *High.* ***Village***, on River Dulnain, in Badenoch and Strathspey district, 7m/11km N of Aviemore. Landmark Visitor Centre and Sculpture Park has exhibition explaining history of local environment. **89 G2** NH9022.
Carrbrook *Gt.Man.* ***Locality***, in small valley, 1m/2km SE of Mossley. SD9801.
Carreg Cennen Castle *Carmar.* ***Castle***, ruined medieval castle (Cadw) on cliff above River Cennen, 3m/5km SE of Llandeilo. **17 K3** SN6619.
Carreg Ddu *Gwyn.* ***Coastal feature***, headland on N coast of Lleyn Peninsula, 1m/2km NW of Morfa Nefyn, forming W extremity of Porth Dinllaen. **36 B1** SH2742.
Carreg Goch *Powys* ***Mountain***, 3m/4km N of Abercraf. Height 1830 feet or 558 metres. **27 H7** SN8116.
Carreg-gwylan-fach *Pembs.* ***Island***, small island off headland between Aberdinas and Porth Tre-wen bays, 1m/2km W of Abereiddy. **16 A2** SM7730.
Carreg Lem *Powys* ***Open space***, craggy hillslope 4m/7km N of Ystradgynlais. **27 G7** SN8017.
Carreg-lwyd *Carmar.* ***Mountain***, 3m/4km NE of Brynamman. Height 2020 feet or 616 metres. **27 G7** SN7317.
Carreg-lwyd *Powys* ***Inland physical feature***, SW facing rocky outcrop, 3m/5km SW of Fan Gyhirych. **27 H7** SN8614.
Carreg Onnen *Pembs.* ***Island***, group of three small islands off Carreg Onnen Bay, on W side of Strumble Head. SM8841.
Carreg Rhoson *Pembs.* ***Island***, rocky island 3m/5km W of Point St. John. One of the larger islands in the group known as Bishops and Clerks. **16 A2** SM6625.
Carreg Ti-pw *Cere.* ***Coastal feature***, headland, 1km N of Llanrhystud. **26 E1** SN5370.
Carreg-wen *Pembs.* ***Settlement***, 4m/6km SE of Cardigan. SN2241.
Carreg y Frân *Powys* ***Open space***, hillslope 4m/6km NW of Llangadfan. **37 J4** SH9514.
Carreg-yr-esgob *Pembs.* ***Island***, at entrance to Porthlysgi Bay, 2m/3km SW of St. David's. SM7222.
Carreg yr Imbill *Gwyn.* ***Coastal feature***, headland on S coast of Lleyn Peninsula forming part of entrance to Pwllheli harbour. **36 C2** SH3834.
Carreglefn *I.o.A.* ***Village***, on Anglesey, 3m/5km S of Cemaes Bay. **46 B4** SH3889.
Carregwastad Point *Pembs.* ***Coastal feature***, headland 3m/5km NW of Fishguard. French invasion force of 1,400 convicts landed here in 1797 and surrendered two days later. **16 C1** SM9340.
Carrick *Arg. & B.* ***Settlement***, 3m/4km E of Lochgilphead. **73 H2** NR9087.
Carrick *Arg. & B.* ***Village***, on W shore of Loch Goil, 2m/3km NW of its junction with Loch Long. **73 K1** NS1994.
Carrick *Fife* ***Hamlet***, 1m/2km NW of Leuchars. **83 F5** NO4422.
Carrick *S.Ayr.* ***Locality***, extensive upland area lying S of River Doon, to S of Ayr. The Prince of Wales, as Steward of Scotland, bears title of Earl of Carrick. **67 G4** NX3095.
Carrick Castle *Arg. & B.* ***Castle***, in Carrick, on W shore of Loch Goil, consisting of keep dating mainly from 15c. **73 K1** NS1994.
Carrick Roads *Cornw.* ***Sea feature***, estuary of River Fal, running from Turnaware Point past Falmouth into English Channel at Pendennis Point. **3 F5** SW8334.
Carrickstone *N.Lan.* ***Suburb***, 1m/2km NW of Cumbernauld town centre. NS7675.
Carriden *Falk.* ***Village***, on S side of Firth of Forth, 1m/2km E of Bo'ness. Site of Roman fort, most easterly fort of Antonine Wall, 1km SE. **75 J2** NT0181.
Carrine *Arg. & B.* ***Settlement***, 7m/11km SW of Campbeltown. **66 A3** NR6708.
Carrington *Gt.Man.* ***Village***, on River Mersey, 3m/5km W of Sale. **49 G3** SJ7392.
Carrington *Lincs.* ***Settlement***, 3m/5km SE of Coningsby. **53 G7** TF3155.
Carrington *Midloth.* ***Village***, 2m/3km W of Gorebridge across River South Esk. **76 B4** NT3160.
Carrington *Notts.* ***Suburb***, 1m/2km N of Nottingham city centre. SK5642.
Carrington Moss *Gt.Man.* ***Open space***, to S of Carrington. **49 G3** SJ7491.
Carroch *D. & G.* ***Settlement***, 6m/10km W of Moniaive. **68 B4** NX6791.

Carrock Fell *Cumb.* ***Mountain***, on N side of River Caldew, 4m/6km S of Caldbeck. Height 2168 feet or 661 metres. **60 E3** NY3433.
Carrog *Conwy* ***Settlement***, 4m/7km E of Blaenau Ffestiniog. SH7647.
Carrog *Denb.* ***Village***, 2m/4km E of Corwen. **38 A1** SJ1143.
Carroglen *P. & K.* ***Settlement***, in Glen Lednock, 3m/4km N of Comrie. **81 J5** NN7626.
Carrol *High.* ***Settlement***, to W of Loch Brora, 2m/3km S of Gordonbush, Sutherland district. **97 F1** NC8407.
Carrol Rock *High.* ***Hill***, with rock outcrops to E, on E side of Loch Brora, 1m/2km S of Gordonbush. Height 682 feet or 208 metres. **97 F1** NC8407.
Carron ***River***, rising on Campsie Fells and flowing E through Carron Valley Reservoir into Firth of Forth on N side of Grangemouth. **74 E2** NS9484.
Carron *Arg. & B.* ***Settlement***, 3m/5km NW of Minard. **73 H1** NR9499.
Carron *Falk.* Population: 3605. ***Locality***, adjoining to N of Falkirk. Iron works founded in 1760. Site of Roman temple. **75 G2** NS8882.
Carron *High.* ***River***, in Sutherland district running E down Strathcarron to Kyle of Sutherland at Bonar Bridge. **96 B3** NH6091.
Carron *Moray* ***Settlement***, with distillery on W bank of River Spey, 5m/8km SW of Craigellachie. **97 K7** NJ2241.
Carron Bridge *Stir.* ***Settlement***, at crossing point of River Carron, 4m/6km NE of Kilsyth. **75 F2** NS7483.
Carron Valley Reservoir *Stir.* ***Reservoir***, on border with North Lanarkshire, 5m/8km NE of Lennoxtown, and almost surrounded by Carron Valley state forest. **74 E2** NS6983.
Carron Water *Aber.* ***River***, rising in hills N of Glenbervie and flowing E to enter North Sea at Stonehaven. **91 F6** NO8785.
Carronbridge *D. & G.* ***Village***, at confluence of River Nith and Carron Water. Site of Roman fort. **68 D4** NX8698.
Carronshore *Falk.* ***Locality***, 2m/3km N of Falkirk. **75 G2** NS8983.
Carrot *Angus* ***Hamlet***, 3m/4km SE of Gateside, on N side of Carrot Hill. **83 F3** NO4641.
Carrot Hill *Angus* ***Hill***, 3m/4km SE of Gateside. Height 850 feet or 259 metres. **83 F3** NO4540.
Carrow Hill *Mon.* ***Hamlet***, 2m/3km W of Caerwent. ST4390.
Carrs Hill *Dur.* ***Mountain***, on Middleton Common, 3m/5km N of Middleton-in-Teesdale. Height 1971 feet or 601 metres. **62 A3** NY9530.
Carrutherstown *D. & G.* ***Village***, 7m/11km NW of Annan. **69 G6** NY1071.
Carruthmuir *Inclyde* ***Settlement***, 3m/5km S of Kilmacolm. **74 B4** NS3564.
Carrville *Dur.* ***Village***, 2m/4km E of Durham. **62 E2** NZ3043.
Carry *Arg. & B.* ***Settlement***, at S end of Cowal peninsula, 4m/6km S of Tighnabruaich. **73 H4** NR9867.
Carsaig *Arg. & B.* ***Locality***, on Carsaig Bay, on S coast of Mull, 2m/3km W of entrance to Loch Buie. **79 G5** NM5321.
Carsaig Bay *Arg. & B.* ***Bay***, on S coast of Mull, 2m/3km W of entrance to Loch Buie. **79 G5** NM5321.
Carsaig Bay *Arg. & B.* ***Bay***, on W coast of Knapdale, 1km NW of Tayvallich in Argyll. **73 F2** NR7387.
Carsaig Island *Arg. & B.* ***Island***, small island on SE side of Sound of Jura, 1m/2km NW of Tayvallich. **73 F2** NR7389.
Carscreugh *D. & G.* ***Settlement***, 2m/3km NE of Glenluce. **64 C4** NX2259.
Carse *Arg. & B.* ***Locality***, on Kintyre, 9m/14km SW of Tarbert. **73 F4** NR7561.
Carse Bay *D. & G.* ***Bay***, at mouth of Kirkbean Burn, 4m/6km N of Southerness. **65 K4** NX9860.
Carse of Ardersier *High.* ***Settlement***, 2m/3km NE of Ardersier. **97 F6** NH8057.
Carse of Balloch *Aber.* ***Open space***, moorland 4m/7km NW of Cruden Bay. **99 J6** NK0441.
Carse of Gowrie *P. & K.* ***Open space***, fertile tract on N side of Firth of Tay, between Perth and Dundee. **82 D5** NO2524.
Carsebreck Loch *P. & K.* ***Lake/loch***, 5m/8km SW of Auchterarder. **81 K6** NN8609.
Carsebridge *Clack.* ***Locality***, 1m/2km NE of Alloa. NS8993.
Carsegowan *D. & G.* ***Settlement***, 2m/4km N of Wigtown. **64 E5** NX4258.
Carseriggan *D. & G.* ***Settlement***, 4m/7km N of Kirkcowan. **64 D4** NX3167.
Carsethorn *D. & G.* ***Village***, on Solway Firth at mouth of River Nith, 10m/16km S of Dumfries. **65 K5** NX9959.
Carsfad Loch *D. & G.* ***Lake/loch***, loch and reservoir in course of Water of Ken 3m/5km N of St. John's Town of Dalry. **68 B5** NX6086.
Carsgailoch Hill *E.Ayr.* ***Mountain***, 4m/6km SW of Cumnock. Height 1194 feet or 364 metres. **67 K2** NS5414.
Carsgoe *High.* ***Settlement***, 3m/4km N of Halkirk. **105 G2** ND1363.
Carshalton *Gt.Lon.* ***Suburb***, in borough of Sutton, 1m/2km E of Sutton town centre. **23 F5** TQ2764.
Carshalton Beeches *Gt.Lon.* ***Suburb***, 1m/2km S of Carshalton. TQ2763.
Carshalton on the Hill *Gt.Lon.* ***Suburb***, 1m/2km S of Carshalton. TQ2863.
Carsie *P. & K.* ***Locality***, 2m/3km S of Blairgowrie. NO1742.
Carsington *Derbys.* ***Village***, 2m/4km W of Wirksworth. **50 E7** SK2553.
Carsington Water *Derbys.* ***Reservoir***, to S of Carsington, 2m/4km SW of Wirksworth. Opened by the Queen in 1992. Noted for brown trout and watersports. Wildlife centre. **50 E7** SK2551.
Carskey Bay *Arg. & B.* ***Bay***, on S coast of Kintyre, 4m/7km E of Mull of Kintyre. **66 A3** NR6607.
Carsluith *D. & G.* ***Hamlet***, on E shore of Wigtown Bay, 2m/4km S of Creetown. **64 E5** NX4854.
Carsluith Castle *D. & G.* ***Castle***, remains of castle (Historic Scotland) with 16c tower house, 1km SE of Carsluith. **64 E5** NX4954.
Carsphairn *D. & G.* ***Village***, 9m/14km SE of Dalmellington. **67 K4** NX5693.
Carstairs *S.Lan.* ***Village***, 4m/6km E of Lanark. **75 H6** NS9346.
Carstairs Junction *S.Lan.* ***Village***, and railway junction, 1m/2km SE of Carstairs. **75 H6** NS9545.
Carswell Marsh *Oxon.* ***Settlement***, 1m/2km NW of Buckland. **21 G2** SU3299.
Carter Bar ***Other feature of interest***, point in Cheviot Hills at which A68 road crosses border between England and Scotland. **70 B3** NT6906.
Carter Fell ***Inland physical feature***, mountain ridge running NE to SW, on border of Cumbria and Scottish Borders, 6m/10km SE of Kielder. Height 1824 feet or 556 metres. **70 B3** NT6603.
Carter's Clay *Hants.* ***Settlement***, 1m/2km SE of Lockerley. **10 E2** SU3024.
Carter's Green *Essex* ***Settlement***, 4m/7km E of Harlow. TL5110.
Carter's Hill *W'ham* ***Settlement***, 1m/2km SW of Winnersh. SU7669.
Carter's Rocks (Also known as Gull Rocks.) *Cornw.* ***Island***, two rock islands off Penhale Point, 4m/6km SW of Newquay. SW7559.
Carterton *Oxon.* Population: 12,421. ***Village***, adjacent to Brize Norton Airfield, 4m/6km SE of Burford. **21 F1** SP2706.
Carterway Heads *Northumb.* ***Settlement***, at crossroads, 4m/6km W of Consett. **62 B1** NZ0451.
Carthagena Bank *P. & K.* ***Coastal feature***, large area of mud, covered at high water, on N side of Firth of Tay, 1m/2km E of Errol. **82 D5** NO2722.
Carthat Hill *D. & G.* ***Hill***, 3m/4km SW of Hightae. Height 794 feet or 242 metres. **69 F6** NY0677.
Carthew *Cornw.* ***Village***, in china clay district, 3m/4km N of St. Austell. **4 A5** SX0056.
Carthorpe *N.Yorks.* ***Village***, 4m/6km SE of Bedale. **57 J1** SE3083.
Cartington *Northumb.* ***Settlement***, 2m/4km NW of Rothbury. Remains of castle dating from 14c. **71 F3** NU0304.
Cartland *S.Lan.* ***Hamlet***, 2m/3km NW of Lanark. NS8646.
Cartledge *Derbys.* ***Settlement***, adjoining to S of Holmesfield. SK3277.
Cartmel *Cumb.* ***Village***, 4m/7km S of Newby Bridge. **55 G2** SD3778.
Cartmel Fell *Cumb.* ***Locality***, 5m/8km N of Lindale. **55 H1** SD4188.
Cartmel Priory *Cumb.* ***Ecclesiastical building***, priory church founded 1188 at Cartmel, with Gatehouse (National Trust), notable stained glass and carved choir stalls. **55 G2** SD3778.
Cartmel Sands *Cumb.* ***Coastal feature***, sands adjoining to W of marshland, 3m/5km E of Ulverston across River Leven estuary. **55 G2** SD3376.
Cartmel Wharf *Cumb.* ***Coastal feature***, large sandbank in Morecambe Bay. **55 G3** SD3568.
Cartworth *W.Yorks.* ***Settlement***, 1km S of Holmfirth. SE1407.
Carway (Carwe). *Carmar.* ***Village***, 5m/7km NW of Llanelli. **17 H4** SN4606.
Carwe *Carmar. Welsh form of Carway, qv.*
Cary *Som.* ***River***, rising near Castle Cary and flowing W to Henley where it becomes King's Sedgemoor Drain, flowing NW into River Parrett at Dunball. **8 C1** ST3140.
Cas-bach *Newport Welsh form of Castleton, qv.*
Cas-blaidd *Pembs. Welsh form of Wolf's Castle, qv.*
Cas-fuwch *Pembs. Welsh form of Castlebythe, qv.*
Cas-gwent *Mon. Welsh form of Chepstow, qv.*
Cas-mael *Pembs. Welsh form of Puncheston, qv.*
Cas-wis *Pembs. Welsh form of Wiston, qv.*
Cascob *Powys* ***Settlement***, 5m/8km SW of Knighton. **28 B2** SO2366.
Cashel *Stir.* ***Settlement***, on E shore of Loch Lomond, 3m/4km NW of Balmaha. **74 C1** NS3994.
Cashel Dhu *High.* ***Locality***, at the mouth of Strathmore River where it flows into Loch Hope. **103 G3** NC4550.
Cashes Green *Glos.* ***Suburb***, W district of Stroud. SO8205.
Cashlie *P. & K.* ***Settlement***, in Glen Lyon, 8m/12km NW of Killin. **81 F3** NN4842.
Cashmoor *Dorset* ***Hamlet***, 3m/5km SE of Tollard Royal. **9 J3** ST9713.
Caskieberran *Fife* ***Suburb***, W district of Glenrothes. NO2500.
Caslllwchwr *Swan. Welsh form of Loughor, qv.*
Casmorys *Pembs. Welsh form of Castle Morris, qv.*
Casnewydd *Newport Welsh form of Newport, qv.*
Casnewydd-bach *Pembs. Welsh form of Little Newcastle, qv.*
Cassencarie *D. & G.* ***Settlement***, 1km S of Creetown. **64 E5** NX4757.
Cassington *Oxon.* ***Village***, 5m/8km NW of Oxford. **31 F7** SP4510.
Cassiobury Park *Herts.* ***Open space***, to W of Watford town centre. **22 D2** TQ0996.
Cassley *High.* ***River***, in Sutherland district, running SE down Glen Cassley into River Oykel 8m/12km SW of Lairg. **96 B1** NC4700.
Cassop *Dur.* ***Village***, 5m/8km SE of Durham. **62 E3** NZ3438.
Castell *Conwy* ***Hamlet***, 1m/2km N of Dolgarrog. SH7669.
Castell Bryn-gwyn *I.o.A.* ***Historic/prehistoric site***, on S part of Anglesey, 1m/2km W of Brynsiencyn. Site dating from Neolithic times, consisting of ditch and rampart with large standing stones nearby. **46 C6** SH4667.
Castell Caereinion *Powys Welsh form of Castle Caereinion, qv.*
Castell Cawr *Conwy See Abergele.*
Castell Coch *Cardiff* ***Historic/prehistoric site***, medieval fortified house (Cadw) restored in 19c, on steep wooded slope overlooking River Taff, 5m/8km NW of Cardiff. **18 E3** ST1382.
Castell Dinas Bran (Also known as Crow Castle.) *Denb.* ***Castle***, 12c castle 1m/2km NE of Llangollen. **38 B1** SJ2243.
Castell du *Powys See Sennybridge.*
Castell Gorfod *Carmar.* ***Settlement***, on W bank of Cynia River, 3m/5km N of St. Clears. **17 F2** SN2620.
Castell Gwalchmai *Pembs. Welsh form of Walwyn's Castle, qv.*
Castell Howell *Cere.* ***Settlement***, 2m/3km SE of Talgarreg. **26 D4** SN4448.
Castell-nedd *N.P.T. Welsh form of Neath, qv.*
Castell Newydd Emlyn *Cere. Welsh form of Newcastle Emlyn, qv.*
Castell-paen *Powys Welsh form of Painscastle, qv.*
Castell Pictwn *Pembs. Welsh form of Picton Castle, qv.*
Castell y Bere *Gwyn.* ***Castle***, ruined castle (Cadw) of uncertain date, to SW of Llanfihangel-y-pennant. **37 F5** SH6608.
Castell-y-bwch *Torfaen* ***Settlement***, 3m/4km SW of Cwmbran. **19 F2** ST2792.
Castell y Geifr *Powys* ***Inland physical feature***, rocky outcrop, 1km SE of Carreg Goch. **27 H7** SN8216.
Castellau *R.C.T.* ***Settlement***, 3m/4km SW of Pontypridd. **18 D3** ST0586.
Castelldwyran *Pembs.* ***Locality***, 4m/6km W of Whitland. SN1418.
Castellhaidd *Pembs. Welsh form of Hayscastle, qv.*
Castellhenri *Pembs. Welsh form of Henry's Moat, qv.*
Castellmartin *Pembs. Welsh form of Castlemartin, qv.*
Casterton *Cumb.* ***Village***, 1m/2km NE of Kirkby Lonsdale across River Lune. **56 B2** SD6279.
Castle Acre *Norf.* ***Village***, 4m/6km N of Swaffham. Remains of 11c-13c castle (English Heritage), and of 12c priory (English Heritage). **44 C4** TF8115.
Castle Acre Castle *Norf.* ***Castle***, remains of large Norman castle (English Heritage) including a fine gateway. **44 C4** TF8215.
Castle Acre Priory *Norf.* ***Ecclesiastical building***, remains of 11c Cluniac priory with Tudor gatehouse and Norman arcading (English Heritage), on SW side of Castle Acre. **44 C4** TF8114.
Castle-an-Dinas *Cornw.* ***Historic/prehistoric site***, hillfort on Castle Downs which attain height of 702 feet or 214 metres. **3 G2** SW9462.
Castle Ashby *Northants.* ***Village***, 6m/10km SW of Wellingborough. **32 B3** SP8659.
Castle Ashby House *Northants.* ***Historic house***, Elizabethan and later, seat of Earl of Northampton at Castle Ashby, 7m/10km E of Northampton. Notable gardens. **32 B3** SP8659.
Castle Bank *Staffs.* ***Suburb***, 1m/2km SW of Stafford. **40 B3** SJ9021.
Castle Bay *W.Isles* ***Bay***, on S coast of Barra. **84 B5** NL6697.
Castle Bolton *N.Yorks.* ***Village***, above Wensleydale to N, 5m/8km W of Leyburn. Ruins of 14c castle. **62 B7** SE0391.
Castle Bromwich *W.Mid.* ***Suburb***, 5m/9km E of Birmingham. Remains of motte-and-bailey castle beside M6 motorway. Hall of 17c. **40 D7** SP1489.
Castle Bytham *Lincs.* ***Village***, 8m/12km N of Stamford. Earthwork remains of Norman castle. **42 C4** SK9818.
Castle Caereinion (Castell Caereinion). *Powys* ***Village***, 4m/6km W of Welshpool. **38 A5** SJ1605.
Castle Campbell (Formerly known as Castle Gloom.) *Clack.* ***Castle***, dating from late 15c (Historic Scotland), in Dollar Glen (National Trust for Scotland) nearly 1m/2km N of Dollar. **75 H1** NS9699.
Castle Camps *Cambs.* ***Village***, 3m/5km SW of Haverhill. Church stands in outer moat of former castle built in 12c. **33 K4** TL6343.
Castle Carrock *Cumb.* ***Village***, 4m/6km S of Brampton. **61 G1** NY5455.
Castle Cary *Som.* Population: 2904. ***Small town***, 3m/5km SW of Bruton. Market hall, partly 17c; remains of castle. **9 F1** ST6332.
Castle Combe *Wilts.* ***Village***, 5m/9km NW of Chippenham. Motor-racing circuit to SE. **20 B4** ST8477.
Castle Dhu *P. & K. See Moulin.*
Castle Donington *Leics.* Population: 6007. ***Village***, 7m/12km NW of Loughborough; East Midlands International Airport 1m/2km SE; Donington motor-racing circuit 2m/3km SW. **41 G3** SK4427.
Castle Douglas *D. & G.* Population: 3697. ***Small town***, at N end of Carlingwark Loch, 9m/14km NE of Kirkcudbright. **65 H4** NX7662.
Castle Drogo *Devon* ***Castle***, granite castle (National Trust) designed by Lutyens. Stands on granite outcrop above gorge of River Teign, 1m/2km SW of Drewsteignton. **7 F6** SX7290.
Castle Eaton *Swin.* ***Village***, on River Thames, 3m/5km E of Cricklade. **20 E2** SU1495.
Castle Eden *Dur.* ***Village***, 2m/3km S of Peterlee. The castle is an 18c house. **63 F3** NZ4238.
Castle Eden Walkway Country Park *Stock.* ***Leisure/recreation***, linear park following course of old railway, 4m/7km NW of Stockton-on-Tees. Visitor centre. **62 E4** NZ4024.
Castle End *Peter.* ***Hamlet***, adjoining to N of Maxey, 1m/2km S of Market Deeping. TF1208.
Castle End *Warks.* ***Settlement***, adjoining to W of Kenilworth. **30 D1** SP2871.
Castle Fraser *Aber.* ***Castle***, baronial tower house (National Trust for Scotland) 6m/10km SW of Inverurie. Built 1575-1636, with notable Great Hall and walled garden. Said to be haunted. **91 F3** NJ7212.
Castle Frome *Here.* ***Village***, 6m/9km S of Bromyard. **29 F4** SO6645.
Castle Gate *Cornw.* ***Settlement***, 3m/4km NE of Penzance. SW4934.
Castle Gloom *Clack. Former name of Castle Campbell, qv.*

Castle Goring *W.Suss.* ***Settlement***, 3m/5km NW of Worthing. TQ1005.
Castle Grant *High.* ***Castle***, former seat of the chiefs of Grant, Earls of Seafield, in Badenoch and Strathspey district 2m/3km N of Grantown-on-Spey. **89 H1** NJ0430.
Castle Green *Cumb.* ***Settlement***, on E side of Kendal. SD5392.
Castle Green *Gt.Lon.* ***Suburb***, in borough of Barking and Dagenham, 2m/3km E of Barking town centre. TQ4783.
Castle Green *Powys* ***Locality***, to NW of Talgarth, opposite Bronllys Castle across River Llynfi. SO1534.
Castle Green *S.Yorks.* ***Suburb***, adjoining to SE of Penistone. SE2502.
Castle Green *Surr.* ***Hamlet***, adjoining to S of Chobham. SU9660.
Castle Gresley *Derbys.* ***Hamlet***, 2m/3km SW of Swadlincote. **40 E4** SK2718.
Castle Haven *Aber.* ***Bay***, shingle and rocky bay between Bowdun Head to N and Dunnottar Castle to S, 1m/2km S of Stonehaven. **91 G6** NO8884.
Castle Heaton *Northumb.* ***Settlement***, 3m/5km NE of Cornhill on Tweed. **77 H6** NT9041.
Castle Hedingham *Essex* ***Small town***, old market town, 4m/6km NW of Halstead. 12c cross in churchyard. Remains of Norman castle. **34 B5** TL7835.
Castle Hill *High.* ***Mountain***, in Badenoch and Strathspey district, 5m/9km SE of Aviemore. Height 2388 feet or 728 metres. **89 G4** NH9505.
Castle Hill *Kent* ***Hamlet***, 2m/4km SE of Paddock Wood. TQ6942.
Castle Hill *Suff.* ***Suburb***, N district of Ipswich. **35 F4** TM1547.
Castle Hill *W.Yorks.* ***Locality***, 1m/2km S of Huddersfield town centre. Ancient hillfort. SE1514.
Castle Hill *Wilts.* ***Locality***, at entrance to Old Sarum, 2m/3km N of Salisbury. SU1432.
Castle House (Sir Alfred Munnings Art Museum) *Essex* ***Other feature of interest***, 1km S of Dedham and 7m/11km NE of Colchester. Home of Sir Alfred Munnings, and displaying his life's work. **34 E5** TM0632.
Castle Howard *N.Yorks.* ***Historic house***, baroque mansion by Vanbrugh in large formal grounds 5m/7km W of Malton. **58 D2** SE7170.
Castle Island *N.Ayr.* ***Island***, small island off E coast of island of Little Cumbrae. Remains of medieval tower at N end. NS1551.
Castle Island *P. & K.* ***Island***, in Loch Leven, 1m/2km E of Kinross. Remains of 15c castle (Historic Scotland). NO1301.
Castle Kennedy *D. & G.* ***Village***, 3m/5km E of Stranraer. Ruins of late 16c castle destroyed by fire in 1715 to N, on isthmus between Black Loch and White Loch within grounds of Lochinch Castle. **64 B5** NX1059.
Castle Kennedy Gardens *D. & G.* ***Garden***, 75 acres of garden laid out by Field Marshall Lord Stair and troops in 18c on isthmus between White Loch and Black Loch, with ruins of Castle Kennedy and Lochinch Castle at either end, 3m/5km E of Stranraer. Contains original specimens from Sir Joseph Hooker's Himalayan expeditions. Famous for rhododendrons, azaleas, magnolias and embothriums. **64 B4** NX1161.
Castle Knowe *Sc.Bord. Alternative name for Fast Castle, qv.*
Castle Lachlan (Also known as Lachlan Castle.) *Arg. & B.* ***Historic house***, in Argyll near mouth of Strathlachlan River. Ruined 16c tower of Maclachlans on shore of Loch Fyne to W. **73 J1** NS0195.
Castle Leod *High.* ***Castle***, 12c tower house, re-modelled in 1606, 1km N of Strathpeffer. Seat of Earls of Cromartie. **96 B6** NH4859.
Castle Levan *Inclyde* ***Hamlet***, 2m/3km SW of Gourock. Castle. **74 A3** NS2176.
Castle Loch *D. & G.* ***Lake/loch***, loch 6m/10km E of Glenluce. Remains of castle on islet near E end of loch. **64 C5** NX2853.
Castle Loch *D. & G.* ***Lake/loch***, to S of Lochmaben. Remains of 14c castle on S shore. With Hightae Mill Loch, 1km further S, it forms nature reserve. **69 F5** NY0881.
Castle Madoc *Powys* ***Settlement***, 5m/8km N of Brecon. **27 K5** SO0236.
Castle Menzies *P. & K.* ***Historic house***, 16c mansion 1m/2km W of Aberfeldy across River Tay. **81 K2** NN8349.
Castle Moil *High. Anglicised form of Caisteal Maol, qv.*
Castle Morris (Casmorys). *Pembs.* ***Village***, 5m/8km SW of Fishguard. **16 C1** SM9031.
Castle O'er *D. & G.* ***Historic/prehistoric site***, ancient earthwork surrounded by Castle O'er Forest, S of Eskdalemuir. **69 H4** NY2492.
Castle O'er Forest *D. & G.* ***Forest/woodland***, to S of Eskdalemuir. **69 H4** NY2393.
Castle of Cobbie Row *Ork. Alternative name for Cubbie Roo's Castle, qv.*
Castle of Old Wick (Also known as Old Man of Wick.) *High.* ***Castle***, ruined 12c-14c tower (Historic Scotland), on E coast of Caithness district, 1m/2km S of Wick. **105 J4** ND3648.
Castle of Park *D. & G.* ***Castle***, castellated late 16c tower house, 1km W of Glenluce across Water of Luce. **64 B5** NX1857.
Castle Park *N.Yorks.* ***Suburb***, W district of Whitby. NZ8810.
Castle Point *Cornw.* ***Coastal feature***, headland to SW of St. Mawes. Above is St. Mawes Castle. **3 F5** SW8332.
Castle Point *Northumb.* ***Coastal feature***, headland at SE corner of Holy Island, near castle. **77 K6** NU1441.
Castle Pulverbatch *Shrop. Alternative name for Pulverbatch, qv.*
Castle Rising *Norf.* ***Village***, 4m/7km NE of King's Lynn. Remains of Norman castle (English Heritage). Trinity Hospital, 17c almshouses. **44 A3** TF6624.
Castle Rising Castle *Norf.* ***Castle***, on S side of Castle Rising, 4m/6km NE of King's Lynn. Massive Norman keep and earthworks (English Heritage). **44 A3** TF6624.
Castle Rock of Muchalls *Aber.* ***Coastal feature***, on North Sea coast, 1m/2km S of Muchalls. **91 G6** NO9090.
Castle Rushen *I.o.M.* ***Castle***, medieval fortress (Manx National Heritage) dating from 1153, standing on site of an original Viking stronghold at Castletown. Last Viking King, Magnus, died here in 1265. **54 B7** SC2667.
Castle Semple Collegiate Church *Renf.* ***Ecclesiastical building***, remains of church (Historic Scotland), founded 1504, at NE end of Castle Semple Loch. **74 B4** NS3760.
Castle Semple Loch *Renf.* ***Lake/loch***, loch on E side of Lochwinnoch. **74 B5** NS3659.
Castle Semple Water Country Park *Renf.* ***Leisure/recreation***, water park and bird sanctuary, at Castle Semple Loch, E of Lochwinnoch. **74 B5** NS3659.
Castle Sowerby *Cumb.* ***Locality***, 1m/2km N of Hutton Roof. NY3836.
Castle Stalker *Arg. & B.* ***Castle***, on islet at entrance to Loch Laich, Argyll, S of Shuna Island. Originally built for James IV, late 15c. **80 A3** NM9247.
Castle Street *W.Yorks.* ***Locality***, adjoining to E of Todmorden. SD9524.
Castle Stuart *High.* ***Castle***, built in 1625 by James Stuart, 3rd Earl of Moray, 5m/8km E of Inverness. **96 E6** NH7449.
Castle Sween *Arg. & B.* ***Castle***, ruined castle (Historic Scotland) of the MacNeils, dating from 11c, on E side of Loch Sween in Argyll, opposite Danna Island. **73 F3** NR7178.
Castle Vale *W.Mid.* ***Suburb***, 5m/8km NE of Birmingham city centre. SP1491.
Castlebay (Gaelic form: Bagh a' Chaisteil.) *W.Isles* ***Small town***, at head of Castle Bay on S coast of Barra. Chief port and settlement of island, although airfield is at N end. **84 B5** NL6698.
Castlebythe (Cas-fuwch). *Pembs.* ***Hamlet***, 7m/11km SE of Fishguard. Remains of motte to E. **16 D2** SN0228.
Castlecary *N.Lan.* ***Hamlet***, 3m/5km SW of Bonnybridge. Site of Roman camp, traversed by railway. **75 F3** NS7878.
Castlecary Roman Fort *Falk.* ***Historic/prehistoric site***, to E of Castlecary. Remains of one of line of forts along Antonine Way; site of camp now traversed by railway. **75 F3** NS7977.
Castlecraig *High.* ***Settlement***, 2m/3km NE of Cromarty across mouth of Cromarty Firth. **97 F5** NH8269.
Castlecraig *Sc.Bord.* ***Settlement***, 1km S of Blyth Bridge. **75 K6** NT1344.
Castlecroft *Staffs.* ***Suburb***, 3m/5km W of Wolverhampton. SO8697.
Castledykes *D. & G. Alternative name for Kirkcudbright, qv.*
Castlefairn *D. & G.* ***Settlement***, 8m/12km NE of St. John's Town of Dalry. **68 C5** NX7387.
Castlefairn Water *D. & G.* ***River***, running NE to join Dalwhat Water and form Cairn Water, 1km SE of Moniaive. **68 C5** NX7890.
Castleford *W.Yorks.* Population: 38,536. ***Town***, former mining town on River Aire, at its confluence with River Calder, 10m/15km SE of Leeds. Town stands on site of Roman Lagentium. RSPB Reserve at Fairburn Ings. **57 K7** SE4225.
Castleford Ings *W.Yorks.* ***Locality***, adjoining to NE of Castleford, on S side of River Aire. SE4326.
Castlehead *Renf.* ***Suburb***, to SW of Paisley town centre. NS4763.
Castlehill *W.Dun.* ***Suburb***, NW district of Dumbarton. NS3876.
Castlehill Point *D. & G.* ***Coastal feature***, headland at E side of estuary of Urr Water, 6m/9km S of Dalbeattie. **65 J5** NX8552.
Castlelaw Fort *Midloth. See Glencorse.*
Castlelaw Hillfort *Midloth.* ***Historic/prehistoric site***, small Iron Age hillfort consisting of three concentric ramparts and souterrain to SW of Castlelaw Hill, 2m/4km N of Penicuik. Occupied into Roman times. **76 A4** NT2263.
Castlemartin (Castellmartin). *Pembs.* ***Village***, 5m/8km SW of Pembroke. Army training area to S. **16 C5** SR9198.
Castlemilk *D. & G.* ***Settlement***, on E side of Water of Milk, 3m/5km NW of Ecclefechan. **69 G6** NY1577.
Castlemilk *Glas.* ***Suburb***, 2m/3km SW of Rutherglen. **74 E5** NS6059.
Castlemorton *Worcs.* ***Village***, 4m/6km SE of Malvern Wells. **29 G5** SO7937.
Castlerigg *Cumb.* ***Hamlet***, 1m/2km SE of Keswick. NY2822.
Castlerigg Stone Circle *Cumb.* ***Historic/prehistoric site***, 1m/2km NE of Castlerigg. Megalithic circle (English Heritage) of thirty-eight stones, 100 feet or 30 metres in diameter, with another ten stones set in a rectangle within. **60 D4** NY2923.
Castleshaw Moor *Gt.Man.* ***Open space***, moorland adjoining to S of Denshaw Moor, 6m/9km NE of Oldham. **49 J1** SD9911.
Castleside *Dur.* Population: 4555. ***Suburb***, 2m/3km SW of Consett. **62 B2** NZ0748.
Castlesteads *Cumb.* ***Settlement***, 1m/2km N of Plumpton, at site of Roman fort of Voreda. NY4938.
Castlesteads *Cumb.* ***Settlement***, 2m/3km NW of Brampton. Site of Roman fort of Uxellodunum to N. NY5163.
Castlethorpe *M.K.* ***Village***, 3m/4km N of Stony Stratford. **32 B4** SP7944.
Castlethorpe *N.Lincs.* ***Locality***, 1m/2km W of Brigg. SE9807.
Castlethorpe Wharf *M.K.* ***Locality***, 1m/2km SW of Castlethorpe, on Grand Union Canal. SP7944.
Castleton *Aber.* ***Settlement***, 4m/6km N of Turriff. **99 F5** NJ7256.
Castleton *Angus* ***Hamlet***, 3m/5km NE of Meigle. **82 E3** NO3346.
Castleton *Arg. & B.* ***Settlement***, 3m/4km SE of Lochgilphead. **73 G2** NR8884.
Castleton *Derbys.* ***Village***, 5m/8km W of Hathersage. Remains of Norman Peveril Castle (English Heritage) on limestone hill to S. Various caves in vicinity, some formerly mined for Blue John, a rare variety of fluorspar. **50 D4** SK1582.
Castleton *Gt.Man.* ***Suburb***, 2m/3km S of Rochdale town centre. **49 H1** SD8810.
Castleton (Cas-bach). *Newport* ***Village***, 5m/7km SW of Newport. **19 F3** ST2583.
Castleton *N.Yorks.* ***Village***, on River Esk, in North York Moors National Park, 8m/12km W of Egton. **63 H6** NZ6808.
Castleton *Sc.Bord.* ***Locality***, in Liddesdale, 3m/4km NE of Newcastleton. **70 A4** NY5190.
Castleton Ridge *N.Yorks.* ***Inland physical feature***, mountain ridge rising to 1069 feet or 326 metres and running N to S, 2m/3km S of Castleton. **63 H6** NZ6707.
Castletown *Cumb.* ***Suburb***, W district of Penrith. NY5030.
Castletown *Dorset* ***Suburb***, to N of Portland. Helicopter station to W. SY6874.
Castletown *High.* ***Settlement***, 5m/8km SE of Inverness. **96 E7** NH7442.
Castletown *High.* Population: 1028. ***Village***, with small harbour on Dunnet Bay, N coast of Caithness district, 5m/8km E of Thurso. **105 G2** ND1968.
Castletown *I.o.M.* ***Small town***, with harbour on Castletown Bay, 9m/14km SW of Douglas. Remains of 12c Castle Rushen (Manx National Heritage). Nautical Museum (Manx National Heritage) with 18c armed yacht in original boathouse. Old Grammar School (Manx National Heritage) with period Victorian classroom. **54 B7** SC2667.
Castletown *Staffs.* ***Suburb***, to W of Stafford town centre. SJ9123.
Castletown *T. & W.* ***Suburb***, 2m/4km W of Sunderland city centre across River Wear. **62 E1** NZ3558.
Castletown Bay *I.o.M.* ***Bay***, 9m/14km SW of Douglas; bay extends W from Langness Point to Scarlett Point. **54 B7** SC2667.
Castletown Nautical Museum *I.o.M.* ***Other feature of interest***, museum (Manx National Heritage) housed in three-storey boathouse dating from late 18c, beside Castletown's harbour. Includes 18c armed yacht, The Peggy. **54 B7** SC2667.
Castleweary *Sc.Bord.* ***Settlement***, 1m/2km S of Teviothead. **69 K3** NT4003.
Castlewigg *D. & G.* ***Settlement***, 4m/6km SW of Garlieston. **64 E6** NX4242.
Castley *N.Yorks.* ***Hamlet***, on N side of River Wharfe, 1m/2km S of Huby and 4m/6km E of Otley. SE2645.
Caston *Norf.* ***Village***, 3m/5km SE of Watton. **44 D6** TL9597.
Castor *Peter.* ***Suburb***, W district of Peterborough. **42 E6** TL1298.
Castra Exploratum *Cumb. See Netherby.*
Castramont *D. & G.* ***Settlement***, 3m/4km N of Gatehouse of Fleet. **65 F4** NX5960.
Caswell *Swan.* ***Suburb***, 3m/5km W of Mumbles Head, above Caswell Bay, which extends SE to Whiteshell Point. SS5987.
Caswell Bay *Swan.* ***Bay***, extends SE from Caswell to Whiteshell Point, 2m/3km W of The Mumbles. SS5987.
Cat Firth *Shet.* ***Sea feature***, inlet on Mainland, to N of Lambgarth Head on E coast. **109 D7** HU4453.
Cat Hill *S.Yorks.* ***Settlement***, 1m/2km N of Penistone. SE2405.
Cat Law *Angus* ***Mountain***, 6m/9km NW of Kirriemuir. Height 2224 feet or 678 metres. **82 E1** NO3161.
Cata Sand *Ork.* ***Coastal feature***, large area of sand with dunes on seaward side, on E coast of Sanday. Overbister lies to W. **106 G3** HY6940.
Catacol *N.Ayr.* ***Hamlet***, on N side of Catacol Bay, on NW coast of Arran. NR9149.
Catacol Bay *N.Ayr.* ***Bay***, on NW coast of Arran. **73 G6** NR9049.
Cataractonium *N.Yorks. See Catterick Bridge.*
Catbrain *S.Glos.* ***Hamlet***, at W end of Filton Airfield, 5m/8km N of Bristol. **19 J3** ST5780.
Catbrook *Mon.* ***Hamlet***, 2m/3km S of Trelleck. SO5102.
Catchall *Cornw.* ***Hamlet***, 3m/4km SW of Penzance. **2 B6** SW4328.
Catchems Corner *W.Mid.* ***Settlement***, adjoining to E of Balsall, 4m/7km NW of Kenilworth. SP2576.
Catchems End *Worcs.* ***Suburb***, to E of Bewdley, 3m/4km W of Kidderminster. SO7976.
Catchgate *Dur.* ***Suburb***, adjoining to NW of Annfield Plain, 2m/3km W of Stanley. NZ1652.
Catcleugh *Northumb.* ***Settlement***, on N bank and at E end of Catcleugh Reservoir, in Cheviot Hills. **70 C3** NT7403.
Catcleugh Reservoir *Northumb.* ***Reservoir***, in upper Redesdale, 3m/5km SE of Carter Bar. **70 C3** NT7403.
Catcleugh Shin *Sc.Bord.* ***Mountain***, 1km W of Carter Bar in Cheviot Hills. Height 1742 feet or 531 metres. **70 B3** NT6806.
Catcliffe *S.Yorks.* ***Village***, 5m/9km E of Sheffield. **51 G4** SK4288.
Catcott *Som.* ***Village***, on N side of Polden Hills, 7m/11km W of Glastonbury. **8 C1** ST3939.
Cateran Hill *Northumb.* ***Hill***, 4m/7km W of North Charlton. Height 876 feet or 267 metres. **71 G1** NU1023.
Caterham *Surr.* Population: 15,089. ***Town***, on North Downs, 6m/10km S of Croydon. **23 G6** TQ3455.
Cater's Beam *Devon* ***Open space***, hillslope in Dartmoor National Park, 4m/7km SE of Princetown. **5 G4** SX6368.
Caterthun *Angus* ***Locality***, includes sites of Brown Caterthun and White Caterthun Iron Age forts, 6m/9km NW of Brechin. NO5566.
Catesby *Northants.* ***Locality***, parish containing hamlets of Upper and Lower Catesby, 4m/6km SW of Daventry. **31 G3** SP5259.
Catfield *Norf.* ***Village***, 2m/4km SE of Stalham. **45 H3** TG3821.
Catfield Common *Norf.* ***Hamlet***, 1m/2km E of Catfield, on W side of Hickling Broad. TG3921.
Catfirth *Shet.* ***Settlement***, at head of Cat Firth inlet. **109 D7** HU4354.

Catford *Gt.Lon.* **Suburb**, in borough of Lewisham, 1m/2km S of Lewisham and 7m/11km SE of Charing Cross. **23 G4** TQ3873.
Catforth *Lancs.* **Village**, 6m/9km NW of Preston. **55 H6** SD4735.
Catforth Gardens *Lancs.* **Garden**, informal country garden with year-round interest, 5m/8km NW of Preston. **55 H6** SD4735.
Catfoss *E.Riding* **Locality**, 2m/3km NE of Brandesburton. TA1448.
Catharine Slack *W.Yorks.* **Locality**, 2m/3km N of Halifax. SE0928.
Cathays *Cardiff* **Suburb**, to N of Cardiff city centre. Cathays Park to W of city centre. ST1877.
Cathcart *Glas.* **Suburb**, 4m/6km S of Glasgow city centre. NS5860.
Cathedin *Powys See Cathedine.*
Cathedine (Cathedin). *Powys* **Hamlet**, 2m/3km S of Llangorse. **28 A6** SO1425.
Catherine de Barnes Heath *W.Mid.* **Suburb**, 2m/3km E of Solihull town centre. SP1780.
Catherington *Hants.* **Locality**, 1m/2km NW of Horndean. **11 H3** SU6914.
Catherston Leweston *Dorset* **Hamlet**, 2m/4km NE of Lyme Regis. SY3794.
Catherton *Shrop.* **Settlement**, 2m/3km NW of Cleobury Mortimer. **29 F1** SO6578.
Cathkin *S.Lan.* **Suburb**, 3m/4km SE of Rutherglen and 3m/4km N of East Kilbride. NS6258.
Catholes *Cumb.* **Hamlet**, on River Dee, 1m/2km S of Sedbergh. SD6590.
Catisfield *Hants.* **Suburb**, 2m/3km W of Fareham. SU5406.
Catley Lane Head *Gt.Man.* **Suburb**, 2m/3km NW of Rochdale town centre. Healey Dell Nature Reserve nearby. SD8715.
Catlodge *High.* **Settlement**, in Badenoch and Strathspey district, 5m/8km N of Dalwhinnie. NN6392.
Catlow *Lancs.* **Settlement**, 2m/3km SE of Nelson. **56 D6** SD8836.
Catlow Fell *Lancs.* **Open space**, moorland, 3m/5km NW of Stocks Reservoir and 6m/10km SE of High Bentham, with border of Lancashire and North Yorkshire separating it from Cold Stone Plain. **56 C3** SD7060.
Catlowdy *Cumb.* **Locality**, 4m/6km E of Canonbie. **69 K6** NY4576.
Catmere End *Essex* **Hamlet**, 3m/5km W of Saffron Walden. TL4939.
Catmore *W.Berks.* **Village**, 8m/13km N of Newbury. **21 H4** SU4580.
Caton *Devon* **Hamlet**, 2m/3km NE of Ashburton. **5 H3** SX7871.
Caton *Lancs.* Population: 2410. **Village**, 4m/6km NE of Lancaster. **55 J3** SD5364.
Caton Green *Lancs.* **Hamlet**, 1m/2km E of Caton, on E side of River Lune. SD5465.
Caton Moor *Lancs.* **Open space**, moorland with highest point of 1184 feet or 361 metres, 7m/11km E of Lancaster. **55 J3** SD5663.
Cator Court *Devon* **Settlement**, 2m/3km W of Widecombe in the Moor. **5 G3** SX6877.
Catrine *E.Ayr.* Population: 2327. **Village**, on River Ayr, 2m/3km SE of Mauchline. Ballochmyle House, 1km NW, is subject of two songs by Burns. **67 K1** NS5225.
Cat's Ash *Newport* **Hamlet**, 2m/3km E of Caerleon across River Usk. ST3790.
Catsfield *E.Suss.* **Village**, 2m/3km SW of Battle. **14 C6** TQ7213.
Catsfield Stream *E.Suss.* **Settlement**, 1km SW of Catsfield. TQ7213.
Catsham *Som.* **Settlement**, 2m/3km N of Keinton Mandeville. ST5533.
Catshaw *S.Yorks.* **Settlement**, 2m/4km W of Penistone, on N side of River Don. SE2003.
Catshill *W.Mid.* **Suburb**, to S of Brownhills town centre. SK0505.
Catshill *Worcs.* Population: 9188. **Locality**, 2m/3km N of Bromsgrove. **29 J1** SO9573.
Catstone *Sc.Bord.* **Mountain**, in Pentland Hills, 3m/5km W of West Linton. Height 1469 feet or 448 metres. **75 J5** NT0952.
Cattadale *Arg. & B.* **Settlement**, on Islay, 4m/7km E of Bowmore. **72 B5** NR3860.
Cattal *N.Yorks.* **Village**, on River Nidd, 3m/4km S of Whixley. **57 K4** SE4454.
Cattawade *Suff.* **Village**, at head of River Stour estuary, 8m/13km SW of Ipswich. **35 F5** TM1033.
Cattedown *Plym.* **Suburb**, 1m/2km SE of Plymouth city centre. SX4953.
Catterall *Lancs.* **Village**, 2m/3km S of Garstang. **55 J5** SD4942.
Catteralslane *Shrop.* **Settlement**, 1m/2km E of Whitchurch. SJ5640.
Catterick *N.Yorks.* Population: 2629. **Village**, 5m/7km SE of Richmond. Airfield to SE. **62 D7** SE2397.
Catterick Bridge *N.Yorks.* **Hamlet**, on River Swale, 1m/2km NW of Catterick, near site of Roman town of Cataractonium. Racecourse. SE2397.
Catterick Camp *N.Yorks.* Population: 8694. **Military establishment**, large military base, 2m/3km S of Richmond. **62 C7** SE1897.
Catterlen *Cumb.* **Hamlet**, 3m/4km NW of Penrith. Hall, 1m/2km S, dates from 16c. **61 F3** NY4833.
Catterline *Aber.* **Village**, on E coast, 5m/8km S of Stonehaven. **91 G7** NO8678.
Catterton *N.Yorks.* **Hamlet**, 2m/4km NE of Tadcaster. **58 B5** SE5145.
Catteshall *Surr.* **Suburb**, to E of Godalming. SU9844.
Catthorpe *Leics.* **Village**, 4m/6km NE of Rugby. **31 G1** SP5578.
Cattishall *Suff.* **Settlement**, 2m/3km E of Bury St. Edmunds town centre. TL8865.
Cattistock *Dorset* **Village**, 1m/2km N of Maiden Newton. **8 E4** SY5999.
Cattle End *Northants.* **Settlement**, adjoining to SW of Silverstone, 4m/6km SW of Towcester. SP6643.
Catto *N.Yorks.* **Settlement**, on E side of Landmoth Wood, 4m/6km E of Northallerton. SE4292.
Catton *Norf.* **Suburb**, 3m/4km N of Norwich. **45 G4** TG2312.
Catton *N.Yorks.* **Village**, 2m/4km NW of Topcliffe. **57 J2** SE3678.
Catton *Northumb.* **Village**, 1m/2km N of Allendale Town. **61 K1** NY8257.
Catton Hall *Derbys.* **Settlement**, 3m/4km E of Alrewas. **40 E4** SK2015.
Catwick *E.Riding* **Village**, 5m/8km W of Hornsea. **59 H5** TA1245.
Catworth *Cambs.* **Village**, 10m/15km W of Huntingdon. **32 D1** TL0873.
Caudle Green *Glos.* **Hamlet**, 6m/10km NE of Stroud. SO9410.
Caudworthy *Cornw.* **Hamlet**, 3m/5km S of Week St. Mary. **4 C1** SX2592.
Caulcott *Beds.* **Settlement**, 4m/6km SW of Kempston. TL0042.
Caulcott *Oxon.* **Hamlet**, 5m/8km W of Bicester. **31 G6** SP5024.
Cauldcleuch Head *Sc.Bord.* **Mountain**, 5m/7km SE of Teviothead. Height 1994 feet or 608 metres. **69 K3** NT4600.
Cauldcots *Angus* **Settlement**, 1m/2km SW of Inverkeilor. **83 H3** NO6547.
Cauldhall Moor *Midloth.* **Open space**, moorland 2m/3km E of Howgate. **76 A5** NT2758.
Cauldhame *Stir.* **Settlement**, 2m/3km E of Dunblane. **81 K7** NN8201.
Cauldhame *Stir.* **Village**, adjoining to SW of Kippen, 9m/15km W of Stirling. **74 E1** NS6494.
Cauldkine Rig *D. & G. Alternative spelling of Calkin Rig, qv.*
Cauldon *Staffs.* **Hamlet**, among quarries, 6m/9km NE of Cheadle. **40 C1** SK0749.
Cauldon Lowe *Staffs.* **Mountain**, with tumulus at summit, 1m/2km S of Cauldon. Height 1191 feet or 363 metres. SK0747.
Cauldron Snout **Waterfall**, in River Tees on border of Cumbria and Durham, below Cow Green Reservoir. Highest waterfall in England, falling in eight cascades. **61 K4** NY8128.
Cauldshiels Hill *Sc.Bord.* **Mountain**, 3m/4km SW of Melrose. Height 1076 feet or 328 metres. **76 D7** NT5131.
Cauldshiels Loch *Sc.Bord.* **Lake/loch**, small loch 2m/4km SW of Melrose. **76 D7** NT5132.
Cauldside *D. & G.* **Settlement**, 4m/7km NE of Canonbie. **69 K5** NY4381.
Caulkerbush *D. & G.* **Settlement**, 7m/11km SE of Dalbeattie. **65 K5** NX9257.
Caultrashal Beag *W.Isles Anglicised form of Calltraiseal Bheag, qv.*
Caultrashal Mòr *W.Isles Anglicised form of Calltraiseal Mhòr, qv.*
Caundle Marsh *Dorset* **Hamlet**, 3m/5km SE of Sherborne. **9 F3** ST6713.
Caundle Wake *Dorset* **Hamlet**, 1km SE of Bishop's Caundle and 5m/8km SE of Sherborne. ST7012.
Caunsall *Worcs.* **Settlement**, 3m/5km NE of Kidderminster. **40 A7** SO8581.
Caunton *Notts.* **Village**, 5m/8km NW of Newark-on-Trent. **51 K6** SK7460.
Causamul *W.Isles* **Island**, group of rocks nearly 2m/3km W of Aird an Rùnair, W coast of North Uist. **92 B4** NF6670.
Causennae *Lincs. See Ancaster.*
Causeway End *Cumb.* **Locality**, S part of Levens, 4m/7km SW of Kendal. SD4885.
Causeway End *D. & G.* **Settlement**, 3m/5km N of Wigtown. **64 E4** NX4260.
Causeway End *Essex* **Hamlet**, 4m/6km SE of Great Dunmow. **33 K7** TL6819.
Causeway End *Lancs.* **Settlement**, 1m/2km S of Rufford and 4m/7km NE of Ormskirk. SD4514.
Causeway Foot *W.Yorks.* **Hamlet**, 1km E of Ogden Water, 2m/3km S of Denholme. SE0730.
Causeway Grain Head **Mountain**, rising to over 490 metres, astride border of Dumfries & Galloway and Scottish Borders, on S edge of Craik Forest, 6m/9km NE of Bentpath. **69 J4** NY3598.
Causeway Green *W.Mid.* **Suburb**, 1m/2km SE of Oldbury town centre. SO9987.
Causewayhead *Cumb.* **Locality**, 1m/2km E of Silloth. **60 C1** NY1253.
Causewayhead *Stir.* **Suburb**, 1m/2km N of Stirling. **75 G1** NS8095.
Causey *Dur.* **Hamlet**, 2m/3km N of Stanley. 18c Causey Arch to SW, along Tanfield Railway. NZ2056.
Causey Park *Northumb.* **Settlement**, 2m/3km E of Longhorsley. **71 G4** NZ1795.
Causey Pike *Cumb.* **Inland physical feature**, ridge rising to over 620 metres, between Coledale Beck and Newlands Beck, overlooking Derwent Water to W. **60 D4** NY2120.
Causeyend *Aber.* **Settlement**, 2m/3km NW of Balmedie. **91 H3** NJ9419.
Cautley *Cumb.* **Locality**, 3m/5km NE of Sedbergh. **61 H7** SD6995.
Cava *Ork.* **Island**, uninhabited island of about 180 acres or 70 hectares lying 1m/2km off E coast of Hoy at SE end of Bring Deeps. Lighthouse at N end of island. **107 C8** ND3299.
Cavendish *Suff.* **Village**, on River Stour, 4m/6km W of Long Melford. **34 C4** TL8046.
Cavendish Bridge *Leics.* **Hamlet**, on River Trent, 2m/3km N of Castle Donington. SK4429.
Cavenham *Suff.* **Village**, 7m/11km NW of Bury St. Edmunds. **34 B2** TL7669.
Cavens *D. & G.* **Settlement**, 3m/4km N of Southerness. **65 K5** NX9758.
Cavers *Sc.Bord.* **Hamlet**, 2m/4km NE of Hawick. NT5315.
Caversfield *Oxon.* **Settlement**, 2m/3km N of Bicester. Site of Roman building 1m/2km E. **31 G6** SP5825.
Caversham *Read.* **Suburb**, N district of Reading across River Thames. **22 A4** SU7274.
Caversham Heights *Read.* **Suburb**, 1m/2km W of Caversham. SU7075.
Caversta *W.Isles Anglicised form of Cabharstadh, qv.*
Caverswall *Staffs.* **Village**, 4m/6km W of Cheadle. **40 B1** SJ9542.
Cavil *E.Riding* **Settlement**, 2m/3km NE of Howden. SE7730.
Caw *Cumb.* **Mountain**, on Dunnerdale Fells, 4m/7km N of Broughton in Furness. Height 1735 feet or 529 metres. **60 D7** SD2394.
Caw Fell *Cumb.* **Mountain**, on ridge to W of Haycock, 4m/7km N of Nether Wasdale. Height 2404 feet or 733 metres. **60 C5** NY1310.
Cawdor *High.* **Village**, in Nairn district, 5m/8km SW of Nairn. Castle dating from 15c and later. **97 F6** NH8449.
Cawdor Castle *High.* **Castle**, on E bank of Allt Dearg across from Cawdor. Central tower built in 1342, fortified in 1454 and surrounded by 16c buildings. Associated with Shakespeare's Macbeth. Grounds contain notable gardens with herbaceous borders plus roses, shrubs, lilies, holly maze, thistle garden and white garden. **97 F6** NH8449.
Cawfields Roman Camps *Northumb.* **Historic/prehistoric site**, cluster of well-preserved Roman remains (English Heritage), 2m/3km N of Haltwhistle. Includes long section of Hadrian's Wall, camps, Vallum and Milecastle 42. Masonry remains are among tallest along Hadrian's Wall. **70 C7** NY7166.
Cawkeld *E.Riding* **Settlement**, with small lake, 1km N of Kilnwick and 3m/4km SW of Hutton Cranswick. SE9950.
Cawkwell *Lincs.* **Settlement**, 6m/9km SW of Louth. **53 F5** TF2879.
Cawood *N.Yorks.* **Village**, on River Ouse, 4m/7km NW of Selby. Gatehouse of former castle dates from 15c. **58 B6** SE5737.
Cawsand *Cornw.* **Hamlet**, 1m/2km SE of Millbrook, adjoining to S of Kingsand on Cawsand Bay. Once famous for smuggling, now anchorage for yachts at mouth of River Tamar. **4 E5** SX4350.
Cawsand Bay *Cornw.* **Bay**, stretches from Picklecombe Point in N to Penlee Point in S, 4m/6km SW of Plymouth across Plymouth Sound. **4 E5** SX4450.
Cawsand Hill *Devon* **Mountain**, 4m/6km SE of Okehampton, in Dartmoor National Park. Numerous cairns and settlements. Height 1804 feet or 550 metres. **6 E6** SX6391.
Cawston *Norf.* **Village**, 4m/7km SW of Aylsham. **45 F3** TG1323.
Cawston *Warks.* **Suburb**, 3m/4km SW of Rugby. SP4773.
Cawthorn *N.Yorks.* **Settlement**, 4m/6km NW of Pickering. Earthworks of Roman camps to NE. SE7789.
Cawthorne *S.Yorks.* **Village**, 4m/6km W of Barnsley. **50 E2** SE2808.
Cawthorpe *Lincs.* **Hamlet**, 1m/2km N of Bourne. **42 D3** TF0922.
Cawton *N.Yorks.* **Hamlet**, 2m/3km W of Hovingham. **58 C2** SE6476.
Caxton *Cambs.* **Village**, 9m/15km W of Cambridge. **33 G3** TL3058.
Caxton End *Cambs.* **Locality**, E end of Eltisley. TL2759.
Caxton End *Cambs.* **Village**, NW end of Bourn. TL3157.
Caxton Gibbet *Cambs.* **Settlement**, and crossroads, 2m/3km N of Caxton. **33 F3** TL2960.
Caynham *Shrop.* **Village**, 3m/5km E of Ludlow. **28 E1** SO5573.
Caynham Camp *Shrop.* **Historic/prehistoric site**, rectangular Iron Age hillfort, possibly dating from 5c-7c, 2m/3km SE of Ludlow. **28 E1** SO5473.
Caythorpe *Lincs.* **Village**, 8m/13km N of Grantham. Agricultural college to E. **42 C1** SK9348.
Caythorpe *Notts.* **Village**, 1m/2km SE of Lowdham. **41 J1** SK6845.
Cayton *N.Yorks.* **Locality**, 2m/3km N of Ripley. SE2963.
Cayton *N.Yorks.* **Village**, 3m/5km S of Scarborough. **59 G1** TA0583.
Cayton Bay *N.Yorks.* **Bay**, on North Sea coast, 1m/2km NE of Cayton and 3m/5km SE of Scarborough. **59 G1** TA0684.
Ceallan (Anglicised form: Kallin.) *W.Isles* **Settlement**, on E coast of Grimsay, between North Uist and Benbecula. **92 D6** NF8755.
Ceann a' Bháigh (Anglicised form: Lingarabay.) *W.Isles* **Settlement**, on S coast of South Harris, 2m/3km NE of Rodel. **93 F3** NG0685.
Ceann a' Bháigh (Anglicised form: Bayhead.) *W.Isles* **Village**, near W coast of North Uist, 5m/9km S of Griminis Point. **92 C5** NF7468.
Ceann a Deas na Hearadh *W.Isles Gaelic form of South Harris, qv.*
Ceann a' Gharaidh *W.Isles* **Coastal feature**, headland at SW point of South Uist. **84 C3** NF7315.
Ceann a' Mhàim *High.* **Mountain**, in Inverness district on S side of Glen Moriston, 6m/10km W of Fort Augustus. Height 2201 feet or 671 metres. **87 J4** NH2708.
Ceann a Tuath na Hearadh *W.Isles Gaelic form of North Harris, qv.*
Ceann Caol *High.* **Inland physical feature**, mountain ridge on Ardgour rising to 1601 feet or 488 metres, forming NE part of Bràigh Bhlàich, 4m/6km W of Fort William across Loch Linnhe. **87 G7** NN0474.
Ceann Ear *W.Isles* **Island**, one of Heisker Islands group. Sands between Ceann Ear and adjoining Ceann Iar to W are fordable at low tide. **92 B5** NF6462.
Ceann Garbh *Arg. & B.* **Mountain**, peak in Argyll to NE of summit of Beinn Bhuidhe and 6m/9km SE of Dalmally. Height 2634 feet or 803 metres. **80 D5** NN2220.

Ceann Iar *W.Isles* ***Island***, one of Heisker Islands group to W of Ceann Ear. **92 B5** NF6162.
Ceann Leathad nam Bò *High.* ***Coastal feature***, headland 4m/6km SW of Dunbeath. **105 G6** ND1323.
Ceann Loch Shiphoirt (Anglicised form: Seaforth Head.) *W.Isles* ***Settlement***, at head of Loch Seaforth, Isle of Lewis, 3m/4km S of Baile Ailein across Loch Erisort. **100 E6** NB2916.
Ceann na Beinne *High.* ***Hill***, 3m/4km NE of Rubh' an Dùnain, Skye. Height 738 feet or 225 metres. **85 K3** NG4217.
Ceann na Circ (Anglicised form: Chicken Head.) *W.Isles* ***Coastal feature***, headland at S end of Eye Peninsula, Isle of Lewis. **101 G5** NB4929.
Ceann-na-Cleithe *W.Isles Gaelic form of Kennacley, qv.*
Ceann Reamhar *W.Isles* ***Mountain***, on South Harris, 2m/3km SW of Tarbert. Height 1532 feet or 467 metres. **93 G2** NG1199.
Ceanna Mòr *High.* ***Coastal feature***, headland on S side of entrance to Loch a' Choire, Lochaber district. **79 K2** NM8551.
Ceannacroc Forest *High.* ***Open space***, deer forest in Inverness district N of Loch Cluanie. Also forest in Glen Moriston to E. Power station for hydro-electricity scheme at Ceannacroc Bridge. **87 H3** NH1713.
Ceardach *Stir.* ***Island***, islet (National Trust for Scotland) in Loch Lomond, 2m/3km W of Balmaha. NS3991.
Cearsiadar (Anglicised form: Kershader.) *W.Isles* ***Village***, on S side of Loch Erisort, Isle of Lewis, opposite Lacasaigh. **101 F5** NB3420.
Ceathramh Garbh *High.* ***Locality***, area to N of Loch a' Chadh-Fi, Sutherland district. **102 E3** NC2252.
Ceathramh Meadhanach (Anglicised form: Middlequarter.) *W.Isles* ***Settlement***, on North Uist, 1km W of Solas. **92 C4** NF7974.
Cecil Higgins Museum and Art Gallery *Beds.* ***Other feature of interest***, mid 19c mansion in Bedford town centre, with exhibitions of various artwork. **32 D4** TL0549.
Cedar House *Surr. See Cobham.*
Cedig *Powys* ***Settlement***, 3m/5km NW of Llanwddyn. **37 J3** SH9922.
Cefn Berain *Conwy* ***Hamlet***, 4m/6km NW of Denbigh. SH9969.
Cefn-brith *Conwy* ***Hamlet***, 2m/3km NW of Cerrigydrudion. **47 H7** SH9350.
Cefn Brwynog *Cere.* ***Mountain***, to W of Claerwen Reservoir. Height 1542 feet or 470 metres. **27 H2** SN8165.
Cefn Bryn *Swan.* ***Large natural feature***, moorland ridge on Gower peninsula, running W from Penmaen for about 4m/6km. Arthur's Stone, large dolmen of millstone grit to N. **17 J6** SS5089.
Cefn-bryn-brain *Carmar.* ***Village***, 2m/3km E of Brynamman. SN7714.
Cefn Bychan *Caerp. Welsh form of Newbridge, qv.*
Cefn Byrle *Powys* ***Locality***, 5m/8km NE of Ystalyfera. SN8311.
Cefn-caer-Ferch *Gwyn.* ***Settlement***, on Lleyn Peninsula, 4m/6km S of Clynnog-fawr. **36 D1** SH4242.
Cefn Canol *Powys* ***Hamlet***, 1km NW of Rhydycroesau. SJ2331.
Cefn Cantref *Powys* ***Settlement***, 1m/2km S of Brecon. **27 K6** SO0426.
Cefn Carn Fadog *Carmar.* ***Mountain***, 3m/4km NE of Cwmllynfell. Height 1656 feet or 505 metres. **27 G7** SN7616.
Cefn Cenarth *Powys* ***Mountain***, 1m/2km NW of Pant-y-dwr. Height 1509 feet or 460 metres. **27 J1** SN9676.
Cefn Clawdd *Powys* ***Mountain***, 7m/11km N of Brecon. Height 1430 feet or 436 metres. **27 K4** SO0440.
Cefn Coch *Denb.* ***Settlement***, 3m/4km S of Llanfair Dyffryn Clwyd. **47 K7** SJ1251.
Cefn Coch *Gwyn.* ***Mountain***, 4m/7km E of Bala. Height 1443 feet or 440 metres. **37 J2** SJ0035.
Cefn Coch *Powys* ***Locality***, 1km NW of Llanllugan. SJ0402.
Cefn-coch *Powys* ***Mountain***, 2m/3km N of Cefn Fannog in Tywi Forest. Height 1640 feet or 500 metres. **27 H3** SN8254.
Cefn-coch *Powys* ***Settlement***, 1m/2km NW of Llanrhaeadr-ym-Mochnant. **38 A3** SJ1026.
Cefn-coed-y-cymmer *M.Tyd.* ***Locality***, 2m/3km NW of Merthyr Tydfil. **18 D1** SO0308.
Cefn Coleshill *Flints.* ***Locality***, 2m/3km W of Flint. Remains of medieval fortress. SJ2173.
Cefn-crib *Torfaen* ***Hamlet***, 3m/5km W of Pontypool. ST2399.
Cefn Cribwr *Bridgend* ***Village***, 4m/6km NW of Bridgend. **18 B3** SS8582.
Cefn-crin *Powys* ***Mountain***, rising to over 450 metres, 4m/7km NE of Rhayader. **27 K1** SO0272.
Cefn Cross *Bridgend* ***Locality***, on E side of Cefn Cribwr. **18 B3** SS8682.
Cefn Crug *Powys* ***Mountain***, 3m/5km N of Llanwrtyd Wells. Height 1515 feet or 462 metres. **27 H3** SN8551.
Cefn Cyff *Powys* ***Inland physical feature***, mountain ridge rising to over 620 metres, running NE in Brecon Beacons, 4m/6km S of Brecon. **27 K6** SO0422.
Cefn-ddwysarn *Gwyn.* ***Settlement***, 3m/5km NE of Bala. **37 J2** SH9638.
Cefn Drum *Swan.* ***Hill***, 2m/3km NE of Pontarddulais. Height 699 feet or 213 metres. **17 K4** SN6104.
Cefn Du *Denb.* ***Inland physical feature***, afforested mountain ridge, rising to 1384 feet or 422 metres, 2m/3km S of Cyffylliog. **47 J7** SJ0454.
Cefn Einion *Shrop.* ***Settlement***, 4m/6km N of Clun. **38 B7** SO2886.
Cefn Fannog *Powys* ***Mountain***, 4m/7km NW of Llanwrtyd Wells, to NE of Llyn Brianne Reservoir in Tywi Forest. Height 1496 feet or 456 metres. **27 H3** SN8251.
Cefn Fforest *Caerp.* ***Suburb***, N district of Blackwood. ST1697.
Cefn Glas *Bridgend* ***Suburb***, NW district of Bridgend. SS8980.
Cefn-gorwydd *Powys* ***Hamlet***, 2m/3km E of Llanwrtyd Wells. **27 J4** SN9045.
Cefn Grug *N.P.T.* ***Inland physical feature***, mountain ridge, 3m/5km E of Resolven. **18 B1** SN8802.
Cefn Gwenffrwd *Carmar.* ***Inland physical feature***, mountain ridge, rising to 1387 feet or 423 metres, 3m/5km W of Llyn Brianne. **27 G4** SN7448.
Cefn Gwrhyd *N.P.T.* ***Hill***, 2m/3km W of Ystalyfera. Height 968 feet or 295 metres. **18 A1** SN7308.
Cefn-gwyn *Powys* ***Settlement***, 4m/6km SE of Newtown. **38 A7** SO1587.
Cefn Gwyngul *R.C.T.* ***Inland physical feature***, mountain ridge, approximately 450 metres high, E of Rhondda Fach valley above Tylorstown. **18 D2** ST0395.
Cefn Hengoed *Caerp.* ***Village***, adjoining to N of Hengoed, 2m/4km S of Bargoed. **18 E2** ST1495.
Cefn-hengoed *Swan.* ***Suburb***, 2m/4km NE of Swansea city centre across River Tawe. SS6895.
Cefn Hill *Here.* ***Mountain***, 4m/6km SE of Hay-on-Wye. Height 1594 feet or 486 metres. **28 B5** SO2738.
Cefn Hir-fynydd *Wrex.* ***Inland physical feature***, mountain ridge rising to over 460 metres, 1m/2km S of Llanarmon Dyffryn Ceiriog. **38 A2** SJ1631.
Cefn Hirgoed *Bridgend* ***Open space***, common 3m/4km NE of Bridgend. **18 C3** SS9383.
Cefn Llechid *Powys* ***Mountain***, 1m/2km SE of Sennybridge. Height 1312 feet or 400 metres. **27 J6** SN9327.
Cefn-llwyd *Cere.* ***Settlement***, 4m/7km E of Aberystwyth. SN6583.
Cefn Llwydlo *Carmar.* ***Inland physical feature***, afforested mountain ridge in Crychan Forest, 3m/5km SW of Llanwrtyd Wells. **27 H4** SN8542.
Cefn Manmoel *B.Gwent* ***Inland physical feature***, mountain ridge running N to S, separating upper part of Ebbw Vale from upper part of Sirhowy Valley. **18 E1** SO1607.
Cefn Mawr *Powys* ***Open space***, hillslope 3m/5km N of Ystradgynlais. **27 G7** SN7915.
Cefn-mawr *Wrex.* Population: 8538. ***Village***, 1m/2km SW of Ruabon. **38 B1** SJ2842.
Cefn Meiriadog *Denb.* ***Hill***, 2m/3km SW of Denbigh. Height 538 feet or 164 metres. **47 J5** SJ0172.
Cefn Merthyr *M.Tyd.* ***Mountain***, rising above River Taff, 1km E of Aberfan. Height 1207 feet or 368 metres. **18 D1** ST0899.
Cefn Morfudd *N.P.T.* ***Mountain***, 2m/3km SE of Tonna. Height 1007 feet or 307 metres. **18 A2** SS7897.
Cefn Onneu *Powys* ***Open space***, hillslope running E to W, 3m/5km SW of Crickhowell. **28 A7** SO1615.
Cefn Padrig *Carmar.* ***Coastal feature***, sandflat 2m/3km E of Burry Port. **17 H5** SN4600.
Cefn Pyllau-duon *B.Gwent* ***Inland physical feature***, mountain ridge rising to 1640 feet or 500 metres and running SE, 3m/4km NW of Tredegar. **27 K7** SO1012.
Cefn Rhigos *R.C.T.* ***Hamlet***, 1m/2km N of Rhigos. SN9106.
Cefn rhudd *Conwy* ***Open space***, plateau area 4m/6km SE of Llanrwst. **47 G7** SH8459.
Cefn Rhyswg *Caerp.* ***Inland physical feature***, SW spur of mountain to E of Abercarn and Ebbw Vale, rising to 1312 feet or 400 metres. **19 F2** ST2393.
Cefn Sidan Sands *Carmar.* ***Coastal feature***, sandflat to S and W of mouth of Gwendraeth estuary, 4m/6km W of Kidwelly. **17 G4** SN3305.
Cefn-y-bedd *Flints.* ***Hamlet***, 4m/6km N of Wrexham. **48 C7** SJ3156.
Cefn-y-bedd *Powys Former name of Cilmery, qv.*
Cefn-y-coed *Powys* ***Locality***, upland area with settlement, 1m/2km S of Llandyssil. **38 A6** SO1993.
Cefn y Cwne *Cere.* ***Mountain***, 6m/9km E of Tregaron. Height 1729 feet or 527 metres. **27 G3** SN7758.
Cefn-y-Garth *Swan.* ***Locality***, 1m/2km SE of Clydach towards Neath. SN7000.
Cefn-y-pant *Carmar.* ***Hamlet***, 2m/3km NW of Llanboidy. **16 E2** SN1925.
Cefn y Rhondda *R.C.T.* ***Mountain***, NE of Treorchy. Height 1578 feet or 481 metres. **18 C2** SS9797.
Cefn yr Arail *B.Gwent* ***Open space***, S slope of ridge, 1m/2km NW of Abertillery. **18 E1** SO1905.
Cefn-yr Esgair *Cere.* ***Mountain***, rising to over 450 metres, 3m/4km NW of Plynlimon and N of Nant-y-moch Reservoir. **37 G7** SN7488.
Cefndeuddwr *Gwyn.* ***Settlement***, in Coed-y-Brenin Forest, 5m/8km N of Dolgellau. **37 G3** SH7225.
Cefneithin *Carmar.* ***Village***, 1m/2km NW of Cross Hands. **17 J3** SN5513.
Cefni Reservoir *I.o.A.* ***Reservoir***, in course of River Cefni on Anglesey, 2m/3km NW of Llangefni. **46 C5** SH4477.
Cefnpennar *R.C.T.* ***Village***, 1m/2km NW of Mountain Ash. SO0300.
Cefntyle-brych *N.P.T.* ***Mountain***, 4m/7km E of Resolven. Height 1758 feet or 536 metres. **18 B1** SN9001.
Ceibwr Bay *Pembs.* ***Bay***, 1m/2km NW of Moylgrove and 5m/8km W of Cardigan. **26 A4** SN1045.
Ceidio *I.o.A.* ***Settlement***, in central Anglesey, 5m/8km SW of Amlwch. **46 C4** SH4085.
Ceidio Fawr *Gwyn.* ***Settlement***, 1m/2km S of Morfa Nefyn. **36 B2** SH2838.
Ceigidfa *Powys Welsh form of Guilsfield, qv.*
Ceinewydd *Cere. Welsh form of New Quay, qv.*
Ceint *I.o.A.* ***Settlement***, on Anglesey, 1m/2km E of Llangefni. **46 C5** SH4874.
Ceiriog ***River***, rising in Berwyn mountain range SE of Corwen and running E by Glyn Ceiriog and Chirk into River Dee 2m/3km NE of Chirk. SJ3139.
Ceirw ***River***, rising 3m/5km S of Pentrefoelas and flowing E into River Alwen on SE side of Maerdy. **37 H1** SJ0244.
Cellan *Cere.* ***Settlement***, 2m/4km E of Lampeter. Model Aircraft Exhibition. **27 F4** SN6149.
Cellar Head (Gaelic form: Rubha an t-Seileir.) *W.Isles* ***Coastal feature***, headland on NE coast of Isle of Lewis, 6m/9km N of Tolsta Head. **101 H2** NB5656.
Cellardyke *Fife* ***Suburb***, central district of Anstruther. **83 G7** NO5703.
Cellarhead *Staffs.* ***Hamlet***, 5m/8km E of Stoke-on-Trent. **40 B1** SJ9547.
Celleron *Cumb.* ***Locality***, 4m/6km S of Penrith. NY4925.
Cemaes *I.o.A.* ***Village***, fishing village and resort on S side of Cemaes Bay, 5m/8km W of Amlwch. Wylfa nuclear power station 1m/2km to W. **46 B3** SH3793.
Cemaes Bay *I.o.A.* ***Bay***, wide bay on N coast of Anglesey, 5m/8km W of Amlwch; E coast of bay, National Trust. **46 B3** SH3793.
Cemaes Head *Pembs.* ***Coastal feature***, headland on W side of mouth of River Teifi, 4m/6km NW of Cardigan. **26 A3** SN1350.
Cemais *Newport See Kemeys Inferior.*
Cemais Comawndwr *Mon. Welsh form of Kemeys Commander, qv.*
Cemlyn Bay *I.o.A.* ***Bay***, on N coast of Anglesey, 3m/4km E of Carmel Head. **46 B3** SH3394.
Cemmaes *Powys* ***Village***, 7m/11km NE of Machynlleth. **37 H5** SH8306.
Cemmaes Road (Glantwymyn). *Powys* ***Hamlet***, 5m/8km NE of Machynlleth. **37 H5** SH8204.
Cenarth *Carmar.* ***Village***, 3m/4km W of Newcastle Emlyn. Location of National Coracle Centre. Salmon-leap on River Teifi, where coracle fishing formerly prospered. **26 B4** SN2641.
Cendl *B.Gwent Welsh form of Beaufort, qv.*
Cennin *Gwyn.* ***Settlement***, at E end of Lleyn Peninsula, 5m/8km S of Penygroes. **36 D1** SH4645.
Central Criminal Courts (Also known as Old Bailey.) *Gt.Lon.* ***Other feature of interest***, situated on site of old Newgate Prison in City of London, 1m/2km NE of Charing Cross. Trials can be viewed from public galleries. TQ3181.
Central Lancashire New Town *Lancs.* ***Locality***, designated 1970. Area of 55 square miles or 142 square km includes Preston in N and Chorley in S. SD5525.
Centre for Alternative Technology *Powys* ***Other feature of interest***, 3m/4km N of Machynlleth. Showcase and research centre for sustainable communities, including water-balanced cliff railway and wind generators. 80 per cent of power here is generated by wind, sun and water, using sustainable technology. Energy-saving houses with organic gardens demonstrate concept. **37 G5** SH7504.
Ceos (Anglicised form: Keose.) *W.Isles* ***Village***, near E coast of Isle of Lewis, 1m/2km of Lacasaigh. **101 F5** NB3521.
Ceredigion Museum *Cere.* ***Other feature of interest***, in Aberystwyth's early 20c music hall. Memorabilia from theatre and cinema, as well as some local hsitory. **36 E7** SN5881.
Ceres *Fife* ***Village***, 3m/4km SE of Cupar. **82 E6** NO4011.
Cerist *Powys* ***Settlement***, on river of same name, 2m/4km N of Llanidloes. SN9688.
Cerne *Dorset* ***River***, rising near Up Cerne and flowing S into River Frome on N side of Dorchester. **9 F5** SY6991.
Cerne Abbas *Dorset* ***Village***, on River Cerne, 7m/11km N of Dorchester. **9 F4** ST6601.
Cerney Wick *Glos.* ***Village***, 2m/3km NW of Cricklade. **20 D2** SU0796.
Cerrig Gwylan *Pembs.* ***Island***, two small islands 1km N of Abereiddi Bay. SM7932.
Cerrigceinwen *I.o.A.* ***Village***, on Anglesey, 2m/4km SW of Llangefni. **46 C5** SH4273.
Cerrigydrudion *Conwy* ***Village***, 12m/20km SW of Ruthin. **37 J1** SH9548.
Cess *Norf.* ***Locality***, 1km W of Martham. TG4417.
Cessford *Sc.Bord.* ***Settlement***, 3m/4km W of Morebattle. **70 C1** NT7323.
Cessnock Water ***River***, rising 3m/5km S of Darvel and running circuitously NW to River Irvine between Galston and Kilmarnock. **74 D7** NS4737.
Ceunant *Gwyn.* ***Hamlet***, 3m/5km E of Caernarfon. SH5361.
Chaceley *Glos.* ***Village***, 3m/5km SW of Tewkesbury across River Severn. **29 H5** SO8530.
Chacewater *Cornw.* ***Village***, 4m/6km NE of Redruth. **2 E4** SW7544.
Chackmore *Bucks.* ***Village***, 1m/2km NW of Buckingham. **31 H5** SP6835.
Chacombe *Northants.* ***Village***, 3m/5km NE of Banbury. **31 F4** SP4943.
Chad Valley *W.Mid.* ***Suburb***, 2m/3km SW of Birmingham city centre. Botanical gardens. **40 C7** SP0485.
Chadderton *Gt.Man.* Population: 34,026. ***Town***, industrial town, 6m/10km NE of Manchester. **49 J2** SD9005.
Chadderton Fold *Gt.Man.* ***Settlement***, 1m/2km NW of Chadderton. SD8906.
Chadderton Heights *Gt.Man.* ***Settlement***, 1m/2km N of Chadderton. SD8907.
Chaddesden *Derby* ***Suburb***, 2m/3km E of Derby city centre. **41 F2** SK3837.
Chaddesley Corbett *Worcs.* ***Village***, 4m/7km SE of Kidderminster. **29 H1** SO8973.
Chaddleworth *W.Berks.* ***Village***, 7m/11km NW of Newbury. **21 H4** SU4177.
Chadlington *Oxon.* ***Village***, 3m/4km NW of Charlbury. **30 E6** SP3221.
Chadshunt *Warks.* ***Hamlet***, 2m/3km NE of Kineton. **30 E3** SP3452.
Chadstone *Northants.* ***Settlement***, 1km SW of Castle Ashby and 7m/11km SW of Wellingborough. SP8558.
Chadwell *Leics.* ***Hamlet***, 4m/6km NE of Melton Mowbray. **42 A3** SK7824.
Chadwell *Shrop.* ***Settlement***, 4m/7km SE of Newport. SJ7814.
Chadwell End *Beds.* ***Settlement***, adjoining to W of Pertenhall, 2m/3km SW of Kimbolton. TL0865.
Chadwell Heath *Gt.Lon.* ***Suburb***, in borough of Barking and Dagenham, 2m/3km W of Romford. TQ4888.
Chadwell St. Mary *Thur.* ***Small town***, 1m/2km N of Tilbury. **24 C4** TQ6478.

Chadwick End *W.Mid.* ***Hamlet***, 4m/6km E of Hockley Heath. **30 D1** SP2073.
Chadwick Green *Mersey.* ***Suburb***, 1m/2km SW of Billinge. SJ5299.
Chaffcombe *Som.* ***Village***, 2m/4km NE of Chard. **8 C3** ST3510.
Chagford *Devon* ***Small town***, on E edge of Dartmoor, 4m/6km NW of Moretonhampstead. An original stannery town where tin was weighed and taxed. 15c church. **7 F7** SX7087.
Chailey *E.Suss.* ***Village***, 6m/10km N of Lewes. **13 G5** TQ3919.
Chain Bridge *Lincs.* ***Locality***, with bridge over New Hammond Beck, 2m/3km SW of Boston. TF3043.
Chainbridge *Cambs.* ***Locality***, on Twenty Foot River, 2m/3km N of March. TF4200.
Chainhurst *Kent* ***Village***, 2m/4km N of Marden. **14 C3** TQ7347.
Chaipaval *W.Isles* ***Mountain***, on South Harris, 2m/3km SE of Toe Head. Height 1197 feet or 365 metres. **92 E2** NF9792.
Chalbury *Dorset* ***Hamlet***, 4m/7km N of Wimborne Minster. SU0106.
Chalbury Common *Dorset* ***Hamlet***, 4m/7km N of Wimborne Minster. **10 B4** SU0206.
Chaldon *Surr.* ***Village***, 2m/3km W of Caterham. **23 G6** TQ3155.
Chaldon Down *Dorset* ***Open space***, downland 1km from coast, 1km S of Chaldon Herring. **9 G6** SY7881.
Chaldon Herring (Also known as East Chaldon.) *Dorset* ***Village***, 4m/7km SW of Wool. **9 G6** SY7983.
Chale *I.o.W.* ***Village***, near S coast, 5m/8km W of Ventnor, and just inland from Chale Bay. **11 F7** SZ4877.
Chale Green *I.o.W.* ***Village***, 1m/2km N of Chale. **11 F7** SZ4879.
Chalfont Common *Bucks.* ***Suburb***, 1m/2km N of Chalfont St. Peter. **22 D2** TQ0092.
Chalfont St. Giles *Bucks.* Population: 4987. ***Small town***, 3m/5km SE of Amersham. Site of Milton's cottage where Paradise Lost was completed. **22 C2** SU9893.
Chalfont St. Peter *Bucks.* Population: 9762. ***Small town***, commuter town 6m/9km NW of Uxbridge. **22 D2** TQ0090.
Chalford *Glos.* Population: 5331. ***Village***, 4m/6km SE of Stroud. **20 B1** SO8902.
Chalford *Wilts.* ***Settlement***, 1km S of Westbury. ST8650.
Chalgrave *Beds.* ***Settlement***, 3m/5km N of Dunstable. TL0027.
Chalgrove *Oxon.* Population: 2832. ***Village***, 4m/6km NW of Watlington. Airfield to N. Site of Civil War battle (1643) to E. **21 K2** SU6396.
Chalk *Kent* ***Suburb***, E district of Gravesend. **24 C4** TQ6772.
Chalk Beck *Cumb.* ***River***, rising to N of Warnell Fell and flowing N into River Wampool just N of West Curthwaite, 3m/5km W of Dalston. **60 E2** NY3348.
Chalk End *Essex* ***Settlement***, 3m/5km SE of Leaden Roding. TL6310.
Chalk Farm *Gt.Lon.* ***Suburb***, in borough of Camden, 3m/4km NW of Charing Cross. TQ2884.
Chalk Hill *Herts.* ***Suburb***, SW district of St. Albans. TL1305.
Chalk Hill *N.Lincs.* ***Locality***, 1m/2km E of Melton Ross. TA0811.
Chalkhouse Green *Oxon.* ***Settlement***, 3m/5km N of Reading. SU7178.
Chalkshire *Bucks.* ***Settlement***, 2m/3km W of Wendover. SP8407.
Chalkstone *Suff.* ***Locality***, adjoining to NE of Haverhill. TL6746.
Chalkwell *Kent* ***Suburb***, W district of Sittingbourne. TQ8964.
Chalkwell *S'end* ***Suburb***, W district of Southend-on-Sea. TQ8585.
Challacombe *Devon* ***Village***, on W side of Exmoor, 5m/8km W of Simonsbath. **6 E1** SS6941.
Challacombe Common *Devon* ***Open space***, moorland at NW side of Exmoor, 1m/2km N of Challacombe. **6 E1** SS6842.
Challister *Shet.* ***Settlement***, on N coast of Whalsay, 1km E of Brough. HU5665.
Challister Ness *Shet.* ***Coastal feature***, headland on N coast of Whalsay, 1m/2km NE of Challister. **109 E6** HU5767.
Challoch *D. & G.* ***Settlement***, 2m/3km NW of Newton Stewart. **64 D4** NX3867.
Challock *Kent* ***Village***, 4m/6km E of Charing. **15 F2** TR0050.
Chalmington *Dorset* ***Settlement***, 2m/3km N of Maiden Newton. **8 E4** ST5900.
Chalton *Beds.* ***Village***, 5m/8km NW of Luton. **32 D6** TL0326.
Chalton *Hants.* ***Village***, 3m/4km NE of Horndean. Sites of Roman buildings 1m/2km E and 1m/2km NW. **11 J3** SU7316.
Chalvey *Slo.* ***Suburb***, SW district of Slough. SU9679.
Chalvington *E.Suss.* ***Village***, 5m/7km W of Hailsham. **13 J6** TQ5209.
Chambercombe Manor *Devon* ***Historic house***, to SE of Ilfracombe. One of England's oldest manor houses, mentioned in Domesday Book, much altered and restored. Present house dates mainly from 16c and 17c. **6 D1** SS5346.
Champany *Falk.* ***Settlement***, 2m/3km NE of Linlithgow. **75 J3** NT0278.
Chancery *Cere.* ***Hamlet***, 3m/5km S of Aberystwyth. SN5876.
Chandler's Cross *Herts.* ***Hamlet***, 3m/4km W of Watford. **22 D2** TQ0698.
Chandler's Ford *Hants.* ***Suburb***, to NW of Eastleigh. **11 F2** SU4320.
Changue Forest *S.Ayr.* ***Forest/woodland***, in Glentrool Forest Park, 2m/3km E of Barr. **67 H4** NX3193.
Changue Hill *E.Ayr.* ***Hill***, 2m/3km S of Darvel. Height 977 feet or 298 metres. **74 D7** NS5635.
Channel's End *Beds.* ***Settlement***, 6m/10km NE of Bedford. TL1156.
Channerwick *Shet.* ***Settlement***, at head of Channer Wick inlet on Mainland, 1km SW of Hoswick. **109 D10** HU4023.
Chanonry Point *High.* ***Coastal feature***, headland with lighthouse in Ross and Cromarty district at entrance to Inner Moray Firth or Inverness Firth opposite Fort George. **96 E6** NH7455.
Chantry *Som.* ***Village***, 4m/6km W of Frome. **20 A7** ST7147.
Chantry *Suff.* ***Suburb***, SW district of Ipswich. **35 F4** TM1443.
Chapel *Cumb.* ***Hamlet***, just S of Bassenthwaite. NY2231.
Chapel *Fife* ***Suburb***, NW district of Kirkcaldy. **76 A1** NT2593.
Chapel Allerton *Som.* ***Village***, 2m/4km NW of Wedmore. **19 H6** ST4050.
Chapel Allerton *W.Yorks.* ***Suburb***, 2m/3km N of Leeds city centre. **57 J6** SE3037.
Chapel Amble *Cornw.* ***Village***, 2m/3km N of Wadebridge. **3 G1** SW9975.
Chapel Brampton *Northants.* ***Village***, 4m/7km NW of Northampton. **31 J2** SP7266.
Chapel Chorlton *Staffs.* ***Village***, 6m/10km NW of Stone. **40 A2** SJ8137.
Chapel Cleeve *Som.* ***Hamlet***, just S of Blue Anchor, 2m/4km W of Watchet. ST0342.
Chapel Cross *E.Suss.* ***Settlement***, adjoining to W of Punnett's Town, 2m/4km E of Heathfield. **13 K4** TQ6120.
Chapel-en-le-Frith *Derbys.* Population: 8715. ***Small town***, market town with medieval chapel, 5m/8km N of Buxton. **50 C4** SK0580.
Chapel End *Beds.* ***Locality***, E end of Wilshamstead, 4m/7km SE of Bedford. TL0743.
Chapel End *Beds.* ***Settlement***, NE end of Houghton Conquest, 3m/4km NE of Ampthill. TL0541.
Chapel End *Beds.* ***Settlement***, E end of Cardington, 3m/5km SE of Bedford. TL0948.
Chapel End *Beds.* ***Settlement***, S end of Colmworth, 3m/5km NE of Bedford. TL1058.
Chapel End *Cambs.* ***Hamlet***, S end of Great Gidding, 3m/5km W of Sawtry. TL1182.
Chapel End *Ches.* ***Settlement***, 1m/2km E of Audlem. SJ6743.
Chapel End *Northants.* ***Hamlet***, E end of Lutton, 3m/5km SW of Stilton. TL1187.
Chapel End *Warks.* ***Locality***, adjoining to S of Hartshill, 3m/4km W of Nuneaton. **41 F6** SP3293.
Chapel Fell *Dur.* ***Open space***, moorland to S of St. John's Chapel. **61 K3** NY8735.
Chapel Field *Gt.Man.* ***Suburb***, 1m/2km SE of Radcliffe. SD7906.
Chapel Field *Norf.* ***Locality***, 1km SW of Stalham. TG3624.
Chapel Fields *W.Mid.* ***Suburb***, 1m/2km W of Coventry city centre. **30 E1** SP3178.
Chapel Finian *D. & G.* ***Historic/prehistoric site***, traces of 10c-11c chapel (Historic Scotland) on E shore of Luce Bay, 5m/8km NW of Port William. **64 C6** NX2748.
Chapel Green *Northants.* ***Locality***, on E edge of Silverstone motor racing circuit, 4m/7km S of Towcester. SP6842.
Chapel Green *Warks.* ***Settlement***, 6m/10km NW of Coventry. SP2685.
Chapel Green *Warks.* ***Settlement***, adjoining to S of Napton on the Hill, 3m/5km SE of Southam. SP4660.
Chapel Haddlesey *N.Yorks.* ***Village***, 4m/7km SW of Selby. **58 B7** SE5826.
Chapel Hill *Aber.* ***Settlement***, near E coast, 2m/3km E of Cruden Bay. **91 J1** NK0635.
Chapel Hill *Lincs.* ***Village***, 3m/5km E of Billinghay. **53 F7** TF2054.
Chapel Hill *Mon.* ***Village***, 4m/6km N of Chepstow. **19 J1** SO5300.
Chapel Hill *N.Yorks.* ***Hamlet***, 2m/3km NE of Harewood, on N side of River Wharfe. SE3446.
Chapel Hill *N.Yorks.* ***Settlement***, 3m/5km NE of Askern. SE5818.
Chapel House *Lancs.* ***Suburb***, in NW part of Skelmersdale. SD4706.
Chapel Island *Cumb.* ***Island***, small island in River Leven estuary, 1m/2km SE of Hammerside Point. Ruin of chapel. SD3275.
Chapel Knapp *Wilts.* ***Hamlet***, adjoining to S of Gastard, 4m/6km SW of Chippenham. ST8868.
Chapel Lawn *Shrop.* ***Hamlet***, 3m/5km S of Clun. **28 C1** SO3176.
Chapel-le-Dale *N.Yorks.* ***Hamlet***, 4m/7km NE of Ingleton. **56 C2** SD7477.
Chapel Leigh *Som.* ***Hamlet***, 2m/4km N of Milverton. ST1229.
Chapel Milton *Derbys.* ***Hamlet***, 1km N of Chapel-en-le-Frith. SK0581.
Chapel Ness *Fife* ***Coastal feature***, headland at W end of bay enclosing Elie harbour. **76 C1** NT4899.
Chapel of Garioch *Aber.* ***Village***, 4m/6km NW of Inverurie. Maiden Stone (Historic Scotland) 1m/2km NW, 9c inscribed Celtic cross. **91 F2** NJ7124.
Chapel Point *Cornw.* ***Coastal feature***, headland at S end of Mevagissey Bay, 1m/2km SE of Mevagissey. **4 A6** SX0243.
Chapel Point *Pembs.* ***Coastal feature***, headland with lighthouse, at SE end of Caldey Island. **16 E5** SS1495.
Chapel Rossan *D. & G.* ***Settlement***, on W coast of Luce Bay, adjoining to S of Ardwell. **64 B6** NX1145.
Chapel Row *Essex* ***Hamlet***, adjoining to NW of Woodham Ferrers, 7m/11km SE of Chelmsford. TL7900.
Chapel Row *W.Berks.* ***Village***, 6m/10km E of Newbury. **21 J5** SU5669.
Chapel St. Leonards *Lincs.* Population: 2884. ***Village***, coastal village, 6m/9km N of Skegness. **53 J5** TF5572.
Chapel Stile *Cumb.* ***Village***, 4m/6km W of Ambleside. **60 E6** NY3205.
Chapel Town *Cornw.* ***Hamlet***, 6m/9km SE of Newquay. **3 F3** SW8855.
Chapelbank *P. & K.* ***Hamlet***, on N bank of River Earn, 3m/4km NW of Dunning. **82 B6** NO0017.
Chapelburn Roman Fort *Cumb.* ***Historic/prehistoric site***, fort on S side of River Irthing at Chapelburn, 4m/7km NW of Brampton. **70 A7** NY5964.
Chapeldonan *S.Ayr.* ***Settlement***, 2m/3km NE of Girvan. **67 F3** NS1900.
Chapelend Way *Essex* ***Village***, 4m/7km NE of Finchingfield. TL7038.
Chapelfell Top *Dur.* ***Mountain***, highest point on Chapel Fell, 2m/3km S of St. John's Chapel. Height 2306 feet or 703 metres. **61 K3** NY8734.
Chapelgate *Lincs.* ***Hamlet***, adjoining to E of Gedney. **43 H3** TF4124.
Chapelhall *N.Lan.* Population: 4405. ***Village***, 2m/3km SE of Airdrie. **75 F4** NS7862.
Chapelhill *High.* ***Settlement***, 3m/4km SW of Balintore. **97 F4** NH8273.
Chapelhill *P. & K.* ***Hamlet***, 3m/5km W of Errol. **82 D5** NO2021.
Chapelhill *P. & K.* ***Settlement***, 3m/4km N of Methven. **82 B4** NO0030.
Chapelhouse *Cumb.* ***Locality***, 2m/4km NW of Carlisle. NY3759.
Chapelknowe *D. & G.* ***Village***, 3m/5km NE of Kirkpatrick-Fleming. **69 J6** NY3173.
Chapels *Cumb.* ***Hamlet***, 1m/2km NE of Kirkby-in-Furness. SD2383.
Chapelthorpe *W.Yorks.* ***Village***, 1km E of Crigglestone. SE3215.
Chapelton *Aber.* ***Settlement***, 3m/5km SW of Stonehaven. **91 G6** NO8582.
Chapelton *Angus* ***Hamlet***, 3m/4km SE of Friockheim. **83 H3** NO6247.
Chapelton *Devon* ***Hamlet***, 5m/8km S of Barnstaple, in River Taw valley. SS5726.
Chapelton *High.* ***Locality***, in Badenoch and Strathspey district, 2m/3km W of Boat of Garten. NH9119.
Chapelton *S.Lan.* ***Village***, 3m/5km NW of Strathaven. **74 E6** NS6848.
Chapeltown *B'burn.* ***Village***, 4m/7km N of Bolton. **49 G1** SD7315.
Chapeltown *Cumb.* ***Settlement***, 1km S of Easton and 4m/6km NE of Longtown. **69 K6** NY4371.
Chapeltown *Moray* ***Settlement***, 5m/8km E of Tomintoul. **89 K2** NJ2421.
Chapeltown *S.Yorks.* Population: 23,479. ***Town***, 5m/9km N of Sheffield. **51 F3** SK3596.
Chapman Sands *Essex* ***Coastal feature***, sandbank in River Thames estuary, to E of Canvey Island. **24 E3** TQ8383.
Chapmans Well *Devon* ***Hamlet***, 6m/9km N of Launceston. **6 B6** SX3593.
Chapmanslade *Wilts.* ***Village***, 4m/6km SW of Westbury. **20 B7** ST8247.
Chapmore End *Herts.* ***Hamlet***, 3m/4km N of Hertford. **33 G7** TL3216.
Chappel *Essex* ***Village***, 5m/7km E of Halstead. **34 C6** TL8928.
Char *Dorset* ***River***, flowing through Marshwood Vale, and into Lyme Bay at Charmouth. **8 D5** SY3693.
Charaton *Cornw.* ***Settlement***, 4m/6km W of Callington. SX3069.
Chard *Som.* Population: 10,770. ***Town***, in elevated position, 12m/19km SE of Taunton. Museum in 16c house. Forde Abbey to S. **8 C4** ST3208.
Chard Junction *Som.* ***Hamlet***, on border with Dorset, 3m/4km SE of Chard, where a branch line (now dismantled) ran to Chard from main line railway. **8 C4** ST3304.
Chardleigh Green *Som.* ***Hamlet***, 1m/2km N of Chard. ST3110.
Chardstock *Devon* ***Village***, 3m/5km S of Chard. **8 C4** ST3104.
Charfield *S.Glos.* Population: 2231. ***Village***, 3m/4km W of Wotton-under-Edge. **20 A2** ST7292.
Charford *Worcs.* ***Suburb***, SW district of Bromsgrove. SO9569.
Charing *Kent* ***Small town***, on hillside below Pilgrims' Way 6m/9km NW of Ashford. Scant remains of former Archbishop's Palace. **14 E3** TQ9549.
Charing Cross *Dorset* ***Hamlet***, adjoining Alderholt and 2m/4km SW of Fordingbridge. SU1112.
Charing Heath *Kent* ***Settlement***, 2m/3km W of Charing. **14 E3** TQ9249.
Charingworth *Glos.* ***Hamlet***, 3m/5km E of Chipping Campden. **30 C4** SP2039.
Charlbury *Oxon.* Population: 2694. ***Small town***, parish and small town, 6m/9km SE of Chipping Norton. Former weaving town. **30 E7** SP3519.
Charlcombe *B. & N.E.Som.* ***Village***, 2m/3km N of Bath. **20 A5** ST7567.
Charlcutt *Wilts.* ***Hamlet***, 3m/5km N of Calne. **20 C4** ST9875.
Charlecote *Warks.* ***Village***, 4m/7km E of Stratford-upon-Avon. **30 D3** SP2656.
Charlecote Park *Warks.* ***Historic house***, 1m/2km W of Wellesbourne. Home of Lucy family since 1247; present house (National Trust) built in 16c. Visited by Queen Elizabeth I. Deer park landscaped by 'Capability' Brown. Shakespeare reputedly poached deer here. **30 D3** SP2556.
Charles *Devon* ***Hamlet***, 5m/8km N of South Molton. **6 E2** SS6832.
Charles Tye *Suff.* ***Hamlet***, 4m/7km SW of Stowmarket. **34 E3** TM0252.
Charlesfield *Sc.Bord.* ***Settlement***, 1m/2km SE of Newtown St. Boswells. **70 A1** NT5829.
Charleshill *Surr.* ***Settlement***, 4m/6km SE of Farnham. **22 B7** SU8944.

Charleston *Angus* ***Village***, 1km S of Glamis. **82 E3** NO3845.
Charleston *Renf.* ***Suburb***, 1m/2km S of Paisley town centre. NS4862.
Charleston Farmhouse *E.Suss.* ***Historic house***, 1m/2km W of Selmeston and 6m/10km E of Lewes. Home of Vanessa Bell and focal point for Bloomsbury set who decorated house and garden with their art and creativity. **13 H6** TQ4906.
Charlestown *Aberdeen* ***Hamlet***, 4m/6km S of Aberdeen. **91 H4** NJ9300.
Charlestown *Aber.* ***Locality***, on NE coast, at N end of St. Combs. **99 J4** NK0563.
Charlestown *Cornw.* ***Village***, adjoining to SE of St. Austell. China clay port with wharves still used for loading clay into vessels. Location for TV series of Poldark and Onedin Line. Shipwreck museum with collection of photographs, relics and tableaux of historical scenes. **4 A5** SX0351.
Charlestown *Derbys.* ***Hamlet***, adjoining to S of Glossop. SK0392.
Charlestown *Dorset* ***Suburb***, 2m/3km W of Weymouth. **9 F7** SY6579.
Charlestown *Fife* ***Village***, small port on N side of Firth of Forth, 3m/5km SW of Dunfermline. **75 J2** NT0683.
Charlestown *Gt.Man.* ***Suburb***, 1m/2km NW of Salford city centre. SD8100.
Charlestown *Gt.Man.* ***Suburb***, 4m/6km NE of Manchester city centre. SD8703.
Charlestown *High.* ***Hamlet***, in Ross and Cromarty district, on N shore of Beauly Firth, 1m/2km W of North Kessock. **96 D7** NH6448.
Charlestown *High.* ***Village***, at head of Gair Loch, W coast of Ross and Cromarty district, 1m/2km S of Gairloch village. **94 E4** NG8074.
Charlestown *Lincs.* ***Hamlet***, adjoining to N of Ancaster. SK9844.
Charlestown *W.Yorks.* ***Suburb***, S district of Baildon. SE1538.
Charlestown *W.Yorks.* ***Village***, on River Calder, 1m/2km W of Hebden Bridge. SD9726.
Charlestown of Aberlour (Also known as Aberlour.) *Moray* ***Small town***, on S bank of River Spey, 4m/6km S of Rothes. Built in 19c by Charles Grant from whom name was taken. **97 K7** NJ2643.
Charlesworth *Derbys.* Population: 2140. ***Village***, 2m/3km W of Glossop. **50 C3** SK0092.
Charlinch (Also spelled Charlynch.) *Som.* ***Hamlet***, 4m/6km W of Bridgwater. **8 B1** ST2337.
Charlotteville *Surr.* ***Suburb***, SE district of Guildford. TQ0049.
Charlton *Gt.Lon.* ***Suburb***, in borough of Greenwich, 7m/12km E of Charing Cross. **23 H4** TQ4177.
Charlton *Hants.* ***Suburb***, in NW part of Andover. **21 G7** SU3547.
Charlton *Herts.* ***Suburb***, in SW part of Hitchin. **32 E6** TL1728.
Charlton *Northants.* ***Village***, 4m/6km W of Brackley. **31 G5** SP5236.
Charlton *Northumb.* ***Settlement***, on N side of River North Tyne, 3m/4km NW of Bellingham. **70 D5** NY8084.
Charlton *Oxon.* ***Suburb***, E district of Wantage. **21 H3** SU4088.
Charlton *R. & C.* ***Hamlet***, 2m/4km E of Guisborough. NZ6415.
Charlton *Som.* ***Hamlet***, astride Bridgwater and Taunton Canal, 4m/7km E of Taunton. ST2926.
Charlton *Som.* ***Hamlet***, 2m/3km S of Radstock. **19 K6** ST6852.
Charlton *Som.* ***Suburb***, E district of Shepton Mallet. ST6343.
Charlton *Surr.* ***Suburb***, on E edge of Queen Mary Reservoir, 2m/3km W of Sunbury. TQ0869.
Charlton *Tel. & W.* ***Hamlet***, 4m/6km W of Wellington. Mound of medieval castle. SJ5911.
Charlton *W.Suss.* ***Village***, 1km E of Singleton. **12 B5** SU8812.
Charlton *Wilts.* ***Hamlet***, 3m/4km SE of Shaftesbury. **9 J2** ST9021.
Charlton *Wilts.* ***Village***, 2m/3km NE of Malmesbury. **20 C3** ST9688.
Charlton *Wilts.* ***Village***, 1m/2km NW of Upavon. **20 E6** SU1156.
Charlton *Worcs.* ***Hamlet***, 1m/2km E of Stourport-on-Severn. SO8371.
Charlton *Worcs.* ***Village***, 2m/3km NW of Evesham. **30 B4** SP0145.
Charlton Abbots *Glos.* ***Hamlet***, 3m/4km S of Winchcombe. **30 B6** SP0324.
Charlton Adam *Som.* ***Village***, 4m/7km NE of Ilchester. **8 E2** ST5328.
Charlton-All-Saints *Wilts.* ***Village***, in River Avon valley, 5m/7km S of Salisbury. **10 C2** SU1723.
Charlton Down *Dorset* ***Open space***, hillslope rising to 407 feet or 124 metres, 4m/6km SW of Blandford Forum. **9 H4** ST8700.
Charlton Down *Wilts.* ***Hill***, 3m/5km W of East Chisenbury. Height 535 feet or 163 metres. **20 D6** SU0852.
Charlton Hill *Shrop.* ***Settlement***, and hill, 3m/4km N of Cressage. SJ5807.
Charlton Horethorne *Som.* ***Village***, 4m/7km SW of Wincanton. **9 F2** ST6623.
Charlton Kings *Glos.* Population: 11,332. ***Village***, adjoining to E of Cheltenham. **29 J6** SO9620.
Charlton Mackrell *Som.* ***Village***, 3m/5km E of Somerton. **8 E2** ST5228.
Charlton Marshall *Dorset* ***Village***, on River Stour, 2m/3km SE of Blandford Forum. **9 H4** ST8806.
Charlton Musgrove *Som.* ***Village***, 1m/2km NE of Wincanton. **9 G2** ST7229.
Charlton-on-Otmoor *Oxon.* ***Village***, 4m/7km S of Bicester. **31 G7** SP5615.
Charlton on the Hill *Dorset* ***Hamlet***, adjoining Charlton Marshall, 2m/3km SE of Blandford Forum. ST8904.
Charlton Park *Wilts.* ***Historic house***, to NW of Charlton, 2m/3km NE of Malmesbury. Built for Earls of Suffolk at beginning of 17c and altered by Matthew Brettingham the Younger in 18c. **20 C3** ST9589.
Charlwood *E.Suss.* ***Locality***, 2m/3km W of Forest Row. TQ3934.
Charlwood *Surr.* ***Village***, on W side of London (Gatwick) Airport, 3m/5km NW of Crawley. **23 F7** TQ2441.
Charlynch *Som.* *Alternative spelling of Charlinch, qv.*
Charminster *Bourne.* ***Suburb***, 3m/4km NE of Bournemouth town centre. SZ1094.
Charminster *Dorset* Population: 1615. ***Village***, 1m/2km N of Dorchester. **9 F5** SY6892.
Charmouth *Dorset* ***Small town***, resort on steep hill on coast, 2m/3km NE of Lyme Regis. **8 C5** SY3693.
Charn a' Ghille Chear ***Mountain***, one of Hills of Cromdale on border of Highland and Moray, 7m/11km E of Grantown-on-Spey. Height 2329 feet or 710 metres. **89 J2** NJ1329.
Charndon *Bucks.* ***Village***, 6m/9km E of Bicester. **31 H6** SP6724.
Charney Bassett *Oxon.* ***Village***, 4m/7km N of Wantage. **21 G2** SU3894.
Charnock Green *Lancs.* ***Hamlet***, 2m/3km W of Chorley. SD5516.
Charnock Richard *Lancs.* ***Village***, 2m/4km SW of Chorley. **48 E1** SD5515.
Charnwood Forest *Leics.* ***Large natural feature***, elevated area, former hunting ground, SW of Loughborough, composed of pre-Cambrian rocks which obtrude above ground at various points. Quarrying is carried on. The area attains height of 916 feet or 279 metres at Bardon Hill, 2m/4km E of Coalville. **41 G4** SK4914.
Charsfield *Suff.* ***Village***, 3m/5km W of Wickham Market. **35 G3** TM2556.
Chart Corner *Kent* ***Hamlet***, 4m/7km SE of Maidstone. **14 C3** TQ7950.
Chart Sutton *Kent* ***Village***, 4m/6km NW of Headcorn. Roman building to N. **14 D3** TQ8049.
Charter Alley *Hants.* ***Hamlet***, 5m/7km NW of Basingstoke. **21 K6** SU5957.
Charterhouse *Som.* ***Hamlet***, on Mendip Hills, 3m/5km NE of Cheddar. **19 H6** ST5055.
Charterville Allotments *Oxon.* ***Locality***, 3m/5km W of Witney. **30 E7** SP3110.
Chartham *Kent* Population: 2464. ***Village***, on Great Stour River, 3m/5km SW of Canterbury. **15 G2** TR1055.
Chartham Hatch *Kent* ***Village***, 3m/5km W of Canterbury. **15 F2** TR1056.
Chartridge *Bucks.* ***Village***, 2m/4km NW of Chesham. **22 C1** SP9303.
Chartway Street *Kent* ***Locality***, 4m/6km N of Headcorn. TQ8350.
Chartwell *Kent* ***Historic house***, National Trust property, formerly the home of Sir Winston Churchill, with grounds 2m/3km S of Westerham. **23 H6** TQ4551.
Charvil *W'ham* ***Village***, 1m/2km W of Twyford. SU7775.
Charwelton *Northants.* ***Village***, 5m/8km SW of Daventry. **31 G3** SP5356.
Charwelton Bridge *Northants.* ***Bridge***, early medieval packhorse bridge over River Cherwell at Charwelton. SP5355.
Chase Cross *Gt.Lon.* ***Suburb***, N district of Romford, in borough of Havering. TQ5191.
Chase End Street *Worcs.* ***Settlement***, 4m/6km SE of Ledbury, below E slope of Chase End Hill, at S end of Malvern Hills. **29 G5** SO7635.
Chase Side *Gt.Lon.* ***Suburb***, in borough of Enfield, to N of Enfield town centre, 11m/17km N of Charing Cross. TQ3297.
Chase Terrace *Staffs.* ***Locality***, 3m/4km N of Brownhills. **40 C4** SK0409.
Chasetown *Staffs.* ***Suburb***, 2m/3km N of Brownhills. **40 C5** SK0408.
Chasewater *W.Mid.* ***Lake/loch***, 1m/2km NW of Brownhills. **40 C5** SK0307.
Chasewater Light Railway *W.Mid.* ***Other feature of interest***, tourist railway which runs for 1km along W and N sides of Chasewater from a terminus 1m/2km NW of Brownhills. **40 C5** SK0307.
Chastleton *Oxon.* ***Village***, 4m/7km NW of Chipping Norton. Early 17c Cotswold manor house. **30 D6** SP2429.
Chastleton House *Oxon.* ***Historic house***, 17c house (National Trust) in Chastleton, 4m/6km SE of Moreton-in-Marsh, displaying collections of rare objects: Elizabethan and Jacobean gardens and topiary. **30 D6** SP2429.
Chasty *Devon* ***Hamlet***, just S of Holsworthy. **6 B5** SS3402.
Chat Hill *W.Yorks.* ***Locality***, adjoins to SE of Thornton, 3m/5km W of Bradford city centre. SE1132.
Chat Moss *Gt.Man.* ***Marsh/bog***, extensive area of peat bog, now largely reclaimed, to W of Eccles. Traversed by Liverpool and Manchester railway (George Stephenson, 1829). **49 F3** SJ7097.
Chatburn *Lancs.* ***Village***, 2m/3km NE of Clitheroe. Extensive quarries between here and Clitheroe. **56 C5** SD7644.
Chatcull *Staffs.* ***Hamlet***, 1m/2km W of Standon. **39 G2** SJ7934.
Chatelherault Country Park *S.Lan.* ***Leisure/recreation***, 500 acre country park on banks of Avon Water, 2m/3km SE of Hamilton. Encompasses Chatelherault Hunting Lodge. **75 F5** NS7353.
Chater ***River***, rising S of Whatborough Hill, E of Tilton and flowing E into River Welland 2m/3km W of Stamford. **42 B5** TF0005.
Chatham *Caerp.* ***Locality***, adjoining to E of Machen. ST2188.
Chatham *Med.* Population: 71,691. ***Town***, former ship-building town, on River Medway between Rochester and Gillingham, 28m/45km E of London. Naval and military base, and tourist centre. Nelson's Victory launched here. Childhood home of Charles Dickens. **24 D5** TQ7567.
Chatham Green *Essex* ***Hamlet***, 5m/8km N of Chelmsford town centre. TL7115.
Chatham Historic Dockyard and Lifeboat Collection *Med.* ***Other feature of interest***, 1m/2km N of Chatham, with early 18c buildings and a ropery exhibition, including longest room in Britain, quarter of a mile long. **24 D5** TQ7569.
Chathill *Northumb.* ***Hamlet***, 4m/6km SW of Seahouses. **71 G1** NU1826.
Chatsworth House *Derbys.* ***Historic house***, 17c-19c house, seat of Duke of Devonshire, in River Derwent valley, 7m/12km W of Chesterfield. Large formal grounds. **50 E5** SK2670.
Chattenden *Med.* ***Village***, 2m/3km N of Rochester. **24 D4** TQ7571.
Chatter End *Essex* ***Settlement***, 3m/4km N of Bishop's Stortford. TL4725.
Chatteris *Cambs.* Population: 7261. ***Small town***, 7m/11km S of March. **43 G7** TL3985.
Chatteris Fen *Cambs.* ***Open space***, fenland, 3m/5km S of Chatteris. **33 G1** TL3879.
Chatterley *Staffs.* ***Locality***, 3m/5km N of Newcastle-under-Lyme. SJ8451.
Chattern Hill *Surr.* ***Suburb***, adjoining to E of Ashford, 3m/5km E of Staines. TQ0871.
Chattisham *Suff.* ***Village***, 4m/7km E of Hadleigh. **34 E4** TM0942.
Chattle Hill *Warks.* ***Suburb***, 1m/2km N of Coleshill. SP1990.
Chatto *Sc.Bord.* ***Settlement***, on Kale Water, 2m/3km SW of Hownam. **70 C2** NT7618.
Chatton *Northumb.* ***Village***, 4m/6km E of Wooler. **71 F1** NU0528.
Chaul End *Beds.* ***Settlement***, 2m/3km W of Luton town centre. TL0521.
Chaulden *Herts.* ***Suburb***, 1m/2km W of Hemel Hempstead town centre. TL0306.
Chavenage *Glos.* ***Historic house***, 16c Elizabethan manor house associated with Oliver Cromwell, 2m/3km NW of Tetbury. **20 B2** ST8795.
Chavey Down *Brack.F.* ***Village***, 1m/2km E of Bracknell. SU8969.
Chawleigh *Devon* ***Village***, 2m/3km SE of Chulmleigh. **7 F4** SS6814.
Chawley *Oxon.* ***Locality***, 3m/5km W of Oxford. **21 H1** SP4704.
Chawston *Beds.* ***Settlement***, 3m/5km SW of St. Neots. **32 E3** TL1556.
Chawton *Hants.* ***Village***, 1m/2km SW of Alton. Jane Austen's house, now a museum situated in village. **11 J1** SU7037.
Chazey Heath *Oxon.* ***Hamlet***, 3m/5km NW of Reading. SU6977.
Cheadle *Gt.Man.* Population: 29,229. ***Town***, 3m/4km W of Stockport. 16c church contains Saxon cross. **49 H4** SJ8588.
Cheadle *Staffs.* Population: 10,833. ***Town***, old market town, 8m/13km E of Stoke-on-Trent. Impressive 19c church, and some interesting buildings. **40 C1** SK0043.
Cheadle Heath *Gt.Man.* ***Suburb***, 1m/2km NE of Cheadle. SJ8789.
Cheadle Hulme *Gt.Man.* ***Suburb***, 1m/2km S of Cheadle. **49 H4** SJ8786.
Cheam *Gt.Lon.* ***Suburb***, in borough of Sutton, 1m/2km W of Sutton town centre. **23 F5** TQ2463.
Cheapside *W. & M.* ***Hamlet***, on SW edge of Windsor Great Park, 1m/2km E of Ascot. **22 C5** SU9469.
Chearsley *Bucks.* ***Village***, 3m/5km N of Thame. **22 A1** SP7110.
Chebsey *Staffs.* ***Village***, 2m/3km E of Eccleshall. **40 A3** SJ8628.
Checkendon *Oxon.* ***Village***, 4m/7km E of Goring. **21 K3** SU6682.
Checkley *Ches.* ***Hamlet***, 2m/4km N of Woore. **39 G1** SJ7346.
Checkley *Here.* ***Hamlet***, 5m/8km E of Hereford. **28 E5** SO5938.
Checkley *Staffs.* ***Village***, 5m/8km NW of Uttoxeter. **40 C2** SK0237.
Checkley Green *Ches.* ***Settlement***, to SW of Checkley. SJ7245.
Chedburgh *Suff.* ***Village***, 6m/10km SW of Bury St. Edmunds. **34 B3** TL7957.
Cheddar *Som.* Population: 4484. ***Small town***, on S slopes of Mendip Hills, 8m/12km NW of Wells, at foot of Cheddar Gorge. Noted for its caves; name given to cheese made in area. **19 H6** ST4553.
Cheddar Caves *Som.* ***Other feature of interest***, limestone caves to NE of Cheddar at W end of Cheddar Gorge, which includes Gough's Cave, Cox's Cave and The Crystal Quest; also Britain's oldest skeleton. **19 H6** ST4653.
Cheddar Cliffs *Som.* ***Inland physical feature***, limestone cliffs above Cheddar Gorge, to NE of Cheddar. **19 H6** ST4754.
Cheddar Gorge *Som.* ***Inland physical feature***, deep limestone gorge, with large caves much visited by tourists. Cliffs on N side of gorge (National Trust). **19 H6** ST4754.
Cheddar Reservoir *Som.* ***Reservoir***, circular reservoir, 1m/2km W of Cheddar. **19 H6** ST4453.
Cheddington *Bucks.* ***Village***, 4m/6km N of Tring. **32 C7** SP9217.
Cheddleton *Staffs.* Population: 3534. ***Village***, 3m/5km S of Leek. **49 J7** SJ9752.
Cheddleton Heath *Staffs.* ***Hamlet***, 1m/2km NE of Cheddleton. SJ9853.
Cheddon Fitzpaine *Som.* ***Village***, 2m/4km NE of Taunton. **8 B2** ST2427.
Chedglow *Wilts.* ***Hamlet***, 4m/6km N of Malmesbury. **20 C2** ST9493.
Chedgrave *Norf.* ***Village***, adjoining to N of Loddon across River Chet, 7m/11km NW of Beccles. **45 H6** TM3699.

Chedington *Dorset* ***Village***, 4m/6km SE of Crewkerne. **8 D4** ST4805.

Chediston *Suff.* ***Village***, 2m/3km W of Halesworth. **35 H1** TM3577.

Chediston Green *Suff.* ***Hamlet***, 1km NW of Chediston. TM3578.

Chedworth *Glos.* ***Village***, 4m/7km SW of Northleach. **30 B7** SP0511.

Chedworth Roman Villa *Glos.* ***Historic/prehistoric site***, well preserved Roman villa (National Trust), 1m/2km N of Chedworth and 7m/11km SE of Cheltenham. Many walls still standing. **30 B7** SP0513.

Chedworth Woods *Glos.* ***Forest/woodland***, 1km N of Chedworth. **30 B7** SP0513.

Chedzoy *Som.* ***Village***, 3m/5km E of Bridgwater. **8 C1** ST3437.

Cheeklaw *Sc.Bord.* ***Suburb***, at S edge of Duns. **77 F5** NT7852.

Cheesden *Gt.Man.* ***Settlement***, 2m/4km SE of Edenfield. **49 H1** SD8216.

Cheeseman's Green *Kent* ***Settlement***, 3m/4km SE of Ashford. **15 F4** TR0238.

Cheetham *Gt.Man.* ***Suburb***, 1m/2km N of Manchester city centre. SD8400.

Cheetham Hill *Gt.Man.* ***Suburb***, 2m/4km N of Manchester city centre. **49 H2** SD8401.

Cheetwood *Gt.Man.* ***Suburb***, 1m/2km N of Manchester city centre. SD8300.

Cheglinch *Devon* ***Hamlet***, 3m/5km S of Ilfracombe. SS5143.

Cheldon *Devon* ***Hamlet***, 3m/5km E of Chulmleigh. **7 F4** SS7313.

Chelford *Ches.* ***Village***, 6m/10km W of Macclesfield. **49 H5** SJ8174.

Chelker Reservoir *N.Yorks.* ***Reservoir***, 1m/2km NW of Addingham. **57 F4** SE0551.

Chellaston *Derby* ***Suburb***, 4m/7km SE of Derby city centre. **41 F2** SK3730.

Chellington *Beds.* ***Hamlet***, 7m/11km NW of Bedford, adjoining to N of Carlton. SP9555.

Chells *Herts.* ***Suburb***, in NE part of Stevenage. TL2625.

Chelmarsh *Shrop.* ***Village***, 3m/5km S of Bridgnorth. Reservoir to E. **39 G7** SO7287.

Chelmarsh Reservoir *Shrop.* ***Reservoir***, 4m/6km S of Bridgnorth. **39 G7** SO7387.

Chelmer *Essex* ***River***, rising near Thaxted, flowing S to Chelmsford, then E to join River Blackwater at Maldon. **33 K6** TL8507.

Chelmondiston *Suff.* ***Village***, 4m/6km NW of Shotley Gate. **35 G5** TM2037.

Chelmorton *Derbys.* ***Village***, 4m/7km SE of Buxton. **50 D6** SK1170.

Chelmsford *Essex* Population: 97,451. ***Town***, cathedral and county town on River Chelmer, 30m/48km NE of London. Cathedral, previously parish church, has 15c tower. 18c mill with craft workshops. Museum includes history of Essex Regiment. Anglia Polytechnic University. **24 D1** TL7006.

Chelmsford and Essex Museum *Essex* ***Other feature of interest***, 1km S of Chelmsford town centre. Exhibits include natural history displays and a Victorian room. Houses Essex Regiment Museum. **24 D1** TL7005.

Chelmsford Cathedral *Essex* ***Ecclesiastical building***, in Chelmsford town centre. Completed in 1424 but collapsed in 1800 and rebuilt. Interesting flintwork on S porch and large tower with flèche spire. **24 D1** TL7007.

Chelmsley Wood *W.Mid.* ***Suburb***, 7m/12km E of Birmingham. SP1886.

Chelsea *Gt.Lon.* ***Suburb***, SW of central London and contained within royal borough of Kensington and Chelsea. Situated on N bank of River Thames, crossed here by Battersea, Albert and Chelsea Bridges. Royal Chelsea Hospital, by Wren, houses pensioners. Chelsea Flower Show takes place in the grounds. Coldstream Guards based at Chelsea Barracks. TQ2778.

Chelsfield *Gt.Lon.* ***Village***, 2m/3km SE of Orpington. **23 H5** TQ4864.

Chelsham *Surr.* ***Hamlet***, 1m/2km E of Warlingham. **23 G6** TQ3759.

Chelston Heath *Som.* ***Hamlet***, 1m/2km E of Wellington. ST1621.

Chelsworth *Suff.* ***Village***, 4m/7km NW of Hadleigh. **34 D4** TL9848.

Cheltenham *Glos.* Population: 91,301. ***Town***, largest town in The Cotswolds, 8m/12km E of Gloucester. Mainly residential, with many Regency and Victorian buildings. Formerly a spa town, Pittville Pump Room overlooks Pittville Park. Hosts Cheltenham Gold Cup race meeting, Cheltenham International Music Festival and Festival of Literature, among other events. Birthplace of composer Gustav Holst. Shopping and tourist centre, with some light industry. **29 J6** SO9422.

Cheltenham *Mon.* ***Locality***, between Blackrock and Clydach, to E of Bryn-mawr. SO2212.

Cheltenham Racecourse *Glos.* ***Racecourse***, in Prestbury Park, 2m/3km NE of Cheltenham. National Hunt course, with sixteen race days a year, including the three-day Cheltenham National Hunt Festival, when Cheltenham Gold Cup is staged. **29 J6** SO9524.

Chelveston *Northants.* ***Village***, 2m/3km E of Higham Ferrers. **32 C2** SP9969.

Chelvey *N.Som.* ***Hamlet***, 4m/7km SE of Clevedon. **19 H5** ST4668.

Chelwood *B. & N.E.Som.* ***Village***, 4m/7km S of Keynsham. **19 K5** ST6361.

Chelwood Common *E.Suss.* ***Village***, 2m/3km E of Horsted Keynes. TQ4128.

Chelwood Gate *E.Suss.* ***Hamlet***, 3m/5km S of Forest Row. **13 H4** TQ4130.

Chelworth *Wilts.* ***Hamlet***, 5m/8km NE of Malmesbury. **20 C2** ST9794.

Chelworth Lower Green *Wilts.* ***Hamlet***, 1m/2km SW of Cricklade. SU0892.

Chelworth Upper Green *Wilts.* ***Hamlet***, 1m/2km W of Cricklade. SU0892.

Cheney Longville *Shrop.* ***Hamlet***, 2m/3km NW of Craven Arms. **38 D7** SO4284.

Chenies *Bucks.* ***Village***, 4m/6km E of Amersham. Site of Roman villa 1m/2km W beside River Chess. **22 D2** TQ0198.

Chenies Manor *Bucks.* ***Historic house***, in Chenies, 4m/6km E of Amersham. 15c manor house with fortified tower. Home to Earls of Bedford and now MacLeod Matthews. **22 D2** TQ0198.

Chepstow (Cas-gwent). *Mon.* Population: 9461. ***Small town***, near mouth of River Wye, 15m/24km E of Newport. Remains of castle (Cadw) partly Norman but mainly of 14c. Racecourse. **19 J2** ST5393.

Chepstow Castle *Mon.* ***Castle***, ruins overlooking River Wye on NE side of Chepstow. Originating in 11c, one of first stone castles in Britain. Built by Earl of Hereford, William FitzOsbern. Previously known as Bigod's tower. **19 J2** ST5294.

Chepstow Museum *Mon.* ***Other feature of interest***, on E side of Chepstow, exhibiting local history. **19 J2** ST5394.

Chepstow Park Wood *Mon.* ***Forest/woodland***, mixed woodland to N of Itton Common. **19 H2** ST4897.

Chequerbent *Gt.Man.* ***Settlement***, 1m/2km E of Westhoughton. SD6706.

Chequerfield *W.Yorks.* ***Suburb***, 1km SE of Pontefract town centre. SE4621.

Chequers Corner *Norf.* ***Locality***, at crossroads 3m/4km E of Wisbech. TF4908.

Cherhill *Wilts.* ***Village***, 3m/4km E of Calne. **20 D4** SU0370.

Cherhill White Horse *Wilts.* ***Historic/prehistoric site***, 1km SE of Cherhill. Carved into N slope of Cherhill Down by Dr. Christopher Alsop in 1780. **20 D4** SU0469.

Cherington *Glos.* ***Village***, 4m/6km E of Nailsworth. **20 C2** ST9098.

Cherington *Warks.* ***Village***, 3m/5km SE of Shipston on Stour. **30 D5** SP2936.

Cheriton *Devon* ***Hamlet***, 2m/3km SE of Lynton. **7 F1** SS7346.

Cheriton *Hants.* ***Village***, 3m/4km S of New Alresford. 1m/2km NE, site of Civil War battle, 1644. **11 G2** SU5828.

Cheriton *Kent* ***Suburb***, W district of Folkestone. **15 H4** TR2036.

Cheriton (Also known as Stackpole Elidor.) *Pembs.* ***Hamlet***, 3m/4km S of Pembroke. **16 C5** SR9897.

Cheriton *Swan.* ***Village***, near W end of Gower peninsula, 2m/4km S of Whitford Point and 13m/20km W of Swansea. **17 H5** SS4593.

Cheriton Bishop *Devon* ***Village***, 6m/10km SW of Crediton. **7 F6** SX7793.

Cheriton Cross *Devon* ***Hamlet***, adjoining Cheriton Bishop, 6m/10km SW of Crediton. **7 F6** SX7793.

Cheriton Fitzpaine *Devon* ***Village***, 4m/7km NE of Crediton. **7 G5** SS8606.

Cherrington *Tel. & W.* ***Village***, 5m/8km W of Newport. **39 F4** SJ6619.

Cherry Burton *E.Riding* ***Village***, 3m/5km NW of Beverley. **59 F5** SE9842.

Cherry Cobb Sands *E.Riding* ***Coastal feature***, sandbank to S of Foulholme Sands in River Humber. **59 J7** TA2020.

Cherry Green *Essex* ***Hamlet***, 3m/4km SW of Thaxted. TL5729.

Cherry Hinton *Cambs.* ***Suburb***, SE district of Cambridge. **33 H3** TL4856.

Cherry Orchard *Worcs.* ***Suburb***, S district of Worcester. SO8553.

Cherry Tree *B'burn.* ***Suburb***, 2m/3km SW of Blackburn. SD6525.

Cherry Tree *Gt.Man.* ***Suburb***, 1m/2km E of Romiley. SJ9590.

Cherry Trees *Herts.* ***Locality***, 2m/3km E of Harpenden. TL1614.

Cherry Willingham *Lincs.* Population: 1265. ***Village***, 4m/6km E of Lincoln. **52 D5** TF0372.

Chertsey *Surr.* Population: 10,016. ***Town***, on right bank of River Thames 3m/5km S of Staines. Seven-arched 18c bridge spans river. Scant remains of 7c abbey. **22 D5** TQ0466.

Cherwell ***River***, rising N of Woodford Halse and flowing S through Banbury into River Thames at Oxford. **31 G3** SP5105.

Cheselbourne *Dorset* ***Village***, 4m/6km N of Puddletown. **9 G5** SY7699.

Chesham *Bucks.* Population: 20,290. ***Town***, London commuter town on S side of Chiltern Hills, 25m/40km NW of London. **22 C1** SP9601.

Chesham *Gt.Man.* ***Suburb***, 1m/2km N of Bury town centre. SD8012.

Chesham Bois *Bucks.* ***Suburb***, between Chesham and Amersham. **22 C2** SU9699.

Cheshunt *Herts.* Population: 51,998. ***Town***, in River Lea Valley 14m/22km N of London. Fruit and vegetables grown under glass. **23 G1** TL3502.

Cheshunt Field *Essex* ***Locality***, 3m/4km SW of Colchester, containing sites of a Roman temple and a Roman theatre. TL9622.

Chesil Bank *Dorset* *Alternative name for Chesil Beach, qv.*

Chesil Beach (Also known as Chesil Bank.) *Dorset* ***Coastal feature***, shingle bank stretching 18m/29km from Abbotsbury to Isle of Portland. Pebbles decrease in size from E to W. **8 E6** SY5882.

Cheslyn Hay *Staffs.* ***Locality***, 2m/3km S of Cannock. **40 B5** SJ9707.

Chess ***River***, rising at Chesham and flowing SE into River Colne to E of Rickmansworth. **22 D2** TQ0694.

Chessetts Wood *Warks.* ***Settlement***, 3m/4km E of Hockley Heath. SP1873.

Chessington *Gt.Lon.* ***Suburb***, in borough of Kingston upon Thames, 4m/6km S of Kingston upon Thames town centre. Chessington World of Adventures lies to S. **22 E5** TQ1863.

Chessington World of Adventures *Gt.Lon.* ***Leisure/recreation***, theme park featuring fairground rides and housing endangered animals, 4m/6km N of Leatherhead. **22 E5** TQ1762.

Chestall *Staffs.* ***Hamlet***, to SE of Cannock Chase, 3m/5km S of Rugeley. SK0512.

Chester *Ches.* Population: 80,110. ***City***, county town and cathedral city on River Dee, 34m/54km SW of Manchester and 15m/24km SE of Birkenhead. Commercial, financial and tourist centre built on Roman town of Deva. Includes biggest Roman amphitheatre in Britain (English Heritage) and well preserved medieval walls (English Heritage). Castle, now county hall, includes 12c Agricola Tower (English Heritage). Cathedral with remains of original Norman abbey. Famed for Tudor timber-framed buildings which include Chester Rows, two-tier galleried shops and Bishop Lloyd's House, with ornate 16c carved façade. Eastgate clock built to commemorate Queen Victoria's diamond jubilee in 1897. Racecourse 1m/2km SW of city centre; zoo 3m/4km N of city centre. **48 D6** SJ4066.

Chester Castle *Ches.* ***Castle***, motte built by William the Conqueror in 11c in Chester city centre; Edward I rebuilt gatehouse and domestic buildings. 12c Agricola Tower (English Heritage) includes vaulted chapel. Castle replaced by neo-classical buildings 1793-1820 and now serves as County Hall and Assize Court. **48 D6** SJ4065.

Chester Cathedral *Ches.* ***Ecclesiastical building***, built of red sandstone in Chester city centre and containing most building styles from Norman foundation up to 19c. Remains of original Norman abbey church built in 1092 are found on N side. Particularly noted for medieval choir stalls. **48 D6** SJ4066.

Chester-le-Street *Dur.* Population: 35,123. ***Town***, on site of Roman military station of Concangium, beside River Wear, 6m/9km N of Durham. Medieval parish church contains Ankers House Museum. Nearby 14c Lumley Castle, is now a hotel. **62 D1** NZ2751.

Chester Moor *Dur.* ***Village***, 1m/2km S of Chester-le-Street. NZ2649.

Chester Zoo *Ches.* ***Leisure/recreation***, set in 100 acres, 3m/4km N of Chester city centre. Second largest zoo in country. Conservation projects are a priority and zoo houses many endangered species. **48 D5** SJ4170.

Chesterblade *Som.* ***Village***, 3m/5km SE of Shepton Mallet. **19 K7** ST6641.

Chesterfield *Derbys.* Population: 71,945. ***Town***, market and industrial town, 10m/16km S of Sheffield. Church has famous twisted spire. Former 16c inn now houses tourist information centre. Tapton House was home to George Stephenson. **51 F5** SK3871.

Chesterfield *Staffs.* ***Hamlet***, 3m/5km E of Brownhills. **40 D5** SK1005.

Chesterfield Canal ***Canal***, formerly linking Chesterfield with River Trent at West Stockwith. Now navigable only from West Stockwith to Worksop. SK7894.

Chesterhill *Midloth.* ***Village***, 3m/5km SE of Dalkeith. NT3765.

Chesterholm *Northumb.* ***Locality***, on site of Roman fort of Vindolanda (English Heritage), 1m/2km NW of Bardon Mill. NY7766.

Chesterhope *Northumb.* ***Locality***, 4m/6km E of Bellingham. NY8985.

Chesters *E.Loth.* ***Historic/prehistoric site***, earthworks of ancient fort (Historic Scotland), 1km S of Drem. Similar site of same name 3m/5km S of Dunbar. **76 D3** NT5078.

Chesters *Sc.Bord.* ***Settlement***, 2m/3km SW of Ancrum. **70 B1** NT6022.

Chesters *Sc.Bord.* ***Village***, 5m/9km NW of Carter Bar. **70 B2** NT6210.

Chesters Roman Fort *Northumb.* ***Historic/prehistoric site***, remains (English Heritage) of Roman cavalry fort of Cilurnum on Hadrian's Wall, 1km W of Chollerford and 2m/3km NE of Fourstones. To E, remains of abutments where Chesters Bridge (English Heritage) crossed River North Tyne. **70 E6** NY9170.

Chesterton *Cambs.* ***Suburb***, NE district of Cambridge. **33 H3** TL4660.

Chesterton *Cambs.* ***Village***, 5m/7km SW of Peterborough. **42 E6** TL1295.

Chesterton *Oxon.* ***Village***, 2m/3km W of Bicester. **31 G6** SP5621.

Chesterton *Shrop.* ***Hamlet***, 5m/8km NE of Bridgnorth. **39 G6** SO7897.

Chesterton *Staffs.* ***Locality***, 3m/4km N of Newcastle-under-Lyme town centre, on site of Roman settlement. **40 A1** SJ8349.

Chesterton *Warks.* ***Hamlet***, 5m/9km SE of Royal Leamington Spa. Site of Roman building to W. SP3558.

Chesterton Green *Warks.* ***Hamlet***, 5m/8km SE of Royal Leamington Spa. **30 E3** SP3458.

Chesterwood *Northumb.* ***Locality***, 1m/2km NW of Haydon Bridge. NY8365.

Chestfield *Kent* ***Suburb***, to SE of Whitstable. **25 H5** TR1365.

Chestnut Street *Kent* ***Settlement***, 2m/3km W of Sittingbourne. TQ8763.

Cheston *Devon* ***Hamlet***, 2m/3km SW of South Brent. SX6858.

Cheswardine *Shrop.* ***Village***, 4m/6km SE of Market Drayton. **39 G3** SJ7129.

Cheswell *Tel. & W.* ***Settlement***, 2m/4km SW of Newport. SJ7117.

Cheswick *Northumb.* ***Hamlet***, 5m/7km SE of Berwick-upon-Tweed. **77 J6** NU0346.

Cheswick Black Rocks *Northumb.* ***Coastal feature***, rocks on Cheswick Sands, between high water mark and low water mark, 1m/2km NE of Cheswick. **77 J6** NU0347.

Cheswick Buildings *Northumb.* ***Hamlet***, 1km SW of Cheswick. NU0245.

Cheswick Green *W.Mid.* ***Village***, 2m/4km NW of Hockley Heath. SP1375.

C

Chet *Norf.* ***River***, rising NW of Poringland and flowing E into River Yare, 3m/5km NE of Loddon. **45 H6** TG4001.
Chetney *Kent* ***Marsh/bog***, 2m/3km NW of Iwade. **24 E4** TQ8871.
Chetnole *Dorset* ***Village***, 6m/9km SE of Yeovil. **9 F4** ST6008.
Chettiscombe *Devon* ***Hamlet***, 2m/3km NE of Tiverton. **7 H4** SS9614.
Chettisham *Cambs.* ***Hamlet***, 2m/3km N of Ely. **43 J7** TL5483.
Chettle *Dorset* ***Village***, 3m/5km S of Tollard Royal. **9 J3** ST9513.
Chettle House *Dorset* ***Historic house***, excellent example of Baroque Queen Anne house by Thomas Archer, located at Chettle, 6m/10km NE of Blandford Forum. **9 J3** ST9513.
Chetton *Shrop.* ***Village***, 4m/6km SW of Bridgnorth. **39 F6** SO6690.
Chetwode *Bucks.* ***Hamlet***, 5m/7km SW of Buckingham. **31 H6** SP6429.
Chetwynd Aston *Tel. & W.* ***Village***, 1m/2km SE of Newport. **39 G4** SJ7517.
Chetwynd End *Tel. & W.* ***Suburb***, in N part of Newport. SJ7419.
Chetwynd Park *Tel. & W.* ***Hamlet***, 1m/2km N of Chetwynd End. SJ7321.
Cheveley *Cambs.* ***Village***, 3m/5km SE of Newmarket. **33 K2** TL6860.
Chevening *Kent* ***Settlement***, 3m/5km NW of Sevenoaks. **23 H6** TQ4857.
Cheverell's Green *Herts.* ***Locality***, at SW end of Markyate, 4m/7km SW of Luton. **32 D7** TL0515.
Chevet *W.Yorks.* ***Locality***, 4m/6km S of Wakefield. SE3415.
Chevington *Suff.* ***Village***, 5m/8km SW of Bury St. Edmunds. **34 B3** TL7859.
Chevington Drift *Northumb.* ***Village***, 3m/5km S of Amble. **71 H4** NZ2699.
Chevinside *Derbys.* ***Locality***, 1km SW of Belper across River Derwent. SK3446.
Cheviot Hills ***Large natural feature***, N end of The Pennines, extending along border of England and Scotland, highest part being The Cheviot at 2673 feet or 815 metres. Hills contain vast areas of moorland, forests and peat and provide pasturage for sheep, especially breed known as Cheviots. **70 B4** NT6804.
Chevithorne *Devon* ***Village***, 2m/4km NE of Tiverton. **7 H4** SS9715.
Chew *B. & N.E.Som.* ***River***, rising at Chewton Mendip and flowing through Chew Valley Lake into River Avon at Keynsham. ST6568.
Chew Green *Northumb.* ***Historic/prehistoric site***, site of Roman camps, Ad Fines, at head of Coquetdale 6m/9km E of Carter Bar. **70 C3** NT7808.
Chew Magna *B. & N.E.Som.* ***Village***, 6m/10km S of Bristol. **19 J5** ST5763.
Chew Moor *Gt.Man.* ***Village***, 3m/5km W of Bolton town centre, just SW of Rumworth Lodge Reservoir. SD6607.
Chew Reservoir *Gt.Man.* ***Reservoir***, near head of Chew Brook valley 5m/7km E of Mossley. **50 C2** SE0301.
Chew Stoke *B. & N.E.Som.* ***Village***, 7m/11km S of Bristol. **19 J5** ST5561.
Chew Valley Lake *B. & N.E.Som.* ***Reservoir***, large reservoir in valley of River Chew 8m/13km S of Bristol. **19 J6** ST5760.
Chewton Keynsham *B. & N.E.Som.* ***Hamlet***, 1m/2km S of Keynsham. **19 K5** ST6566.
Chewton Mendip *Som.* ***Village***, below N slopes of Mendip Hills, 6m/9km NE of Wells. **19 J6** ST5953.
Cheylesmore *W.Mid.* ***Suburb***, 1m/2km S of Coventry city centre. SP3377.
Cheynies *Shet.* ***Island***, uninhabited island of 24 acres or 10 hectares 4m/6km W of Scalloway, Mainland. **109 C9** HU3438.
Chichacott *Devon* ***Hamlet***, 2m/3km NE of Okehampton. SX6096.
Chichele College *Northants.* ***Historic/prehistoric site***, ruins of secular college (English Heritage) in Higham Ferrers. Founded in 1422, only parts of quadrangle remain for secular canons. **32 C2** SP9568.
Chicheley *M.K.* ***Village***, 2m/4km NE of Newport Pagnell. **32 C4** SP9045.
Chichester *W.Suss.* Population: 26,572. ***City***, county town, site of Roman town Noviomagus, 9m/14km E of Havant, near head of Chichester Harbour (Chichester Channel). Ancient cathedral city (Royal Charter granted 1135), sports and tourism centre with some light industry. Cathedral, mainly Norman; 16c market cross; annual drama festival. **12 B6** SU8604.
Chichester Cathedral *W.Suss.* ***Ecclesiastical building***, in centre of Chichester. Mainly Norman, later additions in keeping with this. Detached bell tower built in 1436. The only ancient English cathedral visible from the sea. Noted for tapestry by John Piper (1966). **12 B6** SU8504.
Chichester Channel *See Chichester Harbour.*
Chichester Harbour ***Sea feature***, large inlet of sea to E of Hayling Island. Comprises four main arms, or channels, which are Chichester, Bosham, Thorney and Emsworth Channels. **11 J4** SU7500.
Chicken Head *W.Isles Anglicised form of Ceann na Circ, qv.*
Chicken Rock *I.o.M.* ***Island***, with lighthouse, 1km SW of Caigher Point, Calf of Man. **54 A7** SC1463.
Chicken Rock (Gaelic form: A' Chearc.) *W.Isles* ***Island***, offshore from Ceann na Circ, Isle of Lewis, with beacon. NB4928.
Chickenley *W.Yorks.* ***Suburb***, 1m/2km E of Dewsbury town centre. SE2621.
Chickenley Heath *W.Yorks.* ***Locality***, adjoining to N of Chickenley, 1m/2km E of Dewsbury. SE2621.
Chickerell *Dorset* Population: 2204. ***Village***, 3m/4km NW of Weymouth. **9 F6** SY6480.
Chickering *Suff.* ***Settlement***, 2m/3km NW of Stradbroke. **35 G1** TM2176.
Chicklade *Wilts.* ***Village***, 8m/12km NE of Shaftesbury. **9 J1** ST9134.
Chickney *Essex* ***Settlement***, 3m/5km SW of Thaxted. **33 J6** TL5728.
Chicksands *Beds.* ***Military establishment***, joint services base owned by Ministry of Defence, 1m/2km W of Shefford. Includes remains of Chicksands Priory. **32 E5** TL1239.
Chidden *Hants.* ***Hamlet***, 4m/7km NW of Horndean. **11 H3** SU6517.
Chidden Holt *Hants.* ***Settlement***, 1km SW of Chidden and 1m/2km NE of Hambledon. SU6516.
Chiddingfold *Surr.* Population: 2359. ***Village***, 5m/7km S of Milford. Site of Roman villa 2km E. **12 C3** SU9635.
Chiddingly *E.Suss.* ***Hamlet***, 4m/7km NW of Hailsham. **13 J5** TQ5414.
Chiddingstone *Kent* ***Village***, partly owned by National Trust, 4m/6km E of Edenbridge. Chiddingstone Castle, castellated manor house. **23 H7** TQ5045.
Chiddingstone Castle *Kent* ***Historic house***, 17c manor house, castellated during 19c Gothic revival, at W end of Chiddingstone village. **23 H7** TQ4945.
Chiddingstone Causeway *Kent* ***Village***, 1m/2km NE of Chiddingstone. **23 J7** TQ5246.
Chiddingstone Hoath *Kent* ***Hamlet***, 2m/3km S of Chiddingstone. **23 H7** TQ4942.
Chideock *Dorset* ***Village***, near coast, 3m/5km W of Bridport. **8 D5** SY4292.
Chidham *W.Suss.* ***Village***, opposite Bosham, near head of Chichester Harbour (Bosham Channel). **11 J4** SU7903.
Chidswell *W.Yorks.* ***Suburb***, 1m/2km NE of Dewsbury town centre. SE2623.
Chieveley *W.Berks.* ***Village***, 4m/6km N of Newbury. **21 H4** SU4773.
Chignall St. James *Essex* ***Hamlet***, 4m/6km NW of Chelmsford. **24 C1** TL6709.
Chignall Smealy *Essex* ***Hamlet***, 4m/6km NW of Chelmsford. **33 K7** TL6611.
Chigwell *Essex* Population: 10,332. ***Town***, 12m/19km NE of London. **23 H2** TQ4493.
Chigwell Row *Essex* ***Village***, 2m/3km E of Chigwell. **23 H2** TQ4693.
Chilbolton *Hants.* ***Village***, in River Test valley, 4m/6km NE of Stockbridge. **21 G7** SU3940.
Chilcomb *Hants.* ***Hamlet***, 2m/3km SE of Winchester. **11 G2** SU5028.
Chilcombe *Dorset* ***Hamlet***, 4m/7km E of Bridport. **8 E5** SY5291.
Chilcompton *Som.* Population: 1748. ***Village***, 2m/3km SW of Midsomer Norton. **19 K6** ST6452.
Chilcote *Leics.* ***Village***, 6m/9km SW of Ashby de la Zouch. **40 E4** SK2811.
Child Okeford *Dorset* ***Village***, in Stour valley at SW end of Cranborne Chase, 3m/5km E of Sturminster Newton. **9 H3** ST8312.
Childer Thornton *Ches.* ***Village***, 2m/4km W of Ellesmere Port. **48 C5** SJ3677.
Childerditch *Essex* ***Locality***, 3m/4km SE of Brentwood. **24 C3** TQ6089.
Childerley *Cambs.* ***Locality***, parish with 19c hall on site of earlier building, 6m/10km NW of Cambridge. TL3561.
Childrey *Oxon.* ***Village***, 2m/4km W of Wantage. **21 G3** SU3687.
Child's Ercall *Shrop.* ***Village***, 6m/10km NW of Newport. **39 F3** SJ6625.
Child's Hill *Gt.Lon.* ***Suburb***, in borough of Barnet, 5m/8km NW of Charing Cross. TQ2486.
Childswickham *Worcs.* ***Village***, 2m/3km NW of Broadway. **30 B5** SP0738.
Childwall *Mersey.* ***Suburb***, 5m/7km E of Liverpool city centre. **48 D4** SJ4189.
Childwick Green *Herts.* ***Hamlet***, 2m/4km N of St. Albans. **32 E7** TL1410.
Chilfrome *Dorset* ***Village***, 1m/2km NW of Maiden Newton. **8 E5** SY5898.
Chilgrove *W.Suss.* ***Hamlet***, 3m/5km W of Singleton. **12 B5** SU8214.
Chilham *Kent* ***Village***, 6m/9km SW of Canterbury. Remains of medieval castle. **15 F2** TR0653.
Chilham Castle *Kent* ***Castle***, in Chilham, 2m/3km SW of Shalmsford Street. Medieval banquets held in keep. Landscaped park by 'Capability' Brown. **15 F2** TR0653.
Chilhampton *Wilts.* ***Settlement***, beside River Wylye, 1m/2km N of Wilton. SU0933.
Chilla *Devon* ***Hamlet***, 6m/10km E of Holsworthy. SS4402.
Chilland *Hants.* ***Hamlet***, 1km W of Itchen Abbas and 3m/5km NE of Winchester. SU5232.
Chillaton *Devon* ***Village***, 6m/9km NW of Tavistock. **6 C7** SX4381.
Chillenden *Kent* ***Village***, 3m/5km SE of Wingham. **15 H2** TR2653.
Chillerton *I.o.W.* ***Village***, 3m/5km S of Newport. **11 F6** SZ4984.
Chillesford *Suff.* ***Village***, 3m/4km NW of Orford. **35 H3** TM3852.
Chilley *Devon* ***Hamlet***, 4m/7km NE of Kingsbridge. SX7650.
Chillingham *Northumb.* ***Village***, 4m/7km E of Wooler. Castle, 14c-19c. Chillingham herd of cattle in park. On far side of Park, Ross Castle (National Trust), ancient hillfort. **71 F1** NU0625.
Chillingham Park *Northumb.* ***Leisure/recreation***, 365 acre park with unique herd of wild white cattle, 5m/8km SE of Wooler. Cattle descended from herd trapped in park in 13c and these are the only pure breed examples of their kind. All visits must be accompanied by a warden. **71 F1** NU0725.
Chillington *Devon* ***Village***, 4m/6km E of Kingsbridge. **5 H6** SX7942.
Chillington *Som.* ***Village***, 4m/6km W of Crewkerne. **8 C3** ST3811.
Chillington Hall *Staffs.* ***Historic house***, 18c house in spacious grounds laid out by 'Capability' Brown, 2m/3km S of Brewood. **40 A5** SJ8606.
Chilmark *Wilts.* ***Village***, 8m/12km W of Wilton. **9 J1** ST9732.
Chilson *Oxon.* ***Village***, 3m/4km W of Charlbury. **30 E7** SP3119.
Chilson *Som.* ***Hamlet***, 3m/5km S of Chard. ST3203.
Chilson Common *Som.* ***Hamlet***, 1km N of Chilson, 3m/4km S of Chard. ST3304.
Chilsworthy *Cornw.* ***Village***, 1m/2km W of Gunnislake. **4 E3** SX4172.
Chilsworthy *Devon* ***Village***, 2m/3km NW of Holsworthy. **6 B5** SS3206.
Chiltern Hills ***Large natural feature***, range of chalk hills extending NE from River Thames valley, in vicinity of Goring in SW to Dunstable in NE. Highest point is Haddington Hill, 875 feet or 261 metres, near Wendover. **22 A2** SP8702.
Chiltern Hundreds *Bucks.* ***Locality***, area comprising Burnham, Desborough and Stoke, the Stewardship of which was formerly an office of profit under the Crown, now purely nominal but retained to enable a Member of Parliament voluntarily to resign his seat. **22 B2** SU9490.
Chilthorne Domer *Som.* ***Village***, 3m/5km NW of Yeovil. **8 E3** ST5219.
Chilton *Bucks.* ***Village***, 4m/6km N of Thame. **31 H7** SP6811.
Chilton *Devon* ***Hamlet***, 3m/5km NE of Crediton. SS8604.
Chilton *Dur.* Population: 4250. ***Village***, 2m/3km SW of Ferryhill. **62 D3** NZ2829.
Chilton *Oxon.* ***Village***, 4m/6km SW of Didcot. **21 H3** SU4885.
Chilton *Suff.* ***Hamlet***, 1m/2km NE of Sudbury. Includes Chilton Industrial Estate. TL8942.
Chilton Candover *Hants.* ***Hamlet***, 5m/8km N of New Alresford. **11 G1** SU5940.
Chilton Cantelo *Som.* ***Village***, 4m/7km N of Yeovil. **8 E2** ST5722.
Chilton Foliat *Wilts.* ***Village***, on River Kennet, 2m/3km NW of Hungerford. **21 G4** SU3270.
Chilton Lane *Dur.* ***Locality***, adjoining to SE of Ferryhill Station. NZ3031.
Chilton Moor *T. & W.* ***Locality***, 1m/2km SW of Houghton le Spring. NZ3249.
Chilton Polden *Som.* ***Village***, on N side of Polden Hills, 5m/8km NE of Bridgwater. **8 C1** ST3739.
Chilton Street *Suff.* ***Village***, 1m/2km NW of Clare. **34 B4** TL7546.
Chilton Trinity *Som.* ***Village***, 1m/2km N of Bridgwater. **8 B1** ST2939.
Chilvers Coton *Warks.* ***Suburb***, to S of Nuneaton town centre. **41 F6** SP3590.
Chilwell *Notts.* ***Suburb***, adjoining to SW of Beeston, 5m/8km SW of Nottingham. SK5135.
Chilworth *Hants.* Population: 1675. ***Village***, 4m/6km N of Southampton. **11 F3** SU4018.
Chilworth *Surr.* ***Village***, 2m/4km SE of Guildford. **22 D7** TQ0247.
Chilworth Manor *Surr.* ***Historic house***, 17c house with 18c wing on site of 11c monastery recorded in Domesday Book, 2m/3km SE of Guildford. 17c garden with 18c walled garden added by Sarah, Duchess of Marlborough. **22 D7** TQ0247.
Chimney *Oxon.* ***Settlement***, 6m/9km S of Witney. **21 G1** SP3500.
Chimney Street *Suff.* ***Settlement***, 4m/6km NE of Haverhill. TL7248.
Chineham *Hants.* ***Village***, adjoining to NE of Basingstoke. **21 K6** SU6554.
Chingford *Gt.Lon.* ***Suburb***, in borough of Waltham Forest, 9m/15km NE of London Bridge. Districts of Chingford Green and Chingford Hatch are N and S respectively of centre. **23 G2** TQ3894.
Chingford Green *Gt.Lon.* ***Suburb***, N district of Chingford. TQ3894.
Chingford Hatch *Gt.Lon.* ***Suburb***, S district of Chingford. TQ3892.
Chingle Hall *Lancs.* ***Historic house***, Britain's oldest surviving brick-built house, built 1260, 1km S of Goosnargh and 4m/7km N of Preston. **55 J6** SD5636.
Chinley *Derbys.* ***Village***, 2m/3km NW of Chapel-en-le-Frith. **50 C4** SK0482.
Chinley Head *Derbys.* ***Settlement***, 1m/2km N of Chinley. **50 C4** SK0484.
Chinnor *Oxon.* Population: 5599. ***Village***, 4m/7km SE of Thame. **22 A1** SP7500.
Chinnor and Princes Risborough Railway *Bucks.* ***Other feature of interest***, private railway running for over 3m/5km from Chinnor to Thame Junction, 1km S of Princes Risborough. **22 A1** SP7802.
Chipchase Castle *Northumb.* ***Castle***, 14c tower house and Jacobean manor house above banks of River North Tyne, 2m/3km SE of Wark across river. **70 D6** NY8875.
Chipley *Som.* ***Hamlet***, 2m/4km NW of Wellington. **7 K3** ST1123.
Chipnall *Shrop.* ***Hamlet***, 4m/6km SE of Market Drayton. **39 G2** SJ7231.
Chippenhall Green *Suff.* ***Settlement***, 2m/3km W of Cratfield. TM2875.
Chippenham *Cambs.* ***Village***, 4m/7km N of Newmarket. **33 K2** TL6669.
Chippenham *Wilts.* Population: 25,961. ***Town***, historic former wool town, now popular with London commuters, on River Avon, 12m/19km NE of Bath. **20 C4** ST9173.
Chipperfield *Herts.* ***Village***, 4m/6km S of Hemel Hempstead. **22 D1** TL0401.
Chipping *Herts.* ***Village***, 2m/3km N of Buntingford. **33 G5** TL3532.
Chipping *Lancs.* ***Village***, 4m/6km NE of Longridge. **56 B5** SD6243.

Chipping Barnet *Gt.Lon.* ***Suburb***, in borough of Barnet, 11m/17km N of Charing Cross. TQ2496.
Chipping Campden *Glos.* Population: 1741. ***Small town***, of Cotswold stone 8m/12km SE of Evesham. Former centre of wool trade. Arcaded Jacobean market hall (National Trust). **30 C5** SP1539.
Chipping Hill *Essex* ***Suburb***, in centre of Witham. **34 C7** TL8115.
Chipping Norton *Oxon.* Population: 5386. ***Small town***, old wool town in Cotswolds with splendid 15c church, 18m/29km NW of Oxford. **30 E6** SP3127.
Chipping Ongar *Essex* Population: 5974. ***Small town***, 6m/10km NW of Brentwood. **23 J1** TL5502.
Chipping Sodbury *S.Glos.* Population: 31,973. ***Town***, former market town, 11m/17km NE of Bristol, with 16c church tower. **20 A3** ST7282.
Chipping Warden *Northants.* ***Village***, 6m/9km NE of Banbury. Site of Roman villa 1m/2km SE. **31 F4** SP4948.
Chipstable *Som.* ***Hamlet***, 3m/4km W of Wiveliscombe. **7 J3** ST0427.
Chipstead *Kent* ***Suburb***, to NW of Sevenoaks. **23 H6** TQ5056.
Chipstead *Surr.* ***Village***, 2m/4km SE of Banstead. **23 F6** TQ2757.
Chirbury *Shrop.* ***Village***, 3m/5km N of Church Stoke. **38 B6** SO2698.
Chirdon Burn *Northumb.* ***River***, rising on Wark Forest and flowing NE into River North Tyne, 4m/6km W of Bellingham, below confluence with Tarset Burn. **70 B5** NY7885.
Chirk (Y Waun). *Wrex.* Population: 4264. ***Small town***, above River Ceiriog 5m/8km N of Oswestry. Motte near church marks site of 11c castle. Present castle, 1m/2km W, dates in part from early 14c. **38 B2** SJ2937.
Chirk Castle *Wrex.* ***Castle***, 1m/2km W of Chirk. 13c Mortimers built fortress, transformed into a livable house in 18c (National Trust). Originally square, castle is now rectangular in plan. Interior has decorative styles ranging from 16c to mid 19c. **38 B2** SJ2638.
Chirk Green *Wrex.* ***Suburb***, N part of Chirk. SJ2938.
Chirmorrie *S.Ayr.* ***Settlement***, 4m/6km S of Barrhill. **64 C3** NX2076.
Chirnside *Sc.Bord.* Population: 1253. ***Village***, 6m/9km E of Duns. **77 G5** NT8656.
Chirnsidebridge *Sc.Bord.* ***Village***, 1m/2km W of Chirnside on Whiteadder Water. **77 G5** NT8556.
Chirton *T. & W.* ***Suburb***, 1m/2km W of North Shields town centre. NZ3468.
Chirton *Wilts.* ***Village***, 5m/8km SE of Devizes. **20 D6** SU0757.
Chisbury *Wilts.* ***Hamlet***, 4m/7km SW of Hungerford. 13c Chisbury Chapel (English Heritage) and Chisbury Camp to SE. **21 F5** SU2766.
Chiscan *Arg. & B.* ***Settlement***, on Kintyre, 2m/3km W of Campbeltown. **66 A2** NR6718.
Chiscan Water *Arg. & B.* ***River***, stream on Kintyre, running generally N into Machrihanish Water. **66 A2** NR6820.
Chiselborough *Som.* ***Village***, 6m/9km W of Yeovil. **8 D3** ST4614.
Chiseldon *Swin.* Population: 2651. ***Village***, 4m/6km SE of Swindon. **20 E3** SU1879.
Chislehampton *Oxon.* ***Hamlet***, 7m/11km SE of Oxford. **21 J2** SU5999.
Chislehurst *Gt.Lon.* ***Suburb***, in borough of Bromley, 11m/18km SE of Charing Cross. Caves to W. **23 H4** TQ4469.
Chislehurst Caves *Gt.Lon.* ***Other feature of interest***, Stone Age chalk tunnels and caves, used as air-raid shelter in World War II, 1km SW of Chislehurst. **23 H5** TQ4369.
Chislehurst West *Gt.Lon.* ***Locality***, 1m/2km NW of Chislehurst. TQ4371.
Chislet *Kent* ***Village***, 4m/6km SE of Herne Bay. **25 J5** TR2264.
Chisley *W.Yorks.* ***Village***, 1m/2km NE of Hebden Bridge. SE0028.
Chiswell Green *Herts.* ***Suburb***, 2m/3km SW of St. Albans. **22 E1** TL1304.
Chiswick *Gt.Lon.* ***Suburb***, N of River Thames in borough of Hounslow, 6m/10km W of Charing Cross. Chiswick Bridge over river. Chiswick House (English Heritage), 18c Italianate house. **23 F4** TQ2078.
Chiswick End *Cambs.* ***Hamlet***, adjoining to S of Meldreth, 3m/5km N of Royston. TL3745.
Chiswick Eyot *Gt.Lon.* ***Island***, in River Thames, 2m/3km W of Hammersmith Bridge. TQ2177.
Chiswick House *Gt.Lon.* ***Historic house***, at Chiswick, in borough of Hounslow. One of first 18c Palladian villas (English Heritage) in England, built by third Earl of Burlington from 1725-30 and modelled on Villa Rotunda at Vicenza; interiors and gardens by William Kent. **23 F4** TQ2076.
Chisworth *Derbys.* ***Village***, 3m/4km SW of Glossop. **49 J3** SJ9992.
Chithurst *W.Suss.* ***Hamlet***, 3m/5km W of Midhurst. **12 B4** SU8423.
Chittening Warth *Bristol* ***Locality***, on River Severn estuary, 2m/3km S of Severn Beach. Chittening Trading Estate in vicinity. ST5382.
Chittering *Cambs.* ***Hamlet***, 8m/13km NE of Cambridge. **33 H2** TL4970.
Chitterne *Wilts.* ***Village***, on Salisbury Plain, 8m/12km E of Warminster. **20 C7** ST9944.
Chittlehamholt *Devon* ***Village***, 5m/8km SW of South Molton. **6 E3** SS6421.
Chittlehampton *Devon* ***Village***, 5m/8km W of South Molton. **6 E3** SS6325.
Chittoe *Wilts.* ***Village***, 5m/8km SE of Chippenham. **20 C5** ST9566.
Chivelstone *Devon* ***Hamlet***, 3m/4km N of Prawle Point. **5 H7** SX7838.
Chivenor *Devon* ***Village***, to SE of Braunton. Chivenor Airfield to S of Braunton. SS5034.
Chno Dearg *High.* ***Mountain***, in Lochaber district 3m/5km SE of foot of Loch Treig. Munro: height 3434 feet or 1047 metres. **87 K7** NN3774.
Chobham *Surr.* Population: 3411. ***Village***, 3m/5km NW of Woking, on S side of Chobham Common. **22 C5** SU9761.
Chobham Common *Surr.* ***Open space***, expanse of fairly open heath to S of Windsor Great Park. **22 C5** SU9761.
Chobham Ridges *Surr.* ***Inland physical feature***, at W edge of Westend Common, 2m/3km S of Bagshot. **22 C5** SU9060.
Choicelee *Sc.Bord.* ***Hamlet***, 3m/5km SW of Duns. **77 F5** NT7451.
Cholderton *Wilts.* ***Village***, 5m/7km E of Amesbury. **21 F7** SU2242.
Cholesbury *Bucks.* ***Village***, 4m/6km NW of Chesham. **22 C1** SP9307.
Chollerford *Northumb.* ***Locality***, at road junction and crossing of River North Tyne, 4m/6km N of Hexham. Planetrees Roman Wall (English Heritage) 1m/2km to SE, is narrow section of wall on larger foundations, indicative of rebuilding by Romans. NY9170.
Chollerton *Northumb.* ***Village***, 5m/8km N of Hexham. **70 E6** NY9371.
Cholsey *Oxon.* Population: 3262. ***Village***, 2m/4km SW of Wallingford. **21 J3** SU5886.
Cholsey and Wallingford Railway *Oxon.* ***Other feature of interest***, tourist railway running between Cholsey and Wallingford. **21 J3** SU5987.
Cholstrey *Here.* ***Hamlet***, 2m/3km W of Leominster. **28 D3** SO4659.
Cholwell *B. & N.E.Som.* ***Hamlet***, 4m/7km NW of Midsomer Norton. **19 K6** ST6158.
Cholwell *Devon* ***Settlement***, 3m/5km NW of Tavistock. **4 E3** SX4375.
Chop Gate *N.Yorks.* ***Hamlet***, 6m/10km S of Stokesley. **63 G6** SE5599.
Choppington *Northumb.* ***Village***, 1m/2km N of Bedlington. NZ2583.
Chopwell *T. & W.* Population: 4436. ***Village***, 3m/5km SE of Prudhoe. **62 C1** NZ1158.
Chorley *Ches.* ***Locality***, on SW side of Alderley Edge. SJ8378.
Chorley *Ches.* ***Village***, 5m/9km W of Nantwich. **48 E7** SJ5751.
Chorley *Lancs.* Population: 33,536. ***Town***, market town, 10m/16km NW of Bolton. 16c Astley Hall 1km NW. **48 E1** SD5817.
Chorley *Shrop.* ***Village***, 5m/8km N of Cleobury Mortimer. **39 F7** SO6983.
Chorley *Staffs.* ***Hamlet***, 3m/5km NW of Lichfield. **40 C4** SK0711.
Chorley Green *Ches.* ***Settlement***, to N of Chorley. SJ5751.
Chorleywood *Herts.* Population: 9025. ***Small town***, commuter town, growing with arrival of railway in 1880s, 2m/3km NW of Rickmansworth. **22 D2** TQ0396.
Chorleywood Bottom *Herts.* ***Suburb***, to S of Chorleywood. TQ0295.
Chorleywood West *Herts.* ***Suburb***, to W of Chorleywood. TQ0196.
Chorlton *Ches.* ***Hamlet***, 4m/6km SE of Crewe. **49 G7** SJ7250.
Chorlton-cum-Hardy *Gt.Man.* ***Suburb***, 3m/4km SW of Manchester city centre. **49 H3** SJ8293.
Chorlton Lane *Ches.* ***Hamlet***, 2m/3km W of Malpas. **38 D1** SJ4547.
Chorlton on Medlock *Gt.Man.* ***Suburb***, 1m/2km SE of Manchester city centre. Royal Infirmary. University of Manchester site. SJ8496.
Chorrie Island *High.* *Anglicised form of Eilean Choraidh, qv.*
Chowley *Ches.* ***Settlement***, 1m/2km SW of Tattenhall. **48 D7** SJ4756.
Chrishall *Essex* ***Village***, 6m/9km E of Royston. **33 H5** TL4439.
Chrishall Grange *Cambs.* ***Settlement***, 2m/3km N of Chrishall. **33 H4** TL4442.
Chrisswell *Inclyde* ***Settlement***, 3m/4km SW of Greenock. **74 A3** NS2274.
Christchurch *Cambs.* ***Village***, 3m/4km NW of Welney. **43 H6** TL4996.
Christchurch *Dorset* Population: 36,379. ***Town***, near coast, 5m/8km E of Bournemouth, at confluence of Rivers Avon and Stour. Longest parish church in England. Ruins of Norman house (English Heritage) within bailey of Norman castle (English Heritage). **10 C5** SZ1592.
Christchurch *Glos.* ***Locality***, 2m/3km N of Coleford. **28 E7** SO5713.
Christchurch (Eglwys Y Drindod). *Newport* ***Suburb***, 3m/4km S of Newport. **19 G3** ST3489.
Christchurch Bay *Dorset* ***Bay***, between Hengistbury Head to W and Hurst Point to E. **10 D5** SZ1592.
Christchurch Bridge *Dorset* ***Bridge***, 15c bridge over River Avon at Christchurch. SZ1692.
Christchurch Castle *Dorset* ***Castle***, remains of 12c Norman motte and bailey castle with Constable's house (English Heritage) in Christchurch town centre. **10 C5** SZ1692.
Christchurch Mansion *Suff.* ***Historic house***, Tudor house set in Christchurch Park, Ipswich, with rooms furnished in styles from Tudor to Victorian. Includes Wolsey Art Gallery. **35 F4** TM1645.
Christchurch Priory *Dorset* ***Ecclesiastical building***, longest parish church in England (312 feet or 95 metres) and situated in Christchurch town centre, with some excellent examples of Norman architecture. **10 C5** SZ1692.
Christian Malford *Wilts.* ***Village***, 4m/7km NE of Chippenham. **20 C4** ST9678.
Christianbury Crag *Cumb.* ***Mountain***, on N side of Bewcastle Fells, 7m/11km SE of Newcastleton. Height 1597 feet or 487 metres. **70 A5** NY5782.
Christleton *Ches.* ***Suburb***, 3m/4km E of Chester. **48 D6** SJ4465.
Christmas Common *Oxon.* ***Hamlet***, 2m/3km SE of Watlington. **22 A2** SU7193.
Christon *N.Som.* ***Village***, 5m/7km SE of Weston-super-Mare. **19 G6** ST3757.
Christon Bank *Northumb.* ***Hamlet***, 1m/2km W of Embleton. **71 H1** NU2123.
Christow *Devon* ***Village***, 4m/6km NW of Chudleigh. **7 G7** SX8384.
Christskirk *Aber.* ***Settlement***, with historic Christ's Kirk, 2m/3km SW of Insch. NJ6026.
Chrona Island *High.* *Anglicised form of Eilean Chrona, qv.*
Chryston *N.Lan.* Population: 3057. ***Village***, adjoining to N of Muirhead, 4m/7km NW of Coatbridge. **74 E3** NS6870.
Chuck Hatch *E.Suss.* ***Settlement***, on N slope of Ashdown Forest, 2m/3km S of Hartfield. TQ4733.
Chudleigh *Devon* Population: 3046. ***Small town***, small market town, 5m/8km N of Newton Abbot. Original village almost totally destroyed by fire in early 19c. **5 J3** SX8679.
Chudleigh Knighton *Devon* ***Village***, by River Teign, 4m/6km N of Newton Abbot. **5 J3** SX8477.
Chulmleigh *Devon* ***Small town***, 8m/12km S of South Molton. **6 E4** SS6814.
Chunal *Derbys.* ***Settlement***, 1m/2km S of Glossop. **50 C3** SK0391.
Church *Lancs.* Population: 4277. ***Small town***, adjoining to W of Accrington. Site of settlement since 1200. **56 C7** SD7429.
Church Aston *Tel. & W.* ***Village***, 1m/2km S of Newport. **39 G4** SJ7417.
Church Bay (Porth Swtan). *I.o.A.* ***Bay***, on NW coast of Anglesey, 3m/5km S of Carmel Head. **46 A4** SH2988.
Church Brampton *Northants.* ***Village***, 4m/7km NW of Northampton. **31 J2** SP7165.
Church Brough *Cumb.* ***Village***, adjoining to S of Brough, with Roman fort, Verteris, to W. NY7914.
Church Broughton *Derbys.* ***Village***, 3m/5km NE of Sudbury. **40 E2** SK2033.
Church Charwelton *Northants.* ***Settlement***, to SE of Charwelton, 5m/8km SW of Daventry. SP5455.
Church Clough *Lancs.* ***Locality***, adjoining to S of Colne. SD8839.
Church Common *Hants.* ***Locality***, 1m/2km N of Petersfield. SU7425.
Church Common *Suff.* ***Settlement***, 1km N of Snape. **35 H3** TM3959.
Church Crookham *Hants.* ***Suburb***, 1m/2km S of Fleet. **22 B6** SU8152.
Church Eaton *Staffs.* ***Village***, 6m/9km SW of Stafford. **40 A4** SJ8417.
Church End *Beds.* ***Hamlet***, N end of Husborne Crawley, 2m/3km N of Woburn. SP9536.
Church End *Beds.* ***Hamlet***, SW end of Eversholt, 2m/4km E of Woburn. SP9832.
Church End *Beds.* ***Hamlet***, SE end of Totternhoe, 2m/3km W of Dunstable. Site of Roman villa across road from church. **32 C6** SP9921.
Church End *Beds.* ***Hamlet***, adjoining to N of Colmworth, 4m/7km W of St. Neots. TL1058.
Church End *Beds.* ***Hamlet***, 2m/3km N of Sandy. **32 E3** TL1652.
Church End *Beds.* ***Locality***, W end of Biddenham, 2m/4km W of Bedford. TL0149.
Church End *Beds.* ***Locality***, W end of Thurleigh. TL0558.
Church End *Beds.* ***Village***, W end of Renhold, 3m/5km NE of Bedford. TL0852.
Church End *Beds.* ***Village***, at N end of Arlesey, 5m/8km N of Hitchin. **32 E5** TL1937.
Church End *Bucks.* ***Locality***, surrounding church at Long Crendon, 2m/3km NW of Thame. SP6909.
Church End *Bucks.* ***Settlement***, at Pitstone, 3m/4km NE of Tring. SP9415.
Church End *Cambs.* ***Hamlet***, 1m/2km E of Parson Drove. **43 G5** TF3909.
Church End *Cambs.* ***Locality***, NW end of Over. **33 G1** TL3770.
Church End *Cambs.* ***Locality***, N end of Cherry Hinton. **33 H3** TL4857.
Church End *Cambs.* ***Settlement***, NE part of Catworth. TL0973.
Church End *Cambs.* ***Settlement***, 1m/2km N of Woodwalton, just N of Woodwalton church, 7m/11km N of Huntingdon. TL2082.
Church End *Cambs.* ***Settlement***, N end of Swavesey. TL3669.
Church End *Cambs.* ***Settlement***, S end of Comberton. TL3855.
Church End *Cambs.* ***Village***, NW end of Pidley, 2m/3km SE of Warboys. TL3278.
Church End *E.Riding* ***Settlement***, 1km W of North Frodingham. **59 G4** TA0953.
Church End *Essex* ***Hamlet***, SW of Ashdon, 3m/5km NE of Saffron Walden. **33 J4** TL5841.
Church End *Essex* ***Hamlet***, 4m/6km NW of Braintree. **34 B6** TL7228.
Church End *Essex* ***Settlement***, 5m/7km S of Braintree. TL7316.
Church End *Glos.* ***Hamlet***, 1km NE of Eastington. SO7805.
Church End *Glos.* ***Hamlet***, 1km S of Twyning. SO8936.
Church End *Gt.Lon.* ***Suburb***, to W of Finchley, in borough of Barnet, 7m/11km NW of Charing Cross. TQ2490.
Church End *Hants.* ***Hamlet***, 4m/6km NE of Basingstoke. **21 K6** SU6756.
Church End *Herts.* ***Hamlet***, 3m/4km W of Bishop's Stortford. TL4422.
Church End *Herts.* ***Hamlet***, 3m/4km NW of Rickmansworth. TQ0398.
Church End *Herts.* ***Locality***, adjoining to SW of Redbourn, 4m/6km NE of Hemel Hempstead. **32 E7** TL1011.

Church End *Herts.* ***Settlement***, E end of Weston, 3m/5km SE of Baldock. TL2630.
Church End *Lincs.* ***Hamlet***, 1km N of Quadring. **43 F2** TF2234.
Church End *Lincs.* ***Hamlet***, 1km S of North Somercotes. **53 H3** TF4295.
Church End *Norf.* ***Locality***, between Walpole St. Peter and Walpole Highway, 4m/7km NE of Wisbech. TF5115.
Church End *Surr.* ***Settlement***, adjoining to W of Ockham, 4m/7km E of Woking. TQ0656.
Church End *Warks.* ***Hamlet***, to E of Shustoke, 3m/5km NE of Coleshill. SP2490.
Church End *Warks.* ***Hamlet***, 5m/7km W of Nuneaton. **40 E6** SP2992.
Church End *Wilts.* ***Locality***, forming E part of Lyneham. **20 D4** SU0278.
Church Enstone *Oxon.* ***Village***, 4m/7km E of Chipping Norton. **30 E6** SP3725.
Church Fenton *N.Yorks.* ***Village***, 2m/4km NE of Sherburn in Elmet. Airfield to NE. **58 B6** SE5136.
Church Green *Devon* ***Hamlet***, 3m/5km S of Honiton. **7 K6** SY1796.
Church Gresley *Derbys.* ***Suburb***, 1m/2km SW of Swadlincote. **40 E4** SK2918.
Church Hanborough *Oxon.* ***Village***, 5m/8km NE of Witney. **31 F7** SP4212.
Church Hill *Ches.* ***Hamlet***, 1km S of Winsford. SJ6465.
Church Hill *Derbys.* ***Hamlet***, adjoining to SW of North Wingfield. SK4064.
Church Hill *Staffs.* ***Hamlet***, adjoining to Hednesford, 2m/3km NE of Cannock. SK0011.
Church Hill *Worcs.* ***Suburb***, NE district of Redditch. SP0668.
Church Hougham *Kent* ***Settlement***, 3m/4km W of Dover. TR2740.
Church House *Som.* ***Historic house***, 15c house in Crowcombe, 5m/8km SE of Williton. **7 K2** ST1336.
Church Houses *N.Yorks.* ***Hamlet***, 7m/11km N of Kirkbymoorside. **63 H7** SE6697.
Church Knowle *Dorset* ***Village***, 1m/2km W of Corfe Castle. **9 J6** SY9481.
Church Laneham *Notts.* ***Village***, with church and inn beside River Trent, 1km E of Laneham. SK8176.
Church Langley *Essex* ***Suburb***, residential development 2m/3km E of Harlow town centre. **23 H1** TL4709.
Church Langton *Leics.* ***Village***, 4m/6km N of Market Harborough. **42 A6** SP7293.
Church Lawford *Warks.* ***Village***, 4m/6km W of Rugby. **31 F1** SP4476.
Church Lawton *Ches.* ***Village***, 1m/2km NW of Kidsgrove. **49 H7** SJ8255.
Church Leigh *Staffs.* ***Village***, 5m/7km NW of Uttoxeter. **40 C2** SK0235.
Church Lench *Worcs.* ***Village***, 5m/8km N of Evesham. **30 B3** SP0251.
Church Mayfield *Staffs.* ***Village***, 1km S of Mayfield. SK1544.
Church Minshull *Ches.* ***Village***, on River Weaver, 4m/7km NW of Crewe. **49 F6** SJ6660.
Church Norton *W.Suss.* ***Hamlet***, 2m/3km NE of Selsey. **12 B7** SZ8695.
Church Oakley *Hants. Alternative name for Oakley, qv.*
Church of Plaque (Athelstaneford Church). *E.Loth.* ***Ecclesiastical building***, 3m/4km NE of Haddington. Plaque by church tells of origins of St. Andrew's Cross (the Saltire) first adopted as Scottish symbol here. Book of the Saltire on display in church. **76 D3** NT5377.
Church of St. Mary *Carmar. See Kidwelly Priory.*
Church Preen *Shrop.* ***Village***, 5m/8km W of Much Wenlock. **38 E6** SO5498.
Church Pulverbatch *Shrop.* ***Village***, 7m/12km SW of Shrewsbury. **38 D5** SJ4302.
Church Stoke *Powys* ***Village***, on River Camlad, 3m/5km SE of Montgomery. **38 B6** SO2794.
Church Stowe *Northants.* ***Village***, 5m/8km SE of Daventry. **31 H3** SP6357.
Church Street *Essex* ***Hamlet***, in vicinity of church of Belchamp St. Paul, 2m/4km SE of Clare. TL7943.
Church Street *Kent* ***Hamlet***, 4m/6km N of Rochester. **24 D4** TQ7174.
Church Street *Suff.* ***Locality***, 1km W of Wrentham. TM4883.
Church Stretton *Shrop.* Population: 3435. ***Small town***, former spa town under E slope of Long Mynd, 12m/19km S of Shrewsbury. Nearby Carding Mill Valley (National Trust), cut into slopes of The Long Mynd, has spectacular scenery. **38 D6** SO4593.
Church Town *Cornw.* ***Hamlet***, adjoining to E of Carn Brea Village, 1km SW of Redruth. SW6941.
Church Town *Leics.* ***Hamlet***, 3m/4km E of Ashby de la Zouch. SK3916.
Church Town *N.Lincs.* ***Locality***, part of Belton in which church is situated. SE7806.
Church Town *Surr.* ***Hamlet***, 1km E of Godstone. TQ3551.
Church Village *R.C.T.* Population: 7894. ***Village***, 3m/5km S of Pontypridd. **18 D3** ST0886.
Church Warsop *Notts.* ***Village***, 1km N of Market Warsop and 5m/8km NE of Mansfield. **51 H6** SK5668.
Church Wilne *Derbys.* ***Hamlet***, on River Derwent, 3m/5km SW of Long Eaton. SK4431.
Churcham *Glos.* ***Village***, 4m/7km W of Gloucester. **29 G7** SO7618.
Churchbridge *Staffs.* ***Suburb***, 1m/2km S of Cannock. SJ9808.
Churchdown *Glos.* Population: 9110. ***Village***, 4m/6km E of Gloucester. **29 H6** SO8819.
Churchend *Essex* ***Hamlet***, 1km N of Great Dunmow. **33 K6** TL6222.
Churchend *Essex* ***Village***, on Foulness Island, 9m/14km NE of Southend-on-Sea. **25 G2** TR0093.
Churchend *S.Glos.* ***Hamlet***, 3m/5km SW of Wotton-under-Edge. **20 A2** ST7191.
Churche's Mansion *Ches.* ***Historic house***, Elizabethan timber-framed building, one of three buildings in Nantwich to survive fire of 1583. **49 F7** SJ6551.
Churchfield *W.Mid.* ***Suburb***, 1m/2km NE of West Bromwich town centre. SP0192.
Churchgate *Herts.* ***Suburb***, to W of Cheshunt town centre. **23 G1** TL3402.
Churchgate Street *Essex* ***Suburb***, 3m/4km NE of Harlow town centre. **33 H7** TL4811.
Churchhill *Edin.* ***Suburb***, 1m/2km SW of Edinburgh city centre. NT2471.
Churchill *Devon* ***Hamlet***, 5m/8km NE of Barnstaple. SS5940.
Churchill *Devon* ***Hamlet***, 3m/4km N of Axminster. ST2901.
Churchill *N.Som.* ***Village***, below N slopes of Mendip Hills, 3m/4km S of Congresbury. **19 H6** ST4459.
Churchill *Oxon.* ***Village***, 3m/4km SW of Chipping Norton. **30 D6** SP2824.
Churchill *Worcs.* ***Village***, 3m/5km S of Stourbridge. **29 H1** SO8879.
Churchill *Worcs.* ***Village***, 5m/8km E of Worcester. **29 J3** SO9253.
Churchingford *Som.* ***Village***, 8m/12km S of Taunton. **8 B3** ST2112.
Churchover *Warks.* ***Village***, 4m/6km N of Rugby. **41 H7** SP5180.
Churchstanton *Som.* ***Village***, 5m/8km SE of Wellington. **7 K4** ST1914.
Churchstow *Devon* ***Village***, 2m/3km NW of Kingsbridge. **5 H6** SX7145.
Churchthorpe *Lincs.* ***Locality***, adjoining to N of Fulstow. **53 G3** TF3297.
Churchtown *B'pool* ***Suburb***, 3m/5km N of Blackpool town centre. SD3140.
Churchtown *Derbys.* ***Hamlet***, 3m/4km NW of Matlock. SK3662.
Churchtown *Devon* ***Hamlet***, 1km E of Parracombe. **6 E1** SS6744.
Churchtown (Also known as Lezayre.) *I.o.M.* ***Hamlet***, 2m/3km W of Ramsey. **54 D4** SC4294.
Churchtown *Lancs.* ***Village***, 1m/2km SW of Garstang. **55 H5** SD4842.
Churchtown *Mersey.* ***Suburb***, 2m/3km NE of Southport town centre. **48 C1** SD3618.
Churchtown *Shrop.* ***Settlement***, 5m/8km NW of Clun. SO2687.
Churn ***River***, rising at Seven Springs, 4m/6km S of Cheltenham and flowing S into River Thames at Cricklade. **30 B7** SU0994.
Churnet *Staffs.* ***River***, rising NE of Upper Hulme, flowing through Tittesworth Reservoir then SW towards Leek where it loops to W of town. It then flows SE into River Dove 1m/2km S of Rocester. **40 C1** SK1037.
Churnsike Lodge *Northumb.* ***Settlement***, on N side of River Irthing, in Wark Forest, 6m/10km E of Bewcastle. **70 B6** NY6677.
Churston Ferrers *Torbay* ***Village***, on W outskirts of Brixham. **5 K5** SX9056.
Churt *Surr.* ***Village***, 3m/4km NW of Hindhead. **12 B3** SU8538.
Churton *Ches.* ***Village***, 6m/10km S of Chester. **48 D7** SJ4156.
Churwell *W.Yorks.* ***Village***, 1m/2km NE of Morley. **57 H7** SE2729.
Chute *Wilts.* ***Locality***, parish, 7m/11km NW of Andover, containing village of Upper Chute, hamlets of Chute Cadley and Chute Standen, and part of hamlet of Lower Chute. SU3053.
Chute Cadley *Wilts.* ***Hamlet***, forms part of parish of Chute, along with Chute Standen, 1m/2km E of Upper Chute, 6m/9km NW of Andover. **21 G6** SU3153.
Chute Causeway *Wilts.* ***Open space***, hillslope carrying Roman road, 1km N of Upper Chute. **21 F6** SU2955.
Chute Forest *Wilts.* ***Locality***, parish 5m/8km NW of Andover containing part of hamlet of Lower Chute. SU3151.
Chute Standen *Wilts.* ***Hamlet***, forms part of parish of Chute, along with Chute Cadley, 1km E of Upper Chute, 6m/10km NW of Andover. **21 G6** SU3053.
Chwerfri *Powys* ***River***, rising some 2m/3km SE of Caban Coch Reservoir and flowing SE into River Irfon just above its junction with River Wye near Builth Wells. **27 J3** SO0351.
Chwilog *Gwyn.* ***Village***, 4m/7km W of Criccieth. **36 D2** SH4338.
Chwitffordd *Flints. Welsh form of Whitford, qv.*
Chyandour *Cornw.* ***Suburb***, to NE of Penzance. **2 B5** SW4730.
Chynhalls Point *Cornw.* ***Coastal feature***, headland on E coast of Lizard peninsula, 1km S of Coverack. SW7817.
Chysauster *Cornw.* ***Settlement***, 3m/4km N of Penzance. SW4734.
Chysauster Ancient Village *Cornw.* ***Historic/prehistoric site***, English Heritage property to N of Chysauster. Iron Age village consisting of four pairs of houses either side of a main street. **2 B5** SW4735.
Ciaran Water *High.* ***River***, flowing S from Loch Chiarain into Blackwater Reservoir. **80 E1** NN2860.
Cil *Powys* ***Locality***, 1km NW of Aberriw. SJ1801.
Cilan Uchaf *Gwyn.* ***Settlement***, on SE tip of Lleyn Peninsula, 3m/5km SW of Abersoch. **36 C3** SH2923.
Cilcain *Flints.* ***Village***, 4m/7km W of Mold. **47 K6** SJ1765.
Cilcennin *Cere.* ***Village***, 4m/7km E of Aberaeron. **26 E2** SN5260.
Cilcewydd *Powys* ***Hamlet***, on River Severn, 2m/3km S of Welshpool. SJ2203.
Cilfaesty Hill *Powys* ***Mountain***, 5m/8km S of Newtown. Height 1732 feet or 528 metres. **38 A7** SO1284.
Cilfrew *N.P.T.* ***Village***, 2m/3km NE of Neath. **18 A1** SN7700.
Cilfynydd *R.C.T.* ***Village***, 1m/2km NE of Pontypridd. **18 D2** ST0891.
Cilgerran *Pembs.* ***Village***, on S bank of River Teifi, 2m/3km SE of Cardigan. Ruins of 13c castle (National Trust) on cliff above river. Annual coracle races held on river in August. **26 A4** SN1943.
Cilgerran Castle *Pembs.* ***Castle***, ruins of 13c castle (Cadw and National Trust) on cliff overlooking Cilgerran and River Teifi. **26 A4** SN1943.
Cilgeti *Pembs. Welsh form of Kilgetty, qv.*
Cilgwyn *Carmar.* ***Settlement***, 2m/3km SE of Llanwrda. **27 G6** SN7429.
Cilgwyn *Pembs.* ***Settlement***, 2m/4km SE of Newport. **16 D1** SN0736.
Ciliau Aeron *Cere.* ***Settlement***, 4m/6km SE of Aberaeron. **26 E3** SN5058.
Cilieni *Powys* ***River***, rising on Mynydd Eppynt and flowing S into River Usk, 1m/2km NW of Sennybridge. SN9329.
Cille-Bharra *W.Isles* ***Ecclesiastical building***, on Barra, 1m/2km SE of Scurrival Point on N of island. Ruined church of St. Barr and restored chapel of St. Mary formed part of medieval monastery. Replica of unique Celtic/Norse stone at the site. **84 C4** NF7007.
Cille Bhrighde (Anglicised form: Kilbride.) *W.Isles* ***Village***, at SW end of South Uist. **84 C3** NF7514.
Cille Pheadair (Anglicised form: Kilpheder.) *W.Isles* ***Settlement***, on South Uist, 1m/2km SW of Dalabrog. **84 C3** NF7419.
Cilmaengwyn *N.P.T.* ***Village***, 2m/3km NE of Pontardawe. SN7405.
Cilmeri *Powys Alternative spelling of Cilmery, qv.*
Cilmery (Cilmeri. Formerly known as Cefn-y-bedd.) *Powys* ***Hamlet***, 2m/4km W of Builth Wells. **27 K3** SO0051.
Cilrhedyn *Pembs.* ***Hamlet***, 4m/6km SW of Newcastle Emlyn. **17 F1** SN2734.
Cilrhedyn Bridge *Pembs.* ***Settlement***, with bridge across River Gwaun, 2m/3km SE of Fishguard. **16 D1** SN0034.
Cilsan *Carmar.* ***Hamlet***, 2m/3km W of Llandeilo. SN5922.
Ciltalgarth *Gwyn.* ***Settlement***, 4m/6km NW of Bala. **37 H1** SH8840.
Cilurnum *Northumb. See Chesters Roman Fort.*
Cilwendeg *Pembs.* ***Settlement***, 1m/2km NE of Boncath. **17 F1** SN2238.
Cilybebyll *N.P.T.* ***Village***, 1m/2km E of Pontardawe. **18 A1** SN7404.
Cilycwm *Carmar.* ***Village***, on River Gwenlais, 4m/6km N of Llandovery. **27 G4** SN7540.
Cimla *N.P.T.* ***Suburb***, SE district of Neath. SS7696.
Cinder Hill *W.Mid.* ***Suburb***, on borders of Dudley and Wolverhampton, 3m/5km N of Dudley town centre. SO9294.
Cinderford *Glos.* Population: 9566. ***Small town***, former mining town in Forest of Dean, 11m/18km W of Gloucester. **29 F7** SO6514.
Cinderhill *Derbys.* ***Hamlet***, 2m/3km SE of Belper. SK3746.
Cinderhill *Notts.* ***Suburb***, 3m/5km NW of Nottingham city centre. SK5343.
Cindery Island *Essex* ***Island***, uninhabited island in Brightlingsea Creek, S of Brightlingsea. TM0915.
Cinnamon Brow *Warr.* ***Suburb***, in NE part of Warrington. SJ6291.
Cìoch Mhòr *High.* ***Mountain***, in Ross and Cromarty district, 8m/12km E of Gorstan. Height 1581 feet or 482 metres. **96 C5** NH5063.
Cioch-na-h-Oighe *N.Ayr.* ***Mountain***, on Arran, 6m/9km N of Brodick. Height 2168 feet or 661 metres. **73 H6** NR9943.
Cippenham *Slo.* ***Suburb***, W district of Slough. SU9480.
Cippyn *Pembs.* ***Settlement***, 2m/3km NW of St. Dogmaels. **26 A4** SN1448.
Cir Mhòr *N.Ayr.* ***Mountain***, National Trust for Scotland property on Arran, 3m/5km W of Corrie. Height 2617 feet or 798 metres. **73 H6** NR9743.
Cirbhig (Anglicised form: Kirivick.) *W.Isles* ***Settlement***, 1km SW of Carloway, Isle of Lewis. **100 D3** NB1941.
Cirean Geardail *High.* ***Coastal feature***, headland 1m/2km SW of Point of Stoer, Sutherland district. **102 C5** NC0034.
Cirencester *Glos.* Population: 15,221. ***Town***, market town on site of Roman Corinium, 14m/22km NW of Swindon. In Roman times town was second only to London. Former wool centre. Many notable buildings, including 15c St. John's Church, 13c St. John's Hospital and Corn Hall. Roman history in Corinium Museum. Amphitheatre (English Heritage). Craftwork displays at Brewery Arts centre. Nearby Cirencester Park was established by Lord Bathurst. **20 D1** SP0202.
Cirencester Roman Amphitheatre *Glos.* ***Historic/prehistoric site***, grass-covered amphitheatre (English Heritage) with walls up to 25 feet high, to SW of Cirencester town centre. **20 D1** SP0201.
Cissbury Ring *W.Suss.* ***Historic/prehistoric site***, Iron Age fort (National Trust) on South Downs 1m/2km E of Findon, on site of flint-mining industry of early Neolithic period. Views to Beachy Head and Isle of Wight. **12 E6** TQ1408.
Ciste Dhubh *High.* ***Mountain***, on border of Inverness and Skye and Lochalsh districts, 3m/5km N of head of Loch Cluanie. Munro: height 3221 feet or 982 metres. **87 G3** NH0616.
Citadel *High.* ***Suburb***, to N of Inverness town centre. NH6646.
Citadilla *N.Yorks.* ***Locality***, 1km N of Catterick Bridge. NZ2200.
City *V. of Glam.* ***Hamlet***, 2m/4km N of Cowbridge. SS9878.
City Dulas *I.o.A.* ***Settlement***, on Anglesey, 4m/6km NE of Llanerchymedd. **46 C4** SH4687.

City of London Guildhall *Gt.Lon.* ***Historic house***, in City of London, 2m/3km NE of Charing Cross. 15c Guildhall with alterations to façade by George Dance, 1789, and later restorations by Sir Giles Gilbert Scott. Great Hall is used for ceremonial occasions. Medieval groined vaulting in crypts. Roman amphitheatre excavated in courtyard. Library provides historical information about London, and contains Museum of the Clockmakers Company. TQ3281.
Clabhach *Arg. & B.* ***Settlement***, near NW coast of Coll, 3m/5km NW of Arinagour. **78 C2** NM1858.
Clach Bheinn *Arg. & B.* ***Mountain***, with craggy summit, in Argyll Forest Park, rising above W shore of Loch Eck. Height 2109 feet or 643 metres. **73 K2** NS1288.
Clach-bhreac *Arg. & B.* ***Settlement***, near head of Loch Caolisport, 8m/12km NW of Tarbert. **73 F3** NR7675.
Clach Dhian *Moray Gaelic form of Shelter Stone, qv.*
Clach Leathad (Also known as Clachlet). *High.* ***Mountain***, in Lochaber district, 7m/11km NW of Bridge of Orchy, with skiing facilities. Height 3601 feet or 1098 metres. **80 D3** NN2449.
Clachaig *Arg. & B.* ***Settlement***, on Little Eachaig River in Argyll, 5m/8km NW of Dunoon. **73 K2** NS1181.
Clachaig Water *Arg. & B.* ***River***, on Kintyre, flowing W to enter sea at Muasdale, 4m/6km S of Tayinloan. **72 E6** NR6840.
Clachan *Arg. & B.* ***Locality***, with power station, at head of Loch Fyne, in Argyll. **80 C6** NN1812.
Clachan *Arg. & B.* ***Settlement***, on Lismore, 2m/3km SW of Port Ramsay. **79 K3** NM8643.
Clachan *Arg. & B.* ***Village***, in Kintyre, Argyll, 10m/16km SW of Tarbert. **73 F5** NR7656.
Clachan *High.* ***Hamlet***, on W coast of Raasay, 2m/3km NW of S end of island. **86 B1** NG5436.
Clachan *W.Isles* ***Settlement***, 2m/3km E of Ardivachar Point on South Uist. **92 C7** NF7746.
Clachan-a-Luib *W.Isles* ***Settlement***, near W coast of North Uist, 3m/5km N of Cairinis. NF8163.
Clachan Burn *High.* ***River***, flowing NW into sea at Farr Bay, Caithness district. **104 C3** NC7162.
Clachan Hill *Arg. & B.* ***Mountain***, to N of Loch Fyne, 7m/11km NE of Inveraray. Height 2158 feet or 658 metres. **80 C6** NN1815.
Clachan Mòr *Arg. & B.* ***Settlement***, on N coast of Tiree, 5m/7km NW of Scarinish. NL9847.
Clachan of Campsie (Also known as Campsie.) *E.Dun.* ***Village***, 2m/3km NW of Lennoxtown. **74 E3** NS6179.
Clachan of Glendaruel *Arg. & B.* ***Village***, in Argyll, on River Ruel, 4m/6km N of head of Loch Riddon. **73 J2** NR9984.
Clachan-Seil *Arg. & B.* ***Settlement***, on Seil, nearly 1m/2km S of Clachan Bridge. **79 J6** NM7819.
Clachan Yell *Aber.* ***Mountain***, 6m/10km SE of Ballater. Height 2053 feet or 626 metres. **90 C5** NO4491.
Clachandhu *Arg. & B.* ***Settlement***, 1km N of Balnahard, Mull. **79 F4** NM4535.
Clachaneasy *D. & G.* ***Settlement***, 7m/11km NW of Newton Stewart. **64 D3** NX3574.
Clachanmore *D. & G.* ***Settlement***, 7m/11km SE of Portpatrick. **64 A6** NX0846.
Clachanturn *Aber.* ***Settlement***, 1m/2km SE of Craithie, S of River Dee. **89 K5** NO2794.
Clachlet *High. Alternative name for Clach Leathad, qv.*
Clachnaben *Aber.* ***Mountain***, 2m/3km W of Bridge of Dye. Height 1932 feet or 589 metres. **90 E6** NO6186.
Clachnabrain *Angus* ***Settlement***, in Glen Clova, 2m/3km S of Rottal. **82 E1** NO3766.
Clachnaharry *High.* ***Suburb***, in Inverness district, at N terminus of Caledonian Canal, on NW side of Inverness. **96 D7** NH6446.
Clachtoll *High.* ***Hamlet***, on W coast of Sutherland district, 5m/8km S of Point of Stoer. **102 C6** NC0427.
Clackmannan *Clack.* Population: 3420. ***Small town***, former wool manufacturing town, 2m/3km E of Alloa. Remains of 14-15c tower. **75 H1** NS9191.
Clackmannan Tower *Clack.* ***Historic/prehistoric site***, tall 15c tower to W of Clackmannan. **75 H1** NS9092.
Clackmarras *Moray* ***Settlement***, 3m/5km SE of Elgin. NJ2458.
Clackriach *Aber.* ***Locality***, 1m/2km S of Maud with remains of castle. NJ9246.
Clacton-on-Sea *Essex* Population: 45,065. ***Town***, North Sea resort, developed in 1860s, with pier, 13m/21km SE of Colchester. Seven mile stretch of beach. Holiday and entertainment centre. Living Ocean aquarium. **35 F7** TM1714.
Clacton Pier *Essex* ***Other feature of interest***, 1km S of Clacton-on-Sea town centre. **35 F7** TM1714.
Cladach a' Chaolais (Anglicised form: Claddach Kyles.) *W.Isles* ***Settlement***, on North Uist, 6m/9km SE of Aird an Rùnair. **92 C5** NF7666.
Cladach Chircebost (Anglicised form: Claddach Kirkibost.) *W.Isles* ***Settlement***, on North Uist, 6m/10km SE of Aird an Rùnair. **92 C5** NF7865.
Claddach Kirkibost *W.Isles Anglicised form of Cladach Chircebost, qv.*
Claddach Kyles *W.Isles Anglicised form of Cladach a' Chaolais, qv.*
Cladich *Arg. & B.* ***Settlement***, in Argyll, near E side of Loch Awe, 5m/9km SW of Dalmally. **80 B5** NN0921.
Cladswell *Worcs.* ***Settlement***, 3m/4km NW of Alcester. SP0458.
Claerwen ***River***, rising SE of Cwmystwyth and flowing S to head of Claerwen Reservoir, then SE through reservoir, and on to head of Caban Coch Reservoir. SN9061.
Claerwen Reservoir *Powys* ***Reservoir***, large reservoir in River Claerwen valley, 7m/11km W of Rhayader. **27 H2** SN8663.
Claggain Bay *Arg. & B.* ***Bay***, on E coast of Islay, 4m/6km S of McArthur's Head. **72 C5** NR4653.
Claggan *High.* ***Locality***, in Lochaber district, 4m/6km N of Lochaline. **79 J3** NM6949.
Claggan *High.* ***Settlement***, adjoining to NE of Fort William. **87 H7** NN1274.
Clagh Ouyr *I.o.M.* ***Mountain***, 3m/5km NW of Laxey. Height 1807 feet or 551 metres. **54 D5** SC4188.
Claife Heights *Cumb.* ***Open space***, moorland and woodland, containing several tarns, between Esthwaite Water and Windermere. **60 E7** SD3797.
Claigan *High.* ***Settlement***, on Skye, 2m/3km SW of Rubha Maol. **93 H6** NG2353.
Claines *Worcs.* ***Hamlet***, 3m/4km N of Worcester. **29 H3** SO8558.
Clairinch *Stir.* ***Island***, wooded islet in Loch Lomond, 1km SW of Balmaha. Part of nature reserve also comprising Inchcailloch and Torrinch. NS4189.
Claish Moss *High.* ***Marsh/bog***, 2m/4km NE of Salen, Lochaber district. **79 J1** NM7167.
Clandon Park *Surr.* ***Historic house***, 18c house and grounds (National Trust), 3m/4km E of Guildford. **22 D6** TQ0451.
Clandown *B. & N.E.Som.* ***Locality***, on N side of Radstock. **19 K6** ST6855.
Clanfield *Hants.* ***Locality***, 3m/4km N of Horndean. **11 J3** SU6916.
Clanfield *Oxon.* ***Village***, 4m/7km N of Faringdon. **21 F1** SP2802.
Clannaborough Barton *Devon* ***Hamlet***, 6m/10km W of Crediton. Road junction, Clannaborough Cross, to N. **7 F5** SS7402.
Clanville *Hants.* ***Village***, 4m/6km NW of Andover. Site of Roman villa to W. **21 G7** SU3148.
Clanyard Bay *D. & G.* ***Bay***, on W coast of Rinns of Galloway, 2m/3km S of Port Logan. **64 A7** NX0938.
Claonaig *Arg. & B.* ***Settlement***, in Kintyre, Argyll, 2m/3km W of Skipness. **73 G5** NR8756.
Claonairigh *Arg. & B.* ***Settlement***, 3m/5km SW of Inveraray. **80 B7** NN0504.
Claonel *High.* ***Settlement***, 1m/2km SW of Lairg. **96 C1** NC5604.
Clap Gate *N.Yorks.* ***Settlement***, 4m/6km W of Wetherby. **57 J5** SE3447.
Clapgate *Dorset* ***Settlement***, 2m/3km N of Wimborne Minster. **10 B4** SU0102.
Clapgate *Herts.* ***Hamlet***, 4m/6km NW of Bishop's Stortford. TL4425.
Clapham *Beds.* Population: 3501. ***Village***, on River Great Ouse, 2m/3km NW of Bedford. **32 D3** TL0352.
Clapham *Devon* ***Hamlet***, 4m/6km SW of Exeter. SX8987.
Clapham *Gt.Lon.* ***Suburb***, in borough of Lambeth, 3m/5km S of Charing Cross. Clapham Common is large open space to W; to W again is Clapham Junction, well-known railway junction and station. **23 F4** TQ2975.
Clapham *N.Yorks.* ***Village***, 6m/9km NW of Settle. **56 C3** SD7469.
Clapham *W.Suss.* ***Village***, 4m/7km NW of Worthing. **12 D6** TQ0906.
Clapham Bridge *N.Yorks.* ***Bridge***, stone packhorse bridge over Clapham Beck in village of Clapham, 5m/8km NW of Settle. SD7469.
Clapham Folly *Beds.* ***Suburb***, adjoining to NW of Clapham, 3m/4km NW of Bedford. TL0253.
Clapham Green *Beds.* ***Settlement***, adjoining to E of Clapham, 2m/3km NW of Bedford. TL0352.
Clapham Green *N.Yorks.* ***Hamlet***, 1m/2km W of Hampsthwaite. SE2458.
Clapham Hill *Kent* ***Suburb***, in S part of Whitstable. **25 H5** TR1064.
Clappers *Sc.Bord.* ***Hamlet***, 1m/2km E of Foulden. **77 H5** NT9455.
Clappersgate *Cumb.* ***Settlement***, 1km SW of Ambleside. Remains of 1c-2c Roman fort of Galava (English Heritage). **60 E6** NY3603.
Clapton *Som.* ***Hamlet***, 1m/2km SW of Midsomer Norton. ST6453.
Clapton *Som.* ***Village***, 3m/4km SW of Crewkerne. **8 D4** ST4106.
Clapton Court *Som.* ***Garden***, 3m/5km SW of Crewkerne. Formal terraces, rose and water gardens, and woodland including 200 year-old ash tree. **8 D4** ST4106.
Clapton-in-Gordano *N.Som.* ***Village***, 3m/4km SE of Portishead. **19 H4** ST4774.
Clapton-on-the-Hill *Glos.* ***Village***, 4m/6km NE of Northleach. **30 C7** SP1617.
Clapton Park *Gt.Lon.* ***Suburb***, in borough of Hackney, to S of Hackney Marsh, 1m/2km NE of Hackney. TQ3685.
Clapworthy *Devon* ***Hamlet***, 3m/4km SW of South Molton. **6 E3** SS6724.
Clapworthy Cross *Devon* ***Settlement***, 1m/2km NW of Clapworthy and 4m/6km W of South Molton. SS6525.
Clara Vale *T. & W.* ***Village***, 1m/2km W of Ryton. NZ1364.
Clarach *Cere.* ***Hamlet***, on N side of Llangorwen, 2m/3km NE of Aberystwyth. **37 F7** SN6083.
Clarbeston *Pembs.* ***Village***, 7m/11km NE of Haverfordwest. **16 D2** SN0421.
Clarbeston Road *Pembs.* ***Village***, 2m/3km W of Clarbeston. **16 D2** SN0421.
Clarborough *Notts.* ***Village***, 2m/4km NE of Retford. **51 K4** SK7383.
Clardon *High.* ***Locality***, includes Clardon Hill and scattered settlements to E of Thurso. **105 G2** ND1368.
Clardon Head *High.* ***Coastal feature***, headland on N coast of Caithness district, 3m/4km NE of Thurso. **105 G1** ND1570.
Clare *Suff.* Population: 1976. ***Small town***, market town on River Stour, 7m/11km NW of Sudbury. Many pargeted houses. Scant remains of medieval castle and priory. **34 B4** TL7645.
Clare Castle Country Park *Suff.* ***Leisure/recreation***, country park in Clare, on River Stour. Variety of landscapes from grassland to woodland and ponds, with a variety of birdlife. Also ruins of castle keep. **34 B4** TL7645.
Clare Priory *Essex* ***Ecclesiastical building***, remains of Augustinian priory founded in 1248 at Clare, on River Stour. Burial place of Lionel, Duke of Clarence, Edward III's son. **34 B4** TL7744.
Clarebrand *D. & G.* ***Settlement***, 2m/3km N of Castle Douglas. **65 H4** NX7665.
Clareland *Worcs.* ***Locality***, 1m/2km SE of Stourport-on-Severn. SO8269.
Claremont Park *Surr.* ***Suburb***, to SE of Esher, including Claremont, 18c house now a school, and Claremont Landscape Garden (National Trust), 1m/2km S of Esher. **22 E5** TQ1363.
Clarencefield *D. & G.* ***Village***, 7m/11km W of Annan. **69 F7** NY0968.
Clarendon Park *Leic.* ***Suburb***, 1m/2km S of Leicester city centre. SK5902.
Clarendon Park *Wilts.* ***Locality***, parish 3m/5km E of Salisbury, containing classical mansion, Clarendon House, and remains of medieval Clarendon Palace. SU1830.
Clareton *N.Yorks.* ***Settlement***, 3m/5km NE of Knaresborough. **57 J4** SE3959.
Clarilaw *Sc.Bord.* ***Settlement***, 3m/5km NE of Hawick. **70 A2** NT5218.
Clark Green *Ches.* ***Settlement***, 1m/2km N of Bollington. SJ9379.
Clarken Green *Hants.* ***Locality***, 5m/8km W of Basingstoke and 1km E of Oakley. SU5650.
Clark's Green *Surr.* ***Settlement***, 6m/9km N of Horsham. TQ1739.
Clarkston *E.Renf.* Population: 18,899. ***Suburb***, 5m/8km S of Glasgow. **74 D5** NS5757.
Clashach Point *Moray* ***Coastal feature***, point on N coast 1km NE of Hopeman. Clashnach Cove is bay to E. **97 J4** NJ1570.
Clashban *High.* ***Settlement***, 3m/5km NE of Bonar Bridge. **96 D2** NH6496.
Clashcoig *High.* ***Settlement***, 3m/4km NE of Bonar Bridge. **96 D2** NH6393.
Clashdorran *High.* ***Settlement***, in Ross and Cromarty district, 1m/2km SW of Muir of Ord. NH5148.
Clashgour *Arg. & B.* ***Settlement***, 4m/7km NW of Bridge of Orchy. **80 D3** NN2342.
Clashindarroch *Aber.* ***Settlement***, on W side of Kirkney Water, 3m/4km W of Gartly. **90 C1** NJ4831.
Clashindarroch Forest *Aber.* ***Forest/woodland***, 6m/9km SW of Huntly. **90 C1** NJ4633.
Clashmach Hill *Aber.* ***Mountain***, 4m/7km E of Haugh of Glass. Height 1230 feet or 375 metres. **90 C1** NJ4938.
Clashmore *High.* ***Settlement***, 3m/5km S of Point of Stoer, W coast of Sutherland district. NC0331.
Clashmore *High.* ***Village***, in Sutherland district, 3m/5km W of Dornoch. **96 E2** NH7489.
Clashmore Wood *High.* ***Forest/woodland***, on slopes of Creagan Asdale, 3m/5km W of Dornoch. **96 E2** NH7490.
Clashnessie *High.* ***Hamlet***, on Clashnessie Bay, W coast of Sutherland district, 4m/6km SE of Point of Stoer. **102 C5** NC0530.
Clashnessie Bay *High.* ***Bay***, on W coast of Sutherland district, 4m/6km SE of Point of Stoer. **102 C5** NC0531.
Clashnoir *Moray* ***Locality***, 5m/7km NE of Tomintoul. **89 K2** NJ2222.
Clatford *Wilts.* ***Hamlet***, 2m/3km W of Marlborough. SU1568.
Clatford Oakcuts *Hants.* ***Locality***, 3m/5km NW of Stockbridge. SU3339.
Clathy *P. & K.* ***Settlement***, 6m/9km NE of Auchterarder. **82 A5** NN9920.
Clatt (Also known as Kirktown of Clatt). *Aber.* ***Village***, 3m/5km E of Rhynie. **90 D2** NJ5325.
Clatter *Powys* ***Hamlet***, 3m/4km NW of Caersws. **37 J6** SN9994.
Clattercote *Oxon.* ***Settlement***, 5m/8km N of Banbury. Reservoir to SW. SP4549.
Clatterford *I.o.W.* ***Suburb***, 1m/2km SW of Newport. SZ4887.
Clatterford End *Essex* ***Hamlet***, 2m/3km SW of Chipping Ongar. TL5202.
Clatterford End *Essex* ***Locality***, adjoining to SW of Fyfield, 3m/4km N of Chipping Ongar. **23 J1** TL5606.
Clatterford End *Essex* ***Settlement***, 2m/3km E of Leaden Roding. TL6113.
Clatterin Brig *Aber.* ***Settlement***, 3m/5km N of Fettercairn. **90 E7** NO6678.
Clatteringshaws *D. & G.* ***Settlement***, on E side of Clatteringshaws Loch, 6m/9km W of New Galloway. **65 F3** NX5576.
Clatteringshaws Loch *D. & G.* ***Lake/loch***, large loch and reservoir (Galloway Hydro-electricity Scheme) 5m/9km W of New Galloway. Bruce's Stone (National Trust for Scotland), granite boulder on E shore. Galloway Deer Museum on E shore 1km S of Bruce's Stone. **65 F3** NX5476.
Clatto Country Park *Dundee* ***Leisure/recreation***, 3m/4km N of Dundee city centre. Reservoir is focal point of this 35 acre country park. **82 E4** NO3634.
Clatto Hill *Fife* ***Hill***, 3m/4km N of Kennoway. Height 813 feet or 248 metres. **82 E7** NO3506.
Clatworthy *Som.* ***Hamlet***, 3m/4km NW of Wiveliscombe. **7 J2** ST0530.
Clatworthy Reservoir *Som.* ***Reservoir***, in upper valley of River Tone to W of Clatworthy. **7 J2** ST0431.
Clauchlands Point *N.Ayr.* ***Coastal feature***, headland on E coast of Arran, at N end of Lamlash Bay. **73 J7** NS0532.
Clauchrie Burn *D. & G.* ***River***, stream rising on Auchercairn Height and flowing S to join River Nith, 1km N of Auldgirth. **68 E5** NX9087.
Claughton *Lancs.* ***Hamlet***, 3m/5km SE of Garstang. **55 J5** SD5242.
Claughton *Lancs.* ***Village***, 6m/10km NE of Lancaster. **55 J3** SD5666.
Claughton *Mersey.* ***Suburb***, 1m/2km W of Birkenhead town centre. SJ3088.
Clausentum *S'ham. See Bitterne.*

Clava Cairns *High.* ***Historic/prehistoric site***, group of three Stone Age-Bronze Age burial cairns (Historic Scotland), 6m/9km E of Inverness beyond Culloden. **96 E7** NH7544.
Claverdon *Warks.* ***Village***, 3m/5km E of Henley-in-Arden. **30 C2** SP1964.
Claverham *N.Som.* ***Village***, 2m/3km N of Congresbury. **19 H5** ST4466.
Clavering *Essex* ***Village***, 7m/11km N of Bishop's Stortford. **33 H5** TL4731.
Claverley *Shrop.* ***Village***, 5m/8km E of Bridgnorth. **39 G6** SO7993.
Claverton *B. & N.E.Som.* ***Village***, above River Avon and Kennet and Avon Canal, 3m/4km E of Bath. Museum of American domestic life. **20 A5** ST7864.
Claverton Down *B. & N.E.Som.* ***Settlement***, 1km SW of Claverton. ST7763.
Claverton Manor *B. & N.E.Som.* ***Historic house***, Georgian manor house 3m/4km E of Bath. Houses American Museum with 17c-19c American domestic interiors and folk art. **20 A5** ST7864.
Claw *Devon* ***River***, rising 2m/3km E of Hollacombe and flowing SW through Clawton to River Tamar, to W of Tetcott. SX3296.
Clawdd-côch *V. of Glam.* ***Hamlet***, 4m/7km NE of Cowbridge. ST0577.
Clawdd-ddu-bach *Powys* ***Inland physical feature***, mountain ridge rising to 1679 feet or 512 metres, 2m/3km W of Craig Goch Reservoir. **27 H2** SN8670.
Clawdd-newydd *Denb.* ***Hamlet***, 5m/7km SW of Ruthin. **47 J7** SJ0852.
Clawfin *E.Ayr.* ***Settlement***, 2m/3km NE of Dalmellington. **67 K3** NS5007.
Clawthorpe *Cumb.* ***Settlement***, 1km N of Burton-in-Kendal. **55 J2** SD5377.
Clawton *Devon* ***Village***, 3m/5km S of Holsworthy. **6 B6** SX3599.
Claxby *Lincs.* ***Settlement***, 3m/5km S of Alford. **53 H5** TF4571.
Claxby *Lincs.* ***Village***, 4m/6km N of Market Rasen. **52 E3** TF1194.
Claxby Pluckacre *Lincs.* ***Locality***, 4m/7km SE of Horncastle. **53 G6** TF3064.
Claxton *Hart.* ***Settlement***, 1m/2km NW of Greatham. NZ4728.
Claxton *Norf.* ***Village***, 2m/3km E of Rockland St. Mary. **45 H5** TG3303.
Claxton *N.Yorks.* ***Village***, 3m/5km N of Stamford Bridge. **58 C3** SE6960.
Clay Common *Suff.* ***Settlement***, 4m/6km NW of Southwold. **45 J7** TM4780.
Clay Coton *Northants.* ***Village***, 6m/9km E of Rugby. **31 G1** SP5977.
Clay Cross *Derbys.* Population: 12,135. ***Town***, industrial town, 5m/8km S of Chesterfield. **51 F6** SK3963.
Clay End *Herts.* ***Hamlet***, 4m/7km E of Stevenage. TL3025.
Clay Gates *Staffs.* ***Settlement***, 1m/2km NE of Brewood. SJ9009.
Clay Head *I.o.M.* ***Coastal feature***, headland at S end of Laxey Bay, 5m/8km NE of Douglas. **54 D5** SC4480.
Clay Hill *Bristol* ***Suburb***, 3m/5km NE of Bristol city centre. ST6274.
Clay Hill *Gt.Lon.* ***Suburb***, in borough of Enfield, 1m/2km N of Enfield town centre. TQ3298.
Clay Lake *Lincs.* ***Suburb***, 1km SE of Spalding town centre. TF2521.
Clay Mills *Staffs.* ***Locality***, 3m/4km N of Burton upon Trent, adjoining to NE of Stretton. SK2627.
Clay of Allan *High.* ***Settlement***, 4m/6km SE of Tain. **97 F4** NH8276.
Clay Street *Suff.* ***Settlement***, 1km W of Thornham Magna. TM0970.
Claybrooke Magna *Leics.* ***Village***, 4m/7km NW of Lutterworth. **41 G7** SP4988.
Claybrooke Parva *Leics.* ***Village***, 4m/6km NW of Lutterworth. **41 G7** SP4987.
Claydene *Kent* ***Settlement***, 5m/8km NW of Groombridge. **23 H7** TQ4641.
Claydon *Oxon.* ***Village***, 6m/10km N of Banbury. **31 F3** SP4550.
Claydon *Suff.* Population: 3285. ***Village***, 4m/6km NW of Ipswich. **35 F4** TM1349.
Claydon House *Bucks.* ***Historic house***, seat of Verney family in Middle Claydon, 15m/24km NW of Aylesbury. Built in 1768 and noted for its extravagant interior rococo decoration produced by Luke Lightfoot, carpenter of second Earl Verney. **31 J6** SP7125.
Claygate *Kent* ***Hamlet***, 3m/5km E of Paddock Wood. **14 C3** TQ7144.
Claygate *Surr.* ***Village***, 1m/2km S of Esher. **22 E5** TQ1563.
Claygate Cross *Kent* ***Settlement***, 1m/2km S of Borough Green. **23 K6** TQ6155.
Clayhall *Gt.Lon.* ***Suburb***, in borough of Redbridge, 2m/4km NW of Ilford. TQ4289.
Clayhanger *Devon* ***Village***, 4m/7km E of Bampton. **7 J3** ST0222.
Clayhanger *Som.* ***Hamlet***, 2m/3km N of Chard. ST3111.
Clayhanger *W.Mid.* ***Hamlet***, 1km SW of Brownhills. **40 C5** SK0404.
Clayhidon *Devon* ***Hamlet***, 4m/6km SE of Wellington. **7 K4** ST1615.
Clayhill *E.Suss.* ***Hamlet***, 1m/2km W of Beckley. TQ8423.
Clayhill *Hants.* ***Hamlet***, 1km S of Lyndhurst. SU3007.
Clayhythe *Cambs.* ***Hamlet***, on E bank of River Cam, 5m/8km NE of Cambridge. TL5064.
Clayland Cross *Torbay* ***Suburb***, on SW side of Paignton. SX8759.
Clayock *High.* ***Locality***, 1m/2km E of Georgemas Junction Station. **105 G3** ND1659.
Claypit Hill *Cambs.* ***Hamlet***, 6m/10km SW of Cambridge city centre. TL3554.
Claypits *Glos.* ***Hamlet***, 5m/8km W of Stroud. SO7606.
Claypole *Lincs.* ***Village***, 5m/7km SE of Newark-on-Trent. **42 B1** SK8449.
Claypotts Castle *Dundee* ***Castle***, 16c castle (Historic Scotland), 1km NW of Broughty Ferry. **83 F4** NO4531.
Claythorn *Glas.* ***Suburb***, 3m/5km NW of Glasgow city centre. NS5468.
Claythorpe *Lincs.* ***Settlement***, 3m/5km NW of Alford. **53 H5** TF4179.
Clayton *Gt.Man.* ***Suburb***, 3m/5km E of Manchester city centre. SJ8898.
Clayton *S.Yorks.* ***Village***, 3m/4km SW of South Elmsall. **51 G2** SE4507.
Clayton *Staffs.* ***Suburb***, S district of Newcastle-under-Lyme. **40 A1** SJ8543.
Clayton *W.Suss.* ***Village***, 6m/10km N of Brighton. On South Downs above village are two windmills known as Jack and Jill. **13 F5** TQ2914.
Clayton *W.Yorks.* ***Suburb***, 3m/5km W of Bradford city centre. **57 G6** SE1131.
Clayton Bridge *Gt.Man.* ***Locality***, 1km NE of Clayton. SJ8898.
Clayton Brook *Lancs.* ***Locality***, 2m/4km NE of Leyland. SD5724.
Clayton Green *Lancs.* ***Village***, 2m/4km E of Leyland. SD5723.
Clayton Heights *W.Yorks.* ***Suburb***, of Bradford, 1m/2km E of Queensbury. SE1230.
Clayton-le-Dale *Lancs.* ***Hamlet***, 1km S of Copster Green and 3m/5km N of Blackburn. SD6633.
Clayton-le-Moors *Lancs.* Population: 6961. ***Small town***, 2m/3km NW of Accrington. **56 C6** SD7431.
Clayton-le-Woods *Lancs.* ***Suburb***, to E of Leyland. **55 J7** SD5622.
Clayton West *W.Yorks.* Population: 3994. ***Village***, 6m/10km NW of Barnsley. **50 E1** SE2510.
Clayworth *Notts.* ***Village***, 5m/8km N of Retford. **51 K4** SK7288.
Cleadale *High.* ***Hamlet***, at NW end of Eigg. **85 K6** NM4788.
Cleadon *T. & W.* Population: 5088. ***Suburb***, 3m/5km S of South Shields. **71 J7** NZ3862.
Clearbrook *Devon* ***Hamlet***, on River Meavy, 7m/12km NE of Plymouth. **5 F4** SX5265.
Clearwell *Glos.* ***Village***, 2m/3km S of Coleford. Neo-Gothic castle. To N, Clearwell Caves, ancient iron ore mines. **19 J1** SO5708.
Clearwell Meend *Glos.* ***Locality***, 1m/2km E of Clearwell. SO5708.
Cleasby *N.Yorks.* ***Village***, 3m/4km W of Darlington across River Tees. **62 D5** NZ2513.
Cleasby Hill *N.Yorks.* ***Mountain***, 4m/6km S of Bowes, on W side of Faggergill Moor. Height 1673 feet or 510 metres. **62 A6** NY9707.
Cleat *Ork.* ***Settlement***, near S end of South Ronaldsay, 1m/2km NE of Brough Ness. **107 D9** ND4584.
Cleat *W.Isles* ***Settlement***, on N coast of Barra, 1m/2km E of Greian Head. NF6604.
Cleat Hill *Beds.* ***Hill***, rising to over 60 metres, 3m/4km NE of Bedford town centre. **32 D3** TL0653.
Cleatham *N.Lincs.* ***Locality***, 1m/2km N of Kirton in Lindsey. Extensive quarries. SE9300.
Cleatlam *Dur.* ***Village***, 1m/2km S of Staindrop. **62 C5** NZ1118.
Cleatop *N.Yorks.* ***Settlement***, in Ribble valley, 1m/2km S of Settle. **56 D3** SD8161.
Cleator *Cumb.* ***Village***, 2m/3km N of Egremont. **60 B5** NY0113.
Cleator Moor *Cumb.* Population: 6410. ***Village***, 1m/2km N of Cleator. **60 B5** NY0214.
Cleaves *N.Yorks.* ***Locality***, 1km NE of Sutton-under-Whitestonecliffe. SE4983.
Cleckheaton *W.Yorks.* Population: 13,576. ***Town***, 4m/7km NW of Dewsbury. Formerly a Roman iron-working area. **57 G7** SE1925.
Cledan *Powys* ***River***, flowing NE into River Irfon, 1km E of Llanwrtyd Wells. **27 H4** SN8945.
Cledwen *Conwy* ***River***, running N by Gwytherin to join River Gallen at Llangernyw, forming River Elwy. SH8767.
Clee Hill *Shrop.* *Alternative name for Titterstone Clee Hill, qv.*
Clee St. Margaret *Shrop.* ***Village***, 7m/11km NE of Ludlow. **38 E7** SO5684.
Cleedownton *Shrop.* ***Hamlet***, 6m/9km NE of Ludlow. **38 E7** SO5880.
Cleehill *Shrop.* ***Village***, 5m/8km E of Ludlow. **28 E1** SO5975.
Cleers *Cornw.* ***Settlement***, 5m/7km NW of St. Austell. SW9758.
Cleestanton *Shrop.* ***Hamlet***, 5m/8km NE of Ludlow. SO5779.
Cleethorpes *N.E.Lincs.* Population: 32,719. ***Town***, coastal resort at mouth of River Humber, adjoining to E of Grimsby. Sandy beaches, pier and all-weather leisure centre. Norman church in old part of town. **53 G2** TA3008.
Cleethorpes Coast Light Railway *N.E.Lincs.* ***Other feature of interest***, runs along coast, from S to centre of Cleethorpes, taking in views of Humber estuary. Has rare steam locomotives. **53 G2** TA3207.
Cleeton St. Mary *Shrop.* ***Village***, 5m/7km NW of Cleobury Mortimer. **29 F1** SO6178.
Cleeve *N.Som.* ***Village***, 2m/3km NE of Congresbury. **19 H5** ST4666.
Cleeve *Oxon.* ***Locality***, N district of Goring. **21 K3** SU6081.
Cleeve Abbey *Som.* ***Ecclesiastical building***, remains of 13c Cistercian abbey (English Heritage) in Washford. **7 J1** ST0440.
Cleeve Hill *Glos.* ***Village***, 4m/6km NE of Cheltenham. **29 J6** SO9826.
Cleeve Prior *Worcs.* ***Village***, 5m/8km NE of Evesham. **30 B4** SP0849.
Cleghorn *S.Lan.* ***Settlement***, 2m/3km NE of Lanark. **75 H6** NS8946.
Clehonger *Here.* ***Village***, 3m/5km SW of Hereford. **28 D5** SO4637.
Cleidda Hill *Mon.* *Welsh form of Clytha Hill, qv.*
Cleigh *Arg. & B.* ***Settlement***, in Argyll, 3m/5km S of Oban. **79 K5** NM8725.
Cleirwy *Powys* *Welsh form of Clyro, qv.*
Cleiseval *W.Isles* ***Mountain***, in Forest of Harris, 2m/3km SW of head of Loch Meavaig. Height 1676 feet or 511 metres. **100 C7** NB0708.
Cleish *P. & K.* ***Village***, 3m/5km SW of Kinross at foot of Cleish Hills. **75 J1** NT0998.
Cleish Hills *P. & K.* ***Large natural feature***, hills extend from Saline in W to Kelty in E, SW of Loch Leven. **75 J1** NT0696.
Cleland *N.Lan.* Population: 2945. ***Village***, 3m/5km E of Motherwell. **75 F5** NS7958.
Clement Street *Kent* ***Settlement***, 2m/3km NE of Swanley. TQ5370.
Clement's End *Beds.* ***Settlement***, 4m/7km S of Dunstable. TL0215.
Clench Common *Wilts.* ***Settlement***, 2m/3km S of Marlborough. **20 E5** SU1765.
Clenchwarton *Norf.* Population: 2156. ***Village***, 2m/3km W of King's Lynn across River Great Ouse. **43 J3** TF5820.
Clennell *Northumb.* ***Settlement***, 1km NE of Alwinton. NT9207.
Clent *Worcs.* ***Village***, to S of Clent Hills, 4m/6km SE of Stourbridge. **29 J1** SO9279.
Clent Hills *Worcs.* ***Large natural feature***, National Trust owned, 4m/6km SE of Stourbridge. **29 J1** SO9379.
Clent Hills Country Park *Worcs.* ***Leisure/recreation***, country park 3m/5km SE of Stourbridge, with over 360 acres of woodland featuring variety of wildlife and four standing stones dating from 18c. **40 B7** SO9379.
Cleobury Mortimer *Shrop.* Population: 2164. ***Village***, 10m/16km E of Ludlow. **29 F1** SO6775.
Cleobury North *Shrop.* ***Village***, 7m/11km SW of Bridgnorth. **39 F7** SO6286.
Clephanton *High.* ***Settlement***, 5m/8km SW of Nairn. **97 F6** NH8150.
Clerk Green *W.Yorks.* ***Suburb***, 1km SW of Batley town centre. SE2323.
Clerkenwell *Gt.Lon.* ***Suburb***, in boroughs of Camden and Islington, 1m/2km NE of Charing Cross. TQ3182.
Clerklands *Sc.Bord.* ***Hamlet***, 3m/5km SE of Selkirk. **70 A1** NT5024.
Clermiston *Edin.* ***Suburb***, 4m/6km W of Edinburgh city centre. NT1974.
Clestrain *Ork.* ***Settlement***, in S part of Mainland, E of Skerries of Clestrain. **107 C7** HY3006.
Clestrain Sound *Ork.* ***Sea feature***, sea passage between islands of Mainland and Graemsay. Named after locality on Mainland to E. **107 B7** HY2706.
Clett *High.* ***Island***, islet on W side of Holborn Head, Caithness district, 2m/3km N of Thurso. **105 G1** ND1071.
Clett *High.* ***Island***, islet off NW coast of Skye, 1m/2km S of Ardmore Point. NG2258.
Clett Ard *W.Isles* ***Mountain***, with notable viewpoint, 2m/3km NW of Marvig, to W of Loch Seaforth, North Harris. Height 1076 feet or 328 metres. **100 D7** NB1808.
Clett Head *Shet.* ***Coastal feature***, headland at S end of Whalsay. **109 E6** HU5560.
Clett Nisabost *W.Isles* ***Hill***, near W coast of South Harris, 3m/4km N of Loch Langavat. Height 518 feet or 158 metres. **93 F2** NG0495.
Clettack Skerry *Ork.* ***Island***, one of Pentland Skerries, most easterly of group. ND4877.
Clettwr Fawr *Cere.* ***River***, headwater of River Clettwr, S of Llanarth. Converges with Clettwr Fach at Pontshaen. **26 D4** SN4346.
Cletwr *Cere.* ***River***, rising 4m/6km NE of Talybont and flowing W to Tre'r-ddol, then NW into River Dyfi 2m/3km above Aberdyfi. **37 F6** SN6494.
Cleuch Head *Sc.Bord.* ***Hamlet***, 1m/2km SE of Bonchester Bridge. **70 A2** NT5910.
Cleuchbrae *D. & G.* ***Settlement***, 2m/3km N of Mouswald and 6m/10km W of Dumfries. **69 F6** NY0673.
Clevancy *Wilts.* ***Hamlet***, 4m/7km NE of Calne. **20 D4** SU0575.
Clevedon *N.Som.* Population: 21,670. ***Town***, on River Severn estuary 8m/13km NE of Weston-super-Mare. Shingle beach, small pier 1m/2km E. Clevedon Court (National Trust), manor house of many periods. **19 H4** ST4071.
Clevedon Court *N.Som.* ***Historic house***, 14c manor (National Trust) at E side of Clevedon. Home to Elton family, it has 12c tower, 13c great hall and 18c terraced garden. **19 H4** ST4271.
Cleveland Hills *N.Yorks.* ***Large natural feature***, isolated range of hills in North York Moors National Park, curving round from S of Teeside almost to Thirsk. **63 G7** SE5096.
Cleveland Tontine *N.Yorks.* ***Settlement***, at junction of A19 and A172 roads, 1m/2km NW of Osmotherley. **63 F7** SE4499.
Cleveley *Oxon.* ***Settlement***, 1m/2km E of Enstone and 4m/6km NE of Charlbury. SP3923.
Cleveleys *Lancs.* Population: 14,030. ***Town***, coastal resort, 5m/7km N of Blackpool. **55 G5** SD3143.
Clevelode *Worcs.* ***Hamlet***, on W bank of River Severn, 4m/6km E of Great Malvern. **29 H4** SO8346.
Cleverton *Wilts.* ***Hamlet***, 3m/5km E of Malmesbury. **20 C3** ST9785.
Cleves Cross *Dur.* ***Locality***, on E side of Ferryhill. NZ2932.
Clewer *Som.* ***Hamlet***, 2m/3km SW of Cheddar. **19 H6** ST4451.
Clewer Green *W. & M.* ***Suburb***, SW district of Windsor. SU9475.

Clewer New Town *W. & M.* ***Suburb***, in W part of Windsor. SU9576.
Clewer Village *W. & M.* ***Suburb***, W district of Windsor. **22 C4** SU9577.
Cley *Norf. Familiar form of Cley next the Sea, qv.*
Cley Hill *Wilts.* ***Hill***, chalk hill (National Trust) with Iron Age fort, 2m/4km W of Warminster. Height 804 feet or 245 metres. **20 B7** ST8344.
Cley next the Sea (Commonly referred to as Cley.) *Norf.* ***Village***, 4m/6km NW of Holt. Bird sanctuary on marshes to N. **44 E1** TG0443.
Cliad Bay *Arg. & B.* ***Bay***, on NW coast of Coll, 3m/4km NW of Arinagour. **78 C1** NM1960.
Cliatasay *W.Isles* ***Island***, islet in Loch Roag, W coast of Isle of Lewis, opposite entrance to Little Loch Roag. NB1333.
Cliburn *Cumb.* ***Village***, 6m/9km SE of Penrith. Hall of 16c. **61 G4** NY5824.
Click Mill *Ork.* ***Historic/prehistoric site***, 2m/3km NE of Dounby. Only working specimen of traditional Orcadian horizontal water mill. **106 C5** HY3222.
Clickimin Broch *Shet.* ***Historic/prehistoric site***, broch or castle (Historic Scotland) at end of causeway running out into Loch of Clickimin on W side of Lerwick. **109 D8** HU4640.
Cliddesden *Hants.* ***Village***, 2m/3km S of Basingstoke. **21 K7** SU6349.
Clieves Hills *Lancs.* ***Locality***, 2m/3km W of Ormskirk. SD3808.
Cliff *Carmar.* ***Settlement***, adjoining to S of Ferryside. **17 G4** SN3609.
Cliff *High.* ***Settlement***, on E bank of River Shiel, 1m/2km N of Acharacle, Lochaber district. **79 H1** NM6769.
Cliff End *E.Suss.* ***Village***, coastal village, 5m/8km E of Hastings. **14 D6** TQ8813.
Cliff End *W.Yorks.* ***Suburb***, 1m/2km W of Huddersfield town centre. SE1216.
Cliff Grange *Shrop.* ***Settlement***, 2m/3km SW of Market Drayton. SJ6432.
Cliffe *Lancs.* ***Suburb***, to NW of Great Harwood. SD7232.
Cliffe *Med.* ***Village***, 5m/8km N of Rochester. To N, Cliffe Marshes on S bank of River Thames estuary. **24 D4** TQ7376.
Cliffe *N.Yorks.* ***Hamlet***, on S bank of River Tees, opposite Piercebridge. NZ2115.
Cliffe *N.Yorks.* ***Village***, 3m/5km E of Selby. **58 C6** SE6631.
Cliffe Castle Art Gallery and Museum *W.Yorks.* ***Other feature of interest***, museum housed in Victorian mansion in Keighley. Also gardens, conservatory and small aviary. **57 F5** SE0542.
Cliffe Hill *E.Suss.* ***Hill***, 1m/2km E of Lewes. Height 538 feet or 164 metres. **13 H5** TQ4310.
Cliffe Hill *W.Yorks.* ***Locality***, 1m/2km N of Brighouse. SE1425.
Cliffe Woods *Med.* Population: 2881. ***Village***, 2m/3km S of Cliffe and 3m/5km N of Rochester. **24 D4** TQ7373.
Clifford *Here.* ***Village***, on River Wye, 2m/4km NE of Hay-on-Wye. Remains of 13c castle. **28 B4** SO2445.
Clifford *W.Yorks.* ***Village***, 3m/5km SE of Wetherby. **57 K5** SE4244.
Clifford Castle *Here.* ***Castle***, on SW side of village of Clifford, 3m/4km NE of Hay-on-Wye. Remains of three castles: a motte near Old Castleton, a motte called Newton Tump and a motte which was held by Clifford family and later by Mortimers. **28 B4** SO2445.
Clifford Chambers *Warks.* ***Village***, 2m/3km S of Stratford-upon-Avon. **30 C3** SP1952.
Clifford's Mesne *Glos.* ***Village***, 2m/4km SW of Newent. **29 G6** SO7023.
Clifford's Tower *York* ***Castle***, remains of 13c-14c stone tower (English Heritage) in quatrefoil design, forming part of York Castle fortifications. Built by Henry III to replace William the Conqueror's wooden keep which was razed in 1190, it sits atop a layered Norman motte, dominating York's skyline and affording fine views of city. **58 C4** SE6052.
Cliffs End *Kent* ***Village***, in Pegwell Bay, 2m/3km W of Ramsgate. **25 K5** TR3364.
Cliffsend *Kent* ***Village***, 2m/3km W of Ramsgate. TR3464.
Clifftown *S'end* ***Suburb***, to S of Southend-on-Sea town centre. TQ8785.
Clift Hills *Shet.* ***Large natural feature***, line of hills running N and S on Mainland, on E side of Clift Sound. **109 C9** HU3931.
Clift Sound *Shet.* ***Sea feature***, sea channel S of Scalloway between Mainland and islands of Trondra and East Burra. **109 C9** HU3934.
Clifton *Beds.* ***Village***, 1m/2km E of Shefford. **32 E5** TL1638.
Clifton *Bristol* ***Suburb***, W district of Bristol, largely residential. Suspension bridge by I.K. Brunel spans Avon Gorge. **19 J4** ST5673.
Clifton *Cumb.* ***Village***, 3m/4km SE of Penrith. Clifton Hall (English Heritage), remnant of 15c manor house. **61 G4** NY5326.
Clifton *Derbys.* ***Village***, 1m/2km SW of Ashbourne. **40 D1** SK1644.
Clifton *Devon* ***Hamlet***, 6m/10km NE of Barnstaple. SS6041.
Clifton *Gt.Man.* ***Suburb***, 1m/2km N of Swinton. SD7703.
Clifton *Halton* ***Locality***, 1m/2km S of Runcorn. SJ5280.
Clifton *Lancs.* ***Village***, 5m/8km W of Preston. **55 H6** SD4630.
Clifton *N.Yorks.* ***Hamlet***, 2m/3km N of Otley. SE1948.
Clifton *Northumb.* ***Hamlet***, 2m/3km S of Morpeth. **71 H5** NZ2082.
Clifton *Nott.* ***Suburb***, 3m/4km SW of West Bridgford. **41 H2** SK5534.
Clifton *Oxon.* ***Village***, on River Cherwell, 1m/2km E of Deddington. **31 F5** SP4931.
Clifton *S.Yorks.* ***Suburb***, central district of Rotherham. SK4392.
Clifton *S.Yorks.* ***Village***, 1m/2km S of Conisbrough. SK5196.
Clifton *Stir.* ***Village***, on NW side of Tyndrum. **80 E4** NN3230.
Clifton *W.Yorks.* ***Village***, 1m/2km E of Brighouse. SE1622.
Clifton *Worcs.* ***Hamlet***, 6m/9km S of Worcester. **29 H4** SO8446.
Clifton *York* ***Suburb***, 1m/2km NW of York city centre. SE5953.
Clifton Campville *Staffs.* ***Village***, 5m/8km NE of Tamworth. **40 E4** SK2510.
Clifton Dykes *Cumb.* ***Locality***, 1km E of Clifton and 2m/3km SE of Penrith. NY5427.
Clifton Gardens *E.Riding* ***Suburb***, to NW of Goole. SE7324.
Clifton Green *Cumb.* ***Locality***, adjoining to S of Little Clifton. NY0528.
Clifton Hampden *Oxon.* ***Village***, 3m/5km E of Abingdon. **21 J2** SU5495.
Clifton Junction *Gt.Man.* ***Locality***, 1m/2km NE of Swinton. SD7903.
Clifton Maybank *Dorset* ***Settlement***, 2m/3km SE of Yeovil. ST5713.
Clifton Reynes *M.K.* ***Village***, 5m/8km N of Newport Pagnell. **32 C3** SP9051.
Clifton Suspension Bridge *Bristol* ***Bridge***, elegant suspension bridge by Brunel, built mid 19c, spanning River Avon gorge at Bristol. ST5673.
Clifton upon Dunsmore *Warks.* ***Village***, 2m/3km NE of Rugby. **31 G1** SP5376.
Clifton upon Teme *Worcs.* ***Village***, 6m/9km NE of Bromyard. **29 G2** SO7161.
Cliftonville *Kent* ***Suburb***, E district of Margate. **25 K4** TR3671.
Climping *W.Suss.* ***Village***, 2m/3km W of Littlehampton. **12 D6** TQ0002.
Climpy *S.Lan.* ***Settlement***, 1m/2km NW of Forth. **75 H5** NS9255.
Clink *Som.* ***Suburb***, NE district of Frome. ST7948.
Clint *N.Yorks.* ***Village***, 4m/7km NW of Harrogate. **57 H4** SE2559.
Clint Green *Norf.* ***Village***, 3m/4km SE of East Dereham. **44 E4** TG0210.
Clintburn *Northumb.* ***Forest/woodland***, part of Wark Forest, 9m/15km N of Haltwhistle. **70 C6** NY7179.
Clinterty *Aberdeen* ***Locality***, comprises Little Mill of Clinterty and Haughs of Clinterty, together with nearby Meikle Clinterty and Clinterty Home Farm, to SW of Kirkhill Forest, 3m/4km N of Westhill. **91 G3** NJ8310.
Clintmains *Sc.Bord.* ***Hamlet***, 2m/3km NE of St. Boswells, over River Tweed. **76 E7** NT6132.
Clints Dod *E.Loth.* ***Mountain***, in Lammermuir Hills, 3m/5km NW of Whiteadder Reservoir. Height 1309 feet or 399 metres. **76 E4** NT6268.
Clippesby *Norf.* ***Hamlet***, 3m/4km NE of Acle. **45 J4** TG4214.
Clippings Green *Norf.* ***Hamlet***, 4m/6km E of East Dereham. TG0412.
Clipsham *Rut.* ***Village***, 7m/11km NW of Stamford. Limestone quarries to SE. **42 C4** SK9716.
Clipston *Northants.* ***Village***, 4m/6km SW of Market Harborough. **42 A7** SP7181.
Clipston *Notts.* ***Hamlet***, 6m/9km SE of Nottingham. **41 J2** SK6334.
Clipstone *Notts.* ***Village***, 5m/8km NE of Mansfield. Remains of medieval royal hunting lodge for Sherwood Forest. **51 J6** SK6064.
Clipstone Forest *Notts.* ***Forest/woodland***, part of Sherwood Forest, 4m/7km E of Mansfield. **51 J6** SK6062.
Clisham *W.Isles* ***Mountain***, in North Harris 5m/7km N of Tarbert. Highest point on Isle of Lewis. Height 2621 feet or 799 metres. **100 D7** NB1507.
Clitheroe *Lancs.* Population: 13,548. ***Town***, former market town above River Ribble valley, 10m/15km NE of Blackburn. Remains of 12c castle keep. Church has medieval tower. **56 C5** SD7441.
Clitheroe Castle *Lancs.* ***Castle***, shell of Norman castle on small hill in Clitheroe. **56 C5** SD7441.
Clive *Shrop.* ***Village***, 3m/5km S of Wem. **38 E3** SJ5124.
Cliveden *Bucks.* ***Garden***, in grounds of house (National Trust), now a hotel, 1m/2km E of Cookham across River Thames. Gardens include parterre and water gardens, as well as various walks. **22 C3** SU9185.
Clivocast *Shet.* ***Settlement***, on S coast of Unst, 1km E of Uyeasound. **108 F2** HP6000.
Clixby *Lincs.* ***Hamlet***, 2m/4km N of Caistor. TA1004.
Clocaenog *Denb.* ***Village***, 4m/6km SW of Ruthin. **47 J7** SJ0854.
Clocaenog Forest ***Forest/woodland***, afforested area on border of Conwy and Denbighshire, to W of Clocaenog. **47 J7** SJ0053.
Cloch Point *Inclyde* ***Coastal feature***, headland with lighthouse, on Firth of Clyde opposite Dunoon, 3m/4km SW of Gourock. **73 K3** NS2075.
Clochan *Moray* ***Village***, near N coast, 3m/5km S of Buckie. **98 C4** NJ4060.
Clochtow *Aber.* ***Settlement***, 1km W of Radel Haven, 4m/7km SW of Cruden Bay. **91 J1** NK0530.
Clock Face *Mersey.* ***Locality***, 3m/4km SE of St. Helens. **48 E3** SJ5291.
Clockhill *Aber.* ***Settlement***, 3m/4km SW of Maud. **99 G6** NJ8945.
Cloddach *Moray* ***Settlement***, 3m/4km S of Elgin. **97 J6** NJ1958.
Cloddiau *Powys* ***Hamlet***, 2m/3km NW of Welshpool. SJ2009.
Clodock *Here.* ***Hamlet***, 4m/7km W of Pontrilas. **28 C6** SO3227.
Cloford *Som.* ***Hamlet***, 4m/6km SW of Frome. **20 A7** ST7243.
Cloichran *Stir.* ***Settlement***, 4m/6km SW of Ardeonaig on S bank of Loch Tay. **81 H4** NN6133.
Cloigyn *Carmar.* ***Settlement***, 4m/6km S of Carmarthen. SN4314.
Clola *Aber.* ***Village***, 8m/13km W of Peterhead. **99 J6** NK0043.
Clonrae *D. & G.* ***Settlement***, 6m/10km NE of Moniaive. **68 D4** NX8293.
Clophill *Beds.* Population: 2372. ***Village***, 3m/5km E of Ampthill. **32 D5** TL0837.
Clopton *Northants.* ***Village***, 4m/7km E of Thrapston. **32 D1** TL0680.
Clopton *Suff.* ***Hamlet***, 4m/6km NW of Woodbridge. TM2152.
Clopton *Warks.* ***Suburb***, N district of Stratford-upon-Avon. SP1956.
Clopton Bridge *Warks.* ***Bridge***, stone bridge built over River Avon at Stratford-upon-Avon on site of Saxon ford. Dating from 1480, with subsequent modifications. SP2054.
Clopton Corner *Suff.* ***Hamlet***, 1m/2km N of Clopton. TM2254.
Clopton Green *Suff.* ***Hamlet***, 6m/9km N of Clare. **34 B3** TL7654.
Clopton Green *Suff.* ***Settlement***, 1km N of Rattlesden. TL9760.
Clopton Green *Suff.* ***Settlement***, 1m/2km N of Clopton. TM2154.
Close Clark *I.o.M.* ***Settlement***, 3m/5km N of Ballasalla. **54 B6** SC2775.
Close Houses *Cumb.* ***Settlement***, 2m/3km SE of Milburn. NY6727.
Close Moss *W.Yorks.* ***Open space***, moorland 2m/3km W of Marsden. **50 C1** SE0111.
Closeburn *D. & G.* ***Village***, 2m/4km SE of Thornhill. **68 D4** NX8992.
Closworth *Som.* ***Village***, 4m/6km S of Yeovil. **8 E3** ST5610.
Clothall *Herts.* ***Village***, 2m/3km SE of Baldock. **33 F5** TL2731.
Clothan *Shet.* ***Settlement***, on SW coast of Yell, 1km N of Ulsta. **108 D4** HU4581.
Clotton *Ches.* ***Hamlet***, 2m/3km NW of Tarporley. **48 E6** SJ5263.
Cloud Hill *D. & G.* ***Mountain***, 3m/5km SW of Sanquhar. Height 1479 feet or 451 metres. **68 C3** NS7305.
Clouds Hill *Dorset* ***Historic house***, National Trust property 1m/2km N of Bovington Camp. Home of T.E. Lawrence (Lawrence of Arabia). **9 H5** SY8290.
Clough *Cumb.* ***Settlement***, adjoining to SW of Garsdale Head, with Garsdale Station to SE across Clough River. **61 J7** SD7891.
Clough *Gt.Man.* ***Locality***, 1km NW of Littleborough. **49 J1** SD9317.
Clough *Gt.Man.* ***Suburb***, adjoining to E of Shaw, 3m/4km NE of Oldham. SD9408.
Clough *W.Yorks.* ***Village***, 1m/2km E of Slaithwaite across River Colne. SE0914.
Clough Dene *Dur.* ***Hamlet***, 1m/2km S of Burnopfield. NZ1755.
Clough Field *S.Yorks.* ***Suburb***, 2m/3km W of Sheffield city centre. SK3187.
Clough Fold *Lancs.* ***Suburb***, adjoining to E of Rawtenstall. SD8222.
Clough Foot *W.Yorks.* ***Hamlet***, 2m/3km W of Todmorden. **56 E7** SD9023.
Clough Head *Cumb.* ***Mountain***, on E side of St. John's Vale, 4m/7km E of Keswick. Height 2381 feet or 726 metres. **60 E4** NY3322.
Clough Head *W.Yorks.* ***Hamlet***, 1km S of Sowerby Bridge. SE0622.
Clougha Pike *Lancs.* ***Mountain***, on moorland, 4m/7km SE of Lancaster. Height 1355 feet or 413 metres. **55 J4** SD5459.
Cloughton *N.Yorks.* ***Village***, 4m/7km N of Scarborough. **63 K3** TA0094.
Cloughton Newlands *N.Yorks.* ***Hamlet***, 1km N of Cloughton. **63 K3** TA0195.
Cloughton Wyke *N.Yorks.* ***Bay***, on North Sea coast, 1km E of Cloughton and 4m/7km N of Scarborough. **63 K3** TA0295.
Clounlaid *High.* ***Settlement***, 4m/7km NE of Ardtornish, Lochaber district. **79 J2** NM7552.
Clousta *Shet.* ***Hamlet***, on Mainland, at head of Voe of Clousta. **109 C7** HU3057.
Clouston *Ork.* ***Settlement***, in Stenness, Mainland, 1km S of Loch of Stenness. **107 C6** HY3011.
Clova *Aber.* ***Settlement***, to E of Clova Hill, 4m/6km SW of Rhynie. **90 C2** NJ4522.
Clova *Angus* ***Village***, in Glen Clova, 12m/19km N of Kirriemuir. **90 B7** NO3273.
Clove Lodge *Dur.* ***Settlement***, in Baldersdale, on S side of Blackton Reservoir, 5m/8km W of Cotherstone. **62 A5** NY9317.
Clovelly *Devon* ***Village***, picturesque village on N coast, 9m/14km W of Bideford, crowded around cobbled pedestrian street descending steeply to quay. Associations with author Charles Kingsley and 'A Message from the Sea' by Dickens. **6 B3** SS3124.
Clovelly Bay *Devon* ***Bay***, small area of Barnstaple or Bideford Bay between Clovelly in W and Buck's Mills in E. **6 B3** SS3324.
Clovelly Cross *Devon* ***Settlement***, 1m/2km S of Clovelly. **6 B3** SS3123.
Clovenfords *Sc.Bord.* ***Village***, 3m/4km W of Galashiels. **76 C7** NT4436.
Clovenstone *Aber.* ***Locality***, 3m/4km S of Inverurie. **91 F3** NJ7717.
Cloverhill *Aberdeen* ***Settlement***, 1km inland from coast and 4m/6km N of Aberdeen harbour. **91 H3** NJ9412.
Cloverley *Shrop. Alternative name for Calverhall, qv.*
Cloves *Moray* ***Settlement***, 5m/8km W of Elgin. **97 J5** NJ1361.

Clovullin *High.* ***Hamlet***, on W shore of Loch Linnhe in Lochaber district, 1m/2km NE of Sallachan Point. **80 B1** NN0063.
Clow Bridge *Lancs.* ***Hamlet***, on W side of Clowbridge Reservoir, 3m/5km S of Burnley. SD8228.
Clowbridge Reservoir *Lancs.* ***Reservoir***, to E of Clow Bridge. **56 D7** SD8228.
Clowne *Derbys.* Population: 7234. ***Small town***, 3m/5km NE of Bolsover. **51 G5** SK4975.
Clows Top *Worcs.* ***Village***, 4m/6km SE of Cleobury Mortimer. **29 G1** SO7171.
Cloyntie *S.Ayr.* ***Settlement***, 3m/5km SE of Maybole. **67 H3** NS3305.
Cluanach *Arg. & B.* ***Settlement***, on Islay, 3m/5km E of Bowmore. **72 B5** NR3659.
Cluanie Forest *High.* ***Open space***, deer forest in Skye and Lochalsh district to S and W of head of Loch Cluanie. **87 G3** NH0409.
Cluas Deas *High.* ***Coastal feature***, small headland 3m/4km SW of Point of Stoer, Sutherland district. **102 C5** NC0032.
Clubmoor *Mersey.* ***Suburb***, 3m/5km NE of Liverpool city centre. SJ3893.
Clubworthy *Cornw.* ***Hamlet***, 4m/6km SE of Week St. Mary. **4 C1** SX2792.
Cluddley *Tel. & W.* ***Settlement***, 1m/2km SW of Wellington. SJ6310.
Cluden Water *D. & G.* ***River***, formed by confluence of Cairn Water and Old Water to S of Newtonairds, and running SE to River Nith, 1m/2km N of Dumfries. **68 D5** NX9677.
Cluer *W.Isles* ***Settlement***, on E coast of South Harris, 1m/2km S of Greosabhagh. **93 G2** NG1490.
Clumber Park *Notts.* ***Open space***, late 18c landscape design (National Trust) created out of heathland bordering Sherwood Forest, 4m/6km SE of Worksop. Now a country park. **51 J5** SK6275.
Clun ***River***, rising at Anchor near Welsh border and flowing E to Aston on Clun, then S, to join River Teme at Leintwardine. **28 C1** SO4073.
Clun *Shrop.* ***Village***, 5m/9km N of Knighton and 8m/13km W of Craven Arms. Remains of 12c castle (English Heritage) overlooking River Clun. **38 B7** SO3080.
Clun Castle *Shrop.* ***Castle***, consisting of large low motte with two baileys (English Heritage), at W side of Clun, 5m/8km N of Knighton. Became stone castle in 12c. **38 B7** SO2981.
Clun Forest *Shrop.* ***Open space***, area of hill country, 6m/10km NW of Clun. **38 B7** SO2186.
Clunas *High.* ***Locality***, 3m/5km SE of Cawdor. **97 F7** NH8746.
Clunbury *Shrop.* ***Village***, 4m/7km W of Craven Arms. **38 C7** SO3780.
Clunbury Hill *Shrop.* ***Hill***, 7m/11km NE of Knighton. Height 984 feet or 300 metres. **38 C7** SO3779.
Clunderwen *Carmar.* *Welsh form of Clynderwen, qv.*
Clune *High.* ***Settlement***, in Strathdearn, 2m/3km S of Tomatin. **88 E2** NH7925.
Clune *Moray* ***Settlement***, 2m/3km S of Cullen. **98 D4** NJ5163.
Clunes *High.* ***Hamlet***, in Lochaber district on NW shore of Loch Lochy, 3m/5km NE of foot of loch. **87 H6** NN2088.
Clungunford *Shrop.* ***Village***, on River Clun, 4m/6km SW of Craven Arms. **28 C1** SO3978.
Clunie *Aber.* ***Locality***, comprises Clunie Hill, Backhill of Clunie and Home Farm of Clunie, 1m/2km SE of Aberchirder. **98 E5** NJ6350.
Clunie *P. & K.* ***Settlement***, on W shore of Loch of Clunie, 4m/7km W of Blairgowrie. **82 C3** NO1143.
Clunie Water *Aber.* ***River***, running N down Glen Clunie to River Dee on N side of Braemar. **89 J6** NO1492.
Clunton *Shrop.* ***Village***, 2m/4km E of Clun. **38 C7** SO3381.
Cluny *Aber.* ***Locality***, and castle 3m/4km N of Banchory. NO6899.
Cluny *Fife* ***Settlement***, 3m/5km NW of Kirkcaldy. **76 A1** NT2495.
Cluny House Gardens *P. & K.* ***Garden***, wild woodland garden with wide range of Himalayan plants, 2m/3km NE of Aberfeldy. **81 K2** NN8751.
Clutton *B. & N.E.Som.* Population: 1239. ***Village***, 4m/6km NW of Midsomer Norton. **19 K6** ST6259.
Clutton *Ches.* ***Village***, 4m/6km E of Holt. **48 D7** SJ4654.
Clutton Hill *B. & N.E.Som.* ***Hamlet***, 1m/2km NE of Clutton. ST6359.
Clwt-y-bont *Gwyn.* ***Settlement***, adjoining to W of Deiniolen. **46 D6** SH5763.
Clwyd ***River***, rising in Clocaenog Forest and flowing S to Melin-y-Wig, then NE to Ruthin, then N to coast on W side of Rhyl. SH9980.
Clwydian Hills *Denb.* *Alternative name for Clwydian Range, qv.*
Clwydian Range (Also known as Clwydian Hills.) *Denb.* ***Large natural feature***, line of hills extending N from Llantysilio Mountain to Prestatyn, punctuated by a series of high passes. Highest point is Moel Famau, 1817 feet or 554 metres. **47 J5** SJ1465.
Clwydyfagwyr *M.Tyd.* ***Settlement***, 1m/2km W of Merthyr Tydfil. SO0206.
Clydach *Mon.* ***Village***, 2m/3km E of Bryn-mawr. **28 B7** SO2213.
Clydach *Swan.* ***Small town***, 6m/10km NE of Swansea. Birthplace of Sir Bartle Frere, first High Commissioner for South Africa. Nearby Clydach Gorge, focus of great industrial activity in 18c-19c. **17 K4** SN6901.
Clydach Terrace *B.Gwent* ***Settlement***, 1m/2km N of Bryn-mawr. SO1813.
Clydach Vale *R.C.T.* ***Village***, 1m/2km W of Tonypandy. **18 C2** SS9793.
Clydau *Pembs.* *Welsh form of Clydey, qv.*
Clyde ***River***, rising S of Abington and W of Moffat and flowing NW through Glasgow to Firth of Clyde at Dumbarton. **74 E4** NS3974.
Clyde Law ***Mountain***, on border of Scottish Borders and South Lanarkshire, 5m/8km E of Elvanfoot. Height 1791 feet or 546 metres. **69 F2** NT0217.
Clydebank *W.Dun.* Population: 29,171. ***Town***, industrial town on N bank of River Clyde, 6m/10km NW of Glasgow. Formerly a shipbuilding town, the QEII was built here. **74 D4** NS5069.
Clydesdale ***Valley***, carrying mid section of River Clyde, stretching from confluence with Medwin Water at The Meetings, 1m/2km SE of Carstairs Junction, to urban development S of Motherwell. Valley is broad from The Meetings, before narrowing at Hyndford Bridge and becoming a gorge, with many waterfalls, notably Bonnington Linn and Corra Linn, and nature trails around Lanark. Beyond Crossford, valley broadens again, with steep parallel sides as river meanders NE. **75 G6** NS8249.
Clydey (Clydau). *Pembs.* ***Hamlet***, 5m/8km SW of Newcastle Emlyn. **17 F1** SN2535.
Clyffe Pypard *Wilts.* ***Village***, 4m/6km S of Wootton Bassett. **20 D4** SU0776.
Clynder *Arg. & B.* ***Village***, on W shore of Gare Loch, 3m/4km N of Kilcreggan. **74 A2** NS2484.
Clynderwen (Clunderwen). *Carmar.* ***Village***, 3m/5km N of Narberth. **16 E3** SN1219.
Clyne *N.P.T.* ***Settlement***, 4m/6km NE of Neath. SN8000.
Clyne Common *Swan.* ***Open space***, heath 2m/4km NW of The Mumbles. **17 J5** SS5990.
Clyne Valley Country Park *Swan.* ***Leisure/recreation***, wooded country park in River Clyne valley, 2m/4km SW of Swansea. **17 K5** SS6191.
Clynelish *High.* ***Settlement***, in Sutherland district, 1m/2km NW of Brora. **97 F1** NC8905.
Clynfyw *Pembs.* ***Settlement***, 1km SW of Abercych. **17 F1** SN2439.
Clynnog-fawr *Gwyn.* ***Village***, near coast of Caernarfon Bay, 9m/14km SW of Caernarfon. Fine 16c church of St. Bueno. **36 D1** SH4149.
Clyro (Cleirwy). *Powys* ***Village***, 1m/2km NW of Hay-on-Wye across River Wye. Traces of Roman fort 1m/2km E. Remains of motte and bailey castle. **28 B4** SO2143.
Clyro Hill *Powys* ***Mountain***, 3m/5km NW of Hay-on-Wye. Height 1246 feet or 380 metres. **28 B4** SO1946.
Clyst *Devon* ***River***, rising at Clyst William, 1km E of Plymtree, flowing SW to Broad Clyst, then S into River Exe estuary 1km NW of Exton. SX9785.
Clyst Honiton *Devon* ***Village***, 5m/7km E of Exeter. Exeter Airport to E of village. **7 H6** SX9893.
Clyst Hydon *Devon* ***Village***, 4m/6km S of Cullompton. Paradise Copse (National Trust) is 1m/2km to W. **7 J5** ST0301.
Clyst St. George *Devon* ***Village***, 5m/8km SE of Exeter. **7 H7** SX9888.
Clyst St. Lawrence *Devon* ***Village***, 5m/8km NW of Ottery St. Mary. **7 J5** ST0200.
Clyst St. Mary *Devon* ***Village***, 4m/6km E of Exeter. **7 H6** SX9790.
Clyst William *Devon* ***Hamlet***, 4m/7km SE of Cullompton. ST0602.
Clyth *High.* ***Locality***, near E coast of Caithness district, 2m/3km E of Lybster, containing Upper and Mid Clyth. ND2736.
Clytha Hill (Cleidda Hill). *Mon.* ***Hill***, rising to over 190 metres, 6m/10km SE of Abergavenny. **19 G1** SO3607.
Clywedog *Denb.* ***River***, rising in N part of Clocaenog Forest and flowing E to Bontuchel, then N to join River Clwyd 3m/4km E of Denbigh. SJ0865.
Clywedog *Powys* ***River***, rising 3m/5km SW of Pennant and flowing SE through Clywedog Reservoir to join River Severn at Llanidloes. **37 J7** SN9584.
Cnap Chaochan Aitinn *Moray* ***Mountain***, rising to N above Glen Loin, 6m/9km S of Tomintoul. Height 2342 feet or 714 metres. **89 J4** NJ1409.
Cnewr *Powys* ***Settlement***, 4m/7km SW of Sennybridge. **27 H6** SN8922.
Cnicht *Gwyn.* ***Mountain***, 3m/5km W of Blaenau Ffestiniog. Height 2260 feet or 689 metres. **37 F1** SH6446.
Cnoc (Anglicised form: Knock.) *W.Isles* ***Village***, on Eye Peninsula, Isle of Lewis, 4m/7km E of Stornoway. **101 G4** NB4931.
Cnoc a' Bhaid Bhàin *High.* ***Mountain***, rising to N of Strath an Lòin and E shore of Loch Shin. Height 1207 feet or 368 metres. **103 G7** NC4219.
Cnoc a' Bhaid-rallaich *High.* ***Mountain***, in Ross and Cromarty district, 4m/6km W of Ullapool across Loch Broom. Height 1788 feet or 545 metres. **95 G2** NH0693.
Cnoc a' Bhaile-shios *Arg. & B.* ***Mountain***, on Kintyre, 4m/6km S of Tarbert. Height 1384 feet or 422 metres. **73 G4** NR8662.
Cnoc a' Bharaille *Arg. & B.* ***Mountain***, on Knapdale, 5m/7km NW of Tarbert. Height 1545 feet or 471 metres. **73 F3** NR8072.
Cnoc a' Chapuill *N.Ayr.* ***Mountain***, on Arran, 4m/6km W of Lamlash. Height 1368 feet or 417 metres. **66 D1** NR9629.
Cnoc a' Choire *High.* ***Mountain***, to S of Strath Grudie, 3m/4km NE of Invercassley. Height 1319 feet or 402 metres. **96 C1** NC5004.
Cnoc a' Chraois *High.* ***Mountain***, situated to S of Strath More. Height 1141 feet or 348 metres. **103 G4** NC4540.
Cnoc a' Ghiubhais *High.* ***Hill***, 3m/5km S of Cape Wrath. Height 974 feet or 297 metres. **102 E1** NC2670.
Cnoc a' Ghiubhais *High.* ***Mountain***, S of Srath a' Chràisg, 7m/11km S of Altnaharra, Sutherland district. Height 1135 feet or 346 metres. **103 H6** NC5423.
Cnoc a' Ghriama *High.* ***Mountain***, in Sutherland district, rising to E of Loch a' Ghriama. Height 1220 feet or 372 metres. **103 G6** NC4026.
Cnoc a' Mhadaidh *Arg. & B.* ***Mountain***, in Argyll Forest Park, 1m/2km NE of Orchard. Height 1542 feet or 470 metres. **73 K2** NS1683.
Cnoc a' Mhoid *High.* ***Hill***, 4m/6km SW of S end of Loch Loyal, Caithness district. Height 830 feet or 253 metres. **103 H4** NC5740.
Cnoc Ach'na h-Uai *High.* ***Hill***, in Sutherland district, 1km N of Loch Achnamoine. Height 928 feet or 283 metres. **104 D5** NC8133.
Cnoc an Alaskie *High.* ***Mountain***, 3m/4km SE of S end of Loch Fiag, Sutherland district. Height 1023 feet or 312 metres. **103 G6** NC4926.
Cnoc an dà Chinn *Arg. & B.* ***Mountain***, 3m/4km E of Kilninian, Mull. Height 1282 feet or 391 metres. **79 F3** NM4444.
Cnoc an Daimh Beag *High.* ***Hill***, 1m/2km E of Loch Meadie. Height 968 feet or 295 metres. **103 H4** NC5240.
Cnoc an Daimh Mòr *High.* ***Mountain***, 3m/4km S of Loch an Dherue, Caithness district. Height 1168 feet or 356 metres. **103 H4** NC5342.
Cnoc an Earrannaiche *High.* ***Hill***, 4m/6km N of Lybster. Height 692 feet or 211 metres. **105 H4** ND2441.
Cnoc an Eireannaich *High.* ***Mountain***, on border of Sutherland and Caithness districts, 2m/3km SE of Cnoc Coire na Feàrna. Height 1696 feet or 517 metres. **104 E6** NC9527.
Cnoc an Fhuarain Bhàin *High.* ***Hill***, 4m/6km E of Trantlebeg. Height 797 feet or 243 metres. **104 E3** NC9553.
Cnoc an Liath-bhaid Mhòir *High.* ***Mountain***, 2m/4km S of Loch an Alltan Fheàrna, Sutherland district. Height 1424 feet or 434 metres. **104 C6** NC7529.
Cnoc an t-Sabhail *High.* ***Mountain***, with rounded summit in Ross and Cromarty district, 6m/10km NE of Alness. Height 1243 feet or 379 metres. **96 D4** NH6879.
Cnoc an t-Samhlaidh *Arg. & B.* ***Hill***, on Kintyre, 3m/5km NW of Grogport. Height 866 feet or 264 metres. **73 F6** NR7949.
Cnoc an t-Sìdhein *High.* ***Mountain***, rounded summit in Ross and Cromarty district, 3m/4km S of Achnasheen. Height 1220 feet or 372 metres. **95 H6** NH1553.
Cnoc an t-Soluis *W.Isles* *Gaelic form of Lighthill, qv.*
Cnoc Ard an t-Siùil *High.* ***Hill***, situated just S of Whiten Head. Height 600 feet or 183 metres. **103 G2** NC4967.
Cnoc Badaireach na Gaoithe *High.* ***Hill***, 2m/3km SE of S end of Strathy Forest. Height 699 feet or 213 metres. **104 D3** NC8451.
Cnoc Beithe *P. & K.* ***Mountain***, 3m/5km N of Crieff. Height 1460 feet or 445 metres. **81 K5** NN8626.
Cnoc Breac *High.* ***Hill***, 5m/8km SE of Rubha Réidh, Ross and Cromarty district. Height 961 feet or 293 metres. **94 D3** NG7884.
Cnoc Ceann nam Bad *High.* ***Hill***, 4m/7km S of Lairg, to W of Achany Glen. Height 879 feet or 268 metres. **96 C1** NC5500.
Cnoc Céislein *High.* ***Mountain***, in Ross and Cromarty district, 4m/6km W of Alness. Height 1715 feet or 523 metres. **96 C4** NH5870.
Cnoc Coinnich *Arg. & B.* ***Mountain***, in area of Argyll known as Argyll's Bowling Green, between Loch Goil and Loch Long. Height 2496 feet or 761 metres. **80 D7** NN2300.
Cnoc Coire na Feàrna *High.* ***Mountain***, on border of Sutherland and Caithness districts, 4m/7km E of Burnfoot. Height 1430 feet or 436 metres. **104 E5** NC9329.
Cnoc Corr Guinie *High.* ***Mountain***, rounded summit, in Ross and Cromarty district, 4m/6km NE of Alness. Height 1302 feet or 397 metres. **96 D4** NH6676.
Cnoc Craggie *High.* ***Mountain***, rising above W shore of Loch Craggie. Height 1046 feet or 319 metres. **103 J3** NC6052.
Cnoc Cromuillt *High.* ***Mountain***, on border of Sutherland and Caithness districts, 4m/7km SE of Forsinard. Height 1200 feet or 366 metres. **104 E5** NC9438.
Cnoc Eille Mòr *High.* ***Mountain***, in Inverness district, 5m/7km W of Beauly. Height 1322 feet or 403 metres. **96 B7** NH4548.
Cnoc Fraing *High.* ***Mountain***, in Badenoch and Strathspey district, 6m/9km NW of Aviemore. Height 2444 feet or 745 metres. **89 F3** NH8014.
Cnoc Freiceadain *High.* *See Reay.*
Cnoc Glac na Luachrach *High.* ***Hill***, rising to over 140 metres, 2m/3km S of Broadford Airport, Skye. **86 C2** NG6921.
Cnoc Leamhnachd *High.* ***Hill***, 1km E of Loch Beannach and 2m/4km N of Rhilochan. Height 961 feet or 293 metres. **104 C7** NC7511.
Cnoc Meadhonach *High.* ***Mountain***, in Sutherland district, 5m/8km N of Gordonbush. Height 1128 feet or 344 metres. **104 D7** NC8417.
Cnoc Moy *Arg. & B.* ***Mountain***, rounded summit on S part of Kintyre, 6m/10km NW of Southend. Height 1463 feet or 446 metres. **66 A2** NR6115.
Cnoc Muigh-bhlàraidh *High.* ***Mountain***, in Ross and Cromarty district, 6m/10km SE of Bonar Bridge. Height 1791 feet or 546 metres. **96 D3** NH6382.
Cnoc na Breun-choille *High.* ***Mountain***, 1m/2km SW of Altanduin, Sutherland district. Height 1197 feet or 365 metres. **104 C6** NC7824.
Cnoc na Carriage *Arg. & B.* ***Hill***, at SE end of Cowal peninsula, 3m/5km S of Tighnabruaich. Height 679 feet or 207 metres. **73 H4** NR9768.
Cnoc na Feannaig *High.* ***Mountain***, 2m/4km NW of Dalbreck, on NW side of Srath na Seilge. Height 1260 feet or 384 metres. **104 C7** NC7119.
Cnoc na Glas Choille *High.* ***Mountain***, summit lies 1m/2km SE of Loch Urigill. Height 1007 feet or 307 metres. **95 J1** NC2708.
Cnoc na h-Innse Mòire *High.* ***Mountain***, 3m/5km W of Craggie, Sutherland district. Height 1102 feet or 336 metres. **104 D7** NC8219.
Cnoc na Moine *High.* ***Mountain***, with forested summit in Inverness district, 5m/7km SW of Inverness. Height 1036 feet or 316 metres. **96 C7** NH5942.

Cnoc na Saobhaidhe *High.* ***Hill***, 3m/4km SW of Ben Alisky. Height 951 feet or 290 metres. **105 F5** ND0235.
Cnoc nan Cuilean *High.* ***Mountain***, 1m/2km SW of Lettermore, Caithness district. Height 1827 feet or 557 metres. **103 H4** NC5946.
Cnoc nan Gall *High.* ***Hill***, on border of Sutherland and Caithness districts, 3m/5km E of Forsinard. Height 902 feet or 275 metres. **104 E4** NC9442.
Cnoc nan Sltheag *Stir.* ***Open space***, partly wooded hillslope, 4m/6km N of Aberfoyle. **81 G7** NN5307.
Cnoc nan Tri-chlach *High.* ***Mountain***, rising above W shore of Loch Cròcach, Caithness district. Height 1132 feet or 345 metres. **104 C4** NC7943.
Cnoc Odhar *Arg. & B.* ***Hill***, on S part of Kintyre, 5m/8km SW of Campbeltown. Height 909 feet or 277 metres. **66 A2** NR6612.
Cnoc Reamhar *Arg. & B.* ***Hill***, on S part of Kintyre, 6m/9km NW of Southend. Height 895 feet or 273 metres. **66 A2** NR6013.
Cnoc Reamhar *Arg. & B.* ***Hill***, on Knapdale, 5m/7km W of Cairnbaan. Height 869 feet or 265 metres. **73 F1** NR7691.
Cnoc Reamhar *Arg. & B.* ***Hill***, on Kintyre, 2m/3km NW of Grogport. Height 666 feet or 203 metres. **73 F6** NR7746.
Cnoc Salislade *High.* ***Mountain***, 2m/4km NE of Kildonan Lodge, Sutherland district. Height 1584 feet or 483 metres. **104 E6** NC9423.
Cnoc Uaine *High. Gaelic form of Knock, qv.*
Cnocan Conachreag *High.* ***Hill***, 6m/9km NW of Dunbeath. Height 882 feet or 269 metres. **105 G5** ND1136.
Cnocan Dubh *High.* ***Mountain***, in Lochaber district, between Loch Loyne and Loch Garry. Height 1122 feet or 342 metres. **87 H4** NH1703.
Cnocloisgte Water *High.* ***River***, in Caithness district, running NE and joining Cnocglass Water just S of Loch Calium. **104 E3** ND0251.
Cnwch Coch *Cere.* ***Hamlet***, 4m/6km W of Devil's Bridge. **27 F1** SN6775.
Coachford *Aber.* ***Settlement***, 4m/6km SE of Keith. **98 C6** NJ4645.
Coad's Green *Cornw.* ***Village***, 5m/9km SW of Launceston. **4 C3** SX2976.
Coal Aston *Derbys.* ***Suburb***, adjoining to NE of Dronfield. **51 F5** SK3679.
Coal Pool *W.Mid.* ***Suburb***, 1m/2km N of Walsall town centre. SK0100.
Coal Street *Suff.* ***Locality***, 2m/3km S of Stradbroke. TM2370.
Coalbournbrook *W.Mid.* ***Suburb***, in NW part of Stourbridge. SO8985.
Coalbrookdale *Tel. & W.* ***Village***, in gorge of River Severn, 2m/3km SW of Dawley, Telford. Cradle of iron industry, where Darby discovered the iron smelting process in 1709. **39 F5** SJ6604.
Coalbrookvale *B.Gwent* ***Locality***, 2m/3km S of Bryn-mawr. **18 E1** SO1909.
Coalburn *S.Lan.* Population: 1169. ***Village***, 3m/5km S of Lesmahagow. **75 G7** NS8134.
Coalburns *T. & W.* ***Hamlet***, 3m/4km SW of Ryton. **71 G7** NZ1260.
Coalcleugh *Northumb.* ***Settlement***, 2m/3km NE of Nenthead. **61 K2** NY8045.
Coaley *Glos.* ***Village***, 3m/4km N of Dursley. **20 A1** SO7701.
Coalfell *Cumb.* ***Locality***, 4m/7km E of Brampton. NY5960.
Coalhill *Essex* ***Hamlet***, 3m/5km N of Wickford. TQ7597.
Coalmoor *Tel. & W.* ***Settlement***, 2m/3km W of Dawley. SJ6607.
Coalpit Heath *S.Glos.* ***Locality***, adjoining to S of Frampton Cotterell. **19 K3** ST6780.
Coalpit Hill *Staffs.* ***Locality***, adjoining to SW of Kidsgrove. **49 H7** SJ8253.
Coalport *Shrop.* ***Village***, on River Severn 1m/2km S of Madeley, Telford. **39 G5** SJ6902.
Coalsnaughton *Clack.* ***Village***, 1km S of Tillicoultry across River Devon. **75 H1** NS9295.
Coaltown of Balgonie *Fife* ***Village***, 1m/2km S of Markinch. **76 B1** NT3099.
Coaltown of Wemyss *Fife* ***Village***, 1km N of West Wemyss and 4m/7km NE of Kirkcaldy. **76 B1** NT3295.
Coalville *Leics.* Population: 30,408. ***Town***, on W edge of Charnwood Forest, 12m/19km NW of Leicester. Snibston Discovery Park shows local industrial history. **41 G4** SK4214.
Coalway *Glos.* ***Village***, 1m/2km SE of Coleford. SO5810.
Coanwood *Northumb.* ***Hamlet***, 3m/5km SW of Haltwhistle. NY6859.
Coast *High.* ***Settlement***, 1km W of Second Coast and 1m/2km SE of Laide, in Ross and Cromarty district. **95 F2** NG9291.
Coat *Som.* ***Hamlet***, 1m/2km NW of Martock. **8 D2** ST4520.
Coatbridge *N.Lan.* Population: 43,617. ***Town***, 9m/14km E of Glasgow. Former steel town, with industrial museum. **75 F4** NS7265.
Coate *Swin.* ***Settlement***, 2m/3km SE of Swindon town centre. **20 E3** SU1882.
Coate *Wilts.* ***Village***, 2m/4km E of Devizes. **20 D5** SU0461.
Coates *Cambs.* ***Village***, 3m/4km E of Whittlesey. **43 G6** TL3097.
Coates *Glos.* ***Village***, 3m/5km W of Cirencester. **20 C1** SO9700.
Coates *Lancs.* ***Locality***, adjoining to E of Barnoldswick. SD8847.
Coates *Lincs.* ***Settlement***, 2m/3km NE of Stow. **52 C4** SK9083.
Coates *Notts.* ***Settlement***, 1km N of Cottam. SK8281.
Coates *W.Suss.* ***Hamlet***, 3m/4km SE of Petworth. **12 C5** SU9917.
Coatham *R. & C.* ***Suburb***, on North Sea coast, adjoining to W of Redcar. **63 G4** NZ5925.
Coatham Mundeville *Darl.* ***Hamlet***, 4m/6km N of Darlington. **62 D4** NZ2820.
Cobairdy *Aber.* ***Settlement***, on S side of Fourman Hill, 4m/6km NE of Huntly. **98 D6** NJ5743.
Cobbaton *Devon* ***Hamlet***, 6m/9km SE of Barnstaple. **6 E3** SS6127.
Cobbin's Brook *Essex* ***River***, stream rising N of Epping, and flowing SW to Waltham Abbey where it joins Old River Lea or Lee. **23 H1** TL3799.
Cobbinshaw Reservoir *W.Loth.* ***Reservoir***, 3m/5km S of West Calder. **75 J5** NT0158.
Cobbler's City *W'ham* ***Locality***, 4m/6km E of Reading. SU7773.
Cobbler's Green *Norf.* ***Settlement***, 4m/6km NW of Bungay. TM2892.
Cobbler's Plain *Mon.* ***Hamlet***, 1m/2km N of Devauden. SO4700.
Cobby Syke *N.Yorks.* ***Settlement***, 1m/2km E of Blubberhouses. SE1955.
Cobden *Devon* ***Settlement***, 4m/7km W of Ottery St. Mary. SY0396.
Cober (Also known as Looe or Loe.) *Cornw.* ***River***, rising 3m/5km SE of Camborne and flowing into The Loe. SW6425.
Coberley *Glos.* ***Village***, 4m/6km S of Cheltenham. **29 J7** SO9616.
Cobhall Common *Here.* ***Hamlet***, 4m/7km SW of Hereford. SO4535.
Cobham *Kent* ***Village***, 4m/6km SE of Gravesend. Owletts (National Trust), 17c house. Church has well-known collection of brasses. **24 C5** TQ6768.
Cobham *Surr.* Population: 7627. ***Small town***, on River Mole, 4m/7km NW of Leatherhead. Cedar House (National Trust), 15c house with later alterations and additions. **22 E6** TQ1060.
Cobham Hall *Kent* ***Historic house***, 16c-17c house with 18c alterations and set in 150 acres of landscaped gardens, 4m/6km W of Strood. Now a girls' boarding school. **24 C5** TQ6868.
Cobleland *Stir.* ***Settlement***, on River Forth, 1m/2km NE of Gartmore. **74 D1** NS5398.
Cobler's Green *Essex* ***Hamlet***, 4m/7km SE of Great Dunmow. **33 K7** TL6819.
Cobley Hill *Worcs.* ***Settlement***, 3m/5km NW of Redditch. SP0171.
Cobmarsh Island *Essex* ***Island***, off W end of Mersea Island. **34 D7** TM0012.
Cobnash *Here.* ***Hamlet***, 3m/5km W of Leominster. **28 D2** SO4560.
Cobridge *Stoke* ***Suburb***, in Stoke-on-Trent, between Burslem and Hanley. SJ8748.
Coburty *Aber.* ***Locality***, 3m/4km S of Rosehearty. **99 H4** NJ9264.
Cochno *W.Dun.* ***Settlement***, 3m/4km N of Clydebank. **74 C3** NS4974.
Cochrage Muir *P. & K.* ***Open space***, fairly flat area of hill and moorland, 4m/6km NW of Blairgowrie. **82 C3** NO1249.
Cochran *Aber.* ***Locality***, adjoining to SE of Kincardine O'Neil. NO5999.
Cochrane Pike *Northumb.* ***Mountain***, in Cheviot Hills, 2m/3km SW of Ingram. Height 1096 feet or 334 metres. **71 F2** NU0013.
Cock Alley *Derbys.* ***Hamlet***, 2m/3km E of Chesterfield. **51 G6** SK4170.
Cock and End *Suff.* ***Settlement***, 6m/9km NE of Haverhill. TL7253.
Cock Bank *Wrex.* ***Settlement***, 3m/5km SE of Wrexham. SJ3545.
Cock Beck ***River***, rising to N of Garforth and flowing NE to join River Wharfe, 1km S of Tadcaster. **57 J6** SE4942.
Cock Bevington *Warks.* ***Settlement***, 6m/9km N of Evesham. SP0552.
Cock Bridge *Aber.* ***Settlement***, near road bridge over River Don 8m/12km SE of Tomintoul. 16c-17c Corgarff Castle (Historic Scotland) to SW. **89 K4** NJ2509.
Cock Cairn ***Mountain***, 4m/6km SW of Ballochan. Summit on border of Aberdeenshire and Angus. Height 2385 feet or 727 metres. **90 C6** NO4688.
Cock Clarks *Essex* ***Village***, 4m/6km SW of Maldon. **24 E1** TL8102.
Cock Gate *Here.* ***Settlement***, 4m/7km NW of Leominster. SO4665.
Cock Green *Essex* ***Hamlet***, 5m/7km SW of Braintree. TL6919.
Cock Hill *Aber.* ***Mountain***, 2m/3km SE of Ballochan. Height 1961 feet or 598 metres. **90 D6** NO5387.
Cock Law *N.Ayr.* ***Mountain***, to W of and overlooking Camphill Reservoir. Height 1174 feet or 358 metres. **74 A5** NS2555.
Cock Law *Sc.Bord.* ***Mountain***, rising to over 410 metres and aligned N to S, in Cheviot Hills to E of Kelsocleugh Burn. **70 D2** NT8518.
Cock of Arran *N.Ayr.* ***Coastal feature***, headland at N end of Arran. **73 H5** NR9552.
Cockayne *N.Yorks.* ***Hamlet***, at head of Bransdale, in Cleveland Hills, 9m/15km N of Hemsley. **63 H7** SE6198.
Cockayne Hatley *Beds.* ***Village***, in fruit-growing area, 2m/4km E of Potton. **33 F4** TL2549.
Cockayne Ridge *N.Yorks.* ***Inland physical feature***, mountain ridge rising to 1410 feet or 430 metres and running NW to SE, 1m/2km NW of Cockayne. **63 H6** NZ6100.
Cockburn Law *Sc.Bord.* ***Mountain***, with hillfort at summit, 2m/3km SE of Abbey St. Bathans. Height 1066 feet or 325 metres. **77 F4** NT7659.
Cockburnspath *Sc.Bord.* ***Village***, near coast, 8m/12km SE of Dunbar. **77 F3** NT7771.
Cockden *Lancs.* ***Hamlet***, 2m/3km SE of Nelson. SD8734.
Cockenheugh *Northumb.* ***Hill***, 3m/5km NW of Belford. Height 692 feet or 211 metres. **77 J7** NU0634.
Cockenzie and Port Seton *E.Loth.* Population: 4235. ***Small town***, on Firth of Forth, 4m/6km NE of Musselburgh. Power station to W. Seton Sands beach on coast to E. **76 C3** NT4075.
Cocker *Cumb.* ***River***, rising in Cumbrian Mountains, to N of Great Gable, and flowing N through Buttermere and Crummock Water into River Derwent at Cockermouth. **60 C4** NY1230.
Cocker Bar *Lancs.* ***Settlement***, 3m/4km W of Leyland. SD5022.
Cocker Brook *Lancs.* ***Locality***, 2m/4km SW of Accrington. SD7325.
Cocker Hill *D. & G.* ***Mountain***, 3m/4km NE of Kirkconnel. Height 1650 feet or 503 metres. **68 C2** NS7515.
Cockerham *Lancs.* ***Village***, 6m/10km S of Lancaster. **55 H4** SD4652.
Cockermouth *Cumb.* Population: 7702. ***Small town***, at confluence of Rivers Cocker and Derwent, 8m/13km E of Workington. Remains of 13c-14c castle. In Main Street, 18c house (National Trust), birthplace of Wordsworth, 1770. **60 C3** NY1230.
Cockernhoe *Herts.* ***Hamlet***, 3m/4km NE of Luton. **32 E6** TL1223.
Cockersand Abbey *Lancs.* ***Ecclesiastical building***, on coast at estuary of River Lune, near Plover Scar lighthouse, 6m/10km NW of Garstang. Finely vaulted chapter house built in 13c. **55 H4** SD4253.
Cockersdale *W.Yorks.* ***Settlement***, 1km N of Drighlington, 2m/4km NW of Morley. SE2329.
Cockerton *Darl.* ***Suburb***, 1m/2km W of Darlington town centre. NZ2715.
Cockett *Swan.* ***Suburb***, 2m/3km NW of Swansea city centre. **17 K5** SS6394.
Cockfield *Dur.* Population: 1537. ***Village***, 2m/4km N of Staindrop. **62 C4** NZ1224.
Cockfield *Suff.* ***Village***, 4m/6km N of Lavenham. **34 D3** TL9054.
Cockfosters *Gt.Lon.* ***Suburb***, on borders of Barnet and Enfield boroughs, 10m/16km N of Charing Cross. **23 F2** TQ2796.
Cockholm Burn *Sc.Bord.* ***River***, small stream which rises in mountains 4m/7km NW of Lauder, and flows S to join Gala Water at Stow. **76 C6** NT4444.
Cocking *W.Suss.* ***Village***, 3m/4km S of Midhurst. **12 B5** SU8717.
Cocking Causeway *W.Suss.* ***Hamlet***, 1m/2km S of Midhurst. SU8819.
Cockington *Torbay* ***Village***, of cob and thatch on W side of Torbay, 1m/2km W of Torquay town centre. **5 J4** SX8963.
Cockington Court *Torbay* ***Leisure/recreation***, country park, 2m/3km N of Paignton. Ancient forge and 17c mansion in 287 acres of grounds. **5 J4** SX8963.
Cocklake *Som.* ***Village***, 1m/2km N of Wedmore. **19 H7** ST4349.
Cocklaw *Northumb.* ***Settlement***, on E side of River North Tyne, 4m/7km N of Hexham. NY9371.
Cocklaw Hill *E.Loth.* ***Mountain***, 1m/2km NW of Oldhamstocks. Height 1050 feet or 320 metres. **77 F3** NT7271.
Cockle Park *Northumb.* ***Hamlet***, 3m/5km N of Morpeth. 16c tower. NZ2091.
Cockleford *Glos.* ***Settlement***, 5m/8km S of Cheltenham. SO9614.
Cockleroy *W.Loth.* ***Hill***, with fort and panoramic viewpoint, 2m/3km SW of Linlithgow. Height 912 feet or 278 metres. **75 H3** NS9874.
Cockley Beck *Cumb.* ***Settlement***, on E side of River Duddon, between passes of Hardknott and Wrynose, 8m/13km W of Ambleside. **60 D6** NY2401.
Cockley Cley *Norf.* ***Village***, of North Breckland, 4m/6km SW of Swaffham. Remains of 7c Saxon church. **44 B5** TF7904.
Cockmuir *Aber.* ***Settlement***, 3m/4km E of Strichen. NJ9855.
Cockpen *Midloth.* ***Settlement***, 2m/3km S of Dalkeith. NT3263.
Cockpole Green *W'ham* ***Village***, 3m/5km E of Henley-on-Thames across river. **22 A3** SU7981.
Cocks Hill *Devon* ***Mountain***, in Dartmoor National Park, 4m/6km NW of Princetown. Height 1643 feet or 501 metres. **5 F3** SX5678.
Cockshead *Cere.* ***Settlement***, 4m/6km SW of Tregaron. SN6355.
Cockshut Hill *W.Mid.* ***Suburb***, 5m/8km E of Birmingham city centre. SP1485.
Cockshutt *Shrop.* ***Village***, 4m/7km SE of Ellesmere. **38 D3** SJ4329.
Cockthorpe *Norf.* ***Hamlet***, 4m/7km E of Wells-next-the-Sea. **44 D1** TF9842.
Cockwood *Devon* ***Village***, on W side of River Exe estuary opposite Exmouth. **7 H7** SX9780.
Cockwood *Som.* ***Hamlet***, 1m/2km E of Stogursey. ST2242.
Cockyard *Derbys.* ***Hamlet***, 1m/2km SW of Chapel-en-le-Frith. SK0479.
Cod Beck *N.Yorks.* ***River***, rising on Cleveland Hills near Osmotherley and flowing S through Thirsk into River Swale 1m/2km S of Topcliffe. **57 K2** SE4174.
Codda *Cornw.* ***Settlement***, 1m/2km N of Bolventor. **4 B3** SX1878.
Coddenham *Suff.* ***Village***, 6m/10km N of Ipswich. Site of Romano-British settlement by River Gipping 1m/2km SW. **35 F3** TM1354.
Coddington *Ches.* ***Village***, 8m/12km SE of Chester. **48 D7** SJ4555.
Coddington *Here.* ***Village***, 3m/5km N of Ledbury. **29 G4** SO7142.
Coddington *Notts.* ***Village***, 3m/4km E of Newark-on-Trent. **52 B7** SK8354.
Codford St. Mary *Wilts.* ***Village***, 4m/6km SE of Heytesbury. **9 J1** ST9739.

Codford St. Peter *Wilts.* ***Village***, 3m/4km SE of Heytesbury. **20 C7** ST9640.
Codicote *Herts.* ***Village***, 2m/3km NW of Welwyn. **33 F7** TL2118.
Codmore Hill *W.Suss.* ***Hamlet***, 1m/2km NE of Pulborough. Site of Roman villa 1km E. **12 D5** TQ0520.
Codnor *Derbys.* ***Village***, 2m/3km SE of Ripley. **41 G1** SK4249.
Codnor Gate *Derbys.* ***Locality***, 1m/2km E of Ripley. SK4150.
Codrington *S.Glos.* ***Hamlet***, 2m/3km S of Chipping Sodbury. **20 A4** ST7278.
Codsall *Staffs.* Population: 11,718. ***Suburb***, 4m/7km NW of Wolverhampton. **40 A5** SJ8603.
Codsall Wood *Staffs.* ***Village***, 2m/3km NW of Codsall. **40 A5** SJ8404.
Codsend Moors *Som.* ***Open space***, steep area of Exmoor rising to N of River Quarme, 2m/3km NE of Exford. **7 G1** SS8640.
Coduinn *W.Isles* ***Hill***, 1m/2km SW of head of Little Loch Roag, Isle of Lewis. Height 790 feet or 241 metres. **100 D5** NB1129.
Coed-Cwnwr *Mon.* ***Settlement***, 2m/4km SE of Usk. ST4199.
Coed-duon *Caerp. Welsh form of Blackwood, qv.*
Coed Eva *Torfaen* ***Suburb***, in SW part of Cwmbran. ST2793.
Coed-llai *Flints. Welsh form of Leeswood, qv.*
Coed Mawr *Gwyn.* ***Suburb***, 1m/2km SW of Bangor. SH5670.
Coed Morgan *Mon.* ***Settlement***, 4m/6km SE of Abergavenny. **28 C7** SO3511.
Coed y Brenin Forest Park *Gwyn.* ***Forest/woodland***, large wooded area 3m/5km to 6m/10km N of Dolgellau. **37 G3** SH7326.
Coed-y-bryn *Cere.* ***Hamlet***, 4m/7km NE of Newcastle Emlyn. SN3545.
Coed-y-caerau *Newport* ***Settlement***, 3m/5km E of Caerleon across River Usk. ST3891.
Coed-y-gaer *Powys* ***Mountain***, 3m/5km E of Llanidloes. Height 1184 feet or 361 metres. **37 K7** SO0084.
Coed-y-paen (Coed-y-paun). *Mon.* ***Village***, 3m/5km SW of Usk. **19 G2** ST3398.
Coed-y-parc *Gwyn.* ***Hamlet***, 1km W of Bethesda. SH6166.
Coed-y-paun *Mon. Welsh form of Coed-y-paen, qv.*
Coed-yr-ynys *Powys* ***Locality***, on River Usk, 4m/7km W of Crickhowell. **28 A6** SO1520.
Coed Ystumgwern *Gwyn.* ***Locality***, adjoining to N of Dyffryn Ardudwy. **36 E3** SH5823.
Coedcae *Torfaen* ***Locality***, on NE side of Blaenavon. **19 F1** SO2508.
Coedcernyw *Newport Welsh form of Coedkernew, qv.*
Coedely *R.C.T.* ***Settlement***, 2m/3km S of Tonyrefail. **18 D3** ST0185.
Coedkernew (Coedcernyw). *Newport* ***Settlement***, 4m/6km SW of Newport. **19 F3** ST2783.
Coedpenmaen *R.C.T.* ***Hamlet***, 1km N of Pontypridd. ST0891.
Coedpoeth *Wrex.* Population: 5300. ***Village***, 3m/5km W of Wrexham. **48 B7** SJ2851.
Coedway *Powys* ***Hamlet***, 1m/2km E of Crewgreen. SJ3414.
Coedylade *Powys* ***Settlement***, 1m/2km N of Welshpool. SJ2209.
Coelbren *Powys* ***Village***, 3m/4km NE of Seven Sisters. **27 H7** SN8511.
Coety *Bridgend See Coity.*
Cofcott Green *Devon* ***Settlement***, 3m/5km S of Holsworthy. **6 B6** SX3399.
Coffinswell *Devon* ***Village***, 3m/5km SE of Newton Abbot. **5 J4** SX8968.
Coffle End *Beds.* ***Locality***, at E end of Sharnbrook. TL0059.
Cofton *Devon* ***Hamlet***, 2m/3km N of Dawlish. SX9680.
Cofton Hackett *Worcs.* ***Village***, 6m/9km NW of Redditch. **30 B1** SP0075.
Cogan *V. of Glam.* ***Suburb***, NW district of Penarth. **18 E4** ST1772.
Cogenhoe *Northants.* ***Village***, 5m/8km E of Northampton. **32 B2** SP8360.
Cogges *Oxon.* ***Suburb***, just E of Witney across River Windrush. Cogges Manor Farm contains a working museum of rural Victorian life. SP3609.
Coggeshall *Essex* Population: 3927. ***Village***, 6m/9km E of Braintree. Paycocke's (National Trust), dating from c. 1500, is one of several old houses. **34 C6** TL8522.
Coggeshall Hamlet *Essex* ***Hamlet***, 1km S of Coggeshall. **34 C6** TL8521.
Coggins Mill *E.Suss.* ***Settlement***, 1m/2km NE of Mayfield. **13 J4** TQ5927.
Cogra Moss *Cumb.* ***Lake/loch***, 1m/2km S of Lamplugh. **60 B5** NY0919.
Cóig Peighinnean (Anglicised form: Five Penny Ness.) *W.Isles* ***Village***, 1m/2km S of Butt of Lewis and 1m/2km NW of Port Nis. **101 H1** NB5264.
Cóig Peighinnean Bhuirgh (Anglicised form: Five Penny Borve.) *W.Isles* ***Village***, near NW coast of Isle of Lewis adjoining High Borve and 5m/8km NE of Barvas. **101 F2** NB4056.
Coigach *High.* ***Large natural feature***, upland area in Ross and Cromarty district, 6m/9km N of Ullapool and 6m/9km SE of Achiltibuie. **95 G1** NC1004.
Coignafearn Forest *High.* ***Open space***, deer forest on Monadhliath Mountains in Inverness district, astride upper reaches of River Findhorn. **88 D3** NH6412.
Coilantogle *Stir.* ***Settlement***, 2m/3km W of Callander. **81 G7** NN5906.
Coileitir *High.* ***Settlement***, in Glen Etive, 2m/3km NE of head of Loch Etive. **80 C3** NN1446.
Coilesan *Arg. & B.* ***Settlement***, on NE side, near N end of Loch Long, 3m/5km SW of Arrochar. **80 D7** NN2600.
Coiliochbhar Hill *Aber.* ***Mountain***, 4m/7km W of Alford. Height 1745 feet or 532 metres. **90 D3** NJ5015.
Coillaig *Arg. & B.* ***Settlement***, to N of Loch Awe, 2m/3km SW of Kilchrenan. **80 B5** NN0120.
Coille Coire Chrannaig *High.* ***Forest/woodland***, small wooded area to NW of Loch Laggan, 3m/5km W of Kinloch Laggan. **88 B6** NN4789.
Coille Mhòr *High.* ***Mountain***, W summit of Druim Fhada, 6m/10km NW of Fort William. Height 2083 feet or 635 metres. **87 G6** NN0382.
Coille Mhorgil *High.* ***Settlement***, 13m/21km W of Invergarry. **87 H4** NH1001.
Coille-righ *High.* ***Settlement***, in Glen Elchaig, 5m/8km E of Dornie, Skye and Lochalsh district. **87 F2** NG9627.
Coillore *High.* ***Settlement***, 1km SE of Bracadale across Loch Beag, Skye. **85 J1** NG3537.
Coiltie *High.* ***River***, in Inverness district running NE to Urquhart Bay on NW side of Loch Ness. **88 B2** NH5229.
Coiltry *High.* ***Locality***, in Inverness district, 3m/4km SW of Fort Augustus. NH3506.
Coirc Bheinn *Arg. & B.* ***Mountain***, 3m/4km SE of Balnahard, Mull. Height 1840 feet or 561 metres. **79 F4** NM4832.
Coire a' Chonachair *High.* ***Open space***, hillslope to SW of Mullach Chonachair and 1m/2km W of Lubcroy. **95 K1** NC3302.
Coire Bog *High.* ***River***, rising on NE slope of Sròn na Saobhaidhe and flowing E into Wester Fearn Burn, 3m/5km SW of Kincardine. **96 C3** NH5885.
Coire Ceirsle Hill *High.* ***Mountain***, in Lochaber district, 3m/5km NE of Spean Bridge. Height 2145 feet or 654 metres. **87 J6** NN2485.
Coire Dhuinnid *High.* ***Valley***, carrying An Leth-allt SW into Loch Duich, 3m/4km SE of Dornie. **87 F2** NG9224.
Coire Lochan *High.* ***Lake/loch***, on N slope of Carn Eige and 1m/2km S of W part of Loch Mullardoch. **87 H2** NH1227.
Coire na Beinne *High.* ***Hill***, 6m/10km N of Dunbeath. Height 741 feet or 226 metres. **105 G4** ND1440.
Coire nan Capull *Arg. & B.* ***Mountain***, rounded summit on Kintyre, 3m/5km S of Tarbert. Height 1096 feet or 334 metres. **73 G4** NR8561.
Coire Nochd Mòr *P. & K.* ***Mountain***, 7m/11km NE of Callander. Height 1630 feet or 497 metres. **81 J6** NN7411.
Coire Odhar *High.* ***Inland physical feature***, corrie to W of Meall nan Ruadhag, 9m/14km SE of Fort Augustus. **88 C4** NH5006.
Coire Odhar *P. & K.* ***Locality***, SW slope (National Trust for Scotland) of Ben Lawers, headquarters of Scottish Ski club. NN6140.
Coirefrois Burn *High.* ***River***, flowing E and joining Black Water river to E of Dalbreck. **103 J7** NC7415.
Coity (Coety). *Bridgend* ***Village***, 2m/3km NE of Bridgend. Site of ancient burial-chamber to N. Ruins of Norman castle (Cadw), abandoned in 16c. **18 C3** SS9281.
Coity Castle *Bridgend* ***Castle***, 1m/2km NE of Bridgend. 11c castle belonging to Lord Morgan, made into a stone castle in 12c, with alterations in Tudor times. **18 C3** SS9281.
Coity Mountain *Torfaen* ***Mountain***, 1m/2km SW of Blaenavon. Height 1906 feet or 581 metres. **19 F1** SO2307.
Cokhay Green *Derbys.* ***Hamlet***, 1km SW of Repton. SK2926.
Col (Anglicised form: Coll.) *W.Isles* Population: 1161. ***Village***, near E coast of Isle of Lewis, 5m/8km NE of Stornoway. **101 G3** NB4640.
Col-bheinn *High.* ***Mountain***, 4m/6km W of Lothbeg, Sutherland district. Height 1765 feet or 538 metres. **104 D7** NC8811.
Col Sands (Gaelic form: Tràigh Chuil.) *W.Isles* ***Coastal feature***, beach on E coast of Isle of Lewis, 4m/7km NE of Stornoway. **101 G4** NB4638.
Col Uarach (Anglicised form: Upper Coll.) *W.Isles* ***Village***, 1km SW of Col across Abhainn Chuil. NB4539.
Colaboll *High.* ***Settlement***, on NE shore of Loch Shin, 2m/4km NE of Lairg. **103 H7** NC5610.
Colan *Cornw.* ***Hamlet***, 4m/6km E of Newquay. **3 F2** SW8661.
Colaton Raleigh *Devon* ***Village***, 4m/6km N of Budleigh Salterton. **7 J7** SY0787.
Colbost *High.* ***Settlement***, on W coast of Loch Dunvegan, 3m/4km NW of Dunvegan, Skye. **93 H7** NG2148.
Colburn *N.Yorks.* ***Hamlet***, 2m/4km W of Catterick. SE1999.
Colbury *Hants.* ***Hamlet***, 2m/3km SW of Totton. **10 E3** SU3410.
Colby *Cumb.* ***Village***, 1m/2km W of Appleby-in-Westmorland. **61 H4** NY6620.
Colby *I.o.M.* ***Village***, 2m/4km E of Port Erin. **54 B6** SC2370.
Colby *Norf.* ***Village***, 3m/5km NE of Aylsham. **45 G2** TG2231.
Colby Woodland Garden *Pembs.* ***Garden***, NE of Summerhill. Woodland (National Trust) with rhododendrons and azaleas. **16 E4** SN1507.
Colchester *Essex* Population: 96,063. ***Town***, on River Colne 51m/82km NE of London, dating from Iron Age. First Roman capital of Britain (Camulodunum); many Roman remains. Remains of Norman castle now museum. St. John's Abbey Gate (English Heritage), surviving from Benedictine abbey. Many old buildings. University of Essex 2m/4km SE. Zoo. **34 D6** TL9925.
Colchester Castle *Essex* ***Castle***, in Colchester town centre, 11c castle with first one of great towers built over remains of Roman temple. Tower houses now converted into museums. **34 D6** TL9925.
Colchester Green *Suff.* ***Settlement***, to NE of Cockfield, 7m/11km SE of Bury St. Edmunds. TL9255.
Colchester Zoo *Essex* ***Leisure/recreation***, over 175 species of animals housed in 40 acres of gardens to S of Colchester town centre. **34 D6** TL9823.
Colcot *V. of Glam.* ***Locality***, 1m/2km N of Barry. **18 E5** ST1069.
Cold Ash *W.Berks.* ***Village***, 3m/5km NE of Newbury. **21 J5** SU5169.
Cold Ashby *Northants.* ***Village***, 5m/8km S of Husbands Bosworth. **31 H1** SP6576.
Cold Ashton *S.Glos.* ***Village***, 5m/8km N of Bath. **20 A4** ST7472.
Cold Aston (Also known as Aston Blank.) *Glos.* ***Village***, 3m/5km NE of Northleach. **30 C6** SP1219.
Cold Blow *Pembs.* ***Hamlet***, 1m/2km SE of Narberth. **16 E3** SN1212.
Cold Brayfield *M.K.* ***Village***, in loop of River Great Ouse, 3m/4km E of Olney. **32 C3** SP9352.
Cold Chapel *S.Lan.* ***Settlement***, 1m/2km N of Abington. **68 E1** NS9324.
Cold Cotes *N.Yorks.* ***Hamlet***, 2m/3km SE of Ingleton. SD7171.
Cold Fell *Cumb.* ***Mountain***, to N of King's Forest of Geltsdale, 3m/5km SE of Hallbankgate. Height 2037 feet or 621 metres. **61 H1** NY6055.
Cold Green *Here.* ***Locality***, 4m/6km NW of Ledbury. SO6842.
Cold Hanworth *Lincs.* ***Hamlet***, 2m/4km W of Faldingworth. **52 D4** TF0383.
Cold Harbour *Oxon.* ***Settlement***, 2m/4km E of Goring. SU6379.
Cold Hatton *Tel. & W.* ***Hamlet***, 6m/10km N of Wellington. SJ6221.
Cold Hatton Heath *Tel. & W.* ***Settlement***, 1km E of Cold Hatton. SJ6321.
Cold Hesledon *Dur.* ***Village***, 2m/3km SW of Seaham. **63 F2** NZ4047.
Cold Hiendley *W.Yorks.* ***Hamlet***, 2m/3km N of Royston. SE3714.
Cold Higham *Northants.* ***Village***, 4m/6km NW of Towcester. **31 H3** SP6653.
Cold Inn *Pembs.* ***Hamlet***, 2m/3km W of Saundersfoot. SN1005.
Cold Kirby *N.Yorks.* ***Village***, 5m/8km W of Helmsley. **58 B1** SE5384.
Cold Law *Northumb.* ***Mountain***, 4m/6km NE of The Cheviot. Height 1483 feet or 452 metres. **70 E1** NT9523.
Cold Newton *Leics.* ***Settlement***, 8m/13km E of Leicester, near site of former village. **42 A5** SK7106.
Cold Northcott *Cornw.* ***Hamlet***, 7m/11km E of Camelford. SX2086.
Cold Norton *Essex* ***Village***, 4m/7km S of Maldon. **24 E1** TL8400.
Cold Overton *Leics.* ***Village***, 3m/5km W of Oakham. **42 B5** SK8110.
Cold Row *Lancs.* ***Settlement***, 1m/2km N of Hambleton. SD3744.
Cold Weston *Shrop.* ***Locality***, 6m/9km NE of Ludlow. SO5483.
Coldbackie *High.* ***Village***, to S of Tongue Bay, N coast of Caithness district, 2m/4km NE of Tongue. **103 J2** NC6160.
Coldblow *Gt.Lon.* ***Suburb***, in borough of Bexley, 2m/4km W of Dartford. **23 J4** TQ5073.
Coldean *B. & H.* ***Suburb***, NE district of Brighton. **13 G6** TQ3308.
Coldeast *Devon* ***Hamlet***, 3m/5km NW of Newton Abbot. **5 J3** SX8174.
Coldeaton *Derbys.* ***Settlement***, 3m/4km SE of Hartington. SK1456.
Colden *I.o.M.* ***Mountain***, 6m/10km E of Peel. Height 1597 feet or 487 metres. **54 C5** SC3484.
Colden *W.Yorks.* ***Settlement***, 2m/3km NW of Hebden Bridge. SD9628.
Colden Common *Hants.* Population: 3065. ***Village***, 3m/5km NE of Eastleigh. **11 F2** SU4822.
Coldermeadow *Northants.* ***Suburb***, SW district of Corby. SP8687.
Coldfair Green *Suff.* ***Village***, 1m/2km SW of Leiston. **35 J2** TM4361.
Coldham *Cambs.* ***Hamlet***, 5m/8km SW of Wisbech. **43 H5** TF4302.
Coldharbour *Dorset* ***Settlement***, 2m/3km N of Weymouth town centre. SY6581.
Coldharbour *Glos.* ***Hamlet***, 1km S of St. Briavels. SO5503.
Coldharbour *Gt.Lon.* ***Locality***, on N bank of River Thames on Aveley Marshes, in borough of Havering, 14m/22km E of Charing Cross. TQ5278.
Coldharbour *Surr.* ***Village***, 4m/6km S of Dorking. **22 E7** TQ1443.
Coldingham *Sc.Bord.* ***Village***, 3m/5km NW of Eyemouth. Ruins of 12c priory. **77 G4** NT9066.
Coldingham Bay *Sc.Bord.* ***Bay***, 1m/2km E of Coldingham. **77 H4** NT9066.
Coldingham Loch *Sc.Bord.* ***Lake/loch***, 1m/2km SW of St. Abb's Head. **77 G4** NT8968.
Coldingham Moor *Sc.Bord.* ***Open space***, moorland 2m/4km NW of Coldingham. **77 G4** NT8567.
Coldingham Priory *Sc.Bord.* ***Ecclesiastical building***, in Coldingham, 3m/5km NW of Eyemouth. 13c priory, largely demolished during Civil War, but some features survived and are incorporated into parish church. **77 H4** NT9065.
Coldrain *P. & K.* ***Settlement***, 3m/4km E of Crook of Devon. **82 B7** NO0800.
Coldred *Kent* ***Village***, 5m/7km NW of Dover. **15 H3** TR2746.
Coldrey House *Hants.* ***Historic house***, 16c-17c farmhouse with fine Georgian elevations, 1m/2km W of Bentley. Substantial remains of villa or homestead farm to SW, including finds of pottery, iron implements, bronze ring and a coin. **22 A7** SU7743.
Coldridge *Devon* ***Village***, 4m/7km E of Winkleigh. **6 E5** SS6907.
Coldrife *Northumb.* ***Settlement***, 4m/6km S of Rothbury. **71 F4** NZ0694.
Coldrum Long Barrow *Kent* ***Historic/prehistoric site***, 1km E of Trottiscliffe, Neolithic burial chamber (National Trust) in which skeletal remains have been found. **24 C5** TQ6560.

Coldsmouth Hill *Northumb.* ***Mountain***, in Cheviot Hills, 2m/3km E of Kirk Yetholm. Height 1361 feet or 415 metres. **70 D1** NT8528.
Coldstream *Sc.Bord.* Population: 1746. ***Small town***, on River Tweed 9m/14km NE of Kelso. Coldstream Guards raised here by General Monk, 1660. **77 G7** NT8439.
Coldwaltham *W.Suss.* ***Village***, 2m/3km SW of Pulborough. **12 D5** TQ0216.
Coldwells *Aber.* ***Settlement***, near E coast, 1m/2km W of Murdoch Head. **99 K6** NK1040.
Coldyreath *Cornw.* ***Hamlet***, 4m/7km NW of St. Austell. SW9858.
Cole ***River***, rising near Portway, 9m/14km S of Birmingham, and flowing N and NE into River Tame 2m/3km NE of Coleshill. **40 D7** SP2191.
Cole ***River***, rising at Swindon and flowing N into River Thames 1km below Lechlade. SU2298.
Cole *Som.* ***Village***, 1m/2km SW of Bruton. **9 F1** ST6633.
Cole End *Warks.* ***Suburb***, N end of Coleshill. SP1989.
Cole Green *Herts.* ***Hamlet***, 3m/5km E of Welwyn Garden City. **33 F7** TL2811.
Cole Green *Herts.* ***Settlement***, NW end of Brent Pelham, 5m/7km E of Buntingford. TL4331.
Cole Henley *Hants.* ***Settlement***, 2m/3km N of Whitchurch. SU4650.
Colebatch *Shrop.* ***Hamlet***, 1m/2km S of Bishop's Castle. **38 C7** SO3187.
Colebrook *Devon* ***Hamlet***, 1m/2km SW of Cullompton. **7 J5** ST0006.
Colebrooke *Devon* ***Village***, 4m/7km W of Crediton. **7 F5** SS7700.
Coleburn *Moray* ***Settlement***, 4m/7km S of Elgin. NJ2455.
Coleby *Lincs.* ***Village***, 7m/11km S of Lincoln. **52 C6** SK9760.
Coleby *N.Lincs.* ***Village***, 6m/9km N of Scunthorpe. **52 C1** SE8919.
Coleford *Devon* ***Village***, 4m/7km W of Crediton. **7 F5** SS7701.
Coleford *Glos.* Population: 9567. ***Small town***, in Forest of Dean, 4m/7km SE of Monmouth. **28 E7** SO5710.
Coleford *Som.* Population: 2213. ***Village***, 6m/9km W of Frome. **19 K7** ST6848.
Coleford Water *Som.* ***Hamlet***, 4m/7km NE of Wiveliscombe. ST1133.
Colegate End *Norf.* ***Hamlet***, 1m/2km N of Pulham Market. TM1987.
Colehill *Dorset* ***Village***, adjoining to NE of Wimborne Minster. **10 B4** SU0201.
Coleman Green *Herts.* ***Settlement***, 3m/5km W of Welwyn Garden City. TL1912.
Coleman's Hatch *E.Suss.* ***Hamlet***, on N edge of Ashdown Forest, 2m/3km SE of Forest Row. **13 H3** TQ4533.
Colemere *Shrop.* ***Village***, 3m/4km SE of Ellesmere. **38 D2** SJ4332.
Colemere Country Park *Shrop.* ***Leisure/recreation***, country park consisting chiefly of lakes, woodland and grassland, 2m/3km SE of Ellesmere. Designated Site of Special Scientific Interest due to importance of bogland vegetation and associated birdlife. **38 D2** SJ4233.
Colemore *Hants.* ***Hamlet***, 5m/8km S of Alton. **11 J1** SU7030.
Colemore Green *Shrop.* ***Settlement***, 3m/5km N of Bridgnorth. SO7097.
Colenden *P. & K.* ***Settlement***, 1km E of Luncarty across River Tay. **82 C5** NO1029.
Coleorton *Leics.* ***Village***, 3m/4km NW of Coalville. **41 G4** SK4017.
Coleorton Moor *Leics.* ***Hamlet***, 1km S of Coleorton and 3m/4km NW of Coalville. SK4016.
Coleridge Cottage *Som.* ***Historic house***, National Trust property at Nether Stowey, on E side of Quantock Hills. Home of Coleridge for three years, where he wrote 'Rime of the Ancient Mariner' between 1799 and 1800. **7 K1** ST1940.
Colerne *Wilts.* Population: 2572. ***Village***, 6m/10km W of Chippenham. Airfield to W. Site of Roman villa on N side of airfield. **20 B4** ST8271.
Cole's Common *Norf.* ***Settlement***, 1m/2km N of Pulham Market. TM2088.
Cole's Cross *Devon* ***Settlement***, 3m/5km NE of Kingsbridge. **5 H6** SX7746.
Coles Green *Suff.* ***Hamlet***, 4m/7km W of Ipswich. TM0941.
Cole's Green *Suff.* ***Settlement***, 1km SE of Framlingham. TM2962.
Coles Green *Worcs.* ***Settlement***, 4m/6km N of Great Malvern. SO7651.
Colesbourne *Glos.* ***Village***, 6m/10km SE of Cheltenham. **30 B7** SO9913.
Colesbrook *Dorset* ***Settlement***, 1km N of Gillingham. ST8027.
Colesden *Beds.* ***Hamlet***, 6m/10km NE of Bedford. **32 E3** TL1255.
Coleshill *Bucks.* ***Village***, 1m/2km SW of Amersham. **22 C2** SU9495.
Coleshill *Oxon.* ***Village***, National Trust property, 4m/6km W of Faringdon. **21 F2** SU2393.
Coleshill *Warks.* Population: 6324. ***Small town***, 9m/14km E of Birmingham. Medieval church with fine spire. **40 E7** SP1989.
Colestocks *Devon* ***Hamlet***, 3m/5km N of Ottery St. Mary. **7 J5** ST0900.
Coleton *Devon* ***Settlement***, 2m/3km E of Dartmouth across River Dart. SX9051.
Coleton Fishacre Garden *Devon* ***Garden***, 20 acre garden (National Trust) designed by Rupert and Lady Dorothy D'Oyly Carte in early 20c, 2m/3km E of Kingswear. Contains rare and exotic trees and shrubs in climatically-favoured coastal location. **5 K5** SX9150.
Coley *B. & N.E.Som.* ***Hamlet***, 1m/2km E of East Harptree. ST5855.
Coley *Staffs.* ***Settlement***, 4m/6km NW of Rugeley. SK0122.
Coley *W.Yorks.* ***Settlement***, 1km E of Northowram, 3m/4km NE of Halifax. SE1226.
Colfa *Powys Welsh form of Colva, qv.*
Colfin *D. & G.* ***Settlement***, 4m/6km E of Portpatrick. **64 A5** NX0555.
Colgate *W.Suss.* ***Hamlet***, 4m/6km E of Horsham. **13 F3** TQ2332.
Colgrain *Arg. & B.* ***Settlement***, 2m/4km NW of Cardross. **74 B2** NS3280.
Colgrave Sound *Shet.* ***Sea feature***, sea passage between Yell and Fetlar, S of Hascosay. **108 E4** HU5789.
Colham Green *Gt.Lon.* ***Suburb***, in borough of Hillingdon, 2m/3km SE of Uxbridge. TQ0781.
Colindale *Gt.Lon.* ***Suburb***, in borough of Barnet, 1m/2km NW of Hendon. TQ2189.
Colinsburgh *Fife* ***Village***, built in 18c, 2m/4km NW of Elie. **83 F7** NO4703.
Colinton *Edin.* ***Suburb***, 4m/6km SW of Edinburgh city centre. **76 A4** NT2168.
Colintraive *Arg. & B.* ***Village***, in Argyll on E shore of Kyles of Bute, 2m/3km SE of entrance to Loch Riddon. Car and pedestrian ferry service to Rhubodach on Bute. **73 J3** NS0374.
Colkirk *Norf.* ***Village***, 2m/3km S of Fakenham. **44 D3** TF9126.
Coll *Arg. & B.* ***Island***, sparsely populated island of Inner Hebrides, measuring 12m/20km NE to SW and nearly 4m/6km at greatest width. NE point is 9m/15km W of Ardnamurchan Point on mainland and SW point is 2m/3km NE of neighbouring island of Tiree. Coll is fairly low-lying, and somewhat bleak and windswept. Lochs noted for trout fishing. **78 C2** NM2058.
Coll *W.Isles Anglicised form of Col (village), qv.*
Colla Firth *Shet.* ***Sea feature***, inlet of Yell Sound on NE coast of Mainland. **108 C4** HU3583.
Colla Firth *Shet.* ***Sea feature***, inlet on E coast of Mainland, 4m/6km N of Laxo and head of Dury Voe. **109 D6** HU4369.
Collace *P. & K.* ***Settlement***, 8m/12km NE of Perth. **82 D4** NO2032.
Collafirth *Shet.* ***Locality***, comprises settlements of North and South Collafirth at head of Colla Firth, 1m/2km SW of Housetter, Mainland. **108 C4** HU3583.
Collafirth *Shet.* ***Settlement***, at head of Colla Firth, on E coast of Mainland. **109 D6** HU4368.
Collamoor Head *Cornw.* ***Settlement***, 5m/8km NE of Boscastle. **4 B1** SX1793.
Collaton St. Mary *Torbay* ***Village***, on W edge of Paignton. **5 J4** SX8660.
College Burn *Northumb.* ***River***, rising on The Cheviot and flowing N to Westnewton, where it joins Bowmont Water to form River Glen. **70 D1** NT9030.
College Green *Som.* ***Settlement***, 1km E of Parbrook and 5m/8km SE of Glastonbury. ST5736.
College Milton *S.Lan.* ***Suburb***, and industrial estate, 1m/2km NW of East Kilbride town centre. NS6155.
College Town *Brack.F.* ***Suburb***, adjoining to E of Sandhurst. SU8561.
Collessie *Fife* ***Village***, 6m/9km W of Cupar. **82 D6** NO2813.
Colleton Mills *Devon* ***Settlement***, on River Taw, 1m/2km NW of Chulmleigh. **6 E4** SS6615.
Collett's Green *Worcs.* ***Hamlet***, 3m/5km SW of Worcester. **29 H3** SO8251.
Collie Law *Sc.Bord.* ***Mountain***, 4m/6km NW of Lauder. Height 1250 feet or 381 metres. **76 C5** NT4850.
Collier Law *Dur.* ***Mountain***, 1m/2km NE of Crawleyside. Height 1692 feet or 516 metres. **62 B2** NZ0141.
Collier Row *Gt.Lon.* ***Suburb***, NW district of Romford, in borough of Havering. **23 J2** TQ4990.
Collier Street *Kent* ***Village***, 3m/5km S of Yalding. **14 C3** TQ7145.
Collier's End *Herts.* ***Village***, 4m/7km N of Ware. **33 G6** TL3720.
Collier's Green *E.Suss.* ***Settlement***, 1km E of Staple Cross. TQ7922.
Collier's Wood *Gt.Lon.* ***Suburb***, in borough of Merton, 1m/2km E of Wimbledon. Running S from High Street, on W side of railway station, is Merton Abbey Wall (National Trust). TQ2670.
Colliery Row *T. & W.* ***Suburb***, adjoining to W of Houghton le Spring. **62 E1** NZ3249.
Collieston *Aber.* ***Village***, on E coast, 3m/5km NE of Newburgh across River Ythan and Sands of Forvie. **91 J2** NK0328.
Colliford Lake *Cornw.* ***Reservoir***, on Bodmin Moor, 7m/11km NE of Bodmin. **4 B3** SX1772.
Collin *D. & G.* ***Village***, 4m/6km E of Dumfries. **69 F6** NY0276.
Collin Hags *D. & G.* ***Hill***, 4m/6km NE of Waterbeck. Height 836 feet or 255 metres. **69 J5** NY2980.
Collingbourne Ducis *Wilts.* ***Village***, 2m/4km NW of Ludgershall. **21 F6** SU2453.
Collingbourne Kingston *Wilts.* ***Village***, 4m/6km NW of Ludgershall. **21 F6** SU2355.
Collingham *Notts.* Population: 2801. ***Village***, 6m/9km NE of Newark-on-Trent. **52 B6** SK8361.
Collingham *W.Yorks.* Population: 2714. ***Village***, 2m/3km SW of Wetherby. **57 J5** SE3845.
Collington *Here.* ***Hamlet***, 4m/6km N of Bromyard. **29 F2** SO6460.
Collingtree *Northants.* ***Village***, at S end of Northampton. **31 J3** SP7555.
Collins End *Oxon.* ***Settlement***, 2m/3km NE of Pangbourne. SU6578.
Collins Green *Warr.* ***Village***, 5m/8km NW of Warrington. **48 E3** SJ5594.
Collins Green *Worcs.* ***Settlement***, 6m/9km E of Bromyard. SO7457.
Colliston *Angus* ***Village***, 4m/6km NW of Arbroath. Colliston House, 16c. **83 H3** NO6045.
Colliton *Devon* ***Hamlet***, 4m/7km SE of Cullompton. **7 J5** ST0804.
Collmuir *Aber.* ***Settlement***, 4m/6km NE of Tarland. **90 D4** NJ5306.
Collum Green *Bucks.* ***Locality***, 2m/4km S of Beaconsfield. SU9586.
Collycroft *Warks.* ***Suburb***, N district of Bedworth. **41 F7** SP3587.
Collyhurst *Gt.Man.* ***Suburb***, 2m/3km NE of Manchester city centre. SD8500.
Collynie *Aber.* ***Settlement***, 5m/8km E of Fyvie. **91 G1** NJ8436.
Collyweston *Northants.* ***Village***, 3m/5km SW of Stamford. **42 D5** SK9902.
Colmonell *S.Ayr.* ***Village***, in River Stinchar valley, 5m/7km NE of Ballantrae. **67 F5** NX1486.
Colmworth *Beds.* ***Village***, 7m/11km NE of Bedford. **32 E3** TL1058.
Coln *Glos.* ***River***, rising near Brockhampton and flowing SW into River Thames 1m/2km above Lechlade. **20 E1** SU2199.
Coln Rogers *Glos.* ***Village***, 4m/6km SW of Northleach. **20 D1** SP0809.
Coln St. Aldwyns *Glos.* ***Village***, 2m/3km SE of Bibury. **20 E1** SP1405.
Coln St. Dennis *Glos.* ***Village***, 3m/5km SW of Northleach. **30 B7** SP0810.
Colnabaichin *Aber.* ***Settlement***, near crossing point of River Don, 1m/2km E of Corgarff. **89 K4** NJ2908.
Colnbrook *Slo.* Population: 4955. ***Village***, 4m/6km SE of Slough. **22 D4** TQ0277.
Colne *Cambs.* Population: 1202. ***Village***, 6m/10km S of Chatteris. **33 G1** TL3775.
Colne *Essex* ***River***, rising in NW Essex, to SE of Haverhill, and flowing SE through Sible Hedingham, Halstead and Colchester into North Sea between Brightlingsea and Mersea Island. **34 D6** TM0715.
Colne *Lancs.* Population: 18,776. ***Town***, former cotton town, 6m/9km NE of Burnley. 12c church. **56 D5** SD8840.
Colne Bridge *W.Yorks.* ***Locality***, on River Colne, 2m/3km W of Mirfield across River Calder. SE1720.
Colne Edge *Lancs.* ***Hamlet***, 1km N of Colne. SD8841.
Colne Engaine *Essex* ***Village***, 2m/4km E of Halstead. **34 C5** TL8530.
Colne Point *Essex* ***Coastal feature***, headland, 5m/8km SW of Clacton-on-Sea. **35 F7** TM1012.
Colne Valley *Essex* ***Valley***, carrying River Colne between Halstead and West Bergholt. **34 C6** TL8529.
Colney *Norf.* ***Village***, on River Yare, 3m/5km W of Norwich. **45 F5** TG1807.
Colney Hatch *Gt.Lon.* ***Suburb***, in borough of Barnet, 7m/12km N of Charing Cross. TQ2791.
Colney Heath *Herts.* ***Village***, 3m/4km SW of Hatfield. **23 F1** TL2005.
Colney Street *Herts.* ***Hamlet***, 3m/5km N of St. Albans. Site of Roman villa 1km NW. **22 E1** TL1502.
Colonsay *Arg. & B.* ***Island***, 16 square miles or 40 square km lying 8m/13km NW of Jura in Inner Hebrides. Has rocky coastline interspersed with sandy beaches. Chief settlement is Scalasaig on E coast. Diverse wildlife includes seabirds, seal colonies, otters and wild goats. Joined to Oronsay to S at low tide. **72 B1** NR3793.
Colonsay House *Arg. & B.* ***Other building***, on Colonsay to NE of Kiloran. Woodland garden includes rhododendrons, mimosa, eucalyptus and palm trees. **72 B1** NR3793.
Colpy *Aber.* ***Settlement***, 9m/14km SE of Huntly. **90 E1** NJ6432.
Colquhar *Sc.Bord.* ***Settlement***, with remains of tower, 3m/5km N of Innerleithen. **76 B6** NT3341.
Colsay *Shet.* ***Island***, uninhabited island of 54 acres or 22 hectares lying off W coast of Mainland opposite Bay of Scousburgh. **109 F9** HU3618.
Colscott *Devon* ***Hamlet***, 2m/4km E of Bradworthy. SS3614.
Colsterdale *N.Yorks.* ***Settlement***, 4m/7km S of Middleham. **57 G1** SE1381.
Colsterdale Moor *N.Yorks.* ***Open space***, remote moorland on N side of upper reaches of River Burn, 7m/11km W of Masham. **57 G1** SE1181.
Colsterworth *Lincs.* ***Village***, 7m/12km S of Grantham. **42 C3** SK9324.
Colston *E.Dun.* ***Suburb***, 3m/4km N of Glasgow city centre. NS6069.
Colston Bassett *Notts.* ***Village***, 4m/7km S of Bingham. Old market cross (National Trust). **42 A2** SK7033.
Colt Crag Reservoir *Northumb.* ***Reservoir***, 9m/14km N of Hexham. **70 E6** NY9378.
Colt Hill *D. & G.* ***Mountain***, 7m/11km NW of Moniaive. Height 1961 feet or 598 metres. **68 B4** NX6998.
Coltfield *Moray* ***Settlement***, 3m/5km S of Burghead. **97 J5** NJ1163.
Colthouse *Cumb.* ***Settlement***, adjoining to N of Town End, 1km E of Hawkshead. SD3498.
Coltishall *Norf.* Population: 1992. ***Village***, 8m/12km NE of Norwich. **45 G4** TG2719.
Coltness *N.Lan.* ***Suburb***, 1m/2km N of Wishaw. NS7956.
Colton *Cumb.* ***Hamlet***, 2m/3km N of Greenodd. **55 G1** SD3186.
Colton *Norf.* ***Village***, 5m/8km N of Wymondham. **45 F4** TG1009.
Colton *N.Yorks.* ***Village***, 4m/6km E of Tadcaster. **58 B5** SE5444.
Colton *Staffs.* ***Village***, 2m/3km N of Rugeley. **40 C3** SK0520.
Colton *W.Yorks.* ***Suburb***, 4m/7km E of Leeds city centre. SE3632.
Columbia *T. & W.* ***Suburb***, to SE of Washington town centre. NZ3155.

C

Colva (Colfa). *Powys* ***Settlement***, 6m/10km SW of Hay-on-Wye. **28 B3** SO2053.
Colva Hill *Powys* ***Mountain***, 6m/10km W of Kington. Height 1673 feet or 510 metres. **28 A3** SO1954.
Colvend *D. & G.* ***Locality***, at S end of White Loch, 5m/8km SE of Dalbeattie. **65 J5** NX8654.
Colvister *Shet.* ***Settlement***, on W side of Basta Voe, Yell. **108 E3** HU5196.
Colwall *Here.* ***Hamlet***, 3m/5km NE of Ledbury. SO7342.
Colwall Green *Here.* ***Village***, 3m/5km NE of Ledbury. **29 G4** SO7541.
Colwall Stone *Here.* ***Village***, 3m/5km SW of Great Malvern. **29 G4** SO7542.
Colwell *Northumb.* ***Village***, 7m/11km N of Hexham. **70 E6** NY9575.
Colwell Bay *I.o.W.* ***Bay***, to N of Totland, extending from Warden Point to Cliff End. **10 E6** SZ3288.
Colwich *Staffs.* Population: 1222. ***Village***, on River Trent, 3m/5km NW of Rugeley. **40 C3** SK0121.
Colwick *Notts.* ***Suburb***, 3m/5km E of Nottingham. **41 J1** SK6140.
Colwick Hall *Notts.* ***Historic house***, in Colwick, 1km W of Radcliffe on Trent and 4m/6km E of Nottingham, where Mrs. Musters, Byron's 'Mary Chaworth' lived. **41 J2** SK6239.
Colwinston (Tregolwyn). *V. of Glam.* ***Village***, 4m/6km W of Cowbridge. **18 C4** SS9475.
Colworth *W.Suss.* ***Village***, 3m/5km NW of Bognor Regis. **12 C6** SU9102.
Colwyn Bay (Also known as Rhôs Bay.) *Conwy* ***Bay***, on SE side of Rhôs-on-Sea and N of town of Colwyn Bay. SH8479.
Colwyn Bay (Bae Colwyn). *Conwy* Population: 29,883. ***Town***, popular coastal resort situated 10m/16km W of Rhyl. Sandy beaches. **47 G5** SH8578.
Coly *Devon* ***River***, rising S of Honiton and flowing into River Axe to E of Colyford. SY2592.
Colyford *Devon* ***Village***, 2m/3km N of Seaton. **8 B5** SY2592.
Colyton *Devon* Population: 1684. ***Village***, 3m/4km N of Seaton. **8 B5** SY2493.
Colzium House *N.Lan.* ***Garden***, walled garden of rare shrubs and trees in grounds of Colzium House to NE of Kilsyth. House also contains Kilsyth Heritage Museum. **75 F3** NS7278.
Comb Fell *Northumb.* ***Mountain***, 1m/2km SE of The Cheviot. Height 2132 feet or 650 metres. **70 E2** NT9118.
Comb Hill *Sc.Bord.* ***Mountain***, 3m/5km S of Teviothead. Mast at summit. Height 1686 feet or 514 metres. **69 J3** NT3900.
Comb Law *S.Lan.* ***Mountain***, in Lowther Hills, 2m/3km NE of Ballencleuch Law. Height 2109 feet or 643 metres. **68 E3** NS9407.
Combe *Devon* ***Hamlet***, 2m/3km E of Morebath. SS9725.
Combe *Devon* ***Hamlet***, just W of South Pool, 3m/5km N of Prawle Point. SX7640.
Combe *Devon* ***Settlement***, on River Mardle, below E side of Dartmoor, 3m/4km NW of Buckfastleigh. SX7068.
Combe *Here.* ***Hamlet***, 2m/4km E of Presteigne. **28 C2** SO3463.
Combe *Oxon.* ***Village***, 5m/9km NE of Witney. **31 F7** SP4115.
Combe *Som.* ***Hamlet***, 1km N of Langport. ST4128.
Combe *W.Berks.* ***Hamlet***, 5m/8km N of Hurstbourne Tarrant. **21 G5** SU3760.
Combe Abbey *Warks.* ***Historic house***, in Coombe Abbey Country Park with lake, Coombe Pool, 4m/7km E of Coventry. Abbey was originally a Cistercian monastery, founded in 12c. **30 E1** SP4079.
Combe Common *Surr.* ***Settlement***, adjoining to NW of Chiddingfold, 4m/6km S of Milford. SU9436.
Combe Cross *Devon* ***Settlement***, 2m/3km NE of Ashburton. **5 H3** SX7870.
Combe Down *B. & N.E.Som.* ***Suburb***, SE district of Bath. **20 A5** ST7662.
Combe Florey *Som.* ***Village***, 6m/10km NW of Taunton. **7 K2** ST1531.
Combe Hay *B. & N.E.Som.* ***Village***, 3m/5km S of Bath. **20 A5** ST7359.
Combe Martin *Devon* Population: 2453. ***Village***, running down to Combe Martin Bay, on N coast, 4m/6km E of Ilfracombe. Claims longest village street in England. **6 D1** SS5846.
Combe Martin Bay *Devon* ***Bay***, on North Devon coast, 4m/6km E of Ilfracombe. **6 D1** SS5748.
Combe Martin Wildlife and Dinosaur Park *Devon* ***Leisure/recreation***, 1m/2km SE of Combe Martin. Animated dinosaur display is showpiece attraction, but park also holds wide variety of animals ranging from apes to meerkats, all set in 20 acres of gardens and woodland. **6 E1** SS6045.
Combe Moor *Here.* ***Village***, 4m/6km E of Presteigne. **28 C2** SO3663.
Combe Pafford *Torbay* ***Suburb***, 1m/2km N of Torquay town centre. SX9166.
Combe Raleigh *Devon* ***Village***, 1m/2km N of Honiton. **7 K5** ST1502.
Combe St. Nicholas *Som.* ***Village***, 2m/4km NW of Chard. **8 B3** ST3011.
Combe Sydenham Hall *Som.* ***Historic house***, 3m/4km S of Williton and 3m/5km S of Watchet. 16c home of Elizabeth Sydenham, wife of Sir Francis Drake. Includes a working bakery, Elizabethan gardens, deer park and trout farm. **7 J2** ST0736.
Combeinteignhead *Devon* ***Village***, 3m/4km E of Newton Abbot. **5 K3** SX9071.
Comberbach *Ches.* ***Village***, 3m/4km NW of Northwich. **49 F5** SJ6477.
Comberford *Staffs.* ***Hamlet***, 2m/4km N of Tamworth. **40 D5** SK1907.
Comberton *Cambs.* Population: 2311. ***Village***, 4m/7km W of Cambridge. **33 G3** TL3856.
Comberton *Here.* ***Hamlet***, 5m/9km N of Leominster. **28 D2** SO4967.
Combpyne *Devon* ***Hamlet***, in parish of Combpyne Rousdon, 3m/5km W of Lyme Regis. **8 B5** SY2992.
Combpyne Rousdon *Devon* ***Locality***, parish 3m/5km W of Lyme Regis. SY2992.
Combridge *Staffs.* ***Hamlet***, 3m/4km N of Uttoxeter. SK0937.
Combrook *Warks.* ***Village***, 7m/11km E of Stratford-upon-Avon. **30 E3** SP3051.
Combs *Derbys.* ***Hamlet***, 2m/3km SW of Chapel-en-le-Frith. **50 C5** SK0478.
Combs *Suff.* ***Village***, 2m/3km S of Stowmarket. **34 E3** TM0456.
Combs Ford *Suff.* ***Suburb***, S district of Stowmarket. **34 E3** TM0557.
Combs Reservoir *Derbys.* ***Reservoir***, 1km N of Combs. **50 C5** SK0379.
Combwich *Som.* ***Village***, on tidal reach of River Parrett, 4m/7km NW of Bridgwater. **19 F7** ST2542.
Come-to-Good *Cornw.* ***Hamlet***, 3m/5km S of Truro. SW8140.
Comely Bank *Edin.* ***Suburb***, 1m/2km NW of Edinburgh city centre. NT2374.
Comer *Stir.* ***Settlement***, at NW end of Gleann Dubh, 4m/6km SW of Stronachlachar. **80 E7** NN3804.
Comers *Aber.* ***Settlement***, 8m/12km N of Banchory. **90 E4** NJ6707.
Comfort *Cornw.* ***Locality***, 2m/3km NE of Penryn, adjoining Mylor Bridge. SW8036.
Comhampton *Worcs.* ***Village***, 3m/5km SE of Stourport-on-Severn. SO8366.
Comin Capel Betws *Cere.* ***Settlement***, 4m/7km W of Tregaron. SN6157.
Comins Coch *Cere.* ***Village***, 2m/3km E of Aberystwyth. SN6182.
Comiston *Edin.* ***Suburb***, 3m/5km S of Edinburgh city centre. NT2468.
Comlongon Castle *D. & G.* ***Castle***, 15c castle with dungeons and well-preserved Great Hall, 1km W of Clarencefield. **69 F7** NY0769.
Commercial End *Cambs.* ***Hamlet***, at N end of Swaffham Bulbeck, 6m/9km W of Newmarket. **33 J2** TL5563.
Commins Coch *Powys* ***Hamlet***, 2m/3km SE of Cemmaes Road. **37 H5** SH8403.
Common Edge *B'pool* ***Suburb***, 2m/3km SE of Blackpool town centre. **55 G6** SD3232.
Common End *Cumb.* ***Locality***, adjoining to S of Distington. NY0022.
Common Law *Sc.Bord.* ***Mountain***, 3m/5km SW of Broughton. Height 1545 feet or 471 metres. **75 J7** NT0732.
Common Marsh *Hants. See Stockbridge.*
Common Moor *Cornw.* ***Village***, 3m/5km N of Liskeard. **4 C4** SX2469.
Common of Dunning *P. & K.* ***Open space***, forested mountain area, 3m/5km S of Dunning. **82 B7** NO0109.
Common Platt *Wilts.* ***Hamlet***, adjoining to NW of Swindon. SU1086.
Common Side *Ches.* ***Locality***, 1m/2km SE of Helsby. SJ5074.
Common Side *Derbys.* ***Village***, 1km NW of Barlow. **51 F5** SK3375.
Common Side *S.Yorks.* ***Suburb***, 3m/4km SE of Sheffield city centre. SK3884.
Common Square *Lincs.* ***Hamlet***, 2m/3km E of Washingborough. TF0470.
Commondale *N.Yorks.* ***Village***, 2m/4km NW of Castleton. **63 H5** NZ6610.
Commondale Moor *N.Yorks.* ***Open space***, moorland on Cleveland Hills, 4m/6km NW of Castleton. **63 H5** NZ6411.
Commonedge Hill *Clack.* ***Mountain***, on Ochil Hills, 3m/4km NE of Dollar. Height 1538 feet or 469 metres. **82 A7** NN9801.
Commonside *Derbys.* ***Settlement***, 8m/12km NW of Derby. **40 E1** SK2441.
Commonside *Notts.* ***Locality***, adjoining to S of Huthwaite, 1m/2km W of Sutton in Ashfield. SK4658.
Commonwood *Wrex.* ***Settlement***, 2m/3km W of Holt. SJ3753.
Compass Hill *High.* ***Hill***, near E end of Canna. Height 459 feet or 140 metres. **85 H4** NG2706.
Compstall *Gt.Man.* ***Village***, 2m/3km E of Romiley. **49 J3** SJ9690.
Compton *Devon* ***Hamlet***, 3m/5km W of Torquay. Compton Castle (National Trust) is a restored medieval manor house. **5 J4** SX8664.
Compton *Hants.* ***Hamlet***, 4m/6km S of Stockbridge. SU3429.
Compton *Hants.* ***Village***, 3m/4km S of Winchester. **11 F2** SU4625.
Compton *Plym.* ***Suburb***, 2m/3km NE of Plymouth city centre. SX4956.
Compton *Staffs.* ***Hamlet***, 5m/8km W of Stourbridge. SO8284.
Compton *Surr.* ***Suburb***, adjoining to E of Farnham. SU8546.
Compton *Surr.* ***Village***, 3m/5km SW of Guildford. Norman sanctuary of church has upper chamber unique in Europe. **22 C7** SU9547.
Compton *W.Berks.* ***Village***, 5m/7km W of Streatley. **21 J4** SU5279.
Compton *W.Suss.* ***Village***, 7m/11km NE of Havant. **11 J3** SU7714.
Compton *W.Yorks.* ***Hamlet***, with small lake, 1km SE of Collingham. SE3944.
Compton *Wilts.* ***Hamlet***, on River Avon, 2m/3km S of Upavon. SU1352.
Compton Abbas *Dorset Alternative name for West Compton, qv.*
Compton Abbas *Dorset* ***Village***, on W edge of Cranborne Chase, 3m/5km S of Shaftesbury. **9 H3** ST8618.
Compton Abdale *Glos.* ***Village***, 4m/6km NW of Northleach. **30 B7** SP0616.
Compton Acres Gardens *Poole* ***Garden***, 3m/4km SE of Poole town centre. Cliff-top gardens with colourful displays. **10 B6** SZ0589.
Compton Bassett *Wilts.* ***Village***, 3m/4km E of Calne. **20 D4** SU0372.
Compton Bay *I.o.W.* ***Bay***, extending SE from Freshwater Bay to Hanover Point on SW coast. **10 E6** SZ3684.
Compton Beauchamp *Oxon.* ***Village***, 5m/9km S of Faringdon. **21 F3** SU2887.
Compton Bishop *Som.* ***Village***, 2m/3km W of Axbridge. **19 G6** ST4055.
Compton Castle *Devon* ***Castle***, 14c fortified manor (National Trust), with later additions, 3m/5km W of Torquay. Home of Gilbert family. **5 J4** SX8664.
Compton Chamberlayne *Wilts.* ***Village***, 5m/7km W of Wilton. **10 B2** SU0229.
Compton Common *B. & N.E.Som.* ***Hamlet***, 1km SW of Compton Dando. ST6464.
Compton Dando *B. & N.E.Som.* ***Village***, 7m/11km W of Bath. **19 K5** ST6464.
Compton Down *Wilts.* ***Open space***, hillslope 2m/3km W of Compton. **20 D6** SU0151.
Compton Dundon *Som.* ***Village***, at E end of Sedgemoor, 3m/4km S of Street. **8 D1** ST4832.
Compton Durville *Som.* ***Hamlet***, 4m/7km NE of Ilminster. ST4117.
Compton Martin *B. & N.E.Som.* ***Village***, below N slopes of Mendip Hills, 3m/5km S of Chew Stoke. **19 J6** ST5457.
Compton Pauncefoot *Som.* ***Village***, 3m/4km E of Sparkford. **9 F2** ST6426.
Compton Valence *Dorset* ***Village***, 3m/5km S of Maiden Newton. **8 E5** SY5993.
Compton Verney *Warks.* ***Settlement***, 7m/11km E of Stratford-upon-Avon. SP3152.
Comra *High.* ***Settlement***, 1km E of Kinloch Laggan. **88 C5** NN5490.
Comrie *Fife* ***Village***, 5m/7km W of Dunfermline. NT0189.
Comrie *P. & K.* Population: 1439. ***Village***, at junction of Glen Artney, Glen Lednock, and Strathearn, 6m/10km W of Crieff. Drummond Trout Farm and Fishery. **81 J5** NN7722.
Cona Glen *High.* ***Valley***, carrying Cona River in Lochaber district, running E to River Scaddle, W of Loch Linnhe. **87 F7** NM9472.
Cona' Mheall *High.* ***Mountain***, rocky summit in Ross and Cromarty district, with scree-covered W slope, 1m/2km E of Beinn Dearg and 12m/20km SE of Ullapool. Munro: height 3214 feet or 980 metres. **95 J3** NH2781.
Conachair *W.Isles* ***Mountain***, summit of St. Kilda. Height 1410 feet or 430 metres. NA0900.
Conachcraig *Aber.* ***Mountain***, 2m/3km NW of Spittal of Glenmuick. Height 2827 feet or 862 metres. **89 K6** NO2887.
Conamheall *Clack. Gaelic form of Conival, qv.*
Conamheall *High.* ***Mountain***, with Strath Dionard and River Dionard to W and Loch Dionard to SW. Height 1581 feet or 482 metres. **103 F3** NC3651.
Concangium *Dur. See Chester-le-Street.*
Conchra *Arg. & B.* ***Settlement***, 3m/5km NE of Clachan of Glendaruel. **73 J2** NS0288.
Conchra *High.* ***Settlement***, 1km N of Dornie across Loch Long, Skye and Lochalsh district. **86 E2** NG8827.
Concord *T. & W.* ***Suburb***, to N of Washington. NZ3057.
Concraigie *P. & K.* ***Hamlet***, 3m/4km SE of Butterstone. **82 C3** NO1044.
Condate *Ches. See Northwich.*
Conder *Lancs.* ***River***, rising E of Lancaster and flowing SW into River Lune 1km E of Glasson, 3m/5km SW of Lancaster. **55 J4** SD4556.
Conder Green *Lancs.* ***Settlement***, 4m/6km S of Lancaster. **55 H4** SD4556.
Condercum *Cumb. See Benwell Roman Fort.*
Conderton *Worcs.* ***Village***, 5m/9km NE of Tewkesbury. **29 J5** SO9637.
Condicote *Glos.* ***Village***, 3m/5km NW of Stow-on-the-Wold. **30 C6** SP1528.
Condorrat *N.Lan.* ***Suburb***, 2m/3km SW of Cumbernauld town centre. **75 F3** NS7373.
Condover *Shrop.* ***Village***, 4m/7km S of Shrewsbury. **38 D5** SJ4905.
Condover Green *Shrop.* ***Locality***, 1m/2km SE of Condover. SJ4905.
Coney Hall *Gt.Lon.* ***Suburb***, in borough of Bromley, 3m/5km S of Bromley town centre. TQ3964.
Coney Hill *Glos.* ***Suburb***, SE district of Gloucester. SO8517.
Coney Island *High. Anglicised form of Eilean a' Chonnaidh, qv.*
Coney Weston *Suff.* ***Village***, 5m/8km N of Ixworth. **34 D1** TL9578.
Coneyhurst Common *W.Suss.* ***Hamlet***, 2m/3km SE of Billingshurst. **12 E4** TQ1023.
Coneysthorpe *N.Yorks.* ***Village***, estate village of Castle Howard, 5m/8km W of Malton. **58 D2** SE7171.
Coneythorpe *N.Yorks.* ***Hamlet***, 3m/5km NE of Knaresborough. **57 J4** SE3958.
Conford *Hants.* ***Hamlet***, 1m/2km NW of Liphook. **12 B3** SU8233.
Congash *High.* ***Settlement***, 1m/2km SE of Grantown-on-Spey. **89 H2** NJ0526.
Congdon's Shop *Cornw.* ***Hamlet***, 5m/8km SE of Launceston. **4 C3** SX2878.
Congerstone *Leics.* ***Village***, 7m/11km S of Ashby de la Zouch. **41 F5** SK3605.
Congham *Norf.* ***Village***, 7m/11km E of King's Lynn. **44 B3** TF7123.
Congl-y-wal *Gwyn.* ***Locality***, 1m/2km S of Blaenau Ffestiniog. SH7044.

Conglass Water *Moray* ***River***, flowing NW to join River Avon, 3m/5km NW of Tomintoul. **89 J3** NJ1422.
Congleton *Ches.* ***Town***, on River Dane, 11m/18km N of Stoke-on-Trent. Former cotton-spinning and silk-producing town. Gothic town hall. **49 H6** SJ8562.
Congresbury *N.Som.* Population: 3435. ***Village***, 5m/9km S of Clevedon. **19 H5** ST4363.
Congresbury Yeo (Upper stretch known as (River) Yeo.) ***River***, rising originally as River Yeo at Compton Martin and flowing NW through Blagdon Lake or Yeo Reservoir. Below reservoir it is known as Congresbury Yeo, and it continues NW through Congresbury and into mouth of River Severn 4m/6km SW of Clevedon. **19 H5** ST3666.
Congreve *Staffs.* ***Settlement***, 1m/2km SW of Penkridge. SJ9013.
Conicavel *Moray* ***Settlement***, 4m/7km SW of Forres across River Findhorn. **97 G6** NH9953.
Conie Glen *Arg. & B.* ***Valley***, carrying Conieglen Water to Brunerican Bay on S coast of Kintyre peninsula. **66 A2** NR6907.
Conieglen Water *Arg. & B.* ***River***, on S part of Kintyre, rising on E slopes of The Slate and flowing E, then S through Conie Glen into sea at W end of Brunerican Bay. **66 A2** NR6907.
Coningsby *Lincs.* Population: 5126. ***Village***, 4m/6km SE of Woodhall Spa. Airfield to S. **53 F7** TF2258.
Conington *Cambs.* ***Village***, 2m/4km SE of Stilton. **42 E7** TL1785.
Conington *Cambs.* ***Village***, 9m/15km NW of Cambridge. 18c hall. **33 G2** TL3266.
Conisbrough *S.Yorks.* Population: 16,031. ***Town***, 5m/8km SW of Doncaster. Remains of Norman castle (English Heritage) above River Don. **51 H3** SK5098.
Conisbrough Castle *S.Yorks.* ***Castle***, remains of late 12c castle (English Heritage) built by Hamelin Plantagenet, 5m/8km SW of Doncaster. **51 H3** SK5198.
Conisbrough Parks *S.Yorks.* ***Locality***, adjoining to S of Conisbrough. SK5096.
Conisby *Arg. & B.* ***Settlement***, on Islay, 1km N of Bruichladdich. **72 A4** NR2661.
Conisholme *Lincs.* ***Village***, 7m/11km NE of Louth. **53 H3** TF4095.
Coniston *Cumb.* ***Village***, at N end of Coniston Water, 6m/10km SW of Ambleside. **60 E7** SD3097.
Coniston *E.Riding* ***Village***, 5m/9km NE of Kingston upon Hull. **59 H6** TA1535.
Coniston Cold *N.Yorks.* ***Village***, 6m/10km NW of Skipton. **56 E4** SD9055.
Coniston Water *Cumb.* ***Lake/loch***, 5m/9km long, but less than 1km wide, on W side of Grizedale Forest, with Coniston at its NW end. Donald Campbell was killed on this lake in 1967 while attempting a new world waterspeed record. **60 D7** SD3094.
Conistone *N.Yorks.* ***Village***, in Wharfedale, 2m/4km NW of Grassington. **56 E3** SD9867.
Conistone Moor *N.Yorks.* ***Open space***, moorland containing disused mine workings, 3m/4km SE of Kettlewell. **57 F2** SE0070.
Conival (Gaelic form: Conamheall.) *High.* ***Mountain***, in Sutherland district 4m/6km E of Inchnadamph. Munro: height 3237 feet or 987 metres. **103 F6** NC3019.
Conland *Aber.* ***Settlement***, 5m/8km NE of Huntly. **98 E6** NJ6043.
Connah's Quay *Flints.* Population: 14,443. ***Town***, and port on River Dee, 7m/12km W of Chester and 4m/6km SE of Flint. Power station. **48 B6** SJ2969.
Connel *Arg. & B.* ***Village***, on S side of entrance to Loch Etive, Argyll. Cantilever bridge with span of some 500 feet or 150 metres carries road (formerly railway) across loch. Falls of Lora nearby. **80 A4** NM9134.
Connel Ferry Bridge *Arg. & B.* ***Bridge***, railway bridge across entrance to Loch Etive, built in 1901. Second largest cantilever bridge in Britain. NM9134.
Connel Park *E.Ayr.* ***Village***, 1m/2km SW of New Cumnock. **68 B2** NS6012.
Connor Downs *Cornw.* ***Village***, 2m/4km NE of Hayle. **2 C5** SW5939.
Conock *Wilts.* ***Hamlet***, 5m/8km SE of Devizes. 18c manor house. SU0657.
Conon *High.* ***River***, in Ross and Cromarty district running E from Loch Luichart to head of Cromarty Firth. Falls of Conon below Loch Luichart. NH5658.
Conon Bridge *High.* Population: 2592. ***Village***, in Ross and Cromarty district on River Conon near head of Cromarty Firth. **96 C6** NH5455.
Cononish *Stir.* ***River***, rising on slopes of Ben Lui and running E to River Fillan, 1m/2km SE of Tyndrum. **80 E5** NN3328.
Cononish *Stir.* ***Settlement***, 6m/9km NW of Crianlarich. **80 E5** NN3028.
Cononley *N.Yorks.* ***Village***, 3m/5km S of Skipton. **56 E5** SD9846.
Cononsyth *Angus* ***Hamlet***, 3m/5km SE of Letham. **83 G3** NO5646.
Conostom *W.Isles* ***Hill***, 3m/4km S of Earshader, Isle of Lewis. Height 840 feet or 256 metres. **100 D4** NB1630.
Consall *Staffs.* ***Hamlet***, 7m/11km E of Stoke-on-Trent. **40 B1** SJ9848.
Consett *Dur.* Population: 20,148. ***Town***, 12m/19km SW of Newcastle upon Tyne. Previously an important iron and steel town. **62 C1** NZ1051.
Consett and Sunderland Railway Path *Dur.* ***Other feature of interest***, path and cycle route along disused railway, running E from Consett to Sunderland. **62 C1** NZ1451.
Constable Burton *N.Yorks.* ***Village***, 3m/5km E of Leyburn. **62 C7** SE1690.
Constable Burton Hall Gardens *N.Yorks.* ***Garden***, terraced woodland garden with lilies, roses and wild flowers at 18c Palladian house, Constable Burton Hall, 3m/5km E of Leyburn. **62 C7** SE1691.
Constable Lee *Lancs.* ***Locality***, 1km N of Rawtenstall. SD8123.
Constantine *Cornw.* ***Village***, 5m/8km SW of Falmouth. **2 E6** SW7329.
Constantine Bay *Cornw.* ***Bay***, 1m/2km S of Trevose Head. **3 F1** SW8574.
Constantine Bay *Cornw.* ***Village***, near bay of same name, 3m/5km W of Padstow. SW8674.
Contin *High.* ***Village***, in Ross and Cromarty district, 2m/3km SW of Strathpeffer. **96 B6** NH4556.
Contlaw *Aberdeen* ***Locality***, comprises Nether Contlaw and Contlaw Mains, 1m/2km N of Peterculter. **91 G4** NJ8302.
Contrary Head *I.o.M.* ***Coastal feature***, headland on W coast, 1m/2km SW of Peel. **54 B5** SC2282.
Contullich *High.* ***Settlement***, 1km NW of Alness. **96 D4** NH6370.
Conway *Conwy English form of Conwy, qv.*
Conwil Elvet *Carmar. See Cynwyl Elfed.*
Conwy *Conwy* ***River***, rising at Llyn Conwy, 5m/9km NE of Ffestiniog, and flowing N by Betws-y-coed and Llanrwst into Conwy Bay on N side of town of Conwy. Tidal from Trefriw, near Llanrwst. **47 F5** SH7779.
Conwy (Conway). *Conwy* Population: 3627. ***Small town***, resort and small port on W bank of River Conwy estuary, 3m/5km S of Llandudno across river. One of Europe's best examples of a medieval walled town, with 13c castle built by Edward I (Cadw). Many other historic buildings within town. Road and railway bridges by Telford and Robert Stephenson respectively (road bridge is National Trust property). **47 F5** SH7877.
Conwy Bay *Conwy* ***Bay***, extends from Great Ormes Head westwards to Puffin Island (Priestholm). **46 E5** SH7080.
Conwy Castle *Conwy* ***Castle***, substantial and picturesque ruins (Cadw) on W bank of River Conwy, 1m/2km S of river mouth. Designed for Edward I by Master James of St. George in 13c and is part of walled town to which it is joined. **47 F5** SH7877.
Conwy Falls *Conwy* ***Waterfall***, in course of River Conwy 5m/8km S of Llanrwst. **47 G7** SH8053.
Conwy Sands *Gwyn.* ***Coastal feature***, sands at mouth of Conwy estuary between Conwy and Llandudno. **47 F4** SH7680.
Conwy Suspension Bridge *Gwyn.* ***Bridge***, suspension bridge (National Trust) crossing River Conwy, between Llandudno Junction and Conwy. Designed and built by Thomas Telford in 1826, with restored toll-keeper's house. **47 F4** SH7877.
Conyer *Kent* ***Hamlet***, at head of creek running into The Swale, 4m/6km NW of Faversham. **25 F5** TQ9664.
Conyer's Green *Suff.* ***Hamlet***, adjoining to N of Great Barton, 3m/5km NE of Bury St. Edmunds. TL8868.
Cooden *E.Suss.* ***Suburb***, to W of Bexhill. **14 C7** TQ7107.
Coodham *S.Ayr.* ***Settlement***, 1m/2km NE of Symington. **74 B7** NS3932.
Cooil *I.o.M.* ***Hamlet***, 2m/4km W of Douglas. SC3476.
Cookbury *Devon* ***Village***, 5m/7km NE of Holsworthy. **6 C5** SS4006.
Cookbury Wick *Devon* ***Hamlet***, in SW part of Cookbury parish, 3m/5km E of Holsworthy. SS3805.
Cookham *W. & M.* Population: 6096. ***Small town***, and riverside resort on River Thames, 3m/4km N of Maidenhead. Much National Trust property in vicinity. **22 B3** SU8985.
Cookham Dean *W. & M.* ***Village***, 1m/2km to W of Cookham. **22 B3** SU8684.
Cookham Rise *W. & M.* ***Village***, 1km to W of Cookham. **22 B3** SU8885.
Cookhill *Worcs.* ***Village***, 2m/4km W of Alcester. **30 B3** SP0558.
Cookley *Suff.* ***Hamlet***, 3m/4km SW of Halesworth. **35 H1** TM3475.
Cookley *Worcs.* Population: 2030. ***Village***, 2m/4km N of Kidderminster. **40 A7** SO8480.
Cookley Green *Oxon.* ***Village***, 2m/4km N of Nettlebed. **21 K3** SU6990.
Cookley Green *Suff.* ***Settlement***, 1m/2km NW of Cookley. TM3375.
Cookley Street *Suff.* ***Locality***, 1m/2km E of Cookley. TM3475.
Cookney *Aber.* ***Hamlet***, 3m/4km W of Newtonhill. **91 G5** NO8793.
Cook's Cairn *Moray* ***Mountain***, 5m/8km W of Cabrach. Height 2476 feet or 755 metres. **90 B2** NJ3027.
Cook's Green *Suff.* ***Settlement***, to E of Brettenham, 6m/9km SW of Stowmarket. TL9753.
Cooksbridge *E.Suss.* ***Hamlet***, 2m/4km NW of Lewes. **13 H5** TQ4013.
Cooksey Green *Worcs.* ***Settlement***, 3m/5km W of Bromsgrove. SO9069.
Cookshill *Staffs.* ***Hamlet***, 4m/7km W of Cheadle. **40 B1** SJ9443.
Cooksland *Cornw.* ***Locality***, 1m/2km E of Bodmin. SX0867.
Cooksmill Green *Essex* ***Village***, 4m/7km W of Chelmsford. **24 C1** TL6306.
Cookson Green *Ches.* ***Settlement***, just W of Crowton. SJ5774.
Cookson's Green *Dur.* ***Settlement***, 1m/2km N of Ferryhill. NZ2934.
Cookston *Aber.* ***Settlement***, 2m/3km NW of Ellon. **91 H1** NJ9432.
Cookworthy Museum *Devon* ***Other feature of interest***, at Kingsbridge. Exhibits include local history and costumes in 17c school. **5 H6** SX7344.
Coolham *W.Suss.* ***Village***, 3m/5km SE of Billingshurst. **12 E4** TQ1222.
Cooling *Med.* ***Village***, on edge of Cooling Marshes, 5m/8km N of Rochester. Ruins of 14c castle. **24 D4** TQ7576.
Cooling Street *Med.* ***Hamlet***, 1m/2km SW of Cooling. TQ7474.
Coom Burn *D. & G. See Garroch Burn.*
Coomb Dod ***Mountain***, on border of South Lanarkshire and Scottish Borders, 7m/11km S of Coulter. Height 2083 feet or 635 metres. **69 F1** NT0423.
Coomb Island *High. Alternative name for Neave Island, qv.*
Coombe *Cornw.* ***Hamlet***, 2m/3km NW of Camborne. **2 D4** SW6242.
Coombe *Cornw.* ***Settlement***, near coast, 4m/6km N of Bude. National Trust property to E and W. **6 A4** SS2111.
Coombe *Cornw.* ***Settlement***, 3m/4km S of Truro. SW8340.
Coombe *Cornw.* ***Village***, 4m/6km W of St. Austell. **3 G3** SW9551.
Coombe *Devon* ***Hamlet***, 4m/6km NE of Kingsbridge. **5 H6** SX7848.
Coombe *Devon* ***Hamlet***, 1km S of Christow. **7 G7** SX8384.
Coombe *Devon* ***Hamlet***, E of Tipton St. John, 2m/3km S of Ottery St. Mary. SY1092.
Coombe *Som.* ***Hamlet***, 1km NE of West Monkton. ST2729.
Coombe *Som.* ***Hamlet***, 2m/3km W of Crewkerne. ST4109.
Coombe *Wilts.* ***Settlement***, on River Avon, 3m/5km S of Upavon. SU1550.
Coombe Bissett *Wilts.* ***Village***, on River Ebble, 3m/5km SW of Salisbury. **10 C2** SU1026.
Coombe End *Som.* ***Hamlet***, 3m/5km NW of Wiveliscombe. ST0229.
Coombe Hill *Bucks.* ***Hill***, National Trust property to N of Coombe, 1m/2km SW of Wendover. Viewpoint. Height 843 feet or 257 metres. **22 B1** SP8406.
Coombe Hill *Glos.* ***Hamlet***, 5m/8km NW of Cheltenham. **29 H6** SO8827.
Coombe Keynes *Dorset* ***Village***, 2m/3km S of Wool. **9 H6** SY8484.
Coombe Street *Som.* ***Hamlet***, adjoining to E of Penselwood, 4m/6km NE of Wincanton. ST7631.
Coombe Throop *Som.* ***Locality***, 3m/5km S of Wincanton. ST7123.
Coombes *W.Suss.* ***Settlement***, 2m/3km SE of Steyning. **12 E6** TQ1908.
Coombeswood *W.Mid.* ***Suburb***, in NE part of Halesowen. SO9785.
Coombs *Pembs.* ***Suburb***, E district of Milford Haven. SM9106.
Cooper Street *Kent* ***Locality***, 2m/3km NW of Sandwich. TR3059.
Cooper Turning *Gt.Man.* ***Settlement***, 2m/3km S of Horwich. SD6308.
Cooper's Corner *E.Suss.* ***Settlement***, adjoining to N of Hurst Green. **14 C5** TQ7327.
Cooper's Corner *Kent* ***Settlement***, 1m/2km S of Ide Hill. **23 H7** TQ4849.
Cooper's Green *E.Suss.* ***Settlement***, 1m/2km N of Uckfield. TQ4823.
Cooper's Green *Herts.* ***Settlement***, 3m/4km NW of Hatfield. TL1909.
Cooper's Hill *Glos.* ***Hill***, rising to over 250 metres, 1m/2km SE of Brockworth and 5m/8km E of Gloucester city centre. Site of annual cheese rolling competition. SO8914.
Cooper's Hill *Surr.* ***Settlement***, 1m/2km N of Englefield Green. **22 C4** SU9971.
Coopersale Common *Essex* ***Village***, 1m/2km E of Epping. **23 H1** TL4702.
Coopersale Street *Essex* ***Hamlet***, 1km S of Coopersale Common, 1km SE of Epping. TL4701.
Cooran Lane *D. & G.* ***River***, formed from various burns, flowing S in Silver Flowe valley to E of Craighaw and becoming Black Water of Dee, 1km E of Loch Dee. **67 J5** NX4880.
Cootham *W.Suss.* ***Locality***, adjoining to W of Storrington. **12 D5** TQ0714.
Cop Mere *Staffs.* ***Lake/loch***, 2m/3km W of Eccleshall. **40 A3** SJ8029.
Cop Street *Kent* ***Hamlet***, 1m/2km N of Ash. **15 H2** TR2959.
Copcut *Worcs.* ***Settlement***, 2m/3km SW of Droitwich Spa. SO8861.
Copdock *Suff.* ***Village***, 3m/5km SW of Ipswich. **35 F4** TM1142.
Copeland Forest *Cumb.* ***Large natural feature***, area of fells to N of West Water. **60 C6** NY1307.
Copford Green *Essex* ***Village***, 5m/7km W of Colchester. **34 D6** TL9222.
Copgrove *N.Yorks.* ***Hamlet***, 4m/6km SW of Boroughbridge. **57 J3** SE3463.
Copinsay *Ork.* ***Island***, uninhabited island of about 200 acres or 80 hectares 2m/3km SE of Point of Ayre, Mainland. Steep cliffs on E side, with lighthouse. Bird sanctuary. **107 F7** HY6101.
Copister *Shet.* ***Settlement***, at S end of Yell, to W of Hamna Voe. **108 D5** HU4879.
Cople *Beds.* ***Village***, 4m/6km E of Bedford. **32 E4** TL1048.
Copley *Dur.* ***Village***, 6m/10km NE of Barnard Castle. **62 B4** NZ0825.
Copley *Gt.Man.* ***Suburb***, to E of Stalybridge. SJ9798.
Copley *W.Yorks.* ***Suburb***, on River Calder, 2m/3km S of Halifax town centre. SE0822.
Copley Hill *W.Yorks.* ***Suburb***, 1m/2km NW of Batley town centre. SE2326.
Copley Wood *Som.* ***Forest/woodland***, 4m/6km SE of Street. **8 D1** ST5031.
Coplow Dale *Derbys.* ***Settlement***, just N of Little Hucklow. **50 D5** SK1679.
Copmanthorpe *York* Population: 4125. ***Village***, 4m/7km SW of York. **58 B5** SE5646.
Copmere End *Staffs.* ***Hamlet***, on S side of Cop Mere lake, 2m/3km W of Eccleshall. SJ8029.
Copner *Ports.* ***Suburb***, 1m/2km NE of Portsmouth city centre. SU6602.
Copp *Lancs.* ***Hamlet***, 4m/7km N of Kirkham. SD4239.
Coppathorne *Cornw.* ***Hamlet***, 4m/6km S of Bude. **6 A5** SS2000.
Coppay *W.Isles* ***Island***, small uninhabited island 1m/2km W of Toe Head, W coast of South Harris. NF9393.

Coppenhall *Staffs.* ***Village***, 2m/4km S of Stafford. **40 B4** SJ9019.

Coppenhall Moss *Ches.* ***Suburb***, 2m/3km N of Crewe town centre. **49 G7** SJ7058.

Copperhouse *Cornw.* ***Suburb***, adjoining to E of Hayle. SW5738.

Coppicegate *Shrop.* ***Hamlet***, 5m/8km NE of Cleobury Mortimer. SO7380.

Coppingford *Cambs.* ***Settlement***, 7m/11km NW of Huntingdon. **32 E1** TL1680.

Coppleridge *Dorset* ***Hamlet***, 3m/4km NW of Shaftesbury. **9 H2** ST8426.

Copplestone *Devon* ***Village***, 5m/8km NW of Crediton. **7 F5** SS7702.

Coppull *Lancs.* Population: 7698. ***Village***, 6m/9km N of Wigan. **48 E1** SD5614.

Coppull Moor *Lancs.* ***Hamlet***, adjoining to S of Coppull, 2m/3km N of Standish. **48 E1** SD5512.

Copsale *W.Suss.* ***Village***, 4m/6km S of Horsham. **12 E4** TQ1724.

Copse Hill *Gt.Lon.* ***Suburb***, at S end of Wimbledon Common, in borough of Merton, 8m/13km SW of Charing Cross. TQ2270.

Copster Green *Lancs.* ***Village***, 4m/6km N of Blackburn. **56 B6** SD6734.

Copston Magna *Warks.* ***Hamlet***, 4m/6km SE of Hinckley. **41 G7** SP4588.

Copt Green *Warks.* ***Settlement***, 3m/4km SE of Hockley Heath. SP1769.

Copt Heath *W.Mid.* ***Suburb***, 2m/3km SE of Solihull. **30 C1** SP1777.

Copt Hewick *N.Yorks.* ***Village***, 2m/3km E of Ripon. **57 J2** SE3371.

Copt Oak *Leics.* ***Hamlet***, beside M1 motorway, 4m/6km E of Coalville. **41 G4** SK4812.

Copthall Green *Essex* ***Hamlet***, 3m/4km SW of Epping. TL4200.

Copthill *Dur.* ***Locality***, adjoining to W of Cowshill, 1m/2km N of Wearhead. NY8540.

Copthorne Population: 3930. ***Village***, on border of Surrey and West Sussex, 3m/5km NE of Crawley. **13 G3** TQ3139.

Copthorne *Ches.* ***Hamlet***, adjoining to SW of Audlem. SJ6543.

Copy Lake *Devon* ***Settlement***, 2m/3km W of Chulmleigh. **6 E4** SS6513.

Copy's Green *Norf.* ***Hamlet***, just SE of Wighton across River Stiffkey. Site of Roman fort 1km N. TF9439.

Copythorne *Hants.* ***Village***, 1m/2km NE of Cadnam. **10 E3** SU3014.

Coquet *Northumb.* ***River***, rising in Cheviot Hills, near border of England and Scotland, 4m/6km N of Byrness and flowing E past Rothbury and Warkworth, into North Sea at Amble, opposite Coquet Island. **71 G4** NU2705.

Coquet Island *Northumb.* ***Island***, in North Sea, 1m/2km E of mouth of River Coquet and 2m/3km E of Amble. Lighthouse on SW side. RSPB reserve. **71 H3** NU2904.

Coralhill *Aber.* ***Settlement***, 1m/2km S of St. Combs. **99 J4** NK0561.

Coran of Portmark *D. & G.* ***Mountain***, 1m/2km E of Loch Doon. Height 2040 feet or 622 metres. **67 K4** NX5093.

Corbet Tower *Sc.Bord.* *See Morebattle.*

Corbets Tey *Gt.Lon.* ***Suburb***, in borough of Havering, to S of Upminster. TQ5685.

Corbiegoe *High.* ***Settlement***, 1km SE of Thrumster. **105 J4** ND3444.

Corbridge *Northumb.* Population: 2719. ***Small town***, on N bank of River Tyne 3m/5km E of Hexham. 17c road bridge across river. Remains of Roman military town of Corstopitum (English Heritage), 1km NW. **70 E7** NY9864.

Corbridge Roman Site *Northumb.* ***Historic/prehistoric site***, Corstopitum Roman fort (English Heritage), 1km W of Corbridge, built to guard bridge over River Tyne. Remains of a storehouse and temples; also museum with archaeological finds. **70 E7** NY9864.

Corby *Northants.* Population: 49,053. ***Town***, 7m/11km N of Kettering. New Town designated 1950. Former steel town. **42 B7** SP8988.

Corby Castle *Cumb.* ***Historic house***, incorporating part of medieval peel tower to SE of Wetheral on E bank of River Eden. **61 F1** NY4754.

Corby Glen *Lincs.* ***Village***, 7m/11km NW of Bourne. **42 D3** SK9924.

Corby Hill *Cumb.* ***Locality***, adjacent to E of Warwick Bridge, 4m/7km SW of Brampton. NY4857.

Corby Loch *Aberdeen* ***Lake/loch***, small loch 5m/8km N of Aberdeen. **91 H3** NJ9214.

Corby Pike *Northumb.* ***Mountain***, 3m/4km NE of Rochester. Height 1207 feet or 368 metres. **70 D3** NT8401.

Cordach *Aber.* ***Settlement***, 1m/2km SE of Kincardine O'Neil. **90 E5** NO6097.

Cordwell *Derbys.* ***Settlement***, 1m/2km SW of Holmesfield. SK3176.

Cordwell *Norf.* ***Settlement***, 3m/4km S of Ashwellthorpe. TM1393.

Core Hill *Aber.* ***Hill***, 1km E of Cross of Jackston, and 3m/5km S of Fyvie. Height 804 feet or 245 metres. **91 F1** NJ7633.

Core Hill *P. & K.* ***Mountain***, in Ochil Hills, 8m/12km N of Alloa. Height 1781 feet or 543 metres. **81 K7** NN8804.

Coreley *Shrop.* ***Hamlet***, 4m/6km N of Tenbury Wells. **29 F1** SO6173.

Cores End *Bucks.* ***Locality***, 1km E of Bourne End. SU9087.

Corfe *Dorset* ***River***, rising S of Purbeck Hills, 1m/2km NW of Kimmeridge, flowing E and then N through gap in hills at Corfe Castle and into Poole Harbour. **9 J6** SY9886.

Corfe *Som.* ***Village***, 3m/5km S of Taunton. **8 B3** ST2319.

Corfe Castle *Dorset* ***Castle***, 11c castle to NW of Corfe Castle town centre. Used as a royal prison and partly destroyed during Civil War. **9 J6** SY9582.

Corfe Castle *Dorset* ***Village***, 4m/6km SE of Wareham, in gap of Purbeck Hills. Remains of Norman castle (English Heritage). **9 J6** SY9682.

Corfe Castle Museum *Dorset* ***Other feature of interest***, in centre of Corfe Castle, containing exhibits on local history. **9 J6** SY9582.

Corfe Mullen *Dorset* ***Village***, 3m/4km SW of Wimborne Minster. **9 J5** SY9798.

Corfton *Shrop.* ***Village***, 4m/7km E of Craven Arms. **38 D7** SO4984.

Corgarff *Aber.* ***Hamlet***, 1m/2km E of Cock Bridge. Corgarff Castle (Historic Scotland) to W across River Don. **89 K4** NJ2708.

Corgarff Castle *Aber.* ***Historic house***, derelict tower house (Historic Scotland) dating from 16c or early 17c, to W of Corgarff across River Don. **89 K4** NJ2508.

Corhampton *Hants.* ***Village***, adjoining to N of Meonstoke. **11 H2** SU6120.

Corhampton Down *Hants.* ***Open space***, hillslope 2m/3km W of Corhampton. **11 G2** SU5720.

Corinium Museum *Glos.* ***Other feature of interest***, in Cirencester town centre. Artefacts from Roman times, with reconstructed Roman rooms and workshop. Local history and archaeology exhibitions. **20 D1** SP0102.

Corkerhill *Glas.* ***Suburb***, on W side of Pollok Grounds, 4m/6km SW of Glasgow city centre. NS5462.

Corkindale Law *E.Renf.* ***Hill***, 4m/6km S of Johnstone. Height 850 feet or 259 metres. **74 C5** NS4456.

Corkney Top *Inclyde* ***Mountain***, 1m/2km NE of Creuch Hill. Height 1174 feet or 358 metres. **74 A4** NS2769.

Corlabhadh *W.Isles* ***Hill***, 1m/2km SE of head of Loch Shell, Isle of Lewis. Height 977 feet or 298 metres. **101 F7** NB3018.

Corlarach Hill *Arg. & B.* ***Mountain***, 3m/5km SW of Dunoon. Height 1374 feet or 419 metres. **73 K3** NS1373.

Corley *Warks.* ***Village***, 5m/7km NW of Coventry. **40 E7** SP3085.

Corley Ash *Warks.* ***Village***, 1km NW of Corley. **40 E7** SP2986.

Corley Moor *Warks.* ***Village***, 1m/2km W of Corley. **40 E7** SP2884.

Cormiston *S.Lan.* ***Locality***, 2m/3km W of Biggar. NT0037.

Corn Du *Powys* ***Mountain***, one of two chief peaks of Brecon Beacons, 10m/16km SW of Brecon. Height 2863 feet or 873 metres. **27 K6** SO0021.

Corn Holm *Ork.* ***Island***, small uninhabited island 1km W of Copinsay. **107 E7** HY5901.

Cornaa *I.o.M.* ***Locality***, 3m/5km S of Ramsey. Situated on stream running out to sea at Port Cornaa. SC4689.

Cornabus *Arg. & B.* ***Settlement***, 2m/3km NW of Port Ellen, Islay. **72 B6** NR3346.

Cornard Tye *Suff.* ***Hamlet***, 2m/3km E of Sudbury. TL9041.

Corndon *Devon* ***Hamlet***, 4m/6km W of Moretonhampstead. SX6985.

Corndon Hill *Powys* ***Mountain***, rounded peak close to English border, 3m/5km NE of Church Stoke. Height 1683 feet or 513 metres. **38 C6** SO3096.

Corndon Tor *Devon* ***Mountain***, in Dartmoor National Park, 1m/2km NE of Dartmeet. Height 1414 feet or 431 metres. **5 G3** SX6874.

Corney *Cumb.* ***Settlement***, 2m/3km N of Bootle. **60 C7** SD1191.

Cornforth *Dur.* Population: 2742. ***Village***, 4m/7km NW of Sedgefield. **62 E3** NZ3134.

Cornharrow Hill *D. & G.* ***Mountain***, rising to over 500 metres, 6m/9km W of Moniaive. **68 B4** NX6993.

Cornhill *Aber.* ***Village***, 5m/8km S of Portsoy. **98 D5** NJ5858.

Cornhill *Stoke* ***Suburb***, 2m/3km NE of Burslem. SJ8952.

Cornhill Cross *Staffs.* ***Locality***, 1km S of Leek. SJ9855.

Cornhill on Tweed *Northumb.* ***Village***, opposite Coldstream across River Tweed and 12m/20km SW of Berwick-upon-Tweed. **77 G7** NT8539.

Cornholme *W.Yorks.* Population: 1627. ***Village***, 2m/4km NW of Todmorden. **56 E7** SD9026.

Cornish Engines *Cornw.* ***Other feature of interest***, two preserved Cornish beam engines, located in Pool, 2m/3km W of Redruth. **2 D4** SW6740.

Cornish Hall End *Essex* ***Village***, 2m/4km N of Finchingfield. **33 K5** TL6836.

Cornmeadow Green *Worcs.* ***Suburb***, 2m/3km N of Worcester. SO8558.

Cornquoy *Ork.* ***Settlement***, in far S of Mainland, 8m/13km SE of Kirkwall. **107 E7** HY5299.

Cornriggs *Dur.* ***Settlement***, 1m/2km N of Wearhead. **61 K2** NY8441.

Cornsay *Dur.* ***Village***, 3m/5km SW of Lanchester. **62 C2** NZ1443.

Cornsay Colliery *Dur.* ***Hamlet***, 2m/3km E of Cornsay. **62 C2** NZ1643.

Corntown *High.* ***Settlement***, 1km NE of Conon Bridge. **96 C6** NH5556.

Corntown (Corntwn). *V. of Glam.* ***Hamlet***, 2m/3km SE of Bridgend across Ewenny River. **18 C4** SS9177.

Corntwn *V. of Glam.* *Welsh form of Corntown, qv.*

Cornwall County Museum *Cornw.* ***Other feature of interest***, at Truro, exhibits on minerals and artwork by Cornish painters. **3 F4** SW8145.

Cornwell *Oxon.* ***Hamlet***, 3m/4km W of Chipping Norton. **30 D6** SP2727.

Cornwood *Devon* ***Village***, on S edge of Dartmoor, 3m/5km NW of Ivybridge. **5 G5** SX6059.

Cornworthy *Devon* ***Village***, 4m/6km SE of Totnes. **5 J5** SX8255.

Corodale Bay *W.Isles* ***Bay***, small bay on E coast of South Uist, 3m/4km N of Loch Eynort. To N lies 'Prince's Cave' where Charles Edward Stuart sought refuge after Battle of Culloden, 1746. **84 D1** NF8331.

Corpach *High.* ***Village***, in Lochaber district at entrance to Caledonian Canal, 2m/3km N of Fort William across head of Loch Linnhe. **87 H7** NN0976.

Corpach Bay *Arg. & B.* ***Bay***, on NW coast of Jura, 7m/11km NW of entrance to Loch Tarbert. **72 D1** NR5691.

Corpusty *Norf.* ***Village***, opposite Saxthorpe across River Bure, 5m/9km NW of Aylsham. **45 F3** TG1130.

Corr Eilean *Arg. & B.* ***Island***, in sound of Jura, at seaward end of Loch Sween. **72 E3** NR6775.

Corra-bheinn *Arg. & B.* ***Mountain***, 3m/5km E of Ben More, Mull. Height 2309 feet or 704 metres. **79 G4** NM5732.

Corrachree *Aber.* ***Settlement***, 1m/2km W of Tarland. Symbol Stone nearby. **90 C4** NJ4604.

Corran *Arg. & B.* ***River***, on Jura, rising on slopes of Paps of Jura and flowing E, then S to Loch na Mile on E side of Leargybreck. **72 D3** NR5471.

Corran *Arg. & B.* ***Settlement***, isolated settlement on E shore of Loch Goil, opposite Ardnahein. **74 A1** NS2193.

Corran *High.* ***Settlement***, in Lochaber district, on NE shore of Loch Hourn, 1m/2km SE of Arnisdale. **86 E4** NG8509.

Corran *High.* ***Settlement***, on W shore of Loch Linnhe, in Lochaber district. Vehicle ferry to opposite shore across Corran Narrows. **80 B1** NN0163.

Corran Narrows *High.* ***Sea feature***, narrow neck of Loch Linnhe by Corran. Vehicle ferry operates. **80 B1** NN0163.

Corran Seilebost *W.Isles* ***Coastal feature***, headland on W coast of South Harris, 1km N of Seilebost. **93 F2** NG0698.

Corranbuie *Arg. & B.* ***Settlement***, on SE shore of West Loch Tarbert, near head of loch, 2m/3km SW of Tarbert. **73 G4** NR8465.

Corranmore *Arg. & B.* ***Settlement***, on NW shore of Loch Craignish, 1km SW of Ardfern. **79 J7** NM7903.

Corrany *I.o.M.* ***Settlement***, 4m/6km N of Laxey. **54 D5** SC4589.

Correen Hills *Aber.* ***Large natural feature***, small range of hills between Alford in SE and Rhynie in NW. **90 D2** NJ5122.

Correnie Forest *Aber.* ***Forest/woodland***, 6m/9km SE of Alford. **90 E4** NJ6410.

Correnie Moor *Aber.* ***Open space***, upland area to W of Correnie Forest, 4m/7km SE of Alford. **90 E3** NJ6109.

Corribeg *High.* ***Settlement***, in Lochaber district, on N shore of Loch Eil, 1m/2km E of Kinlocheil. NM9978.

Corrie *N.Ayr.* ***Village***, on E coast of Arran, 4m/7km N of Brodick. **73 J6** NS0243.

Corrie Common *D. & G.* ***Village***, 5m/9km NE of Lockerbie. **69 H5** NY2086.

Corrie na Urisgean *Stir.* *Gaelic form of Goblin's Cave, qv.*

Corrie of Balglass *Stir.* ***Inland physical feature***, N facing corrie, 1m/2km across at back wall, on N edge of Campsie Fells, 4m/6km SE of Balfron. **74 D2** NS5885.

Corrie Water *D. & G.* ***River***, flowing S from Little Whitriggs to join Water of Milk, 3m/5km E of Lockerbie. **69 G5** NY1882.

Corriechrevie *Arg. & B.* ***Settlement***, on Kintyre, 2m/3km SW of Clachan. **73 F5** NR7353.

Corriecravie *N.Ayr.* ***Settlement***, near SW coast of Arran, 3m/5km SE of Blackwaterfoot. Remains of Iron Age fort of Torr a' Chaisteil (Historic Scotland). **66 D1** NR9223.

Corriedoo *D. & G.* ***Settlement***, 4m/6km E of St. John's Town of Dalry. **68 B5** NX6782.

Corriehallie Forest *High.* ***Open space***, deer forest in Ross and Cromarty district S of Orrin Reservoir. **95 K7** NH3748.

Corrielorne *Arg. & B.* ***Settlement***, 3m/5km NE of Melfort. **79 K6** NM8717.

Corriemoillie Forest *High.* ***Open space***, deer forest in Ross and Cromarty district SE of Loch Glascarnoch. **95 K5** NH3567.

Corriemulzie *High.* ***River***, in Sutherland district, running NE down Strath Mulzie into River Einig 4m/6km SW of Oykel Bridge. **95 K2** NH3397.

Corrieshalloch Gorge *High.* ***Inland physical feature***, spectacular gorge (National Trust for Scotland) in Ross and Cromarty district, 5m/8km S of head of Loch Broom. Contains Falls of Measach (National Trust for Scotland). **95 H4** NH2077.

Corrievorrie *High.* ***Settlement***, in Strathdearn, 3m/5km SW of Tomatin. **88 E2** NH7724.

Corrieyairack Forest *High.* ***Open space***, deer forest in Badenoch and Strathspey district, running up to border with Inverness and Lochaber districts 7m/11km SE of Fort Augustus. **88 B5** NN4296.

Corrieyairack Hill *High.* ***Mountain***, peak in Corrieyairack Forest on border of Badenoch and Strathspey and Inverness districts. Height 2939 feet or 896 metres. **88 B5** NN4299.

Corrieyairack Pass *High.* ***Other feature of interest***, carries General Wade's Military Road over to Culachy Forest and Glen Tarff. **88 B5** NN4099.

Corrimony *High.* ***Hamlet***, in Inverness district, 8m/12km W of Drumnadrochit. Prehistoric chambered cairn (Historic Scotland) to E. **87 K1** NH3730.

Corrimony Chambered Cairn *High.* ***Historic/prehistoric site***, well-preserved, roughly circular passage grave 60 feet in diameter and 8 feet high, just E of Corrimony, 3m/4km E of Cannich. **87 K1** NH3830.

Corringham *Lincs.* ***Village***, 4m/6km E of Gainsborough. **52 B3** SK8791.

Corringham *Thur.* Population: 15,373. ***Town***, 4m/6km S of Basildon. **24 D3** TQ7083.

Corris *Denb.* ***River***, running NE to River Clywedog at Cyffylliog. **47 J7** SJ0557.

Corris *Gwyn.* ***Village***, 4m/7km N of Machynlleth. **37 G5** SH7507.

Corris Uchaf (Upper Corris). *Gwyn.* ***Hamlet***, 1m/2km NW of Corris. **37 G5** SH7408.

Corrlarach *High.* ***Settlement***, in Cona Glen, Lochaber district, 4m/7km S of head of Loch Eil. **87 F7** NM9671.

Corrour Forest *High.* ***Forest/woodland***, bordering Loch Ossian in Lochaber district. Also deer forest to SE of loch. **81 F1** NN4167.

Corrour Shooting Lodge *High.* ***Settlement***, at NE end of Loch Ossian, 4m/6km NE of Corrour Station. **81 F1** NN4169.

Corrour Station *High.* ***Other building***, railway station on West Highland line to Fort William, 1m/2km SW of head of Loch Ossian and 11m/17km E of Kinlochleven. **80 E1** NN3566.

Corrow *Arg. & B.* ***Settlement***, at N end of Loch Goil, 1m/2km SW of Lochgoilhead. **80 C7** NN1800.

Corry *High.* ***Settlement***, adjoining to N of Broadford, Skye. **86 C2** NG6424.

Corry Brook *Devon* ***River***, rising N of Dalwood and flowing SE to join River Yarty at Gammons Hill, 1km W of Axminster. **8 B5** SY2898.

Corrychurrachan *High.* ***Settlement***, on E shore of Loch Linnhe, 6m/9km SW of Fort William. **80 B1** NN0466.

Corryhabbie Hill *Moray* ***Mountain***, 6m/10km E of foot of Glenlivet. Height 2562 feet or 781 metres. **89 K2** NJ2828.

Corrykinloch *High.* ***Settlement***, situated at NW end of Loch Shin, Sutherland district. **103 F6** NC3625.

Corrylach *Arg. & B.* ***Settlement***, on Kintyre, on W side of Loch Lussa, 6m/9km N of Campbeltown. **66 B1** NR7030.

Corrymuckloch *P. & K.* ***Settlement***, 1m/2km S of Amulree. **81 K4** NN8934.

Cors Ddyga *I.o.A.* *Welsh form of Malltraeth Marsh, qv.*

Cors Fochno *Cere.* ***Marsh/bog***, large marsh on E side of Borth and S of River Dyfi estuary. **37 F6** SN6391.

Cors-goch Glan Teifi *Cere.* ***Marsh/bog***, 2m/3km N of Tregaron. **27 F2** SN6863.

Corsback *High.* ***Settlement***, 4m/7km E of Halkirk. **105 H2** ND2060.

Corsback *High.* ***Settlement***, near N coast of Caithness district, 1m/2km E of Dunnet. ND2372.

Corscombe *Dorset* ***Village***, 6m/9km SE of Crewkerne. **8 E4** ST5105.

Corse *Aber.* ***Settlement***, 5m/7km E of Huntly. **98 E6** NJ6040.

Corse *Glos.* ***Locality***, 7m/11km N of Gloucester. SO7827.

Corse Hill *E.Renf.* ***Mountain***, 4m/6km SE of Eaglesham. Height 1233 feet or 376 metres. **74 D6** NS5946.

Corse Lawn *Worcs.* ***Hamlet***, 7m/11km N of Gloucester. **29 H5** SO8330.

Corse of Kinnoir *Aber.* ***Settlement***, 3m/5km NE of Huntly. **98 D6** NJ5443.

Corsebank *D. & G.* ***Settlement***, 4m/7km NE of Sanquhar. **68 D2** NS8016.

Corsegight *Aber.* ***Settlement***, 3m/5km NW of New Deer. NJ8450.

Corsehill *D. & G.* ***Settlement***, 2m/3km SE of Boreland. **69 G5** NY1889.

Corsemalzie *D. & G.* ***Settlement***, 4m/7km SW of Wigtown. **64 D5** NX3753.

Corserine *D. & G.* ***Mountain***, summit of Rhinns of Kells, 4m/6km S of S end Loch Doon. Height 2670 feet or 814 metres. **67 J5** NX4987.

Corsewall *D. & G.* ***Settlement***, on W side of Loch Ryan, 6m/9km N of Stranraer. **64 A4** NX0369.

Corsewall Point *D. & G.* ***Coastal feature***, headland with lighthouse, 4m/6km NW of Kirkcolm. Ruins of Corsewall Castle 1m/2km SE. **66 D6** NW9872.

Corsham *Wilts.* Population: 11,359. ***Town***, attractive stone town, 4m/6km SW of Chippenham. Many 17c houses. **20 B4** ST8670.

Corsham Court *Wilts.* ***Historic house***, 16c-18c house with adjoining park on E side of Corsham, 3m/5km SW of Chippenham. Contains 18c furniture and one of oldest art collections of old masters. Gardens designed by 'Capability' Brown and Repton. **20 B4** ST8770.

Corsindae *Aber.* ***Settlement***, 4m/6km NW of Echt. **90 E4** NJ6808.

Corsley *Wilts.* ***Village***, 3m/5km NW of Warminster. **20 B7** ST8246.

Corsley Heath *Wilts.* ***Village***, 1m/2km SW of Corsley. **20 B7** ST8245.

Corsock *D. & G.* ***Village***, 8m/13km E of New Galloway. **65 H3** NX7576.

Corsock Loch *D. & G.* ***Lake/loch***, small loch 1km SW of Corsock. **65 H3** NX7575.

Corston *B. & N.E.Som.* ***Village***, 4m/6km W of Bath. Site of Roman villa 2km E. **19 K5** ST6965.

Corston *Wilts.* ***Village***, 2m/3km S of Malmesbury. **20 C3** ST9284.

Corstopitum *Northumb.* *See Corbridge Roman Site.*

Corstorphine *Edin.* ***Suburb***, 4m/6km W of Edinburgh city centre. **75 K3** NT1972.

Corstorphine Hill *Edin.* ***Suburb***, to NE of Corstophine. NT2073.

Cortachy *Angus* ***Settlement***, and castle, near foot of Glen Clova, 4m/6km N of Kirriemuir. Noted for breeding of Aberdeen Angus cattle. **82 E2** NO3959.

Corton *Suff.* ***Village***, and coastal resort, 3m/4km N of Lowestoft. **45 K6** TM5497.

Corton *Wilts.* ***Village***, 2m/3km SE of Heytesbury. **20 C7** ST9340.

Corton Denham *Som.* ***Village***, 3m/5km SE of Sparkford. **9 F2** ST6322.

Corúna (Anglicised form: Corunna.) *W.Isles* ***Settlement***, near W coast of North Uist, opposite Baleshare. **92 D5** NF8161.

Corunna *W.Isles* *Anglicised form of Corúna, qv.*

Corve *Shrop.* ***River***, rising 3m/4km SW of Much Wenlock and flowing SW through Corve Dale, to E of Wenlock Edge, to join River Teme on W side of Ludlow. **38 D7** SO5075.

Corve Dale *Shrop.* ***Valley***, carrying River Corve below SE slope of Wenlock Edge. **38 E7** SO5489.

Corwar House *S.Ayr.* ***Settlement***, 3m/5km SE of Barrhill. **67 G5** NX2780.

Corwen *Denb.* ***Small town***, on River Dee, 8m/13km W of Llangollen. Has links with Owain Glyndŵr. Iron Age fort 1km to N. **37 K1** SJ0743.

Corwharn *Angus* ***Mountain***, 2m/3km SW of Balnaboth. Height 2004 feet or 611 metres. **82 D1** NO2865.

Coryton *Cardiff* ***Suburb***, 4m/6km NW of Cardiff city centre. ST1481.

Coryton *Devon* ***Hamlet***, 6m/10km N of Tavistock. **6 C7** SX4583.

Coryton *Thur.* ***Town***, industrial town beside River Thames, 5m/8km S of Basildon. **24 D3** TQ7382.

Cosby *Leics.* Population: 3390. ***Village***, 7m/11km SW of Leicester. **41 H6** SP5494.

Coscote *Oxon.* ***Settlement***, 1m/2km S of Didcot. SU5188.

Coseley *W.Mid.* ***Suburb***, N district of Dudley. **40 B6** SO9494.

Cosford *Shrop.* ***Locality***, 1m/2km NW of Albrighton. Site of RAF Cosford and Cosford Airfield. **39 G5** SJ7905.

Cosford *Warks.* ***Settlement***, 2m/4km N of Rugby. SP4979.

Cosgrove *Northants.* ***Village***, on Grand Union Canal, 1m/2km N of Stony Stratford across canal and River Great Ouse. **31 J4** SP7942.

Cosham *Ports.* ***Suburb***, N district of Portsmouth, below Ports Down. **11 H4** SU6505.

Cosheston *Pembs.* ***Village***, 2m/3km NE of Pembroke. **16 D4** SN0003.

Coshieville *P. & K.* ***Settlement***, 3m/4km N of Kenmore. **81 J3** NN7749.

Coskills *N.Lincs.* ***Settlement***, 1m/2km NW of Barnetby le Wold. TA0410.

Cosmeston *V. of Glam.* ***Settlement***, to S of Penarth and 4m/6km E of Barry. ST1769.

Cosmeston Country Park *V. of Glam.* ***Leisure/recreation***, country park with two lakes, 1m/2km SW of Penarth. Reconstructed 14c village is main attraction. **18 E5** ST1769.

Cossal Marsh *Notts.* ***Hamlet***, to N of Cossall, 1m/2km E of Ilkeston. SK4842.

Cossall *Notts.* ***Village***, 6m/9km W of Nottingham. **41 G1** SK4842.

Cossington *Leics.* ***Village***, 6m/10km N of Leicester. **41 J4** SK6013.

Cossington *Som.* ***Village***, 5m/7km NE of Bridgwater. **19 G7** ST3540.

Costa *Ork.* ***Settlement***, at N end of Mainland, 1m/2km E of Loch of Swannay. **106 C5** HY3328.

Costa Beck *N.Yorks.* ***River***, rising on E side of Pickering and flowing S to join River Rye, 3m/5km NW of Malton. **58 D1** SE8076.

Costa Head *Ork.* ***Coastal feature***, headland on N coast of Mainland. **106 C4** HY3130.

Costessey *Norf.* Population: 2203. ***Village***, 4m/6km NW of Norwich. **45 F4** TG1711.

Costock *Notts.* ***Village***, 5m/8km NE of Loughborough. **41 H3** SK5726.

Coston *Leics.* ***Hamlet***, 5m/8km W of Colsterworth. **42 B3** SK8422.

Coston *Norf.* ***Hamlet***, 4m/7km NW of Wymondham. **44 E5** TG0606.

Cot-town *Aber.* ***Settlement***, 1km E of Rhynie. **90 D2** NJ5026.

Cot-town *Aber.* ***Settlement***, 4m/6km NE of Fyvie. **99 G6** NJ8240.

Cote *Oxon.* ***Hamlet***, 4m/7km S of Witney. **21 G1** SP3504.

Cote *Som.* ***Settlement***, 3m/4km SE of Highbridge. **19 G7** ST3444.

Cote Houses *Lincs.* ***Locality***, 1km E of Susworth. SE8401.

Cote Wall *W.Yorks.* ***Locality***, 1km S of Ravensthorpe across River Calder. SE2119.

Cotebrook *Ches.* ***Village***, 2m/3km NE of Tarporley. **48 E6** SJ5765.

Cotehele *Cornw.* ***Historic house***, medieval manor house (National Trust) on W bank of River Tamar, 1km SW of Calstock. Home of Edgcumbe family. House includes original furniture and collection of tapestries. Gardens include dovecot, 18c tower and Victorian summerhouse. **4 E4** SX4268.

Cotehill *Cumb.* ***Village***, 6m/9km SE of Carlisle. **61 F1** NY4650.

Cotes *Cumb.* ***Locality***, 1km N of Levens. **55 H1** SD4886.

Cotes *Leics.* ***Hamlet***, 1m/2km NE of Loughborough. **41 H3** SK5520.

Cotes *Staffs.* ***Settlement***, 1km SW of Swynnerton. **40 A2** SJ8434.

Cotesbach *Leics.* ***Village***, 1m/2km S of Lutterworth. **41 H7** SP5382.

Cotgrave *Notts.* Population: 7364. ***Village***, 6m/9km SE of Nottingham. **41 J2** SK6435.

Cothall *Aber.* ***Settlement***, on N side of River Don, 3m/4km NW of Dyce. **91 G3** NJ8715.

Cotham *Bristol* ***Suburb***, to N of Bristol city centre. ST5874.

Cotham *Notts.* ***Village***, 4m/7km S of Newark-on-Trent. **42 A1** SK7947.

Cothelstone *Som.* ***Hamlet***, at foot of Quantock Hills, 6m/9km NW of Taunton. **7 K2** ST1831.

Cothercott *Shrop.* ***Settlement***, 3m/5km SE of Pontesbury. **38 D5** SJ4201.

Cotheridge *Worcs.* ***Hamlet***, 4m/7km W of Worcester. **29 G3** SO7855.

Cotherstone *Dur.* ***Village***, 3m/5km NW of Barnard Castle. Scant remains of Norman castle to N. **62 B5** NZ0119.

Cotherstone Moor *Dur.* ***Open space***, moorland on S side of Baldersdale, 7m/12km W of Barnard Castle. **62 A5** NY9317.

Cothi *Carmar.* ***River***, rising about 8m/13km E of Lampeter and flowing SW into River Tywi 5m/9km E of Carmarthen. **17 J1** SN5020.

Cothill *Oxon.* ***Hamlet***, 3m/4km NW of Abingdon. **21 H2** SU4699.

Cotleigh *Devon* ***Village***, 3m/5km NE of Honiton. **8 B4** ST2002.

Cotmanhay *Derbys.* ***Suburb***, 1m/2km N of Ilkeston town centre. SK4643.

Coton *Cambs.* ***Village***, 3m/4km W of Cambridge. **33 H3** TL4058.

Coton *Northants.* ***Village***, 9m/14km NW of Northampton. **31 H1** SP6771.

Coton *Shrop.* ***Settlement***, 4m/7km S of Whitchurch. SJ5334.

Coton *Staffs.* ***Hamlet***, 5m/9km E of Stone. **40 B2** SJ9732.

Coton *Staffs.* ***Hamlet***, 2m/3km NW of Tamworth. **40 D5** SK1805.

Coton *Staffs.* ***Settlement***, to E of Gnosall Heath. SJ8120.

Coton Clanford *Staffs.* ***Hamlet***, 3m/5km W of Stafford. **40 A3** SJ8723.

Coton Hayes *Staffs.* ***Settlement***, 1m/2km NE of Coton. SJ9933.

Coton Hill *Shrop.* ***Suburb***, to N of Shrewsbury. SJ4813.

Coton Hill *Staffs.* ***Settlement***, to NE of Coton. SJ9832.

Coton in the Clay *Staffs.* ***Village***, 6m/9km NW of Burton upon Trent. **40 D3** SK1629.

Coton in the Elms *Derbys.* ***Village***, 5m/8km S of Burton upon Trent. **40 E4** SK2415.

Coton Manor Wildlife Garden *Northants.* ***Garden***, 9m/14km NW of Northampton. Garden laid on different levels, including rose, holly, and water gardens; also ornamental birds. **31 H1** SP6572.

Coton Park *Derbys.* ***Hamlet***, 3m/4km SW of Swadlincote. SK2717.

Cotonwood *Shrop.* ***Settlement***, 4m/6km S of Whitchurch. SJ5335.

Cotonwood *Staffs.* ***Settlement***, 2m/3km W of Gnosall. SJ8020.

Cotswold Hills ***Large natural feature***, Jurassic (or oolotic) limestone heights extending from Edge Hill, NW of Banbury, to River Avon valley at Bath. Sometimes name is applied only to central section. SO9807.

Cotswold Water Park *Wilts.* ***Leisure/recreation***, watersport centre on artificial lakes created by gravel extraction, to S of South Cerney. **20 D2** SU0495.

Cotswold Wildlife Park *Oxon.* ***Leisure/recreation***, in Bradwell Grove, 3m/4km S of Burford. Varied collection of animals from around world housed in 120 acres of landscaped parkland surrounding a Victorian Gothic mansion. **21 F1** SP2408.

Cott *Devon* ***Village***, 1m/2km NW of Totnes. SX7861.

Cottage End *Hants.* ***Hamlet***, 1km W of Forton, 3m/5km E of Andover. SU4143.

Cottam *E.Riding* ***Settlement***, 5m/8km N of Great Driffield. Site of former village to N. **59 F3** SE9964.

Cottam *Lancs.* ***Village***, 3m/5km NW of Preston. **55 H6** SD5032.

Cottam *Notts.* ***Hamlet***, 7m/12km E of Retford. **52 B4** SK8179.

Cottartown *High.* ***Settlement***, 2m/3km N of Grantown-on-Spey. **89 H1** NJ0331.

Cottarville *Northants.* ***Suburb***, 3m/4km NE of Northampton town centre. SP7862.

Cottenham *Cambs.* Population: 4486. ***Village***, 6m/9km N of Cambridge. **33 H2** TL4567.

Cottenham Park *Gt.Lon.* ***Suburb***, at S end of Wimbledon Common, 1m/2km W of Wimbledon. TQ2269.

Cotterdale *N.Yorks.* ***Settlement***, 4m/6km NW of Hawes. **61 K7** SD8393.

Cottered *Herts.* ***Village***, 3m/4km W of Buntingford. **33 G6** TL3129.

Cotteridge *W.Mid.* ***Suburb***, 4m/7km S of Birmingham city centre. **40 C7** SP0480.

Cotterstock *Northants.* ***Village***, on River Nene, 2m/3km NE of Oundle. **42 D6** TL0490.

Cottesbrooke *Northants.* ***Village***, 9m/14km N of Northampton. **31 J1** SP7073.

Cottesmore *Rut.* ***Village***, 4m/6km NE of Oakham. **42 C4** SK9013.

Cottingham *E.Riding* ***Town***, adjoining to NW of Kingston upon Hull. **59 G6** TA0432.

Cottingham *Northants.* ***Village***, 3m/5km W of Corby. **42 B6** SP8490.

Cottingley *W.Yorks.* ***Suburb***, 1m/2km S of Bingley town centre. SE1137.

Cottisford *Oxon.* ***Hamlet***, 5m/8km N of Bicester. **31 G5** SP5831.

Cotton *Staffs.* ***Hamlet***, 4m/7km NE of Cheadle. **40 C1** SK0646.

Cotton *Suff.* ***Village***, 5m/9km N of Stowmarket. **34 E2** TM0766.

Cotton End *Beds.* ***Hamlet***, 4m/6km SE of Bedford. **32 D4** TL0845.

Cotton End *Northants.* ***Suburb***, to S of Northampton town centre. SP7559.

Cotton Tree *Lancs.* ***Locality***, on Colne Water, 1m/2km E of Colne. SD9040.

Cottonworth *Hants.* ***Settlement***, 1m/2km SW of Wherwell. SU3739.

Cottown *Aber.* ***Settlement***, 1m/2km SW of Kintore. **91 F3** NJ7615.

Cotts *Devon* ***Hamlet***, 6m/9km SW of Yelverton. SX4365.

Cottwood *Devon* ***Hamlet***, 5m/8km W of Chulmleigh. SS6114.

Cotwall *Tel. & W.* ***Settlement***, 1km E of High Ercall. SJ6017.

Cotwalton *Staffs.* ***Settlement***, 1m/2km W of Hilderstone. **40 B2** SJ9234.

Couch Green *Hants.* ***Settlement***, 1m/2km W of Itchen Abbas and 3m/5km NE of Winchester. SU5233.

Couch's Mill *Cornw.* ***Hamlet***, 3m/5km E of Lostwithiel. **4 B5** SX1459.

Coughton *Here.* ***Hamlet***, 2m/3km S of Ross-on-Wye. **28 E6** SO5921.

Coughton *Warks.* ***Village***, 2m/3km N of Alcester. **30 B2** SP0860.

Coughton Court *Warks.* ***Historic house***, Tudor house (National Trust) of Throckmortons, 2m/3km N of Alcester. **30 B2** SP0860.

Cougie *High.* ***Settlement***, 4m/6km SE of Affric Lodge. **87 J2** NH2421.

Coul Point *Arg. & B.* ***Coastal feature***, headland on W coast of Islay, 2m/3km W of Loch Gorm. **72 A4** NR1864.
Coulaghailtro *Arg. & B.* ***Settlement***, on W of Kintyre, 1m/2km N of Kilberry. **73 F4** NR7165.
Coulags *High.* ***Settlement***, 3m/5km NE of head of Loch Carron. **95 F7** NG9645.
Coulby Newham *Middbro.* ***Suburb***, 4m/6km S of Middlesbrough, to E of Hemlington. **63 G5** NZ5214.
Coulderton *Cumb.* ***Hamlet***, 2m/3km SW of Egremont. NX9808.
Coulin *High.* ***River***, formed by confluence of Easan Dorcha and Allt Doire Bheithe, and flowing N into Loch Coulin. NH0255.
Coulin Forest *High.* ***Open space***, deer forest in Ross and Cromarty district SW of Kinlochewe beyond Loch Clair. **95 F6** NG9954.
Coull *Aber.* ***Settlement***, 3m/4km N of Aboyne. Site of medieval castle. **90 D4** NJ5102.
Coulport *Arg. & B.* ***Settlement***, on E shore of Loch Long, 4m/6km N of Cove. **74 A2** NS2087.
Coulregrain *W.Isles* ***Settlement***, on Isle of Lewis, adjoining to NE of Stornoway. NB4334.
Coulsdon *Gt.Lon.* ***Suburb***, in borough of Croydon, 5m/8km S of Croydon town centre. **23 G6** TQ3158.
Coulston *Wilts.* ***Village***, 6m/9km SW of Devizes. **20 C6** ST9554.
Coulter *S.Lan.* ***Village***, 3m/4km S of Biggar. **75 J7** NT0233.
Coultershaw Bridge *W.Suss.* ***Settlement***, and road bridge over River Rother, 1m/2km S of Petworth. **12 C5** SU9618.
Coultings *Som.* ***Hamlet***, 2m/3km SE of Stogursey. **19 F7** ST2241.
Coulton *N.Yorks.* ***Hamlet***, 2m/3km SW of Hovingham. **58 C2** SE6374.
Coultra *Fife* ***Settlement***, 1m/2km W of Gauldry. **82 E5** NO3523.
Cound *Shrop.* ***Hamlet***, 6m/10km SE of Shrewsbury. **38 E5** SJ5504.
Cound Brook *Shrop.* ***River***, rising on The Long Mynd and flowing N to Condover, then E into River Severn, 1m/2km below Wroxeter. **38 E5** SJ5606.
Coundlane *Shrop.* ***Settlement***, 1km E of Cound. SJ5704.
Coundmoor *Shrop.* ***Settlement***, 2m/3km S of Cound. SJ5502.
Coundon *Dur.* Population: 2524. ***Village***, 2m/3km E of Bishop Auckland. **62 D3** NZ2329.
Coundon *W.Mid.* ***Suburb***, 2m/4km NW of Coventry city centre. SP3181.
Coundon Grange *Dur.* ***Settlement***, 1m/2km SW of Coundon. **62 D4** NZ2228.
Coundongate *Dur.* ***Settlement***, 1m/2km W of Coundon. NZ2229.
Countam *D. & G.* ***Mountain***, 6m/10km SW of Sanquhar. Height 1558 feet or 475 metres. **68 C3** NS7102.
Countam *D. & G.* ***Mountain***, 5m/8km N of Moniaive. Height 1640 feet or 500 metres. **68 C4** NX7698.
Counters End *Herts.* ***Suburb***, to W of Hemel Hempstead town centre. TL0407.
Countersett *N.Yorks.* ***Hamlet***, at N end of Semer Water, 2m/3km SW of Bainbridge. **56 E1** SD9187.
Countess *Wilts.* ***Settlement***, 1km N of Amesbury. **20 E7** SU1542.
Countess Wear *Devon* ***Suburb***, SE district of Exeter. **7 H6** SX9490.
Countesthorpe *Leics.* Population: 6161. ***Village***, 6m/9km S of Leicester. **41 H6** SP5895.
Counthorpe *Lincs.* ***Settlement***, 6m/9km W of Bourne. TF0020.
Countisbury *Devon* ***Hamlet***, on N Devon coast, 2m/3km E of Lynton. **7 F1** SS7449.
Countisbury Cove *Devon* ***Bay***, shingle bay on N coast of Devon, to E of Foreland Point, 1m/2km NE of Countisbury. **18 A6** SS7650.
County Oak *W.Suss.* ***Suburb***, to N of Crawley. **13 F3** TQ2738.
Coup Green *Lancs.* ***Village***, 4m/6km E of Preston. SD5927.
Coupall *High.* ***River***, rising between Buachaille Etive Mòr and Buachaille Etive Beag in Lochaber district and running NE, then E to River Etive at head of Glen Etive. **80 D2** NN2454.
Coupar Angus *P. & K.* Population: 2223. ***Small town***, 4m/7km SE of Blairgowrie. Fragment of 12c abbey. 18c tollbooth. **82 D3** NO2240.
Coupland *Cumb.* ***Settlement***, 2m/3km SE of Appleby-in-Westmorland. **61 J5** NY7118.
Coupland *Northumb.* ***Hamlet***, 4m/6km NW of Wooler. 17c castle. **77 H7** NT9331.
Cour *Arg. & B.* ***Settlement***, on Kintyre, 3m/4km N of Grogport. **73 G6** NR8248.
Cour Bay *Arg. & B.* ***Bay***, on E coast of Kintyre, Argyll, 3m/5km N of Grogport. **73 G6** NR8248.
Court-at-Street *Kent* ***Settlement***, 4m/7km W of Hythe. **15 F4** TR0935.
Court Barton *Devon* ***Hamlet***, 2m/3km S of Crediton. **7 G6** SX8297.
Court Colman *Bridgend* ***Hamlet***, 2m/3km NW of Bridgend. SS8881.
Court Henry *Carmar.* ***Village***, 5m/7km W of Llandeilo. **17 J2** SN5522.
Court Herbert *N.P.T.* ***Locality***, adjoining to W of Neath. SS7497.
Court Hey *Mersey.* ***Suburb***, 5m/8km E of Liverpool city centre. SJ4190.
Court House Green *W.Mid.* ***Suburb***, 2m/4km NE of Coventry city centre. **41 F7** SP3581.
Courteachan *High.* ***Settlement***, in Lochaber district, to E of Mallaig across harbour. NM6897.
Courteenhall *Northants.* ***Village***, 4m/7km S of Northampton. **31 J3** SP7653.
Courtsend *Essex* ***Village***, on Foulness Island, 2m/3km SW of Foulness Point. **25 G2** TR0293.
Courtway *Som.* ***Hamlet***, at foot of Quantock Hills, 4m/6km S of Nether Stowey. **8 B1** ST2034.
Cousland *Midloth.* ***Village***, 3m/5km E of Dalkeith. **76 B4** NT3768.
Cousley Wood *E.Suss.* ***Village***, 1m/2km NE of Wadhurst. **13 K3** TQ6533.
Coustonn *Arg. & B.* ***Settlement***, on W coast of Loch Striven, 2m/3km N of Strone Point. **73 J3** NS0774.
Coutlair Knowe *Sc.Bord.* ***Mountain***, in Craik Forest, 3m/4km NW of Craik. Height 1371 feet or 418 metres. **69 J2** NT3311.
Cove *Arg. & B.* ***Village***, on Cove Bay, on E shore of Loch Long, 1m/2km NW of Kilcreggan. **74 A2** NS2282.
Cove *Devon* ***Village***, on River Exe, 2m/3km S of Bampton. **7 H4** SS9519.
Cove *Hants.* ***Suburb***, 2m/3km NW of Farnborough. **22 B6** SU8455.
Cove *High.* ***Village***, on W shore of Loch Ewe, Ross and Cromarty district, 7m/11km NW of Poolewe. **94 E2** NG8090.
Cove *Sc.Bord.* ***Settlement***, next to small bay on North Sea coast, 1km NE of Cockburnspath. **77 F3** NT7772.
Cove Bay *Aberdeen* Population: 4887. ***Village***, on E coast, 3m/5km S of Aberdeen. **91 H4** NJ9501.
Cove Bottom *Suff.* ***Hamlet***, 1km S of South Cove. TM4979.
Covehithe *Suff.* ***Hamlet***, near coast, 4m/6km NE of Southwold. **45 K7** TM5281.
Covehurst Bay *E.Suss.* ***Bay***, 2m/3km E of Hastings. **14 D6** TQ8510.
Coven *Staffs.* Population: 2230. ***Village***, 5m/8km N of Wolverhampton. **40 B5** SJ9006.
Coven Lawn *Staffs.* ***Settlement***, 1km S of Coven. SJ9005.
Coveney *Cambs.* ***Village***, 4m/6km NW of Ely. **43 H7** TL4882.
Covenham Reservoir *Lincs.* ***Reservoir***, large reservoir 5m/8km N of Louth. **53 G3** TF3495.
Covenham St. Bartholomew *Lincs.* ***Village***, adjoining to N of Covenham St. Mary, 5m/7km N of Louth. **53 G3** TF3394.
Covenham St. Mary *Lincs.* ***Village***, adjoining to S of Covenham St. Bartholomew, 5m/7km N of Louth. **53 G3** TF3394.
Covent Garden *Gt.Lon.* ***Other feature of interest***, fashionable pedestrianised piazza in City of Westminster, 1km N of Charing Cross. Originally designed by Inigo Jones as a residential square in 1630s. Market buildings dating from 1830 by Fowler. Floral Hall added in 1860 by E.M. Barry. In 1974 the famous fruit and vegetable market moved from here to Nine Elms. TQ3080.
Coventry *W.Mid.* Population: 299,316. ***City***, 17m/27km E of Birmingham. Cathedral built 1954-62 beside ruins of medieval cathedral destroyed in air raid in 1940. Centre has been rebuilt, but some old buildings remain, including Bonds Hospital and the medieval Guildhall. A town rich from textile industry in middle ages, Coventry is now known for its motor car industry; other important industries are manufacturing and engineering. Universities. Civil airport at Baginton to S. Coventry Canal runs N to Trent and Mersey Canal at Fradley Junction near Lichfield. **30 E1** SP3379.
Coventry Cathedral *W.Mid.* ***Ecclesiastical building***, modern cathedral in centre of Coventry, designed by Sir Basil Spence to replace building destroyed by German bombs in 1940. Of particular note are stained glass windows, and tapestry by Graham Sutherland which fills the E wall. Remains of old cathedral, dominated by Perpendicular steeple, adjacent to S of new building. **30 E1** SP3379.
Cover *N.Yorks.* ***River***, rising on moors N of Kettlewell and flowing SE down Coverdale into River Ure, 1m/2km E of Middleham. **57 F1** SE1487.
Cover Head Bents *N.Yorks.* ***Locality***, on E side of North Moor near head of Coverdale, 4m/7km NE of Kettlewell. **56 E2** SD9978.
Coverack *Cornw.* ***Village***, fishing village on E coast of Lizard peninsula, 10m/15km SE of Helston. **2 E7** SW7818.
Coverack Bridges *Cornw.* ***Hamlet***, 2m/3km N of Helston. SW6630.
Coverdale *N.Yorks.* ***Valley***, narrow tributary dale to S of Wensleydale, running SW to NE and to S of Leyburn across River Ure. **57 F1** SE0581.
Coverham *N.Yorks.* ***Hamlet***, on River Cover, 2m/3km SW of Middleham. Remains of 13c abbey, partly absorbed into Georgian house. **57 F1** SE1086.
Coverham Abbey *N.Yorks.* ***Ecclesiastical building***, scant remains of Premonstratensian house, 2m/3km SW of Middleham. **57 G1** SE1086.
Covesea *Moray* ***Settlement***, near N coast of region, 3m/5km W of Lossiemouth. Lighthouse (Covesea Skerries) 1m/2km E. **97 J4** NJ1870.
Covesea Skerries *Moray* ***Island***, group of islands off N coast, 3m/4km W of Lossiemouth. **97 J4** NJ1971.
Covingham *Swin.* ***Suburb***, 2m/3km E of Swindon town centre. SU1885.
Covington *Cambs.* ***Village***, 6m/10km E of Higham Ferrers. **32 D1** TL0570.
Covington *S.Lan.* ***Settlement***, 1m/2km N of Thankerton. **75 H7** NS9739.
Cow Castle and Settlement *S.Lan.* ***Historic/prehistoric site***, Iron Age hillfort and large D-shaped settlement, 1m/2km SE of Coulter. **75 J7** NT0433.
Cow Green *Suff.* ***Settlement***, 1m/2km S of Bacton. TM0565.
Cow Green Reservoir ***Reservoir***, large reservoir on border of Cumbria and Durham in upper Teesdale, 9m/14km NW of Middleton-in-Teesdale. **61 J3** NY8129.
Cow Ridge *N.Yorks.* ***Open space***, shoulder of moorland between Snilesworth Moor and Bilsdale West Moor, 6m/9km E of Osmotherley. **63 G7** SE5395.
Cowal *Arg. & B.* ***Large natural feature***, tongue of land in Argyll, between Loch Fyne and Loch Long, 17m/28km SW of Crianlarich. Cowal Hydro-electricity Scheme at head of Loch Striven. NS1090.
Cowan Bridge *Lancs.* ***Village***, 2m/3km SE of Kirkby Lonsdale. **56 B2** SD6376.
Cowan Fell *D. & G.* ***Mountain***, 1km SW of Loch Fell and 4m/6km S of Bodesbeck. Height 1850 feet or 564 metres. **69 G3** NT1603.
Cowbar *R. & C.* ***Locality***, including rocky headland at mouth of Roxby Beck, opposite Staithes on North Sea coast. NZ7818.
Cowbeech *E.Suss.* ***Hamlet***, 4m/6km NE of Hailsham. **13 K5** TQ6114.
Cowbit *Lincs.* ***Village***, 3m/5km S of Spalding. **43 F4** TF2618.
Cowbridge *Som.* ***Hamlet***, just N of Timberscombe, 2m/4km W of Dunster. SS9542.
Cowbridge (Y Bont-faen). *V. of Glam.* Population: 3682. ***Small town***, market town 12m/19km W of Cardiff. **18 D4** SS9974.
Cowcliffe *W.Yorks.* ***Suburb***, 2m/3km N of Huddersfield town centre. SE1318.
Cowden *Kent* ***Village***, 5m/8km E of East Grinstead. **23 H7** TQ4640.
Cowden Pound *Kent* ***Settlement***, 1m/2km N of Cowden. **23 H7** TQ4642.
Cowdenbeath *Fife* Population: 12,126. ***Town***, former coalmining town 5m/8km NE of Dunfermline. **75 K1** NT1691.
Cowdenburn *Sc.Bord.* ***Settlement***, 3m/4km SW of Leadburn. NT2052.
Cowdray House *W.Suss.* ***Historic house***, ruins of Tudor mansion destroyed in fire in 18c, at Cowdray Park 1m/2km E of Midhurst. **12 B4** SU9021.
Cowdray Park *W.Suss. See Midhurst.*
Cowen Head *Cumb.* ***Hamlet***, on either side of River Kent, 3m/5km N of Kendal. SD4997.
Cowers Lane *Derbys.* ***Hamlet***, 3m/4km W of Belper. SK3046.
Cowes *I.o.W.* Population: 16,335. ***Town***, at mouth of River Medina opposite East Cowes (vehicle ferry operates), 4m/7km N of Newport and 9m/15km W of Portsmouth across The Solent. Headquarters of Royal Yacht Squadron. Yachting centre with week-long yearly regatta dating from 1814. **11 F5** SZ4995.
Cowes Maritime Museum *I.o.W.* ***Other feature of interest***, museum in Cowes with model ships, tools and paintings depicting maritime history of town and Medina shipyards. **11 F5** SZ4995.
Cowes Roads *I.o.W.* ***Sea feature***, part of The Solent immediately N of Cowes and River Medina estuary. **11 F5** SZ5097.
Cowesby *N.Yorks.* ***Village***, 5m/9km NE of Thirsk. **63 F7** SE4689.
Cowesfield Green *Wilts.* ***Settlement***, 6m/10km W of Romsey. SU2523.
Cowey Green *Essex* ***Settlement***, 4m/6km S of Manningtree. TM0925.
Cowfold *W.Suss.* Population: 1564. ***Village***, 6m/9km SE of Horsham. **13 F4** TQ2022.
Cowgill *Cumb.* ***Hamlet***, in Dentdale, 3m/5km E of Dent. **56 C1** SD7586.
Cowglen *Glas.* ***Suburb***, 4m/6km SW of Glasgow city centre. NS5361.
Cowhill *Derbys.* ***Suburb***, adjoining to S of Belper. SK3546.
Cowie *Aber.* ***Village***, adjoining to N of Stonehaven, at mouth of Cowie Water. **91 G6** NO8786.
Cowie *Stir.* Population: 2049. ***Village***, 4m/6km SE of Stirling. **75 G2** NS8489.
Cowie Water *Aber.* ***River***, rising on hills to W of Cowie and running E through Fetteresso Forest. Glenury Viaduct is 1km from mouth of river. **91 G6** NO8786.
Cowlairs *Glas.* ***Suburb***, 2m/3km NE of Glasgow city centre. NS6067.
Cowlam Manor *E.Riding* ***Hamlet***, 2m/3km E of Sledmere, near site of former village. **59 F3** SE9665.
Cowlands *Cornw.* ***Settlement***, at head of Cowlands Creek, 3m/4km S of Truro. SW8240.
Cowley *Derbys.* ***Settlement***, 1m/2km SW of Dronfield. SK3377.
Cowley *Devon* ***Hamlet***, at confluence of Rivers Exe and Yeo, 2m/3km N of Exeter. **7 H6** SX9095.
Cowley *Glos.* ***Village***, 4m/6km S of Cheltenham. **29 J7** SO9614.
Cowley *Gt.Lon.* ***Suburb***, in borough of Hillingdon, 1m/2km S of Uxbridge. **22 D3** TQ0582.
Cowley *Oxon.* ***Suburb***, to SE of Oxford. **21 J1** SP5403.
Cowley Peachey *Gt.Lon.* ***Suburb***, adjoins to S of Cowley, in borough of Hillingdon. TQ0581.
Cowling *Lancs.* ***Suburb***, in SE part of Chorley. SD5917.
Cowling *N.Yorks.* ***Hamlet***, 2m/3km W of Bedale. **57 H1** SE2387.
Cowling *N.Yorks.* ***Village***, 5m/9km E of Colne. **56 E5** SD9642.
Cowlinge *Suff.* ***Village***, 6m/10km NE of Haverhill. **34 B3** TL7154.
Cowm Reservoir *Lancs.* ***Reservoir***, just W of Whitworth. **49 H1** SD8818.
Cowmes *W.Yorks.* ***Village***, 2m/4km E of Huddersfield. **50 D1** SE1716.
Cownwy *Powys* ***River***, rising 3m/4km E of Llanymawddwy and running E into River Vyrnwy 1m/2km S of Lake Vyrnwy dam. **37 J4** SJ0217.
Cowpe *Lancs.* ***Hamlet***, on hillside above Rossendale valley, 2m/3km SE of Rawtenstall and 3m/4km SW of Bacup. SD8321.
Cowpen *Northumb.* ***Suburb***, to W of Blyth. **71 H5** NZ2981.
Cowpen Bewley *Stock.* ***Hamlet***, 2m/3km NE of Billingham. **63 F4** NZ4824.
Cowper and Newton Museum *M.K.* ***Other feature of interest***, museum to S of Olney, commemorating poet and hymn writer, William Cowper and Reverend John Newton, set at Orchard Side, Georgian home of Cowper from 1768-1786. Cowper and Newton collaborated on Olney Hymns, 1779, most famous of which is Amazing Grace. **32 B3** SP8951.
Cowplain *Hants.* ***Suburb***, 1m/2km NE of Waterlooville. **11 H3** SU6911.

Cowsden *Worcs.* ***Hamlet***, 5m/8km N of Pershore. SO9453.

Cowshill *Dur.* ***Village***, 1km N of Wearhead. **61 K2** NY8540.

Cowsic Head *Devon* ***River***, source of Cowsic River on Dartmoor, 4m/7km N of Princetown. **6 D7** SX5980.

Cowthorpe *N.Yorks.* ***Village***, 3m/5km NE of Wetherby. **57 K4** SE4252.

Cox Common *Suff.* ***Settlement***, 3m/5km N of Halesworth. **45 H7** TM4082.

Cox Green *Essex* ***Settlement***, adjoining to SE of Ramsden Heath. TQ7195.

Cox Green *T. & W.* ***Locality***, on S bank of River Wear, 5m/7km W of Sunderland. NZ3255.

Cox Tor *Devon* ***Mountain***, on W side of Dartmoor, 3m/5km NE of Tavistock. Height 1450 feet or 442 metres. **5 F3** SX5376.

Coxall *Here.* ***Locality***, 6m/9km E of Knighton. SO3774.

Coxbank *Ches.* ***Village***, 1m/2km S of Audlem. **39 F1** SJ6541.

Coxbench *Derbys.* ***Village***, 5m/8km N of Derby. **41 F1** SK3743.

Coxbridge *Som.* ***Settlement***, 3m/5km SE of Glastonbury. ST5436.

Coxford *Norf.* ***Hamlet***, adjoining to S of Tattersett, 5m/8km W of Fakenham. Remains of 13c priory to S. TF8429.

Coxheath *Kent* Population: 3954. ***Suburb***, 3m/5km SW of Maidstone. **14 C2** TQ7451.

Coxhoe *Dur.* Population: 2395. ***Village***, 5m/8km SE of Durham. **62 E3** NZ3235.

Coxley *Som.* ***Village***, 2m/3km SW of Wells. **19 J7** ST5343.

Coxley *W.Yorks.* ***Hamlet***, 1km E of Middlestown. SE2717.

Coxley Wick *Som.* ***Hamlet***, to NW of Coxley, 2m/3km SW of Wells. ST5243.

Coxlodge *T. & W.* ***Suburb***, 3m/4km N of Newcastle upon Tyne city centre, in district of Gosforth. NZ2368.

Coxpark *Cornw.* ***Settlement***, 2m/3km W of Gunnislake. SX4072.

Coxtie Green *Essex* ***Hamlet***, 3m/4km NW of Brentwood. **23 J2** TQ5695.

Coxwold *N.Yorks.* ***Village***, 5m/8km N of Easingwold. Laurence Sterne, author of Tristram Shandy, was vicar here, and lived at Shandy Hall from 1760 to 1768. **58 B2** SE5377.

Coychurch (Llangrallo). *Bridgend* ***Village***, 2m/3km E of Bridgend. **18 C4** SS9379.

Coylet *Arg. & B.* ***Settlement***, on E shore of Loch Eck, 4m/6km N of Orchard. **73 K2** NS1488.

Coylton *S.Ayr.* Population: 1907. ***Village***, 5m/8km E of Ayr. **67 J2** NS4119.

Coylumbridge *High.* ***Hamlet***, in Badenoch and Strathspey district, 2m/3km SE of Aviemore. **89 G3** NH9110.

Coynach *Aber.* ***Settlement***, 3m/4km W of Tarland. **90 C4** NJ4305.

Coynachie *Aber.* ***Settlement***, 6m/9km SE of Haugh of Glass. **90 C1** NJ4934.

Coytrahen (Y Goetre-hen). *Bridgend* ***Village***, 4m/6km N of Bridgend. **18 B3** SS8985.

Crab Orchard *Dorset* ***Settlement***, 1m/2km S of Verwood. SU0806.

Crab Rocks *N.Yorks.* ***Coastal feature***, rock islet adjacent to coast, 1m/2km N of Bempton. **59 J2** TA2073.

Crabbet Park *W.Suss.* ***Settlement***, 1m/2km S of Copthorne. **13 G3** TQ3037.

Crabbs Cross *Worcs.* ***Suburb***, S district of Redditch. **30 B2** SP0464.

Crabgate *Norf.* ***Hamlet***, 3m/5km N of Reepham. TG0927.

Crabtree *Plym.* ***Suburb***, on River Plym, 3m/4km NE of Plymouth city centre. **5 F5** SX5156.

Crabtree *S.Yorks.* ***Suburb***, 1m/2km N of Sheffield city centre. SK3589.

Crabtree *W.Suss.* ***Village***, 2m/3km N of Cowfold. **13 F4** TQ2225.

Crabtree Green *Wrex.* ***Settlement***, 4m/6km S of Wrexham. SJ3344.

Cracaval *W.Isles* ***Mountain***, near W coast of Isle of Lewis 1m/2km S of Mealisval. Height 1686 feet or 514 metres. **100 C5** NB0225.

Crackaig *Arg. & B.* ***Settlement***, on SE coast of Jura, 1km S of Craighouse. **72 D4** NR5265.

Crackenedge *W.Yorks.* ***Suburb***, to N of Dewsbury town centre. SE2422.

Crackenthorpe *Cumb.* ***Village***, 2m/3km NW of Appleby-in-Westmorland. **61 H4** NY6622.

Crackington *Cornw.* ***Hamlet***, comprising Higher and Middle Crackington, 5m/8km NE of Boscastle. **4 B1** SX1595.

Crackington Haven *Cornw.* ***Village***, and coastal resort, 5m/8km NE of Boscastle. Cove has cliffs rising to 400 feet or 122 metres. **4 B1** SX1496.

Crackley *Staffs.* ***Suburb***, 3m/5km N of Newcastle-under-Lyme town centre. SJ8350.

Crackley *Warks.* ***Suburb***, 1m/2km NE of Kenilworth. SP2973.

Crackleybank *Shrop.* ***Hamlet***, 3m/5km E of Oakengates. **39 G4** SJ7510.

Crackpot *N.Yorks.* ***Hamlet***, 1km SW of Low Row. **62 A7** SD9796.

Crackthorn Corner *Suff.* ***Settlement***, 1km E of Thelnetham. TM0378.

Cracoe *N.Yorks.* ***Village***, 3m/5km SW of Grassington. **56 E3** SD9760.

Craddock *Devon* ***Village***, 1m/2km E of Uffculme and 5m/8km NE of Cullompton. **7 J4** ST0812.

Cradhlastadh (Anglicised form: Crowlista.) *W.Isles* ***Settlement***, near W coast of Isle of Lewis, 1m/2km W of Timsgearraidh. **100 C4** NB0433.

Cradley *Here.* ***Village***, 3m/4km W of Great Malvern. **29 G4** SO7347.

Cradley *W.Mid.* ***Suburb***, NW district of Halesowen. **40 B7** SO9485.

Cradley Heath *W.Mid.* ***Suburb***, 4m/6km W of Warley town centre. SO9486.

Cradoc *Powys* ***Hamlet***, 2m/3km NW of Brecon. SO0130.

Crafthole *Cornw.* ***Village***, 5m/8km W of Torpoint. **4 D5** SX3654.

Crafton *Bucks.* ***Settlement***, 4m/6km SW of Leighton Buzzard. SP8819.

Crag Foot *Lancs.* ***Settlement***, 3m/4km NW of Carnforth. SD4873.

Crag Hill *Cumb.* ***Mountain***, on Barbon High Fell, 3m/4km S of Dent. Height 2237 feet or 682 metres. **56 B1** SD6983.

Crag Houses *Cumb.* ***Settlement***, adjoining to NW of hamlet of Buttermere. NY1717.

Crag Lough *Northumb.* ***Lake/loch***, lake on N side of Hadrian's Wall 2m/4km NW of Bardon Mill. **70 C7** NY7668.

Cragdale Moor *N.Yorks.* ***Open space***, moorland at head of Cragdale Water, 4m/7km S of Bainbridge. **56 E1** SD9182.

Cragg *W.Yorks.* ***Hamlet***, 2m/3km S of Mytholmroyd. **57 F7** SE0023.

Cragg Hill *W.Yorks.* ***Suburb***, 4m/7km NW of Leeds city centre, in district of Horsforth. SE2237.

Craggan *High.* ***Locality***, in Badenoch and Strathspey district, 1m/2km SW of Grantown-on-Spey, comprising Upper Craggan and Wester Craggan. NJ0126.

Craggan *Moray* ***Settlement***, 4m/6km N of Tomnavoulin. **89 J1** NJ1832.

Craggan *P. & K.* ***Settlement***, 4m/7km SE of Comrie. **81 K6** NN8117.

Craggan Hill *Arg. & B.* ***Hill***, elongated hill, aligned SW to NE above E shore of Loch Long and 4m/7km NE of Garelochhead. Height 958 feet or 292 metres. **74 A1** NS2698.

Cragganruar *P. & K.* ***Settlement***, to N of Loch Tay, 10m/16km SW of Kenmore. **81 H3** NN6941.

Craggie *High.* ***Settlement***, 2m/4km SW of Kildonan Lodge, Sutherland district. **104 D6** NC8719.

Craggie *High.* ***Settlement***, 1km E of Daviot across River Nairn. **88 E1** NH7239.

Craggiemore *High.* ***Locality***, in Inverness district, 5m/9km SE of Inverness. NH7339.

Craghead *Dur.* ***Village***, 2m/3km SE of Stanley. **62 D1** NZ2150.

Cragside *Northumb.* ***Historic house***, 19c mansion by Norman Shaw, 1m/2km E of Rothbury. **71 F3** NU0702.

Crai *Powys* *Welsh form of Cray, qv.*

Craibstone *Aberdeen* ***Settlement***, 6m/9km NW of Aberdeen. Site of agricultural college. **91 G3** NJ8712.

Craibstone *Moray* ***Settlement***, 6m/9km SE of Buckie. **98 C5** NJ4959.

Craichie *Angus* ***Hamlet***, 4m/6km SE of Forfar. **83 F3** NO5047.

Craig *Angus* ***Locality***, parish to S of Montrose, including village of Kirkton of Craig. NO7055.

Craig *Arg. & B.* ***Settlement***, on Mull, 3m/4km E of head of Loch Scridain. **79 G5** NM5829.

Craig *Arg. & B.* ***Settlement***, on N shore of Loch Etive, 3m/5km NE of Taynuilt across loch. **80 B4** NN0334.

Craig *D. & G.* ***Settlement***, 2m/4km W of Crossmichael. **65 G4** NX6967.

Craig *High.* ***River***, flowing W to NE shore of Loch Torridon, Ross and Cromarty district. **94 D5** NG7663.

Craig *High.* ***Settlement***, 4m/7km SE of Redpoint, on NE shore of Loch Torridon, Ross and Cromarty district. **94 D5** NG7763.

Craig *High.* ***Settlement***, 9m/15km SW of Achnasheen, Ross and Cromarty district. **95 G7** NH0349.

Craig *S.Ayr.* ***Settlement***, 2m/3km S of Straiton. **67 H3** NS3802.

Craig a Barns *P. & K.* ***Mountain***, 1m/2km NW of Dunkeld. Height 1105 feet or 337 metres. **82 B3** NO0143.

Craig Berthlŵyd *M.Tyd.* ***Village***, 1km S of Treharris. ST0996.

Craig Bhagailteach *P. & K.* ***Mountain***, in Atholl, 5m/7km NW of Blair Atholl. Height 1614 feet or 492 metres. **81 K1** NN8169.

Craig Bron-banog *Denb.* ***Mountain***, in Clocaenog Forest, 3m/4km NE of Llanfihangel Glyn Myfyr. Height 1643 feet or 501 metres. **47 J7** SJ0152.

Craig Castle *Aber.* ***Castle***, 16c castle with 18c portal and wing, overlooking wooded glen 2m/3km N of Lumsden. **90 C2** NJ4724.

Craig-cefn-parc *Swan.* ***Locality***, 1m/2km NW of Clydach. **17 K4** SN6702.

Craig Cwm Silyn *Gwyn.* ***Mountain***, 4m/7km NW of Beddgelert. Height 2408 feet or 734 metres. **46 D7** SH5250.

Craig Ddrwg *Gwyn.* ***Inland physical feature***, craggy edge 3m/5km SW of Trawsfynydd. **37 F2** SH6533.

Craig Ewen *Aber.* ***Coastal feature***, headland on N side of Peterhead. **99 K6** NK1247.

Craig Fan Ddu *Powys* ***Inland physical feature***, cliff running to SE of Brecon Beacons, 8m/12km N of Merthyr Tydfil. **27 K7** SO0119.

Craig Fell *D. & G.* ***Hill***, on E side of Glenwhan Moor and 2m/3km S of New Luce. Height 538 feet or 164 metres. **64 B4** NX1761.

Craig Goch Reservoir *Powys* ***Reservoir***, highest in series of large reservoirs in River Elan valley, 5m/8km W of Rhayader. **27 H1** SN8968.

Craig Gyfynys *Gwyn.* ***Hill***, on N shore of Llyn Trawsfynydd, 3m/4km SE of Ffestiniog. Height 918 feet or 280 metres. **37 F2** SH6838.

Craig Hill *P. & K.* ***Mountain***, 3m/5km SW of Aberfeldy. Height 1843 feet or 562 metres. **81 K3** NN8145.

Craig Hulich *P. & K.* ***Mountain***, 1km N of Amulree. Height 1811 feet or 552 metres. **81 K4** NN8937.

Craig Lea *P. & K.* ***Mountain***, rising to over 510 metres, 8m/13km NE of Crieff. **82 A4** NN9432.

Craig Mellon *Angus* ***Mountain***, 1m/2km NW of Glendoll Lodge. Height 2840 feet or 866 metres. **89 K7** NO2677.

Craig nan Caisean *P. & K.* ***Mountain***, in Tummel Forest, 1m/2km NE of Tummel Bridge. Height 1565 feet or 477 metres. **81 J1** NN7760.

Craig of Bunzeach *Aber.* ***Mountain***, 3m/4km SE of Strathdon. Height 1742 feet or 531 metres. **90 B4** NJ3609.

Craig of Dalfro *Aber.* ***Mountain***, 1m/2km S of Strachan. Height 1040 feet or 317 metres. **90 E6** NO6789.

Craig of Knockgray *D. & G.* ***Mountain***, 1km NE of Carsphairn. Height 1256 feet or 383 metres. **67 K4** NX5794.

Craig Rhiwarth *Powys* ***Hill***, to N of Llangynog. Height 535 feet or 163 metres. **37 K3** SJ0526.

Craig Rossie *P. & K.* ***Mountain***, on N edge of Ochil Hills, 3m/4km E of Auchterarder. Height 1345 feet or 410 metres. **82 A6** NN9811.

Craig Rostan *Stir.* ***Open space***, slopes of Creag a' Bhocain, above E shore of Loch Lomond opposite Tarbet. **80 E7** NN3404.

Craig Siarls *Carmar.* ***Mountain***, 5m/8km SE of Llanddewi-Brefi. Height 1279 feet or 390 metres. **27 G4** SN7048.

Craig Twrch *Carmar.* ***Inland physical feature***, mountain ridge 3m/4km SE of Llanfair Clydogau. **27 F4** SN6649.

Craig Veann ***Mountain***, on border of Aberdeenshire and Moray, 5m/8km S of Tomintoul. Height 2332 feet or 711 metres. **89 J3** NJ1810.

Craig-y-cae *Gwyn.* ***Mountain***, rising to over 520 metres on N slopes of Y Garn, 4m/6km NW of Dolgellau. **37 F3** SH7023.

Craig-y-don *Conwy* ***Suburb***, adjoining to E of Llandudno. SH7981.

Craig y Ffynnon *Gwyn.* ***Mountain***, slopes of Glasgwm, 4m/6km NW of Dinas-Mawddwy. Height 2555 feet or 779 metres. **37 H4** SH8319.

Craig y Llyn ***Inland physical feature***, N facing cliffs and rock outcrops, 2m/4km S of Pontneddfechan, on border of Neath Port Talbot and Rhondda Cynon Taff. **18 B1** SN9003.

Craig-y-nos *Powys* ***Locality***, in River Tawe valley, 6m/10km NE of Ystalyfera. **27 H7** SN8315.

Craig-y-nos Country Park *Powys* ***Leisure/recreation***, in Glyntawe, 3m/4km NE of Abercraf. 44 acres of grounds surrounding a 19c folly under renovation. **27 H7** SN8415.

Craig yr Hyrddod *Gwyn.* ***Open space***, hillslope with craggy NW side, 5m/8km NW of Llanuwchllyn and 2m/3km SW of Llyn Celyn. **37 H2** SH8237.

Craigandaive *Arg. & B.* ***Settlement***, at head of Loch Striven on W shore, 1km NW of Ardtaraig. **73 J2** NS0583.

Craiganour Forest *P. & K.* ***Open space***, upland area and game forest in Atholl to N of Loch Rannoch, 6m/9km NW of Kinloch Rannoch. **81 G1** NN6064.

Craigans *Arg. & B.* ***Settlement***, 4m/7km NE of Lochgilphead. **73 H1** NR9094.

Craigbeg *High.* ***Settlement***, in Glen Spean, 11m/18km E of Spean Bridge. **88 B6** NN4081.

Craigcleuch *D. & G.* ***Settlement***, 2m/3km NW of Langholm. **69 J5** NY3486.

Craigculter *Aber.* ***Settlement***, 2m/3km SE of New Pitsligo. **99 H5** NJ9054.

Craigdallie *P. & K.* ***Settlement***, at foot of Braes of the Carse, 4m/6km N of Errol. **82 D5** NO2428.

Craigdam *Aber.* ***Settlement***, 3m/5km NE of Oldmeldrum. **91 G1** NJ8430.

Craigdarroch *D. & G.* ***Settlement***, 2m/4km W of Moniaive. **68 C4** NX7490.

Craigdarroch *E.Ayr.* ***Settlement***, in Glen Afton, 4m/7km S of New Cumnock. **68 B3** NS6306.

Craigdhu *D. & G.* ***Settlement***, 3m/4km E of Monreith. **64 D6** NX3940.

Craigdhu *High.* ***Settlement***, 6m/10km SW of Beauly. **96 B7** NH4440.

Craigdullyeart Hill *E.Ayr.* ***Mountain***, rising to over 410 metres, 3m/5km NE of New Cumnock. **68 B2** NS6515.

Craigeam *W.Isles* ***Island***, rock island off W coast of Isle of Lewis, 2m/4km W of Carloway. **100 D3** NB1643.

Craigearn *Aber.* ***Hamlet***, 1m/2km SW of Kemnay. Lang Stane o'Craigearn is standing stone to N. **91 F3** NJ7214.

Craigellachie *Moray* ***Village***, at confluence of River Fiddich and River Spey, 3m/5km S of Rothes. **97 K7** NJ2845.

Craigellachie Nature Reserve *High.* ***Nature reserve***, on slopes to W of Aviemore. Noted for variety of habitats which encourage wildlife, especially birds: birchwood on lower slopes supports tree warblers, spotted flycatchers and willow warblers, moorland areas and woodland margins are home to red and black grouse respectively, while cliffs provide breeding sites for kestrels, jackdaws and peregrine falcons. **89 F3** NH8711.

Craigellie *Aber.* ***Settlement***, 3m/5km S of Inverallochy. **99 J4** NK0260.

Craigencallie *D. & G.* ***Settlement***, 2m/3km W of Clatteringshaws Loch. **65 F3** NX5077.

Craigend *Moray* ***Settlement***, on N bank of River Lossie, 1km E of Dallas. **97 J6** NJ1353.

Craigend *P. & K.* ***Settlement***, 2m/3km S of Perth. **82 C5** NO1220.

Craigendoran *Arg. & B.* ***Suburb***, at E end of Helensburgh. Terminus for passenger boat services. **74 B2** NS3081.

Craigengar *W.Loth.* ***Mountain***, in Pentland Hills, 4m/7km NW of West Linton. Height 1699 feet or 518 metres. **75 J5** NT0955.

Craigengillan *E.Ayr.* ***Settlement***, 2m/3km S of Dalmellington. **67 J3** NS4702.

Craigenputtock *D. & G.* ***Settlement***, 5m/9km S of Moniaive. **68 C5** NX7782.

Craigens *Arg. & B.* ***Settlement***, at head of Loch Gruinart, Islay, 4m/6km NW of Bridgend. **72 A4** NR2967.

Craigens *E.Ayr.* ***Village***, 1m/2km SE of Cumnock. NS5818.

Craiggiecat *Aber.* ***Hill***, 4m/6km W of Newtonhill. Height 649 feet or 198 metres. **91 G5** NO8492.

Craigglass *Arg. & B.* ***Settlement***, 1km SE of Cairnbaan. **73 G2** NR8490.
Craiggowrie *High.* ***Mountain***, in Badenoch and Strathspey district, 4m/6km E of Aviemore. Height 2250 feet or 686 metres. **89 G3** NH9613.
Craighall *Fife* ***Settlement***, on Craighall Burn, 3m/5km SE of Cupar. **83 F6** NO4010.
Craighat *Stir.* ***Settlement***, 3m/5km NW of Carbeth. **74 C2** NS4984.
Craighead *Fife* ***Hamlet***, on North Sea coast, next to Fife Ness. **83 H7** NO6309.
Craighead *High.* ***Settlement***, on Black Isle, 4m/6km SW of Cromarty. **96 E5** NH7561.
Craighlaw *D. & G.* ***Settlement***, 1m/2km W of Kirkcowan. **64 D4** NX3060.
Craighoar Hill *D. & G.* ***Mountain***, in Lowther Hills, 5m/8km SW of Moffat. Height 1761 feet or 537 metres. **69 F3** NT0002.
Craighorn *Clack.* ***Mountain***, 4m/7km N of Alloa. Height 2066 feet or 630 metres. **81 K7** NN8800.
Craighouse *Arg. & B.* ***Village***, and small port on E coast of Jura, 3m/5km N of S end of island. **72 D4** NR5267.
Craigie *Aber.* ***Settlement***, 2m/3km E of Newmachar. **91 H3** NJ9119.
Craigie *Dundee* ***Suburb***, 2m/3km NE of Dundee city centre. NO4231.
Craigie *P. & K.* ***Suburb***, SW district of Perth. NO1122.
Craigie *P. & K.* ***Village***, on SE side of Loch of Clunie, 4m/6km W of Blairgowrie. **82 C3** NO1143.
Craigie *S.Ayr.* ***Suburb***, E district of Ayr. NS3521.
Craigie *S.Ayr.* ***Village***, 4m/6km S of Kilmarnock. **74 C7** NS4232.
Craigie Brae *Aber.* ***Settlement***, to E of Upper Lake, 3m/4km NE of Tarves. **91 G1** NJ8834.
Craigie Fell *S.Ayr.* ***Open space***, hillslope of Auchencrosh Hill, 3m/5km SE of Ballantrae. **64 B3** NX1078.
Craigieburn *D. & G.* ***Settlement***, 1m/2km E of Moffat, on W bank of Moffat Water. **69 G3** NT1105.
Craigieholm *P. & K.* ***Settlement***, 3m/4km SW of Burrelton. **82 C4** NO1634.
Craigielaw *E.Loth.* ***Settlement***, 1km W of Aberlady. NT4579.
Craigielaw Point *E.Loth.* ***Coastal feature***, headland to W of Craigielaw, on Firth of Forth at SW end of Aberlady Bay. **76 C3** NT4480.
Craigievar Castle *Aber.* ***Castle***, turreted Baronial 17c castle (National Trust for Scotland) 4m/6km S of Alford. Castle is seven storeys high and surrounded by notable grounds. **90 D4** NJ5609.
Craiglee *E.Ayr.* ***Mountain***, 1m/2km W of Loch Doon. Height 1715 feet or 523 metres. **67 J4** NX4796.
Craigleith *E.Loth.* ***Island***, small island 1m/2km N of North Berwick. Haunt of puffins. **76 D2** NT5587.
Craigleith *Edin.* ***Suburb***, 2m/3km NW of Edinburgh city centre. NT2374.
Craiglich *Aber.* ***Mountain***, 3m/5km E of Tarland. Height 1561 feet or 476 metres. **90 D4** NJ5305.
Craiglockhart *Edin.* ***Suburb***, 3m/5km SW of Edinburgh city centre. **76 A3** NT2270.
Craiglug *Aber.* ***Settlement***, 3m/5km W of Kirkton of Maryculter. **91 G5** NO8197.
Craigluscar Hill *Fife* ***Hill***, 3m/4km SE of Saline. Height 745 feet or 227 metres. **75 J1** NT0690.
Craigmahandle *Aber.* ***Mountain***, 2m/3km W of Ballochan. Height 1883 feet or 574 metres. **90 C5** NO4890.
Craigmaid *Sc.Bord.* ***Mountain***, summit lies 1m/2km S of Fruid Reservoir. Height 1814 feet or 553 metres. **69 F2** NT0717.
Craigmaud *Aber.* ***Settlement***, 2m/3km N of New Pitsligo. **99 G5** NJ8858.
Craigmillar *Edin.* ***Suburb***, 3m/4km SE of Edinburgh city centre. **76 A3** NT2871.
Craigmillar Castle *Edin.* ***Castle***, impressive, mainly medieval, ruined castle (Historic Scotland) to S of Craigmillar. **76 A3** NT2870.
Craigmore *Arg. & B.* ***Settlement***, on Bute, SE of Bogany Point, 1m/2km E of Rothesay. **73 K4** NS1065.
Craigmyle House *Aber.* ***Settlement***, 1km E of Torphins. **90 E4** NJ6301.
Craignafeich *Arg. & B.* ***Settlement***, on Cowal peninsula, 2m/3km SW of Tighnabruaich. **73 H3** NR9571.
Craignair *D. & G.* ***Locality***, 1km W of Dalbeattie. **65 J4** NX8260.
Craignant *Shrop.* ***Hamlet***, 1m/2km NW of Sellatyn. **38 B2** SJ2535.
Craignavie *Stir.* ***Settlement***, 1km SW of Killin. **81 G4** NN5631.
Craignaw *D. & G.* ***Mountain***, 1m/2km SE of Loch Enoch. Height 2116 feet or 645 metres. **67 J5** NX4683.
Craigneil *S.Ayr.* ***Settlement***, 1km SW of Colmonell. **67 F5** NX1485.
Craignelder *D. & G.* ***Mountain***, 2m/3km W of Loch Grannoch and 6m/10km NE of Newton Stewart. Height 1971 feet or 601 metres. **65 F4** NX5069.
Craignethan Castle *S.Lan.* ***Castle***, restored 15c tower house (Historic Scotland), 1km W of Crossford. **75 G6** NS8146.
Craigneuk *N.Lan.* ***Suburb***, 1m/2km E of Motherwell, adjoining to NW of Shieldmuir. NS7756.
Craignish *Arg. & B.* ***Locality***, peninsula parish on W coast of Argyll, including Craignish Castle. NM7701.
Craignish Castle *Arg. & B.* ***Castle***, dating from 16c, near S end of peninsula, W of Loch Craignish in Argyll. **79 J7** NM7701.
Craignish Point *Arg. & B.* ***Coastal feature***, headland at S end of Craignish peninsula and seaward end of Loch Craignish. **73 F1** NR7599.
Craignure *Arg. & B.* ***Hamlet***, on Craignure Bay, E coast of Mull, opposite entrance to Loch Linnhe. Car ferry to Oban. **79 J4** NM7137.
Craignure Bay *Arg. & B.* ***Bay***, on E coast of Mull, opposite entrance to Loch Linnhe. **79 J4** NM7137.
Craigo *Angus* ***Village***, on River North Esk, 5m/7km N of Montrose. **83 H1** NO6864.
Craigoch *S.Ayr.* ***Settlement***, 4m/6km S of Maybole. **67 H3** NS2904.
Craigow *P. & K.* ***Hamlet***, 2m/3km NW of Milnathort. **82 B7** NO0806.
Craigower *P. & K.* ***Mountain***, 1m/2km NW of Pitlochry, rising to over 400 metres. Viewpoint (National Trust for Scotland) looks W across Pass of Killiecrankie towards Loch Tummel. **82 A1** NN9260.
Craigowl Hill *Angus* ***Mountain***, summit of Sidlaw Hills, 6m/10km N of Dundee. Mast at summit. Height 1492 feet or 455 metres. **82 E3** NO3740.
Craigrothie *Fife* ***Village***, 2m/4km S of Cupar. **82 E6** NO3710.
Craigroy *Moray* ***Settlement***, 1m/2km S of Dallas. **97 J6** NJ1250.
Craigroy Farm *Moray* ***Settlement***, on W bank of River Avon, 6m/9km S of Upper Knockando. **89 J1** NJ1834.
Craigruie *Stir.* ***Settlement***, on N shore of Loch Voil, 3m/4km W of Balquhidder. **81 G5** NN4920.
Craig's End *Essex* ***Settlement***, 4m/6km NE of Finchingfield. TL7137.
Craigsanquhar *Fife* ***Settlement***, 3m/5km NE of Cupar. **82 E6** NO3919.
Craigshill *W.Loth.* ***Suburb***, central district of Livingston. NT0668.
Craigside *Dur.* ***Settlement***, 2m/4km W of Crook. NZ1235.
Craigston Castle *Aber.* ***Castle***, 17c castle 4m/7km NE of Turriff. **99 F5** NJ7655.
Craigton *Aberdeen* ***Hamlet***, just NW of Peterculter. **91 G4** NJ8301.
Craigton *Angus* ***Village***, 4m/7km SW of Kirriemuir. **82 E2** NO3250.
Craigton *Angus* ***Village***, 4m/6km NW of Carnoustie. **83 G4** NO5138.
Craigton *Glas.* ***Suburb***, 3m/5km W of Glasgow city centre across River Clyde. NS5464.
Craigton *High.* ***Settlement***, in Ross and Cromarty district, at entrance to Beauly Firth, opposite Inverness. NH6648.
Craigton *Stir.* ***Settlement***, at foot of Fintry Hills, 1m/2km E of Fintry across Endrick Water. **74 E2** NS6286.
Craigton Point *High.* ***Coastal feature***, headland at entrance to Beauly Firth opposite Inverness, with beacon. **96 D7** NH6647.
Craigtoun Country Park *Fife* ***Leisure/recreation***, 50 acre country park 3m/4km SW of St. Andrews. Features range from landscaped gardens and ponds to extensive range of activities including trampolining, crazy golf and adventure playground. **83 F6** NO4714.
Craigtown *High.* ***Settlement***, on E bank of Halladale River, 2m/3km N of Croik. **104 D3** NC8956.
Craigvinean Forest *P. & K.* ***Forest/woodland***, on W side of Strath Tay above Dunkeld. **82 A3** NN9943.
Craik *Aber.* ***Settlement***, 3m/4km SW of Rhynie. **90 C2** NJ4625.
Craik *Sc.Bord.* ***Village***, to N of Borthwick Water, in Craik Forest area, 5m/8km SW of Burnfoot. **69 J3** NT3408.
Craik Cross Hill ***Mountain***, on border of Dumfries & Galloway and Scottish Borders, 5m/9km NE of Eskdalemuir. Site of Roman signal station. Height 1473 feet or 449 metres. **69 H3** NT3004.
Craik Forest *Sc.Bord.* ***Forest/woodland***, 10m/16km W of Hawick. Encloses Crib Law mountain. **69 J2** NT3309.
Craik Moor *Sc.Bord.* ***Open space***, moorland 2m/4km SW of Hownam. **70 D2** NT8018.
Crail *Fife* Population: 1449. ***Small town***, and resort, 2m/4km SW of Fife Ness. Specialises in crab and lobster fishing. 16c tolbooth. Several old houses restored by National Trust for Scotland. **83 H7** NO6107.
Crailing *Sc.Bord.* ***Village***, 4m/6km NE of Jedburgh. **70 B1** NT6824.
Crailinghall *Sc.Bord.* ***Hamlet***, 3m/5km NE of Jedburgh. **70 B1** NT6922.
Crailzie Hill *Sc.Bord.* ***Mountain***, 3m/4km SE of Romannobridge. Height 1561 feet or 476 metres. **75 K6** NT1945.
Craiselound *N.Lincs.* ***Village***, 1m/2km S of Haxey. **51 K3** SK7798.
Crakehill *N.Yorks.* ***Settlement***, 2m/4km SE of Topcliffe. **57 K2** SE4273.
Crakemarsh *Staffs.* ***Hamlet***, 2m/3km N of Uttoxeter. SK0936.
Cralic *High.* *Anglicised form of A' Chràlaig, qv.*
Crambe *N.Yorks.* ***Village***, 6m/9km SW of Malton. **58 D3** SE7364.
Cramlington *Northumb.* Population: 26,238. ***Town***, 8m/12km N of Newcastle upon Tyne. Industrial estate to NW. **71 H6** NZ2676.
Crammag Head *D. & G.* ***Coastal feature***, headland with lighthouse on W coast of Rinns of Galloway, 5m/8km NW of Mull of Galloway. **64 A7** NX0834.
Crammers *Devon* ***Hamlet***, 1m/2km NE of Chudleigh. SX8880.
Cramond *Edin.* ***Suburb***, 5m/7km of Edinburgh city centre. Site of Roman fort to N. **75 K3** NT1976.
Cramond Bridge *Edin.* ***Suburb***, 5m/8km NW of Edinburgh city centre, at road crossing of River Almond. NT1775.
Cramond Island *Edin.* ***Island***, small island 1m/2km N of Cramond in Firth of Forth, accessible across sands at low tide. **75 K3** NT1978.
Cranage *Ches.* ***Village***, 1m/2km NW of Holmes Chapel. **49 G6** SJ7568.
Cranberry *Staffs.* ***Hamlet***, 5m/8km W of Stone. **40 A2** SJ8236.
Cranborne *Dorset* ***Village***, 8m/12km NW of Ringwood. Jacobean manor house. **10 B3** SU0513.
Cranborne Chase ***Large natural feature***, hilly, partly wooded area, formerly a forest and hunting preserve, on border of Dorset and Wiltshire, 6m/10km SE of Shaftesbury. **9 H3** ST9318.
Cranborne Common *Dorset* ***Open space***, heath 1m/2km SW of Alderholt. **10 B3** SU1011.
Cranborne Manor Gardens *Dorset* ***Garden***, in Cranborne, 16m/26km S of Salisbury. 17c historic gardens designed by John Tradescant. Displays include yew hedges, a wild garden, Jacobean mount garden and old roses. **10 B3** SU0513.
Cranbourne *Brack.F.* ***Village***, 3m/4km N of Ascot. **22 C4** SU9272.
Cranbrook *Gt.Lon.* ***Suburb***, NW district of Ilford, in borough of Redbridge. TQ4287.
Cranbrook *Kent* Population: 3522. ***Small town***, on Kentish Weald, 7m/11km W of Tenterden. Formerly a cloth-weaving centre, it has many brick and half-timbered houses. Union Mill, largest working windmill in England, is here. **14 C4** TQ7736.
Cranbrook Common *Kent* ***Hamlet***, 2m/3km NE of Cranbrook. **14 C4** TQ7838.
Crane Islands *Cornw.* ***Island***, group of small islands off N coast, 2m/3km SW of Portreath. **2 D4** SW6344.
Crane Moor *S.Yorks.* ***Hamlet***, 1m/2km E of Thurgoland, and 4m/6km E of Penistone. SE3001.
Crane's Corner *Norf.* ***Hamlet***, 5m/8km W of East Dereham. TF9113.
Cranes Industrial Estate *Essex* ***Locality***, industrial area in NE part of Basildon. TQ7290.
Cranfield *Beds.* Population: 4142. ***Village***, 8m/12km SW of Bedford. Airfield to W. Cranfield University. **32 C4** SP9542.
Cranford *Devon* ***Hamlet***, 1m/2km NE of Woolfardisworthy. **6 B3** SS3421.
Cranford *Gt.Lon.* ***Suburb***, in borough of Hounslow, on E side of London Heathrow Airport, 12m/19km W of Charing Cross. Cranford Park is 1km NW across Grand Union Canal, in borough of Hillingdon. **22 E4** TQ1077.
Cranford *Northants.* ***Locality***, parish containing villages of Cranford St. Andrew and Cranford St. John, 4m/6km E of Kettering. SP9277.
Cranford St. Andrew *Northants.* ***Village***, in parish of Cranford, 4m/6km E of Kettering. **32 C1** SP9277.
Cranford St. John *Northants.* ***Village***, in parish of Cranford, 4m/6km E of Kettering. **32 C1** SP9277.
Cranham *Glos.* ***Village***, 5m/9km SE of Gloucester. **29 H7** SO8912.
Cranham *Gt.Lon.* ***Suburb***, in borough of Havering, 1m/2km E of Upminster. **23 J3** TQ5787.
Crank *Mersey.* ***Village***, 3m/4km N of St. Helens. **48 E2** SJ5099.
Crankwood *Gt.Man.* ***Settlement***, 2m/3km W of Leigh. SD6100.
Cranleigh *Surr.* Population: 9574. ***Small town***, with fine 14c church, 8m/12km SE of Guildford. **12 D3** TQ0639.
Cranley *Suff.* ***Settlement***, 1m/2km SE of Eye. TM1572.
Cranley Gardens *Gt.Lon.* ***Suburb***, in borough of Haringey, 6m/9km N of Charing Cross. TQ2889.
Cranmer Green *Suff.* ***Hamlet***, 1m/2km E of Walsham le Willows. **34 E1** TM0171.
Cranmere Pool *Devon* ***Marsh/bog***, hollow in bog at heart of Dartmoor, 6m/10km S of Okehampton. **6 E7** SX6085.
Cranmore *I.o.W.* ***Settlement***, 3m/4km E of Yarmouth. **11 F5** SZ3990.
Cranmore *Som.* ***Locality***, parish 4m/6km E of Shepton Mallet, containing village of West Cranmore and hamlet of East Cranmore. **19 K7** ST6743.
Cranna *Aber.* ***Locality***, comprises North Cranna, South Cranna and Mains of Cranna, 1m/2km NE of Aberchirder. **98 E5** NJ6353.
Crannach *Moray* ***Settlement***, 4m/7km NE of Keith. **98 C5** NJ4954.
Cranoe *Leics.* ***Village***, 5m/9km N of Market Harborough. **42 A6** SP7695.
Cransford *Suff.* ***Village***, 2m/4km E of Framlingham. **35 H2** TM3164.
Cranshaws *Sc.Bord.* ***Village***, on Whiteadder Water, 8m/12km NW of Duns. **76 E4** NT6961.
Cranshaws Hill *Sc.Bord.* ***Mountain***, 1m/2km W of Cranshaws. Height 1243 feet or 379 metres. **76 E4** NT6761.
Cransley *Northants.* ***Locality***, parish containing village of Great Cransley and locality of Little Cransley, 3m/4km SW of Kettering. SP8376.
Cransmill Hill *Aber.* ***Mountain***, rising to over 420 metres, 4m/6km W of Gartly. **90 C1** NJ4631.
Cranstackie *High.* ***Mountain***, in Sutherland district 3m/4km W of head of Loch Eriboll. Height 2624 feet or 800 metres. **103 F3** NC3555.
Cranstal *I.o.M.* ***Settlement***, 2m/3km S of Point of Ayre. **54 D3** NX4602.
Cranswick *E.Riding* ***Locality***, at S end of Hutton Cranswick, 4m/6km S of Great Driffield. TA0252.
Crantock *Cornw.* ***Village***, attractive village near coast, 2m/3km SW of Newquay across River Gannel. Round Garden (National Trust). **2 E2** SW7960.
Cranwell *Lincs.* ***Village***, 4m/6km NW of Sleaford. Royal Air Force college and airfield to W. **42 D1** TF0349.
Cranwich *Norf.* ***Hamlet***, 2m/3km NW of Mundford. **44 B6** TL7894.
Cranworth *Norf.* ***Village***, 6m/9km S of East Dereham. **44 D5** TF9804.
Craobh Haven *Arg. & B.* ***Settlement***, 2m/3km S of Arduaine. **79 J7** NM7907.
Crapstone *Devon* ***Village***, 5m/7km SE of Tavistock. **5 F4** SX5067.
Crarae *Arg. & B.* ***Village***, on Loch Fyne, 2m/4km SW of Furnace, near Inveraray. **73 H1** NR9897.
Crarae Lodge *Arg. & B.* ***Garden***, overlooking Loch Fyne, 10m/16km NE of Lochgilphead. Noted for rhododendrons, conifers and ornamental shrubs. **73 H1** NR9897.
Craro Island *Arg. & B.* ***Island***, small island off W coast of Gigha, 1m/2km from S end. **72 E6** NR6247.

Crask Inn *High.* ***Settlement***, on N side of Srath a' Chràisg, Sutherland district. **103 H6** NC5224.
Crask of Aigas *High.* ***Settlement***, in wooded area beside River Beauly, 4m/7km SW of Beauly town, in Inverness district. **96 B7** NH4642.
Craskins *Aber.* ***Settlement***, 2m/3km NE of Tarland. **90 D4** NJ5106.
Craster *Northumb.* ***Village***, attractive fishing village on North Sea coast, 6m/10km NE of Alnwick. **71 H1** NU2519.
Craswall *Here.* ***Hamlet***, 5m/8km SE of Hay-on-Wye. **28 B5** SO2736.
Craswall Priory *Here.* ***Ecclesiastical building***, remains of priory, 1m/2km N of Craswall. **28 B5** SO2737.
Crateford *Staffs.* ***Settlement***, 2m/3km E of Brewood. SJ9009.
Cratfield *Suff.* ***Village***, 5m/8km W of Halesworth. **35 H1** TM3175.
Crathes *Aber.* ***Village***, on N side of River Dee, 3m/5km E of Banchory. **91 F5** NO7596.
Crathes Castle *Aber.* ***Castle***, built in 16c with later additions (National Trust for Scotland), 1m/2km W of Crathes. Gardens include early 18c yew hedges. **91 F5** NO7396.
Crathie *Aber.* ***Village***, on River Dee, 1km E of Balmoral Castle. **89 K5** NO2695.
Crathie *High.* ***Settlement***, in valley of River Spey, 9m/13km SW of Newtonmore. **88 C5** NN5894.
Crathie Church *Aber.* ***Ecclesiastical building***, church in Craithie, 1km E of Balmoral Castle and 8m/12km W of Ballater. Used by Royal Family when in residence at Balmoral. **89 K5** NO2694.
Crathorne *N.Yorks.* ***Village***, 4m/6km S of Yarm. **63 F6** NZ4407.
Craufurdland Water ***River***, running SW to confluence with Fenwick Water 1m/2km NE of Kilmarnock. Combined stream, known as Kilmarnock Water, flows through Kilmarnock to River Irvine on S side of town. **74 C6** NS4339.
Craven Arms *Shrop.* ***Small town***, at railway junction, 7m/11km NW of Ludlow. Named after its coaching inn. 13c Stokesay Castle 1m/2km to S. **38 D7** SO4382.
Craw *N.Ayr.* ***Settlement***, on NW coast of Arran, 3m/4km NE of Pirnmill. **73 G6** NR8948.
Crawcrook *T. & W.* ***Village***, 1m/2km W of Ryton. **71 G7** NZ1363.
Crawcwellt *Gwyn.* ***Open space***, hillside area 3m/4km SW of Trawsfynydd. **37 F2** SH6731.
Crawford *Lancs.* ***Hamlet***, 3m/5km SE of Skelmersdale. **48 D2** SD4902.
Crawford *S.Lan.* ***Village***, on River Clyde, 2m/4km SE of Abington. Site of Roman fort and fragment of old castle to N across river. **68 E1** NS9520.
Crawford Bridge *Dorset* ***Bridge***, 15c stone bridge over River Stour at Spetisbury, 4m/6km SE of Blandford Forum. SY9101.
Crawfordjohn *S.Lan.* ***Village***, 3m/5km W of Abington. **68 D1** NS8823.
Crawfordton *D. & G.* ***Settlement***, 1m/2km E of Moniaive. **68 C4** NX7990.
Crawick *D. & G.* ***Village***, 1m/2km NW of Sanquhar. **68 C2** NS7711.
Crawick Water *D. & G.* ***River***, running SW to River Nith, 1km to S of Crawick. **68 D2** NS7711.
Crawley *Devon* ***Hamlet***, 4m/6km W of Chard. ST2608.
Crawley *Hants.* ***Village***, 5m/8km NW of Winchester. **11 F1** SU4234.
Crawley *Oxon.* ***Village***, 2m/3km NW of Witney. **30 E7** SP3412.
Crawley *W.Suss.* Population: 88,203. ***Town***, 27m/43km S of London. Designated New Town 1947. Light industry. Gatwick (London) Airport to N. **13 F3** TQ2736.
Crawley Down *Hants.* ***Open space***, hillslope, 1m/2km NE of Crawley and 5m/8km NW of Winchester. **11 F1** SU4336.
Crawley Down *W.Suss.* Population: 4993. ***Village***, 5m/7km E of Crawley. **13 G3** TQ3437.
Crawley Side *Dur.* ***Locality***, 1km N of Stanhope. NY9940.
Crawleyside *Dur.* ***Hamlet***, 1m/2km N of Stanhope and 4m/6km SE of Rookhope. **62 A2** NY9940.
Crawshawbooth *Lancs.* ***Village***, 2m/3km N of Rawtenstall. Restored 18c Goodshaw Chapel (English Heritage), complete with furnishings. **56 D7** SD8125.
Crawston Hill *D. & G.* ***Hill***, 1m/2km NE of Dunscore. Height 712 feet or 217 metres. **68 D5** NX8885.
Crawton *Aber.* ***Settlement***, on North Sea coast, 4m/6km S of Stonehaven Nature Reserve. Bay to S of settlement. **91 G7** NO8779.
Crawton Bay *Aber.* ***Bay***, small bay, 4m/6km S of Stonehaven. Nature Reserve around headland at E end of bay. **91 G7** NO8779.
Crawyn *I.o.M.* ***Hamlet***, 4m/6km NE of Kirk Michael. **54 C4** SC3496.
Craxe's Green *Essex* ***Locality***, 5m/8km SW of Colchester. TL9519.
Cray *N.Yorks.* ***Hamlet***, 1m/2km N of Buckden. **56 E2** SD9479.
Cray *P. & K.* ***Hamlet***, on Shee Water, in Glen Shee, 4m/7km SE of Spittal of Glenshee. **82 C1** NO1463.
Cray (Crai). *Powys* ***Hamlet***, 3m/5km SW of Sennybridge. **27 H6** SN8924.
Cray Reservoir *Powys* ***Reservoir***, 2m/3km S of Cray. **27 H6** SN8821.
Crayford *Gt.Lon.* ***Suburb***, in borough of Bexley, in River Cray valley, 2m/3km W of Dartford. Crayford Ness on S bank of River Thames to NE beyond Crayford Marshes. **23 J4** TQ5174.
Crayke *N.Yorks.* ***Village***, 2m/3km E of Easingwold. 15c castle, part ruined, part incorporated in 19c house. **58 B2** SE5670.
Crays Hill *Essex* ***Village***, 2m/3km N of Basildon. **24 D2** TQ7192.
Cray's Pond *Oxon.* ***Hamlet***, 2m/4km E of Goring. **21 K3** SU6380.
Crazies Hill *W'ham* ***Hamlet***, 3m/5km N of Twyford. **22 A3** SU7980.
Creach Beinn (Anglicised form: Ben Creach.) *Arg. & B.* ***Mountain***, on Mull 3m/4km NE of Lochbuie. Height 2289 feet or 698 metres. **79 H5** NM6427.
Creach Bheinn *Arg. & B.* ***Mountain***, on Ardmeanach peninsula, Mull, 1m/2km E of Aird na h-Iolaire. Height 1610 feet or 491 metres. **79 F5** NM4129.
Creach Bheinn *Arg. & B.* ***Mountain***, in Argyll, 2m/4km SE of Loch Creran. Height 2657 feet or 810 metres. **80 B3** NN0242.
Creach Bheinn *High.* ***Mountain***, in Lochaber district 3m/5km SE of head of Loch Sunart. Height 2798 feet or 853 metres. **79 K2** NM8757.
Creachan Mòr *Arg. & B.* ***Mountain***, 1km N of Malcolm's Point, Mull. Height 1082 feet or 330 metres. **79 F6** NM4919.
Creachan Mòr *Arg. & B.* ***Mountain***, in Argyll 2m/3km W of junction of Loch Goil with Loch Long. Height 2155 feet or 657 metres. **73 K1** NS1891.
Creacombe *Devon* ***Hamlet***, 3m/5km N of Witheridge. **7 G4** SS8119.
Creag a' Chaorainn *High.* ***Inland physical feature***, mountain ridge 5m/8km E of head of Loch Carron. **95 G7** NH0043.
Creag a' Chlachain *High.* ***Mountain***, in Inverness district, 4m/6km SE of Dores. Height 1197 feet or 365 metres. **88 D1** NH6433.
Creag a' Chrionaich *High.* ***Mountain***, with rock outcrops to E, 1m/2km NW of Lothbeg, Sutherland district. Height 1292 feet or 394 metres. **104 E7** NC9211.
Creag a' Lain *High.* ***Mountain***, 3m/4km S of Beinn Edra, Skye. Height 1998 feet or 609 metres. **93 K6** NG4658.
Creag a' Mhadaidh *P. & K.* ***Mountain***, in Craiganour Forest, 4m/7km NW of Kinloch Rannoch. Height 2007 feet or 612 metres. **81 H1** NN6365.
Creag a' Mhaim *High.* ***Mountain***, rocky summit in Inverness district, 2m/4km S of W end of Loch Cluanie. Munro: height 3106 feet or 947 metres. **87 G4** NH0808.
Creag a' Phuill *Arg. & B.* ***Coastal feature***, headland on SE shore of Loch Fyne, 1m/2km S of Inveraray across loch. **80 B7** NN1005.
Creag an Dail Bheag *Aber.* ***Inland physical feature***, area of cliffs with scree below, above River Gain stream in Grampian Mountains, 4m/7km N of Braemar. **89 J5** NO1498.
Creag an Eunaich *P. & K.* ***Mountain***, 3m/5km NW of Dunkeld. Height 1506 feet or 459 metres. **82 A3** NN9743.
Creag an Funan *Aber.* ***Mountain***, 5m/8km S of Cabrach. Height 2073 feet or 632 metres. **90 B3** NJ3819.
Creag an Lòin *High.* ***Mountain***, in Badenoch and Strathspey district, 1m/2km NW of Newtonmore. Height 1794 feet or 547 metres. **88 D4** NH6901.
Creag an Sgliata *P. & K.* ***Mountain***, 3m/4km S of Acharn. Height 2286 feet or 697 metres. **81 J3** NN7639.
Creag an-t Sithein *P. & K.* ***Mountain***, with crags on E side of summit, 1m/2km N of Glen Brerachan. Height 2083 feet or 635 metres. **82 B1** NO0166.
Creag an Tarmachain ***Mountain***, one of Hills of Cromdale, on border of Highland and Moray, 8m/12km N of Tomintoul. Height 2119 feet or 646 metres. **89 J1** NJ1531.
Creag Beinn nan Eun *P. & K.* ***Inland physical feature***, crag on SW side of Findhu Glen, 7m/11km NE of Callander. **81 J6** NN7213.
Creag Bhalg *Aber.* ***Mountain***, 1m/2km N of Inverey. Height 2191 feet or 668 metres. **89 H5** NO0991.
Creag Bhàn *Arg. & B.* ***Hill***, 1m/2km N of Ardminish, Gigha. Height 328 feet or 100 metres. **72 E5** NR6450.
Creag Bhàn Ard *High.* ***Mountain***, in Morvern, Lochaber district, 4m/6km NW of Lochaline. Height 1112 feet or 339 metres. **79 H3** NM6348.
Creag Bhlag *High.* ***Mountain***, in Badenoch and Strathspey district, 2m/3km NE of Kingussie. Height 1729 feet or 527 metres. **88 E4** NH7603.
Creag Dhubh *High.* ***Mountain***, in Ross and Cromarty district, 1m/2km SE of Corrieshalloch Gorge. Height 1712 feet or 522 metres. **95 J4** NH2176.
Creag Dhubh *High.* ***Mountain***, in Badenoch and Strathspey district, 3m/5km NE of Newtonmore. Height 2578 feet or 786 metres. **88 E4** NH7203.
Creag Dhubh *High.* ***Mountain***, in Badenoch and Strathspey district, 5m/9km S of Aviemore. Height 2781 feet or 848 metres. **89 G4** NH9004.
Creag Dhubh *High.* ***Mountain***, in Lochaber district, on N side of Glen Spean, 3m/5km NE of Roybridge. Height 2158 feet or 658 metres. **87 K6** NN3282.
Creag Dhubh *High.* ***Mountain***, rising to over 740 metres, 2m/3km SW of Newtonmore. **88 D5** NN6797.
Creag Dhubh *P. & K.* ***Inland physical feature***, steep SE flank of Blath Bhalg mountain, 1968 feet or 600 metres high. **82 B1** NO0160.
Creag Dionard *High.* ***Mountain***, to SW of Loch Dionard. Height 2552 feet or 778 metres. **103 F4** NC3348.
Creag Dubh *High.* ***Mountain***, peak in Inverness district 3m/4km NW of dam of Loch Mullardoch. Height 3103 feet or 946 metres. **87 J1** NH1935.
Creag Each *P. & K.* ***Hill***, with craggy summit, 2m/3km NE of Comrie. Height 991 feet or 302 metres. **81 J5** NN7924.
Creag Fhraoch *W.Isles* ***Coastal feature***, cliff 4m/7km SW of Tolsta Head, Isle of Lewis. **101 H3** NB5142.
Creag Gharbh *Stir.* ***Mountain***, on S side of Loch Tay, 6m/10km NE of Lochearnhead. Height 2089 feet or 637 metres. **81 H4** NN6333.
Creag Ghoraidh (Anglicised form: Creagorry.) *W.Isles* ***Settlement***, on S coast of Benbecula, 4m/7km S of Benbecula (Baile a' Mhanaich) Aerodrome. **92 D7** NF7948.
Creag Island *Arg. & B.* ***Island***, islet off S coast of Lismore, nearly 1km S of Eilean Dubh and on W side of Pladda Island. NM8337.
Creag Leacach *Angus* ***Mountain***, 4m/6km NE of Spittal of Glenshee. Munro: height 3237 feet or 987 metres. **89 J7** NO1574.
Creag Liath *High.* ***Mountain***, 3m/4km NW of Grantown-on-Spey. Height 1476 feet or 450 metres. **89 H1** NJ0031.
Creag Liath *P. & K.* ***Mountain***, 3m/4km NW of Comrie. Height 1637 feet or 499 metres. **81 J5** NN7324.
Creag Liath *P. & K.* ***Mountain***, 4m/7km SW of Dunkeld. Height 1397 feet or 426 metres. **82 A4** NN9837.
Creag Loch nan Dearcag *High.* ***Mountain***, in Ross and Cromarty district on N slopes of River Meig valley, and 2m/3km NE of Milltown. Height 1758 feet or 536 metres. **95 K6** NH3356.
Creag Loisgte *High.* ***Mountain***, in Sutherland district, 4m/6km SW of Oykel Bridge. Height 1351 feet or 412 metres. **95 K2** NH3695.
Creag Meagaidh *High.* ***Mountain***, on border of Lochaber and Badenoch and Strathspey districts, 3m/5km N of E end of Loch Moy. Munro: height 3706 feet or 1130 metres. **88 B6** NN4187.
Creag-mheall Beag *High.* ***Mountain***, 6m/9km SE of Laide, Ross and Cromarty district. Height 1138 feet or 347 metres. **95 F3** NG9786.
Creag Mhòr ***Mountain***, on border of Perth & Kinross and Stirling, 5m/8km NE of Tyndrum. Munro: height 3434 feet or 1047 metres. **80 E4** NN3936.
Creag Mhòr *High.* ***Mountain***, 5m/8km SE of Loch Choire, Sutherland district. Height 2339 feet or 713 metres. **103 J6** NC6924.
Creag Mhòr *High.* ***Mountain***, in Sherramore Forest, 10m/16km SE of Fort Augustus. Height 2506 feet or 764 metres. **88 B5** NN4897.
Creag Mhòr *P. & K.* ***Mountain***, to N of Loch Tay, 6m/10km NW of Kenmore. Munro: height 3218 feet or 981 metres. **81 H3** NN6949.
Creag Mhòr *Stir.* ***Mountain***, 4m/6km W of Killin. Height 2358 feet or 719 metres. **81 G4** NN5134.
Creag Mhòr *W.Isles* ***Hill***, on coast, to S of entrance to Loch Carlabhagh, Isle of Lewis. Height 226 feet or 69 metres. **100 D3** NB1741.
Creag na Criche *P. & K.* ***Mountain***, craggy summit, 6m/10km NW of Methven. Height 1492 feet or 455 metres. **82 A4** NN9835.
Creag na h-Iolaire *Arg. & B.* ***Mountain***, 3m/4km N of Lochbuie, Mull. Height 1660 feet or 506 metres. **79 G5** NM6129.
Creag nam Bodach *High.* ***Mountain***, in Badenoch and Strathspey district, 3m/4km S of Dalwhinnie. Height 1574 feet or 480 metres. **88 E5** NN7596.
Creag nam Fiadh *High.* ***Mountain***, 2m/4km SW of Kinbrace, Sutherland district. Height 1269 feet or 387 metres. **104 D6** NC8423.
Creag Nam Fiadh Mòr *Arg. & B.* ***Hill***, on central Jura, 1m/2km SW of Tarbert. Height 859 feet or 262 metres. **72 D2** NR5981.
Creag nam Fitheach *Arg. & B.* ***Mountain***, on Mull, 3m/5km E of Lochbuie. Height 1030 feet or 314 metres. **79 H5** NM6624.
Creag nam Mial *P. & K.* ***Mountain***, 5m/8km E of Ballinluig. Height 1840 feet or 561 metres. **82 B2** NO0554.
Creag nan Caiman *High.* ***Mountain***, in Inverness district, 2m/3km SE of Affric Lodge. Height 2168 feet or 661 metres. **87 H2** NH1920.
Creag nan Damh *High.* ***Mountain***, peak on border of Lochaber and Skye and Lochalsh districts 4m/6km NE of Kinloch Hourn. Munro: height 3011 feet or 918 metres. **87 F3** NG9811.
Creag nan Gabhar *Aber.* ***Mountain***, 4m/7km S of Braemar. Height 2736 feet or 834 metres. **89 J6** NO1584.
Creag nan Gall *Aber.* ***Mountain***, 2m/3km S of Balmoral Castle, with large rock outcrop on NW side. Height 1971 feet or 601 metres. **89 K5** NO2691.
Creag Nay *High.* ***Mountain***, in Inverness district, 1m/2km NE of Drumnadrochit. Height 1240 feet or 378 metres. **88 C1** NH5230.
Creag Pitridh *High.* ***Mountain***, in Badenoch and Strathspey district, 1m/2km E of SW end of Lochan na h-Earba. Munro: height 3031 feet or 924 metres. **88 B6** NN4881.
Creag Rainich *High.* ***Mountain***, in Ross and Cromarty district, 8m/13km S of Dundonnell. Height 2647 feet or 807 metres. **95 G4** NH0975.
Creag Riabhach *High.* ***Mountain***, 7m/11km S of Cape Wrath. Height 1591 feet or 485 metres. **102 E2** NC2763.
Creag Riabhach Bheag *High.* ***Mountain***, 2m/3km NE of Ben Hope. Height 1519 feet or 463 metres. **103 G3** NC4952.
Creag Riabhach na Greighe *High.* ***Mountain***, 4m/6km S of W end of Loch Choire, Sutherland district. Height 1512 feet or 461 metres. **103 J6** NC6120.
Creag Ruadh *High.* ***Mountain***, with twin summits at 2201 feet or 671 metres and 2148 feet or 655 metres on borders of Sutherland and Ross and Cromarty districts, 12m/20km NE of Garve. **96 B3** NH4381.
Creag Scalabsdale *High.* ***Mountain***, on border of Sutherland and Caithness districts, to SE of Loch Scalabsdale. Height 1820 feet or 555 metres. **104 E6** NC9624.
Creag Tharsuinn *Arg. & B.* ***Mountain***, with craggy E face, rising to form W side of Garrachra Glen, 7m/11km S of Strachur. Height 2102 feet or 641 metres. **73 J1** NS0891.
Creag Thoraraidh *High.* ***Mountain***, 2m/3km NE of Helmsdale. Height 1322 feet or 403 metres. **105 F7** ND0318.
Creag Uchdag ***Mountain***, on border of Perth & Kinross and Stirling, 3m/5km SE of Ardeonaig on S shore of Loch Tay. Height 2883 feet or 879 metres. **81 J4** NN7032.
Creagan *Arg. & B.* ***Settlement***, on N shore of Loch Creran, Argyll, 3m/5km E of Portnacroish. NM9744.
Creagan a' Chaise *Moray* ***Mountain***, summit of Hills of Cromdale, 5m/8km SE of Grantown-on-Spey. Height 2368 feet or 722 metres. **89 J2** NJ1024.
Creagan an Eich *Arg. & B.* ***Mountain***, on E side of Loch Fyne, 3m/5km S of Inveraray across the loch. Height 1096 feet or 334 metres. **80 C7** NN1003.
Creagan Asdale *High.* ***Hill***, in Sutherland district, 5m/8km NW of Dornoch. Height 722 feet or 220 metres. **96 E2** NH7292.

C

Creagan Dubha Réidhe Bhig *High.* ***Mountain***, 4m/6km E of Syre, Caithness district. Height 1105 feet or 337 metres. **104 C4** NC7544.
Creagan Glas *High.* ***Mountain***, 2m/3km S of Muie, Sutherland district. Height 1027 feet or 313 metres. **96 D1** NC6701.
Creagan Mòr *High.* ***Mountain***, on SE side of Loch Ericht, 3m/4km SW of Dalwhinnie. Height 2539 feet or 774 metres. **88 D6** NN6180.
Creagan na Beinne *P. & K.* ***Mountain***, 3m/5km SW of Ardtalnaig. Height 2913 feet or 888 metres. **81 J4** NN7436.
Creagbheitheachain *High.* ***Settlement***, in Glen Scaddle, 4m/7km N of Sallachan Point, Lochaber district. **80 A1** NM9868.
Creagorry *W.Isles Anglicised form of Creag Ghoraidh, qv.*
Creake Abbey *Norf.* ***Ecclesiastical building***, remains of abbey founded in 1206, with 14c chapel (English Heritage), 1m/2km N of North Creake. **44 C2** TF8539.
Crealy Park *Devon* ***Other feature of interest***, in Clyst St. Mary, 4m/6km E of Exeter. Attractions include animal park, boats and racetrack. **7 H6** SX9691.
Creamore Bank *Shrop.* ***Settlement***, 1m/2km N of Wem. SJ5130.
Creaton *Northants.* ***Village***, 8m/13km NW of Northampton. **31 J1** SP7071.
Creca *D. & G.* ***Hamlet***, 3m/5km NE of Annan. **69 H6** NY2270.
Credenhill *Here.* Population: 2013. ***Village***, 4m/7km NW of Hereford. **28 D4** SO4543.
Crediton *Devon* Population: 6142. ***Small town***, market town and former seat of Bishops of the South West, 7m/11km NW of Exeter. 7c birthplace of St. Boniface. **7 G5** SS8300.
Cree ***River***, whose headwaters are in Glentrool Forest Park. River then flows S to Newton Stewart and Wigtown Bay. **67 H5** NX4655.
Creebridge *D. & G.* ***Village***, opposite Newton Stewart across River Cree. NX4165.
Creech *Dorset* ***Settlement***, 3m/5km NE of Corfe Castle. SY9183.
Creech Heathfield *Som.* ***Village***, 4m/6km NE of Taunton. ST2727.
Creech St. Michael *Som.* Population: 1901. ***Village***, 3m/5km E of Taunton. **8 B2** ST2725.
Creed *Cornw.* ***Hamlet***, 6m/9km SW of St. Austell. **3 G4** SW9347.
Creedy Park *Devon* ***Settlement***, 1km N of Crediton. **7 G5** SS8301.
Creekmouth *Gt.Lon.* ***Locality***, on River Thames, on E side of Barking Creek, in borough of Barking and Dagenham. **23 H3** TQ4581.
Creeting St. Mary *Suff.* ***Village***, 3m/5km SE of Stowmarket. **34 E3** TM0956.
Creeton *Lincs.* ***Hamlet***, 5m/8km W of Bourne. **42 D3** TF0119.
Creetown *D. & G.* ***Village***, on E side of River Cree estuary at mouth of Moneypool Burn, 6m/10km SE of Newton Stewart. Granite quarries to S. **64 E5** NX4758.
Creggans *Arg. & B.* ***Settlement***, in Argyll, on E shore of Loch Fyne, 1m/2km NW of Strachur. **80 B7** NN0802.
Cregneash *I.o.M.* ***Hamlet***, 1m/2km W of Port St. Mary. Cregneash Village Folk Museum (Manx National Heritage) depicts 19c crofting community. **54 A7** SC1867.
Cregrina *Powys* ***Hamlet***, 5m/8km E of Builth Wells. **28 A3** SO1252.
Creich *Arg. & B.* ***Locality***, at NW end of Ross of Mull, 1m/2km NE of Fionnphort. NM3124.
Creich *Fife* ***Settlement***, 5m/8km NW of Cupar. **82 E5** NO3221.
Creigau *Mon.* ***Hamlet***, 1km N of Devauden. ST4899.
Creigh Hill *Angus* ***Mountain***, comprises two distinct summits over 490 metres, with cairns, at SW end of Backwater Reservoir and 2m/3km NE of Dykend. **82 D2** NO2658.
Creigiau *Cardiff* Population: 2240. ***Village***, 3m/4km E of Llantrisant. **18 D3** ST0881.
Creiglyn Dyfi *Gwyn.* ***Lake/loch***, tarn 5m/8km S of Llanuwchllyn. **37 H3** SH8622.
Creinch *W.Dun.* ***Island***, in Loch Lomond, 2m/3km E of Rossdhu House. NS3988.
Creise *High.* ***Mountain***, peak to S of Stob a' Ghlais Choire, 7m/11km SE of Kinlochleven. Munro: height 3608 feet or 1100 metres. **80 D2** NN2350.
Crelevan *High.* ***Settlement***, in Strathglass, 5m/8km NE of Cannich. **87 K1** NH3837.
Crelly *Cornw.* ***Settlement***, 3m/5km N of Helston. SW6732.
Cremyll *Cornw.* ***Village***, beside River Tamar estuary opposite Stonehouse district of Plymouth. To S, Mount Edgcumbe house and park. **4 E5** SX4553.
Crendell *Dorset* ***Settlement***, 2m/3km E of Cranborne. SU0813.
Cressage *Shrop.* ***Village***, 3m/5km NW of Much Wenlock. **38 E5** SJ5904.
Cressbrook *Derbys.* ***Hamlet***, on River Wye, 4m/6km NW of Bakewell. SK1773.
Cresselly *Pembs.* ***Village***, 6m/9km NE of Pembroke. **16 D4** SN0606.
Cressex *Bucks.* ***Suburb***, SW district of High Wycombe. SU8591.
Cressing *Essex* ***Village***, 3m/4km SE of Braintree. **34 B6** TL7920.
Cresswell *Northumb.* ***Village***, on coast, 4m/6km N of Ashington. **71 H4** NZ2993.
Cresswell *Pembs.* ***River***, rising NW of Saundersfoot and flowing W to Cresswell, where it forms an estuary which continues W to join Carew River and flow into Daugleddau estuary at Jenkins Point. SN0106.
Cresswell *Pembs.* ***Village***, at head of River Cresswell estuary, 6m/10km NW of Tenby. **16 D4** SN0506.
Cresswell *Staffs.* ***Village***, 3m/5km SW of Cheadle. **40 B2** SJ9739.
Creswell *Derbys.* Population: 4655. ***Village***, 4m/7km NE of Bolsover. Model village adjoins to W. Creswell Crags 1km to E. **51 H5** SK5274.
Creswell Crags *Derbys.* ***Historic/prehistoric site***, important archaeological site, 5m/8km NE of Bolsover. Caves in cliffs were early Stone Age dwellings. SK5374.
Creswell Green *Staffs.* ***Hamlet***, 3m/5km W of Lichfield. SK0710.
Cretingham *Suff.* ***Village***, 4m/6km SE of Debenham. **35 G3** TM2260.
Cretshengan *Arg. & B.* ***Settlement***, on W of Kintyre, 2m/3km N of Kilberry. **73 F4** NR7166.
Creuch Hill *Inclyde* ***Mountain***, on NW fringe of Duchal Moor. Height 1446 feet or 441 metres. **74 A4** NS2668.
Crewe *Ches.* Population: 63,351. ***Town***, with important railway station and junction, 12m/20km NW of Stoke-on-Trent. Manchester Metropolitan University. **49 G7** SJ7055.
Crewe *Ches.* ***Village***, 1m/2km E of Holt across River Dee. **48 D7** SJ4253.
Crewe Green *Ches.* ***Hamlet***, 1km E of Crewe town centre. SJ7255.
Crewgreen *Powys* ***Village***, 8m/13km NE of Welshpool. **38 C4** SJ3215.
Crewkerne *Som.* Population: 7142. ***Small town***, market town, largely stone built, 8m/13km SW of Yeovil. **8 D4** ST4409.
Crews Hill *Here.* ***Settlement***, 4m/7km SW of Newent. SO6722.
Crew's Hole *Bristol* ***Suburb***, on N bank of River Avon, 2m/4km E of Bristol city centre. ST6273.
Crewton *Derby* ***Suburb***, 2m/4km SE of Derby city centre. **41 F2** SK3733.
Crianlarich *Stir.* ***Village***, on River Fillan, 12m/20km SW of Killin. Railway junction of Oban and Fort William lines. **80 E5** NN3825.
Crib Law *Sc.Bord.* ***Mountain***, with fire tower in Craik Forest, 1m/2km NW of Craik. Height 1387 feet or 423 metres. **69 J3** NT3309.
Crib Law *Sc.Bord.* ***Mountain***, in Lammermuir Hills, 2m/3km SW of Hopes Reservoir. Height 1670 feet or 509 metres. **76 D4** NT5260.
Cribba Head *Cornw.* ***Coastal feature***, headland to S of Penberth Cove, 2m/3km S of St. Buryan. **2 B6** SW4022.
Cribbs Causeway *S.Glos.* ***Leisure/recreation***, retail complex 5m/8km N of Bristol. **19 J3** ST5780.
Cribden Side *Lancs.* ***Settlement***, below Cribden Hill, 1km NE of Haslingden. SD7924.
Cribin Fawr *Gwyn.* ***Mountain***, 4m/7km SE of Dolgellau. Height 2198 feet or 670 metres. **37 G4** SH7915.
Cribyn *Cere.* ***Hamlet***, 4m/6km NW of Lampeter. **26 E3** SN5251.
Criccieth *Gwyn.* Population: 1720. ***Small town***, resort on Tremadog Bay, 15m/24km S of Caernarfon. Remains of 13c castle (Cadw). **36 D2** SH5038.
Criccieth Castle *Gwyn.* ***Castle***, in Criccieth, on S coast of Lleyn Peninsula. Remains of castle started by Llywelyn the Great in 1230 and largely destroyed by Owain Glyndŵr in 1404. **36 D2** SH4937.
Crich *Derbys.* Population: 1836. ***Village***, 4m/7km N of Belper. **51 F7** SK3554.
Crich Carr *Derbys.* ***Hamlet***, 1km W of Crich. **51 F7** SK3354.
Crich Common *Derbys.* ***Village***, adjoining to S of Crich. SK3553.
Crichie *Aber.* ***Locality***, comprises many dispersed settlements, 1m/2km SW of Stuartfield. **99 H6** NJ9544.
Crichton *Midloth.* ***Hamlet***, 2m/3km S of Pathhead. **76 B4** NT3862.
Crichton Castle *Midloth.* ***Castle***, 14c and later, one of largest castles in Scotland (Historic Scotland), 6m/10km SE of Edinburgh. **76 B4** NT3861.
Crick *Mon.* ***Hamlet***, 4m/7km SW of Chepstow. **19 H3** ST4890.
Crick *Northants.* Population: 1314. ***Village***, 6m/9km E of Rugby. **31 G1** SP5872.
Crick Wharf *Northants.* ***Settlement***, 1km E of Crick across Grand Union Canal. SP5972.
Crickadarn *Powys* ***Hamlet***, 6m/10km SE of Builth Wells. **27 K4** SO0942.
Cricket Hill *Hants.* ***Suburb***, to SE of Yateley. SU8260.
Cricket Malherbie *Som.* ***Hamlet***, 3m/5km NE of Chard. **8 C3** ST3611.
Cricket St. Thomas *Som.* ***Hamlet***, 3m/5km E of Chard, grouped round small mansion. Grounds are now wildlife park. **8 C4** ST3708.
Crickham *Som.* ***Hamlet***, 1m/2km N of Wedmore. ST4349.
Crickheath *Shrop.* ***Hamlet***, 4m/7km S of Oswestry. **38 B3** SJ2922.
Crickheath Wharf *Shrop.* ***Settlement***, to N of Crickheath, on Shropshire Union Canal. SJ2923.
Crickhowell (Crucywel). *Powys* ***Village***, on River Usk, 6m/9km NW of Abergavenny. Scant remains of old castle. **28 B7** SO2118.
Cricklade *Wilts.* Population: 3808. ***Village***, on River Thames, 7m/11km NW of Swindon. Former Saxon town, with town walls still in evidence. Site of Roman building to N. **20 D2** SU1093.
Cricklewood *Gt.Lon.* ***Suburb***, in borough of Brent, 5m/9km NW of Charing Cross. TQ2385.
Crickley Hill *Glos.* ***Hill***, rising to over 260 metres. Partly National Trust property, with country park and Iron Age fort on escarpment of Cotswold Hills, 4m/6km S of Cheltenham. Viewpoint. **29 J7** SO9316.
Crick's Green *Here.* ***Settlement***, 3m/4km SW of Bromyard. SO6351.
Criddlestyle *Hants.* ***Settlement***, 1m/2km E of Fordingbridge. SU1614.
Cridling Stubbs *N.Yorks.* ***Village***, 2m/3km SE of Knottingley. **58 B7** SE5221.
Crieff *P. & K.* Population: 6023. ***Small town***, above E bank of River Earn, 16m/25km W of Perth. Noted for local crafts. **81 K5** NN8621.
Criffell *D. & G.* ***Mountain***, prominent landmark commanding extensive views, 3m/4km S of New Abbey. Height 1866 feet or 569 metres. **65 K4** NX9561.
Criftins *Shrop. Alternative name for Dudleston Heath, qv.*
Crigdon Hill *Northumb.* ***Mountain***, 4m/7km W of Harbottle. Height 1237 feet or 377 metres. **70 D3** NT8605.
Criggan *Cornw.* ***Hamlet***, 5m/8km N of St. Austell. SX0160.
Criggion (Crugion). *Powys* ***Village***, 6m/10km NE of Welshpool. **38 B4** SJ2914.
Crigglestone *W.Yorks.* ***Village***, 3m/5km SW of Wakefield. **51 F1** SE3116.
Crim Rocks *I.o.S.* ***Island***, group of islets, 6m/10km SW of St. Mary's. **2 B2** SV8009.
Crimble *Gt.Man.* ***Settlement***, on N side of River Roch, 2m/3km W of Rochdale. SD8611.
Crimchard *Som.* ***Suburb***, NW district of Chard. ST3109.
Crimdon Park *Dur.* ***Settlement***, 4m/6km NW of Hartlepool. **63 F3** NZ4737.
Crime Rigg *Dur.* ***Locality***, to S of Sherburn Hill, 4m/7km E of Durham. NZ3341.
Crimea Pass *Gwyn. Alternative name for Bwlch y Gorddinan, qv.*
Crimond *Aber.* ***Village***, near NE coast, 8m/13km NW of Peterhead. **99 J5** NK0556.
Crimonmogate *Aber.* ***Settlement***, in woodland near small lake, 3m/5km S of St. Combs. **99 J5** NK0358.
Crimplesham *Norf.* ***Village***, 3m/4km E of Downham Market. **44 A5** TF6503.
Crinan *Arg. & B.* ***Village***, on Crinan Loch, in Argyll, 6m/10km NW of Lochgilphead. **73 F1** NR7894.
Crinan Canal *Arg. & B.* ***Canal***, connects Crinan Loch with Ardrishaig and Loch Fyne, running across N part of Kintyre peninsula. Lighthouse at Ardrishaig entrance to canal. NR8191.
Crinan Ferry *Arg. & B.* ***Settlement***, to E of Crinan across River Add; ferry for pedestrians across river. NR7993.
Crinan Loch (Also known as Loch Crinan.) *Arg. & B.* ***Sea feature***, sea-loch in Argyll, 6m/10km NW of Lochgilphead. **73 F1** NR7895.
Crincoed Point *Pembs.* ***Coastal feature***, headland on W side of Fishguard Bay, 2m/3km N of Fishguard. **16 C1** SM9540.
Crindai *Newport Welsh form of Crindau, qv.*
Crindau (Crindai). *Newport* ***Suburb***, to N of Newport town centre. ST3089.
Crindledyke *N.Lan.* ***Settlement***, 1m/2km E of Newmains. NS8356.
Cringleford *Norf.* Population: 2190. ***Village***, 3m/4km SW of Norwich. **45 F5** TG1905.
Cringletie *Sc.Bord.* ***Settlement***, 3m/4km N of Peebles. **76 A6** NT2344.
Crinkle Crags *Cumb.* ***Mountain***, fell in Lake District S of Bow Fell. Height 2814 feet or 858 metres. **60 D6** NY2404.
Crinkley Bottom *Som.* ***Leisure/recreation***, TV based theme park in grounds of Cricket House at Cricket St. Thomas, 3m/5km E of Chard, featuring wide variety of wildlife and activities including sea lion show and camel trekking. Also Heavy Horse Centre and woodland railway. **8 C4** ST3608.
Crinow (Crynwedd). *Pembs.* ***Hamlet***, 1m/2km E of Narberth. **16 E3** SN1214.
Crionaig *W.Isles* ***Locality***, upland area of S part of Isle of Lewis, rising to over 460 metres, 3m/5km S of head of Loch Shell. **100 E7** NB2906.
Cripplesease *Cornw.* ***Hamlet***, 2m/4km SE of St. Ives. **2 B5** SW5036.
Cripplesty *Dorset* ***Hamlet***, 3m/4km E of Cranborne. SU0912.
Cripp's Corner *E.Suss.* ***Settlement***, 4m/6km NE of Battle. **14 C5** TQ7721.
Critchells' Green *Hants.* ***Settlement***, adjoining to S of Lockerley. SU2926.
Crix *Essex* ***Settlement***, 1km SW of Hatfield Peverel. **34 B7** TL7711.
Crizeley *Here.* ***Settlement***, 7m/11km SW of Hereford. SO4432.
Croachy *High.* ***Locality***, comprising settlement of West Croachy and hamlet of East Croachy, in Inverness district, 5m/9km SE of Dores. NH6427.
Croalchapel *D. & G.* ***Settlement***, 3m/4km SE of Thornhill. **68 E4** NX9091.
Croasdale *Cumb.* ***Settlement***, 2m/3km NE of Ennerdale Bridge. **60 B5** NY0917.
Croasdale Fell *Lancs.* ***Open space***, moorland on E side of Forest of Bowland, 3m/5km NW of Slaidburn. **56 B4** SD6756.
Crochan Hill *P. & K.* ***Mountain***, on N side of Glen Almond, 9m/15km NE of Crieff. Height 1660 feet or 506 metres. **82 A4** NN9533.
Crock Ness *Ork.* ***Coastal feature***, headland on E coast of Hoy opposite Flotta. **107 C8** ND3293.
Crock Street *Som.* ***Settlement***, 1m/2km S of Broadway. **8 C3** ST3213.
Crockenhill *Kent* ***Village***, 1m/2km SE of Swanley. **23 J5** TQ5067.
Crocker End *Oxon.* ***Hamlet***, 1km E of Nettlebed. SU7086.
Crockerhill *Hants.* ***Settlement***, 2m/3km N of Fareham. SU5709.
Crockerhill *W.Suss.* ***Hamlet***, 4m/7km E of Chichester. SU9207.
Crockernwell *Devon* ***Village***, 4m/7km N of Moretonhampstead. **7 F6** SX7592.
Crockerton *Wilts.* ***Village***, 2m/3km S of Warminster. **20 B7** ST8642.
Crockerton Green *Wilts.* ***Hamlet***, to NE of Crockerton, 1m/2km S of Warminster. ST8643.

C

Crocketford (Also known as Nine Mile Bar.) *D. & G.* ***Village***, 7m/12km NE of Castle Douglas. **65 J3** NX8372.
Crockey Hill *York* ***Settlement***, 4m/6km S of York, on road to Selby. **58 C5** SE6246.
Crockham Hill *Kent* ***Village***, 2m/3km S of Westerham. **23 H6** TQ4450.
Crockhurst Street *Kent* ***Settlement***, 2m/4km SE of Tonbridge. **23 K7** TQ6244.
Crockleford Heath *Essex* ***Settlement***, 3m/5km E of Colchester. **34 E6** TM0326.
Crococalana *Notts. See Brough.*
Croe *High.* ***River***, running NW to head of Loch Duich in Skye and Lochalsh district. **87 G3** NG9521.
Croes Hywel *Mon.* ***Settlement***, 2m/3km E of Abergavenny. **28 C7** SO3314.
Croes-lan *Cere.* ***Hamlet***, 3m/5km NW of Llandysul. **26 C4** SN3844.
Croes-y-mwyalch *Torfaen* ***Settlement***, 3m/4km N of Newport. **19 G2** ST3092.
Croes y pant *Mon.* ***Settlement***, 3m/5km NE of Pontypool. **19 G1** SO3104.
Croesau Bach *Shrop.* ***Settlement***, 3m/5km SW of Oswestry. **38 B3** SJ2428.
Croeserw *N.P.T.* Population: 2731. ***Village***, 3m/4km N of Maesteg. **18 B2** SS8695.
Croesgoch *Pembs.* ***Hamlet***, 6m/9km NE of St. David's. **16 B2** SM8230.
Croesor *Gwyn.* ***Hamlet***, 4m/6km N of Penrhyndeudraeth. **37 F1** SH6344.
Croespenmaen *Caerp.* ***Locality***, 1m/2km NW of Newbridge. **18 E2** ST1998.
Croesyceiliog *Carmar.* ***Hamlet***, 2m/4km S of Carmarthen. **17 H3** SN4016.
Croesyceiliog *Torfaen* ***Suburb***, in NE part of Cwmbran. **19 G2** ST3096.
Croesywaun *Gwyn.* ***Village***, 3m/5km SE of Caernarfon. SH5259.
Croford *Som.* ***Settlement***, 2m/3km E of Wiveliscombe. ST1027.
Croft *Here.* ***Settlement***, 5m/8km NW of Leominster. Croft Castle to SE. SO4465.
Croft *Leics.* ***Village***, 6m/9km E of Hinckley. Syenite quarries to N. **41 H6** SP5195.
Croft *Lincs.* ***Village***, 2m/3km NE of Wainfleet All Saints. **53 J6** TF5061.
Croft *Pembs.* ***Settlement***, 2m/4km SW of Cardigan. SN1542.
Croft *Warr.* ***Village***, 4m/6km NE of Warrington. **49 F3** SJ6393.
Croft Ambrey Iron Age Hillfort *Here.* ***Historic/prehistoric site***, Iron Age hillfort within Croft Castle Estate. **28 D2** SO4466.
Croft Castle *Here.* ***Castle***, medieval building (National Trust), with later modifications, 3m/5km NW of Leominster. **28 D2** SO4465.
Croft Head *D. & G.* ***Mountain***, 4m/7km E of Moffat. Height 2086 feet or 636 metres. **69 G3** NT1505.
Croft Marsh *Lincs.* ***Open space***, lowland 2m/3km SW of Skegness. **53 J6** TF5360.
Croft-on-Tees *N.Yorks.* ***Village***, on River Tees, 3m/5km S of Darlington. **62 D5** NZ2809.
Croftamie *Stir.* ***Village***, on Catter Burn, 2m/3km S of Drymen. NS4786.
Croftfoot *Glas.* ***Suburb***, 3m/5km S of Glasgow city centre. NS6060.
Crofthead *Cumb.* ***Settlement***, 1m/2km N of Longtown. **69 J6** NY3870.
Croftmoraig *P. & K.* ***Locality***, with triple stone circle on S side of River Tay near its confluence with River Lyon. NN7947.
Croftmore *P. & K.* ***Settlement***, in valley of River Tilt, 3m/4km N of Blair Atholl. **81 K1** NN8868.
Crofton *Cumb.* ***Locality***, 3m/5km E of Wigton. NY3049.
Crofton *W.Yorks.* Population: 5874. ***Village***, 4m/6km SE of Wakefield. **51 F1** SE3717.
Crofton *Wilts.* ***Settlement***, on Kennet and Avon Canal, and on line of Roman road, 6m/10km SW of Hungerford. **21 F5** SU2662.
Crofts *D. & G.* ***Settlement***, 3m/4km SE of Corsock. **65 H3** NX7974.
Crofts Bank *Gt.Man.* ***Suburb***, to N of Urmston town centre. SJ7695.
Crofts End *Bristol* ***Suburb***, 3m/5km NE of Bristol city centre. ST6274.
Crofts of Benachielt *High.* ***Settlement***, 3m/5km N of Latheron. **105 G5** ND1838.
Crofts of Buinach *Moray* ***Settlement***, 1m/2km NE of Kellas. **97 J6** NJ1855.
Crofts of Haddo *Aber.* ***Locality***, 4m/7km E of Fyvie. **91 G1** NJ8337.
Crofty *Swan.* ***Village***, 1m/2km SE of Salthouse Point. **17 J5** SS5294.
Crogary Mòr *W.Isles* ***Hill***, on North Uist, 1km NE of Maari. Height 590 feet or 180 metres. **92 D4** NF8673.
Crogen *Gwyn.* ***Settlement***, 5m/8km NE of Bala. **37 K2** SJ0036.
Croggan *Arg. & B.* ***Village***, on S side of entrance to Loch Spelve, Mull. **79 J5** NM7027.
Croglin *Cumb.* ***Village***, 9m/15km S of Brampton. **61 G2** NY5747.
Croglin Fell *Cumb.* ***Open space***, moorland on N side of Croglin Water, highest point of which is 1938 feet or 591 metres, 6m/10km NE of Kirkoswald. **61 H2** NY6049.
Croglin Water *Cumb.* ***River***, rising on E side of Scarrowmanwick Fell on Gilderdale Forest, flowing W past Croglin, then SW into River Eden, 2m/3km N of Lazonby. **61 H2** NY5342.
Croic-bheinn *High.* ***Mountain***, in Ross and Cromarty district, 3m/5km SW of Shieldaig. Height 1617 feet or 493 metres. **94 D6** NG7652.
Croick *High.* ***Locality***, in Sutherland district, at foot of Strath Chuilionaich, 10m/15km W of Bonar Bridge. **96 B2** NH4591.
Croick *High.* ***Settlement***, on E side of Halladale River, 1km N of Trantlebeg. **104 D3** NC8954.
Croig *Arg. & B.* ***Settlement***, on N coast of Mull, 3m/5km E of Caliach Point. **79 F2** NM4053.
Crois Dughaill (Anglicised form: Crossdougal.) *W.Isles* ***Settlement***, on South Uist, 1km S of Dalabrog. **84 C3** NF7520.
Croit Bheinn *High.* ***Mountain***, 4m/6km SE of Lochailort, Lochaber district. Height 2175 feet or 663 metres. **86 E7** NM8177.
Croit e Caley *I.o.M.* ***Settlement***, 1m/2km NE of Port St. Mary. **54 B6** SC2269.
Crom Allt *High.* ***River***, flows N into Loch Urigill, Ross and Cromarty district. **95 J1** NC2509.
Cròm Allt *High.* ***River***, rising on NW slopes of Carn na Crìche and flowing N into Allt Odhar, 10m/16km E of Fort Augustus. NH5306.
Crom Loch *High.* ***Lake/loch***, small loch on border of Sutherland and Ross and Cromarty districts, 13m/21km N of Garve. **95 K3** NH3983.
Cromalt Hills *High.* ***Large natural feature***, upland area on border of Ross and Cromarty and Sutherland districts, 4m/6km S of Elphin. **95 J1** NC2106.
Cromar *Aber.* ***Locality***, between Aboyne and Tarland. **90 C4** NJ4704.
Cromarty *High.* ***Small town***, with harbour in Ross and Cromarty district, on S side of entrance to Cromarty Firth, 15m/24km NE of Inverness. Hugh Miller's Cottage (National Trust for Scotland), birthplace of eminent geologist, dates from 1650; contains small museum. **96 E5** NH7867.
Cromarty Bay *High.* ***Bay***, on S side of Cromarty Firth, Ross and Cromarty district, between Balblair and Cromarty. **96 E5** NH7466.
Cromarty Court House *High.* ***Historic house***, in Cromarty, 15m/24km NE of Inverness. Built in 1773, containing reconstruction of trial, animated figures and history of Cromarty. **96 E5** NH7967.
Cromarty Firth *High.* ***Sea feature***, long inlet of Moray Firth extending past Nigg Bay and Invergordon to Dingwall, Ross and Cromarty district. **96 D5** NH6667.
Crombie *Fife* ***Village***, 3m/5km SW of Dunfermline. NT0485.
Crombie Castle *Aber.* ***Castle***, medieval castle 2m/4km W of Aberchirder. **98 D5** NJ5952.
Crombie Country Park *Angus* ***Leisure/recreation***, adjacent to Crombie Reservoir, 2m/3km NE of Monikie. 250 acre park surrounding Victorian reservoir styled to resemble natural loch. **83 G3** NO5240.
Crombie Mill *Angus* ***Settlement***, to SE of Crombie Reservoir, 2m/3km NE of Monikie. **83 G3** NO5340.
Crombie Reservoir *Angus* ***Reservoir***, small reservoir 4m/7km NW of Carnoustie. **83 G3** NO5240.
Cromblet *Aber.* ***Settlement***, 2m/3km SE of Fyvie. **91 F1** NJ7834.
Cromdale *High.* ***Village***, in Badenoch and Strathspey district, 3m/5km E of Grantown-on-Spey. **89 H2** NJ0728.
Cromer *Herts.* ***Village***, 4m/7km W of Buntingford. **33 F6** TL2928.
Cromer *Norf.* Population: 7267. ***Small town***, coastal resort and former fishing town, 21m/33km N of Norwich. **45 G1** TG2142.
Cromer Hyde *Herts.* ***Settlement***, 2m/3km W of Welwyn Garden City. **33 F7** TL2012.
Cromer Point *N.Yorks.* ***Coastal feature***, headland 3m/5km N of Scarborough. **63 K3** TA0392.
Cromford *Derbys.* Population: 1213. ***Village***, 2m/3km N of Wirksworth. **50 E7** SK2956.
Cromhall *S.Glos.* ***Village***, 4m/6km E of Thornbury. Site of Roman villa 1km SW. **19 K2** ST6990.
Cromhall Common *S.Glos.* ***Hamlet***, 1m/2km S of Cromhall. **19 K3** ST6989.
Cromlet *P. & K.* ***Mountain***, rounded summit, 7m/11km N of Dunblane. Height 1328 feet or 405 metres. **81 J6** NN7811.
Cromore *W.Isles Anglicised form of Gleann Ghrabhair, qv.*
Crompton *Gt.Man.* ***Suburb***, including localities of High Crompton and Crompton Fold, 3m/5km N of Oldham. SD9309.
Crompton Fold *Gt.Man.* ***Suburb***, to NE of Shaw, 3m/5km N of Oldham. **49 J2** SD9509.
Cromwell *Notts.* ***Village***, 5m/8km N of Newark-on-Trent. 1km E is site of Roman bridge across River Trent. **52 B6** SK7961.
Cromwell Bottom *W.Yorks.* ***Settlement***, 1m/2km W of Brighouse, on N side of River Calder. SE1222.
Cromwell's Castle *I.o.S.* ***Castle***, mid-17c round tower (English Heritage) built on NW coast of Tresco by Oliver Cromwell to defend New Grimsby harbour. **2 B1** SV8815.
Cronberry *E.Ayr.* ***Village***, 3m/5km NE of Cumnock. **68 B1** NS6022.
Crondall *Hants.* ***Village***, 3m/5km NW of Farnham. Site of Roman villa 1m/2km S. **22 A7** SU7948.
Cronk-y-Voddy *I.o.M.* ***Settlement***, 3m/5km N of St. John's. **54 C5** SC3085.
Cronkley Fell *Dur.* ***Open space***, moorland 3m/5km SE of Cow Green Reservoir. **61 K4** NY8427.
Cronton *Mersey.* ***Village***, 2m/4km NW of Widnes. **48 D4** SJ4988.
Cronwern *Pembs. Welsh form of Crunwere, qv.*
Crook *Cumb.* ***Village***, 4m/6km W of Kendal. **61 F7** SD4695.
Crook *Dur.* Population: 8246. ***Small town***, 5m/8km NW of Bishop Auckland. **62 C3** NZ1635.
Crook Aldersey *Ches.* ***Locality***, adjoining to E of Coddington. SJ4555.
Crook Gate *Lancs.* ***Settlement***, 2m/3km E of Hambleton. SD4042.
Crook of Devon *P. & K.* ***Village***, on bend of River Devon, 5m/9km W of Kinross. **82 B7** NO0300.
Crookdale *Cumb.* ***Locality***, 3m/5km E of Aspatria. NY1943.
Crooke *Gt.Man.* ***Hamlet***, on Leeds and Liverpool Canal, 3m/4km NW of Wigan. SD5507.
Crooked End *Glos.* ***Locality***, adjoining to E of Ruardean, 3m/5km NW of Cinderford. SO6217.
Crooked Oak *Devon* ***River***, rising on S foothills of Exmoor and flowing W through Ash Mill into River Mole at Alswear, 3m/4km S of South Molton. **7 F3** SS7222.
Crooked Soley *Wilts.* ***Settlement***, 3m/5km NW of Hungerford. SU3172.
Crookedholm *E.Ayr.* ***Locality***, 2m/3km E of Kilmarnock town centre. **74 C7** NS4537.
Crookedshaws Hill *Sc.Bord.* ***Mountain***, 2m/3km E of Morebattle. Height 1010 feet or 308 metres. **70 C1** NT8024.
Crookes *S.Yorks.* ***Suburb***, 2m/3km W of Sheffield city centre. SK3287.
Crookesmoor *S.Yorks.* ***Suburb***, 1m/2km W of Sheffield city centre. SK3387.
Crookfoot Reservoir *Hart.* ***Reservoir***, small reservoir on border with Durham, 2m/3km SW of Elwick and 5m/8km W of Hartlepool. **63 F3** NZ4331.
Crookgate Bank *Dur.* ***Locality***, just SE of Burnopfield. NZ1856.
Crookhall *Dur.* ***Locality***, adjoining to SE of Consett. NZ1150.
Crookham *Northumb.* ***Hamlet***, on River Till, 4m/6km E of Cornhill on Tweed. **77 H7** NT9138.
Crookham *W.Berks.* ***Hamlet***, 4m/6km NE of Kingsclare. **21 J5** SU5464.
Crookham Eastfield *Northumb.* ***Settlement***, 1km NW of Crookham. NT9039.
Crookham Village *Hants.* ***Village***, 2m/3km SW of Fleet. **22 A6** SU7952.
Crookhill *T. & W.* ***Suburb***, adjoining to SE of Ryton. NZ1663.
Crooklands *Cumb.* ***Hamlet***, 6m/9km S of Kendal. **55 J1** SD5383.
Crookston *Glas.* ***Suburb***, 2m/4km E of Paisley. NS5263.
Crookston Castle *Glas.* ***Castle***, early 15c castle (Historic Scotland) surrounded by 12c earthworks, 3m/4km SE of Paisley. **74 D4** NS5262.
Croome D'Abitôt *Worcs.* ***Locality***, 7m/11km S of Worcester. SO8844.
Cropredy *Oxon.* ***Village***, 4m/6km N of Banbury. Site of Civil War battle, 1644. **31 F4** SP4646.
Cropston *Leics.* ***Village***, 5m/7km NW of Leicester. **41 H4** SK5510.
Cropston Reservoir *Leics.* ***Reservoir***, to W of Cropston. **41 H4** SK5510.
Cropthorne *Worcs.* ***Village***, on S bank of River Avon, 3m/4km W of Evesham. **29 J4** SO9944.
Cropton *N.Yorks.* ***Village***, 4m/7km NW of Pickering. **58 D1** SE7589.
Cropton Forest *N.Yorks.* ***Forest/woodland***, large area of afforestation between Pickering to S and Wheeldale Moor to N. **63 J7** SE7894.
Cropwell Bishop *Notts.* Population: 1802. ***Village***, 8m/12km SE of Nottingham. **41 J2** SK6835.
Cropwell Butler *Notts.* ***Village***, 8m/12km SE of Nottingham. **41 J2** SK6837.
Cros (Anglicised form: Cross.) *W.Isles* ***Village***, near N end of Isle of Lewis, 2m/4km SW of Port Nis. **101 G1** NB5062.
Crosbie *N.Ayr.* ***Settlement***, 1m/2km NE of West Kilbride. **74 A6** NS2150.
Crosbost (Anglicised form: Crossbost.) *W.Isles* ***Village***, on E coast of Isle of Lewis, on N side of entrance to Loch Leurbost. **101 F5** NB3924.
Crosby *Cumb.* ***Village***, 3m/4km NE of Maryport. **60 B3** NY0738.
Crosby *I.o.M.* ***Village***, 4m/7km NW of Douglas. **54 C6** SC3279.
Crosby *Mersey.* Population: 52,869. ***Town***, on coast opposite Crosby Channel at mouth of River Mersey, 6m/9km N of Liverpool. **48 C3** SJ3198.
Crosby *N.Lincs.* ***Suburb***, NW district of Scunthorpe. **52 B1** SE8711.
Crosby Channel *Mersey.* ***Sea feature***, at mouth of River Mersey, 6m/9km N of Liverpool. **48 B2** SJ2899.
Crosby Court *N.Yorks.* ***Settlement***, 2m/3km SE of Northallerton. **62 E7** SE3991.
Crosby Garrett *Cumb.* ***Village***, 3m/5km W of Kirkby Stephen. **61 J6** NY7209.
Crosby Ravensworth *Cumb.* ***Village***, 5m/9km SW of Appleby-in-Westmorland. Site of ancient settlement of Ewe Close 1m/2km SW. **61 H5** NY6214.
Crosby Ravensworth Fell *Cumb.* ***Open space***, moorland 1m/2km NW of Orton. **61 H5** NY6010.
Crosby Villa *Cumb.* ***Hamlet***, 4m/6km NE of Maryport. NY0939.
Crosby Warren *N.Lincs.* ***Open space***, lowland, containing several lakes, to NE of Scunthorpe. **52 C1** SE9012.
Crosbymoor *Cumb.* ***Locality***, 4m/7km W of Brampton. NY4659.
Croscombe *Som.* ***Village***, 3m/5km E of Wells. **19 J7** ST5944.
Crose Mere *Shrop.* ***Lake/loch***, one of several lakes in district, 3m/5km SE of Ellesmere. **38 D2** SJ4330.
Crosemere *Shrop.* ***Settlement***, adjoining to N of Cockshutt. SJ4329.
Crosland Edge *W.Yorks.* ***Settlement***, 1m/2km NE of Meltham. SE1012.
Crosland Hill *W.Yorks.* ***Suburb***, 2m/3km SW of Huddersfield town centre. SE1114.
Cross *Som.* ***Village***, 1m/2km W of Axbridge. **19 H6** ST4154.
Cross *W.Yorks.* ***Locality***, 1m/2km SW of Cleckheaton. SE1723.
Cross *W.Isles Anglicised form of Cros, qv.*
Cross Ash *Mon.* ***Hamlet***, 3m/5km W of Skenfrith. **28 D7** SO4019.

C

Cross-at-Hand *Kent* ***Hamlet***, 2m/3km N of Staplehurst. **14 C3** TQ7846.
Cross Bank *Worcs.* ***Hamlet***, 3m/4km SW of Bewdley. SO7573.
Cross Bush *W.Suss.* ***Hamlet***, 1m/2km SE of Arundel. **12 D6** TQ0306.
Cross Drain *Lincs.* ***Other water feature***, artificial drainage channel running from NE of Langtoft, SE to River Welland, 3m/4km E of Deeping St. James. **42 E4** TF1514.
Cross End *Beds.* ***Settlement***, 1km E of Thurleigh. TL0658.
Cross End *Essex* ***Settlement***, adjoining to NE of Pebmarsh, 4m/6km NE of Halstead. TL8533.
Cross End *M.K.* ***Settlement***, adjoining to E of Wavendon, 4m/6km NW of Woburn. SP9137.
Cross Fell *Cumb.* ***Mountain***, summit of The Pennines, 4m/6km NE of Milburn. Height 2929 feet or 893 metres. **61 H3** NY6834.
Cross Foxes Inn *Gwyn.* ***Settlement***, 2m/3km SE of Dolgellau. **37 G4** SH7616.
Cross Gates *W.Yorks.* ***Suburb***, 4m/6km E of Leeds city centre. **57 J6** SE3534.
Cross Green *Devon* ***Settlement***, 4m/7km NE of Launceston. **6 B7** SX3888.
Cross Green *Staffs.* ***Settlement***, 1km SE of Coven. SJ9106.
Cross Green *Suff.* ***Hamlet***, 6m/9km SE of Bury St. Edmunds. **34 C3** TL8955.
Cross Green *Suff.* ***Hamlet***, 5m/9km SW of Stowmarket. **34 D3** TL9852.
Cross Green *Suff.* ***Settlement***, just N of Hartest, 5m/7km NW of Long Melford. TL8352.
Cross Green *W.Yorks.* ***Locality***, 2m/3km SE of Leeds city centre. Industrial estate. SE3232.
Cross Hands *Carmar.* Population: 9520. ***Small town***, 8m/13km N of Llanelli. **17 J3** SN5612.
Cross Hands *Pembs.* ***Settlement***, 2m/3km S of Canaston Bridge. **16 D3** SN0712.
Cross Hill *Derbys.* ***Locality***, 2m/3km NW of Heanor. **41 G1** SK4148.
Cross Hill *Sc.Bord.* ***Mountain***, 4m/7km SW of Ettrick. Height 1450 feet or 442 metres. **69 H3** NT2507.
Cross Hills *N.Yorks.* ***Settlement***, in Airedale, 4m/7km NW of Keighley. **57 F5** SE0045.
Cross Houses *Shrop.* ***Settlement***, 1m/2km SW of Bridgnorth. SO6991.
Cross Houses *Shrop.* ***Village***, 4m/7km SE of Shrewsbury. **38 E5** SJ5407.
Cross in Hand *E.Suss.* ***Village***, 1m/2km W of Heathfield. **13 J4** TQ5621.
Cross Inn *Cere.* ***Hamlet***, 5m/9km E of Aberaeron. **26 E2** SN5464.
Cross Inn *Cere.* ***Village***, 2m/3km S of New Quay. **26 C3** SN3857.
Cross Inn *R.C.T.* ***Hamlet***, 5m/7km S of Pontypridd. **18 D3** ST0583.
Cross Keys *Kent* ***Suburb***, in SW part of Sevenoaks. TQ5253.
Cross Keys *Wilts.* ***Locality***, on N side of Corsham. **20 B4** ST8771.
Cross Lane *I.o.W.* ***Suburb***, NE district of Newport. SZ5089.
Cross Lane Head *Shrop.* ***Village***, 2m/3km N of Bridgnorth. **39 G6** SO7095.
Cross Lanes *Bucks.* ***Locality***, 2m/3km W of Princes Risborough. SP7702.
Cross Lanes *Cornw.* ***Settlement***, 4m/7km SE of Helston. **2 D6** SW6921.
Cross Lanes *Cornw.* ***Settlement***, 4m/6km SW of Truro. **2 E4** SW7642.
Cross Lanes *N.Yorks.* ***Settlement***, 3m/5km S of Easingwold. **58 B3** SE5265.
Cross Lanes *Wrex.* ***Village***, 3m/5km SE of Wrexham. **38 C1** SJ3746.
Cross Law *Sc.Bord.* ***Hill***, 3m/4km NW of Coldingham. Height 745 feet or 227 metres. **77 G4** NT8768.
Cross Moor *Cumb.* ***Settlement***, 2m/3km SW of Ulverston. SD2676.
Cross Oak *Powys* ***Locality***, 1m/2km NW of Talybont-on-Usk. SO1023.
Cross of Jackston *Aber.* ***Settlement***, at road junction, 5m/8km NW of Oldmeldrum. **91 F1** NJ7432.
Cross o'th'hands *Derbys.* ***Hamlet***, 4m/7km W of Belper. **40 E1** SK2846.
Cross Rigg *Dur.* ***Mountain***, 1m/2km S of Edmundbyers. Height 1276 feet or 389 metres. **62 B2** NZ0247.
Cross Street *Suff.* ***Village***, 3m/5km NE of Eye. **35 F1** TM1876.
Cross Town *Ches.* ***Suburb***, E district of Knutsford. SJ7578.
Cross Water *S.Ayr.* ***River***, rising in Arecleoch Forest and flowing NE to join Duisk River at Barrhill, 9m/15km E of Ballantrae. **64 C3** NX2382.
Cross Water of Luce ***River***, rising in vicinity of Arecleoch Forest, E of Ballantrae, and flowing S to join Main Water of Luce at New Luce, to form Water of Luce. **64 B4** NX1764.
Crossaig *Arg. & B.* ***Settlement***, on E coast of Kintyre, 5m/7km N of Grogport. **73 G5** NR8351.
Crossapol *Arg. & B.* ***Settlement***, in SW part of Coll, overlooking Crossapol Bay. **78 C2** NM1253.
Crossapol Bay *Arg. & B.* ***Bay***, wide bay on S coast of Coll, near SW end of island. **78 C2** NM1352.
Crossapoll *Arg. & B.* ***Settlement***, on S coast of Tiree, 3m/5km W of Scarinish. **78 A3** NL9943.
Crossbarrow *Cumb.* ***Locality***, 3m/5km E of Workington. NY0428.
Crossbost *W.Isles* *Anglicised form of Crosbost, qv.*
Crossbush *W.Suss.* ***Hamlet***, 1m/2km SE of Arundel. TQ0306.
Crosscanonby *Cumb.* ***Village***, 3m/4km NE of Maryport. **60 B3** NY0639.
Crossdale Street *Norf.* ***Village***, 2m/3km S of Cromer. **45 G2** TG2239.
Crossdougal *W.Isles* *Anglicised form of Crois Dughaill, qv.*
Crossens *Mersey.* ***Suburb***, 3m/4km NE of Southport town centre. **55 G7** SD3719.
Crossflatts *W.Yorks.* ***Suburb***, NW district of Bingley, between River Aire and Leeds and Liverpool Canal. SE1040.
Crossford *D. & G.* ***Settlement***, 4m/6km E of Moniaive. **68 D5** NX8388.
Crossford *Fife* Population: 2756. ***Village***, 2m/3km W of Dunfermline. **75 J2** NT0686.
Crossford *S.Lan.* ***Village***, near confluence of Rivers Nethan and Clyde, 3m/4km SW of Carluke. **75 G6** NS8246.
Crossgate *Lincs.* ***Hamlet***, 1km N of Pinchbeck. **43 F3** TF2426.
Crossgate *Staffs.* ***Settlement***, 4m/6km NE of Stone. SJ9437.
Crossgatehall *E.Loth.* ***Hamlet***, 3m/4km NE of Dalkeith. **76 B4** NT3669.
Crossgates *Cumb.* ***Locality***, 1m/2km W of Lamplugh. NY0721.
Crossgates *Fife* Population: 1937. ***Village***, 2m/3km SW of Cowdenbeath. **75 K2** NT1488.
Crossgates *N.Yorks.* ***Settlement***, 3m/4km S of Scarborough. TA0384.
Crossgates *P. & K.* ***Settlement***, 4m/7km SW of Perth. **82 B5** NO0420.
Crossgates *Powys* ***Hamlet***, at crossroads, 3m/5km NE of Llandrindod Wells. **27 K2** SO0864.
Crossgill *Cumb.* ***Locality***, at confluence of Cross Gill and River South Tyne, 1km SE of Garrigill. NY7440.
Crossgill *Lancs.* ***Hamlet***, 5m/8km E of Lancaster. **55 J3** SD5562.
Crosshands *Carmar.* ***Settlement***, 1m/2km W of Llanboidy. SN1922.
Crosshands *E.Ayr.* ***Settlement***, at road junction, 2m/4km NW of Mauchline. **74 C7** NS4830.
Crosshill *Fife* ***Locality***, adjoining to S of Lochore. **75 K1** NT1796.
Crosshill *Glas.* ***Suburb***, 2m/4km S of Glasgow city centre, in Govanhill district. NS5862.
Crosshill *Glas.* ***Suburb***, 6m/9km E of Glasgow, in Baillieston district. NS6863.
Crosshill *S.Ayr.* ***Village***, 3m/5km SE of Maybole. **67 H3** NS3206.
Crosshouse *E.Ayr.* Population: 2670. ***Village***, 2m/3km W of Kilmarnock. **74 B7** NS3938.
Crosskeys *Caerp.* ***Village***, 1m/2km NW of Risca. **19 F2** ST2291.
Crosskirk *High.* ***Settlement***, near N coast of Caithness district, 5m/9km W of Thurso. Ruined Chapel of St. Mary (Historic Scotland), probably 12c. **105 F1** ND0369.
Crosskirk Bay *High.* ***Bay***, small bay on N coast of Caithness district, to NW of Crosskirk. **105 F1** ND0270.
Crosslands *Cumb.* ***Hamlet***, 3m/4km NW of Newby Bridge. SD3489.
Crosslanes *Shrop.* ***Hamlet***, 7m/12km SE of Oswestry. **38 C4** SJ3218.
Crosslee *Renf.* ***Hamlet***, 2m/4km NW of Johnstone. **74 C4** NS4066.
Crosslee *Sc.Bord.* ***Hamlet***, 3m/5km NE of Ettrick. **69 J2** NT3018.
Crosslet *W.Dun.* ***Suburb***, NE district of Dumbarton. **74 C3** NS4076.
Crossley *W.Yorks.* ***Locality***, 1m/2km N of Mirfield. SE2021.
Crossley Hall *W.Yorks.* ***Suburb***, 2m/3km W of Bradford city centre. SE1333.
Crossmichael *D. & G.* ***Village***, 4m/6km NW of Castle Douglas. **65 H4** NX7366.
Crossmoor *Lancs.* ***Settlement***, 4m/7km N of Kirkham. **55 H6** SD4438.
Crossmyloof *Glas.* ***Suburb***, 2m/4km S of Glasgow city centre. NS5762.
Crossraguel Abbey *S.Ayr.* ***Ecclesiastical building***, mainly 15c to 16c ruins of abbey founded in 1244 (Historic Scotland), 2m/3km SW of Maybole. **67 G3** NS2708.
Crossroads *Aber.* ***Settlement***, 3m/5km SE of Banchory. **91 F5** NO7594.
Crossroads *E.Ayr.* ***Settlement***, at road junction, 4m/6km SE of Kilmarnock. **74 C7** NS4733.
Crossroads *Fife* ***Suburb***, central district of Methil. NT3699.
Crossway *Mon.* ***Settlement***, 1m/2km SW of Skenfrith. **28 D7** SO4419.
Crossway *Powys* ***Hamlet***, 2m/3km S of Llandrindod Wells. **27 K3** SO0457.
Crossway Green *Mon.* ***Suburb***, to NW of Chepstow town centre. ST5294.
Crossway Green *Worcs.* ***Village***, 3m/4km SE of Stourport-on-Severn. **29 H2** SO8468.
Crossways *Dorset* ***Village***, 6m/9km E of Dorchester. SY7788.
Crossways *Glos.* ***Settlement***, 1km NW of Coleford. **28 E7** SO5611.
Crosswell *Pembs.* ***Hamlet***, 2m/3km SW of Eglwyswrw. **16 E1** SN1236.
Crosswood (Trawsgoed). *Cere.* ***Settlement***, 3m/5km SE of Llanilar. SN6672.
Crosswood Reservoir *W.Loth.* ***Reservoir***, 4m/7km SE of West Calder. **75 J5** NT0557.
Crosthwaite *Cumb.* ***Hamlet***, 4m/7km W of Kendal. **60 F7** SD4491.
Croston *Lancs.* Population: 2622. ***Village***, 6m/10km W of Chorley. **48 D1** SD4818.
Crostwick *Norf.* ***Hamlet***, 5m/8km NE of Norwich. **45 G4** TG2516.
Crostwight *Norf.* ***Locality***, 3m/5km E of North Walsham. **45 H3** TG3330.
Crouch *Essex* ***River***, rising W of Basildon and flowing E into North Sea to N of Foulness Island. Estuary well known for yachting. **25 F2** TR0396.
Crouch *Kent* ***Hamlet***, 1m/2km SE of Borough Green. **23 K6** TQ6155.
Crouch End *Gt.Lon.* ***Suburb***, in borough of Haringey, 5m/8km N of Charing Cross. TQ2988.
Crouch Hill *Dorset* ***Hamlet***, 2m/3km S of Bishop's Caundle. **9 G3** ST7010.
Croucheston *Wilts.* ***Hamlet***, adjoining to S of Bishopstone, 4m/7km SW of Wilton. SU0625.
Croughton *Northants.* ***Village***, 4m/6km SW of Brackley. **31 G5** SP5433.
Crovie *Aber.* ***Village***, on E side of Gamrie Bay, 6m/10km E of Macduff. **99 G4** NJ8065.
Crovie Head *Aber.* ***Coastal feature***, headland to N of Crovie. **99 G4** NJ8066.
Crow *Hants.* ***Hamlet***, 1m/2km SE of Ringwood. **10 C4** SU1603.
Crow Castle *Denb.* *Alternative name for Castell Dinas Bran, qv.*
Crow Edge *S.Yorks.* ***Settlement***, 4m/6km W of Penistone. SE1804.
Crow End *Cambs.* ***Village***, N end of Bourn. TL3257.
Crow Green *Essex* ***Hamlet***, 2m/3km NW of Brentwood. TQ5896.
Crow Hill *Here.* ***Village***, 3m/5km NE of Ross-on-Wye. **29 F6** SO6426.
Crow Nest *W.Yorks.* ***Suburb***, to E of Bingley town centre. SE1139.
Crow Rock *Pembs.* ***Island***, islet, 1km SE of Linney Head. **16 B5** SR8894.
Crow Sound *I.o.S.* ***Sea feature***, strait between NE coast of St. Mary's and Eastern Isles. **2 C1** SV9213.
Crowan *Cornw.* ***Village***, 3m/5km S of Camborne. **2 D5** SW6434.
Crowan Beacon *Cornw.* ***Hill***, 1m/2km E of Crowan. Height 728 feet or 222 metres. **2 D5** SW6635.
Crowborough *E.Suss.* Population: 19,563. ***Town***, in elevated position to E of Ashdown Forest, 7m/11km SW of Royal Tunbridge Wells. **13 J3** TQ5131.
Crowborough Town *E.Suss.* ***Suburb***, to NW of Crowborough. TQ5131.
Crowcombe *Som.* ***Village***, at foot at Quantock Hills, 6m/10km SE of Watchet. **7 K2** ST1436.
Crowdecote *Derbys.* ***Hamlet***, 1m/2km E of Longnor. **50 D6** SK1065.
Crowden *Derbys.* ***Hamlet***, on N shore of Torside Reservoir, 4m/6km E of Tintwistle. Mountain rescue post. SK0799.
Crowden *Devon* ***Hamlet***, 7m/11km NW of Okehampton. SX4999.
Crowdhill *Hants.* ***Hamlet***, 2m/4km E of Eastleigh. **11 F2** SU4920.
Crowdundle Beck *Cumb.* ***River***, rising on SE slope of Cross Fell and flowing SW into River Eden between Culgaith and Temple Sowerby. **61 H3** NY6028.
Crowell *Oxon.* ***Hamlet***, 3m/4km NW of Stokenchurch. SU7499.
Crowfield *Northants.* ***Hamlet***, 4m/6km NE of Brackley. **31 H4** SP6141.
Crowfield *Suff.* ***Village***, 4m/7km SW of Debenham. **35 F3** TM1457.
Crowfield Green *Suff.* ***Locality***, 1km N of Crowfield. TM1457.
Crowgate Street *Norf.* ***Settlement***, 3m/5km N of Wroxham. TG3021.
Crowhole *Derbys.* ***Settlement***, adjoining to N of Common Side, 4m/7km NW of Chesterfield. SK3375.
Crowhurst *E.Suss.* ***Village***, 4m/7km NW of Hastings. **14 C6** TQ7512.
Crowhurst *Surr.* ***Hamlet***, 3m/5km S of Oxted. **23 G7** TQ3947.
Crowhurst Lane End *Surr.* ***Hamlet***, 3m/5km SE of Godstone. **23 G7** TQ3748.
Crowland *Lincs.* Population: 3172. ***Small town***, in Fens, 8m/13km NE of Peterborough. Remains of abbey founded in 8c. Triangular bridge of 14c. **43 F4** TF2310.
Crowland *Suff.* ***Hamlet***, 1m/2km SE of Walsham le Willows. **34 E1** TM0170.
Crowland Abbey *Lincs.* ***Ecclesiastical building***, originally one of the great Saxon abbeys in E of England, 8m/12km S of Spalding. Partly 12c, with ruined Norman arch. Bell dates from 15c. **43 F4** TF2410.
Crowland Common *Lincs.* ***Open space***, lowland 2m/3km NW of Crowland. **43 F4** TF2011.
Crowlas *Cornw.* ***Village***, 3m/5km NE of Penzance. **2 C5** SW5133.
Crowle *N.Lincs.* Population: 2916. ***Village***, 8m/12km W of Scunthorpe across River Trent. **51 K1** SE7712.
Crowle *Worcs.* ***Village***, 5m/7km E of Worcester. **29 J3** SO9256.
Crowle Green *Worcs.* ***Hamlet***, adjoining to N of Crowle, 4m/7km NE of Worcester. **29 J3** SO9156.
Crowlin Islands *High.* ***Island***, group of three islands lying close together 1m/2km off W coast of Ross and Cromarty district on N side of entrance to Loch Carron. Total area 420 acres or 170 hectares. Eilean Mòr is largest and nearest to mainland. Eilean Meadhonach lies to its W; Eilean Beag, smallest, is immediately N of Eilean Meadhonach. Beacon on Eilean Beag. **86 C1** NG6934.
Crowlista *W.Isles* *Anglicised form of Cradhlastadh, qv.*
Crowmarsh *Oxon.* *Alternative name for Crowmarsh Gifford, qv.*
Crowmarsh Gifford (Also known as Crowmarsh.) *Oxon.* ***Village***, across River Thames from Wallingford. **21 K3** SU6189.
Crown Corner *Suff.* ***Hamlet***, 3m/5km SE of Stradbroke. TM2570.
Crown Hills *Leic.* ***Suburb***, 2m/3km E of Leicester city centre. SK6204.
Crown Wood *Brack.F.* ***Suburb***, SE district of Bracknell. SU8767.
Crownhill *Plym.* ***Suburb***, 3m/5km N of Plymouth city centre. **4 E5** SX4858.
Crownpits *Surr.* ***Suburb***, to SE of Godalming town centre. SU9743.
Crownthorpe *Norf.* ***Village***, 2m/3km NW of Wymondham. **44 E5** TG0803.
Crowntown *Cornw.* ***Hamlet***, 3m/4km NW of Helston. **2 D5** SW6330.

Crowpill *Som.* ***Suburb***, N district of Bridgwater. ST2937.
Crows-an-wra *Cornw.* ***Hamlet***, 4m/6km NE of Land's End. **2 A6** SW3927.
Crow's Nest *Cornw.* ***Hamlet***, 3m/5km N of Liskeard. SX2669.
Crow's Nest *D. & G.* ***Coastal feature***, headland to NW of Stairhaven, 3m/4km S of Glenluce. **64 B5** NX2053.
Crowsnest *Shrop.* ***Settlement***, 1km SW of Snailbeach. SJ3601.
Crowther *T. & W.* ***Locality***, industrial estate in W part of Washington. NZ2856.
Crowthorne *Brack.F.* Population: 21,500. ***Town***, 4m/6km SW of Bracknell. Important local establishments include Wellington College, Broadmoor Hospital and Road Research Laboratory. **22 B5** SU8464.
Crowton *Ches.* ***Village***, 5m/8km W of Northwich. **48 E5** SJ5774.
Croxall *Staffs.* ***Hamlet***, 6m/10km N of Tamworth. **40 D4** SK1913.
Croxby *Lincs.* ***Hamlet***, 3m/5km NW of Binbrook. TF1998.
Croxby Top *Lincs.* ***Locality***, 1m/2km W of Croxby. TF1698.
Croxdale *Dur.* ***Village***, 2m/3km N of Spennymoor. **62 D3** NZ2636.
Croxden *Staffs.* ***Hamlet***, 4m/7km SE of Cheadle. Remains of Early English abbey (English Heritage). **40 C2** SK0639.
Croxden Abbey *Staffs.* ***Ecclesiastical building***, ruined Cistercian abbey founded in 1176, 5m/8km N of Uttoxeter. Chief survival is magnificent W end of church. **40 C1** SK0639.
Croxley Green *Herts.* ***Locality***, 1m/2km NE of Rickmansworth. **22 D2** TQ0795.
Croxteth Hall *Mersey.* ***Historic house***, 5m/8km NE of Liverpool city centre. Early 20c home of Molyneux family, Earls of Sefton. 500 acre park includes Victorian farm and walled garden, with farm animals and mini-railway. **48 D3** SJ4194.
Croxton *Cambs.* ***Hamlet***, on edge of park, 4m/6km E of St. Neots. **33 F3** TL2459.
Croxton *Norf.* ***Village***, 2m/4km N of Thetford. **44 C7** TL8786.
Croxton *N.Lincs.* ***Village***, 7m/11km NE of Brigg. **52 E1** TA0912.
Croxton *Staffs.* ***Hamlet***, 3m/5km NW of Eccleshall. **39 G2** SJ7831.
Croxton Green *Ches.* ***Settlement***, 7m/11km N of Whitchurch. **48 E7** SJ5452.
Croxton Kerrial *Leics.* ***Village***, 7m/11km SW of Grantham. **42 B3** SK8329.
Croxtonbank *Staffs.* ***Hamlet***, 1km NW of Croxton. **39 G2** SJ7831.
Croy *High.* ***Village***, in Inverness district close to border with Nairn district, 7m/11km SW of Nairn. **96 E7** NH7649.
Croy *N.Lan.* Population: 1148. ***Village***, 1m/2km SE of Kilsyth. **75 F3** NS7275.
Croy Brae *S.Ayr.* ***Open space***, hillslope near coast at N end of Culzean Bay, where by an optical illusion known as 'Electric Brae' a downward slope appears to go upward. **67 G2** NS2513.
Croyde *Devon* ***Village***, 7m/12km SW of Ilfracombe, on stream running down to Croyde Bay, SE of Baggy Point. **6 C2** SS4439.
Croyde Bay *Devon* ***Bay***, SE of Baggy Point, to W of Croyde. **6 C2** SS4239.
Croyde Bay *Devon* ***Hamlet***, on coast, to W of Croyde. SS4339.
Croydon *Cambs.* ***Village***, 6m/10km NW of Royston. **33 G4** TL3149.
Croydon *Gt.Lon.* ***Town***, 9m/15km S of Charing Cross. Former palace of Archbishops of Canterbury, now a school, situated adjacent to 19c parish church. TQ3265.
Croydon Hill *Som.* ***Forest/woodland***, afforested upland area of North Exmoor to S of Dunster. **7 H1** SS9740.
Cruach *Arg. & B.* ***Settlement***, 1m/2km SE of Bowmore, Islay. **72 B5** NR3258.
Cruach a' Bhuic *Arg. & B.* ***Mountain***, partly in Argyll Forest Park, 2m/3km W of Carrick. Height 2083 feet or 635 metres. **73 K1** NS1693.
Cruach a' Ghaill *High.* ***Mountain***, in Moidart, Lochaber district, 3m/4km SE of Ardmolich. Height 1217 feet or 371 metres. **86 D7** NM7570.
Cruach a' Phubuill *Arg. & B.* ***Mountain***, on Knapdale, 5m/8km NW of Tarbert. Height 1565 feet or 477 metres. **73 G3** NR8276.
Cruach Airde *Arg. & B.* ***Hill***, on W of Kintyre, 1m/2km E of Kilberry. Height 699 feet or 213 metres. **73 F4** NR7363.
Cruach Airdeny *Arg. & B.* ***Mountain***, 2m/3km N of head of Loch Nant. Height 1299 feet or 396 metres. **80 A5** NM9927.
Cruach an Eachlaich *Arg. & B.* ***Mountain***, 2m/3km N of Ford. Height 1148 feet or 350 metres. **79 K7** NM8606.
Cruach an Lochain *Arg. & B.* ***Mountain***, 6m/9km SW of Strachur. Height 1666 feet or 508 metres. **73 J1** NS0493.
Cruach an t-Sorchain *Arg. & B.* ***Mountain***, on Kintyre, 2m/3km S of Tarbert. Height 1125 feet or 343 metres. **73 G4** NR8765.
Cruach Ardrain *Stir.* ***Mountain***, 3m/5km SE of Crianlarich. Munro: height 3428 feet or 1045 metres. **81 F5** NN4021.
Cruach Ardura *Arg. & B.* ***Hill***, on Mull, 6m/9km NE of Lochbuie. Height 708 feet or 216 metres. **79 H5** NM6629.
Cruach Bhrochdadail *High.* ***Mountain***, in Moidart, 3m/4km E of Rois-bheinn. Height 1171 feet or 357 metres. **86 D7** NM7176.
Cruach Breacain *Arg. & B.* ***Mountain***, on Knapdale, 2m/3km W of Ardrishaig. Height 1181 feet or 360 metres. **73 G2** NR8286.
Cruach Choireadail *Arg. & B.* ***Mountain***, 4m/6km S of head of Loch Bà, Mull. Height 2027 feet or 618 metres. **79 G4** NM5930.
Cruach Chuilceachan *Arg. & B.* ***Mountain***, on Cowal peninsula, 9m/14km N of Tighnabruaich. Height 1427 feet or 435 metres. **73 H2** NR9887.
Cruach Doire Léithe *Arg. & B.* ***Mountain***, on Kintyre, 3m/5km S of Tarbert. Height 1237 feet or 377 metres. **73 G4** NR8763.
Cruach Doire 'n Dòbhrain *High.* ***Hill***, 3m/4km SW of Arisaig, Lochaber district. Height 338 feet or 103 metres. **86 C6** NM6384.
Cruach Fasgach *Arg. & B.* ***Mountain***, 2m/3km S of Garbhallt. Height 1096 feet or 334 metres. **73 J1** NS0293.
Cruach Ionnastail *Arg. & B.* ***Hill***, in N part of Jura, 3m/4km N of Ardlussa. Height 968 feet or 295 metres. **72 E1** NR6491.
Cruach Lusach *Arg. & B.* ***Mountain***, in Knapdale, 4m/7km SW of Ardrishaig. Height 1528 feet or 466 metres. **73 F2** NR7883.
Cruach Mhic-an-t-Saoir *Arg. & B.* ***Mountain***, on Kintyre, 4m/6km W of Grogport. Height 1194 feet or 364 metres. **73 F6** NR7442.
Cruach Mhic-Gougain *Arg. & B.* ***Hill***, on Kintyre, 5m/8km NW of Grogport. Height 813 feet or 248 metres. **73 F6** NR7550.
Cruach Mhòr *Arg. & B.* ***Mountain***, in Argyll, 4m/7km NW of Inveraray. Height 1932 feet or 589 metres. **80 B6** NN0514.
Cruach na Seilcheig *Arg. & B.* ***Hill***, on Jura, 2m/3km W of Aird of Kinuachdrachd and 7m/11km N of Ardlussa. Height 971 feet or 296 metres. **72 E1** NR6898.
Cruach nam Fearna *Arg. & B.* ***Mountain***, 1m/2km NW of Melfort. Height 1089 feet or 332 metres. **79 K6** NM8215.
Cruach nam Fiadh *Arg. & B.* ***Hill***, on Kintyre, 3m/5km W of Claonaig. Height 882 feet or 269 metres. **73 G5** NR8256.
Cruach nam Miseag *Arg. & B.* ***Mountain***, with craggy summit in Argyll Forest Park, rising above W shore of Loch Goil and 3m/4km SW of Lochgoilhead. Height 1988 feet or 606 metres. **73 K1** NS1898.
Cruach nam Mult *Arg. & B.* ***Mountain***, 4m/7km SE of Inveraray across Loch Fyne. Height 2004 feet or 611 metres. **80 C7** NN1605.
Cruach nan Caorach *Arg. & B.* ***Mountain***, on Cowal peninsula with craggy face, 5m/8km N of Tighnabruaich. Height 1502 feet or 458 metres. **73 H2** NR9980.
Cruach nan Capull *Arg. & B.* ***Mountain***, in Argyll, 4m/6km SE of Inveraray across Loch Fyne. Height 1853 feet or 565 metres. **80 C7** NN1405.
Cruach nan Capull *Arg. & B.* ***Mountain***, 3m/5km SW of Strachur. Height 1578 feet or 481 metres. **73 J1** NS0797.
Cruach nan Capull *Arg. & B.* ***Mountain***, overlooking Loch Striven, 5m/8km W of Dunoon. Height 2004 feet or 611 metres. **73 J3** NS0979.
Cruach nan Con *Arg. & B.* ***Mountain***, 4m/6km E of Pennyghael, Mull. Height 1627 feet or 496 metres. **79 G5** NM5726.
Cruach nan Cuilean *Arg. & B.* ***Mountain***, 1km NW of Loch Striven and 11m/17km SW of Strachur. Height 1417 feet or 432 metres. **73 J2** NS0484.
Cruach nan Gabhar *Arg. & B.* ***Mountain***, on Kintyre, 4m/6km SW of Grogport. Height 1161 feet or 354 metres. **73 F6** NR7541.
Cruach Neuran *Arg. & B.* ***Mountain***, rising above S shore of Loch Tarsan. Height 1991 feet or 607 metres. **73 J2** NS0881.
Cruach Scarba *Arg. & B.* ***Mountain***, highest point on Scarba, 1m/2km NW of Rubha Righinn. Height 1473 feet or 449 metres. **79 H7** NM6904.
Cruach Sganadail *Arg. & B.* ***Mountain***, in N part of Jura, 3m/4km W of Lussagiven. Height 1181 feet or 360 metres. **72 D2** NR5987.
Cruach Sléibhe *Arg. & B.* ***Hill***, 1km NW of Calgary, Mull. Height 544 feet or 166 metres. **78 E2** NM3752.
Cruach Tairbeirt *Arg. & B.* ***Mountain***, between N end of Loch Long and W side of Loch Lomond, 1km N of Tarbet. Height 1361 feet or 415 metres. **80 D7** NN3105.
Cruach Torran Lochain *Arg. & B.* ***Mountain***, 1m/2km E of Gruline, Mull. Height 1138 feet or 347 metres. **79 G3** NM5640.
Cruachan *Stir.* ***Mountain***, on E side of Loch Lomond, 3m/5km NE of Tarbet across the loch. Height 1761 feet or 537 metres. **80 E7** NN3507.
Cruachan Beinn a' Chearcaill *High.* ***Hill***, 5m/8km N of Bracadale, Skye. Height 889 feet or 271 metres. **93 J7** NG3546.
Cruachan Ceann a' Ghairbh *Arg. & B.* ***Hill***, 3m/5km N of Fanmore, Mull. Height 856 feet or 261 metres. **79 F3** NM4248.
Cruachan Dearg *Arg. & B.* ***Mountain***, 3m/4km E of Ben More, Mull. Height 2309 feet or 704 metres. **79 G4** NM5633.
Cruachan Mìn *Arg. & B.* ***Mountain***, 3m/4km N of Rubha nam Bràithrean, Mull. Height 1233 feet or 376 metres. **79 F5** NM4421.
Cruachan Odhar *Arg. & B.* ***Hill***, 1m/2km NW of Kilninian, Mull. Height 840 feet or 256 metres. **78 E3** NM3846.
Cruachan Reservoir *Arg. & B.* ***Reservoir***, 1m/2km SE of Ben Cruachan, in Argyll, with hydro-electric power station. **80 B5** NN0828.
Cruban Beag *High.* ***Mountain***, in Badenoch and Strathspey district, 5m/8km SW of Newtonmore. Height 1935 feet or 590 metres. **88 D5** NN6692.
Cruchie *Aber.* ***Settlement***, 4m/6km NE of Huntly. **98 D6** NJ5842.
Crucifixion Cave *Arg. & B.* *See Davaar Island.*
Cruckmeole *Shrop.* ***Hamlet***, 4m/7km SW of Shrewsbury. **38 D5** SJ4309.
Cruckton *Shrop.* ***Hamlet***, 4m/7km SW of Shrewsbury. Site of Roman villa. **38 D4** SJ4310.
Crucywel *Powys* *Welsh form of Crickhowell, qv.*
Cruden Bay *Aber.* Population: 1708. ***Village***, near mouth of Water of Cruden, 7m/11km S of Peterhead, with Port Erroll adjoining to SE. **91 J1** NK0936.
Crudgington *Tel. & W.* ***Village***, 4m/7km N of Wellington. **39 F4** SJ6318.
Crudgington Green *Tel. & W.* ***Hamlet***, 1km SE of Crudgington. SJ6318.
Crudwell *Wilts.* ***Village***, 4m/6km N of Malmesbury. **20 C2** ST9592.
Cruffell *D. & G.* ***Mountain***, 6m/9km SW of Kirkconnel. Polvaird Loch is small loch to S of summit. Height 1827 feet or 557 metres. **68 B3** NS6804.
Crug *Powys* ***Settlement***, 6m/10km W of Knighton. **28 A1** SO1972.
Crug Mawr *Powys* ***Mountain***, 4m/6km NW of Crickhowell. Height 1804 feet or 550 metres. **28 B6** SO2622.
Cruggleton *D. & G.* ***Locality***, and ruined castle of the Comyns on W side of Wigtown Bay, 3m/5km NE of Whithorn. NX4843.
Cruggleton Bay (Also known as Rigg Bay.) *D. & G.* ***Bay***, to N of Cruggleton, on W side of Wigtown Bay. **64 E6** NX4844.
Cruggleton Castle *D. & G.* ***Castle***, on coast near Cruggleton Point, 2m/3km S of Garlieston. 12c-13c ruins of castle which belonged to Lords of Galloway, who ruled Scotland at this time. **64 E6** NX4843.
Crugion *Powys* *Welsh form of Criggion, qv.*
Crugmeer *Cornw.* ***Hamlet***, 1m/2km NW of Padstow. **3 G1** SW9076.
Crugybar *Carmar.* ***Settlement***, 2m/3km S of Pumsaint. **17 K1** SN6537.
Cruick Water *Angus* ***River***, rising in mountains N of Noranside, and flowing S before turning E to flow through a wide valley and entering West Water, 3m/4km SE of Edzell. **83 F1** NO6265.
Cruim Leacainn *High.* ***Hill***, 6m/9km NE of Fort William. Height 748 feet or 228 metres. **87 H6** NN1680.
Cruinn a' Bheinn *Stir.* ***Mountain***, peak between Ben Lomond and Loch Arklet. Height 2076 feet or 633 metres. **80 E7** NN3605.
Cruinn Bheinn *Stir.* ***Mountain***, on N side of Loch Katrine, 2m/3km NW of Stronachlachar across loch. Height 1788 feet or 545 metres. **81 F6** NN4312.
Cruivie Castle *Fife* ***Castle***, late 15c L-plan tower house, 2m/4km NW of Leuchars. **83 F5** NO4122.
Crùlabhig (Anglicised form: Crulivig.) *W.Isles* ***Settlement***, on W side of Isle of Lewis, 1km SE of bridge connecting Great Bernera with main island. **100 D4** NB1733.
Crulivig *W.Isles* *Anglicised form of Crùlabhig, qv.*
Crumlin (Crymlyn). *Caerp.* ***Locality***, adjoining to N of Newbridge. **19 F2** ST2198.
Crummock Water *Cumb.* ***Lake/loch***, National Trust property, formed by River Cocker between Loweswater and Buttermere, 3m/4km in length and 1km maximum width. **60 C5** NY1519.
Crumpfield *Worcs.* ***Suburb***, 2m/3km SW of Redditch town centre. SP0165.
Crumpsall *Gt.Man.* ***Suburb***, 3m/4km N of Manchester city centre. SD8402.
Crumpsbrook *Shrop.* ***Settlement***, 3m/5km NW of Cleobury Mortimer. SO6278.
Crumpton Hill *D. & G.* ***Mountain***, 4m/7km N of Langholm. Height 1574 feet or 480 metres. **69 J4** NY3491.
Crundale *Kent* ***Village***, 2m/4km NE of Wye. **15 F3** TR0749.
Crundale *Pembs.* ***Village***, 2m/3km NE of Haverfordwest. **16 C3** SM9718.
Crunwere (Cronwern). *Pembs.* ***Hamlet***, 4m/6km S of Whitland. SN1810.
Crutherland *S.Lan.* ***Settlement***, 2m/3km SE of East Kilbride. **74 E5** NS6651.
Cruwys Morchard *Devon* ***Settlement***, 5m/8km W of Tiverton. **7 G4** SS8712.
Crux Easton *Hants.* ***Hamlet***, 4m/6km NE of Hurstbourne Tarrant. **21 H6** SU4256.
Cruys *Angus* ***Mountain***, 3m/4km S of Glenlee. Height 2430 feet or 741 metres. **90 C7** NO4275.
Crwbin *Carmar.* ***Hamlet***, 6m/9km SE of Carmarthen. **17 H3** SN4713.
Crychan *Carmar.* ***River***, flowing SW into River Brân, 2m/3km NE of Llandovery. **27 H5** SN7837.
Crychan Forest ***Forest/woodland***, large afforested area straddling border of Carmarthenshire and Powys to NE of Llandovery. **27 H5** SN8338.
Cryers Hill *Bucks.* ***Village***, 3m/4km N of High Wycombe. **22 B2** SU8796.
Crymlyn *Caerp.* *Welsh form of Crumlin, qv.*
Crymlyn *Gwyn.* ***Settlement***, 3m/5km E of Bangor. **46 E5** SH6371.
Crymych *Pembs.* ***Village***, 8m/12km S of Cardigan. **16 E1** SN1833.
Crynant *N.P.T.* ***Village***, 5m/8km NE of Neath. **18 A1** SN7904.
Crynwedd *Pembs.* *Welsh form of Crinow, qv.*
Crystal Palace *Gt.Lon.* ***Other feature of interest***, site of glass exhibition hall originally erected in Hyde Park for Great Exhibition of 1851, later moved to this site and burnt out in 1936. Site now occupied by television mast and sports centre. Name is also applied to surrounding district. **23 G4** TQ3471.
Cuaig *High.* ***Settlement***, near W coast of Ross and Cromarty district, 1m/2km S of Rubha Chuaig. **94 D6** NG7057.
Cuan Sound *Arg. & B.* ***Sea feature***, narrow stretch of sea separating Seil and Luing. **79 J6** NM7514.
Cubbie Roo's Castle (Also known as Castle of Cobbie Row.) *Ork.* ***Castle***, remains of 12c Norse castle (Historic Scotland) on Wyre. Cubbie Roo or Cobbie Row are corruptions of 'Kolbein Hruga', the name of chieftain who built it. **106 D5** HY4426.

C

Cubbington *Warks.* ***Village***, 2m/4km NE of Royal Leamington Spa. **30 E2** SP3468.
Cubert *Cornw.* ***Village***, 3m/5km SW of Newquay. **2 E3** SW7857.
Cubitt Town *Gt.Lon.* ***Suburb***, on Isle of Dogs, borough of Tower Hamlets, on N bank of River Thames and 5m/8km E of Charing Cross. TQ3878.
Cubley *S.Yorks.* ***Suburb***, adjoining to S of Penistone. SE2402.
Cublington *Bucks.* ***Village***, 6m/9km N of Aylesbury. **32 B6** SP8322.
Cublington *Here.* ***Hamlet***, 7m/11km W of Hereford. SO4038.
Cuckfield *W.Suss.* Population: 2879. ***Small town***, 2m/3km W of Haywards Heath. **13 G4** TQ3024.
Cucklington *Som.* ***Village***, 3m/5km E of Wincanton. **9 G2** ST7527.
Cuckmere *E.Suss.* ***River***, rising near Heathfield and flowing S through gap in South Downs at Alfriston, then into English Channel at Cuckmere Haven. Notable for meanders as it approaches sea. **13 J6** TV5197.
Cuckney *Notts.* ***Village***, 7m/11km N of Mansfield. **51 H5** SK5671.
Cuckney Hill *Notts.* ***Hill***, to S of Cuckney. Height 325 feet or 99 metres. **51 H5** SK5570.
Cuckold's Green *Suff.* ***Settlement***, 1m/2km W of Wrentham. TM4882.
Cuckoo Bridge *Lincs.* ***Settlement***, with bridge over North Drove Drain, 3m/5km SW of Spalding. TF2020.
Cuckoo Oak *Tel. & W.* ***Locality***, 1km E of Madeley. SJ7004.
Cuckoo's Corner *Hants.* ***Settlement***, adjoining to NE of Holybourne, 2m/4km NE of Alton. SU7441.
Cuckoo's Nest *Ches.* ***Settlement***, 4m/7km SW of Chester town centre. **48 C6** SJ3760.
Cudden Point *Cornw.* ***Coastal feature***, headland on Mount's Bay 5m/8km E of Penzance. **2 C6** SW5427.
Cuddesdon *Oxon.* ***Village***, 6m/9km SE of Oxford. Church of England Theological College. **21 J1** SP6003.
Cuddington *Bucks.* ***Village***, 4m/6km NE of Tring. **31 J7** SP7311.
Cuddington *Ches.* Population: 4339. ***Village***, 4m/7km W of Northwich. **49 F5** SJ5972.
Cuddington Heath *Ches.* ***Hamlet***, 1m/2km W of Malpas. **38 D1** SJ4847.
Cuddy Hill *Lancs.* ***Settlement***, 6m/10km NW of Preston. **55 H6** SD4937.
Cudham *Gt.Lon.* ***Village***, in borough of Bromley, 2m/3km E of Biggin Hill. **23 H6** TQ4459.
Cudliptown *Devon* ***Hamlet***, 4m/6km NE of Tavistock. **5 F3** SX5279.
Cudworth *Som.* ***Village***, 4m/6km E of Chard. **8 C3** ST3810.
Cudworth *S.Yorks.* Population: 11,715. ***Town***, 3m/5km NE of Barnsley. **51 F2** SE3808.
Cudworth Common *S.Yorks.* ***Locality***, 1m/2km SE of Cudworth. SE3907.
Cuerdale *Lancs.* ***Locality***, on E side of River Ribble, 3m/4km E of Preston town centre. SD5729.
Cuerden Green *Lancs.* ***Settlement***, 2m/3km N of Leyland. SD5524.
Cuerden Valley Country Park *Lancs.* ***Leisure/recreation***, to NE of Clayton-le-Woods, 4m/7km SE of Preston town centre. Most of park is still farmland but there are areas of woodland, a lake and wildlife sanctuary. **55 J7** SD5623.
Cuerdley Cross *Halton* ***Settlement***, 2m/3km NE of Widnes. SJ5486.
Cuffley *Herts.* Population: 4887. ***Village***, 2m/4km W of Cheshunt. **23 G1** TL3002.
Cuiashader *W.Isles* *Anglicised form of Cuidhaseadair, qv.*
Cuidhaseadair (Anglicised form: Cuiashader.) *W.Isles* ***Settlement***, near E coast of Isle of Lewis, 3m/5km NW of Cellar Head. **101 H2** NB5458.
Cuidhe Cròm *Aber.* *See Lochnagar.*
Cuidhir (Anglicised form: Cuier.) *W.Isles* ***Settlement***, on Barra, 2m/4km W of Ardmhòr. **84 B4** NF6703.
Cuidhtinis (Anglicised form: Quidnish.) *W.Isles* ***Settlement***, on SE coast of South Harris, 4m/6km NE of Rodel. **93 F3** NG0987.
Cuidrach *High.* ***Settlement***, on W coast of Trotternish peninsula, 3m/5km S of Uig, Skye. **93 J6** NG3759.
Cuier *W.Isles* *Anglicised form of Cuidhir, qv.*
Cuil Bay *High.* ***Bay***, on E side of Loch Linnhe, extending SE from Rubha Mòr. **80 A2** NM9754.
Cuil Hill *D. & G.* ***Mountain***, 5m/8km E of Dalbeattie. Height 1378 feet or 420 metres. **65 K4** NX9163.
Cuil-uaine *Arg. & B.* ***Settlement***, 1m/2km SE of Connel. **80 A4** NM9232.
Cuilags *Ork.* ***Mountain***, situated in NW section of Hoy. Height 1420 feet or 433 metres. **107 B7** HY2003.
Cuillin Hills *High.* ***Large natural feature***, group of gabbroic mountains with serrated peaks in S part of Skye, to E and NE of Loch Brittle in district known as Minginish. There are several peaks of over 3000 feet (914 metres), highest being Sgurr Alasdair, 3258 feet or 993 metres. Range is noted for rock climbing. **85 K2** NG4422.
Cuillin Sound *High.* ***Sea feature***, stretch of sea separating Rum, Canna and Sanday from Skye and Soay. **85 J3** NG3612.
Cuilmuich *Arg. & B.* ***Settlement***, on W shore of Loch Goil, to N of Carrick. **73 K1** NS1995.
Cùl a' Bhogha *High.* ***Coastal feature***, hillslope backing small bay, 2m/4km NW of Ullapool in Ross and Cromarty district. **95 H2** NH1098.
Cul Beag *High.* ***Mountain***, 2m/4km SW of Cul Mòr. Height 2522 feet or 769 metres. **95 H1** NC1408.
Cul Mòr *High.* ***Mountain***, in Ross and Cromarty district 8m/13km SW of Inchnadamph. Height 2785 feet or 849 metres. **102 D7** NC1611.
Culachy Forest *High.* ***Open space***, deer forest in Inverness district, 6m/10km S of Fort Augustus. **87 K5** NN3999.
Culag *Arg. & B.* ***Settlement***, on W shore of Loch Lomond, 2m/3km N of Luss. **74 B1** NS3595.
Culardoch *Aber.* ***Mountain***, in Grampian Mountains, 5m/8km N of Bridge of Dee. Height 2952 feet or 900 metres. **89 J5** NO1998.
Culbin Forest *Moray* ***Forest/woodland***, on coast extending W towards Nairn from Findhorn Bay. Planted on drifting sands which buried original farmland. **97 G5** NH9861.
Culblean Hill *Aber.* ***Mountain***, 4m/6km NE of Ballater. Height 1981 feet or 604 metres. **90 B4** NJ3901.
Culbo *High.* ***Settlement***, on N side of Black Isle, 5m/7km N of Munlochy. **96 D5** NH6360.
Culbokie *High.* ***Village***, on Black Isle, Ross and Cromarty district nearly 1m/2km from SE shore of Cromarty Firth and 7m/12km NE of Muir of Ord. **96 D6** NH6059.
Culbone *Som.* ***Locality***, near coast, 3m/5km W of Porlock. **7 G1** SS8348.
Culbone Hill *Som.* ***Mountain***, to S of Culbone on N edge of Exmoor and traversed by main road. Height 1355 feet or 413 metres. **7 G1** SS8247.
Culburnie *High.* ***Settlement***, in Inverness district, 4m/6km SW of Beauly. **96 B7** NH4941.
Culcabock *High.* ***Suburb***, to E of Inverness. **96 D7** NH6844.
Culcharan *Arg. & B.* ***Settlement***, 1km NE of Benderloch. **80 A4** NM9139.
Culcharry *High.* ***Hamlet***, in Nairn district, 4m/7km S of Nairn. **97 F6** NH8650.
Culcheth *Gt.Man.* ***Suburb***, 3m/5km E of Manchester city centre. SJ8899.
Culcheth *Warr.* Population: 5860. ***Small town***, 3m/5km S of Leigh. **49 F3** SJ6595.
Culcreuch Castle *Stir.* ***Castle***, located at foot of Fintry Hills, 1km NE of Fintry. 16c tower house, part of a larger building. **74 E2** NS6287.
Culdrain *Aber.* ***Settlement***, on W bank of River Bogie, 4m/6km S of Huntly. **90 D1** NJ5233.
Culdrose *Cornw.* ***Locality***, to SE of Helston. Culdrose Royal Naval Air Station to S. SW6626.
Culduie *High.* ***Settlement***, 1m/2km N of Toscaig, on W coast of Ross and Cromarty district. **94 D7** NG7140.
Culford *Suff.* ***Village***, 4m/6km N of Bury St. Edmunds. 18c hall in park houses a school. **34 C2** TL8370.
Culfordheath *Suff.* ***Settlement***, 5m/8km S of Thetford. TL8574.
Culgaith *Cumb.* ***Village***, 6m/10km E of Penrith. **61 H4** NY6129.
Culgower *High.* ***Settlement***, 2m/4km NE of Lothbeg, Sutherland district. **104 E7** NC9711.
Culham *Oxon.* ***Village***, 1m/2km S of Abingdon. Atomic energy research establishment. **21 J2** SU5095.
Culindrach *Arg. & B.* ***Settlement***, on E coast of Kintyre, 3m/5km NE of Claonaig. **73 H5** NR9159.
Culkein *High.* ***Village***, 2m/3km SE of Point of Stoer, W coast of Sutherland district. **102 C5** NC0332.
Culkerton *Glos.* ***Hamlet***, 3m/5km NE of Tetbury. **20 C2** ST9395.
Cullachie *High.* ***Settlement***, 2m/3km W of Nethy Bridge. **89 G2** NH9720.
Cullaloe Hills *Fife* ***Large natural feature***, partly wooded hills, 5m/8km E of Dunfermline and 1m/2km N of Dalgety Bay, on Firth of Forth. **75 K2** NT1787.
Cullaloe Reservoir *Fife* ***Reservoir***, small reservoir 1m/2km N of Aberdour. **75 K2** NT1985.
Cullen *Moray* Population: 1420. ***Village***, on Cullen Bay on N coast, 6m/10km E of Buckie. Bin of Cullen, hill 3m/5km SW, commands wide views. **98 D4** NJ5167.
Cullen Bay *Moray* ***Bay***, to N of Cullen, on N coast of Moray, 6m/10km E of Buckie. **98 D4** NJ5067.
Cullen House *Moray* ***Historic house***, partly 13c, 1km SW of Cullen. **98 D4** NJ5066.
Cullercoats *T. & W.* ***Village***, former fishing village between Tynemouth and Whitley Bay, now adjoining both. **71 J6** NZ3670.
Cullerlie Stone Circle (Also known as Garlogie Stone Circle.) *Aber.* ***Historic/prehistoric site***, Bronze Age circle (Historic Scotland) of eight boulders and 30 foot diameter, enclosing excavated burial chambers, nearly 1m/2km S of Garlogie. **91 F4** NJ7804.
Cullernose Point *Northumb.* ***Coastal feature***, headland on North Sea coast 1km S of Craster. **71 H2** NU2618.
Cullicudden *High.* ***Settlement***, scattered settlement on SE side of Cromarty Firth, Ross and Cromarty district, 3m/5km SW of Balblair. **96 D5** NH6564.
Culligran Falls *High.* ***Waterfall***, in River Farrar 1km SW of Culligran. **95 K7** NH3740.
Cullingworth *W.Yorks.* Population: 1955. ***Village***, 2m/3km E of Haworth. **57 F6** SE0636.
Cullipool *Arg. & B.* ***Village***, on NW coast of Luing. **79 J6** NM7313.
Cullivoe *Shet.* ***Village***, on NE coast of Yell, at head of inlet of Culli Voe. **108 E2** HP5402.
Culloch *P. & K.* ***Settlement***, 3m/5km S of Comrie. **81 J6** NN7817.
Culloden *High.* Population: 3669. ***Locality***, includes site of Battle of Culloden (1746), 5m/8km E of Inverness. **96 E7** NH7246.
Culloden Forest *High.* ***Forest/woodland***, to NE and to S of Culloden Muir. **96 E7** NH7647.
Culloden Muir *High.* ***Open space***, tract in Inverness district, 4m/7km E of Inverness. Site of battle in 1746 in which army of Prince Charles Edward was destroyed by Duke of Cumberland's forces. Various sites, museum, and visitor centre, all owned by National Trust for Scotland. **96 E7** NH7445.
Cullompton *Devon* Population: 5676. ***Small town***, former wool town on River Culm, 5m/9km SE of Tiverton. Most of former town destroyed by fire. Fine church of St. Andrew's has fan-vaulted aisle. **7 J5** ST0207.
Culm *Devon* ***River***, rising in Black Down Hills and flowing SW into River Exe below Stoke Canon. **7 J5** SX9396.
Culm Davy *Devon* ***Hamlet***, 2m/3km NE of Culmstock. ST1215.
Culm Valley *Devon* ***Valley***, part of River Culm valley to S of Black Down Hills, running W from Hemyock to Culmstock and then Uffculme. **7 K4** ST1413.
Culmaily *High.* ***Settlement***, 1m/2km W of Golspie. **97 F2** NH8099.
Culmington *Shrop.* ***Village***, 5m/8km N of Ludlow. **38 D7** SO4982.
Culmstock *Devon* ***Village***, below W end of Black Down Hills, 5m/8km SW of Wellington. **7 J4** ST1013.
Culnacraig *High.* ***Settlement***, 1m/2km E of Achduart, Ross and Cromarty district. **95 G1** NC0603.
Culnadalloch *Arg. & B.* ***Settlement***, 2m/3km E of Connel. **80 A4** NM9433.
Culnaknock *High.* ***Settlement***, near NE coast of Skye, 3m/5km S of Staffin. **94 B5** NG5162.
Culnamean *High.* ***Settlement***, at head of Loch Brittle, Skye. **85 K2** NG4120.
Culpho *Suff.* ***Hamlet***, 4m/6km W of Woodbridge. **35 G4** TM2149.
Culquhirk *D. & G.* ***Settlement***, 1km N of Wigtown. **64 E5** NX4256.
Culrain *High.* ***Hamlet***, in Sutherland district, 3m/5km NW of Bonar Bridge. **96 C2** NH5794.
Culross *Fife* ***Small town***, on N side of River Forth 7m/11km W of Dunfermline. Several National Trust for Scotland properties in town, which displays good examples of 16c and 17c Scottish domestic architecture. **75 H2** NS9885.
Culross Palace *Fife* ***Historic house***, situated in Culross and built between 1597 to 1611 for local entrepreneur, Sir George Bruce. **75 H2** NS9885.
Culross Town House *Fife* ***Historic house***, National Trust for Scotland property in Culross, 7m/11km W of Dunfermline. Built in 1626 as a result of wealth generated by coal exports. **75 H2** NS9885.
Culroy *S.Ayr.* ***Settlement***, 3m/5km NE of Maybole. **67 H2** NS3114.
Culsalmond *Aber.* *Alternative name for Kirkton of Culsalmond, qv.*
Culsh *Aber.* ***Settlement***, 2m/3km NW of Ballater. **90 B5** NO3497.
Culsh Earth House *Aber.* ***Historic/prehistoric site***, site of prehistoric earth house or souterrain (Historic Scotland) at settlement of Culsh, 2m/3km E of Tarland. **90 D4** NJ5005.
Culshabbin *D. & G.* ***Settlement***, 5m/8km NW of Port William. **64 D5** NX3050.
Culswick *Shet.* ***Settlement***, on Mainland, 4m/6km W of Garderhouse. **109 B8** HU2745.
Cult Hill *Fife* ***Hill***, 1m/2km SE of Powmill. Height 866 feet or 264 metres. **75 J1** NT0296.
Culter Allers Farm *S.Lan.* ***Settlement***, 2m/3km S of Coulter, in Culter Water valley. **75 J7** NT0331.
Culter Cleuch Shank *S.Lan.* ***Mountain***, 4m/6km SW of Tweedsmuir. Height 1801 feet or 549 metres. **69 F1** NT0322.
Culter Fell ***Mountain***, on border of South Lanarkshire and Scottish Borders, 6m/9km S of Biggar. Height 2453 feet or 748 metres. **69 F1** NT0529.
Culter Water *S.Lan.* ***River***, rising in mountain S of Biggar on slopes of Gathersnow Hill, and flowing NW through Culter Waterhead Reservoir, N to Coulter, joining River Clyde 1km NW of Coulter. **75 J7** NT0135.
Culter Waterhead Reservoir *S.Lan.* ***Reservoir***, 4m/7km S of Coulter. **69 F1** NT0327.
Cultercullen *Aber.* ***Settlement***, 3m/5km SE of Pitmedden. **91 H2** NJ9224.
Culteuchar Hill *P. & K.* ***Mountain***, 2m/3km S of Forgandenny. Height 1027 feet or 313 metres. **82 B6** NO0915.
Cults *Aberdeen* ***Suburb***, 3m/5km SW of Aberdeen city centre. **91 G4** NJ8903.
Cults *Aber.* ***Locality***, to W of Knockandy Hill, 1m/2km SE of Gartly. **90 D1** NJ5330.
Cults *D. & G.* ***Settlement***, 2m/3km S of Garlieston. **64 E6** NX4643.
Cultybraggan Camp *P. & K.* ***Military establishment***, military training camp 1m/2km S of Comrie. **81 J6** NN7619.
Culvennan Fell *D. & G.* ***Hill***, 3m/4km N of Kirkcowan. Height 699 feet or 213 metres. **64 D4** NX3164.
Culver Cliff *I.o.W.* ***Coastal feature***, cliff between Whitecliff Bay and Sandown Bay on SE coast. **11 H6** SZ6385.
Culver Down *I.o.W.* *See Bembridge.*
Culver Hole *Swan.* ***Other feature of interest***, 1km S of Port Eynon. Man-made structure built into cliff; origin uncertain, but associations with smuggling. Also used as an armoury and dovecote. **17 H6** SS4684.
Culverhouse Cross *V. of Glam.* ***Settlement***, 4m/7km N of Barry. **18 E4** ST1174.
Culverlane *Devon* ***Hamlet***, 3m/4km E of South Brent. SX7460.
Culverstone Green *Kent* Population: 3908. ***Village***, 3m/5km N of Wrotham Heath. **24 C5** TQ6362.
Culverthorpe *Lincs.* ***Hamlet***, 4m/7km SW of Sleaford. **42 D1** TF0240.
Culvie *Aber.* ***Settlement***, 2m/3km W of Aberchirder. **98 D5** NJ5953.
Culworth *Northants.* ***Village***, 7m/11km NE of Banbury. **31 G4** SP5446.
Culzean Bay *S.Ayr.* ***Bay***, extends N from Culzean Castle towards Dunure. **67 G2** NS2310.
Culzean Castle *S.Ayr.* ***Historic house***, late 18c mansion (National Trust for Scotland) built around medieval tower of the Kennedys, on coast 4m/7km W of Maybole. Surrounding grounds became Scotland's first country park. **67 G3** NS2311.
Culzean Country Park *S.Ayr.* ***Leisure/recreation***, National Trust for Scotland property of 563 acres surrounding Culzean Castle, 4m/7km W of Maybole. First park in Scotland to become a Country Park. Includes wide variety of terrain, including gardens, woodland and shoreline. **67 G3** NS2309.
Cumberhead *S.Lan.* ***Settlement***, 4m/7km SW of Lesmahagow. **75 F7** NS7734.

Cumberland Stone *High.* ***Historic/prehistoric site***, huge stone (National Trust for Scotland) at road junction to SE of Culloden Muir, 3m/5km E of Inverness, from which Duke of Cumberland is said to have viewed battlefield of Culloden. **96 E7** NH7545.
Cumberlow Green *Herts.* ***Settlement***, 4m/6km W of Buntingford. TL3030.
Cumbernauld *N.Lan.* Population: 48,762. ***Town***, 12m/20km NE of Glasgow. New Town designated 1955. Original village of Cumbernauld 1m/2km N of town centre. **75 F3** NS7674.
Cumberworth *Lincs.* ***Village***, 4m/6km SE of Alford. **53 J5** TF5073.
Cumdivock *Cumb.* ***Locality***, 2m/3km SE of Thursby. NY3448.
Cuminestone *Aber.* *Alternative spelling of Cuminestown, qv.*
Cuminestown *Aber.* ***Village***, 5m/8km E of Turriff. Alternative spellings: Cuminestone, Cummestone, Cumminestown. **99 G5** NJ8050.
Cumloden *D. & G.* ***Settlement***, 1m/2km N of Newton Stewart. **64 E4** NX4167.
Cummersdale *Cumb.* ***Village***, on River Caldew, on S outskirts of Carlisle. **60 E1** NY3953.
Cummertrees *D. & G.* ***Village***, near shore of Solway Firth, 4m/6km W of Annan. **69 G7** NY1366.
Cummestone *Aber.* *Alternative spelling of Cuminestown, qv.*
Cumminestown *Aber.* *Alternative spelling of Cuminestown, qv.*
Cummingstown *Moray* ***Village***, on N coast 1m/2km E of Burghead. **97 J5** NJ1368.
Cumnock (Also known as Cumnock and Holmhead.) *E.Ayr.* Population: 9607. ***Small town***, on Lugar Water 14m/23km E of Ayr. **67 K1** NS5619.
Cumnock and Holmhead *E.Ayr.* *Alternative name for Cumnock, qv.*
Cumnor *Oxon.* ***Village***, 4m/6km W of Oxford. **21 H1** SP4604.
Cumrew *Cumb.* ***Village***, 7m/11km S of Brampton. **61 G1** NY5450.
Cumrue *D. & G.* ***Settlement***, 3m/4km N of Lochmaben. **69 F5** NY0786.
Cumstoun *D. & G.* ***Settlement***, 1m/2km N of Kirkcudbright. **65 G5** NX6853.
Cumwhinton *Cumb.* ***Village***, 4m/6km SE of Carlisle. **61 F1** NY4452.
Cumwhitton *Cumb.* ***Village***, 7m/11km E of Carlisle. **61 G1** NY5052.
Cundall *N.Yorks.* ***Village***, 4m/7km NE of Boroughbridge. **57 K2** SE4272.
Cunndal *W.Isles* ***Bay***, small bay, 1km SW of Butt of Lewis. **101 H1** NB5165.
Cunnigill Hill *Shet.* ***Hill***, 1km S of Collafirth, Mainland. Height 577 feet or 176 metres. **109 D6** HU4367.
Cunning Park *S.Ayr.* ***Suburb***, S district of Ayr. NS3220.
Cunninghame ***Locality***, area of land between West Kilbride and Corse Hill, 5m/8km S of East Kilbride. **74 A6** NS4046.
Cunninghamhead *N.Ayr.* ***Hamlet***, 4m/6km NE of Irvine. **74 B6** NS3741.
Cunningsburgh *Shet.* ***Locality***, on E coast of Mainland, 8m/13km S of Lerwick. HU4329.
Cunnister *Shet.* ***Settlement***, on E side of Basta Voe, 1km SE of Sellafirth, Yell. **108 E3** HU5296.
Cunnoquhie *Fife* ***Settlement***, to W of Fernie. **82 E6** NO3115.
Cupar *Fife* Population: 7545. ***Small town***, royal burgh, with charter from 1363, on River Eden, 9m/14km S of Newport-on-Tay and 10m/16km NE of Glenrothes. Mainly Georgian architecture. **82 E6** NO3714.
Cupar Muir *Fife* ***Hamlet***, 1m/2km SW of Cupar. **82 E6** NO3513.
Cupid Green *Herts.* ***Suburb***, 2m/3km NE of Hemel Hempstead town centre. TL0709.
Cur *Arg. & B.* ***River***, flowing SW then, 1km S of Strachur, SE into head of Loch Eck. **80 C7** NS1296.
Curbar *Derbys.* ***Village***, 4m/7km NE of Bakewell. **50 E5** SK2574.
Curborough *Staffs.* ***Settlement***, 2m/3km N of Lichfield. SK1212.
Curbridge *Hants.* ***Hamlet***, near head of River Hamble estuary, 1m/2km SE of Botley. **11 G3** SU5211.
Curbridge *Oxon.* ***Village***, 2m/3km SW of Witney. **21 G1** SP3308.
Curdridge *Hants.* ***Village***, 1m/2km W of Botley. **11 G3** SU5213.
Curdworth *Warks.* ***Village***, 3m/5km NW of Coleshill. **40 D6** SP1892.
Curland *Som.* ***Village***, scattered village 6m/9km SE of Taunton. **8 B3** ST2717.
Curlew Green *Suff.* ***Settlement***, 2m/3km N of Saxmundham. TM3865.
Curling Tye Green *Essex* ***Settlement***, 2m/3km W of Maldon. TL8207.
Curload *Som.* ***Hamlet***, 5m/8km W of Langport. **8 C2** ST3428.
Curraghs Wildlife Park *I.o.M.* ***Leisure/recreation***, 1m/2km W of Sulby, where animals from all over world mix with indigenous four-horned Loghtan sheep and Manx cats. **54 C4** SC3694.
Curridge *W.Berks.* ***Hamlet***, 3m/5km N of Newbury. **21 H4** SU4871.
Currie *Edin.* ***Suburb***, on Water of Leith, 6m/9km SE of Edinburgh. Heriot-Watt University (Riccarton Campus) 1m/2km NW. **75 K4** NT1866.
Curriott Hill *Som.* ***Suburb***, SW district of Crewkerne. ST4309.
Currock *Cumb.* ***Suburb***, 1m/2km S of Carlisle city centre. NY4054.
Curry Mallet *Som.* ***Village***, 7m/11km E of Taunton. **8 C2** ST3321.
Curry Rivel *Som.* Population: 1899. ***Village***, 2m/3km SW of Langport. **8 C2** ST3925.
Curteis' Corner *Kent* ***Hamlet***, 1km N of Biddenden. **14 D4** TQ8539.
Curthwaite *Cumb.* ***Locality***, comprising East Curthwaite and West Curthwaite, 1m/2km SE of Thursby. NY3348.
Curtisden Green *Kent* ***Hamlet***, 2m/3km NE of Goudhurst. **14 C3** TQ7440.
Curtisknowle *Devon* ***Hamlet***, 6m/9km SW of Totnes. SX7353.
Curtismill Green *Essex* ***Locality***, 5m/8km N of Romford. TQ5196.
Cury *Cornw.* ***Hamlet***, 4m/6km S of Helston. **2 D6** SW6721.
Curyan *Cornw.* ***Hamlet***, in China clay district, 4m/7km NW of St. Austell. SW9656.
Cusgarne *Cornw.* ***Hamlet***, 4m/6km E of Redruth. SW7640.
Cushat Law *Northumb.* ***Mountain***, in Cheviot Hills, 5m/8km N of Alwinton. Height 2020 feet or 616 metres. **70 E2** NT9213.
Cushnie *Aber.* ***Settlement***, 2m/3km S of Gardenstown. **99 F4** NJ7962.
Cushuish *Som.* ***Hamlet***, 4m/7km NW of Taunton. **7 K2** ST1930.
Cusop *Here.* ***Village***, on Welsh border, 1m/2km SE of Hay-on-Wye. **28 B4** SO2341.
Custards *Hants.* ***Locality***, adjoining to NE of Lyndhurst. SU3008.
Cusworth *S.Yorks.* ***Suburb***, 2m/3km NW of Doncaster town centre. Hall is 18c house containing museum, in large grounds with lake. SE5404.
Cusworth Hall *S.Yorks.* ***Other feature of interest***, early Georgian mansion set in country park, containing museum of local history, 2m/3km W of Doncaster. **51 H2** SE5403.
Cut Hill *Devon* ***Mountain***, in Dartmoor National Park, 4m/6km NW of Postbridge. Height 1981 feet or 604 metres. **6 D7** SX5982.
Cutcloy *D. & G.* ***Settlement***, 1km N of Burrow Head and 3m/5km S of Whithorn. **64 E7** NX4535.
Cutcombe *Som.* ***Hamlet***, on Exmoor, 5m/8km SW of Dunster. **7 H2** SS9239.
Cutgate *Gt.Man.* ***Suburb***, 2m/3km W of Rochdale town centre. SD8614.
Cuthill *High.* ***Locality***, on N shore of Dornoch Firth, 3m/5km SW of Dornoch. **96 E3** NH7587.
Cutiau *Gwyn.* ***Settlement***, 2m/3km NE of Barmouth. **37 F4** SH6317.
Cutlers Green *Essex* ***Hamlet***, 1m/2km W of Thaxted. TL5930.
Cutnall Green *Worcs.* ***Village***, 3m/5km N of Droitwich Spa. **29 H2** SO8768.
Cutsdean *Glos.* ***Village***, 4m/7km E of Winchcombe. **30 B5** SP0830.
Cutsyke *W.Yorks.* ***Suburb***, to S of Castleford. SE4224.
Cutthorpe *Derbys.* ***Village***, 3m/4km NW of Chesterfield. **51 F5** SK3473.
Cutthorpe Green *Derbys.* ***Settlement***, to S of Cutthorpe. SK3473.
Cutts *Shet.* ***Settlement***, on NE of Trondra. **109 D9** HU4038.
Cuttyhill *Aber.* ***Settlement***, 6m/10km NW of Peterhead. **99 J5** NK0450.
Cuween Hill *Ork.* ***Historic/prehistoric site***, site of communal burial cairn (Historic Scotland) of c. 1800 BC, 1km S of Finstown, Mainland. **107 C6** HY3612.
Cuxham *Oxon.* ***Village***, 5m/9km NE of Wallingford. **21 K2** SU6695.
Cuxton *Med.* Population: 3273. ***Village***, on a ridge overlooking River Medway, opposite Rochester, 2m/3km SW of Strood. **24 D5** TQ7066.
Cuxwold *Lincs.* ***Village***, 4m/6km E of Caistor. **52 E2** TA1701.
Cwm *B.Gwent* Population: 3047. ***Village***, 3m/4km S of Ebbw Vale. **18 E1** SO1805.
Cwm *Denb.* ***Hamlet***, 3m/5km S of Prestatyn. **47 J5** SJ0677.
Cwm-bach *Carmar.* ***Settlement***, 1m/2km NW of Llanelli. SN4801.
Cwm Capel *Carmar.* ***Settlement***, 1m/2km N of Burry Port. SN4502.
Cwm-celyn *B.Gwent* ***Locality***, on N side of Blaina. SO2008.
Cwm Ceulan *Cere.* ***Valley***, running from a point 2m/3km NW of Nant-y-moch Reservoir in E, to Tal-y-bont in W. **37 F6** SN6790.
Cwm-Cewydd *Gwyn.* ***Settlement***, 1m/2km NE of Mallwyd. **37 H4** SH8713.
Cwm Crawnon *Powys* ***Hamlet***, 1km W of Llangynidr. SO1419.
Cwm Crew *Powys* ***Valley***, carrying Nant Crew, 1km E of Beacons Reservoir. **27 J7** SN9917.
Cwm Croes *Gwyn.* ***Valley***, running NE from Cwm-Ffynnon to River Twrch at Talardd. **37 H3** SH8825.
Cwm Cynllwyd *Gwyn.* ***Valley***, upper valley of River Twrch running SE to NW, 3m/4km SE of Llanuwchllyn. **37 H3** SH9025.
Cwm-Dows *Caerp.* ***Locality***, adjoining to SW of Newbridge. ST2096.
Cwm Einion *Cere.* ***Valley***, carrying River Einion, 4m/6km NE of Tal-y-bont. **37 F6** SN6994.
Cwm Ffrwd-oer *Torfaen* ***Locality***, 1m/2km NW of Pontypool. **19 F1** SO2601.
Cwm Gelli *Caerp.* ***Locality***, adjoining to N of Blackwood, 4m/7km SW of Abertillery. ST1798.
Cwm Gwaun *Pembs.* ***Valley***, carrying River Gwaun SE to NW, towards Fishguard. **16 D1** SN0233.
Cwm Head *Shrop.* ***Settlement***, 4m/6km SW of Church Stretton. SO4288.
Cwm Irfon *Powys* ***Settlement***, on W bank of River Irfon, 3m/4km NW of Llanwrtyd Wells. **27 H4** SN8549.
Cwm-Llinau (Also known as Cwmlline.) *Powys* ***Hamlet***, 3m/5km S of Mallwyd. **37 H5** SH8407.
Cwm-mawr *Carmar.* ***Settlement***, adjoining to NW of Tumble. SN5312.
Cwm-Morgan *Carmar.* ***Hamlet***, 4m/6km S of Newcastle Emlyn. **17 F1** SN2934.
Cwm Owen *Powys* ***Valley***, upper valley of Nant yr Offeiriad, 9m/15km N of Brecon. **27 K4** SO0244.
Cwm-parc *R.C.T.* ***Village***, 1km W of Treorchy. **18 C2** SS9495.
Cwm Penmachno *Gwyn.* ***Hamlet***, 4m/6km E of Blaenau Ffestiniog. SH7547.
Cwm Plysgog *Pembs.* ***Settlement***, adjoining to N of Cilgerran. SN1943.
Cwm Prysor *Gwyn.* ***Valley***, carrying River Prysor W into Llyn Trawsfynydd. **37 G2** SH7435.
Cwm-twrch Isaf *Powys* ***Locality***, 2m/3km SE of Cwmllynfell. **27 G7** SN7610.
Cwm-twrch Uchaf *Powys* ***Village***, 1m/2km SE of Cwmllynfell. SN7511.
Cwm-y-glo *Carmar.* ***Hamlet***, adjoining to N of Cross Hands. SN5513.
Cwm-y-glo *Gwyn.* ***Village***, 2m/4km NW of Llanberis. **46 D6** SH5562.
Cwmafan (Cwmavon). *N.P.T.* Population: 5159. ***Village***, 2m/3km NE of Port Talbot. **18 A2** SS7892.
Cwmafon *Torfaen* *Welsh form of Cwmavon, qv.*
Cwmaman *R.C.T.* ***Village***, 2m/3km S of Aberdare. **18 D2** ST0099.
Cwmann *Carmar.* ***Hamlet***, 1km SE of Lampeter. **26 E4** SN5847.
Cwmavon *N.P.T.* *English form of Cwmafan, qv.*
Cwmavon (Cwmafon). *Torfaen* ***Hamlet***, 2m/3km SE of Blaenavon. SO2706.
Cwmbach *Carmar.* ***Village***, 6m/10km N of St. Clears. **17 F2** SN2525.
Cwmbach *Powys* ***Hamlet***, 2m/3km N of Builth Wells. **27 K3** SO0254.
Cwmbach *Powys* ***Hamlet***, 1km W of Glassbury. **28 A5** SO1639.
Cwmbach *R.C.T.* Population: 4065. ***Village***, 2m/3km SE of Aberdare. **18 D1** SO0201.
Cwmbelan *Powys* ***Settlement***, 2m/3km S of Llanidloes. **37 J7** SN9481.
Cwmbrân *Torfaen* *Welsh form of Cwmbran, qv.*
Cwmbran (Cwmbrân). *Torfaen* Population: 46,021. ***Town***, 4m/7km N of Newport. New Town designated 1949. Residential and industrial. **19 F2** ST2894.
Cwmbrwyno *Cere.* ***Settlement***, 3m/5km NW of Devil's Bridge. **37 G7** SN7080.
Cwmcarfan *Mon.* *Welsh form of Cwmcarvan, qv.*
Cwmcarn *Caerp.* ***Village***, 1m/2km S of Abercarn. **19 F2** ST2193.
Cwmcarvan (Cwmcarfan). *Mon.* ***Hamlet***, 4m/6km SW of Monmouth. **19 H1** SO4707.
Cwmcou *Cere.* *See Cwmcoy.*
Cwmcoy (Cwmcou). *Cere.* ***Village***, 1m/2km NW of Newcastle Emlyn. **26 B4** SN2942.
Cwmdare *R.C.T.* ***Village***, 1m/2km NW of Aberdare. **18 C1** SN9803.
Cwmdu *Carmar.* ***Hamlet***, 5m/8km N of Llandeilo. **17 K1** SN6330.
Cwmdu *Powys* ***Hamlet***, 4m/7km NW of Crickhowell. **28 A6** SO1823.
Cwmdu *Swan.* ***Suburb***, 1m/2km NW of Swansea city centre. SS6494.
Cwmduad *Carmar.* ***Hamlet***, 6m/10km SW of Llandysul. **17 G1** SN3731.
Cwmerfyn *Cere.* ***Settlement***, 5m/7km NW of Devil's Bridge. SN7082.
Cwmfelin *Bridgend* ***Village***, 1m/2km SE of Maesteg. SS8689.
Cwmfelin *M.Tyd.* ***Hamlet***, 3m/4km N of Treharris. SO0900.
Cwmfelin Boeth *Carmar.* ***Village***, 2m/3km N of Whitland. **16 E3** SN1919.
Cwmfelin Mynach *Carmar.* ***Village***, 5m/9km N of Whitland. **17 F2** SN2224.
Cwmfelinfach *Caerp.* Population: 2441. ***Village***, 4m/6km S of Blackwood. **18 E2** ST1891.
Cwmffrwd *Carmar.* ***Hamlet***, 2m/3km S of Carmarthen. **17 H3** SN4217.
Cwmgiedd *Powys* ***Village***, 2m/3km NE of Ystalyfera. **27 G7** SN7811.
Cwmgors *N.P.T.* ***Settlement***, adjoining to S of Gwaun-Cae-Gurwen. **27 G7** SN7010.
Cwmgwili *Carmar.* ***Settlement***, 4m/6km W of Ammanford. SN5710.
Cwmgwrach *N.P.T.* ***Locality***, adjoining to S of Blaengwrach. **18 B1** SN8605.
Cwmgwyn *Swan.* ***Suburb***, 2m/3km W of Swansea city centre. SS6393.
Cwmhiraeth *Carmar.* ***Settlement***, 3m/4km SE of Newcastle Emlyn. SN3337.
Cwmifor *Carmar.* ***Hamlet***, 2m/3km NE of Llandeilo. SN6525.
Cwmiou *Mon.* *Alternative spelling of Cwmyoy, qv.*
Cwmisfael *Carmar.* ***Hamlet***, 1m/2km SW of Llanddarog. **17 H3** SN4915.
Cwmlline *Powys* *Alternative name for Cwm-Llinau, qv.*
Cwmllyfri *Carmar.* ***Settlement***, 2m/3km N of Llanstephan. **17 G3** SN3413.
Cwmllynfell *N.P.T.* Population: 1399. ***Village***, 2m/4km SE of Brynamman. **27 G7** SN7413.
Cwmmiles *Carmar.* ***Hamlet***, 1km S of Login. SN1622.
Cwmnantyrodyn *Caerp.* ***Hamlet***, 2m/3km SW of Newbridge. ST1895.
Cwmpengraig *Carmar.* ***Hamlet***, 4m/6km SE of Newcastle Emlyn. **17 G1** SN3436.
Cwmpennar *R.C.T.* ***Village***, 1km NW of Mountain Ash. SO0400.
Cwmrhos *Powys* ***Locality***, 4m/7km NW of Crickhowell. SO1824.
Cwmrhydyceirw *Swan.* ***Suburb***, 4m/6km N of Swansea city centre. SS6699.
Cwmsychbant *Cere.* ***Hamlet***, 6m/10km W of Lampeter. **26 D4** SN4746.

Cwmsyfiog *Caerp.* ***Hamlet***, 2m/3km N of Bargoed. SO1502.
Cwmsymlog *Cere.* ***Settlement***, 5m/8km NW of Devil's Bridge. **37 F7** SN6983.
Cwmtillery (Cwmtyleri). *B.Gwent* ***Locality***, 1m/2km N of Abertillery. **19 F1** SO2105.
Cwmtudu *Cere.* ***Coastal feature***, headland 3m/5km SW of New Quay. **26 C3** SN3557.
Cwmtyleri *B.Gwent Welsh form of Cwmtillery, qv.*
Cwmwysg *Powys* ***Settlement***, on River Usk, 2m/3km W of Trecastle. Usk Reservoir 1m/2km to W. SN8528.
Cwmynyscoy *Torfaen* ***Settlement***, 1km S of Pontypool. ST2899.
Cwmyoy (Also spelled Cwmiou.) *Mon.* ***Hamlet***, 6m/9km N of Abergavenny. Medieval Church of St. Martin is notably of irregular shape due to rock subsidence. **28 C6** SO2923.
Cwmyrhaiadr *Powys* ***Settlement***, 3m/5km S of Machynlleth. SN7596.
Cwmystwyth *Cere.* ***Hamlet***, 4m/7km SE of Devil's Bridge. **27 G1** SN7873.
Cwrt *Gwyn.* ***Settlement***, 4m/6km W of Machynlleth. **37 F5** SH6800.
Cwrt-newydd *Cere.* ***Village***, 6m/9km W of Lampeter. **26 D4** SN4847.
Cwrt-y-Cadno *Carmar.* ***Settlement***, on River Cothi 3m/5km NE of Pumsaint. SN6944.
Cwrt-y-gollen *Powys* ***Hamlet***, 1m/2km SE of Crickhowell. **28 B7** SO2316.
Cych ***River***, rising S of Newcastle Emlyn and flowing N into River Teifi between Newcastle Emlyn and Cardigan. SN2441.
Cydweli *Carmar. Welsh form of Kidwelly, qv.*
Cyffylliog *Denb.* ***Village***, on River Clywedog, 4m/6km W of Ruthin. **47 J7** SJ0657.
Cymau *Flints.* ***Hamlet***, 4m/7km NW of Wrexham. SJ2955.
Cymdda *Bridgend* ***Suburb***, adjoining to S of Sarn, 2m/3km N of Bridgend. SS9083.
Cymer Abbey *Gwyn.* ***Historic/prehistoric site***, ruined 13c abbey (Cadw) to E of Llanelltyd across River Mawddach. **37 G4** SH7219.
Cymmer *N.P.T.* ***Village***, 3m/5km N of Maesteg. **18 B2** SS8696.
Cymmer *R.C.T.* ***Locality***, 1km S of Porth. **18 D2** ST0290.
Cymyran Bay *I.o.A.* ***Bay***, on W coast of Anglesey, bounded by S coast of Holy Island and adjacent to coast of main island on SW side of Valley Airfield. **46 A5** SH2974.
Cyncoed *Cardiff* ***Suburb***, 3m/4km N of Cardiff city centre. ST1880.
Cyncoed *Mon. Welsh form of Kingcoed, qv.*
Cynfal *Gwyn.* ***River***, running W into River Dwyryd 1m/2km W of Ffestiniog. **37 G1** SH6841.
Cynfal Falls (Rhaeadr Cynfal). *Gwyn.* ***Waterfall***, two waterfalls in course of River Cynfal 1km S of Ffestiniog. **37 G1** SH7041.
Cynffig *Bridgend Welsh form of Kenfig, qv.*
Cynffig (Kenfig). *N.P.T.* ***River***, rising N of Cefn Cribwr and flowing W into Swansea Bay, S of Margam. SS7783.
Cynghordy *Carmar.* ***Hamlet***, 4m/7km NE of Llandovery. **27 H5** SN8039.
Cynheidre *Carmar.* ***Settlement***, 4m/7km N of Llanelli. **17 H4** SN4907.
Cynin *Carmar.* ***River***, rising 1km NE of Trelech and flowing S into River Taf at St. Clears. **17 F2** SN2815.
Cynon *R.C.T.* ***River***, rising N of Hirwaun and flowing SE by Aberdare and Mountain Ash into River Taff at Abercynon. **18 C1** ST0894.
Cynonville *N.P.T.* ***Hamlet***, 1km W of Duffryn. SS8295.
Cyntwell *Cardiff* ***Suburb***, 4m/6km W of Cardiff city centre. ST1275.
Cynwyd *Denb.* ***Village***, in River Dee valley, 2m/3km SW of Corwen. **37 K1** SJ0541.
Cynwyl Elfed (Conwil Elvet). *Carmar.* ***Village***, 5m/8km NW of Carmarthen. **17 G2** SN3727.
Cyprus *Gt.Lon.* ***Suburb***, in borough of Newham, at E end of Royal Albert Dock, 2m/3km S of East Ham. TQ4380.
Cyrn-y-Brain *Denb.* ***Mountain***, 4m/7km SW of Minera. Height 1843 feet or 562 metres. **38 B1** SJ2049.
Cyrnau Bach *Cere.* ***Mountain***, 1m/2km S of Devil's Bridge. Height 1269 feet or 387 metres. **27 G1** SN7475.
Cyrniau Nod *Powys* ***Mountain***, 6m/10km SE of Bala. Height 2184 feet or 666 metres. **37 J3** SH9827.
Cywyn *Carmar.* ***River***, rising 2m/4km E of Trelech and flowing S into River Taf 3m/4km SE of St. Clears. SN3012.

D

Daaey *Shet.* ***Island***, small island off N coast of Fetlar opposite Urie Ness. HU6095.
Dabton *D. & G.* ***Settlement***, 1km SE of Carronbridge, 1m/2km N of Thornhill. **68 D4** NX8796.
Daccombe *Devon* ***Hamlet***, 3m/4km N of Torquay. **5 K4** SX9068.
Dacre *Cumb.* ***Village***, 4m/7km SW of Penrith. **61 F4** NY4526.
Dacre *N.Yorks.* ***Hamlet***, 4m/6km SE of Pateley Bridge. **57 G3** SE1962.
Dacre Banks *N.Yorks.* ***Village***, 1m/2km N of Dacre. **57 G3** SE1962.
Daddry Shield *Dur.* ***Hamlet***, 1km E of St. John's Chapel. **61 K3** NY8937.
Dadford *Bucks.* ***Hamlet***, 3m/5km NW of Buckingham. **31 H5** SP6638.
Dadlington *Leics.* ***Village***, 3m/5km NW of Hinckley. **41 G6** SP4098.
Daer Reservoir *S.Lan.* ***Reservoir***, in course of Daer Water. **68 E3** NS9513.
Dafen *Carmar.* ***Locality***, adjoining to E of Llanelli. **17 J4** SN5201.
Daffy Green *Norf.* ***Settlement***, 3m/5km SW of East Dereham. **44 D5** TF9609.
Dagdale *Staffs.* ***Hamlet***, 3m/4km W of Uttoxeter. SK0534.
Dagenham *Gt.Lon.* ***Suburb***, in borough of Barking and Dagenham, 3m/5km S of Romford. Motor works to S beside River Thames. **23 H3** TQ5084.
Daggons *Dorset* ***Settlement***, adjoining to W of Alderholt. **10 C3** SU1012.
Daglingworth *Glos.* ***Village***, 3m/4km NW of Cirencester. Site of Roman building 1km SE. **20 C1** SO9905.
Dagnall *Bucks.* ***Village***, 4m/6km S of Dunstable. **32 C7** SP9916.
Dagworth *Suff.* ***Settlement***, 2m/3km N of Stowmarket. TM0461.
Dail *Arg. & B.* ***Settlement***, on NE shore of Loch Etive, 6m/9km NE of Taynuilt across loch. **80 B4** NN0539.
Dail Beag (Anglicised form: Dalbeg.) *W.Isles* ***Settlement***, near NW coast of Isle of Lewis, 2m/3km NE of Carloway. **100 E3** NB2245.
Dail Bho Dheas (Anglicised form: South Dell.) *W.Isles* ***Village***, 4m/6km SW of Butt of Lewis. **101 G1** NB4861.
Dail Bho Thuath (Anglicised form: North Dell.) *W.Isles* ***Settlement***, between Dail Bho Dheas and Cros, 3m/5km S of Butt of Lewis. **101 G1** NB4961.
Dail Mòr (Anglicised form: Dalmore.) *W.Isles* ***Settlement***, near NW coast of Isle of Lewis, 2m/3km NE of Carloway. Dalmore Bay on coast to NW. **100 E3** NB2144.
Dailly *S.Ayr.* Population: 1007. ***Village***, on S bank of Water of Girvan, 6m/9km E of Girvan. **67 G3** NS2701.
Dailnamac *Arg. & B.* ***Settlement***, 3m/4km NW of Taynuilt. **80 A4** NM9732.
Dainton *Devon* ***Hamlet***, beside main-line railway, 3m/5km S of Newton Abbot, near summit of steep incline. SX8566.
Dairsie (Also known as Dairsiemuir or Osnaburgh). *Fife* ***Village***, 3m/5km NE of Cupar. Remains of medieval castle 1m/2km S, near 17c bridge over River Eden. **83 F6** NO4117.
Dairsiemuir *Fife Alternative name for Dairsie, qv.*
Dairy Houses *E.Riding* ***Settlement***, 3m/4km E of Hedon. TA2229.
Daisy Bank *W.Mid.* ***Suburb***, in E part of Walsall. SP0497.
Daisy Green *Essex* ***Settlement***, 4m/7km W of Colchester town centre. TL9325.
Daisy Green *Suff.* ***Settlement***, 1m/2km E of Great Ashfield. TM0167.
Daisy Hill *Gt.Man.* ***Locality***, 1m/2km S of Westhoughton. SD6504.
Daisy Hill *W.Yorks.* ***Suburb***, 3m/4km NW of Bradford city centre. SE1334.
Daisy Hill *W.Yorks.* ***Suburb***, 1km NE of Morley town centre. SE2628.
Daisy Nook *Gt.Man.* ***Settlement***, 1m/2km NW of Ashton-under-Lyne. Daisy Nook Country Park to N. SD9100.
Daisy Nook Country Park *Gt.Man.* ***Leisure/recreation***, 85 acres of land, rich in plants and wildlife, set within River Medlock valley and densely populated industrial region, 3m/4km SW of Oldham. Boating, fishing, footpaths. **49 J2** SD9201.
Dalabrog (Anglicised form: Daliburgh.) *W.Isles* ***Village***, near W coast of South Uist, 3m/5km NW of Lochboisdale. **84 C2** NF7521.
Dalavich *Arg. & B.* ***Settlement***, on W shore of Lock Awe, in Argyll, 1km S of mouth of River Avich. **80 A6** NM9612.
Dalballoch *High.* ***Settlement***, in Glen Banchor, 3m/5km W of Newtonmore. **88 D5** NN6598.
Dalbeattie *D. & G.* Population: 4421. ***Small town***, small granite town on Kirkgunzeon Lane, 13m/20km SW of Dumfries. **65 J4** NX8361.
Dalbeattie Forest *D. & G.* ***Forest/woodland***, to S of Dalbeattie. **65 J5** NX8361.
Dalbeg *W.Isles Anglicised form of Dail Beag, qv.*
Dalbeg Bay *W.Isles Anglicised form of Bagh Dail Beag, qv.*
Dalbeth *Glas.* ***Suburb***, on N bank of River Clyde, 3m/5km SE of Glasgow city centre, in Tollcross district. NS6362.
Dalblair *E.Ayr.* ***Settlement***, at confluence of Glenmuir Water and Guelt Water, 4m/7km E of Darvel. **68 B2** NS6419.
Dalbog *Angus* ***Hamlet***, 2m/3km NW of Edzell. **90 D7** NO5871.
Dalbreck *High.* ***Settlement***, at confluence of rivers Black Water and Coirefrois Burn, 5m/9km N of Rhilochan. **104 C7** NC7416.
Dalbury *Derbys.* ***Hamlet***, 6m/9km W of Derby. **40 E2** SK2634.
Dalby *I.o.M.* ***Hamlet***, near W coast, 4m/6km S of Peel. **54 B6** SC2178.
Dalby *Lincs.* ***Hamlet***, 3m/4km N of Spilsby. TF4170.
Dalby *N.Yorks.* ***Settlement***, 2m/3km W of Terrington. SE6471.
Dalby Beck *N.Yorks.* ***River***, upper reaches of Thornton Beck, where it flows through Thornton Dale, 4m/7km NE of Pickering. **58 E1** SE8587.
Dalby Forest *N.Yorks.* ***Forest/woodland***, on S edge of North Riding Forest Park, 4m/7km NW of Snainton. **58 E1** SE8788.
Dalby Mountain *I.o.M.* ***Hill***, 4m/6km S of Peel. Height 918 feet or 280 metres. **54 B6** SC2477.
Dalby Point *I.o.M.* ***Coastal feature***, headland 1km W of Dalby. **54 B6** SC2178.
Dalby Wolds *Leics.* ***Locality***, 2m/3km SW of Old Dalby. SK6522.
Dalcairnie *E.Ayr.* ***Settlement***, 1m/2km SW of Dalmellington. **67 J3** NS4604.
Dalch *Devon* ***River***, rising on Witheridge Moor, 4m/6km E of Witheridge, and flowing W into River Yeo 1km S of Lapford. **7 G4** SS7307.
Dalchalloch *P. & K.* ***Settlement***, in Glen Errochty, adjoining to Trinafour. **81 J1** NN7264.
Dalchalm *High.* ***Settlement***, on E coast of Sutherland district, 1m/2km N of Brora. **97 G1** NC9105.
Dalchenna *Arg. & B.* ***Settlement***, on NE shore of Loch Fyne, 2m/3km SW of Inveraray. **80 B7** NN0705.
Dalchirach *Moray* ***Settlement***, in Avon valley, 9m/14km SW of Dufftown. **89 J1** NJ1934.
Dalchork *High.* ***Settlement***, near mouth of River Tirry, NE of Loch Shin, 2m/4km N of Lairg. **103 H7** NC5710.
Dalchreichart *High.* ***Settlement***, in Glen Moriston, Inverness district, 6m/9km NW of Fort Augustus. **87 J3** NH2912.
Dalchruin *P. & K.* ***Settlement***, in Glen Artney, 8m/12km NE of Callander. **81 J6** NN7116.
Dalchuirn *High.* ***Locality***, in Ross and Cromarty district on NW shore of Loch Carron, adjoining Lochcarron. NG9039.
Dalcross *High.* ***Locality***, 1m/2km SW of Croy. **96 E7** NH7748.
Dalcross Airport *High. Former name of Inverness Airport, qv.*
Dalderby *Lincs.* ***Settlement***, 2m/4km S of Horncastle. **53 F6** TF2466.
Dalditch *Devon* ***Settlement***, 2m/3km NW of Budleigh Salterton. SY0483.
Daldownie *Aber.* ***Settlement***, on S bank of River Gairn, 4m/6km NW of Craithie. **89 K4** NJ2400.
Dale *Cumb.* ***Hamlet***, 2m/3km N of Kirkoswald. NY5444.
Dale *Derbys.* ***Hamlet***, 3m/4km SW of Ilkeston. Slight remains of Norman abbey. **41 G2** SK4338.
Dale *Gt.Man.* ***Settlement***, adjoining to E of Delph. SD9808.
Dale *Pembs.* ***Village***, on Dale Roads, bay at W end of Milford Haven, 2m/3km N of St. Ann's Head. **16 B4** SM8005.
Dale Bottom *Cumb.* ***Locality***, 2m/3km SE of Keswick. NY2921.
Dale End *Derbys.* ***Hamlet***, 1km NW of Elton, 4m/7km S of Bakewell. SK2161.
Dale End *N.Yorks.* ***Hamlet***, 2m/3km W of Cononley, 4m/6km SW of Skipton. SD9646.
Dale Head *Cumb.* ***Hamlet***, 4m/7km SE of Keswick, on E side of Thirlmere. NY3117.
Dale Head *Cumb.* ***Mountain***, at E end of Buttermere Fell, 2m/3km NW of Seatoller. Height 2470 feet or 753 metres. **60 D5** NY2215.
Dale Head *Cumb.* ***Settlement***, on Martindale Common, 3m/5km E of Glenridding. **60 F5** NY4316.
Dale Moor *Derbys.* ***Settlement***, to E of Dale, 3m/4km SW of Ilkeston. SK4438.
Dale of Walls *Shet.* ***Settlement***, adjacent to E of Voe of Dale, on W coast of Mainland. **109 A7** HU1852.
Dale Park *W.Suss.* ***Settlement***, 3m/5km NW of Arundel. **12 C6** SU9709.
Dale Point *Pembs.* ***Coastal feature***, headland 1m/2km E of Dale. **16 B4** SM8005.
Dalebank *Derbys.* ***Settlement***, 2m/3km SW of Clay Cross. SK3661.
Dalebrow *Ches.* ***Suburb***, adjoining to S of Prestbury. SJ9076.
Dalehouse *N.Yorks.* ***Locality***, 1km SW of Staithes. **63 J5** NZ7717.
Dalelia *High.* ***Settlement***, with pier, on N shore of Loch Shiel, in Lochaber district, 3m/4km SE of Kinlochmoidart. **79 J1** NM7369.
Dalemain *Cumb.* ***Historic house***, medieval and Tudor house with Georgian façade set within estate, 3m/5km SW of Penrith. Notable 16c oak panelling and 18c Chinese wallpaper in drawing room. 12c pele tower houses Westmoreland and Cumberland Yeomanry regimental collection. Knot Garden has early Roman fountain. **61 F4** NY4726.
Dales Brow *Gt.Man.* ***Suburb***, 1m/2km S of Swinton town centre. SD7700.
Dales Farm *Aber. See Peterhead.*
Dales Green *Staffs.* ***Settlement***, 2m/3km NE of Kidsgrove. SJ8556.
Dales Voe *Shet.* ***Sea feature***, narrow inlet on NE coast of Mainland, 2m/4km SE of Scatsta. **109 D5** HU4270.
Dales Voe *Shet.* ***Sea feature***, inlet on E coast of Mainland, 3m/5km N of Lerwick. **109 D8** HU4546.
Daless *High.* ***Settlement***, in valley of River Findhorn, 6m/10km NE of Moy. **89 F1** NH8638.
Dalestie *Moray* ***Settlement***, on E bank of River Avon, 4m/7km S of Tomintoul. **89 J3** NJ1610.
Dalfad *Aber.* ***Settlement***, on N side of River Gairn, 4m/7km NW of Ballater. **90 B4** NJ3100.
Dalganachan *High.* ***Settlement***, situated just W of confluence of Rumsdale Water and Glutt Water, where they form River Thurso. **105 F4** ND0040.
Dalgarven *N.Ayr.* ***Settlement***, on River Garnock, 2m/3km N of Kilwinning. **74 A6** NS2945.
Dalgety Bay *Fife* Population: 7860. ***Small town***, housing development on bay of same name 3m/4km E of Inverkeithing. Donibristle Industrial Estate adjoins to NW. On shore of bay is ruined church of St. Bridget (Historic Scotland), dating from 1244. **75 K2** NT1683.
Dalgig *E.Ayr.* ***Settlement***, 4m/6km E of New Cumnock. **67 K2** NS5512.
Dalginross *P. & K.* ***Village***, on S side of River Earn opposite Comrie. Roman sites to S. **81 J5** NN7721.
Dalgonar *D. & G.* ***Settlement***, 6m/9km SW of Sanquhar. **68 C3** NS7003.
Dalguise *P. & K.* ***Settlement***, on W side of Strath Tay, 4m/6km NW of Dunkeld. **82 A3** NN9947.
Dalhalvaig *High.* ***Village***, in Strath Halladale, in Caithness district, 6m/10km S of Melvich. **104 D3** NC8954.
Dalham *Suff.* ***Village***, 5m/8km E of Newmarket. **34 B2** TL7261.
Dalhousie Castle *Midloth.* ***Castle***, dating from mid-15c, 1m/2km W of Newtongrange across River South Esk. Formerly seat of Ramsays. NT3263.
Daliburgh *W.Isles Anglicised form of Dalabrog, qv.*
Daligan *Arg. & B.* ***Settlement***, 2m/4km NE of Helensburgh. **74 B2** NS3284.
Dalinlongart *Arg. & B.* ***Settlement***, 4m/6km NW of Dunoon. **73 K2** NS1482.
Dalivaddy *Arg. & B.* ***Settlement***, on Kintyre, 3m/4km W of Campbeltown. **66 A2** NR6719.
Dalkeith *Midloth.* Population: 11,567. ***Town***, market town astride Rivers North and South Esk, 6m/10km SE of Edinburgh. **76 B4** NT3367.

Dalkeith Country Park *Midloth.* ***Leisure/recreation***, 800 acre country park with nature trails, farm animals and 18c bridge. Situated to N of Dalkeith. Rivers North and South Esk flow through park. **76 B4** NT3367.
Dalkeith House *Midloth.* ***Historic house***, to N of Dalkeith, built c. 1700, formerly seat of Dukes of Buccleuch. **76 B4** NT3367.
Dall *P. & K.* ***Locality***, on S shore of Loch Rannoch, 5m/7km W of Kinloch Rannoch. House (1855) is part of Rannoch boys' public school. NN5956.
Dall Burn *P. & K.* ***River***, running generally NE through Rannoch Forest into Loch Rannoch, 4m/7km W of Kinloch Rannoch. NN5956.
Dallachoilish *Arg. & B.* ***Settlement***, on S side of the narrows of Loch Creran, Argyll. NM9744.
Dallas *Moray* ***Village***, on River Lossie, 9m/14km SW of Elgin. Ruins of Tor Castle to N. **97 J6** NJ1252.
Dallas Forest *Moray* ***Forest/woodland***, to N of Dallas. **97 J6** NJ1252.
Dallaschyle *High.* ***Settlement***, 2m/3km E of Croy. **97 F7** NH8149.
Dallash *D. & G.* ***Settlement***, on W bank of Palnure Burn, 4m/6km NE of Newton Stewart. **64 E4** NX4769.
Dalleagles *E.Ayr.* ***Settlement***, 4m/6km SW of New Cumnock. NS5710.
Dallinghoo *Suff.* ***Village***, 4m/6km N of Woodbridge. **35 G3** TM2654.
Dallington *E.Suss.* ***Village***, 5m/8km E of Heathfield. **13 K5** TQ6519.
Dallington *Northants.* ***Suburb***, NW district of Northampton. **31 J2** SP7362.
Dallow *N.Yorks.* ***Settlement***, 4m/7km NE of Pateley Bridge across Dallow Moor. SE1971.
Dallowgill Moor *N.Yorks.* ***Open space***, moorland, highest point of which is 390 metres, 3m/5km N of Pateley Bridge. **57 G2** SE1571.
Dalmadilly *Aber.* ***Settlement***, 1km N of Kemnay. **91 F3** NJ7317.
Dalmahoy *Edin.* ***Locality***, 1m/2km SE of Ratho. Golf-course. NT1468.
Dalmally *Arg. & B.* ***Village***, on River Orchy in Argyll, 2m/3km E of NE end of Loch Awe. **80 C5** NN1627.
Dalmarnock *Glas.* ***Suburb***, on N bank of River Clyde, 2m/3km SE of Glasgow city centre. NS6163.
Dalmarnock *P. & K.* ***Settlement***, on W side of Strath Tay, 3m/4km NW of Dunkeld. **82 A3** NN9945.
Dalmary *Stir.* ***Settlement***, 1m/2km S of Gartmore. **74 D1** NS5095.
Dalmellington *E.Ayr.* Population: 1597. ***Small town***, on tributary of nearby River Doon, 13m/21km SE of Ayr. Site of 13c priory. **67 J3** NS4805.
Dalmeny *Edin.* ***Village***, 1m/2km E of South Queensferry. **75 K3** NT1477.
Dalmeny House *Edin.* ***Historic house***, 19c home of Earls of Rosebery to E of Dalmeny Park overlooking Firth of Forth, 2m/3km NE of Dalmeny. Scotland's first Gothic Revival house, designed by William Wilkins. Contains important collections of porcelain, paintings and furniture. **75 K3** NT1678.
Dalmichy *High.* ***Settlement***, on E bank of River Tirry, 4m/7km N of Lairg. **103 H7** NC5713.
Dalmigavie *High.* ***Settlement***, 12m/19km N of Kingussie. **8 E3** NH7419.
Dalmilling *S.Ayr.* ***Suburb***, E district of Ayr. NS3622.
Dalmore *High.* ***Locality***, on N shore of Cromarty Firth, Ross and Cromarty district, 1m/2km SE of Alness. **96 D5** NH6668.
Dalmore *W.Isles* *Anglicised form of Dail Mòr, qv.*
Dalmuir *W.Dun.* ***Suburb***, 1km NW of Clydebank town centre. NS4970.
Dalmunzie Hotel *P. & K.* ***Settlement***, 1m/2km NW of Spittal of Glenshee. **89 H7** NO0971.
Dalnabreck *High.* ***Settlement***, in Lochaber district, 3m/5km N of Salen across head of Loch Shiel. **79 J1** NM7069.
Dalnacardoch Forest *P. & K.* ***Open space***, deer forest to N of Dalnacardoch Lodge in Glen Garry. **88 D7** NN6875.
Dalnacarn *P. & K.* ***Settlement***, 6m/9km NE of Pitlochrie. **82 B1** NO0063.
Dalnaglar Castle *P. & K.* ***Hamlet***, in Glen Shee, 1km N of Cray. **82 C1** NO1464.
Dalnaha *Arg. & B.* ***Settlement***, on S shore of Loch Spelve, 5m/8km E of Lochbuie, Mull. **79 H5** NM6826.
Dalnahaitnach *High.* ***Settlement***, 4m/6km SW of Carrbridge. **89 F3** NH8519.
Dalnamain *High.* ***Settlement***, 8m/11km NW of Dornoch. **96 E2** NH7298.
Dalnamein Forest *P. & K.* ***Open space***, upland area in Forest of Atholl, 9m/14km SE of Dalwhinnie. **88 E7** NN7678.
Dalnatrat *High.* ***Settlement***, on SE shore of Loch Linnhe, 1m/2km S of Rubha Mòr. **80 A2** NM9653.
Dalnavie *High.* ***Settlement***, 3m/4km N of Alness. **96 D4** NH6473.
Dalness *High.* ***Settlement***, in Glen Etive, Lochaber district, SW of Buachaille Etive Mòr. Series of waterfalls in River Etive. Mountainous area to N is property of National Trust for Scotland. **80 C2** NN1651.
Dalnessie *High.* ***Settlement***, on River Brora, 12m/20km NE of Lairg. **103 J7** NC6315.
Dalnigap *D. & G.* ***Settlement***, 8m/12km SE of Ballantrae. **64 B3** NX1371.
Dalqueich *P. & K.* ***Hamlet***, 3m/5km NW of Kinross. **82 B7** NO0704.
Dalquharran *S.Ayr.* ***Settlement***, with 15c castle beside Water of Girvan, situated to N of Dailly across river. NS2702.
Dalreoch *S.Ayr.* ***Settlement***, in Stinchar valley, 6m/9km NE of Ballantrae. **67 F5** NX1686.
Dalriech *P. & K.* ***Settlement***, in valley of River Almond, 7m/11km N of Comrie. **81 J4** NN7833.
Dalroy *High.* ***Settlement***, 8m/12km E of Inverness. **96 E7** NH7644.
Dalrulzian *P. & K.* ***Settlement***, at S end of Glen Shee, 5m/8km N of Bridge of Cally. **82 C2** NO1358.
Dalry *D. & G.* *Alternative name for St. John's Town of Dalry.*
Dalry *Edin.* ***Suburb***, 1m/2km SW of Edinburgh city centre. NT2372.
Dalry *N.Ayr.* Population: 5732. ***Small town***, former 18c weaving centre on River Garnock, 6m/10km NE of Ardrossan. **74 A6** NS2949.
Dalrymple *E.Ayr.* Population: 1297. ***Village***, 5m/8km S of Ayr. **67 H2** NS3514.
Dalscote *Northants.* ***Settlement***, 4m/6km N of Towcester. SP6854.
Dalserf *S.Lan.* ***Village***, 2m/4km E of Larkhall. **75 F5** NS8050.
Dalsetter *Shet.* ***Settlement***, on Yell, near head of Basta Voe. HU5099.
Dalshangan *D. & G.* ***Settlement***, 3m/5km SE of Carsphairn. **67 K5** NX5988.
Dalskairth *D. & G.* ***Settlement***, 3m/5km SW of Dumfries. **65 K3** NX9372.
Dalston *Cumb.* ***Village***, on River Caldew, 4m/7km SW of Carlisle. Hall, mainly late 19c, dates partly from 16c and 17c. **60 E1** NY3650.
Dalston *Gt.Lon.* ***Suburb***, in borough of Hackney, 4m/6km NE of Charing Cross. TQ3384.
Dalswinton *D. & G.* ***Village***, 6m/10km N of Dumfries. Site of Roman fort to SW beside railway. **68 E5** NX9385.
Dalswinton Common *D. & G.* ***Open space***, moorland 8m/13km N of Dumfries. **68 E5** NX9488.
Daltomach *High.* ***Settlement***, in Strathdearn, 6m/10km SW of Tomatin. **88 E2** NH7421.
Dalton *Cumb.* ***Hamlet***, on edge of woodland, 1m/2km E of Burton-in-Kendal. SD5476.
Dalton *D. & G.* ***Village***, 7m/11km NW of Annan. **69 G6** NY1174.
Dalton *Lancs.* ***Settlement***, 2m/3km NE of Skelmersdale. **48 D2** SD4908.
Dalton *N.Yorks.* ***Village***, 6m/10km NW of Richmond. **62 C6** NZ1108.
Dalton *N.Yorks.* ***Village***, 2m/3km E of Topcliffe. **57 K2** SE4376.
Dalton *Northumb.* ***Hamlet***, 4m/6km W of Ponteland. **71 G6** NZ1172.
Dalton *Northumb.* ***Settlement***, 4m/6km S of Hexham, between Ham Burn and Rowley Burn. **62 A1** NY9158.
Dalton *S.Yorks.* ***Locality***, adjoining to NE of Rotherham. **51 G3** SK4694.
Dalton Castle *Cumb.* ***Castle***, 14c tower (National Trust) with exhibition, in Market Place at Dalton-in-Furness. **54 E1** SD1282.
Dalton-in-Furness *Cumb.* Population: 7550. ***Small town***, 4m/6km NE of Barrow-in-Furness. Dalton castle (National Trust), restored 14c peel tower in market place. Birthplace of artist George Romney in 1734. **55 F2** SD2374.
Dalton-le-Dale *Dur.* ***Village***, 2m/3km SW of Seaham. **63 F2** NZ4048.
Dalton Magna *S.Yorks.* ***Hamlet***, 1km S of Dalton, 3m/4km E of Rotherham. SK4693.
Dalton-on-Tees *N.Yorks.* ***Village***, 4m/7km S of Darlington. **62 D6** NZ2907.
Dalton Parlours *W.Yorks.* ***Locality***, 3m/4km S of Wetherby. Site of Roman villa. SE4044.
Dalton Parva *S.Yorks.* ***Locality***, 1km SW of Dalton, 2m/3km NE of Rotherham. SK4693.
Dalton Piercy *Hart.* ***Hamlet***, 3m/5km W of Hartlepool. **63 F3** NZ4631.
Daltot *Arg. & B.* ***Settlement***, on SE side of Loch Sween, 3m/5km NE of Achnamara. **73 F2** NR7583.
Daltra *High.* ***Settlement***, 1m/2km SW of Ferness. **97 G7** NH9443.
Dalveen Pass *D. & G.* ***Other feature of interest***, pass carrying A702 road from Carronbridge to Elvanfoot through Lowther Hills. **68 D3** NS9007.
Dalveich *Stir.* ***Settlement***, on N side of Loch Earn, 2m/3km E of Lochearnhead. **81 H5** NN6124.
Dalvennan *E.Ayr.* ***Settlement***, 2m/3km W of Patna. **67 H2** NS3810.
Dalvourn *High.* ***Settlement***, 8m/12km S of Inverness. **88 D1** NH6834.
Dalwhat Water *D. & G.* ***River***, rising on S slopes of Black Hill and flowing SE to join Castlefairn Water and form Cairn Water, 1km SE of Moniaive. **68 C4** NX7890.
Dalwhinnie *High.* ***Village***, on River Truim, in Badenoch and Strathspey district, 12m/20km SW of Kingussie. **88 D6** NN6384.
Dalwood *Devon* ***Village***, 3m/5km NW of Axminster. **8 B4** ST2400.
Dalziel *N.Lan.* ***Locality***, parish between Motherwell and Wishaw on N bank of River Clyde. Contains Dalzell House, with 15c tower. NS7654.
Dam Green *Norf.* ***Settlement***, 1m/2km SE of Kenninghall. TM0585.
Dam Side *Lancs.* ***Locality***, just NE of Pilling, 6m/9km W of Garstang. SD4048.
Damask Green *Herts.* ***Hamlet***, S end of Weston, 3m/4km SE of Baldock. TL2529.
Damerham *Hants.* ***Village***, 3m/5km NW of Fordingbridge. **10 C3** SU1015.
Damflask Reservoir *S.Yorks.* ***Reservoir***, 5m/8km NW of Sheffield. **50 E3** SK2890.
Damgate *Norf.* ***Locality***, 1km N of Martham. TG4519.
Damgate *Norf.* ***Village***, adjoining to S of Acle. **45 J5** TG4009.
Damnaglaur *D. & G.* ***Settlement***, 1km SW of Drummore, on W side of Luce Bay. **64 B7** NX1235.
Damsay *Ork.* ***Island***, in Bay of Firth on E coast of Mainland. **107 C6** HY3914.
Damsbrook *Derbys.* ***Settlement***, 1m/2km S of Clowne. SK4973.
Damside *P. & K.* ***Settlement***, 2m/3km NE of Auchterarder. **82 A6** NN9614.
Dan Caerlan *R.C.T.* ***Hamlet***, 1km NE of Llantrisant. ST0583.
Dan y Graig *Swan.* ***Suburb***, 1m/2km E of Swansea city centre across River Tawe. SS6793.
Dan-yr-Ogof Showcaves *Powys* ***Cave***, extensive cave system 1m/2km N of Pen-y-cae, beyond Craig-y-nos. Includes Europe's largest showcave complex, Dinosaur Iron Age Farm Museum and Morgan Brothers' Shire Horse Centre. **27 H7** SN8316.
Danaway *Kent* ***Hamlet***, 3m/5km W of Sittingbourne. TQ8663.
Danbury *Essex* Population: 3464. ***Village***, 5m/8km E of Chelmsford. Lingwood Common (National Trust) to N. **24 D1** TL7705.
Danbury Park Country Park *Essex* ***Leisure/recreation***, 41 acre country park comprising woodlands, gardens, open grassland and artificial lakes, 1km SW of Danbury. **24 D1** TL7704.
Danby *N.Yorks.* ***Village***, on River Esk, 12m/19km W of Whitby. **63 J6** NZ7008.
Danby Beacon *N.Yorks.* ***Hill***, 2m/3km NW of Danby. Viewpoint and tumulus. Height 981 feet or 299 metres. **63 H6** NZ7309.
Danby Botton *N.Yorks.* ***Locality***, 2m/4km S of Castleton. NZ6904.
Danby High Moor *N.Yorks.* ***Open space***, moorland 4m/6km S of Castleton. **63 H6** NZ6802.
Danby Low Moor *N.Yorks.* ***Open space***, moorland 1m/2km N of Danby. **63 H5** NZ6910.
Danby Wiske *N.Yorks.* ***Village***, 4m/6km NW of Northallerton. **62 E7** SE3398.
Dancers Hill *Herts.* ***Settlement***, 2m/3km SW of Potters Bar. TQ2399.
Dancing Green *Here.* ***Locality***, 3m/5km SE of Ross-on-Wye. SO6320.
Dandaleith *Moray* ***Settlement***, on W bank of River Spey, 1km N of Craigellachie. **97 K7** NJ2845.
Danderhall *Midloth.* Population: 2599. ***Hamlet***, 2m/3km NW of Dalkeith. **76 B4** NT3069.
Dane ***River***, rising SW of Buxton and flowing W to Middlewich, then NW into River Weaver at Northwich. **49 J6** SJ6573.
Dane Bank *Gt.Man.* ***Suburb***, 1m/2km W of Denton. SJ9095.
Dane End *Herts.* ***Hamlet***, 5m/8km N of Ware. **33 G6** TL3321.
Dane End *Herts.* ***Settlement***, 3m/5km S of Royston. TL3435.
Dane Hills *Leic.* ***Suburb***, 2m/3km W of Leicester city centre. **41 H5** SK5604.
Dane in Shaw *Ches.* ***Suburb***, 1m/2km SE of Congleton town centre. SJ8761.
Danebank *Ches.* ***Suburb***, adjoining to SE of Disley. SJ9784.
Danebridge *Ches.* ***Hamlet***, on River Dane, on border with Staffordshire, 1km SE of Wincle. **49 J6** SJ9665.
Danehill *E.Suss.* ***Village***, 5m/8km NE of Haywards Heath. **13 H4** TQ4027.
Danemoor Green *Norf.* ***Settlement***, 4m/7km NW of Wymondham. TG0505.
Dane's Brook ***River***, stream rising on Exmoor between Twitchen and Withypool and forming, for most of its length, part of boundary between Devon and Somerset before joining River Barle 2m/4km NW of Dulverton. **7 G2** SS8829.
Danes Wood *Devon* *See Broadclyst.*
Daneshill *Hants.* ***Suburb***, NE district of Basingstoke. SU6553.
Danesmoor *Derbys.* ***Locality***, 1km E of Clay Cross. **51 G6** SK4063.
Danestone *Aberdeen* ***Locality***, on N side of River Don, 2m/3km SE of Dyce. **91 H3** NJ9110.
Danethorpe Hill *Notts.* ***Hill***, 3m/5km NE of Newark-on-Trent. Height 108 feet or 33 metres. **52 B7** SK8457.
Daneway *Glos.* ***Locality***, 5m/9km W of Cirencester. SO9303.
Dangerous Corner *Gt.Man.* ***Locality***, 2m/3km W of Atherton. SD6402.
Dangerous Corner *Lancs.* ***Locality***, 5m/8km NW of Wigan. SD5210.
Danhiraeth *Carmar.* ***Locality***, 3m/4km SE of Newcastle Emlyn. SN3438.
Daniel's Water *Kent* ***Settlement***, 3m/5km W of Ashford. TQ9641.
Danna Island (Also known as Island of Danna.) *Arg. & B.* ***Coastal feature***, peninsula in Argyll, joined by an isthmus of a road's width to S end of peninsula between Loch Sween and Sound of Jura. **72 E3** NR6978.
Danny *W.Suss.* ***Historic house***, Elizabethan, E-shaped house, built c. 1595, 1m/2km SW of Hassocks. **13 F5** TQ2814.
Danny Burn *P. & K.* ***River***, stream flowing NE into Allan Water at Blackford. **81 K7** NN8805.
Dan's Castle *Dur.* ***Locality***, N part of Tow Law. NZ1239.
Danskine *E.Loth.* ***Settlement***, 3m/4km SE of Gifford. **76 D4** NT5667.
Danthorpe *E.Riding* ***Settlement***, 1m/2km N of Burton Pidsea. TA2432.
Danum *S.Yorks.* *See Doncaster.*
Danygraig *Caerp.* ***Hamlet***, opposite Risca across Ebbw River. ST2390.
Danzey Green *Warks.* ***Settlement***, 3m/5km NW of Henley-in-Arden. SP1269.
Dapple Heath *Staffs.* ***Hamlet***, 1km NE of Newton, 3m/4km NW of Abbots Bromley. SK0426.
Darby End *W.Mid.* ***Suburb***, 2m/3km S of Dudley town centre. SO9587.
Darby Green *Hants.* ***Locality***, 1km S of Sandhurst. **22 B5** SU8360.
Darby Green *Worcs.* ***Hamlet***, 6m/9km E of Bromyard. SO7456.
Darby's Hill *W.Mid.* ***Locality***, 1m/2km W of Oldbury. SO9689.
Darcy Lever *Gt.Man.* ***Suburb***, 1m/2km SE of Bolton town centre. SD7308.

Dare Valley Country Park *R.C.T.* ***Leisure/recreation***, country park 1m/2km W of Aberdare. Built on site of former collieries and disused railway tracks, this park acknowledges its roots with an industrial trail explaining history of area, as well as nature trails. **18 C1** SN9802.
Daren *Powys* ***Locality***, 2m/3km SW of Crickhowell. SO2015.
Daren-felen *Mon.* ***Locality***, 2m/3km E of Bryn-mawr. SO2112.
Darenth *Kent* Population: 3292. ***Village***, on River Darent, 2m/3km SE of Dartford. Site of Roman villa to S. **23 J4** TQ5671.
Daresbury *Halton* ***Village***, 4m/6km SW of Warrington. **48 E4** SJ5782.
Darfield *S.Yorks.* Population: 7723. ***Small town***, 5m/7km E of Barnsley. **51 G2** SE4104.
Dargate *Kent* ***Village***, 4m/6km SW of Whitstable. **25 G5** TR0861.
Dargues *Northumb.* ***Settlement***, on Roman road, 2m/3km W of Otterburn. Site of Roman camp nearby. **70 D4** NY8693.
Darite *Cornw.* ***Village***, 3m/5km N of Liskeard. **4 C4** SX2569.
Darland *Med.* ***Settlement***, to S of Gillingham. TQ7865.
Darland *Wrex.* ***Settlement***, adjoining to NE of Rossett. SJ3757.
Darlaston *Staffs.* ***Locality***, 1m/2km NW of Stone. SJ8735.
Darlaston *W.Mid.* ***Suburb***, SW district of Walsall. **40 B6** SO9796.
Darlaston Green *W.Mid.* ***Suburb***, W district of Walsall. SO9797.
Darley *N.Yorks.* ***Village***, 4m/7km SE of Pateley Bridge. **57 H4** SE2059.
Darley Abbey *Derby* ***Suburb***, 1m/2km N of Derby city centre. SK3438.
Darley Bridge *Derbys.* ***Village***, 2m/3km NW of Matlock. SK2661.
Darley Dale *Derbys.* ***Settlement***, in River Derwent valley, 3m/5km NW of Matlock. **50 E6** SK2663.
Darley Ford *Cornw.* ***Settlement***, 6m/9km N of Liskeard. SX2773.
Darley Head *N.Yorks.* ***Hamlet***, adjoining to W of Darley, 3m/5km NE of Blubberhouses. SE2059.
Darley Hillside *Derbys.* ***Hamlet***, 3m/4km NW of Matlock. SK2763.
Darlingscott *Warks.* ***Village***, 2m/3km NW of Shipston on Stour. **30 D4** SP2342.
Darlington *Darl.* Population: 86,767. ***Town***, on River Skerne, 31m/50km S of Newcastle upon Tyne. Darlington Railway Centre and Museum houses George Stephenson's 'Locomotion' steam engine, which pulled the first train on world's first public passenger railway. Tees Cottage Pumping Station, waterworks museum with early 20c steam beam and gas engines. **62 D5** NZ2914.
Darliston *Shrop.* ***Settlement***, 6m/9km SE of Whitchurch. **38 E2** SJ5833.
Darlton *Notts.* ***Village***, 3m/5km NE of Tuxford. **51 K5** SK7773.
Darn Hill *Gt.Man.* ***Suburb***, 1m/2km W of Heywood town centre. SD8310.
Darnabo *Aber.* ***Settlement***, 3m/4km NE of Fyvie. **99 F6** NJ7841.
Darnall *S.Yorks.* ***Suburb***, 3m/4km E of Sheffield city centre. **51 F4** SK3988.
Darnaw *D. & G.* ***Mountain***, rising to over 470 metres, 2m/3km W of Clatteringshaws Loch. **65 F3** NX5176.
Darnaway Castle *Moray* ***Castle***, seat of Earl of Moray, 1m/2km SW of Forres. Dating from 15c, Great Hall has survived with 19c mansion in front of it. **97 G6** NH9955.
Darnaway Forest ***Forest/woodland***, afforested area on W side of River Findhorn and on border of Highland and Moray, 5m/8km SW of Forres. **97 G6** NH9851.
Darnbrook Fell *N.Yorks.* ***Open space***, moorland, with highest point of 2047 metres or 624 metres, 3m/5km W of Arncliffe, in Littondale. **56 D2** SD8872.
Darnconner *E.Ayr.* ***Settlement***, 2m/4km NE of Auchinleck. **67 K1** NS5723.
Darnford *Aber.* ***Settlement***, 3m/4km S of Crathes. **91 F5** NO7692.
Darngarroch *D. & G.* ***Settlement***, 4m/7km N of Gatehouse of Fleet. **65 G4** NX6263.
Darnick *Sc.Bord.* ***Village***, 1m/2km W of Melrose. 16c peel tower. **76 D7** NT5334.
Darowen *Powys* ***Hamlet***, 2m/3km S of Cemmaes Road. **37 H5** SH8301.
Darra *Aber.* ***Settlement***, 2m/3km SE of Turriff. **99 F6** NJ7447.
Darracott *Devon* ***Village***, 4m/7km SW of Hartland. SS2317.
Darras Hall *Northumb.* ***Suburb***, adjoining to S of Ponteland. **71 G6** NZ1571.
Darrington *W.Yorks.* ***Village***, 2m/3km SE of Pontefract. **51 G1** SE4820.
Darrou *D. & G.* ***Mountain***, rising to over 470 metres, 2m/3km NW of Clatteringshaws Loch. **67 K5** NX5080.
Darrow Green *Norf.* ***Settlement***, 4m/6km N of Harleston. Traces of motte and bailey castle to E. TM2589.
Darsham *Suff.* ***Village***, 2m/3km NE of Yoxford. **35 J2** TM4170.
Dart *Devon* ***River***, rising as East and West Dart Rivers on N Dartmoor. The two streams join at Dartmeet and river then flows generally SE into sea just below Dartmouth. Tidal from Totnes; estuary opens out opposite Stoke Gabriel. **5 J5** SX8949.
Dartfield *Aber.* ***Settlement***, 2m/3km W of Crimond. **99 J5** NK0257.
Dartford *Kent* Population: 59,411. ***Town***, industrial town on River Darent, 2m/3km from S bank of River Thames. Former shipbuilding town. Partly Norman church, and 14c priory. **23 J4** TQ5474.
Dartford Tunnel ***Other feature of interest***, conveys road traffic under River Thames northbound from Dartford on S bank to Purfleet on N bank. See also Queen Elizabeth II Bridge. **23 J4** TQ5676.
Dartington *Devon* ***Village***, 2m/3km NW of Totnes. **5 H4** SX7862.
Dartmeet *Devon* ***Locality***, on Dartmoor, at confluence of East and West Dart Rivers, 6m/9km NW of Ashburton. Clapper bridge over East Dart beside road bridge. **5 G3** SX6773.
Dartmoor *Devon* ***Large natural feature***, between Lydford in W, Crockernwell in N, Bovey Tracey in E and Ivybridge in S. Extensive bare upland area of granite protected by National Park status, with many rocky summits or tors of between 1000 and 2000 feet (300 and 600 metres). Many swift streams as well as boggy areas. Numerous prehistoric and medieval sites (English Heritage) in area surrounding upper Plym valley. **6 D7** SX5880.
Dartmoor Wildlife Park *Devon* ***Leisure/recreation***, on S slopes of Dartmoor, 4m/6km NW of Ivybridge. One of largest collection of big cats in W of England, including some endangered species. Also falconry displays and adventure playground. **5 F5** SX5858.
Dartmouth *Devon* Population: 5676. ***Small town***, small port and resort on River Dart estuary, 7m/12km SE of Totnes. Royal Naval College on hill above town. Castle (English Heritage) at harbour entrance, 1m/2km S. Bayard's Cove Fort (English Heritage), 16c artillery fort protecting harbour. Ferries cross river. **5 J5** SX8751.
Dartmouth Castle *Devon* ***Castle***, earliest surviving 15c coastal fortress (English Heritage) with 16c-17c alterations, to S of Dartmouth overlooking Dart estuary. **5 J5** SX8850.
Dartmouth Museum *Devon* ***Other feature of interest***, in Dartmouth. Maritime museum, in 17c building, with models of ships and some local history. **5 J5** SX8751.
Dartmouth Park *Gt.Lon.* ***Suburb***, in borough of Camden, to E of Highgate Ponds, 4m/7km N of Charing Cross. TQ2886.
Darton *S.Yorks.* Population: 13,819. ***Town***, on River Dearne, 3m/5km NW of Barnsley. **51 F2** SE3110.
Darton Lane Head *S.Yorks.* ***Locality***, 1m/2km NE of Darton. SE3310.
Darvel *E.Ayr.* Population: 3759. ***Small town***, on River Irvine, 9m/14km E of Kilmarnock. Birthplace of Sir Alexander Fleming, 1881-1955, who discovered penicillin. **74 D7** NS5637.
Darvilshill *Bucks.* ***Settlement***, 3m/5km SE of Princes Risborough. SU8399.
Darwell *E.Suss.* ***Settlement***, to SW of Robertsbridge. **14 C5** TQ7222.
Darwell Hole *E.Suss.* ***Settlement***, 4m/6km NW of Battle. TQ6919.
Darwell Reservoir *E.Suss.* ***Reservoir***, 4m/6km NW of Battle. **14 C5** TQ7121.
Darwen ***River***, rising near Darwen and flowing N to Blackburn, then W to River Ribble at Walton-le-Dale, on S side of Preston. **55 K7** SD5428.
Darwen *B'burn.* Population: 29,864. ***Town***, industrial town, 4m/6km S of Blackburn. **56 B7** SD6922.
Datchet *W. & M.* Population: 4947. ***Small town***, on N bank of River Thames, 3m/4km SE of Slough. Queen Mother Reservoir to E. **22 C4** SU9877.
Datchworth *Herts.* ***Village***, 3m/5km NE of Welwyn. **33 F7** TL2619.
Datchworth Green *Herts.* ***Hamlet***, 3m/5km NE of Welwyn. **33 F7** TL2718.
Daubhill *Gt.Man.* ***Suburb***, 2m/3km SW of Bolton town centre. **49 G2** SD7007.
Daufraich *Pembs.* ***Island***, rocky island 2m/3km W of Ramsey Island. One of the larger islands in the group known as Bishops and Clerks. SM6623.
Daugh of Cairnborrow *Aber.* ***Hill***, rising to over 290 metres on N side of River Deveron, 3m/4km NE of Haugh of Glass. **98 C6** NJ4541.
Daugh of Carron *Moray* ***Open space***, tract surrounding Burn of Carron, 4m/6km SW of Charlestown of Aberlour. **89 J1** NJ2139.
Daugh of Invermarkie *Aber.* ***Open space***, on N side of Hill of Talnamounth, 1m/2km NW of Haugh of Glass. **98 C6** NJ4341.
Daugh of Kinermony *Moray* ***Settlement***, 2m/3km SW of Charlestown of Aberlour. **97 K7** NJ2441.
Dauntsey *Wilts.* ***Hamlet***, 4m/7km SE of Malmesbury. **20 C3** ST9882.
Dauntsey Green *Wilts.* ***Hamlet***, 1km E of Dauntsey. ST9882.
Dauntsey Lock *Wilts.* ***Hamlet***, on former Wiltshire and Berkshire Canal, now dry, 5m/8km SW of Wootton Bassett. ST9980.
Dava *High.* ***Settlement***, on border with Moray, 7m/11km NW of Grantown-on-Spey. **89 H1** NJ0038.
Dava Moor *High.* ***Open space***, moorland to SE of Dava. **89 H1** NJ0137.
Davaar *Arg. & B.* ***Settlement***, on S side of Kildalloig Bay, 2m/3km E of Campbeltown. **66 B2** NR7518.
Davaar Island *Arg. & B.* ***Island***, opposite entrance to Campbeltown Loch on E coast of Kintyre. Lighthouse at N point. On SE side is cave known as Crucifixion Cave. **66 B2** NR7520.
Davan *Aber.* ***Settlement***, to N of Loch Davan, 3m/5km SW of Tarland. **90 C4** NJ4401.
Davenham *Ches.* ***Village***, 2m/3km S of Northwich. **49 F5** SJ6571.
Davenport *Gt.Man.* ***Suburb***, 1m/2km S of Stockport town centre. SJ8988.
Davenport Green *Ches.* ***Suburb***, 1m/2km SW of Wilmslow town centre. SJ8379.
Davenport Green *Gt.Man.* ***Settlement***, 3m/4km SE of Altrincham. SJ8086.
Daventry *Northants.* Population: 18,099. ***Town***, market town 12m/19km W of Northampton. Remains of Iron Age fort and site of Roman building. Former coaching stop on London to Holyhead road. 17c Moot Hall now houses museum. **31 G2** SP5762.
Daventry Country Park *Northants.* ***Leisure/recreation***, 150 acre country park surrounding Daventry Reservoir to N of Daventry. Attracts a wide range of birds. **31 G2** SP5764.
Daventry Reservoir *Northants.* ***Reservoir***, to NE of Daventry. **31 G2** SP5863.
David Street *Kent* ***Settlement***, 1m/2km S of Meopham and 4m/6km N of Wrotham Heath. TQ6464.
David's Well *Powys* ***Locality***, 8m/13km SW of Newtown. SO0578.
Davidson's Mains (Formerly known as Muttonhole.) *Edin.* ***Suburb***, 3m/5km NW of Edinburgh city centre. NT2075.
Davidstow *Cornw.* ***Village***, 4m/6km NE of Camelford. **4 B2** SX1587.
Davington *D. & G.* ***Hamlet***, in valley of River White Esk, 3m/5km NW of Eskdalemuir. **69 H3** NT2302.
Daviot *Aber.* ***Village***, 5m/7km NW of Inverurie. Loanhead Stone Circle (Historic Scotland) to N dates from Bronze Age. **91 F2** NJ7528.
Daviot *High.* ***Settlement***, in Inverness district, 5m/8km SE of Inverness. **88 E1** NH7239.
Davoch of Grange *Moray* ***Settlement***, 3m/5km E of Keith. **98 C5** NJ4851.
Davyhulme *Gt.Man.* ***Suburb***, adjoining to NW of Urmston. SJ7595.
Davyshiel Common *Northumb.* ***Locality***, 2m/4km N of Otterburn. **70 D4** NY8997.
Daw Cross *N.Yorks.* ***Locality***, adjoining to W of Pannal, 2m/4km S of Harrogate. SE2951.
Daw End *W.Mid.* ***Suburb***, 2m/3km NE of Walsall. SK0300.
Dawley *Tel. & W.* ***Town***, forming central area of Telford, 3m/5km SE of Wellington. **39 F5** SJ6807.
Dawley Bank *Tel. & W.* ***Suburb***, to N of Dawley. SJ6808.
Dawley Brook *W.Mid.* ***Locality***, 3m/5km N of Stourbridge. SO8889.
Dawlish *Devon* Population: 9648. ***Small town***, 12m/20km S of Exeter. Resort with sands and red cliffs. **5 K3** SX9676.
Dawlish Warren *Devon* ***Coastal feature***, sandy spit at mouth of River Exe, 2m/3km NE of Dawlish. Popular holiday resort. Nature Reserve. SX9879.
Dawlish Water *Devon* ***River***, rising on Haldon, to E of Dawlish, and flowing through town centre. **5 K3** SX9676.
Dawn *Conwy* ***Hamlet***, 4m/6km S of Colwyn Bay. **47 G5** SH8672.
Dawpool Bank *Mersey.* ***Coastal feature***, sandbank on SW side of Wirral opposite Heswall. **48 B4** SJ2281.
Daw's Green *Som.* ***Locality***, 3m/4km SW of Taunton. ST1921.
Daws Heath *Essex* ***Hamlet***, 1m/2km S of Rayleigh. **24 E3** TQ8188.
Daw's House *Cornw.* ***Hamlet***, 2m/3km SW of Launceston. SX3183.
Dawsmere *Lincs.* ***Settlement***, 5m/7km N of Long Sutton. **43 H2** TF4430.
Dawyck House *Sc.Bord.* ***Historic house***, house, park and gardens in River Tweed valley, 6m/10km SW of Peebles. **75 K7** NT1635.
Day Green *Ches.* ***Settlement***, 1km S of Hassall Green. SJ7857.
Dayhills *Staffs.* ***Settlement***, 1m/2km NW of Milwich. SJ9532.
Dayhouse Bank *Worcs.* ***Settlement***, 4m/6km S of Halesowen. SO9678.
Daylesford *Glos.* ***Hamlet***, 4m/6km E of Stow-on-the-Wold. **30 D6** SP2425.
Daywall *Shrop.* ***Settlement***, 1km W of Gobowen. SJ2933.
Ddol *Flints.* ***Settlement***, 1m/2km SE of Caerwys. **47 K5** SJ1471.
Ddol *Wrex.* ***Locality***, 1m/2km SW of Wrexham. SJ3149.
Ddol *Wrex.* ***Settlement***, 4m/7km SE of Wrexham. SJ3845.
Ddol Cownwy *Powys* ***Settlement***, on River Cownwy, 1m/2km S of Lake Vyrnwy dam. SJ0117.
Ddu *Conwy* ***River***, running NE from Llyn Cowlyd Reservoir into River Conwy SE of Dolgarrog. SH7866.
Dduallt *Gwyn.* ***Mountain***, 4m/7km SW of Llanuwchllyn. Height 2155 feet or 657 metres. **37 H3** SH8127.
Ddyle *Powys* ***Mountain***, 9m/14km N of Llandrindod Wells. Height 1591 feet or 485 metres. **27 K1** SO0575.
Deacons *Som.* ***Settlement***, 3m/4km NW of Taunton. ST2028.
Deadman Hill *Hants.* ***Hill***, rising to over 110 metres, 2m/3km E of Woodgreen. **10 C3** SU2016.
Deadman's Cross *Beds.* ***Hamlet***, 3m/4km NW of Shefford. TL1141.
Deadman's Green *Staffs.* ***Hamlet***, 1km E of Checkley, 4m/7km NW of Uttoxeter. SK0337.
Deadwater *Hants.* ***Settlement***, adjoining to E of Bordon, 5m/8km W of Hindhead. SU8035.
Deadwaters *S.Lan.* ***Settlement***, 2m/4km W of Kirkmuirhill. **75 F6** NS7541.
Deaf Hill *Dur.* ***Locality***, to NE of Trimdon Colliery, 4m/6km SW of Peterlee. NZ3736.
Deal *Kent* Population: 28,504. ***Town***, cinque port and resort on E coast, 8m/13km NE of Dover. Castle (English Heritage) built by Henry VIII. **15 J2** TR3752.
Deal Castle *Kent* ***Castle***, 16 castle (English Heritage) formed of large complex of rounded citadels, built on coast at Deal by Henry VIII to guard against invasion after he broke with Church of Rome. **15 J2** TR3752.
Deal Hall *Essex* ***Settlement***, 4m/6km E of Burnham-on-Crouch, 1m/2km NW of Holliwell Point. **25 G2** TR0197.
Dean ***River***, rising 4m/7km E of Macclesfield and flowing NW through Bollington into River Bollin on N side of Wilmslow. **49 H4** SJ8382.
Dean *Cumb.* ***Village***, 5m/7km SW of Cockermouth. **60 B4** NY0725.
Dean *Devon* ***Village***, 1m/2km S of Buckfastleigh. **5 H4** SX7364.
Dean *Dorset* ***Hamlet***, 2m/3km SW of Sixpenny Handley. **9 J3** ST9715.
Dean *Hants.* ***Hamlet***, 1m/2km NE of Bishop's Waltham. **11 G3** SU5619.
Dean *Lancs.* ***Locality***, on Forest of Rossendale, 3m/5km E of Rawtenstall. SD8525.
Dean *Oxon.* ***Hamlet***, 2m/3km NW of Charlbury. **30 E6** SP3422.
Dean *Som.* ***Hamlet***, 3m/5km E of Shepton Mallet. **19 K7** ST6744.

Dean Bank *Dur.* ***Locality***, adjoining to W of Ferryhill. **62 D3** NZ2832.
Dean Burn *Midloth.* ***River***, small stream rising on Fala Moor and flowing N to join East Water 1km SE of Fala. One of numerous streams which join to flow into River Tyne. **76 C5** NT4458.
Dean Castle *E.Ayr.* ***Castle***, 14c stronghold, enlarged and embellished in 15c, with country park on hill overlooking confluence of Fenwick Water and Craufurdland Water, 1m/2km NE of Kilmarnock town centre. Once seat of the Boyds, Lords of Kilmarnock, last of whom lost his head after Battle of Culloden 1746. Collection of armour and medieval musical instruments. **74 C7** NS4339.
Dean Court *Oxon.* ***Suburb***, 3m/4km W of Oxford city centre. SP4705.
Dean Cross *Devon* ***Hamlet***, 3m/5km S of Ilfracombe. SS5042.
Dean Forest and Wye Valley *Glos.* ***Leisure/recreation***, national forest park of oak and beech woodlands and conifer plantations on a steeply edged plateau which stretches from River Severn estuary to valley of lower River Wye as it meanders between Ross-on-Wye and Chepstow. The forest, a former hunting forest, has a history of iron-ore and coal mining from Roman times to mid 20c. Area has many nature reserves, walking and cycling trails. **29 F7** SO6213.
Dean Forest Railway *Glos.* ***Other feature of interest***, tourist railway, running 1m/2km from New Mills in N, to S side of Lydney. **19 K1** SO6204.
Dean Head *S.Yorks.* ***Settlement***, 2m/4km SE of Penistone. SE2600.
Dean Heritage Centre *Glos.* ***Other feature of interest***, depicting past life in Forest of Dean by exhibitions and demonstrations, 2m/3km S of Cinderford. **29 F7** SO6610.
Dean Hill *Wilts.* ***Hill***, 1km S of West Dean. Height 479 feet or 146 metres. **10 D2** SU2426.
Dean Moor *Devon* ***Open space***, moorland in Dartmoor National Park, 4m/6km W of Buckfastleigh. **5 G4** SX6766.
Dean Prior *Devon* ***Village***, on E side of Dartmoor, 2m/3km S of Buckfastleigh. **5 H4** SX7363.
Dean Row *Ches.* ***Hamlet***, 2m/3km E of Wilmslow. **49 H4** SJ8681.
Dean Street *Kent* ***Hamlet***, 2m/3km SW of Maidstone. **14 C2** TQ7452.
Dean Water ***River***, running W from Loch of Forfar, past Glamis Castle, to River Isla 3m/5km SE of Alyth. **82 E3** NO2845.
Deanburnhaugh *Sc.Bord.* ***Hamlet***, 3m/4km SW of Roberton, on Borthwick Water. **69 J2** NT3911.
Deane *Gt.Man.* ***Suburb***, 2m/3km SW of Bolton town centre. SD6808.
Deane *Hants.* ***Hamlet***, 6m/9km W of Basingstoke. **21 J7** SU5450.
Deanend *Dorset* ***Hamlet***, 2m/3km W of Sixpenny Handley. ST9717.
Deanhead *W.Yorks.* ***Hamlet***, 3m/4km S of Ripponden, on W side of Scammonden Water. SE0416.
Deanland *Dorset* ***Hamlet***, 1m/2km NW of Sixpenny Handley. **9 J3** ST9918.
Deanlane End *W.Suss.* ***Settlement***, 4m/6km NE of Havant. SU7412.
Deans *W.Loth.* ***Suburb***, W district of Livingston. NT0269.
Deans Bottom *Kent* ***Settlement***, 1m/2km W of Bredgar and 3m/5km SW of Sittingbourne. TQ8660.
Deans Industrial Estate *W.Loth.* ***Locality***, in Deans suburb of Livingston. NT0269.
Deanscales *Cumb.* ***Hamlet***, 3m/5km SW of Cockermouth. **60 B4** NY0926.
Deansgreen *Warr.* ***Settlement***, 1m/2km SE of Lymm. SJ6985.
Deanshanger *Northants.* Population: 2724. ***Village***, 2m/3km W of Stony Stratford across River Great Ouse. **31 J4** SP7639.
Deanston *Stir.* ***Village***, 1m/2km W of Doune across River Teith. **81 J7** NN7101.
Deard's End *Herts.* ***Locality***, adjoining to W of Knebworth, 2m/4km S of Stevenage. TL2420.
Dearg Sgeir *Arg. & B.* ***Island***, islet midway between Mull and Torran Rocks group, 2m/3km S of Erraid. **78 D6** NM2915.
Dearham *Cumb.* Population: 1414. ***Suburb***, 2m/3km E of Maryport. **60 B3** NY0736.
Dearne ***River***, rising E of Huddersfield and flowing SE through Barnsley and into River Don N of Conisbrough. **51 F2** SK5099.
Dearne *S.Yorks.* ***Locality***, 7m/11km W of Barnsley. Comprises urban area around Goldthorpe and Bolton upon Dearne with surrounding section of Dearne Valley. SE4603.
Dearnley *Gt.Man.* ***Locality***, 1m/2km W of Littleborough. SD9215.
Deasker *W.Isles* ***Island***, islet 3m/5km SW of Aird an Rùnair on North Uist. **92 B5** NF6466.
Debach *Suff.* ***Hamlet***, 4m/6km NW of Woodbridge. **35 G3** TM2454.
Debate *D. & G.* ***Settlement***, 2m/3km SE of Paddockhole. **69 H5** NY2582.
Debdale *Gt.Man.* ***Suburb***, 4m/7km SE of Manchester city centre. SJ8996.
Debden *Essex* ***Village***, 4m/6km SE of Saffron Walden. **33 J5** TL5533.
Debden Cross *Essex* ***Settlement***, 2m/3km NW of Thaxted. TL5732.
Debden Green *Essex* ***Settlement***, 2m/4km W of Thaxted. **33 J5** TL5732.
Debden Green *Essex* ***Settlement***, at N end of Loughton. TQ4398.
Deben *Suff.* ***River***, rising to W of Debenham and flowing SE to Wickham Market, then S to Woodbridge, where it forms estuary flowing S into North Sea at Woodbridge Haven 3m/4km NE of Felixstowe. **35 G2** TM3336.
Debenham *Suff.* Population: 1777. ***Village***, on River Deben near its source, 11m/18km N of Ipswich. **35 F2** TM1763.
Deblin's Green *Worcs.* ***Hamlet***, 4m/6km NE of Great Malvern. SO8249.
Dechmont *W.Loth.* Population: 1134. ***Hamlet***, 1m/2km SW of Uphall. **75 J3** NT0470.
Dechmont Hill *S.Lan.* ***Hill***, 3m/5km N of East Kilbride, with remains of hillfort on S slopes. Height 600 feet or 183 metres. **74 E5** NS6558.
Decker Hill *Shrop.* ***Settlement***, 1m/2km N of Shifnal. SJ7509.
Dedda Skerry *Shet.* ***Coastal feature***, rocky headland on E coast of Mainland, S of Helli Ness. **109 D10** HU4627.
Deddington *Oxon.* ***Village***, built of Cotswold stone, 6m/9km S of Banbury. Remains of castle (English Heritage). **31 F5** SP4631.
Deddington Castle *Oxon.* ***Historic/prehistoric site***, remains of 12c castle (English Heritage) concealed by extensive earthworks, to E of Deddington, 6m/9km S of Banbury. **31 F5** SP4731.
Dedham *Essex* ***Village***, on River Stour, 6m/10km NE of Colchester. **34 E5** TM0533.
Dedham Heath *Essex* ***Hamlet***, 6m/9km NE of Colchester. TM0531.
Dedridge *W.Loth.* ***Suburb***, 1m/2km S of Livingston town centre. NT0666.
Dedworth *W. & M.* ***Suburb***, W district of Windsor. SU9476.
Dee ***River***, major river of NE Scotland rising at Pools of Dee in Cairngorm Mountains and running E past Braemar, Balmoral, Ballater and Banchory for about 90m/145km to North Sea at Aberdeen. **91 G5** NJ9605.
Dee (Dyfrdwy). ***River***, flowing from NE end of Llyn Tegid circuitously by Corwen, Llangollen, and Chester into Irish Sea between Point of Ayr and Hilbre Point. Has a long and wide estuary which divides Wales and England, and forms W edge of Wirral peninsula. **48 B5** SJ1983.
Dee *Cumb.* ***River***, rising on Blea Moor, E of Whernside, and flowing NW to Dent, then into River Rawthey 1m/2km SW of Sedbergh. **56 B1** SD6491.
Dee *D. & G.* ***River***, issuing from Loch Ken to flow S through Tongland Loch and past Kirkcudbright into Kirkcudbright Bay. Stretch above Loch Ken is known as Black Water of Dee or River Dee. **65 H4** NX6746.
Dee Bridge *Ches.* ***Bridge***, red sandstone bridge over River Dee, built 1407, on S side of Chester city centre. Consists of seven arches of various styles. SJ4065.
Deecastle *Aber.* ***Hamlet***, 4m/7km E of Ballater. **90 C5** NO4396.
Deene *Northants.* ***Village***, 4m/6km NE of Corby. **42 C6** SP9492.
Deene Hall *Northants.* ***Historic house***, Tudor home of Brudenells, 6m/10km NE of Corby. **42 C6** SP9492.
Deenethorpe *Northants.* ***Village***, 4m/7km NE of Corby. **42 C6** SP9591.
Deep Dale *Dur.* ***Valley***, carrying Deepdale Beck and running, in its lower regions, through Deepdale Woods 3m/4km E of Barnard Castle. **62 A5** NY9715.
Deep Hayes Country Park *Staffs.* ***Leisure/recreation***, 125 acres of meadows, woodland, pools and marshland 2m/3km E of Endon. Attracts wide variety of plant and animal life. **49 J7** SJ9553.
Deep Pit *S.Yorks.* ***Suburb***, 2m/3km SE of Sheffield city centre. SK3785.
Deepcar *S.Yorks.* ***Locality***, 1m/2km E of Stocksbridge. **50 E3** SK2897.
Deepcut *Surr.* Population: 1451. ***Locality***, 3m/5km SE of Camberley, largely consisting of military barracks. **22 C6** SU9057.
Deepdale *Cumb.* ***Locality***, and valley of Deepdale Beck, running N into Dentdale, SE of Dent. **56 C1** SD7284.
Deepdale *N.Yorks.* ***Settlement***, in Langstrothdale, 4m/6km NW of Buckden. **56 D2** SD8979.
Deepdale Beck *Dur.* ***River***, rising on Bowes Moor and flowing E into River Tees at Barnard Castle. **62 A5** NZ0416.
Deepdene *Surr.* ***Suburb***, residential locality to E of Dorking. TQ1749.
Deepfields *W.Mid.* ***Locality***, 3m/5km SE of Wolverhampton town centre. SO9494.
Deeping Fen *Lincs.* ***Open space***, lowland 5m/8km NE of Market Deeping. **42 E4** TF1816.
Deeping Gate *Cambs.* ***Village***, on S bank of River Welland, 7m/12km N of Peterborough. **42 E5** TF1509.
Deeping St. James *Lincs.* ***Village***, on River Welland, adjoining to E of Market Deeping. **42 E5** TF1509.
Deeping St. Nicholas *Lincs.* ***Village***, 5m/8km SW of Spalding. **43 F4** TF2116.
Deepweir *Mon.* ***Suburb***, SE district of Caldicot. ST4887.
Deer ***River***, rising N of Chilsworthy and flowing S into River Tamar on E side of North Tamerton. **6 B5** SX3197.
Deer Abbey *Aber.* ***Ecclesiastical building***, scant remains of 13c Cistercian monastery, on N bank of South Ugie Water, 1km W of Old Deer. **99 H6** NJ9648.
Deer Hill *Cumb.* ***Hill***, in Spadeadam Forest, 5m/8km N of Greenhead. Height 872 feet or 266 metres. **70 B6** NY6673.
Deer Law *Sc.Bord.* ***Mountain***, 3m/4km NW of St. Mary's Loch. Height 2063 feet or 629 metres. **69 H1** NT2225.
Deer Sound *Ork.* ***Sea feature***, large inlet on N coast of Mainland, between Mull Head to E and Rerwick Head to W. **107 E7** HY5307.
Deerdykes *N.Lan.* ***Settlement***, 3m/5km SW of Cumbernauld town centre. NS7172.
Deerhill *Moray* ***Settlement***, on S side of Aultmore, 4m/6km NE of Keith. **98 C5** NJ4656.
Deerhurst *Glos.* ***Village***, on E bank of River Severn, 7m/11km NW of Cheltenham. Odda's Chapel (English Heritage), 11c. **29 H6** SO8729.
Deerhurst Walton *Glos.* ***Settlement***, 3m/5km S of Tewkesbury. SO8828.
Deerlee Knowe *Sc.Bord.* ***Open space***, steep forested hillside, between 300 and 350 metres, on W of Lamblain Edge in Cheviot Hills, 1m/2km NE of Carter Bar. **70 C3** NT7108.
Deerness *Ork.* ***Locality***, on peninsula at E end of Mainland, 8m/13km SE of Kirkwall beyond Deer Sound. HY5605.
Deerness Valley Walk *Dur.* ***Leisure/recreation***, 8m/13km section of disused railway reclaimed for use by horse riders, cyclists and walkers in River Deerness valley between Durham and Stanley Crook. **62 C2** NZ2042.
Deer's Hill *Aber.* ***Hill***, 3m/5km S of Cuminestown. Height 584 feet or 178 metres. **99 G6** NJ8045.
Deerton Street *Kent* ***Settlement***, 3m/5km W of Faversham. TQ9762.
Defford *Worcs.* ***Village***, 3m/4km SW of Pershore. **29 J4** SO9143.
Defynnog *Powys* ***Village***, 1km S Sennybridge. **27 J6** SN9227.
Deganwy *Conwy* Population: 4665. ***Suburb***, 2m/3km S of Llandudno. Remains of castle on hill. **47 F5** SH7779.
Degnish *Arg. & B.* ***Settlement***, 1km NE of Degnish Point. **79 J6** NM7812.
Degnish Point *Arg. & B.* ***Coastal feature***, headland at N side of entrance to Loch Melfort. **79 J6** NM7712.
Deighton *N.Yorks.* ***Village***, 5m/8km N of Northallerton. **62 E6** NZ3801.
Deighton *W.Yorks.* ***Suburb***, 3m/4km NE of Huddersfield town centre. SE1619.
Deighton *York* ***Village***, 5m/8km S of York. **58 C5** SE6244.
Deil's Caldron *P. & K.* ***Inland physical feature***, chasm containing Falls of Lednock, in course of River Lednock, 1m/2km N of Comrie. **81 J5** NN7623.
Deil's Elbow *S.Ayr.* ***Other feature of interest***, sharp bend on minor road, caused by narrow valley below steep SW slopes of Clauchrie Hill, 5m/7km E of Dailly. **67 H3** NS3401.
Deiniolen *Gwyn.* Population: 1529. ***Village***, 2m/3km N of Llanberis. **46 D6** SH5763.
Delabole *Cornw.* ***Village***, 2m/4km W of Camelford. Old Delabole Slate Quarry on E side of village is 400 years old. **4 A2** SX0784.
Delamere *Ches.* ***Village***, 6m/9km W of Winsford. **48 E6** SJ5668.
Delamere Forest Park *Ches.* ***Forest/woodland***, discontinuous wooded area including former hunting reserve of Delamere Forest, to N and NE of Delamere; Primrosehill Wood, 1m/2km SE of Kelsall; and numerous woodland tracts in between. **48 E5** SJ5668.
Delavorar *Moray* ***Settlement***, on W bank of River Avon, 2m/3km S of Tomintoul. **89 J3** NJ1615.
Delfrigs *Aber.* ***Settlement***, 2m/3km N of Balmedie. **91 H2** NJ9621.
Delgatie Castle (Also spelled Delgaty Castle.) *Aber.* ***Castle***, 11c tower house containing the widest turnpike stair in Scotland, 2m/3km E of Turriff. **99 F5** NJ7550.
Delgatie Forest *Aber.* *Alternative spelling of Delgaty Forest, qv.*
Delgaty Castle *Aber.* *Alternative spelling of Delgatie Castle, qv.*
Delgaty Forest (Also spelled Delgatie Forest.) *Aber.* ***Forest/woodland***, to SE of Delgatie Castle and to E of Turriff. **99 F6** NJ7550.
Dell *W.Isles* ***River***, in N part of Isle of Lewis running N into Atlantic Ocean, 1km N of Dail Bho Dheas and 3m/5km SW of Butt of Lewis. **101 H2** NB4862.
Dell Lodge *High.* ***Settlement***, 1km SE of Nethy Bridge. **89 H3** NJ0119.
Dell Quay *W.Suss.* ***Hamlet***, with quay on Chichester Harbour (Chichester Channel), 2m/3km SW of Chichester. SU8302.
Delliefure *High.* ***Settlement***, 3m/5km NE of Grantown-on-Spey. **89 H1** NJ0730.
Delly End *Oxon.* ***Settlement***, 2m/4km N of Witney. SP3513.
Delmonden Green *Kent* ***Locality***, 2m/3km W of Hawkhurst. TQ7330.
Delnabo *Moray* ***Settlement***, 1m/2km SW of Tomintoul. **89 J3** NJ1617.
Delny *High.* ***Settlement***, in Ross and Cromarty district, 3m/5km NE of Invergordon. **96 E4** NH7372.
Delph ***Other water feature***, artificial drainage channel of River Great Ouse, running from Earith to confluence with New Bedford River, 2m/3km SW of Denver Sluice. **43 J6** TL5798.
Delph *Gt.Man.* Population: 5029. ***Locality***, 4m/7km NE of Oldham. **49 J2** SD9807.
Delph *W.Mid.* ***Suburb***, 3m/5km SW of Dudley town centre. SO9286.
Delph Bank *Lincs.* ***Open space***, lowland 3m/4km SE of Holbeach. **43 G3** TF3821.
Delph Reservoir *B'burn.* ***Reservoir***, on moors 4m/7km N of Bolton. **49 F1** SD7015.
Delphorie *Aber.* ***Settlement***, on W bank of River Don at foot of Ardhuncart Hill, 6m/9km S of Rhynie. **90 C3** NJ4818.
Delting *Shet.* ***Locality***, of Mainland between Dales Voe and Olna Firth. HU4067.
Delves *Dur.* ***Suburb***, SE of Consett. **62 C2** NZ1249.
Delvine *P. & K.* ***Settlement***, 2m/3km E of Caputh. **82 C3** NO1240.
Dembleby *Lincs.* ***Hamlet***, 5m/9km S of Sleaford. **42 D2** TF0437.
Demelza *Cornw.* ***Settlement***, 4m/6km E of St. Columb Major. SW9763.
Denaby *S.Yorks.* ***Village***, 5m/9km NE of Rotherham. **51 G3** SK4899.
Denaby Main *S.Yorks.* ***Village***, 1m/2km E of Denaby. **51 G3** SK4899.
Denbeath *Fife* ***Suburb***, N district of Buckhaven. NT3698.
Denbigh (Dinbych). *Denb.* Population: 8529. ***Small town***, on rocky limestone hill above River Clwyd, 10m/16km S of Rhyl. Remains of 12c-13c castle (Cadw). Birthplace of explorer H.M. Stanley. **47 J6** SJ0566.
Denbigh Castle *Denb.* ***Castle***, built in Edward I's reign in 13c by Henry de Lacy in Denbigh; now a ruin. **47 J6** SJ0565.
Denbigh Friary *Denb.* ***Ecclesiastical building***, Carmelite Friary founded c. 1285 in NE part of Denbigh. Much of the small church survives. **47 J6** SJ0666.
Denbury *Devon* ***Village***, 3m/5km SW of Newton Abbot. **5 J4** SX8268.
Denby *Derbys.* ***Village***, 3m/4km S of Ripley. **41 F1** SK3946.

D

Denby Bottles *Derbys.* ***Village***, 1km W of Denby. SK3946.
Denby Dale *W.Yorks.* Population: 2282. ***Small town***, 8m/12km W of Barnsley. **50 E2** SE2208.
Denchworth *Oxon.* ***Village***, 3m/5km NW of Wantage. **21 G2** SU3891.
Dendron *Cumb.* ***Village***, 3m/5km E of Barrow-in-Furness. **55 F2** SD2470.
Dene Mouth *T. & W.* ***Sea feature***, mouth of River Dene, 2m/3km E of Peterlee. **63 F2** NZ4640.
Denend *Aber.* ***Settlement***, 4m/7km E of Huntly. **90 D1** NJ5937.
Deneside *Dur.* ***Suburb***, W district of Seaham. NZ4148.
Denford *Northants.* ***Village***, 1m/2km S of Thrapston. **32 C1** SP9976.
Denge Beach *Kent* ***Coastal feature***, shingle beach 3m/4km SE of Lydd, with Dungeness at its S tip. **15 F6** TR0717.
Denge Marsh *Kent* ***Marsh/bog***, 1km SE of Lydd. **15 F5** TR0420.
Dengie *Essex* ***Village***, 4m/7km NE of Burnham-on-Crouch. **25 F1** TL9801.
Dengie Flat *Essex* ***Coastal feature***, mud flat on E coast between St. Peter's Flat and Ray Sand, 3m/4km E of Tillingham. **25 G1** TM0404.
Dengie Marshes *Essex* ***Marsh/bog***, 2m/3km W of Ray Sand on E coast. **25 G1** TM0100.
Denham *Bucks.* ***Village***, 2m/3km NW of Uxbridge. **22 D3** TQ0487.
Denham *Suff.* ***Village***, 6m/10km W of Bury St. Edmunds. Earthworks of motte and bailey castle 1m/2km NW. **34 B2** TL7561.
Denham *Suff.* ***Village***, 3m/5km E of Eye. **35 F1** TM1974.
Denham End *Suff.* ***Settlement***, 1m/2km N of Denham. TL7663.
Denham Green *Bucks.* Population: 2091. ***Suburb***, 1m/2km N of Denham. **22 D3** TQ0487.
Denham Green *Suff.* ***Locality***, 1km S of Denham. TM1974.
Denham Street *Suff.* ***Settlement***, 1m/2km SW of Denham. TM1972.
Denhead *Aber.* ***Settlement***, 1m/2km S of Kintore. **91 F3** NJ7914.
Denhead *Aber.* ***Settlement***, 1m/2km S of New Leeds. **99 H5** NJ9952.
Denhead *Angus* ***Settlement***, 2m/3km NW of Arbirlot. **83 G3** NO5742.
Denhead *Dundee* ***Settlement***, 3m/5km to NW of Dundee city centre. **82 E4** NO3431.
Denhead *Fife* ***Settlement***, 3m/5km SW of St. Andrews. **83 F6** NO4613.
Denholm *Sc.Bord.* ***Village***, 5m/8km NE of Hawick. **70 A2** NT5618.
Denholme *W.Yorks.* Population: 2295. ***Village***, 6m/10km W of Bradford. **57 F6** SE0734.
Denholme Clough *W.Yorks.* ***Hamlet***, 1m/2km S of Denholme. **57 F6** SE0732.
Denholme Gate *W.Yorks.* ***Settlement***, 1m/2km S of Denholme. SE0632.
Denio *Gwyn.* ***Locality***, adjoining to N of Pwllheli. **36 C2** SH3735.
Denmans *W.Suss.* ***Garden***, well-designed 20c garden at Fontwell, 5m/8km N of Bognor Regis. Seminars from John Brookes' School of Garden Design. **12 C6** SU9407.
Denmead *Hants.* Population: 5626. ***Village***, 2m/4km NW of Waterlooville. 1m/2km NW, Rookwood Farm, Tudor and earlier. **11 H3** SU6512.
Denmill *Aber.* ***Settlement***, 4m/6km W of Newmachar. **91 G3** NJ8218.
Denmoss *Aber.* ***Settlement***, 4m/6km SE of Inverkeithny. **98 E6** NJ6541.
Denne Park *W.Suss.* ***Open space***, estate surrounding private house 1m/2km SW of Horsham. **12 E4** TQ1629.
Dennington *Suff.* ***Village***, 2m/4km N of Framlingham. **35 G2** TM2867.
Dennis Head *Cornw.* ***Coastal feature***, headland on S side of mouth of Helford River, 8m/13km E of Helston and to E side of St. Anthony-in-Meneage. SW7825.
Dennis Head *Ork.* ***Coastal feature***, headland at E extremity of North Ronaldsay, at NE end of Linklet Bay. HY7955.
Dennis Part *W.Mid.* ***Locality***, 1m/2km N of Stourbridge town centre. SO9085.
Dennistoun *Glas.* ***Suburb***, 1m/2km E of Glasgow city centre. NS6065.
Denny *Falk.* Population: 11,061. ***Town***, industrial town on River Carron, 5m/8km W Falkirk. Forms one town with Dunipace. **75 G2** NS8182.
Denny Abbey *Cambs.* ***Ecclesiastical building***, 2m/3km N of Waterbeach. Founded originally by Benedictines, taken over by Knights Templar and subsequently used by the nuns of St. Clare. Fragments of church and refectory building survive (English Heritage). **33 H2** TL4968.
Denny Hill *Glos.* ***Locality***, on W bank of River Severn, 5m/8km W of Gloucester across river. SO7516.
Denny Island *B. & N.E.Som.* ***Island***, lying towards N end of Chew Valley Lake. ST5760.
Denny Island *Mon.* ***Island***, rock island in Severn estuary on line of demarcation between England and Wales. ST4581.
Denny Lodge *Hants.* ***Locality***, in New Forest, 3m/4km SE of Lyndhurst. SU3305.
Denny Priory *Cambs.* *See Waterbeach.*
Dennyloanhead *Falk.* ***Village***, 2m/3km S of Denny. **75 G2** NS8080.
Denshaw *Gt.Man.* ***Hamlet***, 5m/8km NE of Oldham. **49 J1** SD9710.
Denside *Aber.* ***Settlement***, 2m/3km E of Kirkton of Durris. **91 G5** NO8095.
Densole *Kent* ***Village***, 4m/6km N of Folkestone. **15 H3** TR2141.
Denston *Suff.* ***Village***, 5m/7km N of Clare. **34 B3** TL7652.
Denstone *Staffs.* ***Village***, 5m/8km N of Uttoxeter. **40 C1** SK1040.
Dent *Cumb.* ***Small town***, in valley of River Dee known as Dentdale, 4m/7km SE of Sedbergh. Cobbled streets. **56 C1** SD7087.
Dentdale *Cumb.* ***Valley***, secluded dale, with steep side of Aye Gill Pike rising to N, and through which River Dee flows from E to W, past Cowgill, Dent and Gawthorp. **56 C1** SD7087.
Denton *Cambs.* ***Village***, 1m/2km SW of Stilton. **42 E7** TL1487.
Denton *Darl.* ***Hamlet***, 1m/2km E of Summerhouse. **62 D5** NZ2118.
Denton *E.Suss.* ***Suburb***, 1m/2km N of Newhaven. **13 H6** TQ4502.
Denton *Gt.Man.* Population: 37,785. ***Town***, 4m/6km NE of Stockport. **49 J3** SJ9295.
Denton *Kent* ***Suburb***, E district of Gravesend. TQ6673.
Denton *Kent* ***Village***, 7m/11km N of Folkestone. **15 H3** TR2147.
Denton *Lincs.* ***Village***, 4m/6km SW of Grantham. Site of Roman villa 1m/2km SE. **42 B2** SK8632.
Denton *Norf.* ***Village***, 4m/6km W of Bungay. **45 G7** TM2788.
Denton *N.Yorks.* ***Village***, 2m/3km NE of Ilkley across River Wharfe. **57 G5** SE1448.
Denton *Northants.* ***Village***, 5m/9km E of Northampton. **32 B3** SP8357.
Denton *Oxon.* ***Hamlet***, 6m/9km SE of Oxford. **21 J1** SP5902.
Denton Burn *T. & W.* ***Suburb***, 4m/6km W of Newcastle upon Tyne city centre. NZ1965.
Denton Fell *Cumb.* ***Open space***, wooded area which includes Black Rigg, 836 feet or 255 metres, and Whamoss Rigg, 813 feet or 248 metres, 3m/5km SW of Greenhead. **70 B7** NY6162.
Denton Hall Roman Turret *T. & W.* ***Historic/prehistoric site***, turret foundations and 65 metre wall section (English Heritage) on course of Hadrian's Wall in Denton, 3m/5km W of Newcastle upon Tyne city centre. Turret retains base of platform on which ladder to upper floor was rested. First surviving stretch of wall from Newcastle upon Tyne. **71 G7** NZ1965.
Denton Holme *Cumb.* ***Suburb***, to S of Carlisle city centre. NY4054.
Denton Reservoir *Lincs.* ***Reservoir***, 1km N of Denton. **42 B2** SK8632.
Denton's Green *Mersey.* ***Suburb***, NW district of St. Helens. SJ4996.
Denver *Norf.* ***Village***, 1m/2km S of Downham Market. **44 A5** TF6101.
Denvilles *Hants.* ***Suburb***, E district of Havant. **11 J4** SU7206.
Denwick *Northumb.* ***Hamlet***, 1m/2km E of Alnwick. **71 H2** NU2014.
Deopham *Norf.* ***Village***, 4m/6km W of Wymondham. **44 E5** TG0400.
Deopham Green *Norf.* ***Village***, 1m/2km S of Deopham. **44 E6** TG0400.
Depden *Suff.* ***Settlement***, 6m/10km SW of Bury St. Edmunds. **34 B3** TL7856.
Depden Green *Suff.* ***Settlement***, 1m/2km W of Chedburgh. TL7757.
Deppers Hill *Warks.* ***Settlement***, 2m/3km SW of Southam. SP3959.
Deptford *Gt.Lon.* ***Suburb***, in borough of Lewisham, 5m/8km E of Charing Cross. **23 G4** TQ3777.
Deptford *T. & W.* ***Locality***, 1m/2km NW of Sunderland city centre on S bank of River Wear. NZ3857.
Deptford *Wilts.* ***Hamlet***, 1km NE of Wylye across River Wylye. **10 B1** SU0138.
Deptford Industrial Estate *T. & W.* ***Locality***, on S bank of River Wear, 1km NW of Sunderland city centre. NZ3857.
Derby *Derby* Population: 223,836. ***City***, industrial city and county town on River Derwent, 35m/56km NE of Birmingham. Shopping and entertainment centre. Cathedral mainly by James Gibbs, 1725. Both manufacturing and engineering are important to local economy. University. The porcelain industry also has a presence here. **41 F2** SK3536.
Derby Cathedral *Derby* ***Ecclesiastical building***, in centre of Derby, elevated to cathedral status in 1927. Perpendicular tower is only remnant of medieval church and subsequent building took place in early 18c and mid 20c. **41 F2** SK3536.
Derby Fort *I.o.M.* ***Historic/prehistoric site***, fort on N end of St. Michael's Island, built in 1645 during English Civil War by Earl of Derby to protect Derbyhaven. Fort served as lighthouse in 18c. **54 C7** SC3067.
Derbyhaven *I.o.M.* ***Village***, on bay of Derby Haven, 1m/2km E of Castletown. **54 B7** SC2867.
Dere Street ***Other feature of interest***, discontinuous Roman road running between York and Edinburgh. Present-day roads, including sections of A1, follow its course. **62 D5** NZ2021.
Dererach *Arg. & B.* ***Settlement***, on N shore of Loch Scridain, Mull, 2m/3km N of Pennyghael across loch. **79 G5** NM5129.
Derfyn *Conwy* ***River***, flowing NE from slopes of Moel Maelogen and into River Gallen, 1m/2km S of Llangernyw. **47 G6** SH8665.
Deri *Caerp.* ***Village***, 2m/3km NW of Bargoed. **18 E1** SO1201.
Deri *Mon.* ***Inland physical feature***, mountain ridge rising to over 370 metres, running SE from Sugar Loaf, 1m/2km N of Abergavenny. **28 B7** SO2917.
Dernaglar Loch *D. & G.* ***Lake/loch***, small loch 4m/7km E of Glenluce. **64 C5** NX2658.
Derril *Devon* ***Hamlet***, 2m/4km W of Holsworthy. SS3003.
Derringstone *Kent* ***Village***, 6m/10km SE of Canterbury. **15 G3** TR2049.
Derrington *Staffs.* ***Village***, 2m/3km W of Stafford. **40 A3** SJ8922.
Derriton *Devon* ***Hamlet***, just SW of Holsworthy. SS3303.
Derry *Stir.* ***Settlement***, on N side of Loch Earn, 3m/5km E of Lochearnhead. **81 H5** NN6424.
Derry Burn *Aber.* ***River***, rising in Cairngorm Mountains and flowing S through Glen Derry to join Lui Water at Derry Lodge, 4m/6km NW of Inverey. **89 H5** NO0493.
Derry Cairngorm (Also known as Cairn Gorm of Derry). *Aber.* ***Mountain***, in Cairngorm Mountains, 2m/3km E of Ben Macdui. Munro: height 3788 feet or 1155 metres. **89 H5** NO0198.
Derry Downs *Gt.Lon.* ***Suburb***, in borough of Bromley, 1m/2km NE of Orpington. TQ4767.
Derry Hill *Wilts.* ***Hamlet***, 3m/4km W of Calne. **20 C4** ST9570.
Derrythorpe *N.Lincs.* ***Hamlet***, on W bank of River Trent, 2m/3km S of Keadby. **52 B2** SE8208.
Dersingham *Norf.* Population: 3761. ***Village***, 7m/11km S of Hunstanton. **44 A2** TF6830.
Dervaig *Arg. & B.* ***Village***, on Mull, 5m/8km W of Tobermory. Group of standing stones 1km E. **79 F2** NM4352.
Derventio *Cumb.* *See Papcastle.*
Derventio *Derby* *See Little Chester.*
Derwen *Bridgend* ***Hamlet***, 2m/3km N of Bridgend. SS9182.
Derwen *Denb.* ***Village***, 5m/8km N of Corwen. **47 J7** SJ0750.
Derwen Churchyard Cross *Denb.* ***Historic/prehistoric site***, fine example of Celtic cross (Cadw) in churchyard at Derwen, 5m/8km SW of Ruthin. **47 J7** SJ0750.
Derwen-fawr *Carmar.* *Welsh form of Broad Oak, qv.*
Derwen Fawr *Swan.* ***Suburb***, 3m/5km SW of Swansea city centre, and 2m/3km S of Sketty. SS6292.
Derwen-gam *Cere.* *Welsh form of Oakford, qv.*
Derwenlas *Powys* ***Hamlet***, 2m/3km SW of Machynlleth. **37 G6** SN7299.
Derwent ***River***, formed by confluence of streams near Hunstanworth and flowing NE through Derwent Reservoir and by Shotley Bridge and Ebchester to River Tyne at Derwent Haugh, E of Blaydon. **62 C1** NZ2063.
Derwent ***River***, rising on Fylingdales Moor, S of Whitby and flowing S to Vale of Pickering at Ayton, SW to Malton, then S by Stamford Bridge to join River Ouse, 5m/7km SE of Selby. **58 E2** SE6728.
Derwent ***River***, rising on NE slopes of Bleaklow Hill, 6m/10km E of Glossop, and flowing S through Derwent and Ladybower Reservoirs, Baslow, Matlock, Belper and Derby and into River Trent at Great Wilne, 3m/5km SW of Long Eaton. **41 G2** SK4530.
Derwent *Cumb.* ***River***, rising as Grains Gill below Allen Crags to NE of Scafell and flowing N through Borrowdale into Derwent Water, then NW to Bassenthwaite Lake, then W by Cockermouth to Solway Firth at Workington. **60 D5** NX9829.
Derwent Dale *Derbys.* ***Valley***, part of Upper Derwent Valley, running N to S, and containing Derwent Reservoir, 4m/7km NE of Edale. **50 D3** SK1692.
Derwent Estate *S.Yorks.* ***Open space***, National Trust property, to E of Derwent Reservoir, in Peak District National Park. Part of High Peak Estate (National Trust). SK1893.
Derwent Fells *Cumb.* ***Large natural feature***, mountain range to SW of Derwent Water. **60 D5** NY2117.
Derwent Haugh *T. & W.* ***Locality***, at mouth of River Derwent, 3m/5km W of Gateshead. NZ2063.
Derwent Reservoir ***Reservoir***, large reservoir on border of Durham and Tyne & Wear, in valley of River Derwent, 5m/7km W of Consett. **62 B1** NZ0251.
Derwent Reservoir *Derbys.* ***Reservoir***, in Derwent Dale between Howden and Ladybower Reservoirs, 9m/14km E of Glossop across High Peak. **50 D3** SK1790.
Derwent Water *Cumb.* ***Lake/loch***, lake formed by River Derwent SW of Keswick, about 3m/5km long N to S and up to 1m/2km wide E to W. Part owned by National Trust. **60 D4** NY2521.
Derwentcote Steel Furnace *Dur.* *See Hamsterley.*
Derwydd *Carmar.* ***Locality***, 3m/5km S of Llandeilo. **17 K3** SN6117.
Derybruich *Arg. & B.* ***Settlement***, 3m/5km SW of Tighnabruaich. **73 H3** NR9370.
Desborough *Northants.* Population: 7351. ***Small town***, small manufacturing town 5m/8km NW of Kettering. **42 B7** SP8083.
Desford *Leics.* Population: 3194. ***Village***, 7m/11km E of Leicester. **41 G5** SK4703.
Deskry Water *Aber.* ***River***, rising to E of Mullachdubh and flowing NE before turning N, then W to join River Don 3m/4km E of Strathdon. **90 B4** NJ3812.
Detchant *Northumb.* ***Hamlet***, 2m/3km NW of Belford. **77 J7** NU0836.
Dethenydd *Powys* ***Mountain***, 4m/7km E of Llandiloes. Height 1824 feet or 556 metres. **37 K7** SO0282.
Dethick *Derbys.* ***Settlement***, 2m/3km SE of Matlock. SK3257.
Detling *Kent* ***Village***, 3m/4km NE of Maidstone. County Agricultural Showground 1km NE. **14 C2** TQ7958.
Deuchar Hill *Angus* ***Hill***, 1km S of Auchnacree. Height 977 feet or 298 metres. **83 F1** NO4662.
Deuchar Law *Sc.Bord.* ***Mountain***, 4m/7km NE of St. Mary's Loch. Height 1778 feet or 542 metres. **69 H1** NT2829.
Deuchary Hill *P. & K.* ***Mountain***, 4m/6km N of Dunkeld. Height 1670 feet or 509 metres. **82 B3** NO0348.
Deucheran Hill *Arg. & B.* ***Mountain***, on Kintyre, 3m/5km W of Grogport. Height 1079 feet or 329 metres. **73 F6** NR7644.
Deuchrie Dod *E.Loth.* ***Hill***, 1m/2km S of Stenton. Height 974 feet or 297 metres. **76 E3** NT6272.
Deuddwr *Powys* ***Hamlet***, 6m/10km N of Welshpool. **38 B4** SJ2417.
Deunant *Conwy* ***Locality***, 6m/9km W of Denbigh. **47 H6** SH9665.
Deuxhill *Shrop.* ***Settlement***, 4m/6km S of Bridgnorth. **39 F7** SO6987.

Deva *Ches. See Chester.*
Devauden *Mon.* ***Village***, 4m/7km NW of Chepstow. **19 H2** ST4898.
Deveron ***River***, rising S of Cabrach, and flowing NE by Huntly and Turriff to Banff Bay on E side of Banff. **98 E6** NJ6964.
Devil's Beef Tub *D. & G.* ***Large natural feature***, vast semicircular hollow in hills, 5m/8km N of Moffat. Source of River Annan. **69 F2** NT0613.
Devil's Bridge *Cere.* ***Bridge***, three superimposed bridges in deep valley of River Mynach, 10m/16km SE of Aberystwyth. Lowest bridge is 12c. SN7477.
Devil's Bridge (Pontarfynach). *Cere.* ***Hamlet***, in landscape of crags and wooded glens, 10m/16km E of Aberystwyth. **27 G1** SN7376.
Devil's Bridge *D. & G.* ***Coastal feature***, stack at Burrow Head, 2m/3km SW of Isle of Whithorn. **64 E7** NX4634.
Devil's Dyke *W.Suss.* ***Large natural feature***, steep slope in South Downs above Poynings; the subject of legend. Dyke is below a large Iron Age fort. TQ2611.
Devil's Elbow *P. & K.* ***Other feature of interest***, double hairpin bend, now bypassed, 1km S of Cairnwell Pass on road from Braemar to Spittal of Glenshee. **89 J7** NO1476.
Devil's Staircase *High.* ***Other feature of interest***, on Old Military Road, running down steep SE slope of Stob Mhic Mhartuin, 3m/5km SE of Kinlochleven. **80 D2** NN2157.
Devil's Water *Northumb.* ***River***, rising on Allendale Common, 5m/7km SE of Allendale Town, and flowing NE into River Tyne 1m/2km W of Corbridge. **62 A1** NY9764.
Devitts Green *Warks.* ***Settlement***, 5m/8km E of Coleshill. SP2790.
Devizes *Wilts.* Population: 13,205. ***Town***, market town, 10m/16km SE of Chippenham, on Kennet and Avon Canal at W end of Vale of Pewsey. Large central square and many Georgian buildings. Victorian castle on site of previous medieval one. Museum of Wiltshire prehistory. Kennet and Avon canal to W, has 29 locks in 2m/3km stretch of water on Caen Hill. **20 D5** SU0061.
Devizes Museum *Wilts.* ***Other feature of interest***, in Devizes, displaying Neolithic, Bronze and Iron Age artefacts. **20 D5** SU0061.
Devoke Water *Cumb.* ***Lake/loch***, lake 2m/4km SE of Eskdale Green. **60 C7** SD1596.
Devon ***River***, rising on Ochil Hills and flowing through Glendevon Reservoirs and E down Glen Devon to Glendevon, then SE to Crook of Devon, where it turns sharply to run almost due W to S side of Menstrie, then S to River Forth 2m/4km W of Alloa. **75 H1** NS8493.
Devon ***River***, rising near Eaton and flowing N into River Trent at Newark-on-Trent. **42 A1** SK7853.
Devonport *Plym.* ***Locality***, W district of Plymouth beside stretch of River Tamar Estuary known as Hamoaze. Naval base. Car ferry to Torpoint. **4 E5** SX4555.
Devonside *Clack.* ***Village***, on S bank of River Devon opposite Tillicoultry. **75 H1** NS9296.
Devoran *Cornw.* ***Village***, at head of Restronguet Creek, 4m/6km SW of Truro. **2 E5** SW7939.
Dewar *Sc.Bord.* ***Settlement***, 8m/12km N of Innerleithen. **76 B6** NT3448.
Dewar Burn *Sc.Bord.* ***River***, small stream which rises on Dewar Hill and flows N to become Heriot Water, 1m/2km NE of Dewar. **76 B6** NT3550.
Dewi Fawr *Carmar.* ***River***, rising E of Trelech and flowing S into River Cynin at St. Clears. **17 F3** SN2816.
Dewlish *Dorset* ***Village***, 3m/5km NE of Puddletown. **9 G5** SY7798.
Dewsall *Here.* ***Locality***, 4m/7km SW of Hereford. SO4833.
Dewsall Court *Here.* ***Settlement***, 4m/7km SW of Hereford. **28 D5** SO4833.
Dewsbury *W.Yorks.* Population: 50,168. ***Town***, on River Calder, 8m/13km SW of Leeds. Originally a 'wool' town, textiles still feature prominently in its market. **57 H7** SE2421.
Dewsbury Moor *W.Yorks.* ***Suburb***, adjoining to W of Dewsbury. SE2222.
Dhoon *I.o.M.* ***Settlement***, 2m/3km NE of Laxey. **54 D5** SC4586.
Dhoor *I.o.M.* ***Settlement***, 1m/2km NW of Ramsey. **54 D4** SC4496.
Dhowin *I.o.M.* ***Settlement***, 1m/2km N of Andreas. **54 D3** NX4101.
Dhuhallow *High.* ***Settlement***, 3m/4km E of Inverfarigaig. **88 C2** NH5522.
Diabhal *W.Isles Gaelic form of Diaval, qv.*
Dial *N.Som.* ***Locality***, 2m/3km NE of Bristol International Airport and 5m/9km SW of Bristol. ST5366.
Dial Green *W.Suss.* ***Hamlet***, 5m/7km NE of Midhurst. SU9227.
Dial Post *W.Suss.* ***Village***, 5m/7km NE of Washington. **12 E5** TQ1519.
Diaval (Gaelic form: Diabhal.) *W.Isles* ***Hill***, rising to over 150 metres, 7m/12km NW of Tolsta Head, Isle of Lewis. **101 G2** NB4552.
Dibden *Hants.* ***Village***, 1m/2km N of Dibden Purlieu. **11 F4** SU4107.
Dibden Hill *Bucks.* ***Settlement***, adjoining to S of Chalfont St. Giles. SU9992.
Dibden Purlieu *Hants.* ***Suburb***, adjoining to SW of Hythe, on edge of New Forest. **11 F4** SU4106.
Dibyn Du *Cere.* ***Mountain***, 3m/4km W of Claerwen Reservoir. Height 1738 feet or 530 metres. **27 G2** SN7965.
Dickens Heath *W.Mid.* ***Settlement***, 3m/5km SW of Solihull. SP1176.
Dickleburgh *Norf.* ***Village***, 4m/6km NE of Diss. **45 F7** TM1682.
Dickleburgh Moor *Norf.* ***Hamlet***, 1km N of Dickleburgh. TM1783.
Didbrook *Glos.* ***Hamlet***, 3m/4km NE of Winchcombe. **30 B5** SP0531.
Didcot *Oxon.* Population: 17,691. ***Town***, 10m/16km S of Oxford, with 15c church and centre for railway enthusiasts. **21 J3** SU5290.
Diddington *Cambs.* ***Village***, 4m/6km N of St. Neots. **32 E2** TL1965.
Diddlebury *Shrop.* ***Village***, 5m/8km E of Craven Arms. **38 E7** SO5085.
Didley *Here.* ***Hamlet***, 6m/10km SW of Hereford. **28 D5** SO4532.
Didling *W.Suss.* ***Hamlet***, 4m/6km SW of Midhurst. **12 B5** SU8318.
Didlington *Norf.* ***Locality***, parish with church and park, 3m/4km NW of Mundford. TL7797.
Didmarton *Glos.* ***Village***, 6m/9km SW of Tetbury. **20 B3** ST8287.
Didsbury *Gt.Man.* ***Suburb***, 5m/8km S of Manchester city centre. **49 H3** SJ8490.
Didworthy *Devon* ***Hamlet***, on E bank of River Avon, 2m/3km NW of South Brent. **5 G4** SX6862.
Diebidale *High.* ***River***, in Sutherland district running NE down Glen Diebidale to head of Glen Calvie. **96 B3** NH4686.
Diebidale Forest *High.* ***Open space***, deer forest extending E and W of river Diebidale. **96 B3** NH4686.
Diffwys *Gwyn.* ***Mountain***, 5m/8km NW of Dolgellau. Height 2460 feet or 750 metres. **37 F3** SH6623.
Digby *Lincs.* ***Village***, 6m/9km N of Sleaford. **52 D7** TF0854.
Digg *High.* ***Settlement***, on NE coast of Skye, W of Staffin Bay. **93 K5** NG4669.
Diggle *Gt.Man.* ***Village***, 6m/9km E of Oldham. **50 C2** SE0008.
Dighty Water *Dundee* ***River***, rising in Sidlaw Hills and flowing E by N side of Dundee city, entering Firth of Tay 1km W of Monifieth. **82 E4** NO4831.
Digmoor *Lancs.* ***Suburb***, SE district of Skelmersdale. **48 D2** SD4904.
Digswell *Herts.* ***Locality***, at N end of Welwyn Garden City. **33 F7** TL2515.
Digswell Water *Herts.* ***Settlement***, 1m/2km NE of Welwyn Garden City town centre. TL2514.
Dihewyd *Cere.* ***Hamlet***, 5m/8km SE of Aberaeron. **26 D3** SN4855.
Dildawn *D. & G.* ***Settlement***, 3m/5km SW of Castle Douglas. **65 H5** NX7259.
Dilham *Norf.* ***Village***, 5m/7km SE of North Walsham. **45 H3** TG3325.
Dilhorne *Staffs.* ***Village***, 2m/4km W of Cheadle. **40 B1** SJ9743.
Dillington *Cambs.* ***Hamlet***, 3m/4km SE of Kimbolton. TL1365.
Dilston *Northumb.* ***Hamlet***, 1m/2km SW of Corbridge. **70 E7** NY9763.
Dilton Marsh *Wilts.* ***Village***, 2m/3km W of Westbury. **20 B6** ST8449.
Dilworth *Lancs.* ***Locality***, 1m/2km E of Longridge. SD6137.
Dilwyn *Here.* ***Village***, 6m/9km SW of Leominster. **28 D3** SO4154.
Dilwyn Common *Here.* ***Settlement***, 5m/8km SW of Leominster. **28 D3** SO4255.
Dimple *Gt.Man.* ***Hamlet***, 1km NW of Egerton, on E side of Delph Reservoir. SD7015.
Dimsdale *Staffs.* ***Suburb***, 1m/2km N of Newcastle-under-Lyme town centre. SJ8448.
Din Dryfol Burial Chamber *I.o.A.* ***Historic/prehistoric site***, Megalithic tomb of segmented cist type (Cadw) on SW side of Anglesey, 5m/8km E of Rhosneigr and 3m/5km NE of Aberffraw. Originally about 50 feet in length, but now in poor condition. **46 B5** SH3972.
Din Fell *Sc.Bord.* ***Mountain***, 6m/9km N of Newcastleton. Height 1735 feet or 529 metres. **69 K4** NY4596.
Din Lligwy *I.o.A.* ***Historic/prehistoric site***, remains of 4c village (Cadw) near E coast of Anglesey, 1m/2km W of Moelfre. Capel Lligwy (Cadw) is medieval chapel to E. **46 C4** SH4986.
Dinam *Gwyn.* ***Open space***, partly forested upland area 3m/5km SW of Llandrillo. **37 K2** SJ0133.
Dinas *Carmar.* ***Hamlet***, 7m/11km S of Newcastle Emlyn. **17 F1** SN2730.
Dinas *Gwyn.* ***Hamlet***, 2m/3km E of Tudweiliog. **36 B2** SH2636.
Dinas *Gwyn.* ***Locality***, at W end of Criccieth. SH4937.
Dinas *Gwyn.* ***Settlement***, 2m/3km S of Caernarfon. **46 C7** SH4759.
Dinas *Pembs.* ***Village***, 4m/6km E of Fishguard. **16 D1** SN0138.
Dinas *R.C.T.* ***Locality***, 1km E of Penygraig. ST0091.
Dinas Dinlle *Gwyn.* ***Hamlet***, on coast, 1m/2km W of Llandwrog. Site of ancient British fort to S. **46 C7** SH4356.
Dinas Fach *Pembs.* ***Coastal feature***, headland on St. Brides Bay, 5m/8km E of St. David's. SM8222.
Dinas Fawr *Pembs.* ***Coastal feature***, headland (National Trust) on St. Brides Bay, 4m/6km E of St. David's. **16 B2** SM8122.
Dinas Head *Pembs.* ***Coastal feature***, headland on coast 2m/3km N of Dinas, at N end of promontory of Dinas Island. **16 D1** SN0138.
Dinas Island *Pembs.* ***Coastal feature***, promontory 2m/3km N of Dinas. **16 D1** SN0138.
Dinas-Mawddwy *Gwyn.* ***Hamlet***, 8m/13km E of Dolgellau. **37 H4** SH8514.
Dinas Powis *V. of Glam. See Dinas Powys.*
Dinas Powys (Dinas Powis). *V. of Glam.* Population: 8512. ***Suburb***, 2m/3km W of Penarth. Site of ancient hillfort 1km N. Remains of medieval castle. **18 E4** ST1571.
Dinbych *Denb. Welsh form of Denbigh, qv.*
Dinbych-y-pysgod *Pembs. Welsh form of Tenby, qv.*
Dinckley *Lancs.* ***Settlement***, 3m/4km N of Whalley. SD6835.
Dinder *Som.* ***Village***, 2m/3km SE of Wells. **19 J7** ST5744.
Dinedor *Here.* ***Village***, 3m/4km SE of Hereford. **28 E5** SO5336.
Dinefwr Park *Carmar.* ***Other feature of interest***, parkland on W side of Llandeilo, surrounding Dinefwr Old Castle and overlooking River Tywi. Landscaped in 18c by George Rhys, now has rare white cattle and a nature reserve. **17 K2** SN6122.
Dines Green *Worcs.* ***Suburb***, W district of Worcester. SO8255.
Ding *Som.* ***River***, rising on Black Down Hills to NE of Buckland St. Mary and flowing NE to River Isle, 3m/4km N of Ilminster. **8 B3** ST2814.
Dingestow (Llanddingad). *Mon.* ***Village***, 4m/6km SW of Monmouth. **28 D7** SO4510.
Dingle *Mersey.* ***Suburb***, 3m/4km SE of Liverpool city centre. SJ3687.
Dingleton *Sc.Bord.* ***Suburb***, adjoining to S of Melrose. NT5433.
Dingley *Northants.* ***Village***, 2m/4km E of Market Harborough. **42 A7** SP7787.
Dingwall *High.* Population: 5228. ***Small town***, chief town of Ross and Cromarty district at head of Cromarty Firth, 11m/18km NW of Inverness. **96 C6** NH5458.
Dinlabyre *Sc.Bord.* ***Settlement***, on E bank of Liddel Water, 4m/6km NE of Newcastleton. **70 A4** NY5291.
Dinmael *Conwy* ***Settlement***, 1m/2km W of Maerdy. SJ0044.
Dinmore *Here.* ***Locality***, 7m/11km N of Hereford. SO4850.
Dinmore Manor *Here.* ***Garden***, 500 feet above sea level, includes 12c chapel, 5m/8km S of Leominster. Notable for colours in autumn. **28 D3** SO4850.
Dinnet *Aber.* ***Settlement***, on N side of River Dee, 6m/10km E of Ballater. Muir of Dinnet is flat area to W. **90 C5** NO4598.
Dinnings Hill *D. & G.* ***Mountain***, 2m/3km W of Eskdalemuir. Height 1089 feet or 332 metres. **69 H4** NY2197.
Dinnington *Som.* ***Village***, 3m/5km SE of Ilminster. **8 D3** ST4012.
Dinnington *S.Yorks.* Population: 8845. ***Locality***, 6m/9km NW of Worksop. **51 H4** SK5385.
Dinnington *T. & W.* Population: 1722. ***Village***, 3m/4km E of Ponteland. **71 H6** NZ2073.
Dinorwic *Gwyn. English form of Dinorwig, qv.*
Dinorwig (Dinorwic). *Gwyn.* ***Locality***, 1m/2km SE of Deiniolen. Dinorwig Hydro-electric Pump Storage Scheme is a notable scheme in connection with Marchlyn Mawr Reservoir to NE. **46 D6** SH5961.
Dinting Vale *Derbys.* ***Locality***, 1m/2km NW of Glossop. SK0194.
Dinton *Bucks.* ***Village***, 4m/6km SW of Aylesbury. **31 J7** SP7611.
Dinton *Wilts.* ***Village***, 5m/8km W of Winton. Dinton Park, Phillipps House, and Hyde's House are National Trust properties. **10 B1** SU0131.
Dinton Pastures Country Park *W'ham* ***Leisure/recreation***, 3m/4km NW of Wokingham. 230 acres containing seven lakes, with River Loddon flowing along W side, providing opportunities for watersports and fishing as well as attracting over 100 species of bird. **22 A4** SU7872.
Dinvin *D. & G.* ***Settlement***, 1km NE of Portpatrick. **64 A5** NX0055.
Dinwoodie Mains *D. & G.* ***Settlement***, straddling railway, 6m/9km N of Lockerbie. **69 G4** NY1090.
Dinworthy *Devon* ***Hamlet***, 1m/2km NW of Holsworthy. **6 B4** SS3115.
Diollaid Mhòr *Arg. & B.* ***Mountain***, on Kintyre, 3m/4km NW of Carradale. Height 1187 feet or 362 metres. **73 F7** NR7739.
Dionard *High.* ***River***, in Sutherland district, rising on Reay Forest and running N down Strath Dionard into Kyle of Durness. **103 F3** NC3661.
Dipford *Som.* ***Hamlet***, 2m/3km SW of Taunton. ST2022.
Dipley *Hants.* ***Settlement***, 2m/3km W of Hartley Wintney. SU7457.
Dippen *Arg. & B.* ***Village***, near E coast of Kintyre, 4m/6km N of Saddell. **73 F7** NR7937.
Dippenhall *Surr.* ***Hamlet***, 2m/3km W of Farnham. **22 B7** SU8146.
Dippin *N.Ayr.* ***Settlement***, on Arran, 1km W above Dippin Head. **66 E1** NS0422.
Dippin Head *N.Ayr.* ***Coastal feature***, headland at SE end of Arran 2m/4km S of Whiting Bay. **66 E1** NS0522.
Dipple *Moray* ***Settlement***, 1m/2km W of Fochabers. **98 B5** NJ3258.
Dipple *S.Ayr.* ***Locality***, on coast, 2m/3km S of Turnberry. **67 G3** NS2002.
Dippool Water *S.Lan.* ***River***, rising to W of Auchengray and flowing SW to join Mouse Water, 2m/3km N of Carstairs. **75 H6** NS9448.
Diptford *Devon* ***Village***, 3m/5km SE of South Brent. **5 H5** SX7256.
Dipton *Dur.* ***Village***, 3m/5km NE of Consett. **62 C1** NZ1553.
Dipton Wood *Northumb.* ***Forest/woodland***, roughly circular in shape, 3m/4km SE of Hexham. **70 E7** NY9760.
Diptonmill *Northumb.* ***Locality***, on West Dipton Burn, 2m/3km S of Hexham. NY9260.
Dirdhu *High.* ***Settlement***, 3m/4km W of Bridge of Brown. **89 H2** NJ0720.
Dirleton *E.Loth.* ***Village***, 2m/4km W of North Berwick. Massive ruins of 13c castle (Historic Scotland). **76 D2** NT5184.
Dirleton Castle *E.Loth.* ***Castle***, 3m/4km SW of North Berwick at Dirleton. 13c stone castle (Historic Scotland) built on earlier motte, with alterations in 14c-15c. Damaged on Robert the Bruce's orders in 13c and also during Civil War. 16c and Victorian gardens. **76 D2** NT5183.
Dirrie More *High.* ***Other feature of interest***, pass between Loch Glascarnoch and Strath More, Ross and Cromarty district, carrying road from Dingwall to Ullapool. Height 915 feet or 279 metres. **95 J4** NH2475.
Dirrington Great Law *Sc.Bord.* ***Mountain***, conical hill on Lammermuir, 2m/3km S of Longformacus. Height 1309 feet or 399 metres. **76 E5** NT6954.
Dirrington Little Law *Sc.Bord.* ***Mountain***, conical hill 1m/2km SW of Dirrington Great Law. Height 1191 feet or 363 metres. **76 E5** NT6954.

Dirt Pot *Northumb.* ***Locality***, 1km NW of Allenheads. NY8546.
Discoed *Powys* ***Hamlet***, 2m/4km W of Presteigne. **28 B2** SO2764.
Discovery Point and RRS Discovery *Dundee* ***Other feature of interest***, in Dundee, near Tay Road Bridge, where Captain Scott kept his Antarctic ship. Exhibitions show story of ship, from expeditions up to Russian Revolution and World War I. **83 F5** NO4029.
Diserth *Denb. Welsh form of Dyserth, qv.*
Diseworth *Leics.* ***Village***, 6m/10km NW of Loughborough. **41 G3** SK4524.

D

Disgwylfa Fawr *Cere.* ***Mountain***, 1m/2km SW of Nant-y-moch Reservoir dam. Height 1660 feet or 506 metres. **37 G7** SN7384.
Dishes *Ork.* ***Settlement***, on Stronsay, overlooking Bay of Holland. **106 F5** HY6623.
Dishforth *N.Yorks.* ***Village***, 4m/7km N of Boroughbridge. Airfield to S. **57 J2** SE3873.
Dishig *Arg. & B.* ***Settlement***, 4m/7km SW of Gruline, Mull. **79 F4** NM4935.
Dishley *Leics.* ***Settlement***, 2m/3km NW of Loughborough. SK5121.
Disley *Ches.* Population: 3743. ***Small town***, 2m/3km W of New Mills. **49 J4** SJ9784.
Diss *Norf.* Population: 6538. ***Small town***, on River Waveney 19m/31km SW of Norwich. **45 F7** TM1180.
Disserth *Powys* ***Settlement***, on River Ithon, 2m/4km SW of Llandrindod Wells. **27 K3** SO0358.
Distington *Cumb.* Population: 2318. ***Village***, 3m/5km S of Workington. **60 B4** NY0023.
Distinkhorn *E.Ayr.* ***Mountain***, 3m/5km SE of Darvel. Height 1260 feet or 384 metres. **74 D7** NS5833.
Ditchampton *Wilts.* ***Locality***, adjoining to N of Wilton. SU0831.
Ditcheat *Som.* ***Village***, 3m/5km NW of Castle Cary. **9 F1** ST6236.
Ditchingham *Norf.* Population: 1951. ***Village***, 1m/2km N of Bungay. **45 H6** TM3391.
Ditchley *Oxon.* ***Locality***, 3m/4km NE of Charlbury. Ditchley Park, 18c mansion by James Gibbs, now Anglo-American conference and study centre. Sites of Roman villas to SE. **30 E6** SP3921.
Ditchling *E.Suss.* ***Village***, large village, 3m/4km SE of Burgess Hill. **13 G5** TQ3215.
Ditchling Beacon *E.Suss.* ***Viewpoint***, 1m/2km S of Ditchling on South Downs (partly National Trust), noted viewpoint and hillfort. **13 G5** TQ3215.
Ditchling Beacon Hillfort *E.Suss.* ***Historic/prehistoric site***, remains of hillfort (National Trust) on South Downs at Ditchling Beacon, at a height of 813 feet or 248 metres, 1m/2km S of Ditchling. Magnificent viewpoint across The Weald. **13 G5** TQ3313.
Ditchling Common Country Park *E.Suss.* ***Leisure/recreation***, country park 1m/2km E of Burgess Hill, with 188 acres of woodland, marshland and ponds. Designated Site of Special Scientific Interest due to variety of plants and birds. **13 G5** TQ3318.
Ditherington *Shrop.* ***Suburb***, NE district of Shrewsbury. SJ5014.
Ditteridge *Wilts.* ***Hamlet***, 5m/8km NE of Bath. **20 B5** ST8169.
Dittisham *Devon* ***Village***, to S and W of River Dart estuary, 3m/4km N of Dartmouth. **5 J5** SX8655.
Ditton *Halton* ***Suburb***, 1m/2km W of Widnes town centre. **48 D4** SJ4985.
Ditton *Kent* ***Village***, forming part of industrial and residential development, 3m/5km NW of Maidstone. **14 C2** TQ7157.
Ditton Green *Cambs.* ***Village***, 3m/5km S of Newmarket. **33 K3** TL6558.
Ditton Priors *Shrop.* ***Village***, 7m/11km S of Much Wenlock. **39 F7** SO6089.
Divach Burn *High.* ***River***, formed by tributaries from slopes of Glas-bheinn Beag and flowing NE into River Coiltie, 2m/3km SW of Drumnadrochit. **88 B2** NH4927.
Divie ***River***, rising on Carn Bad na Caorach and flowing N to join Dorback Burn and continue N to River Findhorn 6m/10km S of Forres. **97 H7** NJ0049.
Dixton *Glos.* ***Hamlet***, below W slope of Dixton Hill, 3m/5km NW of Winchcombe. **29 J5** SO9830.
Dixton *Mon.* ***Locality***, adjoining to NE of Monmouth. **28 E7** SO5113.
Dizzard *Cornw.* ***Locality***, near N coast, 6m/9km SW of Bude. Valley running down to sea is National Trust property. SX1698.
Dizzard Point *Cornw.* ***Coastal feature***, headland at S end of Bude Bay, 1km NW of Dizzard. **4 B1** SX1698.
Dobcross *Gt.Man.* ***Village***, 4m/7km E of Oldham, between Delph and Uppermill. SD9906.
Dobwalls *Cornw.* ***Village***, 3m/4km W of Liskeard. **4 C4** SX2165.
Dobwalls Family Adventure Park *Cornw.* ***Leisure/recreation***, family theme park with emphasis on railways, 1km N of Dobwalls. **4 C4** SX2165.
Doc Penfro *Pembs. Welsh form of Pembroke Dock, qv.*
Doccombe *Devon* ***Hamlet***, 2m/3km E of Moretonhampstead. **7 F7** SX7786.
Dochanassie *High.* ***Locality***, on SE shore of Loch Lochy in Lochaber district, opposite Bunarkaig across loch. NN2085.
Dochart *Stir.* ***River***, running NE down Glen Dochart to join River Lochay at head of Loch Tay. **81 G4** NN5733.
Dochgarroch *High.* ***Settlement***, on Caledonian Canal, 4m/7km SW of Inverness. **96 D7** NH6140.
Dochrie Hill *P. & K.* ***Mountain***, 4m/7km NW of Kinross. Height 1197 feet or 365 metres. **82 B7** NO0808.
Dockeney *Norf.* ***Settlement***, adjoining to SW of Geldeston. TM3891.
Dockenfield *Surr.* ***Settlement***, 4m/7km S of Farnham. SU8240.
Docker *Cumb.* ***Hamlet***, 4m/6km NE of Kendal, to NE of Hay Fell. SD5695.
Docker *Lancs.* ***Settlement***, on S side of Docker Moor, 4m/6km SW of Kirkby Lonsdale. SD5774.
Docking *Norf.* Population: 1256. ***Village***, 11m/17km NW of Fakenham. **44 B2** TF7637.
Docklow *Here.* ***Village***, 4m/7km E of Leominster. **28 E3** SO5657.
Dockray *Cumb.* ***Hamlet***, on Aira Beck, 4m/6km S of Troutbeck. **60 E4** NY3921.
Dockray *Cumb.* ***Settlement***, 1m/2km NE of Wigton. NY2649.
Dockroyd *W.Yorks.* ***Locality***, S part of Oakworth, 3m/4km SW of Keighley. SE0338.
Doctor's Gate *Derbys.* ***Valley***, narrow, steep-sided part of Shelf Brook valley, 3m/5km E of Glossop, which was used as course of Roman road. **50 C3** SK0893.
Docwra's Manor *Cambs.* ***Garden***, exuberant garden with many unusual plants, surrounding manor at Shepreth, 8m/13km SW of Cambridge. **33 G4** TL3947.
Dodbrooke *Devon* ***Suburb***, E district of Kingsbridge. SX7344.
Dodd Fell *N.Yorks.* ***Mountain***, 4m/6km SW of Hawes. Height 2191 feet or 668 metres. **56 D1** SD8484.
Dodd Hill *D. & G.* ***Mountain***, 6m/10km NE of Carsphairn. Height 1633 feet or 498 metres. **68 B4** NX6498.
Doddenham *Worcs.* ***Hamlet***, 6m/10km W of Worcester. SO7556.
Doddinghurst *Essex* Population: 3839. ***Village***, 3m/5km N of Brentwood. **23 J2** TQ5999.
Doddington *Cambs.* Population: 1405. ***Village***, 3m/5km N of Chatteris. **43 G6** TL3990.
Doddington *Ches.* ***Locality***, 5m/8km SE of Nantwich. 15c castle and 18c hall. SJ7046.
Doddington *Kent* ***Village***, 4m/7km SE of Sittingbourne. **14 E2** TQ9357.
Doddington *Lincs.* ***Village***, 5m/8km W of Lincoln. **52 C5** SK9070.
Doddington *Northumb.* ***Village***, 3m/4km N of Wooler. **77 H7** NT9932.
Doddington *Shrop.* ***Village***, 4m/6km W of Cleobury Mortimer. **29 F1** SO6176.
Doddington Hall *Lincs.* ***Historic house***, well-preserved Elizabethan house with many original artefacts, 5m/8km SW of Lincoln. **52 B5** SK8970.
Doddiscombsleigh *Devon* ***Village***, 6m/9km SW of Exeter. **7 G7** SX8586.
Doddshill *Norf.* ***Locality***, adjoining to E of Dersingham. TF6930.
Doddycross *Cornw.* ***Hamlet***, 4m/6km SE of Liskeard. SX3062.
Dodford *Northants.* ***Village***, 3m/5km SE of Daventry. **31 H2** SP6160.
Dodford *Worcs.* ***Village***, 2m/3km NW of Bromsgrove. **29 J1** SO9372.
Dodington *Som.* ***Hamlet***, at foot of Quantock Hills, 1m/2km NW of Nether Stowey. **7 K1** ST1740.
Dodington *S.Glos.* ***Locality***, 2m/3km SE of Chipping Sodbury. **20 A3** ST7480.
Dodington Ash *S.Glos.* ***Locality***, 1m/2km S of Dodington. **20 A4** ST7578.
Dodleston *Ches.* ***Village***, 4m/7km SW of Chester. Remains of motte and bailey castle. **48 C6** SJ3661.
Dodman Point *Cornw.* ***Coastal feature***, headland (National Trust) on S coast, 4m/6km S of Mevagissey at E end of Veryan Bay. **3 H5** SX0039.
Dodmarsh *Here.* ***Settlement***, 4m/7km NE of Hereford. SO5743.
Dods Leigh *Staffs.* ***Hamlet***, to SW of Church Leigh, 4m/7km W of Uttoxeter. SK0134.
Dodscott *Devon* ***Hamlet***, 3m/5km E of Great Torrington. SS5419.
Dodworth *S.Yorks.* Population: 4964. ***Small town***, 2m/3km W of Barnsley. **51 F2** SE3105.
Dodworth Bottom *S.Yorks.* ***Locality***, adjoining to SE of Dodworth, 2m/3km SW of Barnsley. SE3204.
Dodworth Green *S.Yorks.* ***Locality***, adjoins to SW of Dodworth. SE3104.
Doe *High.* ***River***, in Inverness district rising on Glenaffric Forest and running SE to Glen Moriston 3m/5km E of dam of Loch Cluanie. **87 H3** NH2211.
Doe Bank *W.Mid.* ***Suburb***, to N of Sutton Coldfield town centre. SP1297.
Doe Green *Warr.* ***Suburb***, in W part of Warrington. SJ5587.
Doe Lea *Derbys.* ***Settlement***, 1km SE of Heath. **51 G6** SK4566.
Doehole *Derbys.* ***Settlement***, 3m/5km E of Matlock. SK3558.
Doffcocker *Gt.Man.* ***Suburb***, 2m/3km NW of Bolton town centre. SD6910.
Dog Bank *P. & K.* ***Coastal feature***, large intertidal area of mud on N side of Firth of Tay, about 3m/4km S of Longforgan. **82 E5** NO3024.
Dog Fall *High.* ***Waterfall***, in Glen Affric 1m/2km E of Loch Beinn a' Mheadhoin, Inverness district. NH2828.
Dog Hill *Gt.Man.* ***Locality***, 3m/5km NE of Oldham. SD9509.
Dog Hillock *Angus* ***Mountain***, 3m/5km E of Rottal in Glen Clova. Height 2368 feet or 722 metres. **83 F1** NO4269.
Dog Lane *Norf.* ***Locality***, 1km W of Horsford. TG1815.
Dog Village *Devon* ***Village***, adjacent to Broadclyst, 5m/8km NE of Exeter. **7 H6** SX9896.
Dogdyke *Lincs.* ***Village***, 3m/5km E of Billinghay. **53 F7** TF2055.
Dogley Lane *W.Yorks.* ***Settlement***, 1km S of Fenay Bridge, 3m/5km SE of Huddersfield. SE1814.
Dogmersfield *Hants.* ***Village***, 3m/5km NE of Odiham. **22 A6** SU7852.
Dogsthorpe *Peter.* ***Suburb***, 2m/3km N of Peterborough city centre. TF1901.
Dogtail End *Worcs.* ***Settlement***, 3m/5km S of Redditch. SP0463.
Dogton Stone *Fife* ***Historic/prehistoric site***, 1m/2km S of Kinglassie. Ancient Celtic cross with traces of human and animal sculpture; now without top and arms. **76 A1** NT2397.
Doire Ban *High.* ***Mountain***, 3m/5km NE of North Ballachulish. Height 1856 feet or 566 metres. **80 B1** NN0964.
Doire Meurach *High.* ***Mountain***, in Monadhliath range, 9m/12km SE of Foyers. Height 2581 feet or 787 metres. **88 C3** NH5611.
Doire Tana *High.* ***Open space***, N facing hillslope in Fasnakyle Forest above E end of Loch Mullardoch. **87 J2** NH2128.
Doirlinn Head *W.Isles* ***Coastal feature***, headland on W coast of Barra, 3m/4km W of Castlebay. **84 B5** NL6299.
Dol Fawr *Powys* ***Settlement***, 3m/5km E of Cemmaes. **37 H5** SH8806.
Dol-gran *Carmar.* ***Settlement***, 1m/2km SW of Pencader. **17 H1** SN4334.
Dolanog *Powys* ***Hamlet***, on River Vyrnwy, 5m/7km NW of Llanfair Caereinion. **37 K4** SJ0612.
Dolau *Powys* ***Settlement***, nearly 1m/2km W of Llanfihangel Rhydithon. **28 A2** SO1467.
Dolau *R.C.T.* ***Village***, forming S part of Llanharan, 6m/10km E of Bridgend. ST0082.
Dolaucothi Estate *Carmar.* ***Locality***, large area of wooded hills (National Trust) astride River Cothi valley, to NE of Pumsaint. Dolaucothi Gold Mines (National Trust) above S bank of river, to E of Pumsaint. SN6640.
Dolaucothi Gold Mines *Carmar.* ***Other feature of interest***, remains of gold mines above S bank of River Cothi, to E of Pumsaint. Worked intermittently from Roman times to 1938. Gold-panning and displays of 1930s mine machinery. **27 F4** SN6640.
Dolbadarn Castle *Gwyn.* ***Castle***, largely 13c remains (Cadw), at NW end of Llyn Peris, 1km SE of Llanberis. **46 D6** SH5859.
Dolbenmaen *Gwyn.* ***Hamlet***, 5m/7km NW of Porthmadog. Motte marks site of Norman castle. **36 E1** SH5043.
Dolebury Warren Hillfort *N.Som.* ***Historic/prehistoric site***, rectangular Iron Age hillfort with commanding views at N edge of Mendip Hills, 2m/3km NE of Winscombe. . **19 H6** ST4458.
Doleham *E.Suss.* ***Locality***, 1m/2km S of Brede. TQ8316.
Dolemeads *B. & N.E.Som.* ***Suburb***, E district of Bath across River Avon from city centre. ST7564.
Doles Wood *Hants.* ***Forest/woodland***, 1km S of Hurstbourne Tarrant. **21 G6** SU3752.
Doley *Staffs.* ***Settlement***, 2m/3km NW of Adbaston. SJ7429.
Dolfach *Powys* ***Settlement***, on E bank of River Wye, 2m/3km S of Llangurig. **27 J1** SN9177.
Dolfor *Powys* ***Hamlet***, 3m/5km S of Newtown. **38 A7** SO1087.
Dolforwyn Castle *Powys* ***Castle***, ruined castle (Cadw), probably 13c, above River Severn 2m/3km SE of Bettws Cedewain. **38 A6** SO1595.
Dolgarreg *Carmar.* ***Settlement***, on S bank of River Tywi, 1m/2km W of Llanwrda. **27 G5** SN7331.
Dolgarrog *Conwy* ***Village***, 6m/10km S of Conwy. **47 F6** SH7667.
Dolgellau *Gwyn.* Population: 2396. ***Small town***, stone-built market town and resort on River Wnion, 17m/27km SW of Bala. **37 G4** SH7217.
Dolgoch *Gwyn.* ***Settlement***, 5m/8km NE of Tywyn. **37 F5** SH6504.
Doll *High.* ***Settlement***, 1m/2km W of Brora, on E coast of Sutherland district. **97 F1** NC8803.
Dollar *Clack.* Population: 2670. ***Small town***, at foot of Ochil Hills, 6m/10km NE of Alloa. Castle Campbell is late 15c. **75 H1** NS9697.
Dollar Law *Sc.Bord.* ***Mountain***, 5m/8km SE of Drumelzier. Height 2680 feet or 817 metres. **69 G1** NT1727.
Dollarbeg *Clack.* ***Settlement***, 1m/2km S of Dollar. **75 H1** NS9796.
Dolley Green *Powys* ***Settlement***, 2m/3km W of Presteigne. SO2865.
Dolleycanney *Powys* ***Settlement***, 3m/4km NW of Painscastle. **28 A4** SO2049.
Dollis Hill *Gt.Lon.* ***Suburb***, in borough of Brent, 6m/10km NW of Charing Cross. TQ2286.
Dollywagon Pike *Cumb.* ***Mountain***, in Lake District 1m/2km S of Helvellyn. Height 2808 feet or 856 metres. **60 E5** NY3413.
Dolphin *Flints.* ***Hamlet***, 1m/2km S of Holywell. SJ1973.
Dolphinholme *Lancs.* ***Hamlet***, 6m/9km SE of Lancaster. **55 J4** SD5153.
Dolphinton *S.Lan.* ***Village***, 7m/11km NE of Biggar. **75 K6** NT1046.
Dolton *Devon* ***Village***, 7m/11km SE of Great Torrington. **6 D4** SS5712.
Dolwen *Cere.* ***Settlement***, on N side of Goginan, 4m/7km NW of Devil's Bridge. SN6881.
Dolwen *Conwy* ***Hamlet***, 4m/6km SE of Colwyn Bay. **47 G5** SH8874.
Dolwen *Powys* ***Settlement***, 3m/5km SW of Llangadfan. **37 J5** SH9707.
Dolwyddelan *Conwy* ***Village***, on River Lledr, 5m/7km SW of Betws-y-coed. To W is keep of Norman castle (Cadw). **47 F7** SH7352.
Dolwyddelan Castle *Conwy* ***Castle***, Norman castle keep (Cadw) in valley of River Lledr, 5m/8km SW of Betws-y-coed. Built 12c, possibly by Iorwerth, father of Llywelyn the Great. Decayed into ruin after 15c, but modern roof and battlements added in 19c. **47 F7** SH7252.
Dolybont *Cere.* ***Locality***, 2m/3km SE of Borth. **37 F7** SN6288.
Dolyhir *Powys* ***Settlement***, 3m/5km NW of Kington. **28 B3** SO2457.
Dolywern *Wrex.* ***Hamlet***, on River Ceiriog, 4m/7km W of Chirk. **38 B2** SJ2237.

Domgay *Powys* ***Settlement***, 1m/2km E of Llandysilio. **38 B4** SJ2819.
Dominion Estate *Leic.* ***Suburb***, housing estate 3m/4km W of Leicester city centre. SK5405.
Don ***River***, major river of NE Scotland which rises 7m/11km S of Tomintoul and flows E by Strathdon, Alford and Inverurie to North Sea at Bridge of Don on N side of Aberdeen. **90 E3** NJ9509.
Don ***River***, rising W of Dunford Bridge and flowing E to Penistone, SE to Sheffield, then NE by Rotherham, Mexborough, and Doncaster to join River Ouse at Goole. **51 G3** SE7422.
Doncaster *S.Yorks.* Population: 71,595. ***Town***, historic crossing point on River Don on site of Roman fort of Danum, 17m/27km NE of Sheffield. Includes one of three Mansion Houses in Britain. Flying Scotsman steam engine built here. Racecourse, famous for St. Leger, on E side of town, with grandstand by Carr of York, 1776. Airport to SE. **51 H2** SE5703.
Dones Green *Ches.* ***Settlement***, 4m/6km NW of Northwich. SJ6077.
Donhead St. Andrew *Wilts.* ***Village***, 4m/6km E of Shaftesbury. **9 J2** ST9124.
Donhead St. Mary *Wilts.* ***Village***, 3m/5km E of Shaftesbury. **9 J2** ST9024.
Donibristle *Fife* ***Settlement***, 3m/4km NW of Aberdour. **75 K2** NT1688.
Donibristle Industrial Estate *Fife* ***Locality***, 2m/3km E of Inverkeithing and 1km N of Donibristle Bay. NT1583.
Doniert Stone *Cornw.* *Alternative name for King Doniert's Stone, qv.*
Doniford *Som.* ***Hamlet***, on coast, 1m/2km E of Watchet. **7 J1** ST0842.
Donington *Lincs.* Population: 2569. ***Village***, 9m/14km N of Spalding. **43 F2** TF2035.
Donington *Shrop.* ***Settlement***, to N of Albrighton. SJ8004.
Donington Collection *Leics.* ***Other feature of interest***, 2m/3km SW of Castle Donington, displaying large collection of Grand Prix race cars. **41 G3** SK4225.
Donington le Heath *Leics.* ***Locality***, 1m/2km S of Coalville. **41 G4** SK4212.
Donington le Heath Manor House *Leics.* ***Historic house***, restored 13c manor house 1m/2km S of Coalville. **41 G4** SK4212.
Donington on Bain *Lincs.* ***Village***, 6m/10km SW of Louth. **53 F4** TF2382.
Donington South Ings *Lincs.* ***Locality***, 1m/2km S of Donington. TF2035.
Donisthorpe *Leics.* Population: 3425. ***Village***, 3m/5km SW of Ashby de la Zouch. **41 F4** SK3114.
Donkey Street *Kent* ***Locality***, just E of Burmarsh. TR1032.
Donkey Town *Surr.* ***Hamlet***, 2m/3km SE of Bagshot. **22 C5** SU9360.
Donna Nook *Lincs.* ***Coastal feature***, promontory on North Sea coast, 2m/3km NE of North Somercotes. **53 H3** TF4399.
Donnington *Glos.* ***Village***, 2m/3km N of Stow-on-the-Wold. **30 C6** SP1928.
Donnington *Here.* ***Settlement***, 2m/4km S of Ledbury. **29 G5** SO7134.
Donnington *Shrop.* ***Settlement***, 1m/2km E of Wroxeter. **38 E5** SJ5807.
Donnington *Tel. & W.* Population: 13,683. ***Suburb***, 2m/3km N of Oakengates. **39 G4** SJ7013.
Donnington *W.Berks.* ***Suburb***, to N of Newbury. **21 H5** SU4668.
Donnington *W.Suss.* ***Hamlet***, 2m/3km S of Chichester. **12 B6** SU8502.
Donnington Castle *W.Berks.* ***Castle***, English Heritage property with 14c gatehouse, 1m/2km NW of Newbury town centre. **21 H5** SU4668.
Donnington Wood *Tel. & W.* ***Locality***, 1m/2km S of Donnington. SJ7012.
Donwell *T. & W.* ***Suburb***, NW district of Washington. NZ2958.
Donyatt *Som.* ***Village***, 1m/2km W of Ilminster. **8 C3** ST3314.
Doon ***River***, issuing from Loch Doon and flowing NW through Bogton Loch, Patna and Dalrymple to Firth of Clyde, at S end of Ayr. **67 J3** NS3219.
Doonfoot *S.Ayr.* ***Suburb***, to S of Ayr, on Firth of Clyde, at mouth of River Doon. NS3219.
Doonie Point *Aber.* ***Coastal feature***, rocky headland, 1km S of Muchalls. **91 H5** NO9090.
Door of Cairnsmore *D. & G.* ***Open space***, craggy hillslope on S side of Cairnsmore of Fleet, 6m/10km E of Newton Stewart. **65 F4** NX5164.
Dorback Burn *High.* ***River***, in Badenoch and Strathspey district running NW to River Nethy, 1m/2km SE of Nethy Bridge. **89 H3** NJ0119.
Dorback Burn *Moray* ***River***, flowing NE from Lochindorb, then N to join River Findhorn 1km S of Logie. **97 G7** NJ0049.
Dorchester *Dorset* Population: 15,037. ***Town***, county town on River Frome, 7m/12km N of Weymouth. Remains of Roman town house in Colliton Park. Home of Thomas Hardy and scene of his novel 'The Mayor of Casterbridge'. **9 F5** SY6990.
Dorchester *Oxon.* ***Village***, Roman town on River Thame, near its confluence with River Thames, 4m/6km NW of Wallingford. Medieval abbey. **21 J2** SU5794.
Dorchester Abbey *Oxon.* ***Ecclesiastical building***, Augustinian priory founded c. 1140, 8m/12km SE of Oxford, with abbey church surviving as parish church. Notable window at E end, including much 14c glass. **21 J2** SU5794.
Dorchester Dinosaur Museum *Dorset* ***Other feature of interest***, museum in Dorchester, with small exhibitions of dinosaurs designed to appeal to children. **9 F5** SY6891.
Dordale *Worcs.* ***Locality***, 3m/5km NW of Bromsgrove. SO9274.
Dordon *Warks.* Population: 4667. ***Village***, 3m/5km NW of Atherstone. **40 E5** SK2600.
Dore *Here.* ***River***, rising E of Hay-on-Wye and flowing SE down Golden Valley into River Monnow, to S of Pontrilas. **28 C5** SO3926.
Dore *S.Yorks.* ***Suburb***, 5m/8km SW of Sheffield city centre. **51 F4** SK3081.
Dore Holm *Shet.* ***Island***, small island off W coast of Mainland to SE of Stenness. HU2176.
Dores *High.* ***Village***, in Inverness district, on E side of Loch Ness, 2m/3km S of NE end of loch. **88 C1** NH5934.
Dorket Head *Notts.* ***Locality***, 5m/8km N of Nottingham. **41 H1** SK5947.
Dorking *Surr.* Population: 15,658. ***Town***, commuter town, dominated by its church spire, 11m/17km E of Guildford, below North Downs. **22 E7** TQ1649.
Dorley's Corner *Suff.* ***Settlement***, 1m/2km N of Saxmundham. TM3865.
Dorlin *High.* ***Locality***, on S side of Loch Moidart in Lochaber district, 5m/8km N of Salen. NM6672.
Dormans Park *Surr.* ***Settlement***, 2m/3km S of Lingfield. **23 G7** TQ3940.
Dormansland *Surr.* ***Village***, 3m/4km N of East Grinstead. **23 H7** TQ4042.
Dormanstown *R. & C.* ***Locality***, adjoining to SW of Redcar. **63 G4** NZ5823.
Dormer's Wells *Gt.Lon.* ***Suburb***, in borough of Ealing, 1m/2km NE of Southall. TQ1380.
Dormington *Here.* ***Village***, 5m/7km E of Hereford. **28 E4** SO5840.
Dormston *Worcs.* ***Hamlet***, 6m/10km W of Alcester. SO9857.
Dorn *Glos.* ***Settlement***, 1m/2km N of Moreton-in-Marsh. SP2034.
Dorn *Oxon.* ***River***, rising N of Heythrop and flowing SE into River Glyme, 2m/3km N of Woodstock. **30 E6** SP4419.
Dorney *Bucks.* ***Village***, 3m/4km W of Slough. **22 C4** SU9279.
Dorney Court *Bucks.* ***Historic house***, to W of Dorney, 2m/3km SW of Slough. 15c manor with furnishings from last 400 years. **22 C4** SU9278.
Dorney Reach *Bucks.* ***Settlement***, on River Thames, 1m/2km W of Dorney. SU9179.
Dornie *High.* ***Village***, in Skye and Lochalsh district on E side of entrance to Loch Long, 8m/12km E of Kyle of Lochalsh. **86 E2** NG8826.
Dornoch *High.* Population: 1196. ***Small town***, in Sutherland district on N shore of Dornoch Firth 12m/19km E of Bonar Bridge. 13c cathedral, rebuilt 19c. **96 E3** NH7989.
Dornoch Cathedral *High.* ***Ecclesiastical building***, in centre of Dornoch, founded in 1224, restored in 17c and 20c, and containing some fine 13c stonework. **96 E2** NH7990.
Dornoch Firth *High.* ***Sea feature***, marks border between Ross and Cromarty and Sutherland districts and runs 22m/36km from Bonar Bridge out to Tarbet Ness. **97 F3** NJ7989.
Dornoch Point *High.* ***Coastal feature***, headland 1m/2km S of Dornoch. **97 F3** NH7989.
Dornoch Sands *High.* ***Coastal feature***, extensive sandy area on N coast of Dornoch Firth, 1m/2km SW of Dornoch. **96 E3** NH7788.
Dornock *D. & G.* ***Village***, 3m/4km E of Annan. **69 H7** NY2366.
Dorothy Clive Garden *Staffs.* ***Garden***, 8m/12km SW of Newcastle-under-Lyme. Rock and scree gardens, rare trees, rhododendrons, azaleas and shrub roses. **39 G1** SJ7540.
Dorrery *High.* ***Settlement***, 1m/2km W of Scotscalder Station. **105 F3** ND0754.
Dorridge *W.Mid.* ***Suburb***, 3m/5km S of Solihull town centre. **30 C1** SP1675.
Dorrington *Lincs.* ***Village***, 5m/7km N of Sleaford. **52 D7** TF0852.
Dorrington *Shrop.* ***Village***, 6m/10km S of Shrewsbury. **38 D5** SJ4702.
Dorsell *Aber.* ***Settlement***, 2m/3km SW of Alford. **90 D3** NJ5414.
Dorset *Dorset* *Alternative name for (River) Piddle, qv.*
Dorset *W.Yorks.* ***Suburb***, 2m/3km NE of Leeds city centre, in Harehills district. SE3235.
Dorset County Museum *Dorset* ***Other feature of interest***, in Dorchester, with exhibits on natural history and geology. **9 F5** SY6991.
Dorsington *Warks.* ***Village***, 6m/9km SW of Stratford-upon-Avon. **30 C3** SP1349.
Dorstone *Here.* ***Village***, 6m/9km E of Hay-on-Wye. Arthur's Stone (English Heritage), burial chamber 1km N. **28 C4** SO3141.
Dorton *Bucks.* ***Village***, 6m/9km NW of Thame. **31 H7** SP6814.
Dorusduain *High.* ***Settlement***, in Skye and Lochalsh district, 4m/6km NE of Shiel Bridge. **87 F2** NG9822.
Doseley *Tel. & W.* ***Suburb***, to SW of Dawley. SJ6706.
Dosthill *Staffs.* ***Suburb***, 3m/4km S of Tamworth town centre. **40 E5** SK2100.
Dotland *Northumb.* ***Settlement***, 3m/5km S of Hexham. **62 A1** NY9259.
Dottery *Dorset* ***Settlement***, 2m/3km N of Bridport. **8 D5** SY4595.
Doublebois *Cornw.* ***Settlement***, 4m/6km W of Liskeard. **4 B4** SX1965.
Douchary *High.* ***River***, on borders of Ross and Cromarty and Sutherland districts, running N down Glen Douchary into Rhiddorach River above Loch Achall, E of Ullapool. **95 J2** NH2593.
Dougalston *E.Dun.* ***Hamlet***, 1km E of Milngavie. **74 D3** NS5673.
Dougarie *N.Ayr.* ***Settlement***, on NW coast of Arran, 8m/12km W of Brodick. **73 G7** NR8837.
Dougarie Point *N.Ayr.* ***Coastal feature***, headland on NW coast of Arran, 4m/6km S of Pirnmill. **73 G7** NR8738.
Dough Crag *Northumb.* ***Mountain***, rocky outcrop on W side of Harwood Forest, to E of Darden Lough, 3m/5km S of Hepple. Height 1266 feet or 386 metres. **70 E4** NY9795.
Doughton *Glos.* ***Hamlet***, 1m/2km SW of Tetbury. **20 B2** ST8791.
Douglas ***River***, rising near Wigan and flowing NW into River Ribble estuary opposite Freckleton. Lower reaches also known as River Asland. **48 D1** SD4326.
Douglas *I.o.M.* ***Town***, port, resort, seat of government and chief town of island, on E coast 19m/30km S of Point of Ayre and 14m/23km NE of Calf of Man. Situated on Douglas Bay. **54 C6** SC3875.
Douglas *S.Lan.* Population: 1616. ***Small town***, with industrial estate, 8m/13km S of Lanark. St. Bride's Church (Historic Scotland) is 12c chancel in churchyard. **75 G7** NS8330.
Douglas and Angus *Dundee* ***Suburb***, 3m/4km NE of Dundee city centre. **83 F4** NO4432.
Douglas Bay *I.o.M.* ***Bay***, extends N from Douglas Head to Onchan Head. **54 D6** SC3875.
Douglas Burn *Sc.Bord.* ***River***, rising in mountains of Ettrick Forest and flowing SE to join Yarrow Water, 1m/2km E of St. Mary's Loch. **69 H1** NT2924.
Douglas Hall *D. & G.* ***Settlement***, 1m/2km E of Colvend and 2m/4km NE of Rockcliffe. **65 J5** NX8855.
Douglas Head *I.o.M.* ***Coastal feature***, headland to S of Douglas, forming S extremity of Douglas Bay. **54 C6** SC3875.
Douglas Hill *Gwyn.* ***Locality***, 1m/2km W of Bethesda. **46 E6** SH6065.
Douglas Water *Arg. & B.* ***River***, in Argyll, running E to Loch Fyne 3m/5km S of Inveraray. **80 B7** NN0704.
Douglas Water *S.Lan.* ***Hamlet***, to E of river of same name, 1m/2km N of Rigside. **75 G7** NS8736.
Douglas Water *S.Lan.* ***River***, rising 7m/11km SW of Douglas and flowing past town and past hamlet of Douglas Water, to River Clyde 3m/4km SE of Lanark. **75 G7** NS8330.
Douglastown *Angus* ***Village***, 3m/5km SW of Forfar. **83 F3** NO4147.
Doulting *Som.* ***Village***, 2m/3km E of Shepton Mallet. **19 K7** ST6443.
Dounan Bay *D. & G.* ***Bay***, 8m/12km NW of Stranraer. **66 D7** NW9668.
Dounby *Ork.* ***Village***, on Mainland, 6m/10km NW of Finstown. **106 B5** HY2920.
Doune *Arg. & B.* ***Settlement***, near N end of Loch Lomond, 1m/2km SE of Ardlui across loch. **80 E6** NN3314.
Doune *Arg. & B.* ***Settlement***, in Glen Douglas, 2m/3km W of Inverbeg. **74 B1** NS3198.
Doune *High.* ***Settlement***, 1km E of Brae, to S of River Oykel. **96 B1** NC4400.
Doune *High.* ***Settlement***, 1m/2km S of Aviemore. **89 F3** NH8910.
Doune *Stir.* Population: 1212. ***Village***, 4m/6km W of Dunblane. 14c Doune Castle (Historic Scotland) to S. **81 J7** NN7201.
Doune Castle *Stir.* ***Castle***, partially restored late 14c courtyard castle (Historic Scotland) built for Regent Albany, to S of Doune beside River Teith. **81 J7** NN7201.
Doune Hill *Arg. & B.* ***Mountain***, 5m/7km S of Arrochar. Height 2408 feet or 734 metres. **74 A1** NS2997.
Doune Motor Museum *Stir.* ***Other feature of interest***, vintage and post-vintage cars collected by Earl of Moray, 1km NE of Doune. **81 J7** NN7102.
Doune Park *Aber.* ***Settlement***, 1m/2km S of Macduff. **99 F4** NJ7162.
Dounepark *S.Ayr.* ***Suburb***, S district of Girvan. NX1897.
Douneside *Aber.* ***Settlement***, 1km N of Tarland. **90 C4** NJ4805.
Dounie *High.* ***Settlement***, 2m/3km W of Ardgay. **96 C2** NH5690.
Dounie *High.* ***Settlement***, 6m/9km NW of Tain. **96 D3** NH6986.
Dounreay *High.* ***Locality***, on N coast of Caithness district, 8m/13km W of Thurso. Site of Experimental Reactor Establishment of Atomic Energy Authority. **104 E2** NC9867.
Dounreay Nuclear Power Development Establishment *High.* ***Other feature of interest***, on N coast of Caithness district, 8m/13km W of Thurso, with exhibitions on processes involved at this decommissioned site which still re-processes spent nuclear fuel. **104 E2** NC9867.
Dousland *Devon* ***Village***, on W edge of Dartmoor, 5m/8km SW of Tavistock. **5 F4** SX5368.
Dovaston *Shrop.* ***Settlement***, 7m/11km SE of Oswestry. **38 C3** SJ3421.
Dove ***River***, rising 4m/6km SW of Buxton and flowing S through Dove Dale, past Ashbourne and on to Uttoxeter, then SE into River Trent at Newton Solney, 3m/5km NE of Burton upon Trent. **50 D7** SK2726.
Dove *N.Yorks.* ***River***, rising on Cleveland Hills, 4m/6km SE of Ingleby Greenhow, and flowing S into River Rye 3m/5km E of Nunnington. **63 H7** SE7178.
Dove *Suff.* ***River***, rising near Mendlesham and flowing NE past Eye into River Waveney 1km N of Hoxne. **35 F1** TM1778.
Dove Cottage *Cumb.* ***Other feature of interest***, home of William Wordsworth, to E of Grasmere lake, with interior preserved much as it was. Nearby museum contains manuscripts and relics. **60 E6** NY3407.
Dove Dale ***Valley***, stretch of River Dove valley between Hartington and Thorpe, in Peak District National Park. The river flows between steep limestone cliffs, wooded in parts. Much National Trust property on both banks. **50 D7** SK1452.
Dove Holes *Derbys.* ***Village***, 3m/5km N of Buxton. **50 C5** SK0777.

Dovecot *Mersey.* ***Suburb***, 5m/8km E of Liverpool city centre. SJ4191.

Dovenby *Cumb.* ***Village***, 3m/4km NW of Cockermouth. **60 B3** NY0933.

Dovendale *Lincs.* ***Hamlet***, 4m/6km SW of Louth. TF3082.

Dover *Kent* Population: 34,179. ***Town***, cinque port, resort and Channel port on Strait of Dover, 15m/24km SE of Canterbury, with large modern docks for freight and passengers. Dominated by high white cliffs and castle (English Heritage). Remains of 12c Knights Templar Church (English Heritage) across valley from castle. Sections of moat of 19c fort at Western Heights (English Heritage), above town on W side of harbour. **15 J3** TR3141.

Dover Castle *Kent* ***Castle***, well preserved castle (English Heritage), excellent example of concentric fortress, built during reign of Henry II on site of original Roman fortress, 1km E of Dover town centre. Miles of secret wartime tunnels (English Heritage) running under castle and cliffs were first used during Napoleonic wars, later becoming World War II headquarters from which evacuation from Dunkirk was directed. **15 J3** TR3241.

Dover Museum *Kent* ***Other feature of interest***, in Dover town centre, with local history exhibits and artefacts. **15 J3** TR3141.

Dovercourt *Essex* ***Suburb***, S district of Harwich. Resort. **35 G6** TM2531.

Doverdale *Worcs.* ***Village***, 3m/5km NW of Droitwich Spa. **29 H2** SO8666.

Doveridge *Derbys.* ***Village***, 2m/3km E of Uttoxeter across River Dove. **40 D2** SK1134.

Doversgreen *Surr.* ***Suburb***, residential district to S of Reigate. **23 F7** TQ2548.

Dovestone Reservoir *Gt.Man.* ***Reservoir***, 6m/10km E of Oldham. **50 C2** SE0103.

Dovey *English form of (River) Dyfi, qv.*

Dovey Forest *English form of Dyfi Forest, qv.*

Dovey Valley *Gwyn. English form of Dyfi Valley, qv.*

Dow Crag *Cumb.* ***Mountain***, rising above small lake of Goat's Water, with cliffs and scree on E side, 1km W of The Old Man of Coniston and 3m/4km W of Coniston. Height 2555 feet or 779 metres. **60 D7** SD2597.

Dowally *P. & K.* ***Hamlet***, in Strath Tay, 3m/5km S of Ballinluig. **82 B3** NO0048.

Dowanhill *Glas.* ***Suburb***, 2m/3km NW of Glasgow city centre. NS5667.

Dowbridge *Lancs.* ***Locality***, adjoining to E of Kirkham. SD4331.

Dowdeswell *Glos.* ***Locality***, comprising Upper and Lower Dowdeswell, 3m/5km SE of Cheltenham. **30 B6** SP0019.

Dowhill *S.Ayr.* ***Settlement***, 2m/3km S of Turnberry. **67 G3** NS2002.

Dowlais *M.Tyd.* ***Locality***, 2m/3km NE of Merthyr Tydfil town centre. SO0707.

Dowland *Devon* ***Hamlet***, 7m/12km SE of Great Torrington. **6 D4** SS5610.

Dowlands *Devon* ***Settlement***, 3m/4km E of Seaton. **8 B5** SY2890.

Dowles *Worcs.* ***Locality***, 1m/2km NW of Bewdley. SO7776.

Dowlish Ford *Som.* ***Hamlet***, 1m/2km W of Dowlish Wake. ST3513.

Dowlish Wake *Som.* ***Village***, 2m/3km SE of Ilminster. **8 C3** ST3712.

Down Ampney *Glos.* ***Village***, 2m/4km N of Cricklade. Birthplace of Vaughan Williams. **20 E2** SU1097.

Down End *Som.* ***Locality***, adjoining to N of Dunball, 3m/5km N of Bridgwater. **19 G7** ST3141.

Down Field *Cambs.* ***Hamlet***, adjoining to SE of Soham. **33 J1** TL5971.

Down Hatherley *Glos.* ***Village***, 4m/6km NE of Gloucester. **29 H6** SO8622.

Down House *Gt.Lon.* ***Historic house***, 18c house (English Heritage) in village of Downe, 2m/3km NE of Biggin Hill, occupied for forty years by Charles Darwin. Includes Darwin's study, where he wrote 'On the Origin of Species by means of Natural Selection' in 1859, period furnishings and instrumentation, Darwin Museum and memorabilia. **23 H5** TQ4361.

Down St. Mary *Devon* ***Village***, 7m/11km NW of Crediton. **7 F5** SS7404.

Down Thomas *Devon* ***Village***, 3m/5km SE of Plymouth across River Plym estuary. **5 F6** SX5050.

Downan Point *S.Ayr.* ***Coastal feature***, headland at S end of Ballantrae Bay. **66 E5** NX0680.

Downderry *Cornw.* ***Town***, small resort on S coast 4m/6km E of Looe. **4 D5** SX3154.

Downe *Gt.Lon.* ***Village***, 2m/3km NE of Biggin Hill. Down House (English Heritage), once home of Charles Darwin, contains Darwin relics. **23 H5** TQ4361.

Downend *I.o.W.* ***Settlement***, 2m/4km SE of Newport. To E, site of Roman villa. **11 G6** SZ5387.

Downend *S.Glos.* ***Suburb***, 5m/8km NE of Bristol city centre, in Mangotsfield district. **19 K4** ST6476.

Downend *W.Berks.* ***Hamlet***, 1km N of Chieveley. **21 H4** SU4774.

Downfield *Cambs.* ***Hamlet***, 1m/2km SE of Soham. TL6071.

Downfield *Dundee* ***Suburb***, NW district of Dundee. **82 E4** NO3833.

Downgate *Cornw.* ***Village***, 2m/3km NE of Callington. **4 D3** SX3772.

Downham *Essex* ***Village***, 2m/3km NW of Wickford. **24 D2** TQ7295.

Downham *Gt.Lon.* ***Suburb***, in borough of Lewisham, 2m/3km SE of Catford. TQ3971.

Downham *Lancs.* ***Village***, 3m/5km NE of Clitheroe. **56 C5** SD7844.

Downham *Northumb.* ***Settlement***, 6m/10km S of Coldstream. **77 G7** NT8634.

Downham Market *Norf.* Population: 5841. ***Small town***, market town near E bank of River Great Ouse, 10m/17km S of King's Lynn. **44 A5** TF6103.

Downhead *Cornw.* ***Settlement***, 2m/4km N of Altarnun. **4 C2** SX2384.

Downhead *Som.* ***Hamlet***, 3m/4km SW of Sparkford. ST5625.

Downhead *Som.* ***Village***, 5m/8km E of Shepton Mallet. **19 K7** ST6945.

Downhill *T. & W.* ***Suburb***, housing estate in NW part of Sunderland. NZ3559.

Downholland Cross *Lancs.* ***Settlement***, 3m/5km W of Ormskirk. **48 C2** SD3606.

Downholme *N.Yorks.* ***Village***, 4m/7km SW of Richmond. **62 C7** SE1197.

Downies *Aber.* ***Village***, on E coast, 7m/11km S of Aberdeen. **91 H5** NO9295.

Downing *Flints.* ***Settlement***, 3m/4km NW of Holywell. **47 K5** SJ1578.

Downing Street *Gt.Lon.* ***Other feature of interest***, 17c street in City of Westminster with houses built by Sir George Downing. Number 10 is official residence of Prime Minister; Number 11 that of Chancellor of the Exchequer. Access is restricted. TQ3079.

Downley *Bucks.* ***Suburb***, 2m/3km NW of High Wycombe. **22 B2** SU8495.

Downs *V. of Glam.* ***Settlement***, 5m/8km W of Cardiff. Television station to S. ST1074.

Downside *N.Som.* ***Hamlet***, to NW of Bristol International Airport, 1m/2km W of Felton. **19 H5** ST4965.

Downside *Som.* ***Hamlet***, 1m/2km N of Shepton Mallet. **19 K7** ST6244.

Downside *Som.* ***Hamlet***, 4m/7km SW of Radstock. 1km E, Downside Abbey, Benedictine monastery and boys' school. **19 K6** ST6450.

Downside *Surr.* ***Hamlet***, 1m/2km S of Cobham. **22 E6** TQ1058.

Downton *Devon* ***Hamlet***, 2m/3km NW of Dartmouth. **5 J5** SX8553.

Downton *Devon* ***Settlement***, 1km NE of Lydford. **6 D7** SX5285.

Downton *Hants.* ***Hamlet***, 4m/6km SW of Lymington. **10 D5** SZ2693.

Downton *Wilts.* Population: 2475. ***Village***, on River Avon, 6m/10km S of Salisbury. **10 C2** SU1821.

Downton on the Rock *Here.* ***Village***, 5m/9km W of Ludlow. **28 D1** SO4273.

Dowsby *Lincs.* ***Village***, 6m/10km N of Bourne. **42 E2** TF1129.

Dowthorpe End *Northants.* ***Locality***, E end of Earls Barton, 4m/6km SW of Wellingborough. SP8563.

Dowthwaitehead *Cumb.* ***Hamlet***, at head of Aira Beck valley, 1m/2km W of Dockray. **60 E4** NY3620.

Doxey *Staffs.* ***Suburb***, in NW part of Stafford. SJ9023.

Doxford *Northumb.* ***Locality***, 3m/5km W of Embleton. NU1823.

Doynton *S.Glos.* ***Village***, 6m/10km N of Bath. **20 A4** ST7174.

Dozmary Pool *Cornw.* ***Lake/loch***, natural lake on Bodmin Moor, 9m/15km NE of Bodmin. Subject of Arthurian legend. **4 B3** SX1974.

Drabblegate *Norf.* ***Settlement***, on E side of River Bure, 1m/2km N of Aylsham. TG2028.

Draethen *Caerp.* ***Hamlet***, 4m/6km E of Caerphilly. **19 F3** ST2287.

Draffan *S.Lan.* ***Settlement***, 4m/6km SE of Larkhall. **75 F6** NS7945.

Dragley Beck *Cumb.* ***Suburb***, S district of Ulverston. SD2977.

Dragonby *N.Lincs.* ***Hamlet***, 2m/3km N of Scunthorpe. Site of former settlement. SE9014.

Dragons Green *W.Suss.* ***Locality***, 4m/6km E of Billingshurst. TQ1423.

Drake Law *S.Lan.* ***Mountain***, with forested summit, 2m/3km SW of Abington. Height 1584 feet or 483 metres. **68 D1** NS9022.

Drakeland Corner *Devon* ***Settlement***, 1km NE of Sparkwell. **5 F5** SX5758.

Drakelow *Worcs.* ***Hamlet***, 3m/4km N of Kidderminster. SO8180.

Drakemire *Sc.Bord.* ***Locality***, 3m/4km S of Grantshouse. **77 F4** NT8061.

Drakemyre *N.Ayr.* ***Village***, 1km N of Dalry. NS2950.

Drakes Broughton *Worcs.* ***Village***, 2m/3km NW of Pershore. **29 J4** SO9248.

Drakes Cross *Worcs.* ***Locality***, 7m/11km S of Birmingham. **30 B1** SP0876.

Drake's Island *Plym.* ***Island***, National Trust property in Plymouth Sound, fortified since 15c. **4 E5** SX4652.

Drakewalls *Cornw.* ***Village***, former tin-mining village, 1km S of Gunnislake. SX4270.

Drambuie *D. & G.* ***Settlement***, 1m/2km SE of Kirkconnel, across River Nith and Kello Water. **68 C2** NS7410.

Draughton *N.Yorks.* ***Village***, 3m/5km E of Skipton. **57 F4** SE0352.

Draughton *Northants.* ***Village***, 7m/11km W of Kettering. **31 J1** SP7676.

Drax *N.Yorks.* ***Village***, 5m/9km SE of Selby. Power station. **58 C7** SE6726.

Draycot Foliat *Swin.* ***Hamlet***, 1m/2km S of Chiseldon. SU1877.

Draycote *Warks.* ***Village***, 5m/8km SW of Rugby. **31 F1** SP4470.

Draycote Water *Warks.* ***Reservoir***, 5m/8km NE of Southam. **31 F2** SP4569.

Draycott *Derbys.* ***Village***, 3m/5km W of Long Eaton. **41 G2** SK4433.

Draycott *Glos.* ***Village***, 3m/4km NW of Moreton-in-Marsh. **30 C5** SP1835.

Draycott *Shrop.* ***Settlement***, 6m/10km E of Bridgnorth. SO8192.

Draycott *Som.* ***Village***, below S slopes of Mendip Hills, 2m/3km SE of Cheddar. **19 H6** ST4750.

Draycott *Worcs.* ***Settlement***, 4m/7km S of Worcester. **29 H4** SO8547.

Draycott Cross *Staffs.* ***Settlement***, 2m/3km SW of Cheadle. SJ9841.

Draycott in the Clay *Staffs.* ***Village***, 5m/8km SE of Uttoxeter. **40 D3** SK1528.

Draycott in the Moors *Staffs.* ***Village***, 3m/5km SW of Cheadle. **40 B2** SJ9840.

Draycott Moor *Oxon.* ***Locality***, 6m/10km W of Abingdon. SU4098.

Drayford *Devon* ***Hamlet***, on Little Dart River, 6m/10km E of Chulmleigh. SS7813.

Draynes *Cornw.* ***Hamlet***, 4m/6km NW of Liskeard. SX2169.

Drayton *Leics.* ***Village***, 5m/8km NW of Corby. **42 B6** SP8392.

Drayton *Lincs.* ***Locality***, 1km SE of Swineshead. **43 F2** TF2439.

Drayton *Norf.* Population: 2240. ***Suburb***, 5m/7km NW of Norwich. **45 F4** TG1813.

Drayton *Oxon.* ***Village***, 2m/3km NW of Banbury. **31 F4** SP4241.

Drayton *Oxon.* ***Village***, 2m/3km SW of Abingdon. **21 H2** SU4794.

Drayton *Ports.* ***Suburb***, N district of Portsmouth, below E end of Ports Down. **11 H4** SU6705.

Drayton *Som.* ***Village***, 2m/3km SW of Langport. **8 D2** ST4024.

Drayton *Warks.* ***Settlement***, 2m/4km W of Stratford-upon-Avon. SP1655.

Drayton *Worcs.* ***Village***, 5m/8km E of Kidderminster. **29 J1** SO9076.

Drayton Bassett *Staffs.* ***Village***, 3m/4km SW of Tamworth. **40 D5** SK1900.

Drayton Beauchamp *Bucks.* ***Village***, 1m/2km W of Tring. **32 C7** SP9012.

Drayton Manor Park *Staffs.* ***Leisure/recreation***, 250 acre theme park, 2m/3km SW of Tamworth. Includes over 50 rides and a 15 acre zoo. **40 D5** SK1801.

Drayton Parslow *Bucks.* ***Village***, 4m/6km SW of Bletchley. **32 B6** SP8328.

Drayton St. Leonard *Oxon.* ***Village***, 4m/7km N of Wallingford. **21 J2** SU5996.

Dre-fach *Cere.* ***Hamlet***, 5m/8km W of Lampeter. **26 E4** SN5045.

Drebley *N.Yorks.* ***Settlement***, above River Wharfe, 2m/3km SE of Burnsall. **57 F4** SE0559.

Dreemskerry *I.o.M.* ***Hamlet***, 2m/3km SE of Ramsey. **54 D4** SC4791.

Dreenhill *Pembs.* ***Hamlet***, 2m/4km SW of Haverfordwest. **16 C3** SM9214.

Drefach *Carmar.* ***Village***, 3m/5km E of Newcastle Emlyn. **17 G1** SN3538.

Drefach *Carmar.* ***Village***, 2m/3km W of Cross Hands. **17 J3** SN5213.

Drefelin *Carmar.* ***Hamlet***, 4m/6km SE of Newcastle Emlyn. SN3637.

Dreghorn *N.Ayr.* Population: 3960. ***Village***, 3m/5km E of Irvine. **74 B7** NS3538.

Drellingore *Kent* ***Settlement***, 3m/5km N of Folkestone, 2m/3km E of Densole. **15 H3** TR2441.

Drem *E.Loth.* ***Village***, 4m/6km N of Haddington. **76 D3** NT5179.

Drenewydd *Bridgend Welsh form of Newton, qv.*

Drenewydd Gelli-farch *Mon. Welsh form of Shirenewton, qv.*

Dresden *Stoke* ***Suburb***, in S part of Longton, Stoke-on-Trent. SJ9042.

Dreswick Point *I.o.M.* ***Coastal feature***, headland with lighthouse at S end of Langness promontory, on E side of Langness Point. **54 B7** SC2865.

Drewsteignton *Devon* ***Village***, 3m/5km N of Moretonhampstead. Castle Drogo (National Trust) 1m/2km SW. **7 F6** SX7390.

Driby *Lincs.* ***Hamlet***, 5m/8km N of Spilsby. **53 G5** TF3874.

Driesh *Angus* ***Mountain***, 4m/6km W of Clova. Munro: height 3106 feet or 947 metres. **89 K7** NO2773.

Driffield *Glos.* ***Village***, 4m/6km SE of Cirencester. **20 D2** SU0799.

Driffield Cross Roads *Glos.* ***Locality***, 1m/2km SW of Driffield. SU0698.

Drift Reservoir *Cornw.* ***Reservoir***, 2m/4km W of Penzance. **2 B6** SW4329.

Drigg *Cumb.* ***Village***, 2m/3km SE of Seascale. **60 B7** SD0699.

Drighlington *W.Yorks.* ***Village***, 3m/4km W of Morley. **57 H7** SE2229.

Drimfern *Arg. & B.* ***Settlement***, in Glen Aray, 4m/7km N of Inveraray. **80 B6** NN0814.

Drimlee *Arg. & B.* ***Settlement***, at head of Glen Shira, 6m/9km NE of Inveraray. **80 C6** NN1416.

Drimnin *High.* ***Village***, on E shore of Sound of Mull, 4m/6km E of Tobermory across sound. **79 G2** NM5554.

Drimore *W.Isles* ***Settlement***, on South Uist, 4m/7km S of Hornish Point. **84 C1** NF7640.

Drimpton *Dorset* ***Village***, 3m/5km SW of Crewkerne. **8 D4** ST4105.

Drimsynie *Arg. & B.* ***Settlement***, at N end of Loch Goil, 1km W of Lochgoilhead. **80 C7** NN1901.

Drimvore *Arg. & B.* ***Settlement***, in valley of River Add, 5m/7km NW of Lochgilphead. **73 G1** NR8394.

Drinan *High.* ***Settlement***, 2m/3km NE of Elgol, Skye. **86 B3** NG5415.

Dringhouses *York* ***Suburb***, 2m/3km SW of York city centre. SE5849.

Drinishader *W.Isles* ***Settlement***, on inlet of East Loch Tarbert, South Harris, 4m/6km SE of Tarbert. NG1794.

Drinkstone *Suff.* ***Village***, 6m/10km NW of Stowmarket. **34 D2** TL9561.

Drinkstone Green *Suff.* ***Village***, 1km S of Drinkstone. **34 D3** TL9561.

Drinkstone Hill *Sc.Bord.* ***Mountain***, 3m/5km NW of Hawick. Height 1043 feet or 318 metres. **69 K2** NT4818.

Drip Moss *Stir.* ***Open space***, low-lying area between Rivers Forth and Teith, 3m/5km NW of Stirling. **75 F1** NS7595.
Drishaig *Arg. & B.* ***Settlement***, on N shore of NE arm of Loch Fyne, 4m/7km NE of Inveraray. **80 C6** NN1510.
Drissaig *Arg. & B.* ***Settlement***, 3m/4km NW of Dalavich, to N of Loch Avich. **80 A6** NM9415.
Driver's End *Herts.* ***Hamlet***, 2m/4km N of Welwyn. TL2219.
Drochaid Mhòr *High.* ***Locality***, on River Dionard, 1m/2km S of head of Kyle of Durness. **103 F2** NC3460.
Drointon *Staffs.* ***Hamlet***, 6m/9km N of Rugeley. **40 C3** SK0226.
Droitwich Spa *Worcs.* Population: 20,966. ***Town***, 6m/10km NE of Worcester. Centre for salt extraction since Bronze Age. Developed spa status due to curative saline springs as salt industry declined at end of 19c. Site of Roman town of Salinae to N. **29 H2** SO8963.
Dron *P. & K.* ***Village***, 5m/8km S of Perth. **82 C6** NO1415.
Dronfield *Derbys.* Population: 22,985. ***Town***, market and industrial town, 5m/8km N of Chesterfield. 14c church. **51 F5** SK3578.
Dronfield Woodhouse *Derbys.* ***Locality***, 2m/3km W of Dronfield. **51 F5** SK3378.
Drongan *E.Ayr.* Population: 2910. ***Village***, 7m/11km E of Ayr. **67 J2** NS4418.
Dronger *Shet.* ***Coastal feature***, rocky headland on NW of Fair Isle. **108 A1** HZ2074.
Dronley *Angus* ***Hamlet***, 1m/2km S of Kirkton of Auchterhouse. **82 E4** NO3435.
Droop *Dorset* ***Hamlet***, 1km SE of Hazelbury Bryan and 4m/7km SW of Sturminster Newton. ST7508.
Drope *V. of Glam.* ***Settlement***, 5m/8km W of Cardiff. ST1075.
Dropmore *Bucks.* ***Settlement***, 2m/3km N of Burnham. **22 C3** SU9286.
Drosgl *Gwyn.* ***Mountain***, in Carneddau range, 6m/9km SE of Bangor. Height 2486 feet or 758 metres. **46 E6** SH6667.
Drosgol *Cere.* ***Mountain***, above N shore of Nant-y-moch Reservoir, 2m/3km NW of Plynlimon summit across reservoir. Height 1804 feet or 550 metres. **37 G7** SN7587.
Droxford *Hants.* ***Village***, on River Meon, 1m/2km SW of Meonstoke. The Old Rectory (National Trust), 18c house next to church. **11 H3** SU6018.
Droylsden *Gt.Man.* Population: 22,666. ***Town***, industrial town, adjoining to E of Manchester. **49 J3** SJ9198.
Drub *W.Yorks.* ***Hamlet***, 1m/2km NE of Cleckheaton. SE1926.
Druid (Y Ddwyryd). *Denb.* ***Hamlet***, 2m/4km W of Corwen. **37 K1** SJ0443.
Druid's Heath *W.Mid.* ***Settlement***, 1km NE of Aldridge. SK0501.
Druidston *Pembs.* ***Hamlet***, 1m/2km S of Nolton. **16 B3** SM8616.
Druie *High.* ***River***, in Badenoch and Strathspey district running NW into River Spey at Aviemore. NH8911.
Druim a' Chùirn *High.* ***Large natural feature***, mountain ridge rising to 1916 feet of 584 metres, 2m/3km NE of Meoble, South Morar, Lochaber district. **86 E6** NM8189.
Druim a' Chuirn *High.* ***Mountain***, 3m/5km NW of Loch Arkaig, Lochaber district. Height 2696 feet or 822 metres. **87 F5** NM9695.
Druim an Fhraoich Mhin *Arg. & B.* ***Mountain***, 4m/7km E of Kilninian. Height 1043 feet or 318 metres. **79 F3** NM4645.
Druim Chòsaidh *High.* ***Inland physical feature***, mountain ridge in Lochaber district running E and W on N side of head of Loch Quoich, and attaining height of 2995 feet or 913 metres at Sgurr a' Choire-bheithe. **87 F4** NG9100.
Druim Dearg *Angus* ***Mountain***, 1m/2km W of Bellaty. Height 1486 feet or 453 metres. **82 D2** NO2158.
Druim Fada *Arg. & B.* ***Mountain***, in Laggan Deer Forest, Mull, 3m/4km SE of Lochbuie. Height 1328 feet or 405 metres. **79 H5** NM6422.
Druim Fada *High.* ***Inland physical feature***, mountain ridge in Lochaber district running E and W on N side of narrow part of Loch Hourn, SE of Arnisdale. Highest point 2327 feet or 709 metres. **86 E4** NG8908.
Druim Fada *High.* ***Inland physical feature***, mountain ridge on Locheil Forest, Lochaber district, 5m/8km N of Fort William. Summit, at E end of ridge, is Stob a' Ghrianain, 2440 feet or 744 metres. **87 G6** NN0882.
Druim Fiaclach *High.* ***Inland physical feature***, mountain ridge in Moidart, Lochaber district, 3m/4km SE of Lochailort. Attains height of 2850 feet or 869 metres. **86 D7** NM7979.
Druim Garbh *High.* ***Inland physical feature***, mountain ridge, 5m/8km NE of Strontian, Lochaber district. **79 K1** NM8668.
Druim Gleann Laoigh *High.* ***Mountain***, 8m/12km NW of Fort William. Height 2289 feet or 698 metres. **87 G6** NN0685.
Druim Hain *High.* ***Inland physical feature***, mountain ridge 1m/2km NE of Loch Coruisk, Skye. **85 K2** NG4922.
Druim Leathad nam Fias *High.* ***Inland physical feature***, mountain ridge and watershed between Cona Glen and Glen Scaddle in Lochaber district, 9m/15km W of Fort William. **80 A1** NM9670.
Druim Mòr *P. & K.* ***Inland physical feature***, mountain ridge rising to 1204 feet or 367 metres to W of Strath Tay, 5m/8km W of Dunkeld. **82 A3** NN9242.
Druim na Cluain-airighe *High.* ***Inland physical feature***, mountain ridge in Knoydart, Lochaber district, 2m/4km NW of Inverie. **86 D4** NG7503.
Druim na h-Achlaise *High.* ***Mountain***, in Skye and Lochalsh district, on S side of Loch Loyne. Height 1771 feet or 540 metres. **87 H4** NH1303.
Druim nam Bad *High.* ***Marsh/bog***, marshy area with number of small lochs. Beinn Direach and Ben Hee lie to W and SW respectively. **103 G5** NC4738.
Druim nan Cliar *High.* ***Locality***, includes a large number of lochs to E of Loch Hope. **103 G3** NC4957.
Druim nan Cnamh *High.* ***Inland physical feature***, mountain ridge on border of Inverness and Skye and Lochalsh districts, between Lochs Cluanie and Loyne. Summit 2555 feet or 779 metres. **87 H4** NH1307.
Druim Shionnach *High.* ***Mountain***, in Inverness district, forming part of Cluanie Forest, 1m/2km S of W end of Loch Cluanie. Munro: height 3237 feet or 987 metres. **87 G4** NH0708.
Druimarbin *High.* ***Settlement***, on E shore of Loch Linnhe, 2m/4km SW of Fort William. **80 B1** NN0771.
Druimavuic *Arg. & B.* ***Settlement***, at head of Loch Creran, 12m/21km NE of Oban. **80 B3** NN0044.
Druimdrishaig *Arg. & B.* ***Settlement***, on NW coast of Kintyre, 4m/6km N of Kilberry. **73 F3** NR7370.
Druimindarroch *High.* ***Locality***, on N side of Loch nan Uamh, 2m/3km SE of Arisaig, in Lochaber district. **86 C6** NM6884.
Druimkinnerras *High.* ***Settlement***, 6m/9km SW of Beauly. **96 B7** NH4639.
Druimyeon Bay *Arg. & B.* ***Bay***, on E side of Gigha, N of Ardminish Point. **72 E5** NR6550.
Drum *Arg. & B.* ***Settlement***, on Cowal peninsula, 4m/6km NW of Tighnabruaich. **73 H3** NR9376.
Drum *Conwy* ***Mountain***, 4m/6km SE of Llanfairfechan. Height 2526 feet or 770 metres. **47 F6** SH7069.
Drum *P. & K.* ***Village***, 5m/7km W of Kinross. **82 B7** NO0400.
Drum Castle *Aber.* ***Castle***, 14c castle tower with house adjoining, 3m/5km W of Peterculter. **91 F4** NJ7900.
Drum-ddu *Powys* ***Mountain***, one of the Mynydd Eppynt peaks, 3m/5km SE of Llangammarch Wells. Height 1555 feet or 474 metres. **27 J4** SN9744.
Drum Ddu *Powys* ***Mountain***, 2m/3km S of Llanwrthwl. Height 1761 feet or 537 metres. **27 J2** SN9760.
Drum Hollistan *High.* ***Open space***, hillslope below N slopes of Beinn Ruadh in Caithness district, 2m/3km W of Reay. **104 E2** NC9263.
Drum Mains *N.Lan.* ***Settlement***, 3m/5km W of Cumbernauld town centre. NS7173.
Drum Peithnant *Cere.* ***Mountain***, 1m/2km SW of Plynlimon summit. Height 2244 feet or 684 metres. **37 G7** SN7785.
Drum yr Eira *Powys* ***Mountain***, rising to over 600 metres, 4m/6km S of Claerwen Reservoir. **27 H3** SN8559.
Drumachloy *Arg. & B.* ***Settlement***, on Bute, 1km N of Ettrick Bay. **73 J4** NS0367.
Drumadoon Bay *N.Ayr.* ***Bay***, on W coast of Arran, extending either side of Blackwaterfoot. **66 C1** NR8927.
Drumbeg *High.* ***Village***, on S side of Eddrachillis Bay, W coast of Sutherland district. **102 D5** NC1232.
Drumblade *Aber.* ***Locality***, 4m/6km E of Huntly. **98 D6** NJ5840.
Drumblair *Aber.* ***Settlement***, 3m/4km S of Inverkeithny. **98 E6** NJ6343.
Drumbreddan Bay *D. & G.* ***Bay***, 9m/13km SE of Portpatrick. **64 A6** NX0743.
Drumbuie *High.* ***Settlement***, in Skye and Lochalsh district, 2m/4km NE of Kyle of Lochalsh. **86 D1** NG7731.
Drumburgh *Cumb.* ***Hamlet***, on line of Hadrian's Wall, 4m/6km W of Burgh by Sands. Various Roman sites in vicinity. **60 D1** NY2659.
Drumchapel *Glas.* ***Suburb***, 5m/8km NW of Glasgow city centre. **74 D3** NS5270.
Drumchardine *High.* ***Settlement***, 3m/5km E of Beauly. **96 C7** NH5644.
Drumchork *High.* ***Settlement***, on E shore of Loch Ewe, 5m/8km N of Poolewe. **94 E3** NG8788.
Drumclog *S.Lan.* ***Village***, 5m/8km E of Darvel. Monument 1m/2km NW commemorates battle of 1679 in which Covenanters defeated Life Guards under Claverhouse, later Viscount Dundee, leading to confrontation at Battle of Bothwell Bridge 1679. **74 E7** NS6338.
Drumcoltran Tower *D. & G.* ***Historic/prehistoric site***, 16c tower (Historic Scotland) 1m/2km N of Kirkgunzeon and 5m/8km NE of Dalbeattie. **65 J4** NX8668.
Drumdelgie *Aber.* ***Settlement***, 6m/9km SE of Keith. **98 C6** NJ4842.
Drumderfit *High.* ***Settlement***, 1m/2km S of Munlochy. **96 D6** NH6551.
Drumderg *P. & K.* ***Mountain***, in Forest of Alyth, 3m/5km NE of Bridge of Cally. Height 1384 feet or 422 metres. **82 C2** NO1754.
Drumeldrie *Fife* ***Hamlet***, 2m/3km E of Lower Largo. **83 F7** NO4403.
Drumelzier *Sc.Bord.* ***Village***, on Drumelzier Burn near its confluence with River Tweed, 8m/13km SW of Peebles. Ruins of Tinnis Castle on hillside to NE. **75 K7** NT1334.
Drumelzier Law *Sc.Bord.* ***Mountain***, 2m/3km SE of Drumelzier. Height 2191 feet or 668 metres. **75 K7** NT1431.
Drumfearn *High.* ***Settlement***, at head of Sleat peninsula, Skye, 3m/4km NW of Eilean Iarmain. **86 C3** NG6715.
Drumfern *High.* ***Settlement***, 1km W of head of Loch Eil, Lochaber district. **87 F7** NM9578.
Drumgarve *Arg. & B.* ***Settlement***, on Kintyre, 3m/5km N of Campbeltown. **66 B1** NR7226.
Drumgley *Angus* ***Hamlet***, 3m/4km W of Forfar. **83 F3** NO4150.
Drumguish *High.* ***Hamlet***, on S side of valley of River Spey, 2m/3km SE of Kingussie. **88 E5** NN7899.
Drumhead *Aber.* ***Settlement***, 6m/10km SW of Banchory. **90 E5** NO6092.
Drumin *Moray* ***Settlement***, 3m/5km NW of Tomnavoulin. **89 J1** NJ1830.
Drumine *High.* ***Settlement***, 6m/10km W of Nairn. **96 E6** NH7951.
Drumine Forest *Moray* ***Forest/woodland***, 5m/8km S of Forres. **97 H6** NJ0250.
Drumjohn *D. & G.* ***Settlement***, 6m/9km SE of Dalmellington. **67 K4** NX5297.
Drumlamford House *S.Ayr.* ***Settlement***, on W side of Loch Dornal, 5m/8km SE of Barrhill. **64 C3** NX2876.
Drumlamford Loch *S.Ayr.* ***Lake/loch***, small loch 4m/7km SE of Barrhill. **64 C3** NX2877.
Drumlanrig Castle *D. & G.* ***Castle***, seat of the Duke of Buccleuch, dating from late 17c, in Nithsdale 3m/5km NW of Thornhill. **68 D4** NX8599.
Drumlasie *Aber.* ***Settlement***, 3m/4km NE of Torphins. **90 E4** NJ6405.
Drumlemble *Arg. & B.* ***Village***, in Kintyre, 4m/6km W of Campbeltown. **66 A2** NR6619.
Drumlithie *Aber.* ***Village***, 6m/10km SW of Stonehaven. **91 F6** NO7880.
Drummoddie *D. & G.* ***Locality***, 4m/6km E of Port William. NX3945.
Drummond *High.* ***Settlement***, 1km S of Evanton across River Sgitheach, Ross and Cromarty district. **96 D5** NH6065.
Drummond *Stir.* ***Settlement***, 3m/4km SE of Callander. **81 H7** NN6706.
Drummond Castle *P. & K.* ***Castle***, founded in 15c, 3m/4km SW of Crieff. Much restored. Surrounded by formal garden, including topiary, terraces and Victorian parterre with fountains. **81 K6** NN8418.
Drummond Hill *P. & K.* ***Mountain***, elongated wooded mass to N of Kenmore, at foot at Loch Tay. Height 1502 feet or 458 metres. **81 J3** NN7646.
Drummore *D. & G.* ***Village***, on Drummore Bay on E coast of Rinns of Galloway, 4m/7km N of Mull of Galloway. **64 B7** NX1336.
Drummossie Muir *High.* ***Large natural feature***, moorland tract in Inverness district, centred on S part of Culloden Forest, 3m/5km SE of Inverness. **88 D1** NH7343.
Drummuir Castle *Moray* ***Castle***, 4m/7km NE of Dufftown. **98 B6** NJ3744.
Drumnadrochit *High.* ***Village***, on River Enrick, 1m/2km W of Urquhart Bay on Loch Ness, Inverness district. **88 C1** NH5029.
Drumnagorrach *Moray* ***Settlement***, 3m/5km NW of Milltown of Rothiemay and 6m/9km E of Keith. **98 D5** NJ5252.
Drumnatorran *High.* ***Settlement***, 1km N of Strontian, Lochaber district. **79 K1** NM8262.
Drumoak *Aber.* ***Village***, 3m/5km W of Peterculter. **91 F5** NO7998.
Drumochter *See Pass of Drumochter.*
Drumore *Arg. & B.* ***Settlement***, on Kintyre, 1m/2km NW of Campbeltown. **66 B1** NR7022.
Drumour *P. & K.* ***Settlement***, 5m/8km SW of Dunkeld. **82 A3** NN9639.
Drumoyne *Glas.* ***Suburb***, 3m/4km W of Glasgow city centre, in Govan district. NS5465.
Drumpellier Country Park *N.Lan.* ***Leisure/recreation***, country park 1m/2km NW of Coatbridge. **75 F4** NS7165.
Drumrash *D. & G.* ***Settlement***, on E bank of Loch Ken, 4m/7km SE of New Galloway. **65 G3** NX6871.
Drumrunie *High.* ***Settlement***, on River Runie, 3m/4km NE of Strathkanaird. **95 H1** NC1605.
Drumrunie Forest *High.* ***Open space***, deer forest in Ross and Cromarty district around Cul Mòr, 10m/16km N of Ullapool. Part of Inverpolly National Nature Reserve. **102 D7** NC1810.
Drumry *Renf.* ***Suburb***, 1km N of Clydebank town centre. NS5070.
Drums *Aber.* ***Settlement***, 2m/3km SW of Newburgh. **91 H2** NJ9822.
Drumsturdy *Angus* ***Hamlet***, 2m/3km N of Monifieth. **83 F4** NO4835.
Drumtassie Burn *Falk.* ***River***, rising on Blawhorn Moss to NW of Blackridge, and flowing NE to join River Avon to W of Avonbridge. Forms part of border with West Lothian. **75 G4** NS9172.
Drumtochty Forest *Aber.* ***Forest/woodland***, to N and S of Drumtochty Castle, 6m/10km N of Laurencekirk. **90 E7** NO6980.
Drumtroddan Standing Stones *D. & G.* ***Historic/prehistoric site***, site of two Bronze Age standing stones (Historic Scotland), with nearby cup and ring marks of similar age, on natural rock face just S of Drumtroddan, 8m/12km SW of Wigtown. **64 D6** NX3644.
Drumuie *High.* ***Settlement***, 3m/4km NW of Portree, Skye. **93 K7** NG4546.
Drumuillie *High.* ***Settlement***, in Badenoch and Strathspey district, 3m/4km NE of Boat of Garten. **89 G2** NH9420.
Drumvaich *Stir.* ***Settlement***, 3m/4km SE of Callander. **81 H7** NN6704.
Drumwhindle *Aber.* ***Locality***, 4m/7km NW of Ellon. **91 H1** NJ9236.
Drumwhirn *D. & G.* ***Settlement***, 7m/11km E of Galloway. **68 C5** NX7480.
Drunkendub *Angus* ***Settlement***, 2m/3km S of Inverkeilor. **83 H3** NO6646.
Druridge *Northumb.* ***Settlement***, 1m/2km E of Widdrington near to North Sea coast at Druridge Bay. NZ2795.
Druridge Bay *Northumb.* ***Bay***, to E of Druridge, extending from Hauxley in N to Snab Point in S. **71 H4** NZ2796.
Druridge Bay Country Park *Northumb.* ***Leisure/recreation***, country park near coast at Druridge Bay with sand dunes adjacent to woodland and meadows surrounding Ladyburn Lake, which is used for watersports in summer. **71 H4** NZ2600.
Drury *Flints.* ***Locality***, 1m/2km E of Buckley. **48 B6** SJ2964.
Drury Square *Norf.* ***Locality***, 2m/3km SE of Litcham and 6m/9km W of East Dereham. TF9014.
Drusillas Park *E.Suss.* ***Leisure/recreation***, small zoo aimed especially at children, 1m/2km NE of Alfriston. **13 J6** TQ5204.
Dry Burn *E.Loth.* ***River***, rising in Lammermuir Hills, and flowing NE to North Sea, 4m/6km SE of Dunbar. **76 E3** NT7375.

Dry Doddington *Lincs.* ***Village***, 6m/9km SE of Newark-on-Trent. **42 B1** SK8546.
Dry Drayton *Cambs.* ***Village***, 5m/8km NW of Cambridge. **33 G2** TL3862.
Dry Harbour *High.* ***Settlement***, in centre of Rona. **94 C6** NG6258.
Dry Hill *Som.* ***Mountain***, on Exmoor, 3m/4km NE of Simonsbath. Height 1456 feet or 444 metres. **7 G1** SS8141.
Dry Sandford *Oxon.* ***Hamlet***, 3m/4km NW of Abingdon. **21 H2** SP4600.
Dry Street *Essex* ***Settlement***, S of Lee Chapel, Basildon. **24 C3** TQ6986.
Drybeck *Cumb.* ***Hamlet***, 3m/5km S of Appleby-in-Westmorland. **61 H5** NY6615.
Drybridge *Moray* ***Settlement***, near N coast on Burn of Buckie, 2m/3km S of Buckie. **98 C4** NJ4362.
Drybridge *N.Ayr.* ***Hamlet***, with standing stone, 2m/3km SE of Irvine, on bend of River Irvine. **74 B7** NS3636.
Drybrook *Glos.* ***Village***, 2m/4km N of Cinderford. **29 F7** SO6417.
Drybrook *Here.* ***Locality***, 4m/6km S of Ross-on-Wye. SO5918.
Dryburgh *Sc.Bord.* ***Village***, 1km N of St. Boswells across River Tweed. Large statue of William Wallace, erected in 1814, to N of village. NT5932.
Dryburgh Abbey *Sc.Bord.* ***Historic/prehistoric site***, remains of abbey (Historic Scotland) founded in 1150, in loop of River Tweed, 1m/2km S of Bemersyde. Burial place of Sir Walter Scott, d. 1832, and of Field-Marshal Lord Haig, d. 1928. **76 D7** NT5931.
Dryden Fell *Sc.Bord.* ***Mountain***, 2m/3km N of Teviothead. Height 1151 feet or 351 metres. **69 K3** NT3908.
Dryfe Water *D. & G.* ***River***, rising on S side of Loch Fell and running S to River Annan, 2m/3km W of Lockerbie. **69 G4** NY1082.
Drygarn Fawr *Powys* ***Mountain***, 4m/7km N of Abergwesyn. Height 2116 feet or 645 metres. **27 H3** SN8658.
Drygrange *Sc.Bord.* ***Settlement***, 2m/3km S of Earlston, next to W bank of Leader Water. **76 D7** NT5735.
Dryhope *Sc.Bord.* ***Hamlet***, at NE end of St. Mary's Loch, 2m/3km NE of Cappercleuch. **69 H1** NT2624.
Drylaw *Edin.* ***Suburb***, 2m/3km NW of Edinburgh city centre. NT2275.
Drymen *Stir.* ***Village***, 7m/11km NE of Balloch. To W is site of Buchanan Castle. **74 C2** NS4788.
Drymuir *Aber.* ***Locality***, 1m/2km SW of Maud. **99 H6** NJ9145.
Drynham *Wilts.* ***Settlement***, 1m/2km S of Trowbridge. ST8656.
Drynoch *High.* ***Settlement***, at head of Loch Harport, Skye. **85 K1** NG4031.
Dryrigs Hill *S.Lan.* ***Mountain***, with forested summit, 4m/7km SE of Muirkirk. Height 1443 feet or 440 metres. **68 C1** NS7424.
Drysgol *Powys* ***Mountain***, 3m/4km W of Pant-y-dwr. Height 1588 feet or 484 metres. **27 J1** SN9474.
Dryslwyn *Carmar.* ***Hamlet***, on River Tywi, 5m/8km W of Llandeilo. Ruins of medieval castle. **17 J2** SN5520.
Dryslwyn Castle *Carmar.* ***Castle***, remains, situated to S of Dryslwyn, on N bank of River Tywi. **17 J2** SN5520.
Dryton *Shrop.* ***Settlement***, 2m/3km NW of Cressage. **38 E5** SJ5806.
Duachy *Arg. & B.* ***Settlement***, 1m/2km SW of Kilninver, on NW shore of Loch Seil. **79 K5** NM8020.
Duad *Carmar.* ***River***, rising 5m/8km S of Llandysul and flowing S into River Gwili 4m/7km NW of Carmarthen. **17 G1** SN3826.
Duart Bay *Arg. & B.* ***Bay***, to W of Duart Point, on E coast of Mull. **79 J4** NM7435.
Duart Castle *Arg. & B.* ***Castle***, on Duart Point, Mull, seat of the chief of the Macleans. **79 J4** NM7435.
Duart Point *Arg. & B.* ***Coastal feature***, headland on E coast of Mull opposite entrance to Loch Linnhe. **79 J4** NM7435.
Dubford *Aber.* ***Settlement***, 1m/2km S of Gardenstown. **99 F4** NJ7963.
Dubh Artach *Arg. & B.* ***Island***, rock lying 16m/26km SW of Mull. NM1203.
Dubh Bheinn *Arg. & B.* ***Mountain***, on Jura, 3m/4km NW of Craighouse. Height 1738 feet or 530 metres. **72 C4** NR4868.
Dubh Bheinn *Arg. & B.* ***Mountain***, on N part of Jura, 4m/6km NW of Lussagiven. Height 1574 feet or 480 metres. **72 D2** NR5889.
Dubh Chreag *Arg. & B.* ***Mountain***, on Knapdale, 5m/7km NW of Tarbert. Height 1574 feet or 480 metres. **73 F4** NR7970.
Dubh Eas *Stir.* ***River***, flowing SE into River Falloch, 3m/4km N of Ardlui. **80 D5** NN3219.
Dubh Eilean *Arg. & B.* ***Island***, rocky island off W coast of Oronsay. **72 B2** NR3388.
Dubh Ghleann *Aber.* ***Valley***, narrow, steep-sided valley in Grampian Mountains to E of Beinn Bhreac, with a stream flowing in a N to S direction to Glen Quoich. **89 H5** NO0697.
Dubh Loch *Aber.* ***Lake/loch***, small loch 2m/3km W of Loch Muick and 7m/12km SE of Braemar. **89 K6** NO2382.
Dubh Loch *Arg. & B.* ***Lake/loch***, small loch in Argyll in course of River Shira, 2m/3km NE of Inveraray. **80 C6** NN1111.
Dubh Loch *High.* ***Lake/loch***, upper part of Loch Bad an Sgalaig, Ross and Cromarty district. **94 E5** NG8470.
Dubh Loch *High.* ***Lake/loch***, in W part of Ross and Cromarty district adjacent to head of Fionn Loch and 1m/2km S of Beinn a' Chàisgein Mòr. **95 F4** NG9876.
Dubh Loch Beag *High.* ***Lake/loch***, small round loch in Benmore Forest, 1km E of River Oykel. **103 F7** NC3216.
Dubh Loch Mòr *High.* ***Lake/loch***, small corrie loch with Ben More Assynt rising steeply to N. **103 F7** NC3119.
Dubh Sgeir *Arg. & B.* ***Island***, rock island in Firth of Lorn, 1m/2km SW of Bach Island. **79 J5** NM7625.
Dubh Sgeirean *High.* ***Island***, group of island rocks 1m/2km off W coast of Sutherland district, 4m/6km SW of Kinlochbervie. NC1654.
Dubhchladach *Arg. & B.* ***Settlement***, at head of West Loch Tarbert, 1m/2km W of Tarbert. **73 G4** NR8468.
Dubheads *P. & K.* ***Settlement***, 6m/9km N of Auchterarder. **82 A5** NN9621.
Dublin *Suff.* ***Settlement***, 1km N of Rishangles. TM1669.
Dubmill Point *Cumb.* ***Coastal feature***, headland at N end of Allonby Bay. **60 B2** NY0745.
Dubton *Angus* ***Hamlet***, 3m/4km NW of Friockheim. **83 G2** NO5652.
Duchal *Inclyde* ***Settlement***, 1m/2km S of Kilmacolm. **74 B4** NS3567.
Duchal Moor *Inclyde* ***Open space***, moorland to E and SE of North Burnt Hill and Creuch Hill respectively. **74 A4** NS2766.
Duchally *High.* ***Settlement***, on E side of Glen Cassley, 6m/9km W of Loch Shin. **103 F7** NC3817.
Duchray Castle *Stir.* ***Castle***, former stronghold of the Grahams, on S bank of Duchray Water in Loch Ard Forest, to W of Aberfoyle. **74 C1** NS4899.
Duchray Hill *P. & K.* *Alternative name for Mealna Letter, qv.*
Duchray Water *Stir.* ***River***, flows E through Loch Ard Forest to join River Forth 1m/2km W of Aberfoyle. **81 F7** NS4899.
Duchrie Burn *Aber.* ***River***, rising on N slopes of Culardoch and flowing SE, then NE, to join River Gairn 1km E of Daldownie. **89 K5** NJ2500.
Duck End *Beds.* ***Settlement***, adjoining to SW of Stevington, 5m/7km NW of Bedford. SP9852.
Duck End *Beds.* ***Settlement***, 4m/6km S of Bedford. TL0644.
Duck End *Bucks.* ***Settlement***, adjoining to NW of Swanbourne, 2m/3km E of Winslow. SP7927.
Duck End *Cambs.* ***Locality***, adjoining to S of Girton, 3m/5km NW of Cambridge. TL4261.
Duck End *Cambs.* ***Settlement***, W end of Graveley, 5m/8km S of Huntingdon. TL2464.
Duck End *Essex* ***Settlement***, 3m/5km NE of Great Dunmow. **33 K6** TL6526.
Duck End *Essex* ***Settlement***, N end of Finchingfield. TL6833.
Duck Street *Hants.* ***Hamlet***, 4m/6km NW of Andover. SU3249.
Duck Street *N.Yorks.* ***Settlement***, adjoining to S of Greenhow Hill. Radio/TV mast. SE1163.
Duck Street *Suff.* ***Hamlet***, 4m/7km NE of Lavenham. TL9554.
Duckend Green *Essex* ***Settlement***, 2m/3km W of Braintree. TL7223.
Duckington *Ches.* ***Settlement***, 3m/5km N of Malpas. **48 D7** SJ4851.
Ducklington *Oxon.* ***Village***, 1m/2km S of Witney. **21 G1** SP3507.
Duckmanton *Derbys.* ***Village***, 2m/3km S of Staveley. SK4472.
Duck's Cross *Beds.* ***Settlement***, 6m/9km NE of Bedford. **32 E3** TL1156.
Ducks Island *Gt.Lon.* ***Suburb***, in borough of Barnet, 1m/2km SW of Chipping Barnet and 10m/16km NW of Charing Cross. TQ2395.
Duckworth Hall *Lancs.* ***Settlement***, 3m/4km SE of Blackburn town centre. SD7226.
Dudden Hill *Gt.Lon.* ***Suburb***, N of Willesden in borough of Brent, 6m/9km NW of Charing Cross. TQ2285.
Duddenhoe End *Essex* ***Hamlet***, 5m/8km W of Saffron Walden. **33 H5** TL4636.
Duddingston *Edin.* ***Suburb***, 3m/5km E of Edinburgh city centre. **76 A3** NT2972.
Duddington *Northants.* ***Village***, 5m/8km SW of Stamford. **42 C5** SK9800.
Duddlestone *Som.* ***Hamlet***, to SW of Taunton Racecourse, 2m/4km S of Taunton. ST2321.
Duddleswell *E.Suss.* ***Hamlet***, on S side of Ashdown Forest, 4m/7km N of Uckfield. **13 H4** TQ4627.
Duddo *Northumb.* ***Hamlet***, 4m/6km SE of Norham. **77 H6** NT9342.
Duddon *Ches.* ***Village***, 3m/5km NW of Tarporley. **48 E6** SJ5164.
Duddon Bridge *Cumb.* ***Hamlet***, at road crossing of River Duddon, 1m/2km NW of Broughton in Furness. **54 E1** SD1988.
Duddon Sands *Cumb.* ***Coastal feature***, sandflat in River Duddon estuary, 4m/6km N of Barrow-in-Furness. **54 E2** SD1675.
Dudleston *Shrop.* ***Hamlet***, 4m/7km NW of Ellesmere. SJ3438.
Dudleston Heath (Also known as Criftins.) *Shrop.* ***Locality***, 3m/4km NW of Ellesmere. **38 C2** SJ3636.
Dudley *T. & W.* Population: 5277. ***Village***, 6m/9km N of Newcastle upon Tyne. **71 H6** NZ2673.
Dudley *W.Mid.* Population: 192,171. ***Town***, 8m/12km W of Birmingham. Remains of castle and 12c priory. Black Country museum, zoo and nature reserve. **40 B6** SO9490.
Dudley Castle *W.Mid.* ***Castle***, 13c castle in centre of Dudley, built on site of earlier motte by Roger and John de Somery, with addition of 14c chapel. Taken over by Dudley family during reign of Henry VIII. **40 B6** SO9490.
Dudley Hill *W.Yorks.* ***Suburb***, 2m/3km SE of Bradford city centre. **57 G6** SE1830.
Dudley Port *W.Mid.* ***Suburb***, to W of West Bromwich. **40 B6** SO9691.
Dudley Wood *W.Mid.* ***Suburb***, 2m/4km S of Dudley town centre. SO9486.
Dudley Zoo *W.Mid.* ***Leisure/recreation***, traditional zoo set in grounds of ruined castle in centre of Dudley. **40 B6** SO9490.
Dudlow's Green *Warr.* ***Suburb***, 3m/5km S of Warrington town centre. SJ6284.
Dudmaston Hall *Shrop.* ***Historic house***, 17c manor (National Trust), 3m/5km SE of Bridgnorth. Contains fine furniture, Dutch flower paintings and modern art. Lakeside garden and extensive estate grounds. **39 G7** SO7488.
Dudsbury *Dorset* ***Locality***, residential locality, 5m/8km N of Bournemouth. **10 B5** SZ0798.
Dudwell *E.Suss.* ***River***, rising to E of Heathfield and flowing E into River Rother below Etchingham. TQ7126.
Dudwell Mountain *Pembs.* ***Hill***, 5m/8km NW of Haverfordwest. Height 584 feet or 178 metres. **16 C2** SM9022.
Duff House *Aber.* ***Historic house***, on SW side of Banff. Fine example of Georgian baroque architecture, designed by William Adam for first Earl of Fife in 1735. Housed German prisoners in World War II. Houses fine National Galleries of Scotland collections of paintings, furniture, tapestries and artefacts. **98 E4** NJ6963.
Duffield *Derbys.* Population: 4514. ***Village***, on River Derwent, 5m/8km N of Derby. Mound of Norman castle. **41 F1** SK3443.
Duffryn *N.P.T.* ***Village***, 3m/5km N of Maesteg. **18 B2** SS8395.
Dufftown *Moray* Population: 1710. ***Small town***, at confluence of Dullan Water and River Fiddich 16m/26km SE of Elgin. Auchindown Castle (Historic Scotland), ruined 15c castle 2m/3km SE. **98 B6** NJ3239.
Dufftown Museum *Moray* ***Other feature of interest***, museum in Dufftown clock tower with exhibits on local history, distilling and a reconstructed laundry. **90 B1** NJ3239.
Duffus *Moray* ***Village***, near N coast, 5m/8km NW of Elgin. St. Peter's Kirk and shaft of 14c cross (Historic Scotland) on E side of village. **97 J5** NJ1768.
Duffus Castle *Moray* ***Castle***, ruined 14c castle (Historic Scotland) standing on earlier motte, 1m/2km SE of Duffus. **97 J5** NJ1768.
Dufton *Cumb.* ***Village***, 3m/5km N of Appleby-in-Westmorland. **61 H4** NY6825.
Dufton Fell *Cumb.* ***Open space***, moorland to W of Cow Green Reservoir. Highest point is Meldon Hill at 2516 feet or 767 metres. **61 J4** NY7428.
Duggleby *N.Yorks.* ***Village***, 6m/10km SE of Malton. Lost medieval village of Wharram Percy (English Heritage) 2m/3km SW. **58 E3** SE8767.
Dugoed *Gwyn.* ***River***, rising 4m/7km NE of Mallwyd and flowing S, then W into River Dyfi on W side of Mallwyd. **37 H4** SH8512.
Duhonw *Powys* ***River***, rising about 6m/9km SW of Builth Wells and running into River Wye 1m/2km E of Builth Wells. **27 K4** SO0651.
Duiar *High.* ***Settlement***, on E bank of River Spey, 7m/11km SW of Upper Knockando. **89 J1** NJ1233.
Duible *High.* ***Settlement***, 2m/3km SE of Kildonan Lodge, to N of River Helmsdale. **104 E6** NC9219.
Duich *Arg. & B.* ***River***, flowing W, then NW, into River Laggan at N end of Laggan Bay, Islay. **72 B5** NR3055.
Duiletter *Arg. & B.* ***Settlement***, 2m/3km N of Dalmally. **80 C5** NN1530.
Duinish *P. & K.* ***Settlement***, 6m/9km NW of Kinloch Rannoch. **81 H1** NN6167.
Duirinish *High.* ***Large natural feature***, mountainous peninsula, including Healabhal Mhòr and Healabhal Beag, in extreme W of Skye. N part separated from Vaternish peninsula by Loch Dunvegan to E, and S part bounded by Loch Bracadale to E. Fine cliff scenery. NG2045.
Duirinish *High.* ***Settlement***, in Skye and Lochalsh district, 3m/5km NE of Kyle of Lochalsh. **86 D1** NG7831.
Duisdalemore *High.* ***Settlement***, on E side of Sleat peninsula, Skye, 1km N of Eilean Iarmain. **86 D3** NG7013.
Duisk *S.Ayr.* ***River***, rising SE of Barrhill and running NW, past Barrhill, to join River Stinchar at Pinwherry. **67 G5** NX1986.
Duisky *High.* ***Settlement***, on S shore of Loch Eil, 6m/10km W of Fort William across Loch Linnhe. **87 G7** NN0076.
Duke End *Warks.* ***Settlement***, 2m/4km E of Coleshill. SP2188.
Duke Street *Suff.* ***Hamlet***, 4m/6km E of Hadleigh. TM0742.
Dukehouse *Norf.* ***Locality***, 1m/2km N of Foulsham. TG0327.
Dukes Pass *Stir.* ***Other feature of interest***, mountain pass at height of 797 feet or 243 metres in Achray Forest, between The Trossachs and Aberfoyle. **81 G7** NN5103.
Dukesfield *Northumb.* ***Locality***, to N of Slaley Forest, 4m/7km S of Hexham. NY9457.
Dukestown *B.Gwent* ***Locality***, on N edge of South Wales coalfield, adjoining to N of Tredegar. **28 A7** SO1310.
Dukinfield *Gt.Man.* Population: 17,917. ***Town***, industrial town, 6m/10km E of Manchester. **49 J3** SJ9497.
Dulais *Carmar.* ***River***, rising NE of Llanfynydd and flowing S into River Tywi 1km E of Rhosmaen. **17 K2** SN6424.
Dulais *N.P.T.* ***River***, rising near Seven Sisters and flowing S into River Neath 2m/3km NE of Neath. **18 A1** SS7799.
Dulas *Carmar.* ***River***, rising 3m/5km NE of Llanfynydd and flowing SW into River Tywi, 1m/2km E of Llanarthney. **17 K2** SN5420.
Dulas *Conwy* ***River***, rising about 5m/8km S of Colwyn Bay and running NE to coast at Llanddulas. SH9178.
Dulas *Gwyn.* ***River***, running S into River Dyfi nearly 1m/2km NE of Machynlleth. SH7501.
Dulas *Here.* ***Locality***, 1m/2km NW of Ewyas Harold. SO3729.
Dulas *I.o.A.* ***Locality***, near NE coast of Anglesey, 3m/5km SE of Amlwch. **46 C4** SH4789.
Dulas *Powys* ***River***, rising in Glaslyn Lake and flowing NW into River Dyfi, 1m/2km NE of Machynlleth. **37 G6** SH7501.
Dulas *Powys* ***River***, running NE by Tirabad into River Irfon 1m/2km W of Llangammarch Wells. SN9146.
Dulas *Powys* ***River***, rising S of Caban Coch Reservoir and flowing S to River Irfon at Garth. **27 J3** SN9549.
Dulas *Powys* ***River***, rising E of Rhayader and flowing S, then SE into River Ithon 2m/3km N of Llandrindod Wells. **27 K2** SO0663.

Dulas Bay *I.o.A.* ***Bay***, to E of Dulas on NE coast of Anglesey. Includes Traeth Dulas. **46 C4** SH4989.
Dulax *Aber.* ***Settlement***, 3m/5km N of Strathdon. **90 B3** NJ3518.
Dulcote *Som.* ***Village***, 1m/2km SE of Wells. Dulcote Hill to SE. **19 J7** ST5644.
Dulford *Devon* ***Hamlet***, 3m/5km E of Cullompton. **7 J5** ST0705.
Dull *P. & K.* ***Village***, 3m/5km W of Aberfeldy. **81 K3** NN8049.
Dullan Water *Moray* ***River***, rising on NW side of Glenfiddich Forest and flowing NE down Glen Rinnes to River Fiddich at Dufftown. **90 A1** NJ3339.
Dullatur *N.Lan.* ***Village***, 2m/3km NW of Cumbernauld. **75 F3** NS7476.
Dullingham *Cambs.* ***Village***, 4m/6km S of Newmarket. **33 K3** TL6357.
Dullingham Ley *Cambs.* ***Hamlet***, 1m/2km SE of Dullingham. TL6456.
Dulnain *High.* ***River***, in Badenoch and Strathspey district rising on Monadhliath Mountains and running NE to River Spey, 1m/2km SE of Dulnain Bridge. **89 F3** NJ0023.
Dulnain Bridge *High.* ***Village***, in Badenoch and Strathspey district, 3m/5km SW of Grantown-on-Spey. **89 G2** NH9924.
Duloe *Beds.* ***Hamlet***, 2m/3km W of St. Neots. **32 E2** TL1560.
Duloe *Cornw.* ***Village***, 4m/6km S of Liskeard. 37 foot diameter stone circle with eight quartz blocks, reputed to pre-date Stonehenge. Church with 13c tower. **4 C5** SX2358.
Dulsie *High.* ***Settlement***, 3m/4km SW of Ferness. **97 G7** NH9341.
Dulverton *Som.* ***Small town***, attractive town on River Barle, on S edge of Exmoor, 10m/16km N of Tiverton. 15c stone bridge. **7 H3** SS9127.
Dulwich *Gt.Lon.* ***Suburb***, large district in borough of Southwark, in SE London, some 5m/8km SE of Charing Cross. Sub-districts are East and West Dulwich, the latter being partly in borough of Lambeth; and Dulwich Village, which still retains something of a village character. There are considerable open spaces, including Dulwich Common, Dulwich Park, and grounds of Dulwich College. **23 G4** TQ3372.
Dulwich Village *Gt.Lon.* ***Locality***, in borough of Southwark, 2m/3km SE of Brixton. Still retains something of a village character. TQ3372.
Dulyn *Conwy* ***River***, rising above Dulyn Reservoir and flowing E into River Conwy 1km E of Tal-y-bont. SH7768.
Dulyn Reservoir *Conwy* ***Reservoir***, 4m/7km W of Dolgarrog. SH7066.
Dumbarton *W.Dun.* Population: 21,962. ***Town***, situated at confluence of River Leven and River Clyde, 14m/22km NW of Glasgow. Previously an important engineering and shipbuilding town; the 'Cutty Sark' was built here in 1869. Ancient castle (Historic Scotland) on basalt rock prominence above River Clyde. **74 C3** NS3975.
Dumbarton Castle *W.Dun.* ***Castle***, ancient castle (Historic Scotland) built on site of Roman fort to S of Dumbarton, on basalt rock prominence overlooking N bank of River Clyde estuary. Castle was a royal seat for Mary, Queen of Scots. Since beginning of 17c has been used as a garrison and artillery fortress. **74 C3** NS4074.
Dumbarton Muir *W.Dun.* ***Open space***, moorland area to NE of Dumbarton. **74 C3** NS4579.
Dumbleton *Glos.* ***Village***, 5m/8km N of Winchcombe. **30 B5** SP0136.
Dumbreck *Glas.* ***Suburb***, 2m/3km SW of Glasgow city centre. NS5663.
Dumcrieff *D. & G.* ***Locality***, on Moffat Water, 1m/2km SE of Moffat. **69 G3** NT1003.
Dumeath *Aber.* ***Settlement***, on W side of River Deveron, 1m/2km S of Haugh of Glass. **90 C1** NJ4237.
Dumfin *Arg. & B.* ***Settlement***, 3m/5km NE of Helensburgh. **74 B2** NS3484.
Dumfries *D. & G.* Population: 32,136. ***Town***, on River Nith, 60m/97km SE of Glasgow and 29m/47km NW of Carlisle across head of Solway Firth. Known for cotton spinning and weaving. Burns lived in town from 1791 to his death in 1796, and town contains many related tourist attractions. **65 K3** NX9776.
Dumfries Museum and Camera Obscura *D. & G.* ***Other feature of interest***, contained in 18c windmill, 1km W of Dumfries town centre, with exhibits on local history. Camera Obscura gives table-top panorama of Dumfries and surrounding area. **65 K3** NX9876.
Dumgoyne *Stir.* ***Settlement***, 4m/6km NW of Strathblane. **74 D2** NS5283.
Dummer *Hants.* ***Village***, 5m/8km SW of Basingstoke. **21 J7** SU5846.
Dumpling Green *Norf.* ***Locality***, 1m/2km SE of East Dereham. TG0011.
Dumplington *Gt.Man.* ***Locality***, 1m/2km N of Urmston. SJ7697.
Dun *Angus* ***Settlement***, 3m/5km NW of Montrose. **83 H2** NO6659.
Dun *W.Isles* ***Island***, steep, rocky, uninhabited island (National Trust for Scotland) in St. Kilda group, about 54m/86km W of South Harris and 35m/56km W of North Uist, lying off SE end of St. Kilda itself. Narrow island nearly 1m/2km wide. Haunt of sea birds. NF1097.
Dùn Bàn *Arg. & B. See Burg.*
Dùn Beag Broch *High.* ***Historic/prehistoric site***, 1km W of Bracadale, Skye. Fine example of Hebridean broch (Historic Scotland), occupied until 18c. **85 J1** NG3438.
Dùn Borve Broch *W.Isles* ***Historic/prehistoric site***, Historic Scotland property on NW coast of Isle of Lewis, 8m/13km SW of Butt of Lewis. **101 G2** NB4158.
Dùn Caan *High.* ***Mountain***, highest point on Raasay, with caves on S side, 4m/6km from S end of island. Height 1453 feet or 443 metres. **86 B1** NG5739.
Dun Carloway *W.Isles* ***Settlement***, near W coast of Isle of Lewis, 1m/2km SW of Carloway village. Here is Iron Age broch or fort (Historic Scotland). **100 D3** NB1841.
Dùn Chonnuill (Also known as Eileach Chonail.) *Arg. & B.* ***Island***, most northerly of Garvellachs group of islands in Firth of Lorn. Ruins of 13c castle. NM6812.
Dun Corr-bhile *Arg. & B.* ***Mountain***, on W side of Loch Shira, 1m/2km NE of Inveraray. Height 1056 feet or 322 metres. **80 B6** NN1010.
Dùn da Ghaoithe *Arg. & B.* ***Mountain***, 3m/5km W of Craignure, Mull. Height 2512 feet or 766 metres. **79 H4** NM6736.
Dun Dornaigil Broch *High.* ***Historic/prehistoric site***, situated on E side of Strath More, 9m/14km NW of Altnaharra. Good example of Iron Age broch. **103 G4** NC4545.
Dun Hill *Arg. & B. Alternative name for Dun I, qv.*
Dun I (Also known as Dun Hill). *Arg. & B.* ***Hill***, summit of Iona, 1km N of Baile Mòr. Height 328 feet or 100 metres. **78 D5** NM2825.
Dun Law *Sc.Bord.* ***Mountain***, on NW flank of Mount Main, 2m/3km E of Dewar. Height 1542 feet or 470 metres. **76 B6** NT3748.
Dun Law *Sc.Bord.* ***Mountain***, 3m/4km SE of Fala. Height 1292 feet or 394 metres. **76 C5** NT4657.
Dun Leacainn *Arg. & B.* ***Mountain***, on N shore of Loch Fyne, 1m/2km NE of Furnace. Height 1178 feet or 359 metres. **80 B7** NN0301.
Dùn-Mòr *Arg. & B.* ***Hill***, rising to over 80 metres on W coast of Seil, to N of Ellanbeich. **79 J6** NM7417.
Dun Rig *E.Ayr.* ***Hill***, above Greenock Water on SW slopes of Meanlour Hill. Height 836 feet or 255 metres. **68 B1** NS6329.
Dun Rig *Sc.Bord.* ***Mountain***, 6m/9km S of Peebles. Height 2437 feet or 743 metres. **76 A7** NT2531.
Dunach *Arg. & B.* ***Settlement***, on N shore of Loch Feochan, 1m/2km SW of Kilmore. **79 K5** NM8624.
Dunadd *Arg. & B.* ***Historic/prehistoric site***, ancient fort (Historic Scotland) of 6c in Argyll 4m/6km N of Lochgilphead. **73 G1** NR8393.
Dunagoil Bay *Arg. & B.* ***Bay***, on SW coast of Bute, to N of Dunagoil. **73 J5** NS0853.
Dunalastair *P. & K.* ***Settlement***, just E of Dunalastair Water, 3m/5km W of Tummel Bridge. **81 J2** NN7159.
Dunalastair Water *P. & K.* ***Reservoir***, in course of River Tummel below Kinloch Rannoch. **81 J2** NN6958.
Dunan *Arg. & B.* ***Locality***, in Argyll, on W shore of Firth of Clyde, adjoining to NE of Innellan. **73 K3** NS1570.
Dunan *High.* ***Settlement***, 1m/2km E of Luib, on W shore of Loch na Cairidh, opposite Scalpay. **86 B2** NG5827.
Dunan Liath *High.* ***Mountain***, in Sutherland district, 14m/23km N of Garve. Height 2266 feet or 691 metres. **96 B3** NH4184.
Dunans *Arg. & B.* ***Settlement***, 6m/9km NE of Clachan of Glendaruel. **73 J1** NS0491.
Dunball *Som.* ***Village***, at confluence of King's Sedgemoor Drain and River Parrett, 3m/4km N of Bridgwater. **19 G7** ST3141.
Dunbar *E.Loth.* Population: 6518. ***Small town***, coastal resort with small harbour, 27m/43km E of Edinburgh. Scant remains of castle on headland. 2m/3km S is site of battle of 1296 in which English defeated Scots. 2m/3km SE is site of battle of 1650 in which Cromwell defeated supporters of Charles II under Leslie. **76 E3** NT6878.
Dunbar Common *E.Loth.* ***Open space***, moorland on N side of Lammermuir Hills, 3m/4km SE of Garvald. **76 E4** NT6369.
Dunbeath *High.* ***Village***, on E coast of Caithness district, 18m/29km SW of Wick, at mouth of Dunbeath Water. Clifftop castle 1m/2km S. **105 G6** ND1629.
Dunbeath Bay *High.* ***Bay***, on E coast of Caithness district, to SE of Dunbeath. **105 G6** ND1629.
Dunbeath Castle *High.* ***Castle***, in Dunbeath, 15c with 17c additions. **105 G6** ND1529.
Dunbeath Heritage Centre *High.* ***Other feature of interest***, on E coast, 1km NE of Dunbeath. Details the life of novelist, Neil Gunn, who was born in Dunbeath. **105 G5** ND1730.
Dunbeath Water *High.* ***River***, rising 11m/17km W of Dunbeath and flowing into sea on E coast of Caithness at Dunbeath. **105 F5** ND1629.
Dunbeg *Arg. & B.* ***Village***, on Dunstaffnage Bay, 2m/3km W of Connel, Argyll. **79 K4** NM8733.
Dunblane *Stir.* Population: 7368. ***City***, ancient cathedral city on Allan Water 5m/8km N of Stirling. 13c cathedral. Site of Roman camp to SW. **81 J7** NN7801.
Dunblane Cathedral *Stir.* ***Ecclesiastical building***, dating mainly from 13c, but incorporating 12c tower. In centre of Dunblane, 5m/8km N of Stirling. **81 J7** NN7701.
Dunbog *Fife* ***Village***, 3m/5km E of Newburgh. **82 D6** NO2818.
Dunbridge *Hants.* ***Hamlet***, 1km SW of Mottisfont. SU3126.
Dunburgh Hill *Norf.* ***Hamlet***, adjoining to W of Gillingham, 1m/2km NW of Beccles. TM4091.
Duncangill Head *S.Lan.* ***Mountain***, one of three summits rising to over 560 metres on upland plateau, 5m/8km E of Abington. **69 F1** NT0025.
Duncansby *High.* ***Locality***, in NE corner of Caithness district. Duncansby Head is headland to NE, Stacks of Duncansby are group of rocks off coast to E and Ness of Duncansby is headland to N. ND3872.
Duncansby Head *High.* ***Coastal feature***, headland with lighthouse, nearly 2m/3km E of John o' Groats. **105 K1** ND3872.
Duncanston *Aber.* ***Village***, 4m/6km W of Insch. **90 D2** NJ5726.
Duncanston *High.* ***Settlement***, 2m/3km SW of Culbokie, on Black Isle, Ross and Cromarty district. **96 C6** NH5856.
Dunchideock *Devon* ***Hamlet***, 4m/7km SW of Exeter. 1m/2km S, Lawrence Castle, prominent belvedere tower erected 1788. **7 G7** SX8787.
Dunchurch *Warks.* Population: 2251. ***Village***, 3m/4km SW of Rugby. **31 F1** SP4871.
Duncombe *Lancs.* ***Settlement***, to SW of Bilsborrow, 4m/6km S of Garstang. SD5139.
Duncombe Park *N.Yorks.* ***Historic house***, mansion, partly 18c, seat of Earls of Feversham, now boarding school for girls, 1m/2km SW of Helmsley. Formal gardens with classical-style temples. **58 C1** SE6083.
Duncote *Northants.* ***Settlement***, 2m/3km NW of Towcester. **31 H3** SP6750.
Duncow *D. & G.* ***Hamlet***, 3m/4km NW of Locharbriggs. **68 E5** NX9683.
Duncow Burn *D. & G.* ***River***, rising on White Hill and flowing generally S to join River Nith 1m/2km W of Locharbriggs. **68 E5** NX9680.
Duncraggan *Stir.* ***Settlement***, 3m/5km N of Aberfoyle. **81 G7** NN5306.
Duncrievie *P. & K.* ***Village***, 3m/5km N of Milnathort. **82 C7** NO1309.
Duncroist *Stir.* ***Settlement***, in Glen Lochay, 3m/5km NW of Killin. **81 G4** NN5336.
Duncrub *P. & K.* ***Hamlet***, 1km NW of Dunning. **82 B6** NO0014.
Duncryne *W.Dun.* ***Locality***, comprises Duncryne Hill and High Duncryne settlement, 1km SE of Gartocharn. **74 C2** NS4385.
Duncton *W.Suss.* ***Village***, at foot of South Downs, 3m/5km S of Petworth. Site of Roman bath house to S of village. **12 C5** SU9617.
Dundarave Point *Arg. & B.* ***Coastal feature***, headland on N shore of Loch Fyne, 3m/5km NE of Inveraray. **80 C7** NN1308.
Dundee *Dundee* Population: 158,981. ***City***, Scotland's fourth largest city, commercial and industrial centre and port, 18m/29km E of Perth on N side of Firth of Tay, crossed here by a 1m/2km road bridge and a 2m/3km railway bridge. Robert the Bruce declared King of the Scots in Dundee in 1309. Sustained severe damage during Civil War and again prior to Jacobite uprising. City recovered in early 19c and became Britain's main processor of jute. One of largest employers in Dundee today is D.C. Thomson, publisher of The Beano and The Dandy. Many museums and art galleries. Cultural centre, occasionally playing host to overflow from Edinburgh Festival. Episcopal cathedral on site of former castle. Universities. Ship 'Discovery' in which Captain Cook travelled to Antarctic has returned to Victoria dock, where she was built. **83 F4** NO4030.
Dundee Airport *Dundee* ***Airport/airfield***, alongside Firth of Tay, 2m/3km W of Dundee city centre. **82 E5** NO3729.
Dundee Law *Dundee* ***Hill***, 1km NW of Dundee city centre. Bears war memorial. Height 571 feet or 174 metres. NO3931.
Dundon *Som.* ***Village***, on W side of Dundon Hill and 3m/4km S of Street. **8 D1** ST4832.
Dundon Hayes *Som.* ***Hamlet***, 1km NW of Dundon and 3m/4km S of Street, overlooking Sedgemoor. ST4832.
Dundonald *S.Ayr.* Population: 2403. ***Village***, 4m/6km NE of Troon. **74 B7** NS3634.
Dundonald Castle *S.Ayr.* ***Castle***, remains of castle (Historic Scotland), mainly 13c, built by Walter Stewart, 5m/8km SW of Kilmarnock. **74 B7** NS3634.
Dundonnell *High.* ***River***, in W part of Ross and Cromarty district, running N through Dundonnell Forest to head of Little Loch Broom. **95 H3** NH0888.
Dundonnell *High.* ***Settlement***, at head of Little Loch Broom, 4m/7km NE of Ullapool across Loch Broom. **95 G3** NH0887.
Dundonnell Forest *High.* ***Open space***, deer forest in W part of Ross and Cromarty district, between Strath na Sealga and Strath More, 8m/13km S of Ullapool. **95 G3** NH1181.
Dundonnell House *High.* ***Garden***, formal garden with aviary and fine collection of bonsai surrounding house by Dundonnell River, 2m/3km SE of Dundonnell. **95 H3** NH1086.
Dundraw *Cumb.* ***Hamlet***, 3m/5km W of Wigton. **60 D2** NY2149.
Dundreggan *High.* ***Settlement***, in Glen Moriston, Inverness district, 7m/11km W of Invermoriston. **87 K3** NH3114.
Dundreggan Forest *High.* ***Open space***, deer forest to NE of Dundreggan. **87 K3** NH3114.
Dundrennan *D. & G.* ***Village***, 5m/7km SE of Kirkcudbright. Ruined 12c abbey (Historic Scotland). **65 H6** NX7447.
Dundrennan Abbey *D. & G.* ***Ecclesiastical building***, substantial Cistercian ruin (Historic Scotland), founded by David I in 1142 at Dundrennan. Mary, Queen of Scots, spent her last night in Scotland here in 1568. **65 H6** NX7447.
Dundridge *Hants.* ***Settlement***, 2m/3km E of Bishop's Waltham. SU5718.
Dundry *N.Som.* ***Village***, on Dundry Hill, 4m/6km SW of Bristol, with extensive view of city. Church tower built as landmark by Merchant Venturers in 1484. **19 J5** ST5566.
Dundry Hill *N.Som.* ***Hill***, 4m/6km SW of Bristol, with extensive view of city. Height 764 feet or 233 metres. **19 J5** ST5566.
Dunduff Castle *S.Ayr.* ***Castle***, ruins of old baronial fortress 1m/2km E of Dunure. **67 G2** NS2716.
Dunearn *Fife* ***Settlement***, 2m/3km NW of Burntisland. **76 A2** NT2187.
Duneaton Water *S.Lan.* ***River***, rising on slopes of Cairn Table and running E to River Clyde 2m/3km N of Abington. **68 D1** NS9326.
Dunecht *Aber.* ***Village***, 2m/4km N of Echt. **91 F4** NJ7509.
Dunfallandy Stone *P. & K.* ***Historic/prehistoric site***, bell cairn, 1m/2km S of Pitlochry. **82 A2** NN9456.

D

Dunfermline *Fife* Population: 55,083. ***Town***, historic town 13m/20km NW of Edinburgh across Firth of Forth. Residence of Scottish kings; burial place of several, including Robert the Bruce. Scottish capital until 1603. Birthplace of Charles I in 1600. Birthplace of Andrew Carnegie, 1835. Abbey and palace (Historic Scotland). **75 J2** NT0987.
Dunfermline Abbey *Fife* ***Ecclesiastical building***, late 11c Benedictine abbey (Historic Scotland) founded by Queen Margaret at Dunfermline. Burial place of Robert the Bruce. **75 J2** NT0887.
Dunfield *Glos.* ***Hamlet***, 2m/4km S of Fairford. **20 E2** SU1497.
Dunford Bridge *S.Yorks.* ***Settlement***, on edge of Peak District National Park, 4m/6km S of Holmfirth. **50 D2** SE1502.
Dungate *Kent* ***Settlement***, 3m/4km S of Sittingbourne. TQ9159.
Dungavel *S.Lan.* ***Other building***, HM prison 5m/8km SW of Strathaven. **74 E7** NS6537.
Dungavel Hill *S.Lan.* ***Mountain***, 1m/2km N of Roberton. Height 1673 feet or 510 metres. **75 H7** NS9430.
Dungeness *Kent* ***Locality***, and headland with lighthouses, at SW end of St. Mary's Bay, 15m/24km SW across bay from Folkestone. Atomic power station. **15 F6** TR0916.
Dungeon Banks *Mersey.* ***Coastal feature***, sandbank in River Mersey estuary, SE of Liverpool Airport, 1km S of Speke. SJ4580.
Dungeon Ghyll Force *Cumb.* ***Waterfall***, in Dungeon Ghyll, 2m/3km NW of Chapel Stile. **60 D6** NY2906.
Dunglass *E.Loth.* ***Settlement***, near coast 7m/11km SE of Dunbar. Collegiate church (Historic Scotland) dates from 15c. **77 F3** NT7671.
Dungworth *S.Yorks.* ***Hamlet***, 5m/8km NW of Sheffield. SK2889.
Dunham *Notts.* ***Village***, on River Trent, 5m/8km E of Tuxford. **52 B5** SK8174.
Dunham Massey *Gt.Man.* ***Historic house***, 18c stately home (National Trust), seat of late Earl of Stamford, 2m/3km SW of Altrincham. House has working Victorian kitchen and fine collection of furniture and Huguenot silver. Fallow deer roam in 250 acre wooded park; 16c deer barn. **49 G4** SJ7387.
Dunham-on-the-Hill *Ches.* ***Village***, 6m/9km NE of Chester. **48 D5** SJ4772.
Dunham Town *Gt.Man.* ***Village***, 2m/3km W of Altrincham. **49 G4** SJ7487.
Dunham Woodhouses *Gt.Man.* ***Hamlet***, 3m/4km W of Altrincham. SJ7288.
Dunhampstead *Worcs.* ***Locality***, 3m/4km SE of Droitwich Spa. SO9160.
Dunhampton *Worcs.* ***Village***, 4m/6km SE of Stourport-on-Severn. **29 H2** SO8466.
Dunheved *Cornw.* *See Launceston.*
Dunholme *Lincs.* Population: 1847. ***Village***, 6m/10km NE of Lincoln. **52 D5** TF0279.
Dunino *Fife* ***Village***, 4m/6km SE of St. Andrews. Site of Roman camp 2km NE. **83 G6** NO5311.
Dunion Hill *Sc.Bord.* ***Mountain***, 1m/2km SW of Jedburgh. Height 1082 feet or 330 metres. **70 B2** NT6218.
Dunipace *Falk.* Population: 2420. ***Small town***, adjoining to NW of Denny across River Carron, 6m/9km W of Falkirk. **75 G2** NS8083.
Dunira *P. & K.* ***Settlement***, 3m/4km NW of Comrie. **81 J5** NN7323.
Dunkeld *P. & K.* ***City***, ancient cathedral city on River Tay, 10m/15km W of Blairgowrie. Dunkeld Cathedral, partly ruined, dates from 12c, though mainly from 14c-15c. Houses (National Trust for Scotland) near cathedral, late 17c, restored. Stanley Hill (National Trust for Scotland), wooded hill to W. **82 B3** NO0242.
Dunkeld Cathedral *P. & K.* ***Ecclesiastical building***, next to River Tay at Dunkeld, in particularly attractive setting. Part is ruined, but choir has been restored and is in use as parish church. **82 B3** NO0242.
Dunkerton *B. & N.E.Som.* ***Village***, 4m/7km SW of Bath. **20 A6** ST7159.
Dunkery Beacon *Som.* ***Mountain***, summit of Dunkery Hill and highest point of Exmoor and Somerset. Height 1702 feet or 519 metres. **7 G1** SS8941.
Dunkery Hill *Som.* ***Open space***, moorland area (National Trust) on Exmoor, 6m/9km SW of Minehead. **7 G1** SS8941.
Dunkeswell *Devon* ***Village***, 5m/8km N of Honiton. 2m/3km N at Abbey is ruined 13c Dunkeswell Abbey. **7 K5** ST1407.
Dunkeswick *W.Yorks.* ***Village***, 5m/8km S of Harrogate. **57 J5** SE3046.
Dunkirk *Ches.* ***Settlement***, 1m/2km SE of Capenhurst. SJ3873.
Dunkirk *Kent* Population: 2705. ***Village***, 5m/8km W of Canterbury. **15 F2** TR0759.
Dunkirk *Staffs.* ***Settlement***, 2m/3km SW of Kidsgrove. SJ8152.
Dunk's Green *Kent* ***Hamlet***, 1m/2km SE of Plaxtol. Site of Roman villa to NE. **23 K6** TQ6152.
Dunlappie *Angus* ***Hamlet***, 1m/2km SW of Edzell. **83 G1** NO5867.
Dunley *Hants.* ***Settlement***, 1km W of Litchfield. SU4553.
Dunley *Worcs.* ***Village***, 2m/4km SW of Stourport-on-Severn. **29 G2** SO7869.
Dunlop *E.Ayr.* ***Village***, 2m/4km N of Stewarton. Gives name to local cheese. **74 C6** NS4049.
Dunloskin *Arg. & B.* ***Settlement***, 1m/2km NW of Dunoon. **73 K3** NS1678.
Dunmail Raise *Cumb.* ***Mountain***, 1km S of S end of Thirlmere. Height 1591 feet or 485 metres. **60 E5** NY3211.
Dunman *D. & G.* ***Hill***, 3m/5km SW of Drummore. Fort on SW slope. Height 525 feet or 160 metres. **64 B7** NX1033.
Dunmere *Cornw.* ***Village***, on River Camel, 1m/2km NW of Bodmin. **4 A4** SX0467.
Dunmoor Hill *Northumb.* ***Mountain***, in Cheviot Hills, 4m/6km NW of Ingram. Height 1860 feet or 567 metres. **70 E2** NT9618.
Dunmore *Arg. & B.* ***Settlement***, on NW side of West Loch Tarbert, 6m/10km SW of Tarbert. **73 F4** NR7961.
Dunmore *Falk.* ***Settlement***, on W bank of River Forth, 1m/2km N of Airth. **75 G2** NS8989.
Dunn *High.* ***Settlement***, 3m/5km W of Watten. **105 G3** ND1955.
Dunn Street *Kent* ***Settlement***, adjoining to S of Bredhurst, 4m/6km S of Gillingham. TQ7961.
Dunnabie *D. & G.* ***Settlement***, 2m/3km SE of Paddockhole. **69 H5** NY2581.
Dunnet *High.* ***Village***, on Dunnet Bay, N coast of Caithness district, 7m/11km E of Thurso. **105 H1** ND2271.
Dunnet Bay *High.* ***Bay***, on N coast of Caithness district, 7m/11km E of Thurso. **105 H1** ND2271.
Dunnet Head *High.* ***Coastal feature***, promontory on N coast of Caithness district, to N of Dunnet, culminating in headland of Easter Head. **105 G1** ND2271.
Dunnet Hill *High.* ***Hill***, 2m/3km SW of Dunnet Head on N coast. Height 397 feet or 121 metres. **105 G1** ND1973.
Dunnichen *Angus* ***Village***, 4m/6km E of Forfar. To E, site of Battle of Dunnichen (or Nechtansmere), 685, in which Picts defeated Angles. **83 G3** NO5048.
Dunning *P. & K.* ***Village***, 5m/8km E of Auchterarder. **82 B6** NO0114.
Dunnington *E.Riding* ***Hamlet***, 4m/7km NW of Hornsea. **59 H4** TA1552.
Dunnington *Warks.* ***Village***, 7m/11km NE of Evesham. **30 B3** SP0653.
Dunnington *York* Population: 2603. ***Village***, 4m/7km E of York. **58 C4** SE6652.
Dunnockshaw *Lancs.* ***Village***, 3m/5km S of Burnley. **56 D7** SD8127.
Dunnose *I.o.W.* ***Coastal feature***, headland on SE coast, 1m/2km NE of Ventnor. **11 G7** SZ5878.
Dunnottar *Aber.* ***Locality***, 1m/2km S of Stonehaven. NO8783.
Dunnottar Castle *Aber.* ***Castle***, on rock on coast to E of Dunnottar, dating in part from late 14c. **91 G6** NO8783.
Dunollie Castle *Arg. & B.* ***Castle***, partly ruined 12c-15c castle on coast, 1m/2km N of Oban. Ancient stronghold of MacDougalls, it is owned by Chief of Clan MacDougall. **79 K4** NM8531.
Dunoon *Arg. & B.* Population: 9038. ***Small town***, and resort in Argyll, 4m/7km W of Gourock across Firth of Clyde. Ferry services for vehicles and pedestrians to Gourock and Wemyss Bay. Traces of medieval castle on conical rock above pier. **73 K3** NS1776.
Dunphail *Moray* ***Locality***, comprising house and castle on E bank of River Divie, 7m/11km S of Forres. NJ0047.
Dunragit *D. & G.* ***Village***, 3m/5km W of Glenluce. **64 B5** NX1557.
Dunragit Moor *D. & G.* ***Open space***, afforested area 1m/2km N of Dunragit and 6m/9km E of Stranraer. **64 B5** NX1559.
Dunrobin Castle *High.* ***Castle***, seat of Sutherland family on E coast of Sutherland district, 1m/2km NE of Golspie. **97 F1** NC8500.
Dunrobin Glen *High.* ***Valley***, carrying Golspie Burn, 3m/5km NW of Golspie. **97 F1** NC8003.
Dunrossness *Shet.* ***Locality***, district on Mainland, in parish of same name, 5m/8km N of Sumburgh Head. HU3915.
Dunrostan *Arg. & B.* ***Settlement***, on SE side of Loch Sween, 5m/7km SW of Achnamara. **73 F2** NR7380.
Dunruchan Hill *P. & K.* ***Hill***, 4m/12km SE of Comrie. Height 997 feet or 304 metres. **81 J6** NN7916.
Duns *Sc.Bord.* Population: 2444. ***Small town***, market town, 13m/21km W of Berwick-upon-Tweed. Nearby Manderston House notable for azalea and rhododendron garden. **77 F5** NT7853.
Duns Castle *Sc.Bord.* ***Historic house***, 19c mansion to NW of Duns. **77 F5** NT7853.
Dun's Dish *Angus* ***Lake/loch***, small loch 3m/5km E of Brechin. **83 H1** NO6460.
Duns Tew *Oxon.* ***Village***, 2m/3km S of Deddington. **31 F6** SP4528.
Dunsa *Derbys.* ***Settlement***, just NW of Edensor, 2m/3km NE of Bakewell. SK2470.
Dunsby *Lincs.* ***Village***, 4m/7km N of Bourne. **42 E3** TF1026.
Dunsby Fen *Lincs.* ***Open space***, lowland 2m/4km E of Dunsby. **42 E3** TF1326.
Dunscaith Castle *High.* ***Castle***, ruined castle of the Barons of Sleat, on S side of entrance to Loch Eishort, Skye. **86 C3** NG5912.
Dunscar *Gt.Man.* ***Locality***, adjoining to W of Egerton, 1m/2km SE of Delph Reservoir. SD7114.
Dunscore *D. & G.* ***Village***, 8m/13km NW of Dumfries. **68 D5** NX8684.
Dunscroft *S.Yorks.* ***Locality***, adjoining to S of Hatfield. **51 J2** SE6509.
Dunsdale *R. & C.* ***Hamlet***, 2m/3km N of Guisborough. **63 H5** NZ6018.
Dunsden Green *Oxon.* ***Hamlet***, 3m/4km NE of Reading. **22 A4** SU7377.
Dunsfold *Surr.* ***Village***, 4m/6km SW of Cranleigh. Airfield to E. **12 D3** TQ0036.
Dunsford *Devon* ***Village***, 4m/7km NE of Moretonhampstead. **7 G7** SX8189.
Dunshelt *Fife* ***Village***, 2m/3km N of Falkland. **82 D6** NO2410.
Dunshill *Worcs.* ***Settlement***, 4m/6km W of Tewkesbury across River Severn. SO8331.
Dunshillock *Aber.* ***Village***, between Old Deer and Mintlaw. NJ9848.
Dunsinane Hill *P. & K.* ***Hill***, rising to over 300 metres in Sidlaw range, 8m/12km NE of Perth. Surmounted by ancient fort identified by Shakespeare with castle of Macbeth. NO2131.
Dunsinnan *P. & K.* ***Settlement***, with adjoining parkland, 3m/5km SW of Burrelton. **82 C4** NO1632.
Dunskey Burn *D. & G.* ***River***, flowing SW into Port Kale, 1km NW of Portpatrick. **64 A5** NW9955.
Dunskey Castle *D. & G.* ***Castle***, ruined early 16c castle on coast of Rinns of Galloway, 1km S of Portpatrick. **64 A5** NX0053.
Dunslair Heights *Sc.Bord.* ***Mountain***, 3m/5km NE of Peebles. Height 1975 feet or 602 metres. **76 A6** NT2843.
Dunsland Cross *Devon* ***Settlement***, 4m/6km E of Holsworthy. **6 C5** SS4003.
Dunsley *N.Yorks.* ***Hamlet***, 3m/4km W of Whitby. **63 K5** NZ8511.
Dunsley *Staffs.* ***Settlement***, 3m/5km W of Stourbridge. SO8583.
Dunsmore *Bucks.* ***Village***, 2m/3km S of Wendover. **22 B1** SP8605.
Dunsmore Heath *Warks.* ***Open space***, heathland 1m/2km E of Stretton-on-Dunsmore. **31 F1** SP4272.
Dunsop Bridge *Lancs.* ***Hamlet***, 8m/12km NW of Clitheroe. **56 B4** SD6650.
Dunstable *Beds.* Population: 49,666. ***Town***, former coaching town at N end of Chiltern Hills, 5m/7km W of Luton, at crossing of Roman Watling Street and more ancient Icknield Way, and on site of Roman Durocobrivae. Once famous as a hat-making centre. **32 D6** TL0121.
Dunstable Downs *Beds.* ***Large natural feature***, high chalk ridge, partly National Trust property, 2m/3km to SW of Dunstable. Popular location for gliding. TL0019.
Dunstaffnage Castle *Arg. & B.* ***Castle***, remains of 13c castle (Historic Scotland) on W side of Dunstaffnage Bay. Ruins of chapel (Historic Scotland) to SW. **79 K4** NM8834.
Dunstall *Staffs.* ***Hamlet***, 4m/6km SW of Burton upon Trent. **40 D3** SK1820.
Dunstall *W.Mid.* ***Suburb***, 1m/2km NW of Wolverhampton town centre. SJ9000.
Dunstall Common *Worcs.* ***Locality***, 6m/10km N of Tewkesbury. SO8842.
Dunstall Green *Suff.* ***Settlement***, 7m/11km E of Newmarket. **34 B2** TL7461.
Dunstall Hill *W.Mid.* ***Suburb***, 1m/2km N of Wolverhampton town centre. SJ9000.
Dunstan *Northumb.* ***Hamlet***, near North Sea coast, 3m/5km N of Longhoughton. **71 H1** NU2419.
Dunstan Steads *Northumb.* ***Hamlet***, 1km SE of Embleton. NU2422.
Dunstanburgh Castle *Northumb.* ***Castle***, ruined 14c castle (National Trust and English Heritage) on headland at S end of Embleton Bay. **71 H1** NU2522.
Dunster *Som.* ***Village***, below Exmoor and near coast, 2m/3km SE of Minehead. Wide main street with old stone houses; Yarn Market, Butter Cross (both English Heritage). Castle (National Trust) dates from 11c. Gallox Bridge (English Heritage and National Trust), stone packhorse bridge. **7 H1** SS9943.
Dunster Castle and Working Watermill *Som.* ***Castle***, medieval castle (National Trust) in Dunster, 3m/5km SE of Minehead. Dating from c. 1070 and held by Luttrells from 1376. Present appearance owes much to 19c embellishments. Terraced gardens and 28 acre park. Restored 18c working watermill (National Trust) nearby, built on site of medieval mill. **7 H1** SS9943.
Dunster Yarn Market *Som.* ***Historic/prehistoric site***, octagonal covered market hall (English Heritage) in Dunster, built 1609. **7 H1** SS9943.
Dunston *Lincs.* ***Village***, 8m/12km SE of Lincoln. **52 D6** TF0662.
Dunston *Norf.* ***Hamlet***, 4m/6km S of Norwich. **45 G5** TG2202.
Dunston *Staffs.* ***Village***, 3m/5km S of Stafford. **40 B4** SJ9217.
Dunston *T. & W.* ***Locality***, 2m/3km W of Gateshead. **71 H7** NZ2262.
Dunston Heath *Staffs.* ***Settlement***, 1m/2km W of Dunston. SJ9117.
Dunston Hill *T. & W.* ***Suburb***, adjoining to S of Dunston, 3m/4km SW of Gateshead. NZ2261.
Dunstone *Devon* ***Hamlet***, 1m/2km E of Yealmpton. **5 F5** SX5951.
Dunstone *Devon* ***Hamlet***, 5m/8km NW of Ashburton. **5 H3** SX7175.
Dunstone *Devon* ***Settlement***, 4m/6km NE of Prawle point. **5 H6** SX7940.
Dunsville *S.Yorks.* ***Locality***, adjoining to SW of Hatfield. **51 J2** SE6407.
Dunswell *E.Riding* ***Village***, 4m/7km N of Kingston upon Hull. **59 G6** TA0735.
Dunsyre *S.Lan.* ***Village***, 6m/9km E of Carnwath. **75 J6** NT0748.
Dunterton *Devon* ***Hamlet***, 5m/7km SE of Launceston. **4 D3** SX3779.
Duntisbourne Abbots *Glos.* ***Village***, 5m/8km NW of Cirencester. **20 C1** SO9707.
Duntisbourne Leer *Glos.* ***Hamlet***, 5m/7km NW of Cirencester. **20 C1** SO9707.
Duntisbourne Rouse *Glos.* ***Village***, 3m/5km NW of Cirencester. **20 C1** SO9806.
Duntish *Dorset* ***Hamlet***, 1km N of Buckland Newton and 7m/12km SE of Sherborne. **9 F4** ST6906.
Duntocher *W.Dun.* Population: 7882. ***Small town***, on line of Antonine Wall, 2m/3km N of Clydebank. Site of Roman fort to E. **74 C3** NS4972.
Dunton *Beds.* ***Village***, 3m/5km E of Biggleswade. **33 F4** TL2344.
Dunton *Bucks.* ***Village***, 4m/7km SE of Winslow. **32 B6** SP8224.
Dunton *Norf.* ***Hamlet***, 2m/4km W of Fakenham. **44 C2** TF8730.
Dunton Bassett *Leics.* ***Village***, 4m/6km N of Lutterworth. **41 H6** SP5490.

Dunton Green *Kent* ***Suburb***, N district of Sevenoaks. **23 J6** TQ5157.
Dunton Hills *Essex* ***Suburb***, W district of Basildon. TQ6688.
Dunton Patch *Norf.* ***Settlement***, 3m/4km W of Fakenham. TF8730.
Dunton Wayletts *Essex* ***Settlement***, 4m/6km W of Basildon. **24 C3** TQ6590.
Duntrune Castle *Arg. & B.* ***Castle***, modernised castle in Argyll on N shore of Crinan Loch. Formerly stronghold of the Campbells, dating from 13c. **73 F1** NR7995.
Duntulm *High.* ***Settlement***, near N coast of Skye, 7m/11km N of Uig. **93 K4** NG4174.
Duntulm Bay *High.* ***Bay***, to NW of Duntulm, Skye. **93 J4** NG4174.
Duntulm Castle *High.* ***Castle***, ancient castle restored 1911, a S end of Duntulm Bay, Skye. **93 K4** NG4174.
Dunure *S.Ayr.* ***Village***, on coast, 5m/8km NW of Maybole. Fragment of old castle. **67 G2** NS2515.
Dunure Castle *S.Ayr.* ***Castle***, on rocky cliff to W of Dunure. 13c tower castle with vaulted basement and 15c additions; now in ruins. **67 G2** NS2415.
Dunure Mains *S.Ayr.* ***Settlement***, 1km S of Dunure. **67 G2** NS2514.
Dunvant (Dynfant). *Swan.* ***Locality***, 4m/7km W of Swansea. **17 J5** SS5893.
Dunvegan *High.* ***Village***, at head of Loch Dunvegan on NW coast of Skye. **93 H7** NG2547.
Dunvegan Castle *High.* ***Castle***, ancient stronghold of the Macleods, 1m/2km N of Dunvegan, Skye. **93 H7** NG2547.
Dunvegan Head *High.* ***Coastal feature***, headland on W side of entrance to Loch Dunvegan, Skye. **93 G6** NG1756.
Dunviden Lochs *High.* ***Lake/loch***, two small lochs in course of Achanellan Burn, which flows into River Naver, Caithness district. **104 C3** NC7451.
Dunwan Dam *E.Renf.* ***Reservoir***, 2m/3km SW of Eaglesham. **74 D6** NS5549.
Dunwich *Suff.* ***Village***, on coast, 4m/6km SW of Southwold. Once thriving port submerged by sea. Remains of medieval priory. **35 J1** TM4770.
Dunwich Heath *Suff.* ***Nature reserve***, important coastal conservation area of Sandlings heathland (National Trust) to S of Dunwich, noted for varied habitat conditions. Undulating heather and bracken heathland is home to yellowhammer and linnet, while low sandy cliffs provide nesting site for sand martins. Shingle plants such as sea campion, sea-kale and yellow horned-poppy, thrive on Minsmere Beach which stretches for 1m/2km. Minsmere RSPB Reserve is to S. **35 J2** TM4768.
Dunwood *Staffs.* ***Settlement***, 3m/4km SW of Leek. SJ9455.
Dupath Well *Cornw.* ***Historic/prehistoric site***, 15c granite well house (English Heritage) at Dupath, 1m/2km SE of Callington. **4 D4** SX3769.
Dupplin Lake *P. & K.* ***Lake/loch***, small lake 2m/3km E of Findo Gask and 6m/9km W of Perth. **82 B5** NO0320.
Dura *Fife* ***Settlement***, on W side of Ceres Burn, 3m/4km E of Cupar. **83 F6** NO4114.
Durdar *Cumb.* ***Hamlet***, 3m/5km S of Carlisle. **60 F1** NY4051.
Durdle Door *Dorset* ***Coastal feature***, natural sea arch of Portland limestone at end of small rock promontory, 1m/2km SW of West Lulworth. SY8080.
Dure Down *Som.* ***Open space***, hillslope on Exmoor, 1m/2km NW of Simonsbath. **7 F1** SS7440.
Durgan *Cornw.* ***Hamlet***, partly National Trust, on N bank of Helford River, 4m/6km SW of Falmouth. National Trust property to N includes Glendurgan House and grounds. SW7727.
Durgates *E.Suss.* ***Suburb***, NW part of Wadhurst. **13 K3** TQ6332.
Durham *Dur.* Population: 36,937. ***City***, cathedral city on River Wear, 14m/22km S of Newcastle upon Tyne. Cathedral, built on site of shrine of St. Cuthbert, is largely Norman. Medieval castle. University. Gulbenkian Museum of Oriental Art. **62 D2** NZ2742.
Durham Botanic Garden *Dur.* ***Garden***, 1m/2km S of Durham city centre, set in 18 acres of woodland, with worldwide selection of trees, shrubs and cacti, as well as a tropical collection. **62 D2** NZ2741.
Durham Castle *Dur.* ***Castle***, situated to N of cathedral, above River Wear. Originated in 11c as a palace of prince-bishops until 19c when it was used as University College. Together with Durham Cathedral, designated World Heritage Site. **62 D2** NZ2742.
Durham Cathedral *Dur.* ***Ecclesiastical building***, to S of Durham Castle, high above and in loop of River Wear. Considered greatest piece of Norman architecture in Britain. Little remains of Saxon cathedral of AD 988, and present building was started in 1093. The Treasury, in 13c undercroft, contains fragments of St. Cuthbert's wooden coffin, made before AD 698. Together with Durham Castle, designated World Heritage Site. **62 D2** NZ2742.
Durinemast *High.* ***Settlement***, in Morvern, Lochaber district, on N shore of Loch Arienas. **79 H2** NM6752.
Durisdeer *D. & G.* ***Village***, 5m/9km N of Thornhill. Sites of Roman camps to S. **68 D3** NS8903.
Durisdeermill *D. & G.* ***Settlement***, 1km W of Durisdeer. NS8804.
Durkar *W.Yorks.* ***Locality***, 1km SW of Pugneys Country Park, 3m/4km SW of Wakefield. SE3117.
Durleigh *Som.* ***Village***, below dam of reservoir, 2m/3km W of Bridgwater. **8 B1** ST2736.
Durleigh Reservoir *Som.* ***Reservoir***, at W side of Bridgwater, 2m/3km from town centre. **8 B1** ST2636.
Durley *Hants.* ***Village***, 2m/4km N of Botley. **11 G3** SU5116.
Durley *Wilts.* ***Village***, 5m/8km SE of Marlborough. **21 F5** SU2364.
Durley Street *Hants.* ***Hamlet***, 2m/3km W of Bishop's Waltham. SU5217.
Durlow Common *Here.* ***Settlement***, 8m/12km E of Hereford. SO6339.
Durlston Bay *Dorset* ***Bay***, extends N from Durlston Head to Peveril Point. **10 B7** SZ0377.
Durlston Country Park *Dorset* ***Leisure/recreation***, 1km S of Swanage town centre. Coastal park with many points of geological interest and a giant stone globe, as well as nature trails and woodland. **10 B7** SZ0277.
Durlston Head *Dorset* ***Coastal feature***, headland 1m/2km S of Swanage at S end of Durlston Bay. **10 B7** SZ0377.
Durn *Gt.Man.* ***Locality***, adjoining to E of Littleborough. SD9416.
Durn Hill *Aber.* ***Hill***, 1km E of Fordyce, and 2m/3km SW of Portsoy. Height 653 feet or 199 metres. **98 D4** NJ5763.
Durnamuck *High.* ***Village***, on SW side of Little Loch Broom, W coast of Ross and Cromarty district. **95 G2** NH0192.
Durness *High.* ***Village***, near N coast of Sutherland district, 3m/4km S of Far Out Head. Smoo Cave 1m/2km SE. **103 F2** NC4067.
Durno *Aber.* ***Hamlet***, 6m/9km NW of Inverurie. **91 F2** NJ7128.
Duror *High.* ***Settlement***, on N bank of River Duror, 1km E of Cuil Bay. **80 A2** NM9854.
Durovernum *Kent* *See Canterbury.*
Durovigutum *Cambs.* *See Godmanchester.*
Durran *Arg. & B.* ***Settlement***, 3m/5km S of Dalavich, on SE shore of Loch Awe. **80 A7** NM9507.
Durran *High.* ***Locality***, 3m/4km S of Castletown. **105 G2** ND1964.
Durrant Green *Kent* ***Settlement***, 2m/3km N of Tenterden. TQ8836.
Durrants *Hants.* ***Settlement***, 2m/4km N of Havant. SU7209.
Durrington *W.Suss.* ***Suburb***, NW district of Worthing. **12 E6** TQ1204.
Durrington *Wilts.* Population: 4738. ***Village***, military village, 2m/3km N of Amesbury. To S, ancient earthwork of Woodhenge (English Heritage). **20 E7** SU1544.
Durris Forest *Aber.* ***Forest/woodland***, 6m/9km E of Banchory across River Dee. Mast. **91 F5** NO7892.
Dursley *Glos.* Population: 13,331. ***Town***, Cotswold town, 7m/12km SW of Stroud. Former cloth-making town with many 18c houses. **20 A2** ST7597.
Dursley Cross *Glos.* ***Hamlet***, 4m/6km SW of Newent. SO6920.
Durston *Som.* ***Village***, 5m/8km NE of Taunton. **8 B2** ST2928.
Durweston *Dorset* ***Village***, on River Stour, 2m/4km NW of Blandford Forum. **9 H4** ST8508.
Dury *Shet.* ***Settlement***, 1km W of Laxfirth, Mainland. **109 D6** HU4560.
Dury Voe *Shet.* ***Sea feature***, large inlet on E coast of Mainland opposite Whalsay. **109 D6** HU4762.
Dusk Water *N.Ayr.* ***River***, flowing SW from Lochlands Hill to join River Garnock 2m/3km N of Kilwinning. **74 B6** NS2946.
Duslic *High.* ***Island***, small rock island 1km NE of Cape Wrath. **102 E1** NC2675.
Duston *Northants.* ***Suburb***, 2m/3km W of Northampton town centre. To N is New Duston. **31 J2** SP7261.
Dutchman Bank *Gwyn.* ***Coastal feature***, sandbank 2m/3km N of coast at Llanfairfechan. SH6678.
Dutchman's Cap *Arg. & B.* *Alternative name for Bac Mòr, qv.*
Duthie Park and Winter Gardens *Aberdeen* ***Garden***, 50-acre park with boating lake by River Dee, 1m/2km S of Aberdeen city centre. Park contains Winter Gardens covering 2 acres, with exotic plants and birds; also cactus house. **91 H4** NJ9304.
Duthil *High.* ***Village***, in Badenoch and Strathspey district, 2m/3km E of Carrbridge. **89 G2** NH9324.
Duthil Burn *High.* ***River***, flowing S from S slopes of Carn Allt Laoigh into River Dulnain, 1m/2km E of Carrbridge. **89 G2** NH9223.
Dutlas *Powys* ***Settlement***, on River Teme, 6m/9km NW of Knighton. **28 B1** SO2177.
Duton Hill *Essex* ***Village***, 3m/5km N of Great Dunmow. **33 K6** TL6026.
Dutson *Cornw.* ***Hamlet***, 1m/2km NE of Launceston. SX3485.
Dutton *Ches.* ***Village***, 4m/6km SE of Runcorn. **48 E5** SJ5779.
Dutton *Lancs.* ***Locality***, 2m/3km NE of Ribchester. SD6637.
Duxford *Cambs.* Population: 1848. ***Village***, 3m/4km NW of Great Chesterford. 13c chapel (English Heritage) near Whittlesford railway station. **33 H4** TL4746.
Dwarfie Stane *Ork.* ***Historic/prehistoric site***, Neolithic communal burial-chamber on Hoy, 3m/5km E of Rackwick. **107 B7** HY2400.
Dwarwick Head *High.* ***Coastal feature***, headland on N side of Dunnet Bay. **105 H1** ND2071.
Dwyfach *Gwyn.* ***River***, flowing S to join River Dwyfor 2m/4km W of Criccieth. **36 D1** SH4637.
Dwyfor *Gwyn.* ***River***, rising in Cwm Dwyfor below Trum y Ddysgl and flowing S into Tremadog Bay to W of Criccieth. **36 D1** SH4737.
Dwygyfylchi *Conwy* Population: 1496. ***Small town***, small resort 1m/2km E of Penmaenmawr. **47 F5** SH7377.
Dwyran *I.o.A.* ***Village***, on Anglesey, 2m/3km E of Newborough. **46 C6** SH4465.
Dyce *Aberdeen* Population: 6359. ***Village***, 5m/9km NW of Aberdeen. Aberdeen (Dyce) Airport on W side of village. **91 G3** NJ8812.
Dyce Airport *Aberdeen* *Former name of Aberdeen Airport, qv.*
Dyce Symbol Stones *Aberdeen* ***Historic/prehistoric site***, two Pictish symbol stones located at Dyce Old Kirk, 2m/3km N of Dyce. **91 G3** NJ8715.
Dye House *Northumb.* ***Hamlet***, 4m/6km S of Hexham. NY9358.
Dye Water ***River***, rising on Lammermuir Hills and running E to Whiteadder Water 2m/4km SE of Cranshaws. **76 E5** NT7159.
Dyer's End *Essex* ***Locality***, S end of Stambourne, 4m/7km NE of Finchingfield. TL7238.
Dyer's Green *Cambs.* ***Settlement***, 3m/5km N of Royston. TL3545.
Dyfatty *Carmar.* ***Locality***, adjoining to E of Burry Port. **17 H4** SN4501.
Dyffryn *Bridgend* ***Village***, 1m/2km N of Maesteg. **18 B2** SS8593.
Dyffryn *Carmar.* ***Settlement***, 2m/3km W of Abernant. SN3122.
Dyffryn *Gwyn.* *Alternative name for Dyffryn Ardudwy, qv.*
Dyffryn *I.o.A.* *Welsh name of Valley, qv.*
Dyffryn *Pembs.* ***Locality***, adjoining to SW of Goodwick, 1m/2km W of Fishguard. **16 C1** SM9437.
Dyffryn *V. of Glam.* ***Hamlet***, 3m/4km NW of Barry. ST0971.
Dyffryn Ardudwy (Also known as Dyffryn.) *Gwyn.* ***Village***, 5m/8km N of Barmouth. Ancient burial-chamber (Cadw) to S. **36 E3** SH5823.
Dyffryn Burial Chamber *Gwyn.* ***Historic/prehistoric site***, on SE edge of Dyffryn Ardudwy, 5m/8km N of Barmouth. Partly restored Neolithic chambered long barrow comprising two separate chambers (Cadw). **36 E3** SH5922.
Dyffryn Castell *Cere.* ***Settlement***, 4m/6km NE of Devil's Bridge. **37 G7** SN7781.
Dyffryn Ceidrych *Carmar.* ***Settlement***, 2m/3km S of Llangadog. **27 G6** SN7025.
Dyffryn Cellwen *N.P.T.* ***Village***, 3m/5km NW of Glyn-neath. Traces of Roman fort to N. **27 H7** SN8509.
Dyffryn Crawnon *Powys* ***Valley***, carrying River Crawnon NE to Llangynidr. **28 A7** SO1117.
Dyffryn Edeirnion (Also known as Vale of Edeyrnion.) *Denb.* ***Valley***, carrying River Dee between Corwen and Carrog. **37 K2** SJ0743.
Dyffryn House Gardens *V. of Glam.* ***Garden***, to N of Dyffryn, 3m/5km NW of Barry. 55 acres of landscaped gardens and heather bank. **18 D4** ST0972.
Dyffryn Tywi *Carmar.* ***Valley***, carrying Tywi river and running SW to NE, with Llandeilo on its N side. **17 K2** SN6321.
Dyfi (Dovey). ***River***, rising as several streams N of Llanymawddwy and flowing SW by Machynlleth into Cardigan Bay to W of Aberdovey. Wide estuary below confluence with River Einion. **37 F6** SN6095.
Dyfi Forest (Dovey Forest). *Gwyn.* ***Forest/woodland***, on border of Gwynedd and Powys, to W of Aberangell in River Dyfi valley. **37 G4** SH8010.
Dyfi Valley (Dovey Valley). *Gwyn.* ***Valley***, wide valley carrying River Dyfi SE to River Dyfi estuary. **37 G6** SH7200.
Dyfnant Forest *Powys* ***Forest/woodland***, afforested area about 3m/5km S of Lake Vyrnwy. **37 J4** SH9915.
Dyfrdwy *Welsh form of (River) Dee, qv.*
Dyke *Devon* ***Locality***, 1km S of Clovelly. **6 B3** SS3123.
Dyke *High.* ***River***, running NE into River Halladale 8m/13km S of Melvich. **104 D4** NC8952.
Dyke *Lincs.* ***Village***, 2m/3km N of Bourne. **42 E3** TF1022.
Dyke *Moray* ***Village***, 6m/10km E of Nairn and 3m/5km W of Forres. **97 G6** NJ9858.
Dykehead *Angus* ***Village***, near foot of Glen Clova, 4m/6km N of Kirriemuir. **82 E1** NO3860.
Dykehead *N.Lan.* ***Locality***, 5m/9km NE of Wishaw. **75 G5** NS8759.
Dykehead *Stir.* ***Settlement***, 3m/4km S of Port of Menteith. **74 D1** NS5997.
Dykelands *Aber.* ***Hamlet***, 2m/3km NE of Marykirk. **83 J1** NO7068.
Dykends *Angus* ***Settlement***, 1m/2km SE of Bellaty. **82 D2** NO2557.
Dykesfield *Cumb.* ***Locality***, on edge of Burgh Marsh, 1m/2km W of Burgh by Sands. NY3059.
Dykeside *Aber.* ***Settlement***, 4m/6km S of Turriff. **99 F6** NJ7243.
Dylife *Powys* ***Settlement***, 3m/4km SW of Pennant. **37 H6** SN8694.
Dymchurch *Kent* Population: 2951. ***Small town***, coastal town at E edge of Romney Marsh, 5m/8km SW of Hythe. Martello tower (English Heritage). Holiday camp to NE. **15 F5** TR1029.
Dymchurch Martello Tower *Kent* ***Other feature of interest***, restored 18c-19c artillery tower (English Heritage) with original gun, on coast at Dymchurch. **15 F5** TR1029.
Dymock *Glos.* ***Village***, 4m/6km NW of Newent. **29 G5** SO7031.
Dynfant *Swan.* *Welsh form of Dunvant, qv.*
Dyrham *S.Glos.* ***Hamlet***, 4m/7km S of Chipping Sodbury. **20 A4** ST7375.
Dyrham Park *S.Glos.* ***Historic house***, 17c-18c house (National Trust) with deer park, 8m/13km N of Bath. **20 A4** ST7375.
Dyrysgol *Gwyn.* ***Mountain***, 3m/5km SW of Llanuwchllyn. Height 1378 feet or 420 metres. **37 H3** SH8328.
Dyrysgol *Gwyn.* ***Mountain***, 5m/7km N of Dinas-Mawddwy. Height 2398 feet or 731 metres. **37 H3** SH8721.
Dysart *Fife* ***Locality***, on Firth of Forth, adjoining to NE of Kirkcaldy. **76 B1** NT3093.
Dyserth (Diserth). *Denb.* Population: 2394. ***Village***, 3m/4km S of Prestatyn. **47 J5** SJ0579.
Dysynni *Gwyn.* ***River***, rising on S slopes of Cadair Idris and flowing SW through Tal-y-llyn Lake to Cardigan Bay to N of Tywyn. **37 F5** SH5603.

E

Eabost *High.* ***Settlement***, on E side of Loch Bracadale, 2m/3km W of Bracadale, Skye. NG3139.
Eachkamish (Gaelic form: Eachcamais.) *W.Isles* ***Coastal feature***, peninsula on S part of Baleshare, with sand dunes. **92 C6** NF7860.
Eachwick *Northumb.* ***Settlement***, 3m/5km SW of Ponteland. NZ1171.
Eadar dha Fhadhail (Anglicised form: Ardroil.) *W.Isles* ***Settlement***, at head of Camas Uig bay, 4m/7km S of Gallan Head, Isle of Lewis. **100 C4** NB0432.

E

Eag na Maoile *Arg. & B.* ***Island***, group of islets lying nearly 1m/2km off NE end of Coll. **78 D1** NM2765.
Eagland Hill *Lancs.* ***Hamlet***, 4m/6km W of Garstang. **55 H5** SD4345.
Eagle *Lincs.* ***Village***, 7m/11km SW of Lincoln. **52 B6** SK8767.
Eagle Barnsdale *Lincs.* ***Hamlet***, 1m/2km S of Eagle, 1m/2km W of Thorpe on the Hill. SK8865.
Eagle Moor *Lincs.* ***Hamlet***, 1km NE of Eagle, 2m/3km NW of Thorpe on the Hill. SK8868.
Eagle Rock (Hunters Craig). *Edin.* ***Historic/prehistoric site***, on S coast of Firth of Forth, 1m/2km NE of Cramond Bridge. Worn sculpture once thought to have been an eagle, now thought to be a statue of Mercury. **75 K3** NT1877.
Eaglescliffe *Stock.* Population: 18,729. ***Suburb***, 3m/5km SW of Stockton-on-Tees. **63 F5** NZ4215.
Eaglesfield *Cumb.* ***Village***, 2m/4km SW of Cockermouth. **60 B4** NY0928.
Eaglesfield *D. & G.* ***Village***, 3m/5km E of Ecclefechan. **69 H6** NY2374.
Eaglesham *E.Renf.* Population: 3382. ***Village***, 4m/7km SW of East Kilbride. **74 D5** NS5751.
Eaglethorpe *Northants.* ***Hamlet***, adjoining village to N of Warmington, 3m/5km NE of Oundle. **42 D6** TL0791.
Eagley *Gt.Man.* ***Locality***, on E side of River Croal, 3m/5km N of Bolton town centre. **49 G1** SD7113.
Eairy *I.o.M.* ***Settlement***, 3m/5km SE of St. John's. **54 C6** SC2977.
Eakley *Northants.* ***Locality***, including Eakley Lanes and Eakley Grange Farm, 2m/4km E of Hartwell. **32 B3** SP8250.
Eakring *Notts.* ***Village***, 4m/6km S of Ollerton. **51 J6** SK6762.
Ealand *N.Lincs.* ***Village***, 1m/2km SE of Crowle. **51 K1** SE7811.
Ealing *Gt.Lon.* ***Suburb***, in borough of Ealing, 8m/13km W of Charing Cross. Famous for its film studios during 1950s. Pitshanger Manor is now a museum. TQ1780.
Eamont *Cumb.* ***River***, flowing NE from Ullswater, passing S of Penrith and running into River Eden 2m/3km SE of Langwathby. **61 F4** NY5831.
Eamont Bridge *Cumb.* ***Village***, with red sandstone bridge dating from 1425 at road crossing of River Eamont, 1m/2km SE of Penrith. Arthur's Round Table (English Heritage), ancient earthwork over 90 metres across. Mayburgh Henge (English Heritage) to SW. **61 G4** NY5228.
Earadale Point *Arg. & B.* ***Coastal feature***, headland on W coast of Kintyre, 4m/6km SW of Machrihanish. **66 A2** NR5917.
Earby *Lancs.* Population: 4957. ***Small town***, 4m/7km N of Colne. **56 E5** SD9046.
Earcroft *B'burn.* ***Locality***, adjoining to N of Darwen. **56 B7** SD6824.
Eardington *Shrop.* ***Village***, 1m/2km S of Bridgnorth. **39 G6** SO7290.
Eardisland *Here.* ***Village***, on River Arrow, 5m/8km W of Leominster. **28 D3** SO4158.
Eardisley *Here.* ***Village***, 5m/8km S of Kington. **28 C4** SO3149.
Eardiston *Shrop.* ***Hamlet***, 6m/9km SE of Oswestry. **38 C3** SJ3625.
Eardiston *Worcs.* ***Village***, 6m/10km E of Tenbury Wells. **29 F2** SO6968.
Earith *Cambs.* ***Village***, on River Great Ouse, 7m/11km S of Chatteris. **33 G1** TL3874.
Earl Seat *N.Yorks.* ***Mountain***, 3m/5km SE of Burnsall. Height 1473 feet or 449 metres. **57 F4** SE0758.
Earl Shilton *Leics.* Population: 18,083. ***Suburb***, 4m/6km NE of Hinckley. **41 G6** SP4697.
Earl Soham *Suff.* ***Village***, 3m/5km W of Framlingham. **35 G2** TM2363.
Earl Sterndale *Derbys.* ***Village***, 4m/7km SE of Buxton. **50 C6** SK0967.
Earl Stonham *Suff.* ***Village***, 4m/6km E of Stowmarket. **35 F3** TM1058.
Earle *Northumb.* ***Settlement***, 1m/2km S of Wooler. **70 E1** NT9826.
Earle's Fields *Lincs.* ***Suburb***, 1m/2km W of Grantham town centre. SK9035.
Earlestown *Mersey.* ***Suburb***, W district of Newton-le-Willows. **48 E3** SJ5794.
Earley *W'ham* ***Suburb***, 2m/4km E of Reading town centre. SU7571.
Earlham *Norf.* ***Suburb***, 2m/3km W of Norwich city centre. Site of University of East Anglia. **45 F5** TG1908.
Earlish *High.* ***Settlement***, 1m/2km S of Uig, Skye. **93 J5** NG3861.
Earls Barton *Northants.* Population: 4917. ***Village***, 4m/6km SW of Wellingborough. **32 B2** SP8563.
Earl's Burn *Stir.* ***River***, rising on Gargunnock Hills and flowing SE through Earlsburn Reservoirs to join River Carron 1km W of Carron Bridge. **75 F2** NS7283.
Earls Colne *Essex* Population: 3420. ***Village***, 3m/5km SE of Halstead. **34 C6** TL8628.
Earl's Common *Worcs.* ***Hamlet***, 5m/7km SE of Droitwich Spa. **29 J3** SO9559.
Earl's Court *Gt.Lon.* ***Suburb***, in borough of Kensington and Chelsea, 3m/5km W of Charing Cross. Exhibition hall. TQ2578.
Earl's Croome *Worcs.* ***Village***, 6m/10km N of Tewkesbury. **29 H4** SO8742.
Earl's Green *Suff.* ***Hamlet***, 1m/2km W of Bacton. **34 E2** TM0366.
Earl's Hill *Stir.* ***Mountain***, with mast at summit, 6m/9km SW of Stirling. Height 1446 feet or 441 metres. **75 F2** NS7188.
Earl's Palace *Ork.* ***Historic/prehistoric site***, impressive remains of 16c palace of Earls of Orkney situated at Birsay on Brough Head, NW Mainland. **106 B5** HY2428.
Earl's Seat *E.Dun.* ***Mountain***, summit of Campsie Fells on border with Stirling, 3m/5km SE of Killearn. Height 1896 feet or 578 metres. **74 D2** NS5683.
Earl's Seat *Northumb.* ***Mountain***, 3m/5km N of Falstone. Height 1302 feet or 397 metres. **70 C4** NY7192.
Earlsburn Reservoirs *Stir.* ***Reservoir***, two small reservoirs 7m/11km SW of Stirling. **74 E2** NS7089.
Earlsdon *W.Mid.* ***Suburb***, SW district of Coventry. **30 E1** SP3177.
Earlsferry *Fife* ***Town***, and resort on Firth of Forth, adjoining to W of Elie. **83 F7** NT4889.
Earlsfield *Gt.Lon.* ***Suburb***, in borough of Wandsworth, 5m/8km SW of Charing Cross. TQ2673.
Earlsford *Aber.* ***Settlement***, 5m/8km SE of Fyvie. **91 G1** NJ8334.
Earlshall Castle *Fife* ***Castle***, 16c Z-plan castle to E of Leuchars, restored by Sir Robert Lorimer. Grounds are noted for topiary. **83 F5** NO4621.
Earlsheaton *W.Yorks.* ***Suburb***, to E of Dewsbury town centre. SE2521.
Earlston *Sc.Bord.* Population: 1629. ***Small town***, in Lauderdale 4m/6km NE of Melrose. **76 D7** NT5738.
Earlstoun Loch *D. & G.* ***Lake/loch***, loch and reservoir 1m/2km N of St. John's Town of Dalry. **68 B5** NX6183.
Earlstrees *Northants.* ***Locality***, industrial estate on N side of Corby. SP8890.
Earlswood *Mon.* ***Settlement***, 5m/8km NW of Chepstow. **19 H2** ST4495.
Earlswood *Surr.* ***Suburb***, to S of Redhill. TQ2749.
Earlswood *Warks.* ***Village***, 4m/7km SW of Solihull. **30 C1** SP1174.
Earn *P. & K.* ***River***, flowing E from Loch Earn down Strath Earn to River Tay 6m/10km SE of Perth. **82 B6** NO1918.
Earn Water *E.Renf.* ***River***, flowing NE to join White Cart Water at Waterfoot, 2m/3km N of Eaglesham. **74 D5** NS5654.
Earncraig Hill *S.Lan.* ***Mountain***, in Lowther Hills on border with Dumfries & Galloway, 7m/11km W of Beattock. Height 2001 feet or 610 metres. **68 E3** NS9701.
Earnley *W.Suss.* ***Village***, 3m/5km NW of Selsey. **12 B7** SZ8196.
Earnscleugh Water *Sc.Bord.* ***River***, rising in Lammermuir Hills and flowing SW to join Leader Water to NE of Lauder. **76 D5** NT5348.
Earnshaw Bridge *Lancs.* ***Suburb***, adjoining to NW of Leyland. SD5322.
Earnsheugh Bay *Aber.* ***Bay***, small bay 1m/2km NE of Portlethen. **91 H5** NO9498.
Earsairidh (Anglicised form: Ersary.) *W.Isles* ***Village***, on E coast of Barra, 3m/5km E of Castlebay. **84 C5** NL7099.
Earsdon *T. & W.* ***Suburb***, 2m/3km W of Whitley Bay. **71 J6** NZ3272.
Earsdon Moor *Northumb.* ***Settlement***, 5m/8km N of Morpeth. **71 G4** NZ1993.
Earshader (Gaelic form: Iarsiadar.) *W.Isles* ***Settlement***, on W side of Isle of Lewis, on S side of bridge connecting Great Bernera with main island. NB1633.
Earsham *Norf.* ***Village***, 1m/2km W of Bungay. **45 H7** TM3289.
Earsham Street *Suff.* ***Hamlet***, 2m/3km W of Fressingfield. TM2378.
Earshaw Hill *D. & G.* ***Open space***, hillslope 1m/2km SW of Langholm. **69 J5** NY3482.
Earswick *York* ***Locality***, 4m/6km N of York. **58 C4** SE6257.
Eartham *W.Suss.* ***Village***, 5m/8km W of Arundel. **12 C6** SU9309.
Earthcote Green *S.Glos.* ***Settlement***, 4m/6km NW of Yate. **19 K3** ST6485.
Eas a' Chùal Aluinn (Also known as Eas Caul Aulin.) *High.* ***Waterfall***, 1m/2km SE of head of Loch Glencoul. Height 658 feet or 201 metres; highest in Britain. **102 E6** NC2827.
Eas Caul Aulin *High.* *Alternative name for Eas a' Chùal Aluinn, qv.*
Eas Daimh *P. & K.* ***River***, flowing E into Loch an Daimh, 8m/12km W of Bridge of Balgie. **81 F3** NN4546.
Easaval *W.Isles* ***Hill***, rising to over 240 metres, 1m/2km N of Ludag, near S coast of South Uist. **84 C3** NF7715.
Easby *N.Yorks.* ***Hamlet***, 2m/3km SE of Great Ayton. Captain Cook's Monument to NE on Easby Moor. **63 G6** NZ5708.
Easby Abbey *N.Yorks.* ***Ecclesiastical building***, remains of 13c-14c abbey (English Heritage) beside River Swale at Easby, 1m/2km SE of Richmond. **62 C6** NZ1800.
Easby Moor *N.Yorks.* ***Open space***, rising to 1063 feet or 324 metres, 2m/3km SE of Great Ayton. **63 G5** NZ5809.
Eascairt *Arg. & B.* ***Settlement***, on Kintyre, 3m/4km SW of Claonaig. **73 G5** NR8453.
Easdale *Arg. & B.* ***Island***, small island off W coast of Seil. Former slate quarries. Ferry to Seil across narrow Easdale Sound. **79 J6** NM7317.
Easdale *Arg. & B.* ***Settlement***, on W coast of Seil, opposite Easdale island. **79 J6** NM7417.
Easdon Tor *Devon* ***Mountain***, 3m/5km SW of Moretonhampstead, in Dartmoor National Park. Height 1440 feet or 439 metres. **7 F7** SX7282.
Easebourne *W.Suss.* ***Village***, estate village of Cowdray Park 1m/2km NE of Midhurst. **12 B4** SU8922.
Easenhall *Warks.* ***Village***, 4m/6km NW of Rugby. **31 F1** SP4679.
Eashing *Surr.* ***Village***, 2m/3km W of Godalming. **22 C7** SU9443.
Easington *Bucks.* ***Hamlet***, 3m/5km NW of Thame. **21 K1** SP6810.
Easington *Dur.* Population: 7593. ***Village***, 2m/4km NW of Peterlee. Seaton Holme, restored 13c manor house. Easington Colliery to E. **63 F2** NZ4143.
Easington *E.Riding* ***Village***, near North Sea coast, 6m/10km SE of Patrington. **53 H1** TA3919.
Easington *Northumb.* ***Settlement***, 1m/2km NE of Belford. **77 K7** NU1234.
Easington *Oxon.* ***Hamlet***, 3m/4km NW of Watlington. **21 K2** SU6697.
Easington *Oxon.* ***Suburb***, S district of Banbury. SP4539.
Easington *R. & C.* ***Village***, 1m/2km E of Loftus. **63 J5** NZ7418.
Easington Colliery *Dur.* ***Locality***, to E of Easington. **63 F2** NZ4143.
Easington Fell *Lancs.* ***Open space***, moorland 4m/7km N of Clitheroe. **56 C5** SD7248.
Easington Lane *T. & W.* ***Village***, 1m/2km SE of Hetton-le-Hole. **62 E2** NZ3646.
Easingwold *N.Yorks.* Population: 2816. ***Small town***, 12m/19km NW of York. **58 B3** SE5269.
Easole Street *Kent* ***Locality***, adjoining to E of Nonington, 4m/6km S of Wingham. **15 H2** TR2652.
Eassie and Nevay *Angus* ***Village***, 4m/6km W of Glamis. **82 E3** NO3345.
Eassie Sculptured Stone *Angus* ***Historic/prehistoric site***, 7m/11km W of Forfar. Good example of elaborately carved early Christian monument. **82 E3** NO3447.
East Aberthaw *V. of Glam.* ***Village***, 5m/8km W of Barry. **18 D5** ST0366.
East Acton *Gt.Lon.* ***Suburb***, in borough of Ealing, to NE of Acton. TQ2180.
East Adderbury *Oxon.* *See Adderbury.*
East Allen *Northumb.* ***River***, rising 2m/3km S of Allenheads and flowing N of Allendale Town, then NW to join River West Allen and form River Allen. **61 K1** NY8058.
East Allington *Devon* ***Village***, 3m/5km NE of Kingsbridge. **5 H6** SX7748.
East Anglia Transport Museum *Suff.* ***Other feature of interest***, 3m/5km SW of Lowestoft town centre. Working street transport museum. **45 J6** TM5090.
East Anstey *Devon* ***Village***, on S edge of Exmoor, 3m/5km SW of Dulverton. **7 G3** SS8626.
East Anton *Hants.* ***Settlement***, 2m/3km N of Andover. SU3747.
East Appleton *N.Yorks.* ***Hamlet***, 1m/2km S of Catterick. **62 D7** SE2395.
East Aquhorthies *Aber.* *Alternative name for Easter Aquhorthies, qv.*
East Ardsley *W.Yorks.* ***Village***, 3m/5km SE of Morley. **57 J7** SE3025.
East Ashey *I.o.W.* ***Settlement***, 2m/3km NW of Brading. **11 G6** SZ5888.
East Ashling *W.Suss.* ***Village***, 3m/5km NW of Chichester. **12 B6** SU8207.
East Aston *Hants.* ***Settlement***, adjoining to NE of Longparish. SU4345.
East Auchronie *Aber.* ***Settlement***, 2m/3km N of Westhill. **91 G4** NJ8109.
East Ayton *N.Yorks.* Population: 1275. ***Village***, 4m/6km SW of Scarborough, on E side of River Derwent. **59 F1** SE9984.
East Bagborough *Som.* ***Hamlet***, 1km SE of West Bagborough, on SW slopes of Quantock Hills. ST1733.
East Barkwith *Lincs.* ***Village***, 3m/5km NE of Wragby. **52 E4** TF1681.
East Barming *Kent* ***Village***, on River Medway, 3m/4km W of Maidstone. Site of Roman Villa to E and to W. **14 C2** TQ7254.
East Barnby *N.Yorks.* ***Village***, 5m/7km W of Whitby. **63 K5** NZ8212.
East Barnet *Gt.Lon.* ***Suburb***, in borough of Barnet, 9m/14km N of Charing Cross. **23 F2** TQ2794.
East Barsham *Norf.* ***Village***, 3m/4km N of Fakenham. Tudor brick manor house. **44 D2** TF9133.
East Barton *Devon* ***Hamlet***, 4m/6km E of Bideford. SS5127.
East Baugh Fell *Cumb.* ***Open space***, moorland on S side of Baugh Fell, 5m/8km E of Sedbergh. **61 J7** SD7391.
East Beckham *Norf.* ***Village***, 2m/3km S of Sheringham. **45 F2** TG1539.
East Bedfont *Gt.Lon.* ***Suburb***, in borough of Hounslow, on S side of London Heathrow Airport. **22 D4** TQ0873.
East Bergholt *Suff.* ***Village***, 7m/12km NE of Colchester. Birthplace of Constable, 1776. Flatford Mill, Willy Lott's Cottage and Bridge Cottage (National Trust) on River Stour to S. Church bells housed in cage in churchyard. **34 E5** TM0634.
East Bierley *W.Yorks.* ***Village***, 3m/5km SE of Bradford. SE1929.
East Bilney *Norf.* ***Village***, 5m/7km NW of East Dereham. **44 D4** TF9519.
East Blatchington *E.Suss.* ***Suburb***, to N of Newhaven. **13 H7** TQ4800.
East Bloxworth *Dorset* ***Settlement***, 1km E of Bloxworth. SY8994.
East Boldon *T. & W.* ***Suburb***, forms town of Boldon, along with West Boldon, 4m/6km S of South Shields. **71 J7** NZ3661.
East Boldre *Hants.* ***Village***, 1m/2km SW of Beaulieu. **10 E4** SU3700.
East Bolton *Northumb.* ***Hamlet***, 4m/6km NW of Alnwick. **71 G2** NU1316.
East Bolton Moor *N.Yorks.* ***Open space***, moorland containing disused mine workings, 2m/4km NW of Castle Bolton. **62 B7** SE0094.
East Bower *Som.* ***Hamlet***, 1m/2km NE of Bridgwater. ST3237.
East Bradenham *Norf.* ***Village***, 5m/8km SW of East Dereham. **44 D5** TF9208.
East Brent *Som.* ***Village***, 3m/5km NE of Burnham-on-Sea. **19 G6** ST3452.
East Bridge *Suff.* ***Hamlet***, 2m/4km N of Leiston. **35 J2** TM4566.
East Bridgford *Notts.* ***Village***, 8m/13km E of Nottingham. **41 J1** SK6943.
East Briscoe *Dur.* ***Locality***, 2m/3km SW of Romaldkirk. NY9719.
East Brora *High.* ***Settlement***, 1km W of Brora, Sutherland district. **97 F1** NC8904.

East Burton *Dorset* ***Hamlet***, 1m/2km W of Wool. **9 H6** SY8387.
East Butsfield *Dur.* ***Settlement***, 4m/6km S of Consett. NZ1145.
East Butterleigh *Devon* ***Hamlet***, 1km NE of Butterleigh. SS9808.
East Butterwick *N.Lincs.* ***Village***, on opposite bank of River Trent to West Butterwick, 5m/8km SW of Scunthorpe. Nearest bridge at Keadby, 3m/5km N. SE8305.
East Cairn Hill *W.Loth.* ***Mountain***, in Pentland Hills, 3m/5km NW of Carlops. Height 1840 feet or 561 metres. **75 K5** NT1159.
East Cairnbeg *Aber.* ***Hamlet***, 2m/3km SW of Auchenblae. **91 F7** NO7076.
East Calder *W.Loth.* Population: 8692. ***Village***, 2m/3km E of Livingston. **75 J4** NT0867.
East Carleton *Norf.* ***Village***, 5m/9km SW of Norwich. **45 F5** TG1701.
East Carlton *Northants.* ***Village***, 4m/7km W of Corby. **42 B7** SP8389.
East Carlton *W.Yorks.* ***Hamlet***, 2m/3km SE of Otley. SE2243.
East Carlton Country Park *Northants.* ***Leisure/recreation***, country park in East Carlton, 3m/5km W of Corby. **42 B7** SP8389.
East Castle *Dur.* ***Settlement***, 3m/4km E of Consett. NZ1452.
East Chaldon *Dorset Alternative name for Chaldon Herring, qv.*
East Challow *Oxon.* ***Village***, 1m/2km W of Wantage. **21 G3** SU3888.
East Charleton *Devon* ***Village***, in parish of Charleton, along with West Charleton, 2m/3km SE of Kingsbridge. **5 H6** SX7542.
East Chelborough *Dorset* ***Hamlet***, 2m/3km NW of Evershot. **8 E4** ST5505.
East Chevington *Northumb.* ***Locality***, 3m/5km S of Amble. NZ2699.
East Chiltington *E.Suss.* ***Hamlet***, 4m/7km NW of Lewes. **13 G5** TQ3715.
East Chinnock *Som.* ***Village***, 4m/6km W of Yeovil. **8 D3** ST4913.
East Chisenbury *Wilts.* ***Village***, on River Avon, 2m/3km S of Upavon. **20 E6** SU1452.
East Cholderton *Hants.* ***Hamlet***, adjoining to E of Thruxton, 4m/7km W of Andover. SU2945.
East Clandon *Surr.* ***Village***, 4m/7km E of Guildford. **22 D6** TQ0651.
East Claydon *Bucks.* ***Village***, 2m/4km SW of Winslow. **31 J6** SP7325.
East Clevedon *N.Som.* ***Suburb***, adjoining to E of Clevedon. ST4171.
East Clyne *High.* ***Hamlet***, in Sutherland district, 1m/2km N of Brora. NC9006.
East Clyth *High.* ***Settlement***, 1m/2km NE of Mid Clyth. **105 H5** ND2939.
East Coker *Som.* ***Village***, 3m/4km SW of Yeovil. **8 E3** ST5412.
East Combe *Som.* ***Hamlet***, 1km E of Combe Florey. **7 K2** ST1631.
East Common *N.Yorks.* ***Suburb***, SE district of Selby. SE6231.
East Compton *Dorset* ***Hamlet***, 1km NE of Compton Abbas and 3m/4km S of Shaftesbury. ST8718.
East Compton *Som.* ***Hamlet***, 1m/2km S of Shepton Mallet. ST6141.
East Coombe *Devon* ***Hamlet***, to E of Stockleigh Pomeroy, 4m/7km NE of Crediton. SS8803.
East Cornworthy *Devon* ***Hamlet***, 1m/2km E of Cornworthy. **5 J5** SX8455.
East Cote *Cumb.* ***Locality***, on Solway Firth, 1m/2km NE of Silloth. Site of small Roman fort. NY1155.
East Cottingwith *E.Riding* ***Village***, 11m/18km W of Market Weighton, at junction of Pocklington Canal and River Derwent. **58 D5** SE7042.
East Cowes *I.o.W.* ***Village***, at mouth of River Medina opposite Cowes (vehicle ferry operates), 4m/7km N of Newport and 9m/15km W of Portsmouth across The Solent. **11 G5** SZ5095.
East Cowick *E.Riding* ***Village***, 1m/2km E of Snaith. **58 C7** SE6621.
East Cowton *N.Yorks.* ***Village***, 7m/11km NW of Northallerton. **62 E6** NZ3003.
East Cramlington *Northumb.* ***Village***, adjoining to E of Cramlington. NZ2876.
East Cranmore *Som.* ***Hamlet***, in parish of Cranmore, 5m/8km E of Shepton Mallet. **19 K7** ST6843.
East Creech *Dorset* ***Hamlet***, 3m/5km S of Wareham. **9 J6** SY9282.
East Croachy *High.* ***Hamlet***, part of Croachy locality, in Inverness district, 5m/9km SE of Dores. **88 D2** NH6527.
East Croft *Cumb.* ***Locality***, adjoining to N of High Harrington, 2m/3km S of Workington town centre. NY0025.
East Darlochan *Arg. & B.* ***Settlement***, to N of airfield, 4m/6km NW of Campeltown. **66 A1** NR6723.
East Dart *Devon* ***River***, rising on Dartmoor at East Dart Head, 5m/8km NW of Postbridge, and flowing SE by Postbridge to join West Dart River, at Dartmeet. **5 G3** SX6773.
East Davoch *Aber.* ***Settlement***, 2m/3km NW of Tarland. **90 C4** NJ4607.
East Dean *E.Suss.* Population: 1487. ***Village***, on South Downs, 4m/6km W of Eastbourne. **13 J7** TV5597.
East Dean *Hants.* ***Village***, 3m/4km NE of Whiteparish. **10 D2** SU2726.
East Dean *W.Suss.* ***Village***, below South Downs, 6m/9km NE of Chichester. **12 C5** SU9013.
East Dene *S.Yorks.* ***Suburb***, 1m/2km E of Rotherham town centre. SK4493.
East Denton *T. & W.* ***Suburb***, 4m/6km W of Newcastle upon Tyne city centre. NZ2065.
East Dereham *Norf.* Population: 12,974. ***Town***, 16m/25km W of Norwich. Large parish church with detached bell tower. Bonner's Cottages, early 16c, pargeted, now museum of local history. Poet William Cowper lived in town. **44 D4** TF9813.
East Didsbury *Gt.Man.* ***Suburb***, to SE of Didsbury, 5m/8km S of Manchester city centre. SJ8490.
East Down *Devon* ***Hamlet***, 6m/10km NE of Barnstaple. **6 E1** SS6041.
East Drayton *Notts.* ***Village***, 4m/6km NE of Tuxford. **51 K5** SK7775.
East Dulwich *Gt.Lon.* ***Suburb***, in borough of Southwark, 1m/2km NE of Dulwich village. TQ3374.
East Dundry *N.Som.* ***Hamlet***, 1m/2km SE of Dundry and 4m/7km S of Bristol. ST5766.
East Ella *Hull* ***Suburb***, 3m/4km W of Kingston upon Hull city centre. TA0529.
East End *Beds.* ***Locality***, E end of Houghton Regis, 1m/2km N of Dunstable. TL0224.
East End *Beds.* ***Settlement***, NE end of Cranfield, 7m/11km SW of Bedford. SP9642.
East End *Beds.* ***Settlement***, E end of Wilden. TL1055.
East End *Bucks.* ***Settlement***, adjoining to E of Weedon, 3m/5km N of Aylesbury. SP8118.
East End *Cambs.* ***Village***, E end of Bluntisham. TL3774.
East End *Cambs.* ***Village***, E end of Isleham. TL6574.
East End *Dorset* ***Hamlet***, 1km E of Corfe Mullen. **9 J5** SY9998.
East End *E.Riding* ***Locality***, adjoining to E of Ulrome. TA1757.
East End *E.Riding* ***Settlement***, 1km NE of Preston. TA1930.
East End *E.Riding* ***Settlement***, 1m/2km E of Halsham. TA2927.
East End *Essex* ***Settlement***, adjoining to E of Bradwell-on-Sea. TM0007.
East End *Hants.* ***Hamlet***, 1km E of West Meon. SU6424.
East End *Hants.* ***Village***, 2m/3km W of Highclere. **21 H5** SU4161.
East End *Hants.* ***Village***, on S edge of Beaulieu Heath, in New Forest, 3m/5km E of Lymington. **10 E5** SZ3697.
East End *Herts.* ***Settlement***, 5m/7km NW of Bishop's Stortford. **33 H6** TL4527.
East End *Kent* ***Hamlet***, 2m/3km NE of Benenden. **14 D4** TQ8335.
East End *Kent* ***Settlement***, on N coast of Isle of Sheppey, 1m/2km E of Minster. TQ9673.
East End *M.K.* ***Settlement***, 1m/2km E of North Crawley and 4m/7km E of Newport Pagnell. SP9444.
East End *N.Som.* ***Suburb***, E district of Nailsea. **19 H4** ST4870.
East End *Oxon.* ***Hamlet***, 4m/7km NE of Witney. Remains of Roman villa (English Heritage) to NW. **30 E7** SP3914.
East End *Som.* ***Hamlet***, 1m/2km S of Chewton Mendip. ST5951.
East End *Som.* ***Hamlet***, 4m/6km NE of Shepton Mallet. ST6746.
East End *Suff.* ***Hamlet***, adjoining to NW of Brantham. **35 F5** TM1034.
East End *Suff.* ***Settlement***, 1m/2km E of Stonham Aspal. TM1559.
East Ermine *Lincs.* ***Suburb***, N district of Lincoln. SK9873.
East Everleigh *Wilts.* ***Hamlet***, to S of Everleigh, 8m/13km NE of Amesbury. SU2053.
East Ewell *Surr.* ***Suburb***, 1m/2km E of Ewell. TQ2362.
East Farleigh *Kent* ***Village***, on River Medway, 2m/3km SW of Maidstone. **14 C2** TQ7353.
East Farleigh Bridge *Kent* ***Bridge***, 14c-15c Kentish ragstone bridge over River Medway at East Farleigh, 2m/3km SW of Maidstone centre. Considered one of finest bridges in S England. TQ7353.
East Farndon *Northants.* ***Village***, 2m/3km SW of Market Harborough. **42 A7** SP7185.
East Fen *Lincs.* ***Open space***, lowland 4m/6km E of Stickney. **53 G7** TF4055.
East Ferry *Lincs.* ***Village***, on E bank of River Trent, 7m/11km N of Gainsborough. **52 B3** SK8199.
East Firsby *Lincs.* ***Settlement***, 1m/2km N of Spridlington and 6m/10km W of Market Rasen. TF0085.
East Fleet *Dorset* ***Lake/loch***, lagoon and nature reserve behind Chesil Beach stretching from Gore Cove to Portland Harbour. **9 F7** SY6180.
East Fleetham *Northumb.* ***Settlement***, 1m/2km NE of West Fleetham. NU2029.
East Flexford *Surr.* ***Locality***, below N side of Hog's Back, 1m/2km E of Wanborough. SU9449.
East Fortune *E.Loth.* ***Locality***, 4m/6km S of North Berwick. Former airfield now museum of flight. **76 D3** NT5579.
East Fortune Museum of Flight *E.Loth.* ***Other feature of interest***, 4m/6km S of North Berwick, exhibiting over 35 aircraft, including a Spitfire and oldest flying machine in Britain. **76 D3** NT5478.
East Garforth *W.Yorks.* ***Suburb***, to NE of Garforth. SE4133.
East Garston *W.Berks.* ***Village***, 3m/5km SE of Lambourn. **21 G4** SU3676.
East Gerinish *W.Isles* ***Locality***, 4m/6km E of Geirninis, South Uist. NF8339.
East Ginge *Oxon.* ***Hamlet***, 3m/5km E of Wantage. **21 H3** SU4486.
East Glen *Lincs.* ***River***, formed by various tributaries in Ingoldsby area, and flowing S to its confluence with West River Glen, 1m/2km W of Baston, forming River Glen. **42 D4** TF0913.
East Goscote *Leics.* Population: 3038. ***Village***, 6m/9km NE of Leicester. **41 J4** SK6413.
East Grafton *Wilts.* ***Village***, 6m/10km SW of Hungerford. **21 F5** SU2560.
East Green *Suff.* ***Settlement***, 5m/8km N of Haverhill. TL6853.
East Green *Suff.* ***Settlement***, 2m/3km NE of Saxmundham. TM4065.
East Grimstead *Wilts.* ***Village***, within parish of Grimstead, 5m/8km SE of Salisbury. **10 D2** SU2227.
East Grinstead *W.Suss.* Population: 27,058. ***Town***, 8m/13km E of Crawley. Previously an important iron-making town. Many medieval buildings. **13 G3** TQ3938.
East Guldeford *E.Suss.* ***Village***, 1m/2km NE of Rye. **14 E5** TQ9321.
East Guldeford Level *E.Suss.* ***Open space***, lowland 2m/3km NE of Rye. **14 E5** TQ9421.
East Haddon *Northants.* ***Village***, 8m/12km NW of Northampton. **31 H2** SP6668.
East Hagbourne *Oxon.* ***Village***, 1m/2km SE of Didcot. **21 J3** SU5388.
East Halton *N.Lincs.* ***Village***, 4m/7km NW of Immingham. **52 E1** TA1319.
East Halton Skitter *N.Lincs.* ***Coastal feature***, low promontory and mudflat on W bank of River Humber, at mouth of East Halton Beck, 2m/3km N of East Halton. **59 H7** TA1319.
East Ham *Gt.Lon.* ***Suburb***, in borough of Newham, 7m/11km E of London Bridge. **23 H3** TQ4283.
East Hampnett *W.Suss.* ***Settlement***, to E of Tangmere, 4m/6km E of Chichester. SU9106.
East Hanney *Oxon.* ***Village***, 4m/6km N of Wantage. **21 H2** SU4193.
East Hanningfield *Essex* ***Village***, 6m/9km SE of Chelmsford. **24 D1** TL7701.
East Hardwick *W.Yorks.* ***Village***, 2m/3km S of Pontefract. **51 G1** SE4618.
East Harling *Norf.* Population: 1923. ***Village***, 6m/10km SW of Attleborough. **44 D7** TL9986.
East Harlsey *N.Yorks.* ***Village***, 5m/8km NE of Northallerton. **63 F7** SE4299.
East Harnham *Wilts.* ***Suburb***, S district of Salisbury. SU1428.
East Harptree *B. & N.E.Som.* ***Village***, 7m/11km N of Wells. **19 J6** ST5655.
East Hartburn *Stock.* ***Suburb***, 1m/2km SW of Stockton-on-Tees town centre. NZ4218.
East Hartford *Northumb.* ***Village***, 2m/3km SE of Bedlington. **71 H6** NZ2679.
East Harting *W.Suss.* ***Village***, in parish of Harting, 3m/5km SE of Petersfield. **11 J3** SU7820.
East Hatch *Wilts.* ***Hamlet***, 5m/9km NE of Shaftesbury. **9 J2** ST9228.
East Hatley *Cambs.* ***Village***, 4m/7km E of Potton. **33 F3** TL2850.
East Hauxwell *N.Yorks.* ***Village***, 4m/6km NE of Leyburn. **62 C7** SE1693.
East Haven *Angus* ***Settlement***, on coast, 2m/3km NE of Carnoustie. **83 G4** NO5836.
East Heckington *Lincs.* ***Village***, 3m/5km E of Heckington. **42 E1** TF1444.
East Hedleyhope *Dur.* ***Hamlet***, 3m/5km N of Crook. **62 C2** NZ1540.
East Helmsdale *High.* ***Settlement***, just N of Helmsdale. **105 F7** ND0316.
East Hendred *Oxon.* ***Village***, 4m/6km E of Wantage. **21 H3** SU4588.
East Herrington *T. & W.* ***Suburb***, 3m/5km SW of Sunderland city centre. NZ3552.
East Heslerton *N.Yorks.* ***Village***, 9m/15km E of Malton. **59 F2** SE9276.
East Hewish *N.Som.* ***Hamlet***, to N of Hewish, 6m/9km E of Weston-super-Mare. ST3964.
East Hill *Hants.* ***Locality***, adjoining to SE of Liss, 4m/6km NE of Petersfield. SU7827.
East Hoathly *E.Suss.* ***Village***, 5m/8km SE of Uckfield. **13 J5** TQ5216.
East Hoevdi *Shet.* ***Coastal feature***, headland on N coast of Foula. **108 B1** HT9541.
East Hogaland *Shet.* ***Settlement***, on Mainland, 1m/2km SW of Ollaberry. HU3579.
East Holme *Dorset* ***Hamlet***, in River Frome valley, 2m/3km SW of Wareham. SY8985.
East Holywell *Northumb.* ***Settlement***, 1m/2km SW of Holywell. NZ3174.
East Hook *Pembs.* ***Locality***, 1m/2km E of Hook. SM9711.
East Horndon *Essex* ***Hamlet***, 4m/6km SE of Brentwood. **24 C3** TQ6389.
East Horrington *Som.* ***Village***, 2m/3km E of Wells. **19 J7** ST5846.
East Horsley *Surr.* Population: 5925. ***Village***, 7m/11km E of Guildford. **22 D6** TQ0952.
East Horton *Northumb.* ***Hamlet***, 3m/5km NE of Wooler. Devil's Causeway Roman road runs N to S at E edge of hamlet. **77 J7** NU0230.
East Howe *Bourne.* ***Suburb***, 3m/4km NW of Bournemouth town centre. SZ0795.
East Hoyle Bank *Mersey.* ***Coastal feature***, sandbank on Wirral between Mockbeggar Wharf and Dawpool Bank. **48 B3** SJ2190.
East Huntington *York* ***Locality***, adjoining to S of Huntington. SE6156.
East Huntspill *Som.* ***Village***, 2m/3km SE of Highbridge. **19 G7** ST3445.
East Hyde *Beds.* ***Hamlet***, on River Lea, 2m/3km N of Harpenden. **32 E7** TL1217.
East Ilkerton *Devon* ***Locality***, 2m/3km S of Lynton. SS7146.
East Ilsley *W.Berks.* ***Village***, 9m/14km N of Newbury. **21 H3** SU4881.
East Kame *Shet.* ***Hill***, 4m/6km SE of Voe, Mainland. Height 558 feet or 170 metres. **109 D7** HU4257.
East Keal *Lincs.* ***Village***, 2m/3km SW of Spilsby. **53 G6** TF3863.
East Kennett *Wilts.* ***Village***, 2m/3km SE of Avebury. **20 E5** SU1167.
East Keswick *W.Yorks.* Population: 1529. ***Village***, 4m/6km SW of Wetherby. **57 J5** SE3644.
East Kilbride *S.Lan.* Population: 70,422. ***Town***, 7m/11km S of Glasgow. New Town designated 1947. **74 E5** NS6354.

East Kimber *Devon* ***Hamlet***, 7m/11km NW of Okehampton. SX4998.
East Kip *Midloth.* ***Mountain***, rising to over 530 metres in Pentland Hills, 1km SW of summit of Scald Law and 3m/5km W of Penicuik. **75 K4** NT1860.
East Kirkby *Lincs.* ***Village***, 5m/8km SW of Spilsby. **53 G6** TF3362.
East Knapton *N.Yorks.* ***Hamlet***, 7m/11km E of Malton. **58 E2** SE8875.
East Knighton *Dorset* ***Hamlet***, 2m/3km W of Wool. **9 H6** SY8185.
East Knowstone *Devon* ***Hamlet***, 1km E of Knowstone. SS8323.
East Knoyle *Wilts.* ***Village***, 5m/8km N of Shaftesbury. **9 H1** ST8830.
East Kyloe *Northumb.* ***Hamlet***, 3m/5km E of Lowick. NU0539.
East Kyo *Dur.* ***Settlement***, 1km N of Annfield Plain. NZ1752.
East Lambrook *Som.* ***Village***, 2m/3km W of Martock. **8 D3** ST4318.
East Lambrook Manor *Som.* ***Garden***, cottage garden of the late Margery Fish, made famous by her gardening programmes, 1m/2km N of South Petherton. Rare and unusual plants; large hellebores collection. **8 D3** ST4318.
East Lancashire Railway *Lancs.* ***Other feature of interest***, tourist railway running from Bury to Ramsbottom, then on to Rawtenstall. **56 D7** SD8010.
East Langdon *Kent* ***Village***, 3m/5km N of Dover. **15 J3** TR3246.
East Langton *Leics.* ***Village***, 4m/6km N of Market Harborough. **42 A6** SP7292.
East Langwell *High.* ***Locality***, in Sutherland district, 8m/13km NW of Golspie. **96 E1** NC7206.
East Laroch *High. Former name of Ballachulish, qv.*
East Lavant *W.Suss.* ***Village***, 2m/4km N of Chichester. **12 B6** SU8608.
East Lavington *W.Suss.* ***Hamlet***, at foot of South Downs, 4m/7km SW of Petworth. **12 C5** SU9416.
East Layton *N.Yorks.* ***Village***, 4m/7km NW of Scotch Corner. **62 C5** NZ1609.
East Leake *Notts.* Population: 5491. ***Village***, 4m/7km N of Loughborough. **41 H3** SK5526.
East Learmouth *Northumb.* ***Settlement***, 1m/2km S of Cornhill on Tweed. **77 G7** NT8637.
East Learney *Aber.* ***Settlement***, 1m/2km NE of Torphins. **90 E4** NJ6303.
East Leigh *Devon* ***Hamlet***, 5m/7km SE of Winkleigh. **7 F5** SS6905.
East Leigh *Devon* ***Hamlet***, 2m/3km NE of Modbury. SX6852.
East Leigh *Devon* ***Hamlet***, 3m/5km SW of Totnes. SX7658.
East Leigh *Devon* ***Settlement***, to E of Leigh, 1m/2km E of Chawleigh. SS7212.
East Lexham *Norf.* ***Village***, 6m/9km NE of Swaffham. **44 C4** TF8516.
East Lilburn *Northumb.* ***Hamlet***, 4m/6km SW of Wooler. Devil's Causeway, course of Roman Road, runs N to S at edge of hamlet. **71 F1** NU0423.
East Linga *Shet.* ***Island***, small uninhabited island 2m/4km E of Whalsay, 3m/5km S of Skaw Taing. **109 F6** HU6162.
East Linton *E.Loth.* Population: 1422. ***Small town***, on River Tyne 6m/9km W of Dunbar. Nesting for several hundred birds at Phantassie Doocot (National Trust for Scotland), to S. 18c cornmill, in working order, to N at Preston. **76 D3** NT5977.
East Liss *Hants.* ***Locality***, forms part of Liss, 3m/5km NE of Petersfield. **11 J2** SU7827.
East Loch Roag *W.Isles* ***Sea feature***, large inlet on W coast of Isle of Lewis, on E side of Great Bernera. **100 D4** NB1837.
East Loch Tarbert *Arg. & B.* ***Sea feature***, inlet of Loch Fyne at N end of Kintyre, Argyll, running up to Tarbert, for which it provides a harbour. **73 G4** NR8769.
East Loch Tarbert *W.Isles* ***Sea feature***, large inlet between E coast of North and South Harris. Village and port of Tarbert on isthmus between this inlet and West Loch Tarbert. **93 G2** NG1896.
East Lockinge *Oxon.* ***Hamlet***, 2m/3km E of Wantage. SU4287.
East Lomond *Fife* ***Mountain***, with viewpoint at summit, 4m/6km NW of Glenrothes. Height 1391 feet or 424 metres. **82 D7** NO2406.
East Looe *Cornw.* ***River***, rising on Bodmin Moor near St. Cleer, flowing S past Liskeard then towards town of Looe, where it joins West Looe River to form Looe River. **4 C4** SX2553.
East Looe *Cornw.* Population: 2511. ***Suburb***, larger part of Looe, divided from West Looe by Looe River, 7m/11km S of Liskeard. Road bridge connection to West Looe. **4 C5** SX2553.
East Lound *N.Lincs.* ***Village***, 1m/2km E of Haxey. **51 K3** SK7899.
East Low *Dur.* ***Hamlet***, 1km SW of Ebchester. NZ0954.
East Lulworth *Dorset* ***Village***, 3m/5km S of Wool. Ruined 16c castle. **9 H6** SY8682.
East Lutton *N.Yorks.* ***Hamlet***, 10m/16km E of Malton. **59 F3** SE9469.
East Lydford *Som.* ***Village***, in parish of Lydford, to E of Keinton Mandeville. **8 E1** ST5631.
East Lyn *Devon* ***River***, rising on N Exmoor and flowing W through Doone Valley into Bristol Channel via confluence with West Lyn River at Lynmouth. Lower reaches are National Trust property. SS7249.
East Lyn *Devon* ***Settlement***, 1m/2km SE of Lynton. SS7348.
East Lyng *Som.* ***Village***, 1m/2km NW of Stoke St. Gregory. ST3329.
East Mains *Aber.* ***Settlement***, 2m/3km NW of Banchory. **90 E5** NO6797.
East Malling *Kent* Population: 16,057. ***Village***, 4m/6km W of Maidstone. **14 C2** TQ7057.
East Malling Heath *Kent* ***Settlement***, 1m/2km S of East Malling. TQ6955.
East March *Angus* ***Settlement***, 1m/2km NW of Kellas. **83 F4** NO4436.
East Marden *W.Suss.* ***Village***, 5m/7km W of Singleton. **12 B5** SU8014.
East Markham *Notts.* ***Village***, 1m/2km N of Tuxford. **51 K5** SK7472.
East Marsh *Carmar.* ***Locality***, 1m/2km S of Laugharne. **17 F4** SN2808.
East Martin *Hants.* ***Hamlet***, 1km E of Martin, 7m/12km SW of Salisbury. SU0719.
East Marton *N.Yorks.* ***Village***, 5m/8km W of Skipton. **56 E4** SD9050.
East Meon *Hants.* ***Village***, 5m/8km W of Petersfield. **11 H2** SU6722.
East Mere *Devon* ***Settlement***, 4m/6km NE of Tiverton. **7 H4** SS9916.
East Mersea *Essex* ***Hamlet***, on Mersea Island, 8m/12km S of Colchester. **34 E7** TM0514.
East Mey *High.* ***Settlement***, 2m/3km NE of Mey. **105 J1** ND3073.
East Midlands International Airport *Leics.* ***Airport/airfield***, 1m/2km SE of Castle Donington and 6m/9km NW of Loughborough. **41 G3** SK4526.
East Molesey *Surr.* Population: 11,650. ***Suburb***, between River Thames and River Mole, 2m/3km W of Kingston upon Thames. **22 E5** TQ1468.
East Monar Forest *High.* ***Open space***, deer forest in Ross and Cromarty district N of lower part of Loch Monar. **95 H7** NH1042.
East Moor *Derbys.* ***Open space***, large area of moorland on E side of Peak District National Park, to E of Chatsworth Park, 6m/10km W of Chesterfield. **50 E5** SK2873.
East Moor *W.Yorks.* ***Suburb***, to E of Wakefield city centre. SE3421.
East Morden *Dorset* ***Hamlet***, 2m/3km W of Lytchett Matravers. **9 J5** SY9195.
East Morriston *Sc.Bord.* ***Hamlet***, 3m/4km SW of Gordon. NT6041.
East Morton *W.Yorks.* ***Village***, 2m/3km N of Bingley. **57 F5** SE0941.
East Mouse (Ynys Amlwch). *I.o.A.* ***Island***, rock lying off N coast of Anglesey opposite Amlwch. SH4494.
East Ness *N.Yorks.* ***Hamlet***, 2m/3km E of Nunnington. **58 C2** SE6978.
East Newbiggin *Darl.* ***Settlement***, 6m/9km NE of Darlington. NZ3618.
East Newton *E.Riding* ***Settlement***, on coast 1m/2km E of Aldbrough. TA2637.
East Newton *N.Yorks.* ***Settlement***, 1m/2km E of Oswaldkirk. SE6479.
East Northwood *Devon* ***Settlement***, 6m/10km NW of Crediton. SS7709.
East Norton *Leics.* ***Village***, 5m/8km W of Uppingham. **42 A5** SK7800.
East Nynehead *Som.* ***Hamlet***, 1km E of Nynehead, 2m/3km NE of Wellington. ST1522.
East Oakley *Hants.* ***Locality***, extensive locality adjoining to E of Oakley or Church Oakley, 4m/6km W of Basingstoke. **21 J7** SU5750.
East Ogwell *Devon* ***Village***, forms locality of Ogwell, along with West Ogwell, 1m/2km SW of Newton Abbot. **5 J3** SX8370.
East Okement *Devon* ***River***, rising on Dartmoor and joining West Okement at Okehampton to form Okement river. **6 E6** SX5895.
East Onny *Shrop.* ***River***, flowing S along W side of The Long Mynd, to join with River West Onny, 3m/5km E of Bishop's Castle, to form River Onny. **38 C6** SO3789.
East Orchard *Dorset* ***Village***, 3m/5km S of Shaftesbury. **9 H3** ST8317.
East Ord *Northumb.* ***Village***, 1m/2km SW of Berwick-upon-Tweed. **77 H5** NT9851.
East Panson *Devon* ***Hamlet***, 3m/4km SW of Ashwater. **6 B6** SX3692.
East Parley *Dorset* ***Settlement***, at W end of Bournemouth International Airport, 3m/4km SE of Ferndown. SZ0997.
East Peckham *Kent* Population: 2874. ***Village***, 2m/4km N of Paddock Wood. **23 K7** TQ6648.
East Pennard *Som.* ***Village***, 4m/6km SW of Shepton Mallet. **8 E1** ST5937.
East Perry *Cambs.* ***Hamlet***, adjoining West Perry on S side of Grafham Water, 4m/7km NW of St. Neots. TL1566.
East Plean *Stir.* ***Village***, adjoining to N of Plean. NS8386.
East Point Pavilion *Suff.* ***Other feature of interest***, play and education, information and history centre, recently built in Edwardian style on coast at Lowestoft. Hi-tech multi-sensory displays on local history. **45 K6** TM5593.
East Poringland *Norf. Former name for Poringland, qv.*
East Portlemouth *Devon* ***Village***, 1km E of Salcombe across Kingsbridge Estuary. Ferry for pedestrians. **5 H7** SX7438.
East Prawle *Devon* ***Village***, 1m/2km NE of Prawle Point. **5 H7** SX7836.
East Preston *W.Suss.* ***Small town***, coastal town, 3m/4km E of Littlehampton. **12 D6** TQ0702.
East Pulham *Dorset* ***Hamlet***, to NE of Pulham, 5m/8km SW of Sturminster Newton. ST7209.
East Putford *Devon* ***Village***, 8m/13km N of Holsworthy. **6 B4** SS3616.
East Quantoxhead *Som.* ***Village***, near coast, 4m/6km E of Watchet. **7 K1** ST1343.
East Rainton *T. & W.* ***Village***, 2m/3km S of Houghton le Spring. **62 E2** NZ3347.
East Ravendale *N.E.Lincs.* ***Village***, 4m/6km NE of Binbrook. **53 F3** TF2399.
East Raynham *Norf.* ***Village***, 3m/5km SW of Fakenam. 17c hall. **44 C3** TF8825.
East Retford *Notts. Alternative name for Retford, qv.*
East Riddlesden Hall *W.Yorks.* ***Historic house***, 17c manor house (National Trust) with fine collection of oak furniture, 1m/2km NE of Keighley. **57 F5** SE0842.
East Rigton *W.Yorks.* ***Village***, 4m/6km SW of Wetherby. **57 J5** SE3643.
East Road *Kent* ***Bay***, extending N from Dungeness and incorporating Littlestone-on-Sea, Greatstone-on-Sea and Lydd-on-Sea. **15 F5** TR0921.
East Roisnish (Gaelic form: Roisnis an Ear.) *W.Isles* ***Coastal feature***, headland on NW coast of Eye Peninsula, Isle of Lewis. **101 H4** NB5034.
East Rolstone *N.Som.* ***Settlement***, 1km SE of Rolstone. **19 G5** ST3962.
East Rounton *N.Yorks.* ***Village***, 7m/11km NE of Northallerton. **63 F6** NZ4203.
East Row *N.Yorks.* ***Hamlet***, on North Sea coast, adjoining to SE of Sandsend. NZ8612.
East Rudham *Norf.* ***Village***, 6m/10km W of Fakenham. **44 C3** TF8228.
East Runton *Norf.* ***Town***, resort 1m/2km W of Cromer. **45 F1** TG1942.
East Ruston *Norf.* ***Village***, 4m/7km SE of North Walsham. **45 H3** TG3427.
East Saltney *Flints.* ***Locality***, 2m/4km SE of Queensferry. SJ3466.
East Saltoun *E.Loth.* ***Village***, 5m/8km SE of Tranent. **76 C4** NT4767.
East Scrafton *N.Yorks.* ***Settlement***, 3m/5km SW of Middleham. SE0884.
East Sheen *Gt.Lon.* ***Suburb***, in borough of Richmond upon Thames, at N end of Richmond Park, 7m/11km SW of Charing Cross. East Sheen Common (National Trust) to SW. TQ2074.
East Shefford *W.Berks.* ***Hamlet***, 5m/8km NE of Hungerford. **21 G4** SU3875.
East Side *B.Gwent* ***Locality***, 1m/2km N of Abertillery. SO2105.
East Sleekburn *Northumb.* ***Hamlet***, 2m/3km NE of Bedlington. **71 H5** NZ2883.
East Somerset Railway *Som.* ***Other feature of interest***, tourist railway running for 2m/3km from a point 2m/3km SE of Shepton Mallet to Cranmore. Replica Victorian engine shed, historic locomotives and art gallery. **19 K7** ST6542.
East Somerton *Norf.* ***Village***, 1m/2km W of Winterton-on-Sea. **45 J4** TG4719.
East Stanley *Dur.* ***Suburb***, 1km E of Stanley. NZ2053.
East Stocklett *W.Isles* ***Hill***, on South Harris 4m/6km SW of Tarbert. Height 574 feet or 175 metres. **93 G2** NG1195.
East Stockwith *Lincs.* ***Village***, on E bank of River Trent, 4m/6km NW of Gainsborough and opposite West Stockwith. **51 K3** SK7994.
East Stoke *Dorset* ***Village***, on River Frome, 3m/5km W of Wareham. **9 H6** SY8786.
East Stoke *Notts.* ***Village***, 4m/6km SW of Newark-on-Trent. Site of Battle of Stoke Field, 1487 (Lambert Simnel's rebellion). **42 A1** SK7549.
East Stoke *Som.* ***Hamlet***, 1km E of Stoke sub Hamdon. ST4817.
East Stour *Dorset* ***Village***, 2m/4km S of Gillingham. **9 G2** ST7922.
East Stour *Kent* ***River***, rising near Brabourne and flowing into River Great Stour at Ashford. **15 F4** TR0142.
East Stourmouth *Kent* ***Village***, in parish of Stourmouth, to NW of Sandwich. **25 J5** TR2562.
East Stowford *Devon* ***Hamlet***, to E of Stowford, 5m/8km W of South Molton. SS6226.
East Stratton *Hants.* ***Village***, 2m/3km E of Micheldever. **11 G1** SU5440.
East Street *Kent* ***Locality***, 2m/3km W of Sandwich. TR3058.
East Street *Som.* ***Hamlet***, 3m/4km E of Glastonbury. ST5338.
East Studdal *Kent* ***Village***, 4m/7km SW of Deal. **15 J3** TR3149.
East Suisnish *High.* ***Settlement***, on S coast of Raasay, 1m/2km W of Eyre Point. **86 B1** NG5634.
East Tanfield *N.Yorks.* ***Settlement***, on E side of River Ure, 1m/2km SE of West Tanfield. Site of former village to N. SE2877.
East Taphouse *Cornw.* ***Village***, 4m/7km W of Liskeard. **4 B4** SX1863.
East Tarbert Bay *Arg. & B.* ***Bay***, one of two bays on either side of Gigha, near N end of island. **72 E5** NR6552.
East Tarbet *D. & G.* ***Locality***, on Mull of Galloway, 3m/5km S of Cailiness Point on W side of Luce Bay. **64 B7** NX1431.
East-the-Water *Devon* ***Suburb***, to E of Bideford town centre across River Torridge. **6 C3** SS4526.
East Thirston *Northumb.* ***Hamlet***, 1m/2km SE of Felton. **71 G4** NZ1999.
East Tilbury *Thur.* ***Village***, 3m/5km E of Tilbury. **24 C4** TQ6877.
East Tisted *Hants.* ***Village***, 4m/7km S of Alton. **11 J1** SU7032.
East Torrington *Lincs.* ***Hamlet***, 5m/7km SE of Market Rasen. **52 E4** TF1382.
East Town *Som.* ***Hamlet***, 3m/5km NE of Wiveliscombe. ST1032.
East Town *Som.* ***Settlement***, to E of Pilton, 2m/3km SW of Shepton Mallet. ST6040.
East Tuddenham *Norf.* ***Village***, 10m/16km W of Norwich. **44 E4** TG0711.
East Tytherley *Hants.* ***Hamlet***, 5m/9km SW of Stockbridge. **10 D2** SU2929.
East Tytherton *Wilts.* ***Village***, 3m/5km E of Chippenham. **20 C4** ST9674.
East Village *Devon* ***Hamlet***, 3m/5km N of Crediton. **7 G5** SS8405.
East Village *V. of Glam.* ***Suburb***, on SE side of Cowbridge. SS9974.
East Wall *Shrop.* ***Hamlet***, 5m/7km E of Church Stretton. **38 E6** SO5293.
East Wall Houses *Northumb.* ***Settlement***, 1km E of Wall Houses. NZ0568.

East Walton *Norf.* ***Village***, 6m/10km NW of Swaffham. **44 B4** TF7416.
East Wear Bay *Kent* ***Bay***, on English Channel, to E of Folkestone. **15 H4** TR2537.
East Webburn *Devon* ***River***, rising on Dartmoor to W of Manaton and flowing S to join with West Webburn River at Lizwell Meet, 1m/2km E of Ponsworthy, to form River Webburn. **5 H3** SX7173.
East Wellow *Hants.* ***Hamlet***, 3m/5km W of Romsey. **10 E2** SU3020.
East Wemyss *Fife* Population: 1762. ***Village***, on Firth of Forth, 5m/8km NE of Kirkcaldy. 14c ruin of Macduff's Castle to E. **76 B1** NT3396.
East Whitburn *W.Loth.* ***Hamlet***, adjoining to E of Whitburn. **75 H4** NS9665.
East Wickham *Gt.Lon.* ***Suburb***, in borough of Bexley, 6m/9km E of Greenwich and 11m/18km E of Charing Cross. **23 H4** TQ4777.
East Williamston *Pembs.* ***Village***, 4m/6km NW of Tenby. **16 D4** SN0904.
East Winch *Norf.* ***Village***, 5m/8km SE of King's Lynn. **44 A4** TF6916.
East Winterslow *Wilts.* ***Settlement***, 1km NE of Middle Winterslow, 6m/10km NE of Salisbury. SU2433.
East Wittering *W.Suss.* Population: 4630. ***Small town***, coastal resort, 4m/7km NW of Selsey. **12 B7** SZ7997.
East Witton *N.Yorks.* ***Village***, 2m/3km SE of Middleham. **57 G1** SE1486.
East Woodburn *Northumb.* ***Hamlet***, 4m/7km S of Otterburn. NY9086.
East Woodburn Common *Northumb.* ***Open space***, hillside to N of Lisles Burn, with Hart Side, 1102 feet or 336 metres, as its highest point, 2m/3km E of West Woodburn. **70 E5** NY9287.
East Woodhay *Hants.* ***Hamlet***, 2m/3km NW of Highclere. **21 H5** SU4061.
East Woodlands *Som.* ***Settlement***, with West Woodlands, forms locality of Woodlands, 3m/4km S of Frome. ST7844.
East Worldham *Hants.* ***Village***, 2m/4km E of Alton. **11 J1** SU7438.
East Worlington *Devon* ***Hamlet***, 6m/9km E of Chulmleigh. **7 F4** SS7713.
East Yell *Shet.* ***Locality***, 1km S of Otterswick, Yell. **108 E4** HU5284.
East Youlstone *Devon* ***Hamlet***, 7m/12km NE of Bude. **6 A4** SS2715.
Eastacott *Devon* ***Hamlet***, 6m/9km W of South Molton. SS6223.
Eastacott Cross *Devon* ***Locality***, to N of Eastacott. SS6223.
Eastbourne *Darl.* ***Suburb***, 1m/2km E of Darlington town centre. **62 E5** NZ3013.
Eastbourne *E.Suss.* Population: 94,793. ***Town***, coastal resort and conference centre, 19m/31km E of Brighton. Towner Art Gallery in 18c manor house. Eastbourne hosts an International Folk Festival and also international tennis at Devonshire Park. **13 K7** TV6199.
Eastbow Hill *P. & K.* ***Mountain***, 3m/5km S of Auchterarder. Height 1561 feet or 476 metres. **82 A7** NN9407.
Eastbrook *V. of Glam.* ***Suburb***, adjoining to N of Dinas Powys. ST1571.
Eastburn *E.Riding* ***Hamlet***, 2m/4km SW of Great Driffield. **59 F4** SE9955.
Eastburn *W.Yorks.* ***Village***, in Airedale, 1km W of Steeton. SE0244.
Eastbury *Herts.* ***Locality***, 3m/5km S of Watford. **22 E2** TQ0992.
Eastbury *W.Berks.* ***Village***, 2m/3km SE of Lambourn. **21 G4** SU3477.
Eastby *N.Yorks.* ***Village***, 3m/5km NE of Skipton. **57 F4** SE0154.
Eastchurch *Kent* ***Village***, on Isle of Sheppey, 2m/4km SE of Minster. **25 F4** TQ9871.
Eastchurch Marshes *Kent* ***Marsh/bog***, on Isle of Sheppey, 3m/5km SE of Minster. **25 F5** TQ9768.
Eastcombe *Glos.* ***Village***, 3m/5km E of Stroud. **20 B1** SO8904.
Eastcote *Gt.Lon.* ***Suburb***, in borough of Hillingdon, 4m/7km NE of Uxbridge. **22 E3** TQ1187.
Eastcote *Northants.* ***Village***, 4m/6km N of Towcester. **31 H3** SP6854.
Eastcote *W.Mid.* ***Hamlet***, 3m/5km E of Solihull. **30 C1** SP1979.
Eastcote Village *Gt.Lon.* ***Suburb***, to NW of Eastcote, in borough of Hillingdon. TQ1088.
Eastcott *Cornw.* ***Settlement***, 7m/11km NE of Bude. **6 A4** SS2515.
Eastcott *Wilts.* ***Hamlet***, 4m/6km S of Devizes. 16c manor house. **20 D6** SU0255.
Eastcotts *Beds.* ***Suburb***, in SE part of Bedford. TL0747.
Eastcourt *Wilts.* ***Hamlet***, adjoining to E of Burbage, 5m/8km E of Pewsey. SU2361.
Eastcourt *Wilts.* ***Village***, 4m/7km NE of Malmesbury. **20 C2** ST9792.
Eastdown *Devon* ***Hamlet***, 3m/5km SW of Dartmouth. SX8249.
Eastend *Essex* ***Settlement***, 2m/3km W of Harlow, 1km E of Roydon. TL4210.
Eastend *Oxon.* ***Settlement***, to E of Chadlington. **30 E6** SP3322.
Eastend Green *Essex* ***Suburb***, E district of Brightlingsea. TM0916.
Eastend Green *Herts.* ***Settlement***, 2m/4km SW of Hertford. TL2910.
Easter Aquhorthies (Also known as East Aquhorthies.) *Aber.* ***Historic/prehistoric site***, site of ancient stone circle (Historic Scotland), 3m/5km W of Inverurie. **91 F2** NJ7320.
Easter Ardross *High.* ***Settlement***, 2m/3km W of Ardross and 3m/5km N of Alness. **96 D4** NH6373.
Easter Balgedie *P. & K.* ***Village***, nearly 1km SE of Wester Balgedie and 3m/5km E of Milnathort. NO1703.
Easter Balloch *Angus* ***Mountain***, 4m/6km W of Glenlee. Height 2736 feet or 834 metres. **90 B6** NO3480.
Easter Balmoral *Aber.* ***Settlement***, on S bank of River Dee, 1m/2km SE of Balmoral Castle. **89 K5** NO2694.
Easter Boleskine *High.* ***Settlement***, 1m/2km NE of Foyers. **88 C2** NH5022.
Easter Borland *Stir.* ***Settlement***, 4m/7km E of Port of Menteith. **81 H7** NN6400.
Easter Brae *High.* ***Settlement***, on Black Isle, 8m/11km NE of Munlochy. **96 D5** NH6663.
Easter Buckieburn *Stir.* ***Settlement***, 6m/9km SW of Stirling. **75 F2** NS7585.
Easter Compton *S.Glos.* ***Village***, 6m/10km N of Bristol. **19 J3** ST5783.
Easter Drummond *High.* ***Settlement***, 4m/6km SE of Invermoriston across Loch Ness. **88 B3** NH4714.
Easter Dullater *Stir.* ***Settlement***, 2m/3km SW of Callander. **81 G7** NN6006.
Easter Elchies *Moray* ***Settlement***, with distillery, 1m/2km W of Craigellachie across River Spey. NJ2744.
Easter Ellister *Arg. & B.* ***Settlement***, on Rinns of Islay, 2m/3km NE of Portnahaven. **72 A5** NR2053.
Easter Fearn *High.* ***Settlement***, 4m/6km SE of Ardgay. **96 D3** NH6486.
Easter Fearn Burn *High.* ***River***, stream running NE into Dornoch Firth at Easter Fearn Point, Ross and Cromarty district. **96 D3** NH6487.
Easter Galcantray *High.* ***Settlement***, 3m/4km SW of Cawdor. **97 F7** NH8148.
Easter Head *High.* ***Coastal feature***, headland in Caithness district with lighthouse, at N end of Dunnet Head, 4m/6km N of Dunnet. Most northerly point of Scottish mainland. **105 G1** ND2076.
Easter Howgate *Midloth.* ***Settlement***, 3m/5km N of Penicuik. NT2464.
Easter Howlaws *Sc.Bord.* ***Settlement***, 3m/4km SE of Greenlaw. **77 F6** NT7242.
Easter Kinkell *High.* ***Hamlet***, on Black Isle, Ross and Cromarty district, 4m/7km NE of Muir of Ord. **96 C6** NH5755.
Easter Knox *Angus* ***Hamlet***, 3m/5km W of Arbroath. **83 G3** NO5839.
Easter Lednathie *Angus* ***Settlement***, in Glen Prosen, 6m/10km NW of Kirriemuir. **82 E1** NO3363.
Easter Moniack *High.* ***Settlement***, 3m/4km SE of Beauly. **96 C7** NH5544.
Easter Ord *Aber.* ***Settlement***, 1m/2km S of Westhill. **91 G4** NJ8304.
Easter Pencaitland *E.Loth.* ***Village***, to S of Tyne Water, 5m/8km SW of Haddington. NT4468.
Easter Poldar *Stir.* ***Settlement***, on N bank of River Forth, 2m/3km N of Kippen. **74 E1** NS6497.
Easter Quarff *Shet.* ***Village***, on E coast of Mainland at head of East Voe of Quarff Bay, 5m/8km SW of Lerwick. **109 D9** HU4235.
Easter Ross *High.* ***Locality***, large area, mainly upland, extending E from Loch Vaich to E coast between Dornoch Firth and Moray Firth, and making up E part of Ross and Cromarty district. **96 A3** NH4979.
Easter Skeld *Shet.* ***Village***, on Mainland, at head of Skelda Voe, to W of Reawick. **109 C8** HU3144.
Easter Slumbay *High.* ***Locality***, forms Slumbay along with adjoining locality Wester Slumbay, on NW of shore of Loch Carron to SW of Lochcarron, Ross and Cromarty district. NG8939.
Easter Suddie *High.* ***Settlement***, on Black Isle, 1m/2km NE of Munlochy. **96 D6** NH6655.
Easter Tulloch *Aber.* ***Hamlet***, 3m/5km E of Laurencekirk. **91 F7** NO7671.
Easter Whyntie *Aber.* ***Settlement***, 1km S of Boyne Bay, 3m/4km E of Portsoy. **98 E4** NJ6265.
Eastergate *W.Suss.* ***Village***, 4m/7km N of Bognor Regis. **12 C6** SU9405.
Easterhouse *Glas.* ***Suburb***, 6m/10km E of Glasgow city centre. NS6865.
Eastern Isles *I.o.S.* ***Island***, most easterly of Isles of Scilly group; uninhabited. **2 C1** SV9414.
Easterside *Middbro.* ***Suburb***, 2m/3km S of Middlesbrough town centre. NZ5016.
Easterton *Wilts.* ***Village***, 4m/7km S of Devizes. **20 D6** SU0255.
Easterton Sands *Wilts.* ***Settlement***, 1km NW of Easterton. SU0155.
Eastertown *Som.* ***Hamlet***, 1km E of Lympsham. **19 G6** ST3454.
Eastfield *Bristol* ***Suburb***, 3m/4km N of Bristol city centre. ST5777.
Eastfield *Fife* ***Locality***, on SE side of Glenrothes. NT2999.
Eastfield *N.Lan.* ***Suburb***, 1m/2km W of Cumbernauld town centre. NS7474.
Eastfield *N.Lan.* ***Village***, 3m/5km W of Whitburn. **75 G4** NS8964.
Eastfield *N.Yorks.* Population: 9708. ***Village***, 3m/4km S of Scarborough. **59 G1** TA0384.
Eastfield Hall *Northumb.* ***Hamlet***, 2m/3km NW of Warkworth. **71 H3** NU2206.
Eastgate *Dur.* ***Village***, on River Wear, 3m/5km W of Stanhope. **62 A3** NY9538.
Eastgate *Lincs.* ***Locality***, adjoining to SE of Bourne. **42 E4** TF1019.
Eastgate *Norf.* ***Hamlet***, 1m/2km SE of Cawston. **45 F3** TG1423.
Eastgrove Cottage Garden *Worcs.* ***Garden***, 4m/6km S of Stourport-on-Severn. Attractive cottage garden with mainly herbaceous plants and associated nursery. **29 G2** SO7964.
Easthall *Herts.* ***Settlement***, 3m/4km SW of Stevenage. TL2022.
Eastham *Mersey.* ***Suburb***, 3m/5km SE of Bebington town centre. **48 C4** SJ3680.
Eastham *Worcs.* ***Hamlet***, 4m/6km E of Tenbury Wells. SO6568.
Eastham Ferry *Mersey.* ***Suburb***, beside River Mersey estuary, 1m/2km N of Eastham. SJ3681.
Eastham Sands ***Coastal feature***, sandbank in estuary of River Mersey, with Liverpool Airport on E side and Eastham on W side. SJ3881.
Eastham Woods Country Park *Mersey.* ***Leisure/recreation***, over 70 acres of woodland and foreshore, 3m/4km SE of Bebington. **48 C4** SJ3681.
Easthampstead *Brack.F.* ***Suburb***, S district of Bracknell. **22 B5** SU8667.
Easthampton *Here.* ***Hamlet***, 6m/10km NW of Leominster. SO4063.
Easthaugh *Norf.* ***Settlement***, 1m/2km E of Lyng. TG0817.
Eastheath *W'ham* ***Suburb***, S district of Wokingham. **22 B5** SU8067.
Easthope *Shrop.* ***Village***, 5m/8km SW of Much Wenlock. **38 E6** SO5695.
Easthorpe *E.Riding* ***Settlement***, 2m/4km N of Market Weighton. Site of former village to W, partly in Londesborough Park. SE8845.
Easthorpe *Essex* ***Hamlet***, 6m/9km W of Colchester. **34 D6** TL9121.
Easthorpe *Leics.* ***Hamlet***, 7m/11km W of Grantham. **42 B2** SK8138.
Easthorpe *N.Yorks.* ***Locality***, 3m/5km W of Malton. SE7371.
Easthorpe *Notts.* ***Locality***, adjoining to E of Southwell. **51 K7** SK7053.
Easthouses *Midloth.* ***Village***, 1m/2km SE of Dalkeith. **76 B4** NT3465.
Eastington *Devon* ***Hamlet***, 5m/8km SE of Chulmleigh. **7 F5** SS7409.
Eastington *Glos.* ***Hamlet***, 1m/2km SE of Northleach. **30 C7** SP1213.
Eastington *Glos.* ***Village***, 5m/8km W of Stroud. **20 A1** SO7705.
Eastleach *Glos.* ***Locality***, parish 4m/6km N of Lechlade, containing villages of Eastleach Martin and Eastleach Turville, connected by bridge over River Leach. SP1905.
Eastleach Martin *Glos.* ***Village***, in parish of Eastleach, 4m/6km N of Lechlade, connected to Eastleach Turville by bridge over River Leach. **21 F1** SP1905.
Eastleach Martin Bridge *Glos.* ***Bridge***, clapper bridge of unknown date over River Leach, 3m/5km NW of Lechlade. SP2005.
Eastleach Turville *Glos.* ***Village***, in parish of Eastleach, 4m/6km N of Lechlade, connected to Eastleach Martin by bridge over River Leach. **21 F1** SP1905.
Eastleigh *Devon* ***Hamlet***, 2m/4km E of Bideford. **6 C3** SS4827.
Eastleigh *Hants.* Population: 49,934. ***Town***, 5m/8km NE of Southampton. Southampton International Airport 1m/2km S. Formerly Victorian railway town, building carriages. **11 F3** SU4519.
Eastling *Kent* ***Village***, 4m/7km SW of Faversham. **14 E2** TQ9656.
Eastmoor *Derbys.* ***Hamlet***, on E edge of Peak District National Park, 5m/8km W of Chesterfield. SK3071.
Eastmoor *Norf.* ***Settlement***, 3m/4km NE of Stoke Ferry. TF7303.
Eastney *Ports.* ***Suburb***, 2m/3km E of Portsmouth city centre. To E, Fort Cumberland (English Heritage), pentagonal coastal defence built by Duke of Cumberland in 1745. **11 H5** SZ6799.
Eastnor *Here.* ***Village***, 1m/2km E of Ledbury. **29 G5** SO7337.
Eastnor Castle *Here.* ***Castle***, 19c medieval-style castle built by Sir Robert Smirke, 2m/3km SE of Ledbury. Richly decorated interior by Pugin and George Fox. **29 G5** SO7336.
Eastoft *N.Lincs.* ***Village***, 3m/4km NE of Crowle. **52 B1** SE8016.
Eastoke *Hants.* ***Suburb***, at E end of South Hayling, on Hayling Island. **11 J5** SZ7398.
Easton *Cambs.* ***Village***, 6m/10km W of Huntingdon. **32 E1** TL1371.
Easton *Cumb.* ***Hamlet***, 3m/5km W of Burgh by Sands. **60 D1** NY2759.
Easton *Cumb.* ***Settlement***, 4m/6km NE of Longtown. **69 K6** NY4371.
Easton *Devon* ***Hamlet***, 3m/5km S of Modbury. SX6747.
Easton *Devon* ***Hamlet***, 3m/5km NW of Moretonhampstead. **7 F7** SX7188.
Easton *Dorset* Population: 3815. ***Village***, 1m/2km S of Fortuneswell, on Isle of Portland. **9 F7** SY6971.
Easton *Hants.* ***Village***, in River Itchen valley, 2m/4km NE of Winchester. **11 G1** SU5132.
Easton *I.o.W.* ***Locality***, 1km S of Freshwater. **10 E6** SZ3486.
Easton *Lincs.* ***Hamlet***, 2m/3km N of Colsterworth. **42 C3** SK9326.
Easton *Norf.* ***Village***, 6m/10km W of Norwich. **45 F4** TG1310.
Easton *Som.* ***Hamlet***, 3m/4km NW of Wells. **19 J7** ST5147.
Easton *Suff.* ***Village***, 2m/4km NW of Wickham Market. **35 G3** TM2858.
Easton *W.Berks.* ***Settlement***, 5m/7km NW of Newbury. SU4172.
Easton *Wilts.* ***Hamlet***, 3m/4km SW of Chippenham. **20 B4** ST8970.
Easton Farm Park *Suff.* ***Other feature of interest***, museum of Victorian model farm and surrounding country park, 1km SW of Easton. Attractions include a dairy centre, rare breeds and a working blacksmith's forge. **35 G3** TM2758.
Easton Grey *Wilts.* ***Village***, 3m/5km W of Malmesbury. Site of Romano-British settlement to S beside River Avon. **20 B3** ST8887.
Easton Hill *Wilts.* ***Hill***, rising to over 240 metres, 1m/2km S of Easton Royal. **21 F6** SU2058.
Easton-in-Gordano *N.Som.* Population: 4870. ***Small town***, 3m/5km E of Portishead. **19 J4** ST5175.

E

Easton Maudit *Northants.* ***Village***, 6m/10km S of Wellingborough. **32 B3** SP8858.
Easton Neston *Northants.* ***Locality***, 1km NE of Towcester. SP7049.
Easton on the Hill *Northants.* ***Village***, 2m/3km SW of Stamford. Priest's house of 15c (National Trust). **42 D5** TF0104.
Easton Royal *Wilts.* ***Village***, 3m/5km E of Pewsey. **21 F5** SU2060.
Eastrea *Cambs.* ***Village***, 2m/3km E of Whittlesey. **43 F6** TL2997.
Eastriggs *D. & G.* Population: 1943. ***Village***, 3m/5km E of Annan. **69 H7** NY2466.
Eastrington *E.Riding* ***Village***, 3m/5km E of Howden. **58 D6** SE7930.
Eastrop *Swin.* ***Locality***, adjoining to E of Highworth. SU2092.
Eastry *Kent* Population: 2273. ***Village***, 3m/4km SW of Sandwich. **15 H2** TR3154.
Eastside *Ork.* ***Settlement***, 2m/3km SE of St. Margaret's Hope, South Ronaldsay. **107 D8** ND4691.
Eastside Heights *Sc.Bord.* ***Mountain***, 3m/5km NE of Colquhar. Height 1945 feet or 593 metres. **76 B6** NT3545.
Eastville *Bristol* ***Suburb***, 2m/4km NE of Bristol city centre. ST6175.
Eastville *Lincs.* ***Hamlet***, 6m/10km W of Wainfleet All Saints. **53 H7** TF4056.
Eastwell *Leics.* ***Village***, 6m/10km N of Melton Mowbray. **42 A3** SK7728.
Eastwell Park *Kent* ***Open space***, 2000 acres of parkland with lake, in parish of Eastwell, 3m/4km N of Ashford. Traversed by Pilgrims' Way. **15 F3** TR0147.
Eastwick *Herts.* ***Village***, 1m/2km NW of Harlow. **33 H7** TL4311.
Eastwood *Notts.* Population: 19,363. ***Town***, 8m/12km NW of Nottingham. Old mining town and birthplace of D.H. Lawrence, 1885. **41 G1** SK4646.
Eastwood *S.Yorks.* ***Suburb***, to NE of Rotherham town centre. Trading estate to NE. SK4393.
Eastwood *S'end* ***Suburb***, NW district of Southend-on-Sea. **24 E3** TQ8488.
Eastwood *W.Yorks.* ***Hamlet***, 2m/3km E of Todmorden. **56 E7** SD9625.
Eastwood End *Cambs.* ***Settlement***, adjoining to NE of Wimblington. TL4292.
Eathorpe *Warks.* ***Village***, 5m/8km N of Southam. **30 E2** SP3969.
Eaton *Ches.* ***Village***, 1m/2km E of Tarporley. **48 E6** SJ5763.
Eaton *Ches.* ***Village***, 2m/3km NE of Congleton. **49 H6** SJ8765.
Eaton *Here.* ***Locality***, 1m/2km SE of Leominster across River Lugg. SO5058.
Eaton *Leics.* ***Village***, 7m/11km NE of Melton Mowbray. **42 A3** SK7929.
Eaton *Norf.* ***Settlement***, 3m/5km SE of Hunstanton. TF6936.
Eaton *Norf.* ***Suburb***, 2m/3km SW of Norwich city centre. **45 G5** TG2006.
Eaton *Notts.* ***Village***, 2m/3km S of Retford. **51 K5** SK7178.
Eaton *Oxon.* ***Hamlet***, 5m/7km W of Oxford. **21 H1** SP4403.
Eaton *Shrop.* ***Hamlet***, 4m/6km SE of Church Stretton. **38 E6** SO4990.
Eaton *Shrop.* ***Settlement***, 3m/5km E of Bishop's Castle. **38 C7** SO3789.
Eaton Bishop *Here.* ***Village***, 4m/7km W of Hereford. **28 D5** SO4439.
Eaton Bray *Beds.* Population: 4042. ***Village***, 3m/5km W of Dunstable. **32 C6** SP9720.
Eaton Constantine *Shrop.* ***Village***, 5m/8km SW of Wellington. **38 E5** SJ5906.
Eaton Ford *Cambs.* ***Locality***, at N end of Eaton Socon, opposite St. Neots across River Great Ouse. **32 E3** TL1760.
Eaton Green *Beds.* ***Hamlet***, 3m/5km W of Dunstable. **32 C6** SP9621.
Eaton Hall *Ches.* ***Settlement***, 4m/6km S of Chester town centre. **48 D6** SJ4160.
Eaton Hastings *Oxon.* ***Hamlet***, on River Thames, 3m/5km E of Lechlade. **21 F2** SU2698.
Eaton Socon *Cambs.* Population: 12,370. ***Village***, 1m/2km SW of St. Neots across River Great Ouse. Traces of medieval castle beside river to E. **32 E3** TL1658.
Eaton upon Tern *Shrop.* ***Hamlet***, 4m/7km SE of Hodnet. **39 F3** SJ6523.
Eau ***River***, rising E of Gainsborough and flowing N, then E into River Trent 2m/3km S of East Butterwick. **52 C3** SE8303.
Eau Brink *Norf.* ***Locality***, 1m/2km NW of Wiggenhall St. Germans across River Great Ouse. TF5816.
Eau Withington *Here.* ***Settlement***, 3m/4km NE of Hereford. SO5442.
Eaval *W.Isles* ***Mountain***, at SE end of North Uist and highest point on the island. Height 1138 feet or 347 metres. **92 D5** NF8960.
Eaves Brow *Warr.* ***Locality***, 1km SE of Croft. SJ6493.
Eaves Green *Lancs.* ***Locality***, 1m/2km NE of Goosnargh, 3m/4km W of Longridge. SD5637.
Eaves Green *W.Mid.* ***Hamlet***, 5m/8km NW of Coventry. SP2682.
Eavestone *N.Yorks.* ***Settlement***, 4m/7km NE of Pateley Bridge. **57 H3** SE2268.
Ebberston *N.Yorks.* ***Village***, 6m/10km E of Pickering. Ebberston Hall to W. **59 F1** SE8982.
Ebberston Hall *N.Yorks.* ***Historic house***, Palladian villa 2m/3km W of Snainton and 6m/10km E of Pickering. Includes water gardens formed by three small lakes joined by cascades. **58 E1** SE8983.
Ebbesborne Wake *Wilts.* ***Village***, 4m/7km SE of Tisbury. **9 J2** ST9924.
Ebble *Wilts.* ***River***, rising to SE of Tisbury and flowing E into River Avon at Bodenham 3m/5km SE of Salisbury. **10 B2** SU1726.
Ebbor Gorge *Som.* ***Inland physical feature***, 3m/4km NW of Wells. Wooded limestone gorge (National Trust) in Mendip Hills. Nature reserve. Public access over footpaths. ST5248.
Ebbw (Ebwy). ***River***, rising about 3m/5km N of town of Ebbw Vale and flowing S along Ebbw Vale into estuary of River Usk, to S of Newport. **19 F2** ST3183.
Ebbw Vale ***Valley***, deeply incised valley of River Ebbw, running S from town of Ebbw Vale, past Newbridge, Abercarn and Risca, to Newport. Valley and its communities were once famous for production of coal, iron and steel. **19 F2** ST2093.
Ebbw Vale (Glynebwy). *B.Gwent* Population: 19,484. ***Town***, in steep-sided valley, 20m/33km N of Cardiff. Once famous for its coal, iron and steel. **18 E1** SO1609.
Ebchester *Dur.* ***Village***, on River Derwent, 3m/4km N of Consett. Site of Roman fort of Vindomora in village. **62 C1** NZ1055.
Ebdon *N.Som.* ***Hamlet***, just S of Wick St. Lawrence, 4m/6km NE of Weston-super-Mare. ST3664.
Ebford *Devon* ***Village***, 5m/8km SE of Exeter. **7 H7** SX9887.
Ebley *Glos.* ***Suburb***, 1m/2km W of Stroud. SO8204.
Ebnal *Ches.* ***Settlement***, 1m/2km NE of Malpas. SJ4948.
Ebnall *Here.* ***Locality***, 1m/2km W of Leominster. SO4758.
Eboracum *York See York.*
Ebrington *Glos.* ***Village***, 2m/4km E of Chipping Campden. **30 C4** SP1840.
Ebsworthy Town *Devon* ***Hamlet***, 1km NW of Bridestowe. SX5090.
Ebwy *Welsh form of Ebbw (River), qv.*
Ecchinswell *Hants.* ***Village***, 2m/3km W of Kingsclere. **21 J6** SU4959.
Ecclaw *Sc.Bord.* ***Settlement***, 2m/3km SW of Cockburnspath. **77 F4** NT7568.
Ecclaw Hill *Sc.Bord.* ***Hill***, 1km S of Ecclaw and 3m/4km SW of Cockburnspath. Height 912 feet or 278 metres. **77 F4** NT7567.
Ecclefechan *D. & G.* ***Small town***, 5m/8km N of Annan. Birthplace of Thomas Carlyle, 1795-1881, in house (National Trust for Scotland) in main street. **69 G6** NY1974.
Eccles *Gt.Man.* Population: 36,000. ***Town***, former cotton-spinning and weaving town, 4m/6km W of Manchester. **49 G3** SJ7798.
Eccles *Kent* ***Village***, 1m/2km N of Aylesford. Site of Roman building to W. **24 D5** TQ7260.
Eccles *Sc.Bord.* ***Village***, 5m/8km W of Coldstream. **77 F6** NT7641.
Eccles Green *Here.* ***Hamlet***, 3m/4km SW of Weobley. SO3748.
Eccles Road *Norf.* ***Hamlet***, named after railway station, 4m/6km SW of Attleborough. **44 E6** TM0190.
Ecclesfield *S.Yorks.* ***Suburb***, 4m/7km N of Sheffield. **51 F3** SK3594.
Ecclesgreig *Aber.* ***Settlement***, 1m/2km NW of St. Cyrus. **83 J1** NO7365.
Eccleshall *Staffs.* Population: 2748. ***Village***, 7m/11km NW of Stafford. **40 A3** SJ8329.
Eccleshall Castle *Staffs.* ***Castle***, to N of Eccleshall. Became a stone castle at beginning of 13c, with remains now of a later tower and wall. **40 A3** SJ8229.
Eccleshill *B'burn.* ***Locality***, 1m/2km NE of Darwen. SD7023.
Eccleshill *W.Yorks.* ***Suburb***, 2m/4km NE of Bradford city centre. SE1736.
Ecclesmachan *W.Loth.* ***Village***, 3m/5km N of Livingston. **75 J3** NT0568.
Eccleston *Ches.* ***Village***, 3m/4km S of Chester. **48 D6** SJ4162.
Eccleston *Lancs.* Population: 5003. ***Small town***, 4m/7km W of Chorley. **48 E1** SD5217.
Eccleston *Mersey.* ***Suburb***, adjoining to W of St. Helens. **48 D3** SJ4895.
Eccup *W.Yorks.* ***Village***, 6m/9km N of Leeds. **57 H5** SE2842.
Eccup Reservoir *W.Yorks.* ***Reservoir***, large reservoir to SE of Eccup. **57 H5** SE2842.
Echnaloch Bay *Ork.* ***Bay***, on NW side of Burray. **107 D8** ND4697.
Echoing Mountain *P. & K. See Ben Lawers.*
Echt *Aber.* ***Village***, 12m/20km W of Aberdeen. **91 F4** NJ7305.
Eckford *Sc.Bord.* ***Village***, 5m/8km NE of Jedburgh. **70 C1** NT7026.
Eckington *Derbys.* Population: 7167. ***Village***, 5m/8km E of Dronfield. **51 G5** SK4379.
Eckington *Worcs.* ***Village***, in loop of River Avon, 3m/5km SW of Pershore. **29 J4** SO9241.
Ecton *Northants.* ***Village***, 5m/8km E of Northampton. **32 B2** SP8263.
Ecton *Staffs.* ***Settlement***, 1km E of Warslow. **50 C7** SK0958.
Edale *Derbys.* ***Village***, 5m/8km NE of Chapel-en-le-Frith, at S end of The Pennine Way, in part of River Noe valley known as Vale of Edale. **50 D4** SK1285.
Edale Moor *Derbys.* ***Open space***, moorland to SE of Kinder Scout, in High Peak area of The Pennines, 2m/3km NW of Edale. **50 D4** SK1087.
Eday *Ork.* ***Island***, 8m/12km long N to S and from 2m/4km to under 1km wide, lying between islands of Stronsay and Westray. Peat is plentiful, and is used as fuel on this and other islands in group. **106 E4** HY5634.
Eday Airfield *Ork.* ***Airport/airfield***, in centre of Eday, between Ferness Bay and Bay of London. **106 E4** HY5634.
Eday Sound *Ork.* ***Sea feature***, strait between islands of Eday and Sanday, to E of Eday. **106 E4** HY5834.
Edburton *W.Suss.* ***Hamlet***, below Edburton Hill, on South Downs, 3m/5km S of Henfield. **13 F5** TQ2311.
Edderside *Cumb.* ***Settlement***, 2m/3km NE of Allonby. **60 C2** NY1045.
Edderthorpe *S.Yorks.* ***Hamlet***, 1m/2km N of Darfield. SE4105.
Edderton *High.* ***Village***, on S side of Dornoch Firth, Ross and Cromarty district, 5m/8km W of Tain. **96 E3** NH7084.
Edderton Burn *High.* ***River***, flowing N from slopes of Cnoc an t-Sabhail into Dornoch Firth, 1km SE of Edderton. **96 E3** NH7181.
Eddington *Kent* ***Suburb***, to S of Herne Bay. TR1867.
Eddington *W.Berks.* ***Locality***, adjoining to N of Hungerford. **21 G5** SU3469.
Eddisbury Hill *Ches.* ***Hill***, rising to over 150 metres, 2m/3km NE of Kelsall. **48 E6** SJ5569.
Eddleston *Sc.Bord.* ***Village***, 4m/7km N of Peebles. **76 A6** NT2447.
Eddleston Water *Sc.Bord.* ***River***, stream running S through Eddleston village to River Tweed at Peebles. **76 A6** NT2447.
Eddlewood *S.Lan.* ***Suburb***, S district of Hamilton. **75 F5** NS7153.
Eddrachillis Bay *High.* ***Bay***, on W coast of Sutherland district, extending NE from Point of Stoer to Badcall. **102 D5** NC1336.
Eddystone Rocks *Plym.* ***Island***, rocks with lighthouse in English Channel, about 13m/21km S of Rame Head. SX3833.
Eden ***River***, rising N of Kinross and flowing E through Fife region to North Sea at St. Andrews Bay. **82 C7** NO4921.
Eden ***River***, rising on Black Fell Moss, 6m/10km S of Kirkby Stephen, and flowing SW to Aisgill then N by Kirkby Stephen, Appleby-in-Westmorland and Carlisle into Solway Firth, W of Bowness-on-Solway. From Burghmarsh Point it forms a wide estuary which joins that of River Esk, N of Bowness-on-Solway. **69 J7** NY1563.
Eden *Gwyn.* ***River***, rising S of Trawsfynydd and flowing S into River Mawddach 3m/5km N of Llanelltyd. SH7224.
Eden Camp *N.Yorks.* ***Other feature of interest***, 1m/2km NE of Malton. Former prisoner of war camp which recreates life in Britain during World War II. **58 D2** SE7973.
Eden Castle *Aber.* ***Castle***, ruins of 16c tower house on E side of River Deveron, 4m/6km S of Banff. **98 E5** NJ6958.
Eden Mount *Cumb.* ***Locality***, adjoining to N of Grange-over-Sands. SD4078.
Eden Mouth *Fife* ***Sea feature***, where River Eden enters North Sea between sandbanks at low water. **83 G5** NO5021.
Eden Park *Gt.Lon.* ***Suburb***, in borough of Bromley, 1m/2km S of Beckenham. **23 G5** TQ3768.
Eden Vale *Dur.* ***Settlement***, 1km S of Castle Eden. NZ4237.
Eden Water *Sc.Bord.* ***River***, rising in hills 4m/7km SE of Lauder, and flowing SE to join River Tweed, 3m/5km NE of Kelso. **76 E6** NT7637.
Edenbridge *Kent* Population: 7196. ***Small town***, 9m/15km W of Tonbridge. **23 H7** TQ4446.
Edendonich *Arg. & B.* ***Settlement***, in Strath of Orchy, 1km N of Dalmally. **80 C5** NN1627.
Edenfield *Lancs.* Population: 2657. ***Village***, 5m/9km N of Bury. **49 H1** SD7919.
Edenhall *Cumb.* ***Hamlet***, 4m/6km NE of Penrith. **61 G3** NY5632.
Edenham *Lincs.* ***Village***, 3m/4km NW of Bourne. **42 D3** TF0621.
Edenhope Hill *Shrop.* ***Mountain***, 4m/7km W of Bishop's Castle. Height 1391 feet or 424 metres. **38 B7** SO2588.
Edensor *Derbys.* ***Village***, estate village of Chatsworth House, 2m/4km E of Bakewell. **50 E6** SK2569.
Edentaggart *Arg. & B.* ***Settlement***, in Glen Luss, 2m/4km W of Luss. **74 B1** NS3293.
Edenthorpe *S.Yorks.* ***Suburb***, 4m/6km NE of Doncaster. **51 J2** SE6206.
Edentown *Cumb.* ***Suburb***, to N of Carlisle city centre, on N side of River Eden. NY3957.
Edern *Gwyn.* ***Village***, 1km SW of Morfa Nefyn. **36 B2** SH2739.
Edford *Som.* ***Settlement***, adjoining to S of Holcombe, 4m/6km S of Radstock. ST6749.
Edgarhope Wood *Sc.Bord.* ***Forest/woodland***, 2m/3km NW of Lauder. **76 D5** NT5450.
Edgarley *Som.* ***Hamlet***, on SE side of Glastonbury. **8 E1** ST5138.
Edgbaston *W.Mid.* ***Suburb***, 2m/3km SW of Birmingham city centre. Contains University of Birmingham. **40 C7** SP0584.
Edgcote *Northants.* ***Settlement***, 5m/8km NE of Banbury. SP5047.
Edgcott *Bucks.* ***Village***, 6m/10km E of Bicester. **31 H6** SP6722.
Edgcott *Som.* ***Hamlet***, on upper reach of River Exe, just N of Exford. SS8438.
Edgcumbe *Cornw.* ***Hamlet***, 3m/4km S of Stithians. **2 E5** SW7233.
Edge *Dur.* ***Locality***, adjoining to E of Woodland. NZ0726.
Edge *Glos.* ***Village***, 1m/2km W of Painswick. **20 B1** SO8409.
Edge *Shrop.* ***Hamlet***, 6m/10km SW of Shrewsbury. **38 C5** SJ3908.
Edge End *Glos.* ***Hamlet***, 2m/3km NE of Coleford. **28 E7** SO5913.
Edge End *Lancs.* ***Locality***, adjoining to W of Great Harwood. SD7232.
Edge Fold *Gt.Man.* ***Settlement***, 2m/3km SW of Bolton town centre. SD7006.
Edge Green *Ches.* ***Settlement***, 2m/4km N of Malpas. SJ4850.
Edge Green *Gt.Man.* ***Settlement***, 1m/2km E of Ashton-in-Makerfield. SJ5999.
Edge Green *Norf.* ***Settlement***, 1m/2km S of Kenninghall. TM0485.
Edge Hill *Mersey.* ***Suburb***, 2m/3km E of Liverpool city centre. SJ3689.
Edge Hill *Warks.* ***Hill***, marlstone escarpment of Cotswold Hills extension, rising to over 210 metres, 7m/11km NW of Banbury. Site of 1642 Civil War battle in plain 1m/2km NW. Quarries on E side of hill. **30 E4** SP3747.
Edgebolton *Shrop.* ***Hamlet***, 5m/8km SW of Hodnet. **38 E3** SJ5721.

Edgefield *Norf.* ***Village***, 3m/5km SE of Holt. **45 F2** TG0934.
Edgefield Green *Norf.* ***Village***, adjacent to Edgefield, 3m/5km SE of Holt. TG0934.
Edgehead *Midloth.* ***Hamlet***, 3m/5km SE of Dalkeith. NT3765.
Edgelaw Reservoir *Midloth.* ***Reservoir***, small reservoir 4m/6km SW of Gorebridge. **76 A5** NT3058.
Edgeley *Shrop.* ***Settlement***, 1m/2km SE of Whitchurch. **38 E1** SJ5540.
Edgerley *Shrop.* ***Locality***, 9m/15km NW of Shrewsbury. **38 C4** SJ3418.
Edgerton *W.Yorks.* ***Suburb***, 1m/2km NW of Huddersfield town centre. SE1217.
Edgeside *Lancs.* ***Locality***, 2m/3km W of Bacup. SD8322.
Edgeworth *Glos.* ***Village***, 5m/9km NW of Cirencester. **20 C1** SO9406.
Edginswell *Torbay* ***Locality***, at NW edge of Torbay, 2m/3km NW of Torquay town centre. **5 J4** SX8866.
Edgiock *Worcs.* ***Settlement***, 4m/6km NW of Alcester. SP0360.
Edgmond *Tel. & W.* Population: 1376. ***Village***, 2m/3km W of Newport. **39 G4** SJ7219.
Edgmond Marsh *Tel. & W.* ***Settlement***, 1m/2km NW of Edgmond. **39 G3** SJ7120.
Edgton *Shrop.* ***Village***, 4m/6km NW of Craven Arms. **38 C7** SO3885.
Edgware *Gt.Lon.* ***Suburb***, in borough of Barnet, 10m/16km NW of Charing Cross. Edgware Road between here and central London follows line of Roman 'Watling Street'. Roman settlement of Sulloniacae 1m/2km NW. **23 F2** TQ1992.
Edgware Bury *Gt.Lon.* ***Suburb***, in borough of Barnet, to N of Edgware. TQ1994.
Edgworth *B'burn.* Population: 1694. ***Village***, 5m/8km N of Bolton. **49 G1** SD7416.
Edial *Staffs.* ***Settlement***, 3m/4km W of Lichfield. **40 C5** SK0708.
Edinample *Stir.* ***Historic house***, old castellated house on S side of Loch Earn, 1m/2km SE of Lochearnhead across head of loch. **81 H5** NN6022.
Edinbain (Also spelled Edinbane.) *High.* ***Village***, at head of Loch Greshornish, on N coast of Skye. **93 J6** NG3450.
Edinbanchory *Aber.* ***Settlement***, 5m/8km S of Rhynie. **90 C3** NJ4819.
Edinbane *High.* *Alternative spelling of Edinbain, qv.*
Edinbarnet *W.Dun.* ***Settlement***, 3m/4km N of Clydebank. **74 D3** NS5074.
Edinburgh *Edin.* Population: 401,910. ***City***, historic city and capital of Scotland, built on a range of rocky crags and extinct volcanoes, on S side of Firth of Forth, 41m/66km E of Glasgow and 334m/537km NNW of London. Administrative, financial and legal centre of Scotland. Medieval castle (Historic Scotland) on rocky eminence overlooks central area and was one of main seats of Royal court since reign of King Malcolm Canmore in 11c, while Arthur's Seat (largest of the volcanoes) guards eastern approaches. Three universities. There is a Port at Leith where Royal Yacht Britannia now docked and open to public. Important industries include brewing, distilling, food and electronics. Edinburgh is second most popular tourist destination in UK. Palace of Holyroodhouse (Historic Scotland) is chief royal residence of Scotland. Numerous literary associations including Sir Arthur Conan Doyle who was born here. Many galleries and museums including National Gallery of Scotland. Annual arts festival attracts over a million visitors each year and is largest such event in the world. **76 A3** NT2573.
Edinburgh (Turnhouse) Airport *Edin.* ***Airport/airfield***, 6m/10km W of city centre. **75 K3** NT1573.
Edinburgh Castle *Edin.* ***Castle***, standing on basalt crag, dominating Edinburgh city centre. Originated in 11c as a wooden fortress, later becoming a palace, treasury, refuge and prison. Existing castle (Historic Scotland) was mainly built after 17c. Houses Scottish crown jewels and 15c gun, Mons Meg. **76 A3** NT2573.
Edinburgh Zoo *Edin.* ***Leisure/recreation***, in Corstorphine, 3m/5km W of Edinburgh city centre. Established in 1913 in parkland now extending over 80 acres and with more than 1000 animals. Attractions include Darwin Maze and world's largest penguin enclosure. **76 A3** NT2073.
Edinchip *Stir.* ***Settlement***, 1m/2km SW of Lochearnhead. **81 G5** NN5722.
Edingale *Staffs.* ***Village***, 5m/8km N of Tamworth. **40 E4** SK2112.
Edingley *Notts.* ***Village***, 3m/4km NW of Southwell. **51 J7** SK6655.
Edingthorpe *Norf.* ***Village***, 3m/5km NE of North Walsham. **45 H2** TG3232.
Edingthorpe Green *Norf.* ***Hamlet***, 2m/3km NE of North Walsham. TG3131.
Edingthorpe Street *Norf.* ***Hamlet***, to W of Edingthorpe. TG3232.
Edington *Som.* ***Village***, on N side of Polden Hills, 7m/11km W of Glastonbury. **8 C1** ST3839.
Edington *Wilts.* ***Village***, 4m/6km E of Westbury. **20 C6** ST9253.
Edington Bugle *Som.* ***Hamlet***, 2m/3km N of Edington across Edington Heath. ST3942.
Edington Priory *Wilts.* ***Ecclesiastical building***, magnificent cruciform priory church built in 14c, 1m/2km NE of Bratton. Demonstrates transition in style from Decorated to Perpendicular. **20 C6** ST9253.
Edin's Hall Broch *Sc.Bord.* ***Historic/prehistoric site***, 2m/3km SE of Abbey St. Bathans. Unusually large Iron Age broch, one of only ten known in lowland Scotland. **77 F4** NT7760.
Edintore *Moray* ***Settlement***, 3m/4km S of Keith. **98 C6** NJ4246.
Edinvale *Moray* ***Settlement***, 6m/10km E of Forres. **97 J6** NJ1153.
Edistone *Devon* ***Hamlet***, 2m/3km SW of Hartland. **6 A3** SS2421.
Edith Weston *Rut.* Population: 1810. ***Village***, on S side of Rutland Water, 5m/8km SE of Oakham. **42 C5** SK9205.
Edithmead *Som.* ***Hamlet***, 1m/2km E of Burnham-on-Sea. **19 G7** ST3249.
Edlaston *Derbys.* ***Hamlet***, 3m/4km S of Ashbourne. **40 D1** SK1842.
Edlesborough *Bucks.* ***Village***, 4m/6km SW of Dunstable. **32 C7** SP9719.
Edlingham *Northumb.* ***Village***, 5m/8km SW of Alnwick. Edlingham Castle (English Heritage). **71 G3** NU1109.
Edlington *Lincs.* ***Village***, 2m/3km NW of Horncastle. **53 F5** TF2371.
Edmondsham *Dorset* ***Village***, 1m/2km S of Cranborne. Manor house 16c-18c. **10 B3** SU0611.
Edmondsham House *Dorset* ***Garden***, in Edmondsham, 9m/14km N of Ringwood, and includes organic and dower house gardens, with a separate 6-acre garden. **10 B3** SU0612.
Edmondsley *Dur.* ***Village***, 5m/8km NW of Durham. **62 D2** NZ2349.
Edmondstown *R.C.T.* ***Settlement***, 1m/2km N of Tonyrefail. ST0090.
Edmondthorpe *Leics.* ***Village***, 6m/9km N of Oakham. **42 B4** SK8517.
Edmonstone *Ork.* ***Settlement***, on NE peninsula of Shapinsay. **106 E5** HY5220.
Edmonton *Cornw.* ***Hamlet***, 2m/3km NW of Wadebridge. SW9672.
Edmonton *Gt.Lon.* ***Suburb***, in borough of Enfield, 9m/14km N of Charing Cross. **23 G2** TQ3493.
Edmund Hill *Som.* ***Suburb***, on N side of Glastonbury. ST5039.
Edmundbyers *Dur.* ***Village***, 5m/8km W of Consett. **62 B1** NZ0150.
Ednam *Sc.Bord.* ***Village***, 2m/3km N of Kelso. **77 F7** NT7337.
Ednaston *Derbys.* ***Hamlet***, 8m/13km NW of Derby. **40 E1** SK2341.
Edney Common *Essex* ***Hamlet***, 3m/5km N of Ingatestone. **24 C1** TL6504.
Ednol *Powys* ***Locality***, 3m/4km SE of Bleddfa. SO2364.
Edra *Stir.* ***Settlement***, on N shore of Loch Katrine, 8m/12km NW of Aberfoyle. **81 F6** NN4610.
Edradour *P. & K.* ***Locality***, 1m/2km E of Pitlochry. Edradour Distillery, smallest in Scotland. NN9558.
Edradynate *P. & K.* ***Settlement***, in upper part of Tay valley, 5m/8km SW of Pitlochry. **81 K2** NN8852.
Edrom *Sc.Bord.* ***Village***, 3m/5km E of Duns. **77 G5** NT8255.
Edrom Norman Arch *Sc.Bord.* ***Historic/prehistoric site***, good example of Norman chancel arch from church built c. 1105, 3m/4km W of Chirnside. **77 G5** NT8255.
Edstaston *Shrop.* ***Hamlet***, 2m/3km N of Wem. **38 E2** SJ5131.
Edstone *Warks.* ***Settlement***, 3m/5km SE of Henley-in-Arden. **30 C2** SP1762.
Edvin Loach *Here.* ***Settlement***, 2m/4km N of Bromyard. Remains of 11c church (English Heritage). **29 F3** SO6658.
Edwalton *Notts.* ***Locality***, adjoining to SE of West Bridgford. **41 H2** SK5935.
Edwardstone *Suff.* ***Settlement***, 4m/7km E of Sudbury. **34 D4** TL9442.
Edwardsville *M.Tyd.* ***Village***, 4m/7km N of Pontypridd. ST0896.
Edwinsford *Carmar.* ***Settlement***, 1m/2km N of Talley. **17 K1** SN6334.
Edwinstowe *Notts.* Population: 4789. ***Village***, 2m/3km W of Ollerton. **51 J6** SK6266.
Edworth *Beds.* ***Village***, 3m/5km SE of Biggleswade. **33 F4** TL2240.
Edwyn Ralph *Here.* ***Village***, 2m/3km N of Bromyard. **29 F3** SO6457.
Edzell *Angus* ***Village***, on River North Esk, 6m/9km N of Brechin. Remains of castle with 16c tower (Historic Scotland), 1m/2km W. **83 G1** NO6068.
Edzell Castle *Angus* ***Castle***, early 16c tower house (Historic Scotland), with 17c alterations and additions by Sir David Lindsay, 1m/2km W of Edzell and 6m/10km N of Brechin. Vandalised after second Jacobite uprising. Includes Lindsay's formal decorated garden, or Pleasaunce. **83 G1** NO5869.
Eel Pie Island *Gt.Lon.* ***Island***, inhabited island on River Thames in borough of Richmond upon Thames. Foot bridge connects island with Twickenham on W bank. TQ1673.
Eela Water *Shet.* ***Lake/loch***, small but deep loch on Mainland 2m/4km SW of Ollaberry. **108 C5** HU3378.
Efail-fâch *N.P.T.* ***Village***, 2m/4km SE of Neath. SS7895.
Efail Isaf *R.C.T.* ***Village***, 4m/6km S of Pontypridd. **18 D3** ST0884.
Efailnewydd *Gwyn.* ***Village***, 2m/3km W of Pwllheli. **36 C2** SH3535.
Efailwen *Carmar.* ***Hamlet***, 2m/4km NW of Login. **16 E2** SN1325.
Efenechtyd *Denb.* ***Hamlet***, 2m/3km S of Ruthin. **47 K7** SJ1155.
Effingham *Surr.* ***Village***, 4m/6km SW of Leatherhead. **22 E6** TQ1153.
Effirth *Shet.* ***Settlement***, on Mainland, near head of small inlet of Effirth Voe, W of Bixter. **109 C7** HU3152.
Efflinch *Staffs.* ***Hamlet***, 1km S of Barton-under-Needwood. SK1917.
Efford *Devon* ***Settlement***, 6m/9km NW of Exeter. **7 G5** SS8801.
Efford *Plym.* ***Suburb***, 2m/4km NE of Plymouth city centre. SX5056.
Egbury *Hants.* ***Settlement***, 3m/5km NW of Whitchurch. **21 H6** SU4352.
Egdean *W.Suss.* ***Settlement***, 2m/3km SE of Petworth. **12 C4** SU9920.
Egdon *Worcs.* ***Settlement***, 5m/8km SE of Worcester. SO9151.
Egel *N.P.T.* ***River***, rising W of Pen Rhiwfawr and flowing S into Upper Clydach River at Rhyd-y-fro. **18 A1** SN7105.
Egerton *Gt.Man.* ***Village***, 4m/6km N of Bolton. **49 G1** SD7014.
Egerton *Kent* ***Village***, 3m/5km W of Charing. **14 E3** TQ9047.
Egerton Forstal *Kent* ***Hamlet***, 4m/7km SW of Charing. **14 D3** TQ8946.
Egerton Green *Ches.* ***Settlement***, 1m/2km NW of Cholmondeley Castle. **48 E7** SJ5252.
Egerton Park *Mersey.* ***Suburb***, 2m/3km S of Birkenhead town centre. SJ3286.
Egg Buckland *Plym.* ***Suburb***, 3m/4km NE of Plymouth city centre. **5 F5** SX5057.
Eggardon Hill *Dorset* ***Hill***, rising to over 240 metres, 4m/6km SW of Maiden Newton. Crowned by Roman camp. **8 E5** SY5494.
Eggerness *D. & G.* ***Settlement***, 1m/2km NE of Garlieston, on W side of Wigtown Bay. **64 E6** NX4947.
Eggesford Barton *Devon* ***Hamlet***, 2m/3km S of Chulmleigh across River Taw. Settlement of Eggesford Fourways 1km SW. **6 E4** SS6811.
Eggington *Beds.* ***Village***, 2m/4km E of Leighton Buzzard. **32 C6** SP9525.
Egginton *Derbys.* ***Village***, 4m/6km NE of Burton upon Trent. **40 E3** SK2628.
Egglescliffe *Stock.* ***Suburb***, 4m/6km S of Stockton-on-Tees. **63 F5** NZ4113.
Eggleston *Dur.* ***Village***, 4m/6km E of Middleton-in-Teesdale. Eggleston Hall Gardens include walled gardens and rare plants and shrubs. **62 B4** NY9923.
Eggleston Common *Dur.* ***Open space***, moorland to SW of Hamsterley Forest. **62 B4** NZ0027.
Egglestone Abbey *Dur.* ***Ecclesiastical building***, ruined 12c abbey (English Heritage) on SW bank of River Tees, 1m/2km SE of Barnard Castle. **62 B5** NZ0615.
Egham *Surr.* Population: 23,816. ***Town***, mainly residential town, 2m/3km W of Staines. Church has fine monument to Sir John Denham. **22 D4** TQ0171.
Egham Wick *Surr.* ***Settlement***, in Windsor Great Park, 2m/3km W of Egham. SU9870.
Egilsay *Ork.* ***Island***, sparsely populated island off E coast of Rousay, 3m/5km long N to S, 2km wide near N end, tapering to a point at S end. Remains of St. Magnus Church. **106 D5** HY4730.
Egilsay *Shet.* ***Island***, uninhabited island of 54 acres or 22 hectares off W coast of Mainland at entrance to Mangaster Voe. HU3169.
Egleton *Rut.* ***Village***, 1m/2km SE of Oakham. **42 B5** SK8707.
Eglingham *Northumb.* ***Village***, 6m/10km NW of Alnwick. **71 G2** NU1019.
Eglinton *N.Ayr.* ***Suburb***, 2m/3km SE of Kilwinning, in N part of Irvine. NS3141.
Eglinton Castle *N.Ayr.* ***Castle***, remains of late 18c castle set in loop of River Lugton, 2m/3km SE of Kilwinning. Eglinton Park includes formal gardens, rock gardens and large rhododendrons. **74 B6** NS3242.
Egloshayle *Cornw.* ***Village***, on River Camel, 1km E of Wadebridge across river. **4 A3** SX0072.
Egloskerry *Cornw.* ***Village***, 4m/6km NW of Launceston. **4 C2** SX2786.
Eglwys-Brewis *V. of Glam.* ***Hamlet***, 3m/4km E of Llantwit Major. **18 D5** ST0069.
Eglwys Cross *Wrex.* ***Hamlet***, 4m/7km W of Whitchurch. **38 D1** SJ4741.
Eglwys Fach *Cere.* ***Hamlet***, 5m/8km SW of Machynlleth. **37 F6** SN6895.
Eglwys Fair y Mynydd *V. of Glam.* *Welsh form of St. Mary Hill, qv.*
Eglwys Nunydd *N.P.T.* ***Settlement***, 4m/7km SE of Port Talbot. Reservoir to W. SS8084.
Eglwys Nunydd Reservoir *N.P.T.* ***Reservoir***, 5m/8km SE of Port Talbot. Nature Reserve. **18 A3** SS7984.
Eglwys Wen *Pembs.* *Welsh form of Whitechurch, qv.*
Eglwys Wythwr *Pembs.* *Welsh form of Monington, qv.*
Eglwys y Drindod *Newport* *Welsh form of Christchurch, qv.*
Eglwysbach *Conwy* ***Village***, 6m/9km N of Llanrwst. **47 G5** SH8070.
Eglwyseg Mountain *Wrex.* ***Mountain***, 4m/7km W of Rhosllanerchrugog. Height 1676 feet or 511 metres. **38 B1** SJ2246.
Eglwyswrw *Pembs.* ***Village***, 5m/8km SW of Cardigan. Remains of motte and bailey castle. **16 E1** SN1438.
Egmanton *Notts.* ***Village***, 1m/2km S of Tuxford. **51 K6** SK7368.
Egmere *Norf.* ***Settlement***, at crossroads 2m/3km W of Little Walsingham. **44 D2** TF9037.
Egremont *Cumb.* Population: 6581. ***Small town***, industrial town, 5m/8km SE of Whitehaven. Norman castle on River Ehen. **60 B5** NY0110.
Egremont *Mersey.* ***Suburb***, to N of Wallasey town centre, beside River Mersey estuary. SJ3192.
Egton *N.Yorks.* ***Village***, 6m/10km SW of Whitby. **63 K6** NZ8006.
Egton Bridge *N.Yorks.* ***Village***, on River Esk, 1km SW of Egton. **63 K6** NZ8006.
Egton High Moor *N.Yorks.* ***Open space***, large area of moorland in North York Moors, 4m/6km NE of Rosedale Abbey. **63 J6** NZ7501.
Egton Low Moor *N.Yorks.* ***Open space***, moorland S of A171 road, 4m/7km W of Whitby. **63 K6** NZ8208.
Egypt *Glas.* ***Suburb***, 3m/5km SE of Glasgow city centre, in Tollcross district. NS6463.
Egypt *Hants.* ***Hamlet***, 5m/8km S of Whitchurch. **21 H7** SU4640.

Ehen *Cumb.* ***River***, rising as River Liza in Cumbrian Mountains on N slopes of Kirk Fell and flowing W into Ennerdale Water, from where it emerges as River Ehen and flows by Ennerdale Bridge and Egremont into Irish Sea with River Calder NW of Seascale. See also (River) Liza. **60 B5** NY0202.

Eidart *High.* ***River***, flowing generally S through Glenfeshie Forest into River Feshie, 9m/13km SW of Beinn MacDuibh. **89 G5** NN9192.

Eididh nan Clach Geala *High.* ***Mountain***, in Ross and Cromarty district 2m/3km N of Beinn Dearg. Munro: height 3044 feet or 928 metres. **95 J3** NH2584.

Eigg *High.* ***Island***, in Inner Hebrides of about 9 square miles or 23 square km lying 4m/7km SE of Rum across Sound of Rum. Rises to 1291 feet or 393 metres (An Sgurr or Scuir of Eigg). Sound of Eigg is sea passage between Eigg and Muck. **85 K6** NM4687.

E

Eight and Forty *E.Riding* ***Locality***, 1m/2km E of Gilberdyke. SE8429.

Eight Ash Green *Essex* ***Village***, 3m/5km W of Colchester. **34 D6** TL9425.

1853 Gallery *W.Yorks.* ***Other feature of interest***, in salt mill at Saltaire. Mid-19c factory, largest in world at the time, now has gallery housing largest collection of David Hockney's work. **57 G6** SE1337.

Eighton Banks *T. & W.* ***Village***, 3m/5km SE of Gateshead. NZ2758.

Eignaig *High.* ***Settlement***, on NW shore of Loch Linnhe, 4m/7km NE of Rubha an Ridire. **79 J3** NM7943.

Eigneig Bheag *W.Isles* ***Coastal feature***, headland on E coast of North Uist, 2m/3km E of Eaval. **92 E6** NF9260.

Eigneig Mhòr *W.Isles* ***Coastal feature***, headland on E coast of North Uist, 1km N of Eigneig Bheag. **92 E5** NF9361.

Eil *High.* ***Settlement***, in River Dulnain valley, 5m/8km NW of Aviemore. **89 F3** NH8217.

Eilanreach *High.* ***Settlement***, on coast of Skye and Lochalsh district, 1km S of Glenelg. **86 E3** NG8017.

Eildon *Sc.Bord.* ***Village***, on E side of Eildon Hills, 2m/3km S of Melrose. NT5732.

Eildon Hills *Sc.Bord.* ***Mountain***, with three conspicuous peaks on S side of Melrose. Middle peak rises to 1384 feet or 422 metres; N peak, 1325 feet or 404 metres, shows traces of prehistoric settlement; S peak rises to 1217 feet or 371 metres. **76 D7** NT5432.

Eileach an Naoimh *Arg. & B.* ***Island***, narrow uninhabited island, 1m/2km long NE to SW, at SW end of Garvellachs group between Jura and Mull. Remains of Celtic monastery (Historic Scotland). Lighthouse at SW end. **79 H7** NM6409.

Eileach an Naoimh Monastery *Arg. & B.* ***Ecclesiastical building***, ruin of monastery (Historic Scotland) on Eileach an Naoimh, most southwesterly of Garvellachs group in Firth of Lorn. **79 H7** NM6409.

Eileach Chonail *Arg. & B. Alternative name for Dùn Chonnuill, qv.*

Eilean a' Bhreitheimh *High.* ***Island***, small island in Eddrachillis Bay, Sutherland district. **102 D5** NC1240.

Eilean a' Chalmain *Arg. & B.* ***Island***, small island off SW end of Mull, nearly 1m/2km S of Erraid. **78 D6** NM3017.

Eilean a' Chaoil *High.* ***Island***, islet at entrance to Tongue Bay, 1km E of Midfield, Caithness district. NC5965.

Eilean a' Chaolais *High.* ***Island***, islet off S side of Rubha Chaolais, 4m/7km SE of Arisaig across entrance to Loch nan Uamh. NM6980.

Eilean a' Chàr *High.* ***Island***, small island in Summer Isles group. Lies 1m/2km W of Tanera Mòr and nearly 4m/6km W of Achiltibuie on NW coast of Ross and Cromarty district. NB9608.

Eilean a' Chléirich *High. Alternative name for Priest Island, qv.*

Eilean a' Chonnaidh (Anglicised form: Coney Island.) *High.* ***Island***, small uninhabited island off W coast of Sutherland district, 1m/2km NW of Kinlochbervie. NC2057.

Eilean a' Chuirn *Arg. & B.* ***Island***, off SE coast of Islay, 1m/2km S of Ardmore Point. **72 C6** NR4749.

Eilean a' Ghobha *W.Isles* ***Island***, one of Flannan Isles group, lying 2m/3km W of main island, Eilean Mòr. NA6946.

Eilean a' Mhuineil *High.* ***Island***, islet in Loch Hourn at E end of Poll a' Mhuineil. NG8406.

Eilean a' Phidhir *High.* ***Island***, wooded island in Loch Morar, Lochaber district, 1m/2km E of dam. **86 D5** NH7092.

Eilean a' Phiobaire *High.* ***Island***, islet in Lochaber district off SW shore of Loch Hourn, 1m/2km SW of Corran across loch. NG8308.

Eilean an Eireannaich *High.* ***Island***, small uninhabited island at junction of Loch Laxford and Loch a' Chadh-Fi near W coast of Sutherland district. NC2050.

Eilean an Fhraoich *High.* ***Island***, islet in Kyle Rona, between Raasay and Rona. NG6153.

Eilean an Ròin Beag *High.* ***Island***, one of two uninhabited islands off W coast of Sutherland district, 3m/5km NW of Kinlochbervie. NC1758.

Eilean an Ròin Mòr *High.* ***Island***, one of two uninhabited islands off W coast of Sutherland district, 3m/5km NW of Kinlochbervie. **102 D3** NC1758.

Eilean an Rubha *Arg. & B.* ***Island***, forming E boundary of Lussa Bay on E coast of Jura. **72 E2** NR6486.

Eilean an Tighe *W.Isles* ***Island***, islet at head of East Loch Roag, W coast of Isle of Lewis. NB2230.

Eilean an Tighe *W.Isles* ***Island***, one of Shiant Islands group to S of Garbh Eilean, to which it is joined by an isthmus. **93 K2** NG4296.

Eilean Annraidh *Arg. & B.* ***Island***, islet off NE point of Iona. NM2926.

Eilean Ard *High.* ***Island***, small uninhabited island in Loch Laxford, on W coast of Sutherland district. NC1850.

Eilean Arsa *Arg. & B.* ***Island***, small island between Shuna and mainland of Argyll. **79 J7** NM7807.

Eilean Balnagowan *High.* ***Island***, nearly 1m/2km off E shore of Loch Linnhe at foot of Salachan Glen. **80 A2** NM9653.

Eilean Bàn *High.* ***Island***, wooded islet in Loch Morar, Lochaber district, 1km E of dam at W end of loch. NM6992.

Eilean Barraigh *W.Isles Gaelic form of Barra, qv.*

Eilean Beag *High.* ***Island***, smallest of Crowlin Islands group, 2m/3km off W coast of Ross and Cromarty district on N side of entrance to Loch Carron. Lighthouse. NG6835.

Eilean Beag a' Bhàigh *W.Isles See Eilean Mòr a' Bhàigh.*

Eilean Bhearnaraigh *W.Isles Gaelic form of Berneray, qv.*

Eilean Bhride *Arg. & B.* ***Island***, rocky islet off SE coast of Islay, 3m/4km NE of Ardbeg. **72 C6** NR4547.

Eilean Bhride *Arg. & B.* ***Island***, most northerly of Small Isles group off E coast of Jura. **72 D4** NR5569.

Eilean Chalaibrigh *W.Isles Gaelic form of Calabrie Island, qv.*

Eilean Chalbha *Arg. & B.* ***Island***, islet off N coast of Iona, 1m/2km W of Eilean Annraidh. **78 D5** NM2826.

Eilean Chaluim Chille *W.Isles* ***Island***, small uninhabited island at entrance to Loch Erisort, E coast of Isle of Lewis. Ruins of St. Columb's Church at S end. **101 F5** NB3821.

Eilean Chasgaidh *High. Alternative name for Eilean Chathastail, qv.*

Eilean Chathastail (Also known as Eilean Chasgaidh.) *High.* ***Island***, small uninhabited island off Galmisdale at SE end of Eigg, with lighthouse on E coast. NM4883.

Eilean Cheois *W.Isles Gaelic form of Keose Island, qv.*

Eilean Choraidh (Anglicised form: Chorrie Island.) *High.* ***Island***, nearly 1m/2km in length in Loch Eriboll, in Sutherland district, 2m/4km from head of loch. **103 G3** NC4258.

Eilean Chrona (Anglicised form: Chrona Island.) *High.* ***Island***, small uninhabited island 1m/2km W of Oldany Island, off W coast of Sutherland district. **102 C5** NC0633.

Eilean Clùimhrig *High.* ***Island***, islet at mouth of Loch Eriboll, N coast of Sutherland district, 1m/2km SE of Eilean Hoan. **103 G2** NC4665.

Eilean Coltair *Arg. & B.* ***Island***, islet near N shore of Loch Melfort, 3m/5km W of Kilmelford in Argyll. NM8012.

Eilean Craobhach *Arg. & B.* ***Island***, off SE coast of Islay, 1m/2km S of Ardmore Point. NR4649.

Eilean Creagach *Arg. & B.* ***Island***, small island between Shuna and mainland. NM7809.

Eilean Creagach *High.* ***Island***, one of Ascrib Islands group in Loch Snizort, 4m/6km E of Vaternish Point, Skye. NG2965.

Eilean Darach *High.* ***Settlement***, in Strath Beag, 1km E of Dundonnell. **95 H3** NH1088.

Eilean Dearg *Arg. & B.* ***Island***, islet in Loch Riddon, Argyll, with ruins of 17c fort. NS0077.

Eilean Dearg *High.* ***Island***, one of the group of islets off shore of Knoydart, Lochaber district, off W end of Sandaig Bay. NG7000.

Eilean Dioghlum *Arg. & B.* ***Island***, islet on S side of entrance to Loch Tuath, Mull, off NW coast of Gometra. **78 E3** NM3542.

Eilean Dìomhain *Arg. & B.* ***Island***, one of Small Isles group off E coast of Jura. NR5468.

Eilean Donan *High.* ***Island***, rocky islet at entrance to Loch Duich, S of Dornie, Skye and Lochalsh district, with restored castle of the Macraes. NG8825.

Eilean Donan Castle *High.* ***Castle***, former Jacobite stronghold of the Macraes on Eilean Donan at entrance to Loch Duich. Destroyed in 1719 and restored in 19c; now contains Jacobite relics. **86 E2** NG8825.

Eilean Dubh *Arg. & B.* ***Coastal feature***, rock at N point of Staffa. **78 E4** NM3236.

Eilean Dubh *Arg. & B.* ***Island***, small island off SW end of Mull between Eilean a' Chalmain and Erraid. Another small island of same name lies off W coast of Erraid. **78 D6** NM3018.

Eilean Dubh *Arg. & B.* ***Island***, islet off N point of Colonsay. **79 F7** NM4201.

Eilean Dubh *Arg. & B.* ***Island***, small island in Loch Craignish, 1m/2km E of Craignish Castle. NM7902.

Eilean Dubh *Arg. & B.* ***Island***, islet off S coast of Lismore, 2m/3km S of Achnacroish. Joined by causeway to Eilean na Cloiche. Other islets in same group are Eilean nan Gamhna, Creag Island and Pladda Island. **79 K4** NM8338.

Eilean Dubh *Arg. & B.* ***Island***, small island in Loch Linnhe between Lismore and mainland to E. **79 K3** NM8742.

Eilean Dubh *Arg. & B.* ***Island***, on SE side of Sound of Jura, 1m/2km E of Tayvallich. **73 F2** NR7187.

Eilean Dubh *Arg. & B.* ***Island***, small island on W side of entrance to Loch Riddon, Argyll. NS0075.

Eilean Dubh *High.* ***Island***, one of Summer Isles group. Lies 2m/3km S of Tanera Mòr. Area about 200 acres or 80 hectares. **95 F1** NB9703.

Eilean Dubh *High.* ***Island***, islet near S shore of Loch Eishort, Skye, 3m/5km NE of Tarskavaig. NG6114.

Eilean Dubh a' Bhàigh *W.Isles See Eilean Mòr a' Bhàigh.*

Eilean Dubh Mòr *Arg. & B.* ***Island***, uninhabited island of about 150 acres or 60 hectares, lying 2m/3km W of Luing. Smaller island, Eilean Dubh Beag, lies across narrow channel to N. **79 H6** NM6910.

Eilean Dùin *Arg. & B.* ***Island***, small island off coast of Argyll, 3m/4km W of Kilninver. **79 J5** NM7821.

Eilean Fada Mòr *High.* ***Island***, one of Summer Isles group, between Tanera Mòr and Tanera Beg. Area about 150 acres or 60 hectares. NB9707.

Eilean Fhianain *High.* ***Island***, islet in the narrows of Loch Shiel in Lochaber district. Ruined chapel of St. Finnan. NM7568.

Eilean Fladday (Also known as Fladday.) *High.* ***Island***, uninhabited island of about 360 acres or 145 hectares lying off W coast of Raasay midway between Manish Point and Eilean Tigh, and separated from Raasay by narrow channel of Caol Fladda. **94 B6** NG5851.

Eilean Flodaigh (Anglicised form: Flodda.) *W.Isles* ***Island***, small low-lying island off N coast of Benbecula 4m/6km E of Benbecula (Baile a' Mhanaich) Aerodrome. **92 D6** NF8455.

Eilean Flodigarry *High.* ***Island***, small uninhabited island 1km off NE coast of Skye, 2m/3km N of Staffin. **93 K4** NG4871.

Eilean Fraoch *Arg. & B.* ***Island***, islet in Loch Awe opposite entrance to arm of loch running NW to Pass of Brander in Argyll. Ruined castle of the Macnaughtons. NN1025.

Eilean Furadh Mòr (Also known as Foura.) *High.* ***Island***, islet off W coast of Ross and Cromarty district 4m/6km E of Rubha Réidh. **94 D2** NG7993.

Eilean Gaineamhach Boreraig *High.* ***Island***, islet off Skye in Loch Eishort, opposite Boreraig and 2m/4km E of Rubha Suisnish. NG6215.

Eilean Gamhna *Arg. & B.* ***Island***, islet at entrance to Loch Melfort, Argyll. **79 J6** NM7810.

Eilean Garave (Also known as Eilean Geary.) *High.* ***Island***, one of Ascrib Islands group in Loch Snizort, 4m/7km E of Vaternish Point, Skye. NG2964.

Eilean Garbh *Arg. & B.* ***Island***, islet in Loch Tuath between Ulva and mainland of Mull. NM4440.

Eilean Garbh *High.* ***Island***, small uninhabited island off W coast of Rona. NG6056.

Eilean Geary *High. Alternative name for Eilean Garave, qv.*

Eilean Ghaoideamal *Arg. & B.* ***Island***, islet off SE coast of Oronsay across Caolas Mòr. **72 B2** NR3787.

Eilean Ghòmain *Arg. & B.* ***Island***, islet off NW end of Erraid at S end of Sound of Iona. NM2820.

Eilean Glas *W.Isles* ***Island***, islet at entrance to Loch Erisort, E coast of Isle of Lewis. NB3922.

Eilean Heast *High.* ***Island***, small uninhabited island near N shore of Loch Eishort 1km S of locality of Heast. **86 C3** NG6416.

Eilean Hoan *High.* ***Island***, small uninhabited island with rocky coast on W side of entrance to Loch Eriboll, N coast of Sutherland district. Island lies 2m/4km E of Durness and 1km from coast of mainland. **103 G2** NC4467.

Eilean Horrisdale *High.* ***Island***, small island in Gair Loch, W coast of Ross and Cromarty district, opposite Badachro. **94 D4** NG7874.

Eilean Iarmain (Also known as Isleornsay or Isle Ornsay.) *High.* ***Village***, on E coast of Sleat peninsula, Skye, 7m/11km SE of Broadford. Harbour formed by coast of Sleat and W coast of Isle Ornsay. **86 C3** NG7012.

Eilean Ighe *High.* ***Island***, small uninhabited island off coast of Lochaber district, 2m/3km W of Arisaig. **86 C6** NM6388.

Eilean Imersay *Arg. & B.* ***Island***, off S coast of Islay, 1km E of Ardbeg across Loch an t-Sàilein inlet. NR4246.

Eilean Iosal *High.* ***Island***, small uninhabited island off W coast of Eilean nan Ròn, off N coast of Caithness district. NC6365.

Eilean Iosal *High.* ***Island***, one of Ascrib Islands group in Loch Snizort, 4m/6km E of Vaternish Point, Skye. NG2865.

Eilean Iubhard *W.Isles* ***Island***, uninhabited island at mouth of Loch Shell, E coast of Isle of Lewis. **101 F6** NB3809.

Eilean Kearstay *W.Isles* ***Island***, small uninhabited island off W coast of Isle of Lewis opposite Callanish. **100 E4** NB1933.

Eilean Leodhais *W.Isles Gaelic form of Isle of Lewis, qv.*

Eilean Loain *Arg. & B.* ***Island***, near E shore of Loch Sween in Knapdale, Argyll, 1m/2km SE of Tayvallich across loch. **73 F2** NR7585.

Eilean Loch Oscair *Arg. & B.* ***Island***, small uninhabited island off NW coast of Lismore, 2m/3km W of Port Ramsay. **79 K3** NM8645.

Eilean Meadhonach *High.* ***Island***, second largest of Crowlin Islands group, in Inner Sound between Skye and Applecross peninsula, to W of Eilean Mòr. **86 C1** NG6834.

Eilean Mhic Chrion *Arg. & B.* ***Island***, narrow island 1m/2km long NE to SW, near W shore of Loch Craignish in Argyll, 1m/2km from head of loch. **79 K7** NM8003.

Eilean Mhic Coinnich *Arg. & B.* ***Island***, off S end of Rinns of Islay, 1km S of Rubha na Faing. NR1652.

Eilean Mhucaig *Arg. & B.* ***Island***, rocky islet to N of Oronsay. **72 B2** NR3589.

Eilean Mhuire *W.Isles* ***Island***, one of Shiant Islands group, 1km E of Garbh Eilean. **93 K2** NG4398.

Eilean Mòineseach *High.* ***Island***, islet in Enard Bay between Eilean Mòr and NW coast of Ross and Cromarty district. NC0617.

Eilean Molach *Stir. Gaelic form of Ellen's Isle, qv.*

Eilean Molach *W.Isles* ***Island***, islet off Aird Mhòr Mangurstadh, headland on W coast of Isle of Lewis 4m/6km W of Timsgearraidh. NA9932.

Eilean Mòr *Arg. & B.* ***Island***, small island, but largest of a group, lying 1km off NE end of Coll. **78 D1** NM2764.

Eilean Mòr *Arg. & B.* ***Island***, small island off S shore of Ross of Mull, 1m/2km W of Rubh' Ardalanish. **78 E6** NM3416.

Eilean Mòr *Arg. & B.* ***Island***, islet opposite Dunstaffnage Bay, 2m/3km W of Connel, Argyll. **79 K4** NM8834.

Eilean Mòr *Arg. & B.* ***Island***, off NW coast of Islay, 10m/15km NW of Bridgend. **72 A4** NR2169.

Eilean Mòr *Arg. & B.* ***Island***, in Sound of Jura lying 2m/3km SE of Danna Island, in Argyll. Remains of St. Cormac's Chapel (Historic Scotland), medieval chapel with upper chamber. **72 E3** NR6675.

Eilean Mòr *Arg. & B.* ***Island***, in Loch Fyne, 3m/5km SE of Lochgilphead, Argyll. **73 G2** NR8883.

Eilean Mòr *High.* ***Island***, small uninhabited island in Enard Bay 1km off NW coast of Ross and Cromarty district. **102 C7** NC0517.

Eilean Mòr *High.* ***Island***, in Inner Sound, between Skye and Applecross peninsula. Largest of Crowlin Islands group and nearest to Scottish mainland. **86 D1** NG6934.

Eilean Mòr *High.* ***Island***, small island opposite Oronsay in Loch Sunart, off S coast of Ardnamurchan peninsula. **79 G1** NM5861.

Eilean Mòr *High.* ***Island***, in Loch Sunart, 5m/8km SE of Salen. **79 J1** NM7560.

Eilean Mòr *W.Isles* ***Island***, largest of Flannan Isles, having an area of some 30 acres or 12 hectares. Lighthouse to N, and to S of this are ruins of small chapel dedicated to St. Flannan. NA7246.

Eilean Mòr a' Bhàigh *W.Isles* ***Island***, small uninhabited island off S coast of Isle of Lewis 1m/2km SE of entrance to Loch Seaforth. Islets of Eilean Dubh a' Bhàigh and Eilean Beag a' Bhàigh lie between island and coast of Isle of Lewis to N. **100 E7** NB2600.

Eilean Mòr Bayble *W.Isles Anglicised form of Eilean Mòr Phabail, qv.*

Eilean Mòr Chapel *Arg. & B.* ***Ecclesiastical building***, chapel and parts of two crosses on Eilean Mòr in Sound of Jura, off NW coast of Kintyre peninsula. **72 E3** NR6675.

Eilean Mòr Laxay *W.Isles* ***Island***, small uninhabited island near N shore of Loch Erisort, Isle of Lewis, S of Lacasaigh. NB3320.

Eilean Mòr Phabail (Anglicised form: Eilean Mòr Bayble.) *W.Isles* ***Island***, islet off Bagh Phabail Iarach, E coast of Eye Peninsula, Isle of Lewis. NB5330.

Eilean Mullagrach *High.* ***Island***, one of Summer Isles group, nearly 2m/3km off NW coast of Ross and Cromarty district near Alltan Dubh. Area about 180 acres or 75 hectares. **102 B7** NB9511.

Eilean Musdile *Arg. & B.* ***Island***, with lighthouse off SW end of Lismore, 2m/3km E of Duart Point on Mull. **79 J4** NM7735.

Eilean na Bà *High.* ***Island***, small uninhabited island off W coast of Ross and Cromarty district, 4m/7km S of Applecross. NG6938.

Eilean na Cloiche *Arg. & B.* ***Island***, islet off S coast of Lismore, 2m/3km SW of Achnacroish. Joined by causeway to Eilean Dubh to S. Other islets in same group are Eilean nan Gamhna, Creag Island and Pladda Island. NM8338.

Eilean na Gàmhna *High.* ***Island***, one of group of islets off shore of Knoydart, Lochaber district, off W end of Sandaig Bay. NG7001.

Eilean na h-Airde *High.* ***Island***, islet off S coast of Skye opposite Rubha na h-Easgainne and 2m/3km S of Elgol. NG5211.

Eilean na h-Aiteig *High.* ***Island***, islet off W coast of Sutherland district 2m/4km NW of Kinlochbervie. NC1958.

Eilean na h-Aon Chaorach *Arg. & B.* ***Island***, islet 1km off S coast of Iona. NM2520.

Eilean na Saille *High.* ***Island***, islet off W coast of Sutherland district 5m/8km W of Rhiconich. NC1753.

Eilean nam Ban *Arg. & B.* ***Island***, small island in Sound of Iona 1km N of Fionnphort. Separated from Ross of Mull by strait of Bull Hole. NM3024.

Eilean nam Breac *High.* ***Island***, wooded islet in Loch Morar, on S side of Eilean a' Phidhir. NM7091.

Eilean nam Feannag *W.Isles* ***Island***, islet in Loch Roag, W coast of Isle of Lewis, 1m/2km NE of entrance to Little Loch Roag. NB1433.

Eilean nam Muc *Arg. & B.* ***Island***, small island off W coast of Erraid at SW end of Mull. NM2819.

Eilean nan Coinein *Arg. & B.* ***Island***, one of Small Isles group off E coast of Jura. NR5468.

Eilean nan Each *High.* ***Island***, small uninhabited island off NW end of Muck, in Inner Hebrides. **85 J6** NM3981.

Eilean nan Gabhar *Arg. & B.* ***Island***, largest and most southerly of Small Isles group off E coast of Jura. **72 D4** NR5367.

Eilean nan Gamhna *Arg. & B.* ***Island***, islet off NW coast of Kerrera. **79 K4** NM8130.

Eilean nan Gamhna *Arg. & B.* ***Island***, islet off S coast of Lismore, 1km S of Kilcheran Loch. In same group of islets are Eilean na Cloiche, Eilean Dubh, Creag Island and Pladda Island. NM8338.

Eilean nan Gillean *High.* ***Island***, small uninhabited island (National Trust for Scotland) 1m/2km NW of Kyle of Lochalsh, Skye and Lochalsh district. NG7428.

Eilean nan Gobhar *High.* ***Island***, islet at entrance to Loch Ailort, Lochaber district. **86 C6** NM6979.

Eilean nan Ron *Arg. & B.* ***Island***, rocky island, just off S end of Oronsay. **72 B2** NR3386.

Eilean nan Ròn (Also known as Roan Island.) *High.* ***Island***, fertile island of about 300 acres or 120 hectares, with rocky coast, at entrance to Tongue Bay, N coast of Caithness district. **103 J2** NC6465.

Eilean Orasaigh *W.Isles Gaelic form of Orasay Island, qv.*

Eilean Orasaigh (Anglicised form: Orinsay Island.) *W.Isles* ***Island***, small uninhabited island off E coast of Isle of Lewis, on S side of entrance to Loch Erisort. **101 G5** NB4121.

Eilean Ornsay *Arg. & B.* ***Island***, small island lying off SE coast of Coll, on W side of entrance to Loch Eatharna. **78 D2** NM2255.

Eilean Ramsay *Arg. & B.* ***Island***, small uninhabited island off N coast of Lismore. **79 K3** NM8845.

Eilean Ràrsaidh *High.* ***Island***, islet off N shore of Loch Hourn in Lochaber district, 2m/3km W of Arnisdale. NG8111.

Eilean Righ *Arg. & B.* ***Island***, narrow island nearly 2m/3km long NE to SW near E shore of Loch Craignish in Argyll. **79 J7** NM8001.

Eilean Rosaidh *W.Isles Gaelic form of Rosay, qv.*

Eilean Ruairidh *High.* ***Island***, islet on S side of entrance to Loch Eishort, Skye. NG5912.

Eilean Ruairidh Mòr *High.* ***Island***, wooded island in Loch Maree, Ross and Cromarty district. **94 E4** NG8973.

Eilean Rubha an Ridire *High.* ***Island***, islet in Sound of Mull lying 1km NW of Rubha an Ridire, Lochaber district. NM7240.

Eilean Scalpaigh *W.Isles Gaelic form of Scalpay, qv.*

Eilean Sgorach *High.* ***Island***, islet off Skye, lying close to Point of Sleat on W side. NM5599.

Eilean Shamadalain *High.* ***Island***, islet off NW coast of Knoydart, Lochaber district, 1m/2km NE of Airor. NG7306.

Eilean Shona *High.* ***Island***, hilly and partly wooded island at entrance to Loch Moidart in Lochaber district. E part of island is known as Shona Beag, joined to rest of island by narrow neck of land. **86 C7** NM6573.

Eilean Sneth Dian *Arg. & B. Alternative name for Frank Lockwood's Island, qv.*

Eilean Sùbhainn *High.* ***Island***, in Loch Maree, Ross and Cromarty district, nearly 1m/2km NE of Talladale. **95 F4** NG9272.

Eilean Tigh *High.* ***Island***, uninhabited island off N end of Raasay. Area about 180 acres or 75 hectares. **94 B6** NG6053.

Eilean Tighe *W.Isles* ***Island***, second in size of the Flannan Isles, lying to S of the largest, Eilean Mòr. NA7246.

Eilean Tioram *High.* ***Island***, islet at head of Loch Alsh, Skye and Lochalsh district, opposite entrance to Loch Duich. NG8726.

Eilean Tràighe *Arg. & B.* ***Island***, at entrance to West Loch Tarbert, Argyll, between Knapdale and Kintyre. NR7457.

Eilean Trodday *High.* ***Island***, small uninhabited island 1m/2km N of Rubha na h-Aiseig, headland at N point of Skye. Used for sheep grazing. **93 K4** NG4478.

Eilean Vow (Also known as Island I Vow). *Arg. & B.* ***Island***, islet in Loch Lomond 2m/3km S of Ardlui. Ruined castle of the Macfarlanes. NN3312.

Eileanan Diraclett *W.Isles* ***Island***, group of islets in East Loch Tarbert, off South Harris coast, 1m/2km SE of Tarbert. NG1698.

Eileanan Glasa *Arg. & B.* ***Island***, group of islets in Sound of Mull 2m/3km NE of Salen. **79 G3** NM5945.

Eileanan Gleann Righ *Arg. & B.* ***Island***, group of islets in Loch Tarbert, Jura, 1m/2km SE of Rubh' an t-Sàilein. NR5182.

Eileanan Iasgaich *W.Isles* ***Island***, group of islets in Loch Baghasdail, South Uist. NF7818.

Eileanan nan Glas Leac (Also known as Na Glas Leacan.) *High.* ***Island***, group of islets off N coast of Sutherland district, 3m/5km W of Faraid Head (or Far Out Head) across entrance to Balnakeil Bay. NC3472.

Eileann Sionnach *High.* ***Island***, islet with lighthouse in Sound of Sleat, off SE coast of Isle Ornsay. NG7112.

Einacleit (Anglicised form: Enaclete.) *W.Isles* ***Settlement***, 1m/2km N of Giosla, Isle of Lewis. **100 D5** NB1228.

Einig *High.* ***River***, in Sutherland district, running E down Glen Einig into River Oykel 1km SE of Oykel Bridge. **95 K2** NC3900.

Eiriosgaigh *W.Isles Gaelic form of Eriskay, qv.*

Eirth ***River***, running SE into River Tanat at Llangynog. **37 K3** SJ0525.

Eisgean (Anglicised form: Eishken.) *W.Isles* ***Settlement***, on Isle of Lewis, on N side of Loch Shell, 4m/6km W of Leumrabhagh. **101 F6** NB3211.

Eishken *W.Isles Anglicised form of Eisgean, qv.*

Eisingrug *Gwyn.* ***Settlement***, 3m/5km NE of Harlech. **37 F2** SH6134.

Eisteddfa Gurig *Cere.* ***Settlement***, 2m/3km S of Plynlimon. **37 G7** SN7984.

Eitshal *W.Isles* ***Hill***, 4m/7km NW of Liurbost, Isle of Lewis. Mast at summit. Height 731 feet or 223 metres. **101 F4** NB3030.

Elai *Welsh form of Ely (River), qv.*

Elan ***River***, rising 2m/3km E of Cwmystwyth and flowing E, then SE to Pont ar Elan at head of Craig Coch Reservoir. It then runs S through Pen-y-garreg and Garreg-ddu Reservoirs to Caban Coch Reservoir, where it turns NE, then finally SE to join River Wye 2m/3km S of Rhayader. **27 H1** SN9665.

Elan Village *Powys* ***Hamlet***, 3m/5km SW of Rhayader. **27 J2** SN9365.

Elberton *S.Glos.* ***Hamlet***, 3m/4km SW of Thornbury. **19 J3** ST6088.

Elburton *Plym.* ***Suburb***, 4m/6km SE of Plymouth city centre. **5 F5** SX5353.

Elchies Forest *Moray* ***Open space***, moorland tract to W of Rothes. **97 K7** NJ2246.

Elcho *P. & K.* ***Hamlet***, with castle, on S bank of River Tay, 3m/4km NE of Bridge of Earn. **82 C5** NO1620.

Elcho Castle *P. & K.* ***Historic/prehistoric site***, 16c stronghold (Historic Scotland) of the Earls of Wemyss. **82 C5** NO1621.

Elcock's Brook *Worcs.* ***Settlement***, 3m/5km SW of Redditch town centre. SP0164.

Elcombe *Swin.* ***Hamlet***, 3m/5km SW of Swindon. **20 E3** SU1380.

Elder Street *Essex* ***Hamlet***, 3m/5km SE of Saffron Walden. TL5734.

Eldernell *Cambs.* ***Settlement***, 3m/5km E of Whittlesey. **43 G6** TL3198.

Eldersfield *Worcs.* ***Village***, 6m/10km W of Tewkesbury. **29 G5** SO8031.

Elderslie *Renf.* Population: 5286. ***Small town***, adjoining to E of Johnstone. Traditional birthplace of William Wallace. **74 C4** NS4462.

Eldmire *N.Yorks.* ***Locality***, 2m/3km SE of Topcliffe. Site of former village. SE4274.

Eldon *Dur.* ***Village***, 1m/2km N of Shildon. NZ2327.

Eldon Hill *Derbys.* ***Mountain***, 3m/4km SW of Castleton. Height 1542 feet or 470 metres. **50 D4** SK1181.

Eldrable Hill *High.* ***Mountain***, 2m/4km NW of Helmsdale, Sutherland district. Height 1368 feet or 417 metres. **104 E7** NC9816.

Eldrick *S.Ayr.* ***Settlement***, 3m/5km E of Barrhill. **67 G5** NX2881.

Eldridge *Essex* ***Hamlet***, 3m/4km W of Newport. TL4832.

Eldroth *N.Yorks.* ***Settlement***, 4m/6km W of Settle. **56 C3** SD7665.

Eldwick *W.Yorks.* ***Locality***, 1m/2km NE of Bingley. **57 G5** SE1240.

Eleanor Cross *Northants.* ***Historic/prehistoric site***, well preserved 13c cross (English Heritage) in Geddington, 4m/6km NE of Kettering town centre. One of three surviving crosses built in 1290 by Edward I to mark overnight stops in Queen Eleanor's funeral procession along route from Nottinghamshire to London. Cross still dominates centre of village. **42 C7** SP8982.

Electric Brae *S.Ayr. See Croy Brae.*

Elemore Vale *T. & W.* ***Hamlet***, adjoining to SW of Easington Lane, 3m/4km S of Houghton-le-Spring. NZ3545.

Elerch *Cere. Alternative name for Bont-goch, qv.*

Elfhowe *Cumb.* ***Locality***, 1m/2km N of Staveley. SD4699.

Elford *Northumb.* ***Settlement***, 2m/3km W of Seahouses. **77 K7** NU1831.

Elford *Staffs.* ***Village***, on River Tame, 4m/7km N of Tamworth. **40 D4** SK1810.

Elford Closes *Cambs.* ***Settlement***, 2m/3km SW of Stretham. TL5072.

Elgin *Moray* Population: 19,027. ***Town***, market town with cathedral on River Lossie, 5m/8km S of Lossiemouth and 36m/59km E of Inverness. Notable ruins of 13c cathedral (Historic Scotland), traces of ancient castle, 16c Bishop's House (Historic Scotland). Much of medieval street layout remains intact. Museum. **97 K5** NJ2162.

Elgin Cathedral *Moray* ***Ecclesiastical building***, remains of 13c cathedral (Historic Scotland) in centre of Elgin. Known as Lantern of the North, it once rivalled St. Andrews Cathedral. Founded in 1224 and rebuilt after fires in 1270 and 1390, it fell into disrepair during the Reformation. Notable features include octagonal chapter house and Pictish slab in the choir. **97 K5** NJ2263.

Elgin Lane *E.Ayr.* ***River***, issuing from Loch Enoch and flowing N to its confluence with Whitespout Lane to form Carrick Lane. **67 J5** NX4693.

Elgin Museum *Moray* ***Other feature of interest***, museum in Elgin with Pictish, geological and local history displays. Most notable are exotic anthropological exhibits, including a mummy from Peru. **97 K5** NJ2063.

Elgol *High.* ***Village***, on E side of Loch Scavaig, on S coast of Skye. **86 B3** NG5214.

Elham *Kent* Population: 1429. ***Village***, 6m/9km NW of Folkestone. **15 G3** TR1743.

Elibank *Sc.Bord.* ***Locality***, and ruined stronghold of Murrays, 4m/7km E of Innerleithen across River Tweed. NT3936.

Elibank and Traquair Forest *Sc.Bord.* ***Forest/woodland***, on S side of River Tweed, to E of Innerleithen. **76 B7** NT3635.

Eliburn *W.Loth.* ***Locality***, 2m/3km W of Livingston. NT0367.

Elidyr Fawr *Gwyn.* ***Mountain***, on NE side of Llyn Peris, 3m/4km NE of Llanberis. Height 3027 feet or 923 metres. **46 E6** SH6161.

Elie *Fife* ***Town***, resort on Firth of Forth, 5m/8km W of Anstruther. Merged with Earlsferry in 1929. Small harbour. **83 F7** NO4900.

Elilaw *Northumb.* ***Settlement***, 4m/6km NE of Alwinton. **70 E3** NT9708.

Elim *I.o.A.* ***Hamlet***, 1km SE of Llanddeusant, on Anglesey. **46 B4** SH3584.

Eling *Hants.* ***Village***, adjoining to S of Totton. **10 E3** SU3612.

Eling *W.Berks.* ***Settlement***, 6m/9km NE of Newbury. SU5275.

Eling Tide Mill *Hants.* ***Other feature of interest***, S of Totton, in Eling. On site of 900-year-old mill which used tidal energy to grind wheat. Current working waterwheel installed at beginning of 20c. **10 E3** SU3612.

Eliock *D. & G.* ***Locality***, straddling River Nith, 2m/3km SE of Sanquhar. **68 D3** NS8007.

Eliseg's Pillar (Also known as Pillar of Eliseg.) *Denb.* ***Historic/prehistoric site***, remains of 9c cross (Cadw), to N of Valle Crucis Abbey, 2m/3km NW of Llangollen. **38 B1** SJ2044.

Elishader *High.* ***Settlement***, near E coast of Skye, 3m/4km NW of Rubha nam Brathairean. **94 B5** NG5065.

Elishaw *Northumb.* ***Locality***, at road junction, 2m/4km NW of Otterburn. **70 D4** NY8695.

Elkesley *Notts.* ***Village***, 4m/6km S of Retford. **51 J5** SK6975.

Elkington *Northants.* ***Settlement***, 2m/3km NE of Yelvertoft. SP6276.

Elkins Green *Essex* ***Settlement***, just E of Blackmore, 3m/5km NW of Ingatestone. TL6002.

Elkstone *Glos.* ***Village***, 6m/10km S of Cheltenham. Site of Roman villa 2km SE. **29 J7** SO9612.

Ellanbeich *Arg. & B.* ***Settlement***, adjoining Easdale, on W coast of Seil, in Argyll. NM7417.

Elland *W.Yorks.* Population: 14,232. ***Town***, on S bank of River Calder, 4m/6km NW of Huddersfield. Developed as a textile town. **57 G7** SE1021.

Elland Lower Edge *W.Yorks.* ***Settlement***, on S side of River Calder, between Elland and Rastrick. SE1221.

Elland Upper Edge *W.Yorks.* ***Settlement***, 1m/2km E of Elland. SE1220.

Ellary *Arg. & B.* ***Settlement***, on NW side of Loch Caolisport, 2m/3km W of Clachbreck across loch. **73 F3** NR7475.

Ellastone *Staffs.* ***Village***, 4m/7km SW of Ashbourne. **40 D1** SK1143.

Ellbridge *Cornw.* ***Settlement***, 3m/5km NW of Saltash. SX4063.

Ellel *Lancs.* ***Village***, adjoining to N of Galgate, 4m/6km S of Lancaster. SD4856.

Ellemford *Sc.Bord.* ***Settlement***, 3m/4km SW of Abbey St. Bathans. **77 F4** NT7260.

Ellen *Cumb.* ***River***, rising on Uldale Fells, SE of Uldale, and flowing NW, then SW, to Solway Firth at Maryport. **60 C2** NY0236.

Ellenborough *Cumb.* ***Suburb***, in SE part of Maryport. **60 B3** NY0435.

Ellenbrook *Gt.Man.* ***Locality***, 2m/4km E of Tyldesley. SD7201.

Ellenbrook *Herts.* ***Suburb***, to W of Hatfield. TL2008.

Ellenhall *Staffs.* ***Village***, 2m/3km SE of Eccleshall. **40 A3** SJ8426.

Ellen's Green *Surr.* ***Hamlet***, 3m/5km SE of Cranleigh. **12 D3** TQ0935.

Ellen's Isle (Gaelic name: Eilean Molach). *Stir.* ***Island***, islet at E end of Loch Katrine. **81 F7** NN4808.

Ellenthorpe *N.Yorks.* ***Locality***, 1m/2km E of Boroughbridge across River Ure. SE4167.

Eller Beck *N.Yorks.* ***River***, stream rising on Embsay Moor and flowing SE to join Haw Beck N of Skipton, then flowing S through Skipton before joining River Aire, 1m/2km S of Skipton town centre. **56 E4** SD9850.

Eller Keld *Cumb.* ***Locality***, 1m/2km E of Workington. NY0128.

Ellerbeck *N.Yorks.* ***Hamlet***, 4m/7km NE of Northallerton. **63 F7** SE4396.

Ellerburn *N.Yorks.* ***Settlement***, 3m/4km E of Pickering. SE8484.

Ellerby *N.Yorks.* ***Hamlet***, near North Sea coast, 3m/5km S of Staithes. **63 J5** NZ7914.

Ellerdine *Tel. & W.* ***Settlement***, 5m/8km S of Hodnet. SJ6020.

Ellerdine Heath *Tel. & W.* ***Hamlet***, 1m/2km NE of Ellerdine. **39 F3** SJ6020.

Ellergreen *Cumb.* ***Settlement***, to W of Burneside, 2m/3km N of Kendal. SD5095.

Ellerhayes *Devon* ***Hamlet***, 5m/7km SW of Cullompton. SS9702.

Elleric *Arg. & B.* ***Settlement***, in Glen Creran, 3m/5km NE of head of Glen Creran. **80 B3** NN0348.

Ellerker *E.Riding* ***Village***, 1m/2km S of South Cave. **59 F7** SE9229.

Ellers *N.Yorks.* ***Settlement***, on hillside, to S of Sutton-in-Craven. SE0143.

Ellerton *E.Riding* ***Village***, 11m/18km W of Market Weighton. **58 D5** SE7039.

Ellerton *N.Yorks.* ***Village***, 1m/2km E of Catterick across River Swale. **62 D7** SE2597.

Ellerton *Shrop.* ***Settlement***, 2m/3km E of Hinstock. **39 G3** SJ7125.

Ellerton Abbey *N.Yorks.* ***Settlement***, 3m/5km SE of Reeth. Scant remains of Cistercian nunnery. SE0797.

Ellerton Priory *N.Yorks.* ***Ecclesiastical building***, scant remains of Cistercian nunnery in Swaledale, 2m/3km E of Grinton. **62 B7** SE0797.

Ellesborough *Bucks.* ***Village***, 2m/4km W of Wendover. **22 B1** SP8306.

Ellesmere *Shrop.* Population: 2967. ***Small town***, 8m/12km NE of Oswestry. The Mere, on E side, one of several in district, is a large lake used for pleasure boating. **38 C2** SJ3934.

Ellesmere Park *Gt.Man.* ***Suburb***, to N of Eccles town centre. SJ7799.

Ellesmere Port *Ches.* Population: 64,504. ***Town***, at SE end of Wirral peninsula, 7m/11km N of Chester. Docks on Manchester Ship Canal. Ellesmere Port Boat Museum includes exhibits of narrowboat crafts. **48 C5** SJ4077.

Ellingham *Hants.* ***Hamlet***, 2m/3km N of Ringwood. **10 C4** SU1408.

Ellingham *Norf.* ***Village***, 2m/4km NE of Bungay. **45 H6** TM3592.

Ellingham *Northumb.* ***Village***, 5m/8km SW of Seahouses. **71 G1** NU1725.

Ellingstring *N.Yorks.* ***Village***, 4m/6km NW of Masham. **57 G1** SE1783.

Ellington *Cambs.* ***Village***, 5m/8km W of Huntingdon. **32 E1** TL1671.

Ellington *Northumb.* Population: 2253. ***Village***, 3m/4km N of Ashington. **71 H4** NZ2791.

Ellington Thorpe *Cambs.* ***Settlement***, 1km S of Ellington and 5m/8km W of Huntingdon. TL1570.

Elliot Water *Angus* ***River***, rising to W of Redford, and flowing SE by Arbirlot into North Sea, 2m/3km SW of Arbroath. **83 G3** NO6239.

Elliot's Green *Som.* ***Hamlet***, 2m/3km SE of Frome. ST7945.

Ellis Crag *Northumb.* ***Inland physical feature***, rock outcrop at height of 1630 feet or 497 metres in Redesdale Forest, 1m/2km SW of Byrness. **70 C3** NT7401.

Ellisfield *Hants.* ***Village***, 4m/6km S of Basingstoke. **21 K7** SU6345.

Ellistown *Leics.* ***Suburb***, 2m/3km S of Coalville. **41 G4** SK4310.

Ellon *Aber.* Population: 8627. ***Small town***, market town on River Ythan, 15m/24km N of Aberdeen. **91 H1** NJ9530.

Ellonby *Cumb.* ***Hamlet***, 1m/2km W of Skelton. **60 F3** NY4235.

Ellough *Suff.* ***Settlement***, 3m/4km SE of Beccles. **45 J7** TM4486.

Ellough Moor *Suff.* ***Hamlet***, 1m/2km N of Ellough. TM4488.

Elloughton *E.Riding* ***Village***, 1m/2km N of Brough. **59 F7** SE9428.

Ellwick *Ork.* *Alternative spelling of Elwick, qv.*

Ellwood *Glos.* ***Hamlet***, 2m/3km SE of Coleford. **19 J1** SO5908.

Elm *Cambs.* ***Village***, 2m/3km S of Wisbech. **43 H5** TF4707.

Elm Green *Essex* ***Locality***, adjoining to W of Danbury, 4m/7km E of Chelmsford. TL7705.

Elm Grove *Norf.* ***Locality***, adjoining to NE of Belton. TG4803.

Elm Park *Gt.Lon.* ***Suburb***, in borough of Havering, 2m/3km SW of Hornchurch. **23 J3** TQ5285.

Elm Tree Hill *S.Yorks.* ***Suburb***, 3m/4km SE of Sheffield city centre. SK3885.

Elmbridge *Glos.* ***Suburb***, E district of Gloucester. SO8519.

Elmbridge *Worcs.* ***Hamlet***, 3m/5km N of Droitwich Spa. **29 J2** SO8967.

Elmdon *Essex* ***Village***, 5m/8km W of Saffron Walden. **33 H5** TL4639.

Elmdon *W.Mid.* ***Hamlet***, 7m/11km E of Birmingham, on S side of Birmingham International Airport. **40 D7** SP1783.

Elmdon Heath *W.Mid.* ***Suburb***, 1m/2km NE of Solihull town centre. **40 D7** SP1680.

Elmer *W.Suss.* ***Suburb***, to E of Middleton-on-Sea, 3m/5km E of Bognor Regis. SU9800.

Elmers End *Gt.Lon.* ***Suburb***, in borough of Bromley, 1m/2km SW of Beckenham. TQ3568.

Elmer's Green *Lancs.* ***Suburb***, in NE part of Skelmersdale. SD4906.

Elmesthorpe *Leics.* ***Village***, 3m/4km NE of Hinckley. **41 G6** SP4696.

Elmfield *I.o.W.* ***Suburb***, 1m/2km SE of Ryde town centre. SZ6091.

Elmhurst *Staffs.* ***Hamlet***, 2m/3km N of Lichfield. **40 D4** SK1112.

Elmley Castle *Worcs.* ***Village***, 4m/6km SW of Evesham. Site of medieval castle 1km S. **29 J4** SO9841.

Elmley Island *Kent* ***Marsh/bog***, area of marshland on Isle of Sheppey bounded by The Swale, The Dray, and Windmill Creek. **25 F5** TQ9468.

Elmley Lovett *Worcs.* ***Village***, 4m/6km E of Stourport-on-Severn. **29 H2** SO8669.

Elmore *Glos.* ***Village***, on E bank of River Severn, 4m/6km SW of Gloucester across loop of river. **29 G7** SO7815.

Elmore Back *Glos.* ***Hamlet***, on E bank of River Severn, 4m/7km W of Gloucester across loop of river. **29 G7** SO7616.

Elms Green *Worcs.* ***Locality***, 6m/10km SW of Stourport-on-Severn. SO7266.

Elmscott *Devon* ***Settlement***, near coast, 10m/16km N of Bude. **6 A3** SS2321.

Elmsett *Suff.* ***Village***, 3m/5km NE of Hadleigh. **34 E4** TM0546.

Elmstead *Essex* ***Settlement***, 4m/7km E of Colchester. TM0626.

Elmstead *Gt.Lon.* ***Suburb***, in borough of Bromley, 2m/3km NE of Bromley town centre. TQ4270.

Elmstead Heath *Essex* ***Settlement***, 2m/3km NE of Wivenhoe. TM0622.

Elmstead Market *Essex* Population: 1886. ***Village***, 4m/7km E of Colchester. **34 E6** TM0624.

Elmstead Row *Essex* ***Locality***, 2m/3km E of Wivenhoe. TM0621.

Elmsted *Kent* ***Hamlet***, 7m/11km NE of Ashford. TR1144.

Elmstone *Kent* ***Hamlet***, 2m/4km NE of Wingham. **25 J5** TR2660.

Elmstone Hardwicke *Glos.* ***Hamlet***, 3m/5km NW of Cheltenham. **29 J6** SO9226.

Elmswell *E.Riding* ***Village***, 2m/3km W of Great Driffield. **59 F4** SE9958.

Elmswell *Suff.* Population: 2760. ***Village***, 5m/8km NW of Stowmarket. **34 D2** TL9863.

Elmton *Derbys.* ***Village***, 3m/4km NE of Bolsover. **51 H5** SK5073.

Elphin *High.* ***Village***, in Sutherland district, 7m/11km S of Inchnadamph. **102 E7** NC2111.

Elphinstone *E.Loth.* ***Village***, 2m/3km S of Tranent. **76 B3** NT3970.

Elrick *Aber.* ***Locality***, 7m/12km W of Aberdeen. **91 G4** NJ8206.

Elrick *Moray* ***Settlement***, 2m/3km E of Cabrach. **90 C2** NJ4225.

Elrick Burn *High.* ***River***, rising on N slope of Meall nan Laogh and flowing N into River Findhorn, 10m/16km N of Newtonmore. **88 D3** NH6714.

Elrick More *P. & K.* ***Mountain***, on W side of Strath Tay, 4m/7km NW of Dunkeld. Height 1696 feet or 517 metres. **82 A3** NN9646.

Elrig *D. & G.* ***Village***, 3m/5km N of Port William. **64 D6** NX3247.

Elrig Loch *D. & G.* ***Lake/loch***, small loch 1km N of Elrig. **64 D6** NX3247.

Elrigbeag *Arg. & B.* ***Settlement***, in Glen Shira, 4m/7km NE of Inveraray. **80 C6** NN1314.

Els Ness *Ork.* ***Coastal feature***, peninsula on S coast of Sanday, 2m/4km W of Tres Ness. **106 F4** HY6737.

Elsdon *Northumb.* ***Village***, on Elsdon Burn, 3m/5km E of Otterburn. Motte and bailey castle. **70 E4** NY9393.

Elsecar *S.Yorks.* ***Locality***, adjoining to E of Hoyland. **51 F3** SE3800.

Elsecar Discovery Centre *S.Yorks.* ***Other feature of interest***, science-based visitor centre in Elsecar, 5m/8km SE of Barnsley. Interactive displays on power and energy. **51 F3** SK3899.

Elsenham *Essex* ***Village***, 4m/7km NE of Bishop's Stortford. **33 J6** TL5326.

Elsfield *Oxon.* ***Village***, 3m/5km NE of Oxford. **21 J1** SP5310.

Elsham *N.Lincs.* ***Village***, 4m/6km NE of Brigg. **52 D1** TA0312.

Elsham Hall Country Park *N.Lincs.* ***Leisure/recreation***, country park situated to SW of Elsham. Among many attractions are a falconry centre, arboretum, children's farmyard and a theatre. **52 D1** TA0311.

Elsing *Norf.* ***Village***, 5m/7km NE of East Dereham. **44 E4** TG0516.

Elslack *N.Yorks.* ***Village***, 4m/7km W of Skipton. **56 E5** SD9349.

Elson *Hants.* ***Suburb***, N district of Gosport. SU6001.

Elson *Shrop.* ***Hamlet***, 1m/2km NW of Ellesmere. **38 C2** SJ3835.

Elsrickle *S.Lan.* ***Village***, 3m/5km N of Biggar. **75 J6** NT0643.

Elstead *Surr.* Population: 2436. ***Village***, 4m/6km W of Godalming. **22 C7** SU9043.

Elstead Marsh *W.Suss.* ***Locality***, 3m/5km W of Midhurst. SU8320.

Elsted *W.Suss.* ***Village***, 5m/8km W of Midhurst. **12 B5** SU8119.

Elsthorpe *Lincs.* ***Hamlet***, 3m/5km NW of Bourne. **42 D3** TF0523.

Elstob *Dur.* ***Settlement***, 4m/6km S of Sedgefield. **62 E4** NZ3423.

Elston *Lancs.* ***Hamlet***, 4m/7km NE of Preston. **55 J6** SD6032.

Elston *Notts.* ***Village***, 5m/7km SW of Newark-on-Trent. **42 A1** SK7647.

Elston *Wilts.* ***Settlement***, adjoining to N of Shrewton, 6m/9km NW of Amesbury. SU0644.

Elstone *Devon* ***Hamlet***, 2m/3km NW of Chulmleigh. **6 E4** SS6716.

Elstow *Beds.* ***Village***, 2m/3km S of Bedford. **32 D4** TL0546.

Elstree *Herts.* Population: 2196. ***Village***, 5m/8km E of Watford. Elstree Airfield 2km NW. Film studios at Borehamwood to E. **22 E2** TQ1795.

Elstronwick *E.Riding* ***Village***, 3m/5km NE of Hedon. **59 J6** TA2232.

Elswick *Lancs.* ***Village***, 4m/6km N of Kirkham. **55 H6** SD4238.

Elswick *T. & W.* ***Suburb***, on N bank of River Tyne, 1m/2km SW of Newcastle upon Tyne city centre. NZ2363.

Elsworth *Cambs.* ***Village***, 7m/11km SE of Huntingdon. **33 G2** TL3163.

Elterwater *Cumb.* ***Village***, 3m/5km W of Ambleside. To SE is Elter Water lake. **60 E6** NY3204.

Eltham *Gt.Lon.* ***Suburb***, in borough of Greenwich, 9m/14km SE of Charing Cross. **23 H4** TQ4274.

Eltham Palace *Gt.Lon.* ***Historic house***, medieval royal palace (English Heritage) to S of Eltham. Presented to Edward II in 1305 and favourite royal Christmas retreat from Henry III to Henry VIII. Fell into disrepair as Greenwich received royal favour; rebuilt from 1930s in Art Deco and modern styles. Principal surviving area is Great Hall, with excellent example of hammerbeam type roof. **23 H4** TQ4274.

Eltisley *Cambs.* ***Village***, 6m/9km E of St. Neots. **33 F3** TL2759.

Elton *Cambs.* ***Village***, 4m/6km S of Wansford. **42 D6** TL0993.

Elton *Ches.* ***Village***, 4m/6km E of Ellesmere Port. **48 D5** SJ4575.

Elton *Derbys.* ***Village***, 5m/8km W of Matlock. **50 E6** SK2260.

Elton *Glos.* ***Settlement***, 2m/3km NE of Newnham. **29 G7** SO7013.

Elton *Gt.Man.* ***Suburb***, to W of Bury town centre. SD7910.

Elton *Here.* ***Hamlet***, 4m/7km SW of Ludlow. **28 D1** SO4570.

Elton *Notts.* ***Village***, 4m/7km E of Bingham. **42 A2** SK7638.

Elton *Stock.* ***Village***, 3m/5km W of Stockton-on-Tees. **63 F5** NZ4017.

Elton Green *Ches.* ***Suburb***, to S of Elton, 3m/5km E of Ellesmere Port. SJ4575.

Elton Hall *Cambs.* ***Historic house***, 17c mansion house of Proby family, with recently restored gardens, located in Elton Park, just S of Elton. **42 D6** TL0892.

Elton's Marsh *Here.* ***Locality***, 3m/5km NW of Hereford. SO4943.

Eltringham *Northumb.* ***Village***, 1km W of Prudhoe. NZ0862.

Eltrington *Northumb.* ***Locality***, 1m/2km SE of Haydon Bridge. NY8663.

Elvan Water *S.Lan.* ***River***, rising on Lowther Hills and flowing E to join River Clyde at Elvanfoot. **68 E2** NS9517.

Elvanfoot *S.Lan.* ***Village***, at confluence of Elvan Water and River Clyde, 4m/7km S of Abington. **68 E2** NS9517.

Elvaston *Derbys.* ***Village***, 4m/7km SE of Derby. **41 G2** SK4132.

Elvaston Castle *Derbys.* ***Castle***, designed in 19c and set in 200 acres of parkland with walled garden, 4m/7km SE of Derby. Adjoining Elvaston Castle Country Park, has picnic areas and nature trails. Also museum with buildings and workshops restored to recreate life on estate in 1910. **41 G2** SK4133.

Elveden *Suff.* ***Village***, 4m/6km SW of Thetford. Hall originally Georgian, Indianised 19c, enlarged 20c. **34 C1** TL8279.

Elvet Hill *Dur.* ***Suburb***, 1m/2km SW of Durham. NZ2641.

Elvetham *Hants.* ***Locality***, 1m/2km E of Hartley Wintney. SU7856.

Elvingston *E.Loth.* ***Settlement***, 3m/5km W of Haddington. **76 C3** NT4674.

Elvington *Kent* ***Village***, 6m/10km NW of Dover. **15 H2** TR2750.

Elvington *York* ***Village***, on W bank of River Derwent, 7m/11km SE of York. **58 D5** SE7047.

Elwick *Hart.* ***Village***, 3m/5km W of Hartlepool. **63 F3** NZ4532.

Elwick *Northumb.* ***Settlement***, 2m/3km N of Belford. **77 K7** NU1136.

Elwick (Also spelled Ellwick.) *Ork.* ***Locality***, on E side of Elwick bay, S coast of Shapinsay. Balfour is situated on W side of bay. HY4816.

Elworth *Ches.* ***Village***, 1m/2km W of Sandbach. **49 G6** SJ7361.

Elworthy *Som.* ***Hamlet***, on E edge of Exmoor National Park, 5m/8km S of Watchet. **7 J2** ST0834.

Elwy ***River***, formed by confluence of Rivers Cledwen and Gallen near Llangernyw and flowing E and finally N into River Clwyd, 1m/2km N of St. Asaph. **47 H5** SJ0376.

Ely (Elai). ***River***, rising near Gilfach Goch and flowing SE into River Severn estuary at Penarth. **18 D3** ST1972.

Ely *Cambs.* Population: 10,329. ***City***, cathedral city on River Great Ouse, 14m/23km NE of Cambridge. Name comes from eeling, which was once an important industry. City is dominated by huge Norman cathedral built on chalk hill. Centre of large fenland agricultural area. City was last stronghold of Anglo-Saxon resistance against Normans, holding out under Hereward the Wake until 1071. **33 J1** TL5380.

Ely (Trelai). *Cardiff* ***Suburb***, to S of Ely River, 3m/4km W of Cardiff city centre. Site of Roman villa in Trelai Park to E. **18 E4** ST1376.

Ely Cathedral *Cambs.* ***Ecclesiastical building***, one of the longest (517 feet or 158 metres) and most architecturally varied churches in England, located in Ely. Originally a Saxon foundation, present building was started in 1083. Notable features are 250 foot or 76 metre long nave, choir and octagon. **33 J1** TL5480.

Ely Valley *V. of Glam.* ***Valley***, carrying River Ely SE from Miskin for about 2m/3km. **18 D4** ST0580.

Em-sger *Pembs. Alternative name for South Bishop, qv.*

Emberton *M.K.* ***Village***, 1m/2km S of Olney. **32 B4** SP8849.

Emblehope Moor *Northumb.* ***Open space***, moorland, with Redesdale Forest to N and Kielder Forest to S, 5m/8km N of Falstone. **70 C4** NY7495.

Embleton *Cumb.* ***Village***, 3m/5km E of Cockermouth. **60 C3** NY1730.

Embleton *Dur.* ***Settlement***, 4m/7km E of Sedgefield. NZ4229.

Embleton *Northumb.* ***Village***, 7m/11km N of Alnwick. **71 H1** NU2322.

Embleton Bay *Northumb.* ***Bay***, National Trust land, 1m/2km E of Embleton, on North Sea coast. **71 H1** NU2322.

Embo *High.* ***Village***, on E coast of Sutherland district, 2m/3km N of Dornoch. **97 F2** NH8192.

Embo Street *High.* ***Settlement***, 1m/2km SW of Embo. **97 F2** NH8091.

Emborough *Som.* ***Hamlet***, 5m/8km N of Shepton Mallet. **19 K6** ST6151.

Embsay *N.Yorks.* Population: 1796. ***Village***, 2m/3km NE of Skipton. **57 F4** SE0053.

Embsay Moor *N.Yorks.* ***Open space***, moorland containing areas of bog, 2m/4km N of Skipton. SD9956.

Embsay Reservoir *N.Yorks.* ***Reservoir***, 1m/2km NW of Embsay. SE0053.

Embsay Steam Railway *N.Yorks.* ***Other feature of interest***, 2m/3km NE of Skipton. Steam trains running along 3m/4km standard gauge line. **57 F4** SE0153.

Emerson Park *Gt.Lon.* ***Suburb***, to N of Hornchurch, in borough of Havering. TQ5488.

Emery Down *Hants.* ***Village***, 1m/2km W of Lyndhurst. **10 D4** SU2808.

Emley *W.Yorks.* Population: 1993. ***Village***, 3m/5km E of Kirkburton. **50 E1** SE2413.

Emley Moor *W.Yorks.* ***Locality***, 1m/2km W of Emley. SE2213.

Emmanuel Head *Northumb.* ***Coastal feature***, headland at NE corner of Holy Island. **77 K6** NU1343.

Emmer Green *Read.* ***Suburb***, 2m/3km N of Reading. **22 A4** SU7276.

Emmets Nest *Brack.F.* ***Locality***, adjoining to S of Binfield, 2m/3km NW of Bracknell. SU8470.

Emmett Carr *Derbys.* ***Hamlet***, 2m/3km SE of Eckington. SK4577.

Emmetts Garden *Kent* ***Garden***, National Trust property, 2m/3km SE of Westerham. 18 acre hillside shrub garden. **23 H6** TQ4752.

Emmington *Oxon.* ***Hamlet***, 3m/5km SE of Thame. **22 A1** SP7402.

Emneth *Norf.* ***Village***, 2m/4km SE of Wisbech. **43 H5** TF4807.

Emneth Hungate *Norf.* ***Settlement***, 2m/3km E of Emneth. **43 J5** TF5107.

Emorsgate *Norf.* ***Locality***, adjoining to W of Terrington St. Clement. TF5320.

Empingham *Rut.* ***Village***, 5m/8km W of Stamford. Rutland Water, large reservoir to W. **42 C5** SK9508.

Empingham Reservoir *Rut. Former name of Rutland Water, qv.*

Empshott *Hants.* ***Village***, 2m/3km SE of Selborne. **11 J1** SU7531.

Empshott Green *Hants.* ***Settlement***, to W of Empshott, 6m/9km W of Liphook. SU7431.

Emsworth *Hants.* Population: 9155. ***Small town***, 2m/3km E of Havant. Yachting centre on Chichester harbour. **11 J4** SU7405.

Emsworth Channel *See Chichester Harbour.*

Enaclete *W.Isles Anglicised form of Einacleit, qv.*

Enard Bay *High.* ***Bay***, on NW coast of Ross and Cromarty district, on E side of Rubha Coigeach, 5m/8km SW of Lochinver. **102 C7** NC0318.

Enborne *W.Berks.* ***Village***, 3m/5km SW of Newbury. **21 H5** SU4365.

Enborne Row *W.Berks.* ***Hamlet***, 3m/5km SW of Newbury. SU4463.

Enchmarsh *Shrop.* ***Hamlet***, 4m/6km NE of Church Stretton. **38 E6** SO5096.

Endcliffe *S.Yorks.* ***Suburb***, 2m/3km W of Sheffield city centre. SK3286.

Enderby *Leics.* Population: 7020. ***Village***, 5m/8km SW of Leicester. **41 H6** SP5399.

Endmoor *Cumb.* ***Village***, 5m/8km S of Kendal. **55 J1** SD5384.

Endon *Staffs.* ***Village***, 4m/7km SW of Leek. **49 J7** SJ9253.

Endon Bank *Staffs.* ***Village***, adjoining to NE of Endon. SJ9253.

Endrick Water ***River***, rising on Fintry Hills and flowing W past Fintry, Balfron and Drymen along an increasingly contorted and meandering course before flowing into Loch Lomond nearly 1m/2km S of Balmaha. **74 D2** NS4289.

Energlyn *Caerp.* ***Locality***, to N of Caerphilly town centre. Industrial estate. ST1588.

Enfield *Gt.Lon.* ***Town***, 10m/16km N of Charing Cross. Forty Hall now a museum. TQ3296.

Enfield *Worcs.* ***Suburb***, N district of Redditch. SP0368.

Enfield Chase *Gt.Lon.* ***Open space***, rural area to NW of Enfield, formerly a forest. **23 F2** TQ2898.

Enfield Highway *Gt.Lon.* ***Suburb***, 2m/3km E of Enfield, in borough of Enfield. TQ3597.

Enfield Lock *Gt.Lon.* ***Suburb***, on River Lea, 3m/5km E of Enfield, in borough of Enfield. TQ3698.

Enfield Wash *Gt.Lon.* ***Suburb***, 2m/4km NE of Enfield, in borough of Enfield. TQ3598.

Enford *Wilts.* ***Village***, on River Avon, 2m/4km S of Upavon. **20 E6** SU1351.

Enford Down *Wilts.* ***Open space***, hillslope 2m/3km SW of Enford. **20 E7** SU1049.

Engedi *I.o.A.* ***Hamlet***, 2m/3km W of Gwalchmai, on Anglesey. SH3676.

Engine Common *S.Glos.* ***Village***, 2m/4km NW of Chipping Sodbury. **19 K3** ST6984.

England's Gate *Here.* ***Locality***, 7m/12km N of Hereford. SO5451.

Englefield *W.Berks.* ***Village***, 6m/10km W of Reading. **21 K4** SU6272.

Englefield Green *Surr.* ***Village***, 3m/5km W of Staines. **22 C4** SU9971.

Englesea-brook *Ches.* ***Hamlet***, 4m/6km SE of Crewe. **49 G7** SJ7551.

English Bicknor *Glos.* ***Village***, 3m/5km N of Coleford. **28 E7** SO5815.

English Frankton *Shrop.* ***Hamlet***, 5m/8km SE of Ellesmere. **38 D3** SJ4529.

Englishcombe *B. & N.E.Som.* ***Village***, 3m/4km SW of Bath. **20 A5** ST7162.

Enham Alamein *Hants.* ***Village***, 3m/4km N of Andover. Name changed from Knight's Enham in 1945. **21 G7** SU3649.

Enmore *Som.* ***Village***, 4m/6km W of Bridgwater. **8 B1** ST2434.

Ennerdale Bridge *Cumb.* ***Hamlet***, astride River Ehen, 1m/2km from W end of Ennerdale Water. **60 B5** NY0615.

Ennerdale Fell *Cumb.* ***Open space***, hillslope rising steeply to S of Ennerdale Water. **60 C5** NY1015.

Ennerdale Water *Cumb.* ***Lake/loch***, 3m/4km in length, running E and W in course of River Liza or Ehen, W end being 1m/2km E of Ennerdale Bridge. **60 C5** NY1015.

Enniscaven *Cornw.* ***Hamlet***, 5m/8km NW of Austell. SW9659.

Ennochdhu (Also spelled Enochdu.) *P. & K.* ***Hamlet***, in Strathardle, 2m/3km NW of Kirkmichael. Field study centre at Kindrogan, below Kindrogan Hill and across River Ardle. **82 B1** NO0662.

Enoch Hill *E.Ayr.* ***Mountain***, above N edge of Carsphairn Forest, 5m/8km E of Dalmellington. Height 1866 feet or 569 metres. **67 K3** NS5606.

Enochdhu *P. & K. Alternative spelling of Ennochdhu, qv.*

Enrick *High.* ***River***, in Inverness district running E down Glen Urquhart to Urquhart Bay on NW side of Loch Ness. **87 K2** NH5229.

Ensay *Arg. & B.* ***Settlement***, on Mull, 3m/5km NW of Kilninian. **78 E3** NM3648.

Ensay *W.Isles* ***Island***, sparsely populated island in Sound of Harris, 2m/4km off W coast of Harris at Leverburgh. Measures nearly 2m/3km N to S and 1km E to W. **92 E3** NF9686.

Ensbury Park *Bourne.* ***Suburb***, N district of Bournemouth. SZ0794.

Ensdon *Shrop.* ***Hamlet***, 1m/2km NE of Shrawardine. **38 D4** SJ4016.

Ensis *Devon* ***Hamlet***, 4m/7km S of Barnstaple. **6 D3** SS5626.

Enson *Staffs.* ***Settlement***, on River Trent, 4m/6km NE of Stafford. SJ9428.

Enstone *Oxon.* ***Village***, 4m/7km E of Chipping Norton. **30 E6** SP3724.

Enterkin Burn *D. & G.* ***River***, joins River Nith at Enterkinfoot, 6m/9km N of Thornhill. **68 D3** NS8504.

Enterkinfoot *D. & G.* ***Locality***, at confluence of River Nith and Enterkin Burn. **68 D3** NS8504.

Enterpen *N.Yorks.* ***Locality***, adjoining to S of Hutton Rudby. **63 F6** NZ4606.

Enton Green *Surr.* ***Hamlet***, 1m/2km SE of Milford. SU9540.

Enville *Staffs.* ***Village***, 5m/8km W of Stourbridge. **40 A7** SO8286.

Eochar *W.Isles Anglicised form of Iochda, qv.*

Eolaigearraidh (Anglicised form: Eoligarry.) *W.Isles* ***Village***, on Barra, 1m/2km S of Scurrival Point. **84 C4** NF7007.

Eoligarry *W.Isles Anglicised form of Eolaigearraidh, qv.*

Eorabus *Arg. & B.* ***Settlement***, on Mull, 1m/2km N of Bunessan. **78 E5** NM3823.

Eorodal *W.Isles* ***Settlement***, 1km S of Port Nis, Isle of Lewis. **101 H1** NB5362.

Eoropaidh (Anglicised form: Eoropie.) *W.Isles* ***Village***, 1m/2km S of Butt of Lewis. **101 H1** NB5164.

Eoropie *W.Isles Anglicised form of Eoropaidh, qv.*

Eorsa *Arg. & B.* ***Island***, uninhabited island in Loch na Keal, W coast of Mull. Area about 250 acres or 100 hectares. Provides grazing for sheep. **79 F4** NM4837.

Epney *Glos.* ***Hamlet***, on W bank of River Severn, 7m/11km SW of Gloucester. SO7611.

Epperstone *Notts.* ***Village***, 7m/12km NE of Nottingham. **41 J1** SK6548.

Epping *Essex* Population: 9922. ***Small town***, at N end of Epping Forest, 17m/27km NE of London. **23 H1** TL4602.

Epping Forest *Essex* ***Forest/woodland***, open woodland 5m/8km long (NE to SW) and 1m/2km wide, traversed by several roads. **23 H2** TL4602.

Epping Green *Essex* ***Village***, forms part of Epping Upland parish, along with locality of Epping Long Green. **23 H1** TL4602.

Epping Green *Herts.* ***Hamlet***, 4m/6km SW of Hertford. **23 F1** TL2906.

Epping Long Green *Essex* ***Locality***, forms part of Epping Upland parish, along with Epping Green. TL4305.

Epping Upland *Essex* ***Locality***, parish, N and W of town of Epping, containing village of same name and village of Epping Green with locality of Epping Long Green. **23 H1** TL4602.

Eppleby *N.Yorks.* ***Village***, 3m/4km SW of Piercebridge. **62 C5** NZ1713.

Eppleworth *E.Riding* ***Settlement***, 2m/3km W of Cottingham. **59 G6** TA0131.

Epsom *Surr.* Population: 32,203. ***Town***, 6m/9km S of Kingston upon Thames. Once a popular spa town, famous for its Epsom Salts. Racecourse to S is venue for The Oaks and The Derby. **23 F5** TQ2060.

Epwell *Oxon.* ***Village***, 7m/11km W of Banbury. **30 E4** SP3540.

Epworth *N.Lincs.* Population: 3359. ***Small town***, on Isle of Axholme 9m/15km N of Gainsborough. Childhood home of John and Charles Wesley. **51 K2** SE7803.

Epworth Turbary *N.Lincs.* ***Hamlet***, 1m/2km W of Epworth. SE7603.

Erbistock (Erbistog). *Wrex.* ***Village***, 1m/2km W of Overton across River Dee. **38 C1** SJ3541.

Erbistog *Wrex. Welsh form of Erbistock, qv.*

Erbusaig *High.* ***Settlement***, in Skye and Lochalsh district, on Erbusaig Bay. **86 D2** NG7629.

Erch *Gwyn.* ***River***, rising near Llanaelhaearn and running S into Pwllheli harbour. **36 D2** SH3835.

Erchless Castle *High.* ***Settlement***, site of 15c seat of The Chisholm, chief of clan owning Strathglass, located at foot of Strathglass and just N of confluence of Rivers Farrar and Glass. **96 B7** NH4040.

Erchless Forest *High.* ***Open space***, deer forest in Inverness district W of Beauly and S of Orrin Reservoir. **95 K7** NH4145.

Erddig Hall *Wrex.* ***Historic house***, 18c house (National Trust) 1m/2km S of Wrexham, with period kitchens and laundry in out-buildings. 18c walled garden, Victorian parterre and yew walk. Garden also features National Collection of Ivies. **38 C1** SJ3247.

Erdington *W.Mid.* ***Suburb***, 5m/7km NE of Birmingham city centre. **40 D6** SP1191.

Eredine *Arg. & B.* ***Historic house***, to S of Loch Awe, near N end of Eredine Forest. **80 A7** NM9609.

Eredine Forest *Arg. & B.* ***Forest/woodland***, on E side of Loch Awe in Argyll above Portinnisherrich. **80 B6** NM9609.

Erewash ***River***, rising S of Kirkby in Ashfield and flowing S into River Trent 2m/3km E of Long Eaton. **41 G1** SK5133.

Eriboll *High.* ***Settlement***, on E side of Loch Eriboll, Sutherland district, 2m/4km NE of head of loch. **103 G3** NC4356.

Ericht *P. & K.* ***River***, issuing from Loch Ericht and flowing S to Loch Rannoch. **81 G1** NN5257.

Ericht *P. & K.* ***River***, formed by River Ardle and Black Water, and running S to Blairgowrie then SE to River Isla 2m/3km NE of Coupar Angus. **82 D3** NO2342.

Ericstane *D. & G.* ***Settlement***, 3m/5km N of Moffat. **69 F2** NT0711.

Eridge Green *E.Suss.* ***Village***, estate village on W side of Eridge Park, 3m/5km SW of Royal Tunbridge Wells. **13 J3** TQ5535.

Eriff *E.Ayr.* ***Settlement***, on S shore of Loch Muck, 4m/6km SE of Dalmellington. **67 K3** NS5100.

Erines *Arg. & B.* ***Settlement***, in Knapdale, on W shore of Loch Fyne, 4m/6km N of Tarbert. **73 G3** NR8675.

Erisey *Cornw.* ***Hamlet***, 4m/6km N of Lizard Point. SW7117.

Erisgeir *Arg. & B.* ***Island***, flat-topped rocky islet 2m/4km NW of Rubha nan Goirteanan on W coast of Mull and 3m/4km S of Little Colonsay. Provides occasional grazing for sheep. **78 E4** NM3832.

Eriska *Arg. & B.* ***Island***, at entrance to Loch Creran. Causeway to mainland on S side. **80 A3** NM9043.

Eriskay (Gaelic form: Eiriosgaigh.) *W.Isles* ***Island***, of about 3 square miles or 8 square km lying 1m/2km S of South Uist and 5m/8km E of N point of Barra. Small village at N end. Prince Charles Edward first landed on Scottish soil here in 1744 at Coilleag a' Phrionnsa. **84 D4** NF7910.

Eriswell *Suff.* ***Village***, 2m/4km NE of Mildenhall. **34 B1** TL7278.

Erith *Gt.Lon.* ***Suburb***, in borough of Bexley, on S bank of River Thames, 13m/21km E of Charing Cross. **23 J4** TQ5177.

Erith Marshes *Gt.Lon.* ***Marsh/bog***, to NW of Erith. **23 H4** TQ5177.

Erlestoke *Wilts.* ***Village***, 6m/9km E of Westbury. **20 C6** ST9653.

Erme *Devon* ***River***, rising on Dartmoor and flowing into Bigbury Bay 2m/3km S of Holbeton. **5 G4** SX6147.

Ermin Way *Glos.* ***Other feature of interest***, Roman road from Gloucester to Silchester. Present-day roads follow route for considerable stretches, particularly between Gloucester and Swindon. **20 C1** SO9808.

Ermine Street ***Other feature of interest***, Roman road which ran from near Pevensey to York, by London and Lincoln. Present-day roads follow line of Ermine Street for considerable stretches. **52 C4** TL1780.

Ermington *Devon* ***Village***, on River Erme, 2m/3km S of Ivybridge. **5 G5** SX6353.

Ernan Water *Aber.* ***River***, flowing E, then SE down Glen Ernan to join River Don, 2m/3km SW of Strathdon. **90 B3** NJ3310.

Erne Stack *Shet.* ***Coastal feature***, rocky promontory on NW coast of Muckle Roe. **109 B6** HU3067.

Ernesettle *Plym.* ***Suburb***, NW district of Plymouth, 4m/6km from city centre. SX4560.

Erocavum *Cumb. See Brougham.*

Erpingham *Norf.* ***Village***, 3m/5km N of Aylsham. **45 F2** TG1931.

Erradale *High.* ***River***, flowing NW to coast of Ross and Cromarty district, 1m/2km N of Redpoint. **94 D5** NG7371.

Erraid *Arg. & B.* ***Island***, sparsely populated island of 1 square mile or 3 square km, lying off W end of Ross of Mull across Erraid Sound. Described in unflattering terms by R.L. Stevenson in 'Kidnapped'. **78 D6** NM2919.

Erringden *W.Yorks.* ***Settlement***, 1m/2km S of Hebden Bridge. SD9826.

Erriottwood *Kent* ***Hamlet***, 3m/5km SE of Sittingbourne. TQ9359.

Errochty Water *P. & K.* ***River***, running E from Loch Errochty down Glen Errochty to River Garry near Calvine. **81 J1** NN8065.

Errogie *High.* ***Settlement***, near NE end of Loch Mhòr, in Inverness district, 3m/4km E of Inverfarigaig. **88 C2** NH5622.

Errol *P. & K.* Population: 1143. ***Village***, in Carse of Gowrie, 8m/13km E of Perth. **82 D5** NO2522.
Errollston *Aber.* ***Settlement***, 1km N of Cruden Bay. **91 J1** NK0837.
Errwood Reservoir *Derbys.* ***Reservoir***, 3m/5km NW of Buxton. **50 C5** SK0175.
Ersary *W.Isles Anglicised form of Earsairidh, qv.*
Erskine *Renf.* Population: 13,186. ***Town***, on S side of River Clyde near Erskine Bridge, 4m/6km NW of Renfrew. **74 C3** NS4571.
Ervie *D. & G.* ***Locality***, 6m/9km NW of Stranraer. **64 A4** NW9967.
Erwarton *Suff.* ***Village***, 2m/3km W of Shotley Gate. **35 G5** TM2134.
Erwood *Powys* ***Village***, 6m/10km SE of Builth Wells. **27 K4** SO0943.
Eryholme *N.Yorks.* ***Village***, 2m/3km E of Croft-on-Tees across loops of River Tees. **62 E6** NZ3208.
Eryrys *Denb.* ***Hamlet***, 5m/7km SW of Mold. **48 B7** SJ2057.
Escart *Arg. & B.* ***Settlement***, 2m/3km SW of Tarbert. **73 G4** NR8466.
Escley Brook *Here.* ***River***, rising SE of Hay-on-Wye and flowing S into River Monnow, to E of Longtown. **28 C5** SO3228.
Esclusham Mountain *Wrex.* ***Mountain***, 5m/8km W of Wrexham. Height 1496 feet or 456 metres. **48 B7** SJ2450.
Escomb *Dur.* ***Village***, 1m/2km W of Bishop Auckland. Restored 7c Saxon church. NZ1830.
Escot *Devon* ***Garden***, 3m/4km N of Ottery St. Mary. Includes parkland landscaped by 'Capability' Brown, a two-acre walled garden and 25-acre shrubbery garden, as well as a pet and aquatic centre. **7 J6** SY0893.
Escrick *N.Yorks.* ***Village***, 6m/10km S of York. **58 C5** SE6243.
Esdale Law *Sc.Bord.* ***Mountain***, 4m/7km NW of Hawick. Height 1168 feet or 356 metres. **69 K2** NT4417.
Esgair *Carmar.* ***Settlement***, 6m/9km NW of Carmarthen. **17 G2** SN3728.
Esgair Ambor *Cere.* ***Inland physical feature***, mountain ridge rising to over 510 metres, 4m/7km E of Tregaron. **27 G3** SN7559.
Esgair Berfa *Gwyn.* ***Mountain***, rounded summit 3m/4km SE of Fairbourne. Height 1640 feet or 500 metres. **37 F5** SH6309.
Esgair Cerrig *Cere.* ***Inland physical feature***, mountain ridge rising to over 490 metres, 6m/9km E of Llanddewi-Brefi. **27 G3** SN7456.
Esgair Cwmowen *Powys* ***Inland physical feature***, mountain ridge rising to over 400 metres, 3m/5km NE of Carno. **37 J6** SO0099.
Esgair Ddu *Powys* ***Mountain***, 1m/2km E of Aberangell. Height 1522 feet or 464 metres. **37 H4** SH8710.
Esgair Elan *Cere.* ***Inland physical feature***, mountain ridge rising to over 490 metres on S side of River Ystwyth, 4m/6km E of Cwmystwyth. **27 H1** SN8374.
Esgair Ferchon *Carmar.* ***Mountain***, 4m/6km NE of Pumsaint. Height 1424 feet or 434 metres. **27 G4** SN7142.
Esgair Fraith *Cere.* ***Inland physical feature***, mountain ridge rising to 485 metres, 2m/4km SE of Tregaron. **27 G3** SN7057.
Esgair Garthen *Powys* ***Inland physical feature***, mountain ridge rising to 508 metres, running E to W, just S of Claerwen Reservoir. **27 H2** SN8364.
Esgair Llethr *Cere.* ***Mountain***, 4m/6km E of Llanddewi-Brefi. Height 1542 feet or 470 metres. **27 G3** SN7254.
Esgair Llyn-du *Cere.* ***Inland physical feature***, mountain ridge in Tywi Forest, rising to over 530 metres. **27 G3** SN7661.
Esgair Priciau *Powys* ***Inland physical feature***, small plateau area 2m/3km NE of Llanbrynmair. **37 J5** SH9204.
Esgair y Maesnant *Powys* ***Inland physical feature***, mountain ridge rising to 504 metres, 2m/4km E of Plynlimon. **37 H7** SN8386.
Esgair Ychion *Powys* ***Inland physical feature***, mountain ridge rising to 562 metres, 3m/5km W of Llangurig. **27 H1** SN8579.
Esgairgeiliog *Powys* ***Village***, 3m/5km N of Machynlleth. **37 G5** SH7505.
Esgairnantau *Powys* ***Inland physical feature***, mountain ridge rising to over 550 metres, running N to S in W part of Radnor Forest. **28 A2** SO1762.
Esgerdawe *Carmar.* ***Settlement***, 3m/5km N of Llansawel. SN6140.
Esgyryn *Conwy* ***Hamlet***, on N side of Llandudno Junction. SH8078.
Esh *Dur.* ***Village***, 5m/8km W of Durham. **62 C2** NZ1944.
Esh Winning *Dur.* Population: 3643. ***Village***, 5m/8km W of Durham. **62 C2** NZ1941.
Esha Ness *Shet.* ***Coastal feature***, peninsula on NW coast of Mainland, 5m/8km W of Hillswick Lighthouse. Skerry of Eshaness is small island to S. **108 B5** HU2178.
Esher *Surr.* Population: 23,299. ***Town***, 4m/6km SW of Kingston upon Thames. 15c Waynflete Tower by River Mole. Claremont Landscape Garden (National Trust) to S. **22 E5** TQ1364.
Esholt *W.Yorks.* ***Village***, 3m/5km NE of Shipley, on N side of River Aire. SE1840.
Eshott *Northumb.* ***Hamlet***, 2m/3km SE of Felton. **71 H4** NZ2097.
Eshton *N.Yorks.* ***Hamlet***, 1m/2km N of Gargrave. **56 E4** SD9356.
Esk ***River***, formed by confluence of North and South Esk Rivers, 1m/2km N of Dalkeith, and flowing N to enter Firth of Forth at Musselburgh. **76 B4** NT3474.
Esk ***River***, rising as Rivers Black Esk and White Esk and flowing SE to Langholm, then S to Canonbie. Continuing S, it passes into England and flows past Longtown to head of Solway Firth, its channel joining that of River Eden SE of Annan. **69 J5** NY2463.
Esk *Cumb.* ***River***, rising at Esk Hause, to E of Scafell Pikes, and flowing SW into Irish Sea SW of Ravenglass. **60 C7** SD0693.
Esk *N.Yorks.* ***River***, rising on Farndale Moor, North York Moors National Park, and flowing N to Castleton, then E into North Sea at Whitby. **63 K6** NZ8911.
Esk Dale *N.Yorks.* ***Valley***, carrying River Esk E in North York Moors National Park between Danby and Sleights. **63 J6** NZ7207.
Esk Hause *Cumb.* ***Mountain***, saddle between Great End and Esk Pike, 1m/2km NE of Scafell Pike. Height 2490 feet or 759 metres. **60 D6** NY2307.
Esk Valley *N.Yorks.* ***Hamlet***, 1km SW of Grosmont. NZ8204.
Eskadale *High.* ***Settlement***, 6m/9km SW of Beauly. **88 B1** NH4439.
Eskbank *Midloth.* ***Suburb***, to SW of Dalkeith. **76 B4** NT3266.
Eskdale *Cumb.* ***Valley***, carrying River Esk and running SW from SE side of Scafell Pike to coast at Ravenglass. **60 C6** NY1900.
Eskdale Fell *Cumb.* ***Open space***, moorland to S of Burnmoor Tarn, 3m/5km SW of Scafell Pike. **60 C6** NY1803.
Eskdale Green *Cumb.* ***Village***, 4m/7km NE of Ravenglass. Outward Bound Mountain School and Mountain Rescue Post. **60 C6** NY1400.
Eskdalemuir *D. & G.* ***Settlement***, and church on River White Esk, 11m/17km NW of Langholm. Traces of Roman fort nearly 1m/2km N at Raeburnfoot. **69 H4** NY2597.
Eskett *Cumb.* ***Locality***, 1m/2km E of Frizington. NY0516.
Eskham *Lincs.* ***Settlement***, 1km SE of Marsh Chapel. **53 G3** TF3698.
Eskielawn *Angus* ***Mountain***, 3m/4km W of Balnaboth. Height 1991 feet or 607 metres. **82 D1** NO2766.
Eskin *High.* ***River***, formed by several tributaries from E slopes of Carn na Làraiche Maoile and flowing E into River Findhorn, 9m/15km NW of Kingussie. **88 D3** NH6512.
Esknish *Arg. & B.* ***Settlement***, on Islay, 3m/4km NE of Bridgend. **72 B4** NR3664.
Esperley Lane Ends *Dur.* ***Hamlet***, 1m/2km SW of Evenwood. NZ1324.
Espley Hall *Northumb.* ***Settlement***, 3m/5km NW of Morpeth. **71 G4** NZ1790.
Esprick *Lancs.* ***Hamlet***, 3m/4km N of Kirkham. **55 H6** SD4036.
Esscroft *W.Yorks.* ***Settlement***, 1m/2km NW of Burley in Wharfedale. SE1547.
Essendine *Rut.* ***Village***, 4m/6km N of Stamford. **42 D4** TF0412.
Essendon *Herts.* ***Village***, 3m/4km E of Hatfield. **23 F1** TL2708.
Essich *High.* ***Settlement***, in Inverness district, 4m/6km S of Inverness. **88 D1** NH6439.
Essington *Staffs.* ***Village***, 5m/7km NW of Walsall. **40 B5** SJ9603.
Esslemont *Aber.* ***Locality***, comprises many dispersed settlements near Bronie Burn, 2m/3km SW of Ellon. **91 H2** NJ9228.
Esthwaite Water *Cumb.* ***Lake/loch***, extending 2m/3km S from Hawkshead. **60 E7** SD3596.
Eston *R. & C.* Population: 18,671. ***Town***, in Teesside urban complex, 4m/6km E of Middlesbrough. Former mining town. **63 G5** NZ5418.
Estover *Plym.* ***Locality***, with industrial estate, 4m/7km NE of Plymouth. SX5159.
Eswick *Shet.* ***Settlement***, near E coast of Mainland, 1km W of headland Moul of Eswick. HU4853.
Etal *Northumb.* ***Village***, estate village on River Till, 8m/13km NW of Wooler. 18c hall. Remains of 14c castle (English Heritage). **77 H7** NT9239.
Etal Castle *Northumb.* ***Castle***, ruined 14c border castle (English Heritage), 2m/3km NW of Ford. **77 H7** NT9239.
Etchilhampton *Wilts.* ***Village***, 3m/5km E of Devizes. **20 D5** SU0460.
Etchingham *E.Suss.* ***Village***, 7m/11km N of Battle. **14 C5** TQ7126.
Etchinghill *Kent* ***Village***, 3m/5km N of Hythe. **15 G4** TR1639.
Etchinghill *Staffs.* ***Village***, 1m/2km W of Rugeley. **40 C4** SK0218.
Etchingwood *E.Suss.* ***Settlement***, 1m/2km SE of Buxted. TQ5022.
Etherdwick *E.Riding* ***Settlement***, 1m/2km SW of Aldbrough. TA2337.
Etherley Dene *Dur.* ***Village***, 1m/2km W of Bishop Auckland. NZ1928.
Etherow ***River***, rising SW of Dunford Bridge and flowing SW through a series of reservoirs in Longendale into River Goyt, to N of Marple. **49 J3** SJ9690.
Etherow Country Park *Gt.Man.* ***Leisure/recreation***, 250 acre country park with marshes, wooded valley slopes, pools and a reservoir 2m/3km NE of Romiley. River Etherow runs through park. **49 J3** SJ9791.
Ethie Mains *Angus* ***Hamlet***, 2m/3km SE of Inverkeilor. **83 H3** NO6948.
Etling Green *Norf.* ***Locality***, 2m/3km E of East Dereham. TG0113.
Eton *W. & M.* Population: 3767. ***Small town***, on N bank of River Thames, opposite Windsor. Boys' boarding school founded in 1440. **22 C4** SU9677.
Eton Wick *W. & M.* Population: 1974. ***Village***, 1m/2km W of Eton and 2m/3km SW of Slough. **22 C4** SU9578.
Etrop Green *Gt.Man.* ***Locality***, 3m/5km SE of Altrincham. SJ8185.
Etruria *Stoke* ***Suburb***, 1m/2km NW of Stoke-on-Trent city centre, at junction of Caldon Canal and Trent and Mersey Canal. Original site of Wedgwood pottery works. SJ8647.
Etterby *Cumb.* ***Suburb***, 1m/2km NW of Carlisle city centre across River Eden. NY3857.
Etteridge *High.* ***Settlement***, 4m/7km SW of Newtonmore. **88 D5** NN6892.
Ettiley Heath *Ches.* ***Village***, 1m/2km W of Sandbach. SJ7360.
Ettingshall *W.Mid.* ***Suburb***, SE district of Wolverhampton. **40 B6** SO9396.
Ettington *Warks.* ***Village***, 6m/9km SE of Stratford-upon-Avon. **30 D4** SP2649.
Etton *E.Riding* ***Village***, 4m/6km NW of Beverley. **59 F5** SE9843.
Etton *Peter.* ***Village***, 6m/10km NW of Peterborough. **42 E5** TF1406.
Ettrick *Sc.Bord.* ***Village***, on Ettrick Water, 15m/24km W of Hawick. Birthplace of James Hogg, poet, 1770-1835. **69 H2** NT2714.
Ettrick Bay *Arg. & B.* ***Bay***, wide bay on W coast of Bute, 3m/5km W of Rothesay. **73 J4** NS0365.
Ettrick Forest *Sc.Bord.* ***Large natural feature***, large area of moorland to S of Peebles, much used for sheep grazing. **69 G1** NT4832.
Ettrick Pen ***Mountain***, on border of Dumfries & Galloway and Scottish Borders, with cairn at summit, 7m/12km E of Moffat. Height 2270 feet or 692 metres. **69 G3** NT1907.
Ettrick Water *Sc.Bord.* ***River***, rising 6m/9km E of Moffat and flowing NE through Ettrick Forest to River Tweed, 3m/4km NE of Selkirk. **69 J1** NT4832.
Ettrickbridge *Sc.Bord.* ***Village***, on Ettrick Water, 6m/9km SW of Selkirk. **69 J1** NT3824.
Ettrickhill *Sc.Bord.* ***Settlement***, 1km W of Ettrick. **69 H2** NT2614.
Etwall *Derbys.* Population: 2534. ***Village***, 6m/10km SW of Derby. **40 E2** SK2631.
Etwall Common *Derbys.* ***Open space***, heath to SE of Etwall, 6m/10km SW of Derby. **40 E2** SK2730.
Euchan Water *D. & G.* ***River***, rising on mountains 9m/14km SW of Sanquhar and running NE to River Nith on S side of Sanquhar. **68 C3** NS7809.
Euden Beck *Dur.* ***River***, rises on Middleton Common and flows E through Hamsterley Forest to its confluence with Bedburn Beck. **62 B4** NZ0630.
Eudon George *Shrop.* ***Settlement***, 3m/5km SW of Bridgnorth. SO6888.
Eunay Mòr *W.Isles* ***Island***, islet in West Loch Roag, W coast of Isle of Lewis, close to W shore of Great Bernera. NB1336.
Eurach *Arg. & B.* ***Settlement***, 2m/3km SW of Ford. **79 K7** NM8401.
Euston *Suff.* ***Village***, 3m/5km SE of Thetford. **34 C1** TL8979.
Euximoor Drove *Cambs.* ***Settlement***, 4m/7km SE of March. TL4798.
Euximoor Fen *Cambs.* ***Open space***, fenland, 4m/6km NE of March. **43 H6** TL4799.
Euxton *Lancs.* ***Village***, 2m/4km NW of Chorley. **48 E1** SD5519.
Evanstown *Bridgend* ***Village***, on NW side of Gilfach Goch. SS9789.
Evanton *High.* Population: 1225. ***Village***, near N shore of Cromarty Firth, Ross and Cromarty district, 6m/9km NE of Dingwall. **96 D5** NH6066.
Eve Hill *W.Mid.* ***Locality***, 1km W of Dudley town centre. SO9390.
Evedon *Lincs.* ***Village***, 2m/3km NE of Sleaford. **42 D1** TF0947.
Evelix *High.* ***River***, in Sutherland district running S into Dornoch Firth at Ferrytown, 5m/8km W of Dornoch. **96 E2** NH7286.
Evelix *High.* ***Settlement***, 2m/3km NW of Dornoch. **96 E2** NH7691.
Even Swindon *Swin.* ***Suburb***, 1m/2km W of Swindon town centre. SU1384.
Evenjobb *Powys* ***Village***, 4m/6km SW of Presteigne. **28 B2** SO2662.
Evenley *Northants.* ***Village***, 1m/2km S of Brackley. **31 G5** SP5834.
Evenlode ***River***, rising near Moreton-in-Marsh and flowing SE into River Thames E of Eynsham. **30 E6** SP4509.
Evenlode *Glos.* ***Village***, 3m/5km NE of Stow-on-the-Wold. **30 D6** SP2229.
Evenwood *Dur.* Population: 1918. ***Village***, 2m/3km SW of West Auckland. **62 C4** NZ1525.
Evenwood Gate *Dur.* ***Hamlet***, 1m/2km SE of Evenwood. NZ1624.
Everbay *Ork.* ***Settlement***, on Stronsay, 1m/2km NE of Dishes. **106 F5** HY6724.
Evercreech *Som.* Population: 1821. ***Village***, 4m/6km SE of Shepton Mallet. **9 F1** ST6438.
Everdon *Northants.* ***Village***, 4m/6km SE of Daventry. **31 G3** SP5957.
Everingham *E.Riding* ***Village***, 5m/8km W of Market Weighton. **58 E5** SE8042.
Everleigh *Wilts.* ***Village***, 5m/8km NW of Ludgershall. **21 F6** SU1954.
Everley *High.* ***Settlement***, 1km N of Freswick. **105 J2** ND3669.
Everley *N.Yorks.* ***Settlement***, 4m/7km W of Scarborough. **59 F1** SE9788.
Eversholt *Beds.* ***Village***, 3m/5km E of Woburn. **32 C5** SP9932.
Evershot *Dorset* ***Village***, 5m/7km N of Maiden Newton. **8 E4** ST5704.
Eversley *Hants.* ***Village***, 5m/8km SW of Wokingham. Burial-place of Charles Kingsley, rector 1844-75. **22 A5** SU7762.
Eversley Cross *Hants.* ***Village***, 1m/2km E of Eversley. **22 A5** SU7762.
Everthorpe *E.Riding* ***Hamlet***, 1m/2km SE of North Cave. **59 F6** SE9031.
Everton *Beds.* ***Village***, 2m/3km NW of Potton. **33 F3** TL2051.
Everton *Hants.* ***Village***, 2m/3km SW of Lymington. **10 D5** SZ2994.
Everton *Mersey.* ***Suburb***, 1m/2km NE of Liverpool city centre. SJ3592.
Everton *Notts.* ***Village***, 3m/5km SE of Bawtry. **51 J3** SK6991.
Everton *Shet.* ***Locality***, on Mainland, 8m/13km N of Sumburgh Head. HU4121.
Evertown *D. & G.* ***Village***, 2m/3km W of Canonbie. **69 J6** NY3576.

Eves Corner *Essex* ***Locality***, adjoining to E of Danbury, 4m/7km W of Maldon. TL7805.
Eves Corner *Essex* ***Settlement***, 1km N of Burnham-on-Crouch. TQ9497.
Evesbatch *Here.* ***Village***, 5m/7km SE of Bromyard. **29 F4** SO6848.
Evesham *Worcs.* Population: 17,823. ***Town***, on River Avon, 13m/21km SE of Worcester. Centre of fruit and vegetable growing area. N of town is site of Battle of Evesham, 1265, marked by obelisk. 16c bell tower, remains of Evesham Abbey. **30 B4** SP0344.
Evesham Abbey *Worcs.* ***Ecclesiastical building***, ruins of large Benedictine abbey in centre of Evesham, founded in 8c. **30 B4** SP0343.
Evie (Also known as Georth.) *Ork.* ***Settlement***, on Mainland, 2m/3km NW of Woodwick. **106 C5** HY3625.
Evington *Leic.* ***Suburb***, 3m/5km SE of Leicester city centre. **41 J5** SK6104.
Ewart Newtown *Northumb.* ***Hamlet***, in valley of River Till, 3m/4km NW of Wooler. **77 H7** NT9631.
Ewden Village *S.Yorks.* ***Village***, 1m/2km S of Stocksbridge. **50 E3** SK2796.
Ewe Burn *High.* ***River***, stream flowing NE to join Halladale River 1km N of Forsinard, Caithness district. NC8945.
Ewe Hill *S.Lan.* ***Mountain***, 2m/3km NE of Biggar. Height 1178 feet or 359 metres. **75 J6** NT0540.
Ewe Hill *W.Berks.* ***Hill***, 1m/2km NE of Lambourn. Height 705 feet or 215 metres. **21 G3** SU3480.
Ewell *Surr.* Population: 32,202. ***Town***, 5m/8km SE of Kingston upon Thames. Site of Nonsuch Palace, huge mansion built by Henry VIII, 1km NE in Nonsuch Park. **23 F5** TQ2162.
Ewell Minnis *Kent* ***Village***, 4m/6km NW of Dover. **15 H3** TR2643.
Ewelme *Oxon.* ***Village***, 3m/5km SW of Watlington. **21 K2** SU6491.
Ewen *Glos.* ***Village***, 3m/5km SW of Cirencester. **20 D2** SU0097.
Ewenni *V. of Glam.* *Welsh form of Ewenny, qv.*
Ewenny (Ewenni). *V. of Glam.* ***Village***, 2m/3km S of Bridgend across Ewenny River. Ruins of 12c priory (Cadw) on river bank. **18 C4** SS9077.
Ewenny Priory *V. of Glam.* ***Ecclesiastical building***, early Norman priory (Cadw) to NE of Ewenny, 1m/2km S of Bridgend. Good example of part ecclesiastical, part defensive building. **18 C4** SS9177.
Ewerby *Lincs.* ***Village***, 4m/6km E of Sleaford. **42 E1** TF1247.
Ewerby Thorpe *Lincs.* ***Settlement***, 1m/2km E of Ewerby. **42 E1** TF1347.
Ewes Water *D. & G.* ***River***, flowing S to River Esk at Langholm. **69 J4** NY3684.
Eweslees Knowe *D. & G.* ***Mountain***, 4m/7km SW of Craik. Height 1469 feet or 448 metres. **69 J3** NT3201.
Ewesley Burn *Northumb.* ***River***, flowing E from Rothley Lake to its confluence with River Font at Netherwitton. **71 F4** NZ0990.
Ewhurst *E.Suss.* ***Village***, 4m/6km E of Robertsbridge. **14 C5** TQ7924.
Ewhurst *Surr.* ***Village***, 2m/3km E of Cranleigh. **22 D7** TQ0940.
Ewhurst Green *Surr.* ***Hamlet***, 1m/2km S of Ewhurst and 2m/3km E of Cranleigh. **12 D3** TQ0939.
Ewloe *Flints.* ***Village***, 1m/2km NW of Hawarden. Remains of 13c castle (Cadw) to NW. **48 B6** SJ2966.
Ewloe Castle *Flints.* ***Castle***, in Connah's Quay, 5m/8km W of Chester. Built by Owain Gwynedd, Prince of Wales, in 12c and converted to stone in early 13c by Llywelyn the Great. **48 B6** SJ2867.
Ewloe Green *Flints.* ***Settlement***, 1km W of Ewloe. SJ2866.
Ewood *B'burn.* ***Suburb***, 1m/2km S of Blackburn town centre. **56 B7** SD6725.
Ewood Bridge *Lancs.* ***Hamlet***, at crossing of River Irwell, 2m/3km S of Haslingden. SD7921.
Eworthy *Devon* ***Hamlet***, 9m/14km W of Okehampton. **6 C6** SX4495.
Ewshot *Hants.* ***Village***, 3m/4km NW of Farnham. **22 B7** SU8149.
Ewyas Harold *Here.* ***Village***, 1m/2km NW of Pontrilas. **28 C6** SO3828.
Exbourne *Devon* ***Village***, 4m/7km NE of Okehampton. **6 E5** SS6002.
Exbury *Hants.* ***Village***, 3m/5km SW of Fawley. Contains 200 acre Exbury Gardens noted for famous Rothschild collection of rhododendrons. **11 F4** SU4200.
Exbury Gardens *Hants.* ***Garden***, woodland gardens, including Rothschild plant collection, at Exbury House on E bank of Beaulieu River, 2m/3km SW of Blackfield. **11 F5** SZ4299.
Exceat *E.Suss.* ***Hamlet***, on Cuckmere River, 1m/2km N of Cuckmere Haven. TV5199.
Exe ***River***, rising on Exmoor and flowing E to Exton, then S through Tiverton to Exeter. Widens out into estuary at Topsham and flows into English Channel at Exmouth. **7 H4** SX9980.
Exe Valley *Devon* ***Valley***, part of River Exe valley, running S from Cove to Tiverton. **7 H4** SS9414.
Exebridge *Som.* ***Village***, on River Exe, 2m/3km NW of Bampton. **7 H3** SS9324.
Exelby *N.Yorks.* ***Village***, 2m/3km SE of Bedale. **57 H1** SE2987.
Exeter *Devon* Population: 94,717. ***City***, county capital on River Exe, 64m/103km SW of Bristol. Major administrative, business and financial centre on site of Roman town Isca Dumnoniorum. Cathedral is Decorated, with Norman towers and façade with hundreds of stone statues. 15c guildhall. Modern buildings in centre built after extensive damage from World War II. Beneath the city lie remains of medieval water-supply system built in 14c to supply fresh water to city centre. Maritime museum at Old Canal docks houses largest collection of boats in world. Early 16c mansion of Bowhill (English Heritage), with preserved Great Hall, 2m/3km SW. University 1m/2km N of city centre. Airport 5m/8km E at Clyst Honiton. **7 H6** SX9292.
Exeter *Northants.* ***Suburb***, S district of Corby. SP8887.
Exeter Canal *Devon* ***Canal***, running from Exeter to River Exe estuary, along W side of River Exe. SX9686.
Exeter Cathedral *Devon* ***Ecclesiastical building***, built on site of Saxon monastery in Exeter city centre. Present building dates from 12c. Roof has longest continuous stretch of Gothic vaulting in world (over 300 feet or 92 metres). **7 H6** SX9292.
Exford *Som.* ***Village***, on Exmoor and River Exe, 9m/15km SW of Dunster. **7 G2** SS8538.
Exfords Green *Shrop.* ***Hamlet***, 5m/8km SW of Shrewsbury. **38 D5** SJ4506.
Exhall *Warks.* ***Locality***, 2m/3km SW of Bedworth. **41 F7** SP3585.
Exhall *Warks.* ***Village***, 2m/3km SE of Alcester. **30 C3** SP1055.
Exlade Street *Oxon.* ***Hamlet***, 4m/6km NE of Pangbourne. **21 K3** SU6581.
Exley *W.Yorks.* ***Suburb***, 2m/3km S of Halifax town centre. SE0922.
Exminster *Devon* Population: 1916. ***Village***, 4m/6km SE of Exeter. **7 H7** SX9487.
Exmoor (Exmoor Forest). ***Large natural feature***, high moorland area bounded on N by Bristol Channel and on S roughly by a line drawn through Ilfracombe, North Molton and Dulverton. Once a royal forest, now designated (with Brendon Hills to E) Exmoor National Park. Majority of land forms large plateau with steep-sided deep valleys covered by woodland. Brendon Hills are typically a lower, more rolling range. **7 F1** SS7540.
Exmoor Forest *See Exmoor.*
Exmouth *Devon* Population: 28,414. ***Town***, resort on E side of mouth of River Exe, 9m/15km SE of Exeter. Ferry to Starcross (foot passengers). To N is 16-sided 18c house of A la Ronde (National Trust). **7 J7** SY0080.
Exnaboe *Shet.* ***Locality***, on Mainland, to N of Sumburgh Airport across Pool of Virkie. **109 G10** HU3911.
Exning *Suff.* Population: 1932. ***Village***, 2m/3km NW of Newmarket. **33 K2** TL6265.
Exted *Kent* ***Settlement***, 1km NW of Elham. TR1644.
Exton *Devon* ***Village***, on E bank of River Exe estuary, 4m/6km N of Exmouth. **7 H7** SX9886.
Exton *Hants.* ***Village***, 1km N of Meonstoke. **11 H2** SU6120.
Exton *Rut.* ***Village***, 4m/7km E of Oakham. **42 C4** SK9211.
Exton *Som.* ***Village***, on River Exe, 4m/6km N of Dulverton. **7 H2** SS9233.
Exwick *Devon* ***Village***, on W bank of River Exe opposite St. David's railway station across river and 1m/2km NW of Exeter city centre. **7 H6** SX9093.
Ey Burn *Aber.* ***River***, running N down Glen Ey to River Dee at Inverey, 4m/7km W of Braemar. **89 H6** NO0889.
Eyam *Derbys.* ***Village***, 5m/8km N of Bakewell. Annual well-dressing ceremony. Saxon cross in churchyard. **50 E5** SK2176.
Eyam Moor *Derbys.* ***Open space***, to N of Eyam, with ancient stone circle (English Heritage). **50 E5** SK2278.
Eydon *Northants.* ***Village***, 8m/13km NE of Banbury. **31 G3** SP5450.
Eye *Here.* ***Hamlet***, 3m/5km N of Leominster. **28 D2** SO4963.
Eye *Leics.* ***River***, rising 2m/3km W of Saltby and flowing E to Saltby, S to Coston, SE by Garthorpe and then E to Melton Mowbray where it becomes River Wreake. **42 B3** SK7518.
Eye *Peter.* Population: 3010. ***Suburb***, 4m/6km NE of Peterborough. **43 F5** TF2202.
Eye *Suff.* Population: 1741. ***Small town***, 4m/7km SE of Diss. Slight remains of castle. **35 F1** TM1473.
Eye Brook ***River***, rising SW of Tilton on the Hill, flowing SE into Eyebrook Reservoir and into River Welland to E of Caldecott. **42 A5** SP8793.
Eye Castle *Suff.* ***Castle***, in Eye, built by William Malet in 11c, with later additions, some of which remain today. **35 F1** TM1473.
Eye Green *Peter.* ***Hamlet***, 1km N of Eye. **43 F5** TF2203.
Eye Peninsula (Gaelic form: An Rubha. Also known as Point.) *W.Isles* ***Coastal feature***, peninsula on E side of Isle of Lewis, 4m/6km E of Stornoway, measuring 7m/11km NE to SW and up to 2m/4km NW to SE. Forms SE arm of Loch a' Tuath. **101 H4** NB5232.
Eye Water ***River***, rising on Lammermuir Hills, 2m/3km SW of Oldhamstocks, and running E by Grantshouse and Ayton to North Sea at Eyemouth. **77 G4** NT9464.
Eyebrook Reservoir *Leics.* ***Reservoir***, large reservoir nearly 2m/3km long, 1m/2km NW of Caldecott and 5m/8km NW of Corby. **42 B6** SP8595.
Eyemouth *Sc.Bord.* Population: 3473. ***Small town***, and resort on coast, 8m/13km NW of Berwick-upon-Tweed. **77 H4** NT9464.
Eyemouth Museum *Sc.Bord.* ***Other feature of interest***, in Eyemouth town centre, dedicated to memory of 129 fishermen who died in 1881, and includes 15 foot Eyemouth tapestry and exhibits on local history. **77 H4** NT9464.
Eyeworth *Beds.* ***Village***, 4m/6km E of Biggleswade. **33 F4** TL2445.
Eyhorne Manor *Kent* ***Historic house***, 15c Wealden yeoman farmer's house with 17c-18c additions, in Hollingbourne to N of Bearsted. **14 D2** TQ8455.
Eyhorne Street *Kent* ***Village***, 5m/8km E of Maidstone. **14 D2** TQ8354.
Eyke *Suff.* ***Village***, 3m/5km NE of Woodbridge across River Deben. **35 H3** TM3151.
Eynesbury *Cambs.* ***Suburb***, S district of St. Neots. **32 E3** TL1859.
Eynhallow *Ork.* ***Island***, uninhabited island, 1km across, in Eynhallow Sound between islands of Mainland and Rousay. Faint remains of medieval monastery (Historic Scotland). **106 C5** HY3529.
Eynhallow Church *Ork.* ***Ecclesiastical building***, largely ruined 12c church on Eynhallow, 1km off NE coast of Mainland. **106 C5** HY3528.
Eynhallow Sound *Ork.* ***Sea feature***, between islands of Mainland and Rousay. **106 C5** HY3529.
Eynort *High.* ***Settlement***, at head of Loch Eynort, Skye. **85 J2** NG3826.
Eynsford *Kent* Population: 1568. ***Village***, on River Darent, 3m/4km SE of Swanley. Remains of Norman castle (English Heritage). To SW across river, Lullingstone Roman villa (English Heritage) and Lullingstone Castle, 18c house with 16c gateway. **23 J5** TQ5465.
Eynsford Castle *Kent* ***Castle***, remains of a flint-walled Norman castle (English Heritage) to W of Eynsford, 2m/4km SE of Swanley. **23 J5** TQ5366.
Eynsham *Oxon.* Population: 4764. ***Small town***, 6m/9km NW of Oxford. Access from S via 18c tollbridge. **21 H1** SP4309.
Eype *Dorset* ***Village***, near coast 1m/2km SW of Bridport. **8 D5** SY4491.
Eype Mouth *Dorset* *See Golden Cap.*
Eyre *High.* ***Settlement***, on Skye, on E side of Loch Snizort Beag at entrance to Loch Eyre, 7m/11km S of Uig. **93 K6** NG4152.
Eythorne *Kent* Population: 1513. ***Village***, 5m/8km N of Dover. **15 H3** TR2849.
Eyton *Here.* ***Village***, 2m/3km NW of Leominster. **28 D2** SO4761.
Eyton *Shrop.* ***Settlement***, 3m/4km SE of Bishop's Castle. **38 C7** SO3787.
Eyton *Wrex.* ***Settlement***, 1km SE of Stryt-yr-hwch and 3m/5km S of Wrexham. SJ3444.
Eyton on Severn *Shrop.* ***Hamlet***, 2m/3km NW of Cressage. SJ5706.
Eyton upon the Weald Moors *Tel. & W.* ***Village***, 2m/3km N of Wellington. **39 F4** SJ6514.
Eywood *Here.* ***Settlement***, 2m/3km NE of Kington. **28 C3** SO3159.

F

Faberstown *Hants.* ***Locality***, adjoining to E of Ludgershall. SU2750.
Faccombe *Hants.* ***Village***, 3m/5km N of Hurstbourne Tarrant. **21 G6** SU3958.
Faceby *N.Yorks.* ***Village***, 4m/6km SW of Stokesley. **63 F6** NZ4903.
Fachwen *Gwyn.* ***Hamlet***, nearly 1m/2km S of Deiniolen. **46 D6** SH5761.
Facit *Lancs.* ***Hamlet***, adjoining to N of Whitworth, 4m/6km N of Rochdale. SD8819.
Fackley *Notts.* ***Hamlet***, 2m/3km NW of Sutton in Ashfield. SK4761.
Faddiley *Ches.* ***Village***, 4m/6km W of Nantwich. **48 E7** SJ5953.
Fadmoor *N.Yorks.* ***Hamlet***, 2m/4km NW of Kirkbymoorside. **58 C1** SE6789.
Faebait *High.* ***Settlement***, 3m/5km W of Muir of Ord. **96 B6** NH4850.
Faerdre *Swan.* *Welsh form of Vardre, qv.*
Fagley *W.Yorks.* ***Suburb***, 2m/3km NE of Bradford city centre. SE1834.
Faifley *W.Dun.* Population: 6087. ***Small town***, 2m/3km N of Clydebank. **74 D3** NS5073.
Fail *S.Ayr.* ***Settlement***, 1m/2km NW of Tarbolton. **67 J1** NS4228.
Failand *N.Som.* ***Village***, 4m/7km W of Bristol. **19 J4** ST5271.
Failford *S.Ayr.* ***Hamlet***, on N bank of meander of River Ayr, 3m/4km W of Mauchline. **67 J1** NS4526.
Failsworth *Gt.Man.* Population: 20,160. ***Town***, industrial and residential town, 5m/7km NE of Manchester. Former cotton town. **49 H2** SD8901.
Fain *High.* ***Settlement***, 6m/9km SE of Dundonnell. **95 H4** NH1379.
Fair Bhuidhe *P. & K.* ***Mountain***, rounded summit 3m/4km NW of Blair Atholl. Height 1515 feet or 462 metres. **81 K1** NN8467.
Fair Cross *Gt.Lon.* ***Suburb***, 1m/2km NE of Barking. TQ4585.
Fair Hill *Cumb.* ***Suburb***, adjoining to N of Penrith. NY5131.
Fair Isle *Shet.* ***Island***, sparsely inhabited island (National Trust for Scotland), about 3m/5km N to S and 1m/2km E to W, lying 24m/39km SW of Sumburgh Head. Harbour at S end of island. **108 A1** HZ2172.
Fair Isle Airstrip *Shet.* ***Airport/airfield***, 1km NE of Stonybreck. **108 A1** HZ2172.
Fair Oak *Devon* ***Hamlet***, 1km SW of Hockworthy. ST0318.
Fair Oak *Hants.* ***Settlement***, 2m/4km NE of Kingsclere. **21 J5** SU5561.
Fair Oak *Hants.* ***Suburb***, 3m/4km E of Eastleigh. **11 F3** SU4918.
Fair Oak Green *Hants.* ***Hamlet***, 6m/10km NE of Basingstoke. SU6660.
Fair Snape Fell *Lancs.* ***Mountain***, on moor on SW side of Forest of Bowland, 6m/10km N of Longridge. Height 1673 feet or 510 metres. **55 J5** SD5946.
Fairbourne *Gwyn.* ***Village***, 2m/3km S of Barmouth across River Mawddach estuary. **37 F4** SH6112.
Fairbourne Heath *Kent* ***Settlement***, 2m/3km S of Harrietsham. TQ8550.
Fairbourne Railway *Gwyn.* ***Other feature of interest***, narrow gauge railway running N from Fairbourne along spit at mouth of Mawddach estuary. Connected to Barmouth by passenger ferry. **37 F4** SH6112.

Fairburn *N.Yorks.* ***Village***, 2m/4km N of Ferrybridge. Lakes to S and W created by coal-mining subsidence. **57 K7** SE4727.

Fairfield *Cumb.* ***Mountain***, in Lake District 2m/4km SE of Helvellyn. Height 2863 feet or 873 metres. **60 E5** NY3511.

Fairfield *Derbys.* ***Suburb***, E district of Buxton. **50 C5** SK0673.

Fairfield *Gt.Man.* ***Suburb***, 2m/3km E of Bury town centre. SD8211.

Fairfield *Gt.Man.* ***Suburb***, 4m/6km E of Manchester. SJ9097.

Fairfield *Kent* ***Settlement***, 2m/3km S of Appledore. TQ9626.

Fairfield *Mersey.* ***Settlement***, 1km SW of Brimstage. SJ2982.

Fairfield *Mersey.* ***Suburb***, 2m/4km E of Liverpool city centre. SJ3791.

Fairfield *Stock.* ***Suburb***, 1m/2km W of Stockton-on-Tees town centre. NZ4119.

Fairfield *Worcs.* ***Suburb***, to S of Evesham town centre across River Avon. SP0342.

Fairfield *Worcs.* ***Village***, 3m/5km N of Bromsgrove. **29 J1** SO9475.

Fairford *Glos.* Population: 2633. ***Small town***, market town, 8m/13km E of Cirencester. Birthplace of John Keble. St. Mary's Church has fine collection of 15c glass. Airfield to S. **20 E1** SP1501.

Fairgirth *D. & G.* ***Settlement***, 1m/2km NW of Sandyhills Bay, 4m/6km SE of Dalbeattie. **65 J5** NX8756.

Fairham Brook ***River***, rising near Old Dalby and flowing NW into River Trent at West Bridgford. **41 H2** SK5636.

Fairhaven *Lancs.* ***Suburb***, to W of Lytham St. Anne's town centre. SD3227.

Fairhaven Garden *Norf.* ***Garden***, on S side of South Walsham Broad, just N of South Walsham. Gardens, with private broad, a water garden and woodland. **45 H4** TG3613.

Fairhill *S.Lan.* ***Suburb***, S district of Hamilton. NS7154.

Fairholm *S.Lan.* ***Suburb***, adjoining to NW of Larkhall. **75 F5** NS7651.

Fairleigh *W.Yorks.* ***Locality***, adjoining to SW of Pontefract. SE4421.

Fairley *Aberdeen* ***Settlement***, 2m/3km E of Westhill. **91 G4** NJ8607.

Fairlie *N.Ayr.* Population: 1516. ***Small town***, resort on Firth of Clyde, 3m/5km S of Largs. Remains of 16c castle inland in Fairlie Glen. **74 A5** NS2055.

Fairlie Roads *N.Ayr.* ***Sea feature***, sea passage between mainland and the Cumbraes. **73 K5** NS2055.

Fairlight *E.Suss.* Population: 1605. ***Village***, 3m/5km E of Hastings. **14 D6** TQ8611.

Fairlight Cove *E.Suss.* ***Village***, on coast, 1m/2km E of Fairlight. **14 D6** TQ8711.

Fairlop *Gt.Lon.* ***Settlement***, in borough of Redbridge, 3m/5km NE of Ilford. TQ4590.

Fairlop Waters Country Park *Gt.Lon.* ***Leisure/recreation***, in borough of Redbridge, 1km S of Hainault. **23 H2** TQ4590.

Fairlynch Arts Centre and Museum *Devon* ***Other feature of interest***, in Budleigh Salterton. Exhibitions on local history and geology. **7 J7** SY0682.

Fairmile *Devon* ***Hamlet***, on River Tale 1m/2km NW of Ottery St. Mary. **7 J6** SY0897.

Fairmile *Surr.* ***Suburb***, 1m/2km NE of Cobham. Fairmile Common to N. TQ1261.

Fairmilehead *Edin.* ***Suburb***, 4m/6km S of Edinburgh city centre. **76 A4** NT2468.

Fairmoor *Northumb.* ***Settlement***, 1m/2km NW of Morpeth. NZ1887.

Fairnington *Sc.Bord.* ***Hamlet***, 3m/4km NE of Ancrum. **70 B1** NT6427.

Fairoak *Caerp.* ***Settlement***, 1m/2km N of Blackwood. ST1799.

Fairoak *Staffs.* ***Hamlet***, 5m/8km NW of Eccleshall. **39 G2** SJ7632.

Fairseat *Kent* ***Village***, on North Downs, 2m/3km NE of Wrotham. **24 C5** TQ6261.

Fairstead *Essex* ***Hamlet***, 4m/6km W of Witham. **34 B7** TL7616.

Fairstead *Norf.* ***Hamlet***, 4m/7km S of North Walsham. **45 G3** TG2823.

Fairwarp *E.Suss.* ***Hamlet***, 4m/6km N of Uckfield. **13 H4** TQ4626.

Fairwater (Tyllgoed). *Cardiff* ***Suburb***, 3m/4km W of Cardiff city centre. ST1377.

Fairwater *Torfaen* ***Suburb***, in SW part of Cwmbran. ST2794.

Fairwater Grove *Cardiff* ***Suburb***, adjoining to E of Fairwater, in Cardiff. ST1477.

Fairwood *Swan.* ***Settlement***, 5m/9km W of Swansea. Swansea Airport at Fairwood Common, to S. SS5693.

Fairy Cross *Devon* ***Hamlet***, 4m/6km SW of Bideford. **6 C3** SS4024.

Fairy Glen *Conwy* ***Valley***, carrying River Conwy between Conwy Falls and confluence with River Lledr. **47 F7** SH8054.

Fairyhill *Swan.* ***Settlement***, 2m/3km SW of Llanrhidian. **17 H5** SS4691.

Fakenham *Norf.* Population: 6471. ***Small town***, on River Wensum, 23m/37km NW of Norwich. Market place with attractive 18c buildings. Museum of Gas and Local History houses substantially complete Victorian gas works, with displays of domestic gas appliances spanning 20c, and life and history of the town. **44 D3** TF9229.

Fal *Cornw.* ***River***, rising on Goss Moor N of St. Dennis and flowing S and SW to form estuary of Carrick Roads below Turnaware Point before flowing past Falmouth into English Channel between Pendennis Point and Zone Point. **3 G4** SW8331.

Fala *Midloth.* ***Village***, to N of Fala Moor, 4m/6km SE of Pathhead. **76 C4** NT4360.

Fala Dam *Midloth.* ***Hamlet***, 1km NW of Fala. **76 C4** NT4261.

Fala Moor *Midloth.* ***Open space***, moorland 6m/9km SE of Gorebridge and 2m/3km SW of Fala. **76 C5** NT4360.

Falahill *Sc.Bord.* ***Hamlet***, on NE side of Moorfoot Hills, 4m/7km SE of Gorebridge. **76 B5** NT3956.

Falconer Museum *Moray* ***Other feature of interest***, in Forres, with local history exhibits and memorabilia on Hugh Falconer. **97 H6** NJ0459.

Faldingworth *Lincs.* ***Village***, 4m/6km SW of Market Rasen. **52 D4** TF0684.

Falfield *Fife* ***Settlement***, 3m/5km SE of Ceres. **83 F7** NO4408.

Falfield *S.Glos.* ***Village***, 4m/6km NE of Thornbury. **19 K2** ST6893.

Falhouse Green *W.Yorks.* ***Hamlet***, 1km N of Grange Moor, 2m/3km NE of Fenay Bridge. SE2117.

Falin-Wnda *Cere.* ***Settlement***, 4m/7km N of Newcastle Emlyn. SN3246.

Falkenham *Suff.* ***Village***, 3m/5km N of Felixstowe. **35 G5** TM2939.

Falkirk *Falk.* Population: 35,610. ***Town***, industrial town 23m/37km W of Edinburgh. Sections of Antonine Wall visible in town and vicinity. Scene of battle in 1746 in which Prince Charles Edward defeated government forces. **75 G3** NS8880.

Falkland *Fife* Population: 1197. ***Small town***, attractive historic town below NE slope of Lomond Hills, 4m/7km N of Glenrothes. Royal Palace (National Trust for Scotland), 16c. **82 D7** NO2507.

Falkland Palace *Fife* ***Historic house***, in Falkland, 11m/18km N of Kirkcaldy. Country hunting lodge of Stuart monarch from 16c (National Trust for Scotland). Good example of Renaissance style, with beautiful gardens and, reputedly, oldest tennis court in world. **82 D7** NO2507.

Fall of Warness *Ork.* ***Sea feature***, stretch of sea dividing Eday from Muckle Green Holm. **106 E5** HY5328.

Falla *Sc.Bord.* ***Hamlet***, 2m/3km E of Camptown. **70 C2** NT7013.

Fallgate *Derbys.* ***Hamlet***, 3m/4km W of Clay Cross. **51 F6** SK3562.

Fallin *Stir.* Population: 2479. ***Village***, 3m/4km SE of Stirling. **75 G1** NS8391.

Falling Foss *N.Yorks.* ***Waterfall***, in course of May Beck, 1m/2km S of Littlebeck and 5m/8km S of Whitby. **63 K6** NZ8803.

Fallings Heath *W.Mid.* ***Locality***, on border of Walsall and West Bromwich, 2m/3km SW of Walsall town centre. SO9896.

Falloch ***River***, rising on W side of Beinn a' Chroin and flowing N, then SW down Glen Falloch and S to head of Loch Lomond. **80 E5** NN3115.

Fallowfield *Gt.Man.* ***Suburb***, 3m/4km SE of Manchester city centre. SJ8593.

Fallowfield *Northumb.* ***Hamlet***, 1m/2km E of Wall, 3m/5km N of Hexham. NY9268.

Fallowlees Burn *Northumb.* ***River***, stream rising in Harwood Forest and flowing generally E into Fontburn Reservoir. **70 E4** NZ0393.

Falls of Acharn *P. & K.* ***Waterfall***, cascade along Acharn Burn, nearly 1km S of where river enters Loch Tay and 2m/3km SW of Kenmore. **81 J3** NN7543.

Falls of Balnaguard *P. & K.* *See Balnaguard Burn.*

Falls of Barvick *P. & K.* ***Waterfall***, in course of Barvick Burn 2m/3km NW of Crieff. **81 K5** NN8524.

Falls of Bracklinn *Stir.* *Alternative name for Bracklinn Falls, qv.*

Falls of Clyde *S.Lan.* ***Waterfall***, series of waterfalls in course of River Clyde in vicinity of Lanark. Former impressiveness modified by hydro-electricity schemes. **75 G6** NS8840.

Falls of Conon *High.* ***Waterfall***, series of cascades in course of River Conon below Loch Luichart, Ross and Cromarty district. **95 K6** NH3857.

Falls of Cruachan *Arg. & B.* ***Waterfall***, in course of stream in Argyll running from Cruachan Reservoir into Loch Awe. Diminished since construction of reservoir. **80 B5** NN0727.

Falls of Drumly Harry *Angus* ***Waterfall***, in Noran Water, 3m/5km NW of Tannadice. **83 F1** NO4562.

Falls of Falloch *Stir.* ***Waterfall***, in Glen Falloch, 4m/7km SW of Crianlarich. **80 E5** NN3320.

Falls of Fender *P. & K.* *See Fender Burn.*

Falls of Garbh Allt *Aber.* ***Waterfall***, in course of stream running N through Ballochbuie Forest to River Dee 3m/5km E of Braemar. **89 J6** NO1989.

Falls of Glomach *High.* ***Waterfall***, National Trust for Scotland property in Allt a' Ghlomaich, Skye and Lochalsh district, 5m/9km SE of Killilan. Height 370 feet or 113 metres. **87 G2** NH0125.

Falls of Keltie *P. & K.* ***Waterfall***, in course of Keltie Burn 1m/2km W of Monzie. **81 K5** NN8625.

Falls of Keltney *P. & K.* *See Keltney Burn.*

Falls of Kirkaig *High.* ***Waterfall***, in course of River Kirkaig, 1km W of Fionn Loch. **102 D7** NC1118.

Falls of Lochay *Stir.* ***Waterfall***, in River Lochay 2m/4km NW of Killin. Hydro-electricity power station to E. **81 G4** NN5435.

Falls of Measach *High.* ***Waterfall***, in course of Abhainn Droma, headstream of River Broom, Ross and Cromarty district. Waterfall (National Trust for Scotland) occurs where river passes through Corrieshalloch Gorge. NH2077.

Falls of Moness *P. & K.* ***Waterfall***, series of three waterfalls in Urlar Burn 1m/2km S of Aberfeldy. **81 K3** NN8547.

Falls of Ness *P. & K.* ***Waterfall***, in course of Machany Water 1m/2km SE of Muthill. **81 K6** NN8815.

Falls of Orrin *High.* ***Waterfall***, in course of River Orrin, 4m/7km SW of Dingwall and 3m/5km SW from confluence of Rivers Orrin and Conon. **96 B6** NH4652.

Falls of Shin *High.* ***Waterfall***, in course of River Shin, 2m/3km above mouth. **96 C2** NH5799.

Falls of Tarf *P. & K.* ***Waterfall***, in course of Tarf Water, 11m/17km NE of Blair Atholl. **89 G6** NN9879.

Falls of the Bruar *P. & K.* ***Waterfall***, in fir plantation in course of Bruar Water, 1km from its outfall into River Garry E of Calvine. **81 K1** NN8166.

Falls of Truim *High.* ***Waterfall***, in Glen Truim, Badenoch and Strathspey district, 3m/5km above mouth of River Truim. **88 D5** NN6792.

Falls of Tummel *P. & K.* ***Waterfall***, in course of River Tummel, 2m/3km NW of Pitlochry. **81 K2** NN9059.

Falls of Turret *P. & K.* ***Waterfall***, in Glen Turret 3m/4km NW of Crieff. **81 K5** NN8324.

Falls of Unich *Angus* *See Water of Unich.*

Fallside *N.Lan.* ***Suburb***, 3m/5km S of Coatbridge. NS7160.

Falmer *E.Suss.* ***Village***, 4m/7km NE of Brighton town centre. **13 G6** TQ3508.

Falmouth *Cornw.* Population: 20,297. ***Town***, largest town in Cornwall, 10m/16km SE of Redruth and 8m/12km S of Truro. Port with large natural anchorage (Carrick Roads). Popular yachting centre. Includes Pendennis Point, with 15c castle. **3 F5** SW8032.

Falmouth Bay *Cornw.* ***Bay***, S of Falmouth, extending from Pendennis Point southwards to Rosemullion Head. **3 F5** SW8129.

Falsgrave *N.Yorks.* ***Suburb***, SW district of Scarborough. **59 G1** TA0387.

Falstone *Northumb.* ***Hamlet***, in Kielder Forest, on River North Tyne, 8m/12km W of Bellingham. **70 C5** NY7287.

Fan Brycheiniog *Powys* *Welsh form of Carmarthen Van, qv.*

Fan Bwlch Chwyth *Powys* ***Mountain***, 2m/3km E of Cray Reservoir. Height 1978 feet or 603 metres. **27 H6** SN9121.

Fan Fawr *Powys* ***Mountain***, summit of Fforest Fawr, 3m/4km SW of Brecon Beacons. Height 2408 feet or 734 metres. **27 J7** SN9619.

Fan Frynych *Powys* ***Mountain***, 4m/7km SE of Sennybridge. Height 2063 feet or 629 metres. **27 J6** SN9522.

Fan Gyhirych *Powys* ***Mountain***, one of the high peaks of Fforest Fawr, 1m/2km S of Cray Reservoir. Height 2378 feet or 725 metres. **27 H7** SN8819.

Fan Hill *Powys* ***Mountain***, 1km E of Llyn Clywedog. Height 1581 feet or 482 metres. **37 J7** SN9388.

Fan Hir *Powys* ***Inland physical feature***, rocky outcrop, 2m/3km NE of Carreg Goch. **27 H7** SN8219.

Fan Llia *Powys* ***Mountain***, one of Fforest Fawr peaks, 4m/6km E of Fan Gyhirych. Height 2070 feet or 631 metres. **27 J7** SN9318.

Fan Nedd *Powys* ***Mountain***, one of Fforest Fawr peaks, 6m/10km N of Pontneddfechan. Height 2175 feet or 663 metres. **27 J7** SN9118.

Fanagmore *High.* ***Settlement***, on S side of Loch Laxford, 4m/6km N of Scourie, in Sutherland district. **102 D3** NC1749.

Fanagoed *Carmar.* ***River***, flowing SW into River Cothi, 2m/3km N of Pumsaint. **27 F4** SN6742.

Fanans *Arg. & B.* ***Settlement***, 2m/3km SE of Taynuilt. **80 B5** NN0329.

Fancott *Beds.* ***Hamlet***, 4m/6km N of Dunstable. **32 D6** TL0227.

Fanellan *High.* ***Locality***, in Inverness district, 4m/6km SW of Beauly. NH4842.

Fangdale Beck *N.Yorks.* ***Hamlet***, 3m/5km S of Chop Gate. **63 G7** SE5694.

Fangfoss *E.Riding* ***Village***, 4m/6km SE of Stamford Bridge. **58 D4** SE7653.

Fankerton *Falk.* ***Village***, 1m/2km W of Denny. NS7883.

Fanmore *Arg. & B.* ***Settlement***, on Mull, on N side of Loch Tuath, 5m/8km S of Dervaig. **79 F3** NM4144.

Fanna Hill *Sc.Bord.* ***Mountain***, in Wauchope Forest area of Cheviot Hills, 1m/2km NW of Singdean. Height 1686 feet or 514 metres. **70 A3** NT5603.

Fanner's Green *Essex* ***Hamlet***, 4m/6km NW of Chelmsford town centre. TL6812.

Fannich Forest *High.* ***Open space***, deer forest in Ross and Cromarty district N of Loch Fannich. **95 H5** NH1969.

Fans *Sc.Bord.* ***Settlement***, 2m/4km SW of Gordon. **76 E6** NT6240.

Faochaig *High.* ***Mountain***, in Killilan Forest, Skye and Lochalsh district. Height 2847 feet or 868 metres. **87 G1** NH0231.

Far Bank *S.Yorks.* ***Locality***, adjoining to W of Fishlake, 3m/4km W of Thorne. SE6413.

Far Banks *Lancs.* ***Settlement***, 1m/2km NE of Banks. SD4121.

Far Bletchley *M.K.* ***Suburb***, adjoining to SW of Bletchley. SP8433.

Far Cotton *Northants.* ***Suburb***, S district of Northampton. **31 J3** SP7459.

Far End *Cumb.* ***Hamlet***, adjoining to N of Coniston, on S side of Coniston Fells. SD3098.

Far Forest *Worcs.* ***Locality***, on S side of Wyre Forest, 4m/6km W of Bewdley. **29 G1** SO7274.

Far Gearstones *N.Yorks.* ***Settlement***, on W side of Gayle Beck, 1m/2km NE of Ribblehead Station. **56 C1** SD7880.

Far Green *Glos.* ***Hamlet***, 2m/4km NE of Dursley. SO7700.

Far Laund *Derbys.* ***Locality***, 1m/2km NE of Belper. SK3648.

Far Moor *Gt.Man.* ***Suburb***, to S of Orrell, 3m/5km W of Wigan. SD5304.

Far Oakridge *Glos.* ***Hamlet***, to E of Oakridge Lynch, 5m/8km E of Stroud. SO9203.

Far Out Head *High.* *Alternative name for Faraid Head, qv.*

Far Royds *W.Yorks.* ***Suburb***, 2m/4km SW of Leeds city centre. SE2631.

Far Sawrey *Cumb.* ***Village***, 2m/4km SE of Hawkshead. SD3795.

Far Thorpe *Lincs.* ***Settlement***, 3m/5km N of Horncastle. TF2673.

Far Thorpe Green *Essex* ***Locality***, 5m/8km N of Clacton-on-Sea. TM1622.

Fara *Ork.* *Alternative spelling of Faray, qv.*

Fara *Ork.* ***Island***, sparsely inhabited island of about 200 acres or 80 hectares between E coast of Hoy and Flotta. **107 C8** ND3295.

Faraclett Head *Ork.* ***Coastal feature***, headland at NE end of Rousay on E side of Saviskaill Bay. **106 D4** HY4433.
Faraid Head (Also known as Far Out Head.) *High.* ***Coastal feature***, headland on N coast of Sutherland district, 3m/4km N of Durness. **103 F1** NC3971.
Faray (Also spelled Fara or Pharay.) *Ork.* ***Island***, narrow uninhabited island less than 2m/3km long N to S, lying 1m/2km W of Eday across Sound of Faray. **106 E4** HY5336.
Farcet *Cambs.* ***Village***, 3m/4km S of Peterborough. **43 F6** TL2094.
Farcet Fen *Cambs.* ***Open space***, fenland, 2m/4km E of Yaxley. **43 F6** TL2292.
Farden *Shrop.* ***Hamlet***, 4m/6km E of Ludlow. **28 E1** SO5775.
Fareham *Hants.* Population: 27,433. ***Town***, 6m/9km NW of Portsmouth across Portsmouth Harbour. Old market town and port now part of Portsmouth conurbation. Fine Georgian houses in High Street. **11 G4** SU5706.
Farewell *Staffs.* ***Hamlet***, 3m/4km NW of Lichfield. **40 C4** SK0811.
Farforth *Lincs.* ***Settlement***, 6m/9km S of Louth. **53 G5** TF3178.
Farhill *Derbys.* ***Hamlet***, 3m/4km W of Clay Cross. SK3563.
Farigaig *High.* ***River***, running N then W into Loch Ness at Inverfarigaig, 2m/4km NE of Foyers, Inverness district. **88 C2** NH5223.
Faringdon *Oxon.* Population: 5235. ***Small town***, 11m/17km NE of Swindon. Medieval church with interesting monuments. **21 F2** SU2895.
Farington *Lancs.* ***Locality***, 2m/3km N of Leyland. SD5325.
Farington *Lancs.* ***Suburb***, to N of Leyland. **55 J7** SD5423.
Farlam *Cumb.* ***Hamlet***, 2m/4km SE of Brampton. **61 G1** NY5558.
Farlam *Cumb.* ***Settlement***, 3m/4km E of Brampton. NY5760.
Farland Head *N.Ayr.* ***Coastal feature***, headland on Firth of Clyde, 5m/8km NW of Ardrossan. **73 K6** NS1748.
Farlary *High.* ***Locality***, 6m/9km NW of Golspie, Sutherland district. **96 E1** NC7705.
Farleigh *N.Som.* ***Village***, 6m/10km SW of Bristol. **19 H5** ST4969.
Farleigh *Surr.* ***Village***, 2m/3km NE of Warlingham. **23 G5** TQ3760.
Farleigh Green *Kent* ***Village***, 3m/5km SW of Maidstone. TQ7252.
Farleigh Hungerford *Som.* ***Village***, 4m/6km W of Trowbridge. Remains of 14c castle (English Heritage). Site of Roman villa 1km NW. **20 A6** ST8057.
Farleigh Hungerford Castle *Som.* ***Castle***, ruins of 14c castle (English Heritage) by River Frome, 3m/5km W of Trowbridge. Chapel includes tomb of builder, Sir Thomas Hungerford. **20 B6** ST8057.
Farleigh Wallop *Hants.* ***Village***, 3m/5km S of Basingstoke. **21 K7** SU6246.
Farlesthorpe *Lincs.* ***Village***, 2m/3km SE of Alford. **53 H5** TF4774.
Farleton *Cumb.* ***Hamlet***, 5m/8km NW of Kirkby Lonsdale. **55 J1** SD5381.
Farleton *Lancs.* ***Hamlet***, 1m/2km SW of Hornby, on W side of River Lune. SD5767.
Farley *Derbys.* ***Hamlet***, 1m/2km N of Matlock. SK2962.
Farley *Shrop.* ***Settlement***, 1m/2km NW of Pontesbury. **38 C5** SJ3807.
Farley *Shrop.* ***Settlement***, 2m/3km NE of Much Wenlock. SJ6302.
Farley *Staffs.* ***Hamlet***, 4m/6km E of Cheadle. **40 C1** SK0644.
Farley *Wilts.* ***Village***, 5m/8km E of Salisbury. **10 D2** SU2229.
Farley Down *Hants.* ***Open space***, hillslope, 5m/8km W of Winchester. **10 E2** SU3929.
Farley Green *Suff.* ***Hamlet***, 6m/10km NE of Haverhill. TL7353.
Farley Green *Surr.* ***Hamlet***, 4m/6km N of Cranleigh. Site of Roman temple 1km W. **22 D7** TQ0645.
Farley Hill *Luton* ***Suburb***, to SW of Luton town centre. TL0720.
Farley Hill *W'ham* ***Village***, 5m/8km SW of Wokingham. **22 A5** SU7564.
Farley Mount Country Park *Hants.* ***Leisure/recreation***, 4m/6km W of Winchester. Over 200 acres of chalk downlands and woods boasting some rare and unusual plantlife. **11 F2** SU4129.
Farleys End *Glos.* ***Hamlet***, 4m/7km SW of Gloucester across loop of River Severn. **29 G7** SO7715.
Farlington *N.Yorks.* ***Village***, 2m/3km E of Stillington. **58 C3** SE6167.
Farlington *Ports.* ***Suburb***, N district of Portsmouth, 2m/3km W of Havant. SU6805.
Farlow *Shrop.* ***Hamlet***, 4m/6km NW of Cleobury Mortimer. **39 F7** SO6480.
Farm Town *Leics.* ***Hamlet***, 2m/3km E of Ashby de la Zouch. SK3916.
Farmborough *B. & N.E.Som.* ***Village***, 4m/6km NW of Radstock. **19 K5** ST6660.
Farmbridge End *Essex* ***Settlement***, 3m/4km SE of Leaden Roding. TL6211.
Farmcote *Glos.* ***Hamlet***, 2m/4km E of Winchcombe. **30 B6** SP0628.
Farmcote *Shrop.* ***Locality***, 4m/7km E of Bridgnorth. SO7791.
Farmington *Glos.* ***Village***, 2m/3km E of Northleach. **30 C7** SP1315.
Farmoor *Oxon.* ***Hamlet***, beside reservoir of same name, 2m/3km SE of Eynsham. **21 H1** SP4507.
Farmoor Reservoir *Oxon.* ***Reservoir***, 4m/6km W of Oxford city centre. **21 H1** SP4405.
Farmtown *Moray* ***Settlement***, at S end of Sillyearn Wood, 3m/5km NW of Milltown of Rothiemay. **98 D5** NJ5051.
Farnah Green *Derbys.* ***Hamlet***, 1km SW of Belper across River Derwent. SK3347.
Farnborough *Gt.Lon.* ***Suburb***, in borough of Bromley, 1m/2km SW of Orpington. **23 H5** TQ4464.
Farnborough *Hants.* Population: 52,535. ***Town***, in military area, 4m/6km S of Camberley. On W side, Royal Aircraft Establishment and airfield; biennial international airshow. Norman and medieval church. **22 B6** SU8754.
Farnborough *Warks.* ***Village***, 6m/10km N of Banbury. Farnborough Hall (National Trust), mid-18c house. **31 F3** SP4349.
Farnborough *W.Berks.* ***Village***, 4m/7km SE of Wantage. **21 H3** SU4381.
Farnborough Green *Hants.* ***Suburb***, to N of Farnborough. **22 B6** SU8757.
Farnborough Hall *Warks.* ***Historic house***, mid-18c house (National Trust), 6m/10km N of Banbury. **31 F4** SP4349.
Farnborough Park *Hants.* ***Suburb***, to N of Farnborough town centre. SU8755.
Farnborough Street *Hants.* ***Suburb***, to N of Farnborough. SU8756.
Farncombe *Surr.* ***Suburb***, to N of Godalming. **22 C7** SU9745.
Farndale *N.Yorks.* ***Valley***, carrying upper reaches of River Dove above Low Mill, 6m/9km NW of Hutton-le-Hole. **63 H7** SE6697.
Farndale Moor *N.Yorks.* ***Open space***, moorland 2m/3km N of Church Houses. **63 H6** NZ6500.
Farndish *Beds.* ***Village***, 4m/6km SE of Wellingborough. **32 C2** SP9263.
Farndon *Ches.* ***Village***, on River Dee, 6m/9km NE of Wrexham. **48 D7** SJ4154.
Farndon *Notts.* Population: 2233. ***Village***, 2m/3km SW of Newark-on-Trent. **51 K7** SK7651.
Farndon Bridge ***Bridge***, 14c bridge spanning River Dee between Farndon and Holt, crossing border between England and Wales. **48 D7** SJ4154.
Farndon Field *Notts.* ***Locality***, 1m/2km NE of Farndon. SK7651.
Farne Islands *Northumb.* ***Island***, about thirty islands (National Trust) between 2m/3km and 5m/8km offshore opposite Bamburgh. Forms E tip of Great Whin Sill. St. Cuthbert and St. Aidan lived here in 7c. Breeding place for seals and some twenty species of sea birds in nature reserve. Lighthouse on Longstone. **77 K7** NU2337.
Farnell *Angus* ***Village***, 3m/5km SE of Brechin. **83 H2** NO6255.
Farnham *Dorset* ***Village***, 2m/3km SE of Tollard Royal. Pitt-Rivers Museum, established by General Pitt-Rivers in 1880. **9 J3** ST9515.
Farnham *Essex* ***Village***, 2m/3km N of Bishop's Stortford. **33 H6** TL4724.
Farnham *N.Yorks.* ***Village***, 2m/4km N of Knaresborough. **57 J3** SE3460.
Farnham *Suff.* ***Village***, 2m/4km SW of Saxmundham. **35 H3** TM3660.
Farnham *Surr.* Population: 36,178. ***Town***, on River Wey 10m/16km W of Guildford. Many Georgian houses at centre. Castle Keep (English Heritage) on hill to N. Town is birthplace of William Cobbett, who is buried in St. Andrew's churchyard. **22 B7** SU8446.
Farnham Castle *Surr.* ***Castle***, motte and bailey castle keep (English Heritage) on N side of Farnham, rebuilt in 12c by Henry of Blois, with later additions and extensions. Former seat of Bishops of Winchester. **22 B7** SU8347.
Farnham Common *Bucks.* ***Village***, 3m/5km N of Slough. **22 C3** SU9685.
Farnham Green *Essex* ***Settlement***, 3m/4km NW of Bishop's Stortford. **33 H6** TL4625.
Farnham Royal *Bucks.* Population: 6148. ***Village***, 2m/3km N of Slough. **22 C3** SU9683.
Farnhill *N.Yorks.* ***Village***, adjoining to W of Kildwick, 4m/7km SE of Skipton. SE0046.
Farningham *Kent* Population: 1568. ***Village***, on River Darent, 5m/7km S of Dartford. Sites of Roman buildings. **23 J5** TQ5466.
Farnley *N.Yorks.* ***Hamlet***, 2m/3km NE of Otley. Hall is 18c house by Carr of York, incorporating Elizabethan house. **57 H5** SE2148.
Farnley *W.Yorks.* ***Suburb***, 3m/5km W of Leeds city centre. SE2532.
Farnley Tyas *W.Yorks.* ***Village***, 3m/4km SE of Huddersfield. **50 D1** SE1612.
Farnsfield *Notts.* Population: 2549. ***Village***, 4m/6km NW of Southwell. **51 J7** SK6456.
Farnworth *Gt.Man.* Population: 25,053. ***Town***, former cotton town, 2m/4km SE of Bolton. **49 G2** SD7306.
Farnworth *Halton* ***Suburb***, 1m/2km N of Widnes. **48 E4** SJ5187.
Farr *High.* ***Settlement***, in Inverness district, 8m/12km S of Inverness. Loch Farr is small loch to S. **88 D1** NH6833.
Farr *High.* ***Settlement***, 5m/8km NE of Kingussie. **89 F4** NH8203.
Farr *High.* ***Village***, near N coast of Caithness district, 1m/2km NE of Bettyhill. **104 C2** NC7263.
Farr Bay *High.* ***Bay***, on N coast of Caithness district, 1km W of Farr. **103 K2** NC7263.
Farr House *High.* ***Settlement***, 9m/14km S of Inverness. **88 D1** NH6831.
Farr Point *High.* ***Coastal feature***, headland on N coast of Caithness district, 1m/2km N of Farr. **104 C2** NC7263.
Farragon Hill *P. & K.* ***Mountain***, 4m/7km N of Aberfeldy. Height 2558 feet or 780 metres. **81 K2** NN8455.
Farraline *High.* ***Settlement***, at NE end of Loch Mhòr, 3m/5km SE of Inverfarigaig across loch. **88 C2** NH5621.
Farrar *High.* ***River***, running E from Loch Monar to join River Glass 1km below Struy Bridge in Inverness district. **87 K1** NH4039.
Farringdon *Devon* ***Village***, 6m/10km E of Exeter. **7 J6** SY0191.
Farringdon *T. & W.* ***Suburb***, 3m/5km SW of Sunderland city centre. NZ3653.
Farringford *I.o.W.* *See Freshwater.*
Farrington Gurney *B. & N.E.Som.* ***Village***, 2m/4km W of Midsomer Norton. **19 K6** ST6255.
Farrmheall *High.* ***Mountain***, 5m/8km NE of Rhiconich. Height 1709 feet or 521 metres. **103 F3** NC3058.
Farsley *W.Yorks.* ***Locality***, 1m/2km N of Pudsey. **57 H6** SE2135.
Farsley Beck Bottom *W.Yorks.* ***Locality***, 1m/2km N of Pudsey town centre. SE2135.
Farther Howegreen *Essex* ***Hamlet***, to NW of Cold Norton, 4m/6km S of Maldon. TL8401.
Farthing Corner *Med.* ***Settlement***, 3m/5km SE of Gillingham. TQ8163.
Farthing Green *Kent* ***Settlement***, 2m/3km NW of Headcorn. TQ8046.
Farthing Street *Gt.Lon.* ***Locality***, 3m/4km N of Biggin Hill. TQ4262.
Farthinghoe *Northants.* ***Village***, 4m/6km NW of Brackley. **31 G5** SP5339.
Farthingloe *Kent* ***Suburb***, in W part of Dover. **15 H3** TR2940.
Farthingstone *Northants.* ***Village***, 5m/9km SE of Daventry. **31 H3** SP6155.
Fartown *W.Yorks.* ***Suburb***, 1m/2km N of Huddersfield town centre. SE1418.
Farway *Devon* ***Village***, 4m/6km S of Honiton. **7 K6** SY1895.
Farway Country Park *Devon* ***Leisure/recreation***, country park 1m/2km W of Southleigh and 4m/6km S of Honiton, with over 100 acres housing nature trails, pony rides and rare breeds of poultry. **7 K6** SY1894.
Fasag *High.* ***Settlement***, adjoining to N of Torridon, Ross and Cromarty district. **94 E6** NG8956.
Fasagrianach *High.* ***Settlement***, in valley of River Broom, 1m/2km NW of Corrieshalloch Gorge. **95 H3** NH1980.
Fascadale *High.* ***Settlement***, on N coast of Ardnamurchan peninsula, 4m/7km N of Kilchoan. **86 B7** NM5070.
Faseny Water *E.Loth.* ***River***, rising on slopes of Meikle Says Law in Lammermuir Hills, and flowing E to Whiteadder Reservoir. **76 D4** NT6463.
Fasheilach ***Mountain***, 3m/4km S of Linn of Muick Cottage, with summit on border of Aberdeenshire and Angus. Height 2365 feet or 721 metres. **90 B6** NO3485.
Fashven *High.* ***Mountain***, 3m/5km W of Achiemore. Height 1499 feet or 457 metres. **103 F2** NC3167.
Faskadale *High.* ***Settlement***, on Faskadale Bay, 3m/5km W of Ockle Point, on N coast of Ardnamurchan peninsula, Lochaber district. NM5070.
Faslane *Arg. & B.* ***Locality***, 1m/2km SE of Garelochhead. **74 A2** NS2589.
Faslane Bay *Arg. & B.* ***Bay***, on E side of Gare Loch, 1m/2km S of Garelochhead. Nuclear submarine base. **74 A2** NS2489.
Fasnacloich *Arg. & B.* ***Settlement***, 2m/3km NE of head of Loch Creran. **80 B3** NN0247.
Fasnakyle *High.* ***Locality***, in Inverness district, where Glen Affric runs into Strathglass. Hydro-electricity power station. **87 K2** NH3128.
Fasnakyle Forest *High.* ***Open space***, deer forest to NW of Fasnakyle. **87 J1** NH3128.
Fasque House *Aber.* ***Historic house***, early 19c home of Gladstone family, 1m/2km N of Fettercairn. Little changed in furnishings and domestic items. **90 E7** NO6475.
Fassfern *High.* ***Settlement***, on N side of Loch Eil, in Lochaber district, 3m/5km E of Kinlocheil. **87 G7** NN0278.
Fast Castle (Also known as Castle Knowe.) *Sc.Bord.* ***Castle***, scant remains of 12c motte castle on cliff, 4m/6km NW of St. Abb's Head. **77 G3** NT8671.
Fastheugh Hill *Sc.Bord.* ***Mountain***, in Ettrick Forest, 5m/8km W of Selkirk. Height 1643 feet or 501 metres. **69 J1** NT3827.
Fatfield *T. & W.* ***Suburb***, S district of Washington. **62 E1** NZ3054.
Fathan Glinne *Stir.* ***Valley***, carrying Allt Fathan Glinne and running E then SE into valley of Calair Burn, 3m/4km SW of Balquhidder. **81 F6** NN4917.
Fattahead *Aber.* ***Settlement***, 4m/6km NE of Aberchirder. **98 E5** NJ6557.
Faugh *Cumb.* ***Hamlet***, 4m/7km S of Brampton. **61 G1** NY5054.
Fauld *Staffs.* ***Locality***, 2m/3km W of Tutbury. SK1828.
Fauldhouse *W.Loth.* Population: 4690. ***Village***, 3m/4km S of Whitburn. **75 H4** NS9360.
Faulds Brow *Cumb.* ***Mountain***, 1m/2km W of Ratten Row and 6m/9km SE of Wigton. Height 1125 feet or 343 metres. **60 D2** NY2940.
Faulkbourne *Essex* ***Hamlet***, 2m/3km NW of Witham. **34 B7** TL7917.
Faulkland *Som.* ***Village***, 3m/5km E of Radstock. **20 A6** ST7354.
Fauls *Shrop.* ***Hamlet***, 3m/5km NW of Hodnet. **38 E2** SJ5932.
Faulston *Wilts.* ***Settlement***, just SE of Bishopstone, 4m/6km SW of Wilton. SU0725.
Faversham *Kent* Population: 17,070. ***Town***, market town and small port at head of creek, running into The Swale and then into Whitstable Bay. Stone Chapel (English Heritage), medieval church with remains of 4c Romano-British mausoleum, 1m/2km W. **25 G5** TR0161.
Favillar *Moray* ***Settlement***, 5m/8km SW of Dufftown. **89 K1** NJ2734.
Faw Hill *Sc.Bord.* ***Mountain***, 3m/5km NE of Bonchester Bridge. Height 1086 feet or 331 metres. **70 B2** NT6213.
Faw Side *D. & G.* ***Mountain***, on uplands to S of Craik Forest, 5m/8km NE of Bentpath. Height 1722 feet or 525 metres. **69 J4** NY3596.
Fawdington *N.Yorks.* ***Settlement***, on E bank of River Swale, 2m/3km N of Brafferton. **57 K2** SE4372.
Fawdon *T. & W.* ***Suburb***, 3m/5km NW of Newcastle upon Tyne city centre. **71 H7** NZ2268.

Fawfieldhead *Staffs.* ***Settlement***, 1m/2km SW of Longnor. **50 C6** SK0763.

Fawkham Green *Kent* ***Village***, in parish of Fawkham, 3m/4km E of Farningham. **23 J5** TQ5865.

Fawler *Oxon.* ***Village***, 2m/3km SE of Charlbury. Sites of Roman buildings. **30 E7** SP3717.

Fawley *Bucks.* ***Village***, 3m/4km N of Henley-on-Thames. **22 A3** SU7586.

Fawley *Hants.* Population: 13,034. ***Village***, on Southampton Water, 5m/7km E of Beaulieu. **11 F4** SU4503.

Fawley *W.Berks.* ***Village***, 4m/7km S of Wantage. **21 G3** SU3981.

Fawley Bottom *Bucks.* ***Settlement***, to W of Fawley. SU7486.

Fawley Chapel *Here.* ***Hamlet***, beside N bank of River Wye, 4m/6km N of Ross-on-Wye across loop of river. **28 E6** SO5929.

Fawley Court *Bucks.* ***Historic house***, 17c manor house designed by Sir Christopher Wren, 1m/2km N of Henley-on-Thames. Gardens designed by 'Capability' Brown. **22 A3** SU7684.

Fawsley *Northants.* ***Locality***, 4m/6km S of Daventry. Fawsley Hall in park dates from Tudor times. SP5656.

Fawsyde *Aber.* ***Hamlet***, adjacent to W of Roadside of Kinneff, 3m/5km N of Inverbervie. **91 G7** NO8477.

Faxfleet *E.Riding* ***Hamlet***, on N bank of River Ouse, at its confluence with River Trent, 7m/12km E of Goole. **58 E7** SE8624.

Faxton *Northants.* ***Village***, deserted village, 6m/9km W of Kettering. **31 J1** SP7875.

Faygate *W.Suss.* ***Hamlet***, 4m/6km NE of Horsham. **13 F3** TQ2134.

Fazakerley *Mersey.* ***Suburb***, 4m/6km NE of Liverpool city centre. SJ3896.

Fazeley *Staffs.* Population: 4548. ***Village***, 2m/3km S of Tamworth, at junction of Birmingham and Fazeley Canal and Coventry Canal. **40 E5** SK2001.

Feadda Ness *Shet.* ***Coastal feature***, southernmost headland on Isle of Noss. **109 E9** HU5438.

Feall Bay *Arg. & B.* ***Bay***, on NW coast of Coll, 2m/3km from SW end of island. **78 C2** NM1354.

Fearby *N.Yorks.* ***Village***, 2m/3km W of Masham. **57 G1** SE1981.

Feardan Burn *Aber.* ***River***, small stream which rises in Grampian Mountains and flows SW, then SE, to join River Dee 1m/2km SW of Balmoral. **89 K5** NO2393.

Fearn *High.* ***Settlement***, near E coast of Ross and Cromarty district, 2m/3km NW of Balintore. **97 F4** NH8377.

Fearn Abbey *High.* ***Ecclesiastical building***, 2m/3km NW of Balintore. Originally founded in 13c and restored after roof fell down in 1742, killing 42 people. Still a parish church. **97 F4** NH8377.

Fearn Station *High.* ***Other building***, railway station on Inverness to Wick line, 3m/5km SE of Tain. **97 F4** NH8178.

Fearnach *Arg. & B.* ***Settlement***, above Bàgh Fearnoch, 3m/5km S of Auchenbreck. **73 J3** NS0276.

Fearnan *P. & K.* ***Village***, on N shore of Loch Tay, 3m/5km W of Kenmore. **81 J3** NN7244.

Fearnbeg *High.* ***Locality***, in Ross and Cromarty district, on SW side of Loch Torridon, 1m/2km SE of Rubha na Fearn. **94 D6** NG7359.

Fearnhead *Warr.* ***Locality***, 3m/4km NE of Warrington. **49 F3** SJ6390.

Fearnmore *High.* ***Settlement***, on SW side of Loch Torridon, Ross and Cromarty district, 1km S of Rubha na Fearn. **94 D5** NG7260.

Fearnoch *Arg. & B.* ***Settlement***, on Cowal peninsula, 5m/8km NW of Tighnabruaich. **73 H3** NR9279.

Fearnoch Forest *Arg. & B.* ***Forest/woodland***, 2m/3km W of Taynuilt, Argyll. **80 A4** NM9631.

Featherbed Moss ***Open space***, moorland on N side of Longdendale and just S of Chew Reservoir, on border of Greater Manchester and Derbyshire. **50 C2** SE0400.

Featherbed Moss *S.Yorks.* ***Open space***, moorland in Peak District National Park, 1m/2km S of Salter's Brook Bridge. **50 D3** SK1498.

Featherbed Top *Derbys.* ***Mountain***, 4m/6km SE of Glossop. Height 1784 feet or 544 metres. **50 C3** SK0891.

Featherstone *Staffs.* Population: 4201. ***Village***, 4m/7km NE of Wolverhampton. **40 B5** SJ9405.

Featherstone *W.Yorks.* Population: 10,496. ***Locality***, 2m/4km W of Pontefract. **51 G1** SE4222.

Featherstone Castle *Northumb.* ***Historic house***, on River South Tyne, 3m/4km SW of Haltwhistle, part dating from 13c but with many later additions and alterations. **70 B7** NY6761.

Feckenham *Worcs.* ***Village***, 6m/9km NW of Alcester. **30 B2** SP0061.

Fedw-ddu *Powys* ***Mountain***, 2m/3km W of Staylittle. Height 1597 feet or 487 metres. **37 H6** SN8691.

Feehlin *High.* ***River***, in Inverness district running N into River Foyers, 2m/3km S of Foyers on Loch Ness. **88 C3** NH4917.

Feering *Essex* ***Village***, 5m/8km NE of Witham. **34 C6** TL8720.

Feetham *N.Yorks.* ***Village***, in Swaledale, 3m/5km W of Reeth. **62 A7** SD9898.

Feinne-bheinn Mhòr *High.* ***Mountain***, 3m/5km SW of S end of Loch Hope. Height 1525 feet or 465 metres. **103 G4** NC4346.

Feirihisval *W.Isles* ***Mountain***, 3m/4km N of head of Loch Shell, Isle of Lewis. Height 1069 feet or 326 metres. **100 E6** NB3014.

Féith a' Chaoruinn *High.* ***River***, flowing SE to join Abhainn Sgeamhaidh 1m/2km E of Rhian. **103 H6** NC5717.

Féith Gaineimh Mhòr *High.* ***River***, in Caithness district, flowing E and joining Féith Chaorunn Mhòr to form Berriedale Water, 5m/8km W of Braemore. **104 E5** NC9831.

Feith-hill *Aber.* ***Settlement***, 3m/5km SE of Inverkeithny. Stone Circle nearby. **98 E6** NJ6643.

Féith Osdail *High.* ***River***, flowing W into River Tirry, 5m/8km N of Lairg. **103 J7** NC5713.

Féith Talachaidh *High.* ***River***, flowing generally SW into River Spey, 6m/9km W of Laggan. **88 C5** NN5396.

Feizor *N.Yorks.* ***Settlement***, 3m/5km NW of Settle. **56 C3** SD7867.

Felbridge *Surr.* ***Suburb***, 2m/3km NW of East Grinstead. **13 G3** TQ3639.

Felbrigg *Norf.* ***Village***, 2m/3km S of Cromer. **45 G2** TG2039.

Felbrigg Hall *Norf.* ***Historic house***, to W of Felbrigg, 17c house (National Trust) in grounds by Repton. **45 F2** TG2039.

Felcourt *Surr.* ***Village***, 2m/3km N of East Grinstead. **23 G7** TQ3841.

Felden *Herts.* ***Suburb***, in SW part of Hemel Hempstead. **22 D1** TL0404.

Felhampton *Shrop.* ***Hamlet***, 3m/5km N of Craven Arms. SO4487.

Felin Puleston *Wrex.* ***Suburb***, 1m/2km SW of Wrexham town centre. SJ3249.

Felin-wen *Carmar.* *Welsh form of White Mill, qv.*

Felindre *Carmar.* ***Hamlet***, 5m/8km W of Llandeilo. **17 J2** SN5521.

Felindre *Carmar.* ***Hamlet***, 1km S of Llangadog. **27 G6** SN7027.

Felindre *Carmar.* ***Settlement***, 2m/3km W of Llanwrda. SN6830.

Felindre (Also spelled Velindre.) *Carmar.* ***Village***, 3m/5km SE of Newcastle Emlyn. **17 G1** SN3538.

Felindre *Cere.* ***Settlement***, 1m/2km NE of Temple Bar. SN5455.

Felindre *Pembs.* *See Velindre.*

Felindre *Powys* *See Velindre.*

Felindre *Powys* ***Hamlet***, on River Teme, 8m/12km SE of Newtown. **38 A7** SO1681.

Felindre *Powys* ***Settlement***, just S of Cwmdu. SO1723.

Felindre *R.C.T.* ***Hamlet***, 1km E of Pencoed. SS9781.

Felindre *Swan.* ***Hamlet***, 3m/5km E of Pontarddulais. **17 K4** SN6302.

Felinfach *Cere.* ***Hamlet***, 1m/2km NW of Temple Bar. SN5255.

Felinfach *Powys* ***Hamlet***, 4m/7km NE of Brecon. **27 K5** SO0933.

Felinfoel *Carmar.* ***Locality***, adjoining to NE of Llanelli. **17 J4** SN5102.

Felingwmisaf *Carmar.* ***Hamlet***, 6m/10km NE of Carmarthen and 1km S of Felingwmuchaf. SN5023.

Felingwmuchaf *Carmar.* ***Hamlet***, 6m/10km NE of Carmarthen. **17 J2** SN5024.

Felinwynt *Cere.* ***Settlement***, 3m/4km W of Aberporth. SN2250.

Felixkirk *N.Yorks.* ***Village***, 3m/5km NE of Thirsk. **57 K1** SE4684.

Felixstowe *Suff.* Population: 28,606. ***Town***, resort and container port, 11m/17km SE of Ipswich. Nature reserve at Landguard Point. Annual folk festival. **35 G5** TM3034.

Felixstowe Ferry *Suff.* ***Hamlet***, at mouth of River Deben, on W side, 3m/4km NE of Felixstowe. Ferry across river for pedestrians. **35 H5** TM3237.

Felkington *Northumb.* ***Settlement***, 1m/2km NE of Duddo. **77 H6** NT9444.

Felkirk *W.Yorks.* ***Settlement***, 2m/3km NE of Royston. SE3812.

Fell Foot Park *Cumb.* ***Leisure/recreation***, at S end of Windermere lake, 1km NE of Newby Bridge. Small park with extensive flower displays, woodland trails and rowing boats for hire. **55 G1** SD3886.

Fell Loch *D. & G.* ***Lake/loch***, small loch 7m/11km E of Glenluce. **64 D5** NX3155.

Fell of Carleton *D. & G.* ***Hill***, near coast 3m/5km SE of Monreith. Height 479 feet or 146 metres. **64 D7** NX4037.

Fell of Fleet *D. & G.* ***Mountain***, 6m/10km SW of New Galloway. Height 1542 feet or 470 metres. **65 F3** NX5670.

Fell Side *Cumb.* ***Locality***, 2m/3km SW of Caldbeck. NY3037.

Felldownhead *Devon* ***Settlement***, 2m/3km NW of Milton Abbot. **6 B7** SX3780.

Felldyke *Cumb.* ***Locality***, 1km S of Lamplugh. NY0819.

Fellgate *T. & W.* ***Suburb***, 2m/3km S of Hebburn. NZ3262.

Fellhouse Fell *Northumb.* ***Open space***, to SE of Plenmeller Common, 3m/5km S of Bardon Mill. **61 J1** NY7559.

Felling *T. & W.* Population: 35,053. ***Town***, industrial town, adjoining to E of Gateshead. Gateshead International Stadium sited here. **71 H7** NZ2861.

Felling Shore *T. & W.* ***Suburb***, within Felling, on S bank of River Tyne. NZ2862.

Fellonmore *Arg. & B.* ***Settlement***, on shore of Loch Spelve, 4m/7km NE of Lochbuie. **79 H5** NM6827.

Felmersham *Beds.* ***Village***, on River Great Ouse, 6m/10km NW of Bedford. **32 C3** SP9957.

Felmingham *Norf.* ***Village***, 2m/4km W of North Walsham. **45 G3** TG2529.

Felmore *Essex* ***Suburb***, to N of Pitsea, adjoining to E of Basildon. TQ7389.

Felpham *W.Suss.* ***Town***, seaside resort and E district of Bognor Regis. Former fishing village. **12 C7** SZ9599.

Felsham *Suff.* ***Village***, 7m/12km SE of Bury St. Edmunds. **34 D3** TL9457.

Felsted *Essex* ***Village***, 3m/5km E of Great Dunmow. **33 K6** TL6720.

Feltham *Gt.Lon.* ***Suburb***, in borough of Hounslow, 1m/2km SW of Hounslow Heath. **22 E4** TQ1073.

Felthamhill *Surr.* ***Suburb***, 1m/2km S of Feltham. TQ0971.

Felthorpe *Norf.* ***Village***, 7m/11km NW of Norwich. **45 F4** TG1618.

Felton *Here.* ***Village***, 7m/11km NE of Hereford. **28 E4** SO5748.

Felton *N.Som.* ***Village***, 1m/2km E of Bristol International Airport and 6m/10km SW of city centre. **19 J5** ST5265.

Felton *Northumb.* ***Village***, on River Coquet, 8m/13km S of Alnwick. **71 G3** NU1800.

Felton Butler *Shrop.* ***Hamlet***, 1m/2km SE of Nesscliffe. **38 C4** SJ3917.

Feltwell *Norf.* Population: 2931. ***Village***, 5m/8km NW of Brandon. **44 B7** TL7190.

Feltwell Fens *Norf.* ***Open space***, fenland 3m/5km W of Feltwell. **44 A7** TL6589.

Fen Ditton *Cambs.* ***Village***, on River Cam, 3m/4km NE of Cambridge. **33 H3** TL4860.

Fen Drayton *Cambs.* ***Village***, 7m/11km SE of Huntingdon. **33 G2** TL3368.

Fen End *Lincs.* ***Locality***, on E bank of New River, 1m/2km S of Spalding. TF2420.

Fen End *W.Mid.* ***Settlement***, 5m/8km NW of Kenilworth. **30 D1** SP2275.

Fen Street *Norf.* ***Hamlet***, 4m/6km W of Attleborough. TL9895.

Fen Street *Norf.* ***Locality***, 3m/4km S of Attleborough. TM0591.

Fen Street *Norf.* ***Settlement***, 3m/5km W of Diss and 1m/2km E of South Lopham. TM0680.

Fen Street *Suff.* ***Settlement***, 7m/11km NE of Ixworth. **34 D1** TL9879.

Fen Street *Suff.* ***Settlement***, 1m/2km NE of Redgrave and 4m/6km W of Diss. TM0579.

Fen Street *Suff.* ***Settlement***, 1km SE of Debenham. TM1862.

Fenay Bridge *W.Yorks.* ***Suburb***, 3m/4km E of Huddersfield. SE1815.

Fence *Lancs.* ***Village***, 2m/4km W of Nelson. **56 D6** SD8237.

Fence *S.Yorks.* ***Locality***, 6m/9km E of Sheffield. SK4485.

Fence Houses *T. & W.* ***Locality***, 2m/3km W of Houghton le Spring. **62 E1** NZ3250.

Fencott *Oxon.* ***Hamlet***, 4m/7km S of Bicester. **31 G7** SP5716.

Fender Burn *P. & K.* ***River***, running SW down Glen Fender to River Tilt, 1m/2km N of Blair Atholl. Falls of Fender near junction with River Tilt. **89 G7** NN8766.

Fendike Corner *Lincs.* ***Hamlet***, 3m/5km NW of Wainfleet All Saints. **53 H6** TF4560.

Fengate *Norf.* ***Hamlet***, adjoining to NW of Marsham, 1m/2km S of Aylsham. TG1924.

Fenham *Northumb.* ***Settlement***, on coast, 5m/7km N of Belford. NU0840.

Fenham *T. & W.* ***Suburb***, 2m/3km NW of Newcastle upon Tyne city centre. Site of Roman fort to S. NZ2265.

Fenham Flats *Northumb.* ***Coastal feature***, mud-flats between mainland and Holy Island. **77 K7** NU0840.

Fenhouses *Lincs.* ***Settlement***, 1m/2km E of Swineshead. **43 F1** TF2540.

Feniscliffe *B'burn.* ***Locality***, 2m/3km SW of Blackburn. SD6526.

Feniscowles *B'burn.* ***Village***, 3m/4km SW of Blackburn. **56 B7** SD6425.

Feniton *Devon* ***Village***, 4m/6km W of Honiton. **7 K6** SY1099.

Fenlake *Beds.* ***Suburb***, in SE part of Bedford. TL0648.

Fenn Green *Shrop.* ***Hamlet***, 6m/9km NW of Kidderminster. SO7783.

Fenn Street *Med.* ***Hamlet***, 1m/2km E of High Halstow, 6m/9km NE of Strood. TQ7975.

Fenney Hill *Leics.* ***Settlement***, 1m/2km SW of Shepshed. SK4718.

Fennifach *Powys* ***Settlement***, 1m/2km W of Brecon. SO0228.

Fenn's Moss *Wrex.* ***Open space***, moorland, 3m/5km NE of Welshampton. **38 D2** SJ4836.

Fenny Bentley *Derbys.* ***Village***, 2m/4km N of Ashbourne. **50 D7** SK1750.

Fenny Bridges *Devon* ***Village***, on River Otter, 2m/3km NE of Ottery St. Mary. **7 K6** SY1198.

Fenny Compton *Warks.* ***Village***, 8m/12km N of Banbury. **31 F3** SP4152.

Fenny Drayton *Leics.* ***Village***, 3m/5km N of Nuneaton. **41 F6** SP3597.

Fenny Stratford *M.K.* ***Suburb***, in E part of Bletchley, beside Grand Union Canal and River Ouzel. Site of Roman settlement of Magiovinium. **32 B5** SP8834.

Fenrother *Northumb.* ***Settlement***, 4m/7km N of Morpeth. **71 G4** NZ1792.

Fenstanton *Cambs.* Population: 2375. ***Village***, 5m/9km SE of Huntingdon. **33 G2** TL3168.

Fenton *Cambs.* ***Hamlet***, 1m/2km SE of Warboys. **33 G1** TL3279.

Fenton *Cumb.* ***Hamlet***, 4m/6km SW of Brampton. NY5056.

Fenton *Lincs.* ***Village***, 8m/13km S of Gainsborough. **52 B5** SK8476.

Fenton *Lincs.* ***Village***, 6m/9km E of Newark-on-Trent. **52 B7** SK8750.

Fenton *Northumb.* ***Hamlet***, 2m/3km NW of Doddington. **77 H7** NT9733.

Fenton *Notts.* ***Hamlet***, 1km SE of Sturton le Steeple. SK7983.

Fenton *Stoke* ***Town***, one of the towns that form city of Stoke-on-Trent: Burslem, Fenton, Hanley, Longton, Stoke-upon-Trent, Tunstall. Fenton lies to E of city centre. **40 A1** SJ8944.

Fenton Barns *E.Loth.* ***Hamlet***, 3m/5km SW of North Berwick. NT5181.

Fenton House *Gt.Lon.* ***Historic house***, late 17c house (National Trust) in Hampstead; outstanding collection of porcelain and early keyboard instruments. Walled garden. **23 F3** TQ2686.

Fenwick *E.Ayr.* Population: 1057. ***Village***, 4m/7km NE of Kilmarnock. **74 C6** NS4643.

Fenwick *Northumb.* ***Hamlet***, 5m/7km NW of Belford. **77 J6** NU0640.

Fenwick *Northumb.* ***Hamlet***, 1m/2km W of Stamfordham. **71 F6** NZ0572.

Fenwick *S.Yorks.* ***Village***, 5m/8km SW of Snaith. **51 H1** SE5916.

Fenwick Water ***River***, running SW to confluence with Craufurdland Water 1m/2km NE of Kilmarnock. Combined stream, known as Kilmarnock Water, flows through Kilmarnock to River Irvine on S side of town. **74 D6** NS4339.

Feoch Burn *S.Ayr.* ***River***, rising in Loch Crongart and flowing SW to join Duisk River, 1m/2km SE of Barrhill. **67 G5** NX2581.
Feochag Bay *High.* ***Bay***, small bay on W coast of Ross and Cromarty district, 1km SW of Rubha Coigeach. **102 B7** NB9717.
Feochaig *Arg. & B.* ***Settlement***, on SE side of S end of Kintyre, 5m/8km SE of Campbeltown. **66 B2** NR7613.
Feock *Cornw.* ***Village***, at head of Carrick Roads (River Fal), 4m/6km S of Truro. Parish church has separate tower. **3 F5** SW8238.
Feolin *Arg. & B.* ***Settlement***, on SE coast of Jura, 1m/2km N of Craighouse. **72 D4** NR5369.
Feolin Ferry *Arg. & B.* ***Locality***, with pier, on W coast of Jura; ferry across Sound of Islay to Port Askaig, 1km W of Islay. **72 C4** NR4469.
Feorlan *Arg. & B.* ***Settlement***, at S end of Kintyre, 3m/5km W of Southend. **66 A3** NR6307.
Feorlin *Arg. & B.* ***Settlement***, 2m/3km NE of Minard. **73 H1** NR9597.
Ferguslie Park *Renf.* ***Suburb***, W district of Paisley. NS4664.
Ferindonald *High.* ***Settlement***, on E side of Sleat peninsula, Skye, 1m/2km SW of Teangue. NG6507.
Feriniquarrie *High.* ***Settlement***, near NW coast of Skye, 4m/7km S of Dunvegan Head. **93 G6** NG1750.
Fern *Angus* ***Settlement***, 2m/4km N of Tannadice. **83 F1** NO4861.
Ferndale *R.C.T.* Population: 17,341. ***Town***, in Rhondda Fach valley, 4m/6km NW of Porth. **18 C2** SS9996.
Ferndown *Dorset* Population: 25,177. ***Suburb***, 6m/9km N of Bournemouth. **10 B4** SU0700.
Ferness *High.* ***Settlement***, in Nairn district, 8m/13km SE of Nairn. **97 G7** NH9644.
Fernham *Oxon.* ***Village***, 2m/4km S of Faringdon. **21 F2** SU2991.
Fernhill *Gt.Man.* ***Suburb***, 1m/2km N of Bury town centre. SD8011.
Fernhill Gate *Gt.Man.* ***Suburb***, 2m/3km SW of Bolton town centre. SD6907.
Fernhill Gate *Hants.* ***Locality***, 1m/2km N of New Milton. SZ2496.
Fernhill Heath *Worcs.* Population: 2869. ***Village***, 3m/5km NE of Worcester. **29 H3** SO8759.
Fernhurst *W.Suss.* ***Village***, 3m/5km S of Haslemere. **12 B4** SU8928.
Fernie *Fife* ***Hamlet***, 4m/6km W of Cupar. **82 E6** NO3114.
Ferniegair *S.Lan.* ***Hamlet***, 1m/2km SE of Hamilton. NS7354.
Ferniehill *Edin.* ***Suburb***, 4m/6km SE of Edinburgh city centre. NT2969.
Fernilea *High.* ***Settlement***, on W side of Loch Harport, Skye, 1m/2km NW of Carbost. **85 J1** NG3633.
Fernilee *Derbys.* ***Hamlet***, 2m/3km S of Whaley Bridge. **50 C5** SK0178.
Fernilee Reservoir *Derbys.* ***Reservoir***, long narrow reservoir to S of Fernilee. **49 J5** SK0178.
Fernwood *Devon* ***Garden***, woodland garden in Ottery St. Mary, notable for rhododendrons, azaleas and spring bulbs. **7 J6** SY0794.
Fernworthy Reservoir *Devon* ***Reservoir***, surrounded on three sides by afforestation on E part of Dartmoor, 6m/9km W of Moretonhampstead. **6 E7** SX6684.
Ferny Common *Here.* ***Locality***, 5m/8km SE of Kington. SO3651.
Fernybank *Angus* ***Settlement***, 3m/5km SE of Tarfside, on N side of River North Esk. **90 D7** NO5378.
Ferrensby *N.Yorks.* ***Village***, 4m/7km SW of Boroughbridge. **57 J3** SE3660.
Ferriby Sluice *N.Lincs.* ***Locality***, at outfall of River Ancholme into River Humber, 1m/2km W of South Ferriby. SE9721.
Ferring *W.Suss.* ***Small town***, coastal town and resort, 3m/5km W of Worthing. **12 D6** TQ0902.
Ferry Bridge *Dorset* ***Coastal feature***, isthmus with road bridge connecting Chesil Beach and Isle of Portland to mainland, S of Weymouth. **9 F7** SY6676.
Ferry Hill *Cambs.* ***Settlement***, 1m/2km S of Chatteris. TL3883.
Ferry Meadows Country Park *Peter.* ***Leisure/recreation***, country park 3m/5km W of Peterborough city centre, on S bank of River Nene. More than 400 acres of woodland, river, meadows and lakes which attract over 180 bird species. **42 E6** TL1497.
Ferrybridge *W.Yorks.* ***Locality***, on S bank of River Aire, adjoining to W of Knottingley. **57 K7** SE4824.
Ferryden *Angus* ***Village***, on S side of River South Esk, opposite Montrose. **83 J2** NO7156.
Ferryhill *Aberdeen* ***Suburb***, to S of Aberdeen city centre. NJ9305.
Ferryhill *Dur.* Population: 11,610. ***Town***, 6m/10km S of Durham. **62 D3** NZ2832.
Ferryhill Station *Dur.* ***Locality***, 1m/2km SE of Ferryhill. NZ3031.
Ferryside *Carmar.* ***Village***, with bathing beach on River Tywi estuary opposite Llanstephan and 7m/11km S of Carmarthen. **17 G3** SN3610.
Ferrytown *High.* ***Locality***, at mouth of River Evelix on N shore of Dornoch Firth, 5m/8km W of Dornoch, Sutherland district. NH7287.
Fers Ness *Ork.* ***Coastal feature***, N facing headland on W coast of Eday, on W side of wide Fersness Bay. **106 E4** HY5334.
Fersfield *Norf.* ***Village***, 4m/6km NW of Diss. **44 E7** TM0683.
Fersit *High.* ***Settlement***, in valley of River Treig, 1m/2km S of Tulloch Station. **87 K7** NN3578.
Fersness Bay *Ork.* ***Bay***, wide bay on W coast of Eday. HY5434.
Feshie *High.* ***River***, in Badenoch and Strathspey district, rising on S side of Glenfeshie Forest and running N down Glen Feshie to River Spey 1km below Kincraig. **89 F6** NH8406.
Feshiebridge *High.* ***Locality***, in Badenoch and Strathspey district, 1m/2km SE of Kincraig. **89 F4** NH8504.
Fetcham *Surr.* ***Suburb***, 1m/2km W of Leatherhead. **22 E6** TQ1455.
Fetlar *Shet.* ***Island***, large sparsely inhabited island of about 14 square miles or 36 square km S of Unst and E of Yell. Nature reserve. **108 F3** HU6391.
Fetterangus *Aber.* ***Village***, 2m/3km N of Mintlaw. **99 H5** NJ9850.
Fettercairn *Aber.* ***Village***, 11m/17km NW of Montrose. Contains shaft of town cross of Kincardine. **90 E7** NO6573.
Fetteresso Forest *Aber.* ***Forest/woodland***, 6m/10km W of Stonehaven. **91 F6** NO7787.
Fetternear House *Aber.* ***Settlement***, 1m/2km NW of Kemnay. Remains of Fetternear House and Bishops Palace. **91 F3** NJ7217.
Fettes College *Edin.* ***Educational establishment***, boys' public school in Edinburgh, 1m/2km NW of city centre. NT2375.
Feus of Caldhame *Aber.* ***Settlement***, 4m/6km SW of Lawrencekirk. **83 H1** NO6567.
Fewcott *Oxon.* ***Locality***, adjoining to N of Ardley, 4m/7km NW of Bicester. **31 G6** SP5427.
Fewston *N.Yorks.* ***Village***, 6m/9km N of Otley. **57 G4** SE1954.
Fewston Bents *N.Yorks.* ***Settlement***, 1m/2km E of Blubberhouses. SE1954.
Fewston Reservoir *N.Yorks.* ***Reservoir***, to W of Fewston. **57 G4** SE1954.
Ffair-Rhos *Cere.* ***Hamlet***, 6m/10km NE of Tregaron. **27 G2** SN7368.
Ffairfach *Carmar.* ***Village***, 1km S of Llandeilo. **17 K2** SN6221.
Ffald-y-Brenin *Carmar.* ***Hamlet***, 3m/4km NW of Pumsaint. SN6344.
Ffarmers *Carmar.* ***Hamlet***, 5m/8km SE of Lampeter. **27 F4** SN6444.
Ffawyddog *Powys* ***Hamlet***, 1m/2km W of Crickhowell across River Usk. **28 B7** SO2018.
Ffestiniog (Llan Ffestiniog). *Gwyn.* ***Village***, 9m/14km E of Porthmadog. **37 G1** SH7042.
Ffestiniog Railway *Gwyn.* ***Other feature of interest***, preserved railway running narrow gauge steam engines, built in 1836 to transport slate from quarries at Blaenau Ffestiniog to Porthmadog. **37 F1** SH6946.
Ffontygari *V. of Glam.* *Welsh form of Font-y-gary, qv.*
Ffordd-las *Denb.* ***Settlement***, 4m/7km N of Ruthin. **47 K6** SJ1264.
Ffordd-las *Flints.* ***Locality***, 1km NW of Hope. SJ3059.
Fforddlas *Powys* ***Settlement***, 3m/4km SW of Hay-on-Wye. SO2038.
Fforest *Carmar.* ***Village***, 1km NW of Pontarddulais. **17 J4** SN5804.
Fforest-fach *Powys* ***Forest/woodland***, in Radnor Forest, 8m/12km NW of Presteigne. **28 A2** SO1967.
Fforest Fach *Powys* ***Inland physical feature***, upland area rising to 381 metres, 2m/3km SW of Sennybridge. **27 J6** SN8925.
Fforest-fach *Swan.* ***Suburb***, 3m/4km NW of Swansea city centre. **17 K5** SS6295.
Fforest Fawr *Powys* ***Large natural feature***, range of moorland hills, between Black Mountain in W and Brecon Beacons in E, attaining height of 2409 feet or 734 metres at Fan Fawr. **27 G7** SN9119.
Fforest Gôch *N.P.T.* ***Settlement***, 3m/5km N of Neath. SN7401.
Ffos Trosol ***Open space***, on border of Ceredigion and Powys, 3m/4km SE of Cwmystwyth. **27 H1** SN8171.
Ffos-y-ffin *Cere.* ***Village***, 2m/3km S of Aberaeron. **26 D2** SN4460.
Ffos-y-go *Wrex.* ***Settlement***, 3m/5km NW of Wrexham. SJ3054.
Ffostrasol *Cere.* ***Hamlet***, 5m/8km NW of Llandysul. **26 C4** SN3747.
Ffridd Fawr *Denb.* ***Mountain***, 4m/6km S of Denbigh. Height 1128 feet or 344 metres. **47 J7** SJ0560.
Ffridd-Rhyd-Ddu *Powys* ***Mountain***, 4m/7km E of Llanbrynmair. Height 1397 feet or 426 metres. **37 J5** SH9602.
Ffridd Trawsgoed *Gwyn.* ***Forest/woodland***, forested area 4m/6km NW of Llanuwchllyn. **37 H2** SH8333.
Ffridd Uchaf *Gwyn.* ***Settlement***, on SW slopes of Snowdon, 3m/4km NW of Beddgelert. **46 D7** SH5751.
Ffrith *Flints.* ***Hamlet***, 4m/7km NW of Wrexham. **48 B7** SJ2855.
Ffrwdgrech *Powys* ***Settlement***, 1m/2km SW of Brecon. **27 K6** SO0227.
Ffwl-y-mwn *V. of Glam.* *Welsh form of Fonmon, qv.*
Ffynnon *Carmar.* ***Settlement***, 4m/7km SW of Carmarthen. SN3516.
Ffynnon-ddrain *Carmar.* ***Settlement***, 1m/2km N of Carmarthen. **17 H2** SN4021.
Ffynnon Gynydd *Powys* ***Hamlet***, 1m/2km NW of Glasbury. SO1641.
Ffynnon Taf *Cardiff* *Welsh form of Taff's Well, qv.*
Ffynnongroew *Flints.* *See Ffynnongroyw.*
Ffynnongroyw (Ffynnongroew). *Flints.* ***Village***, on River Dee estuary, 2m/3km NW of Mostyn. **47 K4** SJ1382.
Fiag *High.* ***River***, in Sutherland district, running Sfrom Loch Fiag, along Glen Fiag, to Loch Shin. NC4620.
Fiarach *Stir.* ***Mountain***, 3m/4km NW of Crianlarich. Height 2139 feet or 652 metres. **80 E5** NN3425.
Fiaray *W.Isles* ***Island***, small uninhabited island off Scurrival Point at N end of Barra. **84 B3** NF7010.
Fiavig Bàgh *W.Isles* ***Bay***, on W coast of Isle of Lewis, 3m/4km SW of Gallan Head. **100 C4** NB0335.
Fibhig (Anglicised form: Fivig.) *W.Isles* ***Settlement***, near NW coast of Isle of Lewis, NE of North Shawbost. **100 E3** NB2648.
Fichlie *Aber.* ***Settlement***, on N side of River Don, 7m/11km E of Strathdon. **90 C3** NJ4513.
Fickleshole *Surr.* ***Hamlet***, 3m/4km NE of Warlingham. TQ3860.
Fidden *Arg. & B.* ***Settlement***, on W coast of Ross of Mull, 1m/2km S of Fionnphort. **78 E5** NM3021.
Fiddich *Moray* ***River***, rising on Corryhabbie Hill, Glenfiddich Forest, and running NE down Glen Fiddich, then W to Dufftown, then NW to River Spey at Craigellachie. **90 B1** NJ2945.
Fiddington *Glos.* ***Hamlet***, 2m/3km SE of Tewkesbury. **29 J5** SO9231.
Fiddington *Som.* ***Village***, 2m/3km NE of Nether Stowey. **19 F7** ST2140.
Fiddleford *Dorset* ***Village***, 1m/2km SE of Sturminster Newton. ST8013.
Fiddleford Manor *Dorset* ***Historic house***, part of medieval manor (English Heritage) dating from 14c, 1m/2km SE of Sturminster Newton across River Stour. **9 G3** ST8013.
Fiddler's Ferry *Warr.* ***Locality***, on St. Helens Canal, 3m/5km E of Widnes. SJ5686.
Fiddler's Green *Glos.* ***Suburb***, in W part of Cheltenham. SO9122.
Fiddler's Green *Here.* ***Settlement***, 5m/8km SE of Hereford. **28 E5** SO5735.
Fiddler's Green *Norf.* ***Settlement***, 1m/2km NE of Castle Acre. TF8216.
Fiddler's Green *Norf.* ***Settlement***, 1m/2km N of Attleborough. TM0496.
Fiddlers Hamlet *Essex* ***Hamlet***, 1m/2km SE of Epping. **23 H1** TL4701.
Fidra *E.Loth.* ***Island***, small island off shore 3m/4km W of North Berwick. Haunt of sea birds. Lighthouse. **76 D2** NT5186.
Field *Staffs.* ***Hamlet***, 4m/7km W of Uttoxeter. **40 C2** SK0233.
Field Assarts *Oxon.* ***Settlement***, 4m/6km NW of Witney. SP3113.
Field Broughton *Cumb.* ***Hamlet***, 2m/3km N of Cartmel. **55 G1** SD3881.
Field Dalling *Norf.* ***Village***, 4m/7km W of Holt. **44 E2** TG0039.
Field Head *Leics.* ***Hamlet***, 1km E of Markfield. **41 G5** SK4909.
Field Place *W.Suss.* *See Broadbridge Heath.*
Fieldhead *Cumb.* ***Locality***, 1m/2km SW of Calthwaite. NY4539.
Fiend's Fell *Cumb.* ***Mountain***, on Gamblesby Allotments, 3m/5km SE of Renwick. Height 2080 feet or 634 metres. **61 H2** NY6340.
Fife Keith *Moray* ***Locality***, adjoining to W of Keith, connected to it by early 17c bridge. **98 C5** NJ4250.
Fife Ness *Fife* ***Coastal feature***, headland at E extremity of Fife, 9m/15km SE of St. Andrews. **83 H7** NO6309.
Fife Regional Park *Fife* ***Large natural feature***, designated park around Lomond Hills, to NW of Glenrothes. **82 D7** NO2405.
Fifehead Magdalen *Dorset* ***Village***, 5m/8km W of Shaftesbury. **9 G2** ST7821.
Fifehead Neville *Dorset* ***Village***, 2m/4km SW of Sturminster Newton. **9 G3** ST7610.
Fifehead St. Quintin *Dorset* ***Hamlet***, 1km SE of Fifehead Neville and 3m/4km SW of Sturminster Newton. ST7710.
Fifield *Oxon.* ***Village***, 4m/7km N of Burford. **30 D7** SP2318.
Fifield *Wilts.* ***Settlement***, 1m/2km S of Enford and 6m/9km N of Amesbury. SU1450.
Fifield *W. & M.* ***Village***, 4m/6km W of Windsor. **22 C4** SU9076.
Fifield Bavant *Wilts.* ***Hamlet***, 7m/11km SW of Wilton. **10 B2** SU0125.
Figheldean *Wilts.* ***Village***, on River Avon, 4m/6km N of Amesbury. **20 E7** SU1547.
Fighting Cocks *Darl.* ***Hamlet***, 3m/5km E of Darlington. NZ3414.
Filby *Norf.* ***Village***, 5m/8km NW of Great Yarmouth. **45 J4** TG4613.
Filching Manor *E.Suss.* ***Historic house***, medieval manor house with motor museum of veteran and vintage cars, 3m/5km E of Alfriston. **13 J6** TQ5602.
Filey *N.Yorks.* Population: 6044. ***Small town***, North Sea coast resort on Filey Bay, 7m/11km SE of Scarborough. **59 H2** TA1180.
Filey Bay *N.Yorks.* ***Bay***, on North Sea coast, 7m/11km SE of Scarborough. **59 H2** TA1180.
Filey Brigg *N.Yorks.* ***Coastal feature***, mile-long reef at N end of Filey Bay, covered at high tide; site of Roman signal station. **59 H1** TA1180.
Filgrave *M.K.* ***Hamlet***, 3m/5km N of Newport Pagnell across loop of River Great Ouse. **32 B4** SP8748.
Filham *Devon* ***Hamlet***, 1km E of Ivybridge. SX6455.
Filkins *Oxon.* ***Village***, 4m/6km NE of Lechlade. **21 F1** SP2304.
Filla *Shet.* ***Island***, small round-shaped island in SW part of Out Skerries group of islands. **109 F6** HU6668.
Filleigh *Devon* ***Settlement***, 1m/2km NE of Lapford. **7 F4** SS7410.
Filleigh *Devon* ***Village***, 3m/5km NW of South Molton. **6 E3** SS6628.
Fillingham *Lincs.* ***Village***, 9m/15km N of Lincoln. **52 C4** SK9485.
Fillongley *Warks.* ***Village***, 6m/10km NW of Coventry. **40 E7** SP2887.
Filmore Hill *Hants.* ***Hamlet***, 3m/4km NE of West Meon. **11 H2** SU6627.
Filton *S.Glos.* ***Suburb***, 4m/6km N of Bristol city centre. **19 J4** ST6079.
Fimber *E.Riding* ***Village***, 2m/3km NE of Fridaythorpe. **59 F3** SE8960.
Fin Glen *E.Dun.* ***Valley***, carrying Finglen Burn, stream rising on Campsie Fells and running SE to Glazert Water, 1m/2km NW of Lennoxtown. **74 D2** NS5980.

Finalty Hill *Angus* ***Mountain***, 4m/6km W of Glendoll Lodge. Height 2968 feet or 905 metres. **89 K7** NO2175.
Finavon *Angus* ***Settlement***, on River South Esk, 5m/8km NE of Forfar. **83 F2** NO4957.
Finavon Castle *Angus* ***Castle***, ruined 16c stronghold of Earls of Crawford, 1km S of Finavon and 4m/6km SW of Brechin. **83 G2** NO4956.
Finbracks *Angus* ***Mountain***, 2m/3km E of Rottal. Height 2480 feet or 756 metres. **90 B7** NO4070.
Finchale Priory *Dur.* ***Ecclesiastical building***, mainly 13c remains of priory founded late 12c (English Heritage), beside River Wear 3m/5km NE of Durham. **62 D2** NZ2947.
Fincham *Norf.* ***Village***, 5m/8km E of Downham Market. **44 A5** TF6806.
Finchampstead *W'ham* ***Village***, 4m/6km SW of Wokingham. **22 A5** SU7963.
Fincharn Castle *Arg. & B.* ***Castle***, remains of former stronghold of the Macdonalds on E shore of Loch Awe in Argyll, 2m/3km E of head of loch. **80 A7** NM8904.
Fincharn Loch *Arg. & B.* ***Lake/loch***, small loch 4m/6km E of Ford. **80 A7** NM9303.
Finchdean *Hants.* ***Village***, 4m/7km N of Havant. **11 J3** SU7312.
Finchingfield *Essex* ***Village***, 8m/12km NW of Braintree. Sites of Roman buildings in vicinity. **33 K5** TL6832.
Finchley *Gt.Lon.* ***Suburb***, in borough of Barnet, 7m/11km N of Charing Cross. **23 F2** TQ2590.
Findern *Derbys.* Population: 1784. ***Village***, 5m/8km SW of Derby. **41 F2** SK3030.
Findhorn ***River***, formed from many tributaries on Monadhliath Mountains, and flowing from Coignafearn Forest NE through Strathdearn, then E from Drynachan Lodge to Dulsie, finally following an increasingly meandering course NE to enter W end of Burghead Bay at Findhorn. **88 E2** NJ0364.
Findhorn *Moray* ***Village***, fishing village on E side of sandy Findhorn Bay at mouth of River Findhorn, N of Forres. **97 H5** NJ0364.
Findhorn Bay *Moray* ***Bay***, sandy bay at mouth of River Findhorn, N of Forres. **97 H5** NJ0364.
Findhorn Bridge *High.* ***Settlement***, on River Findhorn, 1km S of Tomatin. **89 F2** NH8027.
Findhu Glen *P. & K.* ***Valley***, running NW into Glen Artney, 5m/8km SW of Dalginross. **81 J6** NN7314.
Findhuglen *P. & K.* ***Settlement***, 8m/12km NE of Callander. **81 J6** NN7215.
Findlater Castle *Aber.* ***Castle***, ruined castle on cliffs 2m/3km E of Cullen. **98 D4** NJ5467.
Findlay's Seat *Moray* ***Hill***, 3m/4km N of Rothes. Height 859 feet or 262 metres. **97 K6** NJ2853.
Findo Gask *P. & K.* ***Locality***, surrounded by Roman sites, 7m/12km W of Perth. **82 B5** NO0020.
Findochty *Moray* Population: 1092. ***Village***, fishing village and resort at E end of Spey Bay, 3m/5km NE of Buckie. **98 C4** NJ4667.
Findon (Also known as Finnan.) *Aber.* ***Village***, near E coast, 5m/9km S of Aberdeen. Finnan is name from which smoked haddock takes its name. **91 H5** NO9397.
Findon *W.Suss.* Population: 1776. ***Village***, on South Downs, 4m/7km N of Worthing. **12 E6** TQ1208.
Findon Mains *High.* ***Settlement***, 5m/8km NE of Conon Bridge. **96 D5** NH6060.
Findon Ness *Aber.* ***Coastal feature***, headland on coast at Findon. **91 H5** NO9397.
Findon Valley *W.Suss.* ***Suburb***, N district of Worthing, almost adjoining Findon. TQ1206.
Findowie Hill *P. & K.* ***Mountain***, 8m/12km NW of Methven. Height 1912 feet or 583 metres. **82 A4** NN9435.
Findrassie *Moray* ***Settlement***, 2m/3km NW of Elgin. **97 J5** NJ1965.
Findron *Moray* ***Settlement***, 1km E of Tomintoul. **89 J3** NJ1718.
Finedon *Northants.* Population: 4051. ***Small town***, 3m/5km NE of Wellingborough. Splendid 14c church built in local ironstone. **32 C1** SP9272.
Finegand *P. & K.* ***Settlement***, on Shee Water, 3m/5km SE of Spittal of Glenshee. **82 C1** NO1366.
Fineshade *Northants.* ***Settlement***, 6m/10km W of Wansford. SP9797.
Fingal Street *Suff.* ***Hamlet***, 1m/2km NW of Worlingworth. **35 G2** TM2169.
Fingal's Cave *Arg. & B.* ***Cave***, large cave at S end of Staffa with pillars of basalt at entrance. Dimensions: height 66 feet or 20 metres; depth from entrance to back 227 feet or 69 metres; width of entrance 42 feet or 13 metres. **78 E4** NM3235.
Fingask *Aber.* ***Settlement***, 2m/3km W of Oldmeldrum. **91 F2** NJ7727.
Fingerpost *Worcs.* ***Hamlet***, 3m/5km W of Bewdley. **29 G1** SO7373.
Fingest *Bucks.* ***Village***, 5m/9km N of Henley-on-Thames. **22 A2** SU7791.
Finghall *N.Yorks.* ***Village***, 4m/7km E of Leyburn. **62 C7** SE1889.
Fingland *Cumb.* ***Settlement***, 2m/3km E of Kirkbride. **60 D1** NY2557.
Fingland *D. & G.* ***Settlement***, 5m/8km NW of Sanquhar. **68 C2** NS7517.
Fingland *D. & G.* ***Settlement***, 1m/2km N of Davington. **69 H3** NT2304.
Fingland Fell *D. & G.* ***Mountain***, in woodland, 3m/5km NW of Boreland. Height 1273 feet or 388 metres. **69 G4** NY1495.
Fingle Bridge *Devon* ***Bridge***, over River Teign in narrow wooded gorge, 3m/4km N of Moretonhampstead. SX7489.
Finglen Burn *Stir.* ***River***, flowing SW into Loch Tay, just N of Ardeonaig. **81 H4** NN6636.
Finglesham *Kent* ***Hamlet***, 3m/4km S of Sandwich. **15 J2** TR3353.
Fingringhoe *Essex* ***Village***, 4m/6km SE of Colchester. Marshes to S. **34 E7** TM0220.
Finham *W.Mid.* ***Suburb***, 3m/4km S of Coventry city centre. SP3375.
Finkle Street *S.Yorks.* ***Settlement***, just SW of Wortley, 2m/3km NE of Stocksbridge. SK3098.
Finlarig *Stir.* ***Settlement***, 1km N of Killin. **81 G4** NN5733.
Finlarig Castle *Stir.* ***Castle***, early 17c remains of former seat of Earls of Breadalbane in Killin, 10m/16km NW of Callender. **81 G4** NN5733.
Finlaystone House *Inclyde* ***Historic house***, home of Chief of Clan MacMillan, 3m/4km W of Port Glasgow. House contains doll collection and Celtic art displays and is surrounded by notable gardens. **74 B3** NS3673.
Finmere *Oxon.* ***Village***, 4m/6km W of Buckingham. **31 H5** SP6332.
Finnan *Aber.* *Alternative name for Findon, qv.*
Finnart *Arg. & B.* ***Locality***, in Argyll on E side of Loch Long, 3m/4km N of Garelochhead. **74 A1** NS2495.
Finnart *P. & K.* ***Settlement***, on S side of Loch Rannoch, 1km from head of loch. **81 G2** NN5157.
Finnarts Point *S.Ayr.* ***Coastal feature***, headland 1m/2km N of Finnarts Bay. **64 A3** NX0572.
Finney Green *Ches.* ***Suburb***, 1m/2km NE of Wilmslow. SJ8582.
Finnich Glen ***Valley***, on border of Stirling and West Dunbartonshire, carrying Burn Crooks NW from Burncrooks Reservoir. **74 C2** NS4780.
Finnieston *Glas.* ***Suburb***, 1m/2km W of Glasgow city centre. Scottish Exhibition and Conference Centre situated to W. NS5765.
Finningham *Suff.* ***Village***, 7m/11km N of Stowmarket. **34 E2** TM0669.
Finningley *S.Yorks.* Population: 3624. ***Village***, 4m/7km N of Bawtry. Airfield to SW. **51 J3** SK6799.
Finnygaud *Aber.* ***Locality***, 2m/3km NW of Aberchirder. **98 E5** NJ6054.
Finsbay *W.Isles* ***Settlement***, on Loch Finsbay, on SE coast of South Harris, 2m/4km SW of Manais. NG0786.
Finsbury *Gt.Lon.* ***Suburb***, in borough of Islington, about 1m/2km N of Blackfriars Bridge. **23 G3** TQ3182.
Finsbury Park *Gt.Lon.* ***Suburb***, in boroughs of Haringey and Islington, 4m/7km N of Charing Cross. The park itself is to N, in borough of Haringey. TQ3186.
Finstall *Worcs.* ***Hamlet***, 1m/2km E of Bromsgrove. **29 J1** SO9870.
Finsthwaite *Cumb.* ***Hamlet***, 1m/2km N of Newby Bridge. **55 G1** SD3687.
Finstock *Oxon.* ***Village***, 2m/3km S of Charlbury. **30 E7** SP3616.
Finstown *Ork.* ***Village***, on Mainland at head of Bay of Firth, 6m/10km W of Kirkwall. **107 C6** HY3513.
Fintry *Aber.* ***Settlement***, 4m/6km NE of Turriff. **99 F5** NJ7554.
Fintry *Stir.* ***Village***, on Endrick Water, 5m/7km E of Balfron. **74 E2** NS6186.
Fintry Hills *Stir.* ***Large natural feature***, small mountain range 2m/3km NE of Fintry, with highest summit Stronend (511 metres). **74 E2** NS6488.
Finwood *Warks.* ***Settlement***, 3m/5km NE of Henley-in-Arden. SP1968.
Finzean *Aber.* ***Settlement***, 2m/3km SW of Marywell. **90 D5** NO5993.
Fiola Meadhonach *Arg. & B.* ***Island***, small island immediately N of Lunga. NM7109.
Fionn Bheinn (Anglicised form: Foinaven.) *High.* ***Mountain***, in Ross and Cromarty district 2m/4km N of Achnasheen. Munro: height 3060 feet or 933 metres. **95 H5** NH1462.
Fionn Bheinn Mhòr *High.* ***Mountain***, 2m/3km NW of Oykel Bridge. Height 1082 feet or 330 metres. **95 K1** NC3704.
Fionn Loch *High.* ***Lake/loch***, long narrow loch 1m/2km N of Loch Sionascaig and 3m/5km SE of Inverkirkaig. **102 D7** NC1218.
Fionn Loch *High.* ***Lake/loch***, near W coast of Ross and Cromarty district 5m/8km E of Poolewe. Length over 5m/8km NW to SE; width about 1km. **95 F3** NG9478.
Fionn Loch Mòr *High.* ***Lake/loch***, irregular-shaped loch fed by Fionn Allt, to SE of Gorm Loch Mòr, 5m/8km E of Inchnadamph. **103 F6** NC3324.
Fionnphort *Arg. & B.* ***Village***, on Sound of Iona, at W end of Ross of Mull. Ferry to Iona. **78 E5** NM3023.
Fir Island *Cumb.* ***Island***, small wooded island (National Trust) off E shore of Coniston Water, 2m/3km S of Coniston. SD3094.
Fir Tree *Dur.* ***Village***, 2m/3km SW of Crook. **62 C3** NZ1434.
Fir Vale *S.Yorks.* ***Suburb***, 2m/3km N of Sheffield city centre. **51 F4** SK3690.
Firbank *Cumb.* ***Settlement***, in Lune valley, 3m/4km NW of Sedbergh. **61 H7** SD6293.
Firbeck *S.Yorks.* ***Village***, 3m/5km SE of Maltby. **51 H4** SK5688.
Firby *N.Yorks.* ***Hamlet***, 1m/2km S of Bedale. SE2686.
Firby *N.Yorks.* ***Hamlet***, 4m/7km SW of Malton, on E side of River Derwent. SE7466.
Fire Beacon Point *Cornw.* ***Coastal feature***, 1m/2km NE of Boscastle. **4 A1** SX1092.
Firepool *Som.* ***Suburb***, central district of Taunton, to N of River Tone. ST2225.
Firgrove *Gt.Man.* ***Suburb***, to NW of Milnrow, 1m/2km E of Rochdale. **49 J1** SD9213.
Firle Beacon *E.Suss.* ***Viewpoint***, on ridge of South Downs, 1m/2km SE of West Firle. Height: 712 feet or 217 metres. **13 H6** TQ4707.
Firle Place *E.Suss.* ***Historic house***, mainly Georgian house with Tudor core, 4m/6km SE of Lewes. **13 H6** TQ4707.
Firrhill *Edin.* ***Suburb***, 3m/5km SW of Edinburgh city centre. NT2369.
Firs Lane *Gt.Man.* ***Suburb***, with lake, 1m/2km W of Leigh town centre. SD6400.
Firs Road *Wilts.* ***Hamlet***, 5m/8km NE of Salisbury. **10 D1** SU2133.
Firsby *Lincs.* ***Village***, 4m/6km NW of Wainfleet All Saints. **53 H6** TF4563.
Firth *Shet.* ***Settlement***, on NE coast of Mainland, 1m/2km S of Mossbank across Firths Voe inlet. Firth Ness is headland 1m/2km E. **108 D5** HU4473.
Firth of Clyde ***Sea feature***, estuary of River Clyde running from Dumbarton past Gourock, then turning S and continuing between Strathclyde mainland to E and islands of Bute and Arran to W. **67 F2** NS1043.
Firth of Forth ***Sea feature***, estuary of River Forth, running E and widening out into North Sea between Fife Ness and North Berwick. At its narrowest point (1m/2km), between North and South Queensferry, firth is spanned by Forth road and railway bridges. **76 A2** NT2181.
Firth of Lorn *Arg. & B.* ***Sea feature***, sea passage between SE coast of Mull and Scottish mainland. **79 H6** NM7021.
Firth of Tay ***Sea feature***, estuary of River Tay extending E from confluence of Rivers Tay and Earn past Dundee to Buddon Ness. Length about 23m/37km; maximum width nearly 3m/5km at Invergowrie, although channel is comparatively narrow owing to presence of sandbanks. **82 E5** NO3737.
Firths Voe *Shet.* *See Firth.*
Fish Holm *Shet.* ***Island***, small island off NE coast of Mainland 2m/3km E of Mossbank. **108 D5** HU4774.
Fish Lake *Dur.* ***Lake/loch***, small lake on Lune Forest, 1m/2km NW of Grains o' th' Beck Bridge. **61 K4** NY8620.
Fishbourne *I.o.W.* ***Hamlet***, 2m/3km W of Ryde. **11 G5** SZ5692.
Fishbourne *W.Suss.* ***Village***, 2m/3km W of Chichester. Remains of Roman palace. **12 B6** SU8304.
Fishbourne Roman Palace *W.Suss.* ***Historic/prehistoric site***, largest Roman palace in Britain, 2m/3km W of Chichester, with 25 mosaic floors remaining. Museum details life in Roman Britain. **12 B6** SU8304.
Fishburn *Dur.* Population: 2253. ***Village***, 2m/3km N of Sedgefield. **62 E3** NZ3632.
Fishcross *Clack.* ***Hamlet***, 2m/3km NE of Alloa. NS9095.
Fisher *W.Suss.* ***Settlement***, just W of South Mundham, 3m/5km S of Chichester. SU8700.
Fisher Tarn Reservoir *Cumb.* ***Reservoir***, 2m/4km E of Kendal. **61 G7** SD5592.
Fisherfield Forest *High.* ***Open space***, deer forest in Ross and Cromarty district, centre of which is about 8m/13km E of Poolewe. **95 F3** NG9980.
Fisherford *Aber.* ***Settlement***, 9m/15km E of Huntly. **90 E1** NJ6635.
Fisherrow *E.Loth.* ***Locality***, W part of Musselburgh. Small harbour. NT3373.
Fishers Green *Essex* ***Locality***, on River Lea, 1m/2km E of Cheshunt. TL3702.
Fisher's Green *Herts.* ***Suburb***, in NW part of Stevenage. TL2225.
Fisher's Pond *Hants.* ***Village***, 5m/8km NW of Bishop's Waltham. **11 F2** SU4820.
Fisher's Row *Lancs.* ***Locality***, 1km E of Pilling. **55 H5** SD4148.
Fishersgate *W.Suss.* ***Suburb***, E district of Southwick. TQ2505.
Fisherstreet *W.Suss.* ***Settlement***, 3m/5km SE of Haslemere. **12 C3** SU9531.
Fisherton *High.* ***Settlement***, in Inverness district, on E side of Inner Moray Firth, 1m/2km W of Dalcross Airport. **96 E6** NH7451.
Fisherton *S.Ayr.* ***Settlement***, 1km NE of Dunure. **67 G2** NS2616.
Fisherton de la Mere *Wilts.* ***Hamlet***, 1m/2km NW of Wylye across River Wylye. **10 B1** SU0038.
Fisherwick *Staffs.* ***Settlement***, 4m/6km NW of Tamworth. SK1709.
Fishguard (Abergwaun). *Pembs.* Population: 2679. ***Small town***, with attractive old harbour, at S end of Fishguard Bay. Ferry port, to Rosslare in Eire, at new harbour. Holds annual music festival. See also Goodwick. **16 C1** SM9537.
Fishguard Bay *Pembs.* ***Bay***, extending W from Dinas Head to Crincoed Point. Fishguard Harbour, on W side of bay, is a port, with passenger services to Rosslare, Cork, and Waterford. **16 C1** SM9537.
Fishlake *S.Yorks.* ***Village***, 3m/4km N of Hatfield. **51 J1** SE6513.
Fishleigh Barton *Devon* ***Settlement***, 3m/4km N of High Bickington. **6 D3** SS5824.
Fishley *Norf.* ***Hamlet***, 1m/2km N of Acle. TG4011.
Fishley *W.Mid.* ***Settlement***, 3m/5km N of Walsall town centre. SK0003.
Fishmere End *Lincs.* ***Locality***, 2m/3km SW of Kirton. TF2837.
Fishnish *Arg. & B.* ***Locality***, on E coast of Mull; jetty for ferries from Lochaline on Scottish mainland. **79 H3** NM6641.
Fishnish Bay *Arg. & B.* ***Bay***, on Sound of Mull, 4m/7km E of Salen, Mull. **79 H3** NM6442.
Fishnish Point *Arg. & B.* ***Coastal feature***, headland on E side of Fishnish Bay, Mull. **79 H3** NM6442.
Fishpond Bottom *Dorset* ***Settlement***, 5m/7km E of Axminster. **8 C5** SY3698.
Fishponds *Bristol* ***Suburb***, 3m/5km NE of Bristol city centre. **19 K4** ST6376.
Fishpool *Gt.Man.* ***Suburb***, 1m/2km SE of Bury town centre. **49 H1** SD8109.
Fishtoft *Lincs.* ***Village***, 2m/4km SE of Boston. **43 G1** TF3642.
Fishtoft Drove *Lincs.* ***Settlement***, 3m/5km N of Boston. **43 G1** TF3149.
Fishtown of Usan (Also known as Usan.) *Angus* ***Village***, on E coast, 2m/3km S of Montrose. **83 J2** NO7254.

Fishwick *Lancs.* ***Suburb***, 1m/2km E of Preston town centre. **55 J6** SD5629.
Fishwick *Sc.Bord.* ***Hamlet***, 2m/3km SW of Paxton. **77 H5** NT9151.
Fiskavaig *High.* ***Locality***, with small bay on W coast of Skye, on S shore of Loch Bracadale. NG3334.
Fiskerton *Lincs.* ***Village***, 5m/8km E of Lincoln. **52 D5** TF0472.
Fiskerton *Notts.* ***Village***, on River Trent, 3m/5km SE of Southwell. **51 K7** SK7351.
Fistral Bay *Cornw.* ***Bay***, between Towan Head and East Pentire Point, 1m/2km W of Newquay. **2 E2** SW7962.
Fitful Head *Shet.* ***Coastal feature***, headland on W coast of Mainland, 5m/8km NW of Sumburgh Head. The steep cliffs rise to 929 feet or 283 metres. **109 F9** HU3413.
Fitling *E.Riding* ***Settlement***, 3m/4km S of Aldbrough. TA2534.
Fittleton *Wilts.* ***Village***, on River Avon, 5m/8km N of Amesbury. **20 E6** SU1449.
Fittleworth *W.Suss.* ***Village***, 3m/4km SE of Petworth. **12 D5** TQ0119.
Fitton End *Cambs.* ***Settlement***, 3m/5km NW of Wisbech. **43 H4** TF4212.
Fitz *Shrop.* ***Hamlet***, 4m/7km NW of Shrewsbury. **38 D4** SJ4417.
Fitz House *Wilts.* ***Garden***, hillside terraced gardens in Telfont Magna, bordered by yew and beech hedges. Includes bulbs and spring blossom, clematis and old-fashioned roses. **9 J1** ST9932.
Fitzhead *Som.* ***Village***, 2m/3km N of Milverton. **7 K3** ST1228.
Fitzroy *Som.* ***Hamlet***, 3m/5km NW of Taunton. ST1927.
Fitzwilliam *W.Yorks.* Population: 4662. ***Village***, 2m/3km NW of Hemsworth. **51 G1** SE4115.
Fiunary *High.* ***Settlement***, on SW coast of Morvern, Lochaber district, 4m/6km NW of Lochaline. **79 H3** NM6246.
Fiunary Forest *High.* ***Forest/woodland***, in Lochaber district to NW of Lochaline. **79 H3** NM6647.
Five Acres *Glos.* ***Settlement***, 1m/2km N of Coleford. SO5712.
Five Ash Down *E.Suss.* ***Hamlet***, 2m/3km N of Uckfield. **13 H4** TQ4724.
Five Ashes *E.Suss.* ***Village***, 2m/3km SW of Mayfield. **13 J4** TQ5524.
Five Bells *Som.* ***Hamlet***, 1km S of Watchet. ST0642.
Five Bridges *Here.* ***Locality***, 5m/8km S of Bromyard. **29 F4** SO6547.
Five Houses *I.o.W.* ***Hamlet***, 5m/7km W of Newport. SZ4287.
Five Lane Ends *W.Yorks.* ***Suburb***, 3m/4km NE of Bradford city centre, in Eccleshill district. SE1736.
Five Lanes *Mon.* ***Hamlet***, 1m/2km W of Caerwent. ST4490.
Five Mile Hill Cross *Devon* ***Locality***, 5m/8km W of Exeter. SX8493.
Five Oak Green *Kent* ***Village***, 1m/2km W of Paddock Wood. **23 K7** TQ6445.
Five Oaks *W.Suss.* ***Hamlet***, 2m/3km NE of Billingshurst. **12 D4** TQ0928.
Five Penny Borve *W.Isles Anglicised form of Cóig Peighinnean Bhuirgh, qv.*
Five Penny Ness *W.Isles Anglicised form of Cóig Peighinnean, qv.*
Five Roads *Carmar.* ***Hamlet***, 3m/5km N of Llanelli. **17 H4** SN4805.
Five Sisters (Also known as Five Sisters of Kintail.) *High.* ***Large natural feature***, chain of peaks on Kintail Forest (National Trust for Scotland), Skye and Lochalsh district; from N to S, Sgurr na Moraich, Sgurr nan Saighead, Sgurr Fhuaran (or Scour Ouran), Sgurr na Carnach, and Sgurr na Ciste Duibhe. **87 F3** NG9717.
Five Sisters of Kintail *High. Alternative name for Five Sisters, qv.*
Five Turnings *Shrop.* ***Settlement***, 2m/3km N of Knighton. **28 B1** SO2875.
Five Ways *Worcs.* ***Locality***, 3m/5km NE of Kidderminster. SO8780.
Five Wents *Kent* ***Hamlet***, 1m/2km N of Sutton Valence. **14 D2** TQ8050.
Fivehead *Som.* ***Village***, 5m/8km SW of Langport. **8 C2** ST3522.
Fivelanes *Cornw.* ***Hamlet***, on NE edge of Bodmin Moor, 7m/11km SW of Launceston. **4 C2** SX2280.
Fivig *W.Isles Anglicised form of Fibhig, qv.*
Flackley Ash *E.Suss.* ***Settlement***, adjoining to NW of Peasmarsh. TQ8823.
Flack's Green *Essex* ***Settlement***, 3m/5km W of Witham. TL7614.
Flackwell Heath *Bucks.* Population: 6781. ***Suburb***, 3m/5km W of Beaconsfield. **22 B3** SU8990.
Fladbury *Worcs.* ***Village***, 3m/5km NW of Evesham. **29 J4** SO9946.
Fladbury Cross *Worcs.* ***Locality***, 4m/6km NW of Evesham. SO9947.
Fladda *Arg. & B.* ***Island***, one of larger islands of the Treshnish Isles, lying towards NE end of group. **78 E3** NM2943.
Fladda *Arg. & B.* ***Island***, islet with lighthouse 1m/2km off NW coast of Luing. NM7212.
Fladda-chuain *High.* ***Island***, narrow uninhabited island, nearly 1m/2km long NW to SE, 4m/6km NW of Rubha Hunish, Skye. **93 J3** NG3681.
Fladdabister *Shet.* ***Settlement***, on E coast of Mainland, 6m/10km S of Lerwick, near head of small Bay of Fladdabister. **109 D9** HU4332.
Fladday *High. Alternative name for Eilean Fladday, qv.*
Fladday *W.Isles* ***Island***, small uninhabited island off E coast of Scarp opposite entrance to Loch Resort, W coast of Isle of Lewis. NA9915.
Flag Fen *Cambs.* ***Open space***, fenland, 2m/3km SE of Whittlesey. **43 F6** TL2894.
Flagg *Derbys.* ***Village***, 5m/8km W of Bakewell. **50 D6** SK1368.
Flambards Village *Cornw.* ***Leisure/recreation***, theme park based around reconstruction of Victorian village and World War II street, 1m/2km S of Helston. **2 D6** SW6626.
Flamborough *E.Riding* Population: 1741. ***Village***, 4m/6km NE of Bridlington. **59 J2** TA2270.
Flamborough Head *E.Riding* ***Coastal feature***, headland on North Sea coast, 2m/3km E of Flamborough. **59 J2** TA2270.
Flamstead *Herts.* ***Village***, 5m/8km N of Hemel Hempstead. **32 D7** TL0714.
Flamstead End *Herts.* ***Locality***, 1m/2km NW of Cheshunt. **23 G1** TL3403.
Flamsteed House *Gt.Lon. See Old Royal Observatory.*
Flanders Green *Herts.* ***Settlement***, 3m/4km W of Buntingford. TL3228.
Flanders Moss *Stir.* ***Marsh/bog***, boggy area between River Forth and Goodie Water, SW of Thornhill. **74 E1** NS6398.
Flanesford Priory *Here.* ***Ecclesiastical building***, on W bank of River Wye, 3m/5km SW of Ross-on-Wye across river. Ruins of small Augustinian priory founded in 14c. **28 E7** SO5719.
Flannan Isles *W.Isles* ***Island***, group of small uninhabited islands about 21m/34km W of Gallan Head, Isle of Lewis. The main islands, in order of size, are: Eilean Mòr, Eilean Tighe, Eilean a' Ghobha, Soray, Roareim, Sgeir Toman, and Sgeir Righinn. There are several smaller islets and rocks. Larger islands are grass-covered and are used for grazing. Birds abound. NA7246.
Flansham *W.Suss.* ***Village***, 2m/3km NE of Bognor Regis. **12 C6** SU9601.
Flanshaw *W.Yorks.* ***Suburb***, 1m/2km W of Wakefield city centre. SE3120.
Flappit Spring *W.Yorks.* ***Settlement***, at crossroads, 1m/2km E of Haworth. SE0536.
Flasby *N.Yorks.* ***Settlement***, 4m/7km NW of Skipton. **56 E4** SD9456.
Flash *Staffs.* ***Village***, in Peak District National Park, 4m/7km SW of Buxton. Claims to be highest village in England. **50 C6** SK0267.
Flashader *High.* ***Settlement***, on E side of Loch Greshornish, on N coast of Skye. **93 J6** NG3553.
Flask Inn *N.Yorks.* ***Settlement***, 6m/10km SW of Robin Hood's Bay. **63 J2** NZ9300.
Flat Holm *Cardiff* ***Island***, round island about 1m/2km in circumference in Bristol Channel, 3m/4km SE of Lavernock Point. Lighthouse. **19 F5** ST2264.
Flatford Mill and Bridge Cottage *Suff.* ***Historic house***, mill and cottages (National Trust) on N bank of River Stour, 2m/3km NW of Manningtree. Location made famous by featuring in several of John Constable's paintings, including 'The Haywain' and 'Willy Lott's Cottage'. Flatford Mill now leased out as field study centre. Displays of Constable's life and work housed in Bridge Cottage (National Trust), a restored thatched cottage nearby. **34 E5** TM0733.
Flaunden *Herts.* ***Village***, 4m/6km E of Chesham. **22 D1** TL0100.
Flawborough *Notts.* ***Village***, 5m/8km NE of Bingham. **42 A1** SK7842.
Flawith *N.Yorks.* ***Hamlet***, 4m/7km SW of Easingwold. **57 K3** SE4865.
Flax Bourton *N.Som.* ***Village***, 5m/8km W of Bristol. **19 J5** ST5069.
Flax Moss *Lancs.* ***Suburb***, 1m/2km S of Haslingden. SD7822.
Flaxby *N.Yorks.* ***Village***, 3m/5km E of Knaresborough. **57 J4** SE3957.
Flaxholme *Derbys.* ***Hamlet***, adjoining to S of Duffield, 4m/6km N of Derby. SK3442.
Flaxlands *Norf.* ***Settlement***, to N of Carleton Rode, 4m/6km SE of Attleborough. TM1093.
Flaxley *Glos.* ***Hamlet***, 2m/4km N of Newnham. **29 F7** SO6916.
Flaxley Abbey *Glos.* ***Ecclesiastical building***, Cistercian monastery founded in 12c, 2m/3km NE of Cinderford. Present house preserves abbot's hall and refectory. **29 F7** SO6815.
Flaxpool *Som.* ***Hamlet***, 7m/11km SE of Watchet. **7 K2** ST1435.
Flaxton *N.Yorks.* ***Village***, 8m/13km NE of York. **58 C3** SE6762.
Fleckney *Leics.* Population: 4295. ***Village***, 6m/9km N of Husbands Bosworth. **41 J6** SP6493.
Flecknoe *Warks.* ***Village***, 4m/6km W of Daventry. **31 G2** SP5163.
Fledborough *Notts.* ***Hamlet***, 1m/2km SE of Ragnall, to W of River Trent. SK8172.
Fleet *Dorset* ***Hamlet***, at SE end of Chesil Beach, 3m/5km W of Weymouth. SY6380.
Fleet *Hants.* ***Settlement***, on Hayling Island, just S of Stoke. SU7201.
Fleet *Hants.* Population: 30,391. ***Town***, 4m/6km W of Farnborough. Developed with arrival of railway in 1840. **22 B6** SU8154.
Fleet *High.* ***River***, rising near Lairg in Sutherland district and flowing SE to Loch Fleet and coast, 4m/6km N of Dornoch. NH8195.
Fleet *Lincs.* ***Hamlet***, 2m/3km E of Holbeach. **43 G3** TF3823.
Fleet Air Arm Museum *Som.* ***Other feature of interest***, at Royal Naval Air Station, Yeovilton, 4m/7km N of Yeovil. Tells history of Royal Naval Air Service; 40 aircraft and memorabilia of 20c conflicts. **8 E2** ST5322.
Fleet Bay *D. & G.* ***Sea feature***, inlet of Wigtown bay at mouth of Water of Fleet. **65 F5** NX5652.
Fleet Hargate *Lincs.* ***Village***, 2m/3km E of Holbeach. **43 G3** TF3925.
Fleet Moss *N.Yorks.* ***Marsh/bog***, area of bog near summit of pass between Oughtershaw and Hawes. **56 D1** SD8783.
Fleet Pond *Hants.* ***Lake/loch***, traversed by railway at NE edge of Fleet. **22 B6** SU8154.
Fleetville *Herts.* ***Suburb***, to E of St. Albans city centre. TL1607.
Fleetwood *Lancs.* Population: 27,227. ***Town***, port at mouth of River Wyre, 8m/13km N of Blackpool. Passenger ferries to Belfast and Isle of Man. Ferry for pedestrians across river mouth to Knott End-on-Sea. Two lighthouses. **55 G5** SD3247.
Fleisirin *W.Isles Gaelic form of Flesherin, qv.*
Flemingston (Trefflemin). *V. of Glam.* ***Village***, 3m/5km S of Cowbridge. **18 D5** ST0170.
Flemington *S.Lan.* ***Locality***, 3m/5km SE of Rutherglen. **74 E5** NS6659.
Flemington *S.Lan.* ***Suburb***, adjoining to NE of Strathaven. NS7044.
Flempton *Suff.* ***Village***, 5m/7km NW of Bury St. Edmunds. **34 C2** TL8169.
Fleoideabhagh (Anglicised form: Flodabay.) *W.Isles* ***Settlement***, on SE coast of South Harris, 4m/7km NE of Rodel. **93 F3** NG0988.
Flesherin (Gaelic form: Fleisirin.) *W.Isles* ***Settlement***, on Eye Peninsula, Isle of Lewis, 1km SW of Portnaguran. NB5536.
Fleshwick Bay *I.o.M.* ***Sea feature***, inlet at S end of Niarbyl Bay on E side of Bradda Hill. **54 A6** SC2071.
Fletchersbridge *Cornw.* ***Settlement***, 2m/3km E of Bodmin. SX1065.
Fletchertown *Cumb.* ***Hamlet***, 5m/7km SW of Wigton. **60 D2** NY2042.
Fletching *E.Suss.* ***Village***, 3m/5km NW of Uckfield. Burial place of Edward Gibbon, historian. **13 H4** TQ4223.
Flete *Devon* ***Historic house***, 3m/5km E of Yealmpton. Originally an Elizabethan manor house; Norman Shaw made alterations in 1879. **5 G5** SX6251.
Flete *Devon* ***Settlement***, 3m/5km E of Yealmpton. **5 G5** SX6251.
Fleuchats *Aber.* ***Settlement***, below N slopes of Meikle Charsk Hill, 3m/4km S of Strathdon. **90 B4** NJ3309.
Fleur-de-lis *Caerp.* ***Locality***, 1m/2km SW of Blackwood. **18 E2** ST1596.
Flexbury *Cornw.* Population: 2245. ***Suburb***, N district of Bude. **6 A5** SS2107.
Flexford *Surr.* ***Village***, 4m/7km W of Guildford. **22 C6** SU9350.
Flimby *Cumb.* Population: 1775. ***Village***, on coast, 2m/3km S of Maryport. Site of Roman signal station to N. **60 B3** NY0233.
Flimwell *E.Suss.* ***Village***, 2m/3km E of Ticehurst. **14 C4** TQ7131.
Flint (Y Fflint). *Flints.* Population: 11,737. ***Town***, on River Dee estuary, 11m/17km NW of Chester. Remains of 13c castle (Cadw). **48 B5** SJ2472.
Flint Castle *Flints.* ***Castle***, ruins of 13c castle in Flint, 10m/16km NW of Chester. **48 B5** SJ2473.
Flint Cross *Cambs.* ***Settlement***, 4m/6km NE of Royston. **33 H4** TL4143.
Flint Hill *Dur.* ***Locality***, 2m/3km N of Annfield Plain. NZ1654.
Flint Hill *Lincs.* ***Hill***, crossed by A153 road, 4m/7km N of Horncastle. Height 453 feet or 138 metres. **53 F5** TF2776.
Flint Mountain *Flints.* ***Village***, on hill, 2m/3km S of Flint. **48 B5** SJ2370.
Flintham *Notts.* ***Village***, 6m/10km SW of Newark-on-Trent. **42 A1** SK7445.
Flinton *E.Riding* ***Hamlet***, 2m/3km SW of Aldbrough. **59 J6** TA2236.
Flint's Green *W.Mid.* ***Settlement***, 4m/7km W of Coventry. SP2680.
Flishinghurst *Kent* ***Settlement***, 1m/2km NW of Cranbrook. **14 C4** TQ7637.
Flitcham *Norf.* ***Village***, 8m/13km NE of King's Lynn. **44 B3** TF7226.
Flitholme *Cumb.* ***Settlement***, 2m/3km W of Brough. NY7615.
Flitton *Beds.* ***Village***, 2m/4km SE of Ampthill. De Grey Mausoleum (English Heritage), with tombs and monuments relating to de Grey family of Wrest Park, adjoins Flitton Church. **32 D5** TL0535.
Flitwick *Beds.* Population: 11,063. ***Village***, 2m/3km S of Ampthill. **32 D5** TL0334.
Flixborough *N.Lincs.* ***Village***, 3m/5km NW of Scunthorpe. **52 B1** SE8715.
Flixborough Stather *N.Lincs.* ***Locality***, on E bank of River Trent, 1km SW of Flixborough. Industrial estate. SE8614.
Flixton *Gt.Man.* ***Locality***, 1m/2km W of Urmston. **49 G3** SJ7494.
Flixton *N.Yorks.* ***Village***, 5m/8km W of Filey. **59 G2** TA0479.
Flixton *Suff.* ***Locality***, 3m/5km NW of Lowestoft. TM5195.
Flixton *Suff.* ***Village***, 3m/4km SW of Bungay. **45 H7** TM3186.
Flockton *W.Yorks.* ***Village***, 6m/10km E of Huddersfield. **50 E1** SE2314.
Flockton Green *W.Yorks.* ***Hamlet***, 1km E of Flockton. **50 E1** SE2314.
Flodabay *W.Isles Anglicised form of Fleoideabhagh, qv.*
Floday *W.Isles* ***Island***, small uninhabited island in Loch Roag, W coast of Isle of Lewis, 1m/2km SE of Miabhig. **100 D4** NB1033.
Floday *W.Isles* ***Island***, small uninhabited island off W coast of Isle of Lewis, nearly 1m/2km NW of Great Bernera. NB1241.
Flodda *W.Isles Anglicised form of Eilean Flodaigh, qv.*
Flodday *W.Isles* ***Island***, small uninhabited island 3m/5km E of Northbay village, Barra. **84 C4** NF7502.
Flodday *W.Isles* ***Island***, uninhabited island in Loch na Madadh, E coast of North Uist, 1m/2km E of Lochmaddy. NF9469.
Flodday *W.Isles* ***Island***, small uninhabited island 1m/2km W of Sandray and 1m/2km SW of SW point of Vatersay. **84 A5** NL6192.

F

Floddaybeg *W.Isles* ***Island***, small uninhabited island just off SE tip of North Uist. **92 E6** NF9158.

Floddaymore *W.Isles* ***Island***, uninhabited island off SE coast of North Uist, E of Ronay across narrow strait. **92 E6** NF9157.

Flodden *Northumb.* ***Settlement***, 2m/4km SE of Branxton. Site of Battle of Flodden Field 1513 at Branxton. **77 H7** NT9235.

Flodigarry *High.* ***Settlement***, on NE coast of Skye, 5m/8km SE of Rubha Hunish. **93 K4** NG4672.

Flood's Ferry *Cambs.* ***Settlement***, at confluence of Whittlesey Dike and River Nene (old course), 4m/7km SW of March. TL3593.

Flookburgh *Cumb.* ***Village***, 2m/3km S of Cartmel. **55 G2** SD3675.

Floors *Moray* ***Settlement***, 4m/7km E of Keith. **98 C5** NJ4952.

Floors Castle *Sc.Bord.* ***Castle***, seat of Duke of Roxburghe, 1m/2km NW of Kelso. Built by William Adam in 1721, much altered and enlarged in mid 19c. Reputedly largest inhabited castle in Scotland. **77 F7** NT7134.

F

Flora Macdonald's Birthplace *W.Isles* ***Other feature of interest***, ruins of birthplace of Flora Macdonald, 2m/4km SE of Rubha Ardvule, South Uist. Cairn commemorates Flora, who famously helped Charles Edward Stuart (Bonnie Prince Charlie) escape from English troops. **84 C2** NF7426.

Flordon *Norf.* ***Village***, 8m/12km SW of Norwich. **45 F6** TM1897.

Flore *Northants.* ***Village***, 5m/8km E of Daventry. **31 H2** SP6460.

Florence *Stoke* ***Suburb***, in SE part of Longton, Stoke-on-Trent. SJ9142.

Flotta *Ork.* ***Island***, low-lying island of about 4 square miles or 10 square km lying between Hoy and South Ronaldsay. **107 C8** ND3593.

Flotta *Shet.* ***Island***, small island at entrance to Weisdale Voe, Mainland. HU3746.

Flotterton *Northumb.* ***Settlement***, 4m/6km W of Rothbury. **71 F3** NT9902.

Flowers Green *E.Suss.* ***Settlement***, 1km S of Herstmonceux. TQ6311.

Flowton *Suff.* ***Hamlet***, 5m/8km W of Ipswich. **34 E4** TM0846.

Flushdyke *W.Yorks.* ***Suburb***, 1km NE of Ossett town centre. SE2821.

Flushing *Aber.* ***Settlement***, 1km E of Longside and 4m/7km W of Peterhead. **99 J6** NK0546.

Flushing *Cornw.* ***Hamlet***, on S side of Gillan Harbour, 8m/12km E of Helston. SW7825.

Flushing *Cornw.* ***Village***, N of Falmouth across inlet of Carrick Roads. Queen Anne houses and evidence of Dutch influence from 17c. **3 F5** SW8033.

Fluxton *Devon* ***Hamlet***, 2m/3km SW of Ottery St. Mary. SY0892.

Flyford Flavell *Worcs.* ***Village***, 8m/13km E of Worcester. **29 J3** SO9854.

Foals Green *Suff.* ***Settlement***, 2m/4km SE of Stradbroke. TM2571.

Fobbing *Thur.* ***Village***, 4m/6km S of Basildon. **24 D3** TQ7183.

Fochabers *Moray* Population: 1534. ***Village***, on E bank of River Spey, 8m/13km E of Elgin. **98 B5** NJ3458.

Fochriw *Caerp.* ***Village***, 1m/2km SW of Rhymney. **18 E1** SO1005.

Fockerby *N.Lincs.* ***Village***, adjoining to W of Garthorpe, 7m/12km SE of Goole. **52 B1** SE8419.

Fodder Fen *Cambs.* ***Open space***, fenland, 2m/3km W of Littleport. **43 J7** TL5287.

Fodderletter *Moray* ***Locality***, comprises Easter Fodderletter, Mid Fodderletter and Wester Fodderletter, 1m/2km E of Bridge of Brown. **89 J2** NJ1421.

Fodderty *High.* ***Village***, in Ross and Cromarty district, 2m/4km W of Dingwall. **96 C6** NH5159.

Foddington *Som.* ***Hamlet***, 5m/9km NE of Ilchester. ST5829.

Foel *Powys* ***Hamlet***, 1m/2km NW of Llangadfan. **37 J4** SH9911.

Foel Benddin *Gwyn.* ***Mountain***, 1km N of Dinas-Mawddwy. Height 1706 feet or 520 metres. **37 H4** SH8516.

Foel Cwm-Sian-Llŵyd *Gwyn.* ***Mountain***, 5m/8km SE of Bala. Height 2125 feet or 648 metres. **37 J2** SH9931.

Foel Cwmcerwyn (Prescelly Top). *Pembs.* ***Mountain***, summit of Prescelly Mountains, 6m/9km SE of Newport. Height 1758 feet or 536 metres. **16 D1** SN0931.

Foel Ddu *Gwyn.* ***Mountain***, 7m/11km NE of Dolgellau. Height 1525 feet or 465 metres. **37 H3** SH8124.

Foel Drych *Pembs.* ***Mountain***, 10m/16km S of St. Dogmaels. Height 1207 feet or 368 metres. **16 E1** SN1630.

Foel Dugoed *Gwyn.* ***Mountain***, small plateau area 2m/3km NE of Mallwyd. Height 1440 feet or 439 metres. **37 H4** SH8913.

Foel Eryr *Pembs.* ***Mountain***, 4m/7km S of Newport. Height 1535 feet or 468 metres. **16 D1** SN0632.

Foel Figenau *Gwyn.* ***Mountain***, 5m/8km S of Bala. Height 1902 feet or 580 metres. **37 J3** SH9128.

Foel Fraith *Carmar.* ***Mountain***, 4m/6km N of Cwmllynfell. Height 1981 feet or 604 metres. **27 G7** SN7518.

Foel-Fras *Conwy* ***Mountain***, on border with Gwynedd, 4m/7km S of Llanfairfechan. Height 3090 feet or 942 metres. **46 E6** SH6968.

Foel Fynyddau *N.P.T.* ***Mountain***, 1km SW of Pontrhydyfen. Masts at summit. Height 1214 feet or 370 metres. **18 A2** SS7893.

Foel Goch *Cere.* ***Mountain***, 3m/5km NE of Tal-y-bont. Height 1558 feet or 475 metres. **37 F6** SN6992.

Foel Goch *Gwyn.* ***Mountain***, on W side of Nant Ffrancon pass, 3m/5km S of Bethesda. Height 2726 feet or 831 metres. **46 E6** SH6261.

Foel Goch *Gwyn.* ***Mountain***, 4m/7km NE of Bala. Height 2004 feet or 611 metres. **37 J1** SH9542.

Foel Grach *Conwy* ***Mountain***, on border with Gwynedd, 4m/7km E of Bethesda. Height 3195 feet or 974 metres. **46 E6** SH6865.

Foel Gurig *Powys* ***Mountain***, 1km SE of Llangurig. Height 1574 feet or 480 metres. **27 J1** SN9179.

Foel Lus *Conwy* ***Mountain***, near coast 1km E of Penmaenmawr. Height 1187 feet or 362 metres. **47 F5** SH7376.

Foel Offrwm *Gwyn.* ***Mountain***, 2m/3km NE of Dolgellau. Height 1325 feet or 404 metres. **37 G3** SH7420.

Foel Rhiwlas *Powys* ***Mountain***, 2m/3km E of Llanarmon Dyffryn Ceiriog. Height 1489 feet or 454 metres. **38 B2** SJ1933.

Foel Rhudd *Gwyn.* ***Mountain***, 3m/5km N of Llanymawddwy. Height 2198 feet or 670 metres. **37 H3** SH8923.

Foel Trawsnant *N.P.T.* ***Mountain***, 2m/3km N of Maesteg. Height 1210 feet or 369 metres. **18 B2** SS8393.

Foel Wen *Powys* ***Mountain***, 4m/6km W of Llanarmon Dyffryn Ceiriog. Height 2266 feet or 691 metres. **37 K2** SJ0933.

Foel Wyllt *Gwyn.* ***Mountain***, 4m/6km NE of Tywyn. Height 1027 feet or 313 metres. **37 F5** SH6305.

Foel-y-ffridd *Gwyn.* ***Mountain***, 1m/2km NW of Aberangell. Height 1122 feet or 342 metres. **37 H4** SH8211.

Foel y-Geifr *Gwyn.* ***Mountain***, 3m/4km NW of Machynlleth. Height 1640 feet or 500 metres. **37 G5** SH7004.

Foel y Geifr *Gwyn.* ***Mountain***, 5m/8km S of Bala. Height 2053 feet or 626 metres. **37 J3** SH9327.

Foelgastell *Carmar.* ***Settlement***, 2m/3km NW of Cross Hands. SN5414.

Foffarty *Angus* ***Hamlet***, 2m/3km SE of Glamis. **83 F3** NO4145.

Foggathorpe *E.Riding* ***Village***, 8m/13km W of Market Weighton. **58 D6** SE7537.

Foggbrook *Gt.Man.* ***Suburb***, 2m/3km E of Stockport town centre. SJ9289.

Fogla Skerry *Shet.* ***Island***, small island off W coast of Papa Stour. **109 A6** HU1361.

Fogo *Sc.Bord.* ***Settlement***, 2m/3km S of Gavinton. **77 F6** NT7749.

Fogorig *Sc.Bord.* ***Settlement***, 4m/6km NE of Greenlaw. **77 F6** NT7748.

Foinaven *High.* *Anglicised form of Fionn Bheinn, qv.*

Foinaven *High.* ***Large natural feature***, mountain ridge running N to S, in Sutherland district, at N end of Reay Forest. Highest peak is Ganu Mòr. **103 F3** NC3150.

Foindle *High.* ***Locality***, on S side of Loch Laxford, near W coast of Sutherland district. **102 D4** NC1948.

Fold Head *Lancs.* ***Locality***, 1km SW of Whitworth. SD8717.

Fold Hill *Lincs.* ***Locality***, 1km SE of Friskney. TF4654.

Folda *Angus* ***Settlement***, in Glen Isla, 3m/5km NW of Kirkton of Glenisla. **82 C1** NO1864.

Fole *Staffs.* ***Hamlet***, 4m/6km NW of Uttoxeter. **40 C2** SK0437.

Foleshill *W.Mid.* ***Suburb***, N district of Coventry. **41 F7** SP3582.

Folke *Dorset* ***Village***, 3m/4km SE of Sherborne. **9 F3** ST6513.

Folkestone *Kent* Population: 45,587. ***Town***, Channel port and resort, 14m/22km E of Ashford. Channel Tunnel terminal on N side. **15 H4** TR2235.

Folkingham *Lincs.* ***Village***, 8m/12km S of Sleaford. Remains of 'House of Correction' built in classical style in 1825 on site of former castle. **42 D2** TF0733.

Folkington *E.Suss.* ***Hamlet***, on N slope of South Downs, 5m/7km NW of Eastbourne. **13 J6** TQ5503.

Folksworth *Cambs.* ***Village***, 6m/10km SW of Peterborough. **42 E7** TL1489.

Folkton *N.Yorks.* ***Village***, 4m/7km W of Filey. **59 G2** TA0579.

Folla Rule *Aber.* ***Settlement***, 3m/4km NE of Kirktown of Rayne. **91 F1** NJ7333.

Follifoot *N.Yorks.* ***Village***, 3m/5km SE of Harrogate. **57 J4** SE3452.

Folly *Beds.* ***Locality***, 1km N of Harrold. SP9557.

Folly *Dorset* ***Settlement***, 4m/7km NE of Cerne Abbas. **9 G4** ST7203.

Folly *Pembs.* ***Settlement***, just to N of Camrose. **16 C2** SM9220.

Folly Gate *Devon* ***Village***, 2m/3km NW of Okehampton. **6 D6** SX5797.

Fonmon (Ffwl-y-mwn). *V. of Glam.* ***Hamlet***, 4m/6km W of Barry. ST0467.

Font *Northumb.* ***River***, formed by streams running into Font Reservoir to S of Rothbury and flowing SE from reservoir by Netherwitton to River Wansbeck at Mitford, above Morpeth. **71 G5** NZ1785.

Font-y-gary (Ffontygari). *V. of Glam.* ***Suburb***, adjoining to W of Rhoose, 4m/6km W of Barry. ST0566.

Fontburn Reservoir *Northumb.* ***Reservoir***, in course of River Font, 5m/8km S of Rothbury. **71 F4** NZ0493.

Fonthill Bishop (Also known as Bishop's Fonthill). *Wilts.* ***Village***, 2m/4km N of Tisbury. Gateway to Fonthill Park to S dates from 17c. **9 J1** ST9333.

Fonthill Gifford *Wilts.* ***Village***, 7m/11km NE of Shaftesbury. **9 J1** ST9231.

Fontmell Magna *Dorset* ***Village***, on W edge of Cranborne Chase, 4m/6km S of Shaftesbury. **9 H3** ST8617.

Fontmell Parva *Dorset* ***Hamlet***, in River Stour valley, 3m/4km E of Sturminster Newton. ST8214.

Fontwell *W.Suss.* ***Village***, 5m/8km W of Arundel. Racecourse. **12 C6** SU9407.

Foolow *Derbys.* ***Hamlet***, 3m/4km E of Tideswell. **50 D5** SK1976.

Footdee *Aberdeen* ***Locality***, on N side of Aberdeen port at mouth of River Dee at Aberdeen. NJ9505.

Footherley *Staffs.* ***Hamlet***, 1km SW of Shenstone. SK1002.

Foots Cray *Gt.Lon.* ***Locality***, in borough of Bexley, 1m/2km SE of Sidcup. **23 H4** TQ4770.

Fora Ness *Shet.* ***Coastal feature***, headland on SW side of Mainland, extending out into Muckle Sound. **109 F9** HU3518.

Fora Ness *Shet.* ***Coastal feature***, headland on NE coast of Mainland, almost an island, 1m/2km S of Firth. **108 D5** HU4571.

Forbestown *Aber.* ***Settlement***, on N bank of River Don, to E of Strathdon. **90 B3** NJ3612.

Force Forge *Cumb.* ***Settlement***, in S part of Grizedale Forest, 5m/8km N of Penny Bridge. **60 E7** SD3390.

Force Green *Kent* ***Settlement***, 1km N of Westerham. TQ4455.

Forcett *N.Yorks.* ***Hamlet***, 2m/3km W of Aldbrough St. John. **62 C5** NZ1712.

Forches Cross *Devon* ***Settlement***, 1m/2km NE of Lapford. **7 F5** SS7309.

Ford *Arg. & B.* ***Settlement***, nearly 1km SW of head of Loch Awe, in Argyll. **79 K7** NM8603.

Ford *Bucks.* ***Village***, 4m/6km SW of Aylesbury. **22 A1** SP7709.

Ford *Derbys.* ***Hamlet***, 5m/8km SE of Sheffield. SK4080.

Ford *Devon* ***Hamlet***, just N of Holbeton, 2m/4km E of Yealmpton. **5 G5** SX6150.

Ford *Devon* ***Hamlet***, 4m/6km N of Prawle Point. **5 H6** SX7840.

Ford *Devon* ***Village***, 3m/5km SW of Bideford. **6 C3** SS4024.

Ford *Glos.* ***Hamlet***, 4m/7km E of Winchcombe. **30 B6** SP0829.

Ford *Mersey.* ***Locality***, 6m/9km N of Liverpool city centre. **48 C2** SJ3398.

Ford *Mersey.* ***Suburb***, 3m/4km W of Birkenhead town centre. SJ2888.

Ford *Midloth.* ***Settlement***, just W of Pathhead. **76 B4** NT3864.

Ford *Northumb.* ***Village***, 7m/11km NW of Wooler. Much restored 14c castle. **77 H7** NT9437.

Ford *Pembs.* ***Settlement***, just S of Wolf's Castle. **16 C2** SM9526.

Ford *Plym.* ***Suburb***, 1m/2km NW of Plymouth city centre. SX4656.

Ford *Shrop.* ***Village***, 5m/8km W of Shrewsbury. **38 D4** SJ4113.

Ford *Som.* ***Hamlet***, 1m/2km NE of Wiveliscombe. **7 J3** ST0928.

Ford *Staffs.* ***Hamlet***, on River Hamps, 1m/2km W of Grindon. SK0653.

Ford *W.Suss.* ***Village***, 3m/4km SW of Arundel. **12 C6** SU9903.

Ford *Wilts.* ***Village***, 5m/8km W of Chippenham. **20 B4** ST8474.

Ford End *Essex* ***Village***, 5m/7km SE of Great Dunmow. **33 K7** TL6716.

Ford Green *Lancs.* ***Settlement***, 2m/3km NW of Garstang, at bridge over Lancaster Canal. SD4746.

Ford Heath *Shrop.* ***Settlement***, 6m/9km W of Shrewsbury. SJ4011.

Ford Houses *W.Mid.* ***Suburb***, 3m/5km N of Wolverhampton town centre. SJ9103.

Ford Street *Som.* ***Hamlet***, 2m/3km SE of Wellington. **7 K4** ST1518.

Forda *Devon* ***Hamlet***, 5m/7km SW of Okehampton. SX5390.

Fordbridge *W.Mid.* ***Suburb***, 7m/11km E of Birmingham. SP1787.

Fordcombe *Kent* ***Village***, 4m/6km W of Royal Tunbridge Wells. **23 J7** TQ5240.

Forde Abbey *Dorset* ***Historic house***, S of River Axe, on border with Somerset, 3m/5km SE of Chard. House developed from beautiful remains of 12c Cistercian abbey. Abbot's Chapter House now a chapel. Extensive, attractive grounds. **8 C4** ST3504.

Fordell *Fife* ***Village***, 3m/5km NW of Aberdour. **75 K2** NT1588.

Forden *Powys* ***Village***, scattered village about 4m/6km S of Welshpool. **38 B5** SJ2201.

Forder *Cornw.* ***Locality***, 1m/2km SW of Saltash. SX4158.

Forder Green *Devon* ***Hamlet***, 3m/4km SE of Ashburton. **5 H4** SX7867.

Fordgate *Som.* ***Settlement***, on Taunton and Bridgwater Canal, 2m/3km E of North Petherton. ST3232.

Fordham *Cambs.* Population: 2206. ***Village***, 5m/8km N of Newmarket. **33 K1** TL6370.

Fordham *Essex* ***Village***, 5m/8km NW of Colchester. **34 D6** TL9228.

Fordham *Norf.* ***Hamlet***, 2m/4km S of Downham Market. **44 A6** TL6199.

Fordham Abbey *Cambs.* ***Settlement***, 1km S of Fordham. **33 K2** TL6269.

Fordham Heath *Essex* ***Hamlet***, 3m/5km W of Colchester town centre. TL9326.

Fordingbridge *Hants.* Population: 4301. ***Small town***, on River Avon, 6m/9km N of Ringwood. **10 C3** SU1414.

Fordon *E.Riding* ***Hamlet***, 1m/2km N of Wold Newton. **59 G2** TA0475.

Fordoun *Aber.* ***Village***, 2m/4km SE of Auchenblae. In churchyard (adjoining to S of Auchenblae) is fragment of St. Palladius' chapel, 'the mother church of the Mearns'. **91 F7** NO7278.

Ford's Green *Suff.* ***Settlement***, 1km S of Bacton. TM0666.

Fordstreet *Essex* ***Village***, 5m/8km W of Colchester. **34 D6** TL9226.

Fordwells *Oxon.* ***Settlement***, 4m/7km NW of Witney. **30 E7** SP3013.

Fordwich *Kent* ***Village***, on Great Stour River, 2m/4km NE of Canterbury. **15 G2** TR1859.

Fordyce *Aber.* ***Village***, near N coast, 3m/4km SW of Portsoy. **98 D4** NJ5563.

Fordyce Hill *Aber.* ***Hill***, between Burn of Fordyce and Burn of Durn, 1km SE of Fordyce and 3m/4km SW of Portsoy. Height 590 feet or 180 metres. **98 D4** NJ5662.

Forebrae *P. & K.* ***Settlement***, 3m/5km SW of Methven. **82 A5** NN9824.

Forebridge *Staffs.* ***Suburb***, to S of Stafford town centre. SJ9222.

Foredale *N.Yorks.* ***Settlement***, 1m/2km S of Horton in Ribblesdale. Quarries to N. SD8069.
Foredown Tower *B. & H.* ***Other feature of interest***, in Portslade, 1m/2km NW of Brighton. Edwardian water tower, now used as weather station, with exhibitions and displays on countryside. **13 F6** TQ2407.
Foregate *Staffs.* ***Suburb***, to N of Stafford town centre. SJ9123.
Foreland *Arg. & B.* ***Settlement***, on Islay, 4m/7km W of Bridgend. **72 A4** NR2664.
Foreland *I.o.W.* ***Coastal feature***, headland at most easterly point of island. **11 H6** SZ6687.
Foreland Point *Devon* ***Coastal feature***, headland 3m/4km NE of Lynton. **18 A6** SS7551.
Foremark *Derbys.* ***Hamlet***, 2m/3km E of Repton. SK3326.
Foremark Reservoir *Derbys.* ***Reservoir***, 5m/8km E of Burton upon Trent. **41 F3** SK3324.
Foreness Point *Kent* ***Coastal feature***, headland 2m/3km E of Margate. **25 K4** TR3871.
Forest *Dur.* ***Locality***, 5m/9km NW of Middleton-in-Teesdale. NY8629.
Forest *N.Yorks.* ***Hamlet***, 2m/3km E of Scorton. NZ2700.
Forest Coal Pit *Mon.* ***Hamlet***, 4m/7km N of Abergavenny. SO2820.
Forest Gate *Gt.Lon.* ***Suburb***, in borough of Newham, 1m/2km N of West Ham. **23 H3** TQ4085.
Forest Green *Surr.* ***Village***, 4m/7km E of Cranleigh. **22 E7** TQ1241.
Forest Hall *Cumb.* ***Settlement***, 6m/10km E of Kendal. **61 G6** NY5401.
Forest Hall *T. & W.* ***Suburb***, 1m/2km NE of Longbenton. **71 H7** NZ2769.
Forest Head *Cumb.* ***Settlement***, 4m/6km SE of Brampton. **61 G1** NY5857.
Forest Hill *Gt.Lon.* ***Suburb***, in borough of Lewisham, 6m/9km SE of Charing Cross. TQ3573.
Forest Hill *Oxon.* ***Village***, 5m/8km E of Oxford. **21 J1** SP5807.
Forest Holme *Lancs.* ***Locality***, in valley in Forest of Rossendale, 3m/4km NE of Rawtenstall. SD8425.
Forest-in-Teesdale *Dur.* ***Locality***, on N side of River Tees, 4m/6km E of Cow Green Reservoir. **61 K3** NY8629.
Forest Lane Head *N.Yorks.* ***Suburb***, 2m/3km E of Harrogate town centre. SE3356.
Forest Lodge *Arg. & B.* ***Settlement***, 3m/4km NW Of Bridge of Orchy. **80 D3** NN2742.
Forest Lodge *P. & K.* ***Settlement***, in Glen Tilt, 6m/4km NE of Blair Atholl. **89 G7** NN9374.
Forest Mill *Clack.* ***Village***, 3m/5km NE of Clackmannan. **75 H1** NS9593.
Forest Moor *N.Yorks.* ***Open space***, moorland between Blubberhouses and Harrogate. **57 G4** SE2255.
Forest of Ae *D. & G.* ***Forest/woodland***, to N of Ae Village. **68 E4** NX9889.
Forest of Alyth *P. & K.* ***Open space***, moorland area NW of Alyth. **82 C2** NO1855.
Forest of Atholl *P. & K.* ***Open space***, deer and game forest to N of Glen Garry. **88 E7** NN7970.
Forest of Bere *Hants.* ***Locality***, stretch of country, much of it now built up, between Horndean and Ports Down. **11 H3** SU6411.
Forest of Birse *Aber.* ***Open space***, deer forest 4m/7km S of Aboyne. **90 D5** NO5291.
Forest of Bowland *Lancs.* ***Open space***, large area of wild moorland between Rivers Lune and Ribble, 10m/17km NE of Garstang. **56 B4** SD6552.
Forest of Brechfa *Carmar.* *See Brechfa.*
Forest of Clunie *P. & K.* ***Open space***, moorland area W of Bridge of Cally. **82 B2** NO0850.
Forest of Dean *Glos.* ***Forest/woodland***, heavily wooded area, formerly royal hunting-ground, between River Severn and River Wye. Extensive mineral workings. **29 F7** SO6310.
Forest of Deer *Aber.* ***Forest/woodland***, N of Old Deer. **99 H5** NJ9750.
Forest of Glenartney *P. & K.* ***Large natural feature***, mountain area on NW side of Glen Artney. **81 H6** NN6818.
Forest of Glenavon *Moray* ***Open space***, deer forest on E side of Cairngorm Mountains astride Glen Avon. **89 H4** NJ1005.
Forest of Glentanar *Aber.* ***Forest/woodland***, large area of forest SW of Aboyne, on either side of Glen Tanar. **90 D5** NO4593.
Forest of Harris *W.Isles* ***Large natural feature***, area of mountains, streams and lochs in North Harris, between Loch Resort and Loch Seaforth. **100 C7** NB0509.
Forest of Mamlorn *Stir.* ***Large natural feature***, mountainous area between head of Glen Lochay and that of Glen Lyon, 7m/11km NE of Crianlarich. **81 F4** NN4034.
Forest of Rossendale *Lancs.* ***Large natural feature***, moorland area to NE of Rawtenstall. **56 D7** SD8525.
Forest Row *E.Suss.* Population: 3508. ***Village***, 3m/4km SE of East Grinstead, below N edge of Ashdown Forest. **13 H3** TQ4235.
Forest Side *I.o.W.* ***Settlement***, 1m/2km W of Newport. SZ4789.
Forest Town *Notts.* ***Locality***, 2m/3km E of Mansfield Woodhouse. **51 H6** SK5662.
Forest Way ***Other feature of interest***, footpath on disused railway, running 9m/14km from East Grinstead in W to Groombridge in E. **13 H3** TQ4037.
Forestburn Gate *Northumb.* ***Locality***, 3m/5km S of Rothbury. **71 F4** NZ0696.
Forestside *W.Suss.* ***Village***, 4m/7km N of Emsworth. **11 J3** SU7512.
Forfar *Angus* Population: 12,961. ***Town***, market town, 12m/20km N of Dundee. Former jute and linen-milling centre. Ruins of Restenneth Priory, with 11c tower, to N. **83 F2** NO4550.
Forgandenny *P. & K.* ***Village***, 4m/6km SW of Perth. **82 B6** NO0818.
Forge *Powys* ***Hamlet***, 1m/2km SE of Machynlleth. SN7699.
Forge Hammer *Torfaen* ***Locality***, industrial estate in Cwmbran. ST2995.
Forge Side *Torfaen* ***Locality***, on W side of Blaenavon. SO2408.
Forgewood *N.Lan.* ***Suburb***, N district of Motherwell. NS7458.
Forgie *Moray* ***Locality***, 3m/5km NW of Keith. **98 B5** NJ3854.
Forglen *Aber.* ***Locality***, on W bank of River Deveron, 3m/4km NE of Turriff. NJ6951.
Forgue *Aber.* ***Hamlet***, 2m/3km SW of Inverkeithny and 6m/10km NE of Huntly. Glendronach Distillery is 1m/2km SE in Glen Dronach. NJ6045.
Forhill *Worcs.* ***Settlement***, 5m/8km N of Redditch. SP0475.
Formartine *Aber.* ***Locality***, large undulating area to N and NE of Oldmeldrum. **91 G2** NJ8628.
Formby *Mersey.* Population: 25,356. ***Town***, mainly residential town on coast, 11m/17km N of Liverpool. Championship golf course. **48 B2** SD2907.
Formby Hills *Mersey.* ***Coastal feature***, sand dunes, flanked by coniferous woodland, separating new town of Formby from sea. Part of dunes is National Trust property and contains rare plants. **48 B2** SD2707.
Formby Point *Mersey.* ***Coastal feature***, headland, 2m/3km W of Formby, beyond sand dunes. **48 B2** SD2907.
Forncett End *Norf.* ***Village***, 2m/3km W of Forncett St. Mary. **45 F6** TM1693.
Forncett St. Mary *Norf.* ***Village***, 6m/9km SE of Wymondham. **45 F6** TM1693.
Forncett St. Peter *Norf.* ***Village***, adjoining to S of Forncett St. Mary. **45 F6** TM1693.
Forneth *P. & K.* ***Settlement***, 2m/3km E of Butterstone. **82 B3** NO0845.
Fornham All Saints *Suff.* ***Village***, 2m/4km NW of Bury St. Edmunds. **34 C2** TL8367.
Fornham St. Martin *Suff.* ***Village***, 2m/3km N of Bury St. Edmunds. **34 C2** TL8567.
Fornighty *High.* ***Settlement***, 5m/7km SE of Nairn. **97 G6** NH9351.
Forres *Moray* Population: 8531. ***Small town***, 4m/6km S of mouth of River Findhorn, and 12m/19km W of Elgin. On NE side of town is Sueno's Stone, ancient Celtic obelisk (Historic Scotland). 19c Dallas Dhu Distillery (Historic Scotland) 1m/2km S. **97 H6** NJ0358.
Forrest *N.Lan.* ***Settlement***, 1km S of Forrestfield. **75 G4** NS8566.
Forrest Lodge *D. & G.* ***Settlement***, 6m/9km NW of St. John's Town of Dalry. **67 K5** NX5586.
Forrestburn Reservoir *N.Lan.* ***Reservoir***, aligned SW to NE and about 1m/2km in length, 2m/4km W of Harthill. **75 G4** NS8664.
Forret Hill *Fife* ***Hill***, 4m/6km N of Cupar. Height 571 feet or 174 metres. **82 E5** NO3920.
Forsa *Arg. & B.* ***River***, on Mull, running N down Glen Forsa to Sound of Mull 2m/3km E of Salen. Small airfield at mouth of river on W side. **79 H4** NM5943.
Forsbrook *Staffs.* ***Village***, 3m/5km SW of Cheadle. **40 B1** SJ9641.
Forse *High.* ***Settlement***, near E coast of Caithness district, 1m/2km E of Latheron. **105 H5** ND2134.
Forsie *High.* ***Settlement***, 4m/7km SW of Thurso. **105 F2** ND0463.
Forsinain *High.* ***Settlement***, situated in Strath Halladale, 3m/4km S of Trantlebeg. **104 E4** NC9148.
Forsinard *High.* ***Settlement***, with railway station, in Caithness district, 14m/22km S of Melvich. **104 D4** NC8943.
Forsnaval *W.Isles* ***Hill***, 2m/3km S of Gallan Head, Isle of Lewis. Height 672 feet or 205 metres. **100 C4** NB0635.
Forss Water *High.* ***River***, in Caithness district, running N from Loch Shurrey to N coast 6m/9km W of Thurso. **105 F2** ND0279.
Forston *Dorset* ***Settlement***, 4m/6km N of Dorchester. Site of Roman building to S. **9 F5** SY6695.
Fort Augustus *High.* ***Village***, in Inverness district, at entrance to Caledonian Canal from SW end of Loch Ness; lighthouse marks canal entrance. Village grew up around fort built in 1730 by General Wade; fort later incorporated into 19c Benedictine monastery. **87 K4** NH3709.
Fort Augustus Abbey *High.* ***Ecclesiastical building***, 19c abbey, incorporating part of General Wade's 18c fort, located in Fort Augustus at SW end of Loch Ness. Visitor centre includes displays on Benedictine monks in residence at abbey, Loch Ness and Great Glen, Jacobite risings and history of Scottish Highlander. Clansman Centre depicts 17c life. **87 K4** NH3808.
Fort Brockhurst *Hants.* ***Other feature of interest***, in Gosport, 19c fort with exhibition on history of Portsmouth's defences (English Heritage). **11 H4** SU5902.
Fort Charlotte *Shet.* ***Historic/prehistoric site***, 17c pentagonal artillery fort (Historic Scotland) in Lerwick. Burnt by Dutch in 1675 and rebuilt in 1781. **109 D8** HU4740.
Fort George *High.* ***Military establishment***, military depot (Historic Scotland) built after Jacobite rising of 1745, in Inverness district at entrance to Inner Moray Firth, or Inverness Firth, opposite Chanonry Point. Fort remains a garrison and is partly open to public with museum and Grand Magazine Collection. **96 E6** NH7656.
Fort Island *I.o.M.* *Alternative name for St. Michael's Island, qv.*
Fort Victoria Country Park *I.o.W.* ***Leisure/recreation***, country park surrounding Fort Victoria, 1m/2km W of Yarmouth. Fort Victoria, built as coastal defence against French, has good views across The Solent to Hurst Spit and Castle, and contains museum and aquarium. **10 E6** SZ3389.
Fort William *High.* Population: 10,391. ***Town***, in Lochaber district on E side of Loch Linnhe near head of loch. Pulp mill at Annat. Tourist and mountaineering centre. West Highland Museum. **87 H7** NN1073.
Forter *Angus* ***Settlement***, in Glen Isla, 4m/6km NW of Kirkton of Glenisla. **82 C1** NO1864.
Forteviot *P. & K.* ***Village***, 6m/9km SW of Perth. Site of Roman camp to W. **82 B6** NO0517.
Forth ***River***, major river of central Scotland formed by two headstreams rising N of Ben Lomond and meeting 1m/2km W of Aberfoyle. It then flows E by Stirling and Alloa to Kincardine, where it widens into Firth of Forth. **74 E1** NS9287.
Forth *S.Lan.* Population: 2560. ***Village***, 7m/12km NE of Lanark. **75 H5** NS9453.
Forth Bridge *Fife* ***Bridge***, railway bridge across Firth of Forth between Dalmeny Station on S side and North Queensferry. **75 K3** NT1379.
Forth Road Bridge *Fife* ***Bridge***, spanning 1m/2km across Firth of Forth from Queensferry on S bank to North Queensferry. **75 K3** NT1279.
Forthampton *Glos.* ***Village***, 2m/4km W of Tewkesbury. **29 H5** SO8532.
Forthill *Dundee* ***Suburb***, to NE of Broughty Ferry. NO4631.
Forthside *Stir.* ***Locality***, industrial estate on S bank of River Forth to E of Stirling town centre. NS8093.
Fortingall *P. & K.* ***Village***, in Glen Lyon, 7m/12km W of Aberfeldy. Famed for ancient yew trees. **81 J3** NN7347.
Fortingall Yew *P. & K.* *Alternative name for Ancient Yew Tree, qv.*
Fortis Green *Gt.Lon.* ***Suburb***, on borders of Barnet and Haringey boroughs, 6m/9km N of Charing Cross. TQ2789.
Forton *Hants.* ***Village***, on River Test, 4m/6km E of Andover. **21 H7** SU4243.
Forton *Lancs.* ***Village***, 4m/6km N of Garstang. **55 H4** SD4851.
Forton *Shrop.* ***Hamlet***, 5m/7km NW of Shrewsbury. Airfield to N. **38 D4** SJ4216.
Forton *Som.* ***Hamlet***, 1m/2km SE of Chard. **8 C4** ST3307.
Forton *Staffs.* ***Village***, 1m/2km N of Newport. **39 G3** SJ7521.
Forton Heath *Shrop.* ***Hamlet***, 1m/2km NE of Forton. SJ4317.
Fortrie *Aber.* ***Settlement***, 3m/4km SE of Inverkeithny. **98 E6** NJ6645.
Fortrose *High.* Population: 758. ***Small town***, resort in Ross and Cromarty district on Inner Moray Firth 2m/3km W of Fort George across strait. Ruined 14c cathedral. **96 E6** NH7256.
Fortrose Cathedral *High.* ***Ecclesiastical building***, substantial remains of 14c cathedral at Fortrose on S coast of Black Isle. **96 E6** NH7256.
Fortune Green *Gt.Lon.* ***Locality***, on borders of Barnet and Camden boroughs, 5m/8km NW of Charing Cross. TQ2485.
Fortuneswell *Dorset* Population: 4584. ***Small town***, at N end of Portland. HM prison to E. **9 F7** SY6873.
Forty Foot Drain (Also known as Vermuden's Drain.) *Cambs.* ***Other water feature***, fenland drainage channel connecting River Nene (old course), NE of Ramsey, and Old Bedford River at Welches Dam, S of Manea. **43 G7** TL4685.
Forty Green *Bucks.* ***Village***, adjoining to NW of Beaconsfield. **22 C2** SU9291.
Forty Hill *Gt.Lon.* ***Suburb***, in borough of Enfield, 1m/2km NE of Enfield town centre and 11m/18km N of Charing Cross. **23 G2** TQ3397.
Forvie Ness (Also known as Hackley Head.) *Aber.* ***Coastal feature***, headland N of mouth of River Ythan, on seaward side of Sands of Forvie and at S end of Hackley Bay. **91 J2** NK0226.
Forward Green *Suff.* ***Village***, 3m/5km E of Stowmarket. **34 E3** TM0959.
Foryd Bay *Gwyn.* ***Bay***, of marsh and mudflats leading into SW end of Menai Strait, to E of Morfa Dinlle. **46 C7** SH4459.
Fosbury *Wilts.* ***Hamlet***, 3m/5km S of Shalbourne. **21 G6** SU3158.
Foscot *Glos.* ***Settlement***, to S of Bledington. **30 D6** SP2421.
Foscote *Bucks.* ***Settlement***, 2m/3km NE of Buckingham. Site of Roman villa 1km SE. SP7135.
Fosdyke *Lincs.* ***Village***, 7m/11km S of Boston. **43 G2** TF3133.
Fosdyke Bridge *Lincs.* ***Locality***, 1km S of Fosdyke, with road bridge over River Welland. TF3132.
Foss *P. & K.* ***Locality***, on S side of Loch Tummel, 2m/3km SE of Tummel Bridge. **81 J2** NN7958.
Foss Cross *Glos.* ***Settlement***, 6m/9km NE of Cirencester. **20 D1** SP0609.
Foss Way (Also spelled Fosse Way.) ***Other feature of interest***, ancient trackway adapted by Romans and still largely followed by present-day roads, running from near Sidmouth, Devon, to the Humber, by Ilchester, Leicester and Lincoln, thereafter coinciding with Ermine Street. **52 C6** SP2030.
Fossdale *N.Yorks.* ***Settlement***, on hillside, at head of Wensleydale, 2m/3km NW of Hawes. **61 K7** SD8692.
Fosse Way *Alternative spelling of Foss Way, qv.*
Fossebridge *Glos.* ***Hamlet***, 3m/5km SW of Northleach. **30 B7** SP0811.
Fostall *Kent* ***Settlement***, 3m/5km E of Faversham. TR0661.
Foster Street *Essex* ***Village***, 3m/4km E of Harlow. **23 H1** TL4809.
Fosterhouses *S.Yorks.* ***Settlement***, 1m/2km N of Fishlake, 2m/4km NW of Thorne. SE6514.
Foster's Booth *Northants.* ***Settlement***, to SW of Pattishall, 7m/11km SW of Northampton town centre. **31 H3** SP6654.
Foston *Derbys.* ***Hamlet***, 2m/3km E of Sudbury. **40 D2** SK1831.
Foston *Leics.* ***Settlement***, 6m/10km S of Leicester city centre. SP6094.
Foston *Lincs.* ***Village***, 6m/9km NW of Grantham. **42 B1** SK8542.
Foston *N.Yorks.* ***Hamlet***, 1m/2km E of Thornton-le-Clay. **58 C3** SE6965.
Foston Beck *Lincs.* ***River***, rising 4m/6km W of Grantham and flowing N to River Witham, 1m/2km N of Foston. **42 B2** SK8644.
Foston on the Wolds *E.Riding* ***Village***, 5m/8km E of Great Driffield. **59 H4** TA1055.

Fotherby *Lincs.* ***Village***, 3m/5km N of Louth. **53 G3** TF3191.

Fothergill *Cumb.* ***Locality***, on coast, adjoining to N of Flimby, 2m/3km SW of Maryport. NY0234.

Fotheringhay *Northants.* ***Village***, on River Nene, 4m/6km NE of Oundle. Mound marks site of castle where Mary, Queen of Scots was executed in 1587. **42 D6** TL0693.

Fothringham Hill *Angus* ***Hill***, forested hill, with mast at summit, 3m/5km S of Forfar. Height 820 feet or 250 metres. **83 F3** NO4645.

Foubister *Ork.* ***Settlement***, in S of Mainland, 1km S of Bay of Suckquoy. **107 E7** HY5103.

Foul Anchor *Cambs.* ***Locality***, at confluence of River Nene and North Level Main Drain, 5m/8km N of Wisbech. TF4617.

Foul Mile *E.Suss.* ***Settlement***, 4m/7km NE of Hailsham. **13 K5** TQ6215.

Foula *Shet.* ***Island***, sparsely inhabited island of about 6 square miles or 15 square km lying 26m/42km W of Scalloway, Mainland. Foula has high cliffs and is noted as haunt of sea birds. Chief human settlement is Ham, on Ham Voe, on E coast. **108 B1** HT9639.

Foula Airstrip *Shet.* ***Airport/airfield***, landing strip to S of Foula, just NE of Hametoun. **108 B1** HT9737.

Foulbog *D. & G.* ***Settlement***, 3m/5km N of Davington. **69 H3** NT2407.

Foulbridge *Cumb.* ***Locality***, 1m/2km W of Wreay and 4m/7km S of Carlisle. NY4148.

Foulby *W.Yorks.* ***Hamlet***, 1m/2km E of Crofton. SE3917.

Foulden *Norf.* ***Village***, 4m/7km E of Stoke Ferry. **44 B6** TL7699.

Foulden *Sc.Bord.* ***Village***, 5m/8km W of Berwick-upon-Tweed. **77 H5** NT9255.

Foulden Tithe Barn *Sc.Bord.* ***Historic/prehistoric site***, attractive two-storey tithe barn with external stairs, at Foulden, 3m/5km S of Ayton. **77 H5** NT9355.

Foulholme Sands *E.Riding* ***Coastal feature***, sandbank to SE of Paull Holme Sands, on N side of River Humber. **53 F1** TA1921.

Foulmire Heights *Sc.Bord.* ***Open space***, partly wooded moorland 2m/4km W of Kielder. **70 A4** NY5894.

Foulness ***Sea feature***, sea channel off N Norfolk coast between Cromer and Overstrand. **45 G1** TG2342.

Foulness *E.Riding* ***River***, rising near Market Weighton and flowing S in a wide westward loop into Market Weighton Canal, 2m/3km N of Newport, and into River Humber, 1m/2km NE of Faxfleet. **58 E6** SE8624.

Foulness Island *Essex* ***Island***, on E coast bounded by North Sea, River Crouch, River Roach and The Middleway, 8m/13km NE of Southend-on-Sea. Connected to mainland by road at SW end. **25 F2** TR0092.

Foulness Point *Essex* ***Coastal feature***, headland at NE end of Foulness Island. **25 G2** TR0495.

Foulness Sands *Essex* ***Coastal feature***, sandbank on S side of River Crouch estuary, leading into Whitaker Channel. **25 G2** TR0596.

Foulney Island *Cumb.* ***Coastal feature***, head of narrow peninsula, 4m/7km SE of Barrow-in-Furness and 1m/2km E of Piel Island across Piel Channel. **55 F3** SD2463.

Foulride Green *E.Suss.* ***Suburb***, adjoining to S of Polegate. TQ5803.

Foulridge *Lancs.* ***Village***, 1m/2km N of Colne. **56 D5** SD8942.

Foulsham *Norf.* ***Village***, 8m/12km SE of Fakenham. **44 E3** TG0324.

Foulstone *Cumb.* ***Hamlet***, 3m/5km NW of Kirkby Lonsdale. SD5680.

Foulzie *Aber.* ***Settlement***, 3m/5km S of Macduff. **99 F4** NJ7159.

Fountainhall *Sc.Bord.* ***Village***, on Gala Water, 3m/5km N of Stow. **76 C6** NT4349.

Fountains Abbey *N.Yorks.* ***Ecclesiastical building***, remains of medieval abbey (English Heritage) beside River Skell, 3m/5km SW of Ripon. Fountains Hall, nearby, is 17c house largely built with materials from ruins of abbey. **57 H3** SE2768.

Fountains Fell *N.Yorks.* ***Open space***, moorland, highest point of which is 668 metres, 4m/6km E of Horton in Ribblesdale, containing Fountains Fell Tarn. **56 D2** SD8670.

Four Ashes *Staffs.* ***Hamlet***, 6m/10km N of Wolverhampton. **40 B5** SJ9108.

Four Ashes *Staffs.* ***Settlement***, 6m/10km SE of Bridgnorth. SO8087.

Four Ashes *Suff.* ***Village***, adjoining to S of Walsham le Willows. **34 D1** TM0070.

Four Ashes *W.Mid.* ***Settlement***, adjoining to W of Dorridge, 3m/5km S of Solihull town centre. SP1575.

Four Crosses *Denb.* ***Settlement***, 3m/5km W of Corwen. **37 K1** SJ0342.

Four Crosses *Gwyn.* *English form of Y Ffôr, qv.*

Four Crosses *Powys* ***Settlement***, 3m/5km NW of Llanfair Caereinion. **37 K5** SJ0508.

Four Crosses *Powys* ***Village***, 7m/12km NE of Welshpool. **38 B4** SJ2718.

Four Crosses *Staffs.* ***Hamlet***, 2m/3km W of Cannock. **40 B5** SJ9509.

Four Elms *Kent* ***Village***, 2m/3km NE of Edenbridge. **23 H7** TQ4648.

Four Foot *Som.* ***Settlement***, on Fosse Way, 3m/5km NE of Keinton Mandeville. ST5833.

Four Forks *Som.* ***Hamlet***, 4m/7km W of Bridgwater. **8 B1** ST2337.

Four Gates *Gt.Man.* ***Settlement***, 2m/4km S of Horwich. SD6407.

Four Gotes *Cambs.* ***Village***, 4m/7km N of Wisbech. **43 H4** TF4516.

Four Lane End *S.Yorks.* ***Settlement***, 2m/3km E of Penistone. SE2702.

Four Lane Ends *B'burn.* ***Suburb***, 1m/2km N of Blackburn town centre. SD6729.

Four Lane Ends *Ches.* ***Settlement***, 1m/2km S of Tarporley. SJ5561.

Four Lane Ends *Cumb.* ***Settlement***, 3m/5km E of Barrow-in-Furness. SD2468.

Four Lane Ends *Derbys.* ***Hamlet***, 3m/4km NW of Chesterfield. SK3573.

Four Lane Ends *Gt.Man.* ***Settlement***, 3m/4km NW of Bury. SD7612.

Four Lane Ends *Lancs.* ***Hamlet***, just N of Dolphinholme, on W side of River Wyre, 6m/9km N of Garstang. SD5153.

Four Lane Ends *Lancs.* ***Locality***, 1km NW of Poulton-le-Fylde. SD3340.

Four Lane Ends *Lancs.* ***Settlement***, 3m/4km SE of Blackburn. SD7126.

Four Lane Ends *S.Yorks.* ***Locality***, 3m/4km S of Sheffield city centre. SK3483.

Four Lane Ends *S.Yorks.* ***Locality***, 3m/5km SE of Sheffield city centre. SK3984.

Four Lane Ends *W.Yorks.* ***Locality***, 2m/3km W of Bradford city centre. SE1333.

Four Lane Ends *York* ***Hamlet***, 1km S of Dunnington, 5m/7km E of York. SE6751.

Four Lanes *Cornw.* ***Village***, 2m/3km S of Redruth. **2 D5** SW6938.

Four Marks *Hants.* Population: 1921. ***Village***, 4m/6km SW of Alton. **11 H1** SU6735.

Four Mile Bridge *I.o.A.* ***Village***, on Holy Island at SW end of bridge to Anglesey, 1km SW of Valley. **46 A5** SH2878.

Four Oaks *E.Suss.* ***Hamlet***, adjoining to E of Beckley. **14 D5** TQ8624.

Four Oaks *Glos.* ***Settlement***, 2m/4km NW of Newent. SO6928.

Four Oaks *W.Mid.* ***Hamlet***, 6m/9km W of Coventry. **40 E7** SP2480.

Four Oaks *W.Mid.* ***Locality***, 1m/2km N of Sutton Coldfield. **40 D6** SP1099.

Four Oaks Common *W.Mid.* ***Locality***, to NW of Four Oaks. SP1198.

Four Oaks Park *W.Mid.* ***Suburb***, to SE of Four Oaks and 1m/2km NW of Sutton Coldfield. SP1198.

Four Points *W.Berks.* ***Settlement***, 3m/4km SW of Streatley. SU5578.

Four Roads (Pedair-hewl). *Carmar.* ***Hamlet***, 3m/5km NE of Kidwelly. **17 H4** SN4409.

Four Roads *I.o.M.* ***Locality***, 1km N of Port St. Mary. SC2068.

Four Throws *Kent* ***Hamlet***, 1m/2km E of Hawkhurst. **14 C5** TQ7729.

Foura *High.* *Alternative name for Eilean Furadh Mòr, qv.*

Fourcrosses *Gwyn.* *Alternative English form of Y Ffôr, qv.*

Fourlands Hill *N.Yorks.* ***Settlement***, on S side of River Greta, 2m/3km SW of Ingleton. SD6671.

Fourlane Ends *Derbys.* ***Hamlet***, 2m/3km W of Alfreton. **51 F7** SK3855.

Fourlanes End *Ches.* ***Settlement***, 3m/5km E of Sandbach. **49 H7** SJ8059.

Fourman Hill *Aber.* ***Mountain***, on S side of River Deveron, 2m/3km SE of Milltown of Rothiemay. Height 1128 feet or 344 metres. **98 D6** NJ5745.

Fourpenny *High.* ***Settlement***, 3m/4km N of Dornoch. **96 E2** NH8094.

Fourstones *Northumb.* ***Village***, 4m/6km NW of Hexham. **70 D7** NY8867.

Fovant *Wilts.* ***Village***, 4m/6km E of Tisbury. **10 B2** SU0028.

Foveran *Aber.* ***Settlement***, 1km SW of Newburgh. **91 H2** NJ9924.

Foveran Burn *Aber.* ***River***, flowing E to join River Ythan at Newburgh. **91 H2** NK0025.

Fowey *Cornw.* ***River***, rising in heart of Bodmin Moor and flowing through Lostwithiel, where it becomes tidal. **4 A4** SX1059.

Fowey *Cornw.* Population: 1939. ***Small town***, port dating from medieval times on S coast, at mouth of River Fowey. 14c church and many 16c buildings. Yachting centre. St. Catherine's Castle, now a ruin, built by Henry VIII to defend harbour lies 1m/2km SW. **4 B5** SX1251.

Fowley Common *Ches.* ***Locality***, 1km S of Glazebury. SJ6796.

Fowley Island *Hants.* ***Island***, small uninhabited island in Chichester Harbour near head of Emsworth Channel. SU7404.

Fowley Island *Kent* ***Island***, in The Swale off Teynham Level, 4m/7km NW of Faversham. TQ9765.

Fowlis (Also known as Fowlis Easter.) *Angus* ***Village***, 6m/9km NW of Dundee. Early 17c castle. **82 E4** NO3233.

Fowlis Easter *Angus* *Alternative name for Fowlis, qv.*

Fowlis Wester *P. & K.* ***Village***, 4m/7km E of Crieff. 8c cross (Historic Scotland). **82 A5** NN9224.

Fowlis Wester Sculptured Stone *P. & K.* ***Historic/prehistoric site***, Pictish cross slabs at Fowlis Wester. Also Neolithic stone circles, Bronze Age cairn and standing stones in locality. **82 A5** NN9224.

Fowlmere *Cambs.* ***Village***, 5m/9km NE of Royston. **33 H4** TL4245.

Fownhope *Here.* ***Village***, 6m/9km SE of Hereford. **28 E5** SO5834.

Fox Corner *Surr.* ***Hamlet***, 4m/6km NW of Guildford. SU9654.

Fox Green *Derbys.* ***Settlement***, 1km SE of Creswell. SK5273.

Fox Hatch *Essex* ***Settlement***, adjoining to SE of Kelvedon Hatch, 3m/5km NW of Brentwood. TQ5798.

Fox Hill *B. & N.E.Som.* ***Suburb***, 1m/2km S of Bath city centre. ST7562.

Fox Lane *Hants.* ***Locality***, 3m/4km N of Farnborough. **22 B6** SU8557.

Fox Street *Essex* ***Hamlet***, 3m/4km NE of Colchester. **34 E6** TM0227.

Fox Talbot Museum *Wilts.* ***Other feature of interest***, museum dedicated to pioneer photographer, William Henry Fox Talbot, in 15c medieval barn at entrance to Laycock Abbey, 3m/5km S of Chippenham. Fox Talbot is regarded as 'Father of Modern Photography', having invented positive/negative process in 1840. **20 C5** ST9168.

Foxcombe Hill *Oxon.* ***Village***, 3m/4km N of Abingdon. SP4901.

Foxcote *Glos.* ***Hamlet***, 5m/8km SE of Cheltenham. **30 B7** SP0118.

Foxcote *Som.* ***Hamlet***, 2m/3km E of Radstock. ST7155.

Foxcote Reservoir *Bucks.* ***Reservoir***, 2m/3km NE of Buckingham. **31 J5** SP7136.

Foxcotte *Hants.* ***Hamlet***, 2m/3km NW of Andover. SU3447.

Foxdale *I.o.M.* ***Village***, 2m/4km S of St. John's. **54 B6** SC2778.

Foxearth *Essex* ***Village***, 3m/5km NW of Sudbury. **34 C4** TL8344.

Foxfield *Cumb.* ***Hamlet***, 1m/2km S of Broughton in Furness. **55 F1** SD2185.

Foxfield Light Railway *Staffs.* ***Other feature of interest***, tourist steam railway running N from Blythe Bridge to Godleybrook Mine (disused). Museum includes locomotives, rolling stock and memorabilia. **40 B1** SJ9442.

Foxford *W.Mid.* ***Suburb***, 3m/5km N of Coventry city centre. SP3583.

Foxham *Wilts.* ***Hamlet***, 4m/7km NE of Chippenham. **20 C4** ST9777.

Foxhayes *Devon* ***Locality***, on W side of River Exe, 1m/2km W of Exeter city centre. SX9093.

Foxhills *Hants.* ***Settlement***, 2m/3km SW of Totton. SU3411.

Foxhole *Cornw.* Population: 1115. ***Village***, 3m/5km NW of St. Austell. **3 G3** SW9654.

Foxhole *High.* ***Settlement***, 6m/9km N of Drumnadrochit. **88 C1** NH5238.

Foxhole *Swan.* ***Suburb***, to NE of Swansea city centre across River Tawe. SS6694.

Foxholes *N.Yorks.* ***Village***, 10m/15km N of Great Driffield. **59 G2** TA0173.

Foxhunt Green *E.Suss.* ***Hamlet***, 3m/5km SW of Heathfield. **13 J5** TQ5417.

Foxley *Here.* ***Settlement***, 8m/12km NW of Hereford. **28 D4** SO4146.

Foxley *Norf.* ***Village***, 6m/10km NE of East Dereham. **44 E3** TG0321.

Foxley *Northants.* ***Settlement***, 4m/6km NW of Towcester. **31 H3** SP6451.

Foxley *Wilts.* ***Settlement***, 3m/4km W of Malmesbury. **20 B3** ST8986.

Foxley Bridge *Stoke* ***Locality***, 2m/3km NE of Hanley. SJ8949.

Foxley Green *Wilts.* ***Hamlet***, adjoining to E of Foxley, 2m/3km SW of Malmesbury. ST8985.

Foxlydiate *Worcs.* ***Locality***, at W edge of Redditch. SP1067.

Fox's Cross *Kent* ***Locality***, adjoining to N of Yorkletts, 2m/4km SW of Whitstable. TR0963.

Foxt *Staffs.* ***Village***, 1m/2km SE of Ipstones. **40 C1** SK0348.

Foxton *Cambs.* ***Village***, 6m/10km NE of Royston. **33 H4** TL4148.

Foxton *Dur.* ***Settlement***, 3m/4km S of Sedgefield. **62 E4** NZ3624.

Foxton *Leics.* ***Village***, 3m/5km NW of Market Harborough. **42 A6** SP7090.

Foxton *N.Yorks.* ***Hamlet***, 4m/6km NE of Northallerton. SE4296.

Foxton Canal *Leics.* ***Other feature of interest***, museum of canals with 10 working locks, to SE of Foxton, 3m/5km NW of Market Harborough. Remains of steam-powered boat lift and lift trail with outside exhibitions. **42 A7** SP7189.

Foxup *N.Yorks.* ***Settlement***, 1km W of Halton Gill. **56 D2** SD8676.

Foxwist Green *Ches.* ***Settlement***, 3m/4km NW of Winsford. **49 F6** SJ6268.

Foxwood *Shrop.* ***Hamlet***, 3m/5km W of Cleobury Mortimer. SO6276.

Foy *Here.* ***Village***, on W bank of River Wye, 3m/4km N of Ross-on-Wye across loop of river. **28 E6** SO5928.

Foyers *High.* ***River***, formed by confluence of Allt Breineag and River Fechlin and flowing N, entering Loch Ness at Foyers. NH4920.

Foyers *High.* ***Village***, on SE side of Loch Ness in Inverness district, at mouth of River Foyers. **88 B2** NH4921.

Frachadil *Arg. & B.* ***Settlement***, 1km E of Calgary, Mull. **78 E2** NM3851.

Fraddam *Cornw.* ***Settlement***, 2m/4km SE of Hayle. **2 C5** SW5934.

Fraddon *Cornw.* ***Village***, 3m/5km S of St. Columb Major. **3 G3** SW9158.

Fradley *Staffs.* ***Village***, 4m/6km NE of Lichfield. **40 D4** SK1513.

Fradley Junction *Staffs.* ***Other feature of interest***, junction of Coventry and Trent and Mersey Canals, 1m/2km W of Fradley. SK1414.

Fradswell *Staffs.* ***Village***, 7m/11km NE of Stafford. **40 B2** SJ9931.

Fraisthorpe *E.Riding* ***Hamlet***, 4m/6km S of Bridlington. **59 H3** TA1561.

Framfield *E.Suss.* ***Village***, 2m/3km E of Uckfield. **13 H4** TQ4920.

Framingham Earl *Norf.* ***Village***, 5m/8km SE of Norwich. **45 G5** TG2702.

Framingham Pigot *Norf.* ***Village***, 4m/7km SE of Norwich. **45 G5** TG2703.

Framlingham *Suff.* Population: 2697. ***Small town***, 9m/15km N of Woodbridge. Extensive remains of 12c-13c castle with Tudor chimneys (English Heritage). **35 G2** TM2863.

Framlingham Castle *Suff.* ***Castle***, 12c castle (English Heritage) built by Roger Bigod, Earl of Norfolk, at Framlingham. Retains curtain wall, with 13 towers, each topped by a Tudor chimney. **35 G2** TM2863.

Frampton *Dorset* ***Village***, 5m/8km NW of Dorchester. **9 F5** SY6295.

Frampton *Lincs.* ***Village***, 3m/5km S of Boston. 2m/3km SE is Frampton Marsh, saltmarsh nature reserve which protects largest colony of black-headed gulls in Britain. **43 G2** TF3239.

Frampton Cotterell *S.Glos.* Population: 14,176. ***Village***, 4m/7km W of Chipping Sodbury. **19 K3** ST6682.
Frampton Mansell *Glos.* ***Village***, 5m/8km E of Stroud. **20 C1** SO9202.
Frampton on Severn *Glos.* Population: 1383. ***Village***, 7m/11km W of Stroud. **20 A1** SO7407.
Frampton West End *Lincs.* ***Settlement***, 2m/3km NW of Frampton. **43 G1** TF3040.
Framsden *Suff.* ***Village***, 3m/5km SE of Debenham. **35 G3** TM2059.
Framwellgate Moor *Dur.* ***Suburb***, 1m/2km N of Durham. **62 D2** NZ2644.
France Lynch *Glos.* ***Hamlet***, adjoining to E of Chalford. SO9003.
Frances Green *Lancs.* ***Settlement***, 2m/3km E of Longridge. SD6336.
Franche *Worcs.* ***Suburb***, in NW part of Kidderminster. **29 H1** SO8178.
Frandley *Ches.* ***Settlement***, 1m/2km E of Higher Whitley. SJ6379.
Frank Lockwood's Island (Also known as Eilean Sneth Dian.) *Arg. & B.* ***Island***, islet off S coast of Mull, 2m/4km E of entrance to Loch Buie. **79 H6** NM6219.
Frankby *Mersey.* ***Village***, 2m/3km E of West Kirby. **48 B4** SJ2486.
Frankfort *Norf.* ***Hamlet***, 4m/6km SE of North Walsham. TG3024.
Frankley *Worcs.* ***Village***, 6m/10km SW of Birmingham. **40 B7** SO9980.
Frankley Green *Worcs.* ***Hamlet***, to W of Frankley, 3m/4km SE of Halesowen. SO9980.
Frankley Services *Worcs.* ***Other building***, motorway service station on M5 motorway, 3m/4km SE of Halesowen. **40 B7** SO9881.
Frank's Bridge *Powys* ***Hamlet***, on River Edw, 5m/8km NE of Builth Wells. SO1156.
Frankton *Warks.* ***Village***, 5m/9km N of Southam. **31 F1** SP4270.
Frankwell *Shrop.* ***Suburb***, to W of Shrewsbury town centre. SJ4813.
Frans Green *Norf.* ***Locality***, 1m/2km SW of Weston Longville and 4m/6km W of Taverham. TG1014.
Frant *E.Suss.* ***Village***, 3m/4km S of Royal Tunbridge Wells. **13 J3** TQ5935.
Fraoch Bheinn *High.* ***Mountain***, in Lochaber district 2m/3km N of head of Loch Arkaig. Height 2814 feet or 858 metres. **87 F5** NM9894.
Fraoch Eilean *High. Alternative name for Fraochlan, qv.*
Fraochaidh *High.* ***Mountain***, in Appin, 5m/8km S of South Ballachulish. Height 2883 feet or 879 metres. **80 B2** NN0251.
Fraochlan (Also known as Fraoch Eilean.) *High.* ***Island***, islet in Enard Bay 1km off NW coast of Ross and Cromarty district. NC0518.
Fraserburgh *Aber.* Population: 12,843. ***Town***, fishing town and port at W end of Fraserburgh Bay, 15m/24km NW of Peterhead. Once a herring port, now a whitefish port. Kinnaird Head has 16c century castle and Scotland's oldest lighthouse. **99 H4** NJ9966.
Fraserburgh Bay *Aber.* ***Bay***, at NE tip of Buchan district, extending E of Fraserburgh to Cairnbulg Point. **99 J4** NJ9966.
Frating *Essex* ***Settlement***, 4m/6km N of Brightlingsea. TM0822.
Frating Green *Essex* ***Hamlet***, 6m/10km E of Colchester. **34 E6** TM0923.
Fratton *Ports.* ***Suburb***, 1m/2km E of Portsmouth city centre. **11 H4** SU6500.
Freasley *Warks.* ***Settlement***, 3m/5km SE of Tamworth. SP2499.
Freathy *Cornw.* ***Village***, 3m/5km SW of Torpoint. **4 D5** SX3952.
Freckenham *Suff.* ***Village***, 3m/5km SW of Mildenhall. **33 K1** TL6672.
Freckleton *Lancs.* Population: 4136. ***Village***, 2m/3km S of Kirkham. **55 H7** SD4228.
Fredden Hill *Northumb.* ***Mountain***, forested peak 2m/3km S of Akeld. Height 1138 feet or 347 metres. **70 E1** NT9526.
Free Piece *Hants.* ***Locality***, 1km NW of Bordon Camp. SU7937.
Free Town *Gt.Man.* ***Suburb***, 1m/2km NE of Bury town centre. SD8111.
Freebrough Hill *R. & C.* ***Hill***, 3m/5km N of Castleton. Height 820 feet or 250 metres. **63 H5** NZ6812.
Freeby *Leics.* ***Village***, 3m/5km E of Melton Mowbray. **42 B3** SK8020.
Freefolk *Hants.* ***Hamlet***, adjoining Laverstoke, 2m/3km E of Whitchurch. **21 H7** SU4848.
Freefolk Priors *Hants.* ***Hamlet***, to NW of Freefolk across River Test. SU4848.
Freehay *Staffs.* ***Hamlet***, 1m/2km SE of Cheadle. SK0241.
Freehold Land *Torfaen* ***Locality***, 1m/2km NW of Pontypool. SO2702.
Freeland *Oxon.* ***Village***, 4m/7km NE of Witney. **31 F7** SP4112.
Freemantle *S'ham.* ***Suburb***, 1m/2km W of Southampton city centre. **11 F3** SU4012.
Freester *Shet.* ***Settlement***, in South Nesting, Mainland, 1m/2km SW of Skellister. **109 D7** HU4553.
Freethorpe *Norf.* ***Village***, 3m/5km S of Acle. **45 J5** TG4004.
Freethorpe Common *Norf.* ***Village***, adjoining to SW of Freethorpe. **45 J5** TG4004.
Freevater Forest *High.* ***Open space***, deer forest in Sutherland district E of Seana Bhraigh. **95 K3** NH3588.
Freezy Water *Gt.Lon.* ***Suburb***, 3m/5km NE of Enfield, in borough of Enfield. TQ3699.
Freiston *Lincs.* ***Village***, 3m/5km E of Boston. **43 G1** TF3743.
Freiston Shore *Lincs.* ***Settlement***, near coast, 2m/3km SE of Freiston. **43 G1** TF3942.
Fremington *Devon* Population: 3727. ***Village***, 3m/5km W of Barnstaple on road to Bideford. **6 D2** SS5132.
Fremington *N.Yorks.* ***Settlement***, in Swaledale, 1km N of Grinton across River Swale. **62 B7** SE0499.
French Street *Kent* ***Settlement***, 1m/2km SE of Westerham. TQ4552.
Frenchay *Bristol* ***Locality***, 5m/8km NE of Bristol. **19 K4** ST6477.
Frenchbeer *Devon* ***Hamlet***, on E side of Dartmoor, 5m/8km W of Moretonhampstead. **6 E7** SX6785.
Frenches Green *Essex* ***Settlement***, 4m/6km SW of Braintree. TL7020.
Frendraught *Aber.* ***Locality***, comprises Frendraught House and Mains of Frendraught, 3m/5km S of Inverkeithny. **98 E6** NJ6141.
Freni-fawr *Pembs.* ***Mountain***, 1m/2km NE of Crymych. Height 1296 feet or 395 metres. **17 F1** SN2034.
Frenich *Stir.* ***Settlement***, at N end of Loch Chon, 3m/4km SE of Stronachlachar. **81 F7** NN4106.
Frensham *Surr.* ***Village***, 4m/6km S of Farnham, on River Wey. **22 B7** SU8441.
Frensham Common *Surr.* ***Open space***, National Trust land to SE of Frensham. **22 B7** SU8441.
Frensham Little Pond *Surr.* ***Lake/loch***, to E of Frensham. **22 B7** SU8441.
Frenze *Norf.* ***Locality***, 1m/2km E of Diss. TM1480.
Fresgoe *High.* ***Settlement***, with jetty, on W side of Sandside Bay, 10m/16km W of Thurso. **104 E2** NC9566.
Freshbrook *Swin.* ***Suburb***, 3m/5km SW of Swindon town centre. SU1183.
Freshfield *Mersey.* ***Suburb***, in NW part of Formby. **48 B2** SD2808.
Freshford *B. & N.E.Som.* ***Village***, 4m/6km SE of Bath. **20 A5** ST7860.
Freshney *N.E.Lincs.* ***River***, rising SW of Grimsby as Team Gate Drain and Laceby Beck, then flowing through W part of town into River Humber. **53 F2** TA2711.
Freshwater *I.o.W.* Population: 3658. ***Village***, resort 1m/2km E of Totland. To SW, Farringford, formerly home of Tennyson. **10 E6** SZ3487.
Freshwater Bay *I.o.W.* ***Bay***, 1km S of Freshwater, at W end of Isle of Wight. **10 E6** SZ3485.
Freshwater Bay *I.o.W.* ***Village***, on small bay of same name, 1km S of Freshwater. SZ3485.
Freshwater East *Pembs.* ***Hamlet***, to NW of bay of same name, 3m/5km SE of Pembroke. **16 D5** SS0198.
Freshwater West *Pembs.* ***Bay***, off SW coast of Pembrokeshire, 5m/8km NW of Castlemartin. **16 B5** SR8899.
Fressingfield *Suff.* ***Village***, 4m/6km S of Harleston. **35 G1** TM2677.
Freston *Suff.* ***Village***, 4m/6km S of Ipswich. **35 F5** TM1739.
Freswick *High.* ***Settlement***, at head of Freswick Bay, on E coast of Caithness district, 4m/6km S of Duncansby Head. **105 J2** ND3767.
Freswick Bay *High.* ***Bay***, on E coast of Caithness district. **105 J2** ND3767.
Fretherne *Glos.* ***Village***, 8m/12km W of Stroud. SO7309.
Frettenham *Norf.* ***Village***, 6m/10km N of Norwich. **45 G4** TG2417.
Freuchie *Fife* Population: 1033. ***Village***, 4m/6km N of Glenrothes. **82 D7** NO2806.
Freystrop Cross *Pembs.* ***Hamlet***, 3m/4km S of Haverfordwest. **16 C3** SM9511.
Friar Houses *Dur.* ***Locality***, 4m/6km NW of Middleton-in-Teesdale. NY8928.
Friar Park *W.Mid.* ***Suburb***, in N part of West Bromwich. SP0094.
Friars Carse *D. & G.* ***Settlement***, 6m/10km NW of Dumfries. **68 E5** NX9284.
Friar's Gate *E.Suss.* ***Settlement***, below NE slope of Ashdown Forest, 2m/3km NW of Crowborough. **13 H3** TQ4933.
Friarton *P. & K.* ***Suburb***, S district of Perth. **82 C5** NO1121.
Friarton Island (Also known as Moncreiffe Island.) *P. & K.* ***Island***, in River Tay at Perth, to NE of Friarton. NO1121.
Frickley *S.Yorks.* ***Settlement***, 1m/2km E of Clayton. SE4607.
Friday Bridge *Cambs.* ***Village***, 3m/5km S of Wisbech. **43 H5** TF4604.
Friday Hill *Gt.Lon.* ***Suburb***, in borough of Waltham Forest, 1km SE of Chingford town centre. TQ3893.
Friday Street *E.Suss.* ***Locality***, 3m/5km N of Eastbourne. **13 K6** TQ6203.
Friday Street *Suff.* ***Settlement***, 1m/2km SE of Cretingham. TM2459.
Friday Street *Suff.* ***Settlement***, at N edge of Rendlesham Forest, 3m/5km SE of Wickham Market. TM3351.
Friday Street *Suff.* ***Settlement***, 2m/3km S of Saxmundham. TM3760.
Friday Street *Surr.* ***Settlement***, 4m/6km SW of Dorking. **22 E7** TQ1245.
Fridaythorpe *E.Riding* ***Village***, on The Wolds, 9m/15km W of Great Driffield. **58 E4** SE8759.
Friendly *W.Yorks.* ***Locality***, W part of Sowerby Bridge, on N side of River Calder. SE0524.
Friern Barnet *Gt.Lon.* ***Suburb***, in borough of Barnet, 8m/12km N of Charing Cross. **23 F2** TQ2792.
Friesland Bay *Arg. & B.* ***Bay***, on S coast of Coll, 3m/5km SW of Arinagour. **78 C2** NM1853.
Friesthorpe *Lincs.* ***Village***, 4m/7km SW of Market Rasen. **52 D4** TF0783.
Frieston *Lincs.* ***Hamlet***, adjoining to S of Caythorpe. **42 C1** SK9347.
Frieth *Bucks.* ***Village***, 4m/7km NW of Marlow. **22 A2** SU7990.
Frieze Hill *Som.* ***Suburb***, W district of Taunton. ST2125.
Friezeland *Notts.* ***Village***, 3m/4km N of Eastwood. SK4750.
Frilford *Oxon.* ***Village***, 4m/6km W of Abingdon. **21 H2** SU4497.
Frilsham *W.Berks.* ***Village***, 5m/9km NE of Newbury. **21 J4** SU5373.
Frimley *Surr.* Population: 23,060. ***Town***, adjoining to S of Camberley. **22 B6** SU8858.
Frimley Green *Surr.* ***Locality***, 1m/2km S of Frimley. **22 B6** SU8857.
Frindsbury *Med.* ***Suburb***, N of Rochester city centre across River Medway. Site of Roman building near river bank at Limehouse Reach. **24 D5** TQ7469.
Fring *Norf.* ***Hamlet***, 5m/9km SE of Hunstanton. **44 B2** TF7334.
Fringford *Oxon.* ***Village***, 4m/7km NE of Bicester. **31 H6** SP6028.
Friningham *Kent* ***Settlement***, 4m/7km NE of Maidstone. TQ8158.
Frinsted *Kent* ***Village***, 4m/6km S of Sittingbourne. **14 D2** TQ8957.
Frinton-on-Sea *Essex* Population: 7522. ***Small town***, quiet resort adjoining to SW of Walton on the Naze, 5m/8km NE of Clacton-on-Sea. Former fishing village. **35 G7** TM2319.
Friockheim *Angus* ***Village***, 6m/10km NW of Arbroath. **83 G3** NO5949.
Friog *Gwyn.* ***Settlement***, on S side of Fairbourne, 2m/4km NE of Llwyngwril. **37 F4** SH6112.
Frisby on the Wreake *Leics.* ***Village***, 4m/6km W of Melton Mowbray. **41 J4** SK6917.
Friskney *Lincs.* ***Village***, 3m/5km SW of Wainfleet All Saints. **53 H7** TF4655.
Friskney Eaudike *Lincs.* ***Settlement***, 1km NE of Friskney. **53 H7** TF4756.
Friskney Flats *Lincs.* ***Coastal feature***, mudflats on W side of Boston Deeps, 5m/8km E of Wrangle. **53 H7** TF5051.
Friskney Tofts *Lincs.* ***Locality***, 3m/5km SW of Wainfleet All Saints, on land reclaimed from salt marshes with dykes and banks. Coastal walks on innermost bank. TF4654.
Friston *E.Suss.* ***Village***, 4m/7km W of Eastbourne. **13 J7** TV5598.
Friston *Suff.* ***Village***, 3m/4km SE of Saxmundham. **35 J3** TM4160.
Fritchley *Derbys.* ***Locality***, 4m/6km N of Belper. **51 F7** SK3552.
Frith *Kent* ***Settlement***, 1m/2km S of Doddington. **14 E2** TQ9455.
Frith Bank *Lincs.* ***Settlement***, 2m/3km NW of Boston. **43 G1** TF3147.
Frith Common *Worcs.* ***Settlement***, 6m/10km E of Tenbury Wells. **29 F2** SO6969.
Fritham *Hants.* ***Hamlet***, in New Forest, 4m/6km W of Cadnam. **10 D3** SU2314.
Frithelstock *Devon* ***Village***, 2m/3km W of Great Torrington. Remains of 13c priory. **6 C4** SS4619.
Frithelstock Stone *Devon* ***Village***, 1m/2km SW of Frithelstock. **6 C4** SS4619.
Frithsden *Herts.* ***Settlement***, 2m/3km NE of Berkhamsted. TL0109.
Frithville *Lincs.* ***Village***, 4m/7km N of Boston. **53 G7** TF3150.
Frittenden *Kent* ***Village***, 3m/4km SW of Headcorn. **14 D3** TQ8141.
Frittiscombe *Devon* ***Hamlet***, 4m/7km E of Kingsbridge. SX8043.
Fritton *Norf.* ***Village***, 6m/9km SW of Great Yarmouth. **45 J5** TG4600.
Fritton *Norf.* ***Village***, 6m/10km N of Harleston. **45 G6** TM2292.
Fritton Lake Country Park *Norf.* ***Leisure/recreation***, park containing lake, 3m/5km long, with gardens, walks and watersports, 1m/2km SE of St. Olaves. **45 J5** TG4700.
Fritwell *Oxon.* ***Village***, 3m/4km S of Aynho. **31 G6** SP5229.
Frizinghall *W.Yorks.* ***Suburb***, 2m/3km NW of Bradford city centre. SE1436.
Frizington *Cumb.* Population: 2472. ***Village***, 4m/6km E of Whitehaven. **60 B5** NY0317.
Frocester *Glos.* ***Village***, 4m/6km NE of Dursley. **20 A1** SO7803.
Frochas *Powys* ***Settlement***, 4m/6km SW of Halfway House. **38 B4** SJ2810.
Frodesley *Shrop.* ***Village***, 7m/12km S of Shrewsbury. **38 E5** SJ5101.
Frodesley Lane *Shrop.* ***Settlement***, 1m/2km SW of Frodesley. SJ5000.
Frodingham *N.Lincs.* ***Suburb***, to E of Scunthorpe town centre. **52 B1** SE8911.
Frodsham *Ches.* Population: 8903. ***Small town***, former medieval port, 3m/5km S of Runcorn. **48 E5** SJ5177.
Frog End *Cambs.* ***Hamlet***, 5m/7km NE of Royston. TL3946.
Frog End *Cambs.* ***Settlement***, adjoining to NW of Haslingfield. **33 H3** TL4052.
Frog End *Cambs.* ***Settlement***, 1km W of Little Wilbraham. TL5358.
Frog Pool *Worcs.* ***Hamlet***, 4m/6km S of Stourport-on-Severn. **29 G2** SO7965.
Frogden *Sc.Bord.* ***Settlement***, 2m/3km NW of Morebattle. **70 C1** NT7628.
Froggatt *Derbys.* ***Village***, 3m/4km N of Baslow. **50 E5** SK2476.
Froghall *Staffs.* ***Hamlet***, 3m/4km N of Cheadle. Terminus of Caldon Canal. **40 C1** SK0247.
Frogham *Hants.* ***Hamlet***, on edge of New Forest, 2m/3km SE of Fordingbridge. **10 C3** SU1713.
Frogham *Kent* ***Settlement***, 7m/11km NW of Dover. TR2550.
Frogland Cross *S.Glos.* ***Settlement***, 5m/8km W of Chipping Sodbury. ST6483.
Frogmore *Devon* ***Village***, 3m/5km E of Kingsbridge at head of Frogmore Creek. **5 H6** SX7742.
Frogmore *Hants.* Population: 10,189. ***Locality***, 2m/3km W of Camberley. **22 B6** SU8460.
Frogmore *Herts.* ***Hamlet***, 2m/4km S of St. Albans, on W side of Radlett Airfield. **22 E1** TL1503.
Frogpool *Cornw.* ***Village***, 4m/6km E of Redruth. SW7640.
Frogwell *Cornw.* ***Hamlet***, 1m/2km SW of Callington. SX3468.

F

Frolesworth *Leics.* ***Village***, 5m/7km NW of Lutterworth. **41 H6** SP5090.

Frome ***River***, rising 6m/10km S of Frome and flowing N through town to join River Avon 2m/3km W of Bradford-on-Avon. **20 A7** ST7960.

Frome *Bristol* ***River***, rising E of Yate and flowing W through town, then S by Frampton Cotterell to Bristol where it joins River Avon in city centre. **19 K4** ST6172.

Frome *Dorset* ***River***, rising at Evershot and flowing SE to Dorchester, then E to Wareham and on into Poole Harbour. **9 G5** SY9487.

Frome *Here.* ***River***, rising about 6m/10km N of Bromyard and flowing S through town and into River Lugg, 3m/5km E of Hereford. **29 F4** SO5638.

Frome *Som.* Population: 23,159. ***Town***, 11m/17km S of Bath, with steep medieval streets, once known for cloth-making. 18c wool merchants' houses. 19c all-wood railway station survives. **20 A7** ST7747.

Frome Market *Som.* ***Locality***, market and industrial estate, 3m/5km NE of Frome and adjoining to S of Standerwick. ST8250.

Frome St. Quintin *Dorset* ***Village***, 3m/5km N of Maiden Newton. **8 E4** ST5902.

Frome Vauchurch *Dorset* ***Hamlet***, to S of Maiden Newton across River Frome. SY5997.

Frome Whitfield *Dorset* ***Settlement***, 1km N of Dorchester. SY6991.

Fromefield *Som.* ***Suburb***, NE district of Frome. ST7848.

Fromes Hill *Here.* ***Hamlet***, 5m/8km S of Bromyard. **29 F4** SO6746.

Fron *Denb.* ***Suburb***, adjoining to NE of Denbigh. SJ0566.

Fron *Gwyn.* ***Hamlet***, 5m/8km S of Caernarfon. SH5054.

Fron *Gwyn.* ***Settlement***, on Lleyn Peninsula, 3m/5km NW of Pwllheli. **36 C2** SH3539.

Fron *Powys* ***Settlement***, 3m/4km S of Welshpool. **38 B5** SJ2203.

Fron *Powys* ***Settlement***, 3m/5km NE of Llandrindod Wells. **27 K2** SO0865.

Fron *Powys* ***Settlement***, 2m/3km S of Aberriw. SO1797.

Fron-goch *Gwyn.* ***Hamlet***, 3m/4km NW of Bala. **37 J2** SH9039.

Fron Hill *Powys* ***Mountain***, 1m/2km W of New Rador. Height 1738 feet or 530 metres. **28 A2** SO1961.

Fron Isaf *Wrex.* ***Settlement***, 2m/3km NW of Chirk. SJ2740.

Froncysyllte *Wrex.* ***Village***, 3m/4km NW of Chirk at S end of Pont-Cysyllte Aqueduct. **38 B1** SJ2741.

Frontierland *Lancs.* ***Leisure/recreation***, Wild West theme park in Morecambe. **55 H3** SD4464.

Frostenden *Suff.* ***Settlement***, 4m/6km NW of Southwold. **45 J7** TM4781.

Frosterley *Dur.* ***Village***, on River Wear, 2m/4km SE of Stanhope. **62 B3** NZ0236.

Frosty Hill *Aber.* ***Mountain***, on S side of River Don, 4m/7km N of Tarland. Height 1351 feet or 412 metres. **90 C3** NJ4610.

Froxfield *Wilts.* ***Village***, 3m/4km W of Hungerford. **21 F5** SU2968.

Froxfield Green *Hants.* ***Village***, 3m/5km NW of Petersfield. Site of Romano-British settlement 1km SE. **11 J2** SU7025.

Froyle *Hants.* ***Locality***, parish containing villages of Upper and Lower Froyle, about 4m/7km NE of Alton. SU7543.

Fruid Reservoir *Sc.Bord.* ***Reservoir***, in course of Fruid Water, 3m/4km S of Tweedsmuir. **69 F1** NT0820.

Fryerning *Essex* ***Village***, 5m/8km NE of Brentwood. **24 C1** TL6400.

Fryerns *Essex* ***Suburb***, E district of Basildon. TQ7289.

Fryton *N.Yorks.* ***Settlement***, 1km W of Slingsby. **58 C2** SE6875.

Fuam an Tolla *W.Isles* ***Island***, islet off North Harris in East Loch Tarbert to W of Scalpay. NG2096.

Fuar Bheinn *High.* ***Mountain***, in Lochaber district 2m/4km N of Loch a' Choire. Height 2509 feet or 765 metres. **79 K2** NM8556.

Fuar Loch Mòr *High.* ***Lake/loch***, small loch in Ross and Cromarty district, 6m/10km N of head of Loch Maree. **95 F4** NH0076.

Fuar Tholl *High.* ***Mountain***, in Ross and Cromarty district, 2m/3km W of Achnashellach Lodge. Height 2975 feet or 907 metres. **95 F7** NG9748.

Fuday *W.Isles* ***Island***, uninhabited island of about 500 acres or 200 hectares 2m/3km E of Scurrival Point, Barra. Ancient remains at Dùnan Ruadh. **84 C4** NF7308.

Fugglestone St. Peter *Wilts.* ***Locality***, 1km E of Wilton. **10 C1** SU1031.

Fugla Stack *Shet.* ***Coastal feature***, rock adjacent to W coast of West Burra. **109 C9** HU3530.

Fuiay *W.Isles* ***Island***, uninhabited island off North Bay, Barra. **84 C4** NF7402.

Fulbeck *Lincs.* ***Village***, 9m/15km N of Grantham. **52 C7** SK9450.

Fulbeck *Northumb.* ***Hamlet***, 1m/2km NW of Morpeth. NZ1987.

Fulbeck Hall *Lincs.* ***Historic house***, in Fulbeck, 9m/15km N of Grantham. Home of Fane family. 17c origins, with links with the Raj and Wellington. Used as headquarters of 1st Airborne Division during World War II. **52 C7** SK9450.

Fulbourn *Cambs.* Population: 3896. ***Village***, 5m/7km SE of Cambridge. **33 J3** TL5156.

Fulbrook *Oxon.* ***Village***, 1km NE of Burford. **30 D7** SP2513.

Fulflood *Hants.* ***Suburb***, NW district of Winchester. SU4729.

Fulford *Som.* ***Hamlet***, 3m/5km NW of Taunton. **8 B2** ST2129.

Fulford *Staffs.* ***Village***, 4m/7km NE of Stone. **40 B2** SJ9538.

Fulford (Sometimes known as Gate Fulford). *York* ***Village***, 2m/3km S of York city centre. **58 C5** SE6049.

Fulham *Gt.Lon.* ***Suburb***, on N side of River Thames, in borough of Hammersmith and Fulham, N of Putney Bridge. Fulham Palace, 16c-19c, upstream from Putney Bridge, is traditional residence of Bishop of London. **23 F4** TQ2476.

Fulking *W.Suss.* ***Village***, below N slopes of South Downs, 4m/6km E of Henfield. **13 F5** TQ2411.

Full Sutton *E.Riding* ***Village***, 2m/3km E of Stamford Bridge. **58 D4** SE7455.

Fullaford *Devon* ***Hamlet***, 2m/4km E of Bratton Fleming. SS6838.

Fullarton *Glas.* ***Suburb***, 4m/6km E of Glasgow. NS6462.

Fullarton *N.Ayr.* ***Suburb***, S district of Irvine. NS3238.

Fullbrook *W.Mid.* ***Suburb***, in S part of Walsall. SP0196.

Fuller Street *Essex* ***Hamlet***, 5m/7km W of Witham. **34 B7** TL7416.

Fuller's End *Essex* ***Village***, at S end of Elsenham, 4m/7km NE of Bishop's Stortford. TL5325.

Fuller's Moor *Ches.* ***Hamlet***, 2m/4km E of Clutton. **48 D7** SJ4954.

Fullerton *Hants.* ***Hamlet***, 3m/5km NE of Stockbridge. SU3739.

Fulletby *Lincs.* ***Village***, 4m/6km NE of Horncastle. **53 F5** TF2973.

Fullwell Cross *Gt.Lon.* ***Suburb***, in borough of Redbridge, 3m/4km N of Ilford. TQ4490.

Fullwood *E.Ayr.* ***Settlement***, 3m/5km NE of Stewarton. **74 C6** NS4449.

Fullwood *Gt.Man.* ***Settlement***, 1km E Shaw. SD9408.

Fulmer *Bucks.* ***Village***, 4m/7km NE of Slough. **22 C3** SU9985.

Fulmodeston *Norf.* ***Hamlet***, 5m/8km E of Fakenham. **44 D2** TF9930.

Fulnetby *Lincs.* ***Hamlet***, 2m/4km NW of Wragby. **52 E5** TF0979.

Fulney *Lincs.* ***Suburb***, NE district of Spalding. TF2523.

Fulready *Warks.* ***Settlement***, 2m/3km W of Newbold-on-Stour. **30 D4** SP2746.

Fulstone *W.Yorks.* ***Hamlet***, 3m/4km NE of Holmfirth. SE1709.

Fulstow *Lincs.* ***Village***, 6m/10km N of Louth. **53 G3** TF3297.

Fulwell *Oxon.* ***Hamlet***, 1km S of Enstone. **30 E6** SP3723.

Fulwell *T. & W.* ***Suburb***, 1m/2km N of Sunderland city centre. **62 E1** NZ3959.

Fulwood *Lancs.* ***Suburb***, adjoining to N of Preston. **55 J6** SD5331.

Fulwood *Notts.* ***Locality***, adjoining to SW of Sutton in Ashfield. SK4757.

Fulwood *S.Yorks.* ***Suburb***, 3m/5km W of Sheffield city centre. **51 F4** SK3085.

Fulwood Row *Lancs.* ***Locality***, 2m/4km NE of Preston town centre. SD5632.

Fundenhall *Norf.* ***Village***, 4m/6km SE of Wymondham. **45 F6** TM1596.

Fundenhall Street *Norf.* ***Hamlet***, 1m/2km W of Fundenhall. TM1496.

Funtington *W.Suss.* ***Village***, 5m/7km W of Chichester. **12 B6** SU8008.

Funtley *Hants.* ***Hamlet***, 2m/3km NW of Fareham. **11 G4** SU5608.

Funzie *Shet.* ***Settlement***, on Fetlar, 3m/4km E of Houbie. Funzie Bay to SE. **108 F4** HU6690.

Furley *Devon* ***Hamlet***, 4m/7km NW of Axminster. **8 B4** ST2704.

Furnace *Arg. & B.* ***Village***, on W shore of Loch Fyne in Argyll, 7m/11km SW of Inveraray. **80 B7** NN0300.

Furnace *Carmar.* ***Suburb***, to N of Llanelli town centre. SN5001.

Furnace *Cere.* ***Hamlet***, 4m/6km NE of Talybont. **37 F6** SN6895.

Furnace *High.* ***Settlement***, on NE shore of Loch Maree, 1km SE of Letterewe. **95 F4** NG9670.

Furnace Green *W.Suss.* ***Suburb***, SE district of Crawley. TQ2835.

Furner's Green *E.Suss.* ***Hamlet***, 1m/2km S of Danehill. TQ4026.

Furness *Cumb.* ***Locality***, lying S of Wrynose Pass, between Windermere and River Duddon, and narrowing southwards to a peninsula between River Duddon and River Leven estuaries culminating at Barrow-in-Furness, other principal towns being Dalton-in-Furness and Ulverston. SD2690.

Furness Abbey *Cumb.* ***Ecclesiastical building***, remains of medieval abbey (English Heritage), 12c and later, 2m/3km NE of Barrow-in-Furness. Second largest Cistercian abbey in England. Bow Bridge, to W, is medieval stone bridge across Mill Beck. **55 F2** SD2171.

Furness Fells *Cumb.* ***Large natural feature***, mountain range between Little Langdale and Coniston Water. **60 D6** NY2600.

Furness Vale *Derbys.* ***Village***, 1m/2km SE of New Mills. **50 C4** SK0083.

Furneux Pelham *Herts.* ***Village***, 5m/9km NW of Bishop's Stortford. **33 H6** TL4327.

Furnham *Som.* ***Suburb***, N district of Chard. ST3209.

Fursdon House *Devon* ***Historic house***, 2m/3km N of Thorverton. Home of Fursdon family since 13c with Regency library and notable costume and art collections. **7 H5** SS9204.

Further Quarter *Kent* ***Settlement***, 1km N of Middle Quarter. TQ8939.

Furtho *Northants.* ***Settlement***, church and farm, 1m/2km NW of Old Stratford. SP7743.

Furze Green *Norf.* ***Settlement***, 2m/3km W of Harleston. TM2182.

Furze Hill Common *Dorset* ***Hamlet***, 3m/5km NW of Gillingham. ST7830.

Furze Platt *W. & M.* ***Suburb***, N district of Maidenhead. **22 B3** SU8782.

Furzedown *Gt.Lon.* ***Suburb***, in borough of Wandsworth, 6m/10km S of Charing Cross. TQ2871.

Furzehill *Devon* ***Settlement***, 3m/4km S of Lynton. **7 F1** SS7245.

Furzehill *Dorset* ***Hamlet***, 1m/2km N of Wimborne Minster. SU0102.

Furzeley Corner *Hants.* ***Settlement***, 2m/3km W of Waterlooville. SU6510.

Furzey Gardens *Hants.* ***Garden***, 16c cottage, with 8 acres of informal gardens, 1km NW of Minstead. **10 D3** SU2711.

Furzey Island *Dorset* ***Island***, on S side of Poole Harbour, to S of Brownsea Island. SZ0187.

Furzey Lodge *Hants.* ***Settlement***, in New Forest, 1m/2km W of Beaulieu. SU3602.

Furzley *Hants.* ***Hamlet***, on edge of New Forest, 2m/3km N of Cadnam. SU2816.

Fydell House *Lincs.* ***Historic house***, built in 1726 at Boston. Includes notable carved staircase. **43 G1** TF3243.

Fyfett *Som.* ***Settlement***, in parish of Otterford, 6m/10km S of Taunton. **8 B3** ST2314.

Fyfield *Essex* ***Village***, 3m/4km NE of Chipping Ongar. **23 J1** TL5706.

Fyfield *Glos.* ***Settlement***, to N of Southrop, 4m/6km NE of Fairford. **21 F1** SP2003.

Fyfield *Hants.* ***Village***, 4m/7km W of Andover. **21 F7** SU2946.

Fyfield *Oxon.* ***Village***, 5m/8km W of Abingdon. **21 H2** SU4298.

Fyfield *Wilts.* ***Hamlet***, 1m/2km E of Pewsey. SU1760.

Fyfield *Wilts.* ***Village***, 3m/4km W of Marlborough. **20 E5** SU1468.

Fylingdales Moor *N.Yorks.* ***Open space***, moorland area, to SW of Robin Hood's Bay, at E end of North York Moors. **63 J3** SE9299.

Fylingthorpe *N.Yorks.* ***Village***, 1km SW of Robin Hood's Bay. **63 J2** NZ9405.

Fyne *Arg. & B.* ***River***, in Argyll running SW down Glen Fyne to head of Loch Fyne, 6m/10km NE of Inveraray. **80 D6** NN1810.

Fyne Court *Som.* ***Nature reserve***, set in grounds (National Trust) of demolished former home of pioneer electrician Andrew Crosse, 6m/9km SW of Bridgwater. Native woodland and shrubs provide habitat for plants and animals. Headquarters of Somerset Wildlife Trust. **8 B1** ST2232.

Fyning *W.Suss.* ***Settlement***, just E of Rogate, 4m/7km E of Petersfield. SU8123.

Fyvie *Aber.* ***Village***, on River Ythan, 8m/13km S of Turriff. **91 F1** NJ7637.

Fyvie Castle *Aber.* ***Castle***, fortress palace dating from 14c, with late 16c additions and a wheel staircase, 1m/2km N of Fyvie. **91 F1** NJ7637.

G

Gabalfa *Cardiff* ***Suburb***, 2m/3km NW of Cardiff city centre. ST1678.

Gabhsunn Bho Dheas (Anglicised form: South Galson.) *W.Isles* ***Settlement***, adjacent to Gabhsunn Bho Thuath, near NW coast of Isle of Lewis, 7m/11km SW of Port Nis. **101 G2** NB4358.

Gabhsunn Bho Thuath (Anglicised form: North Galson.) *W.Isles* ***Settlement***, adjacent to Gabhsunn Bho Dheas, near NW coast of Isle of Lewis, 7m/11km SW of Port Nis. **101 G2** NB4459.

Gable Head *Hants.* ***Suburb***, of South Hayling, on Hayling Island. SZ7199.

Gablon *High.* ***Settlement***, 6m/10km E of Bonar Bridge. **96 E2** NH7191.

Gabroc Hill *E.Ayr.* ***Settlement***, 4m/6km NE of Stewarton. **74 C5** NS4550.

Gabwell *Devon* ***Locality***, consists of two hamlets, Higher Gabwell and Lower Gabwell, about 3m/5km N of Torquay. SX9169.

Gaddesby *Leics.* ***Village***, 6m/9km SW of Melton Mowbray. **41 J4** SK6813.

Gaddesden Row *Herts.* ***Settlement***, 3m/4km W of Redbourn. **32 D7** TL0512.

Gadebridge *Herts.* ***Suburb***, to NW of Hemel Hempstead town centre. TL0408.

Gadfa *I.o.A.* ***Settlement***, 2m/4km S of Amlwch. SH4589.

Gadie Burn *Aber.* ***River***, rising to N of Correen Hills and flowing E, through Clatt and Auchleven, to join River Urie 1km E of Kirkton of Oyne. **90 D2** NJ6925.

Gadlas *Shrop.* ***Settlement***, 2m/4km NW of Ellesmere. SJ3737.

Gadlys *R.C.T.* ***Suburb***, adjoining to W of Aberdare. SN9902.

Gadlys *V. of Glam.* ***Locality***, adjoining to N of Llanmaes, 1m/2km NE of Llantwit Major. SS9869.

Gads Hill *Kent* ***Settlement***, on S edge of Higham, 3m/4km NW of Rochester. Home of Charles Dickens, 1857-70. TQ7170.

Gaeilavore Island *High.* ***Island***, one of a group of islets 3m/5km NW of Rubha Hunish at N tip of Skye. See also Gearran Island & Lord Macdonald's Table. **93 J4** NG3679.

Gaer *Newport* Population: 8388. ***Suburb***, 1m/2km SW of Newport town centre. ST2986.

Gaer *Powys* ***Settlement***, 4m/6km NW of Crickhowell. **28 A6** SO1721.

Gaer-fawr *Mon.* ***Hamlet***, 1m/2km SE of Llangwm. ST4498.

Gaerllwyd *Mon.* ***Hamlet***, 3m/4km NW of Shirenewton. **19 H2** ST4496.

Gaerwen *I.o.A.* ***Village***, on Anglesey, 5m/8km W of Menai Bridge. **46 C5** SH4871.

Gagingwell *Oxon.* ***Settlement***, 6m/10km E of Chipping Norton. **31 F6** SP4025.

Gaich *High.* ***Settlement***, 2m/3km SW of Grantown-on-Spey. **89 H2** NJ0125.

Gaick *High.* ***Settlement***, 9m/14km S of Inverness. **88 D1** NH6831.

Gaick Forest *High.* ***Open space***, deer forest in Badenoch and Strathspey district, 7m/11km E of Dalwhinnie. **88 E6** NN7584.

Gaick Lodge *High.* ***Settlement***, in Gaick Forest, 8m/12km E of Dalwhinnie. **88 E6** NN7585.

Gailes *N.Ayr.* ***Settlement***, 3m/5km S of Irvine. NS3335.

Gailey *Staffs.* ***Hamlet***, 2m/4km S of Penkridge. **40 B4** SJ9110.
Gailey Wharf *Staffs.* ***Locality***, 1km E of Gailey, on Staffordshire and Worcestershire Canal. SJ9210.
Gain *Gwyn.* ***River***, rising E of Trawsfynydd and flowing S into River Mawddach in Coed y Brenin Forest, 2m/3km N of Ganllwyd. **37 G3** SH7327.
Gainford *Dur.* ***Village***, on River Tees, 8m/12km W of Darlington. Hall of early 17c. **62 C5** NZ1716.
Gainsborough *Lincs.* Population: 19,704. ***Town***, inland port on River Trent, 15m/25km NW of Lincoln. Gainsborough Old Hall (English Heritage). **52 B3** SK8189.
Gainsborough Old Hall *Notts.* ***Historic house***, 15c manor (English Heritage) in Gainsborough, where Richard III was entertained. Rebuilt in 16c. Notable Great Hall and period medieval kitchen. **52 B4** SK8089.
Gainsborough's House *Suff.* ***Historic house***, birthplace of Thomas Gainsborough, 1727, in Sudbury. Georgian façade with Tudor interior, it houses a collection of Gainsborough's minor works. Garden includes 350 year old mulberry tree. **34 C4** TL8742.
Gainsford End *Essex* ***Hamlet***, 3m/5km NE of Finchingfield. TL7235.
Gair Loch *High.* ***Sea feature***, wide inlet on W coast of Ross and Cromarty district, 8m/13km S of Rubha Réidh. **94 D4** NG7775.
Gairbeinn *High.* ***Mountain***, on Corrieyairack Forest, in Badenoch and Strathspey district, 8m/13km SE of Fort Augustus. Height 2939 feet or 896 metres. **88 B5** NN4698.
Gairich *High.* ***Mountain***, in Lochaber district, 3m/5km SW of dam of Loch Quoich. Munro: height 3014 feet or 919 metres. **87 G5** NN0299.
Gairletter Point *Arg. & B.* ***Coastal feature***, headland in Argyll, on W side of Loch Long, 3m/4km N of Strone Point. **74 A2** NS1984.
Gairloch *High.* ***Village***, on W coast of Ross and Cromarty district, at head of Gair Loch. **94 E4** NG8076.
Gairlochy *High.* ***Settlement***, on Caledonian Canal, at SW end of Loch Lochy, in Lochaber district. **87 H6** NN1784.
Gairn *Aber.* ***River***, rising on Invercauld Forest and running E to River Dee 1m/2km NW of Ballater. **90 A4** NO3596.
Gairney Bank *P. & K.* ***Settlement***, 2m/3km S of Kinross. **75 K1** NT1299.
Gairney Water *P. & K.* ***River***, rising near Drum and flowing E to enter Loch Leven 2m/3km SE of Kinross. **75 J1** NT1499.
Gairnshiel Lodge *Aber.* ***Settlement***, on E bank of River Gairn, 6m/9km NW of Ballater. **89 K4** NJ2900.
Gairsay *Ork.* ***Island***, sparsely populated island of about 500 acres or 200 hectares at N end of Wide Firth between Mainland and Shapinsay. **106 D5** HY4422.
Gairsay Sound *Ork.* ***Sea feature***, off E coast of Mainland between Wyre to N and Gairsay to S. **106 D5** HY4223.
Gaisby *W.Yorks.* ***Suburb***, 1m/2km SE of Shipley town centre. SE1536.
Gaisgaer *W.Isles* *Gaelic form of Gasker, qv.*
Gaisgill *Cumb.* ***Locality***, 2m/3km E of Tebay. NY6305.
Gaitsgill *Cumb.* ***Hamlet***, 3m/4km SE of Dalston. **60 E2** NY3846.
Gala Hill *Sc.Bord.* ***Hill***, 1km S of Galashiels. Height 905 feet or 276 metres. **76 C7** NT4934.
Gala Water *Sc.Bord.* ***River***, rising in Moorfoot Hills and flowing SE by Stow and Galashiels to enter River Tweed 2m/3km W of Melrose. **76 C5** NT5134.
Galabank *Sc.Bord.* ***Settlement***, in valley of Gala Water, 1m/2km NW of Stow. **76 C6** NT4445.
Galashiels *Sc.Bord.* Population: 13,753. ***Town***, on Gala Water, 14m/22km N of Hawick. Once known for its wool industry. **76 C7** NT4936.
Galava *Cumb.* *See Clappersgate.*
Galdenoch *D. & G.* ***Settlement***, on E side of Water of Luce, 2m/3km S of New Luce. **64 B4** NX1761.
Gale *Gt.Man.* ***Settlement***, 1km NE of Littleborough. SD9417.
Galgate *Lancs.* ***Village***, 4m/6km S of Lancaster. **55 H4** SD4855.
Galhampton *Som.* ***Village***, 2m/3km S of Castle Cary. **9 F2** ST6329.
Gallan Head *W.Isles* ***Coastal feature***, headland on W coast of Isle of Lewis on W side of entrance to West Loch Roag. **100 C4** NB0539.
Gallanach *Arg. & B.* ***Settlement***, 3m/5km SW of Oban. **79 K5** NM8225.
Gallantry Bank *Ches.* ***Settlement***, at S end of Peckforton Hills, 2m/4km SW of Peckforton. **48 E7** SJ5153.
Gallantry Bower *Devon* ***Coastal feature***, 100 metre high sea cliff, 1m/2km NW of Clovelly. **6 B3** SS3026.
Gallatown *Fife* ***Locality***, adjoining to N of Kirkcaldy. **76 A1** NT2994.
Gallchoille *Arg. & B.* ***Settlement***, on NW coast of Caol Scotnish, 3m/4km SW of Crinan. **73 F2** NR7689.
Gallen *Conwy* ***River***, running N to join River Cledwen at Llangernyw and form River Elwy. SH8767.
Gallery *Angus* ***Settlement***, 1m/2km W of Marykirk across River North Esk. **83 H1** NO6765.
Galley Common *Warks.* ***Locality***, 3m/5km W of Nuneaton. **41 F6** SP3192.
Galley Hill *Kent* ***Locality***, 1m/2km W of Northfleet. TQ6074.
Galleyend *Essex* ***Suburb***, 2m/4km S of Chelmsford. **24 D1** TL7103.
Galleywood *Essex* ***Suburb***, 3m/4km S of Chelmsford. **24 D1** TL7002.
Gallow Hill *Aber.* ***Hill***, 1m/2km NE of Aberchirder. Height 741 feet or 226 metres. **98 E5** NJ6453.
Gallow Hill *Angus* ***Mountain***, 3m/5km S of Glamis. Height 1243 feet or 379 metres. **82 E3** NO3941.
Gallow Hill *D. & G.* ***Hill***, afforested hill rising to N of Moffat. Height 833 feet or 254 metres. **69 F3** NT0806.
Gallow Hill *High.* ***Mountain***, to S of Glen Gheallaidh, 5m/8km SW of Upper Knockando. Height 1227 feet or 374 metres. **89 J1** NJ1336.
Gallow Hill *N.Yorks.* ***Locality***, 1km S of Knaresborough across River Nidd. SE3456.
Galloway Deer Museum *D. & G.* *See Clatteringshaws Loch.*
Galloway House Gardens *D. & G.* ***Garden***, laid out in 1740s, 1m/2km S of Garlieston. **64 E6** NX4845.
Gallowfauld *Angus* ***Hamlet***, 4m/7km SE of Glamis. **83 F3** NO4442.
Gallowhill *Renf.* ***Suburb***, N district of Paisley. NS4965.
Gallows Corner *Gt.Lon.* ***Locality***, at road junction 2m/3km NE of Romford, in borough of Havering. TQ5390.
Gallows Green *Essex* ***Settlement***, 5m/7km W of Colchester town centre. TL9226.
Gallows Green *Staffs.* ***Hamlet***, adjoining to S of Alton, 4m/7km SE of Cheadle. SK0741.
Gallows Green *Worcs.* ***Locality***, 2m/4km E of Droitwich Spa. SO9362.
Gallows Hill *Dorset* ***Hill***, rising to over 80 metres, to W of Bere Heath and 3m/4km S of Bere Regis. Tumulus at summit. **9 H5** SY8490.
Gallows Hill *Suff.* ***Locality***, 1km NE of Redgrave. TM0378.
Gallowsgreen *Torfaen* ***Locality***, 2m/3km SE of Blaenavon. SO2606.
Gallowstree Common *Oxon.* ***Hamlet***, 5m/7km NW of Reading. **21 K4** SU6980.
Gallowstree Elm *Staffs.* ***Locality***, adjoining to N of Kinver, 4m/7km W of Stourbridge. **40 A7** SO8384.
Gallt Melyd *Denb.* *Welsh form of Meliden, qv.*
Gallt-y-foel *Gwyn.* ***Settlement***, 1km SE of Deiniolen. SH5862.
Galltair *High.* ***Settlement***, in Skye and Lochalsh district, 1km N of Glenelg. **86 E3** NG8119.
Gallypot Street *E.Suss.* ***Settlement***, 1km SW of Hartfield. TQ4735.
Galmington *Som.* ***Suburb***, SW district of Taunton. ST2123.
Galmisdale *High.* ***Locality***, on SE coast of Eigg. Landing stage. **85 K6** NM4883.
Galmpton *Devon* ***Village***, 3m/5km W of Salcombe. **5 G6** SX6940.
Galmpton *Torbay* ***Village***, 3m/5km S of Paignton. **5 J5** SX8856.
Galmpton Warborough *Torbay* ***Suburb***, 3m/4km S of Paignton town centre. SX8856.
Galon Uchaf *M.Tyd.* ***Suburb***, in N part of Merthyr Tydfil. SO0508.
Galphay *N.Yorks.* ***Village***, 4m/6km W of Ripon. **57 H2** SE2572.
Galston *E.Ayr.* Population: 5154. ***Small town***, on River Irvine, 5m/8km E of Kilmarnock. Unusual Byzantine-style Roman Catholic church. **74 D7** NS5036.
Galta Mòr *High.* ***Island***, rock islet on NE coast of Skye, 4m/6km SE of Rubha Hunish. **93 K4** NG4673.
Galtrigill *High.* ***Settlement***, 2m/3km S of Dunvegan Head, Skye. **93 G6** NG1854.
Gamallt *Cere.* ***Mountain***, 7m/11km SE of Pontrhydfendigaid. Height 1594 feet or 486 metres. **27 G3** SN7856.
Gamallt *Gwyn.* ***Open space***, National Trust area 3m/5km NE of Ffestiniog. **37 G1** SH7444.
Gamallt *Powys* ***Mountain***, 2m/3km NW of Rhayader. Height 1558 feet or 475 metres. **27 J1** SN9570.
Gamble Hill *W.Yorks.* ***Suburb***, 3m/4km W of Leeds city centre. SE2533.
Gamble's Green *Essex* ***Locality***, 4m/6km W of Witham. **34 B7** TL7614.
Gamblesby *Cumb.* ***Village***, 8m/13km NE of Penrith. **61 H3** NY6039.
Gamelsby *Cumb.* ***Settlement***, 3m/4km N of Wigton. **60 D1** NY2552.
Gamelshiel Castle *E.Loth.* ***Castle***, 11m/17km NW of Duns. **76 E4** NT6464.
Gameshope Loch *Sc.Bord.* ***Lake/loch***, small loch 2m/3km SE of S end of Fruid Reservoir. **69 G2** NT1316.
Gamesley *Derbys.* ***Village***, 1m/2km W of Glossop. Site of Roman fort 1km NW. SK0194.
Gamhna Gigha *Arg. & B.* ***Island***, group of rocks lying nearly 1m/2km E of Rubh' a' Chairn Bhàin near N end of Gigha. NR6854.
Gamhnach Mhòr *Arg. & B.* ***Island***, islet at entrance to Carsaig Bay on S coast of Mull. NM5420.
Gamlan *Gwyn.* ***River***, running E into River Mawddach 3m/5km N of Llanelltyd. SH7224.
Gamlingay *Cambs.* Population: 3391. ***Village***, 2m/3km NE of Potton. **33 F3** TL2352.
Gamlingay Cinques *Cambs.* ***Hamlet***, to NW of Gamlingay. TL2252.
Gamlingay Great Heath *Cambs.* ***Hamlet***, to W of Gamlingay. TL2251.
Gammaton *Devon* ***Settlement***, 2m/3km SE of Bideford. SS4825.
Gammaton Moor *Devon* ***Settlement***, to S of Gammaton. **6 C3** SS4924.
Gammersgill *N.Yorks.* ***Settlement***, 6m/9km SW of Middleham. **57 F1** SE0582.
Gamrie *Aber.* ***Locality***, near N coast, 5m/9km E of Macduff. **99 F4** NJ7962.
Gamrie Bay *Aber.* ***Bay***, 1m/2km N of Gamrie, between Crovie Head and More Head, 9m/13km W of Rosehearty. **99 G4** NJ7965.
Gamston *Notts.* ***Hamlet***, 3m/5km SE of Nottingham. **41 J2** SK6037.
Gamston *Notts.* ***Village***, 3m/5km S of Retford. **51 K5** SK7076.
Gana Hill *S.Lan.* ***Mountain***, in Lowther Hills, 3m/4km SE of Ballencleuch Law. Height 2191 feet or 668 metres. **68 E3** NS9501.
Ganarew *Here.* ***Hamlet***, 2m/4km NE of Monmouth. **28 E7** SO5216.
Ganavan Bay *Arg. & B.* ***Bay***, 2m/3km N of Oban, Argyll. **79 K4** NM8532.
Gang *Cornw.* ***Hamlet***, 3m/5km W of Callington. SX3068.
Ganllwyd *Gwyn.* ***Hamlet***, in Coed y Brenin Forest Park, 4m/7km N of Dolgellau. **37 G3** SH7224.
Gannel *Cornw.* ***River***, rising at Fraddon and running out to sea at East Pentire Point, W of Newquay. Name usually applied to estuary only. SW7861.
Gannochy *Angus* ***Hamlet***, 1m/2km N of Edzell. **90 E7** NO5970.
Gannochy *P. & K.* ***Suburb***, NE district of Perth, on E side of River Tay. NO1224.
Gannow Green *Worcs.* ***Locality***, 3m/5km S of Halesowen. SO9778.
Ganstead *E.Riding* ***Hamlet***, 5m/8km NE of Kingston upon Hull. **59 H6** TA1434.
Ganthorpe *N.Yorks.* ***Hamlet***, 6m/10km W of Malton. **58 C2** SE6870.
Ganton *N.Yorks.* ***Village***, 8m/13km W of Filey. **59 F2** SE9877.
Gantshill *Gt.Lon.* ***Suburb***, in borough of Redbridge, 1m/2km NW of Ilford. TQ4388.
Ganwick Corner *Herts.* ***Settlement***, 1m/2km S of Potters Bar. TQ2599.
Gaodhail *Arg. & B.* ***Settlement***, in Glen Forsa, Mull, 4m/7km SE of Salen. **79 H4** NM6138.
Gaor Bheinn *High.* *Gaelic form of Gulvain, qv.*
Gappah *Devon* ***Hamlet***, 4m/6km N of Newton Abbot. SX8677.
Gara Bridge *Devon* ***Settlement***, on River Avon, 5m/8km SE of South Brent. **5 H5** SX7353.
Gara Point *Devon* ***Coastal feature***, at SE end of Wembury Bay, 1m/2km S of Wembury. **5 F6** SX5246.
Garabal *Arg. & B.* ***Settlement***, 1m/2km N of Ardlui, at N end of Loch Lomond. **80 E6** NN3117.
Garadhban Forest *Stir.* ***Forest/woodland***, at S end of Loch Lomond, 2m/4km N of Drymen. **74 C1** NS4790.
Garadheancal *High.* ***Settlement***, on Tanera Mòr, largest of Summer Isles group, off W coast of Ross and Cromarty district. **95 F1** NB9907.
Garbat *High.* ***Settlement***, 4m/7km NE of Garve. **96 B5** NH4168.
Garbat Forest *High.* ***Open space***, deer forest in Ross and Cromarty district on W side of Ben Wyvis. **96 B5** NH4368.
Garbh Allt *High.* ***River***, headstream of River Nethy rising on E side of Cairn Gorm and flowing N into head of Strath Nethy. **89 H4** NJ0205.
Garbh-bheinn *High.* ***Mountain***, 2m/4km NW of head of Loch Slapin, Skye. Height 2644 feet or 806 metres. **86 B2** NG5323.
Garbh Bheinn *High.* ***Mountain***, 5m/8km E of Strontian, Lochaber district. Height 2903 feet or 885 metres. **80 A1** NM9062.
Garbh Bheinn (Anglicised form: Garven). *High.* ***Mountain***, in Lochaber district 1m/2km SW of Kinlochleven. Height 2844 feet or 867 metres. **80 C2** NN1760.
Garbh Bheinn *High.* ***Mountain***, in Lochaber district, on E side of Loch Treig, 6m/9km S of Tulloch Station. Height 2814 feet or 858 metres. **87 K7** NN3571.
Garbh Chioch Mhòr *High.* ***Mountain***, 3m/5km E of Camusrory, Lochaber district. Munro: height 3323 feet or 1013 metres. **87 F5** NM9195.
Garbh Eileach *Arg. & B.* ***Island***, largest of Garvellachs group of islands in Firth of Lorn. Lies between A' Chùli and Dùn Chonnuill. **79 H6** NM6812.
Garbh Eilean *High.* ***Island***, small uninhabited island off S end of Rona. NG6153.
Garbh Eilean *W.Isles* ***Island***, islet in Loch Erisort, Isle of Lewis, 1km SE of Ceos and 2m/3km E of Lacasaigh. NB3621.
Garbh Eilean *W.Isles* ***Island***, largest of Shiant Islands group, joined to Eilean an Tighe by a narrow neck of land. **93 K2** NG4198.
Garbh Ghaoir *P. & K.* ***River***, running 2m/3km from Loch Laidon to head of Loch Eigheach. NN4456.
Garbh Leac *High.* *Alternative name for A' Chràlaig, qv.*
Garbh Lochan *High.* ***Lake/loch***, to S of Blackwater Reservoir, 10m/16km E of Kinlochleven. **80 E2** NN3259.
Garbh Mheall Mòr *High.* ***Mountain***, in Badenoch and Strathspey district, 4m/6km S of Newtonmore. Height 1945 feet or 593 metres. **88 E5** NN7292.
Garbh Rèisa *Arg. & B.* ***Island***, small island nearly 1km S of Craignish Point at entrance to Loch Craignish in Argyll. NR7597.
Garbh Sgeir *High.* ***Island***, islet to W of Oigh-sgeir and 9m/14km W of Rum. **85 G5** NM1596.
Garbhallt *Arg. & B.* ***Settlement***, on N bank of Strathlachlan River, 5m/8km SW of Strachur. **73 J1** NS0295.
Garboldisham *Norf.* ***Village***, 7m/11km W of Diss. **44 E7** TM0081.
Garcrogo Forest *D. & G.* ***Forest/woodland***, 4m/7km E of Balmaclellan. **65 H3** NX7278.
Garden *Stir.* ***Settlement***, 2m/3km E of Buchlyvie. **74 D1** NS5994.
Garden City *Flints.* ***Locality***, housing estate on N bank of River Dee, opposite Queensferry. **48 C6** SJ3269.
Garden Village *S.Yorks.* ***Suburb***, W district of Stocksbridge. SK2698.
Garden Village *Wrex.* ***Suburb***, N district of Wrexham. SJ3352.
Gardeners Green *W'ham* ***Hamlet***, 2m/3km SE of Wokingham. SU8266.
Gardens of the Rose *Herts.* ***Garden***, 1m/2km W of Chiswell Green, displaying over 30,000 old and new roses, 1650 different varieties. **22 E1** TL1204.
Gardenstown *Aber.* ***Village***, fishing village on Gamrie Bay on N coast, 6m/9km E of Macduff. **99 F4** NJ8064.
Garderhouse *Shet.* ***Settlement***, on Mainland, at head of Seli Voe, 7m/11km NW of Scalloway across entrance to Weisdale Voe. **109 C8** HU3347.
Gardham *E.Riding* ***Settlement***, 5m/8km E of Market Weighton. **59 F5** SE9542.
Gardner Street *E.Suss.* ***Locality***, adjoining to N of Herstmonceux. TQ6312.
Gare Hill *Som.* ***Hamlet***, 2m/3km NW of Maiden Bradley. **20 A7** ST7740.

Gare Loch *Arg. & B.* ***Sea feature***, inlet of River Clyde running S from Garelochhead to Helensburgh. **74 A2** NS2486.

Garelochhead *Arg. & B.* Population: 1298. ***Village***, and resort at head of Gare Loch, 7m/11km NW of Helensburgh. **74 A1** NS2391.

Garenin *W.Isles* *Anglicised form of Gearrannan, qv.*

Garf Water *S.Lan.* ***River***, rising to N of Robert Law and flowing E to join River Clyde, 2m/3km E of Wiston. **75 H7** NS9832.

Garford *Oxon.* ***Village***, 5m/7km W of Abingdon. Site of Roman temple 1km E. **21 H2** SU4296.

Garforth *W.Yorks.* Population: 15,250. ***Town***, 7m/11km E of Leeds. **57 K6** SE4033.

Gargrave *N.Yorks.* Population: 1530. ***Village***, on River Aire and on Leeds and Liverpool Canal, 4m/7km NW of Skipton. Site of Roman building to SE. **56 E4** SD9354.

Gargunnock *Stir.* ***Village***, 6m/9km W of Stirling. **75 F1** NS7094.

Gargunnock Hills *Stir.* ***Large natural feature***, range of hills to S and SW of Gargunnock. **74 E1** NS7094.

Gargunnock House *Stir.* ***Historic house***, ancestral 16c home of Stirling family, 1km E of Gargunnock. **75 F1** NS7194.

Gariannonum *Norf.* *See Burgh Castle.*

Gariob *Arg. & B.* ***Settlement***, 3m/4km S of Crinan. **73 F2** NR7889.

G

Garioch *Aber.* ***Locality***, large area to NE of Inverurie and S of River Urie and Gadie Burn. **90 E2** NJ6824.

Garland Stone *Pembs.* ***Island***, rock off N point of Skomer Island. **16 A3** SM7210.

Garlands *Cumb.* ***Locality***, 3m/4km SE of Carlisle. NY4353.

Garleffin Fell *S.Ayr.* ***Mountain***, 10m/16km E of Girvan. Height 1407 feet or 429 metres. **67 H4** NX3598.

Garleton Hills *E.Loth.* ***Hill***, small group of hills 2m/3km N of Haddington, rising to over 180 metres. Observation towers. Monument commemorates Earl of Hopetoun, Peninsula War hero. **76 D3** NT5076.

Garlic Street *Norf.* ***Settlement***, 2m/3km W of Harleston. TM2183.

Garlick Hill *D. & G.* ***Mountain***, 5m/8km N of Newton Stewart. Height 1460 feet or 445 metres. **64 E3** NX4372.

Garlies Castle *D. & G.* ***Settlement***, 3m/4km N of Newton Stewart. **64 E4** NX4269.

Garlieston *D. & G.* ***Village***, on Garlieston Bay, on W side of Wigtown Bay, 6m/10km SE of Wigtown. **64 E6** NX4746.

Garlinge Green *Kent* ***Settlement***, 4m/7km SW of Canterbury. TR1152.

Garlogie *Aber.* ***Settlement***, 3m/5km E of Echt. Nearly 1m/2km S is Cullerlie Stone Circle (Historic Scotland). **91 F4** NJ7805.

Garlogie Stone Circle *Aber.* *Alternative name for Cullerlie Stone Circle, qv.*

Garmelow *Staffs.* ***Settlement***, 3m/4km W of Eccleshall. SJ7927.

Garmond *Aber.* ***Village***, 5m/9km E of Turriff. **99 G5** NJ8052.

Garmondsway *Dur.* ***Settlement***, near site of former village, 2m/3km W of Trimdon. NZ3434.

Garmony *Arg. & B.* ***Locality***, on Mull, at W end of Sallastle Bay, on Sound of Mull, 7m/11km E of Salen. **79 H3** NM6740.

Garmouth *Moray* ***Village***, near mouth of River Spey, 8m/12km E of Elgin. **98 B4** NJ3364.

Garmsley Camp *Worcs.* ***Historic/prehistoric site***, hillfort covering nine acres and standing on spur, 5m/8km NW of Bromyard. **29 F2** SO6162.

Garmston *Shrop.* ***Settlement***, 1km NW of Leighton. SJ6006.

Garmus Taing *Shet.* ***Coastal feature***, headland on N coast of Mainland, 3m/5km N of North Roe. **108 C3** HU3694.

Garn Boduan *Gwyn.* ***Mountain***, on Lleyn Peninsula, 5m/8km NW of Pwllheli. Height 1050 feet or 320 metres. **36 C2** SH3139.

Garn Caws *Powys* ***Mountain***, 4m/7km N of Tredegar. Height 1692 feet or 516 metres. **28 A7** SO1216.

Garn Ddu *M.Tyd.* ***Mountain***, 4m/6km NW of Merthyr Tydfil. Height 1506 feet or 459 metres. **27 K7** SO0212.

Garn Prys *Conwy* ***Mountain***, 4m/7km W of Cerrigydrudion. Height 1752 feet or 534 metres. **37 H1** SH8848.

Garn-yr-erw *Torfaen* ***Hamlet***, 1m/2km NW of Blaenavon. SO2309.

Garnant *Carmar.* ***Locality***, adjoining to E of Glanaman. **17 K3** SN6813.

Garndiffaith *Torfaen* ***Suburb***, at N end of Abersychan. SO2604.

Garndolbenmaen *Gwyn.* ***Village***, 4m/6km N of Criccieth. **36 D1** SH4944.

Garnedd Uchaf *Conwy* ***Mountain***, in Carneddau range 5m/8km S of Llanfairfechan. Height 3037 feet or 926 metres. **46 E6** SH6866.

Garneddgoch *Gwyn.* ***Mountain***, 5m/8km W of Beddgelert. Height 2296 feet or 700 metres. **36 E1** SH5149.

Garneddwen *Gwyn.* ***Settlement***, 1km NE of Corris. **37 G5** SH7608.

Garneddwen *Powys* ***Mountain***, 2m/3km SW of Llanarmon Dyffryn Ceiriog. Height 1627 feet or 496 metres. **38 A2** SJ1331.

Garnett Bridge *Cumb.* ***Settlement***, at crossing of River Sprint, 4m/7km N of Kendal. **61 G7** SD5299.

Garnfadryn *Gwyn.* ***Settlement***, 4m/6km NW of Llanbedrog. **36 B2** SH2734.

Garngad *Glas.* ***Suburb***, 1m/2km NE of Glasgow city centre. NS6066.

Garnlydan *B.Gwent* ***Locality***, 2m/3km W of Bryn-mawr. SO1612.

Garnock *N.Ayr.* ***River***, rising about 5m/8km E of Largs and flowing S through Kilbirnie and Dalry to River Irvine, close to Irvine Bay. **74 A5** NS3038.

Garnswllt *Swan.* ***Settlement***, 2m/3km S of Ammanford. **17 K4** SN6209.

Garrabost *W.Isles* ***Village***, on Eye Peninsula, Isle of Lewis, 4m/7km SW of Tiumpan Head. **101 H4** NB5133.

Garrachra *Arg. & B.* ***Settlement***, to W of River Massan, 4m/6km NW of Benmore. **73 J2** NS0888.

Garralburn *Moray* ***Settlement***, 3m/5km NE of Keith. **98 C5** NJ4555.

Garras *Cornw.* ***Hamlet***, 4m/6km SE of Helston. **2 D6** SW7023.

Garreg *Flints.* ***Settlement***, 1km SW of Whitford, below Mynydd-y-garreg. SJ1377.

Garreg *Gwyn.* ***Hamlet***, 2m/3km N of Penrhyndeudraeth. **37 F1** SH6141.

Garreg Bank *Powys* ***Settlement***, to N of Trewern. **38 B4** SJ2811.

Garreg Fawr *Conwy* ***Mountain***, 2m/3km SE of Llanfairfechan. Height 1246 feet or 380 metres. **46 E5** SH6872.

Garreg Las *Carmar.* ***Mountain***, 6m/9km NE of Brynamman. Height 2076 feet or 633 metres. **27 G6** SN7720.

Garrett's Green *W.Mid.* ***Suburb***, 6m/9km E of Birmingham city centre. SP1485.

Garrick *P. & K.* ***Settlement***, 3m/5km SW of Muthill. **81 K6** NN8412.

Garrigill *Cumb.* ***Village***, 4m/6km SE of Alston. **61 J2** NY7441.

Garrisdale Point *High.* ***Coastal feature***, headland at westernmost point of Canna. **85 H4** NG2005.

Garrison of Inversnaid *Stir.* *See Inversnaid.*

Garriston *N.Yorks.* ***Settlement***, on S bank of Garriston Beck, 3m/5km NE of Leyburn. SE1592.

Garroch *D. & G.* ***Settlement***, 1m/2km W of St. John's Town of Dalry. **67 K5** NX5981.

Garroch Burn *D. & G.* ***River***, stream rising on E side of Rig of Clenrie and flowing E to confluence with Glenlee Burn, thereafter continuing SE as Coom Burn for about 1km to its confluence with Water of Ken, 1km SW of St. John's Town of Dalry. **67 K5** NX6081.

Garroch Head *Arg. & B.* ***Coastal feature***, headland at S end of Bute. **73 K5** NS0951.

Garrochty *Arg. & B.* ***Settlement***, at S tip of Bute, 1km NW of Garroch Head. **73 J5** NS0952.

Garron Point *Aber.* ***Coastal feature***, headland on E coast, 2m/3km NE of Stonehaven. **91 G6** NO8987.

Garros *High.* ***Settlement***, 3m/5km S of Staffin, Skye. **94 B5** NG4963.

Garrow *P. & K.* ***Settlement***, 5m/8km SW of Aberfeldy. **81 K4** NN8240.

Garrow Tor *Cornw.* ***Mountain***, on Bodmin Moor, 4m/6km SE of Camelford. Height 1086 feet or 331 metres. **4 B3** SX1478.

Garry *High.* ***River***, formed at confluence of River Kingie and Gearr Garry, and flowing E into Loch Garry. NH1600.

Garry *P. & K.* ***River***, running SE from Loch Garry down Glen Garry to River Tummel 2m/3km NW of Pitlochry. **81 K1** NN9159.

Garry-a-siar *W.Isles* ***Coastal feature***, headland on W coast of Benbecula. **92 C6** NF7553.

Garryhorn *D. & G.* ***Settlement***, 1m/2km W of Carsphairn. **67 K4** NX5493.

Garryhorn Burn *D. & G.* ***River***, rising on N slopes of Meaul and flowing E to join Water of Deugh at Carsphairn, 8m/13km N of St. John's Town of Dalry. **67 K4** NX5592.

Garrynamonie *W.Isles* *Anglicised form of Gearraidh na Monadh, qv.*

Garrywhin *High.* *Alternative name for Cairn of Get, qv.*

Gars-bheinn *High.* ***Mountain***, one of the peaks of Cuillin Hills on Skye, at S end of range. Height 2936 feet or 895 metres. **85 K3** NG4618.

Garscadden *Glas.* ***Suburb***, 5m/8km NW of Glasgow city centre. NS5268.

Garsdale *Cumb.* ***Locality***, and valley of River Clough, 6m/10km E of Sedbergh. **61 H7** SD7390.

Garsdale Head *Cumb.* ***Locality***, 1km SW of Moorcock Inn. **61 J7** SD7892.

Garsdon *Wilts.* ***Village***, 2m/4km E of Malmesbury. **20 C3** ST9687.

Garshall Green *Staffs.* ***Hamlet***, 4m/7km E of Stone. **40 B2** SJ9634.

Garsington *Oxon.* Population: 1853. ***Village***, 5m/8km SE of Oxford. **21 J1** SP5802.

Garstang *Lancs.* Population: 5697. ***Small town***, 10m/17km N of Preston. **55 H5** SD4945.

Garston *Mersey.* ***Suburb***, 5m/9km SE of Liverpool city centre. **48 D4** SJ4084.

Garston Park *Herts.* ***Suburb***, 2m/3km NE of Watford town centre. TL1100.

Garswood *Mersey.* ***Village***, 1m/2km W of Ashton-in-Makerfield. **48 E3** SJ5599.

Gartachoil *Stir.* ***Settlement***, 3m/5km N of Balfron. **74 D1** NS5393.

Gartally *High.* ***Locality***, comprises settlements of Upper and Lower Gartally, 2m/3km NW of Drumnadrochit. **88 B1** NH4831.

Gartavaich *Arg. & B.* ***Settlement***, on Kintyre, 2m/3km NW of Claonaig. **73 G5** NR8558.

Gartbreck *Arg. & B.* ***Settlement***, on E coast of Loch Indaal, 2m/3km E of Port Charlotte across loch. **72 A5** NR2858.

Gartcosh *N.Lan.* ***Village***, 3m/4km NW of Coatbridge. **74 E4** NS6968.

Garth *Bridgend* ***Locality***, 1m/2km SE of Maesteg. **18 B2** SS8690.

Garth *Cere.* ***Hamlet***, adjoining to E of Penrhyn-coch, 4m/7km NE of Aberystwyth. SN6484.

Garth *Gwyn.* ***Suburb***, on Menai Strait, adjoining to N of Bangor. **46 D5** SH5873.

Garth *I.o.M.* ***Settlement***, 4m/6km W of Douglas. **54 C6** SC3177.

Garth *Newport* ***Suburb***, 3m/4km W of Newport. ST2687.

Garth *Powys* ***Locality***, on W side of Knighton. SO2772.

Garth *Powys* ***Village***, 6m/9km W of Builth Wells. **27 J4** SN9549.

Garth *Shet.* ***Settlement***, 1km NE of Norby, Mainland. **109 B7** HU2157.

Garth *Shet.* ***Settlement***, in South Nesting, Mainland, 1km SE of Skellister. HU4754.

Garth *Wrex.* ***Village***, 3m/5km E of Llangollen. **38 B1** SJ2542.

Garth Head *Ork.* ***Coastal feature***, headland on S coast of South Walls peninsula, Hoy. **107 C9** ND3188.

Garth Owen *Powys* ***Settlement***, adjoining to S of Newtown. SO1090.

Garth Place *Caerp.* ***Hamlet***, 2m/3km E of Caerphilly. ST1887.

Garth Row *Cumb.* ***Hamlet***, 3m/5km N of Kendal. SD5297.

Garth Trevor *Wrex.* ***Hamlet***, 3m/4km SW of Ruabon. SJ2642.

Garthamlock *Glas.* ***Suburb***, 4m/7km E of Glasgow city centre. NS6666.

Garthbrengy *Powys* ***Hamlet***, 3m/5km N of Brecon. **27 K5** SO0433.

Garthdee *Aberdeen* ***Suburb***, 2m/4km SW of Aberdeen city centre. NJ9103.

Gartheli *Cere.* ***Settlement***, 5m/9km N of Lampeter. **26 E3** SN5856.

Garthmyl *Powys* ***Hamlet***, 1m/2km S of Aberriw. **38 A6** SO1999.

Garthmyn *Conwy* ***Locality***, 1km NW of Capel Garmon. SH8055.

Garthorpe *Leics.* ***Village***, 6m/9km E of Melton Mowbray. **42 B3** SK8320.

Garthorpe *N.Lincs.* ***Village***, adjoining to E of Fockerby, 7m/12km SE of Goole. **52 B1** SE8419.

Garths *Cumb.* ***Settlement***, 3m/4km SE of Kendal. **61 G7** SD5489.

Garthynty *Carmar.* ***Settlement***, 6m/9km SE of Llanddewi-Brefi. **27 G4** SN7147.

Gartincaper *Stir.* ***Settlement***, 2m/3km SW of Doune. **81 H7** NN6900.

Gartly *Aber.* ***Hamlet***, 5m/8km S of Huntly. **90 D1** NJ5232.

Gartmore *Stir.* ***Village***, 3m/4km S of Aberfoyle. **74 D1** NS5297.

Gartmorn Dam *Clack.* ***Lake/loch***, with country park, 2m/3km NE of Alloa. **75 H1** NS9294.

Gartnagrenach *Arg. & B.* ***Settlement***, on Kintyre, 7m/11km SW of Tarbert. **73 F5** NR7959.

Gartnatra *Arg. & B.* ***Settlement***, 1m/2km E of Bowmore, Islay. **72 B5** NR3260.

Gartness *Stir.* ***Settlement***, on Endrick Water, 1m/2km W of Killearn. **74 D2** NS5086.

Gartocharn *W.Dun.* ***Village***, 4m/6km NE of Balloch. **74 C2** NS4286.

Garton *E.Riding* ***Hamlet***, 3m/4km SE of Aldbrough. **59 J6** TA2635.

Garton End *Peter.* ***Suburb***, 1m/2km N of Peterborough city centre. TF1900.

Garton-on-the-Wolds *E.Riding* ***Village***, 3m/5km NW of Great Driffield. **59 F3** SE9859.

Gartymore *High.* ***Settlement***, in Sutherland district, 1m/2km SW of Helmsdale. **105 F7** ND0114.

Garvald *E.Loth.* ***Village***, 8m/12km SW of Dunbar. **76 D3** NT5870.

Garvamore *High.* ***Settlement***, in River Spey valley, 5m/8km W of Laggan. **88 C5** NN5294.

Garvan *High.* ***Settlement***, on S shore of Loch Eil, 1km S of Kinlocheil across loch. **87 F7** NM9777.

Garvard *Arg. & B.* ***Settlement***, at S end of Colonsay, 3m/4km SW of Scalasaig. **72 B1** NR3691.

Garvary Burn *High.* ***River***, rising to E of Creag Mhòr and flowing SE into River Skinsdale, 2m/4km N of Pollie. **104 C6** NC7519.

Garve *High.* ***Settlement***, in Ross and Cromarty district, 10m/15km W of Dingwall. Loch Garve is 1m/2km SE. **5 K5** NH3961.

Garve Island *High.* *Anglicised form of An Garbh-eilean, qv.*

Garveld *Arg. & B.* ***Settlement***, on S tip of Kintyre, 3m/4km W of Southend. **66 A3** NR6507.

Garvellachs (Also known as Isles of the Sea.) *Arg. & B.* ***Island***, chain of small uninhabited islands, comprising of A' Chùli, Dùn Chonnuill, Eileach an Naoimh and Garbh Eileach, at SW end of Firth of Lorn, 5m/8km W of Luing. **79 H6** NM6511.

Garvellan Rocks *D. & G.* ***Island***, group of offshore rocks on W side of entrance to Fleet Bay. NX5551.

Garven *High.* *Anglicised form of Garbh Bheinn, qv.*

Garvery Hill *High.* ***Mountain***, in Caithness district, 2m/4km S of Morven. Height 1092 feet or 333 metres. **104 E6** NC9924.

Garvestone *Norf.* ***Village***, 4m/7km SE of East Dereham. **44 E5** TG0207.

Garvie *Arg. & B.* ***Settlement***, 4m/7km NE of Clachan of Glendaruel. **73 J2** NS0390.

Garvock *Aber.* ***Settlement***, 2m/3km E of Laurencekirk. **91 F7** NO7470.

Garvock *Inclyde* ***Settlement***, on S shore of Loch Thorn, 4m/6km SW of Garvock. **74 A3** NS2571.

Garvock *P. & K.* ***Settlement***, 1m/2km E of Dunning. **82 B6** NO0314.

Garwald *D. & G.* ***Hamlet***, 3m/4km NW of Eskdalemuir. **69 H3** NT2200.

Garwald Water *D. & G.* ***River***, running SE to White Esk 2m/3km N of Eskdalemuir. NT2400.

Garwaldwaterfoot *D. & G.* ***Settlement***, situated where Garwaldwater joins River White Esk, 2m/3km N of Eskdalemuir. **69 H3** NT2400.

Garwall Hill *D. & G.* ***Mountain***, 7m/11km E of Barrhill. Height 1145 feet or 349 metres. **67 H5** NX3483.

Garway *Here.* ***Village***, 5m/8km SE of Pontrilas. Circular dovecote survives from Knights Templars' commandery. **28 D6** SO4522.

Garway Common *Here.* ***Hamlet***, 2m/3km N of Skenfrith. SO4622.

Garway Hill *Here.* ***Settlement***, 2m/3km N of Garway. **28 D6** SO4425.

Garwick Bay *I.o.M.* ***Coastal feature***, inlet of Laxey bay, 1km NW of Clay Head. **54 D5** SC4381.

Garynahine (Gaelic form: Gearraidh na h-Aibhne.) *W.Isles* ***Settlement***, near W coast of Isle of Lewis, 3m/5km SE of Breascleit. **100 E4** NB2331.
Garyvard *W.Isles Anglicised form of Gearraidh Bhaird, qv.*
Gask *Aber.* ***Settlement***, on N side of Burn of Gask, 2m/3km S of Turriff. **99 F6** NJ7247.
Gask *Aber.* ***Settlement***, 3m/4km N of Cruden Bay. **99 J6** NK0840.
Gask *P. & K.* ***Locality***, 4m/7km NE of Auchterarder. **82 A6** NN9918.
Gaskan *High.* ***Settlement***, on N shore of Loch Shiel, 3m/4km N of Pollock, Lochaber district. **86 E7** NM8072.
Gasker (Gaelic form: Gaisgear.) *W.Isles* ***Island***, small uninhabited island 6m/10km W of Hushinish Point, W coast of North Harris. **100 A6** NA8711.
Gasker Beg *W.Isles* ***Island***, sea rock about 1km SE of Gasker. NA8810.
Gasper *Wilts.* ***Hamlet***, 3m/5km W of Mere. ST7633.
Gass *S.Ayr.* ***Settlement***, 2m/3km E of Straiton. **67 J3** NS4105.
Gass Water *E.Ayr.* ***River***, rising to S of Wardlaw Hill and flowing NW to become Bellow Water 4m/7km NE of Cumnock. **68 B1** NS6224.
Gasstown *D. & G.* ***Locality***, 2m/3km E of Dumfries. NX9976.
Gastard *Wilts.* ***Village***, 4m/7km SW of Chippenham. **20 B5** ST8868.
Gasthorpe *Norf.* ***Hamlet***, 7m/11km E of Thetford. **44 D7** TL9780.
Gaston Green *Essex* ***Hamlet***, 3m/5km S of Bishop's Stortford. TL4917.
Gat Sand *Lincs.* ***Coastal feature***, sandbank in SW part of The Wash off Lincolnshire coast to S of Roger Sand across Gat Channel. **43 H2** TF4738.
Gatcombe *I.o.W.* ***Village***, 3m/4km S of Newport. **11 F6** SZ4885.
Gate Burton *Lincs.* ***Hamlet***, 1km N of Marton. 18c hall with gazebo temple in park. **52 B4** SK8382.
Gate Fulford *York Alternative name for Fulford, qv.*
Gate Helmsley *N.Yorks.* ***Village***, 1m/2km W of Stamford Bridge. **58 C4** SE6955.
Gateacre *Mersey.* ***Suburb***, 6m/9km E of city Liverpool centre. **48 D4** SJ4388.
Gatebeck *Cumb.* ***Settlement***, 5m/8km SE of Kendal. **55 J1** SD5485.
Gateford *Notts.* ***Locality***, adjoining to N of Worksop. **51 H4** SK5781.
Gateforth *N.Yorks.* ***Village***, 4m/6km SW of Selby. **58 B7** SE5628.
Gatehead *E.Ayr.* ***Hamlet***, 2m/4km SW of Kilmarnock. **74 B7** NS3936.
Gateholm Island *Pembs.* ***Island***, off S coast of peninsula at S end of St. Brides Bay, 2m/3km SE of Wooltack Point. Accessible on foot at low tide. **16 A4** SM7707.
Gatehouse *Arg. & B.* ***Settlement***, on E side of Jura, 1m/2km SW of Lagg. **72 D3** NR5877.
Gatehouse *P. & K.* ***Settlement***, 2m/3km SE of Aberfeldy. **81 K3** NN8747.
Gatehouse of Fleet *D. & G.* ***Small town***, former cotton town, near mouth of Water of Fleet, 6m/10km NW of Kirkcudbright. **65 G5** NX6056.
Gatelawbridge *D. & G.* ***Locality***, 2m/3km E of Thornhill. **68 E4** NX9096.
Gateley *Norf.* ***Hamlet***, 4m/7km SE of Fakenham. **44 D3** TF9624.
Gateley Hill *Norf.* ***Settlement***, 1km N of Gateley. TF9625.
Gatenby *N.Yorks.* ***Hamlet***, 4m/6km E of Bedale. **57 J1** SE3287.
Gatescarth Pass *Cumb.* ***Other feature of interest***, mountain pass (1948 feet or 594 metres) between Branstree and Harter Fell, 1m/2km S of Haweswater Reservoir. **61 F6** NY4709.
Gatesgarth *Cumb.* ***Settlement***, at SE end of Buttermere lake. NY1915.
Gateshaw *Sc.Bord.* ***Settlement***, 2m/3km S of Morebattle. **70 C1** NT7722.
Gateshead *T. & W.* Population: 83,159. ***Town***, industrial and administrative town on S bank of River Tyne, opposite Newcastle upon Tyne. Former mining town and port. Metrocentre, largest undercover shopping centre in Europe, is sited here. International athletics stadium. Location of Angel of the North, sculpture 65 feet or 20 metres high, wingspan 175 feet or 54 metres, erected 1998. **71 H7** NZ2563.
Gatesheath *Ches.* ***Settlement***, 1m/2km NW of Tattenhall. **48 D6** SJ4760.
Gateside *Aber.* ***Settlement***, 3m/4km E of Alford. **90 E3** NJ6116.
Gateside *Angus* ***Hamlet***, 4m/6km S of Forfar. **83 F3** NO4344.
Gateside *Fife* ***Village***, 2m/3km W of Strathmiglo. **82 C7** NO1809.
Gateside *N.Ayr.* ***Hamlet***, 1m/2km E of Beith. **74 B5** NS3653.
Gateslack *D. & G.* ***Settlement***, 3m/5km NE of Carronbridge. **68 D3** NS8902.
Gathersnow Hill ***Mountain***, on border of South Lanarkshire and Scottish Borders, 6m/9km S of Coulter. Height 2263 feet or 690 metres. **69 F1** NT0525.
Gathurst *Gt.Man.* ***Locality***, 1km S of Shevington. **48 E2** SD5307.
Gatley *Gt.Man.* Population: 29,228. ***Town***, 3m/5km W of Stockport. **49 H4** SJ8488.
Gattonside *Sc.Bord.* ***Hamlet***, with housing development on N side of River Tweed, opposite Melrose. Footbridge across river. **76 D7** NT5435.
Gatwick (London) Airport (Gatwick Airport). *W.Suss.* ***Airport/airfield***, international airport, 1m/2km S of Horley and 24m/39km S of London. Roof-top spectators' gallery at S Terminal, with panoramic views of airfield. **23 F7** TQ2841.
Gatwick Airport *W.Suss. See Gatwick (London) Airport.*
Gatwick Zoo *Surr.* ***Leisure/recreation***, to SW of Charlwood, 3m/4km W of Gatwick Airport. Hundreds of animals housed in 10 acres of grounds, mostly in naturalised settings. Main attraction is Monkey Island. **23 F7** TQ2340.
Gaufron *Powys* ***Settlement***, 2m/3km E of Rhayader. **27 J2** SN9968.
Gaulby *Leics.* ***Village***, 7m/11km E of Leicester. **41 J5** SK6900.
Gaulden Manor *Som.* ***Historic house***, red sandstone manor 3m/5km NE of Wiveliscombe and 9m/12km NW of Taunton. Seat of Thomas Hardy's Turberville family. Contains Great Hall and collection of antique furniture. Bog garden in grounds. **7 K2** ST1031.
Gauldry *Fife* ***Village***, 4m/6km SW of Newport-on-Tay. **82 E5** NO3723.
Gaulkthorn *Lancs.* ***Settlement***, 1m/2km S of Accrington. SD7526.
Gaultree *Norf.* ***Locality***, adjoining to E of Emneth. TF4907.
Gauntons Bank *Ches.* ***Settlement***, 1km E of Norbury. SJ5647.
Gaunt's Common *Dorset* ***Hamlet***, 1m/2km SE of Hinton Martell. **10 B4** SU0205.
Gaunt's Earthcott *S.Glos.* ***Hamlet***, 2m/3km E of Almondsbury. ST6384.
Gaunt's End *Essex* ***Settlement***, 5m/8km NE of Bishop's Stortford. TL5425.
Gaur (Gaelic form: Abhainn Gaoire.) *P. & K.* ***River***, running E from Loch Eigheach to W end of Loch Rannoch. NN5056.
Gautby *Lincs.* ***Hamlet***, 4m/6km NE of Bardney. **52 E5** TF1772.
Gavinton *Sc.Bord.* ***Village***, 2m/3km SW of Duns. **77 F5** NT7652.
Gawber *S.Yorks.* ***Locality***, 1m/2km NW of Barnsley. **51 F2** SE3207.
Gawcott *Bucks.* ***Village***, 1m/2km SW of Buckingham. **31 H5** SP6831.
Gawsworth *Ches.* ***Hamlet***, 3m/5km SW of Macclesfield. **49 H6** SJ8969.
Gawsworth Hall *Ches.* ***Historic house***, Tudor manor house, 6m/10km SW of Macclesfield town centre. Former home of Mary Fitton, Elizabeth I's Maid of Honour. **49 H6** SJ8969.
Gawthorpe *W.Yorks.* ***Hamlet***, 1km N of Fenay Bridge and 3m/4km E of Huddersfield. SE1816.
Gawthorpe *W.Yorks.* ***Locality***, 2m/3km E of Dewsbury town centre. SE2721.
Gawthorpe Hall *Lancs.* ***Historic house***, early 17c house (National Trust), restored in 1850s by Sir Charles Barry, 1m/2km E of Padiham and 3m/5km NW of Burnley. Former home of Shuttleworth family; houses Rachel Kay-Shuttleworth textile collection. **56 D6** SD8034.
Gawthrop *Cumb.* ***Hamlet***, 1m/2km W of Dent. **56 B1** SD6987.
Gawthwaite *Cumb.* ***Hamlet***, 3m/4km NW of Penny Bridge. **55 F1** SD2784.
Gay Bowers *Essex* ***Settlement***, 4m/7km W of Maldon. TL7904.
Gay Street *W.Suss.* ***Settlement***, 3m/4km NE of Pulborough. **12 D4** TQ0820.
Gaydon *Warks.* ***Village***, 10m/16km NW of Banbury. **30 E3** SP3654.
Gayhurst *M.K.* ***Village***, 3m/4km NW of Newport Pagnell. **32 B4** SP8546.
Gayle *N.Yorks.* ***Village***, adjoining to S of Hawes. SD8789.
Gayle Moor *N.Yorks.* ***Open space***, moorland at head of Gayle Beck, 2m/3km S of Wold Fell and 3m/5km SE of Dent Station. **56 C1** SD7982.
Gayles *N.Yorks.* ***Village***, 5m/8km NW of Richmond. **62 C6** NZ1207.
Gayton *Mersey.* ***Locality***, adjoining to S of Heswall. **48 B4** SJ2780.
Gayton *Norf.* ***Village***, 7m/11km E of King's Lynn. Site of Roman building 1km N. **44 B4** TF7219.
Gayton *Northants.* ***Village***, 4m/6km N of Towcester. Site of Roman building to SE. **31 J3** SP7054.
Gayton *Staffs.* ***Village***, 5m/8km NE of Stafford. **40 B3** SJ9828.
Gayton Engine *Lincs.* ***Locality***, 1km W of Theddlethorpe All Saints, 3m/5km NW of Mablethorpe. TF4588.
Gayton le Marsh *Lincs.* ***Village***, 6m/9km N of Alford. **53 H4** TF4284.
Gayton le Wold *Lincs.* ***Locality***, 6m/9km W of Louth. **53 F4** TF2385.
Gayton Thorpe *Norf.* ***Hamlet***, 1m/2km SE of Gayton. **44 B4** TF7219.
Gaywood *Norf.* ***Suburb***, 1km E of King's Lynn town centre. **44 A3** TF6320.
Gazeley *Suff.* ***Village***, 5m/8km E of Newmarket. **34 B2** TL7264.
Geal Charn ***Mountain***, NE extension of Ladder Hills on border of Aberdeenshire and Moray, 6m/10km NW of Strathdon. Height 2240 feet or 683 metres. **90 B2** NJ3121.
Geal Charn *Aber.* ***Mountain***, 2m/3km N of Corgarff. Height 2207 feet or 673 metres. **89 K3** NJ2810.
Geal Charn *High.* ***Mountain***, in Badenoch and Strathspey district, 8m/12km SE of Nethy Bridge. Height 2693 feet or 821 metres. **89 H3** NJ0912.
Geal Charn *High.* ***Mountain***, in Lochaber district, 4m/7km NW of Achnacarry. Height 2637 feet or 804 metres. **87 H5** NN1594.
Geal Charn *High.* ***Mountain***, 11m/17km SW of Kinloch Laggan. Munro: height 3713 feet or 1132 metres. **88 B7** NN4774.
Geal Charn *High.* ***Mountain***, on Ardverikie Forest in Badenoch and Strathspey district, 4m/6km E of SW end of Loch Laggan. Munro: height 3441 feet or 1049 metres. **88 C6** NN5081.
Geal Charn *High.* ***Mountain***, in Monadhliath range in Badenoch and Strathspey district, 4m/7km NW of Laggan Bridge. Munro: height 3037 feet or 926 metres. **88 C5** NN5698.
Geal-chàrn *High.* ***Mountain***, in Badenoch and Strathspey district, on E side of Loch Ericht and 5m/8km S of Dalwhinnie. Munro: height 3008 feet or 917 metres. **88 C7** NN5978.
Geal Chàrn *P. & K.* ***Mountain***, 3m/5km SE of Kinloch Rannoch. Height 2591 feet or 790 metres. **81 H2** NN6854.
Geal-charn Mòr *High.* ***Mountain***, in Badenoch and Strathspey district 4m/6km W of Aviemore. Height 2703 feet or 824 metres. **89 F3** NH8312.
Geallaig Hill *Aber.* ***Mountain***, 3m/5km NE of Crathie. Height 2437 feet or 743 metres. **89 K5** NO2998.
Geanies House *High.* ***Settlement***, 3m/5km NE of Balintore. **97 F4** NH8979.
Gearach *Arg. & B.* ***Settlement***, on Rinns of Islay, 1m/2km W of Port Charlotte. **72 A5** NR2358.
Gearnsary *High.* ***Settlement***, 1m/2km S of Loch Rimsdale, Sutherland district. **104 C5** NC7332.
Gearr Aonach *High. See The Three Sisters.*
Gearr Chreag *High.* ***Mountain***, 6m/10km E of Glenborrodale across Loch Sunart. Height 1115 feet or 340 metres. **79 J1** NM7061.
Gearr Garry *High.* ***River***, flowing SE out of E end of Loch Quoich into Glen Garry by Kingie Pool. NH0900.
Gearradh *High.* ***Settlement***, on NW shore of Loch Linnhe, 2m/3km W of Sallachan Point. **80 A1** NM9560.
Gearraidh Bhailteas (Anglicised form: Milton.) *W.Isles* ***Locality***, near W coast of South Uist 3m/4km S of Rubha Ardvule. Birthplace of Flora MacDonald. **84 C2** NF7326.
Gearraidh Bhaird (Anglicised form: Garyvard.) *W.Isles* ***Settlement***, on S side of Loch Erisort, Isle of Lewis, 2m/3km SE of Lacasaigh across loch. **101 F5** NB3620.
Gearraidh na h-Aibhne *W.Isles Gaelic form of Garynahine, qv.*
Gearraidh na Monadh (Anglicised form: Garrynamonie.) *W.Isles* ***Settlement***, near S end of South Uist, 1m/2km N of Cille Bhrighde. **84 C3** NF7516.
Gearran Island *High.* ***Island***, one of a group of islets 3m/5km NW of Rubha Hunish at N tip of Skye. See Gaeilavore Island; Lord Macdonald's Table. **93 J4** NG3679.
Gearrannan (Anglicised form: Garenin.) *W.Isles* ***Settlement***, 1m/2km NW of Carloway, Isle of Lewis. **100 D3** NB1944.
Geary *High.* ***Settlement***, on Skye, on W side of Loch Snizort, 4m/6km SE of Vaternish Point. **93 H5** NG2661.
Gedding *Suff.* ***Village***, 7m/12km SE of Bury St. Edmunds. **34 D3** TL9557.
Geddington *Northants.* ***Village***, 3m/5km NE of Kettering. In village square, one of three remaining Eleanor crosses (English Heritage); others at Hardingstone and Waltham Cross. **42 B7** SP8983.
Gedgrave Hall *Suff.* ***Settlement***, 1m/2km SW of Orford. **35 J4** TM4048.
Gedintailor *High.* ***Settlement***, on E coast of Skye, 5m/8km SE of Loch Portree. NG5235.
Gedling *Notts.* ***Suburb***, adjoining to N of Carlton, 3m/5km NE of Nottingham. **41 J1** SK6142.
Gedney *Lincs.* ***Village***, 3m/5km E of Holbeach. **43 H3** TF4024.
Gedney Broadgate *Lincs.* ***Hamlet***, 1m/2km S of Gedney. **43 H3** TF4024.
Gedney Drove End *Lincs.* ***Village***, 5m/7km NE of Long Sutton. **43 H3** TF4629.
Gedney Dyke *Lincs.* ***Hamlet***, 1m/2km N of Gedney. **43 H3** TF4024.
Gedney Hill *Lincs.* ***Village***, 6m/10km E of Crowland. **43 G4** TF3311.
Gedney Marsh *Lincs.* ***Open space***, lowland to SW of The Wash, 6m/9km NE of Holbeach. **43 H3** TF4329.
Gee Cross *Gt.Man.* ***Locality***, 1m/2km SE of Hyde. **49 J3** SJ9593.
Geifas *Cere.* ***Mountain***, 5m/8km E of Pont-rhyd-y-groes. Height 1873 feet or 571 metres. **27 H1** SN8172.
Geilston *Arg. & B.* ***Suburb***, adjoining to N of Cardross. NS3477.
Geirninis (Anglicised form: West Geirinish.) *W.Isles* ***Village***, towards N end of South Uist, on S side of Loch Bee. **92 C7** NF7741.
Geisiadar (Anglicised form: Geshader.) *W.Isles* ***Settlement***, in W part of Isle of Lewis, 3m/5km SE of Miabhig. **100 D4** NB1131.
Gelder Burn *Aber.* ***River***, running N down Glen Gelder to River Dee, 1m/2km SW of Balmoral Castle. NO2494.
Geldeston *Norf.* ***Village***, 3m/4km NW of Beccles. **45 H6** TM3991.
Geldie Burn *Aber.* ***River***, running E to River Dee, 4m/6km W of Inverey. **89 G6** NO0288.
Gell *Conwy* ***Locality***, 5m/8km S of Colwyn Bay. **47 G6** SH8469.
Gell *Gwyn.* ***Settlement***, on Lleyn Peninsula, 1m/2km N of Criccieth. **36 D2** SH4939.
Gelli *Pembs. Alternative spelling of Gelly, qv.*
Gelli *R.C.T.* ***Village***, on S side of Rhondda Fawr valley, 2m/3km SE of Treorchy. SS9794.
Gelli Aur Country Park *Carmar.* ***Leisure/recreation***, country park with gardens, nature trail, aboretum and deer park all focused around a baronial mansion dating from 1824, 2m/3km SW of Llandeilo. **17 K2** SN6019.
Gelli-gaer Common *M.Tyd.* ***Open space***, moorland N of Gelli-gaer, and W of Bargoed. **18 E2** ST1298.
Gelli Gynan *Denb.* ***Settlement***, 4m/7km SE of Ruthin. **47 K7** SJ1854.
Gelli-hâf *Caerp.* ***Locality***, 1km E of Hengoed across Rhymney Valley. ST1695.
Gellideg *M.Tyd.* ***Settlement***, 1m/2km W of Merthyr Tydfil. SO0307.
Gelligaer *Caerp.* Population: 15,906. ***Locality***, 6m/10km N of Caerphilly. Remains of small Roman fort of early 2c. **18 E2** ST1396.

Gelligroes *Caerp.* ***Hamlet***, 2m/3km S of Blackwood. ST1794.
Gellilydan *Gwyn.* ***Village***, 1m/2km E of Maentwrog. **37 F2** SH6839.
Gellinudd *N.P.T.* ***Village***, 1m/2km E of Pontardawe. SN7304.
Gellioedd *Conwy* ***Settlement***, 5m/8km N of Bala. **37 J1** SH9344.
Gelly (Also spelled Gelli.) *Pembs.* ***Settlement***, 4m/6km NW of Narberth. **16 D3** SN0819.
Gellyburn *P. & K.* ***Locality***, to NW of Murthly. **82 B4** NO0938.
Gellywen *Carmar.* ***Hamlet***, 5m/7km N of St. Clears. **17 F2** SN2723.
Gelston *D. & G.* ***Village***, 2m/4km S of Castle Douglas. **65 H5** NX7758.
Gelston *Lincs.* ***Hamlet***, 6m/10km N of Grantham. SK9145.
Gelt *Cumb.* ***River***, rising on Geltsdale and flowing NW into River Irthing, 3m/4km W of Brampton. **61 G1** NY4959.
Geltbridge *Cumb.* ***Hamlet***, on River Gelt, 1m/2km SW of Brampton. NY5159.
Geltsdale *Cumb. Alternative name for King's Forest of Geltsdale.*
Geltsdale Middle *Cumb.* ***Open space***, moorland to S of Middle Top and Crookburn Pike in King's Forest of Geltsdale, 3m/5km NE of Newbiggin. **61 G1** NY5951.
Gelyn *Gwyn.* ***River***, stream running SE into N end of Llyn Celyn. **37 H1** SH8441.
Gembling *E.Riding* ***Hamlet***, 6m/9km E of Great Driffield. **59 H4** TA1057.
Gemmil *Arg. & B.* ***Settlement***, 1m/2km NW of Ardfern. **79 J7** NM7805.
Gendros *Swan.* ***Suburb***, 2m/3km NW of Swansea city centre. SS6395.
General Wade's Military Road *High.* ***Other feature of interest***, road built in 18c and traversing part of Highlands of Scotland via Glen Ore, Fort Augustus, and Corrieyairack Pass, with object of facilitating subjugation of Highlanders after Jacobite rising of 1715. **88 C2** NH5325.
Genoch *D. & G.* ***Locality***, including Genoch Mains and Little Genoch, 5m/8km SE of Stranraer. **64 B5** NX1356.
Genoch Square *D. & G.* ***Settlement***, at road junction, 5m/8km SE of Stranraer. **64 B5** NX1355.
Gentlemen's Cave *Ork.* ***Coastal feature***, cave on W coast of Westray, 1m/2km SE of Noup Head. Formerly haunt of Jacobites. **106 C3** HY3948.
Gentleshaw *Staffs.* ***Village***, 5m/7km E of Cannock. **40 C4** SK0512.
Geo Luon *Ork.* ***Coastal feature***, coastal gully on SW coast of Eday. **106 E5** HY5429.
Geo of Markamouth *Shet.* ***Coastal feature***, small indentation situated on W coast of Yell below Hill of Markamouth. **108 D2** HP4701.
Geo of Vigon *Shet.* ***Coastal feature***, small indentation on W coast of Yell at mouth of North Burn of Vigon. **108 D2** HP4704.
Geodh' a' Bhrideoin *High.* ***Coastal feature***, headland 3m/4km SW of Whiten Head. **103 G2** NC4866.
Geodha Mòr *High.* ***Coastal feature***, 1m/2km SE of Culnacraig, Ross and Cromarty district. **95 G1** NC0702.
Geodha Nasavig *W.Isles* ***Coastal feature***, on W coast of Isle of Lewis, 2m/3km SW of Gallan Head. **100 C4** NB0336.
Geodha Ruadh na Fola *High.* ***Coastal feature***, headland 3m/4km S of Cape Wrath. **102 E1** NC2471.
Geordie's Hill ***Mountain***, astride border of Dumfries & Galloway and Scottish Borders, 6m/10km NW of Newcastleton. Height 1522 feet or 464 metres. **69 K4** NY4396.
George Green *Bucks.* ***Village***, 2m/3km NE of Slough. **22 D3** TQ0081.
George Nympton *Devon* ***Village***, 2m/3km SW of South Molton. **7 F3** SS7023.
Georgeham *Devon* ***Village***, 6m/10km SW of Ilfracombe. **6 C2** SS4639.
Georgemas Junction Station *High.* ***Other building***, railway station 1m/2km E of Halkirk, where Thurso spur joins main line. **105 G3** ND1559.
Georgetown *B.Gwent* ***Suburb***, 1km SE of Tredegar. SO1408.
Georgetown *Renf.* ***Settlement***, 3m/5km NW of Paisley. **74 C4** NS4567.
Georgian House *Bristol* ***Historic house***, merchant's house of 1789 with period furnishings in Great George Street, Bristol. **19 J4** ST5974.
Georgian House *Edin.* ***Historic house***, New Town house, typical of late 18c to early 19c (National Trust for Scotland), designed by Robert Adam in Charlotte Square, Edinburgh, 1km W of city centre. Contains period furnishings. **76 A3** NT2473.
Georth *Ork. Alternative name for Evie, qv.*
Gerard's Bridge *Mersey.* ***Suburb***, to NE of St. Helens town centre. SJ5196.
Gerlan *Gwyn.* ***Locality***, adjoining to E of Bethesda. **46 E6** SH6366.
Germansweek *Devon* ***Village***, 9m/15km W of Okehampton. **6 C6** SX4394.
Germoe *Cornw.* ***Village***, 5m/8km W of Helston. **2 C6** SW5829.
Gerrans *Cornw.* ***Village***, on W side of Gerrans Bay, adjoining Portscatho on inland side. **3 F5** SW8735.
Gerrans Bay *Cornw.* ***Bay***, on S coast, extending E from Portscatho to Nare Head. **3 F5** SW9037.
Gerrards Cross *Bucks.* Population: 9762. ***Small town***, 4m/7km NW of Uxbridge. **22 C3** TQ0088.
Gerston *High.* ***Settlement***, on W bank of River Thurso, to W of Halkirk. **105 G3** ND1259.
Geshader *W.Isles Anglicised form of Geisiadar, qv.*
Gestingthorpe *Essex* ***Village***, 4m/7km SW of Sudbury. Site of Roman building 1m/2km E. **34 C5** TL8138.
Geufford *Powys* ***Hamlet***, 4m/7km N of Welshpool. **38 B4** SJ2114.
Geufron *Powys* ***Settlement***, on River Severn, 4m/7km W of Llanidloes. **37 H7** SN8885.
Geur Rubha *High.* ***Coastal feature***, headland on SW coast of Sleat peninsula, Skye, 1m/2km N of Point of Sleat. **86 B4** NG5501.
Ghlas-bheinn *High.* ***Mountain***, 1m/2km SW of head of Kyle of Durness. Height 1089 feet or 332 metres. **103 F2** NC3361.
Ghyllgrove *Essex* ***Suburb***, to N of Basildon town centre. TQ7089.
Gib Bheinn *Arg. & B.* ***Inland physical feature***, craggy cliff face on Ardmeanach, Mull, 2m/3km N of Aird Fada across Loch Scridain. **79 F5** NM4428.
Gib Heath *W.Mid.* ***Suburb***, 1m/2km NW of Birmingham city centre. SP0588.
Gib Hill *Ches.* ***Settlement***, 1m/2km NW of Great Budworth. SJ6478.
Gibbet Hill *Som.* ***Suburb***, W district of Frome. ST7647.
Gibbet Hill *Surr.* ***Hill***, summit of National Trust property near Hindhead, overlooking Devil's Punch Bowl. Name refers to murder of a sailor in this area in 1786 and fate of murderers. Height 892 feet or 272 metres. **12 C3** SU8935.
Gibbon Hill *N.Yorks.* ***Mountain***, on S side of Swaledale, 3m/5km SW of Reeth. Height 1820 feet or 555 metres. **62 B7** SE0095.
Gibbshill *D. & G.* ***Settlement***, 5m/8km E of New Galloway. **65 H3** NX7278.
Gibraltar *Beds.* ***Hamlet***, 1km SW of Kempston. TL0046.
Gibraltar *Lincs.* ***Locality***, S district of Mablethorpe. TF5184.
Gibraltar *Lincs.* ***Settlement***, on edge of dunes and marshland, 3m/5km S of Skegness. **53 J7** TF5558.
Gibraltar *Suff.* ***Settlement***, 3m/5km NW of Grundisburgh. TM1954.
Gibraltar Point *Lincs.* ***Coastal feature***, headland 4m/6km S of Skegness. Nature reserve to N. **53 J7** TF5657.
Gibraltar Point Nature Reserve *Lincs.* ***Nature reserve***, on 1000 acres of dunes and marshes, with visitor centre and bird observatory, 3m/5km S of Skegness. **53 J7** TF5659.
Giddeahall *Wilts.* ***Hamlet***, 4m/6km W of Chippenham. ST8574.
Giddy Green *Dorset* ***Settlement***, 1m/2km W of Wool. SY8386.
Gidea Park *Gt.Lon.* ***Suburb***, 1m/2km NE of Romford town centre, in borough of Havering. **23 J3** TQ5290.
Gidleigh *Devon* ***Hamlet***, on E edge of Dartmoor, 5m/9km NW of Moretonhampstead. **6 E7** SX6788.
Giedd *Powys* ***River***, flowing S into River Tawe at Ystradgynlais. **27 G7** SN7811.
Giffnock *E.Renf.* Population: 16,190. ***Suburb***, 5m/8km S of Glasgow. **74 D5** NS5659.
Gifford *E.Loth.* ***Village***, 4m/6km S of Hadington. 1m/2km SE is Yester House, 18c mansion, seat of Marquess of Tweeddale, beyond which are ruins of 13c Yester Castle. **76 D4** NT5368.
Gifford Water *E.Loth.* ***River***, rising in Lammermuir Hills and flowing NW to become Colstoun Water, 1m/2km NW of Gifford. **76 D4** NT5269.
Giffordland *N.Ayr.* ***Settlement***, 1m/2km W of Dalry. **74 A6** NS2648.
Giffordtown *Fife* ***Hamlet***, 1m/2km NW of Ladybank. NO2811.
Gigg *Gt.Man.* ***Suburb***, 1m/2km SE of Bury town centre. SD8109.
Giggleswick *N.Yorks.* ***Village***, 1km W of Settle across River Ribble. **56 D3** SD8164.
Gigha *Arg. & B.* ***Island***, narrow island of 9 square miles or 23 square km, 6m/10km long N to S, lying about 2m/3km off W coast of Kintyre, Argyll, opposite Rhunahaorine Point across Sound of Gigha. **72 E6** NR6449.
Gighay *W.Isles* ***Island***, uninhabited island at S end of Sound of Barra and 4m/6km E of Barra (Tràigh Mhòr) Airport. **84 C4** NF7604.
Gigmill *W.Mid.* ***Suburb***, 1km W of Stourbridge town centre. SO8983.
Gigolum Island *Arg. & B.* ***Island***, small island lying to E of S end of Gigha. NR6445.
Gilbent *Gt.Man.* ***Suburb***, 2m/3km W of Bramhall. SJ8784.
Gilberdyke *E.Riding* Population: 2030. ***Village***, 5m/8km E of Howden. **58 E7** SE8329.
Gilbert Street *Hants.* ***Settlement***, 1km NE of Ropley and 4m/7km E of New Alresford. SU6532.
Gilbert's End *Worcs.* ***Hamlet***, 3m/5km E of Malvern Wells. SO8242.
Gilbertstone *W.Mid.* ***Suburb***, 5m/7km SE of Birmingham city centre. SP1384.
Gilchriston *E.Loth.* ***Settlement***, 2m/3km S of East Saltoun. **76 C4** NT4865.
Gilcrux *Cumb.* ***Village***, 3m/5km SW of Aspatria. **60 C3** NY1138.
Gilderdale Forest *Cumb.* ***Open space***, wild moorland area 3m/5km SW of Alston. **61 H2** NY7048.
Gildersome *W.Yorks.* ***Village***, 1m/2km NW of Morley. **57 H7** SE2429.
Gildersome Street *W.Yorks.* ***Locality***, 1km S of Gildersome, just NE of junction 27 of M62 motorway. SE2428.
Gildingwells *S.Yorks.* ***Village***, 4m/6km NW of Worksop. **51 H4** SK5585.
Gilesgate Moor *Dur.* ***Suburb***, adjoining to E of Durham. NZ2943.
Gileston (Silstwn). *V. of Glam.* ***Village***, 3m/5km E of Llantwit Major. **18 D5** ST0167.
Gilfach *Caerp.* ***Village***, adjoining to S of Bargoed. **18 E2** ST1598.
Gilfach Goch *R.C.T.* Population: 4589. ***Village***, 2m/3km NW of Tonyrefail. **18 C3** SS9889.
Gilfachrheda *Cere.* ***Hamlet***, 2m/3km SE of New Quay. **26 D3** SN4058.
Gilgarran *Cumb.* ***Hamlet***, 2m/3km E of Distington. **60 B4** NY0323.
Gilkicker Point *Hants.* ***Coastal feature***, headland at E end of The Solent, 1m/2km S of Alverstoke. **11 H5** SZ6097.
Gill *Cumb.* ***Settlement***, 1m/2km SE of Greystoke. NY4429.
Gill Pike *Northumb.* ***Mountain***, with rocky outcrops, on S edge of Kielder Forest, 7m/11km SW of Falstone. Height 1374 feet or 419 metres. **70 B5** NY6183.
Gillamoor *N.Yorks.* ***Village***, 2m/4km N of Kirkbymoorside. **63 H7** SE6890.
Gillan *Cornw.* ***Village***, on S side of Gillan Harbour, at mouth small stream, 8m/13km E of Helston. SW7825.
Gillar's Green *Mersey.* ***Settlement***, 2m/4km W of St. Helens. SJ4794.
Gillcambon Beck *Cumb.* ***River***, rising in Greystoke Forest and flowing SW into River Caldew at Millhouse, 3m/4km SE of Caldbeck. **60 E3** NY3736.
Gillen *High.* ***Settlement***, 5m/8km SE of Vaternish Point, Skye. **93 H5** NG2659.
Gillenbie *D. & G.* ***Settlement***, between Hope Burn and Corrie Water, 4m/6km S of Boreland. **69 G5** NY1785.
Gillerthwaite *Cumb.* ***Locality***, 1m/2km E of Ennerdale Water. NY1414.
Gillfoot *D. & G.* ***Settlement***, 3m/4km N of New Abbey. **65 K3** NX9570.
Gillfoot Bay *D. & G.* ***Bay***, on Solway Firth, 6m/10km S of New Abbey. **65 K5** NX9755.
Gillibrands *Lancs.* ***Locality***, industrial estate in SW part of Skelmersdale. SD4705.
Gilling East *N.Yorks.* ***Village***, 2m/3km S of Oswaldkirk. **58 C2** SE6176.
Gilling West *N.Yorks.* ***Village***, 3m/4km N of Richmond. **62 C6** NZ1805.
Gillingham *Dorset* Population: 6404. ***Small town***, on River Stour, 4m/7km NW of Shaftesbury. Developed with arrival of railway in 1859. **9 H2** ST8026.
Gillingham *Med.* Population: 94,923. ***Town***, large industrial town adjoining to E of Chatham, 30m/48km E of London. **24 D5** TQ7767.
Gillingham *Norf.* ***Village***, 1m/2km NW of Beccles. **45 J6** TM4191.
Gillivoan *High.* ***Settlement***, to N of Latheron. **105 G5** ND1934.
Gillock *High.* ***Settlement***, 5m/8km E of Halkirk. **105 H3** ND2059.
Gillow Heath *Staffs.* ***Locality***, 1m/2km N of Biddulph. **49 H7** SJ8858.
Gills *High.* ***Settlement***, near N coast of Caithness district, 2m/3km S of St. John's Point. **105 J1** ND3272.
Gills Bay *High.* ***Bay***, to NE of Gills, 3m/5km W of John o' Groats. **105 J1** ND3373.
Gill's Green *Kent* ***Settlement***, 1m/2km N of Hawkhurst. **14 C4** TQ7532.
Gilmanscleuch *Sc.Bord.* ***Hamlet***, 4m/6km SW of Ettrickbridge. **69 J1** NT3321.
Gilmerton *Edin.* ***Suburb***, 4m/7km SE of Edinburgh city centre. **76 A4** NT2968.
Gilmerton *P. & K.* ***Village***, 2m/3km NE of Crieff. **81 K5** NN8823.
Gilmilnscroft *E.Ayr.* ***Settlement***, 2m/4km N of Auchinleck. **67 K1** NS5525.
Gilmonby *Dur.* ***Hamlet***, on S side of Bowes across River Greta. **62 A5** NY9913.
Gilmorton *Leics.* ***Village***, 3m/5km NE of Lutterworth. **41 H7** SP5787.
Gilroyd *S.Yorks.* ***Settlement***, 2m/3km SW of Barnsley town centre. SE3204.
Gilsay *W.Isles* ***Island***, small uninhabited island in Sound of Harris, 2m/3km SW of Renish Point. **93 F4** NG0279.
Gilslake *S.Glos.* ***Settlement***, 2m/3km SE of Severn Beach. ST5683.
Gilsland *Northumb.* ***Village***, on River Irthing, 5m/8km W of Haltwhistle. **70 B7** NY6366.
Gilsland Spa *Cumb.* ***Settlement***, on W bank of River Irthing, 1m/2km N of Gilsland. **70 B7** NY6367.
Gilson *Warks.* ***Settlement***, 1m/2km NW of Coleshill. SP1890.
Gilstead *W.Yorks.* ***Suburb***, to E of Bingley town centre. SE1239.
Gilston *Herts.* ***Hamlet***, 1m/2km N of Harlow town centre. TL4412.
Gilston *Sc.Bord.* ***Settlement***, 3m/4km S of Fala. **76 C5** NT4456.
Gilston Park *Herts.* ***Settlement***, 1m/2km NW of Harlow. **33 H7** TL4413.
Giltar Point *Pembs.* ***Coastal feature***, headland 1m/2km S of Tenby opposite Caldey Island. **16 E5** SS1298.
Giltbrook *Notts.* ***Suburb***, adjoining to SE of Eastwood. SK4845.
Gilver's Lane *Worcs.* ***Settlement***, 3m/4km E of Malvern Wells. SO8141.
Gilwern *Mon.* Population: 2311. ***Village***, 3m/5km W of Abergavenny. **28 B7** SO2414.
Gilwern Hill *Powys* ***Mountain***, 5m/8km NE of Builth Wells. Height 1440 feet or 439 metres. **27 K3** SO0857.
Gimingham *Norf.* ***Village***, 4m/7km N of North Walsham. **45 G2** TG2836.
Gin Pit *Gt.Man.* ***Settlement***, 2m/3km E of Leigh. SD6801.
Ginclough *Ches.* ***Settlement***, 3m/5km NE of Macclesfield. SJ9576.
Ginger's Green *E.Suss.* ***Settlement***, 3m/5km NE of Hailsham. TQ6212.
Ginst Point *Carmar.* ***Coastal feature***, headland at mouth of River Taf estuary, 2m/4km SE of Laugharne. **17 G4** SN3208.
Giosla (Anglicised form: Gisla.) *W.Isles* ***Settlement***, at mouth of Gisla River on W shore of Little Loch Roag, Isle of Lewis. **100 D5** NB1225.
Gipping *Suff.* ***River***, rising some 5m/8km NE of Stowmarket and flowing S to Ipswich, where it forms estuary known as River Orwell. **34 E3** TM1544.
Gipping *Suff.* ***Village***, near source of River Gipping, 3m/5km NE of Stowmarket. **34 E2** TM0763.
Gipsey Bridge *Lincs.* ***Hamlet***, 5m/7km NW of Boston. **43 F1** TF2849.

Gipton *W.Yorks.* ***Suburb***, 3m/4km NE of Leeds city centre, in Harehills district. SE3335.
Girdle Fell *Northumb.* ***Mountain***, in Cheviot Hills, 3m/5km SE of Carter Bar. Height 1738 feet or 530 metres. **70 C3** NT7001.
Girdle Ness *Aberdeen* ***Coastal feature***, headland with lighthouse, 2m/3km E of Aberdeen city centre across River Dee. **91 H4** NJ9705.
Girdle Toll *N.Ayr.* ***Suburb***, to NE of Irvine town centre. NS3440.
Girlington *W.Yorks.* ***Suburb***, 2m/3km NW of Bradford city centre. SE1334.
Girlsta *Shet.* ***Settlement***, on E coast of Mainland, at S end of deep freshwater Loch of Girlsta, 6m/10km N of Lerwick. **109 D7** HU4350.
Girnigoe Castle *High.* ***Castle***, on S coast of Sinclair's Bay. **105 J3** ND3754.
Girnock Burn *Aber.* ***River***, running N down Glen Girnock to River Dee 3m/4km W of Ballater. **90 B5** NO3396.
Girsby *N.Yorks.* ***Hamlet***, on River Tees, 5m/8km SW of Yarm. **62 E6** NZ3508.
Girtford *Beds.* ***Locality***, adjoining to NW of Sandy. **32 E4** TL1649.
Girthon *D. & G.* ***Settlement***, 2m/3km S of Gatehouse of Fleet. **65 G5** NX6053.
Girton *Cambs.* Population: 3215. ***Village***, 3m/5km NW of Cambridge. **33 H2** TL4262.
Girton *Notts.* ***Village***, 8m/13km N of Newark-on-Trent. **52 B6** SK8266.
Girvan *S.Ayr.* Population: 7449. ***Small town***, fishing town and resort at mouth of Water of Girvan, 17m/28km SW of Ayr. **67 F4** NX1897.
Gisborough Moor *R. & C.* ***Open space***, moorland 2m/3km S of Guisborough. **63 H5** NZ6113.
Gisburn *Lancs.* ***Village***, 7m/11km NE of Clitheroe. **56 D5** SD8248.
Gisburn Cotes *Lancs.* ***Settlement***, 2m/3km SW of Gisburn. SD8047.
Gisla *W.Isles* *Anglicised form of Giosla (settlement), qv.*
Gisla *W.Isles* ***River***, flowing E from Loch Grunavat, through Loch Coirgavat and into Little Loch Roag at Giosla, Isle of Lewis. NB1225.
Gisleham *Suff.* ***Hamlet***, 4m/6km SW of Lowestoft. **45 K7** TM5188.
Gislingham *Suff.* ***Village***, 6m/10km SW of Diss. **34 E1** TM0771.
Gissing *Norf.* ***Village***, 4m/6km NE of Diss. **45 F7** TM1485.
Gittisham *Devon* ***Village***, 2m/3km SW of Honiton. **7 K6** SY1398.
Giùr-bheinn *Arg. & B.* ***Mountain***, on N of Islay, 4m/6km NW of Port Askaig. Height 1036 feet or 316 metres. **72 B3** NR3872.
Givendale *N.Yorks.* ***Locality***, 2m/3km SE of Ripon across River Ure. SE3369.
Givons Grove *Surr.* ***Settlement***, 1m/2km S of Leatherhead. **22 E6** TQ1754.
Glack *Aber.* ***Settlement***, 1km W of Daviot. **91 F2** NJ7327.
Glackour *High.* ***Settlement***, in valley of River Broom, 9m/13km SE of Ullapool. **95 H3** NH1882.
Glacks of Balloch Pass *Moray* ***Other feature of interest***, road pass at 365 metres, between Meikle Balloch Hill and Little Balloch Hill, 4m/6km SE of Dufftown. **90 B1** NJ3534.
Gladestry (Llanfair Llythynwg). *Powys* ***Village***, 4m/6km W of Kington. **28 B3** SO2355.
Gladhouse Reservoir *Midloth.* ***Reservoir***, large reservoir 5m/8km SE of Penicuik. **76 B5** NT2953.
Gladsmuir *E.Loth.* ***Village***, 4m/6km W of Haddington. **76 C3** NT4573.
Gladsmuir Hills *W.Loth.* ***Large natural feature***, small mountain range rising to height of 1168 feet or 365 metres at Leven Seat, 3m/4km N of Forth. Former mining area. **75 H5** NS9157.
Gladstone Court Museum *S.Lan.* ***Other feature of interest***, in late 19c coach house in Biggar. Authentic shops in rebuilt village street. **75 J7** NT0238.
Glaic *Arg. & B.* ***Settlement***, to W of Strone Point, 3m/5km N of Port Bannatyne. **73 J3** NS0771.
Glais *Swan.* ***Village***, 1km SE of Clydach across River Tawe. **18 A1** SN7000.
Glais Bheinn *High.* ***Mountain***, 2m/3km NE of Ardtornish Point, Lochaber district. Height 1571 feet or 479 metres. **79 J3** NM7243.
Glaisdale *N.Yorks.* ***Valley***, carrying Glaisdale Beck and running NE from Glaisdale Head to S of village of Glaisdale. **63 J6** NZ7503.
Glaisdale *N.Yorks.* ***Village***, 2m/4km W of Egton. **63 J6** NZ7705.
Glaisdale Beck *N.Yorks.* ***River***, rising on Glaisdale Moor and flowing NE to its confluence with River Esk, 1km E of Glaisdale. **63 J6** NZ7805.
Glaisdale Moor *N.Yorks.* ***Open space***, moorland on North York Moors, 4m/6km N of Rosedale Abbey. **63 J6** NZ7001.
Glaisdale Rigg *N.Yorks.* ***Inland physical feature***, mountain ridge rising to 1069 feet or 326 metres and running NE to SW, 3m/5km SW of Lealholm. **63 J6** NZ7404.
Glaister *N.Ayr.* ***Settlement***, on Arran, 5m/8km W of Brodick. **73 H7** NR9334.
Glaisters Burn *D. & G.* ***River***, stream rising on E slopes of Long Fell and flowing N to join Kirkgunzeon Lane, 1km N of Kirkgunzeon and 4m/6km NE of Dalbeattie. **65 J4** NX8767.
Glamaig *High.* ***Mountain***, 2m/3km E of Sligachan, Skye. Height 2542 feet or 775 metres. **86 B2** NG5130.
Glame *High.* ***Settlement***, on Raasay, 4m/6km S of Manish Point. **94 B7** NG5642.
Glamis *Angus* ***Village***, 10m/16km N of Dundee. Angus Folk Museum (National Trust for Scotland). **82 E3** NO3846.
Glamis Castle *Angus* ***Castle***, 1m/2km N of Glamis, mainly 17c but with parts of much earlier date; birthplace of Princess Margaret, 1930. **82 E3** NO3846.
Glan Adda *Gwyn.* ***Suburb***, to SW of Bangor city centre. **46 D5** SH5771.
Glan-bad *R.C.T.* *Welsh form of Upper Boat, qv.*
Glan-Conwy *Conwy* ***Settlement***, 3m/4km W of Pentrefoelas. **47 G7** SH8352.
Glan-Denys *Cere.* ***Settlement***, 2m/3km N of Lampeter. SN5750.
Glan-Duar *Carmar.* ***Settlement***, adjoining to E of Llanybydder. SN5243.
Glan-Dwyfach *Gwyn.* ***Locality***, in River Dwyfach valley, 4m/6km N of Criccieth. **36 D1** SH4843.
Glan-fechan *Gwyn.* ***Settlement***, 1m/2km N of Machynlleth across River Dyfi. SH7502.
Glan-hafon *Powys* ***Mountain***, 3m/4km NW of Llanrhaeadr-ym-Mochnant. Height 1991 feet or 607 metres. **37 K3** SJ0827.
Glan Honddu *Powys* ***Settlement***, 2m/3km NW of Brecon. **27 K5** SO0332.
Glan-rhyd *Powys* ***Village***, 1km E of Ystalyfera. SN7809.
Glan-y-don *Flints.* ***Village***, 1km SE of Mostyn. **47 K5** SJ1679.
Glan-y-llyn *R.C.T.* ***Locality***, 6m/9km NW of Cardiff. **18 E3** ST1284.
Glan-y-nant *Powys* ***Hamlet***, 1m/2km W of Llanidloes. SN9384.
Glan-yr-afon *Gwyn.* ***Hamlet***, 3m/5km W of Corwen. **37 K1** SJ0242.
Glan-yr-afon *Gwyn.* ***Settlement***, 3m/5km NW of Bala. **37 J1** SH9040.
Glan-yr-afon *I.o.A.* ***Settlement***, 3m/5km N of Beaumaris. SH6080.
Glanaber Terrace *Conwy* ***Locality***, 3m/5km E of Blaenau Ffestiniog. **37 G1** SH7547.
Glanaman *Carmar.* Population: 4244. ***Small town***, 3m/5km E of Ammanford, at S end of Black Mountain. **17 K3** SN6713.
Glanarberth *Cere.* ***Locality***, adjoining to E of Llechryd. SN2243.
Glanbran *Carmar.* ***Settlement***, 3m/5km NE of Llandovery. **27 G5** SN7938.
Glanderston *Aber.* ***Settlement***, 3m/5km W of Insch. **90 D2** NJ5829.
Glandford *Norf.* ***Village***, 3m/5km NW of Holt. Museum of shells. **44 E1** TG0441.
Glandwr *B.Gwent* ***Locality***, 1m/2km W of Llanhilleth. **19 F1** SO2001.
Glandwr *Pembs.* ***Hamlet***, 8m/12km N of Whitland. **16 E2** SN1928.
Glangrwyne *Powys* ***Hamlet***, 2m/3km SE of Crickhowell. **28 B7** SO2316.
Glanllynfi *Bridgend* ***Suburb***, on E side of Maesteg, over River Llynfi. **18 B2** SS8691.
Glanmule *Powys* ***Locality***, 4m/6km E of Newtown. **38 A6** SO1690.
Glannaventa *Cumb.* *See Ravenglass.*
Glanrhyd *Pembs.* ***Settlement***, 3m/5km SW of Cardigan. **26 A4** SN1442.
Glanton *Northumb.* ***Village***, 2m/3km N of Whittingham. **71 F2** NU0714.
Glanton Pyke *Northumb.* ***Settlement***, 1km W of Glanton. NU0514.
Glantwymyn *Powys* *Welsh form of Cemmaes Road, qv.*
Glanvilles Wootton (Also known as Wootton Glanville.) *Dorset* ***Village***, 6m/9km SE of Sherborne. **9 F4** ST6708.
Glanwydden *Conwy* ***Hamlet***, 2m/3km S of Little Ormes Head. SH8180.
Glanywern *Cere.* ***Settlement***, 1m/2km SE of Borth. SN6188.
Glapthorn *Northants.* ***Village***, 2m/3km NW of Oundle. Site of Roman villa 1km E. **42 D7** TL0290.
Glapwell *Derbys.* ***Village***, 3m/5km S of Bolsover. **51 G6** SK4766.
Glaramara *Cumb.* ***Mountain***, on E side of Sty Head Pass, 3m/4km NE of Scafell Pike. Height 2562 feet or 781 metres. **60 D5** NY2410.
Glas Bheinn *Arg. & B.* ***Mountain***, 4m/6km NE of Lochbuie, Mull. Height 1610 feet or 491 metres. **79 H5** NM6528.
Glas Bheinn *Arg. & B.* ***Mountain***, near E coast of Islay, 19m/30km NE of Port Ellen. Height 1545 feet or 471 metres. **72 C5** NR4259.
Glas Bheinn *Arg. & B.* ***Mountain***, on Jura, 3m/4km NW of Craighouse. Height 1840 feet or 561 metres. **72 D4** NR5069.
Glas Bheinn *High.* ***Mountain***, 3m/5km N of Inchnadamph. Height 2545 feet or 776 metres. **102 E6** NC2526.
Glas Bheinn *High.* ***Mountain***, in Skye and Lochalsh district, 2m/3km N of Glenelg. Height 1292 feet or 394 metres. **86 E2** NG8122.
Glas Bheinn *High.* ***Mountain***, 3m/5km SE of Strontian, Lochaber district. Height 2043 feet or 623 metres. **79 K2** NM8357.
Glas Bheinn *High.* ***Mountain***, in Lochaber district, 10m/14km NW of Gairlochy. Height 2152 feet or 656 metres. **87 H5** NN1397.
Glas Bheinn *High.* ***Mountain***, in Lochaber district, on N side of E end of Loch Arkaig, 3m/4km N of Achnacarry. Height 2401 feet or 732 metres. **87 H5** NN1791.
Glas Bheinn (Anglicised form: Glasven.) *High.* ***Mountain***, in Lochaber district 1m/2km E of Loch Eilde Mòr. Height 2588 feet or 789 metres. **80 D1** NN2564.
Glas Bheinn Mhòr ***Mountain***, on border of Argyll & Bute and Highland, 3m/5km SE of head of Loch Etive. Munro: height 3270 feet or 997 metres. **80 C3** NN1542.
Glas Bheinn Mhòr *High.* ***Mountain***, 1m/2km SE of head of Loch Ainort, Skye. Height 1870 feet or 570 metres. **86 B2** NG5525.
Glas-charn *High.* ***Mountain***, 1km S of head of Loch Beoraid, Lochaber district. Height 2076 feet or 633 metres. **86 E6** NM8483.
Glas Eilean *Arg. & B.* ***Island***, small uninhabited island off W coast of Luing. **79 J6** NM7311.
Glas Eilean *Arg. & B.* ***Island***, islet off SW shore of Jura 3m/4km S of Feolin Ferry. NR4465.
Glas Eilean *High.* ***Island***, islet at entrance to Loch Nevis, 1m/2km SW of Sandaig Bay, Knoydart, in Lochaber district. NG7000.
Glas Eilean *High.* ***Island***, islet in Loch Alsh, Skye and Lochalsh district, 2m/4km W of Dornie. **86 E2** NG8425.
Glas Eileanan *Arg. & B.* ***Island***, twin islets, the more easterly having a lighthouse, in Sound of Mull 2m/3km E of Scallastle Bay. NM7139.
Glas-leac Beag *High.* ***Island***, small uninhabited island, outlier of Summer Isles group, 6m/9km NE of Greenstone Point on W coast of Ross and Cromarty district. **95 F1** NB9205.
Glas-leac Mòr *High.* ***Island***, one of Summer Isles group. Lies nearly 2m/3km off NW coast of Ross and Cromarty district near Polbain. Area about 150 acres or 60 hectares. **95 F1** NB9509.
Glas Leathad Mòr *High.* ***Mountain***, summit of Ben Wyvis, 5m/8km NE of Garve. Munro: height 3431 feet or 1046 metres. **96 B5** NH4668.
Glas-loch Mòr *High.* ***Lake/loch***, small loch 1m/2km NE of Meallan Liath Mòr, in Ben Armine Forest, 10m/16km NE of Lairg. **103 J6** NC6719.
Glas Maol *Angus* ***Mountain***, 6m/9km NE of Spittal of Glenshee. Munro: height 3503 feet or 1068 metres. **89 J7** NO1676.
Glas Meall Mòr *P. & K.* ***Mountain***, 6m/9km SE of Dalwhinnie. Height 3044 feet or 928 metres. **88 D7** NN6876.
Glas Tulaichean *P. & K.* ***Mountain***, 5m/8km NW of Spittal of Glenshee. Munro: height 3447 feet or 1051 metres. **89 H7** NO0576.
Glasahoile *Stir.* ***Settlement***, on S shore of Loch Katrine, 6m/10km, NW of Aberfoyle. **81 F7** NN4608.
Glasbury (Y Clas-ar-Wy). *Powys* ***Village***, on River Wye, 4m/6km SW of Hay-on-Wye. **28 A5** SO1739.
Glaschoil *High.* ***Settlement***, 3m/4km N of Grantown-on-Spey. **89 H1** NJ0232.
Glascoed *Denb.* ***Locality***, 3m/5km W of St. Asaph. SH9973.
Glascoed (Glasgoed). *Mon.* ***Hamlet***, 3m/5km W of Usk. **19 G1** SO3301.
Glascoed *Wrex.* ***Settlement***, 4m/7km NW of Wrexham. SJ2754.
Glascorrie *Aber.* ***Settlement***, 2m/3km NE of Ballater. **90 B5** NO3997.
Glascote *Staffs.* ***Suburb***, 1m/2km SE of Tamworth town centre. **40 E5** SK2203.
Glascote Heath *Staffs.* ***Suburb***, 1m/2km SE of Tamworth town centre. SK2202.
Glascwm (Also spelled Glasgwm.) *Powys* ***Hamlet***, 8m/12km E of Builth Wells. **28 A3** SO1553.
Glascwm Hill *Powys* ***Mountain***, 4m/6km N of Painscastle. Height 1719 feet or 524 metres. **28 A3** SO1652.
Glasdrum *Arg. & B.* ***Settlement***, 1km NE of head of Loch Creran. **80 B3** NN0146.
Glasfryn *Conwy* ***Hamlet***, 2m/4km NW of Cerrigydrudion. **47 H7** SH9150.
Glasfynydd Forest *Powys* ***Forest/woodland***, 4m/7km SW of Sennybridge. **27 H6** SN8524.
Glasgoed *Mon.* *Welsh form of Glascoed, qv.*
Glasgow *Glas.* Population: 662,954. ***City***, largest city in Scotland. Port and commercial, industrial, cultural and entertainment centre on River Clyde, 41m/66km W of Edinburgh and 346m/557km NW of London. Major industrial port and important trading point with America until War of Independence. During industrial revolution, nearby coal seams boosted Glasgow's importance and its population increased ten-fold between 1800 and 1900. By beginning of 20c shipbuilding dominated the city, although industry went into decline in 1930's and is now a shadow of its former greatness. Glasgow is now seen to be a city of culture and progress. It has a strong performing arts tradition and many museums and galleries including Burrell Collection (set in Pollok Country Park). Cathedral is rare example of an almost complete 13c church. Three universities. Airport 7m/11km W. **74 D4** NS5965.
Glasgow Airport (Formerly known as Abbotsinch Airport.) *Renf.* ***Airport/airfield***, located on site of former locality, Abbotsinch, 2m/3km N of Paisley, to W of Renfrew. **74 C4** NS4766.
Glasgow Botanic Gardens *Glas.* ***Garden***, on S bank of River Kelvin, 2m/3km NW of Glasgow city centre in Kelvinside district. Contains Kibble's glass palace and houses National Begonia Collection. **74 D4** NS5767.
Glasgow Cathedral *Glas.* ***Ecclesiastical building***, impressive medieval cathedral, 1m/2km E of Glasgow city centre. The only intact surviving cathedral of Reformation on Scottish mainland, it contains intricate stone carvings, a vaulted crypt, and incomplete Blackadder aisle. **74 E4** NS6065.
Glasgwm *Powys* *Alternative spelling of Glascwm, qv.*
Glasha Burn *High.* ***River***, flowing from W slope of Bodach Mòr, then NE into Abhainn an t-Srath Chuileannaich, 5m/7km S of Oykel Bridge. **95 K2** NH3793.
Glashmore *Aber.* ***Settlement***, 2m/3km NW of Drumoak. **91 F4** NJ7600.
Glasinfryn *Gwyn.* ***Village***, 2m/3km S of Bangor. **46 D6** SH5868.
Glasllwch *Newport* ***Suburb***, 1m/2km W of Newport town centre. ST2887.
Glaslyn *Gwyn.* ***Lake/loch***, on E side of Snowdon below summit. **46 E7** SH6154.
Glaslyn *Gwyn.* ***River***, rising on E side of Snowdon summit and running E through Glaslyn (lake) and Llyn Llydaw, SW through Llyn Gwynant to Beddgelert, S through Pass of Aberglaslyn to Porthmadog and SW into Tremadog Bay off Harlech Point. SH5434.
Glaslyn *Powys* ***Lake/loch***, 4m/6km SW of Pennant. **37 H6** SN8294.

G

Glasnacardoch *High.* ***Locality***, on N side of Loch Ailort, on Ardnish peninsula in Lochaber district, 1m/2km E of Rubha Chaolais. NM7080.
Glasnacardoch *High.* ***Settlement***, on coast of Lochaber district, 1km S of Mallaig, on Glasnacardoch Bay. **86 C5** NM6795.
Glasnakille *High.* ***Settlement***, on E side of Strathaird Peninsula, Skye, 1m/2km N of Strathaird Point. Spar Cave on shore of Loch Slapin. **86 B3** NG5313.
Glaspant *Carmar.* ***Settlement***, 1km W of Capel Iwan. **17 F1** SN2836.
Glaspwll *Powys* ***Settlement***, 2m/3km S of Machynlleth. **37 G6** SN7397.
Glass *High.* ***River***, in Inverness district, running NE down Strathglass to join River Farrar 1km SE of Struy Bridge. **87 K1** NH4039.
Glass *High.* ***River***, in Ross and Cromarty district, running SE from Loch Glass to Cromarty Firth E of Evanton. **96 C5** NH6265.
Glass *I.o.M.* ***River***, rising on central mountains and flowing S to join River Dhoo on W side of Douglas, where combined stream continues along S side of town into Douglas harbour. **54 C6** SC3875.
Glass Houghton *W.Yorks.* ***Locality***, adjoining to S of Castleford. SE4424.
Glass Moor *Cambs.* ***Open space***, fenland, 3m/5km SE of Whittlesey. **43 F6** TL2992.
Glassaugh *Aber.* ***Settlement***, 3m/4km W of Portsoy. **98 D4** NJ5564.
Glassburn *High.* ***Settlement***, in Strathglass, 3m/4km NE of Cannich. **87 K1** NH3634.
Glassel *Aber.* ***Hamlet***, 1m/2km N of Bridge of Canny. **90 E5** NO6599.
Glassenbury *Kent* ***Settlement***, 2m/3km W of Goudhurst. **14 C4** TQ7536.
Glasserton *D. & G.* ***Locality***, 2m/3km SW of Whithorn. **64 E7** NX4238.
Glassford *S.Lan.* ***Village***, 2m/4km NE of Strathaven. **75 F6** NS7247.
Glasshouse *Glos.* ***Hamlet***, 3m/5km S of Newent. SO7021.
Glasshouse Hill *Glos.* ***Locality***, 4m/6km S of Newent. **29 G6** SO7020.
Glasshouses *N.Yorks.* ***Village***, 1m/2km SE of Pateley Bridge. **57 G3** SE1764.
Glassingall *Stir.* ***Settlement***, in Strathallan, 2m/3km N of Dunblane. **81 J7** NN7904.
Glasslie *Fife* ***Locality***, comprises Wester Glasslie and Easter Glasslie, to NE of Ballo Reservoir. **82 D7** NO2305.
Glasson *Cumb.* ***Village***, on line of Hadrian's Wall, 1m/2km SE of Port Carlisle. **69 H7** NY2560.
Glasson *Lancs.* ***Village***, on S bank of River Lune estuary, 4m/6km SW of Lancaster. Lighthouse. **55 H4** SD4456.
Glassonby *Cumb.* ***Village***, 7m/11km NE of Penrith. **61 G3** NY5738.
Glasterlaw *Angus* ***Settlement***, 1m/2km N of Friockheim. **83 G2** NO5951.
Glaston *Rut.* ***Village***, 2m/3km E of Uppingham. **42 B5** SK8900.
Glastonbury *Som.* Population: 7747. ***Small town***, 13m/21km E of Bridgwater. Ancient centre of Christian culture and pilgrimage; also Arthurian legends. Remains of 13c abbey. Tribunal House (English Heritage). Glastonbury Music Festival. **8 D1** ST5039.
Glastonbury Abbey *Som.* ***Ecclesiastical building***, earliest Christian foundation in England, located in Glastonbury, and now ruined. Burial place of several Saxon kings. Until 1154, abbot was premier abbot of England. In 1184, entire abbey burned to ground; rebuilding completed in 1303. **8 D1** ST5038.
Glastonbury Tor *Som.* ***Hill***, conical hill (National Trust) to E of Glastonbury, topped by ruined church. Height 518 feet or 158 metres. **8 E1** ST5039.
Glastonbury Tribunal *Som.* ***Historic house***, medieval town house (English Heritage), in High Street, Glastonbury. Reputed to have once been courthouse for Glastonbury Abbey. **8 D1** ST4939.
Glasven *High. Anglicised form of Glas Bheinn, qv.*
Glatton *Cambs.* ***Village***, 2m/4km S of Stilton. **42 E7** TL1586.
Glaven *Norf.* ***River***, rising N of Baconsthorpe and flowing in a southward loop by Hunworth to Letheringsett, then N by Glandford to North Sea, 1m/2km N of Cley next the Sea. TG0445.
Glazebrook *Warr.* ***Settlement***, 3m/4km SW of Irlam. SJ6992.
Glazebury *Warr.* ***Village***, 2m/3km SE of Leigh. **49 F3** SJ6797.
Glazeley *Shrop.* ***Village***, 3m/5km S of Bridgnorth. **39 G7** SO7088.
Gleadless *S.Yorks.* ***Suburb***, 3m/4km SE of Sheffield city centre. **51 F4** SK3783.
Gleadless Townend *S.Yorks.* ***Suburb***, adjoining to E of Gleadless, 3m/4km SE of Sheffield city centre. SK3783.
Gleadmoss *Ches.* ***Settlement***, 2m/3km W of Marton. SJ8268.
Gleadsmoss *Ches.* ***Settlement***, 4m/6km NE of Homes Chapel. **49 H6** SJ8268.
Gleann a' Chilleine *P. & K.* ***Valley***, carrying Allt a' Chilleine N towards Ardtalnaig, on SE side of Loch Tay. **81 J4** NN7238.
Gleann a' Choilich *High.* ***Valley***, running NE from Loch Coire nan Dearcag into W end of Loch Mullardoch. **87 G2** NH0723.
Gleann Airigh *Arg. & B.* ***Valley***, central valley of River Add before it reaches flood plain on Mòine Mhòr, 5m/8km NE of Lochgilphead. **73 H1** NR9296.
Gleann an Fhiodh *High.* ***Valley***, carrying River Laroch N to S shore of Loch Leven at Ballachulish. **80 B2** NN0755.
Gleann Aoistail *Arg. & B.* ***Valley***, carrying Abhainn Ghleann Aoistail S into head of Loch Tarbert, Jura. **72 E2** NR5983.
Gleann Asdale *Arg. & B.* ***Valley***, on Jura, running W between Beinn Chaolais and Aonach-bheinn. **72 C3** NR4871.
Gleann Beag *Arg. & B. See Hell's Glen.*
Gleann Beag *High.* ***Valley***, of Abhainn a' Ghlinne Bhig in Lochaber district, running W into Sound of Sleat, 1m/2km SW of Glenelg. **86 E3** NG8018.
Gleann Beag *High.* ***Valley***, carrying Abhainn a' Ghlinne Bhig E from Glenbeg to its junction with Gleann Mòr, just N of Meall a' Chaorainn. **95 K3** NH3283.
Gleann Beag *P. & K.* ***Valley***, carrying Allt a' Ghlinne Bhig S to Glen Shee at Spittal of Glenshee. **89 J7** NO1172.
Gleann Bhruthadail *W.Isles* ***Valley***, 3m/5km SE of Bragar, Isle of Lewis. **101 F3** NB3244.
Gleann Bianasdail *High.* ***Valley***, carrying stream of Abhainn an Fhasaigh SW from S end of Lochan Fada into SE end of Loch Maree. **95 G5** NH0165.
Gleann Camgharaidh *High.* ***Valley***, carrying Allt Camgharaidh NE towards Loch Arkaig, 1m/2km S of head of loch, Lochaber district. **87 F6** NM9788.
Gleann Cia-Aig *High.* ***Valley***, carrying Abhainn Chia-aig S to E end of Lock Arkaig. **87 H5** NN1890.
Gleann Còsaidh *High.* ***Valley***, carrying Abhainn Chòsaidh in Barrisdale Forest, 1m/2km N of W end of Loch Quoich. **87 F4** NG9202.
Gleann Dà-ghob *P. & K.* ***Valley***, carrying Allt Dà-ghob to N of Loch Tay, 5m/8km W of Kenmore. **81 H3** NN6744.
Gleann Domhain *Arg. & B.* ***Valley***, carrying Barbreck River in Argyll, running SW to head of Loch Craignish. **79 K7** NM8508.
Gleann Dorch *Arg. & B.* ***Valley***, on Jura, carrying Abhainn a' Ghleann Duirch SW into head of Loch Tarbert. **72 D2** NR5783.
Gleann Dubh *High.* ***Valley***, carrying River Traligill NW to Loch Assynt. River valley has extensive cave system 1m/2km SE of Inchnadamph. **102 E6** NC2621.
Gleann Dubh (Also known as Glen Dhu.) *High.* ***Valley***, steep-sided valley in Sutherland district running into head of Loch Glendhu, 4m/6km E of Kylesku Ferry. Situated in Glendhu Forest, westerly extension of Reay Forest. **102 E5** NC2833.
Gleann Dubh *High.* ***Valley***, in Morvern, carrying Black Water SW below Beinn Chlaonleud. **79 J2** NM7152.
Gleann Dubh *Stir.* ***Valley***, upper valley of Duchray Water, 4m/7km S of Stronachlachar. **80 E7** NN4003.
Gleann Dubh Lighe *High.* ***Valley***, carrying Dubh Lighe SW, 2m/3km E of Glenfinnan. **87 F6** NM9380.
Gleann Duibhe *P. & K.* ***Valley***, carrying Abhainn Duibhe, running NE to River Gaur below Loch Eigheach. **81 F2** NN4555.
Gleann Einich *High.* ***Valley***, carrying Am Beanaidh running N for 3m/4km from Loch Einich. **89 G4** NH9202.
Gleann Fearnach *P. & K.* ***Valley***, carrying Allt Fearnach, running S to head of Strathardle. **82 B1** NO0468.
Gleann Fhiodhaig *High.* ***Valley***, carrying River Meig E from N slopes of Maoile Lunndaidh to Loch Beannacharain, 2m/4km NW of Inverchoran. **95 H7** NH1247.
Gleann Fionnlighe *High.* ***Valley***, carrying Fionn Lighe SW towards Loch Eil, 4m/6km E of Glenfinnan, Lochaber district. **87 F6** NM9680.
Gleann Geal *High.* ***Valley***, carrying Abhainn a' Ghlinne Ghil in Lochaber district, running W to River Aline 4m/6km N of Lochaline. **79 J2** NM7250.
Gleann Ghrabhair (Anglicised form: Cromore.) *W.Isles* ***Village***, on S side of entrance to Loch Erisort, E coast of Isle of Lewis. Loch Cromore is small loch to S. **101 F5** NB4021.
Gleann Gniomhaidh *High.* ***Valley***, carrying stream Allt Gleann Gniomhaidh and running E from N slopes of Beinn Fhada to River Affric, 5m/7km W of Loch Affric. **87 G2** NH0320.
Gleann Goibhre *High.* ***Valley***, carrying Allt Goibhre, upper part marking boundary between districts of Inverness and Ross and Cromarty. **96 B7** NH4248.
Gleann Leireag (Anglicised form: Glen Leirg.) *High.* ***Valley***, running NW into Loch Nedd and Eddrachillis Bay, W coast of Sutherland district. **102 D5** NC1531.
Gleann Meadail *High.* ***Valley***, carrying Allt Gleann Meadail W to Inverie River, 3m/5km W of Inverie, Lochaber district. **86 D5** NM8298.
Gleann Meadhonach *High.* ***Valley***, running W to W coast of Sleat peninsula, Skye, 3m/4km S of Tarskavaig Point. **86 B4** NG5905.
Gleann Meinich *High.* ***Valley***, running SE between Meallan nan Uan and Meall na Faochaig into River Meig at Glenmeanie. **95 J6** NH2553.
Gleann Mòr *High.* ***Valley***, carrying Abhainn a' Ghlinne Mhòir SE from just N of Meall a' Chaorainn to its convergence with valley of Alladale River. **96 B3** NH4086.
Gleann Mòr *P. & K. See Keltney Burn.*
Gleann Mòr *P. & K.* ***Valley***, narrow valley through which Allt a' Ghlinne Mhòir flows W and N to join numerous other streams to form headwaters of River Tilt, 1km SE of Falls of Tarf. **89 H7** NO0176.
Gleann Mòr Barvas *W.Isles Anglicised form of Gleann Mòr Bharabhais, qv.*
Gleann Mòr Bharabhais (Anglicised form: Gleann Mòr Barvas.) *W.Isles* ***Valley***, carrying River Barvas, near NW coast of Isle of Lewis, to S of Barvas. **101 F3** NB3548.
Gleann na Guiserein (Anglicised form: Glen Guseran.) *High.* ***Valley***, carrying Abhainn Inbhir Ghuiserein stream in Knoydart, Lochaber district, running NW to Sound of Sleat at Inverguseran. **86 D4** NG7703.
Gleann na Muice *High.* ***Valley***, in Ross and Cromarty district, running S from Loch Gleann na Muice at SE of Lochan Fada, and carrying Abhainn Gleann na Muice, which then forms part of Abhainn Bruachaig at Heights of Kinlochewe. **95 G5** NH0666.
Gleann nam Fiadh *High.* ***Valley***, carrying Abhainn Gleann nam Fiadh and running between Tom a' Chòinich and Am Meallan, then turning S to enter W end of Loch Beinn a' Mheadhoin. **87 H2** NH1425.
Gleann Oraid *High.* ***Valley***, carrying River Talisker, running down to Talisker Bay on W coast of Skye. **85 J1** NG3230.
Gleann Sithidh *High.* ***Valley***, in Ross and Cromarty district, carrying Abhainn Sithidh N from N slopes of Sgurr nan Ceathreamhnan to a point 1m/2km W of Loch Mullardoch. **87 G2** NH0727.
Gleann Suileag *High.* ***Valley***, carrying An t-Suileag S into Loch Eil. **87 G6** NN0181.
Gleann Tanagaidh *High.* ***Valley***, running from S slopes of Beinn Bheag, continuing S and joining Strath Chrombuill 4m/6km NE of Kinlochewe. **95 G5** NH0768.
Gleann Tholastaidh (Anglicised form: Glen Tolsta.) *W.Isles* ***Locality***, near E coast of Isle of Lewis, on E side of valley of same name, 3m/4km SW of Tolsta Head. **101 H3** NB5244.
Gleann Udalain *High.* ***Valley***, carrying Allt Gleann Udalain, 3m/4km S of Stromeferry, Skye and Lochalsh district. **86 E1** NG8730.
Gleaston *Cumb.* ***Village***, 3m/4km SE of Dalton-in-Furness. Remains of medieval Gleaston Castle 1km NE. **55 F2** SD2570.
Glebe *T. & W.* ***Suburb***, to SW of Washington town centre. NZ3056.
Glecknabae *Arg. & B.* ***Settlement***, on NW coast of Bute, 6m/9km NW of Rothesay. **73 J4** NS0068.
Gledhow *W.Yorks.* ***Suburb***, 2m/4km NE of Leeds city centre. **57 J6** SE3137.
Gledrid *Shrop.* ***Settlement***, to E of Chirk Bank. **38 B2** SJ2936.
Glem *Suff.* ***River***, rising SW of Stradishall and flowing E then S into River Stour, 1m/2km W of Long Melford. **34 C4** TL8446.
Glemham Hall *Suff.* ***Historic house***, in park on E side of A12 road near Little Glemham. **35 H3** TM3459.
Glemsford *Suff.* Population: 3212. ***Village***, 3m/4km NW of Long Melford. **34 C4** TL8348.
Glen *D. & G.* ***Settlement***, 3m/5km W of Gatehouse of Fleet. **65 F5** NX5457.
Glen *D. & G.* ***Settlement***, to SW of Glenkiln Reservoir, 3m/4km W of Shawhead. **65 J3** NX8376.
Glen *Lincs.* ***River***, rising near Old Somerby as East and West Glen Rivers which join 1m/2km NW of Greatford, and continue as River Glen, flowing across Fens to join River Welland 5m/8km NE of Spalding. **42 E3** TF2829.
Glen *Northumb.* ***River***, rising as Bowmont Water in Scotland near English border SW of The Cheviot and flowing by Town Yetholm and Mindrum to its confluence with College Burn at Westnewton, then continuing as River Glen to its confluence with River Till, 1m/2km W of Doddington. NT9732.
Glen Achall *High.* ***Valley***, in Ross and Cromarty district, to E of Ullapool. **95 J2** NH1795.
Glen Affric *High.* ***Valley***, largely forested valley carrying River Affric NE through Loch Affric and Loch Beinn a' Mheadhoin to River Glass, Inverness district. **87 H2** NH1521.
Glen Albyn *High. See Glen Mòr.*
Glen Aldie *High.* ***Valley***, in Ross and Cromarty district, running down to S shore of Dornoch Firth on E side of Tain. **96 E3** NH7679.
Glen Almond *P. & K.* ***Valley***, to NW of Methven, carrying River Almond about 13m/20km E towards confluence with River Tay at Perth. **82 A5** NN9128.
Glen Ample *Stir.* ***Valley***, carrying Burn of Ample, running N to Loch Earn, 1m/2km E of Lochearnhead. **81 G6** NN5919.
Glen App *S.Ayr.* ***Valley***, carrying Water of App, running SW of Finnarts Bay near N end of Loch Ryan. **64 A3** NX0674.
Glen Aray *Arg. & B.* ***Valley***, carrying River Aray in Argyll, running S to Loch Fyne at Inveraray. **80 B6** NN0812.
Glen Arklet *Stir.* ***Valley***, containing Loch Arklet, located between Loch Lomond and Loch Katrine. **80 E7** NN3609.
Glen Arnisdale *High.* ***Valley***, carrying River Arnisdale, 1m/2km SE of Arnisdale. **86 E4** NG8709.
Glen Aros *Arg. & B.* ***Valley***, on Mull, carrying Aros River. **79 G3** NM5345.
Glen Arroch *High.* ***Valley***, on Skye, 3m/5km SW of Kyleakin. **86 D2** NG7321.
Glen Artney *P. & K.* ***Valley***, carrying Water of Ruchill, running NE to Strathearn at Comrie. **81 J6** NN7217.
Glen Ashdale *N.Ayr.* ***Valley***, on Arran, carrying Glenashdale Burn to Whiting Bay. **66 E1** NS0425.
Glen Auldyn *I.o.M.* ***Hamlet***, in valley of same name, 2m/3km W of Ramsey. **54 D4** SC4393.
Glen Auldyn *I.o.M.* ***Valley***, 2m/3km SW of Ramsey. **54 D4** SC4292.
Glen Avon *Moray* ***Valley***, steep-sided valley which runs NE, then E, on N side of Forest of Glenavon. **89 H4** NJ0906.
Glen Banchor *High.* ***Valley***, carrying River Calder NE to valley end, 1km NW of Newtonmore. **88 D5** NN6397.
Glen Banvie *P. & K.* ***Valley***, carrying Banvie Burn, running SE to River Garry on W side of Blair Atholl. **81 K1** NN8468.
Glen Barrisdale *High.* ***Valley***, carrying River Barrisdale in Lochaber district, to S of Loch Hourn. **86 E4** NG8704.
Glen Barry ***Valley***, between Knock Hill and Barry Hill on border of Aberdeenshire and Moray, 3m/5km SW of Cornhill. Contains settlement of Glenbarry. **98 D5** NJ5654.
Glen Bay *W.Isles Alternative name for Loch a' Ghlinne, qv.*
Glen Beasdale *High.* ***Valley***, steep-sided valley on South Morar carrying Beasdale Burn and running W to sea at Loch nan Uamh. **86 D6** NM7285.
Glen Beich *Stir.* ***Valley***, carrying Beich Burn and running S to Loch Earn, 2m/3km E of Lochearnhead. **81 H5** NN6328.
Glen Bragar *W.Isles* ***Valley***, carrying River Arnol, S of Bragar, Isle of Lewis. **101 F3** NB3042.

Glen Breackerie *Arg. & B.* ***Valley***, carrying Breackerie Water in Kintyre and running S to Carskey Bay, on S coast of peninsula. **66 A2** NR6510.
Glen Brein *High.* ***Valley***, carrying Allt Breinag in Inverness district and running N to River Feehlin at Whitebridge, 3m/5km S of Foyers. **88 B4** NH4809.
Glen Brerachan *P. & K.* ***Valley***, carrying Brerachan Water and running E to head of Strathardle. **82 B1** NO0263.
Glen Brown ***Valley***, on border of Highland and Moray and carrying Burn of Brown, running N into head of Glen Lochy at Bridge of Brown, 3m/5km NW of Tomintoul, on border of Highland and Moray. **89 J3** NJ1219.
Glen Bruar *P. & K.* ***Valley***, carrying Bruar Water and running S to River Garry, 3m/5km W of Blair Atholl. Falls of the Bruar 1m/2km NE of Calvine. **89 F7** NN8272.
Glen Callater *Aber.* ***Valley***, carrying Callater Burn and running N to join Clunie Water, 2m/3km S of Braemar. **89 J6** NO1685.
Glen Calvie *High.* ***Valley***, carrying Water of Glencalvie in Sutherland district and running N into River Carron at Glencalvie Lodge on S side of Amat Forest. **96 B3** NH4687.
Glen Cannich *High.* ***Valley***, in Inverness district, containing Loch Mullardoch and carrying River Cannich E to River Glass. **87 H2** NH1930.
Glen Carron *High.* ***Valley***, carrying River Carron, in Ross and Cromarty district, running down to Loch Carron from Loch Sgamhain. **95 G6** NH0852.
Glen Cassley *High.* ***Valley***, deep U-shaped valley carrying River Cassley, running SE, in Sutherland district. **103 G7** NC3913.
Glen Catacol *N.Ayr.* ***Valley***, running down to Catacol Bay on NW coast of Arran. **73 H6** NR9248.
Glen Chalmadale *N.Ayr.* ***Valley***, running NW to Loch Ranza on NW coast of Arran. **73 H6** NR9550.
Glen Clova *Angus* ***Valley***, steep sided glacial valley carrying River South Esk SE to confluence with Prosen Water and containing village of Clova. **89 K7** NO3570.
Glen Cluanie *High.* ***Valley***, section of Glen Shiel carrying River Cluanie, above head and to W of Loch Cluanie. **87 G3** NH0610.
Glen Clunie *Aber.* ***Valley***, narrow, steep-sided valley, with Clunie Water flowing N to River Dee at Braemar. **89 J6** NO1485.
Glen Cochill *P. & K.* ***Valley***, carrying Cochill Burn and running S to head of Strath Braan. **82 A3** NN9041.
Glen Coe *High.* ***Valley***, carrying River Coe in Lochaber district and running W to Loch Leven, 3m/5km E of Ballachulish. Scene of notorious massacre in 1692. Much of glen and country to S in care of National Trust for Scotland. Mountain peaks of The Three Sisters overlook glen to S. **80 C2** NN1557.
Glen Coiltie *High.* ***Valley***, carrying River Coiltie and running E from lower slopes of Carn a' Bhainne to Urquhart Bay on Loch Ness. **88 B2** NH4526.
Glen Convinth *High.* ***Valley***, carrying Allt Dearg N from NE of Meall Gorm to Kiltarlity. **88 C1** NH5035.
Glen Creran *Arg. & B.* ***Valley***, wooded valley carrying River Creran SW to head of Loch Creran, Argyll. **80 B3** NN0450.
Glen Croe *Arg. & B.* ***Valley***, carrying Croe Water SE to Loch Long, near head of loch on NE side. **80 D7** NN2504.
Glen Cross *W.Isles* ***Valley***, carrying Cross River, 4m/6km S of Butt of Lewis. **101 H1** NB5061.
Glen Dale *High.* ***Valley***, carrying Hamara River, 5m/8km S of Dunvegan Head, Skye. **93 H7** NG1848.
Glen Damff *Angus* ***Valley***, carrying Glendamff Burn S to Backwater Reservoir. **82 D1** NO2466.
Glen Dee *Aber.* ***Valley***, carrying upper River Dee, 10m/16km W of Braemar. **89 G5** NN9894.
Glen Derry *Aber.* ***Valley***, carrying Derry Burn and running in a N to S direction to Glen Lui. **89 H5** NO0396.
Glen Dessarry *High.* ***Valley***, carrying River Dessary in Lochaber district and running E to junction with Glen Pean, 1km above head of Loch Arkaig. **87 F5** NM9592.
Glen Devon *P. & K.* ***Valley***, carrying River Devon between Dollar and Auchterarder. **82 A7** NN9505.
Glen Dhu *High. Alternative name for Gleann Dubh, qv.*
Glen Diebidale *High.* ***Valley***, carrying River Diebidale, in Sutherland district. **96 B3** NH4583.
Glen Dochart *Stir.* ***Valley***, carrying River Dochart and running NE to join Glen Lochay at head of Loch Tay. **81 F5** NN4828.
Glen Docherty *High.* ***Valley***, in Ross and Cromarty district, running from a point 5m/9km W of Achnasheen NW to Kinlochewe. Excellent viewpoint, giving views NW to Loch Maree and surrounding mountains. **95 G5** NH0460.
Glen Doe *High.* ***Valley***, carrying Allt Doe in Inverness district and running N into Loch Ness, 1m/2km below head of loch. **88 B4** NH4108.
Glen Doll *Angus* ***Valley***, carrying White Water in Angus district and running SE to River South Esk at head of Glen Clova. **89 K7** NO2576.
Glen Douchary *High.* ***Valley***, with waterfalls, in Ross and Cromarty district, carrying River Douchary and running S between Glen Achall and Glean a' Chadha Dheirg. **95 J2** NH2593.
Glen Douglas *Arg. & B.* ***Valley***, carrying Douglas Water and running E to Loch Lomond at Inverbeg. **74 B1** NS3198.
Glen Dronach *Aber. See Forgue.*
Glen Drynoch *High.* ***Valley***, carrying River Drynoch and running W to head of Loch Harport, Skye. **85 K1** NG4330.
Glen Duror *High.* ***Valley***, carrying River Duror in Lochaber district and running W to Cuil Bay on E shore of Loch Linnhe. **80 B2** NN0154.
Glen Dye *Aber.* ***Valley***, carrying Water of Dye and running N to Water of Feugh on W side of Strachan. **90 E6** NO6484.
Glen Eagles *P. & K.* ***Valley***, carrying upper reaches of Ruthven Water, to S of Auchterarder. **82 A7** NN9308.
Glen Effock *Angus* ***Valley***, carrying Water of Effock and running NE to Glen Esk, 2m/3km W of Tarfside. **90 C7** NO4477.
Glen Einig *High.* ***Valley***, carrying River Einig and running N from N slopes of Mullach a' Chadha Bhuidhe, then NE into Strath Oykel just SE of Oykel Bridge. **95 K2** NH3498.
Glen Elchaig *High.* ***Valley***, carrying River Elchaig W below Sgùman Coinntich to head of Loch Long, Skye and Lochalsh district. **87 F2** NG9727.
Glen Ernan *Aber.* ***Valley***, carrying Ernan Water and running SE to River Don, 5m/8km E of Cock Bridge. **90 B3** NJ3310.
Glen Errochty *P. & K.* ***Valley***, carrying Errochty Water and running E from Loch Errochty to River Garry, near Calvine. **81 J1** NN7663.
Glen Esk *Angus* ***Valley***, carrying River North Esk in its upper reaches E between Auchronie and Fernybank. **90 C7** NO4678.
Glen Etive *High.* ***Valley***, carrying River Etive, Lochaber district, running SW to head of Loch Etive. **80 D2** NN1751.
Glen Euchar *Arg. & B.* ***Valley***, carrying River Euchar, in Argyll, running W and NW from Loch Scamadale to Loch Feochan. **79 K6** NM8319.
Glen Ey *Aber.* ***Valley***, carrying Ey Burn and running N to River Dee at Inverey, 4m/7km W of Braemar. **89 H6** NO0886.
Glen Ey Forest *Aber.* ***Open space***, deer forest astride Glen Ey. **89 H6** NO0886.
Glen Eynort *High.* ***Valley***, carrying River Eynort and running down to head of Loch Eynort, Skye. NG3828.
Glen Falloch *Stir.* ***Valley***, carrying River Falloch SW towards head of Loch Lomond. Falls of Falloch, 4m/7km SW of Crianlarich. **80 E5** NN3421.
Glen Farg *P. & K.* ***Valley***, carrying River Farg NE to River Earn, 5m/8km SE of Perth. **82 C6** NO1513.
Glen Fenzie *Aber.* ***Valley***, carrying Glenfenzie Burn SE between Clashanruich and Lary Hill, 5m/8km NW of Ballater. **90 B4** NJ3202.
Glen Feshie *High.* ***Valley***, carrying River Feshie in Badenoch and Strathspey district, running N to River Spey 1km below Kincraig. **89 F5** NN8594.
Glen Fiag *High.* ***Valley***, carrying River Fiag S from Loch Fiag to Loch Shin. **103 G6** NC4526.
Glen Fiddich *Moray* ***Valley***, carrying River Fiddich NE to Dufftown. **90 B1** NJ3234.
Glen Finart *Arg. & B.* ***Valley***, carrying stream in Argyll SE to Loch Long at Finart Bay on N side of Ardentinny. **73 K1** NS1790.
Glen Finglas *Stir.* ***Valley***, carrying Finglas Water SE to Black Water between Loch Achray and Loch Venachar, to W of Callander. **81 F6** NN5209.
Glen Finglas Reservoir *Stir.* ***Reservoir***, in course of Finglas Water, within Glen Finglas. **81 G7** NN5209.
Glen Finlet *Angus* ***Valley***, forested valley carrying Finlet Burn S to Newton Burn. **82 D1** NO2267.
Glen Finnan *High.* ***Valley***, carrying River Finnan, in Lochaber district, S to head of Loch Shiel. **87 F6** NM9083.
Glen Forsa *Arg. & B.* ***Valley***, on Mull, carrying River Forsa N to Sound of Mull, 2m/3km E of Salen. **79 H3** NM6039.
Glen Forslan *High.* ***Valley***, in Moidart, carrying Glenforslan River W to Glen Moidart, Lochaber district, 3m/5km S of Lochailort. **86 D7** NM7773.
Glen Fruin *Arg. & B.* ***Valley***, carrying Fruin Water SE to Loch Lomond, 2m/4km N of foot of loch. **74 A2** NS2987.
Glen Fyne *Arg. & B.* ***Valley***, carrying River Fyne SW to head of Loch Fyne, 6m/10km NE of Inveraray, Argyll. **80 D6** NN2215.
Glen Gairn *Aber.* ***Valley***, to NW of Ballater, carrying River Gairn. **90 B4** NJ3100.
Glen Garry *High.* ***Valley***, in Lochaber district, running E from Loch Quoich and containing Gearr Garry, Loch Garry and River Garry. **87 H4** NH1300.
Glen Garry *P. & K.* ***Valley***, carrying River Garry SE from Loch Garry to River Tummel, 2m/3km NW of Pitlochry. **81 J1** NN7569.
Glen Garvan *High.* ***Valley***, carrying North Garvan River NE towards Loch Eil, 2m/3km SW of Kinlocheil across Loch Eil. **87 F7** NM9574.
Glen Gheallaidh ***Valley***, carrying Allt a' Ghealladh and running E between steep hillsides, to NE of Grantown-on-Spey. Border of Highland and Moray follows river down valley. **97 J7** NJ1238.
Glen Girnaig *P. & K.* ***Valley***, carrying Allt Girnaig SW to River Garry at Killiecrankie. **82 A1** NN9466.
Glen Glass *High.* ***Valley***, carrying River Glass, Ross and Cromarty district, to W of Evanton. **96 C5** NH5667.
Glen Gloy *High.* ***Valley***, carrying River Gloy SW to Glenfintaig, 3m/4km N of Spean Bridge. **87 J5** NN2689.
Glen Golly *High.* ***River***, in Sutherland district rising on E side of Reay Forest and running SE down Glen Golly to head of Strath More. **103 G4** NC4442.
Glen Golly *High.* ***Valley***, steep-sided valley in Sutherland district, carrying Glen Golly River SE to head of Strath More. NC4243.
Glen Gour *High.* ***Valley***, carrying River Gour in Lochaber district and running E to Camas Shallachain, on W side of Sallachan Point on Loch Linnhe. **80 A1** NM9464.
Glen Guseran *High. Anglicised form of Gleann na Guiserein, qv.*
Glen Gyle *Stir.* ***Valley***, carrying Glengyle Water SE to head of Loch Katrine. **80 E6** NN3614.
Glen Hurich *High.* ***Valley***, carrying River Hurich in Lochaber district and running SW to Loch Doilet. **79 K1** NM8468.
Glen Iorsa *N.Ayr.* ***Valley***, carrying Iorsa Water, on Arran, SW into Kilbrannan Sound at N end of Machrie Bay. **73 H7** NR9239.
Glen Isla *Angus* ***Valley***, upper valley of River Isla, from source to Airlie Castle. **82 D1** NO2563.
Glen Kerran *Arg. & B.* ***Valley***, on S part of Kintyre, running SW into Conie Glen. **66 B2** NR7112.
Glen Kingie *High.* ***Valley***, carrying River Kingie in Lochaber district and running E into Glen Garry, 2m/3km SE of dam of Loch Quoich. **87 G5** NN0397.
Glen Kinglas *Arg. & B.* ***Valley***, carrying Kinglas Water in Argyll and running W to near head of Loch Fyne at Cairndow. **80 D7** NN2109.
Glen Kinglass *Arg. & B.* ***Valley***, carrying River Kinglass W into Loch Etive, Argyll, on S side of Ardmaddy Bay. **80 C4** NN1235.
Glen Kyllachy *High.* ***Valley***, running E from S slopes of Carn Eitidh into Strathdearn, 5m/7km SW of Tomatin. **88 E2** NH7424.
Glen Lednock *P. & K.* ***Valley***, carrying River Lednock SE to Strathearn at Comrie. Loch Lednock Reservoir near head of glen. **81 J5** NN7327.
Glen Lee *Angus* ***Valley***, carrying Water of Lee and running E to join Water of Mark at head of River North Esk, 3m/4km W of Tarfside. **90 B6** NO4079.
Glen Leirg *High. Anglicised form of Gleann Leireag, qv.*
Glen Ling *High.* ***Valley***, carrying River Ling SW into head of Loch Long, Skye and Lochalsh district. **87 F1** NG9432.
Glen Liver *Arg. & B.* ***Valley***, carrying River Liver W into Loch Etive, Argyll, 7m/11km from head of loch. **81 G4** NN0835.
Glen Loch *P. & K.* ***Valley***, in Forest of Atholl, to S of Loch Loch, 9m/13km NE of Blair Atholl. **89 G7** NN9874.
Glen Lochay *Stir.* ***Valley***, carrying River Lochay W to join Glen Dochart at head of Loch Tay. **81 G4** NN4836.
Glen Lochsie *P. & K.* ***Valley***, carrying Glen Lochsie Burn SE to head of Glen Shee at Spittal of Glenshee. **89 H7** NO0472.
Glen Lochsie Burn *P. & K.* ***River***, stream running SE to head of Glen Shee at Spittal of Glenshee. NO0871.
Glen Lochy *Arg. & B.* ***Valley***, carrying River Lochy W to Glen Orchy, 2m/3km E of Dalmally, Argyll. **80 D5** NN2428.
Glen Logie *Angus* ***Valley***, running S towards Glen Prosen at Balnaboth. **82 E1** NO3069.
Glen Loth *High.* ***Valley***, in Sutherland district, running S towards coast at Lothbeg. **104 E7** NC9412.
Glen Loy *High.* ***Valley***, carrying River Loy in Lochaber district and running SE into River Lochy, 2m/4km SW of Gairlochy. **87 H6** NN1084.
Glen Loyne *High.* ***Valley***, surrounding Loch Loyne, which lies between Loch Cluanie and Loch Garry. **87 G4** NH1006.
Glen Lui *Aber.* ***Valley***, carrying Lui Water SE to River Dee, 5m/8km W of Braemar. **89 H5** NO0592.
Glen Luss *Arg. & B.* ***Valley***, carrying Luss Water and running E to Loch Lomond at Luss village. **74 B1** NS3193.
Glen Lussa *Arg. & B.* ***Valley***, carrying Lussa Water on Kintyre into Ardnacross Bay, 4m/6km NE of Campbeltown. **66 B1** NR7325.
Glen Lyon *P. & K.* ***Valley***, carrying River Lyon E from Loch Lyon to River Tay, 4m/6km W of Aberfeldy. **81 G3** NN5646.
Glen Mallie *High.* ***Valley***, carrying River Mallie, in Lochaber district, E into S side of Loch Arkaig. **87 G6** NN0887.
Glen Mark *Angus* ***Valley***, carrying Water of Mark and running first NE then SE to head of River North Esk, 3m/4km W of Tarfside. **90 B6** NO4979.
Glen Markie *High.* ***Valley***, carry Glenmarkie Burn and running from W slopes of Burrach Mòr SW to River Killin, 10m/16km E of Fort Augustus. **88 C4** NH5507.
Glen Markie *High.* ***Valley***, carrying Markie Burn in Badenoch and Strathspey district and running S to River Spey 1m/2km W of Laggan Bridge. **88 C5** NN5893.
Glen Massan *Arg. & B.* ***Valley***, carrying River Massan in Argyll and running SE to River Eachaig, 2m/4km NW of head of Holy Loch. **73 K2** NS1286.
Glen Mazeran *High.* ***Valley***, running E, then NE, into Strathdearn, 5m/8km SW of Tomatin. **88 E2** NH7121.
Glen Moidart *High.* ***Valley***, carrying River Moidart SW towards Loch Moidart, Lochaber district. **86 D7** NM7572.
Glen Mona *I.o.M.* ***Hamlet***, 1m/2km N of Dhoon and 3m/5km S of Ramsey. SC4588.
Glen Mona *I.o.M.* ***Valley***, short steep valley 3m/4km N of Dhoon, carrying stream SE to E coast. Section of The Manx Electric Railway runs through valley. **54 D5** SC4689.
Glen Mòr (Great Glen). *High.* ***Valley***, large valley extending 60m/97km along Great Glen faultline from Loch Linnhe at Fort William to Moray Firth at Inverness. Contains Lochs Lochy, Oich, and Ness, and is traversed by Caledonian Canal. NE section of valley, which includes Loch Ness, is also known as Glen Albyn. **87 K4** NH3607.
Glen More *Arg. & B.* ***Valley***, on Mull, carrying two rivers: River Coladoir flows W towards Loch Schridain; River Lussa flows NE below Loch Squabain. **79 H4** NM6029.
Glen More *High.* ***Valley***, section of valley to E of Beinn a' Chaionich and 4m/6km E of Glenelg in Lochaber district, carrying River Glenmore E to Glenelg Bay. **86 E3** NG8818.
Glen More *High.* ***Valley***, carrying Allt Mòr in Glenmore Forest Park, Badenoch and Strathspey district, running N then W into head of Loch Morlich. **89 G4** NH9808.
Glen Moriston *High.* ***Valley***, carrying River Moriston, Inverness district, E from Loch Cluanie to Loch Ness. Power station for hydro-electricity scheme at Ceannacroc Bridge. **87 K3** NH4216.
Glen Muick *Aber.* ***Valley***, carrying River Muick NE from Loch Muick to River Dee, 1km S of Ballater. **90 B6** NO3187.
Glen Nant *Arg. & B.* ***Valley***, carrying River Nant S from Taynuilt to Loch Nant. **80 B5** NN0128.
Glen Nevis *High.* ***Valley***, carrying Water of Nevis, in Lochaber district, running down to Loch Linnhe at Fort William. **87 H7** NN1468.

G

G

Glen Noe *Arg. & B.* ***Valley***, carrying River Noe NW to Loch Etive, Argyll, 3m/4km E of Bonawe. **80 B4** NN0733.
Glen of Coachford *Aber.* ***Valley***, to S of The Balloch, 3m/5km SE of Keith. **98 C6** NJ4646.
Glen of Rothes *Moray* ***Valley***, traversed by A941 road and carrying Broad Burn SE to N of Rothes. **97 K6** NJ2552.
Glen Ogil *Angus* ***Valley***, carrying Noran Water, 4m/7km NW of Tannadice. **83 F1** NO4464.
Glen Ogilvy *Angus* ***Valley***, small, wide valley running in a NE direction and containing settlement of Milton of Ogilvie, 2m/3km S of Glamis. **82 E3** NO3743.
Glen Ogle *Stir.* ***Valley***, running SE down to head of Loch Earn at Lochearnhead. **81 G5** NN5726.
Glen Orchy *Arg. & B.* ***Valley***, carrying River Orchy SW to NE end of Loch Awe, Argyll. **80 D4** NN2433.
Glen Orrin *High.* ***Valley***, carrying River Orrin and running E from Am Fiar-Loch to N of Carn Doire Mhurchaidh. Contains Orrin Reservoir. **95 K6** NH3449.
Glen Ose *High.* ***Valley***, on Skye, carrying River Ose SW to Loch Bracadale. **93 J7** NG3241.
Glen Ouirn *W.Isles* ***River***, flowing W into Loch Sgibacleit, Isle of Lewis. **101 F6** NB3216.
Glen Oykel *High.* ***Valley***, carrying upper reaches of River Oykel, Sutherland district, 7m/11km SE of Elphin. **95 K1** NC3207.
Glen Parva *Leics.* ***Suburb***, 4m/7km SW of Leicester. **41 H6** SP5698.
Glen Pean *High.* ***Valley***, in Lochaber district, carrying River Pean E to junction with Glen Dessarry 1km above head of Loch Arkaig. **87 F5** NM9590.
Glen Prosen *Angus* ***Valley***, carrying Prosen Water and running SE of River South Esk at foot of Glen Clova, 3m/5km NE of Kirriemuir. **82 D1** NO2967.
Glen Quoich *Aber.* ***Valley***, in Braemar Forest, and through which flows Quoich Water in a SE direction to River Dee valley, 2m/3km W of Braemar. **89 H5** NO0893.
Glen Quoich *High.* ***Valley***, in Lochaber district, carrying River Quoich S into Loch Quoich. **87 G4** NH0107.
Glen Rinnes *Moray* ***Valley***, carrying Dullan Water and running down to River Fiddich at Dufftown. **89 K1** NJ3339.
Glen Rock *High.* ***Hill***, with rock outcrops on N and E sides, 3m/5km NW of Golspie, on SW side of Dunrobin Glen. Height 886 feet or 270 metres. **96 E1** NC8003.
Glen Rosa *N.Ayr.* ***Valley***, on Arran, carrying Glenrosa Water to Brodick Bay. **73 H6** NS0136.
Glen Roy *High.* ***Valley***, in Lochaber district, carrying River Roy and running down to River Spean at Roybridge. On sides of valley are Parallel Roads of Glen Roy, shelves or terraces marking successive levels of lake dammed by glaciers during Ice Age. **87 K6** NN2780.
Glen Sannox *N.Ayr.* ***Valley***, on Arran running NE from Cir Mhòr to E coast at Sannox Bay. **73 H6** NR9944.
Glen Scaddle *High.* ***Valley***, carrying River Scaddle in Lochaber district and running E to Inverscaddle Bay on Loch Linnhe. **80 A1** NM9668.
Glen Scorrodale *N.Ayr.* ***Valley***, carrying Sliddery Water SW from S of The Ross Valley to 1km E of Sliddery. **66 D1** NR9523.
Glen Shader *W.Isles* ***Valley***, carrying Shader River SE from NW coast of Isle of Lewis at Siadar Uarach. **101 G2** NB3953.
Glen Shee *P. & K.* ***Valley***, deep valley carrying Shee Water S from Spittal of Glenshee towards Bridge of Cally. Below Blacklunans, river becomes Black Water and valley narrows to the confluence with River Ericht. **82 C1** NO1462.
Glen Shiel *High.* ***Valley***, carrying River Shiel, Skye and Lochalsh district, running NW to Shiel Bridge and head of Loch Duich. 5m/8km SE of Shiel Bridge is site of skirmish in course of Jacobite rising, 1719. **87 F3** NG9614.
Glen Shira *Arg. & B.* ***Valley***, carrying River Shira SW into N end of Loch Fyne, 1m/2km NE of Inveraray. **80 C6** NN1112.
Glen Sletdale *High.* ***Valley***, in Sutherland district, running SE then E into Glen Loth, 2m/3km N of Lothbeg. **104 E7** NC9312.
Glen Sligachan *High.* ***Valley***, carrying River Sligachan to head of Loch Sligachan on E coast of Skye. **85 K2** NG4927.
Glen Spean *High.* ***Valley***, carrying River Spean in Lochaber district and running W through Loch Moy to Spean Bridge and River Lochy below Loch Lochy. **87 K6** NN3479.
Glen Strae *Arg. & B.* ***Valley***, carrying River Strae in Argyll and running SW to River Orchy, 2m/3km W of Dalmally. **80 C4** NN1531.
Glen Strathfarrar *High.* ***Valley***, carrying River Farrar and running E from 1m/2km E of E end of Loch Monar to its convergence with Strathglass by Erchless Castle. **87 J1** NH2638.
Glen Suie *Moray* ***Valley***, carrying Black Burn through Blackwater Forest, at S end of which it meets River Livet. **89 K2** NJ2826.
Glen Tanar *Aber.* ***Valley***, to SW of Aboyne, carrying Water of Tanar. **90 C5** NO4795.
Glen Tarbert *High.* ***Valley***, steep-sided valley in Lochaber district, between Loch Linnhe and head of Loch Sunart. From summit of glen, Carnoch River runs W to Loch Sunart, while River Tarbert runs E to Loch Linnhe. **79 K2** NM8960.
Glen Tarff *High.* ***Valley***, carrying River Tarff in Inverness district and running generally NW to Fort Augustus at head of Loch Ness. **87 K4** NH3902.
Glen Tarken *P. & K.* ***Valley***, running S to N edge of Loch Earn, 2m/3km NW of St. Fillans. **81 H5** NN6626.
Glen Tarsan *Arg. & B.* ***Valley***, in Argyll, running S to head of Loch Tarsan. **73 J2** NS0785.
Glen Tennet *Angus* ***Valley***, small, narrow, steep-sided valley through which Burn of Tennet flows in a SW direction to Water of Tarf. **90 D6** NO5183.
Glen Tilt *P. & K.* ***Valley***, carrying River Tilt SW to River Garry at Blair Atholl. **89 G7** NN8870.
Glen Tolsta *W.Isles* *Anglicised form of Gleann Tholastaidh, qv.*
Glen Torridon *High.* ***Valley***, carrying River Torridon W below Liathach peaks to head of Upper Loch Torridon. **95 F6** NG9356.
Glen Tromie *High.* ***Valley***, carrying River Tromie in Badenoch and Strathspey district and running N to River Spey, 1m/2km E of Kingussie. **88 E5** NN7694.
Glen Trool Lodge *D. & G.* ***Settlement***, on N side of Loch Trool, 4m/7km NE of Bargrennan. **67 J5** NX4080.
Glen Truim *High.* ***Valley***, carrying River Truim in Badenoch and Strathspey district and running N from Pass of Drumochter to River Spey, 5m/8km SW of Kingussie. **88 D6** NN6789.
Glen Tulchan *High.* ***Valley***, partly forested steep-sided valley carrying Burn of Tulchan SE to River Spey. **89 H1** NJ1036.
Glen Turret *P. & K.* ***Valley***, carrying Turret Burn and running SE above and below Loch Turret Reservoir to Strathearn at Crieff. Falls of Turret 2m/3km below Loch Turret Reservoir dam. Distillery at Hosh near foot of glen. **81 K5** NN8225.
Glen Uig *Angus* ***Valley***, small, narrow, steep-sided valley which runs SE, 3m/4km W of Easter Lednathie. **82 E1** NO3163.
Glen Ure *Arg. & B.* ***Valley***, carrying River Ure W into Glen Creran, 3m/5km NE of head of Loch Creran, Argyll. **80 B3** NN0647.
Glen Urquhart *High.* ***Valley***, carrying River Enrick, in Inverness district, on W side of Loch Ness above Drumnadrochit. **88 B1** NH4430.
Glen Varragill *High.* ***Valley***, on Skye, carrying Varragill River through Glen Varragill Forest and Portree Forest. **85 K1** NG4735.
Glen Village *Falk.* ***Village***, 1m/2km S of Falkirk, between Callendar Park and Union Canal. NS8878.
Glen Vine *I.o.M.* ***Locality***, 3m/5km NW of Douglas. **54 C6** SC3378.
Glenacardoch Point *Arg. & B.* ***Coastal feature***, headland on W coast of Kintyre, 1m/2km NW of Glenbarr. **72 E7** NR6538.
Glenae *D. & G.* ***Settlement***, 3m/4km N of Locharbriggs. **68 E5** NX9984.
Glenaladale *High.* ***Settlement***, on E bank of Glenaladale River, 1m/2km NW of Scamodale across Loch Shiel. **86 E7** NM8274.
Glenald *Arg. & B.* ***Settlement***, 1km SW of Garelochhead. **74 A1** NS2390.
Glenamachrie *Arg. & B.* ***Settlement***, in Glen Lonan, 4m/6km E of Oban. **80 A5** NM9228.
Glenancross *High.* ***Locality***, near coast of Lochaber district, 3m/5km N of Arisaig. NM6691.
Glenapp Castle *S.Ayr.* ***Historic house***, 19c mansion, 1m/2km S of Ballantrae. **66 E5** NX0980.
Glenarm *Angus* ***Settlement***, 3m/5km N of Dykehead. **82 E1** NO3764.
Glenbarr *Arg. & B.* ***Village***, near W coast of Kintyre, 10m/16km N of Machrihanish. **72 E7** NR6636.
Glenbatrick *Arg. & B.* ***Settlement***, on coast, to N of Jura Forest, 9m/13km N of Craighouse, Jura. **72 D3** NR5179.
Glenbeg *High.* ***Settlement***, 14m/22km SE of Ullapool. Inaccessible by road. **95 K3** NH3183.
Glenbeg *High.* ***Settlement***, 1m/2km W of Grantown-on-Spey. **89 H2** NJ0027.
Glenbeg *High.* ***Settlement***, on Ardnamurchan peninsula, 1m/2km NW of Glenborrodale. **79 G1** NM5862.
Glenbeich *Stir.* ***Settlement***, on N side of Loch Earn, 2m/3km E of Lochearnhead. **81 H5** NN6124.
Glenbervie *Aber.* ***Village***, 7m/12km SW of Stonehaven. **91 F6** NO7680.
Glenbervie *Falk.* ***Locality***, dispersed settlement on E edge of golf course, 1m/2km NW of Larbert. **75 G2** NS8484.
Glenboig *N.Lan.* Population: 2038. ***Village***, 2m/3km N of Coatbridge. **75 F4** NS7268.
Glenborrodale *High.* ***Settlement***, on Ardnamurchan peninsula, in Lochaber district, 5m/9km SW of Salen. **79 H1** NM6161.
Glenbranter *Arg. & B.* ***Hamlet***, 3m/4km SE of Strachur. **73 K1** NS1197.
Glenbreck *Sc.Bord.* ***Settlement***, 3m/4km SW of Tweedsmuir in Tweeddale. **69 F1** NT0621.
Glenbrittle *High.* ***Settlement***, 1km N of head of Loch Brittle, Skye. **85 K2** NG4121.
Glenbuchat *Aber.* ***Locality***, parish in Glen Buchat comprising Kirkton of Glenbuchat, Mains of Glenbuchat and Glenbuchat Castle, 13m/20km W of Alford. NJ3716.
Glenbuchat Castle *Aber.* ***Castle***, stronghold of Gordons, dating from 1590 (Historic Scotland), 4m/6km SW of Kildrummy. **90 B3** NJ3716.
Glenbuck *E.Ayr.* ***Village***, 6m/9km W of Douglas. **68 C1** NS7429.
Glenburn *Renf.* ***Suburb***, 2m/3km S of Paisley. NS4761.
Glenbyre *Arg. & B.* ***Settlement***, on NW shore of Loch Buie, Mull, 2m/3km SW of Lochbuie. **79 G5** NM5823.
Glencairn Castle *D. & G.* *See Maxwelton House.*
Glencalvie Forest *High.* ***Open space***, deer forest to W of Glen Calvie. **96 B3** NH4687.
Glencanisp Forest *High.* ***Open space***, deer forest SE of Lochinver, Sutherland district. Includes mountain of Canisp. **102 D6** NC1419.
Glencannich Forest *High.* ***Open space***, deer forest in Inverness district SE of Loch Monar. **87 J1** NH2433.
Glencaple *D. & G.* ***Village***, on E bank of River Nith estuary, 5m/8km S of Dumfries. **65 K4** NX9968.
Glencarron and Glenuig Forest *High.* ***Open space***, deer forest S of Loch Sgamhain. **95 H7** NH1149.
Glencarse *P. & K.* ***Village***, 5m/8km E of Perth. **82 C5** NO1921.
Glencat *Aber.* ***Settlement***, 3m/5km SW of Marywell. **90 D5** NO5493.
Glenceitlein *High.* ***Settlement***, on SE side of Glen Etive, 3m/4km NE of head of Loch Etive. **80 C3** NN1447.
Glencloy *N.Ayr.* ***Settlement***, on Arran, 1m/2km W of Brodick. **73 J7** NS0035.
Glencoe *High.* ***Village***, at foot of Glen Coe valley. **80 C2** NN1557.
Glencoe (Whitecorries) Chairlift and Ski Area *High.* ***Leisure/recreation***, 8m/13km SE of Kinlochleven. Commercial skiing in Scotland began here. Lift travels approximately 2400 feet or 730 metres to Meall a' Bhùiridh. **80 D2** NN2652.
Glenconglass *Moray* ***Settlement***, 3m/5km E of Bridge of Brown. **89 J2** NJ1722.
Glencorse *Midloth.* ***Locality***, 2m/3km N of Penicuik. Barracks of Royal Scots Regiment. 1m/2km NW, on S side of Castlelaw Hill, is Castlelaw Fort (Historic Scotland), Iron Age fort enclosing an earth house. NT2462.
Glencorse Reservoir *Midloth.* ***Reservoir***, on Pentland Hills 2m/3km W of Glencorse. **76 A4** NT2462.
Glencraig *Fife* ***Village***, 1m/2km N of Lochgelly. **75 K1** NT1895.
Glencripesdale *High.* ***Settlement***, in Morvern, Lochaber district, near S shore of Loch Sunart, 4m/6km SE of Glenborrodale across loch. **79 H2** NM6659.
Glencrosh *D. & G.* ***Settlement***, 1m/2km S of Moniaive. **68 C5** NX7689.
Glencruittein *Arg. & B.* ***Settlement***, 1m/2km E of Oban. **79 K5** NM8729.
Glencuie *Aber.* ***Settlement***, on N side of Kindie Burn, 5m/8km NE of Strathdon. **90 C3** NJ4216.
Glendaruel *Arg. & B.* ***Valley***, carrying River Ruel in Argyll and running S to head of Loch Riddon. **73 H2** NR9985.
Glendearg *D. & G.* ***Settlement***, 2m/3km N of Davington. **69 H3** NT2305.
Glendearg *Sc.Bord.* ***Hamlet***, 2m/3km NE of Galashiels. **76 D7** NT5138.
Glendebadel Bay *Arg. & B.* ***Bay***, on NW coast of Jura, 2m/3km SW of Glengarrisdale Bay. **72 E1** NR6295.
Glenderamackin *Cumb.* ***River***, rising on Mungrisdale Common and flowing SE round White Horse Bent, then N to Mungrisdale. It then turns to flow S towards Hutton Moor End before flowing SW to join St. John's Beck 1km SW of Threlkeld to form River Greta. **60 E4** NY3124.
Glendessary *High.* ***Settlement***, in Glen Dessary, 2m/3km NW of head of Loch Arkaig, Lochaber district. **87 F5** NM9692.
Glendevon *P. & K.* ***Village***, in Glen Devon, 6m/10km SE of Auchterarder. **82 A7** NN9505.
Glendevon Forest *P. & K.* ***Forest/woodland***, to NE of Glendevon. **82 A7** NN9504.
Glendevon Reservoirs *P. & K.* ***Reservoir***, consisting of Upper Glendevon Reservoir and Lower Glendevon Reservoir in Ochil Hills, 3m/5km SE of Blackford. **82 A7** NN9004.
Glendhu Forest *High.* ***Open space***, upland moorland area in Sutherland district to N of Loch Glendhu. **102 E5** NC2634.
Glendhu Hill ***Mountain***, straddling border of Cumbria and Northumberland, 6m/9km E of Newcastleton. Height 1686 feet or 514 metres. **70 A5** NY5686.
Glendoe Forest *High.* ***Open space***, deer forest, on which Allt Doe stream rises, to S of Glendoebeg. **88 B4** NH4108.
Glendoebeg *High.* ***Settlement***, 2m/3km E of Fort Augustus. **88 B4** NH4109.
Glendoick *P. & K.* ***Settlement***, 1m/2km NE of St. Madoes. **82 D5** NO2022.
Glendoll Lodge *Angus* ***Other building***, youth hostel and Mountain Rescue Post at foot of Glen Doll, 4m/6km NW of Clova. **89 K7** NO2776.
Glendoune *S.Ayr.* ***Settlement***, adjoining to SE of Girvan. **67 F4** NX1996.
Glendrissaig *S.Ayr.* ***Settlement***, 1m/2km S of Girvan. **67 F4** NX1994.
Glenduckie *Fife* ***Settlement***, on S side of Glenduckie Hill, 3m/5km E of Newburgh. **82 D6** NO2818.
Glenduckie Hill *Fife* ***Hill***, 3m/5km E of Newburgh. Height 715 feet or 218 metres. **82 D6** NO2819.
Glendue Fell *Northumb.* ***Mountain***, to NE of Kings' Forest of Geltsdale, with Larchet Hill, 1558 feet or 475 metres, as its E shoulder, 3m/5km SW of Lambley. Height 1712 feet or 522 metres. **61 H1** NY6354.
Glenduisk *S.Ayr.* ***Settlement***, on E bank of Duisk River, 3m/4km NW of Barrhill. **67 G5** NX2085.
Glendurgan Garden *Cornw.* ***Garden***, valley garden (National Trust) with trees, shrubs and laurel maze on N side of Helford River, 8m/12km S of Mawnan Smith. **2 E6** SW7627.
Glendurgan House *Cornw.* *See Durgan.*
Glenduror Forest *High.* ***Forest/woodland***, astride Glen Duror, 3m/4km SE of Kentallen. **80 B2** NN0154.
Glendye Lodge *Aber.* ***Settlement***, to NW of Bridge of Dye. **90 E6** NO6486.
Gleneagles *P. & K.* ***Settlement***, at foot of Glen Eagles, 3m/4km SW of Auchterarder. **82 A7** NN9308.
Gleneagles Hotel *P. & K.* ***Other building***, palatial hotel with two well-known golf-courses, to N of Gleneagles, 2m/3km W of Auchterarder. **82 A6** NN9111.
Glenearn *P. & K.* ***Settlement***, 2m/3km SE of Forgandenny. **82 C6** NO1016.
Glenegedale *Arg. & B.* ***Settlement***, on Islay, 4m/7km NW of Port Ellen. To W beside Laggan Bay is Islay (Port Ellen) Airport. **72 B5** NR3351.
Glenelg *High.* ***Village***, in Lochaber district on Glenelg Bay. **86 E3** NG8119.
Glenelg Bay *High.* ***Bay***, on mainland, at head of Sound of Sleat, 5m/8km SE of Kyle of Lochalsh across Loch Alsh. **86 D3** NG8119.
Glenelg Brochs *High.* ***Historic/prehistoric site***, prehistoric fortifications (Historic Scotland), in Gleann Beag 2m/3km SE of Glenelg. **86 E3** NG8119.

Glenfarg *P. & K.* ***Village***, on River Farg, at head of a narrow pass, 8m/13km S of Perth. **82 C6** NO1513.
Glenfarg Reservoir *P. & K.* ***Reservoir***, near source of River Farg, 2m/3km W of Glenfarg. **82 C6** NO1513.
Glenfeochan *Arg. & B.* ***Settlement***, 1km S of Kilmore. **79 K5** NM8824.
Glenfeshie Forest *High.* ***Open space***, deer forest astride head of Glen Feshie. **89 F5** NN8594.
Glenfiddich Forest *Moray* ***Open space***, moorland tract surrounding source of River Fiddich. **90 B1** NJ3030.
Glenfield *Leic.* ***Suburb***, 3m/5km NW of Leicester. **41 H5** SK5406.
Glenfinnan *High.* ***Village***, at foot of Glen Finnan. Glenfinnan Monument (National Trust for Scotland) to E. **87 F6** NM9083.
Glenfinnan Monument *High.* ***Other feature of interest***, to E of Glenfinnan at head of Loch Shiel. Commemorates uprising in 1745 of Jacobites who met at this spot and raised the standard of Charles Edward Stuart (Bonnie Prince Charlie), before challenging English throne. Visitor centre, with exposition of the campaign. **87 F6** NM9080.
Glenfintaig *High.* ***Locality***, with house and lodge in Lochaber district 1m/2km S of SE shore of Loch Lochy at Invergloy. NN2286.
Glenfoot *P. & K.* ***Hamlet***, 1km SW of Abernethy. **82 C6** NO1715.
Glengalmadale *High.* ***Settlement***, in Lochaber district, 1km NW of Rubha na h-Airde Uinnsinn. **79 K2** NM8653.
Glengap *D. & G.* ***Settlement***, 4m/6km NE of Gatehouse of Fleet. **65 G5** NX6559.
Glengarnock *N.Ayr.* ***Hamlet***, 1m/2km SE of Kilbirnie across River Garnock. **74 B5** NS3252.
Glengarrisdale *Arg. & B.* ***Settlement***, on N coast of Jura, 6m/9km N of Ardlussa. No road access. **72 E1** NR6496.
Glengarrisdale Bay *Arg. & B.* ***Bay***, on NW coast of Jura. **72 E1** NR6497.
Glengarry Forest *High.* ***Open space***, deer forest to S of Glen Garry between Lochs Garry and Lochy. **87 J5** NH1300.
Glengavel Reservoir *S.Lan.* ***Reservoir***, at head of Glengavel Water, 5m/8km NW of Muirkirk. **74 E7** NS6634.
Glengavel Water *S.Lan.* ***River***, issuing from Glengavel Reservoir and flowing N to Avon Water 5m/9km E of Darvel. **74 E7** NS6438.
Glengennet *S.Ayr.* ***Settlement***, 2m/3km SE of Penwhapple Reservoir and 6m/10km E of Girvan. **67 G4** NX2895.
Glengenny Muir *D. & G.* ***Open space***, moorland above River Nith, 4m/6km SE of Sanquhar. **68 D3** NS8105.
Glengolly *High.* ***Settlement***, 1m/2km SW of Thurso. **105 G2** ND1066.
Glengrasco *High.* ***Settlement***, on Skye, 3m/4km NW of Portree. **93 K7** NG4444.
Glengyle *Stir.* ***Settlement***, at NW end of Loch Katrine, 2m/3km N of Stronachlachar. **80 E6** NN3813.
Glenhead *D. & G.* ***Settlement***, 2m/4km NE of Dunscore. **68 D5** NX8987.
Glenhead Farm *Angus* ***Settlement***, at N end of Backwater Reservoir at foot of Cuilt Hill, 4m/7km SW of Balnaboth. **82 D1** NO2562.
Glenhurich *High.* ***Settlement***, on N bank of River Hurich, 3m/4km E of Pollock, Lochaber district. **79 K1** NM8368.
Gleniffer Braes *Renf.* ***Open space***, N facing hillslope 3m/4km SW of Paisley. Gleniffer Braes Country Park to E, with extensive views N over lower Clyde area and into Highlands. **74 C4** NS4460.
Glenisla Forest *Angus* ***Forest/woodland***, around head of Backwater Reservoir. **82 D1** NO2563.
Glenkerry *Sc.Bord.* ***Settlement***, 3m/4km S of Ettrick, on Tima Water. **69 H2** NT2810.
Glenkiln *N.Ayr.* ***Settlement***, on Arran, 1km SW of Lamlash. **73 J7** NS0130.
Glenkiln Reservoir *D. & G.* ***Reservoir***, small reservoir 3m/5km N of Crocketford. **65 J3** NX8477.
Glenkin *Arg. & B.* ***Settlement***, in Glen Kin, 2m/3km W of Sandbank. **73 K3** NS1279.
Glenkinchie *E.Loth. See Pencaitland.*
Glenkindie *Aber.* ***Village***, on River Don, 6m/9km SW of Lumsden. **90 C3** NJ4313.
Glenkinnon Burn *Sc.Bord.* ***River***, rising in mountains, 4m/7km NW of Selkirk, and flowing NE to River Tweed 1m/2km W of Caddonfoot. **76 B7** NT4335.
Glenlair *D. & G.* ***Settlement***, 2m/4km S of Corsock. **65 H3** NX7572.
Glenlatterach *Moray* ***Settlement***, 1km N of Glenlatterach Reservoir, 6m/9km S of Elgin. **97 K6** NJ1954.
Glenlatterach Reservoir *Moray* ***Reservoir***, 6m/10km S of Elgin. **97 J6** NJ1953.
Glenlean *Arg. & B.* ***Settlement***, at head of Glen Lean, below SE arm of Loch Tarsan, 2m/3km NE of Ardtaraig. **73 J2** NS0883.
Glenlee *Angus* ***Settlement***, at NW end of Loch Lee, 2m/3km W of Kirkton. **90 C6** NO4179.
Glenlee *D. & G.* ***Settlement***, 1m/2km SW of St. John's Town of Dalry. **68 B5** NX6080.
Glenlichorn *P. & K.* ***Settlement***, 7m/11km N of Dunblane. **81 J6** NN7912.
Glenlivet *Moray* ***Settlement***, 3m/4km NW of Tomnavoulin. **89 J2** NJ1929.
Glenlivet *Moray* ***Valley***, carrying Livet Water, or River Livet, and running NW to River Avon 8m/12km N of Tomintoul. **89 K2** NJ2126.
Glenlochar *D. & G.* ***Locality***, on River Dee, 3m/4km NW of Castle Douglas. Site of Roman fort on E bank of river. **65 H4** NX7364.
Glenlood Hill *Sc.Bord.* ***Mountain***, 3m/4km NW of Tweedsmuir. Height 1856 feet or 566 metres. **69 F1** NT0828.
Glenluce *D. & G.* ***Village***, on E side of Water of Luce near its mouth, and 9m/14km E of Stranraer. 16c Castle of Park 1km W. **64 B5** NX1957.
Glenluce Abbey *D. & G.* ***Ecclesiastical building***, remains of abbey (Historic Scotland), 1m/2km NW of Glenluce, dates in part from 12c; chapter house of 1470. **64 B5** NX1957.
Glenmallan *Arg. & B.* ***Settlement***, with jetty, on E shore of Loch Long, 3m/5km NE of Garelochhead. **74 A1** NS2496.
Glenmanna *D. & G.* ***Settlement***, below steep NE slopes of Dalzean Snout, 5m/8km S of Sanquhar. **68 C3** NS7601.
Glenmavis *N.Lan.* Population: 2332. ***Village***, forming part of New Monkland, 2m/3km NW of Airdrie. **75 F4** NS7467.
Glenmaye *I.o.M.* ***Village***, 3m/4km S of Peel. **54 B5** SC2379.
Glenmeanie *High.* ***Settlement***, in valley of River Muig, 2m/3km SW of Milton. **95 J6** NH2852.
Glenmore *Arg. & B.* ***Settlement***, in Glen More on Bute, 5m/8km NW of Rothesay. **73 J4** NS0269.
Glenmore *High.* ***River***, flowing NW into River Snizort, 1m/2km NE of Loch Duagrich, Skye. NG4240.
Glenmore *High.* ***Settlement***, on Skye, 3m/5km SW of Portree. **93 K7** NG4340.
Glenmore Forest Park *High.* ***Leisure/recreation***, to E of Aviemore, surrounding Glen More. Scottish Centre of Outdoor Training; ski school and camping available. **89 G3** NH9808.
Glenmore Lodge *High.* ***Other building***, in Glenmore Forest Park, 5m/8km SE of Aviemore. Houses National Outdoor Training Centre; includes mountain rescue post. **89 G4** NH9809.
Glenmore Natural History Centre *High.* ***Other feature of interest***, centre with wildlife exhibitions situated at Glenmore on Ardnamurchan peninsula. **79 G1** NM5862.
Glenmoy *Angus* ***Settlement***, next to Burn of Glenmoye, 3m/5km NE of Dykehead. **83 F1** NO4064.
Glenmuck Height *Sc.Bord.* ***Mountain***, 1m/2km W of Tweedsmuir. Height 1519 feet or 463 metres. **69 F1** NT0724.
Glenmuick *High.* ***Settlement***, at confluence of Abhainn Gleann na Muic and River Cassley, 3m/4km S of Duchally. **103 F7** NC3912.
Glenmuir Water *E.Ayr.* ***River***, rising on W slopes of Stony Hill and running W to Dalblair where it is joined by Guelt Water. It then continues NW to join Bellow Water and form Lugar Water 1km E of Lugar. **68 C2** NS5921.
Glennoe *Arg. & B.* ***Settlement***, on SW side of Loch Etive, 4m/6km NE of Taynuilt. **80 B4** NN0534.
Glenochar *S.Lan.* ***Settlement***, 2m/3km S of Elvanfoot. **68 E2** NS9513.
Glenogil *Angus* ***Hamlet***, 4m/7km NE of Dykehead, in valley of Noran Water. **83 F1** NO4463.
Glenprosen *Angus* ***Village***, 1m/2km SE of Balnaboth, in Glen Prosen. **82 E1** NO3265.
Glenquey Reservoir *P. & K.* ***Reservoir***, small reservoir 1m/2km SW of Glendevon. **82 A7** NN9802.
Glenquicken Moor *D. & G.* ***Open space***, moorland 3m/5km E of Creetown. **65 F5** NX5259.
Glenquiech *Angus* ***Settlement***, 3m/4km NE of Dykehead. **83 F1** NO4261.
Glenquoich Forest *High.* ***Open space***, deer forest between Loch Quoich and Loch Loyne. **87 G4** NH0107.
Glenramskill *Arg. & B.* ***Settlement***, on Kintyre, on S shore of Campbeltown Loch, 1m/2km SE of Campbeltown. **66 B2** NR7319.
Glenrazie *D. & G.* ***Settlement***, 3m/5km NW of Newton Stewart. **64 D4** NX3668.
Glenridding *Cumb.* ***Village***, on Ullswater, 1m/2km NW of Patterdale. **60 E5** NY3816.
Glenrigh Forest *High.* ***Forest/woodland***, astride Glen Righ. **80 B1** NN0563.
Glenrisdell *Arg. & B.* ***Settlement***, on Kintyre, 1m/2km N of Claonaig. **73 G5** NR8657.
Glenrossal *High.* ***Settlement***, on E side of River Cassley, 1m/2km NW of Invercassley. **96 B1** NC4604.
Glenrothes *Fife* Population: 38,650. ***Town***, New town, designated 1948, 16m/25km NE of Forth road bridge. **82 D7** NO2600.
Glens of Foudland *Aber.* ***Valley***, carrying Glen Water between Hill of Bainshole to N and Hill of Foudland to S, 6m/9km SE of Huntly. **90 D1** NJ6034.
Glensanda *High.* ***Settlement***, on NW shore of Loch Linnhe opposite Lismore, 5m/8km SW of Rubha na h-Airde Uinnsinn. **79 K3** NM8246.
Glensaugh *Aber.* ***Hamlet***, 3m/5km NE of Fettercairn, to W of Strathfinella Hill. **90 E7** NO6778.
Glensax Burn *Sc.Bord.* ***River***, rising on slopes of Dun Rig, and flowing N to join River Tweed, 2m/3km SE of Peebles. **76 A7** NT2739.
Glensgaich *High.* ***Settlement***, 6m/9km W of Dingwall. **96 B5** NH4561.
Glenshalg *Aber.* ***Settlement***, 1m/2km N of Lumphanan. **90 D4** NJ5806.
Glenshee *P. & K.* ***Settlement***, 6m/9km NW of Methven. **82 A4** NN9834.
Glenshee Chairlifts and Ski Centre *Aber.* ***Other feature of interest***, large skiing area 6m/9km NE of Spittal of Glenshee, particularly good for beginners. **89 J7** NO1378.
Glenshellish *Arg. & B.* ***Settlement***, just to S of Glenbranter. **73 K1** NS1197.
Glenshieldaig Forest *High.* ***Open space***, deer forest in Ross and Cromarty district S of Loch Shieldaig. **94 E6** NG8350.
Glensluan *Arg. & B.* ***Settlement***, 1m/2km S of Strachur. **73 J1** NS0999.
Glentaggart *S.Lan.* ***Settlement***, 2m/4km S of Glespin. **68 D1** NS8125.
Glentanar *Aber.* ***Locality***, near foot of Glen Tanar, to SW of Aboyne. Forest of Glentanar is on either side of glen. NO4795.
Glentenmont Height *D. & G.* ***Mountain***, on S side of woodland, 4m/7km W of Langholm. Height 1351 feet or 412 metres. **69 H5** NY2885.
Glentham *Lincs.* ***Village***, 7m/11km W of Market Rasen. **52 D3** TF0090.
Glenton *Aber.* ***Settlement***, on N bank of River Don, 5m/8km NE of Alford. **90 E2** NJ6420.
Glentress *Sc.Bord.* ***Hamlet***, 3m/4km SE of Peebles. **76 A7** NT2839.
Glentress Forest *Sc.Bord.* ***Forest/woodland***, 2m/3km E of Peebles. **76 A6** NT2742.
Glentrool Village *D. & G.* ***Village***, forestry village, 3m/5km W of Loch Trool. Glen Trool is valley of Water of Trool. **64 D3** NX3578.
Glentruan *I.o.M.* ***Locality***, 1km N of Bride and 9m/14km N of Ramsey. **54 D3** NX4401.
Glentworth *Lincs.* ***Village***, 11m/17km N of Lincoln. **52 C4** SK9488.
Glenuachdarach *High.* ***Settlement***, on Trotternish peninsula, Skye, 4m/6km SE of Uig. **93 K6** NG4258.
Glenuig *High.* ***Settlement***, at head of Glenuig Bay, Lochaber district. NM6777.
Glenuig Bay *High.* ***Bay***, small bay in Lochaber district, on S side of Sound of Arisaig, 2m/4km W of Roshven. **86 C7** NM6777.
Glenuig Hill *High.* ***Hill***, 2m/3km SW of Roshven, Lochaber district. Height 984 feet or 300 metres. **86 C7** NM6876.
Glenure *Arg. & B.* ***Settlement***, in Glen Creran, 3m/5km NE of head of Glen Creran. **80 B3** NN0448.
Glenurquhart *High.* ***Settlement***, on Black Isle, 4m/6km SW of Cromarty. **96 E5** NH7462.
Glenurquhart Forest *High.* ***Forest/woodland***, astride River Enrick. **88 B2** NH4430.
Glenwhappen Rig *Sc.Bord.* ***Inland physical feature***, saddle at height of 1968 feet or 600 metres between Gathersnow Hill and Coomb Hill, 2m/3km NW of Tweedsmuir. **69 F1** NT0625.
Glenwhilly *D. & G.* ***Settlement***, 7m/11km E of Cairnryan. **64 B3** NX1771.
Gleouraich *High.* ***Mountain***, peak on Glenquoich Forest, Lochaber district, 3m/4km NW of dam of Loch Quoich. Munro: height 3395 feet or 1035 metres. **87 G4** NH0305.
Glespin *S.Lan.* ***Hamlet***, 3m/4km SW of Douglas. **68 D1** NS8028.
Glespin Burn *S.Lan.* ***River***, rising to S of Mosscastle Hill, 3m/4km W of Crawfordjohn, and flowing N to Douglas Water 1km E of Glespin. **68 D1** NS8128.
Gletness *Shet.* ***Settlement***, on South Voe of Gletness, to SW of Glet Ness headland, on E coast of Mainland. **109 D7** HU4751.
Glevum *Glos. See Gloucester.*
Glewstone *Here.* ***Village***, 3m/5km SW of Ross-on-Wye. **28 E6** SO5522.
Glimps Holm *Ork.* ***Island***, small uninhabited island between islands of Burray and Mainland, linked to both by Churchill Barrier. **107 D8** ND4799.
Glinton *Peter.* Population: 1663. ***Village***, 5m/9km NW of Peterborough. **42 E5** TF1505.
Globe Town *Gt.Lon.* ***Suburb***, in borough of Tower Hamlets, 2m/4km NE of London Bridge. TQ3582.
Gloddfa Ganol Mining Museum *Gwyn.* ***Other feature of interest***, 1km N of Blaenau Ffestiniog. Underground tours in world's largest working slate mine, with miles of tunnels and displays of machinery. **37 F1** SH6947.
Glodwick *Gt.Man.* ***Suburb***, 1m/2km SE of Oldham town centre. SD9404.
Glog Hill *Powys* ***Mountain***, 6m/10km NW of Presteigne. Height 1335 feet or 407 metres. **28 B2** SO2269.
Glooston *Leics.* ***Village***, 6m/9km N of Market Harborough. Site of Roman building to N. **42 A6** SP7595.
Glororum *Northumb.* ***Settlement***, 1m/2km SW of Bamburgh. **77 K7** NU1633.
Glossop *Derbys.* Population: 15,385. ***Town***, on edge of Peak District National Park, 13m/22km E of Manchester, at foot of Snake Pass. Former cotton town. 17c houses in Old Glossop. Remains of Roman fort of Melandra. **50 C3** SK0394.
Gloster Hill *Northumb.* ***Hamlet***, 1km W of Amble. **71 H3** NU2504.
Gloucester *Glos.* Population: 114,003. ***City***, industrial city on River Severn, on site of Roman town of Glevum, 32m/52km NE of Bristol. Norman era saw Gloucester grow in political importance, from here William the Conqueror ordered survey of his Kingdom which resulted in Domesday Book of 1086. City became a religious centre during middle ages. Cathedral built in mixture of Norman and Perpendicular styles, has cloisters and England's largest stained glass window, dating from 14c. Edward II is buried in cathedral. Remains of 15c-16c Franciscan friary, Greyfriars, (English Heritage). Historic docks, now largely redeveloped, on Gloucester and Sharpness Canal. Three Choirs Festival held every third year. **29 H7** SO8318.
Gloucester Cathedral *Glos.* ***Ecclesiastical building***, in centre of Gloucester, dating from 1089 but particularly noted for its Perpendicular architecture. The E window, largest in country, is said to have been given in commemoration of Battle of Crecy. Other features of note are Lady Chapel, choir stalls and cloisters. Burial place of Edward II. **29 H7** SO8318.
Gloucestershire and Warwickshire Railway *Glos.* ***Other feature of interest***, tourist steam railway based at Toddington, with line extending W past Winchcombe and Gretton, along escarpment of Cotswold Hills. **30 B6** SP0430.
Gloup *Shet.* ***Settlement***, on Yell, on W side of Gloup Voe. **108 E2** HP5004.
Gloup Holm *Shet.* ***Island***, small island off N coast of Yell. **108 D2** HP4806.
Gloup Ness *Shet.* ***Coastal feature***, headland on N coast of Yell, on E side of entrance to Gloup Voe. **108 E2** HP5005.
Glover *T. & W.* ***Locality***, industrial estate in E part of Washington. NZ3157.
Glover's Hill *Staffs.* ***Locality***, 1m/2km SE of Rugeley. SK0516.
Gloweth *Cornw.* ***Settlement***, 2m/3km W of Truro. **2 E4** SW7945.

Glunimore Island *Arg. & B.* ***Island***, islet lying 1km SE of Sheep Island off S coast of Kintyre. NR7405.
Glusburn *N.Yorks.* Population: 6859. ***Locality***, 4m/7km NW of Keighley. **57 F5** SE0044.
Gluss *Shet.* ***Settlement***, comprises North and South Gluss, 1km from E coast of Mainland, near Gluss Voe. **108 C5** HU3477.
Gluss Isle *Shet.* ***Coastal feature***, peninsula on NE coast of Mainland on W side of entrance to Sullom Voe. Narrow neck of land joins it to rest of Mainland and separates Sullom Voe from Gluss Voe, inlet to W. **108 C5** HU3778.
Glutt Water *High.* ***River***, in Caithness district, flowing N and joining Rumsdale Water to form River Thurso 4m/7km S of Altnabreac. **104 E5** ND0039.
Glyder Fach *Conwy* ***Mountain***, 4m/7km W of Capel Curig. Height 3260 feet or 994 metres. **46 E7** SH6558.
Glyder Fawr *Gwyn.* ***Mountain***, 5m/8km W of Capel Curig. Height 3277 feet or 999 metres. **46 E7** SH6457.
Glyme *Oxon.* ***River***, rising E of Chipping Norton and flowing SE to Wootton, then S through lake in park of Blenheim Palace, Woodstock, and into River Evenlode at S edge of park. SP4414.
Glympton *Oxon.* ***Village***, 3m/5km NW of Woodstock. **31 F6** SP4221.
Glyn *Conwy* ***Settlement***, 3m/4km NW of Betws-y-coed. **47 F7** SH7457.
Glyn Ceiriog *Wrex.* ***Village***, on River Ceiriog, 3m/4km S of Llangollen. **38 B2** SJ2037.
Glyn-Cywarch *Gwyn.* ***Settlement***, 3m/4km NE of Harlech. **37 F2** SH6034.
Glyn-neath (Glyn-nedd). *N.P.T.* Population: 4616. ***Village***, 10m/16km NE of Neath. **18 B1** SN8806.
Glyn-nedd *N.P.T. Welsh form of Glyn-neath, qv.*
Glyn Tarell *Powys* ***Valley***, carrying River Tarell, 5m/8km SW of Brecon. **27 J6** SN9723.
Glynarthen *Cere.* ***Hamlet***, 5m/8km N of Newcastle Emlyn. **26 C4** SN3148.
Glyncoch *R.C.T.* Population: 3237. ***Village***, 1m/2km N of Pontypridd. **18 D2** ST0792.
Glyncorrwg *N.P.T.* ***Village***, 5m/8km N of Maesteg. **18 B2** SS8799.
Glynde *E.Suss.* ***Village***, below South Downs, 3m/5km E of Lewes. **13 H6** TQ4509.
Glynde Place *E.Suss.* ***Historic house***, Elizabethan mansion restored in 18c, with fine views of South Downs, 3m/4km E of Lewes. Houses collection of paintings and displays relating to history of house and its occupants. **13 H6** TQ4509.
Glyndebourne *E.Suss.* ***Historic house***, Elizabethan house with 19c and 20c additions, 2m/4km E of Lewes. Annual summer opera season in opera house within gardens, started 1934. New Opera House opened 1994. **13 H5** TQ4510.
Glyndyfrdwy *Denb.* ***Village***, 4m/6km W of Llangollen. **38 A1** SJ1542.
Glynebwy *B.Gwent Welsh form of Ebbw Vale, qv.*
Glynllifon Park *Gwyn.* ***Leisure/recreation***, country park 1m/2km NW of Penygroes. Features country walk, historic country garden, sculpture workshop and visitor centre. **46 C7** SH4554.
Glynogwr *Bridgend* ***Village***, 6m/9km NE of Bridgend. **18 C3** SS9687.
Glyntaff *R.C.T.* ***Locality***, 1m/2km SE of Pontypridd. **18 D3** ST0889.
Glynteg *Carmar.* ***Hamlet***, 4m/6km SE of Newcastle Emlyn. **17 G1** SN3637.
Gnosall *Staffs.* Population: 4338. ***Village***, 6m/10km W of Stafford. **40 A3** SJ8220.
Gnosall Heath *Staffs.* ***Hamlet***, 1km SW of Gnosall. **40 A4** SJ8220.
Goadby *Leics.* ***Village***, 7m/12km N of Market Harborough. **42 A6** SP7598.
Goadby Marwood *Leics.* ***Village***, 5m/8km NE of Melton Mowbray. **42 A3** SK7826.
Goat Fell *N.Ayr.* ***Mountain***, summit (National Trust for Scotland) of Arran, 4m/6km N of Brodick. Height 2867 feet or 874 metres. **73 H6** NR9941.
Goat Lees *Kent* ***Locality***, adjoining to N of Ashford. TR0145.
Goatacre *Wilts.* ***Village***, 4m/6km N of Calne. **20 D4** SU0177.
Goatfield *Arg. & B.* ***Settlement***, adjoining to NW of Furnace, on N shore of Loch Fyne. **80 B7** NN0100.
Goathill *Dorset* ***Hamlet***, 3m/4km E of Sherborne. **9 F3** ST6717.
Goathland *N.Yorks.* ***Village***, below Goathland Moor, 7m/11km SW of Whitby. **63 K6** NZ8301.
Goathurst *Som.* ***Village***, 3m/5km SW of Bridgwater. **8 B1** ST2534.
Goathurst Common *Kent* ***Locality***, 3m/5km SW of Sevenoaks. TQ4952.
Gob na h-Airde Mòire *W.Isles* ***Coastal feature***, headland on W coast of Isle of Lewis N of Loch Resort, opposite Scarp. **100 C6** NB0117.
Gob na Milaid *W.Isles* ***Coastal feature***, headland with beacon on E coast of Isle of Lewis, 1m/2km S of Kebock Head. **101 G6** NB4211.
Gob Rubh' Uisenis *W.Isles* ***Coastal feature***, headland with lighthouse, at SE tip of Isle of Lewis, 4m/7km S of entrance to Loch Shell. **101 F7** NB3503.
Gob y Deigan *I.o.M.* ***Coastal feature***, small point along stretch of shingle beach, 3m/5km NE of Peel. **54 B5** SC2887.
Gobannium *Mon. See Abergavenny.*
Gobernuisgeach *High.* ***Settlement***, in Caithness district, on Berriedale Water, 7m/12km E of Kinbrace. **104 E5** NC9831.
Gobhaig (Anglicised form: Govig.) *W.Isles* ***Settlement***, on coast of North Harris, 2m/4km SE of Huisinis. **100 C7** NB0109.
Goblin's Cave (Gaelic name: Corrie na Urisgean.) *Stir.* ***Cave***, near E end of Loch Katrine. **81 F7** NN4807.
Gobowen *Shrop.* Population: 2823. ***Village***, 3m/4km N of Oswestry. **38 B2** SJ3033.
Gòdag *High.* ***Island***, islet 1km N of Muck. **85 K6** NM4181.
Godalming *Surr.* Population: 20,630. ***Town***, old town with narrow streets, 4m/7km SW of Guildford. Small market house; some half-timbered houses. Once an important wool town. Charterhouse public school on NW outskirts. **22 C7** SU9643.
Goddard's Corner *Suff.* ***Settlement***, 1m/2km N of Dennington. TM2868.
Goddard's Green *Kent* ***Hamlet***, 3m/4km E of Cranbrook. TQ8134.
Goddard's Green *Kent* ***Locality***, adjoining to SW of Cranbrook. TQ7635.
Goddards Green *W.Suss.* ***Hamlet***, 2m/3km W of Burgess Hill. TQ2820.
Godden Green *Kent* ***Hamlet***, 2m/3km E of Sevenoaks. TQ5555.
Goddington *Gt.Lon.* ***Suburb***, in borough of Bromley, 1m/2km E of Orpington. TQ4765.
Godford Cross *Devon* ***Settlement***, 2m/4km NW of Honiton. **7 K5** ST1302.
Godington *Oxon.* ***Settlement***, 5m/8km NE of Bicester. SP6327.
Godley *Gt.Man.* ***Suburb***, adjoining to E of Hyde. SJ9595.
Godleybrook *Staffs.* ***Settlement***, 2m/3km NW of Cheadle. SJ9744.
Godmanchester *Cambs.* Population: 5243. ***Small town***, on River Great Ouse opposite, and S of, Huntingdon. Site of Roman settlement of Durovigutum. Charter granted in 1212. 13c bridge spans river. **33 F2** TL2470.
Godmanstone *Dorset* ***Village***, 4m/7km N of Dorchester. **9 F5** SY6697.
Godmersham *Kent* ***Village***, on Great Stour River, 6m/9km NE of Ashford. **15 F2** TR0650.
Godney *Som.* ***Hamlet***, 3m/4km NW of Glastonbury. ST4842.
Godolphin Cross *Cornw.* ***Hamlet***, 4m/6km NW of Helston. **2 D5** SW6031.
Godolphin House *Cornw.* ***Historic house***, 17c house, former home of Earls of Godolphin, 1km NW of Godolphin Cross. **2 C5** SW6031.
Godor *Powys* ***Settlement***, 4m/7km W of Four Crosses. **38 B4** SJ2018.
Godre'r-graig *N.P.T.* ***Locality***, 2m/3km SW of Ystalyfera. **18 A1** SN7507.
Godrevy Island *Cornw.* ***Island***, with lighthouse off N coast opposite Godrevy Point. **2 C4** SW5743.
Godrevy Point *Cornw.* ***Coastal feature***, headland (National Trust), 5m/8km NW of Camborne. SW5743.
Godshill *Hants.* ***Hamlet***, 2m/3km E of Fordingbridge. **10 C3** SU1714.
Godshill *I.o.W.* ***Village***, 4m/6km W of Shanklin. **11 G6** SZ5281.
Godstone *Staffs.* ***Settlement***, 1m/2km SW of Church Leigh, 4m/7km W of Uttoxeter. SK0134.
Godstone *Surr.* Population: 2399. ***Village***, 5m/7km E of Redhill. **23 G6** TQ3451.
Godwell *Devon* ***Hamlet***, 1km SE of Ivybridge. SX6455.
Godwick *Norf.* ***Settlement***, 1m/2km NE of Tittleshall. TF9022.
Goetre *Mon.* ***Village***, 4m/6km NE of Pontypool. **19 G1** SO3205.
Goff's Oak *Herts.* ***Locality***, residential locality, 3m/4km W of Cheshunt. **23 G1** TL3203.
Gog Magog Hills *Cambs.* ***Large natural feature***, range of low chalk hills 4m/6km SE of Cambridge. Wandlebury earthwork at summit. **33 H3** TL4953.
Gogar *Edin.* ***Hamlet***, 1m/2km SE of Edinburgh (Turnhouse) Airport. **75 K3** NT1672.
Gogar Burn *Edin.* ***River***, rising 2m/3km S of East Calder and flowing NE to Union Canal, under which it passes, then N and W, sometimes underground, to River Almond, 1m/2km E of Kirkliston. **75 J4** NT1374.
Gogarbank *Edin.* ***Locality***, 1m/2km S of Gogar. NT1770.
Gogarth *Conwy* ***Settlement***, 1m/2km NW of Llandudno. **47 F4** SH7682.
Goginan *Cere.* ***Hamlet***, 4m/7km NW of Devil's Bridge. **37 F7** SN6881.
Gogo Water *N.Ayr.* ***River***, rising on hills 4m/6km E of Largs and flowing through town to Firth of Clyde. **74 A5** NS2059.
Goil *Arg. & B.* ***River***, in Argyll flowing S to head of Loch Goil. **80 C7** NN1901.
Goile Chroic *W.Isles* ***Bay***, small bay on NW coast of Isle of Lewis to N of Bru. **101 F2** NB3451.
Goirtean a' Chladaich *High.* ***Settlement***, on NW shore of Loch Linnhe, 3m/5km SW of Fort William across Loch Linnhe. **87 G7** NN0570.
Goirtein *Arg. & B.* ***Settlement***, on SE shore of Loch Fyne, 5m/8km E of Lochgilphead across loch. **73 H2** NR9589.
Golan *Gwyn.* ***Hamlet***, 4m/6km NW of Porthmadog. **36 E1** SH5242.
Golant *Cornw.* ***Village***, on W bank of River Fowey, 2m/3km N of Fowey. **4 B5** SX1254.
Golberdon *Cornw.* ***Village***, 2m/3km NW of Callington. **4 D3** SX3271.
Golborne *Gt.Man.* Population: 21,693. ***Town***, 6m/9km N of Warrington. **49 F3** SJ6097.
Golcar *W.Yorks.* ***Village***, 3m/5km W of Huddersfield. **50 D1** SE0915.
Gold Hill *Bucks.* ***Locality***, to SW of Chalfont St. Peter town centre. SU9990.
Gold Hill *Cambs.* ***Settlement***, on S side of New Bedford River, 1m/2km SE of Welney. **43 J6** TL5392.
Gold Hill *Dorset* ***Village***, adjoining to N of Child Okeford, 2m/4km E of Sturminster Newton. ST8313.
Gold Hill *Here.* ***Locality***, 4m/7km NW of Ledbury. SO6743.
Gold Street *Kent* ***Locality***, adjoining to E of Sole Street and 4m/7km S of Gravesend. TQ6667.
Goldcliff *Newport* ***Village***, near coast, 5m/8km SE of Newport. **19 G3** ST3683.
Golden Cap *Dorset* ***Hill***, summit of Wear Cliffs on coast, 4m/7km E of Lyme Regis across Lyme Bay and midway between Black Ven, W of Charmouth, and Eype Mouth, SW of Bridport. Height 626 feet or 191 metres. **8 D5** SY4092.
Golden Cross *E.Suss.* ***Village***, 4m/6km NW of Hailsham. **13 J5** TQ5312.
Golden Green *Kent* ***Village***, 3m/5km E of Tonbridge. **23 K7** TQ6348.
Golden Grove *Carmar.* ***Hamlet***, 3m/5km SW of Llandeilo. **17 J3** SN5819.
Golden Hill *Bristol* ***Suburb***, 2m/4km N of Bristol city centre. ST5876.
Golden Hill *Pembs.* ***Suburb***, 1km N of Pembroke. SM9802.
Golden Pot *Hants.* ***Hamlet***, 3m/4km N of Alton. **22 A7** SU7143.
Golden Valley *Derbys.* ***Hamlet***, 2m/3km NE of Ripley. SK4251.
Golden Valley *Glos.* ***Locality***, 3m/5km W of Cheltenham. **29 J6** SO9022.
Golden Valley *Here.* ***Locality***, 4m/6km S of Bromyard. SO6549.
Golden Valley *Here.* ***Valley***, carrying River Dore, to N and S of Vowchurch. **28 C5** SO3536.
Goldenacre *Edin.* ***Suburb***, 1m/2km N of Edinburgh city centre. NT2475.
Goldenhill *Stoke* ***Locality***, 1m/2km N of Tunstall. **49 H7** SJ8553.
Golders Green *Gt.Lon.* ***Suburb***, in borough of Barnet, 6m/10km NW of Charing Cross. **23 F3** TQ2488.
Goldhanger *Essex* ***Village***, off Goldhanger Creek, 4m/6km E of Maldon. **24 E1** TL9008.
Goldielea *D. & G.* ***Settlement***, 3m/5km SW of Dumfries. **65 K3** NX9373.
Golding *Shrop.* ***Settlement***, 3m/5km SW of Cressage. **38 E5** SJ5403.
Goldington *Beds.* ***Suburb***, E district of Bedford. **32 D3** TL0750.
Goldrill Beck *Cumb.* ***River***, issuing from Brothers Water and flowing N into Ullswater, 1km N of Patterdale. **60 E5** NY3916.
Golds Green *W.Mid.* ***Suburb***, 2m/3km NW of West Bromwich town centre. SO9893.
Goldsborough *N.Yorks.* ***Hamlet***, near North Sea coast, 5m/7km NW of Whitby. **63 K5** NZ8314.
Goldsborough *N.Yorks.* ***Village***, 2m/3km E of Knaresborough. Hall dates from early 17c. **57 J4** SE3856.
Goldsithney *Cornw.* ***Village***, 4m/7km E of Penzance. **2 C5** SW5430.
Goldstone *Shrop.* ***Settlement***, 1m/2km E of Lockleywood. SJ7028.
Goldthorn Park *W.Mid.* ***Suburb***, S district of Wolverhampton. SO9196.
Goldthorpe *S.Yorks.* ***Town***, 7m/12km W of Doncaster. **51 G2** SE4604.
Goldworthy *Devon* ***Hamlet***, 4m/7km SW of Bideford. **6 B3** SS3922.
Golford *Kent* ***Hamlet***, 1m/2km E of Cranbrook. TQ7936.
Gollanfield *High.* ***Settlement***, 2m/3km SE of Ardersier. **97 F6** NH8053.
Gollinglith Foot *N.Yorks.* ***Settlement***, 4m/7km W of Masham. Ford over River Burn. SE1581.
Golly *Wrex.* ***Settlement***, 2m/3km E of Hope. SJ3358.
Golspie *High.* Population: 1434. ***Village***, on E coast of Sutherland district, 15m/24km SW of Helmsdale. **97 F2** NH8399.
Golspie Burn *High.* ***River***, flowing SE to E coast of Sutherland district, NE of Golspie. **97 F1** NC8300.
Goltho *Lincs.* ***Locality***, site of former village, 1m/2km SW of Wragby. TF1177.
Golval *High.* ***Settlement***, on E bank of Halladale River, 1m/2km SE of Melvich. **104 D2** NC8962.
Gomeldon *Wilts.* ***Village***, 1km SW of Porton and 5m/6km NE of Salisbury. **10 C1** SU1835.
Gomersal *W.Yorks.* ***Small town***, 1m/2km E of Cleckheaton. **57 H7** SE2026.
Gometra *Arg. & B.* ***Island***, small sparsely populated island off W end of Ulva. Steep cliffs with columns of basalt in places. Road bridge connection with Ulva. **78 E3** NM3641.
Gometra House *Arg. & B.* ***Settlement***, on Gometra, 1km NE of Rubha Maol na Mine. **78 E3** NM3540.
Gomshall *Surr.* ***Village***, 6m/9km E of Guildford. **22 D7** TQ0847.
Gonachan *Stir.* ***Settlement***, 1m/2km E of Fintry, at crossing point of Endrick Water. **74 E2** NS6386.
Gonachan Burn *Stir.* ***River***, stream rising on Campsie Fells and flowing down Gonachan Glen to join Endrick Water 1m/2km SE of Fintry. **74 E2** NS6386.
Gonalston *Notts.* ***Village***, 1m/2km NE of Lowdham. **41 J1** SK6747.
Gonerby Hill Foot *Lincs.* ***Village***, 1m/2km NW of Grantham and 1km SE of Great Gonerby. SK9037.
Gonfirth *Shet.* ***Settlement***, at head of Gon Firth, 2m/4km SW of Voe. **109 C6** HU3761.
Good Easter *Essex* ***Village***, 2m/3km E of Leaden Roding. **33 K7** TL6212.
Goodber Common *Lancs.* ***Open space***, moorland between River Roeburn and River Hindburn, 4m/7km S of Low Bentham. **56 B3** SD6263.
Goodbush Hill ***Mountain***, on border of East Ayrshire and South Lanarkshire, 6m/10km S of Strathaven. Height 1558 feet or 475 metres. **75 F7** NS7035.
Gooderstone *Norf.* ***Village***, 4m/6km E of Stoke Ferry. **44 B5** TF7602.
Goodie Water *Stir.* ***River***, flowing SE from Lake of Menteith into River Forth, 6m/10km NW of Stirling. **74 E1** NS7096.

Goodleigh *Devon* ***Village***, 3m/5km E of Barnstaple. **6 E2** SS5934.
Goodmanham *E.Riding* ***Village***, 1m/2km NE of Market Weighton. **58 E5** SE8943.
Goodmanham Wold *E.Riding* ***Open space***, 3m/4km NE of Market Weighton. **59 F5** SE9043.
Goodmayes *Gt.Lon.* ***Suburb***, in borough of Redbridge, 2m/3km E of Ilford. TQ4686.
Goodnestone *Kent* ***Village***, 2m/3km E of Faversham. **25 G5** TR0461.
Goodnestone *Kent* ***Village***, 2m/3km S of Wingham. **15 H2** TR2554.
Goodnestone Park *Kent* ***Garden***, 14 acres of woodland and walled garden with old roses, to S of Goodnestone and 2m/3km NE of Aylesham. **15 H2** TR2554.
Goodrich *Here.* ***Village***, above River Wye, 4m/6km SW of Ross-on-Wye. Goodrich Castle 1km NE. **28 E7** SO5719.
Goodrich Castle *Here.* ***Castle***, massive remains of largely 13c castle (English Heritage), 1km NE of Goodrich beside River Wye. **28 E7** SO5719.
Goodrington *Torbay* ***Locality***, coastal and residential district to S of Paignton, including Goodrington Sands to S of Roundham Head. **5 J5** SX8958.
Goodshaw *Lancs.* ***Village***, 2m/3km N of Rawtenstall. SD8125.
Goodshaw Fold *Lancs.* ***Hamlet***, 1km N of Goodshaw, 3m/4km N of Rawtenstall. SD8026.
Goodwick (Wdig). *Pembs.* Population: 1933. ***Village***, on W side of Fishguard Bay. Terminal for rail and car ferry services to Ireland. **16 C1** SM9438.
Goodwood House *W.Suss.* ***Historic house***, 18c mansion 3m/5km NE of Chichester. Art collection. Racecourse at N end of Goodwood Park. **12 B6** SU8808.
Goodwood Racecourse *W.Suss.* ***Racecourse***, 1m/2km SE of Singleton and 5m/8km NW of Chichester. Flat-racing course, with eighteen race days a year, including five-day Goodwood Festival meeting in July. **12 B5** SU8811.
Goodworth Clatford (Also known as Lower Clatford.) *Hants.* ***Village***, 2m/3km S of Andover. **21 G7** SU3642.
Goodyers End *Warks.* ***Locality***, 2m/3km SW of Bedworth. **41 F7** SP3385.
Goodyhills *Cumb.* ***Settlement***, adjoining to SE of Holme St. Cuthbert, 3m/5km NE of Allonby. NY1046.
Goole *E.Riding* Population: 19,410. ***Town***, inland port on River Ouse at its confluence with River Don, 23m/37km W of Kingston upon Hull. **58 D7** SE7423.
Goole Fields *E.Riding* ***Settlement***, 2m/3km S of Goole. **51 K1** SE7520.
Goole Moors ***Open space***, lowland on border of North Lincolnshire and South Yorkshire, 4m/6km NW of Crowle. **51 K1** SE7317.
Goom's Hill *Worcs.* ***Settlement***, 7m/11km N of Evesham. SP0254.
Goon Piper *Cornw.* ***Hamlet***, 3m/5km S of Truro. SW8139.
Goonbell *Cornw.* ***Village***, on SE side of St. Agnes. **2 E4** SW7249.
Goonhavern *Cornw.* ***Village***, 2m/3km E of Perranporth. World in Miniature model village. **2 E3** SW7853.
Goonhilly Downs *Cornw.* ***Open space***, 5m/8km SE of Helston. Barren uplands on Lizard peninsula, with many ancient earthworks. Nature reserve. Radio station with prominent aerials. **2 D6** SW7319.
Goonvrea *Cornw.* ***Hamlet***, 1m/2km SE of St. Agnes Head. SW7049.
Goose Green *Essex* ***Hamlet***, 6m/10km NW of Clacton-on-Sea. TM1425.
Goose Green *Essex* ***Settlement***, 4m/6km SE of Lawford. TM1327.
Goose Green *Gt.Man.* ***Suburb***, 2m/3km SW of Wigan town centre. SD5603.
Goose Green *Kent* ***Settlement***, 1m/2km NE of Hadlow. **23 K6** TQ6450.
Goose Green *Kent* ***Settlement***, 1km SW of Biddenden. TQ8437.
Goose Green *Norf.* ***Locality***, adjoining to N of Ashill. TF8804.
Goose Green *S.Glos.* ***Hamlet***, 6m/9km E of Bristol. ST6774.
Goose Green *S.Glos.* ***Suburb***, to N of Yate. ST7183.
Goose Green *W.Suss.* ***Hamlet***, 4m/6km N of Washington. TQ1118.
Goose Pool *Here.* ***Settlement***, 4m/6km SW of Hereford. SO4636.
Gooseberry Green *Essex* ***Suburb***, NW district of Billericay. TQ6695.
Gooseham *Cornw.* ***Settlement***, 7m/11km N of Bude. **6 A4** SS2316.
Goosehill *W.Yorks.* ***Locality***, 1m/2km SW of Normanton. SE3721.
Goosehill Green *Worcs.* ***Settlement***, 3m/4km SE of Droitwich Spa. SO9361.
Goosenford *Som.* ***Hamlet***, 3m/4km NE of Taunton. ST2427.
Goosewell *Plym.* ***Suburb***, SE district of Plymouth, 2m/3km beyond River Plym and 4m/6km W of Yealmpton. **5 F5** SX5252.
Goosey *Oxon.* ***Village***, 4m/6km NW of Wantage. **21 G2** SU3591.
Goosnargh *Lancs.* ***Village***, 3m/5km W of Longridge. **55 J6** SD5536.
Goostrey *Ches.* Population: 2796. ***Village***, 2m/3km NE of Holmes Chapel. **49 G5** SJ7770.
Gop Hill *Flints.* ***Hill***, 2m/3km SE of Prestatyn. Height 656 feet or 200 metres. **47 J4** SJ0880.
Gorbals *Glas.* ***Suburb***, on S bank of River Clyde, to S of Glasgow city centre. NS5964.
Gorcott Hill *Warks.* ***Hamlet***, 3m/5km E of Redditch. **30 B2** SP0968.
Gorddinog *Gwyn.* ***Settlement***, 1m/2km SW of Llanfairfechan. **46 E5** SH6773.
Gordon *Sc.Bord.* ***Village***, 8m/13km NW of Kelso. **76 E6** NT6443.
Gordonbush *High.* ***Settlement***, on E coast in Sutherland district, near head of Loch Brora, 5m/8km NW of Brora village. **97 F1** NC8409.
Gordonsburgh *Moray* ***Suburb***, on E side of Buckie, on N coast. Harbour and lighthouse. NJ4366.
Gordonstoun *Moray* ***Educational establishment***, coeducational public school 4m/6km W of Lossiemouth. Attended by Prince Charles. **97 J5** NJ1868.
Gordonstown *Aber.* ***Settlement***, 9m/15km SW of Banff. **98 D5** NJ5656.
Gordonstown *Aber.* ***Village***, 7m/12km S of Turriff. **91 F1** NJ7138.
Gore Cross *Wilts.* ***Settlement***, 1m/2km S of West Lavington. **20 D6** SU0051.
Gore End *Hants.* ***Hamlet***, 4m/7km SW of Newbury. SU4163.
Gore Heath *Dorset* ***Open space***, wooded heath 2m/3km N of Wareham. **9 J5** SY9291.
Gore Houses *Lancs.* ***Locality***, to W of Lydiate across Leeds and Liverpool Canal. SD3604.
Gore Pit *Essex* ***Settlement***, adjoining to NE of Kelvedon, 4m/7km NE of Witham. TL8719.
Gore Sand *Som.* ***Coastal feature***, sandbank in Bristol Channel to N of River Parrett mouth, 3m/5km NE of Burnham-on-Sea. **19 F6** ST2651.
Gore Street *Kent* ***Settlement***, 1m/2km E of Sarre. **25 J5** TR2765.
Gorebridge *Midloth.* Population: 5888. ***Small town***, 4m/6km S of Dalkeith. Situated on Gore Water. **76 B4** NT3461.
Gorefield *Cambs.* ***Village***, 3m/5km NW of Wisbech. **43 H4** TF4111.
Gores *Wilts.* ***Hamlet***, 4m/6km W of Pewsey. SU1058.
Gorgie *Edin.* ***Suburb***, 2m/4km SW of Edinburgh city centre. NT2272.
Gorhambury *Herts.* ***Historic house***, 18c mansion 2m/3km W of St. Albans, containing part of Sir Francis Bacon's library. Ruins of earlier house (English Heritage) in grounds to W. **22 E1** TL1107.
Goring *Oxon.* Population: 3145. ***Small town***, on River Thames, 9m/14km NW of Reading. Fine medieval church. **21 K3** SU6081.
Goring-by-Sea *W.Suss.* ***Suburb***, W district of Worthing. **12 E6** TQ1102.
Goring Heath *Oxon.* ***Settlement***, 2m/4km NE of Pangbourne. SU6579.
Gorlech *Carmar.* ***River***, rising 4m/6km SE of Llanybydder and flowing SE through Forest of Brechfa into River Cothi at Abergorlech. **17 J1** SN5833.
Gorleston *Norf.* *Familiar form of Gorleston-on-Sea, qv.*
Gorleston-on-Sea (Commonly referred to as Gorleston.) *Norf.* ***Suburb***, S district of Great Yarmouth, at mouth of River Yare. **45 K5** TG5203.
Gorllwyn *Carmar.* ***Settlement***, 6m/9km SE of Newcastle Emlyn. **17 G1** SN3533.
Gorllwyn *Powys* ***Mountain***, 5m/8km N of Beulah. Height 2011 feet or 613 metres. **27 J3** SN9159.
Gorm Loch *High.* ***Lake/loch***, small loch 4m/6km E of Scourie, Sutherland district. **102 E4** NC2144.
Gorm-loch Beag *High.* ***Lake/loch***, small loch to E of Ben Armine. **104 C6** NC7027.
Gorm Loch Mòr *High.* ***Lake/loch***, 4m/7km E of Loch Assynt. **103 F6** NC3125.
Gorm-loch Mòr *High.* ***Lake/loch***, small loch in Ben Armine Forest, to E of Creag Mhòr. **104 C6** NC7123.
Gormack Burn ***River***, rising on Hill of Fare and flowing NE through Midmar Forest, before turning E to join River Dee S of Peterculter. NJ8201.
Gornalwood *W.Mid.* ***Suburb***, 2m/3km W of Dudley town centre. **40 B6** SO9190.
Gorple Reservoirs *W.Yorks.* ***Reservoir***, two reservoirs on Heptonstall Moor, to NW of Hebden Bridge. **56 E6** SD9231.
Gorpley Reservoir *W.Yorks.* ***Reservoir***, 2m/3km SW of Todmorden. **56 E7** SD9122.
Gorrachie *Aber.* ***Settlement***, 5m/8km N of Turriff. **99 F5** NJ7358.
Gorran *Cornw.* *Alternative name for Gorran Churchtown, qv.*
Gorran Churchtown (Also known as Gorran.) *Cornw.* ***Village***, 2m/3km SW of Mevagissey. **3 G4** SW9942.
Gorran Haven *Cornw.* ***Village***, 1m/2km SE of Gorran Churchtown on coast. **4 A6** SW9942.
Gors *Cere.* ***Settlement***, 4m/6km SE of Aberystwyth. **27 F1** SN6277.
Gors-goch *Carmar.* ***Settlement***, 1km SE of Gorslas. SN5713.
Gors Goch *Powys* ***Mountain***, wooded summit rising to over 390 metres, 1m/2km N of Llawryglyn. **37 J6** SN9393.
Gorse Hill *Gt.Man.* ***Suburb***, 1m/2km NE of Stretford. SJ8095.
Gorse Hill *Swin.* ***Suburb***, to N of Swindon town centre. SU1586.
Gorsedd *Flints.* ***Village***, 2m/4km W of Holywell. **47 K5** SJ1576.
Gorsedd Bran *Denb.* ***Mountain***, 2m/3km S of Bylchau. Height 1617 feet or 493 metres. **47 H7** SH9760.
Gorseinon *Swan.* Population: 18,917. ***Town***, 5m/9km NW of Swansea. Garden village to SE. Loughor adjoins to W. **17 J5** SS5898.
Gorseness *Ork.* ***Settlement***, 1km NE of Bay of Isbister, Mainland. **107 D6** HY4119.
Gorsey Leys *Derbys.* ***Hamlet***, 1km E of Overseal. SK3015.
Gorseybank *Derbys.* ***Settlement***, 1km SE of Wirksworth. SK2953.
Gorsgoch *Cere.* ***Hamlet***, 6m/10km W of Lampeter. **26 D3** SN4850.
Gorslas *Carmar.* ***Village***, 1m/2km NE of Cross Hands. **17 J3** SN5713.
Gorsley *Glos.* ***Hamlet***, 2m/4km W of Newent. **29 F6** SO6825.
Gorsley Common *Here.* ***Locality***, 3m/5km W of Newent. **29 F6** SO6725.
Gorsley Green *Ches.* ***Locality***, 1km NW of Marton. SJ8469.
Gorslydan *Powys* ***Mountain***, 3m/4km NE of Llanbister. Height 1735 feet or 529 metres. **28 A1** SO1276.
Gorstage *Ches.* ***Settlement***, 3m/5km W of Northwich. SJ6172.
Gorstan *High.* ***Settlement***, in Ross and Cromarty district, 10m/15km W of Dingwall. **95 K5** NH3862.
Gorstanvorran *High.* ***Settlement***, on S shore of Loch Shiel, 2m/3km NE of Pollock, Lochaber district. **86 E7** NM8071.
Gorstey Ley *Staffs.* ***Locality***, within Burntwood, 2m/4km N of Brownhills. SK0609.
Gorsty Common *Here.* ***Village***, 4m/7km SW of Hereford. SO4437.
Gorsty Hill *Staffs.* ***Hamlet***, 3m/5km S of Uttoxeter. SK1029.
Gortantaoid Point *Arg. & B.* ***Coastal feature***, headland on N coast of Islay, on E side of wide bay at entrance to Loch Gruinart. **72 B3** NR3374.
Gorten *Arg. & B.* ***Settlement***, on Mull, 1km N of Grass Point across Loch Don. **79 J4** NM7432.
Gortenbuie *Arg. & B.* ***Settlement***, in Glen Cannel, 1m/2km S of head of Loch Bà, Mull. **79 G4** NM5933.
Gorteneorn *High.* ***Settlement***, on Kentra Bay, 3m/4km W of Acharacle. **79 H1** NM6367.
Gorthleck *High.* *Alternative name for Lyne of Gorthleck, qv.*
Gorthlick *High.* *Alternative name for Lyne of Gorthleck, qv.*
Gorton *Arg. & B.* ***Settlement***, at head of Loch Gorton, on S coast of Coll. **78 C2** NM1753.
Gorton *Gt.Man.* ***Suburb***, 3m/5km SE of Manchester city centre. Reservoirs to E. **49 H3** SJ8896.
Gosbeck *Suff.* ***Village***, 7m/11km N of Ipswich. **35 F3** TM1655.
Gosberton *Lincs.* Population: 1785. ***Village***, 6m/9km N of Spalding. **43 F2** TF2331.
Gosberton Cheal *Lincs.* ***Locality***, 1m/2km SE of Risegate, 4m/7km NW of Spalding. TF2228.
Gosberton Clough *Lincs.* ***Hamlet***, 6m/9km NW of Spalding. TF1929.
Goseland Hill *Sc.Bord.* ***Mountain***, 3m/4km SE of Biggar. Height 1427 feet or 435 metres. **75 J7** NT0735.
Goseley Dale *Derbys.* ***Locality***, 1m/2km E of Swadlincote. **41 F3** SK3220.
Gosfield *Essex* ***Village***, 4m/7km NE of Braintree. **34 B6** TL7829.
Gosfield Hall *Essex* ***Historic house***, in Gosfield, 4m/7km NE of Braintree, with Tudor gallery and court. First English home of Louis XVIII. **34 B6** TL7729.
Gosford *Devon* ***Locality***, 1m/2km N of Ottery St. Mary. SY0997.
Gosford *Here.* ***Settlement***, 4m/6km W of Tenbury Wells. SO5368.
Gosford *Oxon.* ***Village***, adjoining to SE of Kidlington, 4m/7km N of Oxford. SP5013.
Gosford Bay *E.Loth.* ***Bay***, W facing bay on Firth of Forth, 1m/2km SW of Aberlady. **76 C3** NT4478.
Gosford Green *W.Mid.* ***Suburb***, 1m/2km E of Coventry city centre. SP3578.
Gosford House *E.Loth.* ***Historic house***, overlooking Gosford Bay on Firth of Forth, 2m/3km NE of Longniddry. Central block remains but wings destroyed in 19c. House restored following fire in 1940 and gardens are being re-developed. **76 C3** NT4578.
Gosforth *Cumb.* ***Village***, 2m/4km NE of Seascale. **60 B6** NY0603.
Gosforth *T. & W.* Population: 23,315. ***Town***, adjoining to N of Newcastle upon Tyne, 2m/3km from city centre. Racecourse and nature reserve in High Gosforth Park. **71 H7** NZ2468.
Gosland Green *Ches.* ***Settlement***, 1km E of Bunbury. SJ5758.
Gosling Street *Som.* ***Settlement***, 2m/3km NW of Keinton Mandeville. ST5433.
Gosmore *Herts.* ***Hamlet***, 1m/2km S of Hitchin. **32 E6** TL1827.
Gospel End *Staffs.* ***Village***, 3m/5km S of Wolverhampton. **40 B6** SO9093.
Gospel Green *W.Suss.* ***Settlement***, 3m/4km SE of Haslemere. SU9431.
Gospel Oak *Gt.Lon.* ***Suburb***, in borough of Camden, 4m/6km N of Charing Cross. Name recalls tree where gospel was read during beating of bounds. TQ2885.
Gosport *Hants.* ***Settlement***, just S of Ampfield, 3m/5km E of Romsey. SU3922.
Gosport *Hants.* Population: 67,802. ***Town***, 1m/2km W of Portsmouth across entrance to Portsmouth Harbour (ferry for pedestrians). Royal Naval Submarine Museum at Haslar. **11 H5** SZ6199.
Gossa Water *Shet.* ***Lake/loch***, 1km NW of Easter Skeld, Mainland. **109 C8** HU3046.
Gossa Water *Shet.* ***Lake/loch***, 3m/4km SE of Voe, Mainland. **109 D6** HU4360.
Gossa Water *Shet.* ***Lake/loch***, in N part of Yell 1m/2km NW of Dalsetter. **108 D3** HU4899.
Gossabrough *Shet.* ***Settlement***, near E coast of Yell, 2m/4km N of Burravoe. **108 E4** HU5383.
Gossard's Green *Beds.* ***Settlement***, adjoining to N of Cranfield. SP9643.
Gossington *Glos.* ***Hamlet***, 3m/5km NW of Dursley. SO7302.
Gossops Green *W.Suss.* ***Suburb***, W district of Crawley. **13 F3** TQ2536.
Goswick *Northumb.* ***Settlement***, near coast, 6m/10km SE of Berwick-upon-Tweed. **77 J6** NU0545.
Gotham *Notts.* Population: 1638. ***Village***, 6m/10km N of Loughborough. **41 H2** SK5330.
Gotherington *Glos.* ***Village***, 5m/8km N of Cheltenham. **29 J6** SO9629.
Gothers *Cornw.* ***Hamlet***, 5m/8km NW of St. Austell. SW9658.
Gott *Shet.* ***Settlement***, 1km E of Tingwall Airport, Mainland. **109 D8** HU4345.
Gott Bay *Arg. & B.* ***Bay***, wide bay on S coast of Tiree, NE of Scarinish. **78 B3** NM0546.

Gotton *Som.* ***Hamlet***, 1km W of West Monkton, 3m/5km NE of Taunton. ST2428.
Goudhurst *Kent* ***Village***, hilltop Wealden village, 4m/6km NW of Cranbrook. **14 C4** TQ7237.
Goulceby *Lincs.* ***Village***, 6m/10km N of Horncastle. **53 F5** TF2579.
Gourdas *Aber.* ***Locality***, to SE of Steinman Hill, 3m/4km N of Fyvie. **99 F6** NJ7741.
Gourdon *Aber.* ***Village***, fishing village on E coast 1m/2km S of Inverbervie. **91 G7** NO8270.
Gourock *Inclyde* Population: 11,743. ***Town***, resort and passenger boat terminus on Firth of Clyde, 2m/4km W of Greenock and due S of Kilcreggan across firth. Popular yachting centre. **74 A3** NS2477.
Gourock Bay *Inclyde* ***Bay***, to E of Gourock, on S side of Firth of Clyde. **74 A3** NS2477.
Gousam *W.Isles* ***Island***, islet in Loch Roag, W coast of Isle of Lewis, 2m/3km E of Miabhig. NB1033.
Gouthwaite Reservoir *N.Yorks.* ***Reservoir***, large reservoir in Nidderdale, 2m/3km NW of Pateley Bridge. **57 G3** SE1468.
Govan *Glas.* ***Suburb***, on S side of River Clyde, 2m/4km W of Glasgow city centre. Car ferry across river. **74 D4** NS5565.
Govanhill *Glas.* ***Suburb***, 2m/3km S of Glasgow city centre. NS5862.
Goverton *Notts.* ***Hamlet***, 1km NW of Bleasby. SK7050.
Goveton *Devon* ***Hamlet***, 2m/3km NE of Kingsbridge. **5 H6** SX7546.
Govig *W.Isles* *Anglicised form of Gobhaig, qv.*
Govilon *Mon.* ***Village***, 2m/3km W of Abergavenny. **28 B7** SO2613.
Gowanhill *Aber.* ***Settlement***, 3m/5km SE of Fraserburgh. **99 J4** NK0363.
Gowdall *E.Riding* ***Village***, 1m/2km W of Snaith. **58 C7** SE6222.
Gower (Gŵyr). *Swan.* ***Coastal feature***, peninsula of carboniferous limestone, 15m/24km E to W and from 4m to 8m (6km to 13km) N to S, jutting out from W of Swansea W into Bristol Channel. Rocky coast, except to N where salt marshes border Burry Inlet. Much of coast owned by National Trust. Designated an Area of Outstanding Natural Beauty. **17 H6** SS4889.
Gower Rock *Cornw.* ***Island***, rock island off N coast, 1km W of Boscastle, accessible at low water. SX0890.
Gowerton (Tre-gŵyr). *Swan.* ***Small town***, 5m/7km NW of Swansea. **17 J5** SS5896.
Gowkhall *Fife* ***Village***, 3m/4km W of Dunfermline. **75 J2** NT0589.
Gowkthrapple *N.Lan.* ***Locality***, on S side of Wishaw. NS7953.
Gowthams *Lincs.* ***Locality***, 1km W of Orby. TF4867.
Gowthorpe *E.Riding* ***Settlement***, 3m/5km E of Stamford Bridge. **58 D4** SE7654.
Gowy *Ches.* ***River***, rising SE of Peckforton and flowing generally NW into River Mersey at Stanlow, E of Ellesmere Port. SJ4277.
Goxhill *E.Riding* ***Hamlet***, 2m/4km SW of Hornsea. **59 H5** TA1844.
Goxhill *N.Lincs.* ***Village***, 2m/3km SE of New Holland. **59 H7** TA1021.
Goyle Hill *Aber.* ***Mountain***, 3m/5km SE of Bridge of Dye. Height 1522 feet or 464 metres. **90 E6** NO6882.
Goytre *N.P.T.* ***Hamlet***, 2m/3km E of Port Talbot. **18 A3** SS7889.
Goyt's Bridge *Derbys.* ***Other feature of interest***, bridge across dam at N end of Errwood Reservoir, 3m/5km NW of Buxton. **49 J5** SK0175.
Goyt's Moss *Derbys.* ***Open space***, moorland within Peak District National Park and where River Goyt rises, 3m/5km SW of Buxton. **50 C5** SK0072.
Gozzard's Ford *Oxon.* ***Settlement***, on E side of Abingdon Airfield, 2m/3km NW of Abingdon. SU4698.
Grabhair (Anglicised form: Gravir.) *W.Isles* ***Village***, near E coast of Isle of Lewis at head of Loch Odhairn, 3m/5km W of Kebock Head. **101 F6** NB3715.
Graby *Lincs.* ***Settlement***, 6m/10km N of Bourne. TF0929.
Gracemount *Edin.* ***Suburb***, 4m/6km SE of Edinburgh city centre. NT2768.
Gradbach *Staffs.* ***Settlement***, 6m/9km N of Leek. **49 J6** SJ9965.
Graddon Moor *Devon* ***Open space***, moorland 2m/3km S of Black Torrington. **6 C5** SS4602.
Grade *Cornw.* ***Hamlet***, 2m/3km N of Lizard Point. **2 E7** SW7114.
Gradeley Green *Ches.* ***Settlement***, 4m/6km W of Nantwich. SJ5952.
Graemsay *Ork.* ***Island***, sparsely inhabited island of about 250 acres or 100 hectares, situated in Hoy Sound S of Stromness, Mainland. Two lighthouses, at NE and NW ends. **107 B7** HY2605.
Graffham *W.Suss.* ***Village***, below South Downs, 4m/6km SE of Midhurst. **12 C5** SU9217.
Grafham *Cambs.* ***Village***, 5m/8km W of Huntingdon, on NE side of large reservoir, Grafham Water. **32 E2** TL1669.
Grafham *Surr.* ***Hamlet***, 3m/5km NW of Cranleigh. **22 D7** TQ0241.
Grafham Water *Cambs.* ***Reservoir***, large reservoir 6m/10km SW of Huntingdon. **32 E2** TL1669.
Grafton *Here.* ***Hamlet***, 2m/4km S of Hereford. **28 D5** SO4937.
Grafton *N.Yorks.* ***Village***, 2m/4km SE of Boroughbridge. **57 K3** SE4163.
Grafton *Oxon.* ***Hamlet***, 4m/6km E of Lechlade. **21 F1** SP2600.
Grafton *Shrop.* ***Hamlet***, 5m/9km NW of Shrewsbury. **38 D4** SJ4318.
Grafton *Worcs.* ***Hamlet***, 5m/9km W of Leominster. **28 E2** SO5761.
Grafton *Worcs.* ***Hamlet***, 5m/8km SW of Evesham. SO9837.
Grafton Flyford *Worcs.* ***Village***, 7m/11km E of Worcester. **29 J3** SO9655.
Grafton Regis *Northants.* ***Village***, 5m/7km NW of Stony Stratford. **31 J4** SP7546.
Grafton Underwood *Northants.* ***Village***, 4m/6km E of Kettering. **32 C1** SP9280.
Grafty Green *Kent* ***Village***, 5m/8km W of Charing. **14 D3** TQ8748.
Graham Cunninghame Memorial *Stir.* ***Other feature of interest***, cairn (National Trust for Scotland) to N of Gartmore, 2m/3km SW of Aberfoyle, commemorating life of R.B. Graham Cunninghame (1852-1936), a radical politician, writer, traveller and renowned horseman. **74 D1** NS5297.
Graianrhyd *Denb.* ***Hamlet***, 3m/4km SW of Treuddyn. **48 B7** SJ2156.
Graig *Conwy* ***Hamlet***, 5m/9km SW of Colwyn Bay. Bodnant Garden (National Trust) to N. **47 G5** SH8071.
Graig *Denb.* ***Hamlet***, 1km S of Tremeirchion. **47 J5** SJ0872.
Graig Capel *Carmar.* ***Suburb***, adjoining to N of Burry Port. SN4401.
Graig Fawr *Denb.* ***Hill***, National Trust property, with viewpoint, 2m/3km S of Prestatyn. Height 502 feet or 153 metres. SJ0680.
Graig Fawr *Swan.* ***Hill***, rises to E of River Loughor, 2m/3km NE of Pontarddulais. Height 905 feet or 276 metres. **17 K4** SN6106.
Graig-fechan *Denb.* ***Hamlet***, 3m/5km SE of Ruthin. **47 K7** SJ1454.
Graig Goch *Gwyn.* ***Inland physical feature***, rocky ridge to S of Tal-y-llyn Lake, 6m/9km S of Dolgellau. Height 1883 feet or 574 metres. **37 G5** SH7007.
Graig Penllyn *V. of Glam.* ***Hamlet***, 2m/3km NW of Cowbridge. **18 C4** SS9777.
Graig Syfyrddin *Mon.* ***Open space***, steep NW facing mountain slope, 8m/13km NE of Abergavenny. **28 D6** SO4021.
Graig Wen *Gwyn.* ***Mountain***, 3m/4km SE of Ffestiniog. Height 1824 feet or 556 metres. **37 G2** SH7339.
Grain *Med.* ***Village***, at E end of Isle of Grain, opposite Sheerness. **24 E4** TQ8876.
Grain Earth House *Ork.* ***Historic/prehistoric site***, prehistoric earth house (Historic Scotland) opposite Kirkwall, Mainland, across head of Bay of Kirkwall. **107 D6** HY4411.
Grainel *Arg. & B.* ***Settlement***, on Islay, 4m/7km NW of Bridgend. **72 A4** NR2666.
Grainhow *Aber.* ***Settlement***, 2m/3km W of New Deer. **99 G6** NJ8546.
Grains Bar *Gt.Man.* ***Hamlet***, at crossroads, 3m/5km NE of Oldham. SD9608.
Grainsby *Lincs.* ***Village***, 6m/10km S of Grimsby. **53 F3** TF2799.
Grainthorpe *Lincs.* ***Village***, 7m/11km NE of Louth. **53 G3** TF3897.
Gramisdale *W.Isles* *Anglicised form of Gramsdal, qv.*
Grampian Mountains ***Large natural feature***, great mountain system of Scotland, extending from Oban in SW to Huntly in NE, its southern edge forming natural boundary between Highlands and Lowlands, and N edge being Great Glen fault line. Includes several smaller chains and groups. Highest point is Ben Nevis, 4406 feet or 1343 metres. **88 A7** NN7080.
Grampian Transport Museum *Aber.* ***Other feature of interest***, museum in Alford, with historic vehicles of every description. Includes driving simulator and video bus providing histories of road transport and motor sport. **90 D3** NJ5716.
Grampound *Cornw.* ***Village***, on River Fal, 6m/9km SW of St. Austell. **3 G4** SW9348.
Grampound Road *Cornw.* ***Village***, beside railway, 6m/10km W of St. Austell. **3 G3** SW9150.
Gramsdal (Anglicised form: Gramisdale.) *W.Isles* ***Settlement***, at N end of Benbecula, 2m/3km E of Benbecula (Baile a' Mhanaich) Aerodrome. **92 D6** NF8155.
Granborough *Bucks.* ***Village***, 2m/3km S of Winslow. **31 J6** SP7625.
Granby *Notts.* ***Village***, 4m/6km SE of Bingham. **42 A2** SK7536.
Grand Pier *Devon* ***Other feature of interest***, at Teignmouth, originally built to segregate male and female bathers. **5 K3** SX9472.
Grand Union Canal ***Canal***, connecting River Thames in London with River Soar S of Leicester, and thus with River Trent at Trent Junction N of Kegworth. Another branch goes from Norton Junction, SE of Rugby, to Birmingham, by Royal Leamington Spa, Warwick and Solihull. Unique in Britain in that it is composed of at least 8 separate canals. **22 D2** TQ3681.
Grand Western Canal *Devon* ***Canal***, formerly connecting Tiverton and Taunton. Somerset section disused; Devon section still navigable in parts. SS9612.
Grand Western Canal Country Park *Devon* ***Leisure/recreation***, linear country park beside Grand Western Canal, 6m/10km NE of Tiverton. Canal walk extends 11m/18km along towpath of restored canal from Tiverton Canal Basin to Somerset border. Horse-drawn passenger barge. **7 J4** ST0515.
Grandborough *Warks.* ***Village***, 5m/8km S of Rugby. **31 F2** SP4966.
Grandhome *Aberdeen* ***Locality***, comprising Grandhome House, Mains of Grandhome and Grandhome Moss, 4m/7km NW of Aberdeen. NJ9011.
Grandpont *Oxon.* ***Suburb***, to S of Oxford city centre. SP5105.
Grandtully *P. & K.* ***Settlement***, in upper valley of River Tay, 4m/6km SW of Pitlochry. **82 A2** NN9152.
Grandtully Castle *P. & K.* ***Castle***, dating from 1560, with later additions, in Strath Tay 3m/4km NE of Aberfeldy. **81 K2** NN8951.
Grandtully Hill *P. & K.* ***Mountain***, in forested area 3m/5km SE of Aberfeldy. Height 1745 feet or 532 metres. **82 A3** NN9147.
Grange *Cumb.* ***Hamlet***, in Borrowdale, 1m/2km S of Derwent Water. **60 D5** NY2517.
Grange *Cumb.* ***Locality***, 4m/7km SW of Carlisle. NY3551.
Grange *E.Ayr.* ***Suburb***, W district of Kilmarnock. NS4137.
Grange *Edin.* ***Suburb***, 1m/2km S of Edinburgh city centre. NT2571.
Grange *High.* ***Settlement***, in Inverness district, 8m/13km W of Drumnadrochit. **87 K1** NH3730.
Grange *Med.* ***Settlement***, 3m/5km E of Rochester. **24 D5** TQ7968.
Grange *Mersey.* ***Locality***, 1m/2km E of West Kirby. SJ2286.
Grange *Moray* ***Locality***, comprising Davoch of Grange and Haughs of Grange in Strath Isla, 4m/7km E of Keith. NJ4851.
Grange *N.Yorks.* ***Settlement***, at confluence of Raisdale Beck and Ledge Beck, at N end of Bilsdale, 8m/13km N of Hemsley. **63 G7** SE5796.
Grange *P. & K.* ***Settlement***, in Carse of Gowrie, 2m/3km NE of Errol. **82 D5** NO2725.
Grange *Torfaen* ***Locality***, industrial estate in Cwmbran. ST2995.
Grange Art Gallery and Museum *B. & H.* ***Other feature of interest***, in Rottingdean, houses part of National Toy Museum; also a room dedicated to Rudyard Kipling. **13 G6** TQ3602.
Grange Crossroads *Moray* ***Settlement***, at crossroads, 4m/6km NE of Keith. **98 C5** NJ4754.
Grange de Lings *Lincs.* ***Settlement***, 4m/6km N of Lincoln. SK9877.
Grange Estate *Dorset* ***Settlement***, 1m/2km SE of St. Leonards and 3m/5km SW of Ringwood. SU1101.
Grange Fell *D. & G.* ***Mountain***, 3m/5km E of Bankshill. Height 1046 feet or 319 metres. **69 H5** NY2481.
Grange Hall *Moray* ***Settlement***, 2m/3km NE of Forres. **97 H5** NJ0660.
Grange Heath *Dorset* ***Open space***, heath and wooded area on Isle of Purbeck, 3m/5km NW of Corfe Castle. **9 H6** SY9083.
Grange Hill *Essex* ***Suburb***, S district of Chigwell. **23 H2** TQ4492.
Grange Moor *W.Yorks.* ***Village***, 4m/6km SW of Dewsbury. **50 E1** SE2216.
Grange of Lindores *Fife* ***Hamlet***, 2m/3km SE of Newburgh. **82 D6** NO2516.
Grange-over-Sands *Cumb.* Population: 4473. ***Small town***, resort on W bank of River Kent estuary, 9m/14km N of Morecambe across Morecambe Bay. Treacherous sands offshore. **55 H2** SD4077.
Grange Park *Gt.Lon.* ***Suburb***, in borough of Enfield, 1m/2km SW of Enfield town centre and 9m/14km N of Charing Cross. TQ3195.
Grange Scar *Cumb.* ***Open space***, hillslope with rocky outcrop, 2m/3km S of Great Asby. **61 H5** NY6709.
Grange View *Ches.* ***Locality***, 3m/5km W of Northwich. SJ6074.
Grange Villa *Dur.* ***Village***, 3m/4km W of Chester-le-Street. **62 D1** NZ2352.
Grangemill *Derbys.* ***Hamlet***, 4m/6km NW of Wirksworth. **50 E7** SK2457.
Grangemouth *Falk.* Population: 18,739. ***Town***, industrial town and container port on S side of Firth of Forth, 3m/5km E of Falkirk. E terminus of Forth and Clyde Canal (disused). **75 H2** NS9281.
Grangemuir *Fife* ***Hamlet***, 1m/2km NW of Pittenweem. **83 G7** NO5303.
Grangeston *S.Ayr.* ***Locality***, including Girvan distillery, 2m/3km NE of Girvan. **67 G4** NX2099.
Grangetown *Cardiff* ***Suburb***, 1m/2km S of Cardiff city centre, at mouth of River Taff, on W bank. Road bridge to Butetown and docks. **18 E4** ST1874.
Grangetown *R. & C.* ***Suburb***, 4m/6km E of Middlesbrough. **63 G4** NZ5520.
Grangetown *T. & W.* ***Suburb***, 1m/2km S of Sunderland city centre. NZ4054.
Granish *High.* ***Settlement***, 1m/2km NE of Aviemore. **89 G3** NH9014.
Gransmoor *E.Riding* ***Hamlet***, 6m/9km SE of Bridlington. **59 H4** TA1259.
Granston (Treopert). *Pembs.* ***Hamlet***, 5m/7km S of Strumble Head. **16 B1** SM8934.
Granta *See (River) Cam.*
Granta ***River***, rising S of Castle Camps and flowing NW to join River Cam or Granta S of Great Shelford. **33 H3** TL4651.
Grantchester *Cambs.* ***Village***, 2m/3km SW of Cambridge. Associations with poet, Rupert Brooke. **33 H3** TL4355.
Grantham *Lincs.* Population: 33,243. ***Town***, industrial and market town on River Witham, 22m/35km E of Nottingham. Outstanding church with tall spire. Several old buildings. Angel and Royal Hotel, 15c. Margaret Thatcher born here and Sir Isaac Newton educated at King's School. **42 C2** SK9135.
Grantley *N.Yorks.* ***Village***, 5m/8km W of Ripon. **57 H2** SE2370.
Grantlodge *Aber.* ***Settlement***, 1m/2km W of Kemnay. **91 F3** NJ7017.
Granton *Edin.* ***Suburb***, 2m/4km NW of Edinburgh city centre. Harbour on Firth of Forth. NT2376.
Granton House *D. & G.* ***Settlement***, 3m/4km N of Moffat. **69 F3** NT0709.
Grantown-on-Spey *High.* Population: 2391. ***Small town***, market town and resort, 19m/31km S of Forres. Castle Grant, 2m/3km N, dating in part from 16c, was formerly home of chiefs of Grant, Earls of Seafield. **89 H2** NJ0327.
Grantsfield *Here.* ***Settlement***, 3m/4km E of Leominster. SO5260.
Grantshouse *Sc.Bord.* ***Village***, on Eye Water, 8m/13km W of Eyemouth. **77 G4** NT8065.
Grappenhall *Warr.* ***Locality***, 3m/4km SE of Warrington town centre. **49 F4** SJ6486.
Grasby *Lincs.* ***Village***, 3m/5km NW of Caistor. **52 D2** TA0804.

Grasmere *Cumb.* ***Lake/loch***, 3m/4km NW of Ambleside. **60 E6** NY3306.
Grasmere *Cumb.* ***Village***, on River Rothay, to N of Grasmere lake and 3m/5km NW of Ambleside. William Wordsworth lived here from 1799 to 1808 and is buried in village churchyard. **60 E6** NY3307.
Grasmoor *Cumb.* ***Mountain***, in Lake District, 2m/3km N of Buttermere hamlet. Height 2791 feet or 851 metres. **60 C4** NY1720.
Grass Green *Essex* ***Settlement***, 2m/3km W of Great Yeldham. TL7338.
Grass Holm *Ork.* ***Island***, islet off W coast of Shapinsay opposite Salt Ness. HY4719.
Grass Point *Arg. & B.* ***Coastal feature***, headland on E coast of Mull, on S side of entrance to Loch Don. **79 J4** NM7430.
Grasscroft *Gt.Man.* Population: 2795. ***Locality***, 3m/5km E of Oldham. **49 J2** SD9704.
Grassendale *Mersey.* ***Suburb***, 5m/7km SE of Liverpool city centre. **48 C4** SJ3985.
Grassgarth *Cumb.* ***Settlement***, 4m/7km S of Dalston. NY3444.
Grassgarth *Cumb.* ***Settlement***, 2m/3km E of Windermere. SD4499.
Grassholm Island *Pembs.* ***Island***, small island 8m/12km W of Skomer Island. Bird sanctuary; breeding place of gannet. SM5909.
Grassholme *Dur.* ***Settlement***, at W end of Grassholme Reservoir, 3m/5km SW of Middleton-in-Teesdale. **62 A4** NY9221.
Grassholme Reservoir *Dur.* ***Reservoir***, in course of River Lune, 2m/3km S of Middleton-in-Teesdale. **62 A4** NY9422.
Grassington *N.Yorks.* ***Village***, in Wharfedale, 8m/13km N of Skipton. **57 F3** SE0064.
Grassington Moor *N.Yorks.* ***Open space***, moorland 3m/5km NE of Grassington. **57 F3** SE0268.
Grassmoor *Derbys.* ***Village***, 3m/5km SE of Chesterfield. **51 G6** SK4066.
Grassthorpe *Notts.* ***Village***, 4m/7km SE of Tuxford. **51 K6** SK7967.
Grasswell *T. & W.* ***Suburb***, in NW part of Houghton le Spring. NZ3350.
Grateley *Hants.* ***Village***, 6m/10km SW of Andover. **21 F7** SU2741.
Gratton *Devon* ***Hamlet***, 5m/8km NE of Holsworthy. SS3910.
Gratton *Staffs.* ***Settlement***, 3m/5km W of Leek. SJ9356.
Gratwich *Staffs.* ***Hamlet***, 4m/7km W of Uttoxeter. **40 C2** SK0231.
Gravel Hill *Bucks.* ***Suburb***, to NE of Chalfont St. Peter town centre. TQ0091.
Gravel Hole *Gt.Man.* ***Locality***, 3m/5km N of Oldham. SD9109.
Graveley *Cambs.* ***Village***, 5m/8km S of Huntingdon. **33 F2** TL2563.
Graveley *Herts.* ***Village***, 3m/4km N of Stevenage. **33 F6** TL2327.
Gravelhill *Shrop.* ***Suburb***, in N part of Shrewsbury. SJ4813.
Gravelly Hill *W.Mid.* ***Suburb***, 4m/6km NE of Birmingham city centre. **40 D6** SP1090.
Gravelly Way *Staffs.* ***Locality***, 4m/7km W of Cannock. SJ9109.
Gravels *Shrop.* ***Settlement***, 4m/6km SW of Minsterley. **38 C5** SJ3300.
Graven *Shet.* ***Settlement***, on Mainland, at head of Garths Voe. **108 D5** HU4073.
Graveney *Kent* ***Village***, 3m/4km E of Faversham. **25 G5** TR0562.
Gravesend *Kent* Population: 51,435. ***Town***, industrial town on River Thames, 7m/11km NW of Rochester. Ferry for pedestrians to Tilbury. Traditional daily market. Sailing centre. **24 C4** TQ6474.
Gravir *W.Isles Anglicised form of Grabhair, qv.*
Gray Art Gallery and Museum *Hart.* ***Other feature of interest***, to W of Hartlepool Railway Station. Collections of local and natural history, Chinese porcelain and 19c-20c paintings. **63 G3** NZ5032.
Grayingham *Lincs.* ***Village***, 1m/2km S of Kirton in Lindsey. **52 C3** SK9396.
Grayrigg *Cumb.* ***Village***, 5m/8km NE of Kendal. **61 G7** SD5797.
Grays (Also known as Grays Thurrock.) *Thur.* Population: 50,145. ***Town***, commercial centre on N bank of River Thames, 2m/3km NW of Tilbury. **24 C4** TQ6177.
Grays Thurrock *Thur. Alternative name for Grays, qv.*
Grayshott *Hants.* ***Village***, 1m/2km W of Hindhead. Much National Trust property in vicinity. **12 B3** SU8735.
Grayswood *Surr.* ***Village***, 1m/2km NE of Haslemere. **12 C3** SU9134.
Graythorp *Hart.* ***Locality***, 3m/5km S of Hartlepool. Site of nuclear power station. NZ5127.
Graythwaite Hall Gardens *Cumb.* ***Garden***, 19c gardens on W side of Windermere lake, 4m/7km S of Hawkshead. **60 E7** SD3691.
Grazeley *W'ham* ***Hamlet***, 4m/7km S of Reading. **22 A5** SU6966.
Greanamul *W.Isles* ***Island***, islet 2m/3km E of Barra (Tràigh Mhòr) Airport. **84 C4** NF7305.
Greanamul *W.Isles* ***Island***, islet midway between Pabbay and Sandray. NL6289.
Greasbrough *S.Yorks.* ***Suburb***, 2m/3km NW of Rotherham town centre. **51 G3** SK4195.
Greasby *Mersey.* Population: 28,039. ***Village***, 4m/7km W of Birkenhead. **48 B4** SJ2587.
Greasley *Notts.* ***Hamlet***, 2m/3km E of Eastwood. Scant remains of 14c castle. SK4947.
Great Abington *Cambs.* ***Village***, 4m/7km NE of Great Chesterford. **33 J4** TL5348.
Great Addington *Northants.* ***Village***, 6m/10km SE of Kettering. **32 C1** SP9575.
Great Aish *Devon* ***Settlement***, to SW of Aish and W of South Brent, 4m/7km NE of Ivybridge. SX6860.
Great Alne *Warks.* ***Village***, 2m/4km NE of Alcester. **30 C3** SP1159.
Great Altcar *Lancs.* ***Village***, 2m/3km E of Formby. **48 C2** SD3206.
Great Amwell *Herts.* ***Village***, 1m/2km SE of Ware. **33 G7** TL3612.
Great Asby *Cumb.* ***Village***, 5m/7km S of Appleby-in-Westmorland. **61 H5** NY6813.
Great Ashfield *Suff.* ***Village***, 4m/7km SE of Ixworth. **34 D2** TL9967.
Great Ashley *Wilts.* ***Hamlet***, with Little Ashley, forms locality of Ashley, about 1m/2km NW of Bradford-on-Avon. ST8162.
Great Ayton *N.Yorks.* Population: 3592. ***Village***, 5m/8km SW of Guisborough. Group of Iron Age cairns and hut circles on Great Ayton Moor 2m/4km E. **63 G5** NZ5510.
Great Baddow *Essex* ***Suburb***, adjoining to SE of Chelmsford. **24 D1** TL7204.
Great Bardfield *Essex* ***Village***, 2m/3km S of Finchingfield. **33 K5** TL6730.
Great Barford *Beds.* Population: 1754. ***Village***, 3m/5km NW of Sandy. **32 E3** TL1352.
Great Barr *W.Mid.* ***Suburb***, in NE part of West Bromwich. **40 C6** SP0495.
Great Barrington *Glos.* ***Village***, 3m/5km W of Burford, forms parish of Barrington, along with Little Barrington. Site of Roman building 1km SE beside River Windrush. **30 D7** SP2013.
Great Barrow *Ches.* ***Village***, 4m/7km E of Chester. **48 D6** SJ4768.
Great Barton *Suff.* ***Village***, 3m/5km NE of Bury St. Edmunds. **34 C2** TL8967.
Great Barugh *N.Yorks.* ***Village***, 5m/8km NW of Malton. **58 D2** SE7479.
Great Bavington *Northumb.* ***Hamlet***, 3m/4km S of Kirkwhelpington. **70 E5** NY9880.
Great Bealings *Suff.* ***Village***, 3m/4km W of Woodbridge. **35 G4** TM2348.
Great Bedwyn *Wilts.* ***Village***, on Kennet and Avon Canal, 5m/8km SW of Hungerford. **21 F5** SU2764.
Great Bentley *Essex* ***Village***, 6m/9km NW of Clacton-on-Sea. **35 F6** TM1121.
Great Bernera *W.Isles* ***Island***, in Loch Roag, W coast of Isle of Lewis, 6m/9km N to S and from 1m/2km to 2m/4km in width. Connected to Crulabhig on Isle of Lewis by road bridge at S end. **100 D4** NB1030.
Great Billing *Northants.* ***Suburb***, 4m/6km NE of Northampton town centre. **32 B2** SP8062.
Great Bircham *Norf.* ***Village***, 3m/5km S of Docking. **44 B2** TF7632.
Great Blakenham *Suff.* ***Village***, 5m/8km NW of Ipswich. **35 F3** TM1150.
Great Blencow *Cumb.* ***Hamlet***, 4m/6km NW of Penrith. **61 F3** NY4532.
Great Bolas *Tel. & W.* ***Village***, 6m/10km N of Wellington. **39 F3** SJ6421.
Great Bookham *Surr.* ***Suburb***, 2m/3km SW of Leatherhead. **22 E6** TQ1354.
Great Borne *Cumb.* ***Mountain***, on N side of Ennerdale Water, 3m/5km E of Ennerdale Bridge. Height 2020 feet or 616 metres. **60 C5** NY1216.
Great Bourton *Oxon.* ***Village***, 3m/5km N of Banbury. **31 F4** SP4545.
Great Bowden *Leics.* ***Village***, adjoining to NE of Market Harborough. **42 A7** SP7488.
Great Bradley *Som.* ***Hamlet***, on Exmoor, 1m/2km SE of Withypool. SS8534.
Great Bradley *Suff.* ***Village***, 5m/8km N of Haverhill. **33 K3** TL6653.
Great Braxted *Essex* ***Hamlet***, 3m/4km E of Witham. **34 C7** TL8614.
Great Bricett *Suff.* ***Village***, 5m/8km N of Hadleigh. **34 E3** TM0350.
Great Brickhill *Bucks.* ***Village***, 3m/5km SE of Bletchley. **32 C5** SP9030.
Great Bridge *W.Mid.* ***Suburb***, 2m/3km NW of West Bromwich town centre. SO9792.
Great Bridgeford *Staffs.* ***Village***, 4m/6km NW of Stafford. **40 A3** SJ8826.
Great Brington *Northants.* ***Village***, forms parish of Brington, along with Little Brington, 6m/10km NW of Northampton. **31 H2** SP6664.
Great Bromley *Essex* ***Village***, 6m/9km E of Colchester. **34 E6** TM0826.
Great Broughton *Cumb.* ***Village***, 3m/5km W of Cockermouth. **60 B3** NY0731.
Great Broughton *N.Yorks.* ***Village***, 2m/3km SE of Stokesley. **63 G6** NZ5406.
Great Buckland *Kent* ***Hamlet***, 6m/9km SW of Rochester. TQ6664.
Great Budworth *Ches.* ***Village***, 2m/4km N of Northwich. **49 F5** SJ6677.
Great Burdon *Darl.* ***Hamlet***, 2m/4km NE of Darlington. **62 E5** NZ3116.
Great Burgh *Surr.* ***Settlement***, to E of Epsom Racecourse, 1m/2km SW of Banstead. TQ2358.
Great Burstead *Essex* ***Suburb***, 1m/2km S of Billericay. **24 C2** TQ6892.
Great Busby *N.Yorks.* ***Village***, 2m/3km S of Stokesley. **63 G6** NZ5205.
Great Calva *Cumb.* ***Mountain***, 3m/4km NW of Skiddaw. Height 2263 feet or 690 metres. **60 D3** NY2931.
Great Canfield *Essex* ***Hamlet***, 3m/5km SW of Great Dunmow. **33 J7** TL5918.
Great Canney *Essex* ***Settlement***, 1km W of Cold Norton. **24 E1** TL8300.
Great Carlton *Lincs.* ***Village***, 6m/9km E of Louth. **53 H4** TF4185.
Great Casterton *Rut.* ***Village***, 2m/4km NW of Stamford, on site of Roman town. **42 D5** TF0008.
Great Castle Head *Pembs.* ***Coastal feature***, headland on N shore of Milford Haven, 1m/2km SE of St. Ishmael's. SM8405.
Great Central Railway *Leics.* ***Other feature of interest***, tourist railway running Britain's only main line steam railway service, from Loughborough via Quorn and Swithland Reservoir to Birstall, 3m/4km N of Leicester. **41 H4** SK5519.
Great Chalfield *Wilts.* ***Hamlet***, 3m/5km W of Melksham. Great Chalfield Manor is a moated 15c manor house (National Trust). **20 B5** ST8663.
Great Chart *Kent* ***Village***, 2m/3km W of Ashford. **14 E3** TQ9842.
Great Chatwell *Staffs.* ***Hamlet***, 4m/7km SE of Newport. **39 G4** SJ7914.
Great Chell *Stoke* ***Suburb***, 1m/2km NE of Tunstall. SJ8752.
Great Chesterford *Essex* Population: 1369. ***Village***, on River Cam, 3m/5km NW of Saffron Walden. Site of Roman town. **33 J4** TL5042.
Great Chesters Roman Fort (Aesica) *Northumb.* ***Historic/prehistoric site***, one of the great forts of Hadrian's wall, in grounds of 18c mansion, 2m/3km N of Haltwhistle. Museum displays relics including sculptures, weapons and jewellery. Remains of fort include barracks, stables, commandant's house and bath-house. **70 C7** NY7066.

G

Great Cheverell *Wilts.* ***Village***, 5m/8km SW of Devizes. **20 C6** ST9854.
Great Cheviot *Northumb. Alternative name for The Cheviot, qv.*
Great Chishill *Cambs.* ***Village***, 4m/7km E of Royston. **33 H5** TL4238.
Great Clacton *Essex* ***Suburb***, N district of Clacton-on-Sea. **35 F7** TM1716.
Great Cliff *W.Yorks.* ***Hamlet***, on W side of M1 motorway, 2m/3km SE of Horbury across River Calder. SE3015.
Great Clifton *Cumb.* ***Village***, 3m/5km E of Workington. **60 B4** NY0429.
Great Coates *N.E.Lincs.* ***Village***, 2m/4km W of Grimsby. **53 F2** TA2310.
Great Cob Island *Essex* ***Island***, at mouth of Tollesbury Fleet, 2m/3km E of Tollesbury. **34 D7** TL9810.
Great Comberton *Worcs.* ***Village***, overlooking River Avon, 3m/4km S of Pershore. **29 J4** SO9542.
Great Comp Garden *Kent* ***Garden***, seven acres of formal gardens, 2m/3km E of Borough Green, which include woodland walks, lawns and terraces. **23 K6** TQ6356.
Great Corby *Cumb.* ***Village***, on E bank of River Eden, 6m/9km SW of Brampton. **61 F1** NY4754.
Great Cornard *Suff.* ***Village***, adjoining to SE of Sudbury. **34 C4** TL8840.
Great Cowden *E.Riding* ***Hamlet***, 4m/6km SE of Hornsea. **59 J5** TA2242.
Great Coxwell *Oxon.* ***Village***, 2m/3km SW of Faringdon. Huge 13c monastic barn (National Trust). **21 F2** SU2693.
Great Crakehall *N.Yorks.* ***Village***, 2m/3km NW of Bedale. **62 D7** SE2489.
Great Cransley *Northants.* ***Village***, in parish of Cransley, 3m/4km SW of Kettering. **32 B1** SP8376.
Great Cressingham *Norf.* ***Village***, 5m/8km SE of Swaffham. **44 C5** TF8501.
Great Crosby *Mersey.* ***Suburb***, NE district of Crosby. **48 C2** SJ3299.
Great Crosthwaite *Cumb.* ***Hamlet***, adjoining to NW of Keswick. NY2624.
Great Cubley *Derbys.* ***Village***, 4m/6km N of Sudbury. **40 D2** SK1638.
Great Cumbrae *N.Ayr.* ***Island***, in Firth of Clyde, lying about 1m/2km off mainland across Fairlie Roads. Measures about 3m/5km N to S and 2m/3km E to W. Landing stage at Keppel Pier, Millport. **73 K5** NS1656.
Great Dalby *Leics.* ***Village***, 3m/5km S of Melton Mowbray. **42 A4** SK7414.
Great Deep *W.Suss. See Thorney Island.*
Great Dixter *E.Suss.* ***Historic house***, 15c timber-framed manor house and garden at Northiam. Sir Edwin Lutyens restored house and designed gardens. Landscaper Christopher Lloyd has introduced many interesting and unusual plants. **14 D5** TQ8125.
Great Dodd *Cumb.* ***Mountain***, in Lake District 6m/9km SE of Keswick. Height 2808 feet or 856 metres. **60 E4** NY3426.
Great Doddington *Northants.* ***Village***, 2m/4km SW of Wellingborough. **32 B2** SP8864.
Great Doward *Here.* ***Village***, above W bank of River Wye, 4m/6km NE of Monmouth across loops of river. SO5516.
Great Driffield *E.Riding* Population: 9463. ***Small town***, 11m/18km SW of Bridlington. Agricultural town dating from Saxon times, known as 'Capital of the Wolds'. **59 G4** TA0257.
Great Dun Fell *Cumb.* ***Mountain***, on Milburn Forest, 8m/12km N of Appleby-in-Westmorland. Mast at summit. Height 2778 feet or 847 metres. **61 J3** NY7132.
Great Dunham *Norf.* ***Village***, 5m/8km NE of Swaffham. **44 C4** TF8714.
Great Dunmow *Essex* Population: 4907. ***Small town***, on River Chelmer, 9m/14km E of Bishop's Stortford. Medieval church and Tudor market square. Home of Flitch Trials since 1855; a test of marriage vows held in leap years whereby winners are paraded and awarded a side of bacon, or flitch. **33 K6** TL6222.
Great Durnford *Wilts.* ***Village***, on River Avon, 5m/8km N of Salisbury. **10 C1** SU1337.
Great Easton *Essex* ***Village***, 3m/4km NW of Great Dunmow. **33 K6** TL6025.
Great Easton *Leics.* ***Village***, 4m/7km NW of Corby. **42 B6** SP8493.
Great Eau *Lincs.* ***River***, rising S of Driby and flowing NE into North Sea at Saltfleet Haven. **53 H4** TF4793.
Great Eccleston *Lancs.* Population: 1930. ***Village***, 5m/8km E of Poulton-le-Fylde. **55 H5** SD4240.

Great Edstone *N.Yorks.* ***Village***, 2m/3km SE of Kirkbymoorside. **58 D1** SE7084.
Great Ellingham *Norf.* ***Village***, 2m/4km NW of Attleborough. **44 E6** TM0196.
Great Elm *Som.* ***Village***, 2m/3km NW of Frome. **20 A7** ST7449.
Great End *Cumb.* ***Mountain***, 1m/2km NE of Scafell Pike. Height 2985 feet or 910 metres. **60 D6** NY2108.
Great Eppleton *T. & W.* ***Settlement***, 1m/2km E of Hetton-le-Hole. NZ3648.
Great Eversden *Cambs.* ***Village***, 6m/10km SW of Cambridge. **33 G3** TL3653.
Great Fen *Cambs.* ***Open space***, fenland 4m/6km SE of Ely. **33 K1** TL5978.
Great Fencote *N.Yorks.* ***Hamlet***, 4m/6km SE of Catterick. **62 D7** SE2893.
Great Finborough *Suff.* ***Village***, 3m/4km W of Stowmarket. **34 E3** TM0157.
Great Fransham *Norf.* ***Village***, 6m/9km W of East Dereham. **44 C4** TF8913.
Great Gable *Cumb.* ***Mountain***, in Lake District 3m/5km SW of Seatoller. Height 2949 feet or 899 metres. **60 D5** NY2010.
Great Gaddesden *Herts.* ***Village***, 3m/5km NE of Berkhamsted. **32 D7** TL0211.
Great Gidding *Cambs.* ***Village***, 5m/8km SW of Stilton. **42 E7** TL1183.
Great Givendale *E.Riding* ***Hamlet***, 3m/5km N of Pocklington. **58 E4** SE8153.
Great Glemham *Suff.* ***Village***, 3m/5km W of Saxmundham. **35 H2** TM3461.
Great Glen *High.* *See Glen Mòr.*
Great Glen *Leics.* Population: 2963. ***Village***, 6m/10km SE of Leicester. **41 J6** SP6597.
Great Gonerby *Lincs.* Population: 3759. ***Village***, 2m/3km NW of Grantham. **42 B2** SK8938.
Great Gransden *Cambs.* ***Village***, 5m/8km NE of Potton. **33 F3** TL2755.
Great Green *Cambs.* ***Hamlet***, to NE of Guilden Morden, 6m/10km E of Biggleswade. TL2844.
Great Green *Norf.* ***Locality***, adjoining Little Green between Bunwell and Bunwell Street. TM1293.
Great Green *Norf.* ***Settlement***, 1m/2km N of Denton. **45 G6** TM2789.
Great Green *Suff.* ***Hamlet***, 6m/9km SE of Bury St. Edmunds. **34 D3** TL9155.
Great Green *Suff.* ***Hamlet***, 1m/2km NW of Wingfield. TM2178.
Great Green *Suff.* ***Settlement***, 1m/2km W of Norton. TL9465.
Great Green *Suff.* ***Settlement***, 2m/3km S of Diss. TM1277.
Great Habton *N.Yorks.* ***Village***, 3m/5km NW of Malton. **58 D2** SE7576.
Great Haldon *Devon* ***Large natural feature***, wooded ridge running NW to SE between Exeter and Newton Abbot, crossed by two main roads. SX8983.
Great Hale *Lincs.* ***Village***, 1km S of Heckington. **42 E1** TF1442.
Great Hallingbury *Essex* ***Village***, 2m/3km SE of Bishop's Stortford. **33 J7** TL5119.
Great Hameldon *Lancs.* ***Mountain***, 2m/3km E of Accrington. Height 1342 feet or 409 metres. **56 C7** SD7928.
Great Hampden *Bucks.* ***Hamlet***, 3m/5km E of Princes Risborough. SP8401.
Great Hanwood *Shrop.* ***Village***, 4m/7km SW of Shrewsbury. **38 D5** SJ4309.
Great Harrowden *Northants.* ***Village***, 2m/3km N of Wellingborough. **32 B1** SP8870.
Great Harwood *Lancs.* Population: 10,562. ***Town***, 4m/7km NE of Blackburn. Formerly well-known as a textile town. Historic house of Martholme 2m/3km NE. **56 C6** SD7332.
Great Haseley *Oxon.* ***Village***, 5m/8km SW of Thame. **21 K1** SP6401.
Great Hatfield *E.Riding* ***Village***, 3m/5km S of Hornsea. **59 H5** TA1842.
Great Haw *N.Yorks.* ***Mountain***, on W edge of Masham Moor, 6m/9km SW of Middleham. Height 1784 feet or 544 metres. **57 F2** SE0779.
Great Haywood *Staffs.* Population: 2305. ***Village***, on River Trent, 4m/6km NW of Rugeley. Junction of Staffordshire and Worcestershire Canal with Trent and Mersey Canal lies immediately to W. **40 C3** SJ9922.
Great Heath *W.Mid.* ***Suburb***, 1m/2km NE of Coventry city centre. **41 F7** SP3480.
Great Heck *N.Yorks.* ***Village***, 3m/5km W of Snaith. **58 B7** SE5922.
Great Henny *Essex* ***Hamlet***, 2m/4km S of Sudbury. **34 C5** TL8637.
Great Hill *D. & G.* ***Mountain***, with mast at summit, 4m/7km SE of Thornhill. Height 1158 feet or 353 metres. **68 E4** NX9492.
Great Hinton *Wilts.* ***Village***, 3m/4km E of Trowbridge. **20 C6** ST9059.
Great Hivings *Bucks.* ***Suburb***, N district of Chesham. SP9503.
Great Hockham *Norf.* ***Village***, 6m/10km W of Attleborough. **44 D6** TL9592.
Great Holland *Essex* ***Village***, 4m/6km NE of Clacton-on-Sea. **35 G7** TM2119.
Great Hollands *Brack.F.* ***Suburb***, SW district of Bracknell. SU8567.
Great Horkesley *Essex* ***Village***, 4m/6km N of Colchester. **34 D5** TL9730.
Great Hormead *Herts.* ***Village***, 3m/4km E of Buntingford. **33 H5** TL4029.
Great Horrocks *Gt.Man.* ***Suburb***, 1m/2km NE of Manchester city centre. SJ8499.
Great Horton *W.Yorks.* ***Suburb***, 2m/3km SW of Bradford city centre. SE1431.
Great Horwood *Bucks.* ***Village***, 2m/3km N of Winslow. **31 J5** SP7731.
Great Houghton *Northants.* ***Village***, 3m/4km S of Northampton town centre. **31 J3** SP7958.
Great Houghton *S.Yorks.* Population: 2405. ***Village***, 6m/9km E of Barnsley. **51 G2** SE4306.
Great Howarth *Gt.Man.* ***Locality***, 2m/3km W of Littleborough. SD9015.
Great Hucklow *Derbys.* ***Village***, 6m/10km NW of Bakewell. **50 D5** SK1777.
Great Kelk *E.Riding* ***Hamlet***, 3m/5km S of Burton Agnes. **59 H4** TA1058.
Great Kimble *Bucks.* ***Village***, 2m/3km NE of Princes Risborough. **22 B1** SP8206.
Great Kingshill *Bucks.* Population: 2071. ***Village***, 3m/5km N of High Wycombe. **22 B2** SU8798.
Great Kneeset *Devon* ***Mountain***, 5m/8km E of Lydford, in Dartmoor National Park. Height 1863 feet or 568 metres. **6 D7** SX5885.
Great Knoutberry Hill *Cumb.* ***Mountain***, summit of Whiddale Fell, 5m/8km E of Dent. Height 2204 feet or 672 metres. **56 C1** SD7887.
Great Knowles Green *Suff.* ***Settlement***, 1m/2km NW of Chedburgh. TL7758.
Great Lake *N.Yorks.* ***Lake/loch***, just S of Coneysthorpe, 4m/7km W of Malton. **58 D2** SE7170.
Great Lake *Notts.* ***Lake/loch***, in Welbeck Park, 4m/6km S of Worksop. **51 H5** SK5773.
Great Langton *N.Yorks.* ***Village***, on River Swale, 5m/8km NW of Northallerton. **62 D7** SE2996.
Great Law *Sc.Bord.* ***Mountain***, 4m/6km SW of Stow. Height 1666 feet or 508 metres. **76 C6** NT4041.
Great Leighs *Essex* ***Village***, 4m/7km SW of Braintree. **34 B7** TL7217.
Great Lever *Gt.Man.* ***Suburb***, 1m/2km SE of Bolton town centre. SD7207.
Great Limber *Lincs.* ***Village***, 5m/8km N of Caistor. **52 E2** TA1308.
Great Linford *M.K.* ***Village***, 2m/4km E of Wolverton, within area of Milton Keynes. **32 B4** SP8542.
Great Livermere *Suff.* ***Village***, 5m/8km NE of Bury St. Edmunds. **34 C1** TL8871.
Great Longstone *Derbys.* ***Village***, 2m/4km NW of Bakewell. **50 E5** SK2071.
Great Lumley *Dur.* Population: 3274. ***Village***, 2m/3km SE of Chester-le-Street. **62 D2** NZ2949.
Great Lyth *Shrop.* ***Settlement***, 4m/6km SW of Shrewsbury. **38 D5** SJ4507.
Great Malvern *Worcs.* Population: 31,537. ***Town***, on steep E slope of Malvern Hills, 7m/12km SW of Worcester. Developed as spa in 19c. Church has 15c tower and medieval artefacts. **29 G4** SO7845.
Great Maplestead *Essex* ***Village***, 3m/4km N of Halstead. **34 C5** TL8034.
Great Marton *B'pool* ***Suburb***, 1m/2km E of Blackpool town centre. **55 G6** SD3234.
Great Marton Moss *B'pool* ***Locality***, 2m/3km N of Lytham St. Anne's. SD3331.
Great Massingham *Norf.* ***Village***, 9m/14km N of Swaffham. **44 B3** TF7922.
Great Maytham Hall *Kent* ***Historic house***, neo-Georgian house built 1910 by Sir Edwin Lutyens, 1km S of Rolvenden. **14 D4** TQ8430.
Great Mell Fell *Cumb.* ***Mountain***, 3m/4km SW of Penruddock. Height 1761 feet or 537 metres. **60 E4** NY3925.
Great Melton *Norf.* ***Locality***, 4m/6km NE of Wymondham. **45 F5** TG1206.
Great Meols *Mersey.* ***Locality***, adjoining to NE of Hoylake. SJ2390.
Great Mew Stone *Devon* ***Island***, large pyramidal rock island off Wembury Point at W end of Wembury bay, 5m/8km SE of Plymouth. **4 E6** SX5047.
Great Milton *Oxon.* ***Village***, 8m/12km SE of Oxford. **21 K1** SP6202.
Great Mis Tor *Devon* ***Mountain***, in Dartmoor National Park, 3m/4km NW of Princetown. Height 1768 feet or 539 metres. **5 F3** SX5676.
Great Missenden *Bucks.* Population: 3990. ***Village***, 4m/7km W of Chesham. **22 B1** SP8901.
Great Mitton *Lancs.* ***Village***, on River Ribble, 3m/4km SW of Clitheroe. **56 C6** SD7139.
Great Mongeham *Kent* ***Village***, adjoining to W of Deal. **15 J2** TR3451.
Great Moss *Gt.Man.* ***Locality***, adjoining to S of Orrell. SD5203.
Great Moulton *Norf.* ***Village***, 7m/11km NW of Harleston. **45 F6** TM1690.
Great Munden *Herts.* ***Settlement***, 2m/3km W of Puckeridge. **33 G6** TL3524.
Great Musgrave *Cumb.* ***Village***, 2m/3km SW of Brough. **61 J5** NY7613.
Great Ness *Shrop.* ***Village***, 7m/11km NW of Shrewsbury. **38 C4** SJ3918.
Great Nurcot *Som.* ***Hamlet***, on Exmoor, 1m/2km N of Winsford. SS9036.
Great Oak *Mon.* ***Hamlet***, 2m/4km NW of Raglan. **28 C7** SO3809.
Great Oakley *Essex* ***Village***, 5m/8km SW of Harwich. **35 F6** TM1927.
Great Oakley *Northants.* ***Suburb***, S district of Corby, formerly a village. Hall is partly Tudor. **42 B7** SP8685.
Great Offley *Herts.* ***Village***, 3m/5km SW of Hitchin. **32 E6** TL1427.
Great Orme Country Park *Conwy* ***Leisure/recreation***, over 600 acres of coastal headland, grassland and heath on Great Ormes Head to NW of Llandudno. Attracts over 85 species of birds. Accessible by road, tramway and cable car. **47 F4** SH7683.
Great Orme Tramway *Conwy* ***Other feature of interest***, tramway built 1902, from Llandudno to summit of Great Orme via three alternative routes. **47 F4** SH7782.
Great Ormes Head (Pen-y-Gogarth). *Conwy* ***Coastal feature***, limestone headland 2m/3km NW of Llandudno, with spectacular views of Welsh mainland. Evidence of prehistoric and Roman occupation. **47 F4** SH7584.
Great Ormside *Cumb.* ***Hamlet***, 2m/4km SE of Appleby-in-Westmorland across River Eden. **61 J5** NY7017.
Great Orton *Cumb.* ***Village***, 5m/8km W of Carlisle. **60 E1** NY3254.
Great Ouse (Commonly known as (River) Ouse.) ***River***, major river of E England rising SW of Towcester and flowing circuitously to The Wash by Buckingham, Newport Pagnell, Olney, Bedford, St. Neots, Huntingdon, St. Ives, Ely, Littleport, Downham Market and King's Lynn. **44 A4** TF5924.
Great Ouseburn *N.Yorks.* ***Village***, 5m/7km SE of Boroughbridge. **57 K3** SE4461.
Great Oxendon *Northants.* ***Village***, 2m/4km S of Market Harborough. **42 A7** SP7383.
Great Oxney Green *Essex* ***Suburb***, 3m/4km W of Chelmsford. **24 C1** TL6606.
Great Packington *Warks.* ***Locality***, 4m/6km SE of Coleshill. SP2283.
Great Palgrave *Norf.* ***Settlement***, 2m/3km SE of Castle Acre. **44 C4** TF8312.
Great Parndon *Essex* ***Suburb***, SW district of Harlow. **23 H1** TL4308.
Great Paxton *Cambs.* ***Village***, 3m/5km NE of St. Neots. **33 F2** TL2063.
Great Pinseat *N.Yorks.* ***Mountain***, on E side of Arkengarthdale, 5m/8km E of Keld. Height 1912 feet or 583 metres. **62 A6** NY9702.
Great Plumpton *Lancs.* ***Hamlet***, 3m/4km W of Kirkham. **55 G6** SD3833.
Great Plumstead *Norf.* ***Village***, 5m/8km E of Norwich. **45 G5** TG3010.
Great Ponton *Lincs.* ***Village***, 4m/6km S of Grantham. Site of Roman building to E. **42 C2** SK9230.
Great Postland *Lincs.* ***Open space***, fenland to NE of Crowland. **43 F4** TF2512.
Great Potheridge *Devon* ***Hamlet***, forms locality of Potheridge, along with Little Potheridge and Potheridge Gate, 3m/5km SE of Great Torrington. SS5114.
Great Preston *W.Yorks.* Population: 5507. ***Village***, 2m/4km S of Garforth. **57 J7** SE4029.
Great Purston *Northants.* ***Settlement***, 4m/7km E of Banbury. SP5139.
Great Raveley *Cambs.* ***Village***, 3m/5km SW of Ramsey. **43 F7** TL2581.
Great Rhos *Powys* ***Mountain***, summit of Radnor Forest, 3m/4km NW of New Radnor. Height 2165 feet or 660 metres. **28 A2** SO1863.
Great Ridge *Wilts.* ***Open space***, forested hillslope rising to 220 metres, 4m/6km S of Heytesbury. **9 J1** ST9236.
Great Rissington *Glos.* ***Village***, 5m/8km NW of Burford. **30 C7** SP1917.
Great Rollright *Oxon.* ***Village***, 3m/5km N of Chipping Norton. **30 E5** SP3231.
Great Ryburgh *Norf.* ***Village***, 3m/5km SE of Fakenham. **44 D3** TF9527.
Great Ryle *Northumb.* ***Hamlet***, 3m/5km W of Whittingham. **71 F2** NU0212.
Great Ryton *Shrop.* ***Hamlet***, 6m/9km S of Shrewsbury. **38 D5** SJ4803.
Great Saling *Essex* ***Village***, 4m/7km NW of Braintree. **33 K6** TL7025.
Great Salkeld *Cumb.* ***Village***, 5m/8km NE of Penrith. **61 G3** NY5536.
Great Sampford *Essex* ***Village***, 4m/6km NE of Thaxted. **33 K5** TL6435.
Great Sankey *Warr.* Population: 34,025. ***Suburb***, large urban district, 1m/2km W of Warrington town centre. **48 E4** SJ5788.
Great Saredon *Staffs.* ***Settlement***, 2m/3km SW of Cannock. SJ9508.
Great Saxham *Suff.* ***Settlement***, 4m/7km W of Bury St. Edmunds. **34 B2** TL7862.
Great Seabrights *Essex* ***Settlement***, 2m/3km S of Chelmsford town centre. TL7103.
Great Shefford *W.Berks.* ***Village***, 5m/8km NE of Hungerford. **21 G4** SU3875.
Great Shelford *Cambs.* Population: 6522. ***Small town***, 4m/7km S of Cambridge. **33 H3** TL4652.
Great Shunner Fell *N.Yorks.* ***Mountain***, 4m/6km W of Muker. Height 2348 feet or 716 metres. **61 K7** SD8497.
Great Smeaton *N.Yorks.* ***Village***, 7m/11km N of Northallerton. **62 E6** NZ3404.
Great Snoring *Norf.* ***Village***, 3m/5km NE of Fakenham. **44 D2** TF9434.
Great Somerford *Wilts.* ***Village***, on River Avon, 3m/5km SE of Malmesbury. **20 C3** ST9682.
Great Stainton *Darl.* ***Village***, 6m/9km NE of Darlington. **62 E4** NZ3322.
Great Stambridge *Essex* ***Village***, 2m/3km E of Rochford. **24 E2** TQ8991.
Great Staughton *Cambs.* ***Village***, 5m/8km NW of St. Neots. Site of Roman building 2km SE. **32 E2** TL1264.
Great Steeping *Lincs.* ***Village***, 3m/5km SE of Spilsby. **53 H6** TF4364.
Great Stoke *S.Glos.* ***Locality***, NE part of Stoke Gifford, 6m/9km NE of Bristol. ST6280.
Great Stonar *Kent* ***Locality***, to N of Sandwich. **15 J2** TR3359.
Great Stour *Kent* ***River***, rising near Lenham and flowing SE to Ashford, where it is joined by East Stour River. It then flows NE through Canterbury to Plucks Gutter where it joins Little Stour River to form River Stour. **15 F3** TR2663.
Great Strickland *Cumb.* ***Village***, 5m/9km SE of Penrith. **61 G4** NY5522.
Great Stukeley *Cambs.* ***Village***, 2m/4km NW of Huntingdon. **33 F1** TL2174.

Great Sturton *Lincs.* ***Hamlet***, 5m/9km NW of Horncastle. **53 F5** TF2176.
Great Sutton *Ches.* ***Suburb***, 2m/3km SW of Ellesmere Port town centre. **48 C5** SJ3775.
Great Sutton *Shrop.* ***Hamlet***, 5m/8km N of Ludlow. **38 E7** SO5183.
Great Swinburne *Northumb.* ***Hamlet***, 7m/11km N of Hexham. **70 E6** NY9375.
Great Tarpots *Essex* ***Suburb***, to W of Thundersley, 4m/6km E of Basildon. TQ7688.
Great Tew *Oxon.* ***Village***, 5m/9km E of Chipping Norton. **30 E6** SP3929.
Great Tey *Essex* ***Village***, 7m/11km W of Colchester. **34 C6** TL8925.
Great Thorness *I.o.W.* ***Settlement***, 4m/6km SW of Cowes. SZ4592.
Great Thurlow *Suff.* ***Village***, 3m/5km N of Haverhill. **33 K4** TL6750.
Great Torr *Devon* ***Hamlet***, 3m/4km SW of Modbury. SX6348.
Great Torrington (Commonly known as Torrington.) *Devon* Population: 4073. ***Small town***, hilltop town above River Torridge, 5m/9km SE of Bideford. **6 D4** SS4919.
Great Tosson *Northumb.* ***Hamlet***, 2m/3km SW of Rothbury. With Little Tosson, forms parish of Tosson. **71 F3** NU0200.
Great Totham *Essex* ***Village***, 3m/5km N of Maldon. **34 C7** TL8511.
Great Totham *Essex* ***Village***, 3m/5km E of Witham. **34 C7** TL8613.
Great Tows *Lincs.* ***Hamlet***, 3m/4km S of Binbrook. TF2290.
Great Tree *Cornw.* ***Locality***, 1m/2km NE of Looe. SX2655.
Great Urswick *Cumb.* ***Village***, ranged round three sides of Urswick Tarn, 3m/4km E of Dalton-in-Furness. **55 F2** SD2674.
Great Wakering *Essex* Population: 2577. ***Village***, 2m/3km N of Shoeburyness. **25 F3** TQ9487.
Great Waldingfield *Suff.* ***Village***, 3m/5km NE of Sudbury. **34 D4** TL9143.
Great Walsingham *Norf.* ***Village***, 4m/7km S of Wells-next-the-Sea. **44 D2** TF9437.
Great Waltham *Essex* ***Village***, 4m/7km N of Chelmsford. **33 K7** TL6913.
Great Warford *Ches.* ***Locality***, 2m/3km SW of Alderley Edge. SJ8077.
Great Warley *Essex* ***Village***, 2m/4km SW of Brentwood. **23 J2** TQ5890.
Great Washbourne *Glos.* ***Hamlet***, 4m/7km NW of Winchcombe. **29 J5** SO9834.
Great Weeke *Devon* ***Hamlet***, 3m/4km NW of Moretonhampstead. SX7187.
Great Welnetham *Suff.* ***Settlement***, 3m/5km SE of Bury St. Edmunds. **34 C3** TL8759.
Great Wenham *Suff.* ***Village***, 4m/7km SE of Hadleigh. **34 E5** TM0738.
Great Western Railway Museum *Swin.* ***Other feature of interest***, in Swindon. Includes Great Western Railway locomotives and other railway artefacts. **20 E3** SU1484.
Great Whernside *N.Yorks.* ***Mountain***, 2m/4km NE of Kettlewell. Height 2309 feet or 704 metres. **57 F2** SE0073.
Great Whittington *Northumb.* ***Village***, 4m/7km N of Corbridge. **71 F6** NZ0070.
Great Wigborough *Essex* ***Village***, 7m/11km S of Colchester. **34 D7** TL9614.
Great Wigsell *E.Suss.* ***Hamlet***, 3m/4km NE of Robertsbridge. TQ7627.
Great Wilbraham *Cambs.* ***Village***, 6m/10km E of Cambridge. Village of Little Wilbraham to N. **33 J3** TL5457.
Great Wilne *Derbys.* ***Hamlet***, 1km NE of Shardlow and 1km W of junction of Trent and Mersey Canal with Rivers Trent and Derwent. SK4430.
Great Wishford *Wilts.* ***Village***, on River Wylye, 3m/5km N of Wilton. **10 B1** SU0735.
Great Witchingham *Norf.* ***Hamlet***, 2m/3km S of Reepham. TG1019.
Great Witcombe *Glos.* ***Village***, 6m/9km SE of Gloucester. Remains of Roman villa (English Heritage) to W. **29 J7** SO9114.
Great Witcombe Roman Villa *Glos.* ***Historic/prehistoric site***, remains of Roman villa (English Heritage) built round courtyard at Great Witcombe, 5m/8km SE of Gloucester. Bath suite of three rooms has fine mosaics and foundations of other parts of villa remain. **29 H7** SO9013.
Great Witley *Worcs.* ***Village***, 5m/8km SW of Stourport-on-Severn. Ruins of 18c house (English Heritage) 1m/2km SE. **29 G2** SO7566.
Great Wolford *Warks.* ***Village***, 3m/5km NE of Moreton-in-Marsh. **30 D5** SP2434.
Great Wood Country Park *Herts.* ***Leisure/recreation***, country park of nearly 250 acres, 4m/7km SE of Hatfield. Mainly woodland, there is much to interest botanists. **23 F1** TL2804.
Great Woolstone *M.K.* ***Village***, in Woolstone locality, E of Milton Keynes. **32 B5** SP8739.
Great Wratting *Suff.* ***Village***, 2m/3km NE of Haverhill. **33 K4** TL6848.
Great Wymondley *Herts.* ***Village***, 2m/3km E of Hitchin. Site of Roman villa 1km NW. **33 F6** TL2128.
Great Wyrley *Staffs.* Population: 17,604. ***Locality***, 2m/3km S of Cannock. **40 B5** SJ9907.
Great Wytheford *Shrop.* ***Hamlet***, 2m/3km NW of High Ercall. **38 E4** SJ5719.
Great Yarlside *Cumb.* ***Open space***, hillslope on S side of Shap Fells, 5m/8km SW of Shap. **61 G6** NY5207.
Great Yarmouth *Norf.* Population: 56,190. ***Town***, port and resort at mouth of River Yare, 18m/29km E of Norwich. Former centre for herring fishing industry, North Sea gas fields now attract hi-tech industry. Medieval Rows mostly destroyed in World War II; some remain and have been restored. 13c tollhouse. 19c Nelson's Monument has 217 steps. Birthplace of Anna Sewell, author of Black Beauty. Heliport 2m/3km N. **45 K5** TG5207.
Great Yeldham *Essex* Population: 1513. ***Village***, 6m/10km NW of Halstead. **34 B5** TL7638.
Greatford *Lincs.* ***Village***, 5m/8km NE of Stamford. **42 D4** TF0811.
Greatgate *Staffs.* ***Hamlet***, 4m/6km SE of Cheadle. **40 C1** SK0540.
Greatham *Hants.* ***Village***, 4m/6km W of Liphook. **11 J1** SU7730.
Greatham *Hart.* ***Village***, 3m/5km S of Hartlepool. **63 F4** NZ4927.
Greatham *W.Suss.* ***Settlement***, 2m/3km S of Pulborough. **12 D5** TQ0415.
Greathed Manor *Surr.* ***Historic house***, Victorian manor house to E of Dormansland, 2m/3km SE of Lingfield. **23 H7** TQ4142.
Greatmoor Hill *Sc.Bord.* ***Mountain***, 6m/10km SE of Teviothead. Height 1965 feet or 599 metres. **69 K3** NT4800.
Greatness *Kent* ***Suburb***, N district of Sevenoaks. TQ5356.
Greatstone-on-Sea *Kent* ***Town***, resort on St. Mary's Bay, 1m/2km SE of New Romney. **15 F5** TR0823.
Greatworth *Northants.* ***Village***, 4m/6km NW of Brackley. **31 G4** SP5542.
Greave *Gt.Man.* ***Suburb***, 1m/2km NE of Romiley. SJ9491.
Greave *Lancs.* ***Locality***, adjoining to E of Bacup. SD8723.
Greeb Point *Cornw.* ***Coastal feature***, headland 1m/2km S of Portscatho. **3 F5** SW8733.
Greeba Mountain *I.o.M.* ***Mountain***, 3m/4km E of St. John's. Height 1384 feet or 422 metres. **54 C5** SC3181.
Green *Denb.* ***Settlement***, 1m/2km N of Denbigh. SJ0568.
Green Bank *Cumb.* ***Settlement***, 1m/2km N of Cartmel. SD3880.
Green Bottom *Cornw.* ***Locality***, 4m/6km W of Truro. SW7645.
Green Bottom *Glos.* ***Settlement***, 1m/2km NE of Cinderford. SO6715.
Green Cross *Surr.* ***Settlement***, 2m/3km NW of Hindhead. SU8638.
Green End *Beds.* ***Locality***, NE end of Great Barford village, 4m/7km NW of Sandy. **32 E3** TL1252.
Green End *Beds.* ***Settlement***, 3m/4km SW of Bedford town centre across River Great Ouse. TL0147.
Green End *Beds.* ***Settlement***, S end of Pertenhall, 2m/4km SW of Kimbolton. TL0864.
Green End *Beds.* ***Settlement***, N end of Little Staughton, 3m/5km S of Kimbolton. TL1063.
Green End *Bucks.* ***Settlement***, adjoining to N of Great Brickhill, 3m/4km SE of Bletchley. SP9030.
Green End *Cambs.* ***Hamlet***, N end of Comberton, 4m/7km SW of Cambridge. TL3856.
Green End *Cambs.* ***Locality***, S end of Sawtry, 4m/6km S of Stilton. TL1783.
Green End *Cambs.* ***Locality***, 2m/3km E of Cottenham. TL4768.
Green End *Cambs.* ***Locality***, on E bank of River Cam adjoining Fen Ditton. TL4860.
Green End *Cambs.* ***Locality***, S end of Stretham. TL5174.
Green End *Cambs.* ***Settlement***, on E side of Great Stukeley, 2m/3km NW of Huntingdon. TL2274.
Green End *Cambs.* ***Suburb***, N district of St. Ives. TL3172.
Green End *Herts.* ***Hamlet***, 5m/9km E of Baldock. TL3233.
Green End *Herts.* ***Hamlet***, 4m/6km W of Puckeridge. **33 G6** TL3322.
Green End *Herts.* ***Settlement***, N end of Weston, 2m/4km SE of Baldock. TL2630.
Green End *Lancs.* ***Locality***, adjoining to S of Earby. SD9046.
Green End *Warks.* ***Settlement***, 4m/7km SE of Coleshill. SP2686.
Green Fell *Cumb.* ***Open space***, 1m/2km SE of Melmerby Fell and 6m/10km NE of Langwathby. **61 H3** NY6636.
Green Gate *Devon* ***Hamlet***, just NE of Uplowman, 4m/7km NE of Tiverton. ST0115.
Green Hailey *Bucks.* ***Settlement***, 1m/2km E of Princes Risborough. SP8203.
Green Hammerton *N.Yorks.* ***Village***, 7m/12km SE of Boroughbridge. **57 K4** SE4556.
Green Head *Cumb.* ***Locality***, 1km S of Dalston. NY3649.
Green Head *Ork.* ***Coastal feature***, headland on E coast of Hoy opposite Cava. **107 C8** ND3099.
Green Heath *Staffs.* ***Suburb***, 2m/3km NE of Cannock. SJ9913.
Green Hill *Angus* ***Mountain***, 2m/3km NE of Clova. Height 2854 feet or 870 metres. **90 B7** NO3475.
Green Hill *Northumb.* ***Mountain***, 2m/3km N of Allenheads. Height 1729 feet or 527 metres. **61 K2** NY8647.
Green Hill *Wilts.* ***Settlement***, 3m/4km N of Wootton Bassett. SU0686.
Green Hills *Cambs.* ***Locality***, at SE end of Soham. TL6072.
Green Holm *Shet.* ***Island***, rock off Burra Ness on S coast of Yell. HU5178.
Green Island *Dorset* ***Island***, on S side of Poole Harbour. SZ0086.
Green Island *High.* ***Island***, islet in Enard Bay off NW coast of Ross and Cromarty district, 1m/2km S of Eilean Mòr. NC0515.
Green Isle *Shet.* ***Island***, tiny island off E coast of Mainland in Dury Voe. HU4861.
Green Lane *Devon* ***Hamlet***, 2m/3km SW of Bovey Tracey. SX7877.
Green Lane *Worcs.* ***Suburb***, 3m/4km SE of Redditch. SP0664.
Green Law *Sc.Bord.* ***Mountain***, in Wauchope Forest area of Cheviot Hills, 4m/7km SW of Carter Bar. Height 1207 feet or 368 metres. **70 B3** NT6304.
Green Lowther *S.Lan.* ***Mountain***, summit of Lowther Hills, 2m/3km SE of Leadhills. Mast at summit. Height 2401 feet or 732 metres. **68 E2** NS9012.
Green Moor *S.Yorks.* ***Hamlet***, 1km NE of Stocksbridge. SK2899.
Green Ore *Som.* ***Hamlet***, 2m/4km SW of Chewton Mendip. **19 J6** ST5750.
Green Quarter *Cumb.* ***Hamlet***, just E of Kentmere village, 5m/8km E of Ambleside. NY4604.
Green Rigg *Cumb.* ***Hill***, in Spadeadam Forest, 4m/7km NW of Greenhead. Height 869 feet or 265 metres. **70 B6** NY6171.
Green Scar *Pembs.* ***Island***, rock island lying 1m/2km W of Dinas Fawr, between Black Scar and The Mare. **16 A2** SM7922.
Green Side *W.Yorks.* ***Suburb***, 2m/3km SW of Leeds city centre, in district of Wortley. SE2732.
Green Street *E.Suss.* ***Settlement***, 1km SE of Crowhurst. TQ7611.
Green Street *Glos.* ***Locality***, 4m/7km SE of Gloucester. SO8915.
Green Street *Herts.* ***Hamlet***, 2m/3km W of Bishop's Stortford. TL4522.
Green Street *Herts.* ***Locality***, adjoining to N of Borehamwood. **22 E2** TQ1998.
Green Street *Suff.* ***Locality***, adjoining to E of Hoxne. TM1877.
Green Street *W.Suss.* ***Hamlet***, 2m/3km E of Coolham. TQ1422.
Green Street *Worcs.* ***Hamlet***, 4m/6km S of Worcester. SO8649.
Green Street *Worcs.* ***Locality***, 5m/8km N of Tewkesbury. SO8740.
Green Street Green *Gt.Lon.* ***Suburb***, in borough of Bromley, 2m/3km S of Orpington. **23 H5** TQ4563.
Green Street Green *Kent* ***Village***, 4m/6km SE of Dartford. **23 J4** TQ5870.
Green Tye *Herts.* ***Hamlet***, 3m/5km SW of Bishop's Stortford. **33 H7** TL4418.
Greena *Shet.* ***Island***, small island at entrance to Weisdale Voe, Mainland. HU3747.
Greenacres *Gt.Man.* ***Suburb***, 1m/2km E of Oldham town centre. SD9405.
Greenbank *Edin.* ***Suburb***, 3m/4km S of Edinburgh city centre. NT2369.
Greenbooth Reservoir *Gt.Man.* ***Reservoir***, 3m/5km NW of Rochdale town centre. **49 H1** SD8515.
Greenburn *Angus* ***Settlement***, 1m/2km NW of Monikie. **83 F4** NO4839.
Greencroft *Dur.* ***Locality***, including Greencroft Park, 1m/2km NW of Lanchester. **62 C2** NZ1549.
Greencroft *Dur.* ***Locality***, to W of Annfield Plain. NZ1651.
Greencroft *Norf.* ***Locality***, adjoining to W of Blakeney. TG0243.
Greendams *Aber.* ***Settlement***, 3m/4km N of Bridge of Dye. **90 E5** NO6490.
Greendykes *Northumb.* ***Settlement***, 1km E of Chatton. **71 F1** NU0628.
Greenend *Oxon.* ***Settlement***, 3m/4km NW of Charlbury. SP3221.
Greenfaulds *N.Lan.* ***Suburb***, 1m/2km S of Cumbernauld town centre. NS7573.
Greenfield *Beds.* ***Village***, 2m/4km SE of Ampthill. **32 D5** TL0534.
Greenfield (Maes-Glas). *Flints.* Population: 2230. ***Village***, 1m/2km NE of Holywell. Remains of Basingwerk Abbey (Cadw), founded 1131. **47 K5** SJ1977.
Greenfield *Gt.Man.* ***Village***, 2m/3km NE of Mossley. **50 C2** SD9904.
Greenfield *High.* ***Settlement***, on S side of Loch Garry, 6m/10km W of Invergarry. **87 J4** NH2000.
Greenfield *Lincs.* ***Settlement***, with moat, on edge of woodland, 2m/3km NW of Alford. TF4377.
Greenfield *Oxon.* ***Hamlet***, 3m/5km N of Nettlebed. **22 A2** SU7191.
Greenfields *Derbys.* ***Settlement***, 2m/3km SW of Swadlincote. SK2816.
Greenford *Gt.Lon.* ***Suburb***, in borough of Ealing, 10m/16km W of Charing Cross. **22 E3** TQ1482.
Greenford Green *Gt.Lon.* ***Suburb***, in borough of Ealing, to N of Greenford. TQ1482.
Greengairs *N.Lan.* ***Village***, 3m/5km SE of Cumbernauld. **75 F3** NS7870.
Greengate *Gt.Man.* ***Locality***, 2m/3km NE of Rochdale. SD9115.
Greengates *W.Yorks.* ***Suburb***, 3m/5km NE of Bradford city centre. SE1837.
Greengill *Cumb.* ***Settlement***, 1m/2km SW of Gilcrux. NY1037.
Greenhalgh *Lancs.* ***Hamlet***, 3m/4km NW of Kirkham. **55 H6** SD4035.
Greenhall *Aber.* ***Settlement***, 1m/2km NE of Insch. **90 E2** NJ6329.
Greenham *Som.* ***Hamlet***, 4m/6km W of Wellington. **7 J3** ST0820.
Greenham *W.Berks.* ***Village***, 1m/2km SE of Newbury, with disused airfield of Greenham Common to SE. **21 H5** SU4865.
Greenhaugh *Northumb.* ***Hamlet***, 4m/6km NW of Bellingham. Black Middens Bastle House (English Heritage), 16c fortified farmhouse above N bank of Tarset Burn, 3m/4km NW. **70 C5** NY7987.
Greenhays *Gt.Man.* ***Suburb***, 2m/3km SW of Farnworth and 3m/5km S of Bolton. SD7104.
Greenhead *Northumb.* ***Village***, on Tipalt Burn, 3m/5km W of Haltwhistle. Walltown Crags (English Heritage), one of best-preserved sections of Hadrian's Wall, 1m/2km NE. **70 B7** NY6665.
Greenheads *Aber.* ***Settlement***, 1m/2km NW of Hatton. **91 J1** NK0339.
Greenheys *Gt.Man.* ***Suburb***, 1m/2km SE of Manchester city centre. Art gallery. University of Manchester site. SJ8496.
Greenhill *Dur.* ***Locality***, adjoining to E of Murton. NZ4047.
Greenhill *Falk.* ***Settlement***, 1m/2km S of Bonnybridge. NS8278.
Greenhill *Gt.Lon.* ***Suburb***, in borough of Harrow, 10m/16km NW of Charing Cross. **22 E3** TQ1588.

Greenhill *High.* ***Settlement***, 1m/2km N of Brora, Sutherland district. **97 G1** NC9106.
Greenhill *Kent* ***Suburb***, 1m/2km SW of Herne Bay. TR1666.
Greenhill *S.Yorks.* ***Suburb***, 4m/6km S of Sheffield city centre. **51 F4** SK3481.
Greenhill *Worcs.* ***Settlement***, 4m/6km NW of Great Malvern. SO7248.
Greenhill *Worcs.* ***Suburb***, NE district of Kidderminster. SO8477.
Greenhill Bank *Shrop.* ***Hamlet***, 2m/3km NW of Ellesmere. SJ3736.
Greenhill Covenanters' House *S.Lan.* ***Historic house***, in Biggar. 17c farmhouse re-erected in town, now a museum of 17c life, which explores Covenanting movement and religious conflict which resulted. **75 J7** NT0237.
Greenhillocks *Derbys.* ***Suburb***, adjoining to SE of Ripley. SK4049.
Greenhills *S.Lan.* ***Suburb***, S district of East Kilbride. NS6252.
Greenhillstairs *D. & G.* ***Open space***, W facing valley side of Evan Water, below Greenhill, 4m/6km NW of Moffat. **69 F2** NT0410.
Greenhithe *Kent* ***Locality***, 3m/5km E of Dartford. **23 J4** TQ5875.
Greenholm *E.Ayr.* ***Village***, adjoining to E of Newmilns. Dry ski slope to N. **74 D7** NS5337.
Greenholme *Cumb.* ***Locality***, 2m/3km NW of Tebay. **61 G6** NY5905.
Greenhow Hill *N.Yorks.* ***Village***, 3m/5km W of Pateley Bridge. **57 G3** SE1164.
Greenigo *Ork.* ***Settlement***, 3m/5km SW of Kirkwall. **107 D7** HY4107.
Greenknowe Tower *Sc.Bord.* ***Historic/prehistoric site***, 1km W of Gordon. Attractive, well preserved, turreted tower house dating from 1581. **76 E6** NT6342.
Greenland *High.* ***Locality***, in Caithness district, 3m/4km SE of Dunnet. **105 H2** ND2467.
Greenland *S.Yorks.* ***Suburb***, 3m/4km NE of Sheffield city centre. SK3988.
Greenlands *Bucks.* ***Hamlet***, 2m/3km N of Henley-on-Thames. **22 A3** SU7785.
Greenlands *Worcs.* ***Suburb***, 1m/2km SE of Redditch town centre. SP0565.
Greenlaw *Aber.* ***Settlement***, 4m/6km S of Banff. **98 E5** NJ6758.
Greenlaw *Sc.Bord.* ***Village***, on Blackadder Water, 7m/11km SW of Duns. **77 F6** NT7146.
Greenlaw Moor *Sc.Bord.* ***Open space***, moorland 2m/3km N of Greenlaw. **77 F6** NT7048.
Greenlee Lough *Northumb.* ***Lake/loch***, 3m/5km N of Bardon Mill. **70 C6** NY7769.
Greenli Ness *Ork.* ***Coastal feature***, headland on S coast of Stronsay on W side of entrance to Bay of Holland. **106 F5** HY6221.
Greenloaning *P. & K.* ***Settlement***, 5m/8km NE of Dunblane. **81 K7** NN8307.
Greenmeadow *Torfaen* ***Suburb***, in W part of Cwmbran. ST2795.
Greenmoor Hill *Oxon.* ***Settlement***, adjoining to S of Woodcote, 3m/5km E of Goring. SU6481.
Greenmount *Gt.Man.* ***Village***, 3m/5km SW of Bury. **49 G1** SD7714.
Greenmyre *Aber.* ***Settlement***, 4m/6km E of Fyvie. **91 G1** NJ8236.
Greenoak *E.Riding* ***Settlement***, 4m/7km E of Howden. SE8127.
Greenock *Inclyde* Population: 50,013. ***Town***, industrial town and port on S side of Firth of Clyde, 2m/3km W of Glasgow. Birthplace of James Watt, 1736-1819. Large harbour and docks. **74 A3** NS2776.
Greenock Water *E.Ayr.* ***River***, running SW to River Ayr 4m/7km W of Muirkirk. **75 F7** NS6226.
Greenodd *Cumb.* ***Village***, 3m/5km NE of Ulverston. **55 G1** SD3182.
Greenrow *Cumb.* ***Locality***, adjoining to S of Silloth. NY1052.
Greens *Aber.* ***Locality***, 4m/6km W of New Deer. NJ8245.
Greens Norton *Northants.* Population: 1585. ***Village***, 2m/3km NW of Towcester. **31 H3** SP6649.
Greenscares *P. & K.* ***Settlement***, 3m/5km NW of Braco. **81 J6** NN8012.
Greensgate *Norf.* ***Locality***, 1km W of Weston Longville and 4m/6km W of Taverham. TG1015.
Greenside *T. & W.* ***Village***, 2m/3km SW of Ryton. **71 G7** NZ1362.
Greenside *W.Yorks.* ***Suburb***, 2m/3km E of Huddersfield town centre. SE1716.
Greenskares *Aber.* ***Settlement***, 1m/2km SW of Gardenstown. **99 F4** NJ7763.
Greenstead *Essex* ***Suburb***, 2m/3km E of Colchester town centre. TM0225.
Greenstead Green *Essex* ***Village***, 2m/3km S of Halstead. **34 C6** TL8228.
Greensted *Essex* ***Hamlet***, 1m/2km W of Chipping Ongar. Saxon church with nave walls of Oak. **23 J1** TL5302.
Greensted Green *Essex* ***Hamlet***, 2m/3km W of Chipping Ongar. TL5203.
Greenstone Point (Also known as Rubha na Lice Uaine.) *High.* ***Coastal feature***, headland on W coast of Ross and Cromarty district, 11m/18km N of Poolewe. **94 E2** NG8598.
Greenstreet Green *Suff.* ***Settlement***, 5m/8km N of Hadleigh. TM0450.
Greenway *Glos.* ***Settlement***, 3m/5km S of Ledbury. SO7033.
Greenway *Pembs.* ***Settlement***, 8m/12km SE of Fishguard. **16 D1** SN0630.
Greenway *Som.* ***Hamlet***, 3m/4km NE of Taunton. ST2527.
Greenway *Som.* ***Hamlet***, adjoining North Curry, 6m/9km E of Taunton. **8 C2** ST3124.
Greenway *V. of Glam.* ***Hamlet***, 4m/6km E of Cowbridge. ST0574.
Greenway Bank Country Park *Staffs.* ***Leisure/recreation***, country park of over 90 acres comprising woodland, parkland and a reservoir, 1m/2km SE of Biddulph. **49 H7** SJ8955.
Greenwell *Cumb.* ***Hamlet***, on W bank of River Gelt, 3m/5km S of Brampton. NY5356.
Greenwich *Gt.Lon.* Population: 211,141. ***Suburb***, on S bank of River Thames, 6m/9km E of Charing Cross. At Greenwich itself is Royal Naval College on site of former royal palace, National Maritime Museum, and old Royal Observatory. **23 G4** TQ3977.
Greenwich Observatory *Gt.Lon. Former name of Old Royal Observatory, qv.*
Greenwood Lee *W.Yorks.* ***Settlement***, on hillside, above Hebden Water, 2m/3km NW of Hebden Bridge. SD9729.
Greet *Glos.* ***Hamlet***, 1m/2km N of Winchcombe. **30 B5** SP0230.
Greete *Shrop.* ***Village***, 2m/3km NW of Tenbury Wells. **28 E1** SO5770.
Greetham *Lincs.* ***Village***, 3m/5km E of Horncastle. **53 G5** TF3070.
Greetham *Rut.* ***Village***, 6m/9km NE of Oakham. **42 C4** SK9214.
Greetland *W.Yorks.* ***Village***, 1m/2km W of Elland. **57 F7** SE0921.
Greetland Nook *W.Yorks.* ***Hamlet***, 3m/4km W of Elland. SE0620.
Greg Ness *Aberdeen* ***Coastal feature***, headland on E coast at S end of Nigg Bay, Aberdeen. **91 H4** NJ9704.
Gregson Lane *Lancs.* ***Village***, 4m/6km SE of Preston. SD5926.
Greian Head *W.Isles* ***Coastal feature***, headland on NW coast of Barra, 4m/7km SW of Scurrival Point. **84 B4** NF6404.
Greine Sgeir *W.Isles* ***Island***, rock island off W coast of Isle of Lewis opposite entrance to Loch Resort. NB0015.
Greineim *W.Isles* ***Island***, islet nearly 1km off W coast of Isle of Lewis, 1m/2km N of Mealasta Island. NA9824.
Greinetobht (Anglicised form: Grenetote.) *W.Isles* ***Settlement***, at N end of North Uist, 1m/2km E of Solas. **92 D4** NF8275.
Greinton *Som.* ***Village***, on S side of Polden Hills, 5m/7km W of Street. **8 D1** ST4136.
Grenaby *I.o.M.* ***Settlement***, 3m/5km N of Castletown. **54 B6** SC2672.
Grendon *Northants.* ***Village***, 5m/8km S of Wellingborough. **32 B2** SP8760.
Grendon *Warks.* ***Hamlet***, 2m/4km NW of Atherstone. **40 E6** SK2800.
Grendon Common *Warks.* ***Hamlet***, to S of Grendon, 3m/4km NW of Atherstone. **40 E6** SP2798.
Grendon Green *Here.* ***Locality***, 4m/6km W of Bromyard. **28 E3** SO5957.
Grendon Underwood *Bucks.* ***Village***, 6m/10km E of Bicester. **31 H6** SP6820.
Grenetote *W.Isles Anglicised form of Greinetobht, qv.*
Grenofen *Devon* ***Hamlet***, 2m/3km SE of Tavistock. SX4971.
Grenoside *S.Yorks.* ***Suburb***, 5m/7km N of Sheffield. **51 F3** SK3394.
Greosabhagh (Anglicised form: Grosebay.) *W.Isles* ***Settlement***, at head of Loch Grosebay, on SE coast of South Harris, 4m/7km S of Tarbert. **93 G2** NG1592.
Gresffordd *Wrex. Welsh form of Gresford, qv.*
Gresford (Gresffordd). *Wrex.* Population: 4915. ***Small town***, 3m/5km N of Wrexham. Memorial to mining disaster in 1934. **48 C7** SJ3454.
Gresham *Norf.* ***Village***, 3m/5km S of Sheringham. Scant remains of medieval castle. **45 F2** TG1638.
Gresham's School *Norf. See Holt.*
Greshornish *High.* ***Locality***, on W side of Loch Greshornish, N coast of Skye. **93 J6** NG3353.
Greshornish Point *High.* ***Coastal feature***, headland on Skye, 2m/3km NE of Greshornish at entrance to Loch Greshornish. **93 J6** NG3353.
Gress *W.Isles Anglicised form of Griais (village), qv.*
Gressenhall *Norf.* ***Village***, 2m/4km NW of East Dereham. **44 D4** TF9615.
Gressenhall Green *Norf.* ***Village***, 1m/2km NE of Gressenhall. TF9615.
Gressingham *Lancs.* ***Village***, 5m/8km E of Carnforth. **55 J2** SD5769.
Gresty Green *Ches.* ***Locality***, 1m/2km S of Crewe. SJ7053.
Greta ***River***, rising on Stainmore Forest, E of Brough, and flowing E past Bowes and Brignall to Greta Bridge, then N into River Tees at N end of Rokeby Park, 3m/4km SE of Barnard Castle. **62 B5** NZ0814.
Greta ***River***, formed by confluence of Rivers Doe and Twiss at Ingleton, and flowing W into River Lune 1m/2km N of Melling. SD5972.
Greta *Cumb.* ***River***, flowing W, to join River Derwent just W of Keswick. **60 D4** NY2523.
Greta Bridge *Dur.* ***Hamlet***, on River Greta, 3m/5km SE of Barnard Castle, on site of Roman fort. Dickens stayed at coaching inn here. **62 B5** NZ0813.
Gretna *D. & G.* Population: 3149. ***Village***, 8m/12km E of Annan. **69 J7** NY3167.
Gretna Green *D. & G.* ***Village***, 1km N of Gretna, famous for runaway marriages in former times. **69 J7** NY3167.
Gretna Green *Suff.* ***Locality***, 1km E of Eye. TM1573.
Gretton *Glos.* ***Village***, 2m/3km NW of Winchcombe. **30 B5** SP0030.
Gretton *Northants.* ***Village***, 4m/6km N of Corby. Kirby Hall (English Heritage), 2m/3km SE. **42 C6** SP8994.
Gretton *Shrop.* ***Hamlet***, 4m/7km E of Church Stretton. **38 E6** SO5195.
Grewelthorpe *N.Yorks.* ***Village***, 3m/5km S of Masham. **57 H2** SE2376.
Grey Cairns of Camster *High.* ***Historic/prehistoric site***, Stone Age to Bronze Age burial cairns, 1m/2km N of Upper Camster. **105 H4** ND2544.
Grey Green *N.Lincs.* ***Locality***, adjoining to N of Belton, 3m/4km N of Epworth. SE7807.
Grey Head *Ork.* ***Coastal feature***, headland at N end of Calf of Eday. **106 E3** HY5740.
Grey Hill *S.Ayr.* ***Hill***, 3m/5km S of Girvan. Height 974 feet or 297 metres. **67 F4** NX1692.
Grey Mare's Tail *D. & G.* ***Waterfall***, spectacular waterfall (National Trust for Scotland), 200 feet or over 60 metres high, 9m/14km NE of Moffat. **69 G2** NT1815.
Grey Nag *Northumb.* ***Mountain***, to W of Whitley Common, 3m/5km W of Alston. Height 2152 feet or 656 metres. **61 H2** NY6647.
Greygarth *N.Yorks.* ***Settlement***, 4m/7km N of Pateley Bridge. **57 G2** SE1872.
Greylake *Som.* ***Settlement***, on Sedgemoor, 1m/2km N of Othery. **8 C1** ST3833.
Greylake Fosse *Som.* ***Settlement***, 3m/5km NE of Othery. ST4035.
Greymoorhill *Cumb.* ***Locality***, 2m/4km N of Carlisle. NY3959.
Greys Court *Oxon.* ***Historic house***, National Trust property, originally 14c but much added to, 2m/3km NW of Henley-on-Thames. **22 A3** SU7283.
Greys Green *Oxon.* ***Hamlet***, 3m/4km W of Henley-on-Thames. **22 A3** SU7282.
Greysouthen *Cumb.* ***Village***, 3m/5km W of Cockermouth. **60 B4** NY0729.
Greystead *Northumb.* ***Settlement***, in valley of River North Tyne, 5m/7km NW of Bellingham. NY7785.
Greystoke *Cumb.* ***Village***, 5m/8km W of Penrith. Castle is 19c mansion in Elizabethan style by Salvin, added to original 14c peel tower. **60 F3** NY4430.
Greystoke Forest *Cumb.* ***Forest/woodland***, 8m/12km W of Penrith. **60 E3** NY3932.
Greystone *Aber.* ***Settlement***, 2m/3km E of Crathie. **89 K5** NO2995.
Greystone *Angus* ***Village***, 7m/11km W of Arbroath. **83 G3** NO5343.
Greystone *Lancs.* ***Settlement***, 3m/5km NW of Colne, in valley between Burn Moor and White Moor. **56 D5** SD8543.
Greystone Bridge ***Bridge***, fine example of stone bridge, built in 1439 by Bishop Lacey, over River Tamar between Cornwall and Devon, 3m/5km SE of Launceston. SX3860.
Greystone Heath *Warr.* ***Suburb***, in W part of Warrington. SJ5687.
Greystones *S.Yorks.* ***Suburb***, 3m/4km SW of Sheffield city centre. SK3285.
Greywell *Hants.* ***Village***, 1m/2km W of Odiham. **22 A6** SU7151.
Griais (Anglicised form: Gress.) *W.Isles* ***Village***, near E coast of Isle of Lewis, 7m/12km NE of Stornoway. **101 G3** NB4942.
Grianan *W.Isles* ***Settlement***, on Isle of Lewis, 2m/3km N of Stornoway. NB4135.
Gribbin Head *Cornw.* ***Coastal feature***, headland (National Trust) at E limit of St. Austell Bay. **4 A6** SX0949.
Gribthorpe *E.Riding* ***Settlement***, 5m/7km N of Howden. **58 D6** SE7635.
Gribton *D. & G.* ***Settlement***, 5m/8km NW of Dumfries. **68 E5** NX9280.
Gribun *Arg. & B.* ***Locality***, on W coast of Mull, 2m/3km S of entrance to Loch na Keal. Coast road passes below Gribun Rocks. NM4533.
Gridley Corner *Devon* ***Hamlet***, 4m/6km NE of Launceston. **6 B6** SX3690.
Grif Skerry *Shet.* ***Island***, rock island 1km E of East Linga and 3m/5km SE of Skaw Taing, headland at NE end of Whalsay. **109 F6** HU6362.
Griff *Warks.* ***Settlement***, 1m/2km N of Bedworth. **41 F7** SP3588.
Griffithstown *Torfaen* ***Suburb***, 1m/2km S of Pontypool. **19 F2** ST2999.
Griffydam *Leics.* ***Settlement***, 3m/5km N of Coalville. SK4118.
Grigadale *High.* ***Settlement***, on Ardnamurchan peninsula, 1m/2km E of Point of Ardnamurchan. **79 F1** NM4367.
Grigghall *Cumb.* ***Hamlet***, adjoining to S of Underbarrow, 3m/5km W of Kendal. **61 F7** SD4691.
Grim Ness *Ork.* ***Coastal feature***, headland at E extremity of St. Margaret's Hope. **107 D8** ND4992.
Grimbister *Ork.* ***Settlement***, on Mainland, on S side of Bay of Firth, 1m/2km SE of Finstown. HY3712.
Grime Fen *Suff.* ***Open space***, fenland 1km NW of Lakenheath. **44 A7** TL7083.
Grimeford Village *Lancs.* ***Hamlet***, 1m/2km NW of Horwich. **49 F1** SD6112.
Grimersta *W.Isles Anglicised form of Griomarstaidh, qv.*
Grime's Graves *Norf.* ***Historic/prehistoric site***, Neolithic flint mines (English Heritage), 3m/5km NE of Brandon. **44 C7** TL8189.
Grimesthorpe *S.Yorks.* ***Suburb***, 2m/3km NE of Sheffield city centre. SK3790.
Grimethorpe *S.Yorks.* Population: 3460. ***Village***, 2m/3km E of Cudworth. **51 G2** SE4109.
Griminis (Anglicised form: Griminish.) *W.Isles* ***Settlement***, near W coast of Benbecula, 2m/3km S of Balivanich. **92 C6** NF7751.
Griminis Point (Anglicised form: Griminish Point.) *W.Isles* ***Coastal feature***, headland at NW end of North Uist. **92 C4** NF7276.
Griminish *W.Isles Anglicised form of Griminis, qv.*
Griminish Point *W.Isles Anglicised form of Griminis Point, qv.*
Grimister *Shet.* ***Hamlet***, on Yell, on S side of Whale Firth. **108 D3** HU4693.
Grimley *Worcs.* ***Village***, 4m/6km N of Worcester. **29 H2** SO8360.
Grimmet *S.Ayr.* ***Settlement***, 1m/2km E of Maybole. **67 H2** NS3210.
Grimness *Ork.* ***Settlement***, in NE of South Ronaldsay, 2m/3km E of St. Margaret's Hope. **107 D8** ND4893.
Grimoldby *Lincs.* ***Village***, 4m/7km E of Louth. **53 G4** TF3987.

Grimpo *Shrop.* ***Hamlet***, 5m/8km E of Oswestry. **38 C3** SJ3626.
Grimsargh *Lancs.* ***Village***, 4m/7km NE of Preston. Group of small reservoirs to N. **55 J6** SD5834.
Grimsay (Gaelic form: Griomasaigh.) *W.Isles* ***Island***, of about 3 square miles or 8 square km between North Uist and Benbecula, with causeway connection to both. **92 D6** NF8656.
Grimsbury *Oxon.* ***Suburb***, in E part of Banbury. **31 F4** SP4641.
Grimsby *N.E.Lincs.* Population: 90,703. ***Town***, port at mouth of River Humber, 16m/26km SE of Kingston upon Hull across estuary. Important centre for North Sea fishing industry. National Fishing Heritage Centre. **53 F2** TA2709.
Grimscote *Northants.* ***Village***, 4m/6km NW of Towcester. **31 H3** SP6553.
Grimscott *Cornw.* ***Hamlet***, 2m/3km E of Stratton. **6 A5** SS2606.
Grimshader *W.Isles Anglicised form of Grimsiadar, qv.*
Grimshaw *B'burn.* ***Hamlet***, 1m/2km NE of Darwen. SD7024.
Grimshaw Green *Lancs.* ***Settlement***, 1m/2km N of Parbold. SD4812.
Grimsiadar (Anglicised form: Grimshader.) *W.Isles* ***Village***, on E coast of Isle of Lewis, at head of long narrow inlet, Loch Grimsiadar, 5m/8km S of Stornoway. **101 G5** NB4025.
Grimspound *Devon* ***Historic/prehistoric site***, 3m/4km NW of Widecombe in the Moor, to NW of Hameldown Tor. Late Bronze Age settlement (English Heritage) consisting of about 4 acres, with remains of twenty-four huts. Outer granite wall has been restored. **7 F7** SX7080.
Grimstead *Wilts.* ***Locality***, parish 6m/9km SE of Salisbury, containing villages of East and West Grimstead. SU2227.
Grimsthorpe *Lincs.* ***Hamlet***, 4m/6km NW of Bourne. **42 D3** TF0423.
Grimsthorpe Castle *Lincs.* ***Historic house***, adjoining to SW of Grimsthorpe. Large mansion by Vanbrugh in huge park. **42 D3** TF0423.
Grimston *E.Riding* ***Hamlet***, on coast, 3m/5km SE of Aldbrough. TA2835.
Grimston *Leics.* ***Village***, 5m/8km NW of Melton Mowbray. **41 J3** SK6821.
Grimston *Norf.* ***Village***, 7m/11km E of King's Lynn. **44 B3** TF7221.
Grimston *N.Yorks.* ***Locality***, containing Grimston Park, 2m/3km SE of Tadcaster. SE4941.
Grimston *York* ***Locality***, at road junction on A64, 3m/5km E of York. SE6451.
Grimstone *Dorset* ***Hamlet***, beside River Frome, 4m/6km NW of Dorchester. **9 F5** SY6494.
Grimstone End *Suff.* ***Hamlet***, 1m/2km S of Ixworth. TL9369.
Grimwith Reservoir *N.Yorks.* ***Reservoir***, 3m/4km NE of Burnsall. **57 F3** SE0664.
Grindale *E.Riding* ***Village***, 4m/7km NW of Bridlington. Site of Roman building on E side of village. **59 H2** TA1371.
Grindiscol *Shet.* ***Settlement***, near W coast of Bressay. **109 D9** HU4939.
Grindle *Shrop.* ***Settlement***, 1km W of Ryton. **39 G5** SJ7503.
Grindleford *Derbys.* ***Village***, on River Derwent, 3m/4km S of Hathersage. **50 E5** SK2477.
Grindleton *Lancs.* ***Village***, 3m/4km N of Clitheroe. **56 C5** SD7545.
Grindley *Staffs.* ***Settlement***, 5m/8km SW of Uttoxeter. **40 C3** SK0329.
Grindley Brook *Shrop.* ***Hamlet***, 1m/2km NW of Whitchurch. SJ5243.
Grindlow *Derbys.* ***Hamlet***, 2m/4km NE of Tideswell. **50 D5** SK1877.
Grindon *Northumb.* ***Settlement***, 2m/3km SE of Norham. **77 H6** NT9144.
Grindon *Staffs.* ***Village***, 8m/12km NW of Ashbourne. **50 C7** SK0854.
Grindon *Stock.* ***Hamlet***, 5m/8km NW of Stockton-on-Tees. NZ3925.
Grindon *T. & W.* ***Suburb***, 3m/5km SW of Sunderland city centre. NZ3555.
Grindon & Swainsley Estates *Staffs.* ***Open space***, National Trust property to NW of Grindon, with River Manifold flowing through from N to S. SK1056.
Grindstone Law *Sc.Bord.* ***Mountain***, in Cheviot Hills, 3m/5km N of Byrness. Height 1535 feet or 468 metres. **70 C3** NT7607.
Grindstonelaw *Northumb.* ***Hill***, 2m/3km N of Matfen. Height 731 feet or 223 metres. **71 F6** NZ0073.
Gringley on the Hill *Notts.* ***Village***, 6m/9km E of Bawtry. **51 K3** SK7390.
Grinsdale *Cumb.* ***Village***, on River Eden, 2m/4km NW of Carlisle across loop of river. **60 E1** NY3658.
Grinshill *Shrop.* ***Village***, 7m/11km N of Shrewsbury. **38 E3** SJ5223.
Grinton *N.Yorks.* ***Village***, 1km SE of Reeth. **62 B7** SE0498.
Griomarstaidh (Anglicised form: Grimersta.) *W.Isles* ***Settlement***, 1m/2km S of Linisiadar, on W shore of Loch Cean Thulabhaig, Isle of Lewis. **100 E4** NB2130.
Griomasaigh *W.Isles Gaelic form of Grimsay, qv.*
Griomaval *W.Isles* ***Mountain***, near W coast of Isle of Lewis, 4m/6km N of entrance to Loch Resort. Height 1630 feet or 497 metres. **100 C5** NB0122.
Grisdale *Cumb.* ***Settlement***, 1m/2km W of Moorcock Inn, on E side of Baugh Fell. SD7793.
Grisedale *Cumb.* ***Valley***, carrying Grisedale Beck NE to S end of Ullswater, about 1m/2km W of Patterdale. **60 E5** NY3715.
Grisedale Pike *Cumb.* ***Mountain***, in Lake District 4m/7km W of Keswick. Height 2591 feet or 790 metres. **60 C4** NY1922.
Grishipoll *Arg. & B.* ***Locality***, on Coll near NW coast at Grishipoll Bay. **78 C2** NM1959.
Grishipoll Bay *Arg. & B.* ***Bay***, on NW coast of Coll. **78 C2** NM1959.
Griskerry *Shet.* ***Island***, islet close to W coast of Mainland, 1m/2km NW of Bigton. **109 C10** HU3622.
Gristhorpe *N.Yorks.* ***Village***, 2m/3km NW of Filey. **59 G1** TA0882.
Griston *Norf.* ***Village***, 2m/3km SE of Watton. **44 D6** TL9499.
Gritley *Ork.* ***Settlement***, 1km NE of St. Peter's Bay, Mainland. **107 E7** HY5605.
Grittenham *Wilts.* ***Hamlet***, 2m/4km W of Wootton Bassett. **20 D3** SU0382.
Grittleton *Wilts.* ***Village***, 6m/9km NW of Chippenham. **20 B3** ST8580.
Grizebeck *Cumb.* ***Hamlet***, 3m/4km SE of Broughton in Furness. **55 F1** SD2385.
Grizedale *Cumb.* ***Hamlet***, 3m/4km S of Hawkshead in Grizedale Forest Park. **60 E7** SD3394.
Grizedale Forest Park *Cumb.* ***Forest/woodland***, extensive area of coniferous woodland between Coniston Water and Windermere. **60 E7** SD3394.
Grizedale Forest Park Country Park *Cumb.* ***Leisure/recreation***, between Coniston Water and Windermere, visitor and wildlife centre run by The Forestry Commission, with woodland walks. **60 E7** SD3394.
Groay *W.Isles* ***Island***, small uninhabited island at SE end of Sound of Harris, 4m/7km off E coast of North Uist. **92 E4** NG0079.
Grob Bagh *Arg. & B.* ***Bay***, at S end of Gigha. **72 E6** NR6346.
Groban *High.* ***Mountain***, rounded summit in Ross and Cromarty district, 7m/11km NW of Kinlochewe. Height 2453 feet or 748 metres. **95 G4** NH0970.
Grobister *Ork.* ***Settlement***, 1m/2km NW of Dishes, Stronsay. **106 F5** HY6524.
Groby *Leics.* Population: 7183. ***Village***, 5m/7km NW of Leicester. **41 H5** SK5207.
Groes *Conwy* ***Hamlet***, 3m/5km W of Denbigh. **47 J6** SJ0064.
Groes-faen *R.C.T.* ***Hamlet***, 2m/3km SE of Llantrisant. **18 D3** ST0780.
Groes-lwyd *Powys* ***Settlement***, 3m/4km N of Welshpool. **38 B4** SJ2111.
Groes-wen *Caerp.* ***Hamlet***, 2m/3km W of Caerphilly. ST1286.
Groesffordd *Gwyn.* ***Hamlet***, 1m/2km SW of Morfa Nefyn. **36 B2** SH2739.
Groesffordd Marli *Denb.* ***Settlement***, 1m/2km S of Bodelwyddan. **47 J5** SJ0073.
Groeslon *Gwyn.* ***Hamlet***, 4m/6km SE of Caernarfon. SH5260.
Groeslon *Gwyn.* ***Village***, 4m/6km S of Caernarfon. **46 C7** SH4755.
Grogport *Arg. & B.* ***Settlement***, on Garrachcroit Bàgh, on E coast of Kintyre, Argyll, 4m/7km N of Dippen. **73 G6** NR8044.
Groigearraidh *W.Isles* ***Settlement***, 1km S of Drimore, South Uist. **84 C1** NF7739.
Gromford *Suff.* ***Hamlet***, 1km W of Snape. **35 H3** TM3858.
Gronant *Flints.* ***Village***, 1m/2km E of Prestatyn. **47 J4** SJ0682.
Groombridge ***Village***, on border of East Sussex and Kent, 4m/6km W of Royal Tunbridge Wells. **13 J3** TQ5337.
Grosebay *W.Isles Anglicised form of Greosabhagh, qv.*
Grosmont *Mon.* ***Village***, above W bank of River Monnow, 2m/3km S of Pontrilas. Remains of 13c castle (Cadw). **28 D6** SO4024.
Grosmont *N.Yorks.* ***Village***, 6m/9km SW of Whitby. **63 K6** NZ8205.
Grosmont Castle *Mon.* ***Castle***, fragmentary ruin dating from 13c, with work by Hubert de Burgh, in village of Grosmont, 10m/15km NE of Abergavenny. **28 D6** SO4024.
Grosvenor Bridge *Ches.* ***Bridge***, stone bridge over River Dee in Chester, built in 1827 when its single stone arch was largest in world with 200 foot or 63 metre span. SJ4063.
Grotaig *High.* ***Settlement***, 4m/6km SW of Drumnadrochit. **88 B2** NH4923.
Groton *Suff.* ***Village***, 4m/7km W of Hadleigh. **34 D4** TL9541.
Grotton *Gt.Man.* ***Suburb***, 3m/4km E of Oldham town centre. SD9604.
Groundistone Heights *Sc.Bord.* ***Settlement***, 3m/5km N of Hawick. **69 K2** NT4919.
Grove *Bucks.* ***Settlement***, 2m/3km S of Leighton Buzzard. SP9122.
Grove *Dorset* ***Hamlet***, on E side of Portland. **9 F7** SY6972.
Grove *Kent* ***Settlement***, 3m/5km N of Wingham. **25 J5** TR2362.
Grove *Notts.* ***Village***, 2m/4km E of Retford. **51 K5** SK7379.
Grove *Oxon.* Population: 7504. ***Village***, 2m/3km N of Wantage. **21 H2** SU4090.
Grove *Pembs.* ***Suburb***, adjoining to E of Pembroke. SM9900.
Grove End *Kent* ***Settlement***, 2m/3km S of Sittingbourne. TQ8961.
Grove Green *Kent* ***Suburb***, 1m/2km E of Maidstone. TQ7856.
Grove Park *Gt.Lon.* ***Suburb***, in borough of Hounslow, on N bank of River Thames, to N of Chiswick Bridge. TQ2077.
Grove Park *Gt.Lon.* ***Suburb***, in borough of Lewisham, 3m/5km SE of Lewisham and 9m/14km SE of Charing Cross. **23 H4** TQ4072.
Grove Place *W.Yorks.* ***Suburb***, 2m/3km E of Huddersfield town centre. SE1616.
Grove Town *W.Yorks.* ***Suburb***, SE district of Pontefract. SE4621.
Grove Vale *W.Mid.* ***Suburb***, 3m/4km NE of West Bromwich town centre. SP0394.
Grovehill *Herts.* ***Suburb***, 2m/3km NE of Hemel Hempstead town centre. TL0609.
Grovely Wood *Wilts.* ***Forest/woodland***, 3m/5km NW of Wilton. **10 B1** SU0434.
Grovesend *S.Glos.* ***Settlement***, 1m/2km SE of Thornbury. ST6588.
Grovesend (Pengelli-ddrain). *Swan.* ***Village***, 2m/3km S of Pontarddulais. **17 J4** SN5900.
Grub Street *Norf.* ***Locality***, 1km SW of Happisburgh. TG3730.
Grubb Street *Kent* ***Settlement***, 1m/2km NW of Longfield and 4m/7km SW of Gravesend. TQ5869.
Grudie *High.* ***River***, flows E into Kyle of Durness, Sutherland district. **103 F2** NC3562.
Grudie *High.* ***River***, flowing from E end of Loch Fannich SE to its confluence with River Bran, 1km W of Loch Luichart. **95 J5** NH3062.
Grudie Burn *High.* ***River***, in Sutherland district rising between Loch Shin and Glen Cassley and running SE into River Shin 3m/5km S of Lairg. **96 C1** NC5702.
Gruids *High.* ***Locality***, in Sutherland district 2m/3km SW of Lairg. **96 C1** NC5604.
Gruinard *High.* ***River***, flows N into Gruinard Bay from Loch na Sealga. **95 F3** NG9494.
Gruinard Bay *High.* ***Bay***, on W coast of Ross and Cromarty district, between Greenstone Point and Stattic Point. **95 F2** NG9494.
Gruinard Forest *High.* ***Open space***, mountainous and moorland area to S of Little Loch Broom. **95 G3** NH0286.
Gruinard Island *High.* ***Island***, uninhabited island, property of Ministry of Defence, in Gruinard Bay on W coast of Ross and Cromarty district, between Greenstone Point and Stattic Point. Area about 520 acres or 210 hectares. Formerly site of biological warfare testing. **95 F2** NG9494.
Gruinart *Arg. & B.* ***Locality***, at head of Loch Gruinart on Islay. Here in 1598 Macdonalds repelled invasion of Macleans of Mull. NR2866.
Gruinart Flats *Arg. & B.* ***Locality***, to S of Loch Gruinart, Islay. **72 A4** NR2866.
Grula *High.* ***Settlement***, at head of Loch Eynort, SW coast of Skye. NG3826.
Gruline *Arg. & B.* ***Locality***, at head of Loch na Keal, Mull, 3m/5km SW of Salen. Mausoleum in grounds of Gruline House commemorates Lachlan Macquarie, first governor of New South Wales, Australia. **79 G4** NM5440.
Grumbla *Cornw.* ***Settlement***, 2m/4km SE of St. Just. SW4029.
Grumby Rock *High.* ***Hill***, 1m/2km NE of West Langwell, on S side of Strath Brora. Height 981 feet or 299 metres. **104 B7** NC7010.
Gruna Stack *Shet.* ***Island***, rock island off NW coast of Mainland, 1m/2km NE of entrance to Ronas Voe. HU2886.
Grunasound *Shet.* ***Locality***, on West Burra, 1m/2km S of Hamnavoe. HU3733.
Grunay *Shet.* ***Island***, third largest in Out Skerries group of islands, NE of Whalsay. **108 F5** HU6971.
Grundcruie *P. & K.* ***Settlement***, 1m/2km NW of Methven. **82 B5** NO0026.
Grundisburgh *Suff.* ***Village***, 3m/5km W of Woodbridge. **35 G3** TM2250.
Grune Point *Cumb.* ***Coastal feature***, headland at entrance to Moricambe bay, 1m/2km NE of Skinburness. **60 C1** NY1456.
Gruney *Shet.* ***Island***, uninhabited island nearly 1m/2km N of Point of Fethaland. **108 C3** HU3896.
Grunka Hellier *Shet.* ***Coastal feature***, point on NW coast of Unst. **108 E1** HP5815.
Gruting *Shet.* ***Settlement***, in W part of Mainland, on E side of Gruting Voe. **109 B8** HU2749.
Gruting Voe *Shet.* ***Sea feature***, large inlet whose entrance is on E side of Vaila. **109 B8** HU2749.
Grutness *Shet.* ***Settlement***, on SE side of Grutness Voe, 1m/2km N of Sumburgh Head, Mainland. **109 G10** HU4009.
Grwyne Fawr ***River***, rising in Black Mountains, 2m/3km N of Waun Fach, and flowing S to its confluence with Grwyne Fechan, then S again into River Usk, 2m/3km SE of Crickhowell. **28 B6** SO2315.
Grwyne Fawr Reservoir *Powys* ***Reservoir***, near head of Grwyne Fawr River. **28 B5** SO2330.
Grwyne Fechan *Powys* ***River***, rising on Waun Fach and flowing S to join Grwyne Fawr, 2m/3km NE of Crickhowell. **28 B6** SO2419.
Gryfe ***River***, rising on hills S of Greenock and running N to Gryfe Reservoirs, then SE down Strath Gryfe to Bridge of Weir, then E to Black Cart Water 2m/4km NW of Paisley. **74 C4** NS4666.
Gryfe Reservoirs *Inclyde* ***Reservoir***, pair of reservoirs 3m/5km S of Greenock. **74 A3** NS2871.
Gryme's Dyke *Essex* ***Historic/prehistoric site***, 3m/4km W of Colchester town centre. Section of previously massive dyke built for defence, comprising single bank and ditch. **34 D6** TL9624.
Gualachulain *High.* ***Settlement***, at head of Loch Etive, 11m/18km NE of Taynuilt. **80 C3** NN1145.
Gualann *W.Isles* ***Coastal feature***, narrow strip of land 2m/3km long, between Benbecula and South Uist. Joined to latter at low tide. **92 C7** NF7747.
Guanockgate *Lincs.* ***Locality***, 2m/4km S of Sutton St. Edmund. TF3609.
Guardbridge *Fife* ***Village***, at head of River Eden estuary, with modern road bridge across river beside old 15c bridge, 2m/3km S of Leuchars. Large paper mill. **83 F6** NO4518.
Guarlford *Worcs.* ***Village***, 2m/3km E of Great Malvern. **29 H4** SO8145.
Guarsay Mòr *W.Isles* ***Coastal feature***, headland on NW coast of Mingulay. **84 A6** NL5484.
Guay *P. & K.* ***Hamlet***, in Strath Tay, 3m/5km S of Ballinluig. **82 B3** NO0049.
Gubbergill *Cumb.* ***Settlement***, 2m/3km N of Ravenglass, on E side of River Irt. **60 B7** SD0899.
Gubbion's Green *Essex* ***Settlement***, 4m/6km SW of Braintree. TL7317.
Gubblecote *Herts.* ***Settlement***, 3m/4km NW of Tring. SP9014.

Guestling Green *E.Suss.* ***Village***, 4m/7km NE of Hastings. **14 D6** TQ8513.
Guestling Thorn *E.Suss.* ***Hamlet***, 1m/2km N of Guestling Green. **14 D6** TQ8513.
Guestwick *Norf.* ***Village***, 4m/6km NW of Reepham. **44 E3** TG0627.
Guestwick Green *Norf.* ***Hamlet***, 1km SW of Guestwick and 2m/3km NE of Foulsham. TG0526.
Gugh *I.o.S.* ***Island***, joined to St. Agnes by a sand and rock bar at low tide. **2 B2** SV8908.
Guibean Uluvailt *Arg. & B.* ***Mountain***, 2m/3km SE of Ben More, Mull. Height 1076 feet or 328 metres. **79 G4** NM5531.
Guide *Lancs.* ***Hamlet***, 2m/3km SE of Blackburn. SD7025.
Guide Bridge *Gt.Man.* ***Suburb***, 1m/2km SW of Ashton-under-Lyne. SJ9297.
Guide Post *Northumb.* Population: 8691. ***Village***, 4m/6km E of Morpeth. **71 H5** NZ2585.
Guilden Down *Shrop.* ***Settlement***, 1m/2km NE of Clun. SO3082.
Guilden Morden *Cambs.* ***Village***, 5m/8km NW of Royston. **33 F4** TL2744.
Guilden Sutton *Ches.* ***Village***, 3m/5km E of Chester. **48 D6** SJ4468.

G

Guildford *Surr.* Population: 65,998. ***Town***, county town, and former weaving centre, on River Wey, 27m/43km SW of London. Remains of Norman castle keep. Modern cathedral and University of Surrey on Stag Hill to NW of town centre. Royal Grammar School noted for its chained library. **22 C7** SU9949.
Guildford Castle *Surr.* ***Castle***, early Norman keep, built c. 1173, on an 11c motte, in centre of Guildford. Used as county gaol for 400 years. **22 D7** SU9949.
Guildford Cathedral *Surr.* ***Ecclesiastical building***, 1km NW of town centre. Consecrated in 1961 and built of red brick, the interior is designed in a modern Gothic style. **22 C6** SU9850.
Guildford Museum *Surr.* ***Other feature of interest***, local history exhibits and displays in Guildford. **22 D7** SU9949.
Guildtown *P. & K.* ***Village***, 5m/8km N of Perth. **82 C4** NO1331.
Guile Point *Northumb.* ***Coastal feature***, headland on mainland opposite S end of Holy Island. **77 K6** NU1340.
Guillamon Island *High.* ***Island***, islet 1km off SE coast of Scalpay. NG6327.
Guilsborough *Northants.* ***Village***, 9m/15km NW of Northampton. **31 H1** SP6773.
Guilsfield (Ceigidfa). *Powys* ***Village***, 3m/4km N of Welshpool. **38 B4** SJ2111.
Guilthwaite *S.Yorks.* ***Settlement***, 3m/4km SE of Rotherham. SK4589.
Guilton *Kent* ***Settlement***, adjoining to SW of Ash. TR2858.
Guineaford *Devon* ***Hamlet***, 3m/4km N of Barnstaple. SS5437.
Guirasdeal *Arg. & B.* ***Island***, small island off SW shore of Lunga. **79 H7** NM6907.
Guisachan Forest *High.* ***Open space***, deer forest to S of Glen Affric in Inverness district. **87 J2** NH2520.
Guisborough *R. & C.* Population: 18,156. ***Town***, 6m/9km S of Redcar. Remains of 12c Augustinian priory (English Heritage). Working watermill. **63 H5** NZ6116.
Guisborough Museum *R. & C.* ***Other feature of interest***, in Guisborough. Museum of social history. **63 H5** NZ6016.
Guisborough Priory *R. & C.* ***Ecclesiastical building***, scant remains of priory (English Heritage) founded c. 1119 for Augustinian canons, at Guisborough. Includes Decorated E end of 14c church. **63 H5** NZ6116.
Guise Cliff *N.Yorks.* ***Inland physical feature***, cliff below High Crag, on Heyshaw Moor on S side of Guisecliff Wood, 1m/2km S of Pateley Bridge. **57 G3** SE1663.
Guiseley *W.Yorks.* Population: 15,552. ***Town***, stone-built town with green and market cross, 8m/13km NW of Leeds. **57 G5** SE1941.
Guist *Norf.* ***Village***, 6m/9km SE of Fakenham. **44 D3** TF9925.
Guith *Ork.* ***Settlement***, on Eday, overlooking Ferness Bay. **106 E4** HY5536.
Guiting Power *Glos.* ***Village***, 6m/10km W of Stow-on-the-Wold. **30 B6** SP0924.
Gulberwick *Shet.* ***Village***, on Mainland, at head of Gulber Wick. **109 D9** HU4438.
Gulf of Corryvreckan *Arg. & B. See Strait of Corryvreckan.*
Gull Point *N.Ayr.* ***Coastal feature***, headland at S end of Little Cumbrae. **73 K6** NS1450.
Gull Rock *Cornw.* ***Island***, rock off N coast opposite Portreath. SW6445.
Gull Rock *Cornw.* ***Island***, rock lying off Kynance Cove, 1m/2km NW of Lizard. SW6813.
Gull Rock *Cornw.* ***Island***, rock islet, 1km E of Nare Head. SW9336.
Gull Rock *Cornw.* ***Island***, rock off N coast opposite S end of Trebarwith Strand, 2m/3km SW of Tintagel. SX0386.
Gull Rocks *Cornw. Alternative name for Carter's Rocks, qv.*
Gulland Rock *Cornw.* ***Island***, off N coast to W of Padstow, 3m/4km NE of Trevose Head. **3 F1** SW8779.
Gullane *E.Loth.* Population: 2229. ***Small town***, resort on Gullane Bay, on Firth of Forth, 4m/7km SW of North Berwick. Championship golf-course (Muirfield) to N. **76 C2** NT4882.
Gullane Bay *E.Loth.* ***Bay***, on Firth of Forth, 4m/7km SW of North Berwick. **76 C2** NT4882.
Gullane Bents *E.Loth.* ***Other feature of interest***, area of heath and grass adjacent to Gullane Bay on Firth of Forth, 4m/7km SW of North Berwick. **76 C2** NT4783.
Gullane Point *E.Loth.* ***Coastal feature***, headland at W end of Gullane Bay. **76 C2** NT4882.
Gullane Sands *E.Loth.* ***Nature reserve***, to S of Gullane Point in Aberlady Bay. NT4581.
Gully *W.Yorks.* ***Locality***, adjoining to SE of Holmfirth. SE1407.
Gulvain (Gaelic form: Gaor Bheinn.) *High.* ***Mountain***, in Lochaber district 2m/4km S of head of Loch Arkaig. Height of N summit, a Munro, 3237 feet or 987 metres; S summit 3155 feet or 962 metres. **87 G6** NM9986.
Gulval *Cornw.* ***Hamlet***, to NE of Penzance. Heliport to S. **2 B5** SW4831.
Gulworthy *Devon* ***Settlement***, 3m/4km SW of Tavistock. **4 E3** SX4472.
Gumfreston *Pembs.* ***Hamlet***, 2m/3km W of Tenby. **16 E4** SN1001.
Gumley *Leics.* ***Village***, 4m/6km NW of Market Harborough. **41 J7** SP6890.
Gun Hill *Warks.* ***Settlement***, 5m/8km SW of Nuneaton. SP2889.
Gunby *E.Riding* ***Settlement***, 1km S of Bubwith. **58 D6** SE7135.
Gunby *Lincs.* ***Settlement***, adjacent to parkland which contains Gunby Hall (National Trust), built around 1700, 4m/7km E of Spilsby. TF4767.
Gunby *Lincs.* ***Village***, 2m/3km SW of Colsterworth. **42 C3** SK9121.
Gunby Hall *Lincs.* ***Historic house***, red-brick house built 1700 (National Trust), 4m/7km NE of Spilsby. **53 H6** TF4767.
Gundleton *Hants.* ***Hamlet***, 2m/3km E of New Alresford. **11 H1** SU6133.
Gunfleet Sand *Essex* ***Coastal feature***, sandbank off E coast of England, stretching from Frinton-on-Sea to Clacton-on-Sea. **35 G7** TM2611.
Gunn *Devon* ***Hamlet***, 5m/8km E of Barnstaple. **6 E2** SS6333.
Gunna *Arg. & B.* ***Island***, 1m/2km long E to W, lying off SW end of Coll across Caolas Bàn. **78 C2** NM1051.
Gunnels Wood *Herts.* ***Locality***, industrial estate in W part of Stevenage. TL2323.
Gunnersbury *Gt.Lon.* ***Suburb***, in borough of Hounslow, N of Kew Bridge, 7m/11km W of Charing Cross. Gunnersbury Park has recreational facilities and museum. TQ1978.
Gunnerside *N.Yorks.* ***Village***, in Swaledale, 6m/9km W of Reeth. **62 A7** SD9598.
Gunnerside Gill *N.Yorks.* ***River***, rising on Gunnerside Moor and flowing S through Melbecks Moor to join River Swale just S of Gunnerside. **62 A6** NY9303.
Gunnerton *Northumb.* ***Village***, 3m/5km SE of Wark. Remains of motte and bailey castle to N. **70 E6** NY9075.
Gunness *N.Lincs.* ***Village***, 3m/5km W of Scunthorpe. **52 B1** SE8411.
Gunnislake *Cornw.* Population: 2236. ***Village***, former tin-mining village on steep bank overlooking River Tamar, crossed here by 16c bridge. **4 E3** SX4371.
Gunnislake Bridge (New Bridge). ***Bridge***, granite bridge over River Tamar, built in 1520, on N side of Gunnislake. Carries road from Devon to Cornwall. SX4372.
Gunnista *Shet.* ***Settlement***, near N coast of Bressay. **109 D8** HU4943.
Gunnister *Shet.* ***Settlement***, in N part of Mainland, 2m/4km N of Mangaster, at head of Gunnister Voe. HU3274.
Gunnister *Shet.* ***Settlement***, near N coast of Bressay, opposite small island of Holm of Gunnister. HU5043.
Guns Village *W.Mid.* ***Suburb***, to W of West Bromwich town centre. SO9991.
Gunstone *Staffs.* ***Settlement***, 1m/2km N of Codsall. SJ8704.
Gunter's Bridge *W.Suss.* ***Settlement***, 1m/2km N of Petworth. **12 C4** SU9723.
Gunthorpe *Norf.* ***Village***, 5m/8km SW of Holt. **44 E2** TG0134.
Gunthorpe *Notts.* ***Village***, 7m/12km NE of Nottingham. **41 J1** SK6844.
Gunthorpe *Peter.* ***Suburb***, 3m/5km N of Peterborough city centre. TF1802.
Gunthorpe *Rut.* ***Hamlet***, 2m/3km S of Oakham. SK8605.
Gunthwaite *S.Yorks.* ***Settlement***, 2m/3km N of Penistone. SE2306.
Gunton *Norf.* ***Locality***, consisting of 18c house and church in Gunton Park, 4m/7km NW of North Walsham. House partly burnt down, 1882. TG2234.
Gunton *Suff.* ***Suburb***, 2m/3km N of Lowestoft town centre. TM5495.
Gunver Head *Cornw.* ***Coastal feature***, headland, 2m/3km NW of Padstow. **3 F1** SW8977.
Gunville *I.o.W.* ***Locality***, 1m/2km W of Newport. **11 F6** SZ4889.
Gunwalloe *Cornw.* ***Hamlet***, on coast, 3m/5km S of Helston. **2 D6** SW6522.
Gupworthy *Som.* ***Settlement***, 2m/3km S of Luxborough, in Brendon Hills. SS9734.
Gurnard *I.o.W.* ***Village***, adjoining to W of Cowes. Gurnard Bay to W. **11 F5** SZ4795.
Gurnard's Head *Cornw.* ***Coastal feature***, headland on N coast, 5m/9km W of St. Ives. **2 B5** SW4338.
Gurnett *Ches.* ***Settlement***, 1m/2km S of Macclesfield. SJ9271.
Gurney Slade *Som.* ***Village***, 4m/6km N of Shepton Mallet. **19 K7** ST6249.
Gurnos *M.Tyd.* ***Suburb***, in N part of Merthyr Tydfil. SO0408.
Gurnos *Powys* ***Village***, 1km NE of Ystalyfera. **18 A1** SN7709.
Gushmere *Kent* ***Settlement***, 3m/5km SE of Faversham. TR0457.
Gussage All Saints *Dorset* ***Village***, 4m/6km SW of Cranborne. **10 B3** SU0010.
Gussage St. Andrew *Dorset* ***Hamlet***, 2m/4km SW of Sixpenny Handley. ST9714.
Gussage St. Michael *Dorset* ***Village***, 5m/7km W of Cranborne. **9 J3** ST9811.
Guston *Kent* ***Village***, 2m/3km N of Dover. **15 J3** TR3244.
Gutcher *Shet.* ***Settlement***, on Wick of Gutcher, on E coast of Yell. Vehicle ferry to Wick of Belmont, on Unst. **108 E3** HU5499.
Guthram Gowt *Lincs.* ***Settlement***, on River Glen, 5m/7km W of Spalding. TF1722.
Guthrie *Angus* ***Village***, 7m/11km E of Forfar. **83 G2** NO5650.
Guthrie Castle *Angus* ***Castle***, with 15c tower and notable gardens, 4m/6km E of Forfar. NO5650.
Guyhirn *Cambs.* ***Village***, 6m/9km SW of Wisbech. **43 G5** TF3903.
Guyhirn Gull *Cambs.* ***Locality***, on Wisbech High Fen, 1km W of Guyhirn. TF3903.
Guynd *Angus* ***Settlement***, 5m/8km W of Arbroath. **83 G3** NO5641.
Guy's Cliffe *Warks.* ***Settlement***, on River Avon, 1m/2km N of Warwick. SP2966.
Guy's Head *Lincs.* ***Settlement***, on W side of River Nene, 3m/4km N of Sutton Bridge. Two disused lighthouses on River Nene banks. **43 H3** TF4825.
Guy's Marsh *Dorset* ***Hamlet***, 2m/3km SW of Shaftesbury. **9 H2** ST8420.
Guyzance *Northumb.* ***Hamlet***, 3m/5km S of Shilbottle. **71 H3** NU2103.
Gwaelod-y-garth *Cardiff* ***Village***, 6m/10km NW of Cardiff. **18 E3** ST1184.
Gwaenysgor *Flints.* ***Village***, 1m/2km S of Prestatyn. **47 J4** SJ0781.
Gwaithla *Powys* ***Settlement***, 6m/9km W of Hay-on-Wye. **28 B3** SO2056.
Gwalchmai *I.o.A.* ***Village***, on Anglesey, 4m/7km W of Llangefni. **46 B5** SH3876.
Gwash ***River***, rising near Knossington and flowing E through Rutland Water into River Welland 1m/2km E of Stamford. TF0407.
Gwastad *B.Gwent* ***Mountain***, 2m/3km NE of Abertillery. Height 1814 feet or 553 metres. **19 F1** SO2305.
Gwastad *Pembs.* ***Hamlet***, 1km NE of Llys-y-frân. SN0424.
Gwastadnant *Gwyn.* ***Settlement***, in Pass of Llanberis, 3m/4km SE of town of Llanberis. SH6157.
Gwastadros *Gwyn.* ***Mountain***, gently sloping mountain 2m/3km W of Bala. Height 1181 feet or 360 metres. **37 H2** SH8935.
Gwastedyn Hill *Powys* ***Mountain***, 1m/2km SE of Rhayader. Height 1565 feet or 477 metres. **27 J2** SN9866.
Gwaum-tre-Oda *Cardiff* ***Suburb***, 2m/3km NW of Cardiff city centre. ST1679.
Gwaun *Pembs.* ***River***, rising about 4m/6km S of Newport and flowing W into Fishguard Bay at Fishguard. SM9637.
Gwaun-Cae-Gurwen *N.P.T.* Population: 2955. ***Village***, former coalmining village, 5m/8km N of Pontardawe. **27 G7** SN7011.
Gwaun-Leision *N.P.T.* ***Locality***, adjoining to N of Gwaun-Cae-Gurwen, 1m/2km SW of Brynamman. **27 G7** SN7012.
Gwaun Meisgyn *R.C.T.* ***Locality***, at SE of Beddau, 1m/2km NE of Llantrisant. ST0684.
Gwaun Nant Ddu *Powys* ***Open space***, moorland area on S side of Brecon Beacons, 7m/11km NW of Merthyr Tydfil. **27 J7** SO0016.
Gwaunceste Hill *Powys* ***Mountain***, 6m/9km N of Painscastle. Height 1778 feet or 542 metres. **28 A3** SO1555.
Gwaynynog *Denb.* ***Settlement***, 1km SW of Denbigh. **47 J6** SJ0365.
Gwbert *Cere.* ***Hamlet***, on E side of mouth of River Teifi, 3m/4km N of Cardigan. **26 A4** SN1649.
Gweek *Cornw.* ***Village***, picturesque village with quay on Helford River at head of creek, 3m/5km E of Helford. **2 E6** SW7026.
Gwehelog *Mon.* ***Village***, 2m/3km N of Usk. **19 G1** SO3804.
Gwely'r Misgl *Bridgend* ***Island***, rock island on edge of Kenfig Sands, 3m/5km NW of Porthcawl. SS7880.
Gwenddwr *Powys* ***Hamlet***, 4m/7km S of Builth Wells. **27 K4** SO0643.
Gwendraeth *Carmar.* ***Sea feature***, inlet to W of Kidwelly forming estuary of rivers Gwendraeth Fawr and Gwendraeth Fach. **17 G4** SN3706.
Gwendraeth Fach *Carmar.* ***River***, rising SE of Llanarthney and flowing SW to Kidwelly, thereafter forming a common estuary with Gwendraeth Fawr River and flowing W into Carmarthen Bay. **17 H3** SN3906.
Gwendraeth Fawr *Carmar.* ***River***, rising near Gorslas and flowing SW to join Gwendraeth Fach River in a common estuary flowing W into Carmarthen Bay. **17 H4** SN4005.
Gwendreath *Cornw.* ***Settlement***, on S edge of Goonhilly Downs, 4m/6km N of Lizard Point. SW7316.
Gwenfo *V. of Glam. Welsh form of Wenvoe, qv.*
Gwenlais *Carmar.* ***River***, rising 3m/5km NW of Cilycwm, flowing SE to Cilycwm, then into River Tywi 1m/2km SE of village. **27 G4** SN7538.
Gwennap *Cornw.* ***Village***, in former tin and copper-mining area, 3m/4km SE of Redruth. **2 E4** SW7340.
Gwennap Head *Cornw.* ***Coastal feature***, headland 3m/4km SE of Land's End. **2 A6** SW3621.
Gwennol *Carmar.* ***River***, flowing SW into River Gwydderig, 3m/5km E of Llandovery. **27 H5** SN8233.
Gwenter *Cornw.* ***Settlement***, on S edge of Goonhilly Downs, 5m/8km NE of Lizard Point. **2 E7** SW7417.
Gwern Estyn *Flints.* ***Settlement***, 1km SE of Hope. SJ3157.
Gwern-y-Steeple *V. of Glam.* ***Hamlet***, 1km SW of Peterston-super-Ely. ST0775.
Gwernaffield *Flints.* ***Village***, 2m/3km W of Mold. **48 B6** SJ2064.
Gwernesney (Gwerneshi). *Mon.* ***Hamlet***, 3m/4km E of Usk. **19 H1** SO4101.
Gwernesni *Mon. Welsh form of Gwernesney, qv.*
Gwernogle *Carmar.* ***Hamlet***, 2m/4km N of Brechfa. **17 J1** SN5234.
Gwernymynydd *Flints.* ***Village***, 2m/3km SW of Mold. **48 B6** SJ2162.
Gwersyllt *Wrex.* Population: 9860. ***Locality***, 2m/4km NW of Wrexham. **48 C7** SJ3153.
Gwespyr *Flints.* ***Village***, 3m/4km E of Prestatyn. **47 K4** SJ1182.

Gwili *Carmar.* ***River***, rising to E of Llanpumsaint and flowing W to village, then circuitously to join River Tywi to E of Carmarthen. **17 H2** SN4320.

Gwili *Carmar.* ***River***, rising near Cross Hands and flowing S into River Loughor to W of Pontarddulais. SN5803.

Gwili Railway *Carmar.* ***Other feature of interest***, tourist railway running N from Bronwydd Arms, 2m/4km N of Carmarthen. **17 H2** SN4123.

Gwinear *Cornw.* ***Village***, 2m/3km E of Hayle. **2 C5** SW5937.

Gwithian *Cornw.* ***Village***, 4m/6km W of Camborne. **2 C4** SW5841.

Gwndy *Mon. Welsh form of Undy, qv.*

Gwredog *I.o.A.* ***Settlement***, on Anglesey, 2m/3km NW of Llanerchymedd. SH4086.

Gwrhay *Caerp.* ***Hamlet***, 1km N of Oakdale. ST1899.

Gwrhyd *Powys* ***Mountain***, a peak on Mynydd Eppynt, 7m/11km N of Sennybridge. Height 1489 feet or 454 metres. **27 J5** SN9339.

Gwril *Gwyn.* ***River***, running W into Barmouth Bay at Llwyngwril. SH5810.

Gwrych Castle *Conwy* ***Historic house***, 19c Gothic style mansion on hillside, 1km W of Abergele. **47 H5** SH9277.

Gwy *Welsh form of (River) Wye, qv.*

Gwyddelwern *Denb.* ***Village***, 3m/4km N of Corwen. **37 K1** SJ0746.

Gwydderig ***River***, rising as Nant Gwared, N of Trecastle and flowing S to Llywel then NW into River Tywi at Llandovery. SN7734.

Gwyddgrug *Carmar.* ***Hamlet***, 6m/10km SW of Llanybydder. **17 H1** SN4635.

Gwydir Castle *Conwy* ***Castle***, in River Conwy valley opposite Llanrwst, of various dates from 14c to 20c. **47 F6** SH7961.

Gwydyr Forest *Conwy* ***Forest/woodland***, forested area to S and W of Betws-y-coed. Incorporates Gwydyr Forest Park. **47 F7** SH7755.

Gwynfryn *Wrex.* ***Settlement***, 5m/8km W of Wrexham. SJ2552.

Gŵyr *Swan. Welsh form of Gower, qv.*

Gwystre *Powys* ***Settlement***, 3m/5km N of Llandrindod Wells. **27 K2** SO0665.

Gwytherin *Conwy* ***Village***, 4m/6km S of Llangernyw. **47 G6** SH8761.

Gyfelia *Wrex.* ***Settlement***, 3m/5km S of Wrexham. **38 C1** SJ3245.

Gyffin *Conwy* ***Suburb***, on S side of Conwy. **47 F5** SH7776.

Gylchedd *Conwy* ***Mountain***, plateau 3m/5km N of Llyn Celyn dam. Height 2060 feet or 628 metres. **37 H1** SH8645.

Gylen Castle *Arg. & B.* ***Castle***, ruined castle at S end of Kerrera. Destroyed by Cromwell's troops in 1645. **79 K5** NM8026.

Gypsey Race *E.Riding* ***River***, flowing E from 1m/2km W of Wold Newton into Bridlington Bay at Bridlington. **59 H3** TA1866.

Gyre *Ork.* ***Settlement***, to NE of Orphir Bay, on S coast of Mainland. **107 C7** HY3404.

Gyrn Castle *Flints.* ***Castle***, early 18c castle set in woodland 4m/6km SE of Prestatyn. **47 K4** SJ1181.

Gyrn Ddu *Gwyn.* ***Mountain***, on NE part of Lleyn Peninsula, 2m/3km SW of Clynnog-fawr. Height 1712 feet or 522 metres. **36 D1** SH4046.

Gyrn Goch *Gwyn.* ***Settlement***, 1m/2km SW of Clynnog-fawr. **36 D1** SH4048.

Gyrn Moelfre *Powys* ***Mountain***, 1km NE of Moelfre. Height 1715 feet or 523 metres. **38 A3** SJ1829.

H

Haaf Gruney *Shet.* ***Island***, uninhabited island lying nearly 1m/2km off SE coast of Unst. Area about 50 acres or 20 hectares. Nature reserve. **108 F3** HU6398.

Habber Gallows Hill *Oxon.* ***Hill***, to N of Crow's Castle, 2m/3km SW of Shipton under Wychwood. Height 656 feet or 200 metres. **30 D7** SP2416.

Habberley *Shrop.* ***Village***, 8m/13km SW of Shrewsbury. **38 C5** SJ3903.

Habbies Howe *Sc.Bord.* ***Locality***, wooded area along banks of River North Esk, 1km NE of Carlops. **75 K5** NT1756.

Habergham *Lancs.* ***Suburb***, 2m/3km W of Burnley town centre. SD8033.

Habin *W.Suss.* ***Settlement***, 1m/2km S of Rogate and 4m/7km E of Petersfield. SU8022.

Habitancum *Northumb. See West Woodburn.*

Habost *W.Isles Anglicised form of Tabost (Loch Erisort), qv.*

Habost *W.Isles Anglicised form of Tabost (Butt of Lewis), qv.*

Habrough *N.E.Lincs.* ***Village***, 2m/3km W of Immingham. **52 E1** TA1413.

Haccombe *Devon* ***Settlement***, 3m/4km E of Newton Abbot. **5 J3** SX8970.

Hacconby *Lincs.* ***Village***, 3m/5km N of Bourne. **42 E3** TF1025.

Haceby *Lincs.* ***Hamlet***, 7m/12km E of Grantham. Site of Roman villa 1m/2km NW. **42 D2** TF0236.

Hacheston *Suff.* ***Village***, 2m/4km N of Wickham Market. **35 H3** TM3059.

Hackbridge *Gt.Lon.* ***Suburb***, in borough of Sutton, 2m/3km NE of Sutton town centre. TQ2865.

Hackenthorpe *S.Yorks.* ***Suburb***, 5m/8km SE of Sheffield city centre. **51 G4** SK4183.

Hackford *Norf.* ***Village***, 3m/5km W of Wymondham. **44 E5** TG0502.

Hackforth *N.Yorks.* ***Village***, 3m/5km S of Catterick. **62 D7** SE2493.

Hackington *Kent* ***Locality***, adjoining to N of Canterbury. TR1560.

Hackland *Ork.* ***Settlement***, 1m/2km N of Bay of Isbister. **106 C5** HY3920.

Hacklete *W.Isles Anglicised form of Tacleit, qv.*

Hackleton *Northants.* ***Village***, 5m/8km SE of Northampton. **32 B3** SP8055.

Hackley Head *Aber. Alternative name for Forvie Ness, qv.*

Hacklinge *Kent* ***Settlement***, 3m/4km NW of Deal. **15 J2** TR3454.

Hackman's Gate *Worcs.* ***Hamlet***, 4m/6km E of Kidderminster. SO8977.

Hackness *N.Yorks.* ***Village***, 5m/8km W of Scarborough. **63 J3** SE9690.

Hackness *Ork.* ***Settlement***, at NE end of peninsula of South Walls, Hoy. **107 C8** ND3390.

Hackney *Gt.Lon.* ***Suburb***, 4m/6km NW of Charing Cross. TQ3484.

Hackney Wick *Gt.Lon.* ***Suburb***, in borough of Hackney, 1m/2km E of Hackney. TQ3784.

Hackpen Hill *Devon* ***Hill***, 1m/2km SW of Hemyock. Height 846 feet or 258 metres. **7 K4** ST1112.

Hackpen Hill *Wilts.* ***Hill***, on NW edge of Marlborough Downs, 2m/3km SE of Broad Hinton. Height 892 feet or 272 metres. **20 E4** SU1274.

Hackthorn *Lincs.* ***Village***, 7m/11km N of Lincoln. **52 C4** SK9982.

Hackthorpe *Cumb.* ***Village***, 5m/8km S of Penrith. **61 G4** NY5423.

Haco's Ness *Ork.* ***Coastal feature***, headland at SE end of Shapinsay on Shapinsay Sound. **107 E6** HY5214.

Hacton *Gt.Lon.* ***Settlement***, in borough of Havering, 1m/2km SW of Upminster. TQ5485.

Hadden *Sc.Bord.* ***Hamlet***, 2m/3km NE of Sprouston. **77 F7** NT7836.

Haddenham *Bucks.* Population: 4745. ***Village***, 3m/4km NE of Thame. **22 A1** SP7408.

Haddenham *Cambs.* Population: 2556. ***Village***, 6m/9km SW of Ely. **33 H1** TL4674.

Haddenham End *Cambs.* ***Settlement***, adjoining to N of Haddenham. TL4674.

Haddeo *Som.* ***River***, rising 3m/4km W of Clatworthy Reservoir and flowing SW through Wimbleball Lake, then into River Exe 1m/2km N of Exebridge. SS9326.

Haddington *E.Loth.* Population: 8844. ***Small town***, historic town on River Tyne, 16m/26km E of Edinburgh. Birthplace of John Knox, 1505. Renovated church of St. Mary, 14c-15c. St. Martin's Church (Historic Scotland). **76 D3** NT5173.

Haddington *Lincs.* ***Hamlet***, 7m/11km SW of Lincoln. **52 C6** SK9163.

Haddiscoe *Norf.* ***Village***, 4m/7km N of Beccles. **45 J6** TM4496.

Haddo House *Aber.* ***Historic house***, mansion of 1732 by William Adam, 6m/10km NW of Ellon. Seat of Marquess of Aberdeen. **91 G1** NJ8634.

Haddon *Cambs.* ***Village***, 5m/8km SW of Peterborough. **42 E6** TL1392.

Haddon Hall *Derbys.* ***Historic house***, medieval house in River Wye valley 2m/3km SE of Bakewell. **50 E6** SK2366.

Haddon Hill *Som.* ***Mountain***, to S of Wimbleball Lake and 3m/5km E of Dulverton. Height 1164 feet or 355 metres. **7 H3** SS9628.

Hade Edge *W.Yorks.* ***Settlement***, 2m/3km S of Holmfirth. SE1405.

Hademore *Staffs.* ***Settlement***, 3m/5km NW of Tamworth. **40 D5** SK1708.

Hadfield *Derbys.* ***Locality***, 2m/3km NW of Glossop. **50 C3** SK0296.

Hadham Cross *Herts.* ***Locality***, S end of Much Hadham, 4m/7km SE of Bishop's Stortford. **33 H7** TL4218.

Hadham Ford *Herts.* ***Village***, 3m/5km W of Bishop's Stortford. **33 H6** TL4321.

Hadleigh *Essex* ***Small town***, 4m/7km W of Southend-on-Sea. Remains of Norman castle (English Heritage). Buildings date from medieval times, many pargeted. **24 E3** TQ8187.

Hadleigh *Suff.* Population: 6595. ***Small town***, 8m/13km W of Ipswich. 15c guildhall. **34 E4** TM0242.

Hadleigh Castle *Essex* ***Castle***, 1km S of Hadleigh. Originally 13c castle (English Heritage) begun by Hubert de Burgh, minister of Henry III; remains today are 14c. **24 E3** TQ8186.

Hadleigh Guildhall *Suff.* ***Historic house***, in Hadleigh, with 18c assembly room and timber roof. **34 E4** TM0343.

Hadleigh Heath *Suff.* ***Settlement***, 2m/3km W of Hadleigh. TL9941.

Hadley *Gt.Lon.* ***Suburb***, in borough of Barnet, 3m/4km S of Potters Bar. TQ2497.

Hadley *Tel. & W.* Population: 12,508. ***Locality***, 1m/2km E of Wellington. **39 F4** SJ6712.

Hadley *Worcs.* ***Hamlet***, 3m/4km W of Droitwich Spa. SO8663.

Hadley End *Staffs.* ***Village***, 7m/11km N of Lichfield. **40 D3** SK1320.

Hadley Wood *Gt.Lon.* ***Suburb***, in borough of Enfield, 3m/4km S of Potters Bar and 11m/18km N of Charing Cross. **23 F2** TQ2697.

Hadlow *Kent* Population: 3137. ***Village***, 4m/6km NE of Tonbridge. Tower, 170 feet or 52 metres high, is remains of 19c Gothic castle. **23 K7** TQ6349.

Hadlow Down *E.Suss.* ***Village***, 4m/7km NE of Uckfield. **13 J4** TQ5324.

Hadlow Stair (Also known as The Stair.) *Kent* ***Suburb***, in NE part of Tonbridge. TQ6047.

Hadnall *Shrop.* ***Village***, 5m/8km NE of Shrewsbury. **38 E3** SJ5220.

Hadrian's Camp *Cumb.* ***Locality***, 2m/3km NE of Carlisle, on line of Hadrian's Wall. NY4158.

Hadrian's Wall ***Other feature of interest***, well-preserved Roman fortification system (Vallum) dating from 2c, extending 73m/118km from Bowness-on-Solway to Wallsend. Original height of wall was 21 feet or 6 metres. Numerous section are English Heritage property. Designated as a World Heritage Site. **70 B7** NY6666.

Hadspen *Som.* ***Hamlet***, 1m/2km E of Castle Cary. ST6532.

Hadspen House *Som.* ***Garden***, modern garden, 4m/6km NW of Wincanton. **9 F1** ST6631.

Hadstock *Essex* ***Village***, 4m/7km N of Saffron Walden. **33 J4** TL5544.

Hadston Carrs *Northumb.* ***Coastal feature***, flat rocks 3m/4km SE of Amble. **71 H3** NU2800.

Hadyard Hill *S.Ayr.* ***Mountain***, 6m/9km E of Girvan. Height 1059 feet or 323 metres. **67 G4** NX2799.

Hadyhill *Derbys.* ***Suburb***, to E of Chesterfield town centre across River Rother. SK3970.

Hadzor *Worcs.* ***Village***, 1m/2km SE of Droitwich Spa. **29 J2** SO9162.

Haffenden Quarter *Kent* ***Settlement***, 1m/2km S of Smarden. **14 D3** TQ8841.

Hafod Bridge *Carmar.* ***Settlement***, on River Dulais, 3m/5km NW of Llanwrda. SN6936.

Hafod-Dinbych *Conwy* ***Settlement***, 2m/3km NE of Pentrefoelas. **47 G7** SH8953.

Hafod-lom *Conwy* ***Settlement***, 4m/6km S of Colwyn Bay. **47 G5** SH8571.

Hafod Lwyfog *Gwyn.* ***Open space***, National Trust area 4m/7km NE of Beddgelert. SH6551.

Hafodunos *Conwy* ***Settlement***, 1km W of Llangernyw. **47 G6** SH8667.

Hafodyrynys *Caerp.* ***Hamlet***, 2m/3km NE of Newbridge. ST2298.

Hafren *Welsh form of (River) Severn, qv.*

Hag Hill *Derbys.* ***Settlement***, 2m/3km NE of Clay Cross. SK4066.

Haggate *Lancs.* ***Locality***, 2m/3km SE of Nelson. **56 D6** SD8735.

Haggbeck *Cumb.* ***Settlement***, 4m/6km SE of Catlowdy. **69 K6** NY4773.

Haggersta *Shet.* ***Settlement***, on Mainland, between Weisdale Voe and Loch of Strom. HU3848.

Haggerston *Gt.Lon.* ***Suburb***, in borough of Hackney, 3m/5km NE of Charing Cross. TQ3483.

Haggerston *Northumb.* ***Village***, 3m/5km NE of Lowick. Castle keep of uncertain date. NU0443.

Hagget End *Cumb.* ***Locality***, adjoining to SW of Egremont. NY0010.

Haggrister *Shet.* ***Settlement***, on Mainland, on W side of Sullom Voe, near head of inlet. HU3470.

Haggs *Falk.* Population: 1013. ***Locality***, 2m/4km W of Bonnybridge. **75 F3** NS7979.

Haghill *Glas.* ***Suburb***, 3m/4km E of Glasgow city centre in Dennistoun district. NS6265.

Hagley *Here.* Population: 5417. ***Village***, 3m/5km E of Hereford. **28 E4** SO5641.

Hagley *Worcs.* ***Suburb***, 2m/4km S of Stourbridge. **40 B7** SO9180.

Hagley Hall *Worcs.* ***Historic house***, 18c Palladian manor designed by Sanderson Miller, 3m/4km SE of Stourbridge. Features Rococo plasterwork by Vassali and paintings by Van Dyck and Reynolds. **40 B7** SO9180.

Hagmore Green *Suff.* ***Settlement***, to SW of Boxford, 3m/5km N of Nayland. TL9539.

Hagnaby *Lincs.* ***Locality***, 4m/7km SW of Spilsby. **53 G6** TF3462.

Hagnaby *Lincs.* ***Settlement***, 3m/5km NE of Alford. TF4879.

Hague Bar *Derbys.* ***Settlement***, 1m/2km W of New Mills. SJ9885.

Hagworthingham *Lincs.* ***Village***, 5m/9km E of Horncastle. **53 G6** TF3469.

Haigh *Gt.Man.* ***Hamlet***, 3m/4km NE of Wigan. **49 F2** SD6009.

Haigh Hall Country Park *Gt.Man.* ***Leisure/recreation***, 2m/3km NE of Wigan, on E side of Leeds and Liverpool Canal. Woodland walks in park, plus miniature railway, model village and zoo. **48 E2** SD5908.

Haigh Moor *W.Yorks.* ***Village***, 3m/4km SE of Morley. SE2824.

Haighton Green *Lancs.* ***Settlement***, 4m/6km NE of Preston. **55 J6** SD5634.

Hail Weston *Cambs.* ***Village***, 2m/3km NW of St. Neots. **32 E2** TL1662.

Haile *Cumb.* ***Hamlet***, 2m/3km SE of Egremont. **60 B6** NY0308.

Hailes *Glos.* ***Settlement***, 2m/3km NE of Winchcombe. Ruined Cistercian abbey (National Trust and English Heritage). **30 B5** SP0430.

Hailes Abbey *Glos.* ***Ecclesiastical building***, ruined Cistercian abbey (National Trust and English Heritage) 2m/3km NE of Winchcombe, founded in 1246, including fragment of 15c cloister. **30 B5** SP0530.

Hailes Castle *E.Loth.* ***Castle***, ruined castle of 13c-15c on S bank of River Tyne, 1m/2km SW of East Linton. **76 D3** NT5775.

Hailey *Herts.* ***Suburb***, 1m/2km N of Hoddesdon. **33 G7** TL3710.

Hailey *Oxon.* ***Hamlet***, 3m/5km SE of Wallingford. **21 K3** SU6485.

Hailey *Oxon.* ***Village***, 2m/3km N of Witney. **30 E7** SP3512.

Hailsham *E.Suss.* Population: 18,426. ***Town***, 7m/11km N of Eastbourne. Michelham Priory 2m/3km W. **13 J6** TQ5809.

Haimer *High.* ***Settlement***, 1m/2km SE of Thurso. **105 G2** ND1367.

Hainault *Gt.Lon.* ***Suburb***, in borough of Redbridge, 4m/6km N of Ilford. **23 H2** TQ4591.

Hainault Forest Country Park ***Leisure/recreation***, wooded country park on border of Essex and Greater London, 1m/2km NE of Hainault. **23 H2** TQ4793.

Haine *Kent* ***Settlement***, 4m/6km NW of Ramsgate. TR3566.

Haines Hill *Som.* ***Suburb***, S district of Taunton. ST2223.

Hainford *Norf.* ***Village***, 6m/10km N of Norwich. **45 G4** TG2218.

Hainton *Lincs.* ***Village***, 6m/9km SE of Market Rasen. **52 E4** TF1884.

Hainworth *W.Yorks.* ***Hamlet***, on hillside, overlooking Worth valley, 1m/2km S of Keighley. SE0539.

Haisthorpe *E.Riding* ***Village***, 4m/6km SW of Bridlington. **59 H3** TA1264.

Hakin *Pembs.* ***Suburb***, W district of Milford Haven. SM8905.

Halam *Notts.* ***Village***, 1m/2km NW of Southwell. **51 J7** SK6754.

Halbeath *Fife* ***Hamlet***, 2m/4km E of Dunfermline. **75 K2** NT1288.

Halberton *Devon* ***Village***, 3m/5km E of Tiverton. **7 J4** ST0013.

Halcro *High.* ***Locality***, in Caithness district, 5m/8km SE of Castletown. **105 H2** ND2360.

Halcro Head *Ork.* ***Coastal feature***, headland on E coast of South Ronaldsay, 3m/4km NE of Brough Ness. **107 D9** ND4785.

Halden *Herts.* ***Suburb***, NE district of Welwyn Garden City. TL2414.

Haldenby *N.Lincs.* ***Locality***, 4m/7km NE of Crowle. SE8217.

Hale *Cumb.* ***Hamlet***, 2m/3km S of Milnthorpe. SD5078.

Hale *Gt.Man.* Population: 15,868. ***Town***, adjoining to S of Altrincham. **49 G4** SJ7786.

Hale *Halton* ***Village***, 4m/6km SW of Widnes. SJ4682.

Hale *Hants.* ***Village***, 4m/7km NE of Fordingbridge. **10 C3** SU1918.

Hale *Med.* ***Suburb***, in E part of Chatham. TQ7765.

Hale *Surr.* ***Locality***, 1m/2km NE of Farnham. **22 B7** SU8448.

Hale Bank *Halton* ***Locality***, 1m/2km NE of Hale. **48 D4** SJ4883.

Hale End *Gt.Lon.* ***Suburb***, in borough of Waltham Forest, 1m/2km NE of Walthamstow town centre. TQ3891.

Hale Green *Cumb.* ***Settlement***, adjoining to NE of Hale. SD5078.

Hale Green *Gt.Man.* ***Locality***, 1m/2km E of Hale. SJ7786.

Hale Nook *Lancs.* ***Settlement***, 1m/2km NE of Hambleton. SD3944.

Hale Street *Kent* ***Village***, 3m/4km N of Paddock Wood. **23 K7** TQ6749.

Halebarns *Gt.Man.* ***Locality***, 1m/2km SE of Hale. **49 G4** SJ7985.

Hales *Norf.* ***Village***, 2m/3km SE of Loddon. **45 H6** TM3897.

Hales *Staffs.* ***Village***, 3m/4km E of Market Drayton. Site of Roman villa 1km E. **39 G2** SJ7133.

Hales Green *Derbys.* ***Hamlet***, 3m/5km S of Ashbourne. SK1741.

Hales Hall *Norf.* ***Historic house***, recently restored late medieval manor house and barn, 1m/2km SW of Hales. **45 H6** TM3696.

Hales Place *Kent* ***Suburb***, in N of Canterbury. **15 G2** TR1459.

Hales Street *Norf.* ***Settlement***, 3m/4km W of Pulham Market. TM1587.

Halesfield *Tel. & W.* ***Locality***, industrial estate E of Madeley, Telford. SJ7104.

Halesgate *Lincs.* ***Settlement***, adjoining to SE of Moulton Seas End, 3m/4km NW of Holbeach. TF3226.

Halesowen *W.Mid.* Population: 57,918. ***Town***, 7m/11km W of Birmingham. Former nail-making town with medieval parish church. Remains of 13c priory (English Heritage) 1km SE. **40 B7** SO9683.

Halesowen Abbey *W.Mid.* ***Ecclesiastical building***, remains of 13c priory (English Heritage) founded by King John, 1km SE of Halesowen. **40 B7** SO9782.

Halesworth *Suff.* Population: 4575. ***Small town***, 24m/39km NE of Ipswich. Elizabethan timber-framed house in market place. **35 H1** TM3877.

Halewood *Mersey.* ***Locality***, 4m/6km W of Widnes. **48 D4** SJ4485.

Halewood Green *Mersey.* ***Locality***, 1m/2km NW of Halewood. SJ4585.

Half Acre *Gt.Man.* ***Locality***, 1m/2km N of Prestwich. SD8104.

Half Way Inn *Devon* ***Settlement***, 3m/4km SW of West Hill. **7 J6** SY0490.

Halfmerk Hill ***Mountain***, on border of Dumfries & Galloway and East Ayrshire, 3m/5km NW of Kirkconnel. Height 1479 feet or 451 metres. **68 B2** NS7016.

Halford *Devon* ***Hamlet***, on E edge of Dartmoor National Park, 4m/6km NW of Newton Abbot. SX8174.

Halford *Shrop.* ***Hamlet***, just E of Craven Arms across River Onny. **38 D7** SO4383.

Halford *Warks.* ***Village***, 3m/5km N of Shipston on Stour. **30 D4** SP2645.

Halfpenny *Cumb.* ***Settlement***, 4m/6km S of Kendal. SD5387.

Halfpenny Furze *Carmar.* ***Hamlet***, 2m/3km S of St. Clears. SN2713.

Halfpenny Green *Staffs.* ***Hamlet***, 7m/11km SW of Wolverhampton. Airfield to S. **40 A6** SO8291.

Halfway *Carmar.* ***Settlement***, 5m/9km N of Llandeilo. **17 K1** SN6430.

Halfway *Carmar.* ***Suburb***, on E side of Llanelli. SN5200.

Halfway *Powys* ***Hamlet***, 4m/7km E of Llandovery. Earthworks of Roman camps 1m/2km S. **27 H5** SN8332.

Halfway *S.Yorks.* ***Suburb***, 6m/10km SE of Sheffield city centre. **51 G4** SK4381.

Halfway *W.Berks.* ***Hamlet***, 4m/7km W of Newbury. **21 H5** SU4068.

Halfway Bridge *W.Suss.* ***Hamlet***, midway between Midhurst and Petworth. SU9321.

Halfway House *Shrop.* ***Hamlet***, 1m/2km SE of Wollaston. **38 C4** SJ3411.

Halfway Houses *Kent* ***Village***, on Isle of Sheppey, midway between Queenborough and Minster. **25 F4** TQ9373.

Halfway Houses *Lincs.* ***Settlement***, 6m/10km SW of Lincoln, on A46 road (Foss Way). SK8863.

Halfwayhouse *Glas.* ***Suburb***, 4m/6km SW of Glasgow city centre, in Cardonald district. NS5363.

Halghton Mill *Wrex.* ***Settlement***, 2m/3km SE of Bangor on Dee. **38 D1** SJ4143.

Halidon Hill *Northumb.* ***Hill***, 2m/3km NW of Berwick-upon-Tweed, site of English victory over Scots in 1333. Height 535 feet or 163 metres. **77 H5** NT9654.

Halifax *W.Yorks.* Population: 91,069. ***Town***, 7m/11km SW of Bradford. Noted for Piece Hall, a former wool market. Calderdale Industrial Museum displays mill machinery. 15c Shibden Hall contains the Folk Museum of West Yorkshire. **57 F7** SE0925.

Halistra *High.* ***Locality***, on Vaternish peninsula, Skye, comprising settlements of Upper and Lower Halistra, 5m/8km S of Vaternish Point. **93 H6** NG2459.

Halket *E.Ayr.* ***Settlement***, 1m/2km E of Lugton. NS4252.

Halkirk *High.* ***Village***, on River Thurso, 6m/9km S of Thurso, Caithness district. **105 G3** ND1359.

Halkyn (Helygain). *Flints.* ***Village***, 3m/5km SE of Holywell. **48 B5** SJ2171.

Halkyn Mountain *Flints.* ***Inland physical feature***, NW to SE ridge rising to over 360 metres, to W of Halkyn. Remains of lead mines and quarries. **47 K5** SJ1971.

Hall *E.Renf.* ***Settlement***, 1m/2km W of Uplawmoor. **74 C5** NS4154.

Hall Common *Norf.* ***Hamlet***, 1km S of Ludham. TG3817.

Hall Cross *Lancs.* ***Settlement***, 1m/2km S of Kirkham. SD4230.

Hall Dunnerdale *Cumb.* ***Hamlet***, in River Duddon valley, 5m/8km N of Broughton in Furness. **60 D7** SD2195.

Hall End *Beds.* ***Locality***, adjoining to W of Clophill, 2m/4km E of Ampthill. TL0737.

Hall End *Warks.* ***Locality***, adjoining to W of Dordon. SK2500.

Hall Green *Ches.* ***Settlement***, adjoining to S of Scholar Green, 1m/2km E of Alsager. SJ8356.

Hall Green *Lancs.* ***Settlement***, 1m/2km W of Walmer Bridge, 6m/9km SW of Preston. SD4624.

Hall Green *Lancs.* ***Suburb***, 1m/2km E of Skelmersdale town centre. SD5005.

Hall Green *Norf.* ***Hamlet***, 1m/2km SW of Tivetshall St. Mary. TM1585.

Hall Green *Norf.* ***Locality***, 4m/6km W of East Dereham. TF9315.

Hall Green *W.Mid.* ***Suburb***, 4m/7km SE of Birmingham city centre. **40 D7** SP1081.

Hall Green *W.Mid.* ***Suburb***, 3m/5km NE of Coventry city centre. SP3582.

Hall Green *W.Yorks.* ***Locality***, adjoining to E of Hollingthorpe, 1km S of Crigglestone. SE3115.

Hall Grove *Herts.* ***Suburb***, SE district of Welwyn Garden City. TL2511.

Hall i' th' Wood *Gt.Man.* ***Historic house***, 16c house containing museum to N of Tonge Moor in Bolton; childhood home of Samuel Crompton, inventor of spinning mule. **49 G1** SD7211.

Hall of the Forest *Shrop.* ***Settlement***, 6m/9km NW of Clun. **38 B7** SO2083.

Hall Place *Gt.Lon.* ***Historic house***, well-preserved house built in 1540 with wing added in 1650, 1m/2km SE of Bexleyheath. Gardens, museum, art gallery and local studies centre. **23 J4** TQ5074.

Hall Place *Kent* ***Historic house***, Elizabethan red-bricked house to W of Leigh. **23 J7** TQ5446.

Halladale *High.* ***River***, in Caithness district, running N down Strath Halladale to Melvich Bay on N coast. **104 D3** NC8965.

Hallam Head *S.Yorks.* ***Suburb***, 3m/5km W of Sheffield. SK3086.

Halland *E.Suss.* ***Hamlet***, 4m/6km SE of Uckfield. **13 J5** TQ5016.

Halland's Field *N.Lincs.* ***Locality***, 1km SW of Goxhill. TA0920.

Hallaton *Leics.* ***Village***, 7m/11km NE of Market Harborough. Site of motte and bailey castle to W. **42 A6** SP7896.

Hallatrow *B. & N.E.Som.* ***Village***, 3m/4km NW of Midsomer Norton. **19 K6** ST6357.

Hallbankgate *Cumb.* ***Hamlet***, 4m/6km E of Brampton. **61 G1** NY5859.

Hallbeck *Cumb.* ***Hamlet***, 3m/5km SW of Sedbergh. SD6288.

Hallen *S.Glos.* ***Hamlet***, 4m/7km NW of Bristol city centre, just W of M5 motorway. **19 J4** ST5580.

Hallfield Gate *Derbys.* ***Settlement***, adjoining to Shirland, 2m/3km NW of Alfreton. SK3958.

Hallgarth *Dur.* ***Hamlet***, 1km S of Pittington. NZ3243.

Halliggye Fogou *Cornw.* ***Historic/prehistoric site***, Iron Age fogou, or souterrain (English Heritage), 1km S of Mawgan. Best example in Cornwall. **2 E6** SW7123.

Halliman Skerries *Moray* ***Island***, island group with lighthouse, 1km off N coast and 1m/2km W of Lossiemouth. **97 K4** NJ2172.

Hallin *High.* ***Settlement***, near NW coast of Skye, 5m/8km S of Vaternish Point. **93 H6** NG2558.

Halling *Med.* ***Village***, on River Medway, 4m/6km SW of Rochester. **24 D5** TQ7064.

Hallington *Lincs.* ***Hamlet***, 2m/3km SW of Louth. **53 G4** TF3085.

Hallington *Northumb.* ***Hamlet***, 7m/11km N of Corbridge. **70 E6** NY9875.

Hallington Reservoirs *Northumb.* ***Reservoir***, two adjacent reservoirs to W of Hallington. **70 E6** NY9776.

Hallival *High.* ***Mountain***, 2m/3km S of Kinloch, Rum. Height 2371 feet or 723 metres. **85 J5** NM3996.

Halliwell *Gt.Man.* ***Suburb***, 1m/2km NW of Bolton town centre. SD7010.

Halloughton *Notts.* ***Hamlet***, 1m/2km SW of Southwell. **51 J7** SK6851.

Hallow *Worcs.* ***Village***, 3m/4km NW of Worcester. **29 H3** SO8258.

Hallow Heath *Worcs.* ***Locality***, 1km N of Hallow. **29 H3** SO8258.

Hallrule *Sc.Bord.* ***Hamlet***, 1m/2km N of Bonchester Bridge. **70 A2** NT5914.

Halls *E.Loth.* ***Hamlet***, 2m/3km SE of Stenton. **76 E3** NT6572.

Hall's Green *Herts.* ***Hamlet***, 4m/6km NE of Stevenage. **33 F6** TL2728.

Hall's Tenement *Cumb.* ***Settlement***, 3m/4km S of Castle Carrock, with small lake to N. **61 G1** NY5251.

Hallsands *Devon* ***Village***, small fishing village on S coast, 1m/2km NW of Start Point. **5 J7** SX8138.

Hallsgreen *Essex* ***Settlement***, 2m/4km SW of Harlow town centre. TL4108.

Hallthwaites *Cumb.* ***Hamlet***, 3m/5km N of Millom. SD1885.

Halltoft End *Lincs.* ***Hamlet***, 3m/5km E of Boston. **43 G1** TF3645.

Hallwood Green *Glos.* ***Hamlet***, 4m/6km SW of Ledbury. SO6733.

Hallworthy *Cornw.* ***Hamlet***, 6m/9km NE of Camelford. **4 B2** SX1887.

Hallyburton Forest *P. & K.* ***Forest/woodland***, 4m/6km S of Coupar Angus. **82 D4** NO2334.

Hallyne *Sc.Bord.* ***Settlement***, on Lyne Water, 4m/6km W of Peebles. Sites of Roman forts on both sides of river. NT1940.

Halmadarie Burn *High.* ***River***, rising on NE slopes of Meall nan Aighean and flowing into Loch Truderscaig. **103 J5** NC7032.

Halmer End *Staffs.* ***Hamlet***, 4m/6km NW of Newcastle-under-Lyme. **39 G1** SJ8048.

Halmond's Frome *Here.* ***Hamlet***, 5m/7km S of Bromyard. SO6747.

Halmore *Glos.* ***Village***, 2m/4km NE of Berkeley. **19 K1** SO6902.

Halmyre Mains *Sc.Bord.* ***Hamlet***, 2m/3km SE of West Linton. **75 K6** NT1749.

Halnaker *W.Suss.* ***Village***, 4m/6km NE of Chichester. Halnaker House, ruined medieval manor house, to N. **12 C6** SU9008.

Halnaker Hill *W.Suss.* ***Hill***, on which stands Halnaker windmill, dating from 1740, 5m/8km NE of Chichester. Height 417 feet or 127 metres. **12 C6** SU9109.

Halsall *Lancs.* ***Village***, 3m/5km NW of Ormskirk. **48 C1** SD3710.

Halse *Northants.* ***Hamlet***, 3m/4km NW of Brackley. **31 G4** SP5640.

Halse *Som.* ***Village***, in Vale of Taunton Deane, 2m/3km NE of Milverton. **7 K3** ST1427.

Halsetown *Cornw.* ***Village***, just S of St. Ives. Knill Monument to E. **2 C5** SW5038.

Halsham *E.Riding* ***Village***, 4m/7km W of Withernsea. **59 J7** TA2726.

Halsinger *Devon* ***Settlement***, 5m/7km NW of Barnstaple. **6 D2** SS5138.

Halstead *Essex* Population: 9775. ***Small town***, on River Colne, 6m/10km NE of Braintree. Market town with medieval church. **34 C5** TL8130.

Halstead *Kent* ***Village***, 4m/6km SE of Orpington. **23 H5** TQ4861.

Halstead *Leics.* ***Hamlet***, just E of Tilton on the Hill, 8m/13km NW of Uppingham. **42 A5** SK7505.

Halstock *Dorset* ***Village***, 5m/8km S of Yeovil. **8 E4** ST5308.

Halstow Marshes *Med.* ***Marsh/bog***, 2m/3km N of High Halstow. **24 D4** TQ7778.

Halsway *Som.* ***Hamlet***, at foot of Quantock Hills, 5m/8km SE of Watchet. ST1237.

Halsway Manor *Som.* ***Historic house***, comprising medieval and 19c building, 3m/5km SE of Williton. Now used as centre for folk music and dance. **7 K2** ST1238.

Haltcliff Bridge *Cumb.* ***Locality***, on River Caldew, 3m/5km SE of Caldbeck. NY3636.

Haltemprice *E.Riding* ***Settlement***, 4m/6km from Kingston upon Hull city centre. TA0430.

Haltham *Lincs.* ***Village***, 4m/6km S of Horncastle. **53 F6** TF2463.

Halton *Bucks.* ***Village***, 2m/3km N of Wendover. **32 B7** SP8710.

Halton *Halton* ***Suburb***, 1m/2km E of Runcorn town centre. Remains of medieval castle. **48 E4** SJ5381.

Halton *Lancs.* Population: 2332. ***Village***, on N bank of River Lune, 3m/4km NE of Lancaster. **55 J3** SD5064.

Halton *Northumb.* ***Hamlet***, 2m/4km N of Corbridge. **71 F7** NY9967.

Halton *W.Yorks.* ***Suburb***, 3m/5km E of Leeds city centre. SE3433.

Halton *Wrex.* ***Hamlet***, 2m/3km NE of Chirk. **38 C2** SJ3039.

Halton Brook *Halton* ***Suburb***, to NW of Halton. SJ5282.

Halton East *N.Yorks.* ***Village***, 4m/6km NE of Skipton. **57 F4** SE0453.

Halton Fenside *Lincs.* ***Locality***, 2m/4km SE of Spilsby. TF4263.

Halton Gill *N.Yorks.* ***Hamlet***, near head of Littondale, 4m/7km NW of Arncliffe. **56 D2** SD8876.

Halton Green *Lancs.* ***Settlement***, on N side of River Lune, 1km E of Halton and 4m/6km NE of Lancaster. SD5165.

Halton Holegate *Lincs.* ***Village***, 1m/2km SE of Spilsby. **53 H6** TF4165.

Halton Lea Gate *Northumb.* ***Hamlet***, 5m/8km SW of Haltwhistle. **61 H1** NY6558.

Halton Moor *W.Yorks.* ***Suburb***, adjoining to S of Halton, 3m/4km E of Leeds city centre. SE3432.

Halton Park *Lancs.* ***Settlement***, 2m/3km E of Halton. SD5265.

Halton West *N.Yorks.* ***Village***, 2m/3km SW of Hellifield. **56 D4** SD8454.

Haltwhistle *Northumb.* Population: 3773. ***Small town***, market town for former coal-mining area, on River South Tyne, 14m/23km W of Hexham. **70 C7** NY7064.

Halvergate *Norf.* ***Village***, 3m/5km N of Reedham. **45 J5** TG4206.

Halvergate Marshes *Norf.* ***Marsh/bog***, marshland 4m/6km W of Great Yarmouth. **45 J5** TG4607.

Halwell *Devon* ***Village***, 5m/8km SW of Totnes. **5 H5** SX7753.

Halwill *Devon* ***Village***, 6m/10km SE of Holsworthy. **6 C6** SX4299.

Halwill Forest *Devon* ***Open space***, upland area partly wooded to S and SE of Halwill. **6 C5** SX4299.

Halwill Junction *Devon* ***Village***, 1m/2km E of Halwill, site of former railway junction. **6 C6** SX4299.

Ham *Devon* ***Hamlet***, 4m/7km E of Honiton. ST2301.

Ham *Glos.* ***Settlement***, 2m/3km E of Cheltenham. SO9721.

Ham *Glos.* ***Village***, 1km S of Berkeley. **19 K2** ST6798.

Ham *Gt.Lon.* ***Locality***, residential locality in borough of Richmond upon Thames, between Richmond Park and River Thames. **22 E4** TQ1772.

Ham *High.* ***Settlement***, on N coast, 3m/5km SE of Dunnet Head. **105 H1** ND2373.

Ham *Kent* ***Settlement***, 2m/3km S of Sandwich. **15 J2** TR3254.

Ham *Plym.* ***Suburb***, 2m/3km NW of Plymouth city centre. SX4657.

Ham *Shet.* ***Settlement***, chief settlement of Foula. It is situated on E coast on island's only harbour, Ham Voe. **108 B1** HT9738.

Ham *Shet.* ***Settlement***, on Bressay, 1m/2km SE of Lerwick across Bressay Sound. HU4939.

Ham *Som.* ***Settlement***, 4m/7km W of Ilminster. ST2913.

Ham *Som.* ***Village***, 4m/6km E of Taunton. **8 B2** ST2825.

Ham *Wilts.* ***Village***, 4m/6km S of Hungerford. **21 G5** SU3363.

Ham Common *Dorset* ***Hamlet***, 1km SE of Gillingham. ST8126.

Ham Green *Here.* ***Settlement***, 2m/4km W of Great Malvern. SO7444.

Ham Green *Kent* ***Settlement***, 1m/2km N of Upchurch and 5m/7km E of Gillingham. TQ8468.

Ham Green *Kent* ***Settlement***, 1km SW of Wittersham. TQ8926.

Ham Green *N.Som.* ***Locality***, 4m/6km NW of Bristol. **19 J4** ST5375.

Ham Green *Worcs.* ***Hamlet***, 3m/5km SW of Redditch. **30 B2** SP0163.

Ham Hill *Kent* ***Locality***, 1m/2km SW of Snodland. **24 C5** TQ6960.

Ham Hill Country Park *Som.* ***Leisure/recreation***, 150 acres of disused quarries now home to a variety of wildlife, 1km SE of Stoke sub Hamdon. **8 D3** ST4816.

Ham Hillfort *Som.* ***Historic/prehistoric site***, one of largest hillforts (National Trust) in Britain, on W side of Montacute, 3m/5km W of Yeovil. Occupied since Neolithic times, but particularly during Iron Age and Roman period. **8 D3** ST4916.

Ham House *Gt.Lon.* ***Historic house***, 17c house and grounds (National Trust), beside River Thames N of Ham. **22 E4** TQ1772.

Ham Street *Som.* ***Village***, 4m/7km SE of Glastonbury. **8 E1** ST5534.

Hamars Ness *Shet.* ***Coastal feature***, headland at NW corner of Fetlar. **108 E3** HU5894.

Hamarsay *W.Isles* ***Island***, islet off South Harris in East Loch Tarbert, to W of Scalpay. NG2194.

Hamble *Hants.* ***River***, rising near Bishop's Waltham and flowing into Southampton Water between Hamble and Warsash. Site of Roman building on National Trust property at head of estuary near Curbridge. Lower reach noted for yachting. SU4805.

Hamble-le-Rice *Hants.* Population: 3229. ***Village***, near mouth of River Hamble, on E side of Southampton Water, opposite Fawley. **11 F4** SU4806.

Hambleden *Bucks.* ***Village***, 3m/5km NE of Henley-on-Thames. **22 A3** SU7886.

Hambledon *Hants.* ***Village***, 4m/6km SE of Meonstoke. Traditionally the 'home of cricket', the village club being founded in 18c. Site of Roman building SE of village. **11 H3** SU6414.

Hambledon *Surr.* ***Village***, 3m/5km SE of Milford. **12 C3** SU9638.

Hambleton *Lancs.* Population: 2724. ***Village***, 3m/4km S of Preesall. **55 G5** SD3742.

Hambleton *N.Yorks.* Population: 1566. ***Village***, 4m/7km W of Selby. **58 B6** SE5530.

Hambleton Hill *N.Yorks.* ***Mountain***, to N of Fountains Earth Moor, 4m/7km N of Pateley Bridge. Height 1332 feet or 406 metres. **57 G2** SE1473.

Hambleton Hills *N.Yorks.* ***Large natural feature***, hills lying between River Rye valley to E and Thirsk to SW; a SW extension of Cleveland Hills. **63 F7** SE5185.

Hambleton Moss Side *Lancs.* ***Settlement***, 1km E of Hambleton. **55 G5** SD3742.

Hambridge *Som.* ***Settlement***, 4m/7km SW of Shepton Mallet. ST5836.

Hambridge *Som.* ***Village***, 3m/4km S of Curry Rivel. **8 C2** ST3921.

Hambrook *S.Glos.* ***Hamlet***, 5m/8km NE of Bristol. **19 K4** ST6478.

Hambrook *W.Suss.* ***Village***, 1km N of Nutbourne and 5m/8km W of Chichester. **11 J4** SU7807.

Hamel Down *Devon* ***Open space***, hillslope to SE of Hameldown Tor, 1m/2km N of Widecombe in the Moor. **5 H3** SX7079.

Hameldon Hill *Lancs.* ***Mountain***, 3m/4km SW of Burnley. Masts near summit. Height 1309 feet or 399 metres. **56 D7** SD8128.

Hameldown Tor *Devon* ***Mountain***, 3m/4km NW of Widecombe in the Moor, in Dartmoor National Park. Height 1735 feet or 529 metres. **7 F7** SX7080.

Hameringham *Lincs.* ***Village***, 4m/6km SE of Horncastle. **53 G6** TF3167.

Hamerton *Cambs.* ***Village***, 8m/13km NW of Huntingdon. **32 E1** TL1379.

Hamford Water *Essex* ***Sea feature***, stream draining marshes W of The Naze and flowing out into North Sea at Pennyhole Bay. **35 G6** TM2426.

Hamilton *S.Lan.* Population: 49,991. ***Town***, administrative and commercial town, 11m/17km SE of Glasgow and 1m/2km W of confluence of Rivers Avon and Clyde. Formerly a significant coalmining area in Scotland. Racecourse. **75 F5** NS7255.

Hamilton House *E.Loth. See Prestonpans.*

Hamiltonhill *Glas.* ***Suburb***, 1m/2km N of Glasgow city centre. NS5867.

Hamlet *Devon* ***Hamlet***, 1m/2km W of Honiton. **7 K6** SY1499.

Hamlet *Dorset* ***Hamlet***, adjoining to N of Chetnole, 1m/2km S of Yetminster. ST5908.

Hammer *W.Suss.* ***Village***, 2m/3km W of Haslemere. **12 B3** SU8732.

Hammerpot *W.Suss.* ***Settlement***, 3m/5km NE of Littlehampton. **12 D6** TQ0605.

Hammersmith *Derbys.* ***Locality***, 1km N of Ripley. SK3951.

Hammersmith *Gt.Lon.* ***Suburb***, in borough of Hammersmith and Fulham, 5m/8km W of Charing Cross. TQ2278.

Hammerwich *Staffs.* ***Village***, 2m/3km NE of Brownhills. **40 C5** SK0607.

Hammerwich Square *Staffs.* ***Settlement***, adjoining to W of Hammerwich, 2m/3km NE of Brownhills. SK0607.

Hammerwood *E.Suss.* ***Settlement***, 3m/5km E of East Grinstead. **13 H3** TQ4339.

Hammerwood Park *E.Suss.* ***Historic house***, late 18c hunting lodge, 3m/5km E of East Grinstead. Built by Benjamin Latrobe, architect of The White House in Washington DC. **13 H3** TQ4438.

Hammond Street *Herts.* ***Locality***, 2m/3km NW of Cheshunt. **23 G1** TL3304.

Hammoon *Dorset* ***Village***, on River Stour, 2m/3km E of Sturminster Newton. **9 H3** ST8114.

Hamna Voe *Shet.* ***Sea feature***, inlet on S coast of Yell. **108 D5** HU4980.

Hamnavoe *Shet.* ***Settlement***, situated N of Hamna Voe on W coast of Mainland. **108 B4** HU2380.

Hamnavoe *Shet.* ***Settlement***, on W side of Lunna Ness, Mainland. **108 D5** HU4971.

Hamnavoe *Shet.* ***Settlement***, at head of Hamna Voe. **108 D4** HU4980.

Hamnavoe *Shet.* ***Village***, fishing village at N end of West Burra, with natural harbour formed by bay of Hamna Voe. Connected to Mainland via road bridges at either end of Trondra. **109 C9** HU3635.

Hamnish Clifford *Here.* ***Settlement***, 2m/4km E of Leominster. SO5359.

Hamp *Som.* ***Suburb***, S district of Bridgwater. ST3036.

Hampden Park *E.Suss.* ***Suburb***, N district of Eastbourne. **13 K6** TQ6002.

Hampden Row *Bucks.* ***Hamlet***, 3m/4km SE of Princes Risborough. SP8401.

Hamperden End *Essex* ***Hamlet***, 3m/4km W of Thaxted. TL5630.

Hampnett *Glos.* ***Village***, 1m/2km NW of Northleach. **30 C7** SP1015.

Hampole *S.Yorks.* ***Village***, 6m/10km NW of Doncaster. **51 H2** SE5010.

Hampreston *Dorset* ***Village***, 5m/8km NW of Bournemouth. **10 B5** SZ0598.

Hamps *Staffs.* ***River***, rising 4m/6km NE of Leek and flowing S to Winkhill, E to Waterhouses, then N to its confluence with River Manifold 1m/2km E of Grindon. SK1054.

Hampson Green *Lancs.* ***Locality***, 5m/7km S of Lancaster. SD4954.

Hampstead *Gt.Lon.* ***Suburb***, in borough of Camden, 4m/6km NW of Charing Cross. Includes localities of South and West Hampstead and large open space of Hampstead Heath on high ground to N, at N edge of which is 18c Kenwood House (English Heritage). **23 F3** TQ2685.

Hampstead Garden Suburb *Gt.Lon.* ***Suburb***, to N of Hampstead, in borough of Camden. TQ2688.

Hampstead Norreys (Sometimes spelled Hampstead Norris.) *W.Berks.* ***Village***, 6m/10km NE of Newbury. Site of Roman villa 1km S. **21 J4** SU5276.

Hampstead Norris *W.Berks. Occasional spelling of Hampstead Norreys, qv.*

Hampsthwaite *N.Yorks.* ***Village***, 4m/6km NW of Harrogate. 17c road bridge over River Nidd. **57 H4** SE2558.

Hampton *Devon* ***Hamlet***, 3m/4km SW of Axminster. SY2696.

Hampton *Gt.Lon.* ***Suburb***, to N of River Thames, in borough of Richmond upon Thames, 3m/5km W of Kingston upon Thames. Hampton Court Palace is 2m/3km SE. **22 E5** TQ1370.

Hampton *Kent* ***Suburb***, 1m/2km W of Herne Bay. TR1568.

Hampton *Shrop.* ***Village***, on W bank of River Severn, 4m/7km S of Bridgnorth. **39 G7** SO7486.

Hampton *Swin.* ***Hamlet***, 1km W of Highworth. SU1892.

Hampton *Worcs.* ***Suburb***, W district of Evesham. **30 B4** SP0243.

Hampton Bishop *Here.* ***Village***, between River Wye and River Lugg, 3m/5km SE of Hereford. **28 E5** SO5538.

Hampton Court Palace *Gt.Lon.* ***Historic house***, large mansion with extensive Tudor, Baroque and Victorian gardens on N bank of River Thames, 1m/2km W of Kingston Bridge. Building started by Cardinal Wolsey in 1514; 17c additions by Wren. Gardens include famous maze and Great Vine, world's oldest grapevine. Coombe Conduit (English Heritage), built by Henrty VIII to supply water to Palace, to E. **22 E5** TQ1568.

Hampton Fields *Glos.* ***Hamlet***, 2m/4km E of Nailsworth. ST8899.

Hampton Gay *Oxon.* ***Settlement***, on River Cherwell, 7m/11km N of Oxford. SP4816.

Hampton Green *Ches.* ***Settlement***, 1m/2km E of Hampton Heath. SJ5149.

Hampton Heath *Ches.* ***Hamlet***, 2m/3km NE of Malpas. **38 D1** SJ4949.

Hampton Hill *Gt.Lon.* ***Suburb***, in borough of Richmond upon Thames, 1m/2km NE of Hampton. TQ1471.

Hampton in Arden *W.Mid.* Population: 1223. ***Village***, 3m/5km E of Solihull. **40 E7** SP2080.

Hampton Loade *Shrop.* ***Locality***, on E bank of River Severn, opposite Hampton, 4m/7km S of Bridgnorth. SO7486.

Hampton Lovett *Worcs.* ***Village***, 2m/3km N of Droitwich Spa. **29 H2** SO8865.

Hampton Lucy *Warks.* ***Village***, 4m/6km E of Stratford-upon-Avon. **30 D3** SP2557.

Hampton on the Hill *Warks.* ***Village***, 2m/3km W of Warwick. **30 D2** SP2564.

Hampton Park *S'ham.* ***Suburb***, N district of Southampton. SU4315.

Hampton Poyle *Oxon.* ***Village***, 6m/10km N of Oxford. **31 G7** SP5015.

Hampton Wafre *Here.* ***Locality***, 5m/8km E of Leominster. SO5757.

Hampton Wick *Gt.Lon.* ***Suburb***, in borough of Richmond upon Thames, 3m/4km E of Hampton across Bushy Park and on W bank of River Thames opposite Kingston upon Thames. TQ1769.

Hamptworth *Wilts.* ***Hamlet***, 7m/12km W of Romsey. **10 D2** SU2419.

Hamrow *Norf.* ***Locality***, 1km N of Whissonsett. TF9124.

Hamsey *E.Suss.* ***Hamlet***, in River Ouse valley, 2m/3km N of Lewes. **13 H5** TQ4012.

Hamsey Green *Surr.* ***Locality***, adjoining to NW of Warlingham. TQ3559.

Hamstall Ridware *Staffs.* ***Village***, 4m/6km E of Rugeley. Elizabethan manor house. **40 D4** SK1019.

Hamstead *I.o.W.* ***Settlement***, 3m/5km E of Yarmouth. **11 F5** SZ4091.

Hamstead *W.Mid.* ***Suburb***, in NE part of West Bromwich. **40 C6** SP0493.

Hamstead Marshall *W.Berks.* ***Village***, 4m/6km W of Newbury. **21 H5** SU4165.

Hamsteels *Dur.* ***Settlement***, 2m/3km S of Lanchester. NZ1744.

Hamsterley *Dur.* ***Village***, 2m/3km W of Witton-le-Wear. **62 C3** NZ1131.

Hamsterley *Dur.* ***Village***, 1m/2km NE of Ebchester. 18c Derwentcote Steel Furnace (English Heritage), 1m/2km NE on S bank of River Derwent. **62 C1** NZ1156.

Hamsterley Common *Dur.* ***Open space***, moorland area to W of Hamsterley. **62 B3** NZ1131.

Hamsterley Forest *Dur.* ***Forest/woodland***, wooded area planted with conifers to S of Hamsterley Common, 7m/12km N of Barnard Castle. Visitor centre; forest drive and walks. **62 B4** NZ0428.

Hamsterley Mill *Dur.* ***Locality***, 2m/3km E of Hamsterley. NZ1156.

Hamstreet *Kent* Population: 1189. ***Village***, 6m/9km S of Ashford. **15 F4** TR0033.

Hamworthy *Poole* ***Suburb***, 2m/4km W of Poole town centre across Holes Bay. **9 J5** SY9991.

Hanbury *Staffs.* ***Village***, 5m/8km NW of Burton upon Trent. **40 D3** SK1727.

Hanbury *Worcs.* ***Village***, 4m/7km S of Bromsgrove. The Hall (National Trust) is a red-brick house of 1701. **29 J2** SO9664.

Hanbury Hall *Worcs.* ***Historic house***, Queen Anne red-brick house of 1701 (National Trust), 3m/5km E of Droitwich Spa. Staircase and ceilings painted by Thornhill. 18c orangery in formal garden. **29 J2** SO9464.

Hanbury Woodend *Staffs.* ***Hamlet***, 1m/2km SW of Hanbury. **40 D3** SK1626.

Hanby *Lincs.* ***Settlement***, 3m/4km SE of Ropsley, on site of Roman road. TF0232.

Hanch Hall *Staffs.* ***Historic house***, Queen Anne house, 3m/5km NW of Lichfield. Gardens include pools, lake and bird sanctuary. **40 C4** SK1013.

Hanchet End *Suff.* ***Settlement***, 1m/2km NW of Haverhill. TL6546.

Hanchurch *Staffs.* ***Hamlet***, 3m/4km S of Newcastle-under-Lyme. **40 A1** SJ8441.

Hand and Pen *Devon* ***Settlement***, 3m/5km W of Ottery St. Mary. SY0495.

Hand Green *Ches.* ***Settlement***, 1km W of Tiverton. SJ5460.

Handa Island *High.* ***Island***, of about 1 square mile or 3 square km, including bird sanctuary, off W coast of Sutherland district, to W of locality of Tarbet across Sound of Handa. **102 D4** NC1348.

Handale *R. & C.* ***Settlement***, 1m/2km E of Liverton. NZ7215.

Handbridge *Ches.* ***Suburb***, S district of Chester, to S of River Dee. **48 D6** SJ4065.

Handcross *W.Suss.* ***Village***, 5m/7km S of Crawley. **13 F4** TQ2629.

Handfast Point *Dorset Alternative name for The Foreland, qv.*

Handforth *Ches.* ***Locality***, 1m/2km NE of Wilmslow. **49 H4** SJ8583.

Handley *Ches.* ***Village***, 7m/11km SE of Chester. **48 D7** SJ4657.

Handley *Derbys.* ***Hamlet***, 1m/2km SW of Clay Cross. SK3761.

Handley Green *Essex* ***Settlement***, 2m/3km N of Ingatestone. TL6501.

Handley's Cross *Here.* ***Locality***, 6m/10km W of Hereford. SO4140.

Handsacre *Staffs.* ***Village***, 3m/5km SE of Rugeley. **40 C4** SK0916.

Handside *Herts.* ***Suburb***, SW district of Welwyn Garden City. TL2212.

Handsworth *S.Yorks.* ***Suburb***, 4m/6km E of Sheffield city centre. **51 G4** SK4086.

Handsworth *W.Mid.* ***Suburb***, NW district of Birmingham. **40 C6** SP0490.

Handy Cross *Bucks.* ***Settlement***, 2m/3km SW of High Wycombe. **22 B2** SU8590.

Hanford *Dorset* ***Hamlet***, 4m/6km NW of Blandford Forum. ST8411.

Hanford *Stoke* ***Suburb***, 2m/3km S of Stoke-on-Trent city centre. **40 A1** SJ8742.

Hangersley Hill *Hants.* ***Locality***, 2m/3km NE of Ringwood. SU1706.
Hanging Bridge *Derbys.* ***Hamlet***, on border with Staffordshire, named after bridge over River Dove, 1m/2km SW of Ashbourne. **40 D1** SK1545.
Hanging Heaton *W.Yorks.* ***Locality***, 1m/2km SE of Batley. SE2523.
Hanging Houghton *Northants.* ***Hamlet***, 8m/13km N of Northampton. SP7573.
Hanging Langford *Wilts.* ***Village***, in River Wylye valley, 5m/8km NW of Wilton. **10 B1** SU0336.
Hanging Walls of Mark Anthony *Cumb.* ***Locality***, 2m/4km E of Skirwith. NY6532.
Hangingshaw *D. & G.* ***Settlement***, 6m/9km N of Lockerbie. **69 G5** NY1089.
Hangingshaw *Glas.* ***Suburb***, 2m/4km S of Glasgow city centre. NS5961.
Hangingstone Hill *Devon* ***Mountain***, 5m/8km NW of Postbridge in Dartmoor National Park. Height 1981 feet or 604 metres. **6 E7** SX6186.
Hangleton *B. & H.* ***Suburb***, NW district of Hove. **13 F6** TQ2607.
Hangleton *W.Suss.* ***Settlement***, 1m/2km SE of Angmering. TQ0803.
Hangman Hill *Northumb.* ***Mountain***, on Lilswood Moor, 4m/6km SE of Allendale Town. Height 1453 feet or 443 metres. **61 K1** NY8952.
Hanham *S.Glos.* ***Suburb***, S district of Kingswood, 4m/6km E of Bristol. **19 K4** ST6472.
Hanham Abbots *S.Glos.* *See Hanham Green.*
Hanham Green *S.Glos.* ***Hamlet***, in parish of Hanham Abbots, 4m/6km SE of Bristol. ST6470.
Hankelow *Ches.* ***Village***, 1m/2km NE of Audlem. **39 F1** SJ6745.
Hankerton *Wilts.* ***Village***, 3m/5km NE of Malmesbury. **20 C2** ST9690.
Hankham *E.Suss.* ***Hamlet***, on S side of Pevensey Levels, 4m/7km N of Eastbourne. **13 K6** TQ6105.
Hanley *Stoke* ***Town***, one of old pottery towns that form city of Stoke-on-Trent: Burslem, Fenton, Hanley, Longton, Stoke-upon-Trent, Tunstall. Hanley lies 1m/2km N of city centre. Birthplace of John Smith, captain of Titanic. **40 A1** SJ8847.
Hanley Castle *Worcs.* ***Village***, on W bank of River Severn, 1m/2km NW of Upton upon Severn. **29 H4** SO8442.
Hanley Child *Worcs.* ***Hamlet***, 4m/7km SE of Tenbury Wells. **29 F2** SO6565.
Hanley Swan *Worcs.* ***Village***, 3m/4km SE of Great Malvern. **29 H4** SO8142.
Hanley William *Worcs.* ***Hamlet***, 5m/8km E of Tenbury Wells. **29 F2** SO6765.
Hanlith *N.Yorks.* ***Hamlet***, just E of Kirkby Malham. **56 E3** SD9061.
Hanmer *Wrex.* ***Village***, 5m/9km W of Whitchurch. **38 D2** SJ4539.
Hannah *Lincs.* ***Settlement***, 4m/6km NE of Alford and 2m/4km SW of Sutton on Sea. **53 H5** TF5079.
Hanningfield Reservoir *Essex* ***Reservoir***, large reservoir 4m/7km NE of Billericay. **24 D2** TQ7398.
Hanningfields Green *Suff.* ***Settlement***, to E of Lawshall, 5m/8km N of Long Melford. TL8754.
Hannington *Hants.* ***Village***, 2m/4km SE of Kingsclere. **21 J6** SU5355.
Hannington *Northants.* ***Village***, 5m/9km NW of Wellingborough. **32 B1** SP8171.
Hannington *Swin.* ***Village***, 2m/3km W of Highworth. **20 E2** SU1793.
Hannington Wick *Swin.* ***Hamlet***, 1m/2km N of Hannington. Site of Roman villa 1km NE. **20 E2** SU1793.
Hanscombe End *Beds.* ***Settlement***, 3m/5km SE of Clophill. TL1133.
Hanslope *M.K.* Population: 1923. ***Village***, 5m/8km NW of Newport Pagnell. **32 B4** SP8046.
Hanthorpe *Lincs.* ***Hamlet***, 3m/4km N of Bourne. **42 D3** TF0823.
Hanwell *Gt.Lon.* ***Suburb***, in borough of Ealing, 9m/15km W of Charing Cross. **22 E4** TQ1580.
Hanwell *Oxon.* ***Village***, 2m/4km NW of Banbury. **31 F4** SP4343.
Hanwoodbank *Shrop.* ***Settlement***, 3m/5km SW of Shrewsbury. SJ4410.
Hanworth *Brack.F.* ***Suburb***, S district of Bracknell. SU8666.
Hanworth *Gt.Lon.* ***Suburb***, in borough of Hounslow, 3m/5km W of Twickenham. Hanworth Park is large open space to N and E. **22 E4** TQ1171.
Hanworth *Norf.* ***Village***, 4m/7km S of Cromer. **45 F2** TG1935.
Happisburgh *Norf.* ***Town***, coastal resort, 6m/10km E of North Walsham. Lighthouse. 14c church tower. **45 H2** TG3731.
Happisburgh Common *Norf.* ***Village***, 1m/2km S of Happisburgh. **45 H3** TG3731.
Hapsford *Ches.* ***Hamlet***, 1m/2km SW of Helsby. **48 D5** SJ4774.
Hapsford *Som.* ***Settlement***, 1m/2km NW of Frome. ST7549.
Hapton *Lancs.* ***Village***, 1m/2km S of Padiham. 17c Shuttleworth Hall 1m/2km SW. **56 C6** SD7931.
Hapton *Norf.* ***Village***, 6m/9km SE of Wymondham. **45 F6** TM1796.
Harberton *Devon* ***Village***, 2m/3km SW of Totnes. **5 H5** SX7758.
Harbertonford *Devon* ***Village***, 3m/4km S of Totnes. **5 H5** SX7856.
Harbledown *Kent* ***Suburb***, W of Canterbury. **15 G2** TR1358.
Harborne *W.Mid.* ***Suburb***, 3m/5km SW of Birmingham city centre. **40 C7** SP0284.
Harborough Magna *Warks.* ***Village***, 3m/5km NW of Rugby. **31 F1** SP4779.
Harborough Parva *Warks.* ***Settlement***, adjoining to S of Harborough Magna. SP4778.
Harbottle *Northumb.* ***Village***, 1m/2km SE of Alwinton. Remains of 12c castle. **70 E3** NT9304.
Harbourneford *Devon* ***Hamlet***, 3m/4km S of Buckfastleigh. **5 H4** SX7162.
Harbours Hill *Worcs.* ***Locality***, 3m/5km S of Bromsgrove. SO9565.
Harbridge *Hants.* ***Settlement***, 3m/4km S of Fordingbridge. **10 C3** SU1410.
Harbridge Green *Hants.* ***Settlement***, 1km NW of Harbridge. SU1410.
Harburn *W.Loth.* ***Settlement***, 2m/3km SE of West Calder. **75 J4** NT0461.
Harbury *Warks.* Population: 2428. ***Village***, 3m/5km SW of Southam. **30 E3** SP3759.
Harby *Leics.* ***Village***, 8m/12km N of Melton Mowbray. **42 A2** SK7431.
Harby *Notts.* ***Village***, 6m/10km W of Lincoln. **52 B5** SK8770.
Harcombe *Devon* ***Hamlet***, 3m/4km NE of Sidmouth. **7 K6** SY1590.
Harcombe Bottom *Devon* ***Hamlet***, 2m/4km N of Lyme Regis. SY3395.
Hard Level Gill *N.Yorks.* ***River***, rising on Friarfold Moor and flowing SE towards Healaugh in Swaledale. **62 A6** NY9999.
Hardcastle Crags *W.Yorks.* ***Other feature of interest***, rocks in Hebden Water valley eroded by river, with disused mill and old tollbridge, 2m/3km NW of Hebden Bridge. **56 E6** SD9730.
Harden *Northumb.* ***Locality***, 3m/5km NE of Alwinton. NT9609.
Harden *S.Yorks.* ***Settlement***, 3m/5km S of Holmfirth, at N end of Winscar Reservoir. SE1503.
Harden *W.Mid.* ***Suburb***, 2m/3km N of Walsall town centre. SK0101.
Harden *W.Yorks.* ***Village***, 1m/2km SW of Bingley. **57 F6** SE0838.
Harden Park *Ches.* ***Suburb***, 1m/2km S of Wilmslow town centre. SJ8479.
Hardendale *Cumb.* ***Hamlet***, 1m/2km E of Shap. NY5814.
Hardenhuish *Wilts.* ***Locality***, adjoining to NW of Chippenham. **20 C4** ST9074.
Hardgate *Aber.* ***Settlement***, 3m/5km W of Peterculter. **91 F4** NJ7801.
Hardgate *N.Yorks.* ***Hamlet***, 2m/3km NW of Ripley. SE2662.
Hardham *W.Suss.* ***Hamlet***, 1m/2km SW of Pulborough. Remains of 13c priory to SW. **12 D5** TQ0317.
Hardhorn *Lancs.* ***Suburb***, adjoining to S of Poulton-le-Fylde. SD3538.
Hardingham *Norf.* ***Village***, 2m/3km NE of Hingham. **44 E5** TG0403.
Hardings Wood *Staffs.* ***Locality***, adjoining to W of Kidsgrove. **49 H7** SJ8354.
Hardingstone *Northants.* Population: 1743. ***Village***, 2m/3km S of Northampton. One of three remaining Eleanor crosses (English Heritage) is here, other two being at Geddington and Waltham Cross. **31 J3** SP7657.
Hardington *Som.* ***Village***, 4m/6km NW of Frome. **20 A6** ST7452.
Hardington Mandeville *Som.* ***Village***, 4m/6km SW of Yeovil. **8 E3** ST5111.
Hardington Marsh *Som.* ***Hamlet***, 1m/2km S of Hardington Mandeville. **8 E4** ST5111.
Hardington Moor *Som.* ***Hamlet***, 1km NE of Hardington Mandeville. ST5112.
Hardknott Castle *Cumb.* ***Historic/prehistoric site***, site of Roman fort of Mediobogdum (English Heritage), built AD 120 to AD 138 at W end of Hardknott Pass. **60 D6** NY2101.
Hardknott Pass *Cumb.* ***Other feature of interest***, steep pass between valleys of River Duddon and River Esk, traversed by road from Skelwith Bridge to Eskdale Green in Lake District, at height of 1291 feet or 393 metres. **60 D6** NY2301.
Hardley *Hants.* ***Village***, adjoining to N of Holbury. **11 F4** SU4304.
Hardley Street *Norf.* ***Hamlet***, 2m/3km NE of Loddon. **45 H5** TG3801.
Hardmead *M.K.* ***Settlement***, 4m/7km NE of Newport Pagnell. **32 C4** SP9347.
Hardown Hill *Dorset* *See Morcombelake.*
Hardraw *N.Yorks.* ***Hamlet***, 1m/2km N of Hawes across River Ure. **61 K7** SD8691.
Hardsough *Lancs.* ***Locality***, on River Irwell, 2m/3km S of Haslingden. SD7920.
Hardstoft *Derbys.* ***Hamlet***, 3m/5km E of Clay Cross. **51 G6** SK4363.
Hardway *Hants.* ***Suburb***, 1m/2km NW of Gosport town centre. **11 H4** SU6001.
Hardway *Som.* ***Hamlet***, 3m/4km E of Bruton. **9 G1** ST7234.
Hardwick *Bucks.* ***Village***, 4m/6km N of Aylesbury. **32 B7** SP8019.
Hardwick *Cambs.* Population: 2461. ***Village***, 5m/8km W of Cambridge. **33 G3** TL3758.
Hardwick *Lincs.* ***Settlement***, 2m/3km W of Saxilby. SK8675.
Hardwick *Norf.* ***Locality***, and industrial estate adjoining to SE of King's Lynn. TF6318.
Hardwick *Norf.* ***Village***, 4m/7km N of Harleston. **45 G6** TM2289.
Hardwick *Northants.* ***Village***, 3m/5km NW of Wellingborough. Former manor house once housed Knights Templars. **32 B2** SP8569.
Hardwick *Oxon.* ***Hamlet***, 3m/4km SE of Witney. **21 G1** SP3706.
Hardwick *Oxon.* ***Hamlet***, 4m/7km N of Bicester. **31 G6** SP5729.
Hardwick *S.Yorks.* ***Settlement***, 2m/3km N of Wales. SK4886.
Hardwick *W.Mid.* ***Suburb***, 3m/5km NW of Sutton Coldfield. SP0799.
Hardwick Hall *Derbys.* ***Historic house***, 16c mansion (National Trust) built by Bess of Hardwick, 5m/8km NW of Mansfield. Ruins of Hardwick Old Hall (English Heritage) adjacent, with decorative plasterwork. **51 G6** SK4663.
Hardwick Hall Country Park *Dur.* ***Leisure/recreation***, 40 acres of grounds, 1m/2km W of Sedgefield, comprising a small lake, picnic areas and woodland surrounding 18c mansion, now a hotel. **62 E4** NZ3429.
Hardwick Village *Notts.* ***Hamlet***, in Clumber Park, 4m/7km SE of Worksop. **51 J5** SK6375.
Hardwicke *Glos.* ***Hamlet***, 4m/7km NW of Cheltenham. **29 J6** SO9127.
Hardwicke *Glos.* ***Village***, 5m/8km SW of Gloucester. **29 G7** SO7912.
Hardwicke *Here.* ***Hamlet***, 3m/5km E of Hay-on-Wye. **28 B4** SO2743.
Hardy Monument *Dorset* ***Other feature of interest***, monument (National Trust) on Black Down, 5m/8km SW of Dorchester, erected 1846 to commemorate Vice-Admiral Sir Thomas Masterman Hardy, flag-captain of HMS Victory at Battle of Trafalgar. **9 F6** SY6187.
Hardy's Green *Essex* ***Hamlet***, 5m/8km SW of Colchester. **34 D7** TL9320.
Hare Cairn *Angus* ***Mountain***, to NW of Backwater Reservoir, 2m/3km NE of Kirkton of Glenisla. Height 1692 feet or 516 metres. **82 D1** NO2462.
Hare Croft *W.Yorks.* ***Hamlet***, 1m/2km NE of Denholme. SE0835.
Hare Green *Essex* ***Hamlet***, 6m/10km E of Colchester. **34 E6** TM0924.
Hare Hatch *W'ham* ***Village***, 1m/2km NE of Twyford. **22 B4** SU8077.
Hare Hill *Ches.* ***Garden***, 3m/4km SE of Alderley Edge. Woodland garden around a walled garden (National Trust). **49 H5** SJ8776.
Hare Hill *E.Ayr.* ***Mountain***, rising to over 600 metres, 3m/5km SE of New Cumnock. **68 B3** NS6509.
Hare Hill *S.Lan.* ***Mountain***, 2m/3km W of Forth. Height 1030 feet or 314 metres. **75 H5** NS9053.
Hare Park *Cambs.* ***Locality***, 5m/8km SW of Newmarket. TL5859.
Hare Street *Essex* ***Hamlet***, 2m/3km SE of Chipping Ongar. TL5300.
Hare Street *Essex* ***Suburb***, to W of Harlow town centre. TL4309.
Hare Street *Herts.* ***Settlement***, 4m/6km W of Buntingford. **33 G6** TL3128.
Hare Street *Herts.* ***Village***, 2m/3km E of Buntingford. **33 G6** TL3929.
Harebeating *E.Suss.* ***Locality***, in N part of Hailsham. TQ5910.
Hareby *Lincs.* ***Hamlet***, 4m/7km W of Spilsby. **53 G6** TF3365.
Hareden *Lancs.* ***Settlement***, 1m/2km W of Dunsop Bridge. **56 B4** SD6450.
Harefield *Gt.Lon.* Population: 5333. ***Suburb***, in borough of Hillingdon, 3m/4km S of Rickmansworth. **22 D2** TQ0590.
Harefield *S'ham.* ***Suburb***, 3m/5km E of Southampton city centre across River Itchen. SU4613.
Harehill *Derbys.* ***Hamlet***, 2m/4km NE of Sudbury. SK1735.
Harehills *W.Yorks.* ***Suburb***, 2m/3km NE of Leeds city centre. **57 J6** SE3135.
Harehope *Northumb.* ***Settlement***, 1m/2km NW of Eglingham. NU0920.
Harelaw *Dur.* ***Locality***, 1m/2km N of Annfield Plain. NZ1652.
Harelaw *S.Lan.* ***Settlement***, 2m/3km NW of Carstairs. **75 H6** NS9147.
Harelaw Dam *E.Renf.* ***Reservoir***, 2m/4km S of Neilston. **74 C5** NS4753.
Haremere Hall *E.Suss.* ***Historic house***, 17c manor house 1km NE of Etchingham. **14 C5** TQ7226.
Hareplain *Kent* ***Settlement***, 1m/2km NW of Biddenden. TQ8339.
Haresceugh *Cumb.* ***Locality***, 1m/2km E of Renwick. Remains of castle. **61 H2** NY6142.
Harescombe *Glos.* ***Village***, 5m/8km S of Gloucester. **29 H7** SO8310.
Haresfield *Glos.* ***Village***, 4m/7km NW of Stroud. **29 H7** SO8110.
Hareshaw *N.Lan.* ***Settlement***, 4m/7km SE of Airdrie. NS8160.
Hareshaw *S.Lan.* ***Settlement***, 4m/7km SW of Strathaven. **74 E6** NS6241.
Harestock *Hants.* ***Suburb***, NW district of Winchester. SU4631.
Harewood *Here.* ***Locality***, 5m/8km NW of Ross-on-Wye. SO5328.
Harewood *W.Yorks.* ***Village***, estate village, 7m/11km N of Leeds. **57 J5** SE3245.
Harewood End *Here.* ***Hamlet***, 5m/8km NW of Ross-on-Wye. **28 E6** SO5226.
Harewood Forest *Hants.* ***Forest/woodland***, wooded area E of Andover. **21 G7** SU3943.
Harewood House *W.Yorks.* ***Historic house***, 18c-19c mansion with grounds laid out by 'Capability' Brown. Remains of 14c castle overlooking Wharfedale, 6m/10km N of Leeds. **57 J5** SE3245.
Harford *Devon* ***Settlement***, 3m/5km SW of Crediton. SX8196.
Harford *Devon* ***Village***, on River Erme, 2m/3km N of Ivybridge. **5 G5** SX6359.
Harford Moor *Devon* ***Open space***, moorland between River Erme to W and Ugborough Moor to E, 4m/7km N of Ivybridge. **5 G4** SX6463.
Hargate *Norf.* ***Settlement***, 6m/10km S of Wymondham. **45 F6** TM1191.
Hargatewall *Derbys.* ***Hamlet***, 2m/4km W of Tideswell. SK1175.

Hargrave *Ches.* ***Village***, 6m/9km SE of Chester. **48 D6** SJ4862.
Hargrave *Northants.* ***Village***, 5m/8km E of Higham Ferrers. **32 D1** TL0370.
Hargrave *Suff.* ***Hamlet***, 6m/9km W of Bury St. Edmunds. **34 B3** TL7759.
Hargrave Green *Suff.* ***Village***, 1km S of Hargrave. TL7760.
Harker *Cumb.* ***Hamlet***, 3m/5km N of Carlisle. **69 J7** NY3960.
Harkerside Moor *N.Yorks.* ***Open space***, moorland on S side of Swaledale, 2m/3km SW of Reeth across River Swale. **62 B7** SE0296.
Harknett's Gate *Essex* ***Settlement***, 3m/4km SW of Harlow town centre. TL4206.
Harkstead *Suff.* ***Village***, 4m/6km W of Shotley Gate. **35 F5** TM1834.
Harland Hill *N.Yorks.* ***Mountain***, 3m/5km SE of Aysgarth. Height 1758 feet or 536 metres. **57 F1** SE0184.
Harlaston *Staffs.* ***Village***, 4m/7km N of Tamworth. **40 E4** SK2110.
Harlaw Muir *Sc.Bord.* ***Locality***, 4m/7km SW of Penicuik. **75 K5** NT1855.
Harlaw Reservoir *Edin.* ***Reservoir***, 1m/2km SE of Balerno. **75 K4** NT1864.
Harlaxton *Lincs.* ***Village***, 3m/5km SW of Grantham. **42 B2** SK8832.
Harle Syke *Lancs.* ***Locality***, 3m/4km NE of Burnley. **56 D6** SD8635.
Harleburn Head *S.Lan.* ***Mountain***, 3m/5km E of Elvanfoot. Height 1781 feet or 543 metres. **68 E2** NT0017.
Harlech *Gwyn.* Population: 1233. ***Small town***, at S end of Morfa Harlech on E side of Tremadog Bay. Ruined 13c castle (Cadw) stands on rocky eminence above marsh. **36 E2** SH5831.
Harlech Castle *Gwyn.* ***Castle***, ruins of impressively situated castle (Cadw) on W side of Harlech overlooking Tremadog Bay. Started by Edward I in 1285 and taken by Owain Glyndŵr in 1404. **36 E2** SH5731.
Harlech Point *Gwyn.* ***Coastal feature***, headland at NW end of Morfa Harlech at S side of estuary of Rivers Glaslyn and Dwyryd, 3m/5km N of Harlech. **36 E2** SH5635.
Harlequin *Notts.* ***Suburb***, adjoining to E of Radcliffe on Trent. SK6639.
Harlescott *Shrop.* ***Suburb***, to NE of Shrewsbury. SJ5115.
Harlesden *Gt.Lon.* ***Suburb***, in borough of Brent, 6m/9km W of Charing Cross. **23 F3** TQ2183.
Harleston *Devon* ***Hamlet***, 4m/6km E of Kingsbridge. SX7945.
Harleston *Norf.* Population: 3717. ***Small town***, Georgian market town in River Waveney valley, 8m/13km E of Diss. **45 G7** TM2483.
Harleston *Suff.* ***Village***, 3m/4km NW of Stowmarket. **34 E3** TM0160.
Harlestone *Northants.* ***Village***, 4m/7km NW of Northampton. **31 J2** SP7064.
Harley *Shrop.* ***Village***, 2m/3km NW of Much Wenlock. **38 E5** SJ5901.
Harley *S.Yorks.* ***Village***, 1m/2km W of Wentworth. SK3698.
Harleyholm *S.Lan.* ***Hamlet***, 3m/4km SE of Hyndford Bridge. **75 H7** NS9238.
Harley's Mountain *Here.* ***Mountain***, 4m/6km NE of Presteigne. Height 1266 feet or 386 metres. **28 C2** SO3468.
Harlington *Beds.* Population: 2300. ***Village***, 7m/11km NW of Luton. **32 D5** TL0330.
Harlington *Gt.Lon.* ***Suburb***, in borough of Hillingdon, 13m/21km W of Charing Cross and N of Heathrow Airport. TQ0978.
Harlington *S.Yorks.* ***Locality***, adjoining to S of Barnburgh, 1m/2km N of Mexborough across River Dearne. SE4802.
Harlosh *High.* ***Settlement***, on peninsula protruding southwards into Loch Bracadale, Skye, 4m/7km SE of Dunvegan. **93 H7** NG2841.
Harlosh Island *High.* ***Island***, small uninhabited island off headland in Loch Bracadale, Skye. **85 H1** NG2841.
Harlosh Point *High.* ***Coastal feature***, at end of peninsula protruding into Loch Bracadale, Skye. **93 H7** NG2841.
Harlow *Essex* Population: 74,629. ***Town***, New Town designated 1947, 21m/33km NE of London. **33 H7** TL4409.
Harlow Carr Gardens *N.Yorks.* ***Garden***, headquarters of Northern Horticultural Society set in 68 acres, 2m/3km SW of Harrogate. Includes Museum of Gardening and model village. **57 H4** SE2754.
Harlow Green *T. & W.* ***Suburb***, 3m/5km S of Gateshead town centre. NZ2658.
Harlow Hill *Northumb.* ***Hamlet***, 4m/6km W of Heddon-on-the-Wall. **71 F7** NZ0768.
Harlthorpe *E.Riding* ***Hamlet***, 10m/15km W of Market Weighton. **58 D6** SE7437.
Harlton *Cambs.* ***Village***, 6m/9km SW of Cambridge. **33 G3** TL3852.
Harlyn *Cornw.* ***Hamlet***, S of Harlyn Bay, 3m/4km W of Padstow. SW8775.
Harlyn Bay *Cornw.* ***Bay***, to N of Harlyn, 3m/4km W of Padstow on N coast of Cornwall. **3 F1** SW8775.
Harman's Corner *Kent* ***Settlement***, adjoining to E of Borden, 1m/2km SW of Sittingbourne. TQ8862.
Harman's Cross *Dorset* ***Village***, 2m/3km SE of Corfe Castle. **9 J6** SY9880.
Harmans Water *Brack.F.* ***Suburb***, S district of Bracknell. SU8767.
Harmby *N.Yorks.* ***Village***, 1m/2km E of Leyburn. **62 C7** SE1289.
Harmer Green *Herts.* Population: 1683. ***Locality***, 2m/3km E of Welwyn. **33 F7** TL2516.
Harmer Hill *Shrop.* ***Hamlet***, 6m/10km N of Shrewsbury. **38 D3** SJ4922.
Harmondsworth *Gt.Lon.* ***Suburb***, in borough of Hillingdon, on N side of London Heathrow Airport and 15m/25km W of Charing Cross. **22 D4** TQ0577.
Harmston *Lincs.* ***Village***, 6m/9km S of Lincoln. **52 C6** SK9762.
Harnage *Shrop.* ***Hamlet***, 2m/3km NW of Cressage. SJ5604.
Harnham *Northumb.* ***Locality***, 2m/3km NW of Belsay. NZ0780.
Harnham *Wilts.* ***Suburb***, S district of Salisbury. Includes Harnham Hill, East Harnham and West Harnham. **10 C2** SU1328.
Harnham Hill *Wilts.* ***Suburb***, SW district of Salisbury. SU1328.
Harnhill *Glos.* ***Hamlet***, 3m/5km E of Cirencester. **20 D1** SP0600.
Harold Hill *Gt.Lon.* ***Suburb***, in borough of Havering, 3m/4km NE of Romford. **23 J2** TQ5492.
Harold Park *Gt.Lon.* ***Suburb***, in borough of Havering, 3m/5km NE of Romford. TQ5591.
Harold Wood *Gt.Lon.* ***Suburb***, in borough of Havering, 3m/4km NE of Romford. **23 J2** TQ5490.
Harold's Stones *Mon.* *See Trelleck.*
Harold's Wick *Shet.* ***Sea feature***, inlet on E coast of Unst. **108 F1** HP6312.
Haroldston West *Pembs.* ***Hamlet***, near E coast of St. Brides Bay, 5m/9km W of Haverfordwest. **16 B3** SM8615.
Haroldswick *Shet.* ***Village***, fishing village at head of Harold's Wick, Unst. **108 F1** HP6312.
Harome *N.Yorks.* ***Village***, 3m/4km SE of Helmsley. **58 C1** SE6482.
Harpenden *Herts.* Population: 28,097. ***Town***, mainly residential commuter town, 5m/7km N of St. Albans. Rothamsted (agricultural) Experimental Station to SW. **32 E7** TL1314.
Harperleas Reservoir *Fife* ***Reservoir***, small reservoir 3m/5km NW of Leslie. **82 D7** NO2105.
Harperley *Dur.* ***Hamlet***, 1km N of Annfield Plain. NZ1753.
Harperrig Reservoir *W.Loth.* ***Reservoir***, 4m/7km S of Mid Calder. **75 J4** NT0961.
Harper's Brook *Northants.* ***River***, stream rising N of Desborough and flowing E to Brigstock, then SE into River Nene near Aldwincle. **42 C7** TL0181.
Harpford *Devon* ***Village***, 3m/5km NW of Sidmouth. **7 J6** SY0990.
Harpham *E.Riding* ***Village***, 5m/8km NE of Great Driffield. **59 G3** TA0961.
Harpley *Norf.* ***Village***, 9m/14km W of Fakenham. **44 B3** TF7825.
Harpley *Worcs.* ***Village***, 5m/7km NE of Bromyard. **29 F2** SO6861.
Harpole *Northants.* ***Village***, 4m/7km W of Northampton. Site of Roman building 1km SW. **31 H2** SP6960.
Harprigg *Cumb.* ***Settlement***, on E side of Park Hill, 4m/7km SW of Sedbergh. **56 B1** SD6187.
Harpsdale *High.* ***Settlement***, 2m/3km S of Halkirk. **105 G3** ND1356.
Harpsden *Oxon.* ***Hamlet***, 1m/2km S of Henley-on-Thames. Site of Roman villa to SW. **22 A3** SU7680.
Harpswell *Lincs.* ***Village***, 5m/9km S of Kirton in Lindsey. **52 C3** SK9390.
Harpur Hill *Derbys.* ***Suburb***, 1m/2km S of Buxton town centre. **50 C5** SK0671.
Harpurhey *Gt.Man.* ***Suburb***, 3m/4km NE of Manchester city centre. **49 H2** SD8601.
Harrabol *High.* *Alternative name for Harrapool, qv.*
Harraby *Cumb.* ***Suburb***, 2m/3km SE of Carlisle city centre. NY4254.
Harracott *Devon* ***Hamlet***, 4m/6km S of Barnstaple. SS5526.
Harrapool (Also known as Harrabol.) *High.* ***Locality***, on coast of Skye, adjoining to E of Broadford. **86 C2** NG6523.
Harraton *Devon* ***Hamlet***, 1m/2km SE of Modbury. SX6750.
Harray *Ork.* ***Locality***, on Mainland, 3m/5km NW of Finstown. To W is large Loch of Harray. HY3217.
Harrietfield *P. & K.* ***Village***, on N side of River Almond, 9m/15km NE of Crieff. **82 A4** NN9829.
Harrietsham *Kent* ***Village***, 7m/11km E of Maidstone. **14 D2** TQ8652.
Harringay *Gt.Lon.* ***Suburb***, in borough of Haringey, 5m/8km N of Charing Cross. TQ3188.
Harrington *Cumb.* ***Suburb***, on coast, 2m/4km S of Workington town centre. NX9825.
Harrington *Lincs.* ***Village***, 4m/7km NW of Spilsby. **53 G5** TF3671.
Harrington *Northants.* ***Village***, 6m/10km W of Kettering. **31 J1** SP7780.
Harrington Hall *Lincs.* ***Historic house***, 17c house with medieval origins at Harrington, 4m/6km NW of Spilsby. Walled gardens reputed to be High Hall Garden in Tennyson's Maud. **53 G5** TF3671.
Harringworth *Northants.* ***Village***, 6m/9km N of Corby. **42 C6** SP9197.
Harriot's Hayes *Shrop.* ***Settlement***, 2m/3km E of Albrighton. SJ8305.
Harris *High.* ***Settlement***, near SW coast of Rum, 4m/6km NW of Rubha nam Meirleach. **85 J5** NM3395.
Harris Green *Norf.* ***Settlement***, 4m/7km N of Harleston. TM2389.
Harris Museum and Art Gallery *Lancs.* ***Other feature of interest***, in Greek Revival building in Preston, with exhibits ranging from Bronze Age burial urn and Viking coins to 20c paintings. Also some local history displays. **55 J7** SD5328.
Harriseahead *Staffs.* ***Locality***, 1m/2km W of Biddulph. **49 H7** SJ8656.
Harriston *Cumb.* ***Hamlet***, 1m/2km E of Aspatria. NY1641.
Harrogate *N.Yorks.* Population: 66,178. ***Town***, spa town and conference centre, 13m/21km N of Leeds. Many distinguished Victorian buildings and pleasant, tree-lined streets. Royal Pump Room (1842) now a museum. Harlow Carr Gardens 2m/3km SW. **57 J4** SE3055.
Harrold *Beds.* ***Village***, 8m/12km NW of Bedford. **32 C3** SP9456.
Harrop Dale *Gt.Man.* ***Locality***, on N side of Diggle, 6m/9km E of Oldham. SE0008.
Harrop Fold *Lancs.* ***Hamlet***, on E side of Harrop Fell, 3m/4km W of Bolton by Bowland. SD7449.
Harrow *High.* ***Settlement***, on N coast, 5m/8km SE of Dunnet Head. **105 H1** ND2774.
Harrow Green *Suff.* ***Hamlet***, SW of Lawshall, 5m/9km N of Long Melford. TL8554.
Harrow Hill *W.Suss.* ***Hill***, 3m/4km S of Storrington. Height 548 feet or 167 metres. **12 D6** TQ0809.
Harrow on the Hill *Gt.Lon.* ***Suburb***, in borough of Harrow, 1km S of Harrow. Includes Harrow School, well-known boys' public school. **22 E3** TQ1587.
Harrow Weald *Gt.Lon.* ***Suburb***, in borough of Harrow, adjoining to N of Harrow. **22 E2** TQ1590.
Harrowbarrow *Cornw.* ***Village***, 3m/4km E of Callington. **4 E3** SX3969.
Harrowbeer *Devon* ***Suburb***, adjoining to N of Yelverton, 5m/7km SE of Tavistock. SX5168.
Harrowden *Beds.* ***Settlement***, 2m/3km SE of Bedford. **32 D4** TL0747.
Harrowgate Hill *Darl.* ***Suburb***, 2m/3km N of Darlington town centre. NZ2917.
Harrowgate Village *Darl.* ***Suburb***, 2m/3km N of Darlington town centre. NZ2917.
Harrows Law *S.Lan.* ***Mountain***, in Pentland Hills, 3m/5km NW of Dunsyre. Height 1361 feet or 415 metres. **75 J5** NT0553.
Harry Crofts *S.Yorks.* ***Locality***, 1km N of Thorpe Salvin, 4m/6km NW of Worksop. SK5282.
Harry Stoke *S.Glos.* ***Hamlet***, 1m/2km E of Filton. ST6278.
Harsgeir *W.Isles* ***Island***, islet off W coast of Isle of Lewis, at entrance to West Loch Roag. NB1140.
Harston *Cambs.* ***Village***, 6m/9km SW of Cambridge. **33 H3** TL4250.
Harston *Leics.* ***Village***, 5m/9km SW of Grantham. **42 B2** SK8331.
Harswell *E.Riding* ***Hamlet***, 3m/5km W of Market Weighton. SE8240.
Hart *Hart.* ***Village***, 3m/5km NW of Hartlepool. **63 F3** NZ4634.
Hart Burn *Northumb.* ***River***, rising on moors N of Kirkwhelpington and flowing E into River Wansbeck 6m/9km W of Morpeth. **71 F5** NZ1085.
Hart Common *Gt.Man.* ***Settlement***, 1km NE of Hindley. SD6305.
Hart Fell ***Mountain***, on border of Dumfries & Galloway and Scottish Borders, 6m/9km N of Moffat. Height 2650 feet or 808 metres. **69 G2** NT1113.
Hart Fell *D. & G.* ***Mountain***, 4m/6km E of Boreland. Height 1086 feet or 331 metres. **69 H5** NY2388.
Hart Hill *E.Dun.* ***Mountain***, part of Campsie Fells on border with Stirling, 4m/6km NW of Lennoxtown. Height 1699 feet or 518 metres. **74 E2** NS6082.
Hart Hill *Luton* ***Suburb***, to SE of Luton town centre. TL1021.
Hart Hill *Stir.* ***Mountain***, 5m/8km E of Fintry. Height 1430 feet or 436 metres. **74 E2** NS6988.
Hart Station *Hart.* ***Suburb***, 3m/4km NW of Hartlepool town centre. NZ4634.
Harta Corrie *High.* ***Valley***, 1m/2km N of Loch Coruisk, Skye. **85 K2** NG4723.
Hartamul *W.Isles* ***Island***, islet lying nearly 1m/2km off SE point of South Uist and nearly 2m/3km E of Eriskay. **84 D3** NF8311.
Hartaval *High.* ***Mountain***, 1m/2km NW of The Storr, Skye. Height 2191 feet or 668 metres. **93 K6** NG4855.
Hartburn *Northumb.* ***Village***, on Hart Burn, 7m/11km W of Morpeth. Site of small Roman fort 1km NW. **71 F5** NZ0886.
Hartburn *Stock.* ***Suburb***, 1m/2km SW of Stockton-on-Tees. **63 F5** NZ4218.
Harter Fell *Cumb.* ***Mountain***, 1m/2km SW of S end of Haweswater. Height 2509 feet or 765 metres. **61 F6** NY4609.
Harter Fell *Cumb.* ***Mountain***, 3m/4km S of Ravenstonedale. Height 1712 feet or 522 metres. **61 J6** NY7200.
Harter Fell *Cumb.* ***Mountain***, steep-sided mountain between heads of Eskdale and Dunnerdale, 3m/5km E of Boot, in Eskdale. Height 2129 feet or 649 metres. **60 D7** SD2199.
Hartest *Suff.* ***Village***, 4m/7km NW of Long Melford. **34 C3** TL8352.
Hartfield *E.Suss.* ***Village***, 6m/9km SE of East Grinstead. **13 H3** TQ4735.
Hartfield *High.* ***Settlement***, 1m/2km NE of Applecross. **94 D7** NG7246.
Hartford *Cambs.* ***Suburb***, NE district of Huntingdon. **33 F1** TL2572.
Hartford *Ches.* ***Village***, 1m/2km SW of Northwich. **49 F5** SJ6372.
Hartford *Som.* ***Settlement***, beside River Haddeo, 3m/5km NE of Dulverton. SS9529.
Hartford End *Essex* ***Hamlet***, on River Chelmer, 5m/8km SE of Great Dunmow. **33 K7** TL6817.
Hartfordbeach *Ches.* ***Hamlet***, 1m/2km SW of Northwich. SJ6372.
Hartfordbridge *Hants.* ***Hamlet***, 1m/2km NE of Hartley Wintney. **22 A6** SU7757.
Hartforth *N.Yorks.* ***Hamlet***, 3m/5km N of Richmond. NZ1706.
Hartgrove *Dorset* ***Hamlet***, 4m/7km NE of Sturminster Newton. ST8418.
Hartham *Herts.* ***Locality***, in centre of Hertford. TL3213.
Harthill *Ches.* ***Village***, 9m/15km SE of Chester. **48 D7** SJ5055.
Harthill *S.Yorks.* Population: 1834. ***Village***, 6m/10km W of Worksop. **51 G4** SK4980.
Harthill *W.Loth.* Population: 2904. ***Village***, 5m/8km SW of Bathgate. Service area on M8 motorway. **75 H4** NS9064.
Harthope Burn *Northumb.* ***River***, rising on Cheviot Hills and flowing NE through a narrow steep-sided valley to become Wooler Water, S of Wooler. **70 E1** NT9924.

H

Harting *W.Suss.* ***Locality***, parish 3m/5km SE of Petersfield, containing villages of East and South Harting and hamlet of West Harting. SU7820.
Hartington *Derbys.* ***Village***, 9m/15km N of Ashbourne. **50 D6** SK1260.
Hartland *Devon* ***Village***, 4m/6km W of Clovelly. **6 A3** SS2624.
Hartland Abbey *Devon* ***Historic house***, 1m/2km NW of Hartland. Largely 18c mansion incorporating remains of 12c Augustinian monastery, with notable walled and shrub gardens. Contains document exhibition from 1160 and Victorian and Edwardian photographic exhibition. **6 A3** SS2425.
Hartland Moor Nature Reserve *Dorset* ***Nature reserve***, wet and dry heath with diversity of plant, insect and birdlife, to N of Middlebere Heath, 2m/4km NW of Corfe Castle. **9 J6** SY9485.
Hartland Point *Devon* ***Coastal feature***, 3m/5km W of Hartland, headland with lighthouse at W end of Barnstaple (or Bideford) Bay. **6 A3** SS2624.
Hartland Quay *Devon* ***Settlement***, set amongst spectacular coastal scenery on W coast of Devon, 2m/4km W of Hartland. **6 A3** SS2224.
Hartlebury *Worcs.* ***Village***, 2m/3km E of Stourport-on-Severn. **29 H1** SO8470.
Hartlebury Castle *Worcs.* ***Castle***, residence of Bishops of Worcester, mainly medieval with 17c additions, 1km E of Stourport-on-Severn. Bishop's Palace houses Worcestershire Museum. **29 H1** SO8470.
Hartlepool *Hart.* Population: 87,310. ***Town***, port on Hartlepool Bay, 8m/12km N of Middlesbrough. Oil exploration centre, with fishing still an important industry. Marina created from old dockland. **63 G3** NZ5032.
Hartlepool Bay *Hart.* ***Bay***, 8m/12km N of Middlesbrough. **63 G3** NZ5032.
Hartley *Cumb.* ***Village***, 1km E of Kirkby Stephen. **61 J6** NY7808.
Hartley *Kent* ***Village***, now joined to Longfield to N by suburban development which includes Hartley Green, 6m/9km SE of Dartford. **24 C5** TQ6166.
Hartley *Kent* ***Village***, 1m/2km SW of Cranbrook. **14 C4** TQ7534.
Hartley *Northumb.* ***Locality***, near North Sea coast, 3m/4km N of Whitley Bay. **71 J6** NZ3475.
Hartley *Plym.* ***Suburb***, 2m/3km N of Plymouth city centre. SX4857.
Hartley Green *Kent* ***Suburb***, residential locality between Hartley and Longfield, 5m/8km SW of Gravesend. TQ6067.
Hartley Green *Staffs.* ***Settlement***, 1m/2km NW of Gayton. SJ9729.
Hartley Ground *Cumb.* ***Settlement***, 1m/2km N of Broughton in Furness. SD2189.
Hartley Mauditt *Hants.* ***Settlement***, 2m/4km SE of Alton. SU7436.
Hartley Moor *Northumb.* ***Open space***, moorland, highest point of which is 1883 feet or 574 metres, 4m/6km NE of Nenthead. **61 K2** NY8148.
Hartley Wespall *Hants.* ***Village***, 3m/5km NW of Hook. **22 A6** SU6958.
Hartley Wintney *Hants.* Population: 4159. ***Village***, 3m/5km NE of Hook. **22 A6** SU7656.
Hartley's Village *Mersey.* ***Suburb***, 4m/7km NE of Liverpool city centre. SJ3796.
Hartlington *N.Yorks.* ***Settlement***, 1km SE of Burnsall across River Wharfe. SE0361.
Hartlip *Kent* ***Village***, 4m/7km W of Sittingbourne. Site of Roman villa to W. **24 E5** TQ8364.
Hartlip Hill *Kent* ***Settlement***, to N of Hartlip. TQ8465.
Hartoft End *N.Yorks.* ***Settlement***, 4m/7km N of Wrelton. SE7492.
Harton *N.Yorks.* ***Village***, 4m/6km N of Stamford Bridge. **58 D3** SE7062.
Harton *Shrop.* ***Settlement***, 3m/5km SE of Church Stretton. **38 D7** SO4888.
Harton *T. & W.* ***Suburb***, 1m/2km S of South Shields town centre. **71 J7** NZ3764.
Hartpury *Glos.* ***Village***, 5m/7km N of Gloucester. **29 G6** SO7925.
Hartrigge *Sc.Bord.* ***Settlement***, to NW of Jedburgh. **70 B1** NT6621.
Hartsgarth Fell *Sc.Bord.* ***Open space***, moorland at head of Tarras Water, 4m/7km NW of Newcastleton. **69 K4** NY4594.
Hartshead *W.Yorks.* ***Village***, 1m/2km SW of Liversedge. SE1822.
Hartshead Green *Gt.Man.* ***Hamlet***, 1m/2km W of Mossley. SD9501.
Hartshead Moor Side *W.Yorks.* ***Locality***, adjoining to SW of Cleckheaton, 2m/3km NE of Brighouse. SE1724.
Hartshead Moor Top *W.Yorks.* ***Locality***, adjoining to S of Scholes, 2m/3km NE of Brighouse. SE1625.
Hartshill *Warks.* Population: 12,824. ***Village***, adjoining to NW of Nuneaton. **41 F6** SP3293.
Hartshill Hayes Country Park *Warks.* ***Leisure/recreation***, country park 2m/3km S of Atherstone, with over 120 acres of woodland, hills and grassland reputed to be part of Forest of Arden. **41 F6** SP3194.
Hartsholme Country Park *Lincs.* ***Leisure/recreation***, parkland for informal recreation and countryside walks, 3m/4km SW of Lincoln city centre, at N end of Swanholme Lakes. **52 C6** SK9469.
Hartshorn Pike *Sc.Bord.* ***Mountain***, in Cheviot Hills, 3m/5km E of Singdean. Height 1788 feet or 545 metres. **70 B3** NT6201.
Hartshorne *Derbys.* ***Village***, 2m/3km NE of Swadlincote. **41 F3** SK3220.
Hartside Height *Cumb.* ***Mountain***, on SW side of Gilderdale Forest, 3m/5km E of Renwick. Height 2047 feet or 624 metres. **61 H2** NY6542.
Hartsop *Cumb.* ***Settlement***, 2m/3km S of Patterdale. **60 F5** NY4013.
Hartswell *Som.* ***Locality***, adjoining to S of Wiveliscombe. ST0827.
Hartwell *Bucks.* ***Locality***, parish containing hamlet of Lower Hartwell, 2m/3km SW of Aylesbury. **31 J7** SP7812.
Hartwell *E.Suss.* ***Settlement***, 1km N of Hartfield. **13 H3** TQ4736.
Hartwell *Northants.* Population: 1780. ***Village***, 7m/11km NW of Newport Pagnell. **31 J4** SP7850.
Hartwell House *Bucks.* ***Historic house***, Jacobean manor house to E of Lower Hartwell, 1km W of Aylesbury. **31 J7** SP7912.
Hartwith *N.Yorks.* ***Hamlet***, 1m/2km SE of Summer Bridge. SE2161.
Hartwood *N.Lan.* ***Hamlet***, 4m/7km NE of Wishaw. **75 G5** NS8459.
Harvel *Kent* ***Village***, 4m/6km N of Wrotham Heath. **24 C5** TQ6563.
Harvey Hill *Dur.* ***Mountain***, 3m/4km SW of Wolsingham. Height 1046 feet or 319 metres. **62 B3** NZ0335.
Harvills Hawthorn *W.Mid.* ***Suburb***, 1m/2km NW of West Bromwich town centre. SO9893.
Harvington *Worcs.* ***Village***, 3m/5km E of Kidderminster. **29 H1** SO8774.
Harvington *Worcs.* ***Village***, 3m/5km NE of Evesham. **30 B4** SP0548.
Harvington Cross *Worcs.* ***Village***, adjoining to NW of Harvington, 4m/6km N of Evesham. SP0549.
Harvington Hall *Worcs.* ***Historic house***, Elizabethan moated manor with secret hiding places and 18c chapel, 5m/8km NW of Bromsgrove. **29 H1** SO8774.
Harwell *Notts.* ***Hamlet***, 1km NW of Everton. **51 J3** SK6891.
Harwell *Oxon.* Population: 2236. ***Village***, 2m/3km W of Didcot. Atomic Energy Research Establishment 2m/3km SW. **21 H3** SU4989.
Harwich *Essex* Population: 18,436. ***Town***, busy port for Continental passenger and containerised freight traffic, 16m/26km E of Colchester. Long history as post and dockyard. Britain's oldest cinema dating from 1911. **35 G5** TM2531.
Harwich Harbour *Suff.* ***Sea feature***, N of Harwich, where River Stour and River Orwell form an estuary. **35 G5** TM2633.
Harwood *Dur.* ***Locality***, 10m/15km NW of Middleton-in-Teesdale. **61 K3** NY8133.
Harwood *Gt.Man.* ***Suburb***, 2m/3km NE of Bolton town centre. **49 G1** SD7410.
Harwood *Northumb.* ***Settlement***, 4m/6km N of Kirkwhelpington. NZ0090.
Harwood Dale *N.Yorks.* ***Village***, 7m/11km NW of Scarborough. **63 J3** SE9695.
Harwood Forest *Northumb.* ***Forest/woodland***, large afforested area 6m/10km SW of Rothbury, with Simonside Hills on N side. **70 E4** NY9894.
Harwood Lee *Gt.Man.* ***Suburb***, 3m/4km NE of Bolton. SD7412.
Harwood on Teviot *Sc.Bord.* ***Settlement***, 2m/3km SW of Branxholme. **69 K3** NT4409.
Harworth *Notts.* Population: 3907. ***Village***, 2m/3km SE of Tickhill. **51 J3** SK6191.
Hasbury *W.Mid.* ***Suburb***, 1km W of Halesowen town centre. **40 B7** SO9583.
Hascombe *Surr.* ***Village***, 3m/5km SE of Godalming. **12 C3** SU9939.
Hascosay *Shet.* ***Island***, between Yell and Fetlar. Sea birds abound. **108 E3** HU5592.
Hascosay Sound *Shet.* ***Sea feature***, runs between Hascosay and Yell. **108 E3** HU5592.
Haselbech *Northants.* ***Village***, 6m/10km S of Market Harborough. **31 J1** SP7177.
Haselbury Bryan *Dorset* *Alternative spelling of Hazelbury Bryan, qv.*
Haselbury Plucknett *Som.* ***Village***, 2m/3km NE of Crewkerne. **8 D3** ST4710.
Haseley *Warks.* ***Village***, 4m/6km NW of Warwick. **30 D2** SP2367.
Haseley Knob *Warks.* ***Settlement***, 4m/6km W of Kenilworth. SP2371.
Haseley Manor *I.o.W.* ***Historic house***, restored large manor house in many styles, 3m/5km NW of Sandown. Includes largest working pottery studio on island. **11 G6** SZ5485.
Haselor *Warks.* ***Hamlet***, 2m/4km E of Alcester. **30 C3** SP1257.
Hasfield *Glos.* ***Village***, 6m/9km N of Gloucester across River Severn. **29 H6** SO8227.
Hasguard *Pembs.* ***Settlement***, 4m/7km NW of Milford Haven. **16 B4** SM8509.
Haskayne *Lancs.* ***Village***, 4m/6km W of Ormskirk. **48 C2** SD3508.
Haskeir Eagach (Also known as Heisgeir Eagach.) *W.Isles* ***Island***, group of rocks about 1m/2km SW of Haskeir Island. **92 A3** NF6182.
Haskeir Island (Also known as Heisgeir Island.) *W.Isles* ***Island***, small rocky uninhabited island 8m/13km NW of Griminis Point, North Uist. Seal sanctuary. **92 B3** NF6182.
Hasketon *Suff.* ***Village***, 2m/3km NW of Woodbridge. **35 G3** TM2450.
Hasland *Derbys.* ***Village***, 1m/2km SE of Chesterfield town centre. **51 F6** SK3969.
Hasland Green *Derbys.* ***Suburb***, SW district of Chesterfield, adjoining to S of Hasland. SK3969.
Haslemere *Surr.* Population: 12,218. ***Town***, in wooded and hilly area, 8m/13km SW of Godalming. Much National Trust property in surrounding countryside. Annual music festival. **12 C3** SU9033.
Haslingden *Lancs.* Population: 15,024. ***Town***, market town, 4m/6km SE of Accrington. **56 C7** SD7823.
Haslingden Grane *Lancs.* ***Locality***, 1m/2km W of Haslingden. **56 C7** SD7522.
Haslingfield *Cambs.* ***Village***, 5m/8km SW of Cambridge. **33 H3** TL4052.
Haslington *Ches.* Population: 4183. ***Village***, 2m/3km E of Crewe. **49 G7** SJ7355.
Hasluck's Green *W.Mid.* ***Suburb***, 3m/5km W of Solihull town centre. SP1078.
Hassall *Ches.* ***Settlement***, 2m/4km S of Sandbach. **49 G7** SJ7657.
Hassall Green *Ches.* ***Hamlet***, 1m/2km NE of Hassall. **49 G7** SJ7858.
Hassell Street *Kent* ***Settlement***, 3m/4km E of Wye. **15 F3** TR0946.
Hassendean *Sc.Bord.* ***Settlement***, 5m/7km NE of Hawick. **70 A1** NT5420.
Hassingham *Norf.* ***Hamlet***, 4m/6km SW of Acle. **45 H5** TG3605.
Hassocks *W.Suss.* ***Locality***, adjoining to W of Keymer, below South Downs, 2m/4km S of Burgess Hill. **13 F5** TQ3015.
Hassop *Derbys.* ***Hamlet***, 2m/4km N of Bakewell. **50 E5** SK2272.
Haster *High.* ***Settlement***, 3m/4km W of Wick. **105 J3** ND3251.
Hasthorpe *Lincs.* ***Hamlet***, 1m/2km NE of Welton le Marsh. TF4869.
Hastigrow *High.* ***Settlement***, in Caithness district, 6m/10km SE of Castletown. **105 H2** ND2661.
Hastingleigh *Kent* ***Village***, 6m/9km E of Ashford. **15 F3** TR0944.
Hastings *E.Suss.* Population: 81,139. ***Town***, Cinque port and seaside resort, 32m/52km E of Brighton. Remains of Norman castle on cliff top. Battle of 1066 fought at Battle, 6m/9km NW. **14 D7** TQ8109.
Hastings *Som.* ***Hamlet***, 3m/5km NW of Ilminster. ST3116.
Hastings Castle *E.Suss.* ***Castle***, remnants of Norman castle built 1068-1080 on hill in centre of Hastings. Stone structure replaced William the Conqueror's first castle in England, a prefabricated wooden structure. Remains comprise 11c-13c walls and a gatehouse, and houses The 1066 Story which relates history of castle and Norman invasion. **14 D7** TQ8209.
Hastings Country Park *E.Suss.* ***Leisure/recreation***, 3m/5km NE of Hastings town centre. 500 acres of grass and woodland extending over 4m/6km of coastline. **14 D6** TQ8511.
Hastingwood *Essex* ***Village***, 3m/5km SE of Harlow. **23 H1** TL4807.
Hastoe *Herts.* ***Hamlet***, 1m/2km S of Tring. **22 C1** SP9109.
Haswell *Dur.* ***Village***, 3m/4km W of Easington. **62 E2** NZ3743.
Haswell Moor *Dur.* ***Locality***, 1m/2km S of Haswell. NZ3841.
Haswell Plough *Dur.* ***Village***, 1km S of Haswell. NZ3742.
Hatch *Beds.* ***Settlement***, 1m/2km SW of Sandy. **32 E4** TL1547.
Hatch *Hants.* ***Settlement***, adjoining to S of Old Basing. **21 K6** SU6752.
Hatch Beauchamp *Som.* ***Village***, 5m/9km SE of Taunton. **8 B2** ST3020.
Hatch Bottom *Hants.* ***Locality***, residential locality adjoining to N of West End, 4m/6km NE of Southampton. SU4614.
Hatch Court *Som.* ***Historic house***, Palladian 18c mansion with deer park and restored walled garden, 1km N of Hatch Beauchamp and 6m/10km SE of Taunton. **8 C2** ST3021.
Hatch End *Beds.* ***Settlement***, at W end of Keysoe Row. TL0761.
Hatch End *Gt.Lon.* ***Suburb***, in borough of Harrow, 4m/6km SE of Watford. **22 E2** TQ1291.
Hatch Green *Som.* ***Hamlet***, 1km S of Hatch Beauchamp. **8 B3** ST3019.
Hatchet Green *Hants.* ***Settlement***, adjoining to NW of Hale, 4m/7km NE of Fordingbridge. SU1919.
Hatching Green *Herts.* ***Hamlet***, 1m/2km S of Harpenden. **32 E7** TL1312.
Hatchlands *Surr.* ***Historic house***, 18c house (National Trust) to E of East Clandon, 5m/8km E of Guildford. **22 D6** TQ0652.
Hatchmere *Ches.* ***Hamlet***, 7m/11km W of Northwich. **48 E5** SJ5571.
Hatcliffe *N.E.Lincs.* ***Village***, 7m/11km SW of Grimsby. **53 F2** TA2100.
Hatfield *Here.* ***Village***, 6m/10km E of Leominster. **28 E3** SO5959.
Hatfield *Herts.* Population: 31,104. ***Town***, 18m/29km N of London. New Town, designated 1948, to SW of old. Large shopping centre. Hatfield House nearby. University of Hertfordshire. **23 F1** TL2308.
Hatfield *S.Yorks.* Population: 14,067. ***Town***, 7m/11km NE of Doncaster. **51 J2** SE6609.
Hatfield Broad Oak *Essex* ***Village***, 5m/8km SE of Bishop's Stortford. **33 J7** TL5416.
Hatfield Chase *S.Yorks.* ***Open space***, area of fen, 3m/5km E of Hatfield. **51 K2** SE6609.
Hatfield Forest *Essex* ***Forest/woodland***, wooded area and country park, largely National Trust, 3m/5km E of Bishop's Stortford. **33 J7** TL5320.
Hatfield Garden Village *Herts.* ***Suburb***, to N of Hatfield. TL2109.
Hatfield Heath *Essex* ***Village***, 5m/8km SE of Bishop's Stortford. **33 J7** TL5215.
Hatfield House *Herts.* ***Historic house***, 17c house in large park to E of Hatfield. Grounds notable for autumn displays. **23 F1** TL2308.
Hatfield Hyde *Herts.* ***Suburb***, SE district of Welwyn Garden City. **33 F7** TL2511.
Hatfield Moors *S.Yorks.* ***Open space***, lowland 4m/7km W of Epworth. **51 K2** SE7006.
Hatfield Peverel *Essex* Population: 3405. ***Village***, 3m/5km SW of Witham. **34 B7** TL7911.

H

Hatfield Woodhouse *S.Yorks.* ***Village***, 1m/2km SE of Hatfield. **51 J2** SE6609.
Hatford *Oxon.* ***Village***, 3m/5km E of Faringdon. **21 G2** SU3394.
Hatherden *Hants.* ***Village***, 3m/5km NW of Andover. **21 G6** SU3450.
Hatherleigh *Devon* ***Village***, 7m/11km NW of Okehampton. **6 D5** SS5404.
Hatherlow *Gt.Man.* ***Locality***, adjoining to W of Romiley. SJ9390.
Hathern *Leics.* Population: 1791. ***Village***, 3m/4km NW of Loughborough. **41 G3** SK5022.
Hatherop *Glos.* ***Village***, 3m/4km N of Fairford. **20 E1** SP1505.
Hathersage *Derbys.* ***Village***, 8m/13km N of Bakewell. **50 E4** SK2381.
Hathersage Booths *Derbys.* ***Hamlet***, 1km SE of Hathersage. SK2480.
Hathershaw *Gt.Man.* ***Suburb***, 1m/2km S of Oldham town centre. SD9203.
Hatherton *Ches.* ***Hamlet***, 3m/5km NE of Audlem. **39 F1** SJ6847.
Hatherton *Staffs.* ***Hamlet***, 1m/2km W of Cannock. **40 B4** SJ9510.
Hatley St. George *Cambs.* ***Village***, 4m/6km E of Potton. **33 F3** TL2751.
Hatt *Cornw.* ***Village***, 3m/4km NW of Saltash. **4 D4** SX3962.
Hatt Hill *Hants.* ***Settlement***, just W of Mottisfont. SU3126.
Hatterrall Hill *Mon.* ***Mountain***, 6m/10km N of Abergavenny. Height 1742 feet or 531 metres. **28 C6** SO3025.
Hattersley *Gt.Man.* ***Suburb***, 2m/3km E of Hyde. SJ9794.
Hattingley *Hants.* ***Hamlet***, 1m/2km W of Medstead. **11 H1** SU6437.
Hatton *Aber.* ***Village***, near E coast, 8m/12km SW of Peterhead. **91 J1** NK0537.
Hatton *Derbys.* Population: 2823. ***Village***, 5m/8km N of Burton upon Trent. **40 E3** SK2130.
Hatton *Gt.Lon.* ***Hamlet***, at E end of London Heathrow Airport, in borough of Hounslow, 12m/21km W of Charing Cross. **22 D4** TQ0975.
Hatton *Lincs.* ***Hamlet***, 3m/5km E of Wragby. **52 E5** TF1776.
Hatton *Shrop.* ***Hamlet***, 3m/4km S of Church Stretton. **38 D6** SO4690.
Hatton *Warr.* ***Village***, 4m/6km S of Warrington. **48 E4** SJ5982.
Hatton *Warks.* ***Village***, 4m/6km NW of Warwick. **30 D2** SP2367.
Hatton Castle *Aber.* ***Castle***, residence comprising remains of ancient castle of Balquholly, 3m/5km SE of Turriff. **99 F6** NJ7546.
Hatton Heath *Ches.* ***Settlement***, 4m/7km SE of Chester. **48 D6** SJ4561.
Hatton of Fintray *Aber.* ***Village***, 5m/9km SE of Inverurie. **91 G3** NJ8416.
Hattoncrook *Aber.* ***Settlement***, 3m/4km SE of Oldmeldrum. **91 G2** NJ8424.
Haugh *Gt.Man.* ***Settlement***, adjoining to E of Newhey, 1m/2km SE of Milnrow. SD9411.
Haugh *Lincs.* ***Hamlet***, 3m/4km W of Alford. TF4175.
Haugh Head *Northumb.* ***Settlement***, 1m/2km SE of Wooler. **71 F1** NU0026.
Haugh of Glass *Moray* ***Settlement***, 7m/11km W of Huntly. **90 C1** NJ4239.
Haugh of Urr *D. & G.* ***Village***, 4m/6km N of Dalbeattie. **65 J4** NX8066.
Haugham *Lincs.* ***Hamlet***, 4m/6km S of Louth. **53 G4** TF3381.
Haughhead *E.Dun.* ***Settlement***, 2m/3km NW of Lennoxtown. **74 E3** NS6079.
Haughley *Suff.* ***Village***, 3m/4km NW of Stowmarket. Scant remains of Norman castle. **34 E2** TM0262.
Haughley Green *Suff.* ***Village***, 1m/2km N of Haughley. **34 E2** TM0262.
Haughley New Street *Suff.* ***Hamlet***, 1m/2km W of Haughley. **34 E2** TM0262.
Haughmond Abbey *Shrop.* ***Historic/prehistoric site***, remains of 12c abbey (English Heritage) 3m/5km NE of Shrewsbury. **38 E4** SJ5415.
Haughs *Aber.* ***Settlement***, on W bank of River Isla, 1m/2km N of Ruthven. **98 D6** NJ5049.
Haughs of Cromdale *High.* ***Open space***, tract between Cromdale and NW side of Hills of Cromdale, 4m/6km E of Grantown-on-Spey. **89 H2** NJ0726.
Haughton *Notts.* ***Settlement***, 4m/6km NE of Ollerton. **51 J5** SK6772.
Haughton *Powys* ***Settlement***, 2m/4km E of Four Crosses. SJ3018.
Haughton *Shrop.* ***Hamlet***, 5m/9km E of Oswestry. **38 C3** SJ3727.
Haughton *Shrop.* ***Settlement***, 5m/7km NE of Shrewsbury. **38 E4** SJ5516.
Haughton *Shrop.* ***Settlement***, 1km NW of Shifnal. SJ7408.
Haughton *Shrop.* ***Settlement***, 3m/5km NW of Bridgnorth. **39 F6** SO6795.
Haughton *Staffs.* ***Village***, 4m/7km SW of Stafford. **40 A3** SJ8620.
Haughton Common *Northumb.* ***Open space***, heathland with streams and marshes, 6m/9km NW of Haydon Bridge. **70 C6** NY8072.
Haughton Green *Gt.Man.* ***Locality***, 1m/2km SE of Denton. **49 J3** SJ9393.
Haughton House Country Park *Aber.* ***Leisure/recreation***, 48 acre country park surrounding 19c house, 1km NE of Alford. Consists chiefly of woodland with gardens, aviary and adventure playground. **90 D3** NJ5816.
Haughton Le Skerne *Darl.* ***Suburb***, 2m/3km NE of Darlington town centre. **62 E5** NZ3116.
Haughton Moss *Ches.* ***Village***, 6m/9km NW of Nantwich. **48 E7** SJ5756.
Haultwick *Herts.* ***Hamlet***, 3m/5km W of Puckeridge. **33 G6** TL3323.
Haun *W.Isles Anglicised form of Haunn, qv.*
Haunn (Anglicised form: Haun.) *W.Isles* ***Settlement***, on bay of same name, on N coast of Eriskay. Ferry to Ludag on South Uist. **84 C3** NF7912.
Haunton *Staffs.* ***Village***, 5m/7km NE of Tamworth. **40 E4** SK2310.
Hauxley *Northumb.* ***Village***, near North Sea coast, 1m/2km SE of Amble. **71 H3** NU2703.
Hauxley Haven *Northumb.* ***Bay***, small bay, 2m/3km SE of Amble. **71 H3** NU2802.
Hauxton *Cambs.* ***Village***, 4m/7km S of Cambridge. **33 H3** TL4352.
Havannah *Ches.* ***Settlement***, 1m/2km NE of Congleton. SJ8664.
Havant *Hants.* Population: 46,510. ***Town***, in Portsmouth conurbation, 6m/10km NE of Portsmouth across Langstone Harbour. **11 J4** SU7106.
Haven *Here.* ***Settlement***, 7m/11km W of Leominster. **28 D3** SO4054.
Haven Bank *Lincs.* ***Locality***, 3m/5km S on Coningsby. TF2352.
Haven Side *E.Riding* ***Hamlet***, 1m/2km SW of Patrington. **59 K7** TA3021.
Haven Side *E.Riding* ***Locality***, adjoining to S of Hedon, on N bank of Hedon Haven. TA1828.
Havengore Island *Essex* ***Coastal feature***, on E coast 4m/6km NE of Shoeburyness. **25 F3** TQ9789.
Havenstreet *I.o.W.* ***Village***, 3m/4km SW of Ryde. **11 G5** SZ5690.
Havercroft *W.Yorks.* ***Locality***, adjoining to S of Ryhill. SE3914.
Haverfordwest (Hwlffordd). *Pembs.* Population: 13,454. ***Town***, on Western Cleddau River, 28m/45km W of Carmarthen. River navigable for small craft between town and sea (Milford Haven). Town is market and agricultural centre, with fine Georgian buildings. Views from ruins of 12c castle. Scant remains of 12c priory. **16 C3** SM9515.
Haverfordwest Castle Museum and Art Gallery *Pembs.* ***Other feature of interest***, situated in remains of 12c Norman castle overlooking Haverfordwest. Displays of local history and artwork. **16 C3** SM9515.
Havergate Island *Suff.* ***Island***, uninhabited island in River Ore, to SW of Orford. Nature Reserve. TM4147.
Haverhill *Suff.* Population: 19,086. ***Town***, 16m/26km SE of Cambridge. **33 K4** TL6745.
Haverigg *Cumb.* ***Village***, 1m/2km SW of Millom. **54 E2** SD1678.
Haverigg Point *Cumb.* ***Coastal feature***, headland 1m/2km W of Haverigg. **54 E2** SD1678.
Havering-atte-Bower *Gt.Lon.* ***Village***, in borough of Havering, 3m/4km N of Romford. **23 J2** TQ5193.
Havering Park *Gt.Lon.* ***Suburb***, NW district of Romford, in borough of Havering. TQ4992.
Haveringland *Norf.* ***Locality***, 9m/14km NW of Norwich. Remains of Haveringland Hall lie to N. TG1520.
Havering's Grove *Essex* ***Village***, 2m/3km W of Billericay. TQ6494.
Haverscroft Street *Norf.* ***Locality***, 1m/2km SW of Attleborough. TM0393.
Haversham *M.K.* ***Village***, 1m/2km NE of Wolverton. **32 B4** SP8242.
Haverthwaite *Cumb.* ***Village***, 2m/4km SW of Newby Bridge. **55 G1** SD3483.
Haverton Hill *Stock.* ***Locality***, adjoining to E of Billingham. **63 F4** NZ4822.
Haviker Street *Kent* ***Settlement***, 2m/3km NW of Marden. TQ7246.
Havyat *Som.* ***Settlement***, 2m/3km SE of Glastonbury. ST5237.
Hawarden (Penarlag). *Flints.* Population: 11,660. ***Town***, 2m/3km S of Queensferry and 6m/9km W of Chester. Medieval castle, and later castle in park where William Gladstone lived. Hawarden Airport 2m/3km E. **48 C6** SJ3165.
Hawarden Castle *Flints.* ***Castle***, 5m/8km W of Chester. Formerly home of W.E. Gladstone, 19c statesman; remains of 13c castle in grounds. **48 C6** SJ3165.
Hawbridge *Worcs.* ***Settlement***, 5m/8km SE of Worcester. **29 J4** SO9049.
Hawbush Green *Essex* ***Hamlet***, 3m/4km SE of Braintree. **34 B7** TL7820.
Hawcoat *Cumb.* ***Suburb***, in N part of Barrow-in-Furness. **55 F2** SD2072.
Hawen *Cere.* ***Hamlet***, 5m/8km NE of Newcastle Emlyn. **26 C4** SN3446.
Hawerby *N.Lincs.* ***Locality***, 2m/3km W of North Thoresby. TF2697.
Hawes *N.Yorks.* ***Small town***, market town and tourist centre in Wensleydale, 14m/22km SE of Kirkby Stephen. The well known Wensleydale cheese produced nearby. **56 D1** SD8789.
Hawe's Green *Norf.* ***Settlement***, 1km W of Shotesham. TM2399.
Hawes Side *B'pool* ***Suburb***, 1m/2km SE of Blackpool town centre. SD3234.
Haweswater Reservoir *Cumb.* ***Reservoir***, one of lakes of Lake District converted into reservoir. Dam is 4m/6km W of Shap. Reservoir runs SW to NE; length about 4m/7km. **61 F5** NY5015.
Hawford *Worcs.* ***Settlement***, 3m/5km N of Worcester. **29 H2** SO8460.
Hawford Dovecote *Worcs.* ***Other feature of interest***, 16c half-timbered house (National Trust), 3m/5km N of Worcester. **29 H2** SO8480.
Hawick *Sc.Bord.* Population: 15,812. ***Town***, on River Teviot, 39m/63km S of Edinburgh and 37m/59km N of Carlisle. Centre for knitwear and tourism. **70 A2** NT5014.
Hawick Museum and Scott Gallery *Sc.Bord.* ***Other feature of interest***, in Hawick, with exhibitions on local, social and industrial history, with some Scottish artwork on display in gallery. **69 K2** NT4914.
Hawk Green *Gt.Man.* ***Suburb***, adjoining to S of Marple. SJ9587.
Hawk Hill *Cumb.* ***Locality***, 1m/2km NE of Workington across River Derwent. NY0129.
Hawkchurch *Devon* ***Village***, 3m/5km NE of Axminster. **8 C4** ST3400.
Hawkcraig Point *Fife* ***Coastal feature***, headland on Firth of Forth on E side of Aberdour. **76 A2** NT2084.
Hawkedon *Suff.* ***Village***, 6m/10km NW of Long Melford. **34 B3** TL7953.
Hawkehouse Green *S.Yorks.* ***Settlement***, 3m/4km E of Askern. SE6013.
Hawkenbury *Kent* ***Settlement***, 2m/3km NE of Staplehurst. TQ8045.
Hawkenbury *Kent* ***Suburb***, to SE of Royal Tunbridge Wells. **13 J3** TQ5938.
Hawkeridge *Wilts.* ***Village***, 2m/3km N of Westbury. **20 B6** ST8653.
Hawkerland *Devon* ***Settlement***, 4m/7km N of Budleigh Salterton. **7 J7** SY0588.
Hawkes End *W.Mid.* ***Settlement***, 1km N of Allesley, 3m/5km NW of Coventry city centre. **41 F7** SP3083.
Hawkesbury *S.Glos.* ***Village***, 4m/7km NE of Chipping Sodbury. **20 A3** ST7686.
Hawkesbury *Warks.* ***Locality***, at junction of Coventry Canal and Oxford Canal, 4m/7km N of Coventry. SP3684.
Hawkesbury Upton *S.Glos.* ***Village***, 1m/2km E of Hawkesbury. **20 A3** ST7686.
Hawkhill *Northumb.* ***Settlement***, 3m/4km E of Alnwick. **71 H2** NU2212.
Hawkhope *Northumb.* ***Forest/woodland***, part of Kielder Forest, 1m/2km NW of Falstone. **70 C5** NY7189.
Hawkhurst *Kent* Population: 3463. ***Village***, 4m/6km S of Cranbrook. **14 C4** TQ7630.
Hawkinge *Kent* Population: 2224. ***Village***, 3m/4km N of Folkestone. **15 H3** TR2139.
Hawkley *Hants.* ***Village***, 2m/3km NW of Liss. **11 J2** SU7429.
Hawkridge *Som.* ***Village***, 4m/6km NW of Dulverton, Exmoor. **7 G2** SS8630.
Hawkridge Reservoir *Som.* ***Reservoir***, small reservoir at foot of Quantock Hills, 1m/2km SW of Spaxton. **8 A1** ST2036.
Hawks Ness *Shet.* ***Coastal feature***, headland on E coast of Mainland, 5m/8km N of Lerwick. **109 D8** HU4649.
Hawksdale *Cumb.* ***Locality***, 1m/2km S of Dalston. NY3648.
Hawkshaw Lane *Gt.Man.* ***Locality***, to W of Hawkshaw, 4m/6km NW of Bury. SD7515.
Hawkshead *Cumb.* ***Village***, 4m/7km S of Ambleside. **60 E7** SD3598.
Hawkshead Courthouse *Cumb.* ***Other feature of interest***, 15c courthouse (National Trust) to N of Hawkshead. **60 E7** SD3498.
Hawkshead Hill *Cumb.* ***Hamlet***, 1m/2km NW of Hawkshead. SD3398.
Hawksheads *Lancs.* ***Settlement***, on E side of Bolton-le-Sands across Lancaster Canal. SD4968.
Hawksland *S.Lan.* ***Settlement***, 2m/4km E of Lesmahagow. **75 G7** NS8439.
Hawkswick *N.Yorks.* ***Hamlet***, 2m/3km SE of Arncliffe. **56 E2** SD9570.
Hawksworth *Notts.* ***Village***, 4m/6km NE of Bingham. **42 A1** SK7543.
Hawksworth *W.Yorks.* ***Suburb***, 3m/5km NW of Leeds city centre. SE2536.
Hawksworth *W.Yorks.* ***Village***, 6m/9km N of Bradford. **57 G5** SE1641.
Hawkwell *Essex* ***Village***, 1m/2km NW of Rochford. **24 E2** TQ8591.
Hawkwell *Northumb.* ***Hamlet***, on S side of River Pont, 6m/9km W of Ponteland. **71 F6** NZ0771.
Hawley *Hants.* ***Suburb***, 3m/4km N of Farnborough. **22 B6** SU8558.
Hawley *Kent* ***Hamlet***, 2m/3km S of Dartford. **23 J4** TQ5471.
Hawley Lake *Hants.* ***Lake/loch***, surrounded by woods on Hawley Common, 1m/2km W of Hawley. **22 B6** SU8558.
Hawley's Corner *Gt.Lon.* ***Settlement***, at extreme S edge of borough of Bromley, 2m/3km SE of Biggin Hill. TQ4356.
Hawling *Glos.* ***Village***, 4m/7km SE of Winchmore. **30 B6** SP0623.
Hawnby *N.Yorks.* ***Village***, on River Rye, 6m/10km NW of Helmsley. **63 G7** SE5489.
Haworth *W.Yorks.* Population: 4956. ***Small town***, above River Worth valley, 2m/4km SW of Keighley. The Parsonage, former home of Brontë family, is now a museum. Railway Museum at Haworth Station, with standard gauge steam locomotives. **57 F6** SE0237.
Haworth Moor *W.Yorks.* ***Open space***, moorland 2m/4km SW of Haworth containing bleak ruin of Withens, setting for Emily Brontë's Wuthering Heights. **56 E6** SD9935.
Hawsker Bottoms *N.Yorks.* ***Locality***, 1km E of High Hawsker. NZ9307.
Hawstead *Suff.* ***Village***, 3m/5km S of Bury St. Edmunds. **34 C3** TL8559.
Hawstead Green *Suff.* ***Settlement***, 1km S of Hawstead. TL8559.
Hawthorn *Dur.* ***Village***, 1m/2km N of Easington. **63 F2** NZ4145.
Hawthorn *Glas.* ***Suburb***, 2m/3km N of Glasgow city centre. NS5968.
Hawthorn *Hants.* ***Settlement***, 1m/2km S of Four Marks and 4m/7km SW of Alton. SU6733.
Hawthorn (Y Ddraenen Wen). *R.C.T.* ***Village***, adjoining to S of Rhydyfelin, 2m/3km SE of Pontypridd. ST0987.
Hawthorn *Wilts.* ***Village***, 2m/3km SW of Corsham. **20 B5** ST8469.
Hawthorn Hill *Brack.F.* ***Settlement***, 5m/8km S of Maidenhead. **22 B4** SU8773.
Hawthorn Hill *Lincs.* ***Hamlet***, 2m/3km S of Coningsby. **53 F7** TF2155.

H

Hawthornthwaite Fell *Lancs.* ***Open space***, steep moorland area on W side of Forest of Bowland, 6m/10km NE of Garstang. **55 J4** SD5751.
Hawthorpe *Lincs.* ***Settlement***, 6m/9km NW of Bourne. **42 D3** TF0427.
Hawton *Notts.* ***Hamlet***, 2m/3km S of Newark-on-Trent. **51 K7** SK7851.
Haxby *York* Population: 13,234. ***Village***, large village 4m/6km N of York. **58 C4** SE6058.
Haxby Gates *York* ***Locality***, adjoining to S of Haxby. SE6056.
Haxby Moor End *York* ***Locality***, adjoining to N of Haxby. SE6058.
Haxey *N.Lincs.* ***Village***, 3m/4km S of Epworth. **51 K3** SK7699.
Haxey Turbary *N.Lincs.* ***Settlement***, 1m/2km NW of Haxey. SE7601.
Haxted *Surr.* ***Settlement***, 1m/2km W of Edenbridge. Watermill. **23 H7** TQ4245.
Haxton *Wilts.* ***Settlement***, adjoining to S of Fittleton, 5m/8km N of Amesbury. SU1449.
Haxton Down *Wilts.* ***Open space***, hillslope 2m/3km S of Everleigh. **21 F6** SU2050.
Hay Bluff *Powys* ***Mountain***, at N end of Black Mountains, 4m/6km S of Hay-on-Wye. Height 2221 feet or 677 metres. **28 B5** SO2436.
Hay Green *Herts.* ***Hamlet***, S of Therfield, 3m/4km S of Royston. TL3436.
Hay Green *Norf.* ***Hamlet***, 1m/2km S of Terrington St. Clement. TF5418.
Hay Mills *W.Mid.* ***Suburb***, 3m/5km SE of Birmingham city centre. **40 D7** SP1184.
Hay-on-Wye (Y Gelli). *Powys* Population: 1407. ***Small town***, market town at N end of Black Mountains, 15m/24km NE of Brecon. Remains of motte and bailey 1m/2km E. Remains of 12c castle at town centre. Famous for its numerous second hand book shops owned by Richard Booth. **28 B4** SO2242.
Hay Place *Hants.* ***Settlement***, adjoining to S of Binsted, 4m/6km NE of Alton. SU7740.
Hay Stacks *Cumb.* ***Mountain***, peak on ridge, rising to over 580 metres, between Buttermere and Ennerdale, 3m/4km SE of Buttermere village. **60 C5** NY1913.
Hay Street *Herts.* ***Hamlet***, 2m/3km N of Puckeridge. **33 G6** TL3926.
Haybridge *Som.* ***Hamlet***, 1m/2km W of Wells. ST5346.
Haybridge *Tel. & W.* ***Suburb***, 1m/2km E of Wellington. SJ6711.
Haycock *Cumb.* ***Mountain***, on Ennerdale Fell, 7m/11km NE of Gosforth. Height 2614 feet or 797 metres. **60 C5** NY1410.
Hayden Cross *W.Mid.* ***Suburb***, 4m/6km SE of Dudley town centre. SO9685.
Haydock *Mersey.* Population: 16,705. ***Town***, 4m/6km E of St. Helens. Former coalmining town. Racecourse. **48 E3** SJ5696.
Haydock Park *Mersey.* ***Racecourse***, to NE of Haydock, with one mixed, eighteen flat and nine National Hunt race days each year, including evening meetings between June and August. **48 E3** SJ5897.
Haydon *Dorset* ***Village***, 2m/3km E of Sherborne. **9 F3** ST6715.
Haydon *Som.* ***Hamlet***, 2m/3km SE of Taunton. ST2523.
Haydon *Swin.* ***Settlement***, 3m/5km NW of Swindon town centre. SU1288.
Haydon Bridge *Northumb.* Population: 1784. ***Small town***, astride River South Tyne, 6m/10km W of Hexham. Old bridge, with six arches, was formerly gated against invaders. **70 D7** NY8464.
Haydon Dean *Northumb.* ***Valley***, narrow, wooded valley of Dean Burn, 2m/3km SW of Ancroft. **77 H6** NT9743.
Haydon Wick *Swin.* ***Suburb***, 2m/4km NW of Swindon town centre. **20 E3** SU1288.
Haydown Hill *Wilts.* ***Hill***, 2m/3km W of Vernham Dean. Height 846 feet or 258 metres. **21 G6** SU3156.
Haye *Cornw.* ***Settlement***, just W of Callington. **4 D4** SX3469.
Hayes *Gt.Lon.* ***Suburb***, in borough of Hillingdon, 3m/5km SE of Uxbridge. **22 D3** TQ0980.
Hayes *Gt.Lon.* ***Suburb***, in borough of Bromley, 2m/3km S of Bromley town centre. **23 H5** TQ4066.
Hayes End *Gt.Lon.* ***Suburb***, in borough of Hillingdon, 2m/3km SE of Uxbridge. TQ0882.
Hayes Green *Warks.* ***Locality***, 1m/2km SW of Bedworth. SP3485.
Hayes Town *Gt.Lon.* ***Suburb***, in borough of Hillingdon, 4m/6km SE of Uxbridge. TQ1080.
Hayeswater *Cumb.* ***Lake/loch***, small lake 3m/5km SE of Patterdale. **60 F5** NY4312.
Hayfield *Arg. & B.* ***Settlement***, on N side of Loch Awe, 3m/4km E of Kilchrenan. **80 B5** NN0723.
Hayfield *Derbys.* Population: 2293. ***Small town***, 4m/7km S of Glossop. **50 C4** SK0387.
Hayfield *Fife* ***Suburb***, to N of Kirkcaldy town centre. NT2792.
Hayfield *High.* ***Settlement***, 1km S of Castletown. **105 G2** ND1966.
Haygate *Tel. & W.* ***Suburb***, 1m/2km SE of Wellington. SJ6410.
Haygrove *Som.* ***Suburb***, W district of Bridgwater. ST2836.
Hayhillock *Angus* ***Settlement***, 3m/4km NE of Monikie. **83 G3** NO5242.
Haylands *I.o.W.* ***Suburb***, SW district of Ryde. **11 G5** SZ5891.
Hayle *Cornw.* ***River***, rising 3m/5km S of Camborne and flowing into St. Ives Bay. **2 C5** SW5438.
Hayle *Cornw.* Population: 7034. ***Small town***, with harbour, 3m/5km SE of St. Ives across River Hayle estuary. Richard Trevithick built first steam-powered road vehicle here. Paradise Park is set in 14 acres of sub-tropical gardens and is home The World Parrot Trust, Cornish Otter Sanctuary and Eagles of Paradise show. **2 C5** SW5537.

H

Hayley Green *W.Mid.* ***Suburb***, in SW part of Halesowen. SO9482.
Hayling Bay *Hants.* ***Bay***, formed by gently curving S coast of Hayling Island. **11 J5** SZ7198.
Hayling Island *Hants.* ***Island***, S of Havant between Langstone and Chichester Harbours, 4m/6km from N to S and nearly 4m/7km from E to W at its S end although little more than 1km wide at its centre. Connected to mainland by Langstone Bridge, at N end. Ferry for pedestrians to Portsea Island at SW extremity. **11 J4** SU7200.
Haylot Fell *Lancs.* ***Open space***, N facing moorland 7m/11km E of Lancaster. **55 J3** SD5861.
Haymarket *Edin.* ***Locality***, with railway station, 1m/2km W of Edinburgh city centre. NT2473.
Haymoor Green *Ches.* ***Settlement***, 2m/4km SE of Nantwich. SJ6850.
Hayne *Devon* ***Hamlet***, 2m/3km N of Tiverton. SS9515.
Haynes *Beds.* ***Village***, 4m/7km NW of Shefford. **32 E4** TL0841.
Haynes Church End *Beds.* ***Hamlet***, 2m/3km N of Clophill. **32 D4** TL0841.
Haynes West End *Beds.* ***Hamlet***, 2m/3km NW of Clophill. TL0640.
Hayscastle (Castellhaidd). *Pembs.* ***Hamlet***, 8m/13km SW of Fishguard. **16 B2** SM8925.
Hayscastle Cross *Pembs.* ***Hamlet***, 1m/2km E of Hayscastle. **16 C2** SM8925.
Haysden *Kent* ***Hamlet***, 1m/2km W of Tonbridge. TQ5645.
Hayton *Aberdeen* ***Suburb***, N district of Aberdeen. NJ9208.
Hayton *Cumb.* ***Village***, 3m/4km W of Aspatria. **60 C2** NY1041.
Hayton *Cumb.* ***Village***, 3m/4km SW of Brampton. **61 G1** NY5057.
Hayton *E.Riding* ***Village***, 4m/7km NW of Market Weighton. **58 E5** SE8245.
Hayton *Notts.* ***Village***, 3m/4km NE of Retford. **51 K4** SK7284.
Hayton's Bent *Shrop.* ***Settlement***, 4m/6km N of Ludlow. **38 E7** SO5180.
Haytor Vale *Devon* ***Village***, on E edge of Dartmoor, 5m/8km N of Ashburton. **5 H3** SX7777.
Haytown *Devon* ***Hamlet***, 4m/6km E of Bradworthy, to E of River Torridge. SS3814.
Hayward Gallery *Gt.Lon.* *See South Bank Arts Centre.*
Haywards Heath *W.Suss.* Population: 28,923. ***Town***, 12m/19km N of Brighton. Former market town, now with some light industry. **13 G4** TQ3323.
Haywood *Here.* ***Locality***, 4m/6km SW of Hereford. SO4834.
Haywood *S.Yorks.* ***Settlement***, 2m/3km E of Askern. SE5812.
Haywood *S.Yorks.* ***Suburb***, S district of Stocksbridge. SK2797.
Haywood Oaks *Notts.* ***Settlement***, 1m/2km SE of Blidworth. **51 J7** SK6055.
Hazard's Green *E.Suss.* ***Settlement***, 5m/8km NW of Bexhill. TQ6812.
Hazel End *Essex* ***Settlement***, 2m/3km N of Bishop's Stortford. **33 H6** TL4924.
Hazel Grove *Gt.Man.* Population: 19,865. ***Town***, residential town, 3m/4km SE of Stockport. **49 J4** SJ9286.
Hazel Head *N.Yorks.* ***Settlement***, 2m/3km SW of Goathland. SE8099.
Hazel Leys *Northants.* ***Suburb***, to W of Corby town centre. SP8888.
Hazel Street *Kent* ***Hamlet***, 1km SW of Horsmonden. TQ6939.
Hazelbank *Arg. & B.* ***Settlement***, on SE shore of Loch Fyne, 3m/4km S of Inveraray across loch. **80 B7** NN0904.
Hazelbank *S.Lan.* ***Village***, on River Clyde, 3m/5km NW of Lanark. **75 G6** NS8345.
Hazelbeach *Pembs.* ***Settlement***, on Milford Haven estuary, adjoining to W of Llanstadwell. SM9404.
Hazelbury Bryan (Also spelled Haselbury Bryan.) *Dorset* ***Village***, 4m/7km SW of Sturminster Newton. **9 G4** ST7408.
Hazeleigh *Essex* ***Village***, 2m/4km SW of Maldon. **24 E1** TL8203.
Hazeley *Hants.* ***Hamlet***, 2m/3km NW of Hook. **22 A6** SU7459.
Hazelhead *Aberdeen* ***Locality***, 3m/5km W of Aberdeen city centre. **91 G4** NJ8805.
Hazelhead Park and Zoo *Aberdeen* ***Leisure/recreation***, 2m/3km W of Aberdeen, comprising woodland and gardens, with children's area, aviary and maze. **91 G4** NJ8705.
Hazelhurst *Gt.Man.* ***Suburb***, to W of Swinton. SD7501.
Hazelhurst *Gt.Man.* ***Suburb***, 1m/2km SW of Ramsbottom. SD7815.
Hazelhurst *Gt.Man.* ***Suburb***, 2m/3km NE of Ashton-under-Lyne town centre. SD9600.
Hazelmere *Lancs.* ***Suburb***, 3m/5km N of Preston town centre. SD5233.
Hazelshaw *S.Yorks.* ***Hamlet***, 2m/3km N of Grenoside. SK3296.
Hazelside *S.Lan.* ***Settlement***, 1km NE of Glespin and 2m/3km SW of Douglas. **68 D1** NS8128.
Hazelslack *Cumb.* ***Settlement***, 1m/2km E of Arnside, on E side of Kent estuary. SD4778.
Hazelslade *Staffs.* ***Locality***, 3m/5km NE of Cannock. **40 C4** SK0212.
Hazelton Walls *Fife* ***Settlement***, 5m/8km NW of Cupar. **82 E5** NO3321.
Hazeltonrig Hill *Northumb.* ***Mountain***, 2m/3km E of Alnham. Height 1364 feet or 416 metres. **70 E2** NT9610.
Hazelwood *Derbys.* ***Village***, 2m/3km SW of Belper. **41 F1** SK3246.
Hazelwood *Glas.* ***Suburb***, 3m/4km SW of Glasgow city centre. NS5563.
Hazelwood *Gt.Lon.* ***Hamlet***, 3m/4km NE of Biggin Hill. **23 H5** TQ4461.
Hazlefield *D. & G.* ***Locality***, 2m/3km NE of Dundrennan. **65 H6** NX7749.

Hazlehead *S.Yorks.* ***Settlement***, at road bridge over River Don, 3m/5km W of Penistone. SE1902.
Hazlemere *Bucks.* Population: 10,422. ***Village***, 2m/3km NE of High Wycombe. **22 B2** SU8995.
Hazlerigg *T. & W.* ***Locality***, 5m/7km N of Newcastle upon Tyne. **71 H6** NZ2371.
Hazles *Staffs.* ***Settlement***, 1km NW of Kingsley. SK0047.
Hazlescross *Staffs.* ***Hamlet***, 1km N of Kingsley. SK0047.
Hazleton *Glos.* ***Village***, 3m/5km NW of Northleach. **30 B7** SP0718.
Hazon *Northumb.* ***Hamlet***, 3m/4km N of Felton. NU1904.
Heacham *Norf.* Population: 4064. ***Village***, 2m/4km S of Hunstanton. **44 A2** TF6737.
Head Bridge *Devon* ***Bridge***, on River Mole, 3m/4km NW of Chulmleigh. **6 E4** SS6618.
Head of Brough *Shet.* ***Coastal feature***, headland on W coast of Yell, 2m/3km S of West Sandwick. **108 D4** HU4485.
Head of Crees *High.* ***Coastal feature***, headland on N coast, 1km SE of St. John's Point. **105 J1** ND3174.
Head of Garness *Aber.* ***Coastal feature***, headland on N coast, 3m/4km E of Macduff. **99 F4** NJ7464.
Head of Hesta *Shet.* ***Coastal feature***, headland at easternmost point of Fetlar. **108 F3** HU6791.
Head of Holland *Ork.* ***Coastal feature***, headland on Mainland, 3m/4km E of Kirkwall between Bay of Meil and Inganess Bay. **107 D6** HY4912.
Head of Moclett *Ork.* ***Coastal feature***, to S of Papa Westray. **106 E3** HY4949.
Head of Stanshi *Shet.* ***Coastal feature***, small promontory on N coast of Esha Ness, Mainland. **108 B4** HU2180.
Head of Work *Ork.* ***Coastal feature***, headland on coast of Mainland opposite Shapinsay, 3m/5km NE of Kirkwall. HY4813.
Head o'th'Lane *Staffs.* ***Locality***, 2m/3km N of Tunstall. SJ8553.
Headbourne Worthy *Hants.* ***Village***, 2m/3km N of Winchester. **11 F1** SU4832.
Headcorn *Kent* Population: 2295. ***Village***, 9m/14km SE of Maidstone. **14 D3** TQ8344.
Headingley *W.Yorks.* ***Suburb***, 2m/3km NW of Leeds city centre. Contains Yorkshire County Cricket Ground. SE2736.
Headington *Oxon.* ***Suburb***, to E of River Cherwell, 2m/4km E of Oxford city centre. Oxford Brookes University site. **21 J1** SP5407.
Headington Hill *Oxon.* ***Suburb***, E of River Cherwell, 1m/2km NE of Oxford city centre. SP5306.
Headlam *Dur.* ***Village***, 3m/4km NW of Piercebridge. **62 C5** NZ1818.
Headless Cross *Worcs.* ***Suburb***, S district of Redditch. **30 B2** SP0365.
Headley *Hants.* ***Village***, 3m/4km N of Kingsclere. **21 J5** SU5162.
Headley *Hants.* Population: 5176. ***Village***, 4m/6km W of Hindhead. **12 B3** SU8236.
Headley *Surr.* ***Village***, 3m/4km E of Leatherhead. National Trust property on Headley Heath and in vicinity. **23 F6** TQ2054.
Headley Down *Hants.* ***Hamlet***, 3m/5km W of Hindhead. **12 B3** SU8436.
Headley Heath *Worcs.* ***Settlement***, 6m/10km S of Birmingham city centre. SP0676.
Headley Park *Bristol* ***Suburb***, 3m/4km S of Bristol city centre. ST5769.
Headon *Devon* ***Settlement***, 2m/3km SE of Holsworthy. SS3602.
Headon *Notts.* ***Village***, 4m/6km SE of Retford. **51 K5** SK7476.
Heads Nook *Cumb.* ***Village***, 4m/7km SW of Brampton. **61 F1** NY4955.
Heads of Ayr *S.Ayr.* ***Coastal feature***, headland at S end of Firth of Clyde, 4m/7km SW of Ayr. Holiday camp to E. **67 G2** NS2818.
Heady Hill *Gt.Man.* ***Suburb***, 1m/2km W of Heywood town centre. SD8310.
Heage *Derbys.* Population: 3098. ***Village***, 2m/3km W of Ripley. **51 F7** SK3750.
Healabhal Bheag (Macleod's Table South or Healaval Beg.) *High.* ***Mountain***, flat-topped mountain 4m/6km SW of Dunvegan, Skye. Height 1601 feet or 488 metres. **93 H7** NG2242.
Healabhal Mhòr (Macleod's Table North or Healaval More.) *High.* ***Mountain***, flat-topped mountain 3m/5km SW of Dunvegan, Skye. Height 1535 feet or 468 metres. **93 H7** NG2144.
Healaugh *N.Yorks.* ***Village***, in Swaledale, 1m/2km W of Reeth. **62 B7** SE0399.
Healaugh *N.Yorks.* ***Village***, 3m/5km NE of Tadcaster. **58 B5** SE5047.
Healaval Beg *High.* *Anglicised form of Healabhal Bheag, qv.*
Healaval More *High.* *Anglicised form of Healabhal Mhòr, qv.*
Heald Green *Gt.Man.* ***Locality***, 2m/3km S of Gatley. **49 H4** SJ8485.
Heald Moor *Lancs.* ***Open space***, moorland 2m/4km N of Bacup. **56 D7** SD8826.
Heale *Devon* ***Settlement***, near N coast, 5m/8km SW of Lynton. **6 E1** SS6446.
Heale *Som.* ***Hamlet***, 1km NW of Curry Rivel. ST3825.
Heale House and Garden *Wilts.* ***Garden***, 1km S of Upper Woodford and 4m/6km N of Salisbury. Varied collection of plants in formal garden; includes water garden with Japanese tea-house. **10 C1** SU1236.
Healey *Lancs.* ***Locality***, 1m/2km S of Whitworth. **49 H1** SD8815.
Healey *N.Yorks.* ***Village***, 3m/4km W of Masham. **57 G1** SE1880.
Healey *Northumb.* ***Settlement***, 2m/3km S of Riding Mill. **62 B1** NZ0158.
Healey *W.Yorks.* ***Locality***, on River Calder, 1m/2km SW of Ossett. SE2719.
Healey *W.Yorks.* ***Suburb***, W district of Batley. SE2224.

Healey Stones *Gt.Man.* ***Locality***, 1km SE of Healey. SD8814.
Healeyfield *Dur.* ***Hamlet***, 3m/5km SW of Consett. **62 B2** NZ0648.
Healing *N.E.Lincs.* Population: 1979. ***Village***, 4m/6km W of Grimsby. **53 F1** TA2110.
Heamoor *Cornw.* ***Locality***, to N of Penzance. **2 B5** SW4631.
Heaning *Cumb.* ***Settlement***, 1m/2km E of Windermere. SD4399.
Heanish *Arg. & B.* ***Settlement***, on S coast of Tiree, 1km SW of Scarinish. **78 B3** NM0343.
Heanor *Derbys.* Population: 22,180. ***Town***, market town, 3m/5km NW of Ilkeston. 15c tower on Victorian church. **41 G1** SK4346.
Heanor Gate *Derbys.* ***Suburb***, adjoining to W of Heanor. SK4245.
Heanton Punchardon *Devon* ***Village***, 4m/6km NW of Barnstaple. **6 D2** SS5035.
Heanton Satchville *Devon* ***Settlement***, 4m/7km N of Hatherleigh. **6 D4** SS5311.
Heap Bridge *Gt.Man.* ***Settlement***, by River Roch, 1m/2km E of Bury town centre. SD8210.
Heapey *Lancs.* ***Settlement***, 3m/4km N of Chorley. **56 B7** SD6020.
Heapham *Lincs.* ***Village***, 4m/6km E of Gainsborough. **52 B4** SK8788.
Hearn *Hants.* ***Settlement***, 4m/6km NW of Hindhead. SU8337.
Hearnden Green *Kent* ***Settlement***, 2m/3km N of Headcorn. TQ8246.
Hearnish *W.Isles* ***Coastal feature***, headland on Ceann Iar, one of Heisker Islands group to W of North Uist. **92 B5** NF6263.
Heart Law *E.Loth.* ***Mountain***, 4m/6km NW of Abbey St. Bathans. Height 1286 feet or 392 metres. **77 F4** NT7166.
Hearthstane *Sc.Bord.* ***Settlement***, in Tweeddale, 1m/2km N of Tweedsmuir. **69 G1** NT1125.
Heart's Delight *Kent* ***Hamlet***, 2m/3km SW of Sittingbourne. TQ8862.
Heasley Mill *Devon* ***Hamlet***, on SW edge of Exmoor National Park, 4m/7km N of South Molton. **7 F2** SS7332.
Heast *High.* ***Settlement***, 4m/6km S of Broadford, Skye. Uninhabited island of Eilean Heast 1km off shore to S. **86 C3** NG6417.
Heath *Cardiff* ***Suburb***, 2m/3km N of Cardiff city centre. ST1779.
Heath *Derbys.* ***Village***, 5m/8km SE of Chesterfield. **51 G6** SK4466.
Heath *W.Yorks.* ***Settlement***, 2m/3km E of Wakefield across River Calder. SE3520.
Heath and Reach *Beds.* ***Village***, 2m/3km N of Leighton Buzzard. **32 C6** SP9228.
Heath Common *W.Suss.* ***Settlement***, 2m/3km E of Storrington. TQ1114.
Heath End *Bucks.* ***Settlement***, adjoining to E of Great Kingshill, 4m/6km N of High Wycombe. SU8898.
Heath End *Hants.* ***Hamlet***, 5m/8km SW of Newbury. SU4162.
Heath End *Hants.* ***Locality***, 7m/11km NW of Basingstoke. **21 J5** SU5862.
Heath End *Leics.* ***Hamlet***, 3m/5km N of Ashby de la Zouch. SK3621.
Heath End *S.Glos.* ***Hamlet***, 1km S of Cromhall, 2m/3km NW of Wickwar. ST6989.
Heath End *Surr.* ***Suburb***, 1m/2km SW of Aldershot. **22 B7** SU8449.
Heath End *W.Mid.* ***Suburb***, 2m/4km N of Walsall. SK0202.
Heath Hayes *Staffs.* ***Suburb***, 2m/3km E of Cannock. **40 C4** SK0110.
Heath Hill *Shrop.* ***Hamlet***, 4m/6km S of Newport. **39 G4** SJ7614.
Heath House *Som.* ***Hamlet***, 1m/2km SW of Wedmore. **19 H7** ST4146.
Heath Park *Gt.Lon.* ***Suburb***, SE district of Romford, in borough of Havering. TQ5288.
Heath Side *Kent* ***Settlement***, at S edge of Dartford Heath, 2m/3km SW of Dartford. TQ5172.
Heath Town *W.Mid.* ***Suburb***, NE district of Wolverhampton. **40 B6** SO9399.
Heathbrook *Shrop.* ***Settlement***, 1m/2km E of Hodnet. SJ6228.
Heathcot *Aber.* ***Settlement***, 3m/5km E of Peterculter. **91 G4** NJ8900.
Heathcote *Derbys.* ***Hamlet***, 1m/2km E of Hartington. **50 D6** SK1460.
Heathcote *Shrop.* ***Settlement***, 3m/4km E of Hodnet. **39 F3** SJ6528.
Heathencote *Northants.* ***Settlement***, 1m/2km SE of Towcester. SP7147.
Heathend *W.Suss.* ***Settlement***, 2m/3km S of Petworth. SU9618.
Heather *Leics.* ***Village***, 4m/7km SE of Ashby de la Zouch. **41 F4** SK3910.
Heathfield *Ches.* ***Settlement***, just W of Hatherton. SJ6847.
Heathfield *Devon* ***Locality***, 3m/5km NW of Newton Abbot. **5 J3** SX8376.
Heathfield *E.Suss.* Population: 6629. ***Small town***, 11m/18km S of Royal Tunbridge Wells. Sussex Farm Museum at Horam. **13 J4** TQ5821.
Heathfield *N.Yorks.* ***Settlement***, 2m/3km NW of Pateley Bridge. SE1367.
Heathfield *Som.* ***Hamlet***, in Vale of Taunton Deane, 4m/7km NW of Taunton. **7 K3** ST1626.
Heathfield *S.Ayr.* ***Suburb***, N district of Ayr. NS3523.
Heathfield Moor *N.Yorks.* ***Open space***, moorland, marshy in parts, 3m/5km W of Pateley Bridge. Highest point, 1423 feet or 434 metres, is Flout Hill. **57 G3** SE1067.
Heathlands *Devon* ***Settlement***, 1km S of West Hill. SY0692.
Heathrow Airport *Gt.Lon. See London Heathrow Airport.*
Heathton *Shrop.* ***Hamlet***, 6m/10km E of Bridgnorth. **40 A6** SO8192.
Heathwaite *Cumb.* ***Locality***, adjoining to SE of Windermere. SD4197.
Heathy Brow *E.Suss.* ***Locality***, 1m/2km N of English Channel coast at Peacehaven. TQ4002.
Heatley *Warr.* ***Village***, 2m/3km NE of Lymm. **49 G4** SJ7088.
Heaton *Gt.Man.* ***Suburb***, 2m/3km W of Bolton town centre. SD6909.
Heaton *Lancs.* ***Settlement***, 2m/3km E of Heysham. **55 H3** SD4460.
Heaton *Staffs.* ***Hamlet***, 4m/7km NW of Leek. **49 J6** SJ9562.
Heaton *T. & W.* ***Suburb***, 2m/3km NE of Newcastle upon Tyne city centre. **71 H7** NZ2766.
Heaton *W.Yorks.* ***Suburb***, 2m/3km NW of Bradford city centre. SE1335.
Heaton Chapel *Gt.Man.* ***Suburb***, 2m/3km N of Stockport. SJ8892.
Heaton Hall *Gt.Man.* ***Historic house***, 18c house built by James Wyatt and now run by City Art Galleries, in Heaton Park adjoining to NE of Prestwich, 4m/6km N of Manchester city centre. **49 H2** SD8304.
Heaton Mersey *Gt.Man.* ***Suburb***, 2m/3km W of Stockport. SJ8690.
Heaton Moor *Gt.Man.* ***Locality***, 2m/3km NW of Stockport. **49 H3** SJ8791.
Heaton Norris *Gt.Man.* ***Suburb***, 1m/2km NW of Stockport. SJ8890.
Heaton Royds *W.Yorks.* ***Locality***, 1m/2km SW of Shipley. SE1335.
Heaton's Bridge *Lancs.* ***Hamlet***, 2m/4km N of Ormskirk, on S side of Leeds and Liverpool Canal. SD4011.
Heaval *W.Isles* ***Mountain***, on Barra 1m/2km NE of Castlebay. Height 1256 feet or 383 metres. **84 B5** NL6799.
Heaverham *Kent* ***Hamlet***, 4m/6km NE of Sevenoaks. **23 J6** TQ5758.
Heaviley *Gt.Man.* ***Suburb***, 1m/2km SE of Stockport. **49 J4** SJ9088.
Heavitree *Devon* ***Suburb***, E district of Exeter. SX9492.
Hebburn *T. & W.* Population: 18,183. ***Town***, on S bank of River Tyne, 4m/6km E of Gateshead. Formerly a shipbuilding town. **71 J7** NZ3164.
Hebden *N.Yorks.* ***Village***, 1m/2km N of Burnsall. **57 F3** SE0263.
Hebden Bridge *W.Yorks.* Population: 3681. ***Small town***, at confluence of Hebden Water and River Calder, 7m/11km W of Halifax. Former mill town with recently restored buildings. **56 E7** SD9927.
Hebden Green *Ches.* ***Locality***, 2m/3km SW of Winsford. **49 F6** SJ6265.
Hebden Moor *N.Yorks.* ***Open space***, moorland on NW side of Grimwith Reservoir, 3m/5km NE of Grassington. **57 F3** SE0366.
Hebden Water *W.Yorks.* ***River***, formed at confluence of Graining Water and Alcomden Water, and flowing SE through Hebden Bridge to join River Calder. **56 E6** SD9927.
Hebing End *Herts.* ***Hamlet***, 5m/8km E of Stevenage. **33 G6** TL3122.
Hebron *Carmar.* ***Hamlet***, 7m/11km N of Whitland. **16 E2** SN1827.
Hebron *I.o.A.* ***Settlement***, 2m/4km E of Llanerchymedd. SH4584.
Hebron *Northumb.* ***Hamlet***, 2m/4km N of Morpeth. **71 G5** NZ1989.
Heck *D. & G.* ***Settlement***, 2m/3km SE of Lochmaben, beyond Castle Loch. **69 F5** NY0980.
Heckfield *Hants.* ***Village***, 4m/6km N of Hook. **22 A5** SU7260.
Heckfield Green *Suff.* ***Village***, adjoining to E of Cross Street, 3m/5km NW of Eye. **35 F1** TM1875.
Heckfordbridge *Essex* ***Hamlet***, 4m/7km SW of Colchester. **34 D6** TL9421.
Heckingham *Norf.* ***Settlement***, 2m/3km E of Loddon. **45 H6** TM3898.
Heckington *Lincs.* Population: 2723. ***Village***, 5m/8km E of Sleaford. **42 E1** TF1444.
Heckmondwike *W.Yorks.* Population: 9855. ***Small town***, 2m/4km NW of Dewsbury. **57 H7** SE2123.
Hecla *W.Isles* ***Mountain***, on South Uist 2m/4km S of Loch Sgioport. Height 1988 feet or 606 metres. **84 D1** NF8234.
Heddington *Wilts.* ***Village***, 3m/5km S of Calne. **20 C5** ST9966.
Heddle *Ork.* ***Settlement***, 1m/2km S of Finstown. **107 C6** HY3512.
Heddon *Devon* ***River***, Exmoor river flowing N through Parracombe into Bristol Channel at Heddon's Mouth, 4m/7km W of Lynton. SS6549.
Heddon Oak *Som.* ***Settlement***, 5m/8km SE of Watchet. ST1137.
Heddon-on-the-Wall *Northumb.* ***Village***, 7m/12km W of Newcastle upon Tyne. Section of Hadrian's Wall (English Heritage). **71 G7** NZ1366.
Heddon-on-the-Wall Roman Wall *Northumb.* ***Historic/prehistoric site***, section of Hadrian's Wall (English Heritage) at Heddon-on-the-Wall. Remains of medieval kiln to W. To E of village is example of vallum in fine condition, cut through solid rock. **71 G7** NZ1366.
Heddon's Mouth *Devon* ***Coastal feature***, rocky cove to W of Highveer Point on N coast of Devon, 3m/5km N of Parracombe. **6 E1** SS6449.
Hedenham *Norf.* ***Village***, 3m/5km NW of Bungay. **45 H6** TM3193.
Hedge End *Hants.* Population: 16,171. ***Suburb***, large residential locality, 4m/7km E of Southampton. **11 F3** SU4812.
Hedge-end Island *Essex* ***Island***, uninhabited marshy island, 1m/2km W of The Naze. TM2424.
Hedgehope Hill *Northumb.* ***Mountain***, 3m/4km SE of The Cheviot. Height 2342 feet or 714 metres. **70 E2** NT9319.
Hedgerley *Bucks.* ***Village***, 3m/4km SE of Beaconsfield. **22 C3** SU9687.
Hedgerley Green *Bucks.* ***Settlement***, 1km NE of Hedgerley. SU9787.
Hedging *Som.* ***Hamlet***, 1m/2km NE of Durston. **8 B2** ST3029.
Hedingham Castle *Essex* ***Castle***, built c. 1140 by de Veres, to NE of Castle Hedingham. Fire at beginning of 20c damaged Great Tower. **34 B5** TL7835.
Hedley on the Hill *Northumb.* ***Village***, 3m/4km S of Prudhoe. **62 B1** NZ0759.
Hednesford *Staffs.* ***Town***, in Cannock Chase, 2m/3km NE of Cannock. Former mining town. **40 C4** SK0012.
Hedon *E.Riding* Population: 6646. ***Small town***, 6m/9km E of Kingston upon Hull. Former port, with fine church, known as 'King of Holderness' due to its size. **59 H7** TA1828.
Hedsor *Bucks.* ***Hamlet***, 3m/4km SW of Beaconsfield. **22 C3** SU9187.
Hedworth *T. & W.* ***Suburb***, 2m/3km S of Jarrow. NZ3363.
Heeley *S.Yorks.* ***Suburb***, 2m/3km S of Sheffield city centre. **51 F4** SK3584.
Heglibister *Shet.* ***Settlement***, on W side of Weisdale Voe, 1km NE of Sound, Mainland. **109 C7** HU3851.
Heighington *Darl.* ***Village***, 2m/4km SW of Newton Aycliffe. **62 D4** NZ2422.
Heighington *Lincs.* Population: 1401. ***Village***, 4m/6km E of Lincoln. **52 D6** TF0369.
Height End *Lancs.* ***Locality***, on S side of Cribden Hill, 1m/2km W of Rawtenstall. SD7923.
Heightington *Worcs.* ***Hamlet***, 3m/5km W of Stourport-on-Severn. SO7671.
Heights of Brae *High.* ***Settlement***, 2m/3km NW of Dingwall. **96 C5** NH5161.
Heights of Kinlochewe *High.* ***Settlement***, in Ross and Cromarty district, 3m/4km NE of Kinlochewe. **95 G5** NH0764.
Heilam *High.* ***Settlement***, on E side of Loch Eriboll. Ben Sgeireach lies to NW. **103 G2** NC4560.
Heileasbhal Mòr *W.Isles* ***Mountain***, 3m/4km S of Seilebost, South Harris. Height 1260 feet or 384 metres. **93 F2** NG0792.
Heinish *W.Isles* ***Coastal feature***, headland on W coast of Eriskay, 2m/3km S of Haunn. **84 C4** NF7809.
Heisgeir Eagach *W.Isles Alternative name for Haskeir Eagach, qv.*
Heisgeir Island *W.Isles Alternative name for Haskeir Island, qv.*
Heishival Mòr *W.Isles* ***Hill***, highest point on Vatersay. Height 623 feet or 190 metres. **84 B5** NL6296.
Heisker Islands (Also known as Monach Islands.) *W.Isles* ***Island***, group of low-lying islands 8m/13km SW of Aird an Rùnair, W coast of North Uist. Total area about 600 acres or 240 hectares. No permanent population. See Ceann Ear, Ceann Iar, Shillay and Stockay. **92 B5** NF6262.
Heithat *D. & G.* ***Settlement***, 3m/4km SE of Boreland. **69 G5** NY1988.
Heiton *Sc.Bord.* ***Village***, 2m/4km S of Kelso. **77 F7** NT7130.
Heldale Water *Ork.* ***Lake/loch***, on Hoy, 2m/4km N of Tor Ness. Length 1m/2km. **107 B8** ND2592.
Heldon Hill *Moray* ***Hill***, in wooded area, with steep scarp slope to SE, 6m/10km SW of Elgin. Height 768 feet or 234 metres. **97 J6** NJ1257.
Hele *Devon* ***Hamlet***, 4m/7km N of Launceston. SX3391.
Hele *Devon* ***Hamlet***, 1km NW of Ashburton. SX7470.
Hele *Devon* ***Village***, just E of Ilfracombe. **6 D1** SS5347.
Hele *Devon* ***Village***, on River Culm, 4m/6km SW of Cullompton. **7 H5** SS9902.
Hele *Som.* ***Hamlet***, 3m/4km W of Taunton. ST1824.
Hele *Torbay* ***Suburb***, 1m/2km NW of Torquay town centre. SX9165.
Hele Bridge *Devon* ***Bridge***, over River Torridge, 1m/2km N of Hatherleigh. **6 D5** SS5406.
Hele Lane *Devon* ***Settlement***, 3m/5km NE of Morchard Bishop, by River Dalch. **7 F4** SS7910.
Helebridge *Cornw.* ***Settlement***, 2m/3km S of Bude. **6 A5** SS2103.
Helensburgh *Arg. & B.* Population: 15,852. ***Town***, on N shore of Firth of Clyde, 8m/12km NW of Dumbarton. Noted yachting centre. Birthplace of J.L. Baird, 1888-1946, pioneer of television. **74 A2** NS2982.
Helford *Cornw.* ***River***, rising near Helston and flowing E into English Channel between Mawnan and Dennis Head. **2 E6** SW7526.
Helford *Cornw.* ***Village***, attractive village on inlet on S side of Helford River, 6m/10km E of Helston. Yachting centre. Associations with Daphne du Maurier. **2 E6** SW7526.
Helford Passage *Cornw.* ***Hamlet***, on N side of Helford River, opposite Helford. SW7626.
Helhoughton *Norf.* ***Village***, 4m/6km SW of Fakenham. **44 C3** TF8626.
Helions Bumpstead *Essex* ***Village***, 3m/5km SW of Haverhill. **33 K4** TL6541.
Hell Corner *W.Berks.* ***Settlement***, 1m/2km E of Inkpen. SU3864.
Hellabrick's Wick *Shet.* ***Bay***, wide bay to S of Foula. South Ness lies to S. **108 B1** HT9636.
Hellaby *S.Yorks.* ***Suburb***, 1m/2km W of Maltby. SK5092.
Helland *Cornw.* ***Village***, 3m/5km N of Bodmin. **4 A3** SX0771.
Helland *Som.* ***Hamlet***, adjoining North Curry, 6m/10km E of Taunton. ST3224.
Hellandbridge *Cornw.* ***Settlement***, to NW of Helland, at crossing of River Camel. **4 A3** SX0671.
Hellen's *Here.* ***Historic house***, 13c stone fortress built by Earl of March on E side of Much Marcle, 4m/6km SW of Ledbury. **29 F5** SO6633.
Hellescott *Cornw.* ***Hamlet***, 4m/6km NW of Launceston. SX2888.
Hellesdon *Norf.* ***Village***, on River Wensum, 2m/4km NW of Norwich. **45 F4** TG2010.
Helli Ness *Shet.* ***Coastal feature***, headland on E coast of Mainland, 8m/13km S of Lerwick. **109 D10** HU4628.

H

Helliar Holm (Also spelled Hellyar Holm.) *Ork.* ***Island***, small uninhabited island off S coast of Shapinsay opposite Balfour. Lighthouse at S end. **107 D6** HY4815.
Hellidon *Northants.* ***Village***, 5m/7km SW of Daventry. **31 G3** SP5158.
Hellifield *N.Yorks.* ***Village***, 5m/8km SE of Settle. **56 D4** SD8556.
Hellifield Green *N.Yorks.* ***Settlement***, adjoins to S of Hellifield. SD8556.
Hellingly *E.Suss.* ***Village***, 2m/3km N of Hailsham. **13 J5** TQ5812.
Hellington *Norf.* ***Hamlet***, 6m/10km SE of Norwich. **45 H5** TG3103.
Hellir *Shet.* ***Coastal feature***, small promontory on NE coast of Mainland, 2m/3km NE of North Roe. **108 C3** HU3892.
Hellisay *W.Isles* ***Island***, uninhabited island lying 3m/4km E of Northbay, Barra. **84 C4** NF7504.
Hellister *Shet.* ***Village***, on Mainland, on E side of Weisdale Voe. **109 C8** HU3849.
Hellmoor Loch *Sc.Bord.* ***Lake/loch***, small loch 7m/12km W of Hawick. **69 J2** NT3816.
Hell's Glen (Gleann Beag). *Arg. & B.* ***Valley***, running SE into River Goil, 3m/4km N of Lochgoilhead. **80 C7** NN1707.
Hell's Mouth *Gwyn. Alternative name for Porth Neigwl, qv.*
Hellyar Holm *Ork. Alternative spelling of Helliar Holm, qv.*
Helmdon *Northants.* ***Village***, 4m/6km N of Brackley. **31 G4** SP5843.
Helme *W.Yorks.* ***Hamlet***, just S of Blackmoorfoot Reservoir, 1km N of Meltham. SE1911.
Helmingham *Suff.* ***Village***, 4m/7km S of Debenham. **35 F3** TM1857.
Helmingham Hall *Suff.* ***Historic house***, Tudor and later house in deer park 5m/8km S of Debenham. **35 F3** TM1857.
Helmington Row *Dur.* ***Hamlet***, midway between Crook and Willington. NZ1835.
Helmsdale *High.* ***River***, rising from Loch Badanloch and flowing SE to coast of Sutherland district at Helmsdale. **104 D6** ND0215.
Helmsdale *High.* ***Village***, on E coast of Sutherland district, at mouth of River Helmsdale, 15m/24km NE of Golspie. River runs SE from Loch Badanloch down Strath Kildonan. **105 F7** ND0215.
Helmshore *Lancs.* ***Locality***, 1m/2km S of Haslingden. **56 C7** SD7821.
Helmsley *N.Yorks.* ***Small town***, on River Rye with large cobbled square, 12m/19km E of Thirsk. Remains of 12c castle (English Heritage). 18c Duncombe Park, now girls' school, 1m/2km SW. **58 C1** SE6183.
Helmsley Castle *N.Yorks.* ***Castle***, remains of 12c castle (English Heritage) on SW side of Helmsley, 11m/18km W of Pickering. Original 11c earthworks with later stone walls above, and 14c alterations to tower. **58 C1** SE6183.
Helmsley Moor *N.Yorks.* ***Open space***, moorland, partly afforested, on E side of Bilsdale, 5m/8km N of Helmsley. **63 G7** SE5892.
Helperby *N.Yorks.* ***Village***, on River Swale, adjoining to S of Brafferton, 6m/9km W of Easingwold. **57 K2** SE4369.
Helperthorpe *N.Yorks.* ***Village***, 11m/17km E of Malton. **59 F2** SE9570.
Helpringham *Lincs.* ***Village***, 6m/9km SE of Sleaford. **42 E1** TF1340.
Helpston *Peter.* ***Village***, 6m/10km NW of Peterborough. Site of Roman building 1m/2km S. **42 E5** TF1205.
Helsby *Ches.* Population: 4538. ***Village***, 8m/12km NE of Chester. **48 D5** SJ4875.
Helsby Hill *Ches.* ***Hill***, National Trust property on E side of Helsby, with Iron Age hill fort. Height 462 feet or 141 metres. SJ4975.
Helsey *Lincs.* ***Hamlet***, 1m/2km NW of Hogsthorpe. TF5172.
Helston *Cornw.* Population: 8505. ***Small town***, market town of Lizard peninsula, 15m/24km SW of Truro. Unusual granite-built Georgian church. Former stannary town. Poldark Mine, includes museum containing artefacts from mine and collection of machinery from industries around Britain. **2 D6** SW6527.
Helstone *Cornw.* ***Village***, 2m/3km SW of Camelford. **4 A2** SX0881.
Helton *Cumb.* ***Hamlet***, 5m/9km S of Penrith. **61 G4** NY5122.
Helvellyn *Cumb.* ***Mountain***, in Lake District 4m/6km W of Patterdale. Height 3113 feet or 949 metres. **60 E5** NY3415.
Helwith *N.Yorks.* ***Settlement***, 3m/5km NE of Reeth. NZ0702.
Helwith Bridge *N.Yorks.* ***Settlement***, at crossing of River Ribble, 1m/2km N of Stainforth. **56 D3** SD8169.
Helygain *Flints. Welsh form of Halkyn, qv.*
Hem *Powys* ***Settlement***, 5m/8km S of Welshpool. SJ2300.
Hemblington *Norf.* ***Hamlet***, 4m/6km W of Acle. **45 H4** TG3411.
Hemblington Corner *Norf.* ***Locality***, adjoining to E of Blofield Heath, 1m/2km N of Blofield. TG3311.
Hemborough Post *Devon* ***Settlement***, 3m/4km NW of Dartmouth. **5 J5** SX8352.
Hemel Hempstead *Herts.* Population: 79,235. ***Town***, old market and commuter town on River Gade and Grand Union Canal, 7m/11km NW of Watford. New Town, designated 1947, to E of old. Old town has fine Norman church. **22 D1** TL0507.
Hemerdon *Devon* ***Village***, 6m/10km E of Plymouth. SX5657.
Hemingbrough *N.Yorks.* ***Village***, 4m/6km E of Selby. **58 C6** SE6730.
Hemingby *Lincs.* ***Village***, 3m/5km NW of Horncastle. **53 F5** TF2374.
Hemingfield *S.Yorks.* ***Village***, 1m/2km S of Wombwell. SE3901.
Hemingford Abbots *Cambs.* ***Village***, on River Great Ouse, 3m/5km E of Huntingdon. **33 F1** TL2870.
Hemingford Grey *Cambs.* Population: 2420. ***Village***, 1m/2km W of St. Ives. **33 F1** TL2970.
Hemingstone *Suff.* ***Village***, 6m/9km N of Ipswich. **35 F3** TM1453.
Hemington *Leics.* ***Village***, 7m/11km NW of Loughborough. **41 G3** SK4528.
Hemington *Northants.* ***Village***, 4m/6km SE of Oundle. Beaulieu Hall is 17c manor house. **42 D7** TL0985.
Hemington *Som.* ***Village***, 3m/5km SE of Radstock. **20 A6** ST7253.
Hemley *Suff.* ***Village***, near right bank of River Deben estuary, 5m/8km N of Felixstowe. **35 G4** TM2842.
Hemlington *Middbro.* ***Suburb***, 4m/6km S of Middlesbrough. **63 F5** NZ5014.
Hemp Green *Suff.* ***Settlement***, 1m/2km NW of Yoxford. TM3769.
Hempholme *E.Riding* ***Settlement***, 6m/10km SE of Great Driffield. **59 G5** TA0850.
Hempnall *Norf.* ***Village***, 9m/14km S of Norwich. **45 G6** TM2494.
Hempnall Green *Norf.* ***Village***, 1m/2km SE of Hempnall. **45 G6** TM2494.
Hempriggs *Moray* ***Settlement***, 3m/5km S of Burghead. **97 J5** NJ1063.
Hempriggs House *High.* ***Settlement***, on E side of Loch Hempriggs. **105 J4** ND3447.
Hempstead *Essex* ***Village***, 5m/8km N of Thaxted. **33 K5** TL6338.
Hempstead *Kent* ***Suburb***, in S part of Gillingham. TQ7964.
Hempstead *Norf.* ***Hamlet***, 2m/4km SE of Happisburgh. **45 J3** TG4028.
Hempstead *Norf.* ***Village***, 2m/3km SE of Holt. **45 F2** TG1037.
Hempsted *Glos.* ***Suburb***, in SW part of Gloucester. **29 H7** SO8116.
Hempton *Norf.* ***Village***, 1km SW of Fakenham across River Wensum. **44 D3** TF9129.
Hempton *Oxon.* ***Hamlet***, 1m/2km W of Deddington. **31 F5** SP4431.
Hemsby *Norf.* Population: 5109. ***Village***, 1m/2km S of Winterton-on-Sea. **45 J4** TG4917.
Hemsby Hole *Norf.* ***Sea feature***, sea channel off coast at Hemsby. **45 K4** TG5117.
Hemswell *Lincs.* ***Village***, 5m/8km S of Kirton in Lindsey. **52 C3** SK9390.
Hemsworth *W.Yorks.* Population: 9401. ***Small town***, 6m/9km S of Pontefract. **51 G1** SE4213.
Hemsworth Water Park *W.Yorks.* ***Other feature of interest***, at Hemsworth, 6m/10km SE of Wakefield. Parkland, boating lakes and fishing. **51 G1** SE4214.
Hemyock *Devon* ***Village***, under Black Down Hills, 5m/8km S of Wellington. **7 K4** ST1313.
Hen Gerrig *Powys* ***Mountain***, on NW side of Dyfnant Forest, 4m/7km W of Llanwddyn. Height 1699 feet or 518 metres. **37 J4** SH9518.
Hen Gwrt *Mon.* ***Historic house***, medieval moated manor house (Cadw) at Llantilio Crossenny, 6m/10km E of Abergavenny. **28 C7** SO3915.
Henbrook *Worcs.* ***Settlement***, 3m/5km NE of Droitwich Spa. Masts are notable landmark. SO9266.
Henbury *Bristol* ***Suburb***, 4m/6km NW of Bristol city centre. **19 J4** ST5678.
Henbury *Ches.* ***Village***, 3m/4km W of Macclesfield. **49 H5** SJ8873.
Henderland *D. & G.* ***Settlement***, 6m/10km W of Dumfries. **65 J3** NX8774.
Henderson's Rock *Arg. & B.* ***Coastal feature***, rock off W coast of Seil, 1m/2km S of Easdale. **79 J6** NM7415.
Hendersyde Park *Sc.Bord.* ***Settlement***, 1m/2km NE of Kelso. **77 F7** NT7435.
Hendham *Devon* ***Hamlet***, 4m/7km N of Kingsbridge. SX7450.
Hendomen *Powys* ***Hamlet***, 1m/2km NW of Montgomery. SO2198.
Hendon *Gt.Lon.* ***Suburb***, in borough of Barnet, 7m/11km NW of Charing Cross. **23 F3** TQ2289.
Hendon *T. & W.* ***Suburb***, 1m/2km SE of Sunderland city centre. **62 E1** NZ4055.
Hendraburnick *Cornw.* ***Hamlet***, 3m/5km NE of Camelford. SX1287.
Hendre *Bridgend* ***Hamlet***, 2m/4km NE of Bridgend. SS9381.
Hendre *Flints.* ***Settlement***, 2m/4km SE of Nannerch. SJ1967.
Hendre *Gwyn.* ***Settlement***, 4m/6km NW of Llanbedrog. SH3137.
Hendreforgan *R.C.T.* ***Village***, 2m/3km W of Tonyrefail. SS9888.
Hendy *Carmar.* ***Village***, on W side of River Loughor, opposite Pontarddulais. **17 J4** SN5803.
Hendy-gwyn *Carmar. Welsh form of Whitland, qv.*
Heneglwys *I.o.A.* ***Settlement***, on E side of airfield, 2m/4km W of Llangefni, Anglesey. **46 C5** SH4276.
Henfield *S.Glos.* ***Hamlet***, 4m/6km SW of Chipping Sodbury. ST6779.
Henfield *W.Suss.* Population: 4111. ***Small town***, 7m/11km N of Shoreham-by-Sea. Interesting tile-hung houses. **13 F5** TQ2116.
Henford *Devon* ***Settlement***, 7m/11km NE of Launceston. **6 B6** SX3794.
Hengherst *Kent* ***Settlement***, 5m/8km SW of Ashford. **14 E4** TQ9536.
Hengistbury Head *Bourne.* ***Coastal feature***, headland at W end of Christchurch Bay. **10 C5** SZ1790.
Hengistbury Head Tumuli *Bourne.* ***Historic/prehistoric site***, 6m/9km E of Bournemouth town centre. Iron Age barrow associated with hillfort on headland. **10 C5** SZ1890.
Hengoed *Caerp.* ***Village***, 5m/8km N of Caerphilly. **18 E2** ST1595.
Hengoed *Powys* ***Settlement***, 5m/8km SW of Kington. **28 B3** SO2253.
Hengoed *Shrop.* ***Hamlet***, 1m/2km W of Gobowen. **38 B2** SJ2833.
Hengrave *Suff.* ***Village***, 3m/5km NW of Bury St. Edmunds. **34 C2** TL8268.
Hengrove *Bristol* ***Suburb***, 3m/4km SE of Bristol city centre. ST6069.
Hengynwydd-fawr *Powys* ***Valley***, running N from The Cross to River Severn, 3m/4km E of Llanidloes. **37 J7** SN9881.
Henham *Essex* ***Village***, 6m/10km NE of Bishop's Stortford. **33 J6** TL5428.
Heniarth *Powys* ***Settlement***, 1m/2km NE of Llanfair Caereinion. **38 A5** SJ1108.
Henlade *Som.* ***Hamlet***, 3m/5km E of Taunton. **8 B2** ST2723.
Henleaze *Bristol* ***Suburb***, 3m/4km N of Bristol city centre. ST5876.
Henley *Dorset* ***Hamlet***, 1km S of Buckland Newton and 3m/5km N of Piddletrenthide. ST6904.
Henley *Glos.* ***Locality***, 5m/7km SE of Gloucester. SO9016.
Henley *Shrop.* ***Locality***, 2m/3km NE of Ludlow. **28 E1** SO5476.
Henley *Som.* ***Hamlet***, 1m/2km S of Crewkerne. ST4307.
Henley *Som.* ***Hamlet***, on edge of Sedgemoor, 3m/5km E of Othery. **8 D1** ST4332.
Henley *Suff.* ***Village***, 4m/7km N of Ipswich. **35 F3** TM1551.
Henley *W.Suss.* ***Village***, 3m/4km N of Midhurst. **12 B4** SU8925.
Henley Corner *Som.* ***Settlement***, N of Henley, on King's Sedgemoor Drain, 4m/6km SW of Street. **8 D1** ST4332.
Henley Green *W.Mid.* ***Suburb***, 3m/5km NE of Coventry city centre. SP3681.
Henley-in-Arden *Warks.* Population: 2803. ***Village***, 7m/12km NW of Stratford-upon-Avon. **30 C2** SP1565.
Henley-on-Thames *Oxon.* Population: 10,558. ***Town***, on River Thames 6m/10km NE of Reading. Many old buildings, from 15c-18c. Annual rowing regatta first week in July. **22 A3** SU7682.
Henley Park *Surr.* ***Settlement***, 2m/3km S of Pirbright. **22 C6** SU9352.
Henley Street *Kent* ***Settlement***, 1km SE of Sole Street and 5m/7km S of Gravesend. TQ6667.
Henley's Down *E.Suss.* ***Hamlet***, 3m/5km N of Bexhill. **14 C6** TQ7312.
Henllan *Carmar.* ***Hamlet***, 3m/5km E of Newcastle Emlyn. **17 G1** SN3540.
Henllan *Denb.* ***Village***, 2m/3km NW of Denbigh. **47 J6** SJ0268.
Henllan *Mon.* ***Locality***, 1m/2km S of Llanthony. SO2925.
Henllan Amgoed *Carmar.* ***Settlement***, 2m/4km NW of Whitland. **16 E2** SN1720.
Henllys *Torfaen* ***Village***, 1m/2km W of Cwmbran. **19 F2** ST2693.
Henllys Vale *Torfaen* ***Settlement***, 1m/2km SE of Henllys, to S of Cwmbran. ST2792.
Henlow *Beds.* Population: 5696. ***Village***, 2m/4km E of Shefford. **32 E5** TL1738.
Hennock *Devon* ***Village***, 2m/3km NE of Bovey Tracey. **7 G7** SX8380.
Henny Street *Essex* ***Hamlet***, 2m/3km S of Sudbury. **34 C5** TL8738.
Henryd *Conwy* ***Hamlet***, 2m/3km S of Conwy. **47 F5** SH7774.
Henry's Moat (Castellhenri). *Pembs.* ***Hamlet***, 9m/15km NE of Haverfordwest. **16 D2** SN0427.
Hensall *N.Yorks.* ***Village***, 3m/5km W of Snaith. **58 B7** SE5923.
Hensbarrow Downs *Cornw.* ***Mountain***, 3m/4km E of St. Dennis, in centre of China Clay district. Tumulus at summit. Height 1023 feet or 312 metres. **3 G3** SW9957.
Henshaw *Northumb.* ***Village***, 4m/6km E of Haltwhistle. **70 C7** NY7664.
Henshaw *W.Yorks.* ***Suburb***, to SW of Yeadon town centre. SE2040.
Hensingham *Cumb.* ***Suburb***, 1m/2km SE of Whitehaven town centre. **60 A5** NX9816.
Hensington *Oxon.* ***Locality***, in E part of Woodstock. SP4516.
Henstead *Suff.* ***Village***, 2m/4km W of Kessingland. **45 J7** TM4985.
Hensting *Hants.* ***Hamlet***, 3m/5km NE of Eastleigh. **11 F2** SU4922.
Henstridge *Som.* ***Village***, 6m/10km S of Wincanton. **9 G3** ST7219.
Henstridge Ash *Som.* ***Village***, to N of Henstridge, 2m/3km NW of Stalbridge. **9 G2** ST7120.
Henstridge Bowden *Som.* ***Hamlet***, 2m/4km NW of Henstridge. ST6920.
Henstridge Marsh *Som.* ***Hamlet***, 1m/2km NE of Henstridge. **9 G2** ST7420.
Henton *Oxon.* ***Village***, 4m/7km SE of Thame. **22 A1** SP7602.
Henton *Som.* ***Village***, 4m/6km W of Wells. **19 H7** ST4945.
Henwick *Worcs.* ***Suburb***, W district of Worcester. **29 H3** SO8354.
Henwood *Cornw.* ***Village***, 6m/9km N of Liskeard. **4 C3** SX2673.
Henwood Green *Kent* ***Settlement***, adjoining to E of Pembury. TQ6340.
Heogan *Shet.* ***Settlement***, on NW coast of Bressay, on small Bay of Heogan. **109 D8** HU4743.
Heol-ddu *Carmar.* ***Settlement***, 1m/2km NW of Cefneithin. **17 J3** SN5415.
Heol Lly Goden *Powys* ***Settlement***, 3m/5km SE of Talgarth. **28 A6** SO1729.
Heol Senni *Powys* ***Settlement***, 3m/5km S of Sennybridge. **27 J6** SN9223.
Heol-y-Cyw *Bridgend* ***Village***, 4m/6km NE of Bridgend. **18 C3** SS9484.
Heolgaled *Carmar. Welsh form of Salem, qv.*
Heolgerrig *M.Tyd.* ***Settlement***, 1km W of Merthyr Tydfil. SO0306.
Hepburn *Northumb.* ***Settlement***, 3m/4km S of Chatton. **71 F1** NU0624.
Hepburn Bell *Northumb.* ***Settlement***, 3m/5km S of Chatton. NU0523.

Hepple *Northumb.* ***Village***, 5m/7km W of Rothbury. **70 E3** NT9800.
Hepscott *Northumb.* ***Village***, 2m/3km SE of Morpeth. **71 H5** NZ2284.
Hepthorne Lane *Derbys.* ***Village***, adjoining to W of North Wingfield, 1m/2km NE of Clay Cross. SK4064.
Heptonstall *W.Yorks.* ***Village***, preserved moorland village, 1km NW of Hebden Bridge. Present parish has remains of 13c church in churchyard. **56 E7** SD9828.
Heptonstall Moor *W.Yorks.* ***Open space***, moorland, with Gorple Reservoirs to N, 4m/6km NW of Hebden Bridge. **56 E6** SD9330.
Heptonstall Slack *W.Yorks. Alternative name for Slack, qv.*
Hepworth *Suff.* ***Village***, 5m/7km NE of Ixworth. **34 D1** TL9874.
Hepworth *W.Yorks.* ***Village***, 2m/3km SE of Holmfirth. **50 D2** SE1606.
Hepworth South Common *Suff.* ***Settlement***, 1km SE of Hepworth. TL9974.
Herbrandston *Pembs.* ***Village***, 3m/4km W of Milford Haven. **16 B4** SM8707.
Herdicott *Devon* ***Settlement***, 3m/5km S of Holsworthy. **6 B6** SX3499.
Hereford *Here.* Population: 54,326. ***City***, county town and cathedral city on River Wye, 45m/72km SW of Birmingham. Many old buildings and museums, including Waterworks museum and Churchill Gardens museum. Cathedral includes richly ornamented Early English chapel and contains Mappa Mundi. Three Choirs Festival every third year. **28 E4** SO5139.
Hereford Cathedral *Here.* ***Ecclesiastical building***, in centre of Hereford. Built of local sandstone and dating from 11c. Notable features include Lady Chapel, built in Early English style, Mappa Mundi, map of world dating from 1290, and chained library. **28 E5** SO5139.
Hereford Racecourse *Here.* ***Racecourse***, in Westfields, N suburb of Hereford. National hunt course, with fifteen race days per year, including one on Grand National Day. **28 E4** SO5041.
Hergest Croft Gardens *Here.* ***Garden***, on W side of Kington, with kitchen garden and extensive collection of trees and shrubs. Displays national collection of birches, maples and zelkovas. **28 B3** SO2856.
Hergest Ridge *Powys* ***Mountain***, 3m/4km W of Kington. Height 1397 feet or 426 metres. **28 B3** SO2455.
Heriot *Sc.Bord.* ***Locality***, on Heriot Water, 7m/11km NW of Stow. **76 B5** NT3952.
Heriot Water *Sc.Bord.* ***River***, originating in several headstreams on Moorfoot Hills and running E into Gala Water 2m/3km E of Heriot. **76 B5** NT3952.
Herma Ness *Shet.* ***Coastal feature***, headland at NW end of Unst. **108 E1** HP5918.
Herman Law *Sc.Bord.* ***Mountain***, 1km E of Birkhill. Height 2014 feet or 614 metres. **69 H2** NT2115.
Hermetray *W.Isles* ***Island***, small uninhabited island at S end of Sound of Harris, 1km off NE coast of North Uist. **92 E4** NF9874.
Hermiston *Edin.* ***Village***, on outskirts of Edinburgh, 6m/9km SW of city centre. **75 K3** NT1770.
Hermit Hill *S.Yorks.* ***Hamlet***, 1km W of Pilley, 3m/5km W of Hoyland. SE3200.
Hermitage *Dorset* ***Village***, 6m/9km S of Sherborne. **9 F4** ST6407.
Hermitage *D. & G.* ***Settlement***, 1m/2km NW of Haugh of Urr. **65 J4** NX8068.
Hermitage *Sc.Bord.* ***Settlement***, on Whitrope Burn, 5m/8km N of Newcastleton. **70 A4** NY5095.
Hermitage *W.Berks.* Population: 1557. ***Village***, 4m/6km NE of Newbury. **21 J4** SU5072.
Hermitage *W.Suss.* ***Locality***, adjoining to E of Emsworth. **11 J4** SU7505.
Hermitage Castle *Sc.Bord.* ***Castle***, ruined 13c castle (Historic Scotland) on Hermitage Water, 5m/8km N of Newcastleton. **69 K4** NY4996.
Hermitage Green *Warr.* ***Settlement***, 1km N of Winwick. SJ6094.
Hermitage Water *Sc.Bord.* ***River***, flowing E to Hermitage Castle, then S to Liddel Water 2m/3km NE of Newcastleton. **69 K4** NY4996.
Hermon *Carmar.* ***Hamlet***, 7m/11km NW of Carmarthen. **17 G1** SN3630.
Hermon *Carmar.* ***Settlement***, 2m/4km W of Llangadog. SN6728.
Hermon *I.o.A.* ***Hamlet***, on Anglesey, 2m/3km E of Aberffraw. **46 B6** SH3868.
Hermon *Pembs.* ***Village***, 2m/3km SE of Crymych. **17 F1** SN2031.
Herne *Kent* ***Suburb***, S district of Herne Bay. **25 H5** TR1865.
Herne Bay *Kent* Population: 31,861. ***Town***, N coast resort on bay of same name, 7m/11km N of Canterbury. 18c windmill. 19c tower on seafront. **25 H5** TR1768.
Herne Common *Kent* ***Hamlet***, 1km S of Herne. **25 H5** TR1764.
Herne Hill *Gt.Lon.* ***Locality***, 4m/6km S of Charing Cross, on borders of Lambeth and Southwark boroughs. TQ3274.
Herne Pound *Kent* ***Hamlet***, 1km N of Mereworth. TQ6554.
Herner *Devon* ***Hamlet***, 5m/7km SE of Barnstaple. **6 D3** SS5826.
Hernhill *Kent* ***Village***, 3m/5km E of Faversham. **25 G5** TR0660.
Hernston *V. of Glam.* ***Hamlet***, 1m/2km S of Bridgend. SS9178.
Herodsfoot *Cornw.* ***Village***, 4m/6km SW of Liskeard. **4 C4** SX2160.
Herongate *Essex* Population: 1057. ***Village***, 3m/5km SE of Brentwood. **24 C2** TQ6391.
Heron's Ghyll *E.Suss.* ***Locality***, 4m/6km N of Uckfield. **13 H4** TQ4827.
Heronsgate *Herts.* ***Hamlet***, 1m/2km S of Chorleywood. **22 D2** TQ0294.
Herriard *Hants.* ***Hamlet***, 4m/7km SE of Basingstoke. **21 K7** SU6645.
Herringfleet *Suff.* ***Hamlet***, 6m/9km NW of Lowestoft. **45 J6** TM4797.
Herring's Green *Beds.* ***Settlement***, 4m/6km SE of Bedford. **32 D4** TL0844.
Herringswell *Suff.* ***Village***, 3m/5km S of Mildenhall. **34 B2** TL7169.
Herringthorpe *S.Yorks.* ***Suburb***, 1m/2km SE of Rotherham town centre. SK4492.
Herrington *T. & W.* ***Locality***, comprising East and Middle Herrington, together with West and New Herrington. **62 E1** NZ3553.
Herscha Hill *Aber.* ***Hill***, 2m/3km W of Glenbervie. Height 731 feet or 223 metres. **91 F6** NO7380.
Hersden *Kent* ***Village***, 5m/8km NE of Canterbury. **25 H5** TR2062.
Hersham *Cornw.* ***Settlement***, 3m/5km NE of Bude. **6 A5** SS2507.
Hersham *Surr.* ***Locality***, on W bank of River Mole, 1m/2km W of Esher. **22 E5** TQ1164.
Herstmonceux *E.Suss.* ***Village***, 4m/6km NE of Hailsham. Herstmonceux Castle, 2m/3km SE, former home of Royal Observatory. **13 K5** TQ6312.
Herstmonceux Castle *E.Suss.* ***Garden***, 200 acre grounds of 15c moated castle, 1m/2km S of Herstmonceux, including woods, rose garden and herbaceous borders. Royal Greenwich Observatory based at castle after World War II. **13 K5** TQ6410.
Herston *Dorset* ***Suburb***, adjoining to W of Swanage. **10 B7** SZ0178.
Herston *Ork.* ***Settlement***, on SW side of Widewall Bay, South Ronaldsay, 1km W of Widewall across bay. **107 D8** ND4291.
Herston Head *Ork.* ***Coastal feature***, headland on W coast of South Ronaldsay to S of Widewall Bay. **107 D8** ND4191.
Hertburn *T. & W.* ***Suburb***, in E part of Washington. NZ3157.
Hertford *Herts.* Population: 21,665. ***Town***, historic county town on River Lea, 20m/32km N of London. **33 G7** TL3212.
Hertford *N.Yorks.* ***Other water feature***, artificial channel running W from 1m/2km W of Filey into River Derwent 1m/2km NW of Ganton. **59 G2** SE9878.
Hertford Heath *Herts.* ***Village***, 2m/3km NW of Hoddesdon. **33 G7** TL3511.
Hertingfordbury *Herts.* ***Hamlet***, 1m/2km W of Hertford. **33 G7** TL3012.
Hesgyn *Gwyn.* ***River***, stream running S through Llyn Hesgyn into River Tryweryn, 1m/2km E of Llyn Celyn dam. **37 H1** SH8940.
Hesket Newmarket *Cumb.* ***Village***, 8m/13km SE of Wigton. **60 E3** NY3438.
Hesketh Bank *Lancs.* ***Locality***, 2m/3km N of Tarleton. **55 H7** SD4423.
Hesketh Lane *Lancs.* ***Hamlet***, 3m/4km NE of Longridge. **56 B5** SD6141.
Heskin Green *Lancs.* ***Hamlet***, 4m/6km W of Chorley. **48 E1** SD5315.
Hesleden *Dur.* ***Village***, 2m/3km S of Peterlee. **63 F3** NZ4438.
Hesledon Moor East *Dur.* ***Settlement***, just S of Murton. NZ3946.
Hesledon Moor West *Dur.* ***Locality***, 1km SW of Hesledon Moor East. NZ3845.
Hesleyside *Northumb.* ***Settlement***, in parkland, on W side of River North Tyne, 1m/2km W of Bellingham. **70 D5** NY8184.
Heslington *York* ***Village***, 2m/3km SE of York. Location of University of York. **58 C4** SE6250.
Hessay *York* ***Village***, 5m/8km W of York. **58 B4** SE5253.
Hessenford *Cornw.* ***Village***, 6m/9km SE of Liskeard. **4 D5** SX3057.
Hessett *Suff.* ***Village***, 5m/9km E of Bury St. Edmunds. **34 D2** TL9361.
Hessle *E.Riding* ***Town***, on N bank of River Humber, adjoining to W of Kingston upon Hull. 19c Hessle Cliff Mill has surviving tower and machinery. **59 G7** TA0326.
Hessle *W.Yorks.* ***Settlement***, 1m/2km NW of Ackworth Moor Top. SE4317.
Hest Bank *Lancs.* ***Locality***, on Morecambe Bay, 3m/4km NE of Morecambe. **55 H3** SD4766.
Hestan Island *D. & G.* ***Island***, small island with lighthouse at entrance to Auchencairn Bay on Solway Firth, S of Dalbeattie. **65 J5** NX8350.
Hestercombe Gardens *Som.* ***Garden***, 4m/6km N of Taunton. Edwardian gardens, restored by Jekyllian planting to original designs by Sir Edwin Lutyens and Gertrude Jekyll. **8 B2** ST2428.
Hester's Way *Glos.* ***Suburb***, W district of Cheltenham. SO9223.
Hestley Green *Suff.* ***Settlement***, 3m/5km NW of Debenham. TM1567.
Heston *Gt.Lon.* ***Suburb***, in borough of Hounslow, 11m/18km W of Charing Cross. **22 E4** TQ1277.
Heswall *Mersey.* Population: 31,093. ***Town***, commuter town on Wirral peninsula, 5m/7km SE of West Kirby. **48 B4** SJ2682.
Hethe *Oxon.* ***Village***, 5m/7km N of Bicester. **31 G6** SP5929.
Hethelpit Cross *Glos.* ***Hamlet***, 8m/12km NW of Gloucester. SO7729.
Hether Burn *Cumb.* ***River***, flowing W into River Lyne, 3m/4km SE of Longtown. **69 K7** NY4166.
Hetherington *Northumb.* ***Settlement***, 3m/4km W of Wark. **70 D6** NY8278.
Hethersett *Norf.* Population: 4223. ***Village***, 5m/8km SW of Norwich. **45 F5** TG1504.
Hethersgill *Cumb.* ***Hamlet***, 5m/8km NW of Brampton. **69 K7** NY4767.
Hetherside *Cumb.* ***Locality***, 1m/2km NW of Smithfield and 4m/7km SE of Longtown. NY4366.
Hethpool *Northumb.* ***Settlement***, above W bank of College Burn, 2m/3km SW of Kirknewton. Ruined 14c peel tower. **70 D1** NT8928.
Hett *Dur.* ***Village***, 2m/4km NE of Spennymoor. **62 D3** NZ2836.
Hetton *N.Yorks.* ***Village***, 5m/8km N of Skipton. **56 E4** SD9658.
Hetton Downs *T. & W.* ***Suburb***, adjoining to N of Hetton-le-Hole. NZ3548.
Hetton le Hill *T. & W.* ***Hamlet***, 1m/2km SW of Easington Lane. NZ3545.
Hetton-le-Hole *T. & W.* Population: 13,538. ***Town***, residential town, 6m/10km NE of Durham. **62 E2** NZ3547.
Heugh *Northumb.* ***Settlement***, 5m/8km W of Ponteland. **71 F6** NZ0873.
Heugh-head *Aber.* ***Settlement***, 2m/3km SE of Strathdon. **90 B3** NJ3811.
Heugh-head *Aber.* ***Settlement***, 1m/2km W of Aboyne. **90 D5** NO5099.
Hevdadale Head *Shet.* ***Coastal feature***, headland on NW coast of Mainland, 4m/6km W of Burra Voe. **108 C4** HU3089.
Heveningham *Suff.* ***Village***, 5m/8km SW of Halesworth. **35 H1** TM3372.
Hever *Kent* ***Village***, 2m/4km SE of Edenbridge. **23 H7** TQ4744.
Hever Castle *Kent* ***Castle***, former home of Anne Boleyn, dating from 13c, 3m/5km E of Edenbridge. Tudor manor house added to by Boleyn family and renovated in early 20c by the American, Lord Astor of Hever, who also laid out 30 acres of gardens including Italian, rose, Tudor gardens and a maze. **23 H7** TQ4744.
Heversham *Cumb.* ***Village***, 2m/3km S of Levens. **55 H1** SD4983.
Hevingham *Norf.* ***Village***, 8m/13km N of Norwich. **45 F3** TG2021.
Hewas Water *Cornw.* ***Hamlet***, 3m/5km SW of St. Austell. **3 G4** SW9749.
Hewell Lane *Worcs.* ***Settlement***, to E of Tardebigge, 3m/4km SE of Bromsgrove. **30 B2** SP0069.
Hewelsfield *Glos.* ***Village***, 4m/6km W of Lydney. **19 J1** SO5602.
Hewelsfield Common *Glos.* ***Locality***, 1m/2km W of Hewelsfield. **19 J1** SO5402.
Hewenden *W.Yorks.* ***Hamlet***, 1km E of Cullingworth. SE0736.
Hewish *N.Som.* ***Locality***, comprising hamlets of East and West Hewish, 6m/9km E of Weston-super-Mare. **19 G5** ST3964.
Hewish *Som.* ***Hamlet***, 2m/3km SW of Crewkerne. **8 D4** ST4208.
Hewood *Dorset* ***Hamlet***, 5m/8km NE of Axminster. ST3502.
Heworth *T. & W.* ***Suburb***, central district of Felling. NZ2861.
Heworth *York* ***Suburb***, 1m/2km NE of York city centre. SE6152.
Hewton *Devon* ***Settlement***, 5m/8km W of Okehampton. **6 D6** SX5092.
Hexham *Northumb.* Population: 11,008. ***Town***, market town on S bank of River Tyne, 20m/32km W of Newcastle upon Tyne. Medieval priory church; 19c alterations. Weekly market in The Shambles. Racecourse 2m/3km SW, at High Yarridge. **70 E7** NY9364.
Hexham Abbey *Northumb.* ***Ecclesiastical building***, in centre of Hexham, erected in 12c over crypt of abbey built in AD 674, with Saxon throne in chancel. **70 E7** NY9364.
Hexhamshire Common *Northumb.* ***Open space***, moorland to W of Slaley Forest, 3m/5km E of Allendale Town. **61 K1** NY8754.
Hextable *Kent* ***Village***, 1m/2km N of Swanley. **23 J4** TQ5170.
Hexthorpe *S.Yorks.* ***Suburb***, to SW of Doncaster town centre. SE5602.
Hexton *Herts.* ***Village***, 5m/8km W of Hitchin. **32 E5** TL1030.
Hexworthy *Devon* ***Hamlet***, on Dartmoor, 7m/11km W of Ashburton. **5 G3** SX6572.
Hey *Gt.Man.* ***Locality***, 2m/3km E of Oldham. SD9504.
Hey *Lancs.* ***Hamlet***, 2m/3km N of Colne. SD8843.
Hey Houses *Lancs.* ***Suburb***, 1m/2km N of Lytham St. Anne's. SD3429.
Heybridge *Essex* ***Suburb***, adjoining to N of Maldon. **24 E1** TL8508.
Heybridge *Essex* ***Village***, adjoining to SW of Ingatestone, 3m/5km NW of Billericay. **24 C2** TQ6498.
Heybridge Basin *Essex* ***Locality***, with timber wharf, on Collier Reach, 1m/2km SE of Heybridge. **24 E1** TL8707.
Heybrook Bay *Devon* ***Suburb***, on coast, 4m/6km S of Plymouth across River Plym estuary. **5 F6** SX4949.
Heyden Moor *Derbys.* ***Open space***, moorland on either side of Heyden Brook, 5m/8km SW of Holmfirth. **50 C2** SE0902.
Heydon *Cambs.* ***Village***, 5m/8km E of Royston. **33 H4** TL4340.
Heydon *Norf.* ***Village***, 3m/5km N of Reepham. Hall dates from 16c. **45 F3** TG1127.
Heydon Hill *Som.* ***Mountain***, 3m/5km W of Wiveliscombe. Height 1076 feet or 328 metres. **7 J3** ST0328.
Heydour *Lincs.* ***Hamlet***, 1km NE of Oasby. **42 D2** TF0039.
Heyheads *Gt.Man.* ***Suburb***, to S of Mossley. SD9701.
Heylipoll *Arg. & B.* ***Settlement***, on Tiree, 4m/7km W of Scarinish. **78 A3** NL9743.
Heylor *Shet.* ***Settlement***, on Mainland, on S shore of Ronas Voe. **108 B4** HU2980.
Heyop *Powys* ***Settlement***, 3m/5km NW of Knighton. SO2474.

H

Heyrod *Gt.Man.* ***Suburb***, 1m/2km NE of Stalybridge. SJ9799.
Heysham *Lancs.* ***Town***, coastal town at S end of Morecambe Bay, 3m/4km SW of Morecambe, comprising Upper and Lower Heysham. Passenger ferries to Belfast, Dublin, and Londonderry. 10c church, still in use; 8c ruined chapel. **55 H3** SD4161.
Heysham Lake ***Sea feature***, stretch of sea in SE part of Morecambe Bay, W of sandbanks to S of Heysham. **55 G4** SD3757.
Heyshaw *N.Yorks.* ***Settlement***, 3m/4km S of Pateley Bridge. **57 G3** SE1761.
Heyshott *W.Suss.* ***Village***, 2m/4km S of Midhurst. **12 B5** SU8918.
Heyshott Green *W.Suss.* ***Hamlet***, to N of Heyshott, 2m/3km SE of Midhurst. SU8918.
Heyside *Gt.Man.* ***Locality***, 2m/3km N of Oldham. **49 J2** SD9307.
Heytesbury *Wilts.* ***Village***, on River Wylye, 4m/6km SE of Warminster. **20 C7** ST9242.
Heythrop *Oxon.* ***Village***, 2m/4km E of Chipping Norton. **30 E6** SP3527.
Heywood *Gt.Man.* Population: 29,286. ***Town***, former cotton town, 3m/5km E of Bury. **49 H1** SD8510.
Heywood *Wilts.* ***Village***, 2m/3km N of Westbury. **20 B6** ST8753.
Hibaldstow *N.Lincs.* Population: 1782. ***Village***, 3m/5km SW of Brigg. Site of Roman settlement 1m/2km NW. Gainsthorpe Medieval Village 2m/3km SW. **52 C2** SE9702.
Hibb's Green *Suff.* ***Hamlet***, 5m/8km N of Long Melford. TL8753.
Hickleton *S.Yorks.* ***Village***, 6m/10km W of Doncaster. **51 G2** SE4805.
Hickling *Norf.* ***Village***, 3m/4km E of Stalham. **45 J3** TG4124.
Hickling *Notts.* ***Village***, 7m/12km NW of Melton Mowbray. **41 J3** SK6929.
Hickling Broad *Norf.* ***Lake/loch***, large broad or lake 1m/2km S of Hickling. **45 J3** TG4124.
Hickling Green *Norf.* ***Village***, adjoining to S of Hickling, 3m/4km SE of Stalham. **45 J3** TG4124.
Hickling Heath *Norf.* ***Hamlet***, 1m/2km SW of Hickling. **45 J3** TG4022.
Hickmans Green *Kent* ***Locality***, 3m/5km SE of Faversham. TR0558.
Hicks Forstal *Kent* ***Locality***, 3m/4km S of Herne Bay. TR1863.
Hickstead *W.Suss.* ***Hamlet***, 4m/6km SW of Cuckfield. **13 F4** TQ2620.
Hidcote Bartrim *Glos.* ***Hamlet***, 3m/5km NE of Chipping Campden. Hidcote Manor adjoins to W, with a series of formal gardens (National Trust). SP1742.
Hidcote Boyce *Glos.* ***Hamlet***, 3m/4km NE of Chipping Campden. **30 C4** SP1742.
Hidcote Manor Garden *Glos.* ***Garden***, National Trust property, 3m/4km NE of Chipping Campden. Considered to be one of England's great gardens, designed as a series of outdoor rooms by Major Lawrence Johnston. **30 C4** SP1742.
Higginshaw *Gt.Man.* ***Locality***, 1m/2km N of Oldham. SD9306.
High Ackworth *W.Yorks.* ***Village***, forming part of Ackworth parish, 3m/4km S of Pontefract. **51 G1** SE4417.
High Angerton *Northumb.* ***Hamlet***, just S of Hartburn. NZ0985.
High Balantyre *Arg. & B.* ***Settlement***, 3m/4km NW of Inveraray. **80 B6** NN0711.
High Bankhill *Cumb.* ***Hamlet***, 1km NE of Kirkoswald. NY5642.
High Barnet *Gt.Lon.* ***Suburb***, in borough of Barnet, adjoining to NW of Chipping Barnet. TQ2396.
High Beach *Essex* ***Village***, on W edge of Epping Forest, 2m/4km SE of Waltham Abbey. **23 H2** TQ4097.
High Beeches *W.Suss.* ***Garden***, 1m/2km NE of Handcross, includes 20 acres of woodland and water gardens, and 4 acres of wildflower meadows. **13 F3** TQ2730.
High Bentham *N.Yorks.* Population: 2538. ***Village***, 7m/11km SE of Kirkby Lonsdale. **56 B3** SD6669.
High Bickington *Devon* ***Village***, 7m/11km E of Great Torrington. **6 D3** SS6020.
High Birkwith *N.Yorks.* ***Settlement***, at road end, 3m/4km N of Horton in Ribblesdale. **56 D2** SD8076.
High Blantyre *S.Lan.* ***Suburb***, to SW of Blantyre town centre. **74 E5** NS6756.
High Bonnybridge *Falk.* ***Village***, to SE of Bonnybridge across railway, 3m/5km W of Falkirk. **75 G3** NS8379.
High Borgue *D. & G.* ***Settlement***, 2m/4km W of Kirkcudbright. **65 G5** NX6451.
High Borrans *Cumb.* ***Settlement***, 2m/3km NE of Windermere. NY4300.
High Borve *W.Isles* ***Settlement***, near NW coast of Isle of Lewis, 5m/9km NE of Barvas. NB4156.
High Bradfield *S.Yorks.* ***Village***, on moors, 6m/10km NW of Sheffield. Remains of motte and bailey castle. **50 E3** SK2692.
High Bradley *N.Yorks.* ***Settlement***, to N of Low Bradley, 1m/2km SE of Skipton. SE0049.
High Bransholme *Hull* ***Settlement***, to NE of Bransholme. TA1135.
High Bray *Devon* ***Hamlet***, on W Exmoor, 6m/9km NW of South Molton. **6 E2** SS6934.
High Bridge *Cumb.* ***Settlement***, on Roe Beck, 4m/7km S of Dalston. NY3943.
High Bridge *Lincs.* ***Bridge***, 16c stone bridge over River Witham at Lincoln. Oldest bridge in England to have houses built on it. SK9771.
High Brooms *Kent* ***Suburb***, adjoining to N of Royal Tunbridge Wells. **23 J7** TQ5941.
High Bullen *Devon* ***Hamlet***, 3m/4km E of Great Torrington. **6 D3** SS5120.
High Burton *N.Yorks.* ***Settlement***, 1m/2km N of Masham. **57 H1** SE2282.
High Buston *Northumb.* ***Hamlet***, 2m/4km E of Shilbottle. **71 H3** NU2308.
High Callerton *Northumb.* ***Locality***, 2m/3km S of Ponteland. **71 G6** NZ1670.
High Casterton *Cumb.* ***Hamlet***, adjoining to S of Casterton, 1km NE of Kirkby Lonsdale. SD6278.
High Catton *E.Riding* ***Village***, 1m/2km S of Stamford Bridge. **58 D4** SE7153.
High Church *Northumb.* ***Suburb***, SW district of Morpeth. NZ1986.
High Close *Dur.* ***Settlement***, 1m/2km S of Gainford across River Tees. NZ1715.
High Cogges *Oxon.* ***Hamlet***, 1m/2km E of Cogges. **21 G1** SP3709.
High Common *Norf.* ***Locality***, 3m/4km SE of Shipdham. TF9905.
High Common *Norf.* ***Settlement***, 4m/6km E of Diss. TM1781.
High Coniscliffe *Darl.* ***Village***, on River Tees, 4m/6km W of Darlington. **62 D5** NZ2215.
High Crompton *Gt.Man.* ***Suburb***, to NW of Shaw. SD9208.
High Crosby *Cumb.* ***Hamlet***, 1km E of Low Crosby, 4m/6km NE of Carlisle. NY4559.
High Cross *Cornw.* ***Village***, 4m/7km SW of Falmouth. SW7428.
High Cross *Hants.* ***Village***, 3m/5km NW of Petersfield. **11 J2** SU7126.
High Cross *Herts.* ***Village***, 3m/5km N of Ware. **33 G7** TL3618.
High Cross *Leics.* ***Locality***, at intersection of Watling Street and Foss Way, 4m/7km SE of Hinckley, on site of Roman settlement of Venonae. SP4788.
High Cross *Newport* ***Suburb***, 2m/3km W of Newport town centre. ST2887.
High Cross *Warks.* ***Settlement***, 3m/5km E of Henley-in-Arden. SP1967.
High Cross *W.Suss.* ***Settlement***, 2m/3km W of Hurstpierpoint. TQ2417.
High Cross Bank *Derbys.* ***Suburb***, adjoining to S of Swadlincote. **40 E4** SK2817.
High Cup Nick *Cumb.* ***Inland physical feature***, cliff at head of High Cup Gill 4m/6km E of Dufton. **61 J4** NY7426.
High Dubmire *T. & W.* ***Locality***, adjoining to W of Houghton le Spring. NZ3249.
High Dyke *Cumb.* ***Settlement***, 3m/5km NW of Penrith. NY4733.
High Easter *Essex* ***Village***, 2m/3km NE of Leaden Roding. **33 K7** TL6214.
High Eggborough *N.Yorks.* ***Locality***, 1m/2km SE of Low Eggborough across M62 motorway. SE5623.
High Ellington *N.Yorks.* ***Village***, 2m/4km NW of Masham. **57 G1** SE1983.
High Entercommon *N.Yorks.* ***Settlement***, to SE of Low Entercommon, 4m/6km SE of Croft-on-Tees. **62 E6** NZ3306.
High Ercall *Tel. & W.* ***Village***, 5m/8km NW of Wellington. Hall is part of once larger house of early 17c. **38 E4** SJ5917.
High Etherley *Dur.* Population: 1849. ***Village***, 3m/5km W of Bishop Auckland. **62 C4** NZ1628.
High Fell *T. & W.* ***Suburb***, 2m/4km SE of Gateshead town centre. NZ2760.
High Felling *T. & W.* ***Suburb***, within Felling. NZ2861.
High Ferry *Lincs.* ***Settlement***, 1m/2km S of Sibsey, 4m/6km N of Boston. TF3549.
High Flats *W.Yorks.* ***Settlement***, 1m/2km SW of Denby Dale. SE2107.
High Flatts *Dur.* ***Settlement***, 1m/2km NW of Chester-le-Street. NZ2652.
High Force *Dur.* ***Waterfall***, 70 foot or 21 metre waterfall in upper Teesdale, 4m/7km NW of Middleton-in-Teesdale. **61 K4** NY8828.
High Forge *Dur.* ***Settlement***, 2m/3km NE of Stanley. NZ2254.
High Fremington *N.Yorks.* ***Hamlet***, adjoins Low Fremington, just E of Reeth. SE0499.
High Friarside *Dur.* ***Locality***, 1m/2km W of Burnopfield. NZ1656.
High Garrett *Essex* ***Village***, 3m/4km NE of Braintree. **34 B6** TL7726.
High Gate *W.Yorks.* ***Hamlet***, 2m/3km NW of Hebden Bridge. **56 E7** SD9628.
High Grange *Dur.* ***Settlement***, 2m/4km S of Crook. **62 C3** NZ1731.
High Green *Cumb.* ***Locality***, adjoining to N of Troutbeck, 3m/4km E of Ambleside. NY4103.
High Green *Norf.* ***Hamlet***, 3m/5km NE of Wymondham. **45 F5** TG1305.
High Green *Norf.* ***Locality***, W end of Brooke. TM2898.
High Green *Norf.* ***Settlement***, 4m/7km W of East Dereham. TF9214.
High Green *Norf.* ***Settlement***, 2m/3km W of Shipdham. TF9307.
High Green *Norf.* ***Village***, 1km S of Great Moulton. TM1689.
High Green *N.Yorks.* ***Settlement***, adjoining to W of Langthwaite. NZ0002.
High Green *Shrop.* ***Settlement***, adjoining to E of Chorley, 5m/8km N of Cleobury Mortimer. SO7083.
High Green *S.Yorks.* ***Locality***, 7m/11km N of Sheffield. **51 F3** SK3397.
High Green *Suff.* ***Settlement***, 1km W of Nowton. TL8560.
High Green *W.Yorks.* ***Locality***, adjoining to SE of Fenay Bridge, 4m/6km E of Huddersfield. SE1915.
High Green *Worcs.* ***Village***, 5m/8km W of Pershore. **29 H4** SO8745.
High Grindon *T. & W.* ***Suburb***, 2m/4km SW of Sunderland city centre. NZ3655.
High Habberley *Worcs.* ***Locality***, on W edge of Kidderminster. SO8077.
High Halden *Kent* ***Village***, 3m/4km NE of Tenterden. **14 D4** TQ8937.
High Halstow *Med.* ***Village***, 5m/8km NE of Strood. Northward Hill Nature Reserve to N on edge of Cooling Marshes. **24 D4** TQ7875.
High Ham *Som.* ***Village***, on high ground overlooking Sedgemoor, 3m/5km N of Langport. **8 D1** ST4231.
High Harrington *Cumb.* ***Hamlet***, 1m/2km E of Harrington. **60 B4** NY0025.
High Harrogate *N.Yorks.* ***Suburb***, 1m/2km E of Harrogate town centre. **57 J4** SE3055.
High Hartington *Northumb.* ***Settlement***, 3m/5km NE of Kirkwhelpington. NZ0288.
High Haswell *Dur.* ***Locality***, 1km NW of Haswell. NZ3643.
High Hatton *Shrop.* ***Hamlet***, 3m/4km S of Hodnet. **39 F3** SJ6124.
High Hawsker *N.Yorks.* ***Village***, 3m/4km SE of Whitby. **63 J2** NZ9207.
High Hazels *S.Yorks.* ***Suburb***, 3m/5km E of Sheffield city centre, in district of Darnall. SK3987.
High Heath *Shrop.* ***Settlement***, 1km NW of Hinstock. **39 F3** SJ6827.
High Heath *W.Mid.* ***Suburb***, 2m/4km NE of Walsall. SK0202.
High Hesket *Cumb.* ***Village***, 8m/13km SE of Carlisle. **61 F2** NY4744.
High Hesleden *Dur.* ***Village***, 1km E of Hesleden. NZ4438.
High Hoyland *S.Yorks.* ***Village***, 5m/8km NW of Barnsley. **50 E2** SE2710.
High Hunsley *E.Riding* ***Settlement***, 6m/10km SW of Beverley. **59 F6** SE9535.
High Hurstwood *E.Suss.* ***Hamlet***, 2m/3km N of Buxted. **13 H4** TQ4926.
High Hutton *N.Yorks.* ***Village***, 3m/5km SW of Malton. Sites of Roman buildings 1m/2km NE. Parish known as Huttons Ambo. **58 D3** SE7568.
High Ireby *Cumb.* ***Hamlet***, 1m/2km S of Ireby. **60 D3** NY2338.
High Kilburn *N.Yorks.* ***Hamlet***, up hill to E of Kilburn. **58 B1** SE5179.
High Killerby *N.Yorks.* ***Settlement***, above Cayton Bay, 3m/5km SE of Scarborough. TA0683.
High Kingthorpe *N.Yorks.* ***Settlement***, 3m/5km NE of Pickering. SE8386.
High Knipe *Cumb.* ***Settlement***, 4m/6km NW of Shap. NY5219.
High Knowes *Northumb.* ***Mountain***, in Cheviot Hills, 2m/3km NW of Alnham. Height 1292 feet or 394 metres. **70 E2** NT9612.
High Lands *Dur.* ***Hamlet***, 1m/2km E of Butterknowle. NZ1225.
High Lane *Derbys.* ***Settlement***, 2m/3km W of Ilkeston. **41 G1** SK4342.
High Lane *Gt.Man.* Population: 4861. ***Village***, 5m/8km SE of Stockport. SJ9585.
High Lane *Staffs.* ***Locality***, 1m/2km S of Brown Edge. SJ9052.
High Lane *Staffs.* ***Settlement***, adjoining to SE of Alsagers Bank. SJ8048.
High Lane *Worcs.* ***Hamlet***, 4m/7km NE of Bromyard. **29 F2** SO6760.
High Lanes *Cornw.* ***Settlement***, 2m/3km SW of Mevagissey. SW9843.
High Lanes *Cornw.* ***Suburb***, on SE side of Hayle. SW5637.
High Laver *Essex* ***Hamlet***, 4m/6km N of Chipping Ongar. **23 J1** TL5208.
High Legh *Ches.* ***Village***, 5m/8km NW of Knutsford. **49 G4** SJ7084.
High Leven *Stock.* ***Hamlet***, 2m/3km E of Yarm. **63 F5** NZ4412.
High Littleton *B. & N.E.Som.* ***Village***, 3m/5km NW of Midsomer Norton. **19 K6** ST6458.
High Longthwaite *Cumb.* ***Locality***, 1m/2km S of Wigton. NY2546.
High Lorton *Cumb.* ***Village***, 4m/6km SE of Cockermouth. **60 C4** NY1625.
High Marishes *N.Yorks.* ***Hamlet***, 4m/7km N of Malton. SE8178.
High Marnham *Notts.* ***Village***, 3m/4km N of Sutton on Trent. SK8070.
High Melton *S.Yorks.* ***Village***, 4m/7km W of Doncaster. **51 H2** SE5001.
High Mickley *Northumb.* ***Village***, 2m/3km SW of Prudhoe. NZ0761.
High Moor *Derbys.* ***Hamlet***, 1km E of Killamarsh. SK4680.
High Moor *Lancs.* ***Hamlet***, 1m/2km NE of Parbold. SD5011.
High Moor *Lancs.* ***Locality***, 4m/6km NW of Kirkham. SD3836.
High Moor *N.Yorks.* ***Open space***, moorland 3m/5km NW of Richmond. **62 C6** NZ1304.
High Moorsley *T. & W.* ***Hamlet***, 2m/3km SW of Hetton-le-Hole. NZ3345.
High Nash *Glos.* ***Locality***, adjoining to S of Coleford. SO5710.
High Neb *S.Yorks.* ***Mountain***, at SW edge of Hallam Moors, 3m/4km N of Hathersage. Height 1502 feet or 458 metres. **50 E4** SK2384.
High Newport *T. & W.* ***Suburb***, 2m/3km SW of Sunderland city centre. NZ3854.
High Newton *Cumb.* ***Hamlet***, 2m/3km NW of Lindale. **55 H1** SD4082.
High Newton-by-the-Sea *Northumb.* ***Village***, 2m/3km N of Embleton. **71 H1** NU2325.
High Nibthwaite *Cumb.* ***Hamlet***, at S end of Coniston Water. **60 D7** SD2989.

High Offley *Staffs.* ***Village***, 5m/8km NE of Newport. **39 G3** SJ7826.
High Ongar *Essex* ***Village***, 1m/2km NE of Chipping Ongar. **23 J1** TL5603.
High Onn *Staffs.* ***Hamlet***, 1m/2km SW of Church Eaton. **40 A4** SJ8216.
High Onn Wharf *Staffs.* ***Settlement***, on Shropshire Union Canal, 1km NE of High Onn. SJ8316.
High Orchard *Glos.* ***Suburb***, in SW part of Gloucester. SO8217.
High Park Corner *Essex* ***Village***, 4m/6km SE of Colchester. TM0320.
High Peak *Derbys.* ***Large natural feature***, area of millstone grit hills at NW of Peak District National Park, E of Hayfield and NW of Castleton, rising to flat-topped mountain of Kinder Scout, with highest point being The Peak at 2086 feet or 636 metres. **50 C4** SK0687.
High Peak Estate *Derbys.* ***Open space***, National Trust property in High Peak area of The Pennines, to N of Edale. SK1188.
High Pike *Cumb.* ***Mountain***, on Caldbeck Fells, 3m/5km S of Caldbeck. Height 2158 feet or 658 metres. **60 E3** NY3134.
High Possil *Glas.* ***Suburb***, to N of Possil Park, 2m/3km N of Glasgow city centre. NS5968.
High Raise *Cumb.* ***Mountain***, 1m/2km N of Harrison Stickle on Langdale Pikes. Height 2499 feet or 762 metres. **60 D6** NY2809.
High Raise *Cumb.* ***Mountain***, in Lake District, 2m/3km W of Haweswater Reservoir. Height 2631 feet or 802 metres. **60 F5** NY4413.
High Risby *N.Lincs.* ***Settlement***, 2m/3km W of Appleby, 3m/5km NE of Scunthorpe town centre. **52 C1** SE9114.
High Roding *Essex* ***Village***, 3m/5km SW of Great Dunmow. **33 K7** TL6017.
High Row *Cumb.* ***Locality***, 2m/4km SE of Hesket Newmarket. NY3535.
High Salvington *W.Suss.* ***Suburb***, 3m/5km NW of Worthing town centre. **12 E6** TQ1206.
High Scales *Cumb.* ***Locality***, 3m/5km NE of Aspatria. NY1845.
High Seat ***Mountain***, astride border of North Yorkshire and Cumbria, to W of Birkdale Common, 6m/9km W of Keld. Height 2326 feet or 709 metres. **61 K6** NY8001.
High Seat *Cumb.* ***Mountain***, between Derwent Water and Thirlmere, 4m/6km S of Keswick. Height 1994 feet or 608 metres. **60 D5** NY2818.
High Seat *Sc.Bord.* ***Mountain***, 3m/4km N of Teviothead. Height 1138 feet or 347 metres. **69 K3** NT4009.
High Seaton *Cumb.* ***Locality***, adjoining to N of Seaton. NY0130.
High Shaw *N.Yorks.* ***Settlement***, on hillside, just above Hardraw Force, 1m/2km N of Hawes across River Ure. **61 K7** SD8691.
High Side *Cumb.* ***Locality***, 3m/5km SE of Cockermouth. NY1628.
High Spania *Notts.* ***Suburb***, adjoining to N of Kimberley. SK4945.
High Spen *T. & W.* Population: 1757. ***Village***, 3m/5km S of Ryton. **71 G7** NZ1359.
High Stakesby *N.Yorks.* ***Suburb***, W district of Whitby. NZ8810.
High Stile *Cumb.* ***Mountain***, in Lake District, 1m/2km S of Buttermere hamlet. Height 2644 feet or 806 metres. **60 C5** NY1614.
High Stoop *Dur.* ***Settlement***, 2m/3km NW of Tow Law. NZ1040.
High Street *Cambs.* ***Locality***, adjoining to W of Dry Drayton. TL3762.
High Street *Cornw.* ***Settlement***, 3m/5km W of St. Austell. **3 G3** SW9653.
High Street *Cumb.* ***Mountain***, in Lake District, 2m/3km W of S end of Haweswater Reservoir. Height 2716 feet or 828 metres. **60 F5** NY4411.
High Street *Kent* ***Locality***, adjoining to W of Hawkhurst. **14 C4** TQ7430.
High Street *Norf.* ***Locality***, 1km N of Wendling. TF9313.
High Street *Suff.* ***Hamlet***, 4m/6km N of Orford. **35 J3** TM4355.
High Street *Suff.* ***Settlement***, 1km N of Long Melford. TL8647.
High Street *Suff.* ***Settlement***, 4m/6km SE of Bungay. TM3684.
High Street *Suff.* ***Settlement***, 1m/2km NW of Darsham. TM4170.
High Street Green *Suff.* ***Hamlet***, 3m/5km SW of Stowmarket. **34 E3** TM0055.
High Throston *Hart.* ***Suburb***, 2m/3km NW of Hartlepool town centre. **63 F3** NZ4833.
High Town *Cambs.* ***Locality***, S end of Burwell. TL5866.
High Town *Staffs.* ***Suburb***, 1m/2km NE of Cannock. SJ9912.
High Toynton *Lincs.* ***Village***, 2m/3km E of Horncastle. **53 F6** TF2869.
High Trewhitt *Northumb.* ***Settlement***, 4m/6km NW of Rothbury. **71 F3** NU0005.
High Urpeth *Dur.* ***Hamlet***, 3m/5km NW of Chester-le-Street. NZ2353.
High Warden *Northumb.* ***Hamlet***, 3m/4km NW of Hexham. NY9167.
High Westwood *Dur.* ***Hamlet***, 1m/2km E of Ebchester. NZ1155.
High Wham *Dur.* ***Hamlet***, 1km NE of Butterknowle. NZ1126.
High Whinnow *Cumb.* ***Locality***, 2m/3km NW of Thursby. NY3051.
High Wigsell *E.Suss.* ***Hamlet***, 1km to S of Great Wigsell. TQ7626.
High Willhays *Devon* ***Mountain***, summit of Dartmoor, 4m/6km S of Okehampton. Height 2037 feet or 621 metres. **6 D7** SX5889.
High Wincobank *S.Yorks.* ***Suburb***, part of Wincobank suburb of Sheffield, along with Low Wincobank. SK3791.
High Woods Country Park *Essex* ***Leisure/recreation***, country park including woodland, grassland and farmland 1m/2km N of Colchester. Central lake is fed by tributary of River Colne, with marshland developing on S periphery of park. **34 D6** TM0026.
High Woolaston *Glos.* ***Hamlet***, to W of Woolaston, 4m/7km NE of Chepstow. **19 J2** ST5799.
High Worsall *N.Yorks.* ***Hamlet***, 3m/5km SW of Yarm. NZ3809.
High Wray *Cumb.* ***Hamlet***, 2m/3km NE of Hawkshead. **60 E7** SD3799.
High Wych *Herts.* ***Village***, 1m/2km W of Sawbridgeworth. **33 H7** TL4614.
High Wycombe *Bucks.* Population: 71,718. ***Town***, administration and service centre on River Wye, on S side of Chiltern Hills, 28m/45km NW of London. Site of Roman villa 1km SE of town centre. **22 B2** SU8692.
High Yarridge *Northumb.* ***Locality***, on N side of Hexham Racecourse, 2m/3km SW of Hexham. NY9162.
Higham *Derbys.* ***Village***, 3m/4km S of Clay Cross. **51 F7** SK3959.
Higham *Kent* Population: 2670. ***Village***, 3m/5km NW of Rochester. **24 D4** TQ7171.
Higham *Lancs.* ***Village***, 2m/3km NE of Padiham. **56 D6** SD8036.
Higham *S.Yorks.* ***Village***, adjoining to S of Barugh Green, 2m/3km W of Barnsley. SE3107.
Higham *Suff.* ***Village***, 7m/11km W of Bury St. Edmunds. **34 B2** TL7465.
Higham *Suff.* ***Village***, 4m/7km S of Hadleigh. **34 E5** TM0335.
Higham Common *S.Yorks.* ***Locality***, adjoining to S of Higham, 2m/3km W of Barnsley. SE3106.
Higham Cross *M.K.* ***Settlement***, 1km NW of Hanslope. SP7847.
Higham Dykes *Northumb.* ***Settlement***, 3m/4km NW of Ponteland. **71 G6** NZ1375.
Higham Ferrers *Northants.* Population: 5345. ***Small town***, 4m/7km E of Wellingborough. Medieval church with fine spire. Birthplace of Archbishop Chichele. **32 C2** SP9668.
Higham Gobion *Beds.* ***Village***, 4m/6km S of Clophill. **32 E5** TL1032.
Higham Hill *Gt.Lon.* ***Suburb***, in borough of Waltham Forest, 1m/2km NW of Walthamstow town centre. TQ3690.
Higham on the Hill *Leics.* ***Village***, 3m/5km NE of Nuneaton. **41 F6** SP3895.
Higham Wood *Kent* ***Suburb***, in NE part of Tonbridge. **23 K7** TQ6048.
Highampton *Devon* ***Village***, 4m/6km W of Hatherleigh. **6 C5** SS4804.
Highams Park *Gt.Lon.* ***Suburb***, in borough of Waltham Forest, 1m/2km N of Walthamstow town centre. TQ3791.
Highbridge *Hants.* ***Settlement***, on River Itchen, 2m/3km NE of Eastleigh. SU4621.
Highbridge *Som.* Population: 9794. ***Small town***, on River Brue, near its mouth, 2m/3km SE of Burnham-on-Sea. **19 G7** ST3247.
Highbrook *W.Suss.* ***Hamlet***, 2m/3km S of West Hoathly. **13 G3** TQ3630.
Highburton *W.Yorks.* ***Village***, 4m/6km SE of Huddersfield. **50 D1** SE1913.
Highbury *Gt.Lon.* ***Suburb***, in borough of Islington, 4m/6km NE of Charing Cross. TQ3285.
Highbury *Som.* ***Village***, 4m/6km S of Radstock. **19 K7** ST6849.
Highbury Garden *Dorset* ***Garden***, in West Moors, 7m/11km NE of Wimborne. Unusual and rare plants of interest to botanists and plant collectors, set among mature trees. **10 B4** SU0803.
Highbury Vale *Nott.* ***Suburb***, 3m/5km NW of Nottingham city centre. **41 H1** SK5444.
Highclere *Hants.* Population: 2905. ***Village***, 6m/9km NE of Hurstbourne Tarrant. **21 H5** SU4360.
Highclere Castle *Hants.* ***Historic house***, 1m/2km SE of Highclere and 5m/8km S of Newbury. Seat of Carnarvon family. Remodelled in 19c by Charles Barry. Large park. **21 H6** SU4458.
Highcliffe *Dorset* ***Suburb***, seaside district, 4m/6km E of Christchurch town centre. **10 D5** SZ2192.
Highdown Hill *W.Suss.* ***Hill***, 1m/2km E of Angmering. Archaeological site (National Trust), with finds dating back to Late Bronze Age. Height 266 feet or 81 metres. **12 D6** TQ0904.
Higher Alham *Som.* ***Settlement***, 4m/6km N of Bruton. ST6741.
Higher Ansty *Dorset* ***Hamlet***, forms part of Ansty locality in parish of Hilton, 6m/10km N of Puddletown. **9 G4** ST7603.
Higher Ashton *Devon* ***Hamlet***, part of Ashton parish, along with Lower Ashton, 3m/5km N of Chudleigh. **7 G7** SX8584.
Higher Ballam *Lancs.* ***Settlement***, 2m/3km NE of Lytham St. Anne's. **55 G6** SD3630.
Higher Bartle *Lancs.* ***Settlement***, 1km S of Woodplumpton, 3m/5km NW of Preston. SD5033.
Higher Berry End *Beds.* ***Settlement***, on E side of Woburn Park, 4m/7km SW of Ampthill. SP9834.
Higher Blackley *Gt.Man.* ***Suburb***, 4m/6km N of Manchester city centre. **49 H2** SD8404.
Higher Bockhampton *Dorset* ***Hamlet***, 2m/4km NE of Dorchester. Birthplace, in small thatched house (National Trust) of Thomas Hardy, 1840. **9 G5** SY7292.
Higher Boscaswell *Cornw.* ***Settlement***, 2m/3km NE of St. Just. SW3834.
Higher Brixham *Torbay* ***Suburb***, S district of Brixham. **5 K5** SX9155.
Higher Broughton *Gt.Man.* ***Suburb***, 2m/3km NW of Manchester city centre. SD8200.
Higher Burrow *Som.* ***Hamlet***, to NW of Burrow, 2m/4km NW of South Petherton. ST4020.
Higher Burwardsley *Ches.* ***Hamlet***, to E of Burwardsley. SJ5256.
Higher Chalmington *Dorset* ***Settlement***, to N of Chalmington, 2m/3km N of Maiden Newton. ST5901.
Higher Cheriton *Devon* ***Settlement***, 4m/6km W of Honiton. **7 J5** ST1000.
Higher Chieflowman *Devon* ***Hamlet***, 4m/6km NE of Tiverton. ST0015.
Higher Chillington *Som.* ***Hamlet***, to S of Chillington, 3m/5km SE of Ilminster. ST3810.
Higher Combe *Som.* ***Hamlet***, 2m/3km NW of Dulverton. SS9030.
Higher Crackington *Cornw.* *See Crackington.*
Higher Dinting *Derbys.* ***Hamlet***, 1km E of Dinting Vale. SK0294.
Higher Disley *Ches.* ***Locality***, adjoining to SE of Disley. SJ9784.
Higher Downs *Cornw.* ***Hamlet***, 4m/6km S of Hayle. SW5530.
Higher Drift *Cornw.* ***Settlement***, to W of Lower Drift, 2m/3km W of Newlyn. SW4328.
Higher Durston *Som.* ***Hamlet***, to W of Durston, 4m/7km NE of Taunton. ST2828.
Higher Folds *Gt.Man.* ***Locality***, 2m/3km E of Leigh. SD6800.
Higher Gabwell *Devon* ***Hamlet***, forms part of Gabwell locality, along with Lower Gabwell, about 3m/5km N of Torquay. **5 K4** SX9269.
Higher Gamesley *Derbys.* ***Locality***, to S of Gamesley. SK0194.
Higher Gidcott *Devon* ***Hamlet***, 5m/9km NE of Holsworthy. SS4009.
Higher Green *Gt.Man.* ***Locality***, 1m/2km SE of Tyldesley. **49 G3** SD7000.
Higher Halstock Leigh *Dorset* ***Settlement***, 2m/3km W of Halstock. ST5107.
Higher Harpers *Lancs.* ***Village***, 2m/3km W of Nelson. SD8337.
Higher Hurdsfield *Ches.* ***Locality***, 1km NE of Hurdsfield. SJ9274.
Higher Kingcombe *Dorset* ***Settlement***, 4m/6km NW of Maiden Newton. **8 E5** SY5499.
Higher Kinnerton *Flints.* ***Village***, 2m/4km NE of Hope. SJ3261.
Higher Melcombe *Dorset* ***Hamlet***, 1km W of Melcombe Bingham. ST7402.
Higher Metcombe *Devon* ***Hamlet***, 1m/2km W of Metcombe. SY0692.
Higher Muddiford *Devon* ***Hamlet***, to W of Muddiford, 3m/5km N of Barnstaple. SS5638.
Higher Northcott *Devon* ***Settlement***, forms locality of Northcott, along with Northcott Hamlet, 3m/5km SW of Ashwater. SX3492.
Higher Nyland *Dorset* ***Settlement***, 5m/8km SW of Gillingham. ST7322.
Higher Ogden *Gt.Man.* ***Locality***, 2m/3km E of Milnrow. SD9512.
Higher Penwortham *Lancs.* ***Suburb***, 2m/3km W of Preston across River Ribble. SD5128.
Higher Priestacott *Devon* ***Hamlet***, 6m/9km SE of Holsworthy. SX3996.
Higher Runcorn *Halton* ***Suburb***, to S of Runcorn town centre. SJ5182.
Higher Shotton *Flints.* ***Suburb***, S district of Shotton. SJ3067.
Higher Shurlach *Ches.* ***Suburb***, 2m/3km SE of Northwich. SJ6772.
Higher Standen *Lancs.* ***Settlement***, 1m/2km SE of Clitheroe. SD7440.
Higher Street *Som.* ***Locality***, contained within Curry Mallet, 5m/8km NW of Ilminster. ST3321.
Higher Studfold *N.Yorks.* ***Locality***, to N of Studfold, 1m/2km S of Horton in Ribblesdale. SD8170.
Higher Tale *Devon* ***Hamlet***, 4m/7km SE of Cullompton. **7 J5** ST0601.
Higher Thrushgill *Lancs.* ***Settlement***, on edge of wooded area on E side of Goodber Common, 4m/7km S of Low Bentham. **56 B3** SD6562.
Higher Town *Cornw.* ***Hamlet***, 6m/9km N of St. Austell. SX0061.
Higher Town *I.o.S.* ***Village***, on S part of St. Martin's. **2 C1** SV9215.
Higher Walreddon *Devon* ***Settlement***, 2m/3km S of Tavistock. **4 E3** SX4871.
Higher Walton *Lancs.* Population: 5069. ***Village***, 2m/3km E of Walton-le-Dale. **55 J7** SD5827.
Higher Walton *Warr.* ***Village***, 2m/3km S of Warrington. **48 E4** SJ5985.
Higher Wambrook *Som.* ***Hamlet***, 1km N of Wambrook, 2m/3km W of Chard. ST2908.
Higher Waterston *Dorset* ***Locality***, 2m/4km NW of Puddletown. SY7295.
Higher Whatcombe *Dorset* ***Settlement***, forms locality of Whatcombe, along with Lower Whatcombe, 4m/7km SW of Blandford Forum. **9 H4** ST8301.
Higher Wheelton *Lancs.* ***Village***, 1m/2km NE of Wheelton. SD6122.
Higher White Tor *Devon* ***Mountain***, 2m/3km W of Postbridge, in Dartmoor National Park. Height 1722 feet or 525 metres. **5 G3** SX6178.
Higher Whiteleigh *Cornw.* ***Hamlet***, 8m/13km NW of Launceston. SX2494.
Higher Whitley *Ches.* ***Village***, 5m/8km NW of Northwich. **49 F4** SJ6180.
Higher Woodsford *Dorset* ***Settlement***, 1m/2km S of Woodsford. SY7689.
Higher Wraxall *Dorset* ***Hamlet***, 3m/4km NW of Maiden Newton. ST5601.
Higher Wych *Ches.* ***Hamlet***, 3m/5km NW of Whitchurch. **38 D1** SJ4943.

Higherford *Lancs.* ***Locality***, 2m/3km W of Colne across Leeds and Liverpool Canal. SD8640.
Highfield *Devon* ***Locality***, 7m/11km E of Okehampton. SX7097.
Highfield *E.Riding* ***Hamlet***, 5m/8km N of Howden. **58 D6** SE7236.
Highfield *Gt.Man.* ***Suburb***, 2m/3km SW of Wigan town centre. SD5503.
Highfield *Gt.Man.* ***Suburb***, 2m/3km S of Bolton. SD7105.
Highfield *Herts.* ***Suburb***, 1m/2km N of Hemel Hempstead town centre. TL0608.
Highfield *N.Ayr.* ***Settlement***, 1m/2km E of Dalry. **74 B5** NS3050.
Highfield *Northumb.* ***Forest/woodland***, part of Kielder Forest, 3m/4km N of Falstone. **70 C4** NY7391.
Highfield *Oxon.* ***Suburb***, in NW part of Bicester. SP5723.
Highfield *S.Yorks.* ***Suburb***, to S of Sheffield city centre. SK3585.
Highfield *S'ham.* ***Suburb***, N district of Southampton. SU4214.
Highfield *Stock.* ***Locality***, adjoining to N of Egglescliffe. NZ4214.
Highfield *T. & W.* ***Village***, adjoining to W of Rowlands Gill, 4m/6km S of Ryton. **62 C1** NZ1458.
Highfields *Cambs.* ***Village***, 6m/10km W of Cambridge. **33 G3** TL3558.
Highfields *Derbys.* ***Hamlet***, 2m/3km NE of Clay Cross. SK4265.
Highfields *Northumb.* ***Suburb***, N district of Berwick-upon-Tweed. NT9954.
Highfields *S.Yorks.* ***Locality***, adjoining to S of Adwick le Street, 3m/5km NW of Doncaster. SE5406.
Highgate *E.Suss.* ***Settlement***, adjoining to S of Forest Row. TQ4234.
Highgate *Gt.Lon.* ***Suburb***, in borough of Haringey, 5m/8km N of Charing Cross. TQ2887.
Highgate *N.Yorks.* ***Locality***, 3m/4km SE of Whitley, 4m/7km NE of Askern. SE5919.
Highgate *S.Yorks.* ***Locality***, adjoining to W of Goldthorpe, 3m/4km E of Darfield. SE4503.
Highgate Common Country Park *Staffs.* ***Leisure/recreation***, country park with over 280 acres of heathland and scattered woodland 7m/11km W of Dudley. Views S to Kinver Edge. **40 A6** SO8390.
Highgate Howe *N.Yorks.* ***Settlement***, 1m/2km E of Whitby. NZ9110.
Highgreen Manor *Northumb.* ***Settlement***, 3m/4km N of Greenhaugh, on E side of Kielder Forest. **70 D4** NY8091.
Highland Wildlife Park *High.* ***Leisure/recreation***, wildlife park 4m/6km NE of Kingussie, with breeding groups of Scottish mammals and birds, including some now extinct in the wild in Scotland. Visitor Centre includes exhibition on effects on man in region. **89 F4** NH8004.
Highlane *Ches.* ***Settlement***, 4m/6km SW of Macclesfield. **49 H6** SJ8868.
Highlane *Derbys.* Population: 1509. ***Village***, 5m/7km SE of Sheffield. **51 G4** SK4082.
Highlanes *Staffs.* ***Settlement***, 2m/3km W of Slindon. SJ7932.
Highlaws *Cumb.* ***Settlement***, 2m/3km W of Abbeytown. **60 C2** NY1449.
Highleadon *Glos.* ***Hamlet***, 5m/8km NW of Gloucester. **29 G6** SO7723.
Highleigh *Devon* ***Settlement***, 3m/4km S of Dulverton. SS9123.
Highleigh *W.Suss.* ***Village***, 3m/5km N of Selsey. **12 B7** SZ8498.
Highley *Shrop.* Population: 3299. ***Village***, 6m/10km S of Bridgnorth. **39 G7** SO7483.
Highmead *Cere.* ***Locality***, 1m/2km SW of Llanbydder. **26 E4** SN5043.
Highmoor *Cumb.* ***Locality***, 1km SE of Wigton. NY2647.
Highmoor *Oxon.* ***Hamlet***, 4m/7km W of Henley-on-Thames. SU7084.
Highmoor Cross *Oxon.* ***Hamlet***, to S of Highmoor, 4m/7km NW of Henley-on-Thames. **21 K3** SU7084.
Highmoor Hill *Mon.* ***Settlement***, 1m/2km SW of Caerwent. **19 H3** ST4689.
Highnam *Glos.* Population: 2130. ***Village***, scattered village, 3m/4km W of Gloucester. **29 G7** SO7819.
Highnam Green *Glos.* ***Hamlet***, 3m/4km W of Gloucester. SO7920.
Highstead *Kent* ***Settlement***, 3m/4km SE of Herne Bay. **25 J5** TR2166.
Highsted *Kent* ***Hamlet***, 1m/2km S of Sittingbourne. **25 F5** TQ9061.
Highstreet *Kent* ***Hamlet***, 3m/5km SW of Whitstable. TR0862.
Highstreet Green *Essex* ***Hamlet***, 4m/7km NW of Halstead. **34 B5** TL7634.
Highstreet Green *Surr.* ***Hamlet***, 5m/8km E of Haslemere. SU9835.
Hightae *D. & G.* ***Village***, 3m/4km S of Lochmaben. **69 F6** NY0978.
Highter's Heath *W.Mid.* ***Suburb***, 5m/8km S of Birmingham city centre. SP0879.
Hightown *Ches.* ***Suburb***, 1m/2km SE of Congleton town centre. **49 H6** SJ8762.
Hightown *Hants.* ***Settlement***, adjoining to E of Ringwood. SU1704.
Hightown *Mersey.* Population: 2141. ***Village***, 2m/4km S of Formby. **48 B2** SD3003.
Hightown *S'ham.* ***Suburb***, 4m/6km E of Southampton city centre across River Itchen. SU4711.
Hightown *W.Yorks.* ***Locality***, 1m/2km W of Liversedge. SE1824.
Hightown Green *Suff.* ***Hamlet***, 5m/8km W of Stowmarket. TL9756.
Highway *Cornw.* ***Locality***, 1m/2km NE of Redruth. SW7143.
Highway *Here.* ***Locality***, 7m/11km NW of Hereford. SO4549.
Highway *Wilts.* ***Hamlet***, 4m/6km NE of Calne. **20 D4** SU0474.
Highway *W. & M.* ***Suburb***, W district of Maidenhead. SU8681.
Highweek *Devon* ***Suburb***, 1m/2km NW of Newton Abbot town centre. **5 J3** SX8472.
Highwood *Worcs.* ***Hamlet***, 4m/6km E of Tenbury Wells. SO6567.
Highwood Hill *Gt.Lon.* ***Suburb***, in borough of Barnet, 1m/2km N of Mill Hill and 10m/16km NW of Charing Cross. TQ2193.
Highwood Quarter *Essex* ***Hamlet***, 4m/7km SW of Chelmsford. TL6404.
Highworth *Swin.* Population: 8259. ***Small town***, 6m/9km NE of Swindon. Cotswold stone Georgian buildings. Large church with some Norman carvings. **21 F2** SU2092.
Hilborough *Norf.* ***Village***, 6m/9km S of Swaffham. **44 C5** TF8200.
Hilbre Island *Mersey.* ***Island***, one of two small islands at seaward end of River Dee estuary, 1m/2km off Hilbre Point at NW tip of Wirral peninsula. Little Hilbre Island is to SE. **47 K4** SJ1887.
Hilcote *Derbys.* ***Village***, 3m/4km NE of Alfreton. SK4558.
Hilcott *Wilts.* ***Hamlet***, 4m/6km W of Pewsey. **20 E6** SU1158.
Hildasay *Shet.* ***Island***, uninhabited island of 255 acres or 103 hectares 3m/5km W of Scalloway, Mainland. **109 C8** HU3540.
Hilden Park *Kent* ***Settlement***, adjoining to E of Hildenborough. **23 J7** TQ5748.
Hildenborough *Kent* ***Village***, to NW of Tonbridge. **23 J7** TQ5648.
Hildenley *N.Yorks.* ***Settlement***, 3m/4km W of Malton. SE7470.
Hildersham *Cambs.* ***Village***, 4m/7km NE of Great Chesterford. **33 J4** TL5448.
Hilderstone *Staffs.* ***Village***, 3m/5km E of Stone. **40 B2** SJ9434.
Hilderthorpe *E.Riding* ***Suburb***, to S of Bridlington. **59 H3** TA1765.
Hilfield *Dorset* ***Hamlet***, 7m/12km S of Sherborne. **9 F4** ST6305.
Hilgay *Norf.* ***Village***, 3m/5km S of Downham Market. **44 A6** TL6298.
Hilgay Fen *Norf.* ***Open space***, fenland 3m/4km W of Southery. **43 J6** TL5795.
Hill *Cumb.* ***Locality***, adjoining to N of Ings, 2m/3km E of Windermere. SD4498.
Hill *Pembs.* ***Settlement***, 1m/2km NW of Saundersfoot. SN1206.
Hill *S.Glos.* ***Village***, 3m/5km N of Thornbury. **19 K2** ST6495.
Hill *Warks.* ***Hamlet***, 4m/7km NE of Southam. SP4567.
Hill *Worcs.* ***Settlement***, 3m/5km NE of Pershore. SO9848.
Hill Bottom *Oxon.* ***Settlement***, adjoining to N of Whitchurch Hill, 2m/3km N of Pangbourne. SU6479.
Hill Brow ***Village***, on Hampshire and West Sussex border, 4m/6km NE of Petersfield. **11 J2** SU7926.
Hill Chorlton *Staffs.* ***Village***, 5m/8km SW of Newcastle-under-Lyme. **39 G2** SJ7939.
Hill Common *Norf.* ***Settlement***, at N end of Hickling Broad, 3m/5km SE of Stalham. TG4122.
Hill Cottages *N.Yorks.* ***Settlement***, 1m/2km NW of Rosedale Abbey. SE7197.
Hill Court *Here.* ***Garden***, 3m/4km SW of Ross-on-Wye. Bronze and silver fountain garden, herbaceous borders, flowering shrubs and woodland. **28 E6** SO5721.
Hill Crest *Worcs.* ***Locality***, at W edge of Kidderminster. SO8175.
Hill Croome *Worcs.* ***Settlement***, 5m/8km N of Tewkesbury. SO8840.
Hill Dale *Lancs.* ***Village***, 1m/2km N of Parbold. SD4912.
Hill Deverill *Wilts.* ***Hamlet***, adjoining to S of Longbridge Deverill, 3m/5km S of Warminster. ST8640.
Hill Dyke *Lincs.* ***Hamlet***, 3m/4km NE of Boston. **43 G1** TF3447.
Hill End *Dur.* ***Settlement***, 1m/2km SW of Frosterley. **62 B3** NZ0136.
Hill End *Fife* ***Hamlet***, 2m/3km SE of Powmill. **75 J1** NT0395.
Hill End *Glos.* ***Hamlet***, 3m/5km N of Tewkesbury. SO9037.
Hill End *Gt.Lon.* ***Settlement***, in borough of Hillingdon, 2m/3km S of Rickmansworth. TQ0491.
Hill End *N.Yorks.* ***Settlement***, just E of Hazlewood, 1m/2km E of Bolton Abbey. **57 F4** SE0854.
Hill End *W.Yorks.* ***Suburb***, 3m/4km W of Leeds city centre. SE2533.
Hill End *Worcs.* ***Suburb***, in NE part of Droitwich Spa. SO9063.
Hill Green *Essex* ***Hamlet***, adjoining to NE of Clavering, 3m/5km W of Newport. TL4832.
Hill Head *Hants.* ***Locality***, on shore of The Solent, 1m/2km NW of Lee-on-the-Solent. **11 G4** SU5402.
Hill Hook *W.Mid.* ***Suburb***, 3m/5km NW of Sutton Coldfield town centre. SK1000.
Hill House *Arg. & B.* ***Historic house***, National Trust for Scotland property to N of Helensburgh. Built at beginning of 20c for Walter Blackie, an excellent example of domestic architecture by Charles Rennie Mackintosh. **74 A2** NS3088.
Hill Houses *Shrop.* ***Settlement***, 3m/5km NW of Cleobury Mortimer. SO6379.
Hill Mountain *Pembs.* ***Hamlet***, 5m/8km S of Haverfordwest. SM9708.
Hill o' Many Stanes *High.* ***Historic/prehistoric site***, prehistoric arrangement (Historic Scotland) of about 200 stones in parallel rows, situated NE of Mid Clyth on Hill of Mid Clyth, 9m/14km SW of Wick. **105 H5** ND2938.
Hill of Achmore *Moray* ***Mountain***, N flank of Muckle Lapprach, 7m/11km W of Bridgend. Height 1673 feet or 510 metres. **89 K1** NJ2630.
Hill of Aitnoch *High.* ***Mountain***, in Nairn district, 3m/5km S of Ferness. Height 1355 feet or 413 metres. **89 G1** NH9739.
Hill of Alyth *P. & K.* ***Hill***, to N of Alyth. Height 968 feet or 295 metres. **82 D2** NO2450.
Hill of Arisdale *Shet.* ***Hill***, running SW to NE, above Aris Dale valley to E, and 1km SW of Ward of Otterswick. Height 689 feet or 210 metres. **108 D4** HU4984.
Hill of Auchlee *Aber.* ***Hill***, with Boswell's Monument at summit, 2m/3km W of Portlethen. Height 492 feet or 150 metres. **91 G5** NO8897.
Hill of Barra *Aber.* ***Hill***, 1km S of Oldmeldrum. Height 633 feet or 193 metres. **91 G2** NJ8025.
Hill of Beath *Fife* ***Locality***, adjoining to SW of Cowdenbeath. **75 K1** NT1590.
Hill of Berran *Angus* ***Mountain***, 6m/10km NW of Bridgend, above Waterhead. Height 2001 feet or 610 metres. **90 C7** NO4471.
Hill of Carlincraig *Aber.* ***Hill***, 4m/7km SW of Turriff. Height 630 feet or 192 metres. **98 E6** NJ6744.
Hill of Cat ***Mountain***, 3m/5km SW of Ballochan, with summit on border of Aberdeenshire and Angus. Height 2434 feet or 742 metres. **90 C6** NO4887.
Hill of Christ's Kirk *Aber.* ***Mountain***, with ancient hillfort, to N of Christskirk. Height 1020 feet or 311 metres. **90 E2** NJ6027.
Hill of Corsegight *Aber.* ***Hill***, 3m/5km NW of New Deer. Height 617 feet or 188 metres. **99 G5** NJ8550.
Hill of Couternach *Angus* ***Mountain***, 2m/3km E of Glenprosen. Height 1679 feet or 512 metres. **82 E1** NO3565.
Hill of Culbirnie *Aber.* ***Hill***, 4m/6km SW of Banff. Height 518 feet or 158 metres. **98 E4** NJ6360.
Hill of Dudwick *Aber.* ***Hill***, 4m/7km W of Hatton. Height 571 feet or 174 metres. **91 H1** NJ9737.
Hill of Edendocher *Aber.* ***Mountain***, 3m/5km W of Bridge of Dye. Height 1893 feet or 577 metres. **90 D6** NO6085.
Hill of Fare *Aber.* ***Mountain***, 5m/7km N of Banchory. Height 1545 feet or 471 metres. **90 E4** NJ6803.
Hill of Fearn *High.* ***Village***, near E coast of Ross and Cromarty district, 4m/7km SE of Tain. **97 F4** NH8377.
Hill of Finavon *Angus* ***Hill***, 1m/2km S of Finavon. Height 722 feet or 220 metres. **83 F2** NO4855.
Hill of Fingray ***Mountain***, 3m/4km NE of Fernybank, with summit on border of Aberdeenshire and Angus. Height 1558 feet or 475 metres. **90 D6** NO5781.
Hill of Fishrie *Aber.* ***Hill***, 4m/7km S of Gardenstown. Height 745 feet or 227 metres. **99 G5** NJ8257.
Hill of Formal *Angus* ***Mountain***, 1m/2km N of Bridgend, above West Water. Height 1115 feet or 340 metres. **90 D7** NO5370.
Hill of Foudland *Aber.* ***Mountain***, 6m/10km SE of Huntly. Worked-out quarries on N slopes. Glens of Foudland is valley on N side; Skirts of Foudland are S slopes. Height 1532 feet or 467 metres. **90 E1** NJ6033.
Hill of Garbet *Angus* ***Mountain***, 4m/7km W of Bridgend. Height 1906 feet or 581 metres. **83 F1** NO4668.
Hill of Glansie *Angus* ***Mountain***, 4m/6km E of Rottal in Glen Clova. Height 2381 feet or 726 metres. **83 F1** NO4369.
Hill of Goauch *Aber.* ***Mountain***, 1m/2km NW of Strachan and 3m/4km SW of Banchory. Height 1105 feet or 337 metres. **90 E5** NO6694.
Hill of Hobseat *Aber.* ***Hill***, in Fetteresso Forest, 4m/7km N of Glenbervie. Height 813 feet or 248 metres. **91 F6** NO7587.
Hill of John Cairns *Aber.* ***Mountain***, 6m/9km SW of Rhynie. Height 1745 feet or 532 metres. **90 C2** NJ4320.
Hill of Maud *Moray* ***Hill***, 3m/4km SE of Buckie. Height 899 feet or 274 metres. **98 C4** NJ4663.
Hill of Menmuir *Angus* ***Hill***, to NW of Kirkton of Menmuir. Height 889 feet or 271 metres. **83 G1** NO5265.
Hill of Miffia *Ork.* ***Hill***, 3m/4km N of Stromness, Mainland. Height 518 feet or 158 metres. **107 B6** HY2313.
Hill of Mulderie *Moray* ***Mountain***, 3m/4km W of Keith. Height 1020 feet or 311 metres. **98 B5** NJ3851.
Hill of Nigg *High.* ***Hill***, 4m/6km SW of Balintore. Height 656 feet or 200 metres. **97 F4** NH8270.
Hill of Saughs *Angus* ***Mountain***, 3m/5km N of Auchronie. Height 2132 feet or 650 metres. **90 C6** NO4485.
Hill of Skilmafilly *Aber.* ***Hill***, 3m/5km NE of Methlick. Height 577 feet or 176 metres. **99 G6** NJ8940.
Hill of Stake *Renf.* ***Mountain***, summit of hills to NE of Largs. Height 1712 feet or 522 metres. **74 A4** NS2763.
Hill of Stob *Moray* ***Mountain***, 4m/6km W of Rothes. Height 1010 feet or 308 metres. **97 K7** NJ2147.
Hill of Strone *Angus* ***Mountain***, 2m/3km W of Clova. Height 2788 feet or 850 metres. **89 K7** NO2872.
Hill of Tarvit Mansion House *Fife* ***Historic house***, National Trust for Scotland property built late 17c and remodelled early 20c, 2m/3km S of Cupar. Furniture collection, restored Elizabethan laundry house and gardens. 15c Scotstarvit Tower (Historic Scotland) 1km SW. **82 E6** NO3811.
Hill of the Wangie *Moray* ***Mountain***, on N side of River Lossie, 7m/11km SW of Elgin. Height 1046 feet or 319 metres. **97 J6** NJ1353.
Hill of Three Stones *Moray* ***Mountain***, 4m/6km SW of Cabrach. Height 2073 feet or 632 metres. **90 B2** NJ3422.
Hill of Tillymorgan *Aber.* ***Mountain***, 1m/2km N of Kirkton of Culsalmond. Height 1250 feet or 381 metres. **90 E1** NJ6534.
Hill of Tomechole *Moray* ***Mountain***, 6m/10km SE of Forres. Height 1128 feet or 344 metres. **97 H7** NJ0649.
Hill of Towie *Moray* ***Mountain***, 4m/6km SW of Keith. Height 1112 feet or 339 metres. **98 B6** NJ3847.
Hill of Trusta *Aber.* ***Mountain***, surrounded by Fetteresso Forest, 6m/9km W of Stonehaven. Height 1053 feet or 321 metres. **91 F6** NO7886.
Hill of Wirren *Angus* ***Inland physical feature***, mountain ridge 6m/9km NW of Edzell. **90 D7** NO5273.

Hill of Yarrows *High.* ***Hill***, 1km SW of Loch of Yarrows. Height 695 feet or 212 metres. **105 H4** ND2942.
Hill Ridware *Staffs.* ***Village***, 2m/4km E of Rugeley. **40 C4** SK0817.
Hill Row *Cambs.* ***Village***, adjoining to W of Haddenham, 2m/3km S of Sutton. TL4475.
Hill Row Doles *Cambs.* ***Open space***, hillslope 2m/3km NE of Earith. **33 H1** TL4176.
Hill Side *W.Yorks.* ***Village***, adjoining to S of Kirkheaton, 2m/4km E of Huddersfield town centre. SE1717.
Hill Somersal *Derbys.* ***Settlement***, 1km SE of Somersal Herbert, 3m/5km NE of Uttoxeter. SK1434.
Hill Street *Hants.* ***Hamlet***, 2m/3km NW of Totton. SU3416.
Hill Top *Cumb.* ***Historic house***, at Near Sawrey, just E of S end of Esthwaite Water. 17c farmhouse bought by Beatrix Potter in 1905, now National Trust property. **60 E7** SD3695.
Hill Top *Dur.* ***Hamlet***, adjoining to S of Langley Park. NZ2144.
Hill Top *Dur.* ***Locality***, adjoining to N of Eggleston. NY9924.
Hill Top *Gt.Man.* ***Suburb***, with lake, 1m/2km S of Farnworth, 3m/5km SE of Bolton town centre. SD7303.
Hill Top *Hants.* ***Settlement***, 1m/2km NE of Beaulieu. **11 F4** SU4003.
Hill Top *S.Yorks.* ***Hamlet***, 4m/7km W of Sheffield. SK2889.
Hill Top *S.Yorks.* ***Locality***, 2m/3km NE of Penistone. SE2705.
Hill Top *S.Yorks.* ***Settlement***, 1m/2km SW of Conisbrough. SK4997.
Hill Top *S.Yorks.* ***Suburb***, 2m/3km W of Rotherham town centre. SK3992.
Hill Top *W.Mid.* ***Suburb***, 1m/2km NW of West Bromwich town centre. SO9993.
Hill Top *W.Yorks.* ***Settlement***, 1km SW of Slaithwaite. SE0713.
Hill Top *W.Yorks.* ***Settlement***, at N end of Newmillerdam, 1m/2km E of Crigglestone. **51 F1** SE3315.
Hill Top *W.Yorks.* ***Suburb***, 3m/5km W of Leeds city centre. SE2534.
Hill View *Dorset* ***Suburb***, 4m/6km NW of Poole. **9 J5** SY9895.
Hill Wootton *Warks.* ***Hamlet***, 3m/4km SE of Kenilworth. SP3068.
Hillam *N.Yorks.* ***Village***, 3m/5km NE of Ferrybridge. **58 B7** SE5028.
Hillbeck *Cumb.* ***Settlement***, 1km N of Brough. **61 J5** NY7915.
Hillberry *I.o.M.* ***Settlement***, 3m/4km N of Douglas. **54 C5** SC3879.
Hillborough *Kent* ***Hamlet***, 2m/3km E of Herne Bay town centre. **25 J5** TR2168.
Hillbourne *Poole* ***Suburb***, 2m/3km N of Poole town centre. SZ0094.
Hillbrae *Aber.* ***Settlement***, on E side of Hill of Craigmancie, 3m/5km E of Milltown of Rothiemay. **98 E6** NJ6047.
Hillbrae *Aber.* ***Settlement***, 2m/3km NE of Inverurie. **91 F2** NJ7923.
Hillbrae *Aber.* ***Settlement***, 4m/7km SE of Fyvie. **91 G1** NJ8334.
Hillbutts *Dorset* ***Hamlet***, 1m/2km NW of Wimborne Minster. ST9901.
Hillclifflane *Derbys.* ***Hamlet***, 4m/6km W of Belper. SK2947.
Hillcommon *Som.* ***Hamlet***, in Vale of Taunton Deane, 2m/3km E of Milverton. ST1426.
Hillend *Aber.* ***Settlement***, on NW side of Hill of Janetstown, 4m/6km S of Keith. **98 C6** NJ4144.
Hillend *Fife* ***Village***, 1m/2km NE of Inverkeithing. **75 K2** NT1483.
Hillend *Gt.Man.* ***Locality***, just N of Broadbottom. SJ9994.
Hillend *Midloth.* ***Settlement***, at N end of Pentland Hills, 5m/7km S of Edinburgh. Chair lift to artificial ski-slope. **76 A4** NT2566.
Hillend *N.Lan.* ***Settlement***, 1km SE of Caldercruix, at W end of Hillend Reservoir. NS8267.
Hillend *Swan.* ***Settlement***, at W end of Gower peninsula, at N end of Rhossili Down, 4m/7km NW of Port Eynon. SS4190.
Hillend Green *Glos.* ***Settlement***, 2m/3km NW of Newent. SO7028.
Hillend Reservoir *N.Lan.* ***Reservoir***, to E of Caldercruix. **75 G4** NS8267.
Hillersland *Glos.* ***Hamlet***, 3m/4km N of Coleford. SO5614.
Hillesden *Bucks.* ***Village***, 3m/5km S of Buckingham. **31 H6** SP6828.
Hillesley *S.Glos.* ***Village***, 3m/4km S of Wotton-under-Edge. **20 A3** ST7689.
Hillfarrance *Som.* ***Village***, in Vale of Taunton Deane, 4m/6km W of Taunton. **7 K3** ST1624.
Hillfoot *W.Yorks.* ***Suburb***, 1m/2km W of Pudsey town centre. SE2033.
Hillfoot End *Beds.* ***Settlement***, W part of Shillington, 3m/5km SW of Shefford. TL1234.
Hillgreen *W.Berks.* ***Settlement***, 6m/9km N of Newbury. SU4576.
Hillhampton *Worcs.* ***Locality***, 4m/7km SW of Stourport-on-Severn. SO7765.
Hillhead *Devon* ***Hamlet***, 2m/3km SW of Brixham. **5 K5** SX9053.
Hillhead *Glas.* ***Suburb***, 1m/2km NW of Glasgow city centre, to N of University of Glasgow. NS5667.
Hillhead (Also known as Hillhead of New Coylton.) *S.Ayr.* ***Village***, 6m/9km E of Ayr, adjoining to E of Coylton. NS4219.
Hillhead of Auchentumb *Aber.* ***Locality***, 3m/4km NW of Strichen. **99 H5** NJ9258.
Hillhead of Cocklaw *Aber.* ***Settlement***, 3m/4km SW of Peterhead. **99 J6** NK0844.
Hillhead of New Coylton *S.Ayr. Alternative name for Hillhead, qv.*
Hilliard's Cross *Staffs.* ***Settlement***, 3m/4km NE of Lichfield. **40 D4** SK1411.
Hilliclay *High.* ***Locality***, 3m/5km SE of Thurso. **105 G2** ND1764.
Hillingdon Heath *Gt.Lon.* ***Suburb***, to S of Hillingdon. TQ0782.
Hillington *Glas.* ***Suburb***, on S side of River Clyde, 4m/6km W of Glasgow city centre. NS5164.
Hillington *Norf.* ***Village***, 7m/12km NE of King's Lynn. **44 B3** TF7125.
Hillington Industrial Estate *Renf.* ***Locality***, adjoining to N of Hillington, 5m/8km W of Glasgow city centre. NS5165.
Hillis Corner *I.o.W.* ***Settlement***, 2m/4km SW of Cowes. SZ4793.
Hillmoor *Devon* ***Hamlet***, just SE of Culmstock, 5m/8km SW of Wellington. ST1013.
Hillmorton *Warks.* ***Suburb***, SE district of Rugby. **31 G1** SP5374.
Hillock Vale *Lancs.* ***Locality***, adjoining to NE of Accrington. SD7729.
Hillockhead *Aber.* ***Settlement***, 6m/10km SE of Strathdon. **90 B4** NJ3809.
Hillockhead *Aber.* ***Settlement***, 5m/8km N of Tarland. **90 C3** NJ4912.
Hillowton *D. & G.* ***Settlement***, 1km N of Castle Douglas. **65 H4** NX7763.
Hillpark *Glas.* ***Suburb***, in Pollokshaws district of Glasgow, 4m/6km SW of city centre. NS5559.
Hillpound *Hants.* ***Locality***, adjoining to SE of Swanmore. **11 G3** SU5815.
Hills and Holes *Peter. See Barnack.*
Hill's End *Beds.* ***Hamlet***, on E side of Woburn Park, 2m/4km E of Woburn. SP9833.
Hills of Cromdale *Large natural feature*, range of hills on border of Highland and Moray, 3m/4km SE of Cromdale, between River Spey to W and River Avon to E. Highest point is Creagan a' Chaise (2368 feet or 722 metres). **89 H2** NJ1124.
Hills Town *Derbys.* ***Locality***, adjoining to SE of Bolsover. **51 G6** SK4769.
Hillsborough *S.Yorks.* ***Suburb***, 3m/4km NW of Sheffield city centre. SK3290.
Hillsford Bridge *Devon* ***Settlement***, at junction of Farley Water and Hoaroak Water, 1m/2km SE of Lynton. **7 F1** SS7447.
Hillside *Aber.* ***Locality***, near E coast, 5m/8km S of Aberdeen. **91 H5** NO9297.
Hillside *Angus* Population: 1033. ***Village***, 2m/4km N of Montrose. **83 J1** NO7061.
Hillside *Moray* ***Settlement***, 4m/6km W of Elgin. **97 J5** NJ1560.
Hillside *Shet.* ***Settlement***, adjacent to Voe, Mainland. **109 D6** HU4063.
Hillside *Worcs.* ***Settlement***, 3m/5km S of Great Witley. SO7561.
Hillswick *Shet.* ***Village***, on Mainland on W shore of Ura Firth, at neck of peninsula called Ness of Hillswick. **108 B5** HU2877.
Hillway *I.o.W.* ***Settlement***, 1m/2km SW of Bembridge. **11 H6** SZ6386.
Hillwell *Shet.* ***Settlement***, adjacent to Ringasta, in S of Mainland. **109 F9** HU3714.
Hillyfields *Hants.* ***Hamlet***, 3m/5km NW of Southampton. SU3715.
Hilmarton *Wilts.* ***Village***, 3m/5km N of Calne. **20 D4** SU0175.
Hilperton *Wilts.* ***Village***, 1m/2km NE of Trowbridge. **20 B6** ST8759.
Hilperton Marsh *Wilts.* ***Locality***, adjacent to NW of Hilperton, 2m/3km NE of Trowbridge. ST8660.
Hilpsford Point *Cumb.* ***Coastal feature***, rocks on beach at S end of Isle of Walney, 5m/8km S of Barrow-in-Furness. **55 F3** SD2161.
Hilsea *Ports.* ***Suburb***, of Portsmouth, at N end of Portsea Island. **11 H4** SU6503.
Hilston *E.Riding* ***Hamlet***, 5m/8km NW of Withernsea. TA2833.
Hilton *Aber.* ***Settlement***, 3m/4km N of Ellon. **91 H1** NJ9434.
Hilton *Cambs.* ***Village***, 4m/6km SW of St. Ives. **33 F2** TL2866.
Hilton *Cumb.* ***Village***, at foot of fells, 3m/5km E of Appleby-in-Westmorland. **61 J4** NY7320.
Hilton *Derbys.* Population: 1755. ***Village***, 8m/12km SW of Derby. **40 E2** SK2430.
Hilton *Dorset* ***Village***, 6m/9km N of Puddletown. **9 G4** ST7803.
Hilton *Dur.* ***Hamlet***, 3m/4km E of Staindrop. **62 C4** NZ1621.
Hilton *High.* ***Settlement***, 1km NE of Portmahomack. **97 G3** NH9285.
Hilton *Shrop.* ***Village***, 4m/7km E of Bridgnorth. **39 G6** SO7795.
Hilton *Staffs.* ***Hamlet***, 2m/3km E of Brownhills. SK0805.
Hilton *Stock.* ***Village***, 5m/8km S of Stockton-on-Tees. **63 F5** NZ4611.
Hilton Bay *Sc.Bord.* ***Bay***, small rocky cove, 4m/7km NW of Berwick-upon-Tweed. **77 H4** NT9659.
Hilton of Cadboll *High.* ***Village***, on E coast of Ross and Cromarty district, 1km NE of Balintore. **97 F4** NH8776.
Hilton of Delnies *High.* ***Settlement***, 2m/3km W of Nairn. **97 F6** NH8456.
Hilton Park *Gt.Man.* ***Suburb***, in SW part of Prestwich, 3m/5km NW of Manchester city centre. SD8102.
Himbleton *Worcs.* ***Village***, 4m/7km SE of Droitwich Spa. **29 J3** SO9458.
Himley *Staffs.* ***Village***, 5m/8km S of Wolverhampton. **40 A6** SO8891.
Hincaster *Cumb.* ***Hamlet***, 5m/8km S of Kendal. **55 J1** SD5084.
Hinchcliffe Mill *W.Yorks.* ***Settlement***, in valley, between Holmfirth and Holmbridge. SE1207.
Hinchingbrooke House *Cambs.* ***Historic house***, of many periods on W side of Huntingdon. Originally a nunnery. **33 F1** TL2271.
Hinchley Wood *Surr.* ***Suburb***, 1m/2km S of Thames Ditton. TQ1565.
Hinckley *Leics.* Population: 40,608. ***Town***, 12m/19km SW of Leicester. Formerly known for hosiery production. Joseph Hansom built first Hansom cab here. **41 G6** SP4293.
Hindburn *Lancs.* ***River***, rising on N slopes of Forest of Bowland and flowing NW into River Wenning, to E of Hornby. SD5968.
Hinderclay *Suff.* ***Village***, 6m/10km W of Diss. **34 E1** TM0276.
Hinderton *Ches.* ***Settlement***, 1m/2km E of Neston. SJ3078.
Hinderwell *N.Yorks.* ***Village***, near North Sea Coast, 7m/12km NW of Whitby. **63 J5** NZ7916.
Hindford *Shrop.* ***Hamlet***, 1m/2km NE of Whittington. **38 C2** SJ3333.
Hindhead *Surr.* Population: 7473. ***Village***, in elevated position, 2m/3km NW of Haslemere. Much National Trust property in surrounding countryside. **12 B3** SU8835.
Hindhope Law *Northumb.* ***Mountain***, to NE of Emblehope Moor, 4m/7km W of Rochester. Height 1394 feet or 425 metres. **70 C4** NY7697.
Hindle Fold *Lancs.* ***Suburb***, to N of Great Harwood. SD7332.
Hindlethwaite Moor *N.Yorks.* ***Open space***, moorland on E side of Coverdale, 6m/10km SE of Aysgarth. **57 F2** SE0580.
Hindley *Gt.Man.* Population: 22,581. ***Town***, 2m/4km SE of Wigan. **49 F2** SD6104.
Hindley *Northumb.* ***Settlement***, 3m/4km SE of Riding Mill. NZ0459.
Hindley Green *Gt.Man.* ***Locality***, adjoining to SE of Hindley. **49 F2** SD6303.
Hindlip *Worcs.* ***Village***, 3m/5km NE of Worcester. **29 H3** SO8758.
Hindlow Hollow *Derbys.* ***Locality***, 4m/7km SE of Buxton. SK1068.
Hindolveston *Norf.* ***Village***, 7m/11km SW of Holt. **44 E3** TG0329.
Hindon *Som.* ***Settlement***, 2m/4km W of Minehead. SS9346.
Hindon *Wilts.* ***Village***, 7m/11km NE of Shaftesbury. **9 J1** ST9132.
Hindringham *Norf.* ***Village***, 6m/9km NE of Fakenham. Moated 16c hall. **44 D2** TF9836.
Hingham *Norf.* Population: 1995. ***Village***, 6m/9km W of Wymondham. **44 E5** TG0202.
Hingston Down *Cornw.* ***Open space***, hillslope on E side of Kit Hill, 2m/3km NE of Callington. **4 D3** SX3871.
Hinkley Point *Som.* ***Coastal feature***, headland on Bridgwater Bay. Nuclear power station to E. **7 K1** ST1946.
Hinksford *Staffs.* ***Settlement***, 4m/7km NW of Stourbridge. SO8689.
Hinstock *Shrop.* ***Village***, 5m/8km S of Market Drayton. **39 F3** SJ6926.
Hintlesham *Suff.* ***Village***, 4m/7km E of Hadleigh. **34 E4** TM0843.
Hinton *Glos.* ***Settlement***, near River Severn estuary, 1km E of Sharpness. SO6803.
Hinton *Hants.* ***Settlement***, 2m/3km W of New Milton. **10 D5** SZ2195.
Hinton *Here.* ***Hamlet***, 8m/13km NW of Pontrilas. **28 C5** SO3338.
Hinton *Northants.* ***Village***, 6m/10km SW of Daventry. **31 G3** SP5352.
Hinton *Shrop.* ***Hamlet***, 6m/9km SW of Shrewsbury. **38 D5** SJ4008.
Hinton *S.Glos.* ***Hamlet***, 4m/6km NW of Marshfield. **20 A4** ST7376.
Hinton Admiral *Hants.* ***Settlement***, 2m/3km W of New Milton. **10 D5** SZ2095.
Hinton Ampner *Hants.* ***Hamlet***, 3m/5km S of New Alresford. **11 G2** SU6027.
Hinton Ampner Garden *Hants.* ***Garden***, 1m/2km W of Bramdean. 20c formal and informal gardens (National Trust), with restoration work featuring a dell and a sunken garden. **11 G2** SU5927.
Hinton Blewett *B. & N.E.Som.* ***Village***, 2m/3km E of West Harptree. **19 J6** ST5956.
Hinton Charterhouse *B. & N.E.Som.* ***Village***, 4m/7km S of Bath. **20 A6** ST7758.
Hinton-in-the-Hedges *Northants.* ***Village***, 2m/3km W of Brackley. **31 G5** SP5536.
Hinton Marsh *Hants.* ***Locality***, 3m/5km S of New Alresford. SU5827.
Hinton Martell *Dorset* ***Village***, 4m/6km N of Wimborne Minster. **10 B4** SU0106.
Hinton on the Green *Worcs.* ***Village***, 3m/4km S of Evesham. **30 B4** SP0240.
Hinton Parva *Dorset* ***Hamlet***, 3m/4km N of Wimborne Minster. ST9904.
Hinton Parva *Swin.* ***Village***, 5m/8km E of Swindon. **21 F3** SU2283.
Hinton Priory *B. & N.E.Som.* ***Ecclesiastical building***, remains of 13c priory next to Hinton Abbey, 4m/6km SE of Bath. **20 A6** ST7759.
Hinton St. George *Som.* ***Village***, 2m/4km NW of Crewkerne. **8 D3** ST4212.
Hinton St. Mary *Dorset* ***Village***, 1m/2km N of Sturminster Newton. **9 G3** ST7812.
Hinton Waldrist *Oxon.* ***Village***, 6m/10km E of Faringdon. **21 G2** SU3799.
Hints *Shrop.* ***Settlement***, 3m/5km W of Cleobury Mortimer. **29 F1** SO6175.
Hints *Staffs.* ***Village***, 3m/5km W of Tamworth. **40 D5** SK1503.
Hinwick *Beds.* ***Hamlet***, 5m/8km SE of Wellingborough. **32 C2** SP9361.
Hinxhill *Kent* ***Village***, 3m/4km E of Ashford. **15 F3** TR0442.
Hinxton *Cambs.* ***Village***, 2m/3km N of Great Chesterford. **33 H4** TL4945.
Hinxworth *Herts.* ***Village***, 4m/7km N of Baldock. **33 F4** TL2340.

H

Hipperholme *W.Yorks.* ***Village***, 2m/3km NW of Brighouse. **57 G7** SE1325.
Hipswell *N.Yorks.* ***Village***, on NE edge of Catterick Camp, 2m/3km SE of Richmond. SE1898.
Hipswell Moor *N.Yorks.* ***Open space***, moorland, partly wooded, 2m/3km E of Catterick Camp. **62 C7** SE1496.
Hirael *Gwyn.* ***Suburb***, to NE of Bangor. SH5872.
Hiraeth *Carmar.* ***Hamlet***, 3m/5km NW of Whitland. SN1721.
Hirfynydd *N.P.T.* ***Inland physical feature***, mountain ridge rising to 1578 feet or 481 metres, 3m/5km W of Glyn-neath. Afforestation to SE. **18 B1** SN8205.
Hirn *Aber.* ***Settlement***, 3m/5km NE of Banchory. **91 F4** NJ7300.
Hirnant *Powys* ***Hamlet***, 3m/5km NE of Lake Vyrnwy dam. **37 K3** SJ0522.
Hirnant Pass *Gwyn.* ***Other feature of interest***, pass through Penllyn Forest, 3m/5km SE of Bala. **37 J2** SH9430.
Hirst *Northumb.* ***Suburb***, E district of Ashington. **71 H5** NZ2887.
Hirst Courtney *N.Yorks.* ***Village***, 2m/4km NW of Snaith across River Aire. **58 C7** SE6124.
Hirst Head *Northumb.* ***Locality***, on N side of Bedlington. NZ2682.
Hirta *W.Isles Alternative name for St. Kilda, qv.*
Hirwaen *Denb.* ***Settlement***, 2m/3km NE of Ruthin. **47 K6** SJ1361.
Hirwaun *R.C.T.* ***Village***, 4m/6km NW of Aberdare. Industrial estate 2m/3km W. **18 C1** SN9505.
Hirwaun Common *Bridgend* ***Open space***, heath on N side of Cefn Hirgoed, 3m/5km NE of Bridgend. **18 C3** SS9283.
Hirwaun Common *R.C.T.* ***Open space***, 1m/2km SW of Hirwaun. **18 C1** SN9303.
Hiscott *Devon* ***Hamlet***, 5m/7km S of Barnstaple. **6 D3** SS5426.
Histon *Cambs.* Population: 7200. ***Village***, 3m/5km N of Cambridge. **33 H2** TL4363.
Hitcham *Bucks.* ***Locality***, including Hitcham House and Hitcham Park, 1km E of Taplow. **22 C3** SU9282.
Hitcham *Suff.* ***Village***, 6m/10km NW of Hadleigh. Site of Roman building to NW. **34 D3** TL9851.
Hitcham Causeway *Suff.* ***Settlement***, to NE of Hitcham. TL9852.
Hitcham Street *Suff.* ***Hamlet***, to W of Hitcham. TL9851.
Hitchin *Herts.* Population: 32,221. ***Town***, old market town, 8m/13km NE of Luton. Formerly a wool town; Hitchin Museum displays many garments. **32 E6** TL1829.
Hitchin Museum and Art Gallery *Herts.* ***Other feature of interest***, in Hitchin, with exhibits on local social history and a costume display; frequently changing exhibits in art gallery. **32 E6** TL1829.
Hither Green *Gt.Lon.* ***Suburb***, in borough of Lewisham, 1m/2km SE of Lewisham and 7m/11km SE of Charing Cross. **23 G4** TQ3874.
Hittisleigh *Devon* ***Locality***, parish containing localities of Hittisleigh Barton and Hittisleigh Cross, 7m/12km SW of Crediton. **7 F6** SX7395.
Hittisleigh Barton *Devon* ***Hamlet***, within parish of Hittisleigh, 7m/11km SW of Crediton. SX7395.
Hittisleigh Cross *Devon* ***Hamlet***, within parish of Hittisleigh, 8m/12km SW of Crediton. SX7395.
Hive *E.Riding* ***Hamlet***, adjoining to W of Sandholme, 1m/2km NW of Gilberdyke. SE8230.
Hiveland End *E.Riding* ***Locality***, adjoining to W of Sandholme. SE8230.
Hixon *Staffs.* Population: 1392. ***Village***, 6m/9km NW of Rugeley. **40 C3** SK0025.
Hiz ***River***, rising on SW side of Hitchin and flowing through town, then N into River Ivel at Henlow 4m/6km S of Biggleswade. **32 E5** TL1838.
HM Customs and Excise National Museum *Mersey.* ***Other feature of interest***, in Liverpool city centre, hands-on display of modern-day detection techniques, as well as a smuggling exhibition. **48 C4** SJ3389.
Hoaden *Kent* ***Hamlet***, 1m/2km NW of Ash. **25 J5** TR2659.
Hoaldalbert *Mon.* ***Settlement***, 7m/12km NE of Abergavenny. **28 C6** SO3923.
Hoar Cross *Staffs.* ***Hamlet***, 4m/6km E of Abbots Bromley. **40 D3** SK1323.
Hoar Cross Hall *Staffs.* ***Historic house***, 19c neo-Jacobean house 3m/5km SE of Abbots Bromley. Chapel decorations by Bodley. **40 D3** SK1223.
Hoaroak Hill *Som.* ***Mountain***, on Exmoor, 3m/5km NW of Simonsbath. Height 1551 feet or 473 metres. **7 F1** SS7442.
Hoarwithy *Here.* ***Village***, on River Wye, 5m/8km NW of Ross-on-Wye. **28 E6** SO5429.
Hoath *Kent* ***Village***, 3m/5km SE of Herne Bay. **25 H5** TR2064.
Hob Tor *Derbys.* ***Mountain***, on Peak District National Park border, 1km W of Dove Holes and 3m/4km N of Buxton. Height 1663 feet or 507 metres. **50 C5** SK0677.
Hobarris *Shrop.* ***Settlement***, 4m/6km NE of Knighton. **28 C1** SO3078.
Hobbister *Ork.* ***Settlement***, 1km to E of S end of Loch of Kirkbister, Mainland. **107 C7** HY3807.
Hobbles Green *Suff.* ***Settlement***, 5m/8km NE of Haverhill. TL7053.
Hobbs Cross *Essex* ***Settlement***, 3m/5km E of Harlow. TL4910.
Hobbs Cross *Essex* ***Settlement***, 2m/3km SE of Epping. TQ4799.
Hobbs Lots Bridge *Cambs.* ***Settlement***, at road bridge across Twenty Foot River, 3m/5km NW of March. **43 G5** TF3901.
Hobhole Drain *Lincs.* ***Other water feature***, artificial drainage channel running between Cowbridge Drain, 2m/3km E of Boston, and Toynton Fen Side. **43 G1** TF3645.
Hobkirk *Sc.Bord.* ***Settlement***, 1km S of Bonchester Bridge. **70 A2** NT5810.
Hobland Hall *Norf.* ***Settlement***, 4m/6km S of Great Yarmouth town centre. **45 K5** TG5001.
Hobsick *Notts.* ***Locality***, 1km N of Brinsley. SK4549.
Hobson *Dur.* ***Village***, 1km S of Burnopfield. **62 C1** NZ1755.
Hoby *Leics.* ***Village***, 5m/9km W of Melton Mowbray. **41 J4** SK6617.
Hockenden *Gt.Lon.* ***Settlement***, 1m/2km W of Swanley, in borough of Bromley. TQ4968.
Hockerill *Herts.* ***Suburb***, E district of Bishop's Stortford. TL4920.
Hockering *Norf.* ***Village***, 5m/9km E of East Dereham. **44 E4** TG0713.
Hockering Heath *Norf.* ***Settlement***, 1m/2km NE of Hockering and 3m/4km NE of Mattishall. TG0814.
Hockerton *Notts.* ***Village***, 2m/3km NE of Southwell. **51 K7** SK7156.
Hockholler *Som.* ***Hamlet***, 2m/3km E of Wellington. ST1621.
Hockley *Ches.* ***Suburb***, adjoining to E of Poynton. SJ9283.
Hockley *Essex* Population: 14,538. ***Town***, 5m/8km NW of Southend-on-Sea. **24 E2** TQ8492.
Hockley *Staffs.* ***Suburb***, 3m/4km SE of Tamworth town centre. SK2200.
Hockley *W.Mid.* ***Suburb***, 4m/6km W of Coventry city centre. SP2779.
Hockley Heath *W.Mid.* ***Village***, 10m/15km NW of Warwick. **30 C1** SP1572.
Hockliffe *Beds.* ***Village***, 4m/7km NW of Dunstable. **32 C6** SP9726.
Hockwold cum Wilton *Norf.* ***Village***, 4m/6km W of Brandon. **44 B7** TL7388.
Hockwold Fens *Norf.* ***Open space***, fenland, 2m/3km S of Feltwell. **44 A7** TL6987.
Hockworthy *Devon* ***Village***, 7m/11km W of Wellington. **7 J4** ST0319.
Hod Hill *Dorset* ***Hill***, with hillfort (National Trust) at summit, 3m/5km NW of Blandford Forum. Height 469 feet or 143 metres. **9 H3** ST8510.
Hodder *Lancs.* ***River***, rising on Forest of Bowland and flowing S, through Stocks Reservoir and Slaidburn, into River Ribble 3m/5km SW of Clitheroe. **56 C4** SD7138.
Hoddesdon *Herts.* Population: 36,883. ***Town***, market town, 3m/5km S of Ware. Many medieval buildings. RSPB reserve. **23 G1** TL3709.
Hoddlesden *B'burn.* Population: 1666. ***Village***, 1m/2km E of Darwen. **56 C7** SD7122.
Hodge Beck *N.Yorks.* ***River***, rising on Cleveland Hills and flowing S down Bransdale, then into River Dove 2m/3km S of Kirkbymoorside. **63 H7** SE6983.
Hodgefield *Staffs.* ***Settlement***, 1m/2km NW of Endon. SJ9054.
Hodgehill *Ches.* ***Settlement***, 1m/2km SW of Siddington. SJ8369.
Hodgehill *W.Mid.* ***Suburb***, 4m/7km E of Birmingham city centre. SP1388.
Hodgeston *Pembs.* ***Village***, 3m/5km E of Pembroke. **16 D5** SS0399.
Hodley *Powys* ***Locality***, 4m/6km E of Newtown. SO1691.
Hodnet *Shrop.* ***Village***, 5m/9km SW of Market Drayton. 19c hall has landscaped gardens. Mound in park marks site of former castle. **39 F3** SJ6128.
Hodnet Hall *Shrop.* ***Garden***, in Hodnet, 12m/19km NE of Shrewsbury, with 60 acres of lakeside gardens and woodland. **39 F3** SJ6028.
Hodnetheath *Shrop.* ***Settlement***, 1km S of Hodnet. SJ6127.
Hodsall Street *Kent* ***Hamlet***, 3m/5km N of Wrotham Heath. TQ6262.
Hodsock *Notts.* ***Hamlet***, 1m/2km SW of Blyth. SK6185.
Hodsock Priory *Notts.* ***Ecclesiastical building***, 1m/2km SW of Blyth and 5m/8km NE of Worksop. Parish church dating in parts to Benedictine priory founded in 1088. Notable gatehouse and gardens. **51 J4** SK6186.
Hodson *Swin.* ***Hamlet***, 1km E of Chiseldon. SU1780.
Hodthorpe *Derbys.* ***Village***, 1m/2km E of Whitwell. **51 H5** SK5476.
Hoe *Norf.* ***Hamlet***, 2m/3km N of East Dereham. **44 D4** TF9916.
Hoe Gate *Hants.* ***Settlement***, 1m/2km SW of Hambledon. **11 H3** SU6213.
Hoe Rape *High.* ***Coastal feature***, headland on W coast of Skye at S end of Moonen Bay. **93 G7** NG1543.
Hoff *Cumb.* ***Settlement***, on Hoff Beck, 2m/3km S of Appleby-in-Westmorland. **61 H5** NY6717.
Hoff Beck *Cumb.* ***River***, rising 1m/2km S of Great Asby and flowing N through village, then into River Eden at Colby, 1m/2km W of Appleby-in-Westmorland. **61 H4** NY6621.
Hoffleet Stow *Lincs.* ***Locality***, 1m/2km E of Bicker. **43 F2** TF2437.
Hog Fell *D. & G.* ***Mountain***, 4m/6km NE of Langholm. Height 1217 feet or 371 metres. **69 J5** NY3989.
Hog Hatch *Surr.* ***Locality***, residential locality adjoining to W of Hale. SU8348.
Hog Hill *D. & G.* ***Mountain***, to E of Castle O'er Forest, 4m/6km NW of Bentpath. Height 1096 feet or 334 metres. **69 H4** NY2895.
Hogganfield *Glas.* ***Suburb***, 3m/5km NE of Glasgow city centre. NS6466.
Hoggard's Green *Suff.* ***Settlement***, to E of Stanningfield, 5m/8km S of Bury St. Edmunds. TL8856.
Hoggeston *Bucks.* ***Village***, 3m/5km SE of Winslow. **32 B6** SP8025.
Hoggie *Moray* ***Settlement***, 1m/2km SE of Kirktown of Deskford, 4m/7km S of Cullen. **98 D4** NJ5160.
Hoggington *Wilts.* ***Hamlet***, 2m/3km SW of Trowbridge. ST8255.
Hoggrill's End *Warks.* ***Settlement***, 2m/4km NE of Coleshill. SP2291.
Hogh Bay *Arg. & B.* ***Bay***, on NW coast of Coll, 4m/6km W of Arinagour. **78 C2** NM1657.
Hogha Gearraidh (Anglicised form: Hougharry.) *W.Isles* ***Village***, on NW coast of North Uist, 4m/6km S of Griminis Point. **92 C4** NF7071.
Hoghton *Lancs.* ***Village***, 5m/7km W of Blackburn. **56 B7** SD6125.
Hoghton Bottoms *Lancs.* ***Settlement***, 1m/2km NE of Hoghton. SD6125.
Hoghton Tower *Lancs.* ***Historic house***, dating from 16c, 1km NE of Hoghton and 6m/10km SE of Preston. **56 B7** SD6125.
Hognaston *Derbys.* ***Village***, 4m/7km NE of Ashbourne. **50 E7** SK2350.
Hog's Back *Surr.* ***Inland physical feature***, narrow chalk ridge of North Downs running W from River Wey valley at Guildford for about 7m/11km. A31 road runs along top of ridge and Pilgrims Way below it on S side. Ridge commands extensive views N and S. **22 C7** SU9348.
Hogs Law *Sc.Bord.* ***Mountain***, in Lammermuir Hills, 3m/5km NE of Carfraemill. Cairn at summit. Height 1469 feet or 448 metres. **76 D5** NT5555.
Hogspit Bottom *Herts.* ***Settlement***, 4m/6km E of Chesham. TL0101.
Hogsthorpe *Lincs.* ***Village***, 6m/10km N of Skegness. **53 J5** TF5372.
Holbeach *Lincs.* Population: 6088. ***Small town***, Fenland market town, 7m/12km E of Spalding. Markets held here since 13c. Birthplace of William Stukeley. **43 G3** TF3524.
Holbeach Bank *Lincs.* ***Hamlet***, 2m/3km N of Holbeach. **43 G3** TF3527.
Holbeach Clough *Lincs.* ***Locality***, 1m/2km NW of Holbeach. **43 G3** TF3427.
Holbeach Drove *Lincs.* ***Village***, 6m/9km E of Crowland. **43 G4** TF3212.
Holbeach Hurn *Lincs.* ***Hamlet***, 3m/4km NE of Holbeach. **43 G3** TF3524.
Holbeach Marsh *Lincs.* ***Open space***, lowland 3m/5km N of Holbeach. **43 G3** TF3629.
Holbeach St. Johns *Lincs.* ***Village***, 4m/7km S of Holbeach. **43 G4** TF3418.
Holbeach St. Marks *Lincs.* ***Village***, 4m/7km N of Holbeach. **43 G2** TF3731.
Holbeach St. Matthew *Lincs.* ***Hamlet***, 6m/9km NE of Holbeach. **43 H2** TF4132.
Holbeache *Worcs.* ***Settlement***, 3m/5km NW of Kidderminster. SO7879.
Holbeck *Notts.* ***Village***, 4m/7km SW of Worksop. **51 H5** SK5473.
Holbeck *W.Yorks.* ***Suburb***, 1m/2km S of Leeds city centre across River Aire. SE2932.
Holbeck Woodhouse *Notts.* ***Hamlet***, 1km SE of Holbeck, 4m/7km SW of Worksop. SK5473.
Holberrow Green *Worcs.* ***Hamlet***, 4m/7km W of Alcester. **30 B3** SP0259.
Holbeton *Devon* ***Village***, 3m/4km SE of Yealmpton. **5 G5** SX6150.
Holborn *Gt.Lon.* ***Locality***, district of central London at S end of borough of Camden, 1m/2km NE of Charing Cross. TQ3081.
Holborn Head *High.* ***Coastal feature***, headland on N coast of Caithness district, 2m/3km N of Thurso. Lighthouse 1km S at entrance to Thurso Bay. **105 G1** ND1071.
Holborough *Kent* ***Settlement***, adjoining to W of Snodland. **24 D5** TQ7062.
Holbrook *Derbys.* ***Village***, 2m/4km SE of Belper. **41 F1** SK3644.
Holbrook *S.Yorks.* ***Locality***, 7m/11km SE of Sheffield city centre. SK4481.
Holbrook *Suff.* ***Village***, 5m/8km S of Ipswich. **35 F5** TM1736.
Holbrook Bay *Suff.* ***Bay***, to S of Holbrook on River Stour estuary, extending from S of Harkstead to Stutton Ness. **35 F5** TM1736.
Holbrook Moor *Derbys.* ***Village***, adjoining to N of Holbrook, 2m/3km SE of Belper. SK3645.
Holbrooks *W.Mid.* ***Suburb***, N district of Coventry. SP3383.
Holburn *Northumb.* ***Settlement***, 3m/5km SE of Lowick. **77 J7** NU0436.
Holbury *Hants.* ***Village***, adjoining to W of Fawley oil refinery. **11 F4** SU4303.
Holcombe *Devon* ***Village***, 2m/3km NE of Teignmouth. **5 K3** SX9574.
Holcombe *Gt.Man.* ***Settlement***, adjoining to W of Ramsbottom. SD7816.
Holcombe *Som.* ***Village***, 4m/6km S of Radstock. **19 K7** ST6749.
Holcombe Brook *Gt.Man.* ***Suburb***, 1m/2km SW of Ramsbottom. SD7714.
Holcombe Burnell *Devon* ***Hamlet***, 4m/6km W of Exeter. SX8591.
Holcombe Rogus *Devon* ***Village***, 5m/9km W of Wellington. **7 J4** ST0518.
Holcot *Beds.* ***Settlement***, 4m/6km N of Aspley Guise. SP9438.
Holcot *Northants.* ***Village***, 6m/10km NE of Northampton. **31 J2** SP7969.
Holden *Lancs.* ***Hamlet***, 1km W of Bolton by Bowland. **56 C5** SD7749.
Holden Fold *Gt.Man.* ***Suburb***, 1km S of Royton, 1m/2km NW of Oldham. SD9106.
Holden Gate *W.Yorks.* ***Settlement***, on Bacup to Todmorden road, 3m/4km W of Todmorden. SD8923.
Holdenby *Northants.* ***Village***, 6m/10km NW of Northampton. **31 H2** SP6967.
Holdenby House *Northants.* ***Garden***, in Holdenby, 6m/10km NW of Northampton town centre, surrounding 16c hall with rich historical links with Civil War. Gardens feature a falconry centre and 17c farmstead with rare species. **31 H2** SP6967.
Holdenhurst *Bourne.* ***Hamlet***, 4m/6km NE of Bournemouth town centre. **10 C5** SZ1295.

H

Holderness Drain *E.Riding* ***Other water feature***, runs from Leven Canal into River Humber, on W side of Kingston upon Hull. **59 H6** TA1328.
Holder's Green *Essex* ***Settlement***, 2m/3km SE of Thaxted. TL6328.
Holders Hill *Gt.Lon.* ***Suburb***, in borough of Barnet, 1m/2km NE of Hendon. TQ2390.
Holdfast *Worcs.* ***Locality***, 4m/7km NW of Tewkesbury. SO8537.
Holdgate *Shrop.* ***Village***, 8m/12km SW of Much Wenlock. **38 E7** SO5689.
Holdingham *Lincs.* ***Hamlet***, 1m/2km NW of Sleaford. **42 D1** TF0547.
Holditch *Dorset* ***Hamlet***, 4m/6km NE of Axminster. **8 C4** ST3402.
Holdsworth *W.Yorks.* ***Locality***, adjoining to E of Illingworth, 3m/4km N of Halifax. SE0829.
Hole *Devon* ***Settlement***, 6m/10km N of Honiton. ST1611.
Hole Bottom *W.Yorks.* ***Locality***, adjoining to N of Todmorden. SD9325.
Hole-in-the-Wall *Here.* ***Hamlet***, on E bank of River Wye, 3m/5km N of Ross-on-Wye. **29 F6** SO6128.
Hole Park *Kent* ***Garden***, formal garden with topiary, natural gardens and parkland, 1m/2km NW of Rolvenden. **14 D4** TQ8332.
Hole Street *W.Suss.* ***Settlement***, 1m/2km SE of Ashington and 3m/5km NW of Steyning. **12 E5** TQ1414.
Holehouse *Derbys.* ***Hamlet***, 1km SW of Charlesworth. SK0092.
Holehouse Hill *D. & G.* ***Mountain***, on Forest of Ae, 6m/10km SW of Beattock. Height 1305 feet or 398 metres. **69 F4** NY0094.
Holemoor *Devon* ***Hamlet***, 5m/8km E of Holsworthy. SS4205.
Hole's Hole *Devon* ***Settlement***, on E bank of River Tamar, 6m/10km SW of Yelverton. SX4365.
Holford *Som.* ***Village***, 3m/4km NW of Nether Stowey. **7 K1** ST1541.
Holgate *York* ***Suburb***, 1m/2km W of York city centre. SE5851.
Holgate Moor *N.Yorks.* ***Open space***, moorland 3m/5km SW of Barningham. **62 B6** NZ0605.
Holker *Cumb.* ***Village***, 1km N of Cark. **55 G2** SD3677.
Holker Hall *Cumb.* ***Historic house***, part 16c and 17c, part Victorian, has large park and gardens. Lakeland Motor Museum in grounds. **55 G2** SD3677.
Holkham *Norf.* ***Hamlet***, 2m/3km W of Wells-next-the-Sea. **44 C1** TF8943.
Holkham Bay *Norf.* ***Bay***, off N coast of Norfolk, to N of Holkham. **44 C1** TF8943.
Holkham Hall *Norf.* ***Historic house***, 18c house by Kent in Palladian style, standing nearly 1m/2km SW of Holkham in landscaped grounds with lake. **44 C1** TF8943.
Holl Reservoir *Fife* ***Reservoir***, small reservoir 2m/3km NW of Leslie. **82 D7** NO2203.
Hollacombe *Devon* ***Hamlet***, 2m/3km W of Crediton. SS8000.
Hollacombe *Devon* ***Village***, 2m/4km E of Holsworthy. **6 B5** SS3703.
Hollacombe *Devon* ***Village***, 4m/6km SW of Chulmleigh. **6 E4** SS6311.
Hollacombe Hill *Devon* ***Hamlet***, 4m/6km SE of Plymouth across River Plym estuary. SX5250.
Hollacombe Town *Devon* ***Settlement***, to NW of Hollacombe. SS6211.
Holland *Ork.* ***Settlement***, in centre of Papa Westray. **106 D2** HY4851.
Holland *Ork.* ***Settlement***, in S of Stronsay, 1km S of Dishes. **106 F5** HY6622.
Holland *Surr.* ***Locality***, adjoining to S of Hurst Green. **23 H6** TQ4050.
Holland Fen *Lincs.* ***Hamlet***, 7m/11km NW of Boston. TF2349.
Holland Fen *Lincs.* ***Open space***, lowland 6m/10km NW of Boston. **43 F1** TF2347.
Holland Isle *D. & G.* ***Island***, in course of River Dee 2m/3km W of Parton. NX6669.
Holland Lees *Lancs.* ***Settlement***, 3m/4km NE of Skelmersdale. SD5108.
Holland-on-Sea *Essex* ***Suburb***, NE district of Clacton-on-Sea. **35 F7** TM2016.
Holland Park *Gt.Lon.* ***Suburb***, park and district around it in borough of Kensington and Chelsea, 3m/5km W of Charing Cross. TQ2479.
Hollandstoun *Ork.* ***Locality***, near SW end of North Ronaldsay. **106 G2** HY7553.
Hollee *D. & G.* ***Settlement***, on W side of woodland, 1km S of Kirkpatrick-Fleming. **69 H7** NY2769.
Hollesley *Suff.* ***Village***, 6m/9km SE of Woodbridge across River Deben. **35 H4** TM3544.
Hollesley Bay *Suff.* ***Bay***, to SE of Hollesley, extending SW from Orford Ness to Bawdsey. **35 H4** TM3544.
Hollicombe *Torbay* ***Suburb***, NE district of Paignton. SX8962.
Hollin Busk *S.Yorks.* ***Locality***, adjoining to S of Stocksbridge. SK2797.
Hollin Green *Ches.* ***Settlement***, 4m/6km W of Nantwich. SJ5952.
Hollin Hill *N.Yorks.* ***Locality***, 1m/2km SE of Swainby. NZ4900.
Hollingbourne *Kent* ***Village***, 5m/8km E of Maidstone. **14 D2** TQ8455.
Hollingbury *B. & H.* ***Suburb***, N district of Brighton. **13 G6** TQ3108.
Hollingrove *E.Suss.* ***Hamlet***, between Brightling and Darwell Reservoir, 5m/7km NW of Battle. TQ6920.
Hollington *Derbys.* ***Village***, 5m/9km SE of Ashbourne. **40 E2** SK2239.
Hollington *E.Suss.* ***Suburb***, NW district of Hastings. **14 C6** TQ7911.
Hollington *Staffs.* ***Village***, 4m/6km NW of Uttoxeter. **40 C2** SK0538.
Hollingwood Estate *Derbys.* ***Suburb***, 1m/2km W of Staveley. SK4174.
Hollingworth *Gt.Man.* Population: 15,385. ***Locality***, 2m/4km NW of Glossop. **50 C3** SK0096.
Hollingworth Lake *Gt.Man.* ***Lake/loch***, to S of Littleborough, 3m/4km E of Rochdale. Visitor centre of S side of lake with waymarked shore trail, boat trips and bird sanctuary. **49 J1** SD9314.
Hollinlane *Ches.* ***Locality***, 2m/3km N of Wilmslow. SJ8384.
Hollins *Derbys.* ***Hamlet***, 4m/6km W of Chesterfield. SK3271.
Hollins *Derbys.* ***Settlement***, 4m/6km S of Buxton. SK0667.
Hollins *Gt.Man.* ***Suburb***, 2m/3km S of Bury town centre. **49 H2** SD8108.
Hollins *Staffs.* ***Settlement***, 3m/4km N of Cheadle. SJ9947.
Hollins *Staffs.* ***Suburb***, adjoining to S of Kidsgrove. SJ8253.
Hollins End *S.Yorks.* ***Suburb***, 3m/5km SE of Sheffield city centre. SK3884.
Hollins Green *Warr.* ***Village***, 6m/10km E of Warrington. **49 F3** SJ6991.
Hollins Lane *Lancs.* ***Hamlet***, 4m/6km N of Garstang. SD4951.
Hollinsclough *Staffs.* ***Hamlet***, 2m/3km NW of Longnor. **50 C6** SK0666.
Hollinswood *Tel. & W.* ***Locality***, 1m/2km SW of Oakengates. **39 G5** SJ7008.
Hollinthorpe *W.Yorks.* ***Settlement***, 1km N of Swillington. SE3831.
Hollinwood *Gt.Man.* ***Suburb***, 2m/3km SW of Oldham town centre. SD9002.
Hollinwood *Shrop.* ***Hamlet***, 4m/6km S of Whitchurch. **38 E2** SJ5236.
Holliwell Point *Essex* ***Coastal feature***, point on N bank of River Crouch estuary to S of Ray Sand. **25 G2** TR0296.
Hollow Meadows *S.Yorks.* ***Settlement***, 7m/11km W of Sheffield. SK2488.
Holloway *Derbys.* ***Village***, 3m/5km SE of Matlock. **51 F7** SK3256.
Holloway *Gt.Lon.* ***Suburb***, in borough of Islington, 3m/5km N of Charing Cross. Women's prison. TQ3085.
Holloway *W. & M.* ***Settlement***, 3m/5km W of Maidenhead. SU8480.
Holloway End *W.Mid.* ***Suburb***, in N part of Stourbridge. SO8985.
Hollowell *Northants.* ***Village***, 8m/13km NW of Northampton. **31 H1** SP6871.
Hollowell Reservoir *Northants.* ***Reservoir***, to N of Hollowell. **31 H1** SP6871.
Hollows Tower (The Holehouse). *D. & G.* ***Historic house***, tower on W bank of River Esk, 2m/3km N of Canonbie. Dating from 16c, refuge of Johnnie Armstrong, a Borders bandit, later hanged by James V. **69 J6** NY3878.
Holly Bank *Gt.Man.* ***Settlement***, 1m/2km N of Mossley. SD9603.
Holly Bank *W.Mid.* ***Suburb***, 1m/2km S of Brownhills. SK0503.
Holly Bush *Wrex.* ***Settlement***, 3m/4km NE of Overton. SJ4044.
Holly Cross *W. & M.* ***Hamlet***, 3m/5km N of Twyford. SU8080.
Holly End *Norf.* ***Locality***, 3m/5km SE of Wisbech. **43 J5** TF4906.
Holly Green *Bucks.* ***Settlement***, 2m/3km W of Princes Risborough. SP7703.
Holly Green *Worcs.* ***Hamlet***, 1km NE of Upton upon Severn across River Severn. **29 H4** SO8641.
Hollybush *Caerp.* ***Village***, 4m/6km S of Ebbw Vale. **18 E1** SO1602.
Hollybush *E.Ayr.* ***Village***, 3m/5km NW of Patna. **67 H2** NS3914.
Hollybush *Staffs.* ***Suburb***, 1m/2km S of Fenton. SJ8943.
Hollybush *Worcs.* ***Village***, near S end of Malvern Hills, 3m/5km E of Ledbury. **29 G5** SO7636.
Hollybush Corner *Suff.* ***Settlement***, 1km S of Bradfield St. George. TL9159.
Hollyhurst *Ches.* ***Settlement***, 3m/5km NE of Whitchurch. SJ5744.
Hollym *E.Riding* ***Village***, 2m/3km S of Withernsea. **59 K7** TA3425.
Hollywater *Hants.* ***Settlement***, 1m/2km SE of Bordon and 3m/4km NW of Liphook. SU8034.
Hollywood *Worcs.* ***Village***, 6m/10km S of Birmingham. SP0877.
Holm *D. & G.* ***Settlement***, on W side of White Esk River, to NW of Eskdalemuir. **69 H4** NY2598.
Holm *W.Isles* ***Settlement***, on Isle of Lewis, 2m/4km SE of Stornoway. NB4531.
Holm Island *High.* ***Island***, islet off E coast of Skye, 6m/9km NE of Portree. NG5251.
Holm Island *W.Isles* ***Island***, small uninhabited island off Isle of Lewis to E of Holm Point. NB4430.
Holm of Aikerness *Ork.* ***Island***, small island to E of Aikerness peninsula on Westray. HY4652.
Holm of Boray *Ork.* ***Island***, islet off S coast of Gairsay. HY4520.
Holm of Dalry *D. & G.* ***Locality***, low-lying area in loop of Water of Ken, on SW side of St. John's Town of Dalry. NX6180.
Holm of Drumlanrig *D. & G.* ***Settlement***, 3m/5km NW of Thornhill. **68 D4** NX8398.
Holm of Elsness *Ork.* ***Island***, rocky islet off S coast of Sanday to W of Els Ness peninsula. HY6637.
Holm of Faray *Ork.* ***Island***, narrow uninhabited island less than 1m/2km in length N to S, lying between Faray to S and Westray to N. HY5238.
Holm of Grimbister *Ork.* ***Island***, small uninhabited island in Bay of Firth, 1m/2km E of Finstown, Mainland. HY3713.
Holm of Gunnister *Shet.* ***Island***, small island off N coast of Bressay. HU5044.
Holm of Heogland *Shet.* ***Island***, small island at S end of Unst, 1m/2km W of Uyea. HU5799.
Holm of Houton *Ork.* ***Island***, small uninhabited island at entrance to Bay of Houton, 2m/3km NE of coast of Hoy across Bring Deeps. HY3103.
Holm of Huip *Ork.* ***Island***, small uninhabited island off N coast of Stronsay across Huip Sound. **106 F4** HY6231.
Holm of Melby *Shet.* ***Island***, small island to N of Melby in Sound of Papa. HU1958.
Holm of Odness *Ork.* ***Island***, islet off E coast of Stronsay on S side of entrance to Mill Bay. HY6926.
Holm of Papa *Ork.* ***Island***, small uninhabited island off E coast of Papa Westray. Large chambered cairn (Historic Scotland) with triple central chamber. **106 E2** HY5051.
Holm of Papa Chambered Cairn *Ork.* ***Historic/prehistoric site***, situated on Holm of Papa, off E coast of Papa Westray. Cairn with 14 side chambers and rare carvings. **106 E2** HY5051.
Holm of Scockness *Ork.* ***Island***, small uninhabited island at N end of Rousay Sound between Rousay and Egilsay. HY4531.
Holm of Skaw *Shet.* ***Island***, narrowly separated from N coast of Unst. **108 F1** HP6616.
Holm of Tressaness *Shet.* ***Island***, rock off N coast of Fetlar, opposite Tressa Ness. HU6294.
Holm of West Sandwick *Shet.* ***Island***, small uninhabited island 1km offshore of West Sandwick, Yell. HU4389.
Holm Sound *Ork.* ***Sea feature***, strait dividing S part of Mainland from NE coast of Burray. **107 D8** ND4999.
Holman Clavel *Som.* ***Hamlet***, in Black Down Hills, 2m/3km S of Pitminster. ST2216.
Holmbridge *W.Yorks.* ***Village***, with reservoirs to W and S, 2m/3km SW of Holmfirth. SE1206.
Holmbury St. Mary *Surr.* ***Village***, in wooded area, 5m/8km SW of Dorking. **22 E7** TQ1144.
Holmbush *Cornw.* ***Locality***, on E outskirts of St. Austell. **4 A5** SX0352.
Holmbush *W.Suss.* ***Settlement***, 3m/5km NE of Horsham town centre. **13 F3** TQ2233.
Holmcroft *Staffs.* ***Suburb***, N district of Stafford. SJ9125.
Holme *Cambs.* ***Village***, 7m/11km S of Peterborough. **42 E7** TL1987.
Holme *Cumb.* ***Village***, 5m/9km N of Carnforth. **55 J2** SD5278.
Holme *Lancs.* ***Locality***, 1m/2km SE of Haslingden. SD7922.
Holme *N.Lincs.* ***Settlement***, 3m/5km SE of Scunthorpe. SE9206.
Holme *N.Yorks.* ***Hamlet***, 1m/2km SE of Pickhill, 4m/7km W of Thirsk. SE3582.
Holme *Notts.* ***Village***, 3m/5km N of Newark-on-Trent. **52 B7** SK8059.
Holme *W.Yorks.* ***Village***, 3m/4km SW of Holmfirth. **50 D2** SE1206.
Holme Bridge *Derbys.* ***Bridge***, stone packhorse bridge over River Wye at Bakewell, built 1664. SK2168.
Holme Chapel *Lancs.* ***Village***, 4m/6km SE of Burnley. **56 D7** SD8728.
Holme Common *E.Riding* ***Open space***, lowland 1m/2km S of Holme-on-Spalding-Moor. **58 E6** SE8036.
Holme Green *N.Yorks.* ***Hamlet***, just S of Appleton Roebuck, 4m/7km E of Tadcaster. SE5541.
Holme Green *W'ham* ***Hamlet***, 1m/2km SE of Wokingham. SU8267.
Holme Hale *Norf.* ***Village***, 5m/7km E of Swaffham. **44 C5** TF8807.
Holme Island *Cumb.* ***Coastal feature***, peninsula on N bank of River Kent estuary, 1m/2km E of Grange-over-Sands. **55 H2** SD4278.
Holme Lacy *Here.* ***Village***, 4m/6km SE of Hereford. **28 E5** SO5535.
Holme Marsh *Here.* ***Village***, 3m/5km SE of Kington. **28 C3** SO3454.
Holme Mills *Cumb.* ***Hamlet***, 1km S of Holme, 3m/4km SE of Milnthorpe. SD5278.
Holme next the Sea *Norf.* ***Village***, 3m/4km NE of Hunstanton. **44 B1** TF7043.
Holme-on-Spalding-Moor *E.Riding* Population: 2629. ***Village***, 5m/8km SW of Market Weighton. **58 E6** SE8138.
Holme on the Wolds *E.Riding* ***Village***, 6m/10km NE of Market Weighton. **59 F5** SE9646.
Holme Pierrepont *Notts.* ***Village***, 4m/6km E of Nottingham. **41 J2** SK6239.
Holme Pierrepont Country Park *Notts.* ***Leisure/recreation***, country park on S side of River Trent, adjacent to National Water Sports Centre, 3m/5km E of Nottingham. Low hills and grass-covered banks surrounding 2000 metre rowing course and white water canoeing course. Fishing lake. Nature reserve and lake at N end attracts waterfowl. **41 J2** SK6339.
Holme St. Cuthbert *Cumb.* ***Hamlet***, 3m/4km NW of Westnewton. NY1047.
Holme Slack *Lancs.* ***Suburb***, 1m/2km NE of Preston town centre. SD5531.
Holme Wood *S.Yorks.* ***Locality***, 2m/3km E of Armthorpe. SE6505.
Holmebridge *Dorset* ***Settlement***, 2m/4km W of Wareham. **9 H6** SY8986.
Holmer *Here.* ***Suburb***, to N of Hereford. **28 E4** SO5042.
Holmer Green *Bucks.* ***Village***, 4m/6km NE of High Wycombe. **22 C2** SU9097.
Holmes *Lancs.* ***Settlement***, 1km E of Mere Brow, 4m/7km N of Burscough Bridge. SD4319.
Holmes Chapel *Ches.* Population: 5465. ***Village***, 4m/6km E of Middlewich. **49 G6** SJ7667.
Holme's Hill *E.Suss.* ***Locality***, 4m/7km NW of Hailsham. **13 J5** TQ5312.
Holmes Moss *Cumb.* ***Mountain***, to N of Baugh Fell, 6m/9km NE of Sedbergh. Height 1551 feet or 473 metres. **61 J7** SD7395.
Holmescales *Cumb.* ***Hamlet***, 2m/3km NE of Endmoor, 4m/7km SE of Kendal. SD5587.
Holmesfield *Derbys.* ***Village***, 2m/3km W of Dronfield. **51 F5** SK3277.
Holmeswood *Lancs.* ***Village***, 6m/9km N of Ormskirk. **48 D1** SD4316.

Holmethorpe *Surr.* ***Suburb***, NE district of Redhill. TQ2851.
Holmewood *Derbys.* ***Village***, 1m/2km W of Heath. **51 G6** SK4265.
Holmfield *W.Yorks.* ***Locality***, 2m/3km N of Halifax. **57 F7** SE0828.
Holmfirth *W.Yorks.* Population: 10,989. ***Town***, on River Holme, 5m/8km S of Huddersfield. Old mill town and venue for filming of TV series 'Last of the Summer Wine'. Postcard Museum. **50 D2** SE1408.
Holmhead *D. & G.* ***Settlement***, 6m/10km NE of St. John's Town of Dalry. **68 C5** NX7085.
Holmhead *E.Ayr.* ***Locality***, 1km NW of Cumnock across Lugar Water. **67 K1** NS5620.
Holmpton *E.Riding* ***Village***, near coast, 3m/5km SE of Withernsea. **59 K7** TA3623.
Holmrook *Cumb.* ***Village***, 3m/4km E of Seascale. **60 B6** SD0799.
Holms of Ire *Ork.* ***Island***, two small islands off Whale Point at NW end of Sanday. **106 F3** HY6446.
Holms of Spurness *Ork.* ***Island***, three islets off Spur Ness, SW tip of Sanday. HY6032.
Holms Water *Sc.Bord.* ***River***, rising in mountains 3m/5km NW of Tweedsmuir and flowing NE to Biggar Water, 1m/2km SE of Broughton, and into River Tweed. **69 F1** NT1234.
Holmsey Green *Suff.* ***Locality***, adjoining to E of Beck Row. TL6977.
Holmsgarth *Shet.* ***Village***, on Mainland, adjoining to NW of Lerwick. **109 D8** HU4642.
Holmside *Dur.* ***Settlement***, 6m/9km NW of Durham. **62 D2** NZ2149.
Holmsleigh Green *Devon* ***Hamlet***, 3m/5km NE of Honiton. ST2002.
Holmston *S.Ayr.* ***Suburb***, 1m/2km E of Ayr town centre. **67 H1** NS3520.
Holmwrangle *Cumb.* ***Locality***, 2m/3km NW of Ainstable. **61 G2** NY5148.
Holne *Devon* ***Village***, above River Dart, on E side of Dartmoor, 3m/5km W of Ashburton. Birthplace of Charles Kingsley, 1819. **5 H4** SX7069.
Holne Bridge (New Bridge). *Devon* ***Bridge***, 15c granite bridge over River Dart, 3m/5km W of Ashburton. Good specimen of unaltered medieval bridge. Road only 10 feet or 3 metres wide. SX7170.
Holnest *Dorset* ***Hamlet***, 5m/7km SE of Sherborne. **9 F4** ST6509.
Holnicote *Som.* ***Hamlet***, 2m/3km E of Porlock. SS9146.
Holnicote Estate *Som.* ***Open space***, large National Trust area incorporating open spaces around Selworthy Beacon and Dunkery Beacon. SS9148.
Holoman Bay *High.* ***Bay***, on W coast of Raasay, 3m/5km from S end of island. **86 B1** NG5439.
Holoman Island *High.* ***Island***, islet off W coast of Raasay at N end of Holoman Bay. NG5440.
Holsworthy *Devon* Population: 1892. ***Small town***, agricultural centre, 9m/14km E of Bude. **6 B5** SS3403.
Holsworthy Beacon *Devon* ***Hamlet***, 3m/5km N of Holsworthy. **6 B5** SS3508.
Holt *Dorset* ***Village***, 3m/4km NE of Wimborne Minster. **10 B4** SU0203.
Holt *Mersey.* ***Suburb***, in NW part of Rainhill. SJ4891.
Holt *Norf.* Population: 2972. ***Small town***, 10m/15km W of Cromer. Gresham's School, boys' public school founded as grammar school in 1555. **44 E2** TG0738.
Holt *Wilts.* ***Village***, 2m/4km N of Trowbridge. The Courts (National Trust), 18c house. **20 B5** ST8561.
Holt *Worcs.* ***Hamlet***, 5m/8km N of Worcester. **29 H2** SO8262.
Holt *Wrex.* ***Village***, on W bank of River Dee, 5m/8km E of Wrexham. **48 D7** SJ4154.
Holt End *Hants.* ***Settlement***, 1km SW of Bentworth and 3m/5km W of Alton. **11 H1** SU6639.
Holt End *Worcs.* ***Village***, 3m/4km NE of Redditch. **30 B2** SP0769.
Holt Fleet *Worcs.* ***Hamlet***, on River Severn, 5m/8km W of Droitwich Spa. **29 H2** SO8263.
Holt Green *Lancs.* ***Settlement***, adjoining to S of Aughton, 2m/4km SW of Ormskirk. SD3904.
Holt Heath *Dorset* ***Hamlet***, 4m/7km NE of Wimborne Minster. **10 B4** SU0604.
Holt Heath *Worcs.* ***Village***, on River Severn, 5m/9km NW of Worcester. **29 H2** SO8163.
Holt Street *Kent* ***Settlement***, adjoining to S of Nonington, 4m/6km S of Wingham. TR2551.
Holt Town *Gt.Man.* ***Suburb***, 1m/2km E of Manchester city centre. SJ8698.
Holt Wood *Dorset* ***Settlement***, 1m/2km E of Hinton Martell. SU0305.
Holt Woodlands Country Park *Norf.* ***Leisure/recreation***, 96 acre park, 1km S of Holt, consisting chiefly of heath and woodland with picnic areas and nature trails. **44 E2** TG0837.
Holtby *York* ***Village***, 5m/8km E of York. **58 C4** SE6754.
Holton *Lincs.* ***Village***, 2m/4km NW of Wragby. **52 E4** TF1378.
Holton *Oxon.* ***Village***, 6m/9km E of Oxford. **21 K1** SP6006.
Holton *Som.* ***Village***, 2m/3km SW of Wincanton. **9 F2** ST6826.
Holton *Suff.* ***Village***, 1m/2km E of Halesworth. **35 H1** TM4077.
Holton Heath *Dorset* ***Hamlet***, 2m/3km NE of Wareham. **9 J5** SY9490.
Holton le Clay *Lincs.* Population: 3818. ***Village***, 4m/7km S of Grimsby. **53 F2** TA2802.
Holton le Moor *Lincs.* ***Village***, 3m/5km SW of Caistor. **52 D3** TF0897.
Holton St. Mary *Suff.* ***Village***, 4m/7km SE of Hadleigh. **34 E5** TM0536.
Holtspur *Bucks.* ***Suburb***, W district of Beaconsfield. **22 C2** SU9290.
Holtwood *W.Berks.* ***Settlement***, 4m/7km SW of Newbury. SU4164.
Holtye *E.Suss.* ***Settlement***, 4m/7km E of East Grinstead. TQ4539.
Holtye Common *E.Suss.* ***Settlement***, 4m/6km E of East Grinstead. **13 H3** TQ4539.
Holway *Flints.* ***Suburb***, adjoining to NW of Holywell. SJ1776.
Holway *Som.* ***Suburb***, SE district of Taunton. ST2423.
Holwell *Dorset* ***Village***, in Blackmoor Vale, 5m/8km SE of Sherborne. **9 G3** ST7011.
Holwell *Herts.* ***Village***, 3m/5km N of Hitchin. **32 E5** TL1633.
Holwell *Leics.* ***Hamlet***, 3m/5km N of Melton Mowbray. **42 A3** SK7323.
Holwell *Oxon.* ***Village***, 3m/4km SW of Burford. **21 F1** SP2309.
Holwell *Som.* ***Hamlet***, 4m/6km SW of Frome. Disused quarries nearby. **20 A7** ST7245.
Holwick *Dur.* ***Hamlet***, 3m/5km NW of Middleton-in-Teesdale. **62 A4** NY9026.
Holwick Fell *Dur.* ***Open space***, moorland on S side of River Tees, 4m/6km W of Middleton-in-Teesdale. **61 K4** NY8826.
Holworth *Dorset* ***Settlement***, 1m/2km S of Owermoigne. **9 G6** SY7683.
Holy Cross *T. & W.* ***Suburb***, to NE of Wallsend. NZ3167.
Holy Cross *Worcs.* ***Hamlet***, 4m/6km S of Stourbridge. **29 J1** SO9278.
Holy Island (Ynys Gybi). *I.o.A.* ***Island***, on which Holyhead is situated, measuring 7m/12km from NW to SE and from 1km to 3m/5km wide, lying off W coast of Anglesey. Connected to main island by a road bridge and a road and railway embankment. **46 A5** SH2579.
Holy Island *N.Ayr.* ***Island***, sparsely inhabited island lying across entrance to Lamlash Bay, E coast of Arran. Measures 2m/3km N to S and about 1km across. Rises to 1030 feet or 314 metres. Lighthouses on either side of S end of island. **73 J7** NS0632.
Holy Island (Also known as Lindisfarne.) *Northumb.* ***Island***, 3m/5km E to W and 1m/2km N to S off coast, 5m/8km N of Belford. Road connection with mainland by causeway passable at low tide. **77 K6** NU1242.
Holy Island *Northumb.* ***Village***, to SW of Holy Island, 2m/4km from mainland E coast. Ruins of 11c Lindisfarne Priory (English Heritage); 13c Church of St. Mary. Restored 16c Lindisfarne Castle (National Trust) 1km E of village. **77 K6** NU1242.
Holy Island Sands *Northumb.* ***Coastal feature***, sandbank between mainland and E coast of Holy Island. Sandbank is submerged at high water. Nature reserve. **77 J6** NU1042.
Holy Loch *Arg. & B.* ***Sea feature***, inlet in Argyll running up to Ardbeg from between Stone Point and Hunter's Quay, N of Dunoon. **73 K2** NS1780.
Holy Trinity Church *W.Suss.* ***Ecclesiastical building***, in Bosham, 3m/5km W of Chichester. Depicted on Bayeux Tapestry as church where Harold heard mass en route to Normandy. W part of chancel, tower and possibly nave are from time of Edward the Confessor. **12 B6** SU8003.
Holybourne *Hants.* ***Village***, 2m/3km NE of Alton. **22 A7** SU7341.
Holyfield *Essex* ***Settlement***, 2m/3km N of Waltham Abbey. TL3803.
Holyhead (Caergybi). *I.o.A.* Population: 11,796. ***Town***, on Holy Island, Anglesey, of which it is principal town. At end of A5 road from London, it is ferry port for Eire. 13c St. Cybi's Church within remains of Roman fort. **46 A4** SH2482.
Holyhead Bay *I.o.A.* ***Bay***, on which Holyhead, Anglesey, is situated, extending from North Stack to Carmel Head. **46 A4** SH2687.
Holyhead Mountain (Mynydd Twr). *I.o.A.* ***Hill***, granite hill at NW corner of Holy Island, 2m/3km W of Holyhead. Quarries. Iron Age fort of Caer y Twr (Cadw). Height 722 feet or 220 metres. **46 A4** SH2182.
Holyhead Mountain Hut Circles *I.o.A.* ***Historic/prehistoric site***, 2m/3km W of Holyhead. Remains of twenty circular and rectangular huts (Cadw) from Iron Age and Roman period. **46 A4** SH2181.
Holymoorside *Derbys.* Population: 1685. ***Village***, 3m/5km W of Chesterfield. **51 F6** SK3369.
Holyport *W. & M.* ***Village***, 2m/3km S of Maidenhead. **22 B4** SU8977.
Holystone *Northumb.* ***Hamlet***, 3m/5km SE of Alwinton. **70 E3** NT9502.
Holystone Common *Northumb.* ***Open space***, moorland to W of Holystone. **70 E3** NT9301.
Holytown *N.Lan.* Population: 5820. ***Village***, 2m/4km NE of Hamilton. Newhouse Industrial Estate 1km NE. **75 F4** NS7660.
Holywell *Cambs.* ***Village***, on River Great Ouse, 2m/3km E of St. Ives. **33 G1** TL3370.
Holywell *Cornw.* ***Village***, near N coast, 3m/5km N of Perranporth. **2 E3** SW7658.
Holywell *Dorset* ***Hamlet***, 1m/2km E of Evershot. **8 E4** ST5904.
Holywell *E.Suss.* ***Settlement***, adjoining to SW of Eastbourne. **13 J7** TV6096.
Holywell (Treffynnon). *Flints.* Population: 7531. ***Small town***, near River Dee estuary, 14m/23km NW of Chester. Holy well, sacred to name of St. Winefride. **47 K5** SJ1875.
Holywell *Northumb.* ***Village***, adjoining to SE of Seaton Delaval, 3m/4km NW of Whitley Bay. NZ3174.
Holywell Bank *Flints.* ***Coastal feature***, sandbank at estuary of River Dee (Afon Dyfrdwy), 4m/7km W of Neston. **48 B5** SJ2178.
Holywell Bay *Cornw.* ***Bay***, with huge sand dunes to NW of Holywell, extending S from Kelsey Head to Penhale Point. **2 E2** SW7658.
Holywell Green *W.Yorks.* Population: 3041. ***Village***, 4m/6km S of Halifax. **50 C1** SE0819.
Holywell Lake *Som.* ***Village***, 2m/3km W of Wellington. **7 K3** ST1020.
Holywell Row *Suff.* ***Village***, 2m/3km N of Mildenhall. **34 B1** TL7077.
Holywood *D. & G.* ***Village***, 4m/6km NW of Dumfries. **68 E5** NX9480.
Hom Green *Here.* ***Settlement***, 2m/3km SW of Ross-on-Wye. **28 E6** SO5822.
Home End *Cambs.* ***Locality***, SE end of Fulbourn. TL5255.
Home Law *Sc.Bord.* ***Mountain***, 3m/5km E of Ettrick. Height 1351 feet or 412 metres. **69 J2** NT3215.
Homer *Shrop.* ***Hamlet***, 1m/2km N of Much Wenlock. **39 F5** SJ6101.
Homer Green *Mersey.* ***Hamlet***, 3m/5km NE of Crosby. SD3402.
Homersfield *Suff.* ***Village***, on River Waveney, 4m/7km SW of Bungay. **45 G7** TM2885.
Homerton *Gt.Lon.* ***Suburb***, in borough of Hackney, to E of Hackney. TQ3584.
Homington *Wilts.* ***Village***, on River Ebble, 3m/5km SW of Salisbury. **10 C2** SU1226.
Honddu ***River***, rising in Black Mountains, on S slope of Hay Bluff, and flowing S by Llanthony to Llanvihangel Crucorney, then N into River Monnow, 1km N of Pandy. **28 B5** SO3323.
Honddu *Powys* ***River***, rising on Mynydd Eppynt and flowing S into River Usk at Brecon. **27 K5** SO0428.
Honey Hill *Kent* ***Settlement***, 3m/5km NW of Canterbury. **25 H5** TR1161.
Honey Street *Wilts.* ***Hamlet***, astride Kennet and Avon Canal, 4m/6km W of Pewsey. SU1061.
Honey Tye *Suff.* ***Hamlet***, 2m/3km NW of Nayland. **34 D5** TL9535.
Honeyborough *Pembs.* ***Locality***, 1km N of Neyland. **16 C4** SM9506.
Honeybourne *Worcs.* ***Village***, 4m/7km N of Broadway. **30 C4** SP1144.
Honeychurch *Devon* ***Village***, 3m/5km S of Winkleigh. **6 E5** SS6202.
Honicknowle *Plym.* ***Suburb***, N district of Plymouth, 3m/5km from city centre. SX4658.
Honiley *Warks.* ***Hamlet***, 3m/5km W of Kenilworth. **30 D1** SP2472.
Honing *Norf.* ***Village***, 3m/5km NE of North Walsham. **45 H3** TG3227.
Honingham *Norf.* ***Village***, 8m/13km W of Norwich. **45 F4** TG1011.
Honingham Thorpe *Norf.* ***Locality***, adjoining Colton, 1m/2km S of Honingham. TG1011.
Honington *Lincs.* ***Village***, 5m/8km N of Grantham. **42 C1** SK9443.
Honington *Suff.* ***Village***, 3m/5km NW of Ixworth. **34 D1** TL9174.
Honington *Warks.* ***Village***, 1m/2km N of Shipston on Stour. **30 D4** SP2642.
Honister Pass *Cumb.* ***Other feature of interest***, mountain pass, 1m/2km W of Seatoller, carrying road from Seatoller to Buttermere. **60 D5** NY2213.
Honiton *Devon* Population: 7859. ***Small town***, on River Otter, 16m/24km E of Exeter. The famous Honiton lace displayed in town museum. Unusual church dating from 1830s, but built in Norman style. **7 K5** ST1600.
Honkley *Wrex.* ***Settlement***, 2m/3km NW of Rossett. SJ3459.
Honley *W.Yorks.* Population: 10,990. ***Town***, 3m/5km S of Huddersfield. **50 D1** SE1311.
Honnington *Tel. & W.* ***Settlement***, 3m/5km SW of Newport. SJ7215.
Honor Oak *Gt.Lon.* ***Suburb***, in borough of Southwark, 5m/8km SE of Charing Cross. TQ3574.
Hoo *Kent* ***Locality***, 1m/2km W of Minster. TR2964.
Hoo *Med.* Population: 5262. ***Suburb***, 4m/6km NE of Strood. **24 D4** TQ7872.
Hoo *Suff.* ***Hamlet***, 4m/6km NW of Wickham Market. **35 G3** TM2558.
Hoo Green *Ches.* ***Hamlet***, 4m/6km NW of Knutsford. SJ7182.
Hoo Green *Suff.* ***Hamlet***, adjoins to S of Hoo. TM2558.
Hoo Hole *W.Yorks.* ***Settlement***, 1km S of Mytholmroyd. SE0025.
Hoo Meavy *Devon* ***Hamlet***, E of River Meavy, 6m/10km SE of Tavistock. SX5265.
Hoober *S.Yorks.* ***Hamlet***, 1m/2km E of Wentworth and 4m/6km NW of Rotherham. SK4198.
Hoobrook *Worcs.* ***Locality***, 1m/2km S of Kidderminster. SO8374.
Hood Green *S.Yorks.* ***Hamlet***, 3m/5km SW of Barnsley. SE3102.
Hood Hill *S.Yorks.* ***Hamlet***, 1m/2km NE of Chapeltown. SK3697.
Hooe *E.Suss.* ***Village***, at E edge of Pevensey Levels, 4m/6km W of Bexhill. **13 K6** TQ6809.
Hooe *Plym.* ***Suburb***, S district of Plymouth, to S of River Plym. **5 F5** SX5052.
Hooe Common *E.Suss.* ***Hamlet***, 1km N of Hooe. **13 K5** TQ6809.
Hoohill *B'pool* ***Suburb***, 1m/2km NE of Blackpool town centre. SD3237.
Hook *Cambs.* ***Settlement***, 2m/3km SE of March. TL4293.
Hook *E.Riding* ***Village***, 1m/2km NE of Goole. **58 D7** SE7625.
Hook *Gt.Lon.* ***Suburb***, in borough of Kingston upon Thames, 3m/5km S of Kingston upon Thames town centre. **22 E5** TQ1764.
Hook *Hants.* ***Hamlet***, 4m/7km W of Fareham. SU5005.
Hook *Hants.* Population: 6471. ***Village***, 6m/9km E of Basingstoke. **22 A6** SU7254.
Hook *Pembs.* ***Village***, 3m/5km SE of Haverfordwest. **16 C3** SM9711.
Hook *Wilts.* ***Hamlet***, 2m/3km NE of Wootton Bassett. **20 D3** SU0784.

Hook-a-Gate *Shrop.* ***Hamlet***, 3m/5km SW of Shrewsbury. **38 D5** SJ4609.
Hook End *Oxon.* ***Settlement***, 4m/6km NE of Pangbourne. SU6681.
Hook Green *Kent* ***Hamlet***, 2m/4km S of Northfleet. **24 C4** TQ6170.
Hook Green *Kent* ***Hamlet***, 1m/2km W of Lamberhurst. **13 K3** TQ6535.
Hook Green *Kent* ***Settlement***, 2m/3km SW of Dartford. TQ5271.
Hook Green *Kent* ***Settlement***, 1km N of Meopham. **24 C5** TQ6466.
Hook Norton *Oxon.* Population: 1913. ***Village***, 5m/8km NE of Chipping Norton. **30 E5** SP3533.
Hook Park *Hants.* ***Settlement***, 1m/2km S of Warsash and 3m/4km SW of Park Gate. SU4904.
Hooke *Dorset* ***Village***, 4m/7km NW of Maiden Newton. **8 E4** ST5300.
Hooker Gate *T. & W.* ***Locality***, adjoining to S of High Spen, 1m/2km W of Rowlands Gill. NZ1459.
Hookgate *Staffs.* ***Locality***, 7m/11km NW of Eccleshall. **39 G2** SJ7435.
Hook's Cross *Herts.* ***Settlement***, 4m/6km SE of Stevenage town centre. TL2720.
Hookway *Devon* ***Hamlet***, 1m/2km SE of Crediton. **7 G6** SX8598.
Hookwood *Surr.* ***Locality***, adjoining to W of Horley. **23 F7** TQ2642.
Hoole *Ches.* ***Suburb***, NE district of Chester. **48 D6** SJ4267.
Hooley *Surr.* ***Hamlet***, 4m/6km SW of Purley. **23 F6** TQ2856.
Hooley Bridge *Gt.Man.* ***Locality***, on River Roch, 3m/5km W of Rochdale. SD8511.
Hooley Brow *Gt.Man.* ***Locality***, adjoining to N of Heywood. SD8511.
Hooley Hill *Gt.Man.* ***Suburb***, 1m/2km SW of Dukinfield. SJ9296.
Hoop *Mon.* ***Hamlet***, 3m/5km S of Monmouth. SO5107.
Hooper's Point *Pembs.* ***Coastal feature***, headland 3m/4km N of St. Ann's Head at SE end of Marloes Bay. **16 A4** SM7806.
Hooton *Ches.* ***Hamlet***, 3m/4km NW of Ellesmere Port. **48 C5** SJ3678.
Hooton Levitt *S.Yorks.* ***Village***, 1km SW of Maltby. **51 H3** SK5191.
Hooton Pagnell *S.Yorks.* ***Village***, 7m/11km NW of Doncaster. Hall has 14c gatehouse. **51 G2** SE4808.
Hooton Roberts *S.Yorks.* ***Village***, 4m/7km NE of Rotherham. **51 G3** SK4897.
Hop Pole *Lincs.* ***Hamlet***, 3m/4km SW of Deeping St. Nicholas. TF1813.
Hopcroft's Holt *Oxon.* ***Settlement***, 4m/7km S of Deddington. **31 F6** SP4625.
Hope *Derbys.* ***Village***, in Hope Valley, 4m/6km NW of Hathersage. **50 D4** SK1783.
Hope *Devon* ***Small town***, resort just N of Bolt Tail, consisting of Outer Hope and Inner Hope. **5 G7** SX6740.
Hope *Flints.* Population: 2277. ***Village***, 5m/8km N of Wrexham. **48 C7** SJ3058.
Hope *Powys* ***Settlement***, 2m/3km E of Welshpool across River Severn. **38 B5** SJ2507.
Hope *Shrop.* ***Settlement***, 12m/19km SW of Shrewsbury. **38 C5** SJ3401.
Hope *Staffs.* ***Hamlet***, 1km SW of Alstonefield, 3m/4km N of Ilam. SK1255.
Hope Bagot *Shrop.* ***Hamlet***, 4m/6km N of Tenbury Wells. **28 E1** SO5873.
Hope Bowdler *Shrop.* ***Village***, 2m/3km SE of Church Stretton. **38 D6** SO4792.
Hope Bowdler Hill *Shrop.* ***Mountain***, rising to over 390 metres, 1m/2km E of Church Stretton. **38 D6** SO4793.
Hope Dale *Shrop.* ***Valley***, below E slope of Wenlock Edge. **38 D7** SO4887.
Hope End Green *Essex* ***Hamlet***, 4m/6km W of Great Dunmow. **33 J7** TL5720.
Hope Fell *Northumb.* ***Open space***, to SW of Bulbeck Common, 2m/4km W of Blanchland. **62 A1** NY9251.
Hope Green *Ches.* ***Suburb***, to S of Poynton. SJ9182.
Hope Mansell *Here.* ***Village***, 3m/5km SE of Ross-on-Wye. **29 F7** SO6219.
Hope Moor *Dur.* ***Open space***, moorland 5m/8km SE of Bowes. **62 B6** NZ0207.
Hope under Dinmore *Here.* ***Village***, 4m/6km S of Leominster. **28 E3** SO5052.
Hope Valley *Derbys.* ***Valley***, part of Peakshole Water and Noe River valleys, extending from 1km W of Hope to 1m/2km SE of Hope. **50 D4** SK1683.
Hope Woodlands *Derbys.* ***Open space***, area in High Peak, between Upper Derwent Valley and valley of River Ashop, to NW of Ladybower Reservoir. Some conifer afforestation on sides of river valleys. **50 D3** SK1391.
Hopegill Head *Cumb.* ***Mountain***, 3m/5km N of Buttermere. Height 2526 feet or 770 metres. **60 C4** NY1822.
Hopehouse *Sc.Bord.* ***Hamlet***, 2m/3km NE of Ettrick. **69 H2** NT2916.
Hopeman *Moray* Population: 1461. ***Village***, fishing village and resort on N coast, 6m/9km W of Lossiemouth. **97 J5** NJ1469.
Hope's Green *Essex* ***Suburb***, NW district of South Benfleet. **24 D3** TQ7786.
Hope's Nose *Torbay* ***Coastal feature***, headland at N end of Tor Bay, 2m/3km E of Torquay harbour. **5 K4** SX9563.
Hopes Reservoir *E.Loth.* ***Reservoir***, small reservoir on Lammermuir Hills, 4m/6km S of Gifford. **76 D4** NT5462.
Hopes Water *E.Loth.* ***River***, rising in Lammermuir Hills, flowing NE through Hopes Reservoir and then N to join Gifford Water 1m/2km SE of Gifford. **76 D4** NT5567.
Hopesay *Shrop.* ***Village***, 3m/4km W of Craven Arms. **38 C7** SO3983.
Hopetoun House *W.Loth.* ***Historic house***, 17c mansion on S side of Firth of Forth, 2m/4km W of Forth Road Bridge. **75 J3** NT0879.
Hopetown *W.Yorks.* ***Suburb***, to NE of Normanton. SE3923.
Hopkinstown (Trehopcyn). *R.C.T.* ***Suburb***, W district of Pontypridd. **18 D2** ST0690.
Hopley's Green *Here.* ***Settlement***, 4m/6km SE of Kington. SO3452.
Hopperton *N.Yorks.* ***Hamlet***, 2m/3km W of Green Hammerton and 5m/8km N of Wetherby. SE4256.
Hopping Hill *Northants.* ***Suburb***, 3m/4km NW of Northampton town centre. SP7262.
Hopsford *Warks.* ***Settlement***, on site of lost village between Shilton and Withybrook, 6m/10km NE of Coventry. SP4284.
Hopstone *Shrop.* ***Hamlet***, 4m/7km E of Bridgnorth. SO7894.
Hopton *Derbys.* ***Village***, 2m/3km W of Wirksworth. **50 E7** SK2553.
Hopton *Norf.* Population: 1885. ***Village***, and coastal resort, 5m/8km S of Great Yarmouth. **45 K5** TG5200.
Hopton *Shrop.* ***Hamlet***, 1km N of Nesscliffe. SJ3820.
Hopton *Shrop.* ***Settlement***, 2m/3km SW of Hodnet. **38 E3** SJ5926.
Hopton *Staffs.* ***Hamlet***, 2m/4km NE of Stafford. **40 B3** SJ9426.
Hopton *Suff.* ***Village***, 7m/11km NE of Ixworth. **34 D1** TL9979.
Hopton Cangeford *Shrop.* ***Hamlet***, 4m/7km NE of Ludlow. **38 E7** SO5480.
Hopton Castle *Shrop.* ***Castle***, on S side of village of Hopton Castle, 6m/10km NE of Knighton. Remains of 12c motte castle captured by Royalists during Civil War. **28 C1** SO3677.
Hopton Castle *Shrop.* ***Village***, 5m/8km SW of Craven Arms. Remains of castle. **28 C1** SO3678.
Hopton Titterhill *Shrop.* ***Mountain***, 5m/8km NE of Knighton. Height 1299 feet or 396 metres. **28 C1** SO3577.
Hopton Wafers *Shrop.* ***Village***, 2m/4km W of Cleobury Mortimer. **29 F1** SO6376.
Hoptonheath *Shrop.* ***Hamlet***, 5m/8km SW of Craven Arms. **28 C1** SO3877.
Hopwas *Staffs.* ***Village***, 2m/3km W of Tamworth. **40 D5** SK1704.
Hopwood *Gt.Man.* ***Locality***, to SE of Heywood, 3m/5km SW of Rochdale. SD8609.
Hopwood *Worcs.* ***Village***, 5m/8km N of Redditch. **30 B1** SP0275.
Hopworthy *Devon* ***Hamlet***, 3m/4km W of Holsworthy. SS3002.
Horam *E.Suss.* Population: 1962. ***Village***, 3m/4km S of Heathfield. **13 J5** TQ5717.
Horbling *Lincs.* ***Village***, 6m/9km W of Donington. **42 E2** TF1135.
Horbury *W.Yorks.* Population: 9186. ***Small town***, 3m/5km SW of Wakefield. Birth and burial place of John Carr ('Carr of York'), 18c architect. **50 E1** SE2918.
Horbury Bridge *W.Yorks.* ***Locality***, at crossing point of River Calder and of Calder and Hebble Navigation, 1m/2km W of Horbury. SE2818.
Horden *Dur.* ***Village***, adjoining to E of Peterlee, 1km W of North Sea coast. **63 F2** NZ4441.
Horderley *Shrop.* ***Locality***, 3m/5km NW of Craven Arms. **38 D7** SO4086.
Hordle *Hants.* ***Village***, 4m/6km W of Lymington. **10 D5** SZ2695.
Hordley *Shrop.* ***Hamlet***, 3m/5km SW of Ellesmere. **38 C2** SJ3830.
Horeb *Carmar.* ***Hamlet***, 3m/5km N of Llanelli. **17 H4** SN4905.
Horeb *Carmar.* ***Settlement***, 2m/3km SW of Brechfa. SN5128.
Horeb *Cere.* ***Settlement***, 2m/3km NW of Llandysul. **26 C4** SN3942.
Horeb *Flints.* ***Settlement***, 1m/2km SW of Hope. SJ2857.
Horfield *Bristol* ***Suburb***, 3m/4km N of Bristol city centre. **19 J4** ST5976.
Horham *Suff.* ***Village***, 2m/3km SW of Stradbroke. **35 G1** TM2172.
Horkesley Heath *Essex* ***Village***, 3m/4km N of Colchester. **34 D6** TL9829.
Horkstow *N.Lincs.* ***Village***, 4m/6km SW of Barton-upon-Humber and 7m/11km N of Brigg. **52 C1** SE9818.
Horley *Oxon.* ***Village***, 3m/5km NW of Banbury. **31 F4** SP4143.
Horley *Surr.* Population: 19,267. ***Town***, 4m/6km N of Crawley. 14c church. London (Gatwick) Airport 1m/2km S. **23 F7** TQ2843.
Horn Hill *Bucks.* ***Hamlet***, 3m/5km SW of Rickmansworth. **22 D2** TQ0192.
Hornblotton *Som.* ***Hamlet***, 3m/5km NE of Keinton Mandeville. ST5934.
Hornblotton Green *Som.* ***Hamlet***, 1km S of Hornblotton. **8 E1** ST5934.
Hornby *Lancs.* ***Village***, 8m/13km NE of Lancaster. **55 J3** SD5868.
Hornby *N.Yorks.* ***Hamlet***, 8m/12km N of Northallerton. **62 E6** NZ3605.
Hornby *N.Yorks.* ***Hamlet***, 3m/5km S of Catterick. Castle dating partly from 14c. **62 D7** SE2293.
Hornby Castle *Lancs.* ***Castle***, on E side of Hornby, 6m/9km E of Carnforth. Motte castle taken from Roger de Montbegon by King John in 13c. **55 J3** SD5868.
Horncastle *Lincs.* Population: 4994. ***Small town***, on River Bain, 18m/29km E of Lincoln, on site of Roman town of Banovallum, part of whose walls remain. **53 F6** TF2669.
Hornchurch *Gt.Lon.* ***Town***, in borough of Havering, 2m/4km SE of Romford. Traditional leather town. **23 J3** TQ5487.
Horncliffe *Northumb.* ***Village***, on River Tweed, 5m/8km SW of Berwick-upon-Tweed. River spanned to N by Union Bridge, Britain's first suspension bridge (1820). **77 H5** NT9249.
Horndean *Hants.* ***Small town***, 5m/7km N of Havant. **11 J3** SU7013.
Horndean *Sc.Bord.* ***Settlement***, 1m/2km N of Norham. **77 G6** NT8949.
Horndon *Devon* ***Hamlet***, 4m/7km NE of Tavistock. **6 D7** SX5280.
Horndon on the Hill *Thur.* ***Village***, 5m/8km SW of Basildon. **24 C3** TQ6683.
Horne *Surr.* ***Hamlet***, 4m/6km E of Horley. **23 G7** TQ3344.
Horne Row *Essex* ***Settlement***, to S of Danbury, 5m/8km E of Chelmsford. TL7704.
Horner *Som.* ***Hamlet***, largely National Trust, 1m/2km SE of Porlock. Ancient packhorse bridge. SS8945.
Horner's Green *Suff.* ***Settlement***, N of Boxford, 4m/6km W of Hadleigh. TL9641.
Horniehaugh *Angus* ***Settlement***, 2m/3km NE of Dykehead. **83 F1** NO4161.
Horning *Norf.* ***Village***, on E bank of River Bure, 3m/4km E of Hoveton. **45 H4** TG3417.
Horninghold *Leics.* ***Village***, 4m/6km SW of Uppingham. **42 B6** SP8097.
Horninglow *Staffs.* ***Suburb***, 1m/2km N of Burton upon Trent town centre. **40 E3** SK2325.
Horningsea *Cambs.* ***Village***, on E bank of River Cam, 4m/6km NE of Cambridge. **33 H2** TL4962.
Horningsham *Wilts.* ***Village***, at S side of Longleat Park, 5m/7km SW of Warminster. **20 B7** ST8141.
Horningtoft *Norf.* ***Village***, 4m/7km S of Fakenham. **44 D3** TF9323.
Horningtops *Cornw.* ***Settlement***, 3m/5km SE of Liskeard. **4 C4** SX2760.
Hornish *W.Isles* ***Coastal feature***, headland at northernmost point of Fuday. **84 C4** NF7309.
Hornish Point *W.Isles* ***Coastal feature***, headland on N coast of South Uist, 1m/2km NE of Ardivachar Point. **92 C7** NF7547.
Horns Cross *Devon* ***Hamlet***, 5m/7km SW of Bideford. **6 B3** SS3823.
Horns Cross *E.Suss.* ***Settlement***, 2m/3km S of Northiam. **14 D5** TQ8222.
Horns Cross *Kent* ***Locality***, at Stone, 2m/3km E of Dartford. TQ5774.
Horns Green *Gt.Lon.* ***Settlement***, in borough of Bromley, 2m/3km E of Biggin Hill. TQ4558.
Hornsbury *Som.* ***Settlement***, 1m/2km N of Chard. ST3310.
Hornsby *Cumb.* ***Settlement***, 1m/2km S of Cumwhitton. **61 G2** NY5250.
Hornsby Gate *Cumb.* ***Settlement***, on E side of River Eden, 4m/7km SE of Wetheral. **61 G1** NY5250.
Hornsbygate *Cumb.* ***Settlement***, to E of Hornsby, 4m/7km SE of Wetheral. NY5250.
Hornsea *E.Riding* Population: 7573. ***Small town***, coastal resort, 14m/22km NE of Kingston upon Hull. Well-known for Hornsea Pottery. Hornsea Mere has RSPB nature reserve. **59 J5** TA2047.
Hornsea Bridge *E.Riding* ***Locality***, adjoining to S of Hornsea. TA2047.
Hornsea Freeport *E.Riding* ***Leisure/recreation***, on S side of Hornsea. Park offering leisure and shopping opportunities. Attractions include model village, Butterfly World and birds of prey, while over 28 high street chains have shops selling products at discounted prices. **59 J5** TA2147.
Hornsea Mere *E.Riding* ***Lake/loch***, large lake on W side of Hornsea, containing RSPB nature reserve. **59 H5** TA2047.
Hornsey *Gt.Lon.* ***Suburb***, in borough of Haringey, 6m/9km N of Charing Cross. **23 G3** TQ3088.
Hornton *Oxon.* ***Village***, 5m/8km NW of Banbury. **30 E4** SP3945.
Horpit *Swin.* ***Locality***, 4m/6km E of Swindon. SU2184.
Horrabridge *Devon* Population: 1804. ***Village***, 4m/6km SE of Tavistock. **5 F4** SX5169.
Horridge *Devon* ***Settlement***, 3m/4km N of Ashburton. **5 H3** SX7674.
Horringer *Suff.* ***Village***, 3m/4km SW of Bury St. Edmunds. **34 C2** TL8261.
Horringford *I.o.W.* ***Settlement***, 3m/5km W of Sandown. SZ5485.
Horrocks Fold *Gt.Man.* ***Settlement***, 3m/4km NW of Bolton town centre and 1m/2km S of Delph Reservoir. SD7013.
Horrocksford *Lancs.* ***Locality***, 1m/2km N of Clitheroe, between Waddington and Chatburn. Extensive quarries to E and SE. SD7443.
Horsanish *W.Isles* ***Coastal feature***, headland on W coast of North Harris, 2m/3km SE of Huisinis. **100 B7** NA9908.
Horse Bank *Mersey.* ***Coastal feature***, sandbank at N end of Southport. **55 G7** SD3220.
Horse Bridge *Staffs.* ***Settlement***, 2m/4km SW of Leek. **49 J7** SJ9653.
Horse Green *Ches.* ***Locality***, just SW of Norbury. SJ5546.
Horse Hope Hill *Sc.Bord.* ***Mountain***, 6m/9km NW of St. Mary's Loch. Height 1938 feet or 591 metres. **76 A7** NT2030.
Horse Island *High.* ***Island***, one of Summer Isles group. Lies 1m/2km W of NW coast of Ross and Cromarty district across Horse Sound. Area about 350 acres or 140 hectares. **95 G1** NC0204.
Horse Island *Shet.* ***Island***, rock island lying off S coast of Mainland, 1m/2km W of Sumburgh Head. HU3807.
Horse Isle *N.Ayr.* ***Island***, with bird sanctuary, lying 1km out from Ardrossan harbour in Firth of Clyde. **74 A6** NS2142.
Horse of Copinsay *Ork.* ***Island***, turf-covered rocky islet 1km NE of Copinsay. HY6202.

H

Horse Sound *High.* ***Sea feature***, sea passage between Horse Island and NW coast of Ross and Cromarty district, 2m/3km SE of Achiltibuie. **95 G1** NC0304.
Horsea Island *Ports.* ***Island***, in Portsmouth Harbour, with causeway to Portsea Island. **11 H4** SU6304.
Horsebridge *Devon* ***Hamlet***, on River Tamar, 5m/8km W of Tavistock. **4 E3** SX4075.
Horsebridge *Hants.* ***Hamlet***, on River Test, 3m/5km S of Stockbridge. **10 E1** SU3430.
Horsebrook *Staffs.* ***Hamlet***, 3m/5km SW of Penkridge. **40 A4** SJ8810.
Horsecastle *N.Som.* ***Suburb***, N district of Yatton. ST4266.
Horsehay *Tel. & W.* ***Locality***, 1km W of Dawley, Telford. **39 F5** SJ6707.
Horseheath *Cambs.* ***Village***, 4m/6km W of Haverhill. Site of Roman settlement to NW. **33 K4** TL6147.
Horsehouse *N.Yorks.* ***Village***, 7m/11km SW of Middleham. **57 F1** SE0481.
Horseley Fen *Cambs.* ***Open space***, fenland 2m/3km SE of Chatteris. **43 G7** TL3983.
Horseley Heath *W.Mid.* ***Locality***, 2m/4km NW of West Bromwich town centre. SO9692.
Horseley Hill *Sc.Bord.* ***Hill***, with mast and hillfort, 3m/4km SE of Grantshouse. Height 859 feet or 262 metres. **77 G4** NT8362.
Horsell *Surr.* ***Suburb***, to N of Woking town centre. **22 C6** SU9959.
Horseman Side *Essex* ***Settlement***, 4m/6km NW of Brentwood. TQ5496.
Horseman's Green *Wrex.* ***Hamlet***, 6m/10km W of Whitchurch. **38 D1** SJ4441.
Horsenden *Bucks.* ***Hamlet***, 1m/2km SW of Princes Risborough. SP7902.
Horseshoe Common *Norf.* ***Locality***, adjoining to NW of Briston. TG0533.
Horseshoe Green *Kent* ***Hamlet***, just SE of Markbeech, 3m/5km SE of Edenbridge. TQ4742.
Horseshoe Pass *Denb.* ***Other feature of interest***, road pass crossing Maesyrychen Mountain, 3m/5km NW of Llangollen. **38 A1** SJ1846.
Horseshoes *Wilts.* ***Hamlet***, 3m/5km S of Melksham. ST9159.
Horseway *Cambs.* ***Settlement***, 2m/3km NE of Chatteris. **43 H7** TL4286.
Horsey *Norf.* ***Village***, near coast, 9m/14km NE of Acle. **45 J3** TG4622.
Horsey Corner *Norf.* ***Settlement***, 1km N of Horsey and 3m/5km N of Martham. TG4523.
Horsey Island *Essex* ***Island***, among marshes and creeks 2m/4km W of The Naze. **35 G6** TM2324.
Horsey Mere *Norf.* ***Lake/loch***, broad or lake (National Trust), to SW of Horsey. **45 J3** TG4622.
Horsey Windmill *Norf.* ***Other building***, 200-year-old windpump overlooking Horsey Mere, 2m/4km N of Martham. **45 J3** TG4522.
Horsford *Norf.* Population: 2255. ***Village***, 5m/8km NW of Norwich. **45 F4** TG1916.
Horsforth *W.Yorks.* Population: 18,593. ***Suburb***, 4m/7km NW of Leeds. **57 H6** SE2337.
Horsforth Woodside *W.Yorks.* ***Suburb***, adjoining to E of Horsforth, 4m/6km NW of Leeds city centre. SE2337.
Horsham *W.Suss.* Population: 42,552. ***Town***, old market town, 8m/12km SW of Crawley, with impressive Norman church. **12 E3** TQ1730.
Horsham *Worcs.* ***Settlement***, 6m/10km W of Worcester. **29 G3** SO7357.
Horsham St. Faith *Norf.* ***Village***, 4m/7km N of Norwich. Norwich Airport to S. **45 G4** TG2115.
Horsington *Lincs.* ***Village***, 4m/7km W of Horncastle. **52 E6** TF1968.
Horsington *Som.* ***Village***, 3m/5km S of Wincanton. **9 F2** ST7023.
Horsington Marsh *Som.* ***Settlement***, 1km NE of Horsington. ST7124.
Horsley *Derbys.* ***Village***, 4m/7km S of Ripley. **41 F1** SK3844.
Horsley *Glos.* ***Village***, 1m/2km SW of Nailsworth. **20 B2** ST8398.
Horsley *Northumb.* ***Hamlet***, 1m/2km SE of Rochester. **70 D4** NY8496.
Horsley *Northumb.* ***Village***, 2m/4km W of Heddon-on-the-Wall. **71 F7** NZ0966.
Horsley Cross *Essex* ***Settlement***, 3m/5km SE of Manningtree. **35 F6** TM1227.
Horsley Hill *T. & W.* ***Suburb***, 1m/2km SE of South Shields town centre. NZ3865.
Horsley Woodhouse *Derbys.* ***Village***, 4m/6km S of Ripley. **41 F1** SK3944.
Horsleycross Street *Essex* ***Hamlet***, 2m/4km SE of Manningtree. **35 F6** TM1228.
Horsleygate *Derbys.* ***Settlement***, 1km SW of Holmesfield. SK3177.
Horsleyhill *Sc.Bord.* ***Hamlet***, 4m/6km NE of Hawick. NT5319.
Horsleys Green *Bucks.* ***Settlement***, 2m/3km SE of Stokenchurch. SU7895.
Horsmonden *Kent* ***Village***, 4m/6km SE of Paddock Wood. **14 C3** TQ7040.
Horspath *Oxon.* Population: 1417. ***Village***, 4m/6km E of Oxford. **21 J1** SP5704.
Horstead *Norf.* ***Village***, 1km W of Coltishall. **45 G4** TG2619.
Horsted Keynes *W.Suss.* ***Village***, 4m/7km NE of Haywards Heath. N terminus of Bluebell Railway, S end of which is at Sheffield Park. **13 G4** TQ3828.
Horsted Place *E.Suss.* ***Garden***, Victorian garden, 2m/3km S of Uckfield. **13 H5** TQ4618.
Horton *Bucks.* ***Hamlet***, 4m/6km S of Leighton Buzzard. **32 C7** SP9219.
Horton *Dorset* ***Village***, 5m/8km N of Wimborne Minster. **10 B4** SU0307.
Horton *Lancs.* ***Hamlet***, 2m/3km NE of Gisburn. **56 D4** SD8550.
Horton *Northants.* ***Village***, 6m/9km SE of Northampton. **32 B3** SP8154.
Horton *Oxon. See Horton-cum-Studley.*
Horton *Shrop.* ***Hamlet***, 2m/3km NW of Wem. SJ4829.
Horton *Som.* ***Village***, adjoining to S of Broadway, 3m/4km W of Ilminster. **8 C3** ST3214.
Horton *S.Glos.* ***Village***, 3m/5km NE of Chipping Sodbury. **20 A3** ST7685.
Horton *Staffs.* ***Village***, 3m/5km W of Leek. **49 J7** SJ9457.
Horton *Swan.* ***Village***, above Port Eynon Bay, on S coast of Gower peninsula. **17 H6** SS4785.
Horton *Tel. & W.* ***Hamlet***, 3m/4km NE of Wellington. SJ6814.
Horton *Wilts.* ***Village***, 3m/5km NE of Devizes. **20 D5** SU0563.
Horton *W. & M.* ***Village***, 4m/6km SE of Slough. **22 D4** TQ0175.
Horton Common *Dorset* ***Open space***, heath 1m/2km SW of Verwood. **10 B4** SU0706.
Horton Country Park *Surr.* ***Leisure/recreation***, over 200 acres of meadow and woodland, 1m/2km W of Ewell. **22 E5** TQ1962.
Horton Court *S.Glos.* ***Historic house***, Cotswold manor house (National Trust), 3m/5km NE of Chipping Sodbury. **20 A3** ST7685.
Horton Cross *Som.* ***Hamlet***, 1m/2km NE of Horton. **8 C3** ST3315.
Horton-cum-Studley *Oxon.* ***Village***, comprising adjoining hamlets of Horton and Studley, 6m/10km NE of Oxford. **31 G7** SP5912.
Horton Green *Ches.* ***Hamlet***, 3m/4km NW of Malpas. **38 D1** SJ4549.
Horton Heath *Hants.* ***Suburb***, 3m/5km SE of Eastleigh. **11 F3** SU4917.
Horton in Ribblesdale *N.Yorks.* ***Village***, 5m/8km N of Settle. Limestone quarries. **56 D2** SD8172.
Horton Inn *Dorset* ***Settlement***, 5m/8km N of Wimborne Minster. **10 B4** SU0108.
Horton Kirby *Kent* ***Village***, on River Darent, 4m/6km S of Dartford. **23 J5** TQ5668.
Horton Moor *N.Yorks.* ***Open space***, moorland on W side of Pen-y-Ghent, 2m/3km NE of Horton in Ribblesdale. **56 D2** SD8274.
Horwich *Gt.Man.* Population: 18,017. ***Town***, former mill town, 5m/8km W of Bolton. **49 F1** SD6311.
Horwich End *Derbys.* ***Locality***, adjoining to S of Whaley Bridge. **50 C4** SK0180.
Horwood *Devon* ***Village***, 3m/5km E of Bideford. **6 D3** SS5027.
Hoscar *Lancs.* ***Settlement***, with railway station, 2m/3km E of Burscough Bridge. SD4711.
Hose *Leics.* ***Village***, 7m/11km N of Melton Mowbray. **42 A3** SK7329.
Hoses *Cumb.* ***Settlement***, in small valley, 3m/5km N of Broughton in Furness. **60 D7** SD2192.
Hosey Hill *Kent* ***Settlement***, just S of Westerham. TQ4553.
Hosh *P. & K.* ***Village***, with distillery at foot of Glen Turret, 1m/2km NW of Crieff. **81 K5** NN8523.
Hosta *W.Isles* ***Settlement***, near NW coast of North Uist, 3m/4km S of Griminis Point. **92 C4** NF7272.
Hoswick *Shet.* ***Village***, at head of Hos Wick. **109 D10** HU4123.
Hot Point *Cornw.* ***Coastal feature***, headland 1km E of Lizard. **2 E7** SW7112.
Hotham *E.Riding* ***Village***, 5m/8km S of Market Weighton. **58 E6** SE8934.
Hothersall *Lancs.* ***Locality***, 2m/3km W of Ribchester. SD6234.
Hothfield *Kent* ***Village***, 3m/5km NW of Ashford. **14 E3** TQ9644.
Hoton *Leics.* ***Village***, 3m/5km NE of Loughborough. **41 H3** SK5722.
Hoton Hills *Leics.* ***Settlement***, 1km W of Hoton, 3m/4km NE of Loughborough. SK5722.
Hott Hill *Sc.Bord.* ***Mountain***, 3m/4km SW of Branxholme. Height 1023 feet or 312 metres. **69 K2** NT4210.
Houbie *Shet.* ***Settlement***, on S coast of Fetlar, at head of Wick of Houbie. **108 F3** HU6290.
Houdston *S.Ayr.* ***Settlement***, adjoining to E of Girvan. NX1998.
Hough *Ches.* ***Settlement***, 1m/2km E of Alderley Edge. SJ8578.
Hough *Ches.* ***Village***, 3m/4km S of Crewe. **49 G7** SJ7151.
Hough Bay *Arg. & B.* ***Bay***, at W end of Tiree, on N side of Rubha Chràiginis. **78 A3** NL9346.
Hough End *W.Yorks.* ***Suburb***, 3m/5km W of Leeds city centre. SE2433.
Hough Green *Halton* ***Suburb***, 2m/3km W of Widnes town centre. **48 D4** SJ4886.
Hough-on-the-Hill *Lincs.* ***Village***, 7m/11km N of Grantham. **42 C1** SK9246.
Hough Side *W.Yorks.* ***Locality***, adjoining to E of Pudsey. SE2333.
Hough Skerries *Arg. & B.* ***Island***, group of island rocks lying 1m/2km NW of Hough Bay at W end of Tiree. NL9247.
Hougham *Lincs.* ***Village***, 6m/10km N of Grantham. **42 B1** SK8844.
Hougharry *W.Isles Anglicised form of Hogha Gearraidh, qv.*
Houghton *Cambs.* ***Village***, 3m/4km E of Huntingdon. Timber water-mill (National Trust) on River Great Ouse. **33 F1** TL2872.
Houghton *Cumb.* ***Suburb***, 2m/3km N of Carlisle. **60 F1** NY4059.
Houghton *Devon* ***Settlement***, 1km NE of Ringmore. **5 G6** SX6546.
Houghton *Hants.* ***Village***, on River Test, 2m/3km S of Stockbridge. **10 E1** SU3432.
Houghton *Pembs.* ***Hamlet***, 1m/2km S of Llangwm. **16 C4** SM9807.
Houghton *W.Suss.* ***Village***, 3m/5km N of Arundel. **12 D5** TQ0111.
Houghton Bank *Darl.* ***Hamlet***, 4m/6km SW of Newton Aycliffe. **62 D4** NZ2222.
Houghton Conquest *Beds.* ***Village***, 2m/4km N of Ampthill. **32 D4** TL0441.
Houghton Green *E.Suss.* ***Hamlet***, 2m/3km N of Rye. TQ9222.
Houghton Green *Warr.* ***Suburb***, on N edge of Warrington. SJ6291.
Houghton Hall *Norf.* ***Historic house***, 18c house by Sir Robert Walpole, 8m/12km W of Fakenham. One of finest examples of Palladian architecture in England, set in magnificent parkland, including deer park. **44 B3** TF7928.
Houghton House *Beds.* ***Historic house***, ruined 16c house (English Heritage), 1m/2km N of Ampthill. **32 D5** TL0339.
Houghton-le-Side *Darl.* ***Settlement***, 6m/10km NW of Darlington. **62 D4** NZ2221.
Houghton le Spring *T. & W.* Population: 35,100. ***Town***, 6m/9km SW of Sunderland. **62 E2** NZ3450.
Houghton Lodge *Hants.* ***Garden***, on River Test, in Houghton, 1m/2km S of Stockbridge. Contains Hampshire Hydroponicum in kitchen garden, where vegetation grows without soil. **10 E1** SU3433.
Houghton Mill *Cambs.* ***Other building***, large 19c timber-built water-mill (National Trust) on an island in River Great Ouse, to S of Houghton. **33 F1** TL2871.
Houghton on the Hill *Leics.* ***Village***, 6m/9km E of Leicester. **41 J5** SK6703.
Houghton Regis *Beds.* ***Suburb***, 1m/2km N of Dunstable. **32 D6** TL0123.
Houghton St. Giles *Norf.* ***Village***, 4m/6km N of Fakenham. Restored 14c Slipper Chapel. **44 D2** TF9235.
Houlsyke *N.Yorks.* ***Hamlet***, 5m/8km W of Egton. **63 J6** NZ7307.
Hound *Hants.* ***Village***, 1m/2km E of Netley. **11 F4** SU4708.
Hound Green *Hants.* ***Hamlet***, 3m/5km N of Hook. **22 A6** SU7259.
Hound Hillock *Aber.* ***Mountain***, 4m/6km NW of Fettercairn. Height 1699 feet or 518 metres. **90 E7** NO6279.
Hound Point *Edin.* ***Coastal feature***, headland on S side of Firth of Forth, 1m/2km E of Forth Bridge. **75 K3** NT1579.
Hound Tor Medieval Village *Devon* ***Historic/prehistoric site***, 2m/3km NE of Widecombe in the Moor. Deserted medieval village (English Heritage) occupied in 11c with remains of buildings from 13c. Probably abandoned in 14c as climate became harsher. **5 H3** SX7478.
Houndmills *Hants.* ***Locality***, industrial estate in NW part of Basingstoke. SU6252.
Houndslow *Sc.Bord.* ***Hamlet***, 5m/8km W of Greenlaw. **76 E6** NT6247.
Houndsmoor *Som.* ***Hamlet***, just SE of Milverton, 3m/5km N of Wellington. ST1225.
Houndwood *Sc.Bord.* ***Settlement***, on Eye Water, 2m/4km SE of Grantshouse. **77 G4** NT8463.
Hounsdown *Hants.* ***Village***, 1m/2km S of Totton. **10 E3** SU3511.
Hounslow Green *Essex* ***Hamlet***, 3m/4km SE of Great Dunmow. **33 K7** TL6518.
Housay *Shet.* ***Island***, main island in Out Skerries group, NE of Whalsay. Island is connected to Bruray by road bridge. **108 F5** HU6671.
House of Dun *Angus* ***Historic house***, 18c Palladian house (National Trust for Scotland) built for David Erskine, 3m/5km NW of Montrose. **83 H2** NO6759.
House of the Binns *W.Loth. Alternative name for The Binns, qv.*
Housebay *Ork.* ***Settlement***, on Bay of Houseby, on S coast of Stronsay. HY6721.
Housedon Hill *Northumb.* ***Hill***, 2m/3km N of Westnewton. Height 876 feet or 267 metres. **77 G7** NT9032.
Househill *High.* ***Settlement***, 1km from Nairn across River Nairn. **97 F6** NH8855.
Houses Hill *W.Yorks.* ***Hamlet***, 2m/3km S of Mirfield. SE1916.
Houses of Parliament *Gt.Lon.* ***Other building***, Victorian-Gothic building, 1km S of Charing Cross, on W bank of River Thames. Most of present building dates from 1840-1868 design by Sir Charles Barry and A.W.N. Pugin after a fire in 1834. Oldest part, Westminster Hall, was built in 1099 as Great Hall of William Rufus' new royal palace; roof and Jewel Tower (English Heritage) date from 14c. Occupied by monarchy, it was used as forum or parliament from 1295 under Edward I, until 1512 when Henry VIII departed for Whitehall Palace. In 1550 it became main meeting place for parliament members, when Royal Chapel of St. Stephen's was first used as a debating chamber. Since then it has become main seat of government, withstanding attacks by Guy Fawkes, in 1605, and numerous sovereigns, with no member of the monarchy entering House of Commons since Charles I in 1642. Parliament is divided into House of Lords and House of Commons. Clock tower at N tip of Houses of Parliament holds famous bell, Big Ben. Parliament Past and Present exhibition is contained within Jewel Tower. **23 G4** TQ3079.
Housesteads Roman Fort *Northumb.* ***Historic/prehistoric site***, remains of Britain's best preserved Roman fort of Vercovicium (National Trust and English Heritage) on Hadrian's Wall, 3m/4km N of Bardon Mill. 2m/3km to E is Sewingshields Wall (English Heritage), a mainly unexcavated section including turrets of Coesike and Grindon. **70 C7** NY7868.
Housetter *Shet.* ***Settlement***, on Mainland, 1km N of Colla Firth. **108 C4** HU3684.
Housham Tye *Essex* ***Settlement***, 4m/6km E of Harlow. TL5010.
Houss *Shet.* ***Settlement***, on East Burra, 1m/2km S of bridge connection with West Burra. HU3731.
Houss Ness *Shet.* ***Locality***, in S part of East Burra. **109 C10** HU3728.

Houston *Renf.* Population: 5479. ***Village***, 3m/5km NW of Johnstone. **74 C4** NS4066.
Houston Industrial Estate *W.Loth.* ***Locality***, to N of Livingston town centre. NT0569.
Houstry *High.* ***Settlement***, in Caithness district, 3m/5km NW of Latheron. **105 G5** ND1535.
Houstry of Dunn *High.* ***Settlement***, just N of Backlass, 2m/3km W of Watten. **105 H3** ND2054.
Houton *Ork.* ***Settlement***, on Bay of Houton, on S coast of Mainland. **107 C7** HY3104.
Houton Head *Ork.* ***Coastal feature***, headland on Mainland, 2m/3km NE of Scad Head on Hoy across Bring Deeps. To E is Holm of Houton at entrance to Bay of Houton. **107 C7** HY3003.
Hove *B. & H.* Population: 67,602. ***Town***, residential and seaside resort adjoining to W of Brighton. Former fishing village, with Regency and Victorian houses. Notable art gallery. Site of Sussex county cricket ground. **13 F6** TQ2804.
Hove Edge *W.Yorks.* ***Suburb***, 1m/2km NW of Brighouse town centre. SE1324.
Hoveringham *Notts.* ***Village***, 2m/3km E of Lowdham. **41 J1** SK6946.
Hoveton *Norf.* Population: 1623. ***Village***, 8m/12km NE of Norwich. **45 H4** TG3018.
Hovingham *N.Yorks.* ***Village***, 8m/12km W of Malton. **58 C2** SE6675.
How *Cumb.* ***Hamlet***, 3m/5km SW of Brampton. **61 G1** NY5056.
How Caple *Here.* ***Village***, 4m/7km N of Ross-on-Wye across loop of River Wye. **29 F5** SO6030.
How Caple Court *Here.* ***Garden***, 8m/12km SE of Hereford. 11 acres of formal Edwardian gardens, with restored sunken Florentine garden. **28 E5** SO6130.
How End *Beds.* ***Settlement***, 2m/3km N of Ampthill. **32 D4** TL0340.
How Green *Herts.* ***Locality***, W end of Buntingford. TL3529.
How Green *Kent* ***Hamlet***, 2m/3km E of Edenbridge. TQ4746.
How Hill *Norf.* ***Locality***, 1m/2km NW of Ludham, with Nature Reserve and Nature Trail to NW. TG3719.
How Man *Cumb.* ***Settlement***, 1km from coast, 2m/3km W of Egremont. **60 A5** NX9810.
How Stean Beck *N.Yorks.* ***River***, stream formed from numerous tributaries on Riggs Moor and flowing NE to merge with Armathwaite Gill, entering River Nidd just S of Lofthouse. **57 F2** SE1073.
Howardian Hills *N.Yorks.* ***Large natural feature***, range of hills to S of Vale of Pickering, 8m/13km W of Malton. **58 C2** SE6372.
Howat's Hill *D. & G.* ***Hill***, with Torbeckhill Reservoir to NE, 3m/5km NE of Ecclefechan. Height 810 feet or 247 metres. **69 H6** NY2279.
Howber Hill *N.Yorks. Alternative name for Beamsley Beacon, qv.*
Howbrook *S.Yorks.* ***Hamlet***, 2m/3km SE of Wortley. SK3298.
Howden *E.Riding* Population: 3673. ***Small town***, 3m/5km N of Goole across River Ouse. Partly ruined Howden Minster (English Heritage) dates from 14c. **58 D7** SE7428.
Howden *W.Loth.* ***Suburb***, residential area to SW of Livingston town centre. NT0567.
Howden Clough *W.Yorks.* ***Suburb***, 1m/2km N of Batley town centre. SE2326.
Howden Hill *N.Yorks.* ***Settlement***, 3m/4km SW of Darlington. NZ2413.
Howden-le-Wear *Dur.* ***Village***, 1m/2km S of Crook. **62 C3** NZ1633.
Howden Moors *S.Yorks.* ***Open space***, large area of moorland to NW of Sheffield in Peak District National Park, 2m/3km N of Derwent Reservoir and 6m/10km W of Stocksbridge. Includes areas of marsh along with short, steep river valleys. **50 D3** SK1597.
Howden Reservoir *Derbys.* ***Reservoir***, on border with South Yorkshire, in Derwent Dale, 9m/14km E of Glossop across High Peak. **50 D3** SK1792.
Howdon *T. & W.* ***Suburb***, 1m/2km NE of Wallsend. NZ3267.
Howdon Pans *T. & W.* ***Locality***, to SE of Howdon on N bank of River Tyne. NZ3266.
Howe *Cumb.* ***Hamlet***, in Lyth Valley, 4m/7km SW of Kendal. **55 H1** SD4588.
Howe *High.* ***Settlement***, in Caithness district, 8m/13km NW of Wick. Ruthers of Howe is settlement 1km N. **105 J2** ND3062.
Howe *Norf.* ***Hamlet***, 6m/10km SE of Norwich. **45 G5** TM2799.
Howe *N.Yorks.* ***Hamlet***, 1km SE of Ainderby Quernhow. **57 J1** SE3580.
Howe Bridge *Gt.Man.* ***Locality***, adjoining to SW of Atherton. SD6602.
Howe Green *Essex* ***Village***, 4m/6km SE of Chelmsford. **24 D1** TL7403.
Howe of Alford *Aber.* ***Valley***, broad section of valley carrying River Don in vicinity of Alford. **90 D3** NJ5716.
Howe of Fife *Fife* ***Valley***, fertile area astride River Eden, between Strathmiglo and Cupar. **82 D6** NO2910.
Howe of Teuchar *Aber.* ***Locality***, 2m/3km S of Cuminestown. **99 F6** NJ7947.
Howe of the Mearns *Aber.* ***Valley***, fertile tract to E of Fettercairn. **83 H1** NO6974.
Howe Street *Essex* ***Hamlet***, 1m/2km NE of Finchingfield. **33 K5** TL6934.
Howe Street *Essex* ***Village***, 5m/8km N of Chelmsford. **33 K7** TL6914.
Howegreen *Essex* ***Hamlet***, 4m/6km S of Maldon. TL8301.
Howell *Lincs.* ***Hamlet***, 4m/7km E of Sleaford. **42 E1** TF1346.
Howell Wood Country Park *S.Yorks.* ***Leisure/recreation***, planted as woodland in early 19c, now protected reserve with nature trails, 3m/4km S of Hemsworth. **51 G2** SE4309.
Howey *Powys* ***Village***, 1m/2km S of Llandrindod Wells. **27 K3** SO0558.
Howgate *Midloth.* ***Village***, 1m/2km SE of Penicuik. **76 A5** NT2458.
Howgill *Cumb.* ***Locality***, to SE of Lowgill, 3m/5km NW of Sedbergh. SD6396.
Howgill *Lancs.* ***Settlement***, 2m/3km S of Gisburn. SD8246.
Howgill *N.Yorks.* ***Settlement***, above River Wharfe, 1m/2km SE of Appletreewick. **57 F4** SE0659.
Howick *Northumb.* ***Hamlet***, on coast, 5m/9km NE of Alnwick. **71 H2** NU2517.
Howick Hall *Northumb.* ***Garden***, formal and woodland gardens, 5m/8km NE of Alnwick. **71 H2** NU2417.
Howick Haven *Northumb.* ***Sea feature***, small inlet to S of Howick. **71 H2** NU2517.
Howle *Dur.* ***Hamlet***, 1km W of Butterknowle. NZ0925.
Howle *Tel. & W.* ***Hamlet***, 4m/7km NW of Newport. **39 F3** SJ6923.
Howle Hill *Here.* ***Hamlet***, 2m/4km S of Ross-on-Wye. SO6020.
Howlett End *Essex* ***Hamlet***, 3m/5km NW of Thaxted. **33 J5** TL5834.
Howletts Wild Animal Park *Kent* ***Leisure/recreation***, wildlife park 3m/5km SE of Canterbury city centre, containing wide variety of animals including world's largest breeding gorilla colony in captivity. **15 G2** TR1956.
Howley *Som.* ***Hamlet***, 4m/6km W of Chard. **8 B4** ST2609.
Howmore *W.Isles Anglicised form of Tobha Mòr, qv.*
Hownam *Sc.Bord.* ***Village***, on Kale Water, 8m/13km E of Jedburgh. **70 C2** NT7719.
Hownam Law *Sc.Bord.* ***Mountain***, 3m/4km SE of Morebattle. Height 1473 feet or 449 metres. **70 C1** NT7921.
Hownam Mains *Sc.Bord.* ***Settlement***, 3m/5km S of Morebattle. **70 C1** NT7720.
Howpasley *Sc.Bord.* ***Hamlet***, 1km SW of Craik. **69 J3** NT3407.
Howsham *N.Lincs.* ***Village***, 4m/6km SE of Brigg. **52 D2** TA0404.
Howsham *N.Yorks.* ***Village***, 7m/11km SW of Malton. Hall has Jacobean exterior. **58 D3** SE7362.
Howt Green *Kent* ***Settlement***, 2m/3km NW of Sittingbourne. TQ8965.
Howtel *Northumb.* ***Settlement***, 3m/4km W of Milfield. **77 G7** NT8934.
Howton *Here.* ***Settlement***, 2m/3km NE of Pontrilas. **28 D6** SO4129.
Howtown *Cumb.* ***Locality***, close to S shore of Ullswater, 4m/6km SW of Pooley Bridge. NY4419.
Howwood *Renf.* Population: 1036. ***Village***, 3m/4km SW of Johnstone. **74 C4** NS3960.
Hoxa *Ork.* ***Settlement***, on NW peninsula of South Ronaldsay, 2m/3km W of St. Margaret's Hope. **107 D8** ND4293.
Hoxne *Suff.* ***Village***, 3m/5km NE of Eye. **35 F1** TM1877.
Hoxton *Gt.Lon.* ***Suburb***, in borough of Hackney, 3m/4km NE of Charing Cross. TQ3383.
Hoy *High.* ***Settlement***, 3m/4km SE of Castletown. **105 H2** ND2164.
Hoy *Ork.* ***Island***, second largest of Orkney group of islands after Mainland, lying on W side of Scapa Flow and SW of Mainland across Hoy Sound and Bring Deeps. Island is 14m/22km NW to SE and 6m/10km NE to SW. Rugged, rocky landscape of Old Red Sandstone with steep cliffs to W and stack of Old Man of Hoy, rising to 449 feet or 137 metres, on NW coast. **107 B8** ND2597.
Hoy Sound *Ork.* ***Sea feature***, channel to N of Hoy dividing it from Mainland. **107 A7** HY2307.
Hoylake *Mersey.* Population: 12,777. ***Town***, coastal resort at NW end of Wirral peninsula 7m/11km W of Birkenhead. **48 B4** SJ2189.
Hoyland *S.Yorks.* Population: 15,629. ***Town***, 4m/6km S of Barnsley. **51 F2** SE3600.
Hoyland Common *S.Yorks.* ***Locality***, 1km W of Hoyland. SE3600.
Hoyland Swaine *S.Yorks.* ***Village***, 1m/2km NE of Penistone. **50 E2** SE2604.
Hoyle *W.Suss.* ***Settlement***, 2m/4km SE of Midhurst. SU9018.
Hoyle Green *W.Yorks.* ***Hamlet***, 1km N of Sowerby Bridge. SE0524.
Hoyle Mill *S.Yorks.* ***Suburb***, 1m/2km E of Barnsley town centre. SE3606.
Hubberholme *N.Yorks.* ***Settlement***, at foot of Langstrothdale, 1m/2km NW of Buckden. Partly Norman church has rood loft. **56 E2** SD9278.
Hubberston *Pembs.* ***Suburb***, W district of Milford Haven. SM8906.
Hubbersty Head *Cumb.* ***Settlement***, 4m/7km S of Windermere. SD4291.
Hubberton Green *W.Yorks.* ***Settlement***, 2m/3km W of Sowerby Bridge. SE0322.
Hubbert's Bridge *Lincs.* ***Hamlet***, on South Forty Foot Drain, 4m/6km W of Boston. **43 F1** TF2643.
Huby *N.Yorks.* ***Village***, 5m/8km S of Harrogate. **57 H5** SE2747.
Huby *N.Yorks.* ***Village***, 8m/13km N of York. **58 B3** SE5665.
Hucclecote *Glos.* ***Suburb***, E district of Gloucester; also parish to E. Site of Roman villa. **29 H7** SO8717.
Hucclecote Green *Glos.* ***Suburb***, in SE part of Gloucester. SO8716.
Hucking *Kent* ***Hamlet***, 5m/8km SW of Sittingbourne. **14 D2** TQ8458.
Hucknall *Notts.* Population: 29,160. ***Town***, 6m/10km N of Nottingham. Known for textiles and furniture-making industries. Lord Byron buried here. **41 H1** SK5349.
Hud Hey *Lancs.* ***Locality***, 1m/2km N of Haslingden. SD7824.
Huddersfield *W.Yorks.* Population: 143,726. ***Town***, textile town on River Colne, 11m/17km S of Bradford. Many substantial Victorian buildings, including railway station completed in 1850 and said to be one of finest railway buildings in England. University. **50 D1** SE1416.
Hudderstone *S.Lan.* ***Mountain***, 4m/7km S of Coulter. Height 2057 feet or 627 metres. **69 F1** NT0227.
Huddington *Worcs.* ***Village***, 5m/8km SE of Droitwich Spa. **29 J3** SO9457.
Huddlesford *Staffs.* ***Hamlet***, on Coventry Canal, 3m/4km E of Lichfield. SK1509.
Huddleston *N.Yorks.* ***Locality***, 2m/3km W of Sherburn in Elmet. Former quarries here supplied stone for York Minster and parts of King's College Chapel, Cambridge. SE4633.
Hudnall *Herts.* ***Hamlet***, 4m/6km N of Berkhamsted. TL0013.
Hudscott *Devon* ***Settlement***, 4m/6km W of South Molton. **6 E3** SS6424.
Hudswell *N.Yorks.* ***Village***, 2m/3km W of Richmond. **62 C6** NZ1400.
Huggate *E.Riding* ***Village***, in The Wolds, 6m/10km NE of Pocklington. **58 E4** SE8855.
Hugglescote *Leics.* ***Suburb***, in S part of Coalville. **41 G4** SK4212.
Hugh Mill *Lancs.* ***Locality***, 2m/3km E of Rawtenstall. SD8321.
Hugh Town *I.o.S.* ***Town***, capital of Isles of Scilly, situated on St. Mary's. Harry's Walls (English Heritage), incomplete 16c fort overlooking St. Mary's Pool. **2 C1** SV9010.
Hughenden Manor *Bucks.* ***Historic house***, 1m/2km S of Hughenden Valley, home of Disraeli from 1847 to 1881 (National Trust). **22 B2** SU8696.
Hughenden Valley *Bucks.* Population: 2071. ***Village***, 2m/4km N of High Wycombe. **22 B2** SU8696.
Hughley *Shrop.* ***Village***, 4m/6km W of Much Wenlock. **38 E6** SO5697.
Hugmore *Wrex.* ***Settlement***, 3m/5km NE of Wrexham town centre. **48 C7** SJ3751.
Hugus *Cornw.* ***Settlement***, 3m/5km W of Truro. SW7743.
Huilish Point *W.Isles* ***Coastal feature***, headland 1km NE of Veilish Point on North Uist. **92 D4** NF8278.
Huip Ness *Ork.* ***Coastal feature***, headland on N of Stronsay, bending round to almost enclose Oyce of Huip. **106 F4** HY6430.
Huip Sound *Ork.* ***Sea feature***, channel between Holm of Huip and Stronsay. **106 F4** HY6231.
Huish *Devon* ***Hamlet***, 6m/9km SE of Great Torrington. **6 D4** SS5311.
Huish *Wilts.* ***Hamlet***, 3m/4km N of Pewsey. **20 E5** SU1463.
Huish Champflower *Som.* ***Village***, 2m/4km NW of Wiveliscombe. **7 J3** ST0429.
Huish Episcopi *Som.* ***Village***, 1km E of Langport. **8 D2** ST4226.
Huisinis (Anglicised form: Hushinish.) *W.Isles* ***Settlement***, on W coast of North Harris, on Hushinish Bay. **100 B6** NA9812.
Hulam *Dur.* ***Settlement***, 1m/2km N of Sheraton. NZ4436.
Hulcott *Bucks.* ***Village***, 3m/5km NE of Aylesbury. **32 B7** SP8516.
Hule Moss *Sc.Bord.* ***Lake/loch***, tarn on Greenlaw Moor 2m/3km N of Greenlaw. **77 F6** NT7149.
Hulham *Devon* ***Suburb***, 1m/2km N of Exmouth town centre. SY0183.
Hull ***River***, rising at Elmswell and flowing E, on S side of East Driffield, to Wansford, then S past Beverley into River Humber at Kingston upon Hull. **59 G5** TA1028.
Hull *Hull Familiar name of Kingston upon Hull, qv.*
Hull Bridge *E.Riding* ***Locality***, at road crossing of River Hull, 2m/3km NE of Beverley. TA0541.
Hulland *Derbys.* ***Village***, 4m/7km E of Ashbourne. **40 E1** SK2446.
Hullavington *Wilts.* ***Village***, 4m/7km SW of Malmesbury. **20 B3** ST8982.
Hullbridge *Essex* Population: 6630. ***Suburb***, 3m/4km N of Rayleigh. **24 E2** TQ8195.
Hulme *Staffs.* ***Hamlet***, 4m/6km E of Stoke-on-Trent. SJ9345.
Hulme *Warr.* ***Suburb***, 2m/3km N of Warrington town centre. SJ6091.
Hulme End *Staffs.* ***Hamlet***, on River Manifold, 2m/3km W of Hartington. **50 D7** SK1059.
Hulme Walfield *Ches.* ***Hamlet***, 2m/3km NW of Congleton. **49 H6** SJ8465.
Hulne Park *Northumb.* ***Locality***, 2m/3km NW of Alnwick. **71 G2** NU1415.
Hulne Priory *Northumb.* ***Ecclesiastical building***, remains of 13c Carmelite priory in park, 2m/3km NW of Alnwick. **71 G2** NU1615.
Hulseheath *Ches.* ***Settlement***, 4m/6km NW of Knutsford. SJ7283.
Hulton Lane Ends *Gt.Man.* ***Locality***, 3m/4km SW of Bolton. SD6905.
Hulver Street *Norf.* ***Locality***, 4m/6km W of East Dereham. TF9312.
Hulver Street *Suff.* ***Village***, 4m/6km SE of Beccles. **45 J7** TM4686.
Hulverstone *I.o.W.* ***Hamlet***, 2m/3km NW of Brighstone. SZ3984.
Humber ***Sea feature***, estuarial river formed by Rivers Trent and Ouse and flowing into North Sea between Spurn Head and Northcoates Point. Ports of Kingston upon Hull and Grimsby are situated on its N and S banks respectively. **59 F7** TA3807.
Humber *Devon* ***Hamlet***, 3m/5km NW of Teignmouth. SX9075.
Humber *Here.* ***Settlement***, 3m/5km SE of Leominster. **28 E3** SO5356.
Humber Bridge ***Bridge***, bridge to SW of Kingston upon Hull, spanning River Humber from Hessle on N bank to Barton-on-Humber on S bank. Opened 1981. **59 G7** TA0324.
Humber Bridge Country Park *E.Riding* ***Leisure/recreation***, country park located on N side of Humber Bridge, with over 50 acres of woodland, grassland and ponds with views over River Humber. **59 G7** TA0226.
Humberside International Airport *N.Lincs.* ***Airport/airfield***, 1km SW of Kirmington, 3m/4km E of Barnetby le Wold. **52 E1** TA0909.
Humberston *N.E.Lincs.* Population: 6877. ***Suburb***, 4m/6km SE of Grimsby. **53 G2** TA3105.

Humberston Fitties *N.E.Lincs.* ***Settlement***, on coast, to E of Humberston. TA3305.
Humberstone *Leic.* ***Suburb***, 3m/5km E of Leicester city centre. **41 J5** SK6205.
Humberton *N.Yorks.* ***Settlement***, 2m/3km NE of Boroughbridge across River Ure. SE4268.
Humbie *E.Loth.* ***Village***, on Humbie Water, 8m/13km SW of Haddington. **76 C4** NT4562.
Humbleton *Dur.* ***Settlement***, 3m/4km E of Barnard Castle. NZ0917.
Humbleton *E.Riding* ***Village***, 5m/7km NE of Hedon. **59 J6** TA2234.
Humbleton *Northumb.* ***Settlement***, 1m/2km W of Wooler. **70 E1** NT9728.
Humbleton Hill *Northumb. See Battle of Homildon Hill 1402.*
Humby *Lincs.* ***Hamlet***, 6m/10km E of Grantham. **42 D2** TF0032.
Hume *Sc.Bord.* ***Village***, 3m/5km S of Greenlaw. Ruins of 13c castle, formerly seat of Earls of Home. **77 F6** NT7041.
Hume Castle *Sc.Bord.* ***Castle***, ruins of 13c high-walled enclosure castle, 3m/5km S of Greenlaw. **77 F6** NT7041.
Humehall *Sc.Bord.* ***Settlement***, 3m/4km S of Greenlaw. **77 F6** NT7141.
Humla *High.* ***Island***, rock in Inner Hebrides lying 3m/5km S of W end of Canna. **85 H4** NG1900.
Hummer *Dorset* ***Settlement***, 3m/5km NE of Yeovil. ST5819.
Humphrey Head Point *Cumb.* ***Coastal feature***, headland at outfall of River Kent estuary into Morecambe Bay, 2m/4km SE of Flookburgh. **55 G2** SD3973.
Humshaugh *Northumb.* ***Village***, 5m/8km N of Hexham. **70 E6** NY9171.
Huna *High.* ***Settlement***, on N coast of Caithness district, 3m/5km W of Duncansby Head. Ness of Huna is headland to NE. **105 J1** ND3673.
Huncoat *Lancs.* ***Village***, 2m/3km NE of Accrington. **56 C6** SD7730.
Huncote *Leics.* Population: 1855. ***Village***, 6m/10km SW of Leicester. **41 H6** SP5197.
Hunda *Ork.* ***Island***, sparsely populated island of about 56 acres or 23 hectares, off W end of Burray. **107 D8** ND4396.
Hundalee *Sc.Bord.* ***Hamlet***, 1m/2km S of Jedburgh. **70 B2** NT6418.
Hundall *Derbys.* ***Hamlet***, 3m/4km SE of Dronfield. SK3877.
Hunder Holm *Shet.* ***Island***, small uninhabited island off E coast of Mainland at S end of Lunning Sound and 2m/3km NW of Symbister, Whalsay. HU5163.
Hunderthwaite *Dur.* ***Hamlet***, 1m/2km SW of Romaldkirk. **62 A4** NY9821.
Hunderthwaite Moor *Dur.* ***Open space***, moorland on N side of Balderhead Reservoir, 4m/7km SW of Middleton-in-Teesdale. **61 K5** NY9019.
Hundle Houses *Lincs.* ***Locality***, 3m/5km SE of Coningsby. TF2553.
Hundleby *Lincs.* ***Village***, adjoining to W of Spilsby. **53 G6** TF3866.
Hundleshope Heights *Sc.Bord.* ***Mountain***, 4m/7km S of Peebles. Height 2247 feet or 685 metres. **76 A7** NT2333.
Hundleton *Pembs.* ***Village***, 2m/3km W of Pembroke. **16 C4** SM9600.
Hundon *Suff.* ***Village***, 5m/8km NE of Haverhill. **34 B4** TL7348.
Hundred Acres *Hants.* ***Settlement***, 1m/2km E of Wickham. **11 G3** SU5911.
Hundred End *Lancs.* ***Hamlet***, 2m/3km SW of Hesketh Bank. **55 H7** SD4122.
Hundred Foot Drain *Alternative name for New Bedford River, qv.*
Hundred House *Powys* ***Hamlet***, on River Edw, 5m/8km NE of Builth Wells. **28 A3** SO1154.
Hundred Stream *Norf.* ***Other water feature***, drainage channel running into River Thurne 2m/4km W of Winterton-on-Sea. **45 J3** TG4520.
Huney *Shet.* ***Island***, uninhabited island SW of Balta, off E coast of Unst. **108 F2** HP6406.
Hungarton *Leics.* ***Village***, 7m/11km E of Leicester. **41 J5** SK6907.
Hungate End *M.K.* ***Settlement***, 1km W of Hanslope. SP7846.
Hunger Hill *Gt.Man.* ***Locality***, residential locality, 3m/4km SW of Bolton town centre. SD6706.
Hunger Hill *Lancs.* ***Locality***, 5m/8km NW of Wigan. SD5311:
Hungerford *Hants.* ***Hamlet***, on edge of New Forest, 2m/3km SE of Fordingbridge. **10 C3** SU1612.
Hungerford *Shrop.* ***Hamlet***, 8m/12km NE of Craven Arms. SO5389.
Hungerford *Som.* ***Hamlet***, 3m/4km SW of Watchet. ST0440.
Hungerford *W.Berks.* Population: 5046. ***Small town***, market town on River Kennet and on Kennet and Avon Canal, 9m/14km W of Newbury. **21 G5** SU3368.
Hungerford Green *W.Berks.* ***Locality***, at Aldworth, 2m/4km W of Streatley. SU5579.
Hungerford Newtown *W.Berks.* ***Hamlet***, 2m/3km NE of Hungerford. **21 G4** SU3571.
Hungerhill Gardens *Notts.* ***Suburb***, 1m/2km NE of Nottingham city centre. SK5841.
Hungerton *Lincs.* ***Settlement***, 4m/7km SW of Grantham. SK8730.
Hunglader *High.* ***Settlement***, near N coast of Skye, 5m/8km N of Uig. Monument to Flora Macdonald 1m/2km NE. **93 J4** NG3871.
Hungry Hill *Norf.* ***Settlement***, 1km E of Northrepps. TG2539.
Hungry Law *Northumb.* ***Mountain***, in Cheviot Hills, 2m/3km N of Catcleugh. Height 1643 feet or 501 metres. **70 C3** NT7406.
Hunmanby *N.Yorks.* Population: 3068. ***Village***, 3m/4km SW of Filey. **59 H2** TA0977.
Hunningham *Warks.* ***Village***, 5m/8km NW of Southam. **30 E2** SP3768.
Hunny Hill *I.o.W.* ***Locality***, 1km N of Newport. **11 F6** SZ4989.
Hunsdon *Herts.* ***Village***, 4m/6km E of Ware. **33 H7** TL4114.
Hunsingore *N.Yorks.* ***Village***, 4m/6km NE of Wetherby. **57 K4** SE4253.
Hunslet *W.Yorks.* ***Suburb***, 1m/2km S of Leeds city centre. SE3131.
Hunslet Carr *W.Yorks.* ***Suburb***, adjoining to S of Hunslet, 2m/3km S of Leeds city centre. SE3030.
Hunsonby *Cumb.* ***Hamlet***, 1m/2km E of Little Salkeld. **61 G3** NY5835.
Hunspow *High.* ***Settlement***, on N coast, 3m/4km S of Dunnet Head. **105 H1** ND2172.
Hunstanton *Norf.* Population: 4634. ***Small town***, coastal resort on The Wash, 14m/22km NE of King's Lynn. **44 A1** TF6740.
Hunstanworth *Dur.* ***Hamlet***, 1m/2km SW of Blanchland. **62 A2** NY9449.
Hunston *Suff.* ***Village***, 3m/5km SE of Ixworth. **34 D2** TL9768.
Hunston *W.Suss.* ***Village***, 2m/3km S of Chichester. **12 B6** SU8602.
Hunston Green *Suff.* ***Settlement***, 1m/2km S of Hunston. TL9866.
Hunstrete *B. & N.E.Som.* ***Hamlet***, 4m/6km S of Keynsham. **19 K5** ST6462.
Hunsworth *W.Yorks.* ***Village***, 1m/2km N of Cleckheaton, just E of junction 26 of M62 motorway. SE1826.
Hunt End *Worcs.* ***Locality***, on SW edge of Redditch. **30 B2** SP0364.
Hunt Hill *Angus* ***Mountain***, 3m/5km NW of Runtaleave. Height 2408 feet or 734 metres. **89 K7** NO2671.
Hunt Hill *Moray* ***Mountain***, 3m/5km SW of Rothes. Height 1197 feet or 365 metres. **97 K7** NJ2346.
Hunt House *N.Yorks.* ***Settlement***, to E of Wheeldale Moor, 9m/14km SW of Whitby. **63 K7** SE8198.
Hunt Law *Sc.Bord.* ***Mountain***, in Lammermuir Hills, 3m/5km SE of Hopes Reservoir. Height 1624 feet or 495 metres. **76 D5** NT5758.
Huntenhull Green *Wilts.* ***Settlement***, just S of Chapmanslade, 4m/6km NW of Warminster. ST8247.
Huntercombe End *Oxon.* ***Settlement***, 1m/2km NW of Nettlebed. **21 K3** SU6887.
Hunters Forstal *Kent* ***Suburb***, S district of Herne Bay. **25 H5** TR1866.
Hunter's Quay *Arg. & B.* ***Locality***, with landing stage, on W side of Firth of Clyde, at entrance to Holy Loch, 2m/3km N of Dunoon, Argyll. **73 K3** NS1879.
Hunterston *N.Ayr.* ***Locality***, on Firth of Clyde, opposite Little Cumbrae. Site of atomic power station. Castle with 16c tower. **73 K5** NS1851.
Huntford *Sc.Bord.* ***Settlement***, 1m/2km NW of Carter Bar. **70 B3** NT6808.
Huntham *Som.* ***Hamlet***, 1m/2km NE of North Curry. ST3325.
Huntingdon *Cambs.* Population: 15,575. ***Town***, old market town on River Great Ouse, 15m/24km NW of Cambridge. Birthplace of Oliver Cromwell; Cromwell Museum now occupies school which he attended. Two Norman churches survive and town hall is 18c. Hinchingbrooke House to W. **33 F1** TL2371.
Huntingdon Bridge *Cambs.* ***Bridge***, 14c stone bridge over River Great Ouse on S side of Huntingdon. TL2471.
Huntingfield *Suff.* ***Village***, 4m/6km SW of Halesworth. **35 H1** TM3374.
Huntingford *Dorset* ***Hamlet***, 2m/4km N of Gillingham. **9 H1** ST8030.
Huntington *Here.* ***Suburb***, in NW part of Hereford. SO4841.
Huntington *Here.* ***Village***, on Welsh border, 4m/6km SW of Kington. **28 B3** SO2453.
Huntington *Staffs.* ***Village***, 2m/3km N of Cannock. **40 B4** SJ9713.
Huntington *Tel. & W.* ***Settlement***, 2m/4km S of Wellington. SJ6507.
Huntington *York* ***Suburb***, 3m/4km N of York. **58 C4** SE6156.
Huntingtower *P. & K.* ***Village***, 3m/5km NW of Perth. **82 B5** NO0725.
Huntingtower Castle *P. & K.* ***Castle***, Historic Scotland property of unusual construction comprising two 15c round towers only 10 feet or 3 metres apart, united by a late 17c building, 3m/4km NW of Perth. **82 B5** NO0725.
Huntley *Glos.* ***Village***, 7m/11km W of Gloucester. **29 G7** SO7219.
Huntley *Staffs.* ***Locality***, 1m/2km S of Cheadle. SK0041.
Huntly *Aber.* Population: 4230. ***Small town***, near confluence of Rivers Deveron and Bogie, 24m/39km SE of Elgin and 33m/53km NW of Aberdeen. **98 D6** NJ5339.
Huntly Castle *Aber.* ***Castle***, to N of Huntly beside River Deveron are remains of castle (Historic Scotland), partly 12c but mainly 16c. **98 D6** NJ5339.
Huntlywood *Sc.Bord.* ***Hamlet***, 2m/3km W of Gordon. **76 E6** NT6143.
Hunton *Hants.* ***Hamlet***, 2m/3km W of Micheldever. **11 F1** SU4839.
Hunton *Kent* ***Village***, 5m/8km SW of Maidstone. **14 C3** TQ7149.
Hunton *N.Yorks.* ***Village***, 5m/8km E of Leyburn. **62 C7** SE1892.
Hunton Bridge *Herts.* ***Suburb***, 1m/2km SW of Abbots Langley and 3m/5km NW of Watford. **22 D1** TL0800.
Hunt's Cross *Mersey.* ***Suburb***, 6m/10km SE of Liverpool city centre. **48 D4** SJ4285.
Hunts Green *Warks.* ***Settlement***, 4m/7km S of Tamworth. SP1897.
Hunt's Hill *Bucks.* ***Settlement***, 3m/4km N of High Wycombe. SU8496.
Huntscott *Som.* ***Hamlet***, 3m/5km SW of Minehead. SS9243.
Huntsham *Devon* ***Village***, 3m/5km SE of Bampton. **7 J3** ST0020.
Huntshaw *Devon* ***Hamlet***, 2m/4km N of Great Torrington. SS5022.
Huntshaw Cross *Devon* ***Settlement***, 1m/2km SE of Huntshaw. **6 D3** SS5321.
Huntshaw Mill Bridge *Devon* ***Settlement***, 1km W of Huntshaw. SS4922.
Huntshaw Water *Devon* ***Settlement***, 1km N of Huntshaw. SS5023.
Huntspill *Som.* ***Village***, on flat land known as Huntspill Level, 1m/2km S of Highbridge. **19 G7** ST3145.
Huntspill Level *Som.* ***Open space***, artificial drainage plain to E of Huntspill, 3m/4km SE of Burnham-on-Sea. **19 G7** ST3145.
Huntwick Grange *W.Yorks.* ***Settlement***, 1m/2km SW of Featherstone. SE4019.
Huntworth *Som.* ***Village***, 2m/3km SE of Bridgwater. **8 C1** ST3134.
Hunwick *Dur.* ***Village***, 2m/3km S of Willington. **62 C3** NZ1932.
Hunworth *Norf.* ***Village***, 2m/3km SW of Holt. **44 E2** TG0635.
Hunworth Green *Norf.* ***Hamlet***, adjoins to SE of Hunworth, 3m/4km S of Holt. TG0635.
Hurcott *Som.* ***Hamlet***, 1m/2km NE of Somerton. ST5029.
Hurcott *Som.* ***Settlement***, 3m/4km NE of Ilminster. ST3916.
Hurcott *Worcs.* ***Locality***, 2m/3km E of Kidderminster. SO8577.
Hurdley *Powys* ***Settlement***, 2m/3km E of Church Stoke. SO2994.
Hurdsfield *Ches.* ***Suburb***, to NE of Macclesfield. **49 J5** SJ9274.
Hurgin *Shrop.* ***Mountain***, 5m/8km NW of Knighton. Height 1384 feet or 422 metres. **28 B1** SO2379.
Hurlers Stone Circle (Also known as The Hurlers.) *Cornw.* ***Historic/prehistoric site***, row of three prehistoric stone circles (English Heritage) to W of Minions, 9m/15km SW of Launceston. **4 C3** SX2571.
Hurleston *Ches.* ***Locality***, parish, 3m/4km NW of Nantwich. SJ6255.
Hurlet *Glas.* ***Suburb***, 6m/9km SW of Glasgow city centre in Nitshill district. NS5161.
Hurley *Warks.* ***Village***, 4m/7km W of Atherstone. **40 E6** SP2495.
Hurley *W. & M.* Population: 1712. ***Village***, on River Thames, 4m/7km NW of Maidenhead. **22 B3** SU8283.
Hurley Bottom *W. & M.* ***Locality***, adjoins to S of Hurley. **22 B3** SU8283.
Hurley Common *Warks.* ***Hamlet***, to N of Hurley, 5m/8km SE of Tamworth. SP2496.
Hurley Priory *W. & M.* ***Ecclesiastical building***, remains of Benedictine priory on S bank of River Thames, 4m/6km NW of Maidenhead. Nave now used as parish church. Architecture part Saxon, part Norman, restored in 19c. **22 B3** SU8284.
Hurlford *E.Ayr.* Population: 5396. ***Suburb***, 2m/3km E of Kilmarnock across River Irvine. **74 C7** NS4536.
Hurliness *Ork.* ***Settlement***, on Hoy, 1km E of Melsetter. **107 B9** ND2889.
Hurlston *Lancs.* ***Settlement***, 2m/3km NW of Ormskirk. SD4010.
Hurlston Green *Lancs.* ***Village***, 2m/4km NW of Ormskirk. SD4010.
Hurn *Dorset* ***Village***, 5m/8km NE of Bournemouth. 1m/2km NW, Bournemouth International Airport. **10 C5** SZ1297.
Hursley *Hants.* ***Village***, 4m/7km SW of Winchester. **11 F2** SU4225.
Hurst *Gt.Man.* ***Suburb***, 1m/2km NE of Ashton-under-Lyne town centre. **49 J2** SD9400.
Hurst *N.Yorks.* ***Settlement***, 2m/3km N of Reeth. **62 B6** NZ0402.
Hurst *Som.* ***Locality***, on S side of Martock. ST4518.
Hurst *W'ham* ***Village***, 5m/8km E of Reading. **22 A4** SU7973.
Hurst Castle *Hants.* ***Castle***, 15 castle (English Heritage) built by Henry VIII for coastal defence on spit of land, 4m/6km S of Lymington and less than 1m/2km from Cliff End, Isle of Wight. Charles I imprisoned there, 1648. **10 E5** SZ3189.
Hurst Green *E.Suss.* ***Village***, 7m/11km N of Battle. **14 C5** TQ7327.
Hurst Green *Essex* ***Suburb***, E district of Brightlingsea. TM0916.
Hurst Green *Lancs.* ***Village***, 3m/5km NW of Whalley. **56 B6** SD6838.
Hurst Green *Surr.* ***Locality***, adjoining to S of Oxted. **23 G6** TQ3951.
Hurst Green *W.Mid.* ***Suburb***, in NE part of Halesowen. SO9885.
Hurst Hill *W.Mid.* ***Suburb***, in N part of Dudley. SO9394.
Hurst Moor *N.Yorks.* ***Open space***, moorland 3m/4km E of Arkengarthdale. **62 B6** NZ0303.
Hurst Wickham *W.Suss.* ***Settlement***, adjoining to E of Hurstpierpoint. TQ2916.
Hurstbourne Priors *Hants.* ***Village***, 2m/3km SW of Whitchurch. **21 H7** SU4346.
Hurstbourne Tarrant *Hants.* ***Village***, 5m/8km N of Andover. **21 G6** SU3853.
Hurstead *Gt.Man.* ***Locality***, 2m/3km W of Littleborough. SD9115.
Hurstone *Devon* ***Settlement***, 5m/7km SW of South Molton. SS6422.
Hurstpierpoint *W.Suss.* Population: 5943. ***Small town***, 3m/5km SW of Burgess Hill. Site of Roman villa 1m/2km S. **13 F5** TQ2716.
Hurstway Common *Here.* ***Locality***, 2m/3km NW of Willersley. **28 B4** SO2949.
Hurstwood *Lancs.* ***Hamlet***, 3m/5km E of Burnley. **56 D6** SD8831.
Hurstwood Reservoir *Lancs.* ***Reservoir***, to E of Hurstwood. **56 D6** SD8831.
Hurtmore *Surr.* ***Hamlet***, 2m/3km NW of Godalming. **22 C7** SU9545.

H

Hurworth Burn *Dur.* ***Locality***, at S end of Hurworth Burn Reservoir, 4m/7km NE of Sedgefield. NZ4033.
Hurworth Burn Reservoir *Dur.* ***Reservoir***, 4m/6km NE of Sedgefield. **62 E3** NZ4033.
Hurworth-on-Tees *Darl.* Population: 3269. ***Village***, on River Tees, 3m/5km SE of Darlington. **62 E5** NZ3010.
Hury *Dur.* ***Settlement***, on N side of Hury Reservoir, 3m/4km SW of Romaldkirk. **62 A4** NY9519.
Hury Reservoir *Dur.* ***Reservoir***, 3m/4km SW of Romaldkirk. **62 A5** NY9519.
Husabost *High.* ***Settlement***, on W coast of Loch Dunvegan, 4m/6km NW of Dunvegan, Skye. **93 H6** NG2051.
Husbands Bosworth *Leics.* ***Village***, 6m/10km W of Market Harborough. **41 J7** SP6484.
Husborne Crawley *Beds.* ***Village***, 2m/3km N of Woburn. **32 C5** SP9535.
Hushinish *W.Isles Anglicised form of Huisinis, qv.*
Hushinish Bay (Bàgh Huisinis). *W.Isles* ***Bay***, to S of Huisinis, on W coast of North Harris. **100 B6** NA9911.
Hushinish Glorigs *W.Isles* ***Island***, group of rocks 1m/2km S of Hushinish Point, North Harris. NA9809.
Hushinish Point *W.Isles* ***Coastal feature***, headland on W side of Hushinish Bay, North Harris, and 1m/2km S of Scarp. **100 B6** NA9911.
Husival Mòr *W.Isles* ***Mountain***, near W coast of North Harris, 2m/3km E of Huisinis. Height 1604 feet or 489 metres. **100 C6** NB0211.
Huskeiran *W.Isles* ***Island***, small group of islets 2m/3km NW of Heisker Islands group, to W of North Uist. **92 A5** NF5764.
Husthwaite *N.Yorks.* ***Village***, 4m/6km N of Easingwold. **58 B2** SE5175.
Hut Green *N.Yorks.* ***Locality***, adjoining to NE of Low Eggborough. SE5623.
Hutcherleigh *Devon* ***Hamlet***, 5m/8km NE of Kingsbridge. SX7850.
Hutchesontown *Glas.* ***Suburb***, 1m/2km S of Glasgow city centre. NS5963.
Huthwaite *N.Yorks.* ***Locality***, 1m/2km SE of Swainby. NZ4801.
Huthwaite *Notts.* ***Suburb***, adjoining to W of Sutton in Ashfield. **51 G7** SK4659.
Huttock Top *Lancs.* ***Locality***, adjoining to S of Bacup. SD8622.
Huttoft *Lincs.* ***Village***, 4m/6km S of Sutton on Sea. **53 J5** TF5176.
Huttoft Bank *Lincs.* ***Locality***, on coast 2m/3km NE of Huttoft, comprising part of sea defences built in Roman times. TF5477.
Huttoft Grange *Lincs.* ***Settlement***, 1m/2km N of Huttoft. TF5176.
Hutton *Cumb.* ***Hamlet***, 6m/9km W of Penrith. **60 F4** NY4326.
Hutton *D. & G.* ***Locality***, 6m/10km N of Lockerbie. NY1790.
Hutton *E.Riding* ***Village***, adjoining to N of Hutton Cranswick, 3m/4km S of Great Driffield. TA0253.
Hutton *Essex* ***Suburb***, NE district of Brentwood. **24 C2** TQ6295.
Hutton *Lancs.* ***Village***, 3m/5km SW of Preston. **55 H7** SD4926.
Hutton *N.Som.* Population: 2079. ***Village***, 3m/4km SE of Weston-super-Mare. **19 G6** ST3558.
Hutton *Sc.Bord.* ***Village***, 6m/9km W of Berwick-upon-Tweed. **77 H5** NT9053.
Hutton Bonville *N.Yorks.* ***Settlement***, 4m/7km N of Northallerton. **62 E6** NZ3300.
Hutton Buscel *N.Yorks.* ***Village***, 5m/8km SW of Scarborough. **59 F1** SE9784.
Hutton Conyers *N.Yorks.* ***Hamlet***, 1m/2km NE of Ripon across River Ure. **57 J2** SE3273.
Hutton Cranswick *E.Riding* ***Village***, 4m/6km S of Great Driffield. **59 G4** TA0252.
Hutton End *Cumb.* ***Hamlet***, 2m/3km SW of Calthwaite. **60 F3** NY4438.
Hutton Hang *N.Yorks.* ***Settlement***, 1m/2km S of Constable Burton, 3m/4km E of Middleham. SE1788.
Hutton Henry *Dur.* ***Village***, 6m/10km NW of Hartlepool. **63 F3** NZ4236.
Hutton-in-the-Forest *Cumb.* ***Historic house***, 17c house built around medieval pele tower and home of Lord Inglewood since 1605, 5m/8km NW of Penrith. House altered in 18c and 19c but retains 17c façade and Cupid Staircase. Includes gardens and parkland with woodland walk. **61 F3** NY4635.
Hutton John *Cumb.* ***Settlement***, to E of Hutton. NY4326.
Hutton-le-Hole *N.Yorks.* ***Village***, 2m/4km N of Kirkbymoorside. **63 J7** SE7089.
Hutton Lowcross *R. & C.* ***Hamlet***, 1m/2km S of Guisborough. NZ6013.
Hutton Magna *Dur.* ***Village***, 6m/9km SE of Barnard Castle. **62 C5** NZ1212.
Hutton Mount *Essex* ***Suburb***, E district of Brentwood. TQ6194.
Hutton Mulgrave *N.Yorks.* ***Settlement***, 4m/6km W of Whitby. NZ8310.
Hutton Roof *Cumb.* ***Hamlet***, 4m/6km SE of Hesket Newmarket. **60 E3** NY3734.
Hutton Roof *Cumb.* ***Village***, 3m/4km W of Kirkby Lonsdale. **55 J2** SD5778.
Hutton Rudby *N.Yorks.* Population: 1067. ***Village***, on River Leven, 4m/6km W of Stokesley. **63 F6** NZ4606.
Hutton Sessay *N.Yorks.* ***Village***, 5m/7km SE of Thirsk. **57 K2** SE4776.
Hutton Wandesley *N.Yorks.* ***Village***, adjoining to SE of Long Marston, 5m/8km NE of Tadcaster. **58 B4** SE5050.
Huxham *Devon* ***Hamlet***, 4m/6km NE of Exeter. SX9497.
Huxham Green *Som.* ***Settlement***, 5m/8km SW of Shepton Mallet. ST5936.
Huxley *Ches.* ***Village***, 3m/5km W of Tarporley. **48 E6** SJ5061.
Huxter *Shet.* ***Settlement***, 1km N of Hellister, on E side of Weisdale Voe, Mainland. **109 C7** HU3950.
Huxter *Shet.* ***Settlement***, to N of Loch of Huxter, 1m/2km W of Symbister, Whalsay. **109 E6** HU5662.
Huyton *Mersey.* Population: 56,500. ***Town***, 6m/10km E of Liverpool. **48 D3** SJ4491.
Hwlffordd *Pembs. Welsh form of Haverfordwest, qv.*
Hycemoor *Cumb.* ***Hamlet***, at Bootle railway station, 1m/2km NW of Bootle. **54 D1** SD0989.
Hyde *Glos.* ***Settlement***, 1m/2km NE of Minchinhampton. **20 B1** SO8801.
Hyde *Glos.* ***Settlement***, 7m/11km W of Stow-on-the-Wold. SP0828.
Hyde *Gt.Man.* Population: 30,666. ***Town***, old mill town, 5m/7km NE of Stockport. **49 J3** SJ9494.
Hyde End *W.Berks.* ***Settlement***, 1m/2km SW of Brimpton and 4m/6km NE of Kingsclere. SU5563.
Hyde End *W'ham* ***Settlement***, 1m/2km E of Spencers Wood and 4m/7km S of Reading. SU7366.
Hyde Hall *Essex* ***Garden***, 1m/2km W of Woodham Ferrers and 2m/3km E of Rettendon. 24 acres of garden, including bearded irises and climbing roses. **24 D2** TQ7899.
Hyde Heath *Bucks.* ***Village***, 2m/3km W of Chesham. **22 C1** SP9300.
Hyde Lea *Staffs.* ***Hamlet***, 2m/3km S of Stafford. **40 B4** SJ9120.
Hyde Park *Gt.Lon.* ***Open space***, royal park since 1536, once part of forest reserved by Henry VIII for hunting wild boar and bulls. It was a haunt for highwaymen until 1750. Queen Elizabeth I staged military reviews here, and Great Exhibition of 1851 was held opposite Prince of Wales Gate. Hyde Park now has 360 acres of parkland including walks and Rotten Row, for horse-riders. The Serpentine is used for boating, swimming and fishing, with good roach and perch. The Serpentine Bridge is by George Rennie, 1826. Speakers' Corner, where unknown orators make impromptu discourses on Sundays, is near Marble Arch. **23 F4** TQ2780.
Hyde Park *S.Yorks.* ***Suburb***, to SE of Doncaster town centre. SE5702.
Hyde Park Corner *Som.* ***Locality***, on W side of North Petherton. ST2832.
Hyde's House *Wilts. See Dinton.*
Hydestile *Surr.* ***Locality***, 2m/3km S of Godalming. **22 C7** SU9740.
Hydfer *Powys* ***River***, rising on NE side of Carmarthen Van and flowing N into River Usk at Pont ar Hydfer. **27 H6** SN8627.
Hykeham Moor *Lincs.* ***Suburb***, to NW of North Hykeham, 4m/6km SW of Lincoln city centre. SK9466.
Hylton Castle *T. & W.* ***Historic house***, 15c tower house (English Heritage) in NW part of Sunderland. Gives its name to adjacent housing estate. **62 E1** NZ3558.
Hylton Red House *T. & W.* ***Suburb***, housing estate in NW part of Sunderland. NZ3659.
Hyndford Bridge *S.Lan.* ***Bridge***, road bridge over River Clyde 3m/4km SE of Lanark. **75 H6** NS9141.
Hyndland *Glas.* ***Suburb***, 3m/4km NW of Glasgow city centre, in Partick district. NS5567.
Hyndlee *Sc.Bord.* ***Settlement***, in Wauchope Forest area of Cheviot Hills, 3m/4km S of Hobkirk. **70 A3** NT5806.
Hynish *Arg. & B.* ***Settlement***, at SW end of Hynish Bay, Tiree. **78 A4** NL9839.
Hynish Bay *Arg. & B.* ***Bay***, wide bay on S coast of Tiree. **78 B3** NM0042.
Hyskeir *High. Alternative name for Oigh-sgeir, qv.*
Hyssington *Powys* ***Hamlet***, 3m/4km E of Church Stoke. **38 C6** SO3194.
Hythe *Hants.* Population: 18,538. ***Village***, on W bank of Southampton Water, S of Southampton; ferry connection for pedestrians. Urban expansion inland. **11 F4** SU4207.
Hythe *Kent* Population: 14,569. ***Town***, Cinque port and resort, 4m/6km W of Folkestone. **15 G4** TR1634.
Hythe *Surr.* ***Suburb***, adjoining to E of Egham. TQ0270.
Hythe End *W. & M.* ***Hamlet***, 1m/2km NE of Egham. **22 D4** TQ0172.
Hythie *Aber.* ***Settlement***, 5m/7km SE of Strichen. **99 J5** NK0051.
Hyton *Cumb.* ***Settlement***, 1m/2km SW of Bootle. **54 D1** SD0987.
Hyvots Bank *Edin.* ***Suburb***, 4m/7km SE of Edinburgh city centre. NT2868.

I

Ianstown *Moray* ***Suburb***, E district of Buckie, on N coast. **98 C4** NJ4366.
Iarsiadar *W.Isles Gaelic form of Earshader, qv.*
Ibberton *Dorset* ***Village***, 4m/7km S of Sturminster Newton. **9 G4** ST7807.
Ible *Derbys.* ***Hamlet***, 3m/5km NW of Wirksworth. **50 E7** SK2457.
Ibrox *Glas.* ***Suburb***, 2m/3km W of Glasgow city centre in Govan district. NS5564.
Ibsley *Hants.* ***Hamlet***, 3m/4km N of Ringwood. **10 C4** SU1509.
Ibstock *Leics.* Population: 5243. ***Village***, large village, 3m/5km SW of Coalville. **41 G4** SK4010.
Ibstone *Bucks.* ***Village***, 2m/3km S of Stokenchurch. **22 A2** SU7593.
Ibthorpe *Hants.* ***Village***, adjoining to NW of Hurstbourne Tarrant. **21 G6** SU3753.
Iburndale *N.Yorks.* ***Hamlet***, 3m/5km SW of Whitby. NZ8707.
Ibworth *Hants.* ***Hamlet***, 5m/8km NW of Basingstoke. **21 J6** SU5654.
Icelton *N.Som.* ***Hamlet***, just E of Wick St. Lawrence, 5m/7km NE of Weston-super-Mare. **19 G5** ST3765.
Ickburgh *Norf.* ***Village***, 1m/2km NE of Mundford. **44 C6** TL8194.
Ickenham *Gt.Lon.* ***Suburb***, in borough of Hillingdon, 2m/3km NE of Uxbridge. **22 D3** TQ0786.
Ickford *Bucks.* ***Village***, 4m/6km W of Thame. **21 K1** SP6407.
Ickham *Kent* ***Village***, 5m/7km E of Canterbury. **15 H2** TR2258.
Ickleford *Herts.* ***Village***, 1m/2km N of Hitchin. **32 E5** TL1831.
Icklesham *E.Suss.* ***Village***, 2m/3km W of Winchelsea. **14 D6** TQ8716.
Ickleton *Cambs.* ***Village***, 1m/2km NW of Great Chesterford. **33 H4** TL4943.
Icklingham *Suff.* ***Village***, 7m/12km NW of Bury St. Edmunds. Site of Roman villa 1m/2km SE. **34 B1** TL7772.
Icknield Way ***Historic/prehistoric site***, ancient trackway, originally running from The Wash to S coast of England and later adopted in part by the Romans. Today it can be traced from Thetford to Baldock, below N escarpment of Chiltern Hills to Streatley, and then along The Ridgeway to Avebury. **33 G5** TL3037.
Ickwell Green *Beds.* ***Village***, 3m/4km W of Biggleswade. **32 E4** TL1545.
Ickworth *Suff.* ***Historic house***, National Trust property of 18c-19c in form of elliptical rotunda, with formal gardens, standing in large park 3m/5km SW of Bury St. Edmunds. Park notable for autumn colours. **34 C2** TL8161.
Icomb *Glos.* ***Village***, 2m/4km SE of Stow-on-the-Wold. **30 D6** SP2122.
Idbury *Oxon.* ***Village***, 5m/7km SE of Stow-on-the-Wold. **30 D6** SP2319.
Iddesleigh *Devon* ***Village***, 3m/5km NE of Hatherleigh. **6 D5** SS5708.
Iddinshall *Ches.* ***Settlement***, 1m/2km W of Tarporley. SJ5362.
Ide *Devon* ***Village***, 2m/3km SW of Exeter. **7 H6** SX8990.
Ide Hill *Kent* ***Village***, 4m/6km SW of Sevenoaks. Wooded hillside (National Trust) on S side of village overlooking The Weald. **23 H6** TQ4851.
Ideford *Devon* ***Village***, 4m/7km NE of Newton Abbot. **5 J3** SX8977.
Iden *E.Suss.* ***Village***, 2m/4km N of Rye. **14 E5** TQ9123.
Iden Green *Kent* ***Hamlet***, 1m/2km E of Goudhurst. **14 C4** TQ7437.
Iden Green *Kent* ***Village***, 3m/5km E of Hawkhurst. **14 D4** TQ8031.
Idle ***River***, formed by confluence of Rivers Maun and Meden, 4m/6km S of Retford, and flowing N through Retford to Bawtry then E into River Trent at West Stockwith. **51 K4** SK7894.
Idle *W.Yorks.* ***Suburb***, 3m/5km N of Bradford city centre. SE1737.
Idless *Cornw.* ***Hamlet***, 2m/3km N of Truro. SW8247.
Idlicote *Warks.* ***Hamlet***, 3m/5km NE of Shipston on Stour. **30 D4** SP2844.
Idmiston *Wilts.* ***Village***, on River Bourne, 6m/9km NE of Salisbury. **10 C1** SU1937.
Idoch Water *Aber.* ***River***, running SW through Cuminestown and turning NW 2m/3km SE of Turriff, then flowing NW into River Deveron on W side of town. **99 F6** NJ7150.
Idridgehay *Derbys.* ***Village***, 3m/5km S of Wirksworth. **40 E1** SK2848.
Idridgehay Green *Derbys.* ***Hamlet***, adjoining to NW of Idridgehay, 4m/7km NW of Belper. SK2849.
Idrigil *High.* ***Settlement***, 1km W of Uig, Skye. **93 J5** NG3863.
Idrigill Point *High.* ***Coastal feature***, headland on Skye at NW entrance to Loch Bracadale. **85 H1** NG2536.
Idstone *Oxon.* ***Village***, 7m/11km E of Swindon. **21 F3** SU2584.
Idsworth *Hants.* ***Locality***, 5m/8km NE of Havant. SU7414.
Idvies *Angus* ***Hamlet***, 1km S of Letham. **83 G3** NO5347.
Iffley *Oxon.* ***Suburb***, S district of Oxford. **21 J1** SP5203.
Ifield *Kent Alternative name for Singlewell, qv.*
Ifield *W.Suss.* ***Suburb***, W district of Crawley. **13 F3** TQ2437.
Ifieldwood *W.Suss.* ***Settlement***, 2m/3km S of Charlwood. **13 F3** TQ2338.
Ifold *W.Suss.* ***Locality***, dispersed locality, 5m/8km NW of Billingshurst. **12 D3** TQ0231.
Iford *Bourne.* ***Suburb***, beside River Stour, 4m/5km E of Bournemouth town centre. SZ1393.
Iford *E.Suss.* ***Village***, 2m/3km S of Lewes. **13 H6** TQ4007.
Iford Manor Gardens *Wilts.* ***Garden***, terraced Italianate garden surrounding Tudor house, 3m/5km NW of Trowbridge. Designed by Edwardian architect Harold Peto, it includes cloister, ponds and statues in riverside setting. **20 A6** ST8058.
Ifton *Mon.* ***Settlement***, 1km W of Caldicot. ST4687.
Ifton Heath *Shrop.* ***Locality***, 5m/8km W of Ellesmere. **38 C2** SJ3237.
Ightenhill *Lancs.* ***Locality***, to E of Padiham. SD8134.
Ightfield *Shrop.* ***Village***, 4m/6km SE of Whitchurch. **38 E2** SJ5938.
Ightfield Heath *Shrop.* ***Settlement***, 1m/2km S of Ightfield. SJ5937.
Ightham *Kent* ***Village***, 4m/7km E of Sevenoaks. 2m/4km S, Ightham Mote, moated medieval manor house (National Trust). **23 J6** TQ5956.
Ightham Mote *Kent* ***Historic house***, 5m/8km SE of Sevenoaks, moated manor house (National Trust) dating from 1340 onwards, with medieval great hall, gardens and woodland. **23 J6** TQ5853.
Iken *Suff.* ***Village***, on S side of River Alde estuary, 4m/6km N of Orford. **35 J3** TM4155.
Ilam *Staffs.* ***Village***, on River Manifold, 1km above its junction with River Dove and 4m/6km NW of Ashbourne. Partly National Trust property. **50 D7** SK1350.
Ilam Hall Country Park *Staffs.* ***Leisure/recreation***, National Trust property adjacent to E side of River Manifold, to W of Ilam, 4m/7km NW of Ashbourne. **50 D7** SK1350.
Ilchester *Som.* Population: 1733. ***Village***, on Roman Foss Way, at crossing of River Yeo, 5m/8km NW of Yeovil. **8 E2** ST5222.

Ilderton *Northumb.* ***Hamlet***, 4m/7km SE of Wooler. **71 F1** NU0121.

Ilford *Gt.Lon.* ***Town***, in borough of Redbridge, 8m/13km NE of London Bridge. **23 H3** TQ4386.

Ilford *Som.* ***Hamlet***, 2m/3km N of Ilminster. ST3617.

Ilfracombe *Devon* Population: 10,429. ***Town***, Victorian resort on N coast, 9m/15km N of Barnstaple. Fishing harbour with medieval chapel, previously used as a lighthouse. **6 D1** SS5247.

Ilfracombe Museum *Devon* ***Other feature of interest***, in Ilfracombe, 9m/14km NW of Barnstaple. Local history museum which includes natural history exhibits. **6 D1** SS5247.

Ilkeston *Derbys.* Population: 35,134. ***Town***, market town, 8m/12km NE of Derby and 7m/11km W of Nottingham. Former mining and textile town. Annual October Fair dates from 13c. **41 G1** SK4641.

Ilketshall St. Andrew *Suff.* ***Hamlet***, 3m/5km SE of Bungay. **45 H7** TM3787.

Ilketshall St. John *Suff.* ***Hamlet***, 1m/2km W of Ilketshall St. Andrew. TM3687.

Ilketshall St. Lawrence *Suff.* ***Hamlet***, 1m/2km SW of Ilketshall St. Andrew. **45 H7** TM3787.

Ilketshall St. Margaret *Suff.* ***Hamlet***, 2m/4km W of Ilketshall St. Andrew. **45 H7** TM3787.

Ilkley *W.Yorks.* Population: 13,530. ***Town***, spa town and minor resort in Wharfedale, on site of Roman military station of Olicana, 10m/16km N of Bradford. To S, Ilkley Moor, forming part of Rombalds Moor. **57 G5** SE1147.

Ilkley Moor *W.Yorks.* ***Open space***, to S of Ilkley, forming part of Rombalds Moor. Cow and Calf rocks on edge of moor above Ben Rhydding. **57 G5** SE1147.

Ill Bell *Cumb.* ***Mountain***, to W of Kentmere Reservoir, 4m/7km NW of Ambleside. Height 2476 feet or 755 metres. **60 F6** NY4307.

I

Illand *Cornw.* ***Hamlet***, 5m/8km SW of Launceston. SX2878.

Illey *W.Mid.* ***Hamlet***, in SE part of Halesowen. **40 B7** SO9881.

Illidge Green *Ches.* ***Settlement***, 3m/4km NE of Sandbach. SJ7963.

Illington *Norf.* ***Hamlet***, 6m/10km NE of Thetford. **44 D7** TL9490.

Illingworth *W.Yorks.* ***Suburb***, 2m/4km NW of Halifax town centre. **57 F7** SE0728.

Illingworth Moor *W.Yorks.* ***Locality***, to N of Illingworth. SE0729.

Illogan *Cornw.* ***Village***, 2m/3km NW of Redruth. **2 D4** SW6744.

Illogan Highway *Cornw.* ***Locality***, 1m/2km W of Redruth. SW6741.

Illshaw Heath *W.Mid.* ***Hamlet***, 2m/3km NW of Hockley Heath. SP1374.

Illston on the Hill *Leics.* ***Village***, 8m/13km N of Market Harborough. **42 A6** SP7099.

Ilmer *Bucks.* ***Village***, 3m/5km NW of Princes Risborough. **22 A1** SP7605.

Ilmington *Warks.* ***Village***, 4m/6km NW of Shipston on Stour. **30 D4** SP2143.

Ilminster *Som.* Population: 4162. ***Small town***, 10m/16km SE of Taunton. Former cloth-making town with fine 15c church and 17c open market house. **8 C3** ST3614.

Ilsington *Devon* ***Village***, 4m/7km NE of Ashburton. **5 H3** SX7876.

Ilsington *Dorset* ***Settlement***, 1m/2km W of Tincleton and 4m/7km E of Dorchester. SY7591.

Ilston (Llanilltud Gŵyr). *Swan.* ***Village***, to SW of Swansea Airport, 6m/10km W of Swansea. **17 J5** SS5590.

Ilton *N.Yorks.* ***Hamlet***, 3m/4km SW of Masham. **57 G2** SE1978.

Ilton *Som.* ***Village***, 2m/3km N of Ilminster. **8 C3** ST3517.

Imachar *N.Ayr.* ***Locality***, on W side of Arran, 2m/4km S of Pirnmill. **73 G6** NR8640.

Imber *Wilts.* ***Village***, derelict village on Salisbury Plain, 6m/10km NE of Warminster. Situated in Army training area. ST9648.

Immeroin *Stir.* ***Settlement***, on E side of Glen Buckie, 2m/3km S of Balquhidder. **81 G6** NN5317.

Immingham *N.E.Lincs.* Population: 12,278. ***Town***, 7m/11km NW of Grimsby, and once a main port for surrounding area. **52 E1** TA1714.

Immingham Dock *N.E.Lincs.* ***Locality***, to NE of Immingham, on River Humber. **53 F1** TA2016.

Imperial War Museum *Cambs.* ***Other feature of interest***, at Duxford Airfield, 1m/2km W of Duxford, with operations room, aircraft and land warfare exhibition. **33 H4** TL4646.

Impington *Cambs.* ***Village***, adjoining to E of Histon, 3m/5km N of Cambridge. **33 H2** TL4463.

Ince *Ches.* ***Village***, 3m/5km E of Ellesmere Port. **48 D5** SJ4576.

Ince Banks *Ches.* ***Marsh/bog***, to E of Ellesmere Port, with Stanlow Banks to W. **48 D5** SJ4478.

Ince Blundell *Mersey.* ***Village***, 3m/5km SE of Formby. Hall is 18c. **48 C2** SD3203.

Ince-in-Makerfield *Gt.Man.* Population: 10,554. ***Town***, 1m/2km SE of Wigan. Former coalmining town. **48 E2** SD5903.

Inch *Aber.* ***Settlement***, 2m/4km SW of Fettercairn. **90 E7** NO6271.

Inch *Edin.* ***Suburb***, 3m/4km SE of Edinburgh city centre. NT2770.

Inch Buie *Stir.* ***Island***, lower of two islands in River Dochart at Killin. Former burial place of Clan MacNab. NN5732.

Inch Garvie *Edin.* ***Island***, islet with lighthouse in Firth of Forth beneath Forth Railway Bridge. **75 K3** NT1379.

Inch Kenneth *Arg. & B.* ***Island***, of about 200 acres or 80 hectares at entrance to Loch na Keal, W coast of Mull. Remains of 12c chapel (Historic Scotland). **79 F4** NM4335.

Inch Kenneth Chapel *Arg. & B.* ***Ecclesiastical building***, chapel (Historic Scotland), on Inch Kenneth, 1m/2km NW of Balnahard off W coast of Mull. Medieval monuments in graveyard. **79 F4** NM4335.

Inch Talla *Stir.* ***Island***, islet in Lake of Menteith, with remains of medieval castle. NN5700.

Inchaffray Abbey *P. & K.* ***Ecclesiastical building***, scant remains of early 13c abbey, 6m/9km E of Crieff. **82 A5** NN9522.

Inchbae Forest *High.* ***Open space***, deer forest in Ross and Cromarty district E of Loch Vaich. Inchbae Lodge at junction of River Glascarnoch and Strath Rannoch at S end of forest. **95 K4** NH3778.

Inchbae Lodge *High.* ***Settlement***, at junction of River Glascarnoch and Strath Rannoch, at S end of Inchbae Forest. NH3969.

Inchbare *Angus* ***Settlement***, on West Water, 2m/3km S of Edzell. **83 H1** NO6065.

Inchberry *Moray* ***Settlement***, 7m/12km SE of Elgin. **98 B5** NJ3155.

Inchbraoch (Also known as Inchbrayock or Rossie Island.) *Angus* ***Locality***, on S side of Montrose Basin, connected by road and railway bridges to Montrose. **83 J2** NO7056.

Inchbrayock *Angus Alternative name for Inchbraoch, qv.*

Inchcailleach *Stir. Alternative spelling of Inchcailloch, qv.*

Inchcailleoch *Stir. Alternative spelling of Inchcailloch, qv.*

Inchcailliach *Stir. Alternative spelling of Inchcailloch, qv.*

Inchcailloch *Stir.* ***Island***, off E shore of Loch Lomond opposite Balmaha. Part of nature reserve comprising also Clairinch and Torrinch. Other spellings include Inchcailleach, Inchcailleoch, and Inchcailliach. **74 C1** NS4090.

Inchcape Rock (Also known as Bell Rock.) *Angus* ***Coastal feature***, reef with lighthouse off E coast, 11m/18km SE of Arbroath. **83 J5** NO7627.

Inchcolm *Fife* ***Island***, in Firth of Forth 1m/2km E of Dalgety Bay. Ruins of medieval abbey (Historic Scotland) founded in 12c including 13c chapter house. Best preserved group of monastic buildings in Scotland. **75 K2** NT1882.

Inchconnachan *Arg. & B.* ***Island***, in Loch Lomond 1m/2km SE of Luss. **74 B1** NS3792.

Inchcruin *Stir.* ***Island***, in Loch Lomond 2m/3km W of Balmaha. **74 B1** NS3891.

Inchfad *Stir.* ***Island***, in Loch Lomond 1m/2km W of Balmaha. **74 B1** NS3990.

Inchgalbraith *Arg. & B.* ***Island***, islet with remains of castle, in Loch Lomond 1km NE of Rossdhu House. NS3690.

Inchgrundle *Angus* ***Settlement***, at SW end of Loch Lee. **90 C7** NO4179.

Inchindown *High.* ***Settlement***, 3m/5km N of Invergordon. **96 D4** NH6974.

Inchinnan *Renf.* Population: 1815. ***Village***, 3m/5km N of Paisley. **74 C4** NS4868.

Inchkeith *Fife* ***Island***, narrow island, just over 1km long from N to S, in Firth of Forth 3m/4km SE of Kinghorn. Lighthouse near N end. **76 A2** NT2982.

Inchkeith Hill *Sc.Bord.* ***Mountain***, 3m/5km NW of Lauder. Height 1197 feet or 365 metres. **76 C6** NT4848.

Inchkinloch *High.* ***Settlement***, 1km W of S end of Loch Loyal. **103 J4** NC6044.

Inchlaggan *High.* ***Locality***, in Glen Garry, Lochaber district, 8m/13km W of Invergarry. **87 H4** NH1701.

Inchlonaig *Arg. & B.* ***Island***, in Loch Lomond opposite Luss. **74 B1** NS3893.

Inchlumpie *High.* ***Settlement***, 5m/8km NW of Alness. **96 C4** NH5875.

Inchmahome *Stir.* ***Island***, in Lake of Menteith. Remains of 13c priory (Historic Scotland). NN5700.

Inchmahome Priory *Stir.* ***Ecclesiastical building***, remains of Augustinian monastery (Historic Scotland), founded 1238, on Inchmahome in Lake of Menteith. Mary, Queen of Scots lay hidden here, 1547-8. **81 G7** NN5700.

Inchmarlo *Aber.* ***Settlement***, 2m/3km W of Banchory, on N side of River Dee. **90 E5** NO6796.

Inchmarnock *Arg. & B.* ***Island***, sparsely populated low-lying island 1m/2km W of Bute off St. Ninian's Point. Measures about 2m/3km N to S and about 1km across. **73 H5** NS0259.

Inchmickery *Edin.* ***Island***, islet in Firth of Forth, 3m/4km NW of Granton Harbour. **76 A2** NT2080.

Inchmoan *Arg. & B.* ***Island***, in Loch Lomond, 1m/2km NE of Rossdhu House. **74 B1** NS3790.

Inchmurrin *W.Dun.* ***Island***, largest island in Loch Lomond, 3m/4km N of Balloch. Ruins of old Lennox Castle at SW end of island. **74 B2** NS3887.

Inchnabobart *Aber.* ***Settlement***, 2m/3km N of Spittal of Glenmuick, in Glen Muick. **90 B6** NO3087.

Inchnacardoch Hotel *High.* ***Other building***, adjoining to Fort Augustus, at SW end of Loch Ness. **87 K3** NH3710.

Inchnadamph *High.* ***Village***, in Sutherland district, at head of Loch Assynt. Extensive cave system in valley of River Traligill to SE. **102 E6** NC2521.

Inchnadamph Forest *High.* ***Open space***, deer forest to E of Inchnadamph. **102 E6** NC2521.

Inchock *Angus* ***Settlement***, 1m/2km SE of Inverkeilor. **83 H3** NO6848.

Inchrory *Moray* ***Settlement***, on E bank of River Avon, 7m/11km S of Tomintoul. **89 J4** NJ1708.

Inchtavannach *Arg. & B.* ***Island***, close to W shore of Loch Lomond between Luss and Rossdhu House. **74 B1** NS3691.

Inchture *P. & K.* ***Village***, 8m/12km W of Dundee. **82 D5** NO2828.

Inchvuilt *High.* ***Locality***, on River Farrar, in Inverness district, nearly 2m/3km E of dam of Loch Monar. **87 J1** NH2238.

Inchyra *P. & K.* ***Settlement***, on N bank of River Tay, 5m/8km E of Perth. **82 C6** NO1820.

Indian Queens *Cornw.* ***Village***, 3m/5km S of St. Columb Major. Origin of name unknown. **3 G3** SW9159.

Inerval *Arg. & B.* ***Settlement***, on The Oa, Islay, 3m/5km SW of Port Ellen. **72 B6** NR3241.

Inga Ness *Ork.* ***Coastal feature***, headland on W coast of Westray, 4m/7km SE of Noup Head. **106 D3** HY4143.

Ingale Skerry *Ork.* ***Island***, rock island off S coast of Stronsay, 1m/2km SW of Lamb Head and 1m/2km SE of Tor Ness across Ingale Sound. **107 F6** HY6719.

Inganess Bay *Ork.* ***Bay***, large bay on N coast of Mainland, 2m/3km E of Kirkwall. Kirkwall Airport at head of bay. **107 D6** HY4808.

Ingatestone *Essex* Population: 6002. ***Small town***, 5m/8km NE of Brentwood. **24 C1** TQ6499.

Ingbirchworth *S.Yorks.* ***Village***, 2m/3km NW of Penistone. **50 E2** SE2205.

Ingbirchworth Reservoir *S.Yorks.* ***Reservoir***, to W of Ingbirchworth. **50 E2** SE2205.

Ingerthorpe *N.Yorks.* ***Settlement***, 3m/5km SW of Ripon. **57 H3** SE2866.

Ingestre *Staffs.* ***Village***, 4m/6km E of Stafford. **40 B3** SJ9824.

Ingham *Lincs.* ***Village***, 8m/13km N of Lincoln. **52 C4** SK9483.

Ingham *Norf.* ***Village***, 1m/2km NE of Stalham. **45 H3** TG3926.

Ingham *Suff.* ***Village***, 4m/7km N of Bury St. Edmunds. **34 C1** TL8570.

Ingham Corner *Norf.* ***Hamlet***, 1km N of Ingham, 2m/3km NE of Stalham. TG3927.

Ingleborough *Norf.* ***Hamlet***, 4m/6km N of Wisbech. TF4715.

Ingleborough *N.Yorks.* ***Locality***, adjoining to E of Clapham, 6m/9km NW of Settle. SD7469.

Ingleborough *N.Yorks.* ***Mountain***, 3m/5km NE of Ingleton. Traces of ancient fort at summit. Height 2371 feet or 723 metres. **56 C2** SD7474.

Ingleborough Common *N.Yorks.* ***Open space***, moorland on S side of Ingleborough, 3m/4km E of Ingleton. Contains numerous limestone cave systems and potholes, including well-known Ingleborough Cave and Gaping Gill. **56 C2** SD7373.

Ingleby *Derbys.* ***Hamlet***, on River Trent, 3m/4km NW of Melbourne. **41 F3** SK3526.

Ingleby *Lincs.* ***Locality***, 2m/3km N of Saxilby. **52 B5** SK8977.

Ingleby Arncliffe *N.Yorks.* ***Village***, 7m/11km NE of Northallerton. **63 F6** NZ4400.

Ingleby Barwick *Stock.* ***Hamlet***, 3m/5km S of Stockton-on-Tees. **63 F5** NZ4414.

Ingleby Cross *N.Yorks.* ***Locality***, at crossroads, adjoining to SE of Ingleby Arncliffe. **63 F6** NZ4400.

Ingleby Greenhow *N.Yorks.* ***Village***, 4m/6km E of Stockesley. **63 G6** NZ5806.

Ingleigh Green *Devon* ***Hamlet***, 4m/7km NE of Hatherleigh. SS6007.

Inglesbatch *B. & N.E.Som.* ***Hamlet***, 4m/6km SW of Bath. **19 K5** ST7061.

Inglesham *Swin.* ***Hamlet***, on River Thames, 1m/2km SW of Lechlade. **21 F2** SU2098.

Ingleton *Dur.* ***Village***, 3m/5km E of Staindrop. **62 C4** NZ1720.

Ingleton *N.Yorks.* Population: 1979. ***Village***, at confluence of River Twiss and River Doe to W of Ingleborough, 6m/10km SE of Kirkby Lonsdale. Contains Spelaeological centre. **56 B2** SD6972.

Inglewhite *Lancs.* ***Hamlet***, 7m/11km N of Preston. **55 J5** SD5440.

Inglewood Forest *Cumb.* ***Open space***, rural area and former hunting district, between Penrith and Carlisle. **60 E2** NY4344.

Inglismaldie Forest *Aber.* ***Forest/woodland***, midway between Edzell and Marykirk. **83 H1** NO6467.

Ingliston *Edin.* ***Locality***, site of Royal Highland Showground, 7m/11km W of Edinburgh and 1km SW of Edinburgh Airport. Motor-racing circuit. NT1372.

Ingmire Hall *Cumb.* ***Hamlet***, 1m/2km W of Sedbergh. **61 H7** SD6391.

Ingoe *Northumb.* ***Hamlet***, 3m/5km NW of Stamfordham. **71 F6** NZ0374.

Ingol *Lancs.* ***Suburb***, 2m/4km NW of Preston town centre. SD5131.

Ingoldisthorpe *Norf.* ***Village***, 5m/8km S of Hunstanton. **44 A2** TF6832.

Ingoldmells *Lincs.* Population: 2874. ***Village***, 4m/6km N of Skegness. **53 J6** TF5668.

Ingoldmells Point *Lincs.* ***Coastal feature***, headland 1m/2km E of Ingoldmells. **53 J6** TF5668.

Ingoldsby *Lincs.* ***Village***, 7m/11km SE of Grantham. **42 D2** TF0130.

Ingon *Warks.* ***Settlement***, 2m/3km NE of Stratford-upon-Avon. **30 D3** SP2157.

Ingram *Northumb.* ***Village***, 4m/7km NW of Whittingham. **71 F2** NU0116.

Ingrave *Essex* Population: 1058. ***Suburb***, 2m/3km SE of Brentwood. **24 C2** TQ6292.

Ingrow *W.Yorks.* ***Suburb***, S district of Keighley. **57 F6** SE0539.

Ings *Cumb.* ***Hamlet***, 2m/3km E of Windermere. **60 F7** SD4498.

Ingst *S.Glos.* ***Hamlet***, 3m/5km NE of Severn Beach. **19 J3** ST5887.

Ingstag *High. Alternative spelling of Inkstack, qv.*

Ingworth *Norf.* ***Village***, 2m/3km N of Aylsham. **45 F3** TG1929.

Inham's End *Cambs.* ***Locality***, adjoining to SE of Whittlesey. TL2796.

Inhurst *Hants.* ***Settlement***, 4m/6km NE of Kingsclere. SU5761.

Inishail (Sometimes spelled Innishail.) *Arg. & B.* ***Island***, in Loch Awe at entrance to arm of loch running NW to Pass of Brander in Argyll. Ruined church of St. Pindoca. **80 B5** NN1024.

Inistrynich *Arg. & B.* ***Settlement***, on small peninsula, extending into N part of Loch Awe, 4m/6km SW of Dalmally. **80 C5** NN1023.
Injebreck *I.o.M.* ***Settlement***, 6m/9km N of Douglas. **54 C5** SC3584.
Injebreck Reservoir *I.o.M.* ***Reservoir***, 5m/8km N of Douglas. **54 C5** SC3683.
Inkberrow *Worcs.* ***Village***, 5m/7km W of Alcester. **30 B3** SP0157.
Inkerman *Dur.* ***Village***, 1m/2km NW of Tow Law. NZ1139.
Inkersall *Derbys.* ***Settlement***, 1m/2km S of Staveley. SK4272.
Inkersall Green *Derbys.* ***Suburb***, to NW of Inkersall, 2m/3km SW of Staveley. SK4272.
Inkhorn *Aber.* ***Locality***, comprises Milton of Inkhorn and Mains of Inkhorn, 1m/2km S of Auchnagatt. **91 H1** NJ9239.
Inkpen *W.Berks.* ***Village***, 4m/6km SE of Hungerford. **21 G5** SU3664.
Inkstack (Also spelled Ingstag.) *High.* ***Settlement***, near N coast of Caithness district, 4m/7km E of Castletown. **105 H1** ND2570.
Inlands *W.Suss.* ***Settlement***, just NE of Southbourne, 2m/3km E of Emsworth. SU7706.
Inmarsh *Wilts.* ***Settlement***, to S of Seend, 4m/6km W of Devizes. ST9460.
Innellan *Arg. & B.* Population: 1142. ***Village***, and resort in Argyll, on W shore of Firth of Clyde, 4m/7km S of Dunoon. **73 K4** NS1470.
Inner Brigurd Point *N.Ayr.* ***Coastal feature***, small headland 1km NW of Hunterston. **73 K5** NS1852.
Inner Hebrides ***Island***, group of islands off W coast of Scotland, the chief islands being Skye (with Raasay), Canna, Rum, Eigg, Muck, Coll, Tiree, Mull (with Iona), Colonsay, Jura and Islay. **85 G1** NM3950.
Inner Holm *Ork.* ***Island***, islet on E side of Stromness Harbour, Mainland, to N of Outer Holm. HY2508.
Inner Hope *Devon* ***Suburb***, part of Hope, 4m/7km SW of Kingsbridge. SX6739.
Inner Score *Shet.* ***Island***, small uninhabited island between N end of Bressay and Outer Score. HU5145.
Inner Sound *High.* ***Sea feature***, strait dividing N coast of Scottish mainland from Island of Stroma. **105 J1** ND3576.
Inner Sound *High.* ***Sea feature***, sea channel between W coast of Ross and Cromarty district and islands of Raasay and Rona. Width from 4m/7km to 7m/11km. **94 C7** NG6441.
Inner Sound *Northumb.* ***Sea feature***, sea channel between E coast mainland and island of Inner Farne, 1m/2km offshore. **77 K7** NU2035.
Innerdouny Hill *P. & K.* ***Mountain***, in Ochil Hills, 3m/5km NW of Carnbo. Height 1630 feet or 497 metres. **82 B7** NO0307.
Innerdownie *P. & K.* ***Mountain***, in Ochil Hills, 3m/5km N of Dollar. Height 2004 feet or 611 metres. **82 A7** NN9603.
Innergellie *Fife* ***Settlement***, to N of Kilrenny. **83 G7** NO5705.
Innerleithen *Sc.Bord.* Population: 2515. ***Small town***, at confluence of Leithen Water and River Tweed, 6m/9km SE of Peebles. Site of Roman camp on SW side. **76 B7** NT3336.
Innerleven *Fife* ***Locality***, docks area in Methil, at mouth of River Leven. **82 E7** NO3700.
Innermessan *D. & G.* ***Settlement***, on E side of Loch Ryan, 2m/3km NE of Stranraer. **64 A4** NX0863.
Innerpeffray *P. & K.* ***Settlement***, 3m/5km SE of Crieff. Castle is ruined 17c tower house. Several Roman sites in vicinity. NN9018.
Innerpeffray Library *P. & K.* ***Other feature of interest***, oldest public library in Scotland, founded in 1691 and housed in 18c building. **82 A6** NN9018.
Innertown *Ork.* ***Locality***, on Mainland, just W of Stromness. HY2409.
Innerwell Port *D. & G.* ***Bay***, small bay 2m/3km N of Garlieston, on W side of Wigtown Bay. **64 E6** NX4849.
Innerwick *E.Loth.* ***Village***, 4m/6km SE of Dunbar. **77 F3** NT7273.
Innerwick *P. & K.* ***Settlement***, in Glen Lyon, 1km NE of Bridge of Balgie. **81 G3** NN5847.
Innes Canal *Moray* ***Canal***, running from 3m/4km W of Garmouth, then skirting disused airfield, before running parallel to River Lossie and joining river 1m/2km SE of Lossiemouth. **97 K5** NJ2569.
Innes Links *Moray* ***Coastal feature***, forested coastal area, 3m/5km NW of Garmouth. **97 K5** NJ2867.
Inninbeg *High.* ***Settlement***, on Ardtornish Bay, 1km N of Ardtornish Point, Lochaber district. **79 J3** NM6943.
Inninmore Bay *High.* ***Bay***, on Sound of Mull, extending NW from Rubha and Ridire, Lochaber district. **79 J3** NM7241.
Innis Bheag *High.* ***Island***, sandy island 3m/4km W of Portmahomack. **97 F3** NH8684.
Innis Chonain *Arg. & B.* ***Island***, off W shore of Loch Awe in Argyll, 1m/2km SW of Lochawe. Connected to shore by bridge. **80 C5** NN1025.
Innis Chonnell *Arg. & B.* ***Island***, islet near E shore of Loch Awe in Argyll, opposite Dalavich. Ruins of Ardchonnell Castle, 15c stronghold of the Campbells. NM9711.
Innis Mhòr *High.* ***Island***, sandy island at mouth of Dornoch Firth, 5m/8km NE of Tain. **97 F3** NH8586.
Innis Shearraich *Arg. & B.* ***Island***, islet off E shore of Loch Awe in Argyll, opposite Portinnisherrich. Stepping-stones give access at low water. 13c chapel. NM9711.
Innishail *Arg. & B. Occasional spelling of Inishail, qv.*
Innisidgen Burial Chambers *I.o.S.* ***Historic/prehistoric site***, on NE coast of St. Mary's, 1m/2km NE of Hugh Town. Round cairn, sometimes known as Giant's Grave. Lower Innisidgen entrance grave is close by. **2 C1** SV9212.
Innsworth *Glos.* Population: 3036. ***Suburb***, NE district of Gloucester. **29 H6** SO8621.
Inny *Cornw.* ***River***, rising near Davidstow and flowing SE into River Tamar, S of Dunterton. SX3777.
Insch *Aber.* Population: 1541. ***Village***, 10m/16km NW of Inverurie. Picardy Stone (Historic Scotland), 2m/3km NW. **90 E2** NJ6328.
Insh *High.* ***Village***, in Badenoch and Strathspey district, 4m/6km E of Kingussie. **89 F4** NH8101.
Insh Island *Arg. & B.* ***Island***, uninhabited island in Firth of Lorn, 1m/2km W of Seil, from which it is separated by Sound of Insh. **79 J6** NM7319.
Inshegra *High.* ***Settlement***, on N side of Loch Inchard, W coast of Sutherland district. NC2455.
Inshore *High.* ***Settlement***, overlooking Loch Inshore, 2m/3km NW of Achiemore, Sutherland district. **103 F2** NC3269.
Inshriach Forest *High.* ***Forest/woodland***, to NE of Insh. **89 F4** NH8101.
Inskip *Lancs.* ***Village***, 7m/12km NW of Preston. **55 H6** SD4637.
Inskip Moss Side *Lancs.* ***Locality***, 1m/2km NW of Inskip and 4m/7km SW of Garstang. SD4539.
Instoneville *S.Yorks.* ***Locality***, adjoining to S of Askern. SE5512.
Instow *Devon* ***Village***, on E side of River Torridge estuary, 3m/5km N of Bideford. **6 C2** SS4730.
Intake *S.Yorks.* ***Suburb***, 2m/3km E of Doncaster town centre. SE6003.
Intake *S.Yorks.* ***Suburb***, 3m/4km SE of Sheffield city centre. **51 F4** SK3884.
Intwood *Norf.* ***Hamlet***, 1m/2km S of Cringleford, on SW side of Norwich. **45 F5** TG1904.
Inver *Aber.* ***Settlement***, 1m/2km SW of Balmoral Castle, in River Dee valley. **89 K5** NO2293.
Inver *Arg. & B.* ***Settlement***, on N shore of Loch Creran, 1m/2km E of Creagan. **80 A3** NM9945.
Inver *High.* ***River***, in Sutherland district, flowing W from Loch Assynt to Loch Inver. NC0923.
Inver *High.* ***Settlement***, to NE of Dunbeath. **105 G5** ND1630.
Inver *High.* ***Village***, in Ross and Cromarty district, on S shore of Dornoch Firth, 5m/8km E of Tain. **97 F3** NH8682.
Inver *P. & K.* ***Hamlet***, 1km SW of Dunkeld, over River Tay. **82 B3** NO0142.
Inver Bay *High.* ***Sea feature***, inlet on N side of Inver. **97 F3** NH8682.
Inver Dalavil *High.* ***Bay***, on W coast of Sleat peninsula, Skye, 4m/6km N of Point of Sleat. **86 B4** NG5705.
Inver Mallie *High.* ***Settlement***, at mouth of River Mallie on S shore of Loch Arkaig, 4m/6km NW of Gairlochy. **87 H6** NN1388.
Inverailort *High.* ***Settlement***, with jetty, at head of Loch Ailort, Lochaber district. **86 D6** NM7681.
Inveralligin (Alligin). *High.* ***Village***, on N shore of Upper Loch Torridon, Ross and Cromarty district. **94 E6** NG8457.
Inverallochy *Aber.* Population: 1410. ***Village***, on NE coast, 3m/5km E of Fraserburgh. **99 J4** NK0465.
Inveran *High.* ***Locality***, location of power station (Shin Hydro-Electricity Scheme) at confluence of Rivers Shin and Oykel in Sutherland district, 4m/6km NW of Bonar Bridge. **96 C2** NH5797.
Inveraray *Arg. & B.* ***Small town***, in Argyll on W shore of Loch Fyne, 6m/10km SW of head of loch and 19m/31km NE of Lochgilphead. **80 B7** NN0908.
Inveraray Castle *Arg. & B.* ***Castle***, to N of Inverary, seat of the Dukes of Argyll, dates mainly from 18c; damaged by fire in 1975. **80 B7** NN0908.
Inveraray Jail *Arg. & B.* ***Other feature of interest***, in Inveraray, on NW shore of Loch Fyne. An imaginative exhibition re-creating 19c prison and courtroom life. **80 B7** NN0908.
Inverardoch Mains *Stir.* ***Settlement***, 1km SE of Doune. **81 J7** NN7300.
Inverardran *Stir.* ***Settlement***, 1km E of Crianlarich. **80 E5** NN3924.
Inverarish *High.* ***Settlement***, on SW coast of Raasay, 2m/3km NW of Eyre Point. **86 B1** NG5635.
Inverarity *Angus* ***Settlement***, 4m/6km S of Forfar. **83 F3** NO4544.
Inverarnan *Stir.* ***Settlement***, on River Falloch, 2m/3km N of Ardlui, at head of Loch Lomond. **80 E6** NN3118.
Inverasdale *High.* ***Locality***, on W side of Loch Ewe, W coast of Ross and Cromarty district, 4m/7km NW of Poolewe. **94 E3** NG8186.
Inverbain *High.* ***Settlement***, on W coast of Loch Shieldaig, 7m/11km W of Torridon, Ross and Cromarty district. **94 D6** NG7854.
Inverbeg *Arg. & B.* ***Locality***, on W side of Loch Lomond, 3m/5km N of Luss. Ferry for pedestrians to Rowardennan. **74 B1** NS3497.
Inverbervie *Aber.* Population: 1879. ***Small town***, at mouth of Bervie Water, on E coast, 9m/14km S of Stonehaven. A royal burgh since 1342. **91 G7** NO8372.
Inverboyndie *Aber.* ***Locality***, 1m/2km W of Banff. NJ6664.
Inverbroom *High.* ***Settlement***, in valley of River Broom, 1m/2km S of head of Loch Broom. **95 H3** NH1883.
Inverbrough *High.* ***Settlement***, 1m/2km NE of Tomatin. **89 F2** NH8129.
Invercassley *High.* ***Settlement***, 1km N of confluence of River Cassley and River Oykel. **96 B1** NC4702.
Invercauld Bridge *Aber.* ***Historic/prehistoric site***, on River Dee, 2m/3km E of Braemar. Built by Prince Albert when old bridge, dating from 1752, became royal property and road through Balmoral estate was closed. **89 J5** NO1891.
Invercauld Forest *Aber.* ***Open space***, area of mountain and forest on N side of River Dee, opposite Braemar. **89 J5** NO1395.
Inverchaolain *Arg. & B.* ***Locality***, on E shore of Loch Striven, Argyll, 4m/7km N of Ardyne Point. **73 J3** NS0975.
Invercharnan *High.* ***Settlement***, in Glen Etive, 3m/4km NE of head of Loch Etive. **80 C3** NN1448.
Inverchorachan *Arg. & B.* ***Settlement***, in Glen Fyne, 4m/7km NE of head of Loch Fyne. **80 D6** NN2217.
Inverchoran *High.* ***Settlement***, in valley of River Meig, 8m/12km SE of Achnasheen. **95 J6** NH2550.
Invercloy *N.Ayr. Former name of Brodick, qv.*
Invercreran *Arg. & B.* ***Settlement***, 1m/2km NE of head of Loch Creran. **80 B3** NN0146.
Inverdruie *High.* ***Hamlet***, near mouth of River Druie, in Badenoch and Strathspey district, 1m/2km SE of Aviemore. **89 G3** NH9010.
Inverebrie *Aber.* ***Settlement***, on W side of Ebrie Burn, 3m/5km NW of Ellon. **91 H1** NJ9233.
Invereen *High.* ***Settlement***, 3m/5km SE of Moy. **89 F1** NH7931.
Invererne *Moray* ***Settlement***, 1m/2km N of Forres. **97 H5** NJ0360.
Inveresk *E.Loth.* ***Suburb***, to S of Musselburgh, on site of Roman station. **76 B3** NT3472.
Inveresk Lodge Garden *E.Loth.* ***Garden***, National Trust for Scotland property on E bank of River Esk at Inveresk, 1km S of Musselburgh. Specialises in plants for small gardens. **76 B3** NT3471.
Inverewe *High. See Poolewe.*
Inverewe Gardens *High.* ***Garden***, exotic collection of plants in themed gardens designed by Osgood Mackenzie in 19c on his peninsula estate, 1km N of Poolewe, Ross and Cromarty district. Gardens thrived due to temperate local climate resulting from Gulf Stream. After Mackenzie's death in 1922, National Trust for Scotland took over ownership. Features include rhododendrons, Victorian and walled gardens, giant eucalypts and visitor centre. **94 E3** NG8581.
Inverey *Aber.* ***Settlement***, at foot of Glen Ey, 4m/7km W of Braemar. **89 H6** NO0889.
Inverfarigaig *High.* ***Settlement***, on SE shore of Loch Ness, at mouth of River Farigaig, 2m/4km NE of Foyers, Inverness district. **88 C2** NH5123.
Invergarry *High.* ***Village***, at foot of Glen Garry, in Lochaber district. **87 K4** NH3001.
Invergarry Castle *High.* ***Castle***, 17c L-plan ruin on shore of Loch Oich, to SE of Invergarry. **87 K4** NH3001.
Invergelder *Aber.* ***Settlement***, 1m/2km SW of Balmoral Castle. **89 K5** NO2393.
Invergeldie *P. & K.* ***Settlement***, in Glen Lednock, 4m/6km NW of Comrie. **81 J5** NN7427.
Invergeldie Burn *P. & K.* ***River***, stream flowing SW into River Lednock, 3m/5km NW of Comrie. **81 J5** NN7326.
Invergloy *High.* ***Locality***, in Lochaber district, at mouth of River Gloy, on SE shore of Loch Lochy. **87 J6** NN2288.
Invergordon *High.* Population: 3929. ***Small town***, port and former naval base on N shore of Cromarty Firth, Ross and Cromarty district, 11m/18km NE of Dingwall. Development in connection with North Sea oil. **96 E5** NH7068.
Invergowrie *P. & K.* ***Suburb***, 4m/6km W of Dundee city centre, on Firth of Tay. **82 E4** NO3430.
Inverguseran *High.* ***Locality***, on NW coast of Knoydart, Lochaber district, at foot of Glen Guseran. **86 D4** NG7407.
Inverhadden *P. & K.* ***Settlement***, 1km SE of Kinloch Rannoch. **81 H2** NN6757.
Inverhadden Burn *P. & K.* ***River***, flowing N into Dunalastair Water, 1m/2km E of Kinloch Rannoch. NN6758.
Inverharroch *Moray* ***Settlement***, 1km SE of Bridgend. **90 B1** NJ3831.
Inverherive *Stir.* ***Settlement***, in Strath Fillan, 1m/2km NW of Crianlarich. **80 E5** NN3626.
Inverhope *High.* ***Settlement***, at mouth of River Hope, 4m/7km SW of Whiten Head. **103 G2** NC4761.
Inverie *High.* ***River***, flowing W into Inverie Bay 1m/2km SE of Inverie village, Lochaber district. **86 E5** NM7798.
Inverie *High.* ***Village***, in Lochaber district, on S side of Knoydart. Village is situated on Inverie Bay, on N side of Loch Nevis. Inverie River flows W into bay 1m/2km SE of village. **86 D4** NG7600.
Inverie Bay *High.* ***Bay***, on S coast of Knoydart peninsula, on N side of Loch Nevis. **86 D5** NG7600.
Inverinan *Arg. & B.* ***Settlement***, on W side of Loch Awe, in Argyll, surrounded by Inverinan Forest. **80 A6** NM9917.
Inverinan Forest *Arg. & B.* ***Forest/woodland***, surrounding locality of Inverinan on W side of Loch Awe in Argyll and to N of Inverliever Forest. Information centre and nature trails. **80 A6** NM9917.
Inverinate *High.* ***Village***, Forestry Commission village surrounded by woodland on E bank of Loch Duich, Skye and Lochalsh district, 2m/3km from head of loch. **87 F2** NG9122.
Inverkeilor *Angus* ***Village***, 6m/9km N of Arbroath. **83 H3** NO6649.
Inverkeithing *Fife* Population: 6001. ***Small town***, on Inverkeithing Bay on N side of Firth of Forth, 4m/6km SE of Dunfermline. Ancient royal burgh with charter dating from 1165. **75 K2** NT1383.
Inverkeithing Bay *Fife* ***Bay***, on N side of Firth of Forth, 4m/6km SE of Dunfermline. **75 K2** NT1383.
Inverkeithny *Aber.* ***Village***, on Burn of Forgue, near its confluence with River Deveron, 4m/6km S of Aberchirder. **98 E6** NJ6246.
Inverkip *Inclyde* Population: 1258. ***Village***, on Firth of Clyde, 5m/8km SW of Greenock. **74 A3** NS2072.
Inverkirkaig *High.* ***Hamlet***, in Sutherland district, at head of Loch Kirkaig on W coast, 2m/3km SW of Lochinver. **102 C7** NC0719.
Inverlael *High.* ***Settlement***, at head of Loch Broom, Ross and Cromarty district. **95 H3** NH1885.
Inverlael Forest *High.* ***Open space***, deer forest to E of Inverlael. **95 H3** NH1886.
Inverlauren *Arg. & B.* ***Settlement***, 3m/4km NE of Helensburgh. **74 B2** NS3185.
Inverleith *Edin.* ***Suburb***, 1m/2km NW of Edinburgh city centre. Contains Royal Botanic Garden. NT2475.

Inverliever *Arg. & B.* ***Settlement***, 2m/3km NE of Ford, on N shore of Loch Awe. **79 K7** NM8905.
Inverliever Forest *Arg. & B.* ***Forest/woodland***, on W side of Loch Awe in Argyll, to S of Inverinan Forest and Dalavich. Information centre and nature trails. **80 A7** NM9409.
Inverliver *Arg. & B.* ***Settlement***, on Inverliver Bay, E side of Loch Etive, Argyll, 4m/6km NE of Bonawe. Inverliver Bay is small bay on shore of Loch Etive to N. **80 B4** NN0635.
Inverlochlarig *Stir.* ***Settlement***, in valley of River Larig, 6m/9km SE of Crianlarich. **81 F6** NN4317.
Inverlochy *Arg. & B.* ***Settlement***, 2m/3km E of Dalmally. **80 C5** NN1927.
Inverlochy *High.* ***Locality***, at mouth of River Lochy in Lochaber district, 1m/2km NE of Fort William. 13c castle (Historic Scotland) near mouth of river; present-day castle 1m/2km NE. NN1174.
Inverlussa *Arg. & B.* ***Locality***, at mouth of Lussa River, on E coast of Jura. **72 E2** NR6486.
Invermay *P. & K.* ***Settlement***, on S bank of Water of May, 3m/5km NE of Dunning. **82 B6** NO0616.
Invermoriston *High.* ***Village***, in Inverness district, on River Moriston, 1km above mouth of river. **88 B3** NH4216.
Invernaver *High.* ***Settlement***, near N coast of Caithness district, 1m/2km S of Bettyhill. **104 C2** NC7060.
Inverneil *Arg. & B.* ***Settlement***, on W side of Loch Fyne, 3m/4km S of Ardrishaig. **73 G2** NR8481.
Inverness *High.* Population: 41,234. ***Town***, at mouth of River Ness at entrance to Beauly Firth, 105m/169km NW of Aberdeen and 113m/181km NW of Edinburgh. Administrative, commercial and tourist centre. Caledonian Canal passes to W of town. Inverness Museum and Art Gallery depicts history of Highlands. University of the Highlands and Islands. Airport at locality of Dalcross, 7m/11km NE of town. **96 D7** NH6645.
I
Inverness Airport (Formerly known as Dalcross Airport.) *High.* ***Airport/airfield***, airport on E side of Inner Moray Firth, 8m/13km NE of Inverness. **96 E6** NH7752.
Inverness Museum and Art Gallery *High.* ***Other feature of interest***, in centre of Inverness, with exhibitions of archaeology, natural history and culture of the Highlands. **96 D7** NH6644.
Invernettie *Aber.* ***Hamlet***, 1m/2km S of Peterhead. **99 K6** NK1244.
Invernoaden *Arg. & B.* ***Settlement***, 1km E of Glenbranter. **73 K1** NS1297.
Inveroran Hotel *Arg. & B.* ***Other building***, 2m/3km NW of Bridge of Orchy. **80 D3** NN2741.
Inverorar *Arg. & B.* ***Locality***, at SW corner of Loch Tulla in Argyll. NN2741.
Inverpolly Forest *High.* ***Open space***, upland area, part of Inverpolly National Nature Reserve near NW coast of Ross and Cromarty district, 7m/11km S of Lochinver. **102 D7** NC0912.
Inverpolly National Nature Reserve *High.* ***Nature reserve***, 7m/11km S of Shieldaig, a wilderness of mountains, moorland, woodland, lochs and bogs. Over 100 bird species recorded. **102 D7** NC1910.
Inverquharity *Angus* ***Settlement***, 3m/4km N of Kirriemuir. **83 F2** NO4057.
Inverquhomery *Aber.* ***Settlement***, 1m/2km SW of Longside. **99 J6** NK0246.
Inverroy *High.* ***Settlement***, in Lochaber district, between Roybridge and Spean Bridge. **87 J6** NN2581.
Inversanda *High.* ***Settlement***, on W side of Loch Linnhe in Lochaber district, at foot of Glen Tarbert. **80 A2** NM9359.
Inversanda Bay *High.* ***Bay***, to E of Inversanda, at mouth of River Tarbert, on Loch Linnhe. **80 A2** NM9359.
Inverscaddle Bay *High.* ***Bay***, containing marsh, sand and shingle on W shore of Loch Linnhe, Lochaber district, at mouth of River Scaddle. **80 B1** NN0268.
Invershiel *High.* ***Settlement***, in Skye and Lochalsh district, at head of Loch Duich. **87 F3** NG9319.
Invershin *High.* ***Locality***, with railway station, in Sutherland district, at confluence of Rivers Oykel and Shin, 4m/6km NW of Bonar Bridge. **96 C2** NH5796.
Invershore *High.* ***Settlement***, on E coast of Caithness district, 1km SW of Lybster. ND2434.
Inversnaid *Stir.* ***Settlement***, on E shore of Loch Lomond, opposite Inveruglas. Garrison of Inversnaid, to NE up glen towards Loch Arklet, is farm incorporating remains of fort built in 1713 as deterrent to clan Macgregor. NN3308.
Inversnaid Hotel *Stir.* ***Other building***, on E shore of Loch Lomond, 3m/5km NE of Tarbet across loch. **80 E7** NN3308.
Invertrossachs *Stir.* ***Settlement***, on S side of Loch Venachar, 3m/5km NE of Aberfoyle. **81 G7** NN5604.
Inverugie *Aber.* ***Hamlet***, on River Ugie, 2m/4km NW of Peterhead. Ruined castle of the Keiths, Earls Marischal. **99 K6** NK1048.
Inveruglas *Arg. & B.* ***Locality***, on W shore of Loch Lomond, 3m/5km N of Tarbet, at mouth of Inveruglas Water. Power station operated by water conveyed from Loch Sloy by aqueduct. **80 E7** NN3109.
Inveruglas Isle *Arg. & B.* ***Island***, islet in Loch Lomond, with remains of castle. NN3209.
Inveruglas Water *Arg. & B.* ***River***, stream descending from Loch Sloy to W shore of Loch Lomond. **80 E7** NN3109.
Inveruglass *High.* ***Settlement***, 3m/5km E of Kingussie. **89 F4** NH8001.
Inverurie *Aber.* Population: 9567. ***Small town***, near confluence of Rivers Don and Urie, 14m/22km NW of Aberdeen. Stone circle (Historic Scotland) at Easter Aquhorthies, 3m/5km W. **91 F2** NJ7721.
Inverurie Museum *Aber.* ***Other feature of interest***, museum in Inverurie, with archaeological and geological finds. **91 F2** NJ7721.
Invervar *P. & K.* ***Settlement***, at foot of Invervar Burn, on N side of Glen Lyon, 5m/8km W of Fortingall. **81 H3** NN6648.
Invervegain *Arg. & B.* ***Settlement***, on E coast of Loch Striven, 2m/4km N of Inverchaolain. **73 J3** NS0878.
Inverwick Forest *High.* ***Open space***, deer forest in Inverness district, 3m/5km NW of Fort Augustus. **87 K3** NH3413.
Invery House *Aber.* ***Settlement***, 1m/2km S of Banchory, on W side of Water of Feugh. **90 E5** NO6993.
Inverythan *Aber.* ***Settlement***, on W bank of River Ythan, 3m/4km N of Fyvie. **99 F6** NJ7541.
Inwardleigh *Devon* ***Village***, 3m/5km NW of Okehampton. **6 D6** SX5699.
Inworth *Essex* ***Hamlet***, 1m/2km SE of Kelvedon. **34 C7** TL8817.
Inzie Head *Aber.* ***Coastal feature***, headland on NE coast, at NW end of Strathbeg Bay, 2m/3km SE of Inverallochy. **99 J4** NK0662.
Iochda (Anglicised form: Eochar.) *W.Isles* ***Settlement***, 2m/4km E of Ardivachar Point on South Uist. **92 C7** NF7746.
Iona *Arg. & B.* ***Island***, about 3m/5km long NE to SW and over 1m/2km wide, lying nearly 1m/2km off W end of Ross of Mull across Sound of Iona. Site of monastery founded by St. Columba in 6c. Remains of 13c convent. Cathedral mainly 16c, restored. Tombs of the Kings, where several kings lie buried; grave of John Smith, former Labour leader, also on Iona. Island is owned by National Trust for Scotland and is much visited in summer. Ferry connection with Fionnphort on Mull. **78 D5** NM2723.
Iona Abbey *Arg. & B.* ***Ecclesiastical building***, site of monastery founded in AD 563 by St. Columba to N of Baile Mòr on E coast of Iona. Frequently attacked by raiders, it was replaced in 1203 by Benedictine monastery which subsequently became a ruin during Reformation. Mainly 16c cathedral on site has notable carvings and interior. Restoration of monastery and cathedral started in 20c, and buildings are now home to Iona community. Grounds also include Tomb of the Kings, restored St. Oran's Chapel, 10c St. Martin's Cross and Abbey Museum. **78 D5** NM2824.
Iorsa Water *N.Ayr.* ***River***, on Arran rising to W of Casteal Abhail and running SW down Glen Iorsa into Kilbrannan Sound at N end of Machrie Bay. **73 H7** NR8836.
Iping *W.Suss.* ***Village***, on River Rother, 2m/4km NW of Midhurst. **12 B4** SU8522.
Ipplepen *Devon* Population: 2275. ***Village***, 3m/5km SW of Newton Abbot. **5 J4** SX8366.
Ipsden *Oxon.* ***Village***, 3m/5km SE of Wallingford. **21 K3** SU6385.
Ipsley *Worcs.* ***Suburb***, 2m/3km E of Redditch town centre. SP0666.
Ipstones *Staffs.* ***Village***, 4m/7km N of Cheadle. **50 C7** SK0249.
Ipswich *Suff.* Population: 130,157. ***Town***, county town and port at head of River Orwell estuary, 66m/106km NE of London, with an expanding industrial base. Town has some timber-framed houses; 16c Sparrowe's House is an attractive building in the Butter Market; Great White Horse Inn inspired Dickens with a setting for Pickwick Papers. 16c Christchurch Mansion now houses a museum. Cardinal Wolsey was born here. Several medieval churches survive; 15c stone screen in St. Lawrence's Church and Church of St. Mary-le-Tower has pulpit by Grinling Gibbons. Airport 3m/4km SE. **35 F4** TM1644.
Ipswich Museum *Suff.* ***Other feature of interest***, in Ipswich town centre, with exhibits on archaeology, geology and natural history. **35 F4** TM1644.
Irby *Mersey.* ***Suburb***, 2m/3km NW of Heswall. **48 B4** SJ2584.
Irby Hill *Mersey.* ***Hamlet***, 1km N of Irby. SJ2585.
Irby in the Marsh *Lincs.* ***Village***, 4m/6km NW of Wainfleet All Saints. **53 H6** TF4763.
Irby upon Humber *N.E.Lincs.* ***Village***, 6m/9km SW of Grimsby. **52 E2** TA1904.
Irchester *Northants.* Population: 4529. ***Village***, 3m/4km SE of Wellingborough. Site of Roman town to N. **32 C2** SP9265.
Irchester Country Park *Northants.* ***Leisure/recreation***, 200 acres of grass and woodland close to S bank of River Nene, to NW of Irchester. Nature trails. **32 C2** SP9165.
Ireby *Cumb.* ***Village***, 6m/10km S of Wigton. **60 D3** NY2338.
Ireby *Lancs.* ***Village***, 3m/5km NW of Ingleton. **56 B2** SD6575.
Ireland *Beds.* ***Hamlet***, 2m/3km N of Shefford. TL1341.
Ireland *Ork.* ***Locality***, on Mainland, 5m/8km SW of Finstown, on E side of Bay of Ireland. **107 C7** HY3009.
Ireland *Shet.* ***Settlement***, on W coast of Mainland, 9m/14km N of Sumburgh Head. **109 C10** HU3722.
Ireland's Cross *Shrop.* ***Settlement***, 1km SE of Woore. SJ7341.
Ireleth *Cumb.* ***Village***, 2m/4km N of Dalton-in-Furness. **55 F2** SD2277.
Ires Geo *High.* ***Coastal feature***, small indentation on E coast 1m/2km W of Thrumster. **105 J4** ND3545.
Ireshope Moor *Dur.* ***Open space***, moorland on upper reaches of Ireshope Burn, 2m/4km SW of St. John's Chapel. **61 K3** NY8336.
Ireshopeburn *Dur.* ***Hamlet***, 1m/2km SE of Wearhead. **61 K3** NY8638.
Ireton Houses *Derbys.* ***Settlement***, 1m/2km E of Belper. SK3747.
Irfon *Powys* ***River***, rising 2m/4km SW of Claerwen Reservoir dam, it flows S to Llanwrtyd Wells, then E by Llangammarch Wells and Garth to join River Wye on NW side of Builth Wells. **27 J4** SO0351.
Irish Law *N.Ayr.* ***Mountain***, 4m/6km E of Largs. Height 1588 feet or 484 metres. **74 A5** NS2559.
Irlam *Gt.Man.* Population: 18,504. ***Town***, 8m/13km SW of Manchester. **49 G3** SJ7193.
Irlam o'th' Height *Gt.Man.* ***Suburb***, 2m/4km NW of Salford city centre. SD7900.
Irnham *Lincs.* ***Village***, 6m/10km NW of Bourne. Hall, 16c. Manor house, 18c. **42 D3** TF0226.
Iron Acton *S.Glos.* ***Village***, 3m/5km W of Chipping Sodbury. **19 K3** ST6783.
Iron Band *Cumb.* ***Mountain***, 4m/6km NE of Brough. Height 1843 feet or 562 metres. **61 K5** NY8318.
Iron Bridge *Cambs.* ***Settlement***, and bridge over Sixteen Foot Drain, 4m/6km NW of Welney. TL4898.
Iron Bridge *Tel. & W.* ***Bridge***, world's first cold blast iron bridge (English Heritage), built in 1779 by Telford and cast by Abraham Darby III at Coalbrookdale, it spans River Severn gorge. Bridge is still used by pedestrians. SJ6703.
Iron Cross *Warks.* ***Settlement***, 6m/9km N of Evesham. **30 B3** SP0652.
Ironbridge *Tel. & W.* Population: 2184. ***Small town***, in Telford, 3m/4km S of Dawley. Situated on N side of River Severn gorge and named after bridge spanning it. **39 F5** SJ6703.
Ironbridge Gorge Museum *Tel. & W.* ***Other feature of interest***, on River Severn in Ironbridge, to N of Broseley. Features first cast iron bridge in the world. Various sites include china and tile museums, as well as Blists Mill Museum which has a reconstructed late 19c street. **39 F5** SJ6603.
Irons Bottom *Surr.* ***Settlement***, 2m/4km S of Reigate. TQ2546.
Ironside *Aber.* ***Locality***, comprising Upper Ironside and Backhill of Ironside, 1m/2km E of Fedderate Reservoir and 2m/3km S of New Pitsligo. **99 G5** NJ8852.
Ironville *Derbys.* ***Village***, 3m/4km E of Ripley. **51 G7** SK4351.
Irstead *Norf.* ***Hamlet***, 3m/4km NE of Horning, near S end of Barton Broad. **45 H3** TG3620.
Irstead Street *Norf.* ***Settlement***, on E side of Alderfen Broad, 2m/3km NE of Horning. TG3519.
Irt *Cumb.* ***River***, flowing SW from foot of Wast Water and flowing W past Nether Wasdale, then S to Santon Bridge and into River Esk estuary at Ravenglass. **60 C6** SD0896.
Irthing ***River***, formed by confluence of Gair Burn and Tarn Beck, on W side of Wark Forest, and flowing first E, then generally SW into River Eden 5m/7km E of Carlisle. **70 B6** NY4657.
Irthington *Cumb.* ***Village***, 2m/3km W of Brampton across River Irthing. Carlisle Airport to SW. **69 K7** NY4961.
Irthlingborough *Northants.* Population: 5244. ***Small town***, 4m/7km NE of Wellingborough. 14c bridge over River Nene. Medieval church has notable detached tower. **32 C1** SP9470.
Irthlingborough Bridge *Northants.* ***Bridge***, 14c stone bridge with 19 arches over River Nene on S side of Irthlingborough. SP9570.
Irton *N.Yorks.* ***Village***, 3m/5km SW of Scarborough. **59 G1** TA0184.
Irton Moor *N.Yorks.* ***Open space***, moorland, with tumuli, 3m/5km W of Scarborough. **59 G1** SE9987.
Irvine *E.Ayr.* ***River***, flowing W to Galston, and passing S of Kilmarnock to Irvine and Irvine Bay. **74 C7** NS3239.
Irvine *N.Ayr.* Population: 32,988. ***Town***, port (and New Town, designated 1965) on and near mouth of River Irvine, 7m/11km W of Kilmarnock. Originally main port for trade between Scotland and Ireland. **74 B7** NS3239.
Irvine Bay *N.Ayr.* ***Bay***, wide bay to W of Irvine. **74 A7** NS3038.
Isabella Pit *Northumb.* ***Suburb***, in SW part of Blyth. NZ2980.
Isauld *High.* ***Settlement***, near N coast of Caithness district, 1km E of Reay. **104 E2** NC9765.
Isauld Burn *High.* ***River***, rising in Loch Saorach and flowing NW into Sandside Bay on N coast. ND0063.
Isay *High.* ***Island***, uninhabited island in Loch Dunvegan, Skye, 2m/4km E of Dunvegan Head. **93 H6** NG2157.
Isay *W.Isles* ***Island***, islet in West Loch Tarbert 3m/5km NW of Tarbert, North Harris. NB1002.
Isbister *Ork.* ***Locality***, on Mainland, at head of Bay of Isbister. **107 C6** HY3918.
Isbister *Ork.* ***Settlement***, to SE of Loch of Isbister, in NW of Mainland. Disused airfield to S. **106 B5** HY2623.
Isbister *Shet.* ***Settlement***, on Mainland, 3m/4km S of Point of Fethaland. Northern terminus of road. **108 C3** HU3790.
Isbister *Shet.* ***Settlement***, near E coast of Whalsay, 3m/4km SW of Skaw Taing. **109 E6** HU5764.
Isbister Holm *Shet.* ***Island***, small uninhabited island 1m/2km off Whalsay coast to E of Isbister. HU6064.
Isbourne ***River***, rising in Cotswold Hills near Winchcombe and flowing N into River Avon at Evesham. **30 B5** SP0343.
Isca *Newport See Caerleon Roman Fortress and Baths.*
Isca Dumnoniorum *Devon See Exeter.*
Isfield *E.Suss.* ***Village***, in River Ouse valley, 3m/5km SW of Uckfield. **13 H5** TQ4417.
Isham *Northants.* ***Village***, 3m/5km S of Kettering. **32 B1** SP8873.
Ishriff *Arg. & B.* ***Settlement***, 4m/6km N of Lochbuie, Mull. **79 H4** NM6331.
Isington *Hants.* ***Hamlet***, 1m/2km SW of Bentley, 5m/8km SW of Farnham. SU7742.
Isis *See (River) Thames.*
Isla ***River***, rising 3m/4km NE of Dufftown and flowing NE to Keith, then E to Nethermills before turning SE to join River Deveron 5m/8km N of Huntly. Noted for trout. **98 B6** NJ5347.
Isla ***River***, rising S of Braemar and running S down Glen Isla to Airlie Castle, then on to River Tay 4m/7km W of Coupar Angus. **82 D2** NO1637.
Island Carr *N.Lincs.* ***Locality***, adjoining to W of Brigg. SE9907.
Island Hall *Cambs.* ***Historic house***, 18c mansion at Godmanchester, 15m/24km NW of Cambridge. Restored to its original period decor. Formal gardens and ornamental island. **33 F2** TL2569.
Island I Vow *Arg. & B. Alternative name for Eilean Vow, qv.*

Island Macaskin (Macaskin Island). *Arg. & B.* ***Island***, 1m/2km long NE to SW in Loch Craignish in Argyll, near entrance to loch. **73 F1** NR7899.
Island of Danna *Arg. & B. Alternative name for Danna Island, qv.*
Island of Raasay *High. See Raasay.*
Island of Rona *High. Alternative name for Rona, qv.*
Island of Stroma (Stroma). *High.* ***Island***, 2m/3km N to S and 1m/2km E to W, lying in Pentland Firth 2m/3km E of St. John's Point and 4m/6km NW of Duncansby Head. Island is sparsely populated. Disused harbour on S coast. Lighthouse at N point. **105 J1** ND3577.
Islandpool *Worcs.* ***Locality***, 3m/4km NE of Kidderminster. SO8580.
Islands of Fleet *D. & G.* ***Island***, group of small islands comprising the islands of Ardwell, Barlocco and Murray's, on E side of Wigtown Bay, near entrance to Fleet Bay. **65 F6** NX5749.
Islawr-dref *Gwyn.* ***Locality***, on N side of Cadair Idris, 3m/5km SW of Dolgellau. **37 F4** SH6916.
Islay *Arg. & B.* ***Island***, most southerly of Inner Hebrides and third in size, measuring 25m/40km N to S and 20m/32km E to W; lies off SW coast of Jura, from which it is separated by narrow Sound of Islay. Mainly low-lying and fertile. Numerous species of birds; large herds of deer in W. Port Ellen is chief town and port. Airport at Glenegedale. Port Askaig on Sound of Islay has ferries to Kintyre and Jura. **72 A4** NR3760.
Islay Airport *Arg. & B.* ***Airport/airfield***, at Glenegedale, 5m/7km NW of Port Ellen, Islay. **72 B5** NR3251.
Islay House *Arg. & B.* ***Settlement***, adjoining to N of Bridgend, Islay. **72 B4** NR3362.
Isle *Som.* ***River***, rising N of Chard and flowing generally NE into River Parrett 2m/3km S of Langport. **8 C2** ST4123.
Isle Abbotts *Som.* ***Village***, 4m/6km N of Ilminster. **8 C2** ST3520.
Isle Brewers *Som.* ***Village***, 4m/7km N of Ilminster. **8 C2** ST3621.
Isle Martin *High.* ***Island***, uninhabited island, outlier of Summer Isles group, off W coast of Ross and Cromarty district 3m/5km NW of Ullapool. Area about 600 acres or 240 hectares. **95 G2** NH0999.
Isle of Arran Heritage Museum *N.Ayr.* ***Other feature of interest***, 18c farm 1m/2km NW of Brodick, with exhibits including a blacksmith's and local industrial history displays. **73 J7** NS0036.
Isle of Axholme *N.Lincs.* ***Large natural feature***, area of slight elevation above flat and formerly marshy tract bounded by Rivers Trent, Torne and Idle. Towns and villages include Belton, Epworth and Haxey on the higher ground, and Owston Ferry and West Butterwick beside River Trent. **51 K2** SE7006.
Isle of Dogs *Gt.Lon.* ***Locality***, in borough of Tower Hamlets, 5m/8km E of Charing Cross. Though not an island, district is bounded by River Thames on S, E, and W sides, and contains extensive docks at Millwall. TQ3878.
Isle of Ewe *High.* ***Island***, sparsely inhabited island in Loch Ewe, W coast of Ross and Cromarty district, opposite Aultbea on E shore of loch. Area about 900 acres or 365 hectares. **94 E3** NG8588.
Isle of Grain *Med.* ***Coastal feature***, peninsula on W side of mouth of River Medway opposite Isle of Sheppey. **24 E4** TQ8775.
Isle of Gunnister *Shet.* ***Island***, rock island at entrance to Gunnister Voe inlet, Mainland. HU3073.
Isle of Harty *Kent* ***Coastal feature***, SE part of Isle of Sheppey, bounded by The Swale to S, Capel Fleet to N, the sea to E, and mouth of Bells Creek to W. **25 G5** TR0267.
Isle of Lewis (Gaelic form: Eilean Leodhais.) *W.Isles* ***Island***, largest and most northerly island of the Outer Hebrides, measuring 61m/99km NE to SW and a maximum of half that distance NW to SE. The name Lewis is generally applied to N part of island as distinct from North and South Harris, areas forming S part of island. In this sense Isle of Lewis consists largely of peaty uplands containing innumerable, mostly small, lochs and streams in which salmon and trout abound. Some moorland has been reclaimed for farming, with barley and potatoes being main crops. Chief occupations of islanders are fishing and cloth manufacture. Butt of Lewis is most northerly point. Stornoway is chief town. **100 E3** NB3035.
Isle of Man *D. & G.* ***Locality***, to N of Craigs Moss, 2m/4km E of Dumfries. NY0075.
Isle of Man *I.o.M.* ***Island***, 31m/50km long NE to SW, including Calf of Man, and 13m/21km wide E to W. Lies 17m/28km S of Burrow Head, Scotland, 30m/48km W of St. Bees Head, England, and 33m/54km E of Ballyquintin Point, Northern Ireland. Range of mountains runs NE to SW, highest being Snaefell. Douglas on E coast is chief town, seat of government and terminus of passenger-boat services. Airport near Castletown. **54 C4** SC3585.
Isle of Man Airport (Also known as Ronaldsway Airport.) *I.o.M.* ***Airport/airfield***, commercial airport for island, 1m/2km E of Castletown. **54 B7** SC2868.
Isle of Man Steam Railway *I.o.M.* ***Other feature of interest***, original narrow-gauge engines and coaches transport summer visitors between Douglas and Port Erin. **54 C6** SC3775.
Isle of May *Fife* ***Island***, narrow island 1m/2km long NW to SE, lying 6m/10km SE of Anstruther at entrance to Firth of Forth. Ruins of medieval priory. Relic of first Scottish lighthouse (1636). Present lighthouse built 1816 by Robert, father of Robert Louis Stevenson. Bird observatory. **76 E1** NT6599.
Isle of Nibon *Shet.* ***Island***, located off W coast of N part of Mainland. **108 B5** HU3073.
Isle of Noss *Shet.* ***Island***, uninhabited island and bird sanctuary of about 1 square mile or 3 square km, off E coast of Bressay across Noss Sound. **109 E8** HU5440.
Isle of Oxney *Kent* ***Locality***, area of higher ground surrounded by Rother Levels, 5m/7km N of Rye, containing villages of Wittersham and Stone. **14 D5** TQ9127.
Isle of Portland *Dorset* ***Coastal feature***, limestone peninsula 4m/7km N to S and 2m/3km E to W connected to mainland by Chesil Beach, 4m/7km S of Weymouth. Quarries of Portland stone. HM prison. **9 G7** SY6972.
Isle of Purbeck *Dorset* ***Coastal feature***, peninsula bounded E and S by English Channel, N by Poole Harbour and River Frome, and extending W roughly to a line running N from Worbarrow Bay. Traversed E to W by chalk ridge of Purbeck Hills. Quarries for extraction of Purbeck stone. Oil fields on N part; army training area on SW part. **9 J6** SY9681.
Isle of Sheppey *Kent* ***Island***, separated from mainland by The Swale (bridged at Kingsferry Bridge) and River Medway estuary. Sheppey is 9m/15km E to W and 5m/8km N to S at widest point. Nearly all the population is in N half where there is high ground; S half is mostly marshland. **25 F4** TQ9770.
Isle of Stenness *Shet.* ***Island***, to SW of Stenness, off S end of Esha Ness, Mainland. HU2076.
Isle of Thanet *Kent* ***Locality***, area bounded by North Sea, English Channel and Rivers Stour and Wantsum. Contains towns of Margate, Ramsgate and Broadstairs. **25 J5** TR3167.
Isle of Walney (Walney Island). *Cumb.* ***Island***, long narrow island running N and S opposite Barrow-in-Furness. Length about 8m/13km. Airfield near N end. Causeway to Barrow-in-Furness across narrow Walney Channel. N and S coastlines designated international nature reserves with Natterjack toads and Walney geraniums in N, herring gull and eider duck colonies in S. **54 E3** SD1868.
Isle of Whithorn *D. & G.* ***Small town***, small port on rocky coast, 3m/5km SE of Whithorn. St. Ninian's Chapel (Historic Scotland) is nearby. **64 E7** NX4736.
Isle of Wight *I.o.W.* ***Island***, diamond-shaped island, 10m/16km long by 19m/31km wide, off S coast of Britain across The Solent. With picturesque scenery, it was popularised as a holiday resort by Victorian society. Main towns are Newport, Cowes, Ryde, Ventnor, Sandown and Shanklin. Due to its strategic importance to Portsmouth, the island has a strong military and naval tradition, containing remains of many fortifications. Cowes is home of Royal Yacht Squadron and hosts an internationally renowned annual regatta. Island is noted for its diverse sedimentary rock geology, divided by a ridge of chalk which has The Needles as its W tip. The N is dominated by clays and sands which produce gentle hills, and at Alum Bay, create spectacular coloured banding. The S has more dramatic relief, especially along S coast, where clays overlain by sandstones have led to unstable cliffs and landslips, while streams have cut short, wind eroded ravines or 'chines'. Island contains many important fossilised dinosaur and wood remains. **11 F6** SZ5090.
Isle of Wight (Sandown) Airport *I.o.W.* ***Airport/airfield***, local airport 1m/2km W of Sandown. **11 G6** SZ5783.
Isle of Wight Steam Railway *I.o.W.* ***Other feature of interest***, tourist railway running for over 5m/8km from Smallbrook Junction to Wootton Bridge, via Havenstreet. **11 G5** SZ5993.
Isle of Wight Zoo *I.o.W.* ***Leisure/recreation***, zoo 1m/2km NE of Sandown town centre, overlooking Sandown Bay. Main attraction is comprehensive reptile house, which specialises in snakes; regular snake-handling displays in summer. Also has all big wild cats. **11 H6** SZ6085.
Isle Ornsay *High. Alternative name for Eilean Iarmain, qv.*
Isle Ornsay *High.* ***Island***, small uninhabited island off E coast of Sleat peninsula, Skye, opposite village of Eilean Iarmain. Island forms E side of village harbour. **86 D3** NG7112.
Isle Ristol (Ristol). *High.* ***Island***, one of Summer Isles group. Lies close to NW coast of Ross and Cromarty district 4m/7km S of Rubha Coigeach. Area about 560 acres or 225 hectares. **102 B7** NB9711.
Isleham *Cambs.* Population: 1953. ***Village***, 4m/7km W of Mildenhall. Remains of Norman priory (English Heritage). **33 K1** TL6474.
Isleham Fen *Cambs.* ***Open space***, fenland 2m/3km NW of Isleham. **33 K1** TL6276.
Isleornsay *High. Alternative name for Eilean Iarmain, qv.*
Isles of Scilly *I.o.S.* ***Island***, island group in Atlantic Ocean, 28m/45km SW of Land's End. There are over 100 small rocks and islands, of which only five largest are inhabited: St. Mary's, St. Martin's, Tresco, Bryher and St. Agnes. **2 C2** SV9206.
Isles of the Sea *Arg. & B. Alternative name for Garvellachs, qv.*
Islesburgh *Shet.* ***Settlement***, on Mainland, just S of Mangaster Voe. **109 C6** HU3369.
Islesteps *D. & G.* ***Locality***, 2m/4km S of Dumfries. NX9672.
Isleworth *Gt.Lon.* ***Suburb***, on W bank of River Thames, in borough of Hounslow, 9m/15km W of Charing Cross. **22 E4** TQ1675.
Isleworth Ait *Gt.Lon.* ***Island***, in River Thames to E of Isleworth. TQ1675.
Isley Walton *Leics.* ***Hamlet***, 7m/11km NE of Ashby de la Zouch. **41 G3** SK4225.
Islibhig (Anglicised form: Islivig.) *W.Isles* ***Village***, near W coast of Isle of Lewis, 6m/9km SW of Timsgearraidh. **100 B5** NA9927.
Islington *N.Yorks.* ***Locality***, 1m/2km NE of Tadcaster. SE5044.
Islip *Northants.* ***Village***, 1km W of Thrapston. **32 C1** SP9878.
Islip *Oxon.* ***Village***, 5m/8km N of Oxford. **31 G7** SP5214.
Islivig *W.Isles Anglicised form of Islibhig, qv.*
Isombridge *Tel. & W.* ***Settlement***, 1m/2km NW of Wrockwardine. **39 F4** SJ6013.
Istead Rise *Kent* Population: 3755. ***Village***, 3m/4km S of Northfleet. **24 C5** TQ6370.
Isurium Roman Town *N.Yorks.* ***Historic/prehistoric site***, small Roman town (English Heritage) with rectangular layout, on N side of Aldborough, 1km E of Boroughbridge. Some fragments of town wall remain, and some interesting mosaics. **57 K3** SE4066.
Italian Chapel *Ork.* ***Ecclesiastical building***, beautiful chapel on small island of Lamb Holm, which lies between Mainland and Burray. Created from Nissen hut by Italian prisoners of war. **107 D7** HY4800.
Itchen *River*, rising 1km W of Hinton Ampner and flowing N to New Alresford, W to Kings Worthy, then S through Winchester and Eastleigh into Southampton Water at Southampton. A chalk stream famous for trout-fishing in its upper reaches. SU4209.
Itchen *S'ham.* ***Suburb***, on E bank of River Itchen, 1m/2km E of Southampton city centre. Vehicle ferry across river. **11 F3** SU4311.
Itchen *Warks.* ***River***, rising on hills to W of Fenny Compton and flowing N to Bishop's Itchington and Marton, where it joins River Leam. **30 E2** SP4069.
Itchen Abbas *Hants.* ***Village***, on River Itchen, 4m/6km NE of Winchester. 1m/2km N, site of Roman villa. **11 G1** SU5332.
Itchen Stoke *Hants.* ***Village***, beside River Itchen, 2m/3km W of New Alresford. **11 G1** SU5632.
Itchen Valley Country Park *Hants.* ***Leisure/recreation***, country park with 440 acres of varied countryside including wetland, woodland and meadow, 2m/3km S of Eastleigh. **11 F3** SU4616.
Itchingfield *W.Suss.* ***Village***, 3m/5km SW of Horsham. **12 E4** TQ1328.
Itchington *S.Glos.* ***Hamlet***, 3m/4km SE of Thornbury. **19 K3** ST6586.
Ithon *Powys* ***River***, rising 4m/7km S of Newtown and flowing S to Llandrindod Wells, then into River Wye 1m/2km S of Newbridge on Wye. **27 K1** SO0156.
Itteringham *Norf.* ***Village***, 4m/6km NW of Aylsham. **45 F2** TG1430.
Itton *Devon* ***Hamlet***, 2m/3km SE of North Tawton. **6 E6** SX6899.
Itton (Llanddinol). *Mon.* ***Hamlet***, 3m/4km NW of Chepstow. ST4995.
Itton Common *Mon.* ***Hamlet***, 3m/5km NW of Chepstow. **19 H2** ST4895.
Ive *Cumb.* ***River***, rising to NE of Skelton and flowing NE to join Roe Beck just S of Highbridge, 4m/7km SE of Dalton. **60 F3** NY3943.
Ivegill *Cumb.* ***Hamlet***, 8m/13km S of Carlisle. **60 F2** NY4143.
Ivel *River*, rising near Clothall, SE of Baldock, and flowing N past Biggleswade and Sandy into River Great Ouse at Tempsford. **32 E5** TL1653.
Ivelet *N.Yorks.* ***Settlement***, on River Swale, 1m/2km W of Gunnerside. **62 A7** SD9398.
Iver *Bucks.* Population: 3567. ***Village***, in River Colne valley, 4m/7km E of Slough. **22 D3** TQ0381.
Iver Heath *Bucks.* Population: 3567. ***Village***, 1m/2km N of Iver. **22 D3** TQ0283.
Iveston *Dur.* ***Village***, 2m/3km E of Consett. **62 C1** NZ1350.
Ivetsey Bank *Staffs.* ***Hamlet***, 2m/3km SE of Blymhill. SJ8310.
Ivinghoe *Bucks.* Population: 811. ***Village***, below N escarpment of Chiltern Hills, 3m/5km NE of Tring. **32 C7** SP9416.
Ivinghoe Aston *Bucks.* ***Village***, 5m/8km SW of Dunstable. **32 C7** SP9518.
Ivington *Here.* ***Hamlet***, 2m/3km SW of Leominster. **28 D3** SO4756.
Ivington Green *Here.* ***Hamlet***, 3m/4km SW of Leominster. **28 D3** SO4656.
Ivy Hatch *Kent* ***Hamlet***, 2m/3km S of Ightham. **23 J6** TQ5854.
Ivy Todd *Norf.* ***Settlement***, 5m/8km E of Swaffham. **44 C5** TF8909.
Ivybridge *Devon* Population: 9179. ***Small town***, on River Erme, 10m/16km E of Plymouth. Formerly dependent upon paper industry, it has a medieval bridge and a large railway viaduct. **5 G5** SX6356.
Ivychurch *Kent* ***Village***, on Romney Marsh, 3m/5km NW of New Romney. **15 F5** TR0227.
Ivythorn Hill *Som. See Walton.*
Iwade *Kent* ***Village***, 3m/4km N of Sittingbourne. **25 F5** TQ9067.
Iwerne Courtney (Also known as Shroton.) *Dorset* ***Village***, at SW end of Cranborne Chase, 4m/7km N of Blandford Forum. **9 H3** ST8512.
Iwerne Minster *Dorset* ***Village***, on W edge of Cranborne Chase, 5m/8km N of Blandford Forum. **9 H3** ST8614.
Iwerne Stepleton *Dorset* ***Locality***, at SW end of Cranborne Chase, 4m/6km N of Blandford Forum. ST8611.
Iwrch *Powys* ***River***, rising on Cadair Berwyn and running SE into River Tanant 2m/3km SE of Llanrhaeadr-ym-Mochnant. **38 A3** SJ1424.
Ixworth *Suff.* Population: 2011. ***Village***, on site of Romano-British settlement, 6m/10km NE of Bury St. Edmunds. **34 D1** TL9370.
Ixworth Thorpe *Suff.* ***Village***, 2m/3km NW of Ixworth. **34 D1** TL9173.

J

Jack Green *Lancs.* ***Settlement***, 2m/4km E of Bamber Bridge. SD5925.
Jack Hill *N.Yorks.* ***Settlement***, 1km S of Swinsty Reservoir. **57 G4** SE2051.
Jack-in-the-Green *Devon* ***Settlement***, 5m/8km W of Ottery St. Mary. SY0195.
Jackfield *Tel. & W.* ***Settlement***, 1m/2km SE of Ironbridge. SJ6902.
Jack's Green *Glos.* ***Settlement***, 1m/2km E of Painswick. SO8810.
Jack's Hatch *Essex* ***Settlement***, 2m/4km SW of Harlow town centre. TL4306.
Jacksdale *Notts.* ***Village***, 1m/2km SW of Selston. SK4451.

Jackson Bridge *W.Yorks.* ***Locality***, adjoining to N of Hepworth, 2m/3km E of Holmfirth. SE1607.
Jackstown *Aber.* ***Settlement***, 4m/7km S of Fyvie. **91 F1** NJ7531.
Jackton *S.Lan.* ***Settlement***, 3m/4km E of East Kilbride. **74 D5** NS5952.
Jacobstow *Cornw.* ***Village***, 7m/11km S of Bude. **4 B1** SX1995.
Jacobstowe *Devon* ***Village***, 4m/6km N of Okehampton. **6 D5** SS5801.
Jacobswell *Surr.* ***Suburb***, 2m/3km N of Guildford town centre. SU9952.
Jagger Green *W.Yorks.* ***Settlement***, 2m/3km SW of Elland. SE0919.
Jameston *Pembs.* ***Hamlet***, 4m/7km E of Pembroke. **16 D5** SS0598.
Jamestown *D. & G.* ***Settlement***, on W bank of Meggat Water, 4m/7km N of Bentpath. **69 J4** NY2996.
Jamestown *High.* ***Settlement***, in Ross and Cromarty district, 1m/2km S of Strathpeffer. **96 B6** NH4756.
Jamestown *W.Dun.* ***Locality***, 4m/6km N of Dumbarton. **74 B2** NS3981.
Jane Austen's House *Hants.* ***Historic house***, 17c red brick house in Chawton, 1m/2km SW of Alton. Contains memorabilia of Jane Austen who lived here, 1809-1817. **11 J1** SU7037.
Janefield *High.* ***Settlement***, on Black Isle, 1m/2km N of Fortrose. **96 E6** NH7259.
Janetstown *High.* *Alternative name for Latheronwheel, qv.*
Janetstown *High.* ***Settlement***, 2m/3km SW of Thurso. **105 F2** ND0866.
Janetstown *High.* ***Settlement***, in Caithness district, adjoining to W of Wick. ND3550.
Jarlshof *Shet.* ***Historic/prehistoric site***, important site of prehistoric settlement (Historic Scotland) on E side of West Voe of Sumburgh, Mainland. Contains relics of Bronze, Iron, Dark and Middle Ages. **109 G10** HU3909.
Jarrow *T. & W.* Population: 29,325. ***Town***, on S bank of River Tyne 5m/8km E of Gateshead. Road tunnel under river. Famous for Hunger Marches in 1930s. Parish church incorporates remains (English Heritage) of monastery of Venerable Bede (d 735). Church of St. Paul has Saxon stained glass window. **71 J7** NZ3265.
Jarvis Brook *E.Suss.* ***Suburb***, in valley on SE side of Crowborough. **13 J4** TQ5329.
Jasper's Green *Essex* ***Hamlet***, 3m/5km NW of Braintree. **34 B6** TL7226.
Jaw Hill *W.Yorks.* ***Locality***, just NW of Kirkhamgate, 3m/5km NW of Wakefield. SE2923.
Jawcraig *Falk.* ***Settlement***, 2m/3km N of Slamannan. Settlements of Easter and Wester Jawcraig either side. **75 G3** NS8475.
Jayes Park *Surr.* ***Settlement***, 1km NW of Ockley. **22 E7** TQ1440.
Jaywick *Essex* Population: 4146. ***Village***, resort on coast, 2m/3km SW of Clacton-on-Sea. **35 F7** TM1513.
Jealott's Hill *Brack.F.* ***Settlement***, 5m/8km S of Maidenhead. SU8673.
Jeater Houses *N.Yorks.* ***Hamlet***, 4m/7km E of Northallerton. SE4394.
Jed Water *Sc.Bord.* ***River***, rising in Wauchope Forest and flowing N through Jedburgh to River Teviot 3m/4km N of town. **70 B3** NT6624.
Jedburgh *Sc.Bord.* Population: 4118. ***Small town***, on Jed Water, 10m/16km NE of Hawick. Red sandstone ruins (Historic Scotland) of abbey founded in 12c. Site of Roman fort 3m/5km E. **70 B1** NT6520.
Jedburgh Abbey *Sc.Bord.* ***Ecclesiastical building***, one of four great Border abbeys (Historic Scotland) founded by David I for Augustinian canons, situated on W side of Jedburgh. Dates from 1118 and now extensive ruin, including fine rose window on W front. Visitor Centre with exhibition portraying monastic life. **70 B2** NT6420.
Jeffreyston *Pembs.* ***Village***, 5m/8km NW of Tenby. **16 D4** SN0806.
Jemimaville *High.* ***Village***, on S side of Cromarty Firth, Ross and Cromarty district, 4m/7km W of Cromarty. **96 E5** NH7265.
Jenkins' Green *E.Suss.* ***Locality***, on S side of Pevensey Levels, 4m/7km N of Eastbourne. TQ6205.
Jenkyn Place Gardens *Hants.* ***Garden***, designed for plantsmen, in Bentley, 6m/10km SW of Aldershot. **22 A7** SU7844.
Jericho *Gt.Man.* ***Suburb***, 2m/4km E of Bury town centre. SD8311.
Jersay *N.Lan.* ***Settlement***, 3m/5km N of Newmains. **75 G4** NS8361.
Jersey Marine *N.P.T.* ***Village***, on the Tennant Canal, 4m/7km E of Swansea. SS7193.
Jervaulx Abbey *N.Yorks.* ***Ecclesiastical building***, remains of 12c Cistercian monastic house above River Ure, 3m/5km SE of Middleham. **57 G1** SE1785.
Jerviswood *S.Lan.* ***Settlement***, 1m/2km N of Lanark. **75 G6** NS8845.
Jesmond *T. & W.* ***Suburb***, 1m/2km NE of Newcastle upon Tyne city centre. West Jesmond district to W. Jesmond Dene, wooded glen to E. **71 H7** NZ2566.
Jevington *E.Suss.* ***Village***, on South Downs, 4m/6km NW of Eastbourne. **13 J6** TQ5601.
Jingle Street *Mon.* ***Locality***, 3m/4km SW of Monmouth. SO4710.
Jockey End *Herts.* ***Hamlet***, 4m/7km N of Hemel Hempstead. TL0313.
Jock's Pike *Northumb.* ***Inland physical feature***, edge in woodland to S of Kielder Water, 4m/6km SW of Falstone. **70 B5** NY6684.
Jock's Shoulder *D. & G.* ***Mountain***, in Eskdalemuir Forest, 4m/6km W of Davington. Height 1755 feet or 535 metres. **69 G3** NT1702.
Jodrell Bank *Ches.* ***Settlement***, 3m/5km NE of Holmes Chapel. To N is radio telescope and radio astronomy laboratory, part of University of Manchester's Department of Physics and Astronomy. **49 G5** SJ7970.
Jodrell Bank Science Centre and Arboretum *Ches.* ***Other feature of interest***, 3m/5km NE of Holmes Chapel and 7m/12km SW of Macclesfield. Features Lovell radio telescope and hands-on scientific exhibitions and a planetarium. **49 G5** SJ7971.
John Muir Country Park *E.Loth.* ***Leisure/recreation***, adjacent to North Sea coast, 2m/3km W of Dunbar. 1668 acre country park named in honour of one of founders of conservation movement. Park extends over 8m/12km of coast and attracts over 220 species of bird. **76 E3** NT6479.
John o' Gaunts *W.Yorks.* ***Suburb***, NE district of Rothwell, 4m/7km SE of Leeds. SE3529.
John o' Groats *High.* ***Village***, in NE corner of Caithness district, nearly 2m/3km W of Duncansby Head. Traditionally referred to as NE end of British mainland. **105 J1** ND3773.
Johnby *Cumb.* ***Hamlet***, 2m/3km N of Greystoke. Hall dates from 16c. **60 F3** NY4333.
John's Cross *E.Suss.* ***Settlement***, 3m/5km N of Battle. **14 C5** TQ7421.
John's Hole *Kent* ***Locality***, 1m/2km E of Dartford. TQ5673.
Johnshaven *Aber.* ***Village***, on rocky part of E coast, 4m/7km SW of Inverbervie. **83 J1** NO7967.
Johnson's Street *Norf.* ***Hamlet***, 1m/2km SW of Ludham. TG3717.
Johnston *Pembs.* ***Village***, 4m/6km NE of Milford Haven. **16 C3** SM9310.
Johnston Mains *Aber.* ***Hamlet***, 1km S of Laurencekirk. **83 J1** NO7270.
Johnstone *Devon* ***Hamlet***, 2m/3km E of South Molton. SS7325.
Johnstone *Renf.* Population: 18,635. ***Town***, 4m/6km W of Paisley. **74 C4** NS4263.
Johnstone Castle *Renf.* ***Castle***, 1km SW of Johnstone town centre. **74 C4** NS4262.
Johnstonebridge *D. & G.* ***Settlement***, and road bridge over River Annan, 7m/11km N of Lockerbie. **69 F4** NY1092.
Johnstown *Carmar.* ***Locality***, 1m/2km W of Carmarthen. **17 G3** SN3919.
Johnstown *Wrex.* ***Locality***, adjoining to E of Rhosllanerchrugog. **38 C1** SJ3046.
Joppa *Cere.* ***Locality***, 3m/4km SE of Llanrhystud. SN5666.
Joppa *Edin.* ***Suburb***, of Edinburgh, adjoining to SE of Portobello. **76 B3** NT3173.
Joppa *S.Ayr.* ***Hamlet***, 1km W of Coylton. **67 J2** NS4019.
Jordan Hill Roman Temple *Dorset* ***Historic/prehistoric site***, scant remains of Roman temple (English Heritage) at Jordan Hill, to S of Preston, 2m/3km SE of Weymouth. **9 G6** SY7082.
Jordanhill *Glas.* ***Suburb***, 4m/6km NW of Glasgow city centre. NS5368.
Jordans *Bucks.* ***Hamlet***, 2m/3km E of Beaconsfield. Meeting house of early Quakers, including William Penn. **22 C2** SU9791.
Jordans Green *Norf.* ***Settlement***, 2m/3km SW of Reepham. TG0721.
Jordanston (Trefwrdan). *Pembs.* ***Hamlet***, 4m/6km SW of Fishguard. **16 C1** SM9132.
Jordanstone *P. & K.* ***Settlement***, 2m/3km SE of Alyth. **82 D3** NO2747.
Joyford *Glos.* ***Locality***, 2m/3km N of Coleford. SO5713.
Joy's Green *Glos.* ***Village***, 4m/6km NW of Cinderford. SO6016.
Julian Bower *Lincs.* ***Locality***, adjoining to S of Louth. TF3386.
Jumbles Reservoir *Lancs.* ***Reservoir***, and country park, 3m/5km N of Bolton. **49 G1** SD7314.
Jump *S.Yorks.* ***Locality***, adjoining to E of Hoyland. **51 F2** SE3801.
Jumpers Common *Dorset* ***Suburb***, 1m/2km NW of Christchurch town centre. SZ1494.
Jumper's Town *E.Suss.* ***Settlement***, on N edge of Ashdown Forest, 2m/3km SW of Hartfield. TQ4633.
Junction *Gt.Man.* ***Locality***, 5m/8km NE of Oldham. SD9710.
Juniper Green *Edin.* ***Suburb***, 5m/8km SW of Edinburgh city centre. **75 K4** NT1968.
Juniper Hill *Oxon.* ***Settlement***, 3m/5km S of Brackley. SP5732.
Jura *Arg. & B.* ***Island***, fourth in size of Inner Hebrides, measuring 28m/45km NE to SW and 8m/13km at its widest in S, situated between Islay and Scottish mainland. A mountain ridge runs almost entire length, although interrupted by long inlet of Loch Tarbert on W coast, which nearly bisects island. Deer are numerous. Craighouse is chief port. **72 D2** NR5379.
Jura Forest *Arg. & B.* ***Open space***, deer forest around Paps of Jura in S part of Jura. **72 D3** NR5075.
Jura House *Arg. & B.* ***Settlement***, on Jura, 3m/5km SW of Craighouse. **72 C4** NR4863.
Jurby East *I.o.M.* ***Hamlet***, 2m/3km W of Andreas. **54 C4** SC3899.
Jurby Head *I.o.M.* ***Coastal feature***, point on NW coast 4m/6km NW of Sulby. **54 C4** SC3498.
Jurby West *I.o.M.* ***Hamlet***, on W side of Jurby Aerodrome, 3m/5km NW of Sulby. **54 C4** SC3598.
Justicetown *Cumb.* ***Locality***, 6m/9km N of Carlisle, on S side of River Lyne. NY3764.

K

Kaber *Cumb.* ***Hamlet***, 2m/3km S of Brough. **61 J5** NY7911.
Kaber Fell *Cumb.* ***Open space***, moorland 5m/8km E of Kirkby Stephen. **61 K6** NY8608.
Kailzie Gardens *Sc.Bord.* ***Garden***, 3m/4km SE of Peebles, S of River Tweed. Walled garden dates from 1812. **76 A7** NT2738.
Kaim Hill *N.Ayr.* ***Mountain***, 4m/6km SE of Largs. Height 1269 feet or 387 metres. **74 A5** NS2253.
Kaimes *Edin.* ***Suburb***, 4m/6km S of Edinburgh city centre. **76 A4** NT2768.
Kaimhill *Aberdeen* ***Suburb***, 2m/3km SW of Aberdeen city centre. NJ9203.
Kale Water *Sc.Bord.* ***River***, rising on Cheviot Hills and flowing N to Hownam and Morebattle, where it turns W to run into River Teviot 4m/7km S of Kelso. **70 C1** NT7027.
Kallin *W.Isles* *Anglicised form of Ceallan, qv.*
Kalnakill *High.* ***Settlement***, on W coast of Ross and Cromarty district, 3m/5km S of Rubha Chuaig. **94 C6** NG6954.
Kame of Foula *Shet.* *Alternative name for The Kame, qv.*
Kame of Hoy *Ork.* ***Coastal feature***, rocky headland on NW coast of Hoy. **107 A7** HY1905.
Kame of Sandwick *Shet.* ***Hill***, 2m/3km E of West Sandwick. Height 548 feet or 167 metres. **108 D4** HU4787.
Kames *Arg. & B.* ***Settlement***, on S shore of Loch Melfort, 2m/3km SW of Melfort across loch. **79 K6** NM8111.
Kames *Arg. & B.* ***Village***, in Argyll on W side of Kyles of Bute, 5m/8km N of Ardlamont Point. **73 H3** NR9771.
Kames *E.Ayr.* ***Settlement***, 1km S of Muirkirk. **68 B1** NS6926.
Kames Bay *Arg. & B.* ***Bay***, on E coast of Bute, 2m/3km N of Rothesay, with Port Bannatyne on S side. **73 J4** NS0667.
Kames Hill *Arg. & B.* ***Hill***, part of group of hills on N Bute, 4m/6km NW of Rothesay. Height 882 feet or 269 metres. **73 J4** NS0569.
Kanaird *High.* ***River***, running W from Loch a' Chroisg to Loch Kanaird, W coast of Ross and Cromarty district. **95 H1** NH1199.
Kates Hill *W.Mid.* ***Suburb***, to E of Dudley town centre. SO9590.
Katherines *Essex* ***Suburb***, 1m/2km SW of Harlow town centre. TL4308.
Kay Holm *Shet.* ***Island***, small island off E coast of Yell at entrance to Mid Yell Voe. HU5291.
Kaye Lane *W.Yorks.* ***Suburb***, 1m/2km SE of Huddersfield town centre. SE1514.
Kea *Cornw.* ***Village***, 2m/4km SW of Truro. **3 F4** SW8042.
Keadby *N.Lincs.* ***Hamlet***, on W bank of River Trent, 4m/7km E of Crowle. Road and railway bridges across river to S. Junction of Sheffield and South Yorkshire Navigation with River Trent. **52 B1** SE8311.
Keal Cotes *Lincs.* ***Village***, 4m/6km SW of Spilsby. **53 G6** TF3661.
Kealasay *W.Isles* ***Island***, small uninhabited island off W coast of Isle of Lewis, 1m/2km N of Great Bernera, with Little Bernera in between. NB1441.
Keallasay Beg *W.Isles* ***Island***, small island 1m/2km N of Lochmaddy, North Uist. **92 E4** NF9171.
Keallasay More *W.Isles* ***Island***, small island 2m/4km N of Lochmaddy, North Uist. **92 E4** NF9172.
Kearby Town End *N.Yorks.* ***Settlement***, 2m/3km NE of Harewood and 4m/6km SW of Wetherby. SE3447.
Kearnaval *W.Isles* ***Mountain***, 3m/4km NE of head of Loch Langavat. Height 1240 feet or 378 metres. **100 D6** NB1815.
Kearsley *Gt.Man.* Population: 9287. ***Small town***, 4m/6km SE of Bolton. **49 G2** SD7504.
Kearsley Fell *Northumb.* ***Hill***, 1m/2km NW of Ingoe. Height 800 feet or 244 metres. **71 F6** NZ0276.
Kearstay *W.Isles* ***Island***, small uninhabited island off N coast of Scarp. **100 B6** NA9617.
Kearstwick *Cumb.* ***Hamlet***, 1m/2km N of Kirkby Lonsdale. **56 B1** SD6079.
Kearton *N.Yorks.* ***Settlement***, 1m/2km W of Healaugh. **62 B7** SD9999.
Kearvaig *High.* ***Settlement***, 3m/4km SE of Cape Wrath, on N coast of Sutherland district. **102 E1** NC2972.
Keasden *N.Yorks.* ***Settlement***, 2m/4km SW of Clapham. **56 C3** SD7266.
Keava *W.Isles* ***Island***, small uninhabited island in East Loch Roag opposite Breasclete on W coast of Isle of Lewis. NB1935.
Kebholes *Aber.* ***Settlement***, 3m/4km NE of Aberchirder. **98 E5** NJ6455.
Kebister Ness *Shet.* ***Coastal feature***, headland on E coast of Mainland on E side of entrance to Dales Voe, 4m/6km N of Lerwick. **109 D8** HU4746.
Kebock Head *W.Isles* ***Coastal feature***, headland on E coast of Isle of Lewis 12m/19km S of Stornoway. **101 G6** NB4213.
Kebroyd *W.Yorks.* ***Locality***, on W side of River Ryburn, 2m/3km SW of Sowerby Bridge. SE0420.
Keckwick *Halton* ***Hamlet***, 4m/6km E of Runcorn. **48 E4** SJ5683.
Keddington *Lincs.* ***Settlement***, 1m/2km NE of Louth. **53 G4** TF3488.
Keddington Corner *Lincs.* ***Settlement***, at bridge over Louth Canal, 2m/3km NE of Louth. TF3589.
Kedington *Suff.* Population: 1780. ***Village***, 2m/4km E of Haverhill. **34 B4** TL7046.
Kedleston *Derbys.* ***Settlement***, 4m/7km NW of Derby. **41 F1** SK3041.
Keekle *Cumb.* ***River***, rising on High Park and flowing SW, then S into River Ehen, 1m/2km SW of Cleator Moor. **60 B5** NY0112.
Keelby *Lincs.* Population: 2299. ***Village***, 7m/11km W of Grimsby. **52 E2** TA1609.
Keele *Staffs.* ***Village***, 3m/4km W of Newcastle-under-Lyme. University of Keele to E. **40 A1** SJ8045.
Keeley Green *Beds.* ***Locality***, 4m/6km SW of Bedford. **32 D4** TL0046.
Keeley Lane *Beds.* ***Settlement***, 4m/6km SW of Bedford, to N of Wootton. TL0046.
Keelham *W.Yorks.* ***Hamlet***, 1m/2km SE of Denholme. SE0732.
Keelylang Hill *Ork.* ***Hill***, 3m/4km SE of Finstown. Height 725 feet or 221 metres. **107 C6** HY3710.

Keer *River*, rising SW of Kirkby Lonsdale and flowing SW into Morecambe Bay as Keer Channel, to W of Carnforth. **55 J2** SD4368.
Keer Holme *Lancs.* *Locality*, 1m/2km E of Priest Hutton, 4m/7km NE of Carnforth. SD5573.
Keeres Green *Essex* *Hamlet*, 1km N of Leaden Roding. **33 J7** TL5914.
Keeston *Pembs.* *Village*, 4m/6km NW of Haverfordwest. **16 C3** SM9019.
Keevil *Wilts.* *Village*, 4m/7km E of Trowbridge. **20 C6** ST9258.
Kegworth *Leics.* Population: 3405. *Village*, on River Soar, 5m/8km NW of Loughborough. **41 G3** SK4826.
Kehelland *Cornw.* *Hamlet*, 2m/3km NW of Camborne. **2 D4** SW6241.
Keig *Aber.* *Village*, 3m/5km NE of Alford. **90 E3** NJ6119.
Keighley *W.Yorks.* Population: 49,567. *Town*, market town on River Worth, near its confluence with River Aire, 13m/21km NW of Bradford. Former textile town. **57 F5** SE0641.
Keighley and Worth Valley Railway *W.Yorks.* *Other feature of interest*, tourist railway running from Oxenhope to Keighley, in Worth valley. It passes through Oakworth Station which was featured in film, 'The Railway Children'. **57 F5** SE0335.
Keighley Moor *W.Yorks.* *Open space*, moorland 4m/6km W of Keighley. Contains Keighley Moor Reservoir. **56 E6** SD9838.
Keil *Arg. & B.* *Settlement*, 1m/2km SW of Southend on Kintyre peninsula. **66 A3** NR6707.
Keil *High.* *Settlement*, on SE shore of Loch Linnhe, on S side of Cuil Bay, 1m/2km SE of Rubha Mòr. Burial place of James Stewart, known as James of the Glens, wrongly hanged for Appin Murder of 1752. **80 A2** NM9753.
Keilarsbrae *Clack.* *Locality*, between Alloa and New Sauchie. NS8993.
Keilhill *Aber.* *Settlement*, 3m/5km S of Macduff. **99 F5** NJ7159.
Keillmore *Arg. & B.* *Settlement*, on N coast of Loch na Cille, 5m/8km SW of Tayvallich. **72 E2** NR6880.
Keillor *P. & K.* *Hamlet*, 3m/5km E of Coupar Angus. **82 D3** NO2640.
Keillour *P. & K.* *Locality*, 3m/5km W of Methven. **82 A5** NN9725.
Keillour Forest *P. & K.* *Forest/woodland*, tract between Crieff and Methven. **82 A5** NN9523.
Keills *Arg. & B.* *Hamlet*, on E side of Islay, 1m/2km SW of Port Askaig. **72 C4** NR4168.
Keils *Arg. & B.* *Settlement*, on SE coast of Jura, 1km N of Craighouse. **72 D4** NR5267.
Keinton Mandeville *Som.* *Village*, 6m/10km SE of Glastonbury. Birthplace of Sir Henry Irving, 1838. **8 E1** ST5430.
Keir *Stir.* *Settlement*, 4m/6km NW of Stirling. **75 F1** NS7698.
Keir Hills *D. & G.* *Large natural feature*, range of hills, 4m/7km E of Moniaive. **68 D4** NX8490.
Keir Mill *D. & G.* *Village*, 1m/2km SE of Penpont. **68 D4** NX8593.
Keirs Hill *E.Ayr.* *Open space*, partly wooded hillslope on NE side of Green Hill, 1m/2km SW of Waterside. **67 J3** NS4107.
Keirsleywell Row *Northumb.* *Locality*, 5m/8km NE of Alston. NY7751.
Keisby *Lincs.* *Settlement*, 7m/11km NW of Bourne. **42 D3** TF0328.
Keisley *Cumb.* *Settlement*, 3m/4km NE of Appleby-in-Westmorland. **61 J4** NY7024.
Keiss *High.* *Village*, on E coast of Caithness district, 6m/10km N of Wick. Ruined castle. **105 J2** ND3461.
Keith *Moray* Population: 4793. *Small town*, on right bank of River Isla, 15m/24km SE of Elgin. Dating from 8c but rebuilt in mid 18c. Birthplace of 17c cartographer Sir John Ogilvie. **98 C5** NJ4350.
Keith Inch *Aber.* *Island*, former island off coast at Peterhead, bridge connections now making it part of town. Lies on NE side of Peterhead Bay and is most easterly point of Scotland, excluding Shetland. **99 K6** NK1345.
Keithick *P. & K.* *Settlement*, 1m/2km N of Burrelton. **82 D4** NO2038.
Keithmore *Moray* *Settlement*, 2m/3km E of Dufftown. **90 B1** NJ3539.
Keithock *Angus* *Locality*, comprises settlements of Keithock, Little Keithock and East Mains of Keithock, 2m/3km N of Brechin. **83 H1** NO6063.
Kelbrook *Lancs.* *Village*, 3m/5km N of Colne. **56 E5** SD9044.
Kelby *Lincs.* *Hamlet*, 5m/8km SW of Sleaford. **42 D1** TF0041.
Keld *Cumb.* *Settlement*, 1m/2km SW of Shap. **61 G5** NY5514.
Keld *N.Yorks.* *Village*, 2m/4km NW of Muker. **61 K6** NY8901.
Keld Head *N.Yorks.* *Locality*, adjoining to W of Pickering. SE7884.
Keldholme *N.Yorks.* *Hamlet*, 1m/2km E of Kirkbymoorside. **58 D1** SE7086.
Keldy Castle *N.Yorks.* *Settlement*, on S side of Cropton Forest, 5m/8km NW of Pickering. **63 J7** SE7791.
Kelfield *N.Lincs.* *Settlement*, on W bank of River Trent, 3m/5km SE of Epworth. **52 B2** SE8201.
Kelfield *N.Yorks.* *Village*, 1m/2km E of Cawood across River Ouse. **58 B6** SE5938.
Kelham *Notts.* *Village*, 2m/3km NW of Newark-on-Trent. Kelham Hall, red-brick 19c Gothic mansion by G.G. Scott. **51 K7** SK7755.
Kelk Beck *E.Riding* *River*, rising at Kilham, then flowing S to join Old Howe to form Frodingham Beck, 1km NW of North Frodingham. **59 G4** TA0957.
Kella *I.o.M.* *Settlement*, adjoining to N of Sulby. SC3995.
Kellacott *Devon* *Hamlet*, 5m/8km NE of Launceston. SX4088.
Kellan *Arg. & B.* *Settlement*, on Mull, 2m/3km W of Gruline, to N of Loch na Keal. **79 G3** NM5140.
Kellas *Angus* *Village*, 3m/5km N of Broughty Ferry. **83 F4** NO4535.
Kellas *Moray* *Settlement*, 3m/5km E of Dallas. **97 J6** NJ1654.
Kellaton *Devon* *Village*, 2m/4km NW of Start Point. **5 J7** SX8039.
Kellaways *Wilts.* *Settlement*, 2m/4km NE of Chippenham. ST9575.
Kelleth *Cumb.* *Settlement*, 3m/5km E of Tebay. **61 H6** NY6605.
Kelleythorpe *E.Riding* *Locality*, 1m/2km SW of Great Driffield. **59 G4** TA0156.
Kellie Castle *Angus* *See Arbirlot.*
Kellie Castle *Fife* *Historic house*, mainly 16c-17c house (National Trust for Scotland), 2m/4km N of St. Monans. Parts date from 14c; house restored in 19c. Grounds feature herbaceous plants and old roses in late Victorian gardens. **83 G7** NO5105.
Kellie Law *Fife* *Hill*, 3m/5km NW of Pittenweem. Height 597 feet or 182 metres. **83 G7** NO5106.
Kelling *Norf.* *Village*, 3m/4km NE of Holt. **44 E1** TG0942.
Kellingley *N.Yorks.* *Locality*, 1m/2km E of Knottingley, between River Aire and Aire and Calder Navigation. Colliery site. SE5224.
Kellington *N.Yorks.* *Village*, 3m/5km E of Knottingley. **58 B7** SE5524.
Kello Water *River*, rising on N slopes of Blacklorg Hill and flowing NE, then turning E to join River Nith 1m/2km E of Kirkconnel. **68 B3** NS7411.
Kelloe *Dur.* Population: 1645. *Village*, 5m/8km N of Sedgefield. **62 E3** NZ3436.
Kelloholm *D. & G.* *Village*, adjoining to SE of Kirkconnel across River Nith. **68 C2** NS7411.
Kelly *Cornw.* *Settlement*, 2m/3km NE of Wadebridge. **4 A3** SX0173.
Kelly *Devon* *Hamlet*, 5m/7km SE of Launceston. **6 B7** SX3981.
Kelly Bray *Cornw.* *Village*, 1m/2km N of Callington. **4 D3** SX3571.
Kelmarsh *Northants.* *Village*, 5m/8km S of Market Harborough. **31 J1** SP7379.
Kelmscott *Oxon.* *Village*, on River Thames, 3m/4km W of Lechlade. Old gabled manor house, once home of William Morris. **21 F2** SU2599.
Kelsale *Suff.* *Village*, 1m/2km N of Saxmundham. **35 H2** TM3865.
Kelsall *Ches.* Population: 2394. *Village*, 8m/12km E of Chester. **48 E6** SJ5268.
Kelsay *Arg. & B.* *Settlement*, on Rinns of Islay, 3m/4km NE of Portnahaven. **72 A5** NR1956.
Kelsey Head *Cornw.* *Coastal feature*, headland 3m/5km W of Newquay. **2 E2** SW7660.
Kelshall *Herts.* *Village*, 3m/5km SW of Royston. **33 G5** TL3236.
Kelsick *Cumb.* *Hamlet*, 2m/3km E of Abbeytown. **60 C1** NY1950.
Kelso *Sc.Bord.* Population: 5989. *Small town*, market town opposite confluence of Rivers Teviot and Tweed, 18m/29km NE of Hawick and 20m/32km SW of Berwick-upon-Tweed. Large Georgian square. Bridge by Rennie, 1801. Remains of 12c Abbey (Historic Scotland). **77 F7** NT7233.
Kelso Abbey *Sc.Bord.* *Ecclesiastical building*, largest Border abbey founded by David I in 1128, in Kelso. Now a ruin. **77 F7** NT7333.
Kelstedge *Derbys.* *Village*, 3m/5km NE of Matlock. **51 F6** SK3363.
Kelstern *Lincs.* *Village*, 5m/8km W of Louth. **53 F3** TF2590.
Kelsterton *Flints.* *Locality*, 1m/2km NW of Connah's Quay. SJ2770.
Kelston *B. & N.E.Som.* *Village*, 4m/6km NW of Bath. **19 K5** ST7067.
Keltie Water *Stir.* *River*, flowing S into River Teith, 2m/3km SE of Callander. NN6504.
Keltney Burn *P. & K.* *River*, stream which rises as Allt Mòr and runs down Gleann Mòr, then turns S as Keltney Burn to run into River Lyon at Keltneyburn. Falls of Keltney, waterfall near mouth. **81 J2** NN7748.
Keltneyburn *P. & K.* *Settlement*, 5m/8km W of Aberfeldy. **81 J3** NN7749.
Kelton *D. & G.* *Settlement*, on E bank of River Nith, 3m/5km S of Dumfries. **65 K3** NX9970.
Kelton Hill *D. & G.* *Alternative name for Rhonehouse, qv.*
Kelty *Fife* Population: 5461. *Small town*, 2m/3km N of Cowdenbeath and 4m/6km S of Loch Leven. **75 K1** NT1494.
Kelty Water *Stir.* *River*, running E through Loch Ard Forest to River Forth, 3m/5km SE of Aberfoyle. **74 C1** NS5596.
Kelvedon *Essex* Population: 4422. *Village*, 4m/6km NE of Witham. **34 C7** TL8518.
Kelvedon Hatch *Essex* Population: 2738. *Village*, 3m/4km S of Chipping Ongar. **23 J2** TQ5798.
Kelvin *River*, rising 3m/5km E of Kilsyth and flowing W, then SW through NW part of Glasgow to River Clyde, 2m/3km W of city centre. **75 F3** NS5565.
Kelvin *S.Lan.* *Locality*, industrial estate in S part of East Kilbride. NS6352.
Kelvindale *Glas.* *Suburb*, 3m/5km NW of Glasgow city centre, in Kelvinside district. NS5568.
Kelvingrove Art Gallery and Museum *Glas.* *Other feature of interest*, to S of River Kelvin, 1m/2km W of Glasgow city centre. Includes Scottish Natural History display, British and Italian paintings, as well as Scottish and 18c European artists' work and The Glasgow Boys. **74 D4** NS5766.
Kelvingrove Park *Glas.* *See Glasgow.*
Kelvinhaugh *Glas.* *Suburb*, 1m/2km W of Glasgow city centre. NS5666.
Kelvinside *Glas.* *Suburb*, 2m/4km NW of Glasgow city centre. NS5667.
Kelynack *Cornw.* *Hamlet*, to S of St. Just. **2 A5** SW3729.
Kemacott *Devon* *Hamlet*, 4m/6km SW of Lynton. SS6647.
Kemback *Fife* *Village*, 3m/5km E of Cupar. **83 F6** NO4115.
Kemberton *Shrop.* *Village*, 2m/4km SW of Shifnal. **39 G5** SJ7304.
Kemble *Glos.* *Village*, 4m/6km SW of Cirencester. Airfield to W. **20 C2** ST9897.
Kemerton *Worcs.* *Village*, 4m/7km NE of Tewkesbury. **29 J5** SO9437.
Kemeys Commander (Cemais Comawndwr). *Mon.* *Hamlet*, 3m/5km NW of Usk. **19 G1** SO3404.
Kemeys Inferior (Cemais). *Newport* *Locality*, 6m/10km NE of Newport. **19 G2** ST3792.
Kemnay *Aber.* Population: 3157. *Village*, on River Don, 4m/7km SW of Inverurie. **91 F3** NJ7316.
Kemnay Forest *Aber.* *Forest/woodland*, to N of Kemnay, forming part of Bennachie Forest. **91 F3** NJ7316.
Kemp Town *B. & H.* *Suburb*, E district of Brighton, on coast, with Regency squares and terraces. **13 G6** TQ3303.
Kempe's Corner *Kent* *Settlement*, 3m/5km NE of Ashford. TR0346.
Kempley *Glos.* *Village*, 4m/6km NW of Newent. **29 F6** SO6729.
Kempley Green *Glos.* *Village*, 1km SE of Kempley. **29 F6** SO6729.
Kemps Green *Warks.* *Settlement*, 1m/2km SW of Hockley Heath. SP1470.
Kempsey *Worcs.* Population: 3147. *Village*, on River Severn, 4m/6km S of Worcester. **29 H4** SO8549.
Kempsford *Glos.* Population: 1515. *Village*, 3m/5km S of Fairford. **20 E2** SU1696.
Kempshott *Hants.* *Suburb*, SW district of Basingstoke. **21 K7** SU6050.
Kempston *Beds.* Population: 18,233. *Town*, 2m/3km SW of Bedford across River Great Ouse. **32 D4** TL0347.
Kempston Church End *Beds.* *Settlement*, beside River Great Ouse, 3m/4km SW of Bedford across river. **32 D4** TL0147.
Kempston Hardwick *Beds.* *Settlement*, 4m/6km S of Bedford. **32 D4** TL0244.
Kempston West End *Beds.* *Settlement*, 4m/6km W of Bedford across River Great Ouse. SP9947.
Kempstone *Norf.* *Hamlet*, 1m/2km S of Litcham. TF8816.
Kempton *Shrop.* *Hamlet*, 5m/7km W of Craven Arms. **38 C7** SO3582.
Kempton Park *Surr.* *Racecourse*, park containing racecourse 1m/2km N of Sunbury, 4m/6km W of Kingston upon Thames. Sixteen flat and nine National Hunt race days each year, including a two-day National Hunt Festival at Christmas. **22 E5** TQ1170.
Kemsing *Kent* Population: 3420. *Village*, 3m/4km NE of Sevenoaks. **23 J6** TQ5558.
Kemsley *Kent* *Hamlet*, 2m/3km N of Sittingbourne. **25 F5** TQ9066.
Kenardington *Kent* *Village*, 2m/3km W of Hamstreet. **14 E4** TQ9732.
Kenchester *Here.* *Hamlet*, 5m/8km W of Hereford. To S is site of Roman town (Magnis). **28 D4** SO4343.
Kencott *Oxon.* *Village*, 4m/7km NE of Lechlade. **21 F1** SP2504.
Kendal *Cumb.* Population: 25,461. *Town*, former wool town on River Kent, 19m/31km N of Lancaster. Before becoming Queen, Catherine Parr lived at Kendal Castle, now a ruin. Abbot Hall Art Gallery contains work by John Ruskin. **61 G7** SD5192.
Kendal Castle *Cumb.* *Historic/prehistoric site*, ruins of 12c castle on hill in Kendal. Birthplace of Catherine Parr, Henry VIII's last wife. **61 G7** SD5192.
Kendal End *Worcs.* *Settlement*, 4m/6km NE of Bromsgrove. SP0074.
Kenderchurch *Here.* *Locality*, 1km NE of Pontrilas. **28 D6** SO4028.
Kendleshire *S.Glos.* *Hamlet*, 1m/2km SE of Winterbourne and 7m/11km NE of Bristol. ST6679.
Kendoon Loch *D. & G.* *Lake/loch*, meeting point of several streams running into Water of Ken, in Dundeugh Forest, 6m/9km N of St. John's Town of Dalry. **68 A4** NX6090.
Kenfig (Cynffig). *Bridgend* *Village*, 3m/5km N of Porthcawl. Site of ancient Kenfig town to N, and remains of Kenfig Castle. **18 B3** SS8081.
Kenfig *N.P.T.* *English form of Cynffig, qv.*
Kenfig Burrows *Bridgend* *Coastal feature*, sand dune system on coast to W of Kenfig, 4m/6km NW of Porthcawl. National Nature Reserve. **18 A3** SS8081.
Kenfig Hill *Bridgend* *Locality*, to NE of Pyle, 3m/4km E of Kenfig. **18 B3** SS8383.
Kenfig Pool *Bridgend* *Lake/loch*, to W of Kenfig. **18 A3** SS8081.
Kenidjack *Cornw.* *Settlement*, 1km NW of St. Just. SW3632.
Kenilworth *Warks.* Population: 21,623. *Town*, ruins of red sandstone castle (English Heritage), Norman and later, 5m/8km SW of Coventry. **30 D1** SP2872.
Kenilworth Castle *Warks.* *Castle*, 1m/2km NW of Kenilworth town centre. Red sandstone ruins of castle (English Heritage) built in 12c by William de Clinton. Further additions, including a good water defence system, added in 13c. Soldiers Through the Ages exhibition spans from Romans to World War II. **30 D1** SP2772.
Kenknock *P. & K.* *Settlement*, in Glen Lyon, 4m/6km SW of Bridge of Balgie. **81 G3** NN5243.
Kenknock *Stir.* *Settlement*, in Glen Lochay, 7m/11km NW of Killin. **81 F4** NN4636.
Kenley *Gt.Lon.* *Suburb*, in borough of Croydon, 2m/3km SE of Purley. Kenley Airfield to S. **23 G6** TQ3259.
Kenley *Shrop.* *Village*, 4m/7km W of Much Wenlock. **38 E5** SJ5600.
Kenly Burn *Fife* *River*, rising from Cameron and Kinaldy Burns, and flowing NE to North Sea, 4m/6km SE of St. Andrews. **83 G6** NO5411.

K

Kenmore *Arg. & B.* ***Settlement***, on NE side of Loch Fyne, 4m/7km SW of Inveraray. **80 B7** NN0601.
Kenmore *High.* ***Settlement***, on Loch a' Chracaich, on SW side of Loch Torridon, Ross and Cromarty district, 4m/7km NW of Shieldaig. **94 D6** NG7557.
Kenmore *P. & K.* ***Village***, at foot of Loch Tay, 6m/9km SW of Aberfeldy. On islet in loch is a ruined 12c priory. **81 J3** NN7745.
Kenmore *W.Isles* ***Settlement***, on E shore of Loch Seaforth, 2m/3km W of head of Loch Claidh. **100 E7** NB2206.
Kenmore Wood *Arg. & B.* ***Forest/woodland***, on W side of Loch Lomond, and just to N of Loch Long. **80 E7** NN3207.
Kenmure Castle *D. & G.* ***Castle***, of 15c-17c, seat of the Gordons, 1m/2km S of New Galloway. **65 G3** NX6376.
Kenn *Devon* ***River***, rising 1m/2km S of Longdown and flowing SE into River Exe estuary between Powderham and Starcross. **7 H7** SX9783.
Kenn *Devon* ***Village***, 5m/7km S of Exeter. **7 H7** SX9285.
Kenn *N.Som.* ***River***, rising near Brockley and flowing W into mouth of River Severn, 2m/4km SW of Clevedon. **19 G7** ST3868.
Kenn *N.Som.* ***Village***, 2m/3km S of Clevedon. **19 H5** ST4169.
Kennacley (Gaelic form: Ceann-na-Cleithe.) *W.Isles* ***Settlement***, on W shore of East Loch Tarbert, South Harris, 4m/6km SE of Tarbert. NG1794.
Kennacraig *Arg. & B.* ***Settlement***, on SE coast of West Loch Tarbert, 5m/8km SW of Tarbert. **73 G4** NR8262.
Kennards House *Cornw.* ***Settlement***, 3m/5km W of Launceston. **4 C2** SX2883.
Kennavay *W.Isles* ***Settlement***, on S coast of Scalpay. **93 H2** NG2394.
Kennedy's Pass *S.Ayr.* ***Other feature of interest***, small pass through rock adjacent to coast carrying A77(T) road, 3m/5km SW of Girvan. **67 F4** NX1493.
Kenneggy Downs *Cornw.* ***Hamlet***, 6m/9km W of Helston. Kenneggy is a hamlet to S. SW5629.
Kennerleigh *Devon* ***Village***, 5m/8km N of Crediton. **7 G5** SS8207.
Kennerty *Aber.* ***Settlement***, 3m/5km NW of Banchory. **90 E5** NO6799.
Kennessee Green *Mersey.* ***Suburb***, to S of Maghull town centre. SD3701.
Kennet ***River***, rising near Uffcott and running S, at times undergound, to Avebury, then E through Marlborough, Hungerford and Newbury, into River Thames at Reading. **21 F4** SU7373.
Kennet *Clack.* ***Settlement***, 1m/2km SE of Clackmannan. **75 H1** NS9290.
Kennethmont *Aber.* ***Locality***, parish containing village of Kennethmont, 3m/5km NE of Rhynie. **90 D2** NJ5328.
Kennethmont (Also known as Kirkhill of Kennethmont.) *Aber.* ***Village***, 7m/11km S of Huntly. Leith Hall (National Trust for Scotland) 1km NE. **90 D2** NJ5328.
Kennett *Cambs.* ***Hamlet***, 5m/8km NE of Newmarket. **33 K2** TL6968.
Kennett *Suff.* ***River***, rising S of Cowlinge and flowing N by Moulton and Kennett, joining Lee Brook S of Freckenham. **34 B2** TL6671.
Kennford *Devon* ***Village***, 4m/6km S of Exeter. **7 H7** SX9186.
Kennick Reservoir *Devon* ***Reservoir***, on E edge of Dartmoor, 3m/5km E of Moretonhampstead. **7 G7** SX8084.
Kenninghall *Norf.* ***Village***, 6m/9km S of Attleborough. **44 E7** TM0386.
Kennington *Gt.Lon.* ***Suburb***, in borough of Lambeth, to SE of Vauxhall Bridge. The Oval, Test Match cricket ground and headquarters of Surrey County Cricket Club, is located here. TQ3177.
Kennington *Kent* ***Suburb***, N district of Ashford. **15 F3** TR0245.
Kennington *Oxon.* Population: 4290. ***Suburb***, 2m/4km S of Oxford. **21 J1** SP5202.
Kennishead *Glas.* ***Suburb***, 5m/7km SW of Glasgow city centre, in Carnwadric district. NS5460.
Kennoway *Fife* Population: 4609. ***Small town***, 2m/4km NW of Leven. **82 E7** NO3502.
Kenny *Som.* ***Hamlet***, 1km NW of Ashill and 4m/6km NW of Ilminster. ST3117.
Kennyhill *Suff.* ***Hamlet***, 4m/7km NW of Mildenhall. **33 K1** TL6679.
Kennythorpe *N.Yorks.* ***Hamlet***, 4m/6km S of Malton. **58 D3** SE7865.
Kenovay *Arg. & B.* ***Settlement***, on Tiree, 3m/5km W of Scarinish. NL9946.
Kensal Green *Gt.Lon.* ***Suburb***, in borough of Brent, 5m/8km W of Charing Cross. TQ2382.
Kensal Rise *Gt.Lon.* ***Suburb***, to E of Kensal Green, with Kensal Town to SE, in borough of Kensington and Chelsea. TQ2383.
Kensal Town *Gt.Lon.* ***Suburb***, in borough of Kensington and Chelsea, to SE of Kensal Green. TQ2482.
Kensaleyre *High.* ***Settlement***, at head of Loch Eyre, Skye, 7m/11km NW of Portree. **93 K6** NG4251.
Kensey *Cornw.* ***River***, rising near Treneglos and flowing E through N part of Launceston, then into River Tamar 2m/3km E. SX3584.
Kensham Green *Kent* ***Locality***, 2m/3km SW of Rolvenden. TQ8229.
Kensington *Gt.Lon.* ***Suburb***, district in borough of Kensington and Chelsea, to W of central London. Contains Victoria and Albert Museum, and Natural History and Science Museums; Kensington Palace in Kensington Palace Gardens. TQ2579.
Kensington Gardens *Gt.Lon.* ***Open space***, 275 acres of royal park containing William III's Kensington Palace, adjoining to W of Hyde Park. Includes Round Pond, Albert Memorial (English Heritage) and The Broad Walk, lined by limes and maples. Separated from Hyde Park by The Serpentine and The Long Water, both created by Queen Caroline who ordered damming of Westbourne River. Formal ponds and fountains at N end of The Long Water. TQ2680.
Kensington Palace *Gt.Lon.* ***Historic house***, royal residence in Kensington Gardens. Bought by William III in 1689 and altered by Wren, Hawksmoor and William Kent. Queen Victoria and Queen Mary born here in 1819 and 1867 respectively. State apartments and Costume Museum. **23 F4** TQ2580.
Kenson *V. of Glam.* ***Settlement***, to W of Penmark. ST0568.
Kenstone *Shrop.* ***Settlement***, 1m/2km W of Hodnet. SJ5928.
Kensworth *Beds.* ***Village***, 2m/3km SE of Dunstable. **32 D7** TL0319.
Kensworth Common *Beds.* ***Village***, 3m/4km SE of Dunstable. **32 D7** TL0318.
Kent ***River***, rising in Lake District, 1m/2km S of summit of High Street, then flowing S through Kentmere Reservoir and Kendal into Morecambe Bay, off Humphrey Head Point, as Kent Channel. **55 J1** SD4165.
Kent and East Sussex Railway ***Other feature of interest***, preserved tourist railway running for 7m/11km between Tenterden and Northiam. **14 D5** TQ8833.
Kent Green *Ches.* ***Locality***, 2m/3km N of Kidsgrove. SJ8357.
Kent Street *E.Suss.* ***Settlement***, 2m/3km E of Battle. **14 C6** TQ7815.
Kent Street *Kent* ***Settlement***, 1km NE of Mereworth. **23 K6** TQ6654.
Kentallen *High.* ***Settlement***, at head of narrow Kentallen Bay on Loch Linnhe, Lochaber district, 3m/5km SW of Ballachulish. **80 B2** NN0057.
Kentchurch *Here.* ***Hamlet***, 2m/3km SE of Pontrilas. **28 D6** SO4125.
Kentford *Suff.* ***Village***, 5m/8km E of Newmarket. **34 B2** TL7066.
Kentisbeare *Devon* ***Village***, 3m/5km E of Cullompton. **7 J5** ST0608.
Kentisbury *Devon* ***Hamlet***, on W edge of Exmoor, 7m/11km SW of Lynton. **6 E1** SS6243.
Kentisbury Ford *Devon* ***Hamlet***, 1m/2km S of Kentisbury. **6 E1** SS6142.
Kentish Town *Gt.Lon.* ***Suburb***, in borough of Camden, 3m/5km N of Charing Cross. TQ2984.
Kentmere *Cumb.* ***Village***, on River Kent, 4m/6km N of Staveley. **61 F6** NY4504.
Kentmere Reservoir *Cumb.* ***Reservoir***, 3m/4km N of Kentmere. **60 F6** NY4504.
Kenton *Devon* ***Village***, 4m/7km N of Dawlish. **7 H7** SX9583.
Kenton *Gt.Lon.* ***Locality***, on borders of Brent and Harrow boroughs, 9m/15km NW of Charing Cross. TQ1788.
Kenton *Suff.* ***Village***, 2m/3km NE of Debenham. **35 F2** TM1965.
Kenton *T. & W.* ***Suburb***, 2m/4km NW of Newcastle upon Tyne city centre. **71 H7** NZ2267.
Kenton Bank Foot *T. & W.* ***Suburb***, 4m/6km NW of Newcastle upon Tyne. NZ2068.
Kenton Bar *T. & W.* ***Suburb***, 3m/4km NW of Newcastle upon Tyne city centre. NZ2167.
Kenton Corner *Suff.* ***Settlement***, 1m/2km SE of Kenton. TM2065.
Kenton Green *Glos.* ***Locality***, 4m/7km SW of Gloucester across loop of River Severn. SO7714.
Kentra *High.* ***Settlement***, in Lochaber district, on E side of Kentra Bay, 4m/6km NW of Salen. **79 H1** NM6569.
Kentra Bay *High.* ***Bay***, sheltered bay on N coast of Ardnamurchan peninsula, 3m/4km W of Acharacle. Large expanse of sand at low tide. **79 H1** NM6569.
Kentrigg *Cumb.* ***Locality***, adjoining to N of Kendal, 1m/2km SE of Burneside. SD5194.
Kents Bank *Cumb.* ***Hamlet***, on W bank of River Kent estuary, 1m/2km SW of Grange-over-Sands. **55 H2** SD3976.
Kent's Green *Glos.* ***Village***, 2m/3km SE of Newent. **29 G6** SO7423.
Kent's Oak *Hants.* ***Village***, 3m/5km NW of Romsey. **10 E2** SU3224.
Kentwell Hall *Suff.* ***Historic house***, moated redbrick Tudor manor house with surrounding gardens to N of Long Melford. **34 C4** TL8647.
Kenwick *Shrop.* ***Settlement***, 3m/5km SE of Ellesmere. **38 D2** SJ4230.
Kenwick Bar *Lincs.* ***Locality***, with small hill, at crossroads 2m/3km S of Louth. TF3384.
Kenwood House *Gt.Lon.* ***Historic house***, 18c house (English Heritage) by Robert Adam at N edge of Hampstead Heath 5m/8km N of Charing Cross. Contains 18c English paintings, sculpture and furniture, and fine paintings by Rembrandt, Van Dyck and Vermeer. Gardens and wooded estate of 200 acres with panorama of almost whole of London. **23 F3** TQ2787.
Kenwyn *Cornw.* ***Village***, on N outskirts of Truro. Also river rising some 4m/6km W and flowing through Truro to join River Allen and form Truro River. **3 F4** SW8145.
Kenyon *Gt.Man.* ***Settlement***, 2m/3km W of Culcheth. **49 F3** SJ6395.
Keoldale *High.* ***Settlement***, on E side of Kyle of Durness, Sutherland district, 2m/3km SW of Durness. Ancient cairns and standing stones to E. **103 F2** NC3866.
Keose *W.Isles* *Anglicised form of Ceos, qv.*
Keose Glebe *W.Isles* ***Settlement***, on Isle of Lewis, adjoining to E of Ceos. NB3521.
Keose Island (Gaelic form: Eilean Cheois.) *W.Isles* ***Island***, islet 1km SE of Keose Glebe, in Loch Erisort. NB3621.
Kepnal *Wilts.* ***Hamlet***, 1km E of Pewsey. SU1760.
Keppanach *High.* ***Settlement***, 2m/3km NW of North Ballachulish. **80 B1** NN0262.
Keppoch *Arg. & B.* ***Settlement***, 2m/3km NW of Cardross. **74 B3** NS3279.
Keppoch *High.* ***Locality***, in Lochaber district on N side of Loch nan Ceall, W of Arisaig. Back of Keppoch is settlement to N. NM6486.
Keppoch *High.* ***Settlement***, near NE coast of Loch Duich, 2m/3km SE of Dornie. **86 E2** NG9024.
Keprigan *Arg. & B.* ***Settlement***, near S tip of Kintyre, 1m/2km N of Southend. **66 A2** NR6910.
Kepwick *N.Yorks.* ***Village***, 6m/10km N of Thirsk. **63 F7** SE4690.
Kerdiston *Norf.* ***Settlement***, 1m/2km NW of Reepham. TG0724.
Keresley *W.Mid.* ***Village***, 3m/5km NW of Coventry. **41 F7** SP3183.
Kerloch *Aber.* ***Mountain***, 3m/5km NE of Bridge of Dye. Height 1752 feet or 534 metres. **90 E6** NO6987.
Kernborough *Devon* ***Hamlet***, 4m/6km SE of Kingsbridge. SX7941.
Kerne Bridge *Here.* ***Hamlet***, 3m/5km S of Ross-on-Wye. **28 E7** SO5818.
Kerrera *Arg. & B.* ***Island***, 5m/7km long NE to SW and 2m/3km at widest point, lying to SW of Oban, from which it is separated by Kerrera Sound. Ruined Gylen Castle at S end of island. **79 K5** NM8128.
Kerridge *Ches.* ***Suburb***, to S of Bollington. **49 J5** SJ9376.
Kerridge-end *Ches.* ***Settlement***, 2m/3km NE of Macclesfield. SJ9475.
Kerris *Cornw.* ***Hamlet***, 2m/3km SW of Penzance. **2 B6** SW4427.
Kerry *High.* ***River***, in Ross and Cromarty district, flowing W into Loch Kerry, 2m/3km S of Gairloch. **94 E4** NG8173.
Kerry *Powys* ***Village***, 3m/4km SE of Newtown. **38 A7** SO1490.
Kerry Hill *Powys* ***Mountain***, partly afforested, formerly noted for a breed of sheep. Height 1571 feet or 479 metres. **38 A7** SO1385.
Kerrycroy *Arg. & B.* ***Village***, model village on Kerrycroy Bay, on E coast of Bute, 1m/2km S of Ascog and at N entrance to estate of Mountstuart. **73 K4** NS1061.
Kerry's Gate *Here.* ***Settlement***, 8m/13km SW of Hereford. **28 C5** SO3933.
Kerrysdale *High.* ***Settlement***, in Ross and Cromarty district, 3m/4km SE of Gairloch. **94 E4** NG8273.
Kersal *Gt.Man.* ***Suburb***, 3m/4km E of Swinton. SD8101.
Kersall *Notts.* ***Village***, 5m/8km SE of Ollerton. **51 K6** SK7162.
Kersey *Suff.* ***Village***, 2m/3km NW of Hadleigh. **34 E4** TM0044.
Kersey Tye *Suff.* ***Settlement***, 1m/2km SW of Kersey. TM9843.
Kersey Upland *Suff.* ***Settlement***, 1m/2km SW of Kersey. TM9943.
Kersey Vale *Suff.* ***Settlement***, 1km S of Kersey. TM0043.
Kershader *W.Isles* *Anglicised form of Cearsiadar, qv.*
Kershope Burn ***River***, rising on borders of England and Scotland, 5m/8km E of Newcastleton, and flowing SW along border into Liddel Water at Kershopefoot. **70 A5** NY4782.
Kershope Forest *Cumb.* ***Forest/woodland***, area to E of Kershopefoot, largely planted with conifers. **69 K5** NY4782.
Kershopefoot *Cumb.* ***Hamlet***, at confluence of Kershope Burn and Liddel Water, 3m/5km S of Newcastleton. **69 K5** NY4782.
Kerswell *Devon* ***Village***, 4m/6km E of Cullompton. **7 J5** ST0806.
Kerswell Green *Worcs.* ***Village***, 5m/9km S of Worcester. **29 H4** SO8646.
Kerthen Wood *Cornw.* ***Settlement***, 3m/5km SE of Hayle. SW5833.
Kesgrave *Suff.* ***Suburb***, 4m/6km E of Ipswich. **35 G4** TM2145.
Kessingland *Suff.* Population: 3167. ***Village***, 4m/7km SW of Lowestoft. **45 K7** TM5286.
Kessingland Beach *Suff.* ***Village***, coastal resort and caravan park adjoining to E of Kessingland. **45 K7** TM5286.
Kestle *Cornw.* ***Hamlet***, 2m/3km W of Mevagissey. SW9945.
Kestle Mill *Cornw.* ***Hamlet***, 3m/5km SE of Newquay. **3 F3** SW8559.
Keston *Gt.Lon.* ***Suburb***, in borough of Bromley, 3m/5km S of Bromley town centre. Site of Roman villa to S. **23 H5** TQ4164.
Keston Mark *Gt.Lon.* ***Locality***, residential locality 1km NE of Keston. TQ4265.
Keswick *Cumb.* Population: 4836. ***Small town***, former mining town, including graphite for pencil manufacture, at NE end of Derwent Water, 16m/26km W of Penrith. Tourist centre for Lake District and largest town within National Park. **60 D4** NY2623.
Keswick *Norf.* ***Village***, 3m/5km SW of Norwich. **45 G5** TG2004.
Keswick *Norf.* ***Village***, on coast, 1km SE of Bacton. **45 H2** TG3533.
Ketley *Tel. & W.* ***Suburb***, 2m/3km E of Wellington. SJ6710.
Ketleybank *Tel. & W.* ***Suburb***, 1m/2km SW of Oakengates. SJ6910.
Ketsby *Lincs.* ***Hamlet***, 3m/5km NW of Ulceby Cross. **53 G5** TF3676.
Kettering *Northants.* Population: 47,186. ***Town***, market town once famous for its footwear industry, 13m/21km NE of Northampton. **32 B1** SP8678.
Ketteringham *Norf.* ***Village***, 6m/9km SW of Norwich. **45 F5** TG1602.
Kettins *P. & K.* ***Village***, 1m/2km SE of Coupar Angus. **82 D4** NO2339.
Kettla Ness *Shet.* ***Coastal feature***, headland at S end of West Burra. **109 C10** HU3429.
Kettle Corner *Kent* ***Settlement***, on River Medway, 3m/4km SW of Maidstone. TQ7253.
Kettle Ness *N.Yorks.* ***Coastal feature***, headland on North Sea coast at E end of Runswick Bay, 5m/8km NW of Whitby. **63 K5** NZ8316.
Kettlebaston *Suff.* ***Village***, 3m/5km E of Lavenham. **34 D4** TL9650.
Kettlebridge *Fife* ***Hamlet***, 1m/2km S of Ladybank. **82 E7** NO3007.
Kettlebrook *Staffs.* ***Suburb***, to SE of Tamworth town centre. **40 E5** SK2103.

K

Kettleburgh *Suff.* ***Village***, 2m/4km SW of Framlingham. **35 G3** TM2660.
Kettlehill *Fife* ***Hamlet***, 2m/3km SE of Ladybank. NO3207.
Kettleholm *D. & G.* ***Settlement***, 3m/5km S of Lockerbie. **69 G6** NY1476.
Kettleness *N.Yorks.* ***Hamlet***, situated to S of Kettle Ness headland, 5m/8km NW of Whitby. Site of Roman signal station. **63 K5** NZ8316.
Kettleshulme *Ches.* ***Village***, 6m/9km NE of Macclesfield. **49 J5** SJ9879.
Kettlesing *N.Yorks.* ***Hamlet***, 5m/8km W of Harrogate. **57 H4** SE2256.
Kettlesing Bottom *N.Yorks.* ***Village***, 1km NE of Kettlesing. **57 H4** SE2256.
Kettlesing Head *N.Yorks.* ***Settlement***, at crossroads, 3m/5km E of Blubberhouses. SE2156.
Kettlester *Shet.* ***Locality***, near S coast of Yell, adjoining to NW of Burravoe. HU5179.
Kettlestone *Norf.* ***Village***, 3m/5km E of Fakenham. **44 D2** TF9631.
Kettlethorpe *Lincs.* ***Village***, 3m/5km W of Saxilby. **52 B5** SK8475.
Kettletoft *Ork.* ***Settlement***, and promontory on S coast of Sanday, between Backaskail Bay to W and Kettletoft Bay to E. **106 F4** HY6538.
Kettlewell *N.Yorks.* ***Village***, in Upper Wharfedale, 6m/9km N of Grassington. **56 E2** SD9672.
Ketton *Rut.* Population: 1708. ***Village***, 4m/6km SW of Stamford. **42 C5** SK9804.
Kevingtown *Gt.Lon.* ***Settlement***, in borough of Bromley, 1m/2km NE of Orpington. TQ4867.
Kevock *Midloth.* ***Suburb***, in W part of Bonnyrigg and Lasswade. NT2965.
Kew *Gt.Lon.* ***Locality***, on S side of River Thames, crossed by Kew Bridge, 7m/11km W of Charing Cross. Royal Botanic Gardens Kew to W, containing Kew Palace (English Heritage), 17c-18c house with George III relics. **22 E4** TQ1977.
Kew Gardens *Gt.Lon. See Royal Botanic Gardens Kew.*
Kew Palace *Gt.Lon.* ***Historic house***, small Jacobean mansion built in 1631 in Dutch style, situated within Kew Gardens. Once occupied by George III and Queen Charlotte. **22 E4** TQ1877.
Kewstoke *N.Som.* ***Village***, 2m/3km NE of Weston-super-Mare. Viewpoint (National Trust) known as Monk's Steps or St. Kew's Steps. **19 G5** ST3363.
Kexbrough *S.Yorks.* ***Village***, 4m/6km NW of Barnsley. **51 F2** SE3009.
Kexby *Lincs.* ***Village***, 4m/7km SE of Gainsborough. **52 B4** SK8785.
Kexby *York* ***Village***, 6m/10km E of York. **58 D4** SE7051.
Kexwith Moor *N.Yorks.* ***Open space***, moorland 6m/9km SE of Bowes. **62 B6** NZ0305.
Key Green *Ches.* ***Hamlet***, 2m/3km E of Congleton. **49 H6** SJ8963.
Key Green *N.Yorks.* ***Settlement***, 1m/2km SW of Egton. NZ8004.
Key Street *Kent* ***Settlement***, 1m/2km W of Sittingbourne. TQ8864.
Keyford *Som.* ***Suburb***, S district of Frome. ST7747.
Keyham *Leics.* ***Village***, 5m/9km E of Leicester. **41 J5** SK6706.
Keyhaven *Hants.* ***Village***, on coast, 3m/5km S of Lymington. **10 E5** SZ3091.
Keyingham *E.Riding* Population: 2522. ***Village***, 4m/7km SE of Hedon. **59 J7** TA2425.
Keymer *W.Suss.* Population: 5942. ***Small town***, below South Downs, 2m/4km S of Burgess Hill. Noted for hand-made bricks and tiles. **13 G5** TQ3115.
Keynsham *B. & N.E.Som.* Population: 15,193. ***Town***, on River Avon, midway between Bristol and Bath. Notable 17c church tower. **19 K5** ST6568.
Keynsham Hams *B. & N.E.Som.* ***Locality***, on S bank of River Avon, 1km N of Keynsham. Site of Roman villa 1km to NW. ST6569.
Key's Toft *Lincs.* ***Locality***, 1km S of Wainfleet All Saints. **53 H7** TF4957.
Keysers Estate *Essex* ***Suburb***, on River Lea, 2m/3km S of Hoddesdon. TL3706.
Keysley Down *Wilts.* ***Open space***, hillslope 3m/4km N of East Knoyle. **9 H1** ST8634.
Keysoe *Beds.* ***Village***, 8m/13km N of Bedford. **32 D2** TL0762.
Keysoe Row *Beds.* ***Village***, 1m/2km SE of Keysoe. **32 D2** TL0762.
Keyston *Cambs.* ***Village***, 4m/6km SE of Thrapston. **32 D1** TL0475.
Keyworth *Notts.* Population: 7467. ***Village***, 7m/11km SE of Nottingham. **41 J2** SK6130.
Kibblesworth *T. & W.* ***Village***, 2m/3km W of Birtley. Coal-mining, brick manufacture. **62 D1** NZ2456.
Kibworth Beauchamp *Leics.* ***Village***, 5m/8km NW of Market Harborough. **41 J6** SP6893.
Kibworth Harcourt *Leics.* Population: 3973. ***Village***, 5m/9km NW of Market Harborough. **41 J6** SP6894.
Kidbrooke *Gt.Lon.* ***Suburb***, in borough of Greenwich, 8m/12km E of Charing Cross. **23 H4** TQ4176.
Kidbrooke Park *E.Suss.* ***Garden***, including bog garden and parkland laid out by Humphry Repton, to SW of Forest Row, 3m/5km SE of East Grinstead. **13 H3** TQ4134.
Kidburngill *Cumb.* ***Locality***, 2m/3km SW of Ullock. NY0621.
Kiddal Lane End *W.Yorks.* ***Settlement***, 1m/2km N of Barwick in Elmet. **57 J6** SE4039.
Kiddemore Green *Staffs.* ***Settlement***, 7m/12km NW of Wolverhampton. **40 A5** SJ8508.
Kidderminster *Worcs.* Population: 54,644. ***Town***, famous for carpet-making, on River Stour, 16m/27km W of Birmingham. Developed mainly in 19c, but has 1960s town centre. **29 H1** SO8376.
Kiddington *Oxon.* ***Hamlet***, 3m/4km SE of Enstone. **31 F6** SP4122.
Kidd's Moor *Norf.* ***Settlement***, 1m/2km N of Wymondham. TG1103.
Kidlington *Oxon.* Population: 15,156. ***Town***, 5m/8km N of Oxford. Oxford Airport to NW. **31 F7** SP4914.
Kidmore End *Oxon.* ***Village***, 4m/6km N of Reading. **21 K4** SU6979.
Kidnall *Ches.* ***Settlement***, 2m/3km NW of Malpas. SJ4749.
Kidsdale *D. & G.* ***Settlement***, 3m/4km S of Whithorn. **64 E7** NX4336.
Kidsgrove *Staffs.* Population: 27,702. ***Town***, former mining town, 6m/10km NW of Stoke-on-Trent. **49 H7** SJ8354.
Kidstones *N.Yorks.* ***Settlement***, at head of Bishopdale, 3m/5km N of Buckden. **56 E1** SD9581.
Kidsty Pike *Cumb.* ***Inland physical feature***, edge rising to over 2500 feet or 770 metres, between Hayeswater and Haweswater Reservoir, 6m/10km NE of Ambleside. **60 F5** NY4412.
Kidwelly (Cydweli). *Carmar.* Population: 2664. ***Small town***, on River Gwendraeth Fach, 7m/12km NW of Llanelli. Remains of 12c-14c castle (Cadw) on N bank of river. **17 H4** SN4006.
Kidwelly Castle *Carmar.* ***Castle***, well-preserved castle (Cadw) originating from 12c and made into a stone castle in late 13c, in Kidwelly 8m/12km NW of Llanelli. **17 H4** SN4007.
Kidwelly Priory (Church of St. Mary). *Carmar.* ***Ecclesiastical building***, priory originally founded in 12c by Benedictines at Kidwelly, succeeded by Church of St. Mary in 14c. **17 H4** SN4106.
Kiel Crofts *Arg. & B.* ***Settlement***, adjoining to NW of Benderloch. **80 A4** NM9039.
Kielder (Also known as Kielder Forest Village.) *Northumb.* ***Village***, in Kielder Forest, at W end of Kielder Water (Reservoir), 7m/11km NW of Falstone. **70 B4** NY6293.
Kielder Burn *Northumb.* ***River***, rising on Cheviot Hills, 3m/5km SW of Carter Bar, and flowing SW into Kielder Water, 1km SE of Kielder. **70 B4** NY6392.
Kielder Forest *Northumb.* ***Forest/woodland***, large area of conifer forest planted by Forestry Commission, astride upper valley of River North Tyne on Scottish border. **70 B4** NY6691.
Kielder Forest Park *Northumb.* ***Leisure/recreation***, forest park with mixed woodland and mature spruce plantations, about 6m/10km NW of Bellingham. Forest, developed by Forestry Commission, is largest man-made forest in Europe and surrounds Kielder Water (reservoir) which has boating and watersports facilities. Visitor centre and forest trails. **70 B4** NY6092.
Kielder Forest Village *Northumb. Alternative name for Kielder, qv.*
Kielder Water *Northumb.* ***Reservoir***, large reservoir to W of Falstone, on course of River North Tyne in Kielder Forest. **70 B5** NY6787.
Kielderhead Moor *Northumb.* ***Open space***, large area of moorland in Cheviot Hills, 1m/2km S of Carter Fell, and on which rises Kielder Burn. **70 B3** NT6600.
Kiells *Arg. & B.* ***Hamlet***, on Islay, 1m/2km SW of Port Askaig. NR4168.
Kiessimul (Also spelled Kisimul.) *W.Isles* ***Island***, tiny islet in Castle Bay, S coast of Barra, on which stands Kiessimul Castle, ancient stronghold of Clan Macneil of Barra. NL6697.
Kiessimul Castle (Also spelled Kisimul Castle.) *W.Isles* ***Castle***, on tiny islet of Kiessimul in Castle Bay, S coast of Barra. Ancient stronghold of Clan Macneil of Barra. **84 B5** NL6697.
Kiftsgate Court Garden *Glos.* ***Garden***, which includes tree peonies, abutilons and old roses, 1km SE of Mickleton and 3m/5km NE of Chipping Camden. **30 C4** SP1643.
Kilantringan Loch *S.Ayr.* ***Lake/loch***, small loch 2m/4km S of Ballantrae. **64 A3** NX0979.
Kilbarchan *Renf.* Population: 3846. ***Small town***, 2m/3km W of Johnstone, formerly noted for tartan weaving. 18c weaver's cottage (National Trust for Scotland). **74 C4** NS4063.
Kilbeg *High.* ***Locality***, on E coast of Sleat peninsula, Skye, 2m/4km NE of Ardvasar. **86 C4** NG6506.
Kilberry *Arg. & B.* ***Village***, near W coast of Knapdale, Argyll, 4m/6km NW of Ardpatrick Point. **73 F4** NR7164.
Kilberry Crosses *Arg. & B.* ***Historic/prehistoric site***, collection of late medieval sculptured stones (Historic Scotland) gathered from Kilberry estate at Kilberry Castle on W coast of Kintyre, 1km W of Kilberry. **73 F4** NR7064.
Kilberry Head *Arg. & B.* ***Coastal feature***, headland nearly 1m/2km W of Kilberry, to N of Kilberry Bay. **72 E4** NR7164.
Kilbirnie *N.Ayr.* Population: 8060. ***Small town***, with notable medieval church, on River Garnock, 9m/15km NE of Ardrossan. **74 B5** NS3154.
Kilbirnie Loch *N.Ayr.* ***Lake/loch***, 1m/2km E of Kilbirnie. **74 B5** NS3154.
Kilblaan *Arg. & B.* ***Settlement***, in Glen Shira, 4m/6km NE of Inveraray. **80 C6** NN1213.
Kilblaan Burn *Arg. & B.* ***River***, running E into Glen Shira, 4m/6km NE of Inveraray. **80 C6** NN1213.
Kilbowie *Renf.* ***Suburb***, on N side of Clydebank. NS5071.
Kilbrannan Sound *Arg. & B.* ***Sea feature***, sea passage between Arran and Kintyre. Width between 3m/5km and 8m/13km. **66 C1** NR8441.
Kilbraur *High.* ***Settlement***, 1m/2km W of Gordonbush, to S of River Brora. **104 D7** NC8210.
Kilbraur Hill *High.* ***Mountain***, 1m/2km S of Kilbraur, Sutherland district. Height 1059 feet or 323 metres. **97 F1** NC8208.
Kilbrenan *Arg. & B.* ***Settlement***, on Mull, 2m/3km SE of Fanmore. **79 F3** NM4342.
Kilbride *Arg. & B.* ***Settlement***, in Argyll 3m/4km S of Oban. **79 K5** NM8525.
Kilbride *Arg. & B.* ***Settlement***, on lower slopes of Kilbride Hill, 1m/2km N of Ettrick Bay, Bute. **73 J4** NS0367.
Kilbride *High.* ***Settlement***, 1km E of Torrin, Skye. **86 B2** NG5820.
Kilbride *W.Isles Anglicised form of Cille Bhrighde, qv.*
Kilbride Bay *Arg. & B.* ***Bay***, in Argyll at entrance to Loch Fyne, 2m/4km NW of Ardlamont Point. **73 H4** NR9666.
Kilbride Farm *Arg. & B.* ***Settlement***, 3m/5km SW of Tighnabruaich. **73 H4** NR9668.
Kilbride Point *High.* ***Coastal feature***, headland on E shore of Loch Snizort, Skye, 2m/4km NW of Uig. **93 J5** NG3766.
Kilbridemore *Arg. & B.* ***Settlement***, 5m/8km NE of Clachan of Glendaruel. **73 J1** NS0390.
Kilbucho *Sc.Bord.* ***Locality***, 2m/3km SW of Broughton. NT0835.
Kilburn *Derbys.* Population: 4809. ***Village***, 2m/4km SE of Belper. **41 F1** SK3845.
Kilburn *Gt.Lon.* ***Suburb***, in borough of Brent, 4m/6km NW of Charing Cross. TQ2583.
Kilburn *N.Yorks.* ***Village***, 6m/9km E of Thirsk. **58 B2** SE5179.
Kilby *Leics.* ***Village***, 6m/10km S of Leicester. **41 J6** SP6295.
Kilcadzow *S.Lan.* ***Settlement***, 3m/4km SE of Carluke. **75 G6** NS8848.
Kilchattan *Arg. & B.* ***Village***, on S side of the wide Kilchattan Bay on E coast of Bute, 2m/4km N of Garroch Head. **73 K5** NS1055.
Kilchattan Bay *Arg. & B.* ***Bay***, on E coast of Bute, 2m/4km N of Garroch Head. **73 K5** NS1055.
Kilchenzie *Arg. & B.* ***Village***, in Kintyre, 4m/6km NW of Campbeltown. **66 A1** NR6724.
Kilcheran *Arg. & B.* ***Settlement***, on Lismore, 3m/5km NE of Rubha Fiart. **79 K4** NM8238.
Kilchiaran *Arg. & B.* ***Settlement***, near W coast of Rinns of Islay, at Kilchiaran Bay. **72 A5** NR2060.
Kilchiaran Bay *Arg. & B.* ***Bay***, on W coast of Rinns of Islay. **72 A5** NR2060.
Kilchoan *Arg. & B.* ***Settlement***, on N shore of Loch Melfort, 3m/5km W of Kilmelford. **79 J6** NM7913.
Kilchoan *High.* ***Village***, on S side of Ardnamurchan peninsula, in Lochaber district, 5m/8km SE of Point of Ardnamurchan. **79 F1** NM4863.
Kilchoan Bay *High.* ***Bay***, to W of Kilchoan village, on S side of Ardnamurchan peninsula. **79 F1** NM4863.
Kilchoman *Arg. & B.* ***Settlement***, 1km inland from Machir Bay, on W coast of Islay. **72 A4** NR2163.
Kilchrenan *Arg. & B.* ***Village***, in Argyll, 6m/10km SE of Taynuilt. **80 B5** NN0322.
Kilchrist *Arg. & B.* ***Locality***, on Kintyre, 3m/4km SW of Campbeltown. **66 A2** NR6917.
Kilchurn Castle *Arg. & B.* ***Castle***, remains of castle (Historic Scotland), dating partly from 15c, at NE end of Loch Awe 2m/3km W of Dalmally, Argyll. **80 C5** NN1327.
Kilconquhar *Fife* ***Village***, 1m/2km N of Elie. **83 F7** NO4802.
Kilcot *Glos.* ***Village***, 2m/3km W of Newent. **29 F6** SO6925.
Kilcoy *High.* ***Locality***, in Ross and Cromarty district, 3m/5km E of Muir of Ord. **96 C6** NH5751.
Kilcreggan *Arg. & B.* Population: 1586. ***Village***, at S end of peninsula between Gare Loch and Loch Long, opposite Gourock across Firth of Clyde. Ferry for pedestrians to Gourock. **74 A2** NS2380.
Kildale *N.Yorks.* ***Village***, 5m/8km E of Stokesley. **63 H6** NZ6009.
Kildale Moor *N.Yorks.* ***Open space***, moorland 2m/3km SW of Redcar. **63 G6** NZ6108.
Kildalton *Arg. & B.* ***Locality***, at SE end of Islay, 1m/2km NE of Ardbeg. Graveyard of chapel has 8c carved Celtic cross. NR4347.
Kildalton Church and Crosses *Arg. & B.* ***Ecclesiastical building***, 7m/11km NE of Port Ellen, Islay. Churchyard contains one of finest Celtic crosses in Scotland. **72 C6** NR4550.
Kildary *High.* ***Hamlet***, 6m/9km NE of Invergordon. **96 E4** NH7675.
Kildavie *Arg. & B.* ***Settlement***, at S end of Kintyre, 3m/4km NE of Southend. **66 B2** NR7210.
Kildermorie Forest *High.* ***Open space***, deer forest in Ross and Cromarty district to W of Loch Morie. **96 B4** NH4678.
Kildermorie Lodge *High.* ***Settlement***, 9m/15km NW of Alness. **96 C4** NH5177.
Kildonan *N.Ayr.* ***Locality***, at S end of Arran, 1m/2km SW of Dippin Head. **66 E1** NS0321.
Kildonan Burn *High.* ***River***, in Sutherland district, flowing into River Helmsdale, 1km S of Kildonan Lodge. Gold deposits found here in 19c. **104 E6** NC9120.
Kildonan Castle *N.Ayr.* ***Castle***, ruined keep on rocky cliff to E of Kildonan, Arran. **66 E1** NS0320.
Kildonan Lodge *High.* ***Settlement***, in Strath of Kildonan, Sutherland district, 8m/13km NW of Helmsdale. **104 E6** NC9120.
Kildonnan *High.* ***Locality***, on E coast of Eigg. **85 K6** NM4985.
Kildrochet *D. & G.* ***Settlement***, 3m/5km S of Stranraer. **64 A5** NX0856.
Kildrum *N.Lan.* ***Suburb***, to E of Cumbernauld town centre. NS7675.
Kildrummy *Aber.* ***Locality***, 3m/4km S of Lumsden. **90 C3** NJ4717.
Kildrummy Castle *Aber.* ***Castle***, ruined 13c castle (Historic Scotland) 1m/2km SW of Kildrummy, dismantled after Jacobite rising of 1715. Gardens notable for shrubs and alpines, and include ancient quarry and water gardens. **90 C3** NJ4516.
Kildwick *N.Yorks.* ***Village***, 4m/7km NW of Keighley. 17c Kildwick Hall. Medieval bridge across River Aire. **57 F5** SE0145.
Kilennan *Arg. & B.* ***River***, flowing generally W from slopes of Beinn Bheigier into River Laggan, 9m/13km N of Port Ellen, Islay. **72 B5** NR3558.
Kilfinan *Arg. & B.* ***Village***, on E side of Loch Fyne, Argyll, 4m/7km NW of Tighnabruaich on Kyles of Bute. **73 H3** NR9378.

K

Kilfinan Bay *Arg. & B.* ***Bay***, 1m/2km W of Kilfinan, at mouth of Kilfinan Burn, on E side of Loch Fyne. **73 H3** NR9378.
Kilfinichen Bay *Arg. & B.* ***Bay***, on N side of Loch Scridain on Mull, with headland of Aird Kilfinichen to E. **79 F5** NM4828.
Kilfinnan *High.* ***Settlement***, at NE end of Loch Lochy, 1m/2km SW of Laggan. **87 J5** NN2795.
Kilgetty (Cilgeti). *Pembs.* ***Village***, 4m/7km N of Tenby. **16 E4** SN1207.
Kilgwrrwg Common *Mon.* ***Settlement***, 4m/7km NW of Chepstow. **19 H2** ST4797.
Kilham *E.Riding* ***Village***, 5m/8km NE of Great Driffield. Site of Roman villa 2km E. **59 G3** TA0664.
Kilham *Northumb.* ***Settlement***, 2m/4km NW of Kirknewton. **77 G7** NT8832.
Kilham Hill *Northumb.* ***Mountain***, in Cheviot Hills, 1m/2km NW of Westnewton. Height 1109 feet or 338 metres. **77 G7** NT8731.
Kili Holm *Ork.* ***Island***, small uninhabited island lying off N end of Egilsay. **106 D4** HY4732.
Kilkenneth *Arg. & B.* ***Settlement***, 1km NE of Middleton, near W coast of Tiree. **78 A3** NL9444.
Kilkenny *Glos.* ***Settlement***, 2m/3km W of Shipton. **30 B7** SP0018.
Kilkerran *Arg. & B.* ***Settlement***, on Kintyre, adjoining to SE of Campbeltown. **66 B2** NR7219.
Kilkerran *S.Ayr.* ***Locality***, house and estate 4m/7km S of Maybole. **67 H3** NS3002.
Kilkhampton *Cornw.* ***Village***, 4m/7km NE of Bude. **6 A4** SS2511.
Killamarsh *Derbys.* Population: 8872. ***Small town***, 4m/6km NE of Staveley. **51 G4** SK4580.
Killantringan Bay *D. & G.* *See Black Head.*
Killantringan Lighthouse *D. & G.* *See Black Head.*
Killay *Swan.* ***Suburb***, 3m/5km W of Swansea city centre. **17 K5** SS6092.
Killbeg *Arg. & B.* ***Settlement***, on Mull, 2m/3km SE of Salen. **79 H3** NM6041.
Killean *Arg. & B.* ***Settlement***, 4m/6km SW of Inveraray. **80 B7** NN0404.
Killean *Arg. & B.* ***Settlement***, on W side of Kintyre, Argyll, 1km S of Tayinloan. Remains of medieval church. **72 E6** NR6944.

K

Killearn *Stir.* Population: 1816. ***Village***, 5m/8km NW of Strathblane. Obelisk commemorates George Buchanan, 16c reformer, and tutor to James VI of Scotland. **74 D2** NS5286.
Killegray *W.Isles* ***Island***, uninhabited island in Sound of Harris, 3m/5km SW of Leverburgh, W coast of Harris. Nearly 3km long NW to SE and nearly 1km wide. **92 E3** NF9783.
Killellan *Arg. & B.* ***Locality***, on Kintyre, 4m/6km SW of Campbeltown. **66 A2** NR6815.
Killen *High.* ***Settlement***, on Black Isle, Ross and Cromarty district, 3m/5km W of Fortrose. **96 D6** NH6758.
Killerby *Darl.* ***Village***, 7m/11km NW of Darlington. **62 C4** NZ1919.
Killerby *N.Yorks.* ***Locality***, 2m/3km SE of Catterick. SE2595.
Killerby Halls *N.Yorks.* ***Settlement***, 1km SE of Cayton. TA0682.
Killerton *Devon* ***Hamlet***, 5m/8km SW of Cullompton, on E side of Killerton Park (National Trust). SS9700.
Killerton House *Devon* ***Historic house***, to W of Budlake, 5m/8km NE of Exeter. National Trust property containing garden with collection of rare trees and shrubs, surrounded by Killerton Park (National Trust). **7 H5** SS9700.
Killhope Moor *Dur.* ***Open space***, moorland to S of Coalcleugh Moor, 2m/3km E of Nenthead. **61 K2** NY8043.
Killichonan *P. & K.* ***Village***, on N side of Loch Rannoch, 3m/4km from head of reservoir. Waterfall in burn to E. **81 G2** NN5458.
Killichonan Burn *P. & K.* ***River***, flowing SW into Loch Rannoch at Killichonan. **81 G2** NN5457.
Killichronan *Arg. & B.* ***Settlement***, on Mull, 1km N of Gruline. **79 G3** NM5441.
Killiechanate *High.* ***Settlement***, 1m/2km E of Spean Bridge. **87 J6** NN2481.
Killiechonate Forest *High.* ***Open space***, deer forest in Lochaber district NE of Ben Nevis. **87 J7** NN2174.
Killiecrankie *P. & K.* ***Village***, on River Garry, 3m/5km SE of Blair Atholl, at head of Pass of Killiecrankie (National Trust for Scotland), wooded gorge. To NW is site of battle of 1689 in which troops of King William III were defeated by Jacobites under Graham of Claverhouse ('Bonnie Dundee') who, however, was mortally wounded in the battle. **82 A1** NN9162.
Killiehuntly *High.* ***Settlement***, 3m/4km SE of Kingussie. **88 E5** NN7998.
Killiemor *Arg. & B.* ***Settlement***, 3m/4km W of Gruline, Mull. **79 F4** NM5040.
Killilan *High.* ***Settlement***, in Skye and Lochalsh district, 1m/2km E of head of Loch Long. **87 F1** NG9430.
Killilan Forest *High.* ***Open space***, deer forest to E of Killilan. **87 G1** NG9430.
Killimster *High.* ***Locality***, in Caithness district, 5m/8km NW of Wick. **105 J3** ND3156.
Killin *High.* ***River***, formed from confluence of several tributaries between Meall nan Ruadhag and Carn a' Choire Ghlaise, and flowing N into Loch Killin. NH5309.
Killin *High.* ***Settlement***, to E of Loch Brora, 2m/3km SE of Gordonbush, Sutherland district. **97 F1** NC8507.
Killin *Stir.* ***Village***, at confluence of Rivers Dochart and Lochay, at head of Loch Tay. **81 G4** NN5732.
Killin Rock *High.* ***Hill***, with rock outcrops to S and W, 1m/2km SE of Killin. Height 705 feet or 215 metres. **97 F1** NC8605.
Killinallan *Arg. & B.* ***Settlement***, on N coast of Islay, 5m/9km N of Bridgend. **72 B3** NR3171.
Killinallan Point *Arg. & B.* ***Coastal feature***, headland on E side of Loch Gruinart on N coast of Islay, before loch widens out into bay enclosed by Ardnave Point and Gortantaoid Point. **72 A3** NR3072.
Killinghall *N.Yorks.* ***Village***, 2m/4km N of Harrogate. **57 H4** SE2858.
Killington *Cumb.* ***Hamlet***, 3m/5km SW of Sedbergh. **56 B1** SD6189.
Killington *Devon* ***Settlement***, 4m/6km SW of Lynton. SS6646.
Killington Reservoir *Cumb.* ***Reservoir***, large reservoir 2m/3km NW of Killington. **61 G7** SD6189.
Killingworth *T. & W.* Population: 17,315. ***Suburb***, along with Killingworth Township to W, 4m/7km N of Newcastle upon Tyne. **71 H6** NZ2870.
Killingworth Township *T. & W.* ***Suburb***, to W of Killingworth, 4m/7km N of Newcastle upon Tyne. NZ2871.
Killochan Castle *S.Ayr.* ***Historic house***, 16c mansion on N side of Water of Girvan 3m/5km NE of Girvan. **67 G4** NS2200.
Killochyett *Sc.Bord.* ***Locality***, on Gala Water, adjoining to N of Stow. **76 C6** NT4545.
Killocraw *Arg. & B.* ***Settlement***, on W coast of Kintyre, 7m/11km NW of Campbeltown. **66 A1** NR6630.
Killunaig *Arg. & B.* ***Settlement***, on S side of Loch Scridain, 1m/2km W of Pennyghael, Mull. **79 F5** NM4925.
Killundine *High.* ***Settlement***, on E shore on Sound of Mull, 4m/6km SE of Drimnin, Lochaber district. **79 G3** NM5849.
Kilmacolm *Inclyde* Population: 4343. ***Small town***, former weaving centre, 6m/10km SE of Greenock. **74 B4** NS3569.
Kilmaha *Arg. & B.* ***Settlement***, 3m/5km SW of Dalavich. **80 A7** NM9408.
Kilmahog *Stir.* ***Settlement***, on N bank of River Leny, 1m/2km W of Callander. Site of Roman fort on S bank, towards town. **81 H7** NN6108.
Kilmalieu *High.* ***Settlement***, near NW shore of Loch Linnhe, 3m/4km NE of Rubha na h-Airde Uinnsinn. **79 K2** NM8955.
Kilmaluag *High.* ***Locality***, near N coast of Skye, 2m/3km S of Rubha na h-Aiseig. **93 K4** NG4273.
Kilmaluag Bay *High.* ***Bay***, 1m/2km NE of Kilmaluag, Skye. **93 K4** NG4374.
Kilmany *Fife* ***Village***, 4m/7km SW of Newport-on-Tay. **82 E5** NO3821.
Kilmar Tor *Cornw.* ***Mountain***, on Bodmin Moor, 2m/3km W of Bathpool. Height 1279 feet or 390 metres. **4 C3** SX2575.
Kilmarie *High.* ***Locality***, on E side of Strathaird peninsula, Skye, 4m/7km N of Strathaird Point. **86 B3** NG5517.
Kilmarnock *E.Ayr.* Population: 44,307. ***Town***, 19m/31km SW of Glasgow. Once known for a variety of industries, including locomotive-building and distilling. Associations with Robert Burns; Burns monument and museum. Dean Castle, dating from 14c, is now a museum. **74 C7** NS4237.
Kilmarnock Hill *Arg. & B.* ***Mountain***, 2m/3km SW of Black Craig. Height 1296 feet or 395 metres. **73 K3** NS1073.
Kilmartin *Arg. & B.* ***Village***, in Argyll, 3m/5km NE of Crinan Loch. Damaged 9c cross (Historic Scotland) in churchyard. Remains of 16c castle keep. Kilmartin Burn flows S past village to River Add, 3m/5km S. Many prehistoric remains in vicinity. **73 G1** NR8398.
Kilmartin Castle *Arg. & B.* ***Castle***, ruins of castle on edge of Kilmartin village, 7m/11km N of Lochgilphead. **73 G1** NR8399.
Kilmartin Sculptured Stones *Arg. & B.* ***Historic/prehistoric site***, graveyard in Kilmartin containing 16c carved crosses (Historic Scotland), 8m/12km N of Lochgilphead. **73 G1** NR8398.
Kilmaurs *E.Ayr.* Population: 2744. ***Village***, 2m/4km NW of Kilmarnock. **74 C6** NS4141.
Kilmein Hill *E.Ayr.* ***Mountain***, 3m/4km E of Patna. Height 1407 feet or 429 metres. **67 J2** NS4511.
Kilmelford *Arg. & B.* ***Village***, in Argyll, at head of Loch Melfort. **79 K6** NM8413.
Kilmeny *Arg. & B.* ***Settlement***, on Islay, 1km SW of Ballygrant. NR3965.
Kilmersdon *Som.* ***Village***, 2m/3km S of Radstock. **19 K6** ST6952.
Kilmeston *Hants.* ***Village***, 4m/7km S of New Alresford. **11 G2** SU5926.
Kilmichael *Arg. & B.* ***Settlement***, on Kintyre, 2m/3km NW of Campbeltown. **66 A1** NR6922.
Kilmichael Glassary *Arg. & B.* ***Village***, in Argyll, 4m/6km N of Lochgilphead across River Add. Cup and ring marked rocks (Historic Scotland). To NE is moorland area of Kilmichael Forest. **73 G1** NR8593.
Kilmichael of Inverlussa *Arg. & B.* ***Settlement***, on E side of Loch Sween in Knapdale, Argyll, 5m/8km S of Crinan. **73 F2** NR7785.
Kilmington *Devon* ***Village***, 2m/3km W of Axminster. **8 B5** SY2897.
Kilmington *Wilts.* ***Village***, 4m/6km NW of Mere. **9 G1** ST7736.
Kilmington Common *Wilts.* ***Hamlet***, to S of Kilmington, 4m/6km NW of Mere. ST7736.
Kilmington Street *Wilts.* ***Hamlet***, to SE of Kilmington. **9 G1** ST7736.
Kilmorack *High.* ***Village***, on River Beauly, 2m/3km SW of Beauly town, in Inverness district. **96 B7** NH4944.
Kilmore *Arg. & B.* ***Settlement***, in Argyll, 4m/6km SE of Oban. **79 K5** NM8825.
Kilmore *High.* ***Settlement***, on E coast of Sleat peninsula, Skye, 1m/2km SW of Teangue. Site of Sleat parish church. **86 C4** NG6507.
Kilmory *Arg. & B.* ***Settlement***, in Knapdale, Argyll, 2m/3km N of Point of Knap. **73 F3** NR7075.
Kilmory *Arg. & B.* ***Settlement***, on shore of Linne Mhuirich, 3m/4km SW of Tayvallich. **73 F2** NR7283.
Kilmory *High.* ***River***, flowing N into sea on N coast of Rum. **85 J4** NG3603.
Kilmory *High.* ***Settlement***, at mouth of Kilmory River, on N coast of Rum. **85 J4** NG3603.
Kilmory *High.* ***Settlement***, on Ardnamurchan, Lochaber district, 4m/6km SW of Rubha Aird Druimnich. **79 G1** NM5270.
Kilmory *N.Ayr.* ***Hamlet***, near S coast of Arran, 7m/11km SW of Lamlash. NR9621.
Kilmory Bay *Arg. & B.* ***Bay***, small bay to SW of Kilmory, 12m/20km SW of Lochgilphead. **72 E3** NR7075.
Kilmory Chapel *Arg. & B.* ***Historic/prehistoric site***, 13c chapel containing collection of Celtic and later sculptured stones. Macmillan's Cross (Historic Scotland), late 15c sculptured cross outside chapel. **73 F3** NR7075.
Kilmory Water *N.Ayr.* ***River***, running SW past Kilmory to sea 1km to SW. **66 D1** NR9521.
Kilmote *High.* ***Settlement***, 2m/3km NE of Lothbeg, Sutherland district. **104 E7** NC9711.
Kilmuir *High.* ***Settlement***, to SE of Dunvegan, Skye. **93 H7** NG2547.
Kilmuir *High.* ***Settlement***, near N coast of Skye, 5m/7km N of Uig. **93 J4** NG3770.
Kilmuir *High.* ***Settlement***, 2m/4km N of Inverness across Moray Firth. **96 D7** NH6649.
Kilmuir *High.* ***Settlement***, on Nigg Bay, N side of Cromarty Firth, 4m/7km NE of Invergordon, Ross and Cromarty district. **96 E4** NH7573.
Kilmun *Arg. & B.* ***Village***, on N side of Holy Loch, in Argyll, 1m/2km NW of Strone Point. **73 K2** NS1781.
Kilmux *Fife* ***Settlement***, 2m/3km NE of Kennoway. **82 E7** NO3604.
Kiln Green *Gt.Man.* ***Settlement***, adjoining to S of Diggle, 6m/9km E of Oldham. SE0007.
Kiln Green *Here.* ***Hamlet***, 3m/4km S of Ross-on-Wye. SO6019.
Kiln Green *W'ham* ***Hamlet***, 2m/4km NE of Twyford. **22 B4** SU8178.
Kiln Pit Hill *Northumb.* ***Hamlet***, 5m/8km NW of Consett. **62 B1** NZ0355.
Kilnave *Arg. & B.* ***Locality***, on W side of Loch Gruinart, on N coast of Islay. **72 A3** NR2870.
Kilndown *Kent* ***Village***, 2m/3km SW of Goudhurst. **14 C4** TQ7035.
Kilneuair *Arg. & B.* ***Locality***, with ruined church on E side of Loch Awe in Argyll, 1m/2km E of head of loch. NM8803.
Kilnhill *Cumb.* ***Locality***, 1m/2km W of Bassenthwaite. NY2132.
Kilnhouse *Ches.* ***Locality***, 1m/2km W of Winsford. SJ6366.
Kilnhurst *S.Yorks.* ***Locality***, 4m/6km NE of Rotherham. **51 G3** SK4597.
Kilninian *Arg. & B.* ***Village***, on N side of Loch Tuath, Mull, 4m/6km S of Calgary. **79 F3** NM3945.
Kilninver *Arg. & B.* ***Village***, in Argyll, 6m/9km S of Oban across Loch Feochan. **79 K5** NM8221.
Kilnsea *E.Riding* ***Hamlet***, at N end of spit of land running out to Spurn Head, on N side of mouth of River Humber. **53 H1** TA4015.
Kilnsea Clays *E.Riding* ***Coastal feature***, mud flat in mouth of River Humber, bounded by Spurn Head to E. **53 H1** TA4114.
Kilnsey *N.Yorks.* ***Hamlet***, in Wharfedale, 3m/5km NW of Grassington. **56 E3** SD9767.
Kilnwick *E.Riding* ***Village***, 7m/11km N of Beverley. **59 G5** SE9949.
Kilnwick Percy *E.Riding* ***Settlement***, 2m/3km E of Pocklington. SE8249.
Kiloran *Arg. & B.* ***Settlement***, on Colonsay, 2m/3km N of Scalasaig. **72 B1** NR3996.
Kiloran Bay *Arg. & B.* ***Bay***, 1m/2km N of Kiloran, on NW coast of Colonsay. **72 B1** NR3996.
Kiloran Gardens *Arg. & B.* ***Garden***, on N part of Colonsay. Contains sub-tropical plants. **72 B1** NR3996.
Kilpatrick *N.Ayr.* ***Settlement***, on W coast of Arran, at Kilpatrick Point. **66 D1** NR9027.
Kilpatrick Hills *W.Dun.* ***Large natural feature***, range of low hills to E of Dumbarton. Summit is Duncolm, 1316 feet or 401 metres. **74 C3** NS4676.
Kilpeck *Here.* ***Village***, 4m/6km NE of Pontrilas. **28 D5** SO4430.
Kilpheder *W.Isles* *Anglicised form of Cille Pheadair, qv.*
Kilphedir *High.* ***Settlement***, at confluence of Allt Cille Pheadair and River Helmsdale, 3m/5km NW of Helmsdale. **104 E7** NC9818.
Kilpin *E.Riding* ***Village***, 2m/3km SE of Howden. **58 D7** SE7526.
Kilpin Pike *E.Riding* ***Hamlet***, on N bank of River Ouse, 1m/2km SE of Howden. SE7526.
Kilrenny *Fife* ***Village***, 1m/2km NE of Anstruther. Forms part of Royal Burgh of Kilrenny, Anstruther Easter and Anstruther Wester. **83 G7** NO5704.
Kilrie *Ches.* ***Locality***, adjoining to W of Knutsford. SJ7478.
Kilsby *Northants.* ***Village***, 5m/7km SE of Rugby. **31 G1** SP5671.
Kilspindie *P. & K.* ***Village***, 7m/11km E of Perth. **82 D5** NO2225.
Kilstay *D. & G.* ***Settlement***, 1m/2km N of Drummore on W side of Luce Bay. **64 B7** NX1238.
Kilsyth *N.Lan.* Population: 9918. ***Small town***, 3m/5km NW of Cumbernauld. 1m/2km E is site, now submerged by reservoir, of battle of 1645 in which Montrose defeated Covenanters. **75 F3** NS7178.
Kilsyth Hills *N.Lan.* ***Large natural feature***, upland area running NE from Campsie Fells, to NW of Kilsyth. Bounded by Carron Valley Reservoir to N and River Kelvin valley to S. Notable peaks include Garrel Muir at 1502 feet or 458 metres, Tomtain at 1486 feet or 453 metres and Laird's Hill at 1394 feet or 425 metres. **74 E3** NS6679.
Kiltarlity *High.* ***Village***, in Inverness district, 3m/5km S of Beauly. **96 C7** NH5041.

Kilton *Notts.* ***Suburb***, E district of Worksop. SK5979.
Kilton *R. & C.* ***Hamlet***, 1m/2km SE of Brotton. **63 H5** NZ7018.
Kilton *Som.* ***Hamlet***, 3m/5km NE of Nether Stowey. **7 K1** ST1643.
Kilton Thorpe *R. & C.* ***Hamlet***, 1km SW of Kilton. NZ7018.
Kiltyre *P. & K.* ***Settlement***, on N side of Loch Tay, 4m/7km NE of Killin. **81 H4** NN6236.
Kilvaxter *High.* ***Settlement***, on Skye, 4m/7km N of Uig. **93 J5** NG3869.
Kilve *Som.* ***Village***, 3m/5km NW of Nether Stowey. **7 K1** ST1442.
Kilverstone *Norf.* ***Settlement***, 2m/3km NE of Thetford. **44 C7** TL8984.
Kilvey *Swan.* ***Suburb***, to E of Swansea city centre across River Tawe. SS6693.
Kilvey Hill *Swan.* ***Hill***, to E of Kilvey. Height 633 feet or 193 metres. **17 K5** SS6693.
Kilvey Hill Windmill *Swan.* ***Historic/prehistoric site***, remains of windmill situated near summit of Kilvey Hill, 2m/3km NE of Swansea city centre. **17 K5** SS6793.
Kilvington *Notts.* ***Village***, 7m/11km S of Newark-on-Trent. **42 B1** SK8042.
Kilwinning *N.Ayr.* Population: 15,479. ***Town***, 5m/7km E of Ardrossan. Ruined 12c abbey. Dalgaven Mill dates from 1620. **74 B6** NS3043.
Kilwinning Abbey *N.Ayr.* ***Ecclesiastical building***, scant remains of abbey founded in 12c at Kilwinning. **74 B6** NS3043.
Kimberley *Norf.* ***Hamlet***, 3m/5km NW of Wymondham. **44 E5** TG0704.
Kimberley *Notts.* Population: 10,488. ***Town***, 5m/9km NW of Nottingham. **41 H1** SK5044.
Kimberley Street *Norf.* ***Hamlet***, 3m/5km NW of Wymondham. TG0704.
Kimberworth *S.Yorks.* ***Suburb***, 1m/2km W of Rotherham town centre. SK4092.
Kimble Wick *Bucks.* ***Settlement***, 3m/4km N of Princes Risborough. **22 B1** SP8007.
Kimblesworth *Dur.* ***Village***, 3m/5km N of Durham. **62 D2** NZ2547.
Kimbolton *Cambs.* ***Village***, 7m/11km NW of St. Neots. Castle, partly 16c and 17c, but mainly 18c, by Vanbrugh. **32 E2** TL0967.
Kimbolton *Here.* ***Village***, 3m/4km NE of Leominster. **28 E2** SO5261.
Kimbridge *Hants.* ***Settlement***, on River Test, 3m/5km NW of Romsey. SU3225.
Kimcote *Leics.* ***Village***, 4m/6km NW of Husbands Bosworth. **41 H7** SP5886.
Kimmeridge *Dorset* ***Village***, between Purbeck Hills and coast, 5m/8km S of Wareham. **9 J7** SY9179.
Kimmerston *Northumb.* ***Settlement***, 1m/2km SE of Ford. **77 H7** NT9535.
Kimpton *Hants.* ***Village***, 5m/9km W of Andover. **21 F7** SU2846.
Kimpton *Herts.* Population: 2247. ***Village***, 4m/6km NE of Harpenden. **32 E7** TL1718.
Kinaldy *Fife* ***Settlement***, 4m/6km S of St. Andrews. **83 G6** NO5110.
Kinaldy Burn *Fife* ***River***, small stream, which is a continuation of Lathockar Burn, flowing NE to join with Cameron Burn to form Kenly Water, 4m/6km SE of St. Andrews and 3m/5km from where Kenley Water flows into North Sea. **83 G7** NO5411.
Kinblethmont *Angus* ***Locality***, 4m/6km N of Arbroath. **83 H3** NO6346.
Kinbrace *High.* ***Village***, in Sutherland district, 15m/24km NW of Helmsdale. **104 D5** NC8631.
Kinbrace Burn *High.* ***River***, in Sutherland district, flowing W into River Helmsdale, 1m/2km S of Burnfoot. **104 E5** NC8628.
Kinbreack *High.* ***Settlement***, near head of Glen Kingie, 14m/24km NW of Fort William. **87 G5** NN0096.
Kinbuck *Stir.* ***Village***, on Allan Water, 3m/4km N of Dunblane. **81 J7** NN7905.
Kincaldrum *Angus* ***Settlement***, 4m/6km S of Forfar. **83 F3** NO4344.
Kincaple *Fife* ***Settlement***, 3m/5km NW of St. Andrews. **83 F6** NO4618.
Kincardine (Also known as Kincardine-on-Forth.) *Fife* Population: 3184. ***Small town***, former ship-building centre and port on River Forth, 4m/7km SE of Alloa. Ruined Tulliallan Castle dates from 15c. **75 H2** NS9387.
Kincardine *High.* ***Village***, near head of Dornoch Firth, 1m/2km S of Ardgay, Sutherland district. **96 D3** NH6089.
Kincardine Castle *P. & K.* ***Historic house***, 19c mansion beside Ruthven Water, 1m/2km S of Auchterarder. To SW is fragment of old castle, dismantled in 1645. **82 A7** NN9411.
Kincardine-on-Forth *Fife Alternative name for Kincardine, qv.*
Kincardine O'Neil *Aber.* ***Village***, on N side of River Dee, 7m/11km W of Banchory. **90 D5** NO5999.
Kinclaven *P. & K.* ***Settlement***, 1m/2km SW of Meikleour across River Tay. **82 C4** NO1538.
Kincorth *Aberdeen* ***Suburb***, 2m/3km S of Aberdeen city centre across River Dee. **91 H4** NJ9303.
Kincraig *Aber.* ***Settlement***, 3m/4km W of Newburgh. **91 H2** NJ9624.
Kincraig *High.* ***Village***, on River Spey, in Badenoch and Strathspey district, 6m/9km NE of Kingussie. **89 F4** NH8305.
Kincraig Point *Fife* ***Coastal feature***, headland at E end of Largo Bay. **76 C1** NT4699.
Kincraigie *P. & K.* ***Settlement***, on W side of Strath Tay, 6m/10km SE of Pitlochry. **82 A3** NN9849.
Kindallachan *P. & K.* ***Village***, in Strath Tay, 5m/8km N of Dunkeld. **82 A3** NN9949.
Kinder Low *Derbys.* ***Mountain***, SW edge of Kinder Scout, 3m/4km E of Hayfield. Height 2076 feet or 633 metres. **50 C4** SK0787.
Kinder Reservoir *Derbys.* ***Reservoir***, 1m/2km NE of Hayfield, W of Kinder Scout. **50 C4** SK0588.
Kinder Scout *Derbys.* ***Mountain***, summit of High Peak on Edale Moor, 5m/8km SE of Glossop. Height 2086 feet or 636 metres. **50 C4** SK0887.
Kindrochit Castle *Aber.* ***Castle***, ruined 14c castle, originally a hunting lodge at S side of Braemar on E side of Clunie Water. **89 J5** NO1591.
Kinellar *Aber.* ***Locality***, includes Muir of Kinellar and Kinellar House, 1km W of Blackburn. **91 G3** NJ8112.
Kineton *Glos.* ***Hamlet***, 6m/10km W of Stow-on-the-Wold. **30 B6** SP0926.
Kineton *Warks.* Population: 2079. ***Village***, 10m/15km NW of Banbury. Motte and bailey castle. Site of Battle of Edgehill, 1642, 2m/3km SE. **30 E3** SP3351.
Kineton Green *W.Mid.* ***Locality***, 2m/4km NW of Solihull town centre. **40 D7** SP1281.
Kinfare *Staffs. Alternative name for Kinver, qv.*
Kinfauns *P. & K.* ***Village***, 3m/5km E of Perth across River Tay. **82 C5** NO1622.
Kinfauns Forest *P. & K.* ***Forest/woodland***, to NE of Kinfauns. **82 C5** NO1622.
King Charles's Castle *I.o.S.* ***Castle***, on NW coast of Tresco. 16c coastal fort (English Heritage) reinforced during Civil War by Charles I. **2 B1** SV8816.
King Doniert's Stone (Also known as Doniert Stone.) *Cornw.* ***Historic/prehistoric site***, 9c inscribed stone (English Heritage), 1m/2km NW of St. Cleer. **4 C4** SX2369.
King Edward *Aber.* ***Locality***, 4m/7km S of Banff. Castle of King Edward, medieval ruin 1m/2km S. NJ7157.
King Harry Passage (Also known as King Harry's Reach.) *Cornw.* ***River***, reach of River Fal, 3m/5km S of Truro. King Harry Ferry conveys vehicles across river. SW8439.
King Harry's Reach *Cornw. Alternative name for King Harry Passage, qv.*
King John Bridge *Glos.* ***Bridge***, consists of two bridges over Rivers Avon and Mill Avon at Tewkesbury, joined by causeway. Dates from 13c. SO8933.
King John's House *Wilts. See Tollard Royal.*
King John's Hunting Lodge *Som.* ***Historic house***, restored early Tudor merchant's house (National Trust), in Axbridge. **19 H6** ST4354.
King Sterndale *Derbys.* ***Settlement***, 3m/4km E of Buxton. **50 C5** SK0972.
King Water *Cumb.* ***River***, flowing SW to confluence with River Irthing, 1m/2km N of Brampton. **70 A7** NY5263.
Kingarth *Arg. & B.* ***Village***, on Bute 3m/5km N of Garroch Head. **73 J5** NS0956.
Kingates *I.o.W.* ***Hamlet***, 1m/2km N of Niton. SZ5177.
Kingcoed (Cyncoed). *Mon.* ***Hamlet***, 2m/3km SE of Raglan. **19 H1** SO4205.
Kingerby *Lincs.* ***Hamlet***, 4m/7km NW of Market Rasen. **52 D3** TF0592.
Kingham *Oxon.* ***Village***, 4m/6km SW of Chipping Norton. **30 D6** SP2624.
Kingholm Quay *D. & G.* ***Hamlet***, on E bank of River Nith, 2m/3km S of Dumfries. **65 K3** NX9773.
Kinghorn *Fife* Population: 2931. ***Small town***, popular small resort on Firth of Forth, 2m/3km E of Burntisland. Last Celtic King of Scotland, Alexander, died here in 1286. **76 A2** NT2686.
Kinghorn Loch *Fife* ***Lake/loch***, 1km W of Kinghorn. **76 A2** NT2587.
Kingie *High.* ***River***, in Lochaber district running E down Glen Kingie to River Garry, 2m/3km SE of dam of Loch Quoich. **87 G5** NH1000.
Kinglassie *Fife* Population: 1419. ***Village***, 2m/3km SW of Leslie. **76 A1** NT2398.
Kingledores Burn *Sc.Bord.* ***River***, rising on slopes of Coomb Dod, 3m/5km W of Tweedsmuir and flowing NE to River Tweed at Kingledores, 3m/4km N of Tweedsmuir. **69 F1** NT1028.
Kingley Vale Nature Reserve *W.Suss.* ***Nature reserve***, fine yew woodland, 3m/5km SW of West Dean. **12 B5** SU8210.
Kingmoor *Cumb.* ***Locality***, 2m/3km NW of Carlisle. NY3858.
Kingoodie *P. & K.* ***Locality***, on N side of Firth of Tay, 4m/7km W of Dundee. **82 E5** NO3329.
King's Acre *Here.* ***Settlement***, 3m/4km NW of Hereford. SO4741.
King's Bank *E.Suss.* ***Settlement***, 1km S of Beckley. TQ8523.
King's Bromley *Staffs.* ***Village***, on River Trent, 5m/8km N of Lichfield. **40 D4** SK1216.
King's Broom *Warks.* ***Locality***, adjoining to S of Broom, 7m/11km W of Stratford-upon-Avon. SP0953.
Kings Caple *Here.* ***Village***, 4m/6km NW of Ross-on-Wye across loops of River Wye. **28 E6** SO5628.
King's Cave *N.Ayr.* ***Other feature of interest***, cave on Arran, 1km NW of Torbeg and 2m/3km N of Blackwaterfoot. Possible setting for legend of Robert the Bruce and the spider; carvings on walls. **73 G7** NR8830.
King's Cliffe *Northants.* ***Village***, 5m/7km W of Wansford. **42 D6** TL0097.
King's College Chapel *Cambs.* ***Ecclesiastical building***, founded by Henry VI in Cambridge and built in late Perpendicular style. Particularly notable for stained glass windows, fan vaulting and organ screen. **33 H3** TL4457.
King's Coughton *Warks.* ***Hamlet***, 1m/2km N of Alcester. **30 B3** SP0858.
King's Delph *Cambs.* ***Open space***, fenland 3m/5km SE of Peterborough city centre. **43 F6** TL2395.
King's Forest of Geltsdale (Also known as Geltsdale.) *Cumb.* ***Large natural feature***, moorland area to E and NE of Cumrew, 8m/12km NW of Alston. **61 G1** NY5852.
King's Furlong *Hants.* ***Suburb***, S of Basingstoke town centre. SU6251.
King's Green *Glos.* ***Hamlet***, 4m/7km SE of Ledbury. **29 G5** SO7633.
King's Heath *Northants.* ***Suburb***, 1m/2km NW of Northampton town centre. SP7362.
King's Heath *W.Mid.* ***Suburb***, 4m/6km S of Birmingham city centre. **40 C7** SP0781.
King's Hill *Warks.* ***Settlement***, 3m/5km S of Coventry city centre. SP3274.
King's Hill *W.Mid.* ***Locality***, 1km S of Darlaston town centre. **40 B6** SO9896.
Kings Langley *Herts.* Population: 8144. ***Village***, 3m/5km S of Hemel Hempstead. **22 D1** TL0702.
King's Lynn *Norf.* Population: 41,281. ***Town***, and port on River Great Ouse, 39m/63km W of Norwich. 17c Customs House. Market places known as Tuesday Market and Saturday Market. 15c St. George's Guildhall (National Trust). **44 A3** TF6119.
King's Meaburn *Cumb.* ***Village***, on River Lyvennet, 4m/7km W of Appleby-in-Westmorland. **61 H4** NY6221.
King's Men *Oxon. See Little Rollright.*
King's Moss *Gt.Man.* ***Village***, 2m/3km NW of Billinge. SD5001.
Kings Muir *Sc.Bord.* ***Locality***, adjoining to S of Peebles. **76 A7** NT2539.
King's Newnham *Warks.* ***Settlement***, 4m/6km NW of Rugby. SP4577.
King's Newton *Derbys.* ***Hamlet***, 1m/2km NE of Melbourne. **41 F3** SK3926.
King's Norton *Leics.* ***Village***, 7m/11km SE of Leicester. **41 J5** SK6800.
King's Norton *W.Mid.* ***Suburb***, 5m/8km S of Birmingham city centre. N end of Stratford-upon-Avon Canal. **30 B1** SP0478.
King's Nympton *Devon* ***Village***, 3m/5km N of Chulmleigh. **6 E4** SS6819.
King's Park *Glas.* ***Suburb***, 3m/5km S of Glasgow city centre. NS5961.
King's Pyon *Here.* ***Village***, 8m/13km NW of Hereford. **28 D3** SO4350.
Kings Ripton *Cambs.* ***Village***, 3m/5km NE of Huntingdon. **33 F1** TL2676.
King's Seat *P. & K.* ***Mountain***, 3m/5km SE of Burrelton. Height 1237 feet or 377 metres. **82 D4** NO2233.
King's Seat Hill *Clack.* ***Mountain***, on S edge of Ochil Hills, rising steeply 2m/4km NW of Dollar. Height 2125 feet or 648 metres. **75 H1** NS9399.
King's Sedge Moor *Som.* ***Marsh/bog***, part of Sedgemoor, marshy tract intersected by numerous dykes or rhynes cut for drainage purposes, at sea level, 5m/8km SW of Street. **8 D1** ST4033.
King's Sedgemoor Drain *Som. See Cary (river).*
King's Somborne *Hants.* ***Village***, 3m/4km S of Stockbridge. John of Gaunt's Deer Park to W. **10 E1** SU3631.
King's Stag (Sometimes spelled Kingstag.) *Dorset* ***Village***, 5m/8km SW of Sturminster Newton. Here Thomas de la Lynde killed a stag belonging to Henry III. **9 G3** ST7210.
King's Stanley *Glos.* ***Village***, 3m/4km SW of Stroud. **20 B1** SO8103.
King's Sutton *Northants.* Population: 2073. ***Village***, on River Cherwell, 4m/6km SE of Banbury across river. **31 F5** SP4936.
King's Tamerton *Plym.* ***Suburb***, NW district of Plymouth, 3m/5km from city centre. SX4558.
King's Walden *Herts.* ***Village***, 4m/6km SW of Hitchin. **32 E6** TL1623.
Kings Worthy *Hants.* Population: 4451. ***Village***, 2m/3km N of Winchester. **11 F1** SU4932.
Kingsand *Cornw.* ***Village***, on Cawsand Bay, 1m/2km SE of Millbrook. **4 E5** SX4350.
Kingsbarns *Fife* ***Village***, near coast, 3m/5km N of Crail. **83 G6** NO5912.
Kingsbridge *Devon* Population: 5258. ***Small town***, 11m/17km S of Totnes, at head of Kingsbridge Estuary. Medieval complex of Leigh Barton (English Heritage) 2m/3km NW. **5 H6** SX7344.
Kingsbridge *Som.* ***Village***, 4m/6km S of Dunster. **7 H2** SS9837.
Kingsbridge Estuary *Devon* ***Sea feature***, runs past Salcombe and out to sea between Bolt Head and Prawle Point. SX7441.
Kingsburgh *High.* ***Locality***, on E shore of Loch Snizort Beag, Skye. **93 J6** NG3955.
Kingsbury *Gt.Lon.* ***Suburb***, in borough of Brent, 8m/13km NW of Charing Cross. **22 E3** TQ2088.
Kingsbury *Warks.* Population: 4169. ***Village***, 5m/8km N of Coleshill. **40 E6** SP2196.
Kingsbury Episcopi *Som.* ***Village***, on River Parrett, 4m/6km S of Langport. **8 D2** ST4321.
Kingsbury Water Park *Warks.* ***Leisure/recreation***, watersport-based activity park set in 447 acres, to SW of Kingsbury. Shallow lagoons in N section of park form nature reserve, providing habitat for aquatic life and birds. **40 E6** SP2096.
Kingscavil *W.Loth.* ***Settlement***, 2m/3km E of Linlithgow. **75 J3** NT0376.
Kingsclere *Hants.* Population: 3295. ***Village***, 8m/13km NW of Basingstoke. Site of Royal Counties Show. **21 J6** SU5258.
Kingscote *Glos.* ***Village***, 3m/5km SW of Nailsworth. Site of Romano-British settlement 1km SW. **20 B2** ST8196.
Kingscott *Devon* ***Hamlet***, 3m/5km E of Great Torrington. **6 D4** SS5318.
Kingscross *N.Ayr.* ***Settlement***, near E coast of Arran, at S end of Lamlash Bay. **66 E1** NS0528.
Kingscross Point *N.Ayr.* ***Coastal feature***, headland to E of Kingscross on Arran. Site of Viking burial ground. **66 E1** NS0428.
Kingsdale *Fife* ***Suburb***, adjoining to S of Kennoway. **82 E7** NO3401.

K

Kingsdon *Som.* ***Village***, 3m/4km SE of Somerton. To E, Lyte's Cary (National Trust), old manor house. **8 E2** ST5126.
Kingsdon Hill *Som.* ***Hill***, to NW of Kingsdon, 2m/3km SE of Somerton. Height 282 feet or 86 metres. **8 D2** ST5126.
Kingsdown *Kent* ***Locality***, 3m/5km S of Sittingbourne. TQ9258.
Kingsdown *Kent* ***Village***, on coast, 3m/4km S of Deal. **15 J3** TR3748.
Kingsdown *Swin.* ***Suburb***, 2m/3km NE of Swindon town centre. SU1688.
Kingsdown *Wilts.* ***Village***, 4m/7km NE of Bath. ST8167.
Kingseat *Fife* ***Village***, 3m/5km NE of Dunfermline. **75 K1** NT1290.
Kingsey *Bucks.* ***Village***, 3m/4km E of Thame. **22 A1** SP7406.
Kingsfold *Pembs.* ***Settlement***, 1m/2km SW of Pembroke. **16 C5** SR9799.
Kingsfold *W.Suss.* ***Hamlet***, 4m/7km N of Horsham. **12 E3** TQ1636.
Kingsford *Aberdeen* ***Settlement***, 1m/2km E of Westhill. **91 G4** NJ8406.
Kingsford *Aber.* ***Settlement***, 1m/2km SW of Alford. **90 D3** NJ5614.
Kingsford *Aber.* ***Settlement***, 3m/5km S of Turriff. **99 F6** NJ7244.
Kingsford *E.Ayr.* ***Settlement***, 3m/4km NE of Stewarton. **74 C6** NS4448.
Kingsford *Worcs.* ***Hamlet***, 3m/5km N of Kidderminster. **40 A7** SO8181.
Kingsford Country Park *Worcs.* ***Leisure/recreation***, country park with over 180 acres of heathland and coniferous woodland, 3m/5km NE of Kidderminster. **40 A7** SO8281.
Kingsforth *N.Lincs.* ***Settlement***, 1m/2km S of Barton-upon-Humber. **52 D1** TA0319.
Kingsgate *Kent* ***Suburb***, 2m/3km E of Margate town centre. 18c castle on cliffs to E. **25 K4** TR3870.
Kingshall Green *Suff.* ***Settlement***, to NE of Bradfield St. George. TL9160.
Kingshall Street *Suff.* ***Hamlet***, 4m/7km E of Bury St. Edmunds. TL9161.
Kingsheanton *Devon* ***Hamlet***, 2m/4km N of Barnstaple. **6 D2** SS5537.
Kingsholm *Glos.* ***Suburb***, N district of Gloucester. SO8319.
Kingshott *Herts.* ***Locality***, 1m/2km SE of Hitchin. TL1928.
Kingshouse *Stir.* ***Settlement***, 3m/4km SW of Lochearnhead. **81 G5** NN5620.
Kingshouse Hotel *High.* ***Settlement***, on W side of Rannoch Moor, 6m/10km SE of Kinlochleven. **80 D2** NN2654.
Kingshurst *W.Mid.* ***Suburb***, 7m/11km E of Birmingham. SP1788.
Kingside Hill *Cumb.* ***Locality***, 1m/2km W of Abbeytown. NY1551.
Kingskerswell *Devon* Population: 3672. ***Village***, mainly residential district between Newton Abbot and Torbay. **5 J4** SX8868.
Kingskettle *Fife* ***Village***, 1m/2km S of Ladybank. **82 E7** NO3008.
Kingsland *Gt.Lon.* ***Suburb***, in borough of Islington, 4m/6km NE of Charing Cross. TQ3384.
Kingsland *Here.* ***Village***, 4m/6km NW of Leominster. **28 D2** SO4461.
Kingsland *I.o.A.* ***Suburb***, S district of Holyhead, Anglesey. **46 A4** SH2481.
Kingsland *Shrop.* ***Suburb***, SW district of Shrewsbury. SJ4811.
Kingsley *Ches.* ***Village***, 7m/11km W of Northwich. **48 E5** SJ5574.
Kingsley *Hants.* ***Village***, 5m/8km E of Alton. **11 J1** SU7838.
Kingsley (Kingsley Park). *Northants.* ***Suburb***, 1m/2km NE of Northampton town centre. SP7662.
Kingsley *Staffs.* ***Village***, 2m/4km N of Cheadle. **40 C1** SK0146.
Kingsley Green *W.Suss.* ***Village***, 2m/3km S of Haslemere. **12 B3** SU8930.
Kingsley Holt *Staffs.* ***Village***, 1m/2km SE of Kingsley. SK0246.
Kingsley Park *Northants. See Kingsley.*
Kingslow *Shrop.* ***Settlement***, 6m/10km NE of Bridgnorth. SO7998.
Kingsmead *Hants.* ***Settlement***, 2m/3km NE of Wickham. SU5813.
Kingsmoor *Essex* ***Suburb***, 2m/3km SW of Harlow town centre. TL4307.
Kingsmuir *Angus* ***Village***, 2m/3km SE of Forfar. **83 F3** NO4749.
Kingsmuir *Fife* ***Settlement***, 4m/7km W of Crail. NO5308.
Kingsnorth *Kent* ***Village***, 2m/3km S of Ashford. **15 F4** TR0039.
Kingstag *Dorset Occasional spelling of King's Stag, qv.*
Kingstanding *W.Mid.* ***Locality***, 5m/8km N of Birmingham city centre. **40 C6** SP0794.
Kingsteignton *Devon* Population: 8555. ***Small town***, 2m/3km N of Newton Abbot. **5 J3** SX8773.
Kingsteps *High.* ***Settlement***, dispersed settlement, 1m/2km E of Nairn. **97 G6** NH9057.
Kingsthorne *Here.* ***Village***, 5m/8km S of Hereford. **28 E5** SO4931.
Kingsthorpe *Northants.* ***Suburb***, N district of Northampton. **31 J2** SP7563.
Kingsthorpe Hollow *Northants.* ***Suburb***, 1m/2km N of Northampton town centre. SP7562.
Kingston *Cambs.* ***Village***, 7m/11km W of Cambridge. **33 G3** TL3455.
Kingston *Cornw.* ***Settlement***, 4m/6km N of Callington. SX3675.
Kingston *Devon* ***Settlement***, 2m/3km SW of Newton Poppleford. SY0687.
Kingston *Devon* ***Village***, 3m/5km SW of Modbury. **5 G6** SX6347.
Kingston *Dorset* ***Village***, 4m/6km SW of Sturminster Newton. **9 G4** ST7509.
Kingston *Dorset* ***Village***, on Isle of Purbeck, 5m/8km W of Swanage. **9 J7** SY9579.
Kingston *E.Loth.* ***Settlement***, 2m/3km S of North Berwick. Ruins of 16c Fenton Tower. **76 D2** NT5482.
Kingston *Glas.* ***Suburb***, on S side of River Clyde, to SW of Glasgow city centre. Kingston Bridge carries M8 across River Clyde. NS5864.
Kingston *Gt.Man.* ***Suburb***, adjoining to W of Hyde. SJ9395.
Kingston *Hants.* ***Locality***, 2m/3km S of Ringwood. **10 C4** SU1402.
Kingston *I.o.W.* ***Hamlet***, 2m/3km SE of Shorwell. **11 F6** SZ4781.
Kingston *Kent* ***Village***, 5m/8km SE of Canterbury. **15 G2** TR1951.
Kingston *Moray* ***Village***, on Spey Bay, on W side of mouth of River Spey. **98 B4** NJ3365.
Kingston *Suff.* ***Settlement***, 1m/2km S of Woodbridge. TM2647.
Kingston *Warks.* ***Locality***, 6m/10km SE of Royal Leamington Spa. SP3556.
Kingston *W.Suss.* ***Locality***, comprising East Kingston and West Kingston, near coast between East Preston and Ferring, 4m/7km W of Worthing. **12 D6** TQ0802.
Kingston Bagpuize *Oxon.* Population: 2098. ***Village***, 6m/9km W of Abingdon. **21 H2** SU4098.
Kingston Blount *Oxon.* ***Village***, 3m/4km NW of Stokenchurch. **22 A2** SU7399.
Kingston by Sea *W.Suss.* ***Suburb***, E district of Shoreham-by-Sea. **13 F6** TQ2305.
Kingston Deverill *Wilts.* ***Village***, 4m/6km NE of Mere. **9 H1** ST8437.
Kingston Gorse *W.Suss.* ***Settlement***, on coast, 4m/7km W of Worthing. TQ0801.
Kingston House *Oxon.* ***Historic house***, in Kingston Bagpuize, 4m/6km W of Abingdon. 17c manor with well-preserved interior and interesting stables and gardens. **21 H2** SU4097.
Kingston Lacy *Dorset* ***Historic house***, 17c and later house in park 2m/4km NW of Wimborne Minster. **9 J4** ST9701.
Kingston Lisle *Oxon.* ***Village***, 5m/8km W of Wantage. Blowing Stone located here. **21 G3** SU3287.
Kingston Maurward *Dorset* ***Hamlet***, 2m/3km E of Dorchester. SY7191.
Kingston near Lewes *E.Suss.* ***Village***, on South Downs, 2m/3km SW of Lewes. **13 G6** TQ3908.
Kingston on Soar *Notts.* ***Village***, 6m/9km N of Loughborough. **41 H3** SK5027.
Kingston Russell *Dorset* ***Hamlet***, 4m/7km S of Maiden Newton. Stone circle (English Heritage) 2m/3km S of Long Bredy. **8 E5** SY5891.
Kingston Russell Stone Circle *Dorset* ***Historic/prehistoric site***, S of Tenants Hill, 1m/2km N of Abbotsbury. Scant remains of circle of 18 stones (English Heritage), probably dating from 2200-1400 BC. **8 E6** SY5787.
Kingston St. Mary *Som.* ***Village***, below Quantock Hills, 3m/5km N of Taunton. **8 B2** ST2229.
Kingston Seymour *N.Som.* ***Village***, 3m/5km S of Clevedon. **19 G5** ST4066.
Kingston Stert *Oxon.* ***Settlement***, 3m/5km SE of Thame. SP7201.
Kingston upon Hull (Commonly known as Hull.) *Hull* Population: 310,636. ***City***, port at confluence of Rivers Humber and Hull, 50m/80km E of Leeds. Much of town destroyed during bombing of World War II; town centre has been rebuilt. Formerly had a thriving fishing industry. Major industry nowadays is frozen food processing. Universities. Birthplace of William Wilberforce, slavery abolitionist, 1759. Wilberforce Museum. Famous for associations with poets Andrew Marvell, Stevie Smith and Philip Larkin. **59 H7** TA0928.
Kingston upon Thames *Gt.Lon.* ***Town***, market town and shopping centre on S bank of River Thames, 10m/16km SW of Charing Cross, and a royal borough. The busy modern town is of ancient foundation: Saxon kings were crowned there and coronation stone can still be seen outside Guildhall. TQ1769.
Kingston Warren *Oxon.* ***Settlement***, 4m/6km N of Lambourn. **21 G3** SU3185.
Kingstone *Here.* ***Settlement***, 2m/3km E of Ross-on-Wye. SO6324.
Kingstone *Here.* ***Village***, 6m/10km SW of Hereford. **28 D5** SO4235.
Kingstone *Som.* ***Village***, 1m/2km SE of Ilminster. **8 C3** ST3713.
Kingstone *S.Yorks.* ***Suburb***, to SW of Barnsley town centre. SE3305.
Kingstone *Staffs.* ***Village***, 3m/5km SW of Uttoxeter. **40 C3** SK0629.
Kingstone Winslow *Oxon.* ***Settlement***, adjoining to N of Ashbury, 7m/11km E of Swindon. SU2685.
Kingstown *Cumb.* ***Suburb***, 2m/3km N of Carlisle city centre. **60 E1** NY3959.
Kingstreet *Gt.Man.* ***Settlement***, adjoining to W of Woodford. SJ8782.
Kingsway East *Dundee* ***Locality***, industrial estate 2m/3km NE of Dundee city centre. NO4231.
Kingswear *Devon* ***Small town***, on E bank of River Dart estuary, opposite Dartmouth. Ferries cross river. **5 J5** SX8851.
Kingswell *E.Ayr.* ***Settlement***, 5m/8km SW of Eaglesham. **74 D6** NS5047.
Kingswells *Aberdeen* Population: 1120. ***Village***, 5m/7km W of Aberdeen. **91 G4** NJ8606.
Kingswinford *W.Mid.* ***Suburb***, W district of Dudley. **40 A7** SO8888.
Kingswood *Bucks.* ***Hamlet***, 9m/14km NW of Aylesbury. **31 H7** SP6919.
Kingswood *Essex* ***Suburb***, to S of Basildon town centre. TQ7087.
Kingswood *Glos.* ***Village***, 1m/2km SW of Wotton-under-Edge. 14c Cistercian abbey (English Heritage) to N. **20 A2** ST7491.
Kingswood *Kent* ***Hamlet***, 2m/3km SW of Harrietsham. **14 D2** TQ8450.
Kingswood *Northants.* ***Suburb***, SW district of Corby. SP8687.
Kingswood *Powys* ***Settlement***, 3m/5km SE of Welshpool, on E side of River Severn. **38 B5** SJ2402.
Kingswood *Som.* ***Hamlet***, 4m/6km SE of Watchet. ST1037.
Kingswood *S.Glos.* Population: 60,192. ***Suburb***, former coalmining area 4m/6km E of Bristol city centre. **19 K4** ST6473.
Kingswood *Surr.* ***Locality***, residential locality 3m/5km S of Banstead. **23 F6** TQ2455.
Kingswood *Warks.* ***Village***, 2m/4km SE of Hockley Heath. **30 C1** SP1871.
Kingswood Common *Here.* ***Locality***, 2m/3km S of Kington. **28 B3** SO2954.
Kingthorpe *Lincs.* ***Hamlet***, 2m/3km S of Wragby. **52 E5** TF1275.
Kington *Here.* Population: 2197. ***Small town***, on River Arrow, close to Welsh border, 12m/20km W of Leominster. **28 B3** SO2956.
Kington *Worcs.* ***Village***, 6m/10km W of Alcester. **29 J3** SO9955.
Kington Langley *Wilts.* ***Village***, 2m/4km N of Chippenham. **20 C4** ST9277.
Kington Magna *Dorset* ***Village***, 4m/6km SW of Gillingham. **9 G2** ST7623.
Kington St. Michael *Wilts.* ***Village***, 3m/4km N of Chippenham. **20 B4** ST9077.
Kingussie *High.* Population: 1298. ***Small town***, and tourist centre of River Spey 28m/45km S of Inverness. Highland Folk Museum. **88 E4** NH7500.
Kingweston *Som.* ***Village***, 3m/4km NE of Somerton. **8 E1** ST5230.
Kinharrachie *Aber.* ***Locality***, includes West Kinharrachie and East Kinharrachie, 2m/3km W of Ellon. **91 H1** NJ9231.
Kinharvie *D. & G.* ***Settlement***, 3m/4km W of New Abbey. **65 K4** NX9266.
Kinkell *Aber.* ***Locality***, with remains of 16c church (Historic Scotland), 2m/3km S of Inverurie. NJ7819.
Kinkell *E.Dun.* ***Settlement***, 2m/3km NW of Kirkintilloch. **74 E3** NS6375.
Kinkell Bridge *P. & K.* ***Settlement***, in Strathearn, 5m/8km SE of Crieff. **82 A6** NN9317.
Kinkell Ness *Fife* ***Coastal feature***, small rocky headland, 2m/3km SE of St. Andrews. **83 G6** NO5315.
Kinknockie *Aber.* ***Locality***, 4m/7km S of Mintlaw. **99 J6** NK0041.
Kinlet *Shrop.* ***Hamlet***, 4m/6km NE of Cleobury Mortimer. **39 G7** SO7180.
Kinloch *Fife* ***Hamlet***, 2m/3km NW of Ladybank. **82 D6** NO2712.
Kinloch *High.* ***Settlement***, at head of Loch More, Sutherland district. **103 F5** NC3434.
Kinloch *High.* ***Settlement***, at SE end of Loch Glass, 5m/7km NW of Evanton. **96 C4** NH5370.
Kinloch *High.* ***Settlement***, in Morvern, Lochaber district, on N bank of Kinloch River, near head of Loch Teacuis. **79 H2** NM6554.
Kinloch *High.* ***Village***, at head of Loch Scresort, on E coast of Rum. **85 K5** NM4099.
Kinloch *P. & K.* ***Hamlet***, 1m/2km W of Meigle. **82 D3** NO2644.
Kinloch *P. & K.* ***Village***, 2m/3km W of Blairgowrie. **82 C3** NO1444.
Kinloch Castle *High.* ***Castle***, at Kinloch on E coast of Rum. Early 20c red sandstone castle in Gothic style, built by Sir George Bullough, and now a hotel. **85 K5** NM4099.
Kinloch Hourn *High.* ***Locality***, in Lochaber district, at head of Loch Hourn. **87 F4** NG9507.
Kinloch Laggan *High.* ***Settlement***, at NE end of Loch Laggan, in Badenoch and Strathspey district. **88 C6** NN5489.
Kinloch Rannoch *P. & K.* ***Village***, at foot of Loch Rannoch. **81 H2** NN6658.
Kinlochaline Castle *High.* ***Castle***, at head of Loch Aline in Lochaber district. 15c square turreted tower, stronghold of Clan MacInnes. Now a ruin. **79 H3** NM6947.
Kinlochan *High.* ***Settlement***, in Sunart at head of Loch Doilet, 4m/6km N of Strontian. **79 K1** NM8167.
Kinlochard *Stir.* ***Settlement***, at head of Loch Ard, 4m/7km W of Aberfoyle. **81 F7** NN4502.
Kinlocharkaig *High.* ***Settlement***, near head of Loch Arkaig, Lochaber district. **87 F5** NM9890.
Kinlochbeoraid *High.* ***Settlement***, at head of Loch Beoraid, Lochaber district. **86 E6** NM8585.
Kinlochbervie *High.* ***Village***, on N side of Loch Inchard, W coast of Sutherland district. **102 E3** NC2256.
Kinlocheil *High.* ***Village***, in Lochaber district, near head of Loch Eil, on N shore. **87 F7** NM9779.
Kinlochetive *High.* ***Settlement***, near mouth of River Etive, 1km N of head of Loch Etive. **80 C3** NN1245.
Kinlochewe *High.* ***Settlement***, in Ross and Cromarty district, 2m/3km SE of head of Loch Maree. **95 G5** NH0261.
Kinlochewe Forest *High.* ***Open space***, deer forest to N and W of Kinlochewe. **95 G5** NH0261.
Kinlochlaich *Arg. & B.* ***Settlement***, 1m/2km SE of Portnacroish. **80 A3** NM9346.
Kinlochleven *High.* Population: 1076. ***Small town***, in Lochaber district, at head of Loch Leven. Former industry was aluminium smelting. **80 C1** NN1861.
Kinlochluichart Forest *High.* ***Open space***, deer forest in Ross and Cromarty district between Loch Fannich and Loch Glascarnoch. **95 J4** NH2769.
Kinlochmoidart *High.* ***Locality***, at head of Loch Moidart, in Lochaber district. **86 D7** NM7072.
Kinlochmorar *High.* ***Settlement***, at head of Loch Morar, Lochaber district. **86 E5** NM8691.

K

Kinlochmore *High.* ***Village***, in Lochaber district, on E side of Kinlochleven. **80 C1** NN1962.
Kinlochnanuagh *High.* ***Locality***, in Lochaber district, 1km above head of Loch nan Uamh and 5m/8km E of Arisaig. NM7384.
Kinlochspelve *Arg. & B.* ***Settlement***, 3m/5km E of Lochbuie, near head of Loch Spelve, Mull. **79 H5** NM6526.
Kinloss *Moray* Population: 2281. ***Village***, near N coast, 3m/4km NE of Forres. Airfield to N. Ruins of 12c abbey. **97 H5** NJ0661.
Kinmel Bay (Bae Cinmel). *Conwy* ***Locality***, 3m/5km NE of Abergele. **47 H4** SH9880.
Kinmount Gardens *D. & G.* ***Garden***, at Kinmount House, 4m/6km W of Annan. **69 G7** NY1468.
Kinmuck *Aber.* ***Hamlet***, 3m/5km E of Inverurie. **91 G3** NJ8119.
Kinnaber *Angus* ***Settlement***, near E coast, 3m/4km N of Montrose. 1m/2km W is site of former railway junction famous in days of 'Railway race to the North'. NO7261.
Kinnadie *Aber.* ***Settlement***, 2m/3km S of Stuartfield. **99 H6** NJ9743.
Kinnaird *P. & K.* ***Village***, 10m/16km W of Dundee. **82 D5** NO2428.
Kinnairds Head *Aber.* ***Coastal feature***, headland to N of harbour at Fraserburgh. First lighthouse (Historic Scotland) built by Northern Lighthouse Company, contained within 16c castle built for Fraser family. **99 H4** NJ9967.
Kinneff *Aber.* ***Settlement***, on E coast, 2m/4km NE of Inverbervie. **91 G7** NO8574.
Kinneil House *Falk.* ***Historic house***, mansion (Historic Scotland) of 16-17c, 1m/2km SW of Bo'ness. **75 H2** NS9880.
Kinnel Water *D. & G.* ***River***, rising N of Queensberry and running SE to River Annan, 1m/2km NE of Lochmaben. **69 F5** NY0983.
Kinnelhead *D. & G.* ***Settlement***, 4m/6km SW of Moffat. **69 F3** NT0201.
Kinnell *Angus* ***Settlement***, 1km E of Friockheim. **83 H2** NO6050.
Kinnell *Stir.* ***Settlement***, to E of Killin across River Dochart. **81 G4** NN5732.
Kinnerley *Shrop.* ***Village***, 6m/10km SE of Oswestry. **38 C3** SJ3320.
Kinnerley *Tel. & W.* *Alternative spelling of Kynnersley, qv.*
Kinnersley *Here.* ***Village***, 2m/4km NE of Willersley. Tudor castle. **28 C4** SO3449.
Kinnersley *Worcs.* ***Village***, 7m/11km N of Tewkesbury. **29 H4** SO8743.
Kinnerton *Powys* ***Village***, 3m/4km NE of New Radnor. **28 B2** SO2463.
Kinnerton Green *Flints.* ***Settlement***, 3m/5km NW of Rossett. SJ3361.
Kinnesswood *P. & K.* ***Village***, 4m/6km SE of Milnathort. **82 C7** NO1702.
Kinnettles *Angus* ***Locality***, 3m/5km SW of Forfar. **83 F3** NO4346.
Kinning Park *Glas.* ***Suburb***, 1m/2km SW of Glasgow city centre. NS5664.
Kinninvie *Dur.* ***Hamlet***, 3m/5km N of Barnard Castle. **62 B4** NZ0521.
Kinnordy *Angus* ***Settlement***, 1m/2km NW of Kirriemuir. Loch of Kinnordy is marsh to SW. **82 E2** NO3655.
Kinnoull Hill *P. & K.* ***Hill***, 1m/2km E of Perth across River Tay, at SW end of Sidlaw Hills. Noted viewpoint. Height 728 feet or 222 metres. **82 C5** NO1322.
Kinoulton *Notts.* ***Village***, 9m/14km NW of Melton Mowbray. **41 J2** SK6730.
Kinpurney Hill *Angus* ***Mountain***, with tower at summit, and hillfort, 1m/2km E of Newtyle. Height 1132 feet or 345 metres. **82 E3** NO3141.
Kinrara *High.* ***Settlement***, 3m/5km S of Aviemore. **89 F4** NH8708.
Kinross *P. & K.* Population: 4552. ***Small town***, and resort on W side of Loch Leven, 9m/15km N of Dunfermline. **82 C7** NO1102.
Kinross House *P. & K.* ***Historic house***, late 17c house on shore of Loch Leven, to E of Kinross. **82 C7** NO1102.
Kinrossie *P. & K.* ***Village***, 7m/11km NE of Perth. **82 C4** NO1832.
Kinsbourne Green *Herts.* ***Hamlet***, 2m/4km NW of Harpenden. **32 E7** TL1015.
Kinsford Water *Som.* ***River***, small stream which rises on Exmoor, 3m/4km SW of Simonsbath and flows SE to become Sherdon Water and then flows to join River Barle, 3m/4km W of Withypool. **7 F2** SS7834.
Kinsham *Here.* ***Locality***, parish containing hamlets of Lower Kinsham and Upper Kinsham, 3m/5km E of Presteigne. **28 C2** SO3664.
Kinsham *Worcs.* ***Hamlet***, 3m/5km NE of Tewkesbury. SO9335.
Kinsley *W.Yorks.* ***Village***, 1m/2km NW of Hemsworth. **51 G1** SE4114.
Kinson *Bourne.* ***Suburb***, N district of Bournemouth. **10 B5** SZ0696.
Kintail Estate *High.* ***Open space***, mountainous area (National Trust for Scotland) extending N from Glen Shiel in Skye and Lochalsh district. It encompasses Five Sisters, part of Kintail Forest, Beinn Fhada and Falls of Glomach. Regarded as an excellent upland walking area, it is renowned for wildlife and magnificent scenery. NH0218.
Kintail Forest *High.* ***Open space***, mountainous tract in Skye and Lochalsh district, to NE of Glen Shiel. Mostly within Kintail Estate (National Trust for Scotland). Includes Five Sisters and Beinn Fhada. Herds of red deer and wild goats in area. **87 G3** NG9917.
Kintarvie *W.Isles* ***Settlement***, on Isle of Lewis, 3m/4km SW of head of Loch Erisort, to NW of Loch Seaforth. **100 E6** NB2217.
Kintbury *W.Berks.* Population: 2072. ***Village***, 3m/5km E of Hungerford. Site of Roman building 1km E. **21 G5** SU3866.
Kintessack *Moray* ***Settlement***, on edge of Culbin Forest, 3m/4km W of Forres. **97 G5** NJ0060.
Kintillo *P. & K.* ***Suburb***, at S side of Bridge of Earn. **82 C6** NO1317.
Kintocher *Aber.* ***Settlement***, 4m/6km S of Alford. **90 D4** NJ5709.
Kinton *Here.* ***Hamlet***, 1km NE of Leintwardine and 6m/10km W of Ludlow. **28 D1** SO4074.
Kinton *Shrop.* ***Hamlet***, 9m/14km NW of Shrewsbury. **38 C4** SJ3719.
Kintore *Aber.* Population: 2028. ***Village***, on River Don, 4m/6km S of Inverurie. Site of Roman camp on W side of village. **91 F3** NJ7916.
Kintour *Arg. & B.* ***River***, flowing into Aros Bay on E coast of Islay. **72 C5** NR4651.
Kintour *Arg. & B.* ***Settlement***, on SE side of Islay, 8m/11km NE of Port Ellen. **72 C5** NR4551.
Kintra *Arg. & B.* ***Settlement***, 1km SW of Rubha nan Cearc, Mull. **78 E5** NM3125.
Kintra *Arg. & B.* ***Settlement***, at S end of Laggan Bay, Islay. **72 B6** NR3248.
Kintradwell *High.* ***Settlement***, 3m/4km N of Brora, Sutherland district. **97 G1** NC9107.
Kintraw *Arg. & B.* ***Settlement***, at head of Loch Craignish, to E of mouth of Barbreck River. **79 K7** NM8205.
Kintyre *Arg. & B.* ***Coastal feature***, peninsula in Argyll running S to Mull of Kintyre from narrow isthmus between East and West Loch Tarbert. Length 40m/64km; average width 8m/13km. Chief town is Campbeltown. Airfield at Machrihanish. **66 A2** NR7236.
Kinuachdrach *Arg. & B.* ***Locality***, near NE coast of Jura, 2m/3km from N end of island, with headland of Aird of Kinuachdrach to E. **73 F1** NR7098.
Kinuachdrach Harbour *Arg. & B.* ***Bay***, to SE of Kinuachdrach on E coast of Jura, 1m/2km from N end of island and at S end of Aird of Kinuachdrach. **73 F1** NR7098.
Kinveachy *High.* ***Settlement***, in Badenoch and Strathspey district, 4m/6km N of Aviemore. **89 G3** NH9118.
Kinver (Also known as Kinfare.) *Staffs.* Population: 5054. ***Small town***, 4m/6km W of Stourbridge. To W is Kinver Edge (National Trust), area of heath and woodland with Iron Age fort. **40 A7** SO8483.
Kinwarton *Warks.* ***Settlement***, adjoining to NE of Alcester, with 14c dovecote (National Trust). **30 C3** SP1058.
Kip Hill *Dur.* ***Locality***, adjoining to N of Stanley. NZ2054.
Kiplaw Croft *Aber.* ***Settlement***, 3m/4km SW of Cruden Bay. **91 J1** NK0533.
Kiplin *N.Yorks.* ***Settlement***, 1m/2km W of Great Langton. **62 D7** SE2797.
Kiplingcotes *E.Riding* ***Locality***, adjacent to former railway line between Market Weighton and Beverley; Kiplingcotes Railway Station and restored station box remain. **59 F5** SE9243.
Kipp *Stir.* ***Settlement***, in valley of River Balvag, 1km S of Strathyre. **81 G6** NN5516.
Kippax *W.Yorks.* Population: 9236. ***Village***, 2m/3km SE of Garforth. **57 K6** SE4130.
Kippen *P. & K.* ***Settlement***, 1m/2km S of Dunning. **82 B6** NO0112.
Kippen *Stir.* ***Village***, 9m/15km W of Stirling. **74 E1** NS6594.
Kippenross House *Stir.* ***Other building***, Georgian house, now a guest house, adjoining to S of Dunblane. **81 J7** NN7800.
Kippford (Also known as Scaur.) *D. & G.* ***Village***, on E side of Urr Water estuary, 4m/6km S of Dalbeattie. **65 J5** NX8354.
Kipping's Cross *Kent* ***Settlement***, 1m/2km W of Pembury. **23 K7** TQ6440.
Kippington *Kent* ***Suburb***, in SW part of Sevenoaks. TQ5254.
Kippo Burn *Fife* ***River***, small stream flowing NE from 1km W of Kippo Farm to North Sea at Cambo Ness, 3m/4km NW of Fife Ness. **83 G7** NO6011.
Kirbister *Ork.* ***Locality***, on Mainland, on W side of Loch of Stenness. HY2514.
Kirbister *Ork.* ***Locality***, on Mainland, 4m/7km S of Finstown and 6m/9km W of Kirkwall, on W side of Loch of Kirbister. **107 C7** HY3607.
Kirbister *Ork.* ***Settlement***, 1m/2km E of Dishes, Stronsay. **106 F5** HY6824.
Kirbuster *Ork.* ***Settlement***, situated between Loch of Boardhouse and Loch of Hundland, in N Mainland. **106 B5** HY2825.
Kirby Bedon *Norf.* ***Hamlet***, 4m/6km SE of Norwich. **45 G5** TG2705.
Kirby Bellars *Leics.* ***Village***, 3m/4km W of Melton Mowbray. **42 A4** SK7117.
Kirby Cane *Norf.* ***Hamlet***, 4m/6km NW of Beccles. **45 H6** TM3794.
Kirby Corner *W.Mid.* ***Suburb***, 3m/5km SW of Coventry city centre. **30 D1** SP2976.
Kirby Cross *Essex* ***Locality***, adjoining to W of Frinton-on-Sea, 2m/4km W of Walton on the Naze. **35 G7** TM2120.
Kirby Fields *Leics.* ***Suburb***, 4m/6km W of Leicester. SK5203.
Kirby Green *Norf.* ***Settlement***, adjoining to E of Kirby Cane. TM3794.
Kirby Grindalythe *N.Yorks.* ***Village***, 2m/4km NW of Sledmere. **59 F3** SE9067.
Kirby Hall *Northants.* ***Historic house***, partly restored 16c-17c mansion (English Heritage) with garden, 2m/3km SE of Gretton and 4m/6km NE of Corby town centre. **42 C6** SP9292.
Kirby Hill *N.Yorks.* ***Hamlet***, 4m/6km NW of Richmond. **62 C6** NZ1406.
Kirby Hill *N.Yorks.* ***Village***, 1m/2km N of Boroughbridge. **57 J3** SE3868.
Kirby Knowle *N.Yorks.* ***Village***, 4m/7km NE of Thirsk. **57 K1** SE4687.
Kirby le Soken *Essex* ***Village***, 2m/3km W of Walton on the Naze. **35 G6** TM2222.
Kirby Misperton *N.Yorks.* ***Village***, 3m/5km S of Pickering. **58 D2** SE7779.
Kirby Muxloe *Leics.* Population: 7780. ***Village***, 4m/7km W of Leicester. Moated 15c brick castle (English Heritage). **41 H5** SK5204.
Kirby Muxloe Castle *Leics.* ***Castle***, ruins of castle (English Heritage) 4m/6km W of Leicester city centre. Moated red-brick castle begun in 15c by Lord Hastings, but never completed as he was executed. **41 H5** SK5204.
Kirby Row *Norf.* ***Village***, 3m/5km NE of Bungay. **45 H6** TM3792.
Kirby Sigston *N.Yorks.* ***Settlement***, 3m/5km E of Northallerton. **63 F7** SE4194.
Kirby Underdale *E.Riding* ***Village***, in The Wolds, 4m/7km W of Fridaythorpe. **58 E4** SE8058.
Kirby Wiske *N.Yorks.* ***Village***, on River Wiske, 4m/6km NW of Thirsk. **57 J1** SE3784.
Kirdford *W.Suss.* ***Village***, 4m/7km NE of Petworth. **12 D4** TQ0126.
Kirivick *W.Isles* *Anglicised form of Cirbhig, qv.*
Kirk *High.* ***Settlement***, in Caithness district, 4m/6km NE of Watten. **105 H3** ND2859.
Kirk Beck *Cumb.* ***River***, rising on Blakeley Moss to W of Ennerdale Fell, and flowing SW to join River Ehen 1km SW of Beckermet. **60 B5** NY0106.
Kirk Braddan *I.o.M.* ***Locality***, 1m/2km NW of Douglas. SC3676.
Kirk Bramwith *S.Yorks.* ***Village***, on N bank of River Don, 6m/10km NE of Doncaster. **51 J1** SE6211.
Kirk Burn *High.* ***River***, flowing first W then S to Sortat to become Burn of Lyth. **105 H2** ND3164.
Kirk Deighton *N.Yorks.* ***Village***, 1m/2km N of Wetherby. **57 J4** SE3950.
Kirk Ella *E.Riding* ***Village***, 5m/8km W of Kingston upon Hull city centre. **59 G7** TA0229.
Kirk Fell *Cumb.* ***Mountain***, to N of Wasdale Head, 1m/2km W of Great Gable. Height 2631 feet or 802 metres. **60 C5** NY1910.
Kirk Hallam *Derbys.* ***Suburb***, 1m/2km SW of Ilkeston. **41 G1** SK4540.
Kirk Hammerton *N.Yorks.* ***Village***, 9m/14km W of York. **57 K4** SE4655.
Kirk Hill *S.Ayr.* ***Hill***, 2m/3km N of Dailly. Height 817 feet or 249 metres. **67 G3** NS2604.
Kirk Ireton *Derbys.* ***Village***, 3m/4km SW of Wirksworth. **50 E7** SK2650.
Kirk Langley *Derbys.* ***Village***, 4m/7km NW of Derby. **40 E2** SK2838.
Kirk Loch *D. & G.* ***Lake/loch***, small lake on SW side of Lochmaben. **69 F5** NY0782.
Kirk Merrington *Dur.* ***Village***, 1m/2km S of Spennymoor. **62 D3** NZ2631.
Kirk Michael *I.o.M.* ***Village***, near W coast, 6m/10km NE of Peel. **54 C4** SC3190.
Kirk of Mochrum *D. & G.* *Alternative name for Mochrum, qv.*
Kirk of Shotts (Also spelled Kirk o'Shotts.) *N.Lan.* ***Settlement***, 4m/7km W of Harthill. **75 G4** NS8462.
Kirk o'Shotts *N.Lan.* *Alternative spelling of Kirk of Shotts, qv.*
Kirk Sandall *S.Yorks.* Population: 12,078. ***Suburb***, 4m/6km NE of Doncaster. **51 J2** SE6107.
Kirk Smeaton *N.Yorks.* ***Village***, 5m/8km SE of Pontefract. **51 H1** SE5116.
Kirk Yetholm *Sc.Bord.* ***Village***, on E side of Bowmont Water, 7m/12km SE of Kelso. N terminus of The Pennine Way. **70 D1** NT8228.
Kirkabister *Shet.* ***Settlement***, on SW coast of Bressay, 1m/2km S of Grindiscol. **109 D9** HU4837.
Kirkaig *High.* ***River***, on border of Ross and Cromarty and Sutherland districts, flowing NW into inlet of Loch Kirkaig on W coast. NC0719.
Kirkaig Point *High.* ***Coastal feature***, headland on W coast of Sutherland district between Lochs Inver and Kirkaig, 2m/4km SW of Lochinver. **102 C6** NC0521.
Kirkandrews *D. & G.* ***Settlement***, 5m/8km S of Gatehouse of Fleet. Cup and ring marked rock to NE. **65 G6** NX6048.
Kirkandrews-upon-Eden *Cumb.* ***Village***, 3m/5km NW of Carlisle. **60 E1** NY3558.
Kirkapoll *Arg. & B.* ***Locality***, on Gott Bay, Tiree, nearly 2m/3km N of Scarinish. NM0447.
Kirkbampton *Cumb.* ***Village***, 6m/10km W of Carlisle. **60 E1** NY3056.
Kirkbean *D. & G.* ***Village***, near Solway Firth, 11m/17km S of Dumfries. **65 K5** NX9759.
Kirkbride *Cumb.* ***Village***, 5m/9km N of Wigton. **60 D1** NY2256.
Kirkbridge *N.Yorks.* ***Settlement***, 1km E of Great Crakehall, 4m/6km NW of Bedale. **62 D7** SE2590.
Kirkbuddo *Angus* ***Locality***, 4m/6km SW of Letham. **83 F3** NO5043.
Kirkburn *E.Riding* ***Village***, 3m/5km SW of Great Driffield. **59 F4** SE9855.
Kirkburn *Sc.Bord.* ***Locality***, 3m/5km SE of Peebles. **76 A7** NT2938.
Kirkburton *W.Yorks.* Population: 4121. ***Small town***, 4m/7km SE of Huddersfield, dating mainly from 19c. **50 D1** SE1912.
Kirkby *Lincs.* ***Hamlet***, 4m/6km NW of Market Rasen. **52 D3** TF0692.
Kirkby *Mersey.* Population: 43,017. ***Town***, 6m/10km NE of Liverpool. **48 D3** SJ4098.
Kirkby *N.Yorks.* ***Village***, 2m/3km SE of Stokesley. **63 G6** NZ5305.
Kirkby Fell *N.Yorks.* ***Mountain***, 3m/5km E of Settle. Height 1791 feet or 546 metres. **56 D3** SD8763.
Kirkby Fleetham *N.Yorks.* ***Village***, 4m/6km SE of Catterick. **62 D7** SE2894.
Kirkby Green *Lincs.* ***Village***, 8m/12km N of Sleaford. **52 D7** TF0857.

Kirkby in Ashfield *Notts.* Population: 27,014. ***Town***, 4m/7km SW of Mansfield. **51 G7** SK4956.
Kirkby-in-Furness *Cumb.* ***Village***, small village on E side of River Duddon estuary, 3m/5km S of Broughton in Furness. SD2282.
Kirkby Industrial Estate *Mersey.* ***Locality***, to E of Kirkby. SJ4098.
Kirkby la Thorpe *Lincs.* ***Village***, 2m/3km E of Sleaford. **42 E1** TF0945.
Kirkby Lonsdale *Cumb.* ***Small town***, market town on River Lune, 14m/22km NE of Lancaster. 12c Devil's Bridge spans River Lune. **56 B2** SD6178.
Kirkby Malham *N.Yorks.* ***Village***, in Upper Airedale, 5m/8km E of Settle. **56 D3** SD8961.
Kirkby Mallory *Leics.* ***Village***, 5m/8km N of Hinckley. **41 G5** SK4500.
Kirkby Malzeard *N.Yorks.* ***Village***, 5m/8km NW of Ripon. **57 H2** SE2374.
Kirkby Malzeard Moor *N.Yorks.* ***Open space***, moorland 5m/8km SW of Masham. **57 G2** SE1575.
Kirkby Mills *N.Yorks.* ***Hamlet***, 1km SE of Kirkbymoorside. **58 D1** SE7085.
Kirkby on Bain *Lincs.* ***Village***, 3m/5km E of Woodhall Spa. **53 F6** TF2462.
Kirkby Overblow *N.Yorks.* ***Village***, 4m/6km S of Harrogate. **57 J5** SE3249.
Kirkby Stephen *Cumb.* Population: 1619. ***Small town***, on River Eden, 9m/15km SE of Appleby-in-Westmorland. St. Stephen's church was founded in 8c. **61 J6** NY7708.
Kirkby Thore *Cumb.* ***Village***, on site of Roman town of Bravoniacum, 4m/7km NW of Appleby-in-Westmorland. **61 H4** NY6325.
Kirkby Underwood *Lincs.* ***Village***, 5m/8km N of Bourne. **42 D3** TF0727.
Kirkby Wharfe *N.Yorks.* ***Village***, 2m/3km SE of Tadcaster. **58 B5** SE5040.
Kirkby Woodhouse *Notts.* ***Suburb***, adjoining to N of Annesley Woodhouse, 1m/2km S of Kirkby in Ashfield. SK4954.
Kirkbymoorside *N.Yorks.* Population: 2650. ***Small town***, below North York Moors, 7m/11km W of Pickering. Traces of medieval castle. **58 C1** SE6986.
Kirkcaldy *Fife* Population: 47,155. ***Town***, port and resort, 11m/17km N of Edinburgh across Firth of Forth. Former textile and pottery town, with now more varied industries. Birthplace of economist Adam Smith, 1723, and architect Robert Adam, 1728. Links Market, held annually in April. 15c Ravenscraig Castle to N. **76 A1** NT2791.
Kirkcaldy Museum and Art Gallery *Fife* ***Other feature of interest***, in Kirkcaldy town centre. Gallery includes work by Camden Town Group, with local history exhibition in museum. **76 A1** NT2792.
Kirkcambeck *Cumb.* ***Hamlet***, 5m/8km N of Brampton. **70 A7** NY5368.
Kirkcolm *D. & G.* ***Village***, on Rinns of Galloway, 5m/9km N of Stranraer. **64 A4** NX0268.
Kirkconnel *D. & G.* Population: 2329. ***Small town***, on River Nith, 3m/5km NW of Sanquhar. **68 C2** NS7312.
Kirkconnell *D. & G.* ***Settlement***, 2m/3km NE of New Abbey. **65 K4** NX9767.
Kirkconnell Tower *D. & G.* ***Historic house***, 2m/3km NE of New Abbey. Tower originally part of Kirkconnell House built in 1410; rest of house destroyed in 1570 by English army. NY9768.
Kirkcowan *D. & G.* ***Village***, 6m/10km SW of Newton Stewart. **64 D4** NX3260.
Kirkcudbright (Also known as Castledykes.) *D. & G.* Population: 3588. ***Small town***, on River Dee estuary at head of Kirkcudbright Bay. Site of 13c castle to W beside river. Ruins of MacLellan's Castle (Historic Scotland), 16c mansion, near main square. **65 G5** NX6850.
Kirkcudbright Bay *D. & G.* ***Bay***, on River Dee estuary, to S of Kirkcudbright, on N side of Solway Firth. **65 G6** NX6850.
Kirkdale *D. & G.* ***Settlement***, 4m/6km SE of Creetown. **65 F5** NX5153.
Kirkdale *Mersey.* ***Suburb***, 2m/3km N of Liverpool city centre. SJ3493.
Kirkdale *N.Yorks.* ***Locality***, on Hodge Beck, 1m/2km W of Kirkbymoorside. SE6785.
Kirkdean *Sc.Bord.* ***Settlement***, 1m/2km SW of Blyth Bridge. **75 K6** NT1244.
Kirkfield *S.Lan.* ***Locality***, adjoining to NW of Bothwell, 3m/4km NW of Hamilton. NS7059.
Kirkfieldbank *S.Lan.* ***Village***, 1m/2km W of Lanark across River Clyde. **75 G6** NS8643.
Kirkgunzeon *D. & G.* ***Village***, 4m/7km NE of Dalbeattie. **65 J4** NX8666.
Kirkham *Lancs.* Population: 9038. ***Small town***, market town 8m/12km W of Preston. Site of Roman settlement to E side. **55 H6** SD4232.
Kirkham *N.Yorks.* ***Hamlet***, on River Derwent, 5m/8km SW of Malton. Remains of priory (English Heritage); 13c gatehouse. **58 D3** SE7365.
Kirkham House *Torbay* ***Historic house***, well-preserved and restored 15c stone town house (English Heritage) in central Paignton. **5 J4** SX8861.
Kirkham Priory *N.Yorks.* ***Ecclesiastical building***, Augustinian priory dating from 12c (English Heritage), in River Derwent valley, 5m/8km SW of Malton. **58 D3** SE7365.
Kirkhamgate *W.Yorks.* ***Village***, 3m/4km NW of Wakefield. **57 H7** SE2922.
Kirkharle *Northumb.* ***Hamlet***, 2m/3km SE of Kirkwhelpington. Littleharle Tower 1km N. **71 F5** NZ0182.
Kirkhaugh *Northumb.* ***Settlement***, on W side of River South Tyne, 3m/4km NW of Alston. **61 H2** NY6949.
Kirkheaton *Northumb.* ***Village***, 5m/8km W of Belsay. **71 F6** NZ0177.
Kirkheaton *W.Yorks.* ***Village***, 3m/4km E of Huddersfield. **50 D1** SE1818.
Kirkhill *Angus* ***Hamlet***, 3m/4km NW of Montrose. **83 H1** NO6860.
Kirkhill *High.* ***Village***, in Inverness district, 7m/11km W of Inverness. **96 C7** NH5545.
Kirkhill *Moray* ***Settlement***, 2m/3km NE of Rothes, on W side of River Spey. **98 B5** NJ3051.
Kirkhill of Kennethmont *Aber. Alternative name for Kennethmont (village), qv.*
Kirkhope *Sc.Bord.* ***Settlement***, on Ettrick Water, 1km SW of Ettrickbridge. **69 J1** NT3823.
Kirkhouse *Cumb.* ***Locality***, 3m/4km E of Brampton. NY5659.
Kirkhouse Green *S.Yorks.* ***Settlement***, 2m/3km NW of Stainforth. SE6213.
Kirkibost *High.* ***Locality***, on E side of Strathaird peninsula, Skye, 4m/7km N of Strathaird Point. **86 B3** NG5517.
Kirkibost *W.Isles* ***Settlement***, on Great Bernera, opposite Breascleit on W coast of Isle of Lewis, across East Loch Roag. **100 D4** NB1835.
Kirkibost Island *W.Isles* ***Island***, low-lying uninhabited island off W coast of North Uist 5m/8km SE of Aird an Rùnair. **92 C5** NF7565.
Kirkinch *Angus* ***Settlement***, 2m/3km E of Meigle. **82 E3** NO3144.
Kirkinner *D. & G.* ***Village***, 3m/4km S of Wigtown. **64 E5** NX4251.
Kirkintilloch *E.Dun.* Population: 20,780. ***Town***, on line of Antonine Wall, 7m/11km NE of Glasgow. Formerly a weaving and coalmining centre. **74 E3** NS6573.
Kirkland *Cumb.* ***Hamlet***, 1m/2km N of Ennerdale Bridge. **60 B5** NY0718.
Kirkland *Cumb.* ***Locality***, 1m/2km E of Wigton. NY2648.
Kirkland *Cumb.* ***Settlement***, 2m/3km E of Skirwith. **61 H3** NY6432.
Kirkland *D. & G.* ***Settlement***, 2m/3km NW of Kirkconnel. **68 C2** NS7214.
Kirkland *D. & G.* ***Settlement***, to SE of Forest of Ae, 2m/3km NE of Parkgate. **69 F5** NY0389.
Kirkland *D. & G.* ***Village***, 2m/3km E of Moniaive. **68 D4** NX8090.
Kirkland *Fife* ***Suburb***, N district of Methil. NO3600.
Kirkland Guards *Cumb.* ***Locality***, 1m/2km NE of Bothel. NY1840.
Kirkland of Longcastle *D. & G.* ***Settlement***, 4m/7km N of Monreith. **64 D6** NX3747.
Kirkleatham *R. & C.* ***Village***, 2m/3km S of Redcar. **63 G4** NZ5921.
Kirklees Light Railway *W.Yorks.* ***Other feature of interest***, narrow gauge tourist railway running from Skelmanthorpe to Clayton West. **50 E1** SE2411.
Kirklevington *Stock.* ***Village***, 2m/3km SE of Yarm. **63 F5** NZ4309.
Kirkley *Suff.* ***Suburb***, 1m/2km SW of Lowestoft town centre. **45 K6** TM5391.
Kirkleyditch *Ches.* ***Hamlet***, 2m/3km E of Alderley Edge. SJ8778.
Kirklington *N.Yorks.* ***Village***, 6m/9km SE of Bedale. Hall dates from 16c, although much altered. **57 J1** SE3181.
Kirklington *Notts.* ***Village***, 3m/4km NW of Southwell. **51 J7** SK6757.
Kirklinton *Cumb.* ***Hamlet***, 4m/6km E of Longtown. **69 K7** NY4367.
Kirkliston *Edin.* Population: 2739. ***Village***, 3m/4km S of South Queensferry. **75 K3** NT1274.
Kirkmadrine Stones *D. & G.* ***Historic/prehistoric site***, early Christian inscribed stones (Historic Scotland) in churchyard of Kirkmadrine Church on Rinns of Galloway, 1m/2km SW of Sandhead. **64 A6** NX0848.
Kirkmaiden *D. & G.* ***Village***, on Rinns of Galloway, nearly 1m/2km W of Drummore. **64 B7** NX1236.
Kirkmichael *P. & K.* ***Village***, in Strathardle, 9m/14km E of Pitlochry. **82 B1** NO0860.
Kirkmichael *S.Ayr.* ***Village***, 3m/5km E of Maybole. **67 H3** NS3408.
Kirkmuirhill *S.Lan.* Population: 1900. ***Village***, adjoining to S of Blackwood, 6m/9km W of Lanark. **75 F6** NS7943.
Kirknewton *Northumb.* ***Village***, in River Glen valley, 5m/8km W of Wooler. **70 E1** NT9130.
Kirknewton *W.Loth.* Population: 1363. ***Village***, 10m/16km SW of Edinburgh. **75 K4** NT1166.
Kirkney *Aber.* ***Settlement***, 5m/8km S of Huntly. **90 D1** NJ5132.
Kirkney Water *Aber.* ***River***, stream running NE into River Bogie, 1km NE of Kirkney. **90 C1** NJ5133.
Kirkoswald *Cumb.* ***Village***, 7m/11km N of Penrith. Remains of medieval castle to E. **61 G2** NY5541.
Kirkoswald *S.Ayr.* ***Village***, 4m/7km W of Maybole. Souter Johnnie's House (National Trust for Scotland), former home of John Davidson, the original Souter Johnnie of Burns' poem, Tam o' Shanter. **67 G3** NS2307.
Kirkoswald Castle *Cumb.* ***Castle***, ruined castle with 13c moat, to SE of Kirkoswald. **61 G2** NY5540.
Kirkpatrick Durham *D. & G.* ***Village***, 5m/8km N of Castle Douglas. **65 H3** NX7870.
Kirkpatrick-Fleming *D. & G.* ***Village***, 6m/10km SE of Ecclefechan. Bruce's Cave 1km W. **69 H6** NY2770.
Kirksanton *Cumb.* ***Hamlet***, 2m/3km W of Millom. **54 E1** SD1480.
Kirkstall *W.Yorks.* ***Suburb***, 2m/3km NW of Leeds city centre. Remains of 12c Cistercian abbey beside River Aire. **57 H6** SE2635.
Kirkstall Abbey *W.Yorks.* ***Ecclesiastical building***, remains of 12c Cistercian church (English Heritage) by River Aire, 3m/5km NW of Leeds. Gatehouse now a museum. **57 H6** SE2536.
Kirkstead *Lincs.* ***Village***, on River Witham, 7m/11km SW of Woodhall Spa. Scant remains of 12c abbey 1m/2km E. **52 E6** TF1762.
Kirkstead Abbey *Lincs.* ***Ecclesiastical building***, fragment of 13c Cistercian abbey, 1m/2km S of Woodhall Spa. **52 E6** TF1861.
Kirkstile *Aber.* ***Settlement***, 3m/5km S of Huntly. **90 D1** NJ5235.
Kirkstile *D. & G.* ***Village***, on Ewes Water, 4m/6km N of Langholm. **69 J4** NY3690.
Kirkstone Pass *Cumb.* ***Locality***, and pass in Lake District, carrying road from Windermere to Patterdale, 5m/8km S of Patterdale. **60 F6** NY4008.
Kirkstyle *High.* ***Hamlet***, on Pentland Firth, 4m/6km W of Duncansby Head. ND3472.
Kirkthorpe *W.Yorks.* ***Village***, 2m/3km E of Wakefield city centre, on E side of River Calder. SE3620.
Kirkton *Aber.* ***Settlement***, 1m/2km NE of Auchleven. **90 E2** NJ6425.
Kirkton *Aber.* ***Settlement***, 2m/3km W of Turriff. **98 E5** NJ6950.
Kirkton *Aber.* ***Village***, 3m/5km SE of Alford. **90 E3** NJ6113.
Kirkton *Angus* ***Hamlet***, 3m/5km SW of Forfar. **83 F3** NO4246.
Kirkton *Arg. & B.* ***Settlement***, 1km E of Craignish Castle. **79 J7** NM7701.
Kirkton *D. & G.* ***Village***, 4m/6km N of Dumfries. Remains of Roman fort to NW. **68 E5** NX9781.
Kirkton *Fife* ***Settlement***, on Firth of Tay, 2m/4km W of Wormit. **82 E5** NO3625.
Kirkton *High.* ***Locality***, in Inverness district, 1km N of NE end of Loch Ness. **88 D1** NH6038.
Kirkton *High.* ***Settlement***, 1m/2km S of Melvich, Caithness district. **104 D2** NC8962.
Kirkton *High.* ***Settlement***, on N side of Loch Alsh, in Skye and Lochalsh district, 4m/6km W of Dornie. **86 E2** NG8327.
Kirkton *High.* ***Settlement***, 1m/2km N of Ardersier. **96 E6** NH7856.
Kirkton *High.* ***Settlement***, 6m/9km N of Dornoch across Loch Fleet. **96 E2** NH7999.
Kirkton *P. & K.* ***Settlement***, 4m/6km NE of Auchterarder. **82 A6** NN9618.
Kirkton *Sc.Bord.* ***Locality***, 3m/4km E of Hawick. **70 A2** NT5413.
Kirkton *W.Loth.* ***Locality***, in Livingston, 2m/3km SW of town centre. NT0366.
Kirkton Head *Aber.* ***Coastal feature***, headland on NE coast, 3m/5km N of Peterhead. **99 K5** NK1150.
Kirkton Manor *Sc.Bord.* ***Settlement***, 3m/4km SW of Peebles. **76 A7** NT2237.
Kirkton of Airlie *Angus* ***Locality***, 5m/8km W of Kirriemuir. **82 E2** NO3151.
Kirkton of Auchterhouse *Angus* ***Village***, 6m/10km NW of Dundee. **82 E4** NO3438.
Kirkton of Barevan *High.* ***Settlement***, 2m/3km S of Cawdor. **97 F7** NH8347.
Kirkton of Bourtie *Aber.* ***Settlement***, 1m/2km S of Oldmeldrum. **91 G2** NJ8024.
Kirkton of Collace *P. & K.* ***Settlement***, 1km SW of Collace and 7m/11km NE of Perth. **82 C4** NO1931.
Kirkton of Craig *Angus* ***Village***, 1m/2km SW of Montrose. **83 J2** NO7055.
Kirkton of Culsalmond (Also known as Culsalmond.) *Aber.* ***Village***, 9m/14km SE of Huntly. **90 E1** NJ6432.
Kirkton of Durris *Aber.* ***Village***, 5m/8km E of Banchory. **91 F5** NO7796.
Kirkton of Glenbuchat *Aber.* ***Settlement***, on S slopes of Glen Buchat below Ben Newe, 2m/3km NE of Strathdon. **90 B3** NJ3715.
Kirkton of Glenisla *Angus* ***Village***, on River Isla, 8m/12km N of Alyth. **82 D1** NO2160.
Kirkton of Kingoldrum *Angus* ***Village***, 3m/5km W of Kirriemuir. Site of Balfour Castle to S. **82 E2** NO3355.
Kirkton of Largo *Fife Alternative name for Upper Largo, qv.*
Kirkton of Lethendy *P. & K.* ***Settlement***, 4m/6km SW of Blairgowrie. **82 C3** NO1241.
Kirkton of Logie Buchan *Aber.* ***Village***, 2m/3km E of Ellon across River Ythan. **91 H2** NJ9829.
Kirkton of Maryculter (Also known as Maryculter.) *Aber.* ***Village***, 1m/2km SE of Peterculter across River Dee. **91 G5** NO8599.
Kirkton of Menmuir *Angus* ***Village***, 5m/8km NW of Brechin. **83 G1** NO5364.
Kirkton of Monikie *Angus* ***Settlement***, 4m/6km NW of Carnoustie. **83 G4** NO5138.
Kirkton of Oyne *Aber.* ***Locality***, 1km E of Oyne and 6m/9km NW of Inverurie. NJ6825.
Kirkton of Rayne (Also known as Rayne.) *Aber.* ***Village***, 8m/12km NW of Inverurie. **90 E1** NJ6930.
Kirkton of Skene *Aber.* ***Village***, 9m/14km W of Aberdeen. **91 G4** NJ8007.
Kirkton of Strathmartine *Angus* ***Village***, 4m/6km NW of Dundee. **82 E4** NO3735.
Kirkton of Tealing (Also known as Tealing.) *Angus* ***Hamlet***, 5m/7km N of Dundee. Mast to NW. Tealing House to E has unusual dovecote; also souterrain or earth-house (Historic Scotland). **83 F4** NO4138.
Kirktonhill *Aber.* ***Hamlet***, 1km NE of Marykirk. **83 H1** NO6965.
Kirktonhill *W.Dun.* ***Suburb***, W district of Dumbarton. NS3975.
Kirktown *Aber.* ***Locality***, 1m/2km S of Fraserburgh. NJ9965.
Kirktown *Aber.* ***Suburb***, S district of Peterhead. **99 J5** NK1346.
Kirktown of Alvah *Aber.* ***Village***, near N coast, 2m/4km S of Banff. **98 E4** NJ6760.
Kirktown of Auchterless (Also known as Auchterless.) *Aber.* ***Village***, 5m/8km S of Turriff. **99 F6** NJ7141.
Kirktown of Clatt *Aber. Alternative name for Clatt, qv.*
Kirktown of Deskford *Moray* ***Village***, near N coast, 4m/6km S of Cullen. Ruined church (Historic Scotland). **98 D4** NJ5061.
Kirktown of Fetteresso *Aber.* ***Village***, on E side of Fetteresso Forest, 1m/2km W of Stonehaven. **91 G6** NO8585.

K

Kirktown of Slains *Aber.* ***Locality***, adjoining to N of Collieston, 5m/9km E of Ellon. Remains of Old Castle of Slains 1m/2km NE of Collieston. **91 J2** NK0428.
Kirkwall *Ork.* Population: 6469. ***Small town***, chief town and port of Mainland and capital of Orkney, situated at N end of narrow neck of land between Wide Firth to N and Scapa Flow to S, 24m/38km N of Scottish mainland at Duncansby Head. Location of 12c Bishop's Palace (Historic Scotland), with later additions including 16c round tower, and 17c Renaissance style Earl's Palace (Historic Scotland). **107 D6** HY4411.
Kirkwall Airport *Ork.* ***Airport/airfield***, on Mainland, situated 3m/4km SE of Kirkwall, at head of Inganess Bay. **107 D7** HY4808.
Kirkwhelpington *Northumb.* ***Village***, on River Wansbeck, 9m/14km SE of Otterburn. **70 E5** NY9984.
Kirmington *N.Lincs.* ***Village***, 6m/10km N of Caistor. **52 E1** TA1011.
Kirmond le Mire *Lincs.* ***Village***, 6m/9km NE of Market Rasen. **52 E3** TF1892.
Kirn *Arg. & B.* ***Locality***, in Argyll, adjoining to N of Dunoon, on W shore of Firth of Clyde. **73 K3** NS1878.
Kirriemuir *Angus* Population: 5571. ***Small town***, former linen-weaving centre, 5m/8km NW of Forfar. The Thrums of Barrie's novels, whose birthplace here houses a museum (National Trust for Scotland). **82 E2** NO3854.
Kirriereoch Hill *D. & G.* ***Mountain***, in Glentrool Forest Park on border with South Ayrshire, 4m/7km N of Loch Trool and 1m/2km NW of Merrick. Height 2578 feet or 786 metres. **67 J5** NX4287.
Kirriereoch Loch *D. & G.* ***Lake/loch***, in Glentrool Forest, 5m/8km NW of Loch Trool. **67 H5** NX3686.
Kirstead Green *Norf.* ***Village***, 5m/9km NW of Bungay. **45 G6** TM2997.
Kirstead Green Lings *Norf.* ***Village***, 1m/2km NE of Kirstead Green. TM3098.
Kirtle Water *D. & G.* ***River***, rising 6m/10km W of Langholm and running S to Kirtlebridge, then SE to Solway Firth 1m/2km S of Gretna. **69 H6** NY3165.
Kirtlebridge *D. & G.* ***Village***, 3m/5km SE of Ecclefechan. **69 H6** NY2372.
Kirtleton *D. & G.* ***Settlement***, 6m/9km NE of Ecclefechan. NY2680.
Kirtling *Cambs.* ***Hamlet***, 5m/7km SE of Newmarket. Tudor gatehouse survives from former manor house. **33 K3** TL6856.
Kirtling Green *Cambs.* ***Village***, 1m/2km SW of Kirtling. **33 K3** TL6857.
Kirtlington *Oxon.* ***Village***, 6m/9km W of Bicester. **31 F7** SP4919.
Kirtomy *High.* ***Village***, near N coast of Caithness district, 3m/4km E of Bettyhill. **104 C2** NC7463.
Kirtomy Bay *High.* ***Bay***, 1km N of Kirtomy, on N coast of Caithness district, 3m/4km NE of Bettyhill. **104 C2** NC7464.
Kirtomy Point *High.* ***Coastal feature***, headland 1m/2km N of Kirtomy. **104 C2** NC7463.
Kirton *Lincs.* Population: 2588. ***Village***, 4m/6km SW of Boston. **43 G2** TF3038.
Kirton *Notts.* ***Village***, 3m/4km E of Ollerton. **51 J6** SK6969.
Kirton *Suff.* ***Village***, 4m/6km N of Felixstowe. **35 G5** TM2739.
Kirton End *Lincs.* ***Hamlet***, 1m/2km NW of Kirton. **43 F1** TF2940.
Kirton Holme *Lincs.* ***Hamlet***, 4m/7km W of Boston. **43 F1** TF2642.
Kirton in Lindsey *N.Lincs.* Population: 2773. ***Small town***, 8m/13km S of Scunthorpe. Transport museum in 19c windmill. Airfield to SE. **52 C3** SK9398.
Kiscadale *N.Ayr.* ***Locality***, two localities, North and South Kiscadale, on Whiting Bay, E coast of Arran. **66 E1** NS0426.
Kishorn *High.* ***Locality***, in Ross and Cromarty district, at head of Loch Kishorn. NG8340.
Kishorn *High.* ***River***, running S to head of Loch Kishorn. **94 E7** NG8340.
Kishorn Island *High.* ***Island***, small uninhabited island at entrance to Loch Kishorn. NG8037.
Kisimul *W.Isles Alternative spelling of Kiessimul, qv.*
Kisimul Castle *W.Isles Alternative spelling of Kiessimul Castle, qv.*
Kislingbury *Northants.* ***Village***, on River Nene, 4m/6km W of Northampton. **31 H3** SP6959.
Kismeldon Bridge *Devon* ***Bridge***, over River Torridge, 3m/4km NE of Bradworthy. **6 B4** SS3516.
Kit Hill *Cornw.* ***Mountain***, summit of Hingston Down to NE of Callington. Splendid views of Dartmoor and Bodmin Moor. Accessible by road. Height 1092 feet or 333 metres. **4 D3** SX3771.
Kitchener's Monument *Ork.* ***Other feature of interest***, situated on Marwick Head, 1m/2km NW of Marwick on W coast of Mainland. Memorial to crew of HMS Hampshire and Lord Kitchener, whose boat sank off coast in 1916. **106 B5** HY2225.
Kite Green *Warks.* ***Settlement***, 1m/2km E of Henley-in-Arden. SP1666.
Kites Hardwick *Warks.* ***Settlement***, 5m/8km SW of Rugby. **31 F2** SP4768.
Kithurst Hill *W.Suss.* ***Hill***, 1m/2km S of Storrington. Height 699 feet or 213 metres. **12 D5** TQ0812.
Kitnocks *Hants.* ***Settlement***, adjoining to S of Curdridge, 1m/2km E of Botley. SU5213.
Kit's Coty *Kent* ***Settlement***, 1m/2km S of Blue Bell Hill, 3m/5km N of Maidstone. Kit's Coty House (English Heritage) to S. TQ7461.
Kit's Coty House *Kent* ***Historic/prehistoric site***, consisting of three upright stones and a capstone (English Heritage) probably dating from c. 3000 BC, overlooking River Medway valley, 1m/2km S of Blue Bell Hill, midway between Rochester and Maidstone. Little (or Lower) Kit's Coty House (also English Heritage), formerly known as Countless Stones, to S. Site of Roman temple on other side of main road. **24 D5** TQ7460.
Kitt Green *Gt.Man.* ***Suburb***, in W part of Wigan. SD5505.
Kittisford *Som.* ***Hamlet***, 4m/6km NW of Wellington. **7 J3** ST0722.
Kittisford Barton *Som.* ***Hamlet***, 1km N of Kittisford and 3m/4km S of Wiveliscombe. ST0723.
Kittle *Swan.* ***Village***, to W of Bishopston, on Gower peninsula between Bishopston and Pennard, 6m/10km SW of Swansea. SS5789.
Kitts End *Herts.* ***Settlement***, 2m/3km S of Potters Bar. TQ2498.
Kitt's Green *W.Mid.* ***Suburb***, 5m/9km E of Birmingham city centre. SP1587.
Kitt's Moss *Gt.Man.* ***Suburb***, to W of Bramhall town centre. SJ8884.
Kittybrewster *Aberdeen* ***Suburb***, 1m/2km NW of Aberdeen city centre. NJ9207.
Kitwood *Hants.* ***Hamlet***, 1m/2km S of Four Marks and 5m/8km E of New Alresford. **11 H1** SU6633.
Kivernoll *Here.* ***Hamlet***, 6m/9km SW of Hereford. SO4632.
Kiveton Park *S.Yorks.* ***Suburb***, 6m/10km W of Worksop. **51 G4** SK4982.
Kixley Wharf *W.Mid.* ***Locality***, on Grand Union Canal, 3m/5km SE of Solihull. SP1877.
Klibreck *High.* ***Settlement***, 1m/2km SE of Altnaharra, on S shore of Loch Naver. **103 H5** NC5834.
Klibreck Burn *High.* ***River***, flowing NE into Loch Naver, 1m/2km E of Altnaharra. **103 H5** NC5934.
Knabbygates *Moray* ***Settlement***, 3m/4km N of Milltown of Rothiemay. **98 D5** NJ5552.
Knaik *P. & K.* ***River***, running SE to Allan Water, 1m/2km S of Braco. **81 K6** NN8307.
Knaith *Lincs.* ***Hamlet***, 3m/5km S of Gainsborough. **52 B4** SK8284.
Knaith Park *Lincs.* ***Hamlet***, 1m/2km NE of Knaith, 3m/5km SE of Gainsborough. SK8485.
Knap Corner *Dorset* ***Hamlet***, adjoining to NE of East Stour, 2m/3km S of Gillingham. **9 H2** ST8023.
Knap of Howar *Ork.* ***Historic/prehistoric site***, site of prehistoric stone dwellings (Historic Scotland) on W coast of Papa Westray. Remains date from between 2400 BC and 2800 BC. **106 D2** HY4851.
Knap of Trowieglen *Ork.* ***Mountain***, 3m/4km E of Rackwick. Height 1309 feet or 399 metres. **107 B8** ND2498.
Knapdale *Arg. & B.* ***Locality***, area of Argyll, bounded by Crinan Canal to N, and East and West Loch Tarbert to S. Largely moorland, with many small lochs. **73 F4** NR8078.
Knapdale Forest *Arg. & B.* ***Forest/woodland***, at NW end of Knapdale. **73 F2** NR8176.
Knaphill *Surr.* ***Suburb***, 3m/4km W of Woking. **22 C6** SU9658.
Knaplock *Som.* ***Hamlet***, on Exmoor, 2m/3km SE of Withypool. SS8633.
Knapp *Dundee* ***Hamlet***, 2m/3km NW of Longforgan. **82 D4** NO2831.
Knapp *Som.* ***Village***, 5m/8km E of Taunton. **8 B2** ST3025.
Knaps Longpeak *Devon* ***Coastal feature***, point on W coast of Devon, 1m/2km W of Welcombe. **6 A4** SS2018.
Knapthorpe *Notts.* ***Hamlet***, 4m/6km NE of Southwell. SK7458.
Knaptoft *Leics.* ***Settlement***, 4m/6km N of Husbands Bosworth. SP6289.
Knapton *Norf.* ***Village***, 3m/5km NE of North Walsham. **45 H2** TG3034.
Knapton *York* ***Village***, 3m/4km W of York. **58 B4** SE5652.
Knapton Green *Here.* ***Hamlet***, 9m/15km NW of Hereford. **28 D3** SO4452.
Knapwell *Cambs.* ***Village***, 8m/12km NW of Cambridge. **33 G2** TL3362.
Knaresborough *N.Yorks.* Population: 13,380. ***Town***, market town on escarpment above River Nidd, 3m/5km NE of Harrogate. Petrifying well and remains of 12c castle. **57 J4** SE3557.
Knaresborough Castle *N.Yorks.* ***Castle***, ruined 14c castle of John of Gaunt, partly demolished by Roundheads, on cliff top close to market place in Knaresborough. **57 J4** SE3457.
Knarie Burn *D. & G.* ***River***, rising on E side of Brockloch Hill and flowing SW to join Urr Water, 1km SE of Corsock. **65 H3** NX7675.
Knarsdale *Northumb.* ***Hamlet***, near confluence of Knar Burn and River South Tyne, 7m/11km S of Haltwhistle. **61 H1** NY6753.
Knarston *Ork.* ***Settlement***, on Mainland, 1km E of Dounby. HY3020.
Knathole *Derbys.* ***Locality***, adjoining to SW of New Mills. SJ9985.
Knatts Valley *Kent* ***Settlement***, 1m/2km SW of West Kingsdown. TQ5661.
Knaven *Aber.* ***Locality***, comprises many dispersed settlements, 3m/4km S of New Deer. **99 G6** NJ8843.
Knaves' Green *Suff.* ***Settlement***, 1km S of Wetheringsett. TM1266.
Knavesmire *York* ***Suburb***, 2m/3km S of York city centre. Includes York Racecourse. SE5849.
Knayton *N.Yorks.* ***Village***, 4m/6km N of Thirsk. **57 K1** SE4387.
Knebworth *Herts.* Population: 4025. ***Small town***, 3m/4km S of Stevenage. St. Martin's church designed by Lutyens. **33 F7** TL2520.
Knebworth House *Herts.* ***Historic house***, 16c and 19c, in park to N of Old Knebworth. **33 F6** TL2320.
Knedlington *E.Riding* ***Village***, 1m/2km W of Howden. **58 D7** SE7328.
Kneesall *Notts.* ***Village***, 4m/6km SE of Ollerton. **51 K6** SK7064.
Kneesworth *Cambs.* ***Village***, 2m/4km N of Royston. **33 G4** TL3444.
Kneeton *Notts.* ***Village***, 7m/12km SW of Newark-on-Trent. **42 A1** SK7146.
Knelhall *Staffs.* ***Settlement***, 3m/4km NE of Stone. SJ9237.
Knelston *Swan.* ***Village***, on Gower peninsula, 3m/5km N of Port Eynon Point and 12m/19km W of Swansea. **17 H6** SS4688.
Knettishall *Suff.* ***Settlement***, 7m/11km E of Thetford. **34 D1** TL9680.
Knettishall Heath Country Park *Suff.* ***Leisure/recreation***, 180 acre country park with indigenous heathland, situated by S bank of Little Ouse River 1m/2km N of Coney Weston, at S end of Peddar's Way long distance path. **34 D1** TL9480.
Knightacott *Devon* ***Settlement***, 7m/11km NE of Barnstaple. **6 E2** SS6439.
Knightcote *Warks.* ***Village***, 9m/15km N of Banbury. **31 F3** SP4054.
Knightley *Staffs.* ***Settlement***, 3m/5km SW of Eccleshall. SJ8125.
Knightley Dale *Staffs.* ***Settlement***, 1m/2km S of Knightley. SJ8123.
Knighton *Devon* ***Locality***, at N end of Wembury, 4m/6km SW of Yealmpton across River Yealm estuary. **5 F6** SX5249.
Knighton *Dorset* ***Hamlet***, 1m/2km NE of Yetminster and 4m/6km SW of Sherborne. ST6111.
Knighton *Leic.* ***Suburb***, 2m/3km SE of Leicester city centre. **41 J5** SK6001.
Knighton *Poole* ***Settlement***, 4m/7km NE of Poole town centre. SZ0497.
Knighton (Trefyclo). *Powys* Population: 2972. ***Small town***, on River Teme, 14m/23km W of Ludlow. Motte and bailey castle; also remains of later castle, Bryn y Castell, to E. Well-preserved sections of Offa's Dyke near town. **28 B1** SO2872.
Knighton *Som.* ***Hamlet***, 3m/5km N of Nether Stowey. **7 K1** ST1944.
Knighton *Staffs.* ***Hamlet***, 1m/2km S of Woore. **39 G2** SJ7240.
Knighton *Staffs.* ***Village***, 5m/8km N of Newport. **39 G3** SJ7427.
Knighton *Wilts.* ***Settlement***, 3m/5km NW of Hungerford. Site of Roman villa to SE across River Kennet. **21 F4** SU2971.
Knighton Down *Wilts.* ***Open space***, hillslope 3m/5km NW of Amesbury. **20 E7** SU1144.
Knighton on Teme *Worcs.* ***Hamlet***, 3m/4km NE of Tenbury Wells. SO6370.
Knighton Reservoir *Staffs.* ***Reservoir***, 1m/2km NW of Knighton. **39 G3** SJ7427.
Knight's End *Cambs.* ***Locality***, adjoining to S of March. TL4194.
Knight's Green *Glos.* ***Locality***, 4m/6km S of Ledbury. SO7131.
Knightsbridge *Gt.Lon.* ***Locality***, street in West End, running W from Hyde Park Corner down to site of bridge over Westbourne Brook, which now runs in underground pipes. Term also applied to area surrounding Knightsbridge Underground Station. TQ2779.
Knightshayes Court *Devon* ***Garden***, National Trust garden particularly noted for ornamental shrubs, surrounding 19c Gothic mansion, 2m/3km N of Tiverton. **7 H4** SS9615.
Knightsridge *W.Loth.* ***Suburb***, to NW of Livingston town centre. NT0469.
Knightswood *Glas.* ***Suburb***, 4m/7km NW of Glasgow city centre. NS5369.
Knightwick *Worcs.* ***Settlement***, 4m/7km E of Bromyard. **29 G3** SO7255.
Knill *Here.* ***Hamlet***, on Hindwell Brook, 3m/4km N of Kington. **28 B2** SO2960.
Knipoch *Arg. & B.* ***Settlement***, on S shore of Loch Feochan, 2m/3km NE of Kilninver. **79 K5** NM8522.
Knipton *Leics.* ***Village***, 6m/10km SW of Grantham. **42 B2** SK8231.
Knipton Reservoir *Leics.* ***Reservoir***, 1km SW of Knipton. **42 B2** SK8231.
Knitsley *Dur.* ***Settlement***, 1m/2km S of Consett. **62 C2** NZ1148.
Knitsley Fell *Dur.* ***Hill***, rising to over 270 metres, 2m/4km SE of Wolsingham. **62 B3** NZ0834.
Kniveton *Derbys.* ***Village***, 3m/5km NE of Ashbourne. **50 E7** SK2050.
Knock *Arg. & B.* ***Settlement***, on S bank of River Bà, 1km S of Gruline, Mull. **79 G4** NM5438.
Knock *Cumb.* ***Hamlet***, 4m/7km N of Appleby-in-Westmorland. **61 H4** NY6827.
Knock (Gaelic form: Cnoc Uaine.) *High.* ***Settlement***, on Knock Bay, Skye, on E coast of Sleat peninsula, adjoining to E of Teangue. NG6709.
Knock *Moray* ***Settlement***, 7m/12km E of Keith. **98 D5** NJ5452.
Knock *W.Isles Anglicised form of Cnoc, qv.*
Knock Bay *High.* ***Bay***, on E coast of Sleat peninsula, Skye. **86 C4** NG6709.
Knock Castle (Also known as Camus Castle.) *High.* ***Castle***, on Skye, at E end of bay, also called Camus Castle, ruined castle of Barons of Sleat. **86 C4** NG6709.
Knock Fell *Cumb.* ***Open space***, on S side of Milburn Forest, highest point being Knock Old Man, 2604 feet or 794 metres, 4m/7km W of Cow Green Reservoir. **61 J3** NY7230.
Knock Fell *D. & G.* ***Hill***, adjacent to W of Knock of Luce, 4m/6km E of Glenluce. Fort at summit. Height 574 feet or 175 metres. **64 C5** NX2555.
Knock Head *Aber.* ***Coastal feature***, headland on N coast, 2m/4km NW of Banff. **98 E4** NJ6566.
Knock Hill *Aber.* ***Mountain***, to N of Knock. Height 1410 feet or 430 metres. **98 D5** NJ5452.
Knock Hill *Fife* ***Mountain***, 2m/3km NE of Saline. Height 1194 feet or 364 metres. **75 J1** NT0593.
Knock More *Moray* ***Mountain***, in wooded area, 3m/4km E of Rothes. Height 1168 feet or 356 metres. **98 B5** NJ3150.
Knock Moss *D. & G.* ***Open space***, afforested area adjoining to S of Dernaglar Loch, 4m/7km E of Glenluce. **64 C5** NX2657.

Knock of Auchnahannet *High.* ***Settlement***, 4m/6km N of Grantown-on-Spey. **89 H1** NJ0633.
Knock of Balmyle *P. & K.* ***Mountain***, to E of Balmyle, 3m/5km NW of Bridge of Cally. Height 1456 feet or 444 metres. **82 C2** NO1156.
Knock of Braemoray *Moray* ***Mountain***, 2m/3km N of Dava. Height 1496 feet or 456 metres. **97 H7** NJ0141.
Knock of Crieff *P. & K.* ***Hill***, with notable viewpoint, 1m/2km N of Crieff. Height 912 feet or 278 metres. NN8622.
Knock Saul *Aber.* ***Mountain***, surrounded by Whitehaugh Forest, 5m/7km N of Alford. Height 1351 feet or 412 metres. **90 D2** NJ5723.
Knockaird *W.Isles* ***Settlement***, near N end of Isle of Lewis, 1km NW of Port Nis. NB5364.
Knockalava *Arg. & B.* ***Settlement***, 6m/10km NE of Lochgilphead. **73 H1** NR9196.
Knockally *High.* ***Settlement***, 1km SW of Dunbeath. **105 G6** ND1429.
Knockaloe Moar *I.o.M.* ***Settlement***, 1m/2km S of Peel. **54 B5** SC2382.
Knockan *High.* ***Hamlet***, in Sutherland district, adjoining to S of Elphin, 8m/12km S of Inchnadamph. **102 E7** NC2110.
Knockan *Moray* ***Mountain***, 5m/8km NE of Charlestown of Aberlour. Height 1220 feet or 372 metres. **98 B6** NJ3546.
Knockandhu *Moray* ***Village***, 4m/7km NE of Tomintoul. **89 K2** NJ2123.
Knockando *Moray* ***Locality***, on N bank of River Spey, 7m/11km W of Craigellachie. Includes Knockando Distillery. **97 J7** NJ1941.
Knockandy Hill *Aber.* ***Mountain***, 2m/3km SW of Gartly. Height 1424 feet or 434 metres. **90 D1** NJ5431.
Knockarthur *High.* ***Settlement***, in Sutherland district, 7m/11km NW of Golspie. NC7506.
Knockbain *High.* ***Settlement***, 3m/4km NW of Munlochy. **96 D6** NH6256.
Knockban *High.* ***Locality***, in Strath Bran, 4m/7km E of Achnasheen. **95 J5** NH2161.
Knockbreck *High.* ***Settlement***, adjoining to SE of Tain. **96 E3** NH7981.
Knockbrex *D. & G.* ***Settlement***, overlooking Andwall Isle, on E side of Wigtown Bay, 4m/7km S of Gatehouse of Fleet. **65 F6** NX5849.
Knockdamph *High.* ***Settlement***, 10m/16km E of Ullapool. Inaccessible by road. **95 J2** NH2895.
Knockdee *High.* ***Settlement***, 3m/4km NE of Halkirk. **105 G2** ND1661.
Knockdolian *S.Ayr.* ***Hill***, prominent hill 2m/4km NE of Ballantrae. Height 869 feet or 265 metres. **66 E5** NX1184.
Knockdow *Arg. & B.* ***Settlement***, 2m/3km N of Ardyne Point. **73 K3** NS1070.
Knockdown *Glos.* ***Hamlet***, on border with Wiltshire, 5m/7km SW of Tetbury. **20 B3** ST8388.
Knockencorsan *N.Ayr.* ***Mountain***, elongated mass aligned NE to SW, rising to over 330 metres at head of Noddsdale Water, 3m/5km E of Skelmorlie. **74 A4** NS2366.
Knockendon Reservoir *N.Ayr.* ***Reservoir***, 4m/6km NW of Dalry. **74 A5** NS2452.
Knockenkelly *N.Ayr.* ***Settlement***, on E coast of Arran, towards N end of Whiting Bay. **66 E1** NS0427.
Knockentiber *E.Ayr.* ***Hamlet***, 2m/3km NW of Kilmarnock. **74 C7** NS3939.
Knockfin *High.* ***Settlement***, 4m/6km SW of Cannich. **87 J2** NH2926.
Knockfin Heights *High.* ***Open space***, high ground on border of Sutherland and Caithness districts, rising to 428m. Marshland and numerous small lochs. **104 E5** NC9134.
Knockgray *D. & G.* ***Settlement***, 1m/2km E of Carsphairn. **67 K4** NX5793.
Knockhall *Kent* ***Locality***, 3m/5km E of Dartford. TQ5974.
Knockholt *Kent* ***Village***, 3m/5km NE of Westerham. **23 H6** TQ4658.
Knockholt Pound *Kent* ***Settlement***, to NE of Knockholt, 4m/6km NW of Sevenoaks. **23 H6** TQ4658.
Knockin *Shrop.* ***Village***, 5m/8km SE of Oswestry. Mound of medieval castle E of church. **38 C3** SJ3322.
Knockinlaw *E.Ayr.* ***Suburb***, N district of Kilmarnock. NS4239.
Knocklearn *D. & G.* ***Settlement***, 2m/3km N of Corsock. **65 H3** NX7579.
Knockmill *Kent* ***Settlement***, 3m/5km NW of Wrotham. TQ5761.
Knocknagael Boar Stone *High.* ***Historic/prehistoric site***, 7c or 8c Pictish stone (Historic Scotland), bearing outline of wild boar, situated 3m/4km S of Inverness. **96 D7** NH6541.
Knocknaha *Arg. & B.* ***Settlement***, on Kintyre, 3m/4km SW of Campbeltown. **66 A2** NR6818.
Knocknain *D. & G.* ***Settlement***, 6m/9km W of Stranraer. **64 A4** NW9764.
Knocknalling *D. & G.* ***Settlement***, 3m/4km NW of St. John's Town of Dalry. **67 K5** NX5984.
Knockrome *Arg. & B.* ***Settlement***, adjoining to W of Ardfernal, Jura. **72 D3** NR5571.
Knocksharry *I.o.M.* ***Settlement***, 2m/4km NE of Peel. **54 B5** SC2785.
Knockton *Angus* ***Mountain***, in Forest of Alyth, 3m/4km W of Bellaty. Height 1604 feet or 489 metres. **82 C2** NO1958.
Knockville *D. & G.* ***Settlement***, 6m/9km NW of Newton Stewart. **64 D3** NX3672.
Knockvologan *Arg. & B.* ***Settlement***, 3m/4km S of Fionnphort, Ross of Mull. **78 E6** NM3119.
Knodishall *Suff.* ***Village***, 1m/2km W of Leiston. **35 J2** TM4261.
Knodishall Common *Suff.* ***Settlement***, 1m/2km SE of Knodishall. TM4360.
Knodishall Green *Suff.* ***Settlement***, 1m/2km NW of Knodishall. TM4163.

K

Knole *Kent* ***Historic house***, mansion (National Trust) of 15c-17c in large deer park on E side of Sevenoaks. Ancestral seat of Sackvilles. **23 J6** TQ5454.
Knole *Som.* ***Hamlet***, 2m/4km S of Somerton. ST4825.
Knoll Gardens *Dorset* ***Garden***, 6 acres of gardens to SW of Ferndown. Houses National Collection of Ceanothus and Phygelius in informal garden, with over 4000 other plants. **10 B4** SU0600.
Knollbury *Mon.* ***Hamlet***, 1km NE of Magor. ST4388.
Knolls Green *Ches.* ***Village***, 3m/4km W of Alderley Edge. **49 H5** SJ8079.
Knolton *Wrex.* ***Hamlet***, 2m/3km S of Overton. **38 C2** SJ3738.
Knolton Bryn *Wrex.* ***Settlement***, 1km NW of Knolton. SJ3739.
Knook *Wilts.* ***Village***, on E bank of River Wylye, 1m/2km W of Heytesbury. **20 C7** ST9341.
Knossington *Leics.* ***Village***, 4m/6km W of Oakham. **42 B5** SK8008.
Knott *Cumb.* ***Mountain***, 4m/6km NW of Saddleback. Height 2329 feet or 710 metres. **60 D3** NY2932.
Knott End-on-Sea *Lancs.* ***Village***, on E side of mouth of River Wyre, opposite Fleetwood. Ferry for pedestrians across river. **55 G5** SD3548.
Knott Lanes *Gt.Man.* ***Settlement***, 2m/3km S of Oldham, with Crime Lake to SW. SD9201.
Knotting *Beds.* ***Village***, 4m/6km SE of Rushden. **32 D2** TL0063.
Knotting Green *Beds.* ***Hamlet***, 1km S of Knotting. **32 D2** TL0063.
Knottingley *W.Yorks.* Population: 14,690. ***Town***, old mining town on S bank of River Aire, and on Aire and Calder Canal, 11m/18km E of Wakefield. **58 B7** SE5023.
Knotts *Lancs.* ***Settlement***, 4m/6km E of Slaidburn. SD7653.
Knotty Ash *Mersey.* ***Suburb***, 4m/7km E of Liverpool city centre. **48 D3** SJ4091.
Knotty Green *Bucks.* ***Locality***, 2m/3km N of Beaconsfield. **22 C2** SU9392.
Knoutberry Haw *Cumb.* ***Mountain***, highest point on Baugh Fell, 4m/7km E of Sedbergh. Height 2217 feet or 676 metres. **61 J7** SD7392.
Knowbury *Shrop.* ***Village***, 4m/7km E of Ludlow. **28 E1** SO5774.
Knowe *D. & G.* ***Settlement***, 7m/12km NW of Newton Stewart. **64 D3** NX3171.
Knowe of Onstan Chambered Cairn *Ork.* ***Historic/prehistoric site***, chambered cairn (Historic Scotland) at Knowe of Onstan on S side of Loch of Stenness, Mainland, 3m/4km NE of Stromness. **107 B6** HY2811.
Knowe of Yarso Chambered Cairn *Ork.* ***Historic/prehistoric site***, site of Neolithic communal burial-chamber (Historic Scotland) at Knowe of Yarso, on Rousay, 2m/3km W of Brinyan. **106 D5** HY4028.
Knowefield *Cumb.* ***Suburb***, 1m/2km N of Carlisle city centre, on N side of River Eden. NY4057.
Knowes Hill *Sc.Bord.* ***Mountain***, 1m/2km NW of Clovenfords. Height 1220 feet or 372 metres. **76 C7** NT4338.
Knowes of Elrick *Aber.* ***Settlement***, 1m/2km NW of Aberchirder. **98 E5** NJ6053.
Knowesgate *Northumb.* ***Locality***, 1m/2km N of Kirkwhelpington. **70 E5** NY9885.
Knoweside *S.Ayr.* ***Settlement***, 3m/5km NW of Maybole. **67 G2** NS2512.
Knowetownhead *Sc.Bord.* ***Hamlet***, 4m/6km NE of Hawick. **70 A2** NT5418.
Knowhead *Aber.* ***Settlement***, 1m/2km W of Strichen. **99 H5** NJ9255.
Knowl *W.Yorks.* ***Locality***, adjoining to N of Mirfield. SE2020.
Knowl Green *Essex* ***Hamlet***, 3m/4km S of Clare. **34 B4** TL7841.
Knowl Hill *W. & M.* ***Village***, 3m/5km NE of Twyford. Site of Roman building to W. **22 B4** SU8279.
Knowl Wall *Staffs.* ***Settlement***, 1m/2km NW of Tittensor. **40 A2** SJ8539.
Knowle *Bristol* ***Suburb***, 2m/3km SE of Bristol city centre. **19 K4** ST6070.
Knowle *Devon* ***Hamlet***, 1km NE of Budleigh Salterton. **7 J7** SY0582.
Knowle *Devon* ***Village***, 5m/8km NW of Barnstaple. **6 C2** SS4938.
Knowle *Devon* ***Village***, 4m/6km W of Crediton. **7 F5** SS7801.
Knowle *Shrop.* ***Hamlet***, 3m/5km N of Tenbury Wells. **28 E1** SO5973.
Knowle *Som.* ***Hamlet***, 2m/3km W of Dunster. SS9643.
Knowle *W.Mid.* Population: 17,588. ***Suburb***, 3m/4km SE of Solihull town centre. **30 C1** SP1876.
Knowle Cross *Devon* ***Settlement***, 1m/2km N of Whimple. SY0497.
Knowle Fold *B'burn.* ***Locality***, adjoining to N of Darwen. SD6923.
Knowle Green *Lancs.* ***Hamlet***, 2m/3km E of Longridge. **56 B6** SD6338.
Knowle Hall *Som.* ***Settlement***, 3m/5km NE of Bridgwater. **19 G7** ST3340.
Knowle St. Giles *Som.* ***Hamlet***, 2m/4km NE of Chard. ST3411.
Knowle West *Bristol* ***Suburb***, 2m/3km S of Bristol city centre. ST5970.
Knowles Hill *Devon* ***Suburb***, N district of Newton Abbot. SX8571.
Knowlton *Dorset* ***Settlement***, 1m/2km N of Wimborne St. Giles. **10 B3** SU0210.
Knowlton *Kent* ***Hamlet***, 4m/7km SW of Sandwich. **15 H2** TR2853.
Knowlton Church and Earthworks *Dorset* ***Historic/prehistoric site***, complex group of 3 henges (English Heritage), 1m/2km S of Wimbourne St. Giles. Central circle contains ruined 12c Norman church. **10 B3** SU0211.

Knowsley *Mersey.* ***Village***, 7m/11km NE of Liverpool. **48 D3** SJ4395.
Knowsthorpe *W.Yorks.* ***Suburb***, 2m/3km SE of Leeds city centre. SE3132.
Knowstone *Devon* ***Village***, 7m/11km E of South Molton. **7 G3** SS8223.
Knox Bridge *Kent* ***Hamlet***, 2m/3km S of Staplehurst. TQ7840.
Knox Hill *Aber.* ***Hill***, 1m/2km SW of Inverbervie. Height 522 feet or 159 metres. **91 G7** NO8171.
Knox Knowe *Sc.Bord.* ***Mountain***, on W side of Carter Fell in Cheviot Hills, 4m/6km SW of Carter Bar. Height 1637 feet or 499 metres. **70 B3** NT6402.
Knoydart *High.* ***Large natural feature***, mountainous area of Lochaber district between Lochs Hourn and Nevis, bordering Sound of Sleat between Mainland and Isle of Skye. **86 D4** NG8301.
Knucklas *Powys* ***Hamlet***, 3m/4km NW of Knighton. Early British camp on hill to N. **28 B1** SO2574.
Knutsford *Ches.* Population: 13,352. ***Town***, 6m/10km W of Wilmslow. The 'Cranford' of Mrs Gaskell. 18c Tabley House has excellent collection of paintings. **49 G5** SJ7578.
Knutton *Staffs.* ***Suburb***, 1m/2km NW of Newcastle-under-Lyme town centre. SJ8346.
Knuzden Brook *Lancs.* ***Suburb***, 2m/3km E of Blackburn. SD7127.
Knypersley *Staffs.* ***Locality***, adjoining to S of Biddulph. **49 H7** SJ8856.
Kokoarrah *Cumb.* ***Coastal feature***, sandbank off coast, 3m/4km W of Ravenglass. **60 B7** SD0496.
Krumlin *W.Yorks.* ***Hamlet***, 1m/2km S of Barkisland. SE0518.
Kuggar *Cornw.* ***Hamlet***, 4m/6km N of Lizard Point. **2 E7** SW7216.
Kyle *E.Ayr.* ***Locality***, area of land between Ayr in W and Cumnock in E. **74 D7** NS5021.
Kyle *N.Yorks.* ***River***, rising to N of Easingwold and flowing circuitously S into River Ouse at Newton-on-Ouse. **58 B3** SE5060.
Kyle Akin *High.* ***Sea feature***, narrow strait between Kyleakin, village on Skye, and Kyle of Lochalsh on Scottish mainland, at mouth of Loch Alsh. Crossed by toll road bridge. **86 D2** NG7526.
Kyle More (Also known as Caol Mòr.) *High.* ***Sea feature***, sea channel between Raasay and Scalpay. **86 B1** NG5833.
Kyle of Durness *High.* ***Sea feature***, estuary of River Dionard running into Balnakeil Bay on N coast of Sutherland district, to W of Durness. **103 F2** NC3668.
Kyle of Lochalsh *High.* ***Village***, port in Skye and Lochalsh district, on N side of entrance to Loch Alsh. Road bridge to Kyleakin on Skye across narrow strait of Kyle Akin. **86 D2** NG7627.
Kyle of Sutherland *High.* ***Sea feature***, narrows between Invershin and Bonar Bridge, Sutherland district, at head of Dornoch Firth. **96 C2** NH5795.
Kyle of Tongue *High.* ***Sea feature***, estuarial inlet on N coast of Caithness district running out into Tongue Bay. Village of Tongue on E side of inlet. **103 H3** NC5859.
Kyle Rhea *High.* ***Sea feature***, narrow strait between E end of Skye and W coast of Scottish mainland, connecting Loch Alsh to N with Sound of Sleat to S. Vehicle ferry at S end of strait. **86 D2** NG7922.
Kyle Rona (Also known as Caol Rona.) *High.* ***Sea feature***, strait separating islands of Raasay and Rona. **94 C6** NG6154.
Kyleakin *High.* ***Village***, on Skye, 1km SW of Kyle of Lochalsh across Kyle Akin. **86 D2** NG7526.
Kylerhea *High.* ***Settlement***, at E end of Skye, on Kyle Rhea, 4m/7km SE of Kyleakin. Vehicle ferry across strait to Scottish mainland. **86 D2** NG7820.
Kyles of Bute *Arg. & B.* ***Sea feature***, narrow channel surrounding N part of Bute and separating it from mainland of Argyll. **73 J3** NS0175.
Kyles Scalpay *W.Isles* *Anglicised form of Caolas Scalpaigh, qv.*
Kyles Stockinish *W.Isles* ***Village***, on E side of entrance to Loch Stockinish, on SE coast of South Harris, 6m/9km S of Tarbert. NG1391.
Kylesbeg *High.* ***Settlement***, on N shore of Loch Moidart, opposite E end of Shona Beag. **86 C7** NM6773.
Kylesknoydart *High.* ***Locality***, on N shore of Loch Nevis, Lochaber district, at S end of Knoydart. Loch narrows considerably above this point. **86 E5** NM8093.
Kylesku *High.* ***Hamlet***, at W end of Loch Glendhu, 1km NW of Unapool. NC2233.
Kylesmorar *High.* ***Locality***, 1m/2km NE of Tarbet on N side of North Morar, on S shore of Loch Nevis, Lochaber district. **86 E5** NM8093.
Kylestrome *High.* ***Settlement***, on N side of Loch a' Chàirn Bhàin, W coast of Sutherland district. **102 E5** NC2134.
Kyloag *High.* ***Settlement***, 3m/5km E of Bonar Bridge. **96 D2** NH6691.
Kyloe Hills *Northumb.* ***Hill***, rising to over 130 metres, with craggy SE slopes, to W of East Kyloe. Commands wide views of coast. **77 J7** NU0439.
Kym ***River***, rising as River Til SE of Rushden and flowing NE to Tilbrook, then SE as River Kym through Kimbolton and into River Great Ouse on N side of St. Neots. **32 E2** TL1861.
Kymin *Mon.* ***Hamlet***, 1m/2km E of Monmouth across River Wye, on hill (partly National Trust) commanding views of Wye and Monnow valleys, and with 'temple' erected in 1802 in honour of Nelson's admirals. SO5212.
Kynance Cove *Cornw.* ***Coastal feature***, much visited cove of serpentine rock (National Trust), 1m/2km NW of Lizard Point. **2 D7** SW6813.
Kynaston *Shrop.* ***Settlement***, 1m/2km SE of Kinnerley. SJ3520.
Kynnersley (Sometimes spelled Kinnerley.) *Tel. & W.* ***Village***, 4m/6km NE of Wellington. **39 F4** SJ6716.
Kype Muir *S.Lan.* ***Open space***, upland moorland 4m/6km S of Strathaven, below peaks of Middle Rig and Martinside. **75 F7** NS7038.

Kype Water *S.Lan.* ***River***, issuing from Kype Reservoir and flowing N, then NW to Avon Water 1m/2km SE of Strathaven. **75 F7** NS7143.

Kyre Green *Worcs.* ***Settlement***, 4m/6km S of Tenbury Wells. SO6162.

Kyre Park *Worcs.* ***Settlement***, 3m/5km SE of Tenbury Wells. **29 F2** SO6263.

Kyrewood *Worcs.* ***Hamlet***, 1km E of Tenbury Wells. SO6067.

Kyrle *Som.* ***Settlement***, just N of Ashbrittle, 4m/7km SW of Wiveliscombe. ST0522.

L

Labost *W.Isles* ***Settlement***, near NW coast of Isle of Lewis, 1m/2km NW of Bragar. **100 E3** NB2749.

Lacasaigh (Anglicised form: Laxay.) *W.Isles* ***Village***, near E coast of Isle of Lewis, on N side of Loch Erisort. **101 F5** NB3321.

Lacasdal *W.Isles Gaelic form of Laxdale (village), qv.*

Laceby *N.E.Lincs.* Population: 2666. ***Village***, 4m/7km SW of Grimsby. **53 F2** TA2106.

Lacey Green *Bucks.* ***Village***, 3m/4km SE of Princes Risborough. **22 B1** SP8200.

Lacey Green *Ches.* ***Suburb***, adjoining to N of Wilmslow. SJ8482.

Lach Dennis *Ches.* ***Village***, 4m/6km E of Northwich. **49 G5** SJ7072.

Lacharn *Carmar. Welsh form of Laugharne, qv.*

Lachlan Castle *Arg. & B. Alternative name for Castle Lachlan, qv.*

Lackalee *W.Isles Anglicised form of Leac a' Li, qv.*

Lackenby *Middbro.* ***Locality***, in Eston, 4m/7km E of Middlesbrough. NZ5619.

Lackford *Suff.* ***Village***, 6m/9km NW of Bury St. Edmunds. **34 B1** TL7970.

Lackford Green *Suff.* ***Hamlet***, adjoins to NW of Lackford. TL7970.

Lacock *Wilts.* ***Village***, attractive village on River Avon, 3m/5km S of Chippenham. Mostly owned by National Trust. **20 C5** ST9168.

Lacock Abbey *Wilts.* ***Ecclesiastical building***, medieval abbey (National Trust) on W bank of River Avon, near Lacock. **20 C5** ST9168.

Ladbroke *Warks.* ***Village***, 2m/3km S of Southam. **31 F3** SP4158.

Ladder Hills *Aber.* ***Large natural feature***, range of hills, 6m/10km E of Tomintoul. Summit at Carn Mòr, 2636 feet or 804 metres. **89 K3** NJ2718.

Ladderedge *Staffs.* ***Locality***, 2m/3km SW of Leek. SJ9654.

Laddingford *Kent* ***Village***, on River Teise 1m/2km S of Yalding. **23 K7** TQ6948.

Laddus Fens *Cambs.* ***Open space***, fenland 1m/2km SW of Upwell and 4m/7km N of March. **43 H5** TF4701.

Lade Bank *Lincs.* ***Settlement***, 8m/13km NE of Boston. **53 G7** TF3954.

Ladhar Bheinn *High.* ***Mountain***, in Knoydart, in Lochaber district, 4m/7km NE of Inverie. Munro: height 3346 feet or 1020 metres. **86 E4** NG8203.

Ladies Hill *Lancs.* ***Hamlet***, adjoining to N of Pilling, 6m/9km W of Garstang. SD4048.

Ladock *Cornw.* ***Village***, 4m/6km N of Truro. **3 F3** SW8950.

Lady Green *Mersey.* ***Hamlet***, adjoining to NW of Ince Blundell, 2m/4km SE of Formby. SD3103.

Lady Hall *Cumb.* ***Settlement***, 1m/2km SW of Broughton in Furness across River Duddon estuary. **54 E1** SD1986.

Lady Holme *Cumb.* ***Island***, small island (National Trust) on Windermere, 1m/2km SW of Windermere town. Site of pre-Reformation chantry chapel. SD3997.

Lady House *Gt.Man.* ***Suburb***, adjoining to S of Milnrow. SD9211.

Lady Isle *S.Ayr.* ***Island***, small island with lighthouse in Firth of Clyde 3m/5km W of Troon. **67 G1** NS2729.

Lady Park *T. & W.* ***Locality***, 3m/5km S of Gateshead. NZ2458.

Ladybank *Fife* Population: 1373. ***Small town***, 5m/8km SW of Cupar. **82 D6** NO3009.

Ladybower Reservoir *Derbys.* ***Reservoir***, large reservoir 10m/16km W of Sheffield. Has two arms, one in River Derwent valley and one in River Ashop valley. **50 D4** SK1986.

Ladycross *Cornw.* ***Hamlet***, 3m/4km N of Launceston. **6 B7** SX3288.

Ladyfield *Arg. & B.* ***Settlement***, in Glen Aray, 4m/7km N of Inveraray. **80 B6** NN0915.

Ladykirk *Sc.Bord.* ***Village***, on River Tweed, 6m/9km NE of Coldstream. **77 G6** NT8847.

Ladylea Hill *Aber.* ***Mountain***, 3m/4km N of Strathdon. Height 1998 feet or 609 metres. **90 B3** NJ3416.

Lady's Green *Suff.* ***Settlement***, 7m/11km SW of Bury St. Edmunds. **34 B3** TL7559.

Lady's Holm *Shet.* ***Island***, small uninhabited island lying off S coast of Mainland 2m/4km NW of Sumburgh Head. **109 F10** HU3709.

Lady's Rock *Arg. & B.* ***Island***, rock marked by beacon, lying between Eilean Musdile and E coast of Mull. **79 J4** NM7734.

Ladysford *Aber.* ***Settlement***, 7m/12km SW of Fraserburgh. **99 H4** NJ8960.

Ladyside Height *Sc.Bord.* ***Mountain***, on N flank of Eastside Heights, 1m/2km SE of Dewar. Height 1771 feet or 540 metres. **76 B6** NT3647.

Ladywell *Gt.Lon.* ***Suburb***, in borough of Lewisham, 1m/2km SW of Lewisham and 6m/9km SE of Charing Cross. TQ3774.

Ladywell *W.Loth.* ***Suburb***, near Livingston town centre. NT0568.

Ladywood *W.Mid.* ***Suburb***, to W of Birmingham city centre. SP0586.

Ladywood *Worcs.* ***Hamlet***, 2m/4km SW of Droitwich Spa. SO8760.

Lael *High.* ***River***, rising on N slope of Beinn Dearg and flowing NW, then W into Loch Broom. **95 J3** NH1785.

Lag Burn *Aber.* ***River***, rising on N slopes of Long Bank and flowing NE to join River Bogie, 3m/4km S of Huntly. **90 C1** NJ5235.

Laga *High.* ***Settlement***, 1m/2km E of Glenborrodale, Lochaber district. **79 H1** NM6360.

Lagalochan *Arg. & B.* ***Settlement***, 2m/3km SE of Kilmelford. **79 K6** NM8711.

Lagavulin *Arg. & B.* ***Village***, on S coast of Islay, 1km W of Ardbeg. Distillery. **72 C6** NR4045.

Lagentium *W.Yorks. See Castleford.*

Lagg *Arg. & B.* ***Locality***, on Lagg Bay, on E coast of Jura, 3m/5km S of head of Loch Tarbert. **72 D3** NR5978.

Lagg *N.Ayr.* ***Settlement***, near S coast of Arran, 7m/12km SW of Lamlash. **66 D1** NR9521.

Lagg *S.Ayr.* ***Settlement***, 2m/3km NE of Dunure. **67 G2** NS2717.

Laggan *Arg. & B.* ***River***, on Islay rising near E coast and running W to Laggan Bay, 1m/2km E of Laggan Point. **72 B5** NR2955.

Laggan *Arg. & B.* ***Settlement***, on N side of Laggan Bay, Islay. **72 A5** NR2855.

Laggan *High.* ***Settlement***, at NE end of Loch Lochy, 1km N of South Laggan and 3m/5km SW of Invergarry. Laggan Swing Bridge 1km N. **87 J5** NN2997.

Laggan *High.* ***Village***, on River Spey, in Badenoch and Strathspey district, 6m/10km N of Dalwhinnie. **88 D5** NN6194.

Laggan *Moray* ***Settlement***, on W side of River Fiddich, 2m/3km SE of Dufftown. **90 B1** NJ3436.

Laggan *Stir.* ***Settlement***, on W side of Loch Lubnaig, 1m/2km S of Strathyre. **81 G6** NN5614.

Laggan Bay *Arg. & B.* ***Bay***, small bay at SE end of Loch Tuath, W coast of Mull. **79 F3** NM4540.

Laggan Bay *Arg. & B.* ***Bay***, on Islay, 5m/8km wide, extending S from Laggan Point to Rubha Mòr. **72 A5** NR2955.

Laggan Swing Bridge *High.* ***Bridge***, swing bridge carrying road across Caledonian Canal at SW end of Loch Oich. **87 J5** NN2999.

Laggangairn Standing Stones *D. & G.* ***Historic/prehistoric site***, Bronze Age standing stones 7m/11km S of Barrhill. One has Early Christian incised cross. **64 C3** NX2272.

Laggantalluch Head *D. & G.* ***Coastal feature***, headland on W coast of Rinns of Galloway, 3m/5km W of Drummore. **64 A7** NX0836.

Lagganulva *Arg. & B.* ***Settlement***, near head of Loch Tuath, Mull, 4m/7km SE of Kilninian. **79 F3** NM4541.

Lagganvoulin *Moray* ***Settlement***, 1m/2km SE of Tomintoul. **89 J3** NJ1817.

Laglingarten *Arg. & B.* ***Settlement***, 3m/5km E of Inveraray across Loch Fyne. **80 C7** NN1408.

Lagnalean *High.* ***Settlement***, 3m/5km SW of Inverness. **96 D7** NH6241.

Lagrae *D. & G.* ***Settlement***, 2m/3km NW of Kirkconnel. **68 C2** NS7013.

Laguna *P. & K.* ***Settlement***, 3m/4km N of Stanley. **82 C4** NO1036.

Lahill *Fife* ***Locality***, includes Lahill House, Lahill Mains and Lahill Craig, 2m/3km NE of Lower Largo. **83 F7** NO4403.

Laid *High.* ***Settlement***, in Sutherland district, 5m/8km S of Durness. **103 G3** NC4159.

Laide *High.* ***Village***, in Ross and Cromarty district 5m/8km SE of Greenstone Point on W coast. **94 E2** NG8991.

Laig *High.* ***Settlement***, on Eigg, 1km SW of Cleadale. **85 K6** NM4687.

Laighstonehall *S.Lan.* ***Suburb***, SW district of Hamilton. NS7054.

Laight *E.Ayr.* ***Settlement***, 1m/2km SW of New Cumnock. **68 B2** NS6111.

Laiken Forest *High.* ***Forest/woodland***, 3m/4km SE of Nairn. **97 G6** NH9053.

Laimhrig *W.Isles* ***Coastal feature***, headland on E coast of Isle of Lewis, 1m/2km N of Cellar Head. **101 H2** NB5558.

Lainchoil *High.* ***Settlement***, 4m/6km SE of Nethy Bridge. **89 H3** NJ0618.

Laindon *Essex* ***Suburb***, W district of Basildon. **24 C3** TQ6889.

Laindon Barn *Essex* ***Suburb***, of Basildon, to N of Laindon. TQ6889.

Laindon Ponds *Essex* ***Suburb***, of Basildon, to NE of Laindon. TQ6889.

Lair *P. & K.* ***Settlement***, in Glen Shee, over Shee Water from Cray. **82 C1** NO1463.

Lair of Aldararie ***Mountain***, 3m/5km N of Clova. Summit on border of Aberdeenshire and Angus. Height 2729 feet or 832 metres. **90 B7** NO3178.

Laira *Plym.* ***Suburb***, 2m/3km NE of Plymouth city centre. Laira Bridge spans River Plym, 2m/3km E of city centre. SX5055.

Laird's Seat *Moray* ***Mountain***, on W side of Glen Fiddich, 3m/5km S of Dufftown. Height 1499 feet or 457 metres. **90 B1** NJ3134.

Laird's Seat *S.Lan.* ***Mountain***, 4m/7km SE of Eaglesham. Height 1184 feet or 361 metres. **74 E6** NS6045.

Lairg *High.* ***Village***, at SE end of Loch Shin, in Sutherland district, 17m/27km W of Golspie on E coast. **96 C1** NC5806.

Lairg Lodge *High.* ***Settlement***, on NE shore of Loch Shin, 1km NW of Lairg. **96 C1** NC5707.

Lairg Station *High.* ***Other building***, railway station 2m/3km S of Lairg. **96 C1** NC5804.

Lairgs of Tain *High.* ***Open space***, S slopes of Morangie Forest, 4m/6km SW of Tain. **96 E3** NH7279.

Lairig an Laoigh *High.* ***Other feature of interest***, 30m/48km route, part footpath, part mountain pass, traversing Cairngorm Mountains from Braemar to Nethy Bridge. **89 H4** NJ0209.

Lairig Breisleich ***Other feature of interest***, mountain pass on border of Perth & Kinross and Stirling, 4m/6km SW of Bridge of Balgie. **81 G3** NN5541.

Lairig Ghru ***Inland physical feature***, deep defile creating a mountain pass between Braeriach and Cairn Gorm, dividing Cairngorm Mountains into E and W ranges. **89 G4** NH9603.

Lairig Leacach *High.* ***Valley***, carrying Allt na Lairige SE into S end of Loch Treig. **87 J7** NN2874.

Lairigmor *High.* ***Settlement***, on West Highland Way, 4m/7km NW of Kinlochleven. **80 C1** NN1264.

Laisterdyke *W.Yorks.* ***Suburb***, 2m/3km E of Bradford city centre. SE1933.

Laithers *Aber.* ***Locality***, comprises Hill of Laithers, Mains of Laithers and Mill of Laithers on S bank of River Deveron, 3m/5km W of Turriff. **98 E6** NJ6749.

Laithes *Cumb.* ***Settlement***, 4m/6km NW of Penrith. **61 F3** NY4632.

Laithkirk *Dur.* ***Locality***, 1m/2km S of Middleton-in-Teesdale. NY9524.

Lake *Devon* ***Hamlet***, 1m/2km S of Barnstaple. SS5531.

Lake *Devon* ***Hamlet***, 5m/8km SE of Tavistock. SX5368.

Lake *I.o.W.* ***Suburb***, 1km SW of Sandown. SZ5983.

Lake *Wilts.* ***Hamlet***, beside River Avon, 2m/3km SW of Amesbury. **10 C1** SU1339.

Lake District National Park *Cumb.* ***Large natural feature***, area of mountains and lakes in NW England on W side of The Pennines. On its W side rivers flow into Irish Sea from its hills. Glacial action has led to development of distinctive scenery of rounded mountain summits and ribbon lakes. **60 C5** NY3010.

Lake Meadows *Essex* ***Suburb***, N district of Billericay. TQ6795.

Lake of Menteith *Stir.* ***Lake/loch***, to S of Menteith Hills, 5m/8km SW of Callander. Remains of medieval priory (Historic Scotland) on Inchmahome island and ruins of medieval castle on smaller Inch Talla island. **74 D1** NN5700.

Lake Vyrnwy (Llyn Efyrnwy). *Powys* ***Reservoir***, large reservoir about 4m/7km long from NW to SE and about 1m/2km wide at widest point. The dam, at SE end, is 15m/24km NW of Welshpool. Built in 1880s to supply water to Liverpool. **37 J3** SJ0119.

Lakenham *Norf.* ***Suburb***, to S of Norwich city centre. **45 G5** TG2307.

Lakenheath *Suff.* Population: 9226. ***Village***, 5m/8km SW of Brandon. **44 B7** TL7182.

Lakenheath Warren *Suff.* ***Open space***, heath, 4m/6km SE of Lakenheath. **34 B1** TL7680.

Lakesend *Norf.* ***Village***, 2m/3km N of Welney. **43 J6** TL5196.

Lakeside *Cumb.* ***Settlement***, at S end of Windermere. **55 G1** SD3787.

Lakeside and Haverthwaite Railway *Cumb.* ***Other feature of interest***, tourist railway running SW from Lakeside, at S end of Windermere lake, to just W of Haverthwaite, through Backbarrow Gorge. **55 G1** SD3787.

Laleham *Surr.* ***Locality***, on E bank of River Thames, 2m/3km SE of Staines. **22 D5** TQ0568.

Laleston (Trelales). *Bridgend* ***Village***, 2m/3km W of Bridgend. **18 B4** SS8779.

Lamachan Hill *D. & G.* ***Mountain***, in Glentrool Forest Park 2m/4km SE of Loch Trool. Height 2348 feet or 716 metres. **64 E3** NX4377.

Lamahip *Aber.* ***Mountain***, 4m/6km SE of Aboyne. Height 1325 feet or 404 metres. **90 D5** NO5592.

Lamaload Reservoir *Ches.* ***Reservoir***, 4m/6km E of Macclesfield. **49 J5** SJ9774.

Lamancha *Sc.Bord.* ***Settlement***, 3m/5km SW of Leadburn. **76 A5** NT1952.

Lamarsh *Essex* ***Village***, 4m/6km S of Sudbury. **34 C5** TL8935.

Lamas *Norf.* ***Hamlet***, 4m/7km SE of Aylsham. **45 G3** TG2423.

Lamb *E.Loth.* ***Island***, islet 1m/2km W of North Berwick. Haunt of sea birds. **76 D2** NT5386.

Lamb Corner *Essex* ***Hamlet***, 5m/8km NE of Colchester. **34 E5** TM0431.

Lamb Head *Ork.* ***Coastal feature***, headland at SE end of Stronsay. **106 F5** HY6921.

Lamb Hoga *Shet.* ***Coastal feature***, peninsula at SW corner of Fetlar between Wick of Tresta and Colgrave Sound. **108 F4** HU6088.

Lamb Holm *Ork.* ***Island***, small uninhabited island off S coast of Mainland to SE of St. Mary's, joined to Mainland by road causeway, first part of Churchill Barrier. **107 D7** HY4800.

Lamb House *E.Suss.* ***Historic house***, National Trust property in Rye, dating from early 18c. Home of Henry James and later, E.F. Benson. **14 E5** TQ9220.

Lamb Roe *Lancs.* ***Hamlet***, 1m/2km N of Whalley. SD7337.

Lamba *Shet.* ***Island***, uninhabited island in Yell Sound 1m/2km N of entrance to Sullom Voe. Area about 120 acres or 48 hectares. **108 C4** HU3981.

Lamba Ness *Shet.* ***Coastal feature***, headland on NE coast of Unst. **108 F1** HP6715.

Lamba Taing *Shet.* ***Coastal feature***, headland on E coast of Mainland, 1km N of Leebotten. **109 D10** HU4326.

Lambaness *Ork.* ***Village***, on SW coast of Sanday, inland from headland at Lamba Ness. HY6137.

Lambden *Sc.Bord.* ***Hamlet***, 2m/3km NW of Eccles. NT7443.

Lamberhead Green *Gt.Man.* ***Suburb***, 2m/4km W of Wigan town centre. SD5404.

Lamberhurst *Kent* ***Village***, on River Teise, 6m/10km SE of Royal Tunbridge Wells. Former centre of iron-working industry. Scotney Castle 1m/2km E. **13 K3** TQ6736.

Lamberhurst Down *Kent* ***Hamlet***, 1km SW of Lamberhurst. TQ6735.
Lamberhurst Quarter *Kent* ***Locality***, 2m/3km NW of Lamberhurst. **13 K3** TQ6538.
Lamberton *Sc.Bord.* ***Settlement***, 3m/5km NW of Berwick-upon-Tweed. **77 H5** NT9657.
Lamberton Beach *Sc.Bord.* ***Coastal feature***, area of rocky coastline to NE of Lamberton, 4m/6km NW of Berwick-upon-Tweed. **77 H5** NT9758.
Lambert's Castle Hill *Dorset See Marshwood.*
Lambert's End *W.Mid.* ***Suburb***, on W side of West Bromwich town centre. SO9991.
Lambeth Palace *Gt.Lon.* ***Ecclesiastical building***, London residence of Archbishop of Canterbury since 1197, in borough of Lambeth 2m/3km S of Charing Cross. Remarkable Tudor gatehouse, fine medieval crypt. 14c Hall with a splendid roof and portraits of archbishops on its walls. Great Hall, which houses library, was rebuilt in medieval style in 1633 and is noted for its decorated timber roof. TQ3079.
Lambfair Green *Suff.* ***Hamlet***, 6m/9km NE of Haverhill. TL7153.
Lambfell Moar *I.o.M.* ***Settlement***, 4m/6km E of Peel. **54 B5** SC2984.
Lambhill *Glas.* ***Suburb***, 2m/4km N of Glasgow city centre. NS5769.
Lambhoga Head *Shet.* ***Coastal feature***, headland on E coast of Mainland, 1m/2km SE of Boddam. **109 G9** HU4013.
Lamblair Knowe *D. & G.* ***Mountain***, on Eskdalemuir Forest, 4m/7km NE of Eskdalemuir. Height 1332 feet or 406 metres. **69 H3** NT2903.
Lambley *Northumb.* ***Hamlet***, 4m/6km SW of Haltwhistle. **61 H1** NY6758.
Lambley *Notts.* ***Village***, 5m/8km NE of Nottingham. **41 J1** SK6345.
Lambourn *W.Berks.* Population: 2850. ***Small town***, market town, 12m/19km NW of Newbury. Nearby Lambourn Downs are well-known as racehorse training area. **21 G4** SU3278.
Lambourn Country Park *W.Berks.* ***Leisure/recreation***, country park 3m/4km N of Newbury. SU4570.
Lambourn Downs *W.Berks.* ***Large natural feature***, chalk uplands 1m/2km N of Lambourn, extensively used for racehorse training. **21 G3** SU3278.
Lambourn Woodlands *W.Berks.* ***Settlement***, 2m/3km S of Lambourn. **21 G4** SU3275.
Lambourne *Essex* ***Settlement***, 3m/5km E of Loughton. TQ4796.
Lambourne End *Essex* ***Hamlet***, 1m/2km S of Lambourne. **23 H2** TQ4796.
Lambrigg Fell *Cumb.* ***Mountain***, 2m/3km N of Killington Reservoir and 4m/7km E of Kendal. Height 1109 feet or 338 metres. **61 G7** SD5894.
Lambrook *Som.* ***Suburb***, E district of Taunton. ST2425.
Lambs Green *Dorset* ***Locality***, 1m/2km SW of Wimborne Minster. SY9998.
Lambs Green *W.Suss.* ***Hamlet***, 3m/5km W of Crawley. **13 F3** TQ2136.
Lambston *Pembs.* ***Settlement***, 3m/5km W of Haverfordwest. **16 C3** SM9016.
Lambton *T. & W.* ***Suburb***, to SW of Washington town centre. NZ2955.
Lamellion *Cornw.* ***Suburb***, in SW part of Liskeard. **4 C4** SX2463.
Lamerton *Devon* ***Village***, 3m/4km NW of Tavistock. **4 E3** SX4576.
Lamesley *T. & W.* ***Village***, 3m/5km S of Gateshead. **62 D1** NZ2557.
Lamh Dhearg *P. & K.* ***Mountain***, to W of Glen Shee, 1m/2km W of Cray. Height 1886 feet or 575 metres. **82 C1** NO1263.
Lamington *High.* ***Village***, 4m/6km SW of Tain. **96 E4** NH7476.
Lamington *S.Lan.* ***Village***, 6m/9km SW of Biggar. **75 H7** NS9831.
Lamlash *N.Ayr.* ***Village***, and small port on Lamlash Bay, on E coast of Arran, 3m/5km S of Brodick. **73 J7** NS0231.
Lamlash Bay *N.Ayr.* ***Bay***, on E coast of Arran, 3m/5km S of Brodick. **73 J7** NS0231.
Lamloch *D. & G.* ***Settlement***, 6m/10km SE of Dalmellington. **67 K4** NX5296.
Lammer Law *E.Loth.* ***Mountain***, peak on Lammermuir Hills, 4m/6km S of Gifford. Height 1732 feet or 528 metres. **76 D4** NT5261.
Lammermuir ***Locality***, large upland area straddling borders of Lothian and Scottish Borders, extending W from St. Abb's Head and culminating in Lammermuir Hills. **76 E5** NT7560.
Lammermuir Hills ***Large natural feature***, range of hills with SW to NE axis, summit of which is Meikle Says Law, 1755 feet or 535 metres high. **76 C5** NT5861.
Lamonby *Cumb.* ***Hamlet***, 2m/3km W of Skelton. **60 F3** NY4035.
Lamorick *Cornw.* ***Hamlet***, 3m/4km SW of Bodmin. SX0364.
Lamorna *Cornw.* ***Village***, beside steep-sided valley running down to Lamorna Cove, 4m/6km S of Penzance. SW4424.
Lamorna Cove *Cornw.* ***Bay***, with small quay, 4m/6km S of Penzance. **2 B6** SW4424.
Lamorran *Cornw.* ***Hamlet***, on inlet of River Fal, 3m/5km SW of Tregony. **3 F4** SW8741.
Lampay Islands *High.* ***Island***, two islets on E side of Loch Dunvegan, Skye, 3m/5km E of Dunvegan Head. **93 H6** NG2255.
Lampert *Northumb.* ***Settlement***, in Wark Forest, on E bank of River Irthing, 7m/11km N of Haltwhistle. **70 B6** NY6874.
Lampeter (Llanbedr Pont Steffan). *Cere.* Population: 1989. ***Small town***, market town on River Teifi, 20m/32km NE of Carmarthen. University of Wales, originally St. David's College, founded in 1822, is oldest in Wales. **26 E4** SN5748.
Lampeter Velfrey (Llanbedr Felffre). *Pembs.* ***Village***, 3m/5km E of Narberth. **16 E3** SN1514.
Lamphey (Llandyfai). *Pembs.* ***Village***, 2m/3km E of Pembroke. **16 D4** SN0100.
Lamphey Palace *Pembs.* ***Historic/prehistoric site***, remains of medieval Lamphey Palace (Cadw), 1m/2km SE of Pembroke, formerly residence of Bishops of St. David's. **16 D4** SN0100.
Lamplugh *Cumb.* ***Hamlet***, 7m/11km S of Cockermouth. **60 B4** NY0820.
Lamport *Northants.* ***Village***, 9m/14km N of Northampton. **31 J1** SP7574.
Lampton *Gt.Lon.* ***Suburb***, to N of Hounslow town centre, 10m/16km W of Charing Cross. TQ1376.
Lamyatt *Som.* ***Village***, 2m/3km NW of Bruton. **9 F1** ST6535.
Lan Ystenu *Powys* ***Mountain***, rising to over 330 metres, 1km S of Pentre-llwyn-llŵyd. **27 J3** SN9653.
Lana *Devon* ***Hamlet***, 3m/5km NW of Holsworthy. SS3007.
Lana *Devon* ***Hamlet***, 5m/8km S of Holsworthy. **6 B6** SX3496.
Lanark *S.Lan.* Population: 8877. ***Small town***, market town above E bank of River Clyde, 11m/18km SE of Motherwell. **75 G6** NS8843.
Lanarth *Cornw.* ***Settlement***, 1m/2km W of St. Keverne and 8m/12km SE of Helston. SW7621.
Lancaster *Lancs.* Population: 44,497. ***City***, county town on River Lune, 20m/32km N of Preston. Previously a prosperous port receiving mahogany, tobacco, rum and sugar. Norman castle with 14c and 16c additions. Georgian Old Town Hall. University at Bailrigg, 2m/3km S. **55 H3** SD4761.
Lancaster Canal *Lancs.* ***Canal***, navigable from Tewitfield, near Carnforth to Preston. There is a branch to Glasson, on River Lune estuary, providing access to Irish Sea. **55 J6** SD5230.
Lancaster Castle *Lancs.* ***Castle***, medieval castle with Norman keep standing on Castle Hill, once occupied by a Roman fort. Elizabeth I added fortifications as a defence against Spanish Armada. **55 H3** SD4761.
Lancaster City Museum *Lancs.* ***Other feature of interest***, museum housed in Georgian Old Hall in Lancaster, where displays include local Neolithic, Roman and Medieval history. **55 H3** SD4761.
Lancaster Sound ***Sea feature***, sea channel in Morecambe Bay, between Mort Bank and Cartmel Wharf. **55 G3** SD3268.
Lanchester *Dur.* Population: 3599. ***Small town***, 7m/12km NW of Durham. Site of Roman fort of Longovicium 1km SW. **62 C2** NZ1647.
Lanchester Valley Walk *Dur.* ***Leisure/recreation***, 12m/19km countryside walk along disused railway line between Durham and Lydgetts Junction, Consett, via Lanchester. **62 C2** NZ1647.
Land Gate *Gt.Man.* ***Village***, 2m/3km N of Ashton-in-Makerfield. SD5701.
Land of Nod *Hants.* ***Hamlet***, 3m/5km NW of Hindhead. SU8437.
Land Side *Gt.Man.* ***Settlement***, 1m/2km S of Leigh. SJ6598.
Landbeach *Cambs.* ***Village***, 5m/7km NE of Cambridge. **33 H2** TL4765.
Landcross *Devon* ***Hamlet***, on River Torridge, 2m/3km S of Bideford. **6 C3** SS4623.
Landerberry *Aber.* ***Locality***, 1km S of Echt. **91 F4** NJ7404.
Landewednack *Cornw.* ***Village***, 1m/2km NE of Lizard Point. **2 E7** SW7112.
Landford *Wilts.* ***Village***, 6m/10km W of Romsey. **10 D3** SU2519.
Landguard Fort *Suff.* ***Other feature of interest***, 18c fort (English Heritage) with later additions, 2m/3km SW of Felixstowe town centre, on headland opposite Harwich. Museum has displays of local history. **35 G5** TM2831.
Landguard Point *Suff.* ***Coastal feature***, headland at entrance to Harwich Harbour, 2m/4km SW of Felixstowe. **35 G5** TM2831.
Landhallow *High.* ***Settlement***, near E coast of Caithness, 1km W of Latheron. ND1833.
Landican *Mersey.* ***Settlement***, 4m/6km SW of Birkenhead town centre. SJ2885.
Landimor *Swan. Welsh form of Landimore, qv.*
Landimore (Landimor). *Swan.* ***Hamlet***, on Gower peninsula, 1m/2km E of Cheriton and 12m/19km W of Swansea. Remains of castle. 1m/2km E are ruins of Weobley Castle (Cadw), fortified 13c-14c manor house. **17 H5** SS4693.
Landkey *Devon* Population: 1392. ***Village***, 2m/4km SE of Barnstaple. **6 D2** SS5931.
Landkey Newland *Devon* ***Locality***, adjoining to SE of Landkey, 3m/4km SE of Barnstaple. SS5931.
Landmoth *N.Yorks.* ***Settlement***, on E side of Landmoth Wood, 4m/6km E of Northallerton. SE4292.
Landore *Swan.* ***Suburb***, 2m/3km N of Swansea city centre. **17 K5** SS6596.
Landport *Ports.* ***Suburb***, to N of Portsmouth city centre. SU6401.
Landrake *Cornw.* ***Village***, 4m/6km W of Saltash. **4 D4** SX3760.
Land's End *Cornw.* ***Coastal feature***, headland with spectacular cliff scenery 8m/13km SW of Penzance. Traditionally referred to as SW end of British mainland. Includes Land's End Experience theme park with lasers and sound effects, a model village and a miniature railway. Aerodrome near St. Just, 3m/5km NE. **2 A6** SW3425.
Landscove *Devon* ***Locality***, 2m/4km SE of Ashburton. **5 H4** SX7766.
Landshipping *Pembs.* ***Hamlet***, on E side of Daugleddau River, opposite confluence of Rivers Eastern and Western Cleddau, 10m/16km NW of Tenby. **16 D3** SN0111.
Landulph *Cornw.* ***Village***, beside River Tamar, at its junction with River Tavy, N of Saltash. **4 E4** SX4361.
Landwade *Suff.* ***Settlement***, 3m/5km NW of Newmarket. Site of Roman villa to W. **33 K2** TL6267.
Landywood *Staffs.* ***Locality***, 3m/4km S of Cannock. **40 B5** SJ9906.
Lane *W.Yorks.* ***Settlement***, on hillside 1m/2km SW of Holmbridge. SE1005.
Lane Bottom *Lancs.* ***Hamlet***, 2m/3km SE of Nelson. SD8735.
Lane End *Bucks.* Population: 2684. ***Village***, 4m/6km W of High Wycombe. **22 B2** SU8091.
Lane End *Ches.* ***Locality***, 1km SW of Hollins Green. SJ6890.
Lane-end *Cornw.* ***Settlement***, 3m/4km NW of Bodmin. **4 A4** SX0369.
Lane End *Cumb.* ***Hamlet***, 3m/5km N of Bootle. **60 C7** SD1093.
Lane End *Derbys.* ***Village***, adjoining to NE of Tibshelf, 3m/5km NW of Sutton in Ashfield. **51 G6** SK4461.
Lane End *Dorset* ***Hamlet***, 1m/2km S of Bere Regis. **9 H5** SY8592.
Lane End *Gt.Man.* ***Settlement***, 1m/2km SE of Heywood. SD8609.
Lane End *Hants.* ***Hamlet***, 2m/4km SW of Cheriton. SU5525.
Lane End *Here.* ***Hamlet***, 4m/6km SE of Ross-on-Wye. SO6419.
Lane End *Kent* ***Hamlet***, just E of Darenth, 2m/4km SE of Dartford. **23 J4** TQ5671.
Lane End *Lancs.* ***Locality***, at crossroads adjoining to N of Barnoldswick. SD8747.
Lane End *S.Yorks.* ***Locality***, adjoining to N of Chapeltown. SK3596.
Lane End *Wilts.* ***Hamlet***, 4m/6km W of Warminster. ST8145.
Lane Ends *Ches.* ***Settlement***, 1m/2km SE of Disley. SJ9883.
Lane Ends *Derbys.* ***Hamlet***, 1km N of Sutton on the Hill. SK2334.
Lane Ends *Dur.* ***Locality***, 1m/2km S of Willington. NZ1833.
Lane Ends *Gt.Man.* ***Settlement***, 2m/3km NE of Marple. SJ9790.
Lane Ends *Lancs.* ***Hamlet***, 1km S of Hapton, 3m/4km NE of Accrington. SD7930.
Lane Ends *N.Yorks.* ***Hamlet***, 1m/2km NE of Cowling, 2m/3km SW of Cross Hills. SD9743.
Lane Ends *Stoke* ***Settlement***, 2m/4km N of Tunstall. SJ8754.
Lane Green *Staffs.* ***Locality***, adjoining to E of Codsall. **40 A5** SJ8803.
Lane Head *Dur.* ***Hamlet***, 1km NW of Copley. NZ0725.
Lane Head *Dur.* ***Hamlet***, 6m/9km SE of Barnard Castle. **62 C5** NZ1211.
Lane Head *Dur.* ***Settlement***, 1m/2km E of Edmundbyers. NZ0449.
Lane Head *Gt.Man.* ***Locality***, 1m/2km E of Golborne. **49 F3** SJ6296.
Lane Head *W.Mid.* ***Suburb***, 3m/5km NW of Walsall town centre. SJ9700.
Lane Head *W.Yorks.* ***Hamlet***, 3m/5km E of Holmfirth. **50 D2** SE1908.
Lane Heads *Lancs.* ***Settlement***, 1m/2km SE of Great Eccleston, 5m/8km SW of Garstang. SD4339.
Lane Side *Lancs.* ***Suburb***, to S of Haslingden town centre. SD7822.
Laneast *Cornw.* ***Village***, 7m/11km W of Launceston. **4 C2** SX2284.
Laneham *Notts.* ***Village***, 7m/11km SE of Retford. **52 B5** SK8076.
Lanehead *Dur.* ***Hamlet***, 2m/3km NW of Wearhead. NY8441.
Lanehead *Northumb.* ***Locality***, 3m/5km NW of Bellingham. Remains of Tarset Castle, perhaps late 13c. **70 C5** NY7985.
Lanercost Priory *Cumb.* ***Historic/prehistoric site***, remains of medieval priory (English Heritage) on N side of River Irthing, 3m/4km NE of Brampton. Small section of Hadrian's Wall at Hare Hill 1km NE. **70 A7** NY5563.
Lanescot *Cornw.* ***Hamlet***, 3m/5km SW of Lostwithiel. SX0855.
Lanesend *Pembs.* ***Hamlet***, just E of Cresselly. SN0706.
Lanesfield *W.Mid.* ***Suburb***, S district of Wolverhampton. SO9295.
Laneshaw Bridge *Lancs.* ***Hamlet***, on Colne Water, 2m/4km E of Colne. **56 E5** SD9240.
Laneshaw Reservoir ***Reservoir***, small reservoir on border of Lancashire and North Yorkshire, on W side of woodland of Reedshaw Moss, 4m/6km E of Colne. **56 E5** SD9441.
Laney Green *Staffs.* ***Settlement***, 1m/2km W of Cheslyn Hay. SJ9606.
Lang Craig *Angus* ***Coastal feature***, rock headland at S end of Lunan Bay to E of Ethie Haven, 3m/4km E of Inverkeilor. **83 J3** NO7048.
Lang Stane o'Craigearn *Aber. See Craigearn.*
Langais (Anglicised form: Langass.) *W.Isles* ***Settlement***, on North Uist, 1m/2km NW of Locheport. **92 D5** NF8365.
Langaller *Som.* ***Hamlet***, 1km N of Creech St. Michael, 3m/5km NE of Taunton. ST2626.
Langamull *Arg. & B.* ***Settlement***, on Mull, 1m/2km NE of Calgary. **78 E2** NM3853.
Langar *Notts.* ***Village***, 4m/6km S of Bingham. **42 A2** SK7234.
Langass *W.Isles Anglicised form of Langais, qv.*
Langaton Point *High.* ***Coastal feature***, headland at NW end of Stroma in Pentland Firth. **105 J1** ND3479.
Langbank *Renf.* ***Village***, on S bank of River Clyde, opposite Dumbarton. **74 B3** NS3873.
Langbar *N.Yorks.* ***Hamlet***, 3m/4km NW of Ilkley. **57 F4** SE0951.
Langbaurgh *N.Yorks.* ***Settlement***, just N of Great Ayton. NZ5511.
Langcliffe *N.Yorks.* ***Village***, 1m/2km N of Settle. **56 D3** SD8265.
Langdale Burn *High.* ***River***, rising from Loch Syre and flowing E to join River Naver. NC6944.
Langdale End *N.Yorks.* ***Hamlet***, 7m/11km W of Scarborough. **63 J3** SE9391.
Langdale Fell *Cumb.* ***Open space***, mountainous area 5m/8km SW of Ravenstonedale. **61 H6** NY6500.
Langdale Pikes *Cumb.* ***Mountain***, series of jagged peaks at summit of Langdale Fell. Height 2401 feet or 732 metres. **60 D6** NY2807.

Langdon *Cornw.* ***Hamlet***, 2m/3km SE of Jacobstow. **4 C1** SX2092.

Langdon *Cornw.* ***Hamlet***, 4m/6km N of Launceston. SX3089.

Langdon *Kent* ***Locality***, parish containing villages of East and West Langdon, 3m/5km N of Dover. TR3246.

Langdon Beck *Dur.* ***Settlement***, 7m/11km NW of Middleton-in-Teesdale, near confluence of stream of same name with River Tees. **61 K3** NY8531.

Langdon Common *Dur.* ***Open space***, heathland on N side of River Tees, 2m/3km N of Forest-in-Teesdale. **61 K3** NY8533.

Langdon Hills *Essex* ***Suburb***, of Basildon, to S of Laindon. **24 C3** TQ6787.

Langdon House *Devon* ***Settlement***, 1m/2km NW of Dawlish. **5 K3** SX9478.

Langdown *Hants.* ***Suburb***, S district of Hythe. SU4206.

Langdyke *Fife* ***Hamlet***, 2m/3km NW of Kennoway. **82 E7** NO3304.

Langenhoe *Essex* ***Village***, 4m/7km S of Colchester. **34 E7** TM0018.

Langford *Beds.* Population: 2760. ***Village***, 2m/3km S of Biggleswade. **32 E4** TL1841.

Langford *Devon* ***Hamlet***, 3m/5km S of Cullompton. **7 J5** ST0203.

Langford *Essex* ***Village***, 1m/2km NW of Maldon. **24 E1** TL8309.

Langford *Norf.* ***Locality***, on River Wissey, 3m/5km NE of Mundford. TL8396.

Langford *Notts.* ***Village***, 3m/5km NE of Newark-on-Trent. **52 B7** SK8258.

Langford *Oxon.* ***Village***, 3m/5km NE of Lechlade. **21 F1** SP2402.

Langford *Som.* ***Hamlet***, 2m/3km NW of Taunton. ST2027.

Langford Budville *Som.* ***Village***, 2m/4km NW of Wellington. **7 K3** ST1122.

Langford End *Beds.* ***Village***, 3m/5km N of Sandy. TL1653.

Langford Green *Devon* ***Hamlet***, 3m/5km S of Cullompton. ST0203.

Langford Green *N.Som.* ***Locality***, 2m/3km W of Blagdon. ST4759.

Langham *Essex* ***Hamlet***, 6m/9km NE of Colchester. **34 E5** TM0233.

Langham *Norf.* ***Village***, 5m/8km NW of Holt. **44 E1** TG0041.

Langham *Rut.* ***Village***, 2m/3km NW of Oakham. **42 B4** SK8411.

Langham *Suff.* ***Village***, 3m/5km E of Ixworth. **34 D2** TL9769.

Langham Moor *Essex* ***Locality***, 4m/7km N of Colchester. **34 E5** TM0131.

Langham Wick *Essex* ***Hamlet***, 4m/7km NE of Colchester. TM0231.

Langho *Lancs.* Population: 2134. ***Village***, 4m/6km N of Blackburn. **56 B6** SD7034.

Langholm *D. & G.* Population: 2538. ***Small town***, former mill town on River Esk, 15m/24km E of Lockerbie and 18m/29km N of Carlisle. Birthplace of poet, Hugh MacDiarmid. **69 J5** NY3684.

Langhope Burn *Sc.Bord.* ***River***, flowing E from Shaws Under Loch to Ale Water, 2m/3km SW of Ashkirk. **69 K2** NT4520.

Langland *Swan.* ***Suburb***, in The Mumbles district of Swansea, 2m/3km W of Mumbles Head. SS6087.

Langland Bay *Swan.* ***Bay***, to S of Langland, 1km SW of The Mumbles. **17 K6** SS6087.

Langlands *D. & G.* ***Settlement***, 2m/3km W of Kirkcudbright. **65 G5** NX6552.

Langlee *Sc.Bord.* ***Hamlet***, 2m/3km S of Jedburgh. **70 B2** NT6417.

Langlee Crags *Northumb.* ***Inland physical feature***, rock feature 1km E of Langleeford, above Harthope Burn valley. **70 E1** NT9622.

Langleeford *Northumb.* ***Settlement***, on Harthorpe Burn, 4m/6km SW of Middleton Hall. **70 E1** NT9421.

Langley *Ches.* ***Village***, 2m/3km SE of Macclesfield. **49 J5** SJ9471.

Langley *Derbys.* ***Locality***, 1m/2km E of Heanor. **41 G1** SK4446.

Langley *Essex* ***Village***, 6m/10km SE of Royston. Village consists of Upper and Lower Green. **33 H5** TL4334.

Langley *Glos.* ***Settlement***, 1m/2km W of Winchcombe. SP0028.

Langley *Gt.Man.* ***Suburb***, adjoining to NW of Middleton. SD8506.

Langley *Hants.* ***Village***, 2m/3km SW of Fawley. **11 F4** SU4401.

Langley *Herts.* ***Village***, 2m/3km SW of Stevenage. **33 F6** TL2122.

Langley *Kent* ***Village***, 4m/6km SE of Maidstone. **14 D2** TQ8051.

Langley *Northumb.* ***Village***, 2m/3km SW of Haydon Bridge. NY8261.

Langley *Oxon.* ***Hamlet***, 4m/7km NE of Burford. SP3015.

Langley *Slo.* ***Suburb***, E district of Slough. **22 D4** TQ0179.

Langley *Som.* ***Hamlet***, 1km N of Wiveliscombe. ST0828.

Langley *Warks.* ***Village***, 5m/8km N of Stratford-upon-Avon. **30 C2** SP1962.

Langley *W.Mid.* ***Suburb***, to S of Oldbury town centre. SO9988.

Langley *W.Suss.* ***Hamlet***, 3m/4km SW of Liphook. **12 B4** SU8029.

Langley Burrell *Wilts.* ***Village***, 1m/2km NE of Chippenham. **20 C4** ST9375.

Langley Chapel *Shrop.* *See Acton Burnell.*

Langley Corner *Bucks.* ***Settlement***, 4m/6km NE of Slough. TQ0184.

Langley Green *Derbys.* ***Settlement***, 5m/8km NW of Derby. **40 E2** SK2738.

Langley Green *Essex* ***Settlement***, 2m/3km SE of Coggeshall. TL8721.

Langley Green *Norf.* ***Locality***, 3m/5km N of Loddon. TG3503.

Langley Green *Warks.* ***Settlement***, 1km SE of Langley. SP1962.

Langley Green *W.Mid.* ***Suburb***, adjoining to SE of Langley. SO9988.

Langley Green *W.Suss.* ***Suburb***, NW district of Crawley. TQ2638.

Langley Heath *Kent* ***Village***, 4m/7km SE of Maidstone. **14 D2** TQ8151.

Langley Hill *Glos.* ***Hill***, 1m/2km NW of Winchcombe. Height 899 feet or 274 metres. **30 B6** SP0029.

Langley Marsh *Som.* ***Village***, 1m/2km N of Wiveliscombe. **7 J3** ST0729.

Langley Mill *Derbys.* ***Locality***, 1km N of Langley. **41 G1** SK4447.

Langley Moor *Dur.* ***Locality***, adjoining to E of Brandon. **62 D2** NZ2540.

Langley Park *Dur.* Population: 3910. ***Village***, 4m/7km NW of Durham. **62 D2** NZ2144.

Langley Park *Gt.Lon.* *See Park Langley.*

Langley Park Country Park *Bucks.* ***Leisure/recreation***, country park 1m/2km SW of Iver Heath. 136 acres of woodland, parkland and gardens with extensive flowerbeds. **22 D3** TQ0181.

Langley Street *Norf.* ***Hamlet***, 2m/3km N of Loddon. **45 H5** TG3601.

Langleydale Common *Dur.* ***Open space***, moorland 3m/4km E of Eggleston. **62 B4** NZ0425.

Langmere *Norf.* ***Settlement***, 1m/2km E of Dickleburgh. TM1881.

Langness *I.o.M.* ***Coastal feature***, promontory on E side of Castletown Bay, running out to Langness Point. **54 B7** SC2765.

Langney *E.Suss.* ***Suburb***, NE district of Eastbourne. **13 K6** TQ6302.

Langney Point *E.Suss.* ***Coastal feature***, headland on coast 1m/2km SE of Langney, suburb of Eastbourne, at W end of Pevensey Bay. **13 K6** TQ6302.

Langold *Notts.* Population: 2802. ***Village***, 5m/8km N of Worksop. **51 H4** SK5887.

Langore *Cornw.* ***Hamlet***, 2m/4km NW of Launceston. **6 B7** SX2986.

Langport *Som.* Population: 2882. ***Small town***, market town dating from Saxon times, on River Parrett, 7m/11km NW of Ilchester. Muchelney Abbey (English Heritage) 2m/3km to S. **8 D2** ST4226.

Langrick *Lincs.* ***Hamlet***, 5m/8km NW of Boston. **43 F1** TF2648.

Langridge *B. & N.E.Som.* ***Hamlet***, 3m/5km N of Bath. **20 A5** ST7469.

Langridge *Devon* ***Settlement***, 6m/9km NE of Great Torrington. **6 D3** SS5722.

Langridgeford *Devon* ***Settlement***, 7m/11km S of Barnstaple. **6 D3** SS5722.

Langrigg *Cumb.* ***Settlement***, 2m/3km W of Brough. NY7614.

Langrigg *Cumb.* ***Village***, 3m/4km NE of Aspatria. **60 C2** NY1645.

Langrish *Hants.* ***Village***, 3m/4km W of Petersfield. **11 J2** SU7023.

Langriville *Lincs.* ***Hamlet***, 5m/8km NW of Boston. **43 F1** TF2648.

Langsett *S.Yorks.* ***Hamlet***, 3m/5km SW of Penistone, on N shore of Langsett Reservoir. **50 E2** SE2100.

Langsett Reservoir *S.Yorks.* ***Reservoir***, 3m/5km SW of Penistone. **50 E3** SE2100.

Langshaw *Sc.Bord.* ***Settlement***, 3m/4km NE of Galashiels. **76 D7** NT5139.

Langshawburn *D. & G.* ***Settlement***, 4m/6km NE of Garwaldwaterfoot, accessible only by track. **69 H3** NT2904.

Langside *Glas.* ***Suburb***, 3m/4km SW of Glasgow city centre. NS5761.

Langside *P. & K.* ***Settlement***, 8m/12km N of Dunblane. **81 J6** NN7913.

Langskaill *Ork.* ***Settlement***, 1km N of Bakie Skerry, on S coast of Westray. **106 D3** HY4342.

Langstone *Hants.* ***Village***, at S end of Havant, and at N end of Langstone Harbour. Site of Roman villa to N. **11 J4** SU7105.

Langstone *Newport* ***Hamlet***, 4m/7km E of Newport. ST3789.

Langstone Harbour *Hants.* ***Sea feature***, large inlet of sea between Portsea and Hayling Islands. Langstone Bridge connects Hayling Island to mainland. **11 H4** SU7105.

Langstrothdale Chase *N.Yorks.* ***Open space***, large moorland area astride Langstrothdale, 6m/10km S of Hawes. **56 D2** SD8979.

Langthorne *N.Yorks.* ***Village***, 2m/4km N of Bedale. **62 D7** SE2591.

Langthorpe *N.Yorks.* ***Village***, opposite Boroughbridge across River Ure. **57 J3** SE3867.

Langthwaite *N.Yorks.* ***Hamlet***, in Arkengarthdale, 3m/5km NW of Reeth. **62 B6** NZ0002.

Langtoft *E.Riding* ***Village***, 6m/9km N of Great Driffield. **59 G3** TA0166.

Langtoft *Lincs.* ***Village***, 2m/3km NW of Market Deeping. **42 E4** TF1212.

Langton *Dur.* ***Village***, 3m/4km E of Staindrop. **62 C5** NZ1619.

Langton *Lincs.* ***Hamlet***, 2m/3km W of Horncastle. **53 F6** TF2368.

Langton *Lincs.* ***Village***, 3m/5km N of Spilsby. **53 G5** TF3970.

Langton *N.Yorks.* ***Village***, 3m/5km S of Malton. Sites of Roman buildings 1m/2km E. **58 D3** SE7967.

Langton by Wragby *Lincs.* ***Village***, 1m/2km SE of Wragby. **52 E5** TF1476.

Langton Green *Kent* ***Village***, 3m/4km W of Royal Tunbridge Wells. **13 J3** TQ5439.

Langton Green *Suff.* ***Settlement***, adjoining to N of Eye. TM1474.

Langton Hall *Leics.* ***Historic house***, in West Langton. Dates from 1660s, with 18c and 19c additions. **42 A6** SP7193.

Langton Herring *Dorset* ***Village***, 5m/7km NW of Weymouth. **9 F6** SY6182.

Langton Hill *Lincs.* ***Settlement***, 1km W of Horncastle. TF2368.

Langton Long Blandford *Dorset* ***Hamlet***, beside River Stour, 1m/2km SE of Blandford Forum. **9 J4** ST8905.

Langton Matravers *Dorset* ***Village***, 2m/3km W of Swanage. **10 B7** SY9978.

Langton Wold *N.Yorks.* ***Open space***, undulating ground 2m/3km SE of Norton. **58 D3** SE8068.

Langtree *Devon* ***Village***, 4m/6km SW of Great Torrington. **6 C4** SS4515.

Langtree Week *Devon* ***Hamlet***, 1m/2km E of Langtree. SS4715.

Langwathby *Cumb.* ***Village***, on River Eden, 4m/7km NE of Penrith. **61 G3** NY5633.

Langwell *High.* ***Settlement***, on S side of River Oykel, 2m/3km E of Oykel Bridge. **96 B1** NC4101.

Langwell Forest *High.* ***Open space***, moorland area astride Langwell Water, in Caithness district, W and NW of Berriedale. **105 F6** ND0425.

Langwell House *High.* ***Settlement***, 1km W of Berriedale. **105 G6** ND1022.

Langwell Water *High.* ***River***, in Caithness district, rising on Langwell Forest and flowing E to coast at Berriedale. **105 F6** ND1122.

Langwith *Derbys.* ***Village***, adjoining to SW of Nether Langwith, 3m/5km E of Bolsover. SK5270.

Langwood Fen *Cambs.* ***Open space***, fenland 2m/4km E of Chatteris. **43 H7** TL4285.

Langworth *Lincs.* ***Village***, 5m/7km W of Wragby. **52 D5** TF0676.

Lanhydrock *Cornw.* ***Locality***, 2m/4km SE of Bodmin. SX0863.

Lanhydrock House *Cornw.* ***Historic house***, 3m/4km SE of Bodmin. 17c house (National Trust) restored after fire in 1881 to exemplify Victorian grandeur. It is surrounded by rare shrub and tree gardens and set in 450 acres. **4 A4** SX0863.

Lanivet *Cornw.* ***Village***, 3m/5km SW of Bodmin. **4 A4** SX0364.

Lank *Cornw.* ***Hamlet***, 5m/8km S of Camelford. SX0975.

Lank Rigg *Cumb.* ***Mountain***, 3m/4km SE of Ennerdale Bridge. Height 1774 feet or 541 metres. **60 B5** NY0911.

Lanlivery *Cornw.* ***Village***, 2m/3km W of Lostwithiel. **4 A5** SX0859.

Lanlluest *Powys* ***Mountain***, rising to over 470 metres, 7m/11km W of Knighton. **28 A1** SO1874.

Lannacombe Bay *Devon* ***Bay***, between Prawle Point and Start Point, 6m/10km SE of Kingsbridge. **5 J7** SX8036.

Lanner *Cornw.* ***Village***, 2m/3km SE of Redruth. **2 E4** SW7139.

Lanoy *Cornw.* ***Hamlet***, 6m/10km NW of Callington. SX2977.

Lanreath *Cornw.* ***Village***, 5m/8km NW of Looe. **4 B5** SX1856.

Lansallos *Cornw.* ***Village***, 3m/5km E of Fowey across River Fowey estuary. Coast to S owned by National Trust. **4 B5** SX1751.

Lansdown *B. & N.E.Som.* ***Hamlet***, on hill of same name, 3m/5km NW of Bath. Racecourse. Site of Roman building 1km E; site of Battle of Lansdown 1643 to NW. **20 A5** ST7268.

Lansdown *Glos.* ***Locality***, in N part of Bourton-on-the-Water. SP1621.

Lansdown *Glos.* ***Suburb***, central district of Cheltenham. SO9421.

Lanteglos *Cornw.* ***Hamlet***, 1m/2km SW of Camelford. **4 A2** SX0882.

Lanteglos *Cornw.* ***Locality***, church and farm 1m/2km E of Fowey across River Fowey. In N part of parish, which contains much National Trust property, lies hamlet of Lanteglos Highway. SX1451.

Lanteglos Highway *Cornw.* ***Hamlet***, in N part of parish of Lanteglos, 1m/2km E of Fowey across River Fowey. SX1451.

Lantern of the North *Moray* *See Elgin Cathedral.*

Lantern of the West *B. & N.E.Som.* *See Bath Abbey.*

Lantivet Bay *Cornw.* ***Bay***, on S coast, 3m/4km E of Fowey, between Pencarrow Head and Shag Rock. **4 B5** SX1650.

Lanton *Northumb.* ***Hamlet***, 2m/3km SW of Milfield. **77 H7** NT9231.

Lanton *Sc.Bord.* ***Village***, 2m/3km NW of Jedburgh. **70 B1** NT6221.

Lanvean *Cornw.* ***Settlement***, adjoining to N of St. Mawgan, 5m/8km NE of Newquay. SW8766.

Lapal *W.Mid.* ***Suburb***, 1m/2km E of Halesowen town centre. SO9883.

Lapford *Devon* ***Village***, 5m/8km SE of Chulmleigh. **7 F5** SS7308.

Lapford Cross *Devon* ***Hamlet***, to SW of Lapford across River Yeo, 8m/13km NW of Crediton. SS7207.

Laphroaig *Arg. & B.* ***Village***, on S coast of Islay, 1m/2km E of Port Ellen. Distillery. **72 B6** NR3845.

Lapley *Staffs.* ***Village***, 3m/5km W of Penkridge. **40 A4** SJ8712.

Lappa Valley Railway *Cornw.* ***Other feature of interest***, narrow gauge steam railway extending for 1m/2km S from Benny Mill, 3m/5km SE of Newquay. **3 F3** SW8355.

Lapworth *Warks.* ***Village***, 1m/2km SE of Hockley Heath. **30 C1** SP1671.

Larach na Gaibhre *Arg. & B.* ***Settlement***, on W coast of Kintyre, 9m/14km W of Tarbert. **73 F4** NR7269.

Larachbeg *High.* ***Settlement***, 1km N of head of Loch Aline, Lochaber district. **79 H3** NM6948.

Larbert *Falk.* ***Town***, former iron-working town, 2m/4km NW of Falkirk. **75 G2** NS8582.

Larbreck *Lancs.* ***Settlement***, 1m/2km W of Great Eccleston, on S side of River Wyre. SD4040.

Larch How *Cumb.* ***Locality***, on W side of Kendal. SD5092.

Larches *Lancs.* ***Suburb***, 3m/4km W of Preston. SD4930.

Larden Green *Ches.* ***Settlement***, 4m/7km W of Nantwich. **48 E7** SJ5851.

Larg *D. & G.* ***Settlement***, at confluence of Water of Minnoch and River Cree, 7m/11km NW of Newton Stewart. **64 D3** NX3674.

Larg Hill *D. & G.* ***Mountain***, 7m/11km N of Newton Stewart. Height 2214 feet or 675 metres. **64 E3** NX4275.

Largie *Aber.* ***Settlement***, 7m/12km SE of Huntly. **90 E1** NJ6131.

Largiemore *Arg. & B.* ***Hamlet***, on SE coast of Loch Fyne, 5m/8km E of Lochgilphead. **73 H2** NR9486.

Larglear Hill *D. & G.* ***Hill***, 3m/5km W of Corsock. Height 925 feet or 282 metres. **65 H3** NX7176.

Largo *Fife* ***Locality***, consists of two adjacent villages: Lower Largo on Largo Bay, 3m/4km NE of Leven, and Upper Largo, 1km further NE. NO4102.

Largo Bay *Fife* ***Bay***, on Firth of Forth, extending E from Buckhaven and Methil to Kincraig Point. **83 F7** NO4202.

Largo Law *Fife* ***Hill***, 1m/2km N of Upper Largo. Height 951 feet or 290 metres. **83 F7** NO4204.

Largo Ward *Fife Alternative spelling of Largoward, qv.*

Largoward (Also spelled Largo Ward.) *Fife* ***Village***, 4m/6km NE of Upper Largo. **83 F7** NO4607.

Largs *N.Ayr.* Population: 10,925. ***Town***, old weaving town and resort on Largs Bay, on Firth of Clyde opposite N end of Great Cumbrae. Formerly a major fishing port. **74 A5** NS2059.

Largue *Aber.* ***Settlement***, 4m/6km S of Inverkeithny. **98 E6** NJ6441.

Largybaan *Arg. & B.* ***Settlement***, on S part of Kintyre, 6m/9km NW of Southend. **66 A2** NR6114.

Largybeg *N.Ayr.* ***Settlement***, on SE coast of Arran, to W and above Largybeg Point. **66 E1** NS0523.

Largybeg Point *N.Ayr.* ***Coastal feature***, headland on E coast of Arran at S end of Whiting Bay. Standing stones. **66 E1** NS0523.

Largymore *N.Ayr.* ***Settlement***, on E coast of Arran, 1km S of Whiting Bay. **66 E1** NS0424.

Larig Hill *High.* ***Mountain***, 5m/8km E of Dava. Height 1788 feet or 545 metres. **97 H7** NJ0840.

Lark ***River***, rising 6m/9km S of Bury St. Edmunds and flowing N through the town, then NW into River Great Ouse 2m/3km S of Littleport. **34 B1** TL5784.

Lark Hall *Cambs.* ***Settlement***, 2m/3km NW of West Wratting. **33 J3** TL5854.

Larkfield *Inclyde* ***Suburb***, 1m/2km S of Gourock. NS2375.

Larkfield *Kent* ***Suburb***, 4m/6km NW of Maidstone. TQ7058.

Larkhall *S.Lan.* Population: 15,493. ***Town***, 4m/6km SE of Hamilton. **75 F5** NS7651.

Larkhill *Wilts.* Population: 2108. ***Village***, military village and camp, 3m/4km NW of Amesbury. **20 E7** SU1244.

Larkhill *Worcs.* ***Suburb***, to N of Kidderminster town centre. SO8377.

Larklands *Derbys.* ***Suburb***, E district of Ilkeston. SK4741.

Larling *Norf.* ***Hamlet***, 6m/9km SW of Attleborough. **44 D7** TL9889.

Larmer Tree Grounds *Wilts. See Tollard Royal.*

Larnog *V. of Glam. Welsh form of Lavernock, qv.*

Laroch *High.* ***River***, in Lochaber district, flowing NE below Beinn a' Bheithir to S shore of Loch Leven at Ballachulish. **80 B2** NN0858.

Larrick *Cornw.* ***Hamlet***, 4m/7km SW of Launceston. SX3078.

Larriston *Sc.Bord.* ***Settlement***, in valley of Liddel Water, 6m/9km NE of Newcastleton. **70 A4** NY5494.

Larriston Fells *Sc.Bord.* ***Open space***, 4m/6km W of Kielder, on W side of Kielder Forest, with many streams running down W slopes into Larriston Burn. Highest point is 1679 feet or 512 metres. **70 A4** NY5692.

Lartington *Dur.* ***Village***, 2m/4km W of Barnard Castle. **62 B5** NZ0117.

Larton *Mersey.* ***Suburb***, 2m/3km E of West Kirby. SJ2387.

Lary *Aber.* ***Settlement***, at foot of Lary Hill, 3m/5km NW of Ballater. **90 B4** NJ3300.

Lasborough *Glos.* ***Settlement***, 5m/7km W of Tetbury. **20 B2** ST8294.

Lasham *Hants.* ***Village***, 3m/5km NW of Alton. **21 K7** SU6742.

Lashbrook *Devon* ***Hamlet***, 5m/7km NE of Holsworthy. SS4007.

Lashenden *Kent* ***Settlement***, 2m/3km S of Headcorn. TQ8440.

Lassington *Glos.* ***Settlement***, adjacent to N of Highnam, 3m/4km NW of Gloucester. **29 G6** SO7921.

Lassintullich *P. & K.* ***Settlement***, on S side of Dunalastair Water, 2m/3km SE of Kinloch Rannoch. **81 J2** NN6957.

Lassodie *Fife* ***Settlement***, 2m/3km SW of Kelty. **75 K1** NT1292.

Lasswade *Midloth.* ***Town***, adjoining Bonnyrigg 2m/3km SW of Dalkeith. **76 B4** NT3066.

Lastingham *N.Yorks.* ***Village***, below North York Moors, 6m/10km NW of Pickering. Late Norman church incorporates part of 11c abbey. **63 J7** SE7290.

Latcham *Som.* ***Locality***, 1km SE of Wedmore. ST4447.

Latchford *Oxon.* ***Settlement***, 4m/7km SW of Thame. SP6501.

Latchford *Warr.* ***Suburb***, 1m/2km SE of Warrington town centre. **49 F4** SJ6287.

Latchingdon *Essex* ***Village***, 5m/8km SE of Maldon. **24 E1** TL8800.

Latchley *Cornw.* ***Village***, on River Tamar, 2m/3km NW of Gunnislake. **4 E3** SX4073.

Lately Common *Gt.Man.* ***Settlement***, 2m/3km SE of Leigh. **49 F3** SJ6798.

Lathallan Mill *Fife* ***Settlement***, 4m/6km NE of Lower Largo. **83 F7** NO4605.

Lathbury *M.K.* ***Village***, 1m/2km N of Newport Pagnell. **32 B4** SP8745.

Latheron *High.* ***Village***, near E coast of Caithness district, 15m/24km SW of Wick. **105 G5** ND1933.

Latheronwheel (Also known as Janetstown.) *High.* ***Village***, near E coast of Caithness district, 1m/2km SW of Latheron. **105 G5** ND1832.

Lathockar *Fife* ***Settlement***, 4m/6km S of St. Andrews. **83 F6** NO4910.

Lathones *Fife* ***Settlement***, 1m/2km NE of Largoward. **83 F7** NO4708.

Lathrisk *Fife* ***Settlement***, 1m/2km NE of Falkland. **82 D7** NO2708.

Latimer *Bucks.* ***Village***, 3m/5km SE of Chesham. **22 D2** TQ0099.

Latrigg *Cumb.* ***Mountain***, 1m/2km NE of Keswick. Height 1207 feet or 368 metres. **60 D4** NY2724.

Latteridge *S.Glos.* ***Village***, 4m/7km W of Chipping Sodbury. **19 K3** ST6684.

Lattiford *Som.* ***Hamlet***, 2m/3km SW of Wincanton. **9 F2** ST6926.

Latton *Wilts.* ***Village***, 1m/2km NW of Cricklade. **20 D2** SU0995.

Latton Bush *Essex* ***Suburb***, 1m/2km SE of Harlow town centre. TL4608.

Lauchentyre *D. & G.* ***Settlement***, 3m/4km W of Gatehouse of Fleet. **65 F5** NX5557.

Lauchintilly *Aber.* ***Settlement***, 4m/6km SW of Kintore. **91 F3** NJ7512.

Lauder *Sc.Bord.* Population: 1064. ***Small town***, on Leader Water, 9m/14km N of Melrose. Thirlestane Castle to NE. **76 D6** NT5347.

Lauder Common *Sc.Bord.* ***Open space***, moorland 2m/3km SW of Lauder. **76 C6** NT4946.

Lauderdale *Sc.Bord.* ***Valley***, carrying Leader Water and running SE from Oxton, through Lauder and Earlston, to its confluence with River Tweed at Leaderfoot. **76 D5** NT5348.

Laugharne (Lacharn). *Carmar.* ***Village***, on River Taf estuary, 4m/6km S of St. Clears. Burial place of Dylan Thomas. Remains of medieval castle (Cadw). Army training area to S. **17 G3** SN3010.

Laugharne Burrows *Carmar.* ***Coastal feature***, sand dunes 3m/4km S of Laugharne. **17 F4** SN2907.

Laugharne Castle *Carmar.* ***Castle***, 13c-14c tower and gatehouse (Cadw) on W bank of River Taff, 3m/5km SE of St. Clears. Adapted to mansion in 16c by Sir John Perrott. **17 G3** SN3010.

Laugharne Sands *Carmar.* ***Coastal feature***, sandflat 3m/4km SE of Laugharne. **17 F4** SN3106.

Laughing Law *Sc.Bord.* ***Mountain***, 2m/3km NW of Abbey St. Bathans. Height 1010 feet or 308 metres. **77 F4** NT7364.

Laughterton *Lincs.* ***Village***, 9m/14km S of Gainsborough. **52 B5** SK8376.

Laughton *E.Suss.* ***Village***, 6m/9km E of Lewes. **13 J5** TQ5013.

Laughton *Leics.* ***Village***, 5m/8km W of Market Harborough. **41 J7** SP6689.

Laughton *Lincs.* ***Locality***, comprising West Laughton and Laughton Manor, 1m/2km S of Folkingham. **42 D2** TF0731.

Laughton *Lincs.* ***Village***, 5m/9km NE of Gainsborough. **52 B3** SK8497.

Laughton en le Morthen *S.Yorks.* ***Village***, 2m/3km E of Thurcroft. Remains of motte and bailey castle. **51 H4** SK5188.

Launcells *Cornw.* ***Hamlet***, 2m/3km E of Bude. **6 A5** SS2405.

Launcells Cross *Cornw.* ***Settlement***, 2m/4km E of Stratton. **6 A5** SS2606.

Launceston *Cornw.* Population: 6466. ***Small town***, on hill above River Kensey valley, 20m/32km NW of Plymouth. Officially styled 'Dunheved otherwise Launceston', Dunheved being old Celtic name. Formerly county capital. Remains of Norman castle (English Heritage) dominates town. Fine carvings in St. Mary Magdalene church. **6 B7** SX3384.

Launceston Castle *Cornw.* ***Castle***, surviving medieval shell keep and tower (English Heritage) on motte of Norman castle to N of Launceston town centre. Originally built by Robert of Mortain in 12c. **6 B7** SX3284.

Launceston Steam Railway *Cornw.* ***Other feature of interest***, tourist railway runs 1m/2km W from Launceston through Kensey Valley. Workshop and museum at Launceston. **4 C2** SX3285.

Laund *Lancs.* ***Locality***, 1km N of Rawtenstall. SD8023.

Launde *Leics.* ***Locality***, 6m/9km NW of Uppingham. SK7904.

Launde Abbey *Leics.* ***Historic house***, remains of 12c priory, 5m/8km SW of Oakham. 16c-17c house built on site. **42 B5** SK7904.

Launton *Oxon.* ***Village***, 2m/3km E of Bicester. **31 H6** SP6022.

Laurencekirk *Aber.* Population: 1611. ***Small town***, market town 10m/16km NE of Brechin. Formerly noted for manufacture of snuff-boxes. **91 F7** NO7171.

Laurieston *D. & G.* ***Village***, 9m/14km N of Kirkcudbright. **65 G4** NX6864.

Laurieston *Falk.* ***Locality***, 1m/2km E of Falkirk. Site of Roman fort on line of Antonine Wall to E. **75 H3** NS9179.

Lauriston Castle *Edin.* ***Castle***, 4m/6km NW of Edinburgh city centre, dating in part from late 16c. Grounds overlook Firth of Forth. **76 A3** NT2076.

Lavan Sands (Traeth Lafan). *Gwyn.* ***Nature reserve***, part of Conwy Bay lying between Beaumaris, Anglesey, and Welsh mainland; exposed at low tide. Important site for wildfowl, with large numbers of duck; red-breasted merganser and great-crested grebe use sand and mudflats to moult. **46 E5** SH6375.

Lavatrae *Dur. See Bowes.*

Lavendon *M.K.* ***Village***, 2m/4km NE of Olney. Scant remains of Norman castle. **32 C3** SP9153.

Lavenham *Suff.* Population: 1231. ***Small town***, former wool town 6m/9km NE of Sudbury. Many half-timbered houses. Restored 15c Guildhall (National Trust). Famous church. **34 D4** TL9149.

Lavenham Guildhall of Corpus Christi *Suff.* ***Historic house***, restored 15c timber-framed Guildhall of Corpus Christi (National Trust) in historic wool town of Lavenham, 6m/9km NE of Sudbury. Includes displays on local history, farming, railways and wool trade. 19c mortuary and walled garden. **34 D4** TL9048.

Laverhay *D. & G.* ***Settlement***, on hillside, 4m/7km SE of Beattock. **69 G4** NY1498.

Laverhay Height *D. & G.* ***Mountain***, 5m/8km SE of Beattock. Height 1588 feet or 484 metres. **69 G4** NY1598.

Lavernock (Larnog). *V. of Glam.* ***Hamlet***, on coast at Lavernock Point, headland 2m/3km S of Penarth. **18 E5** ST1868.

Lavernock Point *V. of Glam.* ***Coastal feature***, headland 2m/3km S of Penarth. **18 E5** ST1868.

Laversdale *Cumb.* ***Hamlet***, 4m/6km W of Brampton. **69 K7** NY4762.

Laverstock *Wilts.* ***Village***, to E of Salisbury across River Bourne. **10 C1** SU1530.

Laverstoke *Hants.* ***Village***, on River Test, 2m/3km E of Whitchurch. **21 H7** SU4948.

Laverton *Glos.* ***Village***, 2m/3km SW of Broadway. **30 B5** SP0735.

Laverton *N.Yorks.* ***Village***, 5m/9km W of Ripon. **57 H2** SE2273.

Laverton *Som.* ***Hamlet***, 3m/5km N of Frome. **20 A6** ST7753.

Lavister *Wrex.* ***Village***, 1m/2km NE of Rossett. **48 C7** SJ3758.

Law *S.Lan.* Population: 2900. ***Village***, 2m/4km NW of Carluke. **75 G5** NS8152.

Law Kneis *Sc.Bord.* ***Mountain***, 2m/3km SE of Ettrick. Height 1633 feet or 498 metres. **69 H2** NT2913.

Lawers *P. & K.* ***Settlement***, 1m/2km NE of Comrie. **81 J5** NN7923.

Lawers *P. & K.* ***Village***, on N side of Loch Tay, 7m/11km SW of Kenmore, near mouth of Lawers Burn. **81 H4** NN6739.

Lawers Burn *P. & K.* ***River***, on N side of Loch Tay. **81 H3** NN6739.

Lawford *Essex* ***Village***, 7m/11km NE of Colchester. **34 E5** TM0831.

Lawford *Som.* ***Hamlet***, 6m/9km SE of Watchet. ST1336.

Lawhitton *Cornw.* ***Village***, 2m/3km SE of Launceston. **6 B7** SX3582.

Lawkland *N.Yorks.* ***Hamlet***, 3m/5km NW of Settle. **56 C3** SD7766.

Lawkland Green *N.Yorks.* ***Hamlet***, 2m/4km NW of Settle. SD7865.

Lawley *Tel. & W.* ***Village***, 2m/3km W of Telford. **39 F5** SJ6608.

Lawling Creek *Essex* ***Sea feature***, inlet of River Blackwater estuary to S of Osea Island. **25 F1** TL9003.

Lawnhead *Staffs.* ***Settlement***, 6m/9km W of Stafford. **40 A3** SJ8324.

Lawns *W.Yorks.* ***Settlement***, 2m/4km N of Wakefield, on E side of M1 motorway. SE3124.

Lawrence Castle *Devon See Dunchideock.*

Lawrence House *Cornw.* ***Historic house***, large Georgian house (National Trust) to E of Launceston town centre. Now local museum and civic centre. **6 B7** SX3485.

Lawrence Weston *Bristol* ***Suburb***, NW district of Bristol. ST5478.

Lawrenny *Pembs.* ***Village***, near River Cresswell estuary, 8m/12km SW of Narberth. **16 D4** SN0106.

Laws *Angus* ***Hamlet***, 2m/3km N of Monifieth. Prehistoric fort and broch to SW. **83 F4** NO4935.

Lawshall *Suff.* ***Village***, 5m/8km N of Long Melford. **34 C3** TL8654.

Lawshall Green *Suff.* ***Settlement***, 1m/2km E of Lawshall. TL8853.

Lawton *Here.* ***Settlement***, 3m/5km W of Leominster. **28 D3** SO4459.

Lax Firth *Shet.* ***Sea feature***, inlet on E coast of Mainland, 5m/8km N of Lerwick. **109 D8** HU4447.

Laxa Burn *Shet.* ***River***, stream on Yell running N into head of Mid Yell Voe. **108 D4** HU5091.

Laxadale Lochs *W.Isles* ***Lake/loch***, series of three lochs running N from Urgha on N shore of East Loch Tarbert, North Harris. **100 D7** NB1801.

Laxay *W.Isles Anglicised form of Lacasaigh, qv.*

Laxdale *W.Isles* ***River***, rising 5m/8km NW of Laxdale and flowing past village into Loch a' Tuath, Isle of Lewis. **101 F4** NB4234.

Laxdale (Gaelic form: Lacasdal.) *W.Isles* Population: 1258. ***Village***, at head of River Laxdale estuary, 1m/2km N of Stornoway, Isle of Lewis. **101 G4** NB4234.

Laxey *I.o.M.* ***Small town***, resort on E coast 6m/10km NE of Douglas. Former lead mines. Laxey Wheel (Manx National Heritage), 19c waterwheel with 72 foot or 22 metre diameter, is largest working watermill in world; built to pump water from mines. **54 D5** SC4384.

Laxey Bay *I.o.M.* ***Bay***, on E coast of island, stretching from Laxey Head in N to Clay Head in S. **54 D5** SC4384.

Laxey Head *I.o.M.* ***Coastal feature***, headland at N end of Laxey Bay. **54 D5** SC4384.

Laxfield *Suff.* ***Village***, 6m/9km N of Framlingham. **35 G1** TM2972.

Laxfirth *Shet.* ***Settlement***, on Mainland, at head of inlet of Lax Firth. **109 D8** HU4446.

Laxfirth *Shet.* ***Settlement***, on Mainland, on S side of Dury Voe. **109 D7** HU4759.

Laxford Bridge *High.* ***Bridge***, road junction and bridge over River Laxford at head of Loch Laxford on W coast of Sutherland district. **102 E4** NC2346.

Laxo *Shet.* ***Settlement***, on E coast of Mainland, at head of Dury Voe. **109 D6** HU4463.

Laxton *E.Riding* ***Village***, 3m/5km SE of Howden. **58 D7** SE7925.

Laxton *Northants.* ***Village***, 6m/9km NE of Corby. **42 C6** SP9596.

Laxton *Notts.* ***Village***, 4m/7km E of Ollerton. **51 K6** SK7267.

Laycock *W.Yorks.* ***Village***, on hillside, 2m/3km W of Keighley. **57 F5** SE0241.

Layer Breton *Essex* ***Village***, 6m/9km SW of Colchester. **34 D7** TL9418.

Layer de la Haye *Essex* Population: 1811. ***Village***, 4m/7km SW of Colchester. **34 D7** TL9619.

Layer Marney *Essex* ***Hamlet***, 6m/10km SW of Colchester. **34 D7** TL9217.

Layer Marney Tower *Essex* ***Historic house***, in Layer Marney, 2m/3km NE of Tiptree. Tallest 16c Tudor gatehouse in Britain, with superb examples of terracotta work and medieval barns which feature rare breeds of animals. **34 D7** TL9217.

Layerthorpe *York* ***Suburb***, to E of York city centre. SE6151.

Layham *Suff.* ***Village***, 1m/2km S of Hadleigh. **34 E4** TM0340.

Layland's Green *W.Berks.* ***Locality***, adjoining to E of Kintbury, 4m/6km E of Hungerford. SU3866.

Laymore *Dorset* ***Hamlet***, 4m/6km NW of Broadwindsor. ST3804.

Laysters (Also spelled Leysters.) *Here.* ***Locality***, 6m/9km NE of Leominster. SO5663.

Laysters Pole *Here.* ***Village***, 5m/8km NE of Leominster. **28 E2** SO5563.

Layter's Green *Bucks.* ***Settlement***, to W of Chalfont St. Peter. SU9890.

Layter's Green *Essex* ***Settlement***, 4m/7km E of Harlow. TL5110.

Laytham *E.Riding* ***Village***, 8m/13km W of Market Weighton. **58 D6** SE7439.

Layton *B'pool* ***Suburb***, 1m/2km NE of Blackpool town centre. SD3236.

Lazenby *N.Yorks.* ***Locality***, 3m/5km N of Northallerton. SE3498.

Lazenby *R. & C.* ***Hamlet***, 5m/8km E of Middlesbrough. **63 G4** NZ5719.

Lazonby *Cumb.* ***Village***, on River Eden, 6m/10km N of Penrith. **61 G3** NY5439.

Lea (Alternative spelling: Lee.) ***River***, rising at Leagrave to N of Luton and flowing SE through Luton to Hatfield, then E to Hertford and Ware, then S into River Thames at Blackwall. Supplies water to London through large reservoirs S of Waltham Abbey. **23 G2** TQ3980.

Lea *Derbys.* ***Village***, 3m/4km SE of Matlock. **51 F7** SK3257.

Lea *Here.* ***Village***, 4m/7km SE of Ross-on-Wye. **29 F6** SO6621.

Lea *Lincs.* ***Village***, 2m/3km S of Gainsborough. **52 B4** SK8286.

Lea *Shrop.* ***Hamlet***, 2m/3km E of Bishop's Castle. Remains of castle. **38 C7** SO3589.

Lea *Shrop.* ***Settlement***, 5m/8km SW of Shrewsbury. Site of Roman villa. **38 D5** SJ4108.

Lea *Wilts.* ***Village***, 2m/3km E of Malmesbury. **20 C3** ST9586.

Lea Bridge *Derbys.* ***Hamlet***, 3m/4km SE of Matlock. SK3156.

Lea End *Worcs.* ***Settlement***, 5m/8km N of Redditch. SP0475.

Lea Gardens *Derbys.* ***Garden***, to S of Dethick, 3m/4km SE of Matlock, including rhododendrons in a woodland setting. **51 F7** SK3257.

Lea Green *Here.* ***Settlement***, 6m/9km SE of Tenbury Wells. SO6764.

Lea Green *Mersey.* ***Suburb***, 2m/3km S of St. Helens town centre. SJ5092.

Lea Heath *Staffs.* ***Hamlet***, 1km NW of Newton, 5m/8km N of Rugeley. SK0225.

Lea Marston *Warks.* ***Village***, on River Tame, 3m/4km N of Coleshill. **40 E6** SP2093.

Lea Taing *Ork.* ***Coastal feature***, small rocky promontory 1m/2km S of Rerwick Head on Mainland. **107 E6** HY5410.

Lea Town *Lancs.* ***Locality***, 4m/7km W of Preston. **55 H6** SD4731.

Lea Yeat *Cumb.* ***Settlement***, in Dentdale, 4m/6km E of Dent. **56 C1** SD7686.

Leabaidh an Daimh Bhuidhe ***Mountain***, summit of Ben Avon massif, on border of Aberdeenshire and Moray, N of Braemar. Munro: height 3841 feet or 1171 metres. **89 J4** NJ1301.

Leabrooks *Derbys.* ***Village***, 1m/2km S of Alfreton. SK4253.

Leac a' Li (Anglicised form: Lackalee.) *W.Isles* ***Settlement***, 1m/2km W of Greosabhagh, South Harris. **93 G2** NG1292.

Leac Dhonn *High.* ***Coastal feature***, rocky headland at NW end of Annat Bay, 8m/12km NW of Ullapool, Ross and Cromarty district. **95 G2** NH0199.

Leac Mhòr *High.* ***Coastal feature***, flat rock on coast, N of Opinan and 1m/2km SE of Greenstone Point, Ross and Cromarty district. **94 E2** NG8897.

Leac na Hoe *W.Isles* ***Coastal feature***, headland, easternmost point of North Uist, 3m/4km E of Lochportain. **92 E4** NF9872.

Leac nam Faoileann *High.* ***Coastal feature***, headland at westernmost point of Soay, and 1m/2km S of Skye across Soay Sound. **85 K3** NG4214.

Leac Shoilleir *High.* ***Mountain***, 3m/5km N of Glenborrodale. Height 1443 feet or 440 metres. **79 H1** NM6065.

Leac Tressirnish *High.* ***Coastal feature***, headland on E coast of Skye, 3m/4km NE of The Storr. **94 B6** NG5257.

Leacann Doire Bainneir *High.* ***Mountain***, on E side of NE end of Loch Lochy, 2m/3km SE of Laggan. Height 2099 feet or 640 metres. **87 K5** NN3094.

Leacann nan Gall *Arg. & B.* ***Mountain***, at head of Inverchaolain Glen, 4m/7km NW of Dunoon. Height 1863 feet or 568 metres. **73 K3** NS1078.

Leach *Glos.* ***River***, rising near Northleach and flowing SE into River Thames 1km SE of Lechlade. **20 E1** SU2298.

Leachie Hill *Aber.* ***Mountain***, 4m/6km NW of Glenbervie. Height 1299 feet or 396 metres. **91 F6** NO7385.

Leachkin *High.* ***Locality***, in Inverness district, 2m/3km W of Inverness. **96 D7** NH6444.

Leack *Arg. & B.* ***Settlement***, on S shore of Loch Fyne, 4m/6km SW of Strachur. **73 J1** NS0498.

Leacroft *Staffs.* ***Locality***, 1m/2km SE of Cannock. SJ9909.

Lead *N.Yorks.* ***Locality***, 1km W of Saxton, 4m/6km S of Tadcaster. SE4637.

Leadburn *Midloth.* ***Hamlet***, 3m/4km S of Penicuik. **76 A5** NT2355.

Leaden Roding *Essex* ***Village***, 6m/9km SW of Great Dunmow. **33 J7** TL5913.

Leadenham *Lincs.* ***Village***, 8m/13km NW of Sleaford. **52 C7** SK9552.

Leader Water *Sc.Bord.* ***River***, rising on Lammermuir Hills and flowing S down Lauderdale to River Tweed at Leaderfoot, 2m/3km E of Melrose. **76 D6** NT5734.

Leaderfoot *Sc.Bord.* ***Settlement***, 2m/3km E of Melrose, at confluence of Leader Water and River Tweed. NT5734.

Leadgate *Cumb.* ***Settlement***, 2m/3km S of Alston. **61 J2** NY7043.

Leadgate *Dur.* Population: 4736. ***Suburb***, 1m/2km E of Consett. **62 C1** NZ1251.

Leadgate *Northumb.* ***Hamlet***, 2m/4km S of Prudhoe. **62 C1** NZ1159.

Leadhills *S.Lan.* ***Town***, former lead-mining town 6m/10km SW of Abington. **68 D2** NS8815.

Leadingcross Green *Kent* ***Settlement***, 1km SW of Lenham. TQ8951.

Leadmill *Flints.* ***Suburb***, to NE of Mold. SJ2464.

Leadon ***River***, rising 1m/2km NE of Evesbatch and flowing S past Ledbury, then into River Severn 1m/2km NW of Gloucester. **29 G6** SO8119.

Leafield *Oxon.* ***Village***, 4m/7km NW of Witney. **30 E7** SP3115.

Leagach *High.* *Anglicised form of Liathach, qv.*

Leagag *P. & K.* ***Mountain***, rising to over 600 metres in Rannoch district, 2m/3km SE of Bridge of Gaur. **81 G2** NN5153.

Leagrave *Luton* ***Suburb***, NW district of Luton. Source of River Lea between here and Sundon Park to N. **32 D6** TL0523.

Leagrave Marsh *Luton* ***Suburb***, NW district of Luton. TL0624.

Leagreen *Hants.* ***Locality***, 2m/3km NW of Milford on Sea. SZ2793.

Leake *N.Yorks.* ***Locality***, 5m/8km N of Thirsk. SE4390.

Leake Common Side *Lincs.* ***Village***, 7m/11km NE of Boston. **53 G7** TF3952.

Leake Fold Hill *Lincs.* ***Locality***, 1m/2km N of Old Leake. TF4051.

Leake Hurn's End *Lincs.* ***Settlement***, 1m/2km S of Wrangle. **43 H1** TF4249.

Lealands *E.Suss.* ***Settlement***, 2m/3km N of Hailsham. **13 J5** TQ5813.

Lealholm *N.Yorks.* ***Village***, on River Esk, 3m/5km W of Egton. **63 J6** NZ7607.

Lealholm Moor *N.Yorks.* ***Open space***, moorland 1m/2km NW of Lealholm. **63 J6** NZ7509.

Lealholm Side *N.Yorks.* ***Locality***, up hill to NE of Lealholm. NZ7608.

Lealt *Arg. & B.* ***Settlement***, in Glen Lealt, on E coast of Jura, 2m/3km N of Ardlussa. **72 E1** NR6690.

Lealt *High.* ***Settlement***, near NE coast of Skye, 11m/17km N of Portree. **94 B5** NG5060.

Lealt Burn *Arg. & B.* ***River***, running through Glen Lealt into Sound of Jura, on E coast of Jura. **72 E1** NR6690.

Leam ***River***, rising at Hellidon and flowing N, then W into River Avon between Royal Leamington Spa and Warwick. **31 F2** SP3065.

Leam *Derbys.* ***Settlement***, 1m/2km S of Hathersage. SK2379.

Leamington Hastings *Warks.* ***Village***, 4m/7km NE of Southam. **31 F2** SP4467.

Leamington Spa *Warks.* *Familiar form of Royal Leamington Spa, qv.*

Leamonsley *Staffs.* ***Suburb***, W district of Lichfield. SK1009.

Leamoor Common *Shrop.* ***Hamlet***, 3m/4km N of Craven Arms. SO4386.

Leamside *Dur.* ***Hamlet***, on W side of West Rainton. NZ3146.

Leana Mhòr *High.* ***Mountain***, in Lochaber district, on E side of Glen Roy, 4m/7km N of Roybridge. Height 2247 feet or 685 metres. **87 J6** NN2887.

Leana Mhòr *High.* ***Mountain***, on E side of Glen Roy, 5m/8km NE of Roybridge. Height 2224 feet or 678 metres. **87 K6** NN3087.

Leanach *Arg. & B.* ***Settlement***, 4m/7km SW of Strachur. **73 J1** NS0497.

Leanach *High.* ***Locality***, 6m/10km E of Inverness. **96 E7** NH7544.

Leanachan Forest *High.* ***Forest/woodland***, in Lochaber district 4m/6km SW of Spean Bridge. **87 H7** NN1977.

Leanaig *High.* ***Settlement***, 1m/2km SE of Conon Bridge. **96 C6** NH5654.

Leanoch *Moray* ***Settlement***, on W bank of River Lossie, 1m/2km E of Kellas. **97 J6** NJ1954.

Leanoch Burn *Moray* ***River***, stream flowing N down Glen Latterach into Glenlatterach Reservoir, 6m/10km S of Elgin. **97 J6** NJ1852.

Leap Hill *Northumb.* ***Mountain***, in Cheviot Hills, 2m/3km E of Carter Bar. Height 1538 feet or 469 metres. **70 C3** NT7207.

Leap Moor *Inclyde* ***Open space***, moorland area, to E of Wemyss Bay. **74 A4** NS2369.

Leargybreck *Arg. & B.* ***Locality***, on E coast of Jura, 3m/4km N of Craighouse. **72 D3** NR5371.

Lease Rigg *N.Yorks.* ***Locality***, adjoining to SW of Grosmont. NZ8204.

Leasgill *Cumb.* ***Village***, 1m/2km S of Levens. **55 H1** SD4984.

Leasingham *Lincs.* ***Village***, 2m/3km N of Sleaford. **42 D1** TF0548.

Leasingthorne *Dur.* ***Hamlet***, 2m/4km S of Spennymoor. NZ2529.

Leask *Aber.* ***Locality***, comprises many dispersed settlements, 4m/6km E of Ellon. **91 J1** NK0232.

Leason *Swan.* ***Hamlet***, on Gower peninsula, 1km W of Llanrhidian. SS4892.

Leasowe *Mersey.* ***Suburb***, 3m/5km W of Wallasey town centre. SJ2791.

Leat *Cornw.* ***Settlement***, 3m/4km NW of Launceston. SX3087.

Leathad Dail nan Cliabh *High.* ***Mountain***, 1m/2km SW of Duchally, to W of Glen Cassley. Height 1079 feet or 329 metres. **103 F7** NC3715.

Leatherhead *Surr.* Population: 42,903. ***Town***, on River Mole, 8m/13km S of Kingston upon Thames. 13c church with large 15c tower. **22 E6** TQ1656.

Leathley *N.Yorks.* ***Village***, 2m/4km NE of Otley across River Wharfe. **57 H5** SE2347.

Leaton *Shrop.* ***Village***, 4m/7km NW of Shrewsbury. **38 D4** SJ4618.

Leaton *Tel. & W.* ***Settlement***, 3m/4km W of Wellington. SJ6111.

Leaveland *Kent* ***Village***, 5m/8km S of Faversham. **15 F2** TR0054.

Leavenheath *Suff.* ***Hamlet***, 2m/4km NW of Nayland. **34 D5** TL9537.

Leavening *N.Yorks.* ***Village***, 5m/9km S of Malton. **58 D3** SE7863.

Leaves Green *Gt.Lon.* ***Hamlet***, in borough of Bromley, on W side of Biggin Hill airfield. **23 H5** TQ4161.

Leavesden Green *Herts.* ***Suburb***, 3m/4km N of Watford town centre. TL0900.

Leazes *Dur.* ***Village***, adjoining to W of Burnopfield, 3m/5km NW of Stanley. NZ1656.

Lebberston *N.Yorks.* ***Village***, 3m/4km NW of Filey. **59 G1** TA0782.

Lechlade *Glos.* Population: 1638. ***Small town***, on River Thames, 10m/16km NE of Swindon. Site of Roman building 1km N. **21 F2** SU2199.

Lechuary *Arg. & B.* ***Settlement***, in valley of River Add, 4m/7km N of Lochgilphead. **73 G1** NR8795.

Leck *Lancs.* ***Village***, 2m/4km SE of Kirkby Lonsdale. **56 B2** SD6476.

Leck Beck ***River***, rising as Ease Gill on Barbon High Fell and flowing SW, past Leck and Cowan Bridge, into River Lune to W of Nether Burrow. **56 B2** SD6175.

Leck Fell *Lancs.* ***Open space***, moorland containing several potholes and caves, 3m/5km E of Kirkby Lonsdale. **56 B2** SD6678.

Leckby *N.Yorks.* ***Locality***, 2m/3km SE of Topcliffe across River Swale. SE4173.

Lecket Hill *E.Dun.* ***Mountain***, on Campsie Fells, 2m/4km NE of Lennoxtown. Height 1791 feet or 546 metres. **74 E2** NS6481.

Leckford *Hants.* ***Village***, on River Test, 2m/3km NE of Stockbridge. **10 E1** SU3737.

Leckfurin *High.* ***Settlement***, near N coast of Caithness district, 1m/2km S of Bettyhill. **104 C3** NC7059.

Leckgruinart *Arg. & B.* ***Locality***, on Islay, 4m/6km S of Ardnave Point. **72 A4** NR2769.

Leckhampstead *Bucks.* ***Village***, 3m/5km NE of Buckingham. **31 J5** SP7237.

Leckhampstead *W.Berks.* ***Village***, 6m/9km N of Newbury. **21 H4** SU4376.

Leckhampstead Street *W.Berks.* ***Locality***, adjoining to N of Leckhampstead. SU4376.

Leckhampstead Thicket *W.Berks.* ***Hamlet***, 1m/2km NW of Leckhampstead. SU4276.

Leckhampton *Glos.* ***Suburb***, 2m/3km S of Cheltenham. **29 J7** SO9419.

Leckie *High.* ***Settlement***, 4m/7km NE of Kinlochewe. **95 G5** NH0864.

Leckie *Stir.* ***Locality***, comprises Inch of Leckie, Wester Leckie and Old Leckie, 1m/2km W of Gargunnock. **74 E1** NS6894.

Leckmelm *High.* ***Locality***, on E shore of Loch Broom, Ross and Cromarty district, 4m/6km SE of Ullapool. **95 H2** NH1690.

Leckroy *High.* ***Settlement***, in upper part of Glen Roy, 9m/14km NE of Roybridge. **87 K5** NN3592.

Leckwith (Lecwydd). *V. of Glam.* ***Settlement***, 2m/3km SW of Cardiff. **18 E4** ST1574.

Leckwith Moors *Cardiff* ***Locality***, 1m/2km SW of Cardiff, to E of Leckwith across River Ely. Industrial estate. ST1574.

Leconfield *E.Riding* Population: 1436. ***Village***, 3m/4km N of Beverley. **59 G5** TA0143.

Lecwydd *V. of Glam.* *Welsh form of Leckwith, qv.*

Ledaig *Arg. & B.* ***Locality***, adjoining to S of Tobermory, Mull. NM5055.

Ledaig *Arg. & B.* ***Settlement***, on Ardmucknish Bay, 2m/3km N of Connel, Argyll. **80 A4** NM9037.

Ledaig Point *Arg. & B.* ***Coastal feature***, headland on S end of Ardmucknish Bay and on N side of entrance to Loch Etive. NM8935.

Ledard *Stir.* ***Settlement***, on N shore of Loch Ard, 4m/7km NW of Aberfoyle. **81 F7** NN4602.

Ledbeg *High.* ***Settlement***, on Ledbeg River, 1m/2km E of Cam Loch. **102 E7** NC2413.

Ledburn *Bucks.* ***Hamlet***, 2m/4km SW of Leighton Buzzard. **32 B6** SP9021.

Ledbury *Here.* Population: 6216. ***Small town***, old market town 12m/20km E of Hereford. Many half-timbered houses. 17c market hall stands on wooden pillars in market place. **29 G5** SO7137.

Ledcharrie *Stir.* ***Settlement***, in Glen Dochart, 5m/8km SW of Killin. **81 G5** NN5028.

L

Ledgemoor *Here.* ***Village***, 9m/14km NW of Hereford. **28 D3** SO4150.
Ledgowan Forest *High.* ***Open space***, deer forest S of Loch a' Chroisg in Ross and Cromarty district. **95 H6** NH1256.
Ledicot *Here.* ***Hamlet***, 5m/9km W of Leominster. **28 D2** SO4162.
Ledmore *Arg. & B.* ***Settlement***, at S end of Loch Frisa, 4m/6km NW of Salen, Mull. **79 G3** NM5246.
Ledmore *High.* ***Settlement***, in Sutherland district, 6m/10km S of Inchnadamph. **102 E7** NC2412.
Lednagullin *High.* ***Settlement***, 1km E of Armadale, near N coast of Caithness district. **104 C2** NC8064.
Lednock *P. & K.* ***River***, running SE down Glen Lednock to River Earn at Comrie. Falls of Lednock at Deil's Caldron, 1m/2km N of Comrie. **81 J5** NN7722.
Ledsham *Ches.* ***Locality***, 3m/5km SW of Ellesmere Port. **48 C5** SJ3574.
Ledsham *W.Yorks.* ***Village***, 4m/6km NW of Ferrybridge. **57 K7** SE4529.
Ledston *W.Yorks.* ***Village***, 2m/3km N of Castleford. Hall dates in part from 13c, though mainly 16c-17c. **57 K7** SE4328.
Ledstone *Devon* ***Hamlet***, 2m/3km N of Kingsbridge. SX7446.
Ledwell *Oxon.* ***Hamlet***, 4m/6km SW of Deddington. **31 F6** SP4228.
Lee *Alternative spelling of (River) Lea, qv.*
Lee *Arg. & B.* ***Settlement***, on Mull, 1m/2km E of Bunessan. **79 F5** NM4021.
Lee *Devon* ***Village***, in coombe running down to Lee Bay, 2m/3km W of Ilfracombe. **6 C1** SS4846.
Lee *Hants.* ***Hamlet***, in River Test valley, 2m/3km S of Romsey. **10 E3** SU3617.
Lee *Lancs.* ***Settlement***, near bridge over Tarnbrook Wyre, at foot of Dunkenshaw Fell, 7m/11km SE of Lancaster. **55 J4** SD5655.
Lee *Shrop.* ***Settlement***, 2m/3km S of Ellesmere. **38 D2** SJ4032.
Lee Bay *Devon* ***Bay***, 2m/3km W of Ilfracombe. **6 C1** SS4846.
Lee Brockhurst *Shrop.* ***Village***, 3m/4km SE of Wem. **38 E3** SJ5427.
Lee Chapel *Essex* ***Suburb***, to W of Basildon town centre. TQ6988.
Lee Clump *Bucks.* ***Village***, 4m/6km NW of Chesham. **22 C1** SP9004.
Lee Fell *Lancs.* ***Open space***, area of moorland on W side of Forest of Bowland, 6m/10km E of Lancaster. **55 J4** SD5657.
Lee Head *Derbys.* ***Hamlet***, adjoining to SW of Charlesworth. SK0092.
Lee Mill Bridge *Devon* ***Village***, on River Yealm, 2m/4km W of Ivybridge. Industrial estate to E. **5 F5** SX5955.
Lee Moor *Devon* ***Hamlet***, in china clay district, 5m/9km NW of Ivybridge. **5 F4** SX5761.
Lee Moor *W.Yorks.* ***Locality***, 1km E of Lofthouse Gate, 3m/5km N of Wakefield. SE3425.
Lee-on-the-Solent *Hants.* Population: 7259. ***Small town***, resort and residential locality, 4m/6km W of Gosport. Church built in 1930s has impressive interior. **11 G4** SU5600.
Lee Pen *Sc.Bord.* ***Mountain***, 1m/2km N of Innerleithen. Height 1647 feet or 502 metres. **76 B7** NT3238.
Leebotten *Shet.* ***Settlement***, 1km N of Sandwick, on E coast of Mainland. **109 D10** HU4324.
Leebotwood *Shrop.* ***Village***, 4m/6km NE of Church Stretton. **38 D6** SO4798.
Leece *Cumb.* ***Village***, 3m/5km E of Barrow-in-Furness. **55 F3** SD2469.
Leeds *Kent* ***Village***, 4m/7km E of Maidstone. **14 D2** TQ8253.
Leeds *W.Yorks.* Population: 424,194. ***City***, commercial and industrial city on River Aire and on Leeds and Liverpool Canal, 36m/58km NE of Manchester and 170m/274km NW of London. Prospered during Victorian period, the architecture of a series of ornate arcades containing some magnificent clocks reflecting the affluence of this time. Previously important for textile industry. Boasts several fine galleries and museums. Universities. Leeds Bradford International Airport at Yeadon, 7m/11km NW. **57 H6** SE2933.
Leeds and Liverpool Canal ***Canal***, trans-Pennine canal from Leeds to Liverpool by Shipley, Skipton, Nelson, Burnley, Blackburn, Wigan and Bootle. At Leeds, it connects with Aire and Calder Navigation to form waterway linking Irish Sea with North Sea. Branch to Leigh from Wigan. **56 B7** SJ3392.
Leeds Bradford International Airport *W.Yorks.* ***Airport/airfield***, on NE side of Yeadon, 6m/9km NE of Bradford city centre. **57 H5** SE2241.
Leeds Castle *Kent* ***Castle***, impressive and picturesque castle rising from its own lake, 6m/10km E of Maidstone. Original castle built AD 857 with much subsequent rebuilding in 13c and 16c. Gardens include Culpeper Garden, Duckery, greenhouses and vineyard. Grounds notable for autumn displays. Other attractions are rare breed aviary, maze and underground grotto. **14 D2** TQ8253.
Leedstown *Cornw.* ***Village***, 3m/5km SE of Hayle. **2 D5** SW6034.
Leegomery *Tel. & W.* ***Locality***, 1m/2km NE of Wellington. **39 F4** SJ6612.
Leek *Staffs.* Population: 18,167. ***Town***, former textile and silk-weaving town, 10m/15km NE of Stoke-on-Trent. **49 J7** SJ9856.
Leek Wootton *Warks.* ***Village***, 2m/4km N of Warwick. **30 D2** SP2868.
Leekbrook *Staffs.* ***Settlement***, 2m/3km S of Leek. SJ9853.
Leeming *N.Yorks.* Population: 2754. ***Village***, 2m/3km NE of Bedale. Airfield to E. **57 H1** SE2890.
Leeming *W.Yorks.* ***Hamlet***, 2m/3km W of Denholme. **57 F6** SE0334.
Leeming Bar *N.Yorks.* ***Village***, 1km NW of Leeming. **62 D7** SE2890.
Leen ***River***, rising near Newstead Abbey and flowing S into River Trent on W side of Nottingham. **51 H7** SK5538.
Lees *Derbys.* ***Village***, 6m/9km W of Derby. **40 E2** SK2637.
Lees *Gt.Man.* ***Suburb***, 2m/3km E of Oldham. **49 J2** SD9504.
Lees Green *Derbys.* ***Settlement***, adjoining to N of Lees. SK2637.
Lees Hill *Cumb.* ***Locality***, 1m/2km S of Askerton Castle and 4m/7km NE of Brampton. NY5568.
Leeswood (Coed-llai). *Flints.* Population: 2322. ***Village***, 3m/5km SE of Mold. **48 B7** SJ2759.
Leet Water *Sc.Bord.* ***River***, rising N of Whitsome and flowing S to join River Tweed at Coldstream. **77 G6** NT8439.
Leetown *P. & K.* ***Hamlet***, 3m/4km W of Errol. NO2121.
Leez Lodge Lakes *Essex* ***Reservoir***, two small adjacent reservoirs 4m/7km SW of Braintree. **34 B7** TL7018.
Left Law *S.Lan.* ***Mountain***, 2m/3km NW of Dunsyre. Height 1181 feet or 360 metres. **75 J5** NT0550.
Leftwich Green *Ches.* ***Suburb***, 1m/2km S of Northwich. SJ6672.
Legars *Sc.Bord.* ***Settlement***, 4m/6km S of Greenlaw. **77 F6** NT7140.
Legbourne *Lincs.* ***Village***, 3m/5km SE of Louth. **53 G4** TF3684.
Legburthwaite *Cumb.* ***Locality***, 4m/7km SE of Keswick, near N end of Thirlmere. NY3119.
Legerwood *Sc.Bord.* ***Village***, 4m/7km SE of Lauder. **76 D6** NT5843.
Legoland *W. & M.* ***Leisure/recreation***, 150 acre theme park in Windsor Great Park based around Lego bricks, 2m/3km SW of Windsor town centre. Attractions include Boating School, Driving School and Miniland, replicas of cities from around world. **22 C4** SU9374.
Legsby *Lincs.* ***Village***, 3m/5km SE of Market Rasen. **52 E4** TF1385.
Leicester *Leic.* Population: 318,518. ***City***, county town and commercial and industrial centre on River Soar, on site of Roman town of Ratae Coritanorum, 89m/143km NW of London. Industries include hosiery and footwear, alongside more modern industries. Universities. Many historic remains including Jewry Wall (English Heritage), one of largest surviving sections of Roman wall in the country, Roman baths and a medieval guildhall. Home to England's second biggest street festival after Notting Hill Carnival. Joseph Merrick, the 'Elephant Man' born and lived here. **41 H5** SK5804.
Leicester Cathedral *Leic.* ***Ecclesiastical building***, parish church in centre of Leicester, elevated to cathedral status in 1927. Mainly 13c, in Early English style. **41 H5** SK5804.
Leicester Forest East *Leics.* ***Suburb***, 4m/6km W of Leicester. Service area on M1 motorway. **41 H5** SK5202.
Leicester Forest West *Leics.* ***Hamlet***, 2m/3km SE of Desford. SK5002.
Leideag *W.Isles* ***Settlement***, adjoining to SE of Castlebay, Barra. **84 B5** NL6697.
Leidle *Arg. & B.* ***River***, stream on Mull, rising on Beinn na Croise and running S, W, and finally NW down Glen Leidle into Loch Scridain at Pennyghael. **79 G5** NM5126.
Leigh *Devon* ***Hamlet***, 3m/5km SE of Chulmleigh. SS7212.
Leigh *Dorset* ***Suburb***, to E of Wimborne Minster. SZ0299.
Leigh *Dorset* ***Village***, 5m/8km S of Sherborne. **9 F4** ST6108.
Leigh *Glos.* ***Village***, 5m/9km NE of Gloucester. **29 H6** SO8726.
Leigh *Gt.Man.* Population: 43,150. ***Town***, old market town, 12m/19km W of Manchester. Branch of Leeds and Liverpool Canal from Wigan connects here with Bridgewater Canal. **49 F2** SD6500.
Leigh *Kent* ***Village***, with large green, 3m/4km W of Tonbridge. **23 J7** TQ5446.
Leigh *Shrop.* ***Settlement***, 1m/2km S of Worthen. **38 C5** SJ3303.
Leigh *Surr.* ***Village***, 3m/5km SW of Reigate. **23 F7** TQ2246.
Leigh *Wilts.* ***Village***, 3m/4km W of Cricklade. **20 D2** SU0692.
Leigh *Worcs.* ***Village***, at confluence of Leigh Brook and River Teme, 4m/7km W of Worcester. Leigh Court Barn (English Heritage) is timber-framed barn built in 14c for monks of Pershore Abbey. **29 G3** SO7853.
Leigh Beck *Essex* ***Suburb***, E district of Canvey Island. **24 E3** TQ8182.
Leigh Common *Som.* ***Hamlet***, 2m/3km E of Wincanton. **9 G2** ST7429.
Leigh Delamere *Wilts.* ***Village***, 4m/7km NW of Chippenham. Site of Roman villa to E. **20 B4** ST8879.
Leigh Green *Kent* ***Settlement***, 1m/2km SE of Tenterden. **14 E4** TQ9032.
Leigh-on-Mendip *Som.* *Alternative name for Leigh upon Mendip, qv.*
Leigh-on-Sea *S'end* ***Suburb***, W district of Southend-on-Sea. **24 E3** TQ8486.
Leigh Park *Hants.* ***Suburb***, N district of Havant. SU7108.
Leigh Sinton *Worcs.* ***Village***, 3m/5km N of Malvern. **29 G3** SO7850.
Leigh upon Mendip (Also known as Leigh-on-Mendip.) *Som.* ***Village***, 5m/8km W of Frome. **19 K7** ST6947.
Leigh Woods *N.Som.* ***Settlement***, at N end of Ashton Court Estate, 2m/3km W of Bristol. **19 J4** ST5572.
Leigham *Plym.* ***Suburb***, 3m/5km NE of Plymouth city centre. SX5158.
Leighland Chapel *Som.* ***Hamlet***, on Brendon Hills, 5m/8km SW of Watchet. ST0336.
Leighswood *W.Mid.* ***Suburb***, to N of Aldridge. SK0501.
Leighterton *Glos.* ***Village***, 5m/7km W of Tetbury. **20 B2** ST8291.
Leighton *N.Yorks.* ***Settlement***, 4m/7km W of Masham. **57 G2** SE1679.
Leighton *Powys* ***Village***, 2m/3km SE of Welshpool across River Severn. **38 B5** SJ2405.
Leighton *Shrop.* ***Village***, 5m/7km SW of Wellington. **39 F5** SJ6105.
Leighton *Som.* ***Hamlet***, 5m/9km E of Shepton Mallet. **20 A7** ST7043.
Leighton Bromswold *Cambs.* ***Village***, 5m/7km W of Alconbury. **32 E1** TL1175.
Leighton Buzzard *Beds.* Population: 32,610. ***Town***, market and industrial town, 11m/18km NW of Luton. Attractive church with 190 foot or 58 metre spire. **32 C6** SP9225.
Leighton Buzzard Light Railway *Beds.* ***Other feature of interest***, 6m/9km tourist railway to E of Leighton Buzzard, originally built in early 20c to carry sand. Now has fifty trains from around the world and is a centre for narrow gauge presentations. **32 C6** SP9326.
Leighton Hall *Lancs.* ***Historic house***, 13c hall with neo-Gothic façade, 1km W of Yealand Conyers and 3m/4km N of Carnforth. Contains 18c furniture by Gillow of Lancaster. Presently occupied by Reynolds family. **55 H2** SD4974.
Leighton Reservoir *N.Yorks.* ***Reservoir***, to S of Leighton. **57 G2** SE1679.
Leinthall Earls *Here.* ***Village***, 6m/10km NW of Leominster. **28 D2** SO4467.
Leinthall Starkes *Here.* ***Village***, 6m/9km SW of Ludlow. **28 D2** SO4369.
Leintwardine *Here.* ***Village***, at confluence of River Clun and River Teme and on site of Roman Bravonium, 7m/11km W of Ludlow. **28 D1** SO4074.
Leire *Leics.* ***Village***, 4m/6km N of Lutterworth. **41 H7** SP5290.
Leirinmore *High.* ***Hamlet***, near N coast of Sutherland district, 1m/2km SE of Durness. **103 G2** NC4166.
Leiston *Suff.* Population: 5950. ***Small town***, near coast, 4m/6km E of Saxmundham. Ruins of 14c abbey (English Heritage) 1m/2km N. **35 J2** TM4462.
Leiston Abbey *Suff.* ***Ecclesiastical building***, ruins of Premonstratensian abbey (English Heritage) dates from 14c and includes restored chapel, 1m/2km N of Leiston. Earlier abbey, founded 1180, was on a site closer to sea. **35 J2** TM4464.
Leitfie *P. & K.* ***Hamlet***, 2m/3km S of Alyth. **82 D3** NO2545.
Leith *Cumb.* ***River***, rising at Shap and flowing N to Melkinthorpe, then E into River Lyvennet 1m/2km E of Cliburn. **61 G4** NY6024.
Leith *Edin.* ***Suburb***, 2m/3km N of Edinburgh city centre. Harbour and docks on Firth of Forth. **76 A3** NT2676.
Leith Hall *Aber.* ***Historic house***, National Trust for Scotland property built round central courtyard 1km NE of Kirkhill of Kennethmont, and 7m/11km S of Huntly. Home of head of Leith family since 1650. **90 D2** NJ5429.
Leith Hill *Surr.* ***Hill***, wooded hill (National Trust) 4m/7km SW of Dorking, standing 964 feet or 294 metres, highest point in SE England. A 64 feet (20 metres) tower stands on summit. **22 E7** TQ1343.
Leith Hill Tower *Surr.* ***Other feature of interest***, 18c Gothic tower, 64 feet or 20 metres tall, on top of Leith Hill. Highest point in SE England; magnificent views. **22 E7** TQ1343.
Leithen Water *Sc.Bord.* ***River***, rising on Moorfoot Hills, 3m/4km E of Eddleston, and flowing S to River Tweed at Innerleithen. **76 B6** NT3336.
Leitholm *Sc.Bord.* ***Village***, 4m/7km NW of Coldstream. **77 F6** NT7944.
Leithope Forest *Sc.Bord.* ***Forest/woodland***, large area of coniferous forest in Cheviot Hills, to NE of Carter Bar. **70 C3** NT7209.
Lelant *Cornw.* ***Village***, to W of Hayle across River Hayle estuary. 16c abbey. Bird sanctuary on saltings. **2 C5** SW5437.
Lelant Downs *Cornw.* ***Locality***, 3m/5km S of St. Ives. SW5236.
Lelley *E.Riding* ***Hamlet***, 3m/5km NE of Hedon. **59 J6** TA2032.
Lem Hill *Worcs.* ***Hamlet***, 4m/7km W of Bewdley. **29 G1** SO7274.
Lemanis *Kent See Lympne.*
Lemington *T. & W.* ***Locality***, on N bank of River Tyne, 1m/2km SE of Newburn. **71 G7** NZ1864.
Lemnas *Aber.* ***Settlement***, 2m/3km S of Pennan Bay and 3m/4km W of New Aberdour. **99 G4** NJ8462.
Lemon *Devon* ***River***, rising on E slopes of Dartmoor and running E into River Teign at Newton Abbot. **5 H3** SX8671.
Lempitlaw *Sc.Bord.* ***Settlement***, 3m/5km E of Kelso. **77 F7** NT7832.
Lemreway *W.Isles Anglicised form of Leumrabhagh, qv.*
Lemsford *Herts.* ***Village***, 1m/2km W of Welwyn Garden City. **33 F7** TL2112.
Len *Kent* ***River***, rising S of Lenham and flowing W into River Medway at Maidstone. **14 D2** TQ7555.
Lenacre *Cumb.* ***Settlement***, 2m/3km SE of Sedbergh. SD6689.
Lenchwick *Worcs.* ***Village***, 2m/4km N of Evesham. **30 B4** SP0347.
Lendalfoot *S.Ayr.* ***Village***, coastal village, 6m/10km SW of Girvan. **67 F5** NX1390.
Lendrick *Stir.* ***Settlement***, at W end of Loch Venachar, 4m/6km NE of Aberfoyle. **81 G7** NN5406.
Lendrick Hill *P. & K.* ***Mountain***, 2m/3km NE of Pool of Muckhart. Height 1496 feet or 456 metres. **82 B7** NO0103.
Lenham *Kent* Population: 2167. ***Village***, 4m/6km NW of Charing. **14 D2** TQ8952.
Lenham Heath *Kent* ***Settlement***, 2m/3km SE of Lenham. **14 E3** TQ9149.
Lenie *High.* ***Locality***, comprising Upper Lenie and Lower Lenie, on NW shore of Loch Ness, 2m/3km S of Drumnadrochit, Inverness district. **88 C2** NH5126.
Lenimore (Also known as North Thundergay.) *N.Ayr.* ***Settlement***, on NW coast of Arran, 3m/4km NE of Pirnmill. **73 G6** NR8847.
Lennel *Sc.Bord.* ***Village***, on River Tweed, 1m/2km NE of Coldstream. **77 G6** NT8540.

Lennox Forest *E.Dun.* ***Forest/woodland***, 1m/2km W of Lennoxtown. **74 D3** NS6077.
Lennox Plunton *D. & G.* ***Settlement***, 3m/5km S of Gatehouse of Fleet. **65 G5** NX6051.
Lennoxlove House *E.Loth.* ***Historic house***, mansion of 14c with later additions, 1m/2km S of Haddington. **76 D3** NT5172.
Lennoxtown *E.Dun.* Population: 4524. ***Small town***, 8m/13km N of Glasgow. **74 E3** NS6277.
Lent *Bucks.* ***Suburb***, 3m/5km W of Slough. SU9282.
Lent Rise *Bucks.* ***Suburb***, 3m/5km W of Slough. SU9281.
Lenton *Lincs.* ***Hamlet***, 8m/13km NW of Bourne. **42 D2** TF0230.
Lenton *Notts.* ***Suburb***, 1m/2km SW of Nottingham city centre. SK5539.
Lenton Abbey *Notts.* ***Suburb***, on S side of Wollaton Park, 3m/5km SW of Nottingham city centre. SK5338.
Lentran *High.* ***Settlement***, in Inverness district, 5m/8km W of Inverness. NH5845.
Lenwade *Norf.* ***Village***, 2m/4km NW of Attlebridge. **45 F4** TG0918.
Lenzie *E.Dun.* Population: 9924. ***Locality***, adjoining to S of Kirkintilloch. **74 E3** NS6571.
Lenziemill *N.Lan.* ***Suburb***, 1km S of Cumbernauld town centre. NS7673.
Leoch *Angus* ***Hamlet***, 1m/2km SE of Kirkton of Auchterhouse. **82 E4** NO3536.
Leochel-Cushnie *Aber.* ***Village***, 5m/7km SW of Alford. **90 D3** NJ5210.
Leominster *Here.* Population: 9543. ***Small town***, on River Lugg, 12m/19km N of Hereford. Centre of agricultural district. **28 D3** SO4959.
Leominster Priory *Here.* ***Ecclesiastical building***, parish church in Leominster, once part of Benedictine priory. Encompasses all styles from Norman to Perpendicular. Notable Perpendicular window in main nave. **28 E3** SO4959.
Leonach Burn *High.* ***River***, rising on E slopes of Carn an t-Sean-liathanaich and flowing N into River Findhorn, 4m/6km SW of Ferness. Waterfalls in lower course. **89 G1** NH9240.
Leonard Stanley *Glos.* ***Village***, 3m/5km W of Stroud. **20 B1** SO8003.
Leonardslee Gardens *W.Suss.* ***Garden***, 240 acre woodland garden and deer park set in a valley, 3m/5km SW of Hanscross, with six lakes, rock garden and Bonsai. Particularly noted for rhododendron display. **13 F4** TQ2225.
Leorin *Arg. & B.* ***Settlement***, 3m/4km NW of Port Ellen, Islay. **72 B6** NR3548.
Leorin Lochs *Arg. & B.* ***Lake/loch***, group of small lochs at S end of Islay, 2m/3km N of Port Ellen. **72 B6** NR3748.
Leosaval *W.Isles* ***Mountain***, in Forest of Harris, 3m/5km SE of Huisinis. Height 1351 feet or 412 metres. **100 C7** NB0309.
Lepe *Hants.* ***Settlement***, 3m/5km S of Fawley. **11 F5** SZ4498.
Lepe and Calshot Foreshore Country Park *Hants.* ***Leisure/recreation***, to SW of Calshot. 122 acres of cliff top and shoreline situated between New Forest and sea; main attraction is view to Isle of Wight. **11 F4** SU4700.
Lephin *High.* ***Settlement***, near W coast of Skye, 5m/8km W of Dunvegan. NG1749.
Lephinchapel *Arg. & B.* ***Settlement***, on SW side of Loch Fyne, 3m/5km E of Lochgair across loch. **73 H1** NR9690.
Lephinmore *Arg. & B.* ***Settlement***, on N of Cowal peninsula, 12m/19km N of Tighnabruaich. **73 H1** NR9892.
Leppington *N.Yorks.* ***Village***, 5m/9km S of Malton. Site of former castle. **58 D3** SE7661.
Lepton *W.Yorks.* ***Village***, 4m/6km E of Huddersfield. **50 E1** SE2015.
Lerags *Arg. & B.* ***Locality***, 3m/4km NE of Kilninver, on N shore of Loch Feochan. **79 K5** NM8424.
Leri *Cere.* ***River***, rising S of Nant-y-moch Reservoir and flowing W to within 1km of coast at Borth, then N into River Dyfi estuary S of Aberdyfi. **37 F6** SN6194.
Lerryn *Cornw.* ***Village***, 3m/5km SE of Lostwithiel, at head of creek of River Lerryn. **4 B5** SX1457.
Lerwick *Shet.* Population: 7336. ***Small town***, chief town of Mainland and of Shetland, situated on Bressay Sound 22m/35km N of Sumburgh Head. Fishing port, service base for North Sea oilfields and terminus of passenger boat services from Scottish mainland. Annual festival of Up-Helly-Aa, of pagan origin, held on last Tuesday in January. Fort Charlotte (Historic Scotland), 17c fort. **109 D8** HU4741.
Lesbury *Northumb.* ***Village***, 4m/6km E of Alnwick. **71 H2** NU2311.
Lesbury Bridge *Northumb.* ***Bridge***, medieval bridge over River Aln, 1km NW of Alnmouth. NU2311.
Leschangie *Aber.* ***Locality***, 1m/2km S of Kemnay. **91 F3** NJ7314.
Lescrow *Cornw.* ***Settlement***, just NW of Fowey. **4 B5** SX1152.
Leslie *Aber.* ***Village***, 3m/5km SW of Insch. **90 D2** NJ5924.
Leslie *Fife* Population: 3062. ***Small town***, 2m/3km NW of Glenrothes. **82 D7** NO2401.
Lesmahagow (Also known as Abbey Green.) *S.Lan.* Population: 3266. ***Small town***, former mining town on River Nethan, 5m/8km SW of Lanark. Ruins of 12c priory. **75 G7** NS8139.
Lesnes Abbey *Gt.Lon.* ***Ecclesiastical building***, excavated remains of medieval abbey, N of Lesnes Abbey Woods, 2m/3km W of Erith. **23 H4** TQ4778.
Lesnewth *Cornw.* ***Village***, 2m/3km E of Boscastle. **4 B1** SX1390.
Lessendrum *Aber.* ***Settlement***, to N of Newtongarry Hill, 3m/5km NE of Huntly. **98 D6** NJ5741.
Lessingham *Norf.* ***Village***, 2m/3km SE of Happisburgh. **45 H3** TG3928.
Lessness Heath *Gt.Lon.* ***Suburb***, in borough of Bexley, 1m/2km W of Erith and 12m/19km E of Charing Cross. To E, Lesnes Abbey Woods and medieval ruins of Lesnes Abbey. TQ4978.
Lessonhall *Cumb.* ***Hamlet***, 2m/4km NW of Wigton. **60 D1** NY2250.
Leswalt *D. & G.* ***Village***, on Rinns of Galloway, 3m/5km NW of Stranraer. **64 A4** NX0163.
Letchmore Heath *Herts.* ***Village***, 3m/5km E of Watford. **22 E2** TQ1597.
Letchworth *Herts.* Population: 31,418. ***Town***, 5m/9km N of Stevenage. First English garden city, founded 1903. **33 F5** TL2132.
Letcombe Bassett *Oxon.* ***Village***, 2m/4km SW of Wantage. Prehistoric fort to SE. **21 G3** SU3785.
Letcombe Regis *Oxon.* ***Village***, 1m/2km SW of Wantage. **21 G3** SU3886.
Leth Meadhanach (Anglicised form: South Boisdale.) *W.Isles* ***Village***, 1m/2km SE of Baghasdal. **84 C3** NF7417.
Letham *Angus* Population: 1247. ***Village***, 5m/8km E of Forfar. **83 G3** NO5248.
Letham *Falk.* ***Hamlet***, 1m/2km S of Airth. NS8985.
Letham *Fife* ***Village***, 4m/7km W of Cupar. **82 E6** NO3014.
Letham *P. & K.* ***Suburb***, NW district of Perth. NO0924.
Lethanhill *E.Ayr.* ***Locality***, 1m/2km E of Patna. **67 J2** NS4310.
Lethans Muir *Fife* ***Open space***, moorland to NE of Knock Hill, 4m/6km W of Kelty. **75 J1** NT0794.
Lethen Bar *High.* ***Hill***, in Nairn district, 6m/10km SE of Nairn. Height 846 feet or 258 metres. **97 G7** NH9449.
Lethendy *P. & K.* ***Locality***, 2m/3km NW of Meikleour. 17c tower house. NO1341.
Lethendy *P. & K.* ***Settlement***, 1m/2km NW of New Scone. **82 C5** NO1228.
Lethenty *Aber.* ***Settlement***, 3m/5km NE of Fyvie. **99 G6** NJ8041.
Letheringham *Suff.* ***Hamlet***, 2m/4km NW of Wickham Market. **35 G3** TM2757.
Letheringsett *Norf.* ***Village***, 1m/2km W of Holt. **44 E2** TG0638.
Letocetum *Staffs.* *See Wall.*
Letocetum Roman Baths and Museum *Staffs.* ***Historic/prehistoric site***, in Wall, 2m/3km SW of Lichfield. Posting station and prosperous settlement on Watling Street. Preserved bath house is one of most complete in Britain. **40 D5** SK0906.
Lettaford *Devon* ***Locality***, 4m/6km SW of Moretonhampstead. **7 F7** SX7084.
Letter Finlay *High.* ***Settlement***, on SE side of Loch Lochy, 4m/7km SW of Laggan. **87 J5** NN2591.
Letterach *Moray* ***Mountain***, 7m/11km NW of Strathdon. Height 2581 feet or 787 metres. **89 K2** NJ2820.
Letterewe *High.* ***Settlement***, on NE shore of Loch Maree, Ross and Cromarty district, 6m/10km NW of head of loch. **95 F4** NG9571.
Letterfearn *High.* ***Settlement***, on W shore of Loch Duich, Skye and Lochalsh district, 1m/2km from mouth of loch. **86 E2** NG8823.
Lettermorar *High.* ***Settlement***, on S side of Loch Morar, in Lochaber district, 4m/6km SE of Morar. **86 D6** NM7389.
Lettermore *Arg. & B.* ***Settlement***, on NE shore of Loch Frisa, 6m/9km NW of Salen, Mull. **79 G3** NM4948.
Lettermore *High.* ***Settlement***, 2m/3km NE of Inchkinloch, on W side of Loch Loyal. **103 J4** NC6147.
Letters *High.* ***Settlement***, on W side of Loch Broom, Ross and Cromarty district, 2m/3km from head of loch. **95 H3** NH1687.
Lettershaws *S.Lan.* ***Settlement***, 3m/4km SW of Abington. **68 D1** NS9020.
Letterston (Treletert). *Pembs.* ***Village***, 5m/8km S of Fishguard. **16 C2** SM9429.
Lettoch *High.* ***Settlement***, 2m/3km SE of Nethy Bridge. **89 H3** NJ0219.
Lettoch *High.* ***Settlement***, 5m/8km NE of Grantown-on-Spey. **89 H1** NJ0932.
Letton *Here.* ***Settlement***, 6m/10km E of Knighton. **28 C1** SO3770.
Letton *Here.* ***Village***, 1m/2km SE of Willersley. **28 C4** SO3346.
Letton Lake *Here.* ***River***, running SW from Norton Wood to River Wye, 2m/3km NE of Staunton on Wye. **28 C4** SO3345.
Letty Green *Herts.* ***Village***, 3m/4km W of Hertford. **33 F7** TL2810.
Letwell *S.Yorks.* ***Village***, 4m/6km SE of Maltby. **51 H4** SK5687.
Leuchar Burn ***River***, stream running from Loch of Skene and flowing S to Garlogie, then SE to join Gormack Burn 1km W of Peterculter. NJ8400.
Leuchars *Fife* Population: 2991. ***Village***, 5m/7km S of Tayport, on N side of River Eden estuary. **83 F5** NO4521.
Leum Uilleim *High.* ***Mountain***, in Lochaber district 3m/5km S of head of Loch Treig. Height 2972 feet or 906 metres. **80 E1** NN3364.
Leumrabhagh (Anglicised form: Lemreway.) *W.Isles* ***Village***, near E coast of Isle of Lewis, on N side of Loch Shell, 3m/5km SW of Kebock Head. **101 F6** NB3711.
Leurbost *W.Isles* *Anglicised form of Liurbost, qv.*
Leusdon *Devon* ***Settlement***, on E side of Dartmoor, 4m/6km NW of Ashburton. SX7073.
Levedale *Staffs.* ***Hamlet***, 4m/7km SW of Stafford. **40 A4** SJ8916.
Level's Green *Essex* ***Settlement***, 2m/3km NW of Bishop's Stortford. TL4724.
Leven ***River***, issuing from Loch Leven and flowing E to Largo Bay between towns of Leven and Methil. **82 D7** NO3800.
Leven ***River***, rising on Kildale Moor, North York Moors National Park, and flowing W by Kildale, Easby, Little Ayton, Great Ayton, Stokesley, Hutton Rudby and Crathorne into River Tees 1m/2km NE of Yarm. **63 F6** NZ4312.
Leven *E.Riding* Population: 2036. ***Village***, 6m/10km NE of Beverley. **59 H5** TA1045.
Leven *Fife* Population: 8317. ***Small town***, resort and former mining town on W side of Largo Bay. Docks at Methil. **82 E7** NO3800.
Leven *High.* ***River***, in Lochaber district, running W from Blackwater Reservoir to head of Loch Leven at Kinlochleven. **80 D1** NN1762.
Levencorroch *N.Ayr.* ***Settlement***, above rocky cliff on S coast of Arran, 1m/2km NW of Kildonan. **66 E1** NS0021.
Levenhall *E.Loth.* ***Suburb***, on E side of Musselburgh. **76 B3** NT3673.
Levenish *W.Isles* ***Island***, rock islet (National Trust for Scotland) in St. Kilda group lying 2m/3km SE of E end of St. Kilda itself. Haunt of sea birds. NF1396.
Levens *Cumb.* ***Village***, 5m/8km S of Kendal. **55 H1** SD4886.
Levens Green *Herts.* ***Hamlet***, 2m/3km W of Standon. TL3522.
Levens Hall *Cumb.* ***Historic house***, Elizabethan house with topiary gardens, 1km SE of Levens. **55 H1** SD4886.
Levenshulme *Gt.Man.* ***Suburb***, 3m/5km SE of Manchester city centre. **49 H3** SJ8694.
Levenwick *Shet.* ***Village***, on W side of Leven Wick bay, on E coast of mainland. **109 D10** HU4021.
Lever Edge *Gt.Man.* ***Suburb***, 2m/3km SW of Bolton town centre. SD7006.
Leverburgh (Gaelic form: An T-òb. Formerly named Obbe.) *W.Isles* ***Village***, on SW coast of South Harris, 4m/6km NW of Renish Point. Village and harbour date from industrial development of Isle of Lewis by Lord Leverhulme in 1920s. Lighthouse. **93 F3** NG0186.
Leverington *Cambs.* ***Village***, 2m/3km NW of Wisbech. **43 H4** TF4411.
Levers Water *Cumb.* ***Lake/loch***, mountain lake 2m/3km NW of Coniston. **60 D7** SD3097.
Leverstock Green *Herts.* ***Suburb***, E district of Hemel Hempstead. **22 D1** TL0806.
Leverton *Lincs.* ***Village***, 5m/8km E of Boston. **43 H1** TF4047.
Leverton *W.Berks.* ***Locality***, 1m/2km NW of Hungerford across River Kennet. SU3370.
Leverton Lucasgate *Lincs.* ***Settlement***, adjoining Leverton Outgate, 1m/2km E of Leverton, 6m/9km NE of Boston. TF4147.
Leverton Outgate *Lincs.* ***Settlement***, adjoins Leverton Lucasgate, 1m/2km E of Leverton. **43 H1** TF4147.
Levington *Suff.* ***Village***, 6m/9km SE of Ipswich. **35 G5** TM2339.
Levisham *N.Yorks.* ***Village***, 5m/7km NE of Pickering. **63 K7** SE8390.
Levishie *High.* ***Settlement***, 1m/2km NW of Invermoriston. **88 B3** NH4018.
Levishie Forest *High.* ***Open space***, mountainous area on NW side of Loch Ness, 6m/10km N of Fort Augustus. **88 A3** NH4019.
Lew *Devon* ***River***, rising in Halwill Forest and flowing N through Northlew into River Torridge, 1m/2km NW of Hatherleigh. **6 D5** SS5306.
Lew *Oxon.* ***Village***, 3m/5km SW of Witney. **21 G1** SP3206.
Lewannick *Cornw.* ***Village***, 4m/7km SW of Launceston. **4 C2** SX2780.
Lewcombe *Dorset* ***Settlement***, 1m/2km W of Melbury Osmond. ST5507.
Lewdown *Devon* ***Village***, 7m/12km E of Launceston. **6 C7** SX4486.
Lewes *E.Suss.* Population: 15,376. ***Town***, county town in gap of South Downs (River Ouse), 8m/13km NE of Brighton. Formerly an important medieval river port. Norman castle and several old houses. Anne of Cleves House and Museum. **13 H5** TQ4110.
Lewes Castle *E.Suss.* ***Castle***, Norman castle with shell keep and 14c barbican, in centre of Lewes. Adjacent Barbican House contains Museum of Sussex Archaeology. **13 H5** TQ4110.
Lewesdon Hill *Dorset* *See Broadwindsor.*
Leweston *Dorset* ***Locality***, 3m/4km S of Sherborne. ST6312.
Leweston *Pembs.* ***Hamlet***, 4m/6km N of Haverfordwest. **16 C2** SM9322.
Lewis *W.Isles* *See Isle of Lewis.*
Lewis Textile Museum and Art Gallery *B'burn.* ***Other feature of interest***, to N of Blackburn town centre, with local history display; also displays on South Asia and fine art. **56 B7** SD6828.
Lewisham *Gt.Lon.* ***Suburb***, 6m/10km SE of Charing Cross, situated on Ravensbourne River, which runs into Deptford Creek. TQ3875.
Lewiston *High.* ***Village***, on River Coiltie, 1m/2km W of Urquhart Bay on Loch Ness, Inverness district. **88 C2** NH5129.
Lewistown *Bridgend* ***Village***, 1m/2km S of Ogmore Vale. SS9388.
Lewknor *Oxon.* ***Village***, 3m/5km NE of Watlington. **22 A2** SU7197.
Leworthy *Devon* ***Settlement***, 8m/13km NE of Barnstaple. **6 E2** SS6738.
Lews Castle Gardens *W.Isles* ***Garden***, surrounding Lews Castle on W side of Stornoway Harbour, Isle of Lewis. Soil imported from mainland to create gardens also led to formation of large wooded area. **101 G4** NB4133.
Lewson Street *Kent* ***Hamlet***, 3m/5km W of Faversham. TQ9661.
Lewth *Lancs.* ***Settlement***, 2m/3km NW of Woodplumpton, 6m/9km NW of Preston. SD4836.
Lewthorne Cross *Devon* ***Hamlet***, 4m/7km N of Ashburton. SX7776.
Lewtrenchard *Devon* ***Village***, 8m/13km E of Launceston. **6 C7** SX4586.
Lexden *Essex* ***Locality***, 2m/3km W of Colchester town centre. Earthworks, Iron Age and subsequently Roman (English Heritage); also tumulus, with finds displayed in Colchester Museum. TL9725.

Lexworthy *Som.* **Hamlet**, 3m/4km SW of Bridgwater. ST2535.
Ley *Aber.* **Settlement**, 3m/5km SW of Alford. **90 D3** NJ5312.
Ley *Cornw.* **Settlement**, 5m/8km W of Liskeard. **4 B4** SX1766.
Ley Green *Herts.* **Hamlet**, 3m/5km SW of Hitchin. **32 E6** TL1624.
Ley Hill *Bucks.* **Settlement**, adjoining to E of Botley, 2m/3km E of Chesham. SP9802.
Ley Hill *W.Mid.* **Locality**, 1m/2km N of Sutton Coldfield town centre. SP1298.
Leybourne *Kent* **Village**, on W edge of industrial and residential development, 5m/8km W of Maidstone. **23 K6** TQ6858.
Leyburn *N.Yorks.* Population: 1716. **Small town**, market town, 8m/12km SW of Richmond. **62 C7** SE1190.
Leyburn Moor *N.Yorks.* **Open space**, moorland on N side of Wensleydale, 2m/3km NW of Leyburn. **62 B7** SE0892.
Leycett *Staffs.* **Hamlet**, 4m/6km W of Newcastle-under-Lyme. **39 G1** SJ7946.
Leyland *Lancs.* Population: 37,331. **Town**, 5m/8km S of Preston. Developed around car and lorry manufacture. British Commercial Vehicle Museum sited here. **55 J7** SD5421.
Leyland Green *Gt.Man.* **Locality**, 2m/3km NW of Ashton-in-Makerfield. SD5400.
Leylodge *Aber.* **Settlement**, 2m/4km SW of Kintore. **91 F3** NJ7713.
Leymoor *W.Yorks.* **Suburb**, 3m/4km W of Huddersfield town centre. SE1016.
Leys *Aber.* **Settlement**, 1m/2km SW of Tarland. **90 C4** NJ4602.
Leys *Aber.* **Settlement**, 3m/4km N of Mintlaw. **99 J5** NK0052.
Leys *P. & K.* **Settlement**, 3m/4km SE of Coupar Angus. **82 D4** NO2537.
Leys of Cossans *Angus* **Settlement**, 2m/3km N of Glamis. **82 E3** NO3749.
Leysdown-on-Sea *Kent* Population: 2483. **Village**, with holiday camps, at E end of Isle of Sheppey. **25 G4** TR0370.
Leysmill *Angus* **Village**, 5m/8km NW of Arbroath. **83 H3** NO6047.
Leysters *Here.* *Alternative spelling of Laysters, qv.*
Leyton *Gt.Lon.* **Suburb**, in S part of borough of Waltham Forest, 5m/8km NE of London Bridge. **23 G3** TQ3886.
Leytonstone *Gt.Lon.* **Suburb**, NE district of Leyton, in borough of Waltham Forest. TQ3987.
Lezant *Cornw.* **Village**, 4m/6km S of Launceston. **4 D3** SX3379.
Lezayre *I.o.M.* *Alternative name for Churchtown, qv.*
Lezerea *Cornw.* **Settlement**, 4m/6km N of Helston. SW6833.
Lhanbryde *Moray* Population: 1998. **Village**, 4m/6km E of Elgin. **97 K5** NJ2761.
Liath Eilean *Arg. & B.* **Island**, in Loch Fyne, on E side of Eilean Mòr and 3m/5km SE of Lochgilphead, Argyll. NR8883.
Liathach (Anglicised form: Leagach.) *High.* **Large natural feature**, mountain mass in Torridon Forest, Ross and Cromarty district, N of Torridon. Highest point is Spidean a' Choire Leith, a Munro at 3456 feet or 1054 metres. **95 F6** NG9257.
Liatrie *High.* **Settlement**, 6m/9km W of Cannich. **87 J1** NH2432.
Libanus *Powys* **Hamlet**, 4m/6km SW of Brecon. **27 J6** SN9925.
Libberton *S.Lan.* **Village**, 2m/4km S of Carnwath. **75 H6** NS9846.
Libbery *Worcs.* **Settlement**, 6m/10km E of Worcester. SO9555.
Liberton *Edin.* **Suburb**, 3m/5km SE of Edinburgh city centre. **76 A4** NT2769.
Liberty Hill *S.Yorks.* **Suburb**, 3m/4km W of Sheffield city centre. SK3188.
Liceasto (Anglicised form: Likisto.) *W.Isles* **Settlement**, near head of Loch Stockinish, South Harris, 2m/3km W of Greosabhagh. **93 G2** NG1192.
Lichfield *Staffs.* Population: 28,666. **City**, ancient cathedral city (Royal Charter granted 1549), 15m/24km N of Birmingham. Birthplace of Samuel Johnson, 1709. Cathedral 12c-15c. **40 D5** SK1109.
Lichfield Cathedral *Staffs.* **Ecclesiastical building**, built of local red sandstone in centre of Lichfield, and unique among English medieval cathedrals in having three spires. W front is 19c reproduction of 13-14c original. **40 D4** SK1109.
Lickey *Worcs.* **Village**, on Lickey Hills, 4m/6km NE of Bromsgrove. **29 J1** SO9975.
Lickey End *Worcs.* **Village**, 1m/2km NE of Bromsgrove. **29 J1** SO9772.
Lickey Hills *Worcs.* **Large natural feature**, range of hills with country park, 4m/6km NE of Bromsgrove. **29 J1** SO9975.
Lickfold *W.Suss.* **Hamlet**, 4m/6km NE of Midhurst. **12 C4** SU9226.
Liddaton Green *Devon* **Hamlet**, 6m/9km N of Tavistock. SX4582.
Liddel *Ork.* **Locality**, in SE corner of South Ronaldsay, 2m/3km E of Burwick. **107 D9** ND4683.
Liddel Water **River**, rising on Cheviot Hills, 8m/13km SW of Carter Bar, and running SW down Liddesdale to border with England at Kershopefoot. It then continues SW along England-Scotland border to its confluence with River Esk, 2m/3km S of Canonbie. **69 K6** NY3973.
Liddesdale *High.* **Settlement**, on S shore of Loch Sunart, 3m/4km SW of Strontian across loch. **79 J2** NM7759.
Liddesdale *Sc.Bord.* **Valley**, carrying Liddel Water SW from Saughtree, through village of Newcastleton towards Caulside. **69 K5** NY4888.
Liddington *Swin.* **Village**, 4m/6km SE of Swindon. **21 F3** SU2081.
Lidgate *Derbys.* **Hamlet**, 3m/5km W of Dronfield. **51 F5** SK3077.
Lidgate *Suff.* **Village**, 6m/10km SE of Newmarket. Church on site of Norman castle. **34 B3** TL7257.
Lidget *S.Yorks.* **Locality**, adjoining to S of Auckley, 5m/8km E of Doncaster town centre. SE6500.
Lidget Green *W.Yorks.* **Suburb**, 1m/2km W of Bradford city centre. SE1432.
Lidgett *Notts.* **Suburb**, to S of Edwinstowe. SK6365.
Lidgett Park *W.Yorks.* **Suburb**, 3m/5km NE of Leeds city centre. SE3138.
Lidlington *Beds.* **Village**, 3m/5km W of Ampthill. **32 C5** SP9939.
Lidsey *W.Suss.* **Settlement**, 3m/4km N of Bognor Regis. SU9303.
Lidsing *Kent* **Settlement**, 3m/5km S of Gillingham. **24 D5** TQ7862.
Lidstone *Oxon.* **Settlement**, 3m/5km SE of Chipping Norton. **30 E6** SP3524.
Lienassie *High.* **Settlement**, in Skye and Lochalsh district, 3m/4km NE of Shiel Bridge. **87 F2** NG9621.
Lieurary *High.* **Locality**, to N of Loch Calder. **105 F2** ND0662.
Liff *Angus* **Village**, 5m/8km NW of Dundee. **82 E4** NO3333.
Lifford *W.Mid.* **Suburb**, 5m/8km S of Birmingham city centre. Lifford Hall, early 17c house. SP0579.
Lifton *Devon* **Village**, 4m/6km E of Launceston. **6 B7** SX3885.
Liftondown *Devon* **Hamlet**, 3m/4km E of Launceston. **6 B7** SX3685.
Ligger Bay (Also known as Perran Bay.) *Cornw.* **Bay**, extending S from Ligger Point to Perranporth, and enclosing 2m/3km of sandy beach known as Perran Beach, backed by Penhale Sands. **2 E3** SW7556.
Ligger Point *Cornw.* **Coastal feature**, headland at N end of Ligger Bay, 2m/3km N of Perranporth. **2 E3** SW7556.
Light Oaks *Stoke* **Suburb**, 1m/2km SW of Bagnall. SJ9150.
Lightbowne *Gt.Man.* **Suburb**, 3m/4km NE of Manchester city centre. SD8601.
Lightcliffe *W.Yorks.* **Suburb**, 2m/3km N of Brighouse. SE1425.
Lightfoot Green *Lancs.* **Settlement**, 3m/5km N of Preston. SD5133.
Lighthazles *W.Yorks.* **Locality**, 1m/2km NW of Ripponden. SE0220.
Lighthill (Gaelic form: Cnoc an t-Soluis.) *W.Isles* **Settlement**, adjoining to W of Bac, near E coast of Isle of Lewis. NB4740.
Lighthorne *Warks.* **Village**, 6m/10km S of Royal Leamington Spa. **30 E3** SP3355.
Lightwater *Surr.* Population: 6432. **Locality**, residential locality 1m/2km SE of Bagshot. **22 C5** SU9262.
Lightwater Valley Park *N.Yorks.* **Leisure/recreation**, 1km S of North Stainley, 3m/5km NW of Ripon, with rollercoaster, parkland, farm and factory shopping. **57 H2** SE2876.
Lightwood *Staffs.* **Suburb**, to E of Cheadle. SK0143.
Lightwood *Stoke* **Suburb**, 4m/6km SE of Stoke-on-Trent city centre. **40 B1** SJ9241.
Lightwood Green *Ches.* **Settlement**, 2m/3km W of Audlem. **39 F1** SJ6342.
Lightwood Green *Wrex.* **Settlement**, 1m/2km SE of Overton. **38 C1** SJ3840.
Likisto *W.Isles* *Anglicised form of Liceasto, qv.*
Lilbourne *Northants.* **Village**, 4m/6km E of Rugby. **31 G1** SP5676.
Lilburn *Northumb.* **Locality**, comprising hamlets of Lilburn Tower and East Lilburn, with surrounding scattered settlements, 3m/5km SE of Wooler. NU0224.
Lilburn Tower *Northumb.* **Hamlet**, 3m/5km SE of Wooler. **71 F1** NU0224.
Lilford *Northants.* **Locality**, 3m/4km S of Oundle. Includes Lilford Park and Lilford Lodge Farm. TL0384.
Lillesdon *Som.* **Hamlet**, 1m/2km SW of North Curry. ST3023.
Lilleshall *Tel. & W.* **Village**, 3m/4km SW of Newport. Monument to Duke of Sutherland, d. 1833. Ruins of 12c abbey (English Heritage) 1m/2km SE. **39 G4** SJ7513.
Lilleshall Abbey *Tel. & W.* **Ecclesiastical building**, Augustinian abbey (English Heritage) founded c. 1148, 1m/2km SE of Lilleshall. Now a ruin, including part of 12c-13c church and cloisters. **39 G4** SJ7314.
Lilley *Herts.* **Village**, 4m/7km SW of Hitchin. **32 E6** TL1126.
Lilley *W.Berks.* **Locality**, 8m/12km N of Newbury. **21 H4** SU4479.
Lilliesleaf *Sc.Bord.* **Village**, 7m/11km N of Hawick. **70 A1** NT5325.
Lilling Green *N.Yorks.* **Settlement**, 2m/3km NE of Strensall. SE6463.
Lillingstone Dayrell *Bucks.* **Village**, 4m/6km N of Buckingham. **31 J5** SP7039.
Lillingstone Lovell *Bucks.* **Village**, 4m/7km N of Buckingham. **31 J4** SP7140.
Lillington *Dorset* **Village**, 3m/4km S of Sherborne. **9 F3** ST6212.
Lillington *Warks.* **Suburb**, NE district of Royal Leamington Spa. SP3267.
Lilliput *Poole* **Suburb**, 2m/3km E of Poole town centre. **10 B5** SZ0489.
Lilly *Devon* **Settlement**, 2m/3km E of Barnstaple. SS5833.
Lilstock *Som.* **Hamlet**, near coast, 4m/6km NW of Nether Stowey. **7 K1** ST1644.
Lilybank *Inclyde* **Suburb**, between Greenock and Port Glasgow. Site of small Roman fort 1m/2km SW. NS3074.
Lilyhurst *Shrop.* **Settlement**, 4m/6km S of Newport. SJ7413.
Limbrick *Lancs.* **Settlement**, 2m/3km N of Adlington. **49 F1** SD6016.
Limbury *Luton* **Suburb**, N district of Luton. **32 D6** TL0724.
Limden *E.Suss.* **River**, stream rising 1m/2km SE of Wadhurst and flowing SE into River Rother at Etchingham. **13 K4** TQ7126.
Lime Gate *Gt.Man.* **Suburb**, 2m/3km SW of Oldham town centre. SD9102.
Limebrook *Here.* **Locality**, 4m/6km E of Presteigne. Remains of priory. SO3766.
Limefield *Gt.Man.* **Suburb**, 2m/3km N of Bury town centre. **49 H1** SD8013.
Limehillock *Moray* **Settlement**, on W side of Sillyearn Wood, 3m/5km NW of Milltown of Rothiemay. **98 D5** NJ5152.
Limehouse *Gt.Lon.* **Suburb**, in borough of Tower Hamlets, 3m/4km E of London Bridge. TQ3681.
Limehurst *Gt.Man.* **Suburb**, 1m/2km NW of Ashton-under-Lyne town centre. SD9301.
Limekilnburn *S.Lan.* **Locality**, 3m/5km S of Hamilton. **75 F5** NS7050.
Limekilns *Fife* Population: 1620. **Village**, on N bank of Firth of Forth, 3m/5km W of Inverkeithing. **75 J2** NT0783.
Limerigg *Falk.* **Hamlet**, 1m/2km S of Slamannan. **75 G3** NS8570.
Limerstone *I.o.W.* **Hamlet**, 1m/2km W of Shorwell. **11 F6** SZ4482.
Limeslade *Swan.* *Alternative name for Thistleboon, qv.*
Limestone Brae *Northumb.* **Locality**, 4m/6km N of Nenthead. NY7949.
Limington *Som.* **Village**, 1m/2km E of Ilchester. **8 E2** ST5422.
Limpenhoe *Norf.* **Village**, 2m/3km NW of Reedham. **45 H5** TG3903.
Limpley Stoke *Wilts.* **Village**, 3m/5km SE of Bath. **20 A5** ST7860.
Limpsfield *Surr.* **Village**, below North Downs, 3m/5km W of Westerham. **23 H6** TQ4053.
Limpsfield Chart *Surr.* **Village**, 2m/3km SW of Westerham. TQ4251.
Linacre Reservoirs *Derbys.* **Reservoir**, series of three reservoirs in valley of Holme Brook, 3m/5km W of Chesterfield. **51 F5** SK3372.
Linbriggs *Northumb.* **Settlement**, in Upper Coquetdale, 3m/4km NW of Harbottle. **70 D3** NT8906.
Linby *Notts.* **Village**, 1m/2km N of Hucknall. **51 H7** SK5351.
Linch *W.Suss.* **Locality**, 3m/4km SE of Liphook. SU8528.
Linch Down *W.Suss.* **Hill**, 3m/5km SW of Midhurst. Height 813 feet or 248 metres. **12 B5** SU8417.
Linchmere *W.Suss.* **Village**, 2m/3km E of Liphook. **12 B3** SU8631.
Lincluden *D. & G.* **Suburb**, NW district of Dumfries. NX9677.
Lincluden College *D. & G.* **Ecclesiastical building**, remains of medieval abbey at confluence of Cluden Water and River Nith, 1m/2km N of Dumfries. **65 K3** NX9677.
Lincoln *Lincs.* Population: 80,281. **City**, county town and cathedral city on River Witham, on site of Roman town of Lindum, 120m/193km N of London. Many ancient monuments and archaeological features. Castle built by William I. 13c cathedral, with its twin towers on hilltop dominates skyline. Lincoln Bishop's Old Palace (English Heritage) is medieval building on S side of cathedral. Universities. **52 C5** SK9771.
Lincoln Cathedral *Lincs.* **Ecclesiastical building**, in outstanding position in centre of Lincoln. Founded in late 11c, but badly damaged by earthquake in 1185. Particularly impressive are Angel Choir and W front. Considered to be one of the finest English cathedrals. **52 C5** SK9771.
Lincomb *Worcs.* **Hamlet**, 2m/3km S of Stourport-on-Severn. **29 H2** SO8268.
Lincombe *Devon* **Hamlet**, on W side of Kingsbridge Estuary, 1m/2km N of Salcombe. SX7440.
Lincombe *Devon* **Settlement**, 4m/6km SW of Totnes. **5 H5** SX7458.
Lindal in Furness *Cumb.* **Village**, 2m/3km NE of Dalton-in-Furness. **55 F2** SD2575.
Lindale *Cumb.* **Village**, 2m/3km N of Grange-over-Sands. **55 H1** SD4180.
Lindean *Sc.Bord.* **Hamlet**, 2m/3km NE of Selkirk. **76 C7** NT4931.
Linden *Glos.* **Suburb**, S district of Gloucester. SO8216.
Lindertis *Angus* **Settlement**, 3m/5km SW of Kirriemuir. **82 E2** NO3351.
Lindfield *W.Suss.* **Suburb**, NE district of Haywards Heath. **13 G4** TQ3425.
Lindford *Hants.* **Village**, 1km E of Bordon Camp and 5m/8km W of Hindhead. **12 B3** SU8036.
Lindifferon *Fife* **Settlement**, 4m/6km NW of Cupar. **82 E6** NO3116.
Lindisfarne *Northumb.* *Former and alternative name of Holy Island, qv.*
Lindisfarne Castle *Northumb.* **Castle**, 1km W of Holy Island village, 3m/5km from E coast of mainland. Small 16c fort converted into house (National Trust) at beginning of 20c by Sir Edwin Lutyens. **77 K6** NU1341.
Lindisfarne Priory *Northumb.* **Ecclesiastical building**, impressive red sandstone ruins (English Heritage) dating from late 11c, situated in village of Holy Island, on SW side of Holy Island and 3m/4km from mainland E coast. **77 K6** NU1241.
Lindley *W.Yorks.* **Suburb**, 2m/3km NW of Huddersfield town centre. **50 D1** SE1118.
Lindley Green *N.Yorks.* **Hamlet**, 3m/4km NE of Otley. SE2248.
Lindley Wood Reservoir *N.Yorks.* **Reservoir**, 2m/4km N of Otley. **57 H5** SE2045.
Lindores *Fife* **Village**, 2m/3km SE of Newburgh. **82 D6** NO2616.
Lindores Abbey *Fife* **Ecclesiastical building**, scant remains of abbey founded in 1191 and situated on E side of Newburgh. **82 D6** NO2418.
Lindores Loch *Fife* **Lake/loch**, small loch on S side of Lindores. **82 D6** NO2616.
Lindow End *Ches.* **Settlement**, 2m/3km W of Alderley Edge. SJ8178.

Lindrick *N.Yorks.* ***Locality***, 2m/3km W of Ripon. SE2770.
Lindridge *Worcs.* ***Village***, 5m/8km E of Tenbury Wells. **29 F2** SO6769.
Lindsaig *Arg. & B.* ***Settlement***, on Cowal peninsula, 5m/8km NW of Tighnabruaich. **73 H3** NR9379.
Lindsell *Essex* ***Village***, 4m/6km N of Great Dunmow. **33 K6** TL6427.
Lindsey *Suff.* ***Hamlet***, 4m/6km NW of Hadleigh. To S, near remains of motte and bailey castle, is St. James's Chapel (English Heritage), dating from 13c. **34 D4** TL9745.
Lindsey Tye *Suff.* ***Settlement***, to N of Lindsey, 4m/6km NW of Hadleigh. TL9845.
Lindum *Lincs. See Lincoln.*
Line Houses *Staffs.* ***Locality***, 1m/2km NW of Tunstall. SJ8452.
Lineholt *Worcs.* ***Settlement***, 4m/6km S of Stourport-on-Severn. SO8266.
Linfern Loch *S.Ayr.* ***Lake/loch***, 4m/7km S of Straiton. **67 H4** NX3697.
Linfit *W.Yorks.* ***Settlement***, 1m/2km NE of Kirkburton. SE2013.
Linfitts *Gt.Man.* ***Settlement***, adjoining to NW of Delph. SD9708.
Linford *Hants.* ***Settlement***, 2m/3km NE of Ringwood. **10 C4** SU1806.
Linford *Thur.* Population: 5448. ***Village***, 3m/5km NE of Tilbury. **24 C4** TQ6779.
Linford Wood *M.K.* ***Suburb***, to N of Milton Keynes city centre. SP8440.
Ling *High.* ***River***, in Skye and Lochalsh district, running SW to head of Loch Long. **87 F1** NG9330.
Ling Hill *Stir.* ***Mountain***, 4m/6km NE of Fintry. Height 1364 feet or 416 metres. **74 E2** NS6789.
Ling Ness *Shet.* ***Coastal feature***, headland attached to E coast of Mainland by narrow neck of land. **109 D7** HU4954.
Linga *Shet.* ***Island***, small uninhabited island in Vaila Sound between Vaila and Walls, Mainland. HU2348.
Linga *Shet.* ***Island***, uninhabited island of about 170 acres or 70 hectares off W coast of Mainland between Muckle Roe and the entrance to Olna Firth. **109 C6** HU3563.
Linga *Shet.* ***Island***, small uninhabited island off E coast of Mainland opposite Firth Ness. **108 D5** HU4673.
Linga *Shet.* ***Island***, narrow uninhabited island, 1m/2km long, at S end of Bluemull Sound between Yell and Unst. **108 E3** HU5598.
Linga Holm *Ork.* ***Island***, small uninhabited island off W coast of Stronsay at entrance to St. Catherine's Bay. **106 F5** HY6127.
Linga Sound *Shet.* ***Sea feature***, separates West Linga from W coast of Whalsay. **109 E6** HU5364.
Lingague *I.o.M.* ***Settlement***, 3m/4km NE of Port Erin. **54 B6** SC2272.
Lingarabay *W.Isles Anglicised form of Ceann a' Bhàigh, qv.*
Lingarabay Island *W.Isles* ***Island***, islet in Lingara Bay, off SE coast of South Harris. **93 F3** NG0684.
Lingards Wood *W.Yorks.* ***Settlement***, 1m/2km NE of Marsden. SE0612.
Lingay *W.Isles* ***Island***, small uninhabited island 2m/3km SW of Ludag, on S coast of South Uist. **84 C3** NF7511.
Lingay *W.Isles* ***Island***, small uninhabited island off N coast of North Uist nearly 1m/2km SE of Boreray. **92 D4** NF8778.
Lingay *W.Isles* ***Island***, small uninhabited island at SE end of Sound of Harris, 4m/7km off E coast of North Uist. **93 F4** NG0179.
Lingay *W.Isles* ***Island***, small uninhabited island 1km N of Pabbay and 2m/3km SW of Sandray. **84 A6** NL6089.
Lingbob *W.Yorks.* ***Locality***, adjoining to S of Wilsden. SE0935.
Lingdale *R. & C.* ***Village***, 3m/5km S of Saltburn. **63 H5** NZ6716.
Lingen *Here.* ***Village***, 4m/6km NE of Presteigne. **28 C2** SO3667.
Lingfield *Surr.* Population: 2691. ***Village***, 4m/6km N of East Grinstead. Racecourse 1 km S. **23 G7** TQ3843.
Lingfield Common *Surr.* ***Settlement***, 1km N of Lingfield. TQ3844.
Lingholm Gardens *Cumb.* ***Garden***, on W bank of Derwent Water, 2m/3km S of Portinscale. 40 acres of gardens known for rhododendron, blue poppies and specimen trees. **60 D4** NY2522.
Lingley Green *Warr.* ***Suburb***, 3m/5km W of Warrington town centre. SJ5588.
Lingmell *Cumb.* ***Mountain***, rising to over 800 metres to N of Scafell Pike, 1m/2km SE of Wasdale Head. **60 D6** NY2008.
Lings Cross Rows *Derbys.* ***Locality***, 2m/3km NE of Clay Cross. SK4165.
Lings Row *Derbys.* ***Locality***, 2m/3km NE of Clay Cross. SK4165.
Lingwood *Norf.* Population: 2027. ***Village***, 3m/4km W of Acle. **45 H5** TG3608.
Lingyclose Head *Cumb.* ***Locality***, 3m/4km SW of Carlisle. NY3752.
Linhead *Aber.* ***Settlement***, on N side of Rosy Burn, 5m/8km NW of Turriff. **98 E5** NJ6755.
Linhope *Sc.Bord.* ***Settlement***, 3m/4km S of Teviothead, where Linhope Burn joins Frostlie Burn. **69 K3** NT4001.
Linhouse Water *W.Loth.* ***River***, stream running N from Pentland Hills to River Almond on E side of Livingston. **75 J4** NT0767.
Liniclett *W.Isles Anglicised form of Lionacleit, qv.*
Linicro *High.* ***Settlement***, on Skye, 2m/4km N of Uig. **93 J5** NG3867.
Linkend *Worcs.* ***Hamlet***, 4m/7km W of Tewkesbury across River Severn. SO8331.
Linkenholt *Hants.* ***Village***, 3m/5km NW of Hurstbourne Tarrant. **21 G6** SU3658.
Linkhill *Kent* ***Hamlet***, 1m/2km E of Sandhurst. **14 D5** TQ8128.
Linkinhorne *Cornw.* ***Village***, 4m/6km NW of Callington. **4 D3** SX3173.
Linklater *Ork.* ***Settlement***, 1km S of Ward Hill, South Ronaldsay, above Wind Wick bay. **107 D9** ND4587.
Linklet Bay *Ork.* ***Bay***, wide bay on E side of North Ronaldsay, extending SW from Dennis Head. **106 G2** HY7754.
Links Ness *Ork.* ***Coastal feature***, headland at NW end of Stronsay. **106 F5** HY6129.
Links of Dunnet *High.* ***Coastal feature***, undulating sandy area on E shore of Dunnet Bay and to S of Dunnet Head. Partly within Dunnet Forest. **105 H2** ND2270.
Linksness *Ork.* ***Locality***, including headland with landing stage, at N end of Hoy on Burra Sound, opposite Graemsay. **107 B7** HY2403.
Linksness *Ork.* ***Settlement***, 1m/2km SW of Rerwick Head, on Mainland. **107 E6** HY5310.
Linktown *Fife* ***Suburb***, S district of Kirkcaldy. **76 A1** NT2790.
Linkwood *Moray* ***Locality***, 1m/2km SE of Elgin. NJ2361.
Linley *Shrop.* ***Hamlet***, 3m/5km NE of Bishop's Castle. **38 C6** SO3592.
Linley *Shrop.* ***Settlement***, 4m/6km NW of Bridgnorth. SO6898.
Linley Green *Here.* ***Hamlet***, 3m/4km E of Bromyard. **29 F3** SO6953.
Linley Hill *Shrop.* ***Open space***, NW slope of Norbury Hill, 4m/6km NE of Bishop's Castle. **38 C6** SO3594.
Linlithgow *W.Loth.* Population: 11,866. ***Town***, historic town, 16m/26km W of Edinburgh. Formerly an important industrial area. 15c Linlithgow Palace (Historic Scotland) on side of Linlithgow Loch. 18c Annet House contains Linlithgow Story Museum. **75 H3** NS9977.
Linlithgow Bridge *W.Loth.* ***Locality***, adjoining to W of Linlithgow, below high railway viaduct. **75 H3** NS9977.
Linlithgow Palace *W.Loth.* ***Historic/prehistoric site***, ruins (Historic Scotland) stand on high ground in parkland on S side of Linlithgow Loch, to N of Linlithgow. Birthplace in 1542 of Mary, Queen of Scots and home to all Stewart kings. **75 J3** NS9977.
Linn of Barhoise *D. & G.* ***Waterfall***, in course of River Bladnoch, 1m/2km N of Kirkcowan. **64 D4** NX3362.
Linn of Corriemulzie *Aber.* ***Waterfall***, series of small waterfalls in a ravine in course of Corriemulzie Burn, 3m/5km SW of Braemar. **89 H6** NO1189.
Linn of Dee *Aber.* ***Waterfall***, cascades in narrow cleft in course of River Dee, 1m/2km W of Inverey. **89 H6** NO0689.
Linn of Muick Cottage *Aber.* ***Settlement***, 4m/7km SW of Ballater, in Glen Muick. **90 B6** NO3389.
Linn of Pattack *High.* ***Lake/loch***, pool in course of River Pattack, 2m/3km SE of Kinloch Laggan. **88 C6** NN5587.
Linn of Quoich *Aber.* ***Waterfall***, in course of Quoich Water, 1km NW of its confluence with River Dee. **89 J5** NO1191.
Linn of Tummel *P. & K.* ***Waterfall***, National Trust for Scotland property in River Tummel near its confluence with River Garry 2m/3km S of Killiecrankie. **82 A1** NN9060.
Linnels *Northumb.* ***Settlement***, at bridge over Devil's Water, 2m/3km SE of Hexham. **70 E7** NY9561.
Linney *Pembs.* ***Settlement***, 2m/3km SW of Castlemartin, to S of Linney Burrows sand dunes. **16 B5** SR8996.
Linney Head *Pembs.* ***Coastal feature***, headland 3m/4km SW of Castlemartin. **16 B5** SR8895.
Linngeam *W.Isles* ***Island***, islet in Loch Roag, W coast of Isle of Lewis, 1m/2km NE of entrance to Little Loch Roag. NB1433.
Linnvale *Renf.* ***Suburb***, 1m/2km E of Clydebank town centre across Forth and Clyde canal. NS5170.
Linshader *W.Isles Anglicised form of Linsiadar, qv.*
Linshiels *Northumb.* ***Settlement***, in Coquetdale, 2m/3km W of Alwinton. **70 D3** NT8906.
Linsiadar (Anglicised form: Linshader.) *W.Isles* ***Settlement***, 3m/5km SE of Earshader, at entrance to Loch Cean Thulabhig, Isle of Lewis. **100 E4** NB2031.
Linsidemore *High.* ***Settlement***, in Sutherland district, 6m/10km NW of Bonar Bridge. **96 C2** NH5499.
Linslade *Beds.* ***Town***, industrial town adjoining to W of Leighton Buzzard. **32 C6** SP9125.
Linstead Magna *Suff.* ***Locality***, 1m/2km N of Cratfield. TM3176.
Linstead Parva *Suff.* ***Hamlet***, 4m/6km W of Halesworth. **35 H1** TM3377.
Linstock *Cumb.* ***Hamlet***, on N bank of River Eden, 2m/4km NE of Carlisle. **60 F1** NY4258.
Linthorpe *Middbro.* ***Suburb***, 1m/2km SW of Middlesbrough town centre. NZ4818.
Linthurst Newtown *Worcs.* ***Locality***, 2m/3km NE of Bromsgrove. SO9972.
Linthwaite *W.Yorks.* ***Village***, 3m/5km SW of Huddersfield. **50 D1** SE1014.
Lintlaw *Sc.Bord.* ***Village***, 4m/6km NE of Duns. **77 G5** NT8258.
Lintmill *Moray* ***Village***, near N coast 1m/2km S of Cullen. **98 D4** NJ5165.
Linton *Cambs.* Population: 3959. ***Village***, 7m/11km W of Haverhill. Site of Roman villa 1km SE. **33 J4** TL5646.
Linton *Derbys.* ***Village***, 3m/4km SW of Swadlincote. **40 E4** SK2717.
Linton *Here.* ***Village***, 4m/6km E of Ross-on-Wye. **29 F6** SO6626.
Linton *Kent* ***Village***, 4m/6km S of Maidstone. **14 C3** TQ7550.
Linton *N.Yorks.* ***Village***, 1m/2km S of Grassington. **56 E3** SD9962.
Linton *Sc.Bord.* ***Settlement***, nearly 1m/2km N of Morebattle. **70 C1** NT7726.
Linton *W.Yorks.* ***Village***, 1m/2km SW of Wetherby. **57 J5** SE3946.
Linton Colliery *Northumb.* ***Locality***, 3m/4km N of Ashington; disused mine. NZ2691.
Linton Heath *Derbys.* ***Settlement***, adjoining to SE of Linton. SK2816.
Linton Hill *Here.* ***Village***, to SE of Linton, 4m/6km W of Newent. SO6624.
Linton Hill *Sc.Bord.* ***Hill***, 2m/3km W of Town Yetholm. Height 925 feet or 282 metres. **70 C1** NT7827.
Linton-on-Ouse *N.Yorks.* ***Village***, 9m/14km NW of York. **57 K3** SE4960.
Linton Woods *N.Yorks.* ***Locality***, 1m/2km NE of Linton-on-Ouse. SE5062.
Linton Zoo and Gardens *Cambs.* ***Leisure/recreation***, to SW of Linton. 16 acres housing many exotic and rare animals, including Sumatran tigers and Aldabra great tortoises. Conservation and education are priorities of zoo. **33 J4** TL5546.
Lintz *Dur.* ***Locality***, adjoining to SW of Burnopfield, 3m/5km NW of Stanley. NZ1656.
Lintz Green *Dur.* ***Settlement***, 1m/2km W of Burnopfield. NZ1556.
Lintzford *T. & W.* ***Settlement***, on River Derwent, 1m/2km SW of Rowlands Gill and 4m/7km SW of Blaydon. **62 C1** NZ1457.
Lintzgarth *Dur.* ***Locality***, 1km W of Rookhope. NY9242.
Linwood *Hants.* ***Settlement***, 3m/5km NE of Ringwood. **10 C4** SU1809.
Linwood *Lincs.* ***Village***, 2m/3km S of Market Rasen. **52 E4** TF1086.
Linwood *Renf.* Population: 10,183. ***Locality***, large residential development, 1m/2km NE of Johnstone. **74 C4** NS4464.
Lion Bridge *Northumb.* ***Bridge***, sandstone bridge over River Aln at Alnwick, built in 1773 by John Adam. NU1813.
Lionacleit (Anglicised form: Liniclett.) *W.Isles* ***Village***, on SW coast of Benbecula, 4m/6km S of Benbecula (Baile a' Mhanaich) Aerodrome. **92 C7** NF7949.
Lional (Anglicised form: Lionel.) *W.Isles* ***Village***, near N end of Isle of Lewis, 1km W of Port Nis. **101 H1** NB5263.
Lionel *W.Isles Anglicised form of Lional, qv.*
Liongam *W.Isles* ***Island***, small uninhabited island off W coast of Isle of Lewis, 2m/4km NE of Scarp. **100 B6** NA9919.
Liphook *Hants.* Population: 5374. ***Village***, large village, 4m/7km W of Haslemere. **12 B3** SU8331.
Lipley *Shrop.* ***Settlement***, 5m/8km SE of Market Drayton. SJ7431.
Lipyeate *Som.* ***Settlement***, 3m/5km S of Radstock. ST6850.
Liquo *N.Lan. Alternative name for Bowhousebog, qv.*
Liscard *Mersey.* ***Suburb***, 1m/2km NW of Wallasey town centre. SJ3092.
Liscombe *Som.* ***Hamlet***, 4m/6km NW of Dulverton. **7 G2** SS8732.
Liskeard *Cornw.* Population: 7044. ***Small town***, medieval stannary town, 11m/18km E of Bodmin and 12m/19km W of Saltash. Scenic rail link to Looe. **4 C4** SX2564.
Lismore *Arg. & B.* ***Island***, long, narrow and fertile island in Loch Linnhe, extending 10m/15km from Rubha Fiart NE to a point opposite Port Appin on mainland to E. Ferry to Port Appin. **79 K4** NM8440.
Liss *Hants.* Population: 6148. ***Village***, 3m/5km NE of Petersfield. Includes localities of East and West Liss. **11 J2** SU7727.
Liss Forest *Hants.* ***Village***, 1m/2km NE of Liss and 4m/6km SW of Liphook. **11 J2** SU7828.
Lissett *E.Riding* ***Village***, 2m/4km NW of Skipsea. **59 H4** TA1458.
Lissington *Lincs.* ***Village***, 4m/6km S of Market Rasen. **52 E4** TF1083.
Lisson Grove *Gt.Lon.* ***Suburb***, in City of Westminster, 2m/3km NW of Charing Cross. TQ2781.
Listerdale *S.Yorks.* ***Suburb***, 3m/4km E of Rotherham. SK4691.
Liston *Essex* ***Settlement***, 1m/2km SW of Long Melford. **34 C4** TL8544.
Lisvane (Llysfaen). *Cardiff* ***Village***, 4m/7km N of Cardiff. **18 E3** ST1983.
Liswerry *Newport* ***Suburb***, 2m/3km E of Newport town centre. **19 G3** ST3487.
Litcham *Norf.* ***Village***, 7m/11km NE of Swaffham. **44 C4** TF8817.
Litchard *Bridgend* ***Suburb***, N district of Bridgend. SS9081.
Litchborough *Northants.* ***Village***, 6m/10km SE of Daventry. **31 H3** SP6354.
Litchfield *Hants.* ***Village***, 4m/6km N of Whitchurch. **21 H6** SU4653.
Litherland *Mersey.* Population: 20,905. ***Town***, adjoining to N of Bootle. **48 C3** SJ3397.
Litlington *Cambs.* ***Village***, 3m/5km NW of Royston. **33 G4** TL3142.
Litlington *E.Suss.* ***Village***, in valley of Cuckmere River, 1m/2km S of Alfriston. **13 J6** TQ5201.
Little *High.* ***River***, flowing N and then NW to join River Thurso just E of Dalemore. **105 G4** ND1548.
Little Abington *Cambs.* ***Village***, 5m/7km NE of Great Chesterford. **33 J4** TL5349.
Little Addington *Northants.* ***Village***, 1km S of Great Addington and 6m/10km SE of Kettering. **32 C1** SP9573.
Little Airmyn *N.Yorks.* ***Hamlet***, on W bank of River Aire, opposite Airmyn, 1m/2km NW of Goole. SE7225.
Little Alne *Warks.* ***Hamlet***, 3m/5km S of Henley-in-Arden. **30 C2** SP1361.
Little Altcar *Mersey.* ***Suburb***, SE district of Formby. SD3006.
Little Amwell *Herts.* Population: 2218. ***Village***, 2m/3km S of Ware. **33 G7** TL3511.
Little Ann *Hants.* ***Hamlet***, 2m/3km SW of Andover. SU3343.
Little Ansty (Also known as Pleck.) *Dorset* ***Settlement***, forms part of Ansty locality in parish of Hilton, 6m/10km N of Puddletown. ST7604.
Little Asby *Cumb.* ***Hamlet***, 2m/4km SE of Great Asby. NY6813.
Little Ashley *Wilts.* ***Hamlet***, with Great Ashley, forms locality of Ashley, about 1m/2km NW of Bradford-on-Avon. ST8162.
Little Assynt *High.* ***Settlement***, on N side of Lochan an Iasgaich, W of Loch Assynt. **102 D6** NC1525.

L

Little Aston *Staffs.* ***Village***, 3m/5km NW of Sutton Coldfield. **40 C6** SK0900.

Little Atherfield *I.o.W.* ***Settlement***, 2m/3km S of Shorwell. **11 F7** SZ4680.

Little Ayton *N.Yorks.* ***Hamlet***, 1m/2km E of Great Ayton. **63 G5** NZ5510.

Little Baddow *Essex* Population: 3464. ***Village***, 5m/8km E of Chelmsford. **24 D1** TL7807.

Little Badminton *S.Glos.* ***Hamlet***, 1m/2km N of Badminton across Badminton Park. **20 A3** ST8082.

Little Ballinluig *P. & K.* ***Settlement***, on River Tay, 4m/7km W of Ballinluig. **82 A2** NN9152.

Little Bampton *Cumb.* ***Hamlet***, 3m/5km SE of Kirkbride. **60 D1** NY2755.

Little Bardfield *Essex* ***Village***, 3m/5km E of Thaxted. **33 K5** TL6530.

Little Barford *Beds.* ***Village***, 2m/4km S of St. Neots. **32 E3** TL1856.

Little Barningham *Norf.* ***Village***, 5m/9km NW of Aylsham. **45 F2** TG1433.

Little Barrington *Glos.* ***Village***, forms parish of Barrington, along with Great Barrington, 3m/5km to W of Burford. **30 D7** SP2013.

Little Barrow *Ches.* ***Hamlet***, 1m/2km N of Great Barrow. SJ4670.

Little Barugh *N.Yorks.* ***Hamlet***, 5m/8km N of Malton. **58 D2** SE7679.

Little Bavington *Northumb.* ***Settlement***, 4m/6km S of Kirkwhelpington. NY9878.

Little Bayton *Warks.* ***Locality***, 1m/2km S of Bedworth. SP3585.

Little Bealings *Suff.* ***Village***, 3m/5km W of Woodbridge. **35 G4** TM2247.

Little Bedwyn *Wilts.* ***Village***, 4m/6km SW of Hungerford. **21 F5** SU2966.

Little Beeby *Leics.* ***Settlement***, to SE of Beeby, 1m/2km NW of Hungarton. SK6607.

Little Bentley *Essex* ***Village***, 4m/6km S of Manningtree. **35 F6** TM1125.

Little Berkhamsted *Herts.* ***Village***, 4m/6km SW of Hertford. **23 F1** TL2907.

Little Bernera *W.Isles* ***Island***, off W coast of Isle of Lewis between entrances to East and West Loch Roag and off N shore of Great Bernera. Measures about 1m/2km E to W and an average of 1m/2km N to S. **100 D3** NB1440.

Little Billing *Northants.* ***Suburb***, 3m/5km NE of Northampton town centre. **32 B2** SP8061.

Little Billington *Beds.* ***Settlement***, 2m/3km S of Leighton Buzzard. SP9322.

L

Little Birch *Here.* ***Village***, 6m/9km S of Hereford. **28 E5** SO5131.

Little Bispham *B'pool* ***Suburb***, 1m/2km N of Bispham, along shore, and 1m/2km S of Cleveleys. **55 G5** SD3141.

Little Blakenham *Suff.* ***Village***, 5m/7km NW of Ipswich. **35 F4** TM1048.

Little Blencow *Cumb.* ***Hamlet***, adjoining to NW of Great Blencow, 4m/7km NW of Penrith. NY4532.

Little Bloxwich *W.Mid.* ***Suburb***, adjoining to NE of Bloxwich, 3m/4km N of Walsall town centre. SK0003.

Little Bognor *W.Suss.* ***Hamlet***, 2m/3km SE of Petworth. TQ0020.

Little Bolas *Shrop.* ***Settlement***, 1km NW of Great Bolas across River Tern. SJ6422.

Little Bollington *Ches.* ***Village***, 3m/5km E of Lymm. **49 G4** SJ7286.

Little Bolton *Gt.Man.* ***Suburb***, 3m/4km W of Salford city centre. SJ7998.

Little Bookham *Surr.* ***Suburb***, 3m/5km W of Leatherhead. **22 E6** TQ1254.

Little Bourton *Oxon.* ***Hamlet***, 3m/4km N of Banbury. SP4544.

Little Bowden *Leics.* ***Locality***, adjoining to E of Market Harborough. **42 A7** SP7487.

Little Boys Heath *Bucks.* ***Settlement***, 4m/6km W of Amersham. SU9099.

Little Bradley *Suff.* ***Village***, 4m/7km N of Haverhill. **33 K3** TL6852.

Little Brampton *Shrop.* ***Hamlet***, 4m/7km W of Craven Arms. **38 C7** SO3681.

Little Braxted *Essex* ***Hamlet***, 1m/2km E of Witham. **34 C7** TL8314.

Little Brechin *Angus* ***Village***, 2m/3km NW of Brechin. **83 G1** NO5960.

Little Bredy *Dorset Alternative spelling of Littlebredy, qv.*

Little Bricett *Suff.* ***Locality***, 5m/8km N of Hadleigh. TM0549.

Little Brickhill *M.K.* ***Village***, 2m/4km SE of Bletchley. **32 C5** SP9132.

Little Bridgeford *Staffs.* ***Hamlet***, 1km NW of Great Bridgeford. **40 A3** SJ8727.

Little Brington *Northants.* ***Village***, forms parish of Brington, along with Great Brington, 6m/10km NW of Northampton. **31 H2** SP6663.

Little Bristol *S.Glos.* ***Hamlet***, adjoining to S of Charfield, 2m/4km SW of Wotton-under-Edge. ST7291.

Little Bromley *Essex* ***Village***, 2m/3km SW of Manningtree. **34 E6** TM0928.

Little Bromwich *W.Mid.* ***Suburb***, 3m/5km E of Birmingham city centre. SP1186.

Little Broughton *Cumb.* ***Village***, adjoining to N of Great Broughton, 3m/5km W of Cockermouth. **60 B3** NY0731.

Little Budworth *Ches.* ***Village***, 3m/4km NE of Tarporley. **48 E6** SJ5965.

Little Budworth Common Country Park *Ches.* ***Leisure/recreation***, heath and woodland 1km NW of Little Budworth, to N of Oulton Park motor racing circuit. **48 E6** SJ5865.

Little Burdon *Darl.* ***Settlement***, 1m/2km E of Great Burdon. NZ3216.

Little Burstead *Essex* ***Village***, 2m/3km S of Billericay. **24 C2** TQ6692.

Little Burton *E.Riding* ***Settlement***, to W of Brandesburton. **59 H5** TA1147.

Little Bushey *Herts.* ***Suburb***, E district of Bushey. TQ1594.

Little Bytham *Lincs.* ***Village***, 7m/11km N of Stamford. **42 D4** TF0118.

Little Canford *Dorset* ***Settlement***, beside River Stour, 3m/4km E of Wimborne Minster. SZ0499.

Little Carleton *B'pool* ***Suburb***, of Blackpool, 1m/2km W of Poulton-le-Fylde. SD3338.

Little Carleton Motte *S.Ayr.* ***Historic/prehistoric site***, adjoining to E of Little Carleton, 6m/10km SW of Girvan. **67 F5** NX1389.

Little Carlton *Lincs.* ***Village***, 1km W of Great Carlton. **53 H4** TF3985.

Little Carlton *Notts.* ***Hamlet***, 3m/4km NW of Newark-on-Trent. **51 K7** SK7757.

Little Casterton *Rut.* ***Hamlet***, 2m/3km N of Stamford. Site of Roman villa 1km W. **42 D5** TF0009.

Little Catwick *E.Riding* ***Settlement***, adjoining to S of Catwick. **59 H5** TA1244.

Little Catworth *Cambs.* ***Settlement***, 1m/2km SE of Catworth. TL0972.

Little Cawthorpe *Lincs.* ***Village***, 3m/5km SE of Louth. **53 G4** TF3583.

Little Chalfield *Wilts.* ***Hamlet***, 1km W of Great Chalfield, 3m/4km NE of Bradford-on-Avon. ST8563.

Little Chalfont *Bucks.* ***Village***, 2m/4km E of Amersham. **22 C2** SU9997.

Little Charlinch *Som.* ***Settlement***, 1km SE of Charlinch, 4m/6km W of Bridgwater. ST2437.

Little Chart *Kent* ***Village***, 3m/4km S of Charing. Site of Roman bath house to W. **14 E3** TQ9445.

Little Chester *Derby* ***Suburb***, to N of Derby city centre. Site of Roman fort of Derventio. SK3537.

Little Chesterford *Essex* ***Village***, 3m/4km NW of Saffron Walden. **33 J4** TL5141.

Little Chesterton *Oxon.* ***Settlement***, 2m/4km SW of Bicester. SP5520.

Little Cheverell *Wilts.* ***Village***, 5m/8km S of Devizes. **20 C6** ST9853.

Little Chishill *Cambs.* ***Hamlet***, 5m/7km SE of Royston. **33 H5** TL4137.

Little Clacton *Essex* Population: 2915. ***Village***, 3m/4km N of Clacton-on-Sea. **35 F7** TM1618.

Little Clanfield *Oxon.* ***Settlement***, 4m/6km E of Lechlade. SP2701.

Little Clegg *Gt.Man.* ***Locality***, 1m/2km SW of Littleborough, just W of Hollingworth Lake. SD9214.

Little Clifton *Cumb.* ***Village***, 4m/6km E of Workington. **60 B4** NY0528.

Little Coates *N.E.Lincs.* ***Suburb***, 1m/2km W of Grimsby town centre and 1m/2km SE of Great Coates. TA2408.

Little Colonsay *Arg. & B.* ***Island***, uninhabited island of about 200 acres or 80 hectares, lying 1m/2km off SW coast of Ulva. **78 E4** NM3736.

Little Comberton *Worcs.* ***Village***, 2m/4km SE of Pershore. **29 J4** SO9642.

Little Comfort *Cornw.* ***Hamlet***, 3m/4km S of Launceston. SX3480.

Little Common *E.Suss.* ***Suburb***, W district of Bexhill. **14 C7** TQ7108.

Little Common *S.Yorks.* ***Suburb***, 3m/5km SW of Sheffield city centre. SK3283.

Little Compton *Warks.* ***Village***, 4m/6km NW of Chipping Norton. **30 D5** SP2630.

Little Corby *Cumb.* ***Locality***, 5m/8km E of Carlisle. **61 F1** NY4757.

Little Cornard *Suff.* ***Hamlet***, 2m/4km SE of Sudbury. TL9039.

Little Cowarne *Here.* ***Village***, 4m/6km SW of Bromyard. **29 F3** SO6051.

Little Coxwell *Oxon.* ***Village***, 2m/3km S of Faringdon. **21 F2** SU2893.

Little Crakehall *N.Yorks.* ***Hamlet***, adjoining to NW of Great Crakehall, 5m/8km S of Catterick. **62 D7** SE2490.

Little Cransley *Northants.* ***Settlement***, in parish of Cransley, 3m/4km SW of Kettering. SP8376.

Little Crawley *M.K.* ***Settlement***, to N of North Crawley. SP9245.

Little Creaton *Northants.* ***Settlement***, to SE of Creaton. SP7071.

Little Creich *High.* ***Settlement***, in Sutherland district, on N shore of Dornoch Firth, 2m/4km SE of Bonar Bridge. **96 D3** NH6389.

Little Cressingham *Norf.* ***Village***, 2m/3km SE of Great Cressingham. **44 C6** TF8700.

Little Crosby *Mersey.* ***Village***, to N of Crosby, 1m/2km S of Ince Blundell. **48 C2** SD3101.

Little Crosthwaite *Cumb.* ***Settlement***, on E side of Bassenthwaite Lake, 4m/6km NW of Keswick. NY2327.

Little Cubley *Derbys.* ***Hamlet***, 1km SW of Great Cubley. **40 D2** SK1637.

Little Cumbrae *N.Ayr.* ***Island***, lying 1km S of Great Cumbrae. Measures nearly 2m/3km N to S by nearly 1m/2km E to W. Lighthouse on W side. **73 K5** NS1451.

Little Dalby *Leics.* ***Hamlet***, 2m/3km E of Great Dalby. **42 A4** SK7414.

Little Dart *Devon* ***River***, rising on Rackenford Moor N of Rackenford and flowing W into River Taw near Chulmleigh. **7 G4** SS6613.

Little Dawley *Tel. & W.* ***Suburb***, to S of Dawley. SJ6806.

Little Dens *Aber.* ***Settlement***, 4m/6km SW of Peterhead. **99 J6** NK0743.

Little Dewchurch *Here.* ***Village***, 5m/9km S of Hereford. **28 E5** SO5331.

Little Ditton *Cambs.* ***Settlement***, to NE of Woodditton, 3m/5km SE of Newmarket. TL6658.

Little Doward *Here.* ***Hamlet***, 3m/5km NE of Monmouth. SO5316.

Little Down *Hants.* ***Hamlet***, 4m/6km NW of Hurstbourne Tarrant. SU3558.

Little Downham *Cambs.* Population: 1728. ***Village***, 3m/4km N of Ely. Remains of medieval palace of Bishops of Ely on N side. **43 J7** TL5283.

Little Drayton *Shrop.* ***Suburb***, W district of Market Drayton. SJ6633.

Little Driffield *E.Riding* ***Village***, 1m/2km W of Great Driffield. **59 G4** TA0257.

Little Drybrook *Glos.* ***Settlement***, 3m/4km S of Coleford. SO5907.

Little Dunham *Norf.* ***Village***, 1m/2km S of Great Dunham. **44 C4** TF8714.

Little Dunkeld *P. & K.* ***Village***, across River Tay, to S of Dunkeld (road bridge by Telford, 1809). **82 B3** NO0242.

Little Dunmow *Essex* ***Village***, 2m/3km E of Great Dunmow. Original home of ancient Flitch Trials until 1855, when they were revived at Great Dunmow. **33 K6** TL6521.

Little Durnford *Wilts.* ***Hamlet***, on River Avon, 3m/5km N of Salisbury. SU1234.

Little Easton *Essex* ***Village***, 2m/3km NW of Great Dunmow. **33 K6** TL6023.

Little Eaton *Derbys.* Population: 1926. ***Village***, 3m/5km N of Derby. **41 F1** SK3641.

Little Eccleston *Lancs.* ***Hamlet***, adjoining to W of Great Eccleston, on S side of River Wyre. SD4240.

Little Edstone *N.Yorks.* ***Settlement***, 2m/3km SE of Kirkbymoorside. SE7184.

Little Ellingham *Norf.* ***Village***, 2m/3km N of Great Ellingham. **44 E6** TM0196.

Little Elm *Som.* ***Hamlet***, 4m/7km SW of Frome. ST7146.

Little End *Cambs.* ***Locality***, adjoining to NE of Warboys, 7m/11km NE of Huntingdon. TL3180.

Little End *E.Riding* ***Locality***, adjoining to S of Holme-on-Spalding-Moor. SE8137.

Little End *Essex* ***Hamlet***, 2m/3km SW of Chipping Ongar. **23 J1** TL5400.

Little Everdon *Northants.* ***Hamlet***, 3m/5km SE of Daventry. SP5958.

Little Eversden *Cambs.* ***Village***, 6m/9km SW of Cambridge. **33 G3** TL3753.

Little Eye *Mersey.* ***Island***, small island SE of Hilbre Island, in River Dee estuary opposite West Kirby. SJ1986.

Little Eyton *Tel. & W.* ***Locality***, in Dawley, 1m/2km SW of Telford. SJ6807.

Little Fakenham *Suff.* ***Village***, 4m/7km N of Ixworth. **34 D1** TL9076.

Little Faringdon *Oxon.* ***Village***, 1m/2km NE of Lechlade. **21 F1** SP2201.

Little Fell *Cumb.* ***Mountain***, on Burton Fell, 4m/7km N of Brough. Height 2444 feet or 745 metres. **61 J4** NY7821.

Little Fen *Cambs.* ***Open space***, fenland, to N of Burwell. **33 J2** TL5868.

Little Fencote *N.Yorks.* ***Hamlet***, adjoining to S of Great Fencote, 6m/9km W of Northallerton. **62 D7** SE2893.

Little Fenton *N.Yorks.* ***Village***, 2m/3km NE of Sherburn in Elmet. **58 B6** SE5235.

Little Finborough *Suff.* ***Settlement***, 3m/5km SW of Stowmarket. **34 E3** TM0254.

Little France *Edin.* ***Suburb***, 3m/5km SE of Edinburgh city centre. NT2870.

Little Fransham *Norf.* ***Village***, 1m/2km S of Great Fransham. **44 C4** TF8913.

Little Gaddesden *Herts.* ***Village***, 4m/6km N of Berkhamsted. **32 C7** SP9913.

Little Garway *Here.* ***Settlement***, 1m/2km N of Garway. **28 D6** SO4524.

Little Gidding *Cambs.* ***Settlement***, 5m/8km SW of Stilton. **42 E7** TL1281.

Little Glemham *Suff.* ***Village***, 2m/4km S of Great Glemham. **35 H3** TM3458.

Little Gorsley *Here.* ***Hamlet***, 2m/3km SW of Newent. **29 F6** SO6924.

Little Gransden *Cambs.* ***Village***, just S of Great Gransden, 6m/10km SE of St. Neots. **33 F3** TL2755.

Little Green *Cambs.* ***Settlement***, to N of Guilden Morden, 6m/10km E of Biggleswade. TL2844.

Little Green *Norf.* ***Locality***, adjoining Great Green between Bunwell and Bunwell Street. TM1293.

Little Green *Notts.* ***Settlement***, 1km NE of Car Colston, 2m/3km E of East Bridgford. SK7243.

Little Green *Som.* ***Hamlet***, adjoining to S of Mells, 3m/5km W of Frome. ST7248.

Little Green *Suff.* ***Hamlet***, adjoining to W of Gislingham. **34 E1** TM0671.

Little Green *Wrex.* ***Settlement***, between Eglwys Cross and The Chequer, 4m/6km W of Whitchurch. SJ4840.

Little Green Holm *Ork.* ***Island***, islet to S of Muckle Green Holm across narrow Sound of the Green Holms. HY5226.

Little Grimsby *Lincs.* ***Hamlet***, 3m/4km N of Louth. **53 G3** TF3291.

Little Gringley *Notts.* ***Hamlet***, 2m/3km E of Retford. SK7380.

Little Gruinard *High.* ***River***, flows N into Gruinard Bay from Fionn Loch. **95 F3** NG9494.

Little Gruinard *High.* ***Settlement***, on coast of Ross and Cromarty district, 3m/4km SE of Laide. **95 F3** NG9489.

Little Habton *N.Yorks.* ***Settlement***, 4m/7km NW of Malton. **58 D2** SE7477.

Little Hadham *Herts.* ***Village***, 3m/5km W of Bishop's Stortford. **33 H6** TL4322.

Little Haldon *Devon* ***Open space***, hillslope with notable viewpoints, 2m/3km NW of Teignmouth. **5 K3** SX9175.

Little Hale *Lincs.* ***Village***, 1km S of Great Hale. **42 E1** TF1442.

Little Hall *Suff.* ***Historic house***, restored 16c building in Lavenham, with Crown Post roof which represents fortunes of Lavenham's cloth trade. **34 D4** TL9249.

Little Hallam *Derbys.* ***Suburb***, to S of Ilkeston town centre. SK4640.

Little Hallingbury *Essex* ***Village***, 3m/4km S of Bishop's Stortford. **33 H7** TL5017.

Little Hampden *Bucks.* ***Hamlet***, 3m/4km S of Wendover. **22 B1** SP8503.

Little Hanford *Dorset* ***Hamlet***, 5m/7km NW of Blandford Forum. ST8411.

Little Haresfield *Glos.* ***Hamlet***, 1m/2km SW of Haresfield. SO8009.

Little Harrowden *Northants.* ***Village***, 3m/4km NW of Wellingborough. **32 B1** SP8671.

Little Haseley *Oxon.* ***Hamlet***, 5m/9km SW of Thame. **21 K1** SP6400.

Little Hatfield *E.Riding* ***Settlement***, 1m/2km W of Great Hatfield. TA1743.

Little Hautbois *Norf.* ***Settlement***, 2m/3km NW of Coltishall. **45 G3** TG2521.

Little Haven *Pembs.* ***Village***, on St. Brides Bay, 6m/10km W of Haverfordwest. **16 B3** SM8512.

Little Haven *W.Suss.* ***Suburb***, NE district of Horsham. TQ1832.

Little Havra *Shet.* ***Island***, small uninhabited island lying off W coast of South Havra. HU3526.

Little Hay *Staffs.* ***Village***, 4m/6km N of Sutton Coldfield. **40 D5** SK1202.

Little Hayfield *Derbys.* ***Village***, 1km N of Hayfield. **50 C4** SK0387.

Little Haywood *Staffs.* Population: 1222. ***Village***, 1m/2km SE of Great Haywood. **40 C3** SJ9922.

Little Heath *Ches.* ***Settlement***, to NE of Audlem. SJ6644.

Little Heath *Gt.Lon.* ***Suburb***, in borough of Redbridge, 3m/4km NE of Ilford. TQ4688.

Little Heath *Herts.* ***Settlement***, National Trust property, 2m/3km E of Berkhamsted. TL0108.

Little Heath *W.Mid.* ***Suburb***, N district of Coventry. **41 F7** SP3482.

Little Heck *N.Yorks.* ***Settlement***, 1m/2km NE of Great Heck, 3m/5km W of Snaith. SE5922.

Little Henny *Essex* ***Locality***, 2m/3km S of Sudbury. TL8638.

Little Herbert's *Glos.* ***Locality***, in S part of Charlton Kings. SO9620.

Little Hereford *Here.* ***Village***, 3m/4km W of Tenbury Wells. **28 E2** SO5568.

Little Hill *Leics.* ***Locality***, 4m/7km SE of Leicester. SP6198.

Little Hill *Powys* ***Hill***, 4m/6km SE of Llanbister. Height 984 feet or 300 metres. **28 A2** SO1267.

Little Hill *Powys* ***Mountain***, 5m/8km N of Painscastle. Height 1607 feet or 490 metres. **28 A3** SO1453.

Little Hillbre Island *Mersey.* *See Hillbre Island.*

Little Hockham *Norf.* ***Settlement***, 1m/2km S of Great Hockham. TL9490.

Little Holm *Shet.* ***Island***, rock island in Yell Sound 3m/4km SE of Burra Voe. HU4086.

Little Holtby *N.Yorks.* ***Settlement***, on A1 trunk road, 4m/7km SE of Catterick. **62 D7** SE2791.

Little Hoole Moss Houses *Lancs.* ***Settlement***, 1km SE of Walmer Bridge, 3m/5km W of Leyland. SD4823.

Little Horkesley *Essex* ***Village***, 5m/8km NW of Colchester. **34 D5** TL9632.

Little Hormead *Herts.* ***Hamlet***, 3m/4km E of Buntingford. **33 H6** TL4029.

Little Horsted *E.Suss.* ***Hamlet***, 2m/3km S of Uckfield. **13 H5** TQ4718.

Little Horton *W.Yorks.* ***Suburb***, 3m/4km SW of Bradford city centre. SE1431.

Little Horton *Wilts.* ***Hamlet***, 1m/2km SW of Horton and 2m/4km E of Devizes. SU0462.

Little Horwood *Bucks.* ***Village***, 2m/4km NE of Winslow. **31 J5** SP7930.

Little Houghton *Northants.* ***Village***, 3m/5km E of Northampton. **32 B3** SP8059.

Little Houghton *S.Yorks.* ***Hamlet***, 1km SW of Great Houghton. SE4205.

Little Hucklow *Derbys.* ***Village***, 1m/2km NW of Great Hucklow. **50 D5** SK1777.

Little Hulton *Gt.Man.* ***Locality***, 4m/6km S of Bolton. **49 G2** SD7203.

Little Hungerford *W.Berks.* ***Locality***, at Hermitage, 4m/7km NE of Newbury. **21 J4** SU5173.

Little Hutton *N.Yorks.* ***Hamlet***, adjoining to N of Sessay, 3m/5km E of Topcliffe. SE4576.

Little Idoch *Aber.* ***Settlement***, on S side of Idoch Water, 3m/4km E of Turriff. **99 F6** NJ7649.

Little Irchester *Northants.* ***Hamlet***, 1m/2km NW of Irchester and 1m/2km SE of Wellingborough. SP9066.

Little Island *W.Mid.* ***Suburb***, 3m/4km W of Walsall town centre. SO9788.

Little Kelk *E.Riding* ***Locality***, 1m/2km N of Great Kelk. TA1058.

Little Keyford *Som.* ***Hamlet***, to S of Keyford, 1km S of Frome. ST7847.

Little Kimble *Bucks.* ***Village***, 3m/5km W of Wendover. **22 B1** SP8207.

Little Kineton *Warks.* ***Hamlet***, adjoining to S of Kineton. **30 E3** SP3350.

Little Kingshill *Bucks.* ***Village***, 4m/7km NE of High Wycombe. **22 B2** SU8999.

Little Kit's Coty House *Kent* ***Historic/prehistoric site***, prehistoric long barrow to S of Kit's Coty House, 3m/5km N of Maidstone town centre. **14 C2** TQ7460.

Little Knowle *Devon* ***Suburb***, to NW of Budleigh Salterton town centre. SY0582.

Little Langdale *Cumb.* ***Locality***, 2m/3km W of Skelwith Bridge. NY3103.

Little Langford *Wilts.* ***Hamlet***, in River Wylye valley, 5m/7km NW of Wilton. **10 B1** SU0436.

Little Laver *Essex* ***Hamlet***, 4m/7km N of Chipping Ongar. **23 J1** TL5409.

Little Lawford *Warks.* ***Hamlet***, 3m/4km NW of Rugby. **31 F1** SP4677.

Little Layton *B'pool* ***Suburb***, adjoining to N of Layton, 1m/2km NE of Blackpool town centre. SD3237.

Little Leigh *Ches.* ***Village***, 3m/5km NW of Northwich. **49 F5** SJ6175.

Little Leighs *Essex* ***Hamlet***, 5m/8km SW of Braintree. **34 B7** TL7116.

Little Lepton *W.Yorks.* ***Settlement***, to S of Lepton, 1m/2km NE of Highburton. SE2014.

Little Leven *E.Riding* ***Locality***, adjoining to W of Leven. TA1045.

Little Lever *Gt.Man.* Population: 11,589. ***Town***, former coalmining and textile town, 3m/4km SE of Bolton. **49 G2** SD7507.

Little Ley *Aber.* ***Settlement***, 3m/5km SW of Monymusk. **90 E3** NJ6511.

Little Linford *M.K.* ***Hamlet***, 2m/4km W of Newport Pagnell across River Great Ouse. **32 B4** SP8444.

Little Linga *Ork.* ***Island***, small islet off Links Ness at NW point of Stronsay. HY6030.

Little Linga *Shet.* ***Island***, small island among several others between West Linga and Mainland. HU5265.

Little Linton *Cambs.* ***Hamlet***, 1km NW of Linton, 7m/12km W of Haverhill. TL5547.

Little Load *Som.* ***Hamlet***, on N bank of River Yeo, at N end of Long Load and 3m/5km SW of Somerton. ST4623.

Little Loch Broom *High.* ***Sea feature***, inlet to W of Loch Broom, running parallel to it. **95 G2** NH1392.

Little Loch Roag (Gaelic form: Loch Ròg Beag.) *W.Isles* ***Lake/loch***, narrow loch, 5m/8km long, opening at its N end into Loch Roag, W coast of Isle of Lewis. **100 D5** NB1228.

Little London *Bucks.* ***Hamlet***, 6m/9km NW of Thame. SP6412.

Little London *Cambs.* ***Suburb***, to W of March town centre. TL4196.

Little London *E.Suss.* ***Hamlet***, 1m/2km SW of Heathfield. **13 J5** TQ5619.

Little London *Essex* ***Hamlet***, 5m/8km N of Bishop's Stortford. TL4729.

Little London *Glos.* ***Settlement***, 5m/8km S of Newent. SO7018.

Little London *Hants.* ***Hamlet***, 3m/5km N of Andover. **21 G6** SU3749.

Little London *Hants.* ***Village***, 5m/8km N of Basingstoke. **21 K6** SU6259.

Little London *I.o.M.* ***Settlement***, 3m/5km S of Kirk Michael. **54 C5** SC3286.

Little London *Lincs.* ***Hamlet***, 3m/4km SE of Market Rasen. TF1486.

Little London *Lincs.* ***Locality***, 1m/2km SW of Spalding. **43 F3** TF2320.

Little London *Lincs.* ***Locality***, adjoining to N of Long Sutton. **43 H3** TF4323.

Little London *Lincs.* ***Settlement***, adjoining to N of Tetford, 6m/9km NE of Horncastle. **53 G5** TF3375.

Little London *Norf.* ***Hamlet***, 1km SE of Northwold. **44 B6** TL7696.

Little London *Norf.* ***Locality***, 1km E of Terrington St. Clement. **43 J3** TF5520.

Little London *Norf.* ***Locality***, adjoining to NW of Corpusty. TG1030.

Little London *Norf.* ***Locality***, E part of Southery. TL6294.

Little London *Norf.* ***Settlement***, 1m/2km NE of North Walsham. TG2931.

Little London *Oxon.* ***Locality***, at Brightwell, 2m/3km NW of Wallingford. SU5891.

Little London *Oxon.* ***Suburb***, 3m/5km S of Oxford. SP5201.

Little London *Powys* ***Hamlet***, 2m/3km SE of Caersws. SO0489.

Little London *Som.* ***Hamlet***, adjoining to W of Oakhill, 3m/4km N of Shepton Mallet. ST6247.

Little London *Suff.* ***Settlement***, 2m/3km S of Stowmarket. TM0555.

Little London *W.Yorks.* ***Suburb***, S district of Yeadon, to W of Rawdon. SE2039.

Little London *W.Yorks.* ***Suburb***, to NE of Leeds city centre, in Sheepscar district. SE3034.

Little Longstone *Derbys.* ***Hamlet***, 1km W of Great Longstone. **50 D5** SK2071.

Little Lumley *Dur.* ***Locality***, 1km N of Great Lumley. NZ2949.

Little Lyth *Shrop.* ***Settlement***, 1m/2km E of Great Lyth. SJ4706.

Little Madeley *Staffs.* ***Settlement***, 1m/2km NE of Madeley. SJ7745.

Little Malvern *Worcs.* ***Village***, below E side of Malvern Hills, 4m/6km S of Great Malvern. **29 G4** SO7740.

Little Malvern Court *Worcs.* ***Historic house***, 15c Prior's Hall of former Benedictine priory, home of Berington family since Dissolution, 1m/2km S of Malvern Wells. Set in 10 acres of grounds and featuring collection of 18c-19c needlework. **29 G4** SO7640.

Little Malvern Priory *Worcs.* ***Ecclesiastical building***, 14c church which is relic of 12c Benedictine priory, 4m/6km S of Great Malvern. **29 G4** SO7740.

Little Mancot *Flints.* ***Suburb***, on S side of Mancot Royal and Big Mancot, between Hawarden and Queensferry. SJ3266.

Little Maplestead *Essex* ***Village***, 2m/4km N of Halstead. **34 C5** TL8234.

Little Marcle *Here.* ***Village***, 3m/5km W of Ledbury. **29 F5** SO6736.

Little Marland *Devon* ***Hamlet***, 4m/7km S of Great Torrington. SS4911.

Little Marlow *Bucks.* ***Village***, 2m/3km NE of Marlow. **22 B3** SU8787.

Little Marsden *Lancs.* ***Suburb***, in S part of Nelson. SD8537.

Little Marton *B'pool* ***Suburb***, of Blackpool, adjoining to E of Great Marton. SD3434.

Little Massingham *Norf.* ***Village***, 1m/2km N of Great Massingham. **44 B3** TF7922.

Little Mell Fell *Cumb.* ***Mountain***, 2m/3km S of Penruddock. Height 1656 feet or 505 metres. **60 F4** NY4224.

Little Melton *Norf.* ***Village***, 4m/7km W of Norwich. **45 F5** TG1606.

Little Milford *Pembs.* ***Hamlet***, on W bank of Western Cleddau river, 2m/4km S of Haverfordwest. SM9611.

Little Mill *Mon.* ***Hamlet***, 3m/5km NE of Pontypool. **19 G1** SO3202.

Little Milton *Oxon.* ***Village***, 6m/10km SW of Thame. Site of Roman villa to SE. **21 K1** SP6100.

Little Minch ***Sea feature***, sea passage between Western Isles and Skye. **93 F6** NG1060.

Little Minster *Oxon.* ***Settlement***, 3m/5km W of Witney. SP3111.

Little Missenden *Bucks.* ***Village***, 3m/4km NW of Amersham. **22 C2** SU9298.

Little Mitton *Lancs.* ***Locality***, to S of Great Mitton. SD7138.

Little Mongeham *Kent* ***Settlement***, 3m/5km W of Deal. TR3350.

Little Moor End *Lancs.* ***Suburb***, to S of Oswaldtwistle. SD7326.

Little Moreton Hall *Ches.* ***Historic house***, moated black-and-white Tudor house (National Trust) 3m/5km SW of Congleton. **49 H7** SJ8358.

Little Munden *Herts.* ***Locality***, 4m/6km W of Puckeridge. TL3222.

Little Musgrave *Cumb.* ***Hamlet***, 1km SW of Great Musgrave. **61 J5** NY7613.

Little Ness *I.o.M.* ***Coastal feature***, headland 2m/3km SW of Douglas Head. **54 C6** SC3672.

Little Ness *Shrop.* ***Village***, 1m/2km NE of Great Ness. **38 D4** SJ3918.

Little Neston *Ches.* ***Locality***, adjoining to SE of Neston. **48 B5** SJ2976.

Little Newcastle (Casnewydd-bach). *Pembs.* ***Village***, 5m/9km S of Fishguard. **16 C2** SM9828.

Little Newcombe *Devon* ***Hamlet***, 3m/5km E of Crediton. SX8899.

Little Newsham *Dur.* ***Village***, 2m/3km S of Staindrop. **62 C5** NZ1217.

Little Norton *Som.* ***Hamlet***, 1km E of Norton sub Hamdon, 3m/5km SE of South Petherton. ST4715.

Little Norton *S.Yorks.* ***Suburb***, to SW of Norton, 4m/6km S of Sheffield city centre. SK3582.

Little Norton *Staffs.* ***Suburb***, adjoining Norton Canes, 3m/4km NW of Brownhills. SK0207.

Little Oakley *Essex* ***Village***, 3m/5km SW of Harwich. **35 G6** TM2129.

Little Oakley *Northants.* ***Village***, 2m/3km S of Corby. **42 B7** SP8985.

Little Odell *Beds.* ***Settlement***, adjoining to SW of Odell. SP9657.

Little Offley *Herts.* ***Hamlet***, 4m/6km W of Hitchin. TL1328.

Little Onn *Staffs.* ***Hamlet***, 1m/2km S of Church Eaton. SJ8316.

Little Ormes Head (Trwyn y Fuwch). *Conwy* ***Coastal feature***, headland at E end of Ormes Bay or Llandudno Bay. **47 G4** SH8182.

Little Ormside *Cumb.* ***Locality***, 1m/2km SE of Great Ormside and 3m/4km SE of Appleby-in-Westmorland. NY7016.

Little Orton *Cumb.* ***Hamlet***, 3m/5km W of Carlisle. **60 E1** NY3555.

Little Orton *Leics.* ***Settlement***, 1m/2km NE of Orton-on-the-Hill. SK3105.

Little Ossa *Shet.* ***Island***, rock off NW coast of Mainland 2m/4km W of The Faither. Muckle Ossa rock is adjacent to N. HU2184.

Little Ouse ***River***, rising N of Redgrave and flowing W through Thetford and Brandon into River Great Ouse at Brandon Creek, 4m/7km NE of Littleport. **44 A7** TL6091.

Little Ouse *Cambs.* ***Hamlet***, on banks of Little Ouse River, 4m/6km E of Littleport. TL6289.

Little Ouseburn *N.Yorks.* ***Village***, 1km S of Ouseburn. **57 K3** SE4461.

Little Overton *Wrex.* ***Settlement***, to E of Overton. SJ3841.

Little Oxney Green *Essex* ***Settlement***, to W of Writtle. TL6605.

Little Packington *Warks.* ***Settlement***, 3m/5km S of Coleshill. SP2184.

Little Parndon *Essex* ***Suburb***, W district of Harlow. **23 H1** TL4310.

Little Paxton *Cambs.* Population: 3202. ***Village***, 2m/3km N of St. Neots across River Great Ouse. **32 E2** TL1862.

Little Petherick *Cornw.* ***Village***, 4m/7km W of Wadebridge. **3 G1** SW9172.

Little Plumpton *Lancs.* ***Hamlet***, 3m/4km W of Kirkham. SD3832.

Little Plumstead *Norf.* ***Village***, 1m/2km NE of Plumstead. **45 H4** TG3112.

Little Ponton *Lincs.* ***Hamlet***, 1m/2km N of Great Ponton. **42 C2** SK9232.

Little Postbrook *Hants.* ***Settlement***, 1m/2km S of Titchfield and 3m/5km S of Park Gate. SU5304.

Little Potheridge *Devon* ***Hamlet***, forming locality of Potheridge, along with Great Potheridge and Potheridge Gate, 4m/6km SE of Great Torrington. SS5214.

Little Preston *Northants.* ***Settlement***, 1m/2km SE of Preston Capes and 5m/9km S of Daventry. SP5854.

Little Preston *W.Yorks.* ***Locality***, adjoining to E of Swillington, 1m/2km NW of Great Preston. SE3830.

Little Purston *Northants.* ***Settlement***, 4m/6km E of Banbury. SP5139.

Little Rack Wick *Ork.* ***Bay***, on W coast of Hoy, 2m/3km SE of Sneuk Head. **107 B8** ND2392.

Little Raveley *Cambs.* ***Village***, 1m/2km S of Great Raveley. **33 F1** TL2581.

Little Reedness *E.Riding* ***Hamlet***, adjoining to E of Reedness, 4m/6km E of Goole. SE8022.

L

Little Reynoldston *Swan.* ***Hamlet***, on Gower peninsula, 1km SE of Reynoldston. SS4889.
Little Ribston *N.Yorks.* ***Village***, 4m/6km SE of Knaresborough. Ribston Hall dates from 17c. **57 J4** SE3853.
Little Rissington *Glos.* ***Village***, 4m/6km S of Stow-on-the-Wold. **30 C6** SP1919.
Little Roe *Shet.* ***Island***, uninhabited island of about 70 acres or 30 hectares at S end of Yell Sound 2m/4km E of Ollaberry, Mainland. **108 D5** HU4079.
Little Rogart *High.* ***Settlement***, 1m/2km N of Rogart Station, Sutherland district. **96 E1** NC7204.
Little Rollright *Oxon.* ***Hamlet***, 2m/3km W of Great Rollright. King's Men, commonly known as Rollright Stones (English Heritage), is Bronze Age stone circle and Whispering Knights (English Heritage) is burial-chamber, respectively 1km N and 1km NE of Little Rollright. **30 D5** SP2930.
Little Ross *D. & G.* ***Island***, with lighthouse at entrance to Kirkcudbright Bay, at E extremity of Wigtown Bay. **65 G6** NX6543.
Little Rowsley *Derbys.* ***Hamlet***, adjoining to E of Rowsley, in River Derwent valley, 3m/5km SE of Bakewell. SK2565.
Little Ryburgh *Norf.* ***Hamlet***, 1km NE of Great Ryburgh. **44 D3** TF9527.
Little Ryle *Northumb.* ***Settlement***, 1m/2km S of Great Ryle. **71 F2** NU0111.
Little Ryton *Shrop.* ***Settlement***, adjoining to S of Great Ryton. SJ4803.
Little Salkeld *Cumb.* ***Hamlet***, 1m/2km SE of Great Salkeld across River Eden. **61 G3** NY5536.
Little Sampford *Essex* ***Village***, 2m/4km W of Finchingfield. **33 K5** TL6533.
Little Sandhurst *Brack.F.* ***Suburb***, residential locality adjoining to NW of Sandhurst. SU8361.
Little Saredon *Staffs.* ***Locality***, 1m/2km S of Great Saredon. SJ9307.
Little Saughall *Ches.* ***Hamlet***, 1m/2km SE of Saughall. SJ3670.
Little Saxham *Suff.* ***Hamlet***, 4m/6km W of Bury St. Edmunds. **34 B2** TL7862.
Little Scatwell *High.* ***Settlement***, at confluence of Rivers Conan and Meig, below Loch Luichart, Ross and Cromarty district. **95 K6** NH3956.
Little Sessay *N.Yorks.* ***Hamlet***, 1km SE of Sessay, 3m/4km SE of Dalton. SE4674.
Little Shelford *Cambs.* ***Village***, 5m/8km S of Cambridge. **33 H3** TL4551.
Little Shillay *W.Isles* ***Island***, islet to SW of Shillay. NF8790.
Little Shrawardine *Shrop.* ***Hamlet***, to W of Shrawardine across River Severn. Traces of motte and bailey castle. SJ4015.
Little Shurdington *Glos.* ***Settlement***, 4m/6km SW of Cheltenham. Site of Roman villa on hillside 1m/2km E. SO9117.
Little Silver *Devon* ***Hamlet***, 2m/3km NE of Crediton. SS8601.
Little Silver *Devon* ***Hamlet***, W of River Dart, 3m/5km SW of Tiverton. SS9109.
Little Singleton *Lancs.* ***Village***, 2m/3km E of Poulton-le-Fylde. SD3739.
Little Skerry *Ork.* ***Island***, most southerly of Pentland Skerries. ND4776.
Little Skipwith *N.Yorks.* ***Hamlet***, adjoining to NW of Skipwith, 3m/5km SE of Escrick. SE6538.
Little Smeaton *N.Yorks.* ***Settlement***, 1km S of Great Smeaton. NZ3403.
Little Smeaton *N.Yorks.* ***Village***, 6m/9km SE of Pontefract. **51 H1** SE5216.
Little Snoring *Norf.* ***Village***, 2m/3km S of Great Snoring. **44 D2** TF9434.
Little Sodbury *S.Glos.* ***Village***, 2m/3km E of Chipping Sodbury. **20 A3** ST7583.
Little Sodbury End *S.Glos.* ***Hamlet***, 1km NW of Little Sodbury. ST7583.
Little Somborne *Hants.* ***Hamlet***, 3m/4km SE of Stockbridge. **10 E1** SU3832.
Little Somerford *Wilts.* ***Village***, 3m/5km SE of Malmesbury. **20 C3** ST9684.
Little Soudley *Shrop.* ***Settlement***, 1km SW of Soudley. SJ7128.
Little Stainforth *N.Yorks.* ***Hamlet***, across River Ribble from Stainforth, 2m/4km N of Settle. SD8167.
Little Stainton *Darl.* ***Hamlet***, 5m/8km NE of Darlington. **62 E4** NZ3420.
Little Stanney *Ches.* ***Village***, 5m/8km N of Chester. **48 D5** SJ4174.
Little Staughton *Beds.* ***Village***, 3m/5km S of Kimbolton. **32 E2** TL1062.
Little Steeping *Lincs.* ***Hamlet***, 1m/2km S of Great Steeping. **53 H6** TF4362.
Little Stoke *S.Glos.* ***Locality***, adjoining to SE of Bradley Stoke, 6m/9km NE of Bristol city centre. ST6181.
Little Stoke *Staffs.* ***Suburb***, 1m/2km SE of Stone. SJ9132.
Little Stonham *Suff.* ***Village***, 4m/7km E of Stowmarket. **35 F3** TM1160.
Little Street *Cambs.* ***Hamlet***, 1km E of Little Downham. TL5383.
Little Stretton *Leics.* ***Village***, 6m/9km SE of Leicester. **41 J6** SK6600.
Little Stretton *Shrop.* ***Village***, 1m/2km SW of Church Stretton. **38 D6** SO4491.
Little Strickland *Cumb.* ***Village***, 2m/3km S of Great Strickland. **61 G4** NY5522.
Little Stukeley *Cambs.* ***Village***, 1m/2km NW of Great Stukeley. **33 F1** TL2174.
Little Sugnall *Staffs.* ***Settlement***, 1km NE of Sugnall. SJ8031.
Little Sutton *Ches.* ***Locality***, 1m/2km NW of Great Sutton. **48 C5** SJ3777.
Little Sutton *Shrop.* ***Locality***, 5m/8km N of Ludlow. SO5182.
Little Swinburne *Northumb.* ***Hamlet***, below Little Swinburne Reservoir, 1m/2km NE of Great Swinburne. **70 E6** NY9477.
Little Taff *English form of Taf Fechan, qv.*
Little Tangley *Surr.* ***Hamlet***, 3m/5km SE of Guildford. TQ0246.
Little Tarrington *Here.* ***Hamlet***, 7m/11km E of Hereford. SO6241.
Little Tew *Oxon.* ***Village***, 5m/7km E of Chipping Norton. **30 E6** SP3828.
Little Tey *Essex* ***Hamlet***, 2m/3km W of Marks Tey. **34 C6** TL8923.
Little Thetford *Cambs.* ***Village***, 3m/4km S of Ely. **33 J1** TL5376.
Little Thirkleby *N.Yorks.* ***Hamlet***, adjoining to S of Thirkleby. **57 K2** SE4778.
Little Thornage *Norf.* ***Settlement***, on W bank of River Glaven, 1m/2km W of Holt. TG0538.
Little Thorness *I.o.W.* ***Settlement***, 3m/4km SW of Cowes. SZ4593.
Little Thornton *Lancs.* ***Settlement***, adjoining to SE of Thornton. SD3541.
Little Thorpe *Dur.* ***Hamlet***, 1km SE of Easington. **63 F2** NZ4242.
Little Thorpe *W.Yorks.* ***Locality***, adjoining to W of Roberttown, 1m/2km SW of Liversedge. SE1922.
Little Thurlow *Suff.* ***Settlement***, adjoining to N of Great Thurlow, 3m/5km N of Haverhill. **33 K3** TL6751.
Little Thurlow Green *Suff.* ***Settlement***, to NE of Little Thurlow, 4m/6km N of Haverhill. TL6851.
Little Thurrock *Thur.* ***Locality***, 2m/3km NW of Tilbury. **24 C4** TQ6279.
Little Torboll *High.* ***Settlement***, 5m/8km W of Golspie. **96 E2** NH7598.
Little Torrington *Devon* ***Village***, 1m/2km S of Great Torrington. **6 C4** SS4916.
Little Tosson *Northumb.* ***Settlement***, 3m/5km W of Rothbury. With Great Tosson, it forms parish of Tosson. NU0101.
Little Totham *Essex* ***Village***, 2m/3km E of Great Totham. **34 C7** TL8511.
Little Town *Cumb.* ***Settlement***, 1m/2km S of Stair. **60 D5** NY2319.
Little Town *Lancs.* ***Settlement***, 1km E of Ribchester, on W side of River Ribble. SD6535.
Little Town *Warr.* ***Hamlet***, 1m/2km SW of Culcheth. SJ6494.
Little Twycross *Leics.* ***Settlement***, to NE of Twycross. SK3305.
Little Urswick *Cumb.* ***Village***, 1km SW of Urswick. **55 F2** SD2674.
Little Wakering *Essex* Population: 2577. ***Village***, 2m/4km N of Shoeburyness. **25 F3** TQ9388.
Little Walden *Essex* ***Village***, 2m/3km N of Saffron Walden. **33 J4** TL5441.
Little Waldingfield *Suff.* ***Village***, 4m/7km NE of Sudbury. **34 D4** TL9245.
Little Walsingham *Norf.* ***Village***, 1m/2km SW of Great Walsingham. Noted as place of pilgrimage to Shrine of Our Lady of Walsingham. 18c Walsingham Abbey with remains of medieval Augustinian priory. **44 D2** TF9336.
Little Waltham *Essex* ***Village***, 4m/6km N of Chelmsford. **34 B7** TL7112.
Little Warford *Ches.* ***Locality***, to S of Great Warford. SJ8077.
Little Warley *Essex* ***Settlement***, 2m/4km S of Brentwood. **24 C2** TQ6090.
Little Washbourne *Glos.* ***Hamlet***, 4m/6km NW of Winchcombe. SO9933.
Little Water *Aber.* ***River***, running S to join River Ythan near Chapelhaugh, 2m/3km NW of Methlick. **99 G6** NJ8439.
Little Water of Fleet *D. & G.* ***River***, running S from Loch Fleet into Water of Fleet, 3m/5km N of Gatehouse of Fleet. **65 F4** NX5860.
Little Weighton *E.Riding* ***Village***, 8m/12km NW of Kingston upon Hull. **59 F6** SE9833.
Little Welland *Worcs.* ***Settlement***, 6m/10km NW of Tewkesbury. **29 H5** SO8038.
Little Welnetham *Suff.* ***Hamlet***, 1km E of Great Welnetham. **34 C3** TL8960.
Little Welton *Lincs.* ***Hamlet***, 1m/2km W of Louth. TF3087.
Little Wenham *Suff.* ***Hamlet***, 4m/7km SE of Hadleigh. **34 E5** TM0839.
Little Wenlock *Tel. & W.* ***Village***, 3m/5km S of Wellington. **39 F5** SJ6406.
Little Weston *Som.* ***Hamlet***, 1km E of Sparkford. ST6225.
Little Whernside *N.Yorks.* ***Mountain***, on E side of Coverdale head, 5m/8km NE of Kettlewell. Height 1984 feet or 605 metres. **57 F2** SE0277.
Little Whitefield *I.o.W.* ***Hamlet***, 2m/3km S of Ryde. SZ5889.
Little Whittingham Green *Suff.* ***Settlement***, 1m/2km SE of Fressingfield. **35 G1** TM2876.
Little Whittington *Northumb.* ***Settlement***, 3m/5km N of Corbridge. **70 E7** NY9969.
Little Wigborough *Essex* ***Settlement***, 1km E of Great Wigborough. TL9815.
Little Wilbraham *Cambs.* ***Hamlet***, 6m/9km E of Cambridge city centre. **33 J3** TL5458.
Little Wishford *Wilts.* ***Settlement***, 1km N of Great Wishford. SU0736.
Little Witchingham *Norf.* ***Locality***, 1m/2km E of Great Witchingham. TG1020.
Little Witcombe *Glos.* ***Hamlet***, 5m/8km SE of Gloucester. **29 J7** SO9115.
Little Witley *Worcs.* ***Village***, 7m/11km NW of Worcester. **29 G2** SO7863.
Little Wittenham *Oxon.* ***Village***, 4m/6km NW of Wallingford. **21 J2** SU5693.
Little Wittingham Green *Suff.* ***Settlement***, 1m/2km E of Fressingfield. TM2876.
Little Wolford *Warks.* ***Village***, 3m/5km S of Shipston on Stour. **30 D5** SP2635.
Little Woodcote *Gt.Lon.* ***Settlement***, in borough of Sutton, 2m/3km W of Purley. TQ2861.
Little Woolgarston *Dorset* ***Settlement***, 1km SE of Corfe Castle. SY9781.
Little Woolstone *M.K.* ***Village***, in Woolstone locality, E of Milton Keynes. **32 B5** SP8739.
Little Worth *Tel. & W.* ***Settlement***, 3m/5km S of Wellington. SJ6506.
Little Wratting *Suff.* ***Hamlet***, 2m/3km NE of Haverhill. **33 K4** TL6947.
Little Wymington *Beds.* ***Settlement***, adjoining to N of Wymington and to S of Rushden. SP9565.
Little Wymondley *Herts.* ***Village***, 3m/4km SE of Hitchin. **33 F6** TL2127.
Little Wyrley *Staffs.* ***Hamlet***, 1m/2km SE of Great Wyrley. **40 C5** SJ9907.
Little Wytheford *Shrop.* ***Settlement***, 1km NW of Great Wytheford. SJ5619.
Little Wyvis *High.* ***Mountain***, in Strathgarve Forest, Ross and Cromarty district, 3m/5km NE of Garve. Height 2506 feet or 764 metres. **96 B5** NH4264.
Little Yeldham *Essex* ***Village***, 4m/6km S of Clare. **34 B5** TL7739.
Littlebeck *N.Yorks.* ***Settlement***, 4m/6km S of Whitby. **63 K6** NZ8704.
Littleborough *Devon* ***Settlement***, to W of Puddington, 6m/10km N of Crediton. SS8210.
Littleborough *Gt.Man.* Population: 13,638. ***Town***, 3m/5km NE of Rochdale. **49 J1** SD9316.
Littleborough *Notts.* ***Hamlet***, on W bank of River Trent, on site of Roman station of Segelocum, 4m/7km S of Gainsborough. **52 B4** SK8282.
Littlebourne *Kent* ***Village***, 4m/6km E of Canterbury. **15 G2** TR2057.
Littlebredy (Also spelled Little Bredy.) *Dorset* ***Village***, 6m/10km W of Dorchester. **8 E6** SY5889.
Littlebury *Essex* ***Village***, 2m/3km NW of Saffron Walden. **33 J5** TL5139.
Littlebury Green *Essex* ***Hamlet***, 3m/5km W of Saffron Walden. **33 H5** TL4838.
Littlecott *Wilts.* ***Settlement***, across River Avon from Enford, 2m/3km S of Upavon. SU1451.
Littledale *Lancs.* ***Locality***, 6m/9km E of Lancaster. SD5661.
Littledean *Glos.* ***Village***, 1m/2km E of Cinderford. **29 F7** SO6713.
Littledean Hall *Glos.* ***Historic house***, on S side of Littledean, 1m/2km SE of Cinderford. Hall dating from 13c, with 17c interior and restored Roman remains of a 2c-3c water shrine in gardens. **29 F7** SO6712.
Littleferry *High.* ***Locality***, in Sutherland district, on N side of entrance to Loch Fleet, 3m/5km SW of Golspie. **97 F2** NH8095.
Littlefield Green *W. & M.* ***Hamlet***, 3m/5km SW of Maidenhead. SU8676.
Littleham *Devon* ***Village***, 2m/3km S of Bideford. **6 C3** SS4323.
Littleham *Devon* ***Village***, 2m/3km E of Exmouth. **7 J7** SY0281.
Littlehampton *W.Suss.* Population: 50,408. ***Town***, port and coastal resort with sandy beach at mouth of River Arun, 8m/12km W of Worthing. Site of Roman villa 1km NE of town centre. **12 D6** TQ0202.
Littlehempston *Devon* ***Village***, 2m/3km NE of Totnes. **5 J4** SX8162.
Littlehoughton *Northumb.* ***Settlement***, 1m/2km NW of Longhoughton. **71 H2** NU2316.
Littlemill *E.Ayr.* ***Settlement***, 2m/3km S of Drongan. **67 J2** NS4515.
Littlemill *High.* ***Settlement***, in Nairn district, 4m/7km SE of Nairn. **97 G6** NH9150.
Littlemill *Northumb.* ***Locality***, 1m/2km E of Rennington. NU2218.
Littlemoor *Derbys.* ***Suburb***, 1m/2km N of Chesterfield town centre. SK3773.
Littlemoor *Derbys.* ***Village***, 2m/3km W of Clay Cross. SK3662.
Littlemoor *Dorset* ***Village***, 2m/3km N of Weymouth town centre. SY6883.
Littlemore *Oxon.* ***Suburb***, 3m/4km SE of Oxford. **21 J1** SP5302.
Littlemoss *Gt.Man.* ***Settlement***, 1m/2km NW of Ashton-under-Lyne. SJ9199.
Littleover *Derby* ***Suburb***, 2m/3km SW of Derby city centre. **41 F2** SK3334.
Littleport *Cambs.* Population: 5780. ***Village***, 5m/7km NE of Ely. **43 J7** TL5686.
Littleport Bridge *Cambs.* ***Locality***, 1m/2km NE of Littleport. TL5686.
Littler *Ches.* ***Suburb***, 1m/2km W of Winsford. SJ6366.
Littlestead Green *Oxon.* ***Hamlet***, 3m/4km NE of Reading. SU7377.
Littlestone-on-Sea *Kent* ***Town***, resort on St. Mary's Bay, 1m/2km E of New Romney. **15 F5** TR0824.
Littlethorpe *N.Yorks.* ***Village***, 2m/3km S of Ripon. **57 J3** SE3269.
Littleton *Ches.* ***Village***, 2m/4km E of Chester. **48 D6** SJ4466.
Littleton *Dundee* ***Settlement***, in Sidlaw Hills, 4m/6km NW of Longforgan. **82 D4** NO2633.
Littleton *Hants.* ***Village***, 3m/4km NW of Winchester. Flowerdown Barrows (English Heritage), Bronze Age burial site to SE. **11 F1** SU4532.
Littleton *Som.* ***Hamlet***, 1m/2km N of Somerton. **8 D1** ST4930.
Littleton *Surr.* ***Hamlet***, on S edge of Queen Mary Reservoir, 2m/3km NE of Chertsey. **22 D5** TQ0768.
Littleton *Wilts.* ***Locality***, 2m/4km S of Melksham. ST9060.
Littleton Down *Wilts.* ***Open space***, hillslope on Salisbury Plain rising to 193 metres, 2m/4km SW of West Lavington. **20 C6** ST9751.
Littleton Drew *Wilts.* ***Village***, 7m/11km NW of Chippenham. **20 B3** ST8380.
Littleton-on-Severn *S.Glos.* ***Village***, 3m/4km W of Thornbury. **19 J3** ST5989.
Littleton Panell *Wilts.* ***Village***, 5m/7km S of Devizes. **20 C6** ST9953.

Littletown *Devon* ***Suburb***, to S of Honiton town centre. SY1699.
Littletown *Dur.* ***Village***, 1km N of Sherburn Hill. **62 E2** NZ3443.
Littletown *I.o.W.* ***Settlement***, 3m/4km NE of Newport. SZ5390.
Littletown *W.Yorks.* ***Suburb***, to W of Heckmondwike. SE2024.
Littlewick Green *W. & M.* ***Village***, 3m/5km W of Maidenhead. Site of Roman building to S. **22 B4** SU8479.
Littlewindsor *Dorset* ***Hamlet***, 1m/2km N of Broadwindsor. ST4404.
Littlewood *Staffs.* ***Suburb***, 2m/3km S of Cannock. SJ9807.
Littleworth *Beds.* ***Settlement***, 4m/6km SE of Bedford. TL0744.
Littleworth *Glos.* ***Hamlet***, adjoining to W of Chipping Campden. SP1439.
Littleworth *Oxon.* ***Village***, 2m/3km NE of Faringdon. **21 G2** SU3197.
Littleworth *S.Yorks.* ***Settlement***, adjoining to E of Rossington. SK6398.
Littleworth *Staffs.* ***Locality***, 2m/4km NE of Cannock. **40 C4** SK0111.
Littleworth *Staffs.* ***Suburb***, E district of Stafford. SJ9323.
Littleworth *Worcs.* ***Village***, 4m/6km SE of Worcester. **29 H3** SO8850.
Littleworth End *Cambs.* ***Locality***, S end of Offord D'Arcy, 4m/6km SW of Huntingdon. TL2265.
Littleworth End *Warks.* ***Settlement***, 3m/4km NE of Sutton Coldfield. SP1718.
Littley Green *Essex* ***Hamlet***, 5m/9km SE of Great Dunmow. **33 K7** TL6917.
Litton *Derbys.* ***Village***, 1m/2km E of Tideswell. **50 D5** SK1675.
Litton *N.Yorks.* ***Village***, in Littondale, 2m/3km NW of Arncliffe. **56 E2** SD9074.
Litton *Som.* ***Village***, 6m/10km NE of Wells. **19 J6** ST5954.
Litton Cheney *Dorset* ***Village***, 6m/9km E of Bridport. **8 E5** SY5590.
Littondale *N.Yorks.* ***Valley***, deeply incised valley carrying River Skirfare SE from Halton Gill to join River Wharfe in Wharfedale. **56 E2** SD9272.
Liurbost (Anglicised form: Leurbost.) *W.Isles* ***Village***, on Isle of Lewis, 6m/9km SW of Stornoway, near head of long inlet, Loch Leurbost. **101 F5** NB3725.
Liuthaid *W.Isles* ***Mountain***, 1m/2km E of head of Loch Langavat. Height 1614 feet or 492 metres. **100 D6** NB1713.
Liver *Arg. & B.* ***River***, running W down Glen Liver into Loch Etive, Argyll, on S side of Inverliver Bay, 4m/6km NE of Bonawe. **80 C4** NN0635.
Liverpool *Mersey.* Population: 481,786. ***City***, major port and industrial city on River Mersey estuary, 178m/286km NW of London. Originally a fishing village it experienced rapid expansion during early 18c due to transatlantic trade in sugar, spice and tobacco and was involved in slave trade. Docks declined during 20c, now Albert Dock is home to shops, museums and Liverpool's Tate Gallery. In 19c a multicultural city developed as Liverpool docks were point of departure for Europeans emigrating to America and Australia. Also became home to refugees from Irish potato famine of 1845. Present day Liverpool is home to variety of industries and many museums and art galleries. Also home of the Beatles, who performed at Liverpool's Cavern Club. Universities. Modern Anglican and Roman Catholic cathedrals. On Pier Head the famous Royal Liver Building is situated, topped by Liver Birds. Railway tunnel and two road tunnels under River Mersey to Wirral peninsula. Airport at Speke, 6m/10km. **48 C3** SJ3490.
Liverpool (Aintree) Racecourse (Commonly known as Aintree Racecourse.) *Mersey.* ***Racecourse***, to S of Aintree, 6m/10km N of Liverpool. One three-day National Hunt event each year, at which Grand National is staged. **48 C3** SJ3898.
Liverpool Bay *Mersey.* ***Bay***, stretches from Formby Point to Hoylake. **47 J3** SJ3490.
Liverpool Cathedral *Mersey.* ***Ecclesiastical building***, in Liverpool city centre. Built in Gothic Revival style to designs by Sir Giles Gilbert Scott and completed, after 75 years of work, in 1978. Largest church in Britain. **48 C4** SJ3589.
Liverpool Metropolitan Roman Catholic Cathedral *Mersey.* ***Ecclesiastical building***, in Liverpool city centre. Designed by Sir Frederick Gibberd and built 1962-67. Unusual modern design. **48 C3** SJ3590.
Liversedge *W.Yorks.* Population: 13,575. ***Town***, 3m/5km NW of Dewsbury. **57 G7** SE2024.
Liverton *Devon* ***Hamlet***, 4m/7km NW of Newton Abbot. **5 J3** SX8075.
Liverton *R. & C.* ***Village***, 2m/3km S of Loftus. **63 J5** NZ7115.
Liverton Mines *R. & C.* ***Locality***, quarry and disused mine workings, 1m/2km N of Liverton. NZ7017.
Liverton Street *Kent* ***Settlement***, 2m/3km SW of Lenham. **14 D3** TQ8750.
Livesey Street *Kent* ***Settlement***, 1km N of Teston. TQ7054.
Livet (Also known as Livet Water.) ***River***, rising in Blackwater Forest and flowing NW down Glenlivet to River Avon, 8m/12km N of Tomintoul. **89 K2** NJ1830.
Livet Water *Alternative name for (River) Livet, qv.*
Livingston *W.Loth.* Population: 41,647. ***Town***, manufacturing town, 13m/21km W of Edinburgh. New town, designated 1962, now noted for hi-tech industries. Calder House has links with John Knox. **75 J4** NT0568.
Livingston Mill Farm *W.Loth. Alternative name for Almond Valley Heritage Centre*
Livingston Station *W.Loth.* ***Locality***, 2m/4km W of Livingston town centre. NT0568.
Livingston Village *W.Loth.* ***Village***, 1m/2km SW of Livingston. **75 J4** NT0568.
Lixwm *Flints.* ***Hamlet***, 3m/5km S of Holywell. **47 K5** SJ1671.
Liza *Cumb.* ***River***, rising below Windy Gap on Great Gable and flowing W into Ennerdale Water from where it emerges as River Ehen. **60 C5** NY1214.
Lizard *Cornw.* ***Village***, on Lizard peninsula, 1km NE of Lizard Point. **2 D7** SW7012.
Lizard Point *Cornw.* ***Coastal feature***, headland at most southerly point of British mainland. **2 D7** SW6911.
Llafar *Gwyn.* ***River***, running SE into Llyn Tegid. **37 H2** SH8932.
Llaingarreglwyd *Cere.* ***Settlement***, 2m/3km E of New Quay. SN4158.
Llaingoch *I.o.A.* ***Locality***, adjoining to W of Holyhead. **46 A4** SH2382.
Llaithddu *Powys* ***Locality***, 2m/4km NW of Llanbadarn Fynydd. **37 K7** SO0680.
Llampha *V. of Glam.* ***Settlement***, 3m/5km S of Bridgend. SS9275.
Llan *Powys* ***Hamlet***, 1m/2km SW of Llanbrynmair. **37 H5** SH8800.
Llan-dafel *B.Gwent* ***Settlement***, 2m/3km W of Abertillery. **18 E1** SO1804.
Llan-dawg *Carmar. Welsh form of Llandawke, qv.*
Llan-fair *V. of Glam. Welsh form of St. Mary Church, qv.*
Llan Ffestiniog *Gwyn. See Ffestiniog.*
Llan-lwy *Pembs. Welsh form of Llandeloy, qv.*
Llan-mill *Pembs.* ***Hamlet***, 2m/3km E of Narberth. SN1414.
Llan Sain Siôr *Conwy Welsh form of St. George, qv.*
Llan Sain Siôr *V. of Glam. Welsh form of St. George's, qv.*
Llan-soe *Mon. See Llansoy.*
Llan-wen Hill *Powys* ***Mountain***, 2m/3km S of Knighton. Height 1322 feet or 403 metres. **28 C2** SO2969.
Llan-y-pwll *Wrex.* ***Hamlet***, 2m/4km E of Wrexham. **48 C7** SJ3751.
Llanaber *Gwyn.* ***Hamlet***, on coast, 2m/3km NW of Barmouth. **37 F4** SH6017.
Llanaelhaearn *Gwyn.* ***Village***, on pass to E of Yr Eifl, 6m/10km N of Pwllheli. **36 C1** SH3844.
Llanaeron *Cere.* ***Settlement***, 2m/3km SE of Aberaeron. **26 D2** SN4760.
Llanafan *Cere.* ***Hamlet***, 9m/14km SE of Aberystwyth. Remains of Roman fort 1m/2km W. **27 F1** SN6872.
Llanafan-fawr *Powys* ***Hamlet***, 5m/9km NW of Builth Wells. **27 J3** SN9655.
Llanafan-fechan *Powys* ***Settlement***, 1m/2km E of Garth. **27 J3** SN9750.
Llanallgo *I.o.A.* ***Hamlet***, near E coast of Anglesey, 6m/10km SE of Amlwch. **46 C4** SH5085.
Llanandras *Powys Welsh form of Presteigne, qv.*
Llananno *Powys* ***Locality***, 1m/2km NW of Llanbister. SO0974.
Llanarmon *Gwyn.* ***Settlement***, 4m/6km NE of Pwllheli. **36 D2** SH4239.
Llanarmon Dyffryn Ceiriog *Wrex.* ***Village***, on River Ceiriog, 7m/11km SW of Llangollen. **38 A2** SJ1532.
Llanarmon-yn-Ial *Denb.* ***Village***, on River Alun, 4m/7km E of Ruthin. **47 K7** SJ1956.
Llanarth (Llannarth). *Cere.* ***Village***, 3m/4km SE of New Quay. **26 D3** SN4257.
Llanarth *Mon.* ***Village***, 3m/5km NW of Raglan. **28 C7** SO3710.
Llanarthne *Carmar. Welsh form of Llanarthney, qv.*
Llanarthney (Llanarthne). *Carmar.* ***Village***, 6m/10km W of Llandeilo. **17 J2** SN5320.
Llanasa *Flints.* ***Village***, 3m/4km E of Prestatyn. **47 K4** SJ1081.
Llanbabo *I.o.A.* ***Settlement***, on Anglesey, 1m/2km N of Llyn Alaw dam. **46 B4** SH3786.
Llanbadarn Fawr *Cere.* ***Suburb***, 1m/2km SE of Aberystwyth town centre. Llanbadarn Church, founded in 6c by St. Padarn is site of oldest bishopric in Wales. **36 E7** SN6080.
Llanbadarn Fynydd *Powys* ***Village***, 9m/15km S of Newtown. **27 K1** SO0977.
Llanbadarn-y-garreg *Powys* ***Hamlet***, on River Edw, 5m/7km E of Builth Wells. **28 A4** SO1148.
Llanbadoc (Llanbadog). *Mon.* ***Hamlet***, 1km S of Usk across River Usk. **19 G1** SO3700.
Llanbadog *Mon. Welsh form of Llanbadoc, qv.*
Llanbadrig *I.o.A.* ***Settlement***, on N coast of Anglesey, to E of Cemaes Bay. **46 B3** SH3794.
Llanbeder (Llanbedr). *Newport* ***Village***, 3m/5km NW of Magor. **19 G2** ST3890.
Llanbedr *Gwyn.* ***Village***, on River Artro, 3m/5km S of Harlech. **36 E3** SH5826.
Llanbedr *Newport Welsh form of Llanbeder, qv.*
Llanbedr *Powys* ***Settlement***, 2m/3km W of Painscastle. **28 A4** SO1446.
Llanbedr *Powys* ***Village***, 2m/3km NE of Crickhowell. **28 B6** SO2320.
Llanbedr-Dyffryn-Clwyd *Denb.* ***Village***, 1m/2km NE of Ruthin. **47 K7** SJ1459.
Llanbedr Felffre *Pembs. Welsh form of Lampeter Velfrey, qv.*
Llanbedr Gwynllwg *Newport Welsh form of Peterstone Wentlooge, qv.*
Llanbedr Hill *Powys* ***Mountain***, 2m/3km NW of Painscastle. Height 1532 feet or 467 metres. **28 A4** SO1348.
Llanbedr Pont Steffan *Cere. Welsh form of Lampeter, qv.*
Llanbedr-y-cennin *Conwy* ***Village***, 5m/8km S of Conwy. **47 F6** SH7669.
Llanbedr-y-fro *V. of Glam. Welsh form of Peterston-super-Ely, qv.*
Llanbedrgoch *I.o.A.* ***Village***, near E coast of Anglesey, 4m/7km NE of Llangefni. **46 D4** SH5180.
Llanbedrog *Gwyn.* ***Village***, 4m/6km SW of Pwllheli. **36 C2** SH3231.
Llanbedrog Point *Gwyn. English form of Trwyn Llanbedrog, qv.*
Llanberis *Gwyn.* Population: 1859. ***Small town***, in former slate-quarrying district, 6m/10km E of Caernarfon at foot of Pass of Llanberis. Town is N terminus of Snowdon Mountain Railway. Popular centre for climbers and walkers. To SE, overlooking Llyn Peris, are largely 13c remains of Dolbadarn Castle. **46 D6** SH5760.
Llanberis Lake Railway *Gwyn.* ***Other feature of interest***, restored section of former slate-carrying railway running along NE shore of Llyn Padarn. **46 D6** SH5866.
Llanbethery (Llanbydderi). *V. of Glam.* ***Village***, 5m/8km W of Barry. **18 D5** ST0369.
Llanbister *Powys* ***Village***, on River Ithon, 8m/12km N of Llandrindod Wells. **28 A1** SO1073.
Llanblethian (Llanfleiddan). *V. of Glam.* ***Village***, adjoining to SW of Cowbridge. Remains of medieval castle. **18 C4** SS9874.
Llanboidy *Carmar.* ***Village***, 4m/7km N of Whitland. **17 F2** SN2123.
Llanbradach *Caerp.* Population: 3828. ***Village***, 2m/4km N of Caerphilly. **18 E2** ST1490.
Llanbrynmair *Powys* ***Village***, 5m/8km E of Cemmaes Rd. **37 H5** SH8902.
Llanbydderi *V. of Glam. Welsh form of Llanbethery, qv.*
Llancadle (Llancatal). *V. of Glam.* ***Hamlet***, 5m/7km W of Barry. ST0368.
Llancaeach *Caerp. Welsh form of Llancaiach, qv.*
Llancaeo *Mon. Welsh form of Llancayo, qv.*
Llancaiach (Llancaeach). *Caerp.* ***Locality***, 1m/2km SE of Treharris. ST1196.
Llancarfan *V. of Glam.* ***Village***, 4m/7km NW of Barry. **18 D4** ST0570.
Llancatal *V. of Glam. Welsh form of Llancadle, qv.*
Llancayo (Llancaeo). *Mon.* ***Settlement***, 1m/2km N of Usk. **19 G1** SO3603.
Llancillo *Here.* ***Locality***, 3m/4km SW of Pontrilas. SO3625.
Llancloudy *Here.* ***Hamlet***, 5m/8km N of Monmouth. SO4920.
Llancynfelyn *Cere.* ***Settlement***, 2m/3km N of Talybont. **37 F6** SN6492.
Llandaf *Cardiff Welsh form of Llandaff, qv.*
Llandaff (Llandaf). *Cardiff* ***Suburb***, 2m/3km NW of Cardiff city centre. Cathedral of 12c-13c. **18 E4** ST1578.
Llandaff North *Cardiff* ***Suburb***, of Cardiff, to N of Llandaff across River Taff. **18 E4** ST1578.
Llandanwg *Gwyn.* ***Village***, on Tremadog Bay, 2m/3km S of Harlech. **36 E3** SH5728.
Llandarcy *N.P.T.* ***Locality***, 3m/4km SW of Neath. Oil refinery. SS7195.
Llandawke (Llan-dawg). *Carmar.* ***Hamlet***, 3m/5km S of St. Clears. **17 F3** SN2811.
Llanddaniel Fab *I.o.A.* ***Village***, on Anglesey, 4m/6km W of Menai Bridge. **46 C5** SH4970.
Llanddarog *Carmar.* ***Village***, 6m/10km E of Carmarthen. **17 J3** SN5016.
Llanddeiniol *Cere.* ***Hamlet***, 6m/10km S of Aberystwyth. **26 E1** SN5672.
Llanddeiniolen *Gwyn.* ***Hamlet***, 4m/7km SW of Bangor. **46 D6** SH5466.
Llandderfel *Gwyn.* ***Village***, in River Dee valley, 4m/6km E of Bala. **37 J2** SH9837.
Llanddeusant *Carmar.* ***Locality***, 6m/10km S of Llandovery. **27 G6** SN7724.
Llanddeusant *I.o.A.* ***Village***, on Anglesey, 6m/9km S of Cemaes Bay. **46 B4** SH3485.
Llanddew *Powys* ***Village***, 1m/2km NE of Brecon. Scant remains of former palace of Bishops of St. David's. **27 K5** SO0530.
Llanddewi *Swan.* ***Hamlet***, on Gower peninsula, 3m/5km N of Port Eynon Point and 12m/20km W of Swansea. **17 H6** SS4689.
Llanddewi-Brefi *Cere.* ***Village***, 3m/5km SW of Tregaron. **27 F3** SN6655.
Llanddewi Felffre *Pembs. Welsh form of Llanddewi Velfrey, qv.*
Llanddewi Nant Hodni *Mon. Welsh form of Llanthony, qv.*
Llanddewi Rhydderch *Mon.* ***Village***, 3m/5km E of Abergavenny. **28 C7** SO3512.
Llanddewi Velfrey (Llanddewi Felffre). *Pembs.* ***Village***, 3m/5km W of Whitland. **16 E3** SN1416.
Llanddewi Ystradenni *Powys* ***Hamlet***, 6m/9km NE of Llandrindod Wells. **28 A2** SO1068.
Llanddewi'r Cwm *Powys* ***Settlement***, 2m/3km S of Builth Wells. **27 K4** SO0348.
Llanddingad *Mon. Welsh form of Dingestow, qv.*
Llanddinol *Mon. Welsh form of Itton, qv.*
Llanddoged *Conwy* ***Village***, 1m/2km N of Llanrwst. **47 G6** SH8063.
Llanddona *I.o.A.* ***Village***, on Anglesey, 3m/5km NW of Beaumaris. **46 D5** SH5779.
Llanddowror *Carmar.* ***Village***, 2m/3km SW of St. Clears. Site of Roman fort 2km S. **17 F3** SN2514.
Llanddulas *Conwy* ***Village***, 2m/4km W of Abergele. **47 H5** SH9078.
Llanddunwyd *V. of Glam. Welsh form of Welsh St. Donats, qv.*
Llanddwyn Bay *I.o.A.* ***Bay***, to E of Llanddwyn Island, on SW coast of Anglesey. **46 B6** SH3862.
Llanddwyn Island *I.o.A.* ***Coastal feature***, peninsula on SW coast of Anglesey, 3m/5km SW of Newborough. **46 B6** SH3862.
Llanddwywe *Gwyn.* ***Hamlet***, 4m/7km N of Barmouth. **36 E3** SH5822.
Llanddyfnan *I.o.A.* ***Settlement***, 1m/2km W of Pentraeth. **46 C5** SH5078.
Llandecwyn *Gwyn.* ***Locality***, 3m/5km SW of Maentwrog. SH6337.
Llandefaelog Fach *Powys* ***Settlement***, 3m/4km N of Brecon. **27 K5** SO0332.
Llandefalle (Llandyfalle). *Powys* ***Hamlet***, 3m/5km W of Talgarth. **28 A5** SO1035.
Llandegai *Gwyn. See Llandygai.*
Llandegfan *I.o.A.* ***Village***, on Anglesey, 1m/2km NE of Menai Bridge. **46 D5** SH5673.
Llandegfedd *Mon. Welsh form of Llandegveth, qv.*
Llandegfedd Reservoir *Mon.* ***Reservoir***, large reservoir on border with Torfaen, 3m/5km W of Usk. Popular location for water sports. **19 G2** ST3299.
Llandegla *Denb.* ***Hamlet***, 6m/9km SE of Ruthin. **47 K7** SJ1952.

L

Llandegley *Powys* ***Hamlet***, 2m/3km SE of Penybont. **28 A2** SO1362.
Llandegley Rhos *Powys* ***Open space***, area of low hills 1m/2km S of Llandegley. **28 A2** SO1160.
Llandegveth (Llandegfedd). *Mon.* ***Village***, 4m/7km SW of Usk. Llandegfedd Reservoir is 2m/4km N. **19 G2** ST3395.
Llandegwning *Gwyn.* ***Locality***, 3m/5km NW of Abersoch. **36 B2** SH2630.
Llandeilo *Carmar.* Population: 1666. ***Small town***, on River Tywi near its confluence with River Cennen, 14m/22km E of Carmarthen. Interesting single span bridge across river. **17 K2** SN6322.
Llandeilo Abercywyn *Carmar.* ***Settlement***, 1m/2km N of Laugharne, on E bank of River Taf. **17 G3** SN3113.
Llandeilo Bertholau *Mon.* *Welsh form of Llantilio Pertholey, qv.*
Llandeilo Ferwallt *Swan.* *Welsh form of Bishopston, qv.*
Llandeilo Graban *Powys* ***Hamlet***, 5m/8km SE of Builth Wells. **27 K4** SO0944.
Llandeilo Gresynni *Mon.* *Welsh form of Llantilio Crossenny, qv.*
Llandeilo Hill *Powys* ***Mountain***, 4m/7km W of Painscastle. Height 1440 feet or 439 metres. **27 K4** SO1047.
Llandeilo'r-Fan *Powys* ***Hamlet***, 4m/6km NW of Sennybridge. **27 H5** SN8934.
Llandeloy (Llan-lwy). *Pembs.* ***Village***, 7m/11km E of St. David's. **16 B2** SM8526.
Llandenni *Mon.* *Welsh form of Llandenny, qv.*
Llandenny (Llandenni). *Mon.* ***Village***, 3m/5km NE of Usk. **19 H1** SO4103.
Llandevaud *Newport* ***Village***, 3m/4km NW of Magor. ST4090.
Llandevenny *Mon.* ***Hamlet***, 1m/2km W of Magor. **19 H3** ST4186.
Llandilo *Pembs.* ***Hamlet***, 1m/2km W of Llangolman. SN1027.
Llandinabo *Here.* ***Settlement***, 6m/10km NW of Ross-on-Wye. **28 E6** SO5128.
Llandinam *Powys* ***Village***, on River Severn, 2m/4km S of Caersws. **37 K7** SO0288.
Llandissilio *Pembs.* ***Village***, 5m/7km N of Narberth. **16 E2** SN1221.
Llandoche *V. of Glam.* *Welsh form of Llandough, qv.*
Llandogo *Mon.* ***Village***, on River Wye, 6m/10km N of Chepstow. **19 J1** SO5204.
Llandough *V. of Glam.* ***Hamlet***, 1m/2km S of Cowbridge. **18 C4** SS9972.
Llandough (Llandoche). *V. of Glam.* ***Suburb***, N district of Penarth. **18 E4** ST1673.
Llandovery (Llanymddyfri). *Carmar.* Population: 2037. ***Small town***, at confluence of Rivers Brân and Gwydderig; and 1m/2km above confluence of Rivers Brân and Tywi, 17m/28km W of Brecon. Scant remains of Norman castle. **27 G5** SN7634.
Llandow (Llandw). *V. of Glam.* ***Village***, 4m/6km W of Cowbridge. **18 C4** SS9473.
Llandow Industrial Estate *V. of Glam.* ***Locality***, 1m/2km SE of Llandow, in parish of Llantwit Major. SS9572.
Llandre *Carmar.* ***Settlement***, 1km W of Login. **16 E2** SN1523.
Llandre *Carmar.* ***Settlement***, 1m/2km NE of Pumsaint. **27 F4** SN6741.
Llandre (Also known as Llanfihangel Genau'r-glyn.) *Cere.* ***Village***, 4m/7km NE of Aberystwyth. **37 F7** SN6286.
Llandrillo *Denb.* ***Village***, on River Ceidiog, 5m/8km SW of Corwen. **37 K2** SJ0337.
Llandrillo-yn-Rhôs *Conwy* ***Suburb***, NW district of Colwyn Bay. **47 G4** SH8380.
Llandrindod Wells *Powys* Population: 4362. ***Small town***, spa town 30m/48km NW of Hereford. Noted for wealth of Victorian architecture. Roman camp of Castellcollen 1m/2km N. Ruined 13c Cefnllys Castle 2m/3km E. **27 K2** SO0561.
Llandrinio *Powys* ***Village***, 7m/12km NE of Welshpool. **38 B4** SJ2817.
Llandudno *Conwy* ***Town***, Victorian coastal resort at base of peninsula running out to Great Ormes Head. Links with Lewis Carroll and Alice in Wonderland. **47 F4** SH7882.
Llandudno Bay *Conwy* *Alternative name for Ormes Bay, qv.*
Llandudno Junction *Conwy* Population: 4665. ***Suburb***, railway junction and suburb, 3m/5km SE of Llandudno. **47 F5** SH8077.
Llandudoch *Pembs.* *Welsh form of St. Dogmaels, qv.*
Llandw *V. of Glam.* *Welsh form of Llandow, qv.*
Llandwrog *Gwyn.* ***Village***, 5m/7km SW of Caernarfon. **46 C7** SH4556.
Llandybie *Carmar.* Population: 2833. ***Village***, 2m/3km N of Ammanford. **17 K3** SN6115.
Llandyfaelog *Carmar.* ***Village***, 3m/5km N of Kidwelly. **17 H3** SN4111.
Llandyfaelog-tre'r-graig *Powys* ***Settlement***, 1m/2km NW of Llangorse. **28 A6** SO1229.
Llandyfai *Pembs.* *Welsh form of Lamphey, qv.*
Llandyfalle *Powys* *Welsh form of Llandefalle, qv.*
Llandyfalle Hill *Powys* ***Mountain***, 5m/8km NE of Brecon. Height 1214 feet or 370 metres. **27 K5** SO0636.
Llandyfan *Carmar.* ***Settlement***, 3m/5km N of Ammanford. SN6417.
Llandyfeisant *Carmar.* ***Locality***, parish on W side of Llandeilo, with church on edge of Dynevor Park, supposedly on site of Roman temple. SN6222.
Llandyfriog *Cere.* ***Hamlet***, 2m/3km E of Newcastle Emlyn. **26 C4** SN3341.
Llandyfrydog *I.o.A.* ***Settlement***, on Anglesey, 2m/3km NE of Llanerchymedd. **46 C4** SH4485.
Llandygai (Llandegai). *Gwyn.* ***Village***, 1m/2km SE of Bangor. **46 D5** SH5970.
Llandygwydd *Cere.* ***Village***, 4m/7km SE of Cardigan. **26 B4** SN2443.
Llandynan *Denb.* ***Settlement***, 3m/4km NW of Llangollen. SJ1844.
Llandyrnog *Denb.* ***Village***, 4m/6km E of Denbigh. **47 K6** SJ1064.
Llandyry *Carmar.* ***Settlement***, 2m/3km SE of Kidwelly. **17 H4** SN4304.
Llandysilio *Powys* ***Hamlet***, 7m/11km S of Oswestry. **38 B4** SJ2619.
Llandyssil (Also spelled Llandysul.) *Powys* ***Village***, 2m/3km W of Montgomery. **38 A6** SO1995.
Llandysul *Cere.* ***Small town***, on River Teifi 12m/20km N of Carmarthen. **26 D4** SN4140.
Llandysul *Powys* *Alternative spelling of Llandyssil, qv.*
Llanedern *Cardiff* *Welsh form of Llanedeyrn, qv.*
Llanedeyrn (Llanedern). *Cardiff* ***Hamlet***, on Rhymney River, 4m/6km NE of Cardiff. **19 F3** ST2181.
Llanedi *Carmar.* *Welsh form of Llanedy, qv.*
Llanedy (Llanedi). *Carmar.* ***Settlement***, 2m/3km N of Pontarddulais. SN5807.
Llaneglwys *Powys* ***Hamlet***, 3m/5km NE of Lower Chapel. SO0638.
Llanegryn *Gwyn.* ***Village***, 3m/5km N of Tywyn. **37 F5** SH6005.
Llanegwad *Carmar.* ***Village***, 7m/11km E of Carmarthen. **17 J2** SN5121.
Llaneilian *I.o.A.* ***Village***, on N coast of Anglesey, 2m/3km E of Amlwch. **46 C3** SH4692.
Llaneirwg *Cardiff* *Welsh form of St. Mellons, qv.*
Llanelen *Mon.* *Welsh form of Llanellen, qv.*
Llaneleu *Powys* *Welsh form of Llanelieu, qv.*
Llanelian-yn-Rhôs *Conwy* ***Village***, 2m/3km SE of Colwyn Bay. **47 G5** SH8676.
Llanelidan *Denb.* ***Village***, 5m/8km S of Ruthin. **47 K7** SJ1050.
Llanelieu (Llaneleu). *Powys* ***Hamlet***, 2m/3km E of Talgarth. **28 A5** SO1834.
Llanellen (Llanelen). *Mon.* ***Village***, on River Usk, 2m/3km S of Abergavenny. **28 C7** SO3010.
Llanelli *Carmar.* Population: 44,953. ***Town***, industrial town on N bank of Burry Inlet, 10m/16km NW of Swansea across River Loughor. Former steel town. On marshland to S is Wildfowl and Wetlands Centre. **17 J4** SN5000.
Llanelltud *Gwyn.* *See Llanelltyd.*
Llanelltyd (Llanelltud). *Gwyn.* ***Village***, 1m/2km NW of Dolgellau. Ruins of 13c Cymer Abbey (Cadw) to E. **37 G4** SH7119.
Llanelly *Mon.* ***Hamlet***, 1m/2km W of Gilwern. **28 B7** SO2314.
Llanelly Hill *Mon.* ***Village***, 1m/2km E of Bryn-mawr. **28 B7** SO2211.
Llanelwedd *Powys* ***Village***, opposite Builth Wells across River Wye. Venue of annual Royal Welsh Agricultural Show. **27 K3** SO0451.
Llanelwy *Denb.* *Welsh form of St. Asaph, qv.*
Llanenddwyn *Gwyn.* ***Hamlet***, 5m/8km N of Barmouth. **36 E3** SH5723.
Llanengan *Gwyn.* ***Village***, 1m/2km SW of Abersoch. **36 B3** SH2927.
Llanerchaeron *Cere.* ***Historic house***, National Trust property designed by John Nash, built in 1794-96 and partially renovated, within estate near Llanaeron, 2m/3km NW of Cilau Aeron. **26 D3** SN4859.
Llanerchymedd *I.o.A.* ***Village***, on Anglesey, 6m/9km S of Amlwch. **46 C4** SH4184.
Llanerfyl *Powys* ***Village***, 5m/8km NW of Llanfair Caereinion. **37 K5** SJ0309.
Llaneuddog *I.o.A.* ***Settlement***, 4m/6km SE of Amlwch. SH4688.
Llaneurgain *Flints.* *Welsh form of Northop, qv.*
Llanfable *Mon.* *Welsh form of Llanvapley, qv.*
Llanfach *Caerp.* ***Suburb***, on E side of Abercarn. ST2295.
Llanfaches *Newport* *Welsh form of Llanvaches, qv.*
Llanfachraeth *I.o.A.* ***Village***, on Anglesey, 4m/7km E of Holyhead across Holyhead Bay. **46 B4** SH3182.
Llanfachreth *Gwyn.* ***Village***, 3m/5km NE of Dolgellau. **37 G3** SH7522.
Llanfaelog *I.o.A.* ***Village***, near W coast of Anglesey, 5m/8km SE of Valley. Ty Newydd Burial Chamber (Cadw) 1km NE. **46 B5** SH3373.
Llanfaelrhys *Gwyn.* ***Locality***, on SW end of Lleyn Peninsula, 3m/4km E of Aberdaron. **36 B3** SH2126.
Llanfaenor *Mon.* ***Settlement***, 3m/4km SW of Skenfrith. SO4316.
Llanfaes *I.o.A.* ***Settlement***, on Anglesey, 1m/2km N of Beaumaris. **46 E5** SH6077.
Llanfaes *Powys* ***Locality***, adjoining to W of Brecon. **27 K6** SO0328.
Llanfaes *V. of Glam.* *Welsh form of Llanmaes, qv.*
Llanfaethlu *I.o.A.* ***Village***, on Anglesey, 4m/6km S of Carmel Head. **46 B4** SH3186.
Llanfaglan *Gwyn.* ***Hamlet***, 2m/3km SW of Caernarfon. **46 C6** SH4760.
Llanfair *Gwyn.* ***Village***, 1m/2km S of Harlech. **36 E3** SH5729.
Llanfair Caereinion *Powys* ***Small town***, former flannel-making town on River Banwy, 8m/12km W of Welshpool. W terminus of Welshpool and Llanfair Railway. **38 A5** SJ1006.
Llanfair Clydogau *Cere.* ***Village***, at confluence of Rivers Clywedog and Teifi, 4m/6km NE of Lampeter. Silver mines date from Roman times. **27 F3** SN6251.
Llanfair Disgoed *Mon.* *Alternative spelling of Llanvair-Discoed, qv.*
Llanfair Dyffryn Clwyd *Denb.* ***Village***, 2m/3km S of Ruthin. **47 K7** SJ1355.
Llanfair Hill *Shrop.* ***Mountain***, with clearly-marked section of Offa's Dyke on W side, 4m/7km NW of Knighton. Height 1417 feet or 432 metres. **28 B1** SO2579.
Llanfair Isgoed *Mon.* *Welsh form of Llanvair-Discoed, qv.*
Llanfair Kilgeddin *Mon.* ***Hamlet***, 4m/7km NW of Usk. SO3407.
Llanfair Llythynwg *Powys* *Welsh form of Gladestry, qv.*
Llanfair-Nant Gwyn *Pembs.* ***Settlement***, 5m/9km S of Cardigan. **16 E1** SN1637.
Llanfair-Orllwyn *Cere.* ***Locality***, 3m/5km W of Llandysul. **26 C4** SN3641.
Llanfair Talhaiarn *Conwy* ***Village***, on River Elwy, 5m/8km S of Abergele. **47 H5** SH9270.
Llanfair Waterdine *Shrop.* ***Village***, 4m/6km NW of Knighton. **28 B1** SO2476.
Llanfair-ym-Muallt *Powys* *Welsh form of Builth Wells, qv.*
Llanfair-yn-Neubwll *I.o.A.* ***Village***, on Anglesey, at N end of Valley Airfield, 2m/3km SE of Valley. **46 B5** SH3076.
Llanfairfechan *Conwy* Population: 3338. ***Small town***, Victorian resort on Conwy Bay, midway between Bangor and Conwy. **46 E5** SH6874.
Llanfairpwllgwyngyll *I.o.A.* Population: 3101. ***Village***, on Anglesey, 2m/3km W of Menai Bridge. **46 D5** SH5271.
Llanfairynghornwy *I.o.A.* ***Village***, near N coast of Anglesey, 2m/4km SE of Carmel Head. **46 B3** SH3290.
Llanfallteg *Carmar.* ***Hamlet***, 4m/6km NW of Whitland. Hamlet of Llanfallteg West 1km SW. **16 E3** SN1519.
Llanfallteg West *Carmar.* ***Settlement***, 4m/6km NE of Narberth. **16 E3** SN1519.
Llanfaredd *Powys* ***Settlement***, 2m/3km E of Builth Wells across River Wye. **27 K3** SO0650.
Llanfarian *Cere.* ***Village***, 3m/4km S of Aberystwyth. **26 E1** SN5977.
Llanfarthin *Newport* *Welsh form of Llanmartin, qv.*
Llanfechain *Powys* ***Village***, on River Cain, 3m/5km E of Llanfyllin. Motte and bailey castle on W side of village. **38 A3** SJ1820.
Llanfechell *I.o.A.* ***Village***, near N coast of Anglesey, 2m/3km S of Cemaes Bay. **46 B3** SH3691.
Llanfendigaid *Gwyn.* ***Settlement***, 3m/5km NW of Tywyn. **36 E5** SH5605.
Llanferres *Denb.* ***Village***, 4m/6km SW of Mold. **47 K6** SJ1860.
Llanfeuthin *V. of Glam.* *Welsh form of Llanvithyn, qv.*
Llanfflewyn *I.o.A.* ***Settlement***, on Anglesey, 3m/5km S of Cemaes Bay. **46 B4** SH3589.
Llanfigael *I.o.A.* ***Settlement***, on Anglesey, nearly 1m/2km E of Llanfachraeth. **46 B4** SH3282.
Llanfihangel *Powys* *Shortened form of Llanfihangel-yng-Ngwynfa, qv.*
Llanfihangel-ar-arth *Carmar.* ***Village***, 3m/4km E of Llandysul. **17 H1** SN4539.
Llanfihangel-ar-Elai *Cardiff* *Welsh form of Michaelston-super-Ely, qv.*
Llanfihangel Crucornau *Mon.* *Welsh form of Llanvihangel Crucorney, qv.*
Llanfihangel Dyffryn Arwy *Powys* *Welsh form of Michaelchurch-on-Arrow, qv.*
Llanfihangel Genau'r-glyn *Cere.* *Alternative name for Llandre, qv.*
Llanfihangel Glyn Myfyr *Conwy* ***Village***, 3m/4km E of Cerrigydrudion. **37 J1** SH9949.
Llanfihangel Nant Bran *Powys* ***Hamlet***, 7m/11km NW of Brecon. **27 J5** SN9434.
Llanfihangel-nant-Melan *Powys* ***Settlement***, 3m/4km SW of New Radnor. **28 A3** SO1858.
Llanfihangel-Penbedw *Pembs.* ***Locality***, 5m/7km SE of Cardigan. SN2039.
Llanfihangel Rhydithon *Powys* ***Hamlet***, 4m/6km E of Crossgates. **28 A2** SO1566.
Llanfihangel Rogiet *Mon.* ***Hamlet***, 2m/3km W of Caldicot. **19 H3** ST4587.
Llanfihangel Tal-y-llyn *Powys* ***Village***, 4m/7km E of Brecon. **28 A6** SO1128.
Llanfihangel Troddi *Mon.* *Welsh form of Mitchel Troy, qv.*
Llanfihangel-uwch-Gwili *Carmar.* ***Settlement***, 5m/8km E of Carmarthen. **17 H2** SN4822.
Llanfihangel y Bont-faen *V. of Glam.* *Welsh form of Llanmihangel, qv.*
Llanfihangel-y-Creuddyn *Cere.* ***Village***, 5m/8km W of Devil's Bridge. **27 F1** SN6676.
Llanfihangel-y-fedw *Newport* *Welsh form of Michaelston-y-Fedw, qv.*
Llanfihangel-y-gofion *Mon.* *Welsh form of Llanvihangel Gobion, qv.*
Llanfihangel-y-pennant *Gwyn.* ***Settlement***, 5m/7km NW of Porthmadog. **36 E1** SH5244.
Llanfihangel-y-pennant *Gwyn.* ***Settlement***, 8m/12km NE of Tywyn. Ruins of Castell y Bere (Cadw) to SW. **37 F5** SH6708.
Llanfihangel-y-pwll *V. of Glam.* *Welsh form of Michaelston-le-Pit, qv.*
Llanfihangel-y-traethau *I.o.A.* *Former name of Ynys, qv.*
Llanfihangel yn Nhowyn *I.o.A.* ***Village***, 2m/3km SE of Valley, Anglesey. SH3277.
Llanfihangel-yng-Ngwynfa (Often shortened to Llanfihangel.) *Powys* ***Village***, 4m/7km W of Llanfyllin. **37 K4** SJ0816.
Llanfihangel Ystum Llywern *Mon.* *Welsh form of Llanvihangel-Ystern-Llewern, qv.*
Llanfilo *Powys* ***Village***, 2m/4km W of Talgarth. **28 A5** SO1133.
Llanfleiddan *V. of Glam.* *Welsh form of Llanblethian, qv.*
Llanfocha *Mon.* *Welsh form of St. Maughans, qv.*
Llanfoist *Mon.* ***Village***, 1m/2km SW of Abergavenny across River Usk. **28 B7** SO2813.
Llanfor *Gwyn.* ***Hamlet***, 1km E of Bala. **37 J2** SH9336.
Llanfrechfa *Torfaen* ***Village***, 2m/3km E of Cwmbran. **19 G2** ST3193.
Llanfrothen *Gwyn.* ***Settlement***, 2m/3km N of Penrhyndeudraeth. **37 F1** SH6241.
Llanfrynach *Powys* ***Village***, 3m/4km SE of Brecon. Site of Roman bath house to W. **27 K6** SO0725.
Llanfwrog *Denb.* ***Locality***, adjoining to W of Ruthin across River Clwyd. **47 K7** SJ1157.
Llanfwrog *I.o.A.* ***Hamlet***, on Anglesey, 4m/6km E of Holyhead across Holyhead Bay. **46 B4** SH3084.
Llanfyllin *Powys* ***Small town***, historic town on River Cain, 9m/14km NW of Welshpool. Received first charter in 1293. **38 A4** SJ1419.
Llanfynydd *Carmar.* ***Village***, 6m/9km NW of Llandeilo. **17 J2** SN5527.
Llanfynydd *Flints.* ***Village***, on line of Offa's Dyke, 5m/8km NW of Wrexham. **48 B7** SJ2756.

L

Llanfyrnach *Pembs.* ***Village***, 3m/5km SE of Crymych. **17 F1** SN2231.
Llangadfan *Powys* ***Village***, 6m/10km NW of Llanfair Caereinion. **37 K4** SJ0110.
Llangadog *Carmar.* ***Village***, 1m/2km NE of Kidwelly. SN4207.
Llangadog *Carmar.* ***Village***, 5m/9km SW of Llandovery. **27 G6** SN7028.
Llangadwaladr *I.o.A.* ***Hamlet***, on Anglesey, 2m/3km E of Aberffraw. **46 B6** SH3869.
Llangadwaladr *Powys* ***Locality***, 2m/4km NW of Llansilin. **38 A2** SJ1830.
Llangaffo *I.o.A.* ***Village***, on Anglesey, 7m/12km W of Menai Bridge. **46 C6** SH4468.
Llangain *Carmar.* ***Village***, 3m/5km SW of Carmarthen. **17 G3** SN3815.
Llangammarch Wells *Powys* ***Village***, spa village at confluence of Rivers Cammarch and Irfon, 4m/6km E of Llanwrtyd Wells. The mineral springs contain barium chloride, unique in Britain. **27 J4** SN9347.
Llangan *V. of Glam.* ***Village***, 3m/5km NW of Cowbridge. **18 C4** SS9577.
Llangarron *Here.* ***Village***, 5m/9km N of Monmouth. **28 E6** SO5221.
Llangathen *Carmar.* ***Village***, 3m/5km W of Llandeilo. **17 J2** SN5822.
Llangattock (Llangatwg). *Powys* ***Village***, 1km SW of Crickhowell across River Usk. **28 B7** SO2117.
Llangattock Lingoed (Llangatwg Lingoed). *Mon.* ***Village***, 5m/9km NE of Abergavenny. **28 C6** SO3620.
Llangattock nigh Usk *Mon. Alternative name for The Bryn, qv.*
Llangattock-Vibon-Avel (Llangatwg Feibion Afel). *Mon.* ***Settlement***, 4m/6km NW of Monmouth. **28 D7** SO4515.
Llangatwg *N.P.T. Welsh form of Cadoxton-Juxta-Neath, qv.*
Llangatwg *Powys Welsh form of Llangattock, qv.*
Llangatwg Dyffryn Wysg *Mon. Welsh form of The Bryn, qv.*
Llangatwg Feibion Afel *Mon. Welsh form of Llangattock Vibon Avel, qv.*
Llangatwg Lingoed *Mon. Welsh form of Llangattock Lingoed, qv.*
Llangedwyn *Powys* ***Hamlet***, 3m/5km S of Llansilin. **38 A3** SJ1824.
Llangefni *I.o.A.* Population: 4643. ***Small town***, market town on River Cefni, on Anglesey, 7m/11km W of Menai Bridge. Administrative centre for Anglesey. **46 C5** SH4575.
Llangeinor (Llangeinwyr). *Bridgend* ***Village***, 5m/8km N of Bridgend. **18 C3** SS9187.
Llangeinwyr *Bridgend Welsh form of Llangeinor, qv.*
Llangeitho *Cere.* ***Village***, 4m/6km W of Tregaron. **27 F3** SN6159.
Llangeler *Carmar.* ***Village***, 4m/7km E of Newcastle Emlyn. **17 G1** SN3739.
Llangelynin *Gwyn.* ***Hamlet***, on Cardigan Bay, 4m/7km N of Tywyn. **36 E5** SH5707.
Llangendeirne *Carmar.* ***Village***, 5m/7km SE of Carmarthen. **17 H3** SN4514.
Llangennech *Carmar.* ***Village***, 4m/6km E of Llanelli. **17 J4** SN5601.
Llangennith (Llangynydd). *Swan.* ***Village***, near W end of Gower peninsula, 2m/3km E of Burry Holms. **17 H5** SS4291.
Llangenny *Powys* ***Hamlet***, 1m/2km E of Crickhowell. **28 B7** SO2418.
Llangernyw *Conwy* ***Village***, 6m/10km NE of Llanrwst. **47 G6** SH8767.
Llangeview (Llangyfiw). *Mon.* ***Locality***, 1m/2km E of Usk. SO3900.
Llangian *Gwyn.* ***Village***, 1m/2km W of Abersoch. **36 B3** SH2928.
Llangibby *Mon. English form of Llangybi, qv.*
Llangiwa *Mon. Alternative spelling of Llangua, qv.*
Llangiwg *N.P.T.* ***Settlement***, 1m/2km N of Pontardawe. **18 A1** SN7205.
Llangloffan *Pembs.* ***Hamlet***, 1m/2km SE of Granston. SM9032.
Llanglydwen *Carmar.* ***Hamlet***, 6m/10km N of Whitland. **16 E2** SN1826.
Llangoed *I.o.A.* ***Village***, on Anglesey, 2m/3km N of Beaumaris. **46 E5** SH6079.
Llangoedmor *Cere.* ***Hamlet***, 1m/2km E of Cardigan. **26 A4** SN1945.
Llangofen *Mon. Welsh form of Llangovan, qv.*
Llangollen *Denb.* Population: 3267. ***Small town***, on River Dee, at head of Vale of Llangollen, 9m/15km SW of Wrexham. Tourist centre. Annual International Eisteddfod. Canal connection with Shropshire Union Canal (Hurleston Junction). Remains of 13c Valle Crucis Abbey (Cadw), 1m/2km NW. **38 B1** SJ2141.
Llangollen Railway *Denb.* ***Other feature of interest***, tourist railway, travelling from Llangollen to Carrog. Also Great Western Railway station, with displays. **38 B1** SJ2143.
Llangolman *Pembs.* ***Village***, 8m/12km N of Narberth. **16 E2** SN1127.
Llangors *Powys See Llangorse.*
Llangorse (Llangors). *Powys* ***Village***, 4m/7km S of Talgarth. **28 A6** SO1327.
Llangorse Lake (Llyn Syfaddan). *Powys* ***Lake/loch***, large lake, 4m/6km in circumference, to S of Llangorse. **28 A6** SO1327.
Llangorwen *Cere.* ***Locality***, 2m/3km NE of Aberystwyth. **37 F7** SN6083.
Llangovan (Llangofen or Llangoven.) *Mon.* ***Settlement***, 3m/5km SE of Raglan. **19 H1** SO4505.
Llangoven *Mon. Alternative spelling of Llangovan, qv.*
Llangower *Gwyn.* ***Settlement***, on E side of Llyn Tegid, 3m/5km S of Bala. **37 J2** SH9032.
Llangrallo *Bridgend Welsh form of Coychurch, qv.*
Llangrannog *Cere. See Llangranog.*
Llangranog (Llangrannog). *Cere.* ***Village***, on coast, 6m/10km SW of New Quay. **26 C3** SN3154.
Llangristiolus *I.o.A.* ***Village***, on Anglesey, 1m/2km S of Llangefni. **46 C5** SH4473.
Llangrove *Here.* ***Village***, 4m/7km N of Monmouth. **28 E7** SO5219.
Llangua (Also spelled Llangiwa.) *Mon.* ***Settlement***, 1m/2km S of Pontrilas. **28 C6** SO3925.
Llangunllo (Also spelled Llangynllo.) *Powys* ***Village***, in upper reaches of River Lugg valley, 5m/8km W of Knighton. **28 B1** SO2171.
Llangunnor (Llangynnwr). *Carmar.* ***Hamlet***, 1m/2km E of Carmarthen across River Tywi. **17 H2** SN4220.
Llangurig *Powys* ***Village***, on River Wye, 4m/6km SW of Llanidloes. **27 J1** SN9079.
Llangwm *Conwy* ***Village***, 7m/11km W of Corwen. **37 J1** SH9644.
Llangwm *Mon.* ***Village***, 3m/5km E of Usk. **19 H1** SO4200.
Llangwm *Pembs.* ***Village***, 3m/5km NE of Neyland, at head of creek running into Daugleddau estuary. **16 C4** SM9909.
Llangwm-isaf *Mon.* ***Settlement***, 1km NE of Llangwm. SO4201.
Llangwnnadl *Gwyn.* ***Hamlet***, 3m/5km SW of Tudweiliog. **36 B2** SH2033.
Llangwyfan *Denb.* ***Hamlet***, 5m/8km N of Ruthin. **47 K6** SJ1266.
Llangwyllog *I.o.A.* ***Settlement***, on Anglesey, 3m/5km NW of Llangefni. **46 C5** SH4378.
Llangwyryfon *Cere.* ***Village***, 7m/11km S of Aberystwyth. **26 E1** SN5970.
Llangybi *Cere.* ***Village***, 4m/6km NE of Lampeter. **27 F3** SN6053.
Llangybi *Gwyn.* ***Hamlet***, 5m/8km NE of Pwllheli. **36 D1** SH4241.
Llangybi (Llangibby). *Mon.* ***Village***, 3m/4km S of Usk. Ruined keep of Norman castle to NW. **19 G2** ST3796.
Llangyfelach *Swan.* ***Locality***, 4m/6km N of Swansea. **17 K5** SS6498.
Llangyfiw *Mon. Welsh form of Llangeview, qv.*
Llangynhafal *Denb.* ***Hamlet***, 3m/5km N of Ruthin. **47 K6** SJ1263.
Llangynidr *Powys* ***Village***, 4m/6km W of Crickhowell. **28 A7** SO1519.
Llangynin *Carmar.* ***Village***, 3m/5km NW of St. Clears. **17 F3** SN2519.
Llangynllo *Cere.* ***Settlement***, 4m/6km NE of Newcastle Emlyn. SN3543.
Llangynllo *Powys Alternative spelling of Llangunllo, qv.*
Llangynnwr *Carmar. Welsh form of Llangunnor, qv.*
Llangynog *Carmar.* ***Village***, 5m/8km SW of Carmarthen. **17 G3** SN3316.
Llangynog *Powys* ***Village***, 5m/7km W of Llanrhaeadr-ym-Mochnant. Granite quarries. **37 K3** SJ0526.
Llangynwyd *Bridgend* ***Village***, 2m/3km S of Maesteg. **18 B3** SS8588.
Llangynydd *Swan. Welsh form of Llangennith, qv.*
Llanhamlach *Powys* ***Hamlet***, 3m/5km E of Brecon. **27 K6** SO0926.
Llanharan *R.C.T.* Population: 5107. ***Village***, 6m/10km E of Bridgend. **18 D3** ST0083.
Llanhari *R.C.T. Welsh form of Llanharry, qv.*
Llanharry (Llanhari). *R.C.T.* Population: 2336. ***Village***, 3m/5km SW of Llantrisant. **18 D3** ST0080.
Llanhennock *Mon.* ***Village***, 1m/2km NE of Caerleon. **19 G2** ST3592.
Llanhiledd *B.Gwent Welsh form of Llanhilleth, qv.*
Llanhilleth (Llanhiledd). *B.Gwent* Population: 3984. ***Village***, 2m/3km S of Abertillery. **19 F1** SO2100.
Llanidan *I.o.A.* ***Locality***, 1km E of Brynsiencyn. To W are various antiquities, including Bodowyr Burial Chamber and ancient earthworks Caer Leb and Castell Bryn-gwyn (all Cadw). SH4966.
Llanidloes *Powys* Population: 2616. ***Small town***, at confluence of Rivers Clywedog and Severn 11m/17km SW of Newtown. Museum of local history and industry in Tudor Old Market Hall. **37 J7** SN9584.
Llaniestyn *Gwyn.* ***Hamlet***, 4m/7km NW of Abersoch. **36 B2** SH2633.
Llanigon *Powys* ***Village***, 2m/3km SW of Hay-on-Wye. **28 B5** SO2139.
Llanilar *Cere.* ***Village***, 5m/8km SE of Aberystwyth. **27 F1** SN6275.
Llanilid *R.C.T.* ***Hamlet***, 5m/8km E of Bridgend. Traces of medieval castle. **18 C3** SS9781.
Llanilltern *Cardiff See Capel Llanilltern.*
Llanilltud Faerdref *R.C.T. Welsh form of Llantwit Fardre, qv.*
Llanilltud Fawr *V. of Glam. Welsh form of Llantwit Major, qv.*
Llanilltud Gŵyr *Swan. Welsh form of Ilston, qv.*
Llanishen (Llanisien). *Cardiff* ***Suburb***, 3m/5km N of Cardiff city centre. **18 E3** ST1781.
Llanishen (Llanisien). *Mon.* ***Village***, 3m/4km N of Devauden. **19 H1** SO4703.
Llanisien *Cardiff See Llanishen.*
Llanisien *Mon. See Llanishen.*
Llanismel *Carmar. Welsh form of St. Ishmael, qv.*
Llaniwared *Powys* ***Mountain***, 2m/3km SW of Llangurig. Height 1571 feet or 479 metres. **27 H1** SN8977.
Llanllawddog *Carmar.* ***Locality***, 6m/10km NE of Carmarthen. **17 H2** SN4629.
Llanllechid *Gwyn.* ***Village***, 1m/2km N of Bethesda. **46 E6** SH6268.
Llanlleonfel *Powys* ***Locality***, 1m/2km W of Garth. At Caerau, 1m/2km W, is site of Roman fort. **27 J4** SN9349.
Llanllugan *Powys* ***Hamlet***, 4m/6km SW of Llanfair Caereinion. **37 K5** SJ0502.
Llanllwch *Carmar.* ***Hamlet***, 2m/3km SW of Carmarthen. **17 G3** SN3818.
Llanllwchaiarn *Powys* ***Hamlet***, 1m/2km NE of Newtown. Remains of motte and bailey castle across River Severn. **38 A6** SO1292.
Llanllwni *Carmar.* ***Hamlet***, 4m/6km SW of Llanybydder. **26 D4** SN4839.
Llanllyfni *Gwyn.* ***Village***, on S bank of River Llyfni, 7m/11km S of Caernarfon. **46 C7** SH4752.
Llanllywel *Mon.* ***Hamlet***, 2m/3km S of Usk. **19 G2** ST3998.
Llanmadoc (Also spelled Llanmadog.) *Swan.* ***Village***, at W end of Gower peninsula, 13m/22km W of Swansea and 2m/4km S of Whitford Point. Hillfort known as The Bulwark (mostly National Trust) to S. **17 H5** SS4493.
Llanmadog *Swan. Alternative spelling of Llanmadoc, qv.*
Llanmaes (Llanfaes). *V. of Glam.* ***Village***, 1m/2km NE of Llantwit Major. **18 C5** SS9869.
Llanmartin (Llanfarthin). *Newport* ***Village***, 5m/9km E of Newport. **19 G3** ST3989.
Llanmellin *Mon.* ***Locality***, comprising Great Llanmellin, 1m/2km N of Caerwent, and Lower Llanmellin adjacent to SE. ST4592.
Llanmerewig *Powys* ***Settlement***, 3m/5km E of Newtown. **38 A6** SO1592.
Llanmihangel (Llanfihangel y Bont-faen). *V. of Glam.* ***Hamlet***, 2m/3km SW of Cowbridge. **18 C4** SS9871.
Llanmiloe *Carmar.* ***Village***, 4m/6km W of Laugharne. **17 F4** SN2508.
Llanmorlais *Swan.* ***Hamlet***, 8m/13km W of Swansea. **17 J5** SS5294.
Llannarth *Cere. Welsh form of Llanarth, Dyfed, qv.*
Llannefydd *Conwy* ***Village***, 5m/8km NW of Denbigh. **47 H5** SH9870.
Llannerch *Denb.* ***Settlement***, 2m/3km SE of St. Asaph. **47 J5** SJ0572.
Llannerch-y-môr *Flints.* ***Settlement***, 1m/2km SE of Mostyn. **47 K5** SJ1779.
Llannewydd *Carmar. Welsh form of Newchurch, qv.*
Llannon *Carmar.* ***Village***, 5m/9km N of Llanelli. **17 J4** SN5308.
Llannor *Gwyn.* ***Village***, 2m/3km NW of Pwllheli. **36 C2** SH3537.
Llanofer Fawr *Mon. Welsh form of Llanover, qv.*
Llanon *Cere.* ***Village***, 4m/7km NE of Aberaeron. **26 E2** SN5166.
Llanover (Llanofer Fawr). *Mon.* ***Hamlet***, 4m/6km S of Abergavenny. **19 G1** SO3108.
Llanpumsaint *Carmar.* ***Hamlet***, 6m/9km N of Carmarthen. **17 H2** SN4129.
Llanreithan (Llanrheithan). *Pembs.* ***Settlement***, 8m/13km SW of Fishguard. **16 B2** SM8628.
Llanrhaeadr *Denb.* ***Village***, 3m/4km SE of Denbigh. **47 J6** SJ0863.
Llanrhaeadr-ym-Mochnant *Powys* ***Village***, 4m/7km N of Llanfyllin. **38 A3** SJ1226.
Llanrheithan *Pembs. Welsh form of Llanreithan, qv.*
Llanrhian (Also spelled Llanrian.) *Pembs.* ***Hamlet***, 6m/9km NE of St. David's. **16 B1** SM8131.
Llanrhidian *Swan.* ***Village***, on Gower peninsula, 10m/16km W of Swansea. Llanrhidian Marshes (National Trust), extensive salt marshes to N, on S side of Burry Inlet. **17 J5** SS4992.
Llanrhidian Sands *Swan.* ***Coastal feature***, large area of mud and sand flats on S side of River Loughor estuary, to N of Llanrhidian. **17 H5** SS4895.
Llanrhos *Conwy* ***Hamlet***, 1m/2km S of Llandudno. **47 F4** SH7980.
Llanrhyddlad *I.o.A.* ***Village***, near NW coast of Anglesey, 3m/5km SE of Carmel Head. **46 B4** SH3389.
Llanrhymni *Cardiff Welsh form of Llanrumney, qv.*
Llanrhystud *Cere.* ***Village***, 7m/11km NE of Aberaeron. **26 E2** SN5369.
Llanrian *Pembs. Alternative spelling of Llanrhian, qv.*
Llanrothal *Here.* ***Settlement***, in valley of River Monnow, 4m/7km NW of Monmouth. **28 D7** SO4718.
Llanrug *Gwyn.* Population: 2092. ***Village***, 4m/6km E of Caernarfon. **46 D6** SH5363.
Llanrumney (Llanrhymni). *Cardiff* ***Suburb***, 4m/6km NE of Cardiff city centre. **19 F3** ST2280.
Llanrwst *Conwy* Population: 3012. ***Small town***, market town on River Conwy, 11m/18km S of Colwyn Bay. Early 17c bridge, said to have been built by Inigo Jones. 17c Gwydir Uchaf Chapel, adjoining church, has elaborate interior. **47 F6** SH7961.
Llansadurnen *Carmar.* ***Hamlet***, 4m/6km S of St. Clears. **17 F3** SN2810.
Llansadwrn *Carmar.* ***Village***, 5m/8km SW of Llandovery. **17 K1** SN6931.
Llansadwrn *I.o.A.* ***Hamlet***, on Anglesey, 3m/4km N of Menai Bridge. **46 D5** SH5575.
Llansaint *Carmar.* ***Village***, 2m/3km NW of Kidwelly. **17 G4** SN3808.
Llansamlet *Swan.* ***Suburb***, 4m/6km NE of Swansea city centre. **17 K5** SS6897.
Llansanffraid-ar-Elai *V. of Glam. Welsh form of St. Bride's-super-Ely, qv.*
Llansanffraid Glan Conwy *Conwy* Population: 2021. ***Village***, in River Conwy valley, 4m/6km SW of Colwyn Bay. **47 G5** SH8075.
Llansanffraid Gwynllwg *Newport Welsh form of St. Brides Wentlooge, qv.*
Llansannan *Conwy* ***Village***, on River Aled, 7m/12km W of Denbigh. **47 H6** SH9365.
Llansannor (Llansanwyr). *V. of Glam.* ***Hamlet***, 2m/3km N of Cowbridge. **18 C4** SS9977.
Llansantffraed *Cere.* ***Hamlet***, near coast, 4m/7km NE of Aberaeron. **26 E2** SN5167.
Llansantffraed *Powys* ***Hamlet***, on River Usk, 6m/9km SE of Brecon. **28 A6** SO1223.
Llansantffraed-Cwmteuddwr *Powys* ***Village***, opposite Rhayader across River Wye. **27 J2** SN9667.
Llansantffraed-in-Elwell (Llansantffraid-yn-Elfael). *Powys* ***Village***, 4m/7km NE of Builth Wells. **27 K3** SO0954.
Llansantffraid-ym-Mechain *Powys* ***Village***, 5m/8km E of Llanfyllin. **38 B3** SJ2120.
Llansantffraid-yn-Elfael *Powys Welsh form of Llansantffraed-in-Elwell, qv.*
Llansanwyr *V. of Glam. Welsh form of Llansannor, qv.*

Llansawel *Carmar.* ***Village***, 9m/14km N of Llandeilo. **17 K1** SN6136.

Llansawel *N.P.T. Welsh form of Briton Ferry, qv.*

Llansilin *Powys* ***Village***, 6m/9km E of Llanrhaeadr-ym-Mochnant. **38 B3** SJ2028.

Llansoy (Llan-soe). *Mon.* ***Hamlet***, 4m/7km E of Usk. **19 H1** SO4402.

Llanspyddid *Powys* ***Hamlet***, 2m/3km W of Brecon. **27 K6** SO0128.

Llanstadwell *Pembs.* ***Village***, adjoining to W of Neyland, 6m/10km S of Haverfordwest. **16 C4** SM9505.

Llansteffan *Carmar. See Llanstephan.*

Llansteffan *Powys See Llanstephan.*

Llanstephan (Llansteffan). *Carmar.* ***Village***, on River Tywi estuary, 7m/11km SW of Carmarthen. Ruined castle (Cadw) beside river to S. St. Anthony's Well, wishing well to SW of castle, said to have medicinal properties. **17 G3** SN3510.

Llanstephan (Llansteffan). *Powys* ***Settlement***, 8m/12km SE of Builth Wells. **28 A4** SO1141.

Llanstephan Castle *Carmar.* ***Castle***, 12c-13c double enclosed castle (Cadw) to S of Llanstephan, on W side of mouth of River Tywi. **17 G3** SN3510.

Llantarnam *Torfaen* ***Suburb***, SE district of Cwmbran. **19 G2** ST3093.

Llanteg *Pembs.* ***Hamlet***, 4m/7km S of Whitland. **16 E3** SN1810.

Llanthony (Llanddewi Nant Hodni). *Mon.* ***Hamlet***, in River Honddu valley, in Black Mountains, 9m/14km N of Abergavenny. Remains of 12c priory (Cadw). **28 B6** SO2827.

Llanthony Priory *Mon.* ***Ecclesiastical building***, in Vale of Ewyas, 9m/14km N of Abergavenny. Founded c. 1100 by William de Lacy. Now a substantial ruin of 1175 church, 212 feet long, including W front. **28 B6** SO2827.

Llantilio Crossenny (Llandeilo Gresynni). *Mon.* ***Hamlet***, 6m/10km E of Abergavenny. Medieval manor house of Hen Gwrt (Cadw) to W. **28 C7** SO3914.

Llantilio Pertholey (Llandeilo Bertholau). *Mon.* ***Hamlet***, 2m/3km N of Abergavenny. **28 C7** SO3116.

Llantood *Pembs.* ***Settlement***, 3m/5km SW of Cardigan. **26 A4** SN1541.

Llantrisaint *Mon. Alternative spelling of Llantrisant, qv.*

Llantrisant *I.o.A.* ***Settlement***, 2m/3km SE of Llanddeusant. Tregwhelydd Standing Stone (Cadw) 1m/2km W. SH3683.

Llantrisant (Llantrisaint or Llantrissent.) *Mon.* ***Village***, in valley of River Usk, 3m/4km S of Usk. **19 G2** ST3996.

Llantrisant *R.C.T.* Population: 4568. ***Village***, 4m/7km S of Pontypridd. **18 D3** ST0483.

Llantrissent *Mon. Alternative spelling of Llantrisant, qv.*

Llantrithyd *V. of Glam.* ***Village***, 3m/5km E of Cowbridge. **18 D4** ST0472.

Llantwit Fardre (Llanilltud Faerdref). *R.C.T.* Population: 3277. ***Village***, 3m/5km S of Pontypridd. **18 D3** ST0785.

Llantwit Major (Llanilltud Fawr). *V. of Glam.* Population: 12,909. ***Town***, historic town near Bristol Channel coast, 4m/7km SW of Cowbridge. Llandow Industrial Estate 2m/4km N. Motor-racing circuit 2m/3km N at former airfield. Site of Roman villa 1m/2km NW. Site of Bedford Castle to NE. World's first international sixth-form school established at St. Donat's. Norman church has collection of Celtic crosses. **18 C5** SS9668.

Llantydewi *Pembs. Welsh form of St. Dogwells, qv.*

Llantysilio *Denb.* ***Settlement***, 2m/3km NW of Llangollen. **38 A1** SJ1943.

Llantysilio Mountain *Denb.* ***Large natural feature***, to NW of Llantysilio, range of hills, rising to 1897 feet or 578 metres at Moel y Gamelin. **38 A1** SJ1943.

Llanuwchllyn *Gwyn.* ***Hamlet***, 5m/8km SW of Bala. **37 H2** SH8730.

Llanvaches (Llanfaches). *Newport* ***Village***, 7m/11km W of Chepstow. Site of Roman building 1m/2km SE. **19 H2** ST4391.

Llanvair-Discoed (Llanfair Isgoed or Llanfair Disgoed.) *Mon.* ***Village***, 6m/9km W of Chepstow. **19 H2** ST4492.

Llanvapley (Llanfable). *Mon.* ***Village***, 4m/7km E of Abergavenny. **28 C7** SO3614.

Llanvetherine (Llanwytherin). *Mon.* ***Hamlet***, 4m/7km E of Abergavenny. **28 C7** SO3617.

Llanveynoe *Here.* ***Settlement***, 6m/10km NW of Pontrilas. **28 C5** SO3031.

Llanvihangel Court *Mon.* ***Historic house***, 16c manor house to E of Llanvihangel Crucorney. **28 C6** SO3220.

Llanvihangel Crucorney (Llanfihangel Crucornau). *Mon.* ***Village***, 4m/7km N of Abergavenny. **28 C6** SO3220.

Llanvihangel Gobion (Llanfihangel-y-gofion). *Mon.* ***Hamlet***, 4m/7km SE of Abergavenny. **19 G1** SO3409.

Llanvihangel Pontymoel *Torfaen* ***Locality***, 1m/2km E of Pontypool. SO3001.

Llanvihangel-Ystern-Llewern (Llanfihangel Ystum Llywern). *Mon.* ***Settlement***, 4m/7km W of Monmouth. **28 D7** SO4313.

Llanvithyn (Llanfeuthin). *V. of Glam.* ***Settlement***, 1km N of Llancarfan. ST0571.

Llanwarne *Here.* ***Village***, 6m/10km NW of Ross-on-Wye. **28 E6** SO5028.

Llanwarw *Mon. Welsh form of Wonastow, qv.*

Llanwddyn *Powys* ***Village***, at SE end of Lake Vyrnwy, built to replace former village of Llanwddyn, whose site was submerged by construction of reservoir. **37 K4** SJ0219.

Llanwenarth *Mon.* ***Locality***, 1m/2km W of Abergavenny. SO2714.

Llanwenog *Cere.* ***Hamlet***, 6m/9km W of Lampeter. **26 D4** SN4945.

Llanwern *Newport* ***Village***, 4m/6km E of Newport. **19 G3** ST3688.

Llanwinio *Carmar.* ***Hamlet***, 1km NE of Cwmbach. **17 F2** SN2626.

Llanwnda *Gwyn.* ***Village***, 3m/4km S of Caernarfon. **46 C7** SH4758.

Llanwnda *Pembs.* ***Hamlet***, 2m/4km NW of Fishguard. Ancient burial-chambers in vicinity. **16 C1** SM9339.

Llanwnen *Cere.* ***Village***, 3m/5km W of Lampeter. **26 E4** SN5347.

Llanwnog *Powys* ***Village***, 6m/9km W of Newtown. **37 K6** SO0293.

Llanwonno *R.C.T.* ***Locality***, in St. Gwynno Forest, 4m/7km NW of Pontypridd. **18 D2** ST0395.

Llanwrda *Carmar.* ***Village***, 4m/6km SW of Llandovery. **27 G5** SN7131.

Llanwrin *Powys* ***Hamlet***, 3m/5km NE of Machynlleth across River Dyfi. **37 G5** SH7803.

Llanwrthwl *Powys* ***Hamlet***, 3m/5km S of Rhayader. **27 J2** SN9763.

Llanwrtyd *Powys* ***Locality***, 1m/2km NW of Llanwrtyd Wells. **27 H4** SN8647.

Llanwrtyd Wells *Powys* ***Small town***, small spa on River Irfon, 10m/16km NE of Llandovery. Popular pony-trekking centre. Said to be Britain's smallest town. **27 H4** SN8746.

Llanwyddelan *Powys* ***Hamlet***, 4m/6km SW of Llanfair Caereinion. **37 K5** SJ0801.

Llanwytherin *Mon. Welsh form of Llanvetherine, qv.*

Llanyblodwel *Shrop.* ***Village***, 5m/8km SW of Oswestry. **38 B3** SJ2422.

Llanybri *Carmar.* ***Village***, 6m/10km SW of Carmarthen. **17 G3** SN3312.

Llanybydder (Llanybyther). *Carmar.* ***Village***, on River Teifi, 4m/7km SW of Lampeter. Ancient hillfort of Pen-y-gaer to S. **26 E4** SN5244.

Llanybyther *Carmar. English form of Llanybydder, qv.*

Llanycefn *Pembs.* ***Hamlet***, 3m/4km S of Maenclochog. **16 E2** SN0923.

Llanychaer Bridge (Also known as Llanychar.) *Pembs.* ***Hamlet***, at crossing of River Gwaun, 2m/3km SE of Fishguard. **16 C1** SM9835.

Llanychar *Pembs. Alternative name for Llanychaer Bridge, qv.*

Llanycil *Gwyn.* ***Settlement***, on W shore of Llyn Tegid, 1m/2km SW of Bala. **37 J2** SH9134.

Llanycrwys *Carmar.* ***Settlement***, 5m/7km SE of Lampeter. **27 F4** SN6445.

Llanymawddwy *Gwyn.* ***Hamlet***, on River Dyfi, 5m/8km NE of Mallwyd. **37 J4** SH9019.

Llanymddyfri *Carmar. Welsh form of Llandovery, qv.*

Llanymynech *Powys* ***Village***, on English border, 6m/9km S of Oswestry. Quarries to N. **38 B3** SJ2620.

Llanynghenedl *I.o.A.* ***Hamlet***, on Anglesey, 2m/3km NE of Valley. **46 B4** SH3181.

Llanynys *Denb.* ***Hamlet***, 3m/5km N of Ruthin. **47 K6** SJ1062.

Llanyrafon *Torfaen* ***Suburb***, of Cwmbran, on E bank of River Lwyd. ST3094.

Llanyre *Powys* ***Hamlet***, 1m/2km NE of Llandrindod Wells. **27 K2** SO0462.

Llanystumdwy *Gwyn.* ***Village***, on River Dwyfor, 2m/3km W of Criccieth. Formerly home of David Lloyd George, 1863-1945. **36 D2** SH4738.

Llanywern *Powys* ***Hamlet***, 1m/2km W of Llanfihangel Tal-y-llyn. **28 A6** SO1028.

Llawhaden *Pembs.* ***Village***, 3m/5km NW of Narberth. Moated remains of medieval castle (Cadw). **16 D3** SN0617.

Llawhaden Castle *Pembs.* ***Castle***, situated to NE of Llawhaden. Originally fortified palace built by bishops of St. David's in 12c. **16 D3** SN0717.

Llawlech *Gwyn.* ***Inland physical feature***, saddle between two peaks, rising to over 540 metres, 4m/6km NE of Barmouth. **37 F3** SH6321.

Llawndy *Denb.* ***Settlement***, 1m/2km SW of Point of Ayr. SJ1183.

Llawnt *Shrop.* ***Settlement***, 3m/5km NW of Oswestry. **38 B2** SJ2430.

Llawr-y-dref *Gwyn.* ***Settlement***, at S end of Lleyn Peninsula, 2m/3km W of Abersoch. **36 B3** SH2728.

Llawryglyn *Powys* ***Hamlet***, 3m/4km W of Trefeglwys. **37 J6** SN9391.

Llay *Wrex.* Population: 4832. ***Village***, 3m/5km N of Wrexham town centre. **48 C7** SJ3255.

Llechcynfarwy *I.o.A.* ***Settlement***, on Anglesey, 3m/5km SW of Llanerchymedd. **46 B4** SH3881.

Llecheiddior *Gwyn.* ***Hamlet***, 4m/6km N of Criccieth. SH4743.

Llechfaen *Powys* ***Hamlet***, 2m/4km E of Brecon. **27 K6** SO0828.

Llechryd *Caerp.* ***Village***, 2m/3km NW of Rhymney. **18 E1** SO1009.

Llechryd *Cere.* ***Village***, on River Teifi, 3m/5km SE of Cardigan. **26 B4** SN2143.

Llechrydau *Wrex.* ***Settlement***, 5m/8km NW of Oswestry. **38 B2** SJ2234.

Llechwedd *Conwy* ***Locality***, 2m/3km SW of Conwy. SH7676.

Lledrod *Cere.* ***Village***, 8m/13km SE of Aberystwyth. **27 F1** SN6470.

Lledrod *Powys* ***Settlement***, 5m/8km W of Oswestry. **38 B2** SJ2130.

Llethr *Pembs.* ***Settlement***, 3m/5km E of Solva. **16 B2** SM8523.

Llethr Llwyd *Cere.* ***Mountain***, 6m/9km SE of Tregaron. Height 1525 feet or 465 metres. **27 G3** SN7353.

Llethrid *Swan.* ***Hamlet***, 2m/3km E of Llanrhidian, on Gower peninsula. SS5391.

Lleyn Peninsula (The Lleyn. Welsh form: Penrhyn Llŷn.) *Gwyn.* ***Coastal feature***, peninsula with rocky coastline, dividing Caernarfon Bay from Cardigan Bay. **36 B2** SH3337.

Llidiad-Negog *Carmar.* ***Settlement***, 4m/7km S of Llanybydder. **17 J1** SN5437.

Llidiardau *Gwyn.* ***Settlement***, 4m/6km W of Bala. **37 H2** SH8738.

Llidiartywaen *Powys* ***Locality***, 4m/6km SE of Llanidloes. SO0081.

Lliedi *Carmar.* ***River***, rising 4m/6km N of Llanelli and flowing S into River Loughor. **17 J4** SN5105.

Lligwy Bay *I.o.A.* ***Bay***, on NE coast of Anglesey, 5m/8km SE of Amlwch. Bronze Age burial-chamber (Cadw) 1km S. **46 C4** SH4987.

Lligwy Burial Chamber *I.o.A.* ***Historic/prehistoric site***, chambered barrow set in natural rock fissure, 1km W of Moelfre and 5m/8km SE of Amlwch. Capstone, weighing around 25 tons, is one of largest in Britain. **46 C4** SH5086.

Llithfaen *Gwyn.* ***Village***, 4m/6km NE of Nefyn. **36 C1** SH3543.

Lliw *Gwyn.* ***River***, running SE into River Dee 1m/2km W of SW end of Llyn Tegid. **37 H2** SH8730.

Lliw *Swan.* ***River***, rising 3m/5km SE of Ammanford and flowing SW through Upper and Lower Lliw Reservoirs into estuary of River Loughor, 4m/7km NW of Swansea. **17 K4** SS5697.

Lloc *Flints.* ***Hamlet***, 3m/5km W of Holywell. **47 K5** SJ1476.

Llong *Flints.* ***Settlement***, 2m/3km SE of Mold. **48 B6** SJ2662.

Llowes *Powys* ***Village***, 2m/4km W of Hay-on-Wye across River Wye. **28 A4** SO1941.

Lloyd *Northants.* ***Suburb***, 1m/2km NW of Corby town centre. SP8889.

Lloyney *Powys* ***Settlement***, 3m/5km NW of Knighton. **28 B1** SO2475.

Llugwy *Conwy* ***River***, rising on S side of Carnedd Llywelyn and running S through Ffynnon Llugwy Reservoir, then E by Capel Curig into River Conwy 1km N of Betws-y-coed. **47 F7** SH7957.

Llundain-fach *Cere.* ***Settlement***, 1m/2km E of Tal-sarn. SN5556.

Llwchwr *Welsh form of Loughor (river), qv.*

Llwybr-hir *Flints.* ***Settlement***, 2m/3km N of Caerwys. SJ1175.

Llwyd *Powys* ***River***, running E along N edge of Hafren Forest into Clywedog Reservoir. **37 H6** SN8890.

Llwydcoed *R.C.T.* ***Village***, 1m/2km N of Aberdare. **18 C1** SN9904.

Llwydiarth *Powys* ***Hamlet***, on River Vyrnwy, 3m/4km S of Lake Vyrnwy dam. **37 K4** SJ0315.

Llwyn *Shrop.* ***Settlement***, 1km SW of Clun. **38 B7** SO2880.

Llwyn-croes *Carmar.* ***Settlement***, 1m/2km S of Llanpumsaint. SN4127.

Llwyn-du *Mon.* ***Locality***, 1m/2km N of Abergavenny. SO2815.

Llwyn-Madoc *Powys* ***Settlement***, 1m/2km NW of Beulah. **27 J3** SN9052.

Llwyn-on *M.Tyd.* ***Settlement***, beside dam of Llwyn-on Reservoir, 4m/6km NW of Merthyr Tydfil. SO0111.

Llwyn-on Reservoir *R.C.T.* ***Reservoir***, 4m/6km NW of Merthyr Tydfil. **27 J7** SO0111.

Llwyn-onn *Cere.* ***Settlement***, 1km NW of Gilfachreda. **26 D3** SN4059.

Llwyn-y-brain *Carmar.* ***Settlement***, 1m/2km S of Whitland. **17 F3** SN1915.

Llwyn-y-brain *Carmar.* ***Settlement***, 2m/3km NE of Llanwrda. **27 G5** SN7332.

Llwyn-y-groes *Cere.* ***Hamlet***, 1km E of Gartheli and 5m/9km N of Lampeter. SN5956.

Llwyncelyn *Cere.* ***Hamlet***, 2m/4km SW of Aberaeron. **26 D3** SN4459.

Llwyndafydd *Cere.* ***Village***, 3m/5km S of New Quay. **26 C3** SN3755.

Llwynderw *Powys* ***Settlement***, 3m/5km SW of Welshpool. **38 B5** SJ2003.

Llwyndrain *Pembs.* ***Settlement***, 5m/8km SW of Newcastle Emlyn. SN2634.

Llwyndyrys *Gwyn.* ***Settlement***, 4m/6km N of Pwllheli. **36 C1** SH3741.

Llwynein *Wrex.* ***Settlement***, 3m/4km N of Ruabon. SJ2847.

Llwyneliddon *V. of Glam. Welsh form of St. Lythans, qv.*

Llwyngwril *Gwyn.* ***Village***, coastal village at S end of Barmouth Bay, 6m/9km N of Tywyn. **36 E5** SH5909.

Llwynhendy *Carmar.* ***Suburb***, 2m/4km E of Llanelli. **17 J5** SS5499.

Llwynmawr *Wrex.* ***Hamlet***, 4m/7km W of Chirk. **38 B2** SJ2237.

Llwynypia *R.C.T.* ***Village***, in Rhondda Fawr valley, 3m/5km SE of Treorchy. **18 C2** SS9993.

Llwytmor *Gwyn.* ***Mountain***, in Carneddau range 3m/5km S of Llanfairfechan. Height 2785 feet or 849 metres. **46 E6** SH6869.

Llydiard-y-parc *Denb.* ***Hamlet***, 3m/4km E of Corwen. SJ1143.

Llyn Alaw (Also known as Alaw Reservoir.) *I.o.A.* ***Reservoir***, large reservoir on Anglesey in course of River Alaw, 5m/8km S of Cemaes. **46 B4** SH3785.

Llyn Aled *Conwy* ***Lake/loch***, 5m/7km NE of Pentrefoelas. **47 H7** SH9157.

Llyn Alwen *Conwy* ***Lake/loch***, 4m/6km NE of Pentrefoelas. **47 G7** SH8956.

Llyn Arenig Fawr *Gwyn.* ***Lake/loch***, 5m/9km W of Bala. **37 H2** SH8438.

Llyn Berwyn *Cere.* ***Lake/loch***, in Cwm Berwyn Plantation 4m/7km SE of Tregaron. **27 G3** SN7456.

Llyn Bodlyn *Gwyn.* ***Lake/loch***, near head of River Ysgethin, 6m/10km N of Barmouth. **37 F3** SH6423.

Llyn Bran *Denb.* ***Lake/loch***, 3m/4km S of Bylchau. **47 H7** SH9659.

Llyn Brenig (Brenig Reservoir). *Conwy* ***Reservoir***, 4m/7km S of Bylchau. **47 H7** SH9756.

Llyn Brianne *Cere.* ***Reservoir***, large reservoir in valleys of Rivers Tywi and Camddwr, on borders with Powys and Carmarthenshire, 6m/9km W of Llanwrtyd Wells. Partly enclosed by Tywi Forest. **27 G3** SN7948.

Llyn Caer-Euni *Gwyn.* ***Lake/loch***, 4m/7km NE of Bala. **37 J1** SH9840.

Llyn Cau *Gwyn.* ***Lake/loch***, tarn below Penygadair, the summit of Cadair Idris, on S side. **37 G4** SH7112.

L

Llyn Celyn *Gwyn.* ***Reservoir***, large reservoir 4m/6km NW of Bala. **37 H1** SH8740.
Llyn Clywedog Reservoir *Powys* ***Reservoir***, large reservoir in River Clywedog valley, 3m/5km NW of Llanidloes. **37 H7** SN9187.
Llyn Coch-hwyad *Powys* ***Lake/loch***, small lake 4m/6km E of Mallwyd. **37 J4** SH9211.
Llyn Conwy *Conwy* ***Lake/loch***, 5m/9km NE of Ffestiniog. Source of River Conwy. **37 G1** SH7846.
Llyn Coron *I.o.A.* ***Lake/loch***, on Anglesey to W of Bodorgan railway station. **46 B5** SH3770.
Llyn Cowlyd Reservoir *Conwy* ***Reservoir***, large reservoir 2m/3km N of Capel Curig. **47 F6** SH7363.
Llyn Crafnant *Conwy* ***Reservoir***, 3m/5km W of Llanrwst. **47 F6** SH7561.
Llyn Cwellyn *Gwyn.* ***Lake/loch***, in course of River Gwyrfai 4m/7km N of Beddgelert. **46 D7** SH5654.
Llyn Cwm Bychan *Gwyn.* ***Lake/loch***, small lake 4m/6km E of Harlech. **37 F2** SH6431.
Llyn Cwmystradllyn *Gwyn.* ***Lake/loch***, 3m/5km N of Porthmadog. **36 E1** SH5644.
Llyn Cyfynwy *Denb.* ***Lake/loch***, 1m/2km W of Rhydtalog. **48 B7** SJ2154.
Llyn Cynwch *Gwyn.* ***Lake/loch***, small lake 2m/3km N of Dolgellau. **37 G3** SH7320.
Llyn Dinas *Gwyn.* ***Lake/loch***, in course of River Glaslyn, 2m/3km NE of Beddgelert. **37 F1** SH6149.
Llyn-dŵr Hill (Welsh form: Bryn Llyndŵr.) *Powys* ***Mountain***, 6m/10km E of Llandiloes. Height 1391 feet or 424 metres. **37 K7** SO0583.
Llyn Efyrnwy *Powys Welsh form of Lake Vyrnwy, qv.*
Llyn Egnant *Cere.* ***Lake/loch***, 2m/3km W of head of Claerwen Reservoir. **27 G2** SN7967.
Llyn Eiddwen *Cere.* ***Lake/loch***, 2m/4km S of Llangwyryfon. **27 F2** SN6066.
Llyn Eigiau Reservoir *Conwy* ***Reservoir***, 4m/7km N of Capel Curig. **47 F6** SH7264.
Llyn Fawr *R.C.T.* ***Reservoir***, 6m/9km NW of Treorchy. **18 C1** SN9103.
Llyn Frogwy *I.o.A.* ***Lake/loch***, small lake 2m/4km NE of Llangefni, Anglesey. **46 C5** SH4277.
Llyn Fyrddon Fawr *Cere.* ***Lake/loch***, 2m/3km S of Cwmystwyth. **27 H1** SN8070.
Llyn Geirionydd *Conwy* ***Lake/loch***, 2m/4km W of Llanrwst. **47 F6** SH7661.
Llyn Gweryd *Denb.* ***Lake/loch***, small lake 1m/2km SW of Llanarmon-yn-Ial. **47 K7** SJ1755.
Llyn Gwyddior *Powys* ***Lake/loch***, small lake in hills 6m/9km SE of Mallwyd. **37 J5** SH9307.
Llyn Gwynant *Gwyn.* ***Lake/loch***, in course of River Glaslyn 4m/6km NE of Beddgelert. **46 E7** SH6451.
Llyn Gynon *Cere.* ***Lake/loch***, 4m/7km E of Pontrhydfendigaid. **27 G2** SN7964.
Llyn Helyg *Flints.* ***Lake/loch***, 5m/7km W of Holywell. **47 J5** SJ1177.
Llyn Hir *Powys* ***Lake/loch***, small lake 3m/4km S of Llanerfyl. Source of River Einion. **37 K5** SJ0309.
Llyn Hywel *Gwyn.* ***Lake/loch***, small lake 6m/9km SE of Harlech. **37 F3** SH6626.
Llyn Idwal *Gwyn.* ***Lake/loch***, 1km SW of Llyn Ogwen, below N face of Glyder Fawr. Located in Cwm Idwal which is renowned for its mountain flora. SH6459.
Llyn Llydaw *Gwyn.* ***Lake/loch***, 1m/2km E of summit of Snowdon. **46 E7** SH6254.
Llyn Llywenan *I.o.A.* ***Lake/loch***, on Anglesey, 1m/2km NE of Bodedern. Neolithic burial chamber (Cadw) to S. **46 B4** SH3481.
Llyn Mawr *Powys* ***Lake/loch***, small lake 2m/4km N of Llanwnog. **37 J6** SO0097.
Llyn Moelfre *Powys* ***Lake/loch***, small lake 2m/3km W of Llansilin. **38 A3** SJ1728.
Llyn Nantlle Uchaf *Gwyn.* ***Lake/loch***, on SE side of Nantlle, 6m/10km S of Caernarfon. **46 D7** SH5153.
Llyn Ogwen *Gwyn.* ***Lake/loch***, in course of River Ogwen 4m/7km W of Capel Curig. **46 E6** SH6560.
Llyn Padarn *Gwyn.* ***Lake/loch***, ribbon lake to N of Snowdon massif, 7m/11km S of Bangor. **46 D6** SH5760.
Llyn Penrhaiadr ***Lake/loch***, small lake on border of Ceredigion and Powys, 5m/8km S of Machynlleth. **37 G6** SN7593.
Llyn Peris *Gwyn.* ***Lake/loch***, at foot of Pass of Llanberis, 1km SE of Llanberis town. **46 D7** SH5959.
Llyn Syfaddan *Powys Welsh form of Llangorse Lake, qv.*
Llyn Syfydrin *Cere.* ***Lake/loch***, 5m/8km N of Devil's Bridge. **37 G7** SN7284.
Llyn Tegid (Bala Lake). *Gwyn.* ***Lake/loch***, runs SW to NE and is largest natural lake in Wales, nearly 4m/6km long and 1km wide. **37 H2** SH9033.
Llyn Teifi *Cere.* ***Lake/loch***, 3m/5km E of Pontrhydfendigaid. Source of River Teifi. **27 G2** SN7867.
Llyn Trawsfynydd *Gwyn.* ***Reservoir***, large reservoir 2m/4km S of Ffestiniog. Nuclear power station on N shore. **37 F2** SH6936.
Llyn y Cwrt *Conwy* ***Lake/loch***, small lake 2m/4km E of Pentrefoelas. **47 H7** SH9051.
Llyn y Fan Fawr *Powys* ***Lake/loch***, 6m/9km SW of Trecastle. River Tawe rises on E side. **27 H6** SN8321.
Llyn-y-felin *Cere.* ***Locality***, adjoining to N of Cardigan. SN1846.
Llyn-y-pandy *Flints.* ***Settlement***, 3m/4km NW of Mold. SJ2065.
Llynau Diwaunedd *Conwy* ***Lake/loch***, previously two separated lakes, 4m/6km SW of Capel Curig. **46 E7** SH6853.
Llynclys *Shrop.* ***Village***, 4m/6km S of Oswestry. **38 B3** SJ2824.
Llynfaes *I.o.A.* ***Hamlet***, on Anglesey, 4m/6km NW of Llangefni. **46 C5** SH4178.
Llynfi *Bridgend* ***River***, rising N of Maesteg and flowing S through town, then continuing S to join River Ogmore 2m/4km N of Bridgend. SS8983.
Llynfi *Powys* ***River***, rising 1km NW of Bwlch, between Brecon and Crickhowell, flowing N through Llangorse Lake, then continuing N to join River Wye at Glasbury. **28 A5** SO1738.
Llynnau Mymbyr *Conwy* ***Lake/loch***, adjacent lakes in course of Nantygwryd to W of Capel Curig. **47 F7** SH7057.
Llynnon Mill (Melin Llynnon). *I.o.A.* ***Other feature of interest***, working windmill on W side of Anglesey, 3m/5km N of Bodedern. **46 B4** SH3485.
Llynytarw *Powys* ***Lake/loch***, small lake 2m/4km N of Llanwnog. **37 K6** SO0297.
Llys-y-frân *Pembs.* ***Village***, 8m/12km NE of Haverfordwest, at S end of Llys-y-frân Reservoir. **16 D2** SN0424.
Llys-y-frân Reservoir *Pembs.* ***Reservoir***, to N of Llys-y-frân, 8m/12km NE of Haverfordwest. **16 D2** SN0424.
Llysdinam *Powys* ***Locality***, to W of Newbridge on Wye across River Wye. SO0058.
Llysfaen *Cardiff Welsh form of Lisvane, qv.*
Llysfaen *Conwy* ***Village***, 2m/3km SE of Colwyn Bay. **47 G5** SH8977.
Llyswen *Cere.* ***Locality***, 1km S of Aberaeron. SN4561.
Llyswen *Powys* ***Village***, on River Wye, 8m/13km NE of Brecon. Remains of ancient hill settlement above village to W. **28 A5** SO1337.
Llysworney (Llyswyrny). *V. of Glam.* ***Village***, 2m/3km W of Cowbridge. **18 C4** SS9674.
Llyswyrny *V. of Glam. Welsh form of Llysworney, qv.*
Llywel *Powys* ***Hamlet***, 1m/2km NW of Trecastle. **27 H5** SN8730.
Load Brook *S.Yorks.* ***Settlement***, 5m/8km W of Sheffield. SK2788.
Loadpot Hill *Cumb.* ***Mountain***, 5m/8km E of Glenridding. Height 2204 feet or 672 metres. **61 F5** NY4518.
Loam Street *Suff.* ***Locality***, 1m/2km NW of Southwold. TM4977.
Loanan *High.* ***River***, issuing from Loch Awe and flowing N into Loch Assynt. NC2421.
Loandhu *High.* ***Settlement***, 3m/5km SE of Tain. **97 F4** NH8178.
Loanend *Northumb.* ***Hamlet***, 1m/2km E of Horncliffe. NT9450.
Loanhead *Aber.* ***Settlement***, 3m/4km S of Auchnagatt. **91 H1** NJ9138.
Loanhead *Midloth.* Population: 5659. ***Small town***, former mining town with industrial estates, 6m/9km S of Edinburgh. **76 A4** NT2865.
Loanhead Stone Circle *Aber.* ***Historic/prehistoric site***, Bronze Age stone circle enclosing ring cairn, 1km N of Daviot. Small burial enclosure nearby. **91 F2** NJ7428.
Loans *S.Ayr.* ***Village***, 2m/3km E of Troon. **74 B7** NS3431.
Lobb *Devon* ***Hamlet***, to NW of Braunton, 6m/10km NW of Barnstaple. SS4737.
Lobhillcross *Devon* ***Hamlet***, 9m/14km E of Launceston. SX4686.
Lobscombe Corner *Wilts. Alternative spelling of Lopcombe Corner, qv.*
Loch a' Bhaid-luachraich *High.* ***Lake/loch***, near W coast of Ross and Cromarty district 4m/6km NE of Poolewe. **94 E3** NG8986.
Loch a' Bhainne *High.* ***Lake/loch***, small loch 3m/5km NW of Invergarry. **87 J4** NH2704.
Loch a' Bharpa *W.Isles* ***Lake/loch***, small loch on North Uist, 2m/4km NW of Locheport. **92 D5** NF8366.
Loch a' Bhealaich *Arg. & B. See Tayvallich.*
Loch a' Bhealaich (Anglicised form: Loch a' Vellich.) *High.* ***Lake/loch***, in Caithness district running into SW end of Loch Choire. **103 H6** NC5926.
Loch a' Bhealaich (Also known as Loch Vallich.) *High.* ***Lake/loch***, 2m/3km in length E to W, 4m/7km N of Upper Loch Torridon, Ross and Cromarty district. **94 E5** NG8664.
Loch a' Bhealaich *High.* ***Lake/loch***, National Trust for Scotland property 5m/8km E of head of Loch Duich, in Skye and Lochalsh district. **87 G2** NH0221.
Loch a' Bhealaich Bheithe *High.* ***Lake/loch***, mountain loch in Badenoch and Strathspey district between Ben Alder and Loch Ericht. **88 C7** NN5171.
Loch a' Bhlàir *High.* ***Lake/loch***, small loch in Lochaber district, 1m/2km N of Loch Arkaig below W slopes of Meall a' Bhlàir. **87 G5** NN0594.
Loch a' Bhràighe *High.* ***Bay***, facing NW at N end of Rona. **94 C5** NG6260.
Loch a' Bhraoin *High.* ***Lake/loch***, in Ross and Cromarty district 7m/11km S of head of Loch Broom. **95 H4** NH1374.
Loch a' Chàirn Bhàin (Anglicised form: Loch Cairnbawn.) *High.* ***Sea feature***, inlet on W coast of Sutherland district, running out into Eddrachillis Bay. **102 D5** NC1934.
Loch a' Chaorainn *High.* ***Lake/loch***, small loch on Kildermorie Forest 3m/5km W of Loch Morie, Ross and Cromarty district. **96 B4** NH4678.
Loch a' Chaoruinn *Arg. & B.* ***Lake/loch***, small loch in Knapdale, Argyll, 4m/7km W of West Tarbert. **73 F4** NR7866.
Loch a' Chlaidheimh *High.* ***Lake/loch***, small corrie lake on NE slopes of Maoile Lunndaidh. Issuing stream flows into Loch Monar 2m/4km S. **95 H7** NH1446.
Loch a' Chnuic Bhric *Arg. & B.* ***Lake/loch***, small loch near W coast of Jura, 3m/4km W of Beinn a' Chaolais. **72 C3** NR4473.
Loch a' Choire *High.* ***Lake/loch***, small loch in Inverness district 4m/6km SE of Dores. **88 D2** NH6229.
Loch a' Choire *High.* ***Sea feature***, inlet on NW shore of Loch Linnhe, opposite Shuna Island. **79 K2** NM8452.
Loch a' Choire Mhòir *High.* ***Lake/loch***, small loch at head of Strath Mulzie, Sutherland district, to E of Seana Bhraigh. **95 K3** NH3088.
Loch a' Choire Riabhaich *High.* ***Lake/loch***, small loch in South Morar, 4m/6km W of Arisaig. **86 D6** NM7287.
Loch a' Chracaich *High. Gaelic form of Loch a' Creagach, qv.*
Loch a' Chràthaich *High.* ***Lake/loch***, small loch in Inverness district 4m/7km NW of Invermoriston. **87 K2** NH3621.
Loch a' Chroisg (Anglicised form: Loch Rosque.) *High.* ***Lake/loch***, in Ross and Cromarty district, 1m/2km W of Achnasheen. Length 3m/5km E to W. **95 H6** NH1258.
Loch a' Chuilinn (Also known as Loch Culen.) *High.* ***Lake/loch***, small loch in course of River Bran in Ross and Cromarty district, 1m/2km W of head of Loch Luichart. **95 J5** NH2961.
Loch a' Creagach (Gaelic form: Loch a' Chracaich.) *High.* ***Bay***, on SW side of Loch Torridon, Ross and Cromarty district, 4m/6km NW of Shieldaig. **94 D6** NG7657.
Loch a' Gharbh Bhaid Mhòir *High.* ***Lake/loch***, narrow loch 2m/3km SE of Rhiconich, Sutherland district. **102 E4** NC2748.
Loch a' Gharbhrain *High.* ***Lake/loch***, small loch in Strathvaich Forest, 1km NW of W end of Loch Glascarnoch. **95 J4** NH2876.
Loch a' Ghille Ghobaich *High.* ***Lake/loch***, near coast of Lochaber district, 2m/3km S of Mallaig. **86 C5** NM6894.
Loch a' Ghlinne *High.* ***Lake/loch***, small loch 3m/5km N of Aird of Sleat, Skye. **86 B4** NG5905.
Loch a' Ghlinne (Glen Bay). *W.Isles* ***Lake/loch***, on N coast of St. Kilda. NA0800.
Loch a' Ghlinne *W.Isles* ***Lake/loch***, near W coast of North Harris, 1km N of Husival Mòr. **100 C6** NB0212.
Loch a' Ghobha-Dhuibh *High.* ***Lake/loch***, one of two small lochs on E side of Ben Hope. **103 G4** NC4949.
Loch a' Ghobhainn *High.* ***Lake/loch***, small loch in Shieldaig Forest, 5m/8km SW of Talladale, Ross and Cromarty district. **94 E5** NG8365.
Loch a' Ghorm-choire *High.* ***Lake/loch***, 1m/2km N of Loch Fiag. Ben Hee rises steeply to NW. **103 G5** NC4433.
Loch a' Ghriama *High.* ***Lake/loch***, in Sutherland district running N to S at head of Loch Shin. **103 F6** NC3926.
Loch a' Laip *W.Isles* ***Sea feature***, stretch of water separating Benbecula and Wiay. **92 D7** NF8647.
Loch a' Mhadaidh *High.* ***Lake/loch***, corrie loch below Sgurr Mòr in Ross and Cromarty district, 3m/5km S of Corrieshalloch Gorge. **95 H4** NH1973.
Loch a' Mhuilinn *High. Alternative name for Loch a' Mhuillidh, qv.*
Loch a' Mhuilinn *High.* ***Lake/loch***, small loch 3m/4km SE of Altnabreac Station. **105 F4** ND0142.
Loch a' Mhuillidh (Also known as Loch a' Mhuilinn.) *High.* ***Lake/loch***, small loch in course of River Farrar in Inverness district 4m/7km below Loch Monar. **87 J1** NH2738.
Loch a' Phearsain *Arg. & B.* ***Lake/loch***, to NE of Kilmelford. **79 K6** NM8513.
Loch a' Sguirr *High.* ***Bay***, W facing bay at N end of Raasay. **94 B6** NG6052.
Loch a' Tuath (Also known as Broad Bay.) *W.Isles* ***Bay***, large bay on E coast of Isle of Lewis, extending from Tolsta Head to Tiumpan Head on Eye Peninsula, and SW to Laxdale, N of Stornoway. **101 G4** NB4936.
Loch a' Vellich *High. Anglicised form of Loch a' Bhealaich, qv.*
Loch Achaidh na h-Inich *High.* ***Lake/loch***, small loch 2m/3km S of Plockton, Skye and Lochalsh district. **86 E1** NG8130.
Loch Achall *High.* ***Lake/loch***, at foot of Glen Achall, Ross and Cromarty district, 2m/4km E of Ullapool. **95 H2** NH1795.
Loch Achanalt *High.* ***Lake/loch***, small loch in course of River Bran in Ross and Cromarty district 3m/5km W of head of Loch Luichart. **95 J5** NH2761.
Loch Achilty *High.* ***Lake/loch***, small loch in Ross and Cromarty district 3m/5km W of Strathpeffer. **96 B6** NH4356.
Loch Achnamoine *High.* ***Lake/loch***, 1m/2km SE of Badanloch Lodge, in course of River Helmsdale, Sutherland district. **104 D5** NC8032.
Loch Achonachie *High.* ***Lake/loch***, and reservoir in course of River Conon, Ross and Cromarty district, 3m/5km SW of Strathpeffer. **96 B6** NH4354.
Loch Achray *Stir.* ***Lake/loch***, small loch in Achray Forest, within Queen Elizabeth Forest Park, 7m/11km W of Callander. **81 G7** NN5106.
Loch Affric *High.* ***Lake/loch***, in course of River Affric in Inverness district 12m/19km SW of Cannich. **87 H2** NH1522.
Loch Ailort *High.* ***Sea feature***, arm of Sound of Arisaig passing to S of peninsula of Ardnish in Lochaber district. **86 D6** NM7379.
Loch Ailsh *High.* ***Lake/loch***, in Sutherland district 8m/12km SE of Inchnadamph. **103 F7** NC3110.
Loch Ainort *High.* ***Sea feature***, inlet on E coast of Skye opposite Scalpay. **86 B2** NG5528.
Loch Airdeglais *Arg. & B.* ***Lake/loch***, highest and largest of chain of small lochs in upper reaches of Lussa River, Mull, 2m/3km N of Loch Buie. Others, in order of descent, are Loch an Ellen, Loch an Eilein and Loch Sguabain. **79 H5** NM6228.
Loch Airigh a' Phuill *High.* ***Lake/loch***, small loch in Ross and Cromarty district, 2m/3km E of Charlestown and head of Gair Loch. **94 E4** NG8475.
Loch Airigh na Beinne *High.* ***Lake/loch***, small loch at base of E slopes of Fashven, Sutherland district. **103 F2** NC3266.
Loch Airigh na h-Airde *W.Isles* ***Lake/loch***, 4m/7km E of head of Little Loch Roag, Isle of Lewis. **100 E5** NB2123.
Loch Airigh nan Sloc *W.Isles* ***Lake/loch***, small loch 8m/13km W of Stornoway, Isle of Lewis. **100 E4** NB2833.
Loch Akran *High.* ***Lake/loch***, small loch in Sutherland district, 3m/5km SW of Reay. **104 E2** NC9260.
Loch Alsh *High.* ***Sea feature***, arm of sea between Skye and Scottish mainland, penetrating inland to Eilean Donan, where Loch Duich runs into it from SE and Loch Long from NE. **86 D2** NG8125.
Loch Alvie *High.* ***Lake/loch***, small loch in Badenoch and Strathspey district 2m/4km SW of Aviemore. **89 F4** NH8609.

L

Loch an Alltain Duibh *High.* ***Bay***, on W coast of Ross and Cromarty district, 1m/2km NW of Polbain. **102 B7** NB9812.

Loch an Alltan Fheàrna *High.* ***Lake/loch***, 1km S of Loch nan Clàr, Sutherland district. **104 C5** NC7433.

Loch an Daimh *High.* ***Lake/loch***, in Ross and Cromarty district 9m/14km E of Ullapool. **95 J2** NH2794.

Loch an Daimh *P. & K.* ***Lake/loch***, and reservoir 3m/4km NE of Loch Lyon. Formed out of two smaller lochs, Loch Giorra and Loch Daimh, when water level was raised. **81 F3** NN4846.

Loch an Deerie *High. Alternative name for Loch an Dherue, qv.*

Loch an Dherue (Also known as Loch an Deerie.) *High.* ***Lake/loch***, in Caithness district 3m/5km S of head of Kyle of Tongue. **103 H4** NC5448.

Loch an Doire Dhuibh *High.* ***Lake/loch***, just to S of Loch Sionascaig. **102 D7** NC1311.

Loch an Draing *High.* ***Lake/loch***, small loch in Ross and Cromarty district, 3m/5km NE of Melvaig. **94 D2** NG7790.

Loch an Dubh-Lochain *High.* ***Lake/loch***, small loch in Gleann an Dubh-Lochain. NG8200.

Loch an Dùin ***Lake/loch***, small deep loch on border of Highland and Perth & Kinross, 6m/10km SE of Dalwhinnie. **88 E7** NN7279.

Loch an Easain Uaine *High.* ***Lake/loch***, small loch in Reay Forest, Sutherland district, 3m/4km S of Foinaven. **103 F4** NC3246.

Loch an Eilein *Arg. & B. See Loch Airdeglais.*

Loch an Eilein *High.* ***Lake/loch***, small loch in Rothiemurchus Forest, Badenoch and Strathspey district, 3m/5km S of Aviemore. Noted for triple echo. Remains of medieval castle on islet in loch. **89 F4** NH8907.

Loch an Eilein Castle *High.* ***Castle***, ruined 15c castle, later enlarged, in Loch an Eilein, 3m/5km S of Aviemore. **89 F4** NH8908.

Loch an Eircill *High.* ***Lake/loch***, at SE end of Glen Coul. **103 F6** NC3027.

Loch an Ellen *Arg. & B. See Loch Airdeglais.*

Loch an Eòin *High.* ***Lake/loch***, small loch in Ross and Cromarty district, 5m/8km N of head of Loch Carron. **95 F6** NG9251.

Loch an Fhiarlaid *High.* ***Lake/loch***, small loch in Ross and Cromarty district 4m/6km S of Kinlochewe. **95 G6** NH0556.

Loch an Fhir Mhaoil *W.Isles* ***Lake/loch***, small loch on Isle of Lewis, 5m/8km S of Earshader. **100 D5** NB1826.

Loch an Iasaich *High.* ***Lake/loch***, small loch 3m/4km SE of Attadale, Ross and Cromarty district. **87 F1** NG9535.

Loch an Lagain *High.* ***Lake/loch***, small loch 4m/6km NE of Bonar Bridge. **96 D2** NH6595.

Loch an Laig Aird *High.* ***Lake/loch***, small, irregular-shaped loch, 1m/2km NE of Scourie, Sutherland district. **102 D4** NC1746.

Loch an Laoigh *High.* ***Lake/loch***, on border of Ross and Cromarty and Skye and Lochalsh districts, 4m/6km S of Achnashellach Station. **95 G7** NH0241.

Loch an Leathaid Bhuain *High.* ***Lake/loch***, in Sutherland district adjoining Loch na Creige Duibhe, to W of Loch More. **102 E5** NC2736.

Loch an Leoid *Arg. & B.* ***Lake/loch***, small loch in Argyll, 1m/2km NW of Kilchrenan. **80 B5** NN0124.

Loch an Leothaid *High.* ***Lake/loch***, 2m/3km N of Loch Assynt. **102 D5** NC1630.

Loch an Nostarie *High.* ***Lake/loch***, near coast of Lochaber district, 1m/2km SE of Mallaig. **86 C5** NM6995.

Loch an Ruathair *High.* ***Lake/loch***, in Sutherland district 3m/4km N of Kinbrace. **104 D5** NC8636.

Loch an Sgòir *High.* ***Lake/loch***, small mountain loch, 2m/3km N of Ben Alder. **88 B7** NN4975.

Loch an Sgoltaire *Arg. & B.* ***Lake/loch***, small loch on Colonsay 1km SW of Kiloran Bay. **72 B1** NR3897.

Loch an t-Seilg *High.* ***Lake/loch***, in Sutherland district, 3m/4km NE of Loch Merkland. **103 G5** NC4136.

Loch an t-Seilich *High.* ***Lake/loch***, in course of River Tromie on Gaick Forest, in Badenoch and Strathspey district, 9m/14km S of Kingussie. **88 E6** NN7586.

Loch an t-Siob *Arg. & B.* ***Lake/loch***, on Jura, to S of Beinn Shiantaidh in Paps of Jura. **72 D3** NR5173.

Loch an Tachdaidh *High.* ***Lake/loch***, small loch on low plateau, 10m/16km E of Attadale. **87 G1** NH0938.

Loch an Tairbeart *W.Isles* ***Lake/loch***, small loch, almost surrounded by woodland, 3m/4km SE of Breascleit, Isle of Lewis. **100 E4** NB2532.

Loch an Tobair *W.Isles* ***Lake/loch***, small loch 8m/13km N of Stornoway, Isle of Lewis. **101 G3** NB4345.

Loch an Ulbhaidh *High.* ***Lake/loch***, small loch in course of Allt Loch an Ulbhaidh, 2m/3km N of Loch Shin. **103 G6** NC4922.

Loch Ard *Stir.* ***Lake/loch***, 3m/5km W of Aberfoyle. Remains of medieval castle on islet near S shore. **81 F7** NN4601.

Loch Ard Forest *Stir.* ***Forest/woodland***, S of Loch Ard, forming part of Queen Elizabeth Forest Park. **74 C1** NS4898.

Loch Arichlinie *High.* ***Lake/loch***, small loch in Sutherland district, 2m/3km NW of Kinbrace. **104 D5** NC8435.

Loch Arienas *High.* ***Lake/loch***, in Morvern, Lochaber district, 4m/6km N of Lochaline. **79 H2** NM6851.

Loch Arkaig *High.* ***Lake/loch***, in Lochaber district running about 12m/19km W to E from 1km below confluence of Rivers Dessary and Pean to 1m/2km NW of Bunarkaig on Loch Lochy. **87 G5** NN0891.

Loch Arklet *Stir.* ***Lake/loch***, and reservoir between Loch Katrine and Loch Lomond, 1m/2km E of Inversnaid. **80 E7** NN3709.

Loch Arnish *High.* ***Bay***, on W coast of Raasay, 3m/5km from N end of island. **94 B7** NG5948.

Loch Arthur *D. & G.* ***Lake/loch***, small loch 1km E of Beeswing and 6m/10km SW of Dumfries. **65 K4** NX9068.

Loch Ascaig *High.* ***Lake/loch***, in Sutherland district, 2m/4km E of Altanduin. **104 D6** NC8425.

Loch Ascog *Arg. & B.* ***Lake/loch***, small loch on Bute, 1m/2km S of Rothesay. **73 J4** NS0962.

Loch Ashie *High.* ***Lake/loch***, in Inverness district 6m/10km S of Inverness. Area about 390 acres or 160 hectares. **88 D1** NH6234.

Loch Assapol *Arg. & B.* ***Lake/loch***, on Ross of Mull, 1m/2km SE of Bunessan. **79 F5** NM4020.

Loch Assynt *High.* ***Lake/loch***, in Sutherland district, over 6m/10km NW to SE and 282 feet or 86 metres at maximum depth, 5m/7km E of Lochinver. Village of Inchnadamph at head of loch. **102 E6** NC2124.

Loch Aulasary *W.Isles* ***Sea feature***, large inlet on NE coast of North Uist, 1km N of Lochportain. **92 E4** NF9474.

Loch Avich *Arg. & B.* ***Lake/loch***, 2m/3km NW of Dalavich on W side of Loch Awe, Argyll. **80 A6** NM9314.

Loch Avon *Moray* ***Lake/loch***, below SE slope of Cairn Gorm. River Avon flows from foot of loch. **89 H4** NJ0102.

Loch Awe *Arg. & B.* ***Lake/loch***, narrow loch 24m/39km long SW to NE in Argyll. Runs from Ford to Pass of Brander and discharges by River Awe to Loch Etive. Maximum depth over 300 feet or 90 metres. **80 A6** NM9610.

Loch Awe *High.* ***Lake/loch***, at head of River Loanan, 4m/6km S of Loch Assynt. **102 E7** NC2415.

Loch Bà *Arg. & B.* ***Lake/loch***, source of River Bà on Mull, 3m/5km S of Salen. Length 3m/5km SE to NW. **79 G4** NM5638.

Loch Bà *High.* ***Lake/loch***, on Rannoch Moor in Lochaber district, from which River Bà flows into head of Loch Laidon. **80 E3** NN3250.

Loch Bad a' Ghaill (Anglicised form: Loch Baddagyle.) *High.* ***Lake/loch***, near NW coast of Ross and Cromarty district 8m/12km S of Lochinver. **102 C7** NC0710.

Loch Bad an Sgalaig *High.* ***Lake/loch***, near W coast of Ross and Cromarty district 4m/7km SE of Gairloch. Upper part of loch is known as Dubh Loch. **94 E4** NG8470.

Loch Badanloch *High.* ***Lake/loch***, S part of a double loch in Sutherland district 5m/8km W of Kinbrace. N part of loch is known as Loch nan Clàr. **104 C5** NC7734.

Loch Baddagyle *High. Anglicised form of Loch Bad a' Ghaill, qv.*

Loch Baghasdail *W.Isles Gaelic form of Lochboisdale (village), qv.*

Loch Baghasdail (Anglicised form: Loch Boisdale.) *W.Isles* ***Sea feature***, inlet containing several small islands, near S end of South Uist on E side. **84 D3** NF7919.

Loch Baile Mhic Chailein *Arg. & B.* ***Lake/loch***, small loch in course of River Creran, 2m/3km NW of mouth of river at head of Loch Creran, Argyll. **80 B3** NN0247.

Loch Ballygrant *Arg. & B.* ***Lake/loch***, small loch to E of Ballygrant village on Islay, 3m/4km SW of Port Askaig. **72 C4** NR4066.

Loch Baravaig *High. See Baravaig.*

Loch Bay *High.* ***Sea feature***, inlet on NW coast of Skye, 4m/7km N of Dunvegan. **93 H6** NG2655.

Loch Beag *High.* ***Sea feature***, small inlet at head of Loch nan Uamh, on N side of Ardnish peninsula in Lochaber district. **86 D6** NM7283.

Loch Bealach Cùlaidh *High.* ***Lake/loch***, small narrow loch in Wyvis Forest, 7m/11km NE of Gorstan. **96 B4** NH4471.

Loch Beanie *P. & K.* ***Lake/loch***, small loch or tarn, 3m/5km E of Spittal of Glenshee. **82 C1** NO1668.

Loch Beannach *High.* ***Lake/loch***, 3m/5km NE of Lochinver. **102 D6** NC1326.

Loch Beannach *High.* ***Lake/loch***, in Sutherland district, 4m/6km N of Lairg. **103 J7** NC5912.

Loch Beannach *High.* ***Lake/loch***, small loch, N of River Brora and 3m/5km E of Dalnessie. **103 J7** NC6814.

Loch Beannachan (Also known as Loch Beannacharain.) *High.* ***Lake/loch***, small but deep loch in course of River Meig on Strathconon Forest in Ross and Cromarty district. **95 J6** NH2351.

Loch Beannacharain *High. Alternative name for Loch Beannachan, qv.*

Loch Beannacharan (Also known as Loch Bunacharan.) *High.* ***Lake/loch***, small but deep loch in course of River Farrar in Inverness district 6m/9km above Struy Bridge. **87 K1** NH3038.

Loch Bee *W.Isles* ***Lake/loch***, large loch at N end of South Uist. **92 C7** NF7743.

Loch Beg *Arg. & B.* ***Sea feature***, inlet at head of Loch Scridain, Mull. **79 G5** NM5229.

Loch Beinn a' Mheadhoin (Also known as Loch Beneveian.) *High.* ***Lake/loch***, and reservoir in Glen Affric, Inverness district. Length 6m/9km SW to NE. **87 J2** NH2425.

Loch Ben Harrald *High.* ***Lake/loch***, 3m/5km SW of Altnaharra, Sutherland district. **103 H5** NC5133.

Loch Benachally *P. & K.* ***Lake/loch***, small loch 4m/7km W of Bridge of Cally. **82 B2** NO0750.

Loch Beneveian *High. Alternative name for Loch Beinn a' Mheadhoin, qv.*

Loch Benisval *W.Isles* ***Lake/loch***, small loch 1m/2km NW of head of Loch Resort, Isle of Lewis. **100 C6** NB0818.

Loch Beoraid *High.* ***Lake/loch***, narrow but deep loch in South Morar, Lochaber district, between Loch Morar and Loch Eilt. Length 3m/5km E to W. **86 E6** NM8285.

Loch Bhac *P. & K.* ***Lake/loch***, small loch 4m/6km SW of Blair Atholl. **81 K1** NN8262.

Loch Bhad Ghaineamhaich *High.* ***Lake/loch***, small loch 3m/4km NE of Milton. **95 K6** NH3259.

Loch Bharanaichd *High.* ***Lake/loch***, small loch 5m/8km E of Torridon. **95 F6** NG9757.

Loch Bhrodainn *High.* ***Lake/loch***, in Gaick Forest, 7m/11km E of Dalwhinnie. **88 E6** NN7483.

Loch Bhrollum *W.Isles* ***Sea feature***, inlet on SE coast of Isle of Lewis, 2m/4km to E of Loch Claidh. **101 F7** NB3102.

Loch Bhruthaich *High. Alternative name for Loch Bruicheach, qv.*

Loch Bodavat *W.Isles* ***Lake/loch***, small loch 2m/3km E of Aird Bheag and 1km N of Loch Resort, Isle of Lewis. **100 C6** NB0619.

Loch Bog *P. & K. Alternative name for Stormont Loch, qv.*

Loch Boisdale *W.Isles Anglicised form of Loch Baghasdail (sea-loch), qv.*

Loch Boltachan *P. & K.* ***Lake/loch***, small loch or tarn 1m/2km N of St. Fillans. **81 H5** NN6926.

Loch Borralan *High.* ***Lake/loch***, small loch in Sutherland district 7m/11km S of Inchnadamph. **102 E7** NC2610.

Loch Bracadale *High.* ***Sea feature***, wide inlet on SW coast of Skye between Idrigill Point and Rubha nan Clach. **85 H1** NG2837.

Loch Bradan Reservoir *S.Ayr.* ***Reservoir***, within Glen Trool Forest Park, 7m/11km SW of Dalmellington. **67 J4** NX4297.

Loch Brandy *Angus* ***Lake/loch***, mountain loch 1m/2km N of Clova. **90 B7** NO3375.

Loch Breachacha *Arg. & B.* ***Sea feature***, large inlet on S coast of Coll, 5m/7km SW of Arinagour. **78 C2** NM1653.

Loch Breivat *W.Isles* ***Lake/loch***, near NW coast of Isle of Lewis 2m/3km SE of Arnol. **101 F3** NB3345.

Loch Brittle *High.* ***Sea feature***, inlet on SW coast of Skye, 4m/6km SE of Loch Eynort. **85 J3** NG4019.

Loch Broom *High.* ***Sea feature***, long inlet on which small town of Ullapool is situated, on W coast of Ross and Cromarty district. **95 G2** NH1392.

Loch Broom *P. & K.* ***Lake/loch***, small loch 4m/7km E of Pitlochry. **82 B2** NO0057.

Loch Brora *High.* ***Lake/loch***, in course of River Brora, Sutherland district, 4m/6km NW of Brora village. **97 F1** NC8507.

Loch Bruicheach (Also known as Loch Bhruthaich.) *High.* ***Lake/loch***, small loch in Inverness district 5m/8km NW of Drumnadrochit. **88 B1** NH4536.

Loch Buidhe *High.* ***Lake/loch***, small loch 1km E of Coldbackie, Caithness district. **103 J3** NC6359.

Loch Buidhe *High.* ***Lake/loch***, in Sutherland district 5m/8km NE of Bonar Bridge. **96 D2** NH6698.

Loch Buidhe Mòr *High.* ***Lake/loch***, small loch 1m/2km W of Strathy Forest, Caithness district. **104 C3** NC7758.

Loch Buie *Arg. & B.* ***Sea feature***, large inlet on S coast of Mull. **79 H5** NM6025.

Loch Builg *Moray* ***Lake/loch***, small loch, source of Builg Burn, 6m/9km SW of Cock Bridge. **89 J4** NJ1803.

Loch Bunacharan *High. Alternative name for Loch Beannacharan, qv.*

Loch Cairnbawn *High. Anglicised form of Loch a' Chàirn Bhàin, qv.*

Loch Calavie *High.* ***Lake/loch***, small loch in Skye and Lochalsh district 3m/5km SW of head of Loch Monar. **87 G1** NH0538.

Loch Calder *High.* ***Lake/loch***, in Caithness district, 2m/4km long N to S and nearly 1m/2km wide, 5m/8km SW of Thurso. **105 F2** ND0760.

Loch Callater *Aber.* ***Lake/loch***, small loch in Glen Callater 5m/8km S of Braemar. **89 J6** NO1884.

Loch Caluim *High.* ***Lake/loch***, 2m/3km SE of Loch Scye. Loch is approximately 1km N to S. **105 F3** ND0152.

Loch Càm *Arg. & B.* ***Lake/loch***, small loch on Islay, 3m/4km N of Bridgend. **72 B4** NR3466.

Loch Caoldair *High.* ***Lake/loch***, small loch in Badenoch and Strathspey district 3m/5km NW of Dalwhinnie. **88 D6** NN6189.

Loch Caolisport *Arg. & B.* ***Sea feature***, sea-loch in Argyll, running NE from Point of Knap to Achahoish. **73 F3** NR7374.

Loch Caravat *W.Isles* ***Lake/loch***, on S of North Uist, 1m/2km E of Corúna. **92 D5** NF8461.

Loch Carlabhagh (Anglicised form: Loch Carloway.) *W.Isles* ***Sea feature***, inlet and estuary of Carloway River, on W coast of Isle of Lewis, to W of Carloway village. **100 D3** NB1842.

Loch Carloway *W.Isles Anglicised form of Loch Carlabhagh, qv.*

Loch Carnan *W.Isles* ***Sea feature***, inlet on NE coast of South Uist. **92 D7** NF8243.

Loch Caroy *High.* ***Sea feature***, inlet of Loch Bracadale, Skye, 4m/7km NW of Bracadale village. **93 H7** NG3043.

Loch Carrie *High.* ***Lake/loch***, small loch in course of River Cannich 3m/5km below dam of Loch Mullardoch in Inverness district. **87 J1** NH2633.

Loch Carron *High.* ***Sea feature***, long inlet in Ross and Cromarty district, extending from S end of Inner Sound on N side of Kyle of Lochalsh to foot of Glen Carron. Vehicle ferry across narrows at Stromeferry. **87 F1** NG8735.

Loch Casgro *W.Isles* ***Lake/loch***, small loch 3m/5km E of Bragar, Isle of Lewis. **101 F3** NB3347.

Loch Cean Thulabhig (Anglicised form: Loch Ceann Hulavig.) *W.Isles* ***Sea feature***, inlet on NW coast of Isle of Lewis, 3m/4km S of Breascleit. **100 E4** NB2131.

Loch Ceann Dibig *W.Isles* ***Sea feature***, inlet on E coast of South Harris, 1m/2km S of Tarbert. **93 G2** NG1597.

Loch Ceann Hulavig *W.Isles Anglicised form of Loch Cean Thulabhaig, qv.*

Loch Ceo Ghlas *High. Alternative spelling of Loch Ceo Glais, qv.*

Loch Ceo Glais (Also spelled Loch Ceo Ghlas or Loch Ceo Glas.) *High.* ***Lake/loch***, small loch in Inverness district nearly 1km SW of Loch Duntelchaig. **88 C2** NH5828.

Loch Ceo Glas *High. Alternative spelling of Loch Ceo Glais, qv.*

Loch Chaorunn *Arg. & B.* ***Lake/loch***, small loch in Knapdale, Argyll, 3m/4km NW of Tarbert. **73 G3** NR8371.

Loch Choire *High.* ***Lake/loch***, in Caithness district 6m/9km SE of Altnaharra. **103 J6** NC6328.

Loch Choire Forest *High.* ***Open space***, deer forest in Caithness district surrounding Loch Choire. **103 J5** NC6328.

Loch Choire Lodge *High.* ***Settlement***, at NE end of Loch Choire, Sutherland district. **103 J5** NC6530.

Loch Chon *Stir.* ***Lake/loch***, 4m/6km E of Ben Lomond. **81 F7** NN4205.

Loch Ciaran *Arg. & B.* ***Lake/loch***, small loch in Kintyre, Argyll, 1m/2km S of Clachan. **73 F5** NR7754.

Loch Cill Chriosd *High.* ***Lake/loch***, small loch on Skye, 3m/4km SW of Broadford. **86 C2** NG6120.

Loch Claidh *W.Isles* ***Sea feature***, large inlet on S coast of Isle of Lewis, to E of Loch Seaforth. **100 E7** NB2603.

Loch Clàir *High.* ***Lake/loch***, small loch in Ross and Cromarty district, 1m/2km SE of Port Henderson. **94 D4** NG7771.

L

Loch Gaineamhach *Arg. & B.* ***Lake/loch***, 3m/5km SE of Ford. **80 A7** NM9100.
Loch Gaineamhach *High.* ***Lake/loch***, small loch 7m/11km S of Altnaharra, to SW of Loch a' Bhealaich, Sutherland district. **103 H6** NC5824.
Loch Gaineamhach *High.* ***Lake/loch***, small loch in Ross and Cromarty district, 4m/6km W of Shieldaig. **94 D6** NG7553.
Loch Gaineamhach *High.* ***Lake/loch***, small loch in Ross and Cromarty district, 1m/2km NW of Loch a' Ghobhainn. **94 E5** NG8367.
Loch Gaineimh *High.* ***Lake/loch***, small loch 2m/3km N of West Langwell and 4m/6km SW of Dalbreck, Sutherland district. **103 J7** NC6912.
Loch Gair *Arg. & B.* ***Sea feature***, inlet on W side of Loch Fyne in Argyll, 5m/7km E of Lochgilphead. **73 H2** NR9290.
Loch Gamhna *High.* ***Lake/loch***, small loch 4m/6km S of Aviemore. **89 F4** NH8906.
Loch Gaorsaic *High.* ***Lake/loch***, small loch in NE part of Kintail Estate, Skye and Lochalsh district. **87 G2** NH0222.
Loch Garasdale *Arg. & B.* ***Lake/loch***, small loch in Kintyre, Argyll, 3m/5km S of Clachan. **73 F5** NR7651.
Loch Garbhaig *High.* ***Lake/loch***, small loch 3m/4km E of Letterewe, Ross and Cromarty district. **95 G4** NG9970.
Loch Garry *High.* ***Lake/loch***, and reservoir in course of River Garry, Lochaber district, 2m/4km W of Invergarry. Length 5m/7km. **87 J4** NH2302.
Loch Garry *P. & K.* ***Lake/loch***, narrow deep loch 3m/4km long N to S, at head of Glen Garry, Atholl. **88 D7** NN6270.
Loch Garten *High.* ***Lake/loch***, small loch in Abernethy Forest, in Badenoch and Strathspey district, 4m/6km E of Boat of Garten. Nature trail in vicinity. **89 G3** NJ9718.
Loch Garten Nature Reserve *High.* ***Nature reserve***, Royal Society for the Protection of Birds reserve, 2m/3km SE of Boat of Garten. Particularly noted for nesting ospreys which can be observed from a special hide. **89 G3** NH9718.
Loch Garve *High.* ***Lake/loch***, small but deep loch in Ross and Cromarty district 4m/7km W of Strathpeffer. **96 B5** NH4159.
Loch Gelly *Fife* ***Lake/loch***, small loch to SE of Lochgelly. **75 K1** NT1893.
Loch Ghabhaig *High.* ***Lake/loch***, small loch 1m/2km SW of Talladale, Ross and Cromarty district. **95 F5** NG8969.
Loch Ghuilbinn (Anglicised form: Loch Gulbin.) *High.* ***Lake/loch***, small loch in Lochaber district, 3m/4km N of foot of Loch Ossian. **88 B7** NN4174.
Loch Gilp *Arg. & B.* ***Sea feature***, inlet of Loch Fyne, running past Ardrishaig to Lochgilphead in Argyll. **73 G2** NR8584.
Loch Giorra *P. & K.* *See Loch an Daimh.*
Loch Glascarnoch *High.* ***Reservoir***, in Ross and Cromarty district, 14m/23km NW of Dingwall. **95 K4** NH3470.
Loch Glashan *Arg. & B.* ***Lake/loch***, and reservoir in Asknish Forest 4m/7km NE of Lochgilphead, Argyll. **73 H1** NR9193.
Loch Glass *High.* ***Lake/loch***, in Ross and Cromarty district 8m/12km W of Alness. **96 C4** NH5172.
Loch Glassie *P. & K.* ***Lake/loch***, small loch, 2m/3km N of Aberfeldy. **81 K2** NN8552.
Loch Glencoul *High.* ***Lake/loch***, running NW to join Loch Glendhu, past Kylesku into Loch a' Chàirn Bhàin and then into Eddrachillis Bay, W coast of Sutherland district. **102 E5** NC2531.
Loch Glendhu *High.* ***Lake/loch***, running W to join Loch Glencoul, past Kylesku into Loch a' Chàirn Bhàin and then into Eddrachillis Bay, W coast of Sutherland district. **102 E5** NC2533.
Loch Glow *Fife* ***Lake/loch***, small loch in Cleish Hills 3m/5km W of Kelty. **75 J1** NT0895.
Loch Goil *Arg. & B.* ***Sea feature***, sea-loch in Argyll, running 6m/10km N to S from Lochgoilhead to Loch Long. **73 K1** NS2097.
Loch Goosey *S.Ayr.* ***Lake/loch***, small loch 4m/7km E of Barrhill. **67 G5** NX2982.
Loch Gorm *Arg. & B.* ***Lake/loch***, near W coast of Islay 3m/5km NW of Bruichladdich. On islet towards E side of loch are ruins of a Macdonald stronghold. **72 A4** NR2365.
Loch Gorm *High.* ***Lake/loch***, corrie lake to N of An Coileachan, 2m/4km NE of Loch Fannich. **95 J5** NH2369.
Loch Gowan *High.* ***Lake/loch***, small loch 1m/2km S of Achnasheen, Ross and Cromarty district. **95 H6** NH1456.
Loch Grannoch (Also spelled Loch Grennoch.) *D. & G.* ***Lake/loch***, 7m/11km SW of New Galloway. **65 F4** NX5469.
Loch Grennoch *D. & G.* *Alternative spelling of Loch Grannoch, qv.*
Loch Greshornish *High.* ***Sea feature***, inlet of Loch Snizort on N coast of Skye, 6m/10km NE of Dunvegan. **93 J6** NG3454.
Loch Gress *W.Isles* ***Lake/loch***, small loch on Isle of Lewis, 6m/9km E of Barvas. **101 G2** NB4450.
Loch Grimshader *W.Isles* *Anglicised form of Loch Grimsiadar, qv.*
Loch Grimsiadar (Anglicised form: Loch Grimshader.) *W.Isles* ***Sea feature***, long narrow inlet on E coast of Isle of Lewis. Village of Grimsiadar at head of inlet, 5m/8km S of Stornoway. **101 G5** NB4125.
Loch Grosebay *W.Isles* ***Sea feature***, inlet on SE coast of South Harris, 5m/8km S of Tarbert. **93 G2** NG1592.
Loch Gruinart *Arg. & B.* ***Sea feature***, deep inlet on N coast of Islay. **72 A4** NR2971.
Loch Grunavat *W.Isles* ***Lake/loch***, about 2m/4km N to S near W coast of Isle of Lewis, 2m/4km W of Little Loch Roag. **100 C5** NB0827.
Loch Guinach *High.* *Alternative name for Loch Gynack, qv.*
Loch Gulbin *High.* *Anglicised form of Loch Ghuilbinn, qv.*
Loch Gynack (Also known as Loch Guinach.) *High.* ***Lake/loch***, small loch in Badenoch and Strathspey district, 1m/2km NW of Kingussie. **88 E4** NH7402.
Loch Hallan *W.Isles* ***Lake/loch***, small loch near to coast of South Uist, 1m/2km NW of Dalabrog. **84 C2** NF7322.
Loch Haluim *High.* ***Lake/loch***, small irregular-shaped loch 3m/5km W of Loch Loyal, Caithness district. **103 H4** NC5545.
Loch Harport *High.* ***Sea feature***, long narrow inlet of Loch Bracadale on Skye, running up to Drynoch, W of Sligachan. **85 J1** NG3634.
Loch Harrow *D. & G.* ***Lake/loch***, 2m/3km E of Corserine, summit of Rhinns of Kells. **67 K5** NX5866.
Loch Head *D. & G.* ***Settlement***, on NW shore of Elrig Loch, 4m/6km N of Port William. **64 D6** NX3249.
Loch Head *D. & G.* ***Settlement***, at S end of Loch Doon, 5m/8km W of Carsphairn. **67 J4** NX4892.
Loch Heilen *High.* ***Lake/loch***, in Caithness district 3m/4km SE of Dunnet. **105 H2** ND2568.
Loch Hempriggs *High.* ***Lake/loch***, in Caithness district 2m/4km S of Wick. **105 J4** ND3447.
Loch Hirta (Also known as Village Bay.) *W.Isles* ***Bay***, on SE coast of St. Kilda. NF1098.
Loch Hoil *P. & K.* ***Lake/loch***, small loch or tarn 4m/6km S of Aberfeldy. **81 K3** NN8643.
Loch Hope *High.* ***Lake/loch***, narrow loch in Sutherland district, some 6m/10km long N to S, 1m/2km E of Loch Eriboll at nearest point. **103 G3** NC4654.
Loch Horn *High.* ***Lake/loch***, small loch 1km W of Ben Horn, 4m/7km NW of Golspie. **96 E1** NC7906.
Loch Hosta *W.Isles* ***Lake/loch***, small loch near NW coast of North Uist to N of Hosta. **92 C4** NF7272.
Loch Hourn *High.* ***Sea feature***, long inlet of Sound of Sleat, penetrating inland to Kinloch Hourn, 5m/8km N of head of Loch Quoich, Lochaber district. **86 D3** NG8506.
Loch Howie *D. & G.* ***Lake/loch***, 5m/8km E of St. John's Town of Dalry. **68 C5** NX6983.
Loch Humphrey *W.Dun.* ***Lake/loch***, small loch on Kilpatrick Hills 4m/6km E of Dumbarton. **74 C3** NS4576.
Loch Huna *W.Isles* ***Lake/loch***, small loch on North Uist, 5m/8km S of Solas. **92 D5** NF8166.
Loch Hunder *W.Isles* ***Lake/loch***, small loch on North Uist, 2m/3km S of Loch na Madadh inlet. **92 E5** NF9065.
Loch Hunish *High.* ***Bay***, on S side of Rubha Hunish, at N tip of Skye. **93 J4** NG4076.
Loch Inchard *High.* ***Sea feature***, large inlet on W coast of Sutherland district. River Rhiconich flows into head of loch at Rhiconich. **102 E3** NC2355.
Loch Indaal *Arg. & B.* ***Sea feature***, large arm of sea on E side of Rinns of Islay, extending N to within 2m/4km of Loch Gruinart. **72 A5** NR2758.
Loch Insh *High.* ***Lake/loch***, small loch in course of River Spey in Badenoch and Strathspey district, 5m/8km NE of Kingussie. **89 F4** NH8304.
Loch Inshore *High.* ***Lake/loch***, small loch 2m/3km NW of Achiemore, Sutherland district. **103 F2** NC3269.
Loch Inver *High.* ***Sea feature***, inlet on W coast of Sutherland district with port of Lochinver at its head. **102 C6** NC0922.
Loch Iubhair *Stir.* ***Lake/loch***, in course of River Fillan 2m/4km E of Crianlarich. **81 F5** NN4226.
Loch Kanaird *High.* ***Sea feature***, inlet of Loch Broom, W coast of Ross and Cromarty district, into which River Kanaird flows, on E side of Isle Martin. **95 H2** NH1099.
Loch Katrine *Stir.* ***Lake/loch***, 8m/13km W to E, extending from Glen Gyle to the Trossachs 8m/13km W of Callander. Aqueduct conveys water to Glasgow. **81 F7** NN4409.
Loch Keisgaig *High.* ***Lake/loch***, small loch 4m/7km S of Cape Wrath. **102 E2** NC2668.
Loch Kemp *High.* ***Lake/loch***, small loch on SE side of Loch Ness, 3m/5km across loch from Invermoriston. **88 B3** NH4616.
Loch Ken *D. & G.* ***Lake/loch***, long loch extending 9m/15km S from Kenmure Castle, near New Galloway to Glenlochar. N end of loch is fed by Water of Ken, one of two main tributaries, the other being Black Water of Dee or River Dee which flows into loch below Loch Ken Viaduct. Lower section of loch is also known as River Dee. **65 G3** NX7068.
Loch Kennard *P. & K.* ***Lake/loch***, small loch 4m/6km SE of Aberfeldy. **82 A3** NN9046.
Loch Kildonan *W.Isles* ***Lake/loch***, and locality near W coast of South Uist, 2m/3km SE of Rubha Ardvule. Ruined building near S end of loch is Flora Macdonald's birthplace (1722). **84 C2** NF7327.
Loch Killin *High.* ***Lake/loch***, small loch in Inverness district 9m/15km E of Fort Augustus. **88 C3** NH5210.
Loch Kinardochy *P. & K.* ***Lake/loch***, small loch 3m/4km S of Tummel Bridge. **81 J2** NN7755.
Loch Kindar *D. & G.* ***Lake/loch***, 1m/2km S of New Abbey. **65 K4** NX9664.
Loch Kinellan *High.* ***Lake/loch***, small loch on SW edge of Strathpeffer. **96 B6** NH4757.
Loch Kinnabus *Arg. & B.* ***Lake/loch***, small loch on The Oa, Islay, 2m/3km E of Mull of Oa. **72 A6** NR3042.
Loch Kinord *Aber.* ***Lake/loch***, small loch 1m/2km W of Dinnet. **90 C4** NO4499.
Loch Kirkaig *High.* ***Sea feature***, inlet on W coast on border of Ross and Cromarty district and Sutherland district, 2m/4km SW of Lochinver. **102 C7** NC0719.
Loch Kishorn *High.* ***Sea feature***, wide inlet on N side of Loch Carron, Ross and Cromarty district, opposite Plockton. **86 E1** NG8138.
Loch Knockie *High.* ***Lake/loch***, small loch in Inverness district 5m/8km NE of Fort Augustus. **88 B3** NH4513.
Loch Knowe *Sc.Bord.* ***Mountain***, on W edge of Kielder Forest, 3m/5km W of Kielder. Height 1322 feet or 403 metres. **70 A4** NY5893.
Loch Laga *High.* ***Lake/loch***, small loch 2m/4km NW of Glenborrodale. **79 H1** NM6463.
Loch Laggan *High.* ***Lake/loch***, and reservoir in Badenoch and Strathspey district, linked to Loch Moy to SW where Laggan Dam is located (Lochaber district). Length 11m/18km NE to SW (including Loch Moy). **88 B6** NN4886.
Loch Laich *Arg. & B.* ***Sea feature***, inlet on E shore of Loch Linnhe, SW of Portnacroish, Argyll. **80 A3** NM9246.
Loch Laide *High.* ***Lake/loch***, small loch in Inverness district 4m/7km NE of Drumnadrochit. **88 C1** NH5435.
Loch Laidon (Also known as Loch Lydoch.) ***Lake/loch***, narrow loch 5m/8km long SW to NE on border of Highland and Perth & Kinross, 6m/10km W of Loch Rannoch. Rannoch railway station near NE end. **80 E2** NN3854.
Loch Lairig Eala *Stir.* ***Lake/loch***, small loch 3m/5km S of Killin. **81 G5** NN5527.
Loch Langavat *W.Isles* ***Lake/loch***, on Isle of Lewis, midway between Loch Erisort to E and Loch Resort to W. 8m/13km long NE to SW, although nowhere more than 1km wide. **100 D6** NB1819.
Loch Langavat *W.Isles* ***Lake/loch***, small loch near E coast of Isle of Lewis, 3m/4km SW of Cellar Head. **101 H2** NB5254.
Loch Langavat *W.Isles* ***Lake/loch***, on South Harris, some 3m/4km in length N to S and 2m/4km NE of Leverburgh. **93 F3** NG0490.
Loch Laoigh *High.* ***Lake/loch***, small loch 5m/8km NW of Dornoch. **96 E2** NH7395.
Loch Laro *High.* ***Lake/loch***, small loch 5m/7km N of Bonar Bridge. **96 D2** NH6099.
Loch Laxford *High.* ***Sea feature***, large inlet on W coast of Sutherland district, 4m/6km NE of Scourie. **102 D3** NC1950.
Loch Leacann *Arg. & B.* ***Lake/loch***, small loch in Argyll 3m/4km NW of Furnace on Loch Fyne. NN0003.
Loch Leathan *Arg. & B.* ***Lake/loch***, small loch, 6m/10km N of Lochgilphead. **73 G1** NR8798.
Loch Leathan *High.* ***Reservoir***, 5m/8km N of Portree, Skye. **94 B6** NG5051.
Loch Lednock Reservoir *P. & K.* ***Reservoir***, near head of Glen Lednock, 5m/8km NW of Comrie. **81 J4** NN7129.
Loch Lee *Angus* ***Lake/loch***, in course of Water of Lee, 4m/6km W of Tarfside. **90 C7** NO4279.
Loch Leurbost *W.Isles* ***Sea feature***, long inlet on E coast of Isle of Lewis. Village of Liurbost is near head of inlet on N side. **101 F5** NB3724.
Loch Leven *High.* ***Lake/loch***, in Lochaber district, running 11m/17km W from Kinlochleven to Loch Linnhe. **80 C1** NN0859.
Loch Leven *P. & K.* ***Lake/loch***, some 10m/16km in circumference, on E side of Kinross. Nature reserve. Ruins of medieval priory on St. Serf's Island and ruins of 15c castle (Historic Scotland) on Castle Island. **82 C7** NO1401.
Loch Leven Castle *P. & K.* ***Castle***, on Castle Island in Loch Leven, 1km from shore at Kinross. Early 15c tower house (Historic Scotland) famous as castle in which Mary, Queen of Scots, was imprisoned in 1567. **82 C7** NO1301.
Loch Libo *E.Renf.* ***Lake/loch***, small loch 3m/5km SW of Neilston. **74 C5** NS4355.
Loch Linnhe ***Sea feature***, long sea-loch running 22m/35km from Fort William to Mull. **79 K3** NM9354.
Loch Lochy *High.* ***Lake/loch***, in Glen Mòr in Lochaber district, running 10m/16km SW from Laggan to Gairlochy. Caledonian Canal passes through loch. **87 J6** NN2390.
Loch Lomond ***Lake/loch***, on borders of Argyll & Bute, Stirling and West Dunbartonshire, forming largest stretch of inland water in Britain. Extends 24m/39km from Ardlui in N to Balloch in S. Although generally narrow, the loch widens towards S end where there are a number of wooded islands. **74 B2** NS3598.
Loch Lomond Regional Park ***Leisure/recreation***, regional park surrounding Loch Lomond, Britain's largest stretch of inland water, and including Ben Lomond, Scotland's most southerly mountain over 900 metres. Visitor centre at Luss on W side of loch; West Highland Way long distance path passes along E bank; facilities for cruising and boating. **74 B1** NS3599.
Loch Long *Arg. & B.* ***Sea feature***, narrow sea-loch penetrating 16m/27km inland from head of Firth of Clyde at Kilcreggan on S of Rosneath peninsula and extending NE to Arrochar. **74 A1** NS2192.
Loch Long *High.* ***Lake/loch***, narrow loch in Skye and Lochalsh district running into Loch Alsh at Dornie. **87 F2** NG8928.
Loch Losait *High.* ***Bay***, small bay on E coast of Vaternish peninsula, 6m/9km SE of Vaternish Point, Skye. **93 H5** NG2760.
Loch Loskin *Arg. & B.* ***Lake/loch***, small loch 1m/2km N of Dunoon. **73 K3** NS1678.
Loch Lossit *Arg. & B.* ***Lake/loch***, small loch on Islay 3m/5km SW of Port Askaig. **72 C4** NR4065.
Loch Loyal *High.* ***Lake/loch***, large loch, 4m/7km N to S, in Caithness district 4m/7km S of Tongue. **103 J4** NC6247.
Loch Loyne *High.* ***Lake/loch***, and reservoir on border of Lochaber and Skye and Lochalsh districts between Lochs Cluanie and Garry. **87 H4** NH1705.
Loch Luichart *High.* ***Lake/loch***, and reservoir 6m/10km W of Strathpeffer, Ross and Cromarty district. Power station below dam. Length of loch 6m/10km NW to SE. **95 K5** NH3562.
Loch Lundie *High.* ***Lake/loch***, small loch 1m/2km S of Plockton, Skye and Lochalsh district. **86 E1** NG8031.
Loch Lundie *High.* ***Lake/loch***, in Ross and Cromarty district 3m/5km S of Shieldaig. **94 E7** NG8049.
Loch Lundie *High.* ***Lake/loch***, and reservoir 1m/2km N of Invergarry in Lochaber district. **87 J4** NH2903.
Loch Lunndaidh *High.* ***Lake/loch***, in Sutherland district, 2m/4km W of Golspie. **96 E1** NC7800.
Loch Lurgainn *High.* ***Lake/loch***, in Ross and Cromarty district 8m/13km N of Ullapool. **95 H1** NC1108.
Loch Lydoch *P. & K.* *Alternative name for Loch Laidon, qv.*
Loch Lyon *P. & K.* ***Lake/loch***, large loch and reservoir at head of Glen Lyon. **81 F3** NN4141.
Loch ma Stac *High.* ***Lake/loch***, small loch in Inverness district 6m/10km NW of Invermoriston. **87 K2** NH3421.
Loch Maberry *D. & G.* ***Lake/loch***, on border with South Ayrshire, 5m/9km SE of Barrhill. Remains of old castle on islet in loch. **64 C3** NX2875.
Loch Macaterick *E.Ayr.* ***Lake/loch***, 4m/6km N of Merrick. **67 J4** NX4491.

Loch Maddy *W.Isles Anglicised form of Loch na Madadh (sea-loch), qv.*
Loch Magharaidh *High.* ***Lake/loch***, small loch on Kildermorie Forest, Ross and Cromarty district, 3m/5km NW of Loch Glass. **96 B4** NH4576.
Loch Magillie (Also known as Magillie Loch.) *D. & G.* ***Lake/loch***, small loch 2m/4km E of Stranraer. **64 A5** NX0959.
Loch Mahaick *Stir.* ***Lake/loch***, small loch or tarn 4m/6km N of Doune. **81 J7** NN7006.
Loch Mallachie *High.* ***Lake/loch***, small loch on SW edge of Abernethy Forest, 2m/3km SE of Boat of Garten. **89 G3** NH9617.
Loch Maoile *High.* ***Lake/loch***, 1km S of Strath Kanaird, Ross and Cromarty district. **95 H2** NC1500.
Loch Maovally *High.* ***Lake/loch***, 1km W of Moine House, 2m/3km E of N end of Loch Hope. **103 H2** NC5060.
Loch Maree *High.* ***Lake/loch***, in W part of Ross and Cromarty district extending 12m/20km NW from near Kinlochewe to near Poolewe, where it runs out into Loch Ewe. Width is mostly about 1km, although the maximum width is over 2m/3km. Maximum depth 367 feet or 112 metres. **95 F4** NG9570.
Loch Meadaidh *High.* ***Lake/loch***, small loch 2m/3km S of Durness. **103 F2** NC3964.
Loch Meadie *High.* ***Lake/loch***, 3m/5km N to S, in Caithness district 5m/8km NW to Altnaharra. **103 H4** NC5040.
Loch Meadie *High.* ***Lake/loch***, narrow loch, 2m/3km N to S, 1m/2km S of Kirtomy, Caithness district. **104 C2** NC7560.
Loch Meadie *High.* ***Lake/loch***, 1km NE of Loch Mòr, 1m/2km in length N to S. **105 F4** ND0848.
Loch Meala *High.* ***Lake/loch***, small loch on SW edge of Strathy Forest, Caithness district. **104 C3** NC7857.
Loch Mealt *High.* ***Lake/loch***, small loch near NE coast of Skye 7m/11km E of Uig. **94 B5** NG5065.
Loch Meig *High.* ***Lake/loch***, and reservoir in course of River Meig, 1m/2km above its confluence with River Conon in Ross and Cromarty district. **95 K6** NH3555.
Loch Meiklie *High.* ***Lake/loch***, small loch in Glen Urquhart, Inverness district 4m/7km W of Drumnadrochit. **88 B2** NH4330.
Loch Melfort *Arg. & B.* ***Sea feature***, inlet on coast of Argyll, running up towards Kilmelford. **79 K6** NM8112.
Loch Merkland *High.* ***Lake/loch***, in Sutherland district 4m/6km SW of summit of Ben Hee. **103 F5** NC4233.
Loch Mhairc *P. & K.* ***Lake/loch***, small loch in Forest of Atholl, 9m/14km N of Blair Atholl. **89 F7** NN8879.
Loch Mhoicean *High.* ***Lake/loch***, small loch in Skye and Lochalsh district, 2m/3km NW of Loch Mullardoch. **87 G1** NH0731.
Loch Mhòr *High.* ***Lake/loch***, and reservoir in Inverness district on E side of Loch Ness, 10m/16km NE of Fort Augustus. Reservoir used in Foyers Pump Storage Scheme. **88 C3** NH5319.
Loch Mhuilich *High.* ***Lake/loch***, in valley between Bidean an Eòin Deirg and Maoile Lunndaidh, 1km N of W part of Loch Mullardoch. **95 H7** NH1243.
Loch Migdale *High.* ***Lake/loch***, in Sutherland district, 1m/2km E of Bonar Bridge. **96 D2** NH6390.
Loch Moan *D. & G.* ***Lake/loch***, in Glentrool Forest 7m/12km E of Barrhill. **67 H5** NX3485.
Loch Moidart *High.* ***Sea feature***, arm of sea on W coast of Moidart, running up to Kinlochmoidart in Lochaber district. **86 C7** NM6472.
Loch Monar *High.* ***Lake/loch***, and reservoir at head of Glen Farrar on borders of Inverness, Ross and Cromarty, and Skye and Lochalsh districts. Level of loch artificially raised by dam at E end. Length of loch 8m/13km. **95 H7** NH1440.
Loch Mòr *High.* ***Lake/loch***, near W coast of Skye, 7m/11km W of Dunvegan. **93 G7** NG1448.
Loch Mòr an Stàirr *W.Isles* ***Lake/loch***, small loch on Isle of Lewis, 3m/4km E of Beinn Mholach. **101 F4** NB3938.
Loch Mòr Barabhais (Anglicised form: Loch Mòr Barvas.) *W.Isles* ***Lake/loch***, to W of Barvas village, Isle of Lewis, at foot of Gleann Mòr Bharabhais. **101 F2** NB3450.
Loch Mòr Barvas *W.Isles Anglicised form of Loch Mòr Barabhais, qv.*
Loch Mòr na Caorach *High.* ***Lake/loch***, small loch 3m/4km E of Achargary, Caithness district. **104 C3** NC7654.
Loch Mòr Sandavat *W.Isles* ***Lake/loch***, small loch 1km N of Loch an Tobair, Isle of Lewis. **101 G3** NB4346.
Loch Mòr Sandavat *W.Isles* ***Lake/loch***, small loch on Isle of Lewis, 5m/8km NW of Tolsta Head. **101 G2** NB4952.
Loch Moraig *P. & K.* ***Lake/loch***, small loch 2m/4km E of Blair Atholl. **82 A1** NN9066.
Loch Morar *High.* ***Lake/loch***, long, narrow, deep loch and reservoir in Lochaber district. The loch, which divides North Morar from South Morar, runs 11m/18km E to W and almost reaches sea 3m/5km S of Mallaig. Reputed to be deepest loch in Scotland. **86 D5** NM7790.
Loch More *High.* ***Lake/loch***, in Sutherland district 4m/6km long NW to SE, 6m/10km SE of Laxford Bridge. **103 F5** NC3237.
Loch More *High.* ***Lake/loch***, in course of River Thurso, Caithness district, 9m/15km S of Halkirk. **105 F4** ND0745.
Loch Moreef *W.Isles* ***Lake/loch***, near SE coast of South Uist, 4m/6km E of Ludag. **84 D3** NF8314.
Loch Morie *High.* ***Lake/loch***, in Ross and Cromarty district 8m/13km NW of Alness. **96 C4** NH5376.
Loch Morlich *High.* ***Lake/loch***, in The Queen's Forest, Glenmore Forest Park, in Badenoch and Strathspey district, 4m/6km NW of Cairn Gorm. **89 G4** NH9609.
Loch Morsgail *W.Isles* ***Lake/loch***, small loch on Isle of Lewis, 1m/2km S of head of Little Loch Roag. **100 D5** NB1322.
Loch Moy *High.* ***Lake/loch***, in Strathdearn Forest, Inverness district, 9m/15km SE of Inverness. **88 E1** NH7734.
Loch Moy *High.* ***Lake/loch***, and reservoir, partly in Lochaber district and partly in Badenoch and Strathspey district, linked to Loch Laggan to NE. Laggan Dam is sited at SW end. Sometimes loch is considered as part of Loch Laggan. **88 B6** NN4081.
Loch Mudle *High.* ***Lake/loch***, small loch on Ardnamurchan peninsula in Lochaber district, 4m/6km NE of Kilchoan. **79 G1** NM5466.
Loch Muick *Aber.* ***Lake/loch***, at head of Glen Muick, 9m/14km SW of Ballater. **89 K6** NO2882.
Loch Mullardoch *High.* ***Lake/loch***, and reservoir on borders of Inverness and Skye and Lochalsh districts 7m/11km W of Cannich. **87 H1** NH1931.
Loch na Beinne Bàine *High.* ***Lake/loch***, small loch in Inverness district 8m/13km W of Invermoriston. **87 J3** NH2819.
Loch na Béiste *High.* ***Sea feature***, inlet of Loch Alsh 1km S of Kyleakin, Skye. **86 D2** NG7525.
Loch na Caillich *High.* ***Lake/loch***, small loch 4m/6km W of Lairg. **96 C1** NC5108.
Loch na Caoidhe *High.* ***Lake/loch***, small loch in course of River Orrin, Ross and Cromarty district, 6m/10km W of head of Orrin Reservoir. **95 J7** NH2246.
Loch na Cille *Arg. & B.* ***Sea feature***, inlet at S end of peninsula in Argyll, situated between Loch Sween and Sound of Jura. **72 E3** NR6980.
Loch na Claise Càrnaich *High.* ***Lake/loch***, in Sutherland district, 1m/2km E of Rhiconich. **102 E3** NC2752.
Loch na Claise Mòire *High.* ***Lake/loch***, 3m/4km N of Oykel Bridge. **95 K1** NC3805.
Loch na Craige *P. & K.* ***Lake/loch***, small loch or tarn 3m/5km SE of Aberfeldy. **81 K3** NN8845.
Loch na Craobhaig *W.Isles* ***Lake/loch***, small loch 1m/2km E of head of Loch Tamanavay, Isle of Lewis. **100 C5** NB0620.
Loch na Creige Duibhe *High.* ***Lake/loch***, in Sutherland district adjoining Loch an Leathaid Bhuain, to W of Loch More. **102 E5** NC2836.
Loch na Creitheach *High.* ***Lake/loch***, near S coast of Skye 4m/6km N of Elgol. **86 B2** NG5120.
Loch na Cuilce *High.* ***Sea feature***, small inlet on coast of Skye, S of Loch Coruisk. **85 K3** NG4819.
Loch na Curra *High.* ***Lake/loch***, small loch in Ross and Cromarty district, 2m/3km W of Poolewe. **94 E4** NG8280.
Loch na Dal *High.* ***Sea feature***, inlet of Sound of Sleat, at head of Sleat peninsula, Skye. **86 D3** NG7015.
Loch na Dubhcha *W.Isles* ***Lake/loch***, small loch on North Uist, 1km NE of Lochportain. **92 E4** NF9572.
Loch na Fuaralaich *High.* ***Lake/loch***, 6m/9km W of Lairg and to W of Strath Grudie. **96 B1** NC4806.
Loch na Gaineimh *High.* ***Lake/loch***, small loch 2m/3km S of Loch Badanloch, Sutherland district. **104 C5** NC7630.
Loch na Gainimh *High.* ***Lake/loch***, 1m/2km W of Canisp in Glencanisp Forest. **102 D7** NC1719.
Loch na Gainimh *High.* ***Lake/loch***, small loch in Sutherland district 1km NE of Blairmore. **102 E2** NC2061.
Loch na Gainimh *High.* ***Lake/loch***, small loch in Sutherland district, 3m/4km E of Kinlochbervie. **102 E3** NC2656.
Loch na Gainmhich *High.* ***Lake/loch***, 1m/2km S of Loch Glencoul, Sutherland district. **102 E6** NC2429.
Loch na h-Oidhche *High.* ***Lake/loch***, in W part of Ross and Cromarty district 4m/7km N of head of Upper Loch Torridon. **94 E5** NG8865.
Loch na h-Ula *High.* ***Lake/loch***, 1km S of Rhiconich, Sutherland district. **102 E3** NC2550.
Loch na Keal *Arg. & B.* ***Sea feature***, large inlet on W coast of Mull, head of which reaches to within 3m/4km of E coast at Salen. **79 G4** NM5038.
Loch na Lairige *High.* ***Lake/loch***, small loch in Inverness district, 1m/2km N of Geal Charn and 9m/15km W of Newtonmore. **88 C4** NH5601.
Loch na Lathaich *Arg. & B.* ***Bay***, large bay on N coast of Ross of Mull. Village of Bunessan is at SE corner. **78 E5** NM3623.
Loch na Leitreach *High.* ***Lake/loch***, small but deep loch in Skye and Lochalsh district 6m/9km E of head of Loch Long. **87 G2** NH0227.
Loch na Madadh *W.Isles Gaelic form of Lochmaddy (village), qv.*
Loch na Madadh (Anglicised form: Loch Maddy.) *W.Isles* ***Sea feature***, large inlet and anchorage on E coast of North Uist, containing innumerable islets. On W shore is village and port of Lochmaddy. **92 E5** NF9369.
Loch na Mile *Arg. & B.* ***Bay***, on E coast of Jura, at mouth of Corran River, 3m/4km N of Craighouse. **72 D3** NR5470.
Loch na Mòine *High.* ***Lake/loch***, small loch 1km NE of N end of Loch Loyal. **103 J3** NC6251.
Loch na Mòine *High.* ***Lake/loch***, small loch 4m/7km SE of Poolewe, Ross and Cromarty district. **95 F4** NG9278.
Loch na Saobhaidhe *High.* ***Lake/loch***, small loch 1m/2km E of Loch Strathy. **104 D4** NC7947.
Loch na Scaravat *W.Isles* ***Lake/loch***, small loch, 1km N of Beinn Mholach, Isle of Lewis. **101 F3** NB3540.
Loch na Sealga *High.* ***Lake/loch***, in W part of Ross and Cromarty district 4m/7km SW of Little Loch Broom. **95 G3** NH0382.
Loch na Seilg *High.* ***Lake/loch***, one of two small lochs on E side of Ben Hope. **103 G3** NC4951.
Loch na Seilge *High.* ***Lake/loch***, small loch 1m/2km E of Achiemore, Caithness district. **104 E3** NC9158.
Loch na Sgeallaig *High.* ***Lake/loch***, 1km S of W end of Loch Ossian, and 1km SE of Corrour Station. **80 E1** NN3665.
Loch na Sreinge *Arg. & B.* ***Lake/loch***, small loch 1m/2km N of Loch Avich. **80 A6** NM9216.
Loch na Tuadh *High.* ***Lake/loch***, small loch in Reay Forest, Sutherland district, 2m/3km S of Foinaven. **103 F4** NC3147.
Loch nam Bonnach *High.* ***Lake/loch***, small loch in Inverness district 3m/5km NW of Beauly. **96 B7** NH4848.
Loch nam Brac *High.* ***Lake/loch***, in Caithness district, 1km E of Tarbet. **102 D4** NC1748.
Loch nam Breac *High.* ***Lake/loch***, small loch 3m/5km E of Loch Strathy, Caithness district. **104 D4** NC8248.
Loch nam Breac *W.Isles* ***Lake/loch***, small loch 4m/7km E of Breasclete, Isle of Lewis. **100 E4** NB2837.
Loch nam Breac Dearga *High.* ***Lake/loch***, small loch in Inverness district 4m/6km NE of Invermoriston. **88 B2** NH4522.
Loch nam Falcag *W.Isles* ***Lake/loch***, small loch, 4m/6km W of Liurbost, Isle of Lewis. **101 F5** NB2926.
Loch nam Fiadh *High.* ***Lake/loch***, small loch 5m/8km NW of Garve. **95 K5** NH3164.
Loch nam Meur *High.* ***Lake/loch***, small loch in Inverness district, 4m/7km N of Invermoriston. Another small loch of same name 1m/2km N. **87 K2** NH3923.
Loch nam Uamh *High.* ***Lake/loch***, small loch on Sleat peninsula, 3m/4km E of Tarskavaig, Skye. **86 C4** NG6308.
Loch nan Ceall *High.* ***Sea feature***, inlet on coast of Lochaber district, running up to Arisaig. **86 C6** NM6486.
Loch nan Clach *High.* ***Lake/loch***, small loch in afforested area, 1km S of Loch Mòr na Caorach, 4m/6km SE of Skelpick, Caithness district. **104 C3** NC7653.
Loch nan Clach *High.* ***Lake/loch***, small loch in Morvern, Lochaber district, 5m/8km NE of Rubha an Ridire. **79 J3** NM7846.
Loch nan Clàr *High.* ***Lake/loch***, N part of a double loch in Sutherland district, 6m/10km W of Kinbrace. S part of loch is known as Loch Badanloch. **104 C5** NC7635.
Loch nan Cuinne *High. Alternative name for Loch Rimsdale, qv.*
Loch nan Ealachan *High.* ***Lake/loch***, small loch just E of Borgie Forest, Caithness district. **103 J3** NC6752.
Loch nan Eun *High.* ***Lake/loch***, small loch in Ross and Cromarty district, 3m/4km N of Applecross. **94 D7** NG7048.
Loch nan Eun *High.* ***Lake/loch***, small loch in Skye and Lochalsh district, 4m/7km E of Dornie. **87 F2** NG9426.
Loch nan Eun *High.* ***Lake/loch***, small loch in Inverness district 7m/12km NW of Invermoriston. **87 K2** NH3120.
Loch nan Eun *High.* ***Lake/loch***, small loch 5m/8km E of Fort Augustus. **88 B3** NH4510.
Loch nan Eun *High.* ***Lake/loch***, small loch on border of Inverness and Ross and Cromarty districts 4m/6km W of Muir of Ord. **96 B7** NH4648.
Loch nan Eun *W.Isles* ***Lake/loch***, on North Uist, 3m/4km N of Locheport. **92 D5** NF8367.
Loch nan Gall *High.* ***Lake/loch***, small loch 2m/3km W of Achiemore, Caithness district. **104 D3** NC8658.
Loch nan Geireann *W.Isles* ***Lake/loch***, on North Uist, 2m/3km SE of Solas. **92 D4** NF8472.
Loch nan Stearnag *W.Isles* ***Lake/loch***, small loch, 6m/10km E of Breasclete, Isle of Lewis. **101 F4** NB3137.
Loch nan Torran *Arg. & B.* ***Lake/loch***, small loch in Knapdale, Argyll, 3m/4km SE of Ormsary. **73 F4** NR7568.
Loch nan Uamh *High.* ***Sea feature***, inlet of Sound of Arisaig on N side of peninsula of Ardnish, on coast of Lochaber district. **86 C6** NM6982.
Loch nan Uan *High.* ***Lake/loch***, small loch on W slope of Ben Klibreck, 4m/6km S of Altnaharra. **103 H6** NC5629.
Loch Nant *Arg. & B.* ***Lake/loch***, and reservoir 2m/4km NW of Kilchrenan in Argyll. **80 A5** NN0024.
Loch Naver *High.* ***Lake/loch***, in Caithness district extending 6m/10km E from Altnaharra. **103 H5** NC6136.
Loch Neaty *High.* ***Lake/loch***, small loch in Inverness district 3m/5km SE of Struy Bridge. **88 B1** NH4336.
Loch Nedd *High.* ***Sea feature***, inlet on S side of Eddrachillis Bay, W coast of Sutherland district. **102 D5** NC1333.
Loch Neldricken *D. & G.* ***Lake/loch***, in Glentrool Forest Park, 2m/3km SE of Merrick. **67 J5** NX4482.
Loch Nell *Arg. & B.* ***Lake/loch***, in Argyll 2m/4km SE of Oban. **79 K5** NM8927.
Loch Ness *High.* ***Lake/loch***, in Inverness district extending NE from Fort Augustus to a point 6m/10km SW of Inverness. Length 23m/36km. Average width about 1m/2km. Maximum depth 754 feet or 230 metres. Loch forms part of course of Caledonian Canal. **88 B3** NH5023.
Loch Nevis *High.* ***Sea feature***, long inlet of Sound of Sleat, between Knoydart and North Morar in Lochaber district. Narrows considerably above Kylesknoydart. Total length about 13m/21km. **86 D5** NM7695.
Loch Nisreaval *W.Isles* ***Lake/loch***, small loch on Isle of Lewis, 6m/10km SW of Stornoway. **101 F5** NB3326.
Loch Obisary *W.Isles* ***Lake/loch***, in SE part of North Uist, to N and W of Eaval. **92 D5** NF8861.
Loch Ochiltree *D. & G.* ***Lake/loch***, 8m/13km NW of Newton Stewart. **64 D3** NX3174.
Loch Odhairn *W.Isles* ***Sea feature***, inlet on E coast of Isle of Lewis, extending from Grabhair to Kebock Head. **101 G6** NB4014.
Loch of Blairs *Moray* ***Lake/loch***, small loch 2m/3km S of Forres. **97 H6** NJ0255.
Loch of Boardhouse *Ork.* ***Lake/loch***, large loch in NW Mainland 2m/3km SE of Brough Head. Named after locality at its NW end. **106 B5** HY2625.
Loch of Butterstone *P. & K.* ***Lake/loch***, small loch SW of Butterstone and 2m/4km NE of Dunkeld. **82 B3** NO0544.
Loch of Cliff *Shet.* ***Lake/loch***, long narrow loch S of Burrafirth, Unst. **108 E1** HP6012.
Loch of Clunie *P. & K.* ***Lake/loch***, small loch 4m/6km W of Blairgowrie. On island in loch are remains of Clunie Castle, built about 1500. **82 C3** NO1144.
Loch of Craiglush *P. & K.* ***Lake/loch***, small loch 1m/2km NE of Dunkeld. **82 B3** NO0444.
Loch of Drumellie (Also known as Loch of Marlee.) *P. & K.* ***Lake/loch***, small loch 2m/3km W of Blairgowrie. **82 C3** NO1444.
Loch of Forfar *Angus* ***Lake/loch***, small loch on W side of Forfar. **83 F2** NO4450.
Loch of Girlsta *Shet.* ***Lake/loch***, deep freshwater loch on E coast of Mainland 6m/10km N of Lerwick. **109 D7** HU4350.
Loch of Harray *Ork.* ***Lake/loch***, large loch, nearly 5m/8km N to S, to S of Dounby on Mainland. S end is separated from Loch of Stenness by narrow tongue of land and causeway. **107 B6** HY2915.
Loch of Hundland *Ork.* ***Lake/loch***, at N end of Mainland 3m/5km N of Dounby. **106 B5** HY2925.
Loch of Kinnordy *Angus See Kinnordy.*
Loch of Kirbister *Ork.* ***Lake/loch***, 3m/5km S of Finstown, on N side of road running W from Kirkwall. **107 C7** HY3607.

Loch of Lintrathen *Angus* ***Lake/loch***, and reservoir, 6m/10km W of Kirriemuir. **82 D2** NO2754.
Loch of Lowes *P. & K.* ***Lake/loch***, small loch 1m/2km NE of Dunkeld. Reserve of Scottish Wildlife Trust. **82 B3** NO0443.
Loch of Marlee *P. & K. Alternative name for Loch of Drumellie, qv.*
Loch of Mey *High.* ***Lake/loch***, small loch near N coast, 4m/7km SE of Dunnet Head. **105 H1** ND2673.
Loch of Skaill *Ork.* ***Lake/loch***, near W coast of Mainland 1km E of Skara Brae. **107 B6** HY2418.
Loch of Skene *Aber.* ***Lake/loch***, small round loch 9m/15km W of Aberdeen. **91 F4** NJ7807.
Loch of Spiggie *Shet.* ***Lake/loch***, on Mainland 2m/4km NE of Fitful Head. **109 F9** HU3716.
Loch of Stenness *Ork.* ***Lake/loch***, large loch on Mainland 4m/6km W of Finstown. Separated at E end from Loch of Harray by narrow tongue of land and causeway. **107 B6** HY2812.
Loch of Strathbeg *Aber.* ***Lake/loch***, near NE coast behind Strathbeg Bay, 2m/3km long NW to SE. **99 J5** NK0758.
Loch of Strom *Shet.* ***Lake/loch***, long narrow loch on Mainland in course of Burn of Sandwater, emptying into Stromness Voe, E of Weisdale Voe. **109 C8** HU4048.
Loch of Swannay *Ork.* ***Lake/loch***, large loch at N end of Mainland 5m/8km E of Brough Head. **106 C5** HY3128.
Loch of Tankerness *Ork.* ***Lake/loch***, on Mainland 2m/3km SW of Rerwick Head. HY5109.
Loch of the Lowes *Sc.Bord.* ***Lake/loch***, small loch running into head of St. Mary's Loch in Ettrick Forest. **69 H2** NT2319.
Loch of Tingwall *Shet.* ***Lake/loch***, on Mainland 2m/3km N of Scalloway. At N end of loch is small island traditionally held to be site of old Norse open-air parliament. **109 C8** HU4142.
Loch of Toftingall *High.* ***Lake/loch***, in Caithness district 4m/6km W of Watten. **105 G3** ND1952.
Loch of Watlee *Shet.* ***Lake/loch***, on Unst 2m/4km N of Uyeasound. **108 E2** HP5905.
Loch of Wester *High.* ***Lake/loch***, in Caithness district 6m/10km N of Wick. **105 J3** ND3259.
Loch of Winless *High.* ***Lake/loch***, narrow loch to W of Winless. **105 H3** ND2954.
Loch of Yarehouse *High. Alternative name for Loch of Yarrows, qv.*
Loch of Yarrows (Also known as Loch of Yarehouse.) *High.* ***Lake/loch***, in Caithness district 5m/9km SW of Wick. **105 J4** ND3043.
Loch Oich *High.* ***Lake/loch***, narrow loch in Lochaber district between Loch Lochy and Loch Ness. Caledonian Canal passes through loch. NE end of loch is in Inverness district. **87 K4** NH3100.
Loch Olavat *W.Isles* ***Lake/loch***, small loch on Benbecula, 2m/3km N of Creag Ghoraidh. **92 D7** NF8050.
Loch Olavat *W.Isles* ***Lake/loch***, small loch near N coast of Benbecula, 3m/4km E of Balivanich. **92 D6** NF8154.
Loch Olginey *High.* ***Lake/loch***, in Caithness district 3m/5km SW of Halkirk. **105 F3** ND0957.
Loch Orasay *W.Isles* ***Lake/loch***, on Isle of Lewis, 5m/8km E of Achadh Mòr. Contains small island, Eilean Mòr. **101 F5** NB3828.
Loch Ordie *P. & K.* ***Lake/loch***, small loch 4m/6km SE of Ballinluig. **82 B2** NO0350.
Loch Osgaig (Also known as Loch Owskeich.) *High.* ***Lake/loch***, near NW coast of Ross and Cromarty district 1km S of Enard Bay. **102 C7** NC0412.
Loch Ossian *High.* ***Lake/loch***, in Lochaber district between head of Loch Treig and head of Loch Ericht. Deer sanctuary to N. **80 E1** NN3968.
Loch Owskeich *High. Alternative name for Loch Osgaig, qv.*
Loch Park *Moray* ***Lake/loch***, small loch 3m/4km NE of Dufftown. **98 B6** NJ3543.
Loch Pattack *High.* ***Lake/loch***, small loch in Badenoch and Strathspey district, from which River Pattack flows N then W to head of Loch Laggan. **88 C7** NN5379.
Loch Pityoulish *High.* ***Lake/loch***, small loch in Badenoch and Strathspey district, 2m/3km NE of Aviemore across River Spey. **89 G3** NH9213.
Loch Poll *High.* ***Lake/loch***, 1m/2km long N to S, situated 1m/2km SW of Drumbeg, Sutherland district. **102 C5** NC0931.
Loch Poll Dhaidh *High.* ***Lake/loch***, 3m/4km SE of Clashnessie, Sutherland district. **102 C6** NC0729.
Loch Polly *High. Alternative name for Polly Bay, qv.*
Loch Pooltiel *High.* ***Sea feature***, on NW coast of Skye, 4m/6km S of Dunvegan Head. **93 G6** NG1650.
Loch Portain *W.Isles* ***Sea feature***, inlet 2m/4km NE of Lochmaddy, North Uist. **92 E4** NF9471.
Loch Portree *High.* ***Sea feature***, on E coast of Skye. Town of Portree is situated on N side of loch. **93 K7** NG4842.
Loch Quien *Arg. & B.* ***Lake/loch***, small loch on Bute 1km NE of Scalpsie Bay. **73 J5** NS0659.
Loch Quoich *High.* ***Lake/loch***, and reservoir in Lochaber district at head of Glen Garry. Length about 9m/14km. **87 G4** NH0102.
Loch Rangag *High.* ***Lake/loch***, in Caithness district 5m/9km NW of Lybster. **105 G4** ND1741.
Loch Rannoch *P. & K.* ***Lake/loch***, and reservoir, 10m/16km long W to E. Dam at Kinloch Rannoch at E end. **81 G2** NN5957.
Loch Ranza *N.Ayr.* ***Sea feature***, sea-loch on N coast of Arran. Village of Lochranza on SW side of loch. **73 H5** NR9350.
Loch Raonasgail *W.Isles* ***Lake/loch***, small loch on Isle of Lewis, 1km NW of Tahaval. **100 C5** NB0327.
Loch Recar *S.Ayr. Alternative spelling of Loch Riecawr, qv.*
Loch Reraig *High.* ***Sea feature***, small inlet on N shore of Loch Carron, 2m/3km NE of Plockton. **86 E1** NG8135.
Loch Resort *W.Isles* ***Sea feature***, long narrow inlet on W coast of Isle of Lewis, opposite Scarp. **100 C6** NB0616.
Loch Restil *Arg. & B.* ***Lake/loch***, small loch in Argyll immediately N of Rest and be thankful. NN2207.
Loch Riddon (Also known as Loch Ruel.) *Arg. & B.* ***Sea feature***, inlet in Argyll running N from Kyles of Bute opposite Buttock Point. **73 J3** NS0076.
Loch Riecawr (Also spelled Loch Recar.) *S.Ayr.* ***Lake/loch***, 3m/4km W of S end of Loch Doon. **67 J4** NX4393.
Loch Rifa-gil *High.* ***Lake/loch***, small loch 1m/2km SE of Rhifail, Caithness district. **104 C4** NC7448.
Loch Righ Mòr *Arg. & B.* ***Lake/loch***, on Jura 2m/3km N of Loch Tarbert. **72 D2** NR5485.
Loch Rimsdale (Also known as Loch nan Cuinne.) *High.* ***Lake/loch***, adjoining to W of Loch nan Clar, 8m/13km W of Kinbrace. Border between Caithness and Sutherland districts runs down centre of loch. **104 C5** NC7335.
Loch Roag (Gaelic form: Loch Ròg.) *W.Isles* ***Sea feature***, sea-loch off NW coast of Isle of Lewis to SW of Great Bernera, connected to Little, West and East Loch Roag. Contains many islands and islets. NB1233.
Loch Roan *D. & G.* ***Lake/loch***, small loch 4m/7km N of Castle Douglas. **65 H4** NX7469.
Loch Ròg *W.Isles Gaelic form of Loach Roag, qv.*
Loch Ròg Beag *W.Isles Gaelic form of Little Loch Roag, qv.*
Loch Ronald *D. & G.* ***Lake/loch***, 4m/7km NW of Kirkcowan. **64 C4** NX2664.
Loch Rosail *High.* ***Lake/loch***, 1m/2km E of Naver Forest, Caithness district. **104 C4** NC7140.
Loch Rosque *High. Anglicised form of Loch a' Chroisg, qv.*
Loch Ruard *High.* ***Lake/loch***, in Caithness district 8m/13km NW of Lybster. **105 G4** ND1443.
Loch Ruel *Arg. & B. Alternative name for Loch Riddon, qv.*
Loch Rusky *Stir.* ***Lake/loch***, small loch or tarn 3m/5km S of Callander. **81 H7** NN6103.
Loch Ruthven *High.* ***Lake/loch***, in Inverness district 4m/7km S of Dores. **88 D2** NH6127.
Loch Ryan *D. & G.* ***Sea feature***, large inlet and anchorage running from Milleur Point, at N end of Rinns of Galloway, to Stranraer at head of loch. **64 A3** NX0465.
Loch Sand *High.* ***Lake/loch***, in Caithness district 8m/12km NW of Latheron. **105 F4** ND0941.
Loch Scadavay *W.Isles* ***Lake/loch***, on North Uist 4m/6km W of Lochmaddy. **92 D5** NF8668.
Loch Scadavay *W.Isles* ***Lake/loch***, irregular shaped loch on North Uist, 1m/2km NW of Locheport. **92 D5** NF8766.
Loch Scalabsdale *High.* ***Lake/loch***, small loch in Caithness district, 4m/6km SW of Morven. **104 E6** NC9624.
Loch Scammadale *Arg. & B.* ***Lake/loch***, small but deep loch in Argyll, 6m/10km S of Oban. **79 K6** NM8920.
Loch Scarmclate *High.* ***Lake/loch***, in Caithness district 7m/11km SE of Thurso. **105 G3** ND1859.
Loch Scaslavat *W.Isles Anglicised form of Loch Sgaslabhat, qv.*
Loch Scavaig *High.* ***Bay***, large bay on S coast of Skye, between Elgol and Soay. Cuillin Hills rise steeply from N shore. **85 K3** NG4916.
Loch Scaven *High. Alternative name for Loch Sgamhain, qv.*
Loch Scridain *Arg. & B.* ***Sea feature***, long inlet on W coast of Mull, penetrating to foot of Glen More. **79 F5** NM4525.
Loch Scye *High.* ***Lake/loch***, small loch to E of Beinn nam Bad Mòr. **105 F3** ND0055.
Loch Seaforth *W.Isles* ***Sea feature***, narrow inlet 14m/23km long, penetrating deep into SE coast of North Harris, to NE of Tarbert. Contains steep and uninhabited Seaforth Island. **100 E7** NB2107.
Loch Sealg *W.Isles Alternative name for Loch Shell, qv.*
Loch Sgamhain (Also known as Loch Scaven.) *High.* ***Lake/loch***, small loch in Ross and Cromarty district 5m/8km SW of Achnasheen. **95 H6** NH0952.
Loch Sgaslabhat (Anglicised form: Loch Scaslavat.) *W.Isles* ***Lake/loch***, near W coast of Isle of Lewis, 1km S of Camas Uig bay. **100 C4** NB0231.
Loch Sgeireach *High.* ***Lake/loch***, corrie loch below Ben Sgeireach, 3m/5km W of Loch Shin. **103 G7** NC4611.
Loch Sgeireach Mòr *W.Isles* ***Lake/loch***, small loch 2m/3km S of Muirneag and 4m/7km W of Tolsta Head, Isle of Lewis. **101 G3** NB4945.
Loch Sgibacleit *W.Isles* ***Lake/loch***, small loch to E of head of Loch Seaforth, Isle of Lewis. **101 F6** NB3016.
Loch Sgioport (Anglicised form: Loch Skiport.) *W.Isles* ***Sea feature***, inlet on E coast of South Uist, 12m/20km N of Lochboisdale. **84 D1** NF8438.
Loch Sgioport (Anglicised form: Lochskipport.) *W.Isles* ***Settlement***, on South Uist at head of Loch Sgioport, 2m/4km N of Hecla. **84 D1** NF8238.
Loch Sguabain *Arg. & B. See Loch Airdeglais.*
Loch Sguadaig *High.* ***Lake/loch***, to N of Beinn Teallach, 5m/7km N of Tulloch Station. **87 K6** NN3687.
Loch Sguod *High.* ***Lake/loch***, small loch in Ross and Cromarty district, 5m/8km SE of Rubha Réidh. **94 E3** NG8087.
Loch Shanndabhat *W.Isles* ***Lake/loch***, small loch on Isle of Lewis, 2m/3km NW of Leumrabhagh. **101 F6** NB3413.
Loch Sheilavaig *W.Isles* ***Sea feature***, inlet on E coast of South Uist, 1m/2km N of Loch Sgioport. **84 D1** NF8340.
Loch Shell (Also known as Loch Sealg.) *W.Isles* ***Sea feature***, large inlet on E coast of Isle of Lewis to SW of Kebock Head. **101 F6** NB3410.
Loch Shiel *High.* ***Lake/loch***, narrow loch, 17m/27km long, in Lochaber district, extending SW from Glenfinnan to Acharacle, between Moidart and Sunart. **86 E7** NM8072.
Loch Shieldaig *High.* ***Sea feature***, arm of Loch Torridon, W coast of Ross and Cromarty district. Village of Shieldaig at head of loch. **94 D6** NG7955.
Loch Shin *High.* ***Lake/loch***, in Sutherland district, 17m/27km NW to SE at Lairg. Width varies from under 1km to just over 1m/2km. Maximum depth about 195 feet or 60 metres. Water level raised by concrete dam at SE end. **103 G7** NC4816.
Loch Shira *Arg. & B.* ***Sea feature***, inlet of Loch Fyne, to N of Inveraray in Argyll. NN1009.
Loch Shurrery *High.* ***Lake/loch***, in Caithness district 9m/15km SW of Thurso. **105 F3** ND0455.
Loch Sionascaig *High.* ***Lake/loch***, near NW coast of Ross and Cromarty district 5m/8km S of Lochinver. **102 D7** NC1213.
Loch Skealtar *W.Isles* ***Lake/loch***, small loch on North Uist, 4m/6km NE of Locheport. **92 D5** NF8968.
Loch Skeen *D. & G.* ***Lake/loch***, small loch in hills NE of Moffat, 1m/2km N of White Coomb. **69 G2** NT1716.
Loch Skerrow *D. & G.* ***Lake/loch***, 7m/11km N of Gatehouse of Fleet. **65 G4** NX6068.
Loch Skiach *P. & K.* ***Lake/loch***, small loch 4m/6km SW of Ballinluig. **82 A3** NN9547.
Loch Skiport *W.Isles Anglicised form of Loch Sgioport, qv.*
Loch Slaim *High.* ***Lake/loch***, small loch at N end of Loch Craggie, Caithness district. **103 J3** NC6253.
Loch Slapin *High.* ***Sea feature***, inlet on S coast of Skye, on E side of Strathaird peninsula. **86 B3** NG5717.
Loch Sletill *High.* ***Lake/loch***, small loch 2m/3km E of Sletill Hill, 11m/18km S of Reay in Sutherland district. **104 E4** NC9547.
Loch Sligachan *High.* ***Sea feature***, inlet on E coast of Skye, 7m/11km S of Portree. **86 B1** NG5132.
Loch Sloy *Arg. & B.* ***Lake/loch***, and reservoir on W side of Ben Vorlich, 3m/5km SW of Ardlui. Tunnel aqueduct to Inveruglas on W shore of Loch Lomond. **80 D6** NN2812.
Loch Sneosdal *High.* ***Lake/loch***, small loch 1km NE of Suidh' a' Mhinn, Skye. **93 K5** NG4169.
Loch Snigisclett *W.Isles* ***Lake/loch***, small loch on South Uist, 3m/5km W of Mingearraidh. **84 D2** NF8025.
Loch Snizort *High.* ***Sea feature***, on N coast of Skye, between Trotternish and Vaternish. **93 J5** NG3261.
Loch Snizort Beag *High.* ***Sea feature***, long narrow inlet at SE corner of Loch Snizort, penetrating 6m/10km inland. **93 J6** NG3261.
Loch Spallander Reservoir *S.Ayr.* ***Reservoir***, 6m/9km E of Maybole. **67 H3** NS3908.
Loch Spelve *Arg. & B.* ***Sea feature***, large inlet with narrow entrance on SE coast of Mull. **79 H5** NM6927.
Loch Spotal *W.Isles* ***Lake/loch***, small loch on South Uist, 1m/2km N of Hecla. **84 D1** NF8336.
Loch Spynie *Moray* ***Lake/loch***, small loch 3m/4km S of Lossiemouth. **97 K5** NJ2366.
Loch Stack *High.* ***Lake/loch***, in Sutherland district, in course of River Laxford between Loch More and Loch Laxford. **102 E4** NC2942.
Loch Staing *High.* ***Lake/loch***, small loch 3m/5km SW of S end of Loch Loyal, Caithness district. **103 H4** NC5740.
Loch Staoisha *Arg. & B.* ***Lake/loch***, small loch on Islay 2m/3km NW of Port Askaig. **72 B3** NR4071.
Loch Staosnaig *Arg. & B.* ***Bay***, on E coast of Colonsay, to S of Scalasaig. **72 B1** NR3993.
Loch Steisevat *W.Isles* ***Lake/loch***, near SW coast of South Harris on N side of Leverburgh. **93 F3** NG0187.
Loch Stemster *High.* ***Lake/loch***, 8m/13km NE of Dunbeath. **105 G4** ND1842.
Loch Stockinish *W.Isles* ***Sea feature***, inlet on SE coast of South Harris, 5m/8km S of Tarbert. **93 G2** NG1292.
Loch Stornoway *Arg. & B.* ***Sea feature***, on S coast of Knapdale, Argyll, 2m/3km N of Ardpatrick Point. **73 F5** NR7361.
Loch Strandavat *W.Isles* ***Lake/loch***, narrow loch on Isle of Lewis, 1m/2km long N to S and 1m/2km W of head of Loch Erisort. **100 E6** NB2519.
Loch Strathy *High.* ***Lake/loch***, small loch within Caithness district, 3m/5km SE of Rhifail; Meall Bad na Cuaiche rising to W. **104 C4** NC7747.
Loch Striven *Arg. & B.* ***Sea feature***, sea-loch in Argyll, running N for 8m/13km from Strone Point, Kyles of Bute. **73 J2** NS0777.
Loch Stulaval *W.Isles* ***Lake/loch***, on South Uist, 2m/3km N of Lochboisdale. **84 D2** NF8022.
Loch Suainaval *W.Isles* ***Lake/loch***, long narrow loch, nearly 4m/6km N to S, near W coast of Isle of Lewis S of Timsgearraidh. **100 C5** NB0629.
Loch Sunart *High.* ***Sea feature***, long arm of sea on W coast in Lochaber district, between Ardnamurchan and Sunart to N and Morvern to S. **79 H1** NM7262.
Loch Sween *Arg. & B.* ***Sea feature***, sea-loch running NE from Danna Island to Knapdale Forest, Argyll. Afforestation on banks. **73 F3** NR7383.
Loch Syre *High.* ***Lake/loch***, irregular-shaped loch, containing a number of small islands, 2m/3km E of S end of Loch Loyal. **103 J4** NC6645.
Loch Tamanavay (Gaelic form: Loch Tamnabhaigh.) *W.Isles* ***Sea feature***, inlet on W coast of Isle of Lewis, 4m/7km S of Mealisval mountain. Tamanavay River flows into loch from E. **100 C6** NB0320.
Loch Tamnabhaigh *W.Isles Gaelic form of Loch Tamanavay, qv.*
Loch Tanna *N.Ayr.* ***Lake/loch***, on Arran 3m/5km E of Pirnmill. **73 H6** NR9242.
Loch Tarbert *Arg. & B.* ***Sea feature***, long inlet on W coast of Jura, almost bisecting the island. **72 D2** NR5481.
Loch Tarbhaidh *High.* ***Lake/loch***, small loch 3m/5km NE of Rhiconich. **102 E3** NC2955.
Loch Tarff *High.* ***Lake/loch***, small loch in Inverness district 3m/5km E of Fort Augustus. **88 B3** NH4210.
Loch Tarsan *Arg. & B.* ***Lake/loch***, and reservoir in Argyll, 1m/2km E of head of Loch Striven. **73 J2** NS0784.
Loch Tay *P. & K.* ***Lake/loch***, 15m/24km long from Killin in SW to Kenmore in NE, and in places over 500 feet (over 150 metres) deep. Noted for salmon. **81 H4** NN6838.
Loch Teacuis *High.* ***Sea feature***, long inlet on N coast of Morvern, in Lochaber district. **79 H2** NM6356.
Loch Tealasavay *W.Isles Anglicised form of Loch Thealasbhaidh, qv.*
Loch Teàrnait *High.* ***Lake/loch***, small loch in Morvern, Lochaber district, 4m/7km N of Rubha an Ridire. **79 J3** NM7447.
Loch Thealasbhaidh (Anglicised form: Loch Tealasavay.) *W.Isles* ***Sea feature***, inlet on W coast of Isle of Lewis, between Loch Tamanavay and Loch Resort. **100 C6** NB0218.

Loch Thom *Inclyde* ***Lake/loch***, and reservoir 3m/4km SW of Greenock. **74 A3** NS2572.
Loch Thota Bridein *W.Isles* ***Lake/loch***, small loch 6m/10km SW of Stornoway, Isle of Lewis. **101 F5** NB3327.
Loch Thulachan *High. Alternative name for Lochan Thulachan, qv.*
Loch Thùrnaig *High.* ***Sea feature***, inlet on E side of Loch Ewe, 2m/3km N of Poolewe, Ross and Cromarty district. **94 E3** NG8684.
Loch Tollaidh (Also known as Loch Tollie.) *High.* ***Lake/loch***, near W coast of Ross and Cromarty district 3m/5km E of Gairloch. **94 E4** NG8478.
Loch Tollie *High. Alternative name for Loch Tollaidh, qv.*
Loch Torridon *High.* ***Sea feature***, wide inlet on W coast of Ross and Cromarty district between Red Point and Rubha na Fearn. **94 D5** NG7560.
Loch Toscaig *High.* ***Sea feature***, inlet on W coast of Ross and Cromarty district, 4m/7km S of Applecross. **86 D1** NG7137.
Loch Tralaig *Arg. & B.* ***Lake/loch***, small loch and reservoir in Argyll 3m/5km NE of head of Loch Melfort. **79 K6** NM8816.
Loch Trealaval *W.Isles* ***Lake/loch***, large loch 2m/3km NW of Baile Ailein, Isle of Lewis. **100 E5** NB2723.
Loch Treig *High.* ***Lake/loch***, and reservoir in Lochaber district, 5m/9km long N to S, 14m/23km E of Fort William. Supplies water to aluminium works at Fort William by tunnel under Ben Nevis. Glasgow-Fort William railway runs along E side of loch. Length of dam at N end 440 feet or 134 metres. **87 K7** NN3372.
Loch Tromlee *Arg. & B.* ***Lake/loch***, small loch in Argyll, 1m/2km N of Kilchrenan. **80 B5** NN0425.
Loch Trool *D. & G.* ***Lake/loch***, in Glentrool Forest Park 8m/13km N of Newton Stewart. **64 E3** NX4179.
Loch Truderscaig *High.* ***Lake/loch***, small loch 1m/2km SW of Loch Rimsdale. Border of Caithness and Sutherland districts runs down centre of loch. **104 C5** NC7132.
Loch Tuath *Arg. & B.* ***Sea feature***, arm of sea on W of Mull, with main island to N and Gometra and Ulva to S. **78 E3** NM3943.
Loch Tuim Ghlais *High.* ***Lake/loch***, small loch in Caithness district, 4m/7km NW of Altnabreac. **104 E3** NC9752.
Loch Tulla *Arg. & B.* ***Lake/loch***, in Argyll 2m/3km N of Bridge of Orchy. **80 D3** NN2942.
Loch Tummel *P. & K.* ***Lake/loch***, and reservoir 7m/11km long W to E. The dam at E end is 4m/6km NW of Pitlochry. **81 K2** NN8259.
Loch Tungavat *W.Isles* ***Lake/loch***, small loch 3m/5km S of Earshader, Isle of Lewis. **100 D5** NB1529.
Loch Turret Reservoir *P. & K.* ***Reservoir***, in Glen Turret, 5m/8km NW of Crieff. **81 K5** NN8027.
Loch Uidh an Tuim *High.* ***Lake/loch***, small loch 3m/5km SE of Loch Inchard in Sutherland district. **102 E3** NC2949.
Loch Uigeadail *Arg. & B.* ***Lake/loch***, small loch on Islay, 3m/4km N of Ardbeg. **72 C5** NR4050.
Loch Uisg *Arg. & B.* ***Lake/loch***, nearly 2m/3km long between Loch Buie and Loch Spelve, Mull. **79 H5** NM6425.
Loch Uisge *High.* ***Lake/loch***, small loch in Morvern, Lochaber district, 3m/4km NW of Loch a' Choire. **79 K2** NM8055.
Loch Uisgebhagh (Anglicised form: Loch Uskavagh.) *W.Isles* ***Sea feature***, containing numerous islets, on E coast of Benbecula. **92 D6** NF8551.
Loch Uraraidh *Arg. & B.* ***Lake/loch***, small loch on Islay 4m/7km N of Ardbeg. **72 C5** NR4053.
Loch Uraval *W.Isles* ***Lake/loch***, small loch, 7m/12km W of Stornoway, Isle of Lewis. **101 F4** NB3032.
Loch Urigill *High.* ***Lake/loch***, in Sutherland district 7m/11km S of Inchnadamph. **102 E7** NC2410.
Loch Urr *D. & G.* ***Lake/loch***, 4m/7km S of Moniaive. **68 C5** NX7684.
Loch Urrahag *W.Isles* ***Lake/loch***, 1m/2km long N to S, near NW coast of Isle of Lewis, to E and SE of Arnol village. **101 F3** NB3247.
Loch Uskavagh *W.Isles Anglicised form of Loch Uisgebhagh, qv.*
Loch Ussie *High.* ***Lake/loch***, roughly circular in shape, 3m/4km W of Dingwall in Ross and Cromarty district. **96 C6** NH5057.
Loch Vaa *High.* ***Lake/loch***, small loch 3m/5km N of Aviemore. **89 G3** NH9117.
Loch Vaich *High.* ***Reservoir***, in Ross and Cromarty district, 16m/25km NW of Dingwall. **95 K4** NH3475.
Loch Valley *D. & G.* ***Lake/loch***, in Glentrool Forest Park, 2m/3km NE of Loch Trool. **67 J5** NX4481.
Loch Vallich *High. Alternative name for Loch a' Bhealaich, qv.*
Loch Varkasaig *High.* ***Sea feature***, inlet of Loch Bracadale, 3m/5km S of Dunvegan, Skye. **93 H7** NG2542.
Loch Vatandip *W.Isles* ***Lake/loch***, small loch on Isle of Lewis, 4m/6km W of Stornoway. **101 F4** NB3433.
Loch Vatten *High.* ***Sea feature***, on Skye, 3m/5km SE of Dunvegan. **93 H7** NG2843.
Loch Venachar *Stir.* ***Lake/loch***, extending nearly 4m/6km W to E, 2m/4km W of Callander. **81 G7** NN5705.
Loch Veyatie *High.* ***Lake/loch***, narrow loch, 4m/6km long NW to SE, 7m/11km SW of Inchnadamph. Border of Ross and Cromarty and Sutherland districts runs down centre of loch. **102 D7** NC1713.
Loch Voil *Stir.* ***Lake/loch***, narrow loch, nearly 4m/6km long W to E. Village of Balquhidder at E end. **81 G6** NN5019.
Loch Voshimid *W.Isles* ***Lake/loch***, small loch 3m/4km S of head of Loch Resort. **100 D6** NB1013.
Loch Watten *High.* ***Lake/loch***, to N of Watten; 3m/5km long running NW to SE. **105 H3** ND2355.
Loch Wharral *Angus* ***Lake/loch***, small loch or tarn 2m/3km NE of Clova. **90 B7** NO3574.
Loch Whinyeon *D. & G.* ***Lake/loch***, 3m/5km NE of Gatehouse of Fleet. **65 G4** NX6260.
Lochaber *High.* ***Locality***, mountainous moorland region of W Scotland, spanning Great Glen from Knoydart and North and South Morar in W, to Monadliath Mountains and Glen Spean in E. Deeply incised by Lochs Arkaig, Eil, Linnhe, Lochy and Quoich. **87 F5** NM8797.
Lochaber Loch *D. & G.* ***Lake/loch***, small loch 5m/8km SW of Dumfries. **65 K3** NX9270.
Lochailort *High.* ***Locality***, at head of Loch Ailort. **86 D6** NM7682.
Lochaline *High.* ***Village***, in Lochaber district, on W side of entrance to Loch Aline. **79 H3** NM6744.
Lochalsh Woodland Garden *High.* ***Garden***, wooded lochside garden on Balmacara Estate by N shore of Loch Alsh, 2m/3km E of Kyle of Lochalsh. **86 E2** NG8027.
Lochan a' Bhruic *Arg. & B.* ***Lake/loch***, small loch in Inverliever Forest, 6m/9km NE of Ford. **80 A7** NM9109.
Lochan an Tairt *High.* ***Lake/loch***, small loch above N side of Glen Urquhart, 4m/7km NW of Drumnadrochit. **88 B1** NH4433.
Lochan Beannach *High.* ***Lake/loch***, comprises two lochs below Beinn Airigh Mòr, Lochan Beannach Mòr and Lochan Beannach Beag, to W and E respectively. They are connected by narrow stretch of water and drain into Fionn Loch. **95 F4** NG9477.
Lochan Breaclaich *Stir.* ***Reservoir***, small reservoir 3m/5km E of Killin. **81 H4** NN6231.
Lochan Dubh *High.* ***Lake/loch***, in Lochaber district, between Loch Arkaig and Glen Kingie. **87 G5** NN0695.
Lochan Dubh nan Geodh *High.* ***Lake/loch***, 1m/2km NW of Loch More. **105 F4** ND0547.
Lochan Fada *High.* ***Lake/loch***, narrow loch, 1m/2km N of Cam Loch. The summit of Canisp lies 1m/2km N. **102 E7** NC2016.
Lochan Fada *High.* ***Lake/loch***, in W part of Ross and Cromarty, 4m/6km NE of head of Loch Maree. **95 G4** NH0271.
Lochan Fada *High.* ***Lake/loch***, small narrow loch in Erchless Forest, 2m/3km NE of Erchless Castle. **96 B7** NH4243.
Lochan Gaineamhach *High.* ***Lake/loch***, small loch or tarn 2m/3km NW of Loch Bà. **80 D2** NN3053.
Lochan Hakel *High.* ***Lake/loch***, small loch 1km E of S end of Kyle of Tongue. **103 H3** NC5653.
Lochan Loin nan Donnlaich *P. & K.* ***Lake/loch***, small loch 2m/4km NE of Loch Eigheach. **81 F1** NN4661.
Lochan Long *Arg. & B.* ***Lake/loch***, 4m/6km SE of Dalavich across Loch Awe. **80 B7** NN0209.
Lochan Lùnn Dà-Bhrà *High.* ***Lake/loch***, small loch in Lochaber district, 5m/8km S of Fort William. **80 B1** NN0866.
Lochan na Bi *Arg. & B.* ***Lake/loch***, small loch in Argyll in course of River Lochy, 1m/2km NW of Tyndrum. **80 E4** NN3031.
Lochan na h-Achlaise *High.* ***Lake/loch***, small loch on Black Mount in Lochaber district, 2m/3km N of Loch Tulla. **80 E3** NN3148.
Lochan na h-Earba *High.* ***Lake/loch***, narrow loch in Badenoch and Strathspey district running parallel to, and about 1m/2km SE of, Loch Laggan. **88 B6** NN4883.
Lochan na Lairige *P. & K.* ***Reservoir***, 1m/2km long N to S, 4m/6km N of head of Loch Tay. **81 G3** NN5940.
Lochan na Stainge *High.* ***Lake/loch***, small loch in Lochaber district in course of River Bà, between Loch Buidhe and Loch Bà. **80 E3** NN3049.
Lochan na Stairne *High.* ***Lake/loch***, small loch in Glendoe Forest, 4m/7km SE of Fort Augustus. **88 B4** NH4405.
Lochan nam Fiann *High.* ***Lake/loch***, small loch on Ardnamurchan peninsula, 2m/3km N of Glenborrodale. **79 H1** NM6164.
Lochan nan Carn *High.* ***Lake/loch***, 1km E of Borgie Forest, Caithness district. **103 J3** NC6953.
Lochan Shira *Arg. & B.* ***Lake/loch***, and reservoir 4m/6km S of Dalmally in Argyll. **80 C5** NN1620.
Lochan Sròn Mòr *Arg. & B.* ***Lake/loch***, and reservoir in Argyll below dam of Lochan Shira, 8m/13km NE of Inveraray. **80 C6** NN1619.
Lochan Sròn Smeur *P. & K.* ***Lake/loch***, small loch 2m/3km N of Loch Eigheach. **81 F1** NN4560.
Lochan Thulachan (Also known as Loch Thulachan.) *High.* ***Lake/loch***, in Caithness district 8m/12km NW of Latheron. **105 G4** ND1041.
Lochan Uaine *High.* ***Lake/loch***, small loch in Ross and Cromarty district, 4m/7km SE of Torridon. **95 F6** NG9652.
Lochans *D. & G.* ***Village***, 3m/4km S of Stranraer. **64 A5** NX0656.
Lochar Water *D. & G.* ***River***, rising N of Dumfries and flowing into Solway Firth to SW of Cummertrees. Traverses and drains low-lying region of Lochar Moss. **69 F6** NY0371.
Locharbriggs *D. & G.* Population: 5383. ***Small town***, 3m/4km NE of Dumfries. **68 E5** NX9980.
Lochawe *Arg. & B.* ***Village***, on W bank of Loch Awe in Argyll, 3m/4km W of Dalmally. **80 C5** NN1227.
Lochboisdale (Gaelic form: Loch Baghasdail.) *W.Isles* ***Village***, port on N shore of Loch Baghasdail, inlet on E coast of South Uist. **84 C3** NF7919.
Lochbroom Burn *P. & K.* ***River***, flowing SW from Loch Broom into River Tay, 3m/4km SE of Pitlochry. **82 A2** NN9654.
Lochbuie *Arg. & B.* ***Village***, on S coast of Mull, at head of large inlet of Loch Buie. Ruined keep of Castle Moy. Ancient stone circle to E. **79 H5** NM6025.
Lochcarron *High.* ***Village***, on N shore of Loch Carron, 2m/3km below head of loch. **86 E1** NG8735.
Lochcraig Head *Sc.Bord.* ***Mountain***, rising above N shore of Loch Skeen, 5m/8km SW of St. Mary's Loch. Height 2624 feet or 800 metres. **69 G2** NT1618.
Lochdhu Hotel *High.* ***Other building***, hotel situated on E side of Loch Dubh, 1m/2km S of Altnabreac station. **105 F4** ND0144.
Lochdon *Arg. & B.* ***Village***, at head of Loch Don, inlet on E coast of Mull. **79 J4** NM7333.
Lochdrum *High.* ***Settlement***, in Dirrie More, 4m/6km E of Corrieshalloch Gorge. **95 J4** NH2475.
Lochearnhead *Stir.* ***Village***, at head, or W end, of Loch Earn, 6m/10km S of Killin. **81 G5** NN5823.
Lochee *Dundee* ***Suburb***, 2m/3km NW of Dundee city centre. **82 E4** NO3731.
Locheil Forest *High.* ***Open space***, deer forest extending N of Loch Eil to Loch Arkaig. **87 G6** NN0277.
Locheilside Station *High.* ***Other building***, railway station on N shore of Loch Eil, 1km E of Kinlocheil, Lochaber district. **87 F7** NM9978.
Lochend *Edin.* ***Suburb***, 2m/3km NE of Edinburgh city centre. NT2774.
Lochend *High.* ***Settlement***, in Caithness district, on E side of Loch Heilen, 4m/6km SE of Dunnet. **105 H2** ND2668.
Lochend *High.* ***Settlement***, at NE end of Loch Ness, Inverness district. **88 C1** NH5937.
Locheport *W.Isles* ***Settlement***, on North Uist, on S shore of Loch Euphoirt, 5m/7km from mouth. NF8563.
Lochfoot *D. & G.* ***Village***, at N end of Lochrutton Loch, 5m/8km W of Dumfries. **65 K3** NX8973.
Lochgair *Arg. & B.* ***Village***, 4m/6km NE of Lochgilphead, on Loch Gair, a small inlet on Loch Fyne. **73 H1** NR9290.
Lochgarthside *High.* ***Settlement***, in Inverness district, on NW shore of Loch Mhòr. **88 C3** NH5219.
Lochgelly *Fife* Population: 7044. ***Small town***, former mining town, 7m/11km SW of Glenrothes. **75 K1** NT1893.
Lochgilphead *Arg. & B.* Population: 2421. ***Small town***, at head of Loch Gilp in Argyll. Tourist and shopping centre. Former fishing village which developed with opening of Crinan Canal. **73 G2** NR8687.
Lochgoilhead *Arg. & B.* ***Village***, at head of Loch Goil in Argyll. **80 D7** NN1901.
Lochgoin *E.Ayr.* ***Settlement***, 4m/7km SW of Eaglesham. **74 D6** NS5346.
Lochgoin Reservoir *E.Ayr.* ***Reservoir***, 4m/6km SW of Eaglesham. **74 D6** NS5347.
Lochhill *E.Ayr.* ***Settlement***, 2m/3km NW of New Cumnock. **68 B2** NS6015.
Lochhill *Moray* ***Settlement***, 3m/5km W of Garmouth. **97 K5** NJ2965.
Lochinch Castle *D. & G.* ***Historic house***, 19c mansion 3m/5km E of Stranraer. Grounds contain pinetum, two lochs (White Loch and Black Loch, the latter being more easterly), and, on isthmus between them, ruins of Castle Kennedy, late 16c castle destroyed by fire in 1715. **64 B4** NX1061.
Lochindorb *High.* ***Lake/loch***, 8m/13km N of Carrbridge and 6m/10km NW of Grantown-on-Spey. Medieval castle on island in loch. **89 G1** NH9736.
Lochindorb Castle *High.* ***Castle***, ruins of early 13c castle on island in Lochindorb, 6m/10km NW of Grantown-on-Spey. **89 G1** NH9736.
Lochinver *High.* ***Small town***, fishing port and resort on W coast of Sutherland district at head of Loch Inver 18m/29km N of Ullapool. **102 C6** NC0922.
Lochlair *Angus* ***Settlement***, 3m/5km S of Letham. **83 G3** NO5243.
Lochlands Hill *N.Ayr.* ***Hill***, 2m/3km NE of Beith. Height 689 feet or 210 metres. **74 B5** NS3755.
Lochlane *P. & K.* ***Locality***, in valley of River Earn, 1m/2km W of Crieff. **81 K5** NN8321.
Lochlea *S.Ayr.* ***Settlement***, 3m/4km NE of Tarbolton. **67 J1** NS4530.
Lochluichart *High.* ***Settlement***, on N shore of Loch Luichart, at W end of loch, 4m/6km W of Gorstan. **95 K5** NH3363.
Lochluichart Station *High.* ***Other building***, railway station on route from Inverness to Kyle of Lochalsh, 4m/6km W of Gorstan. **95 K5** NH3262.
Lochmaben *D. & G.* Population: 2024. ***Small town***, royal burgh 8m/13km NE of Dumfries, surrounded by several small lochs. Reputed birthplace of Robert the Bruce. Ruined 13c castle on Castle Loch supplied building stone for many of town's houses. **69 F5** NY0882.
Lochmaben Castle *D. & G.* ***Castle***, 14c ruins on S shore of Castle Loch, to S of Lochmaben; said to be birthplace of Robert the Bruce. **69 F5** NY0881.
Lochmaddy (Gaelic form: Loch na Madadh.) *W.Isles* ***Village***, port on W shore of Loch na Madadh. **92 E5** NF9369.
Lochnagar *Aber.* ***Inland physical feature***, mountain ridge with steep NE facing cliffs, comprising four distinct peaks above Lochnagar Loch, 3m/4km NW of Loch Muick. Peaks are Cac Carn Beag, a Munro at 3788 feet or 1155 metres, Cac Carn Mòr at 3772 feet or 1150 metres, Cuidhe Cròm at 3552 feet or 1083 metres and Meikle Pap at 3214 feet or 980 metres. **89 K6** NO2585.
Lochnaw Castle *D. & G.* ***Castle***, mainly 17c castle, incorporating 16c tower, on S side of small loch, 5m/7km W of Stranraer. Former seat of Agnews. **64 A4** NW9962.
Lochore *Fife* ***Town***, former mining town, 3m/5km N of Cowdenbeath. **75 K1** NT1796.
Lochore Meadows Country Park *Fife* ***Leisure/recreation***, on N side of Loch Ore, 1km SW of Lochore. Focal point of park is loch, with emphasis on watersports and fishing, although there is also a golf course and extensive woodlands. **75 K1** NT1695.
Lochportain *W.Isles* ***Settlement***, on North Uist, on N shore of Loch Portain. **92 E4** NF9471.
Lochranza *N.Ayr.* ***Village***, and resort on W side of Loch Ranza, inlet at N end of Arran. Castle (Historic Scotland) dates from 13c. **73 H6** NR9250.
Lochranza Castle *N.Ayr.* ***Castle***, ruined castle built 13c-14c on promontory in Loch Ranza on N coast of Arran. **73 H5** NR9350.
Lochrosque Forest *High.* ***Open space***, deer forest to NE of Loch Rosque. **95 H5** NH1258.
Lochrutton Loch *D. & G.* ***Lake/loch***, 5m/8km W of Dumfries. **65 J3** NX8972.
Lochs of Lumbister *Shet.* ***Lake/loch***, series of lochs in N part of Yell. **108 D3** HU4896.
Lochside *Aber.* ***Hamlet***, 1km W of St. Cyrus. **83 J1** NO7364.
Lochside *D. & G.* ***Suburb***, NW district of Dumfries. NX9577.
Lochside *High.* ***Settlement***, on E shore of N end of Loch Hope. **103 G3** NC4759.
Lochside *High.* ***Settlement***, in Sutherland district, to SE of Loch an Ruathair. **104 D5** NC8735.

Lochside *High.* ***Settlement***, 1m/2km SE of Castletown. **105 H2** ND2165.
Lochskipport *W.Isles Anglicised form of Loch Sgioport (settlement), qv.*
Lochslin *High.* ***Settlement***, 3m/5km E of Tain. **97 F3** NH8380.
Lochton *S.Ayr.* ***Settlement***, 2m/3km SE of Barrhill. **67 G5** NX2580.
Lochty *Fife* ***Settlement***, 4m/6km NW of Anstruther. **83 G7** NO5208.
Lochuisge *High.* ***Settlement***, 1km W of Loch Uisge, Lochaber district. **79 J2** NM7955.
Lochurr *D. & G.* ***Settlement***, 4m/6km S of Moniaive. **68 C5** NX7685.
Lochussie *High.* ***Settlement***, 1m/2km SW of Strathpeffer. **96 B6** NH4956.
Lochwinnoch *Renf.* Population: 2347. ***Small town***, residential town, 12m/19km SW of Paisley, formerly a weaving centre. Clyde Muirshiel Regional Park contains RSPB reserve. **74 B5** NS3558.
Lochy Burn *Alternative name for Burn of Lochy, qv.*
Lockengate *Cornw.* ***Hamlet***, 4m/7km SW of Bodmin. **4 A4** SX0361.
Lockerbie *D. & G.* Population: 3982. ***Small town***, market town founded in 17c, 11m/17km E of Dumfries. Agricultural centre for surrounding area. Lockerbie Air Disaster Memorial, sited at Lockerbie City Cemetery, commemorates all victims who died in Lockerbie Air Disaster, December 1988. **69 G5** NY1381.
Lockeridge *Wilts.* ***Village***, 3m/5km W of Marlborough. Sarsen stones known locally as Grey Wethers (National Trust). **20 E5** SU1467.
Lockerley *Hants.* ***Village***, 5m/8km NW of Romsey. **10 D2** SU2926.
Lockerley Green *Hants.* ***Locality***, adjoining to S of Lockerley. SU2926.
Lockhills *Cumb.* ***Settlement***, between railway line and River Eden, 1m/2km N of Armathwaite and 5m/8km SE of Wetheral. NY5047.
Locking *N.Som.* ***Village***, 3m/5km SE of Weston-super-Mare. **19 G6** ST3659.
Lockinge *Oxon.* ***Locality***, parish containing hamlets of East and West Lockinge, 2m/3km E of Wantage. SU4287.
Lockington *E.Riding* ***Village***, 5m/8km NW of Beverley. **59 G5** SE9947.
Lockington *Leics.* ***Village***, 1m/2km E of Castle Donington. **41 G3** SK4627.
Lockleaze *Bristol* ***Suburb***, NE district of Bristol. ST6076.
Lockleywood *Shrop.* ***Hamlet***, 4m/6km S of Market Drayton. **39 F3** SJ6928.
Locks Heath *Hants.* Population: 29,848. ***Suburb***, large residential locality, 3m/5km W of Fareham. **11 G4** SU5107.
Locksbottom *Gt.Lon.* ***Suburb***, in borough of Bromley, 2m/3km W of Orpington. **23 H5** TQ4365.
Locksgreen *I.o.W.* ***Settlement***, 4m/6km W of Newport. SZ4490.
Lockton *N.Yorks.* ***Village***, 5m/8km NE of Pickering. **63 K7** SE8489.
Lockton High Moor *N.Yorks.* ***Open space***, moorland, 3m/5km SE of Goathland. **63 K7** SE8596.
Lockton Low Moor *N.Yorks.* ***Open space***, moorland in North Riding Forest Park, 6m/10km NE of Pickering. **63 K7** SE8393.
Lockwood Beck Reservoir *R. & C.* ***Reservoir***, small reservoir 1m/2km W of Moorsholm. **63 H5** NZ6814.
Loddington *Leics.* ***Village***, 5m/8km NW of Uppingham. **42 A5** SK7902.
Loddington *Northants.* ***Village***, 4m/6km W of Kettering. **32 B1** SP8178.
Loddiswell *Devon* ***Village***, 3m/4km NW of Kingsbridge, above valley of River Avon. **5 H6** SX7248.
Loddon ***River***, rising E of Basingstoke and flowing NE into River Thames W of Wargrave. SU7778.
Loddon *Norf.* Population: 2901. ***Small town***, former port, now boating centre, on River Chet 6m/10km NW of Beccles. **45 H6** TM3698.
Lode *Cambs.* ***Village***, 6m/10km NE of Cambridge. Anglesey Abbey (National Trust), house built c. 1600 on site of medieval monastery. **33 J2** TL5362.
Lode Heath *W.Mid.* ***Suburb***, to N of Solihull town centre. SP1580.
Loder Head *Shet.* ***Coastal feature***, headland on E coast of Bressay at entrance to Voe of Cullingsburgh. **109 E8** HU5243.
Loders *Dorset* ***Village***, 2m/3km NE of Bridport. **8 D5** SY4994.
Lodge Green *W.Mid.* ***Settlement***, 6m/10km NW of Coventry. SP2583.
Lodge Island *D. & G.* ***Island***, in River Dee, connected to E bank by causeway, 2m/3km SW of Castle Douglas. NX7361.
Lodge Park *Northants.* ***Suburb***, W district of Corby. SP8689.
Lodge Park *Worcs.* ***Suburb***, to S of Redditch town centre. SP0466.
Lodon *Here.* ***River***, rising to W of Bredenbury and flowing S into River Frome, 1m/2km NW of Ashperton. **29 F3** SO6242.
Lodsworth *W.Suss.* ***Village***, 3m/5km NE of Midhurst. **12 C4** SU9223.
Loe *Cornw. Alternative name for (River) Cober, qv.*
Loe Pool *Cornw. Alternative name for The Loe, qv.*
Loft Hill *Northumb.* ***Mountain***, in Cheviot Hills, 2m/3km NE of Blindburn. Height 1509 feet or 460 metres. **70 D2** NT8413.
Lofthouse *N.Yorks.* ***Village***, on River Nidd, 6m/10km NW of Pateley Bridge. **57 F2** SE1073.
Lofthouse *W.Yorks.* Population: 9568. ***Village***, 3m/5km N of Wakefield. **57 J7** SE3325.
Lofthouse Gate *W.Yorks.* ***Locality***, 1m/2km S of Lofthouse, 3m/4km N of Wakefield city centre. SE3325.
Loftus *R. & C.* Population: 5931. ***Small town***, 4m/6km SE of Saltburn. Formerly a centre for alum manufacture, now of agricultural importance. **63 J5** NZ7218.
Logan *D. & G.* ***Locality***, 4m/7km S of Sandhead, at W end of Sands of Luce, including Logan Mains, Tower and Botanic Gardens. **64 A6** NX0943.
Logan *E.Ayr.* Population: 1214. ***Village***, 1m/2km E of Cumnock. **67 K1** NS5820.
Logan Botanic Gardens *D. & G.* ***Garden***, 1m/2km N of Port Logan. Exotic ferns, plants, palms, shrubs and perennials planted outside. **64 A6** NX0942.
Logan Rock *Cornw.* ***Coastal feature***, stack on S coast, 1km SE of Porthcurno. **2 A6** SW3921.
Logan Water *S.Lan.* ***River***, rising on Spirebush Hill and running E to River Nethan 2m/3km SW of Lesmahagow. **75 F7** NS7936.
Loganlea *W.Loth.* ***Hamlet***, adjoining to W of Addiewell, 4m/7km S of Bathgate. **75 H4** NS9862.
Loganlea Reservoir *Midloth.* ***Reservoir***, small reservoir on Pentland Hills, 3m/5km NW of Penicuik. **75 K4** NT1962.
Loggerheads *Staffs.* ***Village***, 4m/7km E of Market Drayton. **39 G2** SJ7335.
Loggerheads Country Park *Denb.* ***Leisure/recreation***, 74 acre country park offering nature trails and forest and riverside walks, 1km W of Cadole. **47 K6** SJ1962.
Loggie *High.* ***Settlement***, on W shore of Loch Broom, Ross and Cromarty district, 4m/6km from head of loch. **95 H2** NH1490.
Logie *Angus* ***Settlement***, 1m/2km S of Kirriemuir. **82 E2** NO3952.
Logie *Angus* ***Settlement***, 4m/6km N of Montrose. **83 H1** NO6963.
Logie *Fife* ***Village***, 3m/5km W of Leuchars. **83 F5** NO4020.
Logie *Moray* ***Settlement***, 5m/8km S of Forres. **97 H6** NJ0150.
Logie Buchan *Aber.* ***Locality***, parish containing Kirkton of Logie Buchan. NJ9829.
Logie Coldstone *Aber.* ***Village***, adjoining to small lake, 7m/11km NE of Ballater. **90 C4** NJ4304.
Logie Head *Aber.* ***Coastal feature***, headland on N coast, 1m/2km NE of Cullen. **98 D4** NJ5268.
Logie Hill *High.* ***Settlement***, 6m/10km NE of Invergordon. **96 E4** NH7676.
Logie Newton *Aber.* ***Settlement***, 4m/6km N of Kirkton of Culsalmond. **90 E1** NJ6638.
Logie Pert *Angus* ***Village***, 5m/8km NW of Montrose. Cottage within parish, to NW of village, is birthplace of James Mill, 1773-1836. **83 H1** NO6664.
Logiealmond *P. & K.* ***Locality***, on N slope of Glen Almond, 8m/12km NW of Perth. **82 A4** NN9930.
Logierait *P. & K.* ***Village***, 4m/7km SE of Pitlochry, near confluence of Rivers Tay and Tummel. **82 A2** NN9651.
Login *Carmar.* ***Village***, 5m/8km NW of Whitland. **16 E2** SN1623.
Loirston Country Park *Aberdeen* ***Leisure/recreation***, country park with 620 acres of coastal walks to S of River Dee, 2m/3km SE of Aberdeen harbour. Attracts a wide variety of seabirds and other wildlife. Includes Girdle Ness lighthouse. **91 H4** NJ9302.
Lolworth *Cambs.* ***Village***, 6m/10km NW of Cambridge. **33 G2** TL3664.
Lomond Hills ***Large natural feature***, range of hills NE of Loch Leven. Summit is West Lomond, 1712 feet or 522 metres. **82 D7** NO2106.
Lon-Ias *Swan.* ***Suburb***, to S of Birchgrove, 3m/5km W of Neath. SS7097.
Lòn Mòr *High.* ***River***, flowing SW and joining River Haultin, 1m/2km E of head of Loch Eyre. **93 K6** NG4351.
Lonan *Arg. & B.* ***River***, in Argyll, running W down Glen Lonan to head of Loch Nell, 3m/5km E of Oban. **80 A5** NM9028.
Lonan *I.o.M.* ***Locality***, 1km S of Laxey. SC4383.
Lonbain *High.* ***Locality***, in Ross and Cromarty district, 6m/9km N of Applecross. **94 C6** NG6853.
Londesborough *E.Riding* ***Village***, 2m/4km N of Market Weighton. **58 E5** SE8645.
Londinium *Gt.Lon. See London.*
London *Gt.Lon.* Population: 6,675,557. ***City***, capital of England and Europe's largest city. Consists of 32 boroughs together with City of London, totalling over 620 square miles, centred on River Thames. Legislative capital of UK. Financial, commercial, distribution and communications centre. Most industries represented except primary industries such as mining. London developed from Roman settlement of Londinium, dating from AD 43. Despite successful attack by Queen Boudicca (AD 61), London became national capital by end of 1c. Major expansion during Norman era after William the Conqueror became first king crowned at Westminster Abbey. Little left from this period as Great Fire of 1666 destroyed over 13,000 buildings. This was followed by period of rebuilding and rapid expansion, giving London many enduring landmarks such as St. Paul's Cathedral. Cosmopolitan city since 17c when French Huguenots fled to London from persecution of Louis XIV. Much of architecture dates from 19c when London was seen as focus of glorious empire. Home to vast array of galleries and museums including Victoria and Albert and British Museums, National and Tate Galleries. Theatres and shopping in West End. Other attractions include Tower of London and Trafalgar Square. Many universities. **23 F3** TQ3079.
London Apprentice *Cornw.* ***Village***, 2m/3km S of St. Austell. SX0050.
London Beach *Kent* ***Settlement***, 2m/3km N of Tenterden. **14 D4** TQ8836.
London Bridge *Gt.Lon.* ***Bridge***, spanning River Thames, 2m/3km E of Charing Cross. Bridge has been replaced many times. Until 12c it was a wooden construction; the famous stone bridge that followed carried houses and shops. Granite bridge built in 1832 by Rennie was shipped off to Lake Havasu City, Arizona in 1971. Latest construction completed 1973. TQ3280.
London City Airport *Gt.Lon.* ***Airport/airfield***, international airport in borough of Newham, 8m/13km E of Charing Cross. **23 H3** TQ4280.
London Colney *Herts.* ***Suburb***, 3m/4km SE of St. Albans. **22 E1** TL1704.
London End *Northants.* ***Locality***, E end of Irchester, 3m/5km SE of Wellingborough. SP9265.
London Fields *W.Mid.* ***Suburb***, 1m/2km W of Dudley town centre. SO9290.
London Heathrow Airport (Heathrow Airport). *Gt.Lon.* ***Airport/airfield***, major international airport, situated in borough of Hillingdon, 14m/23km W of Charing Cross. **22 D4** TQ0775.
London Luton Airport *Luton* ***Airport/airfield***, international airport, 2m/3km E of Luton town centre. **32 E6** TL1220.
London Minstead *Hants.* ***Hamlet***, adjoining to NE of Minstead, 2m/4km NW of Lyndhurst. SU2811.
Londonderry *N.Yorks.* ***Village***, 2m/4km E of Bedale. **57 H1** SE3087.
Londonderry *W.Mid.* ***Suburb***, 1m/2km N of Warley town centre. SP0087.
Londonthorpe *Lincs.* ***Hamlet***, 3m/5km NE of Grantham. **42 C2** SK9537.
Londubh *High.* ***Settlement***, adjoining to E of Poolewe, Ross and Cromarty district. **94 E3** NG8681.
Lonemore *High.* ***Settlement***, on N shore of Dornoch Firth, 2m/3km W of Dornoch. **96 E3** NH7688.
Long Ashton *N.Som.* Population: 4080. ***Village***, 3m/5km SW of Bristol. **19 J4** ST5470.
Long Bank *Worcs.* ***Village***, 2m/3km W of Bewdley. SO7674.
Long Bennington *Lincs.* ***Village***, 7m/12km NW of Grantham. **42 B1** SK8344.
Long Bredy *Dorset* ***Village***, 8m/12km W of Dorchester. **8 E5** SY5690.
Long Buckby *Northants.* Population: 3428. ***Village***, 5m/8km NE of Daventry. **31 H2** SP6267.
Long Clawson *Leics.* ***Village***, 5m/9km N of Melton Mowbray. **42 A3** SK7227.
Long Common *Hants.* ***Hamlet***, 1m/2km N of Botley. **11 G3** SU5014.
Long Compton *Staffs.* ***Hamlet***, 4m/7km W of Stafford. **40 A3** SJ8522.
Long Compton *Warks.* ***Village***, 4m/6km NW of Chipping Norton. **30 D5** SP2832.
Long Crag *Northumb.* ***Mountain***, 3m/5km N of Rothbury. Height 1046 feet or 319 metres. **71 F3** NU0606.
Long Craig *Angus* ***Coastal feature***, small peninsula of rock on North Sea coast, 2m/3km SE of Montrose. **83 J2** NO7254.
Long Crendon *Bucks.* Population: 2505. ***Village***, 2m/3km NW of Thame. 14c courthouse (National Trust). **21 K1** SP6908.
Long Crendon Courthouse *Bucks.* ***Historic house***, 14c partly half-timbered building (National Trust) to E of Long Crendon, 3m/4km NW of Thame. Manorial courts were held here from reign of Henry V until Victorian times. **21 K1** SP6909.
Long Crichel *Dorset* ***Village***, 6m/10km NE of Blandford Forum. **9 J3** ST9710.
Long Cross *Wilts.* ***Hamlet***, 1km NE of Zeals and 2m/3km W of Mere. ST7832.
Long Cross Victorian Gardens *Cornw.* ***Garden***, to SE of Trelights, 4m/6km N of Wadebridge. Garden dating from late Victorian era, with granite and water features. **3 G1** SW9979.
Long Dale *Notts.* ***Locality***, 4m/6km NE of Hucknall. SK5653.
Long Dean *Wilts.* ***Hamlet***, on By Brook, 5m/7km NW of Chippenham. ST8575.
Long Ditton *Surr.* ***Suburb***, 1m/2km SW of Surbiton. **22 E5** TQ1666.
Long Downs (Also spelled Longdowns.) *Cornw.* ***Village***, 2m/4km W of Penryn. **2 E5** SW7434.
Long Drax *N.Yorks.* ***Settlement***, 1m/2km N of Drax. **58 C7** SE6728.
Long Duckmanton *Derbys.* ***Village***, 1km S of Duckmanton and 2m/3km W of Bolsover. **51 G5** SK4471.
Long Eaton *Derbys.* Population: 44,826. ***Town***, market town, once famous for lace-making, 9m/14km E of Derby and 6m/10km SW of Nottingham. **41 G2** SK4933.
Long Geo *Ork.* ***Coastal feature***, on W coast of S part of Mainland, 3m/5km S of Kirkwall. **107 D7** HY4404.
Long Gill *N.Yorks.* ***Settlement***, 3m/5km W of Long Preston. **56 C4** SD7858.
Long Green *Ches.* ***Settlement***, 4m/6km S of Helsby. SJ4770.
Long Green *Essex* ***Hamlet***, 3m/5km E of Coggeshall. TL9023.
Long Green *Suff.* ***Settlement***, adjoining to W of Wortham. TM0777.
Long Green *Worcs.* ***Hamlet***, 3m/5km W of Tewkesbury. SO8433.
Long Hanborough *Oxon.* Population: 2215. ***Village***, 5m/8km NE of Witney. **31 F7** SP4114.
Long Hermiston *Edin.* ***Locality***, 5m/8km SW of Edinburgh. NT1770.
Long Holcombe *Som.* ***Mountain***, on Exmoor, 2m/3km S of Simonsbath. Height 1430 feet or 436 metres. **7 F2** SS7835.
Long Hope *Ork.* ***Sea feature***, strait separating SE coast of Hoy from N coast of South Walls peninsula. ND3091.
Long Island *Cornw.* ***Island***, off N coast, 1km NW of Trevalga. SX0790.
Long Island *Dorset* ***Island***, on S side of Poole Harbour joined by marshland to N of Round Island. SY9887.
Long Island *Hants.* ***Island***, uninhabited island at N end of Langstone Harbour, 1m/2km SW of Langstone. SU7004.
Long Itchington *Warks.* ***Village***, 2m/4km N of Southam. Site of Roman building 2m/3km NW. Cement works to S. **31 F2** SP4165.
Long John's Hill *Norf.* ***Suburb***, 1m/2km S of Norwich city centre. TG2306.

Long Lane *Tel. & W.* ***Settlement***, adjoining to S of Sleapford. SJ6315.
Long Lane Bottom *W.Yorks.* ***Suburb***, 2m/3km E of Huddersfield town centre. SE1617.
Long Lawford *Warks.* Population: 2501. ***Village***, 2m/4km W of Rugby. **31 F1** SP4776.
Long Load *Som.* ***Village***, on S bank of River Yeo, 4m/6km SE of Langport. **8 D2** ST4623.
Long Loch *Angus* ***Lake/loch***, small loch 2m/3km S of Newtyle. **82 D4** NO2838.
Long Loch *E.Renf.* ***Lake/loch***, 3m/5km S of Neilston. **74 C5** NS4752.
Long Marston *Herts.* ***Village***, 3m/5km NW of Tring. **32 B7** SP8915.
Long Marston *N.Yorks.* ***Village***, 7m/11km W of York. **58 B4** SE5051.
Long Marston *Warks.* ***Village***, 5m/8km SW of Stratford-upon-Avon. **30 C4** SP1548.
Long Marton *Cumb.* ***Village***, 3m/5km N of Appleby-in-Westmorland. Site of Roman camp 1m/2km W. **61 H4** NY6624.
Long Meadowend *Shrop.* ***Hamlet***, 1m/2km W of Craven Arms. SO4182.
Long Melford *Suff.* Population: 2808. ***Small town***, 3m/5km N of Sudbury. Large Perpendicular church. Melford Hall (National Trust) and Kentwell Hall are Elizabethan. Many other old houses. **34 C4** TL8646.
Long Mountain *Powys* ***Inland physical feature***, mountain ridge rising to1338 feet or 408 metres above E bank of River Severn opposite Welshpool. On summit is an ancient camp known as Beacon Ring. **38 B5** SJ2605.
Long Newnton *Glos.* ***Village***, 1m/2km E of Tetbury. **20 C2** ST9192.
Long Nose Spit *Kent* ***Coastal feature***, spit at Foreness Point between Palm Bay and Botany Bay on Isle of Thanet. **25 K4** TR3871.
Long Preston *N.Yorks.* ***Village***, 4m/6km S of Settle. Site of Roman fort at SE end of village. **56 D4** SD8358.
Long Reach *Kent* ***Sea feature***, stretch of sea separating Isle of Sheppey from mainland, to W of Queenborough. **24 E4** TQ8971.
Long Riston *E.Riding* ***Village***, 2m/4km SE of Leven. **59 H5** TA1242.
Long Sand *Lincs.* ***Coastal feature***, sandbank in The Wash, between Boston Deeps and Lynn Deeps off Lincolnshire coast. **43 J1** TF5246.
Long Sandall *S.Yorks.* ***Locality***, on W bank of River Dun Navigation, 3m/5km NE of Doncaster town centre. SE6006.
Long Sight *Gt.Man.* ***Suburb***, 1m/2km N of Oldham town centre. SD9206.
Long Sleddale *Cumb.* ***Valley***, narrow sheltered valley, 7m/11km long. From head of valley a 2m/3km mountain track leads over Gatesgarth Pass (1948 feet or 594 metres) to S end of Haweswater Reservoir. **61 F6** NY4903.
Long Stratton *Norf.* Population: 2945. ***Village***, 10m/16km S of Norwich. **45 F6** TM1992.
Long Street *M.K.* ***Hamlet***, 6m/9km NW of Newport Pagnell. **31 J4** SP7947.
Long Sutton *Hants.* ***Village***, 5m/8km N of Alton. **22 A7** SU7347.
Long Sutton *Lincs.* Population: 4185. ***Small town***, Georgian market town, 9m/13km N of Wisbech. Medieval church has oldest lead spire in England. **43 H3** TF4322.
Long Sutton *Som.* ***Village***, 2m/4km SW of Somerton. **8 D2** ST4625.
Long Thurlow *Suff.* ***Hamlet***, 6m/10km NW of Stowmarket. **34 E2** TM0168.
Long Valley *Hants.* ***Valley***, 1m/2km SE of Fleet. **22 B6** SU8352.
Long Waste *Tel. & W.* ***Hamlet***, 4m/6km NW of Wellington. **39 F4** SJ6115.
Long Whatton *Leics.* ***Village***, 4m/6km NW of Loughborough. **41 G3** SK4823.
Long Wittenham *Oxon.* ***Village***, 3m/4km NE of Didcot. **21 J2** SU5493.
Longa Island *High.* ***Island***, uninhabited island of about 360 acres or 145 hectares at mouth of Gair Loch, W coast of Ross and Cromarty district, 1m/2km S of Rubha Bàn. **94 D4** NG7377.
Longacre Green *Suff.* ***Locality***, 6m/10km N of Haverhill. TL6755.
Longay *High.* ***Island***, uninhabited island of about 150 acres or 60 hectares, lying 1m/2km E of Scalpay at S end of Inner Sound. **86 C1** NG6531.
Longbenton *T. & W.* Population: 17,315. ***Town***, 3m/4km N of Newcastle upon Tyne. **71 H7** NZ2668.
Longborough *Glos.* ***Village***, 3m/4km N of Stow-on-the-Wold. **30 C6** SP1729.
Longbridge *Plym.* ***Suburb***, 3m/5km NE of Plymouth city centre. SX5157.
Longbridge *Warks.* ***Hamlet***, 2m/3km SW of Warwick. **30 D2** SP2662.
Longbridge *W.Mid.* ***Suburb***, 7m/11km SW of Birmingham city centre. Developed due to car manufacture. **30 B1** SP0077.
Longbridge Deverill *Wilts.* ***Village***, 3m/4km S of Warminster. **20 B7** ST8640.
Longbridge Hayes *Staffs.* ***Suburb***, 1m/2km W of Burslem. SJ8550.
Longburgh *Cumb.* ***Hamlet***, 1m/2km W of Burgh by Sands. **60 E1** NY3058.
Longburton *Dorset* ***Village***, 3m/4km S of Sherborne. **9 F3** ST6412.
Longcliffe *Derbys.* ***Hamlet***, 4m/6km W of Wirksworth. **50 E7** SK2255.
Longcombe *Devon* ***Hamlet***, 2m/3km E of Totnes. SX8359.
Longcot *Oxon.* ***Village***, 3m/5km SW of Faringdon. **21 F2** SU2790.
Longcroft *Cumb.* ***Locality***, 1m/2km NW of Kirkbride across River Wampool. NY2158.
Longcroft *Falk.* ***Village***, 4m/6km NE of Cumbernauld. NS7979.
Longcross *Devon* ***Settlement***, 2m/3km E of Milton Abbot. **4 E3** SX4379.
Longcross *Surr.* ***Hamlet***, 2m/4km N of Chobham. **22 C5** SU9865.
Longdale *Cumb.* ***Locality***, 2m/3km E of Tebay. NY6405.
Longden *Shrop.* ***Village***, 5m/8km SW of Shrewsbury. **38 D5** SJ4404.
Longden Common *Shrop.* ***Hamlet***, 1m/2km S of Longden. SJ4404.
Longdendale *Derbys.* ***Valley***, in Peak District carrying River Etherow SW from Woodhead to Gamesley. Contains series of five stepped reservoirs. **50 C3** SK0498.
Longdon *Staffs.* ***Village***, 4m/6km SE of Rugeley. **40 C4** SK0814.
Longdon *Worcs.* ***Village***, 4m/7km NW of Tewkesbury. **29 H5** SO8336.
Longdon Green *Staffs.* ***Village***, 1km SE of Longdon. SK0813.
Longdon upon Tern *Tel. & W.* ***Village***, 3m/5km NW of Wellington. **39 F4** SJ6215.
Longdown *Devon* ***Hamlet***, 4m/6km W of Exeter. **7 G6** SX8691.
Longdowns *Cornw.* *Alternative spelling of Long Downs, qv.*
Longdrum *Aber.* ***Settlement***, 3m/5km SE of Newmachar and 2m/4km W of Balmedie. **91 H3** NJ9217.
Longfield *Kent* Population: 8617. ***Small town***, 4m/7km SW of Gravesend. **24 C5** TQ6069.
Longfield *Wilts.* ***Suburb***, E district of Trowbridge. ST8657.
Longfield Hill *Kent* ***Village***, 4m/6km S of Gravesend. **24 C5** TQ6268.
Longfleet *Poole* ***Suburb***, central district of Poole. **10 B5** SZ0191.
Longford *Derbys.* ***Village***, 9m/14km W of Derby. **40 E2** SK2137.
Longford *Glos.* ***Village***, 1m/2km N of Gloucester. **29 H6** SO8320.
Longford *Gt.Lon.* ***Hamlet***, at W end of London Heathrow Airport, 16m/26km W of Charing Cross. **22 D4** TQ0476.
Longford *Shrop.* ***Hamlet***, 2m/3km W of Market Drayton. **39 F2** SJ6433.
Longford *Tel. & W.* ***Hamlet***, 1m/2km W of Newport. **39 G4** SJ7218.
Longford *W.Mid.* ***Suburb***, 3m/5km N of Coventry city centre. **41 F7** SP3583.
Longford Castle *Wilts.* *See Odstock.*
Longforgan *P. & K.* ***Village***, 6m/10km W of Dundee. **82 E5** NO3129.
Longformacus *Sc.Bord.* ***Village***, on Dye Water, 6m/10km W of Duns. **76 E5** NT6957.
Longframlington *Northumb.* ***Village***, 5m/7km E of Rothbury. **71 G3** NU1301.
Longgrain Head *D. & G.* ***Mountain***, on uplands to S of Craik Forest, 5m/8km N of Langholm. Height 1535 feet or 468 metres. **69 J4** NY3592.
Longham *Dorset* ***Suburb***, 5m/8km N of Bournemouth. **10 B5** SZ0698.
Longham *Norf.* ***Village***, 4m/6km NW of East Dereham. **44 D4** TF9415.
Longhill *Aber.* ***Settlement***, just S of New Leeds, 4m/6km N of Mintlaw. **99 H5** NJ9953.
Longhirst *Northumb.* ***Village***, 3m/4km NE of Morpeth. **71 H5** NZ2289.
Longhope *Glos.* ***Village***, 9m/14km W of Gloucester. **29 F7** SO6818.
Longhope *Ork.* ***Settlement***, on N coast of South Walls peninsula, Hoy, overlooking North Bay. **107 C8** ND3090.
Longhorsley *Northumb.* ***Village***, 6m/10km NW of Morpeth. Battlemented tower, probably of 16c. **71 G4** NZ1494.
Longhoughton *Northumb.* ***Village***, 4m/6km E of Alnwick. **71 H2** NU2415.
Longhoughton Steel *Northumb.* ***Coastal feature***, flat rocks, 2m/3km E of Longhoughton. **71 H2** NU2715.
Longlands *Aber.* ***Settlement***, 3m/5km W of Rhynie. **90 C2** NJ4525.
Longlands *Cumb.* ***Settlement***, 1m/2km SE of Uldale. **60 D3** NY2635.
Longlands *Gt.Lon.* ***Suburb***, in borough of Bexley, 1m/2km NW of Sidcup. TQ4472.
Longlane *Derbys.* ***Hamlet***, 7m/11km W of Derby. **40 E2** SK2538.
Longlane *W.Berks.* ***Village***, 3m/5km NE of Newbury. **21 J4** SU5071.
Longleat House *Wilts.* ***Historic house***, 4m/7km W of Warminster. Renaissance mansion in large park, seat of Marquess of Bath. Longleat Safari Park contains lion reserve along with other wild animals. **20 B7** ST8043.
Longleat Safari Park *Wilts.* ***Leisure/recreation***, 4m/6km W of Warminster. Britain's first safari park, situated in grounds of Elizabethan Longleat House. Other attractions include world's largest hedge maze. **20 B7** ST8143.
Longlevens *Glos.* ***Suburb***, NE district of Gloucester. SO8520.
Longley *S.Yorks.* ***Suburb***, 3m/4km N of Sheffield city centre. SK3591.
Longley *W.Yorks.* ***Hamlet***, 1m/2km S of Holmfirth. SE1406.
Longley *W.Yorks.* ***Settlement***, on W side of Norland Moor, 1m/2km SW of Sowerby Bridge. SE0521.
Longley Green *Worcs.* ***Hamlet***, 4m/7km NW of Great Malvern. **29 G3** SO7350.
Longman Point *High.* ***Coastal feature***, shingle point to N of Inverness, extending into Moray Firth. **96 D7** NH6647.
Longmanhill *Aber.* ***Locality***, near N coast, 3m/4km SE of Macduff. **99 F4** NJ7362.
Longmorn *Moray* ***Village***, 3m/5km S of Elgin. **97 K6** NJ2358.
Longmoss *Ches.* ***Suburb***, 1m/2km W of Macclesfield. SJ8874.
Longnewton *Sc.Bord.* ***Settlement***, 3m/4km S of Newtown St. Boswells. **70 A1** NT5827.
Longnewton *Stock.* ***Village***, 4m/7km W of Stockton-on-Tees. **62 E5** NZ3816.
Longney *Glos.* ***Village***, 6m/10km SW of Gloucester. **29 G7** SO7612.
Longniddry *E.Loth.* Population: 2933. ***Village***, 3m/4km SW of Aberlady. **76 C3** NT4476.
Longnor *Shrop.* ***Village***, 8m/12km S of Shrewsbury. **38 D5** SJ4800.
Longnor *Staffs.* ***Village***, above River Manifold, 6m/9km SE of Buxton. **50 C6** SK0864.
Longovicium *Dur.* *See Lanchester.*
Longparish *Hants.* ***Village***, on River Test, 3m/5km SW of Whitchurch. **21 H7** SU4344.
Longpark *Cumb.* ***Locality***, 2m/3km SW of Scaleby and 4m/7km NE of Carlisle. NY4362.
Longport *Stoke* ***Suburb***, in Burslem district of Stoke-on-Trent. SJ8649.
Longridge *Lancs.* Population: 7351. ***Small town***, 7m/11km NE of Preston. Developed as a cotton town. **56 B6** SD6037.
Longridge *Staffs.* ***Settlement***, 1m/2km NW of Penkridge. SJ9115.
Longridge *W.Loth.* ***Village***, 2m/3km S of Whitburn. **75 H4** NS9462.
Longridge End *Glos.* ***Settlement***, 4m/6km N of Gloucester across River Severn. SO8124.
Longridge Fell *Lancs.* ***Inland physical feature***, mountain ridge to NE of Longridge, rising to 1148 feet or 350 metres. **56 B5** SD6037.
Longridge Towers *Northumb.* ***Settlement***, 2m/3km E of Horncliffe. **77 H5** NT9549.
Longriggend *N.Lan.* ***Village***, 5m/8km NE of Airdrie. **75 G3** NS8270.
Longrock *Cornw.* ***Hamlet***, to E of Penzance. **2 B5** SW5031.
Longsdon *Staffs.* ***Village***, 2m/3km SW of Leek. **49 J7** SJ9654.
Longshaw Common *Gt.Man.* ***Locality***, 4m/6km NW of Ashton-in-Makerfield. SD5302.
Longshaw Estate Country Park *Derbys.* ***Leisure/recreation***, 1360 acre country park, 2m/3km NE of Froggatt. Comprises moorland and farms, with areas suitable for rock climbing. **50 E5** SK2678.
Longships *Cornw.* ***Island***, cluster of islands with lighthouse, 1m/2km W of Land's End. **2 A6** SW3225.
Longside *Aber.* ***Village***, 6m/10km W of Peterhead. **99 J6** NK0347.
Longsight *Gt.Man.* ***Suburb***, 2m/3km SE of Manchester city centre. SJ8696.
Longslow *Shrop.* ***Settlement***, 2m/3km NW of Market Drayton. **39 F2** SJ6535.
Longsowerby *Cumb.* ***Suburb***, 1m/2km S of Carlisle city centre. NY3954.
Longstanton *Cambs.* Population: 1583. ***Village***, 6m/10km NW of Cambridge. **33 G2** TL3966.
Longstock *Hants.* ***Village***, on River Test, 1m/2km N of Stockbridge across river. **10 E1** SU3537.
Longstone *Cornw.* ***Settlement***, 4m/6km N of Bodmin. SX0673.
Longstone *Cornw.* ***Suburb***, to S of St. Ives. SW5338.
Longstone *Edin.* ***Suburb***, 3m/5km SW of Edinburgh city centre. NT2170.
Longstone *Northumb.* ***Island***, in Farne Islands group, with lighthouse. NU2438.
Longstowe *Cambs.* ***Village***, 9m/15km NW of Royston. **33 G3** TL3054.
Longstreet *Wilts.* ***Hamlet***, across River Avon from Enford, 2m/4km S of Upavon. **20 E6** SU1451.
Longthorpe *Peter.* ***Suburb***, 2m/3km W of Peterborough city centre. **42 E6** TL1698.
Longthorpe Tower *Peter.* ***Historic house***, English Heritage property containing early 14c murals, 2m/3km W of Peterborough city centre. **42 E6** TL1698.
Longton *Lancs.* Population: 12,101. ***Village***, 5m/7km SW of Preston. **55 H7** SD4725.
Longton *Stoke* ***Town***, one of towns that form city of Stoke-on-Trent: Burslem, Fenton, Hanley, Longton, Stoke-upon-Trent, Tunstall. Longton lies to SE of city centre. Small potteries still exist. Local history in Gladstone Pottery Museum. **40 B1** SJ9043.
Longtown *Cumb.* Population: 2548. ***Small town***, 8m/13km N of Carlisle. **69 J7** NY3868.
Longtown *Here.* ***Village***, 5m/8km W of Pontrilas. Magnificent views to Black Mountains from 13c Longtown Castle (English Heritage). **28 C6** SO3228.
Longtown Castle *Here.* ***Castle***, 11c motte and bailey castle with early 13c tower (English Heritage), within earthworks of Roman fort in Longtown, 10m/16km SE of Hay-on-Wye. **28 C6** SO3128.
Longville in the Dale *Shrop.* ***Village***, below W slope of Wenlock Edge, 6m/9km E of Church Stretton. **38 E6** SO5493.
Longwell Green *S.Glos.* ***Locality***, 2m/3km N of Keynsham. **19 K4** ST6571.
Longwick *Bucks.* ***Village***, 2m/3km NW of Princes Risborough. **22 A1** SP7805.
Longwitton *Northumb.* ***Hamlet***, 8m/13km W of Morpeth. **71 F5** NZ0788.
Longwood *Shrop.* ***Settlement***, 3m/4km W of Little Wenlock. **39 F5** SJ6006.
Longwood *W.Yorks.* ***Suburb***, 3m/4km W of Huddersfield town centre. SE1016.
Longwood Edge *W.Yorks.* ***Locality***, adjoining to N of Longwood, 3m/5km W of Huddersfield town centre. SE1016.
Longwood Warren *Hants.* ***Open space***, downland 3m/5km SE of Winchester. **11 G2** SU5126.
Longworth *Oxon.* ***Village***, 7m/11km W of Abingdon. **21 G2** SU3999.
Longyester *E.Loth.* ***Hamlet***, 2m/3km SE of Gifford. **76 D4** NT5465.

Lonmay *Aber.* ***Settlement***, 5m/8km S of Fraserburgh. NK0158.
Lonmore *High.* ***Settlement***, 1m/2km SE of Dunvegan, Skye. **93 H7** NG2646.
Looe *Cornw.* *Alternative name for (River) Cober, qv.*
Looe *Cornw.* ***Small town***, and resort on S coast, 7m/11km S of Liskeard. Divided by Looe River into East and West Looe and connected by road bridge. Jetty at mouth of river is known as Banjo Pier due to its shape. SX2553.
Looe Bay *Cornw.* ***Bay***, on S coast, 7m/11km S of Liskeard. **4 C5** SX2553.
Looe Island *Cornw.* *Alternative name for St. George's Island, qv.*
Looe Pool *Cornw.* *Alternative name for The Loe, qv.*
Loose *Kent* ***Village***, on S outskirts of Maidstone. **14 C2** TQ7552.
Loosebeare *Devon* ***Hamlet***, 6m/9km E of Winkleigh. SS7105.
Loosegate *Lincs.* ***Settlement***, 1m/2km NE of Moulton. **43 G3** TF3125.
Loosley Row *Bucks.* ***Village***, 2m/3km S of Princes Risborough. **22 B1** SP8100.
Lopcombe Corner (Lobscombe Corner or Lopscombe Corner.) *Wilts.* ***Hamlet***, at junction of A30 and A343 roads, 7m/11km W of Stockbridge. **10 D1** SU2535.
Lopen *Som.* ***Village***, 2m/3km S of South Petherton. **8 D3** ST4214.
Loppington *Shrop.* ***Village***, 3m/5km W of Wem. **38 D3** SJ4729.
Lopscombe Corner *Wilts.* *Alternative spelling of Lopcombe Corner, qv.*
Lorbottle *Northumb.* ***Settlement***, 3m/5km NW of Rothbury. **71 F3** NU0306.
Lorbottle Hall *Northumb.* ***Settlement***, 4m/6km NW of Rothbury. **71 F3** NU0407.
Lord Arthur's Cairn *Aber.* ***Mountain***, 4m/7km NW of Alford. Height 1699 feet or 518 metres. **90 D3** NJ5119.
Lord Hereford's Knob *Powys* *Alternative name for Twmpa, qv.*
Lord Leycester Hospital *Warks.* ***Historic house***, in Warwick town centre. Founded in 16c by Earl of Leicester, Robert Dudley, who combined religious guilds to make asylum for aged retainers and their wives. Consists of Guildhall, Great Hall and Chapel of St. James. **30 D2** SP2866.
Lord Macdonald's Table *High.* ***Island***, one of a group of islets 3m/5km NW of Rubha Hunish at N tip of Skye. See also Gaeilavore Island, and Gearran Island. NG3679.
Lordington *W.Suss.* ***Settlement***, 1km SW of Walderton and 3m/5km NE of Emsworth. SU7809.
Lord's Cricket Ground *Gt.Lon.* *See St. John's Wood.*
Lord's Hill *S'ham.* ***Suburb***, in NW part of Southampton. SU3815.
Lord's Seat *Cumb.* ***Mountain***, overlooking Bassenthwaite Lake, 4m/7km NW of Keswick. Height 1811 feet or 552 metres. **60 C4** NY2026.
Lorgill *High.* ***Locality***, 6m/9km NW of Idrigill Point, Skye. **93 G7** NG1741.
Lorn *Arg. & B.* ***Locality***, area of Argyll bounded by Loch Awe, Loch Etive and W coast adjoining Firth of Lorn. **80 B5** NN0834.
Lorn *W.Dun.* ***Settlement***, above S shore of Loch Lomond, 2m/3km W of Gartocharn. **74 B2** NS3985.
Lornty *P. & K.* ***Settlement***, on Lornty Burn, 1m/2km NW of Blairgowrie. **82 C3** NO1646.
Lornty Burn *P. & K.* ***River***, rising in Forest of Clunie and flowing SE to River Ericht, 1m/2km N of Blairgowrie. **82 C3** NO1746.
Lorton Vale *Cumb.* ***Valley***, carrying River Cocker from N end of Crummock Water to S side of Cockermouth. **60 C4** NY1426.
Loscoe *Derbys.* ***Village***, 1m/2km NW of Heanor. **41 G1** SK4247.
Loscombe *Dorset* ***Settlement***, 3m/4km SE of Beaminster. SY5097.
Lose Hill *Derbys.* ***Mountain***, National Trust property 1m/2km N of Castleton. Ancient burial-chamber at summit. Height 1561 feet or 476 metres. **50 D4** SK1585.
Loseley House *Surr.* ***Historic house***, Elizabethan manor house in parish of Artington 2m/3km N of Godalming. **22 C7** SU9847.
Losgaintir (Anglicised form: Luskentyre.) *W.Isles* ***Settlement***, on W coast of South Harris, 5m/8km W of Tarbert. **93 F2** NG0799.
Lossie *Moray* ***River***, rising at The Seven Sisters below NE slopes of Carn Kitty and flowing N along Glen Lossie to Dallas, then E through Kellas, and N again to Elgin where it turns E, then finally N to enter Moray Firth at Lossiemouth. **97 K5** NJ2370.
Lossie Forest *Moray* ***Forest/woodland***, bordering N coast on E side of Lossiemouth. **97 K5** NJ2767.
Lossiemouth *Moray* Population: 7184. ***Small town***, fishing port and resort on N coast, 5m/8km N of Elgin. Ramsay MacDonald, first Labour prime minister, born here in 1866. **97 K4** NJ2370.
Lossit *Arg. & B.* ***Settlement***, on Rinns of Islay, 3m/4km NE of Portnahaven. **72 A5** NR1856.
Lossit Bay *Arg. & B.* ***Bay***, on W side of Rinns of Islay, 3m/5km N of Rinns Point. **72 A5** NR1756.
Lost Gardens of Heligan *Cornw.* ***Garden***, 1m/2km NW of Mevagissey. 57 acres containing four walled gardens and 19c working kitchen garden which is now a horticulture museum. Also 20 acre sub-tropical Jungle Garden, 100 acres of ornamental woodland, Italian garden and crystal grotto. **3 G4** SW9946.
Lostock *Gt.Man.* ***Locality***, 4m/6km W of Bolton town centre. Includes localities of Lostock Hall and Lostock Junction. SD6708.
Lostock *Lancs.* ***River***, rising near Whittle-le-Woods, and flowing N towards Bamber Bridge, then turning S to pass Leyland on W side, finally flowing generally W to 1km N of Croston where it joins Wymott Brook. **48 E1** SD4819.
Lostock Gralam *Ches.* ***Village***, 3m/4km E of Northwich. **49 F5** SJ6975.
Lostock Green *Ches.* ***Village***, 3m/4km E of Northwich. **49 F5** SJ6973.
Lostock Hall *Lancs.* ***Locality***, residential locality, 2m/3km N of Leyland, 2m/4km S of Preston. SD5425.
Lostock Hall Fold *Gt.Man.* ***Locality***, 1m/2km NW of Lostock Junction and 4m/6km W of Bolton. SD6509.
Lostock Junction *Gt.Man.* ***Suburb***, 3m/4km W of Bolton town centre. **49 F2** SD6708.
Lostwithiel *Cornw.* Population: 2452. ***Small town***, on River Fowey, 5m/8km SE of Bodmin. 15c bridge; ruined Restormel Castle, with 12c keep, to N. **4 B5** SX1059.
Lostwithiel Bridge *Cornw.* ***Bridge***, distinctive Cornish stone bridge dating from 1437 and crossing River Fowey in Lostwithiel. SX1059.
Loth *Ork.* ***Coastal feature***, cliffs on W coast of Spur Ness, Sanday. **106 F4** HY6034.
Lothbeg *High.* ***Settlement***, near E coast of Sutherland district, 6m/10km SW of Helmsdale. **104 E7** NC9410.
Lothbeg Point *High.* ***Coastal feature***, headland on E coast, 1m/2km SE of Lothbeg. **97 G1** NC9410.
Lothersdale *N.Yorks.* ***Village***, 4m/6km SW of Skipton. **56 E5** SD9545.
Lotherton Hall *W.Yorks.* ***Historic house***, home of Lord and Lady Gascoigne, 3m/5km NE of Garforth. Completed at beginning of 20c, it includes museum of decorative arts containing Gascoigne family's collection of paintings, jewellery, porcelain and silver. **57 K6** SE4436.
Lothianbridge *Midloth.* ***Locality***, on River South Esk, 1km NW of Newtongrange. NT3264.
Lothmore *High.* ***Settlement***, near E coast of Sutherland district, 5m/7km SW of Helmsdale. **104 E7** NC9611.
Lothrie Burn *Fife* ***River***, stream which flows E from Holl Reservoir to join River Leven at Glenrothes. NO2601.
Lottisham *Som.* ***Settlement***, 1m/2km E of Ham Street and 5m/8km SE of Glastonbury. ST5734.
Lotus Hill *D. & G.* ***Mountain***, 1km S of Loch Arthur, 6m/10km NE of Dalbeattie. Height 1053 feet or 321 metres. **65 K4** NX9067.
Loudoun Castle Park *E.Ayr.* ***Leisure/recreation***, surrounding ruins of Loudoun Castle, 1km N of Galston. Scotland's largest theme park featuring a variety of rides, including Scotland's highest roller-coaster. 500 acre park also contains large areas of woodland. **74 D7** NS5037.
Loudwater *Bucks.* ***Locality***, 3m/4km SE of High Wycombe. **22 C2** SU9090.
Loudwater *Herts.* ***Locality***, 1m/2km NW of Rickmansworth. TQ0496.
Loughborough *Leics.* Population: 46,867. ***Town***, market and industrial town, 10m/16km N of Leicester. Carillon Tower has forty-seven bells; museum at bell foundry. University of Technology. Street fair, dating from 13c, held each November. Links with Thomas Cook, travel pioneer. **41 H4** SK5319.
Loughor (Llwchwr). ***River***, rising 4m/6km SE of Llandeilo and flowing S to Burry Inlet and Carmarthen Bay. **17 J5** SS4599.
Loughor (Casllwchwr). *Swan.* ***Small town***, at head of Burry inlet, 6m/10km NW of Swansea. Remains of castle (Cadw) beside River Loughor estuary. **17 J5** SS5798.
Loughor Castle *Swan.* ***Castle***, overlooking River Loughor estuary at Loughor, 1m/2km SW of Gorseinon. 13-14c tower, originally a Norman motte sited over remains of Roman fort. **17 J5** SS5697.
Loughton *Essex* Population: 39,553. ***Town***, on E side of Epping Forest 12m/20km NE of London. **23 H2** TQ4296.
Loughton *M.K.* ***Village***, 1m/2km SW of Milton Keynes city centre. **32 B5** SP8337.
Loughton *Shrop.* ***Hamlet***, 6m/10km NW of Cleobury Mortimer. **39 F7** SO6183.
Lound *Lincs.* ***Hamlet***, 2m/3km SW of Bourne. **42 D4** TF0618.
Lound *Notts.* ***Village***, 2m/4km N of Retford. **51 J4** SK6986.
Lound *Suff.* ***Village***, 5m/7km NW of Lowestoft. **45 K6** TM5099.
Lount *Leics.* ***Hamlet***, 3m/4km NE of Ashby de la Zouch. **41 F4** SK3819.
Loup of Fintry *Stir.* ***Mountain***, with steep slope on S side, in SE part of Fintry Hills. Height 1515 feet or 462 metres. **74 E2** NS6687.
Lour *Angus* ***Settlement***, 3m/5km S of Forfar. **83 F3** NO4746.
Louth *Lincs.* Population: 14,248. ***Town***, market town, 14m/23km S of Grimsby. Former wool town, with many Georgian buildings. Church has soaring Perpendicular spire. **53 G4** TF3287.
Louther Skerry *Ork.* ***Island***, one of Pentland Skerries, lying between Little Skerry and Clettack Skerry. ND4777.
Lovaig Bay *High.* ***Bay***, 1km SW of Rubha Maol, Skye. **93 H6** NG2355.
Lovat *Alternative name for (River) Ouzel, qv.*
Love Clough *Lancs.* ***Village***, adjoining to SW of Dunnockshaw, 4m/6km SW of Burnley. **56 D7** SD8127.
Love Green *Bucks.* ***Locality***, 4m/6km E of Slough. TQ0381.
Loveacott (Also known as Lower Loveacott.) *Devon* ***Hamlet***, 5m/7km SW of Barnstaple. **6 D3** SS5227.
Lovedean *Hants.* ***Locality***, on W side of Horndean. **11 H3** SU6812.
Lover *Wilts.* ***Village***, 7m/12km SE of Salisbury. **10 D2** SU2120.
Loversall *S.Yorks.* ***Village***, 3m/5km S of Doncaster. **51 H3** SK5798.
Loves Green *Essex* ***Village***, 3m/5km N of Ingatestone. **24 C1** TL6404.
Lovesome Hill *N.Yorks.* ***Hamlet***, 4m/6km N of Northallerton. SE3599.
Loveston *Pembs.* ***Hamlet***, 6m/9km NW of Tenby. **16 D4** SN0808.
Lovington *Som.* ***Village***, 3m/5km N of Sparkford. **8 E1** ST5930.
Low *Cumb.* ***Settlement***, 4m/7km SW of Kendal across Lyth Valley. **55 H1** SD4588.
Low Ackworth *W.Yorks.* ***Village***, 1m/2km NE of Ackworth Moor Top. SE4417.
Low Alwinton *Northumb.* ***Settlement***, to S of Alwinton, beside River Coquet. NT9205.
Low Angerton *Northumb.* ***Hamlet***, 1km S of High Angerton. NZ0984.
Low Ballivain *Arg. & B.* ***Settlement***, on N edge of Machrihanish Bay, Kintyre, 5m/7km NW of Campbeltown. **66 A1** NR6525.
Low Barlings *Lincs.* ***Settlement***, 1m/2km SE of Barlings. Remains of 12c abbey. TF0873.
Low Barugh *S.Yorks.* ***Locality***, adjoining to N of Barugh, 2m/4km NW of Barnsley. SE3108.
Low Bentham *N.Yorks.* ***Village***, 6m/10km SE of Kirkby Lonsdale. **56 B3** SD6469.
Low Blantyre *S.Lan.* ***Suburb***, to E of Blantyre town centre. NS6957.
Low Bolton *N.Yorks.* ***Settlement***, just SW of Redmire. **62 B7** SE0490.
Low Bradfield *S.Yorks.* ***Village***, in valley, 1km SW of High Bradfield. **50 E3** SK2692.
Low Bradley *N.Yorks.* ***Village***, 2m/3km SE of Skipton. **57 F5** SE0048.
Low Braithwaite *Cumb.* ***Settlement***, 1m/2km SE of Ivegill. **60 F2** NY4242.
Low Bransholme *Hull* ***Settlement***, to NE of Bransholme. TA1135.
Low Brunton *Northumb.* ***Settlement***, on E side of River North Tyne, 4m/6km N of Hexham. **70 E6** NY9270.
Low Burnham *N.Lincs.* ***Hamlet***, 1m/2km S of Epworth. **51 K2** SE7802.
Low Burton *N.Yorks.* ***Hamlet***, 1km NE of Masham across River Ure. **57 H1** SE2382.
Low Buston *Northumb.* ***Hamlet***, 1m/2km SW of High Buston. NU2207.
Low Carlbury *Darl.* ***Locality***, adjoining to E of Carlbury. NZ2115.
Low Catton *E.Riding* ***Village***, 1m/2km W of High Catton. **58 D4** SE7153.
Low Common *Norf.* ***Settlement***, 6m/10km W of Wymondham. TM1461.
Low Coniscliffe *Darl.* ***Locality***, 2m/3km SE of High Coniscliffe. **62 D5** NZ2413.
Low Cotehill *Cumb.* ***Locality***, to NE of Cotehill. NY4750.
Low Craighead *S.Ayr.* ***Settlement***, 3m/5km NE of Girvan. **67 G3** NS2301.
Low Crosby *Cumb.* ***Village***, 4m/6km NE of Carlisle. **60 F1** NY4459.
Low Dinsdale *Darl.* ***Hamlet***, on River Tees, 4m/7km SE of Darlington. **62 E5** NZ3411.
Low Durranhill *Cumb.* ***Suburb***, 2m/3km E of Carlisle city centre. NY4255.
Low Dyke *Cumb.* ***Locality***, adjoining to NE of Catterlen, 3m/4km NW of Penrith. NY4833.
Low Eggborough *N.Yorks.* ***Village***, 4m/6km E of Knottingley. **58 B7** SE5623.
Low Eighton *T. & W.* ***Locality***, 1m/2km N of Birtley. NZ2657.
Low Ellington *N.Yorks.* ***Hamlet***, 1km NE of High Ellington, 3m/4km NW of Masham. SE2083.
Low Entercommon *N.Yorks.* ***Settlement***, to NW of High Entercommon, 4m/6km SE of Croft-on-Tees. **62 E6** NZ3306.
Low Etherley *Dur.* ***Hamlet***, adjoining to N of High Etherley, 3m/4km W of Bishop Auckland. **62 C4** NZ1628.
Low Fell *T. & W.* ***Suburb***, 2m/3km S of Gateshead town centre. NZ2559.
Low Fold *W.Yorks.* ***Suburb***, 5m/8km NW of Leeds city centre, in district of Horsforth. SE2337.
Low Fremington *N.Yorks.* ***Hamlet***, adjoins High Fremington, just E of Reeth. SE0499.
Low Fulney *Lincs.* ***Locality***, 1m/2km SE of Spalding. TF2621.
Low Gate *Northumb.* ***Hamlet***, 2m/3km W of Hexham. **70 E7** NY9064.
Low Grantley *N.Yorks.* ***Hamlet***, adjoining to NE of Grantley, 5m/8km W of Ripon. SE2370.
Low Green *Gt.Man.* ***Locality***, 1m/2km SW of Hindley. SD6003.
Low Green *N.Yorks.* ***Settlement***, adjoining to SE of Darley, 3m/5km NE of Blubberhouses. SE2059.
Low Green *Suff.* ***Settlement***, 1km NE of Nowton. TL8661.
Low Greenside *T. & W.* ***Hamlet***, to N of Greenside, 3m/4km SE of Prudhoe. NZ1462.
Low Habberley *Worcs.* ***Hamlet***, 2m/3km NW of Kidderminster. **29 H1** SO8077.
Low Ham *Som.* ***Village***, 2m/3km NE of Langport. **8 D2** ST4329.
Low Haswell *Dur.* ***Settlement***, 1m/2km NW of Haswell. NZ3644.
Low Hauxley *Northumb.* ***Settlement***, 1km SE of High Hauxley. NU2802.
Low Hawsker *N.Yorks.* ***Settlement***, 3m/4km SE of Whitby. **63 J2** NZ9207.
Low Haygarth *Cumb.* ***Settlement***, in loop of River Rawthey, 4m/6km NE of Sedbergh. **61 H7** SD6996.
Low Hesket *Cumb.* ***Village***, 1m/2km NW of High Hesket; site of Roman signal station to N. **61 F2** NY4744.
Low Hesleyhurst *Northumb.* ***Settlement***, 3m/5km SE of Rothbury. **71 F4** NZ0997.
Low Hutton *N.Yorks.* ***Village***, on River Derwent, 3m/5km SW of Malton. **58 D3** SE7667.
Low Kingthorpe *N.Yorks.* ***Settlement***, 3m/4km NE of Pickering. SE8385.
Low Knipe *Cumb.* ***Locality***, 4m/7km NW of Shap. NY5219.
Low Laithe *N.Yorks.* ***Settlement***, 1m/2km NW of Summer Bridge. **57 G3** SE1963.
Low Langton *Lincs.* ***Settlement***, 2m/3km SE of Wragby. TF1576.
Low Leighton *Derbys.* ***Locality***, on E side of New Mills. **50 C4** SK0085.

Low Longthwaite *Cumb.* **Locality**, 1m/2km SW of Wigton. NY2546.

Low Lorton *Cumb.* **Hamlet**, in Lorton Vale, or valley of River Cocker, to W of High Lorton. NY1525.

Low Marishes *N.Yorks.* **Hamlet**, 4m/7km NE of Malton. **58 E2** SE8177.

Low Marnham *Notts.* **Village**, 1km S of High Marnham. SK8069.

Low Middleton *Northumb.* **Hamlet**, 1km NE of Middleton. NU1036.

Low Mill *N.Yorks.* **Hamlet**, 6m/9km N of Kirkbymoorside. **63 H7** SE6795.

Low Moor *Lancs.* **Locality**, 1m/2km W of Clitheroe. **56 C5** SD7341.

Low Moor *N.Yorks.* **Open space**, moorland 3m/4km SW of Robin Hood's Bay. **63 J2** NZ9103.

Low Moor *W.Yorks.* **Suburb**, 2m/4km S of Bradford city centre. SE1628.

Low Moorsley *T. & W.* **Village**, 1m/2km SW of Hetton-le-Hole. NZ3446.

Low Newton-by-the-Sea *Northumb.* **Hamlet**, 1km SE of High Newton-by-the-Sea. **71 H1** NU2325.

Low Redford *Dur.* **Hamlet**, to N of Bedburn Beck, 2m/3km SW of Bedburn. **62 B3** NZ0731.

Low Risby *N.Lincs.* **Settlement**, 1m/2km W of Appleby, 4m/6km NE of Scunthorpe. **52 C1** SE9314.

Low Row *Cumb.* **Hamlet**, 4m/6km E of Brampton. **70 A7** NY5863.

Low Row *Cumb.* **Locality**, 3m/5km NE of Aspatria. NY1844.

Low Row *Cumb.* **Locality**, 2m/3km SE of Hesket Newmarket. NY3536.

Low Row *N.Yorks.* **Village**, in Swaledale, 4m/6km W of Reeth. **62 A7** SD9897.

Low Santon *N.Lincs.* **Settlement**, 1m/2km SW of Appleby and 3m/5km NE of Scunthorpe. **52 C1** SE9412.

Low Stillaig *Arg. & B.* **Settlement**, on SW tip of Cowal peninsula, 4m/6km SW of Tighnabruaich. **73 H4** NR9267.

Low Street *Norf.* **Hamlet**, 2m/3km E of Harleston. TM2784.

Low Street *Norf.* **Locality**, 2m/3km W of Stalham. **45 H3** TG3423.

Low Street *Norf.* **Locality**, 1km E of Rollesby. TG4515.

Low Street *Norf.* **Settlement**, 5m/8km NW of Wymondham. TG0405.

Low Team *T. & W.* **Suburb**, 1m/2km SW of Gateshead town centre. NZ2462.

Low Tharston *Norf.* **Hamlet**, 1m/2km W of Tasburgh. TM1895.

Low Torry *Fife* **Locality**, 3m/4km E of Culross. **75 J2** NT0186.

Low Town *N.Yorks.* **Locality**, on River Tees, 2m/4km SW of Yarm. NZ3910.

Low Town *Northumb.* **Settlement**, 1m/2km SE of Longframlington. NU1300.

Low Toynton *Lincs.* **Settlement**, 1km NW of High Toynton. **53 F5** TF2770.

Low Valley *S.Yorks.* **Settlement**, adjoining to SW of Darfield, 1m/2km NE of Wombwell. SE4003.

Low Walworth *Dur.* **Settlement**, 1m/2km SE of Walworth. NZ2317.

Low Waters *S.Lan.* **Suburb**, S district of Hamilton. **75 F5** NS7253.

Low Westwood *Dur.* **Hamlet**, on River Derwent, 1km NE of Ebchester. NZ1156.

Low Whinnow *Cumb.* **Locality**, 1m/2km W of Thursby. NY3050.

Low Wincobank *S.Yorks.* **Suburb**, part of Wincobank suburb of Sheffield, along with High Wincobank. SK3791.

Low Wood *Cumb.* **Settlement**, 2m/4km SW of Newby Bridge. **55 G1** SD3483.

Low Worsall *N.Yorks.* **Hamlet**, 3m/4km SW of Yarm. **62 E5** NZ3909.

Low Wray *Cumb.* **Hamlet**, 2m/4km NE of Hawkshead. NY3701.

Lowbands *Glos.* **Settlement**, 6m/9km SE of Ledbury. SO7731.

Lowca *Cumb.* **Locality**, 2m/4km N of Whitehaven. NX9821.

Lowcote Gate *Derbys.* **Settlement**, 1m/2km W of Ilkeston. SK4442.

Lowdham *Notts.* Population: 2225. **Village**, 7m/12km NE of Nottingham. **41 J1** SK6646.

Lowe *Shrop.* **Settlement**, 1m/2km NW of Wem. SJ5030.

Lowe Hill *Staffs.* **Settlement**, 1m/2km SE of Leek. SJ9955.

Lower Aisholt *Som.* **Hamlet**, 1km SE of Aisholt. **7 K2** ST1935.

Lower Altofts *W.Yorks.* **Locality**, adjoining to NE of Altofts, 1m/2km N of Normanton. SE3723.

Lower Ansty *Dorset* **Hamlet**, forms part of Ansty locality in parish of Hilton, 6m/10km N of Puddletown. ST7603.

Lower Apperley *Glos.* **Hamlet**, 6m/9km NE of Gloucester. **29 H6** SO8627.

Lower Arncott *Oxon.* **Settlement**, 3m/5km SE of Bicester. SP6018.

Lower Ashtead *Surr.* **Suburb**, residential locality to W of Ashtead. TQ1758.

Lower Ashton *Devon* **Hamlet**, part of Ashton parish, along with Higher Ashton, 3m/5km N of Chudleigh. **7 G7** SX8584.

Lower Assendon *Oxon.* **Village**, 2m/3km NW of Henley-on-Thames. **22 A3** SU7484.

Lower Auchalick *Arg. & B.* **Settlement**, on W coast of Cowal, 4m/6km W of Tighnabruaich. **73 H3** NR9174.

Lower Ballam *Lancs.* **Settlement**, 1km NE of Higher Ballam and 3m/5km NE of Lytham St. Anne's. SD3630.

Lower Banavie *High.* **Locality**, adjacent to Banavie in Lochaber district, beside Caledonian Canal, 2m/3km N of Fort William. Series of locks on canal. NN1177.

Lower Barden Reservoir *N.Yorks.* **Reservoir**, one of two reservoirs on Barden Moor, 4m/6km NE of Skipton. SE0356.

Lower Barewood *Here.* **Settlement**, 6m/10km E of Kington. **28 C3** SO3956.

Lower Bartle *Lancs.* **Settlement**, 1km W of Higher Bartle, 4m/6km NW of Preston. SD4933.

Lower Barvas *W.Isles* **Settlement**, on Isle of Lewis, 1km W of Barvas. NB3549.

Lower Bayble *W.Isles* *Anglicised form of Pabail Iarach, qv.*

Lower Bayston *Shrop.* **Locality**, 1km SE of Bayston Hill. SJ4908.

Lower Beeding *W.Suss.* **Village**, 4m/6km SE of Horsham. **13 F4** TQ2227.

Lower Belvedere *Gt.Lon.* **Suburb**, forms part of Belvedere locality, along with Upper Belvedere, in borough of Bexley. TQ4978.

Lower Benefield *Northants.* **Village**, 3m/5km W of Oundle. **42 C7** SP9988.

Lower Bentley *Worcs.* **Hamlet**, 3m/5km SE of Bromsgrove. SO9866.

Lower Berry Hill *Glos.* **Hamlet**, 1km N of Coleford. **28 E7** SO5711.

Lower Birchwood *Derbys.* **Settlement**, 2m/3km SE of Alfreton. SK4354.

Lower Bockhampton *Dorset* **Settlement**, beside River Frome, 2m/4km E of Dorchester. **9 G5** SY7290.

Lower Boddington *Northants.* **Village**, 8m/12km N of Banbury. **31 F3** SP4852.

Lower Boscaswell *Cornw.* **Settlement**, near coast, 2m/3km N of St. Just. **2 A5** SW3734.

Lower Bourne *Surr.* **Suburb**, 1m/2km S of Farnham Centre. **22 B7** SU8444.

Lower Brailes *Warks.* **Village**, 4m/6km E of Shipston on Stour. **30 E5** SP3139.

Lower Breakish *High.* **Settlement**, on Skye, to N of Broadford, on inlet of Ob Breakish. **86 C2** NG6723.

Lower Bredbury *Gt.Man.* **Suburb**, to W of Bredbury. SJ9291.

Lower Broadheath *Worcs.* **Village**, 3m/4km NW of Worcester. **29 H3** SO8157.

Lower Broughton *Gt.Man.* **Suburb**, to SE of High Broughton. SJ8299.

Lower Brynamman *N.P.T.* **Hamlet**, adjoining to SW of Brynamman. **27 G7** SN7013.

Lower Buckland *Hants.* **Suburb**, to N of Lymington. SZ3296.

Lower Bullingham *Here.* **Suburb**, SE suburb of Hereford. **28 E5** SO5238.

Lower Bunbury *Ches.* **Hamlet**, adjoining to SW of Bunbury. SJ5657.

Lower Burgate *Hants.* **Hamlet**, in River Avon valley, 1m/2km N of Fordingbridge. **10 C3** SU1515.

Lower Burrow *Som.* **Hamlet**, to N of Burrow, 3m/5km W of Martock. ST4120.

Lower Burton *Here.* **Settlement**, 5m/8km W of Leominster. SO4256.

Lower Bush *Kent* **Settlement**, adjoining Upper Bush, 1m/2km W of Cuxton and 3m/5km W of Rochester. TQ6967.

Lower Caldecote *Beds.* **Hamlet**, 1m/2km S of Sandy. **32 E4** TL1746.

Lower Cam *Glos.* **Village**, 1m/2km N of Cam. **20 A1** ST7400.

Lower Camster *High.* **Settlement**, 1km N of Grey Cairns of Camster. **105 H4** ND2545.

Lower Canada *N.Som.* **Hamlet**, adjoining to E of Hutton, on N slope of Bleadon Hill, 3m/5km SE of Weston-super-Mare. ST3558.

Lower Catesby *Northants.* **Settlement**, forms parish of Catesby, along with Upper Catesby, 4m/6km SW of Daventry. SP5159.

Lower Chapel *Powys* **Village**, 5m/7km N of Brecon. **27 K5** SO0235.

Lower Cheriton *Devon* **Hamlet**, to N of Higher Cheriton, 4m/6km W of Honiton. ST1001.

Lower Chicksgrove *Wilts.* **Hamlet**, on River Nadder, 2m/3km E of Tisbury. ST9730.

Lower Chute *Wilts.* **Hamlet**, partly in parish of Chute Forest, 5m/8km NW of Andover. **21 G6** SU3151.

Lower City Mills *P. & K.* **Other feature of interest**, working Victorian oatmeal mill in central Perth. Massive internal waterwheel and exhibition telling story of Perth town mills. **82 C5** NO1023.

Lower Clapton *Gt.Lon.* **Suburb**, in borough of Hackney, to NE of Hackney. TQ3585.

Lower Clatford *Hants.* *Alternative name for Goodworth Clatford, qv.*

Lower Clent *Worcs.* **Hamlet**, 1km NW of Clent. SO9179.

Lower Clydach **River**, rising about 4m/6km SE of Ammanford and flowing S into River Tawe at Clydach. **17 K4** SN6801.

Lower Cokeham *W.Suss.* **Locality**, 2m/3km E of Worthing. TQ1704.

Lower Common *Hants.* **Hamlet**, 1km W of Eversley. SU7662.

Lower Creedy *Devon* **Hamlet**, on River Creedy, 2m/3km N of Crediton. SS8402.

Lower Crossings *Derbys.* **Locality**, adjoining to W of Chapel-en-le-Frith. **50 C4** SK0480.

Lower Cumberworth *W.Yorks.* **Village**, 1km N of Denby Dale. SE2209.

Lower Darwen *B'burn.* **Suburb**, 2m/3km N of Darwen, in Blackburn. **56 B7** SD6922.

Lower Dean *Beds.* **Hamlet**, 1m/2km NE of Upper Dean. **32 D2** TL0467.

Lower Denby *W.Yorks.* **Settlement**, 1km SE of Denby Dale. SE2307.

Lower Diabaig *High.* **Settlement**, with landing stage on Loch Diabaig, arm on NE side of larger Loch Torridon, Ross and Cromarty district. **94 D5** NG8160.

Lower Dicker *E.Suss.* **Hamlet**, 3m/4km NW of Hailsham. **13 J5** TQ5311.

Lower Dinchope *Shrop.* **Settlement**, 2m/3km NE of Craven Arms. **38 D7** SO4584.

Lower Down *Shrop.* **Hamlet**, 3m/5km S of Bishop's Castle. **38 C7** SO3384.

Lower Drift *Cornw.* **Hamlet**, 2m/3km SW of Penzance. **2 B6** SW4328.

Lower Dunsforth *N.Yorks.* **Village**, 3m/5km SE of Boroughbridge. **57 K3** SE4464.

Lower Durston *Som.* **Hamlet**, to E of Durston, 5m/8km NE of Taunton. ST2928.

Lower Earley *W'ham* **Suburb**, 3m/5km SE of Reading town centre. SU7470.

Lower Eastern Green *W.Mid.* **Suburb**, 3m/5km W of Coventry city centre. SP2979.

Lower Edmonton *Gt.Lon.* **Suburb**, in borough of Enfield, to N of Edmonton. TQ3493.

Lower Egleton *Here.* **Hamlet**, 8m/13km E of Hereford. **29 F4** SO6245.

Lower Elkstone *Staffs.* **Settlement**, 1km SE of Upper Elkstone. SK0658.

Lower Ellastone *Staffs.* **Hamlet**, adjoining to SE of Ellastone, 4m/7km SW of Ashbourne. SK1142.

Lower End *Beds.* **Settlement**, adjoining to NW of Totternhoe, 3m/5km W of Dunstable. SP9722.

Lower End *Bucks.* **Settlement**, adjoining to W of Long Crendon. SP6809.

Lower End *M.K.* **Hamlet**, 3m/5km N of Woburn. SP9337.

Lower End *Northants.* **Hamlet**, N end of Grendon, 5m/7km S of Wellingborough. **32 B2** SP8861.

Lower End *Northants.* **Settlement**, N end of Brafield-on-the-Green, 4m/7km E of Northampton. SP8259.

Lower Ensden *Kent* **Settlement**, 5m/8km W of Canterbury. TR0755.

Lower Everleigh *Wilts.* **Settlement**, to NW of Everleigh. **20 E6** SU1954.

Lower Eythorne *Kent* **Village**, adjoining to NW of Eythorne, 4m/6km SE of Aylesham. TR2749.

Lower Failand *N.Som.* **Hamlet**, 1m/2km NW of Failand. **19 J4** ST5271.

Lower Farringdon *Hants.* **Village**, 3m/4km S of Alton. **11 J1** SU7035.

Lower Feltham *Gt.Lon.* **Suburb**, in borough of Hounslow, 1m/2km SW of Feltham. TQ0971.

Lower Fittleworth *W.Suss.* **Hamlet**, on River Rother, adjoining to S of Fittleworth. TQ0118.

Lower Foxdale *I.o.M.* **Hamlet**, 1m/2km N of Foxdale. SC2779.

Lower Freystrop *Pembs.* **Settlement**, 1km N of Freystrop Cross. **16 C3** SM9512.

Lower Froyle *Hants.* **Village**, within parish of Froyle, about 4m/7km NE of Alton. **22 A7** SU7543.

Lower Gabwell *Devon* **Hamlet**, forming part of Gabwell locality, along with Higher Gabwell, about 3m/5km N of Torquay. **5 K4** SX9269.

Lower Gledfield *High.* **Hamlet**, in Sutherland district, 1m/2km W of Bonar Bridge. **96 C2** NH5990.

Lower Godney *Som.* **Hamlet**, to NW of Godney, 5m/8km SW of Wells. **19 H7** ST4842.

Lower Goldstone *Kent* **Locality**, 3m/5km NW of Sandwich. TR2961.

Lower Gornal *W.Mid.* **Suburb**, 2m/3km W of Dudley town centre. SO9191.

Lower Grange *W.Yorks.* **Suburb**, 3m/4km W of Bradford city centre. SE1233.

Lower Gravenhurst *Beds.* **Hamlet**, 2m/4km SE of Clophill. TL1135.

Lower Green *Essex* **Settlement**, W part of Langley, 6m/10km SE of Royston. TL4334.

Lower Green *Essex* **Settlement**, 4m/6km E of Finchingfield. TL7331.

Lower Green *Gt.Man.* **Settlement**, 1m/2km S of Tyldesley. SJ7099.

Lower Green *Herts.* **Settlement**, 2m/3km N of Hitchin. TL1832.

Lower Green *Kent* **Settlement**, adjoining to N of Pembury. **23 K7** TQ6241.

Lower Green *Norf.* **Hamlet**, 1km NE of Hindringham. **44 D2** TF9937.

Lower Green *Norf.* **Settlement**, adjoining to N of Freethorpe. TG4005.

Lower Green *Staffs.* **Locality**, adjoining to N of Coven, 5m/9km N of Wolverhampton. **40 B5** SJ9007.

Lower Green *Suff.* **Settlement**, N end of Higham, 7m/11km W of Bury St. Edmunds. TL7465.

Lower Green *Warks.* **Settlement**, 4m/7km S of Rugby. SP4968.

Lower Green Bank *Lancs.* **Settlement**, 3m/5km E of Galgate and 6m/9km NE of Garstang. **55 J4** SD5254.

Lower Grinsty *Worcs.* **Suburb**, SW district of Redditch. SP0265.

Lower Hacheston *Suff.* **Settlement**, 1m/2km NE of Wickham Market. TM3156.

Lower Halistra *High.* **Settlement**, adjoining Upper Halistra, 5m/8km S of Vaternish Point, Skye. NG2459.

Lower Halliford *Surr.* **Suburb**, to E of Shepperton, 1m/2km SW of Sunbury. TQ0867.

Lower Halstock Leigh *Dorset* **Hamlet**, 1km W of Halstock. ST5208.

Lower Halstow *Kent* **Village**, on inlet of River Medway estuary, 4m/6km NW of Sittingbourne. **24 E5** TQ8567.

Lower Hamworthy *Poole* **Locality**, on Poole Harbour, 1km SW of Poole town centre. SZ0089.

Lower Hardres *Kent* **Village**, 3m/5km S of Canterbury. **15 G2** TR1552.

Lower Hardwick *Here.* **Locality**, 6m/10km W of Leominster. SO4056.

Lower Harpton *Here.* **Settlement**, 3m/4km NW of Kington. SO2760.

Lower Hartlip *Kent* **Settlement**, to E of Hartlip. TQ8464.

Lower Hartshay *Derbys.* **Hamlet**, 1m/2km NW of Ripley. SK3851.

Lower Hartwell *Bucks.* **Hamlet**, in parish of Hartwell, 2m/3km W of Aylesbury. SP7916.

Lower Hatton *Staffs.* **Settlement**, 5m/8km NW of Stone. SJ8236.

Lower Hawthwaite *Cumb.* **Settlement**, 1m/2km N of Broughton in Furness. **55 F1** SD2189.

Lower Hayton *Shrop.* **Settlement**, 4m/6km N of Ludlow. **38 E7** SO5081.

Lower Heath *Ches.* **Suburb**, to N of Congleton town centre. SJ8664.

Lower Hergest *Here.* **Hamlet**, 2m/3km SW of Kington. **28 B3** SO2755.

Lower Heyford *Oxon.* **Village**, on River Cherwell and Oxford Canal, 6m/10km W of Bicester. **31 F6** SP4824.

Lower Higham *Kent* **Hamlet**, 1m/2km N of Higham and 3m/5km NW of Rochester. **24 D4** TQ7172.

Lower Holbrook *Suff.* **Hamlet**, 4m/7km W of Shotley Gate. **35 F5** TM1734.

Lower Hopton *W.Yorks.* **Suburb**, S district of Mirfield across River Calder. SE2019.

Lower Hordley *Shrop.* **Settlement**, 1m/2km SE of Hordley. **38 C3** SJ3929.

Lower Horncroft *W.Suss.* **Hamlet**, 3m/4km W of Pulborough. TQ0017.

Lower Horsebridge *E.Suss.* **Village**, on Cuckmere River, 1m/2km N of Hailsham. **13 J5** TQ5711.

Lower Houses *Essex* **Settlement**, adjoining to E of Layer de la Haye, 3m/5km S of Colchester, below dam of Abberton Reservoir. TL9820.

Lower Houses *Shrop.* **Settlement**, 1km NE of Whixall. SJ5235.

Lower Houses *W.Yorks.* **Suburb**, 1m/2km SE of Huddersfield town centre. SE1515.

Lower Howsell *Worcs.* **Suburb**, at N end of Great Malvern. SO7848.

Lower Illey *W.Mid.* **Locality**, to SW of Illey, 2m/3km SE of Halesowen centre. SO9781.

Lower Island *Kent* **Suburb**, in W district of Whitstable, S of harbour. TR1066.

Lower Kersal *Gt.Man.* **Suburb**, in loop of River Irwell, adjoining to SE of Kersal, 3m/4km E of Swinton. SD8101.

Lower Kilburn *Derbys.* **Settlement**, adjoining to SW of Kilburn. SK3845.

Lower Kilchattan *Arg. & B.* **Settlement**, adjoining to SW of Upper Kilchattan. **72 B1** NR3694.

Lower Kilcott *S.Glos.* **Hamlet**, 2m/4km NW of Didmarton. ST7889.

Lower Killeyan *Arg. & B.* **Locality**, on W side of The Oa, Islay, 1m/2km N of Mull of Oa. **72 A6** NR2743.

Lower Kinchrackine *Arg. & B.* **Locality**, in Strath of Orchy in Argyll, 1m/2km W of Dalmally. NN1527.

Lower Kingcombe *Dorset* **Settlement**, 3m/5km NW of Maiden Newton. **8 E5** SY5599.

Lower Kingswood *Surr.* **Village**, 1m/2km S of Kingswood, 2m/3km N of Reigate. TQ2453.

Lower Kinnerton *Ches.* **Hamlet**, 5m/8km SW of Chester. **48 C6** SJ3462.

Lower Kinsham *Here.* **Hamlet**, forms locality of Kinsham, along with Upper Kinsham, 3m/5km E of Presteigne. SO3564.

Lower Knapp *Som.* **Hamlet**, on E side of Knapp, 1km W of North Curry. ST3025.

Lower Langford *N.Som.* **Village**, 3m/4km SE of Congresbury. **19 H5** ST4660.

Lower Largo *Fife* **Village**, on Largo Bay, 2m/4km NE of Leven. Forms locality of Largo with adjacent village of Upper Largo. **83 F7** NO4202.

Lower Leigh *Staffs.* **Hamlet**, 1km W of Church Leigh. SK0135.

Lower Lemington *Glos.* **Hamlet**, 2m/3km NE of Moreton-in-Marsh. **30 D5** SP2134.

Lower Ley *Glos.* **Locality**, on W bank of River Severn, 5m/8km NE of Newnham. SO7516.

Lower Llanfadog *Powys* **Locality**, 2m/4km SW of Rhayader. SN9365.

Lower Loveacott *Devon* Alternative name for Loveacott, qv.

Lower Loxhore *Devon* **Hamlet**, to S of Loxhore, 4m/7km NE of Barnstaple. SS6137.

Lower Lydbrook *Glos.* **Village**, adjoining Upper Lydbrook, 4m/6km W of Cinderford. **28 E7** SO5916.

Lower Lye *Here.* **Hamlet**, 7m/12km NW of Leominster. **28 D2** SO4066.

Lower Machen *Newport* **Village**, 1m/2km SE of Machen, on site of Roman settlement. **19 F3** ST2189.

Lower Maes-coed *Here.* **Settlement**, 4m/7km NW of Pontrilas. **28 C5** SO3430.

Lower Mannington *Dorset* **Settlement**, 1km SE of Mannington. SU0605.

Lower Meend *Glos.* **Settlement**, just W of St. Briavels. SO5504.

Lower Merridge *Som.* **Hamlet**, to W of Merridge, 6m/10km SW of Bridgwater. ST2034.

Lower Middleton Cheney *Northants.* **Village**, adjoining to SE of Middleton Cheney, 3m/5km E of Banbury. SP5041.

Lower Milovaig *High.* **Settlement**, on Skye, forming locality of Milovaig, along with Upper Milovaig, 6m/10km W of Dunvegan. NG1450.

Lower Milton *Som.* **Hamlet**, forming Milton, along with Upper Milton, 1m/2km NW of Wells. ST5347.

Lower Moor *Cornw.* **Open space**, moorland to N of Bodmin Moor, 3m/4km SE of Camelford. **4 B2** SX1482.

Lower Moor *Worcs.* **Village**, 3m/4km E of Pershore. **29 J4** SO9747.

Lower Morton *S.Glos.* **Hamlet**, 1m/2km N of Thornbury. ST6491.

Lower Mountain *Flints.* **Settlement**, 1km N of Hope. SJ3159.

Lower Nash *Pembs.* **Hamlet**, 2m/3km NE of Pembroke. SN0103.

Lower Nazeing *Essex* **Suburb**, 1m/2km W of Nazeing. **23 G1** TL4106.

Lower North Dean *Bucks.* **Settlement**, 4m/6km N of High Wycombe. SU8598.

Lower Noverton *Glos.* **Locality**, 2m/3km NW of Cheltenham. SO9723.

Lower Nyland *Dorset* **Settlement**, 5m/7km SW of Gillingham. ST7421.

Lower Oakfield *Fife* **Suburb**, S district of Kelty. **75 K1** NT1493.

Lower Oddington *Glos.* **Settlement**, 3m/4km E of Stow-on-the-Wold. **30 D6** SP2326.

Lower Ollach *High.* **Settlement**, on Skye, nearly 1m/2km NW of Ollach. **86 B1** NG5137.

Lower Penarth *V. of Glam.* **Suburb**, S district of Penarth. **18 E4** ST1870.

Lower Penn *Staffs.* **Village**, 3m/5km of Wolverhampton. **40 A6** SO8696.

Lower Pennington *Hants.* **Hamlet**, 1m/2km SE of Pennington. **10 E5** SZ3193.

Lower Penwortham *Lancs.* **Suburb**, 1m/2km S of Preston town centre. SD5327.

Lower Peover *Ches.* **Village**, 6m/9km E of Northwich. **49 G5** SJ7474.

Lower Place *Gt.Man.* **Suburb**, 1m/2km SE of Rochdale town centre. SD9011.

Lower Pollicott *Bucks.* **Settlement**, 4m/7km N of Thame. SP7013.

Lower Pond Street *Essex* See Pond Street.

Lower Quinton *Warks.* **Village**, forms parish of Quinton, along with Upper Quinton, 5m/8km S of Stratford-upon-Avon. **30 C4** SP1847.

Lower Race *Torfaen* **Settlement**, on W side of Pontypool. SO2700.

Lower Rainham *Med.* **Settlement**, 1m/2km N of Rainham. TQ8167.

Lower Ratley *Hants.* **Hamlet**, 2m/3km NW of Romsey. SU3223.

Lower Raydon *Suff.* **Hamlet**, 3m/5km S of Hadleigh. TM0338.

Lower Redbrook *Glos.* **Village**, 1km S of Redbrook. SO5310.

Lower Roadwater *Som.* **Hamlet**, to NE of Roadwater, 4m/6km SW of Watchet. ST0338.

Lower Sapey *Worcs.* **Settlement**, 4m/7km NE of Bromyard. SO6960.

Lower Seagry *Wilts.* **Hamlet**, 5m/9km NE of Chippenham. **20 C3** ST9581.

Lower Shader *W.Isles* Anglicised form of Siadar Iarach, qv.

Lower Sharpnose Point *Cornw.* **Coastal feature**, W facing headland 4m/7km N of Bude, at N end of Bude Bay. **6 A4** SS1912.

Lower Sheering *Essex* **Locality**, 1m/2km W of Sheering. TL5013.

Lower Shelton *Beds.* **Hamlet**, 6m/9km SW of Bedford. **32 C4** SP9942.

Lower Shiplake *Oxon.* **Village**, 1m/2km NE of Shiplake. **22 A4** SU7678.

Lower Shuckburgh *Warks.* **Village**, 5m/9km W of Daventry. **31 F2** SP4862.

Lower Shurlach *Ches.* **Suburb**, to NW of Northwich. SJ6772.

Lower Slaughter *Glos.* **Village**, 3m/4km SW of Stow-on-the-Wold. The Old Mill is preserved 19c flour mill. **30 C6** SP1622.

Lower Soothill *W.Yorks.* **Suburb**, adjoining to E of Batley. SE2524.

Lower Soudley *Glos.* **Settlement**, 3m/4km S of Cinderford. SO6610.

Lower Standen *Lancs.* **Settlement**, adjoining to S of Clitheroe. SD7440.

Lower Stanton St. Quintin *Wilts.* **Hamlet**, 1m/2km NE of Stanton St. Quintin. **20 C3** ST9180.

Lower Stoke *Med.* **Village**, 4m/6km W of Grain. **24 E4** TQ8375.

Lower Stondon *Beds.* **Hamlet**, E part of Upper Stondon, 3m/4km S of Shefford. Stondon Museum has large collection of transport exhibits. **32 E5** TL1535.

Lower Stone *Glos.* **Hamlet**, 1m/2km SW of Stone. ST6794.

Lower Stonnall *Staffs.* **Hamlet**, 1km E of Stonnall, 2m/3km SW of Shenstone. SK0803.

Lower Stow Bedon *Norf.* **Hamlet**, 1m/2km SE of Stow Bedon. TL9596.

Lower Street *Dorset* **Settlement**, to S of Winterborne Whitechurch. SY8499.

Lower Street *E.Suss.* **Locality**, adjoining to S of Ninfield, 4m/6km NW of Bexhill. **14 C6** TQ7012.

Lower Street *Norf.* **Settlement**, 1m/2km W of Aldborough. TG1634.

Lower Street *Norf.* **Suburb**, in N part of Horning. TG3417.

Lower Street *Norf.* **Village**, 4m/6km N of North Walsham. TG2635.

Lower Street *Som.* **Locality**, contained within Curry Mallet, 5m/8km NW of Ilminster. ST3321.

Lower Street *Suff.* **Hamlet**, 4m/7km N of Clare. TL7851.

Lower Street *Suff.* **Hamlet**, 6m/10km NW of Ipswich. TM1152.

Lower Street *Suff.* **Hamlet**, forms part of Ufford, along with Upper Street. TM2952.

Lower Street *Suff.* **Locality**, at Stutton, 6m/10km S of Ipswich. TM1534.

Lower Strensham *Worcs.* **Settlement**, 5m/8km N of Tewkesbury. SO9040.

Lower Stretton *Ches.* **Settlement**, to S of Stretton. SJ6282.

Lower Sundon *Beds.* **Village**, 4m/7km NW of Luton. **32 D6** TL0527.

Lower Swanwick *Hants.* **Village**, 1m/2km W of Swanwick. **11 F4** SU4909.

Lower Swell *Glos.* **Village**, 1m/2km W of Stow-on-the-Wold. **30 C6** SP1725.

Lower Sydenham *Gt.Lon.* **Suburb**, in borough of Lewisham, 2m/3km NW of Beckenham. TQ3571.

Lower Tadmarton *Oxon.* **Settlement**, 4m/6km SW of Banbury. SP4037.

Lower Tale *Devon* **Hamlet**, 5m/7km SE of Cullompton. ST0601.

Lower Tamar Lake *Devon* **Lake/loch**, on border with Cornwall, to S of Upper Tamar Lake and 3m/4km SW of Bradworthy. **6 B4** SS2911.

Lower Tean *Staffs.* **Village**, 1m/2km SE of Upper Tean. **40 C2** SK0139.

Lower Threapwood *Ches.* **Settlement**, to S of Threapwood. SJ4444.

Lower Thurlton *Norf.* **Village**, 1km NE of Thurlton. **45 J6** TM4198.

Lower Thurnham *Lancs.* **Settlement**, forms locality of Thurnham, along with Upper Thurnham, 1m/2km W of Galgate. **55 H4** SD4554.

Lower Town *Cornw.* **Village**, 1km N of Helston. SW6529.

Lower Town *Devon* **Hamlet**, on E side of Dartmoor, 4m/6km NW of Ashburton. SX7172.

Lower Town *Here.* **Locality**, 8m/13km E of Hereford. SO6342.

Lower Town *I.o.S.* **Hamlet**, at W end of St. Martin's. **2 C1** SV9116.

Lower Town *Pembs.* **Village**, on E side of mouth of River Gwaun, opposite Fishguard. **16 C1** SM9637.

Lower Town *Worcs.* **Locality**, 3m/5km NE of Worcester. SO8659.

Lower Trebullett *Cornw.* **Settlement**, 1km S of Trebullett. SX3277.

Lower Tuffley *Glos.* **Suburb**, in SW part of Gloucester. SO8214.

Lower Tysoe *Warks.* **Village**, 4m/6km S of Kineton. **30 E4** SP3445.

Lower Upcott *Devon* **Hamlet**, 1m/2km NE of Chudleigh. SX8880.

Lower Upham *Hants.* **Village**, 2m/4km NW of Bishop's Waltham. **11 G3** SU5219.

Lower Upnor *Med.* **Hamlet**, on N bank of River Medway, 2m/3km NE of Strood. TQ7671.

Lower Vexford *Som.* **Hamlet**, 6m/9km SE of Watchet. **7 K2** ST1135.

Lower Walkley *S.Yorks.* **Suburb**, to NW of Walkley, 2m/3km NW of Sheffield city centre. SK3388.

Lower Wall *Kent* **Locality**, on Romney Marsh, 3m/5km N of Dymchurch. TR0833.

Lower Wallop *Shrop.* **Settlement**, 4m/6km NW of Minsterley. **38 C5** SJ3207.

Lower Walton *Warr.* **Locality**, adjoining to S of Warrington. **49 F4** SJ6085.

Lower Waterhay *Wilts.* **Settlement**, on River Thames, 3m/4km W of Cricklade. SU0693.

Lower Waterston *Dorset* **Locality**, 1m/2km NW of Puddletown. Waterston Manor is Elizabethan manor house to W. SY7395.

Lower Weald *M.K.* **Settlement**, to S of Calverton. SP7838.

Lower Wear *Devon* **Suburb**, SE district of Exeter, on E bank of River Exe. SX9489.

Lower Weare *Som.* **Village**, on River Axe, 2m/3km W of Axbridge. **19 H6** ST4053.

Lower Welson *Here.* **Hamlet**, 2m/3km NW of Willersley. **28 B3** SO2950.

Lower Westhouse *N.Yorks.* **Hamlet**, 2m/3km W of Ingleton. SD6673.

Lower Westmancote *Worcs.* **Hamlet**, 4m/7km NE of Tewkesbury. SO9337.

Lower Whatcombe *Dorset* **Settlement**, forms locality of Whatcombe, along with Higher Whatcombe, 4m/7km SW of Blandford Forum. ST8301.

Lower Whatley *Som.* **Hamlet**, to E of Whatley, 2m/3km W of Frome. ST7447.

Lower Whitehall *Ork.* **Locality**, adjoining to E of Whitehall, Stronsay. HY6628.

Lower Whitley *Ches.* **Village**, 1km SW of Whitley. **49 F5** SJ6179.

Lower Wick *Glos.* **Settlement**, 3m/4km SE of Berkeley. ST7096.

Lower Wick *Worcs.* **Suburb**, in SW part of Worcester. SO8352.

Lower Wield *Hants.* **Hamlet**, 2m/3km SE of Preston Candover. **21 K7** SU6340.

Lower Winchendon (Also known as Nether Winchendon.) *Bucks.* **Village**, 4m/7km NE of Thame. **31 J7** SP7312.

Lower Withington *Ches.* **Village**, 4m/6km NE of Holmes Chapel. **49 H6** SJ8169.

Lower Woodend *Bucks.* **Settlement**, 2m/3km W of Marlow. **22 B3** SU8187.

Lower Woodford *Wilts.* **Village**, in parish of Woodford on River Avon, along with Upper Woodford and Middle Woodford, 4m/7km SW of Amesbury. **10 C1** SU1235.

Lower Wraxall *Dorset* **Hamlet**, 3m/4km NW of Maiden Newton. **8 E4** ST5700.

Lower Wraxall *Som.* **Settlement**, 1km SE of Wraxall. ST6035.

Lower Wych *Ches.* **Settlement**, 1m/2km NW of Higher Wych. SJ4844.

Lower Wyche *Worcs.* **Suburb**, 1m/2km S of Great Malvern town centre. **29 G4** SO7744.

Lower Wyke *W.Yorks.* **Settlement**, adjoining to S of Wyke. SE1525.

Lowerford *Lancs.* **Suburb**, adjoining to W of Barrowford, 1m/2km N of Nelson. SD8539.

Lowerhouse *Lancs.* **Suburb**, 2m/3km W of Burnley town centre. SD8032.

Lowertown *Ork.* **Settlement**, on N coast of South Ronaldsay, 1m/2km NW of St. Margaret's Hope. ND4394.

Lowesby *Leics.* **Hamlet**, 9m/14km E of Leicester. Site of former village to N. **42 A5** SK7207.

Lowestoft *Suff.* Population: 62,907. **Town**, resort and former fishing port on North Sea coast, 38m/62km NE of Ipswich. Food manufacture now important industry. **45 K6** TM5493.

Lowestoft End *Suff.* **Suburb**, in N part of Lowestoft. **45 K6** TM5394.

Lowestoft Ness *Suff.* **Coastal feature**, headland on N side of Lowestoft. Most easterly point in Great Britain. **45 K6** TM5493.

Loweswater *Cumb.* **Hamlet**, 1km W of N end of Crummock Water. **60 C4** NY1420.

Loweswater *Cumb.* **Lake/loch**, one of smaller lakes in Lake District, 6m/9km S of Cockermouth. Owned by National Trust. Hamlet of Loweswater 1km E of SE end of lake, with hills of Loweswater Fell to S. **60 C4** NY1221.

Loweswater Fell *Cumb.* ***Open space***, hillslope to S of Loweswater lake. **60 C5** NY1221.
Lowfield *S.Yorks.* ***Suburb***, 1m/2km S of Sheffield city centre. SK3585.
Lowfield Heath *W.Suss.* ***Village***, on S edge of Gatwick (London) Airport, 2m/3km N of Crawley. **23 F7** TQ2740.
Lowford *Hants.* ***Locality***, 3m/4km NW of Park Gate, adjoining to N of Bursledon. SU4810.
Lowgate *N.Yorks.* ***Locality***, 2m/3km SW of Pollington, 4m/6km NE of Askern. SE5918.
Lowgill *Cumb.* ***Locality***, on E side of M6 motorway, 4m/6km NW of Sedbergh. **61 H7** SD6297.
Lowgill *Lancs.* ***Settlement***, 3m/5km S of Lower Bentham. **56 B3** SD6564.
Lowhouse Fold *Gt.Man.* ***Locality***, adjoining to N of Milnrow. SD9313.
Lowick *Cumb.* ***Locality***, 5m/8km N of Ulverston. **55 F1** SD2986.
Lowick *Northants.* ***Village***, 2m/3km NW of Thrapston. **42 C7** SP9780.
Lowick *Northumb.* ***Village***, 7m/12km N of Wooler. **77 J7** NU0139.
Lowick Bridge *Cumb.* ***Hamlet***, to N of Lowick, 3m/5km NW of Greenodd. SD2986.
Lowick Green *Cumb.* ***Hamlet***, 1km S of Lowick and 2m/3km NW of Greenodd. SD2985.
Lowland Point *Cornw.* ***Coastal feature***, headland (National Trust) on E coast of Lizard peninsula, 1m/2km SE of St. Keverne. **3 F7** SW8019.
Lowlandman's Bay *Arg. & B.* ***Bay***, with landing stage on E coast of Jura, 4m/6km S of Lagg. Long rocky promontory on SE side almost closes entrance. **72 D3** NR5672.
Lowlands *Torfaen* ***Suburb***, in N part of Cwmbran. ST2896.
Lowman *Devon* ***River***, rising near Hockworthy and flowing SW into River Exe at Tiverton. **7 H4** SS9512.
Lowmoor Row *Cumb.* ***Settlement***, 1m/2km W of Kirkby Thore. NY6226.
Lownie Moor *Angus* ***Hamlet***, 2m/3km SE of Forfar. **83 F3** NO4848.
Lowryhill *Cumb.* ***Suburb***, 2m/3km N of Carlisle city centre. NY3958.
Lowsonford *Warks.* ***Village***, on Stratford-upon-Avon Canal, 3m/4km NE of Henley-in-Arden. **30 C2** SP1867.
Lowther *Cumb.* ***Hamlet***, 4m/7km S of Penrith. **61 G4** NY5323.
Lowther *Cumb.* ***River***, rising on Shap Fells and flowing N into River Eamont, 2m/3km SE of Penrith. **61 G4** NY5329.
Lowther Castle *Cumb.* ***Historic house***, ruined early 19c mansion in park on E bank of River Lowther, to W of Lowther. **61 G4** NY5323.
Lowther Hill *S.Lan.* ***Mountain***, on border with Dumfries & Galloway, 7m/11km E of Sanquhar. Second highest of Lowther Hills. Mast at summit. Height 2378 feet or 725 metres. See also Green Lowther. **68 D2** NS8810.
Lowther Hills ***Large natural feature***, mountain range forming part of Southern Uplands, framed by Nithsdale to W, Tweeddale and Annandale to E. Range is traversed by Roman Roads with notable Mennock and Dalveen Passes. Former centre of lead mining, especially to N of range around Wanlockhead and Leadhills. Southern Upland Way lies along part of range, including Lowther Hill, second highest peak at 2378 feet or 725 metres. Other notable peaks are Green Lowther at 2401 feet or 732 metres; East Mount Lowther, with its excellent viewpoint at 2070 feet or 631 metres; and Ballencleuch Law at 2266 feet or 691 metres. **68 D2** NS8615.
Lowther Wildlife Park *Cumb.* ***Leisure/recreation***, at Lowther Park, 4m/7km S of Penrith. Wide variety of animals in parkland setting with many other family-oriented attractions. **61 G4** NY5322.
Lowthorpe *E.Riding* ***Village***, 4m/7km NE of Great Driffield. **59 G4** TA0860.
Lowthwaite *Cumb.* ***Locality***, 2m/3km NE of Dockray, on SW side of Little Mell Fell. NY4123.
Lowton *Devon* ***Hamlet***, 3m/5km SE of Winkleigh. SS6604.
Lowton *Gt.Man.* ***Locality***, 1km E of Golborne. **49 F3** SJ6197.
Lowton *Som.* ***Hamlet***, below Black Down Hills, 4m/7km SE of Wellington. ST1918.
Lowton Common *Gt.Man.* ***Locality***, 1m/2km E of Lowton. **49 F3** SJ6397.
Lowton St. Mary's *Gt.Man.* ***Suburb***, 1m/2km E of Lowton. SJ6397.
Loxbeare *Devon* ***Hamlet***, 4m/6km NW of Tiverton. **7 H4** SS9116.
Loxford *Gt.Lon.* ***Suburb***, S district of Ilford, in borough of Redbridge. TQ4485.
Loxhill *Surr.* ***Hamlet***, 4m/6km W of Cranleigh. **12 D3** TQ0038.
Loxhore *Devon* ***Hamlet***, 5m/8km NE of Barnstaple. **6 E2** SS6138.
Loxhore Cott *Devon* ***Hamlet***, to SW of Loxhore, 4m/7km NE of Barnstaple. SS6038.
Loxley *S.Yorks.* ***Locality***, 3m/5km NW of Sheffield. SK3089.
Loxley *S.Yorks.* ***River***, rising on moors W of Low Bradfield and flowing E via Strines, Dale Dike, Agden and Damflask Reservoirs, then into River Don in NW part of Sheffield. **51 F4** SK3489.
Loxley *Warks.* ***Village***, 4m/6km SE of Stratford-upon-Avon. **30 D3** SP2552.
Loxley Green *Staffs.* ***Settlement***, 3m/4km SW of Uttoxeter. SK0630.
Loxton *N.Som.* ***Village***, 4m/6km W of Axbridge. **19 G6** ST3755.
Loxwood *W.Suss.* ***Village***, 5m/8km NW of Billingshurst. **12 D3** TQ0331.
Loyn Bridge *Lancs.* ***Bridge***, 16c stone bridge over River Lune at Hornby, 8m/13km NE of Lancaster. SD5869.
Loyne *High.* ***River***, rising on E slopes of Glenquoich Forest and flowing N, then E into Loch Loyne. **87 G4** NH0706.
Lozells *W.Mid.* ***Suburb***, 2m/3km N of Birmingham city centre. SP0689.
Lùb a' Sgiathain *High.* ***Bay***, on N coast of Skye, to E of Rubha Hunish. NG4176.
Lùb Score *High.* *Alternative name for Score Bay, qv.*
Lubachoinnich *High.* ***Settlement***, in Strath Cuileannach, 5m/8km SW of Invercassley. **96 B2** NH4195.
Lubcroy *High.* ***Settlement***, near confluence of River Oykel and Garbh Allt. **95 K1** NC3501.
Lubenham *Leics.* ***Village***, 2m/3km W of Market Harborough. **42 A7** SP7087.
Lubfearn *High.* ***Settlement***, 5m/8km N of Gorstan. **95 K4** NH3870.
Lubmore *High.* ***Settlement***, at W end of Loch a' Chroisg, 4m/6km W of Achnasheen. **95 G6** NH0958.
Lubreoch *P. & K.* ***Settlement***, in Glen Lyon, adjacent to dam at E end of Loch Lyon. **81 F3** NN4441.
Lucas End *Herts.* ***Locality***, 2m/4km W of Cheshunt. TL3203.
Luccombe *Som.* ***Village***, largely National Trust, on N slopes of Exmoor, 2m/3km SE of Porlock. **7 H1** SS9144.
Luccombe Village *I.o.W.* ***Village***, above Luccombe Bay, 1m/2km S of Shanklin. The Landslip, an undercliff ravine, 1km S. **11 G7** SZ5879.
Luce Bay *D. & G.* ***Bay***, large bay on S coast of Scotland, extending E from Mull of Galloway to Burrow Head, and N to mouth of Water of Luce. **64 B6** NX2244.
Lucker *Northumb.* ***Village***, 4m/6km SE of Belford. **77 K7** NU1530.
Luckett *Cornw.* ***Village***, by River Tamar, 3m/5km NE of Callington. **4 D3** SX3773.
Lucking Street *Essex* ***Hamlet***, 3m/4km N of Halstead. TL8134.
Luckington *Wilts.* ***Village***, 7m/11km W of Malmesbury. **20 B3** ST8383.
Lucklawhill *Fife* ***Settlement***, below Lucklaw Hill, 2m/3km W of Leuchars. **83 F5** NO4221.
Luckwell Bridge *Som.* ***Hamlet***, on Exmoor, 6m/10km SW of Dunster. **7 H2** SS9038.
Lucton *Here.* ***Village***, 5m/8km NW of Leominster. **28 D2** SO4364.
Lucy Cross *N.Yorks.* ***Settlement***, 2m/3km S of Piercebridge. NZ2112.
Ludac *W.Isles* *Anglicised form of Ludag, qv.*
Ludag (Anglicised form: Ludac.) *W.Isles* ***Village***, on S coast of South Uist, 1m/2km E of Cille Bhrighde. Ferry for pedestrians to Eriskay. **84 C3** NF7714.
Ludborough *Lincs.* ***Village***, 6m/9km N of Louth. **53 F3** TF2995.
Ludbrook *Devon* ***Hamlet***, 2m/3km N of Modbury. SX6554.
Ludchurch (Yr Eglwys Lwyd). *Pembs.* ***Village***, 3m/5km SE of Narberth. **16 E3** SN1410.
Luddenden *W.Yorks.* ***Village***, 2m/3km E of Mytholmroyd. **57 F7** SE0426.
Luddenden Foot *W.Yorks.* ***Village***, on River Calder, 1m/2km NW of Sowerby Bridge. SE0426.
Luddenham Court *Kent* ***Hamlet***, 2m/3km NW of Faversham. **25 F5** TQ9963.
Luddesdown *Kent* ***Hamlet***, 5m/8km S of Gravesend. **24 C5** TQ6766.
Luddington *N.Lincs.* ***Village***, 4m/7km NE of Crowle. **52 B1** SE8216.
Luddington *Warks.* ***Village***, on River Avon, 3m/4km SW of Stratford-upon-Avon. **30 C3** SP1652.
Luddington in the Brook *Northants.* ***Village***, 5m/8km SE of Oundle. **42 E7** TL1083.
Ludford *Shrop.* ***Village***, just S of Ludlow across River Teme. **28 E1** SO5174.
Ludford Bridge *Shrop.* ***Bridge***, mid 15c bridge over River Teme, built of stone and with massive cutwaters. SO5174.
Ludford Magna *Lincs.* ***Village***, 6m/10km E of Market Rasen. **53 F4** TF2089.
Ludford Parva *Lincs.* ***Village***, adjoining to W of Ludford Magna. **52 E4** TF2089.
Ludgershall *Bucks.* ***Village***, 6m/9km SE of Bicester. **31 H7** SP6617.
Ludgershall *Wilts.* Population: 3664. ***Small town***, 7m/11km NW of Andover. Remains of 11c castle (English Heritage). **21 F6** SU2650.
Ludgershall Castle *Wilts.* ***Castle***, to N of Ludgershall, 6m/10km NW of Andover. Late 11c motte (English Heritage) which now shows signs of having been a series of buildings over several centuries. Late-medieval cross. **21 F6** SU2651.
Ludgvan *Cornw.* ***Village***, 2m/4km NE of Penzance. **2 B5** SW5033.
Ludham *Norf.* ***Village***, 5m/8km E of Hoveton. **45 H4** TG3818.
Ludlow *Shrop.* Population: 9040. ***Small town***, on hill above River Teme, 24m/38km S of Shrewsbury. 11c castle. Large parish church, mainly 15c. Some half-timbered houses, notably 16c Feathers Inn. **28 E1** SO5174.
Ludlow Castle *Shrop.* ***Castle***, in centre of Ludlow, at top of steep slope above River Teme, with remains of 12c Norman chapel modelled on Church of Holy Sepulchre in Jerusalem, as well as various 14c buildings. **28 E1** SO5074.
Ludney *Lincs.* ***Settlement***, 2m/3km W of North Somercotes. **53 G3** TF3995.
Ludstock *Here.* ***Settlement***, 2m/3km SW of Ledbury. **29 F5** SO6835.
Ludstone *Shrop.* ***Settlement***, 5m/9km E of Bridgnorth. SO8094.
Ludwell *Wilts.* ***Village***, 3m/5km E of Shaftesbury. **9 J2** ST9122.
Ludworth *Dur.* ***Village***, 3m/4km E of Sherburn. **62 E2** NZ3641.
Luffincott *Devon* ***Hamlet***, 6m/10km N of Launceston. **6 B6** SX3394.
Luffness *E.Loth.* ***Locality***, to NE of Aberlady, 5m/8km SW of North Berwick. **76 C2** NT4780.
Luffness Castle *E.Loth.* ***Castle***, on S side of Aberlady Bay, W of Luffness. 16c house with castle inside fortifications. **76 C2** NT4680.
Lufton *Som.* ***Hamlet***, 3m/4km W of Yeovil. ST5116.
Lugar *E.Ayr.* ***Village***, 2m/3km E of Cumnock. **67 K1** NS5921.
Lugar Water *E.Ayr.* ***River***, running W past Lugar and Cumnock to Ochiltree, then N to River Ayr 1m/2km S of Mauchline. **67 K1** NS4925.
Lugate Water *Sc.Bord.* ***River***, arising from numerous streams in mountains W of Stow, and flowing SE into Gala Water, 1m/2km S of Stow. **76 C6** NT4543.
Lugg ***River***, rising some 8m/12km W of Knighton and flowing E via Presteigne to Leominster, then S into River Wye 4m/6km SE of Hereford. **28 D2** SO5637.
Lugg Green *Here.* ***Locality***, on River Lugg, 4m/6km NW of Leominster. SO4462.
Luggate *E.Loth.* ***Hamlet***, 2m/3km S of East Linton. NT5974.
Luggate Burn *E.Loth.* ***Hamlet***, S of Luggate, 1m/2km W of Stenton. NT5974.
Luggie Water ***River***, rising on hills S of Cumbernauld, past which river flows, before joining River Kelvin at Kirkintilloch. **74 E3** NS6574.
Luggiebank *N.Lan.* ***Suburb***, 1m/2km S of Cumbernauld town centre. **75 F3** NS7672.
Lugsdale *Halton* ***Locality***, 1m/2km E of Widnes town centre. SJ5285.
Lugton *E.Ayr.* ***Village***, 4m/7km N of Stewarton. **74 C5** NS4152.
Lugwardine *Here.* ***Village***, 3m/4km E of Hereford. **28 E4** SO5541.
Lui Water *Aber.* ***River***, running SE down Glen Lui to River Dee, 5m/8km W of Braemar. **89 H5** NO0789.
Luib *High.* ***Settlement***, on S shore of Loch Ainort, Skye. **86 B2** NG5627.
Luibeilt *High.* ***Settlement***, in Mamore Forest, 6m/10km NE of Kinlochleven. **80 D1** NN2668.
Luineag *High.* ***River***, flowing W from Loch Morlich and into River Druie at Coylumbridge. **89 G3** NH9110.
Luing *Arg. & B.* ***Island***, lying between Seil and Scarba, 6m/9km long N to S and about 1km wide. Formerly noted for slate-quarrying. **79 J6** NM7410.
Luinga Bheag *High.* ***Island***, to NE of Luinga Mhòr, off W coast of Lochaber district, 3m/4km W of Arisaig. NM6187.
Luinga Mhòr *High.* ***Island***, small uninhabited island off W coast of Lochaber district, 3m/5km W of Arisaig. **86 C6** NM6085.
Luinne Bheinn *High.* ***Mountain***, in Knoydart, Lochaber district, 3m/4km S of Barrisdale. Munro: height 3080 feet or 939 metres. **86 E4** NG8600.
Lulham *Here.* ***Hamlet***, 6m/10km W of Hereford. **28 D4** SO4041.
Lullingstone *Kent* *See Eynsford.*
Lullingstone Castle *Kent* ***Historic house***, 1m/2km S of Eynsford, Tudor house behind a Queen Anne façade, set in parkland with lake. **23 J5** TQ5264.
Lullingstone Roman Villa *Kent* ***Historic/prehistoric site***, excavated remains of a Roman nobleman's villa (English Heritage) dating from c. AD 100, 1km SW of Eynsford. Fine mosaic pavements. **23 J5** TQ5265.
Lullington *Derbys.* ***Village***, 6m/10km NE of Tamworth. **40 E4** SK2513.
Lullington *E.Suss.* ***Hamlet***, on South Downs, across Cuckmere River from Alfriston, 4m/6km NE of Seaford. TQ5202.
Lullington *Som.* ***Village***, 3m/4km N of Frome. **20 A6** ST7851.
Lulsgate Bottom *N.Som.* ***Hamlet***, to NE of Bristol International Airport, 1km W of Felton. **19 J5** ST5065.
Lulsley *Worcs.* ***Village***, 7m/11km W of Worcester. **29 G3** SO7455.
Lulworth Castle *Dorset* ***Castle***, 1km NE of Lulworth Camp. Early 16c hunting lodge converted into house in 18c (English Heritage). **9 H6** SY8582.
Lulworth Cove *Dorset* ***Bay***, circular bay almost landlocked by chalk and limestone cliffs, 1km S of West Lulworth. **9 H7** SY8280.
Lumb *Lancs.* ***Locality***, on River Irwell, 2m/3km N of Ramsbotton. SD7819.
Lumb *Lancs.* ***Village***, 2m/4km NE of Rawtenstall. SD8324.
Lumb *W.Yorks.* ***Village***, 1m/2km NW of Ripponden. **57 F7** SE0221.
Lumbutts *W.Yorks.* ***Hamlet***, 1m/2km SE of Todmorden. **56 E7** SD9523.
Lumby *N.Yorks.* ***Hamlet***, 1m/2km SW of South Milford. **57 K6** SE4830.
Lumley Castle *Dur.* ***Castle***, late 14c castle, 1m/2km N of Great Lumley. Now a hotel. **62 D1** NZ2949.
Lumley Moor Reservoir *N.Yorks.* ***Reservoir***, 6m/9km W of Ripon. **57 H2** SE2270.
Lumley Thicks *Dur.* ***Locality***, 1km NE of Great Lumley. NZ3050.
Lumphanan *Aber.* ***Village***, 9m/15km NW of Banchory. Macbeth is supposed to have died here; commemorative cairn 1km NW. Peel Ring of Lumphanan (Historic Scotland), 1km SW, site of medieval castle. **90 D4** NJ5703.
Lumphinnans *Fife* ***Locality***, between Cowdenbeath and Lochgelly. **75 K1** NT1792.
Lumsdaine *Sc.Bord.* ***Hamlet***, 3m/5km NW of Coldingham. **77 G4** NT8769.
Lumsdale *Derbys.* ***Settlement***, 1km NE of Matlock. SK3160.
Lumsden *Aber.* ***Village***, 4m/6km S of Rhynie. **90 C2** NJ4721.
Lunan *Angus* ***Village***, small village near mouth of Lunan Water, 4m/7km SW of Montrose. **83 H2** NO6851.
Lunan Bay *Angus* ***Bay***, 4m/7km S of Montrose. **83 J2** NO6951.
Lunan Burn *P. & K.* ***River***, rising on Craig More, 3m/4km NE of Dunkeld, and flowing E through a series of five small lochs to River Isla, 3m/4km NE of confluence of River Isla with River Tay. **82 C3** NO1839.

Lunan Water *Angus* ***River***, running E to Lunan Bay, 4m/7km S of Montrose. **83 H3** NO6951.
Lunanhead *Angus* ***Village***, 1m/2km NE of Forfar. **83 F2** NO4752.
Luncarty *P. & K.* Population: 1190. ***Village***, 4m/7km N of Perth. Site of battle of 990 in which Scots defeated Danes. **82 B5** NO0929.
Lund *E.Riding* ***Village***, 7m/11km NW of Beverley. **59 F5** SE9748.
Lund *N.Yorks.* ***Hamlet***, 2m/4km E of Selby. **58 C6** SE6532.
Lund *Shet.* ***Settlement***, overlooking Lunda Wick, on W coast of Unst. **108 E2** HP5703.
Lundavra *High.* ***Settlement***, on N shore of Lochan Lùnn Dà-Bhrà, 4m/7km NE of North Ballachulish. **80 B1** NN0866.
Lunderston Bay *Inclyde* ***Bay***, W facing bay on Firth of Clyde, 1m/2km N of Inverkip. **73 K3** NS2073.
Lunderton *Aber.* ***Settlement***, 3m/4km NW of Peterhead. **99 K6** NK1049.
Lundie *Angus* ***Village***, 3m/5km S of Newtyle. **82 D4** NO2936.
Lundie *High.* ***Locality***, on N shore of Loch Cluanie, 10m/15km W of Dalchreichart. **87 H3** NH1410.
Lundin Links *Fife* Population: 2375. ***Village***, on Largo Bay, on W side of Lower Largo. Three large standing stones on golf-course to N of A915 road. **83 F7** NO4002.
Lunds *N.Yorks.* ***Locality***, 1m/2km N of Moorcock Inn, 6m/9km NW of Hawes. SD7994.
Lundwood *S.Yorks.* ***Suburb***, 2m/3km NE of Barnsley town centre. SE3707.
Lundy *Devon* ***Island***, granite island (National Trust) 3m/5km from N to S and about 1km wide, lying at entrance to Bristol Channel, 19m/31km off Morte Point on N Devon coast. Hamlet at S end. Boat trips from Ilfracombe and Bideford in summer. The island is particularly noted for seabirds (especially Puffins), spectacular coastal scenery and issuing own postage stamps. **6 A1** SS1345.
Lundy Green *Norf.* ***Settlement***, 1m/2km E of Hempnall. TM2492.
Lune ***River***, rising on Ravenstonedale Common and flowing W to Tebay, then S to Kirkby Lonsdale, SW to Lancaster and Irish Sea at Sunderland Point, 4m/7km SW of Lancaster. **55 H4** SD3554.
Lune *Dur.* ***River***, rising to S of Lune Forest and flowing E, through Selset Reservoir and Grassholme Reservoir to River Tees, 1m/2km E of Middleton-in-Teesdale. **61 K4** NY9625.
Lune Aqueduct *Lancs.* ***Bridge***, stone aqueduct, built 1793, carrying Lancaster Canal over River Lune on N side of Lancaster. SD4863.
Lune Forest *Dur.* ***Large natural feature***, wild moorland area lying to E of Mickle Fell and N of River Lune, 5m/8km NE of Brough. **61 K4** NY8323.
Lune Moor *Dur.* ***Open space***, moorland on N side of Selset Reservoir, 3m/5km SW of Middleton-in-Teesdale. **61 K4** NY8823.
Lunedale *Dur.* ***Valley***, carrying River Lune and containing reservoirs of Selset and Grassholme, 3m/5km SW of Middleton-in-Teesdale. **62 A4** NY9220.
Lunga *Arg. & B.* ***Island***, largest island in Treshnish Isles group, situated at mid point of chain. Its summit, Cruachan, is also highest point of Treshnish Isles; 337 feet or 103 metres. **78 D3** NM2741.
Lunga *Arg. & B.* ***Island***, uninhabited island immediately N of Scarba, and W of Luing across Sound of Luing. Area about 500 acres or 200 hectares. **79 J7** NM7008.
Lunga *Arg. & B.* ***Settlement***, 3m/4km S of Arduaine. **79 J7** NM7906.
Lunna *Shet.* ***Village***, on Mainland, on narrow neck of land between two small bays of East and West Lunna Voe, 4m/6km SW of Lunna Ness. **109 D6** HU4869.
Lunna Holm *Shet.* ***Island***, small uninhabited island off Lunna Ness on NE coast of Mainland. **108 E5** HU5274.
Lunna Ness *Shet.* ***Coastal feature***, peninsula on E coast of Mainland, extending NE to its headland 4m/6km NE of Lunna. **108 E5** HU5071.
Lunnasting *Shet.* ***Locality***, district of Mainland, extending S from Lunna Ness to Dury Voe on E coast. **109 D6** HU4765.
Lunning *Shet.* ***Settlement***, near E coast of Mainland, 4m/7km NE of Laxo. **109 E6** HU5066.
Lunning Sound *Shet.* ***Sea feature***, sea passage between Mainland and West Linga, to S of Lunning. **109 E6** HU5066.
Lunnister *Shet.* ***Settlement***, on Mainland, 1m/2km S of Sullom, on W side of Sullom Voe. HU3471.
Lunnon *Swan.* ***Hamlet***, on Gower peninsula, to NE of Parkmill. SS5489.
Lunsford *Kent* ***Locality***, residential locality adjoining to W of New Hythe, 2m/3km W of Aylesford. TQ6959.
Lunsford's Cross *E.Suss.* ***Hamlet***, 2m/4km NW of Bexhill. **14 C6** TQ7210.
Lunt *Mersey.* ***Hamlet***, 2m/3km W of Maghull. **48 C2** SD3402.
Luntley *Here.* ***Settlement***, 6m/10km W of Leominster. **28 C3** SO3955.
Luppitt *Devon* ***Village***, 4m/6km N of Honiton. **7 K5** ST1606.
Lupset *W.Yorks.* ***Suburb***, 1m/2km SW of Wakefield city centre. SE3119.
Lupton *Cumb.* ***Hamlet***, 4m/6km NW of Kirkby Lonsdale. **55 J1** SD5581.
Lupton Beck *Cumb.* ***River***, issuing from Wyndhammere and flowing first S, then W, to join Peasey Beck, 2m/3km N of Holme. **55 J1** SD5282.
Lurg Hill *Moray* ***Mountain***, 5m/8km W of Cornhill. Height 1027 feet or 313 metres. **98 D5** NJ5057.
Lurg Mhòr *High.* ***Mountain***, on border of Skye and Lochalsh and Ross and Cromarty districts, 6m/10km SE of Achnashellach Station. Munro: height 3234 feet or 986 metres. **95 G7** NH0640.
Lurg Moor *Inclyde* ***Open space***, moorland 2m/3km SE of Greenock. **74 A3** NS2973.
Lurgashall *W.Suss.* ***Village***, 4m/7km NW of Petworth. **12 C4** SU9327.
Lurignich *Arg. & B.* ***Settlement***, on SE shore of Loch Linnhe, 3m/4km NE of Portnacroish. **80 A2** NM9451.
Lusby *Lincs.* ***Village***, 4m/6km W of Spilsby. **53 G6** TF3367.
Luskentyre *W.Isles* *Anglicised form of Losgaintir, qv.*
Luss *Arg. & B.* ***Village***, on W shore of Loch Lomond, 8m/12km S of Tarbet. **74 B1** NS3592.
Lussa *Arg. & B.* ***River***, on Jura, running S to Lussa Bay on E coast. **72 E1** NR6486.
Lussa Loch *Arg. & B.* ***Lake/loch***, large loch in Kintyre 5m/8km N of Campbeltown. **73 F7** NR7130.
Lussa Point *Arg. & B.* ***Coastal feature***, headland to E of Lussa Bay, on E coast of Jura. **72 E2** NR6486.
Lussagiven *Arg. & B.* ***Settlement***, on E coast of Jura, 3m/5km NE of Tarbert. **72 E2** NR6386.
Lusta *High.* ***Village***, on Vaternish peninsula, Skye, 4m/7km SE of Ardmore Point. **93 H6** NG2756.
Lustleigh *Devon* ***Village***, 4m/6km SE of Moretonhampstead. **7 F7** SX7881.
Luston *Here.* ***Village***, 3m/4km N of Leominster. **28 D2** SO4863.
Luther Water *Aber.* ***River***, rising in Drumtochty Forest and running S to River North Esk, 2m/3km W of Marykirk. **83 H1** NO6566.
Luthermuir *Aber.* ***Village***, on W side of Luther Water, 3m/4km NW of Marykirk. **83 H1** NO6568.
Luthrie *Fife* ***Village***, 4m/7km NW of Cupar. **82 E6** NO3319.
Luton *Devon* ***Hamlet***, 5m/8km SE of Cullompton. **7 J5** ST0802.
Luton *Devon* ***Hamlet***, 5m/7km NE of Newton Abbot. **5 K3** SX9076.
Luton *Luton* Population: 171,671. ***Town***, large industrial town 28m/45km NW of London. Associated with car manufacture. University. International airport 2m/3km E. **32 D6** TL0821.
Luton *Med.* ***Suburb***, SE district of Chatham. **24 D5** TQ7666.
Luton Hoo *Beds.* ***Historic house***, mansion in large park 2m/3km SE of Luton. **32 E7** TL0821.
Lutterworth *Leics.* Population: 7380. ***Small town***, 6m/10km NE of Rugby. **41 H7** SP5484.
Lutton *Devon* ***Village***, 3m/5km NW of Ivybridge. **5 F5** SX5959.
Lutton *Dorset* ***Settlement***, 3m/5km SE of Corfe Castle. SY9080.
Lutton *Lincs.* ***Village***, 2m/3km N of Long Sutton. **43 H3** TF4325.
Lutton *Northants.* ***Village***, 5m/8km E of Oundle. **42 E7** TL1187.
Lutton Marsh *Lincs.* ***Open space***, lowland 3m/4km NE of Long Sutton. **43 H3** TF4426.
Luxborough *Som.* ***Village***, on Exmoor, 4m/6km S of Dunster. **7 H2** SS9737.
Luxhay Reservoir *Som.* ***Reservoir***, small reservoir 4m/6km SE of Wellington. Leigh Reservoir to W. **7 K4** ST2017.
Luxted *Gt.Lon.* ***Settlement***, 1m/2km NE of Biggin Hill. TQ4360.
Luxulyan *Cornw.* ***Village***, 4m/7km NE of St. Austell. **4 A5** SX0558.
Luzley *Gt.Man.* ***Hamlet***, 1km SW of Mossley. SD9601.
Luzley Brook *Gt.Man.* ***Suburb***, 1km E of Royton. SD9207.
Lwyd *Newport* ***River***, rising near Blaenavon and flowing S by Pontypool and Cwmbran into River Usk at Caerleon. ST3490.
Lybster *High.* ***Settlement***, 6m/9km W of Thurso. **105 F2** ND0268.
Lybster *High.* ***Village***, in Caithness district, 12m/20km SW of Wick. **105 H5** ND2435.
Lyd *Devon* ***River***, rising on Dartmoor and running W past Lydford and through Lydford Gorge before joining River Wolf at Lifton and flowing into River Tamar, 3m/4km E of Launceston. SX3985.
Lydacott *Devon* ***Hamlet***, 4m/6km W of Hatherleigh. **6 C5** SS4803.
Lydbury North *Shrop.* ***Village***, 3m/4km SE of Bishop's Castle. **38 C7** SO3585.
Lydcott *Devon* ***Hamlet***, 7m/11km N of South Molton. **6 E2** SS6936.
Lydd *Kent* Population: 3173. ***Small town***, 4m/7km NW of Dungeness. Airport to E. **15 F5** TR0420.
Lydd-on-Sea *Kent* ***Small town***, coastal resort 3m/5km E of Lydd. **15 F5** TR0420.
Lydden *Dorset* ***River***, rising in hills S of Mappowder and flowing N into River Stour SW of Marnhull. **9 G4** ST7617.
Lydden *Kent* ***Village***, 4m/6km NW of Dover. **15 H3** TR2645.
Lyddington *Rut.* ***Village***, 2m/3km S of Uppingham. **42 B6** SP8797.
Lyddington Bede House *Rut.* ***Historic house***, 15c bishop's palace later converted into almshouses (English Heritage), situated in Lyddington, 6m/9km N of Corby. **42 B6** SP8797.
Lyde Green *Hants.* ***Hamlet***, 2m/3km NW of Hook. SU7057.
Lyde Green *S.Glos.* ***Hamlet***, 4m/7km SW of Chipping Sodbury. ST6777.
Lydeard St. Lawrence *Som.* ***Village***, 4m/7km NE of Wiveliscombe. **7 K2** ST1232.
Lydford *Devon* ***Village***, 7m/11km N of Tavistock. Remains of 12c castle (English Heritage). Parish includes a large part of Dartmoor. **6 D7** SX5184.
Lydford *Som.* ***Locality***, parish to E of Keinton Mandeville, astride River Brue, and containing villages of East and West Lydford and hamlets of Lydford-on-Fosse and Lydford Fair Place. ST5631.
Lydford Castle *Devon* ***Castle***, 12c tower house (English Heritage) on site of previous Anglo-Saxon town to SW of Lydford. Great tower restored in 18c and used as courthouse and prison for Stannary Court. Earthworks of original Norman fort to S. **6 D7** SX5084.
Lydford Fair Place *Som.* ***Hamlet***, in parish of Lydford, to E of Keinton Mandeville. ST5732.
Lydford Gorge *Devon* ***Valley***, wooded ravine carrying River Lyd (National Trust), with waterfall to SW of Lydford. **6 C7** SX5184.
Lydford-on-Fosse *Som.* ***Hamlet***, in parish of Lydford, 1m/2km E of Keinton Mandeville. **8 E1** ST5631.
Lydgate *Gt.Man.* ***Hamlet***, 1m/2km N of Mossley. SD9704.
Lydgate *Gt.Man.* ***Settlement***, 1m/2km E of Littleborough. SD9516.
Lydgate *W.Yorks.* ***Village***, 1m/2km NW of Todmorden. **56 E7** SD9225.
Lydham *Shrop.* ***Village***, 2m/3km NE of Bishop's Castle. **38 C6** SO3391.
Lydiard Green *Wilts.* ***Settlement***, 1km W of Lydiard Millicent. SU0886.
Lydiard Mansion *Wilts.* ***Historic house***, restored Georgian house of Viscount Bolingbroke, 3m/5km W of Swindon town centre. Features Lady Diana Spencer Room. **20 D3** SU1084.
Lydiard Millicent *Wilts.* ***Village***, 4m/6km W of Swindon. **20 D3** SU0986.
Lydiard Tregoze *Swin.* ***Hamlet***, adjoining to W of Swindon. SU1084.
Lydiate *Mersey.* Population: 7301. ***Locality***, 1m/2km N of Maghull. **48 C2** SD3604.
Lydiate Ash *Worcs.* ***Settlement***, 3m/5km N of Bromsgrove. SO9775.
Lydlinch *Dorset* ***Village***, in Blackmoor Vale, 3m/4km W of Sturminster Newton. **9 G3** ST7413.
Lydney *Glos.* Population: 7413. ***Small town***, 8m/13km NE of Chepstow. Industrial estate and harbour on River Severn estuary to S. Roman remains. **19 K1** SO6303.
Lydney Park *Glos.* ***Garden***, with woodland and lakes, as well as Roman temple site, 1m/2km SW of Lydney; particularly well-known for rhododendrons. **19 K1** SO6202.
Lydney Sand *Glos.* ***Coastal feature***, sandbank in River Severn, 2m/3km S of Lydney. **19 K2** ST6299.
Lydstep *Pembs.* ***Hamlet***, 3m/5km SW of Tenby. **16 D5** SS0898.
Lye *W.Mid.* ***Suburb***, E district of Stourbridge. **40 B7** SO9284.
Lye Cross *N.Som.* ***Hamlet***, 1m/2km E of Wrington. ST4962.
Lye Green *Bucks.* ***Hamlet***, 2m/3km NE of Chesham. **22 C1** SP9703.
Lye Green *E.Suss.* ***Hamlet***, 2m/3km N of Crowborough. TQ5034.
Lye Green *Warks.* ***Settlement***, 3m/5km E of Henley-in-Arden. SP1965.
Lye Head *Worcs.* ***Settlement***, 2m/4km SW of Bewdley. SO7573.
Lye's Green *Wilts.* ***Hamlet***, 4m/6km NW of Warminster. ST8246.
Lyford *Oxon.* ***Village***, 4m/7km N of Wantage. **21 G2** SU3994.
Lymbridge Green *Kent* ***Hamlet***, 6m/10km N of Hythe. **15 G3** TR1243.
Lyme Bay ***Bay***, stretching from Start Point to Portland Bill, a distance of 55m/88km by land. Much of coast enclosing bay is designated as Area of Outstanding Natural Beauty. **8 B6** SY3585.
Lyme Hall *Ches.* ***Historic house***, Elizabethan house with later additions in large deer park (National Trust) 2m/3km S of Disley. **49 J4** SJ9682.
Lyme Park *Ches.* ***Leisure/recreation***, country park estate (National Trust), 3m/5km SE of Poynton. Includes Elizabethan house, with 18c and 19c additions, home to Legh family for 600 years; English clock collection, Mortlake tapestries and Grinling Gibbons carvings. 1400 acres of parkland has red and fallow deer and formal gardens include sunken Dutch garden and Killtime, with an orangery containing fig tree and two rare camellias over 200 years old. **49 J4** SJ9682.
Lyme Regis *Dorset* Population: 3851. ***Small town***, resort built into cliffs on Lyme Bay, 20m/32km SW of Yeovil. **8 C5** SY3492.
Lyme Regis Museum *Dorset* ***Other feature of interest***, beside Broad Ledge in Lyme Regis, overlooking Lyme Bay. Local history, with fossil and lace displays. **8 C5** SY3491.
Lymekilns *S.Lan.* ***Suburb***, to NW of East Kilbride town centre. **74 E5** NS6254.
Lyminge *Kent* Population: 1468. ***Village***, 4m/6km N of Hythe. **15 G3** TR1640.
Lyminge Forest *Kent* ***Forest/woodland***, large wooded area 3m/5km N of Lyminge. **15 G3** TR1640.
Lymington *Hants.* ***River***, rising in New Forest and flowing SE past town of Lymington and into The Solent. SZ3494.
Lymington *Hants.* Population: 13,508. ***Town***, yachting centre 15m/24km E of Bournemouth. Vehicle ferry to Yarmouth on Isle of Wight. **10 E5** SZ3295.
Lyminster *W.Suss.* ***Village***, 2m/3km N of Littlehampton. **12 D6** TQ0204.
Lymm *Warr.* Population: 9721. ***Small town***, 5m/8km E of Warrington. Developed with expansion of transport networks in 18c and 19c. **49 F4** SJ6887.
Lymore *Hants.* ***Hamlet***, 2m/3km SW of Lymington town centre. **10 E5** SZ3093.
Lympne *Kent* ***Village***, 3m/4km W of Hythe. Restored medieval castle, Stutfall Castle, remains of Roman fort of Lemanis, to S. **15 G4** TR1134.
Lympne Castle *Kent* ***Castle***, rebuilt in 14c and restored early 20c, to S of Lympne, 3m/4km W of Hythe. **15 G4** TR1134.
Lympsham *Som.* ***Village***, 4m/6km NE of Burnham-on-Sea. **19 G6** ST3354.
Lympstone *Devon* Population: 1855. ***Village***, on E side of River Exe estuary, 2m/3km N of Exmouth. **7 H7** SX9984.
Lynaberack *High.* ***Settlement***, in valley of River Tromie, 4m/6km S of Kingussie. **88 E5** NN7694.
Lynbridge *Devon* ***Locality***, adjoining to S of Lynton. SS7248.
Lynch *Hants.* ***Settlement***, 1km W of Overton. SU5049.
Lynch *Som.* ***Hamlet***, adjoining Bossington, 1m/2km NE of Porlock. SS9047.
Lynch Green *Norf.* ***Village***, adjoining to NW of Hethersett, 4m/6km NE of Wymondham. TG1505.
Lynch Hill *Slo.* ***Suburb***, NW district of Slough. SU9482.

Lynch Tor *Devon* ***Mountain***, in Dartmoor National Park, 4m/6km E of Mary Tavy. Height 1696 feet or 517 metres. **6 D7** SX5680.
Lynchat *High.* ***Settlement***, in Badenoch and Strathspey district, 2m/3km NE of Kingussie. **88 E4** NH7801.
Lyndale Point *High.* ***Coastal feature***, headland on Loch Snizort, N coast of Skye, between entrances to Lochs Greshornish and Snizort Beag. **93 J6** NG3657.
Lyndhurst *Hants.* Population: 2381. ***Small town***, 8m/13km N of Lymington and known as 'the capital of the New Forest'. Verderers Court adjudicates on forest rights. Interesting, brick-built 19c church. **10 E4** SU2908.
Lyndon *Rut.* ***Village***, 4m/7km SE of Oakham. **42 C5** SK9004.
Lyndon Green *W.Mid.* ***Suburb***, 5m/8km E of Birmingham city centre. SP1485.
Lyne *Aber.* ***Locality***, comprising Lyne of Linton and Mill of Lyne, 1m/2km S of Sauchen. **91 F4** NJ7008.
Lyne *Cumb.* ***River***, formed by confluence of Rivers Black Lyne and White Lyne, 5m/7km W of Bewcastle, and flowing SW into River Esk 3m/5km SW of Longtown. **69 K6** NY3565.
Lyne *Sc.Bord.* ***Settlement***, 3m/5km W of Peebles. Site of Roman camp. **76 A6** NT2041.
Lyne *Surr.* ***Village***, 2m/3km W of Chertsey. **22 D5** TQ0166.
Lyne Down *Here.* ***Hamlet***, 5m/8km NE of Ross-on-Wye. SO6431.
Lyne of Gorthleck (Also known as Gorthleck or Gorthlick.) *High.* ***Settlement***, on W side of Loch Mhòr, in Inverness district, 3m/5km E of Foyers. **88 C2** NH5420.
Lyne of Skene *Aber.* ***Village***, 4m/7km SW of Kintore. **91 F3** NJ7610.
Lyne Station *Sc.Bord.* ***Hamlet***, 3m/4km W of Peebles. **76 A7** NT2039.
Lyne Water *Sc.Bord.* ***River***, rising on Pentland Hills and flowing S to River Tweed 3m/4km W of Peebles. **75 K6** NT2139.
Lyneal *Shrop.* ***Hamlet***, 3m/5km SE of Ellesmere. **38 D2** SJ4433.
Lynedale House *High.* ***Settlement***, 3m/4km S of Lyndale Point, Skye. **93 J6** NG3654.
Lynegar *High.* ***Settlement***, to N of Loch Watten. **105 H3** ND2257.
Lyneham *Oxon.* ***Village***, 5m/8km SW of Chipping Norton. **30 D6** SP2720.
Lyneham *Wilts.* Population: 4747. ***Village***, 5m/8km N of Calne. Royal Air Force station and airfield to W. **20 D4** SU0279.
Lyneholmeford *Cumb.* ***Settlement***, on S side of White Line river, 3m/4km NW of Kirkcambeck. **70 A6** NY5172.
Lynemore *High.* ***Settlement***, 3m/5km SE of Grantown-on-Spey. **89 H2** NJ0624.
Lynemore *Moray* ***Settlement***, in Glen Gheallaidh, 4m/6km SW of Upper Knockando. **89 J1** NJ1438.
Lynemouth *Northumb.* Population: 2024. ***Village***, near North Sea coast, 2m/4km NE of Ashington. Power station to S. **71 H4** NZ2991.
Lyness *Ork.* ***Settlement***, with oil service base, on Hoy, opposite S end of Fara. **107 C8** ND3094.
Lynford *Norf.* ***Settlement***, 4m/6km NE of Brandon. **44 C6** TL8291.
Lynford Cottages *Norf.* ***Settlement***, 4m/6km NE of Brandon, in Breckland. TL8192.
Lyng *Norf.* ***Village***, 6m/9km NE of East Dereham. **44 E4** TG0717.
Lyng *Som.* ***Village***, 6m/9km W of Langport. **8 C2** ST3329.
Lyngate *Norf.* ***Hamlet***, 1km NE of Worstead. TG3026.
Lyngford *Som.* ***Suburb***, N district of Taunton. ST2326.
Lynher *Cornw.* ***River***, rising on Bodmin Moor near Altarnun and flowing SE into River Tamar below Saltash. From St. Germans, river is usually known as St. Germans River. **4 D4** SX3757.
Lynmouth *Devon* ***Small town***, fishing resort with harbour at foot of cliff below Lynton, on Lynmouth Bay, 10m/16km W of Porlock. Partly destroyed by floods in 1952. **7 F1** SS7249.
Lynmouth Bay *Devon* ***Bay***, on N coast of Devon, W of Foreland Point. **18 A6** SS7249.
Lynn *Staffs.* ***Settlement***, 2m/3km E of Brownhills. SK0704.
Lynn *Tel. & W.* ***Settlement***, 3m/5km SE of Newport. SJ7815.
Lynn Deeps ***Sea feature***, sea channel in central part of The Wash, between Long Sand and Sunk Sand. **43 J1** TF5645.
Lynn of Lorn *Arg. & B.* ***Sea feature***, strait in Loch Linnhe between Lismore and mainland to E. **79 K3** NM8741.
Lynn of Morvern ***Sea feature***, strait in Loch Linnhe running between Morvern in Lochaber district, Highland, and Lismore, Argyll & Bute. **79 J3** NM7740.
Lynsted *Kent* ***Village***, 3m/5km SE of Sittingbourne. **25 F5** TQ9460.
Lynstone *Cornw.* ***Hamlet***, 1km SW of Bude. SS2005.
Lynton *Devon* ***Small town***, clifftop resort on N coast, 14m/22km NE of Barnstaple. Cliff railway dates from 1890. **7 F1** SS7149.
Lynton and Lynmouth Cliff Railway *Devon* ***Other feature of interest***, water-powered two-carriage cliff railway linking Lynton to Lynmouth. Originally steepest railway in world. **7 F1** SS7149.
Lynworth *Glos.* ***Suburb***, NE district of Cheltenham. SO9623.
Lyon *P. & K.* ***River***, running E from Loch Lyon down Glen Lyon to River Tay, 4m/6km W of Aberfeldy. **81 H3** NN7947.
Lyons *T. & W.* ***Locality***, 1km SE of Hetton-le-Hole. NZ3546.
Lyon's Gate *Dorset* ***Hamlet***, 3m/5km N of Cerne Abbas. **9 F4** ST6605.
Lyon's Green *Norf.* ***Locality***, 1m/2km E of Little Fransham. TF9111.
Lyonshall *Here.* ***Village***, 3m/4km E of Kington. **28 C3** SO3355.
Lype Hill *Som.* ***Mountain***, at W end of Brendon Hills, 2m/3km SE of Wheddon Cross. Height 1387 feet or 423 metres. **7 H2** SS9437.
Lypiatt *Glos.* ***Locality***, parish (Bisley-with-Lypiatt) containing localities of Middle and Nether Lypiatt and Lypiatt Park, on E side of Stroud. SO8805.
Lypiatt Park *Glos.* ***Locality***, forms parish of Bisley-with-Lypiatt, along with Middle Lypiatt and Nether Lypiatt, on E side of Stroud. SO8805.
Lyrabus *Arg. & B.* ***Settlement***, on Islay, 3m/5km NW of Bridgend. **72 A4** NR2964.
Lyrawa Burn *Ork.* ***River***, rising in central Hoy and flowing E to Lyrawa Bay on E coast. **107 B8** ND2599.
Lytchett Matravers *Dorset* Population: 2871. ***Village***, 5m/8km NW of Poole. **9 J5** SY9495.
Lytchett Minster *Dorset* ***Village***, 4m/7km NE of Wareham. **9 J5** SY9692.
Lyte's Cary *Som.* ***Historic house***, old manor house (National Trust), 1m/2km NE of Kingsdon. **8 E2** ST5326.
Lyth *High.* ***Settlement***, in Caithness district, 6m/10km SE of Castletown. **105 H2** ND2863.
Lyth Valley *Cumb.* ***Valley***, carrying River Gilpin S into River Kent estuary. **55 H1** SD4687.
Lytham *Lancs.* ***Suburb***, 2m/4km E of Lytham St. Anne's town centre. **55 G7** SD3627.
Lytham St. Anne's *Lancs.* Population: 40,866. ***Town***, coastal resort on N side of mouth of River Ribble estuary, 12m/19km W of Preston. Formerly separate towns of Lytham and St. Anne's have merged, Lytham originally being a fishing village. Royal Lytham and St. Anne's golf course is regular venue for Open Championship. **55 G7** SD3427.
Lythbank *Shrop.* ***Settlement***, 4m/6km SW of Shrewsbury. SJ4607.
Lythe *N.Yorks.* ***Village***, near North Sea coast, 4m/6km NW of Whitby. **63 K5** NZ8413.
Lythe Hill *Surr.* ***Locality***, 1m/2km E of Haslemere. **12 C3** SU9132.
Lythes *Ork.* ***Settlement***, on South Ronaldsay, 2m/4km S of St. Margaret's Hope. **107 D9** ND4589.
Lythmore *High.* ***Settlement***, 4m/6km SW of Thurso. **105 F2** ND0466.
Lyveden *Northants.* ***Settlement***, 2m/3km NE of Brigstock. SP9885.
Lyveden New Bield *Northants.* ***Historic house***, shell of unfinished house of early 17c, built in shape of a cross by Sir Thomas Tresham, 4m/6km SW of Oundle. **42 C7** SP9885.
Lyvennet *Cumb.* ***River***, rising on Crosby Ravensworth Fell and flowing N by Crosby Ravensworth, Maulds Meaburn and King's Meaburn into River Eden, 1km S of Temple Sowerby. **61 H5** NY6026.

M

Maari *W.Isles* ***Hill***, on North Uist, 3m/5km SE of Solas. Height 561 feet or 171 metres. **92 D4** NF8672.
Maaruig *W.Isles Anglicised form of Maruig, qv.*
Maaruig Island *W.Isles* ***Island***, tiny islet to E of Maruig in Loch Seaforth, North Harris. NB2006.
Mabe Burnthouse *Cornw.* ***Village***, 1m/2km W of Penryn. Two reservoirs to S. **2 E5** SW7634.
Mabie Hotel *D. & G.* ***Other building***, 4m/6km SW of Dumfries, at E side of Mabie Forest. **65 K3** NX9470.
Mablethorpe *Lincs.* Population: 4860. ***Small town***, North Sea coast resort developed in late 19c, 11m/18km E of Louth. Extensive sandy beaches. **53 J4** TF5085.
Macaskin Island *Arg. & B. See Island Macaskin.*
Macbeth's Hillock *Moray* ***Hill***, small hill 5m/8km E of Nairn. Height 161 feet or 49 metres. **97 G6** NH9557.
Macclesfield *Ches.* Population: 50,270. ***Town***, 10m/17km S of Stockport. Former centre of silk manufacture, with medieval town centre. Paradise Mill is now part of Macclesfield Silk Museum. **49 J5** SJ9173.
Macclesfield Forest *Ches.* ***Hamlet***, 4m/6km E of Macclesfield, in Peak District National Park. **49 J5** SJ9772.
Macduff *Aber.* Population: 3894. ***Small town***, small fishing town on E side of Banff Bay, 1m/2km E of Banff. **99 F4** NJ7064.
Macduff's Castle *Fife* ***Castle***, late 14c ruin on E side of East Wemyss, supposed former stronghold of Thanes of Fife. **76 B1** NT3497.
Macedonia *Fife* ***Suburb***, W district of Glenrothes. NO2501.
Machan *S.Lan.* ***Locality***, adjoining to S of Larkhall. **75 F5** NS7650.
Machany *P. & K.* ***Settlement***, 3m/5km NE of Auchterarder. **82 A6** NN9015.
Machany Water *P. & K.* ***River***, running E to River Earn 3m/4km N of Auchterarder. **81 K6** NN9412.
Macharioch *Arg. & B.* ***Settlement***, on Kintyre, 3m/5km E of Southend. **66 B3** NR7309.
Machen *Caerp.* ***Small town***, 4m/6km E of Caerphilly. **19 F3** ST2189.
Machir *Arg. & B.* ***Settlement***, on Rinns of Islay, 9m/13km W of Bridgend. **72 A4** NR2063.
Machir Bay *Arg. & B.* ***Bay***, on W coast of Islay, on S side of Coul Point. **72 A4** NR2063.
Machno *Conwy* ***River***, rising 2m/4km NE of Blaenau Ffestiniog and flowing NE by Penmachno to River Conwy below Machno Falls, 2m/3km SE of Betws-y-coed. **47 F7** SH8053.
Machrie *Arg. & B.* ***River***, flowing E into Laggan Bay, Islay, 4m/7km NW of Port Ellen. **72 B6** NR3250.
Machrie *Arg. & B.* ***Settlement***, on Islay, 3m/5km NW of Port Ellen. **72 B6** NR3249.
Machrie *N.Ayr.* ***Locality***, on Machrie Bay, on W coast of Arran, 4m/6km N of Blackwaterfoot. **73 H7** NR8934.
Machrie Bay *N.Ayr.* ***Bay***, on W coast of Arran, 4m/6km N of Blackwaterfoot. **73 G7** NR8934.
Machrie Moor Stone Circles *N.Ayr.* ***Historic/prehistoric site***, remains of six Bronze Age stone circles on Arran, with standing stones (some fallen) 15 feet or 2.5 metres high. 3m/4km N of Blackwaterfoot. **73 H7** NR9132.
Machrie Water *N.Ayr.* ***River***, running W into Machrie Bay. **73 H7** NR8934.
Machrihanish *Arg. & B.* ***Village***, on Machrihanish Bay, on W coast of Kintyre, 5m/8km W of Campbeltown. **66 A2** NR6320.
Machrihanish Bay *Arg. & B.* ***Bay***, on W coast of Kintyre, 5m/8km W of Campbeltown. **66 A1** NR6320.
Machrins *Arg. & B.* ***Settlement***, on Colonsay, 1m/2km W of Scalasaig. **72 B1** NR3693.
Machynlleth *Powys* Population: 2033. ***Small town***, market town and tourist centre in River Dyfi valley, 16m/26km NE of Aberystwyth. 16c timber-framed house reputed to stand on site of first Welsh Parliament, held in early 15c by Welsh nationalist, Owain Glyndŵr. **37 G5** SH7400.
Machynys *Carmar.* ***Locality***, 1m/2km S of Llanelli town centre. SS5098.
Mackerye End *Herts.* ***Settlement***, 2m/3km NE of Harpenden. Associations with Charles Lamb (See Essays of Elia). TL1515.
Mackney *Oxon.* ***Settlement***, 2m/3km W of Wallingford. SU5889.
Mackworth *Derbys.* ***Village***, 3m/5km NW of Derby. Part of 15c gatehouse of former castle survives. **41 F2** SK3137.
Maclean's Cross *Arg. & B.* ***Historic/prehistoric site***, 15c Celtic cross (Historic Scotland) at Baile Mòr, Iona. **78 D5** NM2824.
Maclean's Nose *High.* ***Coastal feature***, headland on S coast of Ardnamurchan peninsula in Lochaber district, 3m/5km SE of Kilchoan. **79 G1** NM5361.
MacLellan's Castle *D. & G.* ***Castle***, elegant 16c L-plan castlellated and turreted mansion (Historic Scotland) overlooking harbour in Kirkcudbright. Ruined since 1752; complete except for roof. **65 G5** NX6851.
MacLeod's Maidens *High.* ***Coastal feature***, three rocks off Idrigill Point on SW coast of Skye. **85 H1** NG2436.
Macleod's Table North *High. Alternative name for Healabhal Mhòr, qv.*
Macleod's Table South *High. Alternative name for Healabhal Bheag, qv.*
Macmerry *E.Loth.* Population: 1173. ***Village***, 2m/3km E of Tranent. **76 C3** NT4372.
Macmillan's Cross *Arg. & B. See Kilmory Chapel.*
Macphee's Hill *W.Isles* ***Hill***, on Mingulay, overlooking NE coast. Height 735 feet or 224 metres. **84 A6** NL5684.
Macterry *Aber.* ***Settlement***, 3m/5km NE of Fyvie. **99 F6** NJ7842.
Mad Wharf *Mersey.* ***Coastal feature***, sandbank adjoining to W of Formby Hills, 1m/2km W of Formby town centre. **48 B2** SD2507.
Madame Tussaud's *Gt.Lon.* ***Leisure/recreation***, museum of waxworks in City of Westminster to S of Regent's Park and 3m/5km NW of Charing Cross. Contains life-size figures of famous historic and contemporary people. TQ2882.
Madderty *P. & K.* ***Locality***, 5m/9km E of Crieff. **82 A5** NN9521.
Maddington *Wilts.* ***Locality***, adjoining to N of Shrewton, 6m/9km NW of Amesbury. SU0644.
Maddiston *Falk.* ***Village***, 4m/6km W of Linlithgow. **75 H3** NS9476.
Madehurst *W.Suss.* ***Settlement***, 3m/4km NW of Arundel. **12 C5** SU9910.
Madeley *Staffs.* Population: 2254. ***Village***, 5m/8km W of Newcastle-under-Lyme. **39 G1** SJ7744.
Madeley *Tel. & W.* Population: 17,909. ***Suburb***, 2m/3km S of Dawley, Telford. **39 G5** SJ6904.
Madeley Heath *Staffs.* ***Hamlet***, 1m/2km NE of Madeley. **39 G1** SJ7845.
Madeley Heath *Worcs.* ***Settlement***, 4m/7km N of Bromsgrove. SO9577.
Madeleywood *Tel. & W.* ***Locality***, adjoining to E of Ironbridge. SJ6703.
Maders *Cornw.* ***Hamlet***, 2m/3km NW of Callington. SX3471.
Madford *Devon* ***River***, rising to SE of Madford and flowing generally N to River Culm, NE of Hemyock. **7 K4** ST1413.
Madford *Devon* ***Settlement***, 2m/3km SE of Hemyock. **7 K4** ST1411.
Madingley *Cambs.* ***Village***, 4m/6km NW of Cambridge. American World War II cemetery. Hall, Tudor and later. **33 G3** TL3960.
Madjeston *Dorset* ***Hamlet***, 1km S of Gillingham. **9 H2** ST8024.
Madley *Here.* ***Village***, 6m/10km W of Hereford. **28 D5** SO4138.
Madresfield *Worcs.* ***Village***, 2m/3km NE of Great Malvern. **29 H4** SO8047.
Madron *Cornw.* ***Village***, 2m/3km NW of Penzance. Trengwainton Garden (National Trust) has exotic trees and shrubs. To N, Madron Well and Baptistry. **2 B5** SW4531.
Mae Ness *Ork.* ***Coastal feature***, headland at easternmost point of Egilsay. **106 D4** HY4831.
Maelienydd *Powys* ***Open space***, hill ridge rising to over 330 metres, 2m/3km SE of Llanbister. **28 A1** SO1270.
Maen Achwyfaen *Flints.* ***Historic/prehistoric site***, 10c-11c cross (Cadw), 1m/2km W of Whitford. At nearly 11 feet or 3 metres it is tallest monument of its type in Britain. **47 K5** SJ1278.
Maen Porth *Cornw.* ***Settlement***, on small, sandy bay in Falmouth Bay, 1m/2km NW of Mawnan Smith. **2 E6** SW7929.
Maen y Bugael *I.o.A. Welsh form of West Mouse, qv.*
Maen-y-groes *Cere.* ***Hamlet***, 1m/2km S of New Quay. SN3858.
Maenaddwyn *I.o.A.* ***Hamlet***, on Anglesey, 3m/4km E of Llanerchymedd. **46 C4** SH4584.
Maenclochog *Pembs.* ***Village***, 9m/15km SE of Fishguard. **16 D2** SN0827.
Maendy *Cardiff* ***Suburb***, 1m/2km N of Cardiff city centre. ST1778.
Maendy *Newport Welsh form of Maindee, qv.*
Maendy *V. of Glam.* ***Hamlet***, 1m/2km NE of Cowbridge. **18 D4** ST0176.
Maenease Point (Also known as Pen-a-maen.) *Cornw.* ***Coastal feature***, headland on SE side of Gorran Haven. **4 A6** SX0141.
Maenorbyr *Pembs. Welsh form of Manorbier, qv.*

Maentwrog *Gwyn.* ***Village***, 3m/4km W of Ffestiniog. **37 F1** SH6640.
Maer *Cornw.* ***Hamlet***, 1m/2km N of Bude. SS2007.
Maer *Staffs.* ***Village***, 6m/9km SW of Newcastle-under-Lyme. **39 G2** SJ7938.
Maerdy *Carmar.* ***Settlement***, 1m/2km S of Llandeilo. **17 K2** SN6220.
Maerdy *Carmar.* ***Settlement***, 3m/5km W of Llangadog. **17 K2** SN6527.
Maerdy *Conwy* ***Village***, 4m/6km W of Corwen. **37 K1** SJ0144.
Maerdy *Mon. Welsh form of Mardy, qv.*
Maerdy *Mon.* ***Locality***, 1m/2km E of Usk. SO4001.
Maerdy *Mon.* ***Settlement***, 4m/6km SE of Abergavenny. **19 G1** SO3208.
Maerdy *R.C.T.* ***Village***, in Rhondda Fach, 2m/3km NW of Ferndale. **18 C2** SS9798.
Maerun *Newport Welsh form of Marshfield, qv.*
Maes-Glas *Flints. Welsh form of Greenfield, qv.*
Maes-glas *Newport* ***Suburb***, 1m/2km S of Newport town centre. **19 F3** ST2985.
Maes Howe *Ork.* ***Historic/prehistoric site***, site of Neolithic communal burial-chamber (Historic Scotland) near S end of Loch of Harray 3m/4km W of Finstown, Mainland. Viking runes carved on walls. Reputed to be finest megalithic tomb in British Isles. **107 C6** HY3112.
Maes-Treylow *Powys* ***Settlement***, 3m/5km NW of Presteigne. **28 B2** SO2665.
Maesbrook *Shrop.* ***Hamlet***, 5m/9km S of Oswestry. **38 B3** SJ3021.
Maesbury *Shrop.* ***Hamlet***, 3m/4km SE of Oswestry. SJ3025.
Maesbury Marsh *Shrop.* ***Village***, on Shropshire Union Canal, 1km SE of Maesbury. **38 C3** SJ3025.
Maesgeirchen *Gwyn.* ***Suburb***, to E of Bangor. SH5871.
Maesgwynne *Carmar.* ***Settlement***, 1km NW of Llanboidy. **17 F2** SN2023.
Maeshafn *Denb.* ***Hamlet***, 3m/5km SW of Mold. **48 B6** SJ2060.
Maesllyn *Cere.* ***Hamlet***, 4m/6km NW of Llandysul. **26 C4** SN3644.
Maesmynis *Powys* ***Settlement***, 3m/4km SW of Builth Wells. **27 K4** SO0147.
Maesteg *Bridgend* Population: 20,576. ***Town***, industrial town, 6m/9km E of Port Talbot. **18 B2** SS8591.
Maesybont *Carmar.* ***Hamlet***, 3m/4km N of Cross Hands. **17 J3** SN5616.
Maesycrugiau *Carmar.* ***Settlement***, on River Teifi, 4m/6km SW of Llanybydder. **26 D4** SN4741.
Maesycwmmer *Caerp.* ***Village***, 5m/8km N of Caerphilly. **18 E2** ST1594.
Maesyfed *Powys Welsh form of New Radnor, qv.*
Maesyrhandir *Powys* ***Locality***, adjoining to SW of Newtown. SO0990.
Maesyrychen Mountain *Denb.* ***Large natural feature***, range of hills 3m/5km NW of Llangollen, to E of Llantysilio Mountain. **38 A1** SJ1846.
Magdalen Bridge *Oxon.* ***Bridge***, stone bridge over River Cherwell in Oxford, built in 1772. SP5206.
Magdalen Laver *Essex* ***Hamlet***, 4m/7km E of Harlow. **23 J1** TL5108.
Maggieknockater *Moray* ***Locality***, 2m/3km E of Craigellachie. **98 B6** NJ3145.
Maggots End *Essex* ***Settlement***, 4m/6km N of Bishop's Stortford. TL4827.
Magham Down *E.Suss.* ***Village***, 2m/3km NE of Hailsham. **13 K5** TQ6011.
Maghannan *W.Isles* ***Open space***, hillslope below Beinn Mheadhonach, 3m/4km E of head of Loch Tamanavay. **100 C5** NB0721.
Maghull *Mersey.* Population: 21,905. ***Town***, 8m/13km N of Liverpool. **48 C2** SD3702.
Magillie Loch *D. & G. Alternative name for Loch Magillie, qv.*
Magna Carta Island *W. & M.* ***Island***, in River Thames, opposite Runnymede, 1m/2km NW of Egham. Said to be actual site of sealing of Magna Carta by King John in 1215. SU9972.
Magor (Magwyr). *Mon.* Population: 3962. ***Village***, 8m/13km SW of Chepstow. **19 H3** ST4287.
Magpie Green *Suff.* ***Settlement***, 3m/5km W of Diss. TM0778.
Magus Muir *Fife* ***Settlement***, 1m/2km SW of Strathkinness. **83 F6** NO4515.
Magwyr *Mon. Welsh form of Magor, qv.*
Maich Water *Renf.* ***River***, rising on SE slopes of Misty Law and flowing SE to Kilbirnie Loch. **74 B4** NS3355.
Maida Vale *Gt.Lon.* ***Suburb***, in City of Westminster, 3m/5km NW of Charing Cross. TQ2582.
Maiden Bradley *Wilts.* ***Village***, 4m/6km N of Mere. **9 G1** ST8038.
Maiden Castle *Dorset* ***Historic/prehistoric site***, large oval prehistoric earthworks (English Heritage), 2m/3km SW of Dorchester. **9 F6** SY6688.
Maiden Head *N.Som.* ***Hamlet***, 1km SE of Dundry and 4m/7km S of Bristol. ST5666.
Maiden Island *Arg. & B.* ***Island***, islet 1m/2km N of Oban, Argyll. **79 K4** NM8431.
Maiden Law *Dur.* ***Hamlet***, 1m/2km N of Lanchester. **62 C2** NZ1749.
Maiden Newton *Dorset* ***Village***, on River Frome, 8m/13km NW of Dorchester. **8 E5** SY5997.
Maiden Pap *High.* ***Mountain***, 3m/4km E of Morven. Height 1588 feet or 484 metres. **105 F6** ND0429.
Maiden Paps *Sc.Bord.* ***Mountain***, 3m/4km SW of Shankend. Height 1676 feet or 511 metres. **69 K3** NT5002.
Maiden Stone *Aber.* ***Historic/prehistoric site***, 10 foot high 9c red granite Pictish symbol stone, 2m/3km E of Oyne. Pictish symbols carved on one side, Celtic cross on other. **91 F2** NJ7024.
Maiden Wells *Pembs.* ***Hamlet***, 1m/2km SW of Pembroke. **16 C5** SR9799.
Maidencombe *Torbay* ***Hamlet***, overlooking Babbacombe Bay, 3m/4km N of Torquay. **5 K4** SX9268.
Maidenhayne *Devon* ***Hamlet***, to N of Musbury, 3m/4km SW of Axminster. SY2795.
Maidenhead *W. & M.* Population: 59,605. ***Town***, on River Thames, 5m/8km W of Slough. 18c river bridge; 19c railway bridge, by Brunel. **22 B3** SU8881.
Maidenhead Bay *S.Ayr.* ***Bay***, between Culzean and Turnberry. **67 G3** NS2108.
Maidens *S.Ayr.* ***Village***, fishing village on Maidenhead Bay, 5m/9km W of Maybole. **67 G3** NS2107.
Maiden's Green *Brack.F.* ***Hamlet***, 1km W of Winkfield and 3m/4km NE of Bracknell. **22 C4** SU9072.
Maidenwell *Cornw.* ***Settlement***, 3m/5km SE of Blisland. **4 B3** SX1470.
Maidenwell *Lincs.* ***Hamlet***, 5m/8km S of Louth. **53 G5** TF3279.
Maidford *Northants.* ***Village***, 6m/9km NW of Towcester. **31 H3** SP6052.
Maids' Moreton *Bucks.* ***Village***, 1m/2km NE of Buckingham. **31 J5** SP7035.
Maidstone *Kent* Population: 90,878. ***Town***, county town on River Medway. Paper manufacture replaced cloth industry and town still has an industrial base. 14c Archbishop's Palace on riverbank. **14 C2** TQ7655.
Maidstone Museum and Art Gallery *Kent* ***Other feature of interest***, local museum housed in Elizabethan building in Maidstone. **14 C2** TQ7556.
Maidwell *Northants.* ***Village***, 7m/11km S of Market Harborough. **31 J1** SP7476.
Mail *Shet.* ***Settlement***, on E coast of Mainland, 1m/2km S of Starkigarth. **109 D10** HU4327.
Main Water of Luce *D. & G.* ***River***, rising 4m/7km SE of Ballantrae, and flowing S to join Cross Water of Luce at New Luce, to form Water of Luce. **64 B4** NX1764.
Maindee (Maendy). *Newport* ***Suburb***, 1m/2km E of Newport town centre. ST3288.
Mainland (Formerly known as Pomona.) *Ork.* ***Island***, largest island of Orkney group, being 26m/42km long from Brough Head in NW to Rose Ness in SE, and of irregular shape. Kirkwall, chief town of island and of group, is 24m/38km N of Duncansby Head on Scottish mainland across Scapa Flow and Pentland Firth. Kirkwall Airport 3m/4km SE of Kirkwall. **107 B6** HY4010.
Mainland *Shet.* ***Island***, largest island of Shetland, containing Lerwick, the capital, on E coast. Island is 56m/90km long N to S, and generally narrow E to W, being much indented by inlets or voes. **109 C6** HU4149.
Mains *S.Lan.* ***Suburb***, comprised of East Mains and West Mains, to N of East Kilbride town centre. NS6354.
Mains of Ardestie *Angus* ***Hamlet***, 1m/2km N of Monifieth. **83 G4** NO5034.
Mains of Balhall *Angus* ***Hamlet***, 1m/2km SW of Kirkton of Menmuir. **83 G1** NO5163.
Mains of Ballindarg *Angus* ***Hamlet***, 2m/3km SE of Kirriemuir. **83 F2** NO4051.
Mains of Burgie *Moray* ***Settlement***, 3m/5km E of Forres. **97 H6** NJ0959.
Mains of Culsh *Aber.* ***Settlement***, 1m/2km N of New Deer. **99 G6** NJ8848.
Mains of Dillavaird *Aber.* ***Settlement***, 2m/3km NW of Glenbervie. **91 F6** NO7381.
Mains of Drum *Aber.* ***Settlement***, 5m/8km W of Peterculter. **91 G4** NO8099.
Mains of Dudwick *Aber.* ***Settlement***, 4m/7km W of Hatton. **91 H1** NJ9737.
Mains of Faillie *High.* ***Settlement***, 2m/3km SW of Daviot. **88 E1** NH7037.
Mains of Fedderate *Aber.* ***Settlement***, 3m/4km NW of Maud. **99 G6** NJ8950.
Mains of Glenbuchat *Aber.* ***Settlement***, on W side of River Don, 3m/5km NE of Strathdon. Ruins of Glenbuchat Castle, built 1590, nearby. **90 B3** NJ3914.
Mains of Linton *Aber.* ***Settlement***, 1km SE of Sauchen. **91 F4** NJ7010.
Mains of Melgund *Angus* ***Hamlet***, 3m/5km E of Finavon. **83 G2** NO5456.
Mains of Pitfour *Aber.* ***Settlement***, 1m/2km NW of Mintlaw. **99 H6** NJ9849.
Mains of Pittrichie *Aber.* ***Settlement***, 4m/6km SE of Oldmeldrum. **91 G2** NJ8624.
Mains of Sluie *Moray* ***Settlement***, on E bank of River Findhorn, 4m/6km SW of Forres. **97 H6** NJ0053.
Mains of Tannachy *Moray* ***Settlement***, near N coast, 1km W of Portgordon. **98 B4** NJ3863.
Mains of Thornton *Aber.* ***Settlement***, 2m/3km SE of Fettercairn. **90 E7** NO6871.
Mains of Tig *S.Ayr.* ***Settlement***, 3m/4km E of Ballantrae. **67 F5** NX1283.
Mains of Watten *High.* ***Settlement***, 1m/2km NE of Watten, on N side of Loch Watten. **105 H3** ND2456.
Mainsforth *Dur.* ***Hamlet***, 3m/5km NW of Sedgefield. NZ3131.
Mainsriddle *D. & G.* ***Settlement***, 2m/3km NW of Southerness. **65 K5** NX9456.
Mainstone *Shrop.* ***Village***, 5m/8km N of Clun. **38 B7** SO2787.
Maisemore *Glos.* ***Village***, on W bank of River Severn, 2m/3km NW of Gloucester. **29 H6** SO8121.
Maisgeir *Arg. & B.* ***Island***, rock island off SW coast of Gometra, Mull. **78 E4** NM3439.
Maison Dieu *Kent* ***Historic house***, 15c house (English Heritage), part of complex of medieval buildings at Ospringe, 1km SW of Faversham. Includes decorative 16c ceiling and museum on Roman Ospringe. **25 G5** TR0060.
Maitland Park *Gt.Lon.* ***Suburb***, in borough of Camden, 3m/5km NW of Charing Cross. TQ2884.
Major's Green *Worcs.* ***Hamlet***, 1m/2km NE of Hollywood and 6m/10km SE of Birmingham city centre. SP1077.
Majorsbarn *Staffs.* ***Suburb***, adjoining to S of Cheadle. SK0042.
Makendon *Northumb.* ***Settlement***, in Cheviot Hills, 2m/3km SW of Blindburn. **70 D3** NT8009.
Makeney *Derbys.* ***Village***, 1km NE of Duffield. SK3544.
Maker-with-Rame *Cornw.* ***Locality***, S of Millbrook. SX4250.
Makerstoun *Sc.Bord.* ***Settlement***, 4m/6km W of Kelso. **76 E7** NT6732.
Malacleit (Anglicised form: Malaclete.) *W.Isles* ***Settlement***, on North Uist, 1m/2km SW of Solas. **92 C4** NF7974.
Malaclete *W.Isles Anglicised form of Malacleit, qv.*
Malasgair *W.Isles* ***Hill***, NE of head of Loch Seaforth, Isle of Lewis. Height 564 feet or 172 metres. **100 E6** NB2917.
Malborough *Devon* ***Village***, 2m/3km W of Salcombe. **5 H7** SX7039.
Malcolm's Head *Shet.* ***Coastal feature***, headland on NW coast of Fair Isle. **108 A1** HZ1970.
Malcolm's Point *Arg. & B.* ***Coastal feature***, headland on S coast of Ross of Mull, 3m/5km SW of Carsaig. **79 F6** NM4918.
Malden Rushett *Gt.Lon.* ***Village***, in borough of Kingston upon Thames, 2m/4km W of Epsom. **22 E5** TQ1761.
Maldon *Essex* Population: 15,841. ***Town***, old port town at head of River Blackwater estuary, 9m/14km E of Chelmsford. Old buildings include 15c moot hall and unique tower on All Saints' Church. Battle of Maldon fought to SE of town in 991. **24 E1** TL8507.
Malham *N.Yorks.* ***Village***, in Upper Airedale, 5m/8km E of Settle across moors. **56 E3** SD9062.
Malham National Park Centre *N.Yorks.* ***Other feature of interest***, tourist and visitor centre for Yorkshire Dales National Park, N of Kirkby Malham, beneath Malham Cove. Has information on Malham Cove, Malham Tarn and Gordale Scar. **56 D3** SD8962.
Malham Tarn *N.Yorks.* ***Lake/loch***, tarn on limestone moors above Malham Cove, 2m/3km N of Malham; probable source of River Aire. **56 D3** SD8966.
Malham Tarn Estate *N.Yorks.* ***Open space***, upland limestone area (National Trust) of Yorkshire Dales to S and E of Malham Tarn, with several large hill farms; diversity of flora and birdlife. The Pennine Way long distance path passes through estate. **56 D3** SD8966.
Maligar *High.* ***Settlement***, 1m/2km S of Staffin, Skye. **93 K5** NG4864.
Malinbridge *S.Yorks.* ***Suburb***, 2m/3km NW of Sheffield city centre. SK3289.
Malins Lee *Tel. & W.* ***Suburb***, to N of Dawley. SJ6808.
Mallaig *High.* ***Town***, small fishing port and railway terminus on coast of Lochaber district at entrance to Sound of Sleat, and S of entrance to Loch Inver. Vehicle ferry to Armadale, Skye. **86 C5** NM6796.
Mallaigmore *High.* ***Settlement***, on N coast of North Morar, 1m/2km W of Mallaig. **86 D5** NM6997.
Mallaigvaig *High.* ***Locality***, on coast of Lochaber district, 1m/2km NE of Mallaig. **86 C5** NM6997.
Mallart *High.* ***River***, running N through Loch Choire into River Naver below Loch Naver in Caithness district. **103 J5** NC6737.
Malleny House *Edin.* ***Garden***, surrounding 17c house at Balerno. Garden (National Trust for Scotland) includes National Collection of Bonsai and display of shrub roses. **75 K4** NT1666.
Malleny Mills *Edin.* ***Hamlet***, 1km SE of Balerno. **75 K4** NT1665.
Mallerstang Common *Cumb.* ***Open space***, moorland to E of Howgill Fells, on either side of River Eden valley, 5m/8km S of Kirkby Stephen. **61 J7** SD7798.
Malletsheugh *E.Renf.* ***Settlement***, 1km W of Newton Mearns. **74 D5** NS5255.
Malling *Stir.* ***Settlement***, on W side of Lake of Menteith, 3m/4km E of Aberfoyle. **81 G7** NN5600.
Mallowdale Fell *Lancs.* ***Open space***, moorland on Forest of Bowland, 6m/9km S of Wray. **56 B4** SD6159.
Mallows Green *Essex* ***Settlement***, 3m/5km N of Bishop's Stortford. TL4726.
Malltraeth (Malltraeth Yard). *I.o.A.* ***Village***, at head of River Cefni estuary on Anglesey. **46 C6** SH4068.
Malltraeth Bay *I.o.A.* ***Bay***, at mouth of River Cefni, extending from Pen-y-parc to Llanddwyn Island. **46 B6** SH3764.
Malltraeth Marsh (Cors Ddyga). *I.o.A.* ***Marsh/bog***, drained wetland in valley of River Cefni on Anglesey, to S of Llangefni. Marshy fringes to NE. **46 C5** SH4471.
Malltraeth Sands *I.o.A.* ***Coastal feature***, sands covering River Cefni estuary at low tide. **46 B6** SH4068.
Malltraeth Yard *I.o.A. See Malltraeth.*
Mallwyd *Gwyn.* ***Hamlet***, 10m/16km NE of Machynlleth. **37 H4** SH8612.
Mallyan Spout *N.Yorks.* ***Waterfall***, in West Beck 1km W of Goathland. **63 K6** NZ8201.
Malmesbury *Wilts.* Population: 4439. ***Small town***, county town on River Avon, 14m/22km W of Swindon. Parish church is remains of medieval abbey. Market cross. Former weaving centre. **20 C3** ST9387.
Malmesbury Abbey *Wilts.* ***Ecclesiastical building***, 12c remains of important Benedictine house founded at Malmesbury. Strikingly sculptured S porch. Contains alleged tomb of King Athelstan. **20 C3** ST9387.
Malmsmead *Devon* ***Hamlet***, 5m/8km E of Lynton. **7 F1** SS7947.
Malpas *Ches.* ***Small town***, 8m/15km E of Wrexham. Some half-timbered houses. **38 D1** SJ4847.
Malpas *Cornw.* ***Village***, 2m/3km SE of Truro, at confluence of Rivers Tresillian and Truro. **3 F4** SW8442.
Malpas *Newport* ***Suburb***, 2m/3km N of Newport. **19 G2** ST3090.
Maltby *Lincs.* ***Settlement***, 2m/4km SW of Louth. TF3183.
Maltby *S.Yorks.* Population: 18,158. ***Town***, 6m/10km E of Rotherham. **51 H3** SK5292.
Maltby *Stock.* ***Village***, 4m/6km S of Stockton-on-Tees. **63 F5** NZ4613.
Maltby le Marsh *Lincs.* ***Village***, 4m/6km SW of Mablethorpe. **53 H4** TF4681.

M

Malting End *Suff.* ***Settlement***, to SW of Wickhambrook, 7m/12km NE of Haverhill. TL7454.
Malting Green *Essex* ***Village***, 3m/5km S of Colchester. TL9720.
Maltman's Hill *Kent* ***Hamlet***, 5m/8km SW of Charing. **14 E3** TQ9043.
Malton *N.Yorks.* Population: 4294. ***Small town***, on River Derwent, on site of Roman station, 17m/27km NE of York. Agricultural centre. **58 D2** SE7871.
Malvern Hills ***Large natural feature***, narrow range of hills, rising sharply from Severn valley and running N and S for 8m/13km. Mainly ancient metamorphic rocks. The inland resort of Great Malvern is to E of N end. Highest point is Worcestershire Beacon, 1394 feet or 425 metres, near N end. S end, at Chase End Hill, is 4m/6km SE of Ledbury. **29 G4** SO7641.
Malvern Link *Worcs.* ***Suburb***, N district of Great Malvern. **29 G4** SO7848.
Malvern Wells *Worcs.* ***Village***, under E slope of Malvern Hills, 2m/4km S of Great Malvern town centre. Three Counties (Agricultural) Showground to E. **29 G4** SO7742.
Mam a' Chullaich *High.* ***Mountain***, 2m/3km N of Rubha an Ridire. Height 1515 feet or 462 metres. **79 J3** NM7443.
Mam na Gualainn *High.* ***Mountain***, in Lochaber district on N side of Loch Leven and 4m/7km W of Kinlochleven. Height 2611 feet or 796 metres. **80 C1** NN1162.
Mam Sodhail (Anglicised form: Mam Soul.) *High.* ***Mountain***, on border of Inverness and Skye and Lochalsh districts 3m/4km NW of Loch Affric. Munro: height 3870 feet or 1180 metres. **87 H2** NH1225.
Mam Soul *High. Anglicised form of Mam Sodhail, qv.*
Màm Suim *High.* ***Open space***, hillslope forming N shoulder of Stac na h-Iolaire, 3m/5km E of Loch Morlich. **89 H4** NJ0108.
Mam Tor (Also known as Shivering Mountain.) *Derbys.* ***Mountain***, National Trust property surmounted by Iron Age fort, 1m/2km W of Castleton. Height 1696 feet or 517 metres. Also known as 'Shivering Mountain' owing to continuous slumping of S face. **50 D4** SK1283.
Mambeg *Arg. & B.* ***Settlement***, on W shore of Gare Loch, 1m/2km SW of Garelochhead. **74 A2** NS2389.
Mamble *Worcs.* ***Village***, 3m/5km S of Cleobury Mortimer. **29 F1** SO6871.
Mamhead *Devon* ***Locality***, parish, with church in grounds of Mamhead House, 3m/5km NW of Dawlish. **7 H7** SX9381.
Mamheilad *Mon. Welsh form of Mamhilad, qv.*
Mamhilad (Mamheilad). *Mon.* ***Hamlet***, 2m/4km NE of Pontypool. **19 G1** SO3003.
Mamore Forest *High.* ***Open space***, mountain tract in Lochaber district between Kinlochleven and Glen Nevis. **80 C1** NN1765.
Man and his man *Cornw. Alternative name for Bawden Rocks, qv.*
Manaccan *Cornw.* ***Village***, 7m/11km E of Helston. **2 E6** SW7625.
Manacle Point *Cornw.* ***Coastal feature***, headland at easternmost point of Lizard peninsula, 7m/11km S of Falmouth across bay. **3 F6** SW8121.
Manadon *Plym.* ***Suburb***, 2m/4km N of Plymouth city centre. SX4858.
Manafon *Powys* ***Hamlet***, on River Rhiw, 3m/4km S of Llanfair Caereinion. **38 A5** SJ1102.
Manais (Anglicised form: Manish.) *W.Isles* ***Settlement***, on SE coast of South Harris, 8m/12km S of Tarbert. **93 G3** NG1089.
Manaton *Devon* ***Village***, on E edge of Dartmoor, 3m/5km S of Moretonhampstead. **7 F7** SX7581.
Manby *Lincs.* ***Village***, 5m/7km E of Louth. Airfield to W. **53 G4** TF3986.
Mancetter *Warks.* ***Village***, adjoining to SE of Atherstone. To E, on Leicestershire border, is site of Roman settlement of Manduessedum. **41 F6** SP3296.
Manchester *Gt.Man.* Population: 402,889. ***City***, important industrial, business, cultural and commercial centre and port, 164m/264km NW of London. Access for ships by River Mersey and Manchester Ship Canal, opened in 1894. 15c cathedral, formerly parish church, has widest nave in England. Experienced rapid growth during industrial revolution. In 1750, Manchester was essentially still a village. During Victorian era, city was global cotton milling capital. Present day city is home to wide range of industries and is unofficial capital of nation's 'youth culture'. Major shopping centres include Arndale and Trafford Centres. Universities. International airport 9m/14km S of city centre. **49 H3** SJ8398.
Manchester Airport *Gt.Man.* ***Airport/airfield***, international airport, 9m/14km S of Manchester city centre and 3m/5km SE of Altrincham. Built to E of Ringway locality. **49 H4** SJ8084.
Manchester Cathedral *Gt.Man.* ***Ecclesiastical building***, largely Perpendicular building dating from late 15c, in Manchester city centre. Elevated to cathedral status in 1827. Notable carved choir stalls. **49 H3** SJ8498.
Manchester City Art Galleries *Gt.Man.* ***Other feature of interest***, in Manchester city centre, exhibiting some major Pre-Raphaelite art and 19c porcelain and furniture. **49 H3** SJ8498.
Mancot Royal *Flints.* ***Locality***, 1m/2km N of Hawarden. **48 C6** SJ3266.
Mandale Marshes *Stock.* ***Locality***, 1m/2km E of Stockton-on-Tees across River Tees. Location of Teesside Retail Park. NZ4618.
Mandally *High.* ***Locality***, containing settlements of Easter Mandally and Wester Mandally across River Garry from Invergarry. **87 J4** NH2900.
Manderston *Sc.Bord.* ***Historic house***, 2m/3km E of Duns. Edwardian country mansion with luxurious interior, unique silver staircase and marble dairy. Includes Biscuit Tin Museum. **77 G5** NT8154.
Manduessedum *Warks. See Mancetter.*
Manea *Cambs.* Population: 1186. ***Village***, 6m/10km E of Chatteris. **43 H7** TL4789.
Maneight *E.Ayr.* ***Settlement***, below Maneight Hill, 4m/7km NE of Dalmellington. **67 K3** NS5409.
Maney *W.Mid.* ***Suburb***, to S of Sutton Coldfield town centre. SP1295.
Manfield *N.Yorks.* ***Village***, 4m/7km W of Darlington. **62 D5** NZ2213.
Mangaster *Shet.* ***Settlement***, in N part of Mainland, on N side of inlet of St. Magnus Bay called Mangaster Voe. **108 C5** HU3270.
Mangersta *W.Isles Anglicised form of Mangurstadh, qv.*
Mangerton *Dorset* ***Settlement***, on Mangerton River, 3m/4km NE of Bridport. SY4895.
Mangotsfield *S.Glos.* Population: 27,860. ***Town***, 5m/8km NE of Bristol. **19 K4** ST6576.
Mangrove Green *Herts.* ***Hamlet***, 3m/4km NE of Luton town centre. TL1223.
Mangurstadh (Anglicised form: Mangersta.) *W.Isles* ***Settlement***, on W coast of Isle of Lewis, 6m/9km SW of Gallan Head. **100 C4** NB0031.
Manifold *Staffs.* ***River***, rising 4m/7km S of Buxton and flowing S through limestone country of Peak District National Park into River Dove at Thorpe, NW of Ashbourne. **50 D7** SK1450.
Manish *W.Isles Anglicised form of Manais, qv.*
Manish Island *High.* ***Island***, islet off Raasay to SW of Manish Point. NG5648.
Manish Point *High.* ***Coastal feature***, N facing headland on W coast of Raasay, Skye, at entrance to Loch Arnish. **94 B7** NG5648.
Manish Point *W.Isles* ***Coastal feature***, headland on North Uist, 2m/3km NE of Aird an Rùnair. **92 C4** NF7173.
Mankinholes *W.Yorks.* ***Hamlet***, 2m/3km E of Todmorden. **56 E7** SD9623.
Manley *Ches.* ***Village***, 3m/4km SE of Helsby. **48 E5** SJ5071.
Manllegwaun *Carmar.* ***Locality***, 4m/6km SE of Newcastle Emlyn. SN3536.
Manmoel *Caerp.* ***Village***, 4m/6km S of Ebbw Vale. **18 E1** SO1703.
Mannamead *Plym.* ***Suburb***, 1m/2km N of Plymouth city centre. SX4856.
Mannel *Arg. & B.* ***Settlement***, on Hynish Bay, Tiree, 1km S of Balemartine. **78 A3** NL9840.
Manningford *Wilts.* ***Locality***, parish adjoining to N of Upavon, and containing villages of Manningford Abbots, Manningford Bohune, Manningford Bruce. SU1457.
Manningford Abbots *Wilts.* ***Village***, within Manningford parish, 1m/2km SW of Pewsey. **20 E6** SU1459.
Manningford Bohune *Wilts.* ***Village***, within Manningford parish, 2m/4km SW of Pewsey. **20 E6** SU1357.
Manningford Bruce *Wilts.* ***Village***, within Manningford parish, 2m/3km SW of Pewsey. **20 E6** SU1358.
Manningham *W.Yorks.* ***Suburb***, 1m/2km NW of Bradford city centre. SE1534.
Mannings Heath *W.Suss.* ***Village***, 2m/4km SE of Horsham. **13 F4** TQ2028.
Mannington *Dorset* ***Hamlet***, 5m/8km NE of Wimborne Minster. **10 B4** SU0605.
Mannington Hall *Norf.* ***Garden***, surrounding moated hall 2m/3km NE of Saxthorpe, with lake, woodlands and heritage rose collection. **45 F2** TG1432.
Manningtree *Essex* Population: 5043. ***Small town***, at head of River Stour estuary 8m/12km NE of Colchester. **35 F5** TM1031.
Mannofield *Aberdeen* ***Suburb***, 2m/3km SW of Aberdeen city centre. **91 H4** NJ9104.
Manor *S.Yorks.* ***Suburb***, 3m/4km SE of Sheffield city centre. SK3885.
Manor Country Park *Kent* ***Leisure/recreation***, over 50 acres of parkland surrounding Douces Manor to E of West Malling, including lake which attracts great numbers of water birds and other wildlife. **23 K6** TQ6857.
Manor House Gallery and Museum *W.Yorks.* ***Other feature of interest***, in Ilkley, giving history of town. Part of Roman wall nearby. **57 G5** SE1147.
Manor Park *Gt.Lon.* ***Suburb***, in borough of Newham, 1m/2km N of East Ham. TQ4285.
Manor Park *Slo.* ***Suburb***, N district of Slough. SU9681.
Manor Water *Sc.Bord.* ***River***, rising 2m/3km SE of Dollar Law in Ettrick Forest and running N to join River Tweed 1m/2km SW of Peebles. **76 A7** NT2239.
Manorbier (Maenorbyr). *Pembs.* ***Village***, near coast, 4m/7km SW of Tenby. Remains of Norman castle to W. **16 D5** SS0697.
Manorbier Castle *Pembs.* ***Castle***, at Manorbier, overlooking Manorbier Bay, 5m/8km SW of Tenby. 11c-13c well-preserved castle, birthplace of Gerald of Wales. **16 D5** SS0697.
Manorbier Newton *Pembs.* ***Hamlet***, 4m/6km E of Pembroke. SN0400.
Manordeifi *Pembs.* ***Settlement***, 4m/6km SE of Cardigan. **26 B4** SN2243.
Manordeilo *Carmar.* ***Hamlet***, 3m/5km NE of Llandeilo. **17 K2** SN6726.
Manorowen *Pembs.* ***Hamlet***, 2m/3km SW of Fishguard. **16 C1** SM9336.
Manselfield *Swan.* ***Locality***, 3m/5km NW of Mumbles Head. SS5988.
Mansell Gamage *Here.* ***Village***, 8m/13km W of Hereford. **28 C4** SO3944.
Mansell Lacy *Here.* ***Village***, 6m/10km NW of Hereford. **28 D4** SO4245.
Manselton *Swan.* ***Suburb***, 1m/2km N of Swansea city centre. SS6595.
Mansergh *Cumb.* ***Settlement***, 3m/4km N of Kirkby Lonsdale. **56 B1** SD6082.
Mansewood *Glas.* ***Suburb***, 3m/5km SW of Glasgow city centre. NS5660.
Mansfield *Notts.* Population: 71,858. ***Town***, 14m/22km N of Nottingham. Previously important for its coalmining, textiles and quarrying and now a commercial and shopping centre. **51 H6** SK5361.
Mansfield Woodhouse *Notts.* Population: 18,204. ***Town***, adjoining to N of Mansfield. **51 H6** SK5463.
Manson Green *Norf.* ***Settlement***, 1m/2km N of Hingham. TG0203.
Mansriggs *Cumb.* ***Settlement***, 2m/3km N of Ulverston. **55 F1** SD2980.
Manston *Dorset* ***Village***, 2m/3km NE of Sturminster Newton. **9 H3** ST8115.
Manston *Kent* Population: 2295. ***Suburb***, in W part of Ramsgate. Airport to W. **25 K5** TR3466.
Manston *W.Yorks.* ***Suburb***, 4m/7km E of Leeds city centre. SE3634.
Manswood *Dorset* ***Hamlet***, 6m/10km E of Blandford Forum. **9 J4** ST9708.
Manthorpe *Lincs.* ***Hamlet***, 3m/5km SW of Bourne. **42 D4** TF0716.
Manthorpe *Lincs.* ***Village***, 1m/2km N of Grantham. **42 C2** SK9237.
Manton *N.Lincs.* ***Hamlet***, 3m/4km N of Kirton in Lindsey. **52 C2** SE9302.
Manton *Notts.* ***Suburb***, SE district of Worksop. SK5978.
Manton *Rut.* ***Village***, 3m/5km S of Oakham. **42 B5** SK8804.
Manton *Wilts.* ***Hamlet***, 1m/2km W of Marlborough. **20 E5** SU1768.
Manuden *Essex* ***Village***, 3m/5km N of Bishop's Stortford. **33 H6** TL4926.
Manwood Green *Essex* ***Settlement***, 3m/5km W of Leaden Roding. TL5412.
Manx Electric Railway *I.o.M.* ***Other feature of interest***, railway line between Douglas and Ramsey, with panoramic view of Douglas Bay. **54 D5** SC4594.
Manx Museum *I.o.M.* ***Other feature of interest***, museum (Manx National Heritage) in Douglas covering all aspects of island life, housing a 4.5 ton whale skeleton and large-scale model of Viking warship. **54 C6** SC3876.
Maodal *W.Isles* ***Hill***, on W coast of South Harris, 3m/4km NW of Leverburgh. Height 823 feet or 251 metres. **93 F2** NF9990.
Maoile Lunndaidh *High.* ***Mountain***, in Ross and Cromarty district 3m/5km N of Loch Monar. Munro: height 3303 feet or 1007 metres. **95 H7** NH1345.
Maol Bàn *Arg. & B.* ***Mountain***, 3m/5km SW of Rubha nan Sailthean, Mull. Height 1109 feet or 338 metres. **79 H5** NM6823.
Maol Breac ***Mountain***, on border of Stirling and Argyll & Bute, 4m/6km W of Ardlui. Height 2116 feet or 645 metres. **80 D6** NN2515.
Maol Buidhe *Arg. & B.* ***Hill***, on The Oa, Islay, 4m/7km W of Port Ellen. Height 541 feet or 165 metres. **72 A6** NR2945.
Maol Chean-dearg *High.* ***Mountain***, on Ben-damph Forest, Ross and Cromarty district, 5m/8km N of head of Loch Carron. Munro: height 3060 feet or 933 metres. **95 F6** NG9249.
Maol Chinn-dearg *High.* ***Mountain***, peak along ridge on border of Lochaber and Skye and Lochalsh district between Loch Quoich and head of Loch Cluanie. Munro: height 3218 feet or 981 metres. **87 G4** NH0308.
Maol Mòr *Stir.* ***Mountain***, 2m/3km NW of Stronachlachar. Height 2250 feet or 686 metres. **80 E6** NN3711.
Maol na Coille Mòire *Arg. & B.* ***Hill***, 3m/4km SW of Ben More, Mull. Height 945 feet or 288 metres. **79 F4** NM4929.
Maol nan Uan *Arg. & B.* ***Hill***, 1m/2km E of Pennyghael, Mull. Height 899 feet or 274 metres. **79 G5** NM5325.
Maol nan Uan *Arg. & B.* ***Mountain***, 3m/5km W of Duart Point, Mull. Radio mast. Height 1407 feet or 429 metres. **79 J4** NM7035.
Maol Odhar *High.* ***Mountain***, rising to over 790 metres, 2m/3km NE of Fuar Bheinn, Lochaber district. **80 A2** NM8857.
Maol Ruadh *High.* ***Inland physical feature***, ridge extending SE to Meall na h-Uamha, 3m/5km S of Port Henderson, in Ross and Cromarty district. **94 D5** NG7568.
Maolachy *Arg. & B.* ***Settlement***, 1m/2km SW of head of Loch Avich. **79 K6** NM8912.
Maovally *High.* ***Hill***, 3m/5km W of mouth of Kyle of Durness. Height 981 feet or 299 metres. **103 F2** NC3069.
Maovally *High.* ***Mountain***, 2m/3km SW of N end of Loch Shin. Height 1679 feet or 512 metres. **103 F6** NC3721.
Maperton *Som.* ***Village***, 3m/5km SW of Wincanton. **9 F2** ST6726.
Maple Cross *Herts.* Population: 2052. ***Hamlet***, 2m/3km SW of Rickmansworth. **22 D2** TQ0392.
Maplebeck *Notts.* ***Village***, 7m/11km NW of Newark-on-Trent. **51 K6** SK7160.
Mapledurham *Oxon.* ***Village***, on River Thames, 4m/6km NW of Reading across river. Tudor manor house. **21 K4** SU6776.
Mapledurham House and Mill *Oxon.* ***Historic house***, late 16c manor with late 18c chapel, 2m/3km E of Pangbourne and 4m/6km NW of Reading. Also fully restored 15c water mill which produces bran and flour. Home of Blount family; now occasionally used as film set. **21 K4** SU6776.
Mapledurwell *Hants.* ***Village***, 3m/5km E of Basingstoke. **21 K6** SU6851.
Maplehurst *W.Suss.* ***Hamlet***, 2m/3km NW of Cowfold. **12 E4** TQ1824.
Maplescombe *Kent* ***Hamlet***, 2m/3km SE of Farningham. TQ5664.
Mapleton (Also spelled Mappleton.) *Derbys.* ***Village***, 1m/2km NW of Ashbourne. **40 D1** SK1647.
Maplin Sands *Essex* ***Coastal feature***, sands off Essex coast at Foulness Island on N side of entrance to River Thames estuary. **25 G3** TR0088.
Mapperley *Derbys.* ***Village***, 2m/3km NW of Ilkeston. **41 G1** SK4343.
Mapperley *Notts.* ***Suburb***, 3m/4km NE of Nottingham city centre. SK5843.

Mapperley Park *Derbys.* ***Settlement***, 1km W of Mapperley and 3m/4km NW of Ilkeston. SK4243.
Mapperley Park *Notts.* ***Suburb***, 1m/2km N of Nottingham city centre. SK5742.
Mapperton *Dorset* ***Hamlet***, 2m/3km SE of Beaminster. **8 E5** SY5099.
Mapperton *Dorset* ***Settlement***, 3m/4km W of Sturminster Marshall. SY9098.
Mapperton Gardens *Dorset* ***Garden***, to W of Mapperton, with Italianate features, fishponds and shrub gardens. **8 E5** SY5099.
Mappleborough Green *Warks.* ***Suburb***, 3m/5km SE of Redditch. **30 B2** SP0765.
Mappleton *Derbys. Alternative spelling of Mapleton, qv.*
Mappleton *E.Riding* ***Village***, on coast, 3m/5km SE of Hornsea. **59 J5** TA2243.
Mapplewell *S.Yorks.* ***Locality***, adjoining to Staincross, 3m/4km NW of Barnsley. **51 F2** SE3209.
Mappowder *Dorset* ***Village***, 6m/10km SW of Sturminster Newton. **9 G4** ST7306.
Mar Forest *Aber.* ***Open space***, deer forest astride Glen Dee on S side of Cairngorm Mountains. **89 H5** NO0291.
Mar Lodge *Aber.* ***Hamlet***, 1m/2km NE of Inverey. **89 H5** NO0990.
Maratz Hill *S.Ayr.* ***Mountain***, rising to over 320 metres, 3m/5km SE of Straiton. **67 J3** NS4302.
Marazion *Cornw.* Population: 1381. ***Small town***, 3m/4km E of Penzance across Mount's Bay. Oldest charter town in Cornwall. Causeway to St. Michael's Mount. **2 C5** SW5130.
Marble Arch *Gt.Lon.* ***Other feature of interest***, arch in City of Westminster, 3m/5km NW of Charing Cross. Designed by John Nash, 1827, based on Arch of Constantine in Rome and intended to be a grand new entrance for Buckingham Palace. Only when finished was it discovered to be too narrow for state coach to pass through, so it had to be moved to its present site. From 14c to 1783, this was location of Tyburn Gallows, the main execution site for London. TQ2780.
Marble Hill *Gt.Lon.* ***Historic house***, 18c Palladian villa (English Heritage) in borough of Richmond upon Thames on N bank of River Thames, 1m/2km SW of Richmond. Built for George II's mistress, Henrietta Howard, it contains period interior and furnishings. Set in 66 acres of parkland, where concerts held during summer. **22 E4** TQ1773.
Marbury *Ches.* ***Settlement***, 2m/3km N of Northwich. SJ6476.
Marbury *Ches.* ***Village***, 3m/5km NE of Whitchurch. **38 E1** SJ5645.
Marbury Country Park *Ches.* ***Leisure/recreation***, 190 acre country park to S of Budworth Mere, 1m/2km N of Northwich. Includes woodland walks, canal and hides from which wide variety of birds can be observed. **49 F5** SJ6576.
March *Cambs.* Population: 16,221. ***Town***, Fenland market town on site of Saxon settlement, 14m/22km E of Peterborough, on River Nene (old course). **43 H6** TL4196.
March Burn *D. & G.* ***River***, rising on E side of Troston Hill, flowing SE to join New Abbey Pow 1m/2km E of New Abbey and just W of confluence with River Nith. NX9766.
March Ghyll Reservoir *N.Yorks.* ***Reservoir***, small reservoir 2m/4km N of Ilkley. **57 G4** SE1251.
Marcham *Oxon.* Population: 1759. ***Village***, 3m/4km W of Abingdon. **21 H2** SU4596.
Marchamley *Shrop.* ***Village***, 6m/9km SW of Market Drayton. **38 E3** SJ5929.
Marchamley Wood *Shrop.* ***Settlement***, 1m/2km N of Marchamley. SJ5931.
Marchington *Staffs.* ***Village***, 3m/5km SE of Uttoxeter. **40 D2** SK1330.
Marchington Woodlands *Staffs.* ***Settlement***, 2m/3km SW of Marchington. **40 D3** SK1128.
Marchmont *Edin.* ***Suburb***, 1m/2km S of Edinburgh city centre. NT2572.
Marchnant *Cere.* ***River***, rising 1m/2km W of Llyn Fyrddon Fach, flowing W, to join River Meurig. Combined river then flows S into River Teifi, 1km W of Pontrhydfendigaid. **27 G2** SN7268.
Marchros *Gwyn.* ***Village***, 1m/2km S of Abersoch. SH3126.
Marchwiel *Wrex.* ***Village***, 2m/4km SE of Wrexham. **38 C1** SJ3547.
Marchwood *Hants.* Population: 4908. ***Village***, 3m/5km SE of Totton. **10 E3** SU3810.
Marcroes *V. of Glam. Welsh form of Marcross, qv.*
Marcross (Marcroes). *V. of Glam.* ***Village***, 3m/4km W of Llantwit Major. **18 C5** SS9269.
Marcus *Angus* ***Settlement***, 1m/2km E of Finavon. **83 G2** NO5157.
Mardale Common *Cumb.* ***Open space***, steep hillside on E side of Haweswater Reservoir, 5m/8km SW of Shap. **61 F5** NY4812.
Marden *Here.* ***Village***, on River Lugg, 4m/7km N of Hereford. **28 E4** SO5147.
Marden *Kent* Population: 1635. ***Village***, 7m/11km S of Maidstone. **14 C3** TQ7444.
Marden *T. & W.* ***Suburb***, adjoining to S of Whitley Bay. **71 J6** NZ3570.
Marden *Wilts.* ***Village***, 5m/8km W of Pewsey. Hatfield Earthworks (English Heritage), Neolithic enclosure with Bronze Age barrow, to NE. **20 D6** SU0857.
Marden Ash *Essex* ***Hamlet***, adjoining to S of Chipping Ongar. TL5502.
Marden Beech *Kent* ***Settlement***, 1m/2km S of Marden. **14 C3** TQ7343.
Marden Thorn *Kent* ***Hamlet***, 1m/2km SE of Marden. **14 C3** TQ7543.
Marden's Hill *E.Suss.* ***Hamlet***, 1m/2km NW of Crowborough. TQ4932.
Mardington *Sc.Bord.* ***Locality***, 4m/6km NW of Berwick-upon-Tweed. NT9456.
Mardon *Northumb.* ***Hamlet***, 1km E of Branxton. NT9037.
Mardy (Maerdy). *Mon.* ***Locality***, 1m/2km N of Abergavenny. **28 C7** SO3015.
Mare Fen *Cambs.* ***Open space***, fenland 1km NW of Littleport. **43 J7** TL5488.
Mare Green *Som.* ***Village***, 1m/2km NE of North Curry. **8 C2** ST3326.
Mare Tail *Lincs.* ***Coastal feature***, sandbank in SW part of The Wash, off Lincolnshire coast. **43 H2** TF4438.
Marefield *Leics.* ***Settlement***, 7m/11km S of Melton Mowbray. **42 A5** SK7407.
Mareham le Fen *Lincs.* ***Village***, 6m/9km S of Horncastle. **53 F6** TF2861.
Mareham on the Hill *Lincs.* ***Village***, 2m/3km SE of Horncastle. **53 F6** TF2867.
Marehay *Derbys.* ***Locality***, 1m/2km S of Ripley. SK3948.
Maresfield *E.Suss.* ***Village***, 2m/3km N of Uckfield. **13 H4** TQ4624.
Marfleet *Hull* ***Suburb***, 3m/5km E of Kingston upon Hull city centre. **59 H7** TA1429.
Marford *Wrex.* ***Village***, 4m/6km N of Wrexham. **48 C7** SJ3556.
Marg na Craige *High.* ***Mountain***, craggy summit, 5m/8km W of Newtonmore. Height 2736 feet or 834 metres. **88 D5** NN6297.
Margadale Hill *Arg. & B.* ***Hill***, near N end of Islay, 4m/7km NW of Port Askaig. Height 928 feet or 283 metres. **72 B3** NR3975.
Margam *N.P.T.* ***Locality***, SE district of Port Talbot. Large steel works. **18 A3** SS7887.
Margam Abbey Church *N.P.T.* ***Ecclesiastical building***, Cistercian foundation of 1147, 1m/2km SE of Margam. Most of original nave survives today as parish church; impressive restored Italianate frontage. **18 B3** SS8086.
Margam Burrows *N.P.T.* ***Coastal feature***, sand dunes to SW of Margam. **18 A3** SS7887.
Margam Country Park *N.P.T.* ***Leisure/recreation***, country park of over 800 acres to E of Margam. Attractions include fallow deer herd, Fairyland, a maze and giant chess and draughts. SS8088.
Margaret Marsh *Dorset* ***Village***, 3m/5km SW of Shaftesbury. **9 H3** ST8218.
Margaret Roding *Essex* ***Settlement***, 1m/2km S of Leaden Roding. **33 J7** TL5912.
Margaretting *Essex* ***Village***, 4m/6km SW of Chelmsford. **24 C1** TL6701.
Margaretting Tye *Essex* ***Hamlet***, 1m/2km SE of Margaretting. TL6800.
Margate *Kent* Population: 56,734. ***Town***, busy resort on Isle of Thanet, 15m/25km NE of Canterbury, with large harbour, sandy beaches and 19c pier. Became one of England's first coastal resorts when Benjamin Beale, a local Quaker, invented bathing machine which transported bathers from beach into sea. **25 K4** TR3570.
Margery Hill *S.Yorks.* ***Mountain***, in The Pennines, 3m/5km SW of Upper Midhope. Height 1791 feet or 546 metres. **50 D3** SK1895.
Margidunum *Notts. See Bingham.*
Margnaheglish *N.Ayr.* ***Village***, on Lamlash Bay on E coast of Arran, adjoining to NE of Lamlash village. **73 J7** NS0331.
Margreig *D. & G.* ***Settlement***, at head of Glenkiln Reservoir, 3m/4km NW of Shawhead. **65 J3** NX8378.
Margrove Park *R. & C.* ***Hamlet***, 3m/4km E of Guisborough. **63 H5** NZ6515.
Marham *Norf.* Population: 2254. ***Village***, 7m/12km W of Swaffham. Remains of 13c abbey. Airfield to SE. **44 B5** TF7009.
Marhamchurch *Cornw.* ***Village***, 2m/3km SE of Bude. **6 A5** SS2203.
Marholm *Peter.* ***Village***, 4m/6km NW of Peterborough. **42 E5** TF1402.
Marian Cwm *Denb.* ***Settlement***, 1m/2km SE of Dyserth. **47 J5** SJ0777.
Marian-glas *I.o.A.* ***Hamlet***, near E coast of Anglesey, 1m/2km S of Moelfre. **46 D4** SH5084.
Mariandyrys *I.o.A.* ***Settlement***, 3m/5km N of Beaumaris. SH6081.
Mariansleigh *Devon* ***Village***, 3m/5km SE of South Molton. **7 F3** SS7422.
Marine Town *Kent* ***Suburb***, to E of Sheerness. TQ9274.
Marishader *High.* ***Settlement***, 3m/5km S of Staffin Bay, Skye. **93 K5** NG4963.
Maristow *Devon* ***Hamlet***, by River Tavy, 6m/10km N of Plymouth. **4 E4** SX4764.
Marjoribanks *D. & G.* ***Locality***, 1km N of Lochmaben. NY0883.
Mark *Som.* ***Village***, 5m/8km E of Burnham-on-Sea. Elongated locality of Mark Causeway, 1m/2km W. **19 G7** ST3847.
Mark Causeway *Som.* ***Locality***, 1m/2km W of Mark. **19 G7** ST3647.
Mark Cross *E.Suss.* ***Village***, 5m/8km S of Royal Tunbridge Wells. **13 J3** TQ5831.
Mark Hall North *Essex* ***Suburb***, 1m/2km NE of Harlow town centre. TL4611.
Mark Hall South *Essex* ***Suburb***, 1m/2km E of Harlow town centre. TL4610.
Markbeech *Kent* ***Village***, 3m/5km SE of Edenbridge. **23 H7** TQ4742.
Markby *Lincs.* ***Village***, 3m/5km NE of Alford. **53 H5** TF4878.
Markdhu *D. & G.* ***Settlement***, 6m/10km SW of Barrhill. **64 B3** NX1873.
Markeaton *Derby* ***Settlement***, 2m/3km NW of Derby city centre. SK3337.
Markenfield Hall *N.Yorks.* ***Historic house***, dating from 14c, 3m/4km S of Ripon. **57 H3** SE2967.
Market Bosworth *Leics.* Population: 2019. ***Small town***, 6m/10km N of Hinckley. Bosworth Field, 2m/3km S, is site of battle in 1485 in which Henry Tudor defeated Richard III. **41 G5** SK4003.
Market Deeping *Lincs.* Population: 12,068. ***Village***, on River Welland, 7m/11km E of Stamford. **42 E4** TF1310.
Market Drayton *Shrop.* Population: 9482. ***Small town***, market town, 18m/28km NE of Shrewsbury. Georgian and timber-framed houses. **39 F2** SJ6734.
Market End *Warks.* ***Locality***, adjoining to W of Bedworth. SP3486.
Market Harborough *Leics.* Population: 16,563. ***Town***, former 18c coaching stop on River Welland, 14m/23km SE of Leicester. 13c weekly market still survives. 19c corset factory is now Harborough Museum, displaying the famous liberty bodice. Church has 14c steeple. **42 A7** SP7387.
Market Lavington *Wilts.* Population: 1731. ***Village***, 5m/7km S of Devizes. **20 D6** SU0154.
Market Overton *Rut.* ***Village***, 5m/8km N of Oakham. Site of Romano-British settlement 1m/2km E. **42 B4** SK8816.
Market Rasen *Lincs.* Population: 2948. ***Small town***, market and agricultural town, 14m/22km NE of Lincoln. Racecourse 1m/2km SE. **52 E4** TF1089.
Market Stainton *Lincs.* ***Village***, 6m/10km E of Wragby. **53 F5** TF2279.
Market Street *Norf.* ***Village***, 3m/5km N of Wroxham. **45 G3** TG2921.
Market Warsop *Notts.* Population: 10,083. ***Town***, 5m/7km NE of Mansfield. **51 H6** SK5667.
Market Weighton *E.Riding* Population: 4371. ***Small town***, 15m/24km NE of Goole. **58 E5** SE8741.
Market Weston *Suff.* ***Village***, 6m/10km NE of Ixworth. **34 D1** TL9877.
Markethill *P. & K.* ***Settlement***, 1km SE of Coupar Angus. **82 D4** NO2239.
Markfield *Leics.* Population: 3897. ***Village***, 7m/12km NW of Leicester. **41 G4** SK4810.
Markham *Caerp.* ***Village***, 2m/3km NE of Bargoed. **18 E1** SO1601.
Markham Moor *Notts.* ***Hamlet***, 2m/4km NW of Tuxford. **51 K5** SK7174.
Markinch *Fife* Population: 2176. ***Small town***, on E side of Glenrothes. 12c tower on St. Drosten's Church. **82 D7** NO2901.
Markington *N.Yorks.* ***Village***, 3m/4km N of Ripley. **57 H3** SE2864.
Markland Hill *Gt.Man.* ***Suburb***, 2m/3km W of Bolton town centre. SD6809.
Marks Gate *Gt.Lon.* ***Locality***, in borough of Barking and Dagenham, 5m/8km NE of Barking town centre. **23 H3** TQ4890.
Marks Tey *Essex* Population: 3593. ***Village***, 5m/8km W of Colchester. **34 D6** TL9123.
Marksbury *B. & N.E.Som.* ***Village***, 4m/6km S of Keynsham. **19 K5** ST6662.
Markwell *Cornw.* ***Hamlet***, 1m/2km S of Landrake. **4 D5** SX3658.
Markyate *Herts.* Population: 2866. ***Village***, 4m/6km SW of Luton. **32 D7** TL0616.
Marl Bank *Worcs.* ***Settlement***, 3m/5km S of Great Malvern. SO7840.
Marl Hill Moor *Lancs.* ***Open space***, moorland 4m/7km NW of Clitheroe. **56 B5** SD6846.
Marlais *Carmar.* ***River***, rising on Mynydd Pencarreg, flowing SE to Llansawel and into River Cothi 1m/2km to E. **17 K1** SN6436.
Marland *Gt.Man.* ***Suburb***, 1m/2km SW of Rochdale town centre. SD8711.
Marlborough *Wilts.* Population: 6429. ***Small town***, on River Kennet, 10m/16km S of Swindon at foot of Marlborough Downs. Noted for fine, wide High Street flanked by attractive buildings, many 18c. **20 E5** SU1869.
Marlborough Downs *Wilts.* ***Large natural feature***, undulating chalk upland area between Swindon in N and Marlborough in S. **20 E4** SU1869.
Marlbrook *Here.* ***Locality***, 3m/4km S of Leominster. SO5154.
Marlbrook *Worcs.* ***Settlement***, 3m/4km NE of Bromsgrove. SO9774.
Marlcliff *Warks.* ***Hamlet***, 6m/9km NE of Evesham. SP0950.
Marldon *Devon* ***Village***, on W side of Torbay district, 2m/4km NW of Paignton. **5 J4** SX8663.
Marle Green *E.Suss.* ***Settlement***, 1m/2km SE of Horam. TQ5916.
Marle Hill *Glos.* ***Suburb***, N district of Cheltenham. SO9523.
Marlesford *Suff.* ***Village***, 2m/3km NE of Wickham Market. **35 H3** TM3258.
Marley *Kent* ***Locality***, 1m/2km W of Barham. TR1850.
Marley Green *Ches.* ***Settlement***, 4m/6km NE of Whitchurch. **38 E1** SJ5845.
Marley Hill *T. & W.* ***Village***, 5m/8km SW of Gateshead. **62 D1** NZ2057.
Marlingford *Norf.* ***Village***, on River Yare, 5m/8km W of Norwich. **45 F5** TG1309.
Marloes *Pembs.* ***Village***, near coast, at S end of St. Brides Bay, 7m/11km W of Milford Haven. Parish includes Skomer Island and Grassholm Island and The Smalls rocks. Marloes Deer Park 2m/4km W. **16 A4** SM7908.
Marlow *Bucks.* Population: 17,771. ***Town***, commuter town on River Thames, with 19c suspension bridge and weir, 4m/7km NW of Maidenhead. Mary Shelley, author of Frankenstein, lived here. **22 B3** SU8586.
Marlow *Here.* ***Settlement***, 5m/7km SW of Craven Arms. SO3976.
Marlpit Hill *Kent* ***Village***, 1m/2km N of Edenbridge. **23 H7** TQ4447.
Marlpool *Derbys.* ***Locality***, adjoining to SE of Heanor. **41 G1** SK4445.
Marnhull *Dorset* Population: 1539. ***Village***, 3m/5km N of Sturminster Newton. **9 G3** ST7818.
Marnoch *Aber.* ***Settlement***, 2m/4km SW of Aberchirder. **98 D5** NJ5950.

M

Marple *Gt.Man.* Population: 19,829. ***Town***, 4m/7km E of Stockport. Early 19c aqueduct takes Peak Forest Canal over River Goyt. **49 J4** SJ9588.
Marple Bridge *Gt.Man.* ***Suburb***, 1m/2km NE of Marple across River Goyt. SJ9689.
Marpleridge *Gt.Man.* ***Suburb***, adjoining to S of Marple. SJ9587.
Marr *S.Yorks.* ***Village***, 4m/6km NW of Doncaster. **51 H2** SE5105.
Marrel *High.* ***Settlement***, in Sutherland district, 1m/2km N of Helmsdale. **105 F7** ND0117.
Marrick *N.Yorks.* ***Village***, 3m/4km E of Reeth. **62 B7** SE0798.
Marrick Moor *N.Yorks.* ***Open space***, moorland 1m/2km NE of Reeth. **62 B6** NZ0500.
Marrister *Shet.* ***Settlement***, close to W coast of Whalsay, 1m/2km NE of Symbister. **109 E6** HU5463.
Marrival *W.Isles* ***Hill***, on North Uist, 3m/5km S of Solas. Height 754 feet or 230 metres. **92 D5** NF8070.
Marros *Carmar.* ***Hamlet***, 2m/3km W of Pendine. **17 F4** SN2008.
Marscalloch Hill *D. & G.* ***Mountain***, 3m/5km E of Carsphairn. Height 1250 feet or 381 metres. **68 B4** NX6192.
Marsco *High.* ***Mountain***, 3m/4km SW of head of Loch Ainort, Skye. Height 2414 feet or 736 metres. **86 B2** NG5025.
Marsden *T. & W.* ***Suburb***, 2m/3km SE of South Shields town centre. **71 K7** NZ3964.
Marsden *W.Yorks.* Population: 3873. ***Small town***, on River Colne, 7m/11km SW of Huddersfield. **50 C1** SE0411.
Marsden Bay *T. & W.* ***Bay***, sandy bay on North Sea coast, to E of Marsden. **71 K7** NZ3964.
Marsden Hall *Lancs.* ***Locality***, adjoining to E of Nelson. SD8738.
Marsden Height *Lancs.* ***Locality***, 1m/2km S of Nelson. SD8636.
Marsden Moor Estate *Gt.Man.* ***Open space***, open moorland (National Trust) and designated Site of Special Scientific Interest, stretching NW from Wessenden Moor to Buckstones Moss and almost surrounding Marsden. Includes several reservoirs. **50 C2** SE0309.
Marsett *N.Yorks.* ***Settlement***, 3m/5km SW of Bainbridge. **56 E1** SD9086.
Marsh *Bucks.* ***Settlement***, 3m/5km S of Aylesbury town centre. SP8109.
Marsh *Devon* ***Hamlet***, 5m/7km W of Chard. **8 B3** ST2510.
Marsh *W.Yorks.* ***Locality***, adjoining to NW of Oxenhope, 4m/6km SW of Keighley. SE0235.
Marsh *W.Yorks.* ***Suburb***, 1m/2km W of Huddersfield town centre. SE1217.
Marsh *W.Yorks.* ***Suburb***, to SE of Cleckheaton. SE1925.
Marsh Baldon *Oxon.* ***Village***, 5m/9km SE of Oxford. **21 J2** SU5699.
Marsh Benham *W.Berks.* ***Hamlet***, 3m/5km W of Newbury. **21 H5** SU4267.
Marsh Chapel *Lincs.* ***Village***, 7m/11km SE of Cleethorpes. **53 G3** TF3599.
Marsh End *Worcs.* ***Locality***, 5m/8km W of Tewkesbury. SO8135.
Marsh Gibbon *Bucks.* ***Village***, 4m/7km E of Bicester. **31 H6** SP6423.
Marsh Green *Ches.* ***Locality***, 1m/2km W of Sandbach. SJ7461.
Marsh Green *Derbys.* ***Settlement***, 1km NW of Ashover, 3m/5km NE of Matlock. SK3463.
Marsh Green *Devon* ***Hamlet***, 4m/6km W of Ottery St. Mary. **7 J6** SY0493.
Marsh Green *Gt.Man.* ***Suburb***, 2m/3km W of Wigan town centre. SD5506.
Marsh Green *Kent* ***Village***, 1m/2km S of Edenbridge. **23 H7** TQ4344.
Marsh Green *Staffs.* ***Suburb***, 1m/2km N of Biddulph. SJ8859.
Marsh Green *Tel. & W.* ***Settlement***, 3m/5km NW of Wellington. **39 F4** SJ6014.
Marsh Lane *Derbys.* ***Village***, 3m/5km E of Dronfield. **51 G5** SK4079.
Marsh Street *Som.* ***Settlement***, 1km N of Dunster, 2m/3km SE of Minehead. **7 H1** SS9944.
Marshall Meadows *Northumb.* ***Settlement***, 3m/4km NW of Berwick-upon-Tweed. NT9756.
Marshall's Cross *Mersey.* ***Suburb***, 2m/3km S of St. Helens town centre. SJ5192.
Marshall's Elm *Som.* ***Locality***, 1m/2km S of Street. ST4834.
Marshall's Heath *Herts.* ***Settlement***, 2m/3km E of Harpenden. **32 E7** TL1615.
Marshalsea *Dorset* ***Hamlet***, 3m/5km E of Hawkchurch. **8 C4** ST3800.
Marshalswick *Herts.* ***Suburb***, 1m/2km NE of St. Albans city centre. TL1609.
Marsham *Norf.* ***Village***, 2m/3km S of Aylsham. Sites of Roman buildings 1km NE. **45 F3** TG1923.
Marshaw *Lancs.* ***Settlement***, 2m/3km W of Trough of Bowland and 4m/7km NW of Dunsop Bridge. **55 J4** SD5953.
Marshborough *Kent* ***Settlement***, 1m/2km SW of Sandwich. **15 H2** TR3057.
Marshbrook *Shrop.* ***Hamlet***, 3m/4km S of Church Stretton. **38 D7** SO4489.
Marshfield (Maerun). *Newport* Population: 1464. ***Village***, 5m/8km W of Newport. **19 F3** ST2682.
Marshfield *S.Glos.* ***Village***, 6m/10km N of Bath. **20 A4** ST7873.
Marshgate *Cornw.* ***Village***, 4m/6km E of Boscastle. **4 B1** SX1591.
Marshland *E.Riding* ***Open space***, lowland on S side of River Ouse, 3m/5km SE of Goole. **51 K1** SE7819.
Marshland *Norf.* ***Open space***, lowland containing orchards and crossed by many drainage ditches, 4m/7km NE of Wisbech. **43 J4** TF5112.
Marshland Fen *Norf.* ***Open space***, fenland 5m/8km E of Wisbech, through which runs Middle Level Main Drain. **43 J5** TF5407.
Marshside *Mersey.* ***Suburb***, 2m/4km NE of Southport town centre. **48 C1** SD3619.
Marshwood *Dorset* ***Village***, 4m/7km SW of Broadwindsor. Lambert's Castle Hill (National Trust), 1m/2km SW, commanding wide views of Marshwood Vale. **8 C5** SY3899.
Marshwood Vale *Dorset* ***Valley***, 2m/3km SE of Marshwood, watered by River Char and tributaries. **8 C5** SY3899.
Marske *N.Yorks.* ***Village***, 4m/7km W of Richmond. **62 C6** NZ1000.
Marske-by-the-Sea *R. & C.* Population: 8936. ***Small town***, residential town and resort with wide sands on North Sea coast, 2m/3km W of Saltburn. **63 H4** NZ6322.
Marske Moor *N.Yorks.* ***Open space***, moorland 4m/7km NW of Richmond. **62 B6** NZ0903.
Marsland Green *Gt.Man.* ***Suburb***, 2m/3km E of Leigh. SJ6899.
Marston *Ches.* ***Hamlet***, 1m/2km N of Northwich. **49 F5** SJ6675.
Marston *Here.* ***Hamlet***, 4m/7km E of Kington. **28 C3** SO3657.
Marston *Lincs.* ***Village***, 5m/8km N of Grantham. **42 B1** SK8943.
Marston *Oxon.* ***Suburb***, 2m/3km NE of Oxford. **21 J1** SP5208.
Marston *Staffs.* ***Hamlet***, 1m/2km NW of Wheaton Aston. **40 A4** SJ8314.
Marston *Staffs.* ***Hamlet***, 3m/5km N of Stafford. **40 B3** SJ9227.
Marston *Warks.* ***Hamlet***, 4m/6km N of Coleshill. **40 E6** SP2094.
Marston *Wilts.* ***Village***, 4m/6km SW of Devizes. **20 C6** ST9656.
Marston Doles *Warks.* ***Settlement***, on Oxford Canal, 4m/6km SE of Southam. SP4658.
Marston Gate *Som.* ***Suburb***, in SW part of Frome. ST7646.
Marston Green *W.Mid.* ***Suburb***, 7m/11km E of Birmingham. **40 D7** SP1785.
Marston Jabbett *Warks.* ***Locality***, 2m/4km S of Nuneaton. SP3788.
Marston Magna *Som.* ***Village***, 5m/8km NE of Yeovil. **8 E2** ST5922.
Marston Meysey *Wilts.* ***Village***, 3m/5km NE of Cricklade. **20 E2** SU1297.
Marston Montgomery *Derbys.* ***Village***, 4m/6km NW of Sudbury. **40 D2** SK1337.
Marston Moor *N.Yorks.* ***Open space***, area to N of Long Marston, 7m/11km W of York. Site of Parliamentarian victory in Civil War, 1644. **57 K4** SE4952.
Marston Moretaine *Beds.* Population: 1946. ***Village***, 6m/10km SW of Bedford. **32 C4** SP9941.
Marston on Dove *Derbys.* ***Village***, 4m/6km N of Burton upon Trent. **40 E3** SK2329.
Marston St. Lawrence *Northants.* ***Village***, 5m/8km E of Banbury. **31 G4** SP5342.
Marston Stannett *Here.* ***Hamlet***, 5m/9km SE of Leominster. **28 E3** SO5755.
Marston Trussell *Northants.* ***Village***, 3m/5km W of Market Harborough. **41 J7** SP6985.
Marstow *Here.* ***Hamlet***, 4m/7km SW of Ross-on-Wye. **28 E7** SO5519.
Marsworth *Bucks.* ***Village***, 2m/3km N of Tring. **32 C7** SP9214.
Marteg *Powys* ***River***, rising about 4m/6km N of Bwlch-y-sarnau and running SW to River Wye, 3m/4km NW of Rhayader. **27 K1** SN9571.
Marten *Wilts.* ***Hamlet***, 6m/10km SW of Hungerford. **21 F5** SU2860.
Marthall *Ches.* ***Hamlet***, 4m/6km SE of Knutsford. **49 H5** SJ7975.
Martham *Norf.* Population: 2917. ***Village***, 3m/4km W of Winterton-on-Sea. **45 J4** TG4518.
Martham Broad *Norf.* ***Lake/loch***, small lake or broad, 2m/4km W of Winterton-on-Sea. **45 J3** TG4520.
Marthig (Anglicised form: Marvig.) *W.Isles* ***Village***, near E coast of Isle of Lewis, 2m/3km S of entrance to Loch Erisort. **101 G6** NB4119.
Marthwaite *Cumb.* ***Settlement***, adjoining to W of Sedbergh. SD6491.
Martin *Hants.* ***Village***, 4m/7km N of Cranborne. **10 B3** SU0619.
Martin *Kent* ***Settlement***, 4m/6km NE of Dover. TR3347.
Martin *Lincs.* ***Hamlet***, 2m/3km SW of Horncastle. TF2366.
Martin *Lincs.* ***Village***, 5m/8km W of Woodhall Spa. **52 E6** TF1259.
Martin Drove End *Hants.* ***Hamlet***, 2m/3km NW of Martin. **10 B2** SU0521.
Martin Hussingtree *Worcs.* ***Village***, 4m/6km NE of Worcester. **29 H2** SO8859.
Martin Mere Wildfowl and Wetlands Trust *Lancs.* ***Nature reserve***, at Martin Mere, 2m/4km NW of Burscough Bridge. Important wintering ground for Bewick's and Whooper swans. Meadows provide winter roost for thousands of waterfowl. **48 D1** SD4214.
Martindale *Cumb.* ***Locality***, to SW of Howtown, 1km SE of Sandwick. NY4319.
Martindale Common *Cumb.* ***Open space***, mountainous area on E side of Ullswater, 3m/5km E of Glenridding. **60 F5** NY4217.
Martinhoe *Devon* ***Village***, on N coast, 3m/5km W of Lynton. **6 E1** SS6648.
Martinscroft *Warr.* ***Locality***, 4m/6km E of Warrington. **49 F4** SJ6589.
Martinstown *Dorset* ***Village***, 3m/5km W of Dorchester. **9 F6** SY6488.
Martlesham *Suff.* Population: 3113. ***Village***, 2m/3km SW of Woodbridge. **35 G4** TM2547.
Martlesham Heath *Suff.* ***Locality***, 5m/8km E of Ipswich town centre. **35 G4** TM2544.
Martletwy *Pembs.* ***Village***, 8m/14km NW of Tenby. **16 D3** SN0310.
Martley *Worcs.* ***Village***, 7m/11km NW of Worcester. **29 G2** SO7559.
Martnaham Loch *E.Ayr.* ***Lake/loch***, 5m/7km SE of Ayr. Remains of castle on islet in loch. **67 J2** NS3917.
Martock *Som.* Population: 4051. ***Small town***, 6m/10km NW of Yeovil. Medieval Treasurer's House; Georgian town hall. **8 D3** ST4619.
Marton *Ches.* ***Settlement***, 2m/3km NW of Winsford. SJ6267.
Marton *Ches.* ***Village***, 3m/5km N of Congleton. **49 H6** SJ8568.
Marton *Cumb.* ***Hamlet***, 3m/5km W of Ulverston. **55 F2** SD2477.
Marton *E.Riding* ***Hamlet***, 7m/11km N of Hedon. **59 H6** TA1839.
Marton *E.Riding* ***Settlement***, 2m/3km W of Flamborough. TA2069.
Marton *Lincs.* ***Village***, 5m/8km S of Gainsborough. **52 B4** SK8381.
Marton *Middbro.* ***Village***, 3m/5km SE of Middlesbrough. Birthplace of Captain Cook, explorer, in 1728. **63 G5** NZ5115.
Marton *N.Yorks.* ***Village***, 3m/4km SE of Boroughbridge. **57 K3** SE4162.
Marton *N.Yorks.* ***Village***, 4m/7km W of Pickering. **58 D1** SE7383.
Marton *Shrop.* ***Hamlet***, 2m/3km NE of Baschurch. SJ4423.
Marton *Shrop.* ***Village***, 5m/9km N of Church Stoke. **38 B5** SJ2802.
Marton *Warks.* ***Village***, 5m/7km N of Southam. **31 F2** SP4068.
Marton Abbey *N.Yorks.* ***Settlement***, 1m/2km N of Stillington. Remains of priory. **58 B3** SE5869.
Marton Grove *Middbro.* ***Suburb***, 1m/2km S of Middlesbrough town centre. NZ4918.
Marton-in-the-Forest *N.Yorks.* ***Settlement***, 1m/2km E of Stillington. SE5968.
Marton-le-Moor *N.Yorks.* ***Village***, 3m/5km NW of Boroughbridge. **57 J2** SE3770.
Marton Moss Side *B'pool* ***Suburb***, 2m/3km SE of Blackpool town centre. SD3333.
Martyr Worthy *Hants.* ***Hamlet***, on River Itchen, 3m/5km NE of Winchester. **11 G1** SU5132.
Martyr's Green *Surr.* ***Hamlet***, 2m/3km SW of Cobham. **22 D6** TQ0857.
Martyrs' Monument *D. & G.* ***Other feature of interest***, memorial stone in Wigtown to two 17c anti-Episcopalian women who were tied to stakes in River Bladnoch to drown in rising tide. **64 E5** NX4355.
Maruig (Anglicised form: Maaruig.) *W.Isles* ***Settlement***, on N side of Loch Maaruig, inlet on W side of Loch Seaforth, North Harris. **100 E7** NB1906.
Marvig *W.Isles Anglicised form of Marthig, qv.*
Marwell Zoological Park *Hants.* ***Leisure/recreation***, 100 acres of parkland, home to over 1000 animals, 1m/2km SW of Owslebury. Zoo has reputation for conservation and breeding rare animals. **11 G2** SU5021.
Marwick *Ork.* ***Settlement***, near W coast of Mainland, 4m/7km NW of Dounby. **106 B5** HY2324.
Marwick Head *Ork.* ***Coastal feature***, headland on NW coast of Mainland, 5m/8km NW of Dounby. Kitchener's Monument commemorates death of Lord Kitchener in 1916 when HMS Hampshire sank after striking a mine in these waters. **106 B5** HY2225.
Marwood *Devon* ***Village***, 3m/4km N of Barnstaple. **6 D2** SS5437.
Marwood *Dur.* ***Locality***, 4m/7km W of Staindrop. NZ0622.
Marwood Hill Gardens *Devon* ***Garden***, 4m/6km E of Braunton. 20 acres, including three small lakes, a wide variety of rare trees and shrubs, and a bog garden; particularly notable for camellias. National Collection of Astilbes. **6 D2** SS5437.
Mary Arden's House *Warks.* ***Historic house***, early 16c house at Wilmcote, 3m/5km NW of Stratford-upon-Avon town centre. Shakespeare's mother lived here; now contains museum of farming and country life. **30 C3** SP1658.
Mary Tavy *Devon* ***Village***, on W side of Dartmoor, 4m/6km NE of Tavistock. **5 F3** SX5079.
Mary, Queen of Scots House *Sc.Bord.* ***Historic house***, 16c house where Mary, Queen of Scots stayed on visit to Jedburgh in 1566. Now museum and visitor centre detailing Mary's life and displaying some of her possessions. **70 B1** NT6520.
Marybank *High.* ***Settlement***, in Ross and Cromarty district, 3m/5km S of Strathpeffer. **96 B6** NH4853.
Maryburgh *High.* ***Village***, in Ross and Cromarty district, 2m/3km S of Dingwall. **96 C6** NH5456.
Maryculter *Aber. Alternative name for Kirkton of Maryculter, qv.*
Maryfield *Cornw.* ***Village***, 1km NW of Torpoint. SX4256.
Maryfield *Shet.* ***Settlement***, on W coast of Bressay, overlooking Bressay Sound towards Lerwick, on Mainland. **109 D8** HU4842.
Marygold *Sc.Bord.* ***Settlement***, 4m/7km NE of Duns. **77 G4** NT8160.
Maryhill *Aber.* ***Settlement***, 3m/5km SE of Cuminestown. **99 G6** NJ8245.
Maryhill *Glas.* ***Suburb***, 3m/4km NW of Glasgow city centre. Aqueduct carries Forth and Clyde Canal over River Kelvin. **74 D4** NS5668.
Marykirk *Aber.* ***Village***, on N side of River North Esk, 4m/6km SW of Laurencekirk. **83 H1** NO6865.
Maryland *Mon.* ***Locality***, 1m/2km E of Trelleck. SO5105.
Marylebone *Gt.Lon.* ***Suburb***, in City of Westminster, lying S and SW of Regents Park. Originally named after parish church, St. Marylebone. **23 F3** TQ2881.
Marylebone *Gt.Man.* ***Suburb***, NE district of Wigan. **48 E2** SD5906.

Marypark *Moray* ***Locality***, 5m/9km SW of Charlestown of Aberlour. **89 J1** NJ1938.
Maryport *Cumb.* Population: 9797. ***Small town***, on Solway Firth, formerly developed as coal port. Site of Roman Fort to N. **60 B3** NY0336.
Maryport *D. & G.* ***Locality***, on Maryport Bay, 3m/4km N of Mull of Galloway. **64 B7** NX1434.
Marystow *Devon* ***Hamlet***, 6m/10km NW of Tavistock. **6 C7** SX4382.
Maryton *Angus* ***Settlement***, 2m/4km W of Montrose. **83 H2** NO6856.
Marywell *Aber.* ***Hamlet***, 1m/2km N of Portlethen. **91 H5** NO9298.
Marywell *Aber.* ***Village***, 4m/6km SE of Aboyne. **90 D5** NO5895.
Marywell *Angus* ***Village***, 2m/3km N of Arbroath. **83 H3** NO6544.
Màs a' Chnoic-chuairtich *W.Isles* ***Mountain***, to W of Loch Ulladale, 5m/8km NE of Huisinis, North Harris. Height 1266 feet or 386 metres. **100 C6** NB0614.
Màs Garbh *W.Isles* ***Hill***, rising to over 300 metres, 1km SW of Loch Langavat, South Harris. **93 F3** NG0487.
Màs Sgeir *W.Isles* ***Island***, islet off W coast of Isle of Lewis, 2m/4km N of Great Bernera. NB1444.
Mascle Bridge *Pembs.* ***Hamlet***, 1km NW of Neyland. SM9505.
Masham *N.Yorks.* ***Small town***, market town above River Ure, 8m/13km NW of Ripon. Market charter granted 1393. **57 H1** SE2280.
Masham Moor *N.Yorks.* ***Open space***, moorland on E margin of Yorkshire Dales National Park, 3m/5km NE of Scar House Reservoir and 7m/12km W of Masham. **57 F2** SE0979.
Mashbury *Essex* ***Locality***, 5m/7km NW of Chelmsford. **33 K7** TL6511.
Mashie *High.* ***River***, flowing NE from Beinn Eildhe into River Spey, 8m/12km SW of Newtonmore. **88 C6** NN6093.
Mason *T. & W.* ***Locality***, adjoining to N of Dinnington, 3m/4km E of Ponteland. NZ2073.
Masongill *N.Yorks.* ***Hamlet***, 2m/4km NW of Ingleton. SD6675.
Massacamber *W.Isles* ***Coastal feature***, headland on NE Berneray. **92 E3** NF9482.
Massacre of Glencoe 1692 *High.* ***Battle site***, where Macdonald clan of Glencoe were killed on orders of Sir James Dalrymple for being six days late in signing their peace with William III. Visitor centre tells story, and there are walks in the glen. **80 C2** NN1255.
Massingham Heath *Norf.* ***Open space***, heathland 3m/5km NE of Gayton. **44 B3** TF7620.
Mastin Moor *Derbys.* ***Village***, 1m/2km NE of Staveley and 6m/10km NE of Chesterfield. SK4575.
Mastrick *Aberdeen* ***Suburb***, 2m/4km W of Aberdeen city centre. **91 G4** NJ9007.
Matchborough *Worcs.* ***Suburb***, 2m/3km SE of Redditch town centre. SP0766.
Matching *Essex* ***Hamlet***, 3m/5km SE of Sawbridgeworth. **33 J7** TL5211.
Matching Green *Essex* ***Village***, 5m/8km N of Chipping Ongar. **33 J7** TL5311.
Matching Tye *Essex* ***Village***, 4m/7km E of Harlow. **33 J7** TL5111.
Matfen *Northumb.* ***Village***, 5m/8km NE of Corbridge. **71 F6** NZ0371.
Matfield *Kent* ***Village***, 2m/3km S of Paddock Wood. **23 K7** TQ6541.
Matharn *Mon.* *Welsh form of Mathern, qv.*
Mathern (Matharn). *Mon.* ***Village***, 2m/3km SW of Chepstow. **19 J2** ST5291.
Mathersgrave *Derbys.* ***Settlement***, 1km W of Brackenfield. SK3658.
Mathon *Here.* ***Village***, 3m/5km W of Great Malvern. **29 G4** SO7345.
Mathri *Pembs.* *Welsh form of Mathry, qv.*
Mathry (Mathri). *Pembs.* ***Village***, 6m/9km SW of Fishguard. **16 B1** SM8732.
Matlaske *Norf.* ***Village***, 5m/9km S of Sheringham. **45 F2** TG1534.
Matlock *Derbys.* Population: 14,680. ***Town***, inland resort and spa in steep-sided limestone stretch of River Derwent valley, 9m/14km SW of Chesterfield. Tourist centre with many amenities. Riber Castle is now a wildlife park. Pavilion contains a Lead Mining Museum. **51 F6** SK2960.
Matlock Bank *Derbys.* ***Suburb***, N district of Matlock, on E side of River Derwent. **50 E6** SK3060.
Matlock Bath *Derbys.* Population: 1213. ***Locality***, adjoining to S of Matlock. **50 E7** SK2958.
Matlock Bridge *Derbys.* ***Suburb***, next to road bridge over River Derwent, adjoining to S of Matlock. SK2960.
Matlock Dale *Derbys.* ***Hamlet***, adjoining to N of Matlock Bath. SK2959.
Matson *Glos.* ***Suburb***, in S part of Gloucester. **29 H7** SO8415.
Matterdale *Cumb.* ***Locality***, 1m/2km N of Dockray. NY3923.
Matterdale Common *Cumb.* ***Open space***, mountainous area 4m/6km N of Helvellyn. **60 E4** NY3421.
Matterdale End *Cumb.* ***Settlement***, 1km N of Matterdale. **60 E4** NY3923.
Mattersey *Notts.* ***Village***, 3m/5km SE of Bawtry. Remains of medieval priory (English Heritage) to E. **51 J4** SK6889.
Mattersey Priory *Notts.* ***Ecclesiastical building***, scant ruins of priory (English Heritage) founded c. 1185, 1km E of Mattersey and 4m/6km SE of Bawtry. **51 K4** SK7089.
Mattersey Thorpe *Notts.* ***Hamlet***, 1km NW of Mattersey. SK6889.
Mattingley *Hants.* ***Village***, 2m/4km N of Hook. **22 A6** SU7358.
Mattishall *Norf.* Population: 2499. ***Village***, 4m/7km E of East Dereham. **44 E4** TG0511.
Mattishall Burgh *Norf.* ***Village***, 1km N of Mattishall. **44 E4** TG0511.
Mauchline *E.Ayr.* Population: 3931. ***Small town***, 8m/13km SE of Kilmarnock. Burns memorial 1km NW. **67 K1** NS4927.
Maud *Aber.* ***Village***, 3m/4km E of Old Deer and 13m/21km W of Peterhead. **99 H6** NJ9247.
Maugerhay *S.Yorks.* ***Suburb***, 3m/5km S of Sheffield city centre. SK3682.
Maugersbury *Glos.* ***Hamlet***, 1km SE of Stow-on-the-Wold. **30 C6** SP2025.
Maughold *I.o.M.* ***Village***, 3m/5km SE of Ramsey. **54 D4** SC4991.
Maughold Head *I.o.M.* ***Coastal feature***, headland (Manx National Trust) 1km SE of Maughold and 3m/5km SE of Ramsey. Lighthouse and nature reserve. **54 D4** SC4991.
Mauld *High.* ***Settlement***, in Strathglass, 6m/9km NE of Cannich. **87 K1** NH3938.
Maulden *Beds.* ***Village***, 1m/2km E of Ampthill. **32 D5** TL0537.
Maulds Meaburn *Cumb.* ***Village***, 1m/2km N of Crosby Ravensworth. **61 H5** NY6216.
Maun *Notts.* ***River***, rising near Mansfield and flowing through town, then NE by Edwinstowe and Ollerton to join River Meden and form River Idle, 4m/6km S of Retford. **51 J6** SK7075.
Maunby *N.Yorks.* ***Village***, on River Swale, 6m/9km NW of Thirsk. **57 J1** SE3586.
Maund Bryan *Here.* ***Hamlet***, 7m/11km NE of Hereford. **28 E3** SO5650.
Maundown *Som.* ***Hamlet***, below Maundown Hill, 2m/3km NW of Wiveliscombe. **7 J3** ST0628.
Maunsel House *Som.* ***Historic house***, ancestral home of Slade family, 2m/3km S of North Petherton and 4m/6km S of Bridgwater. Built partly prior to Norman Conquest. Chaucer wrote part of Canterbury Tales here. **8 C1** ST3030.
Mautby *Norf.* ***Hamlet***, 3m/4km W of Caister-on-Sea. **45 J4** TG4712.
Mavesyn Ridware *Staffs.* ***Hamlet***, 3m/4km E of Rugeley. **40 C4** SK0816.
Mavis Enderby *Lincs.* ***Village***, 2m/4km W of Spilsby. **53 G6** TF4066.
Mavis Grind *Shet.* ***Coastal feature***, narrow isthmus and former portage on Mainland between Sullom Voe and St. Magnus Bay. **109 C6** HU3468.
Maw Green *Ches.* ***Suburb***, 1m/2km N of Crewe town centre. SJ7157.
Maw Green *W.Mid.* ***Locality***, 1m/2km SE of Walsall town centre. **40 C6** SP0297.
Mawbray *Cumb.* ***Village***, 5m/8km S of Silloth. **60 B2** NY0846.
Mawddach *Gwyn.* ***River***, rising about 4m/6km W of Llanuwchllyn and flowing SW into Barmouth Bay on S side of Barmouth. Tidal to Llanelltyd; estuarial below Penmaenpool. **37 F4** SH6014.
Mawdesley *Lancs.* ***Village***, 6m/10km W of Chorley. **48 D1** SD4914.
Mawdlam *Bridgend* ***Village***, 3m/5km N of Porthcawl. **18 B3** SS8081.
Mawgan *Cornw.* ***Village***, 3m/5km SE of Helston. **2 E6** SW7125.
Mawgan-in-Pydar *Cornw.* ***Locality***, parish containing St. Mawgan. SW8765.
Mawgan Porth *Cornw.* ***Bay***, small cove where River Menalhyl enters the sea, 4m/7km NE of Newquay. **3 F2** SW8467.
Mawgan Porth *Cornw.* ***Settlement***, to SW of Trenance across River Menalhyl, 4m/7km NE of Newquay. Mawgan Porth bay to N. SW8467.
Mawla *Cornw.* ***Hamlet***, 3m/4km N of Redruth. **2 D4** SW7045.
Mawnan *Cornw.* ***Village***, above mouth of Helford River, 4m/6km S of Falmouth. **2 E6** SW7827.
Mawnan Smith *Cornw.* ***Village***, to NW of Mawnan. 13c church. **2 E6** SW7827.
Mawthorpe *Lincs.* ***Settlement***, 2m/3km S of Alford. Nature Reserve to E. TF4573.
Maxey *Peter.* ***Village***, 7m/12km NW of Peterborough. **42 E5** TF1208.
Maxstoke *Warks.* ***Village***, 3m/5km SE of Coleshill. Castle (2m/3km NW), priory and church all of 14c. **40 E7** SP2386.
Maxted Street *Kent* ***Settlement***, 7m/11km N of Hythe. TR1244.
Maxton *Kent* ***Suburb***, W district of Dover. **15 H3** TR3040.
Maxton *Sc.Bord.* ***Village***, 5m/8km SE of Melrose. **70 B1** NT6130.
Maxwellheugh *Sc.Bord.* ***Village***, on S side of River Tweed, opposite Kelso. **77 F7** NT7333.
Maxwelltown *D. & G.* ***Suburb***, W part of Dumfries across River Nith. **65 K3** NX9676.
Maxwelton House *D. & G.* ***Historic house***, restored 14c-15c house, incorporating parts of 14c Glencairn Castle, 3m/5km E of Moniaive. House was 17c birthplace of Annie Laurie, immortalised in Scottish ballad of same name. **68 D5** NX8289.
Maxworthy *Cornw.* ***Hamlet***, 7m/11km NW of Launceston. **4 C1** SX2593.
May Bank *Staffs.* ***Suburb***, 1m/2km N of Newcastle-under-Lyme town centre. SJ8547.
May Beck *N.Yorks.* ***River***, stream rising on North York Moors and flowing N to join Little Beck at Littlebeck. **63 K6** NZ8804.
May Hill *Glos.* ***Hill***, National Trust property, commanding wide views, 3m/5km S of Newent. Height 971 feet or 296 metres. **29 F6** SO6921.
May Hill *Mon.* ***Locality***, on E bank of River Wye, opposite Monmouth. SO5112.
Mayals *Swan.* ***Suburb***, 4m/6km SW of Swansea city centre. SS6090.
Mayar *Angus* ***Mountain***, 5m/9km W of Clova. Munro: height 3044 feet or 928 metres. **89 K7** NO2473.
Maybole *S.Ayr.* Population: 4737. ***Small town***, market town 8m/12km S of Ayr. Restored castle. Remains of 15c collegiate church (Historic Scotland). Former centre for weaving and shoe-making. **67 H3** NS3009.
Maybury *Surr.* ***Suburb***, to E of Woking town centre. TQ0158.
Maybush *S'ham.* ***Suburb***, NW district of Southampton. SU3814.
Mayen *Moray* ***Settlement***, in loop of River Deveron, 2m/3km E of Milltown of Rothiemay. **98 D6** NJ5747.
Mayeston *Pembs.* ***Hamlet***, adjoining to E of Cosheston. SN0103.
Mayfair *Gt.Lon.* ***Suburb***, fashionable district of City of Westminster, in central London, bounded by Oxford Street, Bond Street, Piccadilly and Park Lane. TQ2880.
Mayfield *E.Suss.* Population: 1954. ***Village***, 8m/13km S of Royal Tunbridge Wells. Convent incorporates remains of medieval palace of Archbishops of Canterbury. **13 J4** TQ5826.
Mayfield *Midloth.* Population: 12,103. ***Town***, 3m/4km SE of Dalkeith. **76 B4** NT3564.
Mayfield *Staffs.* ***Village***, 2m/3km W of Ashbourne. **40 D1** SK1546.
Mayford *Surr.* ***Suburb***, S district of Woking. **22 C6** SU9956.
Mayhill *Swan.* ***Suburb***, 1km NW of Swansea city centre. SS6494.
Mayland *Essex* ***Locality***, 3m/5km NW of Burnham-on-Crouch. **25 F1** TL9200.
Maylandsea *Essex* Population: 3362. ***Village***, on Mundon Creek, 4m/6km SE of Maldon. **25 F1** TL9002.
Maynard's Green *E.Suss.* ***Hamlet***, 2m/3km S of Heathfield. **13 J5** TQ5818.
Maypole *I.o.S.* ***Hamlet***, on St. Mary's, 1m/2km NE of Hugh Town. **2 C1** SV9211.
Maypole *Kent* ***Hamlet***, 3m/4km SE of Herne Bay. **25 H5** TR2064.
Maypole *Mon.* ***Hamlet***, 3m/5km NW of Monmouth. SO4716.
Maypole *W.Mid.* ***Suburb***, 5m/9km S of Birmingham city centre. SP0878.
Maypole End *Essex* ***Hamlet***, 4m/6km E of Saffron Walden. TL5937.
Maypole Green *Essex* ***Suburb***, 2m/3km S of Colchester town centre. TL9822.
Maypole Green *Norf.* ***Village***, 3m/5km N of Beccles. **45 J6** TM4195.
Maypole Green *Suff.* ***Hamlet***, 1km S of Bradfield St. George. TL9159.
Maypole Green *Suff.* ***Settlement***, 1km W of Dennington. TM2767.
May's Green *N.Som.* ***Hamlet***, 3m/5km W of Congresbury. ST3963.
Mays Green *Oxon.* ***Settlement***, 2m/3km S of Henley-on-Thames. SU7479.
May's Green *Surr.* ***Settlement***, 2m/3km S of Cobham. TQ0957.
Mayton Bridge *Norf.* ***Bridge***, 15c stone bridge over River Bure at Buxton, 8m/12km N of Norwich city centre. Covered seats at each end of bridge. TG2322.
Maywick *Shet.* ***Settlement***, on W coast of Mainland, at head of May Wick Bay. **109 C10** HU3724.
McArthur's Head *Arg. & B.* ***Coastal feature***, headland with lighthouse on E coast of Islay, at S end of Sound of Islay. **72 C5** NR4659.
McFarquhar's Cave *High.* ***Cave***, on NE tip of Black Isle, 2m/3km SE of Cromarty. **97 F5** NH8065.
McPhail's Anvil *Arg. & B.* ***Island***, one of Torran Rocks group, 4m/6km SW of Mull. **78 D6** NM2613.
Meabhag (Anglicised form: Meavag.) *W.Isles* ***Settlement***, on South Harris, 2m/4km S of Tarbert. **93 G2** NG1596.
Meachard *Cornw.* ***Island***, off Penally Point just N of Boscastle. SX0991.
Mead *Devon* ***Hamlet***, near coast, 5m/8km SW of Hartland. SS2217.
Mead End *Hants.* ***Locality***, 1km W of Sway. SZ2698.
Mead End *Wilts.* ***Settlement***, 1km NE of Bowerchalke. **10 B2** SU0223.
Meadgate *B. & N.E.Som.* ***Hamlet***, 3m/4km N of Radstock. ST6858.
Meadle *Bucks.* ***Village***, 2m/3km N of Princes Risborough. **22 B1** SP8005.
Meadow Green *Here.* ***Hamlet***, 4m/7km E of Bromyard. SO7156.
Meadow Head *B'burn.* ***Settlement***, 2m/3km NW of Darwen. SD6723.
Meadowbank *Ches.* ***Settlement***, 1m/2km N of Winsford. SJ6568.
Meadowfield *Dur.* ***Suburb***, adjoining to E of Brandon. NZ2439.
Meadowhall *S.Yorks.* ***Suburb***, 3m/5km NE of Sheffield city centre. Site of large shopping centre. **51 F3** SK3990.
Meadowmill *E.Loth.* ***Hamlet***, 1m/2km SE of Prestonpans. **76 C3** NT4073.
Meadowtown *Shrop.* ***Hamlet***, 1km NE of Rorrington. **38 C5** SJ3101.
Meadwell *Devon* ***Hamlet***, 5m/8km SE of Launceston. SX4081.
Meaford *Staffs.* ***Hamlet***, 1m/2km NW of Stone. SJ8835.
Meal Bank *Cumb.* ***Hamlet***, 3m/4km NE of Kendal. **61 G7** SD5495.
Meal Buidhe *High.* ***Mountain***, in Badenoch and Strathspey district, 5m/7km SE of Kingussie. Height 2060 feet or 628 metres. **88 E5** NN7995.
Meal Fuar-mhonaidh *High.* ***Mountain***, in Inverness district on NW side of Loch Ness, 6m/9km SW of Drumnadrochit. Height 2283 feet or 696 metres. **88 B2** NH4522.
Meal Hill *W.Yorks.* ***Settlement***, 2m/3km SE of Holmfirth. SE1606.
Mealabost (Anglicised form: Melbost Borve.) *W.Isles* ***Settlement***, 1km N of High Borve, near NW coast of Isle of Lewis. **101 G2** NB4157.

Mealasta *W.Isles* ***Settlement***, on W coast of Isle of Lewis, 5m/9km NW of entrance to Loch Resort. **100 B5** NA9924.
Mealasta Island *W.Isles* ***Island***, uninhabited island, 1m/2km by 1km in extent, lying 1km off W coast of Isle of Lewis, 3m/4km S of Breanais. **100 B5** NA9821.
Mealdarroch Point *Arg. & B.* ***Coastal feature***, headland on W side of Loch Fyne, Argyll, 1m/2km E of Loch Tarbert. **73 G4** NR8868.
Mealisval *W.Isles* ***Mountain***, near W coast of Isle of Lewis 3m/5km W of S end of Loch Suainaval. Height 1883 feet or 574 metres. **100 C5** NB0227.
Meall a' Bhainne *High.* ***Mountain***, 1m/2km S of Glenfinnan, Lochaber district. Height 1834 feet or 559 metres. **87 F7** NM9078.
Meall a' Bhata *High.* ***Mountain***, to S of Loch Choire. Height 1906 feet or 581 metres. **103 J6** NC6326.
Meall a' Bhealaich *High.* ***Mountain***, 4m/6km E of Ben Griam Beg, Caithness district. Height 1105 feet or 337 metres. **104 E4** NC8940.
Meall a' Bhealaich *P. & K.* ***Mountain***, peak between Loch Ericht and Loch Ossian. Height 2827 feet or 862 metres. **81 F1** NN4569.
Meall a' Bhlàir *High.* ***Mountain***, in Lochaber district 2m/3km N of Loch Arkaig and 5m/7km S of dam of Loch Quoich. Height 2152 feet or 656 metres. **87 G5** NN0795.
Meall a' Bhobuir *P. & K.* ***Mountain***, in Rannoch district, 3m/5km SE of Bridge of Gaur. Height 2148 feet or 655 metres. **81 G2** NN5152.
Meall a' Bhràghaid *High.* ***Mountain***, at the head of Glen Oykel. Height 2257 feet or 688 metres. **102 E7** NC2914.
Meall a' Bhreacraibh *High.* ***Mountain***, in Inverness district, 5m/8km SE of Daviot. Height 1807 feet or 551 metres. **88 E1** NH7835.
Meall a' Bhroin *High.* ***Hill***, on S shore of Loch Sunart, 5m/8km E of Glenborrodale across the loch. Height 994 feet or 303 metres. **79 H2** NM6860.
Meall a' Bhrollaich *High.* ***Hill***, 2m/3km NE of Altnaharra, Sutherland district. Height 741 feet or 226 metres. **103 H5** NC5837.
Meall a' Bhuachaille *High.* ***Mountain***, on N edge of Glenmore Forest Park, in Badenoch and Strathspey district, 5m/8km N of Cairn Gorm. Height 2657 feet or 810 metres. **89 G3** NH9911.
Meall a' Bhùirich *High.* ***Mountain***, in Lochaber district, 4m/6km W of head of Loch Treig. Height 2755 feet or 840 metres. **87 J7** NN2570.
Meall a' Bhùiridh *High.* ***Mountain***, in Lochaber district, 1m/2km NE of Clach Leathad to E of Glen Etive. Munro: height 3634 feet or 1108 metres. **80 D2** NN2550.
Meall a' Chàise *High.* ***Mountain***, in Morvern, Lochaber district, 6m/9km N of Ardtornish. Height 1712 feet or 522 metres. **79 J2** NM7256.
Meall a' Chaorainn ***Mountain***, on border of Highland and Perth & Kinross, 3m/5km SE of Dalwhinnie. Height 2959 feet or 902 metres. **88 D6** NN6680.
Meall a' Chaorainn *High.* ***Mountain***, in Ross and Cromarty district, 2m/3km NW of Achnasheen. Height 2312 feet or 705 metres. **95 H5** NH1360.
Meall a' Chaorainn *High.* ***Mountain***, 4m/6km NE of Rubha an Ridire. Height 1578 feet or 481 metres. **79 J3** NM7644.
Meall a' Chaorainn Loch Uisge *High.* ***Mountain***, 1km S of Luch Uisge. Height 1679 feet or 512 metres. **79 K2** NM8053.
Meall a' Chathaidh *P. & K.* ***Mountain***, between Glen Garry and Glen Errochty. Height 1709 feet or 521 metres. **81 J1** NN7467.
Meall a' Chòcaire *High.* ***Mountain***, in Badenoch and Strathspey district, 4m/6km N of Kingussie. Height 2345 feet or 715 metres. **88 E4** NH7507.
Meall a' Choire Bhuidhe *P. & K.* ***Mountain***, 3m/5km NW of Spittal of Glenshee. Height 2847 feet or 868 metres. **89 H7** NO0670.
Meall a' Choire Léith *P. & K.* ***Mountain***, 2m/3km NW of Ben Lawers. Munro: height 3037 feet or 926 metres. **81 H3** NN6143.
Meall a' Choirein Luachraich *High.* ***Mountain***, 3m/5km W of Inversander, Lochaber district. Height 1768 feet or 539 metres. **79 K2** NM8959.
Meall a' Chraidh *High.* ***Mountain***, 3m/4km from W side of Loch Eriboll. Height 1607 feet or 490 metres. **103 F3** NC3759.
Meall a' Chrasgaidh *High.* ***Mountain***, in Ross and Cromarty district, 1m/2km NW of Sgurr Mòr. Munro: height 3064 feet or 934 metres. **95 H4** NH1873.
Meall a' Chràthaich *High.* ***Mountain***, in Inverness district, 11m/18km SW of Drumnadrochit. Height 2227 feet or 679 metres. **87 K2** NH3622.
Meall a' Chuaille *High.* ***Mountain***, in Ross and Cromarty district, 12m/20km NW of Gorstan. Height 2060 feet or 628 metres. **95 K3** NH3482.
Meall a' Churain *Stir.* ***Mountain***, 6m/10km W of Killin. Height 3008 feet or 917 metres. **81 F4** NN4632.
Meall a Fheur Loch *High.* ***Mountain***, 2m/3km W of Loch Merkland. Height 2011 feet or 613 metres. **103 F5** NC3631.
Meall a' Ghiubhais *High.* ***Mountain***, 2m/3km W of head of Loch Maree, Ross and Cromarty district. Height 2880 feet or 878 metres. **95 F5** NG9763.
Meall a' Mhadaidh *Stir.* ***Inland physical feature***, mountain ridge rising to over 550 metres on N side of Loch Earn, 1m/2km NE of Lochearnhead. **81 H5** NN6026.
Meall a' Mhaoil *High.* ***Hill***, 3m/4km NE of head of Loch Ainort. Height 932 feet or 284 metres. **86 B1** NG5530.
Meall a' Mhuic *P. & K.* ***Mountain***, 4m/6km S of Dall on S side of Loch Rannoch. Height 2444 feet or 745 metres. **81 G2** NN5750.
Meall a' Phiobaire *High.* ***Mountain***, 1km NE of Loch Beannach, Sutherland district. Height 1220 feet or 372 metres. **103 J7** NC6915.
Meall a' Phubuill *High.* ***Mountain***, on Locheil Forest, Lochaber district, 5m/8km NE of Kinlocheil. Height 2539 feet or 774 metres. **87 G6** NN0285.
Meall Ailein *High.* ***Mountain***, 4m/6km SE of Altnaharra. Height 2365 feet or 721 metres. **103 J5** NC6131.
Meall A'irigh Mhic Craidh *High.* ***Mountain***, 2m/3km E of Gairloch, Ross and Cromarty district. Height 1145 feet or 349 metres. **94 E4** NG8377.
Meall an Aodainn *High.* ***Mountain***, in Lochaber district, 4m/6km S of Ballachulish. Height 2227 feet or 679 metres. **80 B2** NN0852.
Meall an Araich *Arg. & B.* ***Mountain***, in Argyll, 1m/2km N of Loch Dochard. Height 2837 feet or 865 metres. **80 D3** NN2143.
Meall an Doire Shleaghaich *High.* ***Mountain***, 4m/6km S of Kinlocheil, Lochaber district. Height 1335 feet or 407 metres. **87 F7** NM9873.
Meall an Fharaidh *Arg. & B.* ***Mountain***, with craggy E face, above NW shore of Loch Tarsan. Height 1309 feet or 399 metres. **73 J2** NS0786.
Meall an Fheidh *High.* ***Mountain***, 7m/11km E of Scamodale, Lochaber district. Height 1387 feet or 423 metres. **87 F7** NM9473.
Meall an Fheuraich *Arg. & B.* ***Mountain***, on S side of Glen Kinglass, 6m/9km N of Lochawe. Height 1151 feet or 351 metres. **80 B4** NN1036.
Meall an Fhìar Mhàim *Arg. & B.* ***Mountain***, 5m/8km W of Salen, Mull. Height 1066 feet or 325 metres. **79 F3** NM4843.
Meall an Fhiodhain *Stir.* ***Mountain***, at head of Kirkton Glen, 3m/4km NW of Balquhidder. Height 2594 feet or 791 metres. **81 G5** NN5224.
Meall an Fhuarain *High.* ***Hill***, 4m/6km NE of head of Loch Harport. Height 954 feet or 291 metres. **85 K1** NG4535.
Meall an Fhuarain *High.* ***Mountain***, 4m/7km SE of Loch Urigill, Ross and Cromarty district. Height 1896 feet or 578 metres. **95 J1** NC2802.
Meall an Fhuarain *High.* ***Mountain***, in Sutherland district, 4m/7km SW of Altnaharra. Height 1551 feet or 473 metres. **103 H5** NC5130.
Meall an Fhudair *Arg. & B.* ***Mountain***, in Argyll, 7m/11km NE of head of Loch Fyne. Height 2506 feet or 764 metres. **80 D6** NN2719.
Meall an Inbhire *Arg. & B.* ***Hill***, 3m/4km NW of Tobermory, Mull. Mast on summit. Height 866 feet or 264 metres. **79 F2** NM4656.
Meall an Spothaidh *High.* ***Mountain***, 1km S of Borgie Forest, Caithness district. Height 1207 feet or 368 metres. **103 J4** NC6649.
Meall an t-Seallaidh *Stir.* ***Mountain***, 3m/5km W of Lochearnhead. Height 2795 feet or 852 metres. **81 G5** NN5423.
Meall an t-Sithe *High.* ***Mountain***, in Ross and Cromarty district, 4m/6km W of Corrieshalloch Gorge. Height 1971 feet or 601 metres. **95 H4** NH1476.
Meall an t-Slamain *High.* ***Mountain***, in Ardgour, 2m/3km W of Fort William across Loch Linnhe. Height 1532 feet or 467 metres. **87 G7** NN0773.
Meall an Tarmachain *High.* ***Mountain***, on Ardnamurchan peninsula, 1m/2km N of Kilchoan. Height 1325 feet or 404 metres. **79 F1** NM4966.
Meall an Tuirc *High.* ***Mountain***, in Ross and Cromarty district on NE side of Loch Glass, 5m/9km NW of Evanton. Height 2050 feet or 625 metres. **96 C4** NH5372.
Meall Aundrary *High.* ***Mountain***, 4m/6km SE of Gairloch, Ross and Cromarty district. Height 1079 feet or 329 metres. **94 E4** NG8472.
Meall Bàn *Arg. & B.* ***Mountain***, 3m/5km S of Duror. Height 2148 feet or 655 metres. **80 A3** NM9949.
Meall Beag *High.* ***Island***, one of two islets in Eddrachillis Bay off W coast of Sutherland district, 2m/4km offshore. **102 D5** NC1237.
Meall Bhalach *High.* ***Mountain***, on S side of Blackwater Reservoir, 5m/8km SE of Kinlochleven. Height 2322 feet or 708 metres. **80 D2** NN2557.
Meall Bhanabhie *High.* ***Mountain***, in Lochaber district, 3m/5km N of Fort William. Height 1073 feet or 327 metres. **87 H7** NN1178.
Meall Bhenneit *High.* ***Mountain***, on border of Ross and Cromarty and Sutherland districts, 7m/11km SW of Bonar Bridge. Height 1745 feet or 532 metres. **96 C3** NH5483.
Meall Breac *P. & K.* ***Mountain***, 6m/10km NE of Blair Atholl. Height 2214 feet or 675 metres. **82 A1** NN9668.
Meall Buidhe ***Mountain***, on border of Argyll & Bute and Perth & Kinross, 2m/3km W of head of Loch an Daimh. Height 2975 feet or 907 metres. **81 F3** NN4244.
Meall Buidhe *Arg. & B.* ***Mountain***, in Argyll 6m/10km N of Dalmally. Height 2043 feet or 623 metres. **80 C4** NN1837.
Meall Buidhe *Arg. & B.* ***Mountain***, on Kintyre, 8m/12km N of Campbeltown. Height 1227 feet or 374 metres. **73 F7** NR7332.
Meall Buidhe *High.* ***Mountain***, in Skye and Lochalsh district, 3m/5km S of Glenelg. Height 1594 feet or 486 metres. **86 E3** NG8014.
Meall Buidhe *High.* ***Mountain***, in Knoydart, in Lochaber district, 5m/8km E of Inverie on Loch Nevis. Munro: height 3103 feet or 946 metres. **86 E5** NM8498.
Meall Buidhe *P. & K.* ***Mountain***, 2m/3km N of Loch an Daimh. Munro: height 3054 feet or 931 metres. **81 F2** NN4949.
Meall Cala *Stir.* ***Mountain***, N of Glen Finglas Reservoir, 4m/7km NW of Brig o' Turk. Height 2211 feet or 674 metres. **81 G6** NN5012.
Meall Challibost *W.Isles* ***Coastal feature***, headland at southermost point of Scalpay. **93 H2** NG2294.
Meall Chuaich *High.* ***Mountain***, in Badenoch and Strathspey district 5m/9km NE of Dalwhinnie. Munro: height 3119 feet or 951 metres. **88 E6** NN7187.
Meall Coire nan Saobhaidh *High.* ***Mountain***, in Lochaber district 5m/8km N of Bunarkaig on Loch Lochy. Height 2693 feet or 821 metres. **87 H5** NN1795.
Meall Corranaich *P. & K.* ***Mountain***, 1m/2km W of Ben Lawers summit and 6m/9km NE of Killin. Munro: height 3506 feet or 1069 metres. **81 H3** NN6140.
Meall Cruaidh *High.* ***Mountain***, in Badenoch and Strathspey district, 4m/7km SW of Dalwhinnie. Height 2942 feet or 897 metres. **88 C6** NN5780.
Meall Cruinn *P. & K.* ***Mountain***, in Rannoch district, 8m/12km W of Bridge of Balgie. Height 2716 feet or 828 metres. **81 F3** NN4547.
Meall Cuileig *High.* ***Mountain***, in Inverness district, 3m/5km N of Dalchreichart. Height 1453 feet or 443 metres. **87 J3** NH2716.
Meall Daill *P. & K.* ***Mountain***, on N side of Loch Lyon. Height 2857 feet or 871 metres. **81 F3** NN4143.
Meall Damh *High.* ***Mountain***, 3m/4km E of Ardtornish, Lochaber district. Height 1112 feet or 339 metres. **79 J3** NM7348.
Meall Dearg *High.* ***Mountain***, peak towards E end of Aonach Eagach, N of Glen Coe. Munro: height 3119 feet or 951 metres. **80 C2** NN1658.
Meall Dearg *P. & K.* ***Mountain***, 5m/8km SE of Aberfeldy. Height 2263 feet or 690 metres. **81 K3** NN8841.
Meall Dheirgidh *High.* ***Mountain***, in Sutherland district, 10m/16km SW of Lairg. Height 1663 feet or 507 metres. **96 B2** NH4794.
Meall Dola *High.* ***Mountain***, 2m/4km E of Lairg, to S of Loch Craggie. Height 1059 feet or 323 metres. **96 D1** NC6106.
Meall Dubh *Arg. & B.* ***Mountain***, 3m/5km N of Loch Tarsan. Height 1873 feet or 571 metres. **73 J2** NS0789.
Meall Dubh *High.* ***Mountain***, rounded summit in Ross and Cromarty district, 2m/4km E of Leckmelm. Height 2106 feet or 642 metres. **95 J2** NH2089.
Meall Dubh *High.* ***Mountain***, on border of Inverness and Lochaber districts, 3m/5km E of dam of Loch Loyne. Height 2585 feet or 788 metres. **87 J4** NH2407.
Meall Dubh *P. & K.* ***Mountain***, 5m/8km S of Aberfeldy. Height 2020 feet or 616 metres. **81 K3** NN8540.
Meall Dubhag *High.* ***Mountain***, in W part of Cairngorm Mountains, in Badenoch and Strathspey district, 8m/13km SE of Kingussie. Height 3273 feet or 998 metres. **89 F5** NN8895.
Meall Gaothar *High.* ***Mountain***, in Knoydart, Lochaber district, 4m/6km NW of Inverie. Height 1384 feet or 422 metres. **86 D4** NG7405.
Meall Garbh *Arg. & B.* ***Mountain***, in Argyll to E of Glen Kinglass, 6m/9km N of Dalmally. Height 2283 feet or 696 metres. **80 C4** NN1636.
Meall Garbh *High.* ***Mountain***, in Lochaber district 5m/9km NE of head of Loch Etive. Height 2299 feet or 701 metres. **80 C3** NN1948.
Meall Garbh *P. & K.* ***Mountain***, N shoulder of Ben Lawers. Munro: height 3667 feet or 1118 metres. **81 H3** NN6443.
Meall Garbh *P. & K.* ***Mountain***, in Rannoch district, 4m/7km S of Kinloch Rannoch. Munro: height 3175 feet or 968 metres. **81 H2** NN6551.
Meall Geal *W.Isles* ***Coastal feature***, headland on E coast of Isle of Lewis, 3m/5km N of Cellar Head. **101 H1** NB5660.
Meall Ghaordie ***Mountain***, on border of Perth & Kinross and Stirling, 1m/2km S of Stronwich Reservoir. Munro: height 3408 feet or 1039 metres. **81 G4** NN5139.
Meall Giubhais *High.* ***Mountain***, in Strathconon Forest, Ross and Cromarty district, 3m/5km S of Milton. Height 2171 feet or 662 metres. **95 K6** NH3050.
Meall Glas *Stir.* ***Mountain***, 5m/8km NE of Crianlarich. Munro: height 3139 feet or 957 metres. **81 F4** NN4332.
Meall Glass ***Mountain***, on border of Perth & Kinross and Stirling, 5m/8km N of Killin. Height 2886 feet or 880 metres. **81 G4** NN5639.
Meall Gorm *Aber.* ***Mountain***, 2m/3km N of Bridge of Dee. Height 2024 feet or 617 metres. **89 J5** NO1894.
Meall Gorm *High.* ***Mountain***, 5m/8km SE of Applecross, Ross and Cromarty district. Height 2329 feet or 710 metres. **94 D7** NG7740.
Meall Gorm *High.* ***Mountain***, in Ross and Cromarty district 2m/4km N of Fannich Lodge on N shore of Loch Fannich. Munro: height 3113 feet or 949 metres. **95 J5** NH2269.
Meall Gorm *High.* ***Mountain***, in Inverness district, 3m/5km NW of Drumnadrochit. Height 1355 feet or 413 metres. **88 B1** NH4834.
Meall Greigh *P. & K.* ***Mountain***, 3m/5km NE of Ben Lawers. Munro: height 3283 feet or 1001 metres. **81 H3** NN6743.
Meall Horn *High.* ***Mountain***, 1m/2km SE of Creagan Meall Horn. Height 2549 feet or 777 metres. **103 F4** NC3544.
Meall Leacachain *High.* ***Mountain***, in Ross and Cromarty district, 2m/4km E of Corrieshalloch Gorge. Height 2027 feet or 618 metres. **95 J4** NH2477.
Meall Leathad na Craoibhe *High.* ***Mountain***, 1m/2km SE of Tongue, Caithness district. Height 1017 feet or 310 metres. **103 J3** NC6155.
Meall Leathan Dhail *Stir.* ***Mountain***, 3m/5km NE of Callander. Height 1588 feet or 484 metres. **81 H6** NN6611.
Meall Liath Choire *High.* ***Mountain***, in Ross and Cromarty district, 7m/11km E of Ullapool. Height 1797 feet or 548 metres. **95 J2** NH2296.
Meall Liath Mòr *High.* ***Mountain***, 3m/5km SW of Loch Laggan. Height 1686 feet or 514 metres. **88 B7** NN4080.
Meall Lighiche *High.* ***Mountain***, 4m/6km S of Glencoe village. Height 2532 feet or 772 metres. **80 B2** NN0952.
Meall Loch Airigh Alasdair *High.* ***Mountain***, in Ross and Cromarty district, 2m/3km SE of Toscaig. Height 1155 feet or 352 metres. **86 D1** NG7436.
Meall Luaidhe *P. & K.* ***Mountain***, 2m/3km S of Bridge of Balgie. Height 2558 feet or 780 metres. **81 G3** NN5843.
Meall Meadhonach *High.* ***Mountain***, 3m/5km S of Durness. Height 1384 feet or 422 metres. **103 G2** NC4062.
Meall Mheannaidh *High.* ***Mountain***, 2m/3km N of Letterewe, Ross and Cromarty district. Height 2362 feet or 720 metres. **95 F4** NG9574.

Meall Mhic Iomhair *High.* ***Mountain***, rounded summit in Ross and Cromarty district, 6m/10km NW of Garve. Height 1991 feet or 607 metres. **95 K5** NH3167.
Meall Mòr ***Mountain***, on border of Angus and Perth & Kinross, 3m/4km SE of Cray. Height 1807 feet or 551 metres. **82 C1** NO1760.
Meall Mòr *Arg. & B.* ***Mountain***, on Knapdale, 4m/7km NW of Tarbert. Mast on summit. Height 1574 feet or 480 metres. **73 G3** NR8374.
Meall Mòr *High.* ***Island***, one of two islets in Eddrachillis Bay off W coast of Sutherland district, 2m/4km offshore. **102 D5** NC1237.
Meall Mòr *High.* ***Mountain***, in Ross and Cromarty district between Loch Glass and Loch Morie. Height 2421 feet or 738 metres. **96 C4** NH5174.
Meall Mòr *High.* ***Mountain***, in Inverness district, 3m/4km SE of Daviot. Height 1614 feet or 492 metres. **88 E1** NH7335.
Meall Mòr *High.* ***Mountain***, 3m/5km E of Scamodale, Lochaber district. Height 2490 feet or 759 metres. **86 E7** NM8872.
Meall Mòr *High.* ***Mountain***, 2m/3km S of Glencoe village. Height 2217 feet or 676 metres. **80 C2** NN1055.
Meall Mòr *Stir.* ***Mountain***, 1m/2km N of head of Loch Katrine. Height 2450 feet or 747 metres. **80 E6** NN3815.
Meall Moraig *High.* ***Mountain***, in Sutherland district, 4m/6km NE of Bonar Bridge. Height 1089 feet or 332 metres. **96 D2** NH6694.
Meall na Caorach *Arg. & B.* ***Hill***, rising to over 230 metres in Salen Forest, 3m/5km NW of Salen, Mull. **79 G3** NM5347.
Meall na Caorach *High.* ***Mountain***, rising above Berriedale Water, 3m/5km NW of Berriedale. Height 1299 feet or 396 metres. **105 F6** ND0927.
Meall na Drochaide *High.* ***Mountain***, in Ross and Cromarty district, 9m/14km NE of Garve. Height 2309 feet or 704 metres. **96 C4** NH5069.
Meall na Duibhe *High.* ***Mountain***, 3m/4km E of Kinlochleven. Height 1870 feet or 570 metres. **80 D1** NN2262.
Meall na Faochaig *High.* ***Mountain***, in Ross and Cromarty district, 1m/2km N of Inverchoran. Height 2230 feet or 680 metres. **95 J6** NH2552.
Meall na Fhuaid *High.* ***Mountain***, 4m/7km SW of Ardheslaig, Ross and Cromarty district. Height 1699 feet or 518 metres. **94 D6** NG7350.
Meall na h-Aisre *High.* ***Mountain***, on border of Inverness and Badenoch and Strathspey districts, 10m/17km SE of Fort Augustus. Height 2827 feet or 862 metres. **88 C4** NH5100.
Meall na h-Eilrig *High.* ***Mountain***, in Inverness district, 3m/4km NE of Drumnadrochit. Height 1525 feet or 465 metres. **88 C1** NH5332.
Meall na h-Uamha *High.* ***Hill***, 3m/5km SE of Redpoint, Ross and Cromarty district. Height 945 feet or 288 metres. **94 D5** NG7765.
Meall na Leitreach *High.* ***Mountain***, 2m/3km S of Loch More. Height 1856 feet or 566 metres. **103 F5** NC3432.
Meall na Leitreach *P. & K.* ***Mountain***, on E side of Loch Garry. Height 2542 feet or 775 metres. **88 D7** NN6470.
Meall na Mèine *High.* ***Hill***, 3m/5km E of Poolewe. Height 823 feet or 251 metres. **95 F3** NG9081.
Meall na Moine *High.* ***Mountain***, 1m/2km NW of Creag Riabhach, Sutherland district. Height 1522 feet or 464 metres. **102 E2** NC2862.
Meall na Saobhaidhe *High.* ***Mountain***, 1m/2km SW of Beinn Damh, Ross and Cromarty district. Height 1207 feet or 368 metres. **94 E7** NG8748.
Meall na Speireig *High.* ***Mountain***, rising to over 610 metres, in Ross and Cromarty district, 2m/3km SE of Ben Wyvis. **96 B5** NH4966.
Meall na Suiramach *High.* ***Mountain***, 5m/8km SE of Rubha Hunish, Skye. Height 1781 feet or 543 metres. **93 K5** NG4469.
Meall na Teanga *High.* ***Mountain***, bounded by Allt Coire na Saighe Duibhe to N, and Allt an t-Srath a Dhuibh to S, the two main tributaries of River Mudale. Height 1197 feet or 365 metres. **103 G5** NC4834.
Meall na Teanga *High.* ***Mountain***, on NW side of Loch Lochy, 7m/11km N of Spean Bridge across the loch. Munro: height 3008 feet or 917 metres. **87 J5** NN2192.
Meall nam Bràdhan *High.* ***Mountain***, on borders of Ross and Cromarty and Sutherland districts, 6m/10km E of Leckmelm. Height 2221 feet or 677 metres. **95 J2** NH2690.
Meall nam Fiadh *P. & K.* ***Mountain***, 2m/3km N of St. Fillans. Height 2001 feet or 610 metres. **81 H5** NN6927.
Meall nam Fuaran *P. & K.* ***Mountain***, 5m/8km W of Amulree. Height 2640 feet or 805 metres. **81 K4** NN8236.
Meall nan Aighean *High.* ***Mountain***, 2m/3km SE of Loch Choire Lodge. Height 2276 feet or 694 metres. **103 J6** NC6828.
Meall nan Caorach *High.* ***Mountain***, in Inverness district, 4m/6km NW of Drumnadrochit. Height 1404 feet or 428 metres. **88 B1** NH4735.
Meall nan Caoraich *P. & K.* ***Mountain***, 9m/14km NW of Crieff. Height 2043 feet or 623 metres. **82 A4** NN9234.
Meall nan Ceapraichean *High.* ***Mountain***, in Ross and Cromarty district, 10m/16km SE of Ullapool. Munro: height 3205 feet or 977 metres. **95 J3** NH2582.
Meall nan Con *High.* ***Mountain***, summit of Ben Klibreck, situated 4m/6km S of Altnaharra, Sutherland district. Munro: height 3152 feet or 961 metres. **103 H5** NC5829.
Meall nan Con *High.* ***Mountain***, on Ardnamurchan peninsula, 3m/4km N of Kilchoan. Height 1433 feet or 437 metres. **79 G1** NM5068.
Meall nan Damh *High.* ***Mountain***, in Ross and Cromarty district, 6m/10km SW of Garve. Height 2201 feet or 671 metres. **95 K6** NH3552.
Meall nan Damh *High.* ***Mountain***, 4m/6km S of Glenfinnan, Lochaber district. Height 2371 feet or 723 metres. **87 F7** NM9174.
Meall nan Each *High.* ***Mountain***, 3m/4km N of Rubha na h-Airde Uinnsinn, Lochaber district. Height 1938 feet or 591 metres. **79 K2** NM8856.
Meall nan Eun *Arg. & B.* ***Mountain***, in Argyll 5m/8km E of head of Loch Etive. Munro: height 3037 feet or 926 metres. **80 C3** NN1944.
Meall nan Eun *High.* ***Mountain***, 2m/3km E of mouth of River Barrisdale, to S of Loch Hourn. Height 2184 feet or 666 metres. **87 F4** NG9005.
Meall nan Gabhar *High.* ***Island***, small island in Summer Isles group, adjacent to and N of Horse Island, and nearly 1m/2km W of NW coast of Ross and Cromarty district to S of Polglass. NC0205.
Meall nan Ruadhag *High.* ***Mountain***, on NW side of Rannoch Moor, and S of Blackwater Reservoir. Height 2119 feet or 646 metres. **80 D2** NN2957.
Meall nan Sùbh *P. & K.* ***Mountain***, 1m/2km SE of dam of Loch Lyon. Height 2637 feet or 804 metres. **81 F4** NN4639.
Meall nan Tarmachan *P. & K.* ***Mountain***, 4m/6km N of Killin. Munro: height 3421 feet or 1043 metres. **81 G4** NN5839.
Meall nan Tighearn ***Mountain***, on border of Argyll & Bute and Stirling, 5m/9km SE of Dalmally. Height 2424 feet or 739 metres. **80 D5** NN2323.
Meall Odhar ***Mountain***, on border of Perth & Kinross and Stirling, 4m/7km N of Callander. Height 2119 feet or 646 metres. **81 H6** NN6415.
Meall Odhar *High.* ***Mountain***, in Lochaber district, 8m/13km NW of Bridge of Orchy. Height 2873 feet or 876 metres. **80 C3** NN1946.
Meall Odhar *P. & K.* ***Mountain***, on NE side of Loch Tay, 8m/12km SW of Kenmore. Height 1794 feet or 547 metres. **81 H4** NN6640.
Meall Reamhar *Arg. & B.* ***Mountain***, on Kintyre, 5m/8km W of Tarbert. Height 1565 feet or 477 metres. **73 F4** NR7768.
Meall Reamhar *Arg. & B.* ***Mountain***, on Knapdale, 2m/3km NW of Tarbert. Height 1079 feet or 329 metres. **73 G4** NR8369.
Meall Reamhar *P. & K.* ***Mountain***, to S of Loch Earn, 3m/5km SW of St. Fillans. Height 2224 feet or 678 metres. **81 H5** NN6621.
Meall Reamhar *P. & K.* ***Mountain***, rounded summit, 3m/5km N of Blair Atholl. Height 1853 feet or 565 metres. **89 F7** NN8670.
Meall Reamhar *P. & K.* ***Mountain***, on N side of Glen Almond, 3m/5km SW of Amulree. Height 2188 feet or 667 metres. **81 K4** NN8732.
Meall Reamhar *P. & K.* ***Mountain***, 9m/13km S of Pitlochry. Height 1660 feet or 506 metres. **82 A3** NN9346.
Meall Reamhar *P. & K.* ***Mountain***, 4m/7km NE of Ballinluig. Height 1752 feet or 534 metres. **82 B2** NO0356.
Meall Tairneachan *P. & K.* ***Mountain***, 5m/7km NW of Aberfeldy. Height 2558 feet or 780 metres. **81 K2** NN8054.
Meall Tarsuinn *High.* ***Mountain***, in Lochaber district, 5m/8km N of Achnacarry. Height 2165 feet or 660 metres. **87 H5** NN1696.
Meall Tarsuinn *P. & K.* ***Mountain***, 5m/8km N of Crieff. Height 2125 feet or 648 metres. **81 K5** NN8729.
Meall Taurnie ***Mountain***, on border of Perth & Kinross and Stirling, 6m/10km NW of Killin. Height 2578 feet or 786 metres. **81 F4** NN4838.
Meall Thailm *High.* ***Island***, islet off NW coast of Eilean Iosal. NC6266.
Meall Uaine *P. & K.* ***Mountain***, 2m/3km S of Spittal of Glenshee. Height 2604 feet or 794 metres. **82 C1** NO1167.
Meallach Mhòr *High.* ***Mountain***, in Badenoch and Strathspey district 6m/10km S of Kingussie. Height 2522 feet or 769 metres. **88 E5** NN7790.
Meallan a' Chuail *High.* ***Mountain***, rises steeply to N of Loch Dubh a' Chuail, 2m/3km E of Beinn Leòid. Height 2460 feet or 750 metres. **103 F6** NC3429.
Meallan Buidhe *High.* ***Mountain***, rounded summit in Inverness district, 1m/2km S of central part of Loch Monar. Height 1820 feet or 555 metres. **87 H1** NH1337.
Meallan Buidhe *High.* ***Mountain***, in Inverness district, 8m/13km N of Cannich. Height 2512 feet or 766 metres. **95 K7** NH3344.
Meallan Chuaich *High.* ***Mountain***, rounded summit in Ross and Cromarty district, 7m/11km NE of Kinlochewe. Height 2263 feet or 690 metres. **95 H5** NH1168.
Meallan Liath *High.* ***Mountain***, 2m/3km E of Ben Hope. Height 1971 feet or 601 metres. **103 H3** NC5150.
Meallan Liath Beag *High.* ***Mountain***, in Sutherland district, 5m/8km NW of Lothbeg. Height 1571 feet or 479 metres. **104 D7** NC8815.
Meallan Liath Coire Mhic Dhughaill *High.* ***Mountain***, in Reay Forest in Sutherland district, 2m/3km NE of Loch More. Height 2627 feet or 801 metres. **103 F5** NC3539.
Meallan Liath Mòr *High.* ***Mountain***, rises to E of Loch Merkland. Height 2240 feet or 683 metres. **103 G5** NC4032.
Meallan Liath Mòr *High.* ***Mountain***, in Ben Armine Forest, 2m/4km NE of Dalnessie. Height 1512 feet or 461 metres. **103 J7** NC6518.
Meallan nan Uan *High.* ***Mountain***, in Ross and Cromarty district, 3m/4km W of Milton. Height 2755 feet or 840 metres. **95 J6** NH2654.
Meallan Odhar *High.* ***Mountain***, in Inverness district, 2m/3km N of Sgurr na Lapaich. Height 1870 feet or 570 metres. **87 H1** NH1538.
Meallan Odhar *High.* ***Mountain***, rounded summit in Inverness district, 5m/8km N of E end of Loch Cluanie. Height 2004 feet or 611 metres. **87 J3** NH2117.
Meallan Odhar *High.* ***Mountain***, rounded summit in Inverness district, 3m/5km NE of E end of Loch Mullardoch. Height 2276 feet or 694 metres. **87 J1** NH2435.
Mealna Letter (Also known as Duchray Hill.) *P. & K.* ***Mountain***, 4m/6km SE of Spittal of Glenshee. Height 2299 feet or 701 metres. **82 C1** NO1667.
Meals *Lincs.* ***Locality***, adjoining to N of North Somercotes. **53 H3** TF4197.
Mealsgate *Cumb.* ***Settlement***, 5m/8km SW of Wigton. **60 D2** NY2042.
Meanley *Lancs.* ***Settlement***, on W side of Easington Fell, 2m/3km S of Slaidburn. **56 C5** SD7049.
Meanwood *W.Yorks.* ***Suburb***, 2m/4km N of Leeds city centre. SE2837.
Mearbeck *N.Yorks.* ***Settlement***, 2m/3km S of Settle. **56 D3** SD8160.
Meare *Som.* ***Village***, 4m/6km NW of Glastonbury. Abbot's Fish House (English Heritage), 14c. **19 H7** ST4541.
Meare Green *Som.* ***Hamlet***, 3m/4km SW of North Curry. ST2922.
Mearley *Lancs.* ***Locality***, below W slope of Pendle Hill, 2m/3km E of Clitheroe. SD7741.
Mearns *E.Renf.* ***Locality***, adjoining to SE of Newton Mearns, 3m/5km NW of Eaglesham. **74 D5** NS5455.
Mears Ashby *Northants.* ***Village***, 4m/6km W of Wellingborough. **32 B2** SP8366.
Mease ***River***, rising E of Ashby de la Zouch and flowing first S, then W to Harlaston, and finally NW into River Trent 1km N of Croxall. **40 E4** SK1914.
Measham *Leics.* Population: 3656. ***Village***, 3m/5km SW of Ashby de la Zouch. **41 F4** SK3312.
Meath Green *W.Suss.* ***Suburb***, residential locality adjoining to NW of Horley. TQ2744.
Meathop *Cumb.* ***Hamlet***, 1m/2km E of Lindale. **55 H1** SD4380.
Meaul *D. & G.* ***Mountain***, towards N end of Rhinns of Kells, 4m/7km W of Carsphairn. Height 2280 feet or 695 metres. **67 K4** NX5090.
Meaux *E.Riding* ***Locality***, on site of 12c abbey, 4m/6km E of Beverley. TA0939.
Meavag *W.Isles Anglicised form of Meabhag, qv.*
Meavaig *W.Isles Anglicised form of Miabhag, qv.*
Meavy *Devon* ***River***, rising near Princetown and running SW through Burrator Reservoir and village of Meavy. It then turns S and runs into River Plym at N end of Bickleigh Vale. **5 F4** SX5156.
Meavy *Devon* ***Village***, on River Meavy, 6m/10km SE of Tavistock. **5 F4** SX5467.
Meayll Circle *I.o.M.* ***Historic/prehistoric site***, Neolithic chambered tomb 1km SW of Port Erin. Six pairs of chambers built of stone slabs, arranged in 50 foot or 15 metre diameter circle. **54 A7** SC1867.
Medbourne *Leics.* ***Village***, 6m/10km NE of Market Harborough. **42 B6** SP8093.
Medburn *Northumb.* ***Locality***, 3m/4km SW of Ponteland. NZ1370.
Meddon *Devon* ***Hamlet***, 5m/8km SW of Clovelly. **6 A4** SS2717.
Meden ***River***, rising W of Mansfield and flowing NE through Thoresby Park in The Dukeries to join River Maun and form River Idle 4m/6km S of Retford. **51 H6** SK7075.
Meden Vale *Notts.* Population: 2112. ***Village***, 1m/2km NE of Warsop and 6m/10km NE of Mansfield. **51 H6** SK5869.
Medge Hall *S.Yorks.* ***Settlement***, on Stainforth and Keadby Canal, 2m/3km W of Crowle. SE7412.
Medina *I.o.W.* ***River***, rising at Chale Green near S coast and flowing N into The Solent at Cowes. **11 G5** SZ5096.
Mediobogdum *Cumb. See Hardknott Castle.*
Mediolanum *Shrop. See Whitchurch.*
Medlam *Lincs.* ***Locality***, 1m/2km S of New Bolingbroke. TF3155.
Medlar *Lancs.* ***Settlement***, 2m/4km N of Kirkham. SD4135.
Medlock *Gt.Man.* ***River***, rising on W fringes of Saddleworth Moor, 3m/5km E of Oldham. It flows SW past Oldham, through Manchester, passing to S of city centre, before linking into Bridgewater Canal to NE of Old Trafford. SD9682.
Medlock Vale *Gt.Man.* ***Locality***, 2m/3km W of Ashton-under-Lyne. SJ9099.
Medmenham *Bucks.* ***Village***, on River Thames, 3m/5km W of Marlow. **22 B3** SU8084.
Medomsley *Dur.* ***Village***, 2m/3km N of Consett. **62 C1** NZ1154.
Medstead *Hants.* Population: 1922. ***Village***, 4m/6km W of Alton. **11 H1** SU6537.
Medway ***River***, rising near East Grinstead and flowing E through Tonbridge and Maidstone, then N to Rochester and Chatham, where it widens into an estuary flowing E to join River Thames estuary at Sheerness. Tidal to Allington, between Maidstone and Aylesford. **24 E4** TQ9075.
Medwin Water ***River***, rising in Pentland Hills on N slopes of White Craig and flowing S, forming border between South Lanarkshire and Scottish Borders, before joining with other streams to become South Medwin River. **75 J5** NT0949.
Medwin Water *S.Lan.* ***River***, formed by confluence of North and South Medwin Rivers and flowing W to join River Clyde at The Meetings, 1m/2km S of Carnwath. **75 H6** NS9744.
Meer Common *Here.* ***Settlement***, 5m/8km SE of Kington. SO3652.
Meer End *W.Mid.* ***Hamlet***, 4m/6km NW of Kenilworth. **30 D1** SP2474.
Meerbrook *Staffs.* ***Village***, 3m/5km N of Leek. **49 J6** SJ9860.
Meers Bridge *Lincs.* ***Locality***, at crossroads 1m/2km NW of Mablethorpe. TF4886.
Meersbrook *S.Yorks.* ***Suburb***, 2m/3km S of Sheffield city centre. SK3584.
Meesden *Herts.* ***Village***, 5m/7km NE of Buntingford. **33 H5** TL4332.
Meeson *Tel. & W.* ***Settlement***, 1m/2km W of Cherrington. SJ6520.
Meeson Heath *Tel. & W.* ***Settlement***, to SE of Meeson. SJ6520.
Meeth *Devon* ***Village***, 3m/4km N of Hatherleigh. **6 D5** SS5408.
Meeting House Hill *Norf.* ***Hamlet***, 2m/3km SE of North Walsham. TG3028.

Meggat Water *D. & G.* ***River***, running S to River Esk, 6m/10km NW of Langholm. **69 H4** NY2991.
Megget Reservoir *Sc.Bord.* ***Reservoir***, lies on course of Megget Water, 2m/3km W of Cappercleuch. **69 G1** NT2422.
Meggethead *Sc.Bord.* ***Settlement***, at W end of Megget Reservoir. **69 G1** NT1621.
Megginch Castle *P. & K.* ***Castle***, 16c castle in Carse of Gowrie, 1m/2km N of Errol. **82 D5** NO2424.
Meg's Craig *Angus* ***Coastal feature***, rock headland at N end of Castlesea Bay, 3m/5km NE of Arbroath. **83 H3** NO6843.
Meidrim *Carmar.* ***Village***, 3m/5km N of St. Clears. **17 F2** SN2820.
Meifod *Denb.* ***Settlement***, 2m/3km NW of Cyffylliog. **47 J7** SJ0359.
Meifod *Powys* ***Village***, 4m/7km S of Llanfyllin, in valley of River Vyrnwy, here called Dyffryn Meifod. **38 A4** SJ1513.
Meig *High.* ***River***, in Ross and Cromarty district, rising on West Monar Forest and running E to join River Conon 1m/2km below Loch Luichart. **96 A6** NH3956.
Meigle *P. & K.* ***Village***, 4m/6km SE of Alyth. Belmont Castle to S. Roman sites to N across Dean Water. **82 D3** NO2844.
Meigle Bay *N.Ayr.* ***Bay***, on Firth of Clyde 1m/2km S of Skelmorlie. **73 K4** NS1965.
Meigle Hill *Sc.Bord.* ***Mountain***, 1m/2km W of Galashiels. Height 1387 feet or 423 metres. **76 C7** NT4636.
Meigle Sculptured Stones *P. & K.* ***Historic/prehistoric site***, Christian and Pictish inscribed stones (Historic Scotland) in Meigle. Meigle Museum also houses around 30 stones from area, from 7c-10c. **82 D3** NO2844.
Meikle Balloch Hill ***Mountain***, on border of Aberdeenshire and Moray, 3m/4km E of Keith. Height 1200 feet or 366 metres. **98 C6** NJ4749.
Meikle Bin *Stir.* ***Mountain***, above Carron Valley Forest, on NE edge of Campsie Fells, 4m/6km N of Milton of Campsie. Height 1870 feet or 570 metres. **74 E2** NS6682.
Meikle Black Law *Sc.Bord.* ***Hill***, 3m/4km NE of Grantshouse. Height 804 feet or 245 metres. **77 G4** NT8268.
Meikle Carewe Hill *Aber.* ***Hill***, 5m/8km NW of Stonehaven. Height 872 feet or 266 metres. **91 G5** NO8292.
Meikle Conval *Moray* ***Mountain***, 3m/4km SW of Dufftown. Height 1866 feet or 569 metres. **89 K1** NJ2937.
Meikle Earnock *S.Lan.* ***Locality***, adjoining to S of Hamilton. **75 F5** NS7153.
Meikle Firbriggs *Moray* ***Mountain***, rising above E side of Black Water valley, 2m/3km NW of Cabrach. Height 1768 feet or 539 metres. **90 B2** NJ3528.
Meikle Grenach *Arg. & B.* ***Settlement***, on Bute, E of Loch Fad, 3m/4km SW of Rothesay. **73 J4** NS0760.
Meikle Hill *Moray* ***Hill***, 2m/3km SE of Dallas and 8m/13km W of Rothes. Height 932 feet or 284 metres. **97 J6** NJ1450.
Meikle Kilmory *Arg. & B.* ***Settlement***, on Bute, 3m/5km SW of Rothesay. **73 J4** NS0561.
Meikle Law *Sc.Bord.* ***Mountain***, in Lammermuir Hills, 4m/6km SW of Whiteadder Reservoir. Height 1535 feet or 468 metres. **76 D4** NT6059.
Meikle Loch *Aber.* ***Lake/loch***, small loch near E coast, 1m/2km N of Kirktown of Slains. **91 J1** NK0230.
Meikle Millyea *D. & G.* ***Mountain***, in Rhinns of Kells, 3m/5km N of NW corner of Clatteringshaws Loch. Height 2447 feet or 746 metres. **67 K5** NX5182.
Meikle Pap *Aber.* *See Lochnagar.*
Meikle Rahane *Arg. & B.* ***Settlement***, 3m/5km S of Garelochhead. **74 A2** NS2386.
Meikle Says Law *E.Loth.* ***Mountain***, summit of Lammermuir Hills, 5m/8km SE of Gifford. Height 1755 feet or 535 metres. **76 D4** NT5861.
Meikle Strath *Aber.* ***Settlement***, 3m/5km NE of Edzell. **90 E7** NO6471.
Meikle Tarty *Aber.* ***Settlement***, 2m/3km N of Newburgh. **91 H2** NJ9927.
Meikle Wartle *Aber.* ***Hamlet***, 6m/9km NW of Oldmeldrum. **91 F1** NJ7230.
Meikleour *P. & K.* ***Village***, 4m/6km S of Blairgowrie. Beech hedge of Meikleour House borders A93 road S of here for 580 yards or 530 metres. Planted in 1746, it is now 85 feet or 26 metres high. **82 C4** NO1539.
Meinciau *Carmar.* ***Hamlet***, 4m/7km NE of Kidwelly. **17 H3** SN4610.
Meir *Stoke* ***Suburb***, 4m/6km SE of Stoke-on-Trent city centre. **40 B1** SJ9342.
Meirheath *Staffs.* ***Locality***, 3m/4km SE of Longton, Stoke-on-Trent. **40 B2** SJ9339.
Meisgyn *R.C.T. Welsh form of Miskin, qv.*
Meith Bheinn *High.* ***Mountain***, peak in South Morar, Lochaber district, between Loch Morar and Loch Beoraid. Height 2329 feet or 710 metres. **86 E6** NM8287.
Melbecks Moor *N.Yorks.* ***Open space***, moorland straddling Gunnerside Hill, 3m/5km E of Keld. **62 A6** NY9301.
Melbost *W.Isles* ***Village***, on Isle of Lewis, 3m/4km E of Stornoway. Stornoway Airport on W side of village. **101 G4** NB4632.
Melbost Borve *W.Isles Anglicised form of Mealabost, qv.*
Melbost Point *W.Isles* ***Coastal feature***, headland to N of Melbost. **101 G4** NB4632.
Melbost Sands *W.Isles* ***Coastal feature***, on River Laxdale estuary to NW of Melbost, covered at high tide. **101 G4** NB4632.
Melbourn *Cambs.* Population: 4006. ***Village***, 3m/5km NE of Royston. **33 G4** TL3844.
Melbourne *Derbys.* Population: 4316. ***Small town***, 7m/12km S of Derby. Particularly notable for its Norman church. Birthplace of Thomas Cook, travel pioneer. **41 F3** SK3825.
Melbourne *E.Riding* ***Village***, 4m/7km SW of Pocklington. **58 D5** SE7544.
Melbourne Hall *Derbys.* ***Historic house***, 8m/13km S of Derby. Mainly 18c, with formal gardens. **41 F3** SK3825.
Melbury *Devon* ***Settlement***, 6m/10km SW of Bideford. **6 B4** SS3719.
Melbury Abbas *Dorset* ***Village***, 2m/4km SE of Shaftesbury. **9 H3** ST8820.
Melbury Bubb *Dorset* ***Village***, 2m/3km NE of Evershot. **8 E4** ST5906.
Melbury Osmond *Dorset* ***Village***, 5m/8km S of Yeovil. **8 E4** ST5707.
Melbury Sampford *Dorset* ***Settlement***, 1m/2km N of Evershot. Church and 16c house in Melbury Park. **8 E4** ST5706.
Melby *Shet.* ***Village***, on W coast of Mainland, opposite Papa Stour. **109 A7** HU1957.
Melchbourne *Beds.* ***Village***, 5m/7km E of Rushden. **32 D2** TL0265.
Melchet Court *Hants.* ***Settlement***, 2m/4km SE of Whiteparish. **10 D2** SU2722.
Melcombe Bingham *Dorset* ***Village***, 5m/8km N of Puddletown. **9 G4** ST7602.
Melcombe Horsey *Dorset* ***Locality***, 5m/8km N of Puddletown. ST7502.
Melcombe Regis *Dorset* ***Suburb***, N district of Weymouth. **9 F6** SY6880.
Meldon *Devon* ***Hamlet***, 3m/4km SW of Okehampton. **6 D6** SX5692.
Meldon *Northumb.* ***Hamlet***, 5m/8km W of Morpeth. **71 G5** NZ1183.
Meldon Viaduct *Devon* ***Bridge***, iron lattice railway viaduct built in 1871 with track 150 feet or 50 metres above ground, 3m/4km SW of Okehampton. SX5692.
Meldreth *Cambs.* ***Village***, 4m/6km NE of Royston. **33 G4** TL3746.
Meledor *Cornw.* ***Settlement***, in China Clay district, 6m/9km W of St. Austell. SW9254.
Melford Hall *Suff.* ***Historic house***, brick Tudor mansion (National Trust) with surrounding garden, to E of Melford green at N end of Long Melford. Includes Beatrix Potter display. **34 C4** TL8746.
Melfort *Arg. & B.* ***Settlement***, in Argyll, at head of Loch Melfort, 1m/2km NW of Kilmelford. **79 K6** NM8314.
Melgam Water *Angus* ***River***, a continuation of Black Water, which flows SE into Loch of Lintrathen and exits at Bridgend of Lintrathen, then flows S to join River Isla by Airlie Castle, 4m/6km NE of Alyth. **82 D2** NO2952.
Melgarve *High.* ***Settlement***, to S of Corrieyairack Forest, 10m/17km NW of Kinloch Laggan. **88 B5** NN4695.
Melgum *Aber.* ***Settlement***, 1m/2km N of Tarland. **90 C4** NJ4706.
Meliden (Gallt Melyd). *Denb.* ***Village***, 1m/2km S of Prestatyn. **47 J4** SJ0680.
Melin Caiach *M.Tyd.* ***Locality***, on E side of Treharris. ST1097.
Melin Ifan Ddu *Bridgend Welsh form of Blackmill, qv.*
Melin-y-coed *Conwy* ***Hamlet***, 1m/2km SE of Llanrwst. **47 G6** SH8160.
Melin-y-ddol *Powys* ***Settlement***, in River Banwy valley, 1m/2km W of Llanfair Caereinion. **37 K5** SJ0907.
Melin-y-grug *Powys* ***Settlement***, 3m/5km NW of Llanfair Caereinion. **37 K5** SJ0507.
Melin-y-Wig *Denb.* ***Hamlet***, 5m/9km E of Cerrigydrudion. **37 K1** SJ0448.
Melinbyrhedyn *Powys* ***Settlement***, 5m/7km E of Machynlleth. SN8198.
Melincourt *N.P.T.* ***Hamlet***, 6m/10km NE of Neath, where Melin Court Brook joins River Neath from SE. **18 B1** SN8101.
Melincryddan *N.P.T.* ***Suburb***, in S part of Neath. **18 A2** SS7596.
Melinddwr *Carmar.* ***River***, rising 4m/6km SE of Llanybydder and flowing SE by Rhydcymerau into River Marlais at Llansawel. **17 J1** SN6236.
Melkinthorpe *Cumb.* ***Hamlet***, 4m/7km SE of Penrith. **61 G4** NY5525.
Melkridge *Northumb.* ***Village***, 2m/3km E of Haltwhistle. **70 C7** NY7363.
Melksham *Wilts.* Population: 13,074. ***Town***, small industrial town on River Avon, 6m/10km S of Chippenham. Large 15c church. **20 C5** ST9063.
Melksham Forest *Wilts.* ***Suburb***, to E of Melksham. **20 C5** ST9063.
Mell Head *High.* ***Coastal feature***, headland at SW end of Stroma in Pentland Firth. **105 J1** ND3376.
Melldalloch *Arg. & B.* ***Settlement***, in Argyll, 3m/4km S of Kilfinan. **73 H3** NR9274.
Mellerstain House *Sc.Bord.* ***Historic house***, 18c mansion by William and Robert Adam, 6m/10km NW of Kelso. **76 E7** NT6439.
Mellguards *Cumb.* ***Locality***, 2m/3km S of Wreay and 6m/10km SE of Carlisle. NY4445.
Melling *Lancs.* ***Village***, 5m/8km S of Kirkby Lonsdale. **55 J2** SD5971.
Melling *Mersey.* ***Village***, 2m/3km SE of Maghull. **48 C2** SD3900.
Melling Green *Lancs.* ***Locality***, adjoining to SW of Melling. SD5971.
Melling Mount *Mersey.* ***Hamlet***, 1m/2km NE of Melling. **48 D2** SD3900.
Mellis *Suff.* ***Village***, 3m/5km W of Eye. **34 E1** TM1074.
Mellon Charles *High.* ***Settlement***, 2m/3km NW of Aultbea, on W coast of Ross and Cromarty district. **94 E2** NG8591.
Mellon Udrigle *High.* ***Locality***, 3m/4km SE of Greenstone Point, W coast of Ross and Cromarty district. **94 E2** NG8895.
Mellor *Gt.Man.* ***Village***, 2m/3km E of Marple. **49 J4** SJ9888.
Mellor *Lancs.* Population: 2244. ***Village***, 3m/4km NW of Blackburn. **56 B6** SD6530.
Mellor Brook *Lancs.* ***Village***, 1m/2km W of Mellor. **56 B6** SD6530.
Mells *Som.* ***Village***, 3m/5km W of Frome. **20 A7** ST7249.
Mells Green *Som.* ***Hamlet***, 1km SW of Mells, 3m/5km W of Frome. ST7248.
Mellte ***River***, rising on Fforest Fawr and flowing S by Ystradfellte into River Neath, 1m/2km E of Glyn-neath. **27 J7** SN9007.
Melmerby *Cumb.* ***Village***, 8m/12km NE of Penrith. **61 H3** NY6137.
Melmerby *N.Yorks.* ***Village***, 4m/6km SW of Middleham. **57 F1** SE0785.
Melmerby *N.Yorks.* ***Village***, 4m/6km NE of Ripon. **57 J2** SE3376.
Melmerby Fell *Cumb.* ***Mountain***, 3m/4km E of Melmerby. Height 2329 feet or 710 metres. **61 H3** NY6537.
Melmerby Green End *N.Yorks.* ***Locality***, adjoining to S of Melmerby. SE3376.
Melon Green *Suff.* ***Settlement***, 1m/2km SE of Whepstead. TL8457.
Melowther Hill *E.Renf.* ***Hill***, 2m/3km S of Eaglesham. Height 987 feet or 301 metres. **74 D6** NS5648.
Melplash *Dorset* ***Village***, 2m/3km S of Beaminster. **8 D5** SY4898.
Melrose *Aber.* ***Locality***, comprises Mains of Melrose and Mill of Melrose, 3m/4km E of Macduff. **99 F4** NJ7464.
Melrose *Sc.Bord.* Population: 2270. ***Small town***, on S side of River Tweed 4m/6km E of Galashiels. Ruins of 12c abbey (Historic Scotland). See also Old Melrose. **76 D7** NT5434.
Melrose Abbey *Sc.Bord.* ***Ecclesiastical building***, ruins of Cistercian Abbey (Historic Scotland) founded around 1136 by David I. Almost destroyed during Wars of Independence and current remains, largely 15c, are considered to be the most elegant in Scotland. Robert the Bruce bequeathed his heart to abbey. **76 D7** NT5434.
Melsetter *Ork.* ***Settlement***, at S end of Hoy, 1m/2km NE of Tor Ness. **107 B9** ND2689.
Melsonby *N.Yorks.* ***Village***, 2m/4km NW of Scotch Corner. **62 C6** NZ1908.
Meltham *W.Yorks.* Population: 7514. ***Small town***, former textile town 5m/7km SW of Huddersfield. 1m/2km SW is site of ancient fort, probably dating from Iron Age. **50 C1** SE0910.
Meltham Mills *W.Yorks.* ***Locality***, adjoining to E of Meltham. SE1110.
Melton *E.Riding* ***Village***, 1m/2km NW of North Ferriby. SE9726.
Melton *Suff.* ***Village***, adjoining to NE of Woodbridge. **35 G3** TM2850.
Melton Constable *Norf.* ***Village***, 4m/7km SW of Holt. **44 E2** TG0433.
Melton Mowbray *Leics.* Population: 24,348. ***Town***, old market town on River Wreake or Eye, 14m/22km NE of Leicester, famous for its pork pies and Stilton cheese. Former medieval wool town, it has a large 13c church. Anne of Cleves' medieval house. **42 A4** SK7519.
Melton Ross *N.Lincs.* ***Village***, 5m/8km NW of Brigg. **52 D1** TA0610.
Meltonby *E.Riding* ***Settlement***, 2m/3km N of Pockington. **58 D4** SE7952.
Meluncart *Aber.* ***Mountain***, 3m/5km SW of Bridge of Dye. Height 1722 feet or 525 metres. **90 E6** NO6382.
Melvaig *High.* ***Village***, on W coast of Ross and Cromarty district, 3m/5km S of Rubha Réidh. **94 D3** NG7486.
Melverley *Shrop.* ***Hamlet***, 10m/16km W of Shrewsbury. **38 C4** SJ3316.
Melverley Green *Shrop.* ***Hamlet***, 1m/2km NW of Melverley. **38 C4** SJ3316.
Melvich *High.* ***Village***, near N coast of Caithness district, 15m/24km W of Thurso. **104 D2** NC8864.
Melvich Bay *High.* ***Bay***, 1km N of Melvich, on N coast of Caithness district. **104 D2** NC8864.
Melville's Monument *P. & K.* ***Other feature of interest***, obelisk on hill, 1m/2km N of Comrie, commemorating Lord Melville, 1742-1811. **81 J5** NN7623.
Membury *Devon* ***Village***, 3m/5km NW of Axminster. **8 B4** ST2703.
Memsie *Aber.* ***Village***, 3m/5km SW of Fraserburgh. Bronze Age burial cairn (Historic Scotland). **99 H4** NJ9762.
Memsie Cairn *Aber.* ***Historic/prehistoric site***, fine example of large stone cairn, possibly Bronze Age, 3m/5km S of Fraserburgh. **99 H4** NJ9762.
Memus *Angus* ***Village***, 6m/9km NW of Forfar. **83 F2** NO4258.
Men of Mey *High.* ***Coastal feature***, cluster of rocks off St. John's Point on N coast of Caithness district. **105 J1** ND3175.
Menabilly *Cornw.* ***Settlement***, 2m/3km W of Fowey. **4 A5** SX1051.
Menai Bridge (Porthaethwy). *I.o.A.* Population: 3175. ***Small town***, on Anglesey, at N end of road bridge spanning Menai Strait, 1m/2km W of Bangor. Bridge designed by Telford and built early 19c. **46 D5** SH5571.
Menai Strait *Gwyn.* ***Sea feature***, sea channel separating Anglesey from Welsh mainland. Is some 14m/23km long from Beaumaris to Abermenai Point, and spanned by a road bridge, Menai Bridge, and a combined road and railway bridge, Britannia Bridge. **46 C6** SH5370.
Mendham *Suff.* ***Village***, on River Waveney, 2m/3km E of Harleston. **45 G7** TM2782.
Mendick Hill *Sc.Bord.* ***Mountain***, 2m/3km SW of West Linton. Height 1479 feet or 451 metres. **75 K5** NT1250.
Mendip Forest *Som.* ***Open space***, area of Mendip Hills to NE of Cheddar, with only a few copses of woodland. **19 H6** ST4954.
Mendip Hills *Som.* ***Large natural feature***, carboniferous limestone ridge running 27m/42km NW from a line through Bruton and Frome, almost to Weston-super-Mare and Bristol Channel. Contains many potholes and caverns, best known being at Cheddar Gorge and Wookey Hole. **19 H6** ST5254.
Mendlesham *Suff.* ***Village***, 6m/9km NE of Stowmarket. **35 F2** TM1065.
Mendlesham Green *Suff.* ***Village***, 2m/3km S of Mendlesham. **34 E2** TM1065.

Menethorpe *N.Yorks.* ***Settlement***, 3m/5km S of Malton. **58 D3** SE7667.

Mengham *Hants.* ***Suburb***, of South Hayling, on Hayling Island. SZ7399.

Menheniot *Cornw.* ***Village***, 3m/4km SE of Liskeard. **4 C4** SX2862.

Menie House *Aber.* ***Settlement***, near small lake, 2m/3km N of Balmedie. **91 H2** NJ9720.

Menithwood *Worcs.* ***Village***, 7m/11km E of Tenbury Wells. SO7069.

Mennock *D. & G.* ***Village***, 2m/3km SE of Sanquhar, at confluence of River Nith and Mennock Water, which flows SW down Mennock Pass. **68 D3** NS8008.

Mennock Pass *D. & G.* ***Other feature of interest***, pass carrying road over Lowther Hills at height of 676 feet or 206 metres, between Mennock and Wanlockhead. **68 D2** NS8410.

Mennock Water *D. & G.* ***River***, rising 1km S of Wanlockhead and flowing into River Nith at Mennock, 2m/3km SE of Sanquhar. **68 D3** NS8008.

Menston *W.Yorks.* Population: 4888. ***Village***, 6m/10km N of Bradford. **57 G5** SE1743.

Menstrie *Clack.* Population: 2274. ***Small town***, 4m/6km NE of Stirling. 16c castle was home of Sir William Alexander, 1567-1640, founder of Nova Scotia. **75 G1** NS8496.

Menstrie Castle *Clack.* ***Castle***, late 16c L-plan tower house (National Trust for Scotland) at Menstrie. Birthplace of Sir William Alexander, founder of Nova Scotia. **75 G1** NS8596.

Menteith Hills *Stir.* ***Large natural feature***, range of low hills between Aberfoyle and Callander. **81 G7** NN5603.

Menthorpe *N.Yorks.* ***Settlement***, on W side of River Derwent, 2m/3km SE of North Duffield. SE7034.

Mentmore *Bucks.* ***Historic house***, good example of 19c Jacobean revival designed by Sir Joseph Paxton for Rothschilds to W of Mentmore, 4m/6km S of Leighton Buzzard. Presently used as headquarters for Maharishi University of Natural Law. **32 B7** SP9019.

Mentmore *Bucks.* ***Village***, 4m/6km S of Leighton Buzzard. **32 C7** SP9019.

Meoble *High.* ***River***, in South Morar, Lochaber district, running N from foot of Loch Beoraid to Loch Morar. Locality of Meoble on right bank 1m/2km above mouth. **86 E6** NM7889.

Meoble *High.* ***Settlement***, on E bank of River Meoble, 4m/6km NE of Lochailort. **86 D6** NM7987.

Meoir Langwell *High.* ***River***, stream formed by many small tributaries, flowing N from slopes of Coire Buidhe into River Oykel, 3m/5km E of Oykel Bridge. **96 B2** NC4301.

Meole Brace *Shrop.* ***Suburb***, S district of Shrewsbury. **38 D4** SJ4810.

Meon *Hants.* ***River***, rising 1m/2km S of East Meon and flowing NW through East and West Meon, then SW through Wickham and Titchfield into The Solent 1km W of Hill Head. **11 H2** SU5302.

M

Meon *Hants.* ***Settlement***, 1m/2km S of Titchfield. **11 G4** SU5303.

Meon Hill *Warks.* ***Hill***, 1m/2km NE of Mickleton. Height 636 feet or 194 metres. **30 C4** SP1745.

Meon Valley *Hants.* ***Valley***, carrying River Meon SW between Corhampton and Wickham. **11 G3** SU5812.

Meonstoke *Hants.* ***Village***, on River Meon, 4m/7km E of Bishop's Waltham. **11 H3** SU6119.

Meopham *Kent* Population: 4956. ***Village***, 5m/8km S of Gravesend. **24 C5** TQ6466.

Meopham Green *Kent* ***Locality***, to S of Meopham. **24 C5** TQ6466.

Meopham Station *Kent* ***Locality***, residential locality to N of Meopham. TQ6466.

Mepal *Cambs.* ***Village***, 6m/10km W of Ely. **43 H7** TL4480.

Meppershall *Beds.* ***Village***, 2m/3km S of Shefford. **32 E5** TL1336.

Merbach *Here.* ***Settlement***, 5m/8km NE of Hay-on-Wye. **28 C4** SO3045.

Mercaston *Derbys.* ***Settlement***, 7m/11km NW of Derby. **40 E1** SK2643.

Merchant Fields *W.Yorks.* ***Locality***, 1m/2km N of Cleckheaton. SE1926.

Merchants Square *Gt.Man.* ***Locality***, 1km NE of Lowton. SJ6298.

Merchiston *Edin.* ***Suburb***, 1m/2km SW of Edinburgh city centre. NT2472.

Mere *Ches.* ***Village***, 3m/4km NW of Knutsford. **49 G4** SJ7281.

Mere *Wilts.* Population: 2257. ***Village***, 7m/11km NW of Shaftesbury. **9 H1** ST8132.

Mere Brow *Lancs.* ***Village***, 5m/9km E of Southport. **48 D1** SD4118.

Mere Clough *Lancs.* ***Hamlet***, 3m/5km SE of Burnley. SD8730.

Mere Green *W.Mid.* ***Locality***, 2m/3km N of Sutton Coldfield. **40 D6** SP1199.

Mere Green *Worcs.* ***Settlement***, 4m/6km E of Droitwich Spa. SO9562.

Mere Heath *Ches.* ***Hamlet***, 2m/3km S of Northwich. SJ6670.

Mere Side *Cambs.* ***Open space***, fenland on W bank of River Nene (old course), 2m/4km N of Ramsey. **43 F7** TL2989.

Mere Side *Lancs.* ***Locality***, on S side of Holmeswood, 6m/9km E of Southport. SD4316.

Mereside *B'pool* ***Suburb***, 2m/4km SE of Blackpool town centre. SD3434.

Meretown *Staffs.* ***Settlement***, 1m/2km NE of Newport. SJ7520.

Merevale *Warks.* ***Settlement***, 1km SW of Atherstone. Remains of 12c abbey. Early Victorian hall in park. **40 E6** SP2997.

Mereworth *Kent* ***Village***, 6m/10km W of Maidstone. **23 K6** TQ6653.

Mergie *Aber.* ***Settlement***, 1m/2km W of Rickarton. **91 F6** NO7988.

Meriden *W.Mid.* Population: 1781. ***Village***, 6m/10km W of Coventry. **40 E7** SP2482.

Merkadale *High.* ***Settlement***, on S side of Loch Harport, near head of loch, 1m/2km SE of Carbost, Skye. NG3831.

Merkinch *High.* ***Suburb***, NW district of Inverness. NH6546.

Merkland *D. & G.* ***Settlement***, 2m/3km S of Corsock. **65 H3** NX7473.

Merkland Cross *D. & G.* ***Historic/prehistoric site***, 2m/3km NW of Kirkpatrick-Fleming. Cross, 9 feet or 3 metres high, dating from 1494 and thought to commemorate death of member of Maxwell family in battle. **69 H6** NY2472.

Merkland Point *N.Ayr.* ***Coastal feature***, headland on E coast of Arran, at N end of Brodick Bay. **73 J7** NS0238.

Merley *Poole* ***Village***, 4m/6km N of Poole town centre. SZ0298.

Merlin's Bridge *Pembs.* ***Locality***, on Merlin's Brook, 1km SW of Haverfordwest. **16 C3** SM9414.

Merrick *D. & G.* ***Mountain***, in Glentrool Forest Park, 4m/6km N of Loch Trool. Height 2765 feet or 843 metres. **67 J5** NX4285.

Merridge *Som.* ***Hamlet***, at foot of Quantock Hills, 4m/6km S of Nether Stowey. **8 B1** ST2034.

Merrifield *Devon* ***Hamlet***, 4m/7km SE of Bude. SS2601.

Merrifield *Devon* ***Settlement***, 5m/8km SW of Dartmouth. **5 J6** SX8147.

Merrington *Shrop.* ***Settlement***, 5m/9km N of Shrewsbury. **38 D3** SJ4720.

Merrion *Pembs.* ***Hamlet***, 4m/7km SW of Pembroke. **16 C5** SR9396.

Merriott *Som.* Population: 1956. ***Village***, 2m/3km N of Crewkerne. **8 D3** ST4412.

Merrivale *Devon* ***Settlement***, on Dartmoor, 4m/7km E of Tavistock. **5 F3** SX5475.

Merrivale Prehistoric Settlement *Devon* ***Historic/prehistoric site***, to E of Merrivale, 4m/7km E of Tavistock. Early Bronze Age settlement (English Heritage) consisting of hut circles, cairns and stone rows. **5 F3** SX5574.

Merrow *Surr.* ***Suburb***, E district of Guildford. **22 D6** TQ0250.

Merry Field Hill *Dorset* ***Settlement***, 1m/2km NE of Wimborne Minster. SU0201.

Merry Hill *Herts.* ***Settlement***, adjoining to S of Bushey. **22 E2** TQ1394.

Merry Hill *W.Mid.* ***Leisure/recreation***, large shopping centre in Brierley Hill, 2m/4km SW of Dudley. **40 B7** SO9287.

Merry Hill *W.Mid.* ***Suburb***, SW district of Wolverhampton. SO8897.

Merry Lees *Leics.* ***Locality***, 1m/2km S of Thornton. SK4705.

Merry Oak *S'ham.* ***Suburb***, 2m/3km E of Southampton city centre across River Itchen. SU4412.

Merrybent *Darl.* ***Locality***, 3m/5km W of Darlington. NZ2414.

Merryhill Green *W'ham* ***Locality***, residential locality adjoining to N of Winnersh, 2m/4km NW of Wokingham. SU7871.

Merrymeet *Cornw.* ***Hamlet***, 2m/3km NE of Liskeard. **4 C4** SX2866.

Merse *D. & G.* ***Marsh/bog***, marshland on N coast of Solway Firth, on E side of mouth of River Nith. **69 F7** NY0464.

Mersea Flats *Essex* ***Coastal feature***, mud flat on S side of Mersea Island. **34 E7** TM0512.

Mersea Island *Essex* ***Island***, off coast, 6m/10km SE of Colchester, between estuaries of River Blackwater to SW and River Colne to NE. Joined to mainland by causeway across Strood Channel on N side of island. **34 E7** TM0414.

Mersehead Sands *D. & G.* ***Coastal feature***, sandflat in Solway Firth, from Southerness Point in E to Cow's Snout in W. **65 K5** NX9053.

Mersey ***River***, whose source is at confluence of Rivers Goyt and Tame at Stockport, and which flows into Irish Sea at Liverpool. Estuary provides important shipping lane and forms E edge of Wirral peninsula. Tidal from Warrington. **48 C4** SJ3195.

Mersham *Kent* ***Village***, 3m/5km SE of Ashford. **15 F4** TR0539.

Merstham *Surr.* ***Village***, 2m/3km N of Redhill. **23 F6** TQ2953.

Merston *W.Suss.* ***Village***, 2m/3km SE of Chichester. **12 B6** SU8903.

Merstone *I.o.W.* ***Village***, 3m/5km SE of Newport. **11 G6** SZ5285.

Merther *Cornw.* ***Hamlet***, 2m/4km E of Truro across Tresillian River. **3 F4** SW8644.

Merthyr *Carmar.* ***Settlement***, 4m/6km W of Carmarthen. **17 G2** SN3520.

Merthyr Cynog *Powys* ***Hamlet***, 7m/11km NW of Brecon. **27 J5** SN9837.

Merthyr Dyfan *V. of Glam.* ***Locality***, 1m/2km N of Barry. **18 E5** ST1169.

Merthyr Mawr *Bridgend* ***Village***, 2m/3km SW of Bridgend. **18 B4** SS8877.

Merthyr Tydfil *M.Tyd.* Population: 39,482. ***Town***, former iron, steel and coal town, 21m/33km NW of Cardiff. Ruins of Norman Morlais Castle to N. Birthplace of composer Joseph Parry. **18 D1** SO0406.

Merthyr Vale (Ynysowen). *M.Tyd.* Population: 4298. ***Village***, 5m/7km S of Merthyr Tydfil. **18 D2** ST0799.

Merton *Devon* ***Village***, 5m/8km SE of Great Torrington. **6 D4** SS5212.

Merton *Norf.* ***Village***, 1m/2km S of Watton. **44 C6** TL9098.

Merton *Oxon.* ***Village***, 3m/5km S of Bicester. **31 G7** SP5717.

Merton Abbey Wall *Gt.Lon. See Colliers Wood.*

Mertoun House *Sc.Bord.* ***Garden***, on N bank of River Tweed, 3m/4km E of Newtown St. Boswell, with 20 acres of trees and herbaceous plants, as well as walled garden and circular dovecote. **76 E7** NT6131.

Mertyn *Flints.* ***Settlement***, 2m/3km NW of Holywell. **47 K5** SJ1577.

Mervinslaw *Sc.Bord.* ***Settlement***, to SW of Camptown, over Jed Water. **70 B2** NT6713.

Meshaw *Devon* ***Village***, 5m/8km SE of South Molton. **7 F4** SS7519.

Messing *Essex* ***Hamlet***, 2m/4km E of Kelvedon. **34 C7** TL8918.

Messingham *N.Lincs.* Population: 2952. ***Village***, 4m/7km S of Scunthorpe. **52 B2** SE8904.

Mesty Croft *W.Mid.* ***Locality***, 3m/4km N of West Bromwich town centre. SO9994.

Metcombe *Devon* ***Hamlet***, 3m/4km SW of Ottery St. Mary. SY0891.

Metfield *Suff.* ***Village***, 4m/6km SE of Harleston. **45 G7** TM2980.

Metheringham *Lincs.* Population: 2414. ***Village***, 9m/14km SE of Lincoln. **52 D6** TF0661.

Metherwell *Cornw.* ***Village***, 3m/5km E of Callington. SX4069.

Methil *Fife* ***Town***, port on N coast of Firth of Forth, 8m/12km NE of Kirkcaldy. Formerly a joint burgh with Buckhaven and busy coal port. **76 B1** NT3799.

Methilhill *Fife* ***Suburb***, W district of Methil. NO0035.

Methlem *Gwyn.* ***Settlement***, on SW end of Lleyn Peninsula, 2m/3km N of Aberdaron. **36 A2** SH1730.

Methley *W.Yorks.* ***Village***, 5m/8km NE of Wakefield. **57 J7** SE3926.

Methley Junction *W.Yorks.* ***Hamlet***, at railway junction, 1km SW of Mickletown. SE3925.

Methley Lanes *W.Yorks.* ***Settlement***, 1m/2km W of Methley Junction across M62 motorway. SE3725.

Methlick *Aber.* ***Village***, on River Ythan, 6m/10km S of New Deer. **91 G1** NJ8537.

Methven *P. & K.* Population: 1139. ***Village***, 6m/10km W of Perth. **82 B5** NO0225.

Methven Castle *P. & K.* ***Castle***, 17c tower house, where Queen Margaret Tudor died in 1541, 1m/2km E of Methven. NO0425.

Methwold *Norf.* ***Village***, 6m/10km NW of Brandon. **44 B6** TL7394.

Methwold Fens *Norf.* ***Open space***, fenland 2m/3km SE of Southery. **44 A6** TL6493.

Methwold Hythe *Norf.* ***Village***, 1m/2km W of Methwold. **44 B6** TL7394.

Metrocentre *T. & W.* ***Leisure/recreation***, large shopping centre to S of River Tyne, 3m/4km W of Gateshead town centre. **71 H7** NZ2162.

Metroland *T. & W.* ***Leisure/recreation***, Europe's largest indoor amusement park within Metrocentre shopping centre, 3m/4km W of Gateshead town centre. **71 H7** NZ2162.

Mettingham *Suff.* ***Village***, 2m/3km E of Bungay. Remains of 14c castle 1m/2km S. **45 H6** TM3690.

Metton *Norf.* ***Hamlet***, 3m/5km S of Cromer. **45 F2** TG2037.

Meugher *N.Yorks.* ***Mountain***, to E of Conistone Moor, 4m/7km NE of Grassington. Height 1886 feet or 575 metres. **57 F2** SE0370.

Mevagissey *Cornw.* Population: 2272. ***Small town***, fishing port on Mevagissey Bay, 5m/8km S of St. Austell, with inner and outer harbours. Lost Gardens of Heligan 1m/2km NW. **4 A6** SX0144.

Mevagissey Bay *Cornw.* ***Bay***, E facing bay, extending S from Black Head to Chapel Point, 4m/7km S of St. Austell. **4 A6** SX0144.

Mevvy *Devon* ***River***, rising 1km SW of Princetown and flowing S to Burrator Reservoir. **5 F3** SX5669.

Mew Stone *Devon* ***Island***, rock islet S of Outer Froward Point, 3m/4km SE of Dartmouth. **5 K6** SX9149.

Mew Stone *Pembs.* ***Island***, islet just off S coast of Skomer Island. **16 A4** SM7208.

Mewith Head *N.Yorks.* ***Settlement***, 3m/4km SE of High Bentham. SD7066.

Mexborough *S.Yorks.* Population: 15,282. ***Town***, 5m/8km NE of Rotherham. **51 G3** SK4799.

Mey *High.* ***Village***, near N coast of Caithness district, 6m/9km W of John o' Groats. **105 H1** ND2872.

Meynell Langley *Derbys.* ***Locality***, 5m/8km NW of Derby. SK2840.

Meysey Hampton *Glos.* ***Village***, 2m/3km W of Fairford. **20 E1** SP1100.

Miabhag (Anglicised form: Meavaig.) *W.Isles* ***Settlement***, on NE shore of Loch Meavaig, North Harris. **100 C7** NB0905.

Miabhig (Anglicised form: Miavaig). *W.Isles* ***Village***, at head of inlet of Loch Roag, near W coast of Isle of Lewis, 4m/6km SE of Gallan Head. **100 C4** NB0834.

Mial *High.* ***Settlement***, 1km NW of Gairloch, Ross and Cromarty district. **94 D4** NG7978.

Miavaig *W.Isles Anglicised form of Miabhig, qv.*

Michael *I.o.M.* ***Locality***, on coast, adjoining Kirk Michael. SC3190.

Michael Muir *Aber.* ***Settlement***, 4m/6km NW of Ellon. NJ9033.

Michaelchurch *Here.* ***Hamlet***, 5m/8km W of Ross-on-Wye. **28 E6** SO5225.

Michaelchurch Escley *Here.* ***Village***, 7m/11km NW of Pontrilas. **28 C5** SO3134.

Michaelchurch-on-Arrow (Llanfihangel Dyffryn Arwy). *Powys* ***Hamlet***, 5m/8km SW of Kington. **28 B3** SO2450.

Michaelston-le-Pit (Llanfihangel-y-pwll). *V. of Glam.* ***Village***, 3m/5km SW of Cardiff. **18 E4** ST1573.

Michaelston-super-Ely (Llanfihangel-ar-Elai). *Cardiff* ***Hamlet***, 4m/7km W of Cardiff. ST1176.

Michaelston-y-Fedw (Llanfihangel-y-fedw). *Newport* ***Village***, 5m/8km SW of Newport. **19 F3** ST2484.

Michaelstow *Cornw.* ***Village***, 3m/5km SW of Camelford. **4 A3** SX0878.

Michelcombe *Devon* ***Hamlet***, below Dartmoor, 4m/6km W of Ashburton. SX6968.

Micheldever *Hants.* ***Village***, 6m/10km N of Winchester. **11 G1** SU5139.

Micheldever Forest *Hants.* ***Open space***, stretch of open country, 5m/8km NE of Micheldever. **21 J7** SU5139.

Micheldever Wood *Hants.* ***Forest/woodland***, 1m/2km SE of Micheldever. **11 G1** SU5337.

Michelham Priory *E.Suss.* ***Ecclesiastical building***, Elizabethan house in six acres of gardens on medieval moated island, 2m/3km W of Hailsham and 8m/13km NW of Eastbourne. House incorporates part of Augustinian priory founded in 1229. **13 J6** TQ5509.
Michelmersh *Hants.* ***Village***, 3m/5km N of Romsey. **10 E2** SU3426.
Mickfield *Suff.* ***Village***, 3m/4km W of Debenham. **35 F2** TM1361.
Micklam *Cumb.* ***Locality***, 3m/4km N of Whitehaven. NX9822.
Mickle Fell *Dur.* ***Mountain***, in The Pennines, 6m/10km N of Brough. Height 2591 feet or 790 metres. **61 K4** NY8024.
Mickle Trafford *Ches.* Population: 1904. ***Village***, 3m/5km NE of Chester. **48 D6** SJ4469.
Micklebring *S.Yorks.* ***Village***, 1km W of Braithwell. SK5194.
Mickleby *N.Yorks.* ***Village***, 6m/10km W of Whitby. **63 K5** NZ8012.
Micklefield *Bucks.* ***Suburb***, E district of High Wycombe. SU8993.
Micklefield Green *Herts.* ***Settlement***, 3m/4km N of Rickmansworth. TQ0498.
Mickleham *Surr.* ***Village***, in River Mole valley, 2m/3km S of Leatherhead. **22 E6** TQ1753.
Micklehead Green *Mersey.* ***Locality***, 1m/2km E of Rainhill. SJ5090.
Micklehurst *Gt.Man.* ***Suburb***, to E of Mossley. **49 J2** SD9702.
Micklemeadow *Derbys.* ***Settlement***, 4m/6km SW of Derby. SK3132.
Mickleover *Derby* ***Suburb***, 3m/5km SW of Derby city centre. **41 F2** SK3034.
Mickleover Common *Derbys.* ***Suburb***, to N of Mickleover, 3m/4km from Derby city centre. SK3035.
Micklethwaite *Cumb.* ***Settlement***, 2m/4km NE of Wigton. **60 D1** NY2850.
Micklethwaite *W.Yorks.* ***Village***, 2m/3km N of Bingley, on S side of Bingley Moor. SE1041.
Mickleton *Dur.* ***Village***, 2m/3km SE of Middleton-in-Teesdale. **62 A4** NY9623.
Mickleton *Glos.* Population: 1551. ***Village***, 3m/5km N of Chipping Campden. **30 C4** SP1643.
Mickleton Moor *Dur.* ***Open space***, moorland on S side of Selset Reservoir, 3m/5km SW of Middleton-in-Teesdale. **61 K4** NY9019.
Mickletown *W.Yorks.* Population: 2487. ***Village***, 3m/4km NW of Castleford. **57 J7** SE3927.
Mickley *Derbys.* ***Settlement***, 2m/3km W of Dronfield. SK3279.
Mickley *N.Yorks.* ***Village***, 5m/8km NW of Ripon. **57 H2** SE2576.
Mickley Green *Suff.* ***Settlement***, 1km E of Whepstead. TL8457.
Mickley Square *Northumb.* ***Village***, 1m/2km W of Prudhoe. **71 F7** NZ0762.
Mid Ardlaw *Aber.* ***Settlement***, near N coast, 4m/6km SW of Fraserburgh. **99 H4** NJ9463.
Mid Beltie *Aber.* ***Settlement***, 1m/2km S of Torphins. **90 E4** NJ6200.
Mid Cairncross *Angus* ***Settlement***, in Glen Esk, 1km S of Tarfside. **90 D7** NO4979.
Mid Calder *W.Loth.* ***Village***, 1m/2km SE of Livingston. **75 J4** NT0767.
Mid Clyth *High.* ***Settlement***, on E coast of Caithness district, 2m/3km E of Lybster. To N, on small hill, Hill o' Many Stanes (Historic Scotland). **105 H5** ND2937.
Mid-Hants Railway (Also known as Watercress Line.) *Hants.* ***Other feature of interest***, preserved steam tourist railway running between Alton and New Alresford. 10 mile journey previously served local agricultural community and carried watercress from the extensive beds at New Alresford. **11 H1** SU6635.
Mid Hill *Angus* ***Mountain***, 3m/5km NE of Auchavan. Height 2539 feet or 774 metres. **89 K7** NO2270.
Mid Hill *E.Ayr.* ***Mountain***, on E side of Blackside, 4m/7km SE of Darvel. Height 1342 feet or 409 metres. **74 D7** NS5830.
Mid Hill *High.* ***Mountain***, 6m/10km W of Berriedale. Height 1023 feet or 312 metres. **105 F6** ND0223.
Mid Howe *Ork. Alternative spelling of Midhowe, qv.*
Mid Kame *Shet.* ***Inland physical feature***, ridge rising to over 180 metres and running N to S, situated to S of Voe, Mainland. **109 D7** HU4058.
Mid Lambrook *Som.* ***Hamlet***, 1km SW of East Lambrook, 1m/2km NW of South Petherton. ST4218.
Mid Lavant *W.Suss.* ***Village***, to W of East Lavant, 2m/4km N of Chichester. **12 B6** SU8608.
Mid Letter *Arg. & B.* ***Settlement***, on S side of Loch Fyne, 2m/3km SW of Strachur. **80 B7** NN0700.
Mid Lix *Stir.* ***Settlement***, 2m/3km SW of Killin. **81 G5** NN5530.
Mid Mossdale *N.Yorks.* ***Settlement***, 3m/4km NE of Hawes. **61 K7** SD8391.
Mid Sannox *N.Ayr.* ***Locality***, near E coast of Arran, at foot of Glen Sannox. **73 J6** NS0145.
Mid Thorpe *Lincs.* ***Settlement***, 2m/4km N of Horncastle. TF2673.
Mid Thundergay *N.Ayr. Alternative name for Thundergay, qv.*
Mid Yell *Shet.* ***Village***, on S side of Mid Yell Voe, on E coast of Yell. **108 E3** HU5191.
Midbea *Ork.* ***Settlement***, on Westray, 3m/5km S of Pierowall. **106 D3** HY4444.
Middle Assendon *Oxon.* ***Hamlet***, 3m/4km NW of Henley-on-Thames. **22 A3** SU7385.
Middle Aston *Oxon.* ***Village***, 3m/5km S of Deddington. **31 F6** SP4727.
Middle Barton *Oxon.* Population: 1623. ***Village***, 4m/7km SW of Deddington. **31 F6** SP4325.
Middle Bickenhill *W.Mid.* ***Hamlet***, to E of junction 6 of M42 motorway, 4m/6km NE of Solihull. SP2083.
Middle Bockhampton *Dorset* ***Settlement***, part of Bockhampton locality, 3m/4km NE of Christchurch town centre. SZ1796.
Middle Chinnock *Som.* ***Hamlet***, just E of West Chinnock, 4m/6km SE of South Petherton. ST4713.
Middle Claydon *Bucks.* ***Village***, 4m/6km SW of Winslow. **31 J6** SP7225.
Middle Crackington *Cornw. See Crackington.*
Middle Dodd *Cumb.* ***Mountain***, 3m/5km N of Ambleside. Height 2545 feet or 776 metres. **60 E6** NY3909.
Middle Draft *Cornw.* ***Settlement***, 4m/6km NE of Lostwithiel. SX1364.
Middle Drums *Angus* ***Hamlet***, 2m/3km SW of Brechin. **83 G2** NO5957.
Middle Duntisbourne *Glos.* ***Hamlet***, 4m/6km NW of Cirencester. SO9806.
Middle Fell *Cumb.* ***Open space***, flat-topped moorland, 3m/4km SE of Alston. **61 J2** NY7443.
Middle Fen *Cambs.* ***Open space***, fenland, 2m/3km SE of Ely. **33 J1** TL5679.
Middle Gate *W.Yorks.* ***Locality***, 1km W of Liversedge. SE1923.
Middle Green *Bucks.* ***Settlement***, 2m/3km E of Slough. TQ0080.
Middle Green *Som.* ***Hamlet***, 1km S of Wellington. ST1319.
Middle Green *Suff.* ***Settlement***, to S of Higham church, 7m/11km W of Bury St. Edmunds. TL7465.
Middle Hambleton *Rut. See Rutland Water.*
Middle Handley *Derbys.* ***Village***, 3m/5km E of Dronfield. **51 G5** SK4077.
Middle Harling *Norf.* ***Settlement***, 1m/2km SW of East Harling. **44 D7** TL9885.
Middle Herrington *T. & W.* ***Suburb***, 3m/5km SW of Sunderland city centre. NZ3553.
Middle Hope *N.Som.* ***Coastal feature***, anvil-shaped spit of land protruding into Bristol Channel, 3m/5km N of Weston-super-Mare. **19 G5** ST3366.
Middle Kames *Arg. & B.* ***Settlement***, 3m/5km E of Lochgilphead. **73 H2** NR9189.
Middle Level *Cambs.* ***Large natural feature***, between River Nene and New Bedford River; forms part of the Bedford Level. **43 G7** TL3590.
Middle Level Main Drain *Norf.* ***Other water feature***, fenland drainage channel running from junction of Sixteen Foot Drain and Popham's Eau at Three Holes to River Great Ouse 1km below Wiggenhall St. Germans. **43 J5** TF5914.
Middle Littleton *Worcs.* ***Village***, 3m/5km NE of Evesham. **30 B4** SP0746.
Middle Lypiatt *Glos.* ***Locality***, forms parish of Bisley-with-Lypiatt, along with Nether Lypiatt and Lypiatt Park, on E side of Stroud. SO8704.
Middle Madeley *Staffs.* ***Hamlet***, adjoining to NE of Madeley, 4m/7km W of Newcastle-under-Lyme. SJ7745.
Middle Maes-coed *Here.* ***Settlement***, 3m/4km SW of Vowchurch. **28 C5** SO3333.
Middle Marwood *Devon* ***Hamlet***, to NW of Marwood, 4m/6km NW of Barnstaple. SS5338.
Middle Mayfield *Staffs.* ***Hamlet***, 1km SW of Mayfield. SK1444.
Middle Mill *Pembs.* ***Hamlet***, 4m/6km E of St. David's. **16 B2** SM8025.
Middle Moor *Cambs.* ***Open space***, fenland 2m/4km NW of Ramsey. **43 F7** TL2689.
Middle Moor *Northumb.* ***Open space***, moorland 2m/3km NW of North Charlton. **71 G1** NU1423.
Middle Mouse (Ynys Badrig). *I.o.A.* ***Island***, rock lying about 1km NW of Llanlleiana Head, Anglesey. **46 B3** SH3895.
Middle Quarter *Kent* ***Settlement***, 1km N of High Halden. TQ8938.
Middle Rainton *T. & W.* ***Settlement***, 2m/3km SW of Houghton le Spring. NZ3247.
Middle Rasen *Lincs.* ***Village***, 1m/2km W of Market Rasen. **52 D4** TF0889.
Middle Rigg *P. & K.* ***Settlement***, 2m/3km S of Path of Condie. **82 B7** NO0608.
Middle Salter *Lancs.* ***Settlement***, on W side of Goodber Common, 4m/6km S of Hornby. **56 B3** SD6063.
Middle Sontley *Wrex.* ***Settlement***, to W of Sontley. SJ3246.
Middle Stoford *Som.* ***Hamlet***, 3m/4km E of Wellington. ST1821.
Middle Stoke *Med.* ***Hamlet***, adjoining to S of Lower Stoke, 4m/6km W of Grain. TQ8375.
Middle Stoughton *Som.* ***Hamlet***, 1m/2km NW of Wedmore. ST4249.
Middle Taphouse *Cornw.* ***Hamlet***, 1km W of East Taphouse, 5m/8km W of Liskeard. SX1863.
Middle Tongue *N.Yorks.* ***Open space***, moorland on Langstrothdale Chase, highest point being 2109 feet or 643 metres, 3m/5km NW of Buckden. **56 E1** SD9181.
Middle Town *I.o.S.* ***Hamlet***, on St. Martin's, 1km NW of Higher Town. **2 C1** SV9216.
Middle Tysoe *Warks.* ***Village***, 4m/7km S of Kineton. **30 E4** SP3444.
Middle Wallop *Hants.* ***Village***, 7m/11km SW of Andover. **10 D1** SU2937.
Middle Warren *Hart.* ***Locality***, 2m/3km NW of Hartlepool. NZ4934.
Middle Watch *Cambs.* ***Locality***, in Swavesey, S of village centre. TL3668.
Middle Weald *M.K.* ***Settlement***, 2m/3km SE of Old Stratford. SP7938.
Middle Winterslow *Wilts.* ***Village***, 6m/10km NE of Salisbury. **10 D1** SU2332.
Middle Woodford *Wilts.* ***Village***, in parish of Woodford on River Avon, along with Upper Woodford and Lower Woodford, 4m/6km SW of Amesbury. **10 C1** SU1136.
Middlebere Heath *Dorset* ***Open space***, heath S of Harland Moor Nature Reserve, 2m/3km NW of Corfe Castle. **9 J6** SY9484.
Middlebie *D. & G.* ***Village***, 2m/3km NE of Ecclefechan. Site of Roman camp to N, and Roman fort of Blatobulgium to S. **69 H6** NY2176.
Middlecave *N.Yorks.* ***Locality***, adjoining to W of Malton. SE7771.
Middlecliff *S.Yorks.* ***Hamlet***, 1km S of Great Houghton. SE4305.
Middlecott *Devon* ***Hamlet***, 5m/8km NE of Holsworthy. SS4105.
Middlecroft *Derbys.* ***Suburb***, adjoining to SW of Staveley. SK4273.
Middlefield *Aberdeen* ***Suburb***, 3m/4km NW of Aberdeen city centre. NJ9108.
Middlefield Law *E.Ayr.* ***Mountain***, with cairn at summit, 2m/4km N of Muirkirk. Height 1528 feet or 466 metres. **74 E7** NS6830.
Middleham *N.Yorks.* ***Village***, in Wensleydale, 2m/3km SE of Leyburn. Extensive remains of medieval castle (English Heritage). 17c Braithwaite Hall (National Trust) 1m/2km SW. **57 G1** SE1287.
Middleham Castle *N.Yorks.* ***Castle***, on S side of Middleham, 15m/24km NW of Ripon. 12c-13c ruins of massive keep (English Heritage), which featured a moat inside an extra surrounding wall. Once home of Richard III. **57 G1** SE1287.
Middlehill *Aber.* ***Settlement***, 2m/3km SE of Cuminestown. **99 G6** NJ8349.
Middlehill *Cornw.* ***Settlement***, to SW of Pensilva, 4m/6km NE of Liskeard. **4 C4** SX2969.
Middlehope *Shrop.* ***Hamlet***, 5m/9km NE of Craven Arms. **38 D7** SO4988.
Middlehope Moor *Dur.* ***Open space***, moorland at head of Middlehope Burn, 2m/3km SE of Allenheads. **61 K2** NY8742.
Middlemarsh *Dorset* ***Hamlet***, 6m/10km SE of Sherborne. **9 F4** ST6707.
Middlemore *Devon* ***Hamlet***, 1m/2km SE of Tavistock. SX4972.
Middleport *Stoke* ***Suburb***, in Burslem district of Stoke-on-Trent. SJ8649.
Middlequarter *W.Isles Anglicised form of Ceathramh Meadhanach, qv.*
Middlesborough Roman Catholic Cathedral *Middbro.* ***Ecclesiastical building***, at Coulby Newham, 4m/6km S of Middlesbrough. Built in 1870s and somewhat simple in design, without a tower. E wall has a rose window. **63 G5** NZ5014.
Middlesbrough *Middbro.* Population: 147,430. ***Town***, port, with extensive dock area, on S bank of River Tees, forming part of Teesside urban complex. A former iron and steel town, its chief industries now involve oil and petrochemicals. Unusual transporter bridge over River Tees. University of Teesside. **63 F4** NZ4920.
Middlesbrough Transporter Bridge ***Bridge***, transporter bridge over River Tees, built 1911. Vehicles cross river on platform suspended by cables from 565 foot steel span supported on steel piers. Longest of its kind in world. NZ5021.
Middlesceugh *Cumb.* ***Settlement***, 2m/4km E of Sebergham. NY3941.
Middleshaw *Cumb.* ***Hamlet***, 4m/6km SE of Kendal. **55 J1** SD5589.
Middlesmoor *N.Yorks.* ***Village***, 7m/11km NW of Pateley Bridge. **57 F2** SE0974.
Middlestone *Dur.* ***Village***, 3m/5km NE of Bishop Auckland. NZ2531.
Middlestone Moor *Dur.* ***Locality***, adjoining to SW of Spennymoor. **62 D3** NZ2432.
Middlestown *W.Yorks.* Population: 2331. ***Village***, 3m/5km SE of Dewsbury. **50 E1** SE2617.
Middlethorpe *York* ***Locality***, 3m/4km S of York city centre. SE5948.
Middleton *Aber.* ***Settlement***, 3m/4km W of Newmachar. **91 G3** NJ8419.
Middleton *Angus* ***Hamlet***, 1km SW of Friockheim. **83 G3** NO5848.
Middleton *Arg. & B.* ***Settlement***, near W end of Tiree, 2m/3km SE of Rubha Chràiginis. NL9443.
Middleton *Cumb.* ***Settlement***, 5m/8km N of Kirkby Lonsdale. **56 B1** SD6286.
Middleton *Derbys.* ***Village***, 1m/2km SW of Youlgreave. **50 D6** SK1963.
Middleton *Derbys.* ***Village***, 1m/2km NW of Wirksworth. **50 E7** SK2756.
Middleton *Essex* ***Hamlet***, 1m/2km S of Sudbury. **34 C4** TL8739.
Middleton *Gt.Man.* Population: 45,621. ***Town***, 6m/9km N of Manchester. Former cotton town, once famous for clock-making. **49 H2** SD8606.
Middleton *Hants.* ***Village***, on River Test, 4m/7km E of Andover. **21 H7** SU4244.
Middleton *Hart.* ***Suburb***, of Hartlepool, on E side of harbour. **63 G3** NZ5233.
Middleton *Here.* ***Settlement***, 3m/5km W of Tenbury Wells. SO5469.
Middleton *I.o.W.* ***Hamlet***, 1km SE of Totland. SZ3386.
Middleton *Lancs.* ***Hamlet***, 2m/3km SE of Heysham. **55 H4** SD4258.
Middleton *Midloth.* ***Settlement***, 3m/4km SE of Gorebridge. **76 B5** NT3658.
Middleton *Norf.* ***Village***, 4m/6km SE of King's Lynn. **44 A4** TF6616.
Middleton *N.Yorks.* ***Village***, 1m/2km NW of Pickering. **58 D1** SE7885.
Middleton *Northants.* ***Village***, 4m/6km W of Corby. **42 B7** SP8389.
Middleton *Northumb.* ***Hamlet***, 9m/14km W of Morpeth. **71 F5** NZ0685.
Middleton *Northumb.* ***Settlement***, 1m/2km NW of Belford. **77 J7** NU1035.

Middleton *P. & K.* ***Settlement***, 3m/5km N of Kinross. **82 C7** NO1206.
Middleton *P. & K.* ***Settlement***, 3m/5km NW of Blairgowrie. **82 C3** NO1447.
Middleton *Shrop.* ***Hamlet***, 2m/4km NE of Ludlow. **28 E1** SO5377.
Middleton *Shrop.* ***Locality***, 3m/5km NE of Church Stoke. **38 B6** SO2999.
Middleton *Shrop.* ***Settlement***, 2m/3km E of Oswestry. **38 C3** SJ3129.
Middleton *Suff.* ***Village***, 3m/4km E of Yoxford. **35 J2** TM4367.
Middleton *Swan.* ***Hamlet***, on Gower peninsula, 2m/4km E of Worms Head. **17 H6** SS4287.
Middleton *Warks.* ***Village***, 4m/6km SW of Tamworth. **40 D6** SP1798.
Middleton *W.Yorks.* ***Suburb***, 4m/6km S of Leeds city centre. **57 H7** SE3027.
Middleton *W.Yorks.* ***Village***, on border with North Yorkshire, 1m/2km N of Ilkley across River Wharfe. **57 G5** SE1249.
Middleton Baggot *Shrop.* ***Settlement***, 6m/10km S of Much Wenlock. SO6290.
Middleton Bank Top *Northumb.* ***Settlement***, 1m/2km S of Middleton. **71 F5** NZ0583.
Middleton Cheney *Northants.* Population: 3306. ***Village***, 3m/5km E of Banbury. **31 F4** SP4941.
Middleton Common *Dur.* ***Open space***, heathland with River Wear to N and River Tees to S, 4m/7km N of Middleton-in-Teesdale. **62 A3** NY9431.
Middleton Fell *Cumb.* ***Open space***, moorland 4m/6km S of Sedbergh, with highest point of 1924 feet or 592 metres. **56 B1** SD6586.
Middleton Green *Staffs.* ***Settlement***, 3m/5km E of Hilderstone. **40 B2** SJ9935.
Middleton Hall *Northumb.* ***Settlement***, 2m/3km S of Wooler. **70 E1** NT9825.
Middleton-in-Teesdale *Dur.* ***Small town***, former lead-mining town, 8m/13km NW of Barnard Castle. **62 A4** NY9425.
Middleton Junction *Gt.Man.* ***Locality***, 1m/2km SE of Middleton. SD8804.
Middleton Moat *Norf.* ***Locality***, 1m/2km S of Terrington St. Clement. TF5418.
Middleton Moor *Suff.* ***Hamlet***, 1m/2km W of Middleton. TM4167.
Middleton of Potterton *Aber.* ***Settlement***, 1km W of Potterton and 3m/4km SW of Balmedie. **91 H3** NJ9315.
Middleton-on-Leven *N.Yorks.* ***Settlement***, 4m/6km W of Stokesley. **63 F5** NZ4609.
Middleton-on-Sea *W.Suss.* ***Small town***, resort 3m/4km E of Bognor Regis. Extensive sea defences erected to slow down coastal erosion. **12 C7** SU9700.
Middleton on the Hill *Here.* ***Village***, 4m/7km NE of Leominster. **28 E2** SO5464.
Middleton-on-the-Wolds *E.Riding* ***Village***, 7m/11km NE of Market Weighton. **59 F5** SE9449.
Middleton One Row *Darl.* ***Hamlet***, adjoining to E of Middleton St. George, 4m/7km SE of Darlington. **62 E5** NZ3512.
Middleton Park *Aberdeen* ***Suburb***, to NW of Bridge of Don, 3m/5km N of Aberdeen city centre. **91 H3** NJ9211.
Middleton Priors *Shrop.* ***Settlement***, 6m/10km S of Much Wenlock. **39 F7** SO6290.
Middleton Quernhow *N.Yorks.* ***Hamlet***, 5m/8km N of Ripon. **57 J2** SE3378.
Middleton Railway *W.Yorks.* ***Other feature of interest***, tourist railway running from Tunstall Road roundabout to Middleton Park, 2m/3km S of Leeds city centre. It was first railway to run steam locomotives in 1812. Steam and diesel engines on display. **57 J7** SE3029.
Middleton St. George *Darl.* Population: 2286. ***Village***, on River Tees, 4m/6km E of Darlington. Teesside Airport to E. **62 E5** NZ3412.
Middleton Scriven *Shrop.* ***Village***, 4m/7km SW of Bridgnorth. **39 F7** SO6887.
Middleton Stoney *Oxon.* ***Village***, 3m/5km W of Bicester. **31 G6** SP5323.
Middleton Tyas *N.Yorks.* ***Village***, 1m/2km E of Scotch Corner. **62 D6** NZ2205.
Middleton Wold *E.Riding* ***Open space***, plain containing village of Middleton-on-the-Wolds, 5m/8km NE of Market Weighton. **59 F5** SE9248.
Middletown *Cumb.* ***Settlement***, 2m/3km SW of Egremont. **60 A6** NX9908.
Middletown *N.Som.* ***Locality***, 3m/5km E of Clevedon. ST4471.
Middletown *Powys* ***Village***, under S side of Middletown Hill, in Breidden Hills, 6m/9km NE of Welshpool. **38 C4** SJ3012.
Middletown Hill *Powys* ***Mountain***, one of three principal peaks of Breidden Hills, on N side of Middletown village. Height 1194 feet or 364 metres. Remains of ancient camp, Cefn-y-Castell. **38 C4** SJ3013.
Middlewich *Ches.* Population: 10,100. ***Town***, on Trent and Mersey Navigation, 6m/9km SE of Northwich. Supplier of salt to Romans. **49 G6** SJ7066.
Middlewood *Ches.* ***Settlement***, 2m/3km SE of Hazel Grove. **49 J4** SJ9484.
Middlewood *Cornw.* ***Hamlet***, 7m/11km SW of Launceston. SX2775.
Middlewood *S.Yorks.* ***Village***, adjoining Worrall, 1km S of Oughtibridge. SK3092.
Middlewood Green *Suff.* ***Village***, 4m/6km NE of Stowmarket. **34 E2** TM0961.
Middleyard *E.Ayr.* ***Settlement***, 3m/4km S of Galston. **74 D7** NS5132.
Middleyard *Glos.* ***Hamlet***, 3m/4km SW of Stroud. SO8103.
Middlezoy *Som.* ***Village***, on Sedgemoor, 6m/9km SE of Bridgwater. **8 C1** ST3732.
Middop *Lancs.* ***Locality***, 2m/4km S of Gisburn. SD8345.
Middridge *Dur.* ***Suburb***, in NW part of Newton Aycliffe. **62 D4** NZ2526.
Midfield *High.* ***Settlement***, on N coast of Caithness district, on W side of entrance to Tongue Bay. **103 H2** NC5864.
Midford *B. & N.E.Som.* ***Village***, 3m/4km S of Bath. **20 A5** ST7660.
Midge Hall *Lancs.* ***Settlement***, 2m/3km W of Leyland. **55 J7** SD5123.
Midgeholme *Cumb.* ***Locality***, 7m/11km E of Brampton. **61 H1** NY6359.
Midgham *W.Berks.* ***Village***, 5m/8km E of Newbury. **21 J5** SU5567.
Midgley *W.Yorks.* ***Hamlet***, 5m/9km SW of Wakefield. **50 E1** SE2714.
Midgley *W.Yorks.* ***Village***, 1m/2km E of Mytholmroyd. **57 F7** SE0326.
Midhope Moors *S.Yorks.* ***Open space***, moorland at E side of The Pennines, 1m/2km SW of Upper Midhope. **50 E3** SK1998.
Midhopestones *S.Yorks.* ***Village***, 3m/4km S of Penistone. **50 E3** SK2399.
Midhowe (Sometimes spelled Mid Howe.) *Ork.* ***Historic/prehistoric site***, site of Neolithic communal burial-chamber, and nearby broch, on W coast of Rousay. **106 C4** HY3730.
Midhurst *W.Suss.* Population: 6451. ***Small town***, in River Rother valley N of South Downs, 11m/17km N of Chichester. Ruins of Cowdray House, burnt in 1793. Modern house nearby. Polo and golf in park. Many attractive buildings, including timber-framed and Georgian. **12 B4** SU8821.
Midland Isle *Pembs.* ***Island***, small island between Skomer Island and Welsh mainland, at S end of St. Brides Bay. SM7409.
Midland Ness *Ork.* ***Coastal feature***, headland on S coast of Mainland, to E of Bay of Houton. **107 C7** HY3203.
Midland Railway Centre *Derbys.* ***Other feature of interest***, in Butterley, 1km N of Ripley. Working railway section, 4m/6km long, between Butterley station and Riddings. Museum centre at Swanwick Junction. Also features narrow gauge railway and farm park. **51 G7** SK4051.
Midlem *Sc.Bord.* ***Village***, 4m/6km E of Selkirk. **70 A1** NT5227.
Midlock *S.Lan.* ***River***, rising to W of Clyde Law and flowing NW to join River Clyde to N of Crawford. **69 F2** NS9521.
Midloe *Cambs.* ***Settlement***, 3m/5km NW of St. Neots. TL1664.
Midmar *Aber.* ***Locality***, 6m/10km N of Banchory. 16c Midmar Castle and Midmar Forest to SE. NJ6707.
Midmar Forest *Aber.* ***Forest/woodland***, to SE of Midmar. **91 F4** NJ7005.
Midpark *Arg. & B.* ***Settlement***, on E coast of Inchmarnock, 6m/8km SW of Rothesay. **73 J5** NS0259.
Midsomer Norton *B. & N.E.Som.* ***Town***, former coalmining town, 9m/14km SW of Bath. **19 K6** ST6654.
Midton *Inclyde* ***Suburb***, S district of Gourock. NS2376.
Midtown *High.* ***Settlement***, in Caithness district, on W side of Kyle of Tongue. **103 H2** NC5861.
Midtown *High.* ***Village***, on W shore of Loch Ewe, Ross and Cromarty district, 4m/6km NW of Poolewe. Settlement of Brae adjoins to W. **94 E3** NG8284.
Midtown of Barras *Aber.* ***Hamlet***, 2m/3km SW of Stonehaven. **91 G6** NO8480.
Midville *Lincs.* ***Settlement***, 6m/9km S of Spilsby. **53 G7** TF3857.
Midway *Ches.* ***Suburb***, adjoining to S of Poynton. SJ9282.
Midway *Derbys.* ***Suburb***, to NE of Swadlincote town centre. SK3020.
Migdale *High.* ***Settlement***, in Sutherland district, 1m/2km E of Bonar Bridge and on N side of head of Loch Migdale. **96 D2** NH6292.
Migneint *Conwy* ***Open space***, marshy plateau 5m/8km E of Ffestiniog. **37 G1** SH7742.
Migvie *Aber.* ***Settlement***, 3m/5km NW of Tarland. **90 C4** NJ4306.
Milarrochy *Stir.* ***Settlement***, on E shore of Loch Lomond, 1m/2km NW of Balmaha. **74 C1** NS4092.
Milber (Milber Down). *Devon* ***Suburb***, SE district of Newton Abbot. **5 J3** SX8770.
Milber Down *Devon See Milber.*
Milbethill *Aber.* ***Settlement***, 3m/4km SE of Cornhill. **98 E5** NJ6156.
Milborne Port *Som.* Population: 2614. ***Small town***, stone-built town, 3m/5km NE of Sherborne, with large medieval church. **9 F3** ST6718.
Milborne St. Andrew *Dorset* ***Village***, 4m/6km NE of Puddletown. **9 H5** SY8097.
Milborne Wick *Som.* ***Village***, 1m/2km N of Milborne Port. **9 F2** ST6620.
Milbourne *Northumb.* ***Village***, 3m/5km NW of Ponteland. **71 G6** NZ1175.
Milbourne *Wilts.* ***Hamlet***, 1km E of Malmesbury. ST9487.
Milburn *Cumb.* ***Village***, 6m/10km N of Appleby-in-Westmorland. Howgill Castle 1km E. **61 H4** NY6529.
Milburn Forest *Cumb.* ***Open space***, wild moorland area to NE of Milburn. **61 J3** NY6529.
Milbury Heath *S.Glos.* ***Hamlet***, 2m/3km E of Thornbury. **19 K2** ST6690.
Milby *N.Yorks.* ***Hamlet***, 1km NE of Boroughbridge across River Ure. SE4067.
Milcombe *Oxon.* ***Village***, 5m/8km SW of Banbury. **31 F5** SP4134.
Milcote *Warks.* ***Settlement***, 2m/3km SW of Stratford-upon-Avon. SP1952.
Milden *Suff.* ***Hamlet***, 5m/8km NW of Hadleigh. **34 D4** TL9546.
Mildenhall *Suff.* Population: 10,468. ***Village***, on River Lark, 8m/13km NE of Newmarket. Perpendicular church with tall tower. 'Mildenhall Treasure', horde of Roman silver found in 1942, is in British Museum. **34 B1** TL7174.
Mildenhall *Wilts.* ***Village***, on River Kennet, 1m/2km E of Marlborough. Site of Roman town of Cunetio across river. **21 F4** SU2169.
Mildenhall Fen *Suff.* ***Open space***, fenland, 3m/5km NW of Mildenhall. **33 K1** TL6578.
Mile Cross *Norf.* ***Suburb***, 2m/3km NW of Norwich city centre. TG2110.
Mile Elm *Wilts.* ***Settlement***, 1m/2km S of Calne. **20 C5** ST9969.
Mile End *Essex* ***Locality***, 2m/3km N of Colchester. **34 D6** TL9927.
Mile End *Glos.* ***Locality***, 1m/2km NE of Coleford. **28 E7** SO5811.
Mile End *Gt.Lon.* ***Suburb***, in borough of Tower Hamlets, 3m/4km NE of London Bridge. TQ3682.
Mile End *Suff.* ***Locality***, at SW end of Brandon. TL7785.
Mile End *Suff.* ***Locality***, 1m/2km E of Bungay. TM3589.
Mile Hill *Angus* ***Mountain***, 3m/4km NE of Bridgend of Lintrathen. Height 1342 feet or 409 metres. **82 E2** NO3157.
Mile Oak *B. & H.* ***Suburb***, N district of Portslade-by-Sea. TQ2407.
Mile Oak *Kent* ***Settlement***, 1m/2km SE of Paddock Wood. TQ6843.
Mile Town *Kent* ***Suburb***, adjoining to S of Sheerness. TQ9174.
Milebrook *Powys* ***Settlement***, 2m/3km E of Knighton. **28 C1** SO3172.
Milebush *Kent* ***Settlement***, 1m/2km NE of Marden. **14 C3** TQ7545.
Mileham *Norf.* ***Village***, 6m/10km NW of East Dereham. Remains of motte and bailey castle. **44 D4** TF9219.
Miles Green *Staffs.* ***Settlement***, 1km SE of Audley. SJ8049.
Miles Hill *W.Yorks.* ***Suburb***, 2m/3km N of Leeds city centre. SE2936.
Miles Hope *Here.* ***Settlement***, 3m/5km SW of Tenbury Wells. SO5764.
Miles Platting *Gt.Man.* ***Suburb***, 2m/3km E of Manchester city centre. SJ8699.
Milesmark *Fife* ***Village***, 2m/3km NW of Dunfermline. **75 J2** NT0688.
Miles's Green *W.Berks.* ***Settlement***, 5m/7km E of Newbury. SU5469.
Milfield *Northumb.* ***Village***, 5m/8km NW of Wooler. **77 H7** NT9333.
Milford *Derbys.* ***Village***, 1m/2km S of Belper. **41 F1** SK3545.
Milford *Devon* ***Settlement***, near coast, 10m/16km N of Bude. **6 A3** SS2322.
Milford *Powys* ***Locality***, 1m/2km W of Newtown. SO0991.
Milford *Shrop.* ***Settlement***, adjoining to S of Baschurch. **38 D3** SJ4121.
Milford *Staffs.* ***Village***, 4m/6km SE of Stafford. **40 B3** SJ9721.
Milford *Surr.* Population: 3238. ***Locality***, 2m/3km SW of Godalming. To S, Milford Common (National Trust). **22 C7** SU9442.
Milford Haven *Pembs.* ***Sea feature***, large estuary and natural harbour in SW Wales, running out to sea between St. Ann's Head and Sheep Island, and itself fed by many tidal estuaries. **16 B4** SM8504.
Milford Haven (Aberdaugleddau). *Pembs.* Population: 13,194. ***Town***, major port situated on N side of Milford Haven estuary, 7m/11km SW of Haverfordwest. Dominated by oil refineries. Habour has Marina. **16 C4** SM9006.
Milford Heath *Surr.* ***Locality***, adjoining to S of Milford. SU9441.
Milford on Sea *Hants.* Population: 4434. ***Small town***, resort and residential town, 3m/5km SW of Lymington. 13c church. **10 D5** SZ2891.
Milk Hill *Wilts.* ***Hill***, 1m/2km N of Alton Barnes. Height 964 feet or 294 metres. **20 E5** SU1064.
Milkwall *Glos.* ***Village***, 1m/2km S of Coleford. **19 J1** SO5809.
Milkwell *Wilts.* ***Hamlet***, 4m/6km E of Shaftesbury. ST9123.
Mill Bank *W.Yorks.* ***Village***, 1m/2km N of Ripponden. **57 F7** SE0321.
Mill Bay *Ork.* ***Bay***, wide bay on E coast of Stronsay, extending S from Grice Ness to Odness. **106 F5** HY6626.
Mill Brow *Gt.Man.* ***Hamlet***, 2m/3km NE of Marple. SJ9789.
Mill Buie *Moray* ***Mountain***, 6m/10km SE of Forres. Height 1217 feet or 371 metres. **97 H6** NJ0950.
Mill Buie *Moray* ***Mountain***, 2m/3km W of Glenlatterach Reservoir and 1m/2km S of Kellas. Height 1099 feet or 335 metres. **97 J6** NJ1651.
Mill Common *Norf.* ***Locality***, 2m/4km NE of Aylsham. TG2229.
Mill Common *Norf.* ***Village***, adjoining to N of Thurton. TG3201.
Mill Common *Suff.* ***Settlement***, 3m/5km NE of Halesworth. TM4181.
Mill Cottages *E.Riding* ***Locality***, 1m/2km SW of Sledmere. SE9263.
Mill End *Bucks.* ***Village***, on River Thames, 2m/4km NE of Henley-on-Thames. Site of Roman villa to N. **22 A3** SU7885.
Mill End *Cambs.* ***Locality***, E end of Warboys, 7m/11km NE of Huntingdon. TL3180.
Mill End *Cambs.* ***Settlement***, 1m/2km SE of Kirtling. TL6956.
Mill End *Herts.* ***Hamlet***, 3m/5km NW of Buntingford. **33 G5** TL3332.
Mill End *Herts.* ***Suburb***, W district of Rickmansworth. TQ0394.
Mill End *Worcs.* ***Settlement***, adjoining to N side of Bredon, 4m/6km NE of Tewkesbury, on E bank of River Avon. SO9237.
Mill End Green *Essex* ***Hamlet***, 3m/5km N of Great Dunmow. **33 K6** TL6125.

M

Mill Green *Cambs.* ***Hamlet***, 3m/5km W of Haverhill. TL6245.
Mill Green *Essex* ***Hamlet***, 1m/2km N of Ingatestone. **24 C1** TL6301.
Mill Green *Herts.* ***Settlement***, 1m/2km NE of Hatfield town centre. TL2409.
Mill Green *Norf.* ***Hamlet***, 1km N of Burston. TM1384.
Mill Green *Shrop.* ***Settlement***, 1m/2km NW of Hinstock. **39 F3** SJ6828.
Mill Green *Staffs.* ***Settlement***, 1km S of Abbots Bromley. SK0823.
Mill Green *Suff.* ***Hamlet***, to W of Buxhall, about 3m/5km W of Stowmarket. TL9957.
Mill Green *Suff.* ***Hamlet***, 1km NE of Stonham Aspal. TM1360.
Mill Green *Suff.* ***Settlement***, to NE of Edwardstone, 5m/8km W of Hadleigh. TL9542.
Mill Green *Suff.* ***Settlement***, 1m/2km NE of Parham. TM3161.
Mill Green *W.Mid.* ***Settlement***, 1m/2km E of Aldridge. SK0701.
Mill Green Museum *Herts.* ***Other feature of interest***, in working 18c watermill, in NE part of Hatfield, with local social history exhibits. **23 F1** TL2309.
Mill Hill *B'burn.* ***Suburb***, 1m/2km SW of Blackburn town centre. SD6726.
Mill Hill *Cambs.* ***Hamlet***, with disused windmill, 2m/3km NE of Potton. TL2351.
Mill Hill *Dur.* ***Settlement***, 1m/2km E of Wingate. NZ4237.
Mill Hill *E.Suss.* ***Settlement***, 1m/2km W of Pevensey. TQ6205.
Mill Hill *Glos.* ***Locality***, 3m/4km NW of Lydney. SO6006.
Mill Hill *Gt.Lon.* ***Suburb***, in borough of Barnet, 9m/14km NW of Charing Cross. **23 F2** TQ2192.
Mill Hill *Gt.Man.* ***Suburb***, to E of Bolton town centre, on River Croal. SD7209.
Mill Hill *Norf.* ***Locality***, 1km SE of Tivetshall St. Mary. TM1785.
Mill Hill *Suff.* ***Locality***, adjoining to NW of Peasenhall. TM3469.
Mill Hill Estate *T. & W.* ***Suburb***, 3m/5km S of Sunderland city centre. NZ3852.
Mill House Brow *Warr.* ***Locality***, just S of Croft. SJ6393.
Mill Houses *Lancs.* ***Settlement***, on N bank of River Hindburn, 3m/4km SW of Low Bentham. **56 B3** SD6267.
Mill Lane *Hants.* ***Settlement***, 3m/5km E of Odiham. **22 A6** SU7850.
Mill Meads *Gt.Lon.* ***Suburb***, in borough of Newham, 1m/2km W of West Ham. TQ3883.
Mill of Colp *Aber.* ***Settlement***, on S side of Idoch Water, 2m/3km SE of Turriff. **99 F6** NJ7447.
Mill of Elrick *Aber.* ***Settlement***, on E side of Ebrie Burn, 1km S of Auchnagatt. **99 H6** NJ9340.
Mill of Fortune *P. & K.* ***Settlement***, 1m/2km SE of Comrie. **81 J5** NN7820.
Mill of Kingoodie *Aber.* ***Settlement***, 2m/3km SE of Oldmeldrum. **91 G2** NJ8325.
Mill of Monquich *Aber.* ***Hamlet***, 1m/2km N of Netherley. **91 G5** NO8595.
Mill of Uras *Aber.* ***Settlement***, 3m/5km S of Stonehaven. **91 G7** NO8679.
Mill Place *N.Lincs.* ***Locality***, 1m/2km W of Brigg. SE9806.
Mill Rig *S.Lan.* ***Mountain***, partly wooded peak, 5m/8km SE of Darvel. Height 1099 feet or 335 metres. **74 E7** NS6334.
Mill Side *Cumb.* ***Hamlet***, 3m/5km NE of Lindale. SD4484.
Mill Street *Kent* ***Settlement***, adjoining to W of East Malling. TQ6957.
Mill Street *Norf.* ***Hamlet***, on River Wensum, 4m/6km NE of East Dereham. TG0118.
Mill Street *Norf.* ***Hamlet***, on River Wensum, 6m/9km NE of East Dereham. **44 E4** TG0517.
Mill Street *Suff.* ***Hamlet***, adjoining to W of Gislingham. TM0671.
Mill Street *Suff.* ***Locality***, 1m/2km NW of Halesworth. TM3778.
Milland *W.Suss.* ***Hamlet***, 2m/3km S of Liphook. SU8326.
Milland Marsh *W.Suss.* ***Hamlet***, 3m/5km S of Liphook. Site of Roman station 1km SE. **12 B4** SU8327.
Millarston *Renf.* ***Suburb***, W district of Paisley. NS4663.
Millbank *Aber.* ***Settlement***, on N side of River Ugie, 1m/2km N of Longside. **99 J6** NK0449.
Millbeck *Cumb.* ***Settlement***, 2m/3km N of Keswick. **60 D4** NY2526.
Millbounds *Ork.* ***Settlement***, on Eday, 1m/2km NE of Eday Airfield. **106 E4** HY5635.
Millbreck *Aber.* ***Settlement***, 2m/3km S of Mintlaw. **99 J6** NK0045.
Millbridge *Surr.* ***Village***, on River Wey, 3m/5km S of Farnham. **22 B7** SU8442.
Millbrook *Beds.* ***Village***, 2m/3km W of Ampthill. **32 D5** TL0138.
Millbrook *Cornw.* Population: 1891. ***Village***, 2m/3km S of Torpoint across St. John's Lake, at head of Millbrook Lake, a long inlet of River Tamar estuary. Harbour. **4 E5** SX4252.
Millbrook *Devon* ***Suburb***, to NE of Axminster town centre. SY3098.
Millbrook *Gt.Man.* ***Suburb***, 1m/2km NE of Stalybridge. SJ9899.
Millbrook *S'ham.* ***Suburb***, W district of Southampton. **10 E3** SU3813.
Millbuie *High.* ***Locality***, comprises central, mainly forested, area of Black Isle in Ross and Cromarty district. **96 D5** NH6257.
Millbuie Forest *High.* ***Forest/woodland***, on Black Isle, Ross and Cromarty district, NW of Fortrose. **96 D5** NH6960.
Millburn *Aber.* ***Settlement***, 1km E of Suie Hill and 4m/6km N of Alford. **90 D2** NJ5722.
Millburn *Aber.* ***Settlement***, 6m/10km E of Huntly. **90 E1** NJ6236.
Millburn Geo *Shet.* ***Coastal feature***, small indentation on E coast of Bressay. **109 E9** HU5239.
Millcombe *Devon* ***Settlement***, 5m/8km W of Dartmouth. **5 J6** SX8049.
Millcorner *E.Suss.* ***Hamlet***, 1m/2km S of Northiam. **14 D5** TQ8223.
Milldale *Staffs.* ***Hamlet***, on W bank of River Dove, 1km SE of Alstonefield. SK1354.
Millden *Aber.* ***Settlement***, 1km S of Balmedie. **91 H3** NJ9616.
Milldens *Angus* ***Hamlet***, 3m/5km W of Friockheim. **83 G2** NO5450.
Milldoe *Ork.* ***Hill***, 1m/2km NW of Settiscarth, Mainland. Height 725 feet or 221 metres. **106 C5** HY3520.
Millearn *P. & K.* ***Settlement***, in Strathearn, 5m/8km SE of Crieff. **82 A6** NN9316.
Millend *Glos.* ***Locality***, 1m/2km SW of Coleford. SO5609.
Millend *Oxon.* ***Settlement***, adjoining to N of Chadlington, 3m/5km S of Chipping Norton. SP3222.
Millenheath *Shrop.* ***Settlement***, 1km SE of Prees Higher Heath. **38 E2** SJ5735.
Millerhill *Midloth.* ***Village***, 1m/2km N of Dalkeith. **76 B4** NT3269.
Miller's Dale *Derbys.* ***Village***, in River Wye valley 5m/8km E of Buxton; also the valley itself, from here down to Cressbrook. **50 D5** SK1373.
Millers Green *Derbys.* ***Hamlet***, 1km S of Wirksworth. SK2852.
Miller's Green *Essex* ***Settlement***, 4m/6km NE of Chipping Ongar. TL5807.
Millerston *Glas.* ***Locality***, 4m/6km E of Glasgow. NS6467.
Millerton Hill *Sc.Bord.* ***Hill***, 1m/2km SW of Ayton. Height 433 feet or 132 metres. **77 G5** NT9159.
Milleur Point *D. & G.* ***Coastal feature***, headland at N end of Rinns of Galloway, 3m/5km N of Kirkcolm. **64 A3** NX0273.
Millfield *Peter.* ***Suburb***, 1m/2km N of Peterborough city centre. TF1900.
Millfield *T. & W.* ***Suburb***, to W of Sunderland city centre. NZ3857.
Millfire *D. & G.* ***Mountain***, on Rhinns of Kells, 4m/7km N of Clatteringshaws Loch. Height 2348 feet or 716 metres. **67 K5** NX5084.
Millfore *D. & G.* ***Mountain***, 7m/12km NE of Newton Stewart. Height 2152 feet or 656 metres. **64 E3** NX4775.
Millgate *Lancs.* ***Hamlet***, 1km N of Whitworth. SD8819.
Millgate *Norf.* ***Locality***, adjoining to N of Aylsham. TG1927.
Millgreen *Shrop.* ***Settlement***, 1m/2km NW of Hinstock. SJ6828.
Millhalf *Here.* ***Hamlet***, 6m/9km S of Kington. SO2748.
Millhayes *Devon* ***Hamlet***, by River Culm, 4m/6km S of Wellington. ST1314.
Millhayes *Devon* ***Hamlet***, 5m/8km NE of Honiton. ST2303.
Millhead *Lancs.* ***Locality***, adjoining to N of Carnforth. SD4971.
Millheugh *S.Lan.* ***Locality***, adjoining to W of Larkhall. NS7550.
Millholme *Cumb.* ***Hamlet***, 1m/2km W of Killington Reservoir and 3m/5km E of Kendal. **61 G7** SD5690.
Millhouse *Arg. & B.* ***Settlement***, in Argyll, 1m/2km SW of Kames. **73 H3** NR9570.
Millhouse *Cumb.* ***Settlement***, 2m/3km E of Hesket Newmarket. **60 E3** NY3637.
Millhouse *S.Yorks.* ***Village***, 2m/3km W of Penistone on N bank of River Don. SE2203.
Millhousebridge *D. & G.* ***Settlement***, on River Annan, 3m/5km NW of Lockerbie. **69 G5** NY1085.
Millhouses *S.Yorks.* ***Hamlet***, adjoining to E of Darfield across River Dearne. SE4204.
Millhouses *S.Yorks.* ***Suburb***, 3m/4km SW of Sheffield city centre. SK3383.
Milliganton *D. & G.* ***Settlement***, 1m/2km SW of Dunscore. **68 D5** NX8483.
Millikenpark *Renf.* ***Suburb***, residential development adjoining to SW of Johnstone. **74 C4** NS4161.
Millin Cross *Pembs.* ***Hamlet***, at head of Creek running down to Western Cleddau River, 3m/5km E of Haverfordwest. SM9913.
Millington *E.Riding* ***Village***, 3m/4km NE of Pocklington. **58 E4** SE8351.
Millington Green *Derbys.* ***Hamlet***, 1m/2km NE of Hulland, 5m/8km E of Ashbourne. SK2647.
Milljoan Hill *S.Ayr.* ***Mountain***, 4m/6km SE of Ballantrae. Height 1322 feet or 403 metres. **64 B3** NX1176.
Millmeece *Staffs.* ***Hamlet***, 3m/4km N of Eccleshall. **40 A2** SJ8333.
Millness *High.* ***Settlement***, 3m/4km E of Cannich. **87 K1** NH3731.
Millom *Cumb.* Population: 6455. ***Small town***, on W side of River Duddon estuary, 5m/8km SW of Broughton in Furness. Remains of castle dating from 14c 1km N. Developed as coal-mining town. **54 E1** SD2187.
Millom Castle *Cumb.* ***Castle***, 14c ruin, 1km N of Millom. **54 E1** SD1781.
Millow *Beds.* ***Hamlet***, 3m/4km E of Biggleswade. TL2243.
Millpool *Cornw.* ***Village***, 4m/6km NE of Bodmin. SX1270.
Millport *N.Ayr.* Population: 1340. ***Small town***, resort and port on Millport Bay, at S end of Great Cumbrae, 3m/4km W of Fairlie across Fairlie Roads. **73 K5** NS1655.
Millport Bay *N.Ayr.* ***Bay***, at S end of Great Cumbrae, 3m/4km W of Fairlie across Fairlie Roads. Islets in bay are known as The Eileans. **73 K5** NS1655.
Mills *W.Yorks.* ***Locality***, 1km S of Shelley. SE2010.
Mills Hill *Gt.Man.* ***Locality***, 2m/3km E of Middleton. SD8805.
Millstone Edge *Sc.Bord.* ***Mountain***, 2m/3km SE of Linhope. Height 1853 feet or 565 metres. **69 K3** NT4300.
Millstone Hill *Aber.* ***Mountain***, in Bennachie Forest, 3m/5km N of Monymusk. Height 1338 feet or 408 metres. **90 E2** NJ6720.
Millstone Hill *Moray* ***Hill***, in woodlands 4m/7km N of Keith. Height 987 feet or 301 metres. **98 C5** NJ4257.
Millthorpe *Derbys.* ***Village***, 1km S of Holmesfield. SK3176.
Millthrop *Cumb.* ***Hamlet***, 1km S of Sedbergh. **61 H7** SD6691.
Milltimber *Aberdeen* ***Village***, 1m/2km E of Peterculter. **91 G4** NJ8501.
Milltir Gerrig *Powys* ***Mountain***, 3m/5km NW of Llangynog. Height 1594 feet or 486 metres. **37 K2** SJ0230.
Millton of Noth *Aber.* ***Settlement***, 1km N of Rhynie. **90 D2** NJ5028.
Milltown *Aber.* ***Settlement***, just E of Cock Bridge, 11m/17km NW of Ballater. NJ2609.
Milltown *Cornw.* ***Hamlet***, 1km S of Lostwithiel. SX1057.
Milltown *Derbys.* ***Hamlet***, 3m/4km W of Clay Cross. **51 F6** SK3561.
Milltown *Devon* ***Hamlet***, 4m/6km N of Barnstaple. **6 D2** SS5538.
Milltown *D. & G.* ***Settlement***, 4m/6km W of Canonbie. **69 J6** NY3375.
Milltown *High.* ***Settlement***, in Strathconon, Ross and Cromarty district, 2m/4km above head of Loch Meig. **95 K6** NH3055.
Milltown *High.* ***Settlement***, 3m/4km SW of Ferness. **97 G7** NH9441.
Milltown of Aberdalgie *P. & K.* ***Hamlet***, to N of Aberdalgie, 3m/5km SW of Perth. **82 B5** NO0720.
Milltown of Auchindoun *Moray* ***Settlement***, 2m/3km E of Dufftown. **98 B6** NJ3539.
Milltown of Campfield *Aber.* ***Settlement***, 2m/3km SE of Torphins. **90 E4** NJ6400.
Milltown of Craigston *Aber.* ***Settlement***, 4m/7km NE of Turriff. **99 F5** NJ7655.
Milltown of Edinvillie *Moray* ***Village***, 2m/3km S of Charlestown of Aberlour. **97 K7** NJ2640.
Milltown of Kildrummy *Aber.* ***Locality***, 1km S of Kildrummy and 3m/5km S of Lumsden. **90 C3** NJ4716.
Milltown of Rothiemay *Moray* ***Village***, 5m/9km N of Huntly. **98 D6** NJ5448.
Milltown of Towie *Aber.* ***Settlement***, near bridge over River Don, 7m/11km E of Strathdon. **90 C3** NJ4612.
Millwall *Gt.Lon.* ***Suburb***, dock area on Isle of Dogs in borough of Tower Hamlets, on N bank of River Thames, 5m/8km E of Charing Cross. TQ3779.
Millwey Rise *Devon* ***Suburb***, to NE of Axminster town centre. SY3099.
Milnathort *P. & K.* Population: 1368. ***Small town***, with woollen mills, 2m/3km N of Kinross. Burleigh Castle (Historic Scotland) to E. **82 C7** NO1204.
Milnbank *Glas.* ***Suburb***, 2m/3km E of Glasgow city centre, in Dennistoun district. NS6165.
Milne Height *D. & G.* ***Mountain***, 4m/7km N of Boreland. Height 1381 feet or 421 metres. **69 G4** NY1597.
Milners Heath *Ches.* ***Settlement***, adjoining to SE of Waverton. SJ4662.
Milngavie *E.Dun.* Population: 12,592. ***Town***, 6m/10km N of Glasgow. Remains of 15c Mugdock Castle on Mugdock Loch to N. **74 D3** NS5574.
Milnrow *Gt.Man.* Population: 12,541. ***Town***, industrial town, 2m/4km E of Rochdale. **49 J1** SD9212.
Milnsbridge *W.Yorks.* ***Suburb***, 2m/4km W of Huddersfield town centre. **50 D1** SE1116.
Milnshaw *Lancs.* ***Suburb***, to NW of Accrington town centre. SD7529.
Milnthorpe *Cumb.* Population: 1934. ***Village***, 7m/11km S of Kendal. **55 H1** SD4981.
Milnthorpe *W.Yorks.* ***Suburb***, to E of Pugneys Country Park, 3m/4km S of Wakefield city centre. SE3317.
Milovaig *High.* ***Locality***, on Skye, comprising Upper and Lower Milovaig, 6m/10km W of Dunvegan. **93 G6** NG1549.
Milrig *E.Ayr.* ***Settlement***, 2m/3km S of Galston. **74 D7** NS5034.
Milson *Shrop.* ***Village***, 4m/6km NE of Tenbury Wells. **29 F1** SO6373.
Milstead *Kent* ***Village***, 3m/5km S of Sittingbourne. **14 E2** TQ9058.
Milston *Wilts.* ***Village***, on River Avon, 3m/4km N of Amesbury. **20 E7** SU1645.
Milthorpe *Northants.* ***Settlement***, adjoining to W of Weedon Lois, 6m/10km N of Brackley. SP5946.
Milton *Angus* ***Hamlet***, 2m/3km S of Glamis, in Glen Ogilvey. **82 E3** NO3743.
Milton *Cambs.* Population: 3812. ***Village***, 3m/5km NE of Cambridge. **33 H2** TL4762.
Milton *Cumb.* ***Hamlet***, 2m/3km E of Brampton. **70 A7** NY5560.
Milton *Cumb.* ***Hamlet***, 2m/4km NE of Milnthorpe. SD5383.
Milton *Derbys.* ***Village***, 1m/2km E of Repton. **41 F3** SK3226.
Milton *D. & G.* ***Hamlet***, 2m/4km SE of Glenluce. NX2154.
Milton *D. & G.* ***Village***, 2m/3km SE of Crocketford, with Milton Loch to NW. **65 J3** NX8470.
Milton *Glas.* ***Suburb***, 3m/4km N of Glasgow city centre. NS5969.
Milton *High.* ***Locality***, consisting of Easter and Wester Milton, 5m/8km SE of Nairn. **97 G6** NH9553.
Milton *High.* ***Settlement***, 1km W of Wick. **105 J3** ND3451.
Milton *High.* ***Settlement***, on W coast of Ross and Cromarty district, adjoining to S of Applecross. **94 D7** NG7043.
Milton *High.* ***Settlement***, in Ross and Cromarty district, on N shore of Beauly Firth, 3m/5km E of Muir of Ord. **96 C7** NH5749.
Milton *High.* ***Village***, in Glen Urquhart, in Inverness district, 1m/2km W of Drumnadrochit. **88 B1** NH4930.
Milton *High.* ***Village***, in Ross and Cromarty district, 5m/8km NE of Invergordon. **96 E4** NH7674.
Milton *Kent* ***Suburb***, to E of Gravesend. TQ6574.
Milton *Moray* ***Settlement***, near N coast, 3m/4km S of Cullen. **98 D4** NJ5163.

M

Milton *Newport* ***Locality***, 4m/6km E of Newport. **19 G3** ST3688.
Milton *N.Som.* ***Hamlet***, 1m/2km NE of Weston-super-Mare town centre. **19 G5** ST3462.
Milton *Notts.* ***Village***, 2m/3km NW of Tuxford. **51 K5** SK7173.
Milton *Oxon.* ***Village***, 4m/6km S of Banbury. **31 F5** SP4535.
Milton *Oxon.* ***Village***, 3m/5km NW of Didcot. **21 H2** SU4892.
Milton *Pembs.* ***Village***, 4m/6km E of Pembroke. **16 D4** SN0403.
Milton *P. & K.* ***Settlement***, in Glen Cochill, 1m/2km NE of Amulree. **82 A4** NN9138.
Milton *Ports.* ***Suburb***, 2m/3km E of Portsmouth city centre. SZ6699.
Milton *Som.* ***Hamlet***, 1m/2km N of Martock. ST4621.
Milton *Som.* ***Locality***, comprising Lower and Upper Milton about 1m/2km NW and N respectively of Wells. ST5347.
Milton *Stir.* ***Settlement***, 1m/2km W of Aberfoyle. **81 G7** NN5001.
Milton *Stir.* ***Settlement***, on N side of Loch Venachar, 3m/5km SW of Callander. **81 G7** NN5706.
Milton *Stir.* ***Village***, 2m/4km NW of Drymen. **74 C1** NS4490.
Milton *Stoke* ***Locality***, 4m/6km NE of Stoke-on-Trent city centre. **49 J7** SJ9050.
Milton *Surr.* ***Suburb***, S district of Dorking. TQ1647.
Milton *W.Dun.* Population: 1079. ***Village***, 2m/3km E of Dumbarton. **74 C3** NS4274.
Milton *W.Isles Anglicised form of Gearraidh Bhailteas, qv.*
Milton Abbas *Dorset* ***Village***, 6m/9km SW of Blandford Forum. 1km NW, Milton Abbey, 14c-15c, and Milton Abbey boys' school. **9 H4** ST8001.
Milton Abbey *Dorset* ***Historic house***, 18c Gothic-style house (now a boarding school) to NW of Milton Abbas, 6m/9km SW of Blandford Forum. Designed by Sir William Chambers, it stands next to 14c-15c Abbey Church on site of monastery founded in AD 938 by Athelstan. **9 G4** ST7902.
Milton Abbot *Devon* ***Village***, 6m/9km NW of Tavistock. **4 E3** SX4079.
Milton Bridge *Midloth.* ***Locality***, 2m/3km NE of Penicuik. **76 A4** NT2562.
Milton Bryan *Beds.* ***Village***, 2m/3km SE of Woburn. **32 C5** SP9730.
Milton Burn *P. & K.* ***River***, flowing SE into River Almond, 4m/6km NW of Methven. **82 A4** NN9729.
Milton Chantry *Kent* ***Historic house***, Gravesend's oldest building (English Heritage) founded by Earl of Pembroke in 1322 and included chapel for lepers. Became part of fort in 18c and now contains museum. **24 C4** TQ6574.
Milton Clevedon *Som.* ***Village***, 2m/3km NW of Bruton. **9 F1** ST6637.
Milton Coldwells *Aber.* ***Settlement***, 3m/4km SE of Auchnagatt. **91 H1** NJ9538.
Milton Combe *Devon* ***Village***, 6m/9km S of Tavistock. **4 E4** SX4866.
Milton Damerel *Devon* ***Village***, 5m/8km NE of Holsworthy. **6 B4** SS3810.
Milton End *Glos.* ***Settlement***, 1km E of Arlingham. SO7210.
Milton Eonan *P. & K.* ***Locality***, in Glen Lyon above Bridge of Balgie. Waterfall in Allt Bail a' Mhuilinn, stream running into River Lyon here from S. NN5746.
Milton Ernest *Beds.* ***Village***, on River Great Ouse, 5m/7km NW of Bedford. **32 D3** TL0156.
Milton Green *Ches.* ***Hamlet***, 6m/9km SE of Chester. **48 D7** SJ4658.
Milton Heights *Oxon.* ***Settlement***, 3m/4km W of Didcot. SU4891.
Milton Hill *Oxon.* ***Village***, 3m/5km W of Didcot. **21 H2** SU4790.
Milton Inveramsay *Aber.* ***Settlement***, 3m/5km NW of Inverurie. **91 F2** NJ7325.
Milton Keynes *M.K.* Population: 156,148. ***City***, New Town designated 1967. Includes Bletchley in S, Stony Stratford and Wolverton in NW, and original village of Milton Keynes in E. Area about 34 square miles or 98 square km. Site of De Montfort University and home of The Open University. **32 B5** SP8539.
Milton Keynes Village *M.K.* ***Village***, 3m/5km E of Milton Keynes city centre. **32 B5** SP8839.
Milton Lilbourne *Wilts.* ***Village***, 2m/3km E of Pewsey. **20 E5** SU1960.
Milton Loch *D. & G.* ***Lake/loch***, 1km SE of Crocketford. **65 J3** NX8471.
Milton Lockhart *S.Lan.* ***Settlement***, above E bank of River Clyde, 2m/3km W of Carluke. **75 G6** NS8149.
Milton Lodge Gardens *Som.* ***Garden***, mature terraced early 20c gardens, 1km N of Wells, with outstanding views of Wells Cathedral and Vale of Avalon. Also includes 7 acre aboretum. **19 J7** ST5446.
Milton Malsor *Northants.* ***Village***, 4m/6km SW of Northampton. **31 J3** SP7355.
Milton Manor House *Oxon.* ***Historic house***, Georgian manor designed by Inigo Jones, seat of Barrett family, situated 3m/5km S of Abingdon. Gardens contain dovecote, animals, walled garden and woodland. **21 H2** SU4892.
Milton Morenish *P. & K.* ***Settlement***, on N side of Loch Tay, 3m/5km NE of Killin. **81 H4** NN6136.
Milton Ness *Aber.* ***Coastal feature***, headland on E coast, 6m/9km NE of Montrose. **83 J1** NO7764.
Milton of Auchinhove *Aber.* ***Settlement***, 2m/3km W of Lumphanan. **90 D4** NJ5503.
Milton of Balgonie *Fife* ***Village***, 1m/2km E of Markinch. **82 E7** NS3100.
Milton of Cairnborrow *Aber.* ***Settlement***, on N side of River Deveron, 3m/5km E of Haugh of Glass. **98 C6** NJ4740.
Milton of Campsie *E.Dun.* Population: 4056. ***Village***, 2m/3km N of Kirkintilloch. **74 E3** NS6576.
Milton of Cullerlie *Aber.* ***Settlement***, on N side of Gormack Burn, 3m/4km SE of Echt. **91 F4** NJ7602.
Milton of Cushnie *Aber.* ***Village***, 5m/7km SW of Alford. **90 D3** NJ5211.
Milton of Dalcapon *P. & K.* ***Settlement***, 3m/5km SE of Pitlochry. **82 A2** NN9755.
Milton of Tullich *Aber.* ***Settlement***, on Tullich Burn, 2m/3km NE of Ballater. **90 B5** NO3897.
Milton on Stour *Dorset* ***Village***, 1m/2km N of Gillingham. **9 G2** ST8028.
Milton Regis *Kent* ***Suburb***, to W of Sittingbourne. **24 E5** TQ8964.
Milton Street *E.Suss.* ***Hamlet***, 1m/2km NE of Alfriston. TQ5304.
Milton Street *Kent* ***Locality***, 3m/5km W of Gravesend. TQ6074.
Milton Tower *Moray* ***Other feature of interest***, remains of tower in Keith, built 1480, former home of Oliphant family. **98 C5** NJ4251.
Milton-under-Wychwood *Oxon.* ***Village***, 4m/6km N of Burford. **30 D7** SP2618.
Miltonduff *Moray* ***Settlement***, 3m/4km SW of Elgin. **97 J5** NJ1760.
Miltonhill *Moray* ***Settlement***, 1m/2km inland from Burghead Bay and 4m/7km NE of Forres. **97 H5** NJ0963.
Miltonise *D. & G.* ***Settlement***, 6m/10km SW of Barrhill. **64 B3** NX1873.
Milton's Cottage *Bucks.* ***Historic house***, 15c home of John Milton at Chalfont St. Giles, 3m/4km SE of Amersham. **22 C2** SU9893.
Milverton *Som.* ***Small town***, stone-built town, 7m/11km W of Taunton. **7 K3** ST1225.
Milverton *Warks.* ***Suburb***, in NW part of Royal Leamington Spa. SP3066.
Milwich *Staffs.* ***Village***, 5m/8km E of Stone. **40 B2** SJ9732.
Milwr *Flints.* ***Suburb***, 1m/2km SE of Holywell. SJ1974.
Mimbridge *Surr.* ***Settlement***, 1m/2km SE of Chobham. SU9861.
Minard *Arg. & B.* ***Hamlet***, in Argyll, on W shore of Loch Fyne, 4m/6km SW of Furnace. **73 H1** NR9796.
Minard Castle *Arg. & B.* ***Settlement***, on NW coast of Loch Fyne, 1m/2km S of Minard. **73 H1** NR9794.
Minard Forest *Arg. & B.* ***Forest/woodland***, to W of Minard. **73 H1** NR9796.
Minard Point *Arg. & B.* ***Coastal feature***, headland on N side of entrance to Loch Feochan in Argyll, 5m/8km SW of Oban. **79 K5** NM8123.
Minch Moor *Sc.Bord.* ***Mountain***, 3m/5km SE of Innerleithen. Height 1860 feet or 567 metres. **76 B7** NT3533.
Minchington *Dorset* ***Settlement***, 1km SE of Farnham and 3m/4km SE of Tollard Royal. **9 J3** ST9614.
Minchinhampton *Glos.* Population: 3201. ***Village***, 3m/5km SE of Stroud. **20 B1** SO8700.
Mindrum *Northumb.* ***Settlement***, 4m/7km S of Cornhill on Tweed. **77 G7** NT8432.
Mindrummill *Northumb.* ***Settlement***, 5m/8km NW of Kirknewton. NT8433.
Minehead *Som.* Population: 9158. ***Small town***, Victorian resort on Bristol Channel, with extensive sands and small harbour. **7 H1** SS9746.
Minera *Wrex.* ***Village***, 4m/7km W of Wrexham. **48 B7** SJ2751.
Minety *Wilts.* ***Village***, 5m/8km W of Cricklade. **20 D2** SU0290.
Minety Lower Moor *Wilts.* ***Settlement***, 1km N of Minety. SU0290.
Minffordd *Gwyn.* ***Hamlet***, 1km S of Bangor. SH5770.
Minffordd *Gwyn.* ***Settlement***, to NW of Tal-y-Llyn Lake, 4m/6km S of Dolgellau. **37 G4** SH7311.
Minffordd *Gwyn.* ***Village***, 1km W of Penrhyndeudraeth. **36 E2** SH5938.
Mingarry *W.Isles Anglicised form of Mingearraidh, qv.*
Mingary Castle *High.* ***Castle***, ruined 13c castle on S coast Ardnamurchan peninsula in Lochaber district, 1m/2km SE of Kilchoan. **79 G1** NM5063.
Mingay Island *High.* ***Island***, small uninhabited island in Loch Dunvegan, 1m/2km S of Ardmore Point, Skye. **93 H6** NG2257.
Mingearraidh (Anglicised form: Mingary.) *W.Isles* ***Settlement***, on South Uist, 3m/5km SE of Rubha Ardvule. **84 C2** NF7426.
Minginish *High.* ***Locality***, on Skye, lying S of a line from Sligachan to Loch Harport and W of River Sligachan. Includes Cuillin Hills. **85 J2** NG3530.
Mingulay (Gaelic form: Miughalaigh.) *W.Isles* ***Island***, gaunt, uninhabited island of about 6 square km, with high cliffs, 2m/3km SW of Pabbay and 6m/10km SW of Vatersay. Haunt of sea birds. **84 A6** NL5582.
Mingulay Bay *W.Isles* ***Bay***, on E coast of Mingulay. **84 A6** NL5783.
Miningsby *Lincs.* ***Hamlet***, 5m/8km SE of Horncastle. **53 G6** TF3264.
Minions *Cornw.* ***Village***, on moorland 4m/7km N of Liskeard. Hurlers Stone Circle (English Heritage) to W. **4 C3** SX2671.
Minishant *S.Ayr.* ***Settlement***, 3m/5km NE of Maybole. **67 H2** NS3314.
Minley Manor *Hants.* ***Settlement***, 1m/2km S of Yateley. **22 B6** SU8258.
Minllyn *Gwyn.* ***Hamlet***, 1m/2km N of Mallwyd. **37 H4** SH8514.
Minnes *Aber.* ***Locality***, comprises South Minnes, Miltown of Minnes, Mill of Minnes and Hill of Minnes, 4m/6km W of Newburgh. **91 H2** NJ9423.
Minnigaff *D. & G.* ***Village***, on E side on Newton Stewart across River Cree. **64 E4** NX4166.
Minnonie *Aber.* ***Settlement***, 3m/5km SW of Gardenstown. **99 F4** NJ7760.
Minnygap Height *D. & G.* ***Mountain***, on E edge of Forest of Ae, 5m/8km SW of Beattock. Height 1309 feet or 399 metres. **69 F4** NY0296.
Minskip *N.Yorks.* ***Village***, 1m/2km S of Boroughbridge. **57 J3** SE3864.
Minsmere RSPB Reserve *Suff.* ***Nature reserve***, area of meres and marshes on coast at Minsmere Level, 3m/5km NE of Leiston. Important habitat for variety of common and rare wetland birds, including spoonbill, heron, avocet, marsh harrier, black tern, osprey and sandpipers. Around 200 species are recorded annually on the reserve. Surrounding area also provides heath and woodland habitat. TM4766.
Minstead *Hants.* ***Village***, 2m/3km NW of Lyndhurst. **10 D3** SU2811.
Minsted *W.Suss.* ***Hamlet***, 2m/3km W of Midhurst. SU8520.
Minster *Kent* Population: 15,448. ***Suburb***, on Isle of Sheppey, running down to N coast. **25 F4** TQ9573.
Minster *Kent* Population: 2296. ***Village***, on Isle of Thanet, 5m/7km W of Ramsgate. **25 K5** TR3064.
Minster Abbey *Kent* ***Ecclesiastical building***, in Minster, on Isle of Sheppey. Saxon church joined to a 13c church. **25 F4** TQ9573.
Minster Abbey *Kent* ***Ecclesiastical building***, in Minster, 5m/8km W of Ramsgate. 11c-12c abbey now occupied by Benedictine nuns. **25 K5** TR3164.
Minster Lovell *Oxon.* ***Village***, on River Windrush, 3m/4km NW of Witney. Remains of moated manor house (English Heritage). **30 E7** SP3111.
Minster Lovell Hall and Dovecote *Oxon.* ***Historic house***, ruins of 15c manor (English Heritage) which belonged to Lord Lovell, 1km NE of Minster Lovell and 3m/4km NW of Witney. **30 E7** SP3211.
Minsteracres *Northumb.* ***Settlement***, 4m/6km S of Riding Mill. NZ0255.
Minsterley *Shrop.* ***Village***, 9m/14km SW of Shrewsbury. **38 C5** SJ3705.
Minsterworth *Glos.* ***Village***, on N bank of River Severn, 4m/6km W of Gloucester. Good viewpoint for Severn Bore. **29 G7** SO7717.
Minsthorpe *W.Yorks.* ***Locality***, adjoining to N of South Elmsall. SE4712.
Minterne Gardens *Dorset* ***Garden***, to SW of Minterne Magna, 2m/3km N of Cerne Abbas, containing rhododendrons, shrub gardens, rare trees, lakes and streams. **9 F4** ST6604.
Minterne Magna *Dorset* ***Village***, 2m/3km N of Cerne Abbas. **9 F4** ST6504.
Minterne Parva *Dorset* ***Settlement***, 1km SE of Minterne Magna. ST6603.
Minting *Lincs.* ***Village***, 5m/8km NW of Horncastle. **52 E5** TF1873.
Mintlaw *Aber.* Population: 2522. ***Village***, 8m/13km W of Peterhead. **99 J6** NK0048.
Minto *Sc.Bord.* ***Village***, 5m/9km NE of Hawick. **70 A1** NT5620.
Minto Hills *Sc.Bord.* ***Large natural feature***, comprising two distinct summits separated by a saddle, 1km NW of Minto. N summit height is 836 feet or 255 metres, S summit is 905 feet or 276 metres. **70 A1** NT5521.
Minton *Shrop.* ***Village***, 2m/4km SW of Church Stretton. **38 D6** SO4390.
Minwear (Mynwar). *Pembs.* ***Settlement***, 9m/15km NW of Tenby. **16 D3** SN0313.
Minworth *W.Mid.* ***Village***, 4m/6km SE of Sutton Coldfield. **40 D6** SP1592.
Miodar *Arg. & B.* ***Settlement***, on N coast of Tiree, 1km NW of Caolas. **78 B3** NM0749.
Mirbister *Ork.* ***Settlement***, on Mainland, 1m/2km SE of Dounby. **106 C5** HY3019.
Mire of Midgates *Aber.* ***Mountain***, in Correen Hills, 3m/5km SE of Rhynie. Height 1588 feet or 484 metres. **90 D2** NJ5222.
Mirehouse *Cumb.* ***Historic house***, late 18c house on E side of Bassenthwaite Lake, 4m/6km NW of Keswick. Tennyson and Carlyle visited house as guests of James Spedding. **60 D4** NY2328.
Mirehouse *Cumb.* ***Suburb***, 2m/3km S of Whitehaven town centre. NX9815.
Mireland *High.* ***Settlement***, near E coast of Caithness district, 7m/11km NW of Wick. **105 J2** ND3160.
Mirfield *W.Yorks.* Population: 18,459. ***Town***, on River Calder 3m/5km SW of Dewsbury. Medieval church tower. **57 G7** SE2019.
Mirkady Point *Ork.* ***Coastal feature***, headland on Mainland on E side of Deer Sound, 4m/7km SW of Mull Head. **107 E7** HY5306.
Misarden Park Gardens *Glos.* ***Garden***, 6m/10km NW of Stroud, which includes a topiary, partly designed by Sir Edwin Lutyens, a walled garden, roses and 17c manor house. **20 C1** SO9408.
Miserden *Glos.* ***Village***, 7m/11km NW of Cirencester. **20 C1** SO9309.
Mishnish *Arg. & B.* ***Locality***, on Mull, 3m/5km W of Tobermory. **79 F2** NM4656.
Mishnish Lochs *Arg. & B.* ***Lake/loch***, group of three small lochs, 3m/4km SW of Tobermory. In descending order they are, Loch Carnain an Amais, Loch Meadhoin and Loch Peallach. **79 F2** NM4752.
Miskin *R.C.T.* ***Locality***, adjoining to S of Mountain Ash. **18 D2** ST0498.
Miskin (Meisgyn). *R.C.T.* ***Village***, 2m/3km S of Llantrisant. **18 D3** ST0480.
Mislingford *Hants.* ***Settlement***, 3m/5km SE of Bishop's Waltham. SU5814.
Misselfore *Wilts.* ***Settlement***, 1km SW of Bowerchalke. SU0122.
Misson *Notts.* ***Village***, 3m/4km NE of Bawtry. **51 J3** SK6994.
Misterton *Leics.* ***Hamlet***, 1m/2km E of Lutterworth. **41 H7** SP5583.
Misterton *Notts.* Population: 1953. ***Village***, 5m/8km NW of Gainsborough. **51 K3** SK7694.
Misterton *Som.* ***Village***, 1m/2km SE of Crewkerne. **8 D4** ST4508.
Misterton Carr *Notts.* ***Marsh/bog***, flat area at sea level, drained by numerous dykes to S of River Idle and Mather Drain, and W of Misterton, 6m/10km NW of Gainsborough. **51 K3** SK7194.

Misterton Soss *Notts.* ***Settlement***, on River Idle, 1km E of Misterton. SK7795.
Mistley *Essex* ***Village***, on S side of River Stour estuary, 1m/2km E of Manningtree. Mistley Towers (English Heritage) to NW. TM1131.
Mistley Towers *Essex* ***Other feature of interest***, ruined 18c hall and church (English Heritage), in NW Mistley on S bank of River Stour estuary. Church, designed by Robert Adam, is unusual in having two square towers. **35 F5** TM1132.
Misty Law *N.Ayr.* ***Mountain***, 6m/10km NE of Largs. Height 1673 feet or 510 metres. **74 A4** NS2961.
Mitcham *Gt.Lon.* ***Suburb***, in borough of Merton, 4m/6km NW of Croydon. **23 F5** TQ2768.
Mitchel Troy (Llanfihangel Troddi). *Mon.* ***Village***, 2m/3km SW of Monmouth. **28 D7** SO4910.
Mitcheldean *Glos.* Population: 2243. ***Village***, 3m/5km N of Cinderford. **29 F7** SO6618.
Mitchell *Cornw.* ***Village***, 5m/9km SE of Newquay. **3 F3** SW8654.
Mitchelland *Cumb.* ***Settlement***, 3m/4km SE of Bowness-on-Windermere. **60 F7** SD4395.
Mitchell's Fold Stone Circle *Shrop.* ***Historic/prehistoric site***, Bronze Age stone circle (English Heritage), 75 feet in diameter, on moors 1m/2km NE of Priestweston, 3m/5km NE of Church Stoke. **38 C6** SO3098.
Mitcheltroy Common *Mon.* ***Settlement***, 1m/2km S of Mitchel Troy and 2m/4km SW of Monmouth. **19 H1** SO4909.
Mitford *Northumb.* ***Village***, on River Wansbeck, 2m/3km W of Morpeth. Ruined Norman castle. **71 G5** NZ1785.
Mitford Castle *Northumb.* ***Castle***, to S of River Wansbeck, 2m/3km W of Morpeth. Early 12c motte with later stonework; thought to be only 5-sided great tower in England. **71 G5** NZ1785.
Mither Tap *Aber.* ***Mountain***, with panoramic viewpoint, 5m/8km W of Inverurie. Height 1699 feet or 518 metres. **90 E2** NJ6822.
Mithian *Cornw.* ***Village***, 2m/3km E of St. Agnes. **2 E3** SW7450.
Mitton *Staffs.* ***Settlement***, 3m/4km W of Penkridge. **40 A4** SJ8815.
Mitton Green *Lancs.* ***Settlement***, 2m/3km SW of Clitheroe. SD7139.
Miughalaigh *W.Isles Gaelic form of Mingulay, qv.*
Miwl *Powys Welsh form of (River) Mule, qv.*
Mixbury *Oxon.* ***Village***, 3m/4km SE of Brackley. **31 H5** SP6034.
Mixenden *W.Yorks.* ***Village***, 3m/5km NW of Halifax. SE0628.
Mixon *Staffs.* ***Locality***, 2m/3km W of Butterton. SK0457.
Moar *P. & K.* ***Settlement***, in Glen Lyon, 3m/5km SW of Bridge of Balgie. **81 G3** NN5344.
Moat *Cumb.* ***Settlement***, 2m/3km SE of Canonbie. **69 K6** NY4173.
Moat Hall *Suff. See Parham.*
Moats Tye *Suff.* ***Hamlet***, 2m/4km S of Stowmarket. TM0455.
Mobberley *Ches.* Population: 1875. ***Village***, 2m/4km E of Knutsford. **49 G5** SJ7879.
Mobberley *Staffs.* ***Hamlet***, 1m/2km S of Cheadle. SK0041.
Moccas *Here.* ***Hamlet***, on S side of River Wye, 10m/16km W of Hereford. **28 C4** SO3542.
Moccas Court *Here.* ***Historic house***, 18c mansion decorated by Robert Adam, 9m/13km E of Hay-on-Wye. Parkland designed by 'Capability' Brown. **28 C4** SO3543.
Mochdre *Conwy* ***Hamlet***, 1m/2km W of Colwyn Bay. **47 G5** SH8278.
Mochdre *Powys* ***Hamlet***, on Mochdre Brook, 3m/5km SW of Newtown. **37 K7** SO0788.
Mochrum (Also known as Kirk of Mochrum.) *D. & G.* ***Village***, 2m/3km N of Port William. Restored castle, Old Place of Mochrum, on N shore of Mochrum Loch 6m/9km to NW. **64 D6** NX3446.
Mochrum Loch *D. & G.* ***Lake/loch***, 8m/13km W of Wigtown. At NE corner of loch stands restored Old Place of Mochrum. **64 C5** NX3053.
Mockbeggar *Hants.* ***Settlement***, on edge of New Forest, 3m/5km NE of Ringwood. SU1609.
Mockbeggar *Kent* ***Hamlet***, 1km N of Collier Street. **14 C3** TQ7146.
Mockbeggar Wharf *Mersey.* ***Coastal feature***, sands off N coast of Wirral. **48 B3** SJ2591.
Mockerkin *Cumb.* ***Hamlet***, 5m/8km SW of Cockermouth. **60 B4** NY0823.
Modbury *Devon* ***Village***, 7m/11km NW of Kingsbridge. **5 G5** SX6551.
Moddershall *Staffs.* ***Hamlet***, 2m/4km NE of Stone. **40 B2** SJ9236.
Mode Hill *Ches.* ***Suburb***, 1m/2km SW of Bollington. SJ9276.
Modsarie *High.* ***Settlement***, 3m/5km E of Bettyhill, Caithness district. **103 J2** NC6462.
Moel Cors-y-garnedd *Gwyn.* ***Mountain***, rocky summit 5m/8km NE of Dolgellau. Height 1640 feet or 500 metres. **37 G3** SH7723.
Moel-ddu *Gwyn.* ***Mountain***, 3m/5km N of Porthmadog. Height 1811 feet or 552 metres. **36 E1** SH5744.
Moel Eilio *Gwyn.* ***Mountain***, 2m/3km SW of Llanberis. Height 2381 feet or 726 metres. **46 D7** SH5557.
Moel Emoel *Gwyn.* ***Mountain***, 3m/4km N of Bala. Height 1771 feet or 540 metres. **37 J1** SH9340.
Moel Famau *Denb.* ***Mountain***, highest point of Clwydian Range. At summit is ruin of Jubilee Tower, built in 1810 to mark 50th year of reign of George III. Height 1817 feet or 554 metres. **47 K6** SJ1662.
Moel Famau Country Park *Denb.* ***Leisure/recreation***, 2375 acre country park focused around crest of Clwyd Hills and especially popular with hill walkers, 3m/5km NE of Ruthin. At summit of Moel Famau is ruin of Jubilee Tower. **47 K6** SJ1463.
Moel Feity *Powys* ***Mountain***, 6m/9km SW of Sennybridge. Height 1938 feet or 591 metres. **27 H6** SN8423.
Moel Fferna *Wrex.* ***Mountain***, 4m/6km SE of Cynwyd. Height 2066 feet or 630 metres. **38 A2** SJ1139.
Moel Findeg *Denb.* ***Mountain***, rising to over 360 metres, 3m/5km SW of Mold. **48 B6** SJ2061.
Moel Garegog *Denb.* ***Mountain***, 2m/3km SW of Four Crosses. Height 1355 feet or 413 metres. **48 B7** SJ2152.
Moel Gyffylog *Conwy* ***Mountain***, 5m/8km SW of Colwyn Bay. Height 1118 feet or 341 metres. **47 G5** SH8271.
Moel Hafodowen *Gwyn.* ***Mountain***, in Coed y Brenin Forest 6m/10km SE of Trawsfynydd. Height 1427 feet or 435 metres. **37 G3** SH7526.
Moel Hebog *Gwyn.* ***Mountain***, 2m/3km W of Beddgelert. Height 2565 feet or 782 metres. **36 E1** SH5646.
Moel Hen-fache *Powys* ***Mountain***, 1m/2km NW of Llanrhaeadr-ym-Mochnant. Height 1709 feet or 521 metres. **38 A3** SJ1028.
Moel Hywel *Powys* ***Mountain***, 3m/5km NE of Rhayader. Height 1656 feet or 505 metres. **27 K1** SO0071.
Moel Llyfnant *Gwyn.* ***Mountain***, 6m/10km E of Trawsfynydd. Height 2460 feet or 750 metres. **37 H2** SH8035.
Moel Llyn *Conwy* ***Mountain***, 4m/6km NE of Pentrefoelas. Height 1469 feet or 448 metres. **47 G7** SH8957.
Moel Llys-y-coed *Flints.* ***Mountain***, 2m/3km E of Llangwyfan. Height 1525 feet or 465 metres. **47 K6** SJ1565.
Moel Morfydd *Denb.* ***Mountain***, in Llantysilio Mountains, on S side of River Morwynion. Height 1801 feet or 549 metres. **38 A1** SJ1545.
Moel Penamnen *Gwyn.* ***Mountain***, 2m/3km NE of Blaenau Ffestiniog. Height 2043 feet or 623 metres. **37 G1** SH7148.
Moel Seisiog *Conwy* ***Mountain***, 5m/8km SE of Llanrwst. Height 1535 feet or 468 metres. **47 G7** SH8657.
Moel Siabod *Conwy* ***Mountain***, 6m/9km SW of Betws-y-Coed, with Llyn-y-Foel below summit to E. Height 2860 feet or 872 metres. **47 F7** SH7054.
Moel Sych ***Mountain***, summit of Berwyn range, on border of Denbighshire and Powys, 4m/6km SE of Llandrillo. Height 2713 feet or 827 metres. **37 K2** SJ0631.
Moel Ton-mawr *N.P.T.* ***Mountain***, 3m/5km SW of Maesteg. Height 1046 feet or 319 metres. **18 B3** SS8387.
Moel Tryfan *Gwyn.* ***Settlement***, 4m/7km S of Caernarfon. **46 D7** SH5156.
Moel Wilym *Powys* ***Mountain***, 3m/4km N of Llanbister. Height 1568 feet or 478 metres. **28 A1** SO1177.
Moel Wnion *Gwyn.* ***Mountain***, 4m/6km SW of Llanfairfechan. Height 1902 feet or 580 metres. **46 E6** SH6469.
Moel y Feidiog *Gwyn.* ***Mountain***, 5m/8km SE of Trawsfynydd. Height 1847 feet or 563 metres. **37 G2** ST7832.
Moel y Gamelin *Denb.* ***Mountain***, summit of Llantysilio Mountain 2m/3km E of Bryneglwys. Height 1896 feet or 578 metres. **38 A1** SJ1746.
Moel-y-Gest *Gwyn.* ***Hill***, 1km W of Porthmadog. Height 859 feet or 262 metres. **36 E2** SH5538.
Moel y Golfa *Powys* ***Mountain***, largely wooded and highest of three principal peaks of Breidden Hills. Height 1325 feet or 404 metres. **38 B4** SJ2812.
Moel-y-Llyn *Cere.* ***Mountain***, 3m/4km NW of head of Nant-y-moch Reservoir. Height 1709 feet or 521 metres. **37 G6** SN7191.
Moel y Llyn *Powys* ***Mountain***, 5m/8km E of Dinas-Mawddwy. Height 1453 feet or 443 metres. **37 J4** SH9415.
Moel-y-Mor *Cere.* ***Hill***, 4m/6km N of Llandysul. Height 922 feet or 281 metres. SN4146.
Moel y Parc *Flints.* ***Mountain***, 6m/9km SE of St. Asaph. Height 1305 feet or 398 metres. **47 K5** SJ1170.
Moel y Waun *Denb.* ***Mountain***, 3m/4km SE of Llanfair Dyffryn Clwyd. Height 1351 feet or 412 metres. **47 K7** SJ1653.
Moel yr Henfaes *Denb.* ***Mountain***, 3m/4km NE of Llandrillo. Height 1916 feet or 584 metres. **37 K2** SJ0738.
Moel yr Hyrddod *N.P.T.* ***Mountain***, 3m/4km SE of Resolven. Height 1617 feet or 493 metres. **18 B1** SN8500.
Moel Ysgyfarnogod *Gwyn.* ***Mountain***, 4m/6km SE of Penrhyndeudraeth. Height 2043 feet or 623 metres. **37 F2** SH6534.
Moelfre *Carmar.* ***Mountain***, 3m/5km SE of Newcastle Emlyn. Height 1099 feet or 335 metres. **17 G1** SN3236.
Moelfre *Conwy* ***Mountain***, 1m/2km S of Penmaenmawr. Height 1427 feet or 435 metres. **47 F5** SH7174.
Moelfre *Gwyn.* ***Mountain***, 5m/8km SE of Harlech. Height 1932 feet or 589 metres. **37 F3** SH6224.
Moelfre *I.o.A.* ***Village***, fishing village on E coast of Anglesey, 6m/10km SE of Amlwch. **46 D4** SH5186.
Moelfre *Powys* ***Hamlet***, at lower end of Llyn Moelfre, 2m/3km W of Llansilin. **38 A3** SJ1828.
Moelfre *Powys* ***Mountain***, 3m/4km SW of Bont Dolgadfan. Height 1535 feet or 468 metres. **37 H6** SN8498.
Moelfre *Powys* ***Mountain***, 3m/4km SW of Builth Wells. Height 1446 feet or 441 metres. **27 K4** SO0148.
Moelfre Hill *Powys* ***Mountain***, 2m/3km NE of Llanbister. Height 1558 feet or 475 metres. **28 A1** SO1276.
Moelfre Isaf *Conwy* ***Mountain***, steep-sided mountain 3m/4km S of Abergele. Height 1040 feet or 317 metres. **47 H5** SH9573.
Moelfre Uchaf *Conwy* ***Mountain***, 1m/2km SW of Betws-yn-Rhos. Height 1299 feet or 396 metres. **47 G5** SH8971.
Moelwyn Bach *Gwyn.* ***Mountain***, 3m/4km NW of Ffestiniog. Height 2332 feet or 711 metres. **37 F1** SH6643.
Moelwyn Mawr *Gwyn.* ***Mountain***, 3m/5km NW of Ffestiniog. Height 2526 feet or 770 metres. **37 F1** SH6544.
Moffat *D. & G.* Population: 2342. ***Small town***, market town and resort on River Annan, 19m/31km NE of Dumfries. Fashionable as spa town in 18c. **69 F3** NT0805.
Moffat Water *D. & G.* ***River***, running SW to River Annan 2m/3km S of Moffat. **69 G3** NT0805.
Mogerhanger *Beds.* ***Village***, 2m/3km W of Sandy. **32 E4** TL1449.
Mohope Moor *Northumb.* ***Open space***, moorland between River South Tyne and West Allen Dale, 3m/5km NE of Alston. **61 J2** NY7549.
Moidart *High.* ***Locality***, part of Lochaber district lying W of Loch Shiel and S of Loch Eilt. Coastline indented by Lochs Ailort and Moidart. **86 D7** NM7472.
Moin' a' choire *Arg. & B.* ***Settlement***, 2m/4km NE of Bridgend. **72 B4** NR3664.
Moine House *High.* ***Settlement***, 1km E of Loch Maovally, 6m/9km S of Whiten Head. **103 H2** NC5160.
Mòine Mhòr *Arg. & B.* ***Open space***, flood plain of River Add which meanders across area to its mouth at head of Loch Crinan. **73 G1** NR8293.
Moinechoill Chambered Cairn *N.Ayr.* ***Historic/prehistoric site***, long cairn 5m/7km W of Brodick. **73 H7** NR9435.
Moira *Leics.* ***Hamlet***, 3m/4km S of Swadlincote. **41 F4** SK3115.
Moira Baths *Leics.* ***Hamlet***, to W of Moira, 1m/2km E of Overseal. SK3115.
Mol a' Tuath *W.Isles* ***Sea feature***, inlet on E coast of South Uist, 1km S of Rubha Rossel. **84 D1** NF8535.
Mol-chlach *High.* ***Settlement***, on W side of Camas nan Gall inlet, Soay, in Skye and Lochalsh district. **85 K3** NG4513.
Mol Truisg *W.Isles* ***Bay***, small bay on SE coast of Isle of Lewis, 1m/2km N of Gob Rubh' Uisenis. **101 F7** NB3505.
Molash *Kent* ***Village***, 6m/9km N of Ashford. **15 F2** TR0251.
Mold (Yr Wyddgrug). *Flints.* Population: 8745. ***Small town***, 11m/17km NW of Wrexham. Remains of motte and bailey castle. Birthplace of Daniel Owen, novelist. **48 B6** SJ2364.
Moldgreen *W.Yorks.* ***Suburb***, 1km E of Huddersfield town centre. SE1516.
Mole ***River***, rising at Crawley and flowing circuitously past Horley, Dorking, Leatherhead, Cobham and Esher, before running into River Thames at East Molesey opposite Hampton Court Palace. **22 E5** TQ1568.
Mole *Devon* ***River***, rising on Exmoor, 2m/3km N of Bentwichen, and running SW past North and South Molton into River Taw at Junction Pool, 2m/3km SW of King's Nympton. **6 E3** SS6617.
Mole Hall *Essex* ***Leisure/recreation***, 20 acre park 1m/2km E of Widdington, housing wide variety of animals, ranging from exotic and rare to domestic and commonplace. Mole Hall also contains a Butterfly Pavilion complete with a resident insect specialist. **33 J5** TL5431.
Molehill Green *Essex* ***Settlement***, 3m/5km SW of Braintree. TL7120.
Molehill Green *Essex* ***Village***, 4m/7km NW of Great Dunmow. **33 J6** TL5624.
Molescroft *E.Riding* ***Suburb***, 1m/2km NW of Beverley. **59 G5** TA0240.
Molesden *Northumb.* ***Hamlet***, 3m/5km W of Morpeth. NZ1484.
Molesworth *Cambs.* ***Village***, 5m/8km E of Thrapston. **32 D1** TL0775.
Mollance *D. & G.* ***Settlement***, 3m/4km N of Castle Douglas. **65 H4** NX7765.
Molland *Devon* ***Village***, on S slopes of Exmoor, 6m/9km E of South Molton. **7 G3** SS8028.
Molland Common *Devon* ***Open space***, moorland at S side of Exmoor, 1m/2km NE of Molland. **7 G2** SS8130.
Molland Cross *Devon* ***Settlement***, 5m/8km N of South Molton. SS7133.
Mollin Burn *D. & G.* ***River***, flowing S to join Kinnel Water, 3m/5km NE of Parkgate. **69 F4** NY0593.
Mollington *Ches.* ***Village***, 3m/4km NW of Chester. **48 C5** SJ3870.
Mollington *Oxon.* ***Village***, 4m/7km N of Banbury. **31 F4** SP4447.
Mollinsburn *N.Lan.* ***Hamlet***, 4m/6km SW of Cumbernauld. **75 F3** NS7171.
Molls Cleuch Dod *Sc.Bord.* ***Mountain***, 5m/8km SE of Tweedsmuir. Height 2572 feet or 784 metres. **69 G2** NT1518.
Mompesson House *Wilts.* ***Historic house***, 18c Queen Anne house (National Trust) with walled garden in Cathedral Close, Salisbury. **10 C1** SU1429.
Monach Islands *W.Isles Alternative name for Heisker Islands, qv.*
Monachty *Cere.* ***Settlement***, 3m/5km E of Aberaeron. **26 E2** SN5061.
Monachyle Glen *Stir.* ***Valley***, carrying Monachyle Burn S into Loch Voil, 4m/6km W of Balquhidder. **81 F5** NN4722.
Monachylemore *Stir.* ***Settlement***, at W end of Loch Voil, 4m/6km W of Balquhidder. **81 F6** NN4719.
Monadh Fergie *Moray* ***Mountain***, 3m/4km SE of Tomintoul. Height 1889 feet or 576 metres. **89 J3** NJ1914.
Monadh Gorm *High.* ***Mountain***, 2m/3km W of Loch Arkaig, Lochaber district. Height 1568 feet or 478 metres. **87 F5** NM9691.
Monadh Mòr ***Mountain***, in Cairngorm Mountains on border of Highland and Aberdeenshire, 4m/7km SW of Ben Macdui. Munro: height 3651 feet or 1113 metres. **89 G5** NN9394.
Monadh nam Mial *P. & K.* ***Mountain***, 3m/4km S of Aberfeldy. Height 1975 feet or 602 metres. **81 K3** NN8644.
Monadhliath Mountains *High.* ***Large natural feature***, range of mountains running NE to SW, astride border between Inverness and Badenoch and Strathspey districts, on W side of upper Strathspey. Summit is Carn Dearg at a height of 3100 feet or 945 metres, 16m/26km S of Inverness. **88 B4** NH6710.
Monamenach ***Mountain***, on border of Angus and Perth & Kinross, 4m/6km E of Spittal of Glenshee. Height 2647 feet or 807 metres. **89 J7** NO1770.
Monaughty *Powys* ***Settlement***, 4m/6km SW of Knighton. Gabled Tudor farmhouse. SO2368.
Monaughty Forest *Moray* ***Forest/woodland***, 6m/9km SW of Elgin. **97 J6** NJ1358.
Monawee *Angus* ***Mountain***, 4m/6km S of Mount Keen. Height 2283 feet or 696 metres. **90 C6** NO4080.
Moncreiffe *P. & K.* ***Suburb***, S district of Perth. **82 C6** NO1121.
Moncreiffe Hill *P. & K.* ***Hill***, 2m/3km SE of Moncreiffe. Height 725 feet or 221 metres. **82 C6** NO1121.
Moncreiffe Island *P. & K. Alternative name for Friarton Island, qv.*

Monega Hill *Angus* ***Mountain***, to S of Caenlochan Glen, 3m/5km SE of Glenshee Ski Centre. Height 2978 feet or 908 metres. **89 J7** NO1875.
Monevechadan *Arg. & B.* ***Settlement***, at foot of Hell's Glen, 3m/4km N of Lochgoilhead. **80 C7** NN1805.
Monewden *Suff.* ***Village***, 4m/7km NW of Wickham Market. **35 G3** TM2358.
Money Bridge *Lincs.* ***Locality***, 2m/3km W of Pinchbeck. TF2125.
Money Head *D. & G.* ***Coastal feature***, headland 4m/7km SE of Portpatrick. **64 A6** NX0448.
Moneydie *P. & K.* ***Settlement***, 5m/8km NW of Perth. **82 B5** NO0629.
Moneyrow Green *W. & M.* ***Settlement***, 3m/4km S of Maidenhead. SU8977.
Mongour *Aber.* ***Mountain***, 4m/6km S of Crathes. Height 1233 feet or 376 metres. **91 F5** NO7590.
Moniaive *D. & G.* ***Village***, on Dalwhat Water, 7m/11km SW of Thornhill. 3m/5km E is Maxwelton House. **68 C4** NX7790.
Monifieth *Angus* ***Suburb***, on Firth of Tay, 6m/10km E of Dundee. **83 F4** NO4932.
Monikie *Angus* ***Village***, 5m/8km NW of Carnoustie. Reservoir to SE. **83 F4** NO5038.
Monikie Country Park *Angus* ***Leisure/recreation***, at Monikie Reservoir, to SW of Monikie. 185 acre country park with grass and woodland. Watersports on reservoir. **83 F4** NO5038.
Monimail *Fife* ***Village***, 4m/7km W of Cupar. **82 D6** NO2914.
Monington (Eglwys Wythwr). *Pembs.* ***Settlement***, 3m/5km W of Cardigan. **26 A4** SN1343.
Monivey *Ork.* ***Bay***, to S of Noup Head, Westray. **106 D3** HY4047.
Monk Bretton *S.Yorks.* ***Suburb***, 2m/3km NE of Barnsley town centre. Remains of medieval priory (English Heritage) to SE, with restored 14c gatehouse. **51 F2** SE3607.
Monk End *N.Yorks.* ***Settlement***, adjoining to W of Croft-on-Tees. NZ2809.
Monk Fryston *N.Yorks.* ***Village***, 7m/11km W of Selby. Hall partly medieval. **58 B7** SE5029.
Monk Hesleden *Dur.* ***Hamlet***, 1m/2km SE of Hesleden and 4m/7km NW of Hartlepool. NZ4537.
Monk Sherborne *Hants.* ***Village***, 4m/6km NW of Basingstoke. **21 K6** SU6056.
Monk Soham *Suff.* ***Village***, 3m/5km NE of Debenham. **35 G2** TM2165.
Monk Soham Green *Suff.* ***Hamlet***, 1m/2km NE of Monk Soham. TM2165.
Monk Street *Essex* ***Hamlet***, 1m/2km S of Thaxted. **33 K6** TL6128.
Monken Hadley *Gt.Lon.* ***Suburb***, in borough of Barnet, 11m/18km N of Charing Cross. **23 F2** TQ2597.
Monkerton *Devon* ***Suburb***, at E edge of Exeter, 3m/5km from city centre. SX9693.
Monkey Island *W. & M.* ***Island***, in River Thames, 1km SE of Bray. SU9179.
Monkhide *Here.* ***Hamlet***, 7m/11km E of Hereford. SO6144.
Monkhill *Cumb.* ***Hamlet***, 4m/6km NW of Carlisle. **60 E1** NY3458.
Monkhopton *Shrop.* ***Village***, 6m/9km W of Bridgnorth. **39 F6** SO6293.
Monkland *Here.* ***Village***, on River Arrow, 3m/4km W of Leominster. **28 D3** SO4557.
Monkleigh *Devon* ***Village***, 3m/4km NW of Great Torrington. **6 C3** SS4520.
Monknash (Yr As Fawr). *V. of Glam.* ***Hamlet***, 3m/5km NW of Llantwit Major. **18 C4** SS9270.
Monkokehampton *Devon* ***Village***, 3m/4km E of Hatherleigh. **6 D5** SS5805.
Monks Bridge *Derbys.* ***Bridge***, stone-built bridge, dating from early 15c, over River Dove at Egginton, 4m/6km NE of Burton upon Trent. SK2626.
Monks Eleigh *Suff.* ***Village***, 5m/8km NW of Hadleigh. **34 D4** TL9647.
Monks Eleigh Tye *Suff.* ***Settlement***, 1m/2km NW of Monks Eleigh. TL9548.
Monk's Gate *W.Suss.* ***Hamlet***, 3m/4km SE of Horsham. **13 F4** TQ2027.
Monk's Green *Herts.* ***Settlement***, 2m/4km S of Hertford. TL3308.
Monks' Heath *Ches.* ***Hamlet***, 5m/8km W of Macclesfield. **49 H5** SJ8474.
Monk's Hill *Kent* ***Settlement***, 2m/3km NE of Biddenden. TQ8641.
Monks Horton *Kent* ***Locality***, 4m/6km NW of Hythe. TR1239.
Monk's House *E.Suss.* ***Historic house***, small weather-boarded house (National Trust) in Rodmell, 3m/5km SE of Lewes. Home of Leonard and Virginia Woolf. **13 H6** TQ4206.
Monks House Rocks *Northumb.* ***Coastal feature***, rocks (National Trust) on North Sea coast, 1m/2km NW of Seahouses. **77 K7** NU2033.
Monks Kirby *Warks.* ***Village***, 6m/9km NW of Rugby. **41 G7** SP4683.
Monks Moor *Dur.* ***Open space***, moorland to N of Middleton-in-Teesdale. Highest point is 1853 feet or 565 metres. **62 A4** NY9628.
Monks Orchard *Gt.Lon.* ***Suburb***, in borough of Croydon, 3m/4km NE of Croydon town centre. TQ3667.
Monks Risborough *Bucks.* ***Locality***, adjoining to N of Princes Risborough. **22 B1** SP8004.
Monk's Steps *N.Som.* *See Kewstoke.*
Monkscross *Cornw.* ***Hamlet***, 2m/3km NE of Callington. SX3871.
Monkseaton *T. & W.* ***Suburb***, on W side of Whitley Bay. **71 J6** NZ3472.
Monkshill *Aber.* ***Settlement***, 3m/4km NE of Fyvie. **99 F6** NJ7940.
Monkside *Northumb.* ***Mountain***, on N edge of wooded area to N of Kielder Water, 4m/6km E of Kielder. Height 1683 feet or 513 metres. **70 B4** NY6894.
Monksilver *Som.* ***Village***, on edge of Exmoor National Park, 4m/6km S of Watchet. **7 J2** ST0737.
Monkspath Street *W.Mid.* ***Suburb***, 2m/3km SW of Solihull town centre. SP1476.
Monkstadt *High.* ***Settlement***, 3m/4km N of Uig, Skye. **93 J5** NG3767.
Monkstone Point *Pembs.* ***Coastal feature***, E facing headland at SW end of Saundersfoot Bay, 2m/3km NE of Tenby. **16 E4** SN1403.
Monkstown *Fife* ***Suburb***, adjoining to W of Ladybank. NO3009.
Monkswood *Mon.* ***Hamlet***, 2m/4km NW of Usk. **19 G1** SO3402.
Monkton *Devon* ***Village***, 2m/4km NE of Honiton. **7 K5** ST1803.
Monkton *Kent* ***Village***, on Isle of Thanet, 6m/10km W of Ramsgate. **25 J5** TR2865.
Monkton *Pembs.* ***Suburb***, adjoining to W of Pembroke. SM9701.
Monkton *S.Ayr.* ***Hamlet***, on N side of Prestwick Airport, 4m/7km N of Ayr. **67 H1** NS3527.
Monkton *T. & W.* ***Suburb***, to S of Hebburn. **71 J7** NZ3163.
Monkton *V. of Glam.* ***Settlement***, 3m/5km NW of Llantwit Major. SS9271.
Monkton Combe *B. & N.E.Som.* ***Village***, 2m/4km SE of Bath. **20 A5** ST7762.
Monkton Deverill *Wilts.* ***Village***, 4m/7km NE of Mere. **9 H1** ST8537.
Monkton Farleigh *Wilts.* ***Village***, 3m/5km NW of Bradford-on-Avon. **20 A5** ST8065.
Monkton Heathfield *Som.* ***Village***, 3m/4km NE of Taunton. **8 B2** ST2526.
Monkton Up Wimborne *Dorset* ***Hamlet***, 3m/4km W of Cranborne. **10 B3** SU0113.
Monkton Wyld *Dorset* ***Hamlet***, 3m/5km N of Lyme Regis. SY3396.
Monktonhall *E.Loth.* ***Suburb***, SW part of Musselburgh. NT3371.
Monkwearmouth *T. & W.* ***Suburb***, 1m/2km N of Sunderland city centre across River Wear. **62 E1** NZ3958.
Monkwood *Hants.* ***Village***, 2m/3km SE of Ropley. **11 H1** SU6730.
Monkwood Green *Worcs.* ***Settlement***, 4m/7km NW of Worcester. SO8060.
Monmore Green *W.Mid.* ***Suburb***, 1m/2km SE of Wolverhampton town centre. **40 B6** SO9297.
Monmouth (Trefynwy). *Mon.* Population: 7246. ***Small town***, market town at confluence of Rivers Wye and Monnow, 20m/32km NE of Newport. Remains of medieval castle (Cadw); gatehouse astride bridge over River Monnow. Town is thought to be on site of Roman town of Blestium. **28 E7** SO5012.
Monmouth Castle *Mon.* ***Castle***, remains of medieval castle (Cadw) in Monmouth, 10m/15km SW of Ross-on-Wye. Originally 11c, built by William FitzOsbern, with 12c-13c additions. Birthplace of Henry of Monmouth (Henry V). Ruins include Great Tower, Hall and gatehouse astride bridge over River Monnow. **28 E7** SO5013.
Monmouth Museum *Mon.* ***Other feature of interest***, in Monmouth, 9m/15km SW of Ross-on-Wye. Local history centre, with artefacts belonging to Admiral Nelson. **28 E7** SO5013.
Monnington on Wye *Here.* ***Village***, 9m/14km W of Hereford. **28 C4** SO3743.
Monnow (Mynwy). ***River***, rising in Black Mountains, on E side of Hay Bluff, and flowing S through Longtown towards Pandy, NE towards Pontrilas, then SE into River Wye at Monmouth. **28 D7** SO5116.
Monnow Bridge *Mon.* ***Bridge***, stone bridge at Monmouth over River Monnow, built in 1271 with fortified gate tower. SO5012.
Monreith *D. & G.* ***Village***, on Monreith Bay, 2m/3km SE of Port William. **64 D6** NX3541.
Monreith Bay *D. & G.* ***Bay***, 2m/3km SE of Port William. Ancient cross (Historic Scotland) in grounds of Monreith House to N. **64 D6** NX3541.
Monsale *Essex* ***Settlement***, 4m/6km NE of Burnham-on-Crouch, 1m/2km N of River Crouch estuary. **25 G2** TR0097.
Montacute *Som.* ***Village***, estate village built of Ham stone (see Hamdon Hill), 4m/6km W of Yeovil. Montacute House (National Trust), Elizabethan. **8 D3** ST4916.
Montacute House *Som.* ***Historic house***, 16c house (National Trust) designed by Edward Phelips, 3m/5km W of Yeovil, surrounded by formal gardens and parkland. **8 D3** ST4917.
Monteach *Aber.* ***Settlement***, 3m/4km N of Methlick. **99 G6** NJ8640.
Montford *Shrop.* ***Village***, on River Severn, 5m/8km W of Shrewsbury. **38 D4** SJ4114.
Montford Bridge *Shrop.* ***Village***, on River Severn, 4m/7km NW of Shrewsbury. Bridge by Telford. **38 D4** SJ4315.
Montgarrie *Aber.* ***Village***, 1m/2km N of Alford. **90 D3** NJ5717.
Montgomery (Trefaldwyn). *Powys* ***Village***, former county town, now village, 7m/11km S of Welshpool. Birthplace of George Herbert, 17c poet. Site of ancient British camp on hill to NW. Motte and bailey marks probable site of original castle. Present structure (Cadw) dates from early 13c and was largely demolished in 1649. **38 B6** SO2296.
Montgomery Castle *Powys* ***Castle***, ruin with inner and outer bailey, built on green limestone in 1224, on NW side of Montgomery. Site of major excavation work in latter half of 20c century. **38 B6** SO2196.
Montgreenan *N.Ayr.* ***Locality***, 2m/4km E of Kilwinning. **74 B6** NS3444.
Montpelier *Bristol* ***Suburb***, 1m/2km NE of Bristol city centre. ST5974.
Montrave *Fife* ***Settlement***, 3m/5km NW of Kennoway. **82 E7** NO3706.
Montreathmont Forest *Angus* ***Forest/woodland***, Forestry Commission coniferous forest, 3m/5km NW of Friockheim. **83 G2** NO5654.
Montreathmont Moor *Angus* ***Forest/woodland***, wooded tract 4m/6km S of Brechin. Radio/TV mast. **83 G2** NO5854.
Montrose *Angus* Population: 11,440. ***Town***, port on E coast, 26m/42km NE of Dundee. Golf course founded 1810. **83 J2** NO7157.
Montrose Basin *Angus* ***Sea feature***, large tidal lagoon to W of Montrose. **83 H2** NO7157.
Montrose Museum and Art Gallery *Angus* ***Other feature of interest***, local history museum in centre of Montrose, with maritime and natural history exhibits. **83 J2** NO7157.
Monxton *Hants.* ***Village***, 3m/5km W of Andover. **21 G7** SU3144.
Monyash *Derbys.* ***Village***, 4m/7km W of Bakewell. **50 D6** SK1566.
Monymusk *Aber.* ***Village***, 7m/11km SW of Inverurie. **90 E3** NJ6815.
Monynut Edge *E.Loth.* ***Large natural feature***, ridge and watershed in Lammermuir Hills, 7m/11km S of Dunbar. **76 E4** NT7067.
Monynut Water ***River***, running down W side of Monynut Edge to Whiteadder Water at Abbey St. Bathans. **77 F4** NT7067.
Mony's Stone *High.* ***Historic/prehistoric site***, in Corrimony, 9m/14km W of Drumnadrochit. **87 K1** NH3730.
Monzie *P. & K.* ***Village***, 2m/4km N of Crieff. Falls of Monzie 1m/2km N. **81 K5** NN8725.
Mooa *Shet.* ***Island***, small uninhabited island off E coast of Whalsay, 1m/2km S of Skaw Taing. HU6065.
Moodiesburn *N.Lan.* Population: 5979. ***Small town***, 4m/7km SW of Cumbernauld. **74 E3** NS6970.
Moodlaw Loch *D. & G.* ***Lake/loch***, small loch in Craik Forest, 3m/5km W of Craik. **69 H3** NT2907.
Moonen Bay *High.* ***Bay***, S facing bay on W coast of Skye, 8m/12km W of Dunvegan. Headland of Neist Point to W. **93 G7** NG1346.
Moon's Moat North *Worcs.* ***Suburb***, NE district of Redditch. SP0768.
Moon's Moat South *Worcs.* ***Suburb***, NE district of Redditch. SP0768.
Moonzie *Fife* ***Settlement***, 3m/5km NW of Cupar. **82 E6** NO3417.
Moor Allerton *W.Yorks.* ***Suburb***, 4m/6km N of Leeds city centre. **57 J6** SE3038.
Moor Cock *Lancs.* ***Settlement***, on W side of Burn Moor, 3m/4km S of High Bentham. **56 B3** SD6764.
Moor Crichel *Dorset* ***Village***, 5m/9km N of Wimborne Minster. **9 J4** ST9908.
Moor End *Beds.* ***Settlement***, S end of Eaton Bray, 3m/5km W of Dunstable. SP9720.
Moor End *Beds.* ***Settlement***, 1km N of Radwell and 6m/10km NW of Bedford. TL0058.
Moor End *Cambs.* ***Hamlet***, adjoining to SW of Shepreth, 4m/7km NE of Royston. TL3847.
Moor End *Cumb.* ***Settlement***, to E of Hutton Roof Crags, 3m/4km W of Kirkby Lonsdale. **55 J2** SD5677.
Moor End *E.Riding* ***Hamlet***, adjoining to S of Holme-on-Spalding-Moor. **58 E6** SE8137.
Moor End *Lancs.* ***Settlement***, adjoining to SE of Stalmine, 4m/6km SE of Fleetwood across River Wyre estuary. SD3744.
Moor End *N.Yorks.* ***Hamlet***, adjoining to NE of Kelfield, 2m/3km W of Riccall. SE5938.
Moor End *W.Yorks.* ***Hamlet***, adjoining to W of Mixenden, 3m/5km NW of Halifax. SE0528.
Moor End *York* ***Locality***, adjoining to NE of Stockton on the Forest, 5m/7km NE of York. SE6656.
Moor Green *Herts.* ***Settlement***, 3m/5km SW of Buntingford. TL3226.
Moor Green *W.Mid.* ***Suburb***, 3m/5km S of Birmingham city centre. SP0682.
Moor Green *Wilts.* ***Village***, 1m/2km SW of Corsham. ST8568.
Moor Head *W.Yorks.* ***Locality***, adjoining to N of Gildersome, 2m/3km NW of Morley. SE2329.
Moor Head *W.Yorks.* ***Suburb***, W district of Shipley. SE1337.
Moor Monkton *N.Yorks.* ***Village***, on River Nidd, 7m/11km NW of York. **58 B4** SE5056.
Moor Nook *Lancs.* ***Settlement***, 3m/5km E of Longridge. **56 B6** SD6538.
Moor Park *Herts.* ***Locality***, 1m/2km SE of Rickmansworth. Site of Roman building. **22 D2** TQ0793.
Moor Row *Cumb.* ***Hamlet***, 2m/4km N of Egremont. **60 B5** NY0014.
Moor Row *Cumb.* ***Locality***, 3m/5km W of Wigton. NY2049.
Moor Row *Dur.* ***Locality***, 1m/2km SE of Winston. NZ1515.
Moor Side *Cumb.* ***Settlement***, 3m/5km N of Dalton-in-Furness. SD2278.
Moor Side *Lancs.* ***Locality***, 1km E of Walmer Bridge. SD4824.
Moor Side *Lancs.* ***Settlement***, 2m/3km NE of Kirkham. SD4334.
Moor Side *Lancs.* ***Settlement***, 2m/3km W of Broughton, 4m/7km NW of Preston. SD4935.
Moor Side *Lincs.* ***Hamlet***, 5m/8km SE of Woodhall Spa. **53 F7** TF2457.
Moor Side *W.Yorks.* ***Suburb***, 3m/5km S of Bradford city centre. SE1528.
Moor Street *Med.* ***Settlement***, to E of Gillingham. TQ8265.
Moor Street *W.Mid.* ***Suburb***, 5m/8km SW of Birmingham city centre. SO9982.
Moor Top *W.Yorks.* ***Suburb***, 2m/3km W of Leeds city centre, in district of Armley. SE2733.
Moorby *Lincs.* ***Village***, 4m/7km SE of Horncastle. **53 F6** TF2964.

Moorcot *Here.* ***Settlement***, 3m/5km E of Kington. **28 C3** SO3555.
Moordown *Bourne.* ***Suburb***, 2m/3km N of Bournemouth town centre. **10 B5** SZ0894.
Moore *Halton* ***Village***, beside Bridgewater Canal, 3m/5km SW of Warrington. **48 E4** SJ5784.
Moorend *Cumb.* ***Settlement***, 1km NW of Thursby. NY3250.
Moorend *Glos.* ***Hamlet***, 1km SW of Slimbridge. SO7302.
Moorends *S.Yorks.* Population: 8375. ***Village***, 1m/2km N of Thorne. **51 J1** SE6915.
Moorfield *Derbys.* ***Settlement***, at W edge of Peak District National Park, 1m/2km SE of Glossop. SK0492.
Moorfoot Hills ***Large natural feature***, range of hills, mainly grass-covered, running NE to SW between Tynehead and Peebles. Summit is Blackhope Scar, 2136 feet or 651 metres. **76 B5** NT3050.
Moorgreen *Hants.* ***Settlement***, 3m/4km NW of Botley. SU4715.
Moorgreen *Notts.* ***Hamlet***, 1m/2km E of Eastwood. **41 G1** SK4847.
Moorhall *Derbys.* ***Settlement***, 5m/9km NW of Chesterfield. **51 F5** SK3074.
Moorhampton *Here.* ***Settlement***, 9m/14km NW of Hereford. **28 C4** SO3846.
Moorhole *S.Yorks.* ***Settlement***, 5m/8km SE of Sheffield city centre. SK4182.
Moorhouse *Cumb.* ***Hamlet***, 4m/7km W of Carlisle. **60 E1** NY3356.
Moorhouse *Cumb.* ***Locality***, 2m/3km N of Wigton. NY2551.
Moorhouse *Notts.* ***Hamlet***, 3m/5km SE of Tuxford. **51 K6** SK7566.
Moorhouse *S.Yorks.* ***Settlement***, 1m/2km SE of South Emsall. SE4810.
Moorhouse Bank *Surr.* ***Settlement***, 1m/2km E of Limpsfield. TQ4253.
Moorhouses *Lincs.* ***Locality***, 2m/3km W of New Bolingbroke. TF2856.
Moorland *Som. Alternative name for Northmoor Green, qv.*
Moorlands *W.Yorks.* ***Locality***, 4m/6km SE of Bradford. SE2029.
Moorlinch *Som.* ***Village***, on S side of Polden Hills, 5m/9km W of Street. **8 C1** ST3936.
Moorpark *Renf.* ***Suburb***, S district of Renfrew. NS5066.
Moors *Dorset* ***River***, rising as River Crane and flowing SE past Verwood, becoming Moors River to E of Ringwood Forest, then flowing S into River Stour at Blackwater to NE of Bournemouth. **10 C4** SZ1395.
Moors Valley Country Park *Dorset* ***Leisure/recreation***, country park with visitor centre on E bank of Moors River, 1m/2km E of Three Legged Cross. Encompasses part of Ringwood Forest. **10 C4** SU1005.
Moorsholm *R. & C.* ***Village***, 5m/8km S of Saltburn. **63 H5** NZ6814.
Moorsholm Moor *R. & C.* ***Open space***, moorland on Cleveland Hills, 3m/4km N of Castleton. **63 H5** NZ6711.
Moorside *Cumb.* ***Locality***, 1m/2km SE of Gosforth. NY0701.
Moorside *Dorset* ***Hamlet***, 1km E of Marnhull and 3m/5km N of Sturminster Newton. ST7919.
Moorside *Gt.Man.* ***Suburb***, to SW of Swinton town centre. SD7701.
Moorside *Gt.Man.* ***Suburb***, 2m/4km NE of Oldham town centre. **49 J2** SD9507.
Moorside *W.Yorks.* ***Locality***, adjoining to S of Drighlington. SE2228.
Moorside *W.Yorks.* ***Suburb***, 4m/6km NW of Leeds city centre across River Aire. SE2435.
Moorthorpe *W.Yorks.* ***Suburb***, W district of South Elmsall. SE4611.
Moorthwaite *Cumb.* ***Locality***, on E side of River Eden, 4m/6km SE of Wetheral. NY5050.
Moorthwaite *Cumb.* ***Settlement***, at N end of Moorthwaite Lough, 3m/4km W of Wigton. NY2948.
Moortown *I.o.W.* ***Hamlet***, adjoining to N of Brighstone and 2m/3km W of Shorwell. Site of Roman villa to N. **11 F6** SZ4283.
Moortown *Lincs.* ***Hamlet***, 3m/5km SW of Caistor. **52 D3** TF0799.
Moortown *Tel. & W.* ***Settlement***, 2m/3km NE of High Ercall. SJ6118.
Moortown *W.Yorks.* ***Suburb***, 3m/5km N of Leeds city centre. SE3038.
Moota Hill *Cumb.* ***Hill***, 4m/6km N of Cockermouth. Height 823 feet or 251 metres. **60 C3** NY1436.
Mòr Mhonadh *W.Isles* ***Mountain***, on North Harris, 2m/3km NE of Muaithabhal. Height 1315 feet or 401 metres. **100 E6** NB2713.
Morangie *High.* ***Settlement***, in Ross and Cromarty district, on S shore of Dornoch Firth, 1m/2km NW of Tain. **96 E3** NH7683.
Morangie Forest *High.* ***Forest/woodland***, to SW of Morangie. **96 E3** NH7683.
Morar *High.* ***Village***, lies on neck of North Morar, Lochaber district, between foot of Loch Morar and River Morar estuary. **86 C5** NM6792.
Moray Firth *High.* ***Sea feature***, arm of North Sea extending to Inverness from a line drawn from Duncansby Head to Fraserburgh. Above the narrows between Chanonry Point and Fort George, the firth is known as Inner Moray Firth or Inverness Firth, and above Inverness as Beauly Firth, which extends to mouth of River Beauly. Other important inlets on W side of Moray Firth are Dornoch and Cromarty Firths. **97 F5** NH8565.
Morborne *Cambs.* ***Village***, 6m/9km SW of Peterborough. **42 E6** TL1391.
Morchard Bishop *Devon* ***Village***, 6m/10km NW of Crediton. **7 F5** SS7707.
Morcombelake (Also spelled Morecombelake.) *Dorset* ***Village***, 4m/6km W of Bridport. On E side of village is Hardown Hill (National Trust). **8 C5** SY4094.
Morcott *Rut.* ***Village***, 4m/6km E of Uppingham. **42 C5** SK9200.
Morda ***River***, rising 2m/3km S of Dolywern, near Llangollen and following a meandering course S to flow into River Vyrnwy on English-Welsh border, 2m/3km E of Llanymynech. **38 B2** SJ2920.
Morda *Shrop.* ***Village***, 1m/2km S of Oswestry. **38 B3** SJ2827.
Morden *Dorset* ***Village***, 4m/7km E of Bere Regis. To S and W respectively, hamlets of West and East Morden. **9 J5** SY9195.
Morden *Gt.Lon.* ***Suburb***, in borough of Merton, 1m/2km S of Wimbledon. To E, Morden Hall (National Trust) and deer park intersected by River Wandle. **23 F5** TQ2568.
Morden Green *Cambs.* ***Settlement***, adjoining to E of Steeple Morden, 2m/3km SE of Ashwell. TL2942.
Morden Hall Park *Gt.Lon.* ***Garden***, former deer park (National Trust), to E of Morden. Extensive network of waterways, ancient hay meadow and old estate workshop with craftworkers. **23 F5** TQ2668.
Morden Park *Gt.Lon.* ***Suburb***, and park of same name in borough of Merton, 3m/4km S of Wimbledon. TQ2367.
Mordiford *Here.* ***Village***, on River Lugg, 4m/7km SE of Hereford. **28 E5** SO5737.
Mordington *Sc.Bord.* ***Settlement***, 2m/3km E of Foulden. **77 H5** NT9456.
Mordon *Dur.* ***Hamlet***, 2m/4km SW of Sedgefield. **62 E4** NZ3226.
More *Shrop.* ***Village***, 2m/4km NE of Bishop's Castle. **38 C6** SO3491.
Morebath *Devon* ***Village***, 2m/3km N of Bampton. **7 H3** SS9524.
Morebattle *Sc.Bord.* ***Village***, 6m/10km SE of Kelso. 1km SE is Corbet Tower, stronghold of the Kers, destroyed in 16c, restored in 19c. **70 C1** NT7724.
Morecambe *Lancs.* Population: 46,657. ***Town***, popular coastal resort, 3m/5km NW of Lancaster. Fishing, particularly shellfish, is important industry. Guided walk across Morecambe Bay to Grange-over-Sands at certain low tides. **55 H3** SD4364.
Morecambe Bay *Lancs.* ***Bay***, wide, sandy bay extending W from Morecambe to Furness region of Cumbria. **55 G3** SD4364.
Morecombelake *Dorset Alternative spelling of Morcombelake, qv.*
Moredon *Swin.* ***Suburb***, 2m/3km NW of Swindon town centre. SU1387.
Moredun *Edin.* ***Suburb***, 3m/5km SE of Edinburgh city centre. NT2869.
Morefield *High.* ***Settlement***, on Loch Broom, Ross and Cromarty district, 1m/2km NW of Ullapool. **95 H2** NH1195.
Moreleigh *Devon* ***Village***, 5m/9km SW of Totnes. **5 H5** SX7652.
Morenish *P. & K.* ***Settlement***, on N side of Loch Tay, 2m/3km NE of Killin. **81 H4** NN6035.
Moresby *Cumb.* ***Locality***, 2m/3km N of Whitehaven. **60 A4** NX9921.
Moresby Parks *Cumb.* ***Locality***, 2m/3km NE of Whitehaven. NX9919.
Morestead *Hants.* ***Village***, 3m/5km SE of Winchester. **11 G2** SU5025.
Moreton *Dorset* ***Village***, on River Frome, 4m/7km SE of Puddletown. **9 H6** SY8089.
Moreton *Essex* ***Village***, 3m/4km NW of Chipping Ongar. **23 J1** TL5306.
Moreton *Here.* ***Hamlet***, 3m/5km N of Leominster. **28 E2** SO5064.
Moreton *Mersey.* Population: 28,038. ***Suburb***, SW district of Wallasey. **48 B4** SJ2689.
Moreton *Oxon.* ***Village***, 1m/2km SW of Thame. **21 K1** SP6904.
Moreton *Staffs.* ***Hamlet***, 3m/5km SE of Newport. SJ7917.
Moreton *Staffs.* ***Hamlet***, 1m/2km SE of Marchington. SK1429.
Moreton Corbet *Shrop.* ***Village***, 8m/12km NE of Shrewsbury. Ruins of Moreton Corbet Castle (English Heritage). **38 E3** SJ5523.
Moreton Corbet Castle *Shrop.* ***Castle***, ruins of fine Elizabethan mansion incorporating parts of 13c keep (English Heritage), in Moreton Corbet, 1m/2km N of Shawbury. **38 E3** SJ5623.
Moreton-in-Marsh *Glos.* Population: 1895. ***Small town***, built of Cotswold stone, 8m/12km NW of Chipping Norton. **30 D5** SP2032.
Moreton Jeffries *Here.* ***Village***, 5m/8km SW of Bromyard. **29 F4** SO6048.
Moreton Morrell *Warks.* ***Village***, 6m/10km S of Royal Leamington Spa. **30 E3** SP3155.
Moreton on Lugg *Here.* ***Village***, 4m/6km N of Hereford. **28 E4** SO5045.
Moreton Paddox *Warks.* ***Hamlet***, 3m/5km NW of Kineton. SP3054.
Moreton Pinkney *Northants.* ***Village***, 9m/15km NE of Banbury. **31 G4** SP5749.
Moreton Say *Shrop.* ***Village***, 3m/5km W of Market Drayton. **39 F2** SJ6234.
Moreton Valence *Glos.* ***Village***, 5m/8km NW of Stroud. **20 A1** SO7809.
Moretonhampstead *Devon* ***Small town***, on E side of Dartmoor, 11m/18km W of Exeter. 17c almshouses (National Trust). **7 F7** SX7586.
Moretonmill *Shrop.* ***Settlement***, 1m/2km NE of Shawbury. SJ5722.
Morfa *Carmar.* ***Settlement***, 3m/5km W of Ammanford. SN5712.
Morfa *Cere.* ***Settlement***, 1m/2km SW of Llangranog. SN3052.
Morfa Bychan *Gwyn.* ***Village***, 2m/3km SW of Porthmadog. **36 E2** SH5437.
Morfa Dyffryn *Gwyn.* ***Nature reserve***, sand dune area notable for its flora, to S of Shell Island, 5m/7km SW of Harlech. **36 E3** SH5625.
Morfa Glas *N.P.T.* ***Locality***, adjoining to W of Glyn-neath. **18 B1** SN8706.
Morfa Harlech *Gwyn.* ***Coastal feature***, headland to N of Harlech, fringed by sand dunes to W. Land reclaimed from sea, with marshes of Glastraeth to NE. **36 E2** SH5833.
Morfa Nefyn *Gwyn.* ***Village***, 1m/2km W of Nefyn. **36 B1** SH2840.
Morfa Rhuddlan *Conwy* ***Locality***, low-lying area to S of Towyn and W of River Clwyd estuary. **47 H5** SH9778.
Morfil *Pembs. Welsh form of Morvil, qv.*
Morgan's Hill *Wilts.* ***Hill***, 2m/3km E of Heddington. Height 853 feet or 260 metres. **20 D5** SU0266.
Morgan's Vale *Wilts.* ***Locality***, adjoining Redlynch, 7m/11km SE of Salisbury. **10 C2** SU1921.
Morganstown (Treforgan). *Cardiff* ***Village***, adjoining to N of Radyr, 5m/8km NW of Cardiff. ST1281.
Morham *E.Loth.* ***Locality***, 3m/5km E of Haddington. NT5571.
Moriah *Cere.* ***Settlement***, 3m/4km SE of Aberystwyth. SN6279.
Moricambe *Cumb.* ***Bay***, formed by estuaries of Rivers Wampool and Waver, 4m/6km NE of Silloth. **60 C1** NY1656.
Moridunum *Carmar. See Carmarthen.*
Moriston *High.* ***River***, in Inverness district running E from Loch Cluanie down Glen Moriston to Loch Ness. Power station for hydro-electricity scheme at Ceannacroc Bridge. **87 J3** NH4216.
Mork *Glos.* ***Settlement***, 1km NW of St. Briavels. **19 J1** SO5505.
Morlais *Carmar.* ***River***, rising about 1m/2km SE of Pontyberem and flowing S into River Loughor on E side of Llangennech. SN5701.
Morland *Cumb.* ***Village***, 6m/9km W of Appleby-in-Westmorland and 7m/11km SE of Penrith. **61 G4** NY5922.
Morley *Derbys.* ***Village***, 4m/6km NE of Derby. **41 F1** SK3940.
Morley *Dur.* ***Settlement***, 4m/6km W of West Auckland. **62 C4** NZ1227.
Morley *W.Yorks.* Population: 47,579. ***Town***, former cotton town, 4m/7km SW of Leeds. **57 H7** SE2627.
Morley Green *Ches.* ***Hamlet***, 2m/3km NW of Wilmslow. **49 H4** SJ8282.
Morley St. Botolph *Norf.* ***Village***, 3m/4km W of Wymondham. **44 E5** TM0799.
Mormond Hill *Aber.* ***Hill***, 3m/4km NE of Strichen. Height 754 feet or 230 metres. **99 H5** NJ9856.
Mornick *Cornw.* ***Hamlet***, 3m/5km NW of Callington. SX3172.
Morningside *Edin.* ***Suburb***, 1m/2km S of Edinburgh city centre. **76 A3** NT2471.
Morningside *N.Lan.* ***Settlement***, 1m/2km SE of Newmains. **75 G5** NS8355.
Morningthorpe *Norf.* ***Village***, adjoining to W of Fritton, 6m/10km N of Harleston. **45 G6** TM2192.
Mornish *Arg. & B.* ***Locality***, lying E and SE of Caliach Point, Mull. **78 E2** NM3753.
Morpeth *Northumb.* Population: 14,393. ***Town***, on River Wansbeck, 14m/23km N of Newcastle upon Tyne. Remains of motte and bailey castle. Restored 15c gatehouse at Morpeth Castle. Bridge, built by Telford, over River Wansbeck. **71 G5** NZ1986.
Morphie *Aber.* ***Hamlet***, 2m/3km SE of Marykirk. **83 J1** NO7164.
Morrey *Staffs.* ***Hamlet***, 1m/2km W of Yoxall. **40 D4** SK1218.
Morridge *Staffs.* ***Inland physical feature***, mountain ridge at SW edge of Peak District National Park, running N to S and over 400 metres high, 2m/4km E of Leek. **50 C7** SK0257.
Morridge Side *Staffs.* ***Settlement***, 3m/5km SE of Leek. SK0254.
Morrilow Heath *Staffs.* ***Settlement***, 2m/4km E of Hilderstone. SJ9835.
Morris Fen *Peter.* ***Open space***, lowland 2m/3km N of Thorney. **43 F5** TF2806.
Morriston *Sc.Bord.* ***Locality***, formed of East and West Morriston, 2m/3km SE of Legerwood. NT6041.
Morriston *S.Ayr.* ***Settlement***, 1m/2km NE of Maidens. **67 G3** NS2309.
Morriston *Swan.* ***Suburb***, 3m/5km N of Swansea city centre. **17 K5** SS6798.
Morristown *V. of Glam.* ***Suburb***, W district of Penarth. ST1771.
Morroch *High.* ***Settlement***, adjoining to S of Arisaig, Lochaber district. **86 C6** NM6686.
Morrone Hill *Aber.* ***Mountain***, 2m/3km SW of Braemar. Height 2818 feet or 859 metres. **89 J6** NO1388.
Morsgail Forest *W.Isles* ***Forest/woodland***, upland tract, broken up by innumerable streams and small lochs, to W of Loch Langavat, Isle of Lewis. **100 D6** NB1217.
Morston *Norf.* ***Village***, 1m/2km W of Blakeney. **44 E1** TG0043.
Mort Bank *Cumb.* ***Coastal feature***, sandbanks in Morecambe Bay on W side of Lancaster Sound, 6m/10km E of Barrow-in-Furness. **55 G3** SD2966.
Morte Bay *Devon* ***Bay***, W facing bay between Morte Point and Baggy Point on N coast, 5m/8km SW of Ilfracombe. **6 C1** SS4442.
Morte Point *Devon* ***Coastal feature***, headland (National Trust) at N end of Morte Bay, 5m/8km W of Ilfracombe. **6 C1** SS4445.
Mortehoe *Devon* ***Village***, on N coast, 4m/7km W of Ilfracombe. **6 C1** SS4545.
Morthen *S.Yorks.* ***Village***, 4m/6km SE of Rotherham. SK4789.
Mortimer *W.Berks.* Population: 2732. ***Village***, 7m/11km SW of Reading. **21 K5** SU6564.
Mortimer West End *Hants.* ***Village***, 7m/11km N of Basingstoke. **21 K5** SU6363.
Mortimer's Cross *Here.* ***Settlement***, on River Lugg, 5m/9km NW of Leominster. Site of Wars of the Roses battle, 1461. Interesting 18c water mill (English Heritage), still in working order. **28 D2** SO4263.

M

Mortimer's Deep *Fife* ***Sea feature***, passage between Inchcolm and mainland of Fife. **75 K2** NT1883.
Mortlach Church *Moray* ***Ecclesiastical building***, at Kirktown of Mortlach, to S of Dufftown, and believed to be one of oldest churches continually used for public worship. Originally founded c. AD 566 by St. Moluag, building dates from 11c and 12c and includes sculptured stones, fine stained glass, battle stone and old watch tower. **90 B1** NJ3239.
Mortlake *Gt.Lon.* ***Suburb***, on S bank of River Thames, between Chiswick Bridge and Barnes (railway) Bridge, in borough of Richmond upon Thames. **23 F4** TQ2075.
Mortlich *Aber.* ***Mountain***, 2m/3km N of Aboyne. Height 1250 feet or 381 metres. **90 D4** NJ5301.
Mortomley *S.Yorks.* ***Locality***, adjoining to SE of High Green. SK3497.
Morton *Cumb.* ***Locality***, 1m/2km W of Calthwaite. NY4439.
Morton *Cumb.* ***Suburb***, 1m/2km SW of Carlisle city centre. NY3854.
Morton *Derbys.* ***Village***, 3m/5km N of Alfreton. **51 G6** SK4060.
Morton *I.o.W.* ***Hamlet***, 1km S of Brading. SZ6086.
Morton *Lincs.* ***Settlement***, 2m/3km SW of Thorpe on the Hill. SK8863.
Morton *Lincs.* ***Suburb***, 1m/2km N of Gainsborough. **52 B3** SK8091.
Morton *Lincs.* ***Village***, 3m/4km N of Bourne. **42 E3** TF0924.
Morton *Middbro.* ***Locality***, 4m/6km W of Guisborough. NZ5514.
Morton *Norf.* ***Hamlet***, 1km NW of Attlebridge. **45 F4** TG1217.
Morton *Notts.* ***Village***, 2m/4km SE of Southwell. **51 K7** SK7251.
Morton *Shrop.* ***Hamlet***, 4m/6km S of Oswestry. **38 B3** SJ2924.
Morton *S.Glos.* ***Locality***, adjoining to N of Thornbury. **19 K2** ST6490.
Morton Bagot *Warks.* ***Village***, 3m/4km W of Henley-in-Arden. **30 C2** SP1164.
Morton Castle *D. & G.* ***Castle***, ruined castle on S shore of small Morton Loch, 3m/4km N of Thornhill. **68 D4** NX8999.
Morton Fen *Lincs.* ***Open space***, lowland 4m/6km NE of Bourne. **42 E3** TF1324.
Morton Loch *D. & G.* ***Lake/loch***, small loch, 3m/4km N of Thornhill. **68 D4** NX8999.
Morton-on-Swale *N.Yorks.* ***Village***, 3m/5km SW of Northallerton. **62 E7** SE3291.
Morton Tinmouth *Dur.* ***Hamlet***, 4m/6km E of Staindrop. NZ1821.
Morton's Leam *Cambs.* ***River***, leaving River Nene at Peterborough and flowing NE to rejoin it at Rings End. **43 F6** TL3902.
Moruisg *High.* ***Mountain***, on Glencarron and Glenuig Forest, Ross and Cromarty district. Munro: height 3044 feet or 928 metres. **95 H6** NH1050.
Morvah *Cornw.* ***Village***, 3m/5km NE of St. Just. **2 A5** SW4035.
Morval *Cornw.* ***Hamlet***, 2m/3km N of Looe. **4 C5** SX2656.
Morven *Aber.* ***Mountain***, 5m/8km N of Ballater. Height 2857 feet or 871 metres. **90 B4** NJ3704.
Morven *High.* ***Mountain***, in Caithness district 9m/14km N of Helmsdale. Height 2316 feet or 706 metres. **105 F6** ND0028.
Morvern *High.* ***Locality***, large peninsula in Lochaber district, bounded on N by Loch Sunart, on SW by Sound of Mull and on SE by Loch Linnhe. **79 G2** NM6654.
Morvich *High.* ***Locality***, in Skye and Lochalsh district, near mouth of River Croe, on E side of Loch Duih. Camping site (National Trust for Scotland) for tents and caravans. Adventure camp. **87 F2** NG9620.
Morvich *High.* ***Settlement***, on NE side of River Fleet, 2m/3km SE of Rogart station. **96 E1** NC7500.
Morvil (Morfil). *Pembs.* ***Settlement***, 5m/9km S of Newport. **16 D1** SN0330.
Morville *Shrop.* ***Village***, 3m/5km W of Bridgnorth. **39 F6** SO6694.
Morville Heath *Shrop.* ***Locality***, 2m/3km W of Bridgnorth. SO6893.
Morwellham *Devon* ***Village***, on River Tamar, 4m/6km SW of Tavistock. Former port for copper mines. **4 E4** SX4469.
Morwenstow *Cornw.* ***Village***, on coast, 6m/10km N of Bude. Church is part Norman. **6 A4** SS2015.
Morwick *Northumb.* ***Settlement***, 2m/3km W of Amble. NU2303.
Morwick Hall *Northumb.* ***Settlement***, 2m/3km SW of Warkworth. **71 H3** NU2303.
Morwynion *Denb.* ***River***, rising on N side of Llantysilio Mountain and flowing SW into River Dee at Carrog, E of Corwen. SJ1143.
Mosborough *S.Yorks.* Population: 15,222. ***Suburb***, 6m/10km SE of Sheffield city centre. **51 G4** SK4281.
Moscow *E.Ayr.* ***Hamlet***, 4m/7km NE of Kilmarnock. **74 C6** NS4840.
Mosedale *Cumb.* ***Hamlet***, 4m/7km S of Hesket Newmarket. **60 E3** NY3532.
Mosedale Beck *Cumb.* ***River***, rising on Matterdale Common and flowing N to join River Glenderamakin, 2m/3km NE of Threlkeld. **60 E4** NY3526.
Moselden Height *W.Yorks.* ***Settlement***, 3m/4km S of Barkisland. **50 C1** SE0416.
Moseley *W.Mid.* ***Suburb***, 4m/6km N of Wolverhampton town centre. SJ9304.
Moseley *W.Mid.* ***Suburb***, 1m/2km E of Wolverhampton town centre. SO9398.
Moseley *W.Mid.* ***Suburb***, 3m/4km S of Birmingham city centre. **40 C7** SP0783.
Moseley *Worcs.* ***Hamlet***, 4m/6km NW of Worcester. **29 H3** SO8159.
Moseley Old Hall *Staffs.* ***Historic house***, to N of Moseley, house of Elizabethan origin (National Trust), in which Charles II hid after Battle of Worcester, 1651. **40 B5** SJ9304.
Moses Gate *Gt.Man.* ***Suburb***, in N part of Farnworth. SD7306.
Moses Gate Country Park *Gt.Man.* ***Leisure/recreation***, country park of over 600 acres, mostly comprising grassland and woodland, to W of Little Lever and 2m/3km SE of Bolton town centre. Attracts over 120 bird species. **49 G2** SD7307.
Mosley Common *Gt.Man.* ***Locality***, 2m/3km SW of Walkden. SD7101.
Mosleywell *Shrop.* ***Locality***, 5m/8km SW of Whitchurch. SJ5035.
Moss *Arg. & B.* ***Settlement***, 1km NE of Middleton, Tiree. **78 A3** NL9644.
Moss *S.Yorks.* ***Village***, 6m/9km W of Thorne. **51 H1** SE5914.
Moss *Wrex.* ***Locality***, 3m/4km NW of Wrexham. **48 C7** SJ3053.
Moss Bank *Halton* ***Suburb***, 1m/2km E of Widnes town centre. SJ5285.
Moss Bank *Mersey.* ***Suburb***, 1m/2km N of St. Helens town centre. **48 E3** SJ5198.
Moss End *Brack.F.* ***Hamlet***, 2m/4km N of Bracknell. SU8672.
Moss Hill *Aber.* ***Mountain***, 4m/6km NW of Strathdon. Height 2158 feet or 658 metres. **90 B3** NJ3117.
Moss Houses *Ches.* ***Settlement***, 1km E of Warren. SJ8970.
Moss Moor *Gt.Man.* ***Open space***, moorland across which M62 motorway runs, 4m/6km SE of Littleborough. **49 J1** SD9914.
Moss Nook *Gt.Man.* ***Suburb***, 8m/12km S of Manchester city centre and 3m/4km N of Wilmslow. **49 H4** SJ8385.
Moss of Barmuckity *Moray* ***Settlement***, 2m/3km SE of Elgin. **97 K5** NJ2461.
Moss of Belnagoak *Aber.* ***Open space***, moorland 2m/4km S of New Deer. **99 G6** NJ8742.
Moss of Cruden *Aber.* ***Open space***, moorland 2m/3km N of Hatton. **99 J6** NK0340.
Moss Side *Cumb.* ***Locality***, 2m/3km NE of Abbeytown. NY1952.
Moss Side *Gt.Man.* ***Suburb***, 1m/2km S of Manchester city centre. SJ8495.
Moss-side *High.* ***Settlement***, 2m/3km SW of Nairn. **97 F6** NH8654.
Moss Side *Lancs.* ***Settlement***, 3m/5km NE of Lytham St. Anne's. **55 G6** SD3830.
Moss Side *Mersey.* ***Suburb***, adjoining to E of Maghull. SD3902.
Moss-side *Moray* ***Settlement***, 1m/2km N of Milltown of Rothiemay. **98 D5** NJ5450.
Moss Side *Warr.* ***Settlement***, in SW part of Warrington, between River Mersey and Manchester Ship Canal. SJ5685.
Mossat *Aber.* ***Settlement***, 2m/3km S of Lumsden. **90 C3** NJ4719.
Mossbank *Shet.* ***Village***, on NE coast of Mainland, opposite Samphrey. **108 D5** HU4575.
Mossbay *Cumb.* ***Suburb***, S district of Workington, on Moss Bay. NX9927.
Mossblown *S.Ayr.* Population: 2039. ***Village***, 1m/2km N of Annbank. **67 J1** NS4023.
Mossbrae Height *Sc.Bord.* ***Mountain***, 2m/3km E of Newburgh. Height 1528 feet or 466 metres. **69 J2** NT3419.
Mossbrow *Gt.Man.* ***Hamlet***, 4m/6km NW of Altrincham. SJ7089.
Mossburnford *Sc.Bord.* ***Settlement***, 3m/5km S of Jedburgh. **70 B2** NT6616.
Mossdale *D. & G.* ***Locality***, at site of former railway station, 5m/8km S of New Galloway. **65 G3** NX6670.
Mossdale Moor *N.Yorks.* ***Open space***, moorland on NW side of Widdale Fell, 1m/2km SE of Garsdale Station. **61 K7** SD8090.
Mossend *N.Lan.* ***Town***, 2m/4km NW of Hamilton. **75 F4** NS7360.
Mosser *Cumb.* ***Locality***, 4m/6km S of Cockermouth. Mosser Mains and Mossergate to N and S respectively. NY1124.
Mossgiel *E.Ayr.* ***Settlement***, 1m/2km NW of Mauchline. **67 J1** NS4828.
Mosshead *Aber.* ***Settlement***, 3m/4km E of Huntly. **90 D1** NJ5639.
Mosside *Angus* ***Settlement***, 2m/3km NW of Forfar. **83 F2** NO4352.
Mossley *Ches.* ***Suburb***, 2m/3km SE of Congleton town centre. SJ8761.
Mossley *Gt.Man.* Population: 10,569. ***Town***, 4m/6km SE of Oldham. **49 J2** SD9702.
Mossley *Staffs.* ***Suburb***, central district of Rugeley. SK0417.
Mossley Hill *Mersey.* ***Suburb***, 3m/5km SE of Liverpool city centre. **48 C4** SJ3887.
Mosspark *Glas.* ***Suburb***, 3m/5km SW of Glasgow city centre. NS5463.
Mosspaul Hotel *D. & G.* ***Other building***, 4m/6km S of Teviothead, on A74 road. **69 K4** NY4099.
Mosstodloch *Moray* Population: 1066. ***Village***, 1m/2km NW of Fochabers. **98 B4** NJ3360.
Mosston *Angus* ***Hamlet***, 1m/2km W of Redford. **83 G3** NO5444.
Mosstown *Aber.* ***Settlement***, 4m/6km SE of Fraserburgh. NK0362.
Mosswood *Northumb.* ***Settlement***, 3m/5km E of Edmundbyers. NZ0650.
Mossy Lea *Lancs.* ***Village***, 5m/8km NW of Wigan. SD5312.
Mosterton *Dorset* ***Village***, 3m/5km SE of Crewkerne. **8 D4** ST4505.
Moston *Gt.Man.* ***Suburb***, 3m/5km NE of Manchester city centre. SD8701.
Moston *Shrop.* ***Settlement***, 1m/2km SE of Lee Brockhurst. SJ5626.
Moston Green *Ches.* ***Settlement***, 2m/3km W of Sandbach. SJ7261.
Mostyn *Flints.* Population: 1601. ***Village***, with small quay, on River Dee estuary, 3m/5km NW of Holywell. **47 K4** SJ1580.
Mostyn Bank *Flints.* ***Coastal feature***, sandbank running between Point of Ayr and Mostyn Quay. **47 K4** SJ1383.
Mostyn Quay *Flints.* ***Sea feature***, harbour at SE end of Mostyn Bank, facing Salisbury Middle. **47 K4** SJ1581.
Motcombe *Dorset* ***Village***, 2m/3km NW of Shaftesbury. **9 H2** ST8425.
Mote of Mark *D. & G.* ***Historic/prehistoric site***, well preserved Celtic hillfort of 5c or 6c (National Trust for Scotland) just W of Rockcliffe, 4m/7km S of Dalbeattie. One of the most important archaeological sites on Solway Firth. **65 J5** NX8454.
Mote of Urr *D. & G.* ***Historic/prehistoric site***, remains of Saxon-early Norman fortification, on W bank of Urr Water 2m/4km N of Dalbeattie. **65 J4** NX8164.
Mothecombe *Devon* ***Hamlet***, near mouth of River Erme, 5m/9km S of Ivybridge. SX6147.
Mother Shipton's Cave *N.Yorks.* ***Other feature of interest***, on W side of Knaresborough across River Nidd. Legendary prophetess reputed to be born here in 1488, who predicted invention of motor cars and aeroplanes. **57 J4** SE3456.
Motherby *Cumb.* ***Hamlet***, 6m/9km W of Penrith. **60 F4** NY4228.
Motherwell *N.Lan.* Population: 30,717. ***Town***, former steel town, 12m/20km SE of Glasgow. **75 F5** NS7557.
Motspur Park *Gt.Lon.* ***Suburb***, on borders of Kingston upon Thames and Merton boroughs, 3m/5km E of Kingston upon Thames town centre. TQ2267.
Motte of Druchtag *D. & G.* ***Historic/prehistoric site***, early medieval earthwork on NE side of Mochrum. **64 D6** NX3446.
Mottingham *Gt.Lon.* ***Suburb***, in borough of Bromley, 2m/3km N of Bromley town centre and 9m/15km SE of Charing Cross. **23 H4** TQ4272.
Mottisfont *Hants.* ***Village***, on River Test, 4m/6km NW of Romsey. Mottisfont Abbey Gardens and House are National Trust property. **10 E2** SU3226.
Mottisfont Abbey *Hants.* ***Ecclesiastical building***, in tranquil setting on River Test in Mottisfont, 4m/6km NW of Romsey, was 12c priory before Dissolution and remains now incorporated into 18c house (National Trust). Extensive grounds contain walled gardens and National Collection of Roses. **10 E2** SU3226.
Mottistone *I.o.W.* ***Village***, 3m/5km W of Shorwell. 17c manor house, restored after being buried by landslip. **11 F6** SZ4083.
Mottram in Longdendale *Gt.Man.* ***Locality***, 3m/5km E of Hyde. **49 J3** SJ9995.
Mottram St. Andrew *Ches.* ***Settlement***, 2m/3km E of Alderley Edge. **49 H5** SJ8778.
Mott's Mill *E.Suss.* ***Settlement***, 2m/3km SW of Groombridge. TQ5235.
Moughton Fell *N.Yorks.* ***Open space***, moorland, well-covered with rocky outcrops, 1m/2km W of Horton in Ribblesdale. Cliffs of Moughton Scars on W side. **56 C2** SD7981.
Moul of Eswick *Shet.* ***Coastal feature***, headland 1km E of Eswick. Lighthouse. **109 E7** HU4853.
Mouldsworth *Ches.* ***Village***, 3m/5km SE of Helsby. **48 E5** SJ5171.
Moulin *P. & K.* ***Village***, 1km N of Pitlochry. To SE is Caisteal Dubh (or Castle Dhu), ruined former stronghold of the Campbells. **82 A2** NN9459.
Moulsecoomb *B. & H.* ***Suburb***, NW district of Brighton, with North Moulsecoomb. **13 G6** TQ3306.
Moulsford *Oxon.* ***Village***, on River Thames, 2m/3km N of Streatley. **21 J3** SU5983.
Moulsham *Essex* ***Suburb***, to S of Chelmsford town centre. **24 D1** TL7005.
Moulsoe *M.K.* ***Village***, 3m/4km SE of Newport Pagnell. **32 C4** SP9041.
Moulton *Ches.* Population: 5060. ***Village***, 3m/4km S of Northwich. **49 F6** SJ6569.
Moulton *Lincs.* ***Village***, 4m/6km E of Spalding. **43 G3** TF3024.
Moulton *N.Yorks.* ***Village***, 2m/3km SE of Scotch Corner. Manor house and hall of 17c. **62 D6** NZ2303.
Moulton *Northants.* ***Village***, 4m/7km NE of Northampton. **31 J2** SP7866.
Moulton *Suff.* ***Village***, 4m/6km E of Newmarket. Medieval packhorse bridge (English Heritage), with four arches, spans River Kennett. **33 K2** TL6964.
Moulton *V. of Glam.* ***Hamlet***, 2m/3km NW of Barry. Site of Roman building to S. ST0770.
Moulton Chapel *Lincs.* ***Village***, 4m/6km SE of Spalding. **43 F4** TF2918.
Moulton Eaugate *Lincs.* ***Locality***, on Moulton Fen, 3m/4km SE of Cowbit. TF3016.
Moulton Fen *Lincs.* ***Open space***, lowland 4m/7km SE of Spalding. **43 F4** TF2817.
Moulton Leys *Northants.* ***Suburb***, of Northampton, 1m/2km S of Moulton. SP7866.
Moulton Park *Northants.* ***Locality***, with industrial estate, 1m/2km SW of Moulton and 3m/4km N of Northampton. SP7764.
Moulton St. Mary *Norf.* ***Village***, 2m/3km S of Acle. **45 H5** TG3907.
Moulton Seas End *Lincs.* ***Village***, 2m/3km NE of Moulton. **43 G3** TF3024.
Mound Rock *High.* ***Hill***, on NW side of Loch Fleet, 3m/5km W of Golspie. Height 656 feet or 200 metres. **96 E2** NH7798.
Mounie Castle *Aber.* ***Settlement***, 1m/2km E of Daviot and 4m/7km N of Inverurie. **91 F2** NJ7628.

M

Mount *Cornw.* ***Settlement***, 2m/3km NE of Perranporth. **2 E3** SW7856.
Mount *Cornw.* ***Village***, 5m/8km E of Bodmin. **4 B4** SX1468.
Mount *High.* ***Settlement***, 1m/2km NE of Ferness. **97 G7** NH9746.
Mount *Kent* ***Settlement***, 6m/9km N of Hythe. TR1643.
Mount *W.Yorks.* ***Suburb***, 3m/5km W of Huddersfield town centre. SE0918.
Mount Ambrose *Cornw.* ***Suburb***, 1m/2km NE of Redruth town centre. SW7143.
Mount Battock ***Mountain***, on border of Aberdeenshire and Angus, 5m/8km NE of Tarfside. Height 2555 feet or 779 metres. **90 D6** NO5484.
Mount Blair *P. & K.* ***Mountain***, 1m/2km SW of Forter. Height 2440 feet or 744 metres. **82 C1** NO1662.
Mount Bouie *Angus* ***Mountain***, 2m/3km SW of Clova. Height 1919 feet or 585 metres. **90 B7** NO3070.
Mount Bures *Essex* ***Hamlet***, 1m/2km S of Bures. **34 D5** TL9032.
Mount Caburn *E.Suss.* ***Historic/prehistoric site***, Iron Age hillfort, 1km W of Glynde. **13 H6** TQ4409.
Mount Charles *Cornw.* ***Suburb***, E district of St. Austell. SX0252.
Mount Eagle *High.* ***Hill***, on Black Isle in Ross and Cromarty district, 3m/5km N of Munlochy. Height 840 feet or 256 metres. **96 D6** NH6458.
Mount Edgcumbe *Cornw.* ***Historic house***, 16c house set in country park to S of Cremyll, on W side of The Sound, opposite Plymouth. House rebuilt by Adrian Gilbert Scott after World War II fire. **4 E5** SX4552.
Mount Edgcumbe Country Park *Cornw.* ***Leisure/recreation***, country park surrounding Mount Edgcumbe house on W side of The Sound, opposite Plymouth, 2m/3km E of Millbrook. 729 acres extending along 10m/16km of coastline and containing extensive formal gardens designed over 240 years ago in English, French and Italian styles. Park also contains National Camellia Collection. **4 E5** SX4552.
Mount Florida *Glas.* ***Suburb***, 3m/5km S of Glasgow city centre. NS5861.
Mount Gould *Plym.* ***Suburb***, 1m/2km E of Plymouth city centre. SX4955.
Mount Grace Priory *N.Yorks.* ***Ecclesiastical building***, remains of 14c priory (English Heritage and National Trust) 1m/2km NW of Osmotherley. **63 F7** SE4598.
Mount Harry *E.Suss.* ***Hill***, on South Downs, 2m/3km NW of Lewes. Height 640 feet or 195 metres. **13 G5** TQ3812.
Mount Hawke *Cornw.* Population: 1326. ***Village***, 2m/3km S of St. Agnes. **2 E4** SW7147.
Mount Hill *Fife* ***Hill***, 3m/5km NW of Cupar. Height 725 feet or 221 metres. **82 E6** NO3216.
Mount Howe *Devon* ***Locality***, at confluence of Rivers Clyst and Exe below Topsham, 5m/7km SE of Exeter. SX9787.
Mount Keen ***Mountain***, on border of Aberdeenshire and Angus, 6m/10km SE of Ballater. Munro: height 3080 feet or 939 metres. **90 C6** NO4086.
Mount Manisty *Ches.* ***Suburb***, just N of Ellesmere Port. **48 C5** SJ3978.
Mount Meddin ***Mountain***, on border of Aberdeenshire and Moray, 4m/6km S of Cabrach. Height 1935 feet or 590 metres. **90 B2** NJ4021.
Mount Misery *Cornw.* ***Suburb***, W district of Penzance. SW4629.
Mount of Haddoch *Moray* ***Mountain***, 2m/3km NE of Cabrach. Height 1709 feet or 521 metres. **90 C2** NJ4128.
Mount Oliphant *S.Ayr.* ***Settlement***, 3m/5km SE of Ayr. **67 H2** NS3516.
Mount Pleasant *Brack.F.* ***Locality***, 2m/4km NE of Bracknell. SU8972.
Mount Pleasant *Bucks.* ***Suburb***, on S side of Buckingham. SP6933.
Mount Pleasant *Ches.* ***Hamlet***, 2m/3km NE of Kidsgrove. SJ8456.
Mount Pleasant *Cornw.* ***Settlement***, 5m/8km SW of Bodmin. SX0062.
Mount Pleasant *Derbys.* ***Locality***, 3m/4km NE of Alfreton. SK4358.
Mount Pleasant *Derbys.* ***Suburb***, to NW of Belper. **41 F1** SK3448.
Mount Pleasant *Derbys.* ***Village***, 2m/3km SW of Swadlincote. SK2817.
Mount Pleasant *Dur.* ***Suburb***, adjoining to NE of Spennymoor. NZ2634.
Mount Pleasant *E.Suss.* ***Hamlet***, 4m/7km N of Lewes. TQ4216.
Mount Pleasant *Flints.* ***Suburb***, S district of Flint. SJ2372.
Mount Pleasant *Gt.Lon.* ***Settlement***, in River Colne valley, 3m/4km SW of Rickmansworth. TQ0490.
Mount Pleasant *Gt.Man.* ***Suburb***, 3m/5km N of Bury town centre. SD8015.
Mount Pleasant *Hants.* ***Settlement***, 2m/3km NW of Lymington. SZ2997.
Mount Pleasant *M.Tyd.* ***Hamlet***, on River Taff, to S of Merthyr Vale, 5m/8km S of Merthyr Tydfil. ST0798.
Mount Pleasant *M.K.* ***Locality***, adjoining to N of Stoke Goldington, 4m/7km NW of Newport Pagnell. SP8349.
Mount Pleasant *Norf.* ***Settlement***, 4m/6km W of Attleborough. TL9994.
Mount Pleasant *Pembs.* ***Locality***, 1m/2km N of Cosheston. SN0105.
Mount Pleasant *Stock.* ***Suburb***, 1m/2km N of Stockton-on-Tees town centre. NZ4320.
Mount Pleasant *Stoke* ***Suburb***, 1m/2km SE of Stoke-on-Trent city centre. SJ8844.
Mount Pleasant *Suff.* ***Settlement***, to S of Hundon, 4m/7km E of Haverhill. TL7347.
Mount Pleasant *Suff.* ***Suburb***, to N of Southwold. **35 J1** TM5077.
Mount Pleasant *T. & W.* ***Suburb***, 1m/2km SE of Gateshead town centre. NZ2661.
Mount Pleasant *W.Mid.* ***Suburb***, 4m/7km SW of Dudley town centre. SO8887.
Mount Pleasant *W.Yorks.* ***Suburb***, 1m/2km S of Batley town centre. SE2423.
Mount Sion *Wrex.* ***Suburb***, 4m/6km NW of Wrexham. SJ2953.
Mount Skippitt *Oxon.* ***Settlement***, 4m/7km N of Witney. SP3515.
Mount Sorrel *Wilts.* ***Settlement***, 1km W of Broad Chalke. SU0324.
Mount Stuart *S.Lan.* ***Mountain***, on border with Dumfries & Galloway, at head of Nithsdale, 6m/10km NW of Sanquhar. Height 1568 feet or 478 metres. **68 C2** NS7519.
Mount Tabor *W.Yorks.* ***Village***, 3m/5km NW of Halifax. **57 F7** SE0527.
Mount Vernon *Glas.* ***Suburb***, 4m/7km SE of Glasgow. NS6563.
Mountain *W.Yorks.* ***Hamlet***, 1km NW of Queensbury. TV/Radio masts. SE0930.
Mountain Ash (Aberpennar). *R.C.T.* Population: 10,651. ***Town***, former coalmining town, 4m/6km SE of Aberdare. **18 D2** ST0499.
Mountain Cross *Sc.Bord.* ***Settlement***, 3m/5km S of West Linton. **75 K6** NT1446.
Mountain Water *Pembs.* ***Settlement***, 3m/4km SW of Wolf's Castle. **16 C2** SM9224.
Mountbenger *Sc.Bord.* ***Hamlet***, 3m/5km NE of St. Mary's Loch. **69 J1** NT3125.
Mountblairy *Aber.* ***Locality***, includes Hillhead of Mountblairy, Hill of Mountblairy and Newton of Mountblairy, W of River Deveron and 4m/6km NW of Turriff. **98 E5** NJ6954.
Mountblow *W.Dun.* ***Suburb***, 2m/4km NW of Clydebank town centre. NS4771.
Mountfield *E.Suss.* ***Village***, 3m/5km N of Battle. Gypsum mines 2m/3km W. **14 C5** TQ7420.
Mountfleurie *Fife* ***Suburb***, W district of Leven. NO3701.
Mountgerald *High.* ***Settlement***, 3m/4km NE of Dingwall. **96 C5** NH5661.
Mountjoy *Cornw.* ***Hamlet***, 3m/5km SW of St. Columb Major. **3 F2** SW8760.
Mountnessing *Essex* ***Village***, 3m/5km NE of Brentwood. **24 C2** TQ6397.
Mounton *Mon.* ***Hamlet***, 1m/2km W of Chepstow. **19 J2** ST5193.
Mounts *Devon* ***Hamlet***, 3m/5km NE of Kingsbridge. SX7548.
Mount's Bay *Cornw.* ***Bay***, wide bay on S coast, stretching from Gwennap Head in W to Lizard Point in E. **2 C6** SW5423.
Mountsorrel *Leics.* Population: 8563. ***Village***, 4m/7km SE of Loughborough. **41 H4** SK5815.
Mountstuart *Arg. & B.* ***Historic house***, Victorian mansion (1877) near E coast of Bute 4m/6km SE of Rothesay. Seat of Marquess of Bute. **73 K5** NS1059.
Mousa *Shet.* ***Island***, uninhabited island of about 3 square km lying 1km off E coast of Mainland across Mousa Sound in vicinity of Sandwick. Broch of Mousa (Historic Scotland) on W coast. **109 D10** HU4624.
Mousa Sound *Shet.* ***Sea feature***, channel between Mousa and Mainland. **109 D10** HU4624.
Mousehill *Surr.* ***Locality***, adjoining to S of Milford. SU9441.
Mousehole *Cornw.* ***Village***, fishing village 2m/3km S of Penzance across Gwavas Lake. **2 B6** SW4626.
Mousley End *Warks.* ***Settlement***, 5m/9km NW of Warwick. SP2169.
Mouswald *D. & G.* ***Village***, 6m/10km E of Dumfries. **69 F6** NY0672.
Mouth of The Humber ***Sea feature***, mouth of River Humber between Immingham Dock and Spurn Head. Major shipping route. **53 G1** TA3807.
Mouth of the Severn ***Sea feature***, estuary about 9m/14km wide, where River Severn enters Bristol Channel between South Wales and North Somerset. **19 F5** ST2568.
Mow Cop *Staffs.* ***Village***, 2m/3km NE of Kidsgrove. Mow Cop Castle, ruined folly (National Trust) built 1750s on hill, commanding views over Cheshire Plain. Old Man of Mow (National Trust) to N. **49 H7** SJ8557.
Mowden *Darl.* ***Suburb***, 2m/3km NW of Darlington town centre. **62 D5** NZ2615.
Mowhaugh *Sc.Bord.* ***Settlement***, 4m/6km SE of Morebattle. **70 D1** NT8120.
Mowsley *Leics.* ***Village***, 3m/5km N of Husbands Bosworth. **41 J7** SP6489.
Mowtie *Aber.* ***Settlement***, 3m/5km NW of Stonehaven. **91 G6** NO8388.
Moxley *W.Mid.* ***Suburb***, SW district of Walsall. **40 B6** SO9695.
Moy *High.* ***Settlement***, on N side of Caledonian Canal, 1m/2km SW of Gairlochy. **87 H6** NN1682.
Moy *High.* ***Settlement***, in Glen Spean, 9m/14km W of Kinloch Laggan. **88 B6** NN4282.
Moy *High.* ***Village***, in Inverness district, on W side of Loch Moy, 9m/15km SE of Inverness. **88 E1** NH7634.
Moy Burn *High.* ***River***, flowing W from S slopes of Beinn Bhreac, then flowing S into Loch Moy, 4m/7km SE of Daviot. **88 E1** NH7734.
Moy Forest *High.* ***Open space***, upland area on N side of Loch Laggan. **88 B6** NN4183.
Moy House *Moray* ***Settlement***, 1m/2km NW of Forres. **97 H5** NJ0160.
Moycroft *Moray* ***Locality***, E district of Elgin. NJ2362.
Moylgrove (Trewyddel). *Pembs.* ***Village***, 4m/6km W of Cardigan. **26 A4** SN1144.
Mu Ness *Shet.* ***Coastal feature***, headland at SE end of Unst 3m/5km E of Uyeasound. **108 F2** HP6301.
Mu Ness *Shet.* ***Coastal feature***, headland on W coast of Mainland, 4m/6km S of Melby. **109 A7** HU1652.
Muaithabhal *W.Isles* ***Mountain***, 3m/4km W of head of Loch Shell, Isle of Lewis. Height 1391 feet or 424 metres. **100 E6** NB2511.
Muasdale *Arg. & B.* ***Village***, on W coast of Kintyre, 3m/4km N of Glenbarr. **72 E6** NR6740.
Much Birch *Here.* ***Village***, 6m/10km S of Hereford. **28 E5** SO5030.
Much Cowarne *Here.* ***Village***, 5m/8km SW of Bromyard. **29 F4** SO6247.
Much Dewchurch *Here.* ***Village***, 6m/9km S of Hereford. **28 D5** SO4831.
Much Hadham *Herts.* ***Village***, 4m/6km W of Bishop's Stortford. **33 H7** TL4219.
Much Hoole *Lancs.* ***Village***, 6m/10km SW of Preston. **55 H7** SD4622.
Much Hoole Moss Houses *Lancs.* ***Settlement***, 3m/5km W of Leyland. SD4822.
Much Hoole Moss Town *Lancs.* ***Settlement***, adjoining to S of Much Hoole, 4m/7km W of Leyland. SD4722.
Much Marcle *Here.* ***Village***, 7m/11km NE of Ross-on-Wye. **29 F5** SO6532.
Much Wenlock *Shrop.* Population: 1921. ***Small town***, at NE end of Wenlock Edge 8m/12km NW of Bridgnorth. Ruined priory (English Heritage). Half-timbered guildhall. **39 F5** SO6299.
Muchalls *Aber.* ***Village***, on E coast, 4m/7km N of Stonehaven. Red sandstone cliffs. Bridge of Muchalls is settlement 1km S. **91 G5** NO9092.
Muchalls Castle *Aber.* ***Castle***, 1km W of Muchalls. 17c castle burnt in second Jacobite uprising and later rebuilt. **91 G5** NO8991.
Muchelney *Som.* ***Village***, 1m/2km S of Langport. Remains of medieval abbey (English Heritage). Late medieval Priest's House (National Trust). **8 D2** ST4324.
Muchelney Abbey *Som.* ***Ecclesiastical building***, well-preserved remains, including part of 16c abbot's house (English Heritage) 2m/3km S of Langport. **8 D2** ST4224.
Muchelney Ham *Som.* ***Hamlet***, 1km SE of Muchelney, 3m/5km NW of Martock. ST4323.
Muchlarnick *Cornw.* ***Hamlet***, 3m/5km NW of Looe. **4 C5** SX2156.
Muchra *Sc.Bord.* ***Settlement***, 3m/4km S of St. Mary's Loch. **69 H2** NT2217.
Muchrachd *High.* ***Settlement***, in Glen Cannich, 3m/5km NW of Cannich. **87 J1** NH2833.
Muck *High.* ***Island***, sparsely populated island in Inner Hebrides lying 3m/5km SW of Eigg across Sound of Eigg. Area about 2 square miles or 5 square km. Rises to height of 451 feet or 137 metres. **85 K7** NM4179.
Muck Water *S.Ayr.* ***River***, rising on Drumneillie Hill and flowing SW to join Duisk River, 1km SE of Pinwherry. **67 G5** NX2085.
Mucking *Thur.* ***Settlement***, 1km S of Stanford-le-Hope. **24 C3** TQ6881.
Muckingford *Thur.* ***Locality***, 3m/5km NE of Tilbury. TQ6779.
Muckle Burn *Stir.* ***River***, flowing E, then SE into Allan Water 4m/6km NE of Dunblane. **81 J7** NN8106.
Muckle Cairn *Angus* ***Mountain***, 4m/6km NE of Clova. Height 2709 feet or 826 metres. **90 B7** NO3776.
Muckle Flugga *Shet.* ***Island***, small rocky island 1km N of Unst. Lighthouse. **108 E1** HP6019.
Muckle Green Holm *Ork.* ***Island***, small uninhabited island 1m/2km SW of War Ness at S end of Eday. Smaller island of Little Green Holm to S. **106 E5** HY5227.
Muckle Holm *Shet.* ***Island***, small uninhabited island in Yell Sound 2m/3km E of Burra Voe. **108 D4** HU4088.
Muckle Long Hill *Aber.* ***Mountain***, 3m/5km SE of Haugh of Glass. Height 1282 feet or 391 metres. **90 C1** NJ4536.
Muckle Ossa *Shet.* ***Island***, rock off NW coast of Mainland, 2m/4km W of The Faither. Little Ossa rock is adjacent to S. **108 B4** HU2285.
Muckle Roe *Shet.* ***Island***, inhabited island of some 7 square miles or 18 square km off W coast of Mainland in St. Magnus Bay, connected to Mainland by bridge across Roe Sound. Has high, red cliffs. **109 C6** HU3264.
Muckle Skerry *Ork.* ***Island***, largest of Pentland Skerries, with lighthouse. **105 K1** ND4678.
Muckle Skerry *Shet.* ***Island***, isolated group of rock islands 3m/5km off NW coast of Out Skerries island group. **108 F5** HU6273.
Muckle Skerry of Neapaback *Shet.* ***Island***, rock off Heoga Ness at SE end of Yell. HU5378.
Muckle Water *Ork.* ***Lake/loch***, on Rousay, 1m/2km long, aligned NW to SE. **106 C4** HY3930.
Muckleford *Dorset* ***Settlement***, on S side of River Frome, 4m/6km NW of Dorchester. SY6493.
Mucklestone *Staffs.* ***Village***, 4m/6km NE of Market Drayton. **39 G2** SJ7237.
Muckleton *Shrop.* ***Settlement***, 2m/4km E of Shawbury. **38 E3** SJ5921.
Muckletown *Aber.* ***Settlement***, 3m/5km N of Alford. **90 D2** NJ5721.
Muckley *Shrop.* ***Settlement***, 3m/5km SE of Much Wenlock. SO6495.
Muckley Corner *Staffs.* ***Hamlet***, 3m/5km SW of Lichfield. SK0806.
Muckton *Lincs.* ***Village***, 5m/8km SE of Louth. **53 G4** TF3781.
Muckwell *Devon* ***Hamlet***, 2m/3km NW of Start Point. SX8039.
Mudale *High.* ***River***, running E into head of Loch Naver, in Sutherland district. NC5735.
Mudale *High.* ***Settlement***, to N of River Mudale, 3m/4km W of Loch Naver. **103 H5** NC5336.
Mudd *Gt.Man.* ***Settlement***, adjoining to S of Mottram in Longdendale. SJ9994.
Muddiford *Devon* ***Village***, 3m/5km N of Barnstaple. **6 D2** SS5638.
Muddles Green *E.Suss.* ***Hamlet***, 4m/6km NW of Hailsham. **13 J5** TQ5413.
Muddleswood *W.Suss.* ***Settlement***, 3m/5km E of Henfield. **13 F5** TQ2614.
Mudeford *Dorset* ***Suburb***, seaside district, 2m/3km E of Christchurch town centre. **10 C5** SZ1892.
Mudford *Som.* ***Village***, on River Yeo, 3m/4km NE of Yeovil. **8 E3** ST5719.

Mudford Sock *Som.* ***Hamlet***, to W of Mudford, 2m/3km N of Yeovil. ST5519.
Mudgley *Som.* ***Hamlet***, 1m/2km SE of Wedmore. **19 H7** ST4445.
Mudlee Bracks ***Mountain***, 3m/5km SW of Ballochan, with summit on border of Aberdeenshire and Angus. Height 2257 feet or 688 metres. **90 D6** NO5185.
Mugdock *Stir.* ***Hamlet***, 2m/3km N of Milngavie and 2m/3km S of Strathblane. NS5576.
Mugdock Country Park *Stir.* ***Leisure/recreation***, country park surrounding Mugdock Loch and Castle, 1m/2km S of Strathblane. **74 D3** NS5576.
Mugdrum Island *Fife* ***Island***, narrow low-lying island, 1m/2km long E to W, in Firth of Tay NW of Newburgh. **82 D6** NO2218.
Mugeary *High.* ***Settlement***, on Skye, 4m/6km SW of Portree. **85 K1** NG4438.
Mugginton *Derbys.* ***Village***, 6m/10km NW of Derby. **40 E1** SK2843.
Muggintonlane End *Derbys.* ***Settlement***, 1m/2km N of Mugginton, 4m/7km SW of Belper. SK2844.
Muggleswick *Dur.* ***Hamlet***, 4m/6km W of Consett. **62 B1** NZ0450.
Muggleswick Common *Dur.* ***Open space***, heath to S of Edmundbyers, including several small reservoirs. **62 B2** NZ0147.
Mugswell *Surr.* ***Settlement***, 3m/5km N of Reigate. TQ2654.
Muick *Aber.* ***River***, running NE from Loch Muick down Glen Muick to River Dee 1km S of Ballater. **90 B6** NO3694.
Muie *High.* ***Settlement***, in Sutherland district, 6m/9km E of Lairg. **96 D1** NC6704.
Muir *Aber.* ***Settlement***, at bridge over River Dee, 1m/2km W of Inverey. **89 H6** NO0689.
Muir of Dinnet *Aber.* ***Open space***, moorland on N bank of River Dee to W of Dinnet, 5m/8km W of Aboyne. **90 C5** NO4397.
Muir of Fowlis *Aber.* ***Village***, 3m/4km S of Alford. **90 D3** NJ5612.
Muir of Lochs *Moray* ***Settlement***, 3m/4km SW of Garmouth. **98 B4** NJ3062.
Muir of Miltonduff *Moray* ***Locality***, 1km S of Miltonduff and 3m/4km SW of Elgin. NJ1859.
Muir of Orchill *P. & K.* ***Open space***, moorland tract 3m/5km S of Muthill. **81 K6** NN8612.
Muir of Ord *High.* Population: 2033. ***Village***, in Ross and Cromarty district, 3m/4km N of Beauly. **96 C6** NH5250.
Muir of the Clans *High.* ***Open space***, moorland area 4m/6km SW of Nairn. **97 F6** NH8352.
Muir of Thorn *P. & K.* ***Forest/woodland***, wooded area 4m/6km SE of Dunkeld. **82 B4** NO0737.
Muiravonside Country Park *W.Loth.* ***Leisure/recreation***, country park with 170 acres of parkland, woodland and gardens on W bank of River Avon, 3m/5km SW of Linlithgow. Park includes disused mine shaft. **75 H3** NS9575.
Muirden *Aber.* ***Settlement***, on E side of River Deveron, 3m/4km NW of Turriff. **99 F5** NJ7053.
Muirdrum *Angus* ***Village***, 2m/3km N of Carnoustie. **83 G4** NO5637.
Muiredge *Fife* ***Suburb***, W district of Buckhaven. NT3598.
Muirend *Glas.* ***Suburb***, 4m/6km S of Glasgow city centre, in Cathcart district. NS5760.
Muirfield *E.Loth. See Gullane.*
Muirhead *Aber.* ***Settlement***, 3m/5km S of Alford. **90 D3** NJ5611.
Muirhead *Angus* Population: 919. ***Village***, 5m/8km NW of Dundee. **82 E4** NO3434.
Muirhead *Fife* ***Hamlet***, 3m/4km SE of Falkland. **82 D7** NO2805.
Muirhead *Glas.* ***Suburb***, 6m/9km E of Glasgow city centre. NS6763.
Muirhead *Moray* ***Settlement***, 4m/6km NE of Forres. **97 H5** NJ0863.
Muirhead *N.Lan.* Population: 1027. ***Village***, 4m/6km NW of Coatbridge. **74 E4** NS6869.
Muirhead Reservoir *N.Ayr.* ***Reservoir***, 4m/6km SE of Largs. **74 A5** NS2556.
Muirhouse *Edin.* ***Suburb***, 3m/5km NW of Edinburgh city centre. NT2176.
Muirhouses *Falk.* ***Hamlet***, 1m/2km SE of Bo'ness. **75 J2** NT0180.
Muirkirk *E.Ayr.* Population: 1860. ***Small town***, on River Ayr, 9m/15km NE of Cumnock. Cairn to S marks site of McAdam's original tar works. **68 B1** NS6927.
Muirmill *Stir.* ***Settlement***, 1m/2km W of Carron Bridge. **75 F2** NS7283.
Muirneag *W.Isles* ***Hill***, 6m/9km W of Tolsta Head. Height 813 feet or 248 metres. **101 G3** NB4748.
Muirshearlich *High.* ***Locality***, on NW side of Caledonian Canal in Lochaber district, 5m/7km NE of Fort William. NN1380.
Muirshiel Country Park *Renf.* ***Leisure/recreation***, country park with moorland and mixed woodland on slopes above River Calder, 4m/6km NW of Lochwinnoch. Visitor centre, ranger services and walking trails. **74 B4** NS3163.
Muirskie *Aber.* ***Settlement***, 2m/3km NW of Netherley. **91 G5** NO8295.
Muirtack *Aber.* ***Locality***, 3m/5km W of Hatton. **91 H1** NJ9937.
Muirtack *Aber.* ***Settlement***, 3m/4km S of Cuminestown. **99 G6** NJ8146.
Muirton *High.* ***Settlement***, on Black Isle, 4m/5km SW of Cromarty. **96 E5** NH7463.
Muirton *P. & K.* ***Suburb***, N district of Perth. NO1025.
Muirton of Ardblair *P. & K.* ***Village***, 1m/2km S of Blairgowrie. **82 C3** NO1743.
Muirton of Ballochy *Angus* ***Hamlet***, 3m/5km NE of Brechin. **83 H1** NO6462.
Muirtown *High.* ***Locality***, on NW side of Inverness. NH6546.
Muirtown *Moray* ***Settlement***, 3m/4km W of Forres. NH9959.
Muirtown *P. & K.* ***Village***, 2m/3km SW of Auchterarder. **82 A6** NN9211.
Muiryfold *Aber.* ***Settlement***, on N side of Delgaty Forest, 3m/4km E of Turriff. **99 F5** NJ7651.
Muker *N.Yorks.* ***Village***, on Muker Beck, close to its confluence with River Swale and 8m/13km W of Reeth. **62 A7** SD9097.
Mulbarton *Norf.* Population: 2792. ***Village***, with large green, 5m/8km SW of Norwich. **45 F5** TG1901.
Mulben *Moray* ***Settlement***, 5m/8km W of Keith. **98 B5** NJ3550.
Muldoanich *W.Isles* ***Island***, uninhabited island lying 2m/3km E of SE point of Vatersay. NL6893.
Mule (Miwl). *Powys* ***River***, rising 1m/2km S of Dolfor and flowing NE into River Severn at Abermule. **38 A6** SO1594.
Mulhagery *W.Isles* ***Settlement***, on SE coast of Isle of Lewis, 2m/3km S of entrance to Loch Shell. **101 F7** NB3606.
Mull *Arg. & B.* ***Island***, one of Inner Hebrides lying opposite entrance to Loch Linnhe, off W coast of Scottish mainland, separated by Firth of Lorne and the narrow Sound of Mull. Area about 350 square miles or 910 square km. Coastline rugged, and much indented on W side. Terrain mountainous, reaching 3169 feet or 966 metres at Ben More. Chief town is Tobermory. **79 G4** NM6035.
Mull and West Highland Railway *Arg. & B.* ***Other feature of interest***, Scotland's only island passenger tourist railway, on E coast of Mull, operating between Craignure and Torosay Castle. **79 J4** NM7336.
Mull Head *Ork.* ***Coastal feature***, headland at N end of Papa Westray. **106 E2** HY5055.
Mull Head *Ork.* ***Coastal feature***, headland at E extremity of Mainland beyond Deer Sound. **107 E7** HY5909.
Mull of Cara *Arg. & B.* ***Coastal feature***, headland at S end of Cara. **72 E6** NR6343.
Mull of Galloway *D. & G.* ***Coastal feature***, bold headland, with high cliffs and lighthouse, at S extremity of Rinns of Galloway. Southernmost point of Scotland. **64 B7** NX1530.
Mull of Kintyre *Arg. & B.* ***Coastal feature***, headland at SW end of Kintyre, 9m/14km S of Machrihanish. Mull lighthouse to N. **66 A3** NR5907.
Mull of Logan *D. & G.* ***Coastal feature***, headland to N of Port Logan Bay, 9m/14km SE of Portpatrick. **64 A6** NX0741.
Mull of Oa *Arg. & B.* ***Coastal feature***, headland at SW end of The Oa, Islay. Monument commemorates those who died in two American troopships in 1918. **72 A6** NR2641.
Mulla-fo-dheas *W.Isles* ***Mountain***, on North Harris, 3m/5km S of head of Loch Langavat. Height 2437 feet or 743 metres. **100 D7** NB1407.
Mullach a' Ruisg *W.Isles* ***Mountain***, 1km E of head of Loch Langavat. Height 1551 feet or 473 metres. **100 D6** NB1612.
Mullach an Rathain *High.* ***Mountain***, one of the peaks of Liathach, Ross and Cromarty district. Munro: height 3355 feet or 1023 metres. **95 F6** NG9157.
Mullach Buidhe *N.Ayr.* ***Mountain***, on NW of Arran, 2m/3km SE of Pirnmill. Height 2365 feet or 721 metres. **73 H6** NR9042.
Mullach Charlabhaigh (Anglicised form: Upper Carloway.) *W.Isles* ***Settlement***, adjoining to N of Carloway, Isle of Lewis. **100 E3** NB2043.
Mullach Clach a' Bhlàir *High.* ***Mountain***, in Cairngorm Mountains, in Badenoch and Strathspey district, 8m/12km SW of Ben Macdui. Munro: height 3342 feet or 1019 metres. **89 F5** NN8892.
Mullach Coire a' Chuir *Arg. & B.* ***Mountain***, in Argyll, 3m/4km NW of Lochgoilhead. Height 2096 feet or 639 metres. **80 C7** NN1703.
Mullach Coire Ardachaidh *High.* ***Mountain***, in Lochaber district, between Loch Loyne and Loch Garry. Height 1768 feet or 539 metres. **87 J4** NH2004.
Mullach Coire Mhic Fhearchair *High.* ***Mountain***, in W part of Ross and Cromarty district 3m/5km E of head of Lochan Fada. Munro: height 3342 feet or 1019 metres. **95 G4** NH0573.
Mullach Coire nan Geur-oirean *High.* ***Mountain***, on Locheil Forest, Lochaber district, 4m/7km SE of head of Loch Arkaig. Height 2385 feet or 727 metres. **87 G6** NN0489.
Mullach Fraoch-choire *High.* ***Mountain***, on Glenaffric Forest, Inverness district, 4m/6km SW of head of Loch Affric. Munro: height 3615 feet or 1102 metres. **87 G3** NH0917.
Mullach Mòr *High.* ***Hill***, 1m/2km NW of Kinloch, Rum. Height 997 feet or 304 metres. **85 J4** NG3801.
Mullach na Càrn *High.* ***Mountain***, highest point on Scalpay, Skye and Lochalsh district. Height 1299 feet or 396 metres. **86 C2** NG6029.
Mullach na Dheiragain *High.* ***Mountain***, in Skye and Lochalsh district, with craggy summit 2m/4km SW of W end of Loch Mullardoch. Munro: height 3221 feet or 982 metres. **87 G2** NH0825.
Mullach na Reidheachd *W.Isles* ***Hill***, 1m/2km E of Màs a' Chnoic-chuairtich. Height 968 feet or 295 metres. **100 C6** NB0914.
Mullach nan Cadhaichean *High.* ***Hill***, 6m/9km E of Redpoint, Ross and Cromarty district. Height 964 feet or 294 metres. **94 E5** NG8269.
Mullach nan Coirean *High.* ***Mountain***, in Lochaber district 5m/8km S of Fort William. Munro: height 3080 feet or 939 metres. **80 C1** NN1266.
Mullacott Cross *Devon* ***Settlement***, 2m/3km S of Ilfracombe. **6 D1** SS5144.
Mulldonoch *D. & G.* ***Mountain***, 2m/3km SE of Glen Trool Lodge. Height 1827 feet or 557 metres. **64 E3** NX4278.
Mullion *Cornw.* Population: 2040. ***Village***, 5m/8km S of Helston. Coast to W and SW largely National Trust, including Mullion Cove and Mullion Island. Marconi monument on cliffs above nearby Poldhu Cove, from where first transatlantic radio signals were transmitted. **2 D7** SW6719.
Mullion Cove *Cornw.* ***Coastal feature***, part of coast to W of Mullion, National Trust. **2 D7** SW6719.
Mullion Island *Cornw.* ***Island***, between Predannack Head and Mullion Cove, to SW of Mullion. National Trust property. **2 D7** SW6719.
Mulwith *N.Yorks.* ***Locality***, 2m/3km W of Boroughbridge across River Ure. SE3666.
Mumbles Head *Swan.* ***Coastal feature***, headland at W end of Swansea Bay consisting of two island rocks connected to mainland by causeway. Outer rock has lighthouse. **17 K6** SS6387.
Mumby *Lincs.* ***Village***, 4m/6km E of Alford. **53 J5** TF5174.
Mumps *Gt.Man.* ***Suburb***, to E of Oldham town centre. SD9305.
Muncaster *Cumb.* ***Locality***, 1m/2km E of Ravenglass. SD1096.
Muncaster Castle *Cumb.* ***Castle***, 19c castle by Salvin, 1km E of Ravenglass and 15m/24km SE of Whitehaven, incorporating parts of medieval building, including peel tower and home of Pennington family since 13c. Owl aviary and rhododendron gardens, and walks overlooking River Esk valley. **60 C7** SD1096.
Munderfield Row *Here.* ***Hamlet***, 2m/4km S of Bromyard. **29 F3** SO6551.
Munderfield Stocks *Here.* ***Hamlet***, 3m/5km S of Bromyard. **29 F3** SO6550.
Mundesley *Norf.* Population: 2211. ***Small town***, coastal resort with long, sandy beach 4m/7km NE of North Walsham. **45 H2** TG3136.
Mundford *Norf.* ***Village***, 5m/8km N of Brandon. **44 B6** TL8093.
Mundham *Norf.* ***Village***, 2m/4km W of Loddon. **45 H6** TM3297.
Mundon *Essex* ***Village***, 3m/5km SE of Maldon. **24 E1** TL8602.
Mundurno *Aberdeen* ***Settlement***, 1m/2km inland and 4m/6km E of Dyce. **91 H3** NJ9412.
Munerigie *High.* ***Settlement***, at E end of Loch Garry, 3m/4km W of Invergarry. **87 J4** NH2602.
Muness Castle *Shet.* ***Castle***, late 16c castle (Historic Scotland), 1km W of Mu Ness. **108 F2** HP6301.
Mungasdale *High.* ***Settlement***, 4m/7km E of Laide across Gruinard Bay, Ross and Cromarty district. **95 F2** NG9693.
Mungoswells *E.Loth.* ***Settlement***, 3m/5km NW of Haddington. **76 C3** NT4978.
Mungrisdale *Cumb.* ***Hamlet***, 8m/12km NE of Keswick. **60 E3** NY3630.
Munlochy *High.* ***Village***, in Ross and Cromarty district at head of Munlochy Bay, 6m/9km N of Inverness. **96 D6** NH6453.
Munlochy Bay *High.* ***Bay***, inlet on W side of Inner Moray Firth or Inverness Firth, on S side of Black Isle. **96 D6** NH6453.
Munnoch *N.Ayr.* ***Settlement***, 3m/4km W of Dalry. **74 A6** NS2548.
Munnoch Reservoir *N.Ayr.* ***Reservoir***, 4m/6km N of Ardrossan. **74 A6** NS2547.
Munsley *Here.* ***Hamlet***, 4m/6km NW of Ledbury. **29 F4** SO6640.
Munslow *Shrop.* ***Village***, 6m/10km NE of Craven Arms. **38 E7** SO5287.
Munstead Heath *Surr.* ***Locality***, 1m/2km SE of Godalming. SU9842.
Munstone *Here.* ***Settlement***, 2m/3km N of Hereford. SO5142.
Murch *V. of Glam.* ***Suburb***, adjoining to E of Dinas Powys. ST1670.
Murchington *Devon* ***Hamlet***, 5m/7km NW of Moretonhampstead. **6 E7** SX6888.
Murcott *Oxon.* ***Hamlet***, 4m/7km S of Bicester. **31 G7** SP5815.
Murcott *Wilts.* ***Settlement***, 3m/5km NE of Malmesbury. ST9591.
Murdishaw *Halton* ***Suburb***, E district of Runcorn. SJ5681.
Murdoch Head *Aber.* ***Coastal feature***, headland on E coast, 4m/7km S of Peterhead. **91 K1** NK1239.
Murdostoun *N.Lan.* ***Settlement***, 1m/2km N of Newmains across South Calder Water. **75 G5** NS8257.
Murieston *W.Loth.* ***Suburb***, 2m/3km S of Livingston town centre. NT0664.
Murkle *High.* ***Settlement***, near N coast of Caithness district, 3m/5km E of Thurso. **105 G2** ND1668.
Murkle Bay *High.* ***Bay***, small bay on SW side of Dunnet Bay. **105 G2** ND1669.
Murlaganmore *Stir.* ***Settlement***, at SE end of Glen Lochay, 2m/3km NW of Killin. **81 G4** NN5434.
Murlaggan *High.* ***Settlement***, on N shore of Loch Arkaig, 12m/20km NW of Fort William. **87 G5** NN0192.
Murlaggan *High.* ***Settlement***, in valley of River Spean, 3m/4km E of Roybridge. **87 K6** NN3181.
Murra *Ork.* ***Settlement***, 1m/2km NW of Orgil, near to N coast of Hoy. **107 B7** HY2104.
Murrayfield *Edin.* ***Suburb***, 2m/3km W of Edinburgh city centre. Scottish Rugby Union football ground in S part of district. NT2273.
Murray's Hill *P. & K.* ***Hill***, low hill 5m/8km NE of Crieff. Height 807 feet or 246 metres. **82 A5** NN9325.
Murray's Isles *D. & G.* ***Island***, two most northerly of Islands of Fleet, at entrance to Fleet Bay from Wigtown Bay. **65 F5** NX5649.
Murrell Green *Hants.* ***Settlement***, 1m/2km NE of Hook. SU7455.
Murrister *Shet.* ***Locality***, on Mainland, 2m/3km N of Gruting. HU2751.
Murroes *Angus* ***Hamlet***, on Sweet Burn, 3m/4km NW of Monifieth. **83 F4** NO4635.

Murrow *Cambs.* ***Village***, 6m/9km W of Wisbech. **43 G5** TF3707.
Mursley *Bucks.* ***Village***, 3m/5km E of Winslow. **32 B6** SP8128.
Murston *Kent* ***Settlement***, 1m/2km NE of Sittingbourne. **25 F5** TQ9264.
Murthill *Angus* ***Hamlet***, 2m/3km W of Finavon. **83 F2** NO4657.
Murthly *P. & K.* ***Village***, 5m/8km SE of Dunkeld. **82 B4** NO0938.
Murthly Castle *P. & K.* ***Castle***, stands in wooded grounds beside River Tay, 2m/3km NW of Murthly. NO0739.
Murton *Cumb.* ***Village***, at foot of fells, 3m/5km E of Appleby-in-Westmorland. **61 J4** NY7221.
Murton *Dur.* Population: 7374. ***Small town***, 3m/4km SW of Seaham. Agricultural centre. **62 E2** NZ3947.
Murton *N.Yorks.* ***Settlement***, on edge of woodland, 3m/5km E of Boltby and 6m/9km NW of Helmsley. SE5388.
Murton *Northumb.* ***Hamlet***, 2m/3km SE of Horncliffe. **77 H6** NT9648.
Murton *Swan.* ***Village***, to E of Bishopston, on Gower peninsula, 3m/5km NW of Mumbles Head. SS5889.
Murton *York* ***Village***, 3m/5km E of York. **58 C4** SE6452.
Murton Fell *Cumb.* ***Mountain***, 5m/8km NE of Appleby-in-Westmorland. Height 2207 feet or 673 metres. **61 J4** NY7524.
Murton Fell *Cumb.* ***Open space***, hillslope on W side of Loweswater Fell, summit of which is Knock Murton at a height of 446 metres. **60 B5** NY0919.
Musbury *Devon* ***Village***, 3m/5km SW of Axminster. **8 B5** SY2794.
Muscliff *Bourne.* ***Suburb***, 3m/5km NE of Bournemouth town centre. SZ0995.
Muscoates *N.Yorks.* ***Settlement***, 5m/8km SE of Helmsley. **58 C1** SE6880.
Musdale *Arg. & B.* ***Settlement***, 3m/4km NE of head of Loch Scammadale. **80 A5** NM9322.
Museum of Isle of Wight Geology *I.o.W.* ***Other feature of interest***, 1km E from Sandown, overlooking Sandown Bay, with displays of large local ammonites. **11 H6** SZ6084.
Museum of Reading *Read.* ***Other feature of interest***, museum at Reading with exhibits including full-scale replica of Bayeux Tapestry, local history since Saxon times and Roman artefacts unearthed at Silchester. **22 A4** SU7273.
Museum of the Moving Image *Gt.Lon. See South Bank Arts Centre.*
Museum of Welsh Life *Cardiff* ***Other feature of interest***, museum at St. Fagans, 4m/6km W of Cardiff city centre, detailing life, work and traditions of Welsh people since Middle Ages. Site includes St. Fagans Castle along with over thirty re-erected historic buildings, ranging from shops and schools to farm buildings, with associated fixtures and fittings. Other collections include costume and fashions since Middle Ages; agricultural machinery and transport; rural crafts; cultural life and oral traditions. **18 E4** ST1177.
Mushroom Castle *Brack.F.* ***Locality***, 2m/3km NE of Bracknell. SU8970.
Mushroom Green *W.Mid.* ***Suburb***, 2m/4km S of Dudley town centre. SO9386.
Muskna Field *Shet.* ***Hill***, 1m/2km W of Fladdabister, Mainland. Height 859 feet or 262 metres. **109 D9** HU4032.
Mussel End *Glos.* ***Locality***, between Sandhurst and River Severn, 3m/5km N of Gloucester. SO8223.
Musselburgh *E.Loth.* Population: 20,630. ***Town***, former trading and fishing port on Firth of Forth at mouth of River Esk, 6m/9km E of Edinburgh. Town contains boys' public school of Loretto. Tolbooth, late 16c. Racecourse. **76 B3** NT3472.
Mustard Hyrn *Norf.* ***Settlement***, 1m/2km NW of Martham. TG4418.
Muston *Leics.* ***Village***, 6m/9km W of Grantham. **42 B2** SK8237.
Muston *N.Yorks.* ***Village***, 1m/2km SW of Filey. **59 H2** TA0979.
Mustow Green *Worcs.* ***Hamlet***, 3m/5km SE of Kidderminster. **29 H1** SO8874.
Muswell Hill *Gt.Lon.* ***Suburb***, in borough of Haringey, 6m/10km N of Charing Cross. TQ2890.
Mutford *Suff.* ***Village***, 4m/7km E of Beccles. **45 J7** TM4888.
Muthill *P. & K.* ***Village***, 19c conservation village, 3m/5km S of Crieff. Ruined 15c church with 12c tower (Historic Scotland). **81 K6** NN8617.
Muthill Church *P. & K.* ***Historic/prehistoric site***, ruins of 15c church with 12c tower in Muthill, 3m/4km S of Crieff. **81 K6** NN8717.
Mutley *Plym.* ***Suburb***, to N of Plymouth city centre. SX4855.
Mutterton *Devon* ***Settlement***, 2m/3km SE of Cullompton. **7 J5** ST0305.
Muttonhole *Edin. Former name of Davidson's Mains, qv.*
Muxton *Tel. & W.* ***Suburb***, 2m/4km N of Oakengates. SJ7113.
Mwdwl Eithin *Conwy* ***Mountain***, 7m/11km SW of Colwyn Bay. Height 1276 feet or 389 metres. **47 G6** SH8268.
Mwdwl-eithin *Conwy* ***Mountain***, 3m/4km SE of Cerrigydrudion. Height 1542 feet or 470 metres. **37 J1** SH9846.
Mwnt *Cere.* ***Coastal feature***, headland (National Trust), 4m/6km N of Cardigan. SN1952.
Myarth *Powys* ***Hill***, 3m/5km NW of Crickhowell. Height 951 feet or 290 metres. **28 A6** SO1720.
Mybster *High.* ***Settlement***, in Caithness district, 5m/8km W of Watten. **105 G3** ND1652.
Myddfai *Carmar.* ***Hamlet***, 3m/5km S of Llandovery. **27 G5** SN7730.
Myddle *Shrop.* ***Village***, 7m/12km N of Shrewsbury. Slight remains of medieval castle. **38 D3** SJ4623.
Myddlewood *Shrop.* ***Settlement***, 8m/12km NW of Shrewsbury. **38 D3** SJ4523.
Mydroilyn *Cere.* ***Village***, 5m/8km S of Aberaeron. **26 D3** SN4555.
Myerscough *Lancs.* ***Settlement***, 2m/3km NW of Barton, 4m/6km S of Garstang. SD4939.
Myerscough Smithy *Lancs.* ***Hamlet***, 4m/7km NW of Blackburn. SD6131.
Mylor (Sometimes known as Mylor Churchtown.) *Cornw.* ***Village***, situated at mouth of Mylor Creek, 2m/3km NE of Falmouth. **3 F5** SW8235.
Mylor Bridge *Cornw.* Population: 1635. ***Village***, at head of Mylor Creek, 3m/4km N of Falmouth. **3 F5** SW8036.
Mylor Churchtown *Cornw. Occasional name for Mylor, qv.*
Mynachdy *Cardiff* ***Suburb***, 2m/3km NW of Cardiff city centre. ST1679.
Mynachlog-ddu *Pembs.* ***Settlement***, 3m/5km SW of Crymych. **16 E1** SN1430.
Myndtown *Shrop.* ***Hamlet***, 4m/7km E of Bishop's Castle. **38 C7** SO3989.
Mynwar *Pembs. Welsh form of Minwear, qv.*
Mynwent y Crynwyr *M.Tyd. Welsh form of Quaker's Yard, qv.*
Mynwy *Welsh form of (River) Monnow, qv.*
Mynydd Aberdar *R.C.T.* ***Mountain***, 2m/3km W of Merthyr Tydfil. Height 1499 feet or 457 metres. **18 D1** SO0205.
Mynydd Aberyscir *Powys* ***Mountain***, 4m/6km NW of Brecon. Height 1204 feet or 367 metres. **27 J5** SN9932.
Mynydd Allt-y-grug *N.P.T.* ***Mountain***, 1m/2km SW of Ystalyfera. Height 1112 feet or 339 metres. **18 A1** SN7407.
Mynydd Alltir-fach *Newport* ***Settlement***, at S end of Wentwood Reservoir, 1m/2km NW of Llanvair-Discoed. ST4292.
Mynydd Anelog *Gwyn.* ***Hill***, on SW tip of Lleyn Peninsula, 1m/2km W of Aberdaron. Height 626 feet or 191 metres. **36 A3** SH1527.
Mynydd Bach *Cere.* ***Inland physical feature***, mountain ridge rising to 361 metres at Hafod Ithel, 2m/3km W of Bronnant. **26 E2** SN6166.
Mynydd Bach *Cere.* ***Mountain***, 1m/2km NE of Tynygraig. Height 1217 feet or 371 metres. **27 G1** SN7070.
Mynydd Bach *Gwyn.* ***Mountain***, 4m/6km SE of Trawsfynydd. Height 1148 feet or 350 metres. **37 G2** SH7430.
Mynydd-bach *Mon.* ***Hamlet***, just N of Shirenewton, 3m/5km W of Chepstow. **19 H2** ST4894.
Mynydd-bach *Swan.* ***Suburb***, on W side of Morriston, 3m/4km N of Swansea city centre. SS6597.
Mynydd-bach Trecastell *Carmar.* ***Mountain***, rising to over 390 metres, 1m/2km N of Usk Reservoir dam. **27 H5** SN8330.
Mynydd Baedan *Bridgend* ***Hill***, 4m/6km NW of Bridgend. Height 823 feet or 251 metres. **18 B3** SS8884.
Mynydd Bedwelte *B.Gwent* ***Mountain***, 1m/2km S of Tredegar. Height 1594 feet or 486 metres. **18 E1** SO1407.
Mynydd Bodrochwyn *Conwy* ***Hill***, 3m/5km S of Abergele. Height 918 feet or 280 metres. **47 H5** SH9372.
Mynydd Branar *Conwy* ***Mountain***, 4m/7km S of Colwyn Bay. Height 1063 feet or 324 metres. **47 G5** SH8771.
Mynydd Bryn-llech *Gwyn.* ***Mountain***, 4m/7km W of Llanuwchllyn. Height 1771 feet or 540 metres. **37 H2** SH8031.
Mynydd Bwlch-y-Groes *Powys* ***Inland physical feature***, mountain ridge rising to 1450 feet or 442 metres, 6m/10km E of Llandovery. **27 H5** SN8634.
Mynydd Caerau *Bridgend* ***Mountain***, 3m/5km NE of Maesteg. Height 1824 feet or 556 metres. **18 B2** SS8994.
Mynydd Caregog *Pembs.* ***Mountain***, 2m/3km SW of Newport. Height 1020 feet or 311 metres. **16 D1** SN0336.
Mynydd Carn-y-Cefn *B.Gwent* ***Mountain***, 1km W of Blaina. Height 1804 feet or 550 metres. **18 E1** SO1808.
Mynydd Carningli *Pembs.* ***Mountain***, 4m/7km SE of Dinas Head. Height 1138 feet or 347 metres. **16 D1** SN0637.
Mynydd Castlebythe *Pembs.* ***Mountain***, summit lies 1m/2km E of Puncheston. Height 1138 feet or 347 metres. **16 D2** SN0329.
Mynydd Ceiswyn *Gwyn.* ***Mountain***, 3m/4km SE of Dolgellau. Height 1984 feet or 605 metres. **37 G4** SH7713.
Mynydd Cenin *Gwyn.* ***Hill***, at E end of Lleyn Peninsula, 5m/8km S of Penygroes. Height 859 feet or 262 metres. **36 D1** SH4544.
Mynydd Cerrig *Carmar.* ***Hill***, rising to over 210 metres, 3m/5km W of Cross Hands. **17 H3** SN5013.
Mynydd Cilciffeth *Pembs.* ***Mountain***, 4m/7km SE of Fishguard. Height 1096 feet or 334 metres. **16 D1** SN0132.
Mynydd Clogau *Powys* ***Mountain***, 4m/7km N of Caersws. Height 1319 feet or 402 metres. **37 K6** SO0499.
Mynydd Cribau *Conwy* ***Mountain***, 2m/3km W of Betws-y-coed. Height 1132 feet or 345 metres. **47 F7** SH7555.
Mynydd Cricor *Denb.* ***Mountain***, 3m/5km SE of Llanfair Dyffryn Clwyd. Height 1079 feet or 329 metres. **47 K7** SJ1450.
Mynydd Cynros *Carmar.* ***Mountain***, 2m/3km S of Llansawel. Height 1079 feet or 329 metres. **17 K1** SN6232.
Mynydd Dinas *N.P.T.* ***Hill***, 1m/2km N of Port Talbot. Height 846 feet or 258 metres. **18 A2** SS7691.
Mynydd Dolgoed *Gwyn.* ***Inland physical feature***, narrow ridge rising to 1706 feet or 520 metres, 4m/7km SE of Dolgellau. **37 G4** SH7812.
Mynydd Eglwysilan *Caerp.* ***Mountain***, 4m/6km NW of Caerphilly. Height 1164 feet or 355 metres. **18 E2** ST1292.
Mynydd Eppynt *Powys* ***Open space***, wild moorland area SW of Builth Wells. Artillery range. Watershed of rivers running southwards into River Usk. **27 H5** SN9643.
Mynydd Figyn *Carmar.* ***Mountain***, 4m/7km E of Brechfa. Height 1066 feet or 325 metres. **17 J1** SN5930.
Mynydd Garn-fach *Swan.* ***Hill***, rises above Upper Lliw Reservoir, 4m/6km SE of Ammanford. Height 974 feet or 297 metres. **17 K4** SN6506.
Mynydd Garnclochdy *Torfaen* ***Open space***, mountain slope, 1m/2km NE of Abersychan. **19 F1** SO2805.
Mynydd Hiraethog *Denb.* ***Locality***, upland area 4m/7km N of Cerrigydrudion. **47 H7** SH9455.
Mynydd Illtyd *Powys* ***Mountain***, rising to over 380 metres, 3m/5km SE of Sennybridge. **27 J6** SN9626.
Mynydd Isa *Flints.* ***Suburb***, adjoining to W of Buckley. SJ2564.
Mynydd-llan *Flints.* ***Settlement***, 3m/5km SW of Holywell. SJ1472.
Mynydd Llanelian *Conwy* ***Mountain***, 3m/4km SW of Colwyn Bay. Height 1102 feet or 336 metres. **47 G5** SH8474.
Mynydd Llangatwg *Powys* ***Mountain***, mass to N of Bryn-mawr with steep, craggy N slopes. SE peak attains 1735 feet or 529 metres. Numerous cairns on summit. **28 A7** SO1814.
Mynydd Llangeinwyr *Bridgend* ***Inland physical feature***, mountain ridge running N to S, falling steeply to Ogmore valley to E and Garw valley to W. Highest point is 1748 feet or 533 metres. **18 C2** SS9193.
Mynydd Llangorse *Powys* ***Mountain***, 4m/7km S of Talgarth. Height 1666 feet or 508 metres. **28 A6** SO1526.
Mynydd Llangynidr *Powys* ***Mountain***, 3m/5km N of Tredegar. Height 1804 feet or 550 metres. **28 A7** SO1215.
Mynydd Llanllwni *Carmar.* ***Inland physical feature***, mountain ridge rising to 1256 feet or.383 metres, 1m/2km SE of Llanllwni. **17 J1** SN5037.
Mynydd Llanwenarth *Mon.* ***Inland physical feature***, mountain ridge rising to over 400 metres, extending S from Sugar Loaf, 2m/3km NW of Abergavenny. **28 B7** SO2617.
Mynydd Llanybyther *Carmar.* ***Mountain***, 3m/5km S of Llanybydder. Masts at summit. Height 1319 feet or 402 metres. **17 J1** SN5539.
Mynydd Llwydiarth *I.o.A.* ***Hill***, on SE side of Red Wharf Bay, 3m/4km SE of Benllech. Height 518 feet or 158 metres. **46 D5** SH5479.
Mynydd Llyn Coch-hwyad *Powys* ***Mountain***, 4m/6km E of Aberangell. Height 1650 feet or 503 metres. **37 J5** SH9110.
Mynydd Llysiau *Powys* ***Mountain***, 5m/8km NE of Newtown. Height 2171 feet or 662 metres. **28 B6** SO2027.
Mynydd Maen *Torfaen* ***Mountain***, 3m/4km NW of Cwmbran. Height 1548 feet or 472 metres. **19 F2** ST2597.
Mynydd Maendy *R.C.T.* ***Hill***, 2m/3km S of Gilfach Goch. Height 984 feet or 300 metres. **18 C3** SS9886.
Mynydd Maes-teg *Bridgend* ***Inland physical feature***, SE spur of mountain to N of Gilfach Goch. **18 C2** SS9591.
Mynydd Mallaen *Carmar.* ***Mountain***, massif 5m/8km NE of Pumsaint. Height 1469 feet or 448 metres. **27 G4** SN7344.
Mynydd Marchywell *N.P.T.* ***Mountain***, 3m/5km E of Pontardawe. Height 1371 feet or 418 metres. **18 A1** SN7603.
Mynydd Margam *N.P.T.* ***Mountain***, 2m/4km NE of Margam. Height 1128 feet or 344 metres. **18 B3** SS8188.
Mynydd Mawr *Gwyn.* ***Mountain***, 1m/2km W of Llyn Cwellyn. Height 2289 feet or 698 metres. **46 D7** SH5354.
Mynydd Mawr *Powys* ***Mountain***, 2m/3km N of Llanrhaeadr-ym-Mochnant. Height 1752 feet or 534 metres. **38 A3** SJ1328.
Mynydd Melyn *Pembs.* ***Mountain***, 4m/6km E of Fishguard. Height 1007 feet or 307 metres. **16 D1** SN0236.
Mynydd Merddin *Here.* ***Mountain***, 4m/6km W of Pontrilas. Height 1059 feet or 323 metres. **28 C6** SO3327.
Mynydd Merthyr *M.Tyd.* ***Mountain***, 3m/4km E of Aberdare. Height 1610 feet or 491 metres. **18 D1** SO0402.
Mynydd Moel *Gwyn.* ***Mountain***, E peak of Cadair Idris. Height 2804 feet or 855 metres. **37 G4** SH7213.
Mynydd Myddfai *Carmar.* ***Mountain***, 1m/2km N of head of Usk Reservoir. Height 1443 feet or 440 metres. **27 H6** SN8029.
Mynydd Mynyllod *Gwyn.* ***Mountain***, 5m/8km NE of Bala. Height 1279 feet or 390 metres. **37 J2** SH9939.
Mynydd Pen-bre *Carmar.* ***Hill***, 1m/2km N of Burry Port. Height 587 feet or 179 metres. **17 H4** SN4403.
Mynydd Pen-y-fâl *Mon. Welsh form of Sugar Loaf, qv.*
Mynydd Pencarreg *Carmar.* ***Mountain***, 3m/5km SE of Pencarreg. Mast near summit, Pen Tas-eithin. Height 1361 feet or 415 metres. **26 E4** SN5743.
Mynydd Pencoed *Gwyn.* ***Inland physical feature***, SE ridge of Cadair Idris massif rising to 2512 feet or 766 metres. **37 F4** SH6910.
Mynydd Pennant *Gwyn.* ***Mountain***, 4m/6km SE of Fairbourne. Height 1519 feet or 463 metres. **37 F4** SH6610.
Mynydd Perfedd *Gwyn.* ***Mountain***, on W side of Nant Ffrancon pass, 3m/4km S of Bethesda. Height 2667 feet or 813 metres. **46 E6** SH6262.
Mynydd Preseli *Pembs. Welsh form of Prescelly Mountains, qv.*
Mynydd Resolfen *N.P.T.* ***Mountain***, 2m/3km E of Resolven. Height 1256 feet or 383 metres. **18 B1** SN8503.
Mynydd Rhiw *Gwyn.* ***Mountain***, at SW end of Lleyn Peninsula 5m/8km W of Abersoch. Height 1000 feet or 305 metres. **36 B3** SH2329.
Mynydd Rhiw-Saeson *Powys* ***Open space***, hillside area 4m/7km SE of Aberangell. **37 H5** SH9006.
Mynydd Sylen *Carmar.* ***Hill***, 4m/7km SW of Cross Hands. Mast at summit. Height 932 feet or 284 metres. **17 J4** SN5108.
Mynydd Tan-y-coed *Gwyn.* ***Mountain***, 1m/2km E of Dolgoch. Height 1614 feet or 492 metres. **37 F5** SH6604.
Mynydd Tarw *Powys* ***Mountain***, 3m/4km W of Llanarmon Dyffryn Ceiriog. Height 2234 feet or 681 metres. **38 A2** SJ1132.
Mynydd Trawsnant *Carmar.* ***Mountain***, 4m/6km NW of Llanwrtyd Wells. Height 1696 feet or 517 metres. **27 H4** SN8248.
Mynydd Troed *Powys* ***Mountain***, 3m/5km S of Talgarth. Height 1998 feet or 609 metres. **28 A6** SO1629.
Mynydd Twr *I.o.A. Welsh form of Holyhead Mountain, qv.*
Mynydd Tŷ'r-sais *Powys* ***Mountain***, 7m/11km E of Machynlleth. Height 1178 feet or 359 metres. **37 H5** SH8500.
Mynydd Waun Fawr *Powys* ***Mountain***, with boggy plateau, 3m/5km SE of Llangadfan. Height 1279 feet or 390 metres. **37 K5** SJ0005.

Mynydd Wysg *Powys* ***Open space***, wooded hillslope 1m/2km S of Usk Reservoir. **27 H6** SN8226.
Mynydd y Betws *Carmar.* ***Hill***, rising to over 300 metres, 2m/3km S of Glanaman. **17 K3** SN6710.
Mynydd y Cemais *Powys* ***Inland physical feature***, mountain ridge rising to 1427 feet or 435 metres and running 2m/3km N to S, 2m/3km SE of Aberangell. **37 H5** SH8606.
Mynydd y Drum *N.P.T.* ***Hill***, 1m/2km SE of Ystradgynlais. Site of former opencast workings on NE side. Height 977 feet or 298 metres. **18 B1** SN8009.
Mynydd y Gadfa *Powys* ***Mountain***, 3m/4km NW of Llangadfan. Height 1197 feet or 365 metres. **37 J4** SH9914.
Mynydd y Gaer *Bridgend* ***Hill***, 2m/4km SW of Gilfach Goch. Height 968 feet or 295 metres. **18 C3** SS9585.
Mynydd-y-Garreg *Carmar.* ***Hill***, rising to over 170 metres, 3m/4km NE of Kidwelly. **17 H4** SN4409.
Mynydd-y-garreg *Flints. See Whitford.*
Mynydd-y-glog *R.C.T.* ***Mountain***, 3m/4km N of Hirwaun. Height 1276 feet or 389 metres. **18 C1** SN9709.
Mynydd y Gribin *Powys* ***Open space***, hillslope 1m/2km N of Foel. **37 K5** SJ0002.
Mynydd y Groes *Powys* ***Mountain***, on E edge of Hafren Forest, 3m/5km S of Staylittle. Height 1561 feet or 476 metres. **37 H7** SN8787.
Mynydd y Gwair *Swan.* ***Open space***, moorland to N of Upper Lliw Reservoir, 3m/5km SE of Ammanford. **17 K4** SN6507.
Mynyddislwyn *Caerp.* ***Settlement***, 2m/3km SW of Abercarn. ST1994.
Mynyddygarreg *Carmar.* ***Settlement***, 1m/2km NE of Kidwelly. SN4208.
Mynytho *Gwyn.* ***Settlement***, 2m/3km W of Llanbedrog. **36 C2** SH3030.
Myrebird *Aber.* ***Settlement***, 4m/6km NE of Banchory. **91 F5** NO7499.
Mytchett *Surr.* ***Suburb***, 1m/2km NE of Farnborough. **22 B6** SU8855.
Mythe Bridge ***Bridge***, with single arch of 174 feet or 58 metres, built by Telford in 1823 across River Severn, to NW of Tewkesbury on border of Gloucestershire and Worcestershire. SO8833.
Mytholm *W.Yorks.* ***Village***, 1km W of Hebden Bridge. **56 E7** SD9827.
Mytholmes *W.Yorks.* ***Locality***, in Worth valley, 1m/2km NE of Haworth. SE0337.
Mytholmroyd *W.Yorks.* Population: 4114. ***Small town***, on River Calder, 2m/3km SE of Hebden Bridge. Birthplace of Ted Hughes, poet. **57 F7** SE0126.
Mythop *Lancs.* ***Settlement***, 4m/6km E of Blackpool. SD3634.
Myton-on-Swale *N.Yorks.* ***Village***, on S bank of River Swale, near its confluence with River Ure, 2m/4km S of Brafferton. **57 K3** SE4366.
Mytton *Shrop.* ***Hamlet***, 4m/7km NW of Shrewsbury town centre. SJ4417.

N

Na Binneinean *Arg. & B.* ***Mountain***, rising from NE shore of Loch Bà, 3m/4km SE of Gruline. Height 1076 feet or 328 metres. **79 G4** NM5737.
Na Cruachan *High.* ***Mountain***, in Knoydart, 4m/7km N of Inverie. Height 1912 feet or 583 metres. **86 D4** NG7707.
Na Cùiltean *Arg. & B.* ***Island***, group of rocks with lighthouse, about 1m/2km SE of Rubha na Caillich on E coast of Jura. **72 D4** NR5464.
Na Dromannan *High.* ***Mountain***, 1m/2km SE of Strath Kanaird. Height 1338 feet or 408 metres. **95 J1** NC2001.
Na Glas Leacan *High. Alternative name for Eileanan nan Glas Leac, qv.*
Na Gruagaichean *High.* ***Mountain***, on Mamore Forest in Lochaber district 2m/4km NE of Kinlochleven. Munro: height 3460 feet or 1055 metres. **80 D1** NN2065.
Na h-Uamhachan *High.* ***Mountain***, 4m/7km NE of Glenfinnan, Lochaber district. Height 2266 feet or 691 metres. **87 F6** NM9684.
Na Peileirean ***Sea feature***, stretch of sea to N of Nave Island, 9m/15km NW of Bridgend. **72 A3** NR2976.
Na Torrain *Arg. & B.* ***Island***, one of Torran Rocks group, 4m/6km SW of Mull. **78 D6** NM2613.
Naast *High.* ***Settlement***, on W side of Loch Ewe, in Ross and Cromarty district, 3m/4km NW of Poolewe. **94 E3** NG8283.
Nab Wood *W.Yorks.* ***Suburb***, 1m/2km W of Shipley town centre. SE1237.
Nab's Head *Lancs.* ***Hamlet***, 2m/4km SW of Mellor and 4m/6km W of Blackburn town centre. SD6229.
Naburn *York* ***Village***, on E bank of River Ouse, 4m/6km S of York. 1m/2km S is Bell Hall, house dating from 1680. **58 B5** SE5945.
Nackington *Kent* ***Hamlet***, 2m/3km S of Canterbury. **15 G2** TR1554.
Nacton *Suff.* ***Village***, 5m/8km SE of Ipswich. **35 G4** TM2240.
Nadder *Wilts.* ***River***, rising to E of Shaftesbury and flowing E into River Avon at Salisbury. **10 B1** SU1429.
Nadderwater *Devon* ***Hamlet***, beside Nadder Brook, 2m/3km W of Exeter. SX8993.
Naden Reservoirs *Gt.Man.* ***Lake/loch***, adjoining to N of Greenbooth Reservoir, 3m/5km NW of Rochdale. **49 H1** SD8516.
Nafferton *E.Riding* Population: 1979. ***Village***, 2m/3km NE of Great Driffield. **59 G4** TA0559.
Nailbridge *Glos.* ***Village***, 2m/3km N of Cinderford. **29 F7** SO6416.
Nailsbourne *Som.* ***Hamlet***, 3m/4km N of Taunton. ST2128.
Nailsea *N.Som.* Population: 17,919. ***Town***, former coal-mining town, 7m/11km W of Bristol. **19 H4** ST4770.
Nailstone *Leics.* ***Village***, 5m/7km S of Coalville. **41 G5** SK4107.
Nailstone Wiggs *Leics.* ***Locality***, 1m/2km NE of Nailstone. SK4208.
Nailsworth *Glos.* Population: 5242. ***Small town***, former textile town on hillside 4m/6km S of Stroud. **20 B2** ST8599.
Nairn *High.* ***River***, rising on slopes of Coile Mhòr and flowing NE through Strathnairn to Daviot, and continuing NE to enter Moray Firth at Nairn. **97 F6** NH8857.
Nairn *High.* Population: 7892. ***Small town***, royal burgh and resort in Nairn district, at mouth of River Nairn on S side of Moray Firth, 7m/12km E of Fort George. Former fishing port with harbour built by Thomas Telford. **97 F6** NH8856.
Naked Tam *Angus* ***Mountain***, 4m/6km NE of Dykehead. Height 1607 feet or 490 metres. **83 F1** NO4264.
Nan Bield Pass *Cumb.* ***Other feature of interest***, crossroads of mountain paths, just W of Harter Fell, 1m/2km SW of S end of Haweswater Reservoir. **60 F6** NY4509.
Nancegollan *Cornw.* ***Hamlet***, 3m/5km NW of Helston. **2 D5** SW6332.
Nancekuke *Cornw.* ***Hamlet***, 1m/2km NE of Portreath. SW6745.
Nancledra *Cornw.* ***Hamlet***, 3m/5km S of St. Ives. **2 B5** SW4936.
Nanhoron *Gwyn.* ***Settlement***, 6m/10km SW of Pwllheli. **36 B2** SH2831.
Nannau *Gwyn.* ***Settlement***, 2m/3km NE of Dolgellau. **37 G3** SH7420.
Nannerch *Flints.* ***Village***, 4m/7km S of Holywell. **47 K6** SJ1669.
Nanpantan *Leics.* ***Hamlet***, 3m/4km SW of Loughborough. **41 H4** SK5017.
Nanpean *Cornw.* Population: 1115. ***Village***, in china clay district, 4m/7km NW of St. Austell. **3 G3** SW9656.
Nanstallon *Cornw.* ***Village***, 2m/3km W of Bodmin. **4 A4** SX0367.
Nant Brân *Powys* ***River***, rising on Mynydd Eppynt and flowing SE past Llanfihangel Nant Bran and into River Usk at Aberbran, 4m/6km W of Brecon. **27 J5** SN9829.
Nant Cynnen *Carmar.* ***River***, flowing W and joining River Cywyn 3m/5km W of Carmarthen. **17 G2** SN3321.
Nant-ddu *Powys* ***Settlement***, on Taf Fawr River, 6m/10km NW of Merthyr Tydfil. **27 K7** SO0014.
Nant Ffrancon *Gwyn.* ***Valley***, carrying River Ogwen between Llyn Ogwen and Bethesda. **46 E6** SH6362.
Nant-glas *Powys* ***Hamlet***, 3m/4km SE of Rhayader. **27 J2** SN9965.
Nant Gwared *See Gwydderig.*
Nant Hirin *Powys* ***River***, running from Llyn Cerrigllwydion Uchaf, through Llyn Cerrigllwydion Isaf, to join River Elan 1m/2km NW of head of Craig Goch Reservoir. **27 H1** SN8972.
Nant Mawr *Flints.* ***Suburb***, adjoining to S of Buckley. SJ2763.
Nant Peris *Gwyn.* ***Village***, the old village of Llanberis, 2m/3km SE of the present town. **46 E7** SH6058.
Nant-y-Bwch *B.Gwent* ***Locality***, adjoining to NW of Tredegar. SO1210.
Nant-y-Caws *Shrop.* ***Settlement***, 2m/3km S of Oswestry. SJ2826.
Nant-y-ceisiad *Caerp.* ***Hamlet***, adjoining to W of Machen. ST2089.
Nant-y-deri *Mon. Welsh form of Nant-y-derry, qv.*
Nant-y-derry (Nant-y-deri). *Mon.* ***Hamlet***, 5m/9km S of Abergavenny. **19 G1** SO3306.
Nant-y-dugoed *Powys* ***Settlement***, 5m/8km NE of Aberangell. **37 J4** SH9113.
Nant-y-ffin *Carmar.* ***Locality***, 2m/3km SW of Abergorlech. SN5532.
Nant y Garth Pass *Denb.* ***Other feature of interest***, mountain road pass 3m/5km SE of Llanfair Dyffryn Clwyd. **47 K7** SJ1650.
Nant-y-Gollen *Shrop.* ***Settlement***, 3m/5km W of Oswestry. SJ2428.
Nant-y-groes *Powys* ***Settlement***, 1m/2km NW of Llandrindod Wells. **27 K2** SO0462.
Nant-y-moch Reservoir *Cere.* ***Reservoir***, large reservoir 9m/14km S of Machynlleth. **37 G7** SN7586.
Nant-y-moel *Bridgend* ***Village***, 3m/5km SW of Treorchy. **18 C2** SS9392.
Nant-y-pandy *Conwy* ***Locality***, adjoining to SE of Llanfairfechan. **46 E5** SH6874.
Nant yr Eira *Powys* ***Valley***, carrying River Gam NE from Cwmderwen to E of Dolwen, 4m/7km SW of Llangadfan. **37 J5** SH9606.
Nanternis *Cere.* ***Hamlet***, 2m/4km SW of New Quay. **26 C3** SN3756.
Nantgaredig *Carmar.* ***Village***, 5m/8km E of Carmarthen. **17 H2** SN4921.
Nantgarw *R.C.T.* ***Hamlet***, 2m/4km SW of Caerphilly. **18 E3** ST1185.
Nantglyn *Denb.* ***Hamlet***, 4m/6km SE of Denbigh. **47 J6** SJ0062.
Nantgwyn *Powys* ***Hamlet***, 5m/9km N of Rhayader. SN9776.
Nantgwynant *Gwyn.* ***Valley***, carrying River Glaslyn SW between Llyn Gwynant and Llyn Dinas, 3m/5km NE of Beddgelert. SH6250.
Nantithet *Cornw.* ***Hamlet***, 3m/5km SE of Helston. SW6822.
Nantlle *Gwyn.* ***Settlement***, 3m/4km E of Penygroes. **46 D7** SH5053.
Nantmawr *Shrop.* ***Hamlet***, 1m/2km NE of Llanyblodwel. **38 B3** SJ2524.
Nantmel *Powys* ***Hamlet***, 4m/7km E of Rhayader. **27 K2** SO0366.
Nantmor *Gwyn.* ***Hamlet***, 1m/2km S of Beddgelert. **37 F1** SH6046.
Nantwich *Ches.* Population: 11,695. ***Town***, old town on River Weaver, 4m/7km SW of Crewe. Former centre of salt industry. Many black-and-white houses. **49 F7** SJ6552.
Nantycaws *Carmar.* ***Hamlet***, 3m/4km E of Carmarthen. **17 H3** SN4518.
Nantyffyllon *Bridgend* ***Locality***, 1m/2km N of Maesteg. **18 B2** SS8592.
Nantyglo *B.Gwent* ***Locality***, adjoining to S of Bryn-mawr. **18 E1** SO1910.
Nantygwryd *Gwyn.* ***River***, rising in Llyn Cwmffynnon and flowing E through Llynnau Mymbyr to its confluence with River Llugwy at Capel Curig. **46 E7** SH7157.
Naphill *Bucks.* Population: 2146. ***Village***, 3m/5km N of High Wycombe. **22 B2** SU8496.
Napley Heath *Staffs.* ***Settlement***, 1km N of Mucklestone. SJ7138.
Nappa *N.Yorks.* ***Settlement***, 2m/3km S of Hellifield. **56 D4** SD8553.
Napton Hill *Warks.* ***Hill***, rising to over 150 metres, to W of Napton on the Hill and 3m/4km W of Southam. Windmill on W side. **31 F2** SP4561.
Napton on the Hill *Warks.* ***Village***, 3m/5km E of Southam. Series of locks to SW on Oxford Canal. **31 F2** SP4661.
Nar *Norf.* ***River***, rising S of Tittleshall and flowing W through Narborough and finally N into River Great Ouse at King's Lynn. **44 A4** TF6119.
Narachan Hill *Arg. & B.* ***Hill***, on Kintyre, 4m/6km E of Tayinloan. Height 935 feet or 285 metres. **73 F6** NR7547.
Narberth (Arberth). *Pembs.* Population: 1801. ***Small town***, small market town 10m/16km E of Haverfordwest and 9m/14km N of Tenby. Remnants of 13c castle. Good Georgian architecture. **16 E3** SN1014.
Narberth Bridge *Pembs.* ***Locality***, adjoining to S of Narberth. SN1014.
Narborough *Leics.* Population: 6360. ***Village***, 5m/9km SW of Leicester. **41 H6** SP5497.
Narborough *Norf.* ***Village***, 5m/8km NW of Swaffham. **44 B4** TF7413.
Nare Head *Cornw.* ***Coastal feature***, headland (National Trust) on S coast of E end of Gerrans Bay. **3 G5** SW9136.
Nare Point *Cornw.* ***Coastal feature***, headland at NE corner of Meneage district, 5m/8km S of Falmouth across bay. **3 F6** SW8024.
Narford *Norf.* ***Locality***, 5m/7km NW of Swaffham. TF7613.
Narkurs *Cornw.* ***Settlement***, 7m/12km W of Torpoint. SX3255.
Narrachan *Arg. & B.* ***Settlement***, 4m/7km E of Kilmelford, to N of Loch Avich. **80 A6** NM9114.
Narrows of Raasay *High.* ***Sea feature***, strait between Skye and Raasay at S end of Sound of Raasay. Width just over 1km. **86 B1** NG5435.
Nasareth *Gwyn.* ***Hamlet***, 1m/2km S of Llanllyfni. **46 C7** SH4750.
Naseby *Northants.* ***Village***, 6m/10km SW of Market Harborough. 1m/2km N is site of Civil War battle, 1645. **31 H1** SP6878.
Naseby Reservoir *Northants.* ***Reservoir***, to W of Naseby. **31 H1** SP6878.
Nash *Bucks.* ***Village***, 6m/9km E of Buckingham. **31 J5** SP7834.
Nash *Here.* ***Settlement***, 1m/2km S of Presteigne. **28 C2** SO3062.
Nash *Kent* ***Settlement***, 2m/3km NE of Wingham. TR2658.
Nash (Trefonnen). *Newport* ***Village***, 4m/6km SE of Newport. **19 G3** ST3483.
Nash *Shrop.* ***Village***, 2m/4km N of Tenbury Wells. **28 E1** SO6071.
Nash *V. of Glam.* ***Settlement***, 2m/3km SW of Cowbridge. **18 C4** SS9672.
Nash Lee *Bucks.* ***Settlement***, 2m/3km W of Wendover. **22 B1** SP8408.
Nash Point *V. of Glam.* ***Coastal feature***, headland 3m/5km W of Llantwit Major. **18 B5** SS9168.
Nash Street *Kent* ***Settlement***, 3m/5km S of Gravesend. TQ6469.
Nash's Green *Hants.* ***Hamlet***, 5m/8km SE of Basingstoke. SU6745.
Nassington *Northants.* ***Village***, 2m/3km S of Wansford. **42 D6** TL0696.
Nast Hyde *Herts.* ***Suburb***, 2m/3km W of Hatfield town centre. TL2007.
Nasty *Herts.* ***Village***, 2m/3km W of Puckeridge. **33 G6** TL3524.
Nateby *Cumb.* ***Village***, 1m/2km S of Kirkby Stephen. **61 J6** NY7706.
Nateby *Lancs.* ***Hamlet***, 2m/3km W of Garstang. **55 H5** SD4644.
Nately Scures *Hants.* ***Settlement***, 1m/2km SW of Hook. **22 A6** SU7053.
National Coal Mining Museum *W.Yorks.* ***Other feature of interest***, 1km SW of Middlestown. One of Britain's oldest working mine shafts, with exhibits on 19c conditions. **50 E1** SE2516.
National Exhibition Centre *W.Mid.* ***Other feature of interest***, exhibition and conference centre with 16 halls covering 158,000 square metres, to E of Birmingham International Airport. Hosts over 150 trade and public exhibitions annually, including British International Motor Show, Crufts and Clothes Show Live. **40 D7** SP1983.
National Film Theatre *Gt.Lon. See South Bank Arts Centre.*
National Gallery *Gt.Lon.* ***Leisure/recreation***, gallery built 1838 by W. Wilkins in Trafalgar Square, City of Westminster, to W of Charing Cross. Houses national collection of Western European painting, comprising over 2000 pictures dating from 13c to early 20c. Exhibits are rich in early Italian, Dutch and Flemish, Spanish 15c-18c, British 18c-19c and Impressionist works. Sainsbury Wing by R. Venturi, 1991. TQ2980.
National Gallery of Modern Art *Edin.* ***Other feature of interest***, 1m/2km W of Edinburgh city centre, with 20c paintings, and sculptures in the park outside. Artists include Vuillard, Bonnard, Matisse, Léger and Picasso. **76 A3** NT2373.

National Horseracing Museum *Suff.* ***Other feature of interest***, in Newmarket. Equine tours, exhibitions and art gallery. **33 K2** TL6263.
National Maritime Museum *Gt.Lon.* ***Leisure/recreation***, museum in borough of Greenwich, to S of Greenwich Park. Fine maritime collection of paintings, navigational instruments, costumes and weapons. Exhibition on Nelson's epic life and death. Permanent gallery on global seapower with paintings, watercolours, ship models, photographs and medals. TQ3877.
National Motor Museum *Hants.* ***Other feature of interest***, in Beaulieu. Wheels exhibition, motoring memorabilia, a monorail, and a gallery in 16c house with a monastic life exhibition. **10 E4** SU3802.
National Motorcycle Museum *W.Mid.* ***Other feature of interest***, museum at junction 6 of M42, 1m/2km SE of Birmingham International Airport, exhibiting over 650 machines from last hundred years. **40 E7** SP2082.
National Portrait Gallery *Gt.Lon.* ***Leisure/recreation***, art gallery adjacent to National Gallery, City of Westminster, to W of Charing Cross. Historic collection, founded 1856, of contemporary portraits of famous British men and women. Primary collection has over 9000 portraits, all arranged chronologically from medieval period to present day. First floor now taken up by post-war portraits, photography and video galleries. TQ2980.
National Railway Museum *York* ***Other feature of interest***, museum in York, including old steam locomotives and Queen Victoria's personal carriage. **58 B4** SE5951.
National Waterways Museum *Glos.* ***Other feature of interest***, showing history and development of Britain's waterways. Located in Gloucester Docks, to SW of Gloucester city centre. **29 H7** SO8218.
Natland *Cumb.* ***Village***, 2m/4km S of Kendal. **55 J1** SD5289.
Natural History Museum and Geological Museum *Gt.Lon.* ***Leisure/recreation***, museum in borough of Kensington & Chelsea, 3m/4km SW of Charing Cross. Consists of Life Galleries and Earth Galleries. Life Galleries include skeletons, dinosaurs, exhibits on human biology, marine invertebrates, meteorites and arthropods. Earth Galleries include displays on Earth's resources, Britain's fossils and minerals. TQ2679.
Naughton *Suff.* ***Hamlet***, 4m/7km N of Hadleigh. **34 E4** TM0248.
Naunton *Glos.* ***Village***, 5m/8km W of Stow-on-the-Wold. Restored dovecote. **30 C6** SP1123.
Naunton *Worcs.* ***Village***, 4m/7km N of Tewkesbury. **29 H5** SO8739.
Naunton Beauchamp *Worcs.* ***Village***, 4m/7km N of Pershore. **29 J3** SO9652.
Naunton Dovecote *Glos.* ***Other feature of interest***, at Naunton, 3m/5km NW of Bourton-on-the-Water. Believed to date from 15c and built from rubble with a stone roof; restored in 1949. **30 C6** SP1123.
Navax Point *Cornw.* ***Coastal feature***, headland (National Trust) on N coast nearly 1m/2km E of Godrevy Point and 4m/7km NW of Camborne. **2 C4** SW5943.
Nave Island *Arg. & B.* ***Island***, small island off Ardnave Point on N coast of Islay, on W side of entrance to Loch Gruinart. **72 A3** NR2875.
Navenby *Lincs.* ***Village***, 9m/14km S of Lincoln. **52 C7** SK9857.
Naver *High.* ***River***, in Caithness district running N from Loch Naver down Strathnaver to Torrisdale Bay on N coast. **104 C3** NC6962.
Naver Rock *High.* ***Hill***, 2m/3km S of Bettyhill, Caithness district. Height 554 feet or 169 metres. **103 J3** NC7059.
Navestock *Essex* ***Hamlet***, 4m/7km NW of Brentwood. **23 J2** TQ5397.
Navestock Side *Essex* ***Village***, 1m/2km E of Navestock. **23 J2** TQ5397.
Navidale *High.* ***Settlement***, just N of Helmsdale. **105 F7** ND0316.
Navio *Derbys. See Brough.*
Navity *High.* ***Settlement***, 2m/3km S of Cromarty. **96 E5** NH7865.
Naworth Castle *Cumb.* ***Historic house***, mansion in park 2m/4km E of Brampton, on site of 14c castle of which little remains. **70 A7** NY5662.
Nawton *N.Yorks.* ***Village***, 3m/4km E of Helmsley. **58 C1** SE6584.
Nayland *Suff.* ***Small town***, on River Stour 6m/10km N of Colchester. Many old houses. Church contains painting by Constable. **34 D5** TL9734.
Nazeing *Essex* ***Village***, 3m/5km SW of Harlow. **23 H1** TL4106.
Nazeing Gate *Essex* ***Hamlet***, 1m/2km S of Nazeing. TL4105.
Nazeing Long Green *Essex* ***Hamlet***, 1m/2km SW of Nazeing. TL4004.
Neacroft *Hants.* ***Hamlet***, 3m/5km NE of Christchurch. **10 C5** SZ1896.
Nealhouse *Cumb.* ***Locality***, 2m/3km W of Dalston. NY3351.
Neal's Green *Warks.* ***Locality***, 4m/6km N of Coventry. **41 F7** SP3384.
Neap *Shet.* ***Settlement***, 1km E of Housabister, Mainland. **109 E7** HU5058.
Neap House *N.Lincs.* ***Settlement***, on E bank of River Trent, 3m/4km NW of Scunthorpe. SE8613.
Neap of Skea *Shet.* ***Coastal feature***, headland 1km SE of Housetter, Mainland. **108 C4** HU3783.
Near Sawrey *Cumb.* ***Village***, 1km W of Far Sawrey and 2m/3km SE of Hawkshead. About half the village is owned by the National Trust, including house of Beatrix Potter. **60 E7** SD3795.
Nearton End *Bucks.* ***Settlement***, adjoining to SE of Swanbourne, 2m/4km E of Winslow. SP8027.
Neasden *Gt.Lon.* ***Suburb***, in borough of Brent, 7m/11km NW of Charing Cross. TQ2185.
Neasham *Darl.* ***Village***, on River Tees, 4m/6km SE of Darlington. **62 E5** NZ3210.
Neat Enstone *Oxon.* ***Settlement***, just S of Enstone. SP3724.
Neath (Nedd). *N.P.T.* ***River***, rising in Black Mountains SW of Brecon, flowing SW down Vale of Neath to town of Neath and into Bristol Channel at Baglan Bay. SS7292.
Neath (Castell-nedd). *N.P.T.* Population: 45,965. ***Town***, on River Neath, on site of Roman fort of Nidum, 8m/12km NE of Swansea. Neath Abbey (Cadw) 1m/2km W. Penscynor Wildlife Park is now a major tourist attraction. **18 A2** SS7597.
Neath Abbey *N.P.T.* ***Ecclesiastical building***, ruins of abbey founded in 1130 (Cadw), 1km W of Neath. **18 A2** SS7497.
Neatham *Hants.* ***Hamlet***, 2m/3km NE of Alton. **22 A7** SU7440.
Neatishead *Norf.* ***Village***, 4m/6km NE of Wroxham. **45 H3** TG3421.
Neaton *Norf.* ***Locality***, 1km N of Watton. TF9101.
Neaty Burn *High.* ***River***, flowing SE between Carn Bàn and Beinn a' Bha'ach Ard, and into River Farrar 2m/4km SW of Erchless Castles. **95 K7** NH3739.
Neave Island (Also known as Coomb Island.) *High.* ***Island***, small uninhabited island off N coast of Caithness district opposite Skerray. **103 J2** NC6664.
Neb *I.o.M.* ***River***, rising on central mountains E of Little London and running through that locality, then SW down Glen Helen to St. John's, then NW to Peel and Peel Bay. **54 C5** SC2484.
Neban Point *Ork.* ***Coastal feature***, headland on W coast of Mainland, 3m/5km NW of Stromness. **107 B6** HY2113.
Nebo *Cere.* ***Settlement***, 1km N of Cross Inn. **26 E2** SN5465.
Nebo *Conwy* ***Hamlet***, 4m/7km SE of Llanrwst. **47 G7** SH8356.
Nebo *Gwyn.* ***Hamlet***, 1m/2km SE of Llanllyfni. **46 C7** SH4750.
Nebo *I.o.A.* ***Hamlet***, on Anglesey, 2m/4km SE of Amlwch. **46 C3** SH4690.
Nechells *W.Mid.* ***Suburb***, 3m/4km NE of Birmingham city centre. SP0989.
Nechtansmere *Angus See Dunnichen.*
Necton *Norf.* Population: 1819. ***Village***, 4m/6km E of Swaffham. **44 C5** TF8709.
Nedd *High.* ***Village***, at head of Loch Nedd, 1m/2km SE of Drumbeg, W coast of Sutherland district. **102 D5** NC1331.
Nedd *N.P.T. Welsh form of Neath (river), qv.*
Nedderton *Northumb.* ***Village***, 1m/2km W of Bedlington. **71 H5** NZ2381.
Nedging *Suff.* ***Hamlet***, 4m/6km NW of Hadleigh. TL9948.
Nedging Tye *Suff.* ***Hamlet***, 2m/3km NE of Nedging. **34 E4** TL9948.
Needham *Norf.* ***Village***, 2m/3km SW of Harleston. **45 G7** TM2281.
Needham Market *Suff.* Population: 4312. ***Small town***, on River Gipping, 3m/5km SE of Stowmarket. Noted for superb carvings on church ceiling. **34 E3** TM0855.
Needham Street *Suff.* ***Settlement***, 5m/8km E of Newmarket. TL7265.
Needingworth *Cambs.* Population: 1808. ***Village***, 2m/3km E of St. Ives. **33 G1** TL3472.
Needle Rock *Pembs.* ***Island***, rock on SE side of Dinas Head. SN0140.
Needles Eye *Northumb.* ***Coastal feature***, rock formation on coast, 2m/3km N of Berwick-upon-Tweed. **77 H5** NT9955.
Needles Pleasure Park *I.o.W.* ***Leisure/recreation***, amusement park above Alum Bay, 1m/2km E of The Needles Old Battery and 1m/2km SW of Totland. Includes model railway and working pottery. **10 E6** SZ3185.
Needs Law *Sc.Bord.* ***Mountain***, in Wauchope Forest area of Cheviot Hills, 1m/2km SE of Note o' the Gate. Height 1456 feet or 444 metres. **70 B3** NT6002.
Needwood *Staffs.* ***Settlement***, 4m/6km W of Burton upon Trent. SK1724.
Needwood Forest *Staffs.* ***Forest/woodland***, former hunting forest to W of Needwood. **40 D3** SK1724.
Neen Savage *Shrop.* ***Village***, 1m/2km N of Cleobury Mortimer. **29 F1** SO6777.
Neen Sollars *Shrop.* ***Village***, 5m/8km NE of Tenbury Wells. **29 F1** SO6672.
Neenton *Shrop.* ***Village***, 6m/10km SW of Bridgnorth. **39 F7** SO6387.
Nefyn *Gwyn.* Population: 1987. ***Village***, and resort on cliff above Porth Nefyn, Caernarfon Bay, 6m/9km NW of Pwllheli. **36 C1** SH3040.
Neidpath Castle *Sc.Bord.* ***Castle***, 14c-16c L-plan tower house, on N bank of River Tweed, 1km W of Peebles. **76 A7** NT2340.
Neighbourne *Som.* ***Hamlet***, just E of Ashwick, 3m/5km NE of Shepton Mallet. ST6448.
Neilston *E.Renf.* Population: 5260. ***Small town***, 2m/3km SW of Barrhead. **74 C5** NS4757.
Neilston Pad *E.Renf.* ***Hill***, rising to over 260 metres, 1m/2km S of Neilston. Craggy rocks on E face. **74 C5** NS4755.
Neist Point *High.* ***Coastal feature***, headland with lighthouse on W coast of Skye, 8m/13km W of Dunvegan. Most westerly point of Skye. **93 G7** NG1246.
Neithrop *Oxon.* ***Suburb***, W district of Banbury. SP4440.
Nelly's Moss Lakes *Northumb.* ***Lake/loch***, two adjacent lakes 1m/2km E of Rothbury. **71 F3** NU0702.
Nelson *Caerp.* Population: 5654. ***Village***, 2m/3km W of Ystrad Mynach. **18 E2** ST1195.
Nelson *Lancs.* Population: 29,120. ***Town***, former cotton town, 4m/6km N of Burnley. **56 D6** SD8537.
Nelson Village *Northumb.* ***Locality***, adjoining to NW of Cramlington. **71 H6** NZ2577.
Nemphlar *S.Lan.* ***Settlement***, 2m/3km W of Lanark. **75 G6** NS8544.
Nempnett Thrubwell *B. & N.E.Som.* ***Village***, 2m/3km SW of Chew Stoke. **19 J5** ST5360.
Nene *River*, rising about 3m/5km SW of Daventry and flowing E past Northampton and Wellingborough, then NE through Oundle and Peterborough, and across the Fens to Wisbech, Sutton Bridge and The Wash. **43 G7** TF4926.
Nene Valley Railway ***Other feature of interest***, tourist railway running 15m/24km E from Yarwell Junction through Wansford tunnel, past railway's headquarters at Wansford Station and on to Peterborough. **42 E6** TL0997.
Nenthall *Cumb.* ***Settlement***, 2m/3km NW of Nenthead. **61 J2** NY7545.
Nenthead *Cumb.* ***Village***, 4m/7km SE of Alston. **61 J2** NY7843.
Nenthorn *Sc.Bord.* ***Village***, 4m/6km NW of Kelso. **76 E7** NT6837.
Neopardy *Devon* ***Hamlet***, 3m/5km W of Crediton. SX7998.
Neptune's Staircase *High.* ***Other feature of interest***, 2m/3km N of Fort William. A flight of eight locks built 1805-22, raising Caledonian Canal a total of 64 feet or 20 metres. **87 H7** NN1077.
Nercwys *Flints.* ***Village***, 2m/3km S of Mold. **48 B6** SJ2360.
Nereabolls *Arg. & B.* ***Settlement***, on S coast of Rinns of Islay, 3m/4km SW of Port Charlotte. **72 A5** NR2255.
Neriby *Arg. & B.* ***Settlement***, on Islay, 2m/3km E of Bridgend. **72 B4** NR3660.
Nerston *S.Lan.* ***Suburb***, to N of East Kilbride town centre. **74 E5** NS6456.
Nesbit *Northumb.* ***Settlement***, 1m/2km NW of Doddington. **77 H7** NT9833.
Nesbitt *Dur.* ***Hamlet***, 2m/3km E of Hutton Henry. NZ4536.
Nesfield *N.Yorks.* ***Hamlet***, 2m/3km NW of Ilkley across River Wharfe. SE0949.
Ness *Ches.* ***Locality***, 1m/2km SE of Neston. **48 C5** SJ3076.
Ness *High.* ***River***, flowing from Loch Dochfour at NE end of Loch Ness, NE through Inverness and into Moray Firth at South Kessock. NH6646.
Ness *W.Isles* ***Locality***, 3m/5km S of Butt of Lewis. **101 H1** NB5261.
Ness Botanic Gardens *Ches.* ***Garden***, 1m/2km SE of Neston and 10m/16km NW of Chester. Owned by University of Liverpool. Wide variety of trees and plants; heather and herb gardens; bulb meadow; rose garden showing evolution of rose family. **48 C5** SJ3075.
Ness Glen *E.Ayr.* ***Valley***, steep-sided wooded valley carrying River Doon N to Dalmellington from N arm of Loch Doon. **67 J3** NS4703.
Ness Head *High.* ***Coastal feature***, headland on E coast of Caithness district, 5m/7km S of Duncansby Head. **105 J2** ND3866.
Ness of Burgi *Shet.* ***Coastal feature***, headland on W side of West Voe of Sumburgh, opposite Sumburgh Head. Ancient fort (Historic Scotland). **109 F10** HU3808.
Ness of Duncansby *High.* ***Coastal feature***, headland on N coast of Caithness district, 1m/2km W of Duncansby Head. **105 J1** ND3873.
Ness of Litter *High.* ***Coastal feature***, headland on N coast of Caithness district, 3m/5km NW of Thurso. **105 F1** ND0771.
Ness of Ork *Ork.* ***Coastal feature***, headland at NE end of Shapinsay. **106 E5** HY5422.
Ness of Sound *Shet.* ***Coastal feature***, headland with lighthouse on W coast of Yell, 4m/6km S of West Sandwick. **108 D4** HU4482.
Ness of Tenston *Ork.* ***Settlement***, on headland, on W shore of Loch of Harray, Mainland. **107 B6** HY2816.
Ness Point (Also known as North Cheek.) *N.Yorks.* ***Coastal feature***, headland on North Sea coast, 1m/2km NE of Robin Hood's Bay. **63 J2** NZ9506.
Nesscliffe *Shrop.* ***Village***, 8m/13km NW of Shrewsbury. **38 C4** SJ3819.
Nesting *Shet.* ***Locality***, on Mainland, consisting of North and South Nesting and enclosing South Nesting Bay on E coast. HU4554.
Neston *Ches.* Population: 15,585. ***Town***, market town on Wirral peninsula, 7m/11km W of Ellesmere Port. Rare plants in Ness Botanic Gardens, part of Liverpool University. Four-storey windmill. **48 B5** SJ2977.
Neston *Wilts.* ***Village***, 2m/3km S of Corsham. **20 B5** ST8668.
Netchwood *Shrop.* ***Settlement***, 6m/9km W of Bridgnorth. SO6291.
Nether Alderley *Ches.* ***Village***, 2m/3km S of Alderley Edge. Restored 15c water-powered corn-mill (NT). **49 H5** SJ8476.
Nether Alderley Mill *Ches.* ***Other feature of interest***, 15c water-powered corn-mill (National Trust) with waterwheels, timberwork and Victorian machinery, situated in Nether Alderley. **49 H5** SJ8476.
Nether Auchendrane *S.Ayr.* ***Settlement***, 3m/5km S of Ayr. **67 H2** NS3416.
Nether Barr *D. & G.* ***Settlement***, 1m/2km S of Newton Stewart. **64 E4** NX4263.
Nether Blainslie *Sc.Bord.* ***Hamlet***, 3m/4km SE of Lauder. **76 D6** NT5443.
Nether Boyndlie *Aber.* ***Settlement***, forms locality of Boyndlie with Upper Boyndlie, near N coast, 5m/9km SW of Fraserburgh. NJ9263.
Nether Broughton *Leics.* ***Village***, 6m/9km NW of Melton Mowbray. **41 J3** SK6925.
Nether Burrow *Lancs.* ***Hamlet***, 2m/4km S of Kirkby Lonsdale. **56 B2** SD6175.
Nether Cerne *Dorset* ***Hamlet***, 2m/3km S of Cerne Abbas. **9 F5** SY6798.
Nether Compton *Dorset* ***Village***, 3m/5km E of Yeovil. **8 E3** ST5917.
Nether Crimond *Aber.* ***Settlement***, 4m/6km E of Inverurie. **91 G2** NJ8222.
Nether Dalgliesh *Sc.Bord.* ***Settlement***, 3m/5km S of Ettrick on Tima Water. **69 H3** NT2709.
Nether Dallachy *Moray* ***Village***, near N coast, 4m/6km W of Buckie. **98 B4** NJ3663.
Nether Edge *S.Yorks.* ***Suburb***, 2m/3km SW of Sheffield city centre. SK3484.

N

Nether End *Derbys.* ***Hamlet***, adjoining to S of Over End, at N edge of Chatsworth Park, 3m/5km NE of Bakewell. **50 E5** SK2572.
Nether End *W.Yorks.* ***Settlement***, 1m/2km E of Denby Dale. SE2407.
Nether Exe *Devon* ***Hamlet***, on River Exe, 5m/8km N of Exeter. **7 H6** SS9300.
Nether Glasslaw *Aber.* ***Settlement***, 3m/4km SW of New Aberdour. **99 G5** NJ8659.
Nether Hall *Suff.* ***Historic house***, on E side of Cavendish. 15c hall, now museum and gallery, with a vineyard. **34 C4** TL8146.
Nether Hambleton *Rut. See Rutland Water.*
Nether Handley *Derbys.* ***Hamlet***, to S of Middle Handley, 4m/6km NE of Chesterfield. SK4077.
Nether Handwick *Angus* ***Hamlet***, 3m/5km S of Glamis. **82 E3** NO3641.
Nether Haugh *S.Yorks.* ***Village***, 3m/4km N of Rotherham. **51 G3** SK4196.
Nether Headon *Notts.* ***Hamlet***, 1km N of Headon. **51 K5** SK7477.
Nether Heage *Derbys.* ***Village***, 1km W of Heage. SK3750.
Nether Heselden *N.Yorks.* ***Settlement***, in Littondale, 3m/5km NW of Arncliffe. **56 D2** SD8874.
Nether Heyford *Northants.* Population: 1650. ***Village***, 6m/10km W of Northampton. Site of Roman building to E. **31 H3** SP6658.
Nether Kellet *Lancs.* ***Village***, 2m/3km S of Carnforth. **55 J3** SD5068.
Nether Kinmundy *Aber.* ***Settlement***, 6m/9km W of Peterhead. **99 J6** NK0443.
Nether Langwith *Notts.* Population: 3133. ***Village***, 6m/10km N of Mansfield. **51 H5** SK5370.
Nether Lenshie *Aber.* ***Settlement***, 4m/6km NW of Rothienorman. **98 E6** NJ6840.
Nether Levens *Cumb.* ***Locality***, 1km S of Levens. SD4886.
Nether Loads *Derbys.* ***Settlement***, 4m/6km SW of Chesterfield. SK3269.
Nether Lypiatt *Glos.* ***Locality***, forms parish of Bisley-with-Lypiatt, along with Middle Lypiatt and Lypiatt Park, on E side of Stroud. SO8703.
Nether Moor *Derbys.* ***Settlement***, 3m/5km S of Chesterfield. **51 F6** SK3866.
Nether Newton *Cumb.* ***Settlement***, 1km SE of High Newton. SD4082.
Nether Padley *Derbys.* ***Village***, 2m/4km SE of Hathersage. **50 E5** SK2578.
Nether Pitforthie *Aber.* ***Settlement***, 3m/5km SE of Glenbervie. **91 G7** NO8179.
Nether Poppleton *York* Population: 1681. ***Village***, on River Ouse, 3m/5km NW of York. **58 B4** SE5654.
Nether Row *Cumb.* ***Locality***, 1m/2km S of Caldbeck. NY3237.
Nether Silton *N.Yorks.* ***Village***, 6m/9km E of Northallerton. **63 F7** SE4592.
Nether Skyborry *Shrop.* ***Settlement***, 1m/2km NW of Knighton. SO2773.
Nether Stowey *Som.* ***Village***, at foot of Quantock Hills, 10m/16km W of Bridgwater. Coleridge's cottage (National Trust), where the poet lived from 1797 to 1800. **7 K2** ST1939.
Nether Street *Essex* ***Settlement***, 1m/2km SW of Leaden Roding. TL5812.
Nether Urquhart *Fife* ***Settlement***, 2m/3km SW of Strathmiglo. **82 C7** NO1808.
Nether Wallop *Hants.* ***Village***, 4m/6km W of Stockbridge. **10 E1** SU3036.
Nether Wasdale *Cumb.* ***Village***, 1m/2km E of S end of Wast Water and 4m/6km E of Gosforth. **60 C6** NY1204.
Nether Wellwood *E.Ayr.* ***Settlement***, 3m/5km SW of Muirkirk. **68 B1** NS6526.
Nether Welton *Cumb.* ***Hamlet***, 1km N of Welton. NY3545.
Nether Westcote *Glos.* ***Hamlet***, 4m/7km SE of Stow-on-the-Wold. SP2220.
Nether Whitacre *Warks.* ***Village***, 3m/5km NE of Coleshill. **40 E6** SP2392.
Nether Winchendon *Bucks. Alternative name for Lower Winchendon, qv.*
Nether Woodhouse *Derbys.* ***Locality***, to NW of Over Woodhouse and 1m/2km NW of Bolsover. SK4771.
Nether Worton *Oxon.* ***Hamlet***, 3m/4km W of Deddington. **31 F5** SP4230.
Nether Yeadon *W.Yorks.* ***Suburb***, to SW of Yeadon. SE2040.
Netheravon *Wilts.* ***Village***, on River Avon, 5m/7km N of Amesbury. 18c dovecot (English Heritage). **20 E7** SU1448.
Netherbrae *Aber.* ***Settlement***, near N coast, 3m/5km S of Gardenstown. Locality of Overbrae to E. **99 F5** NJ7959.
Netherbrough *Ork.* ***Settlement***, on Mainland, 4m/6km NW of Finstown. **107 C6** HY3116.
Netherburn *S.Lan.* ***Settlement***, 3m/5km N of Blackwood. **75 G6** NS8047.
Netherbury *Dorset* ***Village***, 1m/2km S of Beaminster. **8 D5** SY4799.
Netherby *Cumb.* ***Settlement***, in valley of River Esk, 2m/3km NE of Longtown. Site of Roman fort of Castra Exploratorum. **69 J6** NY3971.
Netherby *N.Yorks.* ***Hamlet***, on N bank of River Wharfe, 5m/8km W of Wetherby. **57 J5** SE3346.
Nethercott *Devon* ***Hamlet***, 6m/9km NW of Barnstaple. SS4839.
Nethercott *Oxon.* ***Village***, 4m/6km NE of Woodstock. **31 F6** SP4820.
Netherend *Glos.* ***Village***, 3m/5km SW of Lydney. **19 J2** SO5900.
Netherfield *E.Suss.* ***Village***, 3m/5km NW of Battle. **14 C6** TQ7118.
Netherfield *Notts.* ***Locality***, adjoining to SE of Carlton. **41 J1** SK6240.
Netherfield *S.Lan.* ***Locality***, 2m/3km NE of Strathaven. **75 F6** NS7245.
Nethergate *N.Lincs.* ***Locality***, adjoining to S of Westwoodside. SK7599.
Netherhall *N.Ayr.* ***Settlement***, 1km N of Largs across Noddsdale Water. **74 A4** NS2060.
Netherhampton *Wilts.* ***Village***, 2m/4km W of Salisbury across valley of River Nadder. **10 C1** SU1029.
Netherhay *Dorset* ***Hamlet***, 3m/5km SW of Crewkerne. ST4105.
Netherland Green *Staffs.* ***Settlement***, 2m/3km SE of Uttoxeter. SK1030.
Netherley *Aber.* ***Locality***, 4m/7km S of Peterculter. **91 G5** NO8493.
Nethermill *D. & G.* ***Settlement***, 4m/6km NW of Lochmaben. **69 F5** NY0487.
Nethermuir *Aber.* ***Settlement***, 2m/3km SE of New Deer. **99 H6** NJ9044.
Netheroyd Hill *W.Yorks.* ***Suburb***, 2m/3km N of Huddersfield town centre. SE1419.
Netherseal *Derbys.* ***Village***, 4m/7km S of Swadlincote. **40 E4** SK2812.
Nethershield *E.Ayr.* ***Settlement***, 2m/3km E of Sorn. **67 K1** NS5826.
Netherstreet *Wilts.* ***Hamlet***, 3m/5km NW of Devizes. **20 C5** ST9865.
Netherthird *D. & G.* ***Settlement***, 1m/2km N of Tongland, on E side of Tongland Loch. **65 H5** NX7155.
Netherthird *E.Ayr.* ***Village***, 1m/2km SE of Cumnock. **67 K2** NS5718.
Netherthong *W.Yorks.* ***Village***, 1m/2km N of Holmfirth. **50 D2** SE1309.
Netherthorpe *Derbys.* ***Suburb***, E district of Staveley. SK4474.
Netherthorpe *S.Yorks.* ***Settlement***, 3m/5km NW of Worksop. **51 H4** SK5380.
Netherton *Angus* ***Hamlet***, 4m/6km W of Brechin. **83 G2** NO5457.
Netherton *Ches.* ***Settlement***, to SW of Frodsham. **48 E5** SJ5077.
Netherton *Cumb.* ***Suburb***, in E part of Maryport. NY0335.
Netherton *Devon* ***Hamlet***, 2m/3km E of Newton Abbot. **5 J3** SX8971.
Netherton *Hants.* ***Settlement***, 3m/5km N of Hurstbourne Tarrant. SU3757.
Netherton *Mersey.* ***Suburb***, 4m/6km NE of Bootle town centre. **48 C2** SD3500.
Netherton *N.Lan.* ***Village***, 1m/2km SW of Wishaw. NS7854.
Netherton *Northumb.* ***Hamlet***, 6m/9km NW of Rothbury. **70 E3** NT9807.
Netherton *Oxon.* ***Locality***, adjoining to N of Fyfield, 5m/8km W of Abingdon. **21 H2** SU4199.
Netherton *P. & K.* ***Settlement***, just N of Bridge of Cally. **82 C2** NO1452.
Netherton *S.Lan.* ***Settlement***, 2m/3km SW of Forth. **75 H5** NS9250.
Netherton *W.Mid.* ***Suburb***, 1m/2km S of Dudley town centre. **40 B7** SO9388.
Netherton *W.Yorks.* ***Suburb***, 3m/4km SW of Huddersfield town centre. SE1213.
Netherton *W.Yorks.* Population: 2437. ***Village***, 2m/3km SW of Horbury. **50 E1** SE2716.
Netherton *Worcs.* ***Hamlet***, 3m/5km SW of Evesham. **29 J4** SO9941.
Netherton Burnfoot *Northumb.* ***Settlement***, 1km SE of Netherton. NT9907.
Netherton Colliery *Northumb.* ***Locality***, 1m/2km NW of Bedlington. NZ2482.
Netherton Northside *Northumb.* ***Settlement***, to NE of Netherton. NT9807.
Nethertown *Cumb.* ***Hamlet***, near coast, 2m/4km SW of Egremont. **60 A6** NX9907.
Nethertown *High.* ***Settlement***, near N end of Island of Stroma, in Pentland Firth. **105 J1** ND3578.
Nethertown *Lancs.* ***Locality***, 1km NW of Whalley. SD7236.
Nethertown *Staffs.* ***Hamlet***, 1m/2km NW of King's Bromley. SK1017.
Netherwitton *Northumb.* ***Village***, on River Font, 7m/11km NW of Morpeth. Hall probably early 18c. **71 G5** NZ1090.
Netherwood *D. & G.* ***Settlement***, 2m/3km S of Dumfries. **65 K3** NX9872.
Netherwood *E.Ayr.* ***Settlement***, on N bank of Greenock Water, 2m/4km NW of Muirkirk. **68 B1** NS6628.
Nethy *High.* ***River***, in Badenoch and Strathspey district, rising in Cairngorm Mountains and running N to River Spey 4m/7km SW of Grantown-on-Spey. **89 H3** NH9922.
Nethy Bridge *High.* ***Village***, on River Nethy, 1m/2km above mouth. **89 H2** NH9922.
Netley *Hants.* Population: 6327. ***Village***, on E bank of Southampton Water, 2m/3km below mouth of River Itchen. Remains of 13c abbey (English Heritage). Tudor castle converted into mansion in 19c. **11 F4** SU4508.
Netley Abbey *Hants.* ***Ecclesiastical building***, founded by Cistercians at Netley in 1239, now a striking ruin (English Heritage). **11 F4** SU4508.
Netley Marsh *Hants.* Population: 1271. ***Village***, 2m/3km W of Totton. **10 E3** SU3313.
Nettle Hill *Cumb.* ***Mountain***, 4m/6km W of Kirkby Stephen. Height 1253 feet or 382 metres. **61 J6** NY7007.
Nettlebed *Oxon.* ***Village***, 5m/7km NW of Henley-on-Thames. **22 A3** SU7086.
Nettlebridge *Som.* ***Hamlet***, 1km E of Ashwick and 4m/6km NE of Shepton Mallet. **19 K7** ST6448.
Nettlecombe *Dorset* ***Hamlet***, just S of Powerstock, 4m/6km NE of Bridport. **8 E5** SY5195.
Nettlecombe *I.o.W.* ***Settlement***, 3m/4km W of Ventnor. SZ5278.
Nettlecombe *Som.* ***Hamlet***, on edge of Exmoor National Park, 4m/6km S of Watchet. **7 J2** ST0537.
Nettleden *Herts.* ***Village***, 3m/4km NE of Berkhamsted. **32 D7** TL0210.
Nettleham *Lincs.* Population: 3152. ***Village***, 3m/5km NE of Lincoln. **52 D5** TF0075.
Nettlehope Hill *Northumb.* ***Mountain***, in Kidland Forest, 4m/6km NW of Alwinton. Height 1558 feet or 475 metres. **70 D2** NT8911.
Nettlestead *Kent* ***Village***, on River Medway, 5m/7km N of Paddock Wood. **23 K6** TQ6852.
Nettlestead *Suff.* ***Settlement***, 1km N of Somersham. **34 E4** TM0849.
Nettlestead Green *Kent* ***Village***, 1m/2km S of Nettlestead. **23 K6** TQ6852.
Nettlestone *I.o.W.* ***Village***, near NE coast, 3m/4km SE of Ryde. **11 H5** SZ6290.
Nettlestone Point *I.o.W.* ***Coastal feature***, headland on NE coast, to N of Nettlestone and 3m/4km E of Ryde. **11 H5** SZ6291.
Nettleswell *Essex* ***Suburb***, to E of Harlow town centre. TL4510.
Nettlesworth *Dur.* ***Village***, 4m/6km N of Durham. NZ2547.
Nettleton *Lincs.* ***Village***, 1m/2km SW of Caistor. **52 E2** TA1000.
Nettleton *Wilts.* ***Village***, 7m/11km NW of Chippenham. **20 B4** ST8178.
Nettleton Green *Wilts.* ***Hamlet***, adjoining to NW of Nettleton. ST8178.
Nettleton Hill *W.Yorks.* ***Hamlet***, 3m/5km W of Huddersfield town centre. SE0917.
Nettleton Shrub *Wilts.* ***Hamlet***, 1km SE of Nettleton. ST8277.
Netton *Devon* ***Settlement***, 4m/6km SW of Yealmpton. **5 F6** SX5546.
Netton *Wilts.* ***Hamlet***, in River Avon valley, 4m/7km N of Salisbury. **10 C1** SU1336.
Neuadd *Cere.* ***Settlement***, 1km W of Oakford. **26 D3** SN4457.
Neuadd *I.o.A.* ***Settlement***, on N coast of Anglesey, 1km E of Cemaes. **46 B3** SH3893.
Neuadd *Powys* ***Settlement***, 4m/6km E of Llangammarch Wells. **27 J4** SN9947.
Neuadd Reservoirs *Powys* ***Reservoir***, two reservoirs in upper valley of Taf fechan River, 2m/3km SE of Brecon Beacons. **27 K7** SO0218.
Nev of Stuis *Shet.* ***Coastal feature***, headland on Yell on W side of entrance to Whale Firth. **108 D3** HU4697.
Nevendon *Essex* ***Settlement***, 1m/2km S of Wickford. **24 D2** TQ7591.
Nevern (Nyfer). *Pembs.* ***Village***, 2m/3km E of Newport. Traces of 11c castle on hill to N. **16 D1** SN0839.
Nevill Holt *Leics.* ***Hamlet***, with medieval hall and church, 5m/8km SW of Uppingham. **42 B6** SP8193.
Nevis Forest *High.* ***Forest/woodland***, in Lochaber district on W side of Glen Nevis, SE of Fort William. **87 H7** NN1172.
New *Cambs.* ***River***, rising to NW of Newmarket and flowing N, then W and joining Wicken Lode 1km SW of Wicken. **33 J2** TL5670.
New Abbey *D. & G. Alternative name for Sweetheart Abbey, qv.*
New Abbey *D. & G.* ***Village***, 6m/10km S of Dumfries. Ruins of Sweetheart Abbey (Historic Scotland). Monument to W of village commemorates Battle of Waterloo. 18c corn mill (Historic Scotland). **65 K4** NX9666.
New Abbey Corn Mill *D. & G.* ***Other feature of interest***, 18c water-powered corn mill (Historic Scotland) in working order, at New Abbey 12m/20km S of Dumfries. **65 K4** NX9666.
New Aberdour *Aber.* ***Village***, 1m/2km S of Aberdour Bay, on N coast, and 4m/7km SW of Rosehearty. **99 G4** NJ8863.
New Addington *Gt.Lon.* Population: 21,445. ***Suburb***, in borough of Croydon, 3m/5km NW of Biggin Hill. **23 G5** TQ3862.
New Alresford *Hants.* Population: 5041. ***Small town***, on River Aire, 7m/11km E of Winchester. Became 'New' in 1200. Attractive main street with 17c and 18c buildings. **11 G1** SU5832.
New Alyth *P. & K.* ***Hamlet***, 1km S of Alyth. **82 D3** NO2447.
New Ancholme *N.Lincs.* ***Other water feature***, artificially straightened section of River Ancholme from Bishopbridge to Ferriby Sluice, 1m/2km W of South Ferriby. Course of Old River Ancholme meanders on either side. See also (River) Ancholme and Old Ancholme. **52 C1** SE9721.
New Annesley *Notts.* ***Suburb***, 2m/3km SE of Kirkby in Ashfield. SK5153.
New Arley *Warks.* Population: 2026. ***Village***, to SE of Old Arley and 4m/7km SW of Nuneaton. **40 E6** SP2989.
New Arram *E.Riding* ***Settlement***, adjoining to NW of Arram, 3m/5km N of Beverley. TA0344.
New Ash Green *Kent* Population: 8617. ***Village***, dormitory village 1m/2km S of Hartley and 6m/9km S of Northfleet. Site of Roman building to S. **24 C5** TQ6065.
New Balderton *Notts.* ***Suburb***, just N of Balderton, to SE of Newark-on-Trent. SK8152.
New Barn *Kent* ***Hamlet***, 4m/6km SW of Gravesend. **24 C5** TQ6168.
New Barnet *Gt.Lon.* ***Suburb***, in borough of Barnet, 10m/16km N of Charing Cross. **23 F2** TQ2695.
New Barnetby *N.Lincs.* ***Hamlet***, 1m/2km NE of Barnetby le Wold. TA0710.
New Barns *Notts.* ***Settlement***, 1km E of Thrumpton. SK5130.
New Barton *Northants.* ***Suburb***, to N of Earls Barton, 4m/6km SW of Wellingborough. SP8564.
New Beckenham *Gt.Lon.* ***Suburb***, in borough of Bromley, to NW of Beckenham. TQ3670.
New Bedford River (Also known as Hundred Foot Drain.) ***Other water feature***, fenland drainage channel running NE from River Great Ouse, 1km E of Earith, to rejoin it at Denver Sluice. **43 H7** TF5801.
New Belses *Sc.Bord.* ***Settlement***, 6m/10km SE of Selkirk. **70 A1** NT5725.
New Bewick *Northumb.* ***Hamlet***, 7m/11km SE of Wooler. **71 F1** NU0620.
New Bolingbroke *Lincs.* ***Village***, 9m/14km N of Boston. **53 G7** TF3058.

N

New Bolsover *Derbys.* ***Suburb***, adjoining to W of Bolsover. SK4670.

New Boston *Mersey.* ***Suburb***, N part of Haydock. SJ5697.

New Boultham *Lincs.* ***Suburb***, SW district of Lincoln, to N of Boultham. SK9670.

New Bradwell *M.K.* ***Suburb***, adjoining to E of Wolverton, 3m/4km NW of Milton Keynes city centre. Grafton Street Aqueduct takes Grand Union Canal over road. **32 B4** SP8241.

New Brampton *Derbys.* ***Suburb***, to SW of Chesterfield town centre. SK3671.

New Brancepeth *Dur.* ***Village***, 3m/5km W of Durham. NZ2241.

New Bridge *D. & G.* ***Hamlet***, at road crossing of Cluden Water, 2m/4km NW of Dumfries. **65 K3** NX9479.

New Bridge *N.Yorks.* ***Settlement***, 1km N of Pickering. SE8085.

New Brighton *Flints.* ***Hamlet***, 1m/2km NE of Mold. SJ2565.

New Brighton *Hants.* ***Suburb***, 1km N of Emsworth town centre. **11 J4** SU7407.

New Brighton *Mersey.* ***Suburb***, N district of Wallesey, on River Mersey estuary. **48 C3** SJ3193.

New Brighton *N.Yorks.* ***Settlement***, 1m/2km W of Gargrave. SD9253.

New Brighton *W.Yorks.* ***Locality***, 1km SE of Cottingley, 2m/3km SW of Shipley. SE1236.

New Brighton *W.Yorks.* ***Suburb***, just N of Morley town centre. SE2528.

New Brighton *Wrex.* ***Hamlet***, on E slope of Esclusham Mountain, 4m/6km W of Wrexham. SJ2750.

New Brimington *Derbys.* ***Suburb***, adjoining to N of Brimington, 3m/4km NE of Chesterfield. SK4074.

New Brinsley *Notts.* ***Locality***, 2m/3km N of Eastwood. **51 G7** SK4650.

New Brotton *R. & C.* ***Locality***, adjoining to N of Brotton. NZ6820.

New Broughton *Wrex.* ***Hamlet***, 1m/2km W of Wrexham. **48 C7** SJ3151.

New Buckenham *Norf.* ***Village***, 4m/7km SE of Attleborough. Remains of 12c castle. **44 E6** TM0890.

New Bury *Gt.Man.* ***Suburb***, adjoining to SW of Farnworth. SD7205.

New Byth *Aber.* ***Village***, 7m/11km NE of Turriff. **99 G5** NJ8253.

New Catton *Norf.* ***Suburb***, 1m/2km N of Norwich city centre. TG2310.

New Charlton *Gt.Lon.* ***Suburb***, on S bank of River Thames at Woolwich Reach, borough of Greenwich, 7m/11km E of Charing Cross. TQ4178.

New Cheriton *Hants.* ***Settlement***, adjoining to SE of Cheriton. **11 G2** SU5827.

New Chesterton *Cambs.* ***Suburb***, N district of Cambridge. TL4459.

New Clipstone *Notts.* ***Village***, 3m/5km NE of Mansfield. **51 H6** SK5863.

New College *Kent* ***Historic house***, 14c almshouses in Cobham, 4m/7km W of Rochester. Partly rebuilt in 16c, endowed by Sir John de Cobham. **24 C5** TQ6667.

New Costessey *Norf.* ***Suburb***, 3m/5km W of Norwich. **45 F5** TG1810.

New Coundon *Dur.* ***Settlement***, 1m/2km E of Bishop Auckland. NZ2230.

New Cowper *Cumb.* ***Locality***, 1m/2km NW of Westnewton. NY1245.

New Crofton *W.Yorks.* ***Locality***, adjoining to SE of Crofton. SE3817.

New Cross *Cere.* ***Settlement***, 4m/7km SE of Aberystwyth. **27 F1** SN6377.

New Cross *Gt.Lon.* ***Suburb***, in borough of Lewisham, 5m/7km SE of Charing Cross. TQ3676.

New Cross *Som.* ***Hamlet***, 3m/5km W of Martock. ST4119.

New Cross Gate *Gt.Lon.* ***Locality***, part of New Cross in the borough of Lewisham, 5m/7km SE of Charing Cross. TQ3676.

New Cubbington *Warks.* ***Suburb***, to W of Cubbington. SP3368.

New Cumnock *E.Ayr.* Population: 3968. ***Small town***, at confluence of Afton Water and River Nith, 5m/8km SE of Cumnock, in former coal-mining area. **68 B2** NS6113.

New Cut *Norf.* ***Other water feature***, waterway flowing E from near Ingham, and then S into Horsey Mere, 3m/4km N of Martham. TG4422.

New Deer *Aber.* ***Village***, 14m/23km SW of Fraserburgh. **99 G6** NJ8846.

New Delaval *Northumb.* ***Suburb***, adjoining to SW of Blyth. NZ2979.

New Delight *W.Yorks.* ***Hamlet***, 2m/3km W of Hebden Bridge. SD9628.

New Delph *Gt.Man.* ***Hamlet***, adjoining to SE of Delph, 4m/7km NE of Oldham. SD9807.

New Denham *Bucks.* ***Settlement***, 1km NW of Uxbridge. TQ0484.

New Downs *Cornw.* ***Locality***, on W side of St. Just. SW3631.

New Duston *Northants.* ***Suburb***, NW district of Northampton. Lodge Farm Industrial Estate adjoins to E. **31 J2** SP7162.

New Earswick *York* ***Suburb***, 2m/3km N of York. **58 C4** SE6055.

New Edlington *S.Yorks.* ***Suburb***, 4m/6km SW of Doncaster. Old Edlington is 1m/2km SW. **51 H3** SK5398.

New Elgin *Moray* ***Locality***, S district of Elgin. **97 K5** NJ2261.

New Ellerby *E.Riding* ***Village***, 7m/11km N of Hedon. **59 H6** TA1739.

New Eltham *Gt.Lon.* ***Suburb***, in borough of Greenwich, 1m/2km SE of Eltham. **23 H4** TQ4372.

New End *Worcs.* ***Hamlet***, 3m/5km NW of Alcester. **30 B2** SP0560.

New England *Essex* ***Settlement***, 3m/5km SE of Haverhill. TL7042.

New England *Peter.* ***Suburb***, 2m/3km N of Peterborough city centre. **42 E5** TF1801.

New England Bay *D. & G.* ***Bay***, 2m/4km S of Ardwell, on W side of Luce Bay. **64 B6** NX1242.

New England Island *Essex* ***Island***, bounded by creeks 4m/6km NE of Shoeburyness. TQ9790.

New Farnley *W.Yorks.* ***Suburb***, to S of Farnley, 4m/6km SW of Leeds city centre. **57 H6** SE2531.

New Ferry *Mersey.* ***Locality***, beside River Mersey estuary, 2m/4km S of Birkenhead. **48 C4** SJ3485.

New Fletton *Peter.* ***Suburb***, to S of Peterborough city centre. TL1997.

New Forest *Hants.* ***Forest/woodland***, area of heath and woodland extending W of Southampton to valley of River Avon at Fordingbridge and Ringwood, of nearly 150 square miles or about 390 square km, of which about two-thirds are Crown lands. The 'forest', or royal hunting ground, was 'new' in the 11c. **10 D3** SU3005.

New Forest Museum and Information Centre *Hants.* ***Other feature of interest***, in Lyndhurst, exhibiting local history and wildlife of area. **10 E4** SU3008.

New Fryston *W.Yorks.* ***Hamlet***, 2m/3km NE of Castleford. **57 K7** SE4527.

New Galloway *D. & G.* ***Small town***, on W side of Water of Ken valley, 17m/27km N of Kirkcudbright. Smallest royal burgh in Scotland. RSPB reserve on Ken Dee Marshes. **65 G3** NX6377.

New Gilston *Fife* ***Hamlet***, 5m/8km SE of Cupar. **83 F7** NO4308.

New Greens *Herts.* ***Suburb***, 1m/2km N of St. Albans city centre. TL1409.

New Grimsby *I.o.S.* ***Village***, with harbour, on W coast of Tresco. **2 B1** SV8815.

New Grounds *Glos.* ***Open space***, reclaimed land on SE side of Severn estuary, 1m/2km NW of Slimbridge village. **20 A1** SO7306.

New Hadley *Tel. & W.* ***Locality***, 2m/3km E of Wellington. SJ6811.

New Hall *W.Suss.* ***Historic house***, near Small Dole, 8m/12km SW of Burgess Hill. **13 F5** TQ2012.

New Hall Hey *Lancs.* ***Suburb***, in S part of Rawtenstall. SD8022.

New Hartley *Northumb.* Population: 1828. ***Village***, 3m/5km S of Blyth. **71 J6** NZ3076.

New Haw *Surr.* ***Locality***, on River Wey Navigation, 3m/4km S of Chertsey. **22 D5** TQ0563.

New Headington *Oxon.* ***Suburb***, 3m/4km E of Oxford city centre. SP5506.

New Heaton *Northumb.* ***Hamlet***, 2m/3km E of Cornhill on Tweed. NT8840.

New Hedges *Pembs.* ***Hamlet***, 1m/2km N of Tenby. **16 E4** SN1202.

New Herrington *T. & W.* ***Village***, 2m/3km N of Houghton le Spring. NZ3352.

New Hinksey *Oxon.* ***Suburb***, 1m/2km S of Oxford city centre. SP5104.

New Holland *N.Lincs.* ***Village***, on S bank of River Humber, opposite Kingston upon Hull. **59 G7** TA0823.

New Horton Grange *T. & W.* ***Settlement***, 3m/4km NE of Ponteland. **71 G6** NZ1975.

New Houghton *Derbys.* ***Village***, 4m/6km NW of Mansfield. **51 H6** SK4965.

New Houghton *Norf.* ***Hamlet***, to S of Houghton Park, 3m/4km W of East Rudham. **44 B3** TF7927.

New Houses *Dur.* ***Locality***, on N side of Hury Reservoir, 3m/5km SW of Hunderthwaite. NY9419.

New Houses *Gt.Man.* ***Locality***, 3m/4km SW of Wigan town centre. SD5502.

New Houses *N.Yorks.* ***Settlement***, in Ribble valley, 1km N of Horton in Ribblesdale. **56 D2** SD8073.

New Humberstone *Leic.* ***Suburb***, 2m/3km NE of Leicester city centre. SK6105.

New Hunstanton *Norf.* ***Suburb***, to N of Hunstanton town centre. TF6741.

New Hunwick *Dur.* ***Hamlet***, 1km N of Hunwick. NZ1833.

New Hutton *Cumb.* ***Hamlet***, 3m/5km E of Kendal. **61 G7** SD5691.

New Hythe *Kent* ***Locality***, on River Medway, 4m/6km NW of Maidstone. **14 C2** TQ7059.

New Ings *E.Riding* ***Locality***, 4m/6km N of Kingston upon Hull city centre. TA0634.

New Inn *Carmar.* ***Village***, 6m/9km SW of Llanybydder. **17 H1** SN4736.

New Inn *Fife* ***Settlement***, 3m/4km SE of Falkland. **82 D7** NO2804.

New Inn *Mon.* ***Settlement***, 5m/8km NW of Chepstow. **19 H1** SO4800.

New Inn *Torfaen* ***Suburb***, 1m/2km SE of Pontypool. **19 F2** ST3099.

New Invention *Shrop.* ***Hamlet***, 3m/5km N of Knighton. **28 B1** SO2976.

New Invention *W.Mid.* ***Suburb***, 3m/5km NW of Walsall town centre. **40 B5** SJ9701.

New Kelso *High.* ***Settlement***, in Ross and Cromarty district, 3m/5km NE of Lochcarron. NG9342.

New Kyo *Dur.* ***Suburb***, adjoining to E of Annfield Plain. NZ1751.

New Lambton *Dur.* ***Settlement***, 3m/4km E of Chester-le-Street. NZ3150.

New Lanark *S.Lan.* ***Village***, 1km S of Lanark. **75 G6** NS8842.

New Lanark World Heritage Village *S.Lan.* ***Other feature of interest***, museum in New Lanark, 1km S of Lanark, commemorates model village designed by 19c industrialist, Robert Owen. Exhibits include re-creations of workers' living conditions. **75 G6** NS8742.

New Lane *Lancs.* ***Settlement***, 1m/2km NW of Burscough Bridge. **48 D1** SD4212.

New Lane End *Warr.* ***Hamlet***, 2m/3km W of Culcheth. SJ6394.

New Leake *Lincs.* ***Hamlet***, 6m/10km W of Wainfleet All Saints. **53 H7** TF4057.

New Leeds *Aber.* ***Village***, 3m/5km E of Strichen. **99 H5** NJ9954.

New Leslie *Aber.* ***Settlement***, on SE side of Hill of Newleslie, 3m/5km SW of Insch. **90 D2** NJ5825.

New Lodge *S.Yorks.* ***Suburb***, 2m/3km N of Barnsley town centre. SE3409.

New Longton *Lancs.* ***Village***, 2m/3km E of Longton. **55 J7** SD5025.

New Luce *D. & G.* ***Village***, 5m/8km N of Glenluce, at confluence of Cross Water of Luce and Main Water of Luce. **64 B4** NX1764.

New Mains *S.Lan.* ***Settlement***, 1m/2km NE of Douglas. **75 G7** NS8431.

New Mains of Ury *Aber.* ***Settlement***, 1m/2km N of Stonehaven. **91 G6** NO8787.

New Malden *Gt.Lon.* ***Suburb***, in borough of Kingston upon Thames, 2m/4km E of Kingston upon Thames town centre. **23 F5** TQ2168.

New Marske *R. & C.* Population: 3646. ***Village***, 1m/2km SW of Marske-by-the-Sea. **63 H4** NZ6221.

New Marston *Oxon.* ***Suburb***, 1m/2km NE of Oxford city centre, to E of River Cherwell. SP5207.

New Marton *Shrop.* ***Settlement***, 3m/4km N of Whittington. **38 C2** SJ3334.

New Micklefield *W.Yorks.* ***Locality***, S part of Micklefield, 3m/4km E of Garforth. SE4432.

New Mill *Aber.* ***Settlement***, 2m/3km NE of Glenbervie. **91 F6** NO7883.

New Mill *Cornw.* ***Hamlet***, 2m/4km N of Penzance. **2 B5** SW4534.

New Mill *Herts.* ***Locality***, 1km N of Tring. **32 C7** SP9212.

New Mill *W.Yorks.* ***Village***, 1m/2km E of Holmfirth. **50 D2** SE1408.

New Mill End *Beds.* ***Settlement***, 3m/4km SE of Luton town centre, on River Lea. **32 E7** TL1217.

New Mills *Cornw.* ***Village***, 7m/11km W of St. Austell. **3 F3** SW8952.

New Mills *Derbys.* Population: 9092. ***Small town***, industrial town 8m/13km NW of Buxton. Developed due to 18c and 19c cotton mills. **49 J4** SK0085.

New Mills *Glos.* ***Settlement***, 1m/2km N of Lydney. SO6304.

New Mills *Mon.* ***Hamlet***, 3m/5km S of Monmouth. **19 J1** SO5107.

New Mills *Powys* ***Hamlet***, 4m/6km S of Llanfair Caereinion. **37 K5** SJ0901.

New Milton *Hants.* Population: 24,324. ***Town***, 5m/8km W of Lymington. Motorcycle museum. Interesting water tower disguised as castle, built 1900. **10 D5** SZ2495.

New Mistley *Essex* Population: 1808. ***Village***, adjoins to E of Mistley on S bank of River Stour estuary. **35 F5** TM1131.

New Moat *Pembs.* ***Village***, 2m/3km SW of Maenclochog. Traces of motte and bailey castle. **16 D2** SN0625.

New Monkland *N.Lan.* ***Village***, 2m/3km NW of Airdrie. NS7567.

New Moston *Gt.Man.* ***Locality***, 1m/2km E of Moston. SD8701.

New Moston *Gt.Man.* ***Suburb***, 4m/7km NE of Manchester city centre. SD8902.

New Normanton *Derby* ***Suburb***, 1m/2km S of Derby city centre. SK3534.

New Ollerton *Notts.* ***Suburb***, residential locality adjoining to N of Ollerton. SK6668.

New Orleans *Arg. & B.* ***Settlement***, at S end of Kintyre, on E coast, 3m/5km SE of Campbeltown. **66 B2** NR7517.

New Oscott *W.Mid.* ***Suburb***, 2m/3km SW of Sutton Coldfield. SP0994.

New Park *Cornw.* ***Settlement***, 4m/6km NW of Altarnun. **4 B2** SX1783.

New Park *N.Yorks.* ***Suburb***, 1m/2km N of Harrogate town centre. SE2956.

New Parks *Leic.* ***Suburb***, 2m/3km NW of Leicester city centre. SK5505.

New Pitsligo *Aber.* Population: 1118. ***Village***, 10m/16km SW of Fraserburgh. Ruins of 15c Pitsligo Castle 1km SE of Rosehearty. **99 G5** NJ8855.

New Polzeath *Cornw.* ***Locality***, adjoining to N of Polzeath. **3 G1** SW9379.

New Prestwick *S.Ayr.* ***Suburb***, 2m/3km NE of Ayr town centre. **67 H1** NS3524.

New Quay (Ceinewydd). *Cere.* ***Small town***, small coastal resort with picturesque stone quay, 19m/30km SW of Aberystwyth across Cardigan Bay. Heritage centre includes information on maritime history and wildlife. **26 C3** SN3859.

New Quay *Essex* ***Locality***, on River Colne in SE part of Colchester. TM0223.

New Quay Bay *Cere.* ***Bay***, to E of New Quay Head between New Quay Head and Little Quay Bay. **26 C2** SN3959.

New Quay Head *Cere.* ***Coastal feature***, headland to N of New Quay. **26 C2** SN3859.

New Quorndon *Leics.* ***Suburb***, adjoining to W of Quorndon, 2m/3km SE of Loughborough. SK5516.

New Rackheath *Norf.* ***Village***, 4m/7km NE of Norwich. **45 G4** TG2812.

New Radnor (Maesyfed). *Powys* ***Village***, 6m/10km NW of Kington. Former county town of Radnorshire. Motte and bailey earthworks mark site of Norman castle. Traces of town walls on SW side of village. **28 B2** SO2160.

New Rent *Cumb.* ***Settlement***, 1m/2km NE of Skelton. **61 F3** NY4536.

New Ridley *Northumb.* ***Hamlet***, 3m/5km SW of Prudhoe. NZ0559.

New River *Lincs.* ***Other water feature***, starts close to River Welland, 2m/3km NE of Glinton and runs NE of Crowland then past Cowbit to enter River Welland on S side of Spalding. **43 F4** TF2421.

New Road Side *N.Yorks.* ***Village***, just E of Cowling, 3m/4km SW of Cross Hills. SD9743.
New Road Side *W.Yorks.* ***Suburb***, of Bradford, adjoining to N of Wyke, 3m/5km N of Brighouse. SE1527.
New Romney *Kent* Population: 8340. ***Small town***, former Cinque Port, now 1m/2km inland from Littlestone-on-Sea on St. Mary's Bay and 9m/14km SW of Hythe. Large Norman church reflects former importance. **15 F5** TR0624.
New Rossington *S.Yorks.* Population: 12,647. ***Locality***, 4m/7km SE of Doncaster. **51 J3** SK6197.
New Row *Cere.* ***Settlement***, 1m/2km NW of Pont-rhyd-y-groes. SN7273.
New Row *Lancs.* ***Settlement***, 5m/9km W of Whalley. **56 B6** SD6438.
New Sarum *Wilts. Former, and official name of Salisbury, qv.*
New Sauchie *Clack.* ***Locality***, adjoining to NE of Alloa. **75 G1** NS9094.
New Sawley *Derbys.* ***Locality***, adjoining to SW of Long Eaton. **41 G2** SK4732.
New Scarbro' *W.Yorks.* ***Suburb***, 3m/5km W of Leeds city centre. SE2434.
New Scone *P. & K.* Population: 4533. ***Village***, 2m/3km NE of Perth. **82 C5** NO1326.
New Sharlston *W.Yorks.* ***Locality***, 1m/2km S of Normanton. SE3820.
New Shawbost *W.Isles* ***Settlement***, near NW coast of Isle of Lewis, forms locality of Siabost along with North and South Shawbost, 2m/4km W of Bragar. NB2646.
New Shoreston *Northumb.* ***Hamlet***, 2m/3km SE of Bamburgh. NU1932.
New Silksworth *T. & W.* ***Suburb***, 3m/4km S of Sunderland city centre. **62 E1** NZ3853.
New Skelton *R. & C.* ***Village***, 1km E of Skelton. NZ6618.
New Somerby *Lincs.* ***Suburb***, SE district of Grantham. SK9235.
New Spilsby *Lincs.* ***Locality***, adjoining to SE of Spilsby. TF4066.
New Springs *Gt.Man.* ***Locality***, 2m/3km NE of Wigan. SD6007.
New Sprowston *Norf.* ***Suburb***, N district of Norwich. TG2311.
New Stapleford *Notts.* ***Suburb***, N district of Stapleford, 5m/8km W of Nottingham. SK4938.
New Stevenston *N.Lan.* ***Suburb***, 2m/3km NE of Motherwell. NS7659.
New Swanage *Dorset* ***Suburb***, 1m/2km N of Swanage town centre. SZ0380.
New Swannington *Leics.* ***Hamlet***, 1m/2km N of Coalville. SK4215.
New Thirsk *N.Yorks.* ***Locality***, adjoining to W of Thirsk. Includes Thirsk Racecourse. SE4282.
New Thundersley *Essex* ***Suburb***, W district of Thundersley, 4m/6km E of Basildon. TQ7789.
New Tolsta *W.Isles Anglicised form of Tolastadh Ùr, qv.*
New Totley *S.Yorks.* ***Suburb***, in Totley, 6m/9km SW of Sheffield city centre. SK3179.
New Town *Beds.* ***Suburb***, N district of Biggleswade. TL1945.
New Town *Cere.* ***Suburb***, E district of Cardigan. SN1846.
New Town *Dorset* ***Hamlet***, 4m/6km NE of Sturminster Newton. ST8318.
New Town *Dorset* ***Hamlet***, 1km NE of Witchampton and 7m/11km E of Blandford Forum. ST9907.
New Town *Dorset* ***Hamlet***, 1km NW of Sixpenny Handley. ST9918.
New Town *E.Loth.* ***Village***, 3m/5km SE of Tranent. **76 C3** NT4470.
New Town *E.Suss.* ***Suburb***, S district of Uckfield. **13 H4** TQ4720.
New Town *Glos.* ***Hamlet***, 3m/4km NE of Winchcombe. **30 B5** SP0432.
New Town *Luton* ***Suburb***, to S of Luton town centre. TL0920.
New Town *T. & W.* ***Suburb***, E district of Houghton le Spring. NZ3449.
New Town *W.Mid.* ***Locality***, 1km N of Brownhills. SK0506.
New Town *W.Mid.* ***Locality***, 2m/3km W of West Bromwich town centre. SO9791.
New Town *Wilts.* ***Hamlet***, adjoining to E of Ramsbury, 4m/7km W of Hungerford. SU2871.
New Town *Worcs.* ***Settlement***, 6m/10km W of Worcester. SO7557.
New Tredegar *Caerp.* Population: 5350. ***Small town***, 2m/4km N of Bargoed. **18 E1** SO1403.
New Ulva *Arg. & B.* ***Settlement***, on S coast of Loch na Cille, 5m/8km SW of Tayvallich. **73 F2** NR7080.
New Valley *W.Isles* ***Village***, on Isle of Lewis, 1m/2km NW of Stornoway. NB4134.
New Village *E.Riding* ***Village***, E part of Newport, 2m/3km E of Gilberdyke. SE8530.
New Village *S.Yorks.* ***Suburb***, adjoining to N of Bentley, 2m/3km N of Doncaster town centre. SE5606.
New Walsoken *Cambs.* ***Suburb***, E district of Wisbech. **43 H5** TF4709.
New Waltham *N.E.Lincs.* Population: 4263. ***Suburb***, 3m/5km S of Grimsby. **53 F2** TA2804.
New Whittington *Derbys.* ***Suburb***, 3m/4km N of Chesterfield, adjoining to NE of Old Whittington. SK3975.
New Wimpole *Cambs.* ***Village***, 6m/9km N of Royston. **33 G4** TL3449.
New Winton *E.Loth.* ***Hamlet***, 2m/3km SE of Tranent. 17c Winton House 1m/2km SE. **76 C3** NT4271.
New World *Cambs.* ***Settlement***, 2m/3km W of Doddington. TL3690.
New Yatt *Oxon.* ***Hamlet***, 3m/4km NE of Witney. **30 E7** SP3713.
New York *Lincs.* ***Hamlet***, 3m/4km SE of Coningsby. **53 F7** TF2455.
New York *T. & W.* ***Locality***, 3m/4km W of Tynemouth. **71 J6** NZ3270.

New Zealand *Derby* ***Suburb***, 1m/2km W of Derby city centre. SK3336.
Newall *W.Yorks.* ***Suburb***, of Otley, on N side of River Wharfe. SE2046.
Newall Green *Gt.Man.* ***Suburb***, 3m/5km E of Altrincham. SJ8187.
Newark *Ork.* ***Settlement***, on Sanday, at N end of Bay of Newark, 4m/7km SW of Tafts Ness. **106 G3** HY7242.
Newark *Peter.* ***Suburb***, 2m/3km NE of Peterborough city centre. **43 F5** TF2100.
Newark Bay *Ork.* ***Bay***, on S coast of Mainland, 1m/2km E of St. Peter's Pool. **107 E7** HY5704.
Newark Castle *Inclyde* ***Historic house***, 16c-17c mansion (Historic Scotland) on E side of Port Glasgow. Incorporates 15c tower. **74 B3** NS3374.
Newark Castle *Notts.* ***Castle***, ruins of castle begun in 12c and where King John died, in Newark-on-Trent. Elaborately decorated Norman gateway remains. **51 K7** SK7954.
Newark-on-Trent *Notts.* Population: 35,129. ***Town***, market and commercial town, 16m/25km SW of Lincoln and 17m/27km NE of Nottingham. Remains of medieval castle. Church, Early English to Perpendicular, has lofty spire. Hosts County Agricultural Show each May. Newark Air Museum at edge of town. **52 B7** SK7953.
Newark Park *Glos.* ***Historic house***, Tudor hunting lodge (National Trust) altered by James Wyatt in 1790, 3m/4km E of Wotton-under-Edge. **20 A2** ST7893.
Newark Priory *Surr.* ***Ecclesiastical building***, remains of priory (Augustinian), 1km NW of Ripley. **22 D6** TQ0457.
Newarthill *N.Lan.* Population: 6585. ***Village***, 3m/5km NE of Motherwell. **75 F5** NS7859.
Newbald Wold *E.Riding* ***Open space***, 4m/6km SE of Market Weighton, across which runs Wolds Way long distance footpath. **59 F6** SE9137.
Newball *Lincs.* ***Settlement***, 1km E of Langworth, 4m/6km W of Wragby. TF0776.
Newbarn *Kent* ***Settlement***, 1km S of Lyminge, 5m/8km NW of Folkestone town centre. **15 G3** TR1539.
Newbarns *Cumb.* ***Suburb***, 1m/2km NE of Barrow-in-Furness town centre. **55 F2** SD2170.
Newbattle *Midloth.* ***Village***, 1km S of Dalkeith. NT3366.
Newbattle Abbey *Midloth.* ***Historic house***, dating mainly from 16c on site of abbey founded in 1140, 1km S of Dalkeith. **76 B4** NT3366.
Newbiggin *Cumb.* ***Hamlet***, 8m/12km S of Brampton. **61 G2** NY5549.
Newbiggin *Cumb.* ***Settlement***, 2m/3km SE of Ravenglass across River Esk estuary. SD0994.
Newbiggin *Cumb.* ***Settlement***, on W shore of Morecambe Bay, 5m/7km E of Barrow-in-Furness. **55 F3** SD2669.
Newbiggin *Cumb.* ***Village***, 3m/5km W of Penrith. **61 F4** NY4729.
Newbiggin *Cumb.* ***Village***, 6m/10km NW of Appleby-in-Westmorland. **61 H4** NY6228.
Newbiggin *Dur.* ***Village***, 2m/4km NW of Middleton-in-Teesdale. **62 A4** NY9127.
Newbiggin *N.Yorks.* ***Settlement***, to NE of Askrigg. **62 A7** SD9591.
Newbiggin *N.Yorks.* ***Village***, 2m/3km S of Aysgarth. **57 F1** SD9985.
Newbiggin *Northumb.* ***Locality***, 1m/2km W of Blanchland. NY9549.
Newbiggin *Northumb.* ***Settlement***, to W of Dipton Wood, 2m/3km S of Hexham. **70 E7** NY9460.
Newbiggin-by-the-Sea *Northumb.* Population: 7100. ***Small town***, fishing town and resort on North Sea coast, 2m/4km E of Ashington. **71 J5** NZ3187.
Newbiggin Common *Dur.* ***Open space***, moorland on upper reaches of Flushiemere Beck, 2m/4km N of Newbiggin. **62 A3** NY9031.
Newbiggin Hall Estate *T. & W.* ***Suburb***, 4m/6km NW of Newcastle upon Tyne. NZ2067.
Newbiggin-on-Lune *Cumb.* ***Hamlet***, 5m/8km SW of Kirkby Stephen. **61 J6** NY7005.
Newbigging *Aber.* ***Settlement***, in Glen Clunie, 4m/6km S of Braemar. **89 J6** NO1485.
Newbigging *Aber.* ***Settlement***, 4m/6km N of Stonehaven. **91 G5** NO8591.
Newbigging *Angus* ***Hamlet***, 4m/6km NE of Broughty Ferry. **83 F4** NO4935.
Newbigging *Angus* ***Settlement***, 1km NW of Newtyle. **82 D3** NO2841.
Newbigging *Angus* ***Settlement***, 5m/8km N of Dundee. **83 F4** NO4237.
Newbigging *S.Lan.* ***Village***, 2m/4km E of Carnwath. **75 J6** NT0145.
Newbold *Derbys.* ***Suburb***, 1m/2km NW of Chesterfield town centre. **51 F5** SK3772.
Newbold *Leics.* ***Hamlet***, 3m/5km NE of Ashby de la Zouch. **41 G4** SK4018.
Newbold on Avon *Warks.* ***Suburb***, in NW part of Rugby, on River Avon and Oxford Canal. **31 F1** SP4877.
Newbold on Stour *Warks.* ***Village***, 4m/6km N of Shipston on Stour. **30 D4** SP2446.
Newbold Pacey *Warks.* ***Village***, 6m/9km S of Royal Leamington Spa. **30 D3** SP2957.
Newbold Verdon *Leics.* Population: 3426. ***Village***, 3m/4km E of Market Bosworth. **41 G5** SK4403.
Newborough *I.o.A.* ***Village***, on Anglesey, 9m/14km SW of Menai Bridge. **46 C6** SH4265.
Newborough *Peter.* ***Village***, 5m/8km N of Peterborough. **43 F5** TF2006.
Newborough *Staffs.* ***Village***, 4m/6km E of Abbots Bromley. **40 D3** SK1325.
Newbottle *Northants.* ***Settlement***, 4m/6km W of Brackley. **31 G5** SP5236.
Newbottle *T. & W.* ***Village***, 1m/2km N of Houghton le Spring. NZ3351.
Newbourne *Suff.* ***Village***, 4m/7km S of Woodbridge. **35 G4** TM2743.

Newbridge (Cefn Bychan). *Caerp.* Population: 7035. ***Small town***, on Ebbw River, 8m/13km NW of Newport. **19 F2** ST2197.
Newbridge *Cere.* ***Settlement***, with road bridge over River Aeron, 4m/6km SE of Aberaeron. SN5059.
Newbridge *Cornw.* ***Hamlet***, 3m/5km W of Penzance. **2 B5** SW4231.
Newbridge *Cornw.* ***Settlement***, on River Lynher, 1m/2km SW of Callington. **4 D4** SX3467.
Newbridge *E.Suss.* ***Settlement***, below N slope of Ashdown Forest, 1m/2km S of Coleman's Hatch. TQ4532.
Newbridge *Edin.* ***Village***, 3m/5km S of Forth Road Bridge. **75 K3** NT1272.
Newbridge *Hants.* ***Hamlet***, 1m/2km N of Cadnam. **10 E3** SU2915.
Newbridge *I.o.W.* ***Village***, 4m/6km E of Yarmouth. **11 F6** SZ4187.
Newbridge *Lancs.* ***Locality***, 1km N of Nelson town centre. SD8538.
Newbridge *Oxon.* ***Settlement***, at confluence of Rivers Thames and Windrush, 5m/8km S of Eynsham. **21 H1** SP4001.
Newbridge *Pembs.* ***Locality***, 4m/6km S of Fishguard. **16 C1** SM9431.
Newbridge *W.Mid.* ***Suburb***, W district of Wolverhampton. SO8999.
Newbridge *Wrex.* ***Hamlet***, 2m/3km SW of Ruabon. **38 B1** SJ2841.
Newbridge Green *Worcs.* ***Hamlet***, 1m/2km SW of Upton upon Severn. SO8439.
Newbridge-on-Usk *Mon.* ***Settlement***, 4m/6km S of Usk. **19 G2** ST3894.
Newbridge on Wye *Powys* ***Village***, 5m/8km N of Builth Wells. **27 K3** SO0158.
Newbrough *Northumb.* ***Village***, 3m/5km NE of Haydon Bridge. Site of Roman fort 1km W. **70 D7** NY8767.
Newbuildings *Devon* ***Hamlet***, 3m/5km NW of Crediton. SS7903.
Newburgh *Aber.* ***Settlement***, to N of Mormond Hill, 3m/4km NE of Strichen. **99 H5** NJ9659.
Newburgh *Aber.* Population: 1401. ***Village***, with quay, on W side of River Ythan estuary, 1m/2km N of Newburgh Bar at mouth of river. Village is 4m/7km SE of Ellon. **91 H2** NJ9925.
Newburgh *Fife* Population: 2032. ***Small town***, former industrial town with small harbour, on S bank of Firth of Tay, 9m/14km W of Cupar. **82 D6** NO2318.
Newburgh *Lancs.* ***Village***, 3m/5km N of Skelmersdale. **48 D1** SD4810.
Newburgh *Sc.Bord.* ***Hamlet***, 5m/8km SW of Ettrickbridge. **69 J2** NT3220.
Newburgh Bar *Aber.* ***Coastal feature***, sand bar at mouth of River Ythan, 1m/2km N of Newburgh. **91 J2** NJ9925.
Newburgh Priory *N.Yorks.* ***Hamlet***, and remains of monastery in grounds of 18c mansion, 1km SE of Coxwold. **58 B2** SE5476.
Newburn *T. & W.* Population: 42,897. ***Suburb***, on N side of River Tyne, 5m/8km W of Newcastle upon Tyne. **71 G7** NZ1665.
Newbury *Som.* ***Hamlet***, 1m/2km NE of Coleford and 3m/5km S of Radstock. ST6950.
Newbury *W.Berks.* Population: 33,273. ***Town***, former cloth town on River Kennet, 16m/25km W of Reading. 15c church, built by a clothier. 17c Cloth Hall houses Newbury District Museum. Site of two Civil War battles. Racecourse to SE. **21 H5** SU4767.
Newbury *Wilts.* ***Settlement***, adjoining to NE of Horningsham, 4m/6km SW of Warminster. ST8241.
Newbury District Museum *W.Berks.* ***Other feature of interest***, museum in Jacobean Cloth Hall at Newbury, with exhibits on costumes and local history. **21 H5** SU4767.
Newbury Park *Gt.Lon.* ***Suburb***, in borough of Redbridge, 1m/2km NE of Ilford. TQ4488.
Newby *Cumb.* ***Village***, 6m/9km W of Appleby-in-Westmorland. **61 G4** NY5921.
Newby *Lancs.* ***Hamlet***, 2m/3km SW of Gisburn. **56 D5** SD8145.
Newby *N.Yorks.* ***Hamlet***, 3m/4km SE of Ingleton. **56 C2** SD7270.
Newby *N.Yorks.* ***Suburb***, adjoining to NW of Scarborough. TA0190.
Newby *N.Yorks.* ***Village***, 3m/4km NW of Stokesley. **63 G5** NZ5012.
Newby Bridge *Cumb.* ***Village***, 8m/12km NE of Ulverston. **55 G1** SD3786.
Newby Cote *N.Yorks.* ***Settlement***, 1km NE of Newby, 1m/2km NW of Clapham. SD7370.
Newby Cross *Cumb.* ***Settlement***, 3m/5km SW of Carlisle. NY3653.
Newby East *Cumb.* ***Hamlet***, 4m/6km SW of Brampton. **61 F1** NY4758.
Newby End *Cumb.* ***Settlement***, adjoining to E of Newby, 7m/11km SE of Penrith. NY5921.
Newby Hall *N.Yorks.* ***Historic house***, 18c house, partly by Adam, in estate with garden bordering River Ure, 3m/5km W of Boroughbridge. **57 J3** SE3567.
Newby Head *Cumb.* ***Locality***, to W of Newby. NY5821.
Newby West *Cumb.* ***Hamlet***, 2m/4km SW of Carlisle. **60 E1** NY3653.
Newby Wiske *N.Yorks.* ***Village***, 4m/6km S of Northallerton. **57 J1** SE3687.
Newcastle *Bridgend* ***Castle***, mid 12c castle (Cadw) in Bridgend with elaborately decorated Norman gateway. **18 C3** SS9080.
Newcastle (Y Castellnewydd). *Bridgend* ***Suburb***, central district of Bridgend on W side of River Ogmore. Ruins of 12c castle (Cadw). **18 C4** SS9079.
Newcastle *Fife* ***Suburb***, W district of Glenrothes. NO2401.
Newcastle *Mon.* ***Hamlet***, 5m/8km NW of Monmouth. **28 D7** SO4417.
Newcastle *Shrop.* ***Village***, on River Clun, 4m/6km W of Clun. **38 B7** SO2482.

Newcastle Emlyn (Castell Newydd Emlyn). *Cere.* Population: 1506. ***Small town***, market town on River Teifi, 9m/14km E of Cardigan. **26 C4** SN3040.
Newcastle Emlyn Castle *Carmar.* ***Castle***, ruined 13c Welsh and English built castle, 8m/12km SE of Cardigan. **26 C4** SN3140.
Newcastle International Airport (Formerly known as Woolsington Airport.) *T. & W.* ***Airport/airfield***, 5m/8km NW of Newcastle upon Tyne, and to N of Woolsington locality. **71 G6** NZ1969.
Newcastle-under-Lyme *Staffs.* Population: 73,731. ***Town***, adjoining to W of Stoke-on-Trent. Many old buildings have survived, including silk mill in Marsh Parade. **40 A1** SJ8445.
Newcastle upon Tyne *T. & W.* Population: 189,150. ***City***, port on River Tyne about 11m/17km upstream from river mouth and 80m/129km N of Leeds. Granted city status in 1882. Area has been settled for 2000 years. The 'new castle' of city's name started in 1080 by Robert Curthose, eldest son of William the Conqueror. 13c castle gatehouse known as 'Black Gate'. Commercial and industrial centre, previously dependent upon coalmining and shipbuilding. In its heyday, 25 percent of world's shipping built here. Cathedral, formerly parish church dates from 14 to 15c. Bessie Surtees House (English Heritage) comprises 16c and 17c merchants' houses. Tyne Bridge, opened in 1928 and longest of its type at the time. Venerable Bede (AD 672-735) who wrote 'History of the English Church and People', an important document on England's early past, born near Jarrow, now on edge of city. Catherine Cookson, writer, also born in Jarrow, many of her novels based in this area. Universities. Newcastle International Airport 5m/8km NW. **71 H7** NZ2464.
Newcastle upon Tyne Cathedral *T. & W.* ***Ecclesiastical building***, in Newcastle city centre. Elevated to cathedral status in 1882. Mainly 14c-15c. Noted for its spire, a Newcastle landmark, and superbly carved font canopy. **71 H7** NZ2464.
Newcastleton *Sc.Bord.* ***Village***, 18c symmetrical village on Liddel Water, 17m/27km S of Hawick. Former weaving centre. **69 K5** NY4887.
Newcastleton Forest *Sc.Bord.* ***Forest/woodland***, to E of Newcastleton forms part of Border Forest Park. **70 A5** NY4887.
Newchapel (Capel Newydd). *Pembs.* ***Hamlet***, 5m/8km W of Newcastle Emlyn. **17 F1** SN2239.
Newchapel *Stoke* ***Locality***, 1m/2km E of Kidsgrove. **49 H7** SJ8654.
Newchapel *Surr.* ***Hamlet***, 3m/5km NW of East Grinstead. **23 G7** TQ3642.
Newchurch *B.Gwent* ***Suburb***, 1m/2km N of Ebbw Vale. SO1710.
Newchurch (Llannewydd). *Carmar.* ***Hamlet***, 3m/5km NW of Carmarthen. **17 G2** SN3824.
Newchurch *I.o.W.* ***Village***, 2m/4km NW of Sandown. **11 G6** SZ5685.
Newchurch *Kent* ***Village***, on Romney Marsh, 4m/7km N of New Romney. **15 F4** TR0531.
Newchurch *Lancs.* ***Hamlet***, 3m/4km NW of Nelson. **56 D6** SD8239.
Newchurch *Lancs.* ***Suburb***, 2m/3km E of Rawtenstall. **56 D7** SD8322.
Newchurch (Yr Eglwys Newydd ar y Cefn). *Mon.* ***Hamlet***, 2m/3km W of Devauden. **19 H2** ST4597.
Newchurch (Yr Eglwys Newydd). *Powys* ***Hamlet***, 5m/9km N of Hay-on-Wye. **28 B3** SO2150.
Newchurch *Staffs.* ***Hamlet***, 6m/9km W of Burton upon Trent. SK1423.
Newcott *Devon* ***Settlement***, 6m/10km NE of Honiton. **8 B4** ST2208.
Newcraighall *Edin.* ***Village***, 1m/2km SE of Portobello. **76 B3** NT3271.
Newdigate *Surr.* ***Village***, 5m/8km S of Dorking. **22 E7** TQ1942.
Newell Green *Brack.F.* ***Village***, 1m/2km NE of Bracknell. **22 B4** SU8871.
Newenden *Kent* ***Village***, on River Rother, 5m/8km SW of Tenterden. **14 D5** TQ8327.
Newent *Glos.* Population: 4111. ***Small town***, 8m/13km NW of Gloucester. Attractive brick and timber-framed buildings, Shambles Museum and interesting medieval church. **29 G6** SO7225.
Newerne *Glos.* ***Locality***, adjoining to NE of Lydney. **19 K1** SO6303.
Newfield *Dur.* ***Village***, 3m/5km W of Spennymoor. **62 D3** NZ2033.
Newfield *Dur.* ***Village***, 2m/3km W of Chester-le-Street. **62 D1** NZ2452.
Newfield *High.* ***Settlement***, in Ross and Cromarty district, 3m/5km S of Tain. **96 E4** NH7877.
Newfound *Hants.* ***Settlement***, 4m/6km W of Basingstoke. SU5851.
Newgale (Niwgwl). *Pembs.* ***Hamlet***, on St. Brides Bay, 3m/5km E of Solva. **16 B2** SM8422.
Newgale Sands *Pembs.* ***Coastal feature***, sandy beach stretching 2m/3km S from Newgale to Rickets Head. **16 B2** SM8422.
Newgate *Lancs.* ***Locality***, adjoining to W of Up Holland, 2m/3km E of Skelmersdale. SD5105.
Newgate *Norf.* ***Locality***, adjoining to S of Cley next the Sea, and containing Cley church. **44 E1** TG0543.
Newgate Street *Herts.* ***Hamlet***, 4m/7km NW of Cheshunt. **23 G1** TL3005.
Newgord *Shet.* ***Settlement***, just N of Westing, on W coast of Unst. **108 E2** HP5705.
Newhailes *E.Loth.* ***Locality***, adjoining to W of Musselburgh. NT3372.
Newhall *Ches.* ***Village***, 5m/8km NE of Whitchurch. **39 F1** SJ6045.
Newhall *Derbys.* ***Suburb***, 1m/2km NW of Swadlincote. **40 E3** SK2920.
Newhall Point *High.* ***Coastal feature***, N point of Udale Bay on Black Isle, 1km S of Invergordon across Cromarty Firth. **96 E5** NH7067.
Newham *Northumb.* ***Settlement***, 4m/6km SW of Seahouses. **71 G1** NU1728.
Newham Hall *Northumb.* ***Settlement***, 1m/2km NW of West Fleetham. **71 G1** NU1729.
Newhampton *Here.* ***Locality***, 4m/7km NW of Bromyard. SO5857.
Newhaven *E.Suss.* Population: 11,208. ***Town***, container and cross-Channel passenger port at mouth of River Ouse, 9m/14km E of Brighton. **13 H6** TQ4401.
Newhaven *Edin.* ***Suburb***, 2m/3km N of Edinburgh city centre. Small harbour on W side of Leith Harbour. NT2577.
Newhey *Gt.Man.* ***Village***, adjoining to SE of Milnrow. **49 J1** SD9311.
Newhill *S.Yorks.* ***Suburb***, S district of Wath upon Dearne. SK4399.
Newholm *N.Yorks.* ***Hamlet***, 2m/3km W of Whitby. **63 K5** NZ8610.
Newhouse *N.Lan.* ***Settlement***, 4m/6km SE of Airdrie. **75 F4** NS7961.
Newhouse *Wilts.* ***Historic house***, 17c house with Georgian wings, 1m/2km E of Redlynch and 9m/14km S of Salisbury. Features costume and document collection. **10 D2** SU2121.
Newhouse Industrial Estate *N.Lan.* *See Holytown.*
Newhouse Moor *Devon* ***Open space***, moorland 2m/3km NW of Witheridge. **7 F4** SS7917.
Newick *E.Suss.* Population: 2445. ***Village***, 4m/6km W of Uckfield. **13 H4** TQ4121.
Newick Park *E.Suss.* ***Garden***, 18c park with two gardens and farmland walk, 1m/2km S of Newick and 4m/6km SW of Uckfield. **13 H5** TQ4118.
Newingreen *Kent* ***Settlement***, 2m/4km NW of Hythe. TR1236.
Newington *Edin.* ***Suburb***, 1m/2km SE of Edinburgh city centre. NT2671.
Newington *Gt.Lon.* ***Suburb***, in borough of Southwark, N of New Kent Road. TQ3279.
Newington *Kent* ***Suburb***, 1m/2km NW of Ramsgate. TR3666.
Newington *Kent* Population: 2454. ***Village***, 3m/5km W of Sittingbourne. Site of Roman villa 1m/2km N. **24 E5** TQ8665.
Newington *Kent* ***Village***, 3m/4km W of Folkestone. **15 G4** TR1837.
Newington *Notts.* ***Hamlet***, 1m/2km NE of Bawtry. SK6694.
Newington *Oxon.* ***Village***, 5m/7km N of Wallingford. **21 K2** SU6096.
Newington Bagpath *Glos.* ***Settlement***, 5m/8km W of Tetbury. **20 B2** ST8194.
Newington House *Oxon.* ***Historic house***, in village of Newington, 4m/7km N of Wallingford. **21 K2** SU6096.
Newkirk ***Village***, 4m/6km NW of Dinnet. NJ4304.
Newland *Cornw.* ***Island***, small island 1km NW of Pentire Point, 4m/6km N of Padstow. **3 F1** SW9181.
Newland *Cumb.* ***Settlement***, 1m/2km NE of Ulverston. SD2979.
Newland *E.Riding* ***Settlement***, 1km SE of Eastrington, 3m/5km E of Howden. SE8029.
Newland *Glos.* ***Village***, 4m/6km SE of Monmouth. **19 J1** SO5509.
Newland *Hull* ***Suburb***, containing University of Hull, 2m/4km NW of Kingston upon Hull city centre. TA0731.
Newland *N.Yorks.* ***Hamlet***, on N bank of River Aire, 7m/11km SE of Selby. **58 C7** SE6924.
Newland *Oxon.* ***Suburb***, adjoining to E of Witney. SP3610.
Newland *Som.* ***Hamlet***, on Exmoor, 2m/3km W of Exford. SS8238.
Newland *Worcs.* ***Village***, 2m/3km NE of Great Malvern. **29 G4** SO7948.
Newland Common *Worcs.* ***Settlement***, 2m/3km S of Droitwich Spa. SO9060.
Newland Hall *W.Yorks.* ***Settlement***, on E bank of River Calder, 1m/2km W of Normanton. SE3622.
Newlandrig *Midloth.* ***Hamlet***, 2m/3km NE of Gorebridge. **76 B4** NT3662.
Newlands *Cumb.* ***Hamlet***, 1m/2km NE of Hesket Newmarket. NY3439.
Newlands *Essex* ***Suburb***, E district of Canvey Island. TQ8183.
Newlands *Glas.* ***Suburb***, 3m/5km S of Glasgow city centre. NS5760.
Newlands *Northumb.* ***Hamlet***, 1km W of Ebchester. **62 B1** NZ0955.
Newlands *Sc.Bord.* ***Settlement***, on E bank of Hermitage Water, 4m/7km N of Newcastleton. **70 A4** NY5094.
Newland's Corner *Surr.* ***Locality***, 3m/5km E of Guildford. **22 D7** TQ0449.
Newlands Hill *E.Loth.* ***Mountain***, 2m/3km SE of Danskine. Height 1387 feet or 423 metres. **76 D4** NT5865.
Newlands of Geise *High.* ***Settlement***, 2m/3km SW of Thurso. **105 F2** ND0865.
Newlands of Tynet *Moray* ***Hamlet***, near N coast, 4m/6km SW of Buckie. NJ3761.
Newlay *W.Yorks.* ***Locality***, on River Aire, 4m/6km NW of Leeds city centre. SE2436.
Newlyn *Cornw.* ***Suburb***, fishing port adjoining to S of Penzance. **2 B6** SW4628.
Newlyn Downs *Cornw.* ***Open space***, hillslope 1m/2km S of St. Newlyn East. **3 F3** SW8254.
Newlyn East *Cornw.* ***Village***, 4m/6km S of Newquay. **3 F3** SW8256.
Newmachar *Aber.* Population: 1504. ***Village***, 9m/14km N of Aberdeen. **91 G3** NJ8819.
Newmains *N.Lan.* Population: 5878. ***Small town***, 2m/3km E of Wishaw. **75 G5** NS8256.
Newman's End *Essex* ***Settlement***, 5m/8km NE of Harlow. TL5112.
Newman's Green *Suff.* ***Hamlet***, 2m/3km NE of Sudbury. TL8843.
Newmarket *Suff.* Population: 16,498. ***Town***, 13m/20km E of Cambridge. Headquarters of British horse-racing. National Horse Racing Museum is next to Jockey Club in High Street. Racecourses. **33 K2** TL6463.
Newmarket *W.Isles* ***Village***, on Isle of Lewis, 2m/3km N of Stornoway, adjoining to N of Laxdale across River Laxdale. **101 G4** NB4235.
Newmarket Heath *Suff.* ***Open space***, heath, 1m/2km W of Newmarket town centre. **33 K2** TL6163.
Newmarket Hill *E.Suss.* ***Hill***, rising to over 200 metres, 1m/2km SE of Falmer. Mast at summit. **13 G6** TQ3606.
Newmarket Racecourse *Cambs.* ***Racecourse***, 2m/3km SW of Newmarket town centre. Two flat-racing courses, with thirty-one race days a year. The 1000 Guineas, the first of English Classics, is staged in May. National Stud. **33 K2** TL6162.
Newmill *Aber.* ***Settlement***, 3m/4km E of Inverurie. **91 G2** NJ8122.
Newmill *Aber.* ***Settlement***, 3m/5km SW of New Deer. **99 G6** NJ8543.
Newmill *Moray* ***Village***, 1m/2km N of Keith. **98 C5** NJ4350.
Newmill *Sc.Bord.* ***Settlement***, in Teviotdale, 4m/7km SW of Hawick, at confluence of Allan Water and River Teviot. **69 K2** NT4510.
Newmill of Inshewan *Angus* ***Settlement***, 2m/3km E of Dykehead. **83 F1** NO4260.
Newmillerdam *W.Yorks.* ***Village***, 3m/5km S of Wakefield. SE3215.
Newmillerdam Country Park *W.Yorks.* ***Leisure/recreation***, mixed woodland and aboretum surrounding lake, 3m/4km NW of Royston at S edge of Wakefield. **51 F1** SE3314.
Newmills *Edin.* ***Locality***, just N of Balerno across Water of Leith. NT1667.
Newmills *High.* ***Settlement***, on Cromarty Firth in Ross and Cromarty district, 2m/3km SW of Balblair. **96 D5** NH6764.
Newmiln *P. & K.* ***Hamlet***, 3m/4km N of New Scone. **82 C4** NO1230.
Newmiln *P. & K.* ***Settlement***, 2m/3km SW of Methven. **82 B5** NO0122.
Newmilns *E.Ayr.* Population: 3436. ***Small town***, on River Irvine, 7m/11km E of Kilmarnock. Once famous for muslim-weaving and lace. **74 D7** NS5337.
Newney Green *Essex* ***Hamlet***, 3m/5km W of Chelmsford town centre. TL6506.
Newnham *Cambs.* ***Suburb***, 1km SW of Cambridge city centre. Newnham College, women's college of Cambridge University, to N. TL4457.
Newnham *Glos.* ***Village***, on W bank of River Severn, 10m/16km SW of Gloucester across loops of river. **29 F7** SO6911.
Newnham *Hants.* ***Village***, 1m/2km W of Hook. **22 A6** SU7054.
Newnham *Herts.* ***Village***, 2m/4km N of Baldock. **33 F5** TL2437.
Newnham *Kent* ***Village***, 5m/8km SW of Faversham. **14 E2** TQ9557.
Newnham *Northants.* ***Village***, 2m/3km S of Daventry. **31 G3** SP5759.
Newnham Bridge *Worcs.* ***Village***, on N bank of River Rea, 3m/5km E of Tenbury Wells. **29 F2** SO6469.
Newnham Murren *Oxon.* ***Locality***, to E of Wallingford across River Thames. SU6189.
Newnham Paddox *Warks.* ***Settlement***, 4m/6km SW of Lutterworth. **41 G7** SP4883.
Newnoth *Aber.* ***Settlement***, to E of Hill of Noth, 1m/2km S of Gartly. **90 D1** NJ5130.
Newport *Cornw.* ***Suburb***, N district of Launceston. **6 B7** SX3385.
Newport *Devon* ***Suburb***, SW district of Barnstaple. **6 D2** SS5632.
Newport *E.Riding* ***Village***, 7m/11km E of Howden. **58 E6** SE8530.
Newport *Essex* Population: 2178. ***Village***, 3m/5km SW of Saffron Walden. **33 J5** TL5234.
Newport *Glos.* ***Village***, 1m/2km SE of Berkeley. **19 K2** ST6997.
Newport *High.* ***Village***, near E coast of Caithness district, 4m/6km SW of Dunbeath. **105 G6** ND1324.
Newport *I.o.W.* Population: 20,574. ***Town***, largest town on Isle of Wight, at head of River Medina estuary, 4m/7km S of Cowes and midway between Yarmouth and Bembridge. Guildhall and town hall both designed by John Nash. Roman villa at edge of town. **11 G6** SZ4989.
Newport (Casnewydd). *Newport* Population: 115,522. ***Town***, industrial county town and port on River Usk, 10m/16km NE of Cardiff. Previously dependent upon steel, town now has a wider variety of industries. Transporter bridge across River Usk above docks area. Cathedral, former parish church. Sparse ruins of 12c castle (Cadw). University. **19 G3** ST3088.
Newport *Norf.* ***Locality***, coastal resort, 6m/10km N of Great Yarmouth. **45 K4** TG5016.
Newport (Trefdraeth). *Pembs.* ***Small town***, at mouth of River Nyfer, 9m/14km SW of Cardigan. Remains of 13c castle. **16 D1** SN0539.
Newport *Som.* ***Hamlet***, 1m/2km S of North Curry. ST3123.
Newport *Tel. & W.* Population: 10,964. ***Town***, market town on Shropshire Union Canal, 8m/12km NE of Wellington. Many Georgian and Victorian buildings. **39 G4** SJ7419.
Newport Bay *Pembs.* ***Bay***, to NW of Newport, extending E from Dinas Head. **16 D1** SN0539.
Newport Castle *Newport* ***Castle***, stone castle (Cadw) built in 1191 on site of early Norman motte and bailey castle. Partly destroyed and rebuilt on several occasions. Ruins partly restored in 1930. **19 G3** SO3188.
Newport Museum and Art Gallery *Newport* ***Other feature of interest***, in central Newport. Museum has local history and natural history exhibits; art gallery has 18c and 19c watercolours, Welsh paintings, porcelain and sculpture. **19 G3** ST3187.

N

Newport-on-Tay *Fife* Population: 4343. ***Small town***, on S bank of Firth of Tay, opposite Dundee, and connected to it by road and rail bridges. **83 F5** NO4228.
Newport Pagnell *M.K.* Population: 12,285. ***Town***, at confluence of River Great Ouse and River Ouzel or Lovat, 6m/10km N of Bletchley. 19c cast-iron Tickford Bridge spans river. **32 B4** SP8743.
Newpound Common *W.Suss.* ***Hamlet***, 2m/3km NW of Billingshurst. **12 D4** TQ0627.
Newquay *Cornw.* Population: 17,390. ***Town***, popular coastal resort with several sandy beaches, 11m/17km N of Truro. A former fishing village, it expanded with coming of railway, and buildings are mostly Victorian or later. Centre of surfing in Britain. **3 F2** SW8161.
Newquay Bay *Cornw.* ***Bay***, N of Newquay, extends W from Trevelgue Head to Towan Head. **3 F2** SW8161.
Newquay Zoo *Cornw.* ***Leisure/recreation***, traditional zoo at Newquay, boasting additional attractions including a maze, oriental garden and activity play park. **3 F2** SW8261.
Newsam Green *W.Yorks.* ***Settlement***, 1m/2km W of Swillington. SE3630.
Newsbank *Ches.* ***Settlement***, 3m/4km NW of Congleton. SJ8366.
Newseat *Aber.* ***Settlement***, 2m/3km N of Kirktown of Rayne. **91 F1** NJ7032.
Newsells *Herts.* ***Settlement***, 3m/5km SE of Royston. TL3837.
Newsham *Lancs.* ***Hamlet***, 5m/8km N of Preston. **55 J6** SD5136.
Newsham *N.Yorks.* ***Settlement***, 4m/6km NW of Thirsk. **57 J1** SE3784.
Newsham *N.Yorks.* ***Village***, 7m/11km NW of Richmond. **62 C5** NZ1010.
Newsham *Northumb.* ***Locality***, adjoining to SW of Blyth. **71 H6** NZ3079.
Newsham *Stock.* ***Settlement***, 3m/4km SW of Yarm. NZ3811.
Newsholme *E.Riding* ***Hamlet***, 2m/3km NW of Howden. **58 D7** SE7229.
Newsholme *Lancs.* ***Settlement***, 2m/3km N of Gisburn. **6 D4** SD8451.
Newsholme *W.Yorks.* ***Hamlet***, between Keighley Moor and Branshaw Moor, 3m/4km W of Keighley. SE0239.
Newsome *W.Yorks.* ***Suburb***, 1m/2km S of Huddersfield town centre. SE1414.
Newstead *Northumb.* ***Hamlet***, 3m/5km NW of North Charlton. **71 G1** NU1527.
Newstead *Notts.* ***Village***, 3m/5km SE of Kirkby in Ashfield. Newstead Abbey 1m/2km NE. **51 H7** SK5152.
Newstead *Sc.Bord.* ***Village***, 1m/2km E of Melrose. Remains of Roman fort of Trimontium to E. **76 D7** NT5634.
Newstead *W.Yorks.* ***Locality***, adjoining to NE of Ryhill. SE3914.
Newstead Abbey *Notts.* ***Historic house***, given to Lord Byron's ancestors during Dissolution and set in 300 acres of parkland, 1m/2km NE of Newstead. Byron memorabilia in abbey. **51 H7** SK5152.
Newthorpe *N.Yorks.* ***Hamlet***, 2m/3km SW of Sherburn in Elmet. **57 K6** SE4732.
Newthorpe *Notts.* ***Suburb***, E district of Eastwood. SK4846.
Newtimber *W.Suss.* ***Locality***, parish on N slopes of South Downs to E of Poynings containing Newtimber Hill (National Trust), with views of sea and The Weald, and Newtimber Place, moated 17c-18c house. TQ2613.
Newton *Aber.* ***Settlement***, 4m/7km SE of Keith. **98 C6** NJ4745.
Newton *Aber.* ***Settlement***, 4m/6km S of Mintlaw. **99 J6** NK0142.
Newton *Arg. & B.* ***Settlement***, on Newton Bay, on S shore of Loch Fyne, Argyll, opposite Furnace. **73 J1** NS0498.
Newton (Drenewydd). *Bridgend* ***Suburb***, 1m/2km NE of Porthcawl town centre. **18 B4** SS8377.
Newton *Cambs.* ***Village***, 4m/6km NW of Wisbech. **43 H4** TF4314.
Newton *Cambs.* ***Village***, 6m/9km S of Cambridge. **33 H4** TL4349.
Newton (Y Drenewydd). *Cardiff* ***Hamlet***, to E of Cardiff, 1m/2km SE of Rumney. ST2378.
Newton *Ches.* ***Hamlet***, 1m/2km NE of Tattenhall. **48 D7** SJ5059.
Newton *Ches.* ***Settlement***, 2m/3km S of Frodsham. **48 E5** SJ5274.
Newton *Ches.* ***Suburb***, NE district of Chester. SJ4268.
Newton *Cumb.* ***Village***, 2m/3km S of Dalton-in-Furness. **55 F2** SD2271.
Newton *Derbys.* ***Village***, 3m/5km NE of Alfreton. SK4459.
Newton *D. & G.* ***Village***, 7m/11km S of Moffat. **69 G4** NY1194.
Newton *Gt.Man.* ***Locality***, 1km NE of Hyde. **49 J3** SJ9596.
Newton *Here.* ***Hamlet***, 4m/6km NW of Ewyas Harold. SO3433.
Newton *Here.* ***Locality***, 4m/6km SW of Leintwardine. **28 C2** SO3769.
Newton *Here.* ***Village***, 3m/5km S of Leominster. SO5053.
Newton *High.* ***Settlement***, on SW side of Loch Glencoul, Sutherland district. **102 E5** NC2331.
Newton *High.* ***Settlement***, 1m/2km W of Watten. **105 H3** ND2153.
Newton *High.* ***Settlement***, in Caithness district, 1m/2km SW of Wick. **105 J4** ND3449.
Newton *High.* ***Settlement***, 3m/5km E of Muir of Ord. **96 C6** NH5850.
Newton *High.* ***Settlement***, in Inverness district, near E shore of Inner Moray Firth or Inverness Firth, 2m/3km E of Alturlie Point. **96 E7** NH7448.
Newton *High.* ***Settlement***, in Ross and Cromarty district, 1m/2km SW of Cromarty. **96 E5** NH7766.
Newton *Lancs.* ***Hamlet***, 3m/4km S of Kirkby Lonsdale. **55 J2** SD5974.
Newton *Lancs.* ***Settlement***, 2m/4km E of Blackpool. SD3436.
Newton *Lancs.* ***Village***, 2m/3km SE of Kirkham. SD4430.
Newton *Lancs.* ***Village***, on River Hodder, 6m/10km NW of Clitheroe. **56 B4** SD6950.
Newton *Lincs.* ***Village***, 6m/10km S of Sleaford. **42 D2** TF0436.
Newton *Moray* ***Settlement***, 1m/2km S of Garmouth. **98 B4** NJ3362.
Newton *Norf.* ***Hamlet***, 4m/7km N of Swaffham. **44 C4** TF8315.
Newton *N.Ayr.* ***Settlement***, on N coast of Arran, 1km NE of Lochranza across Loch Ranza. **73 H5** NR9351.
Newton *Northants.* ***Village***, 3m/5km N of Kettering. **42 B7** SP8883.
Newton *Northumb.* ***Settlement***, 1m/2km E of Alwinton. NT9407.
Newton *Northumb.* ***Village***, 3m/5km E of Corbridge. **71 F7** NZ0364.
Newton *Notts.* ***Village***, 2m/3km NW of Bingham. **41 J1** SK6841.
Newton *Pembs.* ***Locality***, 4m/6km W of Wolf's Castle. Includes Newton Cross and Newton West Farm. **16 C2** SM8927.
Newton *Pembs.* ***Settlement***, 4m/7km W of Pembroke. **16 C4** SM9000.
Newton *P. & K.* ***Settlement***, on N bank of River Almond, 6m/10km N of Crieff. **81 K4** NN8831.
Newton *Sc.Bord.* ***Hamlet***, 3m/5km W of Jedburgh. **70 B1** NT6020.
Newton *Shrop.* ***Settlement***, 1m/2km E of Ellesmere. SJ4234.
Newton *Som.* ***Hamlet***, 4m/6km SE of Watchet. ST1038.
Newton *S.Glos.* ***Hamlet***, 2m/3km N of Thornbury. ST6492.
Newton *S.Lan.* ***Locality***, 6m/9km SE of Glasgow. NS6660.
Newton *S.Lan.* ***Settlement***, 1m/2km W of Wiston. **75 H7** NS9331.
Newton *S.Yorks.* ***Suburb***, 1km W of Doncaster town centre. SE5602.
Newton *Staffs.* ***Village***, 5m/8km N of Rugeley. **40 C3** SK0325.
Newton *Suff.* ***Village***, 3m/5km E of Sudbury. **34 D4** TL9140.
Newton *Swan.* ***Locality***, on W side of The Mumbles. **17 K6** SS6088.
Newton *Warks.* ***Village***, 3m/4km NE of Rugby. **31 G1** SP5378.
Newton *W.Loth.* ***Settlement***, 2m/3km W of S end of Forth Road Bridge. **75 J3** NT0977.
Newton *W.Mid.* ***Suburb***, 3m/4km NE of West Bromwich town centre. SP0393.
Newton *W.Yorks.* ***Locality***, 2m/3km E of Allerton Bywater. **57 K7** SE4427.
Newton *W.Isles Anglicised form of Baile Mhic Phail, qv.*
Newton *Wilts.* ***Hamlet***, 7m/12km SE of Salisbury. **10 D2** SU2322.
Newton Abbot *Devon* Population: 23,801. ***Town***, market town at head of River Teign estuary. Houses of Victorian railway workers survive, and 15c Bradley Manor is National Trust property. Racecourse. **5 J3** SX8671.
Newton Arlosh *Cumb.* ***Village***, 2m/3km SW of Kirkbride. **60 C1** NY1955.
Newton Aycliffe *Dur.* Population: 25,085. ***Town***, New Town designated 1947, 6m/10km N of Darlington. 12c church with Saxon foundations. **62 D4** NZ2724.
Newton Bewley *Hart.* ***Hamlet***, 1m/2km NE of Wolviston. **63 F4** NZ4626.
Newton Blossomville *M.K.* ***Village***, on River Great Ouse, 6m/9km NE of Newport Pagnell. **32 C3** SP9251.
Newton Bromswold *Northants.* ***Village***, 3m/4km E of Rushden. **32 D2** SP9965.
Newton Burgoland *Leics.* ***Village***, 5m/8km S of Ashby de la Zouch. **41 F5** SK3609.
Newton by Toft *Lincs.* ***Village***, 4m/6km W of Market Rasen. **52 D4** TF0587.
Newton Common *Mersey.* ***Suburb***, adjoining to W of Newton-le-Willows. SJ5695.
Newton Dale *N.Yorks.* ***Valley***, narrow valley in S part of North York Moors, on E side of Cropton Forest, and through which runs North Yorkshire Moors Railway. Valley carries Pickering Beck from Goathland Moor in N to Pickering in S. SE8191.
Newton Ferrers *Devon* Population: 1479. ***Village***, 3m/5km SW of Yealmpton, on creek running into River Yealm estuary. Yachting. **5 F6** SX5448.
Newton Flotman *Norf.* ***Village***, 7m/11km S of Norwich. **45 G6** TM2198.
Newton Green *Mon.* ***Village***, 1m/2km SW of Chepstow. ST5191.
Newton Harcourt *Leics.* ***Village***, 6m/9km SE of Leicester. **41 J6** SP6396.
Newton Haven (Also known as St. Mary's Haven.) *Northumb.* ***Bay***, National Trust property on North Sea coast, 1km SE of High Newton-by-the-Sea. Newton Point at N end. **71 H1** NU2424.
Newton Heath *Dorset* ***Open space***, partly afforested area 3m/5km NE of Corfe Castle. **10 B6** SZ0084.
Newton Heath *Gt.Man.* ***Suburb***, 3m/5km NE of Manchester city centre. SD8800.
Newton Hill *W.Yorks.* ***Locality***, 1m/2km N of Wakefield. SE3222.
Newton Ketton *Darl.* ***Settlement***, 4m/7km N of Darlington. NZ3120.
Newton Kyme *N.Yorks.* ***Village***, 2m/3km NW of Tadcaster. **57 K5** SE4644.
Newton-le-Willows *Mersey.* Population: 19,416. ***Town***, 5m/8km E of St. Helens; originally an old farming village. **48 E3** SJ5995.
Newton-le-Willows *N.Yorks.* ***Village***, 3m/5km W of Bedale. **57 H1** SE2189.
Newton Longville *Bucks.* Population: 1979. ***Village***, 2m/4km SW of Bletchley. **32 B5** SP8431.
Newton Mearns *E.Renf.* Population: 19,494. ***Suburb***, 6m/10km SW of Glasgow. **74 D5** NS5355.
Newton Moor *Gt.Man.* ***Locality***, adjoining to N of Newton. SJ9595.
Newton Morrell *N.Yorks.* ***Hamlet***, 3m/5km NE of Scotch Corner. **62 D6** NZ2309.
Newton Morrell *Oxon.* ***Settlement***, 5m/8km NE of Bicester. SP6129.
Newton Mountain *Pembs.* ***Hamlet***, 5m/8km S of Haverfordwest. **16 C4** SM9808.
Newton Mulgrave *N.Yorks.* ***Settlement***, 2m/3km S of Staithes. **63 J5** NZ7815.
Newton Noyes *Pembs.* ***Locality***, 1km E of Milford Haven. SM9205.
Newton of Ardtoe *High.* ***Settlement***, 3m/4km NW of Acharacle, Lochaber district. **86 C7** NM6470.
Newton of Balcanquhal *P. & K.* ***Settlement***, 1m/2km E of Glenfarg. **82 C6** NO1510.
Newton of Dalvey *Moray* ***Settlement***, on E side of River Findhorn, 2m/3km W of Forres. **97 H6** NJ0057.
Newton of Falkland *Fife* ***Village***, 1m/2km E of Falkland. **82 D7** NO2607.
Newton of Leys *High.* ***Settlement***, 3m/5km S of Inverness. **96 D7** NH6739.
Newton-on-Ouse *N.Yorks.* ***Village***, 7m/12km NW of York. **58 B3** SE5160.
Newton-on-Rawcliffe *N.Yorks.* ***Village***, 4m/7km N of Pickering. **63 K7** SE8190.
Newton on the Hill *Shrop.* ***Settlement***, 1m/2km E of Myddle. SJ4823.
Newton-on-the-Moor *Northumb.* ***Village***, 5m/8km S of Alnwick. **71 G3** NU1705.
Newton on Trent *Lincs.* ***Village***, 9m/15km W of Lincoln. **52 B5** SK8374.
Newton Poppleford *Devon* ***Village***, 3m/5km NW of Sidmouth. **7 J7** SY0889.
Newton Purcell *Oxon.* ***Hamlet***, 6m/9km NE of Bicester. **31 H5** SP6230.
Newton Regis *Warks.* ***Village***, 5m/8km NE of Tamworth. **40 E5** SK2707.
Newton Reigny *Cumb.* ***Village***, 2m/4km NW of Penrith. **61 F3** NY4731.
Newton St. Cyres *Devon* ***Village***, 3m/5km SE of Crediton. **7 G6** SX8898.
Newton St. Faith *Norf.* ***Village***, 5m/9km N of Norwich. **45 G4** TG2117.
Newton St. Loe *B. & N.E.Som.* ***Village***, 3m/5km W of Bath. **20 A5** ST7064.
Newton St. Petrock *Devon* ***Village***, 7m/11km SW of Great Torrington. **6 C4** SS4112.
Newton Solney *Derbys.* ***Village***, 3m/5km NE of Burton upon Trent, at confluence of River Dove and River Trent. **40 E3** SK2825.
Newton Stacey *Hants.* ***Hamlet***, 1m/2km E of Chilbolton. **21 H7** SU4140.
Newton Stewart *D. & G.* Population: 3673. ***Small town***, market town on River Cree, 7m/11km N of Wigtown, and popular holiday resort and fishing centre. **64 E4** NX4165.
Newton Tony *Wilts.* ***Village***, on River Bourne, 4m/7km E of Amesbury. **21 F7** SU2140.
Newton Tors *Northumb.* ***Mountain***, 4m/7km N of The Cheviot. Height 1761 feet or 537 metres. **70 E1** NT9027.
Newton Tracey *Devon* ***Village***, 4m/7km SW of Barnstaple. **6 D3** SS5226.
Newton under Roseberry *R. & C.* ***Hamlet***, 3m/5km SW of Guisborough. **63 G5** NZ5713.
Newton Underwood *Northumb.* ***Settlement***, 3m/5km W of Morpeth. NZ1486.
Newton upon Ayr *S.Ayr.* ***Suburb***, N district of Ayr. NS3423.
Newton upon Derwent *E.Riding* ***Village***, 5m/8km W of Pocklington. **58 D5** SE7249.
Newton Valence *Hants.* ***Village***, 4m/6km S of Alton. **11 J1** SU7232.
Newton Wood *Gt.Man.* ***Suburb***, 1m/2km S of Dukinfield. SJ9496.
Newtonairds *D. & G.* ***Settlement***, 3m/4km S of Dunscore. **68 D5** NX8880.
Newtonferry *W.Isles Anglicised form of Port nan Long, qv.*
Newtongarry *Aber.* ***Locality***, comprising Mains of Newtongarry and Newtongarry Hill, 3m/5km E of Huntly. NJ5735.
Newtongrange *Midloth.* ***Town***, former mining town, 2m/3km S of Dalkeith. Scottish Mining Museum at Lady Victoria colliery. **76 B4** NT3364.
Newtonhill *Aber.* Population: 2139. ***Village***, on E coast, 5m/8km NE of Stonehaven. **91 H5** NO9193.
Newtonmill *Angus* ***Settlement***, 3m/4km N of Brechin. **83 H1** NO6064.
Newtonmore *High.* Population: 1044. ***Village***, on River Spey, in Badenoch and Strathspey district, 3m/5km W of Kingussie. Holiday and skiing centre. Clan Macpherson Museum. **88 E5** NN7199.
Newtown *Aber.* ***Suburb***, E district of Macduff. **99 F4** NJ7164.
Newtown *Beds.* ***Locality***, 2m/3km E of Shefford. TL1739.
Newtown *B.Gwent* ***Locality***, adjoining to N of Tredegar. **28 A7** SO1710.
Newtown *Bridgend* ***Suburb***, to N of Bridgend town centre. SS9080.
Newtown *Bucks.* ***Suburb***, NE district of Chesham. **22 C1** SP9602.
Newtown *Caerp.* ***Locality***, adjoining to SW of Crosskeys, 4m/7km NE of Caerphilly. ST2191.
Newtown *Cambs.* ***Suburb***, 1km NE of Huntingdon town centre. TL2472.
Newtown *Ches.* ***Settlement***, 1m/2km SW of Tattenhall. **48 D7** SJ5058.
Newtown *Ches.* ***Suburb***, 1km NE of Frodsham. SJ5278.
Newtown *Ches.* ***Suburb***, adjoining to E of Poynton. SJ9383.
Newtown *Cornw.* ***Hamlet***, 5m/8km W of Helston. SW5729.
Newtown *Cornw.* ***Hamlet***, 5m/7km SW of Launceston. SX2978.

N

Newtown *Cornw.* ***Settlement***, 1m/2km NW of Fowey. SX1052.
Newtown *Cumb.* ***Hamlet***, 2m/3km NW of Brampton. **70 A7** NY5062.
Newtown *Cumb.* ***Locality***, 3m/5km S of Silloth. Site of Roman fort of Bibra on coast of Solway Firth, to NW. NY0948.
Newtown *Cumb.* ***Locality***, adjoining to NE of Aspatria. NY1542.
Newtown *Cumb.* ***Locality***, 4m/6km S of Penrith. NY5224.
Newtown *Cumb.* ***Suburb***, 1m/2km W of Carlisle city centre. NY3855.
Newtown *Derbys.* ***Locality***, adjoining to SW of New Mills. **49 J4** SJ9984.
Newtown *Devon* ***Hamlet***, 3m/5km E of South Molton. SS7625.
Newtown *Devon* ***Settlement***, 3m/5km NW of Ottery St. Mary. SY0699.
Newtown *Dorset* ***Hamlet***, 1km N of Beaminster. ST4802.
Newtown *Glos.* ***Suburb***, E district of Tewkesbury. SO9032.
Newtown *Glos.* ***Village***, adjoining to S of Sharpness, 2m/3km N of Berkeley. SO6701.
Newtown *Gt.Man.* ***Suburb***, 1m/2km W of Wigan town centre. SD5605.
Newtown *Gt.Man.* ***Suburb***, 1km N of Swinton town centre. SD7702.
Newtown *Hants.* ***Hamlet***, in New Forest, 2m/4km NW of Lyndhurst. **10 D3** SU2710.
Newtown *Hants.* ***Hamlet***, 3m/5km NW of Romsey. **10 E2** SU3023.
Newtown *Hants.* ***Locality***, residential locality adjoining to S of Warsash; location of School of Navigation (University of Southampton). SU4905.
Newtown *Hants.* ***Locality***, adjoining to W of Bishop's Waltham. **11 G3** SU5417.
Newtown *Hants.* ***Suburb***, in S part of Liphook. SU8430.
Newtown *Hants.* ***Village***, 3m/4km S of Newsbury. **21 H5** SU4763.
Newtown *Hants.* ***Village***, 4m/7km S of Meonstoke. **11 H3** SU6113.
Newtown *Here.* ***Settlement***, 1m/2km SW of Leominster. SO4757.
Newtown *Here.* ***Suburb***, W district of Ledbury. **29 G5** SO7037.
Newtown *Here.* ***Village***, 7m/11km E of Hereford. **29 F4** SO6144.
Newtown *High.* ***Locality***, in Invernesss district, 3m/5km SW of Fort Augustus. **87 K4** NH3504.
Newtown *I.o.M.* ***Village***, 4m/6km W of Douglas. **54 C6** SC3273.
Newtown *I.o.W.* ***Village***, 5m/8km W of Newport. Formerly a 'rotten borough'; Old Town Hall (National Trust), also Noah's Ark (National Trust), once an inn. **11 F5** SZ4290.
Newtown *Lancs.* ***Locality***, 2m/3km E of Croston, 4m/7km W of Chorley. SD5118.
Newtown *Moray* ***Locality***, on N coast adjoining to W of Hopeman, 6m/9km W of Lossiemouth. NJ1469.
Newtown *Northants.* ***Locality***, W end of Woodford, 3m/4km SW of Thrapston. SP9677.
Newtown *Northumb.* ***Hamlet***, 1m/2km SW of Rothbury. **71 F3** NU0300.
Newtown *Northumb.* ***Hamlet***, 4m/6km SE of Wooler. **71 F1** NU0425.
Newtown *Oxon.* ***Suburb***, S district of Henley-on-Thames. SU7681.
Newtown *Poole* ***Suburb***, 1m/2km NE of Poole town centre. **10 B5** SZ0393.
Newtown (Y Drenewydd). *Powys* Population: 10,548. ***Town***, former textile town on River Severn, 12m/20km SW of Welshpool. New Town designated 1967, extending to W, is a busy commercial centre. Birthplace of Robert Owen (Father of Socialism). **38 A6** SO1091.
Newtown *R.C.T.* ***Village***, adjoining to SE of Mountain Ash. ST0598.
Newtown *Shrop.* ***Hamlet***, 3m/5km NW of Wem. **38 D2** SJ4731.
Newtown *Som.* ***Hamlet***, 1km SE of Buckland St. Mary. ST2712.
Newtown *Som.* ***Suburb***, N district of Bridgwater. ST2937.
Newtown *S'ham.* ***Suburb***, SE district of Southampton across River Itchen. SU4510.
Newtown *Staffs.* ***Hamlet***, 2m/3km SW of Longnor. **50 C6** SK0663.
Newtown *Staffs.* ***Settlement***, 2m/3km NW of Biddulph. **49 J6** SJ9060.
Newtown *Staffs.* ***Settlement***, 4m/6km N of Walsall. SJ9904.
Newtown *Wilts.* ***Hamlet***, 5m/8km NE of Shaftesbury. **9 J2** ST9129.
Newtown *Wilts.* ***Settlement***, 4m/6km SW of Hungerford. SU3063.
Newtown *Worcs.* ***Suburb***, N district of Stourport-on-Severn. SO8172.
Newtown *Worcs.* ***Suburb***, E district of Worcester. SO8755.
Newtown Bay *I.o.W.* ***Bay***, at mouth of Newtown River, 4m/6km NE of Yarmouth. Coast to E and W is National Trust property. **11 F5** SZ4290.
Newtown-in-Saint-Martin *Cornw.* ***Hamlet***, 6m/9km SE of Helston. **2 E6** SW7423.
Newtown Linford *Leics.* ***Village***, 6m/9km NW of Leicester. **41 H4** SK5110.
Newtown of Rockcliffe *Cumb.* ***Locality***, 4m/7km N of Carlisle. NY3862.
Newtown Old Town Hall *I.o.W.* ***Historic house***, 17c town hall (National Trust) at Newtown, 5m/8km NW of Newport. Was seat of Newtown 'rotten borough' until 1832. **11 F5** SZ4290.
Newtown St. Boswells *Sc.Bord.* Population: 1108. ***Village***, 3m/4km SE of Melrose. **76 D7** NT5731.
Newtown Unthank *Leics.* ***Settlement***, to W of Leicester, 1m/2km NE of Desford. **41 G5** SK4904.
Newtyle *Angus* ***Village***, below N side of Newtyle Hill, 9m/15km NW of Dundee. **82 D3** NO2941.
Newtyle Forest *Moray* ***Forest/woodland***, 4m/7km S of Forres. **97 H6** NJ0552.
Newtyle Hill *P. & K.* ***Mountain***, 1m/2km E of Dunkeld. Height 1040 feet or 317 metres. **82 B3** NO0441.
Newyears Green *Gt.Lon.* ***Settlement***, in borough of Hillingdon, 3m/4km NE of Uxbridge. TQ0788.
Neyland *Pembs.* Population: 3006. ***Small town***, and former port opposite Pembroke Dock across Cleddau estuary and 4m/6km E of Milford Haven. **16 C4** SM9605.
Niarbyl Bay *I.o.M.* ***Bay***, on SW side of island, extending S to Bradda Hill. Has small island, Niarbyl Island at N end. **54 B6** SC2077.
Niarbyl Island (Also known as The Niarbyl.) *I.o.M.* ***Island***, small island off W coast at N end of Niarbyl Bay and 1km SW of Dalby. **54 B6** SC2077.
Nibley *Glos.* ***Locality***, adjoining to SW of Blakeney. **19 K1** SO6606.
Nibley *S.Glos.* ***Hamlet***, 2m/3km W of Chipping Sodbury. **19 K3** ST6982.
Nibley Green *Glos.* ***Hamlet***, 2m/3km SW of Dursley. ST7396.
Nibon *Shet.* ***Locality***, on coast in N part of Mainland, 2m/3km NW of Mangaster. Offshore is island called Isle of Nibon. HU3073.
Nicholashayne *Devon* ***Hamlet***, 2m/3km N of Culmstock. **7 K4** ST1016.
Nicholaston *Swan.* ***Hamlet***, on S coast of Gower peninsula, above E end of Oxwich Bay. **17 J6** SS5288.
Nick of Kindram *D. & G.* ***Coastal feature***, cliff indentation 3m/5km W of Mull of Galloway. **64 B7** NX1132.
Nick of the Balloch Pass *S.Ayr.* ***Other feature of interest***, mountain road pass between Pinbreck Hill and Glengap Hill, 4m/7km E of Barr. **67 H4** NX3493.
Nickie's Hill *Cumb.* ***Settlement***, 1m/2km S of Kirkambeck. NY5367.
Nidd *N.Yorks.* ***Hamlet***, 1m/2km E of Ripley. **57 J3** SE3060.
Nidd *N.Yorks.* ***River***, rising on N slope of Great Whernside and flowing E through Angram and Scar House Reservoirs, SE by Pateley Bridge and Knaresborough to Walshford, then E to join River Ouse at Nun Monkton. SE5157.
Nidderdale *N.Yorks.* ***Valley***, upper part of valley of River Nidd, carved out from Millstone Grit rocks and running E from Scar House Reservoir, then S to Gouthwaite Reservoir. **57 F2** SE0976.
Niddrie *Edin.* ***Suburb***, 3m/5km SE of Edinburgh city centre. **76 A3** NT3071.
Niddry Burn *W.Loth.* ***River***, rising to S of Riccarton Hills and flowing E to Union Canal at Winchburgh. **75 J3** NT0874.
Niddry Castle *W.Loth.* *See Winchburgh.*
Nidum *N.P.T.* *See Neath.*
Nigg *Aberdeen* ***Suburb***, 2m/3km S of Aberdeen city centre across River Dee. **91 H4** NJ9403.
Nigg *High.* ***Settlement***, near E side of Nigg Bay, 6m/10km NE of Invergordon, in Ross and Cromarty district. **97 F4** NH8071.
Nigg Bay *Aberdeen* ***Bay***, on E coast between Girdle Ness and Greg Ness, 2m/3km SE of centre of Aberdeen across River Dee. **91 H4** NJ9604.
Nigg Bay *High.* ***Bay***, to E of Invergordon, on N side of Cromarty Firth. At low tide Sands of Nigg are visible. **96 E4** NH8071.
Nightcott *Som.* ***Hamlet***, 2m/3km SW of Dulverton. **7 G3** SS8925.
Nilig *Denb.* ***Settlement***, 3m/5km SW of Cyffylliog. **47 J7** SJ0254.
Nilston Rigg *Northumb.* ***Settlement***, on shore of small reservoir at Langley, 2m/4km SW of Haydon Bridge. NY8260.
Nimble Nook *Gt.Man.* ***Locality***, 2m/3km W of Oldham. SD9004.
Nine Ashes *Essex* ***Village***, 3m/4km E of Chipping Ongar. **23 J1** TL5902.
Nine Barrow Down *Dorset* ***Open space***, downland 3m/4km NW of Swanage. **10 B6** SZ0081.
Nine Elms *Gt.Lon.* ***Suburb***, in borough of Wandsworth on south bank of River Thames. Battersea Power Station. Fruit and vegetable market, removed from Covent Garden in 1974. TQ2977.
Nine Elms *Swin.* ***Hamlet***, 3m/5km W of Swindon. **20 E3** SU1085.
Nine Ladies Stone Circle *Derbys.* ***Historic/prehistoric site***, stone circle (English Heritage) on Stanton Moor, 4m/6km NW of Matlock. Circle is second largest in Derbyshire, measuring 45 feet or 14 metres. Only four of original stones remain. **50 E6** SK2463.
Nine Mile Bar *D. & G.* *Alternative name for Crocketford, qv.*
Nine Mile Burn *Midloth.* ***Hamlet***, 4m/6km SW of Penicuik. **75 K5** NT1857.
Nine Standards Rigg *Cumb.* ***Mountain***, to N of Birkdale Common, 4m/6km SE of Kirkby Stephen. Height 2171 feet or 662 metres. **61 K6** NY8206.
Ninebanks *Northumb.* ***Hamlet***, 4m/6km SW of Allendale Town. **61 J1** NY7853.
Nineveh *Worcs.* ***Hamlet***, 3m/5km SE of Tenbury Wells. SO6264.
Ninfield *E.Suss.* ***Village***, 4m/6km NW of Bexhill. **14 C6** TQ7012.
Ningwood *I.o.W.* ***Village***, 3m/5km E of Yarmouth. **11 F6** SZ4089.
Nisa Mhòr *W.Isles* ***Hill***, 1km NW of Uigen, Isle of Lewis. Height 446 feet or 136 metres. **100 C4** NB0935.
Nisam Point *W.Isles* ***Coastal feature***, headland at easternmost point of Bearnaraigh. **84 A6** NL5780.
Nisbet *Sc.Bord.* ***Village***, 4m/6km N of Jedburgh. **70 B1** NT6725.
Nista *Shet.* ***Island***, small uninhabited island off E coast of Whalsay, 1m/2km S of Skaw Taing. HU6065.
Nith ***River***, rising on Prickery Hill in Carsphairn Forest, 5m/7km E of Dalmellington and flowing through New Cumnock, then past Sanquhar and Thornhill to Dumfries and out to Solway Firth 3m/4km NE of Southerness. **65 K3** NY0057.
Nithsdale *D. & G.* ***Valley***, carrying River Nith from its source, 5m/7km E of Dalmellington, S to Dumfries. **68 D3** NX8791.
Nithside *D. & G.* ***Suburb***, W district of Dumfries. NX9676.
Niton *I.o.W.* ***Village***, 4m/6km W of Ventnor. St. Catherine's Oratory, 14c lighthouse (English Heritage), stands on highest point of island 1km NW. **11 G7** SZ5076.
Nitshill *Glas.* ***Suburb***, 5m/8km SW of Glasgow city centre. **74 D4** NS5260.
Niwgwl *Pembs.* *Welsh form of Newgale, qv.*
Nizels *Kent* ***Settlement***, 4m/6km NW of Tonbridge. **23 J6** TQ5450.
No Man's Heath *Ches.* ***Hamlet***, 2m/3km E of Malpas. **38 E1** SJ5148.
No Man's Heath *Warks.* ***Hamlet***, 6m/10km NE of Tamworth. **40 E5** SK2908.
No Man's Land *Cornw.* ***Hamlet***, 2m/4km NE of Looe. SX2756.
No Man's Land *Hants.* ***Locality***, 2m/3km E of Winchester. SU5029.
No Ness *Shet.* ***Coastal feature***, headland on E coast of Mainland, 1m/2km SW of Mousa. **109 D10** HU4421.
Noah's Ark *Kent* ***Settlement***, 3m/4km NE of Sevenoaks. TQ5557.
Noah's Green *Worcs.* ***Settlement***, 6m/10km NW of Alcester. SP0061.
Noak Bridge *Essex* ***Suburb***, N district of Basildon. TQ6990.
Noak Hill *Gt.Lon.* ***Suburb***, in N part of borough of Havering, 4m/6km NE of Romford. **23 J2** TQ5493.
Nob End *Gt.Man.* ***Locality***, near confluence of River Croal with River Irwell, 3m/4km SE of Bolton. SD7506.
Noblehill *D. & G.* ***Suburb***, E district of Dumfries. **65 K3** NX9976.
Noblethorpe *S.Yorks.* ***Hamlet***, adjoining to S of Silkstone, 4m/6km W of Barnsley. SE2805.
Nobold *Shrop.* ***Suburb***, 2m/3km SW of Shrewsbury town centre. SJ4710.
Nobottle *Northants.* ***Settlement***, 6m/9km NW of Northampton. Site of Roman building E of Nobottle Wood. **31 H2** SP6763.
Nob's Crook *Hants.* ***Settlement***, 2m/3km NE of Eastleigh. SU4821.
Nocton *Lincs.* ***Village***, 7m/11km SE of Lincoln. **52 D6** TF0564.
Nocton Fen *Lincs.* ***Open space***, fenland on N side of Nocton Delph, 2m/4km SW of Bardney. **52 E6** TF1066.
Noctorum *Mersey.* ***Suburb***, 2m/4km SW of Birkenhead town centre. SJ2887.
Noddsdale *N.Ayr.* ***Settlement***, 2m/3km NE of Largs. **74 A4** NS2161.
Noddsdale Water *N.Ayr.* ***River***, rising on NE slopes of Knockencorsan and flowing SW to join sea 1km N of Largs. **74 A4** NS2000.
Noe *Arg. & B.* ***River***, running NW down Glen Noe to Loch Etive, Argyll, 3m/4km E of Bonawe. **80 B4** NN0434.
Noe *Derbys.* ***River***, rising on S slopes of Kinder Scout in High Peak and flowing generally SE past Edale into River Derwent 1km S of Bamford. SK2082.
Noel Park *Gt.Lon.* ***Suburb***, in borough of Haringey, 1km E of Wood Green. TQ3190.
Nog Tow *Lancs.* ***Locality***, 1km NE of Cottam, 3m/5km NW of Preston. SD5032.
Nogdam End *Norf.* ***Hamlet***, 2m/3km SW of Reedham. TG3900.
Noke *Oxon.* ***Village***, 5m/8km NE of Oxford. Site of Roman temple to SW. **31 G7** SP5413.
Noke Street *Med.* ***Settlement***, 2m/3km N of Rochester. TQ7471.
Noltland Castle *Ork.* ***Castle***, ruins of 16c castle (Historic Scotland) on Westray, W of Pierowall. **106 D3** HY4248.
Nolton *Pembs.* ***Village***, near E coast of St. Brides Bay, 5m/9km W of Haverfordwest. **16 B3** SM8618.
Nolton Haven *Pembs.* ***Hamlet***, at head of inlet of same name, on E side of St. Brides Bay, 6m/10km W of Haverfordwest. SM8518.
Nomansland *Devon* ***Hamlet***, 7m/12km W of Tiverton. **7 G4** SS8313.
Nomansland *Wilts.* ***Village***, on edge of New Forest, 4m/6km NW of Cadnam. **10 D3** SU2517.
Noneley *Shrop.* ***Settlement***, 2m/3km W of Wem. **38 D3** SJ4827.
Nonington *Kent* ***Village***, 4m/6km S of Wingham. **15 H2** TR2552.
Nonsuch Mansion House *Surr.* ***Historic house***, 19c mansion located in Nonsuch Park, 2m/3km W of Sutton. Incorporates earlier 18c house in kitchen wing. Gardens designed by Joseph Thompson, famous in 19c. **23 F5** TQ2363.
Nonsuch Palace *Surr.* *See Ewell.*
Nook *Cumb.* ***Settlement***, 1m/2km N of Catlowdy and 4m/7km NE of Canonbie. **69 K6** NY4679.
Nook *Cumb.* ***Settlement***, 5m/8km NW of Kirkby Lonsdale. **55 J1** SD5482.
Nookside *T. & W.* ***Suburb***, 2m/4km W of Sunderland city centre. NZ3655.
Nookton Fell *Dur.* ***Mountain***, 4m/6km NE of Allenheads. Height 1571 feet or 479 metres. **62 A2** NY9148.
Noonsbrough *Shet.* ***Settlement***, situated on Ness of Noonsbrough, adjacent to Voe of Clousta, Mainland. **109 B7** HU2957.
Nor Wick *Shet.* ***Bay***, on NE coast of Unst, on which locality of Norwick is situated. **108 F1** HP6514.
Noran Water *Angus* ***River***, running S down Glen Ogil then SE to River South Esk 4m/6km W of Brechin. Falls of Drumly Harry in course of river, 3m/5km NW of Tannadice. **83 F2** NO5358.

Noranside *Angus* ***Hamlet***, 3m/4km NW of Finavon. HM Prison. **83 F1** NO4761.
Norbiton *Gt.Lon.* ***Suburb***, in borough of Kingston upon Thames, 1m/2km E of Kingston upon Thames town centre. Norbiton Common to S. **22 E5** TQ1969.
Norbreck *B'pool* ***Suburb***, adjacent to coast, 3m/5km N of Blackpool town centre. **55 G5** SD3141.
Norbury *Ches.* ***Hamlet***, 4m/6km N of Whitchurch. **38 E1** SJ5547.
Norbury *Derbys.* ***Village***, 4m/7km SW of Ashbourne. **40 D1** SK1242.
Norbury *Gt.Lon.* ***Suburb***, in borough of Croydon, 3m/5km N of Croydon town centre. TQ3169.
Norbury *Shrop.* ***Village***, 4m/6km NE of Bishop's Castle. **38 C6** SO3692.
Norbury *Staffs.* ***Village***, 4m/6km NE of Newport. **39 G3** SJ7823.
Norbury Common *Ches.* ***Settlement***, 1m/2km NW of Norbury. SJ5548.
Norbury Junction *Staffs.* ***Settlement***, on Shropshire Union Canal where former Newport Canal used to lock down from mainline canal, 1km SE of Norbury. SJ7922.
Norbury Moor *Gt.Man.* ***Suburb***, adjoining to SW of Hazel Grove. SJ9185.
Norby *N.Yorks.* ***Locality***, adjoining to N of Thirsk. SE4282.
Norchard *Pembs.* ***Settlement***, 3m/5km W of Tenby. SS0899.
Norchard *Worcs.* ***Settlement***, 3m/5km SE of Stourport-on-Severn. **29 H2** SO8468.
Norcott Brook *Ches.* ***Settlement***, 5m/8km NW of Northwich. SJ6080.
Norcross *Lancs.* ***Locality***, 2m/3km NW of Poulton-le-Fylde. SD3341.
Nordelph *Norf.* ***Village***, 4m/6km W of Downham Market. **43 J5** TF5500.
Norden *Dorset* ***Settlement***, 1m/2km NW of Corfe Castle. **9 J6** SY9483.
Norden *Gt.Man.* ***Suburb***, 3m/4km NW of Rochdale town centre. SD8514.
Nordley *Shrop.* ***Hamlet***, 3m/5km NW of Bridgnorth. **39 F6** SO6996.
Nordley Common *Shrop.* ***Settlement***, 4m/6km NW of Bridgnorth. SO6897.
Norfolk Broads (The Broads). *Norf.* ***Large natural feature***, series of shallow lakes in E part of county (except Oulton Broad, which is in Suffolk), surrounded by reedy marshes abounding in waterfowl, extending around Rivers Bure, Waveney and Yare, the whole system forming a popular boating area. The Broads National Park was designated in 1988. **45 H4** TG3515.
Norfolk Wildlife Park *Norf.* ***Leisure/recreation***, 40 acres of parkland, 1m/2km NW of Lenwade, featuring wide selection of British and European wildlife, including only team of trained reindeer in Britain. **44 E4** TG0819.
Norham *Northumb.* ***Village***, on River Tweed, 7m/12km SW of Berwick-upon-Tweed. Remains of 12c castle keep (English Heritage) above river. **77 H6** NT8947.
Norham Castle *Northumb.* ***Castle***, ruins of castle (English Heritage) founded by Bishop Flambard in 12c on S bank of River Tweed, to NE of Norham. **77 H6** NT9047.
Nork *Surr.* ***Suburb***, 1m/2km W of Banstead. TQ2359.
Norland Town *W.Yorks.* ***Village***, 1m/2km SE of Sowerby Bridge. **57 F7** SE0722.
Norley *Ches.* ***Village***, 6m/9km W of Northwich. **48 E5** SJ5772.
Norleywood *Hants.* ***Village***, on S edge of Beaulieu Heath and New Forest, 3m/4km NE of Lymington. **10 E5** SZ3597.
Norlington *E.Suss.* ***Settlement***, adjoining to N of Ringmer, 3m/5km NE of Lewes. TQ4413.
Normacot *Stoke* ***Suburb***, 4m/6km SE of Stoke-on-Trent city centre. SJ9242.
Norman Cross *Cambs.* ***Settlement***, and road junction, 5m/8km SW of Peterborough. **42 E6** TL1590.
Normanby *N.Lincs.* ***Village***, 4m/6km N of Scunthorpe. **52 B1** SE8816.
Normanby *N.Yorks.* ***Village***, 4m/6km SE of Kirkbymoorside. **58 D1** SE7381.
Normanby *R. & C.* ***Suburb***, 4m/6km E of Middlesbrough. **63 G5** NZ5518.
Normanby-by-Spital *Lincs.* ***Village***, 7m/11km W of Market Rasen. **52 D4** TF0088.
Normanby by Stow *Lincs.* ***Settlement***, 2m/3km N of Sturton by Stow. **52 B4** SK8883.
Normanby Hall *N.Lincs.* ***Historic house***, Regency house in 350 acres of gardens and deer park, 4m/6km N of Scunthorpe, and 18c home of Sheffield family. Exhibits of period dress and uniforms. **52 B1** SE8816.
Normanby le Wold *Lincs.* ***Village***, 4m/6km N of Market Rasen. **52 E3** TF1295.
Normandy *Surr.* ***Village***, 4m/7km E of Aldershot. **22 C6** SU9251.
Normann's Ruh *Arg. & B.* ***Settlement***, on Mull, 1m/2km SE of Kilninian. **79 F3** NM4144.
Norman's Bay *E.Suss.* ***Settlement***, on coast at Pevensey Sluice, 4m/6km W of Bexhill. **13 K6** TQ6805.
Norman's Green *Devon* ***Hamlet***, 3m/5km SE of Cullompton. **7 J5** ST0503.
Norman's Law *Fife* ***Hill***, with hillfort and settlement, 1m/2km SW of Brunton. Height 935 feet or 285 metres. **82 E5** NO3020.
Normanston *Suff.* ***Suburb***, 1km NW of Lowestoft. TM5393.
Normanton *Derby* ***Suburb***, 2m/3km S of Derby city centre. **41 F2** SK3433.
Normanton *Leics.* ***Hamlet***, 7m/12km NW of Grantham. **42 B1** SK8140.
Normanton *Lincs.* ***Village***, 7m/11km N of Grantham. **42 C1** SK9446.
Normanton *Notts.* ***Hamlet***, 1m/2km NE of Southwell. **51 K7** SK7054.
Normanton *Rut.* ***Settlement***, at SE side of Rutland Water, 6m/9km W of Stamford. **42 C5** SK9306.
Normanton *W.Yorks.* Population: 18,775. ***Town***, former mining town, 4m/6km E of Wakefield. **57 J7** SE3822.
Normanton *Wilts.* ***Settlement***, on River Avon, 2m/3km SW of Amesbury. SU1340.
Normanton Common *Derbys.* ***Locality***, 2m/3km E of Alfreton. SK4456.
Normanton le Heath *Leics.* ***Village***, 3m/5km SE of Ashby de la Zouch. **41 F4** SK3712.
Normanton on Soar *Notts.* ***Village***, 2m/4km NW of Loughborough across River Soar. **41 H3** SK5123.
Normanton-on-the-Wolds *Notts.* ***Village***, 6m/9km SE of Nottingham. **41 J2** SK6232.
Normanton on Trent *Notts.* ***Village***, 4m/6km SE of Tuxford. **51 K6** SK7968.
Normanton Spring *S.Yorks.* ***Suburb***, 4m/6km SE of Sheffield city centre. SK4084.
Normoss *Lancs.* ***Locality***, 1m/2km S of Poulton-le-Fylde. **55 G6** SD3437.
Norrington Common *Wilts.* ***Settlement***, 1m/2km W of Melksham. **20 B5** ST8864.
Norris Green *Cornw.* ***Hamlet***, 2m/3km SW of Gunnislake. SX4169.
Norris Green *Mersey.* ***Suburb***, 4m/6km NE of Liverpool city centre. SJ3894.
Norris Hill *Leics.* ***Hamlet***, 2m/3km W of Ashby de la Zouch. **41 F4** SK3216.
Norristhorpe *W.Yorks.* ***Suburb***, to SW of Heckmondwike, 2m/3km N of Mirfield. SE2022.
Norsey Wood Country Park *Essex* ***Leisure/recreation***, 165 acres of woodland 1km NE of Billericay, featuring many points of archaeological interest including Bronze Age burial mound and Roman smelting furnace. **24 C2** TQ6895.
North Acre *Norf.* ***Hamlet***, 3m/5km SE of Watton. TL9598.
North Acton *Gt.Lon.* ***Suburb***, in borough of Ealing, 1m/2km N of Acton. TQ2082.
North Anston *S.Yorks.* Population: 4423. ***Village***, 5m/8km NW of Worksop. **51 H4** SK5284.
North Ascot *Brack.F.* ***Locality***, residential locality, 2m/3km E of Bracknell. **22 C5** SU9069.
North Ashton *Gt.Man.* ***Locality***, 2m/3km NW of Ashton-in-Makerfield. SD5500.
North Aston *Oxon.* ***Village***, 2m/3km S of Deddington. **31 F6** SP4729.
North Bacton *Norf.* ***Locality***, adjoining to N of Bacton. TG3433.
North Baddesley *Hants.* Population: 6456. ***Village***, 3m/5km E of Romsey. **10 E2** SU4020.
North Ballachulish *High.* ***Village***, on N shore of Loch Leven, in Lochaber district, 8m/13km W of Kinlochleven. Road bridge spans loch. **80 B1** NN0559.
North Balloch *S.Ayr.* ***Settlement***, on N side of River Strinchar, 4m/6km E of Barr. **67 H4** NX3395.
North Barrow *Som.* ***Village***, 2m/3km N of Sparkford. **9 F2** ST6029.
North Barrule *I.o.M.* ***Mountain***, 2m/4km S of Ramsey. Height 1853 feet or 565 metres. **54 D4** SC4490.
North Barsham *Norf.* ***Hamlet***, 1km N of East Barsham. **44 D2** TF9133.
North Bay *N.Yorks.* ***Bay***, between Castle Cliff and Scalby Ness, on N side of Scarborough. **59 G1** TA0489.
North Bay *Ork.* ***Bay***, large bay on W coast of Sanday, divided from Bay of Brough by Ness of Brough. **106 F3** HY6642.
North Bay *Ork.* ***Bay***, on N side of The Ayre, narrow neck of land connecting peninsula of South Walls to S end of Hoy. **107 B8** ND2890.
North Bay *W.Isles* ***Bay***, to E of Northbay, containing numerous small islands. **84 C4** NF7002.
North Benfleet *Essex* Population: 1989. ***Village***, 3m/5km E of Basildon. **24 D3** TQ7589.
North Bersted *W.Suss.* ***Suburb***, 1m/2km NW of Bognor Regis. **12 C6** SU9201.
North Berwick *E.Loth.* Population: 5687. ***Small town***, and resort on S side of entrance to Firth of Forth, 19m/31km E of Edinburgh. **76 D2** NT5585.
North Berwick Law *E.Loth.* ***Hill***, to S of North Berwick, surmounted by ancient fort and ruins of watch-tower built in Napoleonic Wars. Height 613 feet or 187 metres. **76 D2** NT5584.
North Bierley *W.Yorks.* ***Suburb***, 2m/3km S of Bradford city centre. SE1429.
North Binness Island *Hants.* ***Island***, uninhabited island at N end of Langstone Harbour off Farlington Marshes. SU6904.
North Birny Fell *Sc.Bord.* ***Hill***, 3m/4km N of Newcastleton. Height 902 feet or 275 metres. **69 K4** NY4791.
North Bishop *Pembs.* ***Island***, 3m/5km W of St. David's Head. One of the largest in the group of rocky islands known as Bishops and Clerks. **16 A2** SM6728.
North Bitchburn *Dur.* ***Hamlet***, 2m/3km S of Crook. NZ1732.
North Blyth *Northumb.* ***Locality***, to N of Blyth across River Blyth. NZ3182.
North Boarhunt *Hants.* ***Village***, 2m/3km SE of Wickham. **11 H3** SU6010.
North Bockhampton *Dorset* ***Settlement***, within locality of Bockhampton, 3m/4km NE of Christchurch town centre. SZ1797.
North Bogbain *Moray* ***Settlement***, 3m/4km NW of Keith. **98 B5** NJ3952.
North Boisdale *W.Isles* *Anglicised form of Baghasdal, qv.*
North Bovey *Devon* ***Village***, on River Bovey, 2m/3km SW of Moretonhampstead. **7 F7** SX7483.
North Bowood *Dorset* ***Locality***, 3m/4km SW of Beaminster. SY4499.
North Bradley *Wilts.* ***Village***, 2m/3km S of Trowbridge. **20 B6** ST8555.
North Brentor *Devon* ***Village***, 5m/7km N of Tavistock. 1m/2km S is locality of Brentor. **6 C7** SX4881.
North Brewham *Som.* ***Village***, forms parish of Brewham, along with South Brewham, 3m/4km E of Bruton. **9 G1** ST7236.
North Bridge *Surr.* ***Settlement***, 4m/6km S of Milford. SU9636.
North Brook End *Cambs.* ***Settlement***, 1km NE of Guilden Morden, 6m/10km E of Biggleswade. TL2944.
North Broomage *Falk.* ***Suburb***, on N side of Larbert. NS8583.
North Bruton *E.Riding* *Alternative name for Bruton Fleming, qv.*
North Buckland *Devon* ***Hamlet***, 5m/8km SW of Ilfracombe. **6 C1** SS4840.
North Burlingham *Norf.* ***Village***, 2m/4km W of Acle. **45 H4** TG3610.
North Burnt Hill *N.Ayr.* ***Mountain***, at head of Noddsdale Water, 6m/9km NE of Largs. Height 1414 feet or 431 metres. **74 A4** NS2566.
North Cadbury *Som.* ***Village***, 5m/8km W of Wincanton. **9 F2** ST6327.
North Cairn *D. & G.* ***Settlement***, 1m/2km S of Corsewall Point. **64 A3** NW9770.
North Carlton *Lincs.* ***Village***, 4m/7km NW of Lincoln. **52 C5** SK9477.
North Carlton *Notts.* ***Locality***, adjoining to E of Carlton in Lindrick, 3m/5km N of Worksop. **51 H4** SK5984.
North Carr *Fife* ***Coastal feature***, offshore rock with beacon, 1m/2km N of Fife Ness. **83 H6** NO6411.
North Cave *E.Riding* ***Village***, 6m/10km S of Market Weighton. **58 E6** SE8932.
North Cerney *Glos.* ***Village***, 4m/6km N of Cirencester. Cerney House Gardens are of note. **20 D1** SP0107.
North Chailey *E.Suss.* ***Hamlet***, 1m/2km W of Newick. **13 G4** TQ3921.
North Charford *Hants.* ***Hamlet***, 5m/8km NE of Fordingbridge. **10 D2** SU1919.
North Charlton *Northumb.* ***Hamlet***, 6m/10km N of Alnwick. **71 G1** NU1622.
North Cheam *Gt.Lon.* ***Suburb***, 1m/2km N of Cheam. TQ2465.
North Cheek *N.Yorks.* *Alternative name for Ness Point, qv.*
North Cheriton *Som.* ***Village***, 2m/4km SW of Wincanton. **9 F2** ST6925.
North Chideock *Dorset* ***Hamlet***, 1km N of Chideock. SY4294.
North Cliffe *E.Riding* ***Hamlet***, 3m/4km S of Market Weighton. **58 E6** SE8737.
North Clifton *Notts.* ***Village***, 9m/15km W of Lincoln. **52 B5** SK8272.
North Close *Dur.* ***Hamlet***, 1m/2km S of Spennymoor. NZ2632.
North Cockerington *Lincs.* ***Village***, 4m/6km NE of Louth. **53 G3** TF3790.
North Coker *Som.* ***Village***, 1km N of East Coker. **8 E3** ST5413.
North Collafirth *Shet.* ***Settlement***, at head of Colla Firth inlet, 6m/10km N of Sullom, Mainland. HU3583.
North Common *E.Suss.* ***Hamlet***, 2m/3km W of Newick. TQ3921.
North Common *S.Glos.* ***Hamlet***, 6m/9km E of Bristol. ST6872.
North Common *Suff.* ***Settlement***, 1km NW of Hepworth. TL9775.
North Commonty *Aber.* ***Settlement***, 1m/2km NW of New Deer. NJ8648.
North Coombe *Devon* ***Settlement***, 4m/6km NE of Crediton. SS8704.
North Cornelly *Bridgend* ***Village***, 3m/5km N of Porthcawl. **18 B3** SS8181.
North Corner *S.Glos.* ***Hamlet***, adjoining to W of Frampton Cotterell. ST6582.
North Cotes *Lincs.* ***Village***, 7m/12km SE of Grimsby. Airfield on coast, 2m/3km NE. **53 G2** TA3400.
North Country *Cornw.* ***Locality***, 1m/2km N of Redruth. SW6943.
North Cove *Suff.* ***Village***, 3m/5km E of Beccles. **45 J7** TM4689.
North Cowton *N.Yorks.* ***Village***, 7m/11km S of Darlington. **62 D6** NZ2803.
North Crawley *M.K.* ***Village***, 3m/5km E of Newport Pagnell. **32 C4** SP9244.
North Cray *Gt.Lon.* ***Settlement***, in borough of Bexley, 2m/3km E of Sidcup. **23 H4** TQ4872.
North Creake *Norf.* ***Village***, 7m/11km NW of Fakenham. To N are remains of Creake Abbey (English Heritage), mainly 13c. **44 C2** TF8538.
North Crossaig *Arg. & B.* ***Locality***, adjoining to South Crossaig, on road running beside E coast of Kintyre, Argyll, 4m/7km SW of Claonaig. NR8351.
North Curry *Som.* ***Village***, 6m/10km E of Taunton. **8 C2** ST3125.
North Dallens *Arg. & B.* ***Settlement***, on SE shore of Loch Linnhe, opposite Shuna Island. **80 A3** NM9248.
North Dalton *E.Riding* ***Village***, 6m/10km SW of Great Driffield. **59 F4** SE9352.
North Darley *Cornw.* ***Hamlet***, 6m/10km N of Liskeard. SX2773.
North Dawn *Ork.* ***Settlement***, 1m/2km N of St. Mary's, Mainland. **107 D7** HY4703.
North Deep *Fife* ***Sea feature***, channel in River Tay estuary, between Mugdrum Island and N bank. **82 D6** NO2119.
North Deighton *N.Yorks.* ***Village***, 2m/3km N of Wetherby. **57 J4** SE3951.
North Dell *W.Isles* *Anglicised form of Dail Bho Thuath, qv.*
North Devon Maritime Museum *Devon* ***Other feature of interest***, at Appledore. Traces sea-faring heritage of N Devon coast; artefacts and paintings. **6 C2** SS4630.
North District *Norf.* ***Open space***, fenland 1m/2km SE of Outwell across which runs Middle Level Main Drain. **43 J5** TF5101.
North Down *Wilts.* ***Open space***, hillslope 2m/3km N of Bishops Cannings. **20 D5** SU0467.
North Downs ***Large natural feature***, range of chalk hills, running E from vicinity of Basingstoke above 'gap' towns of Guildford, Dorking, Sevenoaks, Maidstone, and Ashford, and terminating at South Foreland, E of Dover. With South Downs they enclose region known as The Weald, and once formed part of a large chalk anticline which stretched across NW Europe. **22 A7** TQ2050.

North Drove Drain *Lincs.* ***Other water feature***, artificial drainage channel running across Deeping Fen from NE of Langtoft to Pode Hole, 2m/3km W of Spalding. **42 E4** TF2121.
North Duffield *N.Yorks.* ***Village***, 5m/9km NE of Selby. **58 C6** SE6837.
North Elham *Kent* ***Settlement***, 1km NE of Elham. TR1844.
North Elkington *Lincs.* ***Settlement***, 3m/5km NW of Louth. **53 F3** TF2890.
North Elmham *Norf.* ***Village***, 5m/8km N of East Dereham. Remains of Saxon cathedral (English Heritage). **44 D3** TF9820.
North Elmham Saxon Cathedral and Earthworks *Norf.* ***Ecclesiastical building***, ruins of 11c cathedral (English Heritage) on N side of North Elmham which was converted to fortified manor house within moated enclosure in late 14c. **44 D3** TF9821.
North Elmsall *W.Yorks.* ***Small town***, 1m/2km N of South Elmsall and 6m/9km S of Pontefract. **51 G1** SE4711.
North End *Beds.* ***Settlement***, 2m/3km E of Sharnbrook. TL0259.
North End *Bucks.* ***Settlement***, to N of Stewkley. **32 B6** SP8427.
North End *Cumb.* ***Locality***, adjoining to N of Burgh by Sands. NY3259.
North End *Dorset* ***Hamlet***, 3m/5km NW of Shaftesbury. ST8427.
North End *E.Riding* ***Settlement***, 1km N of Bewholme. TA1650.
North End *E.Riding* ***Settlement***, 1km N of Withernwick. TA1941.
North End *E.Riding* ***Settlement***, 1km N of Roos. TA2831.
North End *Essex* ***Hamlet***, 3m/5km SE of Great Dunmow. **33 K7** TL6618.
North End *Essex* ***Hamlet***, 2m/3km E of Great Yeldham, 6m/9km W of Sudbury. TL7839.
North End *Gt.Lon.* ***Suburb***, in borough of Bexley, 1m/2km N of Crayford and 14m/22km E of Charing Cross. TQ5176.
North End *Hants.* ***Hamlet***, adjoining to N of Damerham, 3m/5km NW of Fordingbridge. SU1016.
North End *Hants.* ***Settlement***, 3m/5km SE of Kintbury. **21 H5** SU4062.
North End *Hants.* ***Settlement***, adjoining to N of Cheriton. SU5829.
North End *Leics.* ***Hamlet***, adjoining to NW of Mountsorrel, 4m/6km SE of Loughborough. SK5715.
North End *Lincs.* ***Locality***, adjoining to N of Tetney. TA3101.
North End *Lincs.* ***Locality***, adjoining to N of South Kelsey. TF0499.
North End *Lincs.* ***Locality***, adjoining to N of Swineshead. TF2341.
North End *Lincs.* ***Locality***, adjoining to NW of Saltfleetby St. Peter, 3m/4km NE of Manby. TF4289.
North End *Lincs.* ***Settlement***, 1km NW of Alvingham. TF3592.
North End *Mersey.* ***Locality***, 2m/3km SE of Formby. SD3004.
North End *Mersey.* ***Locality***, 1m/2km NW of Halewood. SJ4487.
North End *Norf.* ***Hamlet***, 1km N of Snetterton. **44 E6** TL9992.
North End *N.Lincs.* ***Locality***, adjoining to N of Goxhill. TA1022.
North End *N.Som.* ***Hamlet***, 1m/2km NW of Yatton. **19 H5** ST4167.
North End *Northants.* ***Suburb***, N district of Higham Ferrers. SP9669.
North End *Northumb.* ***Settlement***, 1km N of Longframlington. **71 G3** NU1301.
North End *Ports.* ***Suburb***, 2m/3km N of Portsmouth city centre. **11 H4** SU6502.
North End *W.Suss.* ***Hamlet***, adjoining to N of Yapton, 3m/5km NW of Littlehampton. SU9804.
North End *W.Suss.* ***Settlement***, 1km N of Findon and 2m/3km S of Washington. **12 E5** TQ1109.
North Erradale *High.* ***Village***, near W coast of Ross and Cromarty district, 4m/7km NW of Gairloch. **94 D3** NG7481.
North Esk ***River***, formed by several streams W of Tarfside and running SE down Glen Esk to Edzell, Marykirk and North Sea between Montrose and St. Cyrus. **90 D7** NO7462.
North Esk ***River***, rising on Pentland Hills near North Esk Reservoir, 1m/2km N of Carlops, and flowing NE to join South Esk River 1m/2km N of Dalkeith; combined river then continues N to Firth of Forth at Musselburgh. **75 K5** NT3368.
North Esk Reservoir *Midloth.* ***Reservoir***, small reservoir in Pentland Hills, bordering Scottish Borders region, 1m/2km N of Carlops. **75 K5** NT1558.
North Essie *Aber.* ***Settlement***, 2m/3km SE of Crimond. **99 J5** NK0755.
North Evington *Leic.* ***Suburb***, 2m/3km E of Leicester city centre. SK6104.
North Fambridge *Essex* ***Village***, on N side of River Crouch estuary, 6m/10km W of Burnham-on-Crouch. TQ8597.
North Feltham *Gt.Lon.* ***Suburb***, in borough of Hounslow, on W side of Hounslow Heath, 13m/20km W of Charing Cross. TQ1074.
North Fen *Cambs.* ***Open space***, fenland 2m/4km SE of Chatteris. **33 H1** TL4081.
North Fen *Cambs.* ***Open space***, fenland 3m/5km NE of Waterbeach. **33 J2** TL5169.
North Fen *Peter.* ***Open space***, fenland between Old South Eau and New South Eau, 3m/5km E of Crowland. **43 F5** TF2809.
North Ferriby *E.Riding* Population: 3752. ***Village***, 7m/11km W of Kingston upon Hull. **59 F7** SE9825.
North Foreland *Kent* ***Coastal feature***, headland with lighthouse, at extreme E point of Isle of Thanet, 1m/2km N of Broadstairs. **25 K4** TR4069.
North Frodingham *E.Riding* ***Village***, 6m/9km SE of Great Driffield. **59 H4** TA0953.
North Galson *W.Isles* *Anglicised form of Gabhsunn Bho Thuath, qv.*
North Glen Sannox *N.Ayr.* ***Valley***, to N of Glen Sannox and running E to coast, 1km N of Sannox Bay. **73 H6** NR9944.
North Gorley *Hants.* ***Hamlet***, on E edge of New Forest, 2m/3km SE of Fordingbridge. **10 C3** SU1611.
North Green *Norf.* ***Settlement***, 4m/6km NW of Harleston. **45 G7** TM2288.
North Green *Suff.* ***Hamlet***, 2m/3km SE of Framlingham. TM3162.
North Green *Suff.* ***Settlement***, 1m/2km NW of Cratfield. TM3076.
North Green *Suff.* ***Settlement***, 2m/3km N of Saxmundham. TM3966.
North Greens *Moray* ***Locality***, near N coast, 2m/3km W of Lossiemouth. NJ2070.
North Grimston *N.Yorks.* ***Village***, 4m/7km SE of Malton. **58 E3** SE8467.
North Halling *Kent* ***Settlement***, 1m/2km N of Halling. TQ7065.
North Harby *Notts.* ***Settlement***, 1m/2km N of Harby. SK8872.
North Harris (Gaelic form: Ceann a Tuath na Hearadh.) *W.Isles* ***Large natural feature***, southern and more mountainous part of Isle of Lewis, S of Loch Resort and W of Loch Seaforth. Includes Forest of Harris. **100 D6** NB1010.
North Harrow *Gt.Lon.* ***Suburb***, 1m/2km W of Harrow. TQ1388.
North Hart *Hart.* ***Settlement***, adjoining to N of Hart, 3m/4km NW of Hartlepool town centre. NZ4635.
North Haven *Aber.* ***Bay***, rocky bay, 2m/3km N of Cruden Bay. **91 K1** NK1138.
North Havra *Shet.* ***Island***, small uninhabited island off S end of peninsula of Strom Ness, Mainland. **109 C8** HU3642.
North Hayling *Hants.* ***Village***, near N end of Hayling Island. Site of Roman building to W. **11 J4** SU7303.
North Hazelrigg *Northumb.* ***Settlement***, 4m/6km W of Belford. **77 J7** NU0533.
North Head *High.* ***Coastal feature***, headland to N of Wick Bay. **105 J3** ND3850.
North Heasley *Devon* ***Settlement***, 5m/8km N of South Molton. **7 F2** SS7333.
North Heath *W.Berks.* ***Settlement***, 5m/7km N of Newbury. SU4574.
North Heath *W.Suss.* ***Hamlet***, 2m/3km NE of Pulborough. **12 D4** TQ0621.
North Hele *Devon* ***Settlement***, 1km NE of Clayhanger and 4m/7km SW of Wiveliscombe. ST0223.
North Hessary Tor *Devon* ***Mountain***, on Dartmoor, surmounted by mast, 1km NW of Princetown and 6m/10km E of Tavistock. Height 1696 feet or 517 metres. SX5774.
North Hill *Cornw.* ***Village***, 6m/10km SW of Launceston. **4 C3** SX2776.
North Hill *Dorset* ***Hill***, 2m/3km W of Bridport. Height 377 feet or 115 metres. **8 D5** SY4790.
North Hill *Dorset* ***Locality***, between Winterbourne Abbas and Winterbourne Steepleton, 4m/6km W of Dorchester. SY6290.
North Hill *Som.* ***Hill***, above N Somerset coast, 2m/3km NW of Minehead. Height 843 feet or 257 metres. **7 H1** SS9447.
North Hillingdon *Gt.Lon.* ***Suburb***, NE of Hillingdon. TQ0884.
North Hinksey *Oxon.* ***Suburb***, 2m/3km W of Oxford. Early 17c roofed reservoir (English Heritage) built for Oxford's water mains. **21 H1** SP4905.
North Holme *N.Yorks.* ***Settlement***, 3m/5km S of Kirkbymoorside. SE6981.
North Holms *Shet.* ***Island***, small rocky island off W coast of Unst. HP5611.
North Holmwood *Surr.* ***Suburb***, S district of Dorking. **22 E7** TQ1647.
North Houghton *Hants.* ***Settlement***, 1m/2km SW of Stockbridge. SU3433.
North Huish *Devon* ***Hamlet***, 3m/4km SE of South Brent. **5 H5** SX7156.
North Hyde *Gt.Lon.* ***Suburb***, in borough of Hounslow, 1m/2km S of Southall. TQ1278.
North Hykeham *Lincs.* ***Suburb***, 4m/6km SW of Lincoln. **52 C6** SK9466.
North Hylton *T. & W.* ***Settlement***, on N bank of River Wear, 2m/3km W of Sunderland. NZ3457.
North Isle of Gletness *Shet.* ***Island***, one of two small islands to S of Glet Ness headland on E coast of Mainland. HU4751.
North Johnston *Pembs.* ***Hamlet***, 1km N of Johnston. **16 C3** SM9311.
North Kelsey *Lincs.* ***Village***, 5m/8km W of Caistor. **52 D2** TA0401.
North Kelsey Beck *N.Lincs.* ***River***, rising to W of Caistor and flowing W, where it joins New River Ancholme. **52 D2** TA0002.
North Kelsey Moor *Lincs.* ***Village***, 2m/3km E of North Kelsey, with site of Roman building to S. TA0602.
North Kensington *Gt.Lon.* ***Suburb***, in borough of Kensington and Chelsea, 4m/6km W of Charing Cross. TQ2381.
North Kessock *High.* ***Village***, in Ross and Cromarty district, on N shore of Beauly Firth, opposite Inverness. **96 D7** NH6547.
North Killingholme *N.Lincs.* ***Village***, 3m/5km NW of Immingham. **52 E1** TA1417.
North Kilvington *N.Yorks.* ***Settlement***, 2m/4km N of Thirsk. **57 K1** SE4285.
North Kilworth *Leics.* ***Village***, 2m/3km W of Husbands Bosworth. **41 J7** SP6183.
North Kingston *Hants.* ***Settlement***, 1m/2km NE of Kingston. SU1602.
North Kiscadale *N.Ayr.* ***Settlement***, forms locality of Kiscadale, along with South Kiscadale, on Whiting bay, E coast of Arran. NS0426.
North Kyme *Lincs.* ***Village***, 7m/11km NE of Sleaford. **52 E7** TF1552.
North Lancing *W.Suss.* Population: 9859. ***Suburb***, in parish of Lancing 3m/5km NE of Worthing. Site of Roman temple 1km N. **12 E6** TQ1805.
North Leazes *Dur.* ***Settlement***, 2m/4km SW of Bishop Auckland. NZ1727.
North Lee *Bucks.* ***Hamlet***, 2m/4km W of Wendover. Site of Roman building to SE. **22 B1** SP8308.
North Lee *W.Isles* ***Hill***, on North Uist, 1m/2km NE of South Lee. Height 820 feet or 250 metres. **92 E5** NF9366.
North Lees *N.Yorks.* ***Hamlet***, 2m/3km N of Ripon. SE3073.
North Leigh *Oxon.* ***Village***, 3m/5km NE of Witney. Roman villa (English Heritage) 2m/3m N. **30 E7** SP3813.
North Leigh Roman Villa *Oxon.* ***Historic/prehistoric site***, large courtyard-type villa (English Heritage) 1m/2km NE of North Leigh and 1m/2km NE of Witney. Visible remains include outlines of three wings and some excellent mosaics. **30 E7** SP3915.
North Level ***Large natural feature***, large expanse of fenland between Rivers Welland and Nene; forms part of Bedford Level. **43 F5** TF2605.
North Level Main Drain ***Other water feature***, drainage channel running from Thorney across Fens to River Nene, 1m/2km E of Tydd Gote. TF4618.
North Leverton with Habblesthorpe *Notts.* ***Village***, 5m/8km E of Retford. South Leverton village 1km S. **51 K4** SK7882.
North Littleton *Worcs.* ***Village***, 4m/6km NE of Evesham. **30 B4** SP0847.
North Lobb *Devon* ***Settlement***, to N of Lobb. SS4738.
North Loch *Ork.* ***Lake/loch***, on NE peninsula of Sanday. **106 G3** HY7545.
North Looe *Surr.* ***Locality***, 1m/2km E of Epsom. TQ2360.
North Lopham *Norf.* ***Village***, 5m/9km NW of Diss. Site of Roman building to E. **44 E7** TM0382.
North Luffenham *Rut.* ***Village***, 6m/10km SE of Oakham. **42 C5** SK9303.
North Lynn *Norf.* ***Locality***, and industrial estate adjoining to NW of King's Lynn, next to E bank of River Great Ouse. TF6121.
North Marden *W.Suss.* ***Hamlet***, 6m/10km SE of Petersfield. **12 B5** SU8016.
North Marston *Bucks.* ***Village***, 3m/5km S of Winslow. **31 J6** SP7722.
North Medwin *S.Lan.* ***River***, rising in Pentland Hills and flowing S to join South Medwin River and become Medwin Water before flowing W into River Clyde, 1m/2km S of Carnwath. **75 J6** NS9844.
North Middleton *Midloth.* ***Village***, 1km NW of Middleton. **76 B5** NT3658.
North Middleton *Northumb.* ***Hamlet***, 2m/4km S of Wooler. NU0024.
North Milford *N.Yorks.* ***Settlement***, 3m/4km SE of Tadcaster. SE5039.
North Millbrex *Aber.* ***Settlement***, 5m/8km NE of Fyvie. **99 G6** NJ8243.
North Molton *Devon* ***Village***, 3m/5km NE of South Molton. **7 F3** SS7329.
North Morar *High.* ***Locality***, mountainous coastal area of Lochaber district between Loch Nevis to N and Loch Morar to S. **86 D5** NM7592.
North Moreton *Oxon.* ***Village***, 2m/4km E of Didcot. **21 J3** SU5689.
North Moulsecoomb *B. & H.* ***Suburb***, NW district of Brighton. TQ3307.
North Mount Vernon *Glas.* ***Suburb***, adjoining to N of Mount Vernon, 4m/7km SE of Glasgow city centre. NS6563.
North Mundham *W.Suss.* ***Village***, 2m/3km SE of Chichester. **12 B6** SU8702.
North Muskham *Notts.* ***Village***, on River Trent, 3m/5km N of Newark-on-Trent. **51 K7** SK7958.
North Neaps *Shet.* ***Coastal feature***, promontory on N coast of Yell. **108 D2** HP4805.
North Ness *Fife* ***Coastal feature***, rocky headland at N end of Isle of May (Nature Reserve), which lies 5m/8km SE of Anstruther. **83 H7** NO6400.
North Nesting *Shet.* ***Locality***, forms locality of Nesting on Mainland, along with South Nesting. **109 D7** HU4559.
North Newbald *E.Riding* ***Village***, 4m/6km SE of Market Weighton. **59 F6** SE9136.
North Newington *Oxon.* ***Village***, 3m/4km W of Banbury. **31 F5** SP4239.
North Newnton *Wilts.* ***Village***, 2m/3km N of Upavon. **20 E6** SU1357.
North Newton *N.Ayr.* ***Locality***, at N end of Arran, opposite Lochranza across Loch Ranza. NR9351.
North Newton *Som.* ***Village***, 1m/2km SE of North Petherton. **8 B1** ST3031.
North Nibley *Glos.* ***Village***, 2m/3km SW of Dursley. Monument on Nibley Knoll commemorates William Tyndale, translator of the Bible. **20 A2** ST7495.
North Norfolk Railway *Norf.* ***Other feature of interest***, tourist railway, known as 'Poppy Line', running from Sheringham to Holt. **45 F1** TG1543.
North Oakley *Hants.* ***Hamlet***, 3m/5km S of Kingsclere. **21 J6** SU5354.
North Ockendon *Gt.Lon.* ***Village***, 2m/3km SE of Upminster. **23 J3** TQ5884.
North Ormesby *Middbro.* ***Suburb***, 1m/2km E of Middlesbrough town centre. **63 G4** NZ5019.
North Ormsby *Lincs.* ***Village***, 5m/7km NW of Louth. **53 F3** TF2893.
North Otterington *N.Yorks.* ***Hamlet***, 3m/4km S of Northallerton. **62 E7** SE3689.
North Owersby *Lincs.* ***Village***, 5m/7km NW of Market Rasen. **52 D3** TF0694.
North Perrott *Som.* ***Village***, 2m/4km E of Crewkerne. **8 D4** ST4709.
North Petherton *Som.* Population: 3294. ***Village***, 3m/4km S of Bridgwater. **8 B1** ST2933.

N

North Petherwin *Cornw.* ***Village***, 5m/7km NW of Launceston. **4 C2** SX2889.
North Pickenham *Norf.* ***Village***, 3m/5km SE of Swaffham. **44 C5** TF8606.
North Piddle *Worcs.* ***Village***, 7m/12km E of Worcester. **29 J3** SO9654.
North Plain *Cumb.* ***Settlement***, on coast of Solway Firth, 2m/3km SW of Bowness-on-Solway. NY1961.
North Pool *Devon* ***Hamlet***, in parish of South Pool, 4m/6km N of Prawle Point. SX7741.
North Poorton *Dorset* ***Village***, 3m/5km SE of Beaminster. **8 E5** SY5198.
North Poulner *Hants.* ***Settlement***, adjoining to NE of Ringwood. SU1606.
North Quarme *Som.* ***Hamlet***, above valley of River Quarme, 2m/3km N of Exton. SS9236.
North Queensferry *Fife* Population: 1051. ***Village***, at N end of Forth bridges. **75 K2** NT1380.
North Queich *P. & K.* ***River***, stream rising from smaller streams flowing off Ochil Hills and flowing E to enter Loch Leven to NW of Kinross. **82 B7** NO1303.
North Radworthy *Devon* ***Hamlet***, on Exmoor, 4m/6km SW of Simonsbath. **7 F2** SS7534.
North Rauceby *Lincs.* ***Village***, 3m/5km W of Sleaford. **42 D1** TF0246.
North Reston *Lincs.* ***Hamlet***, 4m/7km SE of Louth. **53 G4** TF3883.
North Riding Forest Park *N.Yorks.* ***Leisure/recreation***, extensive areas of afforestation to N and E of Pickering, separated by Lockton Low Moor and Lockton High Moor across which runs A169 road N of Pickering. **58 E1** SE8888.
North Rigton *N.Yorks.* ***Village***, 4m/7km SW of Harrogate. **57 H5** SE2749.
North Ripley *Hants.* ***Settlement***, 1m/2km NE of Ripley. SZ1699.
North Roddymoor *Dur.* ***Locality***, 1km E of Roddymoor. NZ1536.
North Rode *Ches.* ***Hamlet***, 3m/5km NE of Congleton. **49 H6** SJ8866.
North Roe *Shet.* ***Locality***, area to N of Mainland, comprising an abundance of lochs and rivers. **108 C4** HU3487.
North Roe *Shet.* ***Village***, on Mainland, just N of Burra Voe. **108 C4** HU3689.
North Rona *W.Isles* *Alternative name for Rona, qv*
North Ronaldsay *Ork.* ***Island***, most northerly island of Orkney group, 3m/4km N of Sanday across North Ronaldsay Firth. An airfield provides air link with Scottish mainland. Area of island about 3 square miles or 8 square km. **106 G2** HY7553.
North Ronaldsay Airfield *Ork.* ***Airport/airfield***, to N of Hollandstoun, North Ronaldsay. **106 G2** HY7553.
North Ronaldsay Firth *Ork.* ***Sea feature***, stretch of water separating North Ronaldsay and Sanday. **106 G3** HY7553.
North Row *Cumb.* ***Locality***, 1km W of Bassenthwaite. NY2232.
North Runcton *Norf.* ***Village***, 3m/5km SE of King's Lynn. **44 A4** TF6415.
North Sandwick *Shet.* ***Settlement***, 1m/2km S of Gutcher, Yell. **108 E3** HU5497.
North Scale *Cumb.* ***Hamlet***, towards N end of Isle of Walney, 1m/2km N of causeway to Barrow-in-Furness. **54 E3** SD1870.
North Scarle *Lincs.* ***Village***, 8m/13km W of Lincoln. **52 B6** SK8466.
North Seaton *Northumb.* ***Locality***, 1m/2km E of Ashington. **71 H5** NZ2986.
North Seaton Colliery *Northumb.* ***Locality***, on N bank of River Wansbeck, 1km S of North Seaton. NZ2985.
North Shawbost *W.Isles* ***Settlement***, near NW coast of Isle of Lewis, forms locality of Siabost along with South and New Shawbost, 2m/3km W of Bragar. NB2647.
North Sheen *Gt.Lon.* ***Suburb***, in borough of Richmond upon Thames, to W of Chiswick Bridge. TQ1976.
North Shian *Arg. & B.* ***Locality***, on N shore of Loch Creran, in Argyll. **80 A3** NM9243.
North Shields *T. & W.* Population: 38,119. ***Town***, industrial centre on N bank of River Tyne, opposite South Shields and 7m/11km E of Newcastle upon Tyne. Ferry port for Scandinavia. Fishing also an important industry, with museum at Fishing Experience Centre. **71 J7** NZ3568.
North Shoebury *S'end* ***Hamlet***, in E part of Southend-on-Sea, 1m/2km NW of Shoeburyness. **25 F3** TQ9286.
North Shore *B'pool* ***Suburb***, to N of Blackpool town centre. **55 G6** SD3038.
North Side *Cumb.* ***Suburb***, 1km N of Workington across River Derwent. NY0029.
North Side *Peter.* ***Hamlet***, on River Nene, 5m/8km E of Peterborough. **43 F6** TL2799.
North Skelton *R. & C.* ***Hamlet***, 1m/2km E of Skelton. **63 H5** NZ6718.
North Skirlaugh *E.Riding* ***Hamlet***, adjoining to N of South Skirlaugh, 6m/10km SW of Hornsea. TA1440.
North Somercotes *Lincs.* ***Village***, near coast 3m/4km NW of Saltfleet. **53 H3** TF4296.
North Stack *I.o.A.* ***Island***, small island at NW tip of Holy Island, Anglesey, 2m/3km W of Holyhead. **46 A4** SH2183.
North Stainley *N.Yorks.* ***Village***, 4m/6km N of Ripon. **57 H2** SE2876.
North Stainmore *Cumb.* ***Locality***, 2m/4km E of Brough. **61 K5** NY8315.
North Stifford *Thur.* ***Village***, 2m/3km NW of Grays. **24 C3** TQ6080.
North Stoke *B. & N.E.Som.* ***Village***, 4m/7km NW of Bath. Site of Roman building 1m/2km NE. **19 K5** ST7068.
North Stoke *Oxon.* ***Village***, 2m/3km S of Wallingford across River Thames. **21 K3** SU6186.
North Stoke *W.Suss.* ***Village***, in River Arun valley, 2m/4km N of Arundel. **12 D5** TQ0210.
North Stoneham *Hants.* ***Settlement***, in green belt between Southampton and Eastleigh, 1m/2km SW of Eastleigh. **11 F3** SU4417.
North Street *Cambs.* ***Locality***, N end of Burwell. TL5867.
North Street *Hants.* ***Hamlet***, 4m/6km E of New Alresford. **11 H1** SU6433.
North Street *Hants.* ***Settlement***, 3m/5km N of Fordingbridge. SU1518.
North Street *Kent* ***Hamlet***, 2m/3km S of Faversham. **15 F2** TR0158.
North Street *Med.* ***Settlement***, 2m/3km SE of High Halstow, 6m/9km NE of Rochester. TQ8174.
North Street *W.Berks.* ***Hamlet***, 5m/8km W of Reading. **21 K4** SU6372.
North Sunderland *Northumb.* Population: 1781. ***Village***, adjoining to SW of Seahouses, 3m/5km SE of Bamburgh. **77 K7** NU2131.
North Sutor *High.* ***Coastal feature***, headland on N side of entrance to Cromarty Firth, Ross and Cromarty district. **97 F5** NH8168.
North Tamerton *Cornw.* ***Village***, by River Tamar, 5m/7km SW of Holsworthy. **6 B6** SX3197.
North Tarbothill *Aberdeen* ***Settlement***, 1km inland from coast and 3m/4km S of Balmedie. **91 H3** NJ9513.
North Tawton *Devon* ***Village***, 6m/10km NE of Okehampton. **6 E5** SS6601.
North Third *Stir.* ***Locality***, includes North Third Reservoir, 3m/5km SW of Stirling. **75 F2** NS7489.
North Third Reservoir *Stir.* ***Reservoir***, small reservoir in course of Bannock Burn, 4m/6km SW of Stirling. **75 F2** NS7589.
North Thoresby *Lincs.* ***Village***, 7m/12km N of Louth. **53 F3** TF2998.
North Thundergay *N.Ayr.* *Alternative name for Lenimore, qv.*
North Tidworth *Wilts.* Population: 6778. ***Small town***, military town, 3m/4km SW of Ludgershall. **21 F7** SU2349.
North Togston *Northumb.* ***Settlement***, to N of Togston, 1m/2km N of Broomhill. **71 H3** NU2502.
North Tolsta *W.Isles* *Anglicised form of Tolastadh Bho Thuath, qv.*
North Town *Devon* ***Hamlet***, adjoining Petrockstow, 4m/6km NW of Hatherleigh. **6 D5** SS5109.
North Town *Hants.* ***Suburb***, E district of Aldershot. **22 B6** SU8850.
North Town *Lancs.* ***Locality***, to N of Padiham. SD7936.
North Town *Som.* ***Hamlet***, just N of North Wootton, 3m/4km SE of Wells. ST5642.
North Town *W. & M.* ***Suburb***, N district of Maidenhead. SU8882.
North Tuddenham *Norf.* ***Village***, 3m/5km E of East Dereham. **44 E4** TG0314.
North Tyne *Northumb.* ***River***, rising on Kielder Forest, near Scottish border, and flowing SE by Falstone, Bellingham and Wark to join River South Tyne and form River Tyne 2m/3km NW of Hexham. **70 D6** NY9166.
North Tyneside Steam Railway *T. & W.* ***Other feature of interest***, on N side of River Tyne, 3m/4km SW of Tynemouth. **71 J7** NZ3367.
North Ugie Water *Aber.* ***River***, rising on E side of Windyheads Hill and flowing SE through Strichen to join South Ugie Water 1m/2km NE of Longside, forming River Ugie. **99 H5** NK0548.
North Uist (Gaelic form: Uibhist a Tuath.) *W.Isles* ***Island***, of about 120 square miles or 310 square km, between South Harris and Benbecula, having innumerable lochs and offshore islands. **92 D4** NF8070.
North Wallbottle *T. & W.* ***Suburb***, to W of Newcastle upon Tyne, 1km N of Wallbottle. NZ1767.
North Walsham *Norf.* Population: 9534. ***Small town***, 14m/22km N of Norwich. **45 G2** TG2830.
North Waltham *Hants.* ***Village***, 6m/9km SW of Basingstoke. **21 J7** SU5646.
North Warnborough *Hants.* ***Village***, on Basingstoke Canal, 1km NW of Odiham. Site of Roman villa 1km N. **22 A6** SU7351.
North Waste *W.Mid.* ***Suburb***, 3m/5km W of Coventry city centre. SP2878.
North Water Bridge *Angus* *Alternative spelling of Northwaterbridge, qv.*
North Watten *High.* ***Settlement***, 3m/4km N of Watten. **105 H3** ND2458.
North Weald Bassett *Essex* Population: 4279. ***Village***, 3m/4km NE of Epping. Numerous masts to E. **23 H1** TL4904.
North Wembley *Gt.Lon.* ***Suburb***, in borough of Brent, 1m/2km NW of Wembley. TQ1786.
North West Channel *I.o.S.* ***Sea feature***, sea channel, 2m/3km SW of Samson and 4m/6km W of St. Mary's, running NW to Atlantic Ocean. **2 B1** SV8410.
North West Point *Devon* ***Coastal feature***, headland at NW of Lundy Island. Lighthouse. **6 A1** SS1348.
North Weston *Oxon.* ***Settlement***, 2m/3km W of Thame. SP6805.
North Wharf *Lancs.* ***Coastal feature***, sandbank on N side of Fleetwood. **55 G5** SD3149.
North Wheatley *Notts.* ***Village***, 4m/7km NE of Retford. **51 K4** SK7685.
North Whilborough *Devon* ***Hamlet***, 3m/5km NW of Torquay. **5 J4** SX8766.
North Wick *B. & N.E.Som.* ***Settlement***, 2m/3km N of Chew Magna. **19 J5** ST5865.
North Widcombe *B. & N.E.Som.* ***Settlement***, at SE corner of Chew Valley Lake, 1m/2km NE of West Harptree. **19 J6** ST5758.
North Willingham *Lincs.* ***Village***, 4m/6km E of Market Rasen. **52 E4** TF1688.
North Wingfield *Derbys.* Population: 12,136. ***Village***, 2m/3km NE of Clay Cross. **51 G6** SK4165.
North Witham *Lincs.* ***Village***, 1m/2km S of Colsterworth. **42 C3** SK9221.
North Woolwich *Gt.Lon.* ***Suburb***, on N bank of River Thames, in borough of Newham. TQ4379.
North Wootton *Dorset* ***Village***, 2m/3km SE of Sherborne. **9 F3** ST6514.
North Wootton *Norf.* ***Village***, 3m/5km NE of King's Lynn. **44 A3** TF6424.
North Wootton *Som.* ***Village***, 3m/4km SE of Wells. **19 J7** ST5641.
North Wraxall *Wilts.* ***Village***, 6m/10km W of Chippenham. **20 B4** ST8175.
North Wroughton *Swin.* ***Locality***, adjoining to N of Wroughton. **20 E3** SU1480.
North Yardhope *Northumb.* ***Settlement***, 2m/3km SW of Holystone. **70 E3** NT9201.
North York Moors National Park *N.Yorks.* ***Large natural feature***, 600 square miles or 1968 square km, much of it moorland, extending from Cleveland and Hambleton Hills towards North Yorkshire coast. **63 H6** NZ7401.
North Yorkshire Moors Railway *N.Yorks.* ***Other feature of interest***, tourist railway running from Pickering to Grosmont, with access to moorland at Newtondale Halt. **58 E1** SE8287.
Northacre *Norf.* ***Hamlet***, 3m/4km SE of Watton. **44 D6** TL9598.
Northall *Bucks.* ***Hamlet***, 4m/6km SE of Leighton Buzzard. SP9520.
Northall Green *Norf.* ***Settlement***, 1m/2km NE of East Dereham. **44 E4** TF9914.
Northallerton *N.Yorks.* Population: 13,774. ***Town***, market town, 14m/23km S of Darlington, with 15c almshouse. **62 E7** SE3693.
Northam *Devon* Population: 6167. ***Small town***, 2m/3km N of Bideford. **6 C3** SS4429.
Northam *S'ham.* ***Suburb***, on W bank of River Itchen, 1m/2km E of Southampton city centre. Northam Bridge carries main road over river. **11 F3** SU4312.
Northam Burrows *Devon* ***Coastal feature***, low-lying promontory and country park to N of Northam, extending to mouth of Rivers Taw and Torridge. **6 C2** SS4429.
Northampton *Northants.* Population: 179,596. ***Town***, county town on River Nene, 60m/97km NW of London. New Town designated 1968. Traditional footwear manufacturing town is well illustrated in Central Museum. Two Norman churches survived a fire in 1675 which destroyed much of town's centre. **31 J2** SP7560.
Northampton Central Museum and Art Gallery *Northants.* ***Other feature of interest***, in Northampton town centre, with local and industrial history displays of footwear and Roman history. **31 J2** SP7560.
Northaw *Herts.* ***Village***, 2m/3km E of Potters Bar. **23 F1** TL2702.
Northay *Devon* ***Settlement***, 1m/2km NW of Marshwood and 5m/7km NE of Axminster. ST3600.
Northay *Som.* ***Hamlet***, 3m/5km NW of Chard. **8 B3** ST2811.
Northbay (Also known as Bayherivagh.) *W.Isles* ***Village***, on Barra, 4m/7km S of Scurrival Point. Barra Airport is 1m/2km N on Tràigh Mhòr. Inlet on which village is situated, is known as Bàgh Hirivagh. NF7002.
Northbeck *Lincs.* ***Settlement***, just N of Scredington, 4m/6km SE of Sleaford. TF0941.
Northborough *Peter.* Population: 1255. ***Village***, 7m/11km NW of Peterborough. 14c manor house. **42 E5** TF1507.
Northbourne *Kent* ***Village***, 3m/4km W of Deal. **15 J2** TR3352.
Northbourne *Oxon.* ***Suburb***, S district of Didcot. SU5289.
Northbridge Street *E.Suss.* ***Settlement***, at N end of Robertsbridge. TQ7324.
Northbrook *Hants.* ***Hamlet***, 1km NW of Micheldever. SU5139.
Northbrook *Oxon.* ***Hamlet***, on E side of Oxford Canal, 6m/9km W of Bicester. **31 F6** SP4922.
Northburnhill *Aber.* ***Settlement***, 2m/3km S of Cuminestown. **99 G6** NJ8147.
Northchapel *W.Suss.* ***Village***, 4m/6km SE of Haslemere. **12 C4** SU9529.
Northchurch *Herts.* ***Suburb***, NW district of Berkhamsted. **22 C1** SP9708.
Northcote Manor *Devon* ***Settlement***, 2m/3km SE of High Bickington. **6 E4** SS6218.
Northcott *Devon* ***Locality***, 1km SW of Culmstock and 6m/9km NE of Cullompton. ST0912.
Northcott *Devon* ***Locality***, parish 5m/8km N of Launceston, containing Northcott Hamlet and Higher Northcott. **6 B6** SX3492.
Northcott Hamlet *Devon* ***Hamlet***, together with Higher Northcott forms locality of Northcott, 6m/9km N of Launceston. SX3392.
Northcourt *Oxon.* ***Suburb***, NE district of Abingdon. SU5098.
Northdown *Kent* ***Suburb***, E district of Margate. TR3770.
Northdyke *Ork.* ***Settlement***, situated on W coast of Mainland, to N of Bay of Skaill. **106 B5** HY2320.
Northedge *Derbys.* ***Settlement***, 3m/4km NW of Clay Cross. SK3565.
Northend *B. & N.E.Som.* ***Suburb***, adjoining to NW of Batheaston. **20 A5** ST7769.
Northend *Bucks.* ***Locality***, 3m/5km SE of Watlington. **22 A2** SU7392.
Northend *Essex* ***Settlement***, adjoining to N of Southminster, 2m/4km N of Burnham-on-Crouch. TL9500.
Northend *Warks.* ***Village***, 8m/13km NW of Banbury. **30 E3** SP3952.
Northend Woods *Bucks.* ***Locality***, 3m/5km SE of High Wycombe. SU9089.
Northenden *Gt.Man.* ***Suburb***, 5m/8km S of Manchester city centre. SJ8290.
Northern Common *Derbys.* ***Locality***, adjoining to N of Dronfield Woodhouse. SK3278.
Northern Moor *Gt.Man.* ***Suburb***, 5m/8km SW of Manchester city centre. SJ8190.

N

Northey Island *Essex* ***Island***, at head of River Blackwater estuary, 2m/3km E of Maldon. **24 E1** TL8806.
Northfield *Aberdeen* ***Suburb***, NW district of Aberdeen. **91 G4** NJ9008.
Northfield *Aber.* ***Settlement***, 1km S of Troup Head, 2m/3km NE of Gardenstown. **99 G4** NJ8266.
Northfield *E.Riding* ***Suburb***, N district of Hessle. TA0327.
Northfield *Edin.* ***Suburb***, adjoining to W of Portobello, 2m/3km E of Edinburgh city centre. NT2973.
Northfield *High.* ***Settlement***, 1m/2km SW of Wick. **105 J4** ND3548.
Northfield *Sc.Bord.* ***Settlement***, adjoining to W of St. Abbs. **77 H4** NT9167.
Northfield *Som.* ***Suburb***, W district of Bridgwater. ST2836.
Northfield *W.Mid.* ***Suburb***, 5m/9km SW of Birmingham city centre. **30 B1** SP0279.
Northfields *Lincs.* ***Suburb***, NW district of Stamford. TF0207.
Northfleet *Kent* Population: 21,397. ***Town***, former shipbuilding town on River Thames, 1m/2km W of Gravesend. Norman church with 14c screen. **24 C4** TQ6274.
Northfleet Green *Kent* ***Settlement***, 2m/3km S of Northfleet. TQ6271.
Northgate *W.Suss.* ***Suburb***, N district of Crawley. TQ2737.
Northhouse *Sc.Bord.* ***Settlement***, 3m/4km NE of Teviothead. **69 K3** NT4307.
Northiam *E.Suss.* ***Village***, 7m/11km NW of Rye. **14 D5** TQ8224.
Northill *Beds.* ***Village***, 2m/4km SW of Sandy. **32 E4** TL1446.
Northington *Glos.* ***Settlement***, on River Severn estuary, just N of Awre, 2m/4km NE of Blakeney. SO7008.
Northington *Hants.* ***Hamlet***, 4m/6km NW of New Alresford. The Grange (English Heritage), 1m/2km S. **11 G1** SU5637.
Northlands *Lincs.* ***Village***, 6m/10km N of Boston. **53 G7** TF3453.
Northleach *Glos.* Population: 1462. ***Small town***, historic wool town, 10m/15km NE of Cirencester. Attractions include Cotswold Countryside Collection with displays of rural life, and Keith Harding's World of Mechanical Music. **30 C7** SP1114.
Northleigh *Devon* ***Hamlet***, 3m/5km E of Barnstaple. **6 E2** SS6034.
Northleigh *Devon* ***Village***, 4m/6km SE of Honiton. **7 K6** SY1996.
Northlew *Devon* ***Village***, 6m/9km NW of Okehampton. **6 D6** SX5099.
Northload Bridge *Som.* ***Locality***, on W side of Glastonbury. ST4939.
Northmoor *Oxon.* ***Village***, 4m/7km S of Eynsham. **21 H1** SP4202.
Northmoor Corner *Som.* ***Locality***, 1km SE of North Newton, 1m/2km SE of North Petherton. ST3030.
Northmoor Green (Also known as Moorland.) *Som.* ***Hamlet***, on River Parrett, 4m/6km SE of Bridgwater. **8 C1** ST3332.
Northmuir *Angus* ***Village***, 1m/2km N of Kirriemuir. **82 E2** NO3855.
Northney *Hants.* ***Hamlet***, at N end of Hayling Island. **11 J4** SU7303.
Northolt *Gt.Lon.* ***Suburb***, in borough of Ealing, 11m/18km W of Charing Cross. To W is Northolt Airfield, formerly main airport of London. **22 E3** TQ1384.
Northop (Llaneurgain). *Flints.* ***Village***, 3m/4km N of Mold. **48 B6** SJ2468.
Northop Hall *Flints.* ***Village***, 2m/3km E of Northop. **48 B6** SJ2667.
Northorpe *Lincs.* ***Hamlet***, 1km N of Donington. **43 F2** TF2035.
Northorpe *Lincs.* ***Locality***, 2m/3km S of Bourne. **42 D4** TF0917.
Northorpe *Lincs.* ***Village***, 3m/4km W of Kirton in Lindsey. **52 B3** SK8997.
Northorpe *W.Yorks.* ***Locality***, adjoining to NE of Mirfield. SE2120.
Northover *Som.* ***Locality***, on N bank of River Yeo, 1km NE of Ilchester. **8 E2** ST5223.
Northover *Som.* ***Suburb***, on SW side of Glastonbury. ST4838.
Northowram *W.Yorks.* Population: 4064. ***Village***, 2m/3km NE of Halifax. **57 G7** SE1127.
Northport *Dorset* ***Suburb***, in N district of Wareham. SY9188.
Northpunds *Shet.* ***Settlement***, 1m/2km SW of Hoswick, Mainland. **109 D10** HU4022.
Northrepps *Norf.* ***Village***, 3m/4km SE of Cromer. **45 G2** TG2439.
Northton (Gaelic form: Taobh Tuath.) *W.Isles* ***Village***, on W coast of South Harris, 4m/6km SE of Toe Head. **92 E3** NF9989.
Northtown *Ork.* ***Settlement***, in N part of Burray, on NE side of Echnaloch Bay. **107 D8** ND4797.
Northumberland Heath *Gt.Lon.* ***Suburb***, in borough of Bexley, 1m/2km SW of Erith and 13m/21km E of Charing Cross. TQ5077.
Northumberland National Park *Northumb.* ***Large natural feature***, covering an area from Hadrian's Wall in S to central Cheviot Hills in N, and from Simonside Hills in E to Kielder Water in W. Wild and remote border country consisting of hills and moorland, and upper reaches of Rivers Rede, Coquet and North Tyne. Highest point is The Cheviot at 2673 feet or 815 metres. Total area is 640 square miles or 1030 square km, one-fifth of which is owned by Forestry Commission and another fifth by Ministry of Defence. **70 D3** NY8084.
Northville *Torfaen* ***Suburb***, in NE part of Cwmbran. ST2996.
Northward Hill Nature Reserve *Med.* ***Nature reserve***, situated to N of High Halstow on edge of Cooling Marshes, 6m/9km NE of Rochester. Largest heronry in Britain. **24 D4** TQ7876.
Northwaterbridge (Also spelled North Water Bridge.) *Angus* ***Settlement***, on River North Esk, 5m/8km SW of Laurencekirk. NO6566.
Northway *Glos.* ***Locality***, adjoining to N of Ashchurch, 2m/4km E of Tewkesbury. **29 J5** SO9234.
Northway *Som.* ***Hamlet***, 2m/3km NE of Milverton. ST1329.
Northway *Swan.* ***Locality***, on Gower peninsula, 3m/5km NW of Mumbles Head. SS5889.
Northwich *Ches.* Population: 34,520. ***Town***, on site of Roman town of Condate at confluence of Rivers Dane and Weaver, 20m/31km SW of Manchester. Salt-mining centre with a more recent chemical industry. Salt Museum. **49 F5** SJ6573.
Northwick *Som.* ***Settlement***, 3m/4km NE of Highbridge. ST3548.
Northwick *S.Glos.* ***Hamlet***, 2m/3km NE of Severn Beach. **19 J3** ST5586.
Northwick *Worcs.* ***Suburb***, N district of Worcester. SO8457.
Northwold *Norf.* ***Village***, 4m/6km SE of Stoke Ferry. **44 B6** TL7597.
Northwood *Derbys.* ***Hamlet***, 4m/6km NW of Matlock. SK3664.
Northwood *Devon* ***Settlement***, 6m/10km NW of Crediton. SS7708.
Northwood *Gt.Lon.* ***Suburb***, in borough of Hillingdon, 3m/4km SE of Rickmansworth. **22 D2** TQ0991.
Northwood *I.o.W.* Population: 1961. ***Village***, 2m/3km S of Cowes. **11 F5** SZ4893.
Northwood *Kent* ***Suburb***, 1m/2km N of Ramsgate. TR3767.
Northwood *Mersey.* ***Suburb***, NE district of Kirkby. SJ4299.
Northwood *Shrop.* ***Village***, 4m/7km NW of Wem. **38 D2** SJ4633.
Northwood *Staffs.* ***Suburb***, 2m/3km S of Newcastle-under-Lyme. SJ8542.
Northwood *Stoke* ***Suburb***, 1km NE of Hanley. SJ8948.
Northwood Green *Glos.* ***Hamlet***, 4m/6km NE of Newnham. **29 G7** SO7216.
Northwood Hills *Gt.Lon.* ***Suburb***, 1km SE of Northwood. TQ1090.
Norton *Glos.* ***Village***, 4m/6km NE of Gloucester. **29 H6** SO8524.
Norton *Halton* ***Suburb***, 3m/4km E of Runcorn town centre. **48 E4** SJ5581.
Norton *Herts.* ***Locality***, at N end of Letchworth. **33 F5** TL2234.
Norton *I.o.W.* ***Hamlet***, 1km W of Yarmouth across River Yar. **10 E6** SZ3489.
Norton *Kent* ***Locality***, 3m/5km W of Faversham. TQ9661.
Norton *Mon.* ***Settlement***, 1m/2km W of Skenfrith. SO4420.
Norton *N.Som.* ***Hamlet***, 2m/4km NE of Weston-super-Mare. ST3463.
Norton *N.Yorks.* Population: 6342. ***Small town***, opposite Malton across River Derwent, 17m/27km NE of York. **58 D2** SE7971.
Norton *Northants.* ***Village***, 2m/4km E of Daventry. 1km NE is site of Roman settlement of Bannaventa. **31 H2** SP6063.
Norton *Notts.* ***Village***, 6m/10km NW of Ollerton. **51 H5** SK5771.
Norton *Powys* ***Village***, 2m/3km N of Presteigne. Remains of motte and bailey castle. **28 C2** SO3067.
Norton *Shrop.* ***Settlement***, 1m/2km NE of Wroxeter. **38 E5** SJ5609.
Norton *Shrop.* ***Settlement***, 2m/3km SE of Craven Arms. **38 D7** SO4681.
Norton *Shrop.* ***Village***, 4m/7km N of Bridgnorth. **39 G5** SJ7200.
Norton *S.Yorks.* ***Suburb***, 3m/5km S of Sheffield city centre. **51 F4** SK3582.
Norton *S.Yorks.* Population: 2077. ***Village***, 6m/10km SE of Knottingley. **51 H1** SE5415.
Norton *Stock.* ***Suburb***, 2m/3km N of Stockton-on-Tees town centre. **63 F4** NZ4421.
Norton *Suff.* ***Village***, 3m/5km SE of Ixworth. **34 D2** TL9565.
Norton *Swan.* ***Suburb***, in The Mumbles, 4m/6km SW of Swansea city centre across Swansea Bay. SS6188.
Norton *V. of Glam.* ***Settlement***, 1km NE of Ogmore-by-Sea. SS8775.
Norton *W.Mid.* ***Suburb***, SW district of Stourbridge. **40 A7** SO8982.
Norton *W.Suss.* ***Hamlet***, 1m/2km N of Selsey. **12 B7** SZ8695.
Norton *W.Suss.* ***Village***, 4m/7km E of Chichester. **12 C6** SU9206.
Norton *Wilts.* ***Village***, 4m/6km SW of Malmesbury. **20 B3** ST8884.
Norton *Worcs.* ***Hamlet***, 3m/4km N of Evesham. **30 B4** SP0448.
Norton *Worcs.* ***Village***, 3m/5km SE of Worcester. **29 H3** SO8751.
Norton Bavant *Wilts.* ***Village***, on River Wylye, 3m/4km SE of Warminster. **20 C7** ST9043.
Norton Bridge *Staffs.* ***Village***, 3m/5km SW of Stone. **40 A3** SJ8730.
Norton Bury *Herts.* ***Hamlet***, 1m/2km NW of Baldock. TL2334.
Norton Canes *Staffs.* Population: 6549. ***Village***, 3m/5km NW of Brownhills. **40 C5** SK0107.
Norton Canon *Here.* ***Village***, 9m/15km NW of Hereford. **28 C4** SO3847.
Norton Conyers *N.Yorks.* ***Historic house***, dating from 16c or earlier, 1km S of Wath. **57 J2** SE3176.
Norton Corner *Norf.* ***Locality***, 3m/5km N of Reepham. TG0928.
Norton Creek *Norf.* ***Sea feature***, channel separating Scolt Head from mainland and connecting Brancaster and Burnham Harbours. **44 B1** TF8145.
Norton Disney *Lincs.* ***Village***, 7m/11km NE of Newark-on-Trent. Site of Roman villa 2m/3km W. **52 B7** SK8859.
Norton Ferris *Wilts.* ***Settlement***, 3m/5km NW of Mere. **9 G1** ST7936.
Norton Fitzwarren *Som.* ***Village***, 3m/4km NW of Taunton. **7 K3** ST1925.
Norton Green *Herts.* ***Suburb***, at W edge of Stevenage. TL2223.
Norton Green *I.o.W.* ***Village***, 1m/2km NE of Totland. **10 E6** SZ3488.
Norton Green *Staffs.* ***Locality***, adjoining Norton Canes, 3m/4km NW of Brownhills. SK0207.
Norton Green *Stoke* ***Suburb***, 1m/2km SW of Brown Edge. SJ9052.
Norton Hammer *S.Yorks.* ***Suburb***, 2m/3km S of Sheffield city centre. SK3483.
Norton Hawkfield *B. & N.E.Som.* ***Hamlet***, 2m/3km NE of Chew Magna. **19 J5** ST5964.
Norton Heath *Essex* ***Village***, 3m/5km E of Chipping Ongar. **24 C1** TL6004.
Norton in Hales *Shrop.* ***Village***, 3m/5km NE of Market Drayton. **39 F2** SJ7038.
Norton in the Moors *Stoke* ***Locality***, 2m/3km NE of Burslem. **49 H7** SJ8951.
Norton-Juxta-Twycross *Leics.* ***Village***, 6m/10km S of Ashby de la Zouch. **41 F5** SK3207.
Norton-le-Clay *N.Yorks.* ***Village***, 3m/5km N of Boroughbridge. **57 J2** SE4071.
Norton Lees *S.Yorks.* ***Suburb***, 2m/3km S of Sheffield city centre. SK3583.
Norton Lindsey *Warks.* ***Village***, 4m/6km W of Warwick. **30 D2** SP2263.
Norton Little Green *Suff.* ***Hamlet***, 1m/2km E of Norton. TL9766.
Norton Malreward *B. & N.E.Som.* ***Village***, 5m/8km S of Bristol. **19 J5** ST6065.
Norton Mandeville *Essex* ***Settlement***, 2m/4km NE of Chipping Ongar. **23 J1** TL5704.
Norton Marshes *Norf.* ***Marsh/bog***, wetland area to S of Reedham, containing numerous small dykes and streams, with Boyce's Dyke bisecting it from E to W. **45 J5** TG4100.
Norton Priory *Halton* ***Ecclesiastical building***, remains of 12c priory, 3m/4km E of Runcorn, with good example of Norman doorway. Museum includes exhibition on evolution of Priory over the centuries. **48 E4** SJ5483.
Norton St. Philip *Som.* ***Village***, 5m/8km N of Frome. **20 A6** ST7755.
Norton Street *Norf.* ***Locality***, forming part of Norton Subcourse, 3m/5km E of Loddon. TM4198.
Norton sub Hamdon *Som.* ***Village***, 5m/9km W of Yeovil. To E, Hamdon Hill. **8 D3** ST4715.
Norton Subcourse *Norf.* ***Village***, 3m/5km E of Loddon. **45 J6** TM4098.
Norton Wood *Here.* ***Hamlet***, 3m/5km E of Willersley. **28 C4** SO3648.
Norton Woodseats *S.Yorks.* ***Suburb***, 3m/4km S of Sheffield city centre. SK3582.
Norwell *Notts.* ***Village***, 5m/8km N of Newark-on-Trent. **51 K6** SK7761.
Norwell Woodhouse *Notts.* ***Hamlet***, 2m/3km W of Norwell. **51 K6** SK7761.
Norwich *Norf.* Population: 171,304. ***City***, county town and cathedral city at confluence of River Wensum and River Yare, 98m/158km NE of London. Middle ages saw Norwich become second richest city in country through exporting textiles. Medieval streets and buildings are well preserved. Sections of 14c flint city wall defences still exist, including Cow Tower (English Heritage). Current chief industries are high technology and computer based. Notable buildings include partly Norman cathedral with second highest spire in Britain, Norman castle with keep (now museum and art gallery), 15c guildhall, modern city hall, numerous medieval churches. University of East Anglia 2m/4km W of city centre. Airport 3m/5km N. **45 G5** TG2208.
Norwich Castle Museum *Norf.* ***Other feature of interest***, military museum in Norwich, which includes a reconstruction of a World War I trench and a narrative of 20c conflict, as well as history of Royal Norfolk Regiment. **45 G5** TG2308.
Norwich Cathedral *Norf.* ***Ecclesiastical building***, fine cathedral in Norwich, to S of River Wensum. Started in 11c, with present stone spire added in 15c. Extensively restored. Particularly noted for roof bosses in the nave and cloisters. **45 G5** TG2308.
Norwick *Shet.* ***Hamlet***, on NE coast of Unst, on Nor Wick bay. **108 F1** HP6514.
Norwood *Derbys.* ***Suburb***, adjoining to NE of Killamarsh. SK4681.
Norwood *Gt.Lon.* ***Suburb***, of south London in boroughs of Croydon and Lambeth, consisting of localities of South and West Norwood, Upper Norwood, and Norwood New Town. TQ3271.
Norwood *S.Yorks.* ***Suburb***, 2m/3km N of Sheffield city centre. SK3590.
Norwood End *Essex* ***Settlement***, 4m/6km N of Chipping Ongar. TL5608.
Norwood Green *Gt.Lon.* ***Suburb***, of Southall in borough of Ealing 10m/17km W of Charing Cross. **22 E4** TQ1378.
Norwood Green *W.Yorks.* ***Village***, 3m/4km N of Brighouse. SE1426.
Norwood Hill *Surr.* ***Hamlet***, 3m/5km W of Horley. **23 F7** TQ2443.
Norwood New Town *Gt.Lon.* ***Locality***, forms suburb of Norwood, along with South and West Norwood, and Upper Norwood, 3m/5km N of Croydon town centre. TQ3270.
Norwood Park *Som.* ***Settlement***, 1m/2km E of Glastonbury. ST5239.
Norwoodside *Cambs.* ***Suburb***, on N side of March. TL4198.
Noseley *Leics.* ***Historic house***, 18c hall 7m/11km N of Market Harborough. Site of former village to W. **42 A6** SP7398.
Nose's Point *Dur.* ***Coastal feature***, headland 1m/2km S of Seaham. **63 F2** NZ4347.

Noss Head *High.* ***Coastal feature***, headland with lighthouse on E coast of Caithness district at S end of Sinclair's Bay. **105 J3** ND3855.

Noss Mayo *Devon* ***Village***, 3m/5km SW of Yealmpton, on S side of creek running into River Yealm estuary, opposite Newton Ferrers. Yachting. **5 F6** SX5447.

Nostell Priory *W.Yorks.* ***Historic house***, Palladian house built in 1733 (National Trust) at Nostell, 3m/5km NW of Hemsworth. Grounds contain 16c church, rose gardens and lakeland walks. **51 G1** SE4017.

Nosterfield *N.Yorks.* ***Hamlet***, 3m/5km E of Masham. **57 H1** SE2780.

Nosterfield End *Cambs.* ***Settlement***, 2m/4km W of Haverhill. TL6344.

Nostie *High.* ***Settlement***, on N side of Loch Alsh, Skye and Lochalsh district, 2m/3km W of Dornie. **86 E2** NG8527.

Note o' the Gate *Sc.Bord.* ***Mountain***, in Wauchope Forest area of Cheviot Hills, over which passes B6357 road in a N to S direction. Height 1233 feet or 376 metres. **70 A3** NT5803.

Notgrove *Glos.* ***Village***, 4m/6km N of Northleach. Neolithic long barrow (English Heritage) 2m/3km NW. **30 C6** SP1020.

Nothe Fort *Dorset* ***Castle***, Victorian coastal defence built on S side of entrance to Weymouth Harbour. Now a museum of coastal defence. **9 F7** SY6878.

Notley Abbey *Bucks.* ***Ecclesiastical building***, remains of medieval abbey, 2m/3km N of Thame. **22 A1** SP7109.

Nottage *Bridgend* ***Suburb***, N of Porthcawl. **18 B4** SS8178.

Notting Hill *Gt.Lon.* ***Suburb***, in borough of Kensington and Chelsea, 3m/5km W of Charing Cross. Famed for its annual carnival. TQ2480.

Nottingham *High.* ***Settlement***, 1m/2km NE of Latheron. **105 H5** ND2135.

Nottingham *Nott.* Population: 270,222. ***City***, on River Trent, 45m/72km NE of Birmingham. Originally Saxon town built on one of a pair of hills. In 1068, Normans built castle on other hill and both communities traded in valley between. Important commercial, industrial, entertainment and sports centre. Key industries include manufacture of lace, mechanical products, tobacco and pharmaceuticals. 17c castle, restored 19c, houses museum and art gallery. Two universities. Repertory theatre. **41 H1** SK5740.

Nottingham Castle Museum *Nott.* ***Other feature of interest***, in Nottingham city centre. First provincial museum in late 19c, it includes story of Nottingham Galleries which depicts development of city. **41 H2** SK5639.

Nottingham Heritage Centre *Notts.* ***Other feature of interest***, transport centre at Ruddington, 4m/7km S of Nottingham city centre. Includes collection of road and rail transport, miniature railway and local history museum set within Rushcliffe Country Park. Steam trains are run, with plans to connect to Grand Central Railway at Loughborough. **41 H2** SK5732.

Nottington *Dorset* ***Hamlet***, 2m/3km NW of Weymouth. SY6682.

Notton *W.Yorks.* ***Village***, 5m/8km S of Wakefield. **51 F1** SE3413.

Notton *Wilts.* ***Hamlet***, 3m/4km S of Chippenham. **20 C5** ST9169.

Nottswood Hill *Glos.* ***Settlement***, 5m/8km S of Newent. SO7018.

Nounsley *Essex* ***Hamlet***, 3m/5km SW of Witham. **24 D1** TL7910.

Noup Head *Ork.* ***Coastal feature***, headland with overhanging cliffs at NW end of Westray. Lighthouse. **106 C2** HY3950.

Noutard's Green *Worcs.* ***Hamlet***, 4m/6km S of Stourport-on-Severn. **29 G2** SO7966.

Novers Park *Bristol* ***Suburb***, 2m/3km S of Bristol city centre. ST5869.

Noverton *Glos.* ***Locality***, 2m/4km NE of Cheltenham. SO9723.

Noviomagus *W.Suss.* *See Chichester.*

Nowton *Suff.* ***Hamlet***, 2m/4km S of Bury St. Edmunds. **34 C2** TL8660.

Nox *Shrop.* ***Hamlet***, 5m/9km W of Shrewsbury. **38 D4** SJ4010.

Noyadd Trefawr *Cere.* ***Settlement***, 5m/8km E of Cardigan. **26 B4** SN2546.

Nuffield *Oxon.* ***Village***, 4m/6km E of Wallingford. **21 K3** SU6687.

Number 1, Royal Crescent *B. & N.E.Som.* ***Historic house***, first 18c Palladian house built in Royal Crescent, Bath, by John Wood the Younger. **20 A5** ST7365.

Nun Appleton *N.Yorks.* ***Settlement***, on N side of River Wharfe, 5m/8km SE of Tadcaster. SE5539.

Nun Hills *Lancs.* ***Locality***, in Rossendale, 1m/2km SW of Bacup. SD8521.

Nun Monkton *N.Yorks.* ***Village***, at confluence of River Nidd and River Ouse, 9m/14km SE of Boroughbridge. **58 B4** SE5057.

Nunburnholme *E.Riding* ***Village***, 3m/5km E of Pocklington. **58 E5** SE8447.

Nuncargate *Notts.* ***Suburb***, N district of Annesley Woodhouse, 1m/2km S of Kirkby in Ashfield. SK5054.

Nunclose *Cumb.* ***Locality***, 1m/2km SW of Armathwaite. NY4945.

Nuneaton *Warks.* Population: 66,715. ***Town***, market town, 8m/13km N of Coventry. Formerly a mining and textile town. Museum of local history in Riversley Park. George Eliot was born at Astley, 4m/6km SW. **41 F6** SP3691.

Nuneham Courtenay *Oxon.* ***Village***, 5m/8km SE of Oxford. **21 J2** SU5599.

Nuneham Park *Oxon.* ***Historic house***, 3m/5km E of Abingdon, now a conference centre. **21 J2** SU5497.

Nuney Green *Oxon.* ***Settlement***, 5m/7km NW of Reading. SU6779.

Nunhead *Gt.Lon.* ***Suburb***, in borough of Southwark, 5m/7km SE of Charing Cross. TQ3575.

Nunney *Som.* ***Village***, 3m/5km SW of Frome. Moated 14c castle (English Heritage). **20 A7** ST7345.

Nunney Castle *Som.* ***Castle***, 14c moated castle (English Heritage) 3m/5km SW of Frome, with hole in wall made by Oliver Cromwell's canon during Civil War. **20 A7** ST7345.

Nunnington *Here.* ***Settlement***, 3m/5km NE of Hereford. SO5543.

Nunnington *N.Yorks.* ***Village***, 2m/4km N of Hovingham. Hall (National Trust) is 16c-17c house. **58 C2** SE6679.

Nunnington Hall *N.Yorks.* ***Historic house***, 17c manor (National Trust) on S side of River Rye in Vale of Pickering, 3m/5km SE of Helmsley. Contains Carlisle Collection of Miniature Rooms. 17c walled garden. **58 C2** SE6779.

Nunnington Park *Som.* ***Settlement***, 1km SE of Wiveliscombe. **7 J3** ST0826.

Nunnykirk *Northumb.* ***Settlement***, 2m/3km NW of Netherwitton. Nunnykirk Hall, mansion built in 1825. NZ0892.

Nunraw Abbey *E.Loth.* ***Ecclesiastical building***, built by Cistercian monks in 1948 on site of earlier foundation, 1km SE of Garvald. **76 D3** NT5970.

Nuns' Pass *Arg. & B.* ***Other feature of interest***, pass on S coast of Mull, 1m/2km SW of Carsaig Bay. **79 G5** NM5220.

Nunsfield *Lincs.* ***Locality***, 1m/2km W of Sutton on Sea. TF5081.

Nunsthorpe *N.E.Lincs.* ***Suburb***, 1m/2km S of Grimsby town centre. TA2607.

Nunthorpe *Middbro.* ***Suburb***, 4m/7km SE of Middlesbrough. **63 G5** NZ5314.

Nunthorpe *York* ***Suburb***, on W bank of River Ouse, 1m/2km S of York city centre. SE5949.

Nunton *W.Isles* *Anglicised form of Baile nan Cailleach, qv.*

Nunton *Wilts.* ***Village***, 3m/4km S of Salisbury. **10 C2** SU1526.

Nunwell House *I.o.W.* ***Historic house***, 17c and Georgian house with gardens, 2m/3km N of Sandown. Former home of Oglander family, with royal connections to Henry VIII and Charles I. **11 G6** SZ5987.

Nunwick *N.Yorks.* ***Settlement***, 2m/3km N of Ripon across River Ure. **57 J2** SE3274.

Nunwick *Northumb.* ***Settlement***, on W side of River North Tyne, 2m/3km SE of Wark. **70 D6** NY8774.

Nup End *Bucks.* ***Locality***, adjoining to NW of Wingrave, 5m/7km NE of Aylesbury. **32 B7** SP8619.

Nup End *Glos.* ***Locality***, adjoining to N of Ashleworth, 5m/8km N of Gloucester. **29 H6** SO8125.

Nup End *Herts.* ***Settlement***, 2m/4km N of Welwyn. TL2219.

Nupend *Glos.* ***Village***, 4m/6km W of Stroud. SO7806.

Nuptown *Brack.F.* ***Settlement***, 5m/8km S of Maidenhead. SU8873.

Nursling *Hants.* ***Village***, in River Test valley 3m/4km S of Romsey. Grove Place, Elizabethan house. **10 E3** SU3616.

Nursted *Hants.* ***Settlement***, 2m/3km SE of Petersfield. **11 J2** SU7621.

Nursteed *Wilts.* ***Settlement***, adjoining to SE of Devizes. SU0260.

Nurston *V. of Glam.* ***Settlement***, to W of Cardiff International Airport, 4m/6km W of Barry. ST0567.

Nurton *Staffs.* ***Hamlet***, 5m/8km W of Wolverhampton. **40 A6** SO8399.

Nutberry Hill *S.Lan.* ***Mountain***, 6m/10km SW of Lesmahagow. River Nethan rises on S side. Height 1712 feet or 522 metres. **75 F7** NS7433.

Nutberry Moss *D. & G.* ***Open space***, flat area on N side of Solway Firth, 3m/5km W of Gretna. **69 H7** NY2668.

Nutbourne *W.Suss.* ***Village***, 3m/4km E of Emsworth. **11 J4** SU7805.

Nutbourne *W.Suss.* ***Village***, 2m/3km E of Pulborough. **12 D5** TQ0718.

Nutfield *Surr.* ***Village***, 2m/3km E of Redhill. **23 G6** TQ3050.

Nuthall *Notts.* ***Locality***, 4m/7km NW of Nottingham. **41 H1** SK5144.

Nuthampstead *Herts.* ***Village***, scattered village, 4m/7km NE of Buntingford. **33 H5** TL4034.

Nuthurst *Warks.* ***Hamlet***, 1km SW of Hockley Heath. **30 C1** SP1571.

Nuthurst *W.Suss.* ***Village***, 3m/5km SE of Horsham. **12 E4** TQ1926.

Nutley *E.Suss.* ***Village***, 5m/7km N of Uckfield. **13 H4** TQ4427.

Nutley *Hants.* ***Settlement***, 5m/8km SW of Basingstoke. **21 K7** SU6044.

Nuttall Lane *Gt.Man.* ***Locality***, adjoining to SW of Ramsbottom. SD7816.

Nutter's Platt *Lancs.* ***Settlement***, 2m/4km SW of Preston town centre. SD5226.

Nutwell *S.Yorks.* ***Locality***, adjoining to SE of Armthorpe. **1 J2** SE6304.

Nyadd *Stir.* ***Settlement***, 4m/7km NW of Stirling. **75 F1** NS7497.

Nybster *High.* ***Settlement***, near E coast of Caithness district, 6m/10km S of John o' Groats. **105 J2** ND3663.

Nyetimber *W.Suss.* ***Village***, suburban village, 3m/5km W of Bognor Regis. **12 B7** SZ8998.

Nyewood *W.Suss.* ***Village***, 4m/6km E of Petersfield. **12 B4** SU8021.

Nyfer *Pembs.* *Welsh form of Nevern, qv.*

Nyfer *Pembs.* ***River***, rising S of Boncath and flowing NW to coast at Newport. SN0639.

Nyland Hill *Som.* ***Hill***, small conical hill rising from Somerset Levels, 2m/3km S of Cheddar. Height 249 feet or 76 metres. **19 H6** ST4550.

Nymans Garden *W.Suss.* ***Garden***, to SE of Handcross, 5m/8km S of Crawley. National Trust property since 1954, includes a walled garden, ruined mansion and exotic species from around the world. Notable for autumn colouring. **13 F4** TQ2629.

Nymet Rowland *Devon* ***Village***, 4m/7km SE of Chulmleigh. **7 F5** SS7108.

Nymet Tracey *Devon* ***Hamlet***, 7m/11km W of Crediton. **7 F5** SS7200.

Nympsfield *Glos.* ***Village***, 3m/5km W of Nailsworth. Chambered Neolithic long barrow (English Heritage), 90 feet or 30 metres long, 1m/2km NW. **20 B1** SO8000.

Nynehead *Som.* ***Hamlet***, 1m/2km N of Wellington. **7 K3** ST1322.

Nythe *Som.* ***Hamlet***, on Sedgemoor, 4m/6km W of Street. **8 D1** ST4234.

Nyton *W.Suss.* ***Village***, 4m/7km N of Bognor Regis. **12 C6** SU9305.

O

Oad Street *Kent* ***Hamlet***, 2m/4km SW of Sittingbourne. **24 E5** TQ8662.

Oadby *Leics.* Population: 18,538. ***Town***, adjoining to SE of Leicester. **41 J5** SK6200.

Oak Cross *Devon* ***Hamlet***, 4m/6km NW of Okehampton. **6 D6** SX5399.

Oak Gate *Gt.Man.* ***Locality***, 1m/2km E of Whitefield. SD8205.

Oak Hill *Stoke* ***Suburb***, 1m/2km SW of Stoke-on-Trent city centre. SJ8643.

Oak Hill *Suff.* ***Hamlet***, 6m/10km SE of Woodbridge. TM3645.

Oak Tree *Darl.* ***Village***, 5m/7km E of Darlington. NZ3513.

Oakall Green *Worcs.* ***Settlement***, 4m/7km NW of Worcester. SO8160.

Oakamoor *Staffs.* ***Village***, 3m/5km E of Cheadle. **40 C1** SK0544.

Oakbank *Arg. & B.* ***Settlement***, near head of Loch Don, 2m/3km NE of Grass Point, Mull. **79 J4** NM7232.

Oakbank *W.Loth.* ***Settlement***, 1km S of Mid Calder. **75 J4** NT0866.

Oakdale *Caerp.* Population: 6637. ***Small town***, 4m/7km S of Abertillery. **18 E2** ST1898.

Oakdale *Poole* ***Suburb***, 1m/2km NE of Poole town centre. SZ0292.

Oake *Som.* ***Village***, in Vale of Taunton Deane, 2m/3km E of Milverton. To N, hamlet of Oake Bridge. **7 K3** ST1525.

Oake Green *Som.* ***Hamlet***, to E of Oake, 3m/4km E of Milverton. ST1525.

Oaken *Staffs.* ***Village***, 1m/2km W of Codsall. **40 A5** SJ8502.

Oakenclough *Lancs.* ***Hamlet***, 4m/6km E of Garstang. **55 J5** SD5347.

Oakengates *Tel. & W.* Population: 13,683. ***Town***, 4m/6km E of Wellington, forming part of Telford. **39 F4** SJ7010.

Oakenhead *Moray* ***Settlement***, 1m/2km S of Lossiemouth. **97 K5** NJ2468.

Oakenholt *Flints.* ***Settlement***, 1m/2km SE of Flint. SJ2671.

Oakenshaw *Dur.* ***Village***, 1m/2km N of Willington. **62 D3** NZ2037.

Oakenshaw *Lancs.* ***Suburb***, adjoining to W of Clayton-le-Moors. SD7431.

Oakenshaw *W.Yorks.* ***Village***, 3m/5km S of Bradford. **57 G7** SE1727.

Oakerthorpe *Derbys.* ***Hamlet***, 2m/3km W of Alfreton. Remains of small Roman fort 1km S. SK3854.

Oakes *W.Yorks.* ***Suburb***, 2m/3km W of Huddersfield town centre. SE1117.

Oakfield *Fife* ***Suburb***, adjoining to S of Kelty. NT1493.

Oakfield *I.o.W.* ***Suburb***, 1km SE of Ryde town centre. SZ5991.

Oakfield *Torfaen* ***Suburb***, in S part of Cwmbran. ST2993.

Oakford (Derwen-gam). *Cere.* ***Hamlet***, 3m/5km S of Aberaeron. **26 D3** SN4558.

Oakford *Devon* ***Village***, 3m/5km W of Bampton. **7 H3** SS9121.

Oakfordbridge *Devon* ***Hamlet***, on River Exe, 1km NE of Oakford. **7 H3** SS9121.

Oakgrove *Ches.* ***Settlement***, 3m/4km S of Macclesfield. **49 J6** SJ9169.

Oakham *Rut.* Population: 8691. ***Small town***, in Vale of Catmose 9m/15km SE of Melton Mowbray. 12c great hall survives from former fortified manor house. Market place with butter cross. **42 B5** SK8608.

Oakham *W.Mid.* ***Locality***, 2m/3km W of Oldbury. SO9689.

Oakham Castle *Rut.* ***Castle***, remains of Norman castle, with preserved medieval hall, in Oakham. **42 B5** SK8608.

Oakhanger *Ches.* ***Hamlet***, 4m/6km E of Crewe. SJ7654.

Oakhanger *Hants.* ***Village***, 4m/7km SE of Alton. **11 J1** SU7635.

Oakhill *Som.* ***Village***, 3m/4km N of Shepton Mallet. **19 K7** ST6347.

Oakhill Manor *Som.* ***Historic house***, set in 8 acres of gardens to W of Oakhill, 3m/4km N of Shepton Mallet. Miniature railway and transport model collection. **19 K7** ST6247.

Oakington *Cambs.* Population: 1583. ***Village***, 4m/7km NW of Cambridge. **33 H2** TL4164.

Oaklands *Conwy* ***Settlement***, 3m/4km SE of Llanrwst. **47 G7** SH8158.

Oaklands *Herts.* ***Village***, 2m/3km N of Welwyn Garden City. **33 F7** TL2417.

Oaklands *Powys* ***Locality***, adjoining to E of Builth Wells. SO0450.

Oakle Street *Glos.* ***Hamlet***, 5m/8km W of Gloucester. **29 G7** SO7517.

Oakleigh *Lancs.* ***Suburb***, in S part of Brierfield, 2m/3km SW of Nelson. SD8435.

Oakleigh Park *Gt.Lon.* ***Suburb***, in borough of Barnet, 9m/14km N of Charing Cross. TQ2694.

Oakley *Beds.* Population: 2375. ***Village***, 4m/6km NW of Bedford. **32 D3** TL0053.

Oakley *Bucks.* ***Village***, 6m/9km NW of Thame. **31 H7** SP6312.

Oakley *Fife* Population: 4181. ***Village***, 4m/7km W of Dunfermline. **75 J2** NT0289.

Oakley *(Also known as Church Oakley.)* *Hants.* Population: 5847. ***Village***, 5m/7km W of Basingstoke. **21 J6** SU5650.

Oakley *Oxon.* ***Suburb***, adjoining to SW of Chinnor. SP7400.

Oakley *Poole* ***Hamlet***, adjoining to N of Merley, 1m/2km S of Wimborne Minster. SZ0198.

Oakley *Suff.* ***Hamlet***, 3m/5km E of Diss. **35 F1** TM1677.

Oakley Green *W. & M.* ***Hamlet***, 3m/4km W of Windsor. **22 C4** SU9276.

Oakley Park *Powys* ***Hamlet***, 2m/3km NE of Llanidloes. **37 J7** SN9886.

Oakmere *Ches.* ***Settlement***, 4m/7km N of Tarporley. SJ5769.

Oakridge *Hants.* ***Suburb***, N district of Basingstoke. SU6353.

Oakridge Lynch *Glos.* ***Village***, 4m/7km E of Stroud. **20 C1** SO9103.

Oaks *Dur.* ***Locality***, adjoining to N of Evenwood, 4m/7km SW of Bishop Auckland. NZ1525.

Oaks *Lancs.* ***Locality***, 4m/6km N of Blackburn. SD6733.

Oaks *Shrop.* ***Settlement***, 2m/3km SE of Pontesbury. **38 D5** SJ4204.

Oaks Green *Derbys.* ***Hamlet***, 1km N of Sudbury. SK1533.

Oaksey *Wilts.* ***Village***, 5m/9km NE of Malmesbury. **20 C2** ST9993.

Oakshaw Ford *Cumb.* ***Settlement***, 7m/11km S of Newcastleton. **70 A6** NY5176.

Oakshott *Hants.* ***Settlement***, 3m/5km N of Petersfield. SU7427.

Oakthorpe *Leics.* ***Village***, 3m/5km SW of Ashby de la Zouch. **41 F4** SK3213.

Oaktree Hill *N.Yorks.* ***Settlement***, 3m/5km N of Northallerton. **62 E7** SE3698.

Oakwell *W.Yorks.* ***Locality***, 3m/4km W of Morley, to S side of M62 motorway. SE2227.

Oakwell Hall *W.Yorks.* ***Historic house***, in country park in Birstall, 1m/2km SW of Drighlington across M62 motorway. Built 1583, now restored and refurnished in 17c style. **57 H7** SE2127.

Oakwood *Gt.Lon.* ***Suburb***, in borough of Enfield, 10m/15km N of Charing Cross. TQ2995.

Oakwood *Northumb.* ***Locality***, 1m/2km NE of Hexham. NY9465.

Oakwood *W.Yorks.* ***Suburb***, 3m/4km NE of Leeds city centre. SE3236.

Oakwood Leisure Park *Pembs.* ***Leisure/recreation***, theme park offering variety of rides, including largest wooden roller-coaster in Europe, at Cross Hands, 3m/4km W of Templeton. **16 D3** SN0612.

Oakwoodhill *Surr.* ***Hamlet***, 5m/8km NW of Horsham. **12 E3** TQ1337.

Oakworth *W.Yorks.* ***Village***, on hillside adjoining to SW of Keighley. **57 F6** SE0338.

Oare *Kent* ***Village***, 1m/2km NW of Faversham. **25 G5** TR0063.

Oare *Som.* ***Hamlet***, 6m/9km E of Lynton. **7 G1** SS8047.

Oare *Wilts.* ***Village***, 2m/3km N of Pewsey. **20 E5** SU1563.

Oasby *Lincs.* ***Village***, 6m/9km SW of Sleaford, with small Tudor manor house. **42 D2** TF0039.

Oates Museum and Gilbert White's House *Hants.* ***Leisure/recreation***, museum dedicated to Oates family in restored 18c house at Selborne. Exploits of Victorian explorer, Frank Oates, and Antarctic expeditionist, Captain Lawrence Oates, are told via mementos and illustrations. House itself is former home of 18c naturalist, Reverend Gilbert White, author of 'The Natural History of Selborne'; it includes period furnishings and is surrounded by garden restored to White's original designs. **11 J1** SU7433.

Oatfield *Arg. & B.* ***Settlement***, on Kintyre, 3m/4km SW of Campbeltown. **66 A2** NR6817.

Oath *Som.* ***Hamlet***, 3m/4km W of Langport. ST3827.

Oathlaw *Angus* ***Village***, 4m/6km N of Forfar. **83 F2** NO4756.

Oatlands *Glas.* ***Suburb***, 1m/2km S of Glasgow city centre. NS5963.

Oatlands *N.Yorks.* ***Suburb***, 1m/2km S of Harrogate town centre. SE3053.

Oatlands Park *Surr.* ***Suburb***, 1m/2km E of Weybridge. TQ0964.

Òb Chuaig *High.* ***Bay***, on W coast of Ross and Cromarty district, 2m/3km SW of Rubha na Fearn and entrance to Loch Torridon. NG7059.

Ob na h-Uamha *High.* ***Bay***, small bay near entrance to Loch Torridon, 1km SW of Rubha na Fearn. NG7160.

Oban *Arg. & B.* Population: 8203. ***Small town***, port and resort in Argyll on Oban Bay, Sound of Kerrera, 60m/97km NW of Glasgow (93m/150km by road). Ferry services to Inner and Outer Hebrides. Annual Highland Gathering in September. **79 K5** NM8530.

Oban Bay *Arg. & B.* ***Bay***, in Argyll on Sound of Kerrera, to W of Oban. **79 K4** NM8530.

Obbe *W.Isles* *Former name of Leverburgh, qv.*

Obley *Shrop.* ***Hamlet***, 3m/4km SE of Clun. **28 C1** SO3277.

Obney Hills *P. & K.* ***Mountain***, with steep slopes and rock outcrops to S and E, 3m/5km NW of Bankfoot and 2m/4km S of Dunkeld. Hillfort at summit. Height 1322 feet or 403 metres. **82 B4** NO0238.

Oborne *Dorset* ***Village***, 2m/3km NE of Sherborne. **9 F3** ST6518.

Obridge *Som.* ***Suburb***, N district of Taunton. ST2325.

Obsdale *High.* ***Locality***, on E side of Alness, Ross and Cromarty district. NH6669.

Obthorpe *Lincs.* ***Settlement***, 3m/5km S of Bourne. TF0915.

Occaney *N.Yorks.* ***Settlement***, 1m/2km SW of Staveley, 3m/5km N of Knaresborough. SE3561.

Occlestone Green *Ches.* ***Settlement***, 2m/3km S of Middlewich. **49 F6** SJ6962.

Occold *Suff.* ***Village***, 2m/3km SE of Eye. **35 F1** TM1570.

Occumster *High.* ***Settlement***, on E coast, to E of Lybster. **105 H5** ND2635.

Ochil Hills ***Large natural feature***, range of hills extending from Bridge of Allan, N of Stirling, to Firth of Tay at Newburgh. Summit is Ben Cleuch, 2363 feet or 720 metres. **81 K7** NO0005.

Ochiltree *E.Ayr.* ***Village***, at confluence of Burnock Water and Lugar Water, 4m/7km W of Cumnock. **67 K1** NS5021.

Ochr-y-foel *Denb.* ***Suburb***, adjoining to E of Dyserth. SJ0679.

Ochr-y-Mynydd *M.Tyd.* ***Locality***, 2m/3km W of Merthyr Tydfil. **18 D1** SO0206.

Ochrwyth *Caerp.* ***Locality***, comprising Lower Ochrwyth, 1m/2km SW of Risca, and Upper Ochrwyth, adjacent to W. ST2489.

Ochtermuthill *P. & K.* ***Settlement***, 3m/5km SW of Crieff. **81 K6** NN8316.

Ochtertyre *P. & K.* ***Settlement***, 2m/3km NW of Crieff. **81 K5** NN8323.

Ochtertyre *Stir.* ***Settlement***, 4m/7km NW of Stirling. **75 F1** NS7597.

Ock *Oxon.* ***River***, rising S of Faringdon and flowing E into River Thames at Abingdon. SU4996.

Ockbrook *Derbys.* ***Village***, 4m/7km E of Derby. Moravian settlement on W side, founded in 18c. **41 G2** SK4236.

Ocker Hill *W.Mid.* ***Suburb***, 3m/4km NW of West Bromwich town centre. SO9793.

Ockeridge *Worcs.* ***Settlement***, 7m/11km NW of Worcester. SO7762.

Ockham *Surr.* ***Village***, 5m/8km E of Woking. Disused airfield to N. **22 D6** TQ0756.

Ockle *High.* ***Hamlet***, on Ardnamurchan peninsula, 1km SE of Ockle Point. **86 B7** NM5570.

Ockle Point *High.* ***Coastal feature***, headland on N coast of Ardnamurchan peninsula in Lochaber district, 10m/16km NW of Salen. **86 B7** NM5471.

Ockley *Surr.* ***Village***, 6m/10km N of Horsham. **12 E3** TQ1439.

Ocle Pychard *Here.* ***Village***, 7m/11km NE of Hereford. **28 E4** SO5946.

Octon *E.Riding* ***Locality***, 1m/2km W of Thwing. Former village no longer exists. **59 G3** TA0369.

Odcombe *Som.* ***Village***, 3m/5km W of Yeovil. **8 E3** ST5015.

Odd Down *B. & N.E.Som.* ***Suburb***, SW district of Bath. **20 A5** ST7362.

Oddendale *Cumb.* ***Hamlet***, 2m/4km SE of Shap. NY5914.

Oddingley *Worcs.* ***Village***, 3m/4km S of Droitwich Spa. **29 J3** SO9059.

Oddington *Oxon.* ***Village***, 6m/10km NE of Oxford. **31 G7** SP5514.

Oddsta *Shet.* ***Locality***, 1m/2km N of Brough Lodge, on NW coast of Fetlar. **108 E3** HU5894.

Odell *Beds.* ***Village***, 8m/12km NW of Bedford. **32 C3** SP9657.

Odham *Devon* ***Hamlet***, 4m/7km W of Hatherleigh. SS4702.

Odie *Ork.* ***Settlement***, on Stronsay, 1km SE of Links Ness. **106 F5** HY6229.

Odiham *Hants.* Population: 3531. ***Village***, 7m/11km E of Basingstoke. **22 A6** SU7451.

Odiham Castle *Hants.* ***Castle***, 13c castle built by King John, 1m/2km S of Hook and 6m/10km SW of Fleet. **22 A6** SU7251.

Odin Bay *Ork.* ***Bay***, on E coast of Stronsay, extending N from Burgh Head. **106 F5** HY6924.

Odness *Ork.* ***Coastal feature***, headland on E coast of Stronsay on S side of entrance to Mill Bay. **106 F5** HY6926.

Odsal *W.Yorks.* ***Suburb***, 2m/3km S of Bradford city centre. SE1529.

Odsal Top *W.Yorks.* ***Suburb***, with sports stadium, 3m/4km S of Bradford city centre. SE1529.

Odsey *Cambs.* ***Hamlet***, 2m/3km SE of Ashwell. TL2938.

Odstock *Wilts.* ***Village***, on River Ebble, 3m/4km S of Salisbury. To E beside River Avon, Longford Castle, triangular Tudor house in park. **10 C2** SU1426.

Odstock Down *Wilts.* ***Open space***, hillslope 1km SW of Odstock. **10 C2** SU1324.

Odstone *Leics.* ***Hamlet***, 6m/10km SE of Ashby de la Zouch. **41 F5** SK3907.

Oerfa *Conwy* ***Mountain***, 3m/5km SE of Llanrwst. Height 1312 feet or 400 metres. **47 G7** SH8259.

Offa's Dyke ***Historic/prehistoric site***, entrenchment (English Heritage) built in 8c by Offa, King of Mercia, to mark boundary between Anglo-Saxon and Welsh territory. Runs from Prestatyn on North Wales coast to Chepstow in S. Still visible at various points and long distance footpath runs its entire length. **28 B2** SO2591.

Offchurch *Warks.* ***Village***, 3m/4km E of Royal Leamington Spa. **30 E2** SP3565.

Offenham *Worcs.* ***Village***, 2m/3km NE of Evesham. **30 B4** SP0546.

Offenham Cross *Worcs.* ***Locality***, 2m/3km NE of Evesham. SP0645.

Offerton *Gt.Man.* ***Suburb***, 2m/3km E of Stockport town centre. **49 J4** SJ9288.

Offerton *T. & W.* ***Settlement***, 4m/6km W of Sunderland. NZ3455.

Offerton Green *Gt.Man.* ***Suburb***, 1km E of Offerton. SJ9388.

Offham *E.Suss.* ***Hamlet***, 2m/3km NW of Lewes. **13 H5** TQ4012.

Offham *Kent* ***Village***, 2m/3km W of West Malling. **23 K6** TQ6557.

Offham *W.Suss.* ***Hamlet***, on River Arun, 1m/2km NE of Arundel. TQ0208.

Offleyhay *Staffs.* ***Settlement***, 2m/3km W of Eccleshall. SJ7929.

Offleyhoo *Herts.* ***Settlement***, 3m/5km SW of Hitchin. TL1426.

Offleymarsh *Staffs.* ***Settlement***, 3m/5km W of Eccleshall. SJ7829.

Offord Cluny *Cambs.* ***Village***, 3m/5km SW of Huntingdon. **33 F2** TL2167.

Offord D'Arcy *Cambs.* ***Village***, 4m/6km SW of Huntingdon. **33 F2** TL2166.

Offton *Suff.* ***Village***, 5m/8km NE of Hadleigh. **34 E4** TM0649.

Offwell *Devon* ***Village***, 2m/3km SE of Honiton. **7 K6** SY1999.

Offwell Brook *Devon* ***River***, rising N of Offwell, flowing SE to join River Coly at Barritshayes, 2m/3km NW of Colyton. **8 B5** SY2194.

Ogbourne Maizey *Wilts.* ***Village***, 2m/3km N of Marlborough. **20 E4** SU1871.

Ogbourne St. Andrew *Wilts.* ***Village***, 2m/3km N of Marlborough. **20 E4** SU1872.

Ogbourne St. George *Wilts.* ***Village***, 3m/5km N of Marlborough. **20 E4** SU2074.

Ogden *W.Yorks.* ***Settlement***, 2m/3km S of Denholme. **57 F6** SE0630.

Ogden Reservoir *Lancs.* ***Reservoir***, 2m/3km W of Haslingden. **56 C7** SD7622.

Ogden Reservoirs *Lancs.* ***Reservoir***, two reservoirs on S side of Pendle Hill, 3m/5km NW of Nelson. **56 D5** SD8139.

Ogden Water *W.Yorks.* ***Reservoir***, in woodland on E side of Ovenden Moor, 2m/3km S of Denholme, with visitor centre. **57 F6** SE0630.

Ogil *Angus* ***Locality***, comprises Easter Ogil, Mains of Ogil and Milton of Ogil, in valley of Noran Water, 4m/7km E of Dykehead. **83 F1** NO4561.

Ogle *Northumb.* ***Hamlet***, 2m/4km E of Belsay. **71 G6** NZ1378.

Oglet *Mersey.* ***Settlement***, to S of Speke. SJ4381.

Oglethorpe *W.Yorks.* ***Settlement***, 1m/2km SE of Boston Spa. SE4444.

Ogmore (Ogwr). ***River***, rising from two tributaries in deeply incised valleys: Ogwr Fawr flows S from S side of Craig Ogwr, while Ogwr Fach flows S, then E from E side of Mynydd Maes-teg. Tributaries meet at Blackmill, forming Ogmore River, which flows SW to confluence with Llynfi River, W of Sarn, before flowing S to Bridgend and then SW into sea 3m/4km E of Porthcawl. **18 B4** SS8575.

Ogmore (Ogwr). *V. of Glam.* ***Hamlet***, 3m/4km SW of Bridgend. 12c-13c remains of castle (Cadw) to N. **18 B4** SS8876.

Ogmore-by-Sea (Aberogwr). *V. of Glam.* ***Village***, 4m/6km SW of Bridgend. **18 B4** SS8674.

Ogmore Castle and Stepping Stones *V. of Glam.* ***Castle***, 2m/4km SW of Bridgend. Late 12c castle on banks of River Ogmore, guarding a ford with unique stepping stones from bailey across river. **18 B4** SS8876.

Ogmore Forest *Bridgend* ***Forest/woodland***, hilly wooded area to E of Ogmore Vale. **18 C3** SS9489.

Ogmore Vale *Bridgend* Population: 6693. ***Village***, 7m/11km N of Bridgend. **18 C2** SS9390.

Ogston Reservoir *Derbys.* ***Reservoir***, 2m/3km SW of Clay Cross. **51 F7** SK3760.

Ogwell *Devon* ***Locality***, parish on SW side of Newton Abbot containing village of East Ogwell and hamlet of West Ogwell. SX8370.

Ogwen Cottage *Conwy* *Alternative name for Pont Pen-y-benglog, qv.*

Ogwr *Welsh form of Ogmore (River), qv.*

Ogwr *V. of Glam.* *Welsh form of Ogmore, qv.*

Oh Me Edge *Northumb.* ***Open space***, on N side of East Kielder Moor, 4m/7km SW of Byrness. **70 B4** NY7099.

Oich *High.* ***River***, in Inverness district running NE from Loch Oich to Fort Augustus at head of Loch Ness. **87 K4** NH3809.

Oigh-sgeir (Also known as Hyskeir.) *High.* ***Island***, group of islets in Inner Hebrides, with lighthouse, lying 9m/14km W of Rum. **85 G5** NM1596.

Oisgill Bay *High.* ***Bay***, on W coast of Skye, 7m/12km W of Dunvegan. **93 G7** NG1349.

Oitir Mhòr *W.Isles* ***Coastal feature***, sandbank on North Uist, 5m/8km SE of Aird an Rùnair to N of Kirkibost Island. **92 C5** NF7566.

Oitir Mhòr *W.Isles* ***Coastal feature***, large sandbank, visible at low tide, between North Uist and Benbecula. **92 D6** NF8157.

Oitir Mhòr *W.Isles* ***Sea feature***, stretch of sea separating Fuday and Gighay, NE of Barra. **84 C4** NF7306.

Oitir na Cudaig *W.Isles* ***Coastal feature***, sandbank at small inlet on E coast of South Uist, 4m/6km SE of Lochboisdale. **84 D3** NF8315.

Okeford Fitzpaine *Dorset* ***Village***, 3m/4km SE of Sturminster Newton. **9 H3** ST8010.

Okehampton *Devon* Population: 4841. ***Small town***, market town at confluence of Rivers East and West Okement, below N edge of Dartmoor. Remains of castle (English Heritage). Artillery ranges on moors to S. **6 D6** SX5895.

Okehampton Camp *Devon* ***Military establishment***, army camp with artillery practice range, 1m/2km S of Okehampton. **6 D6** SX5893.

Okehampton Castle *Devon* ***Castle***, ruins of 11c motte (English Heritage), similar to German hilltop castles, 1km S of Okehampton. Devon's largest castle. **6 D6** SX5894.

Okement *Devon* ***River***, rising on Dartmoor as two separate streams, East and West Okement, flowing N and joining at Okehampton. River then continues N and flows into River Torridge 2m/3km N of Hatherleigh. **6 D5** SS5507.

Okement Hill *Devon* ***Mountain***, in Dartmoor National Park, 6m/10km NE of Lydford. Height 1856 feet or 566 metres. **6 D7** SX6087.

Okeover *Staffs.* ***Settlement***, 2m/3km NW of Ashbourne. SK1548.

Okraquoy *Shet.* ***Settlement***, overlooking Bay of Okraquoy, 1km S of Fladdabister, Mainland. **109 D9** HU4331.

Olchard *Devon* ***Hamlet***, 4m/6km N of Newton Abbot. SX8777.

Olchfa *Swan.* ***Suburb***, 3m/4km W of Swansea city centre. SS6193.

Olchon Brook ***River***, rising in Black Mountains, S of Hay Bluff, and flowing SE into River Monnow S of Longtown. **28 B5** SO3228.

Olchon Valley *Here.* ***Valley***, carrying Olchon Brook SE into Escley Brook, just S of Longtown. **28 B5** SO2832.

Old (Sometimes known as Wold.) *Northants.* ***Village***, 6m/10km SW of Kettering. **31 J1** SP7873.

Old Aberdeen *Aberdeen* ***Suburb***, 1m/2km N of Aberdeen city centre. Includes University of Aberdeen. **91 H4** NJ9408.

Old Alresford *Hants.* ***Village***, 1m/2km N of New Alresford. **11 G1** SU5833.

Old Ancholme *N.Lincs.* ***River***, section of Ancholme River below Bishopbridge to Ferriby Sluice, 1m/2km W of South Ferriby. Course is circuitous, meandering either side of artificially straightened New River Ancholme. See also (River) Ancholme and New Ancholme. **52 C1** SE9717.

O

Old Arley *Warks.* ***Village***, 5m/8km W of Nuneaton. **40 E6** SP2890.
Old Bailey *Gt.Lon.* *Alternative name for Central Criminal Courts, qv.*
Old Barns *Northumb.* ***Locality***, 1km SW of Warkworth. NU2405.
Old Basford *Nott.* ***Suburb***, 3m/4km NW of Nottingham city centre. **41 H1** SK5543.
Old Basing *Hants.* Population: 3391. ***Village***, 2m/3km E of Basingstoke. To W, ruins of Basing House, mansion destroyed in Civil War; gatehouse, tithe barn and dovecote remain. **21 K6** SU6652.
Old Beaupre Castle *V. of Glam.* ***Castle***, 16c building on site of fortified house dating from 13c, 1m/2km S of Cowbridge. Present remains (Cadw) largely incorporated into adjacent farmhouse. **18 D4** ST0072.
Old Bedford River ***Other water feature***, fenland drainage channel running NE from Earith to Salters Lode. **43 J6** TF5801.
Old Belses *Sc.Bord.* ***Settlement***, 6m/10km SE of Selkirk. **70 A1** NT5624.
Old Bewick *Northumb.* ***Hamlet***, 6m/10km SE of Wooler. **71 F1** NU0621.
Old Bexley *Gt.Lon.* ***Suburb***, in borough of Bexley, 3m/5km W of Dartford. TQ4973.
Old Blair *P. & K.* ***Settlement***, with ruined church, 1m/2km N of Blair Atholl. Burial place of 'Bonnie Dundee' - see Killiecrankie. NN8666.
Old Blockhouse *I.o.S.* ***Historic/prehistoric site***, 16c gun battery (English Heritage) overlooking bay at Old Grimsby, on E coast of Tresco. **2 B1** SV8915.
Old Bolingbroke *Lincs.* ***Village***, 3m/5km W of Spilsby. Earthworks mark site of 13c hexagonal castle (English Heritage), birthplace of Henry IV, 1367. **53 G6** TF3465.
Old Boston *Mersey.* ***Locality***, adjoining to NE of Haydock. SJ5797.
Old Bradwell *M.K.* *Alternative name for Bradwell, qv.*
Old Bramhope *W.Yorks.* ***Settlement***, 1m/2km W of Bramhope. SE2343.
Old Brampton *Derbys.* ***Village***, 3m/5km W of Chesterfield. **51 F5** SK3371.
Old Brandelhow *Cumb.* *Alternative name for Brandelhow, qv.*
Old Bridge of Urr *D. & G.* ***Settlement***, and road bridge across Urr Water, 4m/6km N of Castle Douglas. **65 H4** NX7767.
Old Buckenham *Norf.* ***Village***, 3m/5km SE of Attleborough. Faint remains of castle and priory to N. **44 E6** TM0691.
Old Burdon *T. & W.* ***Settlement***, 1km SW of Burdon, 2m/3km SW of Ryhope. NZ3850.
Old Burghclere *Hants.* ***Hamlet***, 2m/3km S of Burghclere. **21 H6** SU4657.
Old Byland *N.Yorks.* ***Village***, 4m/7km W of Helmsley. **58 B1** SE5485.
Old Carlisle *Cumb.* ***Locality***, 1m/2km S of Wigton. Site of Roman fort to W. NY2646.
Old Cassop *Dur.* ***Hamlet***, 1m/2km NW of Cassop. NZ3339.
Old Castle Head *Pembs.* ***Coastal feature***, headland 1m/2km SE of Manorbier and 4m/7km SW of Tenby. **16 D5** SS0796.
Old Castle of Slains *Aber.* ***Castle***, remains of old castle destroyed by James VI (James I of England), on E coast 4m/7km NE of Newburgh. See also Slains Castle. NK0529.
Old Church Stoke *Powys* ***Hamlet***, 1m/2km NE of Church Stoke. SO2895.
Old Clee *N.E.Lincs.* ***Suburb***, 1m/2km SE of Grimsby town centre and 1m/2km W of Cleethorpes. TA2908.
Old Cleeve *Som.* ***Village***, 2m/4km SW of Watchet. Remains of Cleeve Abbey (English Heritage), located 1m/2km SE at Washford. **7 J1** ST0341.
Old Colwyn *Conwy* ***Suburb***, 1m/2km E of Colwyn Bay, incorporating original village of Colwyn. **47 G5** SH8678.
Old Coulsdon *Gt.Lon.* ***Locality***, to SE of Coulsdon. TQ3157.
Old Craig *Aber.* ***Settlement***, 1m/2km SE of Pitmedden. **91 H2** NJ9025.
Old Craighall *E.Loth.* ***Settlement***, 1m/2km S of Musselburgh. **76 B3** NT3370.
Old Croft *Norf.* ***River***, rising S of Upwell, formerly flowing S through Christchurch and Littleport to join River Great Ouse. Middle section has now been cut by drainage channels of New Bedford River and Old Bedford River. **43 H6** TL5787.
Old Crombie *Aber.* ***Settlement***, 2m/3km W of Aberchirder. **98 D5** NJ5951.
Old Dailly *S.Ayr.* ***Village***, 3m/4km E of Girvan. **67 G4** NX2299.
Old Dalby *Leics.* ***Village***, 6m/9km NW of Melton Mowbray. **41 J3** SK6723.
Old Dam *Derbys.* ***Hamlet***, adjoining to N of Peak Forest, 3m/5km NW of Tideswell. SK1179.
Old Deer *Aber.* ***Village***, on S side of Forest of Deer, 10m/15km W of Peterhead. Ruined 13c abbey (Historic Scotland) 1km NW. **99 H6** NJ9747.
Old Dilton *Wilts.* ***Hamlet***, 1m/2km SW of Westbury. ST8649.
Old Dolphin *W.Yorks.* ***Suburb***, of Bradford, 1m/2km E of Queensbury. SE1130.
Old Down *Som.* ***Hamlet***, 3m/5km SW of Midsomer Norton. ST6251.
Old Down *S.Glos.* ***Village***, 3m/4km SW of Thornbury. ST6187.
Old Edlington *S.Yorks.* ***Village***, 5m/7km SW of Doncaster. New Edlington is 1m/2km NE. SK5397.
Old Eldon *Dur.* ***Hamlet***, 1m/2km NE of Shildon. NZ2427.
Old Ellerby *E.Riding* ***Village***, 7m/11km NE of Kingston upon Hull. **59 H6** TA1637.
Old Elvet Bridge *Dur.* ***Bridge***, substantial stone bridge over River Wear in Durham, dating from 13c. Houses built on land arches. NZ2742.
Old Felixstowe *Suff.* ***Suburb***, NE district of Felixstowe. **35 H5** TM3135.
Old Field Carr *Lancs.* ***Locality***, adjoining to S of Poulton-le-Fylde. SD3538.
Old Fletton *Peter.* ***Town***, adjoining to S of Peterborough. 9c carvings in St. Margaret's Church. **42 E6** TL1997.
Old Ford *Gt.Lon.* ***Suburb***, in borough of Tower Hamlets, 3m/5km NE of London Bridge. TQ3683.
Old Forge *Here.* ***Hamlet***, on N bank of River Wye, 4m/7km SW of Ross-on-Wye. SO5518.
Old Furnace *Torfaen* ***Settlement***, 1m/2km W of Pontypool. SO2600.
Old Glossop *Derbys.* ***Locality***, 1m/2km NE of Glossop. **50 C3** SK0494.
Old Goginan *Cere.* ***Settlement***, 6m/10km E of Aberystwyth, to N of Goginan across River Melindwr. **37 F7** SN6881.
Old Goole *E.Riding* ***Suburb***, S district of Goole. **58 D7** SE7422.
Old Gore *Here.* ***Settlement***, 3m/5km NE of Ross-on-Wye. **29 F6** SO6328.
Old Grimsbury *Oxon.* ***Suburb***, in NE part of Banbury. SP4641.
Old Grimsby *I.o.S.* ***Hamlet***, on E side of Tresco. **2 B1** SV8915.
Old Hall *E.Riding* ***Settlement***, on N side of Humber estuary, opposite Grimsby. **53 F1** TA2717.
Old Hall Green *Herts.* ***Hamlet***, 1m/2km SW of Puckeridge. TL3722.
Old Hall Street *Norf.* ***Settlement***, 1km SW of Knapton, 2m/4km NE of North Walsham. TG3033.
Old Harlow *Essex* ***Suburb***, 2m/3km NE of Harlow town centre. TL4711.
Old Head *Ork.* ***Coastal feature***, headland at SE end of South Ronaldsay. **107 D9** ND4683.
Old Heath *Essex* ***Suburb***, in SE part of Colchester. **34 E6** TM0122.
Old Heathfield *E.Suss.* ***Village***, 1m/2km SE of Heathfield. TQ5920.
Old Hill *W.Mid.* ***Suburb***, 3m/5km W of Warley town centre. **40 B7** SO9586.
Old Hill *W.Isles* ***Island***, small uninhabited island off W coast of Isle of Lewis, 2m/3km NW of Great Bernera. NB1143.
Old Howe *E.Riding* ***Other water feature***, drainage channel running 1m/2km via a right-angled turn into Frodingham Beck, 1km N of North Frodingham. **59 H4** TA0953.
Old Hutton *Cumb.* ***Hamlet***, 4m/7km SE of Kendal. **55 J1** SD5688.
Old Ingarsby *Leics.* ***Settlement***, on site of former village, 6m/10km E of Leicester. SK6805.
Old Inverlochy Castle *High.* ***Castle***, ruined 13c building with round corner towers, on bank of River Lochy, 2m/3km NE of Fort William. **87 H7** NN1275.
Old Kea *Cornw.* ***Hamlet***, above Truro River, 2m/3km SE of Truro. **3 F4** SW8441.
Old Kilpatrick *W.Dun.* Population: 2408. ***Small town***, on N bank of River Clyde, to N of Erskine Bridge. Site of Roman fort near line of Antonine Wall. **74 C3** NS4673.
Old Kinnernie *Aber.* ***Settlement***, 2m/3km W of Dunecht. **91 F4** NJ7209.
Old Knebworth *Herts.* ***Village***, 2m/4km S of Stevenage. **33 F6** TL2320.
Old Laund Booth *Lancs.* ***Locality***, adjoining to W of Nelson. SD8337.
Old Laxey *I.o.M.* ***Village***, adjoining Laxey, at mouth of Laxey River. SC4483.
Old Leake *Lincs.* ***Village***, 6m/10km NE of Boston. **53 H7** TF4050.
Old Leslie *Aber.* ***Settlement***, 3m/4km SW of Insch. **90 D2** NJ5925.
Old Lynn Channel ***Sea feature***, sea channel in S part of The Wash, between sandbanks of Old South and Thief Sand off N Norfolk coast. **43 J2** TF5133.
Old Malden *Gt.Lon.* ***Suburb***, in borough of Kingston upon Thames, 3m/5km SE of Kingston upon Thames town centre. **23 F5** TQ2166.
Old Malton *N.Yorks.* ***Village***, adjoining to NE of Malton. **58 D2** SE7972.
Old Malton Moor *N.Yorks.* ***Open space***, lowland in Vale of Pickering, 2m/3km NE of Malton. **58 E2** SE7974.
Old Man of Hoy *Ork.* ***Coastal feature***, massive column of rock rising from foot of cliffs on NW coast of Hoy, 1m/2km N of Rora Head. Height 449 feet or 137 metres. **107 A7** HY1700.
Old Man of Mow ***Inland physical feature***, rock pinnacle (National Trust) to N of Mow Cop, on border of Cheshire and Staffordshire, isolated by local quarrying. Mow Cop Castle to S. SJ8557.
Old Man of Wick *High.* *Alternative name for Castle of Old Wick, qv.*
Old Marton *Shrop.* ***Settlement***, 3m/4km NE of Whittington. SJ3434.
Old Melrose *Sc.Bord.* ***Ecclesiastical building***, site of monastery founded in 7c, in loop of River Tweed, 3m/4km E of Melrose. NT5833.
Old Merchant's House and Row 111 House *Norf.* ***Historic house***, two 17c houses (English Heritage) at Great Yarmouth. Type of building unique to town, with original architectural fixtures. Greyfriars' Cloisters (English Heritage) nearby. **45 K5** TG5207.
Old Micklefield *W.Yorks.* ***Village***, 5m/8km N of Castleford. **57 K6** SE4433.
Old Military Road *High.* ***Other feature of interest***, series of military roads traversing the Highlands, built by Caulfeild, Wade's successor, after 1745 Hanoverian campaign. **89 H1** NJ0035.
Old Milton *Hants.* ***Suburb***, 1km N of Barton on Sea. SZ2394.
Old Milverton *Warks.* ***Village***, 2m/3km NW of Royal Leamington Spa. **30 D2** SP2967.
Old Netley *Hants.* ***Hamlet***, 3m/4km NW of Park Gate. **11 F3** SU4610.
Old Newton *Suff.* ***Village***, 3m/4km N of Stowmarket. **34 E2** TM0562.
Old Oswestry Hillfort *Shrop.* ***Historic/prehistoric site***, extensive Iron Age fort (English Heritage), 1m/2km N of Oswestry. **38 B2** SJ2931.
Old Peak (Also known as South Cheek.) *N.Yorks.* ***Coastal feature***, headland at S end of Robin Hood's Bay on North Sea coast, 1km N of Ravenscar. **63 J2** NZ9802.
Old Philpstoun *W.Loth.* ***Hamlet***, nearly 1m/2km E of Philpstoun. **75 J3** NT0577.
Old Place of Mochrum *D. & G.* ***Castle***, restored castle with 15c and 16c towers, on NE bank of Mochrum Loch, 7m/11km NW of Port William. **64 D5** NX3054.
Old Poltalloch *Arg. & B.* ***Settlement***, 3m/4km S of Ardfern across Loch Craignish. **79 K7** NM8000.
Old Portlethen *Aber.* ***Village***, 1km E of Portlethen on North Sea coast. **91 H5** NO9295.
Old Quarrington *Dur.* ***Hamlet***, 1m/2km W of Quarrington Hill. NZ3237.
Old Radnor (Pencraig). *Powys* ***Hamlet***, 3m/4km E of New Radnor. Remains of Norman motte. **28 B3** SO2559.
Old Rattray *Aber.* ***Settlement***, on E side of Loch of Strathbeg, 1m/2km W of Rattray Head. **99 J5** NK0857.
Old Ravensworth *T. & W.* ***Settlement***, 4m/6km S of Gateshead. NZ2357.
Old Rayne *Aber.* ***Village***, 8m/12km NW of Inverurie. **90 E2** NJ6728.
Old Rectory *N.Lincs.* ***Historic house***, at Epworth. John Wesley, founder of Methodism, and his brother Charles were born here in 1703. House rebuilt in 1709 after fire, and has been preserved. **51 K2** SE7903.
Old Romney *Kent* ***Village***, on Romney Marsh, 2m/4km W of New Romney. **15 F5** TR0325.
Old Royal Observatory (Formerly known as Greenwich Observatory.) *Gt.Lon.* ***Other feature of interest***, in borough of Greenwich, situated in Greenwich Park. Designed by Wren and founded by Charles II in 1675. Site of pioneer work in development of astronomy and nautical navigation. Contains astronomical and time instruments, 17c Astronomer Royal's rooms and restored Octagon room by Wren. Location of largest refracting telescope in UK, London's only camera obscura and Meridian Line. Forms part of National Maritime Museum and includes Flamsteed House. TQ3877.
Old Sarum *Wilts.* ***Historic/prehistoric site***, large earthwork (English Heritage) 2m/3km N of Salisbury. Site of original town, castle, and cathedral. **10 C1** SU1332.
Old Scone *P. & K.* ***Hamlet***, 2m/3km N of Perth, on E side of River Tay. **82 C5** NO1126.
Old Shields *N.Lan.* ***Settlement***, 3m/5km NE of Cumbernauld. **75 G3** NS8175.
Old Shirley *S'ham.* ***Suburb***, N district of Southampton. SU3914.
Old Shoreham *W.Suss.* ***Suburb***, to N of Shoreham, extends on to southern slopes of South Downs. TQ2006.
Old Snydale *W.Yorks.* ***Hamlet***, 1m/2km SW of North Featherstone. SE4021.
Old Soar Manor *Kent* ***Historic house***, solar block (National Trust and English Heritage) of late 13c knight's dwelling, 1m/2km E of Plaxtol. **23 K6** TQ6154.
Old Sodbury *S.Glos.* ***Village***, 2m/3km E of Chipping Sodbury. **20 A3** ST7581.
Old Somerby *Lincs.* ***Village***, 3m/5km SE of Grantham. **42 C2** SK9633.
Old Sontley *Wrex.* ***Settlement***, to S of Sontley. SJ3346.
Old South *Lincs.* ***Coastal feature***, sandbank in SW part of The Wash, off Lincolnshire coast. **43 H2** TF4435.
Old Stillington *Stock.* ***Hamlet***, 1km SW of Stillington. NZ3622.
Old Stratford *Northants.* ***Village***, 1km NW of Stony Stratford across River Great Ouse. **31 J4** SP7741.
Old Sunderlandwick *E.Riding* ***Locality***, 2m/3km S of Great Driffield, containing site of former village. **59 G4** TA0155.
Old Swan *Mersey.* ***Suburb***, 3m/5km E of Liverpool city centre. SJ3991.
Old Swarland *Northumb.* ***Hamlet***, 2m/3km NW of Felton. **71 G3** NU1601.
Old Swinford *W.Mid.* ***Suburb***, 1km S of Stourbridge town centre. **40 B7** SO9083.
Old Tame *Gt.Man.* ***Hamlet***, on E side of Crompton Moor, 1km SW of Denshaw and 4m/6km NE of Oldham. SD9609.
Old Tebay *Cumb.* ***Locality***, adjoining to N of Tebay. NY6105.
Old Thirsk *N.Yorks.* ***Suburb***, to NE of Thirsk. SE4382.
Old Thornville (Also known as Thornville.) *N.Yorks.* ***Locality***, on N side of River Nidd, 1km NE of Cattal and 5m/8km NE of Wetherby. SE4554.
Old Town *Cumb.* ***Hamlet***, 3m/5km N of Kirkby Lonsdale. **55 J1** SD5982.
Old Town *Cumb.* ***Locality***, adjoining to S of High Hesket. NY4743.
Old Town *E.Suss.* ***Suburb***, to W of Eastbourne. TV5999.
Old Town *I.o.S.* ***Hamlet***, on St. Mary's, 1km SE of Hugh Town. **2 C1** SV9110.
Old Town *Northumb.* ***Locality***, 1m/2km S of Otterburn. **70 D4** NY8891.
Old Town *S.Yorks.* ***Suburb***, 1m/2km NW of Barnsley town centre. SE3307.
Old Town *W.Yorks.* ***Hamlet***, 1m/2km NE of Hebden Bridge. SD9928.
Old Trafford *Gt.Man.* ***Suburb***, of Manchester and 2m/3km SW of Salford city centre. Docks on Manchester Ship Canal. Cricket and football grounds. SJ8195.
Old Tree *Kent* ***Locality***, 3m/5km SE of Herne Bay. TR2064.
Old Tupton *Derbys.* ***Settlement***, to SW of Tupton, 1m/2km N of Clay Cross. **51 F6** SK3865.
Old Warden *Beds.* ***Village***, 4m/6km W of Biggleswade. Biggleswade (Old Warden) Airfield 1m/2km E. **32 E4** TL1343.
Old Wardour Castle *Wilts.* ***Castle***, remains of 14c castle with later additions (English Heritage), 1m/2km SE of Wardour Castle. **9 J2** ST9326.

Old Water *D. & G.* ***River***, issuing from Glenkiln Reservoir and joining Cairn Water to E, to form Cluden Water, 6m/10km NW of Dumfries. **65 J3** NX8879.
Old Weston *Cambs.* ***Village***, 6m/9km W of Alconbury. **32 E1** TL0977.
Old Whittington *Derbys.* ***Suburb***, adjoining to SW of New Whittington, 2m/3km N of Chesterfield. SK3874.
Old Wick (Also known as Pulteneytown.) *High.* ***Locality***, on S side of Wick, in Caithness district. Ruins of Castle of Old Wick (Historic Scotland), 1m/2km S of Wick. ND3649.
Old Windsor *W. & M.* Population: 7497. ***Small town***, 2m/3km SE of Windsor across Home Park. 13c church by River Thames. **22 C4** SU9874.
Old Wingate *Dur.* ***Locality***, 2m/3km W of Wingate. NZ3737.
Old Wives Lees *Kent* ***Village***, 5m/8km W of Canterbury. **15 F2** TR0754.
Old Woking *Surr.* ***Town***, old market town 1m/2km SE of Woking town centre. **22 D6** TQ0156.
Old Wolverton *M.K.* ***Locality***, to W of Wolverton town centre. **32 B4** SP8141.
Old Woods *Shrop.* ***Settlement***, 2m/3km NW of Bomere Heath. **38 D3** SJ4420.
Old Woodstock *Oxon.* ***Hamlet***, at NW end of Woodstock. SP4417.
Old Yeavering *Northumb.* ***Settlement***, 1km W of Yeavering. NT9230.
Oldany Island *High.* ***Island***, uninhabited island of about 500 acres or 200 hectares at SW side of entrance to Eddrachillis Bay, W coast of Sutherland district. **102 C5** NC0834.
Oldberrow *Warks.* ***Hamlet***, 2m/3km W of Henley-in-Arden. **30 C2** SP1265.
Oldborough *Devon* ***Hamlet***, 1km S of Morchard Bishop. **7 F5** SS7706.
Oldbury *Kent* ***Locality***, adjoining to W of Ightham, 4m/6km E of Sevenoaks. **23 J6** TQ5856.
Oldbury *Shrop.* ***Village***, 1km S of Bridgnorth. **39 G6** SO7192.
Oldbury *Warks.* ***Hamlet***, 2m/3km S of Atherstone. Iron Age fort to N. **41 F6** SP3194.
Oldbury *W.Mid.* Population: 72,771. ***Suburb***, of Warley, 5m/8km W of Birmingham. **40 B6** SO9989.
Oldbury Castle *Wilts.* ***Historic/prehistoric site***, triangular Iron Age hillfort enclosing hilltop of Cherhill Down, 1km SE of Cherhill. **20 D4** SU0469.
Oldbury Naite *S.Glos.* ***Settlement***, 1m/2km NE of Oldbury-on-Severn. **19 K2** ST6293.
Oldbury-on-Severn *S.Glos.* ***Village***, near River Severn estuary, 2m/3km NW of Thornbury. **19 K2** ST6192.
Oldbury on the Hill *Glos.* ***Hamlet***, 1km N of Didmarton. **20 B3** ST8188.
Oldbury Sands *S.Glos.* ***Coastal feature***, large sandbank in River Severn, 2m/3km W of Oldbury-on-Severn. **19 J2** ST5892.
Oldcastle (Yr Hengastell). *Bridgend* ***Suburb***, central district of Bridgend. SS9079.
Oldcastle *Mon.* ***Hamlet***, 3m/4km S of Longtown. **28 C6** SO3224.
Oldcastle Heath *Ches.* ***Settlement***, 1m/2km SW of Malpas. **38 D1** SJ4745.
Oldchapel Hill *Powys* ***Mountain***, 1km NE of Tylwch. Height 1397 feet or 426 metres. **37 J7** SN9780.
Oldcotes *Notts.* ***Village***, 3m/4km S of Tickhill. Site of villa on E side. **51 H4** SK5888.
Oldcroft *Glos.* ***Village***, 2m/3km W of Blakeney. SO6406.
Oldeamere *Cambs.* ***Settlement***, 3m/4km E of Whittlesey. TL3096.
Oldfallow *Staffs.* ***Suburb***, 1km N of Cannock. SJ9711.
Oldfield *W.Yorks.* ***Settlement***, 1m/2km W of Haworth. **57 F6** SE0037.
Oldfield *W.Yorks.* ***Settlement***, 1m/2km N of Holmfirth. SE1310.
Oldfield *Worcs.* ***Hamlet***, 4m/6km W of Droitwich Spa. **29 H2** SO8464.
Oldfield Brow *Gt.Man.* ***Suburb***, 1m/2km NW of Altrincham town centre. SJ7588.
Oldford *Som.* ***Hamlet***, 2m/3km NE of Frome. **20 A6** ST7850.
Oldhall *Aber.* ***Settlement***, 4m/6km W of Aboyne. **90 C5** NO4698.
Oldhall *High.* ***Settlement***, 3m/4km NW of Watten. **105 H3** ND2056.
Oldhall *Renf.* ***Suburb***, 2m/3km E of Paisley. NS5064.
Oldham *Gt.Man.* Population: 103,931. ***Town***, former cotton-spinning and weaving town, 7m/12km NE of Manchester. Reputed to have largest permanent outdoor market (Tommyfield) in England. Winston Churchill first elected as MP here. Oldham Art Gallery contains works by many famous painters. **49 J2** SD9305.
Oldham Edge *Gt.Man.* ***Suburb***, 1km N of Oldham town centre. SD9305.
Oldhamstocks *E.Loth.* ***Village***, 6m/10km SE of Dunbar. **77 F3** NT7470.
Oldhurst *Cambs.* ***Village***, 5m/8km NE of Huntingdon. **33 F1** TL3077.
Oldland *S.Glos.* ***Suburb***, 6m/9km E of Bristol. **19 K4** ST6771.
Oldmeldrum *Aber.* Population: 1976. ***Small town***, 4m/7km NE of Inverurie. **91 G2** NJ8027.
Oldmill *Aber.* ***Settlement***, on S side of Corse Burn, 4m/6km NE of Tarland. **90 D4** NJ5306.
Oldmills Working Mill *Moray* ***Other feature of interest***, 13c oatmeal mill on River Lossie, to W of Elgin. **97 J5** NJ2063.
Oldpark *Tel. & W.* ***Locality***, 1m/2km N of Dawley. **39 F5** SJ6909.
Oldridge *Devon* ***Settlement***, 3m/4km S of Crediton. **7 G6** SX8296.
Oldshore Beg *High.* ***Settlement***, near W coast of Sutherland district, 3m/4km NW of Kinlochbervie. **102 D3** NC1959.
Oldshore More *High.* ***Settlement***, near W coast of Sutherland district, 2m/3km NW of Kinlochbervie. **102 E3** NC2058.
Oldstead *N.Yorks.* ***Hamlet***, 7m/11km E of Thirsk. **58 B1** SE5380.
Oldtown *High.* ***Settlement***, in Sutherland district, 1km S of Ardgay, near head of Dornoch Firth. NH5989.
Oldtown of Aigas *High.* ***Settlement***, 5m/8km SW of Beauly. **96 B7** NH4540.
Oldtown of Ord *Aber.* ***Settlement***, 5m/8km SW of Banff. **98 E5** NJ6259.
Oldwalls *Swan.* ***Hamlet***, 1km W of Llanrhidian. **17 H5** SS4891.
Oldway *Swan.* ***Locality***, to SE of Bishopston on Gower peninsula, 3m/5km NW of Mumbles Head. SS5888.
Oldways End *Som.* ***Hamlet***, on border with Devon, 4m/6km SW of Dulverton. **7 G3** SS8624.
Oldwhat *Aber.* ***Locality***, 3m/5km SW of New Pitsligo. **99 G5** NJ8651.
Oldwich Lane *W.Mid.* ***Settlement***, 5m/9km W of Kenilworth. SP2174.
Oldwood *Shrop.* ***Settlement***, 5m/9km NW of Shrewsbury. SJ4520.
Oldwood Common *Worcs.* ***Locality***, 1m/2km S of Tenbury Wells. SO5866.
Olgrinmore *High.* ***Locality***, to S of Scotscalder Station. **105 F3** ND0955.
Olicana *W.Yorks.* *See Ilkley.*
Oliver *Sc.Bord.* ***Settlement***, just N of Tweedsmuir, in Tweeddale. **69 G1** NT1025.
Oliver's Battery *Hants.* ***Settlement***, 2m/3km NE of Basingstoke. Name taken from Oliver Cromwell. Motte and bailey castle to S. SU6653.
Oliver's Battery *Hants.* ***Suburb***, SW of Winchester. So called because from here Oliver Cromwell bombarded the city. **11 F2** SU4527.
Ollaberry *Shet.* ***Village***, on N side of bay of same name, on NE coast of Mainland, 4m/7km N of Sullom. **108 C4** HU3680.
Ollerton *Ches.* ***Village***, 2m/3km SE of Knutsford. **49 G5** SJ7776.
Ollerton *Notts.* Population: 5220. ***Small town***, (with New Ollerton) in Sherwood Forest, 12m/19km NW of Newark-on-Trent. Early 18c watermill. **51 J6** SK6567.
Ollerton *Shrop.* ***Hamlet***, 3m/5km SE of Hodnet. **39 F3** SJ6525.
Ollerton Fold *Lancs.* ***Settlement***, on E side of Leeds and Liverpool Canal, 2m/3km NW of Abbey Village and 5m/8km SW of Blackburn town centre. SD6223.
Olmarch *Cere.* ***Settlement***, 4m/7km SW of Tregaron. SN6255.
Olmstead Green *Cambs.* ***Settlement***, 4m/6km SW of Haverhill. **33 K4** TL6341.
Olna Firth *Shet.* ***Sea feature***, inlet on W coast of Mainland with village of Voe at its head. **109 C6** HU3864.
Olney *M.K.* Population: 4484. ***Small town***, market town on River Great Ouse, 5m/8km N of Newport Pagnell. Town well-known for its lace industry and famous for its Shrove Tuesday Pancake Race. Site of Roman building to NE. **32 B3** SP8851.
Olney *Northants.* ***Locality***, adjoining to S of Silverstone, 4m/6km SW of Towcester. **31 H4** SP6643.
Olrig House *High.* ***Settlement***, 1m/2km SW of Castletown. **105 G2** ND1866.
Olton *W.Mid.* ***Suburb***, 2m/4km NW of Solihull town centre. **40 D7** SP1282.
Olveston *S.Glos.* ***Village***, 3m/5km SW of Thornbury. **19 J3** ST6087.
Ombersley *Worcs.* ***Village***, 4m/6km W of Droitwich Spa. **29 H2** SO8463.
Ompton *Notts.* ***Village***, 3m/4km SE of Ollerton. **51 J6** SK6865.
Onchan *I.o.M.* ***Suburb***, 2m/3km NE of Douglas. **54 C6** SC3978.
Onchan Head *I.o.M.* ***Coastal feature***, headland at NE end of Douglas Bay to S of Onchan. **54 D6** SC3978.
One Tree Hill Country Park *Thur.* ***Leisure/recreation***, 1m/2km N of Corringham. Over 30 acres of woodland-covered hilltop affording views of Kentish Weald. **24 C3** TQ6985.
Onecote *Staffs.* ***Village***, 4m/7km E of Leek. **50 C7** SK0455.
Onehouse *Suff.* ***Village***, 2m/3km W of Stowmarket. TM0259.
Onen *Mon.* ***Locality***, 6m/9km W of Monmouth. SO4314.
Ongar Hill *Norf.* ***Settlement***, 4m/6km NE of Terrington St. Clement. **43 J3** TF5724.
Ongar Street *Here.* ***Settlement***, 4m/7km S of Leintwardine. **28 C2** SO3967.
Onibury *Shrop.* ***Village***, 3m/4km SE of Craven Arms. **28 D1** SO4579.
Onich *High.* ***Village***, in Lochaber district, on N side of entrance to Loch Leven, 2m/3km W of North Ballachulish. **80 B1** NN0261.
Onley *Northants.* ***Settlement***, 3m/4km S of Rugby. SP5171.
Onllwyn *N.P.T.* ***Village***, 2m/3km NE of Seven Sisters. **27 H7** SN8410.
Onllwyn *R.C.T.* ***Mountain***, 3m/5km NE of Hirwaun. Height 1374 feet or 419 metres. **18 C1** SN9908.
Onneley *Staffs.* ***Village***, 1m/2km E of Woore. **39 G1** SJ7543.
Onslow Village *Surr.* ***Suburb***, W district of Guildford. **22 C7** SU9749.
Openshaw *Gt.Man.* ***Suburb***, 3m/4km E of Manchester city centre. SJ8897.
Openwoodgate *Derbys.* ***Suburb***, 1m/2km E of Belper. SK3647.
Opinan *High.* ***Settlement***, 2m/3km SE of Greenstone Point, Ross and Cromarty district. **94 E2** NG8796.
Opinan *High.* ***Village***, on W coast of Ross and Cromarty district, 4m/7km SW of Gairloch across Gair Loch. **94 D4** NG7472.
Opsay *W.Isles* ***Island***, small uninhabited island in Sound of Harris, 4m/6km off NE coast of North Uist. NF9876.
Orange Lane *Sc.Bord.* ***Settlement***, 4m/7km SE of Greenlaw. **77 F6** NT7742.
Orasay Island *W.Isles* ***Island***, small uninhabited island near head of East Loch Roag, W coast of Isle of Lewis. NB2132.
Orasay Island (Gaelic form: Eilean Orasaigh.) *W.Isles* ***Island***, islet at entrance to Loch Leurbost, E coast of Isle of Lewis. NB4024.
Orbliston *Moray* ***Settlement***, 7m/11km SE of Elgin. **98 B5** NJ3057.
Orbost *High.* ***Locality***, on Skye, 3m/5km S of Dunvegan. **93 H7** NG2543.
Orby *Lincs.* ***Village***, 6m/9km NW of Skegness. **53 H6** TF4967.
Orby Marsh *Lincs.* ***Open space***, lowland 4m/6km NW of Skegness. **53 J6** TF5067.
Orcadia *Arg. & B.* ***Settlement***, on E coast of Bute, 1m/2km E of Rothesay. **73 K4** NS1063.
Orchard *Arg. & B.* ***Settlement***, 1km NW of head of Holy Loch and 4m/7km NW of Dunoon. **73 K2** NS1582.
Orchard Leigh *Bucks.* ***Settlement***, 2m/4km NE of Chesham. SP9803.
Orchard Portman *Som.* ***Village***, 2m/4km SE of Taunton. **8 B2** ST2421.
Orchard Wyndham *Som.* ***Settlement***, 1km S of Williton. **7 J2** ST0739.
Orchardton *D. & G.* ***Historic/prehistoric site***, 12c round tower (Historic Scotland) 1m/2km S of Palnackie and 1km N of Orchardton Bay. **65 J5** NX8155.
Orchardton Bay *D. & G.* ***Bay***, small bay on W side of Wigtown Bay, 4m/6km SE of Wigtown. **64 E5** NX4650.
Orcheston *Wilts.* ***Village***, on Salisbury Plain, 7m/11km NW of Amesbury. **20 D7** SU0545.
Orcheston Down *Wilts.* ***Open space***, hillslope 2m/4km E of Tilshead. **20 D7** SU0748.
Orchy *Arg. & B.* ***River***, in Argyll, running SW from Loch Tulla down Glen Orchy to NE end of Loch Awe. **80 D4** NN1327.
Orcop *Here.* ***Village***, 5m/8km E of Pontrilas. **28 D6** SO4726.
Orcop Hill *Here.* ***Village***, 5m/9km E of Pontrilas. **28 D6** SO4829.
Ord *High.* ***River***, flowing NW into Loch Eishort, Skye, 3m/4km NE of Tarskavaig. **86 C3** NG6113.
Ord *High.* ***Settlement***, on S side of Loch Eishort, Sleat peninsula, Skye, 5m/8km W of Eilean Iarmain. **86 C3** NG6113.
Ordhead *Aber.* ***Village***, 7m/11km SE of Alford. **90 E3** NJ6610.
Ordie *Aber.* ***Village***, 2m/3km N of Dinnet. **90 C4** NJ4501.
Ordie Burn *P. & K.* ***River***, rising on hills W of Bankfoot and flowing SE to join River Tay at Luncarty, 4m/6km N of Perth. **82 B4** NO1029.
Ordiequish *Moray* ***Settlement***, on E side of River Spey, 1m/2km S of Fochabers. **98 B5** NJ3357.
Ordsall *Gt.Man.* ***Suburb***, 1m/2km SW of Salford city centre. SJ8197.
Ordsall *Notts.* ***Suburb***, S district of Retford. **51 K5** SK7079.
Ore *E.Suss.* ***Suburb***, NE district of Hastings. **14 D6** TQ8311.
Ore *Suff.* ***Sea feature***, estuary of River Alde below Blackstakes Reach and inland of Orford Ness. It flows SW parallel to coast, into North Sea 1m/2km E of Hollesley. TM3743.
Oreham Common *W.Suss.* ***Settlement***, 1m/2km S of Henfield. **13 F5** TQ2213.
Oreston *Plym.* ***Suburb***, SE district of Plymouth E of River Plym. **5 F5** SX5053.
Oreton *Shrop.* ***Hamlet***, 3m/5km N of Cleobury Mortimer. **39 F7** SO6580.
Oreval *W.Isles* ***Mountain***, 1m/2km N of Cleiseval in Forest of Harris. Height 2171 feet or 662 metres. **100 C6** NB0810.
Orfasay *Shet.* ***Island***, small uninhabited island off S coast of Yell, separated from it by Sound of Orfasay. **108 D5** HU4977.
Orford *Suff.* ***Village***, on River Ore, 9m/15km E of Woodbridge. Remains of Norman castle (English Heritage). **35 J4** TM4249.
Orford *Warr.* ***Suburb***, 2m/3km NE of Warrington town centre. **49 F3** SJ6190.
Orford Beach *Suff.* ***Coastal feature***, narrow strip of shingle extending 6m/9km from Orford Ness to mouth of River Ore. **35 J4** TM4046.
Orford Castle *Suff.* ***Castle***, remaining great tower (English Heritage) of 12c castle built by Henry II, to W of Orford. **35 J4** TM4149.
Orford Ness *Suff.* ***Coastal feature***, largest vegetated shingle spit in Europe (National Trust), 2m/3km E of Orford across River Alde and 4m/7km S of Aldeburgh. **35 J4** TM4249.
Organford *Dorset* ***Hamlet***, 3m/4km W of Upton. SY9392.
Orgreave *S.Yorks.* ***Locality***, 4m/7km E of Sheffield. SK4287.
Orgreave *Staffs.* ***Hamlet***, 1m/2km W of Alrewas. **40 D4** SK1416.
Orielton *Pembs.* ***Locality***, 3m/4km SW of Pembroke. Decoy pond of Wildfowl Inquiry Committee. SR9599.
Orinsay *W.Isles* ***Settlement***, near E coast of Isle of Lewis, on N side of Loch Shell, 1m/2km W of Leumrabhagh. NB3612.
Orinsay Island *W.Isles* *Anglicised form of Eilean Orasaigh, qv.*
Orka Voe *Shet.* ***Sea feature***, inlet on coast of Mainland at S end of Yell Sound. **108 D5** HU4077.
Orknagable *Shet.* ***Coastal feature***, cliffs on W coast of Unst, towards N of island. **108 E1** HP5713.
Orlestone *Kent* ***Hamlet***, 5m/8km S of Ashford. TR9934.
Orleton *Here.* ***Village***, 5m/8km N of Leominster. **28 D2** SO4967.
Orleton *Worcs.* ***Village***, on River Teme, 7m/11km E of Tenbury Wells. **29 F2** SO6966.
Orleton Common *Here.* ***Locality***, 5m/7km SW of Ludlow. **28 D2** SO4768.
Orlingbury *Northants.* ***Village***, 4m/6km NW of Wellingborough. **32 B1** SP8672.
Ormacleit (Anglicised form: Ormiclate.) *W.Isles* ***Settlement***, 2m/4km NE of Rubha Ardvule, South Uist. **84 C1** NF7431.
Ormathwaite *Cumb.* ***Locality***, 1m/2km N of Keswick. NY2625.

Ormes Bay (Also known as Llandudno Bay.) *Conwy* ***Bay***, on North Wales coast, extending from Little Ormes Head westwards to Pen-trwyn, N of Llandudno. SH7982.
Ormesby *Middbro.* ***Suburb***, 3m/5km SE of Middlesbrough. Hall (National Trust) is mid-18c house. **63 G5** NZ5317.
Ormesby Hall *R. & C.* ***Historic house***, National Trust property, 3m/5km SW of Middlesbrough. 18c Palladian mansion with stable blocks and holly walk in gardens. **63 G5** NZ5216.
Ormesby St. Margaret *Norf.* Population: 2729. ***Village***, 5m/8km N of Great Yarmouth. **45 J4** TG4914.
Ormesby St. Michael *Norf.* ***Village***, 1m/2km W of Ormesby St. Margaret. **45 J4** TG4914.
Ormiclate *W.Isles Anglicised form of Ormacleit, qv.*
Ormidale *Arg. & B.* ***Settlement***, in lower Glendaruel, 2m/3km S of Clachan of Glendaruel. **73 J2** NS0081.
Ormiscaig *High.* ***Settlement***, on E shore of Loch Ewe, Ross and Cromarty district, 1m/2km NW of Aultbea. **94 E2** NG8590.
Ormiston *E.Loth.* Population: 2078. ***Village***, 2m/4km S of Tranent. Market cross (Historic Scotland). **76 C4** NT4169.
Ormiston Hill *Fife* ***Hill***, 1km S of Newburgh. Height 777 feet or 237 metres. **82 D6** NO2316.
Ormiston Market Cross *E.Loth.* ***Historic/prehistoric site***, 15c cross in main street at Ormiston, 2m/3km S of Tranent. **76 C4** NT4169.
Ormlie *High.* ***Locality***, adjacent to SW of Thurso. **105 G2** ND1067.
Ormsaigbeag *High.* ***Locality***, on S coast of Ardnamurchan in Lochaber district, 1km SW of Kilchoan. NM4763.
Ormsaigmore *High.* ***Settlement***, on S coast of Ardnamurchan, in Lochaber district, between Kilchoan and locality of Ormsaigbeag. **79 F1** NM4763.
Ormsary *Arg. & B.* ***Settlement***, in Knapdale, Argyll, on E side of Loch Caolisport, 4m/7km SW of Achahoish. NR7472.
Ormskirk *Lancs.* Population: 23,425. ***Town***, market town, 7m/12km SE of Southport. **48 D2** SD4108.
Ornish Island *W.Isles* ***Island***, small uninhabited island at entrance to Loch Sgioport, E coast of North Uist. **84 D1** NF8538.
Ornsby Hill *Dur.* ***Locality***, adjoining to N of Lanchester. NZ1648.
Oronsay *Arg. & B.* ***Island***, sparsely inhabited island of about 2 square miles or 5 square km off S end of Colonsay, to which it is connected by sands at low tide. Traces of Stone Age settlement. Remains of 14c priory near W coast. **72 B2** NR3588.
Oronsay *High.* ***Island***, small uninhabited island off Ullinish Point, Skye, in Loch Bracadale. **85 J1** NG3136.
Oronsay *High.* ***Island***, small uninhabited island at entrance to Loch Sunart in Lochaber district, W of Carna. **79 G2** NM5959.
Oronsay *W.Isles* ***Island***, low-lying uninhabited island in bay on N coast of North Uist to E of Solas. **92 D4** NF8475.
Oronsay Priory *Arg. & B.* ***Ecclesiastical building***, on Oronsay. Ruins of priory thought to be founded by St. Columba. Present remains are of 14c Augustinian foundation, together with grave slabs and crosses. **72 B2** NR3488.
Orosay *W.Isles* ***Island***, small uninhabited island on E side of Barra (Tràigh Mhòr) Airport. **84 C4** NF7106.
Orosay *W.Isles* ***Island***, small uninhabited island off W coast of South Uist 3m/5km SW of Dalabrog. **84 C3** NF7217.
Orosay *W.Isles* ***Island***, islet off NE coast of Vatersay. NL6497.
Orosay *W.Isles* ***Island***, islet on E side of entrance to Castle Bay on S coast of Barra. NL6697.
Orosay *W.Isles* ***Island***, islet off SE coast of Barra opposite Earsairidh. NL7099.
Orphir *Ork.* ***Locality***, on Mainland, 7m/11km SW of Kirkwall. Scant remains of 11c or 12c round church (Historic Scotland). **107 C7** HY3406.
Orphir Round Church and Earl's Bu *Ork.* ***Ecclesiastical building***, remains of only circular medieval church in Scotland, overlooking Orphir Bay on S coast of Mainland. **107 C7** HY3304.
Orpington *Gt.Lon.* ***Town***, in borough of Bromley, 14m/22km SE of Charing Cross. **23 H5** TQ4665.
Orrell *Gt.Man.* Population: 12,251. ***Town***, 4m/6km W of Wigan. **48 E2** SD5203.
Orrell *Mersey.* ***Suburb***, 4m/6km NE of Liverpool city centre. SJ3496.
Orrell Post *Gt.Man.* ***Locality***, in Orrell, on N side of M58 motorway. SD5304.
Orrin *High.* ***River***, in Ross and Cromarty district, rising on East Monar Forest and running E to River Conon 4m/7km SW of Dingwall. **96 B6** NH5153.
Orrin Reservoir *High.* ***Reservoir***, 5m/8km long and 7m/12km from confluence of River Orrin and River Conon. **95 K7** NH3649.
Orrisdale *I.o.M.* ***Hamlet***, near W coast, 1m/2km W of Ballaugh. **54 C4** SC3293.
Orrisdale Head *I.o.M.* ***Coastal feature***, headland on coast to W of Orrisdale. **54 B4** SC3293.
Orrok House *Aber.* ***Settlement***, 1m/2km N of Balmedie. **91 H3** NJ9619.
Orroland *D. & G.* ***Settlement***, 2m/3km E of Dundrennan. **65 H6** NX7746.
Orsay *Arg. & B.* ***Island***, with lighthouse off S end of Rinns of Islay opposite Port Wemyss. NR1651.
Orsett *Thur.* ***Village***, 4m/6km N of Tilbury. **24 C3** TQ6481.
Orsett Heath *Thur.* ***Hamlet***, 3m/4km N of Tilbury. TQ6479.
Orslow *Staffs.* ***Hamlet***, 2m/3km N of Blymhill. **40 A4** SJ8015.
Orston *Notts.* ***Village***, 4m/7km E of Bingham. **42 A1** SK7641.
Orthwaite *Cumb.* ***Locality***, 2m/3km NE of Bassenthwaite. NY2534.
Orton *Cumb.* ***Village***, 3m/4km N of Tebay. **61 H6** NY6208.
Orton *Northants.* ***Village***, 4m/7km W of Kettering. **32 B1** SP8079.
Orton *Peter.* ***Suburb***, SW district of Peterborough, including former villages of Orton Longueville and Orton Waterville. TL1796.
Orton Longueville *Peter.* ***Village***, along with Orton Waterville forms suburb of Orton, SW district of Peterborough. **42 E6** TL1796.
Orton-on-the-Hill *Leics.* ***Village***, 4m/6km N of Atherstone. **41 F5** SK3003.
Orton Rigg *Cumb.* ***Hamlet***, 3m/5km NW of Dalston. NY3352.
Orton Waterville *Peter.* ***Village***, along with Orton Longueville forms suburb of Orton, SW district of Peterborough. **42 E6** TL1796.
Orval *High.* ***Mountain***, on Rum, 4m/7km W of Kinloch. Height 1873 feet or 571 metres. **85 J5** NM3398.
Orwell *Cambs.* ***Village***, 6m/10km N of Royston. **33 G4** TL3650.
Orwell *Suff.* ***Sea feature***, tidal part of River Gipping from Ipswich where it forms estuary, to its confluence with River Stour at Harwich, then flowing into Harwich Harbour and North Sea. **35 G5** TM2633.
Orwell Bridge *Suff.* ***Bridge***, carrying Ipswich Bypass over River Orwell downstream from Ipswich. Centre span of 623 feet or 192 metres is longest pre-stressed concrete arch in Britain. TM1741.
Osbaldeston *Lancs.* ***Village***, 3m/5km NW of Blackburn. **56 B6** SD6431.
Osbaldeston Green *Lancs.* ***Settlement***, 1m/2km N of Mellor, 4m/6km NW of Blackburn town centre. SD6432.
Osbaldwick *York* ***Suburb***, 2m/3km E of York. **58 C4** SE6351.
Osbaston *Leics.* ***Hamlet***, 2m/3km NE of Market Bosworth. **41 G5** SK4204.
Osbaston *Shrop.* ***Settlement***, 1km NW of Knockin. SJ3222.
Osbaston *Tel. & W.* ***Settlement***, 6m/9km NW of Wellington. **38 E4** SJ5918.
Osbaston Hollow *Leics.* ***Settlement***, 1km NW of Barlestone. SK4106.
Osbaston Lount *Leics.* ***Settlement***, 1km W of Barlestone. SK4105.
Osbaston Toll Gate *Leics.* ***Hamlet***, adjoining to W of Barlestone. SK4105.
Osborne *I.o.W.* ***Settlement***, 1m/2km SE of East Cowes. **11 G5** SZ5194.
Osborne Bay *I.o.W.* ***Bay***, on N coast, to NE of Osborne House. **11 G5** SZ5194.
Osborne House *I.o.W.* ***Historic house***, Queen Victoria's home (English Heritage), designed by Prince Albert, 1m/2km SE of East Cowes. Little altered since Queen Victoria died here in 1901. **11 G5** SZ5194.
Osbournby *Lincs.* ***Village***, 5m/8km S of Sleaford. **42 D2** TF0638.
Oscroft *Ches.* ***Village***, 4m/7km NW of Tarporley. **48 E6** SJ5066.
Ose *High.* ***Settlement***, at mouth of River Ose, Skye, 3m/5km NW of Bracadale. **93 J7** NG3140.
Osea Island *Essex* ***Island***, in River Blackwater estuary, 4m/7km E of Maldon. **25 F1** TL9106.
Osgathorpe *Leics.* ***Village***, 3m/5km N of Coalville. **41 G4** SK4319.
Osgodby *Lincs.* ***Village***, 3m/5km NW of Market Rasen. Site of Roman settlement 1km S. **52 D3** TF0792.
Osgodby *N.Yorks.* ***Village***, 2m/3km NE of Selby. **58 C6** SE6433.
Osgodby *N.Yorks.* ***Village***, 3m/4km S of Scarborough. **59 G1** TA0584.
Osgodby Moor *Lincs.* ***Locality***, 2m/3km N of Middle Rasen. **52 D3** TF0892.
Osgoodby *N.Yorks.* ***Locality***, 4m/6km E of Thirsk, comprising High Osgoodby Grange and Low Osgoodby Grange. Osgodby Hall, to N, dates from 17c. **57 K1** SE4980.
Osidge *Gt.Lon.* ***Suburb***, in borough of Barnet, 9m/14km N of Charing Cross. TQ2894.
Oskaig *High.* ***Settlement***, on W coast of Raasay, 3m/5km from S end of island. **86 B1** NG5438.
Oskaig Point *High.* ***Coastal feature***, headland on W coast of Raasay, 1km N of Clachan. **86 B1** NG5438.
Osleston *Derbys.* ***Hamlet***, 7m/11km W of Derby. SK2437.
Osmaston *Derby* ***Suburb***, 2m/3km SE of Derby city centre. **41 F2** SK3633.
Osmaston *Derbys.* ***Village***, 2m/4km SE of Ashbourne. **40 D1** SK1943.
Osmington *Dorset* ***Village***, 5m/9km SE of Dorchester. **9 G6** SY7283.
Osmington Mills *Dorset* ***Hamlet***, on S coast, 1m/2km SE of Osmington and 4m/6km NE of Weymouth. **9 G6** SY7281.
Osmington White Horse *Dorset* ***Historic/prehistoric site***, figure on horseback, said to represent George III, carved into S slope of White Horse Hill, 1m/2km N of Osmington. **9 G6** SY7184.
Osmondthorpe *W.Yorks.* ***Suburb***, 3m/4km E of Leeds city centre. SE3233.
Osmotherley *N.Yorks.* ***Village***, 6m/10km NE of Northallerton. **63 F7** SE4597.
Osnaburgh *Fife Alternative name for Dairsie, qv.*
Osney *Oxon.* ***Suburb***, W district of Oxford. **21 J1** SP4906.
Ospringe *Kent* ***Hamlet***, on SW side of Faversham. Maison Dieu (English Heritage), 15c house and museum. **15 F2** TR0060.
Ossett *W.Yorks.* Population: 20,405. ***Town***, market town, 3m/5km W of Wakefield. **57 H7** SE2720.
Ossett Spa *W.Yorks.* ***Locality***, adjoining to SE of Ossett. SE2919.
Ossett Street Side *W.Yorks.* ***Suburb***, 1km N of Ossett town centre. SE2721.
Ossian *High.* ***River***, in Lochaber district, running N from Loch Ossian down Strath Ossian to Loch Ghuilbinn. **88 B7** NN4174.
Ossian's Cave *High.* ***Cave***, cleft on N face of Aonach Dubh, Lochaber district, one of The Three Sisters. Ossian, legendary Gaelic warrior and bard, is said to have been born beside Loch Triochatan to W. **80 C2** NN1556.
Ossington *Notts.* ***Village***, 7m/12km N of Newark-on-Trent. **51 K6** SK7564.
Ostem *W.Isles* ***Island***, islet on W side of Kearstay, small island off N coast of Scarp. NA9617.
Ostend *Essex* ***Hamlet***, 1m/2km NW of Burnham-on-Crouch. **25 F2** TQ9397.
Ostend *Norf.* ***Locality***, on coast, adjoining to E of Walcott, 1m/2km NW of Happisburgh. TG3632.
Osterley *Gt.Lon.* ***Suburb***, in borough of Hounslow, 10m/16km W of Charing Cross. To N is Osterley Park, containing Osterley House (National Trust), 18c house by Robert Adam. **22 E4** TQ1477.
Osterley Park *Gt.Lon.* ***Historic house***, National Trust property, originally Tudor, transformed to its present state in 1761 by Robert Adam; set in extensive park, 1m/2km N of Hounslow. Park notable for autumn colours. **22 E4** TQ1477.
Oswaldkirk *N.Yorks.* ***Village***, 3m/5km S of Helmsley. **58 C2** SE6278.
Oswaldtwistle *Lancs.* Population: 12,176. ***Town***, market town, adjoining to SW of Accrington. Former textile town. James Hargreaves, inventor of Spinning Jenny, lived in town. **56 C7** SD7327.
Oswestry *Shrop.* Population: 15,612. ***Town***, market town near Welsh border, 16m/26km NW of Shrewsbury. Birthplace of Wilfrid Owen and Barbara Pym. Iron Age hillfort to N. Transport Museum at old station. **38 B3** SJ2929.
Ot Moor *Oxon.* ***Open space***, tract lying some 6m/10km NE of Oxford. **31 G7** SP5614.
Oteley *Shrop.* ***Settlement***, at Ellesmere, on E side of The Mere. SJ4134.
Otford *Kent* Population: 3420. ***Village***, on River Darent, 3m/4km N of Sevenoaks. Site of Roman villa to E. Remains of archbishop's palace. **23 J6** TQ5259.
Otham *Kent* ***Village***, 3m/4km SE of Maidstone. **14 C2** TQ7953.
Otherton *Staffs.* ***Settlement***, 1m/2km S of Penkridge. SJ9212.
Othery *Som.* ***Village***, on Sedgemoor, 6m/10km SE of Bridgwater. **8 C1** ST3831.
Otley *Suff.* ***Village***, 6m/9km NW of Woodbridge. **35 G3** TM2055.
Otley *W.Yorks.* Population: 13,596. ***Town***, on River Wharfe, 10m/15km NW of Leeds. **57 H5** SE2045.
Otley Green *Suff.* ***Settlement***, 1km NE of Otley. TM2055.
Otley Hall *Suff.* ***Historic house***, 15c moated manor noted for superb architecture to N of Otley. Gardens, partly designed by Francis Inigo Thomas in 19c-20c, include canal mount, rose garden and nutteries. **35 F3** TM2056.
Otter ***River***, rising on S slopes of Black Down Hills and flowing SW through Honiton and Ottery St. Mary into English Channel on E side of Budleigh Salterton. **7 J6** SY0781.
Otter *Arg. & B.* ***Settlement***, on Kilfinan Bay, 5m/8km NW of Tighnabruaich. **73 H3** NR9278.
Otter Ferry *Arg. & B.* ***Settlement***, in Argyll, on E side of Loch Fyne, 4m/6km N of Kilfinan. **73 H2** NR9384.
Otter Rock *Arg. & B.* ***Island***, to S of Torran Rocks group, 4m/7km SW of Mull. **78 D6** NM2811.
Otterbourne *Hants.* ***Village***, 3m/5km N of Eastleigh. **11 F2** SU4623.
Otterburn *N.Yorks.* ***Hamlet***, on edge of Yorkshire Dales National Park, 2m/3km E of Hellifield. **56 D4** SD8857.
Otterburn *Northumb.* ***Village***, on River Rede, 15m/24km SE of Carter Bar. Site of Battle of Chevy Chase, 1388, in which Scots defeated Henry Percy. Military camp 2m/3km N. Artillery range on moors to N. **70 D4** NY8893.
Ottercops Moss *Northumb.* ***Open space***, moorland on E side of Raylees Common, 4m/6km NE of West Woodburn. Masts at summit. **70 E5** NY9589.
Otterden Place *Kent* ***Settlement***, 3m/5km N of Charing. **14 E2** TQ9454.
Otterford *Som.* ***Settlement***, 6m/10km S of Taunton. ST2214.
Otterham *Cornw.* ***Village***, 4m/7km E of Boscastle. **4 B1** SX1690.
Otterham Quay *Kent* ***Hamlet***, at head of Otterham Creek, 3m/5km E of Gillingham. TQ8366.
Otterhampton *Som.* ***Hamlet***, 5m/8km NW of Bridgwater. **19 F7** ST2443.
Otters Wick *Ork.* ***Sea feature***, large inlet on N coast of Sanday. **106 F3** HY6943.
Otters Wick *Shet.* ***Bay***, on E coast of Yell. **108 E4** HU5285.
Ottershaw *Surr.* Population: 4334. ***Village***, 2m/4km SW of Chertsey. **22 D5** TQ0263.
Otterswick *Shet.* ***Settlement***, at head of Otters Wick bay. **108 E4** HU5285.
Otterton *Devon* ***Village***, on River Otter, 2m/3km NE of Budleigh Salterton. **7 J7** SY0885.
Otterwood *Hants.* ***Settlement***, on edge of New Forest, 2m/3km E of Beaulieu. SU4102.
Ottery *Cornw.* ***River***, rising near Jacobstow and flowing SE into River Tamar 2m/3km NE of Launceston. **4 D2** SX3486.
Ottery St. Mary *Devon* Population: 3253. ***Small town***, 11m/18km E of Exeter. Notable large 14c church. Birthplace of Samuel Taylor Coleridge, 1772. **7 J6** SY0995.
Ottinge *Kent* ***Hamlet***, 5m/8km N of Hythe. **15 G3** TR1642.
Ottringham *E.Riding* ***Village***, 3m/5km W of Patrington. **59 J7** TA2624.
Oughterby *Cumb.* ***Hamlet***, 1m/2km SW of Kirkbampton. **60 D1** NY2955.
Oughtershaw *N.Yorks.* ***Settlement***, on Oughtershaw Beck, or upper reach of River Wharfe, 5m/8km NW of Buckden. **56 D1** SD8681.
Oughtershaw Moss *N.Yorks.* ***Open space***, moorland on N side of head of Langstrothdale, 5m/8km S of Hawes. **56 D1** SD8581.
Oughterside *Cumb.* ***Village***, 2m/3km SW of Aspatria. NY1140.

O

Oughtibridge *S.Yorks.* Population: 3021. ***Village***, on River Don, 5m/8km NW of Sheffield. **51 F3** SK3093.
Oulston *N.Yorks.* ***Village***, 3m/5km N of Easingwold. **58 B2** SE5474.
Oulton *Cumb.* ***Village***, 2m/3km N of Wigton. **60 D1** NY2450.
Oulton *Norf.* ***Hamlet***, 4m/6km NW of Aylsham. **45 F3** TG1328.
Oulton *Staffs.* ***Settlement***, 1km S of Norbury. SJ7822.
Oulton *Staffs.* ***Village***, 1m/2km NE of Stone. **40 B2** SJ9135.
Oulton *Suff.* ***Suburb***, 2m/3km NW of Lowestoft. **45 K6** TM5294.
Oulton *W.Yorks.* ***Locality***, 5m/9km SE of Leeds. **57 J7** SE3628.
Oulton Broad *Suff.* ***Locality***, and lake, to S of Oulton. **45 K6** TM5294.
Oulton Grange *Staffs.* ***Settlement***, 1km W of Oulton. SJ9035.
Oulton Heath *Staffs.* ***Settlement***, 1km N of Oulton. SJ9036.
Oulton Street *Norf.* ***Village***, 1m/2km SE of Oulton. **45 F3** TG1328.
Oultoncross *Staffs.* ***Suburb***, 1km S of Oulton. SJ9034.
Oundle *Northants.* Population: 3996. ***Small town***, on River Nene 12m/19km SW of Peterborough. Many old buildings. Boys' public school, founded 1556. **42 D7** TL0388.
Ousby *Cumb.* ***Village***, 7m/11km NE of Penrith. **61 H3** NY6234.
Ousby Fell *Cumb.* ***Open space***, 4m/7km E of Melmerby. Highest point is Rigg End, 1853 feet or 565 metres. **61 H3** NY6838.
Ousdale *High.* ***Settlement***, on Ousdale Burn, 4m/6km SW of Berriedale. **105 F6** ND0620.
Ousden *Suff.* ***Village***, 7m/11km SE of Newmarket. **34 B3** TL7459.
Ouse *Familiar form of (River) Great Ouse, qv.*
Ouse ***River***, formed by confluence of Rivers Swale and Ure to E of Boroughbridge and flowing SE by York, Cawood, Selby and Goole, to join River Trent and form River Humber 7m/12km E of Goole. Main tributaries are Rivers Swale, Ure, Nidd, Wharfe, Aire and Don from W, and River Derwent from E. Tidal to within 1m/2km of Naburn. **58 C6** SE8623.
Ouse ***River***, rising in St. Leonard's Forest to E of Horsham, flowing E then S through Lewes into English Channel at Newhaven. **13 H5** TQ4500.
Ouse Fen *Cambs.* ***Open space***, fenland, 2m/3km NE of Needingworth. **33 G1** TL3773.
Ouse Ness *Ork.* ***Coastal feature***, headland on E coast of Westray, overlooking Papa Sound. **106 D3** HY4549.
Ousefleet *E.Riding* ***Village***, on S side of River Ouse, 5m/9km E of Goole. **58 E7** SE8223.
Ouston *Dur.* Population: 5957. ***Village***, 2m/3km NW of Chester-le-Street. **62 D1** NZ2554.
Ouston *Northumb.* ***Settlement***, 1m/2km S of Stamfordham. Airfield to SE. **71 F6** NZ0770.
Out Elmstead *Kent* ***Locality***, 1km N of Barham. TR2050.
Out Head *Fife* ***Coastal feature***, headland on S side of River Eden estuary, 2m/4km N of St. Andrews. **83 F6** NO4919.
Out Newton *E.Riding* ***Settlement***, near coast, 4m/7km E of Patrington. **59 K7** TA3821.
Out Rawcliffe *Lancs.* ***Hamlet***, 4m/6km SE of Preesall. **55 H5** SD4041.
Out Skerries (Also known as The Skerries.) *Shet.* ***Island***, group of several small islands, some no more than rocks, lying about 5m/8km NE of Whalsay. Housay and Bruray are inhabited and connected by a road bridge. The extreme eastern island, Bound Skerry, has a lighthouse. **108 F5** HU6771.
Out Skerries Airstrip *Shet.* ***Airport/airfield***, situated on Burray, in the Out Skerries group of islands. **108 F5** HU6872.
Out Stack *Shet.* ***Island***, rock about 1km NE of Muckle Flugga and 1m/2km NE of Herma Ness, Unst. Most northerly point of British Isles. **108 F1** HP6120.
Outberry Plain *Dur.* ***Mountain***, to N of Middleton Common, 5m/8km N of Middleton-in-Teesdale. Height 2142 feet or 653 metres. **62 A3** NY9332.
Outcast *Cumb.* ***Settlement***, 1km SE of Ulverston. SD3077.
Outchester *Northumb.* ***Hamlet***, 2m/3km E of Belford. NU1433.
Outer Hebrides *W.Isles See Western Isles administrative area description.*
Outer Holm *Ork.* ***Island***, islet on E side of Stromness Harbour, Mainland. HY2508.
Outer Hope *Devon* ***Suburb***, part of Hope, 4m/7km SW of Kingsbridge. SX6740.
Outer Score *Shet.* ***Island***, small uninhabited island off N end of Bressay. HU5145.
Outertown *Ork.* ***Settlement***, near W coast of Mainland, 1m/2km NW of Stromness. **107 B6** HY2310.
Outgate *Cumb.* ***Hamlet***, 1m/2km N of Hawkshead. **60 E7** SD3599.
Outhgill *Cumb.* ***Hamlet***, 5m/8km S of Kirkby Stephen. **61 J6** NY7801.
Outlands *Staffs.* ***Settlement***, 4m/6km W of Eccleshall. **39 G3** SJ7730.
Outlane *W.Yorks.* ***Village***, 4m/7km W of Huddersfield. Site of Roman fort to S. **50 C1** SE0817.
Outrington *Warr.* ***Settlement***, 1m/2km NE of Lymm. SJ6987.
Outshore Point *Ork.* ***Coastal feature***, headland on W coast of Mainland 2m/3km S of Marwick Head. **106 B5** HY2222.
Outward *Gt.Man.* ***Hamlet***, 1m/2km S of Radcliffe. SD7705.
Outward Gate *Gt.Man.* ***Locality***, to E of Outwood. SD7705.
Outwell *Norf.* Population: 1683. ***Village***, 5m/8km SE of Wisbech. **43 J5** TF5103.
Outwell Basin ***Locality***, on border of Cambridgeshire and Norfolk, 1m/2km NW of Outwell. TF5004.
Outwood *Som.* ***Hamlet***, 1km E of Durston, 2m/3km NW of North Curry. ST3028.
Outwood *Surr.* ***Village***, 3m/5km NE of Horley. **23 G7** TQ3245.
Outwood *W.Yorks.* ***Locality***, 2m/3km N of Wakefield. **57 J7** SE3223.
Outwoods *Leics.* ***Hamlet***, 3m/5km NW of Coalville. SK4018.
Outwoods *Staffs.* ***Hamlet***, 3m/4km SE of Newport. SJ7818.
Ouzel (Also known as (River) Lovat.) ***River***, rising near Dunstable and flowing W, then N past Leighton Buzzard and Bletchley into River Great Ouse at Newport Pagnell. **32 B5** SP8844.
Ouzlewell Green *W.Yorks.* ***Village***, adjoining to NE of Lofthouse, 1m/2km S of Rothwell. SE3326.
Ovenden *W.Yorks.* ***Suburb***, 1m/2km NW of Halifax town centre. **57 F7** SE0827.
Over *Cambs.* Population: 2436. ***Village***, 9m/14km NW of Cambridge. **33 G2** TL3770.
Over *Ches.* ***Locality***, adjoining to W of Winsford. **49 F6** SJ6365.
Over *Glos.* ***Settlement***, 1m/2km NW of Gloucester. SO8119.
Over *S.Glos.* ***Hamlet***, 2m/4km NW of Filton. **19 J3** ST5882.
Over Alderley *Ches.* ***Locality***, to E of Nether Alderley. SJ8575.
Over Bridge *Glos.* ***Bridge***, single-arch stone bridge (English Heritage) built between 1825-1827 by Thomas Telford across River Severn, 1m/2km NW of Gloucester city centre. No longer used for road traffic. **29 H7** SO8119.
Over Burrow *Lancs.* ***Hamlet***, 2m/3km S of Kirkby Lonsdale, on N side of Leck Beck. Site of Calacum Roman fort. SD6175.
Over Burrows *Derbys.* ***Hamlet***, 1m/2km S of Brailsford. SK2639.
Over Compton *Dorset* ***Village***, 2m/4km E of Yeovil. **8 E3** ST5916.
Over Dinsdale *N.Yorks.* ***Hamlet***, in loop of River Tees, 4m/7km SE of Darlington across river. NZ3411.
Over End *Cambs.* ***Settlement***, S part of Elton, 7m/11km SW of Peterborough city centre. TL0993.
Over End *Derbys.* ***Locality***, adjoining to SE of Baslow, 4m/6km NE of Bakewell. **50 E5** SK2572.
Over Green *Warks.* ***Hamlet***, 3m/5km SE of Sutton Coldfield. SP1694.
Over Haddon *Derbys.* ***Village***, 2m/3km SW of Bakewell. **50 E6** SK2066.
Over Kellet *Lancs.* ***Village***, 1m/2km E of Carnforth. **55 J2** SD5270.
Over Kiddington *Oxon.* ***Hamlet***, 3m/4km SE of Enstone. **31 F6** SP4022.
Over Knutsford *Ches.* ***Suburb***, adjoining to SE of Knutsford. SJ7678.
Over Monnow *Mon.* ***Suburb***, 1km SW of Monmouth town centre across River Monnow. SO5012.
Over Norton *Oxon.* ***Village***, 1m/2km N of Chipping Norton. **30 E6** SP3128.
Over Peover *Ches.* ***Hamlet***, 3m/5km SE of Knutsford. **49 G5** SJ7874.
Over Rankeilour *Fife* ***Settlement***, 3m/5km W of Cupar. **82 E6** NO3213.
Over Silton *N.Yorks.* ***Hamlet***, 5m/8km E of Northallerton. **63 F7** SE4593.
Over Stowey *Som.* ***Hamlet***, on lower slopes of Quantock Hills, 1m/2km SW of Nether Stowey and 16m/25km W of Bridgwater. **7 K2** ST1838.
Over Stratton *Som.* ***Village***, 1m/2km S of South Petherton. **8 D3** ST4315.
Over Street *Wilts.* ***Locality***, just W of Stapleford across River Till. SU0637.
Over Tabley *Ches.* ***Settlement***, 2m/3km NW of Knutsford. **49 G4** SJ7280.
Over Wallop *Hants.* ***Village***, 7m/11km SW of Andover. **10 D1** SU2838.
Over Water *Cumb.* ***Lake/loch***, 1m/2km S of Uldale. **60 D3** NY2535.
Over Whitacre *Warks.* ***Village***, 4m/6km E of Coleshill. **40 E6** SP2491.
Over Winchendon *Bucks. Alternative name for Upper Winchendon, qv.*
Over Woodhouse *Derbys.* ***Locality***, 1m/2km N of Bolsover. SK4771.
Over Worton *Oxon.* ***Hamlet***, 3m/4km SW of Deddington. **31 F6** SP4329.
Overbecks Museum and Garden *Devon* ***Other feature of interest***, early 20c house (National Trust), with toy and natural history museum, 1m/2km S of Salcombe. Former home of scientist Otto Overbeck; museum contains memorabilia. 6-acre terraced garden (National Trust) containing rare and exotic plants and shrubs; spectacular views over Kingsbridge Estuary. **5 H7** SX7237.
Overbister *Ork.* ***Village***, in centre of Sanday, with Lamaness Firth to N and Cata Sand to E. **106 F3** HY6840.
Overbrae *Aber.* ***Locality***, near N coast, 3m/5km S of Gardenstown. Locality of Netherbrae to W. **99 G5** NJ8059.
Overbury *Worcs.* ***Village***, 5m/8km NE of Tewkesbury. **29 J5** SO9537.
Overcombe *Dorset* Population: 2483. ***Locality***, on Weymouth Bay, 2m/3km NE of Weymouth. **9 F6** SY6981.
Overgreen *Derbys.* ***Settlement***, 4m/6km NW of Chesterfield. SK3273.
Overleigh *Som.* ***Suburb***, S district of Street. **8 D1** ST4835.
Overley *Staffs.* ***Settlement***, 1km NW of Alrewas. SK1515.
Overmoor *Staffs.* ***Settlement***, 1m/2km E of Werrington. SJ9647.
Overpool *Ches.* ***Suburb***, in N district of Ellesmere Port. **48 C5** SJ3877.
Overscaig Hotel *High.* ***Other building***, on NE side of Loch Shin. **103 G6** NC4123.
Overseal *Derbys.* ***Village***, 3m/4km S of Swadlincote. **40 E4** SK2915.
Overslade *Warks.* ***Suburb***, SW district of Rugby. SP4973.
Oversland *Kent* ***Hamlet***, 4m/6km SE of Faversham. **15 F2** TR0557.
Oversley Green *Warks.* ***Hamlet***, SE of Alcester across River Arrow. **30 B3** SP0956.
Overstone *Northants.* ***Village***, 5m/8km NE of Northampton. **32 B2** SP8066.
Overstrand *Norf.* ***Village***, and coastal resort, 2m/3km E of Cromer. **45 G1** TG2440.
Overthorpe *Northants.* ***Hamlet***, 2m/3km E of Banbury. SP4840.
Overton *Aberdeen* ***Settlement***, to NW of Aberdeen Airport, 2m/3km NW of Dyce. **91 G3** NJ8714.
Overton *Aber.* ***Settlement***, on S side of Gallows Hill, 2m/3km NW of Kemnay. **91 F3** NJ7118.
Overton *Ches.* ***Suburb***, adjoining to SE of Frodsham. SJ5277.
Overton *Hants.* Population: 3660. ***Village***, on River Test, 4m/6km E of Whitchurch. **21 J7** SU5149.
Overton *Lancs.* ***Village***, 2m/4km SE of Heysham. **55 H4** SD4358.
Overton *N.Yorks.* ***Hamlet***, on River Ouse, 4m/6km NW of York. **58 B4** SE5555.
Overton *Shrop.* ***Hamlet***, 2m/3km S of Ludlow. **28 E1** SO5072.
Overton *Swan.* ***Hamlet***, just W of Port Eynon, on Gower peninsula. **17 H6** SS4685.
Overton *W.Yorks.* ***Village***, adjoining to SW of Middlestown. SE2616.
Overton *Wrex.* ***Village***, 6m/9km SE of Wrexham. **38 C1** SJ3741.
Overton Bridge *Wrex.* ***Hamlet***, at road crossing of River Dee, 1m/2km W of Overton. SJ3542.
Overton Green *Ches.* ***Locality***, 4m/7km W of Congleton. SJ7960.
Overtown *Aber.* ***Locality***, just SE of Gordonstown, 9m/15km SW of Banff. NJ5655.
Overtown *Lancs.* ***Hamlet***, 2m/3km SE of Kirkby Lonsdale, on S side of Leck Beck. SD6276.
Overtown *N.Lan.* Population: 1972. ***Village***, 1m/2km S of Wishaw. **75 G5** NS8052.
Overtown *Swin.* ***Settlement***, 3m/5km S of Swindon. SU1579.
Overtown *W.Yorks.* ***Settlement***, adjoining to S of Walton, 3m/5km SE of Wakefield. SE3516.
Overy *Oxon.* ***Settlement***, across River Thame from Dorchester. SU5893.
Overy Staithe *Norf. Alternative name for Burnham Overy Staithe, qv.*
Oving *Bucks.* ***Village***, 5m/8km NW of Aylesbury. **31 J6** SP7821.
Oving *W.Suss.* ***Village***, 3m/4km E of Chichester. **12 C6** SU9005.
Ovingdean *B. & H.* ***Suburb***, of Brighton, 3m/4km E of town centre. **13 G6** TQ3503.
Ovingham *Northumb.* ***Village***, 1m/2km NW of Prudhoe across River Tyne. Road bridge spans river here. **71 F7** NZ0863.
Ovington *Dur.* ***Village***, 5m/8km E of Barnard Castle. **62 C5** NZ1314.
Ovington *Essex* ***Hamlet***, 2m/3km S of Clare. **34 B4** TL7642.
Ovington *Hants.* ***Village***, on River Itchen, 2m/3km W of New Alresford. **11 G1** SU5631.
Ovington *Norf.* ***Village***, 1m/2km NE of Watton. **44 D5** TF9202.
Ovington *Northumb.* ***Village***, 2m/3km W of Prudhoe across River Tyne. **71 F7** NZ0663.
Owen's Bank *Staffs.* ***Locality***, adjoining to W of Tutbury. SK2028.
Ower *Hants.* ***Settlement***, 1m/2km SE of Fawley. SU4701.
Ower *Hants.* ***Village***, 3m/4km NE of Cadnam. **10 E3** SU3216.
Owermoigne *Dorset* ***Village***, 6m/10km SE of Dorchester. **9 G6** SY7685.
Owl End *Cambs.* ***Settlement***, NE end of Great Stukeley, 2m/4km NW of Huntingdon. TL2275.
Owlcotes *Derbys.* ***Settlement***, 3m/4km SW of Bolsover. SK4467.
Owler Bar *Derbys.* ***Settlement***, 4m/6km W of Dronfield. SK2978.
Owlerton *S.Yorks.* ***Suburb***, 2m/3km NW of Sheffield city centre. SK3389.
Owletts *Kent* ***Historic house***, 17c red-brick Charles II house (National Trust) in Cobham, 4m/7km W of Rochester. **24 C5** TQ6668.
Owletts End *Worcs.* ***Suburb***, in SE part of Evesham. SP0443.
Owlpen *Glos.* ***Hamlet***, 3m/4km E of Dursley. ST8098.
Owlpen Manor *Glos.* ***Historic house***, Tudor manor set in terraced yew gardens, 3m/5km E of Dursley. Medieval tithe barn, 17c Court House and 18c mill. Contains 17c wall hangings, Cotswold furniture and beadwork collection. **20 B2** ST8098.
Owl's Green *Suff.* ***Settlement***, 2m/3km N of Dennington. TM2869.
Owlswick *Bucks.* ***Hamlet***, 2m/3km NW of Princes Risborough. **22 A1** SP7906.
Owlthorpe *S.Yorks.* ***Village***, 5m/8km SE of Sheffield city centre. SK4181.
Owmby *Lincs.* ***Hamlet***, 4m/6km NE of Caistor. **52 D2** TA0704.
Owmby-by-Spital *Lincs.* ***Village***, 7m/11km W of Market Rasen. Site of Roman setttlement 2m/3km W. **52 D4** TF0087.
Owslebury *Hants.* ***Village***, 4m/7km SE of Winchester. Site of late Iron Age village at Bottom Pond Farm. **11 G2** SU5123.
Owston *Leics.* ***Village***, 5m/9km W of Oakham. **42 A5** SK7707.
Owston *S.Yorks.* ***Hamlet***, 1km NE of Carcroft. SE5511.
Owston Ferry *N.Lincs.* ***Village***, on W bank of River Trent, 3m/5km SE of Epworth. Traces of medieval castle S of church. **52 B2** SE8000.
Owstwick *E.Riding* ***Hamlet***, 5m/8km NW of Withernsea. **59 J6** TA2732.
Owthorne *E.Riding* ***Locality***, adjoining to W of Withernsea. TA3328.
Owthorpe *Notts.* ***Village***, 8m/12km SE of Nottingham. **41 J2** SK6733.

Oxborough *Norf.* ***Village***, 3m/5km E of Stoke Ferry. Oxburgh Hall (National Trust) is moated house dating from 15c. **44 B5** TF7401.
Oxburgh Hall *Norf.* ***Historic house***, 15c moated manor with fine Tudor gatehouse (National Trust) on S side of Oxborough, 3m/4km E of Stoke Ferry and 8m/12km E of Downham Market. Home of Bedingfeld family. Gardens feature a French parterre, chapel and woodland walks. **44 B5** TF7401.
Oxcars *Fife* ***Island***, islet with lighthouse in Firth of Forth 1km SE of Inchcolm and 2m/3km S of Hawkcraig Point. NT2081.
Oxcliffe Hill *Lancs.* ***Settlement***, 2m/3km SE of Morecambe, on banks of River Lune. **55 H3** SD4461.
Oxclose *T. & W.* ***Suburb***, to W of Washington town centre. NZ2956.
Oxcombe *Lincs.* ***Hamlet***, 6m/9km NE of Horncastle. **53 G5** TF3177.
Oxcroft *Derbys.* ***Settlement***, 2m/3km N of Bolsover. SK4873.
Oxcroft Estate *Derbys.* ***Locality***, 1km S of Oxcroft and 1m/2km N of Bolsover. SK4873.
Oxen End *Essex* ***Settlement***, 3m/5km SE of Thaxted. **33 K6** TL6629.
Oxen Park *Cumb.* ***Hamlet***, 3m/5km N of Greenodd. **55 G1** SD3187.
Oxencombe *Devon* ***Settlement***, below Great Haldon, 2m/3km NE of Chudleigh. SX8882.
Oxenfoord Castle *Midloth.* ***Castle***, 18c castle built on site of older castle in mansion style designed by Robert Adam, to N of Pathhead, 4m/6km SE of Dalkeith. Now a boarding school. **76 B4** NT3865.
Oxenhall *Glos.* ***Settlement***, 1m/2km NW of Newent. SO7126.
Oxenholme *Cumb.* ***Hamlet***, and railway junction, 2m/3km SE of Kendal. **61 G7** SD5389.
Oxenhope *W.Yorks.* ***Village***, 1m/2km S of Haworth. End of Keighley & Worth Valley railway line. **57 F6** SE0335.
Oxenpill *Som.* ***Hamlet***, between Meare and Westhay, 4m/6km NW of Glastonbury. ST4441.
Oxenton *Glos.* ***Village***, below W slope of Oxenton Hill, 6m/9km N of Cheltenham. **29 J5** SO9531.
Oxenwood *Wilts.* ***Hamlet***, 6m/10km NW of Hurstbourne Tarrant. **21 G6** SU3059.
Oxford *Oxon.* Population: 118,795. ***City***, at confluence of Rivers Thames and Cherwell, 52m/84km NW of London. Began as Saxon settlement, flourished under Normans when it was chosen as royal residence. University dating from 13c, recognised as being among best in the world. Many notable buildings create spectacular skyline. Cathedral. Bodleian Library, second largest in UK. Ashmolean museum, oldest public museum in country. Tourist and commercial centre. Ancient St. Giles Fair held every September. Oxford Brookes University at Headington, 2m/4km E of city centre. Airport at Kidlington. **21 J1** SP5106.
Oxford Botanic Gardens *Oxon.* ***Garden***, in Oxford city centre. Oldest in England (17c), built on site of a medieval Jewish cemetery, and with a gateway designed by Nicolas Stone. **21 J1** SP5105.
Oxford Cathedral *Oxon.* ***Ecclesiastical building***, in centre of Oxford, adjacent to Christ Church College. Smallest cathedral in England. Rebuilt 1140-80. Has several windows by William Morris and Burne Jones. **21 J1** SP5105.
Oxford University Colleges *Oxon.* ***Educational establishment***, Oxford University has 35 colleges with total student population of about 9,500. Colleges vary in date of foundation with Balliol, University College and Merton (13c) being the oldest and St. Catherine's (1963) the newest. **21 J1** SP5106.
Oxfordshire County Museum *Oxon.* ***Other feature of interest***, in Woodstock, with displays of local history of Oxfordshire area. **31 F7** SP4416.
Oxgangs *Edin.* ***Suburb***, 4m/6km S of Edinburgh city centre. NT2368.
Oxhey *Herts.* ***Suburb***, SE district of Watford. TQ1295.
Oxhill *Dur.* ***Suburb***, to W of Stanley. NZ1852.
Oxhill *Warks.* ***Village***, 4m/6km S of Kineton. **30 E4** SP3145.
Oxlease *Herts.* ***Suburb***, S district of Hatfield. TL2207.
Oxley *W.Mid.* ***Suburb***, 2m/4km N of Wolverhampton town centre. **40 B5** SJ9002.
Oxley Green *Essex* ***Hamlet***, 2m/3km SE of Tiptree. **34 D7** TL9114.
Oxley's Green *E.Suss.* ***Hamlet***, 1km NE of Brightling. **13 K4** TQ6921.
Oxna *Shet.* ***Island***, uninhabited island of about 180 acres or 73 hectares 4m/6km SE of Skelda Ness, Mainland, across The Deeps. **109 C9** HU3537.
Oxnam *Sc.Bord.* ***Village***, on Oxnam Water, 4m/6km SE of Jedburgh. **70 B2** NT6918.
Oxnam Water *Sc.Bord.* ***River***, rising near Harkers Hill and flowing W, then N through Oxnam and into River Teviot 4m/6km SE of Jedburgh. **70 C2** NT6918.
Oxnead *Norf.* ***Hamlet***, 3m/5km SE of Aylsham. **45 G3** TG2224.
Oxnop Ghyll *N.Yorks.* ***Settlement***, in small valley on S side of Swaledale, 2m/3km SW of Gunnerside. **62 A7** SD9396.
Oxshott *Surr.* Population: 7627. ***Village***, 3m/5km NW of Leatherhead. **22 E5** TQ1460.
Oxspring *S.Yorks.* ***Village***, 2m/3km SE of Penistone. **50 E2** SE2602.
Oxted *Surr.* Population: 11,117. ***Town***, 4m/6km W of Westerham at foot of North Downs. Two distinct centres: new Oxted which is main part adjacent to railway station, and Old Oxted. **23 G6** TQ3852.
Oxton *Mersey.* ***Suburb***, 2m/3km W of Birkenhead town centre. **48 C4** SJ2987.
Oxton *N.Yorks.* ***Settlement***, 1m/2km E of Tadcaster. SE5043.
Oxton *Notts.* ***Village***, 4m/7km NW of Lowdham. **51 J7** SK6251.
Oxton *Sc.Bord.* ***Village***, 4m/7km NW of Lauder. Site of Roman fort 1km N. **76 C5** NT4953.
Oxwich *Swan.* ***Village***, on Gower peninsula, 11m/17km W of Swansea. Sands of the bay, with sand dunes and marshes inland, form Oxwich Nature Reserve. 16c Oxwich Castle (Cadw) to SE. **17 J6** SS4986.
Oxwich Bay *Swan.* ***Bay***, extends NE of Oxwich Point to Great Tor, on S coast of Gower peninsula. **17 J6** SS4986.
Oxwich Castle *Swan.* ***Castle***, 16c manor (Cadw), with remains of 14c buildings, at SE side of Oxwich. **17 J6** SS5086.
Oxwich Green *Swan.* ***Hamlet***, on Gower peninsula, 1km S of Oxwich. **17 J6** SS4986.
Oxwick *Norf.* ***Settlement***, 3m/5km S of Fakenham. **44 D3** TF9125.
Oykel *High.* ***River***, in Sutherland district rising S of Ben More Assynt and running SE to Oykel Bridge, then E down Strath Oykel to join River Shin in Kyle of Sutherland, 4m/6km NW of Bonar Bridge. **95 K1** NH5796.
Oykel Bridge *High.* ***Bridge***, road bridge over River Oykel in Sutherland district 13m/21km W of Lairg. **95 K1** NC3800.
Oykel Forest *High.* ***Forest/woodland***, in Sutherland district 7m/11km W of Lairg. **96 B1** NC4802.
Oyne *Aber.* ***Village***, 7m/11km NW of Inverurie. **90 E2** NJ6725.
Oystermouth *Swan.* ***Suburb***, chief locality in The Mumbles district of Swansea, 4m/7km SW of Swansea city centre across bay. Castle dates from late 13c. SS6188.
Oystermouth Castle *Swan.* ***Castle***, remains of late 13c castle, 1km NW of The Mumbles. **17 K6** SS6188.
Ozleworth *Glos.* ***Settlement***, 2m/4km E of Wotton-under-Edge. **20 A2** ST7993.

P

Pabaidh Mòr (Anglicised form: Pabay Mòr.) *W.Isles* ***Island***, uninhabited island in West Loch Roag, 3m/5km E of Gallan Head, Isle of Lewis. **100 D4** NB1038.
Pabaigh *W.Isles Gaelic form of Pabbay, qv.*
Pabail Iarach (Anglicised form: Lower Bayble.) *W.Isles* ***Village***, on Eye Peninsula, Isle of Lewis, 1m/2km S of Garrabost. Adjacent to Pabail Uarach. **101 H4** NB5231.
Pabail Uarach (Anglicised form: Upper Bayble.) *W.Isles* ***Village***, on Eye Peninsula, Isle of Lewis, 1m/2km SE of Garrabost. Adjacent to Pabail Iarach. **101 H4** NB5231.
Pabay *High.* ***Island***, low-lying island of 360 acres or 145 hectares, sparsely inhabited, 3m/4km NE of Broadford, Skye. **86 C2** NG6727.
Pabay Beag *W.Isles* ***Island***, small uninhabited island in West Loch Roag, 3m/5km E of Gallan Head, Isle of Lewis. NB1038.
Pabay Mòr *W.Isles Anglicised form of Pabaidh Mòr, qv.*
Pabbay *W.Isles* ***Island***, uninhabited island at N end of Sound of Harris 5m/8km SW of Toe Head. Pabbay measures 3m/4km by nearly 2m/3km and rises to a height of 642 feet or 196 metres. **92 D3** NF8988.
Pabbay (Gaelic form: Pabaigh.) *W.Isles* ***Island***, uninhabited island of about 560 acres or 225 hectares midway between Mingulay and Sandray. **84 A6** NL6087.
Pachesham *Surr.* ***Locality***, 1m/2km NW of Leatherhead. TQ1558.
Packington *Leics.* ***Village***, 1m/2km S of Ashby de la Zouch. **41 F4** SK3614.
Packmoor *Stoke* ***Locality***, 2m/3km N of Tunstall. SJ8654.
Packmores *Warks.* ***Suburb***, N district of Warwick. SP2865.
Packwood *W.Mid.* ***Settlement***, 1m/2km E of Hockley Heath. SP1773.
Packwood House *Warks.* ***Historic house***, Tudor house (National Trust) with 17c additions, 2m/3km E of Hockley Heath. **30 C1** SP1772.
Padanaram *Angus* ***Village***, 2m/3km W of Forfar. **83 F2** NO4251.
Padarn Country Park *Gwyn.* ***Leisure/recreation***, 320 acre country park on NE shore of Llyn Padarn, 1km NE of Llanberis across lake. Focal point is now defunct Dinorwig slate quarries, one of largest in world. **46 D6** SH5860.
Padbury *Bucks.* ***Village***, 3m/4km SE of Buckingham. **31 J5** SP7230.
Paddaburn Moor *Northumb.* ***Open space***, wooded area on W side of Wark Forest, 6m/9km NE of Bewcastle. **70 B6** NY6479.
Paddington *Gt.Lon.* ***Suburb***, in City of Westminster, 3m/4km NW of Charing Cross. **23 F3** TQ2681.
Paddington *Warr.* ***Suburb***, 1m/2km E of Warrington town centre. SJ6389.
Paddlesworth *Kent* ***Village***, 3m/5km NW of Folkestone. **15 G3** TR1939.
Paddock *Kent* ***Settlement***, 3m/4km E of Charing. TQ9950.
Paddock *W.Yorks.* ***Suburb***, 1m/2km W of Huddersfield town centre. SE1216.
Paddock Wood *Kent* Population: 6694. ***Small town***, industrial town, 5m/8km E of Tonbridge. Annual Hop Festival. **23 K7** TQ6645.
Paddockhaugh *Moray* ***Settlement***, on E side of River Lossie, 3m/4km S of Elgin. **97 K6** NJ2058.
Paddockhole *D. & G.* ***Settlement***, at bridge over Water of Milk, 3m/4km NE of Bankshill. **69 H5** NY2383.
Paddolgreen *Shrop.* ***Settlement***, 2m/4km N of Wem. **38 E2** SJ5032.
Padeswood *Flints.* ***Settlement***, 3m/4km E of Mold. **48 B6** SJ2762.
Padfield *Derbys.* ***Hamlet***, 1m/2km N of Glossop. SK0396.
Padgate *Warr.* ***Suburb***, 2m/3km NE of Warrington town centre. SJ6390.
Padiham *Lancs.* Population: 12,570. ***Town***, 3m/4km W of Burnley. Former cotton town, with typically terraced streets. Jacobean mansion of Gawthorpe Hall (National Trust) 1m/2km E. **56 C6** SD7933.
Padnal Fen *Cambs.* ***Open space***, fenland 3m/5km NE of Ely. **43 J7** TL5782.
Padon Hill *Northumb.* ***Mountain***, with monument, to E of Blackburn Common, 4m/7km W of Otterburn. Height 1243 feet or 379 metres. **70 D4** NY8192.
Padside *N.Yorks.* ***Settlement***, 4m/6km S of Pateley Bridge. **57 G4** SE1659.
Padside Green *N.Yorks.* ***Settlement***, 3m/4km N of Blubberhouses. SE1659.
Padstow *Cornw.* Population: 2460. ***Small town***, and resort on hillside overlooking estuary of River Camel near N coast, 5m/8km NW of Wadebridge. Many medieval buildings around harbour. 16c Court House of Sir Walter Raleigh. **3 G1** SW9175.
Padstow Bay *Cornw.* ***Bay***, to N of Padstow, extending SW from Pentire Point to Stepper Point. **3 G1** SW9279.
Padworth *W.Berks.* ***Village***, 8m/12km SW of Reading. **21 K5** SU6166.
Paganhill *Glos.* ***Suburb***, W district of Stroud. SO8405.
Page Bank *Dur.* ***Settlement***, on N bank of River Wear, 2m/3km NW of Spennymoor. NZ2335.
Page Moss *Mersey.* ***Suburb***, 5m/8km NE of Liverpool city centre. SJ4291.
Page's Green *Suff.* ***Locality***, 2m/3km NW of Debenham. TM1465.
Pagham *W.Suss.* ***Village***, 4m/6km W of Bognor Regis. **12 B7** SZ8897.
Paglesham Churchend *Essex* ***Village***, 4m/6km NE of Rochford. **25 F2** TQ9293.
Paglesham Eastend *Essex* ***Hamlet***, 5m/7km E of Rochford. **25 F2** TQ9492.
Paibeil (Anglicised form: Paible.) *W.Isles* ***Settlement***, near W coast of North Uist, 3m/5km SE of Aird an Rùnair. **92 C5** NF7367.
Paible *W.Isles Anglicised form of Paibeil, qv.*
Paible *W.Isles* ***Settlement***, on SE coast of Tarasaigh. **93 F2** NG0299.
Paignton *Torbay* Population: 42,989. ***Town***, and resort on Tor Bay with harbour and pier, 3m/5km SW of Torquay. Sandy beaches. Tourist attractions include Paignton Zoo and Paignton and Dartmouth Railway. **5 J4** SX8960.
Paignton and Dartmouth Steam Railway *Devon* ***Other feature of interest***, tourist railway which runs for 7m/11km N from Kingswear to Paignton, connecting with ferry crossing to Dartmouth. **5 J5** SX8851.
Paignton Zoo *Torbay* ***Leisure/recreation***, 75 acre zoo to SW of Paignton town centre, with emphasis on conservation and containing over 60 endangered species. **5 J5** SX8759.
Pailton *Warks.* ***Village***, 5m/7km NW of Rugby. **41 G7** SP4781.
Paine's Cross *E.Suss.* ***Settlement***, 1m/2km W of Burwash Common. TQ6223.
Paines Hill *Surr.* ***Settlement***, 1m/2km S of Limpsfield. TQ4151.
Painleyhill *Staffs.* ***Settlement***, 4m/6km W of Uttoxeter. SK0333.
Painscastle (Castell-paen). *Powys* ***Village***, 4m/7km NW of Hay-on-Wye. Site of Norman castle rebuilt in 13c. **28 A4** SO1646.
Painscastle Castle *Powys* ***Historic/prehistoric site***, 12c motte and bailey castle rebuilt in 13c, 4m/7km NW of Hay-on-Wye. Only earthworks remain. **28 A4** SO1646.
Painshawfield *Northumb.* Population: 3033. ***Suburb***, 3m/4km SW of Prudhoe. **71 F7** NZ0660.
Painsthorpe *E.Riding* ***Hamlet***, on hillside, 1km E of Kirby Underdale and 4m/6km W of Fridaythorpe. SE8158.
Painswick *Glos.* Population: 1628. ***Small town***, built of Cotswold stone, 3m/5km NE of Stroud. Site of Roman villa 1km NW. **20 B1** SO8609.
Painter's Forstal *Kent* ***Hamlet***, 2m/4km SW of Faversham. TQ9958.
Painter's Green *Herts.* ***Hamlet***, adjoining to S of Datchworth, 3m/5km NE of Welwyn. TL2718.
Painthorpe *W.Yorks.* ***Locality***, adjoining to S of Crigglestone. SE3115.
Pairc *W.Isles Gaelic form of Park, qv.*
Paisley *Renf.* Population: 75,526. ***Town***, 7m/11km W of Glasgow. Originally a monastic settlement, with its first church built in 12c; rebuilt 13c church now restored. Formerly known for its linen production, then as a cotton and silk town. University. **74 C4** NS4864.
Paisley Abbey *Renf.* ***Ecclesiastical building***, Cluniac Abbey church founded in Paisley town centre in 1163 and restored following destruction on orders of Edward I. **74 C4** NS4863.
Paisley Museum and Art Gallery *Renf.* ***Other feature of interest***, in Paisley town centre, with collection of shawls, exhibitions on local industrial and natural history, and 19c Scottish art gallery. **74 C4** NS4764.
Pakefield *Suff.* ***Suburb***, S district of Lowestoft. **45 K6** TM5390.
Pakenham *Suff.* ***Village***, 2m/3km S of Ixworth. **34 D2** TL9267.
Palace Fields *Ches.* ***Suburb***, to E of Runcorn town centre. SJ5481.
Palace of Holyroodhouse *Edin.* ***Historic house***, chief royal residence of Scotland dating from 16c, located below Holyrood Park at E end of Royal Mile in Edinburgh city centre. Remains of Holyrood Abbey in grounds. **76 A3** NT2773.
Palace of Spynie *Moray* ***Historic/prehistoric site***, 15c fortress (Historic Scotland) of Bishops of Moray, now in ruins, 3m/4km S of Lossiemouth. Includes 15c David's Tower overlooking Spynie Loch and Moray Firth. **97 K5** NJ2365.
Palacerigg Country Park *N.Lan.* ***Leisure/recreation***, 700 acre country park, 2m/3km SE of Cumbernauld. Home to wide variety of animals from Scotland and N Europe, also wild population of bison, lynx and wildcats. **75 F3** NS7873.
Pale *Gwyn.* ***Settlement***, 1km S of Llandderfel across River Dee. **37 J2** SH9836.
Palehouse Common *E.Suss.* ***Settlement***, 2m/3km SE of Uckfield. TQ4918.

Palestine *Hants.* ***Settlement***, 1m/2km SW of Grateley and 7m/11km SW of Andover. **21 F7** SU2640.
Paley Street *W. & M.* ***Village***, 3m/5km S of Maidenhead. **22 B4** SU8776.
Palfrey *W.Mid.* ***Suburb***, in S part of Walsall. SP0197.
Palgowan *D. & G.* ***Settlement***, on E side of Glentrool Forest, 3m/5km N of Glentrool Village. **67 H5** NX3783.
Palgrave *Suff.* ***Village***, 1m/2km S of Diss. **35 F1** TM1178.
Pallant House *W.Suss.* ***Historic house***, Queen Anne house in Chichester built for local wine merchant, Henry Peckham, in 1712. Includes Edwardian kitchens and a gallery which includes wide collection of modern British art. **12 B6** SU8603.
Pallinsburn House *Northumb.* ***Settlement***, surrounded by parkland, 3m/4km E of Cornhill on Tweed. **77 G7** NT8939.
Pallion *T. & W.* ***Suburb***, 1m/2km W of Sunderland city centre. NZ3757.
Palmarsh *Kent* ***Suburb***, 2m/3km W of Hythe. TR1333.
Palmer Moor *Derbys.* ***Settlement***, 2m/3km NW of Sudbury. SK1333.
Palmers Cross *Surr.* ***Settlement***, 4m/6km SE of Godalming. TQ0240.
Palmer's Flat *Glos.* ***Locality***, 1m/2km SE of Coleford. SO5809.
Palmers Green *Gt.Lon.* ***Suburb***, in borough of Enfield, 2m/4km S of Enfield town centre and 8m/13km N of Charing Cross. TQ3193.
Palmer's Green *Kent* ***Settlement***, 1km E of Brenchley. TQ6841.
Palmerscross *Moray* ***Settlement***, on SW side of Elgin. **97 K5** NJ2061.
Palmerstown *V. of Glam.* ***Locality***, 2m/3km NE of Barry. **18 E5** ST1369.
Palmersville *T. & W.* ***Locality***, adjoining to NE of Longbenton. NZ2870.
Palnackie *D. & G.* ***Village***, 3m/5km S of Dalbeattie. **65 J5** NX8256.
Palnure *D. & G.* ***Settlement***, 3m/5km SE of Newton Stewart. **64 E4** NX4563.
Palnure Burn *D. & G.* ***River***, rising to S of Clatteringshaws Loch and flowing SW, then S into River Cree at Muirfad Flow 3m/5km SE of Newton Stewart. **64 E4** NX4562.
Palterton *Derbys.* ***Village***, 1m/2km S of Bolsover. **51 G6** SK4768.
Pamber End *Hants.* ***Hamlet***, 4m/7km N of Basingstoke. **21 K6** SU6158.
Pamber Green *Hants.* ***Village***, 5m/9km N of Basingstoke. **21 K6** SU6059.
Pamber Heath *Hants.* ***Village***, 7m/11km N of Basingstoke. **21 K5** SU6162.
Pamington *Glos.* ***Hamlet***, 3m/5km E of Tewkesbury. **29 J5** SO9433.
Pamphill *Dorset* ***Village***, 1m/2km W of Wimborne Minster. 17c house of Kingston Lacy in parkland to NW. **9 J4** ST9800.
Pampisford *Cambs.* ***Village***, 4m/6km N of Great Chesterford. **33 H4** TL4948.
Pan *Ork.* ***Settlement***, on S side of Pan Hope, Flotta. **107 C8** ND3794.
Panborough *Som.* ***Hamlet***, 3m/5km SE of Wedmore. **19 H7** ST4745.
Panbride *Angus* ***Village***, 1km N of Carnoustie. **83 G4** NO5634.
Pancrasweek *Devon* ***Hamlet***, 3m/5km NW of Holsworthy. **6 A5** SS2805.
Pancross *V. of Glam.* ***Hamlet***, 1km N of Penmark. ST0469.
Pandy *Gwyn.* ***Hamlet***, 3m/5km NE of Tywyn. **37 F5** SH6203.
Pandy *Gwyn.* ***Locality***, adjoining to SE of Llanuwchllyn. SH8729.
Pandy *Mon.* ***Village***, 6m/9km N of Abergavenny. **28 C6** SO3322.
Pandy *Powys* ***Settlement***, 1m/2km N of Llanbrynmair. **37 J5** SH9004.
Pandy *Wrex.* ***Hamlet***, 4m/7km S of Llangollen. **38 A2** SJ1935.
Pandy Tudur *Conwy* ***Hamlet***, 4m/6km NE of Llanrwst. **47 G6** SH8564.
Pandy'r Capel *Denb.* ***Settlement***, 1m/2km W of Llanelidan. SJ0850.
Panfield *Essex* ***Village***, 2m/3km NW of Braintree. **34 B6** TL7325.
Pang *W.Berks.* ***River***, rising N of Hampstead Norris and flowing into River Thames at Pangbourne. **21 J4** SU6376.
Pangbourne *W.Berks.* Population: 2522. ***Small town***, on River Thames 6m/9km NW of Reading. Nautical College 1m/2km SW. **21 K4** SU6376.
Pannal *N.Yorks.* Population: 2787. ***Village***, 2m/4km S of Harrogate. **57 J4** SE3051.
Pannal Ash *N.Yorks.* ***Suburb***, 2m/3km SW of Harrogate town centre. SE2952.
Pannanich Hill *Aber.* ***Mountain***, 2m/3km SE of Ballater. Height 1971 feet or 601 metres. **90 B5** NO3895.
Panpunton *Shrop.* ***Settlement***, just N of Knighton across River Teme. **28 B1** SO2872.
Panshanger *Herts.* ***Suburb***, E district of Welwyn Garden City. TL2513.
Pant *Essex* ***River***, rising to E of Saffron Walden and flowing SE through Great Bardfield and Shalford to Braintree, where it becomes River Blackwater. TL7624.
Pant *Shrop.* ***Village***, 5m/7km S of Oswestry. **38 B3** SJ2722.
Pant *Wrex.* ***Locality***, 1m/2km NW of Ruabon. **38 B1** SJ2946.
Pant *Wrex.* ***Suburb***, adjoining to NE of Gresford. SJ3555.
Pant-glas *Gwyn.* ***Hamlet***, 9m/15km S of Caernarfon. **36 D1** SH4747.
Pant Gwyn *Gwyn.* ***Settlement***, 3m/4km SW of Llanuwchllyn. **37 H3** SH8426.
Pant-lasau *Swan.* ***Settlement***, 5m/8km N of Swansea. **17 K4** SN6500.
Pant Mawr *Powys* ***Locality***, on River Wye, 4m/7km NW of Llangurig. **37 H7** SN8482.
Pant-pastynog *Denb.* ***Settlement***, 3m/4km S of Denbigh. **47 J6** SJ0461.
Pant Sychbant *R.C.T.* ***Valley***, carrying stream E into River Taf Fawr, 4m/6km NE of Hirwaun. Caves to E and W of valley. **18 C1** SN9709.
Pant-teg *Torfaen Welsh form of Panteg, qv.*
Pant-y-dwr *Powys* ***Village***, 4m/7km N of Rhayader. **27 J1** SN9874.
Pant-y-ffridd *Powys* ***Settlement***, 2m/4km NW of Aberriw. **38 A5** SJ1502.
Pant y Wacco *Flints.* ***Hamlet***, 3m/4km W of Holywell. SJ1476.
Pantasaph *Flints.* ***Village***, Roman Catholic model village, with 19c Franciscan monastery, 2m/3km W of Holywell. **47 K5** SJ1575.
Pantasaph Friary *Flints.* ***Ecclesiastical building***, Roman Catholic community founded in 1852, 2m/3km SW of Holywell. Includes church and Franciscan friary. **47 K5** SJ1676.
Panteg (Pant-teg). *Torfaen* ***Settlement***, 2m/3km SE of Pontypool. ST3199.
Pantersbridge *Cornw.* ***Hamlet***, 6m/9km E of Bodmin. SX1568.
Pantglas *Powys* ***Settlement***, 3m/4km SE of Machynlleth. **37 G6** SN7798.
Pantgwyn *Carmar.* ***Settlement***, 3m/4km SE of Llanfynydd. SN5925.
Pantgwyn *Cere.* ***Settlement***, 4m/6km E of Cardigan. **26 B4** SN2445.
Pantllwyd *Powys* ***Mountain***, 3m/4km N of head of Claerwen Reservoir. Height 1797 feet or 548 metres. **27 H1** SN8370.
Pantmawr *Cardiff* ***Suburb***, 4m/6km NW of Cardiff city centre. ST1481.
Panton *Lincs.* ***Hamlet***, 3m/5km E of Wragby. **52 E5** TF1778.
Pantperthog *Gwyn.* ***Locality***, 2m/4km N of Machynlleth. **37 G5** SH7404.
Pantyffordd *Flints.* ***Settlement***, 1m/2km SW of Treuddyn. **48 B7** SJ2457.
Pantyffynnon *Carmar.* ***Locality***, adjoining to S of Ammanford. **17 K3** SN6210.
Pantygasseg *Torfaen* ***Settlement***, 2m/3km W of Pontypool. ST2599.
Pantygelli *Mon.* ***Hamlet***, 3m/4km N of Abergavenny. SO3017.
Pantymenyn *Carmar.* ***Locality***, 2m/3km NW of Login. SN1426.
Pantymwyn *Flints.* ***Hamlet***, 3m/4km W of Mold. SJ1964.
Pantyscallog *M.Tyd.* ***Locality***, 2m/3km NE of Merthyr Tydfil. SO0609.
Panxworth *Norf.* ***Hamlet***, 4m/6km NW of Acle. **45 H4** TG3413.
Pap of Glencoe (Also known as Sgorr na Ciche.) *High.* ***Mountain***, in Lochaber district nearly 2m/3km E of foot of Glen Coe. Height 2434 feet or 742 metres. **80 C2** NN1259.
Papa *Shet.* ***Island***, small uninhabited island on E side of island of Oxna and 2m/4km W of Scalloway, Mainland. **109 C9** HU3637.
Papa Little *Shet.* ***Island***, situated between Muckle Roe and Mainland, 2m/3km N to S and 1km E to W. **109 C6** HU3360.
Papa Sound *Ork.* ***Sea feature***, sea channel between islands of Westray and Papa Westray. **106 D2** HY4751.
Papa Stour *Shet.* ***Island***, inhabited island 1m/2km off W coast of Mainland at SW end of St. Magnus Bay. It is roughly 3m/4km E to W and 2m/3km N to S, separated from Mainland by Sound of Papa, 1m/2km wide. Coastline noted for caves. **109 A6** HU1760.
Papa Stour Airstrip *Shet.* ***Airport/airfield***, to S of Biggings, on Papa Stour. **109 A6** HU1760.
Papa Stronsay *Ork.* ***Island***, off NE coast of Stronsay, separated from it by Papa Sound. Lighthouse on far side of island. **106 F5** HY6629.
Papa Westray (Papay). *Ork.* ***Island***, N and E of Westray across Papa Sound. It is some 3m/5km N to S and from 1km to 1m/2km E to W. **106 E2** HY4952.
Papa Westray Airfield *Ork.* ***Airport/airfield***, to N of Holland, Papa Westray. **106 D2** HY4852.
Papay *Ork. See Papa Westray.*
Papcastle *Cumb.* ***Village***, 1m/2km NW of Cockermouth across River Derwent. Site of Roman fort of Derventio. **60 C3** NY1031.
Paphrie Burn *Angus* ***River***, stream which flows NE on N side of Hill of Menuir to join West Water 1km S of Bridgend. **83 G1** NO5467.
Papil *Shet.* ***Settlement***, on West Burra, 3m/4km S of Hamnavoe. HU3631.
Papley *Ork.* ***Locality***, on E side of South Ronaldsay, 2m/3km SE of St. Margaret's Hope. ND4691.
Papple *E.Loth.* ***Settlement***, 3m/5km S of East Linton. **76 D3** NT5972.
Papplewick *Notts.* ***Village***, 1m/2km NE of Hucknall. **51 H7** SK5451.
Paps of Jura *Arg. & B.* ***Inland physical feature***, three highest peaks of mountain ridge of Jura, situated 5m/8km N of Craighouse. Peaks are Beinn an Oir, Beinn Shiantaidh and Beinn a' Chaol. **72 C3** NR5074.
Papworth Everard *Cambs.* ***Village***, 6m/10km SE of Huntingdon. **33 F2** TL2862.
Papworth St. Agnes *Cambs.* ***Village***, 5m/8km SE of Huntingdon. **33 F2** TL2664.
Par *Cornw.* Population: 4418. ***Small town***, resort and port 4m/6km E of St. Austell. **4 A5** SX0753.
Paradise *Som.* ***Locality***, on W side of Glastonbury. ST4938.
Paradise *Staffs.* ***Locality***, 1m/2km SE of Coven. SJ9206.
Paradise *Tel. & W.* ***Locality***, 1km N of Ironbridge. SJ6704.
Paradise Copse *Devon See Clyst Hydon.*
Paradise Wildlife Park *Herts.* ***Leisure/recreation***, wildlife park 2m/3km SW of Hoddesdon. **23 G1** TL3306.
Parallel Roads of Glen Roy *High. See Glen Roy.*
Paramour Street *Kent* ***Locality***, 3m/5km NW of Sandwich. TR2861.
Parbold *Lancs.* Population: 2872. ***Village***, 7m/11km NW of Wigan. **48 D1** SD4910.
Parbrook *Som.* ***Village***, 5m/8km SE of Glastonbury. **8 E1** ST5636.
Parbrook *W.Suss.* ***Hamlet***, 1km S of Billingshurst. TQ0825.
Parc *Gwyn.* ***Hamlet***, 4m/6km SW of Bala. **37 H2** SH8733.
Parc Cefn Onn *Caerp.* ***Leisure/recreation***, country park with 200 acres of open country and wooded hillside, 2m/3km SE of Caerphilly. Noted for rhododendrons and azaleas. **18 E3** ST1784.
Parc le Breos Burial Chamber *Swan.* ***Historic/prehistoric site***, burial-chamber (Cadw) on Gower peninsula, to NW of Parkmill. **17 J6** SS5389.
Parc-Seymour *Newport* ***Village***, 3m/5km N of Magor. ST4091.
Parc-y-rhôs *Carmar.* ***Settlement***, 1m/2km S of Lampeter. SN5745.
Parciau *I.o.A.* ***Locality***, near E coast of Anglesey, 1m/2km N of Brynteg. SH4984.
Parcllyn *Cere.* ***Hamlet***, 1m/2km W of Aberporth. **26 B3** SN2451.
Parcrhydderch *Cere.* ***Settlement***, 1m/2km SW of Llangeitho. **27 F3** SN6058.
Pardown *Hants.* ***Locality***, 1m/2km SE of Oakley. SU5749.
Pardshaw *Cumb.* ***Hamlet***, 4m/7km SW of Cockermouth. **60 B4** NY0924.
Parham *Suff.* ***Village***, 2m/4km SE of Framlingham. 1km SE, Moat Hall, 15c moated manor house. **35 H2** TM3060.
Parham *W.Suss.* ***Historic house***, Tudor house in large park below South Downs, 2m/3km W of Storrington. **12 D5** TQ0614.
Paris *W.Yorks.* ***Locality***, 1m/2km SE of Holmfirth. SE1507.
Parish Holm *S.Lan.* ***Settlement***, 3m/5km W of Glespin. **68 C1** NS7628.
Park *Aber.* ***Locality***, 4m/6km SW of Peterculter. NO7898.
Park *Aber.* ***Settlement***, 1km S of Cornhill. **98 D5** NJ5857.
Park *N.Lincs.* ***Locality***, adjoining to N of Westwoodside. SE7400.
Park (Gaelic: Pairc.) *W.Isles* ***Locality***, in SE part of Isle of Lewis, between Loch Erisort and Loch Seaforth. **100 E7** NB3212.
Park Bridge *Gt.Man.* ***Suburb***, 2m/3km N of Ashton-under-Lyne town centre. SD9402.
Park Burn *D. & G.* ***River***, flowing N from Locharbriggs to join Water of Ae, 1m/2km W of Parkgate. **68 E5** NX9987.
Park Close *Lancs.* ***Hamlet***, 1m/2km S of Barnoldswick. SD8844.
Park Corner *B. & N.E.Som.* ***Hamlet***, 1km SW of Freshford and 4m/6km SE of Bath. ST7859.
Park Corner *E.Suss.* ***Settlement***, 1m/2km SE of Groombridge. TQ5336.
Park Corner *Oxon.* ***Settlement***, 1m/2km N of Nettlebed. **21 K3** SU6988.
Park Corner *W. & M.* ***Locality***, 2m/4km NW of Maidenhead. SU8583.
Park End *Beds.* ***Settlement***, adjoining to E of Stevington, 4m/7km NW of Bedford. SP9953.
Park End *Cambs.* ***Settlement***, S end of Swaffham Bulbeck. TL5561.
Park End *Middbro.* ***Suburb***, 2m/4km SE of Middlesbrough town centre. NZ5117.
Park End *Northumb.* ***Settlement***, on W side of River North Tyne, 1m/2km SE of Wark. **70 D6** NY8675.
Park End *Staffs.* ***Settlement***, 1m/2km NW of Audley. SJ7851.
Park End *Worcs.* ***Settlement***, 2m/3km SW of Bewdley. SO7673.
Park Farm *Worcs.* ***Suburb***, 2m/3km SE of Redditch town centre. SP0665.
Park Gate *Hants.* ***Village***, 4m/7km NW of Fareham. **11 G4** SU5108.
Park Gate *W.Yorks.* ***Hamlet***, just N of Skelmanthorpe. SE2311.
Park Gate *W.Yorks.* ***Suburb***, SW district of Guiseley. SE1841.
Park Gate *Worcs.* ***Settlement***, 2m/3km W of Bromsgrove. SO9371.
Park Green *Suff.* ***Settlement***, 3m/4km NW of Debenham. TM1364.
Park Head *Cornw.* ***Coastal feature***, headland (National Trust) on N coast, 4m/6km S of Trevose Head. **3 F1** SW8470.
Park Head *Cumb.* ***Locality***, on S bank of Raven Beck, 2m/3km E of Kirkoswald. NY5841.
Park Head *Derbys.* ***Settlement***, 1km E of Crich. SK3654.
Park Head *W.Yorks.* ***Hamlet***, 2m/3km W of Denby Dale. SE1908.
Park Hill *Lancs.* ***Suburb***, 1m/2km NW of Burnley town centre. SD8133.
Park Hill *S.Yorks.* ***Suburb***, 1km E of Sheffield city centre. SK3687.
Park Lane *Bucks.* ***Locality***, 3m/5km W of High Wycombe. SU8192.
Park Lane *Wrex.* ***Settlement***, 1km SE of Penley. **38 D2** SJ4239.
Park Langley *Gt.Lon.* ***Suburb***, in borough of Bromley, 2m/3km SW of Bromley town centre. Langley Park to S, with golf course. TQ3867.
Park Mill *W.Yorks.* ***Locality***, adjoining to N of Clayton West. SE2611.
Park Royal *Gt.Lon.* ***Suburb***, in borough of Brent, 7m/11km W of Charing Cross. TQ1982.
Park Side *S.Yorks.* ***Suburb***, on S side of Stannington, 3m/5km NW of Sheffield city centre. SK3088.
Park Street *Herts.* ***Hamlet***, 2m/3km S of St. Albans. **22 E1** TL1404.
Park Town *Oxon.* ***Suburb***, 1m/2km N of Oxford city centre. SP5107.
Park Village *W.Mid.* ***Suburb***, 1m/2km NE of Wolverhampton town centre. SJ9200.

P

Parkbroom *Cumb.* ***Settlement***, 3m/4km NE of Carlisle. NY4358.

Parkend *Cumb.* ***Settlement***, 1m/2km SW of Caldbeck. **60 D3** NY3038.

Parkend *Glos.* ***Village***, 4m/6km N of Lydney. **19 K1** SO6108.

Parker's Green *Kent* ***Hamlet***, 2m/3km NE of Tonbridge. TQ6148.

Parkeston *Essex* ***Village***, on S side of River Stour estuary, 1m/2km W of Harwich. **35 G5** TM2332.

Parkfield *Bucks.* ***Suburb***, S part of Princes Risborough. SP8002.

Parkfield *Cornw.* ***Settlement***, 5m/7km NE of Liskeard. SX3167.

Parkfield *S.Glos.* ***Settlement***, 4m/6km SW of Chipping Sodbury. ST6977.

Parkfield *W.Mid.* ***Suburb***, S district of Wolverhampton. SO9296.

Parkfield *Worcs.* ***Locality***, 2m/3km NW of Worcester. SO8257.

Parkford *Angus* ***Settlement***, 2m/3km SW of Finavon. **83 F2** NO4754.

Parkgate *Ches.* ***Locality***, 4m/6km SE of Knutsford. SJ7874.

Parkgate *Ches.* ***Suburb***, 1m/2km NW of Neston. **48 B5** SJ2778.

Parkgate *Cumb.* ***Locality***, 1km SW of Waverton, on opposite side of River Waver. NY2146.

Parkgate *D. & G.* ***Locality***, 5m/8km NW of Lochmaben. **69 F5** NY0187.

Parkgate *Kent* ***Settlement***, 2m/3km W of Tenterden. TQ8534.

Parkgate *S.Yorks.* ***Suburb***, 2m/3km N of Rotherham. **51 G3** SK4395.

Parkgate *Surr.* ***Hamlet***, 4m/7km SE of Dorking. **23 F7** TQ2043.

Parkhall *Renf.* ***Suburb***, 2m/3km NW of Clydebank. NS4872.

Parkhall Country Park *Staffs.* ***Leisure/recreation***, 300 acre country park of heath, woodland and pools 3m/5km E of Stoke-on-Trent city centre. Attracts wide variety of wildlife. **40 B1** SJ9244.

Parkham *Devon* ***Village***, 5m/8km SW of Bideford. **6 B3** SS3821.

Parkham Ash *Devon* ***Hamlet***, 1m/2km W of Parkham, 4m/6km SE of Clovelly. **6 B3** SS3620.

Parkhead *Cumb.* ***Locality***, on E side of River Caldew, 3m/4km S of Welton and 7m/11km SE of Wigton. NY3340.

Parkhead *Glas.* ***Suburb***, 2m/4km E of Glasgow city centre. NS6163.

Parkhead *S.Yorks.* ***Suburb***, 3m/5km SW of Sheffield city centre. SK3183.

Parkhill *Angus* ***Settlement***, 3m/4km N of Arbroath. **83 H3** NO6445.

Parkhill *Notts.* ***Hamlet***, 1km S of Southwell. SK6952.

Parkhill *P. & K.* ***Settlement***, 1m/2km NE of Blairgowrie. **82 C3** NO1846.

Parkhouse *Glas.* ***Suburb***, 2m/3km N of Glasgow city centre. NS5968.

Parkhouse *Mon.* ***Settlement***, 6m/9km S of Monmouth. **19 J1** SO4902.

Parkhouse Green *Derbys.* ***Hamlet***, 2m/3km E of Clay Cross. SK4163.

Parkhurst *I.o.W.* ***Village***, 2m/3km N of Newport. HM Prison. **11 F5** SZ4991.

Parkhurst Forest *I.o.W.* ***Forest/woodland***, 3m/4km NW of Newport. **11 F5** SZ4691.

Parklands *W.Yorks.* ***Suburb***, 3m/4km N of Leeds city centre. SE2937.

Parkmill *Swan.* ***Village***, on Gower peninsula, 6m/9km W of Mumbles Head. **17 J6** SS5489.

Parkmore *Moray* ***Settlement***, 1m/2km NE of Dufftown. **98 B6** NJ3341.

Parkneuk *Aber.* ***Settlement***, 3m/5km NW of Inverbervie. **91 F7** NO7975.

Parkneuk *Fife* ***Suburb***, adjoining to NW of Dunfermline. NT0888.

Parkside *Cumb.* ***Locality***, 1km NE of Cleator Moor. NY0315.

Parkside *Dur.* ***Suburb***, SW district of Seaham. NZ4248.

Parkside *N.Lan.* ***Village***, 3m/4km N of Wishaw. NS8058.

Parkside *Wrex.* ***Settlement***, 2m/3km E of Gresford. SJ3855.

Parkstone *Poole* ***Suburb***, 1m/2km E of Poole town centre. **10 B5** SZ0391.

Parkway *Som.* ***Settlement***, 1km S of Marston Magna. ST5921.

Parkway *Suff.* ***Locality***, at NW edge of Haverhill. TL6646.

Parkwood Springs *S.Yorks.* ***Suburb***, 1m/2km N of Sheffield city centre. SK3489.

Parley Common *Dorset* ***Open space***, heath 1m/2km SE of Ferndown town centre. **10 B5** SZ0899.

Parley Cross *Dorset* ***Hamlet***, 1km SE of West Parley and 4m/7km N of Bournemouth. **10 B5** SZ0898.

Parley Green *Dorset* ***Settlement***, by N bank of River Stour, 1m/2km W of Bournemouth International Airport. SZ0997.

Parlick *Lancs.* ***Mountain***, on SW side of Forest of Bowland, 5m/8km N of Longridge. Height 1417 feet or 432 metres. **55 J5** SD5945.

Parlington *W.Yorks.* ***Settlement***, 2m/3km N of Garforth. SE4236.

Parnham *Dorset* ***Historic house***, Tudor mansion with 19c alterations by Nash, 1km S of Beaminster. Includes furniture workshop and school for craftsmen in wood. **8 D4** ST4700.

Parr Brow *Gt.Man.* ***Locality***, 1m/2km E of Tyldesley. SD7101.

Parr Fold *Gt.Man.* ***Locality***, adjoining to S of Walkden. SD7302.

Parracombe *Devon* ***Village***, on Exmoor, 4m/7km SW of Lynton. **6 E1** SS6645.

Parrett *Som.* ***River***, rising near Cheddington and flowing N to Langport, then NW through Bridgwater and into Bridgwater Bay to W of Burnham-on-Sea. **19 F7** ST2449.

Parrog *Pembs.* ***Locality***, 1km NW of Newport. **16 D1** SN0439.

Parson Cross *S.Yorks.* ***Suburb***, 3m/5km N of Sheffield city centre. SK3592.

Parson Drove *Cambs.* ***Village***, 6m/10km W of Wisbech. **43 G5** TF3708.

Parsonage Green *Essex* ***Suburb***, 2m/3km N of Chelmsford town centre. TL7010.

Parsonby *Cumb.* ***Hamlet***, 2m/3km S of Aspatria. **60 C3** NY1438.

Parsons *T. & W.* ***Locality***, industrial estate in NW part of Washington. NZ2957.

Parsons Green *Gt.Lon.* ***Suburb***, in S part of borough of Hammersmith and Fulham, NE of Putney Bridge. TQ2576.

Parson's Heath *Essex* ***Suburb***, 1m/2km NE of Colchester town centre. TM0126.

Parson's Hills *Derbys.* ***Locality***, 1km W of Repton. SK2926.

Partick *Glas.* ***Suburb***, 2m/3km W of Glasgow city centre. **74 D4** NS5567.

Partickhill *Glas.* ***Suburb***, 3m/4km NW of Glasgow city centre in Partick district. NS5566.

Partington *Gt.Man.* Population: 9109. ***Small town***, 4m/6km NW of Hale. Selected as overspill town in 1950s. **49 G3** SJ7191.

Partney *Lincs.* ***Village***, 2m/3km NE of Spilsby. **53 H6** TF4168.

Parton *Cumb.* ***Village***, on Parton Bay, adjoining to N of Whitehaven. Site of Roman fort to N. **60 A4** NX9720.

Parton *D. & G.* ***Village***, 7m/11km NW of Castle Douglas. **65 G3** NX6970.

Partridge Green *W.Suss.* ***Village***, 3m/4km SW of Cowfold. **12 E5** TQ1919.

Partrishow *Powys* ***Settlement***, in Black Mountains, 5m/8km N of Abergavenny. **28 B6** SO2722.

Parwich *Derbys.* ***Village***, 5m/8km N of Ashbourne. **50 D7** SK1854.

Parys Mountain *I.o.A.* ***Hill***, 2m/3km S of Amlwch. Earthworks mark sites of former copper mines, once world's largest. Windmill at summit. Height 482 feet or 147 metres. **46 C4** SH4490.

Paslow Wood Common *Essex* ***Settlement***, 2m/4km E of Chipping Ongar. TL5801.

Pass of Aberfoyle *Stir.* ***Other feature of interest***, road pass at NE end of Loch Ard, 3m/4km NW of Aberfoyle. **81 F7** NN4801.

Pass of Aberglaslyn *Gwyn.* ***Other feature of interest***, narrow part of River Glaslyn valley, below Beddgelert. **36 E1** SH5946.

Pass of Achray *Stir.* ***Other feature of interest***, section of narrow, steep-sided valley carrying Achray Water E from Loch Katrine to Loch Achray, 4m/6km NW of Aberfoyle. **81 F7** NN4806.

Pass of Balmaha *Stir.* ***Other feature of interest***, pass to W of Balmaha and to N of Craigie Fort, carrying road at height of 92 feet or 28 metres along E shore of Loch Lomond. **74 C1** NS4191.

Pass of Brander *Arg. & B.* ***Other feature of interest***, pass in Argyll, traversed by River Awe, running from foot of Loch Awe, on SW side of Ben Cruachan. **80 B5** NN0528.

Pass of Drumochter ***Other feature of interest***, mountain pass between Glen Truim and Glen Garry, 6m/9km S of Dalwhinnie. Carries the A9 road and the Perth-Inverness railway, the latter rising to 1484 feet or 452 metres, the summit of the British railway system. **88 D7** NN6275.

Pass of Glencoe *High.* ***Other feature of interest***, mountain pass carrying A82(T) between S slopes of A' Chailleach and N slopes of The Three Sisters, at head of Glen Coe, 3m/5km S of Kinlochleven. **80 C2** NN1557.

Pass of Killiecrankie *P. & K.* ***Other feature of interest***, narrow, wooded pass in valley of River Garry, 3m/4km NW of Pitlochry. Visitor centre gives information on local history and wildlife. **82 A1** NN9161.

Pass of Leny *Stir.* ***Other feature of interest***, wooded defile containing Falls of Leny, below Loch Lubnaig 2m/4km W of Callander. **81 G7** NN5908.

Pass of Llanberis *Gwyn.* ***Other feature of interest***, mountain pass between Snowdon and Glyder Fawr. **46 E7** SH5760.

Pass of Melfort *Arg. & B.* ***Other feature of interest***, mountain pass 1km N of Melfort. **79 K6** NM8414.

Passenham *Northants.* ***Village***, on River Great Ouse, 1km SW of Stony Stratford across river. **31 J5** SP7839.

Passfield *Hants.* ***Hamlet***, 2m/3km NW of Liphook. **12 B3** SU8234.

Passingford Bridge *Essex* ***Settlement***, 4m/7km SE of Epping. **23 H2** TQ5097.

Passmores *Essex* ***Suburb***, 1km S of Harlow town centre. TL4408.

Paston *Norf.* ***Hamlet***, near coast, 4m/6km NE of Walsham. **45 H2** TG3234.

Paston *Peter.* ***Suburb***, 2m/4km N of Peterborough city centre. TF1902.

Paston Green *Norf.* ***Settlement***, 1km E of Knapton. TG3133.

Paston Street *Norf.* ***Village***, adjoining to NW of Paston, 1m/2km S of Mundesley. TG3134.

Pasturefields *Staffs.* ***Settlement***, beside River Trent, 2m/3km SE of Weston. SJ9924.

Patchacott *Devon* ***Hamlet***, 7m/12km NW of Okehampton. SX4798.

Patcham *B. & H.* ***Suburb***, N district of Brighton. **13 G6** TQ3009.

Patchetts Green *Herts.* ***Settlement***, 2m/4km E of Watford. TQ1497.

Patching *W.Suss.* ***Village***, 5m/7km NW of Worthing. **12 D6** TQ0806.

Patchole *Devon* ***Settlement***, 7m/11km SE of Ilfracombe. **6 E1** SS6142.

Patchway *S.Glos.* ***Suburb***, 6m/9km N of Bristol. **19 J3** ST6082.

Pateley Bridge *N.Yorks.* ***Small town***, in Nidderdale 11m/18km NW of Harrogate. Disused lead mines on surrounding moors, and remains of Bronze Age settlements. **57 G3** SE1565.

Pateley Moor *N.Yorks.* ***Open space***, moorland 3m/4km NE of Pateley Bridge. **57 G3** SE1967.

Path Head *T. & W.* ***Locality***, 1km W of Blaydon. NZ1763.

Path of Condie *P. & K.* ***Hamlet***, 4m/6km SE of Dunning. **82 B6** NO0711.

Pathe *Som.* ***Hamlet***, 3m/5km SE of Westonzoyland. **8 C1** ST3730.

Pather *N.Lan.* ***Suburb***, S district of Wishaw. NS7954.

Pathfinder Village *Devon* ***Hamlet***, 4m/7km S of Crediton. **7 G6** SX8393.

Pathhead *Aber.* ***Settlement***, 1m/2km SW of St. Cyrus. **83 J1** NO7363.

Pathhead *E.Ayr.* ***Hamlet***, on N bank of River Nith, opposite New Cumnock. **68 B2** NS6114.

Pathhead *Fife* ***Locality***, district of Kirkcaldy, in vicinity of harbour. **76 A1** NT2892.

Pathhead *Midloth.* ***Village***, 4m/7km SE of Dalkeith. **76 B4** NT3964.

Pathlow *Warks.* ***Settlement***, 3m/4km NW of Stratford-upon-Avon. SP1758.

Pathstruie *P. & K.* ***Locality***, 4m/6km SE of Dunning. NO0711.

Patmore Heath *Herts.* ***Settlement***, 4m/6km NW of Bishop's Stortford. **33 H6** TL4425.

Patna *E.Ayr.* Population: 2387. ***Village***, on River Doon, 5m/8km NW of Dalmellington. **67 J2** NS4110.

Patney *Wilts.* ***Village***, 5m/8km SE of Devizes. **20 D6** SU0758.

Patrick *I.o.M.* ***Village***, 1m/2km S of Peel. **54 B5** SC2482.

Patrick Brompton *N.Yorks.* ***Village***, 3m/5km W of Bedale. **62 D7** SE2290.

Patricroft *Gt.Man.* ***Suburb***, to W of Eccles town centre. SJ7698.

Patrington *E.Riding* Population: 1943. ***Village***, 4m/6km SW of Withernsea. Large 14c cruciform church known as 'Queen of Holderness'. **59 K7** TA3122.

Patrixbourne *Kent* ***Village***, 3m/5km SE of Canterbury. **15 G2** TR1855.

Patshull *Staffs.* ***Settlement***, 7m/11km W of Wolverhampton. SJ8000.

Pattack *High.* ***River***, in Badenoch and Strathspey district, running N from Loch Pattack then turning W to head of Loch Laggan. **88 C6** NN5389.

Patterdale *Cumb.* ***Village***, 1km S of SW end of Ullswater. **60 E5** NY3915.

Pattingham *Staffs.* Population: 2283. ***Village***, 6m/9km W of Wolverhampton. **40 A6** SO8299.

Pattinson *T. & W.* ***Locality***, industrial estate in E part of Washington. Wildfowl refuge to E. NZ3255.

Pattishall *Northants.* ***Village***, 4m/6km N of Towcester. **31 H3** SP6754.

Pattiswick *Essex* ***Hamlet***, 3m/4km NW of Coggeshall. **34 C6** TL8124.

Patton *Cumb.* ***Locality***, 3m/5km NE of Kendal. SD5496.

Patton Bridge *Cumb.* ***Hamlet***, 1km S of Whinfell Tarn, 3m/5km NE of Kendal. SD5597.

Paul *Cornw.* ***Village***, on S side of Penzance. **2 B6** SW4627.

Paulerspury *Northants.* ***Village***, 3m/4km SE of Towcester. **31 J4** SP7145.

Paull *E.Riding* ***Village***, on E bank of River Humber, 2m/3km SW of Hedon. **59 H7** TA1626.

Paull Holme *E.Riding* ***Settlement***, 1m/2km SE of Paull. TA1824.

Paull Holme Sands *E.Riding* ***Coastal feature***, sandbank on N side of River Humber, 3m/5km S of Hedon. **59 H7** TA1823.

Paul's Dene *Wilts.* ***Suburb***, N district of Salisbury. SU1431.

Paul's Green *Cornw.* ***Settlement***, 3m/5km SE of Hayle. SW5933.

Paul's Hill *Moray* ***Mountain***, rising to over 450 metres, 4m/7km SW of Upper Knockando. **97 J7** NJ1140.

Paulsgrove *Ports.* ***Suburb***, below Ports Down 4m/6km N of Portsmouth city centre. SU6306.

Paulton *B. & N.E.Som.* Population: 4734. ***Village***, 2m/3km NW of Midsomer Norton. **19 K6** ST6556.

Paulton's Park *Hants.* ***Leisure/recreation***, amusement park, 2m/3km SE of West Wellow, featuring over forty different attractions and set in parkland with extensive 'Capability' Brown gardens. **10 E3** SU3116.

Pauntley *Glos.* ***Settlement***, 3m/4km NE of Newent. SO7429.

Pauperhaugh *Northumb.* ***Settlement***, on N side of River Coquet, 3m/5km SE of Rothbury. **71 G4** NZ1099.

Pave Lane *Tel. & W.* ***Settlement***, 1m/2km SE of Chetwynd Aston. SJ7516.

Pavenham *Beds.* ***Village***, on River Great Ouse, 5m/9km NW of Bedford. **32 C3** SP9955.

Pavenham Bury *Beds.* ***Locality***, to N of Pavenham. SP9855.

Pawlaw Pike *Dur.* ***Mountain***, 1m/2km NW of Hamsterley Forest. Height 1597 feet or 487 metres. **62 B3** NZ0032.

Pawlett *Som.* ***Village***, on flat lands near mouth of River Parrett, 4m/6km N of Bridgwater. **19 F7** ST3042.

Pawston *Northumb.* ***Hamlet***, 4m/7km S of Cornhill on Tweed. **77 G7** NT8532.

Paxford *Glos.* ***Village***, 2m/4km E of Chipping Campden. **30 C5** SP1837.

Paxhill Park *W.Suss.* ***Settlement***, 2m/3km SW of Horsted Keynes. **13 G4** TQ3626.

Paxton *Sc.Bord.* ***Village***, 4m/7km W of Berwick-upon-Tweed. **77 H5** NT9353.

Paxton House *Sc.Bord.* ***Historic house***, Palladian mansion built for daughter of Frederick the Great, 1km S of Paxton on W bank of River Tweed. Designed by Adam family, it is well-preserved, furnished by Chippendale and Trotter, and houses a Regency picture gallery. **77 H5** NT9352.

Paycocke's *Essex* ***Historic house***, merchant's house and garden, now National Trust property. Dating from c. 1500 it is one of several old houses in Coggeshall. **34 C6** TL8422.

Payden Street *Kent* ***Settlement***, 2m/3km NE of Lenham. TQ9254.
Payhembury *Devon* ***Village***, 5m/8km W of Honiton. 2m/3km NE, Hembury Fort, Iron Age earthwork, 884 feet or 269 metres above sea level. **7 J5** ST0801.
Payne End *Herts.* ***Locality***, W part of Sandon, 5m/8km E of Baldock. TL3134.
Paynes Hall *Herts.* ***Settlement***, 2m/3km NW of Ware. **33 G7** TL3316.
Paynter's Lane End *Cornw.* ***Locality***, 2m/3km NW of Redruth. SW6743.
Paythorne *Lancs.* ***Hamlet***, 2m/3km N of Gisburn. **56 D4** SD8251.
Paythorne Bridge *Lancs.* ***Bridge***, medieval stone bridge over River Ribble on S side of Paythorne, 9m/14km W of Skipton. SD8351.
Paythorne Moor *Lancs.* ***Open space***, low moorland 3m/4km SW of Hellifield. **56 D4** SD8353.
Peacehaven *E.Suss.* Population: 16,517. ***Suburb***, on coast, 2m/3km W of Newhaven. **13 H6** TQ4100.
Peacemarsh *Dorset* ***Locality***, adjoining to N of Gillingham. **9 H2** ST8027.
Peachley *Worcs.* ***Locality***, 3m/5km NW of Worcester. **29 H3** SO8057.
Peacock's Heath *Here.* ***Locality***, 1m/2km N of Bromyard. SO6456.
Peak Dale *Derbys.* ***Hamlet***, 3m/5km NE of Buxton. **50 C5** SK0976.
Peak District ***Large natural feature***, hill area and National Park, forming S end of Pennines. Comprises the Peak proper (also known as the High Peak), an area of millstone grit hills E of Hayfield, whose summit, Kinder Scout attains a height of 2088 feet or 636 metres; and a larger but less elevated area of limestone hills between Chapel-en-le-Frith and Ashbourne, intersected by deep valleys and criss-crossed by dry stone walls. **50 D4** SK1365.
Peak Forest *Derbys.* ***Village***, 4m/6km E of Chapel-en-le-Frith. **50 D5** SK1179.
Peak Hill *Lincs.* ***Locality***, on E side of New River, 1m/2km S of Cowbit. TF2616.
Peak Rail *Derbys.* ***Other feature of interest***, tourist railway which runs NW in River Derwent valley for over 4m/7km from Matlock to Rowsley South. **50 E6** SK2861.
Peakirk *Peter.* ***Village***, 5m/8km N of Peterborough. **42 E5** TF1606.
Peakirk Wildlife Refuge *Peter.* ***Nature reserve***, on N side of Peakirk, 4m/7km N of Peterborough town centre. Flooded gravel pit is home to hundreds of waterfowl. **42 E5** TF1707.
Pean *High.* ***River***, in Lochaber district, running E down Glen Pean to join River Dessary 1km above head of Loch Arkaig. **87 F6** NM9791.
Pean Hill *Kent* ***Settlement***, 3m/4km S of Whitstable. **25 H5** TR1062.
Pear Tree *Derby* ***Suburb***, 2m/3km S of Derby city centre. SK3533.
Pearsie *Angus* ***Hamlet***, 4m/6km NW of Kirriemuir. **82 E2** NO3659.
Pearson Fold *W.Yorks.* ***Suburb***, 3m/5km S of Bradford city centre. SE1627.
Pearson's Green *Kent* ***Hamlet***, 2m/3km SE of Paddock Wood. TQ6943.
Peartree *Herts.* ***Suburb***, E district of Welwyn Garden City. TL2412.
Peartree Green *Essex* ***Settlement***, adjoining to S of Doddinghurst, 3m/5km N of Brentwood. TQ5998.
Peartree Green *Here.* ***Settlement***, 5m/9km N of Ross-on-Wye across loops of river. SO5932.
Peartree Green *S'ham.* ***Suburb***, 1m/2km E of Southampton city centre across River Itchen. SU4411.
Peas Hill *Cambs.* ***Suburb***, in NW part of March. TL4097.
Pease Bay *Sc.Bord.* ***Bay***, small sandy bay with rocky headlands, 1m/2km E of Cockburnspath. **77 F3** NT7971.
Pease Pottage *W.Suss.* ***Hamlet***, 3m/4km S of Crawley. **13 F3** TQ2533.
Peasedown St. John *B. & N.E.Som.* Population: 3398. ***Village***, 2m/3km NE of Radstock. **20 A6** ST7057.
Peasehill *Derbys.* ***Hamlet***, 1km SE of Ripley. SK4049.
Peaseland Green *Norf.* ***Settlement***, 1km S of Elsing, 3m/5km N of Mattishall. TG0516.
Peasemore *W.Berks.* ***Village***, 6m/10km N of Newbury. **21 H4** SU4577.
Peasenhall *Suff.* ***Village***, 3m/4km W of Yoxford. **35 H2** TM3569.
Pease's West *Dur.* ***Locality***, 1km N of Crook. NZ1636.
Peaslake *Surr.* ***Village***, 4m/6km N of Cranleigh. **22 D7** TQ0844.
Peasley Cross *Mersey.* ***Suburb***, 1m/2km SE of St. Helens town centre. SJ5294.
Peasmarsh *E.Suss.* ***Village***, 3m/4km NW of Rye. **14 D5** TQ8822.
Peasmarsh *Som.* ***Settlement***, 2m/3km SW of Ilminster. ST3312.
Peasmarsh *Surr.* ***Hamlet***, 2m/3km NE of Godalming. SU9946.
Peaston *E.Loth.* ***Hamlet***, 3m/4km SW of Pencaitland. **76 C4** NT4365.
Peastonbank *E.Loth.* ***Hamlet***, 1m/2km S of Pencaitland. **76 C4** NT4466.
Peat Hill *Aber.* ***Mountain***, 6m/9km NE of Strathdon. Height 1856 feet or 566 metres. **90 C3** NJ4119.
Peat Hill *Angus* ***Mountain***, 3m/5km NW of Kirkton of Menmuir. Height 1578 feet or 481 metres. **83 G1** NO5067.
Peat Hill *N.Ayr.* ***Mountain***, 4m/6km NE of Largs. Height 1378 feet or 420 metres. **74 A4** NS2464.
Peat Inn *Fife* ***Village***, 6m/9km SE of Cupar. **83 F7** NO4509.
Peat Law *Sc.Bord.* ***Mountain***, 2m/3km NW of Selkirk. Height 1397 feet or 426 metres. **76 C7** NT4430.
Peathill *Aber.* ***Village***, 1m/2km S of Rosehearty. **99 H4** NJ9365.
Peathrow *Dur.* ***Settlement***, 1m/2km W of Cockfield. NZ1024.
Peatling Magna *Leics.* ***Village***, 6m/10km NW of Husbands Bosworth. **41 H6** SP5992.
Peatling Parva *Leics.* ***Village***, 4m/7km NE of Lutterworth. **41 H7** SP5889.
Peaton *Shrop.* ***Hamlet***, 6m/10km E of Craven Arms. **38 E7** SO5384.
Peats Corner *Suff.* ***Settlement***, 2m/3km SE of Debenham. TM1960.
Pebble Coombe *Surr.* ***Village***, 3m/5km W of Reigate. **23 F6** TQ2152.
Pebmarsh *Essex* ***Village***, 3m/5km NE of Halstead. **34 C5** TL8533.
Pebworth *Worcs.* ***Village***, 6m/10km NE of Broadway. **30 C4** SP1346.
Pecket Well *W.Yorks.* ***Village***, 1m/2km N of Hebden Bridge. **56 E7** SD9929.
Peckforton *Ches.* ***Hamlet***, 4m/6km S of Tarporley. **48 E7** SJ5356.
Peckforton Castle *Ches.* ***Historic house***, 19c mansion, 1m/2km N of Peckforton, on N end of wooded Peckforton Hills. **48 E7** SJ5358.
Peckforton Hills *Ches.* ***Forest/woodland***, on upland area, 1km W of Peckforton. **48 E7** SJ5256.
Peckham *Gt.Lon.* ***Suburb***, in borough of Southwark, 4m/6km SE of Charing Cross. TQ3476.
Peckham Bush *Kent* ***Hamlet***, 1m/2km N of East Peckham. TQ6649.
Peckham Rye *Gt.Lon.* ***Locality***, S of Peckham. To S towards Dulwich, Peckham Rye Common and Park. TQ3476.
Peckleton *Leics.* ***Village***, 8m/12km W of Leicester. **41 G5** SK4700.
Peckover House *Cambs.* ***Historic house***, National Trust property, 18c, on W side of Wisbech. **43 H5** TF4509.
Pedair-hewl *Carmar.* *Welsh form of Four Roads, qv.*
Pedham *Norf.* ***Hamlet***, 2m/3km N of Blofield. TG3312.
Pedmore *W.Mid.* ***Suburb***, SE district of Stourbridge. **40 B7** SO9182.
Pednormead End *Bucks.* ***Suburb***, SW district of Chesham. SP9501.
Pedwell *Som.* ***Village***, towards E end of Polden Hills, 4m/6km W of Street. **8 D1** ST4236.
Peebles *Sc.Bord.* Population: 7065. ***Small town***, resort on River Tweed, 20m/33km S of Edinburgh. Cross Kirk (Historic Scotland) is ruin dating from 13c. **76 A6** NT2540.
Peel *I.o.M.* ***Small town***, resort with harbour, on W coast, 10m/16km NW of Douglas. Developed around herring trade. Peel Castle (Manx National Heritage) on St. Patrick's Isle, contains 11c church. 19c cathedral. **54 B5** SC2484.
Peel *Lancs.* ***Settlement***, 3m/5km NE of Lytham St. Anne's. SD3531.
Peel Castle *I.o.M.* ***Castle***, on St. Patrick's Isle, to NW of Peel. Group of ruins inside 16c walls (Manx National Heritage) include 11c church and round tower and 13c St. German's Cathedral. Castle was seat of Norse Kingdom of Man and the Isles during 11c. **54 B5** SC2484.
Peel Fell ***Mountain***, on border of Northumberland and Scottish Borders, 4m/6km N of Kielder. Steep-sided to W. Height 1975 feet or 602 metres. **70 B4** NY6399.
Peel Green *Gt.Man.* ***Suburb***, 1m/2km W of Eccles town centre. SJ7497.
Peel Island *Cumb.* ***Island***, small island (National Trust) off E shore of Coniston Water, 1m/2km from S end of lake and 1m/2km N of High Nibthwaite. SD2991.
Peel Ring of Lumphanan *Aber.* ***Historic/prehistoric site***, moated medieval earthwork, 1km SW of Lumphanan, where it is said Macbeth made his last stand. Structure is 120 feet or 36.5 metres in diameter by 18 feet or 5.5 metres high. **90 D4** NJ5703.
Peening Quarter *Kent* ***Settlement***, 1m/2km NW of Wittersham. TQ8828.
Peffer Burn *E.Loth.* ***River***, rising in Garleton Hills, N of Haddington, and flowing NE to North Sea at Pefferside, 4m/7km NW of Dunbar. **76 D3** NT5678.
Pegal Burn *Ork.* ***River***, rising in central Hoy and flowing E into Pegal Bay. **107 B8** ND2598.
Peggs Green *Leics.* ***Hamlet***, 3m/4km N of Coalville. SK4117.
Pegsdon *Beds.* ***Hamlet***, 4m/7km W of Hitchin. TL1230.
Pegswood *Northumb.* Population: 3225. ***Village***, 2m/3km NE of Morpeth. **71 H5** NZ2287.
Pegwell *Kent* ***Suburb***, of Ramsgate, on Pegwell Bay. Hovercraft terminal. Power station to SW. TR3664.
Pegwell Bay *Kent* ***Coastal feature***, cove S of Ramsgate, opening into Sandwich Bay. Traditional site of Roman landing in AD 43, of Saxon landing in AD 449, and of St. Augustine's in AD 597, the last commemorated by a cross (English Heritage). **25 K5** TR3463.
Peighinn nan Aoireann (Anglicised form: Peninerine.) *W.Isles* ***Settlement***, on South Uist, 1m/2km NE of Rubha Aird-mhicheil. **84 C1** NF7434.
Peinchorran *High.* ***Settlement***, on Skye, on N side of Loch Sligachan, near mouth of loch. **86 B1** NG5233.
Peinlich *High.* ***Settlement***, on Skye, 3m/5km S of Uig. **93 K6** NG4158.
Peinmore *High.* ***Settlement***, on Skye, 5m/8km NW of Portree. NG4248.
Pelaw *T. & W.* ***Suburb***, to E of Felling. **71 H7** NZ2962.
Pelcomb (Pencam). *Pembs.* ***Settlement***, to E of Pelcomb Cross, 3m/4km NW of Haverfordwest. SM9218.
Pelcomb Bridge *Pembs.* ***Settlement***, 1m/2km SE of Pelcomb. **16 C3** SM9317.
Pelcomb Cross *Pembs.* ***Hamlet***, to W of Pelcomb, 3m/4km NW of Haverfordwest. **16 C3** SM9117.
Peldon *Essex* ***Village***, 5m/8km S of Colchester. **34 D7** TL9816.
Pell Green *E.Suss.* ***Settlement***, adjoining to N of Wadhurst. TQ6432.
Pellon *W.Yorks.* ***Suburb***, 2m/3km W of Halifax town centre. SE0725.
Pelsall *W.Mid.* Population: 10,007. ***Suburb***, 3m/5km N of Walsall. **40 C5** SK0103.
Pelsall Wood *W.Mid.* ***Suburb***, adjoining to N of Pelsall, 3m/5km N of Walsall. SK0103.
Pelton *Dur.* Population: 5279. ***Village***, 2m/3km NW of Chester-le-Street. **62 D1** NZ2553.
Pelton Fell *Dur.* ***Locality***, 1m/2km S of Pelton. NZ2551.
Pelutho *Cumb.* ***Settlement***, 4m/6km W of Abbeytown. **60 C2** NY1249.
Pelynt *Cornw.* ***Village***, 3m/5km NW of Looe. **4 C5** SX2055.
Pemberton *Carmar.* ***Suburb***, on E side of Llanelli. SN5300.
Pemberton *Gt.Man.* ***Suburb***, 2m/3km W of Wigan town centre. SD5504.
Pembrey (Pen-bre). *Carmar.* ***Village***, adjoining to W of Burry Port. **17 H4** SN4201.
Pembrey Country Park *Carmar.* ***Leisure/recreation***, country park with over 500 acres of parkland, woodland and 7m/11km stretch of award-winning beach, 3m/4km W of Burry Port. Attractions include dry ski slope and toboggan run, adventure playground and narrow gauge railway. **17 H4** SN4000.
Pembrey Forest *Carmar.* ***Forest/woodland***, to W of Pembrey. **17 G4** SN3803.
Pembridge *Here.* ***Village***, 6m/10km E of Kington. Many old half-timbered buildings, including market hall. 'New' Inn is early 16c. **28 C3** SO3958.
Pembridge Castle *Here.* ***Castle***, 4m/7km NW of Monmouth. Early 13c castle, of which a later 17c house remains. **28 D7** SO4819.
Pembroke *Pembs.* ***River***, rising 5m/8km E of Pembroke town, and flowing W to town where it forms an estuary which continues W and finally N into Milford Haven on W side of town of Pembroke Dock. SM9402.
Pembroke (Penfro). *Pembs.* Population: 6773. ***Small town***, on river of same name, 29m/47km SW of Carmarthen. Parts of 13c walls still remain. Ruins of 13c castle on site of earlier building. **16 C4** SM9801.
Pembroke Castle *Pembs.* ***Castle***, 12-13c fortress with 75 foot high round Norman keep. Castle dominates town of Pembroke and sits on S side of Pembroke River. **16 C4** SM9701.
Pembroke Dock (Doc Penfro). *Pembs.* Population: 8651. ***Small town***, and port near head of Milford Haven estuary, on S side opposite Neyland. To W is estuary of Pembroke River. New marina in old docks. To S, Cosmeston Lakes Country Park includes a recreated medieval village. **16 C4** SM9603.
Pembroke Ferry *Pembs.* ***Locality***, at S end of road bridge on S side of Milford Haven estuary, 1m/2km NE of Pembroke Dock. SM9704.
Pembrokeshire Coast National Park *Pembs.* ***Leisure/recreation***, national park encompassing entire Pembrokeshire coastline, from 1m/2km N of St. Dogmaels in N, around coast to Amroth in S. **16 D1** SM8617.
Pembury *Kent* Population: 6016. ***Village***, large village 3m/5km E of Royal Tunbridge Wells. **23 K7** TQ6240.
Pen-a-maen *Cornw.* *Alternative name for Maenease Point, qv.*
Pen Allt-mawr *Powys* ***Mountain***, peak on Black Mountains, 4m/6km N of Crickhowell. Height 2358 feet or 719 metres. **28 B6** SO2024.
Pen-bont Rhydybeddau *Cere.* ***Village***, on Nant Silo, 6m/10km E of Aberystwyth. **37 F7** SN6783.
Pen-bre *Carmar.* *Welsh form of Pembrey, qv.*
Pen Brush *Pembs.* ***Coastal feature***, headland 1m/2km SW of Strumble Head. Group of small islands off shore. **16 B1** SM8839.
Pen-cae *Cere.* ***Hamlet***, 1m/2km SE of Llanarth. SN4356.
Pen-cae-cwm *Conwy* ***Settlement***, 2m/3km SW of Bylchau. SH9461.
Pen Caer *Pembs.* ***Coastal feature***, peninsula rich in prehistoric antiquities NW of Fishguard. **16 B1** SM9040.
Pen-caer-fenny *Swan.* ***Locality***, to S of Salthouse Point, 4m/6km W of Gowerton on Gower peninsula. SS5295.
Pen Carreg Dan *Powys* ***Mountain***, 1m/2km NE of Abergwesyn. Height 1620 feet or 494 metres. **27 H3** SN8654.
Pen Carreg Gopa *Cere.* ***Mountain***, 5m/8km NE of Tal-y-Bont. Height 1466 feet or 447 metres. **37 G6** SN7294.
Pen Cerrig-calch *Powys* ***Mountain***, peak on Black Mountains, 3m/4km N of Crickhowell. Height 2299 feet or 701 metres. **28 B6** SO2122.
Pen-clawdd *Swan.* Population: 3308. ***Village***, 3m/5km W of Gowerton. **17 J5** SS5495.
Pen Coed *Powys* ***Mountain***, 2m/3km SW of Llangadfan. Height 1174 feet or 358 metres. **37 J5** SH9708.
Pen-ffordd *Pembs.* ***Hamlet***, 3m/5km S of Maenclochog. **16 D2** SN0722.
Pen-groes-oped *Mon.* ***Settlement***, 4m/7km S of Abergavenny. **19 G1** SO3107.
Pen Gwyllt Meirch *Powys* ***Open space***, steep W facing hillslope in Black Mountains, 4m/7km NE of Crickhowell. **28 B6** SO2424.
Pen-hw *Newport* *Welsh form of Penhow, qv.*
Pen Llithrig y-wrach *Conwy* ***Mountain***, 3m/4km N of Capel Curig. Height 2621 feet or 799 metres. **47 F6** SH7162.
Pen-llyn *I.o.A.* ***Settlement***, on Anglesey, at N end of Llyn Llywenan. **46 B4** SH3582.
Pen-lôn *I.o.A.* ***Hamlet***, 1km SE of Newborough, near S coast of Anglesey. SH4365.
Pen Maen-wern *Powys* ***Mountain***, 1m/2km S of Claerwen Reservoir dam. Height 1784 feet or 544 metres. **27 H2** SN8661.
Pen Milan *Powys* ***Mountain***, 4m/7km SW of Brecon. Height 1820 feet or 555 metres. **27 J6** SN9923.
Pen Mill *Som.* ***Suburb***, E district of Yeovil. ST5716.
Pen-plaenau *Wrex.* ***Mountain***, 5m/8km E of Llandrillo. Height 1781 feet or 543 metres. **38 A2** SJ1136.
Pen Pumlumon-Arwystli ***Mountain***, on border of Ceredigion and Powys, 2m/3km E of Plynlimon summit. Height 2430 feet or 741 metres. **37 H7** SN8187.

P

Pen Pyrod *Swan. Welsh form of Worms Head, qv.*
Pen Rhiwclochdy *Cere.* ***Mountain***, 6m/10km SE of Tregaron. Height 1414 feet or 431 metres. **27 G3** SN7451.
Pen Rhiwfawr *N.P.T.* ***Village***, 1m/2km S of Cwmllynfell. SN7410.
Pen-sarn *Gwyn.* ***Hamlet***, 3m/4km S of Harlech. **36 E3** SH5828.
Pen-sarn *Gwyn.* ***Settlement***, at end of Lleyn Peninsula, 3m/5km N of Chwilog. **36 D1** SH4344.
Pen Tas-eithin *Carmar.* ***Mountain***, 3m/5km E of Llanybydder. Mast at summit. Height 1361 feet or 415 metres. **26 E4** SN5743.
Pen Trum-gwr *Gwyn.* ***Mountain***, rounded summit 1m/2km S of Dolgoch. Height 1676 feet or 511 metres. **37 F5** SH6502.
Pen-twyn *Caerp.* ***Settlement***, 1km W of Llanhilleth. SO2000.
Pen-twyn *Mon.* ***Village***, 2m/4km S of Monmouth. **19 J1** SO5209.
Pen-'twyn *Torfaen* ***Suburb***, in Abersychan, 2m/3km NW of Pontypool. SO2603.
Pen Twyn Mawr *Powys* ***Mountain***, rising to over 650 metres in Black Mountains, 10m/16km S of Hay-on-Wye. **28 B6** SO2426.
Pen-y-banc *Carmar.* ***Hamlet***, 1m/2km NW of Llandeilo. **17 K2** SN6124.
Pen-y-banc *Carmar.* ***Settlement***, 1m/2km SW of Ammanford. SN6111.
Pen y Bedw *Conwy* ***Mountain***, 5m/8km E of Blaenau Ffestiniog. Height 1729 feet or 527 metres. **37 G1** SH7746.
Pen-y-Bont *B.Gwent* ***Locality***, adjoining to N of Abertillery. SO2105.
Pen-y-bont *Carmar.* ***Hamlet***, 8m/13km NW of Carmarthen. SN3027.
Pen-y-bont *Carmar.* ***Settlement***, on NW bank of River Brân, 1m/2km NE of Llandovery. **27 G5** SN7836.
Pen-y-bont *Powys* ***Hamlet***, 1m/2km E of Llangedwyn. **38 B3** SJ2123.
Pen-y-bont *Powys* ***Settlement***, on bank of Afron Banwy, opposite Llangadfan. **37 K4** SJ0110.
Pen-y-bont *Wrex.* ***Locality***, 1m/2km SE of Rhydtalog. SJ2453.
Pen-y-bont *Wrex.* ***Settlement***, 2m/3km SW of Ruabon. SJ2841.
Pen-y-Bont ar Ogwr *Bridgend Welsh form of Bridgend, qv.*
Pen-y-bryn *Gwyn.* ***Settlement***, at head of Mawddach estuary, 3m/4km NW of Dolgellau. **37 F4** SH6919.
Pen-y-bryn *Pembs.* ***Hamlet***, 2m/3km S of Cardigan. SN1742.
Pen-y-bryn *Wrex.* ***Settlement***, 2m/4km W of Ruabon. SJ2644.
Pen-y-bwlch *Cere.* ***Mountain***, 4m/6km SE of Pontrhydfendigaid. Height 1650 feet or 503 metres. **27 G2** SN7863.
Pen-y-cae *Powys* ***Settlement***, 6m/9km NE of Ystalyfera. **27 H7** SN8413.
Pen-y-cae-mawr *Mon.* ***Locality***, 2m/3km SE of Llantrisant. **19 H2** ST4195.
Pen-y-cefn *Flints.* ***Hamlet***, 2m/4km NE of Tremeirchion. **47 K5** SJ1175.
Pen y Cil *Gwyn.* ***Coastal feature***, headland at W end of Aberdaron Bay. **36 A3** SH1523.
Pen-y-clawdd *Mon.* ***Hamlet***, 3m/4km E of Raglan. **19 H1** SO4507.
Pen-y-coed *Powys* ***Settlement***, 5m/8km N of Welshpool. SJ2414.
Pen-y-coedcae *R.C.T.* ***Village***, 2m/3km SW of Pontypridd. **18 D3** ST0687.
Pen-y-Crug *Powys* ***Mountain***, surmounted by ancient British camps, 1m/2km NW of Brecon. Height 1086 feet or 331 metres. **27 K5** SO0230.
Pen-y-Darren *M.Tyd.* ***Suburb***, 1km N of Merthyr Tydfil town centre. SO0507.
Pen-y-fai *Bridgend* ***Locality***, 1m/2km N of Bridgend. **18 B3** SS8982.
Pen y Fan *Powys* ***Mountain***, one of two chief peaks of Brecon Beacons, 5m/8km SW of Brecon. Height 2906 feet or 886 metres. **27 K6** SO0121.
Pen-y-felin *Flints.* ***Hamlet***, 1km W of Nannerch. SJ1569.
Pen-y-ffordd *Flints.* ***Hamlet***, 2m/3km NW of Mostyn. SJ1381.
Pen y Ffridd Cownwy *Powys* ***Mountain***, to N of Dyfnant Forest 3m/5km SW of Llanwddyn. Height 1630 feet or 497 metres. **37 J4** SH9717.
Pen-y-gaer *Carmar. See Llanybydder.*
Pen y Gaer *Powys* ***Settlement***, 1m/2km W of Tretower. Site of Roman fort. SO1621.
Pen-y-garn *Carmar.* ***Settlement***, 3m/5km E of Brechfa. **17 J1** SN5731.
Pen y Garn *Cere.* ***Mountain***, 4m/6km E of Devil's Bridge. Height 2001 feet or 610 metres. **27 G1** SN7977.
Pen-y-garn *Cere.* ***Settlement***, adjoining to N of Bow Street. SN6285.
Pen y Garn *Gwyn.* ***Mountain***, 1m/2km SE of Fairbourne. Height 1506 feet or 459 metres. **37 F4** SH6210.
Pen-y-garreg *Powys* ***Settlement***, 3m/5km SW of Builth Wells. **27 K4** SO0246.
Pen-y-genffordd *Powys Alternative spelling of Pengenffordd, qv.*
Pen-y-Ghent *N.Yorks.* ***Mountain***, 2m/3km NE of Horton in Ribblesdale. Height 2276 feet or 694 metres. **56 D2** SD8373.
Pen-y-Gogarth *Conwy Welsh form of Great Ormes Head, qv.*
Pen-y-Graig *Gwyn.* ***Hamlet***, on NW side of Llangwnnadl. SH2033.
Pen-y-groes *Cardiff* ***Suburb***, 3m/5km NE of Cardiff. ST2181.
Pen y Gurnos *Cere.* ***Mountain***, 10m/16km N of Llandovery, to W of Llyn Brianne. Height 1496 feet or 456 metres. **27 G3** SN7751.
Pen y Gwely *Powys* ***Mountain***, 3m/4km S of Glyn Ceiriog. Height 1456 feet or 444 metres. **38 B2** SJ2133.
Pen-y-Gwryd *Conwy* ***Open space***, hillslope on border of Conwy and Gwynedd, rising from Llyn Cwmffynnon to Glyder group at E end of Pass of Llanberis, 4m/7km W of Capel Curig. **46 E7** SH6657.
Pen-y-Gwryd *Gwyn.* ***Settlement***, with hotel, 4m/7km E of Capel Curig. Site of Roman camp. **46 E7** SH6655.
Pen-y-lan *Cardiff* ***Suburb***, in Cardiff 1m/2km N of city centre. ST1978.
Pen-y-maes *Flints.* ***Suburb***, adjoining to E of Holywell. SJ1976.
Pen y Manllwyn *Powys* ***Inland physical feature***, ridge extending NW from Waun Fach in Black Mountains, 4m/6km SE of Talgarth. **28 B5** SO2031.
Pen y Mwdwl *Conwy* ***Mountain***, with tumulus, 1km NW of Llansannan. Height 1178 feet or 359 metres. **47 H6** SH9166.
Pen-y-parc *Flints.* ***Settlement***, 1m/2km S of Halkyn. SJ2169.
Pen-y-Park *Here.* ***Settlement***, 3m/5km NE of Hay-on-Wye. **28 B4** SO2744.
Pen-y-Pass *Gwyn.* ***Settlement***, with Youth Hostel at head of Pass of Llanberis, 3m/4km E of Snowdon summit. SH6455.
Pen-y-stryt *Denb.* ***Hamlet***, 6m/10km SE of Ruthin. **47 K7** SJ1951.
Pen-ychain *Gwyn.* ***Coastal feature***, headland on Tremadog Bay, 4m/6km E of Pwllheli. Large holiday camp 1m/2km inland. **36 D2** SH4335.
Pen-yr-afr *Pembs.* ***Coastal feature***, headland on N coast, 4m/6km NW of Cardigan. **26 A4** SN1148.
Pen-yr-englyn *R.C.T.* ***Village***, in Rhondda Fawr valley, 1m/2km NW of Treorchy. SS9497.
Pen-yr-heol *Mon.* ***Settlement***, 3m/4km NE of Raglan. **28 D7** SO4311.
Pen-yr-Heolgerrig *M.Tyd.* ***Settlement***, 1m/2km W of Merthyr Tydfil. SO0206.
Penallt *Mon.* ***Hamlet***, 2m/3km SE of Monmouth. **28 E7** SO5210.
Penally *Pembs.* ***Village***, 1m/2km SW of Tenby. **16 E5** SS1199.
Penalt *Here.* ***Hamlet***, 4m/6km NW of Ross-on-Wye across loop of river. **28 E6** SO5729.
Penaran *Powys* ***Settlement***, 1m/2km SW of Kerry. SO1388.
Penare *Cornw.* ***Settlement***, to N of Dodman Point, 3m/5km S of Mevagissey. National Trust property to N and S. **3 G4** SX0040.
Penare Point *Cornw.* ***Coastal feature***, headland on Mevagissey Bay just N of Mevagissey. **4 A6** SX0245.
Penarlag *Flints. Welsh form of Hawarden, qv.*
Penarth *V. of Glam.* Population: 23,434. ***Town***, port and resort at mouth of River Ely 3m/5km S of Cardiff. **18 E4** ST1871.
Penarth Fawr Medieval House *Gwyn.* ***Historic house***, early 15c hall house (Cadw) on S side of Lleyn Peninsula, 3m/5km NE of Pwllheli. **36 D2** SH4137.
Penboyr *Carmar.* ***Settlement***, 4m/7km SE of Newcastle Emlyn. **17 G1** SN3536.
Penbryn *Cere.* ***Village***, 2m/4km E of Aberporth. **26 B3** SN2952.
Penbwchdy *Pembs.* ***Coastal feature***, headland 3m/4km SW of Strumble Head. **16 B1** SM8737.
Pencader *Carmar.* ***Village***, 3m/5km SE of Llandysul. **17 H1** SN4436.
Pencaenewydd *Gwyn.* ***Hamlet***, 4m/7km NE of Pwllheli. **36 D1** SH4041.
Pencaitland *E.Loth.* Population: 1287. ***Locality***, parish containing villages of Easter and Wester Pencaitland, on either side of Tyne Water, 4m/6km SE of Tranent. **76 C4** NT4468.
Pencam *Pembs. Welsh form of Pelcomb, qv.*
Pencarnisiog *I.o.A.* ***Hamlet***, near W coast of Anglesey, 2m/4km E of Rhosneigr. SH3573.
Pencarreg *Carmar.* ***Hamlet***, 1m/2km NE of Llanbydder. **26 E4** SN5345.
Pencarrow *Cornw.* ***Hamlet***, just S of Camelford. SX1082.
Pencarrow *Cornw.* ***Historic house***, 4m/6km NW of Bodmin. Georgian manor with 50 acres of garden, including a Victorian rockery and an Italian garden. **4 A3** SX0471.
Pencarrow Head *Cornw.* ***Coastal feature***, headland on S coast at W end of Lantivet Bay, 2m/3km E of Fowey. **4 B5** SX1550.
Pencelli *Powys* ***Hamlet***, 4m/6km SE of Brecon. **27 K6** SO0925.
Pencilan Head *Gwyn. English form of Trwyn Cilan, qv.*
Penclegyr *Pembs.* ***Coastal feature***, headland 3m/4km N of St. David's. **16 A1** SM7629.
Penclegyr *Pembs.* ***Coastal feature***, headland 2m/3km NW of Croes-goch. **16 B1** SM8032.
Pencoed *Bridgend* Population: 8331. ***Village***, 4m/6km E of Bridgend. **18 C3** SS9681.
Pencombe *Here.* ***Village***, 4m/6km W of Bromyard. **28 E3** SO6052.
Pencoyd *Here.* ***Hamlet***, 6m/9km W of Ross-on-Wye. **28 E6** SO5126.
Pencraig *Here.* ***Hamlet***, 3m/5km SW of Ross-on-Wye. **28 E6** SO5620.
Pencraig *Powys Welsh form of Old Radnor, qv.*
Pencraig *Powys* ***Settlement***, 1km N of Llangynog. **37 K3** SJ0427.
Pencribach *Cere.* ***Coastal feature***, headland at N end of Cribach Bay, 1m/2km NW of Aberporth. **26 B3** SN2552.
Pendarves Point *Cornw. See St. Eval.*
Pendeen *Cornw.* ***Village***, 2m/3km N of St. Just. **2 A5** SW3834.
Pendeen Watch *Cornw.* ***Coastal feature***, headland with lighthouse, 7m/11km NW of Penzance. **2 A5** SW3735.
Pendennis Castle *Cornw.* ***Castle***, 16c fortress (English Heritage) built by Henry VIII to protect Carrick Roads, situated on peninsula to SE of Falmouth. Held for Charles I during Civil War. **3 F5** SW8231.
Pendennis Point *Cornw.* ***Coastal feature***, headland on W side of entrance to Carrick Roads. 16c Pendennis Castle (English Heritage) underwent five-month siege during Civil War. **3 F5** SW8231.
Penderyn *R.C.T.* ***Village***, 2m/3km N of Hirwaun. **18 C1** SN9408.
Pendeulwyn *V. of Glam. Welsh form of Pendoylan, qv.*
Pendine *Carmar.* ***Village***, on Carmarthen Bay, 5m/8km W of Laugharne. **17 F4** SN2308.
Pendine Sands *Carmar.* ***Coastal feature***, wide stretch of sands, formerly used for car speed trials, to E of Pendine. **17 F4** SN2607.
Pendle Hill *Lancs.* ***Mountain***, prominent limestone hill, 4m/6km E of Clitheroe, in Forest of Pendle. Infamous witches of Pendle lived along lower slopes of hill in early 17c. Height 1827 feet or 557 metres. **56 D5** SD8041.
Pendlebury *Gt.Man.* Population: 21,577. ***Town***, 5m/7km NW of Manchester. Artist L.S. Lowry lived here for many years. **49 G2** SD7802.
Pendleton *Gt.Man.* ***Suburb***, 1m/2km NW of Salford city centre. SJ8199.
Pendleton *Lancs.* ***Village***, 2m/3km SE of Clitheroe. **56 C6** SD7539.
Pendock *Worcs.* ***Village***, 7m/11km W of Tewkesbury. **29 G5** SO7832.
Pendoggett *Cornw.* ***Village***, 5m/8km NE of Wadebridge. **4 A3** SX0279.
Pendomer *Som.* ***Hamlet***, 4m/7km SW of Yeovil. **8 E3** ST5210.
Pendoylan (Pendeulwyn). *V. of Glam.* ***Village***, 4m/7km E of Cowbridge. **18 D4** ST0676.
Pendre *Bridgend* ***Suburb***, 1km N of Bridgend town centre. SS9081.
Penegoes *Powys* ***Village***, 2m/3km E of Machynlleth. **37 G5** SH7700.
Penelewey *Cornw.* ***Hamlet***, 3m/4km S of Truro. SW8140.
Penenden Heath *Kent* ***Suburb***, N district of Maidstone. TQ7657.
Penffordd-Las *Powys Welsh form of Staylittle, qv.*
Penfro *Pembs. Welsh form of Pembroke, qv.*
Pengam *Caerp.* ***Locality***, 1m/2km W of Blackwood. **18 E2** ST1597.
Pengam *Cardiff* ***Suburb***, in Cardiff 2m/3km E of city centre. ST2177.
Pengam *Newport* ***Settlement***, 1km W of Peterstone Wentlooge. ST2679.
Penge *Gt.Lon.* ***Suburb***, in borough of Bromley, 1m/2km S of Crystal Palace. **23 G4** TQ3470.
Pengelli-ddrain *Swan. Welsh form of Grovesend, qv.*
Pengenffordd (Also spelled Pen-y-genffordd.) *Powys* ***Settlement***, 3m/4km SE of Talgarth. **28 A5** SO1730.
Pengorffwysfa *I.o.A.* ***Hamlet***, near N coast of Anglesey, 2m/3km E of Amlwch. **46 C3** SH4692.
Pengover Green *Cornw.* ***Hamlet***, 2m/3km E of Liskeard. **4 C4** SX2865.
Pengwern *Denb.* ***Settlement***, 1m/2km SW of Rhuddlan. **47 J5** SJ0176.
Penhale *Cornw.* ***Hamlet***, 1m/2km SE of Mullion. **2 D7** SW6918.
Penhale Jakes *Cornw.* ***Settlement***, 3m/5km W of Helston. SW6028.
Penhale Point *Cornw.* ***Coastal feature***, headland on N coast, 3m/5km N of Perranporth. **2 E3** SW7559.
Penhale Sands *Cornw.* ***Coastal feature***, sand dunes behind Perran Beach, N of Perranporth. **2 E3** SW7656.
Penhallow *Cornw.* ***Hamlet***, 2m/3km S of Perranporth. **2 E3** SW7651.
Penhalvean *Cornw.* ***Settlement***, 1m/2km S of Lanner. **2 E5** SW7137.
Penhelig (Penhelyg). *Gwyn.* ***Settlement***, 1km E of Aberdyfi. SN6296.
Penhellick *Cornw.* ***Settlement***, 2m/3km E of Camborne. SW6740.
Penhelyg *Gwyn. Welsh form of Penhelig, qv.*
Penhill *N.Yorks.* ***Mountain***, on Melmerby Moor, 1m/2km S of West Witton. Height 1725 feet or 526 metres. **57 F1** SE0486.
Penhill *Swin.* ***Suburb***, 2m/3km N of Swindon town centre. SU1588.
Penhow (Pen-hw). *Newport* ***Hamlet***, 3m/5km W of Caerwent. Castle, now a farmhouse, is a 12c-15c fortified house. **19 H2** ST4290.
Penhow Castle *Newport* ***Castle***, small early 13c enclosure castle built by Sir William St. Maur, with 15c alterations, 4m/6km NW of Caldicot. **19 H2** ST4290.
Penhurst *E.Suss.* ***Settlement***, 4m/6km W of Battle. **13 K5** TQ6916.
Peniarth *Gwyn.* ***Settlement***, 1km E of Llanegryn. **37 F5** SH6105.
Penicuik *Midloth.* Population: 17,173. ***Town***, on River North Esk, 9m/14km S of Edinburgh. Edinburgh Crystal Glass Works and Visitor Centre based here. 12c belfry in parish church. **76 A4** NT2359.
Peniel *Carmar.* ***Hamlet***, 3m/5km NE of Carmarthen. SN4324.
Peniel *Denb.* ***Settlement***, 2m/4km SW of Denbigh. SJ0263.
Peniel Heugh *Sc.Bord.* ***Hill***, 4m/6km N of Jedburgh, bearing monument raised in 1815 to commemorate Battle of Waterloo. Height 777 feet or 237 metres. **70 B1** NT6526.
Penifiler *High.* ***Settlement***, on Skye, 1m/2km S of Portree across Loch Portree. **93 K7** NG4841.
Penilee *Glas.* ***Suburb***, in Hillington district of Glasgow. NS5164.
Peninerine *W.Isles Anglicised form of Peighinn nan Aoireann, qv.*
Peninver *Arg. & B.* ***Settlement***, on E coast of Kintyre, 4m/6km NE of Campbeltown. **66 B1** NR7524.
Penisa'r Waun *Gwyn.* ***Hamlet***, 3m/5km NW of Llanberis. **46 D6** SH5563.
Penisarcwn *Powys* ***Settlement***, 1m/2km SW of Llanwddyn. **37 K4** SJ0018.
Penishawain *Powys* ***Settlement***, 4m/6km NE of Brecon. SO0832.
Penistone *S.Yorks.* Population: 8627. ***Small town***, market town on River Don, 7m/11km W of Barnsley. **50 E2** SE2403.
Penistone Hill *W.Yorks.* ***Mountain***, 1km SW of Haworth. Height 1030 feet or 314 metres. **57 F6** SE0236.
Penjerrick *Cornw.* ***Settlement***, 2m/3km SW of Falmouth. **2 E5** SW7730.

P

Penk *Staffs.* ***River***, rising W of Codsall and flowing N into River Sow 1m/2km E of Stafford. SJ9422.
Penketh *Warr.* ***Suburb***, urban district in W part of Warrington. **48 E4** SJ5587.
Penkill *S.Ayr.* ***Settlement***, 3m/5km E of Girvan. Penkill Castle to S. **67 G4** NX2398.
Penkiln Burn *D. & G.* ***River***, rising on S slopes of Lamachan Hill and running S to River Cree at N end of Newton Stewart. **64 E4** NX4166.
Penkridge *Staffs.* Population: 7212. ***Village***, 6m/9km S of Stafford. **40 B4** SJ9214.
Penlan *Swan.* ***Suburb***, 2m/3km N of Swansea city centre. SS6496.
Penlean *Cornw.* ***Hamlet***, 1km S of Poundstock. SX2098.
Penlee Point *Cornw.* ***Coastal feature***, headland at S end of Cawsand Bay. **4 E6** SX4448.
Penley *Wrex.* ***Village***, 3m/5km E of Overton. **38 D2** SJ4139.
Penllech *Gwyn.* ***Settlement***, 2m/3km SW of Tudweiliog. **36 B2** SH2234.
Penllechwen *Pembs.* ***Coastal feature***, headland 1m/2km NE of St. David's Head. **16 A2** SM7329.
Penlle'rfedwen *N.P.T.* ***Open space***, hillslope 2m/3km E of Gwaun-Cae-Gurwen. **27 G7** SN7211.
Penllergaer *Swan.* ***Village***, 5m/7km NW of Swansea. **17 K5** SS6198.
Penllwyn *Caerp.* ***Suburb***, at W side of Pontllanfraith, 1m/2km S of Blackwood. ST1795.
Penllyn *V. of Glam.* ***Village***, 2m/3km NW of Cowbridge. **18 C4** SS9776.
Penmachno *Conwy* ***Village***, 4m/6km S of Betws-y-coed. **47 F7** SH7950.
Penmaen *Caerp.* ***Locality***, 1km E of Blackwood across Sirhowy River. ST1897.
Penmaen *Swan.* ***Village***, on Gower peninsula, 6m/10km W of Mumbles Head. **17 J6** SS5388.
Penmaen Dewi *Pembs.* *Welsh form of St. David's Head, qv.*
Penmaen-Rhôs *Conwy* ***Suburb***, 2m/3km E of Colwyn Bay. SH8778.
Penmaen Swatch ***Sea feature***, channel between Lavan Sands and Dutchman Bank off coast at Llanfairfechan. **46 E5** SH6577.
Penmaenan *Conwy* ***Settlement***, on W side of Penmaenmawr. SH7076.
Penmaenmawr *Conwy* Population: 2681. ***Small town***, and resort on North Wales coast, 4m/7km W of Conwy. Mountain of Penmaen Mawr to SW (1550 feet or 472 metres). **47 F5** SH7176.
Penmaenpool *Gwyn.* ***Hamlet***, on S bank of River Mawddach, 2m/4km W of Dolgellau. **37 F4** SH6918.
Penmarc *V. of Glam.* *Welsh form of Penmark, qv.*
Penmark (Penmarc). *V. of Glam.* ***Village***, 3m/5km W of Barry. Remains of castle sacked by Owain Glyndŵr. **18 D5** ST0568.
Penmarth *Cornw.* ***Village***, 4m/7km S of Redruth. SW7035.
Penmon *I.o.A.* ***Locality***, 3m/5km NE of Beaumaris. Remains of partly Norman priory (Cadw). St. Seiriol's Well (Cadw), named after founder of original 6c priory. Dovecote (Cadw) of c. 1600 to E. Cross (Cadw) of c. 1100 on hill to NW. **46 E4** SH6380.
Penmon Priory *I.o.A.* ***Ecclesiastical building***, on E tip of Anglesey, 3m/5km NE of Beaumaris. Founded in 6c, with church rebuilt in 12c and now used as parish church. Includes 17c dovecote. **46 E4** SH6380.
Penmorfa *Gwyn.* ***Hamlet***, 2m/3km NW of Porthmadog. **36 E1** SH5440.
Penmorfa *Pembs.* ***Coastal feature***, headland 2m/3km N of Mathry. **16 B1** SM8734.
Penmynydd *I.o.A.* ***Village***, on Anglesey, 3m/5km NW of Menai Bridge. **46 D5** SH5074.
Penn *Bucks.* ***Village***, 3m/4km NW of Beaconsfield. Supposed ancestral home of William Penn, founder of Pennsylvania. **22 C2** SU9193.
Penn *W.Mid.* ***Suburb***, SW district of Wolverhampton. **40 A6** SO8995.
Penn Moor *Devon* ***Open space***, moorland to SW of Dartmoor National Park, 5m/8km NW of Ivybridge. **5 F4** SX6063.
Penn Street *Bucks.* ***Village***, 2m/4km W of Amersham. **22 C2** SU9296.
Pennal *Gwyn.* ***Village***, 3m/5km W of Machynlleth across River Dyfi. **37 F5** SH6900.
Pennal-isaf *Gwyn.* ***Settlement***, 1m/2km N of Pennal. SH7001.
Pennan *Aber.* ***Village***, on N coast, at foot of cliffs on Pennan Bay, W of Pennan Head and 2m/3km SE of Troup Head. **99 G4** NJ8465.
Pennan Head *Aber.* ***Coastal feature***, on W of Pennan Bay and 2m/3km SE of Troup Head. **99 G4** NJ8565.
Pennance *Cornw.* ***Village***, adjoining to N of Lanner. **2 E4** SW7140.
Pennant *Cere.* ***Village***, 4m/6km E of Aberaeron. **26 E2** SN5163.
Pennant *Powys* ***Hamlet***, 4m/6km N of head of Llyn Clywedog Reservoir. **37 H6** SN8797.
Pennant Melangell *Powys* ***Settlement***, 2m/3km W of Llangynog. **37 K3** SJ0226.
Pennar *Pembs.* ***Suburb***, adjoining to S of Pembroke Dock. SM9602.
Pennard *Swan.* ***Village***, on Gower peninsula, 4m/7km W of Mumbles Head. To W is Pennard Castle. **17 J6** SS5688.
Pennerley *Shrop.* ***Hamlet***, 7m/11km N of Bishop's Castle. **38 C6** SO3599.
Penninghame *D. & G.* ***Settlement***, 4m/6km NW of Newton Stewart. **64 D4** NX3869.
Pennington *Cumb.* ***Village***, 2m/3km W of Ulverston. **55 F2** SD2677.
Pennington *Gt.Man.* ***Suburb***, 1km S of Leigh town centre. SJ6599.
Pennington *Hants.* ***Suburb***, 1m/2km SW of Lymington. SZ3194.
Pennington Flash *Gt.Man.* ***Leisure/recreation***, 1m/2km SW of Leigh. The Flash, a 170 acre stretch of water, is focal point of 1000 acre park, a renowned centre for ornithology, attracting over 200 species of bird. Other attractions include sailing, angling and pony-trekking. **49 F2** SJ6399.
Pennington Green *Gt.Man.* ***Hamlet***, 3m/4km E of Wigan. SD6106.
Pennocrucium *Staffs.* *See Water Eaton.*
Pennorth *Powys* ***Hamlet***, 1m/2km W of Llangorse Lake. SO1125.
Pennsylvania *S.Glos.* ***Hamlet***, 2m/4km W of Marshfield. **20 A4** ST7473.
Penny Bridge *Cumb.* ***Village***, 3m/5km NE of Ulverston. **55 G1** SD3082.
Penny Green *Derbys.* ***Settlement***, 1km SE of Whitwell, 3m/5km SW of Worksop. SK5475.
Pennycross *Plym.* ***Suburb***, of Plymouth 2m/3km N of city centre. SX4757.
Pennyfuir *Arg. & B.* ***Settlement***, 1m/2km NE of Oban. **79 K4** NM8732.
Pennygate *Norf.* ***Hamlet***, 5m/8km NE of Wroxham. TG3422.
Pennyghael *Arg. & B.* ***Locality***, on S side of Loch Scridain, Mull, 9m/14km E of Bunessan. **79 G5** NM5126.
Pennyglen *S.Ayr.* ***Settlement***, 2m/3km W of Maybole. **67 G2** NS2710.
Pennygown *Arg. & B.* ***Settlement***, on Sound of Mull, 2m/3km E of Salen. Ruined chapel, with decorated Celtic cross shaft, beside road to E. **79 H3** NM5942.
Pennylands *Lancs.* ***Suburb***, W district of Skelmersdale. SD4706.
Pennymoor *Devon* ***Hamlet***, 6m/9km W of Tiverton. **7 G4** SS8611.
Penny's Green *Norf.* ***Settlement***, 1km NW of Wreningham. TM1599.
Pennyvenie *E.Ayr.* ***Settlement***, 1m/2km NE of Dalmellington. NS4906.
Pennywell *T. & W.* ***Suburb***, 3m/5km W of Sunderland city centre. NZ3555.
Penparc *Cere.* ***Hamlet***, 3m/4km NE of Cardigan. **26 B4** SN2147.
Penparc *Pembs.* ***Village***, 1m/2km NE of Croes-goch. **16 B1** SM8431.
Penparcau *Cere.* ***Locality***, on E side of Pendinas, 1m/2km SE of Aberystwyth across River Rheidol. **36 E7** SN5980.
Penpedairheol *Mon.* ***Settlement***, 3m/5km NW of Usk. SO3303.
Penpedairhoel *Caerp.* ***Village***, 1km NE of Gelligaer. ST1497.
Penperlleni *Mon.* ***Settlement***, 4m/6km NE of Pontypool. **19 G1** SO3204.
Penpethy *Cornw.* ***Hamlet***, 2m/3km NW of Camelford. SX0886.
Penpillick *Cornw.* ***Settlement***, 3m/4km SW of Lostwithiel. **4 A5** SX0856.
Penpol *Cornw.* ***Hamlet***, on inlet of Restronguet Creek, 4m/6km S of Truro. **3 F5** SW8139.
Penpoll *Cornw.* ***Hamlet***, at head of Penpoll Creek, 2m/3km NE of Fowey across River Fowey. **4 B5** SX1454.
Penponds *Cornw.* ***Hamlet***, 1m/2km SW of Camborne. SW6339.
Penpont *D. & G.* ***Village***, on Scaur Water, 2m/4km W of Thornhill. **68 D4** NX8494.
Penpont *Powys* ***Settlement***, 5m/7km W of Brecon. **27 J6** SN9728.
Penprysg *Bridgend* ***Suburb***, adjoining to N of Pencoed, 4m/7km NE of Bridgend. SS9682.
Penquit *Devon* ***Hamlet***, 1m/2km SE of Ivybridge. SX6454.
Penrest *Cornw.* ***Settlement***, 4m/7km S of Launceston. SX3377.
Penrherber *Carmar.* ***Settlement***, 1m/2km SW of Newcastle Emlyn. **17 F1** SN2939.
Penrhiw *Carmar.* ***Village***, 4m/6km W of Newcastle Emlyn. SN2540.
Penrhiw-llan *Cere.* ***Hamlet***, 4m/6km E of Newcastle Emlyn. **26 C4** SN3742.
Penrhiw-pâl *Cere.* ***Hamlet***, 4m/7km NE of Newcastle Emlyn. **26 C4** SN3445.
Penrhiwceiber *R.C.T.* ***Village***, 1m/2km S of Mountain Ash. **18 D2** ST0597.
Penrhiwgarreg *B.Gwent* ***Locality***, on E side of Abertillery. SO2204.
Penrhiwgoch *Carmar.* ***Settlement***, 3m/4km N of Cefneithin. **17 J3** SN5518.
Penrhiwtyn *N.P.T.* ***Suburb***, adjoining to S of Neath. SS7495.
Penrhos *Gwyn.* ***Hamlet***, on stream of same name, 2m/4km W of Pwllheli. **36 C2** SH3433.
Penrhos *I.o.A.* ***Hamlet***, on Holy Island, Anglesey, 2m/3km SE of Holyhead. **46 A4** SH2781.
Penrhos *Mon.* ***Hamlet***, 3m/4km N of Raglan. **28 D7** SO4111.
Penrhos *Powys* ***Locality***, adjoining to NE of Ystradgynlais, 2m/4km NE of Ystalyfera. **27 H7** SN8011.
Penrhos-garnedd *Gwyn.* ***Settlement***, 2m/3km SW of Bangor. **46 D5** SH5570.
Penrhosfeilw Standing Stones *I.o.A.* ***Historic/prehistoric site***, two standing stones (Cadw), about ten feet or three metres high, on Holy Island, 2m/3km SW of Holyhead. **46 A4** SH2280.
Penrhyn Bay (Bae Penryhn). *Conwy* Population: 3589. ***Small town***, resort on E side of Little Ormes Head. Also the name of the surrounding bay which stretches from Little Ormes Head to Rhôs Point. **47 G4** SH8281.
Penrhyn Castle *Gwyn.* ***Historic house***, mansion (National Trust) built in 19c in Norman style, 1m/2km E of Bangor. **46 E5** SH6071.
Penrhyn-coch *Cere.* ***Hamlet***, 4m/6km NE of Aberystwyth. **37 F7** SN6484.
Penrhyn Llŷn *Gwyn.* *Welsh form of Lleyn Peninsula, qv.*
Penrhyn Mawr *Gwyn.* ***Coastal feature***, headland on Caernarfon Bay, 4m/6km N of Aberdaron. **36 A2** SH1632.
Penrhyn Mawr *I.o.A.* ***Coastal feature***, headland on W coast of Holy Island, 3m/5km SW of Holyhead. **46 A5** SH2179.
Penrhyn-side *Conwy* ***Locality***, adjoining to W of resort of Penrhyn Bay. **47 G4** SH8181.
Penrhyn Slate Quarry *Gwyn.* *See Bethesda.*
Penrhyndeudraeth *Gwyn.* Population: 1948. ***Village***, 3m/5km E of Porthmadog and 6m/10km W of Ffestiniog. **37 F2** SH6138.
Penrhys *R.C.T.* ***Hamlet***, on S slopes of Mynydd Ty'n-tyle, between Rhondda Fawr and Rhondda Fach, 1km W of Tylorstown. **18 D2** ST0094.
Penrice *Swan.* ***Hamlet***, on Gower peninsula, 2m/4km NW of Oxwich Point and 11m/17km W of Swansea. Ruins of Norman castle to N in park; annual Gower Agricultural Show held in grounds. **17 H6** SS4987.
Penrith *Cumb.* Population: 12,049. ***Town***, market town, 18m/29km SE of Carlisle. Remains of 14c castle (English Heritage). Norman church. Town hall by Robert Adam. **61 G3** NY5130.
Penrith Castle *Cumb.* ***Castle***, ruined 14c castle (English Heritage) in Penrith, built to defend town against Scottish raiders. **61 G4** NY5129.
Penrose *Cornw.* ***Hamlet***, 5m/9km NW of Launceston. SX2589.
Penrose *Cornw.* ***Village***, 4m/6km SW of Padstow. **3 F1** SW8770.
Penruddock *Cumb.* ***Village***, 6m/9km W of Penrith. **60 F4** NY4227.
Penryn *Cornw.* ***Sea feature***, creek running from Penryn into Falmouth Bay. SW7934.
Penryn *Cornw.* Population: 7027. ***Small town***, granite historic port at head of inlet running down to Carrick Roads (River Fal), 2m/3km NW of Falmouth. Chief medieval port of Cornwall, superseded by Falmouth in 17c. **2 E5** SW7834.
Pensarn *Carmar.* ***Locality***, on S side of Carmarthen across River Tywi. **17 H3** SN4119.
Pensarn *Conwy* ***Village***, 1km N of Abergele. **47 H5** SH9579.
Pensax *Worcs.* ***Village***, 6m/10km W of Stourport-on-Severn. **29 G2** SO7269.
Pensby *Mersey.* ***Locality***, 1m/2km NW of Heswall. **48 B4** SJ2683.
Penselwood *Som.* ***Village***, 4m/6km NE of Wincanton. **9 G1** ST7531.
Pensford *B. & N.E.Som.* ***Village***, 6m/10km S of Bristol. **19 K5** ST6163.
Pensham *Worcs.* ***Settlement***, 1km S of Pershore across River Avon. **29 J4** SO9344.
Penshaw *T. & W.* ***Locality***, 3m/4km N of Houghton le Spring. **62 E1** NZ3253.
Penshaw Monument *T. & W.* ***Historic/prehistoric site***, Doric temple built in 1844 to commemorate 1st Earl of Durham and now National Trust property, 1km NE of Penshaw. NZ3354.
Penshiel Hill *E.Loth.* ***Mountain***, in Lammermuir Hills, 1m/2km SW of Whiteadder Reservoir. Height 1401 feet or 427 metres. **76 E4** NT6362.
Penshurst *Kent* ***Village***, on River Medway, 5m/7km W of Tonbridge. **23 J7** TQ5243.
Penshurst Place *Kent* ***Historic house***, 14c manor house on N side of Penshurst. **23 J7** TQ5243.
Pensilva *Cornw.* Population: 1528. ***Village***, 4m/7km NE of Liskeard. **4 C4** SX2969.
Pensnett *W.Mid.* ***Suburb***, 2m/4km SW of Dudley town centre. **40 B7** SO9188.
Penston *E.Loth.* ***Hamlet***, 1km E of Macmerry. NT4472.
Pentewan *Cornw.* ***Village***, 3m/5km S of St. Austell. **4 A6** SX0147.
Pentir *Gwyn.* ***Village***, 3m/5km S of Bangor. **46 D6** SH5767.
Pentire *Cornw.* ***Suburb***, W district of Newquay. **2 E2** SW7961.
Pentire Point *Cornw.* ***Coastal feature***, headland (National Trust) on N coast at N end of Padstow Bay. **3 G1** SW9280.
Pentireglaze *Cornw.* ***Settlement***, 1km NE of Polzeath. **3 G1** SW9479.
Pentland Firth ***Sea feature***, sea area between Orkney and N coast of Scottish mainland. **107 B9** ND2682.
Pentland Hills ***Large natural feature***, range of grass-covered hills, designated as Regional Park, largely composed of Old Red Sandstone, running some 16m/26km from S of Edinburgh towards Carnwath. Numerous reservoirs. Summit is Scald Law, 1898 feet or 579 metres. **75 J5** NT1055.
Pentland Skerries *Ork.* ***Island***, group of four small uninhabited islands at E end of Pentland Firth, 3m/5km S of South Ronaldsay. Islands are Muckle Skerry (largest, with lighthouse), Little Skerry, Louther Skerry and Clettack Skerry. **105 K1** ND4678.
Pentlepoir *Pembs.* ***Hamlet***, 1m/2km W of Saundersfoot. **16 E4** SN1105.
Pentlow *Essex* ***Hamlet***, on River Stour, opposite Cavendish, 3m/5km W of Long Melford. **34 C4** TL8146.
Pentlow Street *Essex* ***Settlement***, 1km E of Pentlow. TL8246.
Pentney *Norf.* ***Village***, 7m/11km NW of Swaffham. **44 B4** TF7213.
Penton Grafton *Hants.* ***Hamlet***, 3m/4km NW of Andover. SU3247.
Penton Mewsey *Hants.* ***Village***, 3m/4km NW of Andover. **21 G7** SU3347.
Pentonville *Gt.Lon.* ***Suburb***, in borough of Islington, 2m/3km N of Charing Cross. TQ3083.
Pentraeth *I.o.A.* ***Village***, on Anglesey, 5m/8km N of Menai Bridge. **46 D5** SH5278.
Pentre *Flints.* ***Locality***, on SE side of Queensferry. SJ3167.
Pentre *Powys* ***Settlement***, adjoining to S of Llangynog across River Tanat. **37 K3** SJ0525.
Pentre *Powys* ***Settlement***, 4m/7km SW of Newtown. **37 K7** SO0686.
Pentre *Powys* ***Settlement***, 1m/2km SE of Kerry. SO1589.
Pentre *Powys* ***Settlement***, 4m/7km SW of Knighton. **28 B2** SO2366.

P

Pentre *Powys* ***Settlement***, 4m/6km NW of Bishop's Castle. **38 B6** SO2792.

Pentre *R.C.T.* ***Village***, in Rhondda Fawr valley, 1km SE of Treorchy. **18 C2** SS9696.

Pentre *Shrop.* ***Settlement***, 3m/4km S of Clun. SO3076.

Pentre *Shrop.* ***Village***, 9m/14km NW of Shrewsbury. **38 C4** SJ3617.

Pentre *Wrex.* ***Hamlet***, 2m/3km N of Chirk. **38 B1** SJ2840.

Pentre *Wrex.* ***Settlement***, 2m/3km SE of Ruabon. SJ3141.

Pentre Bach *Flints.* ***Locality***, 1m/2km NW of Bagillt. SJ2176.

Pentre-bach *Powys* ***Settlement***, 3m/5km N of Sennybridge. **27 J5** SN9032.

Pentre Berw *I.o.A.* ***Village***, on Anglesey, 2m/4km S of Llangefni across Malltraeth Marsh. **46 C5** SH4772.

Pentre-bont *Conwy* ***Hamlet***, on River Lledr, opposite Dolwyddelan. **47 F7** SH7352.

Pentre-bwlch *Denb.* ***Settlement***, 1m/2km S of Pen-y-stryt. **38 A1** SJ1949.

Pentre-celyn *Denb.* ***Village***, 4m/6km S of Ruthin. **47 K7** SJ1453.

Pentre-celyn *Powys* ***Settlement***, 4m/6km SE of Aberangell. **37 H5** SH8905.

Pentre-chwyth *Swan.* ***Suburb***, 2m/3km NE of Swansea city centre across River Tawe. **17 K5** SS6795.

Pentre-cwrt *Carmar.* ***Village***, 2m/4km SW of Llandysul. **17 G1** SN3838.

Pentre-Dolau-Honddu *Powys* ***Settlement***, 4m/6km SE of Llangammarch Wells. **27 J4** SN9943.

Pentre-dwr *Swan.* ***Suburb***, 4m/6km NE of Swansea. **17 K5** SS6996.

Pentre Ffwrndan *Flints.* ***Suburb***, adjoining to SE of Flint. SJ2572.

Pentre-galar *Pembs.* ***Settlement***, 2m/3km S of Crymych. **16 E1** SN1730.

Pentre Gwenlais *Carmar.* ***Hamlet***, 3m/4km N of Ammanford. **17 K3** SN6016.

Pentre Gwynfryn *Gwyn.* ***Settlement***, 3m/4km SE of Harlech. **36 E3** SH5927.

Pentre Halkyn *Flints.* ***Hamlet***, 1m/2km NW of Halkyn and 2m/4km SE of Holywell. **48 B5** SJ2072.

Pentre Ifan Burial Chamber *Pembs.* ***Historic/prehistoric site***, burial-chamber (Cadw) 3m/5km SE of Newport. **16 E1** SN0936.

Pentre Isaf *Conwy* ***Settlement***, in valley of River Elwy, 6m/9km S of Colwyn Bay. **47 G6** SH8768.

Pentre Llanrhaeadr *Denb.* ***Hamlet***, 4m/6km NW of Ruthin. **47 J6** SJ0862.

Pentre-llwyn-llŵyd *Powys* ***Settlement***, 5m/8km NW of Builth Wells. **27 J3** SN9654.

Pentre-llyn *Cere.* ***Settlement***, just W of Llanilar. SN6175.

Pentre Maelor *Wrex.* ***Settlement***, 3m/4km SE of Wrexham town centre. **38 C1** SJ3749.

Pentre Meyrick (Pentremeurig). *V. of Glam.* ***Hamlet***, 2m/3km NW of Cowbridge. SS9675.

Pentre-piod *Gwyn.* ***Settlement***, at SW end of Llyn Tegid (Bala Lake). **37 H2** SH8931.

Pentre-poeth *Newport* ***Suburb***, 3m/4km W of Newport. **19 F3** ST2686.

Pentre Poeth *Swan.* ***Suburb***, on NW side of Morriston, 4m/6km N of Swansea city centre. SS6698.

Pentre-Poid *Torfaen* ***Locality***, 1m/2km NW of Pontypool. SO2602.

Pentre Saron *Denb.* ***Settlement***, 4m/6km S of Denbigh. **47 J6** SJ0260.

Pentre-tafarn-y-fedw *Conwy* ***Hamlet***, 1m/2km NE of Llanrwst. **47 G6** SH8162.

Pentre-tŷn-gwyn *Carmar.* ***Settlement***, 4m/6km E of Llandovery. **27 H5** SN8135.

Pentrebach *Cere.* ***Settlement***, 2m/3km W of Lampeter. SN5547.

Pentrebach *M.Tyd.* ***Village***, 2m/3km SE of Merthyr Tydfil. **18 D1** SO0603.

Pentrebach *R.C.T.* ***Hamlet***, 1m/2km E of Pontypridd, over River Taff. ST0889.

Pentrebach *Swan.* ***Settlement***, 1m/2km N of Pontarddulais. **17 K4** SN6005.

Pentrecagal *Carmar.* ***Hamlet***, 2m/3km E of Newcastle Emlyn. **26 C4** SN3340.

Pentreclwydau *N.P.T.* ***Settlement***, 2m/3km NE of Resolven. **18 B1** SN8405.

Pentredwr *Denb.* ***Settlement***, 3m/5km S of Pen-y-stryt, 1m/2km E of Horseshoe Pass. **38 A1** SJ1946.

Pentrefelin *Carmar.* ***Settlement***, 2m/3km NW of Llandeilo. **17 J2** SN5923.

Pentrefelin *Cere.* ***Settlement***, 2m/4km E of Lampeter. **27 F4** SN6148.

Pentrefelin *Conwy* ***Village***, 4m/6km SW of Colwyn Bay. Ancient burial chamber 1km W. **47 G5** SH8074.

Pentrefelin *Gwyn.* ***Hamlet***, 2m/3km NE of Criccieth. **36 E2** SH5239.

Pentrefelin *I.o.A.* ***Locality***, 1km S of Amlwch. SH4392.

Pentrefelin *Powys* ***Settlement***, 3m/4km SE of Llanrhaeadr-ym-Mochnant. **38 A3** SJ1524.

Pentrefoelas *Conwy* ***Hamlet***, 8m/12km SE of Llanrwst. **47 G7** SH8751.

Pentregat *Cere.* ***Hamlet***, 3m/5km SE of Llangranog. **26 C3** SN3551.

Pentreheyling *Shrop.* ***Settlement***, 2m/3km SW of Church Stoke. **38 B6** SO2493.

Pentremeurig *V. of Glam.* *Welsh form of Pentre Meyrick, qv.*

Pentre'r beirdd *Powys* ***Settlement***, 5m/8km NW of Welshpool. **38 A4** SJ1813.

Pentre'r Felin *Conwy* ***Hamlet***, 1km S of Eglwysbach. SH8069.

Pentre'r-felin *Powys* ***Settlement***, 1m/2km N of Sennybridge. **27 J5** SN9230.

Pentrich *Derbys.* ***Village***, 1m/2km NW of Ripley. **51 F7** SK3852.

Pentridge *Dorset* ***Village***, 3m/4km E of Sixpenny Handley. **10 B3** SU0317.

Pentridge Hill *Dorset* ***Hill***, topped by Iron Age fort, 1km SE of Pentridge. Height 607 feet or 185 metres. **10 B3** SU0317.

Pentwyn *Caerp.* ***Hamlet***, 2m/3km S of Rhymney. SO1004.

Pentwyn *Cardiff* ***Hamlet***, adjoining to SW of Pentyrch, 6m/10km NW of Cardiff. ST0981.

Pentwyn *Cardiff* ***Suburb***, 4m/6km NE of Cardiff city centre. **19 F3** ST2081.

Pentwyn *Carmar.* ***Settlement***, 1km S of Cross Hands. SN5611.

Pentwyn Berthlŵyd *M.Tyd.* ***Hamlet***, 1km S of Treharris. ST1096.

Pentwyn-mawr *Caerp.* ***Suburb***, 1m/2km SW of Newbridge. Industrial estate to W. ST1996.

Pentwyn Reservoir *Powys* ***Reservoir***, small reservoir, 6m/9km N of Merthyr Tydfil. **27 K7** SO0515.

Pentyrch *Cardiff* Population: 2303. ***Village***, 6m/10km NW of Cardiff. **18 E3** ST1081.

Penuwch *Cere.* ***Settlement***, 6m/9km W of Tregaron. **26 E2** SN5962.

Penvalla *Sc.Bord.* ***Mountain***, 3m/4km NW of Stobo. Height 1765 feet or 538 metres. **75 K7** NT1539.

Penwhapple Reservoir *S.Ayr.* ***Reservoir***, 2m/4km N of Barr. **67 G4** NX2697.

Penwithick *Cornw.* ***Village***, in china clay district, 2m/4km N of St. Austell. **4 A5** SX0256.

Penwood *Hants.* ***Village***, 1m/2km NE of Highclere. SU4461.

Penwortham *Lancs.* ***Small town***, on S side of River Ribble, 2m/3km SW of Preston town centre. **55 J7** SD5128.

Penwortham Lane *Lancs.* ***Suburb***, 2m/3km S of Preston town centre. SD5326.

Penwyllt *Powys* ***Locality***, 7m/11km NE of Ystalyfera. Quarries. **27 H7** SN8515.

Penybont *Cere.* ***Settlement***, 2m/4km SW of Talybont. SN6288.

Penybont *Powys* ***Village***, on River Ithon, 4m/6km NE of Llandrindod Wells. **28 A2** SO1164.

Penybontfawr *Powys* ***Village***, on River Tanat, 5m/8km NW of Llanfyllin. **37 K3** SJ0824.

Penybryn *Caerp.* ***Hamlet***, 1m/2km NW of Ystrad Mynach. **18 E2** ST1396.

Penycae *Wrex.* ***Village***, 2m/3km W of Ruabon. **38 B1** SJ2745.

Penycaerau *Gwyn.* ***Locality***, 2m/3km E of Aberdaron. SH1927.

Penycwm *Pembs.* ***Hamlet***, 6m/10km E of St. David's. **16 B2** SM8423.

Penyffordd *Flints.* Population: 3125. ***Village***, 3m/4km S of Hawarden. **48 C6** SJ3061.

Penyffridd *Gwyn.* ***Hamlet***, 4m/6km S of Caernarfon. SH5056.

Penygadair *Gwyn.* ***Mountain***, central peak and summit of Cadair Idris. Height 2929 feet or 893 metres. **37 G4** SH7113.

Penygarn *Torfaen* ***Suburb***, to NE of Pontypool. SO2801.

Penygarnedd *Powys* ***Hamlet***, 2m/3km SW of Llanrhaeadr-ym-Mochnant. **38 A3** SJ1023.

Penygarreg Reservoir *Powys* ***Reservoir***, one of series of large reservoirs in River Elan valley, 4m/6km W of Rhayader. **27 J2** SN9067.

Penygraig *R.C.T.* ***Small town***, 1km S of Tonypandy. **18 C2** SS9991.

Penygroes *Carmar.* ***Village***, 3m/4km W of Ammanford. **17 J3** SN5813.

Penygroes *Gwyn.* Population: 1796. ***Village***, 6m/10km S of Caernarfon. **46 C7** SH4753.

Penygroes *Pembs.* ***Settlement***, 2m/3km SE of Eglwyswrw. SN1535.

Penymynydd *Flints.* ***Hamlet***, adjoining to N of Penyffordd. SJ3062.

Penyraber *Pembs.* ***Suburb***, in N part of Fishguard, beside Fishguard Harbour. SM9537.

Penyrheol *Caerp.* ***Suburb***, 1m/2km NW of Caerphilly town centre. ST1488.

Penyrheol *Swan.* ***Suburb***, NW district of Gorseinon. SS5899.

Penysarn *I.o.A.* ***Village***, 2m/3km SE of Amlwch, Anglesey. **46 C3** SH4690.

Penywaun *R.C.T.* ***Village***, 2m/4km NW of Aberdare. **18 C1** SN9704.

Penywern *N.P.T.* ***Locality***, adjoining to N of Ystalyfera. SN7609.

Penzance *Cornw.* Population: 19,709. ***Town***, resort and port, 24m/39km SW of Truro. Boat and helicopter services to Isles of Scilly. Interesting buildings include 19c Egyptian House. Tourism now an important industry. Home to Trinity House National Lighthouse Centre. **2 B5** SW4730.

Peopleton *Worcs.* ***Village***, 3m/5km N of Pershore. **29 J3** SO9350.

Peover Heath *Ches.* ***Hamlet***, 4m/7km NE of Holmes Chapel. **49 G5** SJ7973.

Peper Harow *Surr.* ***Hamlet***, 2m/4km W of Godalming. **22 C7** SU9344.

Peplow *Shrop.* ***Hamlet***, 3m/5km SE of Hodnet. Hall is of early 18c. **39 F3** SJ6324.

Pepper Arden *N.Yorks.* ***Hamlet***, 7m/11km NW of Northallerton. NZ2901.

Peppermill Dam *Fife* ***Lake/loch***, 2m/3km NE of Kincardine. **75 H2** NS9489.

Pepper's Green *Essex* ***Settlement***, 3m/4km SE of Leaden Roding. TL6210.

Pepperstock *Beds.* ***Hamlet***, 2m/3km S of Luton town centre. TL0818.

Perceton *N.Ayr.* ***Suburb***, in E part of Irvine. **74 B6** NS3440.

Percie *Aber.* ***Settlement***, 1km W of Finzean. **90 D5** NO5992.

Percuil *Cornw.* ***River***, rising near Treworlas and flowing into Carrick Roads (River Fal) at St. Mawes, opposite Falmouth. **3 F5** SW8533.

Percy Main *T. & W.* ***Suburb***, 1m/2km SW of North Shields. NZ3467.

Percyhorner *Aber.* ***Hamlet***, 2m/4km SW of Fraserburgh. NJ9565.

Percy's Cross *Northumb.* ***Historic/prehistoric site***, shaft of cross, 9m/15km NW of Alnwick, marking spot where leader of Lancastrians was killed in Battle of Hedgeley Moor, 1464. NU0419.

Perdiswell *Worcs.* ***Suburb***, in N part of Worcester. SO8557.

Pergins Island *Poole* ***Island***, small uninhabited island near N end of Holes Bay, to W of Poole town centre. SZ0092.

Perham Down *Wilts.* ***Settlement***, 1m/2km S of Ludgershall. **21 F7** SU2549.

Periton *Som.* ***Suburb***, S district of Minehead. SS9645.

Perivale *Gt.Lon.* ***Suburb***, in borough of Ealing, 9m/14km W of Charing Cross. **22 E3** TQ1683.

Perkhill *Aber.* ***Settlement***, 1m/2km NW of Lumphanan. **90 D4** NJ5705.

Perkins Beach *Shrop.* ***Settlement***, 3m/5km S of Minsterley. **38 C5** SJ3600.

Perkin's Village *Devon* ***Settlement***, 7m/11km E of Exeter. SY0291.

Perkinsville *Dur.* ***Locality***, on N side of Pelton, 2m/3km NW of Chester-le-Street. NZ2553.

Perlethorpe *Notts.* ***Hamlet***, on E edge of Thoresby Park, 2m/4km N of Ollerton. **51 J5** SK6471.

Perran Bay *Cornw.* *Alternative name for Ligger Bay, qv.*

Perran Beach *Cornw.* *See Ligger Bay.*

Perran Downs *Cornw.* ***Village***, 4m/7km S of Hayle. SW5530.

Perran Wharf *Cornw.* ***Settlement***, 3m/4km N of Penryn, on River Kennel. SW7738.

Perranarworthal *Cornw.* ***Village***, 3m/5km N of Penryn. **2 E5** SW7738.

Perranporth *Cornw.* Population: 2611. ***Small town***, coastal resort, 6m/9km SW of Newquay. Large sand dunes at Perran Sands. Popular surfing centre. **2 E3** SW7554.

Perranuthnoe *Cornw.* ***Village***, on S coast, 4m/6km E of Penzance across Mount's Bay. **2 C6** SW5329.

Perranwell Station *Cornw.* ***Hamlet***, 3m/5km N of Penryn. **2 E5** SW7739.

Perranzabuloe *Cornw.* ***Hamlet***, 2m/3km SE of Perranporth. **2 E3** SW7752.

Perrott's Brook *Glos.* ***Hamlet***, 3m/4km N of Cirencester. SP0106.

Perry *Shrop.* ***River***, rising N of Oswestry and flowing generally SE into River Severn 4m/7km NW of Shrewsbury. SJ4416.

Perry *W.Mid.* ***Suburb***, 3m/5km N of Birmingham city centre. SP0792.

Perry Barr *W.Mid.* ***Suburb***, 3m/5km N of Birmingham city centre. **40 C6** SP0791.

Perry Beeches *W.Mid.* ***Suburb***, N district of Birmingham. SP0593.

Perry Crofts *Staffs.* ***Suburb***, to N of Tamworth town centre. SK2105.

Perry Green *Essex* ***Settlement***, 3m/5km E of Braintree. TL8022.

Perry Green *Herts.* ***Hamlet***, 5m/8km N of Ware. **33 H7** TL4317.

Perry Green *Wilts.* ***Hamlet***, adjoining to E of Charlton, 3m/4km NE of Malmesbury. ST9689.

Perry Hall *W.Mid.* ***Suburb***, 3m/4km NE of Wolverhampton town centre. SJ9600.

Perry Street *Kent* ***Suburb***, 1km SE of Northfleet. **24 C4** TQ6373.

Perryfields *Worcs.* ***Suburb***, in N part of Bromsgrove. SO9471.

Perrymead *B. & N.E.Som.* ***Suburb***, 1km S of Bath city centre. ST7563.

Persey *P. & K.* ***Settlement***, 2m/3km N of Bridge of Cally. **82 C2** NO1354.

Pershall *Staffs.* ***Hamlet***, 1m/2km NW of Eccleshall. **40 A3** SJ8129.

Pershore *Worcs.* Population: 7087. ***Small town***, attractive market town on River Avon and centre of a fruit-growing area. Pershore and Hindlip Horticultural College on outskirts. **29 J4** SO9446.

Pershore Abbey *Worcs.* ***Ecclesiastical building***, in centre of Pershore, 7m/11km SE of Worcester. Benedictine abbey and choir built in 12c, now used as parish church. **29 J4** SO9446.

Pershore Bridge (Old Pershore Bridge). *Worcs.* ***Bridge***, stone bridge with brick parapets, dating from 1290, spanning River Avon at Pershore. Now by-passed by new bridge. SO9545.

Persley *Aberdeen* ***Locality***, on River Don, 3m/5km NW of Aberdeen city centre. NJ9010.

Pert *Angus* ***Hamlet***, to S of North Bridge Water, 2m/3km W of Marykirk. **83 H1** NO6565.

Pertenhall *Beds.* ***Village***, 2m/3km SW of Kimbolton. **32 D2** TL0865.

Perth *P. & K.* Population: 41,453. ***City***, ancient cathedral city (Royal Charter granted 1210) on River Tay, 31m/50km N of Edinburgh. Once capital of Medieval Scotland. Centre of livestock trade. Previously cotton manufacturing centre; now important industries include whisky distilling. Airfield (Scone) to NE. **82 C5** NO1123.

Perthcelyn *R.C.T.* ***Village***, 1m/2km S of Mountain Ash. ST0597.

Perthy *Shrop.* ***Hamlet***, 2m/4km W of Ellesmere. **38 C2** SJ3633.

Perton *Staffs.* ***Settlement***, 4m/6km W of Wolverhampton. **40 A6** SO8598.

Perwick Bay *I.o.M.* ***Bay***, S facing bay on S side of Port St. Mary. **54 B7** SC2067.

Pestalozzi Children's Village *E.Suss.* ***Village***, situated at Sedlescombe, 3m/4km NE of Battle. Founded in 1960 for refugee children. TQ7817.

Pested *Kent* ***Locality***, 6m/10km S of Faversham. TR0051.

Peter Black Sand *Norf.* ***Coastal feature***, mudbank in S part of The Wash off N Norfolk coast, 4m/6km E of Dersingham. **44 A2** TF6131.

Peter Hill *Aber.* ***Mountain***, 3m/5km SE of Ballochan. Height 2024 feet or 617 metres. **90 D6** NO5788.
Peter Tavy *Devon* ***Village***, on W side of Dartmoor, 3m/5km NE of Tavistock. **5 F3** SX5177.
Peterborough *Peter.* Population: 134,788. ***City***, on River Nene, 73m/117km N of London. Designated a New Town in 1967. Industrial, commercial and shopping city. Centre of important agricultural area. Cathedral of St. Peter's, Norman and later, gave city its name. 17c guildhall. East of England Agricultural Showground at Alwalton. Flag Fen Excavations, 3m/4km E of city centre, are important archaeological site, with England's earliest wheel housed in Bronze Age museum. **42 E6** TL1998.
Peterborough Cathedral *Peter.* ***Ecclesiastical building***, Saxon foundation as monastery and rebuilt after Conquest, situated in Peterborough city centre. One of most significant Norman buildings in Britain. Memorial stone to Catherine of Aragon, Henry VIII's first wife, who was buried here. Slab marks original burial place in 1587 of Mary, Queen of Scots; her body was subsequently moved to Westminster Abbey by James I in 1612. **42 E6** TL1998.
Peterborough Museum *Peter.* ***Other feature of interest***, in Peterborough city centre, with local history exhibitions. **42 E6** TL1998.
Peterburn *High.* ***Settlement***, on W coast of Ross and Cromarty district, 6m/9km S of Rubha Réidh. **94 D3** NG7483.
Peterchurch *Here.* ***Village***, 8m/12km NW of Pontrilas. **28 C5** SO3438.
Peterculter *Aberdeen* ***Village***, with much housing development, at confluence of Leuchar Burn and River Dee, 7m/11km SW of Aberdeen. **91 G4** NJ8400.
Peterhead *Aber.* Population: 18,674. ***Town***, spa town, port and most easterly town on Scottish mainland, located on NE coast, 27m/44km N of Aberdeen. Largest white fish port in Europe. Industrial estate developments at Dales Farm and Upperton to S. **99 K6** NK1346.
Peterhead Bay *Aber.* ***Bay***, forms large harbour to S of Peterhead. **99 K6** NK1245.
Peterlee *Dur.* Population: 31,139. ***Town***, New Town designated 1948, 7m/11km NW of Hartlepool. **63 F2** NZ4240.
Peter's Green *Herts.* ***Hamlet***, 3m/5km N of Harpenden. **32 E7** TL1419.
Peter's Hill *Aber.* ***Mountain***, 3m/5km N of Ballater. Height 1863 feet or 568 metres. **90 B4** NJ3600.
Peters Marland *Devon* ***Hamlet***, 4m/6km S of Great Torrington. **6 C4** SS4713.
Petersfield *Hants.* Population: 12,177. ***Town***, market town, 11m/18km NE of Portsmouth, with many Georgian houses and a Norman church. **11 J2** SU7423.
Petersfinger *Wilts.* ***Hamlet***, 1m/2km SE of Salisbury. SU1629.
Petersham *Gt.Lon.* ***Locality***, residential locality in borough of Richmond upon Thames, on E bank of River Thames, 1m/2km S of Richmond town centre. TQ1873.
Peterson's Rock *Arg. & B.* ***Island***, rock with beacon lying 1m/2km E of Sanda Island, off S coast of Kintyre. NR7504.
Peterston-super-Ely (Llanbedr-y-fro). *V. of Glam.* ***Village***, 6m/10km W of Cardiff. **18 D4** ST0876.
Peterstone Wentlooge (Llanbedr Gwynllwg). *Newport* ***Village***, near coast, 6m/9km SW of Newport. **19 F3** ST2680.
Peterstow *Here.* ***Village***, 2m/4km W of Ross-on-Wye. **28 E6** SO5624.
Petham *Kent* ***Village***, 4m/7km S of Canterbury. **15 G2** TR1251.
Petherwin Gate *Cornw.* ***Village***, just S of North Petherwin, 4m/7km NW of Launceston. SX2889.
Petre Bank *Ches.* ***Locality***, adjoining to E of Poynton. SJ9383.
Petrockstow *Devon* ***Village***, 4m/6km NW of Hatherleigh. **6 D5** SS5109.
Pett *E.Suss.* ***Village***, 5m/7km NE of Hastings. **14 D6** TQ8713.
Pett Street *Kent* ***Locality***, 2m/3km E of Wye. TR0847.
Petta Water *Shet. See Sand Water.*
Pettaugh *Suff.* ***Village***, 2m/4km S of Debenham. **35 F3** TM1659.
Petteridge *Kent* ***Hamlet***, 1km SW of Brenchley. TQ6641.
Petteril *Cumb.* ***River***, rising at Penruddock, and flowing N into River Eden on E side of Carlisle. **61 F2** NY4156.
Petteril Green *Cumb.* ***Hamlet***, on River Petteril, 2m/3km S of High Hesket. Site of Roman camp to N. NY4741.
Pettinain *S.Lan.* ***Village***, 2m/3km S of Carstairs Junction across River Clyde. **75 H6** NS9543.
Pettistree *Suff.* ***Village***, 1km SW of Wickham Market. **35 G3** TM2954.
Petton *Devon* ***Hamlet***, 3m/5km NE of Bampton. **7 J3** ST0024.
Petton *Shrop.* ***Settlement***, 1m/2km W of Burlton. **38 D3** SJ4326.
Petts Wood *Gt.Lon.* ***Suburb***, in borough of Bromley, 1m/2km NW of Orpington. Named after wood (partly National Trust) to N. TQ4467.
Petty *Aber.* ***Settlement***, 1km S of Fyvie. **91 F1** NJ7636.
Pettycur *Fife* ***Locality***, with small harbour, at S end of Kinghorn. **76 A2** NT2686.
Pettymuick *Aber.* ***Settlement***, 2m/3km SE of Pitmedden. **91 H2** NJ9024.
Petuaria *E.Riding See Brough.*
Petworth *W.Suss.* Population: 2156. ***Small town***, 13m/21km NE of Chichester; Petworth House (National Trust), 17c-19c, with large deer park. **12 C4** SU9721.
Petworth House *W.Suss.* ***Historic house***, late 17c mansion (National Trust) in centre of Petworth, built in French grand style and with 700 acre grounds landscaped by 'Capability' Brown. Impressive collection of paintings includes works by Turner, Van Dyck, Titian, Gainsborough and Reynolds. **12 C4** SU9721.
Petworth Park *W.Suss.* ***Open space***, deer park of over 700 acres (National Trust) to NW of Petworth, landscaped by 'Capability' Brown. **12 C4** SU9622.
Pevensey *E.Suss.* ***Village***, 4m/7km NE of Eastbourne. The Roman Anderida. Remains of Norman castle within walls of Roman fort (English Heritage). **13 K6** TQ6404.
Pevensey Bay *E.Suss.* ***Bay***, wide SE facing bay to N of Langney Point, with coastal resort of same name at its centre. **13 K6** TQ6603.
Pevensey Bay *E.Suss.* Population: 2537. ***Village***, coastal resort extending 2m/3km along coast on bay of same name, 4m/7km NE of Eastbourne. **13 K6** TQ6503.
Pevensey Castle *E.Suss.* ***Castle***, Norman keep within a Roman fort (English Heritage), 4m/6km NE of Eastbourne. **13 K6** TQ6405.
Pevensey Levels *E.Suss.* ***Marsh/bog***, well-drained marshland to N of Pevensey. **13 K6** TQ6307.
Peverell *Plym.* ***Suburb***, of Plymouth N of Central Park. SX4756.
Peveril Castle *Derbys.* ***Castle***, ruined Norman castle (English Heritage) on rocky limestone hill to S of Castleton. **50 D4** SK1482.
Peveril Point *Dorset* ***Coastal feature***, headland at S end of Swanage Bay. **10 B7** SZ0478.
Pewet Island *Essex* ***Island***, marshy island off E bank of River Blackwater estuary. Bradwell Creek passes between island and Bradwell Waterside. TL9908.
Pewit Island *Essex* ***Island***, in Pyefleet Channel on N side of Mersea Island. TM0516.
Pewit Island *Essex* ***Island***, uninhabited marshy island 3m/5km NW of The Naze. TM2226.
Pewit Island *Ports.* ***Island***, small uninhabited island in Portsmouth Harbour. SU6003.
Pewsey *Wilts.* Population: 2452. ***Small town***, on branch of River Avon near its source 6m/10km S of Marlborough. 2km S, Pewsey White Horse cut in chalk on side of Pewsey Hill in 1937. **20 E5** SU1660.
Pewsey Down *Wilts.* ***Open space***, hillslope 2m/3km S of Pewsey. **20 E6** SU1657.
Pewsey Wharf *Wilts.* ***Settlement***, on Kennet and Avon Canal, 1km N of Pewsey. SU1561.
Pewsham *Wilts.* ***Settlement***, 3m/4km SE of Chippenham. ST9470.
Phantassie *E.Loth.* ***Suburb***, on E side of East Linton. Birthplace of Sir John Rennie, 1761-1821, engineer. Notable 16c dovecote (National Trust for Scotland). NT5977.
Pharay *Ork. Alternative spelling of Faray, qv.*
Pheasant's Hill *Bucks.* ***Hamlet***, 4m/7km W of Marlow. SU7887.
Phesdo *Aber.* ***Settlement***, 2m/3km NE of Fettercairn. **90 E7** NO6775.
Philadelphia *T. & W.* ***Locality***, 1m/2km N of Houghton le Spring. NZ3352.
Philham *Devon* ***Hamlet***, 1m/2km S of Hartland. **6 A3** SS2522.
Philip Law *Sc.Bord.* ***Mountain***, in Cheviot Hills, 3m/5km NW of Carter Bar. Height 1358 feet or 414 metres. **70 C2** NT7210.
Philiphaugh *Sc.Bord.* ***Locality***, estate to N of confluence of Ettrick Water and Yarrow Water, 2m/3km W of Selkirk. Site of 1645 Battle of Philiphaugh to E. **69 K1** NT4528.
Philipps House *Wilts.* ***Historic house***, Neo-Grecian house by Jeffry Wyatville, completed 1816 (National Trust), to W of Dinton and 9m/14km W of Salisbury. Home of Wyndham family. **10 B1** SU0032.
Phillack *Cornw.* ***Hamlet***, 1km N of Hayle. **2 C5** SW5638.
Philleigh *Cornw.* ***Village***, 4m/7km NE of St. Mawes. **3 F5** SW8739.
Phillipps House *Wilts. See Dinton.*
Phillipstown *Caerp.* ***Locality***, 3m/4km N of Bargoed. SO1403.
Philorth *Aber.* ***Locality***, comprises Mains of Philorth, Milton of Philorth and Philorth House, 3m/4km S of Fraserburgh. Water of Philorth is stream on E side of locality running NE into Fraserburgh Bay. NK0063.
Philpstoun *W.Loth.* ***Village***, 3m/5km E of Linlithgow. **75 J3** NT0477.
Phocle Green *Here.* ***Hamlet***, 3m/4km NE of Ross-on-Wye. SO6226.
Phoenix Green *Hants.* ***Village***, 2m/4km NE of Hook. **22 A6** SU7555.
Phones *High.* ***Settlement***, 3m/5km S of Newtonmore. **88 E5** NN7094.
Phorp *Moray* ***Settlement***, 4m/6km S of Forres. **97 H6** NJ0452.
Pibsbury *Som.* ***Hamlet***, adjoining Huish Episcopi, 1m/2km E of Langport. **8 D2** ST4426.
Pica *Cumb.* ***Hamlet***, 4m/6km NE of Whitehaven. **60 B4** NY0222.
Picardy Stone *Aber.* ***Historic/prehistoric site***, Pictish inscriptions dating from 7c or 8c on stone (Historic Scotland), 2m/3km NW of Insch. **90 E1** NJ6130.
Piccadilly Corner *Norf.* ***Hamlet***, 3m/4km NE of Harleston. **45 G7** TM2786.
Piccotts End *Herts.* ***Historic house***, 1m/2km N of Hemel Hempstead town centre. **22 D1** TL0509.
Piccotts End *Herts.* ***Suburb***, in N part of Hemel Hempstead. **22 D1** TL0509.
Pickburn *S.Yorks.* ***Hamlet***, 1m/2km W of Adwick le Street. SE5107.
Picken End *Worcs.* ***Locality***, adjoining to E of Hanley Swan, 3m/5km SE of Great Malvern. SO8142.
Pickerells *Essex* ***Settlement***, 1km N of Fyfield, 3m/5km NE of Chipping Ongar. **23 J1** TL5707.
Pickering *N.Yorks.* Population: 5914. ***Small town***, at foot of North York Moors, 16m/25km W of Scarborough. Remains of Norman castle (English Heritage); Pickering Vale Museum and Arts Centre. **58 E1** SE7984.
Pickering Castle *N.Yorks.* ***Castle***, 11c-12c motte and bailey castle (English Heritage), on N side of Pickering. Later converted into stone castle. **58 E1** SE7984.
Pickering Nook *Dur.* ***Hamlet***, adjoining to S of Hobson, 4m/6km NW of Stanley. NZ1755.
Picket Piece *Hants.* ***Settlement***, 2m/3km NE of Andover. **21 G7** SU3947.
Picket Post *Hants.* ***Settlement***, 3m/5km E of Ringwood. **10 C4** SU1906.
Pickford *W.Mid.* ***Settlement***, 4m/7km NW of Coventry city centre. SP2781.
Pickford Green *W.Mid.* ***Hamlet***, adjoins to S of Pickford, 4m/6km NW of Coventry. **40 E7** SP2781.
Pickhill *N.Yorks.* ***Village***, 5m/8km SE of Leeming. **57 J1** SE3483.
Picklescott *Shrop.* ***Hamlet***, 4m/6km N of Church Stretton. **38 D6** SO4399.
Pickletillem *Fife* ***Hamlet***, 3m/4km N of Leuchars. **83 F5** NO4324.
Pickmere *Ches.* ***Village***, 3m/5km NE of Northwich. **49 F5** SJ6977.
Pickney *Som.* ***Hamlet***, 4m/6km NW of Taunton. ST1929.
Pickstock *Tel. & W.* ***Settlement***, 3m/4km NW of Newport. **39 G3** SJ7223.
Pickston *P. & K.* ***Settlement***, 3m/4km NW of Methven. **82 A5** NN9928.
Picktree *Dur.* ***Locality***, 1m/2km NE of Chester-le-Street. NZ2853.
Pickup Bank *B'burn.* ***Settlement***, 2m/3km E of Darwen. SD7222.
Pickwell *Devon* ***Settlement***, near N coast, 6m/9km SW of Ilfracombe. **6 C1** SS4540.
Pickwell *Leics.* ***Village***, 5m/8km SE of Melton Mowbray. **42 A4** SK7811.
Pickworth *Lincs.* ***Village***, 8m/12km S of Sleaford. **42 D2** TF0433.
Pickworth *Rut.* ***Hamlet***, 5m/8km NW of Stamford. **42 C4** SK9913.
Pictish Wheel House *W.Isles* ***Historic/prehistoric site***, near W coast of South Uist, 1m/2km SW of Dalabrog. **84 C3** NF7320.
Picton *Ches.* ***Village***, 4m/6km NE of Chester. **48 D5** SJ4371.
Picton *Denb.* ***Settlement***, 2m/3km S of Point of Ayr. SJ1182.
Picton *N.Yorks.* ***Village***, 3m/5km S of Yarm. **63 F6** NZ4107.
Picton Castle (Castell Pictwn). *Pembs.* ***Castle***, 13c with early 19c additions, 4m/6km E of Haverfordwest. Grounds include 40 acres of woodland and gardens with many mature trees and rhododendrons, as well as a walled garden and fernery. **16 D3** SN0113.
Picton Ferry *Carmar.* ***Locality***, 1km N of St. Clears. SN2717.
Pict's Cross *Here.* ***Locality***, 3m/5km NW of Ross-on-Wye. SO5626.
Piddinghoe *E.Suss.* ***Village***, on River Ouse, 1m/2km NW of Newhaven. **13 H6** TQ4302.
Piddington *Bucks.* ***Village***, 4m/6km W of High Wycombe. SU8094.
Piddington *Northants.* ***Village***, 5m/8km SE of Northampton. **32 B3** SP8054.
Piddington *Oxon.* ***Village***, 5m/8km SE of Bicester. **31 H7** SP6417.
Piddle (Also known as Dorset River and River Trent.) *Dorset* ***River***, rising at Alton Pancras, and flowing generally SE through Puddletown and N of Wareham into Poole Harbour. **9 H6** SY9488.
Piddlehinton *Dorset* ***Village***, 3m/5km NW of Puddletown. **9 G5** SY7197.
Piddletrenthide *Dorset* ***Village***, 6m/10km N of Dorchester. **9 G5** ST7000.
Pidley *Cambs.* ***Village***, 2m/4km SE of Warboys. **33 G1** TL3377.
Pidley Fen *Cambs.* ***Open space***, fenland 2m/3km E of Warboys. **43 G7** TL3480.
Pie Corner *Here.* ***Locality***, 4m/7km N of Bromyard. SO6461.
Piel Bar ***Coastal feature***, sand bar off S coast of Isle of Walney, 6m/9km S of Barrow-in-Furness. **55 F3** SD2361.
Piel Castle *Cumb.* ***Castle***, remains of 14c castle (English Heritage) on Piel Island, 4m/6km SE of Barrow-in-Furness. **55 F3** SD2363.
Piel Island *Cumb.* ***Island***, on S side of Piel Channel, between Roa Island and S end of Isle of Walney. Ferry to Roa Island. Remains of 14c castle. **55 F3** SD2363.
Pield Heath *Gt.Lon.* ***Suburb***, in borough of Hillingdon, 1m/2km S of Uxbridge. TQ0681.
Piercebridge ***Bridge***, early 16c stone bridge over River Tees at Piercebridge village, where it forms boundary between North Yorkshire and Durham. Some fragments of stone piers of 2c timber bridge remain (English Heritage). NZ2115.
Piercebridge *Darl.* ***Village***, on River Tees, 5m/8km W of Darlington, on site of Roman fort. **62 D5** NZ2115.
Pierowall *Ork.* ***Village***, on Bay of Pierowall, on E coast of Westray. **106 D3** HY4348.
Piff's Elm *Glos.* ***Locality***, 4m/6km NW of Cheltenham. SO8926.
Pigdon *Northumb.* ***Settlement***, 3m/5km NW of Morpeth. **71 G5** NZ1588.
Pike Fell *D. & G.* ***Mountain***, 7m/11km NE of Langholm. Height 1637 feet or 499 metres. **69 K4** NY4193.
Pike Hill *Lancs.* ***Suburb***, on W side of River Brun, 1m/2km E of Burnley. SD8632.
Pike Hill *Sc.Bord.* ***Mountain***, 2m/3km S of Craik. Height 1368 feet or 417 metres. **69 J3** NT3505.
Pike Hill Moss *N.Yorks.* ***Mountain***, on North York Moors, 3m/4km S of Glaisdale. Height 1069 feet or 326 metres. **63 J6** NZ7700.
Pike of Blisco *Cumb.* ***Mountain***, in Lake District, 3m/4km SE of Bow Fell and 5m/7km W of Skelwith Bridge. Height 2303 feet or 702 metres. **60 D6** NY2704.
Pikehall *Derbys.* ***Hamlet***, 8m/12km N of Ashbourne. **50 D7** SK1959.
Pikeshill *Hants.* ***Hamlet***, in New Forest, adjoining to NW of Lyndhurst. SU2908.
Pikeston Fell *Dur.* ***Open space***, hillslope to E of Five Pikes and N of Hamsterley Forest. **62 B3** NZ0332.

Pikey Hill *Moray* ***Mountain***, 4m/6km NW of Rothes. Height 1164 feet or 355 metres. **97 K6** NJ2151.
Pilford *Dorset* ***Settlement***, 2m/3km NE of Wimborne Minster. SU0301.
Pilgrims Hatch *Essex* ***Suburb***, NW of Brentwood. **23 J2** TQ5795.
Pilgrims Park *I.o.W.* ***Settlement***, 3m/5km SW of Cowes. SZ4593.
Pilham *Lincs.* ***Hamlet***, 4m/6km NE of Gainsborough. **52 B3** SK8693.
Pill *N.Som.* ***Settlement***, on River Avon, adjoining to E of Easton-in-Gordano. **19 J4** ST5275.
Pillar *Cumb.* ***Mountain***, in Lake District 3m/5km N of NE end of Wast Water. Height 2926 feet or 892 metres. **60 C5** NY1712.
Pillar of Eliseg *Denb. See Eliseg's Pillar.*
Pillaton *Cornw.* ***Village***, 4m/6km S of Callington. **4 D4** SX3664.
Pillaton *Staffs.* ***Settlement***, 1m/2km SE of Penkridge. SJ9413.
Pillerton Hersey *Warks.* ***Village***, 3m/4km SW of Kineton. **30 D4** SP3048.
Pillerton Priors *Warks.* ***Village***, 3m/5km SW of Kineton. **30 D4** SP2947.
Pilleth *Powys* ***Settlement***, 3m/5km SW of Knighton. **28 B2** SO2568.
Pilley *Glos.* ***Suburb***, in S part of Cheltenham. **29 J7** SO9519.
Pilley *Hants.* ***Hamlet***, 2m/3km N of Lymington. **10 E5** SZ3398.
Pilley *S.Yorks.* ***Village***, 2m/3km W of Hoyland. **51 F2** SE3300.
Pillgwenlly *Newport* ***Suburb***, in Newport, on W bank of River Usk, above transporter bridge, 1km S of town centre. ST3186.
Pilling *Lancs.* ***Village***, 3m/4km NE of Preesall. **55 H5** SD4048.
Pilling Lane *Lancs.* ***Settlement***, 2m/3km W of Pilling. **55 G5** SD3749.
Pillowell *Glos.* Population: 1169. ***Village***, 2m/4km N of Lydney. **19 K1** SO6206.
Pilning *S.Glos.* ***Village***, 8m/13km N of Bristol. **19 J3** ST5585.
Pilrig *Edin.* ***Suburb***, 1m/2km NE of Edinburgh city centre. NT2675.
Pilsbury *Derbys.* ***Settlement***, above E bank of River Dove, 2m/3km N of Hartington. **50 D6** SK1263.
Pilsdon *Dorset* ***Hamlet***, 5m/7km W of Beaminster. **8 D5** SY4199.
Pilsdon Pen *Dorset* ***Hill***, with hillfort (National Trust) at SE end of summit, 2m/3km SW of Broadwindsor. Height 909 feet or 277 metres. **8 D4** ST4101.
Pilsgate *Peter.* ***Hamlet***, 3m/4km E of Stamford. **42 D5** TF0605.
Pilsley *Derbys.* ***Village***, 2m/4km NE of Bakewell. **50 E5** SK2471.
Pilsley *Derbys.* Population: 2402. ***Village***, 4m/7km N of Alfreton. **51 G6** SK4262.
Pilsley Green *Derbys.* ***Hamlet***, adjoining to S of Pilsley, 5m/7km N of Alfreton. SK4262.
Pilson Green *Norf.* ***Hamlet***, 1m/2km E of South Walsham. TG3713.
Piltanton Burn *D. & G.* ***River***, rising on Rinns of Galloway, 4m/6km NW of Stranraer, and flowing SE to join Water of Luce at Sands of Luce, S of Glenluce. **64 A5** NX1954.
Piltdown *E.Suss.* ***Hamlet***, 2m/3km NW of Uckfield. **13 H4** TQ4422.
Pilton *Devon* ***Suburb***, N district of Barnstaple. **6 D2** SS5534.
Pilton *Edin.* ***Suburb***, 2m/3km NW of Edinburgh city centre. NT2376.
Pilton *Northants.* ***Village***, 3m/4km SW of Oundle. **42 D7** TL0284.
Pilton *Rut.* ***Hamlet***, 4m/6km NE of Uppingham. **42 C5** SK9102.
Pilton *Som.* ***Village***, 3m/4km SW of Shepton Mallet. **19 J7** ST5840.
Pilton *Swan.* ***Settlement***, on Gower peninsula, 3m/5km E of Worms Head. SS4387.
Pilton Green *Swan.* ***Settlement***, on Gower peninsula, 1km E of Pilton. SS4487.
Pimbo *Lancs.* ***Locality***, industrial estate in SE part of Skelmersdale. SD4904.
Pimhole *Gt.Man.* ***Suburb***, 1m/2km E of Bury town centre. SD8110.
Pimlico *Gt.Lon.* ***Suburb***, residential district of City of Westminster, S of Victoria Station. TQ2978.
Pimlico *Herts.* ***Hamlet***, 3m/5km SE of Hemel Hempstead. TL0905.
Pimperne *Dorset* ***Village***, 2m/4km NE of Blandford Forum. **9 J4** ST9009.
Pimperne Down *Dorset* ***Open space***, hillslope to NW of Pimperne, 3m/4km NE of Blandford Forum. **9 H3** ST8910.
Pin Green *Herts.* ***Suburb***, NE district of Stevenage. TL2425.
Pin Green Industrial Estate *Herts.* ***Locality***, to NE of Pin Green, 1m/2km NE of Stevenage town centre. TL2425.
Pin Mill *Suff.* ***Hamlet***, on S bank of River Orwell, 5m/8km SE of Ipswich. TM2037.
Pinchbeck *Lincs.* Population: 3655. ***Village***, 2m/4km N of Spalding. **43 F3** TF2425.
Pinchbeck Bars *Lincs.* ***Locality***, 3m/4km W of Pinchbeck. **43 F3** TF2425.
Pinchbeck West *Lincs.* ***Hamlet***, 2m/4km W of Pinchbeck. **43 F3** TF2024.
Pincheon Green *S.Yorks.* ***Settlement***, 3m/5km NW of Thorne. SE6517.
Pinchinthorpe *R. & C.* ***Locality***, 3m/4km SW of Guisborough. **63 G5** NZ5714.
Pinchom's Hill *Derbys.* ***Settlement***, 1km SE of Belper. SK3646.
Pinden *Kent* ***Settlement***, 1km W of Longfield and 5m/8km SW of Gravesend. TQ5969.
Pinderachy *Angus* ***Mountain***, 1m/2km NE of Glenogil. Height 1686 feet or 514 metres. **83 F1** NO4564.
Pindon End *M.K.* ***Settlement***, 1m/2km NW of Hanslope. SP7847.
Pineham *Kent* ***Settlement***, 3m/4km N of Dover town centre. TR3145.
Pinehurst *Swin.* ***Suburb***, 1m/2km N of Swindon town centre. SU1587.
Pinfold *Lancs.* ***Hamlet***, 3m/4km NW of Ormskirk. **48 C1** SD3911.
Pinford End *Suff.* ***Settlement***, 3m/5km S of Bury St. Edmunds town centre. TL8459.
Pinged *Carmar.* ***Settlement***, 2m/4km NW of Burry Port. SN4203.
Pinhaw *N.Yorks.* ***Mountain***, on Elslack Moor, 3m/4km E of Earby. Height 1273 feet or 388 metres. **56 E5** SD9447.
Pinhay *Devon* ***Settlement***, 2m/3km SW of Lyme Regis, 1km from S coast. **8 C5** SY3191.
Pinhoe *Devon* ***Suburb***, NE district of Exeter, 3m/5km from city centre. **7 H6** SX9694.
Pinhoe Trading Estate *Devon* ***Locality***, 1km W of Pinhoe. SX9594.
Pink Green *Worcs.* ***Settlement***, 3m/5km NE of Redditch. SP0869.
Pinkery Pond *Som. Alternative name for Pinkworthy Pond, qv.*
Pinkett's Booth *W.Mid.* ***Settlement***, 4m/7km NW of Coventry city centre. SP2781.
Pinkie House *E.Loth.* ***Historic house***, Jacobean mansion on E side of Musselburgh where Prince Charles Edward Stuart spent night after battle of Prestonpans in 1745. House now used by Loretto School. **76 B3** NT3572.
Pinkneys Green *W. & M.* ***Locality***, 2m/3km NW of Maidenhead. National Trust property. **22 B3** SU8582.
Pinkworthy Pond (Also known as Pinkery Pond.) *Som.* ***Lake/loch***, on Exmoor, 4m/6km NW of Simonsbath. **7 F1** SS7242.
Pinley Green *Warks.* ***Hamlet***, 5m/8km W of Warwick. **30 D2** SP2066.
Pinminnoch *S.Ayr.* ***Settlement***, 3m/4km S of Girvan. **67 F4** NX1893.
Pinmore *S.Ayr.* ***Locality***, 5m/8km S of Girvan. **67 G4** NX2091.
Pinn *Devon* ***Settlement***, 2m/3km W of Sidmouth. **7 K7** SY1086.
Pinner *Gt.Lon.* ***Suburb***, in borough of Harrow, 12m/20km NW of Charing Cross. **22 E3** TQ1289.
Pinner Green *Gt.Lon.* ***Suburb***, to NW of Pinner. **22 E2** TQ1190.
Pin's Green *Worcs.* ***Settlement***, 3m/5km NE of Great Malvern. SO8049.
Pinsley Green *Ches.* ***Settlement***, 1m/2km SW of Wrenbury. SJ5846.
Pinvin *Worcs.* ***Village***, 2m/3km N of Pershore. **29 J4** SO9549.
Pinwherry *S.Ayr.* ***Village***, at confluence of River Stinchar and Duisk River, 7m/11km S of Girvan. **67 F5** NX1986.
Pinxton *Derbys.* Population: 4348. ***Village***, 3m/4km E of Alfreton. **51 G7** SK4555.
Pinxton Green *Derbys.* ***Locality***, adjoining to E of Pinxton. SK4555.
Pipe and Lyde *Here.* ***Village***, 3m/4km N of Hereford. **28 E4** SO5044.
Pipe Gate *Shrop.* ***Hamlet***, 1km SE of Woore. **39 G1** SJ7340.
Pipe Ridware *Staffs.* ***Hamlet***, 3m/5km E of Rugeley. **40 C4** SK0917.
Pipehill *Staffs.* ***Hamlet***, 2m/3km SW of Lichfield. SK0908.
Piper Hill *N.Yorks.* ***Locality***, on E side of Catterick Camp, 3m/4km W of Catterick. SE2098.
Piperhall *Arg. & B.* ***Settlement***, on Bute, 4m/6km S of Rothesay. **73 J5** NS0958.
Piperhill *High.* ***Locality***, in Nairn district, 4m/6km S of Nairn. **97 F6** NH8650.
Piper's Ash *Ches.* ***Suburb***, 2m/3km E of Chester. SJ4367.
Pipers Pool *Cornw.* ***Village***, 4m/7km W of Launceston. **4 C2** SX2684.
Pipewell *Northants.* ***Hamlet***, 4m/7km SW of Corby. **42 B7** SP8385.
Pippacott *Devon* ***Settlement***, 3m/5km NW of Barnstaple. **6 D2** SS5237.
Pippin Street *Lancs.* ***Settlement***, 2m/3km N of Whittle-le-Woods. SD5924.
Pipps Hill *Essex* ***Locality***, industrial estate, N of Basildon town centre. TQ6990.
Pipton *Powys* ***Settlement***, 5m/7km SW of Hay-on-Wye. **28 A5** SO1638.
Pirbright *Surr.* ***Village***, 5m/8km NW of Guildford. To NW across railway, Pirbright Camp and firing ranges. **22 C6** SU9455.
Pirnmill *N.Ayr.* ***Village***, on W coast of Arran, opposite Grogport in Kintyre. **73 G6** NR8744.
Pirton *Herts.* ***Village***, 3m/5km NW of Hitchin. **32 E5** TL1431.
Pirton *Worcs.* ***Village***, 5m/8km SE of Worcester. **29 H4** SO8847.
Pisgah *Stir.* ***Locality***, adjoining to SE of Dunblane. **81 J7** NN7900.
Pishill *Oxon.* ***Hamlet***, 3m/4km NE of Nettlebed. **22 A3** SU7290.
Pismire Hill *S.Yorks.* ***Suburb***, 3m/4km NE of Sheffield city centre. SK3791.
Pistyll *Gwyn.* ***Hamlet***, 1m/2km NE of Nefyn. **36 C1** SH3241.
Pistyll *Powys* ***Mountain***, 8m/12km NE of Brecon. Height 1601 feet or 488 metres. **27 K1** SO0177.
Pistyll Rhaeadr *Powys* ***Waterfall***, highest waterfall in Wales (240 feet or 74 metres) at head of River Rhaeadr, 4m/6km NW of Llanrhaeadr-ym-Mochnant. **37 K2** SJ0729.
Pitagowan *P. & K.* ***Settlement***, in valley of River Garry, 3m/5km W of Blair Atholl. **81 K1** NN8265.
Pitblae *Aber.* ***Settlement***, 1m/2km SW of Fraserburgh. **99 H4** NJ9764.
Pitcairley Hill *Fife* ***Hill***, on N edge of Ochil Hills, 1m/2km SE of Abernethy. Height 922 feet or 281 metres. **82 D6** NO2116.
Pitcairngreen *P. & K.* ***Village***, with large green, 4m/6km NW of Perth. **82 B5** NO0627.
Pitcairns *P. & K.* ***Settlement***, 1km SE of Dunning. **82 B6** NO0214.
Pitcalnie *High.* ***Hamlet***, in Ross and Cromarty district, 2m/4km N of N side of entrance to Cromarty Firth. NH8072.
Pitcaple *Aber.* ***Village***, 4m/7km NW of Inverurie. **91 F2** NJ7225.
Pitcaple Castle *Aber.* ***Castle***, Z-plan 16c castle, renovated in 19c, 1km NE of Pitcaple. **91 F2** NJ7226.
Pitcarity *Angus* ***Locality***, in Glen Prosen, 8m/13km NW of Kirriemuir. NO3265.
Pitch Green *Bucks.* ***Hamlet***, 2m/3km W of Princes Risborough. **22 A1** SP7703.
Pitch Place *Surr.* ***Hamlet***, 2m/4km N of Hindhead. SU8939.
Pitch Place *Surr.* ***Locality***, 2m/4km NW of Guildford. **22 C6** SU9752.
Pitchcombe *Glos.* ***Village***, 2m/3km N of Stroud. **20 B1** SO8508.
Pitchcott *Bucks.* ***Village***, 5m/8km NW of Aylesbury. **31 J7** SP7720.
Pitchford *Shrop.* ***Village***, 6m/10km S of Shrewsbury. **38 E5** SJ5303.
Pitcombe *Som.* ***Village***, 1m/2km SW of Bruton. **9 F1** ST6733.
Pitcot *V. of Glam.* ***Locality***, adjoining to S of St. Brides Major, 4m/6km S of Bridgend. **18 B4** SS8974.
Pitcox *E.Loth.* ***Settlement***, 3m/5km SW of Dunbar. **76 E3** NT6475.
Pitcur *P. & K.* ***Locality***, 3m/4km SE of Coupar Angus. Ancient earth-house. **82 D4** NO2537.
Pitfichie *Aber.* ***Settlement***, and ruined castle, 7m/11km SW of Inverurie. **90 E3** NJ6716.
Pitfichie Forest *Aber.* ***Forest/woodland***, to W of Pitfichie and Monymusk. **90 E3** NJ6415.
Pitfour Castle *P. & K.* ***Hamlet***, 5m/8km E of Perth. NO1920.
Pitgrudy *High.* ***Settlement***, 1km NW of Dornoch. **96 E2** NH7991.
Pitinnan *Aber.* ***Locality***, includes Loanhead of Pitinnan, 4m/6km SE of Rothienorman. **91 F1** NJ7430.
Pitkennedy *Angus* ***Settlement***, to W of Montreathmont Forest, 4m/7km NW of Friockheim. **83 G2** NO5454.
Pitkevy *Fife* ***Settlement***, 3m/4km NW of Glenrothes. **82 D7** NO2403.
Pitlessie *Fife* ***Village***, 4m/6km SW of Cupar. **82 E7** NO3309.
Pitlochry *P. & K.* Population: 2541. ***Small town***, and summer resort on River Tummel 5m/8km NW of its confluence with River Tay and 11m/18km NW of Dunkeld. Festival Theatre. Highland Games in August. **82 A2** NN9458.
Pitmachie *Aber.* ***Settlement***, adjoining to W of Old Rayne across River Urie. NJ6728.
Pitman's Corner *Suff.* ***Settlement***, 1m/2km E of Wetheringsett. TM1466.
Pitmedden *Aber.* Population: 1082. ***Village***, 5m/9km E of Oldmeldrum. Remains of Tolquhon Castle (Historic Scotland), 1m/2km NW. **91 G2** NJ8927.
Pitmedden Forest *P. & K.* ***Forest/woodland***, to SE of Abernethy. **82 C6** NO2014.
Pitmedden Garden *Aber.* ***Garden***, National Trust for Scotland property, 1km NW of Pitmedden, includes 17c garden designed by Sir Alexander Seton, Baron of Pitmedden, and Museum of Farming Life. **91 G2** NJ8828.
Pitmiddle Wood *P. & K.* ***Forest/woodland***, coniferous wood with small loch at N end, 2m/3km W of Abernyke. **82 D4** NO2230.
Pitminster *Som.* ***Village***, 4m/6km S of Taunton. **8 B3** ST2219.
Pitmuies *Angus* ***Settlement***, 3m/4km NE of Letham. Includes 18c white harled mansion with gardens featuring kitchen garden, rose garden, trellis walk, hornbeam walk and alpine meadow. **83 G3** NO5649.
Pitmunie *Aber.* ***Settlement***, 1m/2km W of Monymusk. **90 E3** NJ6615.
Pitnacree *P. & K.* ***Settlement***, 3m/5km SW of Pitlochry. **82 A2** NN9253.
Pitney *Som.* ***Village***, 3m/4km W of Somerton. **8 D2** ST4428.
Pitroddie *P. & K.* ***Locality***, 6m/10km E of Perth. **82 D5** NO2125.
Pitscottie *Fife* ***Village***, 3m/5km E of Cupar. **83 F6** NO4113.
Pitsea *Essex* ***Suburb***, SE district of Basildon. **24 D3** TQ7388.
Pitsea Mount *Essex* ***Suburb***, in Basildon adjoining to S of Pitsea. TQ7388.
Pitses *Gt.Man.* ***Suburb***, 2m/3km SE of Oldham town centre. SD9403.
Pitsford *Northants.* ***Village***, 5m/8km N of Northampton. To N is Pitsford Reservoir, over 3m/5km long. **31 J2** SP7568.
Pitsford Hill *Som.* ***Hamlet***, 2m/3km NE of Wiveliscombe. **7 J2** ST0930.
Pitsford Reservoir *Northants.* ***Reservoir***, 6m/9km N of Northampton town centre. **31 J2** SP7669.
Pitsligo *Aber.* ***Locality***, parish on N coast containing ruined Pitsligo Castle, dating from 1424, 1km SE of Rosehearty. NJ9366.
Pitsligo Castle *Aber.* ***Castle***, ruined early 15c castle dating from 1424, 1km SE of Rosehearty. **99 H4** NJ9367.
Pitsmoor *S.Yorks.* ***Suburb***, 1m/2km NE of Sheffield city centre. SK3689.
Pitstone *Bucks.* Population: 1622. ***Hamlet***, 3m/4km N of Tring. **32 C7** SP9315.
Pitstone Green *Bucks.* ***Village***, 1km N of Pitstone. **32 C7** SP9315.
Pitt *Devon* ***Hamlet***, 1m/2km N of Sampford Peverell. **7 J4** ST0316.
Pitt *Hants.* ***Hamlet***, 2m/3km SW of Winchester. **11 F2** SU4528.

Pitt Down *Hants.* ***Open space***, hillslope 2m/3km N of Hursley. **11 F2** SU4228.
Pitt-Rivers Museum *Dorset See Farnham.*
Pittendreich *Moray* ***Settlement***, 1m/2km SW of Elgin. **97 J5** NJ1961.
Pittenheath *Aber.* ***Locality***, inland from Rattray Bay, 2m/3km S of Rattray Head. NK0955.
Pittentrail *High.* ***Settlement***, in Strath Fleet, 1m/2km S of Little Rogart, Sutherland district. **96 E1** NC7202.
Pittenweem *Fife* Population: 1561. ***Small town***, royal burgh and fishing port on Firth of Forth, 1m/2km W of Anstruther. **83 G7** NO5402.
Pitteuchar *Fife* ***Suburb***, in SE part of Glenrothes. NT2799.
Pittington *Dur.* ***Village***, 4m/6km E of Durham. **62 E2** NZ3244.
Pittodrie House *Aber.* ***Other building***, hotel 2m/3km SE of Oyne. **90 E2** NJ7023.
Pitton *Swan.* ***Hamlet***, on Gower peninsula, 2m/4km E of Worms Head. SS4287.
Pitton *Wilts.* ***Village***, 5m/8km E of Salisbury. **10 D1** SU2131.
Pitton Cross *Swan.* ***Settlement***, on Gower peninsula, to E of Pitton, 3m/4km E of Worms Head. SS4387.
Pitts Hill *Stoke* ***Suburb***, 1m/2km NE of Tunstall. SJ8652.
Pittulie *Aber.* ***Settlement***, on N coast, adjoining to W of Sandhaven, 2m/4km W of Fraserburgh. NJ9667.
Pittville *Glos.* ***Suburb***, N district of Cheltenham, includes Pittville Pump Room. SO9523.
Pity Me *Dur.* ***Village***, 2m/3km N of Durham. **62 D2** NZ2645.
Pityme *Cornw.* ***Locality***, 4m/6km NW of Wadebridge. **3 G1** SW9576.
Pixey Green *Suff.* ***Settlement***, 1m/2km NE of Stradbroke. **35 G1** TM2475.
Pixham *Surr.* ***Locality***, residential locality to NE of Dorking. TQ1750.
Pixley *Here.* ***Settlement***, 3m/5km W of Ledbury. SO6638.
Place Fell *Cumb.* ***Mountain***, on E side of Ullswater, 1m/2km E of Glenridding. Height 2155 feet or 657 metres. **60 F5** NY4016.
Place House *Hants. Alternative name for Titchfield Abbey, qv.*
Place Newton *N.Yorks.* ***Settlement***, 1km SE of Wintringham. **58 E2** SE8872.
Pladda *Arg. & B.* ***Island***, one of Small Isles group off E coast of Jura. NR5468.
Pladda *N.Ayr.* ***Island***, small uninhabited island about 1km off S coast of Arran across Sound of Pladda. **66 E2** NS0219.
Pladda Island *Arg. & B.* ***Island***, islet off S coast of Lismore, nearly 1km S of Eilean Dubh, and on E side of Creag Island. **79 K4** NM8337.
Plaidy *Aber.* ***Settlement***, 3m/5km N of Turriff. **99 F5** NJ7255.
Plain Dealings *Pembs.* ***Hamlet***, 1km NW of Llawhaden. SN0518.
Plainfield *Northumb.* ***Settlement***, 4m/7km W of Rothbury. NT9903.
Plains *N.Lan.* Population: 2581. ***Village***, 2m/4km NE of Airdrie. **75 F4** NS7966.
Plains Farm *T. & W.* ***Suburb***, 2m/3km SW of Sunderland city centre. NZ3754.
Plainsfield *Som.* ***Hamlet***, on E slopes of Quantock Hills, 2m/3km S of Nether Stowey. ST1936.
Plaish *Shrop.* ***Hamlet***, 6m/10km W of Much Wenlock. **38 E6** SO5296.
Plaistow *Gt.Lon.* ***Suburb***, in borough of Bromley, 1km N of Bromley town centre. TQ3970.
Plaistow *Gt.Lon.* ***Suburb***, in borough of Newham, 1km S of West Ham. TQ4082.
Plaistow *W.Suss.* ***Village***, 6m/10km NW of Billingshurst. **12 D3** TQ0031.
Plaitford *Hants.* ***Village***, on border with Wiltshire, 5m/8km W of Romsey. **10 D3** SU2719.
Plaitford Green *Hants.* ***Hamlet***, 1m/2km SW of Sherfield English and 4m/7km W of Romsey. SU2821.
Plank Lane *Gt.Man.* ***Suburb***, 2m/3km W of Leigh. SJ6399.
Plas *Carmar.* ***Settlement***, 3m/5km SW of Brechfa. **17 H2** SN4827.
Plas Gogerddan *Cere.* ***Settlement***, 3m/5km NE of Aberystwyth. **37 F7** SN6283.
Plas Gwynant *Gwyn.* ***Settlement***, in Nantgwynant, 3m/5km NE of Beddgelert. **46 E7** SH6350.
Plas Isaf *Denb.* ***Settlement***, 1m/2km N of Cynwyd. **37 K1** SJ0542.
Plas Llwyd *Conwy* ***Settlement***, 2m/3km SW of Rhyl. **47 H5** SH9979.
Plas Llwyngwern *Powys* ***Settlement***, 3m/4km N of Machynlleth. **37 G5** SH7504.
Plas Llysyn *Powys* ***Settlement***, adjoining to N of Carno. **37 J6** SN9597.
Plas Nantyr *Wrex.* ***Settlement***, 7m/12km E of Llandrillo. **38 A2** SJ1537.
Plas Newydd *I.o.A.* ***Historic house***, on N shore of Menai Strait, 1m/2km from Llanfairpwllgwyngyll. Impressive 18c mansion, now National Trust property, designed by James Wyatt and containing Rex Whistler's largest wall painting. Also military museum and fine gardens with woodland walks. **46 D6** SH5269.
Plas-rhiw-Saeson *Powys* ***Settlement***, 1m/2km N of Llanbrynmair and 6m/10km SE of Dinas Mawddy. **37 J5** SH9004.
Plas Teg *Flints.* ***Historic house***, 1610 mansion with decor and furnishings from later centuries, 2m/3km NW of Caergwrle. **48 B7** SJ2859.
Plas-yn-Cefn *Denb.* ***Hamlet***, 2m/4km SW of St. Asaph. Prehistoric caves beside River Elwy to S. **47 J5** SJ0171.
Plas yn Rhiw *Gwyn. See Rhiw.*
Plas-yn-Rhiw *Gwyn.* ***Historic house***, restored part-medieval manor house, National Trust property, 12m/19km SW of Pwllheli. Ornamental gardens, with snowdrop wood. **36 B3** SH2328.
Plashet *Gt.Lon.* ***Suburb***, in borough of Newham, 1km N of East Ham. TQ4284.
Plashett *Carmar.* ***Settlement***, 2m/3km SW of Laugharne. SN2709.
Plasisaf *Conwy* ***Settlement***, in valley of River Aled, 2m/3km NE of Llansannan. **47 H6** SH9567.
Plasterfield *W.Isles* ***Hamlet***, on Isle of Lewis, 1m/2km E of Stornoway. NB4433.
Plastow Green *Hants.* ***Hamlet***, 2m/3km NE of Kingsclere. **21 J5** SU5361.
Platt *Kent* ***Village***, adjoining to E of Borough Green, 9m/14km W of Maidstone. **23 K6** TQ6257.
Platt Bridge *Gt.Man.* ***Village***, 2m/3km SE of Wigan. **49 F2** SD6002.
Platt Hall *Gt.Man.* ***Historic house***, Palladian 18c red-brick building on Wilmslow Road, 3m/4km SE of Manchester city centre. Home of Gallery of English Costume. **49 H3** SJ8594.
Platt Lane *Shrop.* ***Settlement***, 4m/6km SW of Whitchurch. **38 E2** SJ5136.
Platts *S.Yorks.* ***Locality***, adjoining to N of Hoyland. SE3601.
Platt's Heath *Kent* ***Hamlet***, 2m/3km SW of Lenham. TQ8750.
Plawsworth *Dur.* ***Village***, 4m/6km N of Durham. **62 D2** NZ2647.
Plaxtol *Kent* ***Village***, 5m/7km N of Tonbridge. **23 K6** TQ6053.
Play Hatch *Oxon.* ***Hamlet***, 2m/4km NE of Reading. **22 A4** SU7476.
Playden *E.Suss.* ***Village***, 1m/2km N of Rye. **14 E5** TQ9121.
Playford *Suff.* ***Village***, 4m/6km W of Woodbridge. **35 G4** TM2147.
Playing Place *Cornw.* ***Village***, 2m/4km SW of Truro. **3 F4** SW8141.
Playley Green *Glos.* ***Hamlet***, 5m/8km SE of Ledbury. SO7631.
Plealey *Shrop.* ***Hamlet***, 6m/9km SW of Shrewsbury. **38 D5** SJ4206.
Plean *Stir.* Population: 1671. ***Village***, 5m/8km SE of Stirling. **75 G2** NS8386.
Pleasance *Fife* ***Hamlet***, 1km N of Auchtermuchty. **82 D6** NO2312.
Pleasant Valley *Essex* ***Suburb***, in S part of Saffron Walden. TL5337.
Pleasant View *Derbys.* ***Locality***, 1m/2km W of Hayfield. SK0186.
Pleasington *B'burn.* ***Village***, 3m/5km W of Blackburn. **56 B7** SD6426.
Pleasley *Derbys.* ***Village***, 3m/5km NW of Mansfield. **51 H6** SK5064.
Pleasleyhill *Notts.* ***Village***, adjoining to SE of Pleasley, 3m/4km NW of Mansfield. SK5063.
Pleasurewood Hills Theme Park *Suff.* ***Leisure/recreation***, theme park 2m/3km N of Lowestoft town centre, featuring over fifty attractions ranging from roller coasters to roundabouts and landscaped gardens. **45 K6** TM5496.
Pleck *Dorset Alternative name for Little Ansty, qv.*
Pleck *Dorset* ***Hamlet***, 2m/3km SE of Bishop's Caundle, 6m/9km SW of Sturminster Newton. ST7010.
Pleck *W.Mid.* ***Suburb***, 1m/2km SW of Walsall town centre. SO9997.
Pleckgate *Lancs.* ***Suburb***, 2m/3km N of Blackburn town centre. SD6730.
Pledgdon Green *Essex* ***Settlement***, 5m/8km NW of Great Dunmow. TL5626.
Pledwick *W.Yorks.* ***Suburb***, 3m/5km S of Wakefield city centre. SE3316.
Plemstall *Ches.* ***Hamlet***, 4m/7km NE of Chester. SJ4570.
Plenmeller *Northumb.* ***Settlement***, 1m/2km SE of Haltwhistle. **70 C7** NY7163.
Plenmeller Common *Northumb.* ***Open space***, heathland on S side of River South Tyne, 3m/4km SE of Haltwhistle. **70 C7** NY7361.
Pleshey *Essex* ***Village***, 5m/9km NW of Chelmsford. Village surrounded by Norman earthworks. Remains of castle keep. **33 K7** TL6614.
Plessey Woods Country Park *Northumb.* ***Leisure/recreation***, over 100 acres of woodland in River Blyth valley, 2m/3km SW of Bedlington. Park is natural wildlife refuge populated by over 200 species of plants, red squirrels, roe deer and tawny owl. **71 H5** NZ2480.
Pley Moss *E.Ayr.* ***Open space***, plateau, part moorland and part forest, 3m/5km N of Darvel. **74 D6** NS5641.
Plockton *High.* ***Village***, in Skye and Lochalsh district, on S side of Loch Carron, 5m/8km NE of Kyle of Lochalsh. Airfield 1m/2km W. **86 E1** NG8033.
Plodda Falls *High.* ***Waterfall***, formed where Eas Socach falls over 70 feet or 20 metres into pool swelled by confluence with Abhainn Deabhag, 6m/10km SW of Cannich. **87 J2** NH2723.
Plomer's Hill *Bucks.* ***Suburb***, NW district of High Wycombe. SU8494.
Plompton *N.Yorks.* ***Locality***, 2m/3km S of Knaresborough. SE3554.
Plot Gate *Som.* ***Hamlet***, adjoining to NE of Barton St. David, 1m/2km N of Keinton Mandeville. ST5432.
Plot Street *Som.* ***Settlement***, 4m/6km SE of Glastonbury. ST5536.
Plough Hill *Warks.* ***Suburb***, 3m/5km W of Nuneaton. SP3293.
Ploughfield *Here.* ***Village***, 8m/13km W of Hereford. **28 C4** SO3841.
Ploughlands *Cumb.* ***Settlement***, 1m/2km S of Warcop. NY7513.
Ploverfield *Hants.* ***Locality***, adjoining to N of Bursledon, 2m/3km NW of Park Gate. SU4809.
Plowden *Shrop.* ***Hamlet***, 4m/7km NW of Craven Arms. **38 C7** SO3887.
Ploxgreen *Shrop.* ***Hamlet***, 10m/15km SW of Shrewsbury. **38 C5** SJ3603.
Pluckley *Kent* ***Village***, hilltop village, 3m/5km SW of Charing. **14 E3** TQ9245.
Pluckley Thorne *Kent* ***Hamlet***, 1km SW of Pluckley. **14 E3** TQ9244.
Plucks Gutter *Kent* ***Settlement***, on River Stour, 5m/8km NW of Sandwich. TR2663.
Plumbland *Cumb.* ***Village***, 2m/3km S of Aspatria. **60 C3** NY1539.
Plumbley *S.Yorks.* ***Settlement***, 1km W of Mosborough. SK4180.
Plumgarths *Cumb.* ***Settlement***, adjoining to W side of Burneside, 2m/3km NW of Kendal. SD5095.
Plumley *Ches.* ***Village***, 3m/5km SW of Knutsford. **49 G5** SJ7175.
Plumpton *Cumb.* ***Village***, 4m/7km N of Penrith. Site of small Roman fort of Voreda to N. **61 F3** NY4937.
Plumpton *E.Suss.* ***Village***, 4m/7km NW of Lewes, below South Downs. **13 G5** TQ3613.
Plumpton *Northants.* ***Settlement***, 7m/11km N of Brackley. SP5948.
Plumpton End *Northants.* ***Hamlet***, adjoining to E of Paulerspury, 3m/5km SE of Towcester. **31 J4** SP7245.
Plumpton Green *E.Suss.* ***Village***, with racecourse and railway station, 2m/3km N of Plumpton. **13 G5** TQ3613.
Plumpton Head *Cumb.* ***Settlement***, 3m/5km N of Penrith. Site of Roman camp to N. **61 G3** NY5035.
Plumstead *Gt.Lon.* ***Suburb***, in borough of Greenwich, 1km SE of Woolwich and 9m/15km E of Charing Cross. **23 H4** TQ4478.
Plumstead *Norf.* ***Village***, with Plumstead Green, 4m/7km SE of Holt. **45 F2** TG1334.
Plumstead Green *Norf.* ***Settlement***, just SW of Plumstead, 4m/6km SE of Holt. TG1234.
Plumstead Green *Norf.* ***Settlement***, 1km N of Great Plumstead and 2m/3km NW of Brundall. TG3011.
Plumtree *Notts.* ***Village***, 5m/8km SE of Nottingham. **41 J2** SK6133.
Plungar *Leics.* ***Village***, 9m/15km N of Melton Mowbray. **42 A2** SK7633.
Pluscarden Priory *Moray* ***Ecclesiastical building***, 13c priory near locality of Barnhill, 5m/9km SW of Elgin. Occupied and restored by Benedictine monks since 1943. **97 J6** NJ1457.
Plush *Dorset* ***Village***, 2m/3km N of Piddletrenthide. **9 G4** ST7102.
Plusha *Cornw.* ***Settlement***, 6m/9km SW of Launceston. SX2580.
Plushabridge *Cornw.* ***Settlement***, on River Lynher, 4m/6km NW of Callington. SX3072.
Plwmp *Cere.* ***Hamlet***, 5m/8km S of New Quay. **26 C3** SN3652.
Plym ***River***, rising at Plym Head on Dartmoor and flowing SW into Plymouth Sound. **5 F4** SX4853.
Plym Bridge *Plym.* ***Bridge***, over River Plym, 4m/6km NE of Plymouth city centre. **5 F5** SX5258.
Plym Forest *Plym.* ***Forest/woodland***, large woodland area 4m/7km NE of Plymouth, enclosing part of River Plym valley. A small portion is National Trust property. **5 F5** SX5259.
Plymouth *Plym.* Population: 245,295. ***City***, largest city in SW England, 100m/160km SW of Bristol. Port and naval base. Regional shopping centre. City centre rebuilt after bombing in World War II. Has strong commercial and naval tradition. In 1588 Sir Francis Drake sailed from Plymouth to defeat Spanish Armada. Captain Cook's voyages to Australia, South Seas and Antarctica all departed from here. University. Plymouth City Airport to N of city. **4 E5** SX4754.
Plymouth Breakwater *Plym.* ***Coastal feature***, spit at S (seaward) side of The Sound. Beacon at E end and lighthouse at W end. **4 E5** SX4750.
Plymouth City Airport *Plym.* ***Airport/airfield***, international airport 4m/6km N of Plymouth city centre. **5 F4** SX5060.
Plympton *Plym.* ***Suburb***, E district of Plymouth, 4m/7km from city centre. To S, district of Plympton St. Maurice. To W beside River Plym, house and grounds of Saltram (National Trust). **5 F5** SX5356.
Plympton St. Maurice *Plym.* ***Suburb***, of Plymouth to S of Plympton. SX5356.
Plymstock *Plym.* ***Suburb***, SE district of Plymouth, E of River Plym and 3m/5km from city centre. **5 F5** SX5153.
Plymtree *Devon* ***Village***, 3m/5km SE of Cullompton. **7 J5** ST0502.
Plynlimon (Pumlumon). *Cere.* ***Mountain***, 10m/16km W of Llanidloes. Rivers Severn and Wye rise on NE and E slopes respectively. Height 2467 feet or 752 metres. **37 G7** SN7886.
Pocan Smoo *High.* ***Coastal feature***, rock on N coast 1m/2km E of Durness, Sutherland district. **103 G2** NC4267.
Pochin Houses *B.Gwent* ***Settlement***, 3m/5km S of Ebbw Vale. SO1604.
Pock Stones Moor *N.Yorks.* ***Open space***, moorland 4m/7km SW of Pateley Bridge. **57 G3** SE1060.
Pockley *N.Yorks.* ***Village***, 2m/3km NE of Helmsley. **58 C1** SE6386.
Pocklington *E.Riding* Population: 5908. ***Small town***, market town 7m/11km NW of Market Weighton. 13c-15c church known as 'Cathedral of the Wolds'. **58 E5** SE8048.
Pockthorpe *Norf.* ***Locality***, 4m/7km N of Wymondham. TG0907.
Pockthorpe *Norf.* ***Settlement***, adjoining to S of Foulsham. TG0324.
Pockthorpe *Norf.* ***Settlement***, in loop of River Wensum, just NE of Lyng. TG0718.
Pocombe Bridge *Devon* ***Settlement***, 2m/3km SW of Exeter. **7 G6** SX8991.
Pode Hole *Lincs.* ***Settlement***, 2m/3km W of Spalding. **43 F3** TF2122.
Podimore *Som.* ***Village***, 2m/4km NE of Ilchester. **8 E2** ST5425.

P

P

Podington *Beds.* **Village**, 5m/7km SE of Wellingborough. **32 C2** SP9462.

Podmore *Staffs.* **Settlement**, 3m/4km E of Loggerheads. **39 G2** SJ7835.

Pods Brook *Essex* **River**, stream rising SE of Great Bardfield and flowing SE to Braintree, where it joins River Brain. **34 B6** TL7522.

Podsmead *Glos.* **Suburb**, in S part of Gloucester. SO8215.

Poffley End *Oxon.* **Hamlet**, 2m/3km N of Witney. **30 E7** SP3512.

Pogmoor *S.Yorks.* **Suburb**, 1m/2km W of Barnsley town centre. SE3206.

Point *W.Isles* Alternative name for Eye Peninsula, qv.

Point Clear *Essex* **Settlement**, on E bank of Brightlingsea Reach, at mouth of River Colne, 1m/2km SE of Brightlingsea. TM0915.

Point Cranstal *I.o.M.* Alternative name for Shellag Point, qv.

Point Lynas *I.o.A.* **Coastal feature**, headland with lighthouse on N coast of Anglesey, 2m/4km E of Amlwch. **46 C3** SH4793.

Point of Air *Flints.* Alternative spelling of Point of Ayr, qv.

Point of Ardnamurchan *High.* **Coastal feature**, the most westerly point of British mainland. Lighthouse. **79 F1** NM4167.

Point of Ayr (Y Parlwr Du. Also spelled Point of Air.) *Flints.* **Coastal feature**, promontory at W end of River Dee estuary, 4m/6km E of Prestatyn. **47 K4** SJ1285.

Point of Ayre *I.o.M.* **Coastal feature**, northernmost point of island, with two lighthouses, 7m/11km N of Ramsey. **54 D3** NX4605.

Point of Ayre *Ork.* **Coastal feature**, headland on E coast of Mainland, 4m/6km S of Mull Head. **107 E7** HY5903.

Point of Fethaland *Shet.* **Coastal feature**, headland at northernmost point of Mainland, **108 C3** HU3795.

Point of Huro *Ork.* **Coastal feature**, headland at S end of Westray. **106 D4** HY4938.

Point of Knap *Arg. & B.* **Coastal feature**, headland in Knapdale, Argyll, on W side of entrance to Loch Caolisport. **72 E3** NR6972.

Point of Sinsoss *Ork.* **Coastal feature**, in far NE of North Ronaldsay. Dennis Head lies 1km SE. **106 G2** HY7856.

Point of Sleat *High.* **Coastal feature**, headland with beacon at S end of Sleat peninsula. Most southerly point of Skye. **86 B5** NM5699.

Point of Stoer *High.* **Coastal feature**, headland on W coast of Sutherland district, 9m/15km NW of Lochinver. **102 C5** NC0235.

Point of the Graand *Ork.* **Coastal feature**, headland and southernmost point of Egilsay. HY4726.

Point St. John *Pembs.* **Coastal feature**, headland (National Trust) at S end of Whitesand Bay, 2m/4km W of St. David's. **16 A2** SM7125.

Pointon *Lincs.* **Village**, 7m/12km N of Bourne. **42 E2** TF0731.

Pokesdown *Bourne.* **Suburb**, E district of Bournemouth. **10 C5** SZ1392.

Polanach *Arg. & B.* **Settlement**, on SE shore of Loch Linnhe, 4m/6km NE of Port Appin. **80 A2** NM9350.

Polapit Tamar *Cornw.* **Settlement**, 3m/5km N of Launceston. **6 B7** SX3389.

Polbae *D. & G.* **Settlement**, 1m/2km S of Loch Maberry and 6m/10km SE of Barrhill. **64 C3** NX2873.

Polbain *High.* **Village**, near NW coast of Ross and Cromarty district, 2m/3km NW of Achiltibuie. **102 B7** NC0208.

Polbaith Burn *E.Ayr.* **River**, rising on slopes E of Sneddon Law and flowing SW to join River Irvine 1m/2km W of Galston. **74 D6** NS4837.

Polbathic *Cornw.* **Village**, 6m/10km W of Torpoint, at head of creek running into St. Germans River. **4 D5** SX3456.

Polbeth *W.Loth.* Population: 2352. **Hamlet**, 3m/5km SW of Livingston. **75 J4** NT0264.

Polbrock *Cornw.* **Settlement**, on River Camel, 4m/6km NW of Bodmin. SX0169.

Polchar *High.* **Settlement**, 2m/3km S of Aviemore. **89 F4** NH8909.

Poldean *D. & G.* **Settlement**, on hillside, 2m/3km SE of Beattock. **69 G4** NT1000.

Polden Hills *Som.* **Inland physical feature**, hill ridge of low hills rising out of plain between Bridgwater and Glastonbury, running 10m/16km NW to SE. **8 C1** ST4435.

Poldhu Cove *Cornw.* **Bay**, small sandy cove, 1m/2km NW of Mullion. **2 D6** SW6619.

Poldhu Point *Cornw.* **Coastal feature**, point at S end of Poldhu Cove. **2 D7** SW6619.

Pole Elm *Worcs.* **Hamlet**, adjoining to N of Callow End, 3m/5km S of Worcester. SO8349.

Pole Hill *High.* **Hill**, 2m/3km W of Naver Forest, Caithness district. Height 964 feet or 294 metres. **103 J4** NC6441.

Pole Hill *P. & K.* **Hill**, in Braes of the Carse, 3m/5km N of St. Madoes. Height 945 feet or 288 metres. **82 C5** NO1926.

Pole Moor *W.Yorks.* **Settlement**, 5m/8km W of Huddersfield. **50 C1** SE0616.

Polebrook *Northants.* **Village**, 2m/3km E of Oundle. **42 D7** TL0687.

Polegate *E.Suss.* **Suburb**, N of Eastbourne. **13 J6** TQ5804.

Poles *High.* **Settlement**, 2m/3km NW of Dornoch. **96 E2** NH7893.

Polesden Lacey *Surr.* **Historic house**, Regency house and grounds (National Trust) 3m/4km NW of Dorking. **22 E6** TQ1352.

Polesworth *Warks.* Population: 6222. **Village**, 4m/7km NW of Atherstone. **40 E5** SK2602.

Polglass *High.* **Village**, on NW coast of Ross and Cromarty district, 10m/15km NW of Ullapool. **95 G1** NC0307.

Polgooth *Cornw.* Population: 1623. **Village**, 2m/3km SW of St. Austell. **3 G3** SW9950.

Polgown *D. & G.* **Settlement**, 5m/8km SW of Sanquhar. **68 C3** NS7103.

Polharrow Burn *D. & G.* **River**, running E from Loch Harrow to Water of Ken, 2m/4km N of St. John's Town of Dalry. **67 K5** NX6084.

Polin *High.* **Settlement**, near W coast of Sutherland district, 3m/4km NW of Kinlochbervie. NC1959.

Poling *W.Suss.* **Village**, 2m/3km NE of Littlehampton. **12 D6** TQ0404.

Poling Corner *W.Suss.* **Hamlet**, 1km N of Poling. Site of Roman villa to E of Poling. **12 D6** TQ0405.

Polkemmet Country Park *W.Loth.* **Leisure/recreation**, 68 acre country park with woodland, bowling green and golf course, 1m/2km W of Whitburn. **75 H4** NS9265.

Polkemmet Moor *W.Loth.* **Open space**, partly wooded moorland between Fauldhouse and Harthill. **75 H4** NS9162.

Polkerris *Cornw.* **Village**, coastal village on E side of St. Austell Bay, 2m/4km W of Fowey. **4 A5** SX0952.

Poll a' Charra (Anglicised form: Pollachar.) *W.Isles* **Settlement**, near SW coast of South Uist, 4m/6km S of Dalabrog. **84 C3** NF7414.

Poll Creadha *High.* **Sea feature**, inlet on W coast of Ross and Cromarty district, 1m/2km N of Toscaig. **94 C7** NG7140.

Poll na h-Ealaidh *High.* **Sea feature**, small inlet on W coast of Trotternish peninsula, Skye, 3m/5km S of Uig. **93 J6** NG3759.

Polla *High.* **Settlement**, at N end of Strath Beag. **103 F3** NC3854.

Pollachar *W.Isles* Anglicised form of Poll a' Charra, qv.

Pollagach Burn *Aber.* **River**, stream flowing NE to River Dee 4m/6km E of Ballater. **90 C5** NO4296.

Pollard Street *Norf.* **Locality**, 1km SW of Bacton and 4m/6km NE of North Walsham. TG3332.

Pollardras *Cornw.* **Settlement**, 3m/5km NW of Helston. SW6130.

Polldubh *High.* **Settlement**, in Glen Nevis, 5m/8km NW of Kinlochleven. **80 C1** NN1368.

Pollie *High.* **Settlement**, 1m/2km E of Dalbreck, to N of Black Water river, Sutherland district. **104 C7** NC7515.

Pollington *E.Riding* **Village**, 3m/4km SW of Snaith. **51 J1** SE6119.

Polliwilline Bay *Arg. & B.* **Bay**, on E coast of Kintyre, 3m/5km E of Southend. **66 B3** NR7409.

Polloch *High.* **Settlement**, in Lochaber district, on river of same name, which runs NW from Loch Doilet to Loch Shiel. **79 J1** NM7968.

Pollok *Glas.* **Suburb**, 4m/7km SW of Glasgow city centre. NS5362.

Pollok House *Glas.* **Historic house**, dating from 1750, former home of Maxwells is now owned by city of Glasgow. Situated by White Cart Water and surrounded by 361 acres of parkland and gardens to form Pollok Grounds, 3m/5km SW of Glasgow city centre. Stirling Maxwell collection of Spanish paintings is housed here. **74 D4** NS5561.

Pollokshaws *Glas.* **Suburb**, 3m/5km SW of Glasgow city centre. **74 D4** NS5661.

Pollokshields *Glas.* **Suburb**, 2m/3km SW of Glasgow city centre. NS5763.

Polly Bay (Also known as Loch Polly.) *High.* **Sea feature**, inlet in Enard Bay, NW coast of Ross and Cromarty district 2m/4km W of Loch Sionascaig. **102 C7** NC0714.

Polmaddie Hill *S.Ayr.* **Mountain**, 4m/6km SE of Barr. Height 1853 feet or 565 metres. **67 H4** NX3391.

Polmaddy Burn *D. & G.* **River**, rising on E slopes of Corserine and flowing E to Water of Ken, 4m/7km SE of Carsphairn. **67 K5** NX6088.

Polmadie *Glas.* **Suburb**, 2m/3km S of Glasgow city centre in Govanhill district. NS5962.

Polmarth *Cornw.* **Hamlet**, 4m/6km S of Redruth. SW7036.

Polmassick *Cornw.* **Village**, 5m/8km SW of St. Austell. **3 G4** SW9745.

Polmont *Falk.* Population: 18,041. **Town**, 3m/5km E of Falkirk. **75 H3** NS9378.

Polnoon *E.Renf.* **Settlement**, 1m/2km SE of Eaglesham. **74 D5** NS5851.

Polperro *Cornw.* **Small town**, attractive stone-built coastal resort with narrow streets and alleyways, 3m/5km SW of Looe. Many interesting houses. Cars not allowed in village. **4 C5** SX2051.

Polruan *Cornw.* **Village**, at mouth of River Fowey, opposite town of Fowey. **4 B5** SX1250.

Polsham *Som.* **Hamlet**, 3m/4km N of Glastonbury. **19 J7** ST5142.

Polstead *Suff.* **Village**, 4m/6km SW of Hadleigh. **34 D5** TL9938.

Polstead Heath *Suff.* **Hamlet**, 2m/4km SW of Hadleigh. TL9940.

Poltalloch *Arg. & B.* **Locality**, in Argyll, 1m/2km NE of Crinan Loch. Many prehistoric remains (Historic Scotland) in vicinity. **73 G1** NR8196.

Poltesco *Cornw.* **Hamlet**, 3m/5km NE of Lizard Point. SW7215.

Poltimore *Devon* **Village**, 4m/6km NE of Exeter. **7 H6** SX9696.

Polton *Midloth.* **Village**, on River North Esk, 1km SE of Loanhead. **76 A4** NT2864.

Poltross Burn Milecastle *Cumb.* **Historic/prehistoric site**, remains of milecastle (English Heritage) built on S side of Hadrian's Wall to provide Roman troops with living accommodation, 6m/10km NE of Brampton. **70 B7** NY6166.

Polwarth *Edin.* **Suburb**, 1m/2km SW of Edinburgh city centre. NT2372.

Polwarth *Sc.Bord.* **Village**, 4m/6km SW of Duns. **77 F5** NT7450.

Polyphant *Cornw.* **Village**, 5m/7km SW of Launceston. **4 C2** SX2682.

Polzeath *Cornw.* **Village**, on E side of Padstow Bay, 5m/8km NW of Wadebridge. New Polzeath is locality adjoining to N. Fine surfing beach. Associations with John Betjeman. **3 G1** SW9378.

Pomona *Ork.* Former name of Mainland, qv.

Pomphlett *Plym.* **Suburb**, SE district of Plymouth, E of River Plym. SX5153.

Pond Street *Essex* **Hamlet**, comprises Lower Pond Street and to S, Upper Pond Street, 5m/8km W of Saffron Walden. **33 H5** TL4537.

Ponde *Powys* **Locality**, 4m/6km NW of Talgarth. SO1037.

Ponders End *Gt.Lon.* **Suburb**, in borough of Enfield, 2m/3km E of Enfield town. **23 G2** TQ3595.

Pondersbridge *Cambs.* **Hamlet**, 3m/5km S of Whittlesey. **43 F6** TL2692.

Pondtail *Hants.* **Suburb**, E district of Fleet. SU8254.

Ponesk Burn *E.Ayr.* **River**, rising on SW slopes of Hare Craig and flowing S down steep valleys to join River Ayr, 2m/3km E of Muirkirk. **75 F7** NS7130.

Ponsanooth *Cornw.* **Village**, 3m/4km NW of Penryn. **2 E5** SW7537.

Ponsonby *Cumb.* **Locality**, 2m/3km NW of Gosforth. **60 B6** NY0505.

Ponsongath *Cornw.* **Hamlet**, on SE edge of Goonhilly Downs, 8m/13km SE of Helston. SW7517.

Ponsworthy *Devon* **Village**, in steep valley of West Webburn River, 4m/7km NW of Ashburton. **5 H3** SX7073.

Pont *Northumb.* **River**, rising near Little Whittington, N of Corbridge, and flowing E to Ponteland, then N to River Blyth 3m/5km N of Ponteland. **71 G6** NZ1777.

Pont Aber *Carmar.* **Settlement**, 4m/7km SE of Llangadog. **27 G6** SN7322.

Pont Aberglaslyn *Gwyn.* **Settlement**, in valley of River Glaslyn, 1m/2km S of Beddgelert. **36 E1** SH5946.

Pont ar Hydfer *Powys* **Hamlet**, 2m/3km SW of Trecastle. SN8627.

Pont-ar-llechau *Carmar.* **Settlement**, 3m/5km SE of Llangadog. SN7224.

Pont Ceri *Cere.* **Settlement**, 1m/2km NW of Newcastle Emlyn. **26 B4** SN2941.

Pont Clydach *Carmar.* **Bridge**, road bridge over River Clydach, 4m/6km N of Brynamman. **27 G7** SN7319.

Pont Crugnant *Powys* **Settlement**, 3m/4km N of Staylittle. **37 H6** SN8895.

Pont Cwm Pydew *Denb.* **Bridge**, road bridge over Nant Cwm Pydew, 6m/9km SE of Bala. **37 K2** SJ0031.

Pont Cyfyng *Conwy* **Hamlet**, 1m/2km SE of Capel Curig. **47 F7** SH7357.

Pont-Cysyllte Aqueduct *Wrex.* **Bridge**, high iron aqueduct built by Telford in 1795, carrying Llangollen Canal over River Dee valley, 3m/5km E of Llangollen. SJ2741.

Pont Dolgarrog *Conwy* **Settlement**, and bridge over River Ddu, 1m/2km S of Dolgarrog. **47 F6** SH7766.

Pont-faen *Cere.* **Settlement**, 2m/4km E of Lampeter across River Teifi. SN6049.

Pont-faen *Powys* **Hamlet**, 5m/7km NW of Brecon. **27 J5** SN9934.

Pont-Henri (Also spelled Pont Henry.) *Carmar.* **Village**, on River Gwendraeth Fawr, 5m/8km NE of Kidwelly. **17 H4** SN4709.

Pont Henry *Carmar.* Alternative spelling of Pont-Henri, qv.

Pont Hwfa *I.o.A.* **Suburb**, 1m/2km W of Holyhead. SH2382.

Pont Llogel *Powys* **Settlement**, and bridge over River Efyrnwy, 2m/3km S of Llanwddyn. **37 K4** SJ0315.

Pont Pen-y-benglog (Also known as Ogwen Cottage.) *Conwy* **Settlement**, and bridge across River Ogwen on A5 road at W end of Llyn Ogwen, 4m/7km SW of Bethesda. Mountain Rescue Post. **46 E6** SH6460.

Pont Rhyd-sarn *Gwyn.* **Settlement**, on River Dyfrdwy, 1m/2km SW of Llanuwchllyn. **37 H3** SH8528.

Pont Rhyd-y-cyff *Bridgend* **Hamlet**, 2m/3km SE of Maesteg. **18 B3** SS8789.

Pont-rhyd-y-groes *Cere.* **Village**, 3m/5km S of Devil's Bridge. **27 G1** SN7372.

Pont-Rhys-Powell *Mon.* **Locality**, 5m/8km N of Abergavenny. SO3122.

Pont Rhythallt *Gwyn.* **Hamlet**, on River Rhythallt, 3m/5km NW of Llanberis. SH5463.

Pont-rug *Gwyn.* **Hamlet**, on River Seiont, 2m/3km E of Caernarfon. **46 D6** SH5163.

Pont-Siân *Cere.* Welsh form of Pontshaen, qv.

Pont Siôn Norton *R.C.T.* **Locality**, 1m/2km NE of Pontypridd. ST0891.

Pont-tyweli *Carmar.* Welsh form of Pontwelly, qv.

Pont-Walby *N.P.T.* **Locality**, at crossing of River Neath, on E side of Glyn-neath. **18 B1** SN8906.

Pont-y-blew *Wrex.* **Hamlet**, on River Ceiriog, 1m/2km E of Chirk. SJ3138.

Pont-y-pant *Conwy* **Hamlet**, on River Lledr, 3m/5km SW of Betws-y-coed. **47 F7** SH7553.

Pont-y-rhyl *Bridgend* **Hamlet**, in Garw valley, 1m/2km S of Pontycymer. SS9089.

Pont yr Alwen *Conwy* **Locality**, 3m/4km NE of Cerrigydrudion. **47 H7** SH9652.

Pontaman *Carmar.* Alternative spelling of Pontamman, qv.

Pontamman (Pontaman). *Carmar.* **Locality**, 1m/2km E of Ammanford. **17 K3** SN6412.

Pontantwn *Carmar.* **Hamlet**, on River Gwendraeth Fach, 5m/8km S of Carmarthen. **17 H3** SN4413.

Pontardawe *N.P.T.* Population: 18,479. **Town**, 5m/7km NW of Neath. **18 A1** SN7204.

Pontarddulais *Swan.* Population: 7770. **Small town**, former tinplate-manufacturing town on River Loughor, 8m/12km NW of Swansea. **17 J4** SN5903.

Pontarfynach *Cere.* Welsh form of Devil's Bridge, qv.

Pontargothi *Carmar.* **Hamlet**, on River Cothi, 6m/9km E of Carmarthen. **17 J2** SN5021.

Pontarsais *Carmar.* **Hamlet**, 5m/9km N of Carmarthen. **17 H2** SN4428.

Pontblyddyn *Flints.* **Village**, 3m/5km SE of Mold. **48 B6** SJ2760.

Pontbren Llwyd *R.C.T.* **Village**, 1m/2km N of Hirwaun. **18 C1** SN9407.

Pontcanna *Cardiff* ***Suburb***, with large park and recreation ground on W bank of River Taff, 1km W of Cardiff city centre. ST1677.
Pontefract *W.Yorks.* Population: 28,358. ***Town***, 12m/19km SE of Leeds. Famous for its Pontefract Cakes. Remains of Norman castle. Racecourse to NW. Pontefract Museum depicts town's industries, including glass-blowing. **57 K7** SE4522.
Ponteland *Northumb.* Population: 9933. ***Small town***, 7m/11km NW of Newcastle upon Tyne. Remains of Norman castle now incorporated into local inn. **71 G6** NZ1672.
Ponterwyd *Cere.* ***Village***, on River Rheidol, 3m/4km N of Devil's Bridge. Llywernog Silver and Lead Mine Museum 1m/2km W. **37 G7** SN7480.
Pontesbury *Shrop.* Population: 1956. ***Village***, 7m/11km SW of Shrewsbury. **38 D5** SJ3906.
Pontesbury Hill *Shrop.* ***Hamlet***, adjoining to S of Pontesbury. SJ3905.
Pontesford *Shrop.* ***Hamlet***, 6m/10km SW of Shrewsbury. **38 D5** SJ4106.
Pontfadog *Wrex.* ***Village***, 4m/6km W of Chirk. **38 B2** SJ2338.
Pontfaen (Also known as Y Bont-faen.) *Pembs.* ***Hamlet***, on River Gwaun, 4m/6km SW of Newport. **16 D1** SN0234.
Pontgarreg *Cere.* ***Hamlet***, 2m/3km E of Llangranog. SN3354.
Ponthir *Torfaen* ***Village***, 1m/2km N of Caerleon. **19 G2** ST3292.
Ponthirwaun *Cere.* ***Hamlet***, 4m/7km NW of Newcastle Emlyn. **26 B4** SN2645.
Pontllanfraith *Caerp.* Population: 6636. ***Village***, 1m/2km S of Blackwood. **18 E2** ST1895.
Pontlliw *Swan.* ***Village***, 2m/3km SE of Pontarddulais. **17 K4** SN6101.
Pontllyfni *Gwyn.* ***Village***, near mouth of River Llyfni, 7m/11km SW of Caernarfon. **46 C7** SH4352.
Pontlottyn *Caerp.* ***Locality***, 1m/2km S of Rhymney. **18 E1** SO1106.
Pontneathvaughan *Powys English form of Pontneddfechan, qv.*
Pontneddfechan (Pontneathvaughan). *Powys* ***Village***, 1m/2km NE of Glyn-neath. **18 C1** SN9007.
Pontnewydd *Torfaen* ***Suburb***, in N part of Cwmbran. **19 F2** ST2996.
Pontnewynydd *Torfaen* ***Locality***, 1m/2km NW of Pontypool. **19 F1** SO2701.
Pontrhydfendigaid *Cere.* ***Village***, on River Teifi, 5m/8km NE of Tregaron. **27 G2** SN7366.
Pontrhydyfen *N.P.T.* ***Village***, on River Afan, 3m/5km NE of Port Talbot. **18 A2** SS7994.
Pontrhydyrun (Also spelled Pontrhydyrynn.) *Torfaen* ***Locality***, 2m/3km N of Cwmbran. **19 F2** ST2997.
Pontrhydyrynn *Torfaen Alternative spelling of Pontrhydyrun, qv.*
Pontrilas *Here.* ***Village***, on River Dore, near its confluence with River Monnow, 11m/17km SW of Hereford. **28 C6** SO3927.
Pontrobert *Powys* ***Village***, on River Vyrnwy, 4m/6km N of Llanfair Caereinion. **38 A4** SJ1012.
Ponts Green *E.Suss.* ***Hamlet***, 5m/7km W of Battle. **13 K5** TQ6715.
Pontsenni *Powys Welsh form of Sennybridge, qv.*
Pontshaen (Pont-Siân). *Cere.* ***Hamlet***, 4m/6km N of Llandysul. **26 D4** SN4346.
Pontshill *Here.* ***Village***, 3m/5km SE of Ross-on-Wye. **29 F6** SO6321.
Pontsticill *M.Tyd.* ***Village***, 3m/5km N of Merthyr Tydfil. **27 K7** SO0511.
Pontsticill Reservoir (Also known as Tef fechan Reservoir.) *Powys* ***Reservoir***, large reservoir on border with Merthyr Tydfil, in valley of Taf fechan River, 4m/6km N of Merthyr Tydfil. **27 K7** SO0611.
Pontwelly (Pont-tyweli). *Carmar.* ***Village***, just S of Llandysul across River Teifi. **17 H1** SN4140.
Pontyates *Carmar.* ***Village***, 4m/6km E of Kidwelly. **17 H4** SN4608.
Pontyberem *Carmar.* Population: 2349. ***Village***, on River Gwendraeth Fawr, 8m/13km SE of Carmarthen. **17 J3** SN5011.
Pontybodkin *Flints.* ***Village***, 4m/6km SE of Mold. **48 B7** SJ2759.
Pontyclun *R.C.T.* Population: 4568. ***Village***, 1m/2km SW of Llantrisant. **18 D3** ST0381.
Pontycymer *Bridgend* Population: 4439. ***Small town***, 7m/11km N of Bridgend. **18 C2** SS9091.
Pontyglazier *Pembs.* ***Locality***, 1m/2km S of Eglwyswrw. SN1436.
Pontygwaith *R.C.T.* ***Village***, in Rhondda Fach valley, 1km S of Tylorstown. **18 D2** ST0194.
Pontymister *Caerp.* ***Locality***, in Risca, on Ebbw River. **19 F3** ST2490.
Pontymoel *Torfaen* ***Suburb***, in SE part of Pontypool. SO2900.
Pontypool (Pontypŵl). *Torfaen* Population: 35,564. ***Town***, 8m/13km N of Newport. Formerly an iron and tinplate producer. Dry-ski slope. **19 F1** SO2800.
Pontypridd *R.C.T.* Population: 28,487. ***Town***, market town at confluence of River Rhondda and River Taff, 11m/18km NW of Cardiff. 18c single-arched stone bridge. University of Glamorgan. **18 D3** ST0790.
Pontypŵl *Torfaen Welsh form of Pontypool, qv.*
Pontywaun *Caerp.* ***Village***, 1m/2km NW of Risca. **19 F2** ST2292.
Pooksgreen *Hants.* ***Locality***, 2m/3km SE of Totton. **10 E3** SU3710.
Pool *Cornw.* ***Village***, 2m/3km NE of Camborne. **2 D4** SW6641.
Pool *W.Yorks.* ***Village***, on S side of River Wharfe, 3m/4km E of Otley. **57 H5** SE2445.
Pool Bank *Cumb.* ***Settlement***, on W side of Whitbarrow Scar, 4m/6km W of Levens. **55 H1** SD4387.
Pool Dole *Stoke* ***Suburb***, on E side of Fenton. SJ9044.
Pool Green *W.Mid.* ***Suburb***, S district of Aldridge. SK0500.
Pool Head *Here.* ***Hamlet***, 7m/11km NE of Hereford. SO5550.
Pool Hey *Lancs.* ***Settlement***, 2m/4km SE of Southport. SD3615.
Pool Hill *Powys* ***Mountain***, rounded summit, 4m/7km NE of Llanbister. Height 1689 feet or 515 metres. **28 A1** SO1675.
Pool of Muckhart *Clack.* ***Village***, 3m/5km NE of Dollar. **82 B7** NO0000.
Pool Quay *Powys* ***Settlement***, on Shropshire Union Canal, 3m/5km NE of Welshpool. **38 B4** SJ2511.
Pool Street *Essex* ***Hamlet***, 5m/8km NW of Halstead. **34 B5** TL7637.
Poolcray *W.Isles* ***Locality***, near S end of South Uist, 2m/4km N of Cille Bhrighde. NF7717.
Poole *N.Yorks.* ***Settlement***, just S of Burton Salmon, 2m/3km N of Knottingley. SE4927.
Poole *Poole* Population: 138,479. ***Town***, port and manufacturing town on Poole Harbour, 4m/6km W of Bournemouth. Previously known for its boat-building, pottery and fishing, it was badly damaged in World War II. Resort and yachting centre. Waterfront Museum in 15c warehouse recalls its maritime history. **10 B5** SZ0291.
Poole Bay *Poole* ***Bay***, on English Channel, off Poole and Bournemouth, extending E from The Foreland to Hengistbury Head. **10 B6** SZ1089.
Poole Green *Ches.* ***Hamlet***, 3m/4km NW of Nantwich. SJ6355.
Poole Harbour *Dorset* ***Sea feature***, expanse of water open to sea, between Sandbanks and South Haven Point, extending 6m/10km W to mouth of River Frome near Wareham. **9 J6** SZ0089.
Poole Keynes *Glos.* ***Village***, 4m/7km S of Cirencester. **20 C2** SU0095.
Poolend *Staffs.* ***Settlement***, 2m/3km NW of Leek. SJ9658.
Poolewe *High.* ***Village***, at head of Loch Ewe, Ross and Cromarty district, 4m/7km NE of Gairloch. National Trust for Scotland property N and E, including Inverewe gardens to N. **94 E3** NG8580.
Pooley Bridge *Cumb.* ***Village***, at NE end of Ullswater, 5m/7km SW of Penrith. **61 F4** NY4724.
Pooley Street *Norf.* ***Settlement***, 4m/6km W of Diss. TM0580.
Poolfold *Staffs.* ***Hamlet***, 2m/3km NE of Biddulph. SJ8959.
Poolhill *Glos.* ***Hamlet***, 2m/4km N of Newent. **29 G6** SO7329.
Pools of Dee *Aber.* ***Lake/loch***, group of three pools in Cairngorm Mountains at source of River Dee, to NW of Ben Macdui. **89 G4** NH9700.
Poolsbrook *Derbys.* ***Hamlet***, 1km SE of Staveley. SK4473.
Poolstock *Gt.Man.* ***Suburb***, 1km SW of Wigan town centre. SD5704.
Poolthorne *N.Lincs.* ***Settlement***, 1m/2km E of Cadney. TA0303.
Poor Lot Barrows *Dorset* ***Historic/prehistoric site***, large number of Bronze Age mounds, 3m/4km W of Winterbourne Abbas. **8 E5** SY5890.
Poor's End *Lincs.* ***Locality***, adjoining to N of Grainthorpe. TF3897.
Pope Hill *Pembs.* ***Settlement***, 2m/4km SW of Haverfordwest. **16 C3** SM9312.
Popeswood *Brack.F.* ***Village***, 2m/3km W of Bracknell. **22 B5** SU8469.
Popham *Hants.* ***Hamlet***, 4m/7km NE of Micheldever. **21 J7** SU5543.
Poplar *Gt.Lon.* ***Suburb***, in borough of Tower Hamlets, 3m/5km E of London Bridge. **23 G3** TQ3780.
Poplar Street *Suff.* ***Locality***, 2m/3km N of Leiston. TM4465.
Porchester *Notts.* ***Suburb***, 2m/4km NE of Nottingham. SK5942.
Porchfield *I.o.W.* ***Hamlet***, 4m/7km SW of Cowes. **11 F5** SZ4491.
Porin *High.* ***Locality***, in Strathconon, Ross and Cromarty district, 2m/3km above head of Loch Meig. **95 K6** NH3155.
Poringland (Formerly known as East Poringland.) *Norf.* Population: 4684. ***Village***, 5m/8km SE of Norwich. **45 G5** TG2701.
Porkellis *Cornw.* ***Village***, 4m/6km NE of Helston. **2 D5** SW6933.
Porlock *Som.* ***Small town***, resort near coast at foot of steep hill, 4m/7km W of Minehead. Some thatched cottages in town centre. **7 G1** SS8846.
Porlock Bay *Som.* ***Bay***, to N of Porlock, with large stony beach; submarine forest visible at low tide. **7 G1** SS8748.
Porlock Weir *Som.* ***Village***, with small harbour, at W end of Porlock Bay. **7 G1** SS8647.
Port a' Ghàraidh *High.* ***Bay***, small bay on E shore of Sound of Sleat, on coast of Skye and Lochalsh district, 1m/2km SW of Glenelg. **86 D3** NG7917.
Port a' Mhurain *Arg. & B.* ***Sea feature***, inlet on S coast of Coll, to S of Crossapol Bay. **78 C2** NM1251.
Port a' Stoth (Anglicised form: Port Sto.) *W.Isles* ***Sea feature***, small inlet 1km SE of Butt of Lewis. **101 H1** NB5265.
Port Alasdair *W.Isles* ***Sea feature***, small inlet on E coast of Isle of Lewis, 3m/4km N of Cellar Head. **101 H1** NB5560.
Port Allen *D. & G.* ***Bay***, on W side of Wigtown Bay, 2m/3km E of Whithorn. **64 E6** NX4841.
Port Allen *P. & K.* ***Settlement***, on small inlet on N bank of Firth of Tay, 1m/2km S of Errol. **82 D5** NO2521.
Port Allt a' Mhuilinn *High.* ***Sea feature***, small inlet, 1m/2km SW of Strathy Point, Caithness district. **104 D2** NC8068.
Port an Aird Fhada *Arg. & B.* ***Bay***, small bay on S shore of Loch Scridain, Mull, to E of Aird Fada headland. **79 F5** NM4524.
Port an Duine Mhairbh *Arg. & B.* ***Sea feature***, inlet on W coast of Iona, 1m/2km W of Baile Mòr. **78 D5** NM2624.
Port Ann *Arg. & B.* ***Sea feature***, natural harbour on NW shore of Loch Fyne, 3m/4km SE of Lochgilphead. **73 H2** NR9086.
Port Appin *Arg. & B.* ***Village***, in Argyll, on E shore of Loch Linnhe, opposite N end of Lismore. Ferry to Port Ramsay on Lismore. **80 A3** NM9045.
Port Arnol *W.Isles* ***Bay***, on NW coast of Isle of Lewis, 1km NW of Arnol village. **100 E3** NB2949.
Port Askaig *Arg. & B.* ***Village***, and small port on E coast of Islay. Ferry to Feolin Ferry, Jura, on opposite side of Sound of Islay; car ferry service to West Loch Tarbert on mainland. **72 C4** NR4369.
Port Bàn *Arg. & B.* ***Sea feature***, small inlet on NE coast of Tiree. **78 C3** NM0947.
Port Bannatyne *Arg. & B.* Population: 1385. ***Village***, resort on S side of Kames Bay on E coast of Bute, 2m/3km N of Rothesay. **73 J4** NS0767.
Port Bun a' Ghlinne *W.Isles* ***Sea feature***, small inlet on E coast of Isle of Lewis, 3m/5km SW of Tolsta Head. **101 H3** NB5244.
Port Burg *Arg. & B.* ***Bay***, small bay on Loch Tuath, Mull, to S of Burg. **78 E3** NM3845.
Port Carlisle *Cumb.* ***Village***, on River Eden estuary, 11m/17km W of Carlisle. **69 H7** NY2462.
Port Castle Bay *D. & G.* ***Bay***, 2m/4km W of Burrow Head. **64 E7** NX4235.
Port Ceann a' Gharraidh *Arg. & B.* ***Sea feature***, narrow inlet at NE end of Colonsay. **72 C1** NR4298.
Port Charlotte *Arg. & B.* ***Village***, on W side of Loch Indaal, Islay, 7m/11km NE of Rinns Point. **72 A5** NR2558.
Port Chubaird *Arg. & B.* ***Sea feature***, on W coast of The Oa, Islay, 2m/3km SW of Port Ellen. **72 B6** NR3342.
Port Clarence *Stock.* ***Locality***, on N bank of River Tees. Transporter bridge across river to Middlesbrough. **63 G4** NZ4921.
Port Cornaa *I.o.M.* ***Bay***, small bay at mouth of stream, 3m/5km NE of Laxey. **54 D5** SC4787.
Port Dinorwig *Gwyn. Alternative name for Y Felinheli, qv.*
Port Donain *Arg. & B.* ***Bay***, small bay on E coast of Mull, 1m/2km NE of Rubha na Faoilinn. **79 J5** NM7329.
Port Driseach *Arg. & B.* ***Hamlet***, in Argyll, on W shore of Kyles of Bute, 1m/2km NE of Tighnabruaich. **73 H3** NR9873.
Port Dundas *Glas.* ***Suburb***, 1m/2km N of Glasgow city centre. NS5966.
Port e Vullen *I.o.M.* ***Hamlet***, and small bay on SE side of Tableland Point or Gob ny rona. **54 D4** SC4792.
Port Einon *Swan. Welsh form of Port Eynon, qv.*
Port Ellen *Arg. & B.* ***Small town***, and chief port of Islay, on S coast. Ruined Dunyvaig Castle is 14c. Several distilleries, including the well-known Lagavulin and Laphroaig. Airport at Glenegedale, 4m/7km NW. **72 B6** NR3645.
Port Elphinstone *Aber.* ***Hamlet***, 1km S of Inverurie across River Don. **91 F3** NJ7720.
Port Erin *I.o.M.* ***Small town***, port and popular resort on Port Erin Bay, 9m/15km S of Peel. **54 B7** SC1969.
Port Erroll *Aber.* ***Village***, on E coast, adjoining to SE of Cruden Bay, at N end of Bay of Cruden. **91 J1** NK0936.
Port Eynon (Port Einon). *Swan.* ***Village***, on S coast of Gower peninsula, 13m/21km W of Swansea. **17 H6** SS4885.
Port Eynon Bay *Swan.* ***Bay***, on S coast of Gower peninsula, 1km S of Port Eynon, extending E towards Oxwich Point. **17 H6** SS4884.
Port Eynon Point *Swan.* ***Coastal feature***, rocky headland 1km S of Port Eynon. **17 H6** SS4784.
Port Fada *Arg. & B.* ***Sea feature***, on E coast of Kintyre, 2m/3km SW of Claonaig. **73 G5** NR8554.
Port Gaverne *Cornw.* ***Hamlet***, on E side of Port Isaac. **4 A2** SX0080.
Port Geiraha *W.Isles* ***Bay***, small bay on E coast of Isle of Lewis, 3m/4km NW of Tolsta Head. **101 H2** NB5350.
Port Glasgow *Inclyde* Population: 19,693. ***Town***, old port and industrial town on Firth of Clyde, 3m/5km E of Greenock. 16c-17c Newark Castle (Historic Scotland) to E. **74 B3** NS3274.
Port Grenaugh *I.o.M.* ***Sea feature***, inlet 1m/2km W of Santon Head. **54 C6** SC3170.
Port Groudle *I.o.M.* ***Sea feature***, inlet at foot of Groudle Glen, 2m/3km SW of Clay Head. **54 D6** SC4278.
Port Henderson *High.* ***Village***, on W coast of Ross and Cromarty district, 4m/6km SW of Gairloch across Gair Loch. **94 D4** NG7573.
Port Isaac *Cornw.* ***Village***, attractive fishing village on N coast, 5m/8km N of Wadebridge. **4 A2** SW9980.
Port Isaac Bay *Cornw.* ***Bay***, to NE of Port Isaac, extending NW from Varley Point to Penhallic Point. **4 A2** SX0181.
Port Leatham *Arg. & B.* ***Sea feature***, natural harbour at SW tip of Cowal peninsula, 5m/7km SW of Tighnabruaich. **73 H3** NR9267.
Port Lion *Pembs.* ***Hamlet***, 1km S of Llangwm. SM9908.
Port Logan *D. & G.* ***Village***, on W coast of Rinns of Galloway, 4m/6km NW of Drummore. **64 A6** NX0940.
Port Lotha *Arg. & B.* ***Sea feature***, narrow inlet on W coast of Colonsay, 3m/4km W of Scalasaig. **72 B1** NR3492.
Port Lympne *Kent* ***Historic house***, 2m/3km S of Sellindge and 1km N of Royal Military Canal, built at beginning of 20c by Sir Herbert Baker for Sir Philip Sassoon. Treaty of Paris was signed here after World War II. House features Trojan stairway and Moorish patio. 300 acre grounds are home to more than 500 animals, many of them rare, including black rhinoceros and Siberian and Indian tigers. **15 F4** TR1035.
Port Mary *D. & G.* ***Bay***, small bay, 1m/2km S of Dundrennan. **65 H6** NX7545.
Port Mholair *W.Isles Gaelic form of Portvoller, qv.*
Port Min *High.* ***Sea feature***, small inlet on W coast of Ardnamurchan peninsula, 4m/7km NW of Kilchoan. **79 F1** NM4166.
Port Mine *Arg. & B.* ***Sea feature***, small inlet on W coast of Coll, to W of Feall Bay. **78 C2** NM1254.
Port Mooar *I.o.M.* ***Sea feature***, inlet near Booilushag, 3m/5km SE of Ramsey. **54 D4** SC4890.
Port Mòr *Arg. & B.* ***Bay***, with jetty, at N end of Gigha. **72 E5** NR6654.
Port Mòr *Arg. & B.* ***Sea feature***, inlet on S coast of Ross of Mull, 1m/2km NE of Rubh' Ardalanish. **78 E6** NM3617.

Port Mòr *Arg. & B.* ***Sea feature***, inlet on W coast of Colonsay. **72 B1** NR3594.
Port Mòr *High.* ***Coastal feature***, small inlet 2m/3km NE of Portmahomack. **97 G3** NH9287.
Port Mòr *High.* ***Hamlet***, with small harbour, near SE end of Muck, in Inner Hebrides. **85 K7** NM4279.
Port Mulgrave *N.Yorks.* ***Settlement***, 1km N of Hinderwell. **63 J5** NZ7917.
Port na Bà *Arg. & B.* ***Sea feature***, small inlet on N coast of Mull, 3m/4km E of Caliach Point. **78 E2** NM3854.
Port-na-Con *High.* ***Settlement***, on W shore of Loch Eriboll, Sutherland district, 5m/8km S of Durness. Ancient earth-house to N. **103 G2** NC4260.
Port na Craig *P. & K.* ***Settlement***, adjoining to S of Pitlochry across River Tummel. **82 A2** NN9358.
Port na Croise *Arg. & B.* ***Bay***, small bay on N shore of Loch Scridain, Mull, 1km SE of Bearraich. **79 F5** NM4326.
Port na Long *High.* ***Settlement***, on Skye, between Loch Harport and Fiskavaig Bay, 3m/4km NW of Carbost. NG3434.
Port nam Bothag *W.Isles* ***Sea feature***, small inlet, 1km S of Tolastadh bho Thuath, Isle of Lewis. **101 H3** NB5446.
Port nan Giùran *W.Isles Gaelic form of Portnaguran, qv.*
Port nan Long (Anglicised form: Newtonferry.) *W.Isles* ***Settlement***, on N coast of North Uist, 1m/2km N of Beinn Mhòr. **92 D4** NF8978.
Port Nis (Anglicised form: Port of Ness.) *W.Isles* ***Village***, on NE coast of Isle of Lewis, 2m/3km SE of Butt of Lewis. **101 H1** NB5363.
Port o' Warren *D. & G.* ***Settlement***, 6m/9km SE of Dalbeattie. **65 J5** NX8853.
Port of Brims *High.* ***Sea feature***, small inlet to S of Brims Ness on N coast. ND0471.
Port of Menteith *Stir.* ***Village***, at NE corner of Lake of Menteith, 5m/8km SW of Callander. **81 G7** NN5801.
Port of Ness *W.Isles Anglicised form of Port Nis, qv.*
Port of Spittal Bay *D. & G.* ***Bay***, 2m/3km SE of Portpatrick. **64 A5** NX0252.
Port Ohirnie *Arg. & B.* ***Bay***, small bay on SE coast of Mull, 2m/4km E of entrance to Loch Buie. **79 H6** NM6320.
Port Penrhyn *Gwyn.* ***Locality***, dock of former port on Menai Strait, 1m/2km E of Bangor. **46 D5** SH5972.
Port Ramsay *Arg. & B.* ***Settlement***, at N end of Lismore, on Loch Linnhe. Ferry to Port Appin on mainland to E. **79 K3** NM8845.
Port St. Mary *I.o.M.* ***Village***, and resort on Port St. Mary Bay, 2m/4km NE of Spanish Head. **54 B7** SC2067.
Port Skigersta *W.Isles* ***Bay***, small bay near N end of Isle of Lewis, to NE of Sgiogarstaigh. **101 H1** NB5462.
Port Solent *Ports.* ***Settlement***, at head of Portsmouth harbour, 4m/6km N of Portsmouth city centre. **11 H4** SU6305.
Port Sonachan *Arg. & B. Alternative spelling of Portsonachan, qv.*
Port Sto *W.Isles Anglicised form of Port a' Stoth, qv.*
Port Sunlight *Mersey.* ***Locality***, on Wirral peninsula, beside River Mersey estuary, 3m/5km SE of Birkenhead. Originally model village built by Lever family to house factory workers. Lady Lever Art Gallery. **48 C4** SJ3484.
Port Talbot *N.P.T.* Population: 37,647. ***Town***, industrial town and port at mouth of River Afan, 8m/12km E of Swansea across Swansea Bay. **18 A3** SS7690.
Port Tennant *Swan.* ***Suburb***, 1m/2km E of Swansea city centre across River Tawe. SS6793.
Port Vasgo *High.* ***Sea feature***, small inlet near mouth of Tongue Bay. **103 H2** NC5865.
Port Wemyss *Arg. & B.* ***Village***, at S end of Rinns of Islay, opposite Orsay. **72 A5** NR1651.
Port William *D. & G.* ***Town***, small resort with quay, on E shore of Luce Bay, 9m/15km SW of Wigtown. Sandy beaches. Remains of 11c chapel nearby. **64 D6** NX3343.
Portachoillan *Arg. & B.* ***Settlement***, on SE of seaward end of West Loch Tarbert, Kintyre, 1m/2km N of Clachan. **73 F5** NR7657.
Portankill *D. & G.* ***Bay***, small bay 2m/3km S of Cailiness Point. **64 B7** NX1432.
Portavadie *Arg. & B.* ***Village***, on E side of Loch Fyne, opposite Tarbert, 4m/6km SW across peninsula from Tighnabruaich. **73 H4** NR9269.
Portbury *N.Som.* ***Village***, 6m/9km W of Bristol. **19 H4** ST4975.
Portchester *Hants.* Population: 27,433. ***Town***, on N shore of Portsmouth Harbour. Norman castle (English Heritage) with Norman church in precincts, built within walls of Roman fort. **11 H4** SU6105.
Portchester Castle *Hants.* ***Castle***, magnificent castle (English Heritage), 3m/4km NW of Portsmouth across Portsmouth Harbour. Built on Roman and Saxon sites by Henry II in 1160-72, later extended by Edward II and Richard II. Henry V mustered Agincourt expedition here. **11 H4** SU6204.
Portclair Forest *High.* ***Forest/woodland***, in Inverness district 4m/6km N of Fort Augustus. **88 A3** NH3815.
Portencross *N.Ayr.* ***Settlement***, on Firth of Clyde, 5m/9km NW of Ardrossan. Remains of medieval castle. **73 K6** NS1748.
Portencross Castle *N.Ayr.* ***Castle***, on coast at Portencross. Norman castle built on Roman fort and used as a prison in 18c for French prisoners of war. **73 K6** NS1748.
Porter's Fen Corner *Norf.* ***Locality***, 1m/2km S of Wiggenhall St. Mary Magdalen. TF5809.
Portesham *Dorset* ***Village***, 6m/10km NW of Weymouth. **9 F6** SY6085.
Portessie *Moray* ***Suburb***, E district of Buckie on N coast. **98 C4** NJ4466.
Portfield *Arg. & B.* ***Settlement***, on SE coast of Mull, 1km SW of entrance to Loch Spelve. **79 J5** NM7126.
Portfield *W.Suss.* ***Suburb***, on E side of Chichester. SU8704.
Portfield Gate *Pembs.* ***Hamlet***, 2m/3km W of Haverfordwest. **16 C3** SM9215.
Portgate *Devon* ***Hamlet***, 6m/9km E of Launceston. **6 C7** SX4185.
Portgordon *Moray* ***Village***, on Spey Bay, 2m/3km SW of Buckie. **98 B4** NJ3964.
Portgower *High.* ***Settlement***, on E coast of Sutherland district, 2m/3km SW of Helmsdale. **105 F7** ND0013.
Porth *Cornw.* ***Suburb***, to NE of Newquay. **3 F2** SW8362.
Porth *R.C.T.* ***Small town***, at confluence of Rhondda and Little Rhondda Rivers, 3m/5km W of Pontypridd. **18 D2** ST0291.
Porth Ceiriad *Gwyn.* ***Bay***, on S coast of Lleyn Peninsula, 2m/4km S of Abersoch. Extends E from Trwyn Llech-y-doll to Trwyn yr Wylfa. **36 C3** SH3124.
Porth Colmon *Gwyn.* ***Bay***, 1km N of Llangwnnadl, extending from Penrhyn Colmon NE to Penrhyn Melyn. Also locality at SW end of bay. **36 A2** SH2034.
Porth Colmon *Gwyn.* ***Settlement***, on NW coast of Lleyn Peninsula, 5m/8km N of Aberdaron. **36 A2** SH1934.
Porth Dinllaen *Gwyn.* ***Bay***, and hamlet on headland of Trwyn Porth Dinllaen. Bay extends E to Penrhyn Nefyn. **36 B1** SH2741.
Porth Hellick Down Burial Chamber *I.o.S.* ***Historic/prehistoric site***, Neolithic or Bronze Age entrance grave (English Heritage), 1m/2km E of Hugh Town, on St. Mary's. **2 C1** SV9210.
Porth Llechog *I.o.A. See Bull Bay.*
Porth-llwyd *Conwy* ***River***, rising on E side of Carnedd Llywelyn and flowing E into River Conwy on NE side of Dolgarrog. **47 F6** SH7768.
Porth-mawr *Pembs. Welsh form of Whitesands Bay, qv.*
Porth Mellin *Cornw.* ***Village***, above Mullion Cove, 6m/10km S of Helston. **2 D7** SW6617.
Porth Navas *Cornw.* ***Village***, on creek running into Helford River, 5m/8km SW of Falmouth. **2 E6** SW7527.
Porth Neigwl (Also known as Hell's Mouth.) *Gwyn.* ***Bay***, on S side of Lleyn Peninsula, extending E from Trwyn Talfarach to Trwyn y Fulfran, S of Llanengan. **36 B3** SH2626.
Porth Oer *Gwyn.* ***Bay***, sandy bay on NW coast at tip of Lleyn Peninsula, 2m/3km N of Aberdaron. **36 A2** SH1629.
Porth Reservoir *Cornw.* ***Reservoir***, 4m/6km E of Newquay. **3 F2** SW8662.
Porth Sgiwed *Mon. Welsh form of Portskewett, qv.*
Porth Swtan *I.o.A. Welsh form of Church Bay, qv.*
Porth Tywyn *Carmar. Welsh form of Burry Port, qv.*
Porth Wen Bay *I.o.A.* ***Bay***, on N coast of Anglesey, 3m/4km W of Amlwch. **46 C3** SH4094.
Porth-y-felin *I.o.A.* ***Suburb***, adjoining to NW of Holyhead, on cove of same name. SH2483.
Porth-y-waen *Shrop.* ***Settlement***, 4m/7km SW of Oswestry. **38 B3** SJ2523.
Porth Ysgaden *Gwyn.* ***Sea feature***, narrow inlet on N coast of Lleyn Peninsula, 3m/5km N of Llangwnnadl. **36 B2** SH2137.
Porthaethwy *I.o.A. Welsh form of Menai Bridge, qv.*
Porthallow *Cornw.* ***Hamlet***, just inland from Talland Bay, on S coast, 2m/3km SW of Looe. **4 C5** SX2251.
Porthallow *Cornw.* ***Village***, on coast, 9m/14km E of Helston. **2 E6** SW7923.
Porthcawl *Bridgend* Population: 15,922. ***Town***, coastal resort with small harbour, 6m/9km W of Bridgend. Championship golf course. **18 B4** SS8176.
Porthceri *V. of Glam. Welsh form of Porthkerry, qv.*
Porthcothan *Cornw.* ***Hamlet***, on W facing coast, 4m/7km SW of Padstow. **3 F1** SW8572.
Porthcothan Beach *Cornw.* ***Coastal feature***, sandy beach at Porthcothan Bay, where stream enters sea. **3 F1** SW8572.
Porthcurno *Cornw.* ***Village***, 3m/5km SE of Land's End, named after bay to SE. Porthcurno Telegraph Museum. **2 A6** SW3822.
Porthgain *Pembs.* ***Hamlet***, at head of Porthgain inlet, 4m/6km W of Mathry. **16 B1** SM8132.
Porthill *Shrop.* ***Suburb***, W district of Shrewsbury. SJ4712.
Porthill *Staffs.* ***Suburb***, 2m/3km N of Newcastle-under-Lyme town centre. SJ8548.
Porthilly *Cornw.* ***Locality***, above Porthilly Cove on E side of River Camel estuary opposite Padstow. SW9375.
Porthkerry (Porthceri). *V. of Glam.* ***Hamlet***, near coast, 2m/3km SW of Barry. **18 D5** ST0866.
Porthkerry Country Park *V. of Glam.* ***Leisure/recreation***, country park to E of Cardiff International Airport on Bristol Channel coast, 9m/14km SW of Cardiff. Comprises woodland, grassland and cliffs. **18 D5** ST0866.
Porthleven *Cornw.* Population: 3123. ***Small town***, and port 2m/3km SW of Helston. **2 D6** SW6225.
Porthllechog *I.o.A. Welsh form of Bull Bay, qv.*
Porthlysgi Bay *Pembs.* ***Bay***, 2m/3km SW of St. David's. Cliffs are National Trust property. SM7223.
Porthmadog (Portmadoc). *Gwyn.* Population: 3048. ***Small town***, resort on River Glaslyn estuary, 12m/19km E of Pwllheli and 3m/5km W of Penrhyndeudraeth across estuary. Former port for Ffestiniog slate industry. **36 E2** SH5638.
Porthmeor *Cornw.* ***Hamlet***, 5m/8km NW of Penzance. **2 B5** SW4337.
Porthmeor Cove *Cornw.* ***Bay***, to W of Porthmeor, 5m/8km NW of Penzance. SW4237.
Portholland *Cornw.* ***Hamlet***, on Veryan Bay, 4m/7km SW of Mevagissey. **3 G4** SW9641.
Porthoustock *Cornw.* ***Village***, on coast 1m/2km E of St. Keverne. **3 F6** SW8021.
Porthpean *Cornw.* ***Village***, 2m/3km SE of St. Austell. Consists of Higher and Lower Porthpean, running down to St. Austell Bay. **4 A5** SX0350.
Porthscatho *Cornw. Alternative spelling of Portscatho, qv.*
Porthtowan *Cornw.* ***Village***, 4m/6km N of Redruth, named after bay at its NW end. **2 D4** SW6947.
Porthwgan *Wrex.* ***Settlement***, 4m/6km SE of Wrexham. SJ3746.
Porthyrhyd *Carmar.* ***Hamlet***, 4m/7km NW of Llandovery. **27 G5** SN7137.
Porthyrhyd *Carmar.* ***Village***, 3m/5km NW of Cross Hands. **17 J3** SN5115.
Portincaple *Arg. & B.* ***Settlement***, on Loch Long, 1m/2km N of Garelochhead. **74 A1** NS2393.
Portington *E.Riding* ***Hamlet***, 3m/5km NE of Howden. **58 D6** SE7830.
Portinnisherrich *Arg. & B.* ***Locality***, on E shore of Loch Awe, in Argyll, 8m/13km SW of Portsonachan. **80 A6** NM9711.
Portinscale *Cumb.* ***Village***, at N end of Derwent Water, 1m/2km W of Keswick. **60 D4** NY2523.
Portishead *N.Som.* Population: 14,721. ***Town***, port, residential town and holiday resort, 8m/12km W of Bristol. **19 H4** ST4676.
Portknockie *Moray* Population: 1296. ***Village***, and resort on N coast, 4m/7km NE of Buckie. **98 C4** NJ4868.
Portland Bill *Dorset Alternative name for Bill of Portland, qv.*
Portland Castle *Dorset* ***Castle***, 16c-18c castle (English Heritage), at N end of Isle of Portland. **9 F7** SY6874.
Portland Harbour *Dorset* ***Sea feature***, harbour 3m/4km across between Portland and Weymouth. Built by convict labour. **9 F7** SY6876.
Portland Museum *Dorset* ***Other feature of interest***, local history museum in Easton, with World War II German bomb and cottages with memorabilia. **9 F7** SY6971.
Portlethen *Aber.* Population: 6224. ***Village***, on E coast, 6m/10km S of Aberdeen. **91 H5** NO9396.
Portloe *Cornw.* ***Village***, on Veryan Bay, 6m/10km SW of Mevagissey. Coast SW to Nare Head largely National Trust. **3 G5** SW9339.
Portlooe *Cornw.* ***Hamlet***, 1m/2km SW of Looe. SX2452.
Portmadoc *Gwyn. English form of Porthmadog, qv.*
Portmahomack *High.* ***Village***, on S shore of Dornoch Firth, 3m/5km SW of Tarbat Ness, Ross and Cromarty district. **97 G3** NH9184.
Portmeirion *Gwyn.* ***Small town***, fascinating Italian-style village and gardens designed by architect Sir Clough Williams-Ellis, on peninsula on N side of Traeth Bach, 2m/3km SW of Penrhyndeudraeth. Made famous as setting for TV series 'The Prisoner' in 1960s. **36 E2** SH5837.
Portmore *Hants.* ***Hamlet***, 1m/2km NE of Lymington. **10 E5** SZ3397.
Portmore Loch *Sc.Bord.* ***Lake/loch***, small loch 2m/3km NE of Eddleston. NT2650.
Portnacroish *Arg. & B.* ***Village***, on Loch Laich, Argyll, on E side of Loch Linnhe. **80 A3** NM9247.
Portnaguiran New Lands *W.Isles* ***Settlement***, on Eye Peninsula, Isle of Lewis, 1km SW of Portnaguran. NB5536.
Portnaguran (Gaelic form: Port nan Giùran.) *W.Isles* ***Village***, at N end of Eye Peninsula, Isle of Lewis, 1m/2km W of Tiumpan Head. **101 H4** NB5537.
Portnahaven *Arg. & B.* ***Village***, at S end of Rinns of Islay, 1m/2km SE of Rubha na Faing. **72 A5** NR1652.
Portnalong *High.* ***Settlement***, 1m/2km SE of Ardtreck Point, Skye. **85 J1** NG3434.
Portnaluchaig *High.* ***Locality***, on W coast of Lochaber district, 2m/3km N of Arisaig. **86 C6** NM6589.
Portobello *D. & G.* ***Bay***, small inlet 8m/13km N of Portpatrick. **66 D7** NW9666.
Portobello *Edin.* ***Suburb***, on Firth of Forth, 3m/5km E of Edinburgh city centre. Extensive sands. **76 B3** NT3073.
Portobello *T. & W.* ***Locality***, 1m/2km SE of Birtley. NZ2755.
Portobello *W.Mid.* ***Suburb***, to E of Wolverhampton. SO9598.
Portobello *W.Yorks.* ***Suburb***, 1m/2km S of Wakefield city centre across River Calder. SE3318.
Porton *Wilts.* ***Village***, on River Bourne, 5m/8km NE of Salisbury. **10 C1** SU1936.
Portontown *Devon* ***Hamlet***, 4m/6km NW of Tavistock. SX4276.
Portpatrick *D. & G.* ***Small town***, resort with harbour on coast of Rinns of Galloway, 6m/9km SW of Stranraer. Originally developed as port for Ireland, but superseded by Stranraer from mid-19c. **64 A5** NX0054.
Portquin *Cornw.* ***Hamlet***, on N coast, at head of Portquin Bay. **4 A2** SW9780.
Portquin Bay *Cornw.* ***Bay***, inlet extends W from Kellan Head to Rumps Point. Cliffs around bay largely National Trust. At head is hamlet of Portquin. **4 A2** SW9581.
Portreath *Cornw.* ***Village***, popular coastal resort with 18c harbour, 4m/6km NW of Redruth. National Trust owns coast to W. **2 D4** SW6545.
Portree *High.* Population: 2126. ***Small town***, port and chief town of Skye, situated on Loch Portree on E coast, about midway between Rubha Hunish in N and Strathaird Point in S. **93 K7** NG4843.
Ports Down *Hants.* ***Inland physical feature***, chalk ridge running E and W above Portsmouth and Portsmouth Harbour. On ridge are six Palmerston forts built mid-19c for defence against French; also Nelson monument, and 20c naval installations. **11 H4** SU6406.
Portscatho (Also spelled Porthscatho.) *Cornw.* ***Village***, at SW end of Gerrans Bay, 3m/4km NE of St. Mawes. TV drama 'The Camomile Lawn' filmed nearby. **3 F5** SW8735.
Portsea *Ports.* ***Suburb***, on Portsea Island 1km W of Portsmouth city centre. **11 H4** SU6300.
Portsea Island *Ports.* ***Island***, on which most of Portsmouth is situated, between Portsmouth and Langstone Harbours, separated from mainland by tidal creek which is spanned by four bridges. **11 H4** SU6601.
Portskerra *High.* ***Village***, near N coast of Caithness district, adjoining to NW of Melvich. **104 D2** NC8765.
Portskewett (Porth Sgiwed). *Mon.* ***Village***, 4m/7km SW of Chepstow. Site of Roman building to N. **19 J3** ST4988.
Portslade *B. & H.* Population: 17,762. ***Suburb***, of Portslade-by-Sea, N of town centre. **13 F6** TQ2506.
Portslade-by-Sea *B. & H.* ***Town***, 3m/5km W of Brighton. **13 F6** TQ2605.

P

Portslogan *D. & G.* ***Settlement***, 3m/5km N of Portpatrick. **64 A5** NW9858.
Portsmouth *Ports.* Population: 174,690. ***City***, port and naval base (Portsmouth Harbour, on W side of city) 65m/105km SW of London, extending from S end of Portsea Island to S slopes of Ports Down. Various industries, including tourism, financial services and manufacturing. Partly bombed in World War II and now rebuilt; however, some 18c buildings remain. Boat and hovercraft ferries to Isle of Wight. University. Two cathedrals. Nelson's ship, HMS Victory, in harbour, alongside which are remains of Henry VIII's flagship, Mary Rose, which sank in 1545. King James's Gate and Landport Gate were part of 17c defences, and Fort Cumberland is 18c coastal defence at Eastney (all (English Heritage). Royal Garrison Church (English Heritage) was 16c chapel prior to Dissolution. Museums, many with nautical theme. City airport at N end of Portsea Island. **11 H5** SU6400.
Portsmouth *W.Yorks.* ***Hamlet***, on N side of Todmorden Moor, 3m/4km NW of Todmorden. SD9026.
Portsmouth Arms *Devon* ***Settlement***, 2m/3km SE of High Bickerton. Railway station. **6 E4** SS6319.
Portsmouth Cathedral *Ports.* ***Ecclesiastical building***, in Old Portsmouth, 1km S of Portsmouth city centre. Unfinished building, started in 1927, which incorporates chancel and transepts of church of St. Thomas of Canterbury. **11 H5** SZ6399.
Portsmouth Harbour *Ports.* ***Sea feature***, large natural harbour between Portsmouth and Gosport with historic dockyard lying at entrance. Dockyard exhibits famous historic ships, such as the Mary Rose, HMS Warrior and HMS Victory. **11 H4** SU6202.
Portsonachan (Also spelled Port Sonachan.) *Arg. & B.* ***Village***, in Argyll, on E shore of Loch Awe, 8m/13km SW of Dalmally. **80 B5** NN0520.
Portsoy *Aber.* Population: 1822. ***Village***, on N coast, 6m/10km W of Banff. **98 D4** NJ5865.
Portswood *S'ham.* ***Suburb***, NE district of Southampton. **11 F3** SU4314.
Portuairk *High.* ***Settlement***, near W end of Ardnamurchan peninsula, in Lochaber district, 2m/3km E of Point of Ardnamurchan. **79 F1** NM4368.
Portvoller (Gaelic form: Port Mholair.) *W.Isles* ***Settlement***, on Eye Peninsula, Isle of Lewis, 1km S of Tiumpan Head. NB5636.
Portway *Here.* ***Hamlet***, 4m/6km NW of Hereford. SO4845.
Portway *Here.* ***Hamlet***, 3m/5km S of Hereford. SO4935.
Portway *Here.* ***Settlement***, 9m/14km W of Hereford. **28 C4** SO3844.
Portway *Som.* ***Suburb***, SE district of Street. ST4836.
Portway *W.Mid.* ***Locality***, 2m/3km NW of Warley town centre. SO9788.
Portway *Worcs.* ***Hamlet***, 4m/7km NE of Redditch. **30 B1** SP0872.
Portwrinkle *Cornw.* ***Village***, with medieval harbour, on Whitsand Bay, 6m/10km W of Torpoint. **4 D5** SX3553.
Portyerrock *D. & G.* ***Settlement***, on Portyerrock Bay, 2m/4km SE of Whithorn. **64 E7** NX4738.
Posbury *Devon* ***Locality***, 2m/3km SW of Crediton. SX8197.
Posenhall *Shrop.* ***Settlement***, 2m/3km SW of Ironbridge. SJ6501.
Poslingford *Suff.* ***Village***, 2m/3km N of Clare. **34 B4** TL7748.
Possil Park *Glas.* ***Suburb***, 2m/3km N of Glasgow city centre. NS5868.
Possingworth Park *E.Suss.* ***Open space***, 2m/3km W of Heathfield. **13 J4** TQ5420.
Post Green *Dorset* ***Settlement***, to NW of Lytchett Minster. SY9593.
Post Gwyn *Powys* ***Mountain***, 2m/3km N of Llangynog. Height 2181 feet or 665 metres. **37 K3** SJ0429.
Post-mawr *Cere.* *Alternative name for Synod Inn, qv.*
Postbridge *Devon* ***Bridge***, primitive granite clapper bridge over River East Dart, 10m/16km W of Bovey Tracey. Consists of three 15 feet or 5 metre spans made of 6 foot or 2 metre wide slabs supported on piers of five flat stones. SX6478.
Postbridge *Devon* ***Hamlet***, on Dartmoor, 8m/13km SW of Moretonhampstead. Clapper bridge over East Dart River. **5 G3** SX6579.
Postcombe *Oxon.* ***Village***, 4m/6km N of Watlington. **22 A2** SU7099.
Postling *Kent* ***Village***, 3m/5km N of Hythe. **15 G4** TR1439.
Postwick *Norf.* ***Village***, 4m/7km E of Norwich. **45 G5** TG2907.
Potarch *Aber.* ***Settlement***, 2m/3km SE of Kincardine O'Neil. **90 E5** NO6097.
Potheridge *Devon* ***Locality***, consists of three hamlets, Great Potheridge, Little Potheridge, and Potheridge Gate, between 3m/5km and 4m/6km SE of Great Torrington. SS5114.
Potheridge Gate *Devon* ***Hamlet***, forms locality of Potheridge, along with Great Potheridge and Little Potheridge, 3m/5km SE of Great Torrington. SS5114.
Potrail Water *S.Lan.* ***River***, rising on NW slopes between Ballencleuch Law and Scaw'd Law and running NE to join Daer Water and form River Clyde 2m/3km S of Elvanfoot. **68 E3** NS9513.
Potsgrove *Beds.* ***Village***, 2m/3km S of Woburn. **32 C6** SP9529.
Pott Row *Norf.* ***Hamlet***, 1km S of Roydon. **44 B3** TF7021.
Pott Shrigley *Ches.* ***Hamlet***, 1m/2km NE of Bollington. **49 J5** SJ9479.
Potten End *Herts.* ***Village***, 2m/3km E of Berkhamsted. **22 D1** TL0108.
Potter Brompton *N.Yorks.* ***Hamlet***, 1m/2km SW of Ganton. SE9776.
Potter Heigham *Norf.* ***Village***, 10m/16km NW of Great Yarmouth. **45 J3** TG4119.
Potter Hill *S.Yorks.* ***Suburb***, adjoining to SW of High Green, 1m/2km W of Chapeltown. SK3397.
Potter Row *Bucks.* ***Locality***, 1m/2km NE of Great Missenden. SP9002.
Potter Somersal *Derbys.* ***Settlement***, 1km NE of Somersal Herbert, 4m/6km NE of Uttoxeter. SK1435.
Potter Street *Essex* ***Suburb***, E district of Harlow. **23 H1** TL4709.
Pottergate Street *Norf.* ***Settlement***, 1m/2km W of Wacton. TM1591.
Potterhanworth *Lincs.* ***Village***, 6m/10km SE of Lincoln. **52 D6** TF0566.
Potterhanworth Booths *Lincs.* ***Hamlet***, 2m/3km NE of Potterhanworth. **52 D6** TF0767.
Potterne *Wilts.* Population: 1590. ***Village***, 2m/3km S of Devizes. **20 C6** ST9958.
Potterne Wick *Wilts.* ***Hamlet***, to S of Potterne, 2m/3km S of Devizes. **20 C6** SU0057.
Potternewton *W.Yorks.* ***Suburb***, 1m/2km NE of Leeds city centre. SE3036.
Potters Bar *Herts.* Population: 22,414. ***Town***, commuter town, 13m/21km N of London. **23 F1** TL2501.
Potters Brook *Lancs.* ***Settlement***, on E side of Lancaster Canal, 1km N of Forton and 4m/7km N of Garstang. SD4852.
Potter's Cross *Staffs.* ***Settlement***, adjacent to E of Kinver, 3m/5km W of Stourbridge. **40 A7** SO8484.
Potters Crouch *Herts.* ***Hamlet***, 2m/4km SW of St. Albans. **22 E1** TL1105.
Potter's Green *E.Suss.* ***Locality***, on E side of Buxted. TQ5023.
Potter's Green *W.Mid.* ***Suburb***, 3m/5km NE of Coventry city centre. SP3782.
Potters Hill *N.Som.* ***Hamlet***, 1km NE of Bristol International Airport, 6m/10km SW of Bristol. ST5166.
Potters Marston *Leics.* ***Settlement***, 1km NW of Croft. SP4996.
Potterspury *Northants.* ***Village***, 3m/5km NW of Stony Stratford. **31 J4** SP7543.
Potterton *Aber.* Population: 1144. ***Village***, 2m/3km SW of Balmedie. **91 H3** NJ9415.
Potterton *W.Yorks.* ***Hamlet***, 1m/2km N of Barwick in Elmet. SE4038.
Potthorpe *Norf.* ***Locality***, adjoining to NW of Brisley, 6m/10km NW of East Dereham. TF9422.
Pottle Street *Wilts.* ***Hamlet***, adjoining to S of Horningsham, 1m/2km NE of Maiden Bradley. ST8140.
Potto *N.Yorks.* ***Village***, 5m/8km SW of Stokesley. **63 F6** NZ4703.
Potton *Beds.* Population: 4230. ***Small town***, commuter town, 4m/6km NE of Biggleswade, much rebuilt following fire in late 18c. **33 F4** TL2249.
Potton Island *Essex* ***Island***, on S side of River Roach estuary, 4m/6km N of Shoeburyness. **25 F2** TQ9591.
Pott's Green *Essex* ***Settlement***, to S of Marks Tey, 6m/9km W of Colchester town centre. TL9122.
Poughill *Cornw.* ***Village***, 1m/2km NE of Bude. **6 A5** SS2207.
Poughill *Devon* ***Village***, 5m/9km N of Crediton. **7 G5** SS8508.
Poulner *Hants.* ***Locality***, 1m/2km E of Ringwood. **10 C4** SU1605.
Poulshot *Wilts.* ***Village***, 3m/4km SW of Devizes. **20 C6** ST9759.
Poulter ***River***, rising SE of Bolsover and flowing E through Clumber Park in The Dukeries into River Idle, 4m/6km S of Retford. **51 J5** SK7075.
Poulton *Glos.* ***Village***, 5m/8km E of Cirencester. **20 E1** SP1000.
Poulton *Mersey.* ***Suburb***, 1m/2km W of Wallasey town centre. SJ3090.
Poulton-le-Fylde *Lancs.* Population: 18,939. ***Town***, market town, 3m/5km NE of Blackpool. **55 G6** SD3439.
Poulton Priory *Glos.* ***Locality***, and remains of medieval priory 1km SW of Poulton. SU0999.
Poulton Royd *Mersey.* ***Suburb***, 1m/2km S of Bebington. SJ3382.
Pound Bank *Worcs.* ***Hamlet***, 4m/6km W of Bewdley. **29 G1** SO7373.
Pound Bank *Worcs.* ***Suburb***, in E part of Great Malvern. SO7945.
Pound Green *E.Suss.* ***Hamlet***, adjoining to E of Buxted. **13 J4** TQ5023.
Pound Green *Hants.* ***Hamlet***, 3m/5km E of Kingsclere. SU5759.
Pound Green *I.o.W.* ***Suburb***, 1km SW of Freshwater. SZ3386.
Pound Green *Norf.* ***Locality***, adjoining to E of Shipdham. TF9607.
Pound Green *Suff.* ***Hamlet***, 6m/10km NE of Haverhill. TL7154.
Pound Green *Worcs.* ***Hamlet***, 3m/4km NW of Bewdley. SO7578.
Pound Hill *W.Suss.* ***Suburb***, E district of Crawley. **13 F3** TQ2937.
Pound Street *Hants.* ***Settlement***, 1m/2km NE of Highclere. SU4561.
Poundffald *Swan.* ***Village***, 6m/9km W of Swansea. **17 J5** SS5694.
Poundfield *E.Suss.* ***Suburb***, to E of Crowborough. TQ5330.
Poundgate *E.Suss.* ***Hamlet***, 2m/3km SW of Crowborough. **13 H4** TQ4928.
Poundisford Park *Som.* ***Historic house***, 16c Tudor house with well-preserved plaster ceiling in Great Hall, 3m/4km S of Taunton. **8 B3** ST2220.
Poundland *S.Ayr.* ***Settlement***, in Stinchar valley, 7m/11km NE of Ballantrae. **67 F5** NX1787.
Poundon *Bucks.* ***Village***, 4m/7km NE of Bicester. **31 H6** SP6425.
Poundon Hill *Bucks.* ***Settlement***, 1km W of Poundon. SP6325.
Poundsbridge *Kent* ***Settlement***, 3m/5km NW of Royal Tunbridge Wells. **23 J7** TQ5341.
Poundsgate *Devon* ***Hamlet***, on E side of Dartmoor, 4m/6km NW of Ashburton. **5 H3** SX7072.
Poundstock *Cornw.* ***Village***, 4m/7km S of Bude. **4 C1** SX2099.
Povey Cross *W.Suss.* ***Village***, 1m/2km SW of Horley. **23 F7** TQ2642.
Pow Burn ***River***, rising E of Cowie and flowing SE, then NE into River Forth, 1km NW of Kincardine Bridge. **75 G2** NS9187.
Pow Green *Here.* ***Settlement***, 4m/6km N of Ledbury. **29 G4** SO7044.
Pow Hill Country Park *Dur.* ***Leisure/recreation***, 44 acres of moor and woodland overlooking S shore of Derwent Reservoir. **62 B1** NZ0151.
Powburn *Northumb.* ***Village***, 1m/2km N of Glanton. **71 F2** NU0616.
Powderham *Devon* ***Hamlet***, on W bank of River Exe estuary, 5m/8km N of Dawlish. Castle, home of Courtenays since 14c; present house mainly 18c. Deer park. **7 H7** SX9684.
Powderham Castle *Devon* ***Historic house***, 14c home of Earl of Devon, with ancient deer park, rose garden and woodland garden, 1km NE of Kenton. **7 H7** SX9683.
Powerstock *Dorset* ***Village***, 4m/6km NE of Bridport. **8 E5** SY5196.
Powfoot *D. & G.* ***Village***, on Solway Firth, 3m/5km W of Annan. **69 G7** NY1465.
Powick *Worcs.* ***Village***, 3m/4km SW of Worcester. **29 H3** SO8351.
Powis Castle *Powys* ***Castle***, medieval castle (National Trust) in park on S side of Welshpool. Clive Museum contains Indian treasures. Gardens (National Trust) contain lead statues and are terraced with yews, herbaceous plants and some rare trees. **38 B5** SJ2106.
Powler's Piece *Devon* ***Settlement***, 3m/5km SE of Woolfardisworthy. **6 B4** SS3718.
Powmill *P. & K.* ***Village***, 4m/6km E of Dollar. **75 J1** NT0198.
Powysland Museum *Powys* ***Other feature of interest***, in Welshpool. Exhibits include history of railway and canal, as well as agricultural history. **38 B5** SJ2207.
Poxwell *Dorset* ***Hamlet***, 5m/9km SE of Dorchester. **9 G6** SY7484.
Poyle *Slo.* ***Locality***, with trading estate at W end of London (Heathrow) Airport, 3m/5km N of Staines. **22 D4** TQ0376.
Poynders End *Herts.* ***Settlement***, 3m/5km S of Hitchin. TL1924.
Poynings *W.Suss.* ***Village***, below Devil's Dyke, on South Downs, 6m/10km NW of Brighton. **13 F5** TQ2612.
Poyntington *Dorset* ***Village***, 2m/4km N of Sherborne. **9 F2** ST6520.
Poynton *Ches.* Population: 14,768. ***Town***, former mining town, 5m/7km S of Stockport. **49 J4** SJ9283.
Poynton *Tel. & W.* ***Settlement***, 6m/10km NE of Shrewsbury. **38 E4** SJ5717.
Poynton Green *Tel. & W.* ***Hamlet***, 1km N of Poynton. **38 E4** SJ5618.
Poyntzfield *High.* ***Settlement***, on Black Isle, 5m/8km SW of Cromarty. **96 E5** NH7164.
Poys Street *Suff.* ***Hamlet***, 3m/4km W of Yoxford. **35 H1** TM3570.
Poyston *Pembs.* ***Hamlet***, 3m/5km NE of Haverfordwest. SM9619.
Poyston Cross *Pembs.* ***Settlement***, 1m/2km E of Poyston. **16 C3** SM9719.
Poystreet Green *Suff.* ***Hamlet***, 1km S of Rattlesden. **34 D3** TL9858.
Praa Sands *Cornw.* ***Village***, 5m/8km W of Helston, named after mile-long sandy beach to S. **2 C6** SW5828.
Pratis *Fife* ***Settlement***, 3m/5km NW of Kennoway. **82 E7** NO3806.
Pratling Street *Kent* ***Locality***, 1m/2km E of Aylesford. TQ7459.
Pratt's Bottom *Gt.Lon.* ***Village***, in borough of Bromley, 2m/3km SE of Orpington. **23 H5** TQ4762.
Prawle Point *Devon* ***Coastal feature***, headland (National Trust) at southernmost point of Devon, 3m/5km SE of Salcombe across Kingsbridge Estuary. Cliffs along coast to NW are also National Trust property. **5 H7** SX7735.
Praze-an-Beeble *Cornw.* ***Village***, 3m/4km S of Camborne. **2 D5** SW6335.
Predannack Head *Cornw.* ***Coastal feature***, headland on W side of Lizard peninsula, 4m/6km NW of Lizard Point. SW6616.
Predannack Wollas *Cornw.* ***Hamlet***, 2m/3km S of Mullion. **2 D7** SW6616.
Prees *Shrop.* ***Village***, 5m/8km S of Whitchurch. **38 E2** SJ5533.
Prees Green *Shrop.* ***Village***, 4m/6km NE of Wem. **38 E2** SJ5631.
Prees Higher Heath *Shrop.* ***Village***, forms locality of Prees, along with Prees Lower Heath, 2m/3km N of Prees. **38 E2** SJ5636.
Prees Lower Heath *Shrop.* ***Hamlet***, forms locality of Prees, along with Prees Higher Heath, 1m/2km SE of Prees. SJ5732.
Preesall *Lancs.* Population: 5168. ***Village***, 3m/4km E of Fleetwood across River Wyre estuary. **55 G5** SD3647.
Preesgweene *Shrop.* ***Locality***, adjoining to E of Weston Rhyn. **38 B2** SJ2936.
Pren Croes *Powys* ***Mountain***, with partly forested summit, 2m/3km N of Llangadfan. Height 1050 feet or 320 metres. **37 K4** SJ0013.
Pren-gwyn *Cere.* ***Hamlet***, 2m/4km N of Llandysul. **26 D4** SN4244.
Prenbrigog *Flints.* ***Settlement***, to W of Buckley. **48 B6** SJ2664.
Prendergast *Pembs.* ***Locality***, adjoining to NE of Haverfordwest. **16 C3** SM9516.
Prendwick *Northumb.* ***Hamlet***, 4m/7km W of Whittingham. **71 F2** NU0012.
Prenteg *Gwyn.* ***Hamlet***, 2m/3km NE of Porthmadog. **36 E1** SH5841.

Prenton *Mersey.* ***Suburb***, 3m/4km SW of Birkenhead town centre. **48 C4** SJ3086.
Presaddfed Burial Chambers *I.o.A.* ***Historic/prehistoric site***, on W side of Anglesey, 1km E of Bodedern. Two Neolithic chambers, one collapsed, one still with capstone and uprights. **46 B4** SH3480.
Prescelly Mountains (Welsh form: Mynydd Preseli.) *Pembs.* ***Large natural feature***, ridge running E to W for some 6m/10km, to S and SE of Newport. Highest point is Foel Cwmcerwyn (Prescelly Top), 1758 feet or 536 metres. **16 D1** SN1032.
Prescelly Top *Pembs. English form of Foel Cwmcerwyn, qv.*
Prescot *Mersey.* Population: 37,486. ***Town***, 4m/6km SW of St. Helens. **48 D3** SJ4692.
Prescott *Devon* ***Hamlet***, 2m/3km NE of Uffculme, 6m/10km NE of Cullompton. ST0814.
Prescott *Glos.* ***Locality***, 2m/4km W of Winchcombe. Car hill climbs take place here. SO9829.
Prescott *Shrop.* ***Hamlet***, 7m/11km NW of Shrewsbury. **38 D3** SJ4221.
Preshute *Wilts.* ***Locality***, adjoining to W of Marlborough. Site of Roman building on Barton Down to NW. SU1868.
Presley *Moray* ***Settlement***, 5m/8km S of Forres. **97 H6** NJ0151.
Press *Derbys.* ***Settlement***, 2m/3km NW of Clay Cross. SK3665.
Press Castle *Sc.Bord.* ***Castle***, 2m/3km W of Coldingham. **77 G4** NT8765.
Pressen *Northumb.* ***Settlement***, 3m/4km SW of Cornhill on Tweed. **77 G7** NT8335.
Pressendye *Aber.* ***Mountain***, 3m/4km N of Tarland. Height 2030 feet or 619 metres. **90 C4** NJ4908.
Pressmennan Lake *E.Loth.* ***Lake/loch***, 1m/2km SE of Stenton. **76 E3** NT6373.
Prestatyn *Denb.* Population: 15,020. ***Town***, resort near North Wales coast, 4m/6km E of Rhyl. Situated at N end of Clwydian Hills and of Offa's Dyke long distance path. **47 J4** SJ0682.
Prestbury *Ches.* Population: 3346. ***Village***, 2m/4km NW of Macclesfield. **49 H5** SJ9077.
Prestbury *Glos.* ***Village***, 2m/3km NE of Cheltenham. Reputed to be one of most haunted villages in England. **29 J6** SO9723.
Presteigne (Llanandras). *Powys* Population: 1815. ***Small town***, on River Lugg, 5m/8km S of Knighton. 17c bridge spans river. **28 C2** SO3164.
Presthope *Shrop.* ***Hamlet***, 3m/5km SW of Much Wenlock. **38 E6** SO5897.
Prestleigh *Som.* ***Hamlet***, 2m/3km SE of Shepton Mallet. Site of Agricultural Show Ground. **19 K7** ST6340.
Prestolee *Gt.Man.* ***Locality***, 3m/5km SE of Bolton. **49 G2** SD7505.
Preston *B. & H.* ***Suburb***, 1m/2km N of Brighton town centre. **13 G6** TQ3006.
Preston *Devon* ***Hamlet***, 2m/3km N of Newton Abbot. **5 J3** SX8574.
Preston *Dorset* Population: 2483. ***Locality***, 3m/5km NW of Weymouth. Site of Roman villa to S. Slight remains of Roman temple (English Heritage) at Jordan Hill, to SW. **9 G6** SY7083.
Preston *E.Loth.* ***Village***, adjoining to N of East Linton. Mill (National Trust for Scotland) on banks of River Tyne dates from 18c; still in working order. Phantassie Doocot (National Trust for Scotland) dates from 16c. **76 D3** NT5977.
Preston *E.Riding* Population: 2040. ***Village***, 1m/2km N of Hedon. **59 H6** TA1830.
Preston *Glos.* ***Settlement***, 3m/4km SW of Ledbury. **29 F5** SO6734.
Preston *Glos.* ***Village***, 1m/2km SE of Cirencester. **20 D1** SP0400.
Preston *Gt.Lon.* ***Suburb***, in borough of Brent, 9m/14km NW of Charing Cross and 1m/2km N of Wembley. TQ1887.
Preston *Herts.* ***Village***, 3m/5km S of Hitchin. **32 E6** TL1824.
Preston *Kent* ***Suburb***, in SE part of Faversham. **25 G5** TR0260.
Preston *Kent* ***Village***, 2m/3km N of Wingham. **25 J5** TR2560.
Preston *Lancs.* Population: 177,660. ***Town***, on N bank of River Ribble, 27m/45km NW of Manchester. Former major engineering and cotton-spinning town. The Preston Guild, a celebration of merchants' trade, has been held every 20 years from possibly as early as 1179. University of Central Lancashire. **55 J7** SD5429.
Preston *Northumb.* ***Hamlet***, 1m/2km E of Ellingham. Medieval tower house. **71 G1** NU1725.
Preston *Rut.* ***Village***, 2m/3km N of Uppingham. **42 B5** SK8702.
Preston *Sc.Bord.* ***Village***, 2m/4km N of Duns. **77 F5** NT7957.
Preston *Shrop.* ***Settlement***, 2m/3km W of Upton Magna. SJ5211.
Preston *Som.* ***Hamlet***, 5m/8km SE of Watchet. ST1035.
Preston *Suff.* ***Village***, 2m/3km NE of Lavenham. **34 D3** TL9450.
Preston *Torbay* ***Suburb***, N district of Paignton. SX8861.
Preston *T. & W.* ***Suburb***, 1m/2km W of Tynemouth. **71 J7** NZ3569.
Preston *Wilts.* ***Hamlet***, 4m/6km SW of Wootton Bassett. **20 D4** SU0377.
Preston Bagot *Warks.* ***Hamlet***, 2m/3km E of Henley-in-Arden. **30 C2** SP1765.
Preston Bissett *Bucks.* ***Village***, 4m/6km SW of Buckingham. **31 H6** SP6529.
Preston Bowyer *Som.* ***Hamlet***, in Vale of Taunton Deane, 1km NE of Milverton. ST1326.
Preston Brockhurst *Shrop.* ***Village***, 3m/5km SE of Wem. **38 E3** SJ5324.
Preston Brook *Halton* ***Hamlet***, 3m/5km E of Runcorn. Junction of Trent and Mersey Canal and Bridgewater Canal. **48 E4** SJ5680.
Preston Candover *Hants.* ***Village***, 6m/10km N of New Alresford. **21 K7** SU6041.
Preston Capes *Northants.* ***Village***, 5m/8km S of Daventry. **31 G3** SP5754.
Preston Deanery *Northants.* ***Settlement***, 4m/6km SE of Northampton. **31 J3** SP7855.
Preston Grange *T. & W.* ***Locality***, 1km NW of Preston and 1m/2km SW of Whitley Bay. NZ3470.
Preston Green *Warks.* ***Hamlet***, 1m/2km E of Henley-in-Arden. SP1665.
Preston Gubbals *Shrop.* ***Village***, 4m/7km N of Shrewsbury. **38 D4** SJ4919.
Preston Hill *Northumb.* ***Mountain***, 3m/4km NE of The Cheviot. Height 1722 feet or 525 metres. **70 E1** NT9223.
Preston Law *Sc.Bord.* ***Mountain***, 3m/5km S of Peebles. Height 1863 feet or 568 metres. **76 A7** NT2535.
Preston-le-Skerne *Dur.* ***Hamlet***, 2m/3km E of Newton Aycliffe. NZ3024.
Preston Manor *B. & H.* ***Historic house***, 1m/2km N of centre of Brighton; old manor house built 1250, rebuilt 1738. **13 G6** TQ3006.
Preston Market Cross *E.Loth.* ***Historic/prehistoric site***, excellent example of 17c Scottish market cross, 1km S of Prestonpans and 3m/5km NE of Musselburgh. **76 B3** NT3874.
Preston Merse *D. & G.* ***Coastal feature***, lowland coastal strip adjacent to Mersehead Sands to W of Southerness. **65 K5** NX9455.
Preston Mill and Phantassie Dovecot *E.Loth.* ***Historic house***, National Trust for Scotland property to NE of East Linton. 16c mill, one of oldest working watermills in Scotland. Dovecote or Doocot of beehive type, once having 544 pigeon nests. **76 D3** NT5977.
Preston Montford *Shrop.* ***Settlement***, 4m/6km W of Shrewsbury. SJ4314.
Preston Moor *N.Yorks.* ***Open space***, moorland containing disused mine workings, 4m/6km NW of Leyburn. **62 B7** SE0694.
Preston on Stour *Warks.* ***Village***, 3m/5km S of Stratford-upon-Avon. **30 D3** SP2049.
Preston-on-Tees *Stock.* ***Locality***, 2m/3km S of Stockton-on-Tees. NZ4315.
Preston on the Hill *Halton* ***Hamlet***, 4m/6km E of Runcorn. **48 E4** SJ5780.
Preston on Wye *Here.* ***Village***, on S side of River Wye, 8m/13km W of Hereford. **28 C4** SO3842.
Preston Patrick *Cumb.* ***Locality***, 1km S of Endmoor, 6m/10km S of Kendal. SD5483.
Preston Plucknett *Som.* ***Suburb***, W district of Yeovil. **8 E3** ST5316.
Preston Richard *Cumb.* ***Locality***, 5m/9km S of Kendal. SD5384.
Preston Street *Kent* ***Settlement***, adjoining to N of Preston. TR2560.
Preston Tower *Northumb.* ***Historic/prehistoric site***, late 14c peel tower situated in hamlet of Preston, 2m/3km NE of North Charlton. **71 G1** NU1825.
Preston Tower and Hamilton House *E.Loth.* ***Other feature of interest***, part-ruined 15c tower with 16c additions and 17c house (National Trust for Scotland) on S side of Prestonpans. **76 B3** NT3974.
Preston-under-Scar *N.Yorks.* ***Village***, 3m/5km W of Leyburn. Quarries on moors to N. **62 B7** SE0791.
Preston upon the Weald Moors *Tel. & W.* ***Village***, 3m/5km NE of Wellington. **39 F4** SJ6815.
Preston Wynne *Here.* ***Village***, 5m/8km NE of Hereford. **28 E4** SO5547.
Prestonfield *Edin.* ***Suburb***, of Edinburgh 2m/3km SE of city centre. NT2771.
Prestonpans *E.Loth.* Population: 7014. ***Small town***, on Firth of Forth, 3m/5km NE of Musselburgh. Hamilton House (National Trust for Scotland), built 1628. On E side of town is site of battle of 1745 in which Prince Charles Edward Stuart defeated government forces under Sir John Cope. **76 B3** NT3874.
Prestwich *Gt.Man.* Population: 31,801. ***Town***, 4m/6km NW of Manchester. 18c Heaton Hall stands in parkland. **49 H2** SD8203.
Prestwick *Northumb.* ***Hamlet***, 1m/2km E of Ponteland. **71 G6** NZ1872.
Prestwick *S.Ayr.* Population: 13,705. ***Town***, and resort on Firth of Clyde, adjoining to N of Ayr. International airport. Golf's first Open Championship held here in 1860. Ruins of 12c Church of St. Nicholas. **67 H1** NS3525.
Prestwick International Airport *S.Ayr.* ***Airport/airfield***, international airport to NE of Prestwick. **67 H1** NS3626.
Prestwold *Leics.* ***Settlement***, 3m/4km E of Loughborough. Consists of hall and church. **41 H3** SK5721.
Prestwood *Bucks.* Population: 3990. ***Suburb***, 2m/3km W of Great Missenden. **22 B1** SP8700.
Prestwood *Staffs.* ***Hamlet***, 2m/3km N of Rocester. SK1042.
Price Town *Bridgend* ***Village***, 8m/13km N of Bridgend. **18 C2** SS9392.
Prickwillow *Cambs.* ***Village***, on River Lark, 4m/6km E of Ely. **43 J7** TL5982.
Priddy *Som.* ***Village***, on Mendip Hills, 4m/6km NW of Wells. **19 J6** ST5251.
Prideaux Place *Cornw.* ***Historic house***, Elizabethan mansion on N side of Padstow, with recently restored Italian gardens. **3 G1** SW9175.
Priest Hill *Lancs.* ***Settlement***, 1m/2km N of Longridge. **56 B6** SD6039.
Priest Hutton *Lancs.* ***Village***, 3m/5km NE of Carnforth. **55 J2** SD5373.
Priest Island (Also known as Eilean a' Chleirich.) *High.* ***Island***, uninhabited island, outlier of Summer Isles group, 4m/7km NE of Greenstone Point on W coast of Ross and Cromarty district. Area about 500 acres or 200 hectares. **95 F1** NB9202.
Priest Thorpe *W.Yorks.* ***Suburb***, NE district of Bingley. SE1139.
Priestacott *Devon* ***Hamlet***, 6m/9km NE of Holsworthy. SS4206.
Priestcliffe *Derbys.* ***Settlement***, 1m/2km N of Taddington. SK1371.
Priestfield *W.Mid.* ***Locality***, 2m/3km SE of Wolverhampton town centre. SO9397.
Priestfield *Worcs.* ***Locality***, 3m/4km E of Great Malvern. SO8244.
Priesthill Height ***Mountain***, on border of East Ayrshire and South Lanarkshire, 4m/6km NE of Muirkirk. Height 1614 feet or 492 metres. **75 F7** NS7232.
Priestholm *I.o.A. Alternative name for Puffin Island, qv.*
Priesthope Hill *Sc.Bord.* ***Mountain***, 3m/4km NE of Innerleithen. Height 1801 feet or 549 metres. **76 B7** NT3539.
Priestland *E.Ayr.* ***Settlement***, 1km E of Darvel. **74 D7** NS5737.
Priestley Green *W.Yorks.* ***Settlement***, 3m/4km E of Halifax. SE1326.
Priest's House *Som.* ***Historic house***, National Trust property in Muchelney, 1m/2km S of Langport. Late medieval hall, originally home for parish priests. **8 D2** ST4225.
Priest's House Museum *Dorset* ***Historic house***, medieval town house in Wimborne Minster, with walled garden, working kitchen and award-winning museum. **10 B4** SU0000.
Priestweston *Shrop.* ***Village***, 2m/4km NE of Church Stoke. Mitchell's Fold Stone Circle (English Heritage) 1m/2km NE. **38 B6** SO2997.
Priestwood *Brack.F.* ***Suburb***, of Bracknell to W of town centre. SU8669.
Priestwood *Kent* ***Settlement***, 1m/2km S of Meopham. TQ6564.
Priestwood Green *Kent* ***Settlement***, adjoining to S of Priestwood. TQ6564.
Primethorpe *Leics.* ***Locality***, 5m/9km N of Lutterworth. **41 H6** SP5292.
Primrose *T. & W.* ***Suburb***, 1m/2km S of Jarrow. NZ3263.
Primrose Green *Norf.* ***Settlement***, 1m/2km E of Elsing. **44 E4** TG0616.
Primrose Hill *Bucks.* ***Locality***, 3m/5km NE of High Wycombe. SU8897.
Primrose Hill *Derbys.* ***Locality***, 2m/3km NE of Alfreton. SK4155.
Primrose Hill *Glos.* ***Locality***, adjoining to N of Lydney. SO6303.
Primrose Hill *Gt.Lon.* ***Suburb***, in borough of Camden, N of Regents Park and 3m/4km NW of Charing Cross. Also open space to W, opposite Zoological Gardens. TQ2883.
Primrose Hill *Lancs.* ***Settlement***, 2m/3km NW of Ormskirk. SD3809.
Primrose Hill *W.Yorks.* ***Suburb***, E district of Bingley. SE1238.
Primrosehill *Herts.* ***Village***, 3m/5km SE of Hemel Hempstead. TL0803.
Primrosehill *W.Mid.* ***Suburb***, 2m/3km S of Dudley town centre. SO9487.
Prince Charles's Cave *High.* ***Cave***, 1m/2km S of Elgol, Skye. Reputed to be one of many hiding places of Charles Edward Stuart (Bonnie Prince Charlie) while evading English pursuers following Battle of Culloden. **86 B3** NG5112.
Prince Charles's Cave *High.* ***Cave***, on E coast of Skye, 4m/6km NE of Portree. Reputed to be one of many hiding places of Charles Edward Stuart (Bonnie Prince Charlie) while evading English pursuers following Battle of Culloden. **94 B7** NG5148.
Prince Charlie's Cave *High.* ***Cave***, on E side of Loch Ericht, 8m/12km N of Bridge of Gaur. Reputed to be one of many hiding places of Charles Edward Stuart (Bonnie Prince Charlie) while evading English pursuers following Battle of Culloden. **81 F1** NN4968.
Prince Royd *W.Yorks.* ***Suburb***, 2m/3km NW of Huddersfield town centre. SE1218.
Princes End *W.Mid.* ***Locality***, 4m/6km NW of West Bromwich town centre. **40 B6** SO9593.
Princes Gate *Pembs.* ***Settlement***, 2m/3km SE of Narberth. **16 E3** SN1312.
Princes Risborough *Bucks.* Population: 8021. ***Small town***, below NW edge of Chiltern Hills, 7m/10km S of Aylesbury. Manor house of 17c (National Trust) opposite church. **22 B1** SP8003.
Princethorpe *Warks.* ***Village***, 6m/9km N of Southam. **31 F1** SP4070.
Princetown *Caerp.* ***Locality***, 2m/3km N of Rhymney. **28 A7** SO1109.
Princetown *Devon* ***Town***, on central Dartmoor 7m/11km E of Tavistock. Built beside prison originally founded to accommodate French prisoners in Napoleonic wars. **5 F3** SX5873.
Prinknash Abbey and Park *Glos.* ***Other feature of interest***, 4m/6km SE of Gloucester. Benedictine monastery rebuilt in 16c and now part of major new building started in 1930s. Area of parkland adjacent to abbey is tourist attraction with wildfowl and deer. Also pottery, developed by monks with viewing gallery and shop. **29 H7** SO8713.
Prinsted *W.Suss.* ***Settlement***, at head of Chichester Harbour (Thorney Channel), adjoining to S of Southbourne. SU7605.
Prion *Denb.* ***Hamlet***, 2m/4km S of Denbigh. SJ0562.
Prior Muir *Fife* ***Settlement***, 3m/4km SE of St. Andrews. **83 G6** NO5313.
Prior Park *B. & N.E.Som.* ***Garden***, to SE of Bath, landscaped by Ralph Allen in 18c. Gardens include lakes and a Palladian bridge. **20 A5** ST7563.
Prior Park *Cumb.* ***Open space***, moorland on W side of Buck Barrow, 5m/8km NW of Broughton in Furness. **60 C7** SD1390.
Priors Fen *Peter.* ***Open space***, lowland 4m/7km E of Peterborough. **43 F5** TF2500.

Prior's Frome *Here.* ***Village***, 4m/7km E of Hereford. **28 E5** SO5739.
Priors Halton *Shrop.* ***Settlement***, 1m/2km W of Ludlow. SO4975.
Priors Hardwick *Warks.* ***Village***, 5m/8km SE of Southam. **31 F3** SP4756.
Priors Marston *Warks.* ***Village***, 5m/8km SE of Southam. **31 F3** SP4857.
Prior's Norton *Glos.* ***Hamlet***, 4m/7km NE of Gloucester. SO8624.
Priors Park *Glos.* ***Suburb***, S district of Tewkesbury. SO8931.
Priorslee *Tel. & W.* ***Suburb***, 1km S of Oakengates. SJ7110.
Priorswood *Som.* ***Suburb***, N district of Taunton. ST2326.
Priorwood Garden *Sc.Bord.* ***Garden***, National Trust for Scotland property in Melrose, adjacent to 15c ruins of abbey. Grows flowers specifically for drying. **76 D7** NT5433.
Priory Country Park *Beds.* ***Leisure/recreation***, country park with lakes, trees and wildflower meadows, 1m/2km E of Bedford town centre. Visitor centre and nature trails. **32 D4** TL0749.
Priory Wood *Here.* ***Hamlet***, 3m/5km NE of Hay-on-Wye. **28 B4** SO2545.
Prisk *V. of Glam.* ***Settlement***, 2m/3km NE of Cowbridge. ST0176.
Priston *B. & N.E.Som.* ***Village***, 4m/6km N of Radstock. **19 K5** ST6960.
Pristow Green *Norf.* ***Settlement***, 1km S of Tibenham. TM1388.
Prittlewell *S'end* ***Suburb***, 1m/2km NW of Southend-on-Sea town centre. **24 E3** TQ8787.
Prittlewell Priory *S'end* ***Other feature of interest***, ruins of 12c priory, to N of Southend-on-Sea, now housing museum of local and natural history. **24 E3** TQ8787.
Privett *Hants.* ***Hamlet***, 3m/5km NE of West Meon. **11 H2** SU6726.
Privett *Hants.* ***Locality***, 2m/3km W of Gosport town centre. SZ5999.
Prixford *Devon* ***Hamlet***, 2m/3km N of Barnstaple. **6 D2** SS5436.
Proaig *Arg. & B.* ***Settlement***, on E coast of Islay, 10m/15km NE of Port Ellen. **72 C5** NR4557.
Probus *Cornw.* Population: 1827. ***Village***, 5m/8km NE of Truro. Granite church tower dating from 1523 is tallest in Cornwall at 125 feet or 38 metres. **3 F4** SW8947.
Prosen Water *Angus* ***River***, flowing SE down Glen Prosen to join River South Esk 3m/5km NE of Kirriemuir. **82 E1** NO4058.
Prospect Hill *Fife* ***Hill***, rising to over 180 metres, 5m/8km NW of Cupar and S of Firth of Tay. **82 E6** NO3118.
Protsonhill *Aber.* ***Settlement***, 1m/2km E of Gardenstown. **99 G4** NJ8164.
Provan Hall *Glas.* ***Historic house***, 15c mansion (National Trust for Scotland), 5m/8km E of Glasgow city centre. **74 E4** NS6666.
Provanmill *Glas.* ***Suburb***, 3m/4km NE of Glasgow city centre. NS6367.
Provost Ross's House *Aberdeen See Aberdeen Maritime Museum.*
Provost Skene's House *Aberdeen* ***Other feature of interest***, example of early burgh architecture in Guestrow, Aberdeen. This 16c house contains period rooms, museum and painted gallery. **91 H4** NJ9306.
Prudhoe *Northumb.* Population: 11,204. ***Town***, on S side of River Tyne 10m/16km W of Gateshead. 12c-14c castle. **71 G7** NZ0962.
Prudhoe Castle *Northumb.* ***Castle***, originally a Norman castle (English Heritage) belonging to Percy family since 14c, on N side of Prudhoe. Improvements made in 12c-14c. Extensive remains include gatehouse and keep. **71 F7** NZ0963.
Prussia Cove *Cornw.* ***Settlement***, on S coast, 6m/10km W of Helston. Haunt of 18c smuggler John Carter. SW5527.
Prysor *Gwyn.* ***River***, rising above Llyn Conglog-mawr and running into SE end of Llyn Trawsfynydd. **37 G2** SH7034.
Pubil *P. & K.* ***Settlement***, at W end of Glen Lyon, 9m/14km NW of Killin. **81 F3** NN4642.
Public Record Office *Gt.Lon.* ***Other feature of interest***, in borough of Richmond upon Thames at Kew, 2m/3km NE of Richmond. Permanent display of records on major events in English history. Houses Domesday Book of 1086 and one of four existing Magna Cartas. TQ1977.
Publow *B. & N.E.Som.* ***Village***, 3m/5km SW of Keynsham. **19 K5** ST6264.
Puckeridge *Herts.* ***Village***, 6m/10km N of Ware. Site of Roman town to N. **33 G6** TL3823.
Puckington *Som.* ***Village***, 3m/4km NE of Ilminster. **8 C3** ST3718.
Pucklechurch *S.Glos.* Population: 2524. ***Village***, 4m/7km SW of Chipping Sodbury. **19 K4** ST6976.
Pucknall *Hants.* ***Settlement***, 1km E of Braishfield, 3m/5km NE of Romsey. SU3824.
Puckrup *Glos.* ***Settlement***, 3m/4km N of Tewkesbury. SO8836.
Pudding Green *Essex* ***Locality***, 5m/8km SW of Colchester. TL9419.
Puddinglake *Ches.* ***Locality***, adjoining to NE of Byley. **49 G6** SJ7269.
Puddington *Ches.* ***Village***, 7m/11km NW of Chester. **48 C5** SJ3273.
Puddington *Devon* ***Village***, 7m/11km N of Crediton. **7 G4** SS8310.
Puddle Dock *Gt.Lon.* ***Settlement***, 2m/4km E of Upminster, in borough of Havering. TQ5987.
Puddlebrook *Glos.* ***Village***, 3m/5km N of Cinderford. **29 F7** SO6418.
Puddledock *Norf.* ***Settlement***, 2m/3km S of Attleborough. **44 E6** TM0592.
Puddletown *Dorset* ***Village***, 5m/8km NE of Dorchester. **9 G5** SY7594.
Puddletown Down *Dorset* ***Hill***, with tumuli at summit, 2m/3km N of Puddletown. Height 400 feet or 122 metres. **9 G5** SY7597.
Pudd's Cross *Herts.* ***Settlement***, 4m/6km E of Chesham. TL0002.
Pudleston *Here.* ***Village***, 4m/7km E of Leominster. **28 E3** SO5659.
Pudsey *W.Yorks.* Population: 31,636. ***Town***, 4m/6km E of Bradford and 6m/9km W of Leeds. Former industries included wool and shoe-making. Cricketers Herbert Sutcliffe and Len Hutton lived here. **57 H6** SE2233.
Puffin Island (Also known as Priestholm or Ynys Seiriol.) *I.o.A.* ***Island***, 1km long NE to SW, lying less than 1km off E coast of Anglesey, 5m/7km NE of Beaumaris. There are remains of a monastic settlement. **46 E4** SH6582.
Pug Street *Norf.* ***Locality***, 1m/2km NE of Thurne. TG4117.
Pugneys Country Park *W.Yorks.* ***Leisure/recreation***, watersports teaching centre 2m/3km S of Wakefield across River Calder. **51 F1** SE3217.
Pulborough *W.Suss.* Population: 3497. ***Small town***, on River Arun N of South Downs, 12m/19km NW of Worthing. Site of Roman building 1km E of town centre. **12 D5** TQ0418.
Pulborough Brooks RSPB Nature Reserve *W.Suss.* ***Leisure/recreation***, family-orientated nature reserve and country park consisting of 2-mile nature trails leading to viewing hides, 1m/2km SW of Pulborough. **12 D5** TQ0617.
Puldagon *High.* ***Settlement***, 3m/4km SW of Wick. **105 J4** ND3248.
Puleston *Tel. & W.* ***Settlement***, 2m/3km N of Newport. **39 G3** SJ7322.
Pulford *Ches.* ***Village***, 5m/8km SW of Chester. **48 C7** SJ3758.
Pulham *Dorset* ***Village***, 7m/11km SE of Sherborne. **9 G4** ST7008.
Pulham Market *Norf.* ***Village***, 4m/6km NW of Harleston. **45 F7** TM1986.
Pulham St. Mary *Norf.* ***Village***, 3m/4km NW of Harleston. **45 G7** TM2185.
Pulley *Shrop.* ***Settlement***, 3m/4km SW of Shrewsbury. SJ4709.
Pulloxhill *Beds.* ***Village***, 3m/5km SE of Ampthill. **32 D5** TL0533.
Pulniskie Burn *D. & G.* ***River***, flowing generally W, to join Water of Minnoch near Larg, 7m/11km NW of Newton Stewart. **64 D3** NX3674.
Pulrose *I.o.M.* ***Locality***, 1m/2km W of Douglas. SC3675.
Pulrossie *High.* ***Settlement***, 5m/7km W of Dornoch. **96 E3** NH7288.
Pulteney Bridge *B. & N.E.Som.* ***Bridge***, stone bridge over River Avon in Bath, built in 1769 by Robert Adam. Lined with houses, now mainly converted to shops. ST7564.
Pulteneytown *High. Alternative name for Old Wick, qv.*
Pulverbatch (Also known as Castle Pulverbatch.) *Shrop.* ***Hamlet***, with motte and baileys, 1km SW of Church Pulverbatch. **38 D5** SJ4202.
Pumlumon *Cere. Welsh form of Plynlimon, qv.*
Pumpherston *W.Loth.* ***Village***, adjoining to NE of Livingston. **75 J4** NT0669.
Pumpsaint *Carmar. Alternative spelling of Pumsaint, qv.*
Pumsaint (Also spelled Pumpsaint.) *Carmar.* ***Hamlet***, 7m/11km SE of Lampeter. Site of Roman bath house to S. **27 F4** SN6540.
Puncheston (Cas-mael). *Pembs.* ***Village***, 5m/9km SE of Fishguard. **16 D2** SN0029.
Puncknowle *Dorset* ***Village***, 5m/8km SE of Bridport. **8 E6** SY5388.
Punnett's Town *E.Suss.* ***Village***, 3m/4km E of Heathfield. **13 K4** TQ6220.
Purbeck Hills *Dorset* ***Large natural feature***, range of chalk hills running E and W, from Ballard Down N of Swanage to West Lulworth, and traversing Isle of Purbeck. **9 J6** SY9382.
Purbrook *Hants.* ***Village***, adjoining to SW of Waterlooville. **11 H4** SU6708.
Purcell Room *Gt.Lon. See South Bank Arts Centre.*
Purewell *Dorset* ***Suburb***, 1m/2km E of Christchurch town centre. SZ1692.
Purfleet *Thur.* ***Locality***, on N bank of River Thames, 3m/5km W of Grays. **23 J4** TQ5677.
Puriton *Som.* Population: 1986. ***Village***, 3m/5km NE of Bridgwater. **19 G7** ST3241.
Purleigh *Essex* ***Village***, 3m/5km S of Maldon. **24 E1** TL8402.
Purley *Gt.Lon.* ***Town***, in borough of Croydon, 3m/4km S of Croydon town centre. **23 G5** TQ3161.
Purley *W.Berks. Familiar form of Purley on Thames, qv.*
Purley on Thames (Commonly known as Purley.) *W.Berks.* ***Suburb***, 4m/6km NW of Reading. **21 K4** SU6576.
Purlogue *Shrop.* ***Settlement***, 3m/5km N of Knighton. **28 B1** SO2877.
Purlpit *Wilts.* ***Hamlet***, 3m/4km NW of Melksham. ST8766.
Purls Bridge *Cambs.* ***Settlement***, 1m/2km S of Manea. **43 H7** TL4787.
Purse Caundle *Dorset* ***Village***, 2km SE of Milborne Port and 4m/6km E of Sherborne. **9 F3** ST6917.
Purse Caundle Manor *Dorset* ***Historic house***, 15c-16c manor house used as family home, 4m/6km E of Sherborne. **9 F3** ST6917.
Purshull Green *Worcs.* ***Settlement***, 4m/6km W of Bromsgrove. SO9071.
Purslow *Shrop.* ***Hamlet***, 4m/6km E of Clun. **38 C7** SO3680.
Purston Jaglin *W.Yorks.* ***Locality***, 2m/3km SW of Pontefract. **51 G1** SE4319.
Purtington *Som.* ***Hamlet***, 3m/5km W of Crewkerne. ST3909.
Purton *Glos.* ***Settlement***, on W bank of River Severn estuary, 2m/3km S of Blakeney. SO6704.
Purton *Glos.* ***Village***, on E bank of River Severn estuary, 3m/5km N of Berkeley. **19 K1** SO6904.
Purton *Wilts.* Population: 3879. ***Village***, 5m/8km NW of Swindon. **20 D3** SU0887.
Purton Stoke *Wilts.* ***Village***, 2m/3km S of Cricklade. **20 D2** SU0990.
Purves Hall *Sc.Bord.* ***Settlement***, 3m/5km SE of Greenlaw. **77 F6** NT7644.
Pury End *Northants.* ***Village***, 2m/4km SE of Towcester. **31 J4** SP7045.
Pusey *Oxon.* ***Village***, 4m/7km E of Faringdon. **21 G2** SU3596.
Pusey House Gardens *Oxon.* ***Garden***, in Pusey, 8m/12km W of Abingdon. Herbaceous borders, water and pleasure garden, shrubberies and fine trees. **21 G2** SU3596.
Putley *Here.* ***Village***, 4m/6km W of Ledbury. **29 F5** SO6437.
Putley Green *Here.* ***Hamlet***, 4m/6km W of Ledbury. SO6537.
Putloe *Glos.* ***Hamlet***, 5m/8km NW of Stroud. **20 A1** SO7809.
Putney *Gt.Lon.* ***Suburb***, S of River Thames in borough of Wandsworth, 5m/8km SW of Charing Cross. **23 F4** TQ2375.
Putsborough *Devon* ***Hamlet***, near N coast, 6m/10km SW of Ilfracombe. **6 C1** SS4440.
Puttenham *Herts.* ***Village***, 3m/5km NW of Tring. **32 B7** SP8814.
Puttenham *Surr.* ***Village***, below S slope of Hog's Back, 4m/7km W of Guildford. **22 C7** SU9347.
Puttock End *Essex* ***Settlement***, 1m/2km W of Belchamp Walter, 3m/5km NE of Great Yeldham. **34 C4** TL8040.
Putts Corner *Devon* ***Settlement***, 3m/5km SW of Honiton. **7 K6** SY1496.
Puxton *N.Som.* ***Village***, 2m/3km W of Congresbury. **19 H5** ST4063.
Pwll *Carmar.* ***Hamlet***, 2m/3km W of Llanelli. **17 H4** SN4801.
Pwll-glas *Denb.* ***Hamlet***, 2m/3km S of Ruthin. SJ1154.
Pwll-Mawr *Cardiff* ***Suburb***, adjoining to SE of Rumney, 3m/5km NE of Cardiff city centre. ST2278.
Pwll-trap *Carmar.* ***Hamlet***, 1m/2km W of St. Clears. **17 F3** SN2616.
Pwll-y-glaw *N.P.T.* ***Hamlet***, 3m/4km NE of Port Talbot. **18 A2** SS7993.
Pwllcrochan *Pembs.* ***Settlement***, 3m/5km N of Castlemartin. **16 C4** SM9202.
Pwlldefaid *Gwyn.* ***Settlement***, on SW tip of Lleyn Peninsula, 1m/2km W of Aberdaron. **36 A3** SH1526.
Pwlldu Head *Swan.* ***Coastal feature***, limestone headland (National Trust) on S coast of Gower peninsula, 4m/7km W of Mumbles Head. **17 J6** SS5786.
Pwllgloyw *Powys* ***Hamlet***, 3m/5km N of Brecon. **27 K5** SO0333.
Pwllheli *Gwyn.* Population: 3974. ***Small town***, with harbour, almost land-locked, on Tremadog Bay, 8m/12km W of Criccieth. **36 C2** SH3735.
Pwllmeyric *Mon.* ***Village***, 1m/2km SW of Chepstow. **19 J2** ST5192.
Pwllygranant *Pembs.* ***Bay***, on N coast, 3m/4km NW of St. Dogmaels. **26 A4** SN1247.
Pwllypant *Caerp.* ***Suburb***, 1m/2km N of Caerphilly town centre. ST1588.
Pydew *Conwy* ***Village***, 1m/2km NE of Llandudno Junction. SH8079.
Pye Corner *Herts.* ***Hamlet***, 1m/2km N of Harlow. **33 H7** TL4412.
Pye Corner *Kent* ***Hamlet***, 3m/5km N of Headcorn. TQ8548.
Pye Corner *Newport* ***Settlement***, 3m/5km SE of Newport. **19 G3** ST3485.
Pye Green *Staffs.* ***Locality***, 3m/4km N of Cannock. **40 B4** SJ9814.
Pye Hill *Notts.* ***Hamlet***, adjoining to NE of Jacksdale, 1m/2km SW of Selston. SK4451.
Pyecombe *W.Suss.* ***Village***, on South Downs, 6m/9km N of Brighton. **13 F5** TQ2812.
Pyefleet Channel *Essex* ***Sea feature***, inlet of River Colne joining with Strood Channel to W and thus separating Mersea Island from mainland. **34 E7** TM0416.
Pyewipe *N.E.Lincs.* ***Locality***, adjoining to NW of Grimsby. TA2511.
Pykestone Hill *Sc.Bord.* ***Mountain***, 3m/5km SE of Drumelzier. Height 2417 feet or 737 metres. **75 K7** NT1731.
Pyle (Y Pil). *Bridgend* Population: 12,331. ***Town***, 5m/8km W of Bridgend. **18 B3** SS8282.
Pyle *I.o.W.* ***Settlement***, 3m/4km NW of Niton. **11 F7** SZ4778.
Pyleigh *Som.* ***Hamlet***, 1m/2km W of Combe Florey, 4m/6km NE of Wiveliscombe. ST1230.
Pylle *Som.* ***Village***, 3m/5km S of Shepton Mallet. **9 F1** ST6038.
Pymore *Cambs.* ***Village***, 4m/7km W of Littleport. **43 H7** TL4986.
Pymore *Dorset* ***Hamlet***, 1m/2km N of Bridport. SY4794.
Pyrford *Surr.* ***Hamlet***, 2m/3km E of Woking. **22 D6** TQ0458.
Pyrford Green *Surr.* ***Hamlet***, 1km NE of Pyrford. TQ0458.
Pyrland *Som.* ***Suburb***, N district of Taunton. ST2326.
Pyrton *Oxon.* ***Village***, 1m/2km N of Watlington. Elizabethan manor house. **21 K2** SU6895.
Pysgotwr Fawr *Cere.* ***River***, rising 4m/6km E of Llanddewi-Brefi and flowing SE into River Tywi, 1m/2km S of Llyn Brianne. **27 G3** SN7351.
Pytchley *Northants.* ***Village***, 3m/4km S of Kettering. Gives name to famous hunt; kennels at Brixworth. **32 B1** SP8574.
Pythouse *Wilts.* ***Historic house***, Georgian mansion built in Palladian style, 3m/5km W of Tisbury. **9 J2** ST9028.
Pyworthy *Devon* ***Village***, 2m/3km SW of Holsworthy. **6 B5** SS3102.

Q

Quabbs *Shrop.* ***Settlement***, 3m/5km W of Newcastle. **38 B7** SO2080.
Quadring *Lincs.* ***Village***, 7m/11km N of Spalding. **43 F2** TF2433.
Quadring Eaudike *Lincs.* ***Hamlet***, 3m/4km SE of Donington. **43 F2** TF2433.
Quaich *P. & K.* ***River***, running SE down Glen Quaich through Loch Freuchie, then E by Amulree to join Cochill Burn and form River Braan. **81 J4** NN9238.
Quainton *Bucks.* ***Village***, 6m/10km NW of Aylesbury. **31 J7** SP7420.

Quair Water *Sc.Bord.* ***River***, rising in Ettrick Forest and flowing NE into River Tweed, 1m/2km S of Innerleithen. **76 B7** NT3335.
Quaker's Yard (Mynwent y Crynwyr). *M.Tyd.* ***Suburb***, on site of former burial ground on S side of Treharris. ST0996.
Quaking Houses *Dur.* ***Locality***, 1m/2km S of Stanley. NZ1850.
Quality Corner *Cumb.* ***Locality***, 1m/2km NE of Whitehaven. NX9819.
Quantock Forest *Som.* ***Forest/woodland***, wooded area on Quantock Hills between West Bagborough and Nether Stowey. **7 K2** ST1736.
Quantock Hills *Som.* ***Large natural feature***, granite and limestone ridge running NW and SE, extending from West Quantoxhead in NW to Kingston St. Mary in SE, attaining height of 1260 feet or 384 metres on Bagborough Hill, 1m/2km N of West Bagborough. **7 K1** ST1437.
Quarley *Hants.* ***Village***, 6m/10km W of Andover. **21 F7** SU2743.
Quarmby *W.Yorks.* ***Suburb***, 2m/3km W of Huddersfield town centre. **50 D1** SE1117.
Quarme *Som.* ***River***, rising on Exmoor 2m/3km N of Exford and flowing E and then S into River Exe near Exton. **7 G2** SS9234.
Quarndon *Derbys.* ***Village***, 3m/5km N of Derby. **41 F1** SK3341.
Quarr Hill *I.o.W.* ***Locality***, 1m/2km W of Ryde. To W, remains of medieval abbey; early 20c abbey lies beyond. **11 G5** SZ5792.
Quarrelton *Renf.* ***Suburb***, S district of Johnstone. NS4262.
Quarrendon *Bucks.* ***Suburb***, NW district of Aylesbury. SP8014.
Quarrier's Village *Inclyde* ***Village***, 2m/3km NW of Bridge of Weir. **74 B4** NS3666.
Quarrington *Lincs.* ***Village***, 1m/2km SW of Sleaford. **42 D1** TF0544.
Quarrington Hill *Dur.* ***Village***, 5m/8km SE of Durham. **62 E3** NZ3337.
Quarry Bank *W.Mid.* ***Suburb***, S district of Dudley. **40 B7** SO9386.
Quarry Bank Mill *Ches.* ***Historic house***, late 18c working cotton mill owned by Greg family, with restored Apprentice House, in Styal, 1m/2km N of Wilmslow. **49 H4** SJ8382.
Quarry Burn *Dur.* ***Locality***, 2m/3km SE of Crook. NZ1833.
Quarry Head *Aber.* ***Coastal feature***, headland on N coast, 2m/3km SW of Rosehearty. **99 H4** NJ9066.
Quarry Hill *Aber.* ***Mountain***, surrounded by woodland, 4m/6km W of Gartly. Height 1443 feet or 440 metres. **90 C1** NJ4631.
Quarrybank *Ches.* ***Locality***, 2m/3km N of Tarporley. **48 E6** SJ5465.
Quarrywood *Moray* ***Locality***, 2m/4km W of Elgin. **97 J5** NJ1864.
Quartalehouse *Aber.* ***Settlement***, adjoining Stuartfield to N, 10m/16km W of Peterhead. NJ9746.
Quarter *S.Lan.* ***Village***, 3m/4km S of Hamilton. **75 F5** NS7251.
Quatford *Shrop.* ***Village***, on River Severn, 2m/3km SE of Bridgnorth. **39 G6** SO7390.
Quatt *Shrop.* ***Village***, 4m/6km SE of Bridgnorth. **39 G7** SO7588.
Quebec *Dur.* ***Village***, 3m/4km S of Lanchester. **62 C2** NZ1843.
Quebec House *Kent* ***Historic house***, red-brick 17c house, property of The National Trust, in Westerham. Childhood home of General Wolfe. **23 H6** TQ4454.
Quedgeley *Glos.* ***Village***, 3m/5km SW of Gloucester. **29 H7** SO8014.
Queen Adelaide *Cambs.* ***Village***, 2m/3km NE of Ely. **43 J7** TL5681.
Queen Camel *Som.* ***Village***, 1m/2km SW of Sparkford. **8 E2** ST5924.
Queen Charlton *B. & N.E.Som.* ***Hamlet***, 2m/3km SW of Keynsham. **19 K5** ST6367.
Queen Dart *Devon* ***Hamlet***, above Little Dart River, 3m/4km NE of Witheridge. SS8316.
Queen Elizabeth Country Park *Hants.* ***Leisure/recreation***, 3m/5km SW of Petersfield. 1147 acres of woodland and chalk downland covered in nature trails and with facilities for pony-trekking. Also hang-gliding and para-gliding on Butser Hill. **11 J3** SU7219.
Queen Elizabeth Forest Park *Stir.* ***Forest/woodland***, area of forest, moor and mountainside extending from Aberfoyle to Loch Lomond and including Achray and Loch Ard Forests, Ben Lomond and part of The Trossachs. Total area about 70 square miles or 180 square km. **74 C1** NS4798.
Queen Elizabeth Hall *Gt.Lon.* *See South Bank Arts Centre.*
Queen Elizabeth II Bridge ***Bridge***, conveys road traffic southbound across River Thames from Purfleet on N bank to Dartford on S bank. See also Dartford Tunnel. **23 J4** TQ5775.
Queen Elizabeth II Country Park *Northumb.* ***Leisure/recreation***, parkland, woodland and lake 1m/2km N of Ashington. Activities include windsurfing, coarse fishing and nature trails. Light railway connects to Woodhorn Colliery Museum. **71 H5** NZ2888.
Queen Oak *Dorset* ***Village***, between Bourton and Zeals, 3m/5km NW of Gillingham. ST7831.
Queen Street *Kent* ***Hamlet***, 1m/2km E of Paddock Wood. **23 K7** TQ6845.
Queen Street *Suff.* ***Hamlet***, 6m/10km NE of Haverhill. TL7154.
Queen Street *Wilts.* ***Locality***, 6m/10km E of Malmesbury. SU0387.
Queenborough *Kent* Population: 3689. ***Locality***, industrial area at W end of Isle of Sheppey, 2m/3km S of Sheerness. **25 F4** TQ9172.
Queenhill *Worcs.* ***Locality***, 3m/5km NW of Tewkesbury. SO8636.
Queen's Bower *I.o.W.* ***Hamlet***, 2m/3km W of Sandown. SZ5684.
Queen's Cairn *High.* ***Mountain***, in Wyvis Forest, 8m/12km NE of Gorstan. Height 2116 feet or 645 metres. **96 B4** NH4672.
Queen's Ground *Norf.* ***Open space***, fenland 3m/4km NW of Feltwell. **44 A6** TL6793.
Queen's Head *Shrop.* ***Hamlet***, 4m/6km SE of Oswestry. **38 C3** SJ3426.
Queen's Park *Northants.* ***Suburb***, 1m/2km N of Northampton town centre. SP7562.
Queen's Park *Wrex.* ***Suburb***, E district of Wrexham. SJ3550.
Queen's Sedge Moor *Som.* ***Marsh/bog***, marshy area at sea level, cut by dyke for drainage, 2m/3km NE of Glastonbury. **19 J7** ST5241.
Queensberry *D. & G.* ***Mountain***, in Lowther Hills, 6m/10km W of Beattock. Height 2286 feet or 697 metres. **68 E4** NX9899.
Queensbury *Gt.Lon.* ***Suburb***, in borough of Brent, 2m/4km W of Hendon. TQ1889.
Queensbury *W.Yorks.* Population: 7424. ***Small town***, 3m/5km N of Halifax. Developed as a textile centre in 19c. **57 G6** SE1130.
Queensferry *Flints.* Population: 8887. ***Small town***, on S bank of River Dee, 6m/9km W of Chester. **48 C6** SJ3168.
Queenside Muir *Renf.* ***Open space***, moorland area 5m/8km NE of Largs. **74 A4** NS2764.
Queenslie Industrial Estate *Glas.* ***Locality***, 4m/7km E of Glasgow city centre. NS6665.
Queenstown *B'pool* ***Suburb***, 1m/2km NE of Blackpool town centre. SD3137.
Queensville *Staffs.* ***Suburb***, SE district of Stafford. SJ9322.
Queensway *Fife* ***Locality***, industrial estate on NE side of Glenrothes. NO2701.
Queenswood Country Park *Here.* ***Leisure/recreation***, woodland area with waymarked walks and visitor centre, 5m/8km S of Leominster. **28 E3** SO5051.
Queenzieburn *N.Lan.* ***Village***, 2m/3km W of Kilsyth. **74 E3** NS6977.
Quemerford *Wilts.* ***Locality***, adjoining to SE of Calne. **20 D4** SU0069.
Quendale *Shet.* ***Settlement***, on Bay of Quendale, on S coast of Mainland, 4m/6km NW of Sumburgh Head. **109 F9** HU3713.
Quendon *Essex* ***Village***, 6m/10km N of Bishop's Stortford. **33 J5** TL5130.
Queniborough *Leics.* Population: 2387. ***Village***, 6m/10km NE of Leicester. **41 J4** SK6412.
Quenington *Glos.* ***Village***, 2m/3km N of Fairford. **20 E1** SP1404.
Quernmore *Lancs.* ***Locality***, 3m/4km E of Lancaster. **55 J3** SD5160.
Queslett *W.Mid.* ***Locality***, 5m/8km N of Birmingham city centre. **40 C6** SP0694.
Quethiock *Cornw.* ***Village***, 4m/6km E of Liskeard. **4 D4** SX3164.
Quex House and Gardens *Kent* ***Historic house***, on Isle of Thanet, 1m/2km SE of Birchlington. Home of P.H.G. Powell-Cotton, displaying Chinese Imperial porcelain, as well as a collection of African ethnography and local archaeological finds. Gardens include a Victorian walled kitchen garden. **25 K5** TR3168.
Quey Firth *Shet.* ***Sea feature***, inlet on NE coast of Mainland to S of Colla Firth. **108 C4** HU3682.
Quholm *Ork.* ***Settlement***, 1m/2km to W of Loch of Stenness, Mainland. **107 B6** HY2412.
Quick Edge *Gt.Man.* ***Locality***, on hillside, 1km N of Mossley. SD9703.
Quick's Green *W.Berks.* ***Settlement***, 3m/5km W of Pangbourne. SU5876.
Quidenham *Norf.* ***Hamlet***, 5m/8km S of Attleborough. **44 E7** TM0287.
Quidhampton *Hants.* ***Hamlet***, 1km N of Overton near source of River Test. **21 J6** SU5150.
Quidhampton *Wilts.* ***Suburb***, to W of Salisbury. **10 C1** SU1131.
Quidnish *W.Isles* *Anglicised form of Cuidhtinis, qv.*
Quies *Cornw.* ***Island***, group of small islands 1m/2km W of Trevose Head on N coast. **3 F1** SW8376.
Quilquox *Aber.* ***Locality***, comprising settlements of North Quilquox and South Quilquox, 3m/5km E of Methlick. **91 H1** NJ9038.
Quilva Taing *Shet.* ***Coastal feature***, small promontory on W coast of Mainland, 1m/2km SW of Melby. **109 A7** HU1657.
Quin *Herts.* ***River***, rising NE of Barkway and flowing S into River Rib 1km SW of Braughing. **33 G5** TL3824.
Quina Brook *Shrop.* ***Settlement***, 3m/4km NE of Wem. **38 E2** SJ5233.
Quinag *High.* ***Mountain***, in Sutherland district 2m/3km N of Loch Assynt. Height 2650 feet or 808 metres. **102 E6** NC2029.
Quindry *Ork.* ***Settlement***, on NE side of Widewall Bay, South Ronaldsay, 2m/3km SW of St. Margaret's Hope. **107 D8** ND4392.
Quine's Hill *I.o.M.* ***Hamlet***, 2m/4km SW of Douglas. **54 C6** SC3473.
Quinhill *Arg. & B.* ***Settlement***, on Kintyre, adjoining to N of Clachan. **73 F5** NR7656.
Quinish *Arg. & B.* ***Locality***, on Mull, 5m/8km W of Tobermory. **79 F2** NM4254.
Quinish *W.Isles* ***Coastal feature***, rocks off SW coast of Pabbay. **92 D3** NF8886.
Quinish Point *Arg. & B.* ***Coastal feature***, headland at NW end of Quinish locality on Mull, 6m/10km NW of Tobermory. **79 F2** NM4057.
Quinton *Northants.* ***Village***, 4m/6km S of Northampton. **31 J3** SP7754.
Quinton *Warks.* ***Locality***, parish containing village of Lower Quinton and hamlet of Upper Quinton, 5m/8km S of Stratford-upon-Avon. SP1847.
Quinton *W.Mid.* ***Suburb***, in E part of Halesowen. **40 B7** SO9984.
Quinton Green *Northants.* ***Settlement***, 1m/2km E of Courteenhall. SP7853.
Quintrell Downs *Cornw.* ***Hamlet***, 3m/4km SE of Newquay. **3 F2** SW8460.
Quiraing *High.* ***Locality***, area of boulders, screes and rock pinnacles created by largest and most spectacular landslipping in Britain, 6m/9km SE of Rubha Hunish, Skye. **93 K4** NG4569.
Quixhill *Staffs.* ***Hamlet***, in valley of River Churnet, 1m/2km NW of Rocester. SK1041.
Quoditch *Devon* ***Hamlet***, 6m/9km SE of Holsworthy. **6 C6** SX4097.
Quoich Water *Aber.* ***River***, in Cairngorm Mountains, running S to River Dee 2m/3km W of Braemar. **89 H5** NO1290.
Quoig *P. & K.* ***Settlement***, 3m/4km W of Crieff. **81 K5** NN8222.
Quoigs *P. & K.* ***Locality***, 1km SW of Greenloaning. **81 K7** NN8305.
Quoisley *Ches.* ***Settlement***, 1m/2km W of Marbury. SJ5445.
Quorn (Also known as Quorndon.) *Leics.* Population: 4614. ***Village***, 3m/4km SE of Loughborough. The Quorn hunt was founded here. **41 H4** SK5616.
Quorndon *Leics.* *Alternative name for Quorn, qv.*
Quothquan *S.Lan.* ***Settlement***, 3m/5km NW of Biggar. **75 H7** NS9939.
Quoy Ness *Ork.* ***Coastal feature***, rocky cliff on E side of Els Ness peninsula on S coast of Sanday. Quoyness Chambered Cairn. **106 F4** HY6738.
Quoyloo *Ork.* ***Settlement***, on Mainland, 3m/5km W of Dounby. **106 B5** HY2420.
Quoyness Chambered Cairn *Ork.* ***Historic/prehistoric site***, large chambered cairn (Historic Scotland) at Quoy Ness on Els Ness, Sanday. **106 F4** HY6737.
Quoys *Shet.* ***Settlement***, on Unst, to E of Loch of Cliff, 3m/4km N of Baltasound. **108 F1** HP6112.
Quoys of Reiss *High.* ***Settlement***, 1km E of Killimster. **105 J3** ND3357.

R

Raasay (Island of Raasay). *High.* ***Island***, sparsely inhabited island, 13m/21km N to S and up to 3m/5km wide, lying off E coast of Skye opposite Portree. **94 B7** NG5640.
Rabbit Islands *High.* ***Island***, group of islands in Tongue Bay off N coast of Caithness district. Inhabited by rabbits. **103 J2** NC6063.
Rabbit's Cross *Kent* ***Locality***, 2m/4km N of Staplehurst. TQ7847.
Rableyheath *Herts.* ***Settlement***, 2m/3km N of Welwyn. TL2319.
Raby *Cumb.* ***Locality***, 1m/2km NE of Abbeytown. NY1951.
Raby *Mersey.* ***Hamlet***, 2m/3km NE of Neston. **48 C5** SJ3179.
Raby Castle *Dur.* ***Historic house***, mainly 14c, with later additions, 1m/2km N of Staindrop. Home to Lord Barnard's family for over 350 years. Stables house collection of horse drawn carriages. Gardens include yew hedges, formal walled garden and rose garden. **62 C4** NZ1221.
Rachan *Sc.Bord.* ***Settlement***, 1m/2km S of Broughton. **75 K7** NT1134.
Rachub *Gwyn.* ***Village***, 1m/2km N of Bethesda. **46 E6** SH6268.
Rack Wick *Ork.* ***Bay***, on W coast of Hoy, 2m/3km E of Rora Head. Settlement of Rackwick on the bay. **107 A8** ND2099.
Rackenford *Devon* ***Village***, 4m/6km NE of Witheridge. **7 G4** SS8518.
Rackenford Moor *Devon* ***Open space***, moorland 2m/3km NW of Rackenford. **7 G3** SS8220.
Rackham *W.Suss.* ***Hamlet***, below South Downs (Rackham Hill), 2m/4km W of Storrington. **12 D5** TQ0513.
Rackheath *Norf.* ***Hamlet***, 5m/8km NE of Norwich. **45 G4** TG2814.
Racks *D. & G.* ***Village***, on Lochar Moss, 4m/6km E of Dumfries. **69 F6** NY0374.
Rackwick *Ork.* ***Settlement***, on Westray, 1m/2km N of Pierowall. **106 D2** HY4449.
Rackwick *Ork.* ***Settlement***, on bay of Rack Wick, on W cost of Hoy, 2m/3km E of Rora Head. **107 B8** ND2099.
Radbourne *Derbys.* ***Hamlet***, 4m/7km W of Derby. On S side is parkland surrounding 18c house. **40 E2** SK2836.
Radbourne Common *Derbys.* ***Open space***, heath to NE of Radbourne, 4m/6km W of Derby. **40 E2** SK2937.
Radcliffe *Gt.Man.* Population: 32,567. ***Town***, on River Irwell, 2m/4km SW of Bury. **49 G2** SD7807.
Radcliffe *Northumb.* ***Village***, 1m/2km S of Amble. **71 H3** NU2602.
Radcliffe on Trent *Notts.* Population: 7387. ***Small town***, 5m/8km E of Nottingham. Developed from site of Roman river crossing. **41 J2** SK6439.
Radclive *Bucks.* ***Village***, on River Great Ouse, 1m/2km W of Buckingham. **31 H5** SP6734.
Radcot *Oxon.* ***Settlement***, on River Thames, 3m/4km N of Faringdon. **21 F2** SU2899.
Raddington *Som.* ***Hamlet***, 4m/6km SW of Wiveliscombe. ST0226.
Radernie *Fife* ***Settlement***, 5m/8km SE of St. Andrews. NO4609.
Radford *B. & N.E.Som.* ***Hamlet***, 2m/4km NW of Radstock. ST6757.
Radford *Notts.* ***Suburb***, 1m/2km NW of Nottingham city centre. SK5440.
Radford *Oxon.* ***Hamlet***, 5m/8km NW of Woodstock. **31 F6** SP4023.
Radford *W.Mid.* ***Suburb***, 1m/2km NW of Coventry city centre. **41 F7** SP3280.
Radford Semele *Warks.* ***Village***, 2m/3km E of Royal Leamington Spa. **30 E2** SP3464.

Radipole *Dorset* ***Suburb***, N district of Weymouth. **9 F6** SY6681.
Radlett *Herts.* Population: 7619. ***Small town***, residential town, 5m/8km S of St. Albans. Disused Radlett Airfield 2m/3km N. **22 E1** TQ1699.
Radley *Oxon.* ***Village***, 2m/4km NE of Abingdon. **21 J2** SU5199.
Radley Green *Essex* ***Hamlet***, 6m/9km W of Chelmsford. TL6205.
Radmore Green *Ches.* ***Settlement***, 4m/7km NW of Nantwich. SJ5955.
Radnage *Bucks.* ***Hamlet***, 2m/3km NE of Stokenchurch. SU7897.
Radnage Common *Bucks.* ***Locality***, 2m/3km E of Stokenchurch. SU7996.
Radnor Forest *Powys* ***Large natural feature***, wild upland area (although partly afforested) between Presteigne and Penybont, with New Radnor to S. Highest point is Great Rhos, 2165 feet or 660 metres. Mast on Black Mixen. Sheep-grazing on open hills. **28 A2** SO1664.
Radnor Park *Renf.* ***Suburb***, 1m/2km NW of Clydebank town centre. NS4971.
Radstock *B. & N.E.Som.* ***Small town***, former coalmining town, 8m/12km SW of Bath. **19 K6** ST6854.
Radstone *Northants.* ***Village***, 2m/4km N of Brackley. **31 G4** SP5840.
Radur *Cardiff Welsh form of Radyr, qv.*
Radur *Mon. See Rhadyr.*
Radway *Warks.* ***Village***, 7m/11km NW of Banbury. Site of Battle of Edgehill, 1642, 1m/2km NW. **30 E4** SP3748.
Radway Green *Ches.* ***Locality***, 2m/3km SW of Alsager. **49 G7** SJ7754.
Radwell *Beds.* ***Village***, 6m/9km NW of Bedford. **32 D3** TL0057.
Radwell *Herts.* ***Village***, 2m/3km NW of Baldock. **33 F5** TL2335.
Radwinter *Essex* ***Village***, 4m/7km E of Saffron Walden. **33 K5** TL6037.
Radwinter End *Essex* ***Settlement***, 2m/3km NE of Radwinter. TL6239.
Radyr (Radur). *Cardiff* Population: 4335. ***Village***, 4m/6km NW of Cardiff. **18 E3** ST1380.
Rae Burn *D. & G.* ***River***, flowing SW from Raeburnhead to join River White Esk 1km N of Eskdalemuir. **69 J3** NY2598.
Raeburnfoot *D. & G. See Eskdalemuir.*
Raechester *Northumb.* ***Settlement***, on Kirkwhelpington Common, 2m/3km NW of Kirkwhelpington. **70 E5** NY9787.
Raemoir House *Aber.* ***Settlement***, 3m/4km N of Banchory. **90 E5** NO6999.
Raerinish Point *W.Isles* ***Coastal feature***, headland on E coast of Isle of Lewis, 2m/3km E of Crosbost. **101 G5** NB3924.
Raes Knowes *D. & G.* ***Mountain***, on S side of Glentenmont Burn, 4m/7km W of Langholm. Height 997 feet or 304 metres. **69 H5** NY2983.
RAF Museum *Gt.Lon.* ***Other feature of interest***, 1km NW of Hendon. 70 full-size aircraft, displayed in former hangars. **23 F3** TQ2290.
Raffin *High.* ***Settlement***, 2m/3km S of Point of Stoer, Sutherland district. **102 C5** NC0132.
Rafford *Moray* ***Village***, 2m/3km SE of Forres. **97 H6** NJ0656.
Ragdale *Leics.* ***Village***, 6m/9km W of Melton Mowbray. **41 J4** SK6619.
Ragged Appleshaw *Hants.* ***Hamlet***, 1km E of Appleshaw and 4m/7km NW of Andover. SU3148.
Raggra *High.* ***Locality***, in Caithness district, 5m/8km S of Wick. ND3144.
Raglan (Rhaglan). *Mon.* ***Village***, 7m/11km SW of Monmouth. Remains of 15c castle (Cadw) to N. **19 H1** SO4107.
Raglan Castle *Mon.* ***Castle***, well-preserved 15c castle (Cadw) on site of 11c castle to N of Raglan, 8m/12km SE of Abergavenny. **19 H1** SO4108.
Ragley Hall *Warks.* ***Historic house***, large 17c-18c mansion in park, 2m/3km SW of Alcester. **30 B3** SP0755.
Ragnall *Notts.* ***Village***, 13m/20km N of Newark-on-Trent. **52 B5** SK8073.
Rahoy *High.* ***Settlement***, on NE shore of Loch Teacuis, 1m/2km from head of loch. **79 H2** NM6356.
Rain Shore *Gt.Man.* ***Hamlet***, on W side of Greenbooth Reservoir, 3m/5km NW of Rochdale town centre. SD8515.
Rainberg Mòr *Arg. & B.* ***Mountain***, in N part of Jura, 4m/7km W of Lussagiven. Height 1486 feet or 453 metres. **72 D2** NR5687.
Rainford *Mersey.* Population: 6362. ***Small town***, 4m/6km NW of St. Helens. **48 D2** SD4700.
Rainham *Gt.Lon.* ***Town***, in borough of Havering, 5m/8km S of Romford. **23 J3** TQ5381.
Rainham *Med.* ***Suburb***, SE district of Gillingham. **24 E5** TQ8165.
Rainhill *Mersey.* ***Town***, 3m/5km SW of St. Helens. Site of 19c locomotive trials, which featured George Stephenson's Rocket. **48 D3** SJ4991.
Rainhill Stoops *Mersey.* ***Village***, 1m/2km SE of Rainhill. **48 E3** SJ4991.
Rainigadale *W.Isles Anglicised form of Reinigeadal, qv.*
Rainigadale Island *W.Isles* ***Island***, islet in Loch Trollamarig to S of Reinigeadal. NB2201.
Rainow *Ches.* ***Village***, 3m/4km NE of Macclesfield. **49 J5** SJ9575.
Rainsough *Gt.Man.* ***Suburb***, on W side of River Irwell, 1m/2km SW of Prestwich. SD8002.
Rainthorpe Hall and Gardens *Norf.* ***Garden***, large gardens surrounding Elizabethan manor house on River Tas, 1km N of Tasburgh and 7m/12km S of Norwich. Features trees and bamboos. **45 G6** TM2097.
Rainton *N.Yorks.* ***Village***, 4m/7km NE of Ripon. **57 J2** SE3775.
Rainton Bridge *T. & W.* ***Suburb***, adjoining to S of Houghton le Spring. NZ3448.
Rainton Gate *Dur.* ***Locality***, adjoining to S of West Rainton. NZ3146.
Rainworth *Notts.* Population: 7401. ***Village***, 4m/6km SE of Mansfield. **51 H7** SK5958.
Raisbeck *Cumb.* ***Settlement***, 2m/3km SE of Orton. **61 H6** NY6407.
Raise *Cumb.* ***Hamlet***, just W of Alston across River South Tyne. **61 J2** NY7146.
Rait *P. & K.* ***Village***, 7m/12km E of Perth. **82 D5** NO2226.
Raithby *Lincs.* ***Hamlet***, 2m/3km SW of Louth. **53 G4** TF3184.
Raithby *Lincs.* ***Village***, 2m/3km W of Spilsby. **53 G6** TF3767.
Raithwaite *N.Yorks.* ***Locality***, 2m/3km W of Whitby. NZ8711.
Raitts Burn *High.* ***River***, flowing from E slopes of Beinn Bhreac and SE into River Spey, 2m/3km NE of Kingussie. **88 E4** NH7901.
Rake *W.Suss.* ***Village***, 3m/5km SW of Liphook. **12 B4** SU8027.
Rake End *Staffs.* ***Hamlet***, adjoining to NW of Hill Ridware, 2m/3km E of Rugeley. SK0718.
Rake Head *Lancs.* ***Settlement***, 2m/3km SW of Bacup. SD8421.
Rakes Dale *Staffs.* ***Settlement***, 4m/6km E of Cheadle. SK0642.
Rakeway *Staffs.* ***Settlement***, 1km SE of Cheadle. SK0142.
Rakewood *Gt.Man.* ***Locality***, 1m/2km S of Littleborough, just SE of Hollingworth Lake. SD9414.
Raleigh's Cross *Som.* ***Settlement***, in Brendon Hills, 5m/8km SW of Williton. **7 J2** ST0334.
Ralfland Forest *Cumb.* ***Open space***, moorland, highest point of which is Langhowe Pike at 1328 feet or 405 metres, 2m/3km SW of Shap. **61 G5** NY5313.
Ram *Carmar.* ***Settlement***, 1m/2km SE of Lampeter. **26 E4** SN5846.
Ram Alley *Wilts.* ***Settlement***, 4m/7km NE of Pewsey. SU2263.
Ram Hill *S.Glos.* ***Hamlet***, 4m/6km SW of Chipping Sodbury. ST6779.
Ram Lane *Kent* ***Hamlet***, 2m/3km SE of Charing. **14 E3** TQ9646.
Ramasaig *High.* ***Locality***, near W coast of Skye, 8m/13km S of Dunvegan Head. **93 G7** NG1644.
Ramasaig Bay *High.* ***Bay***, on Skye, to W of Ramasaig. **93 G7** NG1644.
Rame *Cornw.* ***Village***, 4m/6km W of Penryn. **2 E5** SW7234.
Rame *Cornw.* ***Village***, in parish of Maker-with-Rame, 2m/3km S of Millbrook. **4 E6** SX4249.
Rame Head *Cornw.* ***Coastal feature***, headland at SE end of Whitsand Bay, to S of Rame. **4 E6** SX4249.
Rammerscales *D. & G.* ***Garden***, with wooded walks at Palladian house built in 1760, 1m/2km SW of Hightae. **69 F6** NY0877.
Ramna Stacks *Shet.* ***Island***, group of island rocks some 1m/2km N of Point of Fethaland. Nature reserve. **108 C3** HU3797.
Ramp Holme *Cumb.* ***Island***, small island (National Trust) on Windermere, 1m/2km S of Bowness-on-Windermere. SD3995.
Rampisham *Dorset* ***Village***, 4m/6km NW of Maiden Newton. **8 E4** ST5602.
Rampside *Cumb.* ***Village***, on W shore of Morecambe Bay, 3m/5km SE of Barrow-in-Furness. **55 F3** SD2466.
Rampton *Cambs.* ***Village***, 6m/10km N of Cambridge. **33 H2** TL4267.
Rampton *Notts.* ***Village***, 6m/10km E of Retford. **52 B5** SK7978.
Ramridge End *Luton* ***Suburb***, NE district of Luton. TL1023.
Rams Ness *Shet.* ***Coastal feature***, headland at SW end of Fetlar. **108 F4** HU6087.
Ramsbottom *Gt.Man.* Population: 17,318. ***Town***, market town, 4m/7km N of Bury. **49 G1** SD7916.
Ramsbury *Wilts.* ***Village***, on River Kennet, 6m/9km E of Marlborough. **21 F4** SU2771.
Ramscraigs *High.* ***Settlement***, near E coast of Caithness, 2m/3km SW of Dunbeath. **105 G6** ND1427.
Ramsdean *Hants.* ***Hamlet***, 3m/4km W of Petersfield. **11 J2** SU7022.
Ramsdell *Hants.* ***Village***, 5m/8km NW of Basingstoke. **21 J6** SU5857.
Ramsden *Gt.Lon.* ***Suburb***, in borough of Bromley, 1m/2km E of Orpington. TQ4766.
Ramsden *Oxon.* ***Village***, 4m/6km N of Witney. **30 E7** SP3515.
Ramsden *W.Yorks.* ***Locality***, 1m/2km S of Holmbridge. SE1105.
Ramsden Bellhouse *Essex* ***Village***, 2m/3km W of Wickford. **24 D2** TQ7194.
Ramsden Heath *Essex* Population: 2110. ***Village***, 3m/4km E of Billericay. **24 D2** TQ7195.
Ramsey *Cambs.* Population: 7577. ***Small town***, Fenland town 10m/16km SE of Peterborough. Remains of Benedictine abbey with 15c gatehouse (National Trust). **43 F7** TL2885.
Ramsey *Essex* ***Village***, 3m/5km W of Harwich. **35 G6** TM2130.
Ramsey *I.o.M.* ***Town***, resort on E coast, 7m/11km S of Point of Ayre. Former ship-building town situated on Ramsey Bay. Sandy beach; pier; small harbour. Grove Museum (Manx National Heritage). Model Tudor village on nearby hill. Heritage Festival held every August at harbour. **54 D4** SC4594.
Ramsey Bay *I.o.M.* ***Bay***, on E coast, extending N from Maughold Head to Shellag Point. Ramsey is situated on bay. **54 D4** SC4594.
Ramsey Forty Foot *Cambs.* ***Hamlet***, 2m/4km NE of Ramsey. **43 G7** TL3087.
Ramsey Heights *Cambs.* ***Hamlet***, 2m/4km W of Ramsey. **43 F7** TL2585.
Ramsey Hollow *Cambs.* ***Open space***, fenland 2m/3km NE of Ramsey. **43 G7** TL3186.
Ramsey Island *Essex* ***Village***, on River Blackwater estuary, 6m/9km N of Burnham-on-Crouch. **25 F1** TL9505.
Ramsey Island (Ynys Dewi). *Pembs.* ***Island***, 2m/3km long N to S and 1m/2km wide, lying 2m/3km SW of St. David's Head, much of it protected by National Trust. Haunt of sea birds. **16 A2** SM7023.
Ramsey Mereside *Cambs.* ***Hamlet***, 2m/4km N of Ramsey. **43 F7** TL2889.
Ramsey St. Mary's *Cambs.* ***Hamlet***, 3m/5km NW of Ramsey. **43 F7** TL2588.
Ramsey Sound *Pembs.* ***Sea feature***, narrow strait with dangerous currents. Separates Ramsey Island from mainland. **16 A2** SM7023.
Ramsgate *Kent* Population: 37,895. ***Town***, resort with large harbour on Isle of Thanet, 15m/24km E of Canterbury. Municipal airport; airport also at Manston. Hovercraft terminal at Pegwell Bay (cross-Channel service). **25 K5** TR3865.
Ramsgate Street *Norf.* ***Hamlet***, 4m/6km SE of Holt. **44 E2** TG0933.
Ramsgill *N.Yorks.* ***Village***, on River Nidd, 4m/7km NW of Pateley Bridge. **57 G2** SE1171.
Ramsgreave *Lancs.* ***Locality***, 2m/3km N of Blackburn. SD6731.
Ramshaw *Dur.* ***Locality***, 2m/3km SW of Blanchland. NY9547.
Ramsholt *Suff.* ***Locality***, on E bank of River Deben estuary, 5m/8km SE of Woodbridge across river. **35 H4** TM3042.
Ramshorn *Staffs.* ***Village***, 5m/8km E of Cheadle. **40 C1** SK0845.
Ramsley *Devon* ***Hamlet***, to NW of South Zeal, 4m/6km SE of Okehampton. SX6493.
Ramsnest Common *Surr.* ***Hamlet***, 3m/5km E of Haslemere. **12 C3** SU9533.
Ranachan *High.* ***Settlement***, 2m/3km W of Strontian, Lochaber district. **79 J1** NM7961.
Ranby *Lincs.* ***Hamlet***, 6m/10km N of Horncastle. **53 F5** TF2378.
Ranby *Notts.* ***Village***, 4m/6km W of Retford. **51 J4** SK6480.
Rand *Lincs.* ***Village***, 2m/3km NW of Wragby. **52 E5** TF1078.
Randlawfoot *Cumb.* ***Locality***, 1km W of Cumwhitton and 2m/3km SE of Wetheral. NY4952.
Randlay *Tel. & W.* ***Suburb***, of Telford, to E of Dawley. SJ7007.
Randolph's Leap *Moray* ***Other feature of interest***, gorge in valley of River Findhorn, 8m/13km SE of Nairn. **97 G7** NH9949.
Randwick *Glos.* ***Village***, 2m/3km NW of Stroud. **20 B1** SO8206.
Ranfurly *Renf.* ***Settlement***, adjoining to S of Bridge of Weir. NS3964.
Rangely Kip *E.Loth.* ***Mountain***, 3m/4km E of Danskine. Height 1312 feet or 400 metres. **76 E4** NT6067.
Rangemore *Staffs.* ***Village***, 4m/6km W of Burton upon Trent. **40 D3** SK1822.
Ranger's House *Gt.Lon.* ***Historic house***, fine red-brick house (English Heritage) at SW edge of Greenwich Park. Built in 1700 and now home to Suffolk collection of paintings. **23 G4** TQ3876.
Rangeworthy *S.Glos.* ***Village***, 3m/5km NW of Chipping Sodbury. **19 K3** ST6886.
Rankinston *E.Ayr.* ***Village***, 3m/5km NE of Patna. **67 J2** NS4514.
Rankle Burn *Sc.Bord.* ***River***, rising in mountains of Craik Forest, flowing N to Buccleuch and into Ettrick Water 2m/4km NE of Ettrick. **69 J2** NT3017.
Rank's Green *Essex* ***Settlement***, 3m/5km S of Braintree. **34 B7** TL7417.
Ranmoor *S.Yorks.* ***Suburb***, 3m/4km W of Sheffield city centre. SK3186.
Ranmore Common *Surr.* ***Locality***, settlement and common land (National Trust), 2m/3km W of Dorking. TQ1450.
Rann *Lancs.* ***Village***, 3m/5km SE of Blackburn. SD7124.
Rannerdale *Cumb.* ***Locality***, on E shore of Crummock Water. NY1618.
Rannoch ***Large natural feature***, mountainous area between Loch Rannoch and Glen Lyon, spanning Highland and Perth & Kinross. Rannoch railway station on Glasgow to Fort William line is near NE end of Loch Laidon. **81 G2** NN5055.
Rannoch *High.* ***River***, in Lochaber district, running W to head of Loch Aline. **79 J3** NM7047.
Rannoch Forest *P. & K.* ***Large natural feature***, mountainous area to N of Rannoch, on W side of foot of Loch Ericht; also forests to S and SW of Loch Rannoch. **81 F1** NN4565.
Rannoch Moor ***Large natural feature***, upland tract to W of Rannoch spanning Highland and Perth & Kinross. Includes Loch Laidon, Loch Bà, and many small lochs or tarns, as well as a nature reserve. **80 E2** NN4050.
Rannoch School *P. & K.* ***Settlement***, on S side of Loch Rannoch, 4m/7km SW of Kinloch Rannoch. **81 G2** NN5956.
Rannoch Station *P. & K.* ***Other building***, station on West Highland line to Fort William, 15m/24km W of Kinloch Rannoch. **81 F2** NN4257.
Ranochan *High.* ***Settlement***, on N shore of Loch Eilt, 3m/5km E of Lochailort. **86 E6** NM8282.
Ranscombe *Som.* ***Hamlet***, 3m/4km W of Dunster. SS9443.
Ranskill *Notts.* ***Village***, 2m/3km E of Blyth. **51 J4** SK6587.
Ranson Moor *Cambs.* ***Open space***, fenland, 3m/5km SW of March. **43 G6** TL3892.
Ranton *Staffs.* ***Village***, 4m/7km W of Stafford. **40 A3** SJ8524.
Ranton Green *Staffs.* ***Settlement***, 1m/2km SW of Ranton. SJ8422.
Ranworth *Norf.* ***Village***, 4m/7km NW of Acle. **45 H4** TG3514.
Rapaire *W.Isles* ***Mountain***, on North Harris, 1m/2km W of head of Loch Langavat. Height 1486 feet or 453 metres. **100 D6** NB1313.
Raploch *Stir.* ***Suburb***, NW district of Stirling. NS7894.

R

Rapness *Ork.* ***Settlement***, on Westray, 6m/10km SE of Pierowall. **106 E3** HY5141.

Rapness Sound *Ork.* ***Sea feature***, stretch of sea dividing Faray from S end of Westray. **106 E4** HY5138.

Rappach *High.* ***Locality***, to N of Strath nan Lòn and containing many tributaries of Allt nan Luibean Molach. **95 J1** NC2302.

Rappach Water *High.* ***River***, formed from several streams in Rhidorroch Forest and flowing E into River Einig at W end of Glen Einig. **95 J2** NH3397.

Rapps *Som.* ***Hamlet***, 2m/3km NW of Ilminster. ST3317.

Rascarrel *D. & G.* ***Settlement***, at Rascarrell Bay, 3m/5km E of Dundrennan. **65 J6** NX7948.

Rascarrel Bay *D. & G.* ***Bay***, 4m/6km E of Dundrennan. **65 J6** NX8048.

Rash *Cumb.* ***Settlement***, 1m/2km S of Sedbergh. SD6689.

Rashwood *Worcs.* ***Hamlet***, 2m/3km NE of Droitwich Spa. SO9165.

Rashy Height *D. & G.* ***Mountain***, 4m/6km NE of Thornhill. Height 1246 feet or 380 metres. **68 E4** NX9398.

Raskelf *N.Yorks.* ***Village***, 3m/4km NW of Easingwold. **57 K2** SE4971.

Rassau *B.Gwent* ***Locality***, 2m/4km W of Bryn-mawr. **28 A7** SO1512.

Rastrick *W.Yorks.* ***Locality***, 1km SW of Brighouse. **57 G7** SE1321.

Rat Island *Devon* ***Island***, off SE point of Lundy. **6 A1** SS1443.

Rat Island *Essex* ***Island***, at mouth of Geedon Creek 6m/10km SE of Colchester. TM0517.

Ratae Coritanorum *Leic. See Leicester.*

Ratagan *High.* ***Settlement***, in Skye and Lochalsh district, on SW shore of Loch Duich, 1m/2km NW of Shiel Bridge, at head of loch. NG9119.

Ratby *Leics.* Population: 3601. ***Village***, 5m/8km W of Leicester. **41 H5** SK5105.

Ratcher Hill *Notts.* ***Hill***, 3m/4km SE of Mansfield. Height 394 feet or 120 metres. **51 H6** SK5760.

Ratcliff *Gt.Lon.* ***Suburb***, in borough of Tower Hamlets, 2m/3km E of London Bridge. TQ3680.

Ratcliffe Culey *Leics.* ***Village***, 2m/3km NE of Atherstone. **41 F6** SP3299.

Ratcliffe on Soar *Notts.* ***Village***, 6m/10km NW of Loughborough. Site of Roman building 1m/2km to W of power station. **41 G3** SK4928.

Ratcliffe on the Wreake *Leics.* ***Village***, 7m/11km NE of Leicester. **41 J4** SK6314.

Ratford Bridge *Pembs.* ***Settlement***, 3m/5km SW of Haverfordwest. **16 C3** SM9012.

Ratfyn *Wilts.* ***Settlement***, 1km NE of Amesbury. Bronze Age cemetery of Ratfyn Barrows (English Heritage), 1m/2km E, has various styles of burial mounds. SU1642.

Rathen *Aber.* ***Village***, 4m/6km S of Fraserburgh. **99 J4** NK0060.

Rathillet *Fife* ***Settlement***, 4m/7km N of Cupar. **82 E5** NO3620.

Rathliesbeag *High.* ***Settlement***, 3m/4km NW of Spean Bridge. **87 J6** NN2185.

Rathmell *N.Yorks.* ***Village***, 2m/3km NW of Long Preston. **56 D3** SD8059.

Ratho *Edin.* Population: 1620. ***Village***, 8m/12km W of Edinburgh. **75 K3** NT1370.

Ratho Station *Edin.* Population: 1159. ***Hamlet***, 1m/2km N of Ratho. **75 K3** NT1372.

Rathven *Moray* ***Village***, near N coast 1m/2km E of Buckie. **98 C4** NJ4465.

Ratley *Warks.* ***Village***, on E side of Edge Hill, 6m/10km NW of Banbury. **30 E4** SP3847.

Ratling *Kent* ***Settlement***, 1m/2km N of Aylesham. TR2453.

Ratlinghope *Shrop.* ***Village***, 4m/6km NW of Church Stretton across The Long Mynd. **38 D6** SO4096.

Ratsloe *Devon* ***Hamlet***, 4m/7km NE of Exeter. SX9597.

Rattar *High.* ***Settlement***, near N coast of Caithness district, 4m/6km SE of Dunnet Head. **105 H1** ND2673.

Ratten Row *Cumb.* ***Locality***, adjoining to NW of Caldbeck. NY3140.

Ratten Row *Cumb.* ***Settlement***, 2m/3km E of Dalston. NY3949.

Ratten Row *Lancs.* ***Settlement***, on N bank of River Wyre, 2m/3km W of St. Michael's on Wyre. **55 H5** SD4241.

Ratten Row *Norf.* ***Locality***, adjoining to W of Walpole Highway, 4m/6km NE of Wisbech. TF5113.

Rattery *Devon* ***Village***, 4m/6km W of Totnes. **5 H4** SX7461.

Rattlesden *Suff.* ***Village***, 5m/7km W of Stowmarket. **34 D3** TL9758.

Ratton Village *E.Suss.* ***Suburb***, 2m/3km NW of Eastbourne town centre. TQ5801.

Rattray *P. & K.* ***Town***, on River Ericht opposite Blairgowrie. **82 C3** NO1845.

Rattray Bay *Aber.* ***Bay***, extends S from Rattray Head to Scotstown Head, 6m/9km N of Peterhead. **99 K5** NK1057.

Rattray Head *Aber.* ***Coastal feature***, headland with lighthouse on NE coast, 7m/12km N of Peterhead. **99 K5** NK1057.

Raughton *Cumb.* ***Locality***, 2m/3km SE of Dalston. NY3947.

Raughton Head *Cumb.* ***Settlement***, 2m/3km S of Raughton. **60 E2** NY3845.

Raunds *Northants.* Population: 7493. ***Small town***, 6m/10km NE of Wellingborough. Footwear manufacture is main industry. Important archaeological site. Medieval church with 15c wall paintings. **32 D1** SP9972.

Ravelston *Edin.* ***Suburb***, 2m/3km W of Edinburgh city centre. NT2274.

Raven Seat *N.Yorks.* ***Locality***, 2m/4km NW of Keld. NY8603.

Ravenfield *S.Yorks.* ***Village***, 4m/6km E of Rotherham. **51 G3** SK4895.

Ravenglass *Cumb.* ***Village***, on River Esk estuary, 4m/7km SE of Seascale. Site of Roman fort of Glannaventa. **60 B7** SD0896.

Ravenglass and Eskdale Railway *Cumb.* ***Other feature of interest***, narrow gauge tourist railway running 7m/11km from Ravenglass to Dalegarth Station in Eskdale valley. Museum displays memorabilia and photographs from railway. **60 B7** SD0896.

Ravenglass Roman Bath House *Cumb.* ***Historic/prehistoric site***, remains of Roman bath house (English Heritage) on 4-acre site of Roman fort of Glannaventa, at Ravenglass. **60 B7** SD0895.

Raveningham *Norf.* ***Village***, 4m/7km NW of Beccles. **45 H6** TM3996.

Raven's Green *Essex* ***Hamlet***, 5m/8km W of Thorpe-le-Soken. TM1024.

Ravens Knowe *Northumb.* ***Mountain***, in Cheviot Hills, along route of The Pennine Way long distance footpath, 3m/4km NE of Byrness. Height 1729 feet or 527 metres. **70 C3** NT7706.

Ravenscar *N.Yorks.* ***Settlement***, above cliffs on North Sea coast, 3m/5km SE of Robin Hood's Bay. **63 J2** NZ9801.

Ravenscraig Castle *Fife* ***Castle***, ruined 15c castle beside sea, in N part of Kirkcaldy. **76 A1** NT2992.

Ravensdale *I.o.M.* ***Settlement***, 1m/2km S of Ballaugh. **54 C4** SC3592.

Ravensden *Beds.* ***Village***, 4m/6km NE of Bedford. **32 D3** TL0754.

Ravensdowne Barracks *Northumb.* ***Other feature of interest***, 18c barracks (English Heritage) on cliff top, just E of Berwick-upon-Tweed town centre. Houses Museum of King's Own Scottish Borderers and Borough Museum. **77 J5** NU0053.

Ravenshaw *N.Yorks.* ***Settlement***, on W side of Rive Aire, 2m/4km SW of Skipton. **56 E5** SD9849.

Ravenshayes *Devon* ***Settlement***, 1m/2km NW of Silverton. **7 H5** SS9404.

Ravenshead *Notts.* Population: 5490. ***Village***, 4m/6km NE of Hucknall. **51 H7** SK5654.

Ravensmoor *Ches.* ***Hamlet***, 2m/4km SW of Nantwich. **49 F7** SJ6250.

Ravensthorpe *Northants.* ***Village***, 8m/13km NW of Northampton. Ravensthorpe Reservoir to E. **31 H1** SP6670.

Ravensthorpe *Peter.* ***Suburb***, NW district of Peterborough. Industrial area astride railway to E. TF1700.

Ravensthorpe *W.Yorks.* ***Suburb***, 2m/3km SW of Dewsbury town centre. **50 E1** SE2220.

Ravensthorpe Reservoir *Northants.* ***Reservoir***, N of Ravensthorpe. **31 H1** SP6770.

Ravenstone *Leics.* ***Village***, 2m/3km W of Coalville. **41 G4** SK4013.

Ravenstone *M.K.* ***Village***, 3m/4km W of Olney. **32 B4** SP8450.

Ravenstonedale *Cumb.* ***Village***, 4m/7km SW of Kirkby Stephen. **61 J6** NY7204.

Ravenstonedale Common *Cumb.* ***Open space***, moorland 3m/5km SW of Ravenstonedale. **61 H6** NY6801.

Ravenstown *Cumb.* ***Settlement***, adjoining to SW of Flookburgh. SD3675.

Ravenstruther *S.Lan.* ***Locality***, 3m/5km E of Lanark. **75 H6** NS9245.

Ravensworth *N.Yorks.* ***Village***, 5m/8km NW of Richmond. Remains of medieval castle. **62 C6** NZ1407.

Raw *N.Yorks.* ***Settlement***, 1m/2km W of Robin Hood's Bay. **63 J2** NZ9305.

Raw Green *S.Yorks.* ***Settlement***, adjoining to SW of Cawthorne, 3m/5km E of Denby Dale. SE2707.

Rawcliffe *E.Riding* ***Village***, on S bank of River Aire, 4m/6km W of Goole. **58 C7** SE6822.

Rawcliffe *York* ***Suburb***, 3m/4km NW of York. **58 B4** SE5855.

Rawcliffe Bridge *E.Riding* ***Village***, 1m/2km SE of Rawcliffe, on Aire and Calder Canal. **58 C7** SE7021.

Rawdon *W.Yorks.* ***Locality***, adjoining to S of Yeadon. **57 H6** SE2039.

Rawfolds *W.Yorks.* ***Locality***, 1km SE of Cleckheaton. SE1924.

Rawmarsh *S.Yorks.* Population: 18,085. ***Town***, residential town, 2m/3km N of Rotherham. **51 G3** SK4396.

Rawnsley *Staffs.* ***Hamlet***, 3m/5km NE of Cannock. SK0212.

Rawreth *Essex* ***Village***, 2m/4km E of Wickford. **24 D2** TQ7893.

Rawridge *Devon* ***Hamlet***, 4m/6km NE of Honiton. **7 K5** ST2006.

Rawtenstall *Lancs.* Population: 21,933. ***Town***, on River Irwell, 6m/10km S of Burnley. Former wool town, before being superseded by cotton industry. **56 D7** SD8122.

Rawyards *N.Lan.* ***Settlement***, adjoining to NE of Airdrie. **75 F4** NS7766.

Raxton *Aber.* ***Settlement***, 1m/2km NE of Tarves. **91 G1** NJ8732.

Ray ***River***, rising SW of Winslow and flowing W into River Cherwell at Islip. **31 G7** SP5213.

Ray ***River***, rising S of Swindon and flowing N into River Thames 1m/2km below Cricklade. SU1293.

Ray Fell *Northumb.* ***Mountain***, 3m/4km W of Kirkwhelpington. Height 994 feet or 303 metres. **70 E5** NY9585.

Ray Sand *Essex* ***Coastal feature***, mud flat S of Dengie Flat at mouth of River Crouch. **25 G1** TM0400.

Raydon *Suff.* ***Village***, 3m/5km SE of Hadleigh. **34 E5** TM0538.

Raylees *Northumb.* ***Settlement***, 1m/2km SW of Elsdon. **70 E4** NY9291.

Raylees Common *Northumb.* ***Open space***, partly wooded moorland containing Blaxter Lough, 2m/4km S of Elsdon. **70 E5** NY9189.

Rayleigh *Essex* Population: 28,912. ***Town***, old market town, 6m/9km NW of Southend-on-Sea. Remains of Norman castle (National Trust). **24 E2** TQ8090.

Raymond's Hill *Devon* ***Hamlet***, 2m/3km SE of Axminster. **8 C5** SY3296.

Rayne *Aber. Alternative name for Kirkton of Rayne, qv.*

Rayne *Essex* Population: 2185. ***Village***, 2m/3km W of Braintree. **34 B6** TL7222.

Rayners Lane *Gt.Lon.* ***Suburb***, in borough of Harrow, 12m/19km NW of Charing Cross. TQ1287.

Raynes Park *Gt.Lon.* ***Suburb***, in borough of Merton, 3m/5km E of Kingston upon Thames. TQ2268.

Rea ***River***, rising as Rea Brook on N side of Brown Clee Hill and flowing S through Cleobury Mortimer into River Teme near Newnham Bridge, 2m/4km E of Tenbury Wells. **29 F1** SO6368.

Rea *Glos.* ***Locality***, on E bank of River Severn, in SW part of Gloucester. SO8015.

Rea Brook ***River***, rising on Long Mountain, E of Welshpool, and flowing NE into River Severn at Shrewsbury. **38 C5** SJ4912.

Rea Hill *Torbay* ***Suburb***, of Brixham just E of town centre. SX9256.

Reach *Cambs.* ***Village***, 5m/8km W of Newmarket. Site of Roman villa 1km SE. **33 J2** TL5666.

Read *Lancs.* ***Village***, 2m/3km W of Padiham. **56 C6** SD7634.

Reading *Read.* Population: 213,474. ***Town***, county and industrial town and railway centre on River Thames, 36m/58km W of London. During Victorian times Reading was an important manufacturing town, particularly for biscuit-making and brewing. University. Remains of Norman abbey, founded by Henry I who lies buried there. **22 A4** SU7173.

Reading Green *Suff.* ***Settlement***, 2m/3km W of Stradbroke. TM2074.

Reading Street *Kent* ***Hamlet***, 3m/5km SE of Tenterden. **14 E4** TQ9230.

Reading Street *Kent* ***Suburb***, 3m/4km N of Broadstairs. TR3869.

Readings *Glos.* ***Locality***, 3m/5km NW of Cinderford. SO6116.

Read's Island *N.Lincs.* ***Island***, uninhabited island in River Humber, 1m/2km NW of South Ferriby. **59 F7** SE9622.

Reagill *Cumb.* ***Hamlet***, 5m/9km W of Appleby-in-Westmorland. **61 H5** NY6017.

Rearquhar *High.* ***Locality***, in Sutherland district, 4m/7km NW of Dornoch. **96 E2** NH7492.

Rearsby *Leics.* ***Village***, 7m/11km SW of Melton Mowbray. **41 J4** SK6514.

Reasby *Lincs.* ***Locality***, 2m/3km N of Langworth. TF0679.

Rease Heath *Ches.* ***Settlement***, 2m/3km N of Nantwich. **49 F7** SJ6454.

Reaster *High.* ***Locality***, in Caithness district, 4m/7km SE of Castletown. **105 H2** ND2565.

Reaveley *Northumb.* ***Settlement***, 3m/5km NW of Powburn. **71 F2** NU0217.

Reawick *Shet.* ***Village***, on Mainland, on small bay of Rea Wick, 2m/3km S of Garderhouse. **109 C8** HU3244.

Reay *High.* ***Village***, near N coast of Caithness district, 10m/15km W of Thurso. Cnoc Freiceadain (Historic Scotland), prehistoric chambered cairn 3m/5km E. **104 E2** NC9664.

Reay Burn *High.* ***River***, flowing N into centre of Sandside Bay, on N coast of Caithness district. **104 E2** NC9665.

Reay Forest *High.* ***Large natural feature***, mountain area and deer forest in Sutherland district, extending from Foinaven SE to Ben Hee, and from Loch More NE to Glen Golly. Clan country of the Mackays. **102 E5** NC3039.

Reculver *Kent* ***Village***, N coast village, 3m/5km E of Herne Bay. Remains of Regulbium, Roman fort of the Saxon shore (English Heritage). **25 J5** TR2269.

Reculver Towers and Roman Fort *Kent* ***Historic/prehistoric site***, Roman fort (English Heritage), first occupied in 3c, in Reculver 3m/5km E of Herne Bay. 12c towers survive from church established initially in AD 669. **25 J5** TR2269.

Red *Cornw.* ***River***, rising 2m/4km SE of Camborne and flowing into St. Ives Bay 1km S of Godrevy Point. **2 D4** SW5842.

Red Ball *Devon* ***Hamlet***, 4m/6km SW of Wellington. ST0817.

Red Brow *Mersey.* ***Locality***, 1m/2km N of Kirkby. SJ4099.

Red Bull *Ches.* ***Settlement***, 1km NW of Kidsgrove. SJ8355.

Red Castle *Angus* ***Castle***, 2m/3km NE of Inverkeilor, on S bank of Lunan Water estuary. Also known as Ederdover, ruins of 16c L-plan tower house. **83 H2** NO6850.

Red Craig *Aber.* ***Mountain***, 5m/8km SE of Ballater. Height 1965 feet or 599 metres. **90 C5** NO4290.

Red Cross *Cambs.* ***Suburb***, 3m/4km SE of Cambridge city centre. TL4755.

Red Dial *Cumb.* ***Settlement***, 1m/2km S of Wigton. **60 D2** NY2546.

Red Down *Cornw.* ***Open space***, hillslope 1km S of Egloskerry. **4 C2** SX2685.

Red Hall *Lincs.* ***Historic house***, 1620 brick building on SW side of Bourne. **42 D4** TF0919.

Red Head *Angus* ***Coastal feature***, small rock headland below hillfort, 3m/4km SE of Inverkeilor. **83 J3** NO7047.

Red Head *High.* ***Coastal feature***, headland on W coast of Island of Stroma. **105 J1** ND3477.

Red Head *Ork.* ***Coastal feature***, headland at N end of Eday. **106 E3** HY5640.

Red Hill *Bourne.* ***Suburb***, 3m/5km N of Bournemouth town centre. SZ0895.

Red Hill *Hants.* ***Locality***, adjoining to S of Rowland's Castle, 3m/4km N of Havant. **11 J3** SU7210.

Red Hill *Powys* ***Mountain***, 3m/4km NE of Painscastle. Height 1670 feet or 509 metres. **28 A4** SO1550.

Red Hill *Warks.* ***Settlement***, 4m/7km W of Stratford-upon-Avon town centre. **30 C3** SP1356.

Red Hill *W.Yorks.* ***Locality***, 1km E of Castleford town centre. SE4425.

Red Hill *Worcs.* ***Suburb***, SE district of Worcester. SO8653.

Red Holm *Ork.* ***Island***, islet between Eday and Westray at N end of Sound of Faray. HY5439.

Red Lion Hill *Powys* ***Mountain***, 9m/15km N of Llandrindod Wells. Height 1617 feet or 493 metres. **27 K1** SO0576.

Red Lodge *Bristol* ***Historic house***, 16c house located just off Park Row in centre of Bristol, with fine stone-carving and woodwork. Museum with collection of furnishings. **19 J4** ST5873.
Red Lodge (Also known as Redlodge Warren.) *Suff.* ***Hamlet***, 6m/9km NE of Newmarket. **33 K1** TL6970.
Red Lumb *Gt.Man.* ***Suburb***, 4m/6km NW of Rochdale town centre, between reservoirs of Ashworth Moor and Greenbooth. SD8415.
Red Oaks Hill *Essex* ***Settlement***, 4m/6km NE of Saffron Walden. **33 J5** TL6039.
Red Pike *Cumb.* ***Mountain***, on ridge between Stirrup Crag and Steeple, with Stoat Tarn below on W side, 3m/4km N of Wast Water. Height 2476 feet or 755 metres. **60 C5** NY1415.
Red Point *High. Alternative name for Rubha Ruadh, qv.*
Red Point *High.* ***Coastal feature***, headland on N coast of Caithness district, 3m/4km W of Reay. **104 E2** NC9366.
Red Point *High.* ***Coastal feature***, headland on W coast of Ross and Cromarty district, on N side of entrance to Loch Torridon. **94 D5** NG7267.
Red Post *Cornw.* ***Hamlet***, 2m/4km SE of Stratton. **6 A5** SS2605.
Red Post *Devon* ***Settlement***, 3m/4km NE of Totnes. **5 J4** SX8363.
Red Rail *Here.* ***Settlement***, on River Wye, 4m/7km NW of Ross-on-Wye. SO5428.
Red Rock *Gt.Man.* ***Settlement***, 3m/5km N of Wigan. **48 E1** SD5809.
Red Roses (Rhos-goch). *Carmar.* ***Hamlet***, 3m/5km S of Whitland. **17 F3** SN2011.
Red Row *Northumb.* ***Village***, 3m/5km S of Amble. **71 H4** NZ2599.
Red Street *Staffs.* ***Locality***, 4m/6km N of Newcastle-under-Lyme. **49 H7** SJ8251.
Red Wharf Bay *I.o.A.* ***Bay***, N facing bay with wide sands on E coast of Anglesey, 6m/9km N of Menai Bridge. Also small resort on W side of bay. **46 D4** SH5481.
Red Wharf Bay *I.o.A.* ***Hamlet***, on W side of bay of same name, 1km SE of Benllech. **46 D4** SH5281.
Redberth *Pembs.* ***Village***, 4m/6km NW of Tenby. **16 D4** SN0804.
Redbourn *Herts.* Population: 4843. ***Village***, 4m/7km NW of St. Albans. **32 E7** TL1012.
Redbourne *N.Lincs.* ***Village***, 5m/8km SW of Brigg. Hall dates from 18c. **52 C2** SK9799.
Redbridge *S'ham.* ***Suburb***, W district of Southampton at head of River Test estuary opposite Totton. SU3713.
Redbrook *Glos.* ***Village***, on River Wye, 3m/4km SE of Monmouth. **19 J1** SO5310.
Redbrook *Wrex.* ***Hamlet***, 2m/3km W of Whitchurch. SJ5040.
Redbrook Street *Kent* ***Settlement***, 6m/9km SW of Ashford. **14 E4** TQ9336.
Redburn *High.* ***Settlement***, 2m/3km W of Evanton. **96 C5** NH5767.
Redburn *High.* ***Settlement***, in Nairn district, 7m/11km SE of Nairn. **97 G7** NH9447.
Redburn *Northumb.* ***Locality***, just W of Bardon Mill, on N bank of River South Tyne. NY7764.
Redburn Common *Dur.* ***Open space***, with disused quarry, 2m/4km W of Rookhope. **62 A2** NY9044.
Redcar *R. & C.* Population: 35,877. ***Town***, resort on North Sea coast, 8m/12km NE of Middlesbrough. Wide sands. Racecourse. Lifeboat Museum contains world's oldest lifeboat. **63 H4** NZ6025.
Redcastle *Angus* ***Hamlet***, to S of Red Castle, 2m/3km NE of Inverkeilor. **83 H2** NO6850.
Redcastle *High.* ***Settlement***, in Ross and Cromarty, district on N shore of Beauly Firth, 4m/6km E of Muir of Ord. **96 C7** NH5849.
Redcleuch Edge *Sc.Bord.* ***Mountain***, in Craik Forest, 2m/3km N of Craik. Height 1279 feet or 390 metres. **69 J2** NT3410.
Redcliff Bay *N.Som.* ***Suburb***, SW district of Portishead. **19 H4** ST4375.
Redcliff Channel *E.Riding* ***Sea feature***, sea strait in Humber estuary, between Redcliff Middle Sand and mainland at North Ferriby. **59 F7** SE9724.
Redcloak *Aber.* ***Settlement***, 1m/2km NW of Stonehaven. **91 G6** NO8586.
Reddicap Heath *W.Mid.* ***Suburb***, 1m/2km E of Sutton Coldfield. SP1495.
Redding *Falk.* ***Suburb***, 2m/4km SE of Falkirk. NS9278.
Reddingmuirhead *Falk.* ***Village***, 2m/4km SE of Falkirk. NS9177.
Reddish *Gt.Man.* ***Locality***, 2m/3km N of Stockport. **49 H3** SJ8993.
Redditch *Worcs.* Population: 73,372. ***Town***, 12m/19km S of Birmingham. New Town designated 1964. Needle Museum recalls past industry. **30 B2** SP0467.
Rede *Northumb.* ***River***, rising near Carter Bar on English-Scottish border, flowing SE through Catcleugh Reservoir, by Rochester to Otterburn, then S into River North Tyne at Redesmouth, 2m/3km SE of Bellingham. **70 D4** NY8582.
Rede *Suff.* ***Village***, 6m/10km SW of Bury St. Edmunds. **34 C3** TL8055.
Redenhall *Norf.* ***Village***, 1m/2km NE of Harleston. **45 G7** TM2684.
Redenham *Hants.* ***Hamlet***, 1km NW of Appleshaw and 5m/8km NW of Andover. SU3049.
Redesdale *Northumb.* ***Valley***, carrying River Rede and running SE from Catcleugh Reservoir to Otterburn, then S to Redesmouth. **70 C4** NY7999.
Redesdale Forest *Northumb.* ***Forest/woodland***, large area of coniferous forest to S of Catcleugh Reservoir and Rede Water in Cheviot Hills. **70 C3** NT7401.
Redesmouth *Northumb.* ***Hamlet***, near confluence of River Rede and River North Tyne, 2m/3km SE of Bellingham. **70 D5** NY8682.
Redford *Aber.* ***Settlement***, 3m/4km E of Laurencekirk. **83 J1** NO7570.
Redford *Angus* ***Village***, 6m/9km NW of Arbroath. **83 G3** NO5644.
Redford *Edin.* ***Suburb***, 4m/6km S of Edinburgh city centre. NT2268.
Redford *W.Suss.* ***Hamlet***, 3m/5km NW of Midhurst. **12 B4** SU8626.
Redgrave *Suff.* ***Village***, 5m/8km W of Diss. **34 E1** TM0477.
Redheugh *Angus* ***Settlement***, 4m/7km NE of Dykehead, to N of Glenogil, in valley of Noran Water. **83 F1** NO4463.
Redhill *Aber.* ***Locality***, 2m/3km S of Loch of Skene and 4m/7km NW of Peterculter. **91 F4** NJ7704.
Redhill *Aber.* ***Settlement***, 3m/4km W of Rothienorman. **90 E1** NJ6836.
Redhill *Moray* ***Settlement***, on NW side of Fourman Hill, 1m/2km SE of Milltown of Rothiemay. **98 D6** NJ5646.
Redhill *N.Som.* ***Village***, 4m/6km E of Congresbury. **19 H5** ST4963.
Redhill *Notts.* ***Suburb***, 4m/7km N of Nottingham city centre. **41 H1** SK5846.
Redhill *Surr.* Population: 23,801. ***Town***, adjoining to E of Reigate. Airfield and heliport 2m/3km SE. **23 F6** TQ2750.
Redhill *Tel. & W.* ***Settlement***, 2m/3km NW of Shifnal. **39 G4** SJ7310.
Redhills *Devon* ***Suburb***, 1m/2km W of Exeter city centre across River Exe. SX9092.
Redhouse *Aber.* ***Settlement***, 3m/4km N of Alford. **90 D2** NJ5820.
Redhouse *Arg. & B.* ***Settlement***, 5m/8km SW of Tarbert. **73 G4** NR8261.
Redhouses *Arg. & B.* ***Settlement***, on Islay, 1m/2km E of Bridgend. **72 B4** NR3562.
Redhythe Point *Aber.* ***Coastal feature***, headland on N coast, 1m/2km NW of Portsoy. **98 D4** NJ5767.
Redisham *Suff.* ***Village***, 4m/6km S of Beccles. **45 J7** TM4084.
Redlake *Shrop.* ***River***, rising W of New Invention and flowing E into River Clun, 1km NW of Leintwardine. **28 C1** SO3974.
Redland *Bristol* ***Suburb***, 1m/2km N of Bristol city centre. **19 J4** ST5875.
Redland *Ork.* ***Settlement***, on Mainland, 1m/2km NW of Woodwick. **106 C5** HY3725.
Redlingfield *Suff.* ***Village***, 3m/5km SE of Eye. **35 F1** TM1871.
Redlingfield Green *Suff.* ***Locality***, 1km NE of Redlingfield. TM1871.
Redlodge Warren *Suff. Alternative name for Red Lodge, qv.*
Redlynch *Som.* ***Hamlet***, 2m/3km SE of Bruton. **9 F1** ST7033.
Redlynch *Wilts.* Population: 2255. ***Village***, 7m/11km SE of Salisbury. **10 D2** SU2021.
Redmain *Cumb.* ***Locality***, 1m/2km SW of Blindcrake and 3m/4km NE of Cockermouth. NY1333.
Redmarley D'Abitot *Glos.* ***Village***, 5m/8km SE of Ledbury. **29 G5** SO7531.
Redmarshall *Stock.* ***Village***, 4m/6km W of Stockton-on-Tees. **62 E4** NZ3821.
Redmile *Leics.* ***Village***, 7m/12km W of Grantham. **42 B2** SK7935.
Redmire *N.Yorks.* ***Village***, 4m/7km W of Leyburn. **62 B7** SE0491.
Redmire Moor *N.Yorks.* ***Open space***, moorland 2m/3km N of Redmire, with viewpoint on roadside and rocky outcrop of Redmire Scar on S side. **62 B7** SE0493.
Redmires Dam *W.Yorks.* ***Reservoir***, small reservoir on Stansfield Moor, 2m/3km N of Todmorden. **56 E7** SD9227.
Redmires Reservoirs *S.Yorks.* ***Reservoir***, three adjacent reservoirs on moors, 6m/9km W of Sheffield city centre. **50 E4** SK2685.
Redmoor *Cornw.* ***Settlement***, 2m/3km NW of Lostwithiel. **4 A4** SX0761.
Rednal *Shrop.* ***Settlement***, 5m/8km SE of Oswestry. **38 C3** SJ3628.
Rednal *W.Mid.* ***Suburb***, 8m/12km SW of Birmingham city centre. **30 B1** SP0076.
Redpath *Sc.Bord.* ***Settlement***, 3m/5km E of Melrose. **76 D7** NT5835.
Redpoint *High.* ***Settlement***, on W coast of Ross and Cromarty district, 3m/5km SW of Port Henderson. **94 D5** NG7369.
Redruth *Cornw.* Population: 17,958. ***Town***, 8m/13km W of Truro. Developed with tin-mining industry; now market town with light industry. **2 D4** SW6941.
Redscarhead *Sc.Bord.* ***Settlement***, 2m/4km N of Peebles. **76 A6** NT2444.
Redshaw *S.Lan.* ***Settlement***, 2m/4km SE of Douglas. **68 D1** NS8628.
Redshin Cove *Northumb.* ***Bay***, small rocky bay, 2m/3km SE of Berwick-upon-Tweed. **77 J5** NU0150.
Redstone Bank *Pembs.* ***Settlement***, 1km N of Narberth. **16 E3** SN1115.
Redwick *Newport* ***Village***, near shore of River Severn estuary, 7m/11km E of Newport. **19 H3** ST4184.
Redwick *S.Glos.* ***Hamlet***, 1m/2km NE of Severn Beach. **19 J3** ST5486.
Redworth *Darl.* ***Hamlet***, 6m/10km NW of Darlington. **62 D4** NZ2423.
Reed *Herts.* ***Village***, 3m/5km S of Royston. **33 G5** TL3636.
Reed End *Herts.* ***Hamlet***, 3m/5km S of Royston. TL3436.
Reed Point *Sc.Bord.* ***Coastal feature***, small rocky headland on North Sea coast, 1m/2km NE of Cockburnspath. **77 F3** NT7872.
Reedham *Norf.* ***Village***, in Norfolk Broads, 6m/9km S of Acle. Across Reedham Marshes to NE is Berney Arms Mill (English Heritage). **45 J5** TG4201.
Reedley *Lancs.* ***Suburb***, in S part of Brierfield, 2m/3km N of Burnley. SD8435.
Reedley Hallows *Lancs.* ***Locality***, 2m/3km N of Burnley. SD8335.
Reedness *E.Riding* ***Village***, on S bank of River Ouse, 3m/5km E of Goole. **58 D7** SE7923.
Reeds Holme *Lancs.* ***Locality***, 1m/2km N of Rawtenstall. SD8024.
Reeker Pike *Northumb.* ***Mountain***, in afforested area to S of Kielder Water, 4m/7km SW of Falstone. Height 1210 feet or 369 metres. **70 B5** NY6682.
Reekie Linn *Angus* ***Waterfall***, in River Isla below Bridge of Craigisla, 4m/6km N of Alyth. **82 D2** NO2553.
Reepham *Lincs.* ***Village***, 4m/7km E of Lincoln. **52 D5** TF0373.
Reepham *Norf.* Population: 2405. ***Village***, 6m/10km SW of Aylsham. **45 F3** TG1022.
Reeth *N.Yorks.* ***Village***, in Swaledale, at foot of Arkengarthdale, 9m/14km W of Richmond. **62 B7** SE0399.
Reeves Green *W.Mid.* ***Settlement***, 5m/8km W of Coventry. SP2677.
Refail *Powys* ***Settlement***, 1km SE of Aberriw. SJ1900.
Regaby *I.o.M.* ***Village***, 3m/4km NW of Ramsey. **54 D4** SC4397.
Regents Park *Gt.Lon.* ***Open space***, on border of Westminster and Camden boroughs, 2m/3km NW of Charing Cross. Royal park of 472 acres, originally part of Henry VIII's great hunting forest. Includes Regent's Canal, London Zoo and London Mosque. **23 F3** TQ2882.
Regil (Formerly known as Ridgehill.) *N.Som.* ***Village***, 1m/2km NW of Chew Stoke. **19 J5** ST5362.
Regoul *High.* ***Settlement***, 3m/5km S of Nairn. **97 F6** NH8851.
Réidh Eilean *Arg. & B.* ***Island***, islet 2m/3km off NW coast of Iona. **78 D5** NM2426.
Reiff *High.* ***Settlement***, on NW coast of Ross and Cromarty district, 3m/4km S of Rubha Coigeach. **102 B7** NB9614.
Reigate *Surr.* Population: 23,801. ***Town***, market town below North Downs, 9m/14km N of Crawley. Once an important coaching town on London to Brighton road. 13c priory. Nearby windmill containing a church. **23 F6** TQ2550.
Reighton *N.Yorks.* ***Village***, 4m/6km S of Filey. **59 H2** TA1375.
Reighton Sands *N.Yorks.* ***Coastal feature***, beach at S end of Filey Bay. **59 H2** TA1376.
Reinigeadal (Anglicised form: Rainigadale.) *W.Isles* ***Settlement***, with youth hostel, in North Harris, on W side of entrance to Loch Seaforth. **100 E7** NB2201.
Rèisa an t-Sruith *Arg. & B.* ***Island***, small island midway between Craignish Point on mainland of Argyll and Aird of Kinuachdrach on NE coast of Jura. **73 F1** NR7399.
Rèisa Mhic Phaidean *Arg. & B.* ***Island***, small island 1m/2km W of Craignish Castle on mainland of Argyll. **79 J7** NM7500.
Reisgill *High.* ***Settlement***, 1km NW of Lybster. **105 H5** ND2336.
Reisgill Burn *High.* ***River***, stream in Caithness district, running S into Lybster Bay on E coast. **105 H5** ND2434.
Reiss *High.* ***Village***, in Caithness district, 3m/5km NW of Wick. **105 J3** ND3354.
Rejerrah *Cornw.* ***Settlement***, 4m/6km S of Newquay. **2 E3** SW8056.
Releath *Cornw.* ***Hamlet***, 3m/5km N of Helston. SW6633.
Relubbus *Cornw.* ***Hamlet***, 3m/5km S of Hayle. **2 C5** SW5631.
Relugas *Moray* ***Settlement***, in Darnaway Forest, 7m/11km S of Forres. **97 G7** NH9948.
Remenham *W'ham* ***Village***, 1m/2km NE of Henley-on-Thames across River Thames. **22 A3** SU7784.
Remenham Hill *W'ham* ***Village***, 1m/2km SE of Remenham. **22 A3** SU7784.
Remony *P. & K.* ***Settlement***, on SE shore of Loch Tay, 1m/2km SW of Kenmore. **81 J3** NN7644.
Rempstone *Notts.* ***Village***, 4m/6km NE of Loughborough. **41 H3** SK5724.
Rendcomb *Glos.* ***Village***, 5m/8km N of Cirencester. **30 B7** SP0209.
Rendham *Suff.* ***Village***, 3m/4km NW of Saxmundham. **35 H2** TM3464.
Rendham Green *Suff.* ***Locality***, adjoins to N of Rendham. TM3464.
Rendlesham *Suff.* ***Hamlet***, 3m/4km SE of Wickham Market. **35 H3** TM3353.
Rendlesham Forest *Suff.* ***Forest/woodland***, to S of Rendlesham, large area planted with conifers (Forestry Commission). **35 H4** TM3353.
Renfrew *Renf.* Population: 20,764. ***Town***, old port and former ship-building town on S side of River Clyde, 5m/9km W of Glasgow. Car ferry across river to Yoker. Glasgow Airport to W. **74 D4** NS5067.
Renhold *Beds.* ***Village***, 4m/6km NE of Bedford. **32 D3** TL0952.
Renish Point *W.Isles* ***Coastal feature***, headland at S end of Harris, 7m/11km NE of North Uist across Sound of Harris. **93 F3** NG0482.
Renishaw *Derbys.* ***Village***, 6m/9km NE of Chesterfield. Hall, seat of the Sitwells, dates partly from early 17c. **51 G5** SK4477.
Rennibister Earth House *Ork.* ***Historic/prehistoric site***, prehistoric earth house (Historic Scotland) on S side of Bay of Firth, Mainland, 4m/6km W of Kirkwall. **107 C6** HY3912.
Rennington *Northumb.* ***Village***, 4m/6km NE of Alnwick. **71 H2** NU2118.
Renton *W.Dun.* Population: 2072. ***Small town***, on W bank of River Leven, 2m/3km N of Dumbarton. Industrial estate across river. **74 B3** NS3878.
Renwick *Cumb.* ***Village***, 10m/16km NE of Penrith. **61 G2** NY5943.
Renwick Fell *Cumb.* ***Open space***, moorland which includes Thack Moor at 1998 feet or 609 metres and Watch Hill at 1975 feet or 602 metres, 2m/3km NE of Renwick and 5m/8km NE of Kirkoswald. **61 H2** NY6145.
Repps *Norf.* ***Hamlet***, 2m/4km W of Martham. **45 J4** TG4216.

Repton *Derbys.* Population: 2012. ***Small town***, historic town 5m/8km NE of Burton upon Trent. Boys' public school founded in 16c. Medieval church incorporating parts of original Saxon building. **41 F3** SK3026.
Rerwick Head *Ork.* ***Coastal feature***, headland on N coast of Mainland, 6m/9km E of Kirkwall. **107 E6** HY5411.
Rescobie *Angus* ***Settlement***, 3m/5km E of Forfar. **83 G2** NO5052.
Rescobie Loch *Angus* ***Lake/loch***, small loch 4m/6km E of Forfar. **83 G2** NO5151.
Rescorla *Cornw.* ***Hamlet***, 3m/5km N of St. Austell. SX0257.
Resipole *High.* ***Settlement***, on N shore of Loch Sunart, 2m/3km E of Salen. **79 J1** NM7264.
Resolis *High.* ***Settlement***, on S side of Cromarty Firth, Ross and Cromarty district, 2m/3km W of Balblair. **96 D5** NH6765.
Resolven *N.P.T.* Population: 2274. ***Village***, 6m/9km NE of Neath. **18 B1** SN8302.
Resourie *High.* ***Settlement***, 2m/3km SE of Scamodale, Lochaber district. **86 E7** NM8670.
Rest and be thankful *Arg. & B.* ***Locality***, in Argyll, at head of Glen Croe, 4m/6km NW of Ardgartan. **80 D7** NN2207.
Restalrig *Edin.* ***Suburb***, 2m/3km E of Edinburgh city centre. NT2874.
Restenneth Priory *Angus* ***Ecclesiastical building***, ruined medieval priory, 2m/3km E of Forfar. **83 F2** NO4851.
Reston *Cumb.* ***Settlement***, 1m/2km W of Staveley, on S side of Hugill Fell. SD4598.
Reston *Sc.Bord.* ***Village***, on Eye Water, 4m/6km W of Eyemouth. **77 G4** NT8862.
Restormel *Cornw.* ***Hamlet***, on W bank of River Fowey, 1m/2km N of Lostwithiel. Restormel Castle (English Heritage) on hill to NW. SX1061.
Restormel Castle *Cornw.* ***Castle***, medieval ruin (English Heritage) on top of hill to NW of Restormel. **4 B4** SX1061.
Restronguet *Cornw.* ***Locality***, 2m/4km NE of Penryn. SW8136.
Restronguet Creek *Cornw.* ***Sea feature***, to N of Restronguet, running down past Restronguet Point to Carrick Roads (River Fal). SW8137.
Reswallie *Angus* ***Settlement***, 3m/5km E of Forfar. **83 G2** NO5051.
Reterth *Cornw.* ***Settlement***, 2m/3km E of St. Columb Major. SW9463.
Retew *Cornw.* ***Settlement***, 1m/2km S of Indian Queens. **3 G3** SW9257.
Retford (Also known as East Retford.) *Notts.* Population: 20,679. ***Town***, market town on River Idle, 27m/43km NE of Nottingham. Georgian buildings; museum in 18c Amcott House. **51 K4** SK7080.
Rettendon *Essex* ***Village***, 3m/5km NE of Wickford. **24 D2** TQ7698.
Rettendon Place *Essex* ***Hamlet***, 3m/5km S of East Hanningfield. **24 D2** TQ7796.
Retyn *Cornw.* ***Settlement***, 2m/3km W of Indian Queens. **3 F3** SW8858.
Revesby *Lincs.* ***Village***, 6m/9km SE of Horncastle. To S, site of medieval abbey. **53 F6** TF2961.
Revesby Bridge *Lincs.* ***Settlement***, at confluence of three fen drains, 1m/2km SE of Revesby. TF3060.
Rew *Devon* ***Hamlet***, 1km N of Ashburton. **5 H3** SX7571.
Rew *Devon* ***Hamlet***, 3m/5km E of Crediton. SX8899.
Rew Street *I.o.W.* ***Hamlet***, 2m/3km SW of Cowes. SZ4794.
Rewe *Devon* ***Village***, on River Culm, 5m/8km NE of Exeter. **7 H6** SX9499.
Rexon *Devon* ***Locality***, including hamlets of Rexon Cross and Rexon, 6m/9km NE of Launceston. SX4188.
Reybridge *Wilts.* ***Hamlet***, on River Avon, 3m/4km S of Chippenham. ST9169.
Reydon *Suff.* ***Hamlet***, 1m/2km NW of Southwold. **35 J1** TM4977.
Reydon Smear *Suff.* ***Settlement***, to N of Reydon. TM4978.
Reymerston *Norf.* ***Village***, 5m/8km S of East Dereham. **44 E5** TG0106.
Reynalton *Pembs.* ***Village***, 6m/9km NW of Tenby. **16 D4** SN0908.
Reynoldston *Swan.* ***Village***, on Gower peninsula, 4m/6km NW of Oxwich Point and 11m/18km W of Swansea. **17 H6** SS4889.
Rezare *Cornw.* ***Hamlet***, 5m/8km N of Callington. **4 D3** SX3677.
Rha *High.* ***River***, on Skye, running SW into Uig Bay. **93 K5** NG3963.
Rhadyr (Radur). *Mon.* ***Hamlet***, 1m/2km NW of Usk. Agricultural college. SO3602.
Rhaeadr Cynfal *Gwyn.* *Welsh form of Cynfal Falls, qv.*
Rhaeadr Ewynnol *Conwy* *Welsh form of Swallow Falls, qv.*
Rhaeadr Fawr *Gwyn.* *Welsh form of Aber Falls, qv.*
Rhaeadr Gwy *Powys* *Welsh form of Rhayader, qv.*
Rhaglan *Mon.* *Welsh form of Raglan, qv.*
Rhandirmwyn *Carmar.* ***Village***, on E side of River Tywi valley, 6m/9km N of Llandovery. **27 G4** SN7843.
Rhaoine *High.* ***Settlement***, in Strath Fleet, 4m/7km E of Lairg. **96 D1** NC6405.
Rhayader (Rhaeadr Gwy). *Powys* Population: 1793. ***Small town***, on River Wye 11m/18km N of Builth Wells. Centre for angling and pony-trekking. **27 J2** SN9768.
Rhedyn *Gwyn.* ***Settlement***, on S part of Lleyn Peninsula, 3m/5km NW of Abersoch. **36 B2** SH2932.
Rhee *See (River) Cam.*
Rhegreanoch *High.* ***Settlement***, 1km NW of Loch Sionascaig. **102 C7** NC0916.
Rheidol *Cere.* ***River***, flowing from Nant-y-moch Reservoir and running S through Dinas Reservoir to Devil's Bridge, then W into Cardigan Bay with River Ystwyth on S side of Aberystwyth. Hydro-electric power station with visitor centre below Rheidol Falls. **27 G1** SN5780.
Rheidol Falls *Cere.* ***Waterfall***, in Cwm Rheidol 2m/3km NW of Devil's Bridge. Hydro-electric power station and visitor centre below waterfall. **27 G1** SN7178.
Rheindown *High.* ***Settlement***, in Ross and Cromarty district, 2m/3km S of Muir of Ord. **96 C7** NH5247.
Rhelonie *High.* ***Settlement***, 5m/8km NW of Bonar Bridge. **96 C2** NH5597.
Rhemore *High.* ***Settlement***, in Lochaber district, 3m/5km SE of Drimnin. **79 G2** NM5750.
Rhencullen *I.o.M.* ***Locality***, 1m/2km NE of Kirk Michael. SC3291.
Rheola *N.P.T.* ***Settlement***, 7m/11km NE of Neath. SN8304.
Rheola Forest *N.P.T.* ***Forest/woodland***, wooded area astride River Neath to NE of Neath. **18 B1** SN8304.
Rhes-y-cae *Flints.* ***Village***, 3m/5km S of Holywell. **47 K6** SJ1870.
Rhewl *Denb.* ***Hamlet***, on N bank of River Dee, 3m/5km NW of Llangollen. **38 A1** SJ1844.
Rhewl *Denb.* ***Village***, on River Clywedog, 2m/3km NW of Ruthin. **47 K6** SJ1060.
Rhewl *Shrop.* ***Locality***, 3m/5km NE of Oswestry. **38 C2** SJ3034.
Rhewl-fawr *Flints.* ***Settlement***, 2m/3km NW of Mostyn. SJ1281.
Rhian *High.* ***Settlement***, 7m/11km N of Lairg. **103 H7** NC5616.
Rhiangoll *Powys* ***River***, rising in Black Mountains on N side of Waun Fach and flowing S into River Usk, 2m/3km NW of Crickhowell. **28 A6** SO1919.
Rhicarn *High.* ***Locality***, in Sutherland district, 2m/3km NW of Lochinver. **102 C6** NC0825.
Rhiconich *High.* ***Settlement***, at head of Loch Inchard, W coast of Sutherland district. **102 E3** NC2552.
Rhicullen *High.* ***Settlement***, in Ross and Cromarty district, 2m/3km N of Invergordon. **96 D4** NH6971.
Rhidorroch *High.* ***River***, running W into Loch Achall, Ross and Cromarty district, E of Ullapool, through Rhidorroch Forest. **95 J2** NH1994.
Rhidorroch *High.* ***Settlement***, on N side of Loch Achall, 3m/5km E of Ullapool. **95 H2** NH1795.
Rhidorroch Forest *High.* ***Open space***, deer forest in Ross and Cromarty district, E of Ullapool. **95 J2** NH1994.
Rhifail *High.* ***Settlement***, in Strathnaver, overlooking River Naver, Caithness district. **104 C4** NC7249.
Rhigos *R.C.T.* ***Village***, 2m/4km W of Hirwaun. **18 C1** SN9205.
Rhilean Burn *High.* ***River***, rising on N slopes of Carn an t-Sean-liathanaich and flowing NE into Leonach Burn, then into River Findhorn, 4m/6km SW of Ferness. Waterfalls in lower course. **89 G1** NH9139.
Rhilochan *High.* ***Locality***, in Sutherland district, 7m/11km NW of Golspie. **96 E1** NC7407.
Rhinduie *High.* ***Settlement***, 4m/6km E of Beauly. **96 C7** NH5845.
Rhinefield *Hants.* ***Locality***, parish in New Forest, N of New Milton. SU2502.
Rhinns of Galloway *D. & G.* *Alternative spelling of Rinns of Galloway, qv.*
Rhinns of Islay *Arg. & B.* *Alternative spelling of Rinns of Islay, qv.*
Rhinns of Kells (Also spelled Rinns of Kells.) *D. & G.* ***Large natural feature***, mountain range running N and S between Loch Doon and Clatteringshaws Loch. Summit is Corserine, 2670 feet or 814 metres. **67 J5** NX5083.
Rhinog Fach *Gwyn.* ***Mountain***, 1m/2km to S of Rhinog Fawr. Height 2332 feet or 711 metres. **37 F3** SH6528.
Rhinog Fawr *Gwyn.* ***Mountain***, with steep scarp slopes 5m/8km SE of Harlech. Height 2362 feet or 720 metres. **37 F3** SH6528.
Rhireavach *High.* ***Settlement***, near E shore of Little Loch Broom, Ross and Cromarty district, 1m/2km SE of Scoraig. **95 G2** NH0295.
Rhiroy *High.* ***Settlement***, 1m/2km W of Leckmelm across Loch Broom. **95 H3** NH1489.
Rhisga *Caerp.* *Welsh form of Risca, qv.*
Rhiston *Shrop.* ***Settlement***, on border with Powys, 1m/2km NW of Church Stoke. SO2595.
Rhiw *Caerp.* ***Suburb***, adjoining to N of Newbridge. ST2098.
Rhiw (Also known as Bwlch-y-Rhiw or Y Rhiw.) *Gwyn.* ***Hamlet***, 4m/6km E of Aberdaron. To E is Plas-yn-Rhiw (National Trust), medieval and later manor house. **36 B3** SH2227.
Rhiw *Powys* ***River***, rising as several streams W of Llanllugan, which form two main streams both named River or Afon Rhiw, flowing E and joining 2m/3km W of Manafon. Single river so formed continues E and runs into River Severn 1m/2km SE of Berriew. SJ1900.
Rhiw-garn *R.C.T.* ***Settlement***, 1m/2km NE of Tonyrefail. ST0289.
Rhiw Gwraidd *Powys* ***Mountain***, with elongated summit, 3m/5km NW of Llandrindod Wells. Height 1446 feet or 441 metres. **27 K2** SO0163.
Rhiwabon *Wrex.* *Welsh form of Ruabon, qv.*
Rhiwaedog-is-afon *Gwyn.* ***Mountain***, 4m/6km SE of Bala. Height 1640 feet or 500 metres. **37 J2** SH9632.
Rhiwargor *Powys* ***Settlement***, at N end of Lake Vyrnwy. **37 J3** SH9624.
Rhiwbeina *Cardiff* *Alternative spelling of Rhiwbina, qv.*
Rhiwbina (Also spelled Rhiwbeina.) *Cardiff* ***Suburb***, 3m/5km NW of Cardiff city centre. Rhiwbina Garden settlement lies 1m/2km SE. ST1581.
Rhiwbryfdir *Gwyn.* ***Locality***, adjoining to N of Blaenau Ffestiniog. **37 F1** SH6946.
Rhiwderin (Rhiwderyn). *Newport* ***Hamlet***, 3m/5km W of Newport. **19 F3** ST2687.
Rhiwderyn *Newport* *Welsh form of Rhiwderin, qv.*
Rhiwen *Gwyn.* ***Locality***, below Moel Rhiwen, 1km NW of Deiniolen and 5m/8km S of Bangor. SH5763.
Rhiwiau Hill *Carmar.* ***Mountain***, 2m/3km N of Twynllanan. Height 1161 feet or 354 metres. **27 G6** SN7526.
Rhiwinder *R.C.T.* ***Settlement***, 1km E of Tonyrefail. ST0188.
Rhiwlas *Gwyn.* ***Settlement***, 1km N of Bala. **37 J2** SH9237.
Rhiwlas *Gwyn.* ***Village***, 4m/6km S of Bangor. **46 D6** SH5765.
Rhiwlas *Powys* ***Settlement***, 3m/4km E of Llanarmon Dyffryn Ceiriog. **38 B2** SJ1932.
Rhiwsaeson *R.C.T.* ***Settlement***, 2m/3km E of Llantrisant. ST0782.
Rhobell Fawr *Gwyn.* ***Mountain***, 6m/9km NE of Dolgellau. Height 2408 feet or 734 metres. **37 G3** SH7825.
Rhode *Som.* ***Hamlet***, 2m/3km SW of Bridgwater. ST2734.
Rhoden Green *Kent* ***Hamlet***, 1m/2km E of Paddock Wood. TQ6845.
Rhodes *Gt.Man.* ***Suburb***, 1m/2km SW of Middleton. SD8505.
Rhodes Minnis *Kent* ***Hamlet***, 5m/8km N of Hythe. **15 G3** TR1543.
Rhodesia *Notts.* ***Hamlet***, 1m/2km W of Worksop. **51 H5** SK5680.
Rhodiad *Pembs.* ***Settlement***, 2m/3km NE of St. David's. **16 A2** SM7627.
Rhodmad *Cere.* ***Settlement***, 2m/3km W of Llanilar. **26 E1** SN5974.
Rholben *Mon.* ***Inland physical feature***, mountain ridge rising to over 350 metres, extending S from Sugar Loaf, 1m/2km NW of Abergavenny. **28 B7** SO2816.
Rhonadale *Arg. & B.* ***Settlement***, on Kintyre, 2m/3km W of Carradale. **73 F7** NR7838.
Rhondda *R.C.T.* ***Locality***, former heart of Welsh coal-mining industry. A mountainous area, 7m/11km NW of Pontypridd, deeply incised by two narrow river valleys, Rhondda Fawr and Rhondda Fach which join at Porth. Along each valley there is near-continuous built-up area: Treherbert, Treorchy, Llwynpia, Tonypandy and Trealaw occupy Rhondda Fawr along Rhondda River, and Maerdy, Ferndale, Tylorstown, Ynyshir occupy Rhondda Fach along Little Rhondda River to E. **18 C2** SS9896.
Rhondda *R.C.T.* ***River***, whose two branches, Rhondda River (Rhondda Fawr) and Little Rhondda River (Rhondda Fach) rise on high ground W of Aberdare and flow SE in roughly parallel courses until joining at Porth and flowing into River Taff at Pontypridd. ST0789.
Rhondda Fach *R.C.T.* ***Valley***, narrow, steep-sided, urbanised valley carrying Little Rhondda River (Rhondda Fach) SE to Porth. **18 C1** SO0195.
Rhondda Fawr *R.C.T.* ***Valley***, narrow, steep-sided, urbanised valley carrying Rhondda River (Rhondda Fawr) SE to River Taff at Pontypridd. **18 C2** SS9794.
Rhonehouse (Also known as Kelton Hill.) *D. & G.* ***Village***, 2m/3km SW of Castle Douglas. **65 H5** NX7459.
Rhoose (Y Rhws). *V. of Glam.* Population: 3574. ***Locality***, 3m/5km W of Barry. Cardiff International Airport to N. Rhoose Point to S. **18 D5** ST0666.
Rhos *Carmar.* ***Village***, 4m/7km SW of Llandysul. **17 G1** SN3735.
Rhôs *Denb.* ***Settlement***, 2m/4km N of Ruthin. SJ1261.
Rhos *N.P.T.* ***Village***, 1m/2km SE of Pontardawe. **18 A1** SN7303.
Rhos *Powys* ***Settlement***, 1km SE of Four Crosses. SJ2717.
Rhos *Shrop.* ***Settlement***, 1m/2km NE of Sellatyn. SJ2735.
Rhôs Bay *Conwy* *Alternative name for Colwyn Bay (bay), qv.*
Rhos-berse *Wrex.* ***Settlement***, to S of Coedpoeth, 3m/5km W of Wrexham. **48 B7** SJ2850.
Rhos Common *Powys* ***Settlement***, to N of Rhos. SJ2818.
Rhos-ddu *Wrex.* ***Suburb***, 1km N of Wrexham town centre. **48 C7** SJ3351.
Rhos Dirion *Powys* ***Open space***, N facing hillslope of Black Mountains, 6m/9km S of Hay-on-Wye. **28 B5** SO2133.
Rhos-fawr *Gwyn.* ***Settlement***, on Lleyn Peninsula, 3m/4km NE of Pwllheli. **36 C2** SH3839.
Rhos-goch *Carmar.* *Welsh form of Red Roses, qv.*
Rhos Haminiog *Cere.* ***Settlement***, 1km N of Cross Inn. SN5464.
Rhos-hill (Rhos-hyl). *Pembs.* ***Hamlet***, 4m/6km S of Cardigan. **26 A4** SN1940.
Rhos-hyl *Pembs.* *Welsh form of Rhos-hill, qv.*
Rhôs Lligwy *I.o.A.* ***Settlement***, on Anglesey, 5m/8km SE of Amlwch. SH4886.
Rhôs-on-Sea *Conwy* ***Small town***, resort at E end of Penrhyn Bay, adjoining to NW of Colwyn Bay. **47 G4** SH8481.
Rhos-y-brithdir *Powys* ***Settlement***, 2m/4km N of Llanfyllin. SJ1323.
Rhos-y-brwyner *Flints.* ***Settlement***, 2m/3km SE of Buckley. **48 B6** SJ2961.
Rhos-y-garth *Cere.* ***Locality***, 2m/3km S of Llanilar. **27 F1** SN6372.
Rhos-y-gwaliau *Gwyn.* ***Hamlet***, 1m/2km SE of Bala. **37 J2** SH9434.
Rhos-y-llan *Gwyn.* ***Settlement***, 1km N of Tudweiliog. **36 B2** SH2337.
Rhos-y-llyn *Pembs.* ***Locality***, 6m/10km SW of Newcastle Emlyn. SN2432.
Rhos-y-mawn *Conwy* ***Settlement***, 1m/2km SW of Llangernyw. **47 G6** SH8566.
Rhos-y-meirch *Powys* ***Settlement***, 2m/3km S of Knighton. **28 B2** SO2769.
Rhosaman *Carmar.* ***Settlement***, 7m/11km E of Ammanford. SN7313.
Rhoscefnhir *I.o.A.* ***Village***, on Anglesey, 1m/2km S of Pentraeth. SH5276.
Rhoscolyn *I.o.A.* ***Village***, small village and resort at S end of Holy Island, Anglesey. **46 A5** SH2675.
Rhoscrowdder *Pembs.* *Welsh form of Rhoscrowther, qv.*
Rhoscrowther (Rhoscrowdder). *Pembs.* ***Village***, 2m/4km N of Castlemartin. **16 C4** SM9002.
Rhosesmor *Flints.* ***Village***, 2m/3km W of Northop. **48 B6** SJ2168.
Rhosfach *Pembs.* ***Hamlet***, 1m/2km N of Llangolman. SN1128.
Rhosgadfan *Gwyn.* ***Hamlet***, 4m/6km S of Caernarfon. **46 D7** SH5057.
Rhosgoch *I.o.A.* ***Hamlet***, 3m/5km SW of Amlwch, Anglesey. **46 C4** SH4089.
Rhosgoch *Powys* ***Hamlet***, 4m/7km NW of Hay-on-Wye. **28 A4** SO1847.

Rhoshirwaun *Gwyn.* ***Hamlet***, 2m/4km NE of Aberdaron. **36 A3** SH1929.

Rhoslan *B.Gwent* ***Locality***, 1m/2km NE of Tredegar. SO1410.

Rhoslan *Gwyn.* ***Hamlet***, 2m/3km NW of Criccieth. **36 D1** SH4840.

Rhoslefain *Gwyn.* ***Hamlet***, 4m/6km N of Tywyn. **36 E5** SH5705.

Rhosllanerchrugog *Wrex.* Population: 12,879. ***Suburb***, urban locality 4m/6km SW of Wrexham. **38 B1** SJ2946.

Rhosmaen *Carmar.* ***Village***, 1m/2km NE of Llandeilo. **17 K2** SN6222.

Rhosmeirch *I.o.A.* ***Hamlet***, on Anglesey, 1m/2km N of Llangefni. **46 C5** SH4677.

Rhosneigr *I.o.A.* ***Small town***, small resort on W coast of Anglesey to SE of Valley Airfield. **46 B5** SH3173.

Rhosnesni *Wrex.* ***Suburb***, 1m/2km E of Wrexham town centre. **48 C7** SJ3551.

Rhosrobin *Wrex.* ***Suburb***, 1m/2km N of Wrexham. SJ3252.

Rhossili *Swan.* ***Village***, at W end of Gower peninsula, near S end of Rhossili Bay. **17 H6** SS4188.

Rhossili Bay *Swan.* ***Bay***, sandy bay on W end of Gower peninsula, extending N from Worms Head to Burry Holms. Rhossili village is near its S end. **17 H6** SS4188.

Rhossili Down *Swan.* ***Large natural feature***, National Trust property, inland from Rhossili Bay, dominant feature of W end of Gower. **17 H6** SS4290.

Rhosson *Pembs.* ***Hamlet***, 1m/2km W of St. David's. **16 A2** SM7225.

Rhostryfan *Gwyn.* ***Village***, 3m/5km S of Caernarfon. **46 C7** SH4957.

Rhostyllen *Wrex.* Population: 1803. ***Village***, 2m/3km SW of Wrexham. **38 C1** SJ3148.

Rhosybol *I.o.A.* ***Village***, on Anglesey, 3m/5km S of Amlwch. **46 C4** SH4288.

Rhosycaerau *Pembs.* ***Hamlet***, 2m/4km W of Fishguard. SM9137.

Rhosygilwen *Pembs.* ***Settlement***, 4m/6km SE of Cardigan. SN2040.

Rhu *Arg. & B.* Population: 1282. ***Village***, and resort on E side of Gare Loch, 2m/3km NW of Helensburgh. **74 A2** NS2683.

Rhuallt *Denb.* ***Village***, 2m/4km E of St. Asaph. **47 J5** SJ0775.

Rhubodach *Arg. & B.* ***Locality***, on NE coast of Bute, opposite Colintraive, Argyll, across Kyles of Bute. Car and pedestrian ferry service to Colintraive. **73 J3** NS0273.

Rhuddall Heath *Ches.* ***Hamlet***, adjoining to SE of Tarporley. SJ5562.

Rhuddlan *Cere.* ***Locality***, 2m/3km W of Llanybydder. SN4943.

Rhuddlan *Denb.* Population: 3182. ***Small town***, 2m/4km SE of Rhyl. Formerly a port at mouth of River Clwyd. Remains of 13c castle (Cadw). Twt Hill (Cadw), to S, is motte of earlier Norman castle. **47 J5** SJ0278.

Rhuddlan Castle and Twt Hill *Denb.* ***Castle***, 13c castle (Cadw) built by Edward I on site of 11c motte and bailey in Rhuddlan, 2m/4km S of Rhyl. Besieged by Roundheads during Civil War and has been ruin since 1648. Twt Hill (Cadw) is small hill to SW with motte of Norman castle at summit. **47 J5** SJ0277.

Rhue *High.* ***Settlement***, on N shore of Loch Broom, 2m/4km NW of Ullapool. **95 G2** NH0997.

Rhulen *Powys* ***Settlement***, 3m/5km NW of Painscastle. **28 A4** SO1349.

Rhulen Hill *Powys* ***Mountain***, 3m/4km NW of Painscastle. Height 1509 feet or 460 metres. **28 A4** SO1348.

Rhum *High.* *Former spelling of Rum, qv.*

Rhumach *High.* ***Settlement***, 2m/3km SW of Arisaig, Lochaber district. **86 C6** NM6385.

Rhunahaorine *Arg. & B.* ***Settlement***, on W side of Kintyre, 2m/3km NE of Tayinloan. **73 F6** NR7048.

Rhunahaorine Point *Arg. & B.* ***Coastal feature***, headland on W coast of Kintyre, Argyll, opposite Gigha. **72 E6** NR6849.

Rhuthun *Denb.* *Welsh form of Ruthin, qv.*

Rhuthun *V. of Glam.* *Welsh form of Ruthin, qv.*

Rhyd *Gwyn.* ***Hamlet***, 2m/3km NW of Maentwrog. **37 F1** SH6341.

Rhyd *Powys* ***Settlement***, in Cwm Llŵyd, 3m/4km NE of Carno. **37 J5** SH9700.

Rhyd-Ddu *Gwyn.* ***Hamlet***, 3m/5km N of Beddgelert. **46 D7** SH5652.

Rhyd-Rosser *Cere.* ***Settlement***, 2m/3km SE of Llanrhystud. **26 E2** SN5667.

Rhyd-uchaf *Gwyn.* ***Hamlet***, 2m/3km NW of Bala. **37 J2** SH9037.

Rhyd-wen *Gwyn.* ***Settlement***, 4m/6km S of Bala. **37 J3** SH9229.

Rhyd-y-ceirw *Denb.* ***Settlement***, 2m/3km SW of Treuddyn. SJ2356.

Rhyd-y-clafdy *Gwyn.* ***Hamlet***, 3m/5km W of Pwllheli. **36 C2** SH3234.

Rhyd-y-foel *Conwy* ***Village***, 2m/4km W of Abergele. Hillfort to SE. **47 H5** SH9176.

Rhyd-y-fro *N.P.T.* ***Village***, 1m/2km NW of Pontardawe. **18 A1** SN7105.

Rhyd-y-groes *Gwyn.* ***Hamlet***, 3m/5km S of Bangor. SH5766.

Rhyd-y-gwin *Swan.* ***Settlement***, 2m/3km NW of Clydach. SN6703.

Rhyd-y-meirch *Mon.* ***Locality***, 4m/6km S of Abergavenny. **19 G1** SO3107.

Rhyd-y-pandy *Swan.* ***Settlement***, 2m/3km W of Clydach. SN6601.

Rhyd-y-sarn *Gwyn.* ***Hamlet***, 1km W of Ffestiniog. SH6942.

Rhyd-yr-onnen *Gwyn.* ***Settlement***, 2m/3km NE of Tywyn. **37 F5** SH6102.

Rhydaman *Carmar.* *Welsh form of Ammanford, qv.*

Rhydargaeau *Carmar.* ***Hamlet***, 4m/7km N of Carmarthen. **17 H2** SN4326.

Rhydcymerau *Carmar.* ***Hamlet***, 6m/9km S of Lampeter. **17 J1** SN5738.

Rhydd *Worcs.* ***Settlement***, 3m/5km E of Great Malvern. **29 H4** SO8345.

Rhydd Green *Worcs.* ***Locality***, on W bank of River Severn, 3m/5km E of Great Malvern. SO8345.

Rhyddhywel *Powys* ***Open space***, between three low summits, 5m/8km SE of Llandiloes. **37 K7** SO0280.

Rhydding *N.P.T.* ***Locality***, on N side of Neath across River Neath. **18 A2** SS7498.

Rhydgaled *Conwy* ***Settlement***, 4m/6km W of Denbigh. SH9964.

Rhydlanfair *Conwy* ***Locality***, 3m/5km W of Pentrefoelas. **47 G7** SH8252.

Rhydlewis *Cere.* ***Hamlet***, 5m/8km NE of Newcastle Emlyn. **26 C4** SN3447.

Rhydlios *Gwyn.* ***Settlement***, 3m/4km N of Aberdaron. **36 A2** SH1830.

Rhydlydan *Conwy* ***Hamlet***, 1m/2km E of Pentrefoelas. **47 G7** SH8950.

Rhydlydan *Powys* ***Settlement***, 2m/3km NE of Caersws. **37 K6** SO0593.

Rhydolion *Gwyn.* ***Settlement***, at SW end of Lleyn Peninsula, 2m/3km W of Abersoch. **36 B3** SH2827.

Rhydowen *Carmar.* ***Locality***, just E of Glandwr, 3m/5km SE of Crymych. SN1928.

Rhydowen *Cere.* ***Hamlet***, 3m/5km NE of Llandysul. **26 D4** SN4445.

Rhydri *Caerp.* *Welsh form of Rudry, qv.*

Rhydspence *Here.* ***Settlement***, 3m/5km N of Hay-on-Wye. **28 B4** SO2447.

Rhydtalog *Flints.* ***Settlement***, 7m/11km NW of Wrexham. **48 B7** SJ2355.

Rhydwaedlyd *Cardiff* ***Suburb***, 3m/5km N of Cardiff city centre. ST1681.

Rhydwyn *I.o.A.* ***Hamlet***, in N part of Anglesey, 4m/7km SW of Cemaes. **46 B4** SH3188.

Rhydycroesau *Shrop.* ***Hamlet***, on Welsh border, 3m/5km W of Oswestry. **38 B2** SJ2430.

Rhydyfelin *Cere.* ***Hamlet***, 2m/3km S of Aberystwyth. **26 E1** SN5979.

Rhydyfelin *R.C.T.* ***Locality***, 2m/3km SE of Pontypridd. **18 D3** ST0988.

Rhydymain *Gwyn.* ***Hamlet***, 6m/9km NE of Dolgellau. **37 G3** SH8022.

Rhydymeudwy *Denb.* ***Settlement***, 1m/2km E of Llanelidan. SJ1251.

Rhydymwyn *Flints.* ***Village***, 3m/4km NW of Mold. **48 B6** SJ2066.

Rhydywrach *Carmar.* ***Settlement***, 3m/5km NW of Whitland. **16 E3** SN1619.

Rhyl *Denb.* Population: 24,909. ***Town***, resort on North Wales coast, 8m/12km W of Point of Ayr, with many facilities for leisure and entertainment. Long, sandy beach. Botanical Gardens. Mouth of River Clwyd on W side of town. **47 J4** SJ0081.

Rhymney (Rhymni). ***River***, rising to N of Rhymney, flowing S down deeply incised Rhymney Valley. To N of Caerphilly river turns E, then meanders S below Machen, before flowing into mouth of River Severn on E side of Cardiff. **19 F3** ST2275.

Rhymney (Rhymni). *Caerp.* Population: 7991. ***Small town***, former industrial town based on local iron and coal deposits, on River Rhymney 4m/7km E of Merthyr Tydfil. **18 E1** SO1107.

Rhymney Valley ***Valley***, deeply incised valley carrying River Rhymney from Rhymney in N, past Bargoed and Hengoed, to Cardiff in S. **18 E2** ST1592.

Rhymni *Welsh form of Rhymney (river), qv.*

Rhymni *Caerp.* *Welsh form of Rhymney (town), qv.*

Rhyn *Shrop.* ***Settlement***, 1m/2km NE of Weston Rhyn. **38 C2** SJ3037.

Rhynd *P. & K.* ***Village***, 3m/5km SE of Perth. **82 C5** NO1520.

Rhynie *Aber.* ***Village***, 8m/13km S of Huntly. **90 C2** NJ4927.

Rhynie *High.* ***Settlement***, near E coast of Ross and Cromarty district, 1m/2km NE of Hill of Fearn. **97 F4** NH8479.

Ri Cruin Cairn *Arg. & B.* ***Historic/prehistoric site***, flat, circular cairn (Historic Scotland) of large water-washed stones at Slockavullin, 6m/10km NW of Lochgilphead. One of several cairns and ancient monuments in vicinity. **73 G1** NR8297.

Rib *Herts.* ***River***, rising N of Buntingford and flowing S into River Lea E of Hertford. **33 G7** TL3313.

Ribbesford *Worcs.* ***Village***, 1m/2km S of Bewdley. **29 G1** SO7874.

Ribble ***River***, rising on Gayle Moor to NE of Ribblehead Viaduct and flowing S to Settle and Long Preston, then SW to Preston and Irish Sea between Southport and Lytham St. Anne's. Tidal and navigable to seagoing vessels from Preston. **55 H7** SD2824.

Ribblehead Viaduct *N.Yorks.* ***Bridge***, tallest viaduct in Britain (156 feet or 53 metres high) carrying Settle to Carlisle railway line, 2m/3km NE of Chapel-le-Dale. SD7579.

Ribblesdale *N.Yorks.* ***Valley***, carrying River Ribble S from Horton in Ribblesdale to Hellifield. **56 D4** SD8062.

Ribbleton *Lancs.* ***Suburb***, 2m/4km NE of Preston town centre. **55 J6** SD5631.

Ribby *Lancs.* ***Settlement***, adjoining to E of Wrea Green, 1m/2km W of Kirkham. SD4031.

Ribchester *Lancs.* ***Village***, on River Ribble, 5m/8km N of Blackburn. Site of Roman fort of Bremetennacum. Museum of Roman antiquities (National Trust). **56 B6** SD6535.

Ribchester Roman Fort and Museum *Lancs.* ***Historic/prehistoric site***, Bremetennacum Roman fort to SW of Ribchester, on W side of River Ribble, 3m/5km SE of Longridge. Pillars at White Bull Inn are probably from Roman bath-house. Museum with fort relics. **56 B6** SD6435.

Riber Castle Wildlife Park *Derbys.* ***Leisure/recreation***, wildlife park surrounding ruins of 19c Riber Castle, 1km SE of Matlock. Includes collection of animals, rare and endangered, common and domestic, from around world. **51 F7** SK3059.

Ribigill *High.* ***Settlement***, 2m/3km SW of Tongue, Caithness district. **103 H3** NC5854.

Riby *Lincs.* ***Hamlet***, 6m/9km W of Grimsby. **52 E2** TA1807.

Riccal *N.Yorks.* ***River***, rising on North York Moors N of Helmsley and flowing SE into River Rye, 3m/4km E of Nunnington. **58 C1** SE7079.

Riccall *N.Yorks.* Population: 1949. ***Village***, 4m/6km N of Selby. **58 C6** SE6237.

Riccarton *E.Ayr.* ***Suburb***, on S side of Kilmarnock. **74 C7** NS4236.

Riccarton Hills *W.Loth.* ***Large natural feature***, small range of hills rising to 833 feet or 254 metres, SE of Linlithgow. **75 J3** NT0173.

Richards Castle *Here.* ***Village***, 3m/5km S of Ludlow. **28 D2** SO4969.

Richborough Castle *Kent* ***Castle***, remains of Roman fort (English Heritage), 2m/3km NW of Sandwich. Built on site of Rutupiae, Roman fort of the Saxon Shore, traditional landing place of Roman army. **25 K5** TR3260.

Richborough Roman Amphitheatre *Kent* ***Historic/prehistoric site***, unimposing feature (English Heritage) beyond Richborough castle fort walls, 1m/2km NW of Sandwich. **25 K5** TR3259.

Richings Park *Bucks.* Population: 1808. ***Village***, 4m/7km E of Slough. **22 D4** TQ0379.

Richmond *Gt.Lon.* ***Town***, on S bank of River Thames, 8m/13km SW of Charing Cross. Shopping centre, with two theatres. Henry VII died here, at royal palace, and Edward VIII was born at 18c White Lodge. Richmond Park, large open space where deer roam, to SE of town. TQ1774.

Richmond *N.Yorks.* Population: 7862. ***Small town***, attractive market town above River Swale, 11m/18km SW of Darlington. Remains of large Norman castle (English Heritage). Late 18c Georgian theatre is oldest in England. **62 C6** NZ1701.

Richmond *S.Yorks.* ***Suburb***, 3m/5km SE of Sheffield city centre. SK4085.

Richmond Castle *N.Yorks.* ***Castle***, Norman castle (English Heritage) with 100 foot towers, on N bank of River Swale on S side of Richmond. One of earliest stone halls in England, Scolland's Hall was built in 11c. **62 C6** NZ1700.

Richmond Hill *I.o.M.* ***Locality***, 3m/4km W of Douglas. SC3374.

Richmond Hill *S.Yorks.* ***Suburb***, on W side of Doncaster across River Don. SE5503.

Richmond Park *Gt.Lon.* ***Open space***, largest of royal parks at 2358 acres, created by Charles I in 1637, 1km SE of Richmond. **22 E4** TQ1973.

Richmond's Green *Essex* ***Hamlet***, 1m/2km SE of Thaxted. TL6229.

Rich's Holford *Som.* ***Hamlet***, 2m/3km S of Crowcombe. ST1434.

Rickarton *Aber.* ***Settlement***, 4m/7km NW of Stonehaven. **91 G6** NO8189.

Rickerby *Cumb.* ***Locality***, on N bank of River Eden, 1m/2km NE of Carlisle across river. NY4156.

Rickerscote *Staffs.* ***Suburb***, S district of Stafford. SJ9220.

Rickets Head *Pembs.* ***Coastal feature***, headland on E side of St. Brides Bay, 6m/10km W of Haverfordwest. **16 B3** SM8518.

Rickford *N.Som.* ***Village***, below N slopes of Mendip Hills, 1m/2km W of Blagdon. **19 H6** ST4859.

Rickinghall *Suff.* ***Village***, comprised of adjoining hamlets of Rickinghall Superior and Rickinghall Inferior, 6m/9km SW of Diss. **34 E1** TM0475.

Rickinghall Inferior *Suff.* *See Rickinghall.*

Rickinghall Superior *Suff.* *See Rickinghall.*

Rickleton *T. & W.* ***Suburb***, SW district of Washington. NZ2853.

Rickling *Essex* ***Village***, 6m/10km N of Bishop's Stortford. **33 H5** TL4931.

Rickling Green *Essex* ***Hamlet***, 6m/9km N of Bishop's Stortford. **33 J6** TL5029.

Rickmansworth *Herts.* Population: 10,767. ***Town***, commuter town on River Colne, 17m/28km NW of London. Moor Park is 18c mansion. **22 D2** TQ0594.

Riddell *Sc.Bord.* ***Hamlet***, 4m/6km SE of Selkirk. **70 A1** NT5124.

Riddings *Cumb.* ***Locality***, 4m/7km N of Longtown. NY4075.

Riddings *Derbys.* ***Locality***, 2m/4km SE of Alfreton. **51 G7** SK4252.

Riddlecombe *Devon* ***Village***, 5m/8km W of Chulmleigh. **6 E4** SS6114.

Riddlesden *W.Yorks.* ***Village***, 1m/2km NE of Keighley across River Aire. **57 F5** SE0842.

Riddlesworth *Norf.* ***Locality***, including Riddlesworth Hall School and Stud, 6m/10km E of Thetford. TL9681.

Riddrie *Glas.* ***Suburb***, 3m/4km E of Glasgow city centre. Contains HM prison (Barlinnie). NS6366.

Ridge *Dorset* ***Hamlet***, 1m/2km S of Wareham. **9 J6** SY9386.

Ridge *Herts.* ***Village***, 3m/4km W of Potters Bar. **23 F1** TL2100.

Ridge *Wilts.* ***Hamlet***, 2m/3km N of Tisbury. **9 J1** ST9531.

Ridge Green *Surr.* ***Village***, 2m/3km SE of Redhill. **23 G7** TQ3048.

Ridge Hill *Gt.Man.* ***Suburb***, 1km N of Stalybridge town centre. SJ9699.

Ridge Hill *Here.* ***Hill***, elongated hill rising to over 140 metres, 3m/4km S of Hereford. **28 E5** SO5035.

Ridge Lane *Warks.* ***Settlement***, 2m/3km SW of Atherstone town centre. **40 E6** SP2995.

Ridge Way ***Other feature of interest***, ancient trackway, running from Vale of Pewsey along N edge of Wiltshire and Berkshire Downs to River Thames valley at Streatley. SU3584.

Ridgebourne *Powys* ***Locality***, adjoining to S of Llandrindod Wells. **27 K2** SO0560.

Ridgehill *N.Som.* *Former name of Regil, qv.*

Ridgeway *Bristol* **Suburb**, 3m/4km NE of Bristol city centre. ST6275.
Ridgeway *Derbys.* **Settlement**, 3m/4km N of Belper. SK3651.
Ridgeway *Derbys.* **Village**, 5m/8km SE of Sheffield. **51 G4** SK4081.
Ridgeway *Newport* **Suburb**, 1m/2km W of Newport town centre. ST2988.
Ridgeway *Pembs.* **Locality**, adjoining to NW of Saundersfoot. SN1305.
Ridgeway *Stoke* **Settlement**, 2m/4km S of Biddulph. SJ8953.
Ridgeway Cross *Here.* **Settlement**, 4m/6km W of Great Malvern. **29 G4** SO7147.
Ridgeway Moor *Derbys.* **Village**, adjoining to S of Ridgeway, 5m/8km SE of Sheffield. SK4081.
Ridgewell *Essex* **Village**, 5m/8km SE of Haverhill. Site of Roman villa to SW. **34 B4** TL7340.
Ridgewood *E.Suss.* **Locality**, residential district to S of Uckfield. **13 H5** TQ4719.
Ridgmont *Beds.* **Village**, at N end of Woburn Park, 3m/4km NE of Woburn. **32 C5** SP9736.
Ridgway *Surr.* **Locality**, 1km S of West Byfleet, 2m/3km E of Woking. TQ0459.
Riding Gate *Som.* **Settlement**, 2m/3km NE of Wincanton. ST7329.
Riding Mill *Northumb.* **Village**, 3m/4km SE of Corbridge. **71 F7** NZ0161.
Ridley *Kent* **Settlement**, 3m/5km S of Longfield. **24 C5** TQ6163.
Ridley *Northumb.* **Locality**, 3m/5km W of Haydon Bridge. Morralee Wood (National Trust) are opposite, on far side of River Allen. NY7963.
Ridley Green *Ches.* **Settlement**, 2m/3km E of Bulkeley. SJ5554.
Ridleywood *Wrex.* **Hamlet**, 2m/3km S of Holt. **48 C7** SJ4051.
Ridlington *Norf.* **Village**, 2m/4km W of Happisburgh. **45 H2** TG3431.
Ridlington *Rut.* **Village**, 2m/4km NW of Uppingham. **42 B5** SK8402.
Ridlington Street *Norf.* **Hamlet**, 4m/6km E of North Walsham. TG3430.
Ridsdale *Northumb.* **Hamlet**, 6m/9km S of Otterburn. **70 E5** NY9084.
Riechip *P. & K.* **Settlement**, 1m/2km N of Butterstone. **82 B3** NO0647.
Rienachait *High.* **Settlement**, near W coast of Sutherland district, 1m/2km N of Stoer village. NC0429.
Riereach Burn *High.* **River**, rising as Allt Creag a' Chait on Carn nan Tri-tighearnan and flowing N past Creag an Daimh, then into Allt Dearg just S of Cawdor. **97 F7** NH8449.
Rievaulx *N.Yorks.* **Village**, 2m/4km W of Helmsley. Ruins of 12c-13c Cistercian abbey (English Heritage). **58 B1** SE5785.
Rievaulx Abbey *N.Yorks.* **Ecclesiastical building**, well-preserved ruins of 12c Cistercian abbey (English Heritage) in River Rye valley, 3m/4km W of Hemsley. **58 B1** SE5784.
Rievaulx Terrace *N.Yorks.* **Garden**, National Trust property above River Rye, with 18c garden temples and viewpoint, 2m/4km W of Hemsley. Garden also has display on 18c English landscaping, as well as terrace and woodlands. **58 B1** SE5784.
Rifail Loch *High.* **Lake/loch**, small loch 2m/3km SE of Syre, Caithness district. **104 C4** NC7142.
Rift House *Hart.* **Suburb**, in SW district of Hartlepool 1m/2km SW of town centre. NZ4930.
Rigg *D. & G.* **Village**, 2m/3km SW of Gretna Green. **69 H7** NY2966.
Rigg *High.* **Settlement**, 3m/4km NE of The Storr, Skye. **94 B6** NG5156.
Rigg Bay *D. & G.* *Alternative name for Cruggleton Bay, qv.*
Riggend *N.Lan.* **Settlement**, 3m/5km N of Airdrie. **75 F4** NS7670.
Riggs Moor *N.Yorks.* **Open space**, remote moorland between Wharfedale and Nidderdale, 4m/7km E of Kettlewell. **57 F2** SE0273.
Righoul *High.* **Settlement**, in Nairn district, 3m/5km S of Nairn. NH8851.
Rigifa *High.* **Settlement**, near N coast of Caithness district, 2m/3km S of St. John's Point. ND3072.
Rigmaden Park *Cumb.* **Settlement**, on W side of River Lune, 4m/6km N of Kirkby Lonsdale. **56 B1** SD6084.
Rigsby *Lincs.* **Hamlet**, 2m/3km W of Alford. **53 H5** TF4275.
Rigside *S.Lan.* **Hamlet**, 1m/2km S of Douglas Water. **75 G7** NS8734.
Riley Green *Lancs.* **Hamlet**, 2m/3km NW of Abbey Village and 4m/6km SW of Blackburn town centre. SD6225.
Rileyhill *Staffs.* **Settlement**, 1m/2km S of King's Bromley. **40 D4** SK1115.
Rilla Mill *Cornw.* **Village**, on River Lynher, 5m/7km NW of Callington. **4 C3** SX2973.
Rillaton *Cornw.* **Hamlet**, 5m/7km NW of Callington. SX2973.
Rillington *N.Yorks.* **Village**, 5m/7km E of Malton. **58 E2** SE8574.
Rimbleton *Fife* **Suburb**, central district of Glenrothes. NO2600.
Rimington *Lancs.* **Village**, 3m/4km SW of Gisburn. **56 D5** SD8045.
Rimpton *Som.* **Village**, 3m/5km S of Sparkford. **9 F2** ST6021.
Rimsdale Burn *High.* **River**, rising N of Lochan Sgeireach and flowing S into Loch Rimsdale, Caithness district. **104 C4** NC7339.
Rimswell *E.Riding* **Village**, 2m/3km W of Withernsea. **59 K7** TA3128.
Rinaston *Pembs.* **Settlement**, 2m/3km E of Wolf's Castle. **16 C2** SM9825.
Ring o' Bells *Lancs.* **Hamlet**, 1m/2km SE of Burscough Bridge, on Leeds and Liverpool Canal. SD4510.
Ring of Brodgar *Ork.* **Historic/prehistoric site**, ancient stone circle (Historic Scotland) on tongue of land between Loch of Harray and Loch of Stenness 4m/7km W of Finstown, Mainland. Twenty-seven stones are still standing out of an estimated original number of sixty. **107 B6** HY2913.
Ringdoo Point *D. & G.* **Coastal feature**, point on E side of Wigtown Bay, 6m/9km SW of Kirkcudbright. **65 F6** NX6045.
Ringford *D. & G.* **Village**, 4m/7km N of Kirkcudbright. **65 G5** NX6857.
Ringinglow *S.Yorks.* **Hamlet**, 4m/7km SW of Sheffield city centre. SK2983.
Ringland *Newport* **Suburb**, 3m/5km E of Newport town centre. ST3588.
Ringland *Norf.* **Village**, 7m/11km NW of Norwich. **45 F4** TG1314.
Ringles Cross *E.Suss.* **Locality**, 1m/2km N of Uckfield. **13 H4** TQ4722.
Ringley *Gt.Man.* **Locality**, 1m/2km E of Kearsley. SD7605.
Ringmer *E.Suss.* Population: 3119. **Village**, below South Downs, 3m/4km NE of Lewes. **13 H5** TQ4412.
Ringmore *Devon* **Suburb**, on S side of River Teign estuary, on W side of Shaldon, 4m/7km E of Newton Abbot. SX9272.
Ringmore *Devon* **Village**, 4m/6km S of Modbury. **5 G6** SX6545.
Ringorm *Moray* **Locality**, comprises Upper Ringorm and Nether Ringorm, 1m/2km NW of Charlestown of Aberlour. **97 K7** NJ2644.
Ring's End *Cambs.* **Hamlet**, 1km S of Guyhirn. **43 G5** TF3902.
Ringsfield *Suff.* **Village**, 2m/3km SW of Beccles. **45 J7** TM4088.
Ringsfield Corner *Suff.* **Hamlet**, 1m/2km S of Ringsfield and 3m/4km SW of Beccles. **45 J7** TM4088.
Ringshall *Herts.* **Settlement**, 4m/7km NE of Tring. **32 C7** SP9814.
Ringshall *Suff.* **Hamlet**, 4m/6km S of Stowmarket. **34 E3** TM0452.
Ringshall Stocks *Suff.* **Hamlet**, 5m/7km S of Stowmarket. **34 E3** TM0551.
Ringstead *Norf.* **Village**, 2m/4km E of Hunstanton. **44 B1** TF7040.
Ringstead *Northants.* **Village**, 2m/4km S of Thrapston. **32 C1** SP9875.
Ringstead Bay *Dorset* **Bay**, 1km NW of White Nothe and 5m/8km NE of Weymouth. Bay surrounded by steep cliffs (National Trust), and below Burning Cliff. **9 G6** SY7581.
Ringwood *Hants.* Population: 11,959. **Town**, market town on E bank of River Avon, with expansion eastwards, 10m/16km NE of Bournemouth. 18c chapel is now a museum. **10 C4** SU1405.
Ringwood Forest **Forest/woodland**, on border of Dorset and Hampshire, 2m/3km NW of Ringwood. 4m/6km long, N to S, and 2m/3km wide. **10 C4** SU1108.
Ringwould *Kent* **Village**, 3m/5km S of Deal. **15 J3** TR3648.
Rinloan *Aber.* **Settlement**, 6m/9km NW of Ballater. **89 K4** NJ2900.
Rinmore *Aber.* **Settlement**, 5m/8km NE of Strathdon. **90 C3** NJ4117.
Rinn Druim Tallig *W.Isles* **Coastal feature**, headland on NW coast of Isle of Lewis, 2m/3km NE of Bragar. **100 E2** NB3150.
Rinn Thorbhais *Arg. & B.* **Coastal feature**, headland at SW end of Tiree. **78 A4** NL9340.
Rinnigill *Ork.* **Settlement**, on E coast of Hoy, 1m/2km SW of Fara across strait. **107 C8** ND3193.
Rinns of Galloway (Also spelled Rhinns of Galloway.) *D. & G.* **Coastal feature**, anvil-shaped peninsula at SW extremity of Scotland, running some 28m/45km N to S. Isthmus 6m/10km wide, from Loch Ryan to Luce Bay, connects peninsula to rest of mainland. **64 A5** NX0552.
Rinns of Islay (Also spelled Rhinns of Islay.) *Arg. & B.* **Coastal feature**, peninsula on W side of Islay, with headland Rinns Point at its S end. **72 A5** NR2157.
Rinns of Kells *D. & G.* *Alternative spelling of Rhinns of Kells, qv.*
Rinns Point *Arg. & B.* **Coastal feature**, headland at S end of Rinns of Islay. **72 A5** NR2157.
Rinsey *Cornw.* **Hamlet**, 3m/4km NW of Porthleven. **2 C6** SW5927.
Rinsey Croft *Cornw.* **Hamlet**, 4m/6km W of Helston. SW6028.
Rip Row *Lancs.* **Locality**, adjoining to N of Whittle-le-Woods. SD5822.
Ripe *E.Suss.* **Village**, 5m/8km W of Hailsham. **13 J6** TQ5110.
Ripley *Derbys.* Population: 18,310. **Town**, market town, 10m/15km N of Derby. Former industries included coalmining, iron and clay. **51 G7** SK3950.
Ripley *Hants.* **Hamlet**, 4m/6km N of Christchurch. **10 C5** SZ1698.
Ripley *N.Yorks.* **Village**, 18c estate village, 3m/5km N of Harrogate. Castle rebuilt 16c-18c; gatehouse dates from 15c. **57 H3** SE2860.
Ripley *Surr.* **Village**, 4m/7km SW of Cobham. **22 D6** TQ0556.
Ripley Castle *N.Yorks.* **Castle**, in Ripley Park, 4m/6km N of Harrogate. Re-built in 1780, with gardens designed by 'Capability' Brown. 15c gatehouse and 16c tower remain. Grounds contain National Collection of Hyacinths, spring bulbs and tropical plants. **57 H3** SE2860.
Riplingham *E.Riding* **Settlement**, 3m/4km E of South Cave. **59 F6** SE9631.
Ripon *N.Yorks.* Population: 13,806. **City**, ancient cathedral city (Royal Charter granted 886) at confluence of Rivers Laver, Skell, and Ure, 10m/16km N of Harrogate. Some light industry. Cathedral, in mixture of styles, built above 7c crypt which is considered to be oldest in England. Many Georgian and medieval buildings. Racecourse 1m/2km SE. **57 J2** SE3171.
Ripon Cathedral *N.Yorks.* **Ecclesiastical building**, in Ripon, 12c, with Saxon crypt. Noted for choir stalls and range of building styles from Saxon to Perpendicular. **57 J2** SE3171.
Rippingale *Lincs.* **Village**, 5m/8km N of Bourne. **42 E3** TF0927.
Ripple *Kent* **Village**, 2m/4km SW of Deal. **15 J2** TR3550.
Ripple *Worcs.* **Village**, 3m/5km N of Tewkesbury. **29 H5** SO8637.
Rippon Tor *Devon* **Mountain**, 2m/3km SE of Widecombe in the Moor, in Dartmoor National Park. Height 1551 feet or 473 metres. **5 H3** SX7475.
Ripponden *W.Yorks.* Population: 2855. **Small town**, on River Ryburn, 5m/8km SW of Halifax. **50 C1** SE0319.
Risabus *Arg. & B.* **Settlement**, on The Oa, Islay, 3m/5km NE of Mull of Oa. **72 B6** NR3143.
Risay *W.Isles* **Island**, islet at entrance to Loch Leurbost, E coast of Isle of Lewis. NB3923.
Risbury *Here.* **Hamlet**, 4m/7km SE of Leominster. **28 E3** SO5455.
Risby *E.Riding* **Settlement**, 1m/2km SW of Bentley. TA0034.
Risby *N.Lincs.* **Locality**, 1m/2km W of Appleby, 4m/6km NE of Scunthorpe. SE9314.
Risby *Suff.* **Village**, 4m/7km NW of Bury St. Edmunds. **34 B2** TL7966.
Risby Warren *N.Lincs.* **Open space**, containing two small lakes, 3m/5km NE of Scunthorpe. **52 C1** SE9213.
Risca (Rhisga). *Caerp.* Population: 15,124. **Town**, 5m/7km NW of Newport. **19 F2** ST2391.
Rise *E.Riding* **Hamlet**, 5m/8km SW of Hornsea. **59 H5** TA1542.
Rise End *Derbys.* **Settlement**, 1km NW of Wirksworth. SK2855.
Riseden *Kent* **Hamlet**, 1km NE of Kilndown. TQ7035.
Risegate *Lincs.* **Village**, 5m/8km N of Spalding. **43 F2** TF2129.
Riseholme *Lincs.* **Hamlet**, 3m/4km N of Lincoln. Late 18c hall, enlarged in 19c. Lake in park. SK9875.
Risehow *Cumb.* **Locality**, 1m/2km S of Maryport. NY0234.
Riseley *Beds.* **Village**, 8m/13km N of Bedford. **32 D2** TL0462.
Riseley *W'ham* **Village**, 6m/10km S of Reading. **22 A5** SU7263.
Risga *High.* **Island**, islet in Loch Sunart in Lochaber district, between islands of Carna and Oronsay. **79 H2** NM6160.
Rishangles *Suff.* **Village**, 4m/6km N of Debenham. **35 F2** TM1668.
Rishton *Lancs.* Population: 6773. **Small town**, 3m/5km NE of Blackburn. Saxon origin. **56 C6** SD7230.
Rishworth *W.Yorks.* **Village**, below E slopes of Rishworth Moor, 1m/2km S of Ripponden. **50 C1** SE0318.
Rishworth Moor *W.Yorks.* **Open space**, moorland to S of Soyland Moor and containing Green Withens Reservoir, 3m/5km E of Littleborough. **49 J1** SD9817.
Rising Bridge *Lancs.* **Locality**, 1m/2km N of Haslingden. SD7825.
Rising Sun *Cornw.* **Hamlet**, 3m/4km E of Callington. SX3970.
Risinghurst *Oxon.* **Suburb**, 3m/5km E of Oxford city centre. SP5607.
Risley *Derbys.* **Village**, 2m/4km NW of Long Eaton. **41 G2** SK4635.
Risley *Warr.* Population: 12,800. **Suburb**, in NE part of Warrington. **49 F3** SJ6692.
Risley Moss Country Park *Warr.* **Leisure/recreation**, 4m/7km NE of Warrington town centre. Demonstration peat bog is main attraction of this park which also boasts woodland, pools, nature trails and wide variety of wildlife. **49 F3** SJ6691.
Rispain *D. & G.* **Historic/prehistoric site**, earthworks of ancient rectangular camp (Historic Scotland), 1m/2km W of Whithorn. **64 E7** NX4239.
Risplith *N.Yorks.* **Hamlet**, 1km NW of Sawley. **57 H3** SE2468.
Rispond *High.* **Settlement**, on Rispond Bay, W side of mouth of Loch Eriboll, N coast of Sutherland district. **103 G2** NC4565.
Ristol *High.* *See Isle Ristol.*
Rivacre Valley Country Park *Ches.* **Leisure/recreation**, 300 acre linear park in NW district of Ellesmere Port. Opportunities for walking and orienteering. **48 C5** SJ3777.
Rivar *Wilts.* **Settlement**, 1m/2km S of Shalbourne. **21 G5** SU3161.
Rivenhall *Essex* **Hamlet**, 2m/3km N of Witham. Site of Roman settlement. **34 C7** TL8217.
Rivenhall End *Essex* **Hamlet**, 1km SE of Rivenhall and 1m/2km NE of Witham. **34 C7** TL8316.
River *Kent* **Suburb**, of Dover, 2m/3km NW of town centre. TR2943.
River *W.Suss.* **Hamlet**, 2m/4km NW of Petworth. **12 C4** SU9422.
River Bank *Cambs.* **Settlement**, on E bank of River Cam, 8m/13km NE of Cambridge. **33 J2** TL5368.
River Bridge *Som.* **Settlement**, by River Brue, 4m/7km NE of Puriton. **19 G7** ST3744.
Riverford Bridge *Devon* **Settlement**, on River Dart, 3m/4km NW of Totnes. **5 H4** SX7763.
Riverhead *Kent* **Suburb**, to NW of Sevenoaks. **23 J6** TQ5156.
River's Vale *Derbys.* **Suburb**, 1km W of Buxton town centre. SK0473.
Riverside *Cardiff* **Suburb**, of Cardiff 1km SW of city centre across River Taff. ST1776.
Riverside *Plym.* **Suburb**, NW district of Plymouth beside River Tamar, just below the road and railway bridges connecting Plymouth and Saltash. SX4358.
Riverside *Stir.* **Suburb**, to E of Stirling town centre and bordering S bank of River Forth. NS8094.
Riverton *Devon* **Settlement**, 5m/8km NW of South Molton. SS6330.
Riverview Park *Kent* **Suburb**, SE district of Gravesend. TQ6671.
Rivington *Lancs.* **Village**, 2m/3km N of Horwich. **49 F1** SD6214.
Roa Island *Cumb.* **Locality**, at end of peninsula, 3m/5km SE of Barrow-in-Furness. **55 F3** SD2364.

R

Roach *Essex* ***River***, rising to W of Rochford and flowing E to W side of Foulness Island, then N into River Crouch. **25 F2** TQ9894.
Roach Bridge *Lancs.* ***Settlement***, at crossing of River Darwen, 3m/5km E of Preston town centre. SD5928.
Road Green *Norf.* ***Settlement***, 1m/2km E of Hempnall. TM2693.
Road Research Laboratory *Brack.F.* *See Crowthorne.*
Road Weedon *Northants.* ***Hamlet***, adjoining to NE of Weedon Bec, 4m/7km SE of Daventry. SP6359.
Roade *Northants.* Population: 2239. ***Village***, 5m/9km S of Northampton. **31 J3** SP7551.
Roadford Reservoir *Devon* ***Reservoir***, 3m/5km SE of Ashwater. **6 C6** SX4291.
Roadhead *Cumb.* ***Hamlet***, 9m/14km N of Brampton. **70 A6** NY5174.
Roadside *High.* ***Settlement***, in Caithness district, 5m/9km SE of Thurso. **105 G2** ND1560.
Roadside *Ork.* ***Settlement***, on Sanday, 6m/10km SW of Tafts Ness. **106 F3** HY6841.
Roadside of Garlogie *Aber.* ***Locality***, strung out along road leading E from Garlogie, 3m/5km E of Echt. NJ7805.
Roadside of Kinneff *Aber.* ***Village***, near E coast, 3m/5km N of Inverbervie. **91 G7** NO8476.
Roadwater *Som.* ***Village***, on Exmoor, 4m/6km SW of Watchet. **7 J2** ST0338.
Roag *High.* ***Settlement***, on Skye, 3m/4km SE of Dunvegan. **93 H7** NG2744.
Roan Fell ***Mountain***, straddling border of Dumfries & Galloway and Scottish Borders, 4m/7km NW of Newcastleton. Height 1863 feet or 568 metres. **69 K4** NY4593.
Roan Head *Ork.* ***Coastal feature***, headland on NE coast of Flotta. **107 C8** ND3896.
Roan Island *High.* *Alternative name for Eilean nan Ròn, qv.*
Roana Bay *Ork.* ***Bay***, 1m/2km N of Point of Ayre, Mainland. **107 E7** HY5805.
Roanheads *Aber.* ***Suburb***, coastal district of Peterhead. NK1346.
Roareim *W.Isles* ***Island***, one of Flannan Isles group, lying 2m/3km W of main island, Eilean Mòr, and on N side of Eilean a' Ghobha. NA6946.
Roast Green *Essex* ***Hamlet***, 4m/7km W of Newport. TL4532.
Roath (Y Rhath). *Cardiff* ***Suburb***, 1m/2km NE of Cardiff city centre. **19 F4** ST1977.
Rob Roy's Grave *Stir.* ***Other feature of interest***, grave of Rob Roy who died in 1734 in Balquhidder, 4m/6km SW of Lochearnhead. **81 G5** NN5321.
Robert Law *S.Lan.* ***Mountain***, 3m/5km NE of Douglas. Height 1332 feet or 406 metres. **75 G7** NS8732.
Roberton *Sc.Bord.* ***Village***, on Borthwick Water, 5m/7km W of Hawick. **69 K2** NT4314.
Roberton *S.Lan.* ***Village***, in Upper Clydedale, 4m/6km N of Abington. **68 E1** NS9428.
Roberton Burn *S.Lan.* ***River***, rising as Standing Burn between Scaur Hill and Wildshaw Hill, and flowing E to join River Clyde to E of Roberton. **68 D1** NS9528.
Robertsbridge *E.Suss.* Population: 1923. ***Village***, 5m/8km N of Battle. **14 C5** TQ7323.
Robertstown *Moray* ***Settlement***, 3m/5km W of Craigellachie. **97 K7** NJ2444.
Robertstown *R.C.T.* ***Suburb***, in N part of Aberdare. SO0003.
Roberttown *W.Yorks.* ***Village***, 1m/2km SW of Liversedge. **57 G7** SE1922.
Robeston Back *Pembs.* ***Hamlet***, 1m/2km W of Robeston Wathen and 3m/4km NW of Narberth. SN0715.
Robeston Cross *Pembs.* ***Settlement***, 2m/3km NW of Milford Haven. **16 B4** SM8809.
Robeston Wathen *Pembs.* ***Village***, 2m/3km NW of Narberth. **16 D3** SN0815.
Robeston West *Pembs.* ***Hamlet***, adjoining to NW of Robeston Cross, 3m/5km NW of Milford Haven. SM8809.
Robin Hill *Staffs.* ***Settlement***, 1m/2km E of Biddulph. SJ9057.
Robin Hill Country Park *I.o.W.* ***Leisure/recreation***, 80 acres of downland, 3m/4km E of Newport. Includes an open animal park, woodland and outdoor pursuits. **11 G6** SZ5388.
Robin Hood *Derbys.* ***Settlement***, 2m/3km E of Baslow. **50 E5** SK2772.
Robin Hood *Lancs.* ***Hamlet***, 3m/5km W of Standish. SD5211.
Robin Hood *W.Yorks.* ***Hamlet***, 4m/7km N of Wakefield. **57 J7** SE3227.
Robin Hood's Bay *N.Yorks.* ***Village***, small North Sea coast resort and fishing village on bay of same name, 5m/8km SE of Whitby. **63 J2** NZ9505.
Robinhood End *Essex* ***Settlement***, 3m/4km NE of Finchingfield. TL7036.
Robins *W.Suss.* ***Settlement***, 3m/5km NW of Midhurst. **12 B4** SU8425.
Robinson *Cumb.* ***Mountain***, on Derwent Fells, 3m/5km NW of Seatoller. Height 2417 feet or 737 metres. **60 D5** NY2016.
Robinson's End *Warks.* ***Suburb***, in W part of Nuneaton. SP3191.
Robinswood Hill Country Park *Glos.* ***Leisure/recreation***, country park adjacent to S of Gloucester. Waymarked walks and wildlife information centre. **29 H7** SO8314.
Roborough *Devon* ***Village***, 5m/9km SE of Great Torrington. **6 D4** SS5717.
Roborough *Plym.* ***Village***, 5m/8km NE of Plymouth. Plymouth City Airport to S. **5 F4** SX5062.
Robroyston *Glas.* ***Suburb***, 3m/5km NE of Glasgow city centre. NS6368.
Roby *Mersey.* ***Town***, 6m/10km E of Liverpool. **48 D3** SJ4390.
Roby Mill *Lancs.* ***Hamlet***, 4m/7km W of Wigan. **48 E2** SD5107.
Rocester *Staffs.* Population: 1432. ***Village***, on River Dove, 4m/6km N of Uttoxeter, on site of Roman settlement. **40 D2** SK1139.
Roch ***River***, rising N of Littleborough and flowing SW, through Littleborough and Rochdale, into River Irwell, S of Bury. SD8007.
Roch (Y Garn). *Pembs.* ***Village***, 6m/10km NW of Haverfordwest. Restored 13c castle or tower house. **16 B2** SM8821.
Roch Bridge *Pembs.* ***Hamlet***, on Brandy Brook, 1m/2km N of Roch. SM8722.
Roch Gate *Pembs.* ***Settlement***, adjoining to W of Roch. SM8720.
Rochallie *P. & K.* ***Settlement***, 1km E of Bridge of Cally. **82 C2** NO1551.
Rochdale *Gt.Man.* Population: 94,313. ***Town***, former cotton town on River Roch, 10m/16km NE of Manchester. Restored 12c parish church. Birthplace of Co-operative movement, with first Co-op opened in Toad Lane in 1844 by Rochdale Pioneers. Headquarters of Co-operative Retail Services. **49 H1** SD8913.
Roche *Cornw.* ***Village***, on N edge of china clay district, 5m/8km N of St. Austell. **3 G2** SW9860.
Roche Abbey *S.Yorks.* ***Ecclesiastical building***, 12c Cistercian abbey (English Heritage) in grounds laid out in 18c by 'Capability' Brown, 2m/3km SE of Maltby. **51 H4** SK5489.
Rochester *Med.* Population: 23,971. ***City***, ancient port, cathedral and commercial city on River Medway, 28m/46km E of London. Ruined keep (English Heritage) of Norman castle. Cathedral displays architectural styles of many periods. **24 D5** TQ7468.
Rochester *Northumb.* ***Hamlet***, 4m/7km NW of Otterburn. Site of Roman fort of Bremenium to N. **70 D4** NY8398.
Rochester Castle *Med.* ***Castle***, Norman fortress (English Heritage), begun in 1087, in centre of Rochester. Two ruined towers remain. **24 D5** TQ7368.
Rochester Cathedral *Med.* ***Ecclesiastical building***, in Rochester. Begun in 1080, with additions from 12c and 14c. **24 D5** TQ7468.
Rochford *Essex* Population: 15,081. ***Town***, old market town, 3m/5km N of Southend-on-Sea. Parish contains most of London Southend Airport. **24 E2** TQ8790.
Rochford *Worcs.* ***Village***, on River Teme, 2m/3km E of Tenbury Wells. **29 F2** SO6268.
Rock *Caerp.* ***Settlement***, 1km N of Blackwood. **18 E2** ST1798.
Rock *Cornw.* ***Village***, opposite Padstow across estuary of River Camel. **3 G1** SW9476.
Rock *Northumb.* ***Village***, 5m/7km N of Alnwick. **71 H1** NU2020.
Rock *Worcs.* Population: 1283. ***Village***, 4m/7km SW of Bewdley. **29 G1** SO7371.
Rock Ferry *Mersey.* ***Suburb***, 2m/3km S of Birkenhead town centre, on banks of River Mersey. **48 C4** SJ3386.
Rock Hill *Worcs.* ***Suburb***, in SW part of Bromsgrove. SO9569.
Rock Savage *Halton* ***Suburb***, 1m/2km S of Runcorn. SJ5180.
Rockall *W.Isles* ***Island***, small uninhabited island lying 186m/300km W of St. Kilda. Height is about 63 feet or 19 metres, summit being surmounted by a navigation light installed in 1972.
Rockbeare *Devon* ***Village***, 5m/8km W of Ottery St. Mary. **7 J6** SY0195.
Rockbourne *Hants.* ***Village***, 3m/5km NW of Fordingbridge. **10 C3** SU1118.
Rockbourne Down *Hants.* ***Open space***, hillslope 2m/3km NW of Rockbourne. **10 B2** SU1021.
Rockbourne Roman Villa *Hants.* ***Historic/prehistoric site***, 1km SE of Rockbourne. Extensive courtyard villa with over 70 rooms. Dates from 1c, with stone construction in 2c. **10 C3** SU1217.
Rockcliffe *Cumb.* ***Village***, 4m/7km NW of Carlisle. **69 J7** NY3561.
Rockcliffe *D. & G.* ***Village***, on E side of Rough Firth, 5m/8km S of Dalbeattie. National Trust for Scotland properties in vicinity include Mote of Mark, site of ancient hillfort, and Rough Island, bird sanctuary in Rough Firth to S of village. **65 J5** NX8453.
Rockcliffe Cross *Cumb.* ***Hamlet***, 1m/2km NW of Rockcliffe. NY3462.
Rockcliffe Marsh *Cumb.* ***Marsh/bog***, marshland at head of Solway Firth, 2m/3km S of Gretna. **69 J7** NY3263.
Rocken End *I.o.W.* ***Coastal feature***, headland at SE end of Chale Bay. **11 F7** SZ4975.
Rockfield *Arg. & B.* ***Settlement***, on Kintyre, 1km SW of Claonaig. **73 G5** NR8655.
Rockfield *High.* ***Settlement***, on E coast of Ross and Cromarty district, 4m/6km SW of Tarbat Ness. **97 G3** NH9282.
Rockfield *Mon.* ***Village***, 2m/3km NW of Monmouth. **28 D7** SO4814.
Rockford *Hants.* ***Settlement***, on edge of New Forest, 2m/3km NE of Ringwood. SU1608.
Rockgreen *Shrop.* ***Locality***, 1m/2km NE of Ludlow. SO5275.
Rockham Bay *Devon* ***Bay***, on N coast, between Bull Point and Morte Point. **6 C1** SS4546.
Rockhampton *S.Glos.* ***Village***, 2m/4km NE of Thornbury. **19 K2** ST6593.
Rockhead *Cornw.* ***Hamlet***, 2m/3km NW of Camelford. **4 A2** SX0784.
Rockingham *Northants.* ***Village***, above River Welland valley, 3m/4km NW of Corby. Remains of Norman castle. **42 B6** SP8691.
Rockingham Castle *Northants.* ***Castle***, in Rockingham, to NW of Corby. Motte built by William the Conqueror, and mentioned in Domesday Book. Present building is mainly Elizabethan, but Norman gateway with crenellated round towers survives. Includes 12 acres of formal and wild gardens. **42 B6** SP8691.
Rockland All Saints *Norf.* ***Village***, 4m/6km W of Attleborough. **44 D6** TL9996.
Rockland St. Mary *Norf.* ***Village***, 6m/10km SE of Norwich. **45 H5** TG3104.
Rockland St. Peter *Norf.* ***Village***, 4m/6km NW of Attleborough. **44 D6** TL9997.
Rockley *Notts.* ***Hamlet***, 2m/4km NW of Tuxford. SK7174.
Rockley *Wilts.* ***Hamlet***, 3m/4km NW of Marlborough. **20 E4** SU1671.
Rockliffe *Lancs.* ***Locality***, adjoining to SE of Bacup. SD8722.
Rockside *Arg. & B.* ***Settlement***, on Rinns of Islay, 1m/2km S of Loch Gorm. **72 A4** NR2263.
Rockvilla *Glas.* ***Suburb***, 1m/2km N of Glasgow city centre. NS5867.
Rockwell End *Bucks.* ***Settlement***, 3m/5km W of Marlow. **22 A3** SU7988.
Rockwell Green *Som.* Population: 1681. ***Locality***, 1m/2km W of Wellington. **7 K4** ST1220.
Rococo Garden *Glos.* ***Garden***, of Painswick House, 1km N of Painswick and 5m/9km S of Gloucester. Designed in early 18c, now restored; particularly noted for its snowdrops. **29 H7** SO8610.
Rodborough *Glos.* ***Suburb***, S district of Stroud. **20 B1** SO8404.
Rodbourne *Swin.* ***Suburb***, 1m/2km NW of Swindon town centre. SU1486.
Rodbourne *Wilts.* ***Village***, 3m/4km S of Malmesbury. **20 C3** ST9383.
Rodbridge Corner *Suff.* ***Settlement***, 2m/3km NW of Sudbury town centre. **34 C4** TL8643.
Rodd *Here.* ***Settlement***, 1m/2km S of Presteigne. **28 C2** SO3262.
Roddam *Northumb.* ***Settlement***, 1m/2km W of Wooperton. **71 F1** NU0220.
Rodden *Dorset* ***Hamlet***, 6m/9km NW of Weymouth. **9 F6** SY6184.
Roddlesworth *Lancs.* ***Settlement***, 2m/3km E of Withnell, 3m/5km W of Darwen. SD6521.
Roddymoor *Dur.* ***Locality***, adjoining to SW of Billy Row. NZ1536.
Rode *Som.* ***Village***, 4m/7km NE of Frome. **20 B6** ST8053.
Rode Heath *Ches.* Population: 2078. ***Village***, 1m/2km N of Alsager. **49 H7** SJ8057.
Rode Hill *Som.* ***Settlement***, adjoining to NE of Rode, 4m/7km NE of Frome. ST8053.
Rodeheath *Ches.* ***Settlement***, 3m/5km NE of Congleton. **49 H6** SJ8767.
Rodel (Gaelic form: Roghadal.) *W.Isles* ***Settlement***, at S end of South Harris, 1m/2km N of Renish Point across inlet of Loch Rodel. **93 F3** NG0483.
Roden ***River***, rising near Northwood and flowing SE through Wem, then S into River Tern 1m/2km SE of Withington. **38 E3** SJ5912.
Roden *Tel. & W.* ***Hamlet***, 6m/9km NW of Wellington. **38 E4** SJ5716.
Roderick Mackenzie's Memorial *High.* ***Other feature of interest***, in valley of River Moriston, 13m/21km W of Invermoriston. Commemorates Roderick Mackenzie who, in 1746, pretended to be Prince Charles Edward Stuart, and was killed by soldiers searching for the Prince after Culloden. **87 J3** NH2311.
Rodhuish *Som.* ***Hamlet***, on edge of Exmoor National Park, 3m/5km SE of Dunster. **7 J2** ST0139.
Rodington *Tel. & W.* ***Village***, on River Roden, 5m/7km NW of Wellington. **38 E4** SJ5814.
Rodington Heath *Shrop.* ***Settlement***, to NW of Rodington. SJ5714.
Rodley *Glos.* ***Hamlet***, on N bank of River Severn, 3m/4km SE of Westbury-on-Severn. **29 G7** SO7411.
Rodley *W.Yorks.* ***Locality***, 1m/2km SW of Horsforth across River Aire. SE2236.
Rodmarton *Glos.* ***Village***, 5m/8km NE of Tetbury. Site of Roman villa 1km NE. **20 C2** ST9498.
Rodmell *E.Suss.* ***Village***, 3m/4km S of Lewes. **13 H6** TQ4106.
Rodmersham *Kent* ***Village***, 2m/3km SE of Sittingbourne. **25 F5** TQ9261.
Rodmersham Green *Kent* ***Hamlet***, 1km W of Rodmersham and 1m/2km SE of Sittingbourne. TQ9161.
Rodney Stoke *Som.* ***Village***, below S slopes of Mendip Hills, 3m/4km SE of Cheddar. **19 H6** ST4850.
Rodsley *Derbys.* ***Village***, 4m/7km SE of Ashbourne. **40 E1** SK2040.
Rodway *Som.* ***Locality***, 3m/5km NW of Bridgwater. **19 F7** ST2540.
Rodway Hill *S.Glos.* ***Suburb***, S district of Mangotsfield, 5m/9km NE of Bristol. ST6675.
Rodwell *Dorset* ***Suburb***, at N end of Portland Harbour, 1km S of Weymouth town centre. SY6778.
Roe *Conwy* ***River***, rising 3m/5km S of Penmaenmawr and flowing E by Rowen into River Conwy to S of Caerhun. **47 F5** SH7769.
Roe Beck *Cumb.* ***River***, rising to NW of Skelton and flowing N to join River Caldew 2m/3km S of Dalston. **60 F3** NY3847.
Roe Cross *Gt.Man.* ***Hamlet***, 2m/3km SE of Stalybridge. SJ9896.
Roe Green *Gt.Man.* ***Suburb***, 2m/3km W of Swinton. SD7501.
Roe Green *Herts.* ***Hamlet***, 5m/7km E of Baldock. **33 G5** TL3133.
Roe Green *Herts.* ***Suburb***, of Hatfield near town centre. TL2208.
Roe Lee *B'burn.* ***Suburb***, 1m/2km N of Blackburn town centre. SD6830.
Roe Ness *Shet.* ***Coastal feature***, headland 2m/3km SE of Easter Skeld, Mainland. **109 C8** HU3242.
Roebuck Low *Gt.Man.* ***Settlement***, on hillside, to E of Strine Dale, 3m/4km NE of Oldham. SD9607.
Roecliffe *N.Yorks.* ***Village***, 1m/2km W of Boroughbridge. **57 J3** SE3765.
Roefield *Lancs.* ***Locality***, 1km W of Clitheroe. SD7341.
Roehampton *Gt.Lon.* ***Suburb***, in borough of Wandsworth, 6m/10km SW of Charing Cross. **23 F4** TQ2274.
Roer Water *Shet.* ***Lake/loch***, in N part of Mainland, 2m/3km NW of North Collafirth. **108 C4** HU3386.

R

Roesound *Shet.* ***Settlement***, on NE of Muckle Roe, at its connection to Mainland. **109 C6** HU3465.
Roestock *Herts.* ***Hamlet***, 2m/3km SW of Hatfield. TL2105.
Roffey *W.Suss.* ***Suburb***, NE district of Horsham. **12 E3** TQ1932.
Rogan's Seat *N.Yorks.* ***Mountain***, 3m/5km N of Muker. Height 2201 feet or 671 metres. **62 A6** NY9103.
Rogart *High.* ***Locality***, in Sutherland district, 4m/7km NW of head of Loch Fleet, on E coast. **96 E1** NC7303.
Rogart Station *High.* ***Other building***, railway station in Strath Fleet, 1m/2km SW of Rogart, Sutherland district. **96 E1** NC7202.
Rogate *W.Suss.* ***Village***, 4m/6km E of Petersfield. **12 B4** SU8023.
Roger Ground *Cumb.* ***Settlement***, in Lake District, just S of Hawkshead. SD3597.
Roger Sand *Lincs.* ***Coastal feature***, sandbank in W side of The Wash off Lincolnshire coast, 9m/15km E of Boston. **43 H1** TF4943.
Rogerstone (Tŷ-dû). *Newport* ***Village***, 3m/4km W of Newport. **19 F3** ST2688.
Roghadal *W.Isles Gaelic form of Rodel, qv.*
Rogie Burn *High.* ***River***, flowing from S of Carn Gorm, then SW into Black Water, 3m/4km W of Strathpeffer. **96 B5** NH4459.
Rogie Falls *High.* ***Waterfall***, salmon leap in course of Black Water, Ross and Cromarty district, 2m/4km W of Strathpeffer. **96 B6** NH4458.
Rogiet *Mon.* ***Village***, 1m/2km W of Caldicot. **19 H3** ST4587.
Rohallion *P. & K.* ***Locality***, and castle 3m/4km SE of Dunkeld. NO0439.
Roineabhal *W.Isles Gaelic form of Roneval, qv.*
Roineval *High.* ***Mountain***, 3m/4km N of head of Loch Harport. Height 1440 feet or 439 metres. **85 K1** NG4135.
Roineval *W.Isles* ***Hill***, 3m/4km W of Baile Ailein, Isle of Lewis. Height 922 feet or 281 metres. **100 E5** NB2321.
Roinn a' Bhuic *W.Isles* ***Coastal feature***, headland on NW coast of Isle of Lewis, 1km N of Cóig Peighinnean Bhuirgh. **101 F2** NB4057.
Roinn na Beinne *High.* ***Mountain***, in Knoydart, Lochaber district, 3m/4km NW of Inverie. Height 1446 feet or 441 metres. **86 D4** NG7302.
Rois-bheinn *High.* ***Mountain***, in Moidart, Lochaber district, 3m/5km S of Lochailort. Height 2893 feet or 882 metres. **86 D7** NM7577.
Roishal Mòr *W.Isles* ***Hill***, 8m/13km E of Carloway, Isle of Lewis. Height 571 feet or 174 metres. **101 F3** NB3341.
Roisnis an Ear *W.Isles Gaelic form of East Roisnish, qv.*
Rokeles Hall *Norf. See Watton.*
Rokemarsh *Oxon.* ***Settlement***, 1km N of Benson. SU6292.
Roker *T. & W.* ***Suburb***, 1m/2km N of Sunderland city centre, to N of River Wear and harbour. **63 F1** NZ4059.
Rollesby *Norf.* ***Village***, 7m/11km NW of Great Yarmouth. **45 J4** TG4415.
Rolleston *Leics.* ***Village***, 8m/13km N of Market Harborough. **42 A5** SK7300.
Rolleston *Notts.* ***Village***, 4m/6km W of Newark-on-Trent across River Trent. **51 K7** SK7452.
Rolleston *Staffs.* Population: 3203. ***Village***, 3m/4km N of Burton upon Trent. **40 E3** SK2327.
Rolleston on Dove *Staffs.* ***Hamlet***, 1km E of Rolleston. SK2427.
Rollestone *Wilts.* ***Locality***, adjoining to S of Shrewton, 5m/9km W of Amesbury. **20 D7** SU0743.
Rollright Stones *Oxon. See Little Rollright.*
Rolston *E.Riding* ***Hamlet***, near coast, 2m/3km S of Hornsea. **59 J5** TA2145.
Rolstone *N.Som.* ***Settlement***, 4m/7km E of Weston-super-Mare. ST3962.
Rolvenden *Kent* ***Village***, 3m/5km SW of Tenterden. **14 D4** TQ8431.
Rolvenden Layne *Kent* ***Village***, 1m/2km SE of Rolvenden. **14 D4** TQ8431.
Romach Hill *Moray* ***Mountain***, 5m/8km SE of Forres. Height 1027 feet or 313 metres. **97 H6** NJ0650.
Romaldkirk *Dur.* ***Village***, 5m/8km NW of Barnard Castle. **62 A4** NY9922.
Roman *Essex* ***River***, rising 2m/3km E of Coggeshall and flowing E into River Colne opposite Wivenhoe. **34 D6** TM0321.
Roman Army Museum *Northumb.* ***Other feature of interest***, museum at Carvoran with lifelike figures of Roman troops and a large-scale model of fort, 1km NE of Greenhead. **70 B7** NY6665.
Roman Baths and Pump Room *B. & N.E.Som.* ***Other feature of interest***, in central Bath, next to hot spring which was once a sacred site. Restaurant in Pump Room. **20 A5** ST7463.
Roman Hill *Suff.* ***Suburb***, in central Lowestoft. TM5493.
Roman Ridge ***Other feature of interest***, Roman road running from Great North Road, 2m/3km E of Upton, through Castleford and Tadcaster, to York. **57 K6** SE4229.
Roman Steps *Gwyn.* ***Inland physical feature***, staircase of unhewn rock slabs on track leading from head of Llyn Cwm Bychan towards Rhinog Fawr. Origin unknown. **37 F3** SH6530.
Romanby *N.Yorks.* ***Suburb***, adjoining to SW of Northallerton. **62 E7** SE3693.
Romannobridge *Sc.Bord.* ***Village***, on Lyne Water, 3m/4km S of West Linton. **75 K6** NT1648.
Romansleigh *Devon* ***Village***, 4m/6km SE of South Molton. **7 F3** SS7220.
Rombalds Moor *W.Yorks.* ***Large natural feature***, stretch of moorland between Wharfedale and Airedale, extending from Addingham in N to Baildon in S, attaining height of 1321 feet or 403 metres, 1m/2km S of Ilkley. Includes Ilkley Moor. **57 F5** SE1145.
Rome Hill *S.Lan.* ***Mountain***, 3m/5km E of Abington. Height 1853 feet or 565 metres. **68 E1** NS9724.
Romesdal *High.* ***Settlement***, on E side of Loch Snizort Beag, Skye, 6m/10km S of Uig. River Romesdal runs W into loch here. NG4053.
Romford *Dorset* ***Settlement***, 1m/2km E of Woodlands. **10 B4** SU0709.
Romford *Gt.Lon.* ***Town***, market town in borough of Havering, 14m/23km E of Charing Cross. Shopping centre with busy market. **23 J3** TQ5189.
Romiley *Gt.Man.* Population: 14,102. ***Town***, residential town, 3m/4km E of Stockport. **49 J3** SJ9390.
Romney Marsh *Kent* ***Marsh/bog***, area of well-drained marshland lying to W of Dymchurch, extensively used for sheep-grazing. **15 F4** TR0430.
Romney Sands *Kent* ***Coastal feature***, beach 1m/2km SE of New Romney, between Littlestone-on-Sea and Greatstone-on-Sea. **15 F5** TR0823.
Romney Street *Kent* ***Settlement***, 2m/3km NE of Otford. **23 J5** TQ5561.
Romney, Hythe and Dymchurch Railway *Kent* ***Other feature of interest***, narrow gauge tourist railway, beginning in Hythe, 4m/7km W of Folkestone, and travelling SW through Dymchurch, St. Mary's Bay, New Romney and ending in Dungeness. **15 G4** TR1534.
Romsey *Hants.* Population: 17,032. ***Town***, market town on River Test, 7m/11km NW of Southampton. 10c-12c abbey. King John's hunting box, 13c house now museum. 1km S, Broadlands, 18c mansion, now home to Mountbatten family. **10 E2** SU3521.
Romsey Abbey *Hants.* ***Ecclesiastical building***, Norman building dating from early 12c, in Romsey. Treasures include Saxon sculpture of Crucifixion. **10 E2** SU3421.
Romsey Town *Cambs.* ***Suburb***, 1m/2km E of Cambridge city centre. TL4757.
Romsley *Shrop.* ***Village***, 5m/7km NW of Kidderminster. **39 G7** SO7882.
Romsley *Worcs.* ***Village***, 3m/4km S of Halesowen. **40 B7** SO9679.
Rona (Also known as Island of Rona or South Rona.) *High.* ***Island***, uninhabited island of about 1600 acres or 650 hectares lying N of Raasay between W coast of Ross and Cromarty district and Trotternish on mainland of Skye. Lighthouse at N end. Island is nearly 5m/8km long N to S. **94 C6** NG6258.
Rona (Gaelic form: Rònaidh. Also known as North Rona.) *W.Isles* ***Island***, uninhabited island of about 300 acres or 120 hectares lying 44m/70km NNE of Butt of Lewis and NW of Cape Wrath. Nature reserve; breeding-ground of grey seals. HW8132.
Ronachan *Arg. & B.* ***Settlement***, on Kintyre, 1m/2km SW of Clachan. **73 F5** NR7454.
Ronachan Point *Arg. & B.* ***Coastal feature***, headland on W coast of Kintyre, Argyll, on S side of entrance to West Loch Tarbert. **73 F5** NR7455.
Ronague *I.o.M.* ***Settlement***, 4m/6km NE of Port Erin. **54 B6** SC2472.
Rònaidh *W.Isles Gaelic form of Rona, qv.*
Rònaigh *W.Isles Gaelic form of Ronay, qv.*
Ronaldsvoe *Ork.* ***Settlement***, at N end of South Ronaldsay, adjoining to W of St. Margaret's Hope. ND4493.
Ronaldsway Airport *I.o.M. Alternative name for Isle of Man Airport, qv.*
Ronas Hill *Shet.* ***Mountain***, summit of Shetland Islands on Mainland between Ronas Voe and Colla Firth. Height 1476 feet or 450 metres. **108 C4** HU3083.
Ronas Voe *Shet.* ***Sea feature***, long inlet on NW coast of Mainland, on S side of Ronas Hill. **108 B4** HU2882.
Ronay (Gaelic form: Rònaigh.) *W.Isles* ***Island***, sparsely populated island of about 2 square miles or 5 square km off SE coast of North Uist, on E side of Grimsay. **92 E6** NF8956.
Roneval *W.Isles* ***Hill***, near S coast of South Uist, 4m/6km SE of Lochboisdale. Height 659 feet or 201 metres. **84 D3** NF8114.
Roneval (Gaelic form: Roineabhal.) *W.Isles* ***Mountain***, on South Harris, 2m/3km E of Leverburgh. Height 1509 feet or 460 metres. **93 F3** NG0486.
Ronkswood *Worcs.* ***Suburb***, E district of Worcester. SO8655.
Ronnachmore *Arg. & B.* ***Settlement***, on Islay, 1m/2km SW of Bowmore. **72 B5** NR3058.
Rood End *W.Mid.* ***Suburb***, 1m/2km N of Warley town centre. SP0088.
Rookhope *Dur.* ***Village***, 4m/7km NW of Stanhope. **62 A2** NY9342.
Rookhope Burn *Dur.* ***River***, rising on N side of Wolfcleugh Common, to N of St. John's Chapel, and flowing SE past Rookhope into River Wear at Eastgate. **61 K2** NY9538.
Rookley *I.o.W.* ***Village***, 3m/5km S of Newport. **11 G6** SZ5084.
Rookley Country Park *I.o.W.* ***Leisure/recreation***, country park E of Rookley, 3m/5km SE of Newport town centre. **11 G6** SZ5183.
Rookleygreen *I.o.W.* ***Hamlet***, just S of Rookley, 1m/2km NW of Godshill. SZ5183.
Rooks Bridge *Som.* ***Village***, 4m/7km W of Axbridge. **19 G6** ST3652.
Rook's Nest *Som.* ***Hamlet***, 4m/6km N of Wiveliscombe. ST0833.
Rookwith *N.Yorks.* ***Settlement***, 4m/7km W of Bedale. **57 H1** SE2086.
Rookwood *W.Suss.* ***Locality***, 1m/2km N of West Wittering. SZ7899.
Rookwood *W.Yorks.* ***Suburb***, 2m/3km E of Leeds city centre. SE3233.
Rookwood Farm *Hants. See Denmead.*
Roos *E.Riding* ***Village***, 4m/6km NW of Withernsea. Site of castle near church to S. **59 J6** TA2930.
Roose *Cumb.* ***Suburb***, in Barrow-in-Furness 2m/3km E of town centre. SD2269.
Roosebeck *Cumb.* ***Settlement***, on W shore of Morecambe Bay, 4m/6km E of Barrow-in-Furness. SD2567.
Roosecote *Cumb.* ***Suburb***, 2m/3km E of Barrow-in-Furness town centre. **55 F3** SD2268.
Rootham's Green *Beds.* ***Hamlet***, 6m/10km NE of Bedford. TL1057.
Rootpark *S.Lan.* ***Settlement***, 1m/2km NE of Forth. **75 H5** NS9554.
Rope *Ches.* ***Settlement***, 2m/3km S of Crewe. SJ6852.
Ropley *Hants.* ***Village***, 4m/6km E of New Alresford. **11 H1** SU6431.
Ropley Dean *Hants.* ***Village***, 3m/4km E of New Alresford. **11 H1** SU6332.
Ropley Soke *Hants.* ***Settlement***, 4m/7km E of New Alresford. **11 H1** SU6533.
Ropsley *Lincs.* ***Village***, 5m/8km E of Grantham. **42 C2** SK9934.
Rora *Aber.* ***Village***, on E side of Rora Moss, 5m/8km NW of Peterhead. **99 J5** NK0650.
Rora Head *Ork.* ***Coastal feature***, headland on W coast of Hoy. **107 A8** ND1799.
Rora Moss *Aber.* ***Open space***, moorland 6m/10km NE of Mintlaw. **99 J5** NK0351.
Rorandle *Aber.* ***Settlement***, to N of Cairn William, 5m/8km W of Kemnay. **90 E3** NJ6518.
Rorrington *Shrop.* ***Hamlet***, 5m/8km NE of Church Stoke. **38 B5** SJ3000.
Rosarie *Moray* ***Settlement***, 3m/5km W of Keith. **98 B5** NJ3850.
Rosarie Forest *Moray* ***Forest/woodland***, 5m/8km N of Dufftown. **98 B6** NJ3548.
Rosay (Gaelic form: Eilean Rosaidh.) *W.Isles* ***Island***, small uninhabited island on S side of entrance to Loch Erisort, E coast of Isle of Lewis. NB4220.
Rose *Cornw.* ***Hamlet***, 1m/2km E of Perranporth. **2 E3** SW7754.
Rose Ash *Devon* ***Village***, 5m/9km SE of South Molton. **7 F3** SS7821.
Rose Green *Essex* ***Hamlet***, 6m/10km NW of Colchester. **34 C6** TL9028.
Rose Green *Suff.* ***Settlement***, 4m/6km NW of Hadleigh. TL9744.
Rose Green *W.Suss.* ***Suburb***, 3m/4km W of Bognor Regis. SZ9099.
Rose Grove *Lancs.* ***Suburb***, 1m/2km W of Burnley town centre. SD8132.
Rose Hill *E.Suss.* ***Settlement***, 5m/8km NE of Lewes. TQ4516.
Rose Hill *Lancs.* ***Suburb***, 1km S of Burnley town centre. SD8331.
Rose Hill *Oxon.* ***Suburb***, 2m/3km SE of Oxford city centre. SP5303.
Rose Hill *Suff.* ***Suburb***, 1m/2km SE of Ipswich town centre. TM1843.
Rose Lands *E.Suss.* ***Suburb***, 1m/2km N of Eastbourne town centre. TQ6100.
Rose Ness *Ork.* ***Coastal feature***, headland at SE end of Mainland, 9m/14km SE of Kirkwall. Lighthouse. **107 E8** ND5298.
Roseacre *Kent* ***Suburb***, 2m/3km E of Maidstone. TQ7955.
Roseacre *Lancs.* ***Settlement***, 3m/5km N of Kirkham. **55 H6** SD4336.
Rosebank *S.Lan.* ***Locality***, on River Clyde, 3m/5km E of Larkhall. **75 G6** NS8049.
Roseberry Topping ***Mountain***, conical peak on border of Redcar & Cleveland and North Yorkshire, 4m/6km SW of Guisborough. Height 1050 feet or 320 metres. **63 G5** NZ5712.
Rosebery *Midloth.* ***Locality***, 4m/6km SW of Gorebridge. NT3057.
Rosebery Reservoir *Midloth.* ***Reservoir***, 1km SE of Rosebery. **76 B5** NT3057.
Rosebrough *Northumb.* ***Settlement***, 3m/5km NW of North Charlton. **71 G1** NU1326.
Roseburn *Edin.* ***Suburb***, 2m/3km W of Edinburgh city centre. NT2273.
Rosebush *Pembs.* ***Hamlet***, 1m/2km N of Maenclochog. **16 D2** SN0729.
Rosecare *Cornw.* ***Hamlet***, 5m/8km NE of Boscastle. SX1695.
Rosecliston *Cornw.* ***Settlement***, 2m/3km S of Newquay. SW8159.
Rosedale *N.Yorks.* ***Valley***, carrying River Seven and running NW to SE on N side of Spaunton Moor, 4m/7km N of Hutton-le-Hole. **63 J7** SE7197.
Rosedale Abbey *N.Yorks.* ***Village***, 6m/10km N of Kirkbymoorside. Remains of 12c priory. Disused lead mines on surrounding moors. **63 J7** SE7295.
Rosedale Moor *N.Yorks.* ***Open space***, moorland on S edge of North York Moors, 8m/13km N of Kirkbymoorside. **63 J7** SE7199.
Roseden *Northumb.* ***Settlement***, 1m/2km E of Ilderton. **71 F1** NU0321.
Rosehall *Aber.* ***Locality***, 1m/2km W of Turriff. NJ7149.
Rosehall *High.* ***Settlement***, at foot of Glen Cassley, in Sutherland district, 8m/12km W of Lairg. **96 B1** NC4702.
Rosehearty *Aber.* Population: 1202. ***Village***, fishing village on N coast, 4m/7km W of Fraserburgh. **99 H4** NJ9367.
Roseheath *Mersey.* ***Locality***, 1km SW of Halewood. SJ4485.
Rosehill *Aber.* ***Settlement***, 1m/2km NE of Aboyne, on E side of Loch of Aboyne. **90 D5** NO5399.
Rosehill *Shrop.* ***Settlement***, 2m/4km NW of Shrewsbury. SJ4715.
Rosehill *Shrop.* ***Settlement***, 3m/4km S of Market Drayton. **39 F2** SJ6630.
Rosehill *T. & W.* ***Suburb***, on E side of Wallsend. NZ3166.
Roseisle *Moray* ***Locality***, 2m/3km SE of Burghead. **97 J5** NJ1367.
Roseisle Forest *Moray* ***Forest/woodland***, bordering Burghead Bay to W of Roseisle. **97 J5** NJ1367.

R

Rosemarket *Pembs.* ***Village***, 2m/4km N of Neyland. Traces of ancient fort at S end. **16 C4** SM9508.
Rosemarkie *High.* Population: 757. ***Village***, and resort on W side of Moray Firth, in Ross and Cromarty district, opposite Fort George. **96 E6** NH7357.
Rosemarkie Bay *High.* ***Bay***, extends to Chanonry Point on S coast of Black Isle. Masts above bay. **96 E6** NH7357.
Rosemary Lane *Devon* ***Hamlet***, 4m/7km SE of Wellington. **7 K4** ST1514.
Rosemoor Garden *Devon* ***Garden***, in Torridge valley, 1km SE of Great Torrington. Royal Horticultural Society garden, particularly noted for roses. **6 D4** SS5018.
Rosemount *P. & K.* ***Locality***, 1m/2km SE of Blairgowrie. **82 C3** NO1843.
Rosemount *S.Ayr.* ***Settlement***, 3m/4km NE of Prestwick. **67 H1** NS3728.
Rosemullion Head *Cornw.* ***Coastal feature***, headland (National Trust) at S end of Falmouth Bay, 3m/5km S of Falmouth. **2 E6** SW7927.
Rosenannon *Cornw.* ***Hamlet***, 3m/5km NE of St. Columb Major. SW9566.
Roseneath *Arg. & B. Alternative spelling of Rosneath, qv.*
Rosenithon *Cornw.* ***Hamlet***, to E of St. Keverne, 10m/15km SE of Helston. SW8021.
Rosepool *Pembs.* ***Settlement***, 1km W of Walwyn's Castle. **16 B3** SM8611.
Rosevean *Cornw.* ***Hamlet***, in China clay district, 4m/6km N of St. Austell. SX0258.
Roseville *W.Mid.* ***Suburb***, in N part of Dudley. SO9393.
Rosevine *Cornw.* ***Settlement***, above W side of Gerrans Bay, 1km N of Portscatho. SW8736.
Rosewarne *Cornw.* ***Settlement***, 3m/5km SW of Camborne. **2 D5** SW6136.
Rosewell *Midloth.* Population: 1063. ***Village***, 4m/6km SW of Dalkeith. **76 A4** NT2862.
Roseworth *Stock.* ***Suburb***, 2m/3km NW of Stockton-on-Tees town centre. NZ4221.
Roseworthy *Cornw.* ***Settlement***, 2m/3km W of Camborne. **2 D5** SW6139.
Rosgill *Cumb.* ***Hamlet***, 2m/3km NW of Shap. **61 G5** NY5316.
Roshven *High.* ***Locality***, in Lochaber district, on S side of entrance to Loch Ailort. **86 D7** NM7078.
Roskhill *High.* ***Settlement***, on Skye, 2m/4km SE of Dunvegan. **93 H7** NG2745.
Roskorwell *Cornw.* ***Settlement***, just N of Porthallow, 9m/14km E of Helston. SW7923.
Rosley *Cumb.* ***Hamlet***, 5m/8km SE of Wigton. **60 E2** NY3245.
Roslin *Midloth.* Population: 1761. ***Village***, 2m/3km S of Loanhead. **76 A4** NT2763.
Roslin Castle *Midloth. Alternative spelling of Rosslyn Castle, qv.*
Roslin Glen Country Park *Midloth.* ***Leisure/recreation***, adjacent to River North Esk, 1km SW of Roslin and 3m/4km NE of Penicuik. Over 40 acres of woodland in steep-sided valley. **76 A4** NT2662.
Rosliston *Derbys.* ***Village***, 4m/7km S of Burton upon Trent. **40 E4** SK2416.
Rosneath (Also spelled Roseneath.) *Arg. & B.* Population: 1393. ***Village***, on W side of Gare Loch, 2m/3km NE of Kilcreggan. **74 A2** NS2583.
Rosneath Bay *Arg. & B.* ***Bay***, to SE of Rosneath, 2m/3km W of Helensburgh across Gare Loch. **74 A2** NS2682.
Rosneath Point *Arg. & B.* ***Coastal feature***, headland on Firth of Clyde, 2m/3km SE of Rosneath. **74 A2** NS2583.
Ross *D. & G.* ***Settlement***, on Ross Bay, on W side of Kirkcudbright Bay, 4m/7km S of Kirkcudbright. **65 G6** NX6444.
Ross *Northumb.* ***Settlement***, near coast, 3m/4km NE of Belford. **77 K7** NU1337.
Ross *P. & K.* ***Settlement***, adjacent to S of Comrie across River Earn. **81 J5** NN7621.
Ross Castle *Northumb.* ***Historic/prehistoric site***, hillfort (National Trust), probably Iron Age, on E side of Chillingham Park. NU0825.
Ross Moor *E.Riding* ***Open space***, lowland on S side of Pocklington Canal, 1m/2km W of Melbourne. **58 D5** SE7343.
Ross of Mull *Arg. & B.* ***Coastal feature***, long granite peninsula at SW end of Mull, running out to Sound of Iona. **78 E5** NM3920.
Ross-on-Wye *Here.* Population: 9606. ***Small town***, market town on River Wye, 9m/14km NE of Monmouth. Old market hall and many interesting Georgian and timber-framed houses. **29 F6** SO5924.
Ross Point *Stir.* ***Inland physical feature***, wooded headland on E side of Loch Lomond, 2m/3km S of Rowardennan. **74 B1** NS3695.
Ross Priory *W.Dun.* ***Settlement***, on S shore of Loch Lomond, 1m/2km NW of Gartocharn. **74 C2** NS4187.
Rossall Point *Lancs.* ***Coastal feature***, headland 1m/2km W of Fleetwood. **55 G5** SD3147.
Rossay *W.Isles* ***Island***, small uninhabited island off South Harris in East Loch Tarbert to W of Scalpay. NG2095.
Rossdhu House *Arg. & B.* ***Castle***, seat of the Colquhouns on W shore of Loch Lomond, 2m/3km S of Luss. **74 B2** NS3689.
Rossett (Yr Orsedd). *Wrex.* Population: 1986. ***Village***, 5m/8km N of Wrexham. 17c water-mill. **48 C7** SJ3657.
Rossett Green *N.Yorks.* ***Suburb***, 1m/2km S of Harrogate town centre. SE3053.
Rosside *Cumb.* ***Settlement***, 1m/2km W of Ulverston. SD2778.
Rossie Farm School *Angus* ***Settlement***, 3m/4km N of Inverkeilor. **83 H2** NO6653.
Rossie Island *Angus Alternative name for Inchbraoch, qv.*
Rossie Moor *Angus* ***Open space***, includes small areas of woodland and several small lochs, above 100 metres high, 4m/7km SW of Montrose. **83 H2** NO6554.
Rossie Ochill *P. & K.* ***Settlement***, 1m/2km NE of Path of Condie. **82 B6** NO0813.
Rossie Priory *P. & K.* ***Settlement***, at foot of Rossie Hill, 2m/3km NW of Longforgan. **82 D4** NO2830.
Rossington *S.Yorks.* ***Village***, 4m/7km SE of Doncaster. **51 J3** SK6298.
Rosskeen *High.* ***Settlement***, in Ross and Cromarty district, 2m/3km W of Invergordon. **96 D5** NH6869.
Rossland *Renf.* ***Hamlet***, adjoining to SE of Bishopton, 5m/8km NW of Paisley. NS4470.
Rosslyn Castle (Also spelled Roslin Castle). *Midloth.* ***Castle***, faint remains of 14c castle, rebuilt 16c-17c, above loop of River North Esk to SE of Roslin. **76 A4** NT2763.
Rossmore *Poole* ***Suburb***, 3m/5km NE of Poole town centre. SZ0593.
Roster *High.* ***Settlement***, 3m/4km N of Lybster. **105 H5** ND2539.
Rostherne *Ches.* ***Village***, 3m/5km N of Knutsford. **49 G4** SJ7483.
Rostholme *S.Yorks.* ***Suburb***, adjoining to N of Bentley, 2m/4km N of Doncaster town centre. SE5606.
Rosthwaite *Cumb.* ***Hamlet***, in Borrowdale, 3m/4km S of Derwent Water. **60 D5** NY2514.
Rosthwaite *Cumb.* ***Settlement***, 3m/4km NE of Broughton in Furness. **55 F1** SD2490.
Roston *Derbys.* ***Village***, 5m/7km SW of Ashbourne. **40 D1** SK1341.
Rostrehwfa *I.o.A.* ***Hamlet***, 1m/2km SW of Llangefni. SH4374.
Rosudgeon *Cornw.* ***Village***, 6m/10km W of Helston. SW5529.
Rosyth *Fife* ***Town***, adjoining to NW of Inverkeithing. Naval base on Firth of Forth to S. **75 K2** NT1183.
Rothbury *Northumb.* Population: 1805. ***Small town***, market town on River Coquet, 11m/17km SW of Alnwick. Surrounding hills known as Rothbury Forest. Nearby Cragside House, built 1865, was first house in world to have electric lighting. **71 F3** NU0501.
Rothbury Forest *Northumb.* ***Open space***, large area of moorland and forest to E of Rothbury. **71 F4** NZ0397.
Rother ***River***, rising near Clay Cross, and flowing N through Chesterfield and Staveley into River Don at Rotherham. SK4292.
Rother ***River***, rising S of Selborne and flowing S to Sheet, near Petersfield, then E past Midhurst to join River Arun 1m/2km W of Pulborough. **12 D5** TQ0318.
Rother ***River***, rising S of Rotherfield and flowing into English Channel 3m/4km SE of Rye. TQ9517.
Rother Levels ***Marsh/bog***, area of well-drained marshland to N of Rye near mouth of River Rother. **14 D5** TQ9025.
Rother Valley Country Park *S.Yorks.* ***Leisure/recreation***, country park on former open-cast coalmining site at E side of River Rother, 6m/10km SE of Sheffield. Contains woodland, grassland, marsh and scrub as well as five lakes which attract great variety of aquatic birds. Facilities for wide variety of sporting activities. **51 G4** SK4582.
Rotherby *Leics.* ***Village***, 5m/8km W of Melton Mowbray. **41 J4** SK6716.
Rotherfield *E.Suss.* ***Village***, 3m/5km E of Crowborough. **13 J4** TQ5529.
Rotherfield Greys *Oxon.* ***Village***, 2m/3km W of Henley-on-Thames. **22 A3** SU7282.
Rotherfield Peppard *Oxon.* ***Village***, 3m/5km W of Henley-on-Thames. **22 A3** SU7181.
Rotherham *S.Yorks.* Population: 121,380. ***Town***, industrial town, 6m/10km NE of Sheffield, at confluence of Rivers Don and Rother. Formerly a heavy industry town, with mining and engineering. Parish church is 15c. Clifton Park Museum, in 18c Clifton House, contains Rockingham Pottery, made in this area. **51 G3** SK4292.
Rotherhithe *Gt.Lon.* ***Suburb***, 4m/6km E of Charing Cross, in borough of Southwark, on S bank of River Thames. Road tunnel under river to Shadwell in borough of Tower Hamlets. TQ3579.
Rotherhope Fell *Cumb.* ***Mountain***, 6m/10km E of Melmerby. Height 1955 feet or 596 metres. **61 J3** NY7139.
Rothersthorpe *Northants.* ***Village***, 4m/6km SW of Northampton. **31 J3** SP7156.
Rotherwick *Hants.* ***Village***, 2m/3km NW of Hook. **22 A6** SU7156.
Rothes *Moray* Population: 1345. ***Small town***, near left bank of River Spey 9m/15km SE of Elgin. Ruined medieval castle of the Leslies. **97 K7** NJ2749.
Rothesay *Arg. & B.* Population: 5264. ***Small town***, chief town and port of Bute, situated on Rothesay Bay on E coast, 7m/11km W of Wemyss Bay across Firth of Clyde. **73 J4** NS0864.
Rothesay Bay *Arg. & B.* ***Bay***, on E coast of Bute, extending from Bogany Point in E to Ardbeg Point in N. **73 J4** NS0864.
Rothesay Castle *Arg. & B.* ***Castle***, mainly 14c castle (Historic Scotland), though parts are earlier, near Rothesay town centre. **73 J4** NS0864.
Rothiebrisbane *Aber.* ***Settlement***, 1m/2km W of Fyvie. **91 F1** NJ7437.
Rothiemurchus *High.* ***Locality***, in Badenoch and Strathspey district, 2m/3km S of Aviemore. Rothiemurchus Forest is deer forest to S. **89 G4** NH9308.
Rothienorman *Aber.* ***Village***, 9m/14km S of Turriff. **91 F1** NJ7235.
Rothiesholm *Ork.* ***Settlement***, in S of Stronsay, between Bay of Bomasty and Bight of Doonatown. **106 F5** HY6223.
Rothiesholm Head *Ork.* ***Coastal feature***, headland at SW end of Stronsay. **106 F5** HY6121.
Rothley *Leics.* ***Village***, on Rothley Brook, 5m/8km N of Leicester. Site of Roman villa 1m/2km W. **41 H4** SK5812.
Rothley *Northumb.* ***Settlement***, 4m/6km NE of Kirkwhelpington. **71 F5** NZ0488.
Rothley Lakes *Northumb.* ***Lake/loch***, two small lakes to N of Rothley. **71 F4** NZ0488.
Rothney *Aber.* ***Hamlet***, adjoining to S of Insch. NJ6227.
Rothwell *Lincs.* ***Village***, 2m/4km SE of Caistor. **52 E3** TF1599.
Rothwell *Northants.* Population: 7070. ***Small town***, historic market town, 4m/6km NW of Kettering. Bone crypt in 13c church. **42 B7** SP8181.
Rothwell *W.Yorks.* Population: 18,336. ***Town***, 5m/7km SE of Leeds. **57 J7** SE3428.
Rothwell Haigh *W.Yorks.* ***Suburb***, 1km N of Rothwell town centre. SE3428.
Rotsea *E.Riding* ***Settlement***, 5m/7km SE of Great Driffield. **59 G4** TA0651.
Rottal *Angus* ***Settlement***, in Glen Clova, 6m/10km N of Dykehead. **82 E1** NO3769.
Rotten Green *Hants.* ***Settlement***, 2m/3km SE of Hartley Wintney. SU7855.
Rotten Row *Bucks.* ***Settlement***, 3m/5km W of Marlow. SU7986.
Rotten Row *Norf.* ***Locality***, on River Tud, 1km NE of East Tuddenham. TG0812.
Rotten Row *W.Mid.* ***Settlement***, 3m/5km SE of Solihull town centre. SP1875.
Rottingdean *B. & H.* Population: 10,744. ***Locality***, coastal locality, 4m/6km E of Brighton town centre. **13 G6** TQ3602.
Rottington *Cumb.* ***Hamlet***, 1m/2km NW of St. Bees. **60 A5** NX9613.
Roud *I.o.W.* ***Settlement***, 4m/6km NW of Ventnor. **11 G6** SZ5180.
Roudham *Norf.* ***Settlement***, 6m/10km NE of Thetford. **44 D7** TL9587.
Rough Castle *Falk.* ***Historic/prehistoric site***, Roman fort on Antonine Wall, 1m/2km E of Bonnybridge. **75 G3** NS8479.
Rough Close *Staffs.* ***Hamlet***, 4m/6km NE of Stone. **40 B2** SJ9239.
Rough Common *Kent* ***Suburb***, 2m/3km NW of Canterbury. **15 G2** TR1259.
Rough Firth *D. & G.* ***Sea feature***, estuary of Urr Water, 5m/8km S of Dalbeattie. Bird sanctuary on Rough Island (National Trust for Scotland), to S of Rockcliffe. **65 J5** NX8353.
Rough Hay *Staffs.* ***Hamlet***, 3m/4km W of Burton upon Trent. SK2023.
Rough Island *D. & G. See Rockcliffe.*
Rough Pike *Northumb.* ***Inland physical feature***, wooded edge rising to over 350 metres, 3m/5km W of Kielder Water. **70 B5** NY6386.
Rough Tor *Cornw.* ***Mountain***, granite tor (National Trust) on Bodmin Moor, 3m/5km SE of Camelford. Height 1312 feet or 400 metres. **4 B2** SX1480.
Rough Tor *Devon* ***Mountain***, in Dartmoor National Park, 3m/4km NW of Postbridge. Height 1791 feet or 546 metres. **5 F3** SX6079.
Rougham *Norf.* ***Village***, 7m/12km N of Swaffham. **44 C3** TF8320.
Rougham *Suff.* ***Hamlet***, 4m/6km SE of Bury St. Edmunds town centre. **34 D2** TL9161.
Rougham Green *Suff.* ***Village***, 4m/6km SE of Bury St. Edmunds. **34 D2** TL9061.
Roughbirchworth *S.Yorks.* ***Hamlet***, 2m/3km SE of Penistone. SE2601.
Roughburn *High.* ***Settlement***, at W end of Loch Laggan, 10m/15km E of Spean Bridge. **87 K6** NN3781.
Roughcote *Staffs.* ***Hamlet***, 4m/7km E of Stoke-on-Trent. SJ9444.
Roughlee *Lancs.* ***Hamlet***, 2m/3km NW of Nelson. **56 D5** SD8440.
Roughley *W.Mid.* ***Locality***, 2m/3km NE of Sutton Coldfield. **40 D6** SP1399.
Roughrigg Reservoir *N.Lan.* ***Reservoir***, 3m/5km E of Airdrie. **75 G4** NS8164.
Roughton *Lincs.* ***Village***, 3m/5km E of Woodhall Spa. **53 F6** TF2464.
Roughton *Norf.* ***Village***, 3m/5km S of Cromer. **45 G2** TG2137.
Roughton *Shrop.* ***Village***, 3m/4km E of Bridgnorth. **39 G6** SO7594.
Round Bush *Herts.* ***Hamlet***, 3m/5km E of Watford. TQ1498.
Round Church of Kilarrow *Arg. & B.* ***Ecclesiastical building***, built by Campbells of Shawfield as part of a planned village, and thought to be a copy of an Italian design. At Bowmore, 11m/18km NW of Port Ellen, Islay. **72 B5** NR3159.
Round Fell *D. & G.* ***Mountain***, 2m/3km S of Clatteringshaws Loch. Height 1319 feet or 402 metres. **65 F3** NX5372.
Round Green *Luton* ***Suburb***, 1m/2km NE of Luton town centre. TL1022.
Round Green *S.Yorks.* ***Hamlet***, 1km W of Worsbrough Reservoir, 2m/3km SW of Barnsley. SE3303.
Round Hill *Cumb.* ***Mountain***, 5m/8km NW of Cow Green Reservoir. Height 2247 feet or 685 metres. **61 J3** NY7436.
Round Hill *Moray* ***Mountain***, 6m/9km SW of Cabrach. Height 2188 feet or 667 metres. **90 B2** NJ3022.
Round Hill *Moray* ***Mountain***, to E of Black Water valley, 3m/4km W of Cabrach. Height 1873 feet or 571 metres. **90 B2** NJ3427.
Round Hill *N.Yorks.* ***Mountain***, 1m/2km E of Urra. Cleveland Way long distance footpath crosses summit. Height 1489 feet or 454 metres. **63 G6** NZ5901.
Round Hill *N.Yorks.* ***Mountain***, 3m/5km SW of Blubberhouses. Height 1342 feet or 409 metres. **57 G4** SE1253.
Round Hill *Notts.* ***Suburb***, SE district of Sutton in Ashfield. SK5158.
Round Hill *Torbay* ***Suburb***, N district of Paignton. SX8962.
Round Oak *Shrop.* ***Hamlet***, 3m/4km NW of Craven Arms. SO3984.
Round Oak *W.Berks.* ***Locality***, 8m/12km SW of Reading. SU6265.
Round Oak *W.Mid.* ***Suburb***, 2m/4km SW of Dudley town centre. SO9287.

R

Round Top *Northumb.* ***Mountain***, in Wark Forest, 8m/12km N of Haltwhistle. Height 1066 feet or 325 metres. **70 C6** NY7077.

Roundbush Green *Essex* ***Hamlet***, 1m/2km N of Leaden Roding. TL5914.

Roundham *Som.* ***Hamlet***, 1m/2km W of Crewkerne. ST4209.

Roundhay *W.Yorks.* ***Suburb***, 3m/5km NE of Leeds city centre. Contains large public park with golf course and lake. **57 J6** SE3337.

Roundhill Reservoir *N.Yorks.* ***Reservoir***, on Masham Moor, 5m/8km SW of Masham. **57 G2** SE1577.

Round's Green *W.Mid.* ***Locality***, 1m/2km W of Oldbury. SO9889.

Rounds Street *Kent* ***Settlement***, adjoining to N of Sole Street, 4m/6km S of Gravesend. TQ6568.

Roundstreet Common *W.Suss.* ***Settlement***, 3m/5km NW of Billingshurst. **12 D4** TQ0528.

Roundthorn *Gt.Man.* ***Suburb***, of Manchester, 3m/4km E of Altrincham. SJ8088.

Roundthwaite *Cumb.* ***Locality***, 1m/2km SW of Tebay. NY6003.

Roundway *Wilts.* ***Village***, 1m/2km NE of Devizes. **20 D5** SU0163.

Roundway Hill *Wilts.* ***Hill***, 1m/2km W of Bishops Cannings. Height 794 feet or 242 metres. **20 D5** SU0264.

Roundyhill *Angus* ***Settlement***, 2m/4km S of Kirriemuir. NO3750.

Rous Lench *Worcs.* ***Village***, 6m/10km N of Evesham. **30 B3** SP0153.

Rousay *Ork.* ***Island***, hilly island of about 16 square miles or 41 square km, lying 1m/2km off N coast of Mainland across Eynhallow Sound. **106 C4** HY4130.

Rousay Sound *Ork.* ***Sea feature***, sea passage between E coast of Rousay and Egilsay. **106 D4** HY4529.

Rousdon *Devon* ***Hamlet***, 3m/5km W of Lyme Regis, in parish of Combpyne Rousdon. **8 B5** SY2991.

Rousham *Oxon.* ***Hamlet***, 4m/6km W of Middleton Stoney. **31 F6** SP4724.

Rousham Gap *Oxon.* ***Settlement***, 1m/2km SW of Rousham. **31 F6** SP4622.

Rousham House *Oxon.* ***Historic house***, 16c-18c, with gardens laid out by William Kent, 4m/7km W of Bicester. **31 F6** SP4724.

Routenburn *N.Ayr.* ***Settlement***, adjoining to N of Netherhall, 1m/2km N of Largs. **74 A4** NS1961.

Routh *E.Riding* ***Village***, 4m/7km NE of Beverley. **59 G5** TA0942.

Rout's Green *Bucks.* ***Settlement***, adjoining to NW of Bledlow Ridge, 2m/4km NE of Stokenchurch. SU7898.

Row *Cornw.* ***Village***, 4m/7km S of Camelford. **4 A3** SX0976.

Row *Cumb.* ***Hamlet***, 6m/10km SE of Windermere. **55 H1** SD4589.

Row *Cumb.* ***Settlement***, just E of Ousby. **61 H3** NY6234.

Row Ash *Hants.* ***Settlement***, between Curdridge and Shedfield, 2m/3km E of Botley. SU5413.

Row Green *Essex* ***Settlement***, 2m/3km SW of Braintree. TL7420.

Row Head *Ork.* ***Coastal feature***, headland on W coast of Mainland to N of Bay of Skaill. **107 B6** HY2218.

Row Heath *Essex* ***Settlement***, 3m/5km NW of Clacton-on-Sea. **35 F7** TM1419.

Row-of-Trees *Ches.* ***Suburb***, to W of Wilmslow. SJ8279.

Row Town *Surr.* ***Locality***, 2m/4km S of Chertsey. **22 D5** TQ0463.

Rowallan Castle *E.Ayr.* ***Castle***, mainly 16c castle (Historic Scotland), 3m/5km N of Kilmarnock. **74 C6** NS4342.

Rowanburn *D. & G.* ***Village***, 1m/2km E of Canonbie. **69 K6** NY4077.

Rowanfield *Glos.* ***Suburb***, W district of Cheltenham. SO9222.

Rowantree Hill *N.Ayr.* ***Mountain***, 3m/5km NE of Largs. Height 1404 feet or 428 metres. **74 A4** NS2362.

Rowardennan *Stir.* ***Locality***, including Rowardennan Lodge to N and Rowardennan Forest to SE, on E shore of Loch Lomond opposite Inverbeg. Ferry for pedestrians. NS3698.

Rowardennan Lodge *Stir.* ***Settlement***, with youth hostel, on E shore of Loch Lomond, 1m/2km NE of Inverbeg across loch. **74 B1** NS3699.

Rowarth *Derbys.* ***Hamlet***, 2m/3km NW of Hayfield. SK0189.

Rowbarton *Som.* ***Suburb***, N district of Taunton. ST2225.

Rowberrow *Som.* ***Hamlet***, 4m/6km S of Congresbury. **19 H6** ST4558.

Rowchoish *Stir.* ***Settlement***, on E side of Loch Lomond, 1m/2km E of Tarbet across loch. **80 E7** NN3304.

Rowde *Wilts.* ***Village***, 2m/3km NW of Devizes. **20 C5** ST9762.

Rowden *Devon* ***Hamlet***, 4m/7km NE of Okehampton. SX6498.

Rowden *N.Yorks.* ***Settlement***, 1km S of Hampsthwaite. SE2557.

Rowen *Conwy* ***Village***, 4m/6km S of Conwy. **47 F5** SH7571.

Rowfield *Derbys.* ***Settlement***, 2m/3km NE of Ashbourne. SK1949.

Rowfoot *Northumb.* ***Hamlet***, 3m/4km SW of Haltwhistle. **70 B7** NY6860.

Rowhedge *Essex* Population: 1749. ***Village***, on River Colne, opposite Wivenhoe. **34 E6** TM0221.

Rowhook *W.Suss.* ***Settlement***, 4m/6km NW of Horsham, on course of Roman Stane Street. Site of Roman station 1m/2km SW. **12 E3** TQ1234.

Rowington *Warks.* ***Village***, 6m/10km NW of Warwick. **30 D2** SP2069.

Rowington Green *Warks.* ***Hamlet***, to N of Rowington. **30 D1** SP2070.

Rowland *Derbys.* ***Hamlet***, 3m/4km N of Bakewell. **50 E5** SK2172.

Rowland's Castle *Hants.* ***Village***, 3m/5km N of Havant. Site of Roman building to S. **11 J3** SU7310.

Rowlands Gill *T. & W.* Population: 6603. ***Village***, on River Derwent 3m/5km SW of Blaydon. **62 C1** NZ1658.

Rowledge *Surr.* ***Suburb***, SW suburb of Farnham. **22 B7** SU8243.

Rowley *Devon* ***Settlement***, 4m/7km S of South Molton. **7 F4** SS7319.

Rowley *Dur.* ***Settlement***, 1km SE of Castleside. **62 B2** NZ0848.

Rowley *E.Riding* ***Hamlet***, 8m/12km NW of Kingston upon Hull. **59 F6** SE9732.

Rowley *Shrop.* ***Settlement***, 5m/8km E of Welshpool. **38 C5** SJ3006.

Rowley Hill *W.Yorks.* ***Locality***, adjoining to S of Fenay Bridge, 3m/5km E of Huddersfield. SE1914.

Rowley Park *Staffs.* ***Suburb***, 1km S of Stafford town centre. SJ9122.

Rowley Regis *W.Mid.* ***Suburb***, W district of Warley. **40 B7** SO9687.

Rowley's Green *W.Mid.* ***Suburb***, 3m/5km N of Coventry city centre. SP3483.

Rowlstone *Here.* ***Village***, 1m/2km W of Pontrilas. **28 C6** SO3727.

Rowly *Surr.* ***Settlement***, 2m/3km NW of Cranleigh. **22 D7** TQ0440.

Rownall *Staffs.* ***Settlement***, 1m/2km NW of Wetley Rocks. SJ9549.

Rowner *Hants.* ***Suburb***, of Gosport 2m/4km NW of town centre. **11 G4** SU5801.

Rowney Green *Worcs.* ***Village***, 3m/4km N of Redditch. **30 B1** SP0471.

Rownhams *Hants.* ***Village***, 4m/6km NW of Southampton. **10 E3** SU3817.

Rowrah *Cumb.* ***Hamlet***, 2m/3km NW of Ennerdale Bridge. **60 B5** NY0518.

Rowridge *I.o.W.* ***Locality***, with television station mast, 4m/6km SW of Newport. SZ4486.

Rowsham *Bucks.* ***Village***, 3m/5km NE of Aylesbury. **32 B7** SP8518.

Rowsley *Derbys.* ***Village***, 3m/5km SE of Bakewell. **50 E6** SK2565.

Rowson Green *Derbys.* ***Village***, 2m/3km SE of Belper. SK3746.

Rowstock *Oxon.* ***Hamlet***, 3m/5km W of Didcot. **21 H3** SU4789.

Rowston *Lincs.* ***Village***, 7m/11km N of Sleaford. **52 D7** TF0856.

Rowthorne *Derbys.* ***Hamlet***, 5m/7km NW of Mansfield. **51 G6** SK4764.

Rowton *Ches.* ***Village***, 3m/5km SE of Chester. **48 D6** SJ4564.

Rowton *Shrop.* ***Locality***, 2m/4km SW of Craven Arms. SO4080.

Rowton *Shrop.* ***Settlement***, 8m/13km W of Shrewsbury. **38 C4** SJ3612.

Rowton *Tel. & W.* ***Hamlet***, 6m/9km NW of Wellington. **39 F4** SJ6119.

Roxburgh *Sc.Bord.* ***Village***, 3m/5km SW of Kelso. **76 E7** NT7030.

Roxby *N.Lincs.* ***Village***, 4m/7km NE of Scunthorpe. **52 C1** SE9116.

Roxby *N.Yorks.* ***Locality***, 1m/2km SW of Pickhill. Site of Roman settlement to N. SE3282.

Roxby *N.Yorks.* ***Village***, 2m/3km SW of Staithes. **63 J5** NZ7616.

Roxby Beck *N.Yorks.* ***River***, rising on Roxby High Moor and flowing NW, then NE into North Sea at Staithes. **63 J5** NZ7819.

Roxby High Moor *N.Yorks.* ***Open space***, moorland 1km S of Scaling Dam Reservoir. **63 J5** NZ7511.

Roxby Low Moor *N.Yorks.* ***Open space***, small area of moorland, 1km NW of Scaling Dam Reservoir. **63 J5** NZ7613.

Roxeth *Gt.Lon.* ***Suburb***, in borough of Harrow, 1m/2km W of Harrow on the Hill. TQ1486.

Roxholm *Lincs.* ***Locality***, 3m/4km N of Sleaford. TF0550.

Roxton *Beds.* ***Village***, 4m/6km N of Sandy. **32 E3** TL1554.

Roxwell *Essex* ***Village***, 4m/6km W of Chelmsford. **24 C1** TL6408.

Roy *High.* ***River***, in Lochaber district, rising on N side of Creag Meagaidh and running down to Loch Roy, then continuing N for 3m/5km before turning SW and running down Glen Roy to River Spean, on S side of Roybridge. **87 K5** NN2780.

Royal Albert Bridge ***Bridge***, railway bridge built by Brunel in 1859 over River Tamar at Saltash. SX4358.

Royal Bath and Wells Showground *Som.* ***Other feature of interest***, agricultural showground, 3m/4km SE of Shepton Mallet. **9 F1** ST6339.

Royal Botanic Gardens *Edin.* ***Garden***, 1m/2km NW of Edinburgh city centre. Rock garden, Pringle Chinese Collection and glasshouses in 70 acres of landscaped gardens. **76 A3** NT2475.

Royal Botanic Gardens Kew (Kew Gardens). *Gt.Lon.* ***Garden***, 300 acre botanic gardens, founded in 1759 by Princess Augusta on S bank of River Thames 1m/2km N of Richmond. Incorporates rare and exotic plants from all over the world and is famous for its economic collections, identification of rare plants, economic botany and scientific research. Includes arboretum, alpine, water and rhododendron gardens, plus 17c Queen's Garden with formal rosebed. Magnificent tropical orchid, palm, temperate and Australasian houses, plus Princess of Wales Conservatory with 10 climatic zones. Herbarium contains Sir Joseph Hooker's famous HMS Erebus and Indian plant collections. Lake, aquatic garden and pagoda were designed by Sir William Chambers in 1760, while curved glass Palm House and Temperate House, 1844-8, are by Decimus Burton. Kew's scientific aspect was developed by its two directors Sir William and Sir Joseph Hooker. **22 E4** TQ1876.

Royal British Legion Village *Kent* ***Village***, rehabilitation centre, 3m/4km NW of Maidstone. **14 C2** TQ7257.

Royal Citadel *Plym.* ***Castle***, in Plymouth. 17c fortress (English Heritage) built to defend coast from Dutch. **4 E5** SX4853.

Royal Festival Hall *Gt.Lon.* *See South Bank Arts Centre.*

Royal Forest *High.* ***Large natural feature***, mountain area (National Trust for Scotland) N of Glen Etive, Lochaber district. Includes Buachaille Etive Mòr. **80 D2** NN2053.

Royal Hill *Devon* ***Mountain***, 2m/3km SE of Princetown, in Dartmoor National Park. Height 1335 feet or 407 metres. **5 G3** SX6172.

Royal Leamington Spa (Commonly referred to as Leamington Spa.) *Warks.* Population: 55,396. ***Town***, spa town on River Leam, 8m/13km S of Coventry. Full style conferred on town in 1838, following visit by Queen Victoria. Many Regency and Victorian buildings. **30 E2** SP3165.

Royal Merchant Navy School *W'ham* *See Sindlesham.*

Royal Museum of Scotland *Edin.* ***Other feature of interest***, in Chambers Street, Edinburgh, with exhibitions including natural history, technology and geology. **76 A3** NT2572.

Royal National Theatre *Gt.Lon.* *See South Bank Arts Centre.*

Royal Oak *Darl.* ***Locality***, named after public house, 4m/6km S of Bishop Auckland. NZ2023.

Royal Oak *Lancs.* ***Settlement***, 4m/6km W of Skelmersdale. SD4103.

Royal Observatory Visitor Centre *Edin.* ***Other feature of interest***, on Blackford Hill, 2m/3km S of Edinburgh city centre. Contains exhibitions on work of Observatory, tour of space and time, and collection of telescopes. **76 A3** NT2570.

Royal Opera House *Gt.Lon.* ***Leisure/recreation***, in City of Westminster, 1km N of Charing Cross. Designed by E.M. Barry in 1858, it is home of world-famous Royal Opera and Royal Ballet companies. TQ3081.

Royal Pavilion *B. & H.* ***Historic house***, exotic early 19c seaside palace in Brighton. Built for Prince Regent, designed by John Nash. Includes restored Regency gardens. **13 G6** TQ3104.

Royal Tunbridge Wells (Commonly known as Tunbridge Wells.) *Kent* Population: 60,272. ***Town***, largely residential town and shopping centre 31m/50km SE of London. Formerly a spa (chalybeate springs). Officially 'Royal' since 1909. **13 J3** TQ5839.

Royal Tweed Bridge *Northumb.* ***Bridge***, built over River Tweed in 1925 at Berwick-upon-Tweed to relieve traffic on existing bridges. Constructed of reinforced concrete, one arch of 361 feet being largest reinforced concrete arch in Britain at time of construction. NT9952.

Royal Victoria Country Park *Hants.* ***Leisure/recreation***, 1m/2km NW of Hamble. 143 acres of parkland, woodland and coastline based around remains of famous Royal Victoria Military Hospital built after Crimean War in 1856. **11 F4** SU4607.

Royal's Green *Ches.* ***Settlement***, 2m/4km W of Audlem. SJ6242.

Roybridge *High.* ***Village***, in Glen Spean, at foot of Glen Roy, in Lochaber district, 3m/5km E of Spean Bridge. **87 J6** NN2781.

Royd *S.Yorks.* ***Locality***, 1km SE of Stocksbridge. SK2797.

Royd Moor *S.Yorks.* ***Settlement***, 2m/3km NW of Penistone. SE2204.

Roydhouse *W.Yorks.* ***Hamlet***, 2m/3km E of Highburton. SE2112.

Roydon *Essex* Population: 1689. ***Village***, 2m/4km W of Harlow. **33 H7** TL4010.

Roydon *Norf.* Population: 1393. ***Village***, 6m/10km E of King's Lynn. **44 B3** TF7022.

Roydon *Norf.* ***Village***, 1m/2km W of Diss. **44 E7** TM0980.

Roydon Hamlet *Essex* ***Village***, 2m/4km SW of Harlow. **23 H1** TL4107.

Royds Green Lower *W.Yorks.* ***Locality***, 1km S of Royds Green Upper. SE3526.

Royds Green Upper *W.Yorks.* ***Locality***, 1m/2km SE of Rothwell. SE3526.

Royl Field *Shet.* ***Hill***, 2m/3km W of Mail, Mainland. Height 961 feet or 293 metres. **109 C10** HU3928.

Royley *Gt.Man.* ***Locality***, adjoining to W of Royton. SD9107.

Roy's Hill *Moray* ***Mountain***, 3m/4km SW of Upper Knockando. Height 1692 feet or 516 metres. **97 J7** NJ1440.

Royston *Herts.* Population: 14,087. ***Town***, market town at crossing of Icknield Way and Roman Ermine Street, 12m/20km SW of Cambridge, and formerly an important coaching stop. **33 G4** TL3540.

Royston *S.Yorks.* Population: 9638. ***Small town***, 3m/5km N of Barnsley. **51 F1** SE3611.

Royston Water *Som.* ***Hamlet***, 1km E of Churchingford. ST2213.

Royton *Gt.Man.* Population: 21,475. ***Town***, old cotton town, 2m/3km N of Oldham. **49 J2** SD9207.

Ru Bornaskitaig *High.* ***Coastal feature***, headland on N coast of Skye, 6m/9km N of Uig. **93 J4** NG3771.

Ru Stafnish *Arg. & B.* ***Coastal feature***, headland on E coast of Kintyre, 6m/9km SE of Campbeltown. **66 B2** NR7713.

Ruabon (Rhiwabon). *Wrex.* Population: 2828. ***Small town***, industrial town, 5m/7km SW of Wrexham. **38 C1** SJ3043.

Ruabon Mountain *Wrex.* ***Mountain***, 3m/5km W of Rhosllanerchrugog. Height 1378 feet or 420 metres. **38 B1** SJ2446.

Ruadh Mheall ***Mountain***, on border of Perth & Kinross and Stirling, 1m/2km NW of head of Loch Lednoch. Height 2237 feet or 682 metres. **81 H4** NN6731.

Ruadh-phort Mòr *Arg. & B.* ***Village***, on E coast of Islay, just N of Port Askaig. NR4269.

Ruadh Sgeir *Arg. & B.* ***Island***, 2m/3km SW of Ross of Mull. **78 D6** NM3014.

Ruadh-stac Mòr *High.* ***Mountain***, summit of Beinn Eighe, 5m/8km W of Kinlochewe in Ross and Cromarty district. Munro: height 3313 feet or 1010 metres. **95 F5** NG9561.

Ruadh Stac Mòr *High.* ***Mountain***, in Ross and Cromarty district, 8m/13km N of Kinlochewe. Munro: height 3011 feet or 918 metres. **95 G4** NH0175.

Ruaig *Arg. & B.* ***Settlement***, near E end of Tiree, 2m/3km W of Rubha Dubh. **78 B3** NM0647.
Ruan Lanihorne *Cornw.* ***Village***, on Ruan River, 5m/8km SE of Truro across Tresillian River. **3 F4** SW8942.
Ruan Major *Cornw.* ***Hamlet***, 3m/5km N of Lizard Point. **2 D7** SW7016.
Ruan Minor *Cornw.* ***Village***, 3m/5km NE of Lizard Point. **2 E7** SW7215.
Ruanaich *Arg. & B.* ***Settlement***, on Iona, 1km SW of Baile Mòr. **78 D5** NM2723.
Ruardean *Glos.* ***Village***, 3m/5km NW of Cinderford. **29 F7** SO6117.
Ruardean Hill *Glos.* ***Village***, 2m/4km NW of Cinderford. SO6317.
Ruardean Woodside *Glos.* ***Village***, 3m/4km NW of Cinderford. **29 F7** SO6216.
Rubers Law *Sc.Bord.* ***Mountain***, 2m/3km SE of Denholm. Height 1391 feet or 424 metres. **70 A2** NT5815.
Rubery *Worcs.* ***Suburb***, 8m/13km SW of Birmingham, on border with West Midlands. **29 J1** SO9877.
Rubh' a' Bhaid Bheithe *Arg. & B.* ***Coastal feature***, headland at N end of Appin, on S side of mouth of Loch Leven. **80 B2** NN0259.
Rubh' a' Bhàigh Uaine *W.Isles* ***Coastal feature***, headland on E coast of Isle of Lewis, 3m/4km S of Stornoway. **101 G5** NB4229.
Rubh a' Bhaird *W.Isles* ***Coastal feature***, headland on S coast of Isle of Lewis, at W entrance to Loch Bhrollum. **101 F7** NB3101.
Rubh' a' Bhearnaig *Arg. & B.* ***Coastal feature***, headland at N end of Kerrera, 1m/2km NW of Oban, Argyll, across Sound of Kerrera. **79 K4** NM8431.
Rubh' a' Bhinnein *Arg. & B.* ***Coastal feature***, headland on NW coast of Coll, 4m/6km N of Arinagour. **78 D1** NM2263.
Rubh' a' Bhrocaire *High.* ***Island***, small uninhabited island (a headland at low tide) off NW coast of Ross and Cromarty district in Enard bay, to E of Eilean Mòr. NC0717.
Rubh' a' Chamais *Arg. & B.* ***Coastal feature***, headland on S side of Lagg Bay, on E side of Jura. **72 E3** NR5978.
Rubh' a' Chaoil *Arg. & B.* ***Coastal feature***, headland on W coast of Mull, on N side of entrance to Loch Tuath. **78 E3** NM3346.
Rubh' a' Choin *High.* ***Coastal feature***, headland on S side of Enard Bay. **102 C7** NC0314.
Rubh' a' Chrois-aoinidh *Arg. & B.* ***Coastal feature***, headland on W coast of Jura on S side of entrance to Loch Tarbert. **72 C2** NR5080.
Rubh' a' Geodha *Arg. & B.* ***Coastal feature***, headland on NE coast of Colonsay. **72 C1** NR4399.
Rubh' a' Mhàil *Arg. & B.* ***Coastal feature***, headland with lighthouse at N extremity of Islay. **72 C3** NR4279.
Rubh' a' Mhill Dheirg *High.* ***Coastal feature***, promontory 4m/7km S of Point of Stoer, Sutherland district. **102 C6** NC0229.
Rubh' a' Mhucard *High.* ***Coastal feature***, headland at N end of Eddrachillis Bay, Sutherland district. **102 D5** NC1538.
Rubh' Aird an t-Sionnaich *High.* ***Coastal feature***, headland on W coast of Sutherland district, 1m/2km SW of Scourie. **102 D4** NC1443.
Rubh' an Dùnain *High.* ***Coastal feature***, headland on SW coast of Skye, on S side of entrance to Loch Brittle. Ancient galleried chamber 1km E, on Soay Sound. **85 J3** NG3816.
Rubh' an Dùnain *W.Isles* ***Coastal feature***, headland on NW coast of Isle of Lewis, 1km N of South Shawbost. **100 E3** NB2448.
Rubh' an Fhir Leithe *High.* ***Coastal feature***, headland on W coast of Sutherland district, 5m/8km NW of Kinlochbervie. **102 D2** NC1863.
Rubh' an Leanachais *Arg. & B.* ***Coastal feature***, headland on E coast of Jura, 1m/2km S of Lowlandman's Bay. **72 D3** NR5570.
Rubh 'an Leim *Arg. & B.* ***Coastal feature***, narrow rocky promontory forming E side of Lowlandman's Bay, Jura, 1km NE of Ardfernal across bay. **72 D3** NR5772.
Rubh' an Lochain *High.* ***Coastal feature***, headland on N coast of Scalpay, Skye and Lochalsh district. **86 C1** NG6132.
Rubh' an t-Sàilein *Arg. & B.* ***Coastal feature***, headland on W coast of Jura on N side of entrance to Loch Tarbert. **72 C2** NR5082.
Rubh' an t-Suibhein *Arg. & B.* ***Coastal feature***, headland on Mull, on N side of entrance to Loch Tuath. **78 E3** NM3645.
Rubh Ard Slisneach *High.* ***Coastal feature***, headland at NW point of Knoydart, Lochaber district, on S side of entrance to Loch Hourn. **86 D4** NG7409.
Rubh' Ardalanish (Anglicised form: Ardalanish Point.) *Arg. & B.* ***Coastal feature***, headland 1m/2km S of Ardalanish Bay. **78 E6** NM3719.
Rubh' Arisaig *High.* ***Coastal feature***, headland on coast of Lochaber district 3m/5km W of Arisaig. **86 C6** NM6184.
Rubh' Leam na Làraich *High.* ***Coastal feature***, headland on westernmost point of Muck. **85 J7** NM3979.
Rubha Aird Druimnich *High.* ***Coastal feature***, headland on N side of Ardnamurchan peninsula in Lochaber district, 9m/14km NW of Salen. **86 B7** NM5772.
Rubha Aird-mhicheil *W.Isles* ***Coastal feature***, headland on W coast of South Uist, 3m/4km N of Rubha Ardvule. **84 C1** NF7233.
Rubha Airigh Bheirg *N.Ayr.* ***Coastal feature***, on NW coast of Arran, 3m/4km NE of Pirnmill. **73 G6** NR8847.
Rubha an Dùine *W.Isles* *Gaelic form of Scarts Rock, qv.*
Rubha an Fhasaidh *High.* ***Coastal feature***, headland on W coast of Eigg, 4m/6km NE of Galmisdale. **85 K6** NM4387.
Rubha an Ridire *High.* ***Coastal feature***, headland at S end of Morvern, Lochaber district. **79 J4** NM7340.
Rubha an t-Seileir *W.Isles* *Gaelic form of Cellar Head, qv.*
Rubha an t-Siùmpain *W.Isles* *Gaelic form of Tiumpan Head, qv.*
Rubha Ardvule *W.Isles* ***Coastal feature***, headland on W coast of South Uist, 10m/16km S of Ardivachar Point. **84 C2** NF7030.
Rubha Bàn *Arg. & B.* ***Coastal feature***, headland on NE corner of Oronsay. **72 B2** NR3889.
Rubha Beag *Arg. & B.* ***Coastal feature***, headland on W coast of Cowal, 5m/8km NW of Tighnabruaich. **73 H3** NR9179.
Rubha Beag *High.* ***Coastal feature***, headland 2m/3km E of Greenstone Point, Ross and Cromarty district. **94 E2** NG8997.
Rubha Bhataisgeir (Anglicised form: Vatisker Point.) *W.Isles* ***Coastal feature***, headland on coast 1km E of Vatisker, Isle of Lewis. **101 G4** NB4839.
Rubha Bhilidh *W.Isles* ***Coastal feature***, headland on E coast of South Uist, 2m/4km E of Ben Corodale. **84 D1** NF8632.
Rubha Bholsa *Arg. & B.* ***Coastal feature***, headland on N coast of Islay, 3m/5km W of Rubh' a' Mhàil. **72 B3** NR3778.
Rubha Bhrollum *W.Isles* ***Coastal feature***, headland on S coast of Isle of Lewis, at E of entrance to Loch Bhrollum. **101 F7** NB3202.
Rubha Bhuic *W.Isles* ***Coastal feature***, headland on W coast of North Harris, 3m/4km SE of Huisinis. **100 C7** NB0108.
Rubha Bocaig *W.Isles* ***Coastal feature***, headland on E coast of South Harris, 3m/4km E of Greosabhagh. **93 G2** NG1891.
Rubha Bolum *W.Isles* ***Coastal feature***, headland on E coast of South Uist, 4m/6km SE of Beinn Mhòr. **84 D2** NF8328.
Rubha Cam nan Gall *W.Isles* ***Coastal feature***, headland at northernmost point of Wiay. **92 D7** NF8847.
Rubha Chaolais *High.* ***Coastal feature***, headland at W end of peninsula of Ardnish, Sound of Arisaig, on coast of Lochaber district. **86 C6** NM6980.
Rubha Chorachan *High.* ***Coastal feature***, headland at S end of Uig Bay, Skye. **93 J5** NG3761.
Rubha Chulinish *Arg. & B.* ***Coastal feature***, headland on N coast of Ulva. **78 E3** NM3942.
Rubha Cluer *W.Isles* ***Coastal feature***, headland on E coast of South Harris, 2m/3km S of Greosabhagh. **93 G3** NG1589.
Rubha Coigeach *High.* ***Coastal feature***, headland on NW coast of Ross and Cromarty district at NW point of Coigach and W point of Enard Bay. **102 B7** NB9818.
Rubha Cruitiridh *Arg. & B.* ***Coastal feature***, headland on S coast of Knapdale, Argyll, on W side of Loch Stornoway. **73 F4** NR7160.
Rubha Deas *W.Isles* ***Coastal feature***, headland on E coast of Eye Peninsula, Isle of Lewis, 1m/2km S of Tiumpan Head. **101 H4** NB5735.
Rubha Dubh *Arg. & B.* ***Coastal feature***, headland at E end of Tiree. **78 C3** NM0948.
Rubha Dubh *Arg. & B.* ***Coastal feature***, headland on S coast of Mull, on W side of entrance to Loch Buie. **79 G5** NM5621.
Rubha Dubh *Arg. & B.* ***Coastal feature***, headland on E coast of Colonsay nearly 2m/3km S of Scalasaig. Another headland with lighthouse at Scalasaig itself has same name. **72 B1** NR3991.
Rubha Dùin Bhàin *Arg. & B.* ***Coastal feature***, headland on W coast of Kintyre, 5m/8km N of Mull of Kintyre. **66 A2** NR5914.
Rubha Fasachd *Arg. & B.* ***Coastal feature***, headland on E side of Loch Breachacha, Coll. **78 C2** NM1652.
Rubha Fiola *Arg. & B.* ***Island***, small island N of Lunga and 1km E of Eilean Dubh Mòr. NM7110.
Rubha Garbh-àird *Arg. & B.* ***Coastal feature***, headland at W end of Ardmucknish Bay, Benderloch, Argyll. **80 A4** NM8736.
Rubha Garbh Airde *Arg. & B.* ***Coastal feature***, headland on N coast of Seil, 2m/3km N of Balvicar. **79 J6** NM7620.
Rubha Garbh-ard *Arg. & B.* ***Coastal feature***, headland on N side of mouth of Loch Crinan. **73 F1** NR7895.
Rubha Garbhaig *High.* ***Coastal feature***, headland on NE coast of Skye, 4m/6km NW of Rubha nam Brathairean. **94 B5** NG4968.
Rubha Hellisdale *W.Isles* ***Coastal feature***, headland on E coast of South Uist, 2m/3km E of Beinn Mhòr. **84 D1** NF8430.
Rubha Hunish *High.* ***Coastal feature***, headland at N end of Skye, 9m/14km N of Uig. **93 J4** NG4077.
Rubha Idrigil *High.* ***Coastal feature***, headland to N of Uig Bay, Skye. **93 J5** NG3763.
Rubha Iosal *W.Isles* ***Coastal feature***, headland on E coast of Isle of Lewis, 1m/2km N of Kebock Head. **101 G6** NB4216.
Rubha Lagganroaig *Arg. & B.* ***Coastal feature***, headland on NE coast of Kintyre, 4m/6km SE of Tarbert. **73 H4** NR9163.
Rubha Lamanais *Arg. & B.* ***Coastal feature***, headland on W coast of Islay, 2m/3km NW of Loch Gorm. **72 A4** NR2068.
Rubha Leathann *W.Isles* ***Coastal feature***, headland on NW coast of Isle of Lewis, 1m/2km W of Siadar Uarach. **101 F2** NB3654.
Rubha Leumair *High.* ***Coastal feature***, headland 3m/4km N of Loch Inver, Sutherland district. **102 C6** NC0326.
Rubha Liath *Arg. & B.* ***Coastal feature***, stack off S coast of NE Tiree. **78 B3** NM0846.
Rubha Liath *Arg. & B.* ***Coastal feature***, on E coast of Islay, 9m/14km NE of Port Ellen. **72 C5** NR4755.
Rubha Liath *W.Isles* ***Coastal feature***, headland on SE coast of Eriskay, 2m/3km SE of Haunn. **84 D4** NF8009.
Rubha Maol *High.* ***Coastal feature***, headland on NW coast of Skye, on W side of entrance to Loch Bay. **93 H6** NG2456.
Rubha Maol na Mine *Arg. & B.* ***Coastal feature***, headland on SW coast of Gometra. **78 E3** NM3440.
Rubha Màs a' Chnuic *W.Isles* ***Coastal feature***, headland on South Harris, 1m/2km E of Toe Head. **92 E2** NF9794.
Rubha Meall na Hoe *W.Isles* ***Coastal feature***, headland on E coast of South Uist, 2m/4km SE of Lochboisdale. **84 D3** NF8217.
Rubha Mhic Gille-mhìcheil *W.Isles* ***Coastal feature***, headland on E coast of North Uist, 2m/3km N of Eigneig Bheag. **92 E5** NF9366.
Rubha Mòr *Arg. & B.* ***Coastal feature***, headland on N coast of Coll, 1m/2km W of NE end of island. **78 D1** NM2464.
Rubha Mòr *Arg. & B.* ***Coastal feature***, headland on W coast of Islay at S end of Laggan Bay. **72 A6** NR2948.
Rubha Mòr *High.* ***Coastal feature***, peninsula on W coast of Ross and Cromarty district, to W of Enard Bay. **102 B7** NB9814.
Rubha Mòr *High.* ***Coastal feature***, large peninsula in Ross and Cromarty district separating Loch Ewe from Gruinard Bay. **94 E2** NG8696.
Rubha Mòr *High.* ***Coastal feature***, headland on E side of Loch Linnhe in Lochaber district, at NW end of Cuil Bay. **80 A2** NM9655.
Rubha Mòr *W.Isles* ***Coastal feature***, headland on SE coast of Barra, 2m/3km E of Castlebay. **84 B5** NL6997.
Rubha na Bearnaich *W.Isles* ***Coastal feature***, headland on SE coast of Eye Peninsula, Isle of Lewis. **101 H4** NB5531.
Rubha na Brèige *High.* ***Coastal feature***, headland to N of Enard Bay. **102 C7** NC0519.
Rubha na Caillich *Arg. & B.* ***Coastal feature***, headland on E coast of Jura, 1km S of Craighouse. **72 D4** NR5366.
Rubha na Carraig-géire *Arg. & B.* ***Coastal feature***, headland at S end of Iona. **78 D5** NM2621.
Rubha na Creige Mòire *W.Isles* ***Coastal feature***, headland on E coast of South Uist, 2m/4km E of Lochboisdale. **84 D3** NF8320.
Rubha na Cruibe *W.Isles* ***Coastal feature***, headland on E coast of South Uist, 2m/3km E of Lochboisdale. **84 D3** NF8219.
Rubha na Faing *Arg. & B.* ***Coastal feature***, headland at SW point of Rinns of Islay. **72 A5** NR1553.
Rubha na Faoilinn *Arg. & B.* ***Coastal feature***, headland on SE coast of Mull, on NE side of entrance to Loch Spelve. **79 J5** NM7227.
Rubha na Fearn *High.* ***Coastal feature***, headland on W coast of Ross and Cromarty district, on S side of entrance to Loch Torridon. **94 D5** NG7261.
Rubha na Feola *High.* ***Coastal feature***, small bay on S shore of Upper Loch Torridon, 4m/6km SW of Torridon. **94 E6** NG8354.
Rubha na Gainmhich *Arg. & B.* ***Coastal feature***, headland on promontory of Ard Imersay, S coast of Islay, 4m/7km E of Port Ellen. **72 C6** NR4346.
Rubha na Gibhte *W.Isles* ***Coastal feature***, headland on E coast of South Uist, 4m/7km NE of Lochboisdale. **84 D2** NF8225.
Rubha na Greine *W.Isles* ***Coastal feature***, headland on E coast of Eye Peninsula, Isle of Lewis, 3m/5km S of Tiumpan Head. **101 H4** NB5633.
Rubha na h-Airde Uinnsinn *High.* ***Coastal feature***, headland on W side of Loch Linnhe in Lochaber district, 1m/2km W of entrance to Loch a' Choire. NM8752.
Rubha na h-Aiseig *High.* ***Coastal feature***, headland at northern point of Skye, 9m/14km N of Uig. **93 K4** NG4476.
Rubha na h-Easgainne (Anglicised form: Strathaird Point.) *High.* ***Coastal feature***, headland on S coast of Skye at S end of Strathaird peninsula. **86 B3** NG5211.
Rubha na h-Ordaig *W.Isles* ***Coastal feature***, headland at SE end of South Uist, 3m/5km SE of entrance to Loch Baghasdail. **84 D3** NF8414.
Rubha na' Leac *High.* ***Coastal feature***, headland on Raasay, 3m/5km N of Eyre Point. **86 C1** NG6038.
Rubha na Leacaig *High.* ***Coastal feature***, headland 1km W of Kinlochbervie, Sutherland district. **102 E3** NC2056.
Rubha na Lice *Arg. & B.* ***Coastal feature***, headland on NW coast of Kerrera. **79 J5** NM8029.
Rubha na Lice Uaine *High.* *Alternative name for Greenstone Point, qv.*
Rubha na Rodagrich *W.Isles* ***Coastal feature***, headland at southernmost point of Ronay. **92 E6** NF8953.
Rubha na Roinne *High.* ***Coastal feature***, headland on E coast of Rum, N of entrance to Loch Scresort. **85 K4** NG4200.
Rubha na Tràille *Arg. & B.* ***Coastal feature***, headland near southernmost point of Jura, 3m/5km S of Craighouse. **72 D4** NR5162.
Rubha nam Barr *Arg. & B.* ***Coastal feature***, on SE side of Sound of Jura, 3m/4km SW of Crinan. **73 F1** NR7591.
Rubha nam Bràithrean *Arg. & B.* ***Coastal feature***, headland on S coast of Ross of Mull, 4m/7km SW of Bunesssan. **79 F6** NM4317.
Rubha nam Brathairean *High.* ***Coastal feature***, headland on NE coast of Skye, 8m/13km E of Uig. **94 B5** NG5262.
Rubha nam Meirleach *High.* ***Coastal feature***, headland on Rum, near southernmost point of island. **85 J5** NM3691.
Rubha nan Cearc *Arg. & B.* ***Coastal feature***, headland at NW end of Ross of Mull. **78 E5** NM3125.
Rubha nan Clach *High.* ***Coastal feature***, headland on W coast of Skye, on SE side of entrance to Loch Bracadale. **85 H1** NG3033.
Rubha nan Còsan *High.* ***Coastal feature***, headland on W coast of Oldany Island, Sutherland district. **102 C5** NC0734.
Rubha nan Gall *Arg. & B.* ***Coastal feature***, headland on N coast of Ulva, 1m/2km E of Rubha Chulinish. **79 F3** NM4141.
Rubha nan Leacan *Arg. & B.* ***Coastal feature***, headland at S end of The Oa, Islay. Most southerly point of island. **72 B7** NR3140.
Rubha nan Oirean *Arg. & B.* ***Coastal feature***, headland on W coast of Mull, 2m/3km W of Calgary. **78 E2** NM3551.
Rubha Port Scolpaig *W.Isles* ***Coastal feature***, headland on North Uist, 1km S of Aird an Rùnair. **92 C5** NF6868.

R

Rubha Quidnish *W.Isles* ***Coastal feature***, headland on SE coast of South Harris, 2m/3km S of Manais. **93 G3** NG1086.
Rubha Raonuill *High.* ***Coastal feature***, headland on N side of entrance to Loch Nevis, on coast of Knoydart, Lochaber district. **86 D5** NM7399.
Rubha Raouill *W.Isles* ***Coastal feature***, rock off SW coast of North Uist, 3m/5km SE of Aird an Rùnair. **92 C5** NF7166.
Rubha Réidh *High.* ***Coastal feature***, headland with lighthouse on W coast of Ross and Cromarty district 10m/16km NW of Poolewe. **94 D2** NG7391.
Rubha Righinn *Arg. & B.* ***Coastal feature***, headland at S point of Scarba. **79 J7** NM7002.
Rubha Robhanais *W.Isles Gaelic form of Butt of Lewis, qv.*
Rubha Rodha *High.* ***Coastal feature***, headland 3m/4km W of Lochinver. **102 C6** NC0523.
Rubha Romagi *W.Isles* ***Coastal feature***, headland on W coast of South Harris, 6m/10km N of Leverburgh. **93 F2** NG0396.
Rubha Rossel *W.Isles* ***Coastal feature***, headland on E coast of South Uist, 2m/4km NE of Hecla. **84 D1** NF8536.
Rubha Ruadh (Also known as Red Point.) *High.* ***Coastal feature***, headland on W coast of Sutherland district, on W side of entrance to Loch Laxford. **102 D3** NC1651.
Rubha Seanach *Arg. & B.* ***Coastal feature***, headland at S end of Kerrera. **79 K5** NM8025.
Rubha Sgeirigin *W.Isles* ***Coastal feature***, headland at southernmost point of Taransay. **92 E2** NF9998.
Rubha Sgor an t-Snidhe *High.* ***Coastal feature***, headland on SW coast of Rum, 2m/3km NW of Rubha nam Meirleach. **85 J5** NM3493.
Rubha Sgor-Innis *Arg. & B.* ***Coastal feature***, headland on NE coast of Coll, looking NE towards Eilean Mòr. **78 D1** NM2763.
Rubha Shamhnan Insir *High.* ***Coastal feature***, headland at northernmost point of Rum. **85 J4** NG3704.
Rubha Suisnish *High.* ***Coastal feature***, headland on S coast of Skye between Loch Eishort and Loch Slapin. **86 B3** NG5815.
Rubha Thearna Sgurr *High.* ***Coastal feature***, headland on SW coast of Skye, 1m/2km NW of entrance to Loch Brittle. **85 J3** NG3619.
Rubha Thormaid *High.* ***Coastal feature***, headland on N coast, 3m/5km NW of mouth of Tongue Bay. **103 H2** NC5468.
Rubha Vallarip *W.Isles* ***Coastal feature***, headland on S coast of South Harris, 1km E of Rodel. **93 F3** NG0682.
Ruchazie *Glas.* ***Suburb***, 4m/6km E of Glasgow city centre. NS6566.
Ruchill *Glas.* ***Suburb***, 2m/3km N of Glasgow city centre. NS5768.
Ruchill Water *P. & K. See Water of Ruchill.*
Ruckcroft *Cumb.* ***Settlement***, 3m/4km NW of Kirkoswald. **61 G2** NY5344.
Ruckhall Common *Here.* ***Locality***, 4m/6km W of Hereford. SO4439.
Ruckinge *Kent* ***Village***, 2m/3km E of Hamstreet. **15 F4** TR0233.
Ruckland *Lincs.* ***Settlement***, 6m/9km S of Louth. **53 G5** TF3378.
Rucklers Green *Herts.* ***Hamlet***, 2m/3km S of Hemel Hempstead. TL0604.
Ruckley *Shrop.* ***Hamlet***, 6m/9km W of Much Wenlock. **38 E5** SJ5300.
Rudbaxton *Pembs.* ***Settlement***, 3m/5km N of Haverfordwest. **16 C2** SM9620.
Rudby *N.Yorks.* ***Village***, opposite Hutton Rudby across River Leven, 4m/6km W of Stokesley. **63 F6** NZ4706.
Rudchester *Northumb.* ***Settlement***, next to Roman fort of Vindobala on Hadrian's Wall, 1m/2km W of Heddon-on-the-Wall. **71 G7** NZ1167.
Rudchester Roman Fort *Northumb.* ***Historic/prehistoric site***, Roman fort of Vindobala on Hadrian's Wall, 1m/2km W of Heddon-on-the-Wall. **71 G7** NZ1167.
Ruddington *Notts.* Population: 6476. ***Village***, 3m/5km S of West Bridgford. **41 H2** SK5733.
Ruddlemoor *Cornw.* ***Settlement***, in China Clay district, 2m/3km N of St. Austell. **4 A5** SX0055.
Ruddons Point *Fife* ***Coastal feature***, headland on E side of Largo Bay. **83 F7** NO4500.
Rudford *Glos.* ***Settlement***, 4m/7km NW of Gloucester. **29 G6** SO7721.
Rudge *Shrop.* ***Locality***, 6m/10km W of Wolverhampton. SO8197.
Rudge *Som.* ***Village***, 3m/5km W of Westbury. **20 B6** ST8251.
Rudge Heath *Shrop.* ***Settlement***, 5m/8km E of Bridgnorth. SO7995.
Rudgeway *S.Glos.* ***Village***, 2m/4km S of Thornbury. **19 K3** ST6286.
Rudgwick *W.Suss.* ***Village***, 4m/6km SE of Cranleigh. **12 D3** TQ0934.
Rudhall *Here.* ***Settlement***, 1m/2km E of Ross-on-Wye. **29 F6** SO6225.
Rudheath *Ches.* ***Hamlet***, 2m/4km NW of Holmes Chapel. SJ7470.
Rudheath *Ches.* ***Village***, adjoining to E of Northwich. **49 F5** SJ6773.
Rudland Rigg *N.Yorks.* ***Other feature of interest***, track across moorland with highest point of 1233 feet or 376 metres, 6m/10km NW of Kirkbymoorside. Disused workings and numerous tumuli on moor. **63 H7** SE6595.
Rudley Green *Essex* ***Hamlet***, 3m/5km SW of Maldon. **24 E1** TL8303.
Rudloe *Wilts.* ***Suburb***, 1m/2km E of Corsham. ST8469.
Rudry (Rhydri). *Caerp.* ***Hamlet***, 3m/4km E of Caerphilly. **18 E3** ST1986.
Rudston *E.Riding* ***Village***, 5m/8km W of Bridlington. Site of Roman villa 1km SW. **59 G3** TA0967.
Rudyard *Staffs.* ***Village***, 2m/4km NW of Leek. **49 J7** SJ9557.
Rudyard Reservoir *Staffs.* ***Reservoir***, 2m/3km in length, to N of Rudyard. Recreational facilities include fishing, boat hire, picnic area and visitor centre. **49 J6** SJ9557.
Rue Point *I.o.M.* ***Coastal feature***, promontory on N coast, 2m/4km N of Andreas. **54 C3** NX4003.
Rueval *W.Isles* ***Hill***, highest point on Benbecula, 3m/5km SE of Benbecula (Baile a' Mhanaich) Aerodrome. Height 407 feet or 124 metres. **92 D6** NF8253.
Rufford *Lancs.* ***Village***, 6m/9km NE of Ormskirk. **48 D1** SD4615.
Rufford *Notts.* ***Locality***, 2m/3km S of Ollerton. SK6464.
Rufford Abbey *Notts.* ***Ecclesiastical building***, remains of 17c restoration of 12c Cistercian abbey (English Heritage), 2m/3km S of Ollerton within Sherwood Forest. Surrounded by country park with 182 acres of parkland, gardens and orangery. **51 J6** SK6464.
Rufford Old Hall *Lancs.* ***Historic house***, late medieval house (National Trust) with later additions, 7m/11km N of Ormskirk. **48 D1** SD4615.
Rufforth *York* ***Village***, 5m/7km W of York. **58 B4** SE5251.
Ruffside *Dur.* ***Settlement***, 2m/3km E of Blanchland. **62 A1** NY9951.
Rugby *Warks.* Population: 61,106. ***Town***, commercial town, 11m/17km E of Coventry, on River Avon. Best known for its railway engineering works, now replaced by a wider range of industries. Boys' public school, founded 1567. Radio transmitting station to E. **31 G1** SP5075.
Rugeley *Staffs.* Population: 22,975. ***Town***, on River Trent, 8m/13km SE of Stafford, with fine 19c church. Former industrial town with power stations nearby. **40 C4** SK0418.
Ruilick *High.* ***Settlement***, 1m/2km NW of Beauly. **96 C7** NH5046.
Ruins *Gt.Man.* ***Locality***, 3m/4km NE of Bolton. SD7411.
Ruinsival *High.* ***Mountain***, on Rum, 4m/7km SW of Kinloch. Height 1732 feet or 528 metres. **85 J5** NM3593.
Ruisgarry *W.Isles Anglicised form of Ruisigearraidh, qv.*
Ruishton *Som.* ***Village***, on River Tone, 3m/4km E of Taunton. **8 B2** ST2625.
Ruisigearraidh (Anglicised form: Ruisgarry.) *W.Isles* ***Settlement***, on Berneray, 1m/2km NE of Borve. **92 E3** NF9282.
Ruislip *Gt.Lon.* ***Suburb***, in borough of Hillingdon, 3m/5km NE of Uxbridge. **22 D3** TQ0987.
Ruislip Common *Gt.Lon.* ***Suburb***, to N of Ruislip. **22 D3** TQ0987.
Ruislip Gardens *Gt.Lon.* ***Suburb***, 1km S of Ruislip. TQ0986.
Ruislip Manor *Gt.Lon.* ***Suburb***, 1m/2km SE of Ruislip. TQ0886.
Ruleos *W.Isles* ***Open space***, on Barra 3m/5km NE of Castlebay. **84 B4** NF7000.
Rum (Formerly spelled Rhum.) *High.* ***Island***, mountainous island of 42 square miles or 109 square km, roughly diamond-shaped, lying 7m/11km S of Rubh' an Dùnain on SW coast of Skye. Island is a National Nature Reserve and is owned by the Nature Conservancy Council, providing opportunities for geological and biological research. **85 J5** NM3798.
Rumble *Shet.* ***Island***, rock island off E coast of Whalsay, 3m/5km E of Clett Head. HU6060.
Rumbling Bridge *P. & K.* ***Village***, on River Devon, 4m/6km E of Dollar. **75 J1** NT0199.
Rumburgh *Suff.* ***Village***, 4m/6km NW of Halesworth. **45 H7** TM3481.
Rumburgh Common *Suff.* ***Locality***, 1km S of Rumburgh. TM3481.
Rumburgh Street *Suff.* ***Hamlet***, 1m/2km E of Rumburgh and 5m/8km S of Bungay. TM3481.
Rumby Hill *Dur.* ***Locality***, 1m/2km SE of Crook. NZ1634.
Rumer Hill *Staffs.* ***Suburb***, 1km SE of Cannock. SJ9809.
Rumford *Cornw.* ***Village***, 4m/6km SW of Padstow. **3 F1** SW8970.
Rumleigh *Devon* ***Hamlet***, by River Tamar, 5m/7km SW of Tavistock. SX4468.
Rumney (Tredelerch). *Cardiff* ***Suburb***, of Cardiff 3m/5km NE of city centre. **19 F4** ST2179.
Rumps Point *Cornw.* ***Coastal feature***, headland (National Trust) on N coast, 4m/7km W of Port Isaac. Ruins of cliff castle. **3 G1** SW9381.
Rumsdale Water *High.* ***River***, in Caithness district, flowing E and joining Glutt Water to form River Thurso, 4m/6km S of Altnabreac. **104 E4** ND0039.
Rumster Forest *High.* ***Forest/woodland***, large coniferous forest on E coast, 2m/3km NW of Lybster. **105 H5** ND2037.
Rumwell *Som.* ***Hamlet***, 2m/3km SW of Taunton. **7 K3** ST1923.
Runacraig *Stir.* ***Settlement***, on NE side of Loch Lubnaig, 2m/3km SE of Strathyre. **81 G6** NN5714.
Runcorn *Halton* Population: 64,154. ***Town***, New Town, designated 1964, on S Bank of River Mersey, 2m/3km S of Widnes, to which it is connected by railway and road bridges. **48 E4** SJ5182.
Runcorn Bridge *Halton* ***Bridge***, built in 1956 to replace transporter bridge over River Mersey between Runcorn and Widnes. Single arch span of 1080 feet or 300 metres; largest steel arch in Europe when first built. SJ5083.
Runcton *W.Suss.* ***Village***, 2m/3km SE of Chichester. **12 B6** SU8802.
Runcton Bottom *Norf.* ***Settlement***, 4m/6km NE of Downham Market. TF6408.
Runcton Holme *Norf.* ***Village***, 4m/6km N of Downham Market. **44 A5** TF6109.
Rundlestone *Devon* ***Hamlet***, 1m/2km NW of Princetown. **5 F3** SX5775.
Runfold *Surr.* ***Hamlet***, 2m/3km E of Farnham. **22 B7** SU8747.
Runhall *Norf.* ***Village***, 5m/8km NW of Wymondham. **44 E5** TG0507.
Runham *Norf.* ***Suburb***, 1km N of Great Yarmouth town centre. TG5108.
Runham *Norf.* ***Village***, 4m/6km W of Caister-on-Sea. **45 J4** TG4611.
Runie *High.* ***River***, in Ross and Cromarty district, flowing SW to join River Kanaird 5m/7km N of Ullapool. **95 H1** NC1301.
Runner End *E.Riding* ***Locality***, W end of Holme-on-Spalding-Moor. SE8038.
Running Waters *Dur.* ***Settlement***, 4m/6km SE of Durham. NZ3340.
Runnington *Som.* ***Hamlet***, on River Tone, 2m/3km NW of Wellington. **7 K3** ST1121.
Runsell Green *Essex* ***Locality***, 4m/6km W of Maldon. **24 D1** TL7905.
Runshaw Moor *Lancs.* ***Hamlet***, 1m/2km W of Euxton, 3m/5km NW of Chorley. SD5319.
Runswick *N.Yorks.* ***Village***, holiday and fishing village on W side of Runswick Bay, 6m/10km NW of Whitby. **63 K5** NZ8016.
Runswick Bay *N.Yorks.* ***Bay***, 6m/10km NW of Whitby. On W side of bay lies Runswick village. **63 K5** NZ8016.
Runtaleave *Angus* ***Settlement***, in Glen Prosen, 2m/3km NW of Balnaboth. **82 D1** NO2867.
Runwell *Essex* ***Village***, adjoining to NE of Wickford. **24 D2** TQ7594.
Ruscombe *Glos.* ***Hamlet***, 2m/3km NW of Stroud. SO8307.
Ruscombe *W'ham* ***Village***, adjoining to E of Twyford. **22 A4** SU7976.
Rush Green *Bucks.* ***Settlement***, 2m/3km NW of Uxbridge. TQ0285.
Rush Green *Gt.Lon.* ***Suburb***, in borough of Havering, 1m/2km S of Romford. **23 J3** TQ5187.
Rush Green *Herts.* ***Settlement***, 2m/3km W of Stevenage. TL2123.
Rush Hill *B. & N.E.Som.* ***Suburb***, 2m/3km SW of Bath city centre. ST7362.
Rushall *Here.* ***Hamlet***, 5m/8km W of Ledbury. **29 F5** SO6434.
Rushall *Norf.* ***Village***, 3m/5km W of Harleston. **45 F7** TM1982.
Rushall *W.Mid.* Population: 5871. ***Locality***, 2m/3km NE of Walsall. **40 C5** SK0201.
Rushall *Wilts.* ***Village***, 1m/2km NW of Upavon. **20 E6** SU1255.
Rushbrooke *Suff.* ***Village***, 3m/5km SE of Bury St. Edmunds. **34 C2** TL8961.
Rushbury *Shrop.* ***Village***, 4m/7km E of Church Stretton. **38 E6** SO5191.
Rushden *Herts.* ***Village***, 4m/7km SE of Baldock. **33 G5** TL3031.
Rushden *Northants.* Population: 23,854. ***Town***, 4m/7km E of Wellingborough. Footwear manufacturing town, with fine 13c parish church. **32 C2** SP9566.
Rushen Abbey *I.o.M.* ***Ecclesiastical building***, founded 1134 by Viking, Olaf I, King of Man, 2m/3km N of Castletown. **54 B6** SC2870.
Rushenden *Kent* ***Locality***, adjoining to S of Queenborough. TQ9071.
Rushford *Devon* ***Hamlet***, 3m/4km NW of Tavistock. SX4476.
Rushford *Norf.* ***Hamlet***, on Suffolk border, 4m/6km E of Thetford. **44 D7** TL9281.
Rushgreen *Warr.* ***Settlement***, 1m/2km E of Lymm. SJ6987.
Rushlake Green *E.Suss.* ***Village***, 4m/6km SE of Heathfield. **13 K5** TQ6218.
Rushley Island *Essex* ***Island***, bounded by creeks, 3m/5km NE of Shoeburyness. TQ9688.
Rushmere *Suff.* ***Hamlet***, 2m/3km W of Kessingland. **45 J7** TM4987.
Rushmere St. Andrew *Suff.* ***Locality***, 2m/4km E of Ipswich. **35 F4** TM1946.
Rushmere Street *Suff.* ***Hamlet***, adjoining to E of Rushmere St. Andrew, 3m/5km E of Ipswich. TM2046.
Rushmoor *Surr.* ***Village***, 3m/5km N of Hindhead. **22 B7** SU8740.
Rushmoor *Tel. & W.* ***Settlement***, 1m/2km NW of Wrockwardine. **39 F4** SJ6113.
Rushock *Worcs.* ***Village***, 5m/8km N of Droitwich Spa. **29 H1** SO8871.
Rusholme *Gt.Man.* ***Suburb***, 2m/3km SE of Manchester city centre. **49 H3** SJ8695.
Rushton *Ches.* ***Settlement***, 2m/3km NE of Tarporley. **48 E6** SJ5864.
Rushton *Northants.* ***Village***, 3m/5km NW of Kettering. Rushton Hall is 16c-17c house with curious triangular lodge (English Heritage). **42 B7** SP8482.
Rushton *Shrop.* ***Settlement***, 4m/6km SW of Wellington. **39 F5** SJ6008.
Rushton Spencer *Staffs.* ***Village***, 5m/8km NW of Leek. **49 J6** SJ9362.
Rushton Triangular Lodge *Northants.* ***Historic house***, three-sided late 16c building (English Heritage) 1m/2km W of Rushton and 4m/7km SW of Corby. Built by Sir Thomas Tresham to symbolize the Holy Trinity, it comprises three-floors, is 33 feet or 10 metres wide, with three gables on each side. **42 B7** SP8383.
Rushup Edge *Derbys.* ***Inland physical feature***, steep mountain slope, 3m/4km W of Castleton. **50 D4** SK1082.
Rushwick *Worcs.* ***Village***, 2m/3km W of Worcester. **29 H3** SO8253.
Rushy Green *E.Suss.* ***Settlement***, on SE side of Ringmer, 3m/4km NE of Lewes. TQ4512.
Rushy Knowe *Northumb.* ***Mountain***, 4m/6km N of Elsdon. Height 1066 feet or 325 metres. **70 E4** NY9299.
Rushyford *Dur.* ***Hamlet***, 3m/4km N of Newton Aycliffe. **62 D4** NZ2828.
Rusk Holm *Ork.* ***Island***, islet lying midway between Fers Ness, Eday and Point of Huro, Westray. **106 E4** HY5136.
Ruskie *Stir.* ***Settlement***, 3m/4km W of Thornhill. **81 H7** NN6200.

Ruskington *Lincs.* Population: 3530. ***Village***, 4m/6km N of Sleaford. **52 D7** TF0850.
Rusko *D. & G.* ***Settlement***, 2m/3km N of Gatehouse of Fleet. **65 F5** NX5858.
Rusland *Cumb.* ***Hamlet***, 3m/4km NW of Newby Bridge. **55 G1** SD3488.
Rusper *W.Suss.* ***Village***, 4m/7km W of Crawley. **13 F3** TQ2037.
Ruspidge *Glos.* ***Village***, adjoining to S of Cinderford. **29 F7** SO6511.
Russ Hill *Surr.* ***Hamlet***, 1km SW of Charlwood. TQ2340.
Russel *High.* ***Settlement***, on N shore of Loch Kishorn, Ross and Cromarty district. **94 E7** NG8240.
Russell Green *Essex* ***Settlement***, 4m/7km NE of Chelmsford town centre. TL7412.
Russell's Green *E.Suss.* ***Settlement***, 1m/2km S of Ninfield. TQ7011.
Russell's Water *Oxon.* ***Village***, 2m/3km N of Nettlebed. **22 A3** SU7089.
Russel's Green *Suff.* ***Settlement***, 2m/3km SE of Stradbroke. TM2572.
Russland *Ork.* ***Locality***, on E side of Loch of Harray, Mainland, 2m/3km S of Dounby. HY3017.
Rusthall *Kent* ***Suburb***, 2m/3km W of Royal Tunbridge Wells. **23 J7** TQ5539.
Rustington *W.Suss.* ***Small town***, coastal town with good sandy beach, 1m/2km E of Littlehampton. **12 D6** TQ0502.
Ruston *N.Yorks.* ***Village***, 6m/10km SW of Scarborough. **59 F1** SE9583.
Ruston Parva *E.Riding* ***Village***, 4m/6km NE of Great Driffield. **59 G3** TA0661.
Rust's Green *Norf.* ***Settlement***, just SW of Barnham Broom. TG0706.
Ruswarp *N.Yorks.* ***Village***, 1m/2km SW of Whitby. **63 K6** NZ8809.
Rutherend *S.Lan.* ***Settlement***, 3m/5km SE of East Kilbride. **74 E5** NS6649.
Rutherford *Sc.Bord.* ***Village***, 6m/9km SW of Kelso. **70 B1** NT6430.
Rutherglen *S.Lan.* ***Town***, on S bank of River Clyde adjoining to SE of Glasgow. **74 E4** NS6161.
Ruthernbridge *Cornw.* ***Hamlet***, 4m/6km W of Bodmin. **4 A4** SX0166.
Ruthers of Howe *High.* ***Settlement***, in Caithness district, 8m/13km NW of Wick. ND3063.
Ruthin (Rhuthun). *Denb.* Population: 5029. ***Small town***, on hill above River Clwyd, 14m/23km W of Wrexham. Remains of 13c castle in grounds of hotel. Range of architectural styles in town include medieval, Tudor and Georgian. Market centre for Vale of Clwyd. **47 K7** SJ1258.
Ruthin (Rhuthun). *V. of Glam.* ***Hamlet***, 4m/6km NW of Cowbridge. SS9779.
Ruthin Castle *Denb.* ***Castle***, in Ruthin, 16m/26km SE of Rhyl. 13c castle built under orders of Edward I as part of conquest of Wales. **47 K7** SJ1257.
Ruthrieston *Aberdeen* ***Suburb***, 1m/2km SW of Aberdeen city centre. **91 H4** NJ9204.
Ruthven *Aber.* ***Village***, 5m/7km N of Huntly. **98 D6** NJ5046.
Ruthven *Angus* ***Village***, on River Isla, 3m/5km E of Alyth. **82 D3** NO2848.
Ruthven *High.* ***Settlement***, 3m/5km SE of Moy. **89 F1** NH8133.
Ruthven *High.* ***Settlement***, 1km S of Kingussie across River Spey. **88 E5** NN7699.
Ruthven Barracks *High.* ***Other feature of interest***, remains of 18c military installations (Historic Scotland) built to keep Highlanders in check, 1m/2km S of Kingussie. **88 E4** NN7699.
Ruthven Water *P. & K.* ***River***, running NE to River Earn 4m/6km NE of Auchterarder. **82 A6** NN9717.
Ruthvoes *Cornw.* ***Village***, 2m/3km S of St. Columb Major. **3 G2** SW9260.
Ruthwaite *Cumb.* ***Settlement***, 1m/2km S of Ireby. **60 D3** NY2336.
Ruthwell *D. & G.* ***Village***, near shore of Solway Firth, 6m/10km W of Annan. Cross (Historic Scotland) probably dating from early 8c, preserved in church. **69 G7** NY1067.
Ruthwell Cross *D. & G.* ***Historic/prehistoric site***, 7c cross in Ruthwell Church, 2m/4km S of Carrutherstown. 18 feet high and carved with figures and verses. **69 G7** NY1068.
Rutland County Museum *Rut.* ***Other feature of interest***, local history museum in Oakham. **42 B5** SK8608.
Rutland Water (Formerly known as Empingham Reservoir.) *Rut.* ***Reservoir***, large reservoir 1km W of Empingham and 5m/9km W of Stamford. Waterfowl nature reserve of national importance. When reservoir was formed the villages of Middle Hambleton and Nether Hambleton were completely submerged. 1m/2km N, Barnsdale Gardens, collection of gardens designed by late Geoff Hamilton. **42 C5** SK9207.
Rutupiae *Kent See Richborough Castle.*
Ruxley *Gt.Lon.* ***Suburb***, in borough of Bexley, 1m/2km SE of Sidcup. TQ4870.
Ruxton Green *Here.* ***Settlement***, 4m/7km NE of Monmouth. SO5419.
Ruyton-XI-Towns *Shrop.* ***Village***, 9m/14km NW of Shrewsbury. Remains of 14c castle keep. **38 C3** SJ3922.
Ryal *Northumb.* ***Hamlet***, 6m/10km N of Corbridge. **71 F6** NZ0174.
Ryal Fold *B'burn.* ***Settlement***, 2m/3km W of Darwen. Nature Trail in woods to W. **56 B7** SD6621.
Ryall *Dorset* ***Village***, on N side of Hardown Hill (see Morcombelake), 4m/6km W of Bridport. **8 D5** SY4094.
Ryall *Worcs.* ***Village***, 1km E of Upton upon Severn across River Severn. SO8640.
Ryarsh *Kent* ***Village***, 2m/3km N of West Malling. **23 K6** TQ6759.
Rycote *Oxon.* ***Settlement***, 3m/4km W of Thame. Restored 15c chapel (English Heritage) with fine carvings and two roofed pews. **21 K1** SP6604.
Rydal *Cumb.* ***Hamlet***, at E end of Rydal Water, 1m/2km NW of Ambleside. Rydal was home of Wordsworth from 1817 to 1850. **60 E6** NY3606.
Rydal Fell *Cumb.* ***Mountain***, on ridge between Great Rigg and Heron Pike, 3m/5km NW of Ambleside. Height 2017 feet or 615 metres. **60 E6** NY3509.
Rydal Mount *Cumb.* ***Historic house***, 1m/2km NW of Ambleside. Home of William Wordsworth, who also designed garden of around 5 acres; this includes two terraces, rare trees and shrubs. **60 E6** NY3606.
Rydal Water *Cumb.* ***Lake/loch***, 1m/2km NW of Ambleside. Hamlet of Rydal lies at E end. **60 E6** NY3506.
Ryde *I.o.W.* Population: 20,502. ***Town***, resort on NE coast, 5m/8km SW of Portsmouth. Many Regency and Victorian houses. Boat and hovercraft ferries across Solent. Long pier, with railway. **11 G5** SZ5992.
Ryde Roads *I.o.W.* ***Sea feature***, part of The Solent immediately N of Ryde. **11 G5** SZ5893.
Ryder's Hill *Devon* ***Mountain***, in Dartmoor National Park, 5m/8km NW of Buckfastleigh. Height 1689 feet or 515 metres. **5 G4** SX6569.
Rydon *Devon* ***Settlement***, 1km W of Holsworthy. **6 B5** SS3304.
Rye *E.Suss.* Population: 3708. ***Small town***, on River Rother, 9m/15km NE of Hastings. Former port, now 2m/3km from sea (Rye Bay). Many picturesque old buildings. 14c Landgate, only surviving town gate. Lamb House (National Trust), 18c, once home of Henry James. 15c Mermaid Inn. **14 E5** TQ9220.
Rye *N.Yorks.* ***River***, rising on Cleveland Hills, 3m/4km E of Osmotherley, and flowing SE past Rievaulx, Helmsley and Nunnington, into River Derwent 4m/6km NE of Malton. **58 D2** SE8275.
Rye Bay *E.Suss.* ***Bay***, 2m/3km SE of Rye. **14 E6** TQ9220.
Rye Dale *N.Yorks.* ***Valley***, carrying River Rye SE from Hawnby to River Dove. **58 B1** SE7079.
Rye Foreign *E.Suss.* ***Village***, 2m/3km NW of Rye. **14 D5** TQ8922.
Rye Harbour *E.Suss.* ***Village***, 1m/2km SE of Rye, near mouth of River Rother. **14 E6** TQ9220.
Rye House *Herts.* ***Historic house***, on River Lea to E of Hoddesdon. Scene of attempt to assassinate Charles II in 1683. Only 15c gatehouse remains. TL3809.
Rye Park *Herts.* ***Suburb***, NE district of Hoddesdon. **23 G1** TL3709.
Rye Street *Worcs.* ***Hamlet***, 5m/8km E of Ledbury. SO7835.
Ryebank *Shrop.* ***Settlement***, 2m/3km N of Wem. SJ5131.
Ryecroft *W.Yorks.* ***Hamlet***, 1km W of Harden, 2m/3km SW of Bingley. SE0738.
Ryeford *Glos.* ***Locality***, 2m/3km W of Stroud. SO8104.
Ryeford *Here.* ***Settlement***, 3m/4km E of Ross-on-Wye. SO6422.
Ryeish Green *W'ham* ***Hamlet***, 4m/6km S of Reading. SU7267.
Ryhall *Rut.* ***Village***, on loop of River Gwash, 2m/4km N of Stamford. **42 D4** TF0310.
Ryhill *Aber.* ***Settlement***, 1km SW of Oyne and 6m/10km NW of Inverurie. NJ6625.
Ryhill *E.Riding* ***Hamlet***, 3m/5km SE of Hedon. TA2225.
Ryhill *W.Yorks.* Population: 4632. ***Village***, 3m/4km NE of Royston. **51 F1** SE3814.
Ryhope *T. & W.* ***Suburb***, 3m/5km S of Sunderland city centre. Ryhope Engines Museum. **63 F1** NZ4052.
Ryhope Colliery *T. & W.* ***Suburb***, to N of Ryhope, 3m/4km S of Sunderland. NZ4053.
Ryknild Street ***Other feature of interest***, Roman road with original course running from Bourton-on-the-Water to Rotherham via Redditch, Birmingham, Lichfield, Derby and Chesterfield. Present-day roads follow some parts of its course. **30 C4** SP0951.
Rylah *Derbys.* ***Settlement***, 2m/3km S of Bolsover. SK4667.
Ryland *Lincs.* ***Hamlet***, adjoining to E of Welton. **52 D4** TF0280.
Rylands *Notts.* ***Suburb***, 1km SE of Beeston town centre and 3m/5km SW of Nottingham. SK5335.
Rylstone *N.Yorks.* ***Village***, 5m/8km N of Skipton. **56 E4** SD9758.
Ryme Intrinseca *Dorset* ***Village***, 4m/6km SE of Yeovil. **8 E3** ST5810.
Rysa Little *Ork.* ***Island***, small uninhabited island off E coast of Hoy and 1km NW of Fara. **107 C8** ND3197.
Ryther *N.Yorks.* ***Village***, on S bank of River Wharfe, 2m/3km NW of Cawood. **58 B6** SE5539.
Ryton ***River***, rising W of Worksop and flowing E through Worksop to Ranby, then N past Blyth into River Idle 1km SE of Bawtry. SK6592.
Ryton *Glos.* ***Settlement***, 4m/6km N of Newent. **29 G5** SO7332.
Ryton *N.Yorks.* ***Settlement***, 3m/4km N of Malton. **58 D2** SE7975.
Ryton *Shrop.* ***Village***, 3m/5km S of Shifnal. **39 G5** SJ7602.
Ryton *T. & W.* Population: 15,952. ***Town***, on S side of River Tyne, 6m/10km W of Newcastle upon Tyne. 13c Holy Cross Church has Jacobean woodwork. Power station to E. **71 G7** NZ1564.
Ryton *Warks.* ***Suburb***, to E of Bulkington, 3m/4km E of Bedworth. SP3986.
Ryton-on-Dunsmore *Warks.* ***Village***, 4m/7km SE of Coventry. **30 E1** SP3874.
Ryton Woodside *T. & W.* ***Hamlet***, 1m/2km SW of Ryton. NZ1463.

S

'S Airdhe Beinn *Arg. & B.* ***Hill***, 2m/3km W of Tobermory, Mull. Height 958 feet or 292 metres. **79 F2** NM4753.
Saasaig *High.* ***Settlement***, to S of Teangue, on E side of Sleat peninsula, Skye. NG6608.
Sabden *Lancs.* ***Village***, 4m/6km SE of Clitheroe. **56 C6** SD7737.
Sabden Fold *Lancs.* ***Settlement***, on S side of Pendle Hill, 2m/3km E of Sabden. SD8038.
Sabhal Beag *High.* ***Mountain***, 4m/7km E of Loch Stack and 3m/5km S of Loch Dionard. Height 2391 feet or 729 metres. **103 F4** NC3742.
Sabhal Mòr *High.* ***Mountain***, 4m/6km NE of Loch Stack, Sutherland district. Height 2306 feet or 703 metres. **103 F4** NC3544.
Sabine's Green *Essex* ***Settlement***, 4m/6km NW of Brentwood. TQ5496.
Sackers Green *Suff.* ***Settlement***, 3m/4km SE of Sudbury. **34 D5** TL9139.
Sackville College *W.Suss.* ***Historic house***, Jacobean almshouse, with fine furniture, in centre of East Grinstead. **13 H3** TQ3938.
Sacombe *Herts.* ***Village***, 4m/6km NW of Ware. **33 G7** TL3319.
Sacombe Green *Herts.* ***Hamlet***, 4m/6km NW of Ware. TL3419.
Sacquoy Head *Ork.* ***Coastal feature***, headland at NW end of Rousay. **106 C4** HY3835.
Sacriston *Dur.* Population: 4726. ***Village***, 3m/5km NW of Durham. **62 D2** NZ2447.
Sadberge *Darl.* ***Village***, 4m/6km NE of Darlington. **62 E5** NZ3416.
Saddell *Arg. & B.* ***Village***, near E coast of Kintyre, 8m/13km N of Campbeltown. **73 F7** NR7832.
Saddell Abbey *Arg. & B.* ***Ecclesiastical building***, in hamlet of Saddall, 5m/7km SW of Carradale. Built in 12c by one of the Lords of the Isles. Only the walls now remain. **73 F7** NR7832.
Saddell Bay *Arg. & B.* ***Bay***, to E of Saddell village, on E side of Kintyre peninsula. **73 F7** NR7832.
Saddell Forest *Arg. & B.* ***Forest/woodland***, astride Saddell Glen to W of Saddell, Kintyre. **73 F7** NR7733.
Saddington *Leics.* ***Village***, 6m/9km NW of Market Harborough. Reservoir 1km SE. **41 J6** SP6591.
Saddington Reservoir *Leics.* ***Reservoir***, 2m/3km SW of Kibworth Beauchamp. **41 J6** SP6691.
Saddle Bow *Norf.* ***Hamlet***, 1m/2km NE of Wiggenhall St. Germans. **44 A4** TF6015.
Saddle Head *Pembs.* ***Coastal feature***, headland on S coast of Pembrokeshire, 1m/2km W of St. Govan's Head. **16 C5** SR9592.
Saddle Hill *High.* ***Mountain***, in Nairn district, 4m/6km S of Croy. Height 1233 feet or 376 metres. **96 E7** NH7843.
Saddle Yoke *D. & G.* ***Mountain***, to E of Blackhope Burn, 5m/8km NE of Moffat. Height 2411 feet or 735 metres. **69 G2** NT1312.
Saddleback (Also known as Blencathra.) *Cumb.* ***Mountain***, in Lake District, 4m/7km NE of Keswick. Height 2847 feet or 868 metres. **60 E4** NY3227.
Saddleworth Moor *Gt.Man.* ***Open space***, moorland on either side of reservoirs of Greenfield and Yeoman Hey, on edge of Peak District National Park, 6m/9km E of Oldham. **50 C2** SE0305.
Sadgill *Cumb.* ***Settlement***, 2m/3km NE of Kentmere. **61 F6** NY4805.
Saffron Walden *Essex* Population: 13,201. ***Town***, old market town, 12m/19km N of Bishop's Stortford. Formerly main growing area for saffron crocus. Many interesting buildings and pargeted houses. Church of St. Mary the Virgin is one of largest in Essex, with a 193 foot or 59 metre spire. Remains of Norman castle. 1m/2km W, Audley End house. **33 J5** TL5338.
Saffron Walden Museum *Essex* ***Other feature of interest***, in Saffron Walden. Exhibits on local history, with a Great Hall Gallery displaying archaeological finds. **33 J5** TL5338.
Sageston *Pembs.* ***Hamlet***, 5m/8km E of Pembroke. **16 D4** SN0503.
Saham Hills *Norf.* ***Hamlet***, adjoining to N of Saham Toney. TF9003.
Saham Toney *Norf.* ***Village***, 1m/2km NW of Watton. **44 C5** TF8902.
Saighdinis (Anglicised form: Sidinish.) *W.Isles* ***Settlement***, 1m/2km E of Locheport, North Uist. **92 D5** NF8763.
Saighton *Ches.* ***Village***, 4m/6km SE of Chester. Saighton Grange, now housing Abbey Gate College, is former grange with 15c gatehouse. **48 D6** SJ4462.
Sàil Chaorainn *High.* ***Mountain***, on Glenaffric Forest, Inverness district, 4m/6km S of head of Loch Affric. Munro: height 3287 feet or 1002 metres. **87 H3** NH1315.
Sàil Gorm *High.* ***Mountain***, situated between Loch a' Chàirn Bhàin and Loch Assynt. Height 2545 feet or 776 metres. **102 D5** NC1930.
Sàil Mhòr *High.* ***Mountain***, one of the peaks of Beinn Eighe, Ross and Cromarty district. Height 3218 feet or 981 metres. **95 F5** NG9360.
Sàil Mhòr *High.* ***Mountain***, in Ross and Cromarty district 4m/6km W of Auchtascailt at head of Little Loch Broom. Height 2516 feet or 767 metres. **95 G3** NH0388.
Saileag *High.* ***Mountain***, in Ross and Cromarty district, on N side of Glen Shiel. Munro: height 3146 feet or 959 metres. **87 G3** NH0114.
Sain Dunwyd *V. of Glam. Welsh form of St. Donats, qv.*
Sain Ffagan *Cardiff Welsh form of St. Fagans, qv.*
Sain Ffred *Pembs. Welsh form of St. Brides, qv.*
Sain Nicolas *Pembs. Welsh form of St. Nicholas, qv.*
Sain Nicolas *V. of Glam. Welsh form of St. Nicholas, qv.*
Sain Pedrog *Pembs. Welsh form of St. Petrox, qv.*
Sain Silian *Newport Welsh form of St. Julians, qv.*
Sain Tathan *V. of Glam. Welsh form of St. Athan, qv.*
St. Abbs *Sc.Bord.* ***Village***, coastal village with small harbour, 3m/4km NW of Eyemouth. **77 H4** NT9167.
St. Abb's Head *Sc.Bord.* ***Coastal feature***, rocky headland with lighthouse, 1m/2km N of St. Abbs. **77 H3** NT9167.
St. Aethans *Moray* ***Locality***, on N coast adjoining to E of Burghead. Site of St. Aethan's Well. NJ1168.

St. Agnes *Cornw.* Population: 2899. ***Small town***, resort near N coast 6m/9km N of Redruth, with beach at Trevaunance Cove. Former tin mining town with steep street of miners' cottages. **2 E3** SW7250.
St. Agnes *I.o.S.* ***Island***, southernmost of five inhabited Isles of Scilly. **2 B2** SV8808.
St. Agnes Beacon *Cornw.* ***Hill***, National Trust property and landmark commanding coastal and inland views, to W of St. Agnes. Height 626 feet or 191 metres. SW7150.
St. Agnes Head *Cornw.* ***Coastal feature***, headland 6m/10km N of Redruth. **2 D3** SW6951.
St. Agnes Leisure Park *Cornw.* ***Leisure/recreation***, amusement park set in several acres of landscaped gardens to S of St. Agnes. Attractions include Cornwall in miniature, haunted house and Jurassic monsters. **2 E3** SW7250.
St. Albans *Herts.* Population: 80,376. ***City***, cathedral city, 19m/31km NW of London. Existing city extends E from remains of Roman town of Verulamium, one of first British cities established by Romans. 1km to S is section of Roman wall (English Heritage) with remains of towers and gateway. Queen Boudicca razed it to the ground in AD 62, but it was quickly rebuilt due to its importance as a trading centre. Currently shopping, business and administrative centre. Comprises mixture of medieval and Victorian buildings. Cathedral Norman and later. Various industries. **22 E1** TL1407.
St. Albans Cathedral *Herts.* ***Ecclesiastical building***, second largest church in England, dating from 11c, in St. Albans city centre. Some Early English and 19c additions. **22 E1** TL1407.
St. Alban's Head (Also known as St. Aldhelm's Head.) *Dorset* ***Coastal feature***, headland at S end of Isle of Purbeck, 5m/8km SW of Swanage. **9 J7** SY9675.
St. Albans Verulamium Roman Town *Herts.* ***Historic/prehistoric site***, on W side of St. Albans. One of finest Roman towns in Britain. Much is covered over, but theatre and other remains are visible. Much interesting and important material in adjacent museum. **22 E1** TL1407.
St. Aldhelm's Head *Dorset Alternative name for St. Alban's Head, qv.*
St. Allen *Cornw.* ***Hamlet***, 4m/6km N of Truro. **3 F3** SW8250.
St. Andras *V. of Glam. Welsh form of St. Andrews Major, qv.*
St. Andrews *Fife* Population: 11,136. ***Town***, historic town standing on rocky promontory on St. Andrews Bay, 11m/17km SE of Dundee across Firth of Tay and 9m/14km E of Cupar. University, founded 1411, is Scotland's oldest and third oldest in Britain. Royal and Ancient Golf Club based here, and is ruling authority on game of golf. Several golf courses, including famous Old Course. Remains of cathedral, priory and castle (Historic Scotland). **83 G6** NO5016.
St. Andrews Bay *Fife* ***Bay***, 11m/17km SE of Dundee across Firth of Tay, and 9m/14km E of Cupar. St. Andrews historic town stands on rocky promontory on bay. **83 G6** NO1516.
St. Andrews Castle *Fife* ***Castle***, ruins of 13c castle (Historic Scotland) on rocky promontory overlooking sea at St. Andrews. Most of ruins date from later periods, including bottle-shaped dungeon in Sea Tower. Visitor Centre. **83 G6** NO5116.
St. Andrews Cathedral *Fife* ***Ecclesiastical building***, once largest church in Scotland (Historic Scotland), dating from 12c-13c, in St. Andrews. Remains include well-preserved precinct walls. **83 G6** NO5116.
St. Andrews Major (St. Andras). *V. of Glam.* ***Hamlet***, adjoining to W of Dinas Powys, 3m/5km W of Penarth. **18 E4** ST1371.
St. Andrew's Well *Dorset* ***Suburb***, 3m/4km NE of Bridport town centre on W bank of Mangerton River. SY4793.
St. Anne's *Lancs.* ***Suburb***, of Lytham St. Anne's, 5m/8km S of Blackpool town centre. **55 G7** SD3128.
St. Anne's Park *Bristol* ***Suburb***, of Bristol on S bank of River Avon, 3m/4km E of city centre. ST6272.
St. Ann's *D. & G.* ***Locality***, 6m/10km S of Beattock. **69 F4** NY0793.
St. Ann's Chapel *Cornw.* ***Village***, 1m/2km SW of Gunnislake. **4 E3** SX4170.
St. Ann's Chapel *Devon* ***Hamlet***, 3m/5km S of Modbury. **5 G6** SX6647.
St. Ann's Head *Pembs.* ***Coastal feature***, headland on W side of entrance to Milford Haven, 2m/3km S of Dale. **16 A4** SM8002.
St. Ann's Hill *Cumb.* ***Suburb***, 1m/2km NW of Carlisle city centre across River Eden. NY3957.
St. Anns Hill *Luton* ***Suburb***, E district of Luton. TL0921.
St. Anthony *Cornw.* ***Hamlet***, on S bank of River Percuil, opposite St. Mawes. **3 F5** SW8532.
St. Anthony Head *Cornw.* ***Coastal feature***, headland (National Trust) to SW of St. Anthony, at entrance to Carrick Roads, 3m/4km SE of Falmouth. SW8431.
St. Anthony-in-Meneage *Cornw.* ***Hamlet***, on N side of Gillan Harbour, 8m/13km E of Helston. **2 E6** SW7825.
St. Anthony's *T. & W.* ***Suburb***, on N bank of River Tyne, 3m/4km SE of Newcastle upon Tyne city centre. NZ2863.
St. Anthony's Hill *E.Suss.* ***Suburb***, NE of Eastbourne. TQ6301.
St. Arvans *Mon.* ***Village***, 2m/3km NW of Chepstow. **19 J2** ST5196.
St. Asaph (Llanelwy). *Denb.* Population: 3399. ***City***, ancient cathedral city on ridge between Rivers Clwyd and Elwy, 5m/8km S of Rhyl. Main industries include printing, light engineering, law, tourism and financial services. Britain's smallest medieval cathedral. Site of first translation of Bible into Welsh. Named after St. Asaph, who became abbot in AD 570 and eventually became city's first bishop. **47 J5** SJ0374.
St. Asaph Cathedral *Denb.* ***Ecclesiastical building***, in St. Asaph, dating from 13c with several restorations. Britain's smallest medieval cathedral. Cruciform, with large central tower. **47 J5** SJ0374.
St. Athan (Sain Tathan). *V. of Glam.* ***Village***, 3m/5km E of Llantwit Major. **18 D5** ST0168.
St. Audries *Som.* ***Settlement***, adjoining to N of West Quantoxhead, 3m/4km SE of Watchet. **7 K1** ST1042.
St. Augustine's Abbey *Kent* ***Ecclesiastical building***, ruined Benedictine abbey (English Heritage) founded in AD 568 by St. Augustine in Canterbury city centre, to E of Canterbury Cathedral. Remains date from 1073. Nearby Conduit House (English Heritage) supplied water to abbey. **15 G2** TR1557.
St. Augustine's Cross *Kent* ***Historic/prehistoric site***, in Cliffs End, 3m/5km SW of Ramsgate. Cross (English Heritage) erected in 1884 to commemorate St. Augustine's landing in AD 597. **25 K5** TR3464.
St. Austell *Cornw.* Population: 21,622. ***Town***, busy town 13m/20km NE of Truro. Former industries were tin and copper mining, and some quarrying. Later, china clay became a main industry. 15c Holy Trinity church. **4 A5** SX0152.
St. Austell Bay *Cornw.* ***Bay***, near which St. Austell town is situated, extends W from Gribbin Head to Black Head. **4 A5** SX0152.
St. Baldred's Boat *E.Loth.* ***Coastal feature***, rock on North Sea coast, 3m/4km NE of Whitekirk. **76 E2** NT6085.
St. Baldred's Cradle *E.Loth.* ***Coastal feature***, rock formation on North Sea coast, 3m/5km NW of Dunbar. **76 E2** NT6381.
St. Bees *Cumb.* Population: 1655. ***Village***, 4m/6km S of Whitehaven. **60 A5** NX9711.
St. Bees Head *Cumb.* ***Coastal feature***, headland on Irish Sea, close to W extremity of county, 2m/3km NW of St. Bees. **60 A5** NX9711.
St. Blazey *Cornw.* Population: 4419. ***Small town***, 4m/6km NE of St. Austell, in district producing china clay. **4 A5** SX0654.
St. Blazey Gate *Cornw.* ***Locality***, adjoins to SW of St. Blazey. **4 A5** SX0653.
St. Boswells *Sc.Bord.* Population: 1128. ***Village***, 4m/6km SE of Melrose. **76 D7** NT5931.
St. Botolph's Priory *Essex* ***Ecclesiastical building***, first Augustinian priory in England (English Heritage) in centre of Colchester. Founded c. 1100 and mainly constructed from Roman brick. **34 D6** TL9924.
St. Breock *Cornw.* ***Village***, just W of Wadebridge. **3 G1** SW9771.
St. Breock Downs *Cornw.* ***Open space***, hillslope rising to 689 feet or 210 metres, 4m/7km NE of St. Columb Major. **3 G2** SW9668.
St. Breock Downs Monolith *Cornw.* ***Historic/prehistoric site***, prehistoric standing stone (English Heritage) 4m/7km NE of St. Columb Major. **3 G2** SW9668.
St. Breward *Cornw.* ***Village***, typical Cornish village on moorland 4m/6km S of Camelford. **4 A3** SX0977.
St. Briavels *Glos.* ***Village***, 5m/7km W of Lydney. **19 J1** SO5504.
St. Briavels Castle *Glos.* ***Castle***, 12c enclosure castle with two 13c gatehouses remaining (English Heritage) on N side of St. Briavels, 4m/6km S of Coleford. Now a youth hostel. **19 J1** SO5504.
St. Brides (Sain Ffred). *Pembs.* ***Hamlet***, on St. Brides Bay, 7m/11km NW of Milford Haven, at S end of small creek in St. Brides Haven. **16 B3** SM8010.
St. Brides Bay *Pembs.* ***Bay***, large W facing bay, extending from Ramsey Sound in N to Skomer Island in S, and to Rickets Head in E, and enclosed by the Pembrokeshire Coast National Park. **16 A3** SM8016.
St. Brides Major (Saint-y-brid). *V. of Glam.* ***Village***, 3m/4km S of Bridgend. **18 B4** SS8974.
St. Bride's Netherwent (Saint-y-brid). *Mon.* ***Locality***, 3m/4km W of Caerwent. Remains of medieval village to W. **19 H3** ST4289.
St. Bride's-super-Ely (Llansanffraid-ar-Elai). *V. of Glam.* ***Village***, 5m/9km W of Cardiff. **18 D4** ST0977.
St. Brides Wentlooge (Llansanffraid Gwynllwg). *Newport* ***Village***, near coast, 4m/6km S of Newport. **19 F3** ST2982.
St. Budeaux *Plym.* ***Suburb***, NW district of Plymouth, 3m/5km from city centre. **4 E5** SX4458.
St. Buryan *Cornw.* ***Village***, 4m/7km E of Land's End. 15c church with rood screen. **2 B6** SW4025.
St. Catherine *B. & N.E.Som.* ***Settlement***, 4m/7km NE of Bath. **20 A4** ST7770.
St. Catherines *Arg. & B.* ***Settlement***, on E shore of Loch Fyne, in Argyll, opposite Inveraray (ferry for pedestrians). **80 C7** NN1207.
St. Catherine's Bay *Ork.* ***Bay***, wide bay on W coast of Stronsay. Linga Holm is at entrance to bay. **106 F5** HY6326.
St. Catherine's Castle *Cornw.* ***Castle***, on coast 1km SW of Fowey. Henry VIII's 16c coastal fort (English Heritage) erected during middle of his reign to defend harbour. **4 B5** SX1150.
St. Catherine's Chapel *Dorset* ***Ecclesiastical building***, 15c chapel (English Heritage) built on hill top as landmark for sailors, to S of Abbotsbury. **8 E6** SY5784.
St. Catherine's Dub *Aber.* ***Coastal feature***, headland at Collieston with views along the rocky coastline. **91 J2** NK0327.
St. Catherine's Island *Pembs.* ***Island***, small island off Castle Hill at Tenby. **16 E4** SN1300.
St. Catherine's Point *I.o.W.* ***Coastal feature***, headland with lighthouse at southernmost point of island. **11 F7** SZ4975.
St. Clears (Sancler). *Carmar.* ***Village***, 9m/14km W of Carmarthen. Traces of motte and bailey castle. **17 F3** SN2716.
St. Cleer *Cornw.* ***Village***, on Bodmin moor, 2m/4km N of Liskeard. King Doniert's Stone (English Heritage), 9c inscribed stone, 1m/2km NW. **4 C4** SX2468.
St. Clement *Cornw.* ***Village***, 2m/3km E of Truro. **3 F4** SW8543.
St. Clement's Church *W.Isles* ***Ecclesiastical building***, cruciform church dating from c. 1500 situated in settlement of Rodel, South Harris. Sculptured slabs and highly decorated. **93 F3** NG0483.
St. Clement's Isle *Cornw.* ***Island***, rocky island off Mousehole, 2m/3km S of Penzance across bay. **2 B6** SW4726.
St. Clether *Cornw.* ***Village***, 8m/12km W of Launceston. **4 C2** SX2084.
St. Colmac *Arg. & B.* ***Settlement***, on Bute, 2m/3km W of Port Bannatyne. Celtic cross, standing stone and stone circles in vicinity. NS0467.
St. Colm's Abbey *Fife* ***Ecclesiastical building***, well preserved monastic building, including 13c octagonal chapter house, on Inchcolm, 1km offshore from N bank of Firth of Forth. **75 K2** NT1882.
St. Columb Major *Cornw.* Population: 2119. ***Village***, 6m/10km E of Newquay. **3 G2** SW9163.
St. Columb Minor *Cornw.* ***Suburb***, E district of Newquay. **3 F2** SW8462.
St. Columb Road *Cornw.* Population: 2458. ***Village***, developed beside railway, 3m/4km S of St. Columb Major. **3 G3** SW9159.
St. Columba's Cave *Arg. & B.* ***Other feature of interest***, cave 1m/2km NW of Ellary, containing rock-shelf with an altar, above which are carved crosses. Occupied from Middle Stone Age. **73 F3** NR7576.
St. Columba's Church *W.Isles* ***Ecclesiastical building***, medieval chapel at Aignis, at W end of Eye Peninsula, Isle of Lewis. **101 G4** NB4832.
St. Columb's Church *W.Isles See Eilean Chaluim Chille.*
St. Combs *Aber.* ***Village***, on NE coast, 4m/7km SE of Fraserburgh. **99 J4** NK0563.
St. Cormac's Chapel *Arg. & B. See Eilean Mòr.*
St. Cross South Elmham *Suff.* ***Village***, 4m/7km SW of Bungay. **45 G7** TM2984.
St. Cybi's Well *Gwyn.* ***Other feature of interest***, ancient well with noted curative properties and unusual vaulted structure (Cadw), at E end of Lleyn Peninsula, N of Llangybi and 2m/3km N of Chwilog. **36 D1** SH4241.
St. Cyrus *Aber.* ***Village***, near coast, 5m/8km NE of Montrose. **83 J1** NO7464.
St. Davids *Fife* ***Settlement***, on St. David's Harbour, 1km SE of Inverkeithing. **75 K2** NT1482.
St. David's (Tyddewi). *Pembs.* Population: 1627. ***City***, ancient cathedral city (considered to be Britain's smallest city) near coast, 3m/4km SE of St. David's Head (Penmaen Dewi), headland at N end of Whitesand Bay. Named after patron saint of Wales who founded it in AD 550. St. David's Cathedral, dates in part from 12c and has been place of pilgrimage for over fifteen hundred years. Cathedral precincts contain Bishop's Palace (Cadw) with surviving buildings dating from 14c; noted for Bishop Henry de Gower's arcaded parapet. **16 A2** SM7525.
St. David's *P. & K.* ***Settlement***, 5m/8km N of Auchterarder. **82 A5** NN9420.
St. David's Cathedral *Pembs.* ***Ecclesiastical building***, in St. David's. Built on the site where St. David was reputed to have founded a monastic settlement in 6c. It became an important site for Pilgrims and dates from 12c with later alterations. Noted for Irish oak nave roof and 116 foot tower. **16 A2** SM7525.
St. David's Head (Penmaen Dewi). *Pembs.* ***Coastal feature***, headland at N end of Whitesand Bay. St. David's is 3m/4km SE of headland. **16 A2** SM7525.
St. Day *Cornw.* Population: 1971. ***Village***, former mining village 2m/3km E of Redruth. **2 E4** SW7342.
St. Decumans *Som.* ***Hamlet***, adjoining to SW of Watchet. **7 J1** ST0642.
St. Dennis *Cornw.* Population: 1974. ***Village***, in china clay district, 5m/8km NW of St. Austell. **3 G3** SW9557.
St. Denys *S'ham.* ***Suburb***, on W bank of River Itchen, 1m/2km NE of Southampton city centre. SU4313.
St. Devereux *Here.* ***Locality***, 7m/11km SW of Hereford. SO4431.
St. Dials *Torfaen* ***Suburb***, in town of Cwmbran. ST2894.
St. Dogmaels (Llandudoch). *Pembs.* ***Village***, on W bank of River Teifi estuary, 1m/2km W of Cardigan across river. Scant ruins of 12c abbey (Cadw). **26 A4** SN1646.
St. Dogmaels Abbey *Pembs.* ***Ecclesiastical building***, ruined abbey (Cadw) founded in 1115 by Benedictines, 1m/2km W of Cardigan. Adjacent church contains inscribed Sagranus stone. Working watermill nearby. **26 A4** SN1645.
St. Dogwells (Llantydewi). *Pembs.* ***Settlement***, 6m/9km S of Fishguard. **16 C2** SM9627.
St. Dominick *Cornw.* ***Village***, 3m/5km SE of Callington. **4 E4** SX3967.
St. Donats (Sain Dunwyd). *V. of Glam.* ***Village***, 2m/3km W of Llantwit Major. Castle dates from 11c. To S, St. Donat's Bay. **18 C5** SS9368.
St. Duthus Chapel *High.* ***Ecclesiastical building***, built between 1065 and 1256 in Tain and containing remains of St. Duthus, transferred there 200 years after his death in 1065. Heritage Centre in grounds. **96 E3** NH7882.
St. Edith's Marsh *Wilts.* ***Hamlet***, 3m/5km NW of Devizes. **20 C5** ST9764.
St. Endellion *Cornw.* ***Hamlet***, 4m/6km N of Wadebridge. **3 G1** SW9978.
St. Enoder *Cornw.* ***Hamlet***, 4m/7km SW of St. Columb Major. **3 F3** SW8957.
St. Erme *Cornw.* ***Village***, 4m/6km NE of Truro. **3 F4** SW8449.
St. Erney *Cornw.* ***Hamlet***, 4m/6km W of Saltash. SX3759.
St. Erth *Cornw.* ***Village***, just S of Hayle. **2 C5** SW5535.
St. Erth Praze *Cornw.* ***Hamlet***, 2m/3km SE of Hayle. **2 C5** SW5735.
St. Ervan *Cornw.* ***Village***, 4m/6km SW of Padstow. **3 F1** SW8970.
St. Eval *Cornw.* ***Hamlet***, 6m/10km NE of Newquay. To W on coast, Pendarves Point (National Trust), overlooking Bedruthan Steps, sandy beach with rocks and caves. **3 F2** SW8868.

St. Ewe *Cornw.* ***Village***, 5m/7km SW of St. Austell. 14c church with octagonal spire. **3 G4** SW9746.
St. Fagans (Sain Ffagan). *Cardiff* ***Village***, 4m/6km W of Cardiff. Welsh Folk Museum, including the castle, an Elizabethan mansion with 13c curtain wall. **18 E4** ST1277.
St. Fagans Castle *Cardiff* ***Castle***, site of small castle, thought to be 13c, in grounds of 16c mansion, 4m/6km W of Cardiff city centre. Site is part of Museum of Welsh Life complex. **18 E4** ST1177.
St. Fergus *Aber.* ***Village***, near NE coast, 4m/7km N of Peterhead. **99 K5** NK0952.
St. Fergus Moss *Aber.* ***Open space***, moorland 2m/3km S of Crimond. **99 J5** NK0553.
St. Fillans *P. & K.* ***Village***, at foot, or E end, of Loch Earn, 5m/8km W of Comrie. **81 H5** NN6924.
St. Florence *Pembs.* ***Village***, 3m/5km W of Tenby. **16 D4** SN0801.
St. Gabriels *T. & W.* ***Suburb***, 1m/2km W of Sunderland city centre. NZ3756.
St. Gennys *Cornw.* ***Village***, 7m/11km SW of Bude across corner of Bude Bay. Some of coast is National Trust property. **4 B1** SX1497.
St. George *Bristol* ***Suburb***, 3m/4km E of Bristol city centre. ST6273.
St. George (Llan Sain Siôr). *Conwy* ***Hamlet***, 2m/4km SE of Abergele. Hillfort of Dinorben to W. **47 H5** SH9775.
St. Georges *N.Som.* ***Village***, 4m/6km E of Weston-super-Mare. **19 G5** ST3762.
St. George's (Llan Sain Siôr). *V. of Glam.* ***Village***, 5m/8km W of Cardiff. **18 D4** ST1076.
St. George's Guildhall *Norf.* ***Historic house***, 15c guildhall (National Trust) at King's Lynn, with adjoining medieval warehouse. Largest remaining example in England, now in use as Arts Centre. **44 A3** TF6120.
St. George's Island (Also known as Looe Island.) *Cornw.* ***Island***, off S coast, 1m/2km S of Looe. **4 C5** SX2551.
St. Germans *Cornw.* ***Sea feature***, estuarine part of River Lynher below St. Germans village, flowing E to join River Tamar S of Saltash. See also (River) Lynher. **4 D5** SX4257.
St. Germans *Cornw.* ***Village***, 8m/13km SE of Liskeard. Interesting church and 16c almshouses. **4 D5** SX3657.
St. German's Cathedral *I.o.M.* ***Ecclesiastical building***, 13c ruins within walls of Peel Castle (Manx National Heritage) at Peel, on St. Patrick's Isle. **54 B5** SC2484.
St. Germans Quay *Cornw.* ***Locality***, at head of St. Germans River, to SE end of St. Germans village. SX3657.
St. Giles House *Dorset* *See Wimborne St. Giles.*
St. Giles in the Wood *Devon* ***Village***, 3m/4km E of Great Torrington. **6 D4** SS5319.
St. Giles on the Heath *Devon* ***Hamlet***, 4m/7km NE of Launceston. **6 B6** SX3590.
St. Giles's Hill *Hants.* ***Suburb***, E district of Winchester. SU4929.
St. Govan's Head *Pembs.* ***Coastal feature***, headland 5m/9km S of Pembroke. **16 C5** SR9792.
St. Gwynno Forest *R.C.T.* ***Forest/woodland***, wooded area NW of Pontypridd. **18 C2** ST0396.
St. Harmon *Powys* ***Village***, 3m/5km N of Rhayader. **27 J1** SN9872.
St. Helen Auckland *Dur.* ***Village***, 2m/4km SW of Bishop Auckland. **62 C4** NZ1827.
St. Helena *Norf.* ***Village***, adjoining to NW of Horsford, 6m/9km NW of Norwich. **45 F4** TG1916.
St. Helena *Warks.* ***Village***, 1km S of Polesworth. SK2601.
St. Helens *Cumb.* ***Locality***, on coast 1m/2km SW of Flimby. NY0132.
St. Helen's *E.Suss.* ***Suburb***, N district of Hastings. **14 D6** TQ8212.
St. Helens *I.o.W.* ***Village***, on Bembridge Harbour, 3m/5km SE of Ryde. To E, 1km offshore, St. Helens Fort. **11 H6** SZ6289.
St. Helen's *I.o.S.* ***Island***, uninhabited island, 1km off NE coast of Tresco. **2 B1** SV8917.
St. Helens *Mersey.* Population: 106,293. ***Town***, 11m/18km E of Liverpool. Traditionally a glass-producing town, this is still main industry. Pilkington plc has its own glass museum here. Transport Museum. **48 E3** SJ5195.
St. Helen's *S.Yorks.* ***Locality***, adjoining to E of Hoyland. SE3800.
St. Helier *Gt.Lon.* ***Suburb***, in borough of Sutton, 2m/3km NE of Sutton town centre. TQ2766.
St. Hilary *Cornw.* ***Hamlet***, 4m/6km S of Hayle. **2 C5** SW5531.
St. Hilary *V. of Glam.* ***Village***, 2m/3km SE of Cowbridge. **18 D4** ST0173.
St. Hill *W.Suss.* ***Settlement***, 2m/3km SW of East Grinstead. **13 G3** TQ3835.
St. Ibbs *Herts.* ***Settlement***, 2m/3km SE of Hitchin. TL1926.
St. Illtyd *B.Gwent* ***Hamlet***, with traces of Norman castle, 1m/2km S of Abertillery. **19 F1** SO2101.
St. Ippollitts *Herts.* ***Village***, 2m/3km SE of Hitchin. **33 F6** TL1927.
St. Ishmael (Llanismel). *Carmar.* ***Settlement***, on River Tywi estuary, 3m/5km W of Kidwelly. **17 G4** SN3608.
St. Ishmael's *Pembs.* ***Village***, 5m/7km W of Milford Haven across Sandyhaven Pill. **16 B4** SM8307.
St. Issey *Cornw.* ***Village***, 4m/6km W of Wadebridge. **3 G1** SW9271.
St. Ive *Cornw.* ***Village***, 4m/6km NE of Liskeard. **4 D4** SX3067.
St. Ive Cross *Cornw.* ***Village***, 5m/7km NE of Liskeard. SX3167.
St. Ives *Cambs.* Population: 16,510. ***Town***, on River Great Ouse, 5m/8km E of Huntingdon, named after Ivo, a Persian bishop whose bones were said to have been found locally. 15c chapel bridge crosses river. **33 G1** TL3171.
St. Ives *Cornw.* Population: 10,092. ***Town***, attractive resort on N coast, on W side of St. Ives Bay, 7m/12km NE of Penzance. Former industries were mainly tin mining and pilchard fishing. Now a tourist centre. Popular with artists for almost a century. Barbara Hepworth lived here, and many of her sculptures can be seen at her studio. **2 C4** SW5140.
St. Ives *Dorset* ***Locality***, 2m/3km SW of Ringwood. **10 C4** SU1204.
St. Ives Bay *Cornw.* ***Bay***, on N coast surrounding St. Ives. **2 C4** SW5140.
St. Ives Bridge *Cambs.* ***Bridge***, Barnack stone bridge over River Great Ouse, on S side of St. Ives, built 1414 to replace wooden bridge. Chantry chapel, consecrated 1426, built on S side of central pier. TL3171.
St. Ives Head *Cornw.* *Alternative name for The Island, qv.*
St. James *Norf.* ***Hamlet***, 1km NE of Coltishall. TG2720.
St. James *Northants.* ***Locality***, industrial estate towards E side of Corby. SP8988.
St. James (St. James's End). *Northants.* ***Suburb***, to W of Northampton town centre. SP7461.
St. James South Elmham *Suff.* ***Village***, 5m/8km NW of Halesworth. **45 H7** TM3281.
St. James's End *Northants.* *See St. James.*
St. James's Palace *Gt.Lon.* ***Historic house***, royal residence in City of Westminster, N of St. James's Park and 1m/2km SW of Charing Cross. Built by Henry VIII with many later additions; ceiling of Chapel Royal possibly by Holbein. TQ2980.
St. Jidgey *Cornw.* ***Hamlet***, 4m/7km NE of St. Columb Major. SW9469.
St. John *Cornw.* ***Village***, 2m/3km SW of Torpoint. **4 E5** SX4053.
St. John's *Dur.* ***Settlement***, 2m/3km S of Wolsingham. **62 B3** NZ0634.
St. John's *Gt.Lon.* ***Suburb***, in borough of Lewisham, 1km NW of Lewisham and 5m/8km SE of Charing Cross. TQ3776.
St. John's *I.o.M.* ***Village***, 3m/4km SE of Peel. Ancient mound of Tynwald Hill to N. **54 B5** SC2781.
St. John's *Kent* ***Suburb***, N district of Sevenoaks. TQ5356.
St. John's *Surr.* ***Suburb***, to W of Woking. **22 C6** SU9857.
St. John's *Worcs.* ***Suburb***, SW district of Worcester. **29 H3** SO8354.
St. John's Beck *Cumb.* ***River***, issuing from Thirlmere and flowing N to join with River Glenderamakin, 1km SW of Threlkeld, to form River Greta. **60 E4** NY3124.
St. John's Chapel *Devon* ***Settlement***, 3m/5km SW of Barnstaple. **6 D3** SS5329.
St. John's Chapel *Dur.* ***Village***, on River Wear, 7m/11km W of Stanhope. **61 K3** NY8838.
St. John's Fen End *Norf.* ***Hamlet***, 5m/8km E of Wisbech. **43 J4** TF5311.
St. John's Head *Ork.* ***Coastal feature***, lofty headland on NW coast of Hoy, rising to 1140 feet or 347 metres, 3m/5km N of Rora Head. **107 A7** HY1803.
St. John's Highway *Norf.* ***Village***, 6m/10km SW of King's Lynn. **43 J4** TF5314.
St. John's Jerusalem *Kent* *See Sutton at Hone.*
St. John's Kirk *S.Lan.* ***Settlement***, 1m/2km NW of Symington. **75 H7** NS9835.
St. John's Lake *Cornw.* ***Sea feature***, tidal mudflats to E of St. John, on W side of River Tamar estuary. Stream flows into inlet. SX4254.
St. John's Loch *High.* ***Lake/loch***, loch on NE side of Dunnet village, S of Dunnet Head on N coast of Caithness district. **105 H1** ND2272.
St. John's Point *High.* ***Coastal feature***, headland on N coast of Caithness district 6m/10km W of Duncansby Head. **105 J1** ND3175.
St. John's Town of Dalry (Also known as Dalry). *D. & G.* ***Village***, on Water of Ken, 2m/4km N of New Galloway. Its name comes from a former church of the Knights Templars. **68 B5** NX6281.
St. John's Wood *Gt.Lon.* ***Suburb***, in City of Westminster, to W of Regents Park, 3m/4km NW of Charing Cross. Includes Lord's Cricket Ground. TQ2683.
St. Judes *I.o.M.* ***Village***, 4m/6km W of Ramsey. **54 C4** SC3996.
St. Julians *Herts.* ***Suburb***, 1m/2km S of St. Albans city centre. TL1405.
St. Julians (Sain Silian). *Newport* ***Suburb***, 1m/2km NE of Newport town centre. ST3289.
St. Juliot *Cornw.* ***Locality***, 2m/3km E of Boscastle. SX1291.
St. Just *Cornw.* Population: 2092. ***Small town***, 4m/6km N of Land's End. Large 15c church. Bronze Age chambered cairn, Ballowall Barrow (English Heritage), 1m/2km W. Land's End Airport 1m/2km to S. **2 A5** SW3731.
St. Just in Roseland *Cornw.* ***Village***, on E side of Carrick Roads, 2m/3km N of St. Mawes. 13c church. **3 F5** SW8435.
St. Katherines *Aber.* ***Settlement***, 5m/8km NW of Oldmeldrum. **91 F1** NJ7834.
St. Keverne *Cornw.* ***Village***, near coast, 9m/14km SE of Helston. **2 E6** SW7921.
St. Kew *Cornw.* ***Village***, 4m/6km NE of Wadebridge. **4 A3** SX0276.
St. Kew Highway *Cornw.* ***Hamlet***, 1m/2km SE of St. Kew. **4 A3** SX0276.
St. Kew's Steps *N.Som.* *See Kewstoke.*
St. Keyne *Cornw.* ***Village***, 2m/4km S of Liskeard. **4 C4** SX2461.
St. Kilda (Also known as Hirta.) *W.Isles* ***Island***, steep rocky island, lying some 54m/86km W of South Harris and 35m/56km W of North Uist. Area about 3 square miles or 8 square km. Uninhabited since 1930, except for Army personnel manning radar stations. Ruined village on Village Bay at SE end. Cliffs below Conachair are highest sea cliffs in Great Britain. Island is chief island of St. Kilda group (all National Trust for Scotland, and collectively forming a nature reserve). See also Boreray, Dun and Soay. NF0999.
St. Lawrence *Cornw.* ***Settlement***, 1m/2km W of Bodmin. **4 A4** SX0466.
St. Lawrence *Essex* ***Hamlet***, to S of St. Lawrence Bay, on S side of River Blackwater estuary, 5m/8km N of Burnham-on-Crouch. **25 F1** TL9604.
St. Lawrence *I.o.W.* ***Village***, near S coast, 2m/3km W of Ventnor. **11 G7** SZ5376.
St. Lawrence *Kent* ***Suburb***, 1m/2km W of Ramsgate. TR3665.
St. Lawrence Green *Suff.* ***Hamlet***, 4m/6km SE of Bungay. TM3784.
St. Leonards *Bucks.* ***Village***, 3m/5km E of Wendover. **22 C1** SP9107.
St. Leonards *Dorset* Population: 6136. ***Locality***, 3m/5km SW of Ringwood. **10 C4** SU1103.
St. Leonards *E.Suss.* ***Town***, coastal town adjoining to W of Hastings. **14 D7** TQ8009.
St. Leonards *Edin.* ***Suburb***, 1m/2km SE of Edinburgh city centre. NT2672.
St. Leonards *S.Lan.* ***Suburb***, to E of East Kilbride town centre. NS6554.
St. Leonard's Forest *W.Suss.* ***Forest/woodland***, wooded area E of Horsham. **13 F3** TQ2131.
St. Leonards Grange *Hants.* ***Settlement***, 6m/9km NE of Lymington. **11 F5** SZ4098.
St. Leonards Priory *Glos.* ***Ecclesiastical building***, site of former Augustinian priory in Leonard Stanley, 1m/2km S of Stonehouse and 3m/5km W of Stroud. Site now occupied by 12c Church of St. Leonard. **20 B1** SO8003.
St. Leonard's Street *Kent* ***Hamlet***, 1km SW of West Malling. **23 K6** TQ6756.
St. Leonard's Tower *Kent* ***Historic/prehistoric site***, remains of Norman keep (English Heritage), 1km SW of West Malling. **23 K6** TQ6756.
St. Levan *Cornw.* ***Hamlet***, 3m/5km SE of Land's End. **2 A6** SW3822.
St. Luke's *Gt.Lon.* ***Suburb***, in borough of Islington, to E of Finsbury. TQ3282.
St. Lythans (Llwyneliddon). *V. of Glam.* ***Hamlet***, 3m/5km N of Barry. Neolithic burial-chamber (Cadw) 1km SW. **18 E4** ST1072.
St. Lythans Burial Chamber (Gwâl-y-Filiart). *V. of Glam.* ***Historic/prehistoric site***, 1km SW of St. Lythans and 5m/8km NW of Barry. Chambered long barrow consisting of three mudstone uprights supporting a large capstone. **18 D4** ST1072.
St. Mabyn *Cornw.* ***Village***, 3m/5km E of Wadebridge. **4 A3** SX0473.
St. Machar's Cathedral *Aberdeen* ***Ecclesiastical building***, twin-towered 14c granite building on ancient site of worship in Aberdeen. Features include 16c oak ceiling and notable stained glass. The nave, dated 1520, still used as parish church. **91 H4** NJ9308.
St. Magnus Bay *Shet.* ***Bay***, large bay on W of coast of Mainland, extending from Esha Ness (N) to Ness of Melby and Papa Stour (S), and penetrating E, through Swarbacks Minn and Olna Firth, as far as Voe. **109 B6** HU2568.
St. Magnus Cathedral *Ork.* ***Ecclesiastical building***, at Kirkwall, on Mainland. Built between 1137 and 1200, though additional work went on over the next 300 years. Contains some fine examples of Norman architecture. **107 D6** HY4410.
St. Magnus Church *Ork.* ***Ecclesiastical building***, remains of church (Historic Scotland), probably of 12c, towards W side of Egilsay. Dedicated to Christian Norse ruler murdered on island in 1116. **106 D4** HY4630.
St. Margaret South Elmham *Suff.* ***Village***, 4m/6km SW of Bungay. **45 H7** TM3183.
St. Margarets *Gt.Lon.* ***Suburb***, to SW of Twickenham Bridge in borough of Richmond upon Thames. TQ1674.
St. Margarets *Here.* ***Village***, 5m/8km NW of Pontrilas. **28 C5** SO3533.
St. Margarets *Herts.* ***Village***, 2m/3km SE of Ware. **33 G7** TL3811.
St. Margarets *Wilts.* ***Suburb***, SE district of Marlborough. SU1968.
St. Margaret's at Cliffe *Kent* Population: 2415. ***Small town***, resort, 4m/6km NE of Dover, on St. Margaret's Bay. Best known as starting point for cross-Channel swimmers. **15 J3** TR3544.
St. Margaret's Bay *Kent* ***Bay***, 4m/6km NE of Dover. **15 J3** TR3544.
St. Margaret's Hope *Fife* ***Sea feature***, anchorage for Rosyth naval base on Firth of Forth. **75 J2** NT1882.
St. Margaret's Hope *Ork.* ***Village***, chief settlement on N coast of South Ronaldsay, at head of bay of same name. **107 D8** ND4493.
St. Margaret's Island *Pembs.* ***Island***, small island off W end of Caldey Island. **16 E5** SS1297.
St. Mark's *Glos.* ***Suburb***, W district of Cheltenham. SO9222.
St. Mark's *I.o.M.* ***Village***, 5m/8km N of Castletown. **54 C6** SC2974.
St. Martin *Cornw.* ***Hamlet***, 1m/2km N of Looe. **4 C5** SX2655.
St. Martin *Cornw.* ***Village***, 5m/9km SE of Helston. **2 E6** SW7323.
St. Martin's *I.o.S.* ***Island***, one of the five inhabited islands. **2 C1** SV9315.
St. Martin's *N.Yorks.* ***Locality***, on S side of Richmond across River Swale. NZ1700.
St. Martins *P. & K.* ***Settlement***, 5m/7km NE of Perth. **82 C4** NO1530.
St. Martin's *Shrop.* Population: 2513. ***Village***, 2m/3km SE of Chirk. **38 C2** SJ3236.
St. Martins *Wilts.* ***Suburb***, NE district of Marlborough. SU1969.
St. Martin's Moor *Shrop.* ***Hamlet***, 1km SW of St. Martin's. SJ3135.
St. Mary Bourne *Hants.* ***Village***, 3m/5km NW of Whitchurch. **21 H6** SU4250.
St. Mary Church (Llan-fair). *V. of Glam.* ***Village***, 2m/3km S of Cowbridge. **18 D4** ST0071.
St. Mary Cray *Gt.Lon.* ***Suburb***, in borough of Bromley, 1m/2km N of Orpington. **23 H5** TQ4667.
St. Mary Hill (Eglwys Fair y Mynydd). *V. of Glam.* ***Locality***, 3m/5km NW of Cowbridge. **18 C4** SS9678.

S

St. Mary in the Marsh *Kent* ***Village***, on Romney Marsh, 2m/3km N of New Romney. **15 F5** TR0627.

St. Marychurch *Torbay* ***Suburb***, N district of Torbay, 1m/2km N of Torquay town centre. **5 K4** SX9166.

St. Marylebone *Gt.Lon. See Marylebone.*

St. Mary's *I.o.S.* ***Island***, largest of the Isles of Scilly. Terminus of air and sea services from mainland. Bronze Age Innisidgen Burial Chambers (English Heritage) 2m/3km NE of Hugh Town. **2 C1** SV9111.

St. Mary's *Ork.* ***Village***, on S coast of Mainland, 6m/10km S of Kirkwall. **107 D7** HY4701.

St. Mary's *W.Suss.* ***Historic house***, good example of timber-framed house with rare 16c painted wall leather at Bramber, 10m/16km NW of Brighton. Library contains private works by poet Thomas Hood. Gardens feature topiary and living fossil tree. **12 E6** TQ1909.

St. Mary's Abbey *Gwyn.* ***Ecclesiastical building***, 13c remains of Augustinian abbey, including bell tower and Celtic crosses, on Bardsey Island, SW of tip of Lleyn Peninsula, 4m/7km SW of Aberdaron across Bardsey Sound. **36 A3** SH1222.

St. Mary's Airport *I.o.S.* ***Airport/airfield***, local airport on SE part of St. Mary's. **2 C1** SV9210.

St. Mary's Bay *Kent* Population: 3163. ***Village***, 2m/4km N of New Romney, 1m/2km S of Dymchurch. **15 F5** TR0827.

St. Mary's Bay *Torbay* ***Bay***, to E of Brixham, stretching S from Durl Head to Sharkham Point. SX9355.

St. Mary's Chapel *High.* ***Ecclesiastical building***, in Crosskirk on N coast, 6m/9km W of Thurso. Irish style chapel with low doors, probably dating from 12c. **105 F1** ND0270.

St. Mary's Croft *D. & G.* ***Settlement***, on W side of Loch Ryan, 4m/6km NW of Stranraer. **64 A4** NX0365.

St. Mary's Episcopal Cathedral *Edin.* ***Ecclesiastical building***, 1m/2km W of Edinburgh city centre. Built in 1879, with W towers added in 1917. Interesting interior and 276 foot or 84 metre high spire. **76 A3** NT2373.

St. Mary's Grove *N.Som.* ***Settlement***, 1km S of Nailsea. **19 H5** ST4669.

St. Mary's Haven *Northumb. Alternative name for Newton Haven, qv.*

St. Mary's Hoo *Med.* ***Village***, 6m/10km NE of Rochester. **24 D4** TQ8076.

St. Mary's Island (Also known as Bait Island.) *T. & W.* ***Island***, rock off North Sea coast, with lighthouse, 2m/3km N of Whitley Bay. **71 J6** NZ3575.

St. Mary's Isle *D. & G.* ***Coastal feature***, peninsula running out from head of Kirkcudbright Bay. **65 G6** NX6749.

St. Mary's Loch *Sc.Bord.* ***Lake/loch***, loch in Ettrick Forest 13m/21km W of Selkirk. 3m/5km long SW to NE; maximum depth over 150 feet or 45 metres. **69 H1** NT2422.

St. Mary's Marshes *Med.* ***Marsh/bog***, 2m/3km W of Allhallows-on-Sea. **24 D4** TQ8078.

St. Mary's Pleasance *E.Loth.* ***Garden***, restored 17c garden on SE side of Haddington next to River Tyne. **76 D3** NT5173.

St. Mary's Sound *I.o.S.* ***Sea feature***, strait dividing SW of St. Mary's from Gugh. **2 B1** SV8809.

St. Maughans (Llanfocha). *Mon.* ***Locality***, 2m/3km S of Skenfrith. SO4716.

St. Maughans Green *Mon.* ***Hamlet***, 1km E of St. Maughans. SO4716.

St. Mawes *Cornw.* ***Town***, on N bank of Percuil River at confluence with River Fal (Carrick Roads). 16c castle (English Heritage) on Castle Point built as twin to Pendennis Castle (English Heritage). Fashionable yachting centre; ferries to Falmouth in summer. **3 F5** SW8433.

St. Mawes Castle *Cornw.* ***Castle***, coastal fort (English Heritage) built by Henry VIII on Castle Point, to SW of St. Mawes. Faces sister castle of Pendennis (English Heritage). **3 F5** SW8333.

St. Mawgan *Cornw.* ***Village***, in parish of Mawgan-in-Pydar, 5m/7km NE of Newquay. **3 F2** SW8765.

St. Mellion *Cornw.* ***Village***, 3m/5km SE of Callington. **4 D4** SX3865.

St. Mellons (Llaneirwg). *Cardiff* ***Suburb***, 4m/6km NE of Cardiff. **19 F3** ST2281.

St. Merryn *Cornw.* ***Village***, 2m/3km W of Padstow. **3 F1** SW8874.

St. Mewan *Cornw.* ***Village***, just W of St. Austell. **3 G3** SW9951.

St. Michael Caerhays *Cornw.* ***Hamlet***, 4m/6km SW of Mevagissey. **3 G4** SW9642.

St. Michael Church *Som.* ***Settlement***, 1km S of North Newton. ST3030.

St. Michael Penkevil *Cornw.* ***Village***, 3m/5km SE of Truro across Truro River estuary. **3 F4** SW8542.

St. Michael South Elmham *Suff.* ***Hamlet***, 4m/6km S of Bungay. **45 H7** TM3483.

St. Michaels *Kent* ***Locality***, adjoining to N of Tenterden. **14 D4** TQ8835.

St. Michaels *Worcs.* ***Hamlet***, 2m/3km SW of Tenbury Wells. **28 E2** SO5865.

St. Michael's Island (Also known as Fort Island.) *I.o.M.* ***Island***, connected by narrow causeway to N end of Langness promontory, at entrance to Derby Haven. Includes ruins of 12c Norse-Celtic chapel and 17c Derby Fort. Spectacular views of coastline. **54 B7** SC2967.

St. Michael's Mount *Cornw.* ***Island***, in Mount's Bay opposite Marazion, 3m/4km E of Penzance and connected to shore by causeway accessible at low tide. Contains castle and remains of 12c monastery now private residence (National Trust). **2 C5** SW5129.

St. Michael's on Wyre *Lancs.* ***Village***, 3m/5km SW of Garstang. **55 H5** SD4641.

St. Minver *Cornw.* ***Village***, 3m/5km NW of Wadebridge. **3 G1** SW9677.

St. Monance *Fife Alternative spelling of St. Monans, qv.*

St. Monans (Also spelled St. Monance.) *Fife* Population: 1373. ***Small town***, fishing town on Firth of Forth, 3m/5km W of Anstruther. Many old houses. **83 G7** NO5201.

St. Mungo *D. & G.* ***Locality***, 3m/5km S of Lockerbie. NY1476.

St. Neot *Cornw.* ***Village***, former wool centre, 5m/8km NW of Liskeard. 15c church with fine stained glass. **4 B4** SX1867.

St. Neots *Cambs.* Population: 13,471. ***Town***, market town on River Great Ouse, 8m/13km SW of Huntingdon, founded in 10c by Benedictine monks. **32 E3** TL1860.

St. Nicholas (Sain Nicolas). *Pembs.* ***Village***, 4m/6km W of Fishguard. **16 C1** SM9035.

St. Nicholas (Sain Nicolas). *V. of Glam.* ***Village***, 6m/10km W of Cardiff. **18 D4** ST0974.

St. Nicholas at Wade *Kent* ***Village***, on Isle of Thanet, 6m/10km W of Margate. **25 J5** TR2666.

St. Nicholas South Elmham *Suff.* ***Hamlet***, 4m/7km S of Bungay. TM3282.

St. Ninians *Stir.* ***Locality***, S district of Stirling. **75 F1** NS7991.

St. Ninian's Cave *D. & G.* ***Cave***, said to have been used as oratory by St. Ninian in 5c (Historic Scotland), at Port Castle Bay, 4m/6km W of Isle of Whithorn. **64 E7** NX4236.

St. Ninian's Chapel *D. & G.* ***Ecclesiastical building***, ruins of 13c chapel (Historic Scotland) at Isle of Whithorn, 3m/5km SE of Whithorn. **64 E7** NX4836.

St. Ninian's Chapel *Moray* ***Ecclesiastical building***, restored chapel built in 1755 at Tynet, 3m/5km NE of Fochabers. Oldest Scottish post-Reformation Catholic church still in use. **98 B4** NJ3761.

St. Ninian's Isle *Shet.* ***Coastal feature***, peninsula on W coast of Mainland, 9m/14km N of Sumburgh Head, joined to rest of Mainland by narrow spit of land at head. **109 C10** HU3620.

St. Ninian's Isle Church *Shet.* ***Ecclesiastical building***, remains of church on W side of Bigton Wick, 1km W of Bigton. **109 C10** HU3620.

St. Ninian's Point *Arg. & B.* ***Coastal feature***, headland on W side of St. Ninian's Bay. **73 J4** NS0361.

St. Olaf's Church *Shet.* ***Ecclesiastical building***, in Lund, overlooking Lunda Wick on W coast of Unst. Ruined 12c church, in use until 1785. **108 E2** HP5604.

St. Olaves *Norf.* ***Village***, 1km SW of Fritton. Remains of 13c priory (English Heritage) named after patron saint of Norway. **45 J5** TM4599.

St. Orland's Stone *Angus* ***Other feature of interest***, symbol stone (Historic Scotland) depicting hunting and boating scenes, 4m/6km W of Forfar. **83 F3** NO4050.

St. Osyth *Essex* Population: 2073. ***Village***, 3m/5km W of Clacton-on-Sea. Remains of 12c abbey with late 15c flint gatehouse. **35 F7** TM1215.

St. Osyth Marsh *Essex* ***Marsh/bog***, 4m/6km SW of Clacton-on-Sea. **35 F7** TM1113.

St. Osyth Priory *Essex* ***Ecclesiastical building***, in St. Osyth, 5m/8km W of Clacton-on-Sea. Remains include fine 15c gatehouse. **35 F7** TM1115.

St. Owen's Cross *Here.* ***Hamlet***, 4m/6km W of Ross-on-Wye. **28 E6** SO5324.

St. Palladius' Chapel *Aber. See Fordoun.*

St. Pancras *Gt.Lon.* ***Suburb***, in borough of Camden, in N part of central London. TQ3082.

St. Patrick's Isle *I.o.M.* ***Island***, connected by causeway to W arm of Peel harbour. On island is Peel Castle (Manx National Heritage); a group of ruins inside 16c walls. **54 B5** SC2484.

St. Paul's Cathedral *Gt.Lon.* ***Ecclesiastical building***, 1m/2km E of Charing Cross in City of London. Built by Christopher Wren and completed in 1710, replacing previous cathedral destroyed in Great Fire. Superb dome, porches and funerary monuments. Contains magnificent stalls by Grinling Gibbons, ironwork by Tijou, paintings by Thornhill and mosaics by Salviati and Sir William Richmond. Reaching a height of 355 feet or 108 metres, via 530 steps, Golden Gallery affords a view over City of London, Wren churches, Tower of London and London Pool. En route to top are Whispering Gallery and Stone Gallery. Nelson and Wellington are among famous buried here. **23 G3** TQ3281.

St. Paul's Cray *Gt.Lon.* ***Suburb***, in borough of Bromley, 1m/2km E of Chislehurst. **23 H5** TQ4669.

St. Paul's Walden *Herts.* ***Village***, 3m/5km W of Stevenage. **32 E6** TL1922.

St. Peter's *Kent* ***Suburb***, W district of Broadstairs (officially Broadstairs and St. Peter's). **25 K5** TR3868.

St. Peter's Church *High.* ***Ecclesiastical building***, situated in Thurso on N coast. Ruins of medieval origin. Present church dates from 17c. **105 G2** ND1168.

St. Peter's Church *Moray* ***Ecclesiastical building***, remains of 13c church with 14c parish cross, to E of Duffus on approach to Gordonstoun School. Formerly centre of village until new Duffus planned in 19c. **97 J5** NJ1768.

St. Peter's Flat *Essex* ***Coastal feature***, mud flat N of Dengie Flat on E coast. **25 G1** TM0408.

St. Petrox (Sain Pedrog). *Pembs.* ***Settlement***, 3m/4km S of Pembroke. **16 C5** SR9797.

St. Philip's Marsh *Bristol* ***Suburb***, of Bristol to E of Temple Meads railway station. ST6072.

St. Pinnock *Cornw.* ***Hamlet***, 3m/5km W of Liskeard. **4 C4** SX2063.

St. Quivox *S.Ayr.* ***Hamlet***, 3m/5km NE of Ayr. **67 H1** NS3724.

St. Radigund's Abbey *Kent* ***Ecclesiastical building***, remains of Premonstratensian abbey, 3m/4km W of Dover town centre. **15 H3** TR2741.

St. Ronan's Church *W.Isles* ***Ecclesiastical building***, situated in SE section of Rona. HW8032.

St. Ruan *Cornw.* ***Hamlet***, 3m/4km NE of Lizard Point. SW7115.

St. Sampson *Cornw.* ***Hamlet***, above E bank of River Fowey, 2m/3km N of Fowey. SX1255.

St. Seirol's Well *I.o.A.* ***Historic/prehistoric site***, adjacent to Penmon Priory on SE tip of Anglesey, 3m/5km NE of Beaumaris. Small building covering well dates in part from 18c, but much older part may include part of original chapel dating from 6c. **46 E4** SH6380.

St. Serf's Island *P. & K.* ***Island***, in Loch Leven, towards SE corner. Ruins of medieval priory. **82 C7** NO1600.

St. Serf's Priory *P. & K.* ***Ecclesiastical building***, on SE of St. Serf's Island in Loch Leven, 3m/5km SE of Kinross. Ruins of priory founded on site of earlier Culdee settlement. **82 C7** NO1600.

St. Stephen *Cornw.* ***Village***, 4m/7km W of St. Austell. **3 G3** SW9453.

St. Stephens *Cornw.* ***Suburb***, N district of Launceston. **6 B7** SX3285.

St. Stephens *Cornw.* ***Suburb***, SW district of Saltash. **4 E5** SX4158.

St. Stephens *Herts.* ***Suburb***, SW district of St. Albans. **22 E1** TL1406.

St. Teath *Cornw.* ***Village***, 3m/5km SW of Camelford. **4 A2** SX0680.

St. Thomas *Devon* ***Suburb***, W district of Exeter, on W side of River Exe. SX9191.

St. Thomas *Swan.* ***Suburb***, 1km E of Swansea city centre across River Tawe. SS6693.

St. Tredwell's Chapel *Ork.* ***Ecclesiastical building***, on E bank of Loch of St. Tredwell, Papa Westray. Ruined chapel of unknown age where Christianity is supposed to be have been initiated in Orkney. **106 D2** HY4950.

St. Tudwal's Island East *Gwyn. See St. Tudwal's Islands.*

St. Tudwal's Island West *Gwyn. See St. Tudwal's Islands.*

St. Tudwal's Islands *Gwyn.* ***Island***, island group comprising two small islands of St. Tudwal's Island East and West, lying off S coast of Lleyn Peninsula to SE of St. Tudwal's Road. **36 C3** SH3425.

St. Tudwal's Road *Gwyn.* ***Bay***, E facing bay with Abersoch at its centre, on W side of larger Tremadog Bay. **36 C3** SH3228.

St. Tudy *Cornw.* ***Village***, 5m/9km NE of Wadebridge. **4 A3** SX0676.

St. Twynnells *Pembs.* ***Hamlet***, 3m/5km SW of Pembroke. **16 C5** SR9497.

St. Veep *Cornw.* ***Hamlet***, 4m/6km SE of Lostwithiel. **4 B5** SX1455.

St. Vigeans *Angus* ***Village***, 1m/2km N of Arbroath. Airfield to NW. **83 H3** NO6342.

St. Wenn *Cornw.* ***Village***, 4m/6km E of St. Columb Major. **3 G2** SW9664.

St. Weonards *Here.* ***Village***, 7m/11km N of Monmouth. **28 D6** SO4924.

St. Winifred's Holy Well and Chapel *Flints.* ***Ecclesiastical building***, in S district of Holywell. Well forms chapel basement, with steps to descend into water. Late 15c origin. **47 K5** SJ1876.

St. Winnow *Cornw.* ***Hamlet***, on E bank of River Fowey, 2m/3km S of Lostwithiel. SX1157.

St. Woollos *Newport* ***Suburb***, of Newport to S of town centre. ST3087.

St. Woolos Cathedral *Newport* ***Ecclesiastical building***, in centre of Newport. Magnificent Norman building work with later additions in Gothic style. Restored mid 19c, while later work has revealed interesting woodwork in roof. **19 G3** ST3087.

Saint-y-brid *Mon. Welsh form of St. Bride's Netherwent, qv.*

Saint-y-brid *V. of Glam. Welsh form of St. Brides Major, qv.*

St. y Nyll *V. of Glam.* ***Hamlet***, just N of St. Bride's-super-Ely, 5m/9km W of Cardiff. ST0978.

Saintbridge *Glos.* ***Suburb***, in SE part of Gloucester. SO8416.

Saintbury *Glos.* ***Village***, 2m/3km NE of Broadway. **30 C4** SP1139.

Salachail *Arg. & B.* ***Settlement***, in Glen Creran, 5m/8km S of Ballachulish. **80 B2** NN0551.

Salachan Glen *High.* ***Valley***, carries Salachan Burn into Loch Linnhe opposite Eilean Balnagowan. **80 A2** NM9653.

Salcey Forest *Northants.* ***Forest/woodland***, wooded area, 7m/11km NW of Newport Pagnell. **32 B3** SP8052.

Salcombe *Devon* Population: 1921. ***Small town***, resort near mouth of Kingsbridge Estuary, 3m/5km S of Kingsbridge (distance by road 6m/10km). Yachting. **5 H7** SX7439.

Salcombe Museum *Devon* ***Other feature of interest***, at Salcombe, includes a shipwreck and shipbuilding exhibitions. **5 H7** SX7339.

Salcombe Regis *Devon* ***Village***, 2m/3km NE of Sidmouth. **7 K7** SY1488.

Salcott *Essex* ***Village***, at head of Salcott Creek, 8m/12km SW of Colchester. **34 D7** TL9513.

Salcott Channel *Essex* ***Sea feature***, inlet at Salcott, flowing into estuary of River Blackwater. **34 D7** TL9513.

Sale *Gt.Man.* Population: 56,052. ***Town***, mainly residential town, 5m/8km SW of Manchester. **49 G3** SJ7892.

Sale Ees *Gt.Man.* ***Locality***, 1km NE of Sale town centre. SJ7892.

Sale Green *Worcs.* ***Hamlet***, 4m/6km SE of Droitwich Spa. **29 J3** SO9358.

Saleby *Lincs.* ***Village***, 2m/3km N of Alford. **53 H5** TF4578.

Salehurst *E.Suss.* ***Village***, 5m/8km N of Battle. Parish contains the larger village of Robertsbridge. **14 C5** TQ7424.

Salem (Heolgaled). *Carmar.* ***Hamlet***, 3m/4km N of Llandeilo. **17 K2** SN6226.

Salem *Cere.* ***Settlement***, 3m/5km E of Bow Street. **37 F7** SN6684.

Salem *Gwyn.* ***Hamlet***, 5m/9km SE of Caernarfon. **46 D7** SH5456.

Salen *Arg. & B.* ***Village***, on bay of same name on Sound of Mull, 9m/14km SE of Tobermory, Mull. **79 G3** NM5743.

Salen *High.* ***Village***, on bay of same name, on N shore of Loch Sunart, in Lochaber district. **79 H1** NM6864.

Salen Bay *Arg. & B.* ***Bay***, small bay at Salen, on coast of Mull. **79 G3** NM5744.

Salen Forest *Arg. & B.* ***Forest/woodland***, stretching SE from head of Loch Frisa, along its NE shore and towards coast and Sound of Mull, 2m/3km NW of Salen, Mull. **79 G3** NM5047.

Salendine Nook *W.Yorks.* ***Suburb***, 3m/4km W of Huddersfield town centre. SE1017.

Sales Point *Essex* ***Coastal feature***, point at N of St. Peter's Flat at mouth of River Blackwater. **25 G1** TM0309.
Salesbury *Lancs.* ***Village***, 3m/5km N of Blackburn. **56 B6** SD6732.
Saleway *Worcs.* ***Settlement***, 3m/5km SE of Droitwich Spa. SO9259.
Salford *Beds.* ***Village***, 5m/8km SE of Newport Pagnell. **32 C5** SP9339.
Salford *Gt.Man.* Population: 79,755. ***City***, adjoining to W of Manchester. Previously a textile centre and major inland port. Docks on Manchester Ship Canal now converted into a leisure and residential centre. Roman Catholic cathedral of mid-19c. Birthplace and subject matter of L.S. Lowry, commemorated at Lowry Centre in Salford Art Gallery. University. **49 H3** SJ8298.
Salford *Oxon.* ***Village***, 2m/3km NW of Chipping Norton. **30 D6** SP2828.
Salford Priors *Warks.* ***Village***, 5m/8km NE of Evesham. **30 B3** SP0751.
Salfords *Surr.* Population: 5813. ***Village***, 3m/4km S of Redhill. **23 F7** TQ2846.
Salhouse *Norf.* ***Village***, 6m/10km NE of Norwich. **45 H4** TG3014.
Saligo Bay *Arg. & B.* ***Bay***, on W coast of Islay, 1m/2km W of Loch Gorm. **72 A4** NR2066.
Saline *Fife* Population: 1235. ***Village***, 5m/8km NW of Dunfermline. **75 J1** NT0292.
Saline Hill *Fife* ***Mountain***, 1m/2km NE of Saline. Height 1178 feet or 359 metres. **75 J1** NT0393.
Saling Hall Garden *Essex* ***Garden***, 12 acres surrounding hall in Great Saling, 4m/6km NW of Braintree. Includes late 17c walled garden, water gardens and aboretum. **33 K6** TL6925.
Salisbury *Edin.* ***Suburb***, 1m/2km SE of Edinburgh city centre. NT2672.
Salisbury (Former, and official name: New Sarum.) *Wilts.* Population: 39,268. ***City***, cathedral city at confluence of Rivers Avon and Nadder, 21m/34km NW of Southampton. Shopping centre and market town, with buildings ranging from medieval to Victorian; several medieval churches. Cathedral, in Early English style, has 404 foot or 123 metre spire, tallest in Britain. **10 C1** SU1429.
Salisbury Cathedral *Wilts.* ***Ecclesiastical building***, on S side of Salisbury city centre. Built between 1220 and 1260, it is the only English cathedral built all in one style (Early English). Spire, tallest in England at 404 feet or 123 metres, was added in 1334. **10 C1** SU1429.
Salisbury Plain *Wilts.* ***Large natural feature***, large tract of chalk upland extending from Westbury and Warminster in W to River Bourne valley and North Tidworth in E, and from Vale of Pewsey in N to River Wylye valley in S. Much used for military training. Ancient earthworks abound. **20 C6** SU1040.
Salkeld Dykes *Cumb.* ***Hamlet***, just W of Great Salkeld. **61 G3** NY5436.
Sallachan *High.* ***Settlement***, near mouth of River Gour, 1m/2km NW of Sallachan Point, Lochaber district. **80 A1** NM9863.
Sallachan Point *High.* ***Coastal feature***, low-lying promontory with beacon on W shore of Loch Linnhe in Lochaber district. **80 A1** NM9861.
Sallachry *Arg. & B.* ***Settlement***, 3m/4km NW of Inveraray. **80 B6** NN0712.
Sallachy *High.* ***Locality***, in Skye and Lochalsh district, on N shore of Loch Long, 3m/5km NE of Dornie. **87 F1** NG9130.
Sallachy *High.* ***Settlement***, on SW shore of Loch Shin, 3m/5km NW of Lairg. **96 C1** NC5508.
Salle *Norf.* ***Hamlet***, 1m/2km NE of Reepham. **45 F3** TG1024.
Salmeston Grange *Kent* ***Historic house***, well-preserved monastic grange, 1km S of Margate town centre. **25 K5** TR3569.
Salmonby *Lincs.* ***Village***, 5m/8km NE of Horncastle. **53 G5** TF3273.
Salmond's Muir *Angus* ***Settlement***, 2m/3km NE of Carnoustie. **83 G4** NO5737.
Salperton *Glos.* ***Hamlet***, 4m/7km NW of Northleach. **30 B6** SP0720.
Salph End *Beds.* ***Hamlet***, 3m/4km NE of Bedford. **32 D3** TL0752.
Salsburgh *N.Lan.* Population: 1398. ***Village***, 5m/7km E of Airdrie. **75 G4** NS8262.
Salt *Staffs.* ***Hamlet***, 4m/6km NE of Stafford. **40 B3** SJ9527.
Salt Cotes *Cumb.* ***Locality***, 2m/3km NE of Abbeytown. NY1853.
Salt Hill *Slo.* ***Suburb***, of Slough, to W of town centre. **22 C4** SU9680.
Salt Holme *Middbro.* ***Settlement***, 2m/3km N of Middlesbrough across River Tees. NZ5023.
Salt Island *I.o.A.* ***Island***, in Holyhead harbour, joined by isthmus to Holy Island just off Holyhead. **46 A4** SH2582.
Salta *Cumb.* ***Locality***, 2m/3km N of Allonby. NY0845.
Saltaire *W.Yorks.* ***Suburb***, W district of Shipley on River Aire, originally built in 19c by Sir Titus Salt as model village for workers at his worsted and alpaca mills. SE1437.
Saltash *Cornw.* Population: 14,139. ***Town***, medieval port beside narrow stretch of River Tamar estuary, 4m/6km NW of Plymouth city centre, crossed by 19c railway bridge and 20c road bridge. **4 E5** SX4358.
Saltburn *High.* ***Village***, on N shore of Cromarty Firth, Ross and Cromarty district, 1m/2km NE of Invergordon. Development in connection with North Sea oil. **96 E4** NH7269.
Saltburn-by-the-Sea *R. & C.* Population: 6145. ***Small town***, North Sea coast resort 4m/7km E of Redcar. Wide sands and only pier in NE. **63 H4** NZ6621.
Saltby *Leics.* ***Village***, 7m/11km SW of Grantham. **42 B3** SK8526.
Saltcoats *Cumb.* ***Settlement***, 1km NW of Ravenglass across River Esk estuary. SD0796.
Saltcoats *N.Ayr.* Population: 11,865. ***Town***, salt town and resort on Firth of Clyde, adjoining to SE of Ardrossan. Harbour, with 19c Martello tower. **74 A6** NS2441.
Saltcotes *Lancs.* ***Locality***, at E end of Lytham St. Anne's. **55 G7** SD3727.
Saltdean *B. & H.* Population: 10,743. ***Village***, 5m/8km E of Brighton. **13 G6** TQ3802.
Salter *Lancs.* ***Locality***, in valley of River Roeburn, 3m/5km S of Hornby, comprising High, Middle, and Lower Salter. SD6063.
Salter Fell *Lancs.* ***Open space***, moorland on E side of upper reaches of River Roeburn, 6m/10km S of Low Bentham. **56 B3** SD6359.
Salter Houses *Hart.* ***Locality***, 2m/4km NW of Wolviston. NZ4227.
Salter Street *W.Mid.* ***Settlement***, 3m/4km NW of Hockley Heath. SP1274.
Salterbeck *Cumb.* ***Suburb***, S district of Workington. NX9926.
Salterforth *Lancs.* ***Village***, 1m/2km SE of Barnoldswick. **56 D5** SD8845.
Saltergate *N.Yorks.* ***Open space***, moorland on S side of Saltergate Moor, 7m/12km NE of Pickering. **63 K7** SE8594.
Salterhill *Moray* ***Settlement***, 3m/4km N of Elgin. **97 K5** NJ2067.
Salter's Bank *Lancs.* ***Coastal feature***, sandbank to SW of Lytham St. Anne's. **55 G7** SD3027.
Salter's Brook Bridge ***Other feature of interest***, mountain pass on border of Derbyshire and South Yorkshire, where A628(T) crosses Salter's Brook, 7m/11km SW of Penistone. Height 1312 feet or 400 metres. **50 D3** SE1300.
Salters Lode *Norf.* ***Locality***, 2m/3km SW of Downham Market across River Great Ouse. TF5801.
Salterswall *Ches.* ***Locality***, 2m/3km W of Winsford. **49 F6** SJ6267.
Saltfleet *Lincs.* ***Village***, coastal village, 9m/14km NE of Louth. **53 H3** TF4593.
Saltfleetby All Saints *Lincs.* ***Hamlet***, 5m/8km NW of Mablethorpe. **53 H3** TF4590.
Saltfleetby St. Clements *Lincs.* ***Hamlet***, 1m/2km N of Saltfleetby All Saints. **53 H3** TF4590.
Saltfleetby St. Peter *Lincs.* ***Village***, 1m/2km SW of Saltfleetby All Saints. **53 H4** TF4590.
Saltford *B. & N.E.Som.* Population: 4340. ***Village***, on River Avon, 2m/3km SE of Keynsham. **19 K5** ST6867.
Salthaugh Grange *E.Riding* ***Settlement***, 2m/3km S of Keyingham. **59 J7** TA2321.
Salthouse *Norf.* ***Village***, 3m/5km N of Holt. **44 E1** TG0743.
Saltinish *W.Isles* ***Locality***, on Barra, 1m/2km SE of Scurrival Point. NF7007.
Saltley *W.Mid.* ***Suburb***, 2m/3km E of Birmingham city centre. **40 C7** SP0987.
Saltmarsh *Newport* ***Settlement***, 1m/2km E of Uskmouth. ST3582.
Saltmarshe *E.Riding* ***Village***, on N bank of River Ouse, 4m/6km SE of Howden. **58 D7** SE7824.
Saltmead *Cardiff* ***Suburb***, 1km SW of Cardiff city centre across River Taff. ST1775.
Saltness *Ork.* ***Settlement***, at S end of Hoy, 1km N of Melsetter. ND2790.
Saltney *Flints.* Population: 4144. ***Suburb***, 2m/3km SW of Chester across River Dee. **48 C6** SJ3764.
Saltom Bay *Cumb.* ***Bay***, on Irish Sea, extending S from Whitehaven to North Head. **60 A5** NX9516.
Salton *N.Yorks.* ***Village***, 4m/7km S of Kirkbymoorside. **58 D1** SE7180.
Saltram *Plym.* ***Historic house***, 18c house built over a Tudor mansion and set within grounds (National Trust) on E side of River Plym, 3m/4km NE of Plymouth city centre. Includes rooms designed by Robert Adam, art gallery in stables and orangery in gardens. **5 F5** SX5255.
Saltrens *Devon* ***Hamlet***, 3m/4km S of Bideford. SS4521.
Saltwell *T. & W.* ***Suburb***, 1m/2km S of Gateshead town centre. NZ2561.
Saltwick *Northumb.* ***Settlement***, 4m/6km SW of Morpeth. **71 G5** NZ1780.
Saltwick Bay *N.Yorks.* ***Bay***, on North Sea coast, 1m/2km E of Whitby. At N end of bay is Saltwick Nab (National Trust), a low, rocky headland. **63 J1** NZ9110.
Saltwood *Kent* ***Suburb***, N of Hythe. Restored medieval castle. **15 G4** TR1535.
Saltwood Castle *Kent* ***Castle***, built 12c by Henry of Essex, 2m/4km W of Folkestone. Home of contemporary art historian, Lord Clarke. **15 G4** TR1636.
Salum *Arg. & B.* ***Settlement***, on Tiree, on E side of Salum Bay, on N coast, 2m/3km W of Rubha Dubh. NM0648.
Salum Bay *Arg. & B.* ***Bay***, on N coast of Tiree. **78 B3** NM0648.
Salvington *W.Suss.* ***Suburb***, N district of Worthing. **12 E6** TQ1205.
Salwarpe *Worcs.* ***Village***, on River Salwarpe, 2m/3km SW of Droitwich Spa. **29 H2** SO8761.
Salway Ash *Dorset Alternative spelling of Salwayash, qv.*
Salwayash (Also spelled Salway Ash.) *Dorset* ***Hamlet***, 2m/4km N of Bridport. **8 D5** SY4596.
Samala *W.Isles Anglicised form of Samhla, qv.*
Samalaman Island *High.* ***Island***, low-lying islet on S side of Sound of Arisaig, 3m/5km W of Roshven, Lochaber district. **86 C7** NM6678.
Samalan Island *Arg. & B.* ***Island***, islet at entrance to Loch na Keal, W coast of Mull, lying 1km NE of Inch Kenneth. **79 F4** NM4536.
Sambourne *Warks.* ***Village***, 3m/5km NW of Alcester. **30 B2** SP0661.
Sambrook *Tel. & W.* ***Village***, 4m/6km NW of Newport. **39 G3** SJ7124.
Samhla (Anglicised form: Samala.) *W.Isles* ***Settlement***, on E side of Baleshare. **92 C5** NF7962.
Samlesbury *Lancs.* ***Village***, on River Ribble, 3m/5km E of Preston. **55 J6** SD5930.
Samlesbury Bottoms *Lancs.* ***Settlement***, on River Darwen, 2m/3km SE of Samlesbury. **56 B7** SD6229.
Samlesbury Hall *Lancs.* ***Historic house***, timber-framed house dating partly from 14c, 4m/6km NW of Blackburn. **56 B6** SD5930.
Sampford Arundel *Som.* ***Village***, 2m/4km SW of Wellington. **7 K4** ST1018.
Sampford Brett *Som.* ***Village***, 2m/3km SE of Watchet. **7 J1** ST0840.
Sampford Courtenay *Devon* ***Village***, 5m/8km NE of Okehampton. **6 E5** SS6301.
Sampford Peverell *Devon* ***Village***, 5m/8km E of Tiverton. **7 J4** ST0314.
Sampford Spiney *Devon* ***Hamlet***, of SW Dartmoor, 4m/6km E of Tavistock. **5 F3** SX5372.
Samphire Island *Cornw.* ***Island***, small island off N coast opposite Carvannel Downs, 1m/2km SW of Portreath. SW6344.
Samphrey *Shet.* ***Island***, uninhabited island of about 200 acres or 80 hectares lying between SW end of Yell and NE coast of Mainland. **108 D5** HU4676.
Sampton Moor *Som.* ***Village***, 1km S of Sampford Arundel and 3m/4km SW of Wellington. ST1117.
Samson *I.o.S.* ***Island***, largest of uninhabited islands of Isles of Scilly, lying S of Bryher. **2 B1** SV8712.
Samson's Lane *Ork.* ***Settlement***, at centre of Stronsay. HY6525.
Samuel's Corner *Essex* ***Hamlet***, 2m/3km NE of Shoeburyness. TQ9587.
Samuelston *E.Loth.* ***Settlement***, on River Tyne, 3m/4km SW of Haddington. **76 C3** NT4870.
Sanaigmore *Arg. & B.* ***Settlement***, on N coast of Islay, 8m/12km NW of Bridgend. **72 A4** NR2370.
Sancler *Carmar. Welsh form of St. Clears, qv.*
Sancreed *Cornw.* ***Village***, 3m/5km W of Penzance. **2 B6** SW4229.
Sancton *E.Riding* ***Village***, 2m/3km SE of Market Weighton. **59 F6** SE9039.
Sand *Devon* ***Historic house***, built in 1594 by Roland Huyshe in Sidbury, with oak-panelled rooms and sculptured stone windows. Includes late 15c Sand Lodge and fine gardens. **7 K6** SY1592.
Sand *Shet.* ***Settlement***, at head of Sand Voe, Mainland. **109 C8** HU3447.
Sand *Som.* ***Hamlet***, 1km S of Wedmore. ST4346.
Sand Bay *N.Som.* ***Bay***, facing W on Bristol Channel and extending S from Sand Point to Birnbeck Island, 3m/4km N of Weston-super-Mare. **19 G5** ST3264.
Sand Beds *W.Mid.* ***Suburb***, in W part of Walsall. SO9799.
Sand Hill *Moray* ***Mountain***, 3m/5km S of Cabrach. Height 1797 feet or 548 metres. **90 B2** NJ3821.
Sand Hills *W.Yorks.* ***Hamlet***, 1km SW of Thorner. SE3739.
Sand Hole *E.Riding* ***Hamlet***, 1m/2km S of Holme-on-Spalding-Moor. **58 E6** SE8137.
Sand Hutton *N.Yorks.* ***Village***, 2m/4km NW of Stamford Bridge. **58 C4** SE6958.
Sand Point *N.Som.* ***Coastal feature***, headland at W end of Middle Hope and N end of Sand Bay on N side of Weston-super-Mare. **19 G5** ST3165.
Sand Side *Cumb.* ***Village***, on E side of River Duddon estuary, 5m/8km N of Dalton-in-Furness. **55 F1** SD2282.
Sand Water *Shet.* ***Lake/loch***, on Mainland in course of Burn of Sandwater, which rises as Burn of Pettawater above small lake of Petta Water, 2m/4km S of Voe. Stream flows S through Petta Water, Sand Water and Loch of Strom into Stromness Voe to E of Weisdale Voe. **109 D7** HU4154.
Sand Wick *Shet.* ***Bay***, wide sandy bay off E coast of Unst. **108 F2** HP6202.
Sanda Island *Arg. & B.* ***Island***, lying nearly 2m/3km off S coast of Kintyre across Sanda Sound. Measures 1m/2km E to W and 1km N to S. Lighthouse at S point. **66 B3** NR7204.
Sanda Sound *Arg. & B.* ***Sea feature***, divides Sanda Island from S coast of Kintyre. Nearly 2m/3km wide. **66 B3** NR7204.
Sandaig *Arg. & B.* ***Settlement***, adjoining to W of Middleton, near W coast of Tiree. **78 A3** NL9443.
Sandaig *High.* ***Locality***, at W end of Knoydart, Lochaber district, on Sandaig Bay, on N side of entrance to Loch Nevis. **86 D4** NG7101.
Sandaig *High.* ***Settlement***, on coast of Skye and Lochalsh district, 4m/6km SW of Glenelg. **86 D3** NG7714.
Sandaig Bay *High.* ***Bay***, on N side of entrance to Loch Nevis. Locality of Sandaig lies on bay. **86 D4** NG7101.
Sandaig Islands *High.* ***Island***, group of islets in Sound of Sleat off N side of entrance to Loch Hourn in Lochaber district. Lighthouse on Eilean Mòr, the islet farthest from mainland shore. **86 D3** NG7614.
Sandal Magna *W.Yorks.* ***Suburb***, 2m/3km S of Wakefield city centre across River Calder. SE3418.
Sandale *Cumb.* ***Locality***, 1m/2km E of Boltongate. NY2440.
Sanday *High.* ***Island***, in Inner Hebrides at SE end of Canna, to which it is connected at low tide. Sanday is 2m/3km E to W and has a maximum width N to S of 1km. Its N coast forms S shore of Canna Harbour. **85 H4** NG2704.
Sanday *Ork.* ***Island***, low-lying island some 14m/23km NE to SW and of varying width, in places less than 1km, lying 3m/4km S of North Ronaldsay and N of Stronsay at nearest points. Spur Ness at extreme SW of island is 17m/28km NE of Kirkwall, Mainland. Airfield near centre of island. **106 G3** HY6840.
Sanday Airfield *Ork.* ***Airport/airfield***, 1km W of Overbister, Sanday. **106 F3** HY6740.
Sanday Sound *Ork.* ***Sea feature***, sea area between islands of Sanday and Stronsay. **106 F4** HY6734.
Sandbach *Ches.* Population: 15,839. ***Town***, market town, 5m/8km NE of Crewe. Two large Saxon crosses (English Heritage) in market place. **49 G6** SJ7760.

S

Sandbach Crosses *Ches.* ***Historic/prehistoric site***, two reconstructed sandstone Saxon crosses (English Heritage) in Sandbach town centre. Believed to have been built in 8c or 9c as Christianity was introduced to area. **49 G6** SJ7560.
Sandbach Heath *Ches.* ***Suburb***, 1m/2km E of Sandbach. SJ7760.
Sandbank *Arg. & B.* Population: 1543. ***Village***, on S side of Holy Loch, Argyll, 2m/4km N of Dunoon. **73 K2** NS1680.
Sandbanks *Poole* ***Suburb***, of Poole on spit of land at N entrance to Poole Harbour. **10 B6** SZ0487.
Sandend *Aber.* ***Village***, on Sandend Bay, N coast, which is 3m/4km E of Cullen. **98 D4** NJ5566.
Sandend Bay *Aber.* ***Bay***, 3m/4km E of Cullen. Sandend village lies on the bay. **98 D4** NJ5566.
Sanderstead *Gt.Lon.* ***Suburb***, in borough of Croydon, 2m/3km E of Purley. **23 G5** TQ3461.
Sandfields *Glos.* ***Suburb***, NW district of Cheltenham. SO9323.
Sandfields *N.P.T.* ***Suburb***, NW district of Port Talbot. SS7490.
Sandford *Cumb.* ***Village***, 4m/6km SE of Appleby-in-Westmorland. **61 J5** NY7216.
Sandford *Devon* Population: 1972. ***Village***, 2m/3km NW of Crediton. **7 G5** SS8202.
Sandford *Dorset* ***Village***, 1m/2km N of Wareham. **9 J5** SY9289.
Sandford *I.o.W.* ***Hamlet***, 3m/4km W of Shanklin. **11 G6** SZ5481.
Sandford *N.Som.* ***Village***, 3m/5km N of Axbridge. Quarries on sides of Sandford Hill. **19 H6** ST4259.
Sandford *Shrop.* ***Settlement***, 1m/2km NE of Knockin. SJ3423.
Sandford *Shrop.* ***Settlement***, 5m/9km SE of Whitchurch. SJ5834.
Sandford *S.Lan.* ***Hamlet***, 1m/2km SE of Strathaven. **75 F6** NS7143.
Sandford Batch *N.Som.* ***Hamlet***, 1km S of Sandford. ST4259.
Sandford Bay *Aber.* ***Bay***, on E coast S of Peterhead, between Burnhaven and Boddam. **99 K6** NK1243.
Sandford Hill *Stoke* ***Suburb***, in Stoke-on-Trent, NE of Longton. SJ9144.
Sandford-on-Thames *Oxon.* ***Village***, 3m/5km SE of Oxford. **21 J1** SP5301.
Sandford Orcas *Dorset* ***Village***, 3m/4km N of Sherborne. **9 F2** ST6220.
Sandford St. Martin *Oxon.* ***Village***, 7m/11km E of Chipping Norton. **31 F6** SP4226.
Sandfordhill *Aber.* ***Settlement***, near E coast, 3m/5km S of Peterhead. **99 K6** NK1142.
Sandgarth *Ork.* ***Settlement***, on SE end of Shapinsay, 6m/9km NE of Kirkwall across Shapinsay Sound. **107 E6** HY5215.
Sandgate *Kent* ***Suburb***, W district of Folkestone. **15 H4** TR2035.
Sandgreen *D. & G.* ***Settlement***, on E shore of Fleet Bay, 3m/5km SW of Gatehouse of Fleet. **65 F5** NX5752.
Sandhaven *Aber.* ***Village***, on N coast, 2m/3km W of Fraserburgh. **99 H4** NJ9667.
Sandhead *D. & G.* ***Village***, coastal village on Sandhead Bay, on W side of Luce Bay, 7m/11km S of Stranraer. **64 A5** NX0949.
Sandhill *S.Yorks.* ***Suburb***, NE district of Rawmarsh, 3m/5km NE of Rotherham. SK4497.
Sandhills *Dorset* ***Hamlet***, 5m/8km SE of Sherborne. **9 F3** ST6810.
Sandhills *Dorset* ***Settlement***, 2m/3km N of Maiden Newton. ST5800.
Sandhills *Oxon.* ***Suburb***, 3m/5km NE of Oxford city centre. SP5607.
Sandhills *Surr.* ***Village***, 3m/5km S of Milford. **12 C3** SU9337.
Sandhills *W.Mid.* ***Locality***, 1km SE of Brownhills. SK0604.
Sandhoe *Northumb.* ***Village***, 2m/3km NW of Corbridge. **70 E7** NY9766.
Sandholme *E.Riding* ***Village***, 5m/8km E of Howden. **58 E6** SE8230.
Sandholme *Lincs.* ***Settlement***, 4m/7km S of Boston. **43 G2** TF3337.
Sandhurst *Brack.F.* Population: 19,153. ***Town***, 3m/4km W of Camberley. Royal Military Academy to E. **22 B5** SU8361.
Sandhurst *Glos.* ***Village***, 3m/5km N of Gloucester. **29 H6** SO8223.
Sandhurst *Kent* ***Village***, 3m/4km SE of Hawkhurst. **14 C5** TQ7928.
Sandhurst Cross *Kent* ***Hamlet***, 1m/2km SW of Sandhurst. TQ7927.
Sandhutton *N.Yorks.* ***Village***, 3m/5km W of Thirsk. **57 J1** SE3882.
Sandiacre *Derbys.* ***Locality***, 2m/3km N of Long Eaton. **41 G2** SK4736.
Sandilands *Lincs.* ***Hamlet***, on coast, 1m/2km S of Sutton on Sea. **53 J4** TF5280.
Sandiway *Ches.* ***Village***, 4m/6km SW of Northwich. **49 F5** SJ6070.
Sandleheath *Hants.* ***Village***, 1m/2km W of Fordingbridge. **10 C3** SU1214.
Sandleigh *Oxon.* ***Village***, 3m/4km N of Abingdon. **21 H1** SP4701.
Sandling *Kent* ***Locality***, adjoining to N of Maidstone. **14 C2** TQ7558.
Sandlow Green *Ches.* ***Settlement***, 2m/3km SE of Holmes Chapel. SJ7866.
Sandness *Shet.* ***Village***, near W coast of Mainland, adjoining to E of Melby. **109 A7** HU1957.
Sandness Hill *Shet.* ***Hill***, to S of Sandness. Height 817 feet or 249 metres. **109 A7** HU1957.
Sandon *Essex* ***Village***, 3m/5km SE of Chelmsford. **24 D1** TL7404.
Sandon *Herts.* ***Village***, 5m/8km E of Baldock. **33 G5** TL3234.
Sandon *Staffs.* ***Village***, 4m/7km NE of Stafford. **40 B3** SJ9429.
Sandown *I.o.W.* Population: 5768. ***Small town***, resort on Sandown Bay, 5m/8km S of Ryde and 2m/3km NE of Shanklin, to which it is joined. Long Victorian pier; good beach. Isle of Wight (Sandown) Airport to W. **11 G6** SZ5984.
Sandown Bay *I.o.W.* ***Bay***, 5m/8km S of Ryde. Resort of Sandown lies on the bay. **11 H6** SZ5984.
Sandown Park *Surr.* ***Racecourse***, park and racecourse on N side of Esher. One mixed, fifteen flat and eleven National Hunt race days each year. **22 E5** TQ1365.
Sandpit Hill *S.Yorks.* ***Locality***, adjoining to W of Branton, 4m/6km E of Doncaster town centre. SE6301.
Sandpits *Shrop.* ***Suburb***, in NE part of Ludlow. SO5175.
Sandplace *Cornw.* ***Hamlet***, 2m/3km N of Looe. **4 C5** SX2555.
Sandquoy *Ork.* ***Settlement***, on Bay of Sandquoy, on N coast of Sanday, 2m/3km SW of Tafts Ness. **106 G3** HY7445.
Sandray (Gaelic form: Sanndraigh.) *W.Isles* ***Island***, uninhabited island of about 4 square km, 1km S of Vatersay and 3m/5km S of Barra. **84 B5** NL6491.
Sandridge *Devon* ***Hamlet***, to N of River Dart estuary, 3m/5km SW of Paignton. SX8656.
Sandridge *Herts.* ***Village***, 3m/4km NE of St. Albans. **32 E7** TL1710.
Sandridge *Wilts.* ***Hamlet***, 3m/4km NE of Melksham. **20 C5** ST9464.
Sandringham *Norf.* ***Village***, estate village of royal residence of Sandringham House, mid 19c mansion in large grounds, 7m/11km NE of King's Lynn. **44 A3** TF6928.
Sandringham House *Norf.* ***Historic house***, mid 19c mansion within royal country estate, 2m/3km S of Dersingham and 8m/13km NE of King's Lynn. Grounds include lakes, flower and shrub gardens. **44 A3** TF6928.
Sandrocks *W.Suss.* ***Settlement***, adjoining to S of Haywards Heath. **13 G4** TQ3322.
Sands End *Gt.Lon.* ***Suburb***, on N bank of River Thames in borough of Hammersmith and Fulham, between Wandsworth and Battersea Bridges. TQ2676.
Sands of Forvie *Aber.* ***Coastal feature***, sandy waste on E coast between Collieston and Newburgh. Forvie Ness Nature Reserve located here. **91 J2** NK0227.
Sands of Luce *D. & G.* ***Coastal feature***, extensive sands along NW coast of Luce Bay, 1m/2km S of Glenluce. **64 B5** NX1654.
Sands of Nigg *High.* ***Coastal feature***, extensive sands in Nigg Bay, 3m/4km N of Cromarty across Cromarty Firth. Sands stretch for up to 3m/4km from N coast of Nigg Bay. **96 E4** NH7872.
Sandsend *N.Yorks.* ***Village***, and resort on North Sea coast, 3m/4km NW of Whitby, on bay called Sandsend Wyke. **63 K5** NZ8612.
Sandsend Ness *N.Yorks.* ***Coastal feature***, headland at N end of Sandsend bay. **63 K5** NZ8612.
Sandside *Cumb.* ***Settlement***, 1m/2km SE of Ulverston. SD3077.
Sandside *Cumb.* ***Settlement***, on E bank of River Kent estuary, 1m/2km W of Milnthorpe. SD4780.
Sandside Bay *High.* ***Bay***, 1m/2km N of Reay, on N coast of Caithness district, with Sandside Head on W side of entrance to bay. **104 E2** NC9665.
Sandside Burn *High.* ***River***, flowing N into W side of Sandside Bay, on N coast of Caithness district. **104 E3** NC9665.
Sandside House *High.* ***Settlement***, 1km NW of Reay, Caithness district. **104 E2** NC9565.
Sandsound *Shet.* ***Settlement***, on E shore of Sandsound Voe. **109 C8** HU3548.
Sandtoft *N.Lincs.* ***Hamlet***, 4m/6km NW of Epworth. **51 K2** SE7408.
Sanduck *Devon* ***Settlement***, 2m/3km SE of Moretonhampstead. **7 F7** SX7683.
Sandway *Dorset* ***Locality***, adjoining to E of Bourton, 4m/6km NW of Gillingham. ST7730.
Sandway *Kent* ***Hamlet***, 1m/2km SW of Lenham. **14 D2** TQ8851.
Sandwell *W.Mid.* ***Suburb***, in NE part of Warley. SP0289.
Sandwell Valley Country Park *W.Mid.* ***Leisure/recreation***, 1700 acre or 688 hectare country park on E side of West Bromwich, including 94 acres or 38 hectares of lakes and woodland with facilities for watersports, riding and nature trails. **40 C6** SP0192.
Sandwich *Kent* Population: 4164. ***Small town***, an original Cinque port on River Stour, 2m/3km from sea (Sandwich Bay), 11m/18km E of Canterbury. Resort, with well-known golf courses. **15 J2** TR3358.
Sandwich Bay *Kent* ***Bay***, 11m/18km E of Canterbury. **15 J2** TR3660.
Sandwich Flats *Kent* ***Coastal feature***, sandflat in Sandwich Bay, 3m/4km S of Ramsgate. **25 K5** TR3561.
Sandwick *Cumb.* ***Settlement***, near S shore of Ullswater, 3m/5km NE of Patterdale. **60 F5** NY4219.
Sandwick *Shet.* ***Settlement***, at head of Sand Wick, S facing bay on E coast of Mainland, 11m/18km S of Lerwick. **109 D10** HU4323.
Sandwick (Gaelic form: Sanndabhaig.) *W.Isles* ***Village***, on Isle of Lewis, 1m/2km E of Stornoway. Mast to N. **101 G4** NB4432.
Sandwith *Cumb.* ***Hamlet***, 2m/4km S of Whitehaven. **60 A5** NX9614.
Sandwood Bay *High.* ***Bay***, on NW coast of Sutherland district, between headlands of Rubh' an t-Socaich Ghlais and Rubh' a Bhuachaille. **102 E2** NC2266.
Sandwood Loch *High.* ***Lake/loch***, near NW coast of Sutherland district at foot of Strath Shinary, draining into Sandwood Bay. **102 E2** NC2264.
Sandy *Beds.* Population: 8554. ***Small town***, on River Ivel, 8m/12km E of Bedford. Market-gardening in vicinity. Headquarters of RSPB, The Lodge, set in 107 acre nature reserve. **32 E4** TL1749.
Sandy *Carmar.* ***Settlement***, adjoining to W of Llanelli. SN4900.
Sandy Bank *Lincs.* ***Settlement***, 3m/5km SE of Coningsby. TF2654.
Sandy Cross *E.Suss.* ***Locality***, residential locality in S part of Heathfield. TQ5820.
Sandy Cross *Here.* ***Locality***, 2m/3km NE of Bromyard. SO6756.
Sandy Cross *Surr.* ***Hamlet***, 3m/5km E of Farnham. SU8847.
Sandy Edge *Sc.Bord.* ***Inland physical feature***, wooded ridge, 1312 feet or 400 metres high, to E of Leap Hill, 9m/14km S of Hawick. **70 A3** NT5201.
Sandy Gate *Devon* ***Locality***, around junction 30 of M5 motorway, 3m/5km E of Exeter. SX9691.
Sandy Haven *Pembs.* ***Settlement***, 1m/2km E of St. Ishmael's, on W side of Sandyhaven Pill. **16 B4** SM8507.
Sandy Lane *W.Yorks.* ***Suburb***, 4m/6km NW of Bradford city centre. **57 G6** SE1135.
Sandy Lane *Wilts.* ***Village***, 3m/5km SW of Calne. Site of Roman town of Verlucio to SE. **20 C5** ST9668.
Sandy Lane *Wrex.* ***Settlement***, 2m/3km SE of Overton. SJ4040.
Sandy Point *Suff.* ***Coastal feature***, point between Holland Gap and Chevaux de frise Point, 2m/3km SW of Frinton-on-Sea. **35 G7** TM2218.
Sandy Way *I.o.W.* ***Hamlet***, just S of Shorwell. SZ4582.
Sandycroft *Flints.* ***Locality***, 1m/2km SE of Queensferry. **48 C6** SJ3367.
Sandyford *Stoke* ***Suburb***, 1m/2km N of Tunstall. SJ8552.
Sandygate *Devon* ***Locality***, 2m/3km N of Newton Abbot. **5 J3** SX8675.
Sandygate *I.o.M.* ***Hamlet***, 2m/3km NW of Sulby. **54 C4** SC3797.
Sandyhaven Pill *Pembs.* ***Sea feature***, estuary running S into Milford Haven between Great Castle Head and South Hook Point. Sandy Haven lies on W side. SM8507.
Sandyhills *D. & G.* ***Locality***, on Sandyhills Bay, small bay 5m/9km SE of Dalbeattie. NX8855.
Sandyhills *Glas.* ***Suburb***, 4m/7km E of Glasgow. NS6563.
Sandylands *Lancs.* ***Suburb***, SW district of Morecambe. **55 H3** SD4263.
Sandylane *Staffs.* ***Locality***, 2m/3km NE of Market Drayton. SJ7035.
Sandylane *Swan.* ***Locality***, on Gower peninsula, adjoining to E of Parkmill. SS5588.
Sandymoor *Halton* ***Locality***, industrial area in NE part of Runcorn. SJ5683.
Sandypark *Devon* ***Hamlet***, 4m/6km NW of Moretonhampstead. SX7189.
Sandyway *Here.* ***Settlement***, 8m/13km N of Monmouth. **28 D6** SO4925.
Sangamore *High.* ***Settlement***, adjoining to SE of Durness, N coast of Sutherland district. NC4067.
Sango Bay *High.* ***Bay***, 3m/4km SE of Faraid Head, adjacent to Durness. **103 G2** NC4068.
Sangobeg *High.* ***Locality***, in Sutherland district, 2m/3km SE of Durness. **103 G2** NC4266.
Sankey Bridges *Warr.* ***Suburb***, in W part of Warrington. SJ5887.
Sankyn's Green *Worcs.* ***Settlement***, 4m/7km S of Stourport-on-Severn. SO7964.
Sanna *High.* ***Settlement***, on Ardnamurchan peninsula, 4m/6km NW of Kilchoan. **79 F1** NM4469.
Sanna Bay *High.* ***Bay***, in Lochaber district, with Sanna Point headland at its N end. **79 F1** NM4370.
Sanna Point *High.* ***Coastal feature***, headland in Lochaber district, at N end of Sanna Bay and 2m/4km NE of Point of Ardnamurchan. **79 F1** NM4370.
Sannaig *Arg. & B.* ***Settlement***, on Jura, 2m/3km S of Craighouse. **72 D4** NR5164.
Sannan *Carmar.* ***River***, rising near Llanfynydd and flowing S into River Dulas, 4m/7km W of Llandeilo. SN5623.
Sanndabhaig *W.Isles Gaelic form of Sandwick, qv.*
Sanndraigh *W.Isles Gaelic form of Sandray, qv.*
Sannox Bay *N.Ayr.* ***Bay***, on NE coast of Arran, to E of Mid Sannox. **73 J6** NS0145.
Sanquhar *D. & G.* Population: 2095. ***Small town***, former mining and cotton town on River Nith, 10m/16km NW of Thornhill and same distance E of New Cumnock. Remains of castle to S. Tolbooth dating from 1735. World's oldest post office, in use since 1738. **68 C3** NS7809.
Santon *Cumb.* ***Locality***, 1km W of Santon Bridge. NY1001.
Santon Bridge *Cumb.* ***Village***, on River Irt 3m/5km SE of Gosforth. **60 C6** NY1101.
Santon Downham *Suff.* ***Village***, 2m/4km NE of Brandon. **44 C7** TL8187.
Santon Head *I.o.M.* ***Coastal feature***, headland 4m/7km SW of Douglas. **54 C6** SC3370.
Sapcote *Leics.* Population: 2628. ***Village***, 4m/6km E of Hinckley. Site of Roman villa 1km E. **41 G6** SP4893.
Sapey Common *Here.* ***Hamlet***, 7m/11km NE of Bromyard. **29 G2** SO7063.
Sapiston *Suff.* ***Village***, 3m/5km N of Ixworth. **34 D1** TL9175.
Sapley *Cambs.* ***Suburb***, in N part of Huntingdon. TL2474.
Sapperton *Derbys.* ***Settlement***, 2m/3km NE of Sudbury. SK1834.
Sapperton *Glos.* ***Village***, 5m/8km W of Cirencester. **20 C1** SO9403.
Sapperton *Lincs.* ***Hamlet***, 7m/11km E of Grantham. **42 D2** TF0133.
Saracen's Head *Lincs.* ***Hamlet***, 2m/3km NW of Holbeach. **43 G3** TF3427.
Sarclet *High.* ***Settlement***, on E coast of Caithness district, 5m/8km S of Wick. **105 J4** ND3443.
Sarclet Head *High.* ***Coastal feature***, headland to SE of Sarclet. **105 J4** ND3443.
Sardis *Pembs.* ***Hamlet***, 4m/6km NE of Milford Haven. **16 C4** SM9608.
Sardis Mountain *Pembs.* ***Hamlet***, 1m/2km N of Saundersfoot. SN1306.
Sarisbury *Hants.* ***Village***, 1m/2km NW of Park Gate. **11 G4** SU5008.

S

Sark ***River***, rising on Leaheads Hill and flowing S along border of England and Scotland to head of Solway Firth, 1km SE of Gretna. **69 J6** NY3266.
Sarkfoot Point *Cumb.* ***Coastal feature***, marshy promontory at head of Solway Firth, 1m/2km S of Gretna. **69 J7** NY3265.
Sarn *Bridgend* ***Village***, 2m/4km N of Bridgend. **18 C3** SS9083.
Sarn *Powys* ***Hamlet***, 6m/9km E of Newtown. **38 B6** SO2090.
Sarn Bach *Gwyn.* ***Settlement***, 1m/2km S of Abersoch. **36 C3** SH3026.
Sarn Cynfelyn *Cere.* ***Coastal feature***, spit of sand and shingle, visible at low tide, 3m/5km S of Borth. **36 E7** SN5885.
Sarn Helen ***Other feature of interest***, name (perhaps derived from Welsh 'sarn hoelen', a paved causeway) given to several sections of Roman road in Wales which may once have formed a continuous link between Caernarfon and Carmarthen. **27 F2** SH5160.
Sarn Meyllteyrn *Gwyn.* ***Village***, 6m/9km NE of Aberdaron. **36 B2** SH2332.
Sarnau *Carmar.* ***Settlement***, 4m/7km W of Carmarthen. **17 G3** SN3318.
Sarnau *Cere.* ***Hamlet***, 2m/3km S of Llangranog. **26 C3** SN3151.
Sarnau *Gwyn.* ***Settlement***, 3m/5km NE of Bala. **37 J2** SH9739.
Sarnau *Powys* ***Hamlet***, 5m/8km N of Welshpool. **38 B4** SJ2315.
Sarnau *Powys* ***Hamlet***, 3m/4km N of Brecon. SO0232.
Sarnesfield *Here.* ***Village***, 11m/18km NW of Hereford. **28 C3** SO3750.
Saron *Carmar.* ***Hamlet***, 3m/5km SW of Llandysul. **17 G1** SN3737.
Saron *Carmar.* ***Village***, 2m/3km W of Ammanford. **17 K3** SN6012.
Saron *Gwyn.* ***Hamlet***, 1m/2km NW of Llanwnda. SH4658.
Saron *Gwyn.* ***Village***, 4m/6km NE of Caernarfon. **46 D6** SH5265.
Sarratt *Herts.* ***Village***, 3m/5km N of Rickmansworth. Site of Roman villa 1m/2km W. **22 D2** TQ0499.
Sarre *Kent* ***Village***, 4m/6km SW of Birchington. **25 J5** TR2565.
Sarsden *Oxon.* ***Hamlet***, 3m/5km SW of Chipping Norton. **30 D6** SP2823.
Sarsgrum *High.* ***Settlement***, on E side of Kyle of Durness, 1m/2km S of Keoldale. **103 F2** NC3764.
Sarson *Hants.* ***Locality***, between Amport and Monxton, 4m/6km W of Andover. SU3044.
Sartfell *I.o.M.* ***Mountain***, 3m/4km SE of Kirk Michael. Height 1489 feet or 454 metres. **54 C5** SC3287.
Sartfield *I.o.M.* ***Settlement***, near coast, 4m/6km NW of Sulby. **54 C4** SC3599.
Satley *Dur.* ***Village***, 3m/5km N of Tow Law. **62 C2** NZ1143.
Satron *N.Yorks.* ***Hamlet***, 1km SW of Gunnerside across River Swale. SD9497.
Satterleigh *Devon* ***Hamlet***, 4m/6km SW of South Molton. **6 E3** SS6622.
Satterthwaite *Cumb.* ***Village***, in Grizedale Forest Park, 4m/6km S of Hawkshead. **60 E7** SD3392.
Sauchar Point *Fife* ***Coastal feature***, headland on E side of Elie Ness 1km SE of Elie town. **76 C1** NT4999.
Sauchen *Aber.* ***Village***, 4m/6km SW of Kemnay. **90 E3** NJ6911.
Saucher *P. & K.* ***Hamlet***, 3m/4km S of Burrelton. **82 C4** NO1933.
Sauchie Law *Sc.Bord.* ***Mountain***, in Craik Forest, 3m/5km SE of Ettrick. Height 1450 feet or 442 metres. **69 H2** NT2910.
Sauchieburn *Aber.* ***Settlement***, 3m/4km S of Fettercairn. **83 H1** NO6669.
Sauchrie *S.Ayr.* ***Settlement***, 3m/4km N of Maybole. **67 H2** NS3014.
Saugh Hill *S.Ayr.* ***Hill***, 2m/3km E of Girvan. Height 971 feet or 296 metres. **67 G4** NX2197.
Saughall *Ches.* Population: 3242. ***Village***, 4m/6km NW of Chester. **48 C6** SJ3670.
Saughall Massie *Mersey.* ***Suburb***, 5m/8km SW of Wallasey town centre. **48 B4** SJ2588.
Saughton *Edin.* ***Suburb***, 3m/5km SW of Edinburgh city centre. NT2071.
Saughtonhall *Edin.* ***Suburb***, to N of Saughton across railway. NT2172.
Saughtree *Sc.Bord.* ***Settlement***, 8m/12km NE of Newcastleton. **70 A4** NY5696.
Saughtree Fell *Sc.Bord.* ***Mountain***, with steep sides, to W of Dawston Burn, 5m/8km NW of Kielder. Height 1424 feet or 434 metres. **70 A4** NY5498.
Saul *Glos.* ***Village***, 7m/11km W of Stroud. **20 A1** SO7409.
Saundby *Notts.* ***Village***, 2m/4km SW of Gainsborough. **51 K4** SK7888.
Saundersfoot *Pembs.* Population: 3221. ***Small town***, small coastal resort with harbour and long sandy beach, 3m/4km N of Tenby and situated on Saundersfoot Bay. **16 E4** SN1304.
Saundersfoot Bay *Pembs.* ***Bay***, extending from Monkstone Point NE to Ragwen Point. Small coastal resort Saundersfoot is on bay. **16 E4** SN1304.
Saunderton *Bucks.* ***Village***, 1m/2km SW of Princes Risborough. Site of Roman villa near church. **22 A1** SP7901.
Saunton *Devon* ***Hamlet***, at N end of Braunton Burrows, 7m/11km NW of Barnstaple. **6 C2** SS4537.
Saunton Sands *Devon* ***Coastal feature***, stretch of sand to SW of Saunton; runs for about 3m/4km to Crow Point and backed by Braunton Burrows. **6 C2** SS4537.
Sausthorpe *Lincs.* ***Village***, 2m/3km NW of Spilsby. **53 G6** TF3869.
Savalbeg *High.* ***Locality***, to SE of Savalmore. Numerous ancient cairns in vicinity. **96 C1** NC5907.
Savalmore *High.* ***Settlement***, in Sutherland district, 1m/2km N of Lairg. **96 C1** NC5808.
Saverley Green *Staffs.* ***Hamlet***, 1m/2km NE of Fulford. SJ9638.
Savernake *Wilts.* ***Locality***, parish lying to S and SE of Marlborough and containing most of Savernake Forest. SU2166.
Savernake Forest *Wilts.* ***Forest/woodland***, wooded area extending from Marlborough 4m/6km south eastwards. **21 F5** SU2166.
Savile Place *W.Yorks.* ***Locality***, 1m/2km N of Mirfield. SE2021.
Savile Town *W.Yorks.* ***Suburb***, to S of Dewsbury town centre across River Calder. SE2420.
Savill Gardens *Surr.* ***Garden***, in Windsor Great Park, 1m/2km W of Englefield Green. 35 acres of woodland featuring many varieties of flowers in springtime. **22 C4** SU9770.
Saviskaill *Ork.* ***Locality***, on N coast of Rousay, 1m/2km S of headland of Saviskaill Head on shore of Saviskaill Bay. HY4033.
Saviskaill Bay *Ork.* ***Bay***, wide bay on Rousay, extending E from Saviskaill Head. On shore of the bay is locality of Saviskaill. **106 D4** HY4133.
Saviskaill Head *Ork.* ***Coastal feature***, headland on N coast of Rousay, 1m/2km N of Saviskaill and to W of Saviskaill Bay. **106 D4** HY4034.
Saw Mill *Powys* ***Settlement***, 1km E of Kerry. SO1589.
Sawbridge *Warks.* ***Settlement***, 5m/8km NW of Daventry. SP5065.
Sawbridgeworth *Herts.* Population: 9432. ***Small town***, on W bank of River Stort, 4m/6km NE of Harlow. **33 H7** TL4814.
Sawddle (Sawdde). *Carmar.* ***River***, rising in Llyn y Fan fach, Black Mountain and flowing NW into River Tywi 1m/2km W of Llangadog. **27 G6** SN6928.
Sawdon *N.Yorks.* ***Hamlet***, 7m/11km W of Scarborough. **59 F1** SE9485.
Sawley *Derbys.* ***Locality***, adjoining to SW of Long Eaton. **41 G2** SK4731.
Sawley *Lancs.* ***Village***, on River Ribble, 4m/6km NE of Clitheroe. Remains of 12c Cistercian abbey (English Heritage). **56 C5** SD7746.
Sawley *N.Yorks.* ***Village***, 5m/7km SW of Ripon. **57 H3** SE2467.
Sawley Abbey *Lancs.* ***Ecclesiastical building***, scant remains of Cistercian abbey (English Heritage), founded 1148, on E side of River Ribble at Sawley, 3m/5km NE of Clitheroe. **56 C5** SD7746.
Sawston *Cambs.* Population: 7172. ***Suburb***, 6m/10km SE of Cambridge. **33 H4** TL4849.
Sawtry *Cambs.* Population: 4766. ***Village***, 4m/6km S of Stilton. Site of Romano-British settlement on E side of village. **42 E7** TL1683.
Saxa Vord *Shet.* ***Hill***, to E of Burra Firth in N part of Unst. Height 935 feet or 285 metres. **108 F1** HP6316.
Saxby *Leics.* ***Village***, 4m/7km E of Melton Mowbray. **42 B4** SK8219.
Saxby *Lincs.* ***Village***, 7m/11km W of Market Rasen. **52 D4** TF0086.
Saxby All Saints *N.Lincs.* ***Village***, 6m/10km N of Brigg. **52 C1** SE9916.
Saxelbye *Leics.* ***Hamlet***, 4m/6km NW of Melton Mowbray. **42 A3** SK7021.
Saxham Street *Suff.* ***Settlement***, 1km NW of Middlewood Green. TM0861.
Saxilby *Lincs.* Population: 3086. ***Village***, on Fossdyke Navigation, 6m/9km NW of Lincoln. **52 B5** SK8975.
Saxlingham *Norf.* ***Village***, 3m/5km W of Holt. **44 E2** TG0239.
Saxlingham Green *Norf.* ***Village***, 1km SE of Saxlingham Nethergate. **45 G6** TM2297.
Saxlingham Nethergate *Norf.* ***Village***, 7m/12km S of Norwich. **45 G6** TM2297.
Saxlingham Thorpe *Norf.* ***Village***, 1m/2km W of Saxlingham Nethergate. **45 G6** TM2297.
Saxmundham *Suff.* Population: 2529. ***Small town***, 18m/29km NE of Ipswich. **35 H2** TM3863.
Saxon Street *Cambs.* ***Village***, 3m/5km SE of Newmarket. **33 K3** TL6759.
Saxondale *Notts.* ***Hamlet***, 7m/11km E of Nottingham. **41 J2** SK6839.
Saxtead *Suff.* ***Hamlet***, 2m/3km NW of Framlingham. TM2565.
Saxtead Green *Suff.* ***Village***, 3m/4km SW of Dennington. 18c post mill (English Heritage). **35 G2** TM2564.
Saxtead Green Post Mill *Suff.* ***Other feature of interest***, 18c post mill (English Heritage) at Saxtead, 3m/4km SW of Dennington. Restored to working order; windmill body rotates to present sails to face wind. **35 G2** TM2564.
Saxtead Little Green *Suff.* ***Village***, 1km W of Saxtead. **35 G2** TM2665.
Saxthorpe *Norf.* ***Village***, opposite Corpusty across River Bure, 6m/9km SE of Holt. **45 F2** TG1130.
Saxton *N.Yorks.* ***Village***, 4m/6km S of Tadcaster. **57 K6** SE4736.
Sayers Common *W.Suss.* ***Village***, 3m/5km W of Burgess Hill. **13 F5** TQ2618.
Scabbacombe Head *Devon* ***Coastal feature***, headland 3m/4km E of Kingswear. **5 K5** SX9251.
Scackleton *N.Yorks.* ***Village***, 2m/3km SW of Hovingham. **58 C2** SE6472.
Scad Hill *P. & K.* ***Mountain***, in Ochil Hills, 3m/5km NW of Dollar. Height 1922 feet or 586 metres. **82 A7** NN9302.
Scadabay *W.Isles* *Anglicised form of Scadabhagh, qv.*
Scadabhagh (Anglicised form: Scadabay.) *W.Isles* ***Settlement***, at head of Loch Scadabay, off SE coast of South Harris, 5m/8km S of Tarbert. **93 G2** NG1792.
Scafell *Cumb.* ***Mountain***, in Lake District 2m/3km SE of Wasdale Head. Height 3162 feet or 964 metres. **60 D6** NY2006.
Scafell Pike *Cumb.* ***Mountain***, highest mountain in England, 1km NE of Scafell in Lake District. Height 3205 feet or 977 metres. **60 D6** NY2006.
Scaftworth *Notts.* ***Village***, 1m/2km SE of Bawtry. **51 J3** SK6691.
Scagglethorpe *N.Yorks.* ***Village***, 3m/5km E of Malton. **58 E2** SE8372.
Scaitcliffe *Lancs.* ***Suburb***, 1km SW of Accrington town centre. SD7528.
Scaladale *W.Isles* *Anglicised form of Sgaladal, qv.*
Scalasaig *Arg. & B.* ***Settlement***, on E coast of Colonsay, and chief settlement on island. Pier and lighthouse. **72 B1** NR3994.
Scalaval *W.Isles* ***Hill***, 3m/4km S of head of Little Loch Roag, Isle of Lewis. Height 853 feet or 260 metres. **100 D6** NB1419.
Scalby *E.Riding* ***Village***, 6m/9km E of Howden. **58 E7** SE8329.
Scalby *N.Yorks.* Population: 9019. ***Small town***, 2m/4km NW of Scarborough. **59 G1** TA0090.
Scalby Mills *N.Yorks.* ***Locality***, 1m/2km E of Scalby. TA0090.
Scalby Ness Rocks *N.Yorks.* ***Coastal feature***, rocky headland on North Sea coast 2m/3km E of Scalby. **63 K3** TA0090.
Scald Law *Midloth.* ***Mountain***, summit of Pentland Hills, 3m/5km W of Penicuik. Height 1899 feet or 579 metres. **75 K4** NT1961.
Scaldwell *Northants.* ***Village***, 8m/12km N of Northampton. **31 J1** SP7672.
Scale Force *Cumb.* ***Waterfall***, National Trust property in course of Scale Beck, 1m/2km W of S end of Crummock Water. **60 C5** NY1517.
Scale Hall *Lancs.* ***Suburb***, between Lancaster and Morecambe, on W side of River Lune. SD4662.
Scale Houses *Cumb.* ***Settlement***, 2m/3km SE of Croglin. **61 G2** NY5845.
Scaleby *Cumb.* ***Village***, 5m/9km NE of Carlisle. **69 K7** NY4463.
Scalebyhill *Cumb.* ***Hamlet***, 1km NW of Scaleby. **69 K7** NY4463.
Scales *Cumb.* ***Hamlet***, 5m/9km NE of Keswick. **60 E4** NY3426.
Scales *Cumb.* ***Village***, 3m/5km E of Dalton-in-Furness. **55 F2** SD2772.
Scales *Lancs.* ***Settlement***, adjoining to E of Newton, 2m/3km SE of Kirkham. SD4530.
Scales Moor *N.Yorks.* ***Open space***, moorland, with rocky outcrops on SE side, 3m/5km N of Ingleton. **56 C2** SD7177.
Scalesceugh *Cumb.* ***Locality***, 5m/8km SE of Carlisle, on E side of River Petteril. NY4449.
Scalford *Leics.* ***Village***, 3m/5km N of Melton Mowbray. **42 A3** SK7624.
Scaling *R. & C.* ***Hamlet***, 4m/7km SW of Staithes. **63 J5** NZ7413.
Scaling Dam *R. & C.* ***Locality***, to S of Scaling, below dam of Scaling Reservoir, 4m/6km SE of Loftus. NZ7412.
Scaling Reservoir *N.Yorks.* ***Reservoir***, on border of North Yorkshire and Redcar & Cleveland, 4m/7km SW of Staithes. **63 J5** NZ7413.
Scaliscro *W.Isles* *Anglicised form of Scealascro, qv.*
Scalla Field *Shet.* ***Hill***, 1m/2km E of East Burrafirth, Mainland. Height 922 feet or 281 metres. **109 C7** HU3857.
Scallasaig *High.* ***Settlement***, 3m/5km E of Glenelg, Skye and Lochalsh district. **86 E3** NG8619.
Scallastle *Arg. & B.* ***Settlement***, on N bank of Scallastle River, 2m/3km NW of Craignure. Standing stone to NE. **79 J4** NM6938.
Scallastle Bay *Arg. & B.* ***Bay***, on Sound of Mull, extending SE from Garmony Point, Mull. **79 H4** NM6939.
Scalloway *Shet.* Population: 1056. ***Small town***, with harbour on W coast of Mainland, 5m/7km W of Lerwick. Remains of early 17c castle (Historic Scotland). **109 C9** HU4039.
Scalloway Castle *Shet.* ***Castle***, in Scalloway, Mainland, overlooking East Voe of Scalloway. Tower house (Historic Scotland) built by Patrick Stewart, Earl of Orkney, in 1600 and abandoned fifteen years later. Garret and roof now missing. **109 D9** HU4039.
Scalpay *High.* ***Island***, of about 9 square miles or 23 square km and roughly circular in shape, lying off E coast of Skye mainland opposite Loch Ainort. Sparsely inhabited. Rises to height of 1298 feet or 396 metres. **86 C1** NG6030.
Scalpay (Gaelic form: Eilean Scalpaigh.) *W.Isles* ***Island***, 3m/4km by 1m/2km, at entrance to East Loch Tarbert, off North Harris, separated from main island by the narrow Sound of Scalpay. Village with N and S harbours at NW end; lighthouse at SE end. **93 H2** NG2395.
Scalpsie Bay *Arg. & B.* ***Bay***, S facing bay on W coast of Bute, 3m/4km NW of Kingarth. **73 J5** NS0557.
Scamadale *Arg. & B.* ***Settlement***, on N shore of Loch Scammadale. **79 K5** NM8820.
Scamblesby *Lincs.* ***Village***, 6m/9km N of Horncastle. **53 F5** TF2778.
Scammonden *W.Yorks.* ***Locality***, 6m/10km W of Huddersfield. SE0415.
Scamodale *High.* ***Locality***, in Lochaber district, halfway along SE shore of Loch Shiel. **86 E7** NM8373.
Scampston *N.Yorks.* ***Village***, 5m/8km NE of Malton. **58 E2** SE8675.
Scampton *Lincs.* ***Village***, 5m/9km N of Lincoln. Airfield to E. Site of Roman villa 1km SE. **52 C5** SK9579.
Scanport *High.* ***Settlement***, in Inverness district, 4m/6km SW of Inverness. **88 D1** NH6339.
Scapa *Ork.* ***Settlement***, 1km S of Kirkwall, Mainland. **107 D7** HY4408.
Scapa Bay *Ork.* ***Bay***, with sheltered anchorage on S coast of Mainland, at NE corner of Scapa Flow. Bay extends inland to within less than 2m/3km of Bay of Kirkwall to N, on which Kirkwall town is situated. Pier on E side of bay provides landing facilities. **107 D7** HY4308.
Scapa Flow *Ork.* ***Sea feature***, large natural anchorage surrounded by islands of Hoy, Mainland, Burra, South Ronaldsay and Flotta, some 10m/16km E to W and 8m/13km N to S. Eastern approaches blocked by Churchill Barrier. **107 C7** HY4000.

Scapegoat Hill *W.Yorks.* ***Village***, 4m/6km W of Huddersfield. SE0816.
Scar *Ork.* ***Settlement***, on N coast of Sanday, with Roos Wick 1km to W. **106 F3** HY6645.
Scar Hill *Aber.* ***Hill***, 2m/3km S of Tarland. Height 981 feet or 299 metres. **90 C4** NJ4801.
Scar Hill *Aber.* ***Mountain***, 4m/7km N of Tarland. Height 1722 feet or 525 metres. **90 C3** NJ4811.
Scar House Reservoir *N.Yorks.* ***Reservoir***, on River Nidd, below Angram Reservoir, 9m/15km NW of Pateley Bridge. **57 F2** SE0676.
Scar Nose *Moray* ***Coastal feature***, headland on N coast on NE side of Portknockie. **98 D4** NJ4968.
Scaraben *High.* ***Mountain***, on Langwell Forest, Caithness, 4m/7km NW of Berriedale. Height 2053 feet or 626 metres. **105 F6** ND0626.
Scarastavore *W.Isles Anglicised form of Sgarasta Mhòr, qv.*
Scaravay *W.Isles* ***Island***, small uninhabited island at SE end of Sound of Harris, 4m/6km off E coast of North Uist. **93 F4** NG0177.
Scarba *Arg. & B.* ***Island***, uninhabited moorland island measuring about 5 square miles or 13 square km, lying 1km N of Jura across Strait of Corryvreckan. **79 H7** NM7004.
Scarborough *N.Yorks.* Population: 38,809. ***Town***, old North Sea fishing port and spa town built on steep cliff side, now large resort and conference town, 35m/57km NE of York. Remains of 12c castle (English Heritage) and of Roman signal station on Castle Cliff, between North Bay and South Bay. **59 G1** TA0488.
Scarborough Castle *N.Yorks.* ***Castle***, 12c castle (English Heritage) built by William LeGros, Earl of Aumale, on headland between North Bay and South Bay at Scarborough. Beseiged in Civil War and damaged by German naval bombardment in World War II, principal remains are keep, 13c barbican and buttressed walls. Affords spectacular coastal views. **59 G1** TA0588.
Scarcewater *Cornw.* ***Settlement***, 6m/10km W of St. Austell. **3 G3** SW9154.
Scarcliffe *Derbys.* ***Village***, 2m/3km SE of Bolsover. **51 G6** SK4968.
Scarcroft *W.Yorks.* ***Hamlet***, 6m/10km NE of Leeds. **57 J5** SE3541.
Scardroy *High.* ***Settlement***, at W end of Loch Beannacharain, 3m/5km NW of Inverchoran. **95 J6** NH2151.
Scares *D. & G.* ***Coastal feature***, group of rocks at entrance to Luce Bay, including Big Scare and Little Scares, about 7m/11km E of Mull of Galloway. NX2533.
Scarff *Shet.* ***Settlement***, 1km SE of Hamnavoe, Mainland. **108 B4** HU2480.
Scarfskerry *High.* ***Settlement***, on N coast of Caithness district, 7m/11km W of John o' Groats. **105 H1** ND2674.
Scargill *Dur.* ***Hamlet***, 4m/6km S of Barnard Castle. Remains of medieval castle, including 15c gatehouse. **62 B5** NZ0510.
Scargill High Moor *Dur.* ***Open space***, moorland to W of The Stang, 3m/4km S of Bowes. **62 A6** NY9809.
Scargreen *Cumb.* ***Settlement***, 1m/2km N of Gosforth. NY0605.
Scarinish *Arg. & B.* ***Village***, principal village and port of Tiree, situated on S coast between Hynish and Gott Bays. Lighthouse. Landing stage on Gott Bay. **78 B3** NM0444.
Scarisbrick *Lancs.* ***Village***, 4m/6km SE of Southport. **48 C1** SD3713.
Scarletts *W'ham* ***Locality***, 2m/3km NE of Twyford. SU8178.
Scarness *Cumb.* ***Locality***, on E side of Bassenthwaite Lake, 1m/2km SW of Bassenthwaite village. NY2230.
Scarning *Norf.* ***Village***, 2m/4km W of East Dereham. **44 D4** TF9512.
Scarp *W.Isles* ***Island***, rugged island, 3m/4km by 2m/3km, lying off W coast of North Harris across narrow strait of Caolas an Scarp. Small village at SE end of island. Scarp rises to height of 1012 feet or 308 metres. **100 B6** NA9615.
Scarrington *Notts.* ***Village***, 2m/3km NE of Bingham. Noted for the 17 foot high mound of horseshoes outside the old forge. **42 A1** SK7341.
Scarrowhill *Cumb.* ***Hamlet***, 1m/2km S of Cumwhitton and 4m/6km SE of Wetheral. NY5150.
Scarth Gap Pass *Cumb.* ***Other feature of interest***, mountain path between High Crag and Hay Stacks, 1m/2km S of Buttermere lake. **60 C5** NY1813.
Scarth Hill *Lancs.* ***Settlement***, 1m/2km SE of Ormskirk. **48 D2** SD4206.
Scarthingwell *N.Yorks.* ***Hamlet***, on lakeside, 1km N of Barkston Ash. SE4936.
Scartho *N.E.Lincs.* ***Village***, 2m/3km S of Grimsby town centre. **53 F2** TA2605.
Scarts Rock (Gaelic form: Rubha an Dùine.) *W.Isles* ***Coastal feature***, on E coast of North Uist, 2m/3km E of Lochportain. **92 E4** NF9771.
Scarva Taing *Ork.* ***Coastal feature***, headland 1m/2km SW of Mull Head, Mainland. **107 E7** HY5708.
Scarwell *Ork.* ***Settlement***, near W coast of Mainland, 3m/5km W of Dounby. HY2420.
Scatraig *High.* ***Settlement***, 1m/2km SW of Daviot. **88 E1** NH7137.
Scatsta *Shet.* ***Locality***, on Mainland on E side of Sullom Voe, adjacent to Scatsta Airfield. HU3972.
Scaur *D. & G. Alternative name for Kippford, qv.*
Scaur Farm *D. & G.* ***Settlement***, 1km E of Glenkiln Reservoir, 7m/11km W of Dumfries. **65 J3** NX8677.
Scaur Hill *S.Lan.* ***Mountain***, rising to over 380 metres, 3m/4km E of Douglas. **75 G7** NS8830.
Scaur Water *D. & G.* ***River***, rising to N of Ox Hill and flowing E, then running SE to River Nith, 2m/3km S of Thornhill. **68 D4** NX8792.
Scawby *N.Lincs.* Population: 1958. ***Village***, 2m/4km SW of Brigg. Site of Roman building 1m/2km W. **52 C2** SE9605.
Scawby Brook *N.Lincs.* ***Village***, 1m/2km NE of Scawby across Scawby Park. SE9806.
Scawsby *S.Yorks.* ***Suburb***, 2m/3km NW of Doncaster town centre. SE5404.
Scawthorpe *S.Yorks.* ***Suburb***, 2m/3km NW of Doncaster town centre. SE5505.
Scawton *N.Yorks.* ***Hamlet***, 4m/7km W of Helmsley. **58 B1** SE5483.
Scawton Moor *N.Yorks.* ***Open space***, moorland at W end of Vale of Pickering, 3m/5km W of Hemsley. **58 B1** SE5582.
Scayne's Hill *W.Suss.* ***Village***, 2m/4km E of Haywards Heath. **13 G4** TQ3623.
Scealascro (Anglicised form: Scaliscro.) *W.Isles* ***Settlement***, on E shore of Little Loch Roag, 2m/3km N of head of loch. **100 D5** NB1327.
Scethrog (Sgethrog). *Powys* ***Hamlet***, 4m/7km SE of Brecon. **28 A6** SO1025.
Schaw *E.Ayr.* ***Settlement***, 1m/2km N of Drongan. **67 J1** NS4420.
Schiehallion *P. & K.* ***Mountain***, conical mountain of quartzite, 4m/7km SE of Kinloch Rannoch. Munro: height 3552 feet or 1083 metres. **81 J2** NN7154.
Scholar Green *Ches.* ***Hamlet***, 1m/2km NE of Kidsgrove. **49 H7** SJ8356.
Scholemoor *W.Yorks.* ***Suburb***, 2m/3km W of Bradford city centre. SE1332.
Scholes *Gt.Man.* ***Suburb***, E district of Wigan. SD5905.
Scholes *S.Yorks.* ***Hamlet***, 3m/5km NW of Rotherham. SK3995.
Scholes *W.Yorks.* ***Village***, 1m/2km E of Holmfirth. **50 D2** SE1607.
Scholes *W.Yorks.* ***Village***, 2m/3km W of Cleckheaton. SE1625.
Scholes *W.Yorks.* Population: 2603. ***Village***, 5m/8km E of Leeds. **57 J6** SE3736.
Scholey Hill *W.Yorks.* ***Settlement***, 1m/2km W of Methley Junction. SE3825.
School Green *Ches.* ***Suburb***, 2m/3km SW of Winsford. SJ6464.
School Green *Essex* ***Settlement***, 3m/5km E of Finchingfield. TL7331.
School Green *I.o.W.* ***Suburb***, 1km W of Freshwater. SZ3386.
School Green *W.Yorks.* ***Locality***, adjoining to E of Thornton, 3m/5km W of Bradford city centre. SE1132.
School House *Dorset* ***Hamlet***, 1km SW of Thorncombe. ST3602.
School Lane *Lancs.* ***Suburb***, adjoining to E of Bamber Bridge, 2m/4km SE of Preston town centre. SD5626.
Schoolgreen *W'ham* ***Settlement***, adjoining to S of Shinfield, 4m/6km S of Reading. SU7367.
Schoose *Cumb.* ***Suburb***, 1m/2km E of Workington town centre. NY0128.
Sciberscross *High.* ***Settlement***, to N of River Brora, 4m/7km W of Gordonbush, Sutherland district. **104 C7** NC7710.
Science Museum *Gt.Lon.* ***Leisure/recreation***, museum in borough of Kensington & Chelsea, 3m/4km SW of Charing Cross. Large collection of very fine engineering models, steam engines, early motor cars, aeroplanes and all aspects of applied physics and chemistry. Displays on history of printing, textiles, medicine and many other industries shown using working models. Special features include space exploration, with actual Apollo 10 space capsule. TQ2679.
Scissett *W.Yorks.* ***Village***, adjoining to SW of Clayton West, 2m/3km NE of Denby Dale. SE2410.
Scleddau *Pembs.* ***Village***, 2m/3km S of Fishguard. **16 C1** SM9434.
Sco Ruston *Norf.* ***Settlement***, 3m/5km N of Wroxham. **45 G3** TG2821.
Scofton *Notts.* ***Hamlet***, 3m/5km E of Worksop. **51 J4** SK6380.
Scole *Norf.* ***Village***, 2m/4km E of Diss. **35 F1** TM1579.
Scolpaig *W.Isles* ***Settlement***, on North Uist, 1km S of Griminis Point. **92 C4** NF7275.
Scolt Head *Norf.* ***Island***, National Trust property of marsh, sand dune, and shingle, off N coast at E end of Brancaster Bay. Nature reserve. Access by boat from Brancaster Staithe. TF8146.
Scolton *Pembs.* ***Settlement***, 1km SE of Spittal. Scolton Manor Country Park to S. **16 C2** SM9822.
Scolton Manor Country Park *Pembs.* ***Leisure/recreation***, country park 4m/6km NE of Haverfordwest. Includes 40 acres of woodland, grassland, formal gardens and nature trails. Park is set around 19c mansion, Scolton Manor, which houses Pembrokeshire County Museum. **16 C2** SM9821.
Scolty *Aber.* ***Hill***, 1m/2km SW of Banchory. Height 981 feet or 299 metres. **90 E5** NO6793.
Sconce Point *I.o.W.* ***Coastal feature***, headland at W end of The Solent, 1m/2km W of Yarmouth. **10 E5** SZ3389.
Scone Palace *P. & K.* ***Historic house***, castellated early 19c mansion on site of medieval abbey and palace, 2m/3km N of Perth across River Tay. Site has historical associations dating from 8c. Locality of Old Scone to E; village of New Scone 2m/3km to E, beyond Old Scone. Scone Airfield 2m/3km NE of New Scone. **82 C5** NO1126.
Sconser *High.* ***Settlement***, on Skye, on S side of Loch Sligachan. **86 B1** NG5131.
Scoonie *Fife* ***Suburb***, NW district of Leven. NO3801.
Scoor *Arg. & B.* ***Settlement***, near S coast of Ross of Mull, 3m/4km SE of Bunessan. **79 F6** NM4119.
Scootmore Forest *Moray* ***Forest/woodland***, afforested area astride Allt a' Gheallaidh immediately above its confluence with River Spey 11m/17km NE of Grantown-on-Spey. **89 J1** NJ1638.
Scopwick *Lincs.* ***Village***, 8m/12km N of Sleaford. **52 D7** TF0658.
Scoraig *High.* ***Settlement***, on NE side of Little Loch Broom, 2m/3km SE of Cailleach Head, on W coast of Ross and Cromarty district. **95 G2** NH0096.
Scorborough *E.Riding* ***Village***, 4m/6km N of Beverley. **59 G5** TA0145.
Score Bay (Also known as Lùb Score.) *High.* ***Bay***, between Rubha Hunish and Ru Bornaskitaig, N coast of Skye. **93 J4** NG3973.
Score Head *Shet.* ***Coastal feature***, headland at E end of Outer Score, off N end of Bressay. **109 E8** HU5145.
Scorrier *Cornw.* ***Village***, 2m/3km NE of Redruth. **2 E4** SW7244.
Scorriton *Devon* ***Village***, on E edge of Dartmoor, 3m/4km NW of Buckfastleigh. **5 H4** SX7068.
Scorton *Lancs.* ***Village***, 3m/4km N of Garstang. **55 J5** SD5048.
Scorton *N.Yorks.* ***Village***, 2m/3km E of Catterick Bridge. **62 D6** NZ2500.
Scot Hay *Staffs.* ***Hamlet***, 3m/5km W of Newcastle-under-Lyme. SJ7947.
Scot Lane End *Gt.Man.* ***Locality***, 1m/2km SE of Blackrod. SD6209.
Scotasay *W.Isles Anglicised form of Sgeotasaigh, qv.*
Scotby *Cumb.* ***Suburb***, 3m/4km E of Carlisle. **60 F1** NY4455.
Scotch Corner *N.Yorks.* ***Locality***, and road junction, 4m/6km NE of Richmond. **62 D6** NZ2105.
Scotforth *Lancs.* ***Suburb***, 1m/2km S of Lancaster city centre. **55 H4** SD4859.
Scothern *Lincs.* ***Village***, 5m/9km NE of Lincoln. **52 D5** TF0377.
Scotland *Leics.* ***Settlement***, 4m/6km NE of Ashby de la Zouch. SK3822.
Scotland *Lincs.* ***Settlement***, just W of Ingoldsby, 6m/9km NE of Colsterworth. TF0030.
Scotland End *Oxon.* ***Settlement***, adjoining to W of Hook Norton, 5m/7km NE of Chipping Norton. SP3433.
Scotland Gate *Northumb.* ***Locality***, 1m/2km N of Bedlington. **71 H5** NZ2584.
Scotland Street *Suff.* ***Settlement***, adjoining to E of Stoke-by-Nayland, 4m/7km SW of Hadleigh. TL9936.
Scotlandwell *P. & K.* ***Village***, 4m/6km W of Leslie. **82 C7** NO1801.
Scotney Castle *Kent* ***Castle***, moated ruins of medieval and later manor house in grounds of 19c mansion of same name, 1m/2km E of Lamberhurst. Surrounded by picturesque gardens (National Trust), containing rhododendrons, azaleas and wisteria. **13 K3** TQ6835.
Scotnish *Arg. & B.* ***Settlement***, 4m/6km SW of Crinan. **73 F2** NR7588.
Scots' Gap *Northumb.* ***Hamlet***, 10m/16km W of Morpeth. **71 F5** NZ0386.
Scotsburn *High.* ***Locality***, 4m/6km N of Invergordon. **96 E4** NH7275.
Scotsburn *Moray* ***Settlement***, 3m/5km E of Forres. NJ0860.
Scotscalder *High.* ***Locality***, with railway station, in Caithness district, 8m/13km S of Thurso. **105 F3** ND0956.
Scotstarvit Tower *Fife* ***Historic house***, 15c tower house (Historic Scotland), 1km SW of Hill of Tarvit Mansion House and 1km NW of Gauldry. Remodelled in mid 16c and home of Sir John Scot, author of Scot of Scotstarvit's Staggering State of the Scots Statesmen. **82 E6** NO3711.
Scotston *Aber.* ***Hamlet***, 2m/3km NE of Laurencekirk. **91 F7** NO7373.
Scotston *P. & K.* ***Settlement***, in Glen Cochill, 5m/8km SE of Aberfeldy. **82 A3** NN9042.
Scotstoun *Glas.* ***Suburb***, on N bank of River Clyde, 3m/5km NW of Glasgow city centre. NS5368.
Scotstounhill *Glas.* ***Suburb***, to N of Scotstoun, 3m/5km NW of Glasgow city centre. NS5367.
Scotstown *High.* ***Village***, in Sunart, Lochaber district, 1m/2km N of Strontian. **79 K1** NM8263.
Scotstown Head *Aber.* ***Coastal feature***, headland at S end of Rattray Bay, 4m/6km N of Peterhead. **99 K5** NK1151.
Scotswood *T. & W.* ***Suburb***, 3m/5km W of Newcastle upon Tyne city centre on N bank of River Tyne. NZ2064.
Scott Willoughby *Lincs.* ***Settlement***, 1m/2km SW of Osbournby, 5m/8km S of Sleaford. TF0537.
Scottarie Burn *High.* ***River***, flowing NE into River Brora at NW end of Loch Brora, Sutherland district. **96 E1** NC8209.
Scotter *Lincs.* Population: 2415. ***Village***, on River Eau, 6m/10km S of Scunthorpe. **52 B2** SE8800.
Scotterthorpe *Lincs.* ***Hamlet***, 1m/2km NW of Scotter. **52 B2** SE8701.
Scottish Maritime Museum *N.Ayr.* ***Other feature of interest***, in Irvine town centre. Exhibits include vessels in harbour and early 20c shipworker's house. **74 B7** NS3138.
Scottish National Portrait Gallery *Edin.* ***Other feature of interest***, part of Royal Museum of Scotland in Queen Street, Edinburgh. Exhibits history of Scotland from 16c to present, with paintings of famous people involved in major events, including Mary, Queen of Scots and Robert Burns. Also contains National Collection of Photography. **76 A3** NT2574.
Scottlethorpe *Lincs.* ***Settlement***, 3m/4km W of Bourne. **42 D3** TF0520.
Scotton *Lincs.* ***Village***, 7m/12km S of Scunthorpe. **52 B3** SK8899.
Scotton *N.Yorks.* ***Village***, on S side of Catterick Camp, 4m/6km S of Richmond. **62 C7** SE1995.
Scotton *N.Yorks.* ***Village***, 2m/3km NW of Knaresborough. **57 J4** SE3259.
Scottow *Norf.* ***Hamlet***, 4m/6km S of North Walsham. **45 G3** TG2723.
Scoughall *E.Loth.* ***Hamlet***, on rocky coast, 4m/7km SE of North Berwick. NT6183.
Scoulton *Norf.* ***Village***, 5m/8km NW of Attleborough. **44 D5** TF9800.
Scoulton Mere *Norf.* ***Lake/loch***, to N of Scoulton, lake with wooded island. **44 D5** TF9800.
Scounslow Green *Staffs.* ***Hamlet***, 3m/4km S of Uttoxeter. SK0929.
Scour Ouran *High. Anglicised form of Sgurr Fhuaran, qv.*
Scoured Rig *Sc.Bord.* ***Mountain***, 4m/7km NE of Lauder. Height 1191 feet or 363 metres. **76 D5** NT5851.

Scourie *High.* ***Village***, on W coast of Sutherland district, at head of Scourie Bay, 5m/8km W of Laxford Bridge. **102 D4** NC1544.
Scourie Bay *High.* ***Bay***, 5m/8km W of Laxford Bridge. Scourie village on W coast of Sutherland district at head. **102 D4** NC1544.
Scourie More *High.* ***Settlement***, 1km W of Scourie, on W coast of Sutherland district. **102 D4** NC1444.
Scousburgh *Shet.* ***Village***, near W coast of Mainland, 6m/10km N of Sumburgh Head. **109 F9** HU3717.
Scout Hill *Cumb.* ***Hill***, 4m/6km NW of Kirkby Lonsdale. Height 932 feet or 284 metres. **55 J1** SD5682.
Scouthead *Gt.Man.* ***Hamlet***, 3m/4km E of Oldham. SD9705.
Scowles *Glos.* ***Hamlet***, 1m/2km W of Coleford. SO5610.
Scrabster *High.* ***Village***, and small port on W side of Thurso Bay, 2m/3km NW of Thurso, Caithness district. **105 F1** ND1070.
Scrafield *Lincs.* ***Hamlet***, 3m/4km E of Horncastle. TF3068.
Scrainwood *Northumb.* ***Settlement***, 5m/8km NE of Alwinton. **70 E3** NT9909.
Scrane End *Lincs.* ***Hamlet***, 4m/7km SE of Boston. **43 G1** TF3841.
Scraptoft *Leics.* ***Village***, 4m/6km E of Leicester. **41 J5** SK6405.
Scratby *Norf.* ***Village***, and coastal resort, 5m/8km N of Great Yarmouth. **45 K4** TG5015.
Scrayingham *N.Yorks.* ***Village***, 3m/5km NE of Stamford Bridge. **58 D3** SE7360.
Scredington *Lincs.* ***Village***, 4m/6km SE of Sleaford. **42 D1** TF0940.
Screel Hill *D. & G.* ***Mountain***, 4m/7km S of Castle Douglas. Height 1125 feet or 343 metres. **65 H5** NX7755.
Scremby *Lincs.* ***Village***, 3m/5km E of Spilsby. **53 H6** TF4467.
Scremerston *Northumb.* ***Village***, 3m/4km S of Berwick-upon-Tweed. **77 J6** NU0049.
Screveton *Notts.* ***Village***, 3m/5km NE of Bingham. **42 A1** SK7343.
Scrinadle *Arg. & B.* ***Mountain***, on Jura, 7m/11km N of Craighouse. Height 1660 feet or 506 metres. **72 C3** NR5077.
Scrivelsby *Lincs.* ***Locality***, including deer park at Scrivelsby Court, 2m/4km S of Horncastle. TF2666.
Scriven *N.Yorks.* ***Village***, 1m/2km N of Knaresborough. **57 J4** SE3458.
Scrooby *Notts.* ***Village***, 1m/2km S of Bawtry. **51 J3** SK6590.
Scropton *Derbys.* ***Village***, 2m/4km SE of Sudbury. **40 D2** SK1930.
Scrot Mòr *W.Isles* ***Island***, islet at S end of Heisker Islands group, to W of North Uist. **92 B5** NF6360.
Scrub Hill *Lincs.* ***Hamlet***, 2m/3km S of Coningsby. **53 F7** TF2355.
Scruton *N.Yorks.* ***Village***, 4m/6km NE of Bedale. **62 D7** SE3092.
Scuir of Eigg *High. Alternative name for An Sgurr, qv.*
Scuir Vullin *High. Anglicised form of Sgurr a' Mhuilinn, qv.*
Sculcoates *Hull* ***Suburb***, 1m/2km N of Kingston upon Hull city centre. TA0930.
Sculthorpe *Norf.* ***Village***, 2m/3km NW of Fakenham. Airfield to W. **44 C2** TF8930.
Scunthorpe *N.Lincs.* Population: 75,982. ***Town***, old iron and steel town, 21m/33km E of Doncaster, now with a more varied industrial base. Restored church of St. Lawrence dates from 12c. **52 B1** SE8910.
Scurdie Ness *Angus* ***Coastal feature***, headland with lighthouse on S side of mouth of River South Esk, 1m/2km E of Montrose. **83 J2** NO7356.
Scurlage *Swan.* ***Hamlet***, on Gower peninsula, 2m/3km N of Port Eynon Point. **17 H6** SS4687.
Scurrival Point *W.Isles* ***Coastal feature***, headland at N extremity of Barra. **84 B4** NF6909.
Scuthvie Bay *Ork.* ***Bay***, large wide bay on NE coast of Sanday, to NW of Start Point. **106 G3** HY7644.
Sea *Som.* ***Settlement***, 1m/2km SW of Ilminster. ST3412.
Sea Mills *Bristol* ***Suburb***, 3m/5km NW of Bristol city centre. ST5576.
Sea of the Hebrides ***Sea feature***, stretch of sea between Outer Hebrides and Inner Hebrides groups of islands. **85 F6** NM1287.
Sea Palling *Norf.* ***Village***, and coastal resort, 4m/7km SE of Happisburgh. **45 J3** TG4226.
Seabank *Arg. & B.* ***Settlement***, 1m/2km N of Benderloch. **80 A3** NM9041.
Seaborough *Dorset* ***Hamlet***, 2m/4km S of Crewkerne. **8 D4** ST4206.
Seabridge *Staffs.* ***Suburb***, 1m/2km SW of Newcastle-under-Lyme town centre. SJ8343.
Seaburn *T. & W.* ***Suburb***, on Whitburn Bay, 2m/3km N of Sunderland city centre. NZ4060.
Seacombe *Mersey.* ***Suburb***, in S part of Wallasey. **48 B3** SJ3190.
Seacombe Cliff *Dorset* ***Coastal feature***, 1m/2km SE of Worth Matravers, 3m/5km W of Durlston Head. **9 J7** SY9876.
Seacroft *Lincs.* ***Settlement***, on coast, 2m/3km S of Skegness. **53 J6** TF5660.
Seacroft *W.Yorks.* ***Suburb***, 4m/7km E of Leeds city centre. **57 J6** SE3635.
Seadyke *Lincs.* ***Settlement***, 2m/3km SE of Kirton. TF3236.
Seafar *N.Lan.* ***Suburb***, central area of Cumbernauld. NS7574.
Seafield *Arg. & B.* ***Settlement***, at head of Loch Sween, 5m/8km W of Lochgilphead. **73 F2** NR7787.
Seafield *S.Ayr.* ***Suburb***, S district of Ayr. **67 H1** NS3320.
Seafield *W.Loth.* ***Hamlet***, 1m/2km E of Blackburn. **75 J4** NT0066.
Seaford *E.Suss.* Population: 19,622. ***Town***, resort on bay of same name, 3m/5km SE of Newhaven. The old harbour was left dry following a storm in 16c, when a new harbour was created at Newhaven. **13 H7** TV4899.
Seaforth *Mersey.* ***Suburb***, S district of Crosby. **48 C3** SJ3297.
Seaforth Head *W.Isles Anglicised form of Ceann Loch Shiphoirt, qv.*
Seaforth Island *W.Isles* ***Island***, uninhabited island, over 1m/2km by over 1km, rising sheer out of Loch Seaforth, Isle of Lewis, to a height of 712 feet or 217 metres. **100 E6** NB2010.
Seagrave *Leics.* ***Village***, 5m/9km E of Loughborough. **41 J4** SK6117.
Seagry Heath *Wilts.* ***Hamlet***, 6m/9km NE of Chippenham. ST9581.
Seaham *Dur.* Population: 22,130. ***Town***, 5m/8km S of Sunderland. **63 F2** NZ4249.
Seaham Grange *Dur.* ***Hamlet***, 1m/2km NW of Seaham. NZ4051.
Seahouses *Northumb.* ***Village***, former fishing village, now resort on North Sea coast, 3m/5km SE of Bamburgh. Sands to N (National Trust). **77 K7** NU2132.
Seal *Kent* ***Village***, 2m/3km NE of Sevenoaks. **23 J6** TQ5556.
Seal Chart *Kent* ***Locality***, 1m/2km SE of Seal. TQ5655.
Seal Sand *Norf.* ***Coastal feature***, large sandbank in S part of The Wash, to NE of Breast Sand off North Norfolk coast. **43 J2** TF5634.
Seal Sands *Stock.* ***Coastal feature***, large area of mud and sand in an inlet at E side of River Tees estuary. **63 G4** NZ5226.
Sealand *Flints.* ***Village***, 4m/6km W of Chester. **48 C6** SJ3568.
Seale *Surr.* ***Village***, 4m/6km E of Farnham. **22 B7** SU8947.
Sealyham *Pembs.* ***Settlement***, 6m/9km S of Fishguard. Gives name to breed of terriers. SM9627.
Seamer *N.Yorks.* ***Village***, 2m/3km NW of Stokesley. **63 F5** NZ4910.
Seamer *N.Yorks.* Population: 2178. ***Village***, 4m/6km SW of Scarborough. Site of Mesolithic settlement 2m/3km S. **59 G1** TA0183.
Seamill *N.Ayr.* ***Town***, summer resort on Firth of Clyde, adjoining to S of West Kilbride. **74 A6** NS2047.
Seana Bhraigh *High.* ***Mountain***, in Sutherland district, 4m/6km S of head of Loch an Daimh. Munro: height 3041 feet or 927 metres. **95 J3** NH2887.
Seana Mheallan *High.* ***Mountain***, in Ross and Cromarty district, 2m/3km E of Torridon. Height 1430 feet or 436 metres. **95 F6** NG9255.
Searby *Lincs.* ***Village***, 4m/7km NW of Caistor. **52 D2** TA0705.
Seasalter *Kent* ***Locality***, on coast, at W end of Whitstable. **25 G5** TR0965.
Seascale *Cumb.* Population: 1766. ***Small town***, Victorian coastal resort, 12m/19km S of Whitehaven. **60 B6** NY0301.
Seat Robert *Cumb.* ***Mountain***, 1m/2km W of Wet Sleddale Reservoir and 3m/5km SW of Shap. Height 1689 feet or 515 metres. **61 G5** NY5212.
Seat Sandal *Cumb.* ***Mountain***, rising above Grisedale Tarn, 3m/4km S of Helvellyn. Height 2414 feet or 736 metres. **60 E5** NY3411.
Seatallan *Cumb.* ***Mountain***, in Copeland Forest, 3m/5km N of Nether Wasdale. Height 2270 feet or 692 metres. **60 C6** NY1308.
Seater *High.* ***Locality***, near N coast of Caithness district, 3m/5km W of Duncansby Head. ND3572.
Seathope Law *Sc.Bord.* ***Mountain***, 4m/7km NE of Innerleithen. Height 1778 feet or 542 metres. **76 B6** NT3740.
Seathorne *Lincs.* ***Settlement***, on coast, 2m/3km N of Skegness. TF5766.
Seathwaite *Cumb.* ***Hamlet***, in River Duddon valley, 6m/9km N of Broughton in Furness. **60 D7** SD2296.
Seathwaite *Cumb.* ***Locality***, in Borrowdale, 1m/2km SW of Seatoller. **60 D5** NY2312.
Seathwaite Tarn *Cumb.* ***Lake/loch***, tarn 1m/2km NW of The Old Man of Coniston and 3m/5km W of Coniston. **60 D7** SD2598.
Seatle *Cumb.* ***Settlement***, 2m/3km S of Newby Bridge. SD3783.
Seatoller *Cumb.* ***Settlement***, in Borrowdale, 3m/5km S of Derwent Water, at foot of Honister Pass. **60 D5** NY2413.
Seaton *Cornw.* ***River***, rising 3m/4km NE of Liskeard and flowing S to S coast at Seaton. **4 C4** SX3054.
Seaton *Cornw.* ***Village***, on S coast, 3m/5km E of Looe, at mouth of river of same name which rises near Darite, N of Liskeard. **4 D5** SX3054.
Seaton *Cumb.* Population: 4380. ***Suburb***, 2m/3km NE of Workington. **60 B3** NY0130.
Seaton *Devon* Population: 7579. ***Small town***, small resort at mouth of River Axe, 6m/10km SW of Axminster. **8 B5** SY2490.
Seaton *Dur.* ***Locality***, 2m/3km W of Seaham. **63 F2** NZ3949.
Seaton *E.Riding* ***Village***, 3m/5km W of Hornsea. **59 H5** TA1646.
Seaton *Northumb.* ***Hamlet***, 1m/2km W of Seaton Sluice. **71 J6** NZ3276.
Seaton *Rut.* ***Village***, 3m/4km SE of Uppingham. **42 C6** SP9098.
Seaton Bank Top *Dur.* ***Locality***, 1km SW of Seaton. NZ3949.
Seaton Bay *Devon* ***Bay***, extending from Beer Head (W) to Culverhole Point (E). Resort of Seaton on N shore of bay. **8 B6** SY2490.
Seaton Burn *T. & W.* ***Locality***, 6m/10km N of Newcastle upon Tyne. **71 H6** NZ2373.
Seaton Carew *Hart.* ***Village***, on North Sea coast, 2m/3km S of Hartlepool. **63 G3** NZ5229.
Seaton Delaval *Northumb.* Population: 7333. ***Small town***, 4m/6km S of Blyth. **71 J6** NZ3075.
Seaton Delaval Hall *Northumb.* ***Historic house***, 18c house by Vanbrugh in Palladian style. Situated in hamlet of Seaton. **71 J6** NZ3276.
Seaton Junction *Devon* ***Hamlet***, at former railway junction, 4m/7km N of Seaton. **8 B5** SY2496.
Seaton Ross *E.Riding* ***Village***, 6m/10km W of Market Weighton. **58 D5** SE7841.
Seaton Sluice *Northumb.* Population: 3292. ***Village***, on North Sea coast, at mouth of Seaton Burn, 3m/5km N of Whitley Bay. **71 J6** NZ3376.
Seaton Terrace *Northumb.* ***Locality***, between Seaton Delaval and Holywell, 3m/5km NW of Whitley Bay. NZ3175.
Seaton Tramway *Devon* ***Other feature of interest***, tourist railway which leaves Seaton Bay and travels N to Colyford and Kingsdon, E of Colyton. **8 B5** SY2590.
Seatown *Aber.* ***Settlement***, near E coast, W of Rattray Head. **99 K5** NK1057.
Seatown *Dorset* ***Settlement***, on S coast, 1km S of Chideock, 3m/4km SW of Bridport. **8 D5** SY4291.
Seatown *Moray* ***Locality***, harbour district of Lossiemouth. NJ2370.
Seatown *Moray* ***Settlement***, on coast, adjoining to W of Cullen. **98 D4** NJ5067.
Seatown *Moray* ***Suburb***, to E of Buckie town centre, on coast between Buckpool and Gordonsburgh. **98 C4** NJ4266.
Seave Green *N.Yorks.* ***Hamlet***, 6m/9km SE of Stokesley. **63 G6** NZ5601.
Seaview *I.o.W.* Population: 2181. ***Village***, on NE coast of Isle of Wight, 2m/4km E of Ryde. **11 H5** SZ6291.
Seaville *Cumb.* ***Hamlet***, 2m/3km NW of Abbeytown. **60 C1** NY1553.
Seavington St. Mary *Som.* ***Village***, 3m/4km E of Ilminster. **8 D3** ST4014.
Seavington St. Michael *Som.* ***Village***, 3m/5km E of Ilminster. **8 D3** ST4015.
Seawick *Essex* ***Hamlet***, 3m/5km SW of Clacton-on-Sea. **35 F7** TM1212.
Sebastopol *Torfaen* ***Suburb***, locality in S part of Griffithstown, 1m/2km S of Pontypool. **19 F2** ST2898.
Sebergham *Cumb.* ***Village***, on River Caldew, 8m/12km SE of Wigton. **60 E2** NY3541.
Seckington *Warks.* ***Village***, 4m/6km NE of Tamworth. **40 E5** SK2607.
Second Coast *High.* ***Settlement***, on S shore of Gruinard Bay, 6m/10km SE of Greenstone Point. **95 F2** NG9290.
Second Severn Crossing ***Bridge***, carrying M4 motorway across River Severn estuary between England and Wales, 3m/5km downstream from Severn Road Bridge. Opened in 1996, it has total length of 3m/5km. The main span, suspended between two towers, measures 1496 feet or 456 metres. ST5186.
Sedbergh *Cumb.* Population: 1670. ***Small town***, on N slope of River Rawther valley, 9m/14km E of Kendal. Boys' boarding school. **61 H7** SD6592.
Sedbury *Glos.* Population: 1680. ***Village***, 1m/2km E of Chepstow across River Wye. **19 J2** ST5493.
Sedbusk *N.Yorks.* ***Hamlet***, 1m/2km NE of Hawes across River Ure. **61 K7** SD8891.
Seddington *Beds.* ***Settlement***, 1m/2km S of Sandy. TL1747.
Sedgeberrow *Worcs.* ***Village***, 4m/6km S of Evesham. **30 B5** SP0238.
Sedgebrook *Lincs.* ***Village***, 4m/6km W of Grantham. **42 B2** SK8537.
Sedgefield *Dur.* Population: 4424. ***Village***, 8m/13km NW of Stockton-on-Tees. Racecourse to SW. **62 E4** NZ3528.
Sedgeford *Norf.* ***Village***, 4m/6km SE of Hunstanton. **44 B2** TF7136.
Sedgehill *Wilts.* ***Village***, 3m/5km N of Shaftesbury. **9 H2** ST8628.
Sedgeletch *T. & W.* ***Suburb***, in NW part of Houghton le Spring. NZ3350.
Sedgemere *W.Mid.* ***Settlement***, 5m/8km NW of Kenilworth. SP2275.
Sedgemoor *Som.* ***Marsh/bog***, marshy tract intersected by numerous dykes or rhynes cut for drainage purposes, extending roughly from Bridgwater in W to a line through Street and Somerton in E, and from Polden Hills in N to River Parrett mouth in S. Site of Battle of Sedgemoor in 1685 to N of Westonzoyland. ST3735.
Sedgley *W.Mid.* ***Suburb***, NW district of Dudley. **40 B6** SO9193.
Sedgley Park *Gt.Man.* ***Suburb***, in S part of Prestwich. SD8202.
Sedgwick *Cumb.* ***Village***, 4m/6km S of Kendal. **55 J1** SD5187.
Sedlescombe *E.Suss.* ***Village***, 3m/4km NE of Battle. The name Sedlescombe is usually applied to both Sedlescombe and Sedlescombe Street, which are virtually adjoining. **14 C6** TQ7718.
Sedlescombe Street *E.Suss.* ***Village***, 1km SE of Sedlescombe. **14 C6** TQ7718.
Seed Green *Lancs.* ***Settlement***, 3m/4km E of Longridge. SD6437.
Seedley *Gt.Man.* ***Suburb***, 1m/2km W of Salford city centre. SJ8098.
Seend *Wilts.* ***Village***, 4m/6km W of Devizes. **20 C5** ST9461.
Seend Cleeve *Wilts.* ***Village***, 1m/2km W of Seend. **20 C5** ST9461.
Seenes Law *Sc.Bord.* ***Mountain***, in Lammermuir Hills, 2m/3km SE of Hopes Reservoir. Height 1683 feet or 513 metres. **76 D4** NT5560.
Seer Green *Bucks.* Population: 2969. ***Village***, 2m/3km NE of Beaconsfield. **22 C2** SU9691.
Seething *Norf.* ***Village***, 5m/9km N of Bungay. **45 H6** TM3197.
Sefton *Mersey.* ***Village***, 3m/5km NE of Crosby. **48 C2** SD3501.
Sefton Town *Mersey.* ***Locality***, 1km SW of Sefton. SD3501.
Segelocum *Notts. See Littleborough.*
Seghill *Northumb.* Population: 2681. ***Village***, 6m/10km NW of Tynemouth. **71 H6** NZ2874.
Segontium Roman Fort and Museum *Gwyn.* ***Historic/prehistoric site***, on SE side of Caernarfon. Fort founded c. AD 78 and largely rebuilt in 4c. Allegedly birthplace of Emperor Constantine. **46 C6** SH4862.
Seighford *Staffs.* ***Village***, 3m/5km NW of Stafford. Airfield to W. **40 A3** SJ8824.

S

Seil *Arg. & B.* ***Island***, on E side of Firth of Lorn connected with mainland of Argyll by Clachan Bridge. Island is 5m/7km long N to S and 2m/3km wide. **79 J6** NM7617.
Seil Sound *Arg. & B.* ***Sea feature***, strait between Seil and mainland. **79 J6** NM7617.
Seilebost *W.Isles* ***Locality***, on South Harris, 1m/2km NE of Buirgh. **93 F2** NG0696.
Seion *Gwyn.* ***Hamlet***, 4m/6km SW of Bangor. **46 D6** SH5467.
Seisdon *Staffs.* ***Village***, 5m/9km SW of Wolverhampton. **40 A6** SO8394.
Seisiadar (Anglicised form: Sheshader.) *W.Isles* ***Village***, on Eye Peninsula, Isle of Lewis, 3m/4km SW of Tiumpan Head. **101 H4** NB5534.
Selattyn *Shrop.* ***Village***, 3m/5km NW of Oswestry. **38 B2** SJ2633.
Selborne *Hants.* ***Village***, 4m/6km SE of Alton. **11 J1** SU7433.
Selby *N.Yorks.* Population: 15,292. ***Town***, market town and port on River Ouse, 13m/20km S of York. Abbey church dominates town. 18c toll bridge. Flour mills. Canal connects River Ouse here with River Aire to SW. **58 C6** SE6132.
Selby Abbey *N.Yorks.* ***Ecclesiastical building***, 11c limestone abbey with three towers, in Selby. **58 C6** SE6132.
Selham *W.Suss.* ***Village***, 3m/5km E of Midhurst. **12 C4** SU9320.
Selhurst *Gt.Lon.* ***Suburb***, in borough of Croydon, 1m/2km N of Croydon town centre. TQ3267.
Selker Bay *Cumb.* ***Bay***, shingle bay 1m/2km W of Bootle Station and 8m/13km NW of Millom. **54 D1** SD0789.
Selkirk *Sc.Bord.* Population: 5922. ***Small town***, royal burgh on hill above Ettrick Water, 9m/15km N of Hawick. Town has associations with Sir Walter Scott, and with Mungo Park, African explorer. Centre for touring Borders. **69 K1** NT4728.
Sellack *Here.* ***Village***, 3m/4km NW of Ross-on-Wye. **28 E6** SO5627.
Sellafield *Cumb.* ***Settlement***, 1km N of Sellafield Station and 2m/3km NW of Seascale. Nuclear reprocessing plant to SE. **60 B6** NY0204.
Sellafirth *Shet.* ***Settlement***, on Yell, 3m/5km NW of Burra Ness. **108 E3** HU5198.
Sellick's Green *Som.* ***Hamlet***, 4m/6km S of Taunton. ST2119.
Sellindge *Kent* ***Village***, 5m/8km NW of Hythe. **15 F4** TR0938.
Sellindge Lees *Kent* ***Settlement***, 1m/2km E of Sellindge. TR0937.
Selling *Kent* ***Village***, 3m/5km SE of Faversham. **15 F2** TR0456.
Sells Green *Wilts.* ***Hamlet***, 3m/5km E of Melksham. **20 C5** ST9562.
Selly Oak *W.Mid.* ***Suburb***, 3m/5km SW of Birmingham city centre. **40 C7** SP0482.
Selmeston *E.Suss.* ***Village***, at foot of South Downs, 3m/4km N of Alfriston. **13 J6** TQ5006.
Selsdon *Gt.Lon.* ***Suburb***, in borough of Croydon, 3m/5km SE of Croydon town centre. **23 G5** TQ3562.
Selset Reservoir *Dur.* ***Reservoir***, in course of River Lune, 3m/5km SW of Middleton-in-Teesdale. **61 K4** NY9121.
Selsey *Glos.* ***Village***, 1m/2km SW of Stroud. SO8303.
Selsey *W.Suss.* Population: 8754. ***Small town***, seaside resort extending along coast and inland from Selsey Bill, 7m/12km S of Chichester. **12 B7** SZ8593.
Selsey Bill *W.Suss.* ***Coastal feature***, headland on English Channel, 8m/13km S of Chichester. **12 B7** SZ8593.
Selsfield Common *W.Suss.* ***Settlement***, 1km SE of Turners Hill. **13 G3** TQ3434.
Selside *Cumb.* ***Hamlet***, 4m/7km N of Kendal. Hall dates from 14c. SD5399.
Selside *N.Yorks.* ***Hamlet***, 3m/5km NW of Horton in Ribblesdale. **56 C2** SD7875.
Selsmore *Hants.* ***Suburb***, of South Hayling on Hayling Island. SZ7398.
Selstead *Kent* ***Hamlet***, 6m/9km N of Folkestone. **15 H3** TR2144.
Selston *Notts.* Population: 3917. ***Village***, 3m/5km SW of Kirkby in Ashfield. **51 G7** SK4653.
Selston Green *Notts.* ***Hamlet***, adjoining to W of Selston. SK4553.
Selworthy *Som.* ***Village***, largely National Trust, 2m/3km E of Porlock. **7 H1** SS9146.
Selworthy Beacon *Som.* ***Mountain***, National Trust property to N of Selworthy, commanding view over Bristol Channel. Height 1010 feet or 308 metres. **7 H1** SS9148.
Semblister *Shet.* ***Settlement***, overlooking The Firth, 1m/2km N of Garderhouse, Mainland. **109 C7** HU3350.
Semer *Suff.* ***Hamlet***, 3m/5km NW of Hadleigh. **34 D4** TM0046.
Semer Water *N.Yorks.* ***Lake/loch***, 2m/3km SW of Bainbridge. **56 E1** SD9287.
Semere Green *Norf.* ***Settlement***, 1m/2km SW of Pulham Market. TM1884.
Semington *Wilts.* ***Village***, 2m/3km S of Melksham. **20 B5** ST8960.
Semley *Wilts.* ***Village***, 3m/5km NE of Shaftesbury. **9 H2** ST8926.
Sempringham *Lincs.* ***Locality***, remains of Gilbertine monastery 8m/13km N of Bourne. Birthplace of St. Gilbert (d. 1189), founder of only English order of monks and nuns. TF1133.
Sence ***River***, rising near Billesdon and flowing SW, then W into River Soar at Enderby to SW of Leicester. **41 J6** SP5598.
Sence *Leics.* ***River***, rising on W slopes of Charnwood Forest and flowing SW into River Anker 1m/2km NE of Atherstone. **41 F5** SP3199.
Send *Surr.* Population: 4102. ***Village***, 3m/4km SE of Woking. **22 D6** TQ0255.
Send Marsh *Surr.* ***Village***, 5m/8km NE of Guildford. **22 D6** TQ0455.
Senghenydd *Caerp.* ***Village***, 4m/6km NW of Caerphilly. **18 E2** ST1190.
Sennen *Cornw.* ***Village***, 1km E of Land's End. **2 A6** SW3525.
Sennen Cove *Cornw.* ***Village***, on coast 1km NW of Land's End. Beach popular with surfers. **2 A6** SW3525.
Sennybridge (Pontsenni). *Powys* ***Village***, at confluence of Rivers Senni and Usk, 8m/12km W of Brecon. Slight remains of Castell du, 14c stronghold, to W. **27 J6** SN9228.
Senwick Hotel *D. & G.* ***Other building***, 3m/5km S of Kirkcudbright. **65 G6** NX6446.
Seph *N.Yorks.* ***River***, formed from waters of Raisdale Beck and Ledge Beck, and flowing S down Bilsdale to River Rye, 1m/2km SE of Hawnby. **63 G7** SE5588.
Sequer's Bridge *Devon* ***Settlement***, 3m/4km S of Ivybridge. **5 G5** SX6351.
Serlby *Notts.* ***Hamlet***, 2m/3km NE of Blyth. SK6389.
Serpentine Bridge *Gt.Lon.* ***Bridge***, stone bridge in Hyde Park, built in 1824 by George Rennie. TQ2680.
Serrington *Wilts.* ***Settlement***, across River Till from Stapleford, 4m/7km NW of Wilton. SU0637.
Serw *Conwy* ***River***, rising on Migneint and flowing NE into River Conwy 3m/4km SW of Ysbyty Ifan. **37 H1** SH8145.
Sessay *N.Yorks.* ***Village***, 4m/6km E of Topcliffe. **57 K2** SE4575.
Setchey *Norf.* ***Hamlet***, 4m/6km S of King's Lynn. Site of Roman building to N. **44 A4** TF6313.
Setley *Hants.* ***Hamlet***, 1m/2km S of Brockenhurst, on edge of New Forest. **10 E4** SU3000.
Seton Mains *E.Loth.* ***Hamlet***, 3m/4km E of Prestonpans. NT4275.
Setter *Shet.* ***Settlement***, at head of Weisdale, Mainland. **109 C7** HU3954.
Setter *Shet.* ***Settlement***, on E coast of Bressay, overlooking Voe of Cullingsburgh. **109 E8** HU5141.
Settiscarth *Ork.* ***Settlement***, on Mainland, 3m/5km N of Finstown and 2m/3km W of Bay of Isbister. **107 C6** HY3618.
Settle *N.Yorks.* Population: 3082. ***Small town***, on River Ribble, 13m/21km NW of Skipton. S end of Settle to Carlisle Railway. Interesting 18c shops, and many Georgian buildings. **56 D3** SD8163.
Settrington *N.Yorks.* ***Village***, 3m/5km E of Malton. **58 E2** SE8370.
Seumas Cleite *W.Isles* ***Island***, islet at entrance to Loch Leurbost, E coast of Isle of Lewis. NB4123.
Seven *N.Yorks.* ***River***, rising on Cleveland Hills, 5m/7km NW of Rosedale Abbey, and flowing S into River Rye 1km SE of Brawby. **58 D1** SE7477.
Seven Ash *Som.* ***Hamlet***, 1m/2km W of West Bagborough. ST1533.
Seven Bridges *Wilts.* ***Settlement***, 1m/2km SE of Cricklade. Site of Roman building. **20 E2** SU1292.
Seven Kings *Gt.Lon.* ***Suburb***, NE district of Ilford, in borough of Redbridge. **23 H3** TQ4587.
Seven Sisters (Blaendulais). *N.P.T.* Population: 2343. ***Village***, 8m/13km NE of Neath. **18 B1** SN8208.
Seven Sisters Country Park *E.Suss.* ***Leisure/recreation***, comprises cliffs, known as Seven Sisters, and South Downs behind (partly National Trust), together with Cuckmere Haven, 3m/5km E of Seaford. **13 J7** TV5396.
Seven Springs *Glos.* ***Settlement***, at cross roads, 4m/6km S of Cheltenham. **29 J7** SO9617.
Seven Star Green *Essex* ***Settlement***, 4m/6km W of Colchester town centre. TL9325.
Seven Stones *I.o.S.* ***Island***, cluster of seven islets 19m/30km W of Land's End and 11m/18km NE of St. Mary's. SW0523.
Sevenhampton *Glos.* ***Village***, 5m/9km E of Cheltenham. **30 B6** SP0321.
Sevenhampton *Swin.* ***Village***, 1m/2km S of Highworth. **21 F2** SU2090.
Sevenoaks *Kent* Population: 24,489. ***Town***, 21m/34km SE of London. Contains large mansion of Knole to E. **23 J6** TQ5255.
Sevenoaks Weald (Also known as Weald.) *Kent* ***Village***, 3m/4km S of Sevenoaks. **23 J6** TQ5350.
Severn (Hafren). ***River***, major river of Wales and W England, rising on Plynlimon in Cambrian Mountains and flowing into Bristol Channel. River course is circuitous, flowing NE via Newtown and Welshpool before turning SE at Shrewsbury, past Ironbridge, then S at Bridgnorth. It then meanders S via Stourport-on-Severn and Worcester and is joined by River Avon at Tewkesbury. It continues to meander S through Vale of Gloucester, past Gloucester, and into a long funnel-shaped estuary which widens to 1m/2km and 3m/4km by old and new Severn Bridges respectively. Estuary widens into Mouth of the Severn, separating Wales from England, before becoming part of Bristol Channel. River is about 180m/290km long, is tidal to Maisemore, NW of Gloucester, and boasts world's second highest tide. It is noted for its autumnal tidal bore which reaches weirs at Gloucester, and can produce a water level rise of up to 2 metres. **19 J2** ST5085.
Severn Beach *S.Glos.* Population: 1468. ***Village***, on River Severn estuary, 8m/13km NW of Bristol. **19 J3** ST5485.
Severn Road Bridge ***Bridge***, motorway bridge carrying M48 across River Severn, to S of Chepstow and 3m/5km N of Second Severn Crossing. Also includes foot and cycle path. **19 J2** ST5590.
Severn Stoke *Worcs.* ***Village***, on E side of River Severn, 7m/11km S of Worcester. **29 H4** SO8544.
Severn Tunnel ***Other feature of interest***, 4m/7km railway tunnel beneath River Severn, between South Wales (SE of Caldicot) and England (NW of Bristol). **19 J3** ST5186.
Severn Valley Railway *Shrop.* ***Other feature of interest***, tourist steam railway, running for 16m/26km from Kidderminster, through Bewdley and along valley of River Severn to Bridgnorth. **39 G6** SO7192.
Sevick End *Beds.* ***Settlement***, 4m/7km NE of Bedford. TL0954.
Sevington *Kent* ***Village***, 2m/3km SE of Ashford. **15 F3** TR0340.
Sewards End *Essex* ***Village***, 2m/3km E of Saffron Walden. **33 J5** TL5738.
Sewardstone *Essex* ***Locality***, 2m/3km S of Waltham Abbey. **23 G2** TQ3897.
Sewerby *E.Riding* ***Village***, adjoining to NE of Bridlington. **59 J3** TA1968.
Sewerby Hall *E.Riding* ***Historic house***, to NE of Bridlington, containing Museum of East Yorkshire and surrounded by 50 acres of landscaped gardens. **59 J3** TA2068.
Seworgan *Cornw.* ***Hamlet***, 4m/6km NE of Helston. **2 E5** SW7030.
Sewstern *Leics.* ***Village***, 3m/5km SW of Colsterworth. **42 B3** SK8821.
Sexhow *N.Yorks.* ***Locality***, 3m/5km SW of Stokesley. **63 F6** NZ4706.
Seymour Villas *Devon* ***Hamlet***, just E of Woolacombe, 4m/6km SW of Ilfracombe. SS4644.
Sezincote *Glos.* ***Hamlet***, 2m/4km W of Moreton-in-Marsh. SP1730.
Sezincote House *Glos.* ***Historic house***, early 19c house in Indian style, 2m/3km SW of Moreton-in-Marsh. **30 C5** SP1730.
Sgairneach Mhòr *P. & K.* ***Mountain***, 3m/5km W of Dalnaspidal Lodge. Munro: height 3250 feet or 991 metres. **88 C7** NN5973.
Sgaith Chùil *Stir.* ***Mountain***, on N side of Glen Dochart, 6m/10km W of Killin. Munro: height 3014 feet or 919 metres. **81 F4** NN4631.
Sgaladal (Anglicised form: Scaladale.) *W.Isles* ***River***, on North Harris, flowing E into Loch Seaforth at Ardvourlie Castle. NB1910.
Sgaorishal *High.* ***Hill***, 3m/4km SW of northernmost point of Rum. Height 912 feet or 278 metres. **85 J4** NG3501.
Sgaoth Aird *W.Isles* ***Mountain***, 3m/4km N of Tarbert, North Harris. Height 1834 feet or 559 metres. **100 D7** NB1604.
Sgaraman nam Fiadh *High.* ***Mountain***, in Monadhliath range in Inverness district 8m/12km NW of Newtonmore. Height 2814 feet or 858 metres. **88 D4** NH6106.
Sgarasta Mhòr (Anglicised form: Scarastavore.) *W.Isles* ***Locality***, on W coast of South Harris, 4m/6km N of Leverburgh. **93 F2** NG0092.
Sgarbh Breac *Arg. & B.* ***Mountain***, on NE corner of Islay, 6m/9km N of Port Askaig. Height 1194 feet or 364 metres. **72 C3** NR4076.
Sgeir a' Bhuic *High.* ***Island***, rock island at mouth of Loch Eriboll, N coast of Sutherland district, 2m/3km SE of Rispond. NC4763.
Sgeir a' Chaisteil *Arg. & B.* ***Island***, one of the Treshnish Isles group, lying immediately N of Lunga. **78 D3** NM2742.
Sgeir an Eirionnaich *Arg. & B.* ***Island***, one of the Treshnish Isles group, lying 1km NE of Lunga and 1km W of Fladda. NM2843.
Sgeir an Fheòir *Arg. & B.* ***Island***, small island of the Treshnish Isles group, lying between Fladda and Lunga. NM2843.
Sgeir Bharrach *Arg. & B.* ***Coastal feature***, headland on W side of Vaul Bay, on N coast of Tiree. **78 B3** NM0449.
Sgeir Eirin *High.* ***Island***, rock island off NE coast of Skye, 4m/6km SE of Rubha na h-Aiseig. **93 K4** NG4872.
Sgeir Fhada *High.* ***Island***, islet in Loch Carron, 1m/2km E of Lochcarron. **86 E1** NG9139.
Sgeir Ghobhlach *Arg. & B.* ***Island***, one of Torran Rocks group, 4m/6km SW of Mull. **78 D6** NM2712.
Sgeir Mhòr a' Bhrein-phuirt *Arg. & B.* ***Coastal feature***, rock off W coast of Jura, 1km N of Rubh' an t-Sàilein. **72 C2** NR5084.
Sgeir Moil Duinn *W.Isles* ***Coastal feature***, rock on NW coast of Scarp, 4m/6km NW of Huisinis, North Harris. **100 B6** NA9516.
Sgeir na Capaill *High.* ***Island***, one of Ascrib Islands group in Loch Snizort, 5m/8km E of Vaternish Point, Skye. NG3064.
Sgeir na h-Eigheach *W.Isles* ***Coastal feature***, on E side of entrance to Loch Claidh, Isle of Lewis, 8m/13km E of Tarbert. **100 E7** NB2800.
Sgeir na h-Iolaire *Arg. & B.* ***Island***, small island of the Treshnish Isles group, to W of Fladda. NM2843.
Sgeir nan Gall *High.* ***Island***, small island just off N coast of Oldany Island. **102 C5** NC0835.
Sgeir nan Gillean *High.* ***Island***, rock near W shore of Loch Linnhe off Rubha na h-Earba, 3m/5km NE of Rubha na h-Airde Uinnsinn, Lochaber district. NM9054.
Sgeir Toman *W.Isles* ***Island***, one of Flannan Isles group, lying 1m/2km S of main island, Eilean Mòr. NA7245.
Sgeirean nan Torran *High.* ***Island***, group of island rocks near W shore of Loch Linnhe, nearly 2m/3km SW of Inversanda Bay, Lochaber district. NM9356.
Sgeotasaigh (Anglicised form: Scotasay.) *W.Isles* ***Island***, off North Harris in East Loch Tarbert, 3m/4km SE of Tarbert. **93 G2** NG1897.
Sgethrog *Powys Welsh form of Scethrog, qv.*
Sgianait *W.Isles* ***Mountain***, near W coast of North Harris, 3m/4km NE of Huisinis. Height 1394 feet or 425 metres. **100 C6** NB0313.
Sgiath Bhuidhe ***Mountain***, on border of Stirling and Perth & Kinross, 8m/12km NW of Killin. Height 2526 feet or 770 metres. **81 F4** NN4638.
Sgiogarstaigh (Anglicised form: Skigersta.) *W.Isles* ***Village***, near N end of Isle of Lewis, 1m/2km S of Port Nis. Port Skigersta is small bay to NE. **101 H1** NB5461.
Sgitheach (Anglicised form: Skiack.) *High.* ***River***, in Ross and Cromarty district, flowing E into Cromarty Firth just S of Evanton. **96 C5** NH6165.
Sgiwen *N.P.T. Welsh form of Skewen, qv.*
Sgodachail *High.* ***Settlement***, in Strathcarron, 7m/11km W of Bonar Bridge. **96 B2** NH4892.

S

Sgor an Lochain Uaine *Aber.* ***Mountain***, to NW of Cairn Toul summit within Cairngorms National Nature Reserve, 13m/21km NW of Braemar. Munro: height 4126 feet or 1258 metres. NN9597.
Sgòr Gaibhre ***Mountain***, on border of Highland and Perth & Kinross, 4m/7km SW of Ben Alder. Munro: height 3123 feet or 952 metres. **81 F1** NN4467.
Sgor Gaoith *High.* ***Mountain***, at W end of Cairngorm Mountains in Badenoch and Strathspey district, 6m/10km SE of Kincraig. Munro: height 3667 feet or 1118 metres. **89 G5** NN9098.
Sgòr Gaoithe *High.* ***Mountain***, at S end of Hills of Cromdale, and 3m/4km W of Bridge of Brown. Height 2060 feet or 628 metres. **89 H2** NJ0721.
Sgòr Mòr *Aber.* ***Mountain***, 5m/8km NW of Inverey, in Grampian Mountains. Height 2667 feet or 813 metres. **89 H5** NO0091.
Sgòr Mòr *Aber.* ***Mountain***, 6m/10km S of Braemar. Height 2909 feet or 887 metres. **89 J6** NO1182.
Sgor na Diollaid *High.* ***Mountain***, in Inverness district on S side of Glen Strathfarrar, 5m/7km NW of Cannich. Height 2683 feet or 818 metres. **87 J1** NH2836.
Sgor na h-Ulaidh *High.* ***Mountain***, in Lochaber district near border with Argyll & Bute, 5m/7km S of foot of Glen Coe. Munro: height 3260 feet or 994 metres. **80 C2** NN1151.
Sgor Reidh *High.* ***Coastal feature***, area of steep slopes, screes and rock outcrops near SW coast of Rum. **85 J5** NM3198.
Sgòrach Breac *High.* ***Hill***, on Sleat peninsula, 6m/10km NE of Tokavaig. Height 981 feet or 299 metres. **86 C3** NG6513.
Sgorach Mòr *Arg. & B.* ***Mountain***, with rounded summit, rising above E shore of Loch Tarsan. Height 1971 feet or 601 metres. **73 K2** NS0984.
Sgòran Dubh Mòr *High.* ***Mountain***, at W end of Cairngorm Mountains in Badenoch and Strathspey district, 6m/9km SE of Kincraig. Height 3644 feet or 1111 metres. **89 G4** NH9000.
Sgorr a' Choise *High.* ***Mountain***, in Lochaber district, 2m/3km S of Ballachulish. Height 2175 feet or 663 metres. **80 B2** NN0854.
Sgorr an Iubhair *High.* ***Mountain***, one of The Mamores, 2m/4km NW of Kinlochmore. Height 3283 feet or 1001 metres. **80 C1** NN1665.
Sgorr Bhogachain *Arg. & B.* ***Hill***, rocky hilltop on Islay, 4m/7km NE of Port Ellen. Height 918 feet or 280 metres. **72 B5** NR3951.
Sgorr Craobh a' Chaorainn *High.* ***Mountain***, 3m/5km S of Glenfinnan, Lochaber district. Height 2542 feet or 775 metres. **86 E7** NM8975.
Sgorr Dhearg *High.* ***Mountain***, peak of Beinn a' Bheithir in Lochaber district, 2m/4km S of Ballachulish. Munro: height 3359 feet or 1024 metres. **80 B2** NN0555.
Sgorr Dhonuill *High.* ***Mountain***, central peak of Beinn a' Bheithir, 3m/5km SW of Ballachulish. Munro: height 3283 feet or 1001 metres. **80 B2** NN0455.
Sgorr na Ciche *High.* *Alternative name for Pap of Glencoe, qv.*
Sgorr nam Faoileann *Arg. & B.* ***Mountain***, on E coast of Islay, 6m/9km S of Port Askaig. Height 1407 feet or 429 metres. **72 C4** NR4260.
Sgorr nam Fiannaidh *High.* ***Mountain***, summit of Aonach Eagach in Lochaber district, at W end of ridge. Munro: height 3172 feet or 967 metres. **80 C2** NN1458.
Sgorr Ruadh *High.* ***Mountain***, in Ross and Cromarty district 3m/5km NW of Achnashellach Lodge. Munro: height 3149 feet or 960 metres. **95 F6** NG9550.
Sgreadan Hill *Arg. & B.* ***Mountain***, on Kintyre, 6m/9km N of Campbeltown. Height 1302 feet or 397 metres. **66 B1** NR7429.
Sgribhis-bheinn *High.* ***Mountain***, 4m/7km SE of Cape Wrath, Sutherland district. Height 1217 feet or 371 metres. **103 F1** NC3171.
Sguide an Leanna *Arg. & B.* ***Sea feature***, narrow inlet on SW coast of Colonsay, 4m/6km SW of Scalasaig. **72 B1** NR3391.
Sgùman Coinntich *High.* ***Mountain***, in Killilan Forest, Skye and Lochalsh district. Height 2883 feet or 879 metres. **87 F1** NG9730.
Sgurr a' Bhealaich Dheirg *High.* ***Mountain***, on Kintail Forest (National Trust for Scotland) on border of Skye and Lochalsh and Inverness districts, 3m/4km NW of head of Loch Cluanie. Munro: height 3405 feet or 1038 metres. **87 G3** NH0314.
Sgurr a' Bhuic *High.* ***Mountain***, 3m/4km SW of Rhuba na h-Airde Uinnsinn, Lochaber district. Height 1866 feet or 569 metres. **79 K3** NM8350.
Sgurr a' Chaorachain *High.* ***Inland physical feature***, mountain ridge in Ross and Cromarty district, 3m/5km W of head of Loch Kishorn, rising to 776 metres. Radio mast. **94 D7** NG7842.
Sgurr a' Chaorachain *High.* ***Mountain***, peak on West Monar Forest, Ross and Cromarty district. Munro: height 3454 feet or 1053 metres. **95 G7** NH0844.
Sgurr a' Chlaidheimh *High.* ***Mountain***, 3m/4km S of Kinloch Hourn, Lochaber district. Height 2758 feet or 841 metres. **87 F4** NG9403.
Sgurr a' Choinnich *Arg. & B.* ***Mountain***, above E shore of Loch Eck and 3m/5km SE of Glenbranter. Height 2168 feet or 661 metres. **73 K1** NS1595.
Sgurr a' Choire-bheithe *High.* ***Mountain***, peak at W end of Druim Chòsaidh, in Lochaber district. Height 2995 feet or 913 metres. **86 E4** NG8901.
Sgurr a' Choire Ghlais *High.* ***Mountain***, peak on border of Inverness and Ross and Cromarty districts, 4m/7km NE of dam of Loch Monar. Munro: height 3552 feet or 1083 metres. **95 J7** NH2543.
Sgurr a' Gharaidh *High.* ***Mountain***, 3m/5km N of Lochcarron, Ross and Cromarty district. Height 2394 feet or 730 metres. **94 E7** NG8844.
Sgurr a' Gharg Gharaidh *High.* ***Mountain***, mass in Glenshiel Forest, 3m/4km SW of Shiel Bridge. Height 2234 feet or 681 metres. **87 F3** NG9115.
Sgurr a' Ghlas Leathaid *High.* ***Mountain***, on Strathconon Forest, Ross and Cromarty district. Height 2768 feet or 844 metres. **95 J6** NH2456.
Sgurr a' Ghreadaidh *High.* ***Mountain***, peak of Cuillin Hills on Skye, to N of Sgurr Alasdair. Munro: height 3191 feet or 973 metres. **85 K2** NG4423.
Sgurr a' Mhadaidh *High.* ***Mountain***, in Cuillin Hills, Skye, 2m/3km NW of head of Loch Coruisk. Munro: height 3011 feet or 918 metres. **85 K2** NG4523.
Sgurr a' Mhaim *High.* ***Mountain***, in Lochaber district, on Mamore Forest S of Glen Nevis. Munro: height 3601 feet or 1098 metres. **80 C1** NN1666.
Sgurr a' Mhaoraich *High.* ***Mountain***, peak in Lochaber district 2m/3km E of Kinloch Hourn. Munro: height 3369 feet or 1027 metres. **87 F4** NG9806.
Sgurr a' Mhuidhe *High.* ***Mountain***, rising to over 480 metres, 1km NE of head of Loch Eilt, Lochaber district. **86 E6** NM8582.
Sgurr a' Mhuilinn (Anglicised form: Scuir Vuillin.) *High.* ***Mountain***, on Strathconon Forest, Ross and Cromarty district. Height 2883 feet or 879 metres. **95 J6** NH2655.
Sgurr a' Phollain *High.* ***Mountain***, on border of Ross and Cromarty and Inverness districts, 4m/6km NW of Erchless Castle. Height 2801 feet or 854 metres. **95 K7** NH3644.
Sgurr Alasdair *High.* ***Mountain***, on Skye, highest peak of the Cuillin Hills, due E of mountain rescue post at foot of Glen Brittle. Munro: height 3257 feet or 993 metres. **85 K2** NG4520.
Sgurr an Airgid *High.* ***Mountain***, in Skye and Lochalsh district, 1m/2km N of head of Loch Duich. Height 2758 feet or 841 metres. **87 F2** NG9422.
Sgurr an Doire Leathain *High.* ***Mountain***, on border of Inverness and Skye and Lochalsh districts, on S side of Glen Shiel. Munro: height 3313 feet or 1010 metres. **87 G4** NH0109.
Sgurr an Eilein Ghiubhais *High.* ***Mountain***, 3m/5km E of Mallaig. Height 1712 feet or 522 metres. **86 D5** NM7297.
Sgurr an Fhuarain *High.* ***Mountain***, in Lochaber district between Loch Quoich and head of Glen Kingie. Height 2962 feet or 903 metres. **87 F5** NM9897.
Sgurr an Iubhair *High.* ***Mountain***, 7m/11km N of Sallachan Point, Lochaber district, 6m/10km W of Fort William. Height 2368 feet or 722 metres. **87 F7** NN0072.
Sgurr an Lochain *High.* ***Mountain***, peak on border of Lochaber and Skye and Lochalsh districts, 4m/7km N of Loch Quoich at foot of Glen Quoich. Munro: height 3293 feet or 1004 metres. **87 G3** NH0010.
Sgurr an Tarmachain *High.* ***Mountain***, 3m/5km NE of Pollock, Lochaber district. Height 2480 feet or 756 metres. **86 E7** NM8470.
Sgurr an Ursainn *High.* ***Mountain***, 2m/3km NE of head of Loch Beoraid, Lochaber district. Height 2680 feet or 817 metres. **86 E6** NM8887.
Sgurr an Utha *High.* ***Mountain***, peak in Lochaber district 2m/4km NW of Glenfinnan. Height 2611 feet or 796 metres. **86 E6** NM8883.
Sgurr Ban *High.* ***Mountain***, in W part of Ross and Cromarty district, 3m/4km NE of Lochan Fada. Munro: height 3244 feet or 989 metres. **95 G4** NH0574.
Sgurr Bhuidhe *High.* ***Mountain***, 3m/5km SE of Mallaig. Height 1443 feet or 440 metres. **86 D5** NM7294.
Sgurr Breac *High.* ***Hill***, 1m/2km N of Loch a' Ghlinne. Height 817 feet or 249 metres. **86 B4** NG5907.
Sgurr Breac *High.* ***Mountain***, in Ross and Cromarty district, 10m/15km NE of Kinlochewe. Munro: height 3280 feet or 1000 metres. **95 H4** NH1571.
Sgurr Breac *High.* ***Mountain***, in North Morar, Lochaber district, 3m/5km E of Tarbet. Height 2388 feet or 728 metres. **86 E5** NM8492.
Sgurr Chòinich *High.* ***Mountain***, in Lochaber district, 5m/8km NW of foot of Loch Arkaig. Height 2450 feet or 747 metres. **87 H5** NN1295.
Sgurr Choinnich *High.* ***Mountain***, peak on West Monar Forest, Ross and Cromarty district. Munro: height 3277 feet or 999 metres. **95 G7** NH0744.
Sgurr Chòinnich Mòr *High.* ***Mountain***, in Lochaber district 4m/6km E of Ben Nevis. Munro: height 3592 feet or 1095 metres. **87 J7** NN2271.
Sgurr Coire Choinnichean *High.* ***Mountain***, in Knoydart, Lochaber district, 2m/3km NE of Inverie. Height 2611 feet or 796 metres. **86 D4** NG7901.
Sgurr Coire nan Eun *High.* ***Mountain***, in Ross and Cromarty district 5m/8km N of lower end of Loch Monar. Height 2588 feet or 789 metres. **95 H7** NH1946.
Sgurr Coire nan Gobhar *High.* ***Mountain***, 3m/4km SE of Inverie, Lochaber district. Height 2424 feet or 739 metres. **86 E5** NM7997.
Sgurr Dearg *Arg. & B.* ***Mountain***, 4m/6km SW of Craignure, Mull. Height 2430 feet or 741 metres. **79 H4** NM6633.
Sgurr Dearg *High.* ***Mountain***, on Skye, peak of the Cuillin Hills. Munro: height 3234 feet or 986 metres. **85 K2** NG4421.
Sgurr Dhomhnuill *High.* ***Mountain***, in Ardgour, Lochaber district, 6m/10km NE of Strontian. Height 2913 feet or 888 metres. **79 K1** NM8867.
Sgurr Dhomhuill Mòr *High.* ***Mountain***, 3m/5km NE of Ardmolich, Lochaber district. Height 2339 feet or 713 metres. **86 D7** NM7475.
Sgurr Dubh *High.* ***Mountain***, peak in Coulin Forest, Ross and Cromarty district, 5m/8km SW of Kinlochewe. Height 2565 feet or 782 metres. **95 F6** NG9755.
Sgurr Dubh Mòr *High.* ***Mountain***, peak of Cuillin Hills on Skye. Munro: height 3096 feet or 944 metres. **85 K2** NG4520.
Sgurr Eilde Mòr *High.* ***Mountain***, on Mamore Forest in Lochaber district, 4m/6km NE of Kinlochleven. Munro: height 3306 feet or 1008 metres. **80 D1** NN2365.
Sgurr Eireagoraidh *High.* ***Mountain***, 3m/4km E of Mallaig. Height 1797 feet or 548 metres. **86 D5** NM7196.
Sgurr Fhuar-thuill *High.* ***Mountain***, on border of Inverness and Ross and Cromarty districts, 4m/6km NE of dam of Loch Monar. Munro: height 3441 feet or 1049 metres. **95 J7** NH2343.
Sgurr Fhuaran (Anglicised form: Scour Ouran.) *High.* ***Mountain***, peak on Kintail Forest (National Trust for Scotland) in Skye and Lochalsh district, 3m/5km SE of Shiel Bridge. One of the Five Sisters. Munro: height 3503 feet or 1068 metres. **87 F3** NG9716.
Sgurr Finnisg-aig *High.* ***Mountain***, in Leanachan Forest, 4m/6km SW of Spean Bridge. Height 2175 feet or 663 metres. **87 H7** NN1876.
Sgurr Fiona *High.* ***Mountain***, one of the peaks of An Teallach, in Ross and Cromarty district. Munro: height 3474 feet or 1059 metres. **95 G3** NH0683.
Sgurr Ghiubhsachain *High.* ***Mountain***, in Lochaber district, 4m/6km S of Glenfinnan. Height 2785 feet or 849 metres. **86 E7** NM8775.
Sgurr Marcasaidh *High.* ***Mountain***, in Ross and Cromarty district, 6m/10km NW of Contin. Height 1902 feet or 580 metres. **95 K5** NH3559.
Sgurr Mhic Bharraich *High.* ***Mountain***, on border of Lochaber and Skye and Lochalsh districts, 2m/3km SW of Shiel Bridge. Height 2562 feet or 781 metres. **87 F3** NG9117.
Sgurr Mhic Choinnich *High.* ***Mountain***, in Cuillin Hills, Skye, 1m/2km W of head of Loch Coruisk. Munro: height 3109 feet or 948 metres. **85 K2** NG4521.
Sgurr Mhòr *High.* ***Mountain***, a peak of Beinn Alligin. Munro: height 3231 feet or 985 metres. **94 E5** NG8661.
Sgurr Mhurlagain *High.* ***Mountain***, in Lochaber district, 3m/4km NE of head of Loch Arkaig. Height 2886 feet or 880 metres. **87 G5** NN0194.
Sgurr Mòr *High.* ***Mountain***, in Ross and Cromarty district 4m/6km NE of head of Loch Fannich. Munro: height 3641 feet or 1110 metres. **95 J4** NH2071.
Sgurr Mòr *High.* ***Mountain***, peak in Lochaber district between Loch Quoich and head of Glen Kingie. Munro: height 3290 feet or 1003 metres. **87 F5** NM9698.
Sgurr na Banachdich *High.* ***Mountain***, peak of Cuillin Hills on Skye. Munro: height 3165 feet or 965 metres. **85 K2** NG4422.
Sgurr na Cairbe *High.* ***Mountain***, in Inverness district, 2m/3km W of W end of Orrin Reservoir. Height 2394 feet or 730 metres. **95 J7** NH3046.
Sgurr na Ciche *High.* ***Mountain***, in Lochaber district 3m/4km SW of head of Loch Quoich. Munro: height 3411 feet or 1040 metres. **87 F5** NM9096.
Sgurr na Ciste Duibhe *High.* ***Mountain***, peak on Kintail Forest (National Trust for Scotland) in Skye and Lochalsh district, 4m/6km SE of Shiel Bridge. One of the Five Sisters. Munro: height 3369 feet or 1027 metres. **87 F3** NG9814.
Sgurr na Coinnich *High.* ***Mountain***, 3m/4km S of Kyleakin near E end of Skye. Height 2424 feet or 739 metres. **86 D2** NG7622.
Sgurr na Feartaig *High.* ***Inland physical feature***, mountain ridge rising to 2827 feet or 862 metres on Achnashellach Forest, Ross and Cromarty district. **95 G7** NH0545.
Sgurr na Greine *High.* ***Mountain***, 2m/3km N of head of Loch Doilet, Lochaber district. Height 1630 feet or 497 metres. **79 K1** NM8170.
Sgurr na h-Aide *High.* ***Mountain***, in Lochaber district 2m/3km NE of head of Loch Morar. Height 2818 feet or 859 metres. **86 E5** NM8893.
Sgurr na h-Eanchainne *High.* ***Mountain***, 3m/5km N of Sallachan Point, Lochaber district. Height 2394 feet or 730 metres. **80 A1** NM9965.
Sgurr na h-Iolaire *High.* ***Hill***, on Sleat peninsula, Skye, 2m/3km E of Tarskavaig. Height 958 feet or 292 metres. **86 C4** NG6109.
Sgurr na Lapaich *High.* ***Mountain***, peak in Inverness district, 1m/2km N of Loch Affric. Height 3398 feet or 1036 metres. **87 H2** NH1524.
Sgurr na Lapaich *High.* ***Mountain***, on border of Inverness and Ross and Cromarty districts, 5m/7km NW of dam of Loch Mullardoch. Munro: height 3772 feet or 1150 metres. **87 H1** NH1635.
Sgurr na Moraich *High.* ***Mountain***, peak on Kintail Forest (National Trust for Scotland) in Skye and Lochalsh district, 2m/3km E of Shiel Bridge. One of the Five Sisters. Height 2873 feet or 876 metres. **87 F3** NG9619.
Sgurr na Muice *High.* ***Mountain***, on border of Inverness and Ross and Cromarty districts 2m/4km NE of dam of Loch Monar. Height 2922 feet or 891 metres. **95 J7** NH2241.
Sgurr na Paite *High.* ***Mountain***, 4m/6km E of Lochailort, to S of Loch Eilt. Height 1059 feet or 323 metres. **86 E6** NM8281.
Sgurr na Ruaidhe (Also known as Sgurr Ruadh.) *High.* ***Mountain***, on border of Inverness and Ross and Cromarty districts, 4m/7km SW of head of Orrin Reservoir. Munro: height 3257 feet or 993 metres. **95 J7** NH2842.
Sgurr na Sgine *High.* ***Mountain***, peak on border of Lochaber and Skye and Lochalsh districts, 3m/5km N of Kinloch Hourn. Munro: height 3100 feet or 945 metres. **87 F3** NG9411.
Sgurr na Stri *High.* ***Mountain***, 4m/6km N of Elgol, and 1km E of Loch na Cuilce, Skye. Height 1630 feet or 497 metres. **86 B3** NG5019.
Sgurr nan Caorach *High.* ***Hill***, 1m/2km N of Aird of Sleat, Skye. Height 918 feet or 280 metres. **86 B4** NG5802.
Sgurr nan Ceannaichean *High.* ***Mountain***, peak on Glencarron and Glenuig Forest, Ross and Cromarty district. Munro: height 3001 feet or 915 metres. **95 G7** NH0848.
Sgurr nan Ceathreamhnan *High.* ***Mountain***, on border of Inverness and Ross and Cromarty districts, 6m/9km W of W end of Loch Affric. Munro: height 3775 feet or 1151 metres. **87 G2** NH0522.

Sgurr nan Clach Geala *High.* ***Mountain***, in Ross and Cromarty district 3m/5km NE of head of Loch Fannich. Munro: height 3585 feet or 1093 metres. **95 H4** NH1871.
Sgurr nan Cnamh *High.* ***Mountain***, 5m/8km NE of Strontian, Lochaber district. Height 2299 feet or 701 metres. **79 K1** NM8864.
Sgurr nan Coireachan *High.* ***Mountain***, in Lochaber district 3m/4km SE of head of Loch Morar. Munro: height 3136 feet or 956 metres. **87 F6** NM9088.
Sgurr nan Coireachan *High.* ***Mountain***, peak in Lochaber district 2m/4km S of head of Loch Quoich. Munro: height 3126 feet or 953 metres. **87 F5** NM9395.
Sgurr nan Conbhairean *High.* ***Mountain***, peak on border of Inverness and Skye and Lochalsh districts, 4m/7km NW of dam of Loch Cluanie. Munro: height 3641 feet or 1110 metres. **87 H3** NH1213.
Sgurr nan Each *High.* ***Mountain***, in Ross and Cromarty district, 2m/3km NE of head of Loch Fannich. Munro: height 3027 feet or 923 metres. **95 H5** NH1869.
Sgurr nan Eag *High.* ***Mountain***, S peak of Cuillin Hills on Skye. Munro: height 3031 feet or 924 metres. **85 K3** NG4519.
Sgurr nan Gillean *High.* ***Mountain***, peak of Cuillin Hills on Skye. Munro: height 3165 feet or 965 metres. **85 K2** NG4725.
Sgurr nan Gillean *High.* ***Mountain***, 1m/2km NE of Rubha nam Meirleach, Rum. Height 2506 feet or 764 metres. **85 J5** NM3893.
Sgurr of Eigg *High.* *Alternative name for An Sgurr, qv.*
Sgurr Ruadh *High.* *Alternative name for Sgurr na Ruaidhe, qv.*
Sgurr Sgiath Airigh *High.* ***Mountain***, peak in Lochaber district 2m/3km SW of Kinloch Hourn. Height 2890 feet or 881 metres. **87 F4** NG9205.
Sgurr Shalachain *High.* ***Mountain***, 2m/3km NE of Beinn Mheadhoin, Lochaber district. Height 1742 feet or 531 metres. **79 K2** NM8052.
Sgurr Thuilm *High.* ***Mountain***, on Skye, peak of the Cuillin Hills. Height 2883 feet or 879 metres. **85 K2** NG4324.
Sgurr Thuilm *High.* ***Mountain***, in Lochaber district 4m/6km SW of head of Loch Arkaig. Munro: height 3159 feet or 963 metres. **87 F6** NM9387.
Shabbington *Bucks.* ***Village***, 3m/4km NW of Thame. **21 K1** SP6606.
Shackerley *Shrop.* ***Hamlet***, 4m/7km E of Shifnal. **40 A5** SJ8106.
Shackerstone *Leics.* ***Village***, 6m/10km S of Ashby de la Zouch. **41 F5** SK3706.
Shackleford *Surr.* ***Village***, 3m/4km NW of Godalming. **22 C7** SU9345.
Shackleton *W.Yorks.* ***Hamlet***, on S side of Shackleton Moor, 2m/3km N of Hebden Bridge. SD9829.
Shacklewell *Gt.Lon.* ***Suburb***, in borough of Hackney, 4m/7km NE of Charing Cross. TQ3385.
Shade *W.Yorks.* ***Locality***, adjoining to SW of Todmorden. SD9323.
Shadfen *Northumb.* ***Settlement***, 2m/3km SE of Morpeth. **71 H5** NZ2285.
Shadforth *Dur.* ***Village***, 5m/7km E of Durham. **62 E2** NZ3441.
Shadingfield *Suff.* ***Village***, 4m/7km S of Beccles. **45 J7** TM4384.
Shadoxhurst *Kent* ***Village***, 4m/7km SW of Ashford. **14 E4** TQ9737.
Shadsworth *B'burn.* ***Suburb***, 2m/3km E of Blackburn town centre. SD7027.
Shadwell *Gt.Lon.* ***Suburb***, in borough of Tower Hamlets, 1m/2km E of Tower Bridge. TQ3580.
Shadwell *Norf.* ***Hamlet***, on S bank of River Thet, 4m/7km E of Thetford. 19c house in park, with large lake, to W. **44 D7** TL9383.
Shadwell *W.Yorks.* ***Village***, 5m/8km NE of Leeds city centre. SE3439.
Shaftenhoe End *Herts.* ***Hamlet***, SE of Barley, 4m/6km SE of Royston. TL4037.
Shaftesbury *Dorset* Population: 6203. ***Small town***, historic town on hillside overlooking Blackmoor Vale, 18m/29km W of Salisbury. Well-known for its steep cobbled street, Gold Hill. Medieval town had twelve churches, of which three remain. **9 H2** ST8622.
Shaftholme *S.Yorks.* ***Settlement***, 3m/4km NE of Adwick le Street. SE5708.
Shafton *S.Yorks.* ***Village***, 4m/7km NE of Barnsley. **51 F1** SE3910.
Shafton Two Gates *S.Yorks.* ***Locality***, adjoining to S of Shafton, 3m/4km SW of Hemsworth. SE3910.
Shaggie Burn *P. & K.* ***River***, flowing SE, then SW near Falls of Monzie, into Turret Burn, 1km NW of Crieff. **81 K5** NN8523.
Shaggs *Dorset* ***Locality***, 2m/4km S of Wool. SY8583.
Shakerley *Gt.Man.* ***Locality***, residential locality adjoining to N of Tyldesley. SD6903.
Shakespeare's Birthplace *Warks.* ***Historic house***, half-timbered house in Stratford-upon-Avon. Now a national memorial. **30 C3** SP1856.
Shalbourne *Wilts.* ***Village***, 4m/6km SW of Hungerford. **21 G5** SU3163.
Shalcombe *I.o.W.* ***Settlement***, 4m/6km SE of Yarmouth. **11 F6** SZ3985.
Shalden *Hants.* ***Village***, 2m/4km NW of Alton. **21 K7** SU6941.
Shalden Green *Hants.* ***Settlement***, 1m/2km N of Shalden. SU6943.
Shaldon *Devon* Population: 1581. ***Small town***, small resort on S side of River Teign estuary. Bridge connects with Teignmouth. **5 K3** SX9372.
Shalfleet *I.o.W.* ***Village***, 4m/6km E of Yarmouth. **11 F6** SZ4189.
Shalford *Essex* ***Village***, 5m/7km NW of Braintree. **34 B6** TL7229.
Shalford *Surr.* ***Village***, adjoining to S of Guildford. 18c water-mill (National Trust). **22 D7** TQ0047.
Shalford Green *Essex* ***Hamlet***, 4m/7km NW of Braintree. **34 B6** TL7127.
Shalloch *S.Ayr.* ***Mountain***, 4m/6km W of Loch Macaterick. Height 1778 feet or 542 metres. **67 H4** NX3792.
Shalloch on Minnoch *S.Ayr.* ***Mountain***, 9m/14km S of Straiton. Height 2522 feet or 769 metres. **67 H4** NX4090.
Shallowford *Devon* ***Settlement***, 3m/4km S of Lynton on Exmoor. **7 F1** SS7144.
Shallowford *Staffs.* ***Settlement***, 1m/2km S of Norton Bridge. SJ8729.
Shalmsford Street *Kent* ***Village***, 4m/6km SW of Canterbury. **15 F2** TR0954.
Shalmstry *High.* ***Settlement***, 2m/3km SE of Thurso. **105 G2** ND1264.
Shalom Hall *Essex* ***Historic house***, 19c house with collections of French furniture and porcelain and English portraits, at Lower Breton, 3m/5km NE of Tiptree. **34 D7** TL9418.
Shalstone *Bucks.* ***Village***, 4m/6km E of Brackley. **31 H5** SP6436.
Shalunt *Arg. & B.* ***Settlement***, on Bute, 5m/8km NW of Rothesay. **73 J3** NS0471.
Shalver *Gt.Man.* ***Suburb***, 2m/3km NE of Oldham town centre. SD9407.
Shambellie Grange *D. & G.* ***Settlement***, 1km N of New Abbey. **65 K4** NX9667.
Shamley Green *Surr.* ***Village***, 4m/7km SE of Guildford. **22 D7** TQ0343.
Shandon *Arg. & B.* Population: 1282. ***Hamlet***, on E shore of Gare Loch, 3m/5km S of Garelochhead. **74 A2** NS2586.
Shandwick *High.* ***Locality***, on Shandwick Bay, E coast of Ross and Cromarty district, 1km S of Balintore. **97 F4** NH8575.
Shandy Hall *N.Yorks.* ***Garden***, mid-15c house on W side of Coxwold, 4m/7km N of Easingwold and 15m/24km N of York. House was home of 18c parson Lawrence Sterne, author of 'Tristram Shandy', between 1860 and 1868. Includes walled garden containing old roses and a wild garden in an old quarry. **58 B2** SE5377.
Shangton *Leics.* ***Village***, 6m/9km N of Market Harborough. **42 A6** SP7196.
Shankend *Sc.Bord.* ***Settlement***, on Lang Burn, at foot of N end of Shankend Hill, 6m/10km S of Hawick. **70 A3** NT5205.
Shankhouse *Northumb.* ***Locality***, 3m/5km SW of Blyth. **71 H6** NZ2778.
Shanklin *I.o.W.* Population: 11,537. ***Town***, resort on Sandown Bay, 7m/11km SE of Newport and 2m/3km SW of Sandown. Town is separated from shore by a vertical cliff. **11 G6** SZ5881.
Shanklin Chine *I.o.W.* ***Valley***, steep-sided ravine including a 12 metre (40 feet) waterfall, 1km S of Shanklin. **11 G6** SZ5881.
Shannochie *N.Ayr.* ***Settlement***, at S end of Arran, 6m/10km SW of Lamlash. **66 D1** NR9721.
Shantron *Arg. & B.* ***Settlement***, by Finlas Water, 5m/7km NE of Helensburgh. **74 B2** NS3487.
Shantullich *High.* ***Settlement***, on Black Isle, 1km NW of Munlochy. **96 D6** NH6353.
Shanzie *P. & K.* ***Settlement***, 2m/3km NE of Alyth. **82 D2** NO2750.
Shap *Cumb.* ***Small town***, 9m/15km S of Penrith. 15c Keld Chapel is National Trust property. **61 G5** NY5615.
Shap Abbey *Cumb.* ***Ecclesiastical building***, remains of 13c-16c monastery (English Heritage), 1m/2km W of Shap. **61 G5** NY5615.
Shap Fells *Cumb.* ***Open space***, moorland to S of Wet Sleddale Reservoir, 4m/7km SW of Shap. **61 G6** NY5208.
Shap Summit *Cumb.* ***Other feature of interest***, highest point on London (Euston) to Carlisle railway line, 3m/4km S of Shap. Height 1036 feet or 316 metres. **61 G5** NY5615.
Shapinsay *Ork.* ***Island***, low-lying island of 10 square miles or 26 square km lying to N and E of Mainland, its SW corner being 1m/2km N of Car Ness across strait, The String, at W end of Shapinsay Sound. **107 E6** HY5017.
Shapinsay Sound *Ork.* ***Sea feature***, strait dividing Shapinsay from S of Mainland. **107 E6** HY5113.
Shapridge *Glos.* ***Locality***, 2m/3km NE of Cinderford. SO6716.
Shapwick *Dorset* ***Village***, on River Stour, 5m/7km SE of Blandford Forum. **9 J4** ST9301.
Shapwick *Som.* ***Village***, on N side of Polden Hills, 5m/8km W of Glastonbury. **8 D1** ST4138.
Sharcott *Wilts.* ***Settlement***, 1m/2km SW of Pewsey. SU1559.
Shard End *W.Mid.* ***Suburb***, 6m/9km E of Birmingham city centre. SP1588.
Shardlow *Derbys.* ***Village***, 6m/10km SE of Derby. Situated on River Trent and on Trent and Mersey Canal. **41 G2** SK4330.
Shareshill *Staffs.* ***Village***, 5m/9km NE of Wolverhampton. **40 B5** SJ9406.
Sharkham Point *Torbay* ***Coastal feature***, headland at S end of St. Mary's Bay, 1m/2km SE of Brixham. **5 K5** SX9354.
Sharlston *W.Yorks.* Population: 2448. ***Village***, 4m/7km E of Wakefield. **51 F1** SE3918.
Sharlston Common *W.Yorks.* ***Village***, 1m/2km NE of Crofton. SE3819.
Sharman's Cross *W.Mid.* ***Suburb***, 1m/2km W of Solihull town centre. SP1379.
Sharnal Street *Med.* ***Settlement***, 5m/8km NE of Strood. TQ7974.
Sharnbrook *Beds.* Population: 1984. ***Village***, 7m/12km NW of Bedford. **32 D3** SP9959.
Sharneyford *Lancs.* ***Settlement***, 1m/2km NE of Bacup. SD8824.
Sharnford *Leics.* ***Village***, 4m/6km SE of Hinckley. **41 G6** SP4891.
Sharnhill Green *Dorset* ***Hamlet***, 1km E of Buckland Newton and 8m/12km SW of Sturminster Newton. ST7005.
Sharoe Green *Lancs.* ***Suburb***, 2m/3km N of Preston. **55 J6** SD5332.
Sharow *N.Yorks.* ***Village***, 1m/2km E of Ripon across River Ure. **57 J2** SE3271.
Sharp Street *Norf.* ***Hamlet***, 1m/2km S of Catfield. TG3820.
Sharpenhoe *Beds.* ***Village***, 6m/10km N of Luton. Sharpenhoe Clappers (National Trust) to SE. **32 D5** TL0630.
Sharper's Head *Northumb.* ***Coastal feature***, headland 1km NE of Berwick-upon-Tweed. **77 J5** NU0054.
Sharperton *Northumb.* ***Hamlet***, 3m/5km SE of Alwinton. **70 E3** NT9503.
Sharpham *Som.* ***Settlement***, 3m/4km SW of Glastonbury. ST4737.
Sharpham House *Devon* ***Hamlet***, on W bank of River Dart, 2m/3km SE of Totnes. **5 J5** SX8257.
Sharpness *Glos.* ***Hamlet***, on River Severn estuary, 11m/18km W of Stroud. Terminus of The Gloucester and Sharpness Canal. Docks. **19 K1** SO6702.
Sharp's Green *Cambs.* ***Locality***, 1m/2km S of Kirtling. TL6855.
Sharpstone *B. & N.E.Som.* ***Hamlet***, adjoining to SW of Freshford, 4m/6km SE of Bath. ST7859.
Sharpthorne *W.Suss.* ***Village***, on a ridge, 1km E of West Hoathly. **13 G3** TQ3732.
Sharrington *Norf.* ***Village***, 3m/5km W of Holt. **44 E2** TG0336.
Sharston *Gt.Man.* ***Suburb***, 6m/9km S of Manchester city centre. SJ8388.
Shatterford *Worcs.* ***Village***, 4m/6km NW of Kidderminster. **39 G7** SO7981.
Shatterling *Kent* ***Settlement***, 1m/2km E of Wingham. TR2658.
Shaugh Prior *Devon* ***Village***, at SW corner of Dartmoor, 7m/11km NE of Plymouth. **5 F4** SX5463.
Shave Cross *Dorset* ***Settlement***, 5m/7km NW of Bridport. SY4198.
Shaver's End *W.Mid.* ***Locality***, 1km NW of Dudley town centre. SO9391.
Shavington *Ches.* Population: 4780. ***Village***, 2m/4km S of Crewe. **49 F7** SJ6951.
Shaw *Gt.Man.* Population: 19,348. ***Town***, market town, adjoining to S of Crompton, 3m/4km N of Oldham. Former cotton town. **49 J2** SD9308.
Shaw *N.Yorks.* ***Locality***, 3m/4km NE of Reeth. NZ0602.
Shaw *Swin.* ***Locality***, 2m/3km W of Swindon. **20 E3** SU1185.
Shaw *W.Berks.* ***Suburb***, NE of Newbury. **21 H5** SU4768.
Shaw *Wilts.* ***Village***, 2m/3km NW of Melksham. **20 B5** ST8865.
Shaw Green *Herts.* ***Settlement***, 4m/6km SE of Baldock. TL2932.
Shaw Green *Lancs.* ***Locality***, 4m/6km W of Chorley. SD5218.
Shaw Green *N.Yorks.* ***Settlement***, just S of Beckwithshaw, 3m/4km SW of Harrogate. SE2652.
Shaw Heath *Ches.* ***Suburb***, adjoining to NE of Knutsford. SJ7679.
Shaw Hill *D. & G.* ***Mountain***, on S side of Black Water of Dee, 5m/7km SW of New Galloway. Height 1263 feet or 385 metres. **65 F3** NX5872.
Shaw Mills *N.Yorks.* ***Village***, 2m/3km NW of Ripley. **57 H3** SE2562.
Shaw Side *Gt.Man.* ***Suburb***, adjoining to E of Shaw. SD9308.
Shawbost *W.Isles* *Anglicised form of Siabost, qv.*
Shawbury *Shrop.* Population: 2289. ***Village***, 7m/11km NE of Shrewsbury. Airfield to N. **38 E3** SJ5521.
Shawclough *Gt.Man.* ***Suburb***, 1m/2km NW of Rochdale town centre. **49 H1** SD8814.
Shawell *Leics.* ***Village***, 4m/7km NE of Rugby. **41 H7** SP5480.
Shawfield *Gt.Man.* ***Settlement***, 2m/3km NW of Rochdale town centre. SD8714.
Shawfield *Staffs.* ***Settlement***, 3m/4km SW of Longnor. SK0661.
Shawford *Hants.* ***Village***, on River Itchen, 3m/5km S of Winchester. **11 F2** SU4725.
Shawford *Som.* ***Settlement***, 1km SW of Rode and 4m/6km N of Frome. ST7953.
Shawforth *Lancs.* ***Hamlet***, 1m/2km N of Whitworth. **56 D7** SD8920.
Shawhead *D. & G.* ***Village***, 6m/10km W of Dumfries. **65 J3** NX8775.
Shawlands *Glas.* ***Suburb***, 3m/4km SW of Glasgow city centre. NS5661.
Shaw's Corner *Herts.* ***Historic house***, Edwardian villa in Ayot St. Lawrence, 3m/5km NE of Harpenden. Former home of playwright George Bernard Shaw; contains memorabilia and revolving summerhouse in which he used to write. **32 E7** TL1916.
Shaw's Hill *Sc.Bord.* ***Mountain***, 2m/3km S of Ettrickbridge. Height 1289 feet or 393 metres. **69 J1** NT3721.
Shaws Under Loch *Sc.Bord.* ***Lake/loch***, small loch 7m/12km NW of Hawick. **69 J2** NT3919.
Shawtonhill *S.Lan.* ***Settlement***, 4m/6km SE of East Kilbride. **74 E6** NS6749.
Shawwood *E.Ayr.* ***Locality***, adjoining to SE of Catrine. NS5325.
Sheanachie *Arg. & B.* ***Settlement***, at S end of Kintyre, 5m/7km NE of Southend. **66 B2** NR7512.
Sheandow *Moray* ***Settlement***, 3m/5km W of Dufftown. **89 K1** NJ2739.
Shear Cross *Wilts.* ***Settlement***, 3m/4km SW of Warminster. **20 B7** ST8542.
Shearington *D. & G.* ***Locality***, 7m/11km SE of Dumfries. **69 F7** NY0366.
Shearsby *Leics.* ***Village***, 4m/7km N of Husbands Bosworth. **41 J6** SP6290.
Sheaval *W.Isles* ***Hill***, 1m/2km E of Mingearraidh, South Uist. Height 731 feet or 223 metres. **84 C2** NF7627.

S

Shebbear *Devon* ***Village***, 7m/11km NE of Holsworthy. **6 C5** SS4309.

Shebdon *Staffs.* ***Hamlet***, 4m/7km N of Newport. **39 G3** SJ7625.

Shebster *High.* ***Settlement***, in Caithness district, 7m/11km SW of Thurso. **105 F2** ND0164.

Shedfield *Hants.* ***Village***, 3m/5km E of Botley. **11 G3** SU5513.

Shee Water *P. & K.* ***River***, rising from numerous streams flowing S from Grampian Mountains and flowing S from Spittal of Glenshee through Glen Shee to become Black Water about 5m/7km SE of Kirkmichael. **82 C1** NO1169.

Sheen *Staffs.* ***Village***, 3m/5km SE of Longnor. **50 D6** SK1161.

Sheep Hill *Dur.* ***Village***, 4m/6km S of Blaydon. NZ1757.

Sheep Island *Arg. & B.* ***Island***, small island off S coast of Kintyre across Sanda Sound, to N of Sanda Island. **66 B3** NR7305.

Sheep Island *Cumb.* ***Island***, small island on sandbank on E side of Isle of Walney, 4m/6km S of Barrow-in-Furness. **55 F3** SD2163.

Sheep Island *Pembs.* ***Island***, small island on E side of entrance to Milford Haven at S end of Castles Bay. **16 B4** SM8401.

Sheep Rock *Shet.* ***Coastal feature***, rocky promontory on E coast of Fair Isle, connected to Mainland by narrow neck of land. **108 A1** HZ2270.

Sheepbridge *Derbys.* ***Locality***, 3m/4km N of Chesterfield town centre. SK3774.

Sheepridge *W.Yorks.* ***Suburb***, 2m/3km N of Huddersfield town centre. SE1519.

Sheepscar *W.Yorks.* ***Suburb***, 1km NE of Leeds city centre. SE3034.

Sheepscombe *Glos.* ***Village***, 2m/3km E of Painswick. **29 H7** SO8910.

Sheepstor *Devon* ***Village***, on SW Dartmoor, 4m/7km SW of Princetown. **5 F4** SX5667.

Sheepwash *Devon* ***Village***, 4m/6km NW of Hatherleigh. **6 C5** SS4806.

Sheepwash *Northumb.* ***Locality***, on River Wansbeck, 2m/3km SW of Ashington. **71 H5** NZ2585.

Sheepway *N.Som.* ***Hamlet***, 2m/3km E of Portishead. **19 H4** ST4976.

Sheepy Magna *Leics.* ***Village***, 3m/4km NE of Atherstone. **41 F5** SK3301.

Sheepy Parva *Leics.* ***Hamlet***, to E of Sheepy Magna across River Sence. **41 F5** SK3301.

Sheering *Essex* ***Village***, 2m/3km E of Sawbridgeworth. **33 J7** TL5013.

Sheerness *Kent* Population: 11,653. ***Town***, port and resort at NW point of Isle of Sheppey. Former naval dockyard and barracks converted to industrial use. **25 F4** TQ9175.

Sheet *Hants.* ***Village***, 1m/2km NE of Petersfield. **11 J2** SU7524.

Sheffield *S.Yorks.* Population: 431,607. ***City***, on River Don, 144m/232km NW of London. Former centre of heavy steel industry, now largely precision steel and cutlery industries. University of Sheffield and Sheffield Hallam University. Various museums dedicated to Sheffield's industrial past. Meadowhall shopping centre and Sheffield City Airport, 3m/5km NE of city centre. **51 F4** SK3587.

Sheffield Botanical Gardens *S.Yorks.* ***Garden***, 1m/2km SW of Sheffield city centre. 19 acres, featuring original 19c range of conservatories designed by Robert Marnock, and a wide range of yews. **51 F4** SK3386.

Sheffield Bottom *W.Berks.* ***Settlement***, 1km S of Theale. **21 K5** SU6569.

Sheffield Green *E.Suss.* ***Settlement***, 2m/3km S of Danehill. **13 H4** TQ4125.

Sheffield Lane Top *S.Yorks.* ***Suburb***, 3m/4km N of Sheffield city centre. SK3691.

Sheffield Park Garden *E.Suss.* ***Garden***, 18c lansdcaped garden (National Trust) laid out by 'Capability' Brown, including lakes linked by cascades and waterfalls, 5m/8km E of Haywards Heath. Sheffield Park Station, 1km SW, is S terminus of Bluebell Railway which runs N to Horsted Keynes. **13 H4** TQ4124.

Shefford *Beds.* Population: 5695. ***Small town***, 9m/14km SE of Bedford. Site of Roman building at W end. **32 E5** TL1439.

Shefford Woodlands *W.Berks.* ***Hamlet***, 3m/5km NE of Hungerford. **21 G4** SU3673.

Sheigra *High.* ***Settlement***, near W coast of Sutherland district, 4m/6km NW of Kinlochbervie. **102 D2** NC1860.

Sheinton *Shrop.* ***Village***, 3m/4km N of Much Wenlock. **39 F5** SJ6103.

Shelderton *Shrop.* ***Hamlet***, 4m/6km SW of Craven Arms. **28 D1** SO4077.

Sheldon *Derbys.* ***Village***, 3m/4km W of Bakewell. **50 D6** SK1768.

Sheldon *Devon* ***Village***, 6m/9km NW of Honiton. **7 K5** ST1208.

Sheldon *W.Mid.* ***Suburb***, 6m/10km E of Birmingham city centre. **40 D7** SP1584.

Sheldon Manor *Wilts.* ***Historic house***, award-winning Plantagenet manor house dating from late 13c, 2m/3km W of Chippenham. Good collection of furniture and interesting garden which includes an edible plant maze. Medieval village it surrounded no longer exists. **20 B4** ST8874.

Sheldwich *Kent* ***Village***, 3m/5km S of Faversham. **15 F2** TR0156.

Sheldwich Lees *Kent* ***Hamlet***, to SE of Sheldwich, 3m/5km S of Faversham. TR0156.

Shelf *Bridgend* ***Hamlet***, 2m/3km E of Bridgend. SS9380.

Shelf *W.Yorks.* Population: 4237. ***Locality***, 4m/6km SW of Bradford. **57 G7** SE1228.

Shelfanger *Norf.* ***Village***, 3m/4km N of Diss. **45 F7** TM1083.

Shelfield *Warks.* ***Settlement***, 3m/4km SW of Henley-in-Arden. SP1262.

Shelfield *W.Mid.* Population: 7079. ***Locality***, 3m/4km NE of Walsall. **40 C5** SK0302.

Shelfield Green *Warks.* ***Settlement***, 1km SW of Shelfield. SP1261.

Shelford *Notts.* ***Village***, 6m/10km E of Nottingham. **41 J1** SK6642.

Shelford *Warks.* ***Settlement***, 3m/5km S of Hinckley. SP4288.

Shell Bay *Fife* ***Bay***, small bay on E side of Largo Bay, between Ruddons Point and Kincraig Point. NO4500.

Shell Green *Halton* ***Suburb***, 1m/2km NE of Widnes. SJ5386.

Shell Ness *Kent* ***Coastal feature***, headland at E extremity of Isle of Sheppey. **25 G5** TR0567.

Shell Top *Devon* ***Mountain***, in Dartmoor National Park, 5m/8km NW of Ivybridge. Height 1558 feet or 475 metres. **5 F4** SX5963.

Shellachan *Arg. & B.* ***Settlement***, on S shore of River Euchar, 3m/5km S of Kilmore. **79 K6** NM8720.

Shellachan *Arg. & B.* ***Settlement***, 3m/5km SE of Taynuilt. **80 B5** NN0326.

Shellag Point (Also known as Point Cranstal.) *I.o.M.* ***Coastal feature***, promontory on E coast, 3m/5km S of Point of Ayre. **54 D4** SC4699.

Shelland *Suff.* ***Settlement***, 3m/5km NW of Stowmarket. TM0060.

Shellbrook *Leics.* ***Hamlet***, 1km W of Ashby de la Zouch. SK3416.

Shellbrook Hill *Shrop.* ***Settlement***, 2m/3km SW of Overton. **38 C1** SJ3540.

Shelley *Essex* ***Hamlet***, 1m/2km N of Chipping Ongar. **23 J1** TL5505.

Shelley *Suff.* ***Hamlet***, 3m/4km S of Hadleigh. **34 E5** TM0338.

Shelley *W.Yorks.* Population: 2212. ***Village***, 5m/8km SE of Huddersfield. **50 E1** SE2011.

Shelley Far Bank *W.Yorks.* ***Locality***, 1km W of Shelley. SE2011.

Shellingford *Oxon.* ***Village***, 2m/4km SE of Faringdon. **21 G2** SU3193.

Shellow Bowells *Essex* ***Hamlet***, 4m/6km S of Leaden Roding. **24 C1** TL6007.

Shelsley Beauchamp *Worcs.* ***Village***, 7m/11km NE of Bromyard. **29 G2** SO7362.

Shelsley Walsh *Worcs.* ***Village***, 7m/11km NE of Bromyard. **29 G2** SO7263.

Shelswell *Oxon.* ***Settlement***, 5m/8km NE of Bicester. SP6030.

Shelter Stone (Gaelic form: Clach Dhian.) *Moray* ***Inland physical feature***, large block of granite at head of Loch Avon, which broke away from crags above and is estimated to weigh over 1300 tons. **89 H4** NJ0001.

Shelthorpe *Leics.* ***Suburb***, 1m/2km S of Loughborough town centre. SK5317.

Shelton *Beds.* ***Village***, 5m/7km E of Higham Ferrers. **32 D2** TL0368.

Shelton *Norf.* ***Hamlet***, 5m/8km N of Harleston. **45 G6** TM2291.

Shelton *Notts.* ***Village***, 10m/16km NW of Grantham. **42 A1** SK7844.

Shelton *Shrop.* ***Suburb***, in W part of Shrewsbury. **38 D4** SJ4513.

Shelton Green *Norf.* ***Settlement***, 1m/2km E of Shelton. **45 G6** TM2390.

Shelton Lock *Derby* ***Suburb***, 4m/6km SE of Derby city centre. SK3731.

Shelve *Shrop.* ***Village***, 7m/11km N of Bishop's Castle. **38 C6** SO3399.

Shelwick *Here.* ***Hamlet***, 2m/3km N of Hereford. **28 E4** SO5243.

Shelwick Green *Here.* ***Hamlet***, adjoining to E of Shelwick, 2m/3km NE of Hereford. SO5243.

Shenfield *Essex* ***Suburb***, E district of Brentwood. **24 C2** TQ6094.

Shenington *Oxon.* ***Village***, 6m/9km W of Banbury. **30 E4** SP3742.

Shenley *Herts.* Population: 2025. ***Village***, 5m/8km SE of St. Albans. **22 E1** TL1900.

Shenley Brook End *M.K.* ***Village***, in Milton Keynes, 3m/4km NW of Bletchley. **32 B5** SP8335.

Shenley Church End *M.K.* ***Village***, 2m/3km SW of Milton Keynes city centre. **32 B5** SP8336.

Shenley Fields *W.Mid.* ***Suburb***, 5m/8km SW of Birmingham city centre. SP0281.

Shenleybury *Herts.* ***Settlement***, 4m/7km SE of St. Albans. **22 E1** TL1801.

Shenmore *Here.* ***Hamlet***, 8m/12km W of Hereford. **28 C5** SO3938.

Shennanton *D. & G.* ***Settlement***, on River Bladnoch, 2m/3km NE of Kirkcowan. **64 D4** NX3463.

Shenstone *Staffs.* Population: 2798. ***Village***, 3m/5km S of Lichfield. Site of Roman building 1km N: finds at museum at Wall. **40 D5** SK1104.

Shenstone *Worcs.* ***Village***, 3m/5km SE of Kidderminster. **29 H1** SO8673.

Shenstone Woodend *Staffs.* ***Settlement***, 2m/3km S of Shenstone. **40 D5** SK1102.

Shenton *Leics.* ***Village***, 2m/4km SW of Market Bosworth. **41 F5** SK3800.

Shenval *Moray* ***Settlement***, 2m/3km N of Tomnavoulin. **89 K2** NJ2129.

Shepeau Stow *Lincs.* ***Hamlet***, 4m/7km E of Crowland. **43 G4** TF3012.

Shephall *Herts.* ***Suburb***, SE district of Stevenage. **33 F6** TL2522.

Shepherd's Bush *Gt.Lon.* ***Suburb***, in borough of Hammersmith and Fulham, 5m/8km W of Charing Cross. TQ2280.

Shepherd's Gate *Norf.* ***Locality***, 1m/2km S of Terrington St. Clement. TF5517.

Shepherd's Green *Oxon.* ***Hamlet***, 3m/5km W of Henley-on-Thames. **22 A3** SU7183.

Shepherd's Patch *Glos.* ***Hamlet***, on The Gloucester and Sharpness Canal, 4m/7km NE of Berkeley. SO7204.

Shepherdshield *Northumb.* ***Forest/woodland***, on S side of Wark Forest, 6m/9km N of Bardon Mill. **70 C6** NY7674.

Shepherdswell (Also known as Sibertswold.) *Kent* Population: 1810. ***Village***, 6m/9km NW of Dover. **15 H3** TR2548.

Shepley *W.Yorks.* Population: 2212. ***Village***, 3m/5km E of Holmfirth. **50 D2** SE1909.

Sheppardstown *High.* ***Settlement***, 4m/6km NW of Lybster. **105 H5** ND2039.

Shepperdine *S.Glos.* ***Settlement***, 5m/8km NE of Severn Road Bridge. **19 K2** ST6295.

Shepperton *Surr.* Population: 9554. ***Suburb***, on N bank of River Thames, opposite Walton-on-Thames. **22 D5** TQ0867.

Shepperton Green *Surr.* ***Suburb***, to NW of Shepperton. TQ0768.

Shepreth *Cambs.* ***Village***, 5m/8km NE of Royston. **33 G4** TL3947.

Shepshed *Leics.* Population: 12,961. ***Town***, industrial town, 4m/6km W of Loughborough. Formerly main industry was footwear and hosiery. **41 G4** SK4719.

Shepton Beauchamp *Som.* ***Village***, 3m/5km NE of Ilminster. **8 D3** ST4017.

Shepton Mallet *Som.* Population: 7581. ***Small town***, 18m/29km S of Bristol. Market place with 15c shambles. Church has splendid panelled wagon roof. **19 K7** ST6143.

Shepton Montague *Som.* ***Village***, 2m/4km S of Bruton. **9 F1** ST6731.

Shepway *Kent* ***Suburb***, SE district of Maidstone. **14 C2** TQ7753.

Sheraton *Hart.* ***Hamlet***, 5m/7km NW of Hartlepool. **63 F3** NZ4435.

Sherborne *Dorset* Population: 7606. ***Small town***, attractive stone-built town with many ancient buildings, 5m/8km E of Yeovil. Medieval abbey and adjacent school. To E, Sherborne Old Castle (English Heritage) and present castle in park beside Sherborne Lake. **9 F3** ST6316.

Sherborne *Glos.* ***Village***, 5m/8km W of Burford. **30 C7** SP1714.

Sherborne Abbey *Dorset* ***Ecclesiastical building***, church of former Benedictine abbey at Sherborne, dating mainly from 15c with good examples of fan vaulting. **9 F3** ST6315.

Sherborne Castle *Dorset* ***Historic house***, built at end of 16c by Sir Walter Raleigh, to SE of Sherborne Old Castle across Sherborne Lake, 5m/8km E of Yeovil. 50 acre lake is surrounded by grounds landscaped by 'Capability' Brown. **9 F3** ST6515.

Sherborne Causeway *Dorset* ***Locality***, 2m/3km W of Shaftesbury. ST8323.

Sherborne Old Castle *Dorset* ***Castle***, rectangular enclosed castle (English Heritage) originating in 12c, with L-plan great tower, to SE of Sherborne, 5m/8km E of Yeovil. Owned by Sir Walter Raleigh in late 16c. **9 F3** ST6416.

Sherborne St. John *Hants.* ***Village***, 3m/5km NW of Basingstoke. 2km NE, The Vyne (National Trust). **21 K6** SU6255.

Sherbourne *Warks.* ***Village***, 3m/5km SW of Warwick. **30 D2** SP2661.

Sherbourne Street *Suff.* ***Settlement***, to NW of Boxford, 5m/7km W of Hadleigh. TL9541.

Sherburn *Dur.* Population: 2832. ***Village***, 3m/5km E of Durham. **62 E2** NZ3142.

Sherburn *N.Yorks.* ***Village***, 11m/18km E of Malton. **59 F2** SE9576.

Sherburn Hill *Dur.* ***Village***, 1m/2km E of Sherburn. NZ3342.

Sherburn in Elmet *N.Yorks.* Population: 5396. ***Village***, 6m/10km S of Tadcaster. **57 K6** SE4933.

Sherburn Wold *N.Yorks.* ***Open space***, undulating ground to S of Sherburn, highest point of which is around 525 feet or 160 metres, with Sherburn Brow on its N side. **59 F2** SE9674.

Shere *Surr.* ***Locality***, parish and village, 5m/8km E of Guildford. **22 D7** TQ0747.

Shereford *Norf.* ***Hamlet***, 2m/3km W of Fakenham. **44 C3** TF8829.

Sherfield English *Hants.* ***Village***, 4m/6km W of Romsey. **10 D2** SU2922.

Sherfield on Loddon *Hants.* Population: 1233. ***Village***, 5m/8km NE of Basingstoke. **21 K6** SU6758.

Sherfin *Lancs.* ***Settlement***, 1m/2km N of Haslingden. SD7825.

Sherford *Devon* ***Village***, 3m/5km E of Kingsbridge. **5 H6** SX7744.

Sherford *Som.* ***Suburb***, S district of Taunton. ST2223.

Sheriff Hutton *N.Yorks.* ***Village***, 4m/6km NE of Strensall. Remains of 14c castle. **58 C3** SE6566.

Sheriff Muir (Also spelled Sheriffmuir.) *Stir.* ***Open space***, moor to E of Dunblane. Scene of indecisive battle in 1715 between government troops and those of Old Pretender. **81 K7** NN8303.

Sheriffhales *Shrop.* ***Village***, 3m/5km N of Shifnal. **39 G4** SJ7512.

Sheriffmuir *Stir.* *Alternative spelling of Sheriff Muir, qv.*

Sheringham *Norf.* Population: 7620. ***Small town***, coastal resort 22m/35km N of Norwich. Former fishing port with small flint-built fishermen's cottages and attractive Georgian buildings. **45 F1** TG1543.

Sherington *M.K.* ***Village***, 2m/3km NE of Newport Pagnell. **32 B4** SP8846.

Shermanbury *W.Suss.* ***Settlement***, 2m/3km N of Henfield. TQ2118.

Shernal Green *Worcs.* ***Settlement***, 2m/3km SE of Droitwich Spa. SO9161.

Shernborne *Norf.* ***Hamlet***, 6m/9km S of Hunstanton. **44 B2** TF7132.

Sherramore *High.* ***Settlement***, in valley of River Spey, 4m/6km W of Laggan. **88 C5** NN5593.

Sherrington *Wilts.* ***Village***, on River Wylye, 3m/5km SE of Heytesbury. **9 J1** ST9639.

Sherston *Wilts.* Population: 1202. ***Village***, 5m/8km W of Malmesbury. **20 B3** ST8586.

Sherwood *Notts.* ***Suburb***, 2m/3km N of Nottingham city centre. SK5743.
Sherwood Country Park *Notts.* ***Leisure/recreation***, country park in Sherwood Forest to N of Edwinstowe, 6m/10km NE of Mansfield. 450 acres of oak and birch trees, forming focal point of Robin Hood legend. Most famous landmark is huge 'Major Oak' which is claimed to be Robin Hood's favourite hideout. Sherwood Forest Amusement Park located at Edwinstowe entrance to park includes giant Astroglide. Visitor centre holds Robin Hood's Sherwood Forest exhibition. **51 J6** SK6267.
Sherwood Forest *Notts.* ***Forest/woodland***, ancient demesne of the Crown, lying between Nottingham and Worksop. Associated with the, perhaps legendary, exploits of Robin Hood. Still well-wooded in N part, known as The Dukeries and consisting of parks of Welbeck, Worksop, Clumber (National Trust) and Thoresby. **51 J6** SK6163.
Sherwood Green *Devon* ***Hamlet***, 4m/7km E of Great Torrington. **6 D3** SS5520.
Sheshader *W.Isles Anglicised form of Seisiadar, qv.*
Shetland Museum *Shet.* ***Other feature of interest***, museum in Lerwick town centre, Mainland, with local history artefacts. **109 D8** HU4741.
Shettleston *Glas.* ***Suburb***, 3m/5km E of Glasgow city centre. **74 E4** NS6464.
Shevington *Gt.Man.* Population: 5650. ***Suburb***, 3m/5km NW of Wigan. **48 E2** SD5408.
Shevington End *Essex* ***Hamlet***, 5m/8km W of Haverhill. TL5942.
Shevington Moor *Gt.Man.* ***Hamlet***, 1m/2km N of Shevington. **48 E1** SD5410.
Shevington Vale *Gt.Man.* ***Village***, 1m/2km NW of Shevington, 4m/6km NW of Wigan. SD5408.
Sheviock *Cornw.* ***Village***, 4m/7km W of Torpoint. **4 D5** SX3755.
Shewalton *N.Ayr.* ***Locality***, 3m/5km SE of Irvine. NS3436.
Shian Bay *Arg. & B.* ***Bay***, on NW coast of Jura, 3m/5km NW of entrance to Loch Tarbert. **72 D2** NR5287.
Shian Island *Arg. & B.* ***Island***, islet to N of Shian Bay on Jura. NR5288.
Shiant Islands *W.Isles* ***Island***, uninhabited group of islands and islets, 4m/6km off SE coast of Isle of Lewis. Garbh Eilean and Eilean an Tighe form one island as they are connected by a narrow neck of land. Eilean Mhuire lies 1km E. There are several islets to W. **93 K2** NG4198.
Shiaram Mòr *W.Isles* ***Island***, islet near W shore of West Loch Roag, W coast of Isle of Lewis. NB1036.
Shibden Hall *W.Yorks.* ***Historic house***, timber-framed house probably from early 15c, 2m/3km down Shibden Dale. **57 G7** SE0929.
Shibden Head *W.Yorks.* ***Hamlet***, at head of Shibden Dale, 2m/4km N of Halifax. SE0929.
Shibden Hill *Sc.Bord.* ***Mountain***, 3m/5km W of Hownam. Height 1007 feet or 307 metres. **70 C2** NT7319.
Shide *I.o.W.* ***Suburb***, 1m/2km S of Newport town centre. SZ5088.
Shiel *High.* ***River***, in Skye and Lochalsh district running NW down Glen Shiel to Shiel Bridge and head of Loch Duich. Kintail Forest (National Trust for Scotland) rises steeply from right bank. **87 F3** NG9319.
Shiel Bridge *High.* ***Village***, in Skye and Lochalsh district, at foot of Glen Shiel and at head of Loch Duich where A87 road crosses River Shiel. **87 F3** NG9318.
Shiel Burn *Moray* ***River***, rising to S of Knock Hill and flowing SW to join River Isla, 3m/4km NW of Milltown of Rothiemay. **98 D5** NJ5149.
Shiel Hill *S.Ayr.* ***Hill***, on N side of Arecleoch Forest, 3m/4km W of Barrhill. Height 754 feet or 230 metres. **67 F5** NX1981.
Shiel Hill *S.Ayr.* ***Mountain***, 2m/3km S of Loch Bradan. Height 1666 feet or 508 metres. **67 J4** NX4194.
Shiel Muir *Moray* ***Open space***, moorland 4m/6km SE of Buckie. **98 C4** NJ4760.
Shield Row *Dur.* ***Suburb***, to NE of Stanley. NZ2053.
Shield Water *Cumb. Alternative name for Black Burn, qv.*
Shieldaig *High.* ***Settlement***, in Ross and Cromarty district, 3m/4km S of Gairloch. **94 E4** NG8072.
Shieldaig *High.* ***Village***, on E shore of Loch Shieldaig, Ross and Cromarty district. **94 E6** NG8153.
Shieldaig Forest *High.* ***Open space***, deer forest in W part of Ross and Cromarty district to N of Upper Loch Torridon. **94 E5** NG8564.
Shieldaig Island *High.* ***Island***, small island (National Trust for Scotland) in Loch Shieldaig, Ross and Cromarty district, almost entirely covered in Scots pine. **94 E6** NG8154.
Shieldhall *Glas.* ***Suburb***, on S side of River Clyde, 4m/6km W of Glasgow city centre. NS5365.
Shieldhill *Falk.* Population: 2071. ***Village***, 2m/3km S of Falkirk. **75 G3** NS8976.
Shieldmuir *N.Lan.* ***Suburb***, 2m/3km SE of Motherwell. NS7755.
Shielfoot *High.* ***Settlement***, on W bank of River Shiel, 1m/2km NW of Acharacle. **86 C7** NM6670.
Shielhill *Angus* ***Hamlet***, 3m/5km NE of Kirriemuir. **83 F2** NO4257.
Shiels *Aber.* ***Locality***, comprises Mains of Shiels and Nether Shiels, 3m/4km SW of Sauchen. **90 E4** NJ6509.
Shifford *Oxon.* ***Settlement***, 5m/8km S of Witney. **21 G1** SP3701.
Shifnal *Shrop.* Population: 5893. ***Small town***, 7m/12km S of Newport. Many interesting buildings, and large church with very interesting Norman and medieval architecture. **39 G5** SJ7407.
Shilbottle *Northumb.* ***Village***, 3m/5km S of Alnwick. Medieval peel tower forms part of vicarage. **71 G3** NU1908.
Shilbottle Grange *Northumb.* ***Hamlet***, adjoining to E of Shilbottle. NU2008.
Shildon *Dur.* Population: 11,136. ***Town***, 2m/4km SE of Bishop Auckland. Former centre for railway carriage building and repair. Timothy Hackworth Victorian and Railway Museum includes working replica of engine. **62 D4** NZ2226.
Shill Moor *Northumb.* ***Mountain***, in Cheviot Hills, 4m/6km SE of The Cheviot. Height 1732 feet or 528 metres. **70 E2** NT9415.
Shillay *W.Isles* ***Island***, westernmost of Heisker Islands group. Lighthouse has been disused since World War II. **92 A5** NF5962.
Shillay *W.Isles* ***Island***, small uninhabited island 5m/8km SW of Toe Head, W coast of South Harris. **92 D2** NF8891.
Shillay Mòr *W.Isles* ***Island***, uninhabited island in Loch Sgioport, E coast of South Uist. NF8438.
Shillingford *Devon* ***Village***, 2m/3km NE of Bampton. **7 H3** SS9823.
Shillingford *Oxon.* ***Village***, 2m/4km N of Wallingford. **21 J2** SU5992.
Shillingford Abbot *Devon* ***Hamlet***, 3m/4km S of Exeter. SX9188.
Shillingford St. George *Devon* ***Village***, 3m/5km S of Exeter. **7 H7** SX9087.
Shillingstone *Dorset* ***Village***, in River Stour valley, 3m/5km SE of Sturminster Newton. **9 H3** ST8211.
Shillington *Beds.* ***Village***, 3m/5km SW of Shefford. **32 E5** TL1234.
Shillmoor *Northumb.* ***Settlement***, in Upper Coquetdale, where Barrow Burn joins River Coquet, 4m/6km NW of Harbottle. **70 D3** NT8807.
Shilstone *Devon* ***Settlement***, on E side of River Okement, 4m/6km N of Okehampton. **6 D5** SS6000.
Shilton *Oxon.* ***Village***, 3m/4km SE of Burford. **21 F1** SP2608.
Shilton *Warks.* ***Village***, 5m/9km NE of Coventry. **41 G7** SP4084.
Shilvinghampton *Dorset* ***Locality***, 4m/7km NW of Weymouth. SY6284.
Shimpling *Norf.* ***Hamlet***, 3m/5km NE of Diss. Site of Roman building 1m/2km NE. **45 F7** TM1583.
Shimpling *Suff.* ***Hamlet***, 3m/5km N of Long Melford. **34 C3** TL8651.
Shimpling Street *Suff.* ***Village***, 4m/7km N of Long Melford. **34 C3** TL8752.
Shin *High.* ***River***, in Sutherland district running S from foot of Loch Shin to Invershin, 4m/6km NW of Bonar Bridge. NH5796.
Shin Forest *High.* ***Forest/woodland***, 3m/5km S of Lairg in Sutherland district. **96 C1** NC5701.
Shincliffe *Dur.* ***Village***, 2m/3km SE of Durham. **62 D2** NZ2940.
Shiney Row *T. & W.* ***Locality***, 2m/3km NW of Houghton le Spring. **62 E1** NZ3252.
Shinfield *W'ham* ***Village***, 4m/6km S of Reading. **22 A5** SU7268.
Shingay *Cambs.* ***Settlement***, 5m/8km NW of Royston. **33 G4** TL3046.
Shingham *Norf.* ***Settlement***, 1km E of Beachamwell, 5m/8km NE of Stoke Ferry. TF7605.
Shingle Street *Suff.* ***Settlement***, on coast, 7m/11km SE of Woodbridge. **35 H4** TM3642.
Shining Tor *Derbys.* ***Mountain***, 3m/4km E of Walker Barn. Height 1834 feet or 559 metres. **49 J5** SJ9973.
Shinnel Water *D. & G.* ***River***, rising on Trostan Hill and running SE past Tynron, then NE to Scaur Water on SW side of Penpont. **68 C4** NX8494.
Shinner's Bridge *Devon* ***Settlement***, 2m/3km NW of Totnes. **5 H4** SX7862.
Shinness *High.* ***Locality***, on E shore of Loch Shin, Sutherland district, 6m/10km NW of Lairg. NC5314.
Shinness Lodge *High.* ***Settlement***, in Shinness locality, on NE shore of Loch Shin, Sutherland district. **103 H7** NC5314.
Shipbourne *Kent* ***Village***, 4m/6km N of Tonbridge. **23 J6** TQ5952.
Shipbrookhill *Ches.* ***Settlement***, 2m/3km SE of Northwich. SJ6771.
Shipdham *Norf.* Population: 2105. ***Village***, 4m/7km SW of East Dereham. **44 D5** TF9507.
Shipham *Som.* ***Village***, on W slope of Mendip Hills, 3m/4km N of Cheddar. **19 H6** ST4457.
Shiphay *Torbay* ***Suburb***, of Torbay, 2m/3km NW of Torquay harbour. **5 J4** SX8965.
Shiplake *Oxon.* ***Village***, on River Thames, 3m/4km S of Henley-on-Thames. **22 A4** SU7678.
Shiplake Row *Oxon.* ***Hamlet***, 1km W of Shiplake. SU7578.
Shipley *Northumb.* ***Settlement***, 3m/5km NW of Alnwick. **71 G2** NU1416.
Shipley *Shrop.* ***Settlement***, 7m/11km W of Wolverhampton. **40 A6** SO8095.
Shipley *W.Suss.* ***Village***, 4m/7km W of Cowfold. **12 E4** TQ1421.
Shipley *W.Yorks.* Population: 28,165. ***Town***, on River Aire and on Leeds and Liverpool Canal, 3m/5km NW of Bradford. **57 G6** SE1437.
Shipley Bridge *Devon* ***Settlement***, on River Avon, 2m/3km NW of South Brent. **5 G4** SX6862.
Shipley Bridge *Surr.* ***Hamlet***, 2m/3km SE of Horley. **23 G7** TQ3040.
Shipley Common *Derbys.* ***Suburb***, 1m/2km N of Ilkeston. SK4543.
Shipley Country Park *Derbys.* ***Leisure/recreation***, over 800 acres of parkland, lakes and woodland to SW of Shipley, 1m/2km S of Heanor. Walking and riding trails and bird hide at Mapperley Reservoir. **41 G1** SK4344.
Shipmeadow *Suff.* ***Village***, 3m/4km W of Beccles. **45 H6** TM3890.
Shippea Hill *Suff.* ***Settlement***, 8m/13km W of Brandon. TL6183.
Shipping *Pembs.* ***Locality***, adjoining to N of Begelly. SN1108.
Shippon *Oxon.* ***Village***, 1m/2km NW of Abingdon. **21 H2** SU4898.
Shipston on Stour *Warks.* Population: 3882. ***Small town***, market town, and former wool town, 12m/20km W of Banbury. **30 D4** SP2540.
Shipton *Glos.* ***Village***, 5m/9km NW of Northleach. **30 B7** SP0318.
Shipton *N.Yorks.* ***Village***, 5m/8km NW of York. **58 B4** SE5558.
Shipton *Shrop.* ***Village***, 6m/10km SW of Much Wenlock. **38 E6** SO5691.
Shipton Bellinger *Hants.* ***Village***, 6m/9km NE of Amesbury. **21 F7** SU2345.
Shipton Gorge *Dorset* ***Village***, 2m/4km SE of Bridport. **8 D5** SY4991.
Shipton Green *W.Suss.* ***Village***, 2m/3km NE of West Wittering. **12 B7** SZ8099.
Shipton Hall *Shrop.* ***Historic house***, 16c house with some interesting Tudor and Georgian features, 6m/10km E of Church Stretton. Built by Richard Lutwyche as dowry for his daughter marrying into Mytton family. **38 E6** SO5692.
Shipton Moyne *Glos.* ***Village***, 2m/4km S of Tetbury. **20 B3** ST8989.
Shipton Oliffe *Glos.* ***Hamlet***, adjoining Shipton, 5m/9km NW of Northleach. SP0318.
Shipton-on-Cherwell *Oxon.* ***Village***, 7m/11km N of Oxford. **31 F7** SP4716.
Shipton Solers *Glos.* ***Settlement***, adjoining to W of Shipton, 5m/9km NW of Northleach. SP0318.
Shipton-under-Wychwood *Oxon.* Population: 2785. ***Village***, 4m/6km NE of Burford. **30 D7** SP2717.
Shiptonthorpe *E.Riding* ***Village***, 2m/3km NW of Market Weighton. **58 E5** SE8543.
Shira *Arg. & B.* ***Locality***, near head of Glen Shira, 7m/11km NE of Inverary. **80 C6** NN1518.
Shira *Arg. & B.* ***River***, flowing SW from Loch Shira into Loch Fyne 1m/2km NE of Inveraray. **80 C6** NN1110.
Shirburn *Oxon.* ***Village***, 1m/2km NE of Watlington. **21 K2** SU6995.
Shirdley Hill *Lancs.* ***Hamlet***, 1m/2km W of Scarisbrick. **48 C1** SD3612.
Shire *Cumb.* ***Locality***, adjoining to NW of Ousby, 2m/3km N of Skirwith. NY6135.
Shire Lodge *Northants.* ***Suburb***, 2m/3km NW of Corby town centre. SP8790.
Shire Oak *W.Mid.* ***Locality***, 1m/2km S of Brownhills. **40 C5** SK0504.
Shirebrook *Derbys.* Population: 10,413. ***Town***, former mining town, 4m/7km N of Mansfield. Site of Roman building, 1km N of town centre. **51 H6** SK5267.
Shirecliffe *S.Yorks.* ***Suburb***, 2m/3km N of Sheffield city centre. SK3590.
Shiregreen *S.Yorks.* ***Suburb***, 3m/5km N of Sheffield city centre. SK3792.
Shirehall Museum *Norf.* ***Other feature of interest***, at Little Walsingham. Georgian courtroom with lock-up and local history exhibition. **44 D2** TF9336.
Shirehampton *Bristol* ***Suburb***, NW district of Bristol. **19 J4** ST5377.
Shiremoor *T. & W.* Population: 6054. ***Suburb***, 2m/4km W of Whitley Bay. **71 J6** NZ3171.
Shirenewton (Drenewydd Gelli-farch). *Mon.* ***Village***, 4m/6km W of Chepstow. **19 H2** ST4793.
Shireoaks *Notts.* ***Village***, 2m/3km NW of Worksop. **51 H4** SK5580.
Shirl Heath *Here.* ***Hamlet***, 4m/6km W of Leominster. **28 D3** SO4359.
Shirland *Derbys.* Population: 3339. ***Village***, 3m/5km S of Clay Cross. **51 G7** SK3958.
Shirlaw Pike *Northumb.* ***Mountain***, 3m/5km NE of Rothbury. Height 1010 feet or 308 metres. **71 F3** NU1003.
Shirley *Derbys.* ***Village***, 4m/7km E of Ashbourne. **40 E1** SK2141.
Shirley *Gt.Lon.* ***Suburb***, in borough of Croydon, 2m/3km E of Croydon town centre. **23 G5** TQ3565.
Shirley *Hants.* ***Settlement***, 4m/7km NE of Christchurch. **10 C5** SZ1798.
Shirley *S'ham.* ***Suburb***, 1m/2km NW of Southampton city centre. **11 F3** SU4013.
Shirley *W.Mid.* ***Suburb***, 2m/4km W of Solihull town centre. **30 C1** SP1178.
Shirley Heath *W.Mid.* ***Suburb***, 3m/4km SW of Solihull. SP1177.
Shirley Moor *Kent* ***Marsh/bog***, area of marshland forming N part of Rother Levels to E of Tenterden. **14 E4** TQ9232.
Shirley Warren *S'ham.* ***Suburb***, N district of Southampton. SU3914.
Shirleywich *Staffs.* ***Settlement***, 1m/2km SE of Weston. SJ9825.
Shirmers Burn *D. & G.* ***River***, flowing S into Loch Ken at Ringbane 3m/5km SW of New Galloway. **65 G3** NX6573.
Shirrell Heath *Hants.* ***Village***, 5m/8km N of Fareham. **11 G3** SU5714.
Shirwell *Devon* ***Village***, 4m/6km NE fo Barnstaple. **6 D2** SS5937.
Shirwell Cross *Devon* ***Hamlet***, to SW of Shirwell and 3m/5km NE of Barnstaple. **6 D2** SS5937.
Shiskine *N.Ayr.* ***Village***, on Arran, 1m/2km NE of Blackwaterfoot. **66 D1** NR9129.
Shittlehope *Dur.* ***Settlement***, 1m/2km SE of Stanhope. NZ0038.
Shivering Mountain *Derbys. Alternative name for Mam Tor, qv.*
Shobdon *Here.* ***Village***, 6m/10km W of Leominster. **28 C2** SO4062.
Shobley *Hants.* ***Settlement***, 3m/4km E of Ringwood. SU1806.
Shobnall *Staffs.* ***Locality***, 1km W of Burton upon Trent town centre. SK2323.
Shobrooke *Devon* ***Village***, 2m/3km NE of Crediton. **7 G5** SS8601.

Shochie Burn *P. & K.* ***River***, flowing SE to join Ordie Burn nearly 1km from confluence with River Tay, 4m/6km N of Perth. **82 B4** NO0930.
Shocklach *Ches.* ***Village***, 3m/5km NW of Malpas. **38 D1** SJ4349.
Shocklach Green *Ches.* ***Settlement***, 1km W of Shocklach. SJ4349.
Shoebury Ness *S'end* ***Coastal feature***, headland at mouth of River Thames estuary, 3m/5km E of Southend-on-Sea town centre. **25 F3** TQ9383.
Shoeburyness *S'end* ***Suburb***, E district of Southend-on-Sea, 4m/6km E of town centre and 1km NE of Shoebury Ness, headland at mouth of River Thames estuary. **25 F3** TQ9384.
Sholden *Kent* ***Suburb***, W of Deal. **15 J2** TR3552.
Sholing *S'ham.* ***Suburb***, E district of Southampton across River Itchen. **11 F3** SU4511.
Shona Beag *High.* ***Island***, E part of Eilean Shona, and joined to it by narrow neck of land. **86 C7** NM6673.
Shoot Hill *Shrop.* ***Settlement***, 5m/8km W of Shrewsbury. **38 D4** SJ4112.
Shooters Hill *Gt.Lon.* ***Suburb***, in borough of Greenwich, 1m/2km S of Woolwich and 9m/15km E of Charing Cross. **23 H4** TQ4376.
Shooting House Hill *Cumb.* ***Mountain***, in moorland area 3m/4km NW of Ulverston. Height 1089 feet or 332 metres. **55 F1** SD2581.
Shop *Cornw.* ***Village***, 6m/9km N of Bude. **6 A4** SS2214.
Shop *Cornw.* ***Village***, 3m/4km W of Padstow. **3 F1** SW8873.
Shop Corner *Suff.* ***Settlement***, 3m/4km NW of Shotley Gate. **35 G5** TM2033.
Shop Street *Suff.* ***Village***, 1km W of Worlingworth. TM2268.
Shopford *Cumb.* ***Locality***, adjoining to S of Bewcastle. NY5674.
Shopnoller *Som.* ***Hamlet***, 1km SW of West Bagborough. ST1632.
Shore *Gt.Man.* ***Village***, adjoining to W of Clough, 1km NW of Littleborough. SD9216.
Shoreditch *Gt.Lon.* ***Suburb***, in borough of Hackney, 1m/2km N of London Bridge. **23 G3** TQ3382.
Shoreham *Kent* ***Village***, on River Darent, 4m/7km N of Sevenoaks. Site of Roman building downstream to N. **23 J5** TQ5161.
Shoreham-by-Sea *W.Suss.* Population: 17,332. ***Town***, container port and resort at mouth of River Adur, 6m/10km W of Brighton. A major shipbuilding centre in Middle Ages. Airport to W. Marlpins Museum housed in building dating from Norman times. **13 F6** TQ2105.
Shoremill *High.* ***Settlement***, on S shore of Cromarty Bay, 3m/4km SW of Cromarty. **96 E5** NH7466.
Shoresdean *Northumb.* ***Settlement***, 4m/6km E of Norham. **77 H6** NT9546.
Shoreston Hall *Northumb.* ***Settlement***, 1m/2km NW of Seahouses. NU2032.
Shoreswood *Northumb.* ***Settlement***, 3m/4km E of Norham. **77 H6** NT9446.
Shoretown *High.* ***Settlement***, 6m/10km NE of Conon Bridge. **96 D5** NH6162.
Shorley *Hants.* ***Hamlet***, 1m/2km S of Cheriton. SU5826.
Shorncliffe *Kent* ***Suburb***, with military barracks 2m/3km W of Folkestone town centre. TR1935.
Shorncote *Glos.* ***Hamlet***, 3m/5km S of Cirencester. **20 D2** SU0296.
Shorne *Kent* ***Village***, 4m/6km SE of Gravesend. **24 C4** TQ6971.
Shorne Ridgeway *Kent* ***Village***, adjoining to S of Shorne, 4m/6km SE of Gravesend. **24 C4** TQ6970.
Short Cross *Powys* ***Settlement***, 3m/5km SE of Welshpool. **38 B5** SJ2605.
Short Green *Norf.* ***Settlement***, 4m/7km N of Diss. **44 E7** TM0986.
Short Heath *Derbys.* ***Hamlet***, 1km E of Overseal. **41 F4** SK3015.
Short Heath *W.Mid.* ***Locality***, 4m/7km N of Birmingham city centre. **40 C6** SP0993.
Short Island *Cornw.* ***Island***, off N coast, 1km NW of Trevalga. SX0790.
Shorta Cross *Cornw.* ***Settlement***, 4m/6km NE of Looe. SX2957.
Shortacombe *Devon* ***Settlement***, 1m/2km NE of Lydford. **6 D7** SX5286.
Shortbridge *E.Suss.* ***Hamlet***, 1m/2km W of Uckfield. TQ4521.
Shortfield Common *Surr.* ***Settlement***, 3m/5km S of Farnham. SU8442.
Shortgate *E.Suss.* ***Settlement***, 6m/10km NE of Lewes. **13 H5** TQ4915.
Shortgrove *Essex* ***Settlement***, 2m/3km SW of Saffron Walden. **33 J5** TL5235.
Shorthampton *Oxon.* ***Settlement***, 2m/3km W of Charlbury. SP3220.
Shortheath *Hants.* ***Settlement***, adjoining to N of Oakhanger, 4m/6km SE of Alton. SU7736.
Shortlands *Gt.Lon.* ***Suburb***, to W of Bromley town centre. TQ3968.
Shortlanesend *Cornw.* ***Village***, 2m/3km NW of Truro. **3 F4** SW8047.
Shorton *Torbay* ***Suburb***, N district of Paignton. SX8862.
Shortroads *Renf.* ***Suburb***, N district of Paisley. NS4765.
Shortstanding *Glos.* ***Hamlet***, 2m/3km N of Coleford. SO5713.
Shortstown *Beds.* ***Hamlet***, 2m/4km SE of Bedford. TL0746.
Shorwell *I.o.W.* ***Village***, 5m/8km SW of Newport. **11 F6** SZ4582.
Shoscombe *B. & N.E.Som.* ***Village***, 2m/3km NE of Radstock. **20 A6** ST7156.
Shotatton *Shrop.* ***Settlement***, 2m/3km W of Ruyton-XI-Towns and 6m/9km SE of Oswestry. SJ3622.
Shotesham *Norf.* ***Village***, 6m/10km S of Norwich. **45 G6** TM2499.
Shotgate *Essex* ***Suburb***, adjoining to E of Wickford. **24 D2** TQ7692.
Shotley *Northants.* ***Settlement***, adjoining to E of Harringworth, 6m/9km NE of Corby. SP9297.
Shotley *Suff.* ***Village***, on W side of River Orwell estuary, 7m/11km SE of Ipswich. **35 G5** TM2335.
Shotley Bridge *Dur.* ***Locality***, on River Derwent, adjoining to NW of Consett. **62 B1** NZ0952.
Shotley Gate *Suff.* ***Village***, at mouth of River Stour opposite Parkeston, 4m/6km W of Felixstowe. Mast of HMS Ganges, former naval training establishment, on E side of village opposite Harwich. **35 G5** TM2433.
Shotley Street *Suff.* ***Village***, 1m/2km NW of Shotley Gate and 7m/12km SE of Ipswich. TM2335.
Shotleyfield *Northumb.* ***Settlement***, 3m/5km NW of Consett. **62 B1** NZ0653.
Shotover Country Park *Oxon.* ***Leisure/recreation***, country park 4m/6km E of Oxford city centre. Both fallow and muntjac deer are amongst animals found in this park, formerly part of royal hunting forest. Still contains woodlands as well as heath, scrub and grassland. **21 J1** SP5605.
Shottenden *Kent* ***Village***, 7m/11km W of Canterbury. **15 F2** TR0454.
Shottermill *Surr.* ***Locality***, 1m/2km W of Haslemere. **12 B3** SU8832.
Shottery *Warks.* ***Suburb***, in W part of Stratford-upon-Avon, containing Anne Hathaway's Cottage. **30 C3** SP1854.
Shottesbrooke *W. & M.* ***Locality***, 3m/5km E of Twyford. SU8477.
Shotteswell *Warks.* ***Village***, 4m/6km NW of Banbury. **31 F4** SP4245.
Shottisham *Suff.* ***Village***, 4m/7km SE of Woodbridge across River Deben. **35 H4** TM3244.
Shottle *Derbys.* ***Hamlet***, 3m/4km NW of Belper. **51 F7** SK3149.
Shottlegate *Derbys.* ***Hamlet***, 2m/3km W of Belper. **41 F1** SK3247.
Shotton *Dur.* ***Settlement***, 3m/4km S of Sedgefield, on Shotton Beck and near site of ancient Shotton village. NZ3625.
Shotton *Dur.* ***Suburb***, in SW part of Peterlee. Hall is of late 18c. **63 F3** NZ4139.
Shotton *Flints.* Population: 11,659. ***Town***, on River Dee, adjoining to Queensferry. **48 C6** SJ3068.
Shotton *Northumb.* ***Settlement***, 2m/3km NE of Kirk Yetholm. **77 G7** NT8430.
Shotton *Northumb.* ***Settlement***, 1m/2km SE of Stannington. NZ2278.
Shotton Colliery *Dur.* Population: 4287. ***Locality***, 1m/2km NW of Shotton. **62 E2** NZ4040.
Shotts *N.Lan.* Population: 8756. ***Locality***, 6m/9km NE of Wishaw. **75 G4** NS8760.
Shotwick *Ches.* ***Village***, 5m/9km NW of Chester. Hall of 17c. **48 C5** SJ3371.
Shoughlaige-e-Caine *I.o.M.* ***Settlement***, 2m/3km S of Kirk Michael. **54 C5** SC3187.
Shouldham *Norf.* ***Village***, 6m/9km NE of Downham Market. **44 A5** TF6708.
Shouldham Thorpe *Norf.* ***Village***, 1m/2km SW of Shouldham. **44 A5** TF6708.
Shoulsbarrow Common *Devon* ***Open space***, moorland at E side of Exmoor, 1m/2km SE of Challacombe. **7 F2** SS6939.
Shoulton *Worcs.* ***Hamlet***, 4m/6km NW of Worcester. **29 H3** SO8158.
Shover's Green *E.Suss.* ***Locality***, 1m/2km SE of Wadhurst. **13 K3** TQ6530.
Shraleybrook *Staffs.* ***Settlement***, 1m/2km W of Audley. SJ7849.
Shrawardine *Shrop.* ***Village***, 6m/10km W of Shrewsbury. Scant remains of medieval castle. **38 C4** SJ4015.
Shrawley *Worcs.* ***Village***, 4m/7km S of Stourport-on-Severn. **29 H2** SO8064.
Shreding Green *Bucks.* ***Settlement***, 3m/5km E of Slough. TQ0281.
Shrewley *Warks.* ***Village***, 5m/8km NW of Warwick. **30 D2** SP2167.
Shrewsbury *Shrop.* Population: 64,219. ***Town***, busy county town, 39m/63km NW of Birmingham, in loop of River Severn. Many timber-framed buildings in town centre, and also some notable Tudor, Jacobean and Georgian buildings. Castle dates from 12c. Boys' public school, founded 1552. Birthplace of Charles Darwin, 1809. **38 D4** SJ4912.
Shrewsbury Abbey *Shrop.* ***Ecclesiastical building***, in Shrewsbury town centre. Founded in 1080. Interesting Perpendicular window in W tower. **38 D4** SJ4912.
Shrewsbury Castle *Shrop.* ***Castle***, in Shrewsbury town centre. Ruins of 11c castle built by Roger de Montgomery; 13c gatehouse put in by Henry III. **38 D4** SJ4812.
Shrewton *Wilts.* Population: 1780. ***Village***, on Salisbury Plain, 6m/9km W of Amesbury. **20 D7** SU0643.
Shrine of Our Lady of Walsingham *Norf.* ***Ecclesiastical building***, shrine at Little Walsingham commemorating apparition of Virgin Mary to local lady of manor in 1061. Major centre of pilgrimage from 1153 until Reformation. New Anglican shrine dates from 1930s and contains statue of Our Lady of Walsingham. **44 D2** TF9336.
Shripney *W.Suss.* ***Village***, 2m/3km N of Bognor Regis. **12 C6** SU9302.
Shrivenham *Oxon.* Population: 3567. ***Village***, 6m/10km NE of Swindon. Royal Military College of Science. **21 F3** SU2489.
Shropham *Norf.* ***Village***, 4m/7km W of Attleborough. **44 D6** TL9893.
Shropshire Union Canal ***Canal***, connecting River Mersey at Ellesmere Port with Staffordshire and Worcestershire Canal at Autherley Junction, near Wolverhampton. **38 B3** SJ4077.
Shroton *Dorset Alternative name for Iwerne Courtney, qv.*
Shrub End *Essex* ***Suburb***, in SW part of Colchester. **34 D6** TL9723.
Shrub Hill *Kent* ***Settlement***, 2m/3km SE of Whitstable town centre. TR1364.
Shucknall *Here.* ***Village***, 5m/8km E of Hereford. **28 E4** SO5842.
Shudy Camps *Cambs.* ***Village***, 3m/5km W of Haverhill. **33 K4** TL6244.
Shugborough *Staffs.* ***Historic house***, 17c-18c house (National Trust) in park, 5m/7km E of Stafford. **40 B3** SJ9922.
Shulishader *W.Isles Anglicised form of Siulaisiadar, qv.*
Shuna *Arg. & B.* ***Island***, sparsely inhabited island of about 2 square miles or 5 square km, lying 1m/2km SW of entrance to Loch Melfort on coast of Argyll and 1km E of Luing across Shuna Sound. **79 J7** NM7608.
Shuna Island *Arg. & B.* ***Island***, sparsely populated island of about 300 acres or 120 hectares in Loch Linnhe, near E shore to NW of Portnacroish. Ruined castle at S end. **80 A3** NM9149.
Shuna Point *Arg. & B.* ***Coastal feature***, headland at S end of Shuna. **79 J7** NM7606.
Shuna Sound *Arg. & B.* ***Sea feature***, sea passage dividing Shuna from Luing. **79 J7** NM7608.
Shurdington *Glos.* Population: 2242. ***Village***, 3m/5km SW of Cheltenham. **29 J7** SO9218.
Shurlock Row *W. & M.* ***Village***, 3m/5km SE of Twyford. **22 B4** SU8374.
Shurnock *Worcs.* ***Settlement***, 4m/7km NW of Alcester. SP0260.
Shurrery *High.* ***Locality***, in Caithness district, 8m/12km SW of Thurso. **105 F3** ND0357.
Shurrery Lodge *High.* ***Settlement***, on W bank of Loch Shurrery. **105 F3** ND0356.
Shurton *Som.* ***Village***, 8m/12km NW of Bridgwater. **7 K1** ST2044.
Shustoke *Warks.* ***Village***, 2m/3km NE of Coleshill. Shustoke Reservoir N of village. **40 E6** SP2290.
Shut End *W.Mid.* ***Locality***, 3m/5km W of Dudley town centre. SO9089.
Shut Heath *Staffs.* ***Hamlet***, 4m/6km W of Stafford. **40 A3** SJ8621.
Shute *Devon* ***Hamlet***, 3m/5km E of Crediton. SS8900.
Shute *Devon* ***Village***, 3m/5km W of Axminster. **8 B5** SY2597.
Shutford *Oxon.* ***Village***, 5m/7km W of Banbury. **30 E4** SP3840.
Shuthonger *Glos.* ***Hamlet***, 2m/3km N of Tewkesbury. **29 H5** SO8835.
Shutlanehead *Staffs.* ***Settlement***, 1m/2km NE of Whitmore. SJ8242.
Shutlanger *Northants.* ***Village***, 3m/4km E of Towcester. **31 J3** SP7249.
Shutt Green *Staffs.* ***Settlement***, 1m/2km NW of Brewood. SJ8709.
Shutter Rock *Devon* ***Coastal feature***, rocks at SW tip of Lundy Island, Great Shutter Rock and Little Shutter Rock. **6 A1** SS1343.
Shuttington *Warks.* ***Village***, 3m/5km E of Tamworth. **40 E5** SK2505.
Shuttlewood *Derbys.* ***Village***, 2m/3km N of Bolsover. **51 G5** SK4672.
Shuttlewood Common *Derbys.* ***Locality***, to N of Shuttlewood, 2m/3km N of Bolsover. SK4672.
Shuttleworth *Gt.Man.* ***Village***, 5m/7km N of Bury. **49 H1** SD8017.
Siabost (Anglicised form: Shawbost.) *W.Isles* ***Locality***, comprises settlements of New, South and North Shawbost, 4m/6km NE of Carloway, Isle of Lewis. **100 E3** NB2546.
Siadar Iarach (Anglicised form: Lower Shader.) *W.Isles* ***Village***, adjacent to Siadar Uarach, near NW coast of Isle of Lewis, between Barvas and Borve. **101 F2** NB3854.
Siadar Uarach (Anglicised form: Upper Shader). *W.Isles* ***Village***, adjacent to Siadar Iarach, near NW coast of Isle of Lewis, between Barvas and Borve. **101 F2** NB3854.
Sibbaldbie *D. & G.* ***Settlement***, on Dryfe Water, 4m/6km N of Lockerbie. **69 G5** NY1487.
Sibbertoft *Northants.* ***Village***, 3m/4km SE of Husbands Bosworth. Site of motte and bailey castle to NE. **41 J7** SP6882.
Sibdon Carwood *Shrop.* ***Village***, 1m/2km W of Craven Arms. **38 D7** SO4183.
Sibertswold *Kent Alternative name for Shepherdswell, qv.*
Sibford Ferris *Oxon.* ***Village***, 7m/11km W of Banbury. **30 E5** SP3537.
Sibford Gower *Oxon.* ***Village***, 7m/11km W of Banbury. **30 E5** SP3537.
Sible Hedingham *Essex* Population: 3947. ***Small town***, 3m/5km NW of Halstead. **34 B5** TL7834.
Sibley's Green *Essex* ***Settlement***, 2m/3km S of Thaxted. TL6128.
Siblyback Reservoir *Cornw.* ***Reservoir***, on S edge of Bodmin Moor, 4m/7km NW of Liskeard. **4 C3** SX2370.
Sibsey *Lincs.* ***Village***, 5m/7km NE of Boston. **53 G7** TF3550.
Sibsey Fen Side *Lincs.* ***Locality***, 1m/2km NW of Sibsey. TF3452.
Sibsey Trader Windmill *Lincs.* ***Other feature of interest***, restored brick-built, six-sail mill (English Heritage) dating from 1877, 1km W of Sibsey. **53 G7** TF3451.
Sibson *Cambs.* ***Hamlet***, 2m/3km SE of Wansford. **42 D6** TL0997.
Sibson *Leics.* ***Village***, 6m/9km N of Nuneaton. **41 F5** SK3500.
Sibster *High.* ***Settlement***, in Caithness district, 3m/4km NW of Wick. **105 J3** ND3252.
Sibthorpe *Notts.* ***Village***, 6m/9km SW of Newark-on-Trent. **42 A1** SK7645.
Sibton *Suff.* ***Locality***, 2m/3km W of Yoxford. Remains of 12c abbey. **35 H2** TM3669.
Sibton Green *Suff.* ***Settlement***, 1m/2km NE of Sibton. TM3671.

Siccar Point *Sc.Bord.* ***Coastal feature***, small rocky headland on North Sea coast, 3m/4km E of Cockburnspath. **77 G3** NT8171.
Sicklesmere *Suff.* ***Village***, 3m/4km SE of Bury St. Edmunds. **34 C3** TL8760.
Sicklinghall *N.Yorks.* ***Village***, 3m/4km W of Wetherby. **57 J5** SE3648.
Sid Cop *S.Yorks.* ***Locality***, adjoining to N of Cudworth. SE3809.
Sidbrook *Som.* ***Settlement***, 3m/5km NE of Taunton. ST2527.
Sidbury *Devon* ***Village***, 3m/5km N of Sidmouth. **7 K6** SY1391.
Sidbury *Shrop.* ***Village***, 5m/8km SW of Bridgnorth. **39 F7** SO6885.
Sidcot *N.Som.* ***Hamlet***, 2m/3km N of Axbridge. **19 H6** ST4257.
Sidcup *Gt.Lon.* ***Suburb***, in borough of Bexley, 5m/8km W of Dartford and 12m/19km SE of Charing Cross. **23 H4** TQ4671.
Siddal *W.Yorks.* ***Suburb***, 1m/2km S of Halifax town centre. SE1023.
Siddick *Cumb.* ***Locality***, 1m/2km N of Workington. NY0031.
Siddington *Ches.* ***Hamlet***, 5m/8km N of Congleton. **49 H5** SJ8470.
Siddington *Glos.* ***Village***, 1m/2km SE of Cirencester. **20 D2** SU0399.
Siddington Heath *Ches.* ***Settlement***, 1m/2km SW of Siddington. SJ8370.
Side of the Moor *Gt.Man.* ***Suburb***, adjoining to E of Bradshaw, 3m/4km NE of Bolton. SD7412.
Sidemoor *Worcs.* ***Suburb***, in N part of Bromsgrove. **29 J1** SO9571.
Sidestrand *Norf.* ***Village***, near coast, 3m/5km SE of Cromer. **45 G2** TG2639.
Sideway *Stoke* ***Locality***, 1m/2km S of Stoke-on-Trent city centre. SJ8743.
Sidford *Devon* ***Suburb***, of Sidmouth, 2m/3km N of sea front. **7 K6** SY1390.
Sidhean an Airgid *W.Isles* ***Mountain***, to E of Loch Seaforth, 6m/10km SW of Cearsiadar. Height 1250 feet or 381 metres. **100 E6** NB2513.
Sìdhean Mòr *High.* ***Mountain***, 4m/7km E of Arisaig, Lochaber district. Height 1971 feet or 601 metres. **86 D6** NM7286.
Sidhean na Raplaich *High.* ***Mountain***, in Morvern, Lochaber district, 2m/3km W of head of Loch Arienas. Height 1804 feet or 550 metres. **79 H2** NM6351.
Sidinish *W.Isles Anglicised form of Saighdinis, qv.*
Sidlaw Hills *P. & K.* ***Large natural feature***, range of hills on SE side of Strathmore, extending from Perth to vicinity of Forfar. Summit is Craigowl Hill, 1492 feet or 455 metres. **82 C5** NO2735.
Sidlesham *W.Suss.* ***Village***, 4m/6km N of Selsey. Site of Roman villa 2km S. **12 B7** SZ8598.
Sidley *E.Suss.* ***Suburb***, N district of Bexhill. **14 C7** TQ7309.
Sidlowbridge *Surr.* ***Settlement***, 2m/4km SW of Redhill. **23 F7** TQ2546.
Sidmouth *Devon* Population: 10,767. ***Town***, attractive S coast resort at mouth of River Sid, 13m/21km E of Exeter, with several Regency buildings. International Folk Festival every August. **7 K7** SY1287.
Sidown Hill *Hants.* ***Hill***, rising to over 260 metres, 2m/3km S of Highclere. **21 H6** SU4457.
Siefton *Shrop.* ***Settlement***, 3m/5km E of Craven Arms. **38 D7** SO4883.
Sigford *Devon* ***Settlement***, 3m/5km NE of Ashburton. **5 H3** SX7773.
Siggar Ness *Shet.* ***Coastal feature***, headland on SW coast of Mainland. **109 F10** HU3411.
Sigglesthorne *E.Riding* ***Village***, 3m/5km W of Hornsea. **59 H5** TA1646.
Sighthill *Edin.* ***Suburb***, of Edinburgh, 4m/7km SW of city centre. College of Commerce. NT1971.
Sighthill Industrial Estate *Edin.* ***Locality***, in Edinburgh, to W of Sighthill. NT1970.
Sighty Crag *Cumb.* ***Mountain***, to E of Bewcastle Fells, 6m/9km SW of Kielder Water. Height 1699 feet or 518 metres. **70 A5** NY6080.
Sigingstone *V. of Glam.* ***Hamlet***, 2m/4km SW of Cowbridge. **18 C4** SS9771.
Signet *Oxon.* ***Settlement***, 1m/2km S of Burford. SP2410.
Sike Moor *N.Yorks.* ***Open space***, moorland on W side of wooded area, 4m/6km N of Horton in Ribblesdale. **56 D2** SD8078.
Silbury Hill *Wilts.* ***Historic/prehistoric site***, ancient earthwork (English Heritage), 1m/2km S of Avebury. Largest artificial mound in Europe. **20 D5** SU1068.
Silchester *Hants.* ***Village***, 7m/11km N of Basingstoke, 1m/2km E, site of Roman town of Calleva. **21 K5** SU6262.
Silchester Roman City Walls *Hants.* ***Historic/prehistoric site***, one of best preserved Roman walls (English Heritage), 1km NE of Silchester and 8m/12km SW of Reading, dating from 2c-3c, with perimeter of one-and-a-half miles and with height reaching 14 foot in places. Also recently restored amphitheatre. **21 K5** SU6462.
Sileau Ruy *I.o.M.* ***Mountain***, 5m/8km E of Peel. Height 1571 feet or 479 metres. **54 C5** SC3282.
Sileby *Leics.* Population: 7190. ***Village***, 5m/8km SE of Loughborough. **41 J4** SK6015.
Silecroft *Cumb.* ***Village***, 3m/5km W of Millom. **54 E1** SD1381.
Silfield *Norf.* ***Settlement***, 1m/2km SE of Wymondham. **45 F6** TM1299.
Sili *V. of Glam. Welsh form of Sully, qv.*
Silian *Cere.* ***Settlement***, 2m/3km N of Lampeter. **26 E3** SN5751.
Silk Willoughby *Lincs.* ***Village***, 2m/3km S of Sleaford. **42 D1** TF0542.
Silkstead *Hants.* ***Settlement***, 1m/2km SE of Hursley. SU4424.
Silkstone *S.Yorks.* ***Village***, 4m/6km W of Barnsley. **50 E2** SE2905.
Silkstone Common *S.Yorks.* ***Village***, 1m/2km S of Silkstone. **50 E2** SE2905.
Silksworth *T. & W.* ***Suburb***, 3m/5km SW of Sunderland city centre. **62 E1** NZ3752.
Sill Field *Cumb.* ***Hamlet***, 1m/2km E of Endmoor, 5m/9km NW of Kirkby Lonsdale. SD5585.
Silloth *Cumb.* Population: 2942. ***Small town***, port on Solway Firth, 10m/15km NW of Wigton. **60 C1** NY1153.
Sills *Northumb.* ***Settlement***, 2m/3km NW of Rochester. **70 D3** NT8200.
Sillyearn *Moray* ***Settlement***, to SW of Knock Hill, 4m/7km SW of Cornhill. Sillyearn Wood on hill adjacent to SW. **98 D5** NJ5254.
Siloh *Carmar.* ***Settlement***, 2m/4km NW of Llandovery. SN7437.
Silpho *N.Yorks.* ***Hamlet***, 5m/8km NW of Scarborough. **63 J3** SE9692.
Silsden *W.Yorks.* Population: 6284. ***Small town***, in Airedale, 4m/6km N of Keighley across River Aire. **57 F5** SE0446.
Silsoe *Beds.* Population: 1553. ***Village***, 1m/2km S of Clophill. **32 D5** TL0835.
Silstwn *V. of Glam. Welsh form of Gileston, qv.*
Silton *Dorset* ***Hamlet***, 3m/4km NW of Gillingham. **9 G2** ST7829.
Silver End *Beds.* ***Hamlet***, 4m/6km NW of Shefford. TL1042.
Silver End *Essex* Population: 3438. ***Village***, planned village built in 1920s by Francis Crittal, philanthropic metal window manufacturer, 4m/6km SE of Braintree. **34 C7** TL8119.
Silver Green *Norf.* ***Settlement***, 6m/9km NW of Ditchingham. TM2593.
Silver Hill *E.Suss.* ***Settlement***, 1m/2km S of Hurst Green. **14 C5** TQ7425.
Silver Hill *E.Suss.* ***Suburb***, 1m/2km NW of Hastings town centre. **14 D6** TQ8010.
Silver Street *Kent* ***Settlement***, adjoining to W of Bredgar. TQ8760.
Silver Street *Som.* ***Hamlet***, 2m/4km E of Wellington. ST1721.
Silver Street *Som.* ***Hamlet***, 1m/2km NW of Keinton Mandeville. ST5432.
Silver Street *Som.* ***Locality***, contained within Curry Mallet, 5m/8km NW of Ilminster. ST3321.
Silverbank *Aber.* ***Suburb***, E district of Banchory, on N bank of River Dee. NO7196.
Silverburn *Midloth.* ***Hamlet***, 2m/3km W of Penicuik. **76 A4** NT2060.
Silvercraigs *Arg. & B.* ***Settlement***, 3m/4km SE of Lochgilphead. **73 G2** NR8984.
Silverdale *Lancs.* Population: 1551. ***Village***, 4m/6km NW of Carnforth. **55 H2** SD4675.
Silverdale *Staffs.* ***Suburb***, 2m/3km W of Newcastle-under-Lyme town centre. **40 A1** SJ8146.
Silverdale Green *Lancs.* ***Locality***, adjoining to E of Silverdale, 3m/5km NW of Carnforth. SD4675.
Silverdale RSPB Nature Reserve *Lancs.* ***Nature reserve***, on marshland between Silverdale and Yealand Conyers, 3m/5km N of Carnforth. Site for many breeding birds. **55 H2** SD4875.
Silvergate *Norf.* ***Hamlet***, 1m/2km NW of Aylsham. TG1727.
Silverknowes *Edin.* ***Suburb***, 3m/5km NW of Edinburgh city centre. NT2076.
Silverlace Green *Suff.* ***Settlement***, 3m/5km SE of Framlingham. TM3260.
Silverley's Green *Suff.* ***Settlement***, 1m/2km NW of Cratfield. **35 G1** TM2975.
Silvermoss *Aber.* ***Settlement***, 5m/8km SE of Fyvie. **91 G1** NJ8333.
Silverstone *Northants.* ***Village***, 3m/5km SW of Towcester. Motor-racing circuit to S. **31 H4** SP6744.
Silverstone Motor Racing Circuit *Northants.* ***Motor racing circuit***, venue for British Grand Prix, 1km S of Silverstone and 4m/7km SW of Towcester. **31 H4** SP6742.
Silverton *Devon* Population: 1222. ***Village***, 5m/8km SW of Cullompton. **7 H5** SS9502.
Silverton *W.Dun.* ***Suburb***, E district of Dumbarton. NS4075.
Silvertown *Gt.Lon.* ***Suburb***, in borough of Newham, on N bank of River Thames (Woolwich Reach). TQ4179.
Silverwell *Cornw.* ***Locality***, 2m/4km SE of St. Agnes. SW7448.
Silvington *Shrop.* ***Village***, 4m/7km NW of Cleobury Mortimer. **29 F1** SO6279.
Silwick *Shet.* ***Settlement***, 1km SE of Westerwick, Mainland. **109 B8** HU2942.
Simene *Dorset* ***River***, rising N of Filford, flowing S into River Brit in Bridport and into Lyme Bay. **8 D5** SY4692.
Simister *Gt.Man.* ***Village***, 2m/3km E of Whitefield. SD8305.
Simmondley *Derbys.* ***Suburb***, 1m/2km SW of Glossop. SK0293.
Simm's Cross *Ches.* ***Suburb***, to N of Widnes town centre. SJ5185.
Simon Fell *N.Yorks.* ***Open space***, moorland on E shoulder of Ingleborough, 3m/5km W of Horton in Ribblesdale. **56 C2** SD7574.
Simonburn *Northumb.* ***Village***, 7m/11km NW of Hexham. Slight remains of medieval castle in wood 1km W. **70 D6** NY8773.
Simons Burrow *Devon* ***Hamlet***, on Black Down Hills, 2m/3km N of Hemyock. ST1416.
Simon's Seat *Cumb.* ***Mountain***, in Howgill Fells, 5m/8km N of Sedburgh. Height 1925 feet or 587 metres. **61 H6** SD6699.
Simon's Seat *N.Yorks.* ***Mountain***, moorland summit 3m/5km E of Burnsall. Height 1591 feet or 485 metres. **57 F4** SE0859.
Simonsbath *Som.* ***Village***, on Exmoor, 7m/12km SE of Lynton. **7 F2** SS7739.
Simonside *Northumb.* ***Mountain***, in Northumberland National Park, 3m/5km SW of Rothbury. Height 1407 feet or 429 metres. **71 F4** NZ0298.
Simonside *T. & W.* ***Suburb***, 1m/2km SE of Jarrow. NZ3463.
Simonstone *Bridgend* ***Suburb***, 1m/2km E of Bridgend. SS9280.
Simonstone *Lancs.* ***Village***, adjoining to E of Read. **56 C6** SD7734.
Simonswood *Mersey.* ***Locality***, 2m/3km NE of Kirkby. SD4200.
Simprim *Sc.Bord.* ***Settlement***, 4m/6km N of Coldstream. **77 G6** NT8545.
Simpson *M.K.* ***Village***, in Milton Keynes 3m/4km SE of the centre. **32 B5** SP8836.
Simpson Green *W.Yorks.* ***Suburb***, 3m/5km NW of Bradford city centre. SE1838.
Sim's Hill *P. & K.* ***Mountain***, 6m/10km NE of Dollar, in Ochil Hills. Height 1581 feet or 482 metres. **82 A7** NN9907.
Sinclair Castle *High.* ***Castle***, early 17c castle, residence of Earls of Caithness, on S coast of Sinclair's Bay, 1km W of Noss Head. **105 J3** ND3754.
Sinclair's Bay *High.* ***Bay***, on E coast of Caithness district, extending N from Noss Head to Brough Head. **105 J3** ND3658.
Sinclair's Hill *Sc.Bord.* ***Settlement***, 3m/4km SE of Duns. **77 G5** NT8150.
Sinclairston *E.Ayr.* ***Settlement***, 2m/3km SE of Drongan. **67 J2** NS4716.
Sinclairtown *Fife* ***Suburb***, 2m/3km NE of Kirkcaldy town centre. NT2993.
Sinderby *N.Yorks.* ***Village***, 6m/10km SE of Bedale. **57 J1** SE3481.
Sinderhope *Northumb.* ***Settlement***, 2m/4km S of Allendale Town. **61 K1** NY8451.
Sinderland *Gt.Man.* ***Locality***, 1m/2km SE of Partington. SJ7390.
Sindlesham *W'ham* ***Village***, adjoining to S of Winnersh. **22 A5** SU7769.
Sinfin *Derby* ***Suburb***, 3m/4km S of Derby city centre. SK3532.
Singdean *Sc.Bord.* ***Settlement***, in Wauchope Forest area of Cheviot Hills, 4m/6km N of Saughtree. **70 A3** NT5801.
Single Street *Gt.Lon.* ***Settlement***, in borough of Bromley, 1m/2km E of Biggin Hill. TQ4359.
Singleton *Lancs.* ***Village***, 2m/4km E of Poulton-le-Fylde. **55 G6** SD3838.
Singleton *W.Suss.* ***Village***, below South Downs, 5m/9km N of Chichester. **12 B5** SU8713.
Singlewell (Also known as Ifield.) *Kent* ***Suburb***, S district of Gravesend. **24 C4** TQ6570.
Singret *Wrex.* ***Settlement***, 3m/5km N of Wrexham. SJ3455.
Sinkhurst Green *Kent* ***Settlement***, 2m/3km SW of Headcorn. TQ8142.
Sinnahard *Aber.* ***Locality***, 5m/9km S of Lumsden. **90 C3** NJ4713.
Sinnington *N.Yorks.* ***Village***, 4m/6km W of Pickering. **58 D1** SE7485.
Sinton Green *Worcs.* ***Hamlet***, 4m/7km NW of Worcester. **29 H2** SO8160.
Sior Loch *Arg. & B.* ***Lake/loch***, small loch in Argyll 8m/13km SE of Oban. **80 A5** NM9623.
Sipson *Gt.Lon.* ***Suburb***, in borough of Hillingdon, on N side of London Heathrow Airport and 14m/23km W of Charing Cross. **22 D4** TQ0777.
Sir Edward's Lake *Northumb. See Capheaton.*
Sir Harold Hillier Gardens *Hants.* ***Garden***, in Ampfield, 3m/5km NE of Romsey. Large collection of 20c plants belonging to Sir Harold Hillier, set in 166 acres of garden. Notable for colours in autumn. **10 E2** SU3723.
Sirhowy (Sirhywi). ***River***, rising N of Tredegar and flowing S by Tredegar and Blackwood into Ebbw River 1m/2km W of Risca. **18 E1** ST2291.
Sirhowy *B.Gwent* ***Locality***, 1km NE of Tredegar. **28 A7** SO1410.
Sirhowy Valley ***Valley***, carrying Sirhowy River SE from Tredegar to its confluence with Ebbw River at Crosskeys. **18 E1** SO1507.
Sirhowy Valley Country Park *Caerp.* ***Leisure/recreation***, 1000 acre country park based around disused railway in wooded area of Sirhowy Valley, 2m/4km NW of Machen. **18 E2** ST1891.
Sirhywi *Welsh form of Sirhowy (River), qv.*
Sisland *Norf.* ***Settlement***, 1m/2km W of Loddon. **45 H6** TM3498.
Sissinghurst *Kent* ***Village***, 1m/2km NE of Cranbrook. **14 C4** TQ7937.
Sissinghurst Castle Garden *Kent* ***Garden***, National Trust property surrounding Tudor house of Sissinghurst Castle, 1m/2km NE of Sissinghurst. Originally designed to be a perfectly English garden by Vita Sackville-West and Sir Harold Nicolson in 1930s, it contains themes including a white garden, Spring garden, wild garden and Nuttery. Gardens are dominated by a profusion of roses, including a fine old rose collection. **14 D4** TQ8038.
Siston *S.Glos.* ***Village***, 7m/11km E of Bristol. **19 K4** ST6875.
Sithean Achadh nan Eun *High.* ***Mountain***, 2m/3km S of Dalnessie, Sutherland district. Height 1040 feet or 317 metres. **103 J7** NC6311.
Sithean Bhealaich Chumhaing *High.* ***Mountain***, 3m/4km NE of Portree, Skye. Height 1286 feet or 392 metres. **94 B7** NG5046.
Sìthean Freiceadain *High.* ***Mountain***, 3m/4km SE of W end of Loch Craggie. Height 1594 feet or 486 metres. **103 J6** NC6323.
Sithney *Cornw.* ***Village***, 2m/3km NW of Helston. **2 D6** SW6329.
Sithney Green *Cornw.* ***Hamlet***, 1km to E of Sithney. SW6429.
Sittaford Tor *Devon* ***Mountain***, 3m/4km N of Postbridge, in Dartmoor National Park. Height 1761 feet or 537 metres. **6 E7** SX6383.

Sittingborne and Kemsley Light Railway *Kent* ***Other feature of interest***, tourist narrow-gauge railway to NE of Sittingbourne. **25 F5** TQ9064.
Sittingbourne *Kent* Population: 38,771. ***Town***, old market town, 8m/13km E of Gillingham. **25 F5** TQ9063.
Siulaisiadar (Anglicised form: Shulishader.) *W.Isles* ***Village***, on Eye Peninsula, Isle of Lewis, 1m/2km NE of Garrabost. **101 H4** NB5335.
Six Ashes *Shrop.* ***Hamlet***, on border with Staffordshire, 5m/9km SE of Bridgnorth. **39 G7** SO7988.
Six Bells *B.Gwent* ***Locality***, adjoining to S of Abertillery. SO2203.
Six Hills *Leics.* ***Hamlet***, and road junction, 7m/11km W of Melton Mowbray. SK6420.
Six Mile Bottom *Cambs.* ***Village***, 6m/9km SW of Newmarket. **33 J3** TL5756.
Six Roads End *Staffs.* ***Settlement***, and junction, 1km S of Draycott in the Clay. SK1527.
Sixhills *Lincs.* ***Village***, 4m/7km E of Market Rasen. **52 E4** TF1787.
Sixmile Cottages *Kent* ***Settlement***, 6m/10km N of Hythe. **15 G3** TR1344.
Sixpenny Handley *Dorset* ***Village***, 5m/8km NW of Cranborne. **9 J3** ST9917.
Sixteen Foot Drain ***Other water feature***, fenland drainage channel connecting Forty Foot Drain, NE of Chatteris, with Middle Level Drain, S of Upwell. **43 H6** TF5000.
Sizergh Castle *Cumb.* ***Castle***, 14c castle (National Trust) with later additions, 3m/5km S of Kendal. Dutch, rose and limestone rock gardens, as well as extensive walks in grounds. **55 H1** SD4987.
Sizewell *Suff.* ***Settlement***, on coast, 2m/3km E of Leiston. Nuclear power station to N. **35 J2** TM4762.
Skail *High.* ***Settlement***, in Caithness district, 9m/15km S of Bettyhill. Chambered cairn and broch nearby. **104 C4** NC7146.
Skaill *Ork.* ***Locality***, on W coast of Mainland, between Bay of Skaill and Loch of Skaill, 4m/6km W of Dounby. **107 B6** HY2318.
Skaill *Ork.* ***Settlement***, on W side of Egilsay. HY4630.
Skaill *Ork.* ***Settlement***, on coast at E end of Mainland, 2m/3km S of Mull Head. **107 E7** HY5806.
Skara Brae *Ork.* ***Historic/prehistoric site***, remains of Neolithic settlement (Historic Scotland) on W coast of Mainland 4m/7km W of Dounby. **107 B6** HY2218.
Skares *Aber.* ***Settlement***, on NW side of Hill of Skares, 1m/2km NW of Kirkton of Culsalmond. **90 E1** NJ6334.
Skares *E.Ayr.* ***Village***, 3m/5km SW of Cumnock. **67 K2** NS5217.
Skarfskerry Point *High.* ***Coastal feature***, headland on N coast, 4m/6km SE of Dunnet Head. **105 H1** ND2574.
Skarpigarth *Shet.* ***Settlement***, to N of Voe of Footabrough, on W coast of Mainland. **109 A7** HU1950.
Skate Point *W.Isles* ***Coastal feature***, headland at W tip of Bearnaraigh. **84 A6** NL5480.
Skateraw *E.Loth.* ***Settlement***, 4m/7km SE of Dunbar. **77 F3** NT7375.
Skateraw Harbour *E.Loth.* ***Sea feature***, on rocky coast to NE of Skateraw. **77 F3** NT7375.
Skaw *Shet.* ***Settlement***, at head of small bay of Skaw Voe, on N coast of Whalsay, 1m/2km W of Skaw Taing. **109 E6** HU5966.
Skaw Taing *Shet.* ***Coastal feature***, headland at NE end of Whalsay. **109 F6** HU6066.
Skaylock Hill *Dur.* ***Mountain***, on Muggleswick Common, rising to NE of Waskerley Reservoir. Height 1342 feet or 409 metres. **62 B2** NZ0345.
Skea *Ork.* ***Coastal feature***, headland on N coast of Mainland. **106 B4** HY2930.
Skea Skerries *Ork.* ***Island***, rocks 1km off S coast of Bakie Skerry, Westray. **106 D3** HY4440.
Skeabost *High.* ***Locality***, on Skye, 5m/8km NW of Portree. **93 K7** NG4148.
Skeabrae *Ork.* ***Settlement***, 1m/2km NW of Dounby. Disused airfield to W. **106 B5** HY2720.
Skeckling *E.Riding* ***Locality***, adjoining to N of Burstwick. TA2228.
Skeeby *N.Yorks.* ***Village***, 2m/3km NE of Richmond. **62 C6** NZ1902.
Skeeby Beck *N.Yorks.* ***River***, rising to NW of Skeeby and flowing S to River Swale at Brompton-on-Swale. **62 C6** SE2199.
Skeffington *Leics.* ***Village***, 8m/13km W of Uppingham. **42 A5** SK7402.
Skeffling *E.Riding* ***Village***, on N side of River Humber estuary, 4m/7km SE of Patrington. **53 G1** TA3719.
Skeffling Clays *E.Riding* ***Coastal feature***, mud flat on N side of mouth of River Humber. **53 G1** TA3617.
Skegby *Notts.* ***Suburb***, 1m/2km N of Sutton in Ashfield. **51 H6** SK5060.
Skegness *Lincs.* Population: 15,149. ***Town***, coastal resort, 19m/30km NE of Boston. Formerly a fishing and agricultural village, it now provides many facilities for leisure and entertainment. **53 J6** TF5663.
Skelberry *Shet.* ***Settlement***, on Mainland, 1m/2km SE of Scousburgh. **109 G9** HU3916.
Skelberry *Shet.* ***Settlement***, on N shore of Dury Voe, 2m/3km E of Laxo, Mainland. HU4763.
Skelbo *High.* ***Settlement***, on S side of Loch Fleet, near E coast of Sutherland district, 4m/6km N of Dornoch. **96 E2** NH7995.
Skelbo Castle *High.* ***Castle***, ancient seat of the Sutherlands, to N of Skelbo on S side of Loch Fleet. **96 E2** NH7995.
Skelbo Street *High.* ***Settlement***, to SE of Skelbo. NH7994.
Skelbrooke *S.Yorks.* ***Village***, 3m/4km E of South Elmsall. SE5112.
Skelda Ness *Shet.* ***Coastal feature***, headland on Mainland, 6m/10km W of Scalloway across The Deeps. **109 C8** HU3041.
Skelding *N.Yorks.* ***Locality***, 4m/7km NE of Pateley Bridge. SE2169.
Skeldon *E.Ayr.* ***Locality***, on N bank of River Doon, comprising Skeldon Hills, Skeldon House and Skeldon Mains, 1m/2km E of Dalrymple. **67 H2** NS3813.
Skeldyke *Lincs.* ***Hamlet***, 4m/7km S of Boston. **43 G2** TF3337.
Skelfhill Pen *Sc.Bord.* ***Mountain***, 3m/4km SE of Teviothead. Height 1745 feet or 532 metres. **69 K3** NT4403.
Skellingthorpe *Lincs.* Population: 2776. ***Village***, 3m/5km W of Lincoln. **52 C5** SK9272.
Skellister *Shet.* ***Settlement***, near E coast of Mainland, at head of South Nesting Bay. **109 D7** HU4654.
Skellorn Green *Ches.* ***Settlement***, 1m/2km S of Poynton. SJ9281.
Skellow *S.Yorks.* ***Locality***, 5m/8km NW of Doncaster. **51 H1** SE5310.
Skelly Rock *Aber.* ***Coastal feature***, rock on sands 2m/3km S of Balmedie. **91 H3** NJ9614.
Skelmanthorpe *W.Yorks.* Population: 3994. ***Small town***, 2m/3km N of Denby Dale. **50 E1** SE2310.
Skelmersdale *Lancs.* Population: 42,104. ***Town***, New Town, designated 1961, developed around former mining village. **48 D2** SD4806.
Skelmonae *Aber.* ***Settlement***, 2m/3km NE of Methlick. **91 G1** NJ8839.
Skelmorlie *N.Ayr.* Population: 1736. ***Small town***, resort on Firth of Clyde, adjoining to S of Wemyss Bay, and 5m/9km N of Largs. **73 K4** NS1967.
Skelmorlie Aisle *N.Ayr.* ***Historic/prehistoric site***, 1km SE of Largs. Fine mausoleum of 1636 with painted roof and interesting tombs and monuments. **74 A5** NS2158.
Skelmuir *Aber.* ***Settlement***, 2m/3km S of Stuartfield. **99 H6** NJ9842.
Skelmuir Hill *Aber.* ***Hill***, 3m/5km E of Auchnagatt. Height 489 feet or 149 metres. **99 H6** NJ9841.
Skelpick *High.* ***Hamlet***, in Caithness district, 4m/6km S of Bettyhill. NC7255.
Skelpick Burn *High.* ***River***, flowing NW to join River Naver 3m/4km S of Bettyhill, Caithness district. **104 C3** NC7157.
Skelsmergh *Cumb.* ***Locality***, 2m/4km NE of Kendal. SD5395.
Skelton *Cumb.* ***Village***, 6m/9km NW of Penrith. **60 F3** NY4335.
Skelton *E.Riding* ***Village***, on E bank of River Ouse, 2m/3km SE of Howden. **58 D7** SE7625.
Skelton *N.Yorks.* ***Settlement***, 5m/8km W of Richmond. **62 B6** NZ0900.
Skelton *N.Yorks.* ***Village***, 2m/4km NW of Boroughbridge. **57 J3** SE3668.
Skelton *R. & C.* Population: 5353. ***Village***, 2m/3km S of Saltburn. Castle of late 18c. **63 H5** NZ6518.
Skelton *York* ***Village***, 4m/6km NW of York. **58 B4** SE5656.
Skelton Castle *R. & C.* ***Castle***, 18c Gothic castle on W side of Skelton, built on site of Norman castle of King Robert I and frequented by Laurence Sterne. **63 H5** NZ6519.
Skelton Green *R. & C.* ***Hamlet***, 1km S of Skelton. **63 H5** NZ6518.
Skelton High Green *R. & C.* ***Locality***, 1km S of Skelton. NZ6518.
Skelton Wood End *Cumb.* ***Locality***, 3m/4km NW of Skelton. NY4038.
Skelwick *Ork.* ***Locality***, on Westray, 4m/6km SE of Pirowall. **106 D3** HY4844.
Skelwith Bridge *Cumb.* ***Hamlet***, 2m/4km W of Ambleside. **60 E6** NY3403.
Skendleby *Lincs.* ***Village***, 3m/5km NE of Spilsby. **53 H6** TF4369.
Skendleby Psalter *Lincs.* ***Hamlet***, 3m/5km SW of Alford. TF4371.
Skenfrith (Ynysgynwraidd). *Mon.* ***Village***, on River Monnow, 6m/9km NW of Monmouth. Remains of small 13c castle (National Trust). **28 D6** SO4520.
Skenfrith Castle *Mon.* ***Castle***, remains of small 13c castle (National Trust), 5m/8km NW of Monmouth. **28 D6** SO4520.
Skeoch Hill *D. & G.* ***Hill***, rising to over 270 metres, 1m/2km E of Glenkiln Reservoir and 7m/11km W of Dumfries. **65 J3** NX8678.
Sker Point (Y Sger). *Bridgend* ***Coastal feature***, headland 3m/4km NW of Porthcawl. SS7879.
Skerne ***River***, rising N of Trimdon and flowing E into Hurworth Burn Reservoir, then circuitously SW to Darlington and into River Tees at Croft-on-Tees. NZ2810.
Skerne *E.Riding* ***Village***, 2m/3km SE of Great Driffield. **59 G4** TA0455.
Skeroblingarry *Arg. & B.* ***Settlement***, on Kintyre, 3m/5km N of Campbeltown. **66 B1** NR7026.
Skerray *High.* ***Settlement***, near N coast of Caithness district, 6m/10km NE of Tongue. **103 J2** NC6563.
Skerry of Eshaness *Shet.* ***Island***, rocky island off S end of Esha Ness on NW coast of Mainland. HU2076.
Skerton *Lancs.* ***Suburb***, of Lancaster, N of River Lune. SD4763.
Skervuile *Arg. & B.* ***Island***, rock with lighthouse, lying 2m/4km off E coast of Jura opposite Lowlandman's Bay. NR6071.
Sketchley *Leics.* ***Suburb***, S district of Hinckley. SP4292.
Sketchley Hill *Leics.* ***Suburb***, SE district of Hinckley. SP4392.
Sketty *Swan.* ***Suburb***, 2m/3km W of Swansea city centre. **17 K5** SS6292.
Skeun *W.Isles* ***Hill***, 2m/3km W of head of Little Loch Roag, Isle of Lewis. Height 869 feet or 265 metres. **100 D5** NB1024.
Skewen (Sgiwen). *N.P.T.* ***Locality***, 2m/3km W of Neath. **18 A2** SS7296.
Skewsby *N.Yorks.* ***Hamlet***, 7m/11km N of Strensall. **58 C2** SE6271.
Skeyton *Norf.* ***Settlement***, 4m/6km E of Aylsham. **45 G3** TG2425.
Skeyton Corner *Norf.* ***Hamlet***, 3m/4km SW of North Walsham. TG2527.
Skiack *High.* *Anglicised form of Sgitheach, qv.*
Skibo Castle *High.* ***Castle***, built in 1898 by Andrew Carnegie on site of former castle, 4m/6km W of Dornoch. **96 E3** NH7389.
Skidbrooke *Lincs.* ***Settlement***, 1m/2km SW of Saltfleet. **53 H3** TF4492.
Skidbrooke North End *Lincs.* ***Settlement***, 1m/2km NW of Saltfleet. TF4494.
Skidby *E.Riding* ***Village***, 6m/10km NW of Kingston upon Hull. **59 G6** TA0133.
Skiddaw *Cumb.* ***Mountain***, in Skiddaw Forest, 4m/6km N of Keswick. Height 3054 feet or 931 metres. **60 D4** NY2629.
Skiddaw Forest *Cumb.* ***Large natural feature***, mountain region in Lake District, to N of Keswick, in which Skiddaw mountain is situated. **60 D4** NY2629.
Skigersta *W.Isles* *Anglicised form of Sgiogarstaigh, qv.*
Skilgate *Som.* ***Village***, on S slopes of Exmoor, 4m/6km NE of Bampton. **7 H3** SS9827.
Skillington *Lincs.* ***Village***, 2m/4km NW of Colsterworth. **42 C3** SK8925.
Skinburness *Cumb.* ***Village***, on Solway Firth, 2m/3km NE of Silloth. Site of small Roman fort at landward end of peninsula running out to Grune Point. **60 C1** NY1255.
Skinidin *High.* ***Settlement***, on Skye, 2m/3km W of Dunvegan across head of Loch Dunvegan. **93 H7** NG2247.
Skinners Green *W.Berks.* ***Settlement***, 2m/3km SW of Newbury. SU4465.
Skinnet *High.* ***Settlement***, 1m/2km N of Halkirk. **105 G2** ND1261.
Skinningrove *R. & C.* ***Locality***, on North Sea coast, 1m/2km NW of Loftus. **63 J4** NZ7119.
Skinsdale *High.* ***River***, in Sutherland district, running S from Borrobol Forest to Black Water, 11m/18km NW of Brora. **104 C6** NC7615.
Skip Bridge *Darl.* ***Settlement***, 3m/4km SE of Darlington. NZ3111.
Skipness *Arg. & B.* ***Village***, on Skipness Bay, on E coast of Kintyre, Argyll. **73 H5** NR9057.
Skipness Castle *Arg. & B.* ***Castle***, ruined 13c castle with later additions, 15m/24km SE of Tarbert on E coast of Kintyre. **73 H5** NR9057.
Skipness Point *Arg. & B.* ***Coastal feature***, headland at entrance to Loch Fyne, 1m/2km E of Skipness. **73 H5** NR9057.
Skipper Island *Essex* ***Island***, uninhabited marshy island 3m/5km W of The Naze. TM2124.
Skippool *Lancs.* ***Village***, adjoining to NE of Poulton-le-Flyde. SD3540.
Skiprigg *Cumb.* ***Settlement***, 3m/5km SE of Dalston. NY3845.
Skipsea *E.Riding* ***Village***, near coast, 5m/8km NW of Hornsea. Remains of motte and bailey castle (English Heritage). **59 H4** TA1655.
Skipsea Brough *E.Riding* ***Settlement***, 1km SW of Skipsea. TA1654.
Skipsea Castle *E.Riding* ***Castle***, motte surrounded by ditch and rampart (English Heritage), separated from bailey by a marsh, to W of Skipsea. Destruction of castle ordered by Henry III. **59 H4** TA1654.
Skipton *N.Yorks.* Population: 13,583. ***Town***, market town on River Aire and on Leeds and Liverpool Canal, 16m/26km NW of Bradford. There has been a settlement here since 7c. Interesting castle, which dominates town, dates from 11c but is mainly of 14c-15c. **56 E4** SD9851.
Skipton Castle *N.Yorks.* ***Castle***, in Skipton. Mostly 14c-17c, but one gateway of original Norman castle remains. **56 E4** SD9952.
Skipton-on-Swale *N.Yorks.* ***Village***, 4m/7km W of Thirsk. **57 J1** SE3679.
Skipwith *N.Yorks.* ***Village***, 5m/8km NE of Selby. **58 C6** SE6638.
Skirbeck *Lincs.* ***Locality***, 1m/2km SE of Boston. **43 G1** TF3443.
Skirbeck Quarter *Lincs.* ***Suburb***, 1m/2km S of Boston town centre. TF3242.
Skirfare *N.Yorks.* ***River***, rising on moors N of Pen-y-ghent and flowing SE through Halton Gill, Litton and Arncliffe into River Wharfe 2m/3km S of Kettlewell. Valley of River Skirfare is known as Littondale. SD9769.
Skirling *Sc.Bord.* ***Village***, 2m/4km E of Biggar. **75 J7** NT0739.
Skirmett *Bucks.* ***Village***, 5m/8km N of Henley-on-Thames. **22 A3** SU7790.
Skirpenbeck *E.Riding* ***Village***, 2m/4km E of Stamford Bridge. **58 D4** SE7155.
Skirrid Fawr *Mon.* *English form of Ysgyryd Fawr, qv.*
Skirts of Foudland *Aber.* *See Hill of Foudland.*
Skirwith *Cumb.* ***Village***, 7m/11km E of Penrith. **61 H3** NY6132.
Skirwith *N.Yorks.* ***Locality***, 1m/2km NE of Ingleton. **56 C2** SD7073.
Skirza *High.* ***Settlement***, near E coast of Caithness district, 3m/5km S of Duncansby Head. **105 J2** ND3868.
Skirza Head *High.* ***Coastal feature***, headland 1km E of Skirza. **105 J2** ND3868.
Skitby *Cumb.* ***Settlement***, 1km E of Smithfield and 4m/7km SE of Longtown. NY4465.
Skittle Green *Bucks.* ***Settlement***, 2m/3km W of Princes Risborough. SP7702.
Skokholm Island *Pembs.* ***Island***, off SW coast of Wales 2m/3km S of Skomer Island and 4m/7km W of St. Ann's Head. Bird sanctuary. **16 A4** SM7305.
Skomer Island *Pembs.* ***Island***, and nature reserve at S end of St. Brides Bay, opposite Wooltack Point and 11m/18km W of Milford Haven. **16 A4** SM7209.
Skronkey *Lancs.* ***Settlement***, 1m/2km SE of Pilling, 5m/8km W of Garstang. SD4147.

Skroo *Shet.* ***Coastal feature***, indentation on NE coast of Fair Isle. **108 A1** HZ2274.
Skuda Sound *Shet.* ***Sea feature***, sea passage between Uyea and S coast of Unst, to E of Clivocast. **108 F2** HP6000.
Skulamus *High.* ***Settlement***, on Skye, 1m/2km E of Broadford. **86 C2** NG6622.
Skullomie *High.* ***Settlement***, on Tongue Bay, Caithness district, 3m/5km NE of Tongue. **103 J2** NC6161.
Skutterskelfe *N.Yorks.* ***Locality***, 3m/4km W of Stokesley. NZ4807.
Skyborry Green *Shrop.* ***Settlement***, 2m/3km NW of Knighton. SO2674.
Skye *High.* ***Island***, largest of Hebridean islands, 535 square miles or 1386 square km, separated from Scottish mainland by Sound of Sleat between Kyleakin and Kyle of Lochalsh, here less than 1km in width. The coastline is much indented. The island is mountainous, with Cuillin Hills rising to 3257 feet or 993 metres, and climate is moist. **85 J1** NG4532.
Skye Green *Essex* ***Settlement***, 1m/2km SE of Coggeshall. TL8722.
Skye of Curr *High.* ***Settlement***, in Badenoch and Strathspey district, 1km SW of Dulnain Bridge. **89 G2** NH9924.
Skyre Burn *D. & G.* ***River***, rising on W slopes of Meikle Bennan and flowing S to Fleet Bay via Skyreburn Bay, 3m/4km SW of Gatehouse of Fleet. **65 F5** NX5754.
Skyreholme *N.Yorks.* ***Settlement***, 1m/2km E of Appletreewick. SE0660.
Skythorns *N.Yorks.* ***Settlement***, 1m/2km W of Grassington. SD9863.
Slack *Aber.* ***Settlement***, 4m/6km E of Gartly. **90 D1** NJ5730.
Slack *Derbys.* ***Settlement***, 3m/5km NE of Matlock. SK3362.
Slack (Also known as Heptonstall Slack.) *W.Yorks.* ***Settlement***, 1m/2km NW of Hebden Bridge. SD9728.
Slack Head *Cumb.* ***Locality***, surrounded by woodland, 1km SW of Beetham and 2m/3km S of Milnthorpe. SD4978.
Slack Side *W.Yorks.* ***Suburb***, 3m/4km SW of Bradford city centre. SE1330.
Slackcote *Gt.Man.* ***Settlement***, 2m/3km E of Shaw. SD9709.
Slackhall *Derbys.* ***Settlement***, 1km NE of Chapel-en-le-Frith. **50 C4** SK0781.
Slackhead *Moray* ***Settlement***, 2m/3km SW of Buckie. **98 C4** NJ4063.
Slackholme End *Lincs.* ***Settlement***, 1m/2km S of Hogsthorpe. TF5370.
Slad *Glos.* ***Village***, 2m/3km NE of Stroud. **20 B1** SO8707.
Slade *Devon* ***Hamlet***, 5m/9km NW of Honiton. ST1108.
Slade *Devon* ***Village***, 1m/2km SW of Ilfracombe. **6 D1** SS5046.
Slade *Pembs.* ***Hamlet***, 1m/2km NW of Haverfordwest. SM9316.
Slade *Swan.* ***Hamlet***, above Port Eynon Bay, on S coast of Gower peninsula, 1km SW of Oxwich. SS4885.
Slade End *Oxon.* ***Locality***, 2m/3km NW of Wallingford, adjoining to E of Brightwell-cum-Sotwell. SU5890.
Slade Field *Cambs.* ***Locality***, adjoining to N of Chatteris. TL3887.
Slade Green *Gt.Lon.* ***Suburb***, in borough of Bexley, 1m/2km SE of Erith and 14m/23km E of Charing Cross. **23 J4** TQ5276.
Slade Heath *Staffs.* ***Settlement***, 5m/8km N of Wolverhampton. SJ9206.
Slade Hooton *S.Yorks.* ***Hamlet***, 2m/3km S of Maltby. SK5289.
Slades Green *Worcs.* ***Settlement***, 3m/5km NW of Tewkesbury. SO8534.
Sladesbridge *Cornw.* ***Hamlet***, 2m/3km SE of Wadebridge. SX0171.
Slaggan Bay *High.* ***Bay***, W facing bay at entrance to Loch Ewe, Ross and Cromarty district, 4m/6km N of Aultbea. To E, ruined village of Slaggan. **94 E2** NG8394.
Slaggyford *Northumb.* ***Hamlet***, 5m/7km NW of Alston. **61 H1** NY6752.
Slaid Hill *W.Yorks.* ***Locality***, 1m/2km W of Shadwell, 5m/8km NE of Leeds city centre. SE3340.
Slaidburn *Lancs.* ***Village***, at confluence of River Hodder and Croasdale Brook, below Forest of Bowland, 7m/11km N of Clitheroe. **56 C4** SD7152.
Slains Castle *Aber.* ***Other feature of interest***, site of 19c castle, now demolished, on granite headland above Port Erroll, on E coast 7m/11km S of Peterhead. See also Old Castle of Slains. **91 K1** NK1036.
Slains Park *Aber.* ***Hamlet***, 3m/4km NE of Inverbervie. **91 G7** NO8575.
Slaithwaite *W.Yorks.* ***Town***, in steep-sided valley of River Colne, 4m/7km W of Huddersfield. **50 C1** SE0714.
Slaley *Derbys.* ***Hamlet***, 3m/4km SW of Matlock. SK2757.
Slaley *Northumb.* ***Village***, 5m/7km SE of Hexham. **62 A1** NY9757.
Slaley Forest *Northumb.* ***Forest/woodland***, to SW of Slaley, area planted with conifers. **62 A1** NY9757.
Slamannan *Falk.* Population: 1430. ***Village***, 5m/8km SW of Falkirk. **75 G3** NS8573.
Slapton *Bucks.* ***Village***, 3m/5km S of Leighton Buzzard. **32 C6** SP9320.
Slapton *Devon* ***Village***, 5m/9km SW of Dartmouth. **5 J6** SX8245.
Slapton *Northants.* ***Village***, 4m/6km W of Towcester. **31 H4** SP6446.
Slapton Ley *Devon* ***Lake/loch***, 1m/2km long freshwater lagoon behind Slapton Sands. Wildlife haunt. **5 J6** SX8245.
Slapton Sands *Devon* ***Coastal feature***, to E of Slapton, with raised sand and shingle beach backed by Slapton Ley, a freshwater lake. SX8244.
Slat Bheinn *High.* ***Mountain***, in Barrisdale Forest, 3m/4km NW of W end of Loch Quoich. Height 2299 feet or 701 metres. **87 F4** NG9102.
Slate Haugh *Moray* ***Settlement***, 3m/5km SE of Buckie. **98 C4** NJ4662.
Slatenber *N.Yorks.* ***Settlement***, 1m/2km SE of Ingleton. **56 C2** SD7172.
Slatepit Dale *Derbys.* ***Hamlet***, 3m/5km SW of Chesterfield. SK3468.
Slattadale *High.* ***Settlement***, on SW shore of Loch Maree, 6m/10km SE of Gairloch. **94 E4** NG8871.
Slattocks *Gt.Man.* ***Hamlet***, 3m/5km S of Rochdale. **49 H2** SD8808.
Slaty Law *N.Ayr.* ***Mountain***, 4m/6km E of Largs. Height 1584 feet or 483 metres. **74 A4** NS2661.
Slaugham *W.Suss.* ***Village***, 1m/2km S of Handcross. **13 F4** TQ2528.
Slaughden *Suff.* ***Locality***, at S end of Aldeburgh, on narrow neck of land separating River Alde estuary from sea. Slaughden Quay is anchorage for small craft. **35 J3** TM4655.
Slaughter Hill *Ches.* ***Suburb***, adjoining to S of Haslington, 2m/3km E of Crewe. SJ7355.
Slaughterford *Wilts.* ***Village***, 5m/8km W of Chippenham. **20 B4** ST8473.
Slawston *Leics.* ***Village***, 5m/9km NE of Market Harborough. **42 A6** SP7794.
Slay Pits *S.Yorks.* ***Locality***, 1m/2km E of Hatfield. SE6709.
Slea *Lincs.* ***River***, rising on Willoughby Heath, SW of Ancaster, and flowing E through Sleaford into River Witham 3m/4km S of Tattershall. TF2054.
Sleach Water *High.* ***River***, in Caithness district, flowing into Loch More 4m/7km E of Altnabreac. **105 F4** ND0746.
Sleaford *Hants.* ***Hamlet***, 5m/9km W of Hindhead. **12 B3** SU8038.
Sleaford *Lincs.* Population: 10,388. ***Town***, market town, 11m/18km NE of Grantham. Remains of 12c castle. Many interesting buildings, including 17c Cogglesford Mill. **42 D1** TF0645.
Sleagill *Cumb.* ***Hamlet***, 3m/5km NE of Shap. **61 G5** NY5919.
Sleap *Shrop.* ***Settlement***, 2m/4km SW of Wem. SJ4826.
Sleapford *Tel. & W.* ***Hamlet***, 3m/5km N of Wellington. **39 F4** SJ6315.
Sleapshyde *Herts.* ***Settlement***, 2m/4km SW of Hatfield. TL2006.
Sleat *High.* ***Locality***, parish and peninsula in SE Skye. Peninsula is connected to rest of island by isthmus between Loch Eishort and Loch na Dal and extends 14m/22km south-westwards to Point of Sleat, most southerly point of Skye. **86 C4** NG6309.
Slebech (Slebets). *Pembs.* ***Locality***, 5m/8km E of Haverfordwest. Park contains ruined church of Knights Templars. SN0314.
Slebets *Pembs.* *Welsh form of Slebech, qv.*
Sledge Green *Worcs.* ***Settlement***, 5m/8km W of Tewkesbury. **29 H5** SO8134.
Sledmere *E.Riding* ***Village***, 7m/12km NW of Great Driffield. **59 F3** SE9364.
Sledmere House *E.Riding* ***Historic house***, Georgian mansion in Sledmere, 7m/12km NW of Great Driffield. Seat of Sykes family, with grounds by 'Capability' Brown. **59 F3** SE9364.
Sleightholme Moor *Dur.* ***Open space***, moorland on S side of Stainmore Forest and over which The Pennine Way passes, 5m/8km N of Keld. **62 A6** NY9108.
Sleights *N.Yorks.* Population: 2061. ***Village***, running down to River Esk, 3m/5km SW of Whitby. **63 K6** NZ8607.
Sleights Moor *N.Yorks.* ***Open space***, moorland 2m/4km SW of Sleights. **63 K6** NZ8504.
Sléiteachal Mhòr *W.Isles* ***Hill***, 4m/6km W of head of Loch Erisort, Isle of Lewis. Height 813 feet or 248 metres. **100 E6** NB2118.
Sleningford *N.Yorks.* ***Locality***, 1m/2km SE of West Tanfield, 4m/7km NW of Ripon. Former village no longer exists. SE2777.
Slepe *Dorset* ***Settlement***, 4m/6km N of Wareham. **9 J5** SY9293.
Slerra *Devon* ***Hamlet***, 1km SW of Clovelly. SS3124.
Sletill Hill *High.* ***Hill***, in Sutherland district, 3m/5km NE of Forsinard. Height 918 feet or 280 metres. **104 E4** NC9246.
Sliabh Bainneach *Moray* ***Mountain***, 5m/8km NE of Dava. Height 1584 feet or 483 metres. **97 H7** NJ0741.
Slickly *High.* ***Settlement***, in Caithness district, 7m/11km SW of John o' Groats. **105 H2** ND2966.
Sliddery *N.Ayr.* ***Settlement***, near SW coast of Arran, 4m/6km SE of Blackwaterfoot. **66 D1** NR9322.
Slieau Curn *I.o.M.* ***Mountain***, 2m/3km E of Kirk Michael. Height 1151 feet or 351 metres. **54 C4** SC3490.
Slieau Dhoo *I.o.M.* ***Mountain***, 3m/4km E of Kirk Michael. Height 1391 feet or 424 metres. **54 C5** SC3589.
Slieau Freoaghane *I.o.M.* ***Mountain***, 2m/3km SE of Kirk Michael. Height 1601 feet or 488 metres. **54 C5** SC3488.
Slieau Lhean *I.o.M.* ***Mountain***, 2m/3km N of Laxey. Height 1538 feet or 469 metres. **54 D5** SC4287.
Slieau Managh *I.o.M.* ***Mountain***, 3m/4km S of Sueby. Height 1256 feet or 383 metres. **54 C4** SC3990.
Sliemore *High.* ***Settlement***, 2m/3km E of Nethy Bridge. **89 H2** NJ0320.
Sligachan *High.* ***Locality***, at head of Loch Sligachan, Skye, 8m/13km S of Portree. **85 K2** NG4829.
Sligga Skerry *Shet.* ***Island***, rock group lying off NW coast of Bigga, at S end of Yell Sound. HU4380.
Sligrachan Hill *Arg. & B.* ***Mountain***, in Argyll Forest Park, rising above E shore of Loch Eck. Height 1804 feet or 550 metres. **73 K1** NS1590.
Slimbridge *Glos.* ***Village***, 4m/6km N of Dursley. Wildfowl and Wetlands Trust nature reserve 1m/2km NW, near River Severn estuary. **20 A1** SO7403.
Slimbridge Wildfowl and Wetlands Trust *Glos.* ***Nature reserve***, on marshland at Slimbridge, on E side of Severn estuary, providing a sanctuary for migrant birds together with a permanent collection of waterfowl from around the world. **20 A1** SO7204.
Slindon *Staffs.* ***Village***, 2m/3km N of Eccleshall. **40 A2** SJ8232.
Slindon *W.Suss.* ***Village***, 4m/6km W of Arundel. 17c flint and brick cottages. Associations with Hillaire Belloc. **12 C6** SU9608.
Slindon Estate *W.Suss.* ***Other feature of interest***, 3521 acre or 1425 hectare estate (National Trust), 5m/9km N of Bognor Regis. Includes most of Slindon village, Slindon Park, Bignor Hill and a section of Roman road, Stane Street. Access by public footpaths and bridleways, with magnificent views. **12 C5** SU9608.
Slinfold *W.Suss.* ***Village***, 4m/6km W of Horsham. **12 E3** TQ1131.
Sling *Glos.* ***Village***, 3m/4km NE of St. Briavels. SO5807.
Slingley Hill *Dur.* ***Settlement***, 3m/5km W of Seaham. NZ3848.
Slingsby *N.Yorks.* ***Village***, 6m/10km W of Malton. **58 C2** SE6974.
Slioch *Aber.* ***Settlement***, 3m/4km SE of Huntly. **90 D1** NJ5638.
Slioch *High.* ***Mountain***, in Ross and Cromarty district 3m/5km N of head of Loch Maree. Munro: height 3214 feet or 980 metres. **95 G5** NH0068.
Slip End *Beds.* ***Village***, 2m/3km S of Luton. **32 D7** TL0718.
Slip End *Herts.* ***Settlement***, 2m/3km SE of Ashwell. **33 F5** TL2837.
Slipton *Northants.* ***Village***, 3m/5km W of Thrapston. **32 C1** SP9579.
Slitrig Water *Sc.Bord.* ***River***, a continuation of Lang Burn, flowing N to join River Teviot at Hawick. **70 A3** NT5014.
Slitting Mill *Staffs.* ***Hamlet***, 1m/2km SW of Rugeley. SK0217.
Sloc Caol *W.Isles* ***Sea feature***, small inlet on E coast of Eriskay, 1m/2km E of Haunn. **84 D3** NF8012.
Slochd *High.* ***Locality***, in Badenoch and Strathspey district, 4m/6km W of Carrbridge. **89 F2** NH8424.
Slochd Mòr *High.* ***Other feature of interest***, mountain pass on A9 between Aviemore and Inverness, 9m/13km NW of Aviemore. **89 F2** NH8325.
Slockavullin *Arg. & B.* ***Settlement***, in Argyll, 1m/2km SW of Kilmartin. Many prehistoric remains in vicinity. **73 G1** NR8297.
Slogarie Farm *D. & G.* ***Settlement***, 3m/4km NW of Laurieston. **65 G4** NX6567.
Sloley *Norf.* ***Hamlet***, 4m/6km S of North Walsham. **45 G3** TG2924.
Slongaber *D. & G.* ***Settlement***, 4m/6km NE of Corsock. **65 J3** NX8079.
Sloothby *Lincs.* ***Village***, 4m/7km SE of Alford. **53 H5** TF4970.
Slough *Slo.* Population: 110,708. ***Town***, commercial and industrial town on N side of River Thames valley, 21m/33km W of London. Developed in 19c with arrival of railway. Thames Valley University. **22 C4** SU9780.
Slough Green *Som.* ***Hamlet***, 2m/3km W of Hatch Beauchamp. ST2720.
Slough Green *W.Suss.* ***Hamlet***, 2m/3km NW of Cuckfield. TQ2826.
Slough Trading Estate *Slo.* ***Suburb***, NW district of Slough. SU9581.
Sluggan *High.* ***Settlement***, 6m/10km N of Aviemore. **89 F2** NH8721.
Sluggan Pass *High.* ***Other feature of interest***, mountain pass following course of Milton Burn past W slopes of Craigowrie, connecting Glenmore Forest Park with Strathspey. **89 G3** NH9414.
Slumbay *High.* ***Locality***, two adjoining localities, Easter and Wester Slumbay, on NW shore of Loch Carron to SW of Lochcarron, Ross and Cromarty district. NG8939.
Slungie Hill *P. & K.* ***Mountain***, in Ochil Hills, 3m/5km N of Carnbo. Height 1355 feet or 413 metres. **82 B7** NO0507.
Slwch Tump *Powys* *See Brecon.*
Slyfield Green *Surr.* ***Suburb***, 2m/3km N of Guildford. SU9952.
Slymaback ***Open space***, hillslope on border of Perth & Kinross and Stirling, 6m/9km NE of Doune. **81 J6** NN7510.
Slyne *Lancs.* ***Village***, 3m/4km N of Lancaster. **55 H3** SD4765.
Sma' Glen *P. & K.* ***Other feature of interest***, stony defile in Glen Almond, at SE edge of Highlands, 6m/9km N of Crieff. Traditional burial place of Ossian. **82 A4** NN9029.
Smailholm *Sc.Bord.* ***Village***, 5m/8km W of Kelso. **76 E7** NT6436.
Smailholm Tower *Sc.Bord.* ***Historic/prehistoric site***, well-preserved 16c tower on isolated hillock, beside small loch 1m/2km SW of Smailholm. Contains tapestries and costume figures. **76 E7** NT6436.
Small Dole *W.Suss.* ***Village***, 2m/3km S of Henfield. **13 F5** TQ2112.
Small Heath *W.Mid.* ***Suburb***, 3m/4km SE of Birmingham city centre. SP0985.
Small Hythe *Kent* ***Hamlet***, 2m/3km S of Tenterden. **14 D4** TQ8930.
Small Isles *Arg. & B.* ***Island***, group of small uninhabited islands off E coast of Jura between Rubha na Caillich and Rubh' an Leanachais. From S to N they are: Eilean nan Gabhar, Eilean nan Coinein, Eilean Dìomhain, Pladda and Eilean Bhrìde. **72 D4** NR5468.
Small Way *Som.* ***Settlement***, 1m/2km S of Castle Cary. ST6330.
Small Wood Hey *Lancs.* ***Locality***, adjoining to W of Pilling, 6m/10km W of Garstang. SD3948.
Smallacombe Downs *Cornw.* ***Open space***, forested hill area on SE side of Bodmin Moor, 4m/6km S of Altarnun. **4 C3** SX2275.
Smallbridge *Gt.Man.* ***Locality***, 2m/3km NE of Rochdale. **49 J1** SD9115.
Smallbrook *Devon* ***Hamlet***, 2m/3km SE of Crediton. SX8698.
Smallburgh *Norf.* ***Village***, 5m/8km SE of North Walsham. **45 H3** TG3324.

S

Smallburn *Aber.* ***Settlement***, 3m/5km NW of Hatton. **99 J6** NK0141.
Smallburn *E.Ayr.* ***Village***, 1km SW of Muirkirk. **68 B1** NS6826.
Smalldale *Derbys.* ***Hamlet***, just NE of Peak Dale, 3m/5km NE of Buxton. SK0977.
Smalldale *Derbys.* ***Locality***, 1m/2km SE of Castleton. SK1681.
Smalley *Derbys.* ***Village***, 6m/10km NE of Derby. **41 G1** SK4044.
Smalley Common *Derbys.* ***Settlement***, 1m/2km S of Smalley. SK4042.
Smalley Green *Derbys.* ***Settlement***, 1km S of Smalley. SK4043.
Smallfield *Surr.* Population: 2578. ***Village***, 2m/3km E of Horley. **23 G7** TQ3143.
Smallford *Herts.* ***Settlement***, 3m/4km E of St. Albans. TL1907.
Smallhythe Place *Kent* ***Historic house***, 15c half-timbered house (National Trust) 1m/2m S of Tenterden. Formerly home of Victorian actress, Ellen Terry. **14 D4** TQ8930.
Smallridge *Devon* ***Hamlet***, 2m/3km N of Axminster. **8 B4** ST3001.
Smallthorne *Stoke* ***Locality***, 1m/2km E of Burslem. **49 H7** SJ8850.
Smallworth *Norf.* ***Hamlet***, 1km S of Garboldisham. **44 E7** TM0080.
Smannell *Hants.* ***Hamlet***, 3m/4km N of Andover. **21 G7** SU3849.
Smardale *Cumb.* ***Settlement***, 3m/4km W of Kirkby Stephen. **61 J6** NY7308.
Smarden *Kent* ***Village***, 7m/11km SW of Charing. **14 D3** TQ8842.
Smaull *Arg. & B.* ***Settlement***, on NW coast of Islay, 9m/13km NW of Bridgend. **72 A4** NR2168.
Smeale *I.o.M.* ***Settlement***, 2m/3km N of Andreas. **54 D3** NX4102.
Smeatharpe *Devon* ***Hamlet***, 7m/11km N of Honiton. **7 K4** ST1910.
Smeaton *Fife* ***Suburb***, 1m/2km N of Kirkcaldy town centre. NT2893.
Smedlay *Gt.Man.* ***Suburb***, 1m/2km NE of Manchester city centre. SD8400.
Smedmore House *Dorset* ***Historic house***, early 17c manor house with walled garden 1km N of Kimmeridge Ledges on S coast of Isle of Purbeck, 2m/3km SW of Kingston. **9 J7** SY9278.
Smeeth *Kent* ***Village***, 5m/7km SE of Ashford. **15 F4** TR0739.
Smeeton Westerby *Leics.* ***Village***, 5m/8km NW of Market Harborough. **41 J6** SP6792.
Smelthouses *N.Yorks.* ***Settlement***, 2m/4km E of Pateley Bridge. **57 G3** SE1964.
Smerclett *W.Isles* ***Locality***, near S end of South Uist, 2m/3km NW of Ludag. NF7415.
Smerral *High.* ***Settlement***, near E coast of Caithness district, 1m/2km NW of Latheronwheel. **105 G5** ND1733.
Smestow *Staffs.* ***Hamlet***, 6m/9km SW of Wolverhampton. SO8591.
Smethwick *W.Mid.* Population: 72,771. ***Suburb***, 2m/3km NE of Warley town centre. **40 C7** SP0288.
Smethwick Green *Ches.* ***Settlement***, 4m/6km W of Congleton. SJ8063.
Smiddy Shaw Reservoir *Dur.* ***Reservoir***, on Muggleswick Common, 3m/5km SE of Edmundbyers. **62 B2** NZ0446.
Smigel Burn *High.* ***River***, in Sutherland district, flowing W into Halladale River, 2m/3km N of Dalhalvaig. **104 E3** NC8957.
Smirisary *High.* ***Settlement***, near coast of Lochaber district, 5m/8km NW of Kinlochmoidart. **86 C7** NM6477.
Smisby *Derbys.* ***Village***, 2m/3km N of Ashby de la Zouch. **41 F4** SK3519.
Smith End Green *Worcs.* ***Hamlet***, 5m/8km W of Worcester. **29 G3** SO7752.
Smith Green *Lancs.* ***Settlement***, 4m/7km S of Lancaster. SD4954.
Smith Sound *I.o.S.* ***Sea feature***, strait with St. Agnes to E and Annet and Hellweathers to W. **2 B2** SV8608.
Smithey Fen *Cambs.* ***Open space***, fenland 3m/5km E of Willingham. **33 H1** TL4570.
Smithfield *Cumb.* ***Hamlet***, 6m/10km NW of Brampton. **69 K7** NY4465.
Smithies *S.Yorks.* ***Suburb***, 1m/2km N of Barnsley town centre across River Dearne. SE3508.
Smithill's Hall *Gt.Man.* ***Historic house***, half-timbered 14c house in Bolton 2m/3km NW of town centre. **49 F1** SD7011.
Smithincott *Devon* ***Hamlet***, 1m/2km SW of Uffculme and 4m/6km NE of Cullompton. **7 J4** ST0611.
Smithley *S.Yorks.* ***Settlement***, 1m/2km W of Wombwell. SE3803.
Smith's End *Herts.* ***Hamlet***, S of Barley, 3m/5km SE of Royston. TL4037.
Smith's Green *Essex* ***Hamlet***, 4m/6km S of Haverhill. TL6740.
Smith's Green *Essex* ***Locality***, adjoining to E of Takeley, 4m/6km W of Great Dunmow. **33 J6** TL5621.
Smithstone *N.Lan.* ***Settlement***, 2m/3km W of Cumbernauld town centre. NS7275.
Smithstown *High.* ***Settlement***, on W coast of Ross and Cromarty district, 1km NW of Gairloch. NG7977.
Smithtown *High.* Population: 1530. ***Village***, in Inverness district, 3m/5km E of Inverness. **96 E7** NH7145.
Smithy Bridge *Gt.Man.* ***Locality***, on River Roch, 1m/2km SW of Littleborough, with Hollingworth Lake to E. SD9315.
Smithy Brow *Warr.* ***Locality***, adjoining to W of Croft. SJ6293.
Smithy Gate *Flints.* ***Settlement***, 1km SW of Holywell. SJ1775.
Smithy Green *Ches.* ***Settlement***, 6m/9km E of Northwich. **49 G5** SJ7474.
Smithy Green *Cumb.* ***Settlement***, 3m/5km N of Ulverston, adjoining to S of Penny Bridge. SD3082.
Smithy Green *Gt.Man.* ***Suburb***, 1m/2km W of Bramhall. SJ8785.
Smithy Houses *Derbys.* ***Hamlet***, 3m/4km E of Belper. SK3847.
Smithy Lane Ends *Lancs.* ***Settlement***, 3m/5km N of Ormskirk, on N side of Leeds and Liverpool Canal. SD4012.
Smockington *Leics.* ***Settlement***, 3m/5km SE of Hinckley. SP4589.
Smoky Row *Bucks.* ***Settlement***, 1m/2km N of Princes Risborough. SP8106.
Smoo Cave *High.* ***Cave***, large limestone cavern near N coast of Sutherland district, 1m/2km SE of Durness, containing waterfall from Allt Smoo. **103 G2** NC4167.
Smug Oak *Herts.* ***Locality***, 4m/6km NE of Watford. **22 E1** TL1302.
Smyrton *S.Ayr.* ***Settlement***, 2m/3km SE of Ballantrae. **67 F5** NX1080.
Smythe's Green *Essex* ***Hamlet***, 6m/10km SW of Colchester. **34 D7** TL9218.
Snab Point *Northumb.* ***Coastal feature***, headland on North Sea coast, 3m/5km N of Newbiggin-by-the-Sea. **71 J4** NZ3092.
Snaefell *I.o.M.* ***Mountain***, highest point on Isle of Man, 3m/5km NW of Laxey. Electric railway to summit. Views to England, Scotland, Wales and Ireland in clear weather. Height 2037 feet or 621 metres. **54 C5** SC3988.
Snaefell Mountain Railway *I.o.M.* ***Other feature of interest***, mountain railway takes electric tram on 4m/6km journey from Laxey to Snaefell, island's highest point, 2037 feet or 621 metres above sea level. **54 D5** SC4384.
Snailbeach *Shrop.* ***Hamlet***, 10m/16km SW of Shrewsbury. **38 C5** SJ3702.
Snailswell *Herts.* ***Settlement***, 2m/3km N of Hitchin. TL1732.
Snailwell *Cambs.* ***Village***, 3m/5km N of Newmarket. **33 K2** TL6467.
Snainton *N.Yorks.* ***Village***, 8m/12km E of Pickering. **59 F1** SE9282.
Snaip Hill *S.Lan.* ***Mountain***, 3m/5km S of Biggar. Height 1187 feet or 362 metres. **75 J7** NT0232.
Snaith *E.Riding* Population: 2748. ***Village***, 6m/10km W of Goole. **58 C7** SE6422.
Snake Pass *Derbys.* ***Other feature of interest***, pass over The Pennines, 3m/5km N of Kinder Scout, traversed by A57 road between Glossop and Ladybower Reservoir. Summit 1680 feet or 512 metres. **50 C3** SK0892.
Snape *N.Yorks.* ***Village***, 2m/4km S of Bedale. Castle, partly ruined Tudor house. **57 H1** SE2684.
Snape *Suff.* ***Village***, 3m/4km S of Saxmundham. **35 H3** TM3959.
Snape Green *Lancs.* ***Settlement***, 1km N of Scarisbrick. **48 C1** SD3814.
Snape Hill *S.Yorks.* ***Locality***, adjoining to W of Darfield. SE4004.
Snape Street *Suff.* ***Village***, 1m/2km S of Snape. TM3959.
Snape Watering *Suff.* ***Settlement***, 1m/2km NW of Snape. TM3859.
Snapper *Devon* ***Settlement***, 3m/4km NE of Barnstaple. SS5934.
Snar Water *S.Lan.* ***River***, rising on N slopes of Wanlock Dod, 1km N of Wanlockhead, and flowing N to join Duneaton Water 1m/2km SW of Crawfordjohn. **68 D2** NS8622.
Snaresbrook *Gt.Lon.* ***Suburb***, in borough of Redbridge, 1m/2km N of Wanstead. TQ4089.
Snarestone *Leics.* ***Village***, 5m/8km S of Ashby de la Zouch. **41 F5** SK3409.
Snarford *Lincs.* ***Hamlet***, 6m/9km SW of Market Rasen. **52 D4** TF0582.
Snargate *Kent* ***Hamlet***, on Romney Marsh, 2m/3km E of Appledore. **14 E5** TQ9928.
Snatchwood *Torfaen* ***Suburb***, 1km S of Abersychan. SO2602.
Snave *Kent* ***Hamlet***, 2m/3km S of Hamstreet. **15 F4** TR0129.
Sneachill *Worcs.* ***Hamlet***, 4m/6km E of Worcester. **29 J3** SO9053.
Snead *Powys* ***Settlement***, 2m/3km N of Bishop's Castle. **38 C6** SO3192.
Snead's Green *Worcs.* ***Settlement***, 4m/6km NW of Droitwich Spa. SO8667.
Sneath Common *Norf.* ***Hamlet***, 3m/5km NW of Pulham Market. TM1589.
Sneaton *N.Yorks.* ***Village***, 2m/3km S of Whitby. **63 K6** NZ8907.
Sneatonthorpe *N.Yorks.* ***Settlement***, 1m/2km SE of Sneaton, 3m/5km S of Whitby. **63 J2** NZ8907.
Snelland *Lincs.* ***Village***, 4m/6km NW of Wragby. **52 D4** TF0780.
Snellings *Cumb.* ***Settlement***, 1m/2km W of Thornhill and 4m/6km SW of Egremont. **60 A6** NX9908.
Snelsmore Common *W.Berks.* ***Open space***, 3m/4km N of Newbury. **21 H4** SU4570.
Snelston *Derbys.* ***Village***, 3m/4km SW of Ashbourne. **40 D1** SK1543.
Snetterton *Norf.* ***Hamlet***, 4m/7km SW of Attleborough. Motor-racing circuit on Snetterton Heath to S. **44 D6** TL9991.
Snettisham *Norf.* Population: 2229. ***Village***, 4m/7km S of Hunstanton. **44 A2** TF6834.
Sneuk Head *Ork.* ***Coastal feature***, headland on W coast of Hoy, 3m/5km SE of Rora Head. **107 B8** ND2095.
Sneyd Green *Stoke* ***Suburb***, 1m/2km NE of Hanley. SJ8949.
Sneyd Park *Bristol* ***Suburb***, of Bristol, 2m/4km NW of city centre. ST5575.
Snibston *Leics.* ***Settlement***, 1m/2km NW of Coalville. **41 G4** SK4113.
Snig's End *Glos.* ***Hamlet***, adjoining to S of Staunton, 7m/11km N of Gloucester. **29 G6** SO7929.
Snilesworth Moor *N.Yorks.* ***Open space***, moorland in Cleveland Hills, 4m/6km E of Osmotherley. **63 G7** SE5298.
Snipeshill *Kent* ***Suburb***, E district of Sittingbourne. TQ9263.
Snishival *W.Isles* ***Settlement***, on South Uist, 4m/7km NE of Rubha Ardvule. **84 C1** NF7634.
Snitter *Northumb.* ***Hamlet***, 2m/4km NW of Rothbury. **71 F3** NU0203.
Snitterby *Lincs.* ***Village***, 4m/6km SE of Kirton in Lindsey. **52 C3** SK9894.
Snitterfield *Warks.* ***Village***, 3m/5km N of Stratford-upon-Avon. **30 D3** SP2159.
Snitterton *Derbys.* ***Hamlet***, 1m/2km W of Matlock. SK2760.
Snittlegarth *Cumb.* ***Settlement***, 3m/4km E of Bothel. NY2137.
Snitton *Shrop.* ***Settlement***, 3m/4km E of Ludlow. **28 E1** SO5575.
Snodhill *Here.* ***Settlement***, 6m/9km E of Hay-on-Wye. **28 C4** SO3140.
Snodland *Kent* Population: 8814. ***Village***, on River Medway, 5m/8km NW of Maidstone. **24 D5** TQ7061.
Snook Point *Northumb.* ***Coastal feature***, headland on North Sea coast at S end of Beadnell Bay. **71 H1** NU2426.
Snow End *Herts.* ***Hamlet***, adjoining to S of Anstey, 3m/5km NE of Buntingford. TL4032.
Snow Street *Norf.* ***Settlement***, 2m/3km NW of Diss. TM0981.
Snowden Hill *S.Yorks.* ***Hamlet***, 2m/3km SE of Penistone. SE2600.
Snowdon (Yr Wyddfa). *Gwyn.* ***Mountain***, 4m/6km N of Beddgelert. S terminus of Snowdon Mountain Railway. Highest mountain in Wales at height of 3559 feet or 1085 metres. Snowdon gives its name to horseshoe-shaped mountain range of which it forms part, and to region of Snowdonia, surrounding it. **46 E7** SH6054.
Snowdon Mountain Railway *Gwyn.* ***Leisure/recreation***, narrow gauge rack and pinion railway running 4m/7km S from Llanberis to summit of Snowdon. **46 D7** SH5859.
Snowdonia National Park *Gwyn.* ***Large natural feature***, in NW Wales, comprising upland region surrounding Snowdon summit, and extending N to coast at Conwy, S to Machynlleth and Dyfi estuary, and E towards Bala. National Park status awarded in 1951. **37 G2** SH6054.
Snowhope Hill *Dur.* ***Mountain***, on Snowhope Moor, 4m/7km SW of Stanhope. Height 1991 feet or 607 metres. **62 A3** NY9434.
Snowshill *Glos.* ***Village***, 3m/4km S of Broadway. **30 B5** SP0933.
Snowshill Manor *Glos.* ***Historic house***, Tudor house (National Trust) situated in the village of Snowshill. Former home of Charles Paget Wade whose passion for collecting all manner of items meant that he had to live in one of the outbuildings due to lack of room in the main house. **30 B5** SP0933.
Snuff Hill *Worcs.* ***Settlement***, 3m/5km N of Bromsgrove. SO9474.
Snydale *W.Yorks.* ***Locality***, 2m/3km W of Featherstone. SE4020.
Soa *Arg. & B.* ***Island***, lying off E end of Gott Bay on S coast of Tiree. **78 B3** NM0746.
Soa *Arg. & B.* ***Island***, small island lying off S coast of Coll, opposite entrance to Loch Breachacha. **78 C2** NM1551.
Soa Island *Arg. & B.* ***Island***, small island, 2m/3km SW of Rubha na Carraig-géire, at S end of Iona. **78 D6** NM2419.
Soake *Hants.* ***Hamlet***, 1m/2km NW of Waterlooville. SU6611.
Soar *Cardiff* ***Hamlet***, 2m/3km W of Taff's Well. ST0983.
Soar *Carmar.* ***Settlement***, 5m/8km S of Llansawel. **17 K2** SN6128.
Soar *Devon* ***Hamlet***, 2m/3km SW of Salcombe. **5 H7** SX7137.
Soar *Powys* ***Locality***, 2m/4km SE of Llanfihangel Nant Bran. SN9732.
Soay *High.* ***Island***, of about 4 square miles or 10 square km lying off S coast of Skye across Soay Sound. Island is mainly flat, but rises to 455 feet or 108 metres in Beinn Bhreac. Literary associations with Gavin Maxwell, Ted Geddes and Lilian Beckwith. **85 K3** NG4514.
Soay *W.Isles* ***Island***, steep, rocky, uninhabited island (National Trust for Scotland) in St. Kilda group about 56m/89km W of North Harris and 37m/59km NW of North Uist, lying off NW end of St. Kilda itself. Area about 240 acres or 97 hectares. Haunt of sea birds. NA0601.
Soay Beag *W.Isles* ***Island***, small uninhabited island in West Loch Tarbert off coast of North Harris, to NW of, and adjacent to, Soay Mòr. **100 C7** NB0605.
Soay Mòr *W.Isles* ***Island***, small uninhabited island in West Loch Tarbert, off W coast of North Harris. **100 C7** NB0605.
Soay Sound *High.* ***Sea feature***, stretch of sea separating Soay and Skye. **85 K3** NG4416.
Soay Sound *W.Isles* ***Sea feature***, stretch of sea separating North Harris from Soag Beag and Soay Mòr. **100 C7** NB0606.
Soay Stac *W.Isles* ***Island***, islet (National Trust for Scotland) situated between Soay and St. Kilda. NA0701.
Soberton *Hants.* ***Village***, 2m/3km S of Meonstoke. Site of Roman building 2km SE. **11 H3** SU6116.
Soberton Heath *Hants.* ***Hamlet***, 1m/2km S of Soberton and 4m/6km S of Meonstoke. **11 H3** SU6014.
Society *W.Loth.* ***Settlement***, on S side of Firth of Forth, 2m/3km W of Forth Road Bridge. NT0979.
Sockbridge *Cumb.* ***Hamlet***, adjoining to N of Tirril, 2m/4km SW of Penrith. NY5026.
Sockburn *Darl.* ***Hamlet***, in loop of River Tees, 6m/9km SE of Darlington. **62 E6** NZ3407.

S

Sodom *Denb.* ***Settlement***, 1m/2km N of Bodfari. SJ0971.
Sodylt Bank *Shrop.* ***Settlement***, 2m/4km SW of Overton. **38 C2** SJ3439.
Softley *Dur.* ***Hamlet***, 1m/2km NW of Butterknowle. NZ0926.
Soham *Cambs.* Population: 6639. ***Village***, 5m/8km SE of Ely. **33 J1** TL5973.
Soham Cotes *Cambs.* ***Settlement***, 2m/3km NW of Soham. TL5774.
Soham Mere *Cambs.* ***Open space***, lowland 1km W of Soham. **33 J1** TL5773.
Soho *Gt.Lon.* ***Locality***, district in City of Westminster, bounded, roughly, by Oxford Street, Regent Street, Shaftesbury Avenue and Charing Cross Road. TQ2981.
Solas (Anglicised form: Sollas.) *W.Isles* ***Village***, near N end of North Uist, 5m/8km E of Griminis Point. **92 D4** NF8074.
Soldon *Devon* ***Hamlet***, to E of Soldon Cross, 4m/7km N of Holsworthy. SS3210.
Soldon Cross *Devon* ***Hamlet***, at crossroads, to W of Soldon. **6 B4** SS3210.
Soldridge *Hants.* ***Hamlet***, 5m/8km SW of Alton. **11 H1** SU6534.
Sole Burn *D. & G.* ***River***, rising in hills 3m/4km W of Kirkcolm and flowing S, then E, into Loch Ryan at Soleburn. **64 A4** NX0364.
Sole Street *Kent* ***Hamlet***, 3m/5km NE of Wye. **15 F3** TR0949.
Sole Street *Kent* ***Village***, 4m/7km S of Gravesend. **24 C5** TQ6567.
Soleburn Bridge *D. & G.* ***Locality***, on W side of Loch Ryan, 3m/4km NW of Stranraer. Road crosses Sole Burn where it enters Loch Ryan. **64 A4** NX0364.
Solent Breezes *Hants.* ***Settlement***, on E shore of Southampton Water, 4m/7km NW of Lee-on-the-Solent. SU5003.
Solfach *Pembs. Welsh form of Solva, qv.*
Solihull *W.Mid.* Population: 94,531. ***Town***, 7m/11km SE of Birmingham. Home of Land Rover. Impressive medieval church. **30 C1** SP1479.
Solihull Lodge *W.Mid.* ***Suburb***, 4m/6km W of Solihull town centre. **30 B1** SP0978.
Sollas *W.Isles Anglicised form of Solas, qv.*
Sollers Dilwyn *Here.* ***Hamlet***, 5m/8km SW of Leominster. **28 D3** SO4255.
Sollers Hope *Here.* ***Village***, 6m/9km N of Ross-on-Wye. **29 F5** SO6133.
Sollom *Lancs.* ***Settlement***, 7m/12km E of Southport. **48 D1** SD4518.
Solomon's Tump *Glos.* ***Settlement***, to NE of Huntley, 6m/10km W of Gloucester. SO7319.
Solsgirth *P. & K.* ***Settlement***, 2m/4km SE of Dollar. **75 H1** NS9895.
Solva *Pembs.* ***River***, rising 1m/2km S of Mathry and flowing W, then S into sea at Solva on N side of St. Brides Bay. SM8023.
Solva (Solfach). *Pembs.* ***Village***, near coast, 3m/5km E of St. David's. **16 A2** SM8024.
Solway Firth ***Sea feature***, arm of Irish Sea between coasts of Cumbria (England) and Dumfries & Galloway (Scotland). Receives waters of Rivers Nith, Annan, Esk, Eden, Wampool, Waver and Derwent. Largely occupied by broad sands and notorious for dangerous tides. **65 H7** NY0050.
Solwaybank *D. & G.* ***Settlement***, 5m/8km W of Canonbie, on S side of Allfornought Hill. **69 J6** NY3077.
Somerby *Leics.* ***Village***, 5m/8km W of Oakham. **42 A4** SK7710.
Somerby *Lincs.* ***Village***, 1km S of Bigby. Site of Roman building 1km W. TA0606.
Somercotes *Derbys.* ***Locality***, 1m/2km SE of Alfreton. **51 G7** SK4253.
Somerford *Dorset* ***Suburb***, 2m/3km E of Christchurch town centre. SZ1793.
Somerford *Staffs.* ***Settlement***, 1m/2km E of Brewood. SJ8908.
Somerford Keynes *Glos.* ***Village***, 4m/7km S of Cirencester. **20 D2** SU0195.
Somerley *W.Suss.* ***Village***, 4m/7km NW of Selsey. **12 B7** SZ8198.
Somerleyton *Suff.* ***Village***, 5m/8km NW of Lowestoft. **45 J6** TM4897.
Somerleyton Hall *Suff.* ***Historic house***, built in 1844 by John Thomas for Sir Morton Peto, a railway entrepreneur, 1m/2km W of Blundeston. Fine panelling and carvings. **45 J6** TM4997.
Somers Town *Gt.Lon.* ***Suburb***, in borough of Camden, N of St. Pancras in central London. TQ2983.
Somersal Herbert *Derbys.* ***Village***, 2m/4km NW of Sudbury. **40 D2** SK1335.
Somersby *Lincs.* ***Village***, 6m/9km E of Horncastle. Birthplace of Lord Tennyson, 1809. **53 G5** TF3472.
Somerset County Museum *Som.* ***Other feature of interest***, in castle at Taunton, with 16c almshouse and various displays. **8 B2** ST2224.
Somersham *Cambs.* Population: 3257. ***Village***, 5m/9km SW of Chatteris. **33 G1** TL3677.
Somersham *Suff.* ***Village***, 5m/8km NW of Ipswich. **34 E4** TM0848.
Somersham High North Fen *Cambs.* ***Open space***, fenland 3m/5km SW of Chatteris. **43 G7** TL3581.
Somerstown *W.Suss.* ***Suburb***, to N of Chichester city centre. SU8605.
Somerton *Newport* ***Suburb***, 1m/2km E of Newport town centre. ST3387.
Somerton *Oxon.* ***Village***, on River Cherwell, 3m/5km S of Aynho. **31 F6** SP4928.
Somerton *Som.* Population: 4489. ***Small town***, 4m/7km NW of Ilchester. 17c almshouses and Georgian buildings. **8 D2** ST4828.
Somerton *Suff.* ***Village***, 5m/9km NW of Long Melford. **34 C3** TL8153.
Sompting *W.Suss.* Population: 9858. ***Village***, 2m/3km NE of Worthing. **12 E6** TQ1705.
Sompting Abbots *W.Suss. Alternative spelling of Sompting Abbotts, qv.*
Sompting Abbotts (Also spelled Sompting Abbots.) *W.Suss.* ***Hamlet***, 1km NW of Sompting. Includes Sompting church, whose Saxon tower is only tower of 'Rhenish helm' type in Britain. TQ1605.
Sonning *W'ham* ***Village***, 2m/3km W of Twyford. Remains of medieval Bishop's Palace, and 19c Deanery Gardens by Lytons. **22 A4** SU7575.
Sonning Common *Oxon.* Population: 4496. ***Village***, 4m/7km N of Reading. **22 A3** SU7080.
Sonning Eye *Oxon.* ***Hamlet***, 1km NW of Sonning across River Thames. **22 A4** SU7575.
Sontley *Wrex.* ***Settlement***, 2m/4km S of Wrexham. SJ3346.
Sookholme *Notts.* ***Hamlet***, 4m/6km N of Mansfield. SK5466.
Soonhope Burn *Sc.Bord.* ***River***, small stream rising in Lammermuir Hills and flowing S to join Cleekhimin Burn 1m/2km E of Carfraemill. **76 D5** NT5253.
Sopley *Hants.* ***Village***, in River Avon valley, 3m/4km N of Christchurch. **10 C5** SZ1597.
Sopworth *Wilts.* ***Village***, 2m/3km W of Sherston. **20 B3** ST8286.
Sor Brook ***River***, rising NW of Banbury and flowing SE around town before joining River Cherwell 2m/3km SE of Adderbury. **31 F5** SP4933.
Soray *W.Isles* ***Island***, one of Flannan Isles group, lying nearly 1m/2km S of main island, Eilean Mòr. NA7245.
Sorbie *D. & G.* ***Village***, 4m/7km N of Whithorn. **64 E6** NX4346.
Sordale *High.* ***Settlement***, in Caithness district, 4m/7km SE of Thurso. **105 G2** ND1462.
Sorisdale *Arg. & B.* ***Locality***, on bay of same name, 1km S of NE end of Coll. **78 D1** NM2763.
Sorn *E.Ayr.* ***Village***, on River Ayr, 4m/6km E of Mauchline. **67 K1** NS5526.
Sorne Point *Arg. & B.* ***Coastal feature***, headland on N coast of Mull, 3m/5km W of Ardmore Point. **79 F2** NM4257.
Sornhill *E.Ayr.* ***Settlement***, 1m/2km S of Galston. **74 D7** NS5134.
Soroba *Arg. & B.* ***Settlement***, adjoining to S of Oban. **79 K5** NM8628.
Sortat *High.* ***Settlement***, in Caithness district, 6m/10km SE of Castletown. **105 H2** ND2863.
Sotby *Lincs.* ***Hamlet***, 7m/11km NW of Horncastle. **53 F5** TF2078.
Sotherton *Suff.* ***Settlement***, 3m/5km N of Blythburgh. TM4479.
Sots Hole *Lincs.* ***Hamlet***, 10m/16km SE of Lincoln. **52 E6** TF1264.
Sotterley *Suff.* ***Hamlet***, 4m/7km SE of Beccles. To N, Sotterley Hall is 18c house in large undulating park. **45 J7** TM4584.
Sotwell *Oxon. See Brightwell-cum-Sotwell.*
Soudley *Shrop.* ***Village***, 5m/8km SE of Market Drayton. **39 G3** SJ7228.
Soughton (Sychdyn). *Flints.* ***Village***, 1m/2km N of Mold. **48 B6** SJ2466.
Soulbury *Bucks.* ***Village***, 3m/5km NW of Leighton Buzzard. **32 B6** SP8827.
Soulby *Cumb.* ***Locality***, 1km NW of Pooley Bridge. NY4625.
Soulby *Cumb.* ***Village***, 2m/4km NW of Kirkby Stephen. **61 J5** NY7411.
Souldern *Oxon.* ***Village***, 7m/11km NW of Bicester. **31 G5** SP5231.
Souldrop *Beds.* ***Village***, 4m/6km SE of Rushden. **32 C2** SP9861.
Soulseat Loch *D. & G.* ***Lake/loch***, 3m/4km SE of Stranraer. **64 A5** NX1058.
Sound *Ches.* ***Locality***, 4m/6km SW of Nantwich. **39 F1** SJ6148.
Sound *Shet.* ***Settlement***, on Mainland, on W side of Weisdale Voe, 1m/2km E of Tresta. **109 C7** HU3850.
Sound *Shet.* ***Village***, on Mainland, 1m/2km SW of Lerwick, near head of large inlet, Voe of Sound. **109 D8** HU4640.
Sound Gruney *Shet.* ***Island***, small island 1m/2km E of Burra Ness, Yell. **108 E3** HU5796.
Sound Heath *Ches.* ***Settlement***, part of locality of Sound, 3m/5km SW of Nantwich. SJ6148.
Sound of Arisaig *High.* ***Sea feature***, large inlet on coast of Lochaber district, with two arms, Loch nan Uamh and Loch Ailort, passing to N and S respectively of peninsula of Ardnish. **86 C6** NM6580.
Sound of Barra *W.Isles* ***Sea feature***, sea passage between South Uist and Barra. **84 C3** NF7509.
Sound of Berneray *W.Isles* ***Sea feature***, strait separating Berneray and North Uist. **92 E4** NF9079.
Sound of Berneray *W.Isles* ***Sea feature***, stretch of sea separating Bearnaraigh and Mingulay. **84 A6** NL5681.
Sound of Bute *Arg. & B.* ***Sea feature***, sea area between Bute and N end of Arran. **73 H5** NS0155.
Sound of Canna *High.* ***Sea feature***, stretch of sea separating Sanday and Canna from Rum. **85 J4** NG3002.
Sound of Eigg *High.* ***Sea feature***, sea passage between islands of Eigg and Muck, in Inner Hebrides. **85 K6** NM4382.
Sound of Eriskay *W.Isles* ***Sea feature***, strait, about 1m/2km wide, between South Uist and Eriskay. **84 C3** NF7913.
Sound of Faray *Ork.* ***Sea feature***, channel between islands of Faray and Eday. **106 E4** HY5336.
Sound of Gigha *Arg. & B.* ***Sea feature***, sea passage between Gigha and Kintyre. **72 E6** NR6749.
Sound of Handa *High.* ***Sea feature***, narrow sea channel separating Handa Island from W coast of Sutherland district. **102 D4** NC1547.
Sound of Harris *W.Isles* ***Sea feature***, sea passage between South Harris and North Uist containing innumerable small islands and rocks. The four larger islands are Berneray, Ensay, Killegray and Pabbay. **92 E3** NF9681.
Sound of Hellisay *W.Isles* ***Sea feature***, strait separating numerous islets off NE coast of Barra from Hellisay, 1m/2km S of Balivanich. **84 C4** NF7403.
Sound of Hoxa *Ork.* ***Sea feature***, sea passage between Flotta and South Ronaldsay. **107 C8** ND3893.
Sound of Insh *Arg. & B.* ***Sea feature***, passage in Firth of Lorn between Insh Island and Seil. **79 J6** NM7419.
Sound of Iona *Arg. & B.* ***Sea feature***, sea strait between Iona and Ross of Mull. **78 D5** NM2822.
Sound of Islay *Arg. & B.* ***Sea feature***, narrow strait between Islay and Jura. **72 C3** NR3875.
Sound of Jura *Arg. & B.* ***Sea feature***, sea passage between Jura and Scottish mainland. **72 E3** NR6480.
Sound of Kerrera *Arg. & B.* ***Sea feature***, stretch of sea separating Kerrera from Scottish mainland. **79 K5** NM8227.
Sound of Luing *Arg. & B.* ***Sea feature***, sea passage to W of Luing, separating it from Scarba, Lunga, and neighbouring islands. **79 J7** NM7208.
Sound of Mingulay *W.Isles* ***Sea feature***, stretch of sea separating Mingulay and Pabbay. **84 A6** NL5986.
Sound of Monach *W.Isles* ***Sea feature***, sea passage between Heisker Islands group and W coast of North Uist. **92 B5** NF7063.
Sound of Mull ***Sea feature***, narrow sea passage between Mull and Morven on Scottish mainland. Width varies from 1m/2km to 3m/5km. **79 G2** NM5945.
Sound of Pabbay *W.Isles* ***Sea feature***, sea channel separating Pabbay and Berneray. **92 E3** NF9085.
Sound of Pabbay *W.Isles* ***Sea feature***, sea channel separating Pabbay and Sandray. **84 B6** NL6289.
Sound of Papa *Shet.* ***Sea feature***, strait 1m/2km wide separating Papa Stour island from Mainland. **109 A7** HU1758.
Sound of Pladda *N.Ayr.* ***Sea feature***, strait between Pladda and SE tip of Arran. **66 E2** NS0220.
Sound of Raasay *High.* ***Sea feature***, sea channel between Raasay and Skye. **94 B7** NG5654.
Sound of Rum *High.* ***Sea feature***, sea passage between Rum and Eigg, in Inner Hebrides. **85 J6** NM4390.
Sound of Sandray *W.Isles* ***Sea feature***, stretch of sea separating Sandray and Vatersay. **84 B5** NL6393.
Sound of Scalpay *W.Isles* ***Sea feature***, narrow strait between Scalpay and SE coast of North Harris. **93 H2** NG2297.
Sound of Shiant *W.Isles* ***Sea feature***, sea passage between Shiant Islands and SE coast of Isle of Lewis. **93 J2** NB3701.
Sound of Shillay *W.Isles* ***Sea feature***, sea channel separating Pabbay and Shillay. **92 D3** NF8890.
Sound of Shuna *Arg. & B.* ***Sea feature***, strait in Loch Linnhe between Shuna Island and mainland to E. **80 A3** NM9249.
Sound of Sleat *High.* ***Sea feature***, stretch of sea separating Scottish mainland from Sleat peninsula, Skye. **86 C4** NG6602.
Sound of Taransay *W.Isles* ***Sea feature***, stretch of sea separating Tarasaigh from South Harris. **93 F2** NG0498.
Sound of Ulva *Arg. & B.* ***Sea feature***, narrow strait between Ulva and Mull. **79 F4** NM3640.
Soundwell *S.Glos.* ***Suburb***, S district of Mangotsfield 5m/8km E of Bristol. **19 K4** ST6575.
Source of River Wye *Cere.* ***Other water feature***, on E slopes of Plynlimon, 1km from summit. **37 G7** SN8087.
Source of The Thames *Glos.* ***Other water feature***, disputed source of River Thames to NW of Thames Head, 3m/5km SW of Cirencester. **20 C2** ST9899.
Sourhope *Sc.Bord.* ***Hamlet***, 2m/3km SE of Mowhaugh. **70 D1** NT8420.
Sourin *Ork.* ***Locality***, at E end of Rousay, 2m/3km N of Brinyan. **106 D4** HY4330.
Sourton *Devon* ***Village***, 5m/7km SW of Okehampton. **6 D7** SX5390.
Souter Head *Aberdeen* ***Coastal feature***, headland on E coast, 3m/5km SE of Aberdeen city centre. **91 H4** NJ9601.
Souter Johnnie's Cottage *S.Ayr.* ***Historic house***, National Trust for Scotland property in Kirkoswald. Home of original Souter (cobbler), John Davidson, as described in Burns' poem, Tam o' Shanter. Contains Burns relics, a restored workshop and a reconstructed ale-house with life-size stone figures from poem. **67 G3** NS2406.
Souter Johnnie's House *S.Ayr. See Kirkoswald.*
Soutergate *Cumb.* ***Hamlet***, 5m/8km N of Dalton-in-Furness. **55 F1** SD2281.
South Acre *Norf.* ***Hamlet***, 4m/6km N of Swaffham. **44 C4** TF8114.
South Acton *Gt.Lon.* ***Suburb***, in borough of Ealing, 1km SW of Acton. TQ1979.
South Alkham *Kent* ***Settlement***, 1km SW of Alkham. TR2441.
South Allington *Devon* ***Hamlet***, 3m/4km NE of Prawle Point. **5 H7** SX7938.
South Alloa *Falk.* ***Settlement***, on S bank of River Forth, 1km SW of Alloa across river. **75 G1** NS8791.
South Ambersham *W.Suss.* ***Hamlet***, 2m/3km E of Midhurst. **12 C4** SU9120.
South Anston *S.Yorks.* Population: 4423. ***Village***, adjoins to S of North Anston. **51 H4** SK5284.
South Ascot *W. & M.* ***Locality***, to S of Ascot. **22 C5** SU9267.
South Ascrib *High.* ***Island***, most southerly of Ascrib Islands group in Loch Snizort. **93 J5** NG3064.
South Baddesley *Hants.* ***Hamlet***, 2m/3km E of Lymington. SZ3596.
South Ballachulish *High.* ***Settlement***, on S side of mouth of Loch Leven, 3m/5km W of Glencoe village. **80 B2** NN0459.
South Balloch *S.Ayr.* ***Settlement***, on S side of River Strinchar, 3m/5km E of Barr. **67 H4** NX3295.
South Bank *R. & C.* Population: 18,672. ***Suburb***, 3m/4km E of Middlesbrough. **63 G4** NZ5420.
South Bank *York* ***Suburb***, 1m/2km SW of York city centre. SE5950.

South Bank Arts Centre *Gt.Lon.* ***Leisure/recreation***, complex on S bank of River Thames in borough of Lambeth, 1m/2km E of Charing Cross. Developed around and after Royal Festival Hall, built for 1951 Festival of Britain. Subsequent additions were Royal National Theatre, Queen Elizabeth Hall, Purcell Room, Hayward Gallery, National Film Theatre and Museum of the Moving Image. TQ3080.
South Barrow *Som.* ***Village***, 4m/6km SW of Castle Cary. **9 F2** ST6027.
South Barrule *I.o.M.* ***Mountain***, 5m/9km N of Castletown. Height 1584 feet or 483 metres. **54 B6** SC2575.
South Bay *N.Yorks.* ***Bay***, sandy bay, at Scarborough. **59 G1** TA0587.
South Bay *Ork.* ***Bay***, wide bay on S coast of North Ronaldsay. **106 G2** HY7452.
South Beddington *Gt.Lon.* ***Locality***, in borough of Sutton, 1km S of Beddington. **23 F5** TQ2963.
South Benfleet *Essex* Population: 47,712. ***Town***, at head of Benfleet Creek, 6m/10km W of Southend-on-Sea. Formerly an old fishing village. **24 D3** TQ7786.
South Bents *T. & W.* ***Suburb***, on North Sea coast, 1km S of Whitburn. NZ4060.
South Bersted *W.Suss.* ***Suburb***, N district of Bognor Regis. **12 C7** SU9300.
South Binness Island *Hants.* ***Island***, 1m/2km SE of North Binness Island, in Langstone Harbour. SU6903.
South Bishop (Also known as Em-sger.) *Pembs.* ***Island***, 3m/4km W of Ramsey Island. Southernmost, and one of largest, in group of rocky islands known as Bishops and Clerks. Lighthouse. SM6522.
South Blackbog *Aber.* ***Settlement***, 4m/6km SE of Fyvie. **91 F1** NJ7932.
South Bockhampton *Dorset* ***Settlement***, part of Bockhampton locality, 3m/4km NE of Christchurch town centre. SZ1795.
South Boisdale *W.Isles* *Anglicised form of Leth Meadhanach, qv.*
South Bowood *Dorset* ***Settlement***, 3m/5km SW of Beaminster. **8 D5** SY4498.
South Bramwith *S.Yorks.* ***Hamlet***, 1m/2km W of Stainforth. SE6211.
South Brent *Devon* Population: 2087. ***Village***, below S edge of Dartmoor, 5m/7km SW of Buckfastleigh. **5 G4** SX6960.
South Brentor *Devon* ***Settlement***, 1km S of North Brentor. **6 C7** SX4780.
South Brewham *Som.* ***Village***, forms parish of Brewham along with North Brewham, 3m/4km E of Bruton. **9 G1** ST7236.
South Bromley *Gt.Lon.* ***Suburb***, 1m/2km SE of Bromley-by-Bow, in borough of Tower Hamlets. TQ3881.
South Broomage *Falk.* ***Suburb***, on S side of Larbert. NS8681.
South Broomhill *Northumb.* ***Village***, 1m/2km S of Broomhill. **71 H4** NZ2599.
South Burlingham *Norf.* ***Village***, 2m/3km S of Burlingham. **45 H5** TG3707.
South Cadbury *Som.* ***Village***, 2m/3km E of Sparkford. Iron Age camp of Cadbury Castle to SW. **9 F2** ST6325.
South Cairn *D. & G.* ***Settlement***, 4m/6km W of Kirkcolm. **64 A4** NW9769.
South Calder Water *N.Lan.* ***River***, rising on hills to E of Shotts and flowing W, passing Motherwell to N and flowing through Strathclyde Loch and into River Clyde. **75 F5** NS7257.
South Carbrain *N.Lan.* ***Locality***, industrial area in Cumbernauld to S of Carbrain. NS7674.
South Cardonald *Glas.* ***Suburb***, adjoining to S of Cardonald, 4m/6km SW of Glasgow city centre. NS5264.
South Carlton *Lincs.* ***Village***, 1km S of North Carlton. **52 C5** SK9576.
South Carlton *Notts.* ***Village***, S part of Carlton in Lindrick. SK5983.
South Cave *E.Riding* Population: 2669. ***Village***, 2m/3km SE of North Cave. **59 F6** SE8932.
South Cerney *Glos.* Population: 2145. ***Village***, 4m/6km SE of Cirencester. Airfield to N. **20 D2** SU0497.
South Chailey *E.Suss.* ***Settlement***, 1m/2km S of Chailey. TQ3917.
South Channel ***Sea feature***, sea channel N of Margate, including Margate Hook. **25 J4** TR3172.
South Channel *N.Lincs.* ***Sea feature***, sea strait in Humber estuary between Read's Island and mainland at Ferriby Sluice, 4m/7km W of Barton-upon-Humber. **59 F7** SE9522.
South Chard *Som.* ***Village***, 2m/3km S of Chard. **8 C4** ST3205.
South Charlton *Northumb.* ***Hamlet***, 5m/7km N of Alnwick. **71 G1** NU1620.
South Cheek *N.Yorks.* *Alternative name for Old Peak, qv.*
South Cheriton *Som.* ***Village***, 3m/4km SW of Wincanton. **9 F2** ST6924.
South Church *Dur.* ***Village***, 1m/2km SE of Bishop Auckland. NZ2128.
South Cleatlam *Dur.* ***Hamlet***, 1km S of Cleatham. NZ1218.
South Cliffe *E.Riding* ***Hamlet***, 1km S of North Cliffe. **58 E6** SE8737.
South Clifton *Notts.* ***Village***, 1m/2km S of North Clifton. **52 B5** SK8270.
South Cockerington *Lincs.* ***Village***, 1m/2km S of North Cockerington. **53 G4** TF3888.
South Collafirth *Shet.* ***Settlement***, at head of Colla Firth inlet, 6m/10km N of Sullom, Mainland. HU3482.
South Collingham *Notts.* ***Village***, adjoining to S of Collingham, 5m/8km N of Newark-on-Trent. SK8261.
South Common *E.Suss.* ***Settlement***, adjoining to W of South Chailey, 1m/2km S of Chailey. **13 G5** TQ3817.
South Common *Som.* ***Open space***, moorland on N side of Exmoor, 2m/3km S of Oare. **7 G1** SS8044.
South Cornelly *Bridgend* ***Village***, 2m/3km N of Porthcawl. **18 B4** SS8180.
South Corrygills *N.Ayr.* ***Settlement***, on Arran, 2m/3km SE of Brodick. **73 J7** NS0334.
South Cove *Suff.* ***Hamlet***, 3m/5km N of Southwold. **45 J7** TM4980.
South Cowton *N.Yorks.* ***Locality***, 1m/2km SE of North Cowton. Parish contains Cowton Castle. NZ2902.
South Creagan *Arg. & B.* ***Settlement***, 1km S of Creagan across Loch Creran. **80 A3** NM9743.
South Creake *Norf.* ***Village***, 1m/2km S of Creake. **44 C2** TF8536.
South Crosland *W.Yorks.* ***Village***, 1km E of Blackmoorfoot Reservoir, 3m/5km SW of Huddersfield town centre. SE1112.
South Crossaig *Arg. & B.* ***Locality***, one of two adjoining localities S of Crossaig Glen, on road running beside E coast of Kintyre, Argyll, 4m/7km SW of Claonaig. NR8351.
South Croxton *Leics.* ***Village***, 7m/12km NE of Leicester. **41 J4** SK6910.
South Dalton *E.Riding* ***Village***, 6m/10km E of Market Weighton. **59 F5** SE9645.
South Darenth *Kent* Population: 2402. ***Village***, on River Darent, 1m/2km S of Darenth and 3m/5km SE of Dartford. **23 J5** TQ5669.
South Deep *Fife* ***Sea feature***, channel in River Tay estuary, between Mugdrum Island and S bank. **82 D6** NO2218.
South Dell *W.Isles* *Anglicised form of Dail Bho Dheas, qv.*
South Devon Railway *Devon* ***Other feature of interest***, steam railway running for 7m/11km along E bank of River Dart from Totnes to Buckfastleigh. **5 H4** SX7466.
South District *Norf.* ***Open space***, fenland 3m/5km S of Outwell. **43 J6** TL5198.
South Downs ***Large natural feature***, range of chalk hills running E, from vicinity of Petersfield in Hampshire parallel and close to Sussex coast, terminating at Beachy Head, W of Eastbourne. Maximum height 888 feet or 271 metres at Butser Hill, 3m/4km SW of Petersfield. With North Downs they enclose region known as The Weald and once formed part of a large chalk anticline which stretched across NW Europe. **12 B5** TQ3010.
South Drove Drain *Lincs.* ***Other water feature***, artificial drainage channel running from Cross Drain, 3m/4km E of Market Deeping, to Pode Hole, 2m/3km W of Spalding. **43 F4** TF2121.
South Duffield *N.Yorks.* ***Village***, 2m/4km S of North Duffield. **58 C6** SE6837.
South Elkington *Lincs.* ***Village***, 1m/2km SE of North Elkington. **53 F4** TF2890.
South Ella *E.Riding* ***Locality***, adjoining to S of Kirk Ella. TA0229.
South Elmsall *W.Yorks.* Population: 9152. ***Small town***, 1m/2km S of North Elmsall and 7m/11km S of Pontefract. **51 G1** SE4711.
South End *Beds.* ***Suburb***, S district of Bedford. TL0448.
South End *Bucks.* ***Hamlet***, to S of Stewkley. **32 B6** SP8525.
South End *Cumb.* ***Settlement***, near S end of Isle of Walney, 4m/7km S of Barrow-in-Furness. **55 F3** SD2063.
South End *E.Riding* ***Locality***, 1km S of Easington. TA3918.
South End *Hants.* ***Settlement***, adjoining to S of Damerham. SU1015.
South End *Norf.* ***Settlement***, 1km S of Snetterton. TL9990.
South End *N.Lincs.* ***Settlement***, 1m/2km SE of Goxhill. **52 E1** TA1120.
South End *W.Berks.* ***Village***, 4m/7km SW of Pangbourne. SU5970.
South Erradale *High.* ***Settlement***, on W coast of Ross and Cromarty district, 3m/4km N of Red Point. **94 D4** NG7471.
South Esk ***River***, rising SE of Braemar and running SE down Glen Clova, then E to Brechin and into North Sea at Montrose. **89 K7** NO7356.
South Esk *Midloth.* ***River***, rising on Moorfoot Hills and flowing N through Gladhouse and Rosebery Reservoirs to confluence with North Esk River, 1m/2km N of Dalkeith. **76 B4** NT3369.
South Fambridge *Essex* ***Hamlet***, on S side of River Crouch estuary, 4m/6km N of Rochford. **24 E2** TQ8595.
South Fawley *W.Berks.* ***Hamlet***, 4m/7km E of Lambourn. **21 G3** SU3980.
South Ferriby *N.Lincs.* ***Village***, 3m/4km W of Barton-upon-Humber. Site of Roman settlement to NE. **59 F7** SE9820.
South Field *E.Riding* ***Suburb***, to S of Hessle, near to N end of Humber Bridge. TA0225.
South Flobbets *Aber.* ***Settlement***, 3m/5km SE of Fyvie. **91 F1** NJ7934.
South Foreland *Kent* ***Coastal feature***, headland with lighthouse 3m/5km E of Dover. **15 J3** TR3643.
South Forty Foot Drain *Lincs.* ***Other water feature***, fenland drainage cut running from Guthram Gowt, 5m/8km W of Spalding, to River Witham on S side of Boston. **42 E2** TF3242.
South Galson *W.Isles* *Anglicised form of Gabhsunn Bho Dheas, qv.*
South Galson *W.Isles* ***River***, on Isle of Lewis, passing between Gabhsunn Bho Thuath and Gabhsunn Bho Dheas and flowing out to sea to N. **101 G2** NB4358.
South Garth *Shet.* ***Settlement***, just N of Gutcher, Yell. **108 E3** HU5499.
South Godstone *Surr.* ***Village***, 2m/3km S of Godstone. **23 G7** TQ3648.
South Gorley *Hants.* ***Hamlet***, on edge of New Forest, 3m/5km N of Ringwood. **10 C3** SU1610.
South Green *Essex* ***Settlement***, at head of Geedon Creek, 5m/7km SE of Colchester. TM0319.
South Green *Essex* ***Suburb***, SE district of Billericay. **24 C2** TQ6893.
South Green *Kent* ***Hamlet***, 4m/7km SW of Sittingbourne. TQ8560.
South Green *Norf.* ***Hamlet***, 1km S of Mattishall. **44 E4** TG0510.
South Green *Norf.* ***Locality***, SW part of Terrington St. Clement. TF5419.
South Green *Norf.* ***Locality***, adjoining to S of East Dereham. TF9912.
South Green *Norf.* ***Settlement***, 1m/2km S of Pulham St. Mary. TM2083.
South Green *Suff.* ***Hamlet***, 2m/3km NE of Eye. TM1775.
South Hackney *Gt.Lon.* ***Suburb***, in borough of Hackney, 1km SE of Hackney. TQ3584.
South Hall *Arg. & B.* ***Settlement***, to W of Inverneil Burn, 1m/2km W of Strone Point. **73 J3** NS0672.
South Ham *Hants.* ***Suburb***, W district of Basingstoke. SU6151.
South Hampstead *Gt.Lon.* ***Suburb***, in borough of Camden, 1m/2km S of Hampstead. TQ2684.
South Hanningfield *Essex* ***Village***, on SE side of Hanningfield Reservoir, 3m/4km N of Wickford. **24 D2** TQ7497.
South Hanningfield Tye *Essex* ***Hamlet***, adjoins to E of South Hanningfield. TQ7497.
South Harbour *Shet.* ***Bay***, on S coast of Fair Isle. **108 A1** HZ2069.
South Harefield *Gt.Lon.* ***Village***, in borough of Hillingdon, 1m/2km S of Harefield. TQ0589.
South Harris (Gaelic form: Ceann a Deas na Hearadh.) *W.Isles* ***Large natural feature***, S part of Isle of Lewis, joined to North Harris by narrow neck of land to SW of Tarbert, with West and East Loch Tarbert on either side. South Harris is dominated by craggy mountains, especially surrounding Beinn Dhubh in N part at 1660 feet or 506 metres, and the central An Coileach at 1266 feet or 386 metres, with cnoc and lochan terrain to E. **93 F2** NG0792.
South Harris Forest *W.Isles* ***Open space***, upland area on South Harris, to SW of Tarbert. **93 F2** NG1098.
South Harrow *Gt.Lon.* ***Suburb***, 2m/3km SW of Harrow. TQ1386.
South Harting *W.Suss.* ***Village***, in parish of Harting, 3m/5km SE of Petersfield. **11 J3** SU7820.
South Hatfield *Herts.* ***Suburb***, S district of Hatfield. TL2206.
South Havra *Shet.* ***Island***, uninhabited island of about 150 acres or 60 hectares lying 1m/2km W of coast of Mainland and about 1m/2km S of East and West Burra. **109 C10** HU3627.
South Hayling *Hants.* ***Town***, at S end of Hayling Island stretching across almost the entire width of the island. **11 J5** SZ7299.
South Hazelrigg *Northumb.* ***Settlement***, 1m/2km S of North Hazelrigg and 3m/4km N of Chatton. **77 J7** NU0532.
South Head *High.* ***Coastal feature***, headland to S of Wick Bay. **105 J4** ND3749.
South Heath *Bucks.* ***Hamlet***, 1m/2km E of Great Missenden. **22 C1** SP9101.
South Heighton *E.Suss.* ***Village***, 1m/2km N of Newhaven. **13 H6** TQ4502.
South Hetton *Dur.* Population: 2799. ***Village***, 3m/4km NW of Easington. **62 E2** NZ3745.
South Hiendley *W.Yorks.* ***Village***, 7m/11km SW of Pontefract. **51 F1** SE3912.
South Hill *Cornw.* ***Hamlet***, 3m/4km NW of Callington. **4 D3** SX3372.
South Hill *Som.* ***Locality***, 1m/2km SW of Somerton. ST4726.
South Hinksey *Oxon.* ***Village***, 1m/2km S of Oxford. **21 J1** SP5004.
South Hole *Devon* ***Settlement***, near coast, 9m/14km N of Bude. **6 A4** SS2220.
South Holland Main Drain *Lincs.* ***Other water feature***, fenland drainage channel running from Cowbit to River Nene, 1m/2km S of Sutton Bridge. **43 H3** TF4719.
South Holme *N.Yorks.* ***Settlement***, 2m/3km N of Slingsby. SE6977.
South Holms *Shet.* ***Island***, small island 1m/2km S of North Holms. **108 E1** HP5711.
South Holmwood *Surr.* ***Village***, 3m/4km S of Dorking. **22 E7** TQ1745.
South Hook Point *Pembs.* ***Coastal feature***, headland on N shore of Milford Haven, 2m/4km W of Milford Haven town. Oil refinery to NE, with jetty terminal. SM8605.
South Hornchurch *Gt.Lon.* ***Suburb***, in borough of Havering, 3m/4km SW of Hornchurch. **23 J3** TQ5487.
South Hourat *N.Ayr.* ***Settlement***, 2m/3km W of Kilbirnie. **74 A5** NS2853.
South Huish *Devon* ***Settlement***, 3m/5km NW of Salcombe. **5 G6** SX6941.
South Hykeham *Lincs.* ***Hamlet***, 1m/2km SW of North Hykeham. **52 C6** SK9466.
South Hylton *T. & W.* ***Suburb***, 3m/4km W of Sunderland city centre. **62 E1** NZ3556.
South Inch *Aber.* ***Coastal feature***, beach with large pools, 1km SE of St. Combs. **99 J4** NK0662.
South Isle of Gletness *Shet.* ***Island***, one of two small islands to S of Glet Ness headland on E coast of Mainland. **109 D7** HU4751.
South Kelsey *Lincs.* ***Village***, 5m/8km SW of Caistor. **52 D3** TF0498.
South Kensington *Gt.Lon.* ***Suburb***, in borough of Kensington and Chelsea, running SW from Victoria and Albert Museum. TQ2678.
South Kessock *High.* ***Suburb***, of Inverness on S bank of Beauly Firth. **96 D7** NH6547.
South Killingholme *N.Lincs.* ***Village***, 1m/2km SE of Killingholme. **52 E1** TA1417.
South Kilvington *N.Yorks.* ***Village***, 1m/2km N of Thirsk. **57 K1** SE4283.
South Kilworth *Leics.* ***Village***, 4m/7km SE of Lutterworth. **41 J7** SP6081.
South Kirkby *W.Yorks.* Population: 9152. ***Small town***, adjoining to W of South Elmsall. **51 G1** SE4511.
South Kirkton *Aber.* ***Settlement***, adjacent to S of Echt. **91 F4** NJ7305.
South Kiscadale *N.Ayr.* ***Settlement***, forms locality of Kiscadale, along with North Kiscadale, and adjoins to W of Whiting Bay. NS0425.

South Knighton *Devon* ***Hamlet***, 3m/5km NW of Newton Abbot. SX8172.

South Knighton *Leic.* ***Suburb***, adjoining to E of Knighton, 3m/4km SE of Leicester city centre. SK6001.

South Kyme *Lincs.* ***Village***, 3m/4km SE of North Kyme. **42 E1** TF1552.

South Kyme Fen *Lincs.* ***Open space***, lowland 1m/2km SE of South Kyme. **42 E1** TF1748.

South Lakes Wild Animal Park *Cumb.* ***Leisure/recreation***, conservation zoo 1m/2km NW of Dalton-in-Furness. Rare species include both Sumatran and Siberian tigers. **55 F2** SD2375.

South Lancing *W.Suss.* Population: 9858. ***Suburb***, on coast in parish of Lancing, 2m/4km E of Worthing. **12 E6** TQ1804.

South Ledaig *Arg. & B.* ***Settlement***, 1km N of North Connel. **80 A4** NM9035.

South Lee *W.Isles* ***Hill***, on North Uist, 2m/4km S of Lochmaddy. Height 922 feet or 281 metres. **92 E5** NF9165.

South Leigh *Oxon.* ***Village***, 3m/4km SE of Witney. **21 G1** SP3908.

South Level ***Large natural feature***, between New Bedford River and Brandon; forms part of Bedford Level. **43 J7** TL5080.

South Leverton *Notts.* ***Village***, 5m/8km E of Retford. **51 K4** SK7881.

South Littleton *Worcs.* ***Village***, 3m/5km NE of Evesham. **30 B4** SP0746.

South Lochboisdale *W.Isles Anglicised form of Taobh a' Deas Loch Baghasdail, qv.*

South Lopham *Norf.* ***Village***, 1m/2km S of North Lopham. **44 E7** TM0382.

South Luffenham *Rut.* ***Village***, 1m/2km S of North Luffenham. **42 C5** SK9303.

South Malling *E.Suss.* ***Suburb***, E district of Lewes. **13 H5** TQ4210.

South Marston *Swin.* ***Village***, 4m/6km NE of Swindon. **20 E3** SU1987.

South Medwin *S.Lan.* ***River***, rising from streams flowing off Pentland Hills, flowing SW through a wide valley and joining North Medwin River to become Medwin Water before flowing into River Clyde, 1m/2km S of Carnwath. **75 J6** NS9844.

South Merstham *Surr.* ***Locality***, adjoining to S of Merstham. TQ2953.

South Middleton *Northumb.* ***Hamlet***, 3m/5km S of Wooler. NT9923.

South Milford *N.Yorks.* Population: 1477. ***Village***, 5m/8km N of Ferrybridge. **57 K6** SE4931.

South Milton *Devon* ***Village***, 3m/4km W of Kingsbridge. **5 H6** SX6942.

South Mimms *Herts.* ***Village***, 2m/3km W of Potters Bar. **23 F1** TL2201.

South Molton *Devon* Population: 4066. ***Small town***, market town with square of Georgian and Regency buildings, 11m/17km SE of Barnstaple. **7 F3** SS7125.

South Moor *Dur.* ***Suburb***, SW district of Stanley. **62 C1** NZ1851.

South Morar *High.* ***Locality***, mountainous coastal area of Lochaber district between Loch Morar to N and Loch nan Uamh to S. **86 D6** NM7587.

South Moreton *Oxon.* ***Village***, 3m/4km SE of Didcot. **21 J3** SU5688.

South Mundham *W.Suss.* ***Village***, 3m/5km S of Chichester. **12 B6** SU8700.

South Muskham *Notts.* ***Village***, 1m/2km S of North Muskham. **51 K7** SK7958.

South Ness *Fife* ***Coastal feature***, headland on SE coast of Isle of May. **76 E1** NT6698.

South Ness *Shet.* ***Coastal feature***, headland and southernmost point of Foula. **108 B1** HT9636.

South Nesting *Shet.* ***Locality***, forms locality of Nesting on Mainland, along with North Nesting. **109 D7** HU4554.

South Nesting Bay *Shet.* ***Bay***, enclosed by Nesting on E coast. The bay extends S from Hill of Neap to N end of Moul of Eswick. **109 D7** HU4956.

South Nevi *Ork.* ***Coastal feature***, on S coast of small island of Copinsay, off SE coast of Mainland. **107 F7** HY6000.

South Newbald *E.Riding* ***Hamlet***, 1km S of N Newbald. **59 F6** SE9136.

South Newington *Oxon.* ***Village***, 6m/9km SW of Banbury. **31 F5** SP4033.

South Newsham *Northumb.* ***Locality***, to S of Newsham. NZ3079.

South Newton *N.Ayr.* ***Locality***, one of two adjoining localities at N end of Arran, opposite Lochranza across Loch Ranza. NR9351.

South Newton *Wilts.* ***Village***, on River Wylye, 2m/4km N of Wilton. **10 B1** SU0834.

South Normanton *Derbys.* Population: 8696. ***Village***, 2m/3km E of Alfreton. **51 G7** SK4456.

South Norwood *Gt.Lon.* ***Locality***, forms suburb of Norwood, along with West Norwood, Upper Norwood, and Norwood New Town, 2m/4km NE of Croydon town centre. **23 G5** TQ3368.

South Nutfield *Surr.* Population: 2271. ***Village***, 2m/3km E of Redhill. **23 G7** TQ3049.

South Ockendon *Thur.* Population: 15,514. ***Suburb***, 3m/4km NW of Grays. **23 J3** TQ5881.

South Ormsby *Lincs.* ***Village***, 3m/5km NW of Ulceby Cross. **53 G5** TF3775.

South Ossett *W.Yorks.* ***Suburb***, adjoining to S of Ossett. SE2819.

South Otterington *N.Yorks.* ***Village***, 4m/6km S of Northallerton. **57 J1** SE3787.

South Owersby *Lincs.* ***Settlement***, 3m/5km NW of Middle Rasen. TF0693.

South Oxhey *Herts.* Population: 16,133. ***Suburb***, 1m/2km S of Oxhey. **22 E2** TQ1295.

South Park *Gt.Lon.* ***Locality***, in borough of Redbridge, 1km E of Ilford. TQ4586.

South Park *Surr.* ***Suburb***, residential district SW of Reigate. **23 F7** TQ2448.

South Parks *Fife* ***Suburb***, in centre of Glenrothes. NO2601.

South Peak Estate *Derbys.* ***Open space***, National Trust property encompassing Dove Dale to NE of Ilam, 4m/7km NW of Ashbourne. SK1452.

South Perrott *Dorset* ***Village***, 3m/5km SE of Crewkerne. **8 D4** ST4706.

South Petherton *Som.* Population: 2523. ***Small town***, 5m/8km E of Ilminster. **8 D3** ST4316.

South Petherwin *Cornw.* ***Village***, 2m/3km SW of Launceston. **6 B7** SX3081.

South Pickenham *Norf.* ***Village***, 2m/3km S of North Pickenham. **44 C5** TF8504.

South Pill *Cornw.* ***Suburb***, N district of Saltash. SX4259.

South Point *Arg. & B.* ***Coastal feature***, rocky headland on W side of S tip of Kintyre peninsula, 6m/10km W of Southend. **66 A3** NR5807.

South Pool *Devon* ***Village***, 3m/5km N of Prawle Point, at head of Southpool Creek, which runs into Kingsbridge Estuary. **5 H6** SX7740.

South Poorton *Dorset* ***Hamlet***, adjoining North Poorton, 5m/7km NE of Bridport. SY5297.

South Quarme *Som.* ***Settlement***, to S of North Quarme. SS9236.

South Queensferry *Edin.* ***Locality***, with harbour and lighthouse, at S end of Forth bridges. **75 K3** NT1278.

South Queich *P. & K.* ***River***, stream rising in Ochil Hills and flowing E to enter Loch Leven to S of Kinross. **82 B7** NO0112.

South Radworthy *Devon* ***Hamlet***, on Exmoor, 5m/8km NE of South Molton. **7 F2** SS7432.

South Rauceby *Lincs.* ***Village***, 1km S of North Rauceby. **42 D1** TF0246.

South Raynham *Norf.* ***Village***, 1m/2km SW of East Raynham across River Wensum. **44 C3** TF8825.

South Redbriggs *Aber.* ***Settlement***, to E of Wood of Hatton, 4m/7km SE of Turriff. **99 F6** NJ7945.

South Reston *Lincs.* ***Village***, 1m/2km E of North Reston. **53 H4** TF3883.

South Rona *High. Alternative name for Rona, qv.*

South Ronaldsay *Ork.* ***Island***, most southerly of main islands of Orkney group, measuring about 8m/12km N to S and 2m/4km E to W. Linked by Churchill Barrier to Burray, Glimps Holm, Lamb Holm and Mainland. **107 D9** ND4590.

South Ruislip *Gt.Lon.* ***Suburb***, 2m/3km SE of Ruislip. TQ1185.

South Runcton *Norf.* ***Hamlet***, 4m/6km N of Downham Market. **44 A5** TF6308.

South Scarle *Notts.* ***Village***, 7m/11km NE of Newark-on-Trent. **52 B6** SK8464.

South Shawbost *W.Isles* ***Settlement***, near NW coast of Isle of Lewis, forms locality of Siabost along with North and New Shawbost, 3m/5km W of Bragar. NB2546.

South Shian *Arg. & B.* ***Locality***, on S shore of Loch Creran, in Argyll. **80 A3** NM9041.

South Shields *T. & W.* Population: 83,704. ***Town***, former mining town and Victorian resort on S bank of River Tyne, 7m/12km E of Gateshead and 7m/11km N of Sunderland. Remains of Roman fort. Long stretch of sands on seaward side of town. **71 J7** NZ3666.

South Shore *B'pool* ***Suburb***, to S of Blackpool town centre. **55 F6** SD3033.

South Side *Dur.* ***Hamlet***, 1km N of Butterknowle. NZ1026.

South Skirlaugh *E.Riding* ***Village***, 7m/12km NE of Kingston upon Hull. **59 H6** TA1439.

South Somercotes *Lincs.* ***Village***, 2m/3km S of North Somercotes. **53 H3** TF4296.

South Somercotes Fen Houses *Lincs.* ***Settlement***, 3m/5km SW of North Somercotes. TF3992.

South Sound *Shet.* ***Sea feature***, sea passage between Hascosay and Ness of Vatsetter, Yell. **108 E3** HU5490.

South Stack *I.o.A.* ***Island***, small island with lighthouse off W coast of Holy Island, Anglesey, 3m/4km W of Holyhead. Island is connected to main island by small suspension bridge. **46 A4** SH2082.

South Stainley *N.Yorks.* ***Village***, 2m/3km NE of Ripley. **57 J3** SE3063.

South Stainmore *Cumb.* ***Locality***, 1m/2km SE of North Stainmore. NY8413.

South Stanley *Dur.* ***Suburb***, 1km S of Stanley. NZ1953.

South Stifford *Thur.* ***Locality***, on N bank of River Thames, 1m/2km W of Grays. TQ5977.

South Stoke *Oxon.* ***Village***, 2m/3km N of Goring. **21 K3** SU6083.

South Stoke *W.Suss.* ***Village***, in River Arun valley, 2m/3km N of Arundel. **12 D6** TQ0210.

South Stour *Kent* ***Locality***, 3m/5km SE of Ashford. TR0338.

South Street *E.Suss.* ***Hamlet***, 1km S of Chailey. **13 G5** TQ3918.

South Street *Gt.Lon.* ***Settlement***, in borough of Bromley, adjoining to SE of Biggin Hill. TQ4357.

South Street *Kent* ***Hamlet***, 4m/6km SE of Faversham. TR0557.

South Street *Kent* ***Settlement***, 1m/2km S of Meopham. **24 C5** TQ6363.

South Street *Kent* ***Settlement***, 5m/8km SE of Gillingham. TQ8361.

South Street *Kent* ***Suburb***, 1m/2km SE of Whitstable town centre. TR1265.

South Tarbrax *S.Lan.* ***Locality***, 1m/2km S of Tarbrax. NT0254.

South Tawton *Devon* ***Village***, 4m/7km E of Okehampton. **6 E6** SX6594.

South Thoresby *Lincs.* ***Village***, 4m/6km W of Alford. **53 H5** TF4076.

South Thorpe *Dur.* ***Settlement***, 1m/2km S of Whorlton. NZ1013.

South Thundergay *N.Ayr. Alternative name for Auchamore, qv.*

South Tidworth *Wilts.* ***Village***, adjoining to S of North Tidworth, 3m/4km SW of Ludgershall. **21 F7** SU2348.

South Top *Aber.* ***Mountain***, in Grampian Mountains, 6m/9km NW of Braemar. Height 3861 feet or 1177 metres. **89 H5** NO0997.

South Tottenham *Gt.Lon.* ***Suburb***, to S of Tottenham. TQ3388.

South Town *Devon* ***Hamlet***, adjoining to SE of Kenton, 4m/6km N of Dawlish. SX9683.

South Town *Hants.* ***Hamlet***, 1km S of Medstead and 4m/6km SW of Alton. **11 H1** SU6536.

South Twerton *B. & N.E.Som.* ***Suburb***, 1m/2km W of Bath city centre. ST7364.

South Tyne ***River***, rising on Tynehead Fell and flowing N by Alston to Haltwhistle, then E by Haydon Bridge to join River North Tyne and form River Tyne 2m/3km NW of Hexham. **70 D7** NY9166.

South Tynedale Railway *Cumb.* ***Other feature of interest***, tourist railway running for over 1m/2km from Alston through River South Tyne valley. **61 J2** NY7148.

South Ugie Water *Aber.* ***River***, rising to W of Maud and flowing E through Old Deer to join River North Ugie 1m/2km NE of Longside, forming River Ugie. **99 H6** NK0548.

South Uist (Gaelic form: Uibhist a Deas.) *W.Isles* ***Island***, of about 140 square miles or 365 square km between Benbecula (causeway connection) and Barra. Contains numerous lochs, especially on W side; mountains on E side rise to 2034 feet or 620 metres. **84 D1** NF7932.

South Upper Barrack *Aber.* ***Settlement***, 2m/3km W of Auchnagatt and 3m/5km SE of New Deer. **99 H6** NJ9042.

South View *Hants.* ***Suburb***, of Basingstoke to N of town centre. SU6352.

South View *Shet.* ***Settlement***, on White Ness, Mainland, 2m/4km NW of Scalloway across Whiteness Voe. **109 C8** HU3842.

South Walls *Ork.* ***Coastal feature***, peninsula at SE end of Hoy, over 3m/5km E to W and nearly 2m/3km N to S, and joined to the rest of Hoy by narrow neck of land, The Ayre, carrying a road. **107 C9** ND3189.

South Walsham *Norf.* ***Village***, 3m/5km NW of Acle. **45 H4** TG3613.

South Warnborough *Hants.* ***Village***, 5m/8km N of Alton. Site of Roman building 1m/2km S. **22 A7** SU7247.

South Weald *Essex* ***Village***, 2m/3km W of Brentwood. **23 J2** TQ5793.

South Weston *Oxon.* ***Village***, 3m/4km N of Watlington. **22 A2** SU7098.

South Wheatley *Cornw.* ***Village***, 7m/12km NW of Launceston. **4 C1** SX2492.

South Wheatley *Notts.* ***Village***, adjoins to SE of North Wheatley. **51 K4** SK7685.

South Wick *Shet.* ***Bay***, on NW coast of Mainland, bounded by Fugla Ness to N. **108 C3** HU3190.

South Widcombe *B. & N.E.Som.* ***Hamlet***, 1m/2km W of Hinton Blewett. **19 J6** ST5856.

South Wigston *Leics.* ***Suburb***, 4m/6km S of Leicester. **41 H6** SP5898.

South Willesborough *Kent* ***Suburb***, forms suburb of Willesborough, along with Willesborough Lees and Willesborough Street. **15 F3** TR0341.

South Willingham *Lincs.* ***Village***, 4m/6km SE of North Willingham. **52 E4** TF1688.

South Wimbledon *Gt.Lon.* ***Suburb***, 1km E of Wimbledon town centre. TQ2570.

South Wingate *Dur.* ***Settlement***, 2m/3km SE of Wingate. **63 F3** NZ4135.

South Wingfield *Derbys.* ***Village***, 3m/4km W of Alfreton. Ruins of medieval Wingfield Manor (English Heritage) 1km S. **51 F7** SK3755.

South Witham *Lincs.* ***Village***, 2m/3km S of North Witham. **42 C4** SK9221.

South Wonston *Hants.* Population: 2402. ***Village***, 4m/7km N of Winchester. **11 F1** SU4635.

South Woodford *Gt.Lon.* ***Suburb***, to S of Woodford Green. TQ4090.

South Woodham Ferrers *Essex* Population: 16,032. ***Town***, modern market town 5m/7km NE of Wickford. **24 E2** TQ8097.

South Wootton *Norf.* ***Suburb***, 2m/3km NE of King's Lynn. **44 A3** TF6422.

South Wraxall *Wilts.* ***Village***, 3m/4km N of Bradford-on-Avon. **20 B5** ST8364.

South Yardley *W.Mid.* ***Locality***, 1m/2km S of Yardley. **40 D7** SP1284.

South Zeal *Devon* ***Village***, on N edge of Dartmoor, 4m/7km E of Okehampton. **6 E6** SX6593.

Southall *Gt.Lon.* ***Suburb***, in borough of Ealing, 11m/18km W of Charing Cross. **22 E4** TQ1280.

Southall Green *Gt.Lon.* ***Suburb***, in borough of Ealing, 11m/18km W of Charing Cross. TQ1279.

Southam *Glos.* ***Village***, 3m/4km NE of Cheltenham. **29 J6** SO9725.

Southam *Warks.* Population: 5304. ***Small town***, market town, 7m/11km SE of Royal Leamington Spa. **31 F2** SP4161.

Southampton *S'ham.* Population: 210,138. ***City***, at confluence of Rivers Itchen and Test at head of Southampton Water, 70m/113km SW of London. Southern centre for business, culture and recreation. Container and transatlantic passenger port, dealing with 7 percent of UK's seaborne trade. Site of many famous departures: Henry V's army bound for Agincourt; the Pilgrim Fathers sailed to America on the Mayflower in 1620; maiden voyage of Queen Mary and only voyage of Titanic. Remains of medieval town walls. Medieval Merchant's House (English Heritage) has authentically recreated furnishings. Boat and helicopter ferries to Isle of Wight. Host to many international boating events including Southampton International Boat Show, Whitbread Round the World, and BT Global Challenge. Southampton International Airport 1m/2km S of Eastleigh. University. **11 F3** SU4112.

Southampton International Airport *Hants.* ***Airport/airfield***, international airport 1m/2km S of Eastleigh. **11 F3** SU4517.
Southampton Water *Hants.* ***Sea feature***, arm of sea extending 6m/10km NW from Calshot Castle to confluence of Rivers Test and Itchen at Southampton. Average width at high tide about 1m/2km. **11 F4** SU4506.
Southay *Som.* ***Hamlet***, adjoining East Lambrook, 2m/3km W of Martock. ST4319.
Southbar *Renf.* ***Settlement***, 1km S of Erskine. **74 C4** NS4669.
Southborough *Gt.Lon.* ***Suburb***, in borough of Kingston upon Thames, 2m/3km S of Kingston upon Thames town centre. TQ1866.
Southborough *Gt.Lon.* ***Suburb***, in borough of Bromley, 2m/3km SE of Bromley town centre. TQ4267.
Southborough *Kent* ***Town***, adjoining to N of Royal Tunbridge Wells. **23 J7** TQ5842.
Southbourne *Bourne.* ***Suburb***, seaside district of Bournemouth 3m/5km E of town centre. **10 C5** SZ1391.
Southbourne *W.Suss.* Population: 9155. ***Village***, 1m/2km E of Emsworth. **11 J4** SU7605.
Southbrook *Devon* ***Settlement***, 3m/4km E of Broadclyst. SY0296.
Southburgh *Norf.* ***Village***, 2m/3km NW of Hingham. **44 E5** TG0004.
Southburn *E.Riding* ***Village***, 3m/5km SW of Great Driffield. **59 F4** SE9854.
Southchurch *S'end* ***Suburb***, E district of Southend-on-Sea. **25 F3** TQ9085.
Southcott *Beds.* ***Suburb***, SW district of Linslade. SP9024.
Southcott *Devon* ***Hamlet***, 3m/4km W of Okehampton. **6 D6** SX5495.
Southcott *Wilts.* ***Settlement***, 1km SE of Pewsey. SU1759.
Southcourt *Bucks.* ***Suburb***, S district of Aylesbury. SP8112.
Southdean *Sc.Bord.* ***Locality***, 5m/7km NW of Carter Bar. **70 B3** NT6309.
Southdene *Mersey.* ***Suburb***, S district of Kirkby. SJ4197.
Southdown *B. & N.E.Som.* ***Suburb***, SW district of Bath, 2m/3km from city centre. ST7263.
Southease *E.Suss.* ***Village***, in River Ouse valley, 3m/5km S of Lewes. **13 H6** TQ4205.
Southend *Aber.* ***Settlement***, 1m/2km SW of Turriff. **99 F6** NJ7148.
Southend *Arg. & B.* ***Village***, in Kintyre, 8m/13km S of Campbeltown. **66 A3** NR6908.
Southend *Bucks.* ***Hamlet***, 5m/7km N of Henley-on-Thames. SU7589.
Southend *Gt.Lon.* ***Suburb***, in borough of Lewisham, 2m/4km S of Lewisham and 7m/12km SE of Charing Cross. TQ3871.
Southend *Oxon.* ***Settlement***, adjoining to S of Garsington, 5m/9km SE of Oxford. SP5801.
Southend *W.Berks.* ***Village***, 1m/2km SW of Bradfield. **21 K4** SU5970.
Southend *Wilts.* ***Hamlet***, 1km SW of Ogbourne St. George, 3m/4km N of Marlborough. SU1973.
Southend-on-Sea *S'end* Population: 158,517. ***Town***, resort on N side of Thames estuary, 35m/57km E of London. Pier over 1m/2km long. London Southend Airport 2m/3km N. **24 E3** TQ8786.
Southerfield *Cumb.* ***Settlement***, 2m/3km SW of Abbeytown. NY1648.
Southerly *Devon* ***Hamlet***, 6m/9km SW of Okehampton. SX5288.
Southern Cross *W.Suss.* ***Suburb***, E district of Southwick. TQ2505.
Southern Green *Herts.* ***Hamlet***, 4m/6km NW of Buntingford. TL3131.
Southernby *Cumb.* ***Locality***, 2m/3km E of Hesket Newmarket. NY3639.
Southerndown *V. of Glam.* ***Village***, 4m/7km S of Bridgend. **18 B4** SS8873.
Southerness *D. & G.* ***Village***, small village and resort with disused lighthouse at Southerness Point, headland on Solway Firth, 3m/5km S of Kirkbean. **65 K5** NX9754.
Southerness Point *D. & G.* ***Coastal feature***, headland on Solway Firth, 3m/5km S of Kirkbean. **65 K5** NX9754.
Southerton *Devon* ***Locality***, 1km N of Newton Poppleford. SY0790.
Southery *Norf.* ***Village***, 5m/8km S of Downham Market. **44 A6** TL6294.
Southery Fens *Norf.* ***Open space***, fenland 4m/7km NE of Littleport. **43 J6** TL5993.
Southey Green *S.Yorks.* ***Suburb***, 3m/4km N of Sheffield city centre. SK3491.
Southfield *Edin.* ***Suburb***, of Edinburgh, 1m/2km S of Portobello. NT3072.
Southfield *Fife* ***Suburb***, on S side of Glenrothes. NT2699.
Southfield *Torbay* ***Suburb***, NW district of Paignton. SX8861.
Southfield Reservoir *E.Riding* ***Reservoir***, 2m/3km S of Snaith. **51 J1** SE6519.
Southfields *Gt.Lon.* ***Suburb***, in borough of Wandsworth, 2m/3km SE of Putney Bridge. TQ2573.
Southfleet *Kent* ***Village***, 3m/5km SW of Gravesend. **24 C4** TQ6171.
Southgate *Cere.* ***Suburb***, 1m/2km SE of Aberystwyth town centre. SN5980.
Southgate *Ches.* ***Suburb***, of Runcorn, SE of town centre. SJ5381.
Southgate *Gt.Lon.* ***Suburb***, in borough of Enfield, 2m/3km SW of Enfield town centre and 9m/14km N of Charing Cross. **23 F2** TQ2994.
Southgate *Norf.* ***Locality***, adjoining to S of Snettisham. Site of Roman building to E. **44 A2** TF6833.
Southgate *Norf.* ***Settlement***, 1km N of Cawston. **45 F3** TG1324.
Southgate *Swan.* Population: 2054. ***Village***, near S coast of Gower peninsula, 5m/8km W of Mumbles Head. **17 J6** SS5588.
Southgate *W.Suss.* ***Suburb***, S district of Crawley. TQ2635.
Southhouse *Edin.* ***Suburb***, 4m/7km S of Edinburgh city centre. NT2767.
Southill *Beds.* ***Village***, 2m/3km N of Shefford. **32 E4** TL1542.
Southington *Hants.* ***Hamlet***, 1km W of Overton. **21 J7** SU5049.
Southleigh *Devon* ***Village***, 3m/5km NW of Seaton. **8 B5** SY2093.
Southmarsh *Som.* ***Hamlet***, 2m/3km NE of Wincanton. ST7330.
Southminster *Essex* Population: 3374. ***Village***, 2m/4km N of Burnham-on-Crouch. **25 F2** TQ9599.
Southmuir *Angus* ***Locality***, adjoining to S of Kirriemuir. **82 E2** NO3853.
Southoe *Cambs.* ***Village***, 3m/4km N of St. Neots. **32 E2** TL1864.
Southolt *Suff.* ***Village***, 4m/6km NE of Debenham. **35 F2** TM1968.
Southorpe *Peter.* ***Village***, 4m/7km SE of Stamford. **42 D5** TF0803.
Southover *Dorset* ***Settlement***, on S side of River Frome, opposite Frampton, 5m/8km NW of Dorchester. SY6294.
Southowram *W.Yorks.* ***Village***, 2m/3km SE of Halifax. **57 G7** SE1123.
Southport *Mersey.* Population: 90,959. ***Town***, coastal resort, 16m/25km N of Liverpool. An attractive shopping centre, it has a long pier and largest marine lake in Britain. Royal Birkdale Golf Club regularly hosts the Open Championship, and Southport Flower Show has been held annually for over 150 years. **48 C1** SD3317.
Southport Zoo and Conservation Trust *Mersey.* ***Leisure/recreation***, variety of animals located in 5 acres of landscaped gardens in Southport. Regular snake-handling sessions. **48 C1** SD3217.
Southpunds *Shet.* ***Locality***, on Mainland, 8m/13km N of Sumburgh Head. HU4020.
Southrepps *Norf.* ***Village***, 4m/7km SE of Cromer. **45 G2** TG2536.
Southrey *Lincs.* ***Village***, on River Witham, 2m/3km SE of Bardney. **52 E6** TF1366.
Southrop *Glos.* ***Village***, 3m/4km N of Lechlade. **20 E1** SP2003.
Southrope *Hants.* ***Hamlet***, 5m/8km SE of Basingstoke. **21 K7** SU6744.
Southsea *Ports.* ***Suburb***, residential and holiday district of Portsmouth, 1m/2km S of city centre. Hovercraft ferry for pedestrians to Isle of Wight from Clarence Pier. **11 H5** SZ6498.
Southsea *Wrex.* ***Locality***, 2m/4km W of Wrexham. **48 B7** SJ3051.
Southstoke *B. & N.E.Som.* ***Village***, 3m/4km S of Bath. **20 A5** ST7461.
Southtown *Norf.* ***Suburb***, 1km S of Great Yarmouth town centre across River Yare. **45 K5** TG5206.
Southtown *Ork.* ***Settlement***, in S of Burray, 1km E of Burray village. **107 D8** ND4895.
Southtown *Som.* ***Settlement***, 3m/4km NW of Ilminster. ST3216.
Southville *Torfaen* ***Suburb***, near centre of Cwmbran. ST2995.
Southwaite *Cumb.* ***Settlement***, 3m/5km S of Kirkby Stephen. **61 J6** NY7803.
Southwaite *Cumb.* ***Village***, 2m/3km W of High Hesket, on E side of M6 motorway service area. **61 F2** NY4445.
Southwark Cathedral *Gt.Lon.* ***Ecclesiastical building***, fine restored Gothic cathedral to S of River Thames, 2m/3km E of Charing Cross. Originally built by Augustinian Canons but destroyed by fire in 1206. Beautiful Early English choir and retrochoir. Tower built c. 1520, nave by Blomfield 1894-7. Work by Comper includes altar screen. Parish church until elevated to cathedral status in 1905. **23 G4** TQ3279.
Southwater *W.Suss.* Population: 5536. ***Village***, 3m/5km S of Horsham. **12 E4** TQ1526.
Southwater Street *W.Suss.* ***Hamlet***, 1m/2km N of Southwater. TQ1527.
Southway *Plym.* ***Suburb***, N district of Plymouth, 4m/7km from city centre. SX4860.
Southway *Som.* ***Settlement***, 2m/4km NE of Glastonbury. **19 J7** ST5142.
Southwell *Dorset* ***Hamlet***, on Portland, 1m/2km N of Bill of Portland. **9 F7** SY6870.
Southwell *Notts.* Population: 6498. ***Small town***, 6m/10km W of Newark-on-Trent. Norman to Perpendicular cathedral, or minster, surrounded by attractive Georgian houses. **51 K7** SK7053.
Southwell Minster *Notts.* ***Ecclesiastical building***, in Southwell, 6m/10km W of Newark-on-Trent. Church dates from 1108; cathedral status late 19c. Chapter House famed for carved foliage decoration. **51 K7** SK7053.
Southwick *D. & G.* ***Settlement***, to NE of Caulkerbush, 7m/11km SE of Dalbeattie. NX9357.
Southwick *Hants.* ***Village***, 3m/5km NW of Cosham. **11 H4** SU6208.
Southwick *Northants.* ***Village***, 3m/4km NW of Oundle. Hall is Tudor and earlier. Site of Roman building 2m/3km W. **42 D6** TL0292.
Southwick *Som.* ***Hamlet***, 3m/4km E of Highbridge. ST3546.
Southwick *T. & W.* ***Suburb***, 1m/2km NW of Sunderland city centre across River Wear. **62 E1** NZ3858.
Southwick *W.Suss.* Population: 11,067. ***Town***, on coast, on E side of Shoreham-by-Sea. Site of Roman villa. **13 F6** TQ2405.
Southwick *Wilts.* ***Village***, 2m/3km SW of Trowbridge. **20 B6** ST8355.
Southwick Burn *D. & G.* ***River***, rising on W slopes of Maidenpap, flowing SE and joining with numerous other streams to flow through Caulkerbush and into Solway Firth on Mersehead Sands. **65 J4** NX9059.
Southwold *Suff.* Population: 3905. ***Small town***, and coastal resort at mouth of River Blyth 8m/12km E of Halesworth. Lighthouse among houses at cliff top. **35 K1** TM5076.
Southwood *Norf.* ***Settlement***, 1m/2km W of Freethorpe. **45 H5** TG3905.
Southwood *Som.* ***Hamlet***, 2m/3km N of Keinton Mandeville. **8 E1** ST5533.
Soutra Hill *Sc.Bord.* ***Mountain***, 2m/3km SE of Fala. Height 1207 feet or 368 metres. **76 C5** NT4559.
Sow *Staffs.* ***River***, rising 1m/2km NW of Fairoak and flowing SE through Stafford into River Trent, 5m/8km to E. **40 A3** SJ9922.
Sowden *Devon* ***Hamlet***, 2m/3km N of Exmouth. SX9983.
Sowe ***River***, rising W of Bedworth and flowing S through E parts of Coventry into River Avon, 3m/4km E of Kenilworth. SP3272.
Sower Carr *Lancs.* ***Hamlet***, 1m/2km N of Hambleton. SD3743.
Sowerby *N.Yorks.* ***Village***, adjoining to S of Thirsk. **57 K1** SE4381.
Sowerby *W.Yorks.* ***Village***, 1m/2km W of Sowerby Bridge and 3m/5km SW of Halifax. **57 F7** SE0423.
Sowerby Bridge *W.Yorks.* ***Town***, on River Calder, 2m/4km SW of Halifax. Rushbearing Festival held annually. **57 F7** SE0423.
Sowerby Row *Cumb.* ***Hamlet***, 2m/3km E of Sebergham. **60 E2** NY3940.
Sowerhill *Som.* ***Hamlet***, 3m/4km SW of Dulverton. SS8924.
Sowley Green *Suff.* ***Settlement***, 4m/7km NE of Haverhill. TL7050.
Sowood *W.Yorks.* ***Hamlet***, 1km S of Stainland, 4m/7km W of Huddersfield town centre. SE0718.
Sowood Green *W.Yorks.* ***Settlement***, adjoining to N of Sowood, 4m/7km W of Huddersfield town centre. SE0718.
Sowton *Devon* ***Village***, on River Clyst, 4m/6km E of Exeter. **7 H6** SX9792.
Soyal *High.* ***Locality***, 3m/4km W of Bonar Bridge. **96 C2** NH5791.
Soyea Island *High.* ***Island***, small uninhabited island off W coast of Sutherland district opposite mouth of Loch Inver. **102 C6** NC0422.
Soyland Moor *W.Yorks.* ***Open space***, moorland with White Holme Reservoir to NW and Blackstone Edge Reservoir to SW, 3m/5km NE of Littleborough. **49 J1** SD9819.
Soyland Town *W.Yorks.* ***Hamlet***, 1km N of Ripponden. SE0320.
Spa Common *Norf.* ***Hamlet***, 1m/2km E of North Walsham. **45 G2** TG2930.
Spa Valley Railway *E.Suss.* ***Other feature of interest***, preserved tourist railway, headquarters in Royal Tunbridge Wells. **13 J3** TQ5738.
Spacey Houses *N.Yorks.* ***Locality***, adjoining to SE of Pannal, 3m/4km S of Harrogate. SE3151.
Spadeadam *Cumb.* ***Settlement***, 3m/5km SE of Bewcastle. **70 A6** NY5870.
Spadeadam Forest *Cumb.* ***Forest/woodland***, large area, mainly afforested, on SW side of Wark Forest, 5m/8km N of Greenhead. **70 B6** NY6372.
Spalding *Lincs.* Population: 18,731. ***Town***, on River Welland, 14m/23km SW of Boston. Centre of bulb-growing area; annual flower festival in May. 15c Ayscoughfee Hall houses interesting museum. **43 F3** TF2422.
Spalding Marsh *Lincs.* ***Open space***, fenland on E side of River Welland, 3m/5km NE of Spalding. Standing isolated in area are ruins of Wykeham Chapel, built in 1311 by Prior Clement Hatfield to be private chapel of his country house (of which line of moat survives). **43 F3** TF2726.
Spaldington *E.Riding* ***Village***, 3m/5km N of Howden. **58 D6** SE7633.
Spaldwick *Cambs.* ***Village***, 7m/11km W of Huntingdon. **32 E1** TL1272.
Spalefield *Fife* ***Settlement***, 2m/3km N of Anstruther. **83 G7** NO5506.
Spalford *Notts.* ***Village***, 9m/14km W of Lincoln. **52 B6** SK8369.
Span Head *Devon* ***Mountain***, on Exmoor, 3m/5km SW of Simonsbath. Height 1617 feet or 493 metres. **7 F2** SS7336.
Spanby *Lincs.* ***Hamlet***, 5m/8km S of Sleaford. **42 D2** TF0938.
Spango Water ***River***, running E to Crawick Water at Spango Bridge, 6m/9km NE of Sanquhar. **68 C2** NS8217.
Spanish Head *I.o.M.* ***Coastal feature***, headland (Manx National Trust) at SW end of island, 2m/4km SW of Port St. Mary. **54 A7** SC1865.
Spar Cave (Also known as Uamh Altrumain.) *High.* ***Cave***, on Skye, on W shore of Loch Slapin, 1m/2km N of Strathaird Point. **86 B3** NG5312.
Sparham *Norf.* ***Village***, 7m/11km NE of East Dereham. **44 E4** TG0719.
Sparhamhill *Norf.* ***Settlement***, 1m/2km NE of Lyng. TG0819.
Spark Bridge *Cumb.* ***Hamlet***, 1m/2km N of Greenodd. **55 G1** SD3084.
Sparket *Cumb.* ***Locality***, 3m/4km W of Pooley Bridge. NY4325.
Sparkford *Som.* ***Village***, 4m/7km SW of Castle Cary. **9 F2** ST6026.
Sparkhill *W.Mid.* ***Suburb***, 3m/4km SE of Birmingham city centre. SP0983.
Sparkwell *Devon* ***Village***, 4m/6km W of Ivybridge. **5 F5** SX5857.
Sparnon Gate *Cornw.* ***Locality***, 1m/2km NW of Redruth. SW6843.
Sparrow Green *Norf.* ***Settlement***, 3m/4km NW of East Dereham. TF9514.
Sparrowpit *Derbys.* ***Hamlet***, 2m/3km E of Chapel-en-le-Frith. **50 C4** SK0980.
Sparrow's Green *E.Suss.* ***Suburb***, N part of Wadhurst. **13 K3** TQ6332.

S

Sparsholt *Hants.* ***Village***, 3m/5km NW of Winchester. Site of Roman building 1m/2km SW. **11 F1** SU4331.
Sparsholt *Oxon.* ***Village***, 3m/5km W of Wantage. **21 G3** SU3587.
Spartleton Edge *E.Loth.* ***Inland physical feature***, ridge running NW to SE in Lammermuir Hills 6m/10km S of Stenton. **76 E4** NT6565.
Spartylea *Northumb.* ***Settlement***, 2m/4km N of Allenheads. **61 K2** NY8548.
Spath *Staffs.* ***Hamlet***, 1m/2km N of Uttoxeter. SK0835.
Spaunton *N.Yorks.* ***Hamlet***, 3m/5km NE of Kirkbymoorside. **63 J7** SE7289.
Spaunton Moor *N.Yorks.* ***Open space***, moorland on N side of Vale of Pickering, 4m/7km N of Kirkbymoorside. **63 J7** SE7094.
Spaxton *Som.* ***Village***, 5m/7km W of Bridgwater. **8 B1** ST2237.
Spean *High.* ***River***, in Lochaber district, running W down Glen Spean to River Lochy, below Loch Lochy. **87 H6** NN1783.
Spean Bridge *High.* ***Village***, on River Spean in Lochaber district, 3m/5km E of foot of Loch Lochy at Gairlochy. Bridge built by Telford. Commandos trained hereabouts in World War II; Commando Memorial 1m/2km W. **87 J6** NN2281.
Spear Hill *W.Suss.* ***Hamlet***, 3m/5km N of Washington. TQ1317.
Speckington *Som.* ***Locality***, at E end of Yeovilton airfield, 3m/4km E of Ilchester. ST5623.
Speddoch *D. & G.* ***Settlement***, 2m/3km SW of Dunscore. **68 D5** NX8582.
Speedwell *Bristol* ***Suburb***, of Bristol, 3m/5km E of city centre. ST6374.
Speedwell Cavern *Derbys.* ***Cave***, former lead mine with underground gallery and pothole in limestone cliff, 1km W of Castleton. Most of cave system is only accessible by boat. **50 D4** SK1482.
Speen *Bucks.* ***Village***, 3m/5km SE of Princes Risborough. **22 B1** SU8499.
Speen *W.Berks.* ***Suburb***, 1m/2km W of Newbury. **21 H5** SU4568.
Speeton *N.Yorks.* ***Village***, 4m/7km SE of Filey. **59 H2** TA1474.
Speinne Mòr *Arg. & B.* ***Mountain***, rising from NE shore of Loch Frisa, 3m/5km S of Tobermory, Mull. Height 1456 feet or 444 metres. **79 G3** NM5049.
Speke *Mersey.* ***Suburb***, 7m/11km SE of Liverpool city centre. Liverpool Airport to W. **48 D4** SJ4283.
Speke Hall *Mersey.* ***Historic house***, half-timbered house (National Trust) dating from 16c, 1m/2km SW of Speke and 6m/10km SE of Liverpool city centre. **48 D4** SJ4283.
Speldhurst *Kent* ***Village***, 2m/4km NW of Royal Tunbridge Wells. **23 J7** TQ5541.
Spellbrook *Herts.* ***Village***, 3m/4km S of Bishop's Stortford. **33 H7** TL4817.
Spelsbury *Oxon.* ***Village***, 2m/3km N of Charlbury. **30 E6** SP3521.
Spen *W.Yorks.* ***Settlement***, between Cleckheaton and Gomersal. SE1925.
Spen Green *Ches.* ***Hamlet***, 3m/5km SW of Congleton. **49 H6** SJ8160.
Spencers Wood *W'ham* Population: 2765. ***Village***, 4m/7km S of Reading. **22 A5** SU7166.
Spennithorne *N.Yorks.* ***Village***, 2m/3km SE of Leyburn. Spennithorne Hall dates partly from 16c. **57 G1** SE1389.
Spennymoor *Dur.* Population: 17,381. ***Town***, former mining town, 4m/6km NE of Bishop Auckland. Trading estate 1m/2km E. **62 D3** NZ2533.
Spernall *Warks.* ***Settlement***, on River Arrow, 3m/5km N of Alcester. SP0862.
Spetchley *Worcs.* ***Village***, 3m/5km E of Worcester. **29 H3** SO8953.
Spetchley Park *Worcs.* ***Garden***, 30 acres of plantsman's garden, with rare plants, formal and kitchen gardens, 2m/3km E of Worcester. **29 H3** SO8953.
Spetisbury *Dorset* ***Village***, on River Stour, 3m/5km SE of Blandford Forum. **9 J4** ST9102.
Spexhall *Suff.* ***Hamlet***, 2m/3km N of Halesworth. **45 H7** TM3780.
Spey ***River***, major river of NE Scotland rising in Loch Spey on Corrieyairack Forest, 10m/16km S of Fort Augustus, and fed by many tributaries before flowing E past Laggan, then NE through Newtonmore and Kingussie through to Strathspey and into Loch Insh. It continues NE, following a winding course by Aviemore and Grantown-on-Spey, before turning N at Charlestown of Aberlour and continuing past Rothes to Spey Bay on Moray Firth at Kingston. Length 107m/172km. Lower course is noted for its profusion of distilleries, forming heart of Highland whisky industry. **98 B5** NJ3465.
Spey Bay *Moray* ***Village***, on bay of same name, on N coast, on E side of mouth of River Spey. **98 B4** NJ3565.
Spey Mouth *Moray* ***Sea feature***, River Spey mouth emptying into Spey Bay, 1km N of Garmouth, with Kingston on its E side. **98 B4** NJ3465.
Speybridge *High.* ***Settlement***, in Badenoch and Strathspey district, 1m/2km S of Grantown-on-Spey. **89 H2** NJ0326.
Speymouth Forest *Moray* ***Forest/woodland***, to S of Fochabers. **98 B5** NJ3657.
Speyview *Moray* ***Settlement***, to SW of Charlestown of Aberlour across Burn of Aberlour. **97 K7** NJ2642.
Spidean a' Choire Leith *High.* ***Mountain***, summit of Liathach, Ross and Cromarty district. Munro: height 3457 feet or 1054 metres. **95 F6** NG9257.
Spidean Còinich *High.* ***Mountain***, with summit 1m/2km N of Loch Assynt. Height 2506 feet or 764 metres. **102 E6** NC2027.
Spidean Coire nan Clach *High.* ***Mountain***, summit of Beinn Eighe, 4m/7km SW of Kinlochewe in Ross and Cromarty district. Munro: height 3188 feet or 972 metres. NG9659.
Spidean Dhomhuill Bhric *High.* ***Mountain***, peak on border of Lochaber and Skye and Lochalsh districts, 4m/6km S of Shiel Bridge and nearly 1m/2km W of The Saddle. Height 3083 feet or 940 metres. **87 F3** NG9212.
Spidean Mialach *High.* ***Mountain***, peak on Glenquoich Forest, Lochaber district, 1m/2km N of dam of Loch Quoich. Munro: height 3267 feet or 996 metres. **87 G4** NH0604.
Spilsby *Lincs.* Population: 2324. ***Small town***, 11m/17km W of Skegness. Birthplace of Sir John Franklin, explorer, 1768. **53 H6** TF4066.
Spindlestone *Northumb.* ***Settlement***, 3m/4km E of Belford. **77 K7** NU1533.
Spindrift *Bucks.* ***Garden***, at Jordans, 2m/3km NE of Beaconsfield. Rare trees, fine herbaceous border, terraced. Model vegetable and fruit garden. **22 C2** SU9892.
Spinkhill *Derbys.* ***Village***, 8m/13km SE of Sheffield. **51 G5** SK4578.
Spinners *Hants.* ***Garden***, on wooded slope between Boldre and Pilley, 1m/2km N of Lymington. Many choice shrubs and plants. **10 E5** SZ3398.
Spinney Hills *Leic.* ***Suburb***, 1m/2km E of Leicester city centre. SK6004.
Spinningdale *High.* ***Village***, on N shore of Dornoch Firth, Sutherland district, 8m/12km W of Dornoch. **96 D2** NH6789.
Spirthill *Wilts.* ***Hamlet***, 3m/5km N of Calne. **20 C4** ST9975.
Spital *High.* ***Settlement***, in Caithness district, 5m/8km W of Wattern. **105 G3** ND1654.
Spital *Mersey.* ***Settlement***, 1m/2km S of Bebington. SJ3383.
Spital *W. & M.* ***Suburb***, S district of Windsor. **22 C4** SU9675.
Spital Hill *S.Yorks.* ***Hamlet***, 1m/2km E of Tickhill. SK6193.
Spital in the Street *Lincs.* ***Settlement***, 9m/14km W of Market Rasen. **52 C3** SK9690.
Spital Tongues *T. & W.* ***Suburb***, 1m/2km W of Newcastle upon Tyne city centre. NZ2365.
Spitalbrook *Herts.* ***Suburb***, in S part of Hoddesdon. **23 G1** TL3607.
Spitalfields *Gt.Lon.* ***Suburb***, in borough of Tower Hamlets, to E of Liverpool Street railway station, 1m/2km NE of London Bridge. TQ3381.
Spithurst *E.Suss.* ***Settlement***, 5m/8km N of Lewes. **13 H5** TQ4217.
Spittal *D. & G.* ***Settlement***, 4m/7km W of Wigtown. **64 D5** NX3557.
Spittal *D. & G.* ***Settlement***, on E side of River Cree, 1m/2km N of Creetown. **64 E4** NX4760.
Spittal *E.Loth.* ***Settlement***, 2m/3km NE of Longniddry. **76 C3** NT4677.
Spittal *E.Riding* ***Settlement***, 3m/5km NW of Pocklington. SE7652.
Spittal *Northumb.* ***Suburb***, of Berwick-upon-Tweed, on S side of harbour. **77 J5** NU0051.
Spittal *Pembs.* ***Village***, 5m/8km N of Haverfordwest. **16 C2** SM9723.
Spittal Hill *High.* ***Hill***, 1km N of Spittal. Height 577 feet or 176 metres. **105 G3** ND1655.
Spittal of Glenmuick *Aber.* ***Hamlet***, 1km N of Loch Muick. Mountain Rescue Post. **90 B6** NO3085.
Spittal of Glenshee *P. & K.* ***Settlement***, on Shee Water, 13m/21km S of Braemar. **82 C1** NO1169.
Spittalfield *P. & K.* ***Village***, 5m/8km SW of Blairgowrie. Remains of Roman fortress at Inchtuthill, 1m/2km SE. **82 C3** NO1040.
Spixworth *Norf.* Population: 3863. ***Village***, 4m/7km N of Norwich. **45 G4** TG2415.
Splatt *Cornw.* ***Locality***, 7m/12km NW of Launceston. SX2288.
Splaynens Green *E.Suss.* ***Hamlet***, 1km N of Fletching. TQ4324.
Splott (Y Sblot.) *Cardiff* ***Suburb***, 1m/2km E of Cardiff city centre. ST2076.
Spo Ness *Ork.* ***Coastal feature***, rocky headland on W coast of Westray. **106 D3** HY4846.
Spodegreen *Ches.* ***Locality***, 1m/2km SE of Little Bollington. SJ7385.
Spofforth *N.Yorks.* ***Village***, 3m/5km NW of Wetherby. Spofforth Castle (English Heritage), ruined 14c fortified house. **57 J4** SE3651.
Spofforth Castle *N.Yorks.* ***Castle***, remains of 14c fortified manor house owned by Percy family (English Heritage) on W side of Spofforth, 4m/6km SE of Harrogate. **57 J4** SE3651.
Spon End *W.Mid.* ***Suburb***, 1m/2km W of Coventry city centre. SP3279.
Spon Green *Flints.* ***Suburb***, adjoining to SE of Buckley. SJ2863.
Spondon *Derby* ***Suburb***, 4m/6km E of Derby city centre. **41 G2** SK4035.
Spoo Ness *Shet.* ***Coastal feature***, rocky headland on W coast of Unst, 1m/2km NW of Newgord. **108 E2** HP5607.
Spooner Row *Norf.* ***Village***, 3m/4km SW of Wymondham. **44 E6** TM0997.
Spoonley *Shrop.* ***Settlement***, 1km N of Market Drayton. **39 F2** SJ6635.
Sporle *Norf.* ***Village***, 2m/4km NE of Swaffham. **44 C4** TF8411.
Spotland Bridge *Gt.Man.* ***Suburb***, 1m/2km W of Rochdale town centre. SD8813.
Spott *E.Loth.* ***Village***, 2m/3km S of Dunbar. **76 E3** NT6775.
Spott Burn *E.Loth.* ***River***, rising 1m/2km E of Stenton and flowing NE via Spott to North Sea, 1m/2km E of Dunbar. **76 E3** NT6978.
Spout Rolla *P. & K.* ***Waterfall***, in River Lednock to S of Loch Lednock Reservoir and 4m/6km NE of St. Fillans. **81 J5** NN7328.
Spratton *Northants.* ***Village***, 6m/10km NW of Northampton. **31 J2** SP7170.
Spreakley *Surr.* ***Village***, 3m/5km S of Farnham. **22 B7** SU8441.
Spreyton *Devon* ***Village***, 7m/11km E of Okehampton. **6 E6** SX6996.
Spriddlestone *Devon* ***Hamlet***, to SE of Plymouth, 3m/5km W of Yealmpton. SX5351.
Spridlington *Lincs.* ***Village***, 9m/14km N of Lincoln. **52 D4** TF0084.
Spring Gardens *Dur.* ***Hamlet***, 1km NW of West Auckland. NZ1726.
Spring Gardens *Shrop.* ***Suburb***, to NE of Shrewsbury town centre. SJ5013.
Spring Grove *Gt.Lon.* ***Suburb***, in borough of Hounslow, 1m/2km NE of Hounslow town centre. TQ1576.
Spring Head *Kent* ***Settlement***, 1m/2km S of Northfleet. Site of Roman settlement to W. TQ6172.
Spring Head *W.Yorks.* ***Locality***, 4m/6km W of Huddersfield. SE0816.
Spring Hill *Gt.Man.* ***Suburb***, 2m/3km NE of Oldham town centre. SD9506.
Spring Hill *W.Mid.* ***Suburb***, SW district of Wolverhampton. SO8895.
Spring Mill Reservoir *Lancs.* ***Lake/loch***, on border with Greater Manchester, 3m/4km NW of Rochdale. **49 H1** SD8717.
Spring Mire *W.Mid.* ***Locality***, 1m/2km W of Dudley town centre. SO9389.
Spring Park *Gt.Lon.* ***Suburb***, in borough of Croydon, 3m/4km E of Croydon town centre. TQ3665.
Spring Vale *I.o.W.* ***Hamlet***, on NE coast, 2m/3km SE of Ryde. SZ6291.
Spring Vale *S.Yorks.* ***Village***, in River Don valley, 1km E of Penistone. SE2503.
Spring Valley *I.o.M.* ***Locality***, 1m/2km W of Douglas. SC3575.
Springboig *Glas.* ***Suburb***, 3m/5km E of Glasgow city centre. NS6564.
Springburn *Glas.* ***Suburb***, 2m/3km N of Glasgow city centre. **74 E4** NS6068.
Springfield *Arg. & B.* ***Settlement***, on E coast of Loch Riddon, 2m/3km S of Auchenbreck. **73 J3** NS0179.
Springfield *Caerp.* ***Suburb***, E district of Pontllanfraith, 2m/3km SW of Newbridge. ST1895.
Springfield *D. & G.* ***Village***, adjoining to E of Gretna Green. **69 J7** NY3268.
Springfield *Essex* ***Suburb***, 2m/3km to NE of Chelmsford town centre. TL7208.
Springfield *Fife* ***Village***, 3m/4km SW of Cupar. **82 E6** NO3411.
Springfield *Gt.Man.* ***Suburb***, 1m/2km SE of Bolton town centre. SD7208.
Springfield *Moray* ***Settlement***, adjoining to N of Forres. **97 H6** NJ0460.
Springfield *P. & K.* ***Settlement***, 1m/2km S of Burrelton. **82 C4** NO1935.
Springfield *Som.* ***Suburb***, W district of Wellington. ST1321.
Springfield *W.Mid.* ***Suburb***, 2m/3km W of Oldbury. SO9688.
Springfield *W.Mid.* ***Suburb***, 3m/5km SE of Birmingham city centre. **40 C7** SP0982.
Springfield Reservoir *S.Lan.* ***Reservoir***, small reservoir 4m/6km E of Carluke. **75 H5** NS9052.
Springfields Gardens *Lincs.* ***Garden***, 25 acre garden 1m/2km NE of Spalding, containing spring flowers, roses and dahlias. Tropical house. Signposted paths through woodland to lake. **43 F3** TF2624.
Springhill *Staffs.* ***Hamlet***, 1m/2km E of Brownhills. SK0705.
Springhill *Staffs.* ***Settlement***, 4m/7km NW of Walsall. SJ9704.
Springholm *D. & G.* ***Village***, 6m/9km NE of Castle Douglas. **65 J4** NX8070.
Springkell *D. & G.* ***Settlement***, on E side of Kirtle Water, 4m/6km E of Ecclefechan. **69 H6** NY2575.
Springleys *Aber.* ***Settlement***, 2m/3km E of Rothienorman. **91 F1** NJ7437.
Springside *N.Ayr.* Population: 1364. ***Hamlet***, 3m/5km E of Irvine. **74 B7** NS3738.
Springthorpe *Lincs.* ***Village***, 4m/6km E of Gainsborough. **52 B4** SK8789.
Springwell *T. & W.* Population: 2603. ***Village***, 4m/6km SE of Gateshead. **62 D1** NZ2858.
Sprint *Cumb.* ***River***, rising S of Haweswater and flowing S into River Kent at Burneside. **61 F6** SD5095.
Sproatley *E.Riding* ***Village***, 4m/6km N of Hedon. **59 H6** TA1934.
Sproston Green *Ches.* ***Hamlet***, 2m/3km E of Middlewich. **49 G6** SJ7366.
Sprotbrough *S.Yorks.* ***Village***, 3m/4km W of Doncaster. **51 H2** SE5302.
Sproughton *Suff.* ***Village***, 3m/4km W of Ipswich. **35 F4** TM1244.
Sprouston *Sc.Bord.* ***Village***, on S side of River Tweed, 2m/3km NE of Kelso. **77 F7** NT7535.
Sprowston *Norf.* ***Suburb***, 2m/4km NE of Norwich. **45 G4** TG2411.
Sproxton *Leics.* ***Village***, 5m/8km W of Colsterworth. **42 B3** SK8524.
Sproxton *N.Yorks.* ***Village***, 2m/3km S of Helmsley. **58 C1** SE6181.
Sprunston *Cumb.* ***Settlement***, 2m/3km SE of Dalston. NY3948.
Sprytown *Devon* ***Hamlet***, 5m/8km E of Launceston. SX4185.
Spur Ness *Ork.* ***Coastal feature***, headland at SW end of Sanday. **106 F4** HY6033.
Spurlands End *Bucks.* ***Settlement***, 4m/6km NE of High Wycombe. SU8997.
Spurn Head *E.Riding* ***Coastal feature***, headland at end of long spit of land on N side of mouth of River Humber. Lighthouse 1km NE; lightship to SW. **53 H1** TA3910.
Spurstow *Ches.* ***Village***, 4m/6km S of Tarporley. **48 E7** SJ5557.
Spy Rigg *Northumb.* ***Mountain***, in Wark Forest on E side of River Irthing, 7m/11km N of Greenhead. Height 1027 feet or 313 metres. **70 B6** NY6875.

Spynie *Moray* ***Locality***, 2m/3km NE of Elgin. To N are ruins of Palace of Spynie (Historic Scotland), formerly castle of Bishops of Moray, dominated by massive 15c tower. NJ2265.
Spynie Canal *Moray* ***Canal***, extension of Terchick Burn cut to serve as a transport link for merchants in Elgin. Canal flows E from near Gilston to NW side of Loch Spynie, then N into sea at Lossiemouth. **97 K5** NJ2370.
Spyway *Dorset* ***Settlement***, to N of Askerswell, 4m/7km E of Bridport. SY5293.
Square Point *D. & G.* ***Settlement***, 1km NE of Walton Park. **65 H3** NX7771.
Squerryes Court *Kent* ***Historic house***, 17c William and Mary manor house with landscaped gardens, 1km SW of Westerham. **23 H6** TQ4453.
Squires Gate *B'pool* ***Suburb***, adjoining to S of South Shore, district of Blackpool, with Blackpool Airport to S. **55 G6** SD3132.
Srath a' Chràisg *High.* ***Valley***, to S of Strath Vagastie in Sutherland district and carrying Allt Domhain. **103 H6** NC5325.
Srath na Seilge *High.* ***Valley***, carrying Black Water river and running SE in Ben Armine Forest. **103 J7** NC6820.
Srath nan Caran *High.* ***Valley***, running W into Loch na Creige Duibhe. **103 F5** NC2836.
Srianach *W.Isles* ***Coastal feature***, promontory on N side of entrance to Loch Shell. **101 G6** NB4010.
Sròn a' Chlaonaidh *P. & K.* ***Mountain***, on E side of S end of Loch Ericht, 4m/7km N of Bridge of Ericht. Height 2050 feet or 625 metres. **81 G1** NN5065.
Sròn a' Chleirich *P. & K.* ***Mountain***, on Dail-na-mine Forest, Forest of Atholl, 9m/14km NW of Blair Atholl. Height 2676 feet or 816 metres. **88 E7** NN7876.
Sròn a' Choire Ghairbh *High.* ***Mountain***, in Lochaber district, 9m/13km N of Spean Bridge across Loch Lochy. Munro: height 3067 feet or 935 metres. **87 J5** NN2294.
Sròn Ach' a' Bhacaidh *High.* ***Hill***, in Sutherland district, 4m/6km N of Bonar Bridge. Height 928 feet or 283 metres. **96 D2** NH6198.
Sròn an Dùin *W.Isles* ***Coastal feature***, headland on W coast of Mingulay. **84 A6** NL5480.
Sròn an t-Sluichd *High.* ***Mountain***, 3m/4km S of head of Loch Eil, Lochaber district. Height 1204 feet or 367 metres. **87 F7** NM9674.
Sròn Bheag *High.* ***Coastal feature***, headland on S coast of Ardnamurchan peninsula, 2m/3km SW of Kilchoan. **79 F1** NM4662.
Sròn Bheag *P. & K.* ***Mountain***, rounded summit in Rannoch district, 3m/4km N of Bridge of Ericht. Height 1689 feet or 515 metres. **81 G1** NN5262.
Sròn Choin *P. & K.* ***Mountain***, to N of Loch Errochty, 3m/4km NW of Trinafour. Height 1856 feet or 566 metres. **81 H1** NN6866.
Sròn Doire *Arg. & B.* ***Settlement***, in Knapdale, 7m/11km N of Tarbert. **73 G3** NR8478.
Sròn Garbh *Arg. & B.* ***Coastal feature***, rocky headland to E of Ardfernal, Jura. **72 D3** NR5670.
Sròn Gharbh *Stir.* ***Mountain***, on SE side of Glen Falloch, 3m/4km S of Crianlarich. Height 2322 feet or 708 metres. **80 E5** NN3721.
Sròn Gun Aran *High.* ***Inland physical feature***, rounded ridge between the steep-sided valleys of Gleann Mòr and Alladale River. **96 B3** NH4088.
Sròn Mhòr *Arg. & B.* ***Mountain***, rising above River Massan, 1m/2km SW of Beinn Mhòr. Height 1670 feet or 509 metres. **73 J2** NS0989.
Sròn Mòr *P. & K.* ***Inland physical feature***, mountain ridge on W side of Glen Tarken rising to 2204 feet or 672 metres, 3m/4km NW of St. Fillans. **81 H5** NN6525.
Sròn na h-Airde Baine *High.* ***Coastal feature***, headland on W coast of Ross and Cromarty district, 1m/2km NW of Toscaig. **94 C7** NG6939.
Sròn nan Saobhaidh *High.* ***Mountain***, in Ross and Cromarty district, at NE end of Orrin Reservoir, 9m/13km W of Muir of Ord. Height 1338 feet or 408 metres. **96 B6** NH3951.
Sròn Ocrhulan *High.* ***Hill***, 3m/4km SE of Vaternish Point, Skye. Height 823 feet or 251 metres. **93 H5** NG2463.
Sròn Raineach *High.* ***Coastal feature***, headland on N coast of North Morar, 2m/3km E of Mallaig. **86 D5** NM7098.
Sròn Romul *W.Isles* ***Mountain***, highest point of Scarp, 3m/4km NW of Huisinis, North Harris. Height 1010 feet or 308 metres. **100 B6** NA9615.
Sròn Ruadh *W.Isles* ***Coastal feature***, headland on E coast of Isle of Lewis, 3m/5km NE of Stornoway. **101 G4** NB4636.
Sròn Ruail *High.* ***Coastal feature***, headland on Canna, to S of Garrisdale Point. **85 H4** NG2104.
Sròn Thoraraidh *High.* ***Mountain***, 3m/4km NE of Lochailort to N of Loch Eilt. Height 1256 feet or 383 metres. **86 E6** NM8083.
Sronphadruig Lodge *P. & K.* ***Settlement***, 6m/10km SE of Dalwhinnie. **88 E7** NN7178.
Stableford *Shrop.* ***Hamlet***, 5m/7km NE of Bridgnorth. SO7598.
Stableford *Staffs.* ***Settlement***, 5m/8km SW of Newcastle-under-Lyme. **40 A2** SJ8138.
Stac a' Bhothain *High.* ***Coastal feature***, headland on E coast of Vaternish peninsula, 6m/10km SE of Vaternish Point, Skye. **93 H6** NG2859.
Stac an Aoineidh *Arg. & B.* ***Island***, islet off SW coast of Iona. **78 D5** NM2522.
Stac an Armin *W.Isles* ***Island***, islet (National Trust for Scotland) lying off N end of Boreray, about 52m/83km W of North Harris. Attains height of 643 feet or 196 metres. Haunt of sea birds. NA1506.
Stac Lee *W.Isles* ***Island***, islet (National Trust for Scotland) lying off W side of Boreray, about 52m/83km W of North Harris. Attains height of 1259 feet or 384 metres. Haunt of sea birds. NA1404.
Stac Mhic Mhurchaidh *Arg. & B.* ***Island***, islet on W side of Réidh Eilean, off NW coast of Iona. NM2426.
Stac na Cathaig *High.* ***Mountain***, in Inverness district, 9m/14km S of Inverness. Height 1463 feet or 446 metres. **88 D1** NH6330.
Stac Pollaidh (Anglicised form: Stac Polly.) *High.* ***Mountain***, well-known landmark in Ross and Cromarty district to N of Loch Lurgainn. Height 2011 feet or 613 metres. **102 D7** NC1010.
Stac Polly *High. Anglicised form of Stac Pollaidh, qv.*
Stacashal *W.Isles* ***Hill***, 6m/9km E of Breascleit, Isle of Lewis. Height 708 feet or 216 metres. **101 F4** NB3037.
Stacey Bank *S.Yorks.* ***Hamlet***, 5m/7km NW of Sheffield. SK2890.
Stack Clo Kearvaig *High.* ***Coastal feature***, stack just off N coast of Sutherland district, 3m/4km SE of Cape Wrath. **102 E1** NC2973.
Stack Islands *W.Isles* ***Island***, group of islets off S coast of Eriskay in Sound of Barra. **84 C4** NF7807.
Stack of Skudiburgh *High.* ***Coastal feature***, headland on W coast of Trotternish peninsula, Skye, 1m/2km NW of Uig. **93 J5** NG3465.
Stack of the Horse *Shet.* ***Coastal feature***, rocky promontory with natural arches on E coast of Yell, 1m/2km SE of Gassabrough. **108 E4** HU5381.
Stack of Ulbster *High.* ***Coastal feature***, stack on E coast, 2m/3km S of Thrumster. **105 J4** ND3341.
Stack Rock *Pembs.* ***Island***, rock in Milford Haven off South Hook Point. Included in parish of Herbrandston. SM8604.
Stack Rocks *Pembs.* ***Coastal feature***, group of rocks off S shore of St. Brides Bay, 2m/3km NE of The Nab Head. **16 A3** SM8113.
Stackhouse *N.Yorks.* ***Settlement***, in Ribble valley, 1m/2km N of Settle. **56 D3** SD8165.
Stackpole *Pembs.* ***Hamlet***, 3m/5km S of Pembroke. **16 C5** SR9896.
Stackpole Elidor *Pembs. Alternative name for Cheriton, qv.*
Stackpole Head *Pembs.* ***Coastal feature***, headland 2m/3km SE of Stackpole. **16 C5** SR9896.
Stacks of Duncansby *High.* ***Coastal feature***, group of offshore rocks 1m/2km S of Duncansby Head. **105 K1** ND3971.
Stacksteads *Lancs.* ***Locality***, 1m/2km SW of Bacup. **56 D7** SD8421.
Staddiscombe *Plym.* ***Hamlet***, at most southerly point of Plymouth, 4m/7km W of Yealmpton. **5 F5** SX5151.
Staddlethorpe *E.Riding* ***Locality***, adjoining to SE of Gilberdyke. **58 E7** SE8328.
Staden *Derbys.* ***Settlement***, 1m/2km SE of Buxton. SK0772.
Stadhampton *Oxon.* ***Village***, 6m/9km N of Wallingford. **21 K2** SU6098.
Stadhlaigearraidh (Anglicised form: Stilligarry.) *W.Isles* ***Village***, on South Uist, on W side of Loch Druidibeg. **84 C1** NF7638.
Staffa *Arg. & B.* ***Island***, uninhabited island of basaltic rock in Inner Hebrides, lying 5m/7km SE of Lunga in the Treshnish Isles group and 6m/9km N of Iona. Area 70 acres or 28 hectares. Island is owned by National Trust for Scotland. Among several notable caves the best known is Fingal's Cave. Various sea birds are to be seen. **78 E4** NM3235.
Staffield *Cumb.* ***Hamlet***, 1m/2km NW of Kirkoswald. **61 G2** NY5541.
Staffin *High.* ***Village***, near NE coast, 6m/10km E of Uig. **93 K5** NG4867.
Staffin Bay *High.* ***Bay***, on NE coast of Skye, 6m/10km SE of Rubha Hunish. **93 K5** NG4868.
Staffin Island *High.* ***Island***, small uninhabited island to E of Staffin Bay, Skye. **93 K5** NG4969.
Stafford *Staffs.* Population: 61,885. ***Town***, of Saxon origin, on River Sow, 14m/23km S of Stoke-on-Trent. Stafford Castle is unfinished 19c structure on site of earlier castle 1m/2km SW of town centre. Izaac Walton was born here in 1593. Town Mill has two waterwheels. **40 B3** SJ9223.
Stafford Ancient High House *Staffs.* ***Historic house***, Elizabethan house built 1595 in Stafford town centre, reputed to be largest timber-framed house in England. Was home to Richard Sneyd and Charles I stayed here in 1642. Houses museum of Staffordshire Yeomanry (Queen's Own Royal Regiment). **40 B3** SJ9123.
Stafford Castle *Staffs.* ***Castle***, 1m/2km SW of Stafford town centre. 11c motte built by William I, with 14c stone castle added. Demolished during Civil War and partly rebuilt in Gothic style in 19c. **40 B3** SJ9022.
Stafford Park *Tel. & W.* ***Locality***, industrial estate 1m/2km NE of Telford town centre. SJ7109.
Staffordlake *Surr.* ***Settlement***, 1km S of Bisley. SU9458.
Stagden Cross *Essex* ***Settlement***, 4m/7km S of Great Dunmow. **33 K7** TL6314.
Stagsden *Beds.* ***Village***, 4m/7km W of Bedford. **32 C4** SP9849.
Stagshaw Bank *Northumb.* ***Settlement***, 2m/3km N of Corbridge. **70 E7** NY9867.
Stagshaw Garden *Cumb.* ***Garden***, National Trust property, 1km S of Ambleside, designed by Cubby Acland. Colourful gardens in woodland setting. **60 E6** NY3803.
Stain *High.* ***Settlement***, on E coast, 1km S of Keiss. **105 J2** ND3460.
Stain Dale *N.Yorks.* ***Valley***, carrying Staindale Beck before it becomes Dalby Beck, 1m/2km E of Lockton. **63 K7** SE8689.
Stainborough *S.Yorks.* ***Locality***, 3m/5km SW of Barnsley. SE3102.
Stainburn *Cumb.* ***Locality***, 1m/2km E of Workington. NY0128.
Stainburn *N.Yorks.* ***Village***, 4m/6km NE of Otley. **57 H5** SE2448.
Stainby *Lincs.* ***Village***, 2m/3km SW of Colsterworth. **42 C3** SK9022.
Staincliffe *W.Yorks.* ***Suburb***, 1m/2km NW of Dewsbury. SE2323.
Staincross *S.Yorks.* ***Locality***, 2m/4km N of Barnsley. **51 F2** SE3310.
Staindrop *Dur.* ***Village***, 5m/9km NE of Barnard Castle. **62 C4** NZ1220.
Staines *Surr.* Population: 51,167. ***Town***, on site of old Roman town of Pontes, on River Thames, 17m/28km W of London. Staines Reservoirs, pair of reservoirs separated by causeway, to N; other reservoirs in vicinity. London (Heathrow) Airport 4m/6km NE. **22 D4** TQ0371.
Staines Green *Herts.* ***Settlement***, 2m/3km W of Hertford. TL2911.
Stainfield *Lincs.* ***Settlement***, 3m/5km N of Bourne. **42 D3** TF0825.
Stainfield *Lincs.* ***Settlement***, 2m/3km N of Bardney. **52 E5** TF1173.
Stainforth *N.Yorks.* ***Village***, on River Ribble, 2m/4km N of Settle. 17c bridge (National Trust). **56 D3** SD8267.
Stainforth *S.Yorks.* Population: 6756. ***Small town***, attractive town on River Don, 7m/11km NE of Doncaster. **51 J1** SE6411.
Stainforth Bridge *N.Yorks.* ***Bridge***, 17c packhorse bridge over River Ribble, between Stainforth and Little Stainforth, 3m/4km N of Settle. Just below the bridge is waterfall in wooded ravine. **56 D3** SD8167.
Staining *Lancs.* ***Village***, 3m/4km E of Blackpool. **55 G6** SD3436.
Stainland *W.Yorks.* ***Village***, 2m/3km SW of Elland. **50 C1** SE0719.
Stainmore Common *Cumb.* ***Open space***, moorland area to N of Stainmore. **61 K5** NY8315.
Stainmore Forest *Dur.* ***Open space***, moorland area on border of Cumbria and Durham, to SE of Stainmore. **62 A5** NY8315.
Stainsacre *N.Yorks.* ***Village***, 2m/3km SE of Whitby. **63 J2** NZ9108.
Stainsby *Derbys.* ***Hamlet***, 1km S of Heath. SK4565.
Stainsby *Lincs.* ***Settlement***, 1m/2km W of Hagworthingham. TF3371.
Stainton *Cumb.* ***Locality***, 1m/2km W of Carlisle across River Eden. NY3856.
Stainton *Cumb.* ***Village***, 3m/4km SW of Penrith. **61 F4** NY4828.
Stainton *Cumb.* ***Village***, 4m/7km S of Kendal. **55 J1** SD5285.
Stainton *Dur.* ***Village***, 2m/3km NE of Barnard Castle. **62 B5** NZ0718.
Stainton *Middbro.* ***Village***, 4m/6km S of Middlesbrough. **63 F5** NZ4814.
Stainton *N.Yorks.* ***Hamlet***, 4m/6km N of Leyburn. **62 B7** SE1096.
Stainton *S.Yorks.* ***Village***, 2m/3km NE of Maltby. **51 H3** SK5593.
Stainton by Langworth *Lincs.* ***Village***, 4m/7km W of Wragby. **52 D5** TF0677.
Stainton Fell *Cumb.* ***Open space***, below and to W of cliffs of Stainton Pike, 4m/6km E of Ravenglass. **60 C7** SD1494.
Stainton le Vale *Lincs.* ***Village***, 2m/4km W of Binbrook. **52 E3** TF1794.
Stainton Moor *N.Yorks.* ***Open space***, moorland with highest point being Whit Fell (1336 feet or 411 metres), 3m/5km NW of Leyburn. **62 B7** SE0795.
Stainton with Adgarley *Cumb.* ***Village***, 2m/3km SE of Dalton-in-Furness. **55 F2** SD2472.
Staintondale *N.Yorks.* ***Village***, 7m/11km NW of Scarborough. **63 J3** SE9998.
Stair *Cumb.* ***Settlement***, 2m/4km SW of Keswick across Derwent Water. **60 D4** NY2321.
Stair *E.Ayr.* ***Village***, on River Ayr, 7m/11km E of Ayr. **67 J1** NS4323.
Stairfoot *S.Yorks.* ***Suburb***, 2m/3km E of Barnsley town centre. SE3705.
Staith *Norf.* ***Settlement***, on River Waveney, 4m/6km SE of Haddiscoe. TM4993.
Staithes *N.Yorks.* ***Village***, surrounded by high cliffs on North Sea coast, 9m/14km NW of Whitby. **63 J5** NZ7818.
Stake Fell *N.Yorks.* ***Open space***, moorland on S side of Wensleydale, 3m/5km SW of Aysgarth. **56 E1** SD9586.
Stake Hill *Gt.Man.* ***Locality***, 3m/5km S of Rochdale. Series of locks on Rochdale Canal on W side. SD8808.
Stake Pass *Cumb.* ***Other feature of interest***, mountain footpath, part of Cumbrian Way, between Borrowdale and Great Langdale. **60 D6** NY2608.
Stake Pool *Lancs.* ***Hamlet***, 1km SE of Pilling. **55 H5** SD4147.
Stakeford *Northumb.* ***Village***, 1m/2km S of Ashington. **71 H5** NZ2685.
Stakes *Hants.* ***Suburb***, S district of Waterlooville. Site of Roman villa to S. SU6808.
Stalbridge *Dorset* Population: 2344. ***Village***, 7m/11km W of Wincanton. **9 G3** ST7317.
Stalbridge Weston *Dorset* ***Hamlet***, 1m/2km SW of Stalbridge. **9 G3** ST7317.
Stalham *Norf.* Population: 4034. ***Village***, 7m/11km SE of North Walsham. **45 H3** TG3725.
Stalham Green *Norf.* ***Locality***, adjoining to E of Stalham. **45 H3** TG3824.
Stalisfield Green *Kent* ***Village***, 2m/3km N of Charing. **14 E2** TQ9552.
Stall Moor *Devon* ***Open space***, moorland to S of Dartmoor, 5m/8km N of Ivybridge. **5 G4** SX6264.
Stalling Busk *N.Yorks.* ***Settlement***, 3m/5km S of Bainbridge. **56 E1** SD9185.
Stallingborough *N.E.Lincs.* ***Village***, 5m/8km W of Grimsby. **53 F1** TA1911.
Stallington *Staffs.* ***Hamlet***, 4m/7km NE of Stone. SJ9439.
Stalmine *Lancs.* ***Village***, 1m/2km SE of Preesall. **55 G5** SD3745.
Stalmine Moss Side *Lancs.* ***Settlement***, adjoining to SE of Stalmine. SD3745.
Stalybridge *Gt.Man.* Population: 22,921. ***Town***, old cotton town, 8m/12km E of Manchester. Many interesting Victorian buildings. **49 J3** SJ9698.

Stalyhill *Gt.Man.* ***Locality***, 2m/3km SE of Stalybridge. SJ9897.
Stambourne *Essex* ***Village***, 4m/7km NE of Finchingfield. **34 B5** TL7238.
Stamford *Lincs.* Population: 17,492. ***Town***, ancient stone-built town designated England's first conservation area in 1967, on River Welland 12m/19km NW of Peterborough. Former industries were pottery, iron-working and cloth. On edge of town is Burghley House, a 16c building by William Cecil, in parkland where famous horse trials take place annually. **42 D5** TF0307.
Stamford *Northumb.* ***Hamlet***, 1m/2km NE of Rennington. **71 H2** NU2219.
Stamford Bridge *Ches.* ***Hamlet***, 4m/7km E of Chester. SJ4667.
Stamford Bridge *E.Riding* Population: 3099. ***Village***, at crossing of River Derwent, 7m/12km E of York. Site of battle in 1066 in which King Harold of England defeated Harald Hardrada of Norway. **58 D4** SE7155.
Stamford Hill *Gt.Lon.* ***Suburb***, in borough of Hackney, 5m/8km NE of Charing Cross. TQ3387.
Stamford Museum *Lincs.* ***Other feature of interest***, museum with local history exhibits, in Stamford. Site of tourist information centre. **42 D5** TF0307.
Stamfordham *Northumb.* ***Village***, 6m/9km N of Prudhoe. **71 F6** NZ0772.
Stamshaw *Ports.* ***Suburb***, 1m/2km N of Portsmouth city centre. SU6402.
Stanage Edge *S.Yorks.* ***Inland physical feature***, mountain cliff edge extending for 3m/4km to W of Hallam Moors, 2m/3km NE of Bamford. Popular climbing area. **50 E4** SK2384.
Stanah *Lancs.* ***Hamlet***, on W side of River Wyre estuary, 2m/3km N of Poulton-le-Fylde. SD3542.
Stanborough *Herts.* ***Hamlet***, 1m/2km SW of Welwyn Garden City. **33 F7** TL2211.
Stanbridge *Beds.* ***Village***, 3m/5km E of Leighton Buzzard. **32 C6** SP9624.
Stanbridge *Dorset* ***Hamlet***, 2m/3km N of Wimborne Minster. **10 B4** SU0003.
Stanbridge Earls *Hants.* ***Educational establishment***, 15c-16c house with later additions, 1m/2km NW of Romsey. Now used as school. **10 E2** SU3323.
Stanbury *W.Yorks.* ***Hamlet***, 1m/2km W of Haworth. **57 F6** SE0137.
Stand *Gt.Man.* ***Suburb***, adjoining to SW of Whitefield. SD7905.
Stand *N.Lan.* ***Settlement***, 2m/4km N of Airdrie. **75 F4** NS7668.
Standburn *Falk.* ***Village***, 4m/7km SE of Falkirk. **75 H3** NS9274.
Standeford *Staffs.* ***Village***, 6m/9km N of Wolverhampton. **40 B5** SJ9107.
Standen *Kent* ***Settlement***, 1m/2km N of Biddenden. **14 D3** TQ8540.
Standen *Lancs.* ***Locality***, on S side of Clitheroe, comprising Higher and Lower Standen. SD7440.
Standen *W.Suss.* ***Historic house***, Victorian house and garden (National Trust) 2m/3km S of East Grinstead. **13 G3** TQ3835.
Standen Street *Kent* ***Settlement***, 3m/5km E of Hawkhurst. TQ8030.
Standerwick *Som.* ***Hamlet***, 3m/5km NE of Frome. ST8250.
Standford *Hants.* ***Village***, 5m/8km W of Hindhead. **12 B3** SU8134.
Standford Bridge *Tel. & W.* ***Settlement***, 1km SW of Sambrook. SJ7024.
Standingstone *Cumb.* ***Hamlet***, adjoining to W of Broughton Moor. NY0533.
Standingstone *Cumb.* ***Locality***, adjoining to N of Wigton. NY2549.
Standish *Glos.* ***Settlement***, 4m/6km NW of Stroud. SO8008.
Standish *Gt.Man.* Population: 12,196. ***Town***, medieval town, 3m/5km NW of Wigan. **48 E1** SD5610.
Standish Lower Ground *Gt.Man.* ***Locality***, on N side of Leeds and Liverpool Canal, 2m/3km NW of Wigan town centre. SD5507.
Standish Moreton *Glos.* ***Locality***, to W of Standish. SO7908.
Standlake *Oxon.* ***Village***, on River Windrush, 5m/8km SE of Witney. **21 G1** SP3903.
Standon *Hants.* ***Hamlet***, 4m/6km SW of Winchester. **11 F2** SU4226.

S

Standon *Herts.* Population: 2731. ***Village***, 6m/10km W of Bishop's Stortford. **33 G6** TL3922.
Standon *Staffs.* ***Village***, 4m/6km N of Eccleshall. **40 A2** SJ8134.
Standon Green End *Herts.* ***Hamlet***, 4m/6km N of Ware. TL3619.
Standwell Green *Suff.* ***Locality***, adjoining to NW of Thorndon. TM1370.
Stane *N.Lan.* ***Village***, 1m/2km SE of Shotts. **75 G5** NS8859.
Stane Street ***Other feature of interest***, Roman road, built by Roman engineer Belinus, running from Chichester to London. Present day A29 road follows course for considerable stretches. **12 D4** TQ0926.
Stanecastle *N.Ayr.* ***Suburb***, adjoining Irvine to E. NS3340.
Stanegate *Northumb.* ***Other feature of interest***, Roman road built c. AD 80, course of which originally ran from Carlisle to Corbridge. **70 D7** NY8167.
Stanerandy Standing Stones *Ork.* ***Historic/prehistoric site***, mound and two standing stones at Stanerandy in N part of Mainland. **106 B5** HY2627.
Staneydale Temple *Shet.* ***Historic/prehistoric site***, heel-shaped Stone Age temple (Historic Scotland) enclosed by stone circle, 1km S of Stanydale, Mainland. Provided central point of previously sizeable Stone Age community. **109 B7** HU2850.
Stanfield *Norf.* ***Village***, 6m/9km NW of East Dereham. **44 D3** TF9320.
Stanfield *Stoke* ***Suburb***, 1km NE of Burslem. SJ8750.
Stanford *Beds.* ***Village***, 2m/3km NE of Shefford. **32 E4** TL1641.
Stanford *Kent* ***Village***, 3m/5km NW of Hythe. **15 G4** TR1238.
Stanford *Norf.* ***Locality***, 4m/6km E of Mundford. TL8594.
Stanford *Shrop.* ***Settlement***, 1m/2km SW of Alberbury. SJ3312.
Stanford Bishop *Here.* ***Village***, 3m/5km SE of Bromyard. **29 F3** SO6851.
Stanford Bridge *Worcs.* ***Village***, on River Teme, 7m/11km SW of Stourport-on-Severn. **29 G2** SO7165.
Stanford Dingley *W.Berks.* ***Village***, 5m/8km SW of Pangbourne. **21 J4** SU5771.
Stanford End *W'ham* ***Settlement***, 1m/2km W of Riseley. SU7063.
Stanford Hall *Leics.* ***Historic house***, 1m/2km E of Swinford and 6m/9km NE of Rugby. 15c home of Cave family, with example of work of 16c Warwick architect, Smith, on Hall. Grounds include rose garden and early ha-ha. **31 G1** SP5879.
Stanford in the Vale *Oxon.* ***Village***, 5m/8km NW of Wantage. **21 G2** SU3493.
Stanford-le-Hope *Thur.* Population: 15,374. ***Town***, 5m/8km NE of Tilbury. **24 C3** TQ6882.
Stanford on Avon *Northants.* ***Village***, 6m/10km NE of Rugby. Stanford Reservoir to NE. **31 G1** SP5878.
Stanford on Soar *Notts.* ***Village***, 1m/2km N of Loughborough. **41 H3** SK5422.
Stanford on Teme *Worcs.* ***Village***, 7m/11km E of Tenbury Wells. **29 G2** SO7065.
Stanford Rivers *Essex* ***Settlement***, 2m/3km SW of Chipping Ongar. **23 J1** TL5300.
Stanford's End *Kent* ***Locality***, 1m/2km S of Edenbridge. TQ4544.
Stanfree *Derbys.* ***Village***, 3m/4km N of Bolsover. SK4774.
Stanger Head *Ork.* ***Coastal feature***, headland on E coast of Westray, N of Rapness. **106 E3** HY5142.
Stanghow *R. & C.* ***Village***, 4m/6km S of Saltburn. **63 H5** NZ6715.
Stanground *Peter.* ***Suburb***, SE district of Peterborough. **43 F6** TL2097.
Stanhill *Lancs.* ***Locality***, 2m/3km W of Accrington. SD7227.
Stanhoe *Norf.* ***Village***, 2m/4km E of Docking. **44 C2** TF8037.
Stanhope *Dur.* Population: 1342. ***Small town***, former lead-mining town on River Wear, 5m/8km W of Wolsingham. **62 A3** NY9939.
Stanhope *Sc.Bord.* ***Settlement***, situated where Stanhope Burn enters River Tweed valley, 3m/5km S of Drumelzier. **69 G1** NT1229.
Stanhope Bretby *Derbys.* ***Locality***, 1m/2km SW of Bretby. SK2822.
Stanhope Burn *Sc.Bord.* ***River***, rising on slopes of Dollar Law and flowing NW to River Tweed, 3m/4km SW of Drumelzier. **69 G1** NT1130.
Stanhope Common *Dur.* ***Open space***, moorland to E of Rookhope. **62 A2** NY9542.
Stanion *Northants.* ***Village***, 2m/3km SE of Corby. **42 C7** SP9186.
Stank *Cumb.* ***Settlement***, 2m/4km E of Barrow-in-Furness. SD2370.
Stanklyn *Worcs.* ***Hamlet***, 3m/4km SE of Kidderminster. SO8574.
Stanks *W.Yorks.* ***Suburb***, 4m/7km E of Leeds city centre. SE3635.
Stanley *Derbys.* ***Village***, 5m/8km NE of Derby. **41 G1** SK4140.
Stanley *Dur.* Population: 18,905. ***Town***, former coal-mining town, 5m/8km W of Chester-le-Street. Nearby is Beamish North of England Open Air Museum. **62 C1** NZ1953.
Stanley *Dur.* ***Village***, 2m/3km N of Crook. NZ1637.
Stanley *Lancs.* ***Suburb***, NW district of Skelmersdale. SD4707.
Stanley *Notts.* ***Hamlet***, 3m/5km NW of Sutton in Ashfield. SK4662.
Stanley *P. & K.* Population: 1274. ***Village***, on River Tay, 8m/12km SE of Dunkeld and 6m/9km N of Perth. **82 C4** NO1033.
Stanley *Shrop.* ***Settlement***, in River Severn valley, 5m/9km NW of Bewdley. SO7483.
Stanley *Staffs.* ***Village***, 6m/9km NE of Stoke-on-Trent. **49 J7** SJ9352.
Stanley *W.Yorks.* Population: 9568. ***Locality***, 1m/2km NE of Wakefield. **57 J7** SE3423.
Stanley *Wilts.* ***Settlement***, 3m/4km E of Chippenham. Site of medieval abbey 1km SE. **20 C4** ST9572.
Stanley Burn *T. & W.* ***River***, rising S of Prudhoe and flowing N to join River Tyne at Wylam, 2m/3km NE of Prudhoe. **71 F7** NZ1264.
Stanley Common *Derbys.* ***Locality***, 1m/2km N of Stanley. **41 G1** SK4142.
Stanley Crook *Dur.* ***Locality***, adjoining to N of Billy Row, 2m/3km N of Crook. NZ1638.
Stanley Downton *Glos.* ***Settlement***, 3m/6km W of Stroud. SO8004.
Stanley Ferry *W.Yorks.* ***Locality***, to E of Stanley, at road crossing of Aire and Calder Canal, 2m/3km NE of Wakefield city centre. SE3522.
Stanley Force *Cumb.* ***Waterfall***, on Stanley Ghyll 1m/2km S of Boot. **60 C7** SD1799.
Stanley Gate *Lancs.* ***Village***, 2m/3km W of Skelmersdale. SD4405.
Stanley Green *Gt.Man.* ***Locality***, 2m/3km W of Bramhall. SJ8684.
Stanley Green *Poole* ***Suburb***, 1m/2km N of Poole town centre, beside Holes Bay. SZ0192.
Stanley Hill *Here.* ***Hamlet***, 5m/8km NW of Ledbury. SO6744.
Stanley Hill *P. & K.* *See Dunkeld.*
Stanley Lane Ends *W.Yorks.* ***Locality***, to N of Stanley. SE3422.
Stanley Moor *Staffs.* ***Settlement***, 1km SW of Stanley. SJ9251.
Stanleygreen *Shrop.* ***Hamlet***, 4m/7km S of Whitchurch. SJ5235.
Stanleytown *R.C.T.* ***Hamlet***, in Rhondda Fach valley, above Pontygwaith, 1km S of Tylorstown. ST0194.
Stanlow *Ches.* ***Locality***, site of large oil refinery, 1m/2km E of Ellesmere Port. SJ4376.
Stanlow *Shrop.* ***Settlement***, 6m/10km NE of Bridgnorth. SO7999.
Stanlow Banks *Mersey.* ***Coastal feature***, sandbank to N of Ellesmere Port. **48 D5** SJ4178.
Stanmer *B. & H.* ***Village***, 4m/6km NE of Brighton town centre. University of Sussex in Stanmer Park to SE. **13 G6** TQ3309.
Stanmore *Gt.Lon.* ***Suburb***, in borough of Harrow, 11m/17km NW of Charing Cross. **22 E2** TQ1692.
Stanmore *Hants.* ***Suburb***, SW district of Winchester. SU4628.
Stanmore *Shrop.* ***Locality***, 2m/3km E of Bridgnorth. SO7492.
Stanmore *W.Berks.* ***Hamlet***, 2m/3km SW of E Ilsley. **21 H4** SU4778.
Stannergate *Dundee* ***Suburb***, 2m/3km E of Dundee city centre, adjacent to Firth of Tay. NO4330.
Stannersburn *Northumb.* ***Hamlet***, at E end of Kielder Water, 1km S of Falstone. **70 C5** NY7286.
Stannery Knowe *E.Ayr.* ***Mountain***, with forested summit, 5m/8km NE of Patna. Height 1191 feet or 363 metres. **67 J2** NS4813.
Stanningfield *Suff.* ***Hamlet***, 5m/8km S of Bury St. Edmunds. **34 C3** TL8756.
Stanningley *W.Yorks.* ***Suburb***, adjoining to N of Pudsey. SE2234.
Stannington *Northumb.* ***Village***, 4m/7km S of Morpeth. **71 H6** NZ2179.
Stannington *S.Yorks.* ***Suburb***, 3m/5km W of Sheffield. **51 F4** SK3088.
Stanpit *Dorset* ***Suburb***, 1m/2km E of Christchurch town centre. SZ1792.
Stansbatch *Here.* ***Hamlet***, 3m/5km SE of Presteigne. **28 C2** SO3461.
Stansfield *Suff.* ***Village***, 5m/7km N of Clare. **34 B3** TL7852.
Stanshope *Staffs.* ***Hamlet***, 2m/3km N of Ilam. SK1254.
Stanstead *Suff.* ***Village***, 3m/4km NW of Long Melford. **34 C4** TL8449.
Stanstead Abbots *Herts.* ***Village***, on River Lea, 3m/4km SE of Ware. **33 G7** TL3911.
Stanstead St. Margarets *Herts.* ***Locality***, containing village of St. Margarets, 2m/3km SE of Ware. TL3811.
Stanstead Street *Suff.* ***Hamlet***, to S of Stanstead. TL8449.
Stansted *Essex* *Familiar form of Stansted Mountfitchet, qv.*
Stansted *Kent* ***Village***, 2m/3km N of Wrotham. **24 C5** TQ6062.
Stansted Airport *Essex* ***Airport/airfield***, international airport 2m/3km SE of Stansted Mountfitchet and 3m/4km E of Bishop's Stortford. Functions as airport for London. **33 J6** TL5124.
Stansted Mountfitchet (Commonly known as Stansted.) *Essex* Population: 4943. ***Village***, 3m/5km NE of Bishop's Stortford. **33 J6** TL5124.
Stansted Park *W.Suss.* ***Historic house***, 2m/3km E of Rowland's Castle and 8m/12km NW of Chichester. Built in Wren style at beginning of 20c. Features ancient chapel, walled gardens and arboretum. **11 J3** SU7610.
Stanthorne *Ches.* ***Locality***, 1m/2km W of Middlewich. SJ6865.
Stanton *Derbys.* ***Settlement***, 2m/3km W of Swadlincote. **40 E4** SK2719.
Stanton *Glos.* ***Village***, 3m/4km SW of Broadway. **30 B5** SP0634.
Stanton *Mon.* ***Hamlet***, 1m/2km NW of Llanvihangel Crucorney. SO3121.
Stanton *Northumb.* ***Settlement***, 4m/6km NW of Morpeth. **71 G4** NZ1390.
Stanton *Staffs.* ***Village***, 4m/6kmW of Ashbourne. **40 D1** SK1246.
Stanton *Suff.* Population: 2131. ***Village***, 3m/5km NE of Ixworth. Site of Roman villa 1m/2km NW. **34 D1** TL9673.
Stanton Butts *Cambs.* ***Suburb***, in NW part of Huntingdon. TL2372.
Stanton by Bridge *Derbys.* ***Village***, 2m/3km NW of Melbourne. The bridge referred to in the name is Swarkestone Bridge. **41 F3** SK3727.
Stanton by Dale *Derbys.* ***Village***, 2m/4km S of Ilkeston. **41 G2** SK4638.
Stanton Drew *B. & N.E.Som.* ***Village***, 6m/10km S of Bristol. **19 J5** ST5963.
Stanton Drew Stone Circles *B. & N.E.Som.* ***Historic/prehistoric site***, 1m/2km E of Chew Magna. Second largest stone circle in Britain (after Avebury), comprising three stone circles and also a cove of three stones (English Heritage). **19 J5** ST5963.
Stanton Fitzwarren *Swin.* ***Village***, 2m/3km SW of Highworth. Site of Roman building to SW. **20 E2** SU1790.
Stanton Ford *Derbys.* ***Settlement***, on River Derwent, 1km N of Baslow. SK2473.
Stanton Harcourt *Oxon.* ***Village***, 3m/4km SW of Eynsham. **21 H1** SP4105.
Stanton Hill *Notts.* ***Village***, 1m/2km NW of Sutton in Ashfield. **51 G6** SK4860.
Stanton in Peak *Derbys.* ***Village***, 1m/2km SW of Rowsley. **50 E6** SK2464.
Stanton Lacy *Shrop.* ***Village***, on River Corve, 3m/5km N of Ludlow. **28 D1** SO4978.
Stanton Lees *Derbys.* ***Hamlet***, 3m/5km NW of Matlock. SK2563.
Stanton Long *Shrop.* ***Village***, 7m/11km SW of Much Wenlock. **38 E6** SO5790.
Stanton-on-the-Wolds *Notts.* ***Village***, 7m/12km SE of Nottingham. **41 J2** SK6330.
Stanton Prior *B. & N.E.Som.* ***Village***, 5m/8km W of Bath. **19 K5** ST6762.

Stanton St. Bernard *Wilts.* ***Village***, 6m/9km E of Devizes. **20 D5** SU0962.
Stanton St. John *Oxon.* ***Village***, 5m/7km E of Oxford. **21 J1** SP5709.
Stanton St. Quintin *Wilts.* ***Village***, 4m/6km N of Chippenham. **20 C3** ST9079.
Stanton Street *Suff.* ***Hamlet***, 3m/4km SE of Ixworth. **34 D2** TL9566.
Stanton under Bardon *Leics.* ***Village***, 4m/6km SE of Coalville. **41 G4** SK4610.
Stanton upon Hine Heath *Shrop.* ***Village***, 4m/7km SW of Hodnet. **38 E3** SJ5624.
Stanton Wick *B. & N.E.Som.* ***Hamlet***, 3m/4km E of Chew Magna. **19 K5** ST6161.
Stanwardine in the Fields *Shrop.* ***Settlement***, 9m/14km NW of Shrewsbury. **38 D3** SJ4124.
Stanwardine in the Wood *Shrop.* ***Settlement***, 5m/8km S of Ellesmere. SJ4227.
Stanway *Essex* ***Village***, 4m/6km W of Colchester. **34 D6** TL9324.
Stanway *Glos.* ***Village***, 4m/6km NE of Winchcombe. **30 B5** SP0632.
Stanway *Shrop.* ***Locality***, 5m/8km E of Church Stretton. SO5391.
Stanway Green *Essex* ***Suburb***, 3m/5km SW of Colchester town centre. TL9523.
Stanway Green *Suff.* ***Settlement***, 3m/4km S of Stradbroke. TM2470.
Stanway House *Glos.* ***Historic house***, 16c home of Lord Neidpath with notable gatehouse, 3m/5km NE of Winchcombe and 9m/14km W of Stow-on-the-Wold. Old brewery, tithe barn and formal gardens in grounds. Village cricket field with pavilion built by Sir James Barrie, author of Peter Pan. **30 B5** SP0632.
Stanwell *Surr.* ***Suburb***, between Staines Reservoir and London (Heathrow) Airport. **22 D4** TQ0574.
Stanwell Moor *Surr.* ***Hamlet***, 2m/3km N of Staines. **22 D4** TQ0474.
Stanwick *Northants.* ***Village***, 2m/4km NE of Higham Ferrers. Site of Roman building to W. **32 C1** SP9871.
Stanwick Camp *N.Yorks.* ***Historic/prehistoric site***, remains of extensive military earthworks (English Heritage) which covered an area of around 850 acres, 6m/10km N of Richmond. Remains, dating from 1c, include excavated section of ditch and rampart which were used by Brigantes against Romans. **62 C5** NZ1811.
Stanwick St. John *N.Yorks.* ***Hamlet***, 1m/2km W of Aldbrough St. John. NZ1811.
Stanwix *Cumb.* ***Suburb***, 1km N of Carlisle city centre. Site of Roman fort. **60 F1** NY3957.
Stanycliffe *Gt.Man.* ***Suburb***, 1m/2km NE of Middleton. SD8707.
Stanydale *Shet.* ***Settlement***, on Mainland, 1m/2km N of Gruting. Neolithic remains (Historic Scotland). **109 B7** HU2850.
Staoinebrig (Anglicised form: Stoneybridge.) *W.Isles* ***Village***, near W coast of South Uist, 3m/5km NE of Rubha Ardvule. **84 C1** NF7433.
Stape *N.Yorks.* ***Hamlet***, 6m/9km N of Pickering. **63 J7** SE7993.
Stapehill *Dorset* ***Hamlet***, 3m/5km E of Wimborne Minster. **10 B4** SU0500.
Stapeley *Ches.* ***Hamlet***, 3m/4km SE of Nantwich. **39 F1** SJ6849.
Stapeley Water Gardens and Palms Tropical Oasis *Ches.* ***Garden***, world's largest water garden centre, set within 64 acres, 1m/2km SE of Nantwich. Houses National Collection of Nymphaea, and tropical and mediterranean animals in Palms Tropical Oasis. **49 F7** SJ6651.
Stapenhill *Staffs.* ***Suburb***, 1m/2km SE of Burton upon Trent town centre. SK2521.
Staple *Kent* ***Village***, 2m/3km E of Wingham. **15 H2** TR2756.
Staple *Som.* ***Hamlet***, 3m/4km SE of Watchet, at N end of Quantock Hills. ST1141.
Staple Cross *Devon* ***Hamlet***, 1km NW of Hockworthy. ST0320.
Staple Cross *E.Suss.* ***Village***, 5m/7km NE of Battle. **14 C5** TQ7822.
Staple Fitzpaine *Som.* ***Village***, 5m/7km SE of Taunton. **8 B3** ST2618.
Staple Hill *Som.* ***Mountain***, eastward extension of Black Down Hills. Height 1033 feet or 315 metres. **8 B3** ST2416.
Staple Hill *S.Glos.* ***Suburb***, S district of Mangotsfield 5m/8km NE of Bristol. ST6576.
Staple Hill *Worcs.* ***Locality***, 2m/3km N of Bromsgrove. SO9773.
Staple Lees *Kent* ***Locality***, 2m/3km SE of Wye. Nature reserve to W. TR0845.
Staple Sound *Northumb.* ***Sea feature***, sound between Inner and Outer Farne Islands, 3m/4km off mainland. **77 K7** NU2336.
Staplefield *W.Suss.* ***Village***, 1m/2km SE of Handcross. **13 F4** TQ2728.
Stapleford *Cambs.* ***Suburb***, 4m/7km S of Cambridge. **33 H3** TL4751.
Stapleford *Herts.* ***Village***, 3m/5km N of Hertford. **33 G7** TL3116.
Stapleford *Leics.* ***Hamlet***, 4m/6km E of Melton Mowbray. Stapleford Park to SE includes 17c hall which is now a hotel. **42 B4** SK8118.
Stapleford *Lincs.* ***Village***, 6m/10km E of Newark-on-Trent. **52 B7** SK8857.
Stapleford *Notts.* Population: 33,313. ***Town***, 3m/4km W of Beeston, with New Stapleford 1m/2km N. Church contains shaft of 11c Saxon cross. **41 G2** SK4837.
Stapleford *Wilts.* ***Village***, on River Till, 4m/7km N of Wilton. **10 B1** SU0737.
Stapleford Abbotts *Essex* ***Village***, 4m/7km N of Romford. **23 H2** TQ5096.
Stapleford Tawney *Essex* ***Settlement***, 3m/5km SE of Epping. **23 J2** TQ5099.
Staplegrove *Som.* ***Suburb***, NW of Taunton. **8 B2** ST2126.
Staplehay *Som.* ***Village***, adjoining Trull, 2m/3km S of Taunton. ST2121.
Staplehurst *Kent* Population: 4879. ***Village***, 5m/8km N of Cranbrook. **14 C3** TQ7843.
Staplers *I.o.W.* ***Hamlet***, 1m/2km E of Newport. **11 G6** SZ5189.
Staplestreet *Kent* ***Hamlet***, 3m/5km E of Faversham. TR0560.
Stapleton *Bristol* ***Suburb***, of Bristol, 3m/4km NE of city centre. **19 J4** ST6076.
Stapleton *Cumb.* ***Locality***, 7m/11km N of Brampton. **70 A6** NY5071.
Stapleton *Here.* ***Village***, 1m/2km NE of Presteigne. **28 C2** SO3265.
Stapleton *Leics.* ***Village***, 3m/5km N of Hinckley. **41 G6** SP4398.
Stapleton *N.Yorks.* ***Village***, on River Tees, 2m/3km SW of Darlington. **62 D5** NZ2612.
Stapleton *Shrop.* ***Village***, 5m/8km S of Shrewsbury. **38 D5** SJ4704.
Stapleton *Som.* ***Hamlet***, 1m/2km N of Martock. **8 D2** ST4621.
Stapley *Som.* ***Hamlet***, 5m/9km SE of Wellington. **7 K4** ST1813.
Staploe *Beds.* ***Village***, 3m/4km W of St. Neots. **32 E2** TL1460.
Staplow *Here.* ***Hamlet***, 3m/4km NW of Ledbury. **29 F4** SO6941.
Star *Fife* ***Village***, 2m/3km NE of Markinch. **82 E7** NO3103.
Star *Pembs.* ***Hamlet***, 3m/5km SE of Boncath. **17 F1** SN2435.
Star *Som.* ***Hamlet***, 1m/2km NE of Winscombe. **19 H6** ST4358.
Star Castle *I.o.S.* ***Castle***, 8-pointed castle built in 1593, 1km W of Hugh Town on St. Mary's. **2 C1** SV8910.
Starbotton *N.Yorks.* ***Village***, in Upper Wharfedale, 2m/3km N of Kettlewell. **56 E2** SD9574.
Starcross *Devon* ***Village***, on W side of River Exe estuary opposite Exmouth. Ferry to Exmouth (foot pasengers). **7 H7** SX9781.
Stareton *Warks.* ***Settlement***, 4m/6km N of Royal Leamington Spa. SP3371.
Stargate *T. & W.* ***Locality***, adjoining to SE of Ryton, 1m/2km W of Blaydon. NZ1663.
Starkholmes *Derbys.* ***Village***, 1m/2km S of Matlock. SK3058.
Starkigarth *Shet.* ***Settlement***, 2m/3km S of Fladdabister, Mainland. **109 D10** HU4229.
Starling *Gt.Man.* ***Suburb***, 2m/3km W of Bury. SD7710.
Starling's Green *Essex* ***Hamlet***, 4m/7km SW of Newport. **33 H5** TL4531.
Starr *E.Ayr.* ***Settlement***, at S end of Loch Doon, just S of mouth of Carrick Lane. **67 J4** NX4893.
Starr's Green *E.Suss.* ***Locality***, adjoining to SE of Battle. TQ7615.
Starston *Norf.* ***Village***, 1m/2km NW of Harleston. **45 G7** TM2384.
Start Bay *Devon* ***Bay***, on S coast, extending S from mouth of River Dart to Start Point. **5 J6** SX8443.
Start Point *Cornw.* ***Coastal feature***, 2m/3km SW of Tintagel. **4 A2** SX0485.
Start Point *Devon* ***Coastal feature***, E facing headland on S coast, at S end of Start Bay. **5 J7** SX8337.
Start Point *Ork.* ***Coastal feature***, headland with lighthouse at E end of Sanday. **106 G3** HY7843.
Startforth *Dur.* ***Village***, on W bank of River Tees, opposite Barnard Castle. **62 B5** NZ0416.
Startley *Wilts.* ***Village***, 3m/5kmS of Malmesbury. **20 C3** ST9482.
Startop's End *Bucks.* ***Settlement***, at Marsworth, 2m/3km N of Tring. SP9214.
Statham *Warr.* ***Locality***, adjoining to W of Lymm. **49 F4** SJ6787.
Stathe *Som.* ***Village***, on River Parrett, 3m/5km NW of Langport. **8 C2** ST3729.
Stathern *Leics.* ***Village***, 8m/12km N of Melton Mowbray. **42 A2** SK7731.
Station Hill *Cumb.* ***Locality***, adjoining to N of Wigton. NY2549.
Station Town *Dur.* ***Locality***, adjoining to S of Wingate, built round former railway station. **63 F3** NZ4036.
Stattic Point *High.* ***Coastal feature***, headland on SW side of entrance to Little Loch Broom, W coast of Ross and Cromarty district. **95 F2** NG9796.
Staughton Green *Cambs.* ***Village***, to NE of Staughton. **32 E2** TL1264.
Staughton Highway *Cambs.* ***Village***, to E of Staughton. **32 E2** TL1264.
Staunton *Glos.* ***Village***, 2m/3km NW of Coleford. **28 E7** SO5412.
Staunton *Glos.* ***Village***, 7m/11km N of Gloucester. **29 G6** SO7829.
Staunton Green *Here.* ***Hamlet***, 4m/6km SE of Kington. SO3661.
Staunton Harold *Leics.* ***Settlement***, 3m/5km NE of Ashby de la Zouch. SK3720.
Staunton Harold Hall *Leics.* ***Historic house***, National Trust property 10m/16km S of Derby. Mainly Palladian house, with surrounding estate houses and church. **41 F3** SK3720.
Staunton Harold Reservoir *Derbys.* ***Reservoir***, to N of Staunton Harold and 1m/2km SW of Melbourne. **41 F3** SK3723.
Staunton in the Vale *Notts.* ***Village***, 2m/3km SW of Long Bennington, in the Vale of Belvoir. SK8043.
Staunton on Arrow *Here.* ***Village***, 5m/8km NE of Kington. **28 C2** SO3660.
Staunton on Wye *Here.* ***Village***, 4m/6km SE of Willersley. **28 C4** SO3745.
Staupes *N.Yorks.* ***Settlement***, 3m/5km NE of Blubberhouses. SE2257.
Stava Ness *Shet.* ***Coastal feature***, headland on E coast of Mainland, on S side of entrance to Dury Voe. **109 E6** HU5060.
Staveley *Cumb.* Population: 1240. ***Village***, 4m/6km E of Windermere. **61 F7** SD4698.
Staveley *Derbys.* Population: 27,665. ***Town***, former iron and coal town, 4m/6km NE of Chesterfield. **51 G5** SK4374.
Staveley *N.Yorks.* ***Village***, 3m/5km SW of Boroughbridge. **57 J3** SE3662.
Staveley Head Fell *Cumb.* ***Open space***, moorland between Kent valley and Long Sleddale, 4m/6km E of Troutbeck. **61 F6** NY4601.
Staveley-in-Cartmel *Cumb.* ***Village***, 1km E of Newby Bridge. **55 G1** SD3786.
Staverton *Devon* ***Village***, 2m/4km N of Totnes. 15c bridge over River Dart. **5 H4** SX7964.
Staverton *Glos.* ***Village***, 4m/6km W of Cheltenham. Airport 1m/2km S. **29 H6** SO8923.
Staverton *Northants.* ***Village***, 2m/4km W of Daventry. **31 G2** SP5361.
Staverton *Wilts.* ***Village***, 2m/3km N of Trowbridge. **20 B5** ST8560.
Staverton Bridge *Devon* ***Bridge***, unaltered early 15c stone bridge over River Dart at Staverton, 3m/4km NW of Totnes. SX7863.
Staverton Bridge *Glos.* ***Locality***, 4m/6km W of Cheltenham. Airport to S. **29 H6** SO8922.
Stavordale Priory *Som.* ***Ecclesiastical building***, small priory founded in 13c and rebuilt in 15c, 3m/4km NE of Wincanton. Excellent fan vaulted chapel in NE corner of church. **9 G1** ST7332.
Stawell *Som.* ***Village***, on S side of Polden Hills, 5m/7km E of Bridgwater. **8 C1** ST3638.
Stawley *Som.* ***Hamlet***, 5m/8km W of Wellington. **7 J3** ST0622.
Staxigoe *High.* ***Village***, on E coast of Caithness district, 2m/3km NE of Wick. **105 J3** ND3852.
Staxton *N.Yorks.* ***Village***, 6m/10km W of Filey. **59 G2** TA0179.
Staylittle (Penffordd-Las). *Powys* ***Hamlet***, at head of Llyn Clywedog Reservoir, 7m/11km S of Llanbrynmair. **37 H6** SN8892.
Staynall *Lancs.* ***Hamlet***, on E bank of River Wyre estuary, 2m/3km S of Preesall. **55 G5** SD3643.
Staythorpe *Notts.* ***Hamlet***, 3m/5km W of Newark-on-Trent. **51 K7** SK7554.
Stean *N.Yorks.* ***Hamlet***, 1km SW of Middlesmoor, on NE side of Stean Moor. **57 F2** SE0873.
Stean Moor *N.Yorks.* ***Open space***, moorland to W of Nidderdale, 6m/10km NW of Pateley Bridge. **57 F2** SE0671.
Steane *Northants.* ***Hamlet***, 3m/4km NW of Brackley. **31 G5** SP5539.
Stearsby *N.Yorks.* ***Hamlet***, 5m/9km E of Easingwold. **58 C2** SE6171.
Steart *Som.* ***Village***, on W side of River Parrett estuary, 2m/4km NE of Stockland Bristol. **19 F7** ST2745.
Stebbing *Essex* ***Village***, 3m/4km NE of Great Dunmow. **33 K6** TL6624.
Stebbing Green *Essex* ***Hamlet***, 1m/2km E of Stebbing; site of Roman building to E of hamlet. **33 K6** TL6624.
Stechford *W.Mid.* ***Suburb***, 4m/6km E of Birmingham city centre. SP1287.
Stedham *W.Suss.* ***Village***, 2m/3km W of Midhurst. **12 B4** SU8622.
Steel Bank *S.Yorks.* ***Suburb***, 1m/2km NW of Sheffield city centre. SK3388.
Steel Cross *E.Suss.* ***Hamlet***, 1m/2km E of Crowborough. **13 J3** TQ5331.
Steel Green *Cumb.* ***Hamlet***, 1km S of Millom. SD1678.
Steel Heath *Shrop.* ***Settlement***, 3m/5km S of Whitchurch. SJ5436.
Steele Road *Sc.Bord.* ***Settlement***, on S side of Arnton Hill, 4m/6km NW of Newcastleton. **70 A4** NY5293.
Steele's Knowe *P. & K.* ***Mountain***, in Ochil Hills, 6m/10km N of Dollar. Height 1591 feet or 485 metres. **82 A7** NN9607.
Steen's Bridge *Here.* ***Hamlet***, 3m/5km E of Leominster. **28 E3** SO5457.
Steep *Hants.* ***Village***, 1m/2km N of Petersfield. Location of Bedales co-educational boarding school, founded 1893. **11 J2** SU7425.
Steep Holm *N.Som.* ***Island***, uninhabited island in Bristol Channel 6m/9km W of Weston-super-Mare, measuring about 1km from E to W and 300 metres from N to S. **19 F5** ST2260.
Steep Lane *W.Yorks.* ***Hamlet***, 2m/3km W of Sowerby Bridge. SE0323.
Steep Marsh *Hants.* ***Hamlet***, 2m/3km NE of Petersfield. **11 J2** SU7526.
Steephill *I.o.W.* ***Locality***, 1km W of Ventnor. SZ5577.
Steeping *Lincs.* ***River***, rising as River Lymm near Salmonby, and flowing SE through Wainfleet All Saints into North Sea on W side of Gibraltar Point. **53 J6** TF5557.
Steeple *Cumb.* ***Mountain***, in Lake District, 3m/5km N of Wast Water. Height 2758 feet or 841 metres. **60 C5** NY1511.
Steeple *Dorset* ***Hamlet***, to S of Purbeck Hills, 4m/6km S of Wareham. **9 J6** SY9181.
Steeple *Essex* ***Village***, 4m/7km N of Burnham-on-Crouch. **25 F1** TL9302.
Steeple Ashton *Wilts.* ***Village***, 3m/5km E of Trowbridge. **20 C6** ST9056.
Steeple Aston *Oxon.* ***Village***, 4m/6km S of Deddington. **31 F6** SP4726.
Steeple Barton *Oxon.* ***Hamlet***, 4m/7km SW of Deddington. **31 F6** SP4425.
Steeple Bumpstead *Essex* ***Village***, 3m/5km S of Haverhill. **33 K4** TL6741.
Steeple Claydon *Bucks.* Population: 2269. ***Village***, 5m/7km S of Buckingham. **31 H6** SP7026.
Steeple Court *Hants.* *See Botley.*

S

Steeple Gidding *Cambs.* ***Village***, 5m/9km SW of Stilton. **42 E7** TL1381.
Steeple Langford *Wilts.* ***Village***, on River Wylye, 5m/8km NW of Wilton. **10 B1** SU0337.
Steeple Morden *Cambs.* ***Village***, 4m/7km W of Royston. **33 F4** TL2842.
Steeple View *Essex* ***Suburb***, NW district of Basildon. TQ6890.
Steeplechase Terrace *Suff.* ***Hamlet***, 4m/7km NE of Haverhill. TL7249.
Steeraway *Tel. & W.* ***Settlement***, 1m/2km S of Wellington. SJ6509.
Steeton *N.Yorks.* ***Locality***, 3m/5km E of Tadcaster. Hall dates partly from 14c. SE5344.
Steeton *W.Yorks.* Population: 3793. ***Village***, in Airedale, 4m/6km NW of Keighley. **57 F5** SE0344.
Steeton Hall *N.Yorks.* ***Historic house***, remains of medieval castle, 1km W of South Milford. Gatehouse (English Heritage), probably dating from 14c, is well-preserved. **57 K6** SE4831.
Stein *High.* ***Settlement***, on W coast of Vaternish peninsula, Skye, 4m/6km SE of Ardmore Point. **93 H6** NG2656.
Steinacleit *W.Isles* ***Historic/prehistoric site***, burial cairn and stone circle (Historic Scotland) near NW coast of Isle of Lewis, 4m/6km NE of Barvas. **101 F2** NB3954.
Steinmanhill *Aber.* ***Settlement***, on S side of Steinman Hill, 3m/4km N of Fyvie. **99 F6** NJ7642.
Stell Hill *D. & G.* ***Mountain***, 3m/5km NE of Davington. Height 1263 feet or 385 metres. **69 H3** NT2705.
Stella *T. & W.* ***Locality***, 1m/2km E of Ryton. **71 G7** NZ1763.
Stelling Minnis *Kent* ***Village***, 7m/11km S of Canterbury. **15 G3** TR1446.
Stelvio *Newport* ***Suburb***, of Newport to SW of town centre. ST2987.
Stembridge *Som.* ***Village***, 4m/7km S of Langport. ST4220.
Stembridge Tower Mill *Som.* ***Other feature of interest***, last thatched windmill in England (National Trust), to SE of High Ham and 5m/8km SW of Street. Dates from 1822 and was in use until 1910. **8 D1** ST4330.
Stemster *High.* ***Settlement***, 3m/5km NE of Halkirk. **105 G2** ND1762.
Stemster *High.* ***Settlement***, 1m/2km N of Loch Stemster. **105 G4** ND1844.
Stemster Hill *High.* ***Hill***, 1km E of Loch Stemster. Height 813 feet or 248 metres. **105 G4** ND1941.
Stemster House *High.* ***Settlement***, 1km N of Loch Scarmclate. **105 G2** ND1860.
Stenalees *Cornw.* Population: 1347. ***Village***, in china clay district, 3m/5km N of St. Austell. **4 A5** SX0157.
Stenbury Down *I.o.W.* ***Open space***, downland 2m/4km NE of Niton. **11 G7** SZ5378.
Stenhill *Devon* ***Hamlet***, 3m/5km NE of Cullompton. ST0510.
Stenhouse *Edin.* ***Suburb***, 3m/5km SW of Edinburgh city centre. NT2171.
Stenhousemuir *Falk.* Population: 16,711. ***Town***, 2m/3km NW of Falkirk. Scotland's largest livestock market sited here. **75 G2** NS8682.
Stenigot *Lincs.* ***Locality***, 6m/10km SW of Louth. **53 F4** TF2581.
Stenness *Ork.* ***Locality***, on Mainland at SE end of Loch of Stenness, 4m/6km SW of Finstown. HY3010.
Stenness *Shet.* ***Settlement***, on Mainland, at S end of Esha Ness, 2m/4km SW of Braehoulland. **108 B5** HU2177.
Stenscholl *High.* ***Settlement***, on Skye, 1m/2km NW of Staffin. **93 K5** NG4767.
Stenson *Derbys.* ***Hamlet***, on Trent and Mersey Canal, 4m/7km SW of Derby. SK3230.
Stenton *E.Loth.* ***Village***, 5m/7km SW of Dunbar. Ruins of Old Parish Church. **76 E3** NT6274.
Stenton *P. & K.* ***Settlement***, 3m/5km SE of Dunkeld. **82 B3** NO0640.
Steornabhagh *W.Isles* *Gaelic form of Stornoway, qv.*
Stepaside *Pembs.* ***Village***, 2m/3km N of Saundersfoot. **16 E4** SN1307.
Stepaside *Powys* ***Hamlet***, 2m/3km SW of Newtown. SO0889.
Stephen Moor *Lancs.* ***Locality***, 2m/4km NE of Slaidburn. **56 C4** SD7453.
Stephenson *T. & W.* ***Suburb***, N district of Washington. NZ3058.
Stephenson's Birthplace *Northumb.* ***Historic house***, 1km W of Wylam, on N side of River Tyne. Small stone tenement (National Trust) built c. 1760 where George Stephenson was born in 1781. **71 G7** NZ1265.
Stepney *Gt.Lon.* ***Suburb***, in borough of Tower Hamlets, 2m/3km E of London Bridge. **23 G3** TQ3581.
Stepper Point *Cornw.* ***Coastal feature***, headland at SW end of Padstow Bay, 2m/3km N of Padstow. SW9178.
Steppingley *Beds.* ***Village***, 2m/4km SW of Ampthill. **32 D5** TL0135.
Stepps *N.Lan.* Population: 4336. ***Suburb***, 5m/8km NE of Glasgow. **74 E4** NS6568.
Sternfield *Suff.* ***Village***, 1m/2km S of Saxmundham. **35 H2** TM3961.
Sterridge *Devon* ***Locality***, along length of Sterridge Valley, 3m/4km SE of Ilfracombe. **6 D1** SS5546.
Stert *Wilts.* ***Village***, 2m/3km SE of Devizes. **20 D6** SU0359.
Stert Flats *Som.* ***Coastal feature***, covered at high water, SW of Burnham-on-Sea. **19 F7** ST2546.
Stert Island *Som.* ***Island***, in Bridgwater Bay, 1m/2km SW of Burnham-on-Sea. **19 F7** ST2948.
Sterte *Poole* ***Locality***, 1km NW of Poole town centre, beside Holes Bay. SZ0091.
Stetchworth *Cambs.* ***Village***, 3m/5km S of Newmarket. **33 K3** TL6458.
Stetchworth Ley *Cambs.* ***Settlement***, 1m/2km SE of Stetchworth. TL6457.
Stevenage *Herts.* Population: 76,064. ***Town***, New Town designated 1946, 28m/45km N of London. Old town to N. **33 F6** TL2324.
Stevenston *N.Ayr.* Population: 10,153. ***Town***, industrial and former mining town, 2m/4km E of Ardrossan. **74 A6** NS2642.
Steventon *Hants.* ***Village***, 6m/10km SW of Basingstoke. Birthplace of Jane Austen, 1775. **21 J7** SU5448.
Steventon *Oxon.* ***Village***, 4m/6km W of Didcot. Priory Cottages (National Trust), part of former monastic buildings. **21 H2** SU4691.
Stevington *Beds.* ***Village***, 4m/7km NW of Bedford. **32 C3** SP9853.
Stewards *Essex* ***Suburb***, 1m/2km S of Harlow town centre. TL4407.
Stewartby *Beds.* ***Village***, 3m/5km N of Ampthill. **32 D4** TL0142.
Stewarton *D. & G.* ***Settlement***, 4m/6km S of Wigtown. **64 E6** NX4449.
Stewarton *E.Ayr.* Population: 6481. ***Small town***, 5m/8km N of Kilmarnock. Town once famous for hat-making. **74 C6** NS4145.
Stewkley *Bucks.* Population: 1530. ***Village***, 5m/7km W of Leighton Buzzard. **32 B6** SP8526.
Stewley *Som.* ***Hamlet***, 4m/6km NW of Ilminster. ST3118.
Stewponey Junction *Staffs.* ***Locality***, junction of Stourbridge Canal with Staffordshire and Worcestershire Canal, 3m/4km W of Stourbridge. SO8684.
Stewton *Lincs.* ***Settlement***, 2m/4km E of Louth. **53 G4** TF3686.
Steyne Cross *I.o.W.* ***Suburb***, 1km SE of Bembridge. SZ6487.
Steyning *W.Suss.* Population: 4346. ***Small town***, market town and former port on River Adur, below South Downs, 5m/7km NW of Shoreham-by-Sea. **12 E5** TQ1711.
Steynton *Pembs.* ***Village***, 1m/2km NE of Milford Haven. **16 C4** SM9107.
Stibb *Cornw.* ***Hamlet***, 3m/5km N of Bude. **6 A4** SS2210.
Stibb Cross *Devon* ***Hamlet***, 5m/8km SW of Great Torrington. **6 C4** SS4214.
Stibb Green *Wilts.* ***Village***, 5m/8km SE of Marlborough. **21 F5** SU2262.
Stibbard *Norf.* ***Village***, 4m/7km E of Fakenham. **44 D3** TF9828.
Stibbington *Cambs.* ***Village***, 1m/2km SE of Wansford. Jacobean hall. **42 D6** TL0898.
Stichill *Sc.Bord.* ***Village***, 3m/5km N of Kelso. **77 F7** NT7138.
Sticker *Cornw.* ***Village***, 3m/4km SW of St. Austell. **3 G3** SW9850.
Stickford *Lincs.* ***Village***, 5m/8km SW of Spilsby. **53 G6** TF3560.
Sticklepath *Devon* ***Village***, 4m/6km E of Okehampton. **6 E6** SX6494.
Sticklepath *Som.* ***Hamlet***, 1km N of Combe St. Nicholas. ST3012.
Stickling Green *Essex* ***Hamlet***, 3m/5km SW of Newport. TL4732.
Stickney *Lincs.* ***Village***, 8m/13km N of Boston. **53 G7** TF3456.
Stidd *Lancs.* ***Settlement***, 1km NE of Ribchester. SD6535.
Stiff Street *Kent* ***Settlement***, 3m/4km SW of Sittingbourne. TQ8761.
Stiffkey *Norf.* ***River***, rising near Swanton Novers and flowing generally W to East Barsham, then NE to village of Stiffkey and North Sea at Blakeney Harbour. **44 D2** TF9944.
Stiffkey *Norf.* ***Village***, 4m/6km E of Wells-next-the-Sea. **44 D1** TF9743.
Stifford's Bridge *Here.* ***Settlement***, at road bridge over Leigh Brook, 3m/5km NW of Great Malvern. **29 G4** SO7348.
Stilamair *W.Isles* ***Island***, islet off South Harris, to SW of Scalpay at entrance to East Loch Tarbert. NG2194.
Stileway *Som.* ***Hamlet***, 3m/5km NW of Glastonbury. ST4641.
Stilligarry *W.Isles* *Anglicised form of Stadhlaigearraidh, qv.*
Stillingfleet *N.Yorks.* ***Village***, 2m/4km NE of Cawood. **58 B5** SE5940.
Stillington *N.Yorks.* ***Village***, 4m/6km E of Easingwold. **58 B3** SE5867.
Stillington *Stock.* ***Village***, 4m/6km S of Sedgefield, 5m/8km NW of Stockton-on-Tees. **62 E4** NZ3723.
Stilton *Cambs.* Population: 2219. ***Village***, 6m/10km SW of Peterborough. The famous cheese of same name was formerly distributed from the Bell Inn here, although made in Leicestershire. **42 E7** TL1689.
Stinchar *S.Ayr.* ***River***, rising in Glentrool Forest Park and flowing N then W through Carrick Forest, then turning SW and running by Barr, Pinwherry and Colmonell to Ballantrae Bay on S side of Ballantrae. **67 F5** NX0781.
Stinchcombe *Glos.* ***Village***, 2m/3km W of Dursley. Site of Roman villa 2km SE. **20 A2** ST7298.
Stingwern Hill *Powys* ***Mountain***, 3m/5km NW of Aberriw. Height 1174 feet or 358 metres. **38 A5** SJ1301.
Stinsford *Dorset* ***Village***, 1m/2km E of Dorchester. **9 G5** SY7191.
Stiperstones *Shrop.* ***Inland physical feature***, hill ridge above locality of same name, 1m/2km SW of Snailbeach. **38 C6** SJ3600.
Stirchley *Tel. & W.* ***Locality***, 1m/2km SE of Dawley, Telford. **39 G5** SJ6906.
Stirchley *W.Mid.* ***Suburb***, 4m/6km S of Birmingham city centre. **40 C7** SP0581.
Stirkoke House *High.* ***Settlement***, 3m/4km W of Wick. **105 J3** ND3150.
Stirling *Aber.* ***Locality***, adjoining to W of Boddam, 3m/4km S of Peterhead. Quarry to S. **99 K6** NK1242.
Stirling *Stir.* Population: 30,515. ***Town***, historic town on slope of rocky eminence above S bank of River Forth, 21m/34km NE of Glasgow. Now a commercial and tourist centre. Medieval castle (Historic Scotland). Cambuskenneth Abbey (Historic Scotland), 1km NE. Some important battles during Wars of Independence fought here. University at Airthrey, 2m/3km N. **75 F1** NS7993.
Stirling Castle *Stir.* ***Castle***, impressive medieval and later castle (Historic Scotland) in Stirling's historic centre, built on site of earlier castle. Mary, Queen of Scots was crowned here in 1543. **75 F1** NS7994.
Stirton *N.Yorks.* ***Hamlet***, on edge of Yorkshire Dales National Park, 1m/2km NW of Skipton. **56 E4** SD9752.
Stisted *Essex* ***Village***, 3m/5km E of Braintree. **34 B6** TL8024.
Stitchcombe *Wilts.* ***Settlement***, on River Kennet, 3m/4km E of Marlborough. SU2269.
Stithians *Cornw.* ***Village***, 3m/5km NW of Penryn. Watersports on large reservoir to W. **2 E5** SW7336.
Stithians Reservoir *Cornw.* ***Reservoir***, 1m/2km W of Stithians. **2 E5** SW7136.
Stittenham *High.* ***Settlement***, 3m/5km N of Alness. **96 D4** NH6574.
Stiughay *W.Isles* ***Island***, islet off North Harris in East Loch Tarbert, to W of Scalpay. NG2096.
Stiughay na Leum *W.Isles* ***Island***, islet off South Harris in East Loch Tarbert, on S side of Stiughay. NG2095.
Stivichall *W.Mid.* ***Suburb***, S district of Coventry. **30 E1** SP3376.
Stix *P. & K.* ***Settlement***, 2m/3km NE of Kenmore. **81 J3** NN7947.
Stixwould *Lincs.* ***Village***, 2m/4km NW of Woodhall Spa. **52 E6** TF1765.
Stixwould Ferry *Lincs.* ***Locality***, on River Witham, 1m/2km SW of Stixwould. TF1564.
Stoak *Ches.* ***Village***, 4m/7km N of Chester. **48 D5** SJ4273.
Stob a' Choin *Stir.* ***Mountain***, 3m/4km NE of head of Loch Katrine. Height 2837 feet or 865 metres. **81 F6** NN4116.
Stob a' Choire Mheadhoin *High.* ***Mountain***, in Lochaber district, 1km NE of Stob Coire Easain and 1m/2km W of Loch Treig. Munro: height 3628 feet or 1106 metres. **87 K7** NN3173.
Stob a' Choire Odhair *High.* ***Mountain***, on border of Argyll and Lochaber districts on NW side of Beinn Toaig and 2m/3km E of Stob Ghabhar. Munro: height 3106 feet or 947 metres. **80 D3** NN2546.
Stob a' Ghrianain *High.* ***Mountain***, summit of Druim Fada, 5m/8km N of Fort William. Height 2440 feet or 744 metres. **87 G6** NN0882.
Stob an Aonaich Mhòir *P. & K.* ***Mountain***, on SE side of Loch Ericht, 11m/18km SW of Dalwhinnie. Height 2804 feet or 855 metres. **81 G1** NN5369.
Stob an Duine Ruaidh *Arg. & B.* ***Mountain***, 1m/2km SW of Ben Starav, Argyll, on E side of Loch Etive. Height 2696 feet or 822 metres. **80 C3** NN1140.
Stob an Eas *Arg. & B.* ***Mountain***, in Argyll 4m/6km N of Lochgoilhead. Height 2401 feet or 732 metres. **80 C7** NN1807.
Stob an Fhàinne *Stir.* ***Mountain***, to N of Loch Arklet, 5m/8km NE of Tarbet across Loch Lomond. Height 2148 feet or 655 metres. **80 E6** NN3511.
Stob an t-Sluichd *Moray* ***Mountain***, 6m/9km E of Loch Avon. Height 3628 feet or 1106 metres. **89 J4** NJ1003.
Stob Bàn *High.* ***Mountain***, in Lochaber district, 3m/5km NW of Kinlochleven. Munro: height 3277 feet or 999 metres. **80 C1** NN1465.
Stob Bàn *High.* ***Mountain***, in Lochaber district, 4m/6km NW of head of Loch Treig. Munro: height 3205 feet or 977 metres. **87 J7** NN2672.
Stob Binnein (Also known as Stobinian and Ben A'an.) *Stir.* ***Mountain***, 1m/2km S of Ben More and 4m/6km SE of Crianlarich. Munro: height 3821 feet or 1165 metres. **81 F5** NN4322.
Stob Breac *Stir.* ***Mountain***, 7m/11km SE of Crianlarich. Height 2250 feet or 686 metres. **81 F6** NN4416.
Stob Choire Claurigh *High.* ***Mountain***, in Lochaber district 4m/7km NW of head of Loch Treig. Munro: height 3861 feet or 1177 metres. **87 J7** NN2673.
Stob Coir' an Albannaich ***Mountain***, on border of Argyll & Bute and Highland, 4m/6km E of head of Loch Etive. Munro: height 3424 feet or 1044 metres. **80 C3** NN1644.
Stob Coire a' Chairn *High.* ***Mountain***, in Mamore Forest, 3m/4km N of Kinlochleven. Munro: height 3218 feet or 981 metres. **80 C1** NN1866.
Stob Coire a' Chearcaill *High.* ***Mountain***, on Ardgour, 5m/8km W of Fort William across Loch Linnhe. Height 2526 feet or 770 metres. **87 G7** NN0172.
Stob Coire an Laoigh *High.* ***Mountain***, 6m/9km S of Spean Bridge. Munro: height 3660 feet or 1116 metres. **87 J7** NN2472.
Stob Coire Easain *High.* ***Mountain***, in Lochaber district 3m/4km N of head of Loch Treig. Munro: height 3660 feet or 1116 metres. **87 K7** NN3073.
Stob Coire nan Cearc *High.* ***Mountain***, in Lochaber district 3m/5km NE of Glenfinnan. Height 2909 feet or 887 metres. **87 F6** NM9385.
Stob Coire Raineach *High.* ***Mountain***, summit at NE end of Buachaille Etive Beag, 1m/2km SE of Pass of Glencoe. Munro: height 3031 feet or 924 metres. NN1954.
Stob Coire Sgreamhach *High.* ***Mountain***, 2m/4km SW of Pass of Glencoe. Munro: height 3510 feet or 1070 metres. NN1553.
Stob Coire Sgriodain *High.* ***Mountain***, in Lochaber district between Loch Treig and Chno Dearg. Munro: height 3201 feet or 976 metres. **87 K7** NN3574.
Stob Dearg *High.* ***Mountain***, summit at NE end of Buachaille Etive Mòr, 3m/5km SE of Pass of Glencoe. Munro: height 3352 feet or 1022 metres. **80 D2** NN2254.
Stob Diamh *Arg. & B.* ***Mountain***, in Ben Cruachan massif, 4m/7km NW of Dalmally. Munro: height 3273 feet or 998 metres. **80 B4** NN0930.
Stob Dubh *High.* ***Mountain***, in Lochaber district on E side of Glen Etive, 4m/6km NE of head of Loch Etive. Height 2896 feet or 883 metres. **80 C3** NN1648.
Stob Dubh *High.* ***Mountain***, summit at SW end of Buachaille Etive Beag in Lochaber district, 2m/3km S of Pass of Glencoe. Munro: height 3142 feet or 958 metres. **80 C2** NN1753.

S

Stob Garbh *Stir.* ***Mountain***, peak 1km N of summit of Cruach Ardrain. Height 3149 feet or 960 metres. **81 F5** NN4122.
Stob Ghabhar *High.* ***Mountain***, in Argyll 6m/9km NW of Bridge of Orchy. Munro: height 3565 feet or 1087 metres. **80 D3** NN2345.
Stob Law *Sc.Bord.* ***Mountain***, 5m/8km SW of Peebles. Height 2050 feet or 625 metres. **76 A7** NT2233.
Stob Mhic Bheathain *High.* ***Mountain***, 6m/9km S of Glenfinnan, Lochaber district. Height 2365 feet or 721 metres. **87 F7** NM9170.
Stob na Broige *High.* ***Mountain***, summit at SW end of Buachaille Etive Mòr, 3m/4km SE of Pass of Glencoe. Munro: height 3132 feet or 955 metres. NN1952.
Stob na Cruaiche ***Mountain***, summit of A' Chruach on border of Highland and Perth & Kinross, between Blackwater Reservoir and Loch Laidon. Height 2424 feet or 739 metres. **80 E2** NN3657.
Stob Odham *Arg. & B.* ***Mountain***, on Knapdale, 5m/8km NW of Tarbert. Height 1843 feet or 562 metres. **73 G3** NR8174.
Stob Poite Coire Ardair *High.* ***Mountain***, rising to NW above Lochan a' Choire, 1m/2km NE of Creag Meagaidh. Steep, craggy SE slopes. Munro: height 3454 feet or 1053 metres. **88 B6** NN4288.
Stobinian *Stir. Alternative name for Stob Binnein, qv.*
Stobo *Sc.Bord.* ***Village***, on River Tweed, 5m/8km SW of Peebles. **75 K7** NT1837.
Stoborough *Dorset* ***Village***, in River Frome valley, 1km S of Wareham. **9 J6** SY9285.
Stoborough Green *Dorset* ***Hamlet***, 1km S of Stoborough and 1m/2km S of Wareham, on N edge of Stoborough Heath. **9 J6** SY9285.
Stobs *Sc.Bord.* ***Settlement***, 4m/6km S of Hawick. NT5009.
Stobwood *S.Lan.* ***Settlement***, 1m/2km SE of Forth. **75 H5** NS9552.
Stock *Essex* Population: 2097. ***Village***, 3m/5km N of Billericay. **24 C2** TQ6898.
Stock Green *Worcs.* ***Village***, 6m/10km SE of Droitwich Spa. **29 J3** SO9758.
Stock Hill *Sc.Bord.* ***Mountain***, 4m/6km SW of Craik. Height 1565 feet or 477 metres. **69 J3** NT3203.
Stock Lane *Wilts.* ***Settlement***, 2m/3km SW of Aldbourne. **21 F4** SU2374.
Stock Wood *Worcs.* ***Hamlet***, 6m/9km W of Alcester. **30 B3** SP0058.
Stockay *W.Isles* ***Island***, easternmost of Heisker Islands group. **92 B5** NF6663.
Stockbridge *Edin.* ***Suburb***, 1km NW of Edinburgh city centre. NT2474.
Stockbridge *Hants.* ***Village***, on River Test, 6m/10km S of Andover. To S, Common Marsh (National Trust). **10 E1** SU3535.
Stockbridge *Stir.* ***Settlement***, adjoining to W of Dunblane. **81 J7** NN7601.
Stockbridge *W.Suss.* ***Suburb***, 1m/2km S of Chichester. SU8503.
Stockbury *Kent* ***Village***, 4m/7km W of Sittingbourne. **24 E5** TQ8461.
Stockcross *W.Berks.* ***Village***, 3m/4km W of Newbury. **21 H5** SU4368.
Stockdale *Cornw.* ***Hamlet***, 2m/3km N of Penryn. SW7937.
Stockdalewath *Cumb.* ***Settlement***, 4m/6km SE of Dalston. **60 E2** NY3844.
Stockeld Park *N.Yorks.* ***Historic house***, small mansion designed by James Paine in Palladian style for Middleton family in 18c and set in large estate, 1m/2km SE of Spofforth and 2m/3km N of Wetherby. **57 J5** SE3749.
Stocker's Head *Kent* ***Settlement***, 1m/2km NE of Charing. TQ9650.
Stockerston *Leics.* ***Village***, 2m/4km SW of Uppingham. **42 B6** SP8397.
Stockghyll Force *Cumb.* ***Waterfall***, on Stock Ghyll 1km E of Ambleside. **60 E6** NY3804.
Stockgrove Country Park *Beds.* ***Leisure/recreation***, country with 59 acres of open hillsides and woodland straddling small valley, 3m/4km N of Leighton Buzzard town centre. **32 C6** SP9129.
Stockheath *Hants.* ***Suburb***, N district of Havant. SU7107.
Stockholes Turbary *N.Lincs.* ***Settlement***, 3m/4km NW of Epworth. SE7607.
Stocking *Here.* ***Hamlet***, 4m/7km NE of Ross-on-Wye. SO6230.
Stocking Green *Essex* ***Settlement***, 3m/5km E of Saffron Walden. TL5938.
Stocking Green *M.K.* ***Settlement***, adjoining to N of Hanslope. SP8047.
Stocking Pelham *Herts.* ***Village***, 5m/9km NW of Bishop's Stortford. **33 H6** TL4529.
Stockingford *Warks.* ***Suburb***, W district of Nuneaton. **41 F6** SP3391.
Stockinish Island *W.Isles* ***Island***, uninhabited island at entrance to Loch Stockinish, SE coast of South Harris, 6m/10km S of Tarbert. NG1390.
Stockland *Cardiff* ***Settlement***, 5m/8km W of Cardiff. ST1078.
Stockland *Devon* ***Village***, 5m/8km NW of Axminster. **8 B4** ST2404.
Stockland Bristol *Som.* ***Village***, 6m/9km NW of Bridgwater. **19 F7** ST2443.
Stockland Green *Kent* ***Settlement***, 2m/4km NW of Royal Tunbridge Wells. TQ5642.
Stockland Hill *Devon* ***Inland physical feature***, hill ridge 728 feet or 222 metres high, running N to S, 4m/7km NE of Honiton. **8 B4** ST2203.
Stockleigh English *Devon* ***Village***, 4m/7km N of Crediton. **7 G5** SS8506.
Stockleigh Pomeroy *Devon* ***Village***, 4m/6km NE of Crediton. **7 G5** SS8703.
Stockley *Wilts.* ***Hamlet***, 2m/3km S of Calne. **20 C5** ST9967.
Stockley Hill *Here.* ***Locality***, 1m/2km E of Peterchurch. SO3638.
Stocklinch *Som.* ***Village***, 2m/3km NE of Ilminster. **8 C3** ST3817.
Stockport *Gt.Man.* Population: 132,813. ***Town***, 6m/10km SE of Manchester, where Rivers Goyt and Tame unite to form River Mersey. Traditionally a hat-making and textile town; now other industries are important. Parish church chancel dates from 14c. Stockport Railway Viaduct, built in 1840, is largest brick structure in Europe and has 27 arches. The Pyramid is landmark office block. **49 H4** SJ8989.
Stocks Reservoir *Lancs.* ***Reservoir***, in River Hodder valley, 2m/3km N of Slaidburn. **56 C4** SD7255.
Stocksbridge *S.Yorks.* Population: 13,182. ***Town***, former steel town, on Little Don River, 8m/14km NW of Sheffield. **50 E3** SK2798.
Stocksfield *Northumb.* ***Village***, on S side of River Tyne, 3m/4km W of Prudhoe. **71 F7** NZ0561.
Stockton *Here.* ***Village***, 2m/3km NE of Leominster. **28 E2** SO5161.
Stockton *Norf.* ***Village***, 3m/5km NW of Beccles. **45 H6** TM3894.
Stockton *Shrop.* ***Settlement***, 2m/3km SW of Marton. SJ2601.
Stockton *Shrop.* ***Village***, 4m/7km N of Bridgnorth. **39 G6** SO7299.
Stockton *Tel. & W.* ***Settlement***, 2m/4km SE of Newport. SJ7716.
Stockton *Warks.* ***Village***, 2m/3km NE of Southam. **31 F2** SP4363.
Stockton *Wilts.* ***Village***, on River Wylye, 5m/7km SE of Heytesbury. **9 J1** ST9838.
Stockton Brook *Staffs.* ***Suburb***, 1m/2km SW of Endon. SJ9152.
Stockton Heath *Warr.* Population: 11,411. ***Suburb***, 1m/2km S of Warrington town centre. **49 F4** SJ6186.
Stockton-on-Tees *Stock.* Population: 83,576. ***Town***, old port, mainly on W bank of River Tees, forming part of Teesside urban complex. Town had been main port on River Tees for hundreds of years until building of larger ships put port into decline. The town then prospered with arrival of railway. Buildings now are very much a mixture of old and new. **63 F4** NZ4418.
Stockton on Teme *Worcs.* ***Village***, 6m/10km SE of Cleobury Mortimer. **29 G2** SO7167.
Stockton on the Forest *York* ***Village***, 4m/7km NE of York. **58 C4** SE6556.
Stockval *High.* ***Mountain***, 1m/2km E of Talisker, Skye. Height 1364 feet or 416 metres. **85 J2** NG3529.
Stockwell *Glos.* ***Settlement***, 5m/8km S of Cheltenham. SO9414.
Stockwell *Gt.Lon.* ***Suburb***, in borough of Lambeth, 3m/4km S of Charing Cross. TQ3076.
Stockwell End *W.Mid.* ***Suburb***, 2m/3km NW of Wolverhampton town centre. SJ8800.
Stockwell Heath *Staffs.* ***Hamlet***, 2m/3km N of Rugeley. SK0521.
Stockwitch Cross *Som.* ***Settlement***, at NE end of Yeovilton airfield, 3m/4km NE of Ilchester. ST5524.
Stockwood *Bristol* ***Suburb***, 4m/6km SE of Bristol city centre. ST6268.
Stockwood *Dorset* ***Hamlet***, 2m/3km NE of Evershot. **8 E4** ST5906.
Stodday *Lancs.* ***Settlement***, 2m/3km SW of Lancaster. **55 H4** SD4658.
Stodmarsh *Kent* ***Village***, 5m/8km E of Canterbury. **25 J5** TR2160.
Stody *Norf.* ***Hamlet***, 3m/4km SW of Holt. **44 E2** TG0535.
Stoer *High.* ***Village***, on W coast of Sutherland district, 5m/8km NW of Lochinver. To N is peninsula of Stoer, culminating in the headland Point of Stoer. Lighthouse on W point of peninsula nearly 4m/6km NW of village. **102 C6** NC0328.
Stoford *Som.* ***Village***, 2m/3km S of Yeovil. **8 E3** ST5613.
Stoford *Wilts.* ***Hamlet***, across River Avon from Great Wishford, 3m/4km N of Wilton. **10 B1** SU0835.
Stogumber *Som.* ***Village***, 4m/6km SE of Watchet. **7 J2** ST0937.
Stogursey *Som.* ***Village***, 7m/11km NW of Bridgwater. **19 F7** ST2042.
Stoke *Devon* ***Village***, 5m/8km W of Clovelly. **6 A3** SS2324.
Stoke *Hants.* ***Village***, 2m/3km SE of Hurstbourne Tarrant. **21 H6** SU4051.
Stoke *Hants.* ***Village***, on Hayling Island, 1m/2km S of Langstone Bridge. **11 J4** SU7202.
Stoke *Med.* ***Village***, 4m/7km W of Grain, on N side of Stoke Saltings and River Medway estuary. **24 E4** TQ8275.
Stoke *Plym.* ***Suburb***, of Plymouth, 1km NW of city centre. SX4655.
Stoke *Suff.* ***Suburb***, 1km S of Ipswich town centre. TM1643.
Stoke *W.Mid.* ***Suburb***, E district of Coventry. **30 E1** SP3779.
Stoke Abbott *Dorset* ***Village***, 2m/3km W of Beaminster. **8 D4** ST4500.
Stoke Albany *Northants.* ***Village***, 5m/7km E of Market Harborough. **42 B7** SP8087.
Stoke Ash *Suff.* ***Village***, 3m/5km SW of Eye. **35 F1** TM1170.
Stoke Bardolph *Notts.* ***Village***, 5m/8km E of Nottingham. **41 J1** SK6441.
Stoke Bishop *Bristol* ***Suburb***, of Bristol, 2m/4km NW of city centre. ST5675.
Stoke Bliss *Worcs.* ***Hamlet***, 5m/8km N of Bromyard. **29 F2** SO6562.
Stoke Bruerne *Northants.* ***Village***, at S end of long tunnel on Grand Union Canal, 4m/6km E of Towcester. **31 J3** SP7449.
Stoke by Clare *Suff.* ***Village***, 5m/7km E of Haverhill. **34 B4** TL7443.
Stoke-by-Nayland *Suff.* ***Village***, 5m/8km SW of Hadleigh. **34 D5** TL9836.
Stoke Canon *Devon* ***Village***, on River Culm, 4m/6km NE of Exeter. **7 H6** SX9398.
Stoke Charity *Hants.* ***Village***, 6m/10km N of Winchester. **11 F1** SU4839.
Stoke Climsland *Cornw.* ***Village***, 3m/5km N of Callington. **4 D3** SX3674.
Stoke Cross *Here.* ***Hamlet***, 3m/5km SW of Bromyard. SO6250.
Stoke Cross *Worcs.* ***Locality***, 1m/2km SE of Bromsgrove. SO9869.
Stoke D'Abernon *Surr.* ***Village***, 3m/5km NW of Leatherhead. Church contains oldest brass in Britain (1277). **22 E6** TQ1259.
Stoke Doyle *Northants.* ***Village***, 1m/2km SW of Oundle. **42 D7** TL0286.
Stoke Dry *Rut.* ***Village***, on E side of Eyebrook Reservoir, 2m/3km S of Uppingham. **42 B6** SP8596.
Stoke Edith *Here.* ***Village***, 6m/9km E of Hereford. SO6040.
Stoke Farthing *Wilts.* ***Hamlet***, on River Ebble, 5m/7km SW of Wilton. SU0525.
Stoke Ferry *Norf.* ***Village***, 6m/10km SE of Downham Market. **44 A6** TF7000.
Stoke Fleming *Devon* ***Village***, on S coast, 2m/3km SW of Dartmouth. **5 J6** SX8648.
Stoke Gabriel *Devon* ***Village***, on inlet of River Dart estuary, 3m/5km SW of Paignton. **5 J5** SX8457.
Stoke Gifford *S.Glos.* Population: 7694. ***Village***, 5m/8km NE of Bristol. **19 K4** ST6279.
Stoke Golding *Leics.* ***Village***, 3m/5km NW of Hinckley. **41 F6** SP3997.
Stoke Goldington *M.K.* ***Village***, 4m/7km NW of Newport Pagnell. **32 B4** SP8348.
Stoke Green *Bucks.* ***Settlement***, 2m/3km NE of Slough. SU9882.
Stoke Hammond *Bucks.* ***Village***, 3m/4km S of Bletchley. **32 B6** SP8829.
Stoke Heath *Shrop.* ***Hamlet***, 3m/5km SW of Market Drayton. **39 F3** SJ6529.
Stoke Heath *W.Mid.* ***Suburb***, 2m/3km NE of Coventry city centre. SP3580.
Stoke Heath *Worcs.* ***Village***, 1m/2km SW of Bromsgrove. SO9468.
Stoke Holy Cross *Norf.* ***Village***, 4m/7km S of Norwich. **45 G5** TG2301.
Stoke Lacy *Here.* ***Village***, 4m/7km SW of Bromyard. **29 F3** SO6249.
Stoke Lyne *Oxon.* ***Village***, 4m/6km N of Bicester. SP5628.
Stoke Mandeville *Bucks.* ***Village***, 3m/4km SE of Aylesbury. **22 B1** SP8310.
Stoke Newington *Gt.Lon.* ***Suburb***, in borough of Hackney, 4m/7km NE of Charing Cross. **23 G3** TQ3386.
Stoke on Tern *Shrop.* ***Village***, 2m/3km E of Hodnet. **39 F3** SJ6428.
Stoke-on-Trent *Stoke* Population: 266,543. ***City***, on River Trent, 135m/217km NW of London. Centre for employment, shopping and leisure. Capital of The Potteries (largest claywear producer in the world), now largely a finishing centre for imported pottery. Many pottery factories and workshops open to public. Created by an amalgamation of former Stoke-upon-Trent and the towns of Burslem, Fenton, Hanley, Longton and Tunstall in 1910. Wide range of industries including steel, engineering, paper, rubber, textile and glass. Many museums devoted to city's industrial heritage. Staffordshire University. **40 A1** SJ8745.
Stoke Orchard *Glos.* ***Village***, 4m/7km NW of Cheltenham, with church containing wall paintings dating from 12c, discovered in 1928. Church was important point for pilgrims on journey to Santiago de Compostella in Spain. **29 J6** SO9228.
Stoke Park Pavilions *Northants.* ***Historic house***, two 17c pavilions by Inigo Jones, 3m/5km E of Towcester. **31 J4** SP7448.
Stoke Pero *Som.* ***Settlement***, on Exmoor, 2m/3km S of Porlock. SS8743.
Stoke Poges *Bucks.* Population: 4851. ***Suburb***, 3m/4km N of Slough. **22 C3** SU9883.
Stoke Point *Devon* ***Coastal feature***, headland at NW end of Bigbury Bay, to SE of Newton Ferrers. **5 F6** SX5645.
Stoke Pound *Worcs.* ***Settlement***, 2m/3km S of Bromsgrove. SO9667.
Stoke Prior *Here.* ***Village***, 2m/4km SE of Leominster. **28 E3** SO5256.
Stoke Prior *Worcs.* ***Village***, 2m/4km S of Bromsgrove. **29 J2** SO9567.
Stoke Rivers *Devon* ***Village***, 5m/8km E of Barnstaple. **6 E2** SS6335.
Stoke Rochford *Lincs.* ***Village***, 5m/9km S of Grantham. **42 C3** SK9227.
Stoke Row *Oxon.* ***Village***, 5m/8km W of Henley-on-Thames. **21 K3** SU6883.
Stoke St. Gregory *Som.* ***Village***, 8m/12km E of Taunton. **8 C2** ST3427.
Stoke St. Mary *Som.* ***Village***, 3m/4km SE of Taunton. **8 B2** ST2622.
Stoke St. Michael *Som.* ***Village***, 4m/6km NE of Shepton Mallet. **19 K7** ST6646.
Stoke St. Milborough *Shrop.* ***Village***, 6m/10km NE of Ludlow. **38 E7** SO5682.
Stoke sub Hamdon *Som.* ***Village***, 5m/8km W of Yeovil. 15c Priory (National Trust). Quarries on Hamdon Hill to S, source of local building stone known as Ham stone. **8 D3** ST4717.
Stoke sub Hamdon Priory *Som.* ***Ecclesiastical building***, 15c priory (National Trust), including great hall, 5m/8km NW of Yeovil. **8 D3** ST4717.
Stoke Talmage *Oxon.* ***Village***, 3m/5km N of Watlington. **21 K2** SU6799.
Stoke Trister *Som.* ***Village***, 2m/3km E of Wincanton. **9 G2** ST7328.

S

Stoke Villice *B. & N.E.Som.* ***Settlement***, on W side of Chew Valley Lake, 1km S of Chew Stoke. ST5560.
Stoke Wake *Dorset* ***Hamlet***, 5m/8km S of Sturminster Newton. **9 G4** ST7606.
Stokeford *Dorset* ***Hamlet***, 4m/6km W of Wareham. **9 H6** SY8687.
Stokeford Bridge *Wilts.* ***Bridge***, four-arched bridge of Bath stone with prominent cutwaters, on E side of Limpley Stoke, 4m/8km SE of Bath. ST7861.
Stokeham *Notts.* ***Village***, 6m/9km SE of Retford. **51 K5** SK7876.
Stokeinteignhead *Devon* ***Village***, 4m/6km E of Newton Abbot. **5 K3** SX9170.
Stokenchurch *Bucks.* Population: 3775. ***Village***, 7m/11km W of High Wycombe. **22 A2** SU7696.
Stokenham *Devon* ***Village***, 5m/8km E of Kingsbridge. **5 J6** SX8042.
Stokes Bay *Hants.* ***Bay***, extending NW from Gilkicker Point, S of Gosport. **11 G5** SZ5998.
Stokesay *Shrop.* ***Village***, 1km S of Craven Arms. Stokesay Castle (English Heritage) is 13c fortified manor house. **38 D7** SO4381.
Stokesay Castle *Shrop.* ***Castle***, fortified 13c manor house (English Heritage) in hamlet of Stokesay, built by Lawrence of Ludlow, 1km S of Craven Arms and 7m/11km NW of Ludlow. **38 D7** SO4381.
Stokesby *Norf.* ***Village***, 2m/3km E of Acle across River Bure. **45 J4** TG4310.
Stokesley *N.Yorks.* Population: 4008. ***Small town***, 8m/12km S of Middlesbrough. **63 G6** NZ5208.
Stolford *Som.* ***Village***, 3m/4km NE of Stogursey. **19 F7** ST2245.
Ston Easton *Som.* ***Village***, 3m/4km W of Midsomer Norton. **19 K6** ST6253.
Stonar Cut *Kent* ***Settlement***, 2m/3km N of Sandwich. **25 K5** TR3361.
Stondon Massey *Essex* ***Village***, 3m/4km SE of Chipping Ongar. **23 J1** TL5800.
Stone *Bucks.* Population: 1972. ***Village***, 2m/4km W of Aylesbury. **31 J7** SP7812.
Stone *Glos.* ***Village***, 3m/4km S of Berkeley. **19 K2** ST6895.
Stone *Kent* ***Locality***, 2m/3km W of Faversham. TQ9861.
Stone *Kent* ***Village***, on River Thames, 2m/3km E of Dartford. **23 J4** TQ5774.
Stone *Kent* ***Village***, in parish of Stone-cum-Ebony on Isle of Oxney, 2m/3km SW of Appledore. **14 E5** TQ9327.
Stone *Som.* ***Settlement***, 2m/3km E of Ham Street. ST5834.
Stone *S.Yorks.* ***Hamlet***, 2m/3km SE of Maltby. SK5589.
Stone *Staffs.* Population: 12,305. ***Town***, market town on River Trent, 7m/11km N of Stafford, with some attractive Georgian buildings. **40 A2** SJ9034.
Stone *Worcs.* ***Village***, 2m/3km SE of Kidderminster. **29 H1** SO8575.
Stone Allerton *Som.* ***Village***, 3m/5km NW of Wedmore. **19 G6** ST4051.
Stone Bridge Corner *Peter.* ***Locality***, 2m/3km S of Thorney. TF2700.
Stone Chair *W.Yorks.* ***Locality***, adjoining to SW of Shelf, 3m/4km NE of Halifax. SE1127.
Stone Cross *Dur.* ***Hamlet***, 2m/4km N of Barnard Castle. NZ0419.
Stone Cross *E.Suss.* ***Settlement***, 2m/3km S of Crowborough. TQ5128.
Stone Cross *E.Suss.* ***Village***, 3m/5km N of Eastbourne. **13 K6** TQ6104.
Stone Cross *Kent* ***Settlement***, 4m/7km W of Royal Tunbridge Wells. **13 J3** TQ5239.
Stone Cross *Kent* ***Settlement***, 4m/7km S of Ashford. **15 F4** TR0236.
Stone Cross *Kent* ***Settlement***, to S of Sandwich. TR3257.
Stone Cross *W.Mid.* ***Suburb***, 2m/3km N of West Bromwich town centre. SP0194.
Stone-edge Batch *N.Som.* ***Hamlet***, 1m/2km NW of Nailsea. ST4671.
Stone Fold *Lancs.* ***Settlement***, 2m/3km N of Haslingden. SD7825.
Stone Hill *S.Lan.* ***Mountain***, 2m/3km NE of Rigside. Height 1030 feet or 314 metres. **75 G7** NS8936.
Stone Hill *S.Yorks.* ***Hamlet***, adjoining to NE of Hatfield Woodhouse. SE6808.
Stone House *Cumb.* ***Settlement***, 1m/2km SE of Lea Yeat. **56 C1** SD7785.
Stone House Cottage Garden *Worcs.* ***Garden***, walled garden with rare wall shrubs and climbing plants, 2m/3km SE of Kidderminster. **29 H1** SO8675.
Stone of Setter *Ork.* ***Historic/prehistoric site***, Bronze Age standing stone in N of Eday, just N of Mill Loch. **106 E4** HY5637.
Stone Point *Essex* ***Coastal feature***, N point of Stone Marsh on S side of Pennyhole Bay, 2m/3km NW of The Naze. **35 G6** TM2425.
Stone Point *Hants.* ***Coastal feature***, headland at SW end of Stanswood Bay, 3m/5km S of Fawley. Includes Lepe Country Park. **11 F5** SZ4598.
Stone Rows *Leics.* ***Hamlet***, 1km E of Donisthorpe. SK3114.
Stone Street *Kent* ***Hamlet***, 3m/4km E of Sevenoaks. **23 J6** TQ5754.
Stone Street *Kent* ***Other feature of interest***, Roman road originally running from Lympne to Canterbury. Present day B2068 road follows long section of its course. **15 G3** TR1344.
Stone Street *Suff.* ***Hamlet***, 1km S of Boxford and 3m/5km N of Nayland. TL9639.
Stone Street *Suff.* ***Hamlet***, 3m/5km N of Halesworth. **45 H7** TM3882.
Stone Street *Suff.* ***Locality***, 1m/2km NW of Hadleigh. TM0143.
Stone Street *Suff.* ***Other feature of interest***, section of Roman road running from Bungay to Halesworth. Present day A144 road follows its course. **45 H7** TM3685.

S

Stonea *Cambs.* ***Settlement***, 3m/5km SE of March. TL4593.
Stoneacre *Kent* ***Historic house***, 15c half-timbered yeoman's house with small garden (National Trust) in Otham, 3m/5km SE of Maidstone. **14 D2** TQ8053.
Stonebow *Worcs.* ***Locality***, 2m/4km N of Pershore. SO9349.
Stonebridge *E.Suss.* ***Settlement***, adjoining to SW of Blackboys. **13 J4** TQ5220.
Stonebridge *Norf.* ***Locality***, 1km NE of Wretham. TL9290.
Stonebridge *N.Som.* ***Hamlet***, adjoining to NW of Banwell, 5m/7km E of Weston-super-Mare. ST3959.
Stonebridge *Warks.* ***Locality***, at major road junction, 4m/6km S of Coleshill. **40 E7** SP2183.
Stonebroom *Derbys.* ***Village***, 2m/4km N of Alfreton. **51 G7** SK4159.
Stoneclough *Gt.Man.* ***Suburb***, 1km NE of Kearsley. SD7505.
Stonecross Green *Suff.* ***Settlement***, 1km W of Whepstead. TL8257.
Stoneferry *Hull* ***Suburb***, 2m/3km N of Kingston upon Hull city centre. **59 H6** TA1031.
Stonefield *Arg. & B.* ***Settlement***, in Knapdale, 2m/3km N of Tarbert. **73 G3** NR8671.
Stonefield *S.Lan.* ***Locality***, 2m/4km NW of Hamilton. **74 E5** NS6957.
Stonefield *Staffs.* ***Suburb***, in N part of Stone. SJ8934.
Stonegate *E.Suss.* ***Village***, 3m/4km SE of Wadhurst. **13 K4** TQ6628.
Stonegate *N.Yorks.* ***Hamlet***, 3m/4km NW of Egton. NZ7709.
Stonegrave *N.Yorks.* ***Village***, 2m/3km NW of Hovingham. **58 C2** SE6577.
Stonehaugh *Northumb.* ***Hamlet***, 4m/7km W of Wark. **70 C6** NY7976.
Stonehaven *Aber.* Population: 9445. ***Small town***, port on Stonehaven Bay, on E coast, 13m/21km S of Aberdeen. **91 G6** NO8785.
Stonehaven Bay *Aber.* ***Bay***, on E coast 13m/21km S of Aberdeen. Stonehaven port lies on bay. NO8786.
Stonehenge *Wilts.* ***Historic/prehistoric site***, remains of Neolithic-Bronze Age earthwork and stone circle (English Heritage and World Heritage Site) on Salisbury Plain, 2m/3km W of Amesbury. Considered to be greatest creation of prehistoric man in Europe. Successive construction phases led to final ceremonial circle, formed of 30 sarsen uprights topped by continuous ring of lintels, an inner horseshoe of five sarsen trilithons and a sandstone Altar Stone; Welsh Bluestones were set within the sarsen circle and horseshoe. All building materials were transported to the site, indicating a resourceful and sophisticated society dedicated to completing the monument. However, exact purpose behind construction of Stonehenge is unknown: theories relate it to a sun-worshipping culture or an astronomical calendar. Stonehenge continues to attract large numbers of visitors, especially for midsummer solstice. It remains the focal point of an archaeologically significant area (much of it National Trust), which includes numerous relics, barrows, earthworks, such as The Cursus, and Woodhenge, a contemporary of early Stonehenge, 1m/2km NE. **20 E7** SU1242.
Stonehill *Surr.* ***Settlement***, 3m/5km N of Woking. SU9963.
Stonehill Green *Kent* ***Settlement***, 1m/2km NW of Swanley. TQ5070.
Stonehouse *Ches.* ***Hamlet***, 1km N of Ashton. SJ5070.
Stonehouse *D. & G.* ***Settlement***, 2m/3km NE of Haugh of Urr. **65 J4** NX8268.
Stonehouse *Glos.* ***Small town***, 3m/5km W of Stroud. **20 B1** SO8005.
Stonehouse *Northumb.* ***Settlement***, 4m/6km S of Haltwhistle. **61 H1** NY6958.
Stonehouse *Plym.* ***Suburb***, 1m/2km W of Plymouth city centre. **4 E5** SX4654.
Stonehouse *S.Lan.* Population: 5328. ***Village***, 3m/5km S of Larkhall. **75 F6** NS7546.
Stonehouses *Staffs.* ***Settlement***, 3m/5km SW of Cheadle. SJ9740.
Stoneleigh *Surr.* ***Suburb***, 1m/2km N of Ewell. TQ2264.
Stoneleigh *Warks.* ***Village***, 3m/5km E of Kenilworth. **30 E1** SP3372.
Stoneleigh Abbey *Warks.* ***Ecclesiastical building***, Cistercian abbey founded c. 1150, 2m/3km SW of Stoneleigh and 1m/2km E of Kenilworth. 14c gateway still remains, together with other fragments now incorporated in Italianate mansion. Royal Agricultural Show is held in grounds. **30 E1** SP3171.
Stoneley Green *Ches.* ***Settlement***, 2m/4km W of Nantwich. SJ6151.
Stonely *Cambs.* ***Village***, adjoining to SE of Kimbolton. **32 E2** TL1067.
Stoner Hill *Hants.* ***Settlement***, 2m/3km NW of Petersfield. **11 J2** SU7226.
Stones *W.Yorks.* ***Settlement***, in valley, 1m/2km SW of Todmorden. SD9223.
Stones Green *Essex* ***Hamlet***, 3m/5km N of Thorpe-le-Soken. **35 F6** TM1626.
Stones of Stenness *Ork.* ***Historic/prehistoric site***, 1km N of Stenness, four standing stones (Historic Scotland) remain out of an estimated original twelve erected in Neolithic times. **107 C6** HY3011.
Stonesby *Leics.* ***Village***, 6m/9km NE of Melton Mowbray. **42 B3** SK8224.
Stonesdale Moor *N.Yorks.* ***Open space***, moorland on upper reaches of West Stones Dale over which The Pennine Way passes, 3m/4km N of Keld. **61 K6** NY8805.
Stonesfield *Oxon.* ***Village***, 3m/4km SE of Charlbury. Site of Roman villa to E. **30 E7** SP3917.
Stoneside Hill *Cumb.* ***Mountain***, 4m/7km W of Broughton in Furness. Height 1384 feet or 422 metres. **54 E1** SD1389.
Stonestreet Green *Kent* ***Settlement***, 5m/8km SE of Ashford. **15 F4** TR0637.
Stonethwaite *Cumb.* ***Settlement***, 1m/2km E of Seatoller. **60 D5** NY2613.

Stoneton *Warks.* ***Settlement***, 9m/14km N of Banbury. SP4654.
Stoney Cross *Hants.* ***Settlement***, 3m/5km NW of Lyndhurst. **10 D3** SU2611.
Stoney Hill *Worcs.* ***Suburb***, E district of Bromsgrove. SO9670.
Stoney Littleton Long Barrow *B. & N.E.Som.* ***Historic/prehistoric site***, to N of Stoney Littleton, 2m/3km E of Peasedown St. John. Fine example of Neolithic chambered burial mound (English Heritage), 100 feet long. **20 A6** ST7357.
Stoney Middleton *Derbys.* ***Village***, 5m/7km N of Bakewell. **50 E5** SK2375.
Stoney Stanton *Leics.* Population: 3113. ***Village***, 4m/7km E of Hinckley. **41 G6** SP4994.
Stoney Stoke *Som.* ***Hamlet***, 2m/4km N of Wincanton. **9 G1** ST7032.
Stoney Stratton *Som.* ***Village***, 1km E of Evercreech. **9 F1** ST6539.
Stoney Stretton *Shrop.* ***Hamlet***, 7m/11km W of Shrewsbury. **38 C5** SJ3809.
Stoneybridge *W.Isles* *Anglicised form of Staoinebrig, qv.*
Stoneyburn *W.Loth.* ***Village***, 4m/6km S of Bathgate. **75 H4** NS9762.
Stoneyford *Devon* ***Settlement***, 1m/2km SW of Newton Poppleford. SY0688.
Stoneygate *Leic.* ***Suburb***, 2m/3km SE of Leicester city centre. **41 J5** SK6002.
Stoneyhills *Essex* ***Hamlet***, 1km N of Burnham-on-Crouch. **25 F2** TQ9597.
Stoneykirk *D. & G.* ***Village***, 5m/8km S of Stranraer. **64 A5** NX0853.
Stoneywood *Aberdeen* ***Village***, on NW outskirts of Aberdeen. **91 G3** NJ8911.
Stonganess *Shet.* ***Settlement***, on E coast of Yell, adjacent to Culli Voe. **108 E2** HP5402.
Stonham Aspal *Suff.* ***Village***, 4m/6km SW of Debenham. **35 F3** TM1359.
Stonnall *Staffs.* ***Village***, 2m/3km SE of Brownhills. **40 C5** SK0603.
Stonor *Oxon.* ***Village***, 4m/7km NW of Henley-on-Thames. **22 A3** SU7388.
Stonor Park *Oxon.* ***Historic house***, originating from 12c, home of Lord and Lady Camoys and Stonor family for over 800 years, 1km NE of Stonor and 4m/7km N of Henley-on-Thames. Includes rare furniture and artefacts from Europe and America, with exhibition on life of St. Edmund Campion who founded sanctuary here. **22 A3** SU7489.
Stonton Wyville *Leics.* ***Village***, 5m/8km N of Market Harborough. **42 A6** SP7395.
Stony Cross *Devon* ***Hamlet***, 4m/6km E of Bideford. SS5125.
Stony Cross *Here.* ***Locality***, 3m/5km W of Tenbury Wells. SO5466.
Stony Cross *Here.* ***Locality***, 3m/5km W of Great Malvern. SO7247.
Stony Dale *Notts.* ***Locality***, 2m/3km NE of East Bridgford. SK7244.
Stony Gate *T. & W.* ***Hamlet***, 1m/2km NE of Houghton le Spring. NZ3551.
Stony Heap *Dur.* ***Settlement***, 2m/4km E of Consett. NZ1451.
Stony Hill *B'pool* ***Suburb***, 2m/3km S of Blackpool town centre. SD3032.
Stony Hill *E.Ayr.* ***Mountain***, 4m/7km SE of Muirkirk. Height 1843 feet or 562 metres. **68 C1** NS7221.
Stony Houghton *Derbys.* ***Village***, 4m/7km NW of Mansfield. **51 G6** SK4966.
Stony Lea *Staffs.* ***Locality***, 1km NE of Cannock. SJ9810.
Stony Stratford *M.K.* ***Small town***, former coaching stop on Watling Street, on River Great Ouse, in NW part of Milton Keynes. Numerous inns. **31 J4** SP7940.
Stonybreck *Shet.* ***Settlement***, 1km SW of Fair Isle Airstrip. **108 A1** HZ2071.
Stonybridge *Pembs.* ***Hamlet***, 1m/2km W of Saundersfoot. SN1104.
Stoodleigh *Devon* ***Hamlet***, 5m/9km NW of South Molton. SS6532.
Stoodleigh *Devon* ***Village***, 5m/7km NW of Tiverton. **7 H4** SS9218.
Stoodleigh Beacon *Devon* ***Hill***, 6m/9km NW of Tiverton. Mast at summit. Height 987 feet or 301 metres. **7 G4** SS8818.
Stopes *S.Yorks.* ***Locality***, 4m/7km W of Sheffield. SK2888.
Stopham *W.Suss.* ***Village***, 1m/2km W of Pulborough. Medieval bridge spans River Arun. **12 D5** TQ0219.
Stopsley *Luton* ***Suburb***, NE district of Luton. **32 E6** TL1023.
Stoptide *Cornw.* ***Locality***, on E side of River Camel estuary, opposite Padstow. **3 G1** SW9475.
Stores Corner *Suff.* ***Locality***, 6m/9km SE of Woodbridge. TM3545.
Storeton *Mersey.* ***Hamlet***, 2m/3km W of Bebington. **48 C4** SJ3084.
Stormont Loch (Also known as Loch Bog.) *P. & K.* ***Lake/loch***, small loch 2m/3km S of Blairgowrie. **82 C3** NO1942.
Stornoway (Gaelic form: Steornabhagh.) *W.Isles* Population: 5975. ***Small town***, port and chief town of Isle of Lewis, situated on E coast, 22m/35km S of Butt of Lewis and 13m/22km E of Breascleit on W coast. Airport 2m/3km E towards Melbost. **101 G4** NB4232.
Stornoway Airport *W.Isles* ***Airport/airfield***, local airport, 2m/3km E of Stornoway, Isle of Lewis. **101 G4** NB4533.
Stornoway Harbour *W.Isles* ***Sea feature***, large natural harbour on S side of Stornoway, Isle of Lewis. **101 G4** NB4232.
Storridge *Here.* ***Hamlet***, 2m/4km NW of Great Malvern. **29 G4** SO7548.
Storrington *W.Suss.* Population: 7429. ***Small town***, old market town below South Downs, 4m/6km SE of Pulborough. Nearby Elizabethan house of Parkham Park, set in large deer park. **12 D5** TQ0814.

Storrs *S.Yorks.* ***Hamlet***, 4m/7km NW of Sheffield. SK2889.
Storrs Bridge *S.Yorks.* ***Locality***, on River Loxey, 1km N of Storrs and 4m/7km NW of Sheffield. SK2889.
Stort ***River***, rising about 7m/11km W of Saffron Walden and flowing S into River Lea 4m/6km SE of Ware. **33 H5** TL3909.
Storth *Cumb.* ***Village***, 1m/2km NE of Arnside. **55 H1** SD4779.
Storwood *E.Riding* ***Hamlet***, 3m/4km W of Melbourne. **58 D5** SE7144.
Stotfield *Moray* ***Suburb***, W district of Lossiemouth. **97 K4** NJ2270.
Stotfold *Beds.* Population: 6524. ***Suburb***, 3m/4km NW of Baldock. **33 F5** TL2236.
Stotfold Green *Beds.* ***Locality***, at N end of Stotfold. TL2236.
Stottesdon *Shrop.* ***Village***, 4m/7km N of Cleobury Mortimer. **39 F7** SO6782.
Stoughton *Leics.* ***Village***, 4m/6km E of Leicester. **41 J5** SK6402.
Stoughton *Som.* ***Locality***, formed of hamlets of Middle Stoughton, West Stoughton and Stoughton Cross, 1m/2km NW of Wedmore. ST4249.
Stoughton *Surr.* ***Suburb***, NW district of Guildford. **22 C6** SU9851.
Stoughton *W.Suss.* ***Village***, 5m/8km NE of Emsworth. Site of Roman building 2km E. **12 B5** SU8011.
Stoughton Cross *Som.* ***Hamlet***, 1m/2km NW of Wedmore. ST4249.
Stoul *High.* ***Settlement***, on SW shore of Loch Nevis, 5m/8km E of Mallaig. **86 D5** NM7594.
Stoulton *Worcs.* ***Village***, 5m/8km SE of Worcester. **29 J3** SO9049.
Stour ***River***, rising on Cotswold Hills N of Chipping Norton and flowing W to Burmington, then N through Shipston on Stour and into River Avon, 2m/3km SW of Stratford-upon-Avon. **30 D4** SP1853.
Stour ***River***, rising near Stourhead and flowing S to Sturminster Newton, then SE through Blandford Forum and Wimborne Minster into Christchurch Harbour. **9 H4** SZ1692.
Stour ***River***, rising some 4m/7km NW of Haverhill and flowing SE by Clare, Cavendish, Sudbury, Bures, Nayland and Dedham to form estuary at Manningtree, then E to Harwich, where it joins River Orwell to flow into Harwich Harbour and North Sea. **34 D5** TM2633.
Stour *Kent* ***River***, running from confluence of Great and Little Stour Rivers at Plucks Gutter into sea at Pegwell Bay. **25 J5** TR3462.
Stour *Worcs.* ***River***, rising S of Dudley and flowing SW, through Stourbridge and Kidderminster, into River Severn at Stourport-on-Severn. **29 H1** SO8170.
Stour Provost *Dorset* ***Village***, 3m/5km S of Gillingham. **9 G2** ST7921.
Stour Row *Dorset* ***Village***, 3m/5km W of Shaftesbury. **9 H2** ST8221.
Stourbridge *W.Mid.* Population: 55,624. ***Town***, with history of glass-making, on River Stour, 10m/17km W of Birmingham. **40 A7** SO9084.
Stourbrough Hill *Shet.* ***Hill***, 3m/4km NW of Walls, Mainland. Height 567 feet or 173 metres. **109 B7** HU2152.
Stourhead *Wilts.* ***Historic house***, 18c house and pleasure grounds (National Trust), 3m/4km NW of Mere. **9 G1** ST7734.
Stourmouth *Kent* ***Locality***, parish, 6m/9km NW of Sandwich, containing villages of East and West Stourmouth. TR2562.
Stourpaine *Dorset* ***Village***, at confluence of River Iwerne with River Stour, at SW end of Cranborne Chase, 3m/4km NW of Blandford Forum. **9 H4** ST8609.
Stourport-on-Severn *Worcs.* Population: 18,283. ***Town***, canal town, at confluence of River Stour and River Severn and on Staffordshire and Worcestershire Canal, 3m/5km SW of Kidderminster. Main dock, surrounded by 18c buildings, now a marina. **29 H1** SO8171.
Stourton *Staffs.* ***Hamlet***, 3m/5km W of Stourbridge. Stewponey Junction on Stourbridge Canal and Staffordshire and Worcestershire Canal to E. **40 A7** SO8585.
Stourton *Warks.* ***Village***, adjoining to E of Cherington, 6m/10km N of Chipping Norton. **30 D5** SP2936.
Stourton *W.Yorks.* ***Locality***, on River Aire, 3m/5km SE of Leeds city centre. Power station on opposite side of river. SE3230.
Stourton *Wilts.* ***Village***, 3m/4km NW of Mere. 18c Stourhead (National Trust) in parkland on N side of village. **9 G1** ST7734.
Stourton Caundle *Dorset* ***Village***, in Blackmoor Vale, 5m/8km E of Sherborne. **9 G3** ST7115.
Stove *Ork.* ***Settlement***, on Bay of Stove, in SW of Sanday. **106 F4** HY6135.
Stoven *Suff.* ***Village***, 5m/8km NE of Halesworth. **45 J7** TM4481.
Stover *S.Glos.* ***Locality***, 2m/3km W of Chipping Sodbury. ST6982.
Stover Country Park *Devon* ***Leisure/recreation***, country park with lake and woodland, 3m/4km SE of Bovey Tracey. **5 J3** SX8375.
Stow *Lincs.* ***Village***, 4m/7km N of Saxilby. Large Saxon/Norman church is notable landmark. **52 B4** SK8881.
Stow *Sc.Bord.* ***Village***, on Gala Water, 5m/8km W of Lauder. **76 C6** NT4544.
Stow Bardolph *Norf.* ***Village***, 2m/3km NE of Downham Market. **44 A5** TF6205.
Stow Bardolph Fen *Norf.* ***Open space***, lowland between Middle Level Main Drain to W and River Great Ouse to E, 4m/6km W of Downham Market. **43 J5** TF5404.
Stow Bedon *Norf.* ***Village***, 4m/6km SE of Watton. Mere on W side of village. **44 D6** TL9596.
Stow cum Quy *Cambs.* ***Village***, 5m/8km E of Cambridge. **33 J2** TL5260.
Stow Longa *Cambs.* ***Village***, 8m/13km W of Huntingdon. **32 E1** TL1070.
Stow Maries *Essex* ***Village***, 5m/8km S of Maldon. **24 E2** TQ8399.
Stow-on-the-Wold *Glos.* Population: 1999. ***Small town***, attractive town, highest in Cotswolds, 8m/12km W of Chipping Norton. Site of Roman villa to NW. **30 C6** SP1925.
Stow Pasture *Lincs.* ***Settlement***, 1km E of Stow. SK8982.
Stowbridge *Norf.* ***Hamlet***, on W bank of River Great Ouse, 3m/4km N of Downham Market. **44 A5** TF6007.
Stowe *Bucks.* ***Locality***, and parish 3m/4km NW of Buckingham, containing Stowe School, boys' public school housed in 18c house in large park. SP6737.
Stowe *Glos.* ***Settlement***, 1m/2km N of St. Briavels. **19 J1** SO5606.
Stowe *Shrop.* ***Hamlet***, 2m/3km NE of Knighton. **28 C1** SO3173.
Stowe *Staffs.* ***Suburb***, 1km NE of Lichfield. SK1210.
Stowe *Staffs.* ***Village***, 6m/10km NE of Stafford. **40 C3** SK0027.
Stowe Landscape Gardens *Bucks.* ***Garden***, large landscaped garden of Georgian era (National Trust) surrounding Stowe School, 3m/4km NW of Buckingham. Notable for arches, temples, Palladian bridge and other monuments by Vanbrugh, Gibbs and Kent. **31 H5** SP6636.
Stowehill *Northants.* ***Settlement***, 5m/8km SE of Daventry. SP6458.
Stowell *Glos.* ***Settlement***, 2m/3km SW of Northleach. **30 B7** SP0813.
Stowell *Som.* ***Village***, 4m/7km SW of Wincanton. **9 F2** ST6822.
Stowell Hill *Som.* ***Garden***, to SE of Templecombe, 6m/9km NE of Sherborne, with rhododendrons, azaleas, magnolias and Japanese cherries. **9 G2** ST7121.
Stowey *B. & N.E.Som.* ***Hamlet***, 3m/4km SE of Chew Magna. **19 J6** ST5959.
Stowford *Devon* ***Hamlet***, 6m/9km W of South Molton. SS6226.
Stowford *Devon* ***Suburb***, 2m/3km N of Sidmouth town centre. SY1189.
Stowford *Devon* ***Village***, 7m/11km E of Launceston. **6 C7** SX4386.
Stowlangtoft *Suff.* ***Village***, 2m/4km SE of Ixworth. **34 D2** TL9568.
Stowmarket *Suff.* Population: 13,229. ***Town***, old market town on River Gipping, 11m/18km NW of Ipswich. Notable as a wool centre in 17c and 18c. The Museum of East Anglian Life is contained in Abbot's Hall. **34 E3** TM0458.
Stowting *Kent* ***Village***, 5m/8km NW of Hythe. **15 G3** TR1241.
Stowting Common *Kent* ***Settlement***, 1m/2km N of Stowting. TR1243.
Stowupland *Suff.* ***Suburb***, 1m/2km NE of Stowmarket. **34 E3** TM0760.
Straad *Arg. & B.* ***Settlement***, near W coast of Bute, 3m/5km SW of Rothesay. NS0462.
Stracathro *Angus* ***Locality***, 2m/4km SE of Edzell. Site of Roman fort. **83 H1** NO6265.
Strachan *Aber.* ***Village***, on Water of Feugh, 3m/4km SW of Banchory. **90 E5** NO6792.
Strachur *Arg. & B.* ***Village***, 1km E of Strachur Bay, on E shore of Loch Fyne, in Argyll. **80 C7** NN0901.
Strachur Bay *Arg. & B.* ***Bay***, on E shore of Loch Fyne in Argyll. 1km E is village of Strachur. **80 B7** NN0801.
Stradbroke *Suff.* ***Village***, 7m/12km NW of Framlingham. **35 G1** TM2373.
Stradbrook *Wilts.* ***Locality***, adjoining to W of Bratton, 3m/5km E of Westbury. ST9152.
Stradishall *Suff.* ***Village***, 7m/11km NE of Haverhill. Airfield to SW. **34 B3** TL7452.
Stradsett *Norf.* ***Hamlet***, 4m/6km E of Downham Market. Hall is Elizabethan, altered early 19c; large lake in park. **44 A5** TF6605.
Strae *Arg. & B.* ***River***, in Argyll, running SW down Glen Strae to River Orchy 2m/3km W of Dalmally. **80 C4** NN1328.
Stragglethorpe *Lincs.* ***Hamlet***, 7m/12km E of Newark-on-Trent. **52 C7** SK9152.
Stragglethorpe *Notts.* ***Locality***, 1m/2km S of Radcliffe on Trent. SK6537.
Straiaval *W.Isles* ***Mountain***, 1km NE of Laxadale Lochs, North Harris. Height 1276 feet or 389 metres. **100 D7** NB1904.
Straight Soley *Wilts.* ***Settlement***, 2m/4km N of Hungerford. SU3272.
Strait of Corryvreckan (Also known as Gulf of Corryvreckan.) *Arg. & B.* ***Sea feature***, sea passage between Scarba and Jura. Notorious for tidal races and whirlpools. **79 H7** NM6902.
Strait of Dover ***Sea feature***, narrow part of English Channel between coasts of England and France. **15 J5** TR4030.
Straiton *Edin.* ***Suburb***, 5m/8km S of Edinburgh city centre. **76 A4** NT2766.
Straiton *S.Ayr.* ***Village***, on Water of Girvan, 6m/10km SE of Maybole. **67 H3** NS3804.
Straits Green *W.Mid.* ***Locality***, 3m/4km W of Dudley town centre. SO9091.
Straloch *Aber.* ***Settlement***, 2m/3km NW of Newmachar. **91 G2** NJ8521.
Straloch *P. & K.* ***Settlement***, in Glen Brerachan, 3m/5km NW of Kirkmichael. **82 B1** NO0463.
Stramshall *Staffs.* ***Village***, 2m/3km NW of Uttoxeter. **40 C2** SK0835.
Strandburgh Ness *Shet.* ***Coastal feature***, headland at NE point of Fetlar. **108 F3** HU6793.
Strands *Cumb.* ***Hamlet***, 4m/6km E of Gosforth. NY1204.
Strands *Cumb.* ***Settlement***, 1km SE of The Green, 3m/4km N of Millom. SD1884.
Strang *I.o.M.* ***Hamlet***, 2m/3km NW of Douglas. **54 C6** SC3678.
Strangeways *Gt.Man.* ***Suburb***, 1m/2km N of Manchester city centre. HM prison. SJ8399.
Strangford *Here.* ***Hamlet***, in loop of River Wye, 3m/4km NW of Ross-on-Wye across river. SO5828.
Strangways *Wilts.* ***Locality***, 2m/3km NW of Amesbury. SU1443.
Strannda (Anglicised form: Strond.) *W.Isles* ***Settlement***, on South Harris, 2m/3km SE of Leverburgh. **93 F3** NG0384.
Stranraer *D. & G.* Population: 11,348. ***Town***, port and resort at head of Loch Ryan, 23m/37km W of Wigtown. Passenger and car ferry service to Larne in Northern Ireland, and also from Cairnryan on E side of loch. Castle House was home of Arctic explorer, John Ross. 16c Stranraer Castle. **64 A4** NX0660.
Strata Florida (Ystrad-fflur). *Cere.* ***Settlement***, 1m/2km SE of Pontrhydfendigaid. Slight remains of 12c abbey (Cadw). **27 G2** SN7465.
Strata Florida Abbey *Cere.* ***Ecclesiastical building***, ruin of important Welsh abbey (Cadw) dating from late 12c to early 13c, 6m/10km NE of Tregaron. Burial place of some princes and princesses of Wales. **27 G2** SN7465.
Stratfield Mortimer *W.Berks.* ***Village***, 6m/9km SW of Reading. **21 K5** SU6664.
Stratfield Saye *Hants.* ***Village***, 8m/12km SW of Reading. **21 K5** SU6861.
Stratfield Saye House *Hants.* ***Historic house***, 1m/2km E of Stratfield Saye and 5m/8km S of Reading. 19c home to Dukes of Wellington. Features Duke of Wellington (Arthur Wellesley) exhibition, with wildfowl centre and gardens in grounds. **21 K5** SU7061.
Stratfield Turgis *Hants.* ***Village***, 6m/10km NE of Basingstoke, along with Turgis Green. **21 K6** SU6960.
Stratford *Beds.* ***Settlement***, 1m/2km SE of Sandy. TL1847.
Stratford *Glos.* ***Settlement***, 4m/6km NW of Tewkesbury. **29 H5** SO8738.
Stratford *Gt.Lon.* ***Suburb***, in borough of Newham, 5m/7km NE of London Bridge. TQ3884.
Stratford Marsh *Gt.Lon.* ***Suburb***, 1km W of Stratford, in River Lea valley. TQ3883.
Stratford New Town *Gt.Lon.* ***Suburb***, 1km N of Stratford. TQ3884.
Stratford-on-Avon *Warks.* *Alternative spelling of Stratford-upon-Avon, qv.*
Stratford St. Andrew *Suff.* ***Village***, 3m/4km SW of Saxmundham. **35 H3** TM3560.
Stratford St. Mary *Suff.* ***Village***, 6m/10km NE of Colchester. **34 E5** TM0434.
Stratford sub Castle *Wilts.* ***Suburb***, in N part of Salisbury below Old Sarum. **10 C1** SU1332.
Stratford Tony *Wilts.* ***Village***, 3m/5km S of Wilton. **10 B2** SU0926.
Stratford-upon-Avon (Also spelled Stratford-on-Avon.) *Warks.* Population: 22,231. ***Town***, on River Avon, 8m/13km SW of Warwick. Birthplace of Shakespeare. Tourist centre. Shakespeare Memorial Theatre. Many attractive 16c buildings and impressive medieval church. Anne Hathaway's Cottage to W, at Shottery. **30 C3** SP2054.
Stratford-upon-Avon Canal ***Canal***, beginning in King's Norton, to S of Birmingham, and flowing S through Hockley Heath and Wootton Wawen to Stratford-upon-Avon, where it joins River Avon. **30 C2** SP1955.
Strath *High.* ***Settlement***, 2m/3km SE of Watten. **105 H3** ND2552.
Strath an Lòin *High.* ***Valley***, carrying Allt Car and running W to E into Loch Shin. **103 G7** NC4117.
Strath Ascaig *High.* ***Valley***, carrying Allt Cadh an Eas, 1km S of Stromeferry, Skye and Lochalsh district. **86 E1** NG8633.
Strath Avon *Moray* ***Valley***, on SE side of Hills of Cromdale, 3m/5km N of Bridge of Brown. **89 J2** NJ1424.
Strath Bay *High.* ***Bay***, small bay to NE of Gairloch, Ross and Cromarty district. **94 D4** NG7977.
Strath Beag *High.* ***Valley***, running N to S from the head of Loch Eriboll. **103 F3** NC3854.
Strath Beag *High.* ***Valley***, in W part of Ross and Cromarty district, carrying Dundonell River N into head of Little Loch Broom. **95 G3** NH0988.
Strath Bogie *Aber.* ***Valley***, below E slopes of Clashmach Hill, carrying River Bogie N towards Huntly. **90 D1** NJ5138.
Strath Braan *P. & K.* ***Valley***, carrying River Braan NE to Strath Tay at Dunkeld. **82 A4** NN9840.
Strath Bran *High.* ***Valley***, carrying River Bran E from Achnasheen to Loch Luichart. **95 J6** NH2461.
Strath Brora *High.* ***Valley***, carrying River Brora, in Sutherland district, to Brora on E coast. **96 E1** NC7609.
Strath Burn *High.* ***River***, rising as Camster Burn and becoming Rowens Burn, then Strath Burn to N of Scorridet. It flows N and joins with Burn of Acharole, where it becomes Wick River 1km S of Watten. **105 H3** ND2350.
Strath Chrombuill *High.* ***Valley***, running E to W from N slopes of Fionn Bheinn and converging with Gleann Tanagaidh, 4m/6km NE of Kinlochewe. **95 H5** NH1164.
Strath Dionard *High.* ***Valley***, in Sutherland district to E of Foinaven, carrying River Dionard N from Loch Dionard. **103 F3** NC3661.
Strath Dores *High.* ***Valley***, on SE side of N end of Loch Ness. **88 D1** NH5935.
Strath Earn *P. & K.* ***Valley***, carrying River Earn E from Loch Earn to head of Firth of Tay below Perth. **81 J5** NN9517.
Strath Fillan *Stir.* ***Valley***, carrying River Fillan SE towards Crianlarich. **80 E5** NN3428.
Strath Finella *Aber.* ***Valley***, to N of Strathfinella Hill, cutting through mountains of Drumtochty Forest in a W to E direction, 4m/7km NE of Fettercairn. **90 E7** NO6879.
Strath Fleet *High.* ***Valley***, in Sutherland district, carrying River Fleet to E coast, N of Dornoch. **96 D1** NC6702.
Strath Gairloch *High.* ***Settlement***, in Ross and Cromarty district, 1km NW of Gairloch. NG7977.
Strath Gartney *Stir.* ***Locality***, land on N shore of Loch Katrine. **81 F6** NN4610.

Strath Gryfe *Inclyde* ***Valley***, carrying River Gryfe, or Gryfe Water, between Gryfe Reservoir and Bridge of Weir. **74 B3** NS3370.

Strath Halladale *High.* ***Valley***, carrying Halladale River in Caithness district, 6m/10km S of Melvich. **104 D4** NC8953.

Strath Isla *Moray* ***Valley***, carrying River Isla from Towiemore, through Keith, to Nethermills. **98 C5** NJ4250.

Strath Kanaird *High.* ***Valley***, running NE to SW and carrying River Kanaird, which flows into sea just S of Camas Mòr. **95 H1** NC1200.

Strath Lungard *High.* ***Valley***, carrying Allt Strath Lungard, 4m/6km S of Talladale. **95 F5** NG9164.

Strath Melness Burn *High.* ***River***, flowing NE into sea, 1m/2km W of mouth of Tongue Bay. **103 H2** NC5764.

Strath Mòr *High.* ***Valley***, carrying Abhainn an t-Stratha Mhòir N from head of Loch Slapin, Skye, and containing Loch na Sguabaidh and Lochain Stratha Mhòir. **86 B2** NG5624.

Strath More *High.* ***Valley***, in Sutherland district, carrying Strathmore river into Loch Hope. **103 G4** NC4550.

Strath More *High.* ***Valley***, carrying River Broom above Loch Broom, about 2m/3km S of head of loch, Ross and Cromarty district. Lael Forest runs down E side of valley. **95 H3** NH1882.

Strath Mulzie *High.* ***Valley***, in Sutherland district, carrying Corriemulzie River NE to confluence with River Einig. **95 J2** NH3192.

Strath na Sealga *High.* ***Valley***, carrying Abhainn Srath na Sealga NW into head of Loch na Sealga, in W part of Ross and Cromarty district. **95 G3** NH0680.

Strath nan Lòn *High.* ***Valley***, running SE to NW, carrying Allt nan Luibean Molach and containing several small lochs. **95 J1** NC2102.

Strath of Appin *Arg. & B.* ***Valley***, in Argyll, running across SW part of Appin from Loch Linnhe to Loch Creran. **80 A3** NM9445.

Strath of Appin (Also known as Appin of Dull.) *P. & K.* ***Valley***, broad valley carrying River Tay from its confluence with River Lyon E towards Aberfeldy. Upper section is narrow valley carrying lower course of Keltney Burn S to its confluence with River Lyon. **81 J2** NN7948.

Strath of Kildonan *High.* ***Valley***, in Sutherland district, carrying River Helmsdale between Kinbrace and Helmsdale. **104 D6** NC8923.

Strath of Orchy *Arg. & B.* ***Valley***, carrying River Orchy W to Loch Awe in vicinity of Dalmally, Argyll. **80 D5** NN1627.

Strath Ossian *High.* ***Valley***, carrying River Ossian between Loch Ghuilbinn and Loch Ossian. **88 B7** NN4172.

Strath Oykel *High.* ***Valley***, carrying River Oykel, Sutherland district, between Oykel Bridge and Invershin. **96 B1** NC4300.

Strath Peffer *High.* ***Valley***, carrying River Peffery E from Strathpeffer to Dingwall on Cromarty Firth. **96 C6** NH4958.

Strath Rannoch *High.* ***Valley***, in Ross and Cromarty district, carrying Allt Coire a' Chùndrain S to Black Water at Inchbae Lodge, at S end of Inchbae Forest. **95 K4** NH3972.

Strath Rory *High.* ***Valley***, carrying Strathrory River, Ross and Cromarty district and runs E into Balnagown River, 5m/7km N of Invergordon. **96 D4** NH6776.

Strath Rusdale *High.* ***Valley***, carrying Black Water in Ross and Cromarty district and running SE to River Averon, 5m/8km NW of Alness. **96 C4** NH5775.

Strath Sgitheach *High.* ***Valley***, carrying Abhainn Sgitheach E from W slopes of Cnoc na Gearraisich to Cromarty Firth at Evanton. **96 C5** NH5262.

Strath Shinary *High.* ***Valley***, carrying Lón Mòr NW into Sandwood Loch, 4m/6km NE of Oldshoremore, Sutherland district. **102 E2** NC2362.

Strath Skinsdale *High.* ***Valley***, carrying River Skinsdale in Sutherland district, 14m/22km NW of Brora. **104 C6** NC7518.

Strath Stack *High.* ***Valley***, running from NW to SE in Sutherland district below S slopes of Ben Stack and carrying Allt Achadh Fairidh. **102 E4** NC2540.

Strath Suardal *High.* ***Valley***, carrying Broadford River, 2m/3km SW of Broadford. **86 C2** NG6120.

Strath Tay *P. & K.* ***Valley***, broad valley below Loch Tay, carrying River Tay E past Aberfeldy. Valley turns S towards Dunkeld below confluence of Rivers Tay and Tummel. **82 A2** NO0043.

Strath Tirry *High.* ***Valley***, carrying River Tirry and running SE parallel with Loch Shin, in Sutherland district. **103 H7** NC4922.

Strath Tollaidh *High.* ***Valley***, 4m/6km SW of Rogart, running SE from Cregan Glas, Sutherland district. **96 D1** NC6800.

Strath Vagastie *High.* ***Valley***, carrying Allt a' Chràisg, in Caithness district, NE to head of Loch Naver. **103 H6** NC5430.

Strath Vaich *High.* ***Valley***, in Ross and Cromarty district carrying Abhainn Strath a' Bhàthaich and running S from Loch Vaich to join River Glascarnoch at Black Bridge, 2m/3km W of Inchbae Lodge. **95 K4** NH3573.

Strathaird *High.* ***Coastal feature***, peninsula on S coast of Skye between Loch Scavaig and Loch Slapin. **86 B2** NG5319.

Strathaird Point *High.* *Anglicised form of Rubha na h-Easgainne, qv.*

Strathallan ***Valley***, carrying Allan Water, NE of Dunblane, marking southern limit of Scottish Highlands in this area. **81 K7** NN8005.

Strathan *High.* ***Settlement***, near W coast of Sutherland district, 1m/2km SW of Lochinver. **102 C6** NC0821.

Strathan *High.* ***Settlement***, in Lochaber district, at head of Loch Arkaig. **87 F5** NM9791.

Strathardle *P. & K.* ***Valley***, carrying River Ardle SE to foot of Glen Shee, below Bridge of Cally. **82 B2** NO1054.

Strathaven *S.Lan.* Population: 6384. ***Small town***, former weaving centre 7m/11km S of Hamilton. **75 F6** NS7044.

Strathbeg Bay *Aber.* ***Bay***, wide bay on NE coast, extending NW from Rattray Head to Inzie Head and to N and E of Loch of Strathbeg. **99 J4** NK0760.

Strathblane *Stir.* ***Valley***, carries Blane Water NW from Strathblane, between NE edge of Kilpatrick Hills and SW edge of Campsie Fells. **74 D2** NS5182.

Strathblane *Stir.* Population: 1981. ***Village***, at head of Strathblane, 9m/14km N of Glasgow. **74 D3** NS5679.

Strathblane Hills *Stir.* ***Mountain***, massif with craggy S and SW slopes, on SW slopes of Campsie Fells to N of Strathblane. Summit is named Slackdhu. Height 1624 feet or 495 metres. **74 D2** NS5581.

Strathbogie *Aber.* ***Locality***, large area to S of Huntly, extending E and W of River Bogie and including its valley, Strath Bogie. **90 C1** NJ5237.

Strathbungo *Glas.* ***Suburb***, 2m/3km S of Glasgow city centre. NS5762.

Strathcarron *High.* ***Locality***, with railway station, at foot of Glen Carron, Ross and Cromarty district. **95 F7** NG9442.

Strathcarron *High.* ***Valley***, carrying River Carron E to Kyle of Sutherland at Bonar Bridge in Sutherland district. **96 C2** NH5192.

Strathclyde Country Park *N.Lan.* ***Leisure/recreation***, country park on E shore of Strathclyde Loch, 1m/2km W of Motherwell. 1000 acres of mixed woodland and parkland with artificial lakes, sandy beaches, accommodation, Scotland's first theme park and remains of Roman bathhouse. **75 F5** NS7357.

Strathconon *High.* ***Valley***, in Ross and Cromarty district, carrying River Conon E to Conon Bridge at head of Cromarty Firth. **96 B6** NH4055.

Strathconon Forest *High.* ***Open space***, deer forest astride River Meig. **95 J7** NH4055.

Strathdearn *High.* ***Valley***, carrying River Findhorn NE through NE section of Monadhliath Mountains towards lowlands SW of Forres. Upper section of valley typically has a broad valley floor, while middle and lower sections are gorge-like; this is most apparent at Streens section. Valley containing Funtack Burn and Loch Moy, to NW of Tomatin, is also referred to as Strathdearn. **88 E2** NH7724.

Strathdon *Aber.* ***Village***, on River Don, 12m/19km E of Tomintoul. **90 B3** NJ3512.

Stratherrick *High.* ***Valley***, carrying Loch Mhòr, E of Loch Ness, in Inverness district. **88 B3** NH5017.

Strathfinella Hill *Aber.* ***Mountain***, rising steeply to E of Glensaugh and Loch Saugh, 3m/5km NE of Fettercairn. Height 1246 feet or 380 metres. **91 F7** NO6777.

Strathgarve Forest *High.* ***Open space***, with forested lower slopes, to N of Loch Garve. **96 B5** NH4063.

Strathgirnock *Aber.* ***Settlement***, 2m/3km W of Ballater. **90 B5** NO3395.

Strathglass *High.* ***Valley***, carrying River Glass, Inverness district, to its confluence with River Farrar near Struy Bridge. **87 K1** NH3835.

Strathkanaird *High.* ***Village***, in Ross and Cromarty district on N side of Strath Kanaird, valley of River Kanaird, 5m/8km N of Ullapool. **95 H1** NC1501.

Strathkinness *Fife* ***Village***, 3m/5km W of St. Andrews. **83 F6** NO4516.

Strathlachlan *Arg. & B.* ***Locality***, in Argyll including Strathlachlan Forest, Lachlan Bay and Castle Lachlan, and surrounding Strathlachlan River 6m/9km SW of Strachur. River flows SW to Loch Fyne via Lachlan Bay. NS0295.

Strathlethan Bay *Aber.* ***Bay***, on E coast, 1km S of Stonehaven. **91 G6** NO8884.

Strathmiglo *Fife* ***Small town***, founded in 15c, 2m/3km SW of Auchtermuchty. **82 D7** NO2110.

Strathmore ***Valley***, great fertile valley separating highlands of Scotland from central lowlands and extending from foot of Loch Lomond to Stonehaven, although term is more generally applied to part between Methven and Brechin. **82 B5** NO4050.

Strathmore *High.* ***River***, in Sutherland district, rising on Reay Forest and running N down Strath More into Loch Hope, where it emerges as River Hope. **103 G4** NC4550.

Strathnairn *High.* ***Valley***, carrying River Nairn NE from Aberarder House to Daviot. **88 D1** NH6733.

Strathnasheallag Forest *High.* ***Open space***, deer forest to E of Loch na Sealga in Ross and Cromarty district. **95 G3** NH0483.

Strathnaver *High.* ***Valley***, carrying River Naver, 10m/16km SE of Tongue, Caithness district. **104 C4** NC7045.

Strathord Forest *P. & K.* ***Forest/woodland***, 2m/3km S of Bankfoot. **82 B4** NO0632.

Strathpeffer *High.* ***Village***, in Ross and Cromarty district, 4m/7km W of Dingwall. Resort, with mineral springs. **96 B6** NH4858.

Strathrannoch *High.* ***Settlement***, in Strath Rannoch, 8m/12km N of Gorstan. **95 K4** NH3874.

Strathspey *High.* ***Valley***, central area of River Spey valley from Kingussie, past Grantown-on-Spey, to Charlestown of Aberlour. Separates Monadhliath Mountains from Cairngorm Mountains and provides a natural transport conduit through the Highlands. Popular tourist destination, providing outdoor activities, water and winter sports, with wilderness areas of surrounding estates and forest parks. Area noted for its wildlife, especially salmon and ospreys. **89 G3** NJ0025.

Strathspey Railway *High.* ***Other feature of interest***, tourist railway running 5m/8km from Aviemore to Boat of Garten, where there is a small railway museum. **89 G3** NH9115.

Strathtay *P. & K.* ***Settlement***, in upper valley of River Tay, 4m/6km SW of Pitlochry. **82 A2** NN9153.

Strathvaich Forest *High.* ***Open space***, deer forest in Ross and Cromarty district to S and W of Loch Vaich. **95 K4** NH3474.

Strathwhillan *N.Ayr.* ***Settlement***, on Arran, adjoining to SE of Brodick. **73 J7** NS0235.

Strathy *High.* ***River***, rising in mountains to S of Loch Strathy and flowing N through Strathy Forest. It then follows E side of forest and flows past Strathy village to N coast and into Strathy Bay. NC8465.

Strathy *High.* ***Village***, near N coast of Caithness district and mouth of River Strathy, 17m/28km W of Thurso. **104 D2** NC8465.

Strathy Bay *High.* ***Bay***, on N coast, 1km N of Strathy. **104 D2** NC8465.

Strathy Forest *High.* ***Forest/woodland***, afforested area astride River Strathy, 6m/9km S of Strathy village. **104 D2** NC8465.

Strathy Point *High.* ***Coastal feature***, headland with lighthouse, 3m/5km N of Strathy. **104 D1** NC8465.

Strathyre *Stir.* ***Village***, in middle of Strathyre Forest, 7m/11km NW of Callander. **81 G6** NN5617.

Strathyre Forest *Stir.* ***Forest/woodland***, in valley of River Balvag. Strathyre Forest Information centre and picnic area to S of Strathyre village. **81 G6** NN5617.

Stratton *Cornw.* ***Town***, on River Neet, forming part of resort of Bude-Stratton, 15m/24km NW of Launceston. Fine medieval church. 1km N is site of Battle of Stamford Hill, where Parliamentarians were defeated in 1643. **6 A5** SS2306.

Stratton *Dorset* ***Village***, 3m/5km NW of Dorchester. **9 F5** SY6593.

Stratton *Glos.* Population: 2298. ***Village***, 1m/2km NW of Cirencester. **20 D1** SP0103.

Stratton Audley *Oxon.* ***Village***, 3m/5km NE of Bicester. **31 H6** SP6026.

Stratton Hall *Suff.* ***Settlement***, by E bank of River Orwell, 5m/7km NW of Felixstowe. TM2438.

Stratton-on-the-Fosse *Som.* ***Village***, on Foss Way, 3m/5km SW of Radstock. On W side of village, Downside Abbey, Benedictine monastery and boys' school. **19 K6** ST6550.

Stratton St. Margaret *Swin.* ***Suburb***, 2m/3km NE of Swindon town centre. **20 E3** SU1787.

Stratton St. Michael *Norf.* ***Village***, 9m/15km S of Norwich. **45 G6** TM2093.

Stratton Strawless *Norf.* ***Village***, 8m/12km N of Norwich. **45 G3** TG2220.

Stravanan *Arg. & B.* ***Settlement***, on Bute, 1km N of Stravanan Bay. **73 J5** NS0857.

Stravanan Bay *Arg. & B.* ***Bay***, on SW coast of Bute, 1m/2km W of Kingarth. **73 J5** NS0756.

Stravithie *Fife* ***Settlement***, 4m/6km SE of St. Andrews. **83 G6** NO5311.

Strawberry Hill *Gt.Lon.* ***Suburb***, in borough of Richmond upon Thames, on left bank of River Thames, S of Twickenham. TQ1572.

Stream *Som.* ***Settlement***, 2m/3km S of Watchet. ST0639.

Streap *High.* ***Mountain***, in Lochaber district 4m/7km NE of Glenfinnan. Height 2982 feet or 909 metres. **87 F6** NM9486.

Streat *E.Suss.* ***Village***, 5m/8km NW of Lewes. **13 G5** TQ3515.

Streatham *Gt.Lon.* ***Suburb***, in borough of Lambeth, 6m/10km S of Charing Cross. **23 F4** TQ2971.

Streatham Hill *Gt.Lon.* ***Suburb***, 1m/2km N of Streatham. TQ3073.

Streatham Park *Gt.Lon.* ***Suburb***, 1km W of Streatham. TQ2971.

Streatham Vale *Gt.Lon.* ***Suburb***, 1km SW of Streatham. TQ2970.

Streatley *Beds.* ***Village***, 5m/8km N of Luton. **32 D6** TL0728.

Streatley *W.Berks.* Population: 1048. ***Village***, on River Thames, 4m/6km NW of Pangbourne. **21 J3** SU5980.

Streens *High.* ***Valley***, gorge-like section of River Findhorn valley, part of larger Strathdearn, below E slopes of Carn nan Tri-tighearnan. Valley is deeply entrenched with River Findhorn meandering across narrow valley floor, creating spurs and steep valley sides. **89 F1** NH8637.

Street *Devon* ***Hamlet***, 4m/7km NE of Sidmouth. SY1888.

Street *Lancs.* ***Settlement***, at crossroads near bridge over River Wyre, 4m/7km NE of Garstang. **55 J4** SD5252.

Street *N.Yorks.* ***Settlement***, 3m/4km SW of Lealholm. **63 J6** NZ7304.

Street *Som.* ***Settlement***, 2m/3km E of Chard. ST3507.

Street *Som.* Population: 10,539. ***Town***, 2m/3km SW of Glastonbury. Town is well-known for its shoe-making industry; original Clark factory is now a Shoe Museum. **8 D1** ST4836.

Street Ashton *Warks.* ***Settlement***, 5m/9km NW of Rugby. SP4582.

Street Dinas *Shrop.* ***Hamlet***, 4m/6km SW of Overton. **38 C2** SJ3338.

Street End *Kent* ***Hamlet***, 3m/5km S of Canterbury. **15 G2** TR1453.

Street End *W.Suss.* ***Hamlet***, 1km N of Sidlesham and 3m/5km S of Chichester. **12 B7** SZ8599.

Street Gate *T. & W.* ***Village***, 4m/6km SW of Gateshead. NZ2159.

Street Houses *N.Yorks.* ***Settlement***, 3m/5km NE of Tadcaster, on A64 road. SE5245.

Street Houses *R. & C.* ***Locality***, 2m/3km E of Loftus. NZ7419.

Street Lane *Derbys.* ***Hamlet***, 1m/2km SW of Ripley. SK3848.

Street Lane *W.Yorks.* ***Suburb***, 4m/6km NE of Leeds city centre. SE3038.

Street on the Fosse *Som.* ***Hamlet***, 3m/5km S of Shepton Mallet. **9 F1** ST6138.

Streethay *Staffs.* ***Village***, 2m/3km E of Lichfield. **40 D4** SK1410.

Streethouse *W.Yorks.* ***Village***, 1m/2km SE of Normanton. SE3920.

Streetlam *N.Yorks.* ***Hamlet***, 5m/8km NW of Northallerton. **62 E7** SE3199.

Streetly *W.Mid.* ***Village***, large suburban village, 3m/4km NW of Sutton Coldfield. **40 C6** SP0898.

Streetly End *Cambs.* ***Hamlet***, 4m/7km NW of Haverhill. TL6148.

Strefford *Shrop.* ***Hamlet***, 2m/3km N of Craven Arms. **38 D7** SO4485.
Strelley *Notts.* ***Village***, 4m/6km W of Nottingham city centre. SK5141.
Strem Ness *Shet.* ***Coastal feature***, headland on NE coast of Foula. **108 B1** HT9741.
Strensall *York* Population: 4432. ***Village***, 6m/9km N of York. **58 C3** SE6360.
Strensall Common *York* ***Open space***, partly wooded lowland 1m/2km E of Strensall. **58 C3** SE6460.
Strensham *Worcs.* ***Settlement***, on W bank of River Avon, 5m/8km N of Tewkesbury. **29 J4** SO9140.
Stretch Down *Devon* ***Hamlet***, 1km SE of Witheridge and 9m/14km W of Tiverton. SS8013.
Stretcholt *Som.* ***Hamlet***, on Pawlett Level, 1m/2km NW of Pawlett and 3m/4km SW of Highbridge. **19 F7** ST2944.
Strete *Devon* ***Village***, on S coast, 4m/6km SW of Dartmouth. **5 J6** SX8446.
Stretford *Gt.Man.* Population: 43,953. ***Town***, residential town, 4m/6km SW of Manchester. **49 G3** SJ7994.
Stretford *Here.* ***Hamlet***, 4m/6km SW of Leominster. SO4455.
Stretford *Here.* ***Settlement***, 2m/4km SE of Leominster. SO5257.
Stretford Court *Here.* ***Settlement***, 4m/6km SW of Leomister. **28 D3** SO4455.
Strethall *Essex* ***Village***, 4m/6km W of Saffron Walden. **33 H5** TL4839.
Stretham *Cambs.* Population: 1471. ***Village***, 4m/6km SW of Ely. Site of Roman building 1m/2km SE. **33 J1** TL5174.
Strettington *W.Suss.* ***Village***, 3m/4km NE of Chichester. **12 B6** SU8907.
Stretton *Ches.* ***Settlement***, 3m/4km E of Holt across River Dee. **48 D7** SJ4452.
Stretton *Derbys.* ***Village***, 1m/2km S of Clay Cross. **51 F6** SK3961.
Stretton *Rut.* ***Village***, 8m/12km NW of Stamford. **42 C4** SK9415.
Stretton *Staffs.* ***Suburb***, 2m/3km NE of Burton upon Trent. **40 E3** SK2526.
Stretton *Staffs.* ***Village***, 6m/10km W of Cannock. Site of Roman fort 1m/2km E. **40 A4** SJ8811.
Stretton *Warr.* ***Village***, 4m/6km S of Warrington. **49 F4** SJ6182.
Stretton en le Field *Leics.* ***Settlement***, 4m/7km SW of Ashby de la Zouch. **41 F4** SK3011.
Stretton Grandison *Here.* ***Village***, 6m/10km NW of Ledbury. **29 F4** SO6344.
Stretton Heath *Shrop.* ***Settlement***, 1m/2km NE of Westbury. **38 C4** SJ3710.
Stretton-on-Dunsmore *Warks.* ***Village***, 6m/10km W of Rugby. **31 F1** SP4072.
Stretton-on-Fosse *Warks.* ***Village***, 4m/6km N of Moreton-in-Marsh. **30 D5** SP2238.
Stretton Sugwas *Here.* ***Village***, 4m/6km NW of Hereford. **28 D4** SO4642.
Stretton under Fosse *Warks.* ***Village***, 5m/8km NW of Rugby. **41 G7** SP4581.
Stretton Westwood *Shrop.* ***Hamlet***, 2m/3km SW of Much Wenlock. **38 E6** SO5998.
Stribers *Cumb.* ***Settlement***, at foot of Speel Bank, 4m/6km NW of Grange-over-Sands. **55 G1** SD3581.
Strichen *Aber.* Population: 1112. ***Village***, 8m/13km S of Fraserburgh. Situated on northern branch of River Ugie known as North Ugie Water. **99 H5** NJ9455.
Striding Edge *Cumb.* ***Inland physical feature***, narrow ridge running up to summit of Helvellyn from E. **60 E5** NY3415.
Strines *Gt.Man.* ***Settlement***, 2m/3km NW of New Mills. SJ9786.
Strines Reservoir *S.Yorks.* ***Reservoir***, below Strines Moor, 3m/5km SW of High Bradfield. **50 E3** SK2390.
Stringston *Som.* ***Village***, 2m/3km NW of Nether Stowey. **7 K1** ST1742.
Strixton *Northants.* ***Village***, 4m/6km S of Wellingborough. **32 C2** SP9061.
Stroan Loch *D. & G.* ***Lake/loch***, small loch in course of River Dee, 5m/8km S of New Galloway. **65 G4** NX6470.
Stroat *Glos.* ***Hamlet***, 4m/6km NE of Chepstow. **19 J2** ST5797.
Stròc-bheinn *High.* ***Mountain***, 3m/5km SW of Portree, Skye. Height 1312 feet or 400 metres. **85 K1** NG4539.
Stroin Vuigh *I.o.M.* ***Coastal feature***, headland 3m/5km N of Port Erin. **54 B6** SC2174.
Strom Ness *Ork.* ***Coastal feature***, southernmost headland on North Ronaldsay. **106 G2** HY7651.
Strom Ness *Shet.* ***Coastal feature***, headland on S coast of Vaila, off Mainland. **109 B8** HU2245.
Strom Ness *Shet.* ***Coastal feature***, headland on W coast of Muckle Roe. **109 B6** HU2965.
Stroma *High.* *See Island of Stroma.*
Stromay *W.Isles* ***Island***, small uninhabited island off NE coast of North Uist, 4m/6km N of Lochmaddy. **92 E4** NF9374.
Strome Castle *High.* ***Castle***, ruins of ancient castle (National Trust for Scotland), destroyed 1602, on N shore of Loch Carron, Ross and Cromarty district, opposite Stromeferry. **86 E1** NG8635.
Stromeferry *High.* ***Village***, on S side of Loch Carron, Skye and Lochalsh district, 8m/13km NE of Kyle of Lochalsh. Vehicle ferry to N shore. **86 E1** NG8634.
Stromemore *High.* ***Settlement***, on N shore of Loch Carron, 1km N of Stromeferry across loch. **86 E1** NG8635.
Stromness *Ork.* Population: 1890. ***Small town***, fishing port with ferry terminal, on inlet of Hoy Sound, 12m/20km W of Kirkwall, Mainland. **107 B7** HY2509.
Stronachlachar *Stir.* ***Settlement***, on S shore of Loch Katrine, 2m/4km SE of head of loch. **81 F7** NN4010.
Stronchullin Hill *Arg. & B.* ***Mountain***, in Argyll Forest Park, 3m/4km NE of Orchard. Height 1797 feet or 548 metres. **73 K2** NS1786.
Strond *W.Isles* *Anglicised form of Strannda, qv.*
Strondeval *W.Isles* ***Hill***, near SW coast of South Harris, 1m/2km SE of Leverburgh. Height 692 feet or 211 metres. **93 F3** NG0384.
Strone *Arg. & B.* ***Village***, resort at Strone Point, Argyll, on W side of entrance to Loch Long. **73 K2** NS1980.
Strone *High.* ***Settlement***, on Urquhart Bay, on NW shore of Loch Ness, Inverness district. **88 C2** NH5228.
Strone *High.* ***Settlement***, in valley of River Lochy, 6m/9km NW of Fort William. **87 H6** NN1481.
Strone *Stir.* ***Settlement***, on N shore of Loch Katrine, 6m/9km NW of Brig o' Turk. **81 F6** NN4510.
Strone Glen *Arg. & B.* ***Valley***, in Kintyre, carrying Strone Water SE to Carskey Bay. **66 A3** NR6507.
Strone Point *Arg. & B.* ***Coastal feature***, headland at N end of Loch Fyne, 1m/2km NE of Inveraray. **80 C7** NN1108.
Strone Point *Arg. & B.* ***Coastal feature***, headland on Kyles of Bute on W side of entrance to Loch Striven, Argyll. **73 J3** NS0671.
Strone Point *Arg. & B.* ***Coastal feature***, headland on W side of entrance to Loch Long. **73 K2** NS1980.
Strone Point *High.* ***Coastal feature***, headland on Loch Ness, to SE of Strone, with ruins of Urquhart Castle (Historic Scotland). NH5328.
Stronechrubie *High.* ***Settlement***, on River Loanan, 2m/3km S of S end of Loch Assynt. **102 E7** NC2419.
Stronenaba *High.* ***Settlement***, in Lochaber district, 2m/3km NW of Spean Bridge. **87 J6** NN2084.
Stronlonag *Arg. & B.* ***Settlement***, above S bank of River Massan, 2m/4km NW of Benmore. **73 K2** NS1186.
Stronmilchan *Arg. & B.* ***Village***, in Argyll, 1m/2km NW of Dalmally. **80 C5** NN1528.
Stronsay *Ork.* ***Island***, irregularly shaped island, 7m/11km in length from NW to SE, and 12m/20km NE of Kirkwall on Mainland. **106 F5** HY6525.
Stronsay Airfield *Ork.* ***Airport/airfield***, close to N coast of Stronsay. **106 F5** HY6329.
Stronsay Firth *Ork.* ***Sea feature***, sea area between Stronsay and Shapinsay. **106 E5** HY5720.
Strontian *High.* ***River***, rising on W side of Sgurr Dhomhnuill and flowing NW, then SW to enter Loch Sunart at Strontian near head of loch. **79 K1** NM8161.
Strontian *High.* ***Village***, on N shore of Loch Sunart, Lochaber district, at mouth of Strontian River, which rises on W side of Sgurr Dhomhnuill. **79 K1** NM8161.
Strontoiller *Arg. & B.* ***Settlement***, 3m/5km E of Oban. **80 A5** NM9028.
Stronuich Reservoir *P. & K.* ***Reservoir***, small reservoir in course of River Lyon, 3m/5km E of Loch Lyon. **81 G3** NN5041.
Stronvar *Stir.* ***Settlement***, at head of Loch Voil, adjoining to SW of Balquhidder. **81 G6** NN5319.
Strood *Med.* Population: 31,803. ***Suburb***, industrial and residential district on NW side of Rochester across River Medway. Beside river to S is Temple Manor (English Heritage). **24 D5** TQ7369.
Strood Green *Surr.* ***Hamlet***, 2m/4km SE of Dorking. TQ2048.
Strood Green *W.Suss.* ***Hamlet***, 3m/4km NW of Horsham. TQ1332.
Strood Green *W.Suss.* ***Settlement***, 4m/6km NE of Petworth. **12 D4** TQ0224.
Stroquhan *D. & G.* ***Settlement***, 2m/3km W of Dunscore. **68 D5** NX8483.
Stroud *Glos.* Population: 38,835. ***Town***, on River Frome, 8m/13km S of Gloucester. Traditionally a centre of wool cloth manufacture and weaving. **20 B1** SO8505.
Stroud *Hants.* ***Village***, 1m/2km W of Petersfield. Site of Roman villa on E side of village. **11 J2** SU7223.
Stroud Common *Surr.* ***Settlement***, 1m/2km SE of Shamley Green. **22 D7** TQ0442.
Stroud Green *Essex* ***Hamlet***, 1m/2km W of Rochford. TQ8590.
Stroud Green *Glos.* ***Hamlet***, 3m/5km NW of Stroud. **20 B1** SO8007.
Stroud Green *Gt.Lon.* ***Suburb***, in borough of Haringey, 5m/8km N of Charing Cross. TQ3188.
Stroude *Surr.* ***Settlement***, 3m/4km SW of Staines. TQ0068.
Stroul *Arg. & B.* ***Hamlet***, on W shore of Gare Loch, adjoining to NW of Rosneath. **74 A2** NS2483.
Stroxton *Lincs.* ***Hamlet***, 3m/5km S of Grantham. Stone manor house of 17c. **42 C2** SK9031.
Struan *High.* ***Settlement***, 1km W of Bracadale, Skye. **85 J1** NG3438.
Struan *P. & K.* ***Village***, at confluence of Errochty Water and River Garry, 4m/6km W of Blair Atholl. Small museum of items of historical interest associated with the Clan Donnachaidh. **81 K1** NN8165.
Strubby *Lincs.* ***Settlement***, 2m/3km E of Wragby. TF1677.
Strubby *Lincs.* ***Village***, 4m/6km N of Alford. Airfield to S. **53 H4** TF4582.
Struie *High.* ***Mountain***, in Ross and Cromarty district, 5m/8km SE of Bonar Bridge. Height 1217 feet or 371 metres. **96 D3** NH6685.
Struie Hill *High.* ***Mountain***, rocky summit rising to over 380 metres, in Ross and Cromarty district, 5m/8km SE of Bonar Bridge. **96 D3** NH6786.
Strumble Head *Pembs.* ***Coastal feature***, headland 5m/8km NW of Fishguard. Lighthouse on rock island of Ynysmeicel. **16 B1** SM8941.
Strumpshaw *Norf.* ***Village***, 4m/6km SW of Acle. **45 H5** TG3407.
Strutherhill *S.Lan.* ***Suburb***, adjoining to S of Larkshall. NS7649.
Struthers *Fife* ***Hamlet***, 3m/5km S of Cupar. **82 E7** NO3709.
Struy *High.* ***Settlement***, at N end of Strathglass, 9m/14km SW of Beauly. **96 B7** NH4040.
Struy Forest *High.* ***Open space***, deer forest to SW of Struy Bridge. **87 K1** NH4040.
Stryd *I.o.A.* ***Suburb***, to S of Holyhead town centre. SH2482.
Stryd y Facsen *I.o.A.* ***Settlement***, on Anglesey, 1m/2km NE of Llanfachraeth. SH3383.
Stryt-cae-rhedyn *Flints.* ***Settlement***, 3m/4km SE of Mold. SJ2660.
Stryt-issa *Wrex.* ***Locality***, 1m/2km NW of Ruabon. **38 B1** SJ2845.
Stryt-yr-hwch *Wrex.* ***Settlement***, 3m/4km S of Wrexham. **38 C1** SJ3346.
Stuabhal *W.Isles* *Gaelic form of Stulaval, qv.*
Stuartfield *Aber.* ***Village***, 10m/16km W of Peterhead. **99 H6** NJ9745.
Stuarton *High.* ***Locality***, in Inverness district adjoining to S of Ardersier, on E shore of Inner Moray Firth or Inverness Firth. NH7854.
Stub Place *Cumb.* ***Settlement***, on coast, 1m/2km NW of Bootle Station and 4m/6km S of Ravenglass. **60 B7** SD0890.
Stubb *Norf.* ***Settlement***, 1km S of Hickling, 3m/5km SE of Stalham. TG4122.
Stubber's Green *W.Mid.* ***Settlement***, 2m/4km NE of Walsall. SK0401.
Stubbin *S.Yorks.* ***Locality***, 3m/5km N of Rotherham. SK4297.
Stubbington *Hants.* Population: 13,665. ***Village***, 3m/4km SW of Fareham. **11 G4** SU5503.
Stubbins *Lancs.* ***Village***, 1km N of Ramsbottom. **49 G1** SD7918.
Stubbins Estate *Lancs.* ***Open space***, agricultural land (National Trust) with public footpaths, to N of Ramsbottom. SD7818.
Stubb's Cross *Kent* ***Settlement***, 3m/5km SW of Ashford. TQ9838.
Stubb's Green *Norf.* ***Settlement***, 1km SE of Shotesham. TM2598.
Stubbs Green *Norf.* ***Settlement***, to S of Loddon. TM3597.
Stubhampton *Dorset* ***Locality***, on SE side of Cranborne Chase, 5m/8km NE of Blandford Forum. **9 J3** ST9113.
Stubley *Derbys.* ***Locality***, 1m/2km W of Dronfield. **51 F5** SK3478.
Stubshaw Cross *Gt.Man.* ***Suburb***, adjoining to NE of Ashton-in-Makerfield. SD5800.
Stubton *Lincs.* ***Village***, 6m/9km SE of Newark-on-Trent. **42 B1** SK8748.
Stùc a' Chroin ***Mountain***, on border of Perth & Kinross and Stirling, 1m/2km SW of Ben Vorlich. Munro: height 3198 feet or 975 metres. **81 H6** NN6117.
Stuc Scardan *Arg. & B.* ***Mountain***, in Argyll, 4m/6km NE of Inveraray. Height 1597 feet or 487 metres. **80 C6** NN1114.
Stuchd an Lochain *P. & K.* ***Mountain***, 2m/3km SW of dam of Loch an Daimh. Munro: height 3149 feet or 960 metres. **81 F3** NN4844.
Stuck *Arg. & B.* ***Settlement***, above NE coast of Bute, 4m/6km NW of Rothesay. **73 J4** NS0670.
Stuck *Arg. & B.* ***Settlement***, 3m/5km SE of Glenbranter. **73 K1** NS1393.
Stuckbeg *Arg. & B.* ***Settlement***, on E shore of Loch Goil, 2m/4km S of Lochgoilhead. **74 A1** NS2197.
Stuckgowan *Arg. & B.* ***Settlement***, on W shore of Loch Lomond, 1m/2km S of Tarbet. **80 E7** NN3202.
Stuckindroin *Arg. & B.* ***Settlement***, at N end of Loch Lomond, 1m/2km N of Ardlui. **80 E6** NN3214.
Stuckreoch *Arg. & B.* ***Settlement***, on S shore of Loch Fyne, 3m/5km SW of Strachur. **73 J1** NS0599.
Stuckton *Hants.* ***Hamlet***, 1m/2km SE of Fordingbridge. **10 C3** SU1613.
Stud Green *W. & M.* ***Settlement***, 2m/4km S of Maidenhead. **22 B4** SU8877.
Studd Hill *Kent* ***Suburb***, 1m/2km W of Herne Bay. TR1567.
Studdal *Kent* ***Settlement***, adjoining to SW of East Studdal. TR3149.
Studdon *Northumb.* ***Locality***, including Studdon Park and High Studdon, 2m/3km S of Allendale Town. **61 K1** NY8454.
Studfold *N.Yorks.* ***Settlement***, 1m/2km S of Horton in Ribblesdale. **56 D2** SD8170.
Studham *Beds.* ***Village***, 6m/9km SW of Luton. **32 D7** TL0115.
Studholme *Cumb.* ***Settlement***, 2m/3km E of Kirkbride. **60 D1** NY2556.
Studland *Dorset* ***Village***, on Studland Bay, at SW end of Poole Bay, 3m/4km N of Swanage. **10 B6** SZ0382.
Studland Bay *Dorset* ***Bay***, at SW end of Poole Bay. Village of Studland on the bay. **10 B6** SZ0382.
Studley *Oxon.* *See Horton-cum-Studley.*
Studley *Warks.* Population: 5883. ***Suburb***, 4m/6km SE of Redditch. **30 B2** SP0763.
Studley *Wilts.* ***Village***, 2m/3km W of Calne. **20 C4** ST9671.
Studley Common *Warks.* ***Locality***, adjoining to E of Studley. **30 B2** SP0663.
Studley Green *Bucks.* ***Settlement***, 2m/3km E of Stokenchurch. SU7995.
Studley Roger *N.Yorks.* ***Hamlet***, 2m/3km SW of Ripon. **57 H2** SE2970.
Studley Royal *N.Yorks.* ***Hamlet***, 2m/4km W of Ripon. Remains of manor house burnt down in 1945. 18c park contains lakes, temples, statues. St. Mary's Church (English Heritage), with highly decorated interior and fine organ, was designed in 1870s by William Burges and is no longer used for worship. **57 H3** SE2770.
Stuggadhoo *I.o.M.* ***Settlement***, 4m/7km W of Douglas. **54 C6** SC3175.
Stulaval (Gaelic form: Stuabhal.) *W.Isles* ***Mountain***, in North Harris, 1m/2km W of S end of Loch Langavat. Height 1899 feet or 579 metres. **100 D6** NB1312.
Stulaval *W.Isles* ***Mountain***, on South Uist 4m/6km N of Lochboisdale. Height 1227 feet or 374 metres. **84 D2** NF8024.
Stuley *W.Isles* ***Island***, uninhabited island off E coast of South Uist, 4m/6km NE of Lochboisdale. Island separated from coast by narrow Stuley Sound. **84 D2** NF8323.

Stump Cross *Essex* ***Locality***, road junction 1m/2km N of Great Chesterford. TL5044.
Stump Cross *Lancs.* ***Settlement***, 2m/3km W of Longridge. SD5737.
Stump Cross *W.Yorks.* ***Locality***, 1m/2km NE of Halifax town centre. SE1026.
Stuntney *Cambs.* ***Village***, 2m/3km SE of Ely. **33 J1** TL5578.
Stunts Green *E.Suss.* ***Hamlet***, 3m/5km NE of Hailsham. **13 K5** TQ6213.
Sturbridge *Staffs.* ***Hamlet***, 1m/2km N of Eccleshall. **40 A2** SJ8330.
Sturdy Hill *Aber.* ***Mountain***, 6m/9km N of Edzell. Height 1784 feet or 544 metres. **90 D7** NO5977.
Sturgate *Lincs.* ***Hamlet***, 4m/6km E of Gainsborough. SK8789.
Sturmer *Essex* ***Village***, 2m/3km SE of Haverhill. **34 B4** TL6943.
Sturminster Common *Dorset* ***Village***, 1m/2km S of Sturminster Newton. **9 G3** ST7812.
Sturminster Marshall *Dorset* ***Village***, on River Stour, 4m/6km W of Wimborne Minster. **9 J4** ST9500.
Sturminster Newton *Dorset* Population: 2155. ***Small town***, market town on River Stour, at SE end of Blackmoor Vale, 8m/13km NW of Blandford Forum. Large market each Monday. 17c mill in working order. **9 G3** ST7814.
Sturry *Kent* Population: 4847. ***Village***, 3m/4km NE of Canterbury. **25 H5** TR1760.
Sturton *N.Lincs.* ***Locality***, adjoining to S of Scawby, 2m/4km SW of Brigg. Site of Roman villa. SE9704.
Sturton by Stow *Lincs.* ***Village***, 4m/6km N of Saxilby. **52 B4** SK8980.
Sturton Grange *W.Yorks.* ***Settlement***, 1m/2km E of Garforth. SE4233.
Sturton le Steeple *Notts.* ***Village***, 6m/9km E of Retford. **51 K4** SK7883.
Stuston *Suff.* ***Village***, 2m/3km SE of Diss. **35 F1** TM1378.
Stutfall Castle *Kent See Lympne.*
Stutton *N.Yorks.* ***Village***, 1m/2km S of Tadcaster. **57 K5** SE4741.
Stutton *Suff.* ***Village***, 6m/10km S of Ipswich. **35 F5** TM1534.
Sty Head *Cumb.* ***Other feature of interest***, mountain pass where footpaths from Borrowdale, Wasdale, Eskdale and Great Langdale meet at a height of 1601 feet or 488 metres. **60 D6** NY2209.
Sty Wick *Ork.* ***Bay***, large wide bay on S coast of Sanday, bounded by Els Ness to W and Lang Taing to E. **106 F4** HY6839.
Styal *Ches.* ***Village***, 1m/2km N of Wilmslow. **49 H4** SJ8383.
Styal Country Park *Ches.* ***Leisure/recreation***, 63 acre or 25 hectacre country park combining nature with history, on River Bollin at Styal, 1m/2km N of Wilmslow. Woodlands and river rub shoulders with Quarry Bank Mill and factory village of Styal. **49 H4** SJ8383.
Stybarrow Dodd *Cumb.* ***Mountain***, in Lake District 2m/3km N of Helvellyn. Height 2755 feet or 840 metres. **60 E5** NY3418.
Styrrup *Notts.* ***Village***, 2m/3km SE of Tickhill. **51 J3** SK6090.
Suainaval *W.Isles* ***Mountain***, 6m/9km S of Gallan Head, and E of northernmost point of Loch Suainaval. Height 1407 feet or 429 metres. **100 C4** NB0730.
Suainebost (Anglicised form: Swanibost.) *W.Isles* ***Village***, near N end of Isle of Lewis, 2m/3km SW of Port Nis. **101 H1** NB5162.
Suardail (Anglicised form: Swordale.) *W.Isles* ***Village***, on Eye Peninsula, Isle of Lewis, 2m/3km SW of Garrabost. **101 G4** NB4930.
Succoth *Aber.* ***Settlement***, on lower slopes of Red Hill, 3m/4km S of Haugh of Glass. **90 C1** NJ4235.
Succoth *Arg. & B.* ***Hamlet***, at head of Loch Long, 1km N of Arrochar. **80 D7** NN2905.
Succothmore *Arg. & B.* ***Settlement***, 1m/2km E of Strachur. **80 C7** NN1201.
Suckley *Worcs.* ***Village***, 5m/8km NW of Great Malvern. **29 G3** SO7251.
Suckley Green *Worcs.* ***Hamlet***, 4m/7km E of Bromyard. SO7153.
Suckley Hills *Worcs.* ***Large natural feature***, range of hills, 5m/8km SE of Bromyard. **29 G3** SO7252.
Suckley Knowl *Worcs.* ***Hamlet***, 4m/6km E of Bromyard. SO7153.
Sudborough *Northants.* ***Village***, 3m/5km NW of Thrapston. **42 C7** SP9682.
Sudbourne *Suff.* ***Village***, on E edge of Tunstall Forest, 2m/3km N of Orford. Sudbourne Marshes to E beside River Alde estuary. **35 J3** TM4153.
Sudbrook *Lincs.* ***Village***, 6m/10km W of Sleaford. **42 C1** SK9744.
Sudbrook *Mon.* ***Village***, on shore River Severn estuary, 4m/7km SW of Chepstow. Severn Railway Tunnel passes underneath. **19 J3** ST5087.
Sudbrooke *Lincs.* ***Village***, 5m/7km NE of Lincoln. **52 D5** TF0376.
Sudbury *Derbys.* ***Village***, 5m/7km E of Uttoxeter. **40 D2** SK1632.
Sudbury *Gt.Lon.* ***Suburb***, in borough of Brent, 9m/15km NW of Charing Cross. **22 E3** TQ1685.
Sudbury *Suff.* Population: 19,512. ***Town***, market town on River Stour, 13m/21km NW of Colchester. Former wool town more recently noted for silk weaving. Birthplace of Thomas Gainsborough in 1727; includes Gainsborough statue on Market Hill and Gainsborough's House. St. Gregory's church contains skull of Simon of Sudbury, Archbishop of Canterbury, beheaded during Peasants Revolt of 1381. **34 C4** TL8741.
Sudbury Hall *Derbys.* ***Historic house***, 17c National Trust property 6m/10km E of Uttoxeter. **40 D2** SK1632.
Sudden *Gt.Man.* ***Suburb***, 1m/2km SW of Rochdale town centre. SD8811.
Sudeley *Glos.* ***Locality***, 1km SE of Winchcombe. SP0327.
Sudeley Castle *Glos.* ***Castle***, to SE of Winchcombe, 8m/13km NE of Cheltenham. Medieval building, much altered and restored, once home of Katherine Parr, sixth wife of Henry VIII. Remains of Roman villa 1m/2km S of castle. Queen's Garden is one of eight gardens surrounding castle; also collection of old roses and a specialist plant centre. **30 B6** SP0327.
Sudgrove *Glos.* ***Settlement***, 7m/11km NW of Cirencester. **20 C1** SO9307.
Sudley Art Gallery and Museum *Mersey.* ***Other feature of interest***, located in Sudley House, 4m/6km SE of Liverpool city centre. Houses collection of 18c and 19c art amassed by Victorian shipowner, George Holt. **48 C4** SJ3886.
Sueno's Stone *Moray* ***Historic/prehistoric site***, glass encased ancient sandstone obelisk, 23 feet or 7 metres high and bearing Celtic symbols, on NE side of Forres. **97 H6** NJ0459.
Suffield *Norf.* ***Hamlet***, 4m/6km NW of North Walsham. **45 G2** TG2232.
Suffield *N.Yorks.* ***Hamlet***, 4m/6km NW of Scarborough. **63 J3** SE9890.
Suffolk Wildlife and Country Park *Suff.* ***Leisure/recreation***, country park to S of Kessingland, with 100 acres or 40 hectacres of exotic animals, including the only aardvarks in Britain. **45 K7** TM5286.
Sugar Loaf (Mynydd Pen-y-fâl) *Mon.* ***Mountain***, conical peak (National Trust) in Black Mountains, 3m/5km NW of Abergavenny. Height 1955 feet or 596 metres. **28 B7** SO2718.
Sugarloaf *Kent* ***Settlement***, 1m/2km N of Hamstreet. **14 E4** TQ9935.
Sugdon *Tel. & W.* ***Settlement***, 4m/6km NW of Wellington. SJ6014.
Sugnall *Staffs.* ***Hamlet***, 2m/4km NW of Eccleshall. **39 G2** SJ7930.
Sugwas Pool *Here.* ***Hamlet***, 4m/7km W of Hereford. SO4541.
Suidh' a' Mhinn *High.* ***Mountain***, 3m/5km N of Uig, Skye. Height 1148 feet or 350 metres. **93 K5** NG4068.
Suidhe Ghuirmain *High.* ***Mountain***, in Inverness district, 4m/7km SE of Cannich. Height 1896 feet or 578 metres. **87 K2** NH3827.
Suie Hill *Aber.* ***Mountain***, surrounded by woodland, 4m/7km N of Alford. Height 1361 feet or 415 metres. **90 D2** NJ5523.
Sùil Ghorm *Arg. & B.* ***Island***, islet with lighthouse, lying 1m/2km off NE end of Coll. NM2865.
Suilven *High.* ***Mountain***, near W coast of Sutherland district 5m/7km SE of Lochinver. Height 2398 feet or 731 metres. **102 D7** NC1518.
Suisgill Burn *High.* ***River***, in Sutherland district, flowing S and joining River Helmsdale 2m/3km N of Kildonan Lodge. **104 E6** NC8924.
Suisnish *High.* ***Settlement***, on Skye, near S coast between Loch Eishort and Loch Slapin. NG5916.
Suisnish Point *High.* ***Coastal feature***, headland at SW corner of Raasay, opposite Balmeanach Bay on Skye. **86 B1** NG5534.
Sula Sgeir *W.Isles* ***Island***, uninhabited island, nearly 1km long NE to SW, and nowhere more than 200 metres wide, situated about 41m/65km N of Butt of Lewis. Nature reserve. Several islets and rocks in vicinity. HW6230.
Sulby *I.o.M.* ***Hamlet***, 3m/5km N of Douglas. SC3780.
Sulby *I.o.M.* ***Village***, 4m/7km W of Ramsey. **54 C4** SC3894.
Sulby Bridge *I.o.M.* ***Locality***, adjoining to E of Sulby. SC3994.
Sulby Reservoir *I.o.M.* ***Reservoir***, 1m/2km W of Snaefell and 4m/6km E of Kirk Michael. **54 C5** SC3788.
Sulby Reservoir *Northants.* ***Reservoir***, adjoining Welford Reservoir 2m/4km S of Husbands Bosworth. **41 J7** SP6581.
Sule Skerry *Ork.* ***Island***, islet with lighthouse, some 37m/60km W of Mainland. HX6224.
Sule Stack *Ork.* ***Island***, islet some 41m/66km W of Mainland. HX5617.
Sulgrave *Northants.* ***Village***, 6m/9km N of Brackley. **31 G4** SP5545.
Sulgrave *T. & W.* ***Suburb***, NE district of Washington. NZ3157.
Sulgrave Manor *Northants.* ***Historic house***, home of George Washington's great-grandfather, 8m/12km NE of Banbury. **31 G4** SP5545.
Sulham *W.Berks.* ***Village***, 2m/3km S of Pangbourne. **21 K4** SU6474.
Sulhamstead *W.Berks.* ***Village***, 6m/10km SW of Reading. **21 K5** SU6368.
Sulhamstead Abbots *W.Berks.* ***Settlement***, in parish of Sulhamstead, along with Sulhamstead Bannister Upper End, 1km NW of Burghfield Common. SU6467.
Sulhamstead Bannister *W.Berks.* ***Locality***, 5m/8km S of Reading. SU6866.
Sulhamstead Bannister Upper End *W.Berks.* ***Settlement***, in parish of Sulhamstead, along with Sulhamstead Abbots, 1m/2km NW of Burghfield Common. SU6368.
Sullington *W.Suss.* ***Hamlet***, below South Downs, 1m/2km W of Washington. **12 D5** TQ0913.
Sullom *Shet.* ***Settlement***, in N part of Mainland, on W shore of Sullom Voe. **108 C5** HU3573.
Sullom Voe *Shet.* ***Sea feature***, inlet some 8m/12km long and almost separating N part of Mainland from the rest. The voe, which runs N into Yell Sound, provides shelter for shipping. **108 C5** HU3573.
Sullom Voe Oil Terminal *Shet.* ***Other feature of interest***, 3m/5km NW of Firth, Mainland. **108 C5** HU3975.
Sulloniacae *Gt.Lon. See Edgware.*
Sully (Sili). *V. of Glam.* ***Suburb***, on coast 3m/4km E of Barry. Sully Island, small island off shore to SE, accessible on foot at low tide. **18 E5** ST1568.
Sully Island *V. of Glam.* ***Island***, at E end of Sully Bay, 3m/5km E of Barry. Accessible at low water. **18 E5** ST1666.
Sulma Water *Shet.* ***Lake/loch***, 3m/4km N of Bridge of Walls, Mainland. Approximately 1m/2km long, N to S. **109 B7** HU2554.
Sumburgh *Shet.* ***Settlement***, on Mainland, 1m/2km N of headland of Sumburgh Head (lighthouse), at S extremity of island. **109 G10** HU4009.
Sumburgh Airport *Shet.* ***Airport/airfield***, airport for Shetland, to N of Sumburgh, at S end of Mainland. **109 G10** HU4009.
Sumburgh Head *Shet.* ***Coastal feature***, headland at S extremity of Mainland. Sumburgh settlement 1m/2km N. Lighthouse. **109 G10** HU4009.
Sumburgh Roost *Shet.* ***Sea feature***, area of sea to S of Sumburgh Head, off S coast of Mainland. **109 F10** HU3906.
Summer Bridge *N.Yorks.* ***Village***, in Nidderdale, 3m/5km SE of Pateley Bridge. **57 H3** SE2062.
Summer Down *Wilts.* ***Open space***, hillslope at NW of Salisbury Plain, rising to 689 feet or 210 metres, 3m/5km SE of Westbury. **20 C7** ST9048.
Summer Hill *W.Mid.* ***Suburb***, 3m/5km NW of West Bromwich town centre. SO9693.
Summer Isles *High.* ***Island***, group of uninhabited islands off NW coast of Ross and Cromarty district between Rubha Coigeach and Greenstone Point. **95 F1** NB9607.
Summer Lodge *N.Yorks.* ***Settlement***, on stream of same name, 2m/3km SE of Gunnerside. SD9695.
Summercourt *Cornw.* ***Village***, 6m/9km SE of Newquay. **3 F3** SW8856.
Summerfield *Norf.* ***Settlement***, 1m/2km NW of Docking. **44 B2** TF7438.
Summerfield *Worcs.* ***Settlement***, 2m/3km NE of Stourport-on-Severn. SO8473.
Summergangs *Hull* ***Suburb***, 2m/3km NE of Kingston upon Hull city centre. TA1130.
Summerhill *Aberdeen* ***Suburb***, 2m/4km W of Aberdeen city centre. NJ9006.
Summerhill *D. & G.* ***Suburb***, W district of Dumfries. NX9576.
Summerhill *Worcs.* ***Suburb***, W district of Kidderminster. SO8176.
Summerhill *Wrex.* ***Locality***, 3m/4km NW of Wrexham. **48 C7** SJ3153.
Summerhouse *Darl.* ***Village***, 6m/10km NW of Darlington. **62 D5** NZ2019.
Summerlands *Cumb.* ***Hamlet***, 4m/7km S of Kendal. SD5386.
Summerlands *Som.* ***Suburb***, W district of Yeovil. ST5416.
Summerleaze *Newport* ***Settlement***, 4m/6km SW of Caldicot. **19 H3** ST4284.
Summersdale *W.Suss.* ***Suburb***, N district of Chichester. SU8606.
Summerseat *Gt.Man.* ***Hamlet***, 3m/4km N of Bury. **49 G1** SD7914.
Summerstown *Gt.Lon.* ***Suburb***, in borough of Wandsworth, 2m/3km S of Wandsworth Bridge. TQ2672.
Summertown *Oxon.* ***Suburb***, 1m/2km N of Oxford city centre. **21 J1** SP5109.
Summerville *D. & G.* ***Suburb***, NW district of Dumfries. NX9676.
Summit *Gt.Man.* ***Hamlet***, 1m/2km NE of Littleborough. **49 J1** SD9418.
Summit *Gt.Man.* ***Locality***, adjoining to W of Gravel Hole, 2m/4km S of Rochdale. SD9109.
Sumners *Essex* ***Suburb***, 2m/3km SW of Harlow town centre. TL4307.
Sun Green *Gt.Man.* ***Settlement***, 1m/2km NE of Stalybridge. SJ9899.
Sunadale *Arg. & B.* ***Settlement***, on W coast of Kintyre, 1km N of Grogport. **73 G6** NR8144.
Sunart *High.* ***Locality***, in Lochaber district, between Loch Shiel and Loch Sunart. **79 H1** NM7966.
Sunbiggin *Cumb.* ***Hamlet***, on S side of Great Asby Scar, 2m/4km E of Orton. NY6508.
Sunbury *Surr.* Population: 27,392. ***Town***, on N bank of River Thames, 4m/7km E of Chertsey. Interesting 18c church. Kempton Park Racecourse nearby. **22 E5** TQ1068.
Sundaywell *D. & G.* ***Settlement***, 3m/5km W of Dunscore. **68 D5** NX8184.
Sunderland *Cumb.* ***Hamlet***, 2m/3km S of Bothel. **60 C3** NY1735.
Sunderland *Lancs.* ***Hamlet***, on W bank of River Lune estuary, 1m/2km SW of Overton and 4m/7km SW of Lancaster. SD4255.
Sunderland *T. & W.* Population: 183,310. ***City***, industrial city and seaport at mouth of River Wear, 11m/17km SE of Newcastle upon Tyne. Previously largest shipbuilding town in the world; coalmining was also important. Several museums celebrate city's industrial past. Service sector and manufacturing account for largest contribution to local economy. National Glass Centre commemorates importance of stained glass to area. Crowtree is popular leisure complex. University. Airport 4m/6km W. **62 E1** NZ3956.
Sunderland Bank *Lancs.* ***Coastal feature***, sandbank on N side of River Lune estuary, 3m/4km S of Heysham harbour. **55 G4** SD3856.
Sunderland Bridge *Dur.* ***Bridge***, stone bridge with substantial cutwaters over River Wear, 3m/5km S of Durham. NZ2637.
Sunderland Bridge *Dur.* ***Village***, at crossing of River Wear, 3m/5km S of Durham. **62 D3** NZ2637.
Sunderland Point *Lancs.* ***Coastal feature***, on N bank of River Lune estuary, 1km S of Sunderland village. **55 G4** SD4255.
Sundhope *Sc.Bord.* ***Hamlet***, 2m/3km SW of Yarrow. **69 J1** NT3325.
Sundhope Height *Sc.Bord.* ***Mountain***, 3m/5km W of Ettrickbridge. Height 1683 feet or 513 metres. **69 J1** NT3423.

Sundon Hills Country Park *Beds.* ***Leisure/recreation***, country park above ridge, 2m/3km SE of Harlington. Designated as both Site of Special Scientific Interest and Area of Outstanding Natural Beauty. **32 D6** TL0529.
Sundon Park *Luton* ***Suburb***, large housing estate at N end of Luton. **32 D6** TL0525.
Sundridge *Gt.Lon.* ***Suburb***, in borough of Bromley, 1km NE of Bromley town centre. TQ4170.
Sundridge *Kent* ***Village***, 3m/5km W of Sevenoaks. **23 H6** TQ4855.
Sundrum *S.Ayr.* ***Settlement***, 1km N of Joppa, with Sundrum Castle to N by Water of Coyle. **67 J1** NS4120.
Sunhill *Glos.* ***Settlement***, 3m/4km NW of Fairford. **20 E1** SP1102.
Sunipol *Arg. & B.* ***Settlement***, near N coast of Mull, 1m/2km E of Caliach Point. **78 E2** NM3753.
Sunk Island *E.Riding* ***Settlement***, on N side of River Humber estuary, 4m/6km SW of Patrington. **53 F1** TA2618.
Sunk Island Sands *E.Riding* ***Coastal feature***, sandbank on N side of Humber estuary. **53 G1** TA3016.
Sunken Island *Essex* ***Island***, at mouth of Salcott Channel, 1m/2km W of West Mersea. TL9912.
Sunningdale *W. & M.* Population: 7881. ***Locality***, residential locality 6m/9km SW of Staines. **22 C5** SU9567.
Sunninghill *W. & M.* ***Locality***, residential district, 4m/7km E of Bracknell. **22 C5** SU9367.
Sunningwell *Oxon.* ***Village***, 2m/4km N of Abingdon. **21 H2** SP4900.
Sunniside *Dur.* ***Village***, 1m/2km E of Tow Law. **62 C3** NZ1438.
Sunniside *T. & W.* Population: 3456. ***Village***, 2m/3km S of Whickham. **62 D1** NZ2058.
Sunny Bank *Cumb.* ***Settlement***, on W side of Coniston Water, 1m/2km S of Torver. **60 D7** SD2892.
Sunny Bank *Lancs.* ***Locality***, 2m/3km S of Haslingden. SD7720.
Sunny Brow *Dur.* ***Suburb***, adjoining to S of Willington. NZ1934.
Sunny Hill *Derby* ***Suburb***, 3m/4km SW of Derby city centre. SK3332.
Sunnyfields *S.Yorks.* ***Suburb***, 2m/3km NW of Doncaster town centre. SE5405.
Sunnyhurst *B'burn.* ***Locality***, 1m/2km W of Darwen. SD6722.
Sunnylaw *Stir.* ***Hamlet***, 3m/5km N of Stirling. **75 F1** NS7998.
Sunnymead *Oxon.* ***Suburb***, N district of Oxford. **21 J1** SP5009.
Sunnymede *Essex* ***Suburb***, E district of Billericay. TQ6894.
Sunnyside *Aber.* ***Settlement***, 2m/3km NW of Portlethen. **91 G5** NO8998.
Sunnyside *Northumb.* ***Settlement***, 1m/2km SE of Hexham. **70 E7** NY9562.
Sunnyside *S.Yorks.* ***Suburb***, 4m/6km E of Rotherham. SK4893.
Sunnyside *W.Suss.* ***Suburb***, residential district to S of East Grinstead. **13 G3** TQ3937.
Sunton *Wilts.* ***Settlement***, 1km N of Collingbourne Ducis, 3m/4km NW of Ludgershall. SU2454.
Sunwick *Sc.Bord.* ***Settlement***, 3m/4km W of Paxton. **77 G5** NT8952.
Surbiton *Gt.Lon.* ***Suburb***, in borough of Kingston upon Thames, 1m/2km S of Kingston upon Thames town centre. **22 E5** TQ1867.
Surby *I.o.M.* ***Locality***, 1m/2km NE of Port Erin. SC2070.
Surfleet *Lincs.* ***Village***, 4m/6km N of Spalding. **43 F3** TF2528.
Surfleet Seas End *Lincs.* ***Hamlet***, 1m/2km E of Surfleet. **43 F3** TF2728.
Surlingham *Norf.* ***Village***, 6m/9km E of Norwich. **45 H5** TG3106.
Surrey Hill ***Hill***, on border of Surrey and Bracknell Forest, 2m/3km N of Camberley. Height 426 feet or 130 metres. **22 B5** SU8864.
Sursay *W.Isles* ***Island***, small uninhabited island in Sound of Harris, 2m/3km off NE coast of North Uist. NF9576.
Sustead *Norf.* ***Village***, 4m/6km SW of Cromer. **45 F2** TG1837.
Susworth *Lincs.* ***Hamlet***, on E bank of River Trent, 3m/5km W of Scotter. **52 B2** SE8302.
Sutcombe *Devon* ***Village***, 5m/8km N of Holsworthy. **6 B4** SS3411.
Sutcombemill *Devon* ***Hamlet***, to S of Sutcombe, on River Waldon. SS3411.
Suton *Norf.* ***Settlement***, 2m/3km SW of Wymondham. **44 E6** TM0999.
Suton Street *Norf.* ***Locality***, 1km S of Suton. TM0999.
Sutor Stacks *High.* ***Coastal feature***, headland on NE tip of Black Isle, 1m/2km E of Cromarty. **97 F5** NH8167.
Sutors of Cromarty *High.* ***Settlement***, 1km E of Cromarty. **97 F5** NH8066.
Sutterby *Lincs.* ***Hamlet***, 4m/7km N of Spilsby. TF3872.
Sutterton *Lincs.* ***Village***, 6m/10km SW of Boston. **43 F2** TF2835.
Sutton *Beds.* ***Village***, 1m/2km S of Potton. **33 F4** TL2247.
Sutton *Bucks.* ***Settlement***, 4m/6km E of Slough. TQ0278.
Sutton *Cambs.* Population: 3076. ***Village***, 6m/10km W of Ely. **33 H1** TL4478.
Sutton *Devon* ***Settlement***, 7m/12km W of Crediton. SS7202.
Sutton *Devon* ***Settlement***, adjacent to South Milton, 3m/4km SW of Kingsbridge. SX7042.
Sutton *E.Suss.* ***Suburb***, to E of Seaford. TV4999.
Sutton *Essex* ***Locality***, 2m/3km N of Southend-on-Sea. TQ8889.
Sutton *Gt.Lon.* ***Town***, administrative and business centre in borough of Sutton, 10m/17km S of Charing Cross and 4m/7km W of Croydon. TQ2564.
Sutton *Kent* ***Village***, 3m/5km SW of Deal. **15 J3** TR3349.
Sutton *Lincs.* ***Settlement***, 5m/8km E of Newark-on-Trent. **52 B7** SK8752.
Sutton *Mersey.* ***Suburb***, 2m/3km SE of St. Helens town centre. SJ5393.
Sutton *Norf.* ***Village***, 1m/2km SE of Stalham. **45 H3** TG3823.
Sutton *N.Yorks.* ***Settlement***, 1m/2km N of Knottingley across River Aire. SE4925.
Sutton *Notts.* ***Hamlet***, 4m/6km SE of Bingham. **42 A2** SK7637.
Sutton *Notts.* ***Village***, 3m/5km N of Retford. **51 J4** SK6884.
Sutton *Oxon.* ***Locality***, adjoining to N of Stanton Harcourt, 2m/4km SW of Eynsham. **21 H1** SP4106.
Sutton *Pembs.* ***Hamlet***, 3m/4km W of Haverfordwest. **16 C3** SM9015.
Sutton *Peter.* ***Village***, 2m/3km E of Wansford. Site of Roman camp to E across Ermine Street. **42 E6** TL0998.
Sutton *Shrop.* ***Settlement***, 4m/7km E of Oswestry. SJ3527.
Sutton *Shrop.* ***Settlement***, 2m/3km S of Market Drayton. **39 F2** SJ6631.
Sutton *Shrop.* ***Suburb***, in S part of Shrewsbury. **38 E4** SJ5010.
Sutton *Shrop.* ***Village***, 4m/7km S of Bridgnorth. **39 G7** SO7286.
Sutton *S.Yorks.* ***Hamlet***, 6m/10km N of Doncaster. **51 H1** SE5512.
Sutton *Staffs.* ***Hamlet***, 2m/4km NE of Newport. **39 G3** SJ7622.
Sutton *Suff.* ***Village***, 3m/5km SE of Woodbridge across River Deben. **35 H4** TM3046.
Sutton *Surr.* ***Settlement***, 1m/2km SE of Gomshall. **22 E7** TQ1045.
Sutton *W.Suss.* ***Village***, 4m/7km S of Petworth. **12 C5** SU9715.
Sutton at Hone *Kent* Population: 2403. ***Village***, 3m/4km S of Dartford. On E side by River Darent is St. John's Jerusalem (National Trust), moated 16c-18c house with remains of Knights Hospitallers chapel. **23 J4** TQ5570.
Sutton Bassett *Northants.* ***Village***, 3m/5km NE of Market Harborough. **42 A7** SP7790.
Sutton Benger *Wilts.* ***Village***, 4m/6km NE of Chippenham. **20 C4** ST9478.
Sutton Bingham *Som.* ***Hamlet***, 3m/5km S of Yeovil, on W shore of Sutton Bingham Reservoir. ST5411.
Sutton Bingham Reservoir *Som.* ***Reservoir***, 3m/5km S of Yeovil. **8 E3** ST5411.
Sutton Bonington *Notts.* ***Village***, 4m/7km NW of Loughborough. **41 H3** SK5025.
Sutton Bridge *Lincs.* Population: 3457. ***Small town***, on River Nene, 9m/14km W of King's Lynn. Victorian knapped flint church. **43 H3** TF4721.
Sutton Broad *Norf.* ***Other water feature***, channel flanked by marsh, to W of Sutton. **45 H3** TG3823.
Sutton Cheney *Leics.* ***Village***, 2m/3km S of Market Bosworth. **41 G5** SK4100.
Sutton Coldfield *W.Mid.* Population: 106,001. ***Town***, former weaving town, 7m/11km NE of Birmingham. Notable buildings include 16c weavers' cottages. Sutton Park to W. **40 D6** SP1296.
Sutton Courtenay *Oxon.* Population: 2327. ***Village***, 3m/5km NW of Didcot. **21 H2** SU5093.
Sutton Crosses *Lincs.* ***Settlement***, 1m/2km S of Long Sutton. **43 H3** TF4321.
Sutton Farm *Worcs.* ***Suburb***, SW district of Kidderminster. SO8175.
Sutton Grange *N.Yorks.* ***Hamlet***, 3m/4km NW of Ripon. **57 H2** SE2874.
Sutton Green *Oxon.* ***Hamlet***, adjoining to N of Stanton Harcourt, 2m/3km SW of Eynsham. SP4106.
Sutton Green *Surr.* ***Hamlet***, 3m/5km S of Woking. **22 D6** TQ0054.
Sutton Green *Wrex.* ***Settlement***, 5m/8km SE of Wrexham. SJ4048.
Sutton Heath *Mersey.* ***Suburb***, 2m/3km S of St. Helens town centre. SJ5092.
Sutton Hill *Tel. & W.* ***Suburb***, S district of Telford, to E of Coalport. SJ7003.
Sutton Holms *Dorset* ***Settlement***, 2m/3km S of Cranborne. **10 B3** SU0510.
Sutton Hoo *Suff.* ***Historic/prehistoric site***, 1m/2km E of Woodbridge across River Deben. Remarkable ship-burial of a Saxon chieftain dating to mid 7c. Many treasures uncovered are now in British Museum. **35 G4** TM2848.
Sutton Howgrave *N.Yorks.* ***Village***, 5m/8km N of Ripon. **57 J2** SE3179.
Sutton in Ashfield *Notts.* Population: 37,890. ***Town***, market and textile town, 3m/5km SW of Mansfield. **51 G7** SK5058.
Sutton-in-Craven *N.Yorks.* ***Locality***, 4m/6km NW of Keighley. **57 F5** SE0044.
Sutton in the Elms *Leics.* ***Hamlet***, 8m/13km SW of Leicester. **41 H6** SP5293.
Sutton Ings *Hull* ***Suburb***, 3m/4km NE of Kingston upon Hull city centre. TA1231.
Sutton Lane Ends *Ches.* ***Hamlet***, 2m/3km S of Macclesfield. **49 J5** SJ9271.
Sutton le Marsh *Lincs.* ***Settlement***, adjoining to S of Sutton on Sea. **53 J4** TF5180.
Sutton Leach *Mersey.* ***Locality***, adjoining to S of Sutton. **48 E3** SJ5292.
Sutton Maddock *Shrop.* ***Village***, 5m/9km N of Bridgnorth. **39 G5** SJ7201.
Sutton Mallet *Som.* ***Hamlet***, 5m/8km E of Bridgwater. **8 C1** ST3737.
Sutton Mandeville *Wilts.* ***Village***, 3m/4km E of Tisbury. **9 J2** ST9828.
Sutton Manor *Mersey.* ***Suburb***, 2m/3km E of Rainhill. SJ5190.
Sutton Marsh *Here.* ***Settlement***, 4m/6km NE of Hereford. SO5444.
Sutton Montis *Som.* ***Village***, 2m/3km SE of Sparkford. **9 F2** ST6224.
Sutton on Derwent *E.Riding* *Alternative spelling of Sutton upon Derwent, qv.*
Sutton-on-Hull *Hull* ***Suburb***, 3m/5km NE of Kingston upon Hull city centre. **59 H6** TA1132.
Sutton on Sea *Lincs.* Population: 4859. ***Small town***, North Sea coast resort, adjoining to S of Mablethorpe. **53 J4** TF5282.
Sutton-on-the-Forest *N.Yorks.* ***Village***, 8m/13km N of York. **58 B3** SE5864.
Sutton on the Hill *Derbys.* ***Village***, 8m/12km W of Derby. **40 E2** SK2333.
Sutton on Trent *Notts.* ***Village***, 8m/12km N of Newark-on-Trent. **51 K6** SK7965.
Sutton Park *N.Yorks.* ***Garden***, parkland designed by 'Capability' Brown in grounds of Georgian house, with lily canal and woodland walks, on S side of Sutton-on-the-Forest, 8m/13km N of York. **58 B3** SE5864.
Sutton Park *W.Mid.* ***Open space***, 2400 acres or 971 hectacres of heath, woodland and lakes to W of Sutton Coldfield town centre. **40 D6** SP1296.
Sutton Poyntz *Dorset* ***Hamlet***, 4m/6km NE of Weymouth. **9 G6** SY7083.
Sutton St. Edmund *Lincs.* ***Village***, 7m/11km N of Guyhirn. **43 G4** TF3613.
Sutton St. James *Lincs.* ***Village***, 4m/6km SW of Long Sutton. **43 H4** TF3918.
Sutton St. Michael *Here.* ***Hamlet***, 4m/7km N of Hereford. SO5246.
Sutton St. Nicholas *Here.* ***Village***, 4m/6km NE of Hereford. **28 E4** SO5345.
Sutton Scarsdale *Derbys.* ***Village***, 3m/4km SW of Bolsover. Shell of 18c Sutton Scarsdale Hall (English Heritage) 2m/3km S of Arkwright. **51 G6** SK4468.
Sutton Scotney *Hants.* ***Village***, 5m/9km S of Whitchurch. **11 F1** SU4639.
Sutton-under-Brailes *Warks.* ***Village***, 3m/5km SE of Shipston on Stour. **30 D5** SP3037.
Sutton-under-Whitestonecliffe *N.Yorks.* ***Village***, below Sutton Bank, 3m/5km E of Thirsk. **57 K1** SE4882.
Sutton upon Derwent (Also spelled Sutton on Derwent.) *E.Riding* ***Village***, on E side of River Derwent, 7m/12km SE of York. **58 D5** SE7046.
Sutton Valence *Kent* ***Village***, on S edge of North Downs, 4m/6km NW of Headcorn. Ruins of 12c Sutton Valence Castle (English Heritage), built to protect road between Maidstone and Rye. **14 D3** TQ8149.
Sutton Veny *Wilts.* ***Village***, 2m/3km W of Heytesbury and 3m/4km SE of Warminster. **20 B7** ST9041.
Sutton Waldron *Dorset* ***Village***, on W edge of Cranborne Chase, 5m/8km S of Shaftesbury. **9 H3** ST8615.
Sutton Walls *Here.* ***Historic/prehistoric site***, Iron Age hillfort, 3m/5km N of Hereford. Consists of single massive bank and ditch with rampart being erected in 3c or 4c. Relics from site in Hereford Museum. **28 E4** SO5246.
Sutton Warblington *Hants.* ***Hamlet***, adjoining Long Sutton, 5m/8km N of Alton. SU7347.
Sutton Weaver *Ches.* ***Village***, 3m/4km SE of Runcorn. **48 E5** SJ5479.
Sutton Wick *B. & N.E.Som.* ***Hamlet***, on E side of Chew Valley Lake, 2m/3km NE of West Harptree. ST5758.
Sutton Wick *Oxon.* ***Locality***, adjoining to N of Drayton, 2m/3km SW of Abingdon. **21 H2** SU4894.
Swaby *Lincs.* ***Village***, 7m/12km SE of Louth. **53 G5** TF3877.
Swadlincote *Derbys.* Population: 36,859. ***Town***, 5m/7km SE of Burton upon Trent. Former prosperity from coal and clay industries. Dry-ski slope. **41 F4** SK3019.
Swaffham *Norf.* Population: 5332. ***Small town***, old market town, 14m/22km SE of King's Lynn. Palladian market cross. Church has double-hammerbeam angel roof. **44 C5** TF8109.
Swaffham Bulbeck *Cambs.* ***Village***, 6m/9km W of Newmarket. **33 J2** TL5562.
Swaffham Heath *Norf.* ***Open space***, partly wooded area 2m/4km SW of Swaffham. **44 B5** TF7807.
Swaffham Prior *Cambs.* ***Village***, 5m/8km W of Newmarket. **33 J2** TL5764.
Swafield *Norf.* ***Village***, 1m/2km N of North Walsham. **45 G2** TG2832.
Swainby *N.Yorks.* ***Locality***, 4m/6km SE of Leeming. SE3385.
Swainby *N.Yorks.* ***Village***, 5m/8km SW of Stokesley. **63 F6** NZ4702.
Swainshill *Here.* ***Locality***, 3m/5km W of Hereford. **28 D4** SO4641.
Swainsthorpe *Norf.* ***Village***, 5m/9km S of Norwich. **45 G5** TG2100.
Swainswick *B. & N.E.Som.* ***Village***, 3m/4km N of Bath. **20 A5** ST7568.
Swaithe *S.Yorks.* ***Settlement***, 1km E of Worsbrough Dale, 3m/4km SE of Barnsley town centre. SE3704.
Swalcliffe *Oxon.* ***Village***, 5m/8km W of Banbury. Site of ancient camp to NE. **30 E5** SP3737.
Swale *N.Yorks.* ***River***, rising on moors W of Keld and flowing SE down Swaledale by Reeth, Richmond and Catterick Bridge to join River Ure, 2m/4km E of Boroughbridge, and form River Ouse. **57 K2** SE4365.
Swalecliffe *Kent* ***Suburb***, E district of Whitstable. **25 H5** TR1367.
Swallow *Lincs.* ***Village***, 4m/7km NE of Caistor. **52 E2** TA1702.
Swallow Beck *Lincs.* ***Suburb***, 3m/4km SW of Lincoln city centre. **52 C6** SK9567.
Swallow Falls (Rhaeadr Ewynnol). *Conwy* ***Waterfall***, spectacular waterfall and rapids, with viewing areas for salmon-jumping, 1m/2km NW of Betws-y-coed on River Llugwy. **47 F7** SH7657.
Swallowcliffe *Wilts.* ***Village***, 2m/3km SE of Tisbury. **9 J2** ST9627.
Swallowfield *W'ham* ***Village***, 6m/9km S of Reading. **22 A5** SU7264.
Swallowfield Park *W'ham* ***Historic house***, 2m/3km S of Shinfield. Built in 1678 by William Talman, architect of Chatsworth, but now much altered. Walled garden. **22 A5** SU7365.

Swallownest *S.Yorks.* ***Locality***, adjoining to S of Aughton, 5m/8km S of Rotherham. SK4585.
Swallows Cross *Essex* ***Settlement***, 3m/4km W of Ingatestone. TQ6198.
Swalwell *T. & W.* ***Locality***, adjoining to N of Whickham, 3m/5km W of Gateshead. **71 H7** NZ2062.
Swampton *Hants.* ***Locality***, adjoining to NW of St. Mary Bourne. **21 H6** SU4150.
Swan Green *Ches.* ***Hamlet***, 5m/8km NE of Middlewich. SJ7373.
Swan Green *Suff.* ***Settlement***, 1m/2km W of Cratfield. TM2974.
Swan Street *Essex* ***Settlement***, 7m/11km W of Colchester. **34 C6** TL8927.
Swan Village *W.Mid.* ***Locality***, 2m/3km N of Dudley town centre. SO9393.
Swan Village *W.Mid.* ***Suburb***, 1m/2km NW of West Bromwich town centre. SO9891.
Swanage *Dorset* Population: 9947. ***Small town***, coastal resort on Swanage Bay, at E end of Isle of Purbeck, 9m/14km SE of Wareham. **10 B7** SZ0278.
Swanage Bay *Dorset* ***Bay***, on E side of Isle of Purbeck, extending from Ballard Point (N) to Peveril Point (S). Coastal resort of Swanage lies on the bay. **10 B6** SZ0278.
Swanage Railway *Dorset* ***Other feature of interest***, tourist railway running NW from Swanage to Norden Station, to N of Corfe Castle. **10 B7** SZ0278.
Swanbach *Ches.* ***Settlement***, 1km S of Audlem. **39 F1** SJ6542.
Swanbister *Ork.* ***Locality***, on Mainland, 1m/2km SW of Kirkbister. HY3405.
Swanbister Bay *Ork.* ***Bay***, to SE of Swanbister, with landing stage on W side. **107 C7** HY3505.
Swanbourne *Bucks.* ***Village***, 2m/3km E of Winslow. **32 B6** SP8027.
Swanbridge *V. of Glam.* ***Settlement***, on coast, opposite Sully Island. **18 E5** ST1667.
Swancote *Shrop.* ***Settlement***, 2m/3km E of Bridgnorth. **39 G6** SO7494.
Swanibost *W.Isles* *Anglicised form of Suainebost, qv.*
Swanland *E.Riding* Population: 3209. ***Village***, 6m/10km W of Kingston upon Hull. **59 F7** SE9927.
Swanlaws *Sc.Bord.* ***Settlement***, 2m/3km S of Hownam. **70 C2** NT7716.
Swanley *Kent* Population: 21,081. ***Town***, industrial town, 4m/6km S of Dartford. **23 J5** TQ5168.
Swanley Village *Kent* ***Village***, 1m/2km NE of Swanley. TQ5269.
Swanmore *Hants.* Population: 2675. ***Village***, 2m/3km SE of Bishop's Waltham. **11 G3** SU5716.
Swanmore *I.o.W.* ***Suburb***, 1km S of Ryde. SZ5891.
Swannay *Ork.* ***Locality***, at N end of Mainland, 4m/6km E of Brough Head. Loch of Swannay is large loch to E. HY2929.
Swannington *Leics.* ***Village***, 1m/2km NW of Coalville. **41 G4** SK4116.
Swannington *Norf.* ***Village***, 9m/14km NW of Norwich. **45 F4** TG1319.
Swanpool Garden Suburb *Lincs.* ***Suburb***, SW district of Lincoln. SK9569.
Swanscombe *Kent* Population: 5973. ***Small town***, 1m/2km from S bank of River Thames and 3m/4km W of Gravesend. Church is partly Saxon. **24 C4** TQ6074.
Swansea (Abertawe). *Swan.* Population: 171,038. ***City***, port on Swansea Bay at mouth of River Tawe, and Wales' second city, 35m/57km W of Cardiff. Settlement developed next to Norman castle built in 1099, but claims made that a Viking settlement existed before this date. Previously a port for local metal smelting industries. Bombed in World War II, and city centre rebuilt. Birthplace of Dylan Thomas, who described it as 'an ugly, lovely town'. Remains of 14c castle (Cadw) or fortified manor house. University of Wales. Tropical plant and wildlife leisure centre, Plantasia. Airport 5m/9km W at Fairwood Common. **17 K5** SS6593.
Swansea Bay ***Bay***, on N side of Bristol Channel, extending E from Mumbles Head to Sker Point, NW of Porthcawl. **17 K6** SS6878.
Swansea Castle *Swan.* ***Castle***, 13c-14c castle ruins on 12c site, E of Swansea city centre. **17 K5** SS6593.
Swansea Valley *N.P.T.* ***Valley***, carrying River Tawe between Pontardawe and Ystalyfera. **18 A1** SN7304.
Swanston *Edin.* ***Suburb***, 4m/7km S of Edinburgh city centre. Swanston Cottage was once a summer home of R.L. Stevenson. NT2367.
Swanton Abbot *Norf.* ***Village***, 3m/5km SW of North Walsham. **45 G3** TG2625.
Swanton Morley *Norf.* ***Village***, 3m/5km NE of East Dereham. **44 E4** TG0116.
Swanton Novers *Norf.* ***Village***, 6m/9km SW of Holt. **44 E2** TG0232.
Swanton Street *Kent* ***Settlement***, 1km S of Bredgar and 3m/5km SW of Sittingbourne. TQ8759.
Swanwick *Derbys.* ***Village***, 2m/3km N of Ripley. **51 G7** SK4053.
Swanwick *Hants.* ***Village***, 1m/2km N of Park Gate. **11 G4** SU5109.
Swanwick Green *Ches.* ***Settlement***, 1km NW of Norbury. SJ5547.
Swarbacks Minn *Shet.* ***Sea feature***, strait between Muckle Roe and islands of Vementry and Papa Little, off W coast of Mainland. **109 B6** HU3161.
Swarby *Lincs.* ***Village***, 4m/6km S of Sleaford. **42 D1** TF0440.
Swardeston *Norf.* ***Village***, 4m/7km S of Norwich. **45 F5** TG2002.
Swarkestone *Derbys.* ***Village***, on River Trent, 5m/8km S of Derby. **41 F3** SK3628.
Swarland *Northumb.* ***Hamlet***, 2m/3km NW of Felton. **71 G3** NU1601.
Swarland Estate *Northumb.* ***Locality***, 1m/2km S of Swarland. NU1601.
Swarraton *Hants.* ***Hamlet***, adjoining to SE of Northington, 3m/5km NW of New Alresford. SU5637.
Swarth Fell *Cumb.* ***Inland physical feature***, mountain ridge of moorland rising to 2234 feet or 681 metres on S side of Mallerstang Common, 3m/5km NW of Garsdale Head. **61 J7** SD7596.
Swartz Geo *Shet.* ***Coastal feature***, small indentation on SE coast of Fair Isle. **108 A1** HZ2170.
Swaton *Lincs.* ***Village***, 5m/8km W of Donington. **42 E2** TF1337.
Swatte Fell *D. & G.* ***Mountain***, 4m/6km NE of Moffat. Height 2388 feet or 728 metres. **69 G2** NT1111.
Swavesey *Cambs.* ***Village***, 9m/14km NW of Cambridge. **33 G2** TL3668.
Sway *Hants.* Population: 2072. ***Small town***, 3m/4km SW of Brockenhurst. 19c Sway Tower (218 feet or 66 metres) is local landmark. **10 D5** SZ2798.
Swayfield *Lincs.* ***Village***, 4m/6km E of Colsterworth. **42 C3** SK9922.
Swaythling *S'ham.* ***Suburb***, NE district of Southampton. **11 F3** SU4415.
Swaythorpe *E.Riding* ***Settlement***, 1m/2km SW of Thwing. Former village no longer exists. **59 G3** TA0368.
Sweet Green *Worcs.* ***Locality***, 5m/8km N of Bromyard. SO6462.
Sweetham *Devon* ***Village***, 3m/5km SE of Crediton. SX8898.
Sweethay *Som.* ***Hamlet***, 3m/4km SW of Taunton. ST2021.
Sweetheart Abbey (Also known as New Abbey.) *D. & G.* ***Ecclesiastical building***, ruin of 13c abbey dating from Early English-Decorated period (Historic Scotland) at New Abbey. Lady Devorgilla and embalmed heart of husband John de Baliol are buried here. **65 K4** NX9666.
Sweethope Hill *Sc.Bord.* ***Hill***, 1m/2km NW of Stichill. Height 731 feet or 223 metres. **76 E7** NT6939.
Sweethope Loughs *Northumb.* ***Lake/loch***, one large and one small lake, 4m/6km W of Kirkwhelpington. **70 E5** NY9482.
Sweetlands Corner *Kent* ***Locality***, adjoining to N of Staplehurst. TQ7845.
Sweetshouse *Cornw.* ***Hamlet***, 4m/6km S of Bodmin. **4 A4** SX0861.
Swefling *Suff.* ***Village***, 3m/4km W of Saxmundham. **35 H2** TM3463.
Swell *Som.* ***Hamlet***, 4m/6km SW of Langport. **8 C2** ST3623.
Swepstone *Leics.* ***Village***, 4m/6km S of Ashby de la Zouch. **41 F4** SK3610.
Swere *Oxon.* ***River***, rising near Hook Norton and flowing E into River Cherwell 5m/8km SE of Banbury. SP4933.
Swerford *Oxon.* ***Village***, 5m/7km NE of Chipping Norton. **30 E5** SP3731.
Swettenham *Ches.* ***Village***, 3m/4km E of Holmes Chapel. **49 H6** SJ8067.
Sweyn Holm *Ork.* ***Island***, small uninhabited island off NE coast of Gairsay. **106 D5** HY4522.
Swffryd *B.Gwent* ***Hamlet***, 1m/2km N of Newbridge. **19 F2** ST2198.
Swift *Warks.* ***River***, rising NW of Husbands Bosworth and flowing SW into River Avon at Brownsover, on N side of Rugby. **41 H7** SP5077.
Swift's Green *Kent* ***Settlement***, 2m/4km E of Headcorn. TQ8744.
Swiftsden *E.Suss.* ***Settlement***, 1m/2km N of Hurst Green. **14 C5** TQ7328.
Swilland *Suff.* ***Village***, 5m/9km N of Ipswich. **35 F3** TM1852.
Swillbrook *Lancs.* ***Hamlet***, 5m/8km NW of Preston. **55 H6** SD4834.
Swillington *W.Yorks.* Population: 3350. ***Village***, 6m/10km SE of Leeds. **57 J6** SE3830.
Swillington Common *W.Yorks.* ***Locality***, 1m/2km N of Swillington. SE3832.
Swimbridge *Devon* ***Village***, 5m/8km SE of Branstaple. **6 E3** SS6230.
Swimbridge Newland *Devon* ***Hamlet***, 2m/3km SE of Barnstaple. **6 E2** SS6230.
Swinbrook *Oxon.* ***Village***, 2m/3km E of Burford. **30 D7** SP2812.
Swincliffe *N.Yorks.* ***Hamlet***, 4m/6km NW of Harrogate. **57 H4** SE2558.
Swincliffe *W.Yorks.* ***Locality***, 1m/2km N of Gomersal across M62 motorway. SE2027.
Swincombe *Devon* ***Hamlet***, on E edge of Exmoor, 5m/8km NW of Simonsbath. SS6941.
Swindale Beck *Cumb.* ***River***, rising on NE side of Selside Pike, and flowing NE into River Lowther, 2m/3km NW of Shap. **61 G5** NY5012.
Swinden *N.Yorks.* ***Hamlet***, in Ribblesdale, 1m/2km S of Hellifield. SD8654.
Swinderby *Lincs.* ***Village***, 8m/13km SW of Lincoln. **52 B6** SK8663.
Swindon *Staffs.* ***Village***, 5m/8km W of Dudley. **40 A6** SO8690.
Swindon *Swin.* Population: 145,236. ***Town***, industrial and commercial centre, 70m/113km W of London. Large, modern shopping centre. Town expanded considerably in 19c with arrival of railway and now houses Great Western Railway Museum. **20 E3** SU1584.
Swindon and Cricklade Railway *Swin.* ***Other feature of interest***, tourist railway, 2m/3km W of Blunsdon St. Andrew. **20 E3** SU1089.
Swindon Village *Glos.* ***Village***, 2m/3km N of Cheltenham. **29 J6** SO9325.
Swine *E.Riding* ***Village***, 5m/8km NE of Kingston upon Hull. **59 H6** TA1335.
Swinefleet *E.Riding* ***Village***, on S bank of River Ouse, 2m/3km SE of Goole across loop of river. **58 D7** SE7622.
Swineford *S.Glos.* ***Hamlet***, on River Avon, which is tidal to this point, 4m/6km SE of Kingswood. ST6969.
Swineshead *Beds.* ***Village***, 10m/16km N of Bedford. **32 D2** TL0565.
Swineshead *Lincs.* Population: 1576. ***Village***, 6m/10km SW of Boston. **43 F1** TF2340.
Swineshead Bridge *Lincs.* ***Hamlet***, with bridge over South Forty Foot Drain, 2m/3km NW of Swineshead. **43 F1** TF2142.
Swineside *N.Yorks.* ***Settlement***, 1m/2km SW of West Scrafton and 5m/8km SW of Middleham. SE0682.
Swiney *High.* ***Settlement***, in Caithness district, 1m/2km W of Lybster. **105 H5** ND2335.
Swinford *Leics.* ***Village***, 5m/8km NE of Rugby. **31 G1** SP5679.
Swinford *Oxon.* ***Hamlet***, on River Thames, 1km SE of Eynsham. **21 H1** SP4408.
Swingate *Notts.* ***Village***, 1km S of Kimberley. SK5043.
Swingfield Minnis *Kent* ***Village***, 5m/7km N of Folkestone. **15 H3** TR2143.
Swingfield Street *Kent* ***Hamlet***, 4m/7km N of Folkestone. St. John's Commandery (English Heritage), medieval chapel converted to farmhouse in 16c, 1km N. TR2343.
Swingleton Green *Suff.* ***Hamlet***, 5m/8km NW of Hadleigh. TL9647.
Swinhill *S.Lan.* ***Settlement***, 2m/3km S of Larkhall. NS7748.
Swinhoe *Northumb.* ***Hamlet***, 3m/4km S of Seahouses. **71 H1** NU2128.
Swinhoe Burn *Northumb.* ***River***, flowing into North Sea 1km SE of Seahouses. **71 H1** NU2231.
Swinhope *Lincs.* ***Settlement***, 1m/2km N of Binbrook. **53 F3** TF2196.
Swining *Shet.* ***Settlement***, overlooking Swining Voe, Mainland. **109 D6** HU4566.
Swinithwaite *N.Yorks.* ***Hamlet***, 3m/4km E of Aysgarth. **57 F1** SE0489.
Swinmore Common *Here.* ***Locality***, 3m/5km NW of Ledbury. SO6741.
Swinnow *W.Yorks.* ***Suburb***, to NE of Pudsey, 4m/6km W of Leeds city centre. SE2334.
Swinscoe *Staffs.* ***Hamlet***, 3m/5km NW of Ashbourne. **40 D1** SK1348.
Swinside Hall *Sc.Bord.* ***Settlement***, 2m/3km SE of Oxnam. **70 C2** NT7216.
Swinstead *Lincs.* ***Village***, 5m/8km W of Bourne. **42 D3** TF0122.
Swinsty Reservoir *N.Yorks.* ***Reservoir***, in River Washburn valley, 5m/8km N of Otley. **57 G4** SE1953.
Swinthorpe *Lincs.* ***Locality***, 3m/5km E of Welton. TF0680.
Swinton *Gt.Man.* Population: 21,578. ***Town***, 5m/7km NW of Manchester. **49 G2** SD7701.
Swinton *N.Yorks.* ***Village***, 1m/2km SW of Masham. **57 H1** SE2179.
Swinton *N.Yorks.* ***Village***, 2m/3km NW of Malton. **58 D2** SE7573.
Swinton *Sc.Bord.* ***Village***, 5m/8km N of Coldstream. **77 G6** NT8347.
Swinton *S.Yorks.* Population: 15,936. ***Town***, 4m/6km N of Rotherham. **51 G3** SK4599.
Swinton Bridge *S.Yorks.* ***Locality***, on River Don, 1km E of Swinton. SK4699.
Swinton Quarter *Sc.Bord.* ***Settlement***, 1km NE of Swinton. NT8447.
Swintonmill *Sc.Bord.* ***Hamlet***, 2m/3km SW of Swinton. **77 G6** NT8146.
Swiss Garden *Beds.* ***Garden***, 3m/4km E of Biggleswade, designed early 19c, and containing formal gardens, woodland walks, tiny thatched buildings and a fairytale grotto. **32 E4** TL1444.
Switha *Ork.* ***Island***, small uninhabited island 1m/2km E of South Walls peninsula at SE end of Hoy. Traces of Bronze Age settlements. **107 C8** ND3690.
Swithland *Leics.* ***Village***, 4m/7km S of Loughborough. **41 H4** SK5413.
Swona *Ork.* ***Island***, of about 60 acres or 25 hectares, 3m/5km W of Burwick, near S end of South Ronaldsay. Beacon at SW end. **107 C9** ND3884.
Swordale *High.* ***Settlement***, 2m/3km W of Evanton. **96 C5** NH5765.
Swordale *W.Isles* *Anglicised form of Suardail, qv.*
Swordland *High.* ***Settlement***, on N shore of Loch Morar, 1km S of Tarbert, Lochaber district. **86 D5** NM7891.
Swordle *High.* ***Locality***, near N coast of Ardnamurchan peninsula, 1km S of Ockle Point. **79 G1** NM5470.
Swordly *High.* ***Settlement***, near N coast of Caithness district, 2m/3km E of Bettyhill. **104 C2** NC7363.
Sworland *High.* ***Settlement***, in North Morar, on N shore of Loch Morar in Lochaber district, 1km S of Tarbet. NM7891.
Sworton Heath *Ches.* ***Settlement***, 2m/3km S of Lymm. **49 F4** SJ6884.
Swyddffynnon *Cere.* ***Village***, 4m/7km N of Tregaron. **27 F2** SN6966.
Swyncombe *Oxon.* ***Suburb***, estate 2m/4km NW of Nettlebed. **21 K2** SU6890.
Swynnerton *Staffs.* ***Village***, 3m/5km NW of Stone. **40 A2** SJ8535.
Swyre *Dorset* ***Village***, 5m/8km SE of Bridport. **8 E6** SY5288.
Sychdyn *Flints.* *Welsh form of Soughton, qv.*
Sychnant *Powys* ***Settlement***, 6m/9km N of Rhayader. SN9777.
Sydallt *Wrex.* ***Settlement***, 4m/6km N of Wrexham. SJ3155.
Syde *Glos.* ***Village***, 5m/8km E of Painswick. **29 J7** SO9410.
Sydenham *Gt.Lon.* ***Suburb***, in borough of Lewisham, 7m/11km SE of Charing Cross, comprising Upper and Lower Sydenham. **23 G4** TQ3671.
Sydenham *Oxon.* ***Village***, 3m/5km SE of Thame. **22 A1** SP7301.
Sydenham *Som.* ***Suburb***, E district of Bridgwater. ST3137.
Sydenham Damerel *Devon* ***Village***, 5m/8km W of Tavistock. **4 E3** SX4076.
Syderstone *Norf.* ***Village***, 6m/9km W of Fakenham. **44 C2** TF8332.

S

Sydling St. Nicholas *Dorset* ***Village***, 2m/4km NE of Maiden Newton. **9 F5** SY6399.
Sydmonton *Hants.* ***Hamlet***, 3m/4km W of Kingsclere. **21 H6** SU4857.
Sydnal Lane *Shrop.* ***Locality***, 1m/2km N of Albrighton. SJ8005.
Sydney *Ches.* ***Suburb***, 1m/2km NE of Crewe town centre. SJ7256.
Syerston *Notts.* ***Village***, 5m/8km SW of Newark-on-Trent. **42 A1** SK7447.
Syfynwy *Pembs.* ***River***, rising on Prescelly Mountains, N of Rosebush, and flowing S through Rosebush and Llys-y-frân Reservoirs into Eastern Cleddau River, 3m/5km N of Canaston Bridge. **16 D2** SN0819.
Syke *Gt.Man.* ***Suburb***, 2m/3km N of Rochdale town centre. **49 H1** SD8915.
Sykehouse *S.Yorks.* ***Village***, 4m/7km NW of Throne. **51 J1** SE6216.
Sykemoor *Pembs.* ***Locality***, adjoining to S of Pembroke Dock. SM9602.
Sykes *Lancs.* ***Settlement***, 2m/3km NW of Dunsop Bridge. **56 B4** SD6351.
Sykes Fell *Lancs.* ***Open space***, steep moorland on either side of Langdon Brook, 3m/5km W of Dunsop Bridge. **55 K5** SD6150.
Syleham *Suff.* ***Hamlet***, 4m/6km SW of Harleston. TM2178.
Sylen *Carmar.* ***Settlement***, 4m/7km N of Llanelli. **17 J4** SN5107.
Sylfaen *Powys* ***Locality***, and station on Welshpool and Llanfair Light Railway, 3m/5km W of Welshpool. SJ1706.
Symbister *Shet.* ***Village***, chief harbour of Whalsay, near SW end of island. **109 E6** HU5362.
Symington *S.Ayr.* Population: 1145. ***Village***, 4m/7km NE of Prestwick. **74 B7** NS3831.
Symington *S.Lan.* ***Village***, 3m/5km SW of Biggar. **75 H7** NS9935.
Symonds Green *Herts.* ***Suburb***, W district of Stevenage. TL2225.
Symonds Yat *Here.* ***Locality***, well-known beauty spot on River Wye, 4m/6km NE of Monmouth across loops of river. **28 E7** SO5516.
Symondsbury *Dorset* ***Village***, 1m/2km W of Bridport. **8 D5** SY4493.
Synod Inn (Also known as Post-mawr.) *Cere.* ***Settlement***, at crossroads, 4m/6km S of New Quay. **26 D3** SN4054.
Syon House *Gt.Lon.* ***Historic house***, 18c house with Robert Adam interiors, set in grounds on N bank of River Thames opposite Royal Botanic Gardens Kew, 1km SW of Brentford in borough of Hounslow. **22 E4** TQ1776.
Syre *High.* ***Settlement***, in Strathnaver, 11m/18km S of Bettyhill, Caithness district. **103 J4** NC6943.
Syreford *Glos.* ***Hamlet***, 5m/8km E of Cheltenham. **30 B6** SP0220.
Syresham *Northants.* ***Village***, 4m/6km NE of Brackley. **31 H4** SP6341.
Syston *Leics.* ***Suburb***, 5m/8km NE of Leicester. **41 J4** SK6211.
Syston *Lincs.* ***Village***, 3m/5km N of Grantham. **42 C1** SK9240.
Sytchampton *Worcs.* ***Village***, 4m/6km SE of Stourport-on-Severn. **29 H2** SO8466.
Sywell *Northants.* ***Village***, 5m/7km W of Wellingborough. **32 B2** SP8267.

T

T.T. Course *I.o.M. See Tourist Trophy Course.*
Taagan *High.* ***Settlement***, 1m/2km NW of Kinlochewe, at SE end of Loch Maree. **95 G5** NH0163.
Taberon Law *Sc.Bord.* ***Mountain***, 2m/3km SE of Stanhope. Height 2057 feet or 627 metres. **69 G1** NT1428.
Tabhaidh Bheag *W.Isles Gaelic form of Tavay Beag, qv.*
Tabhaigh Mhòr (Anglicised form: Tavay Mòr.) *W.Isles* ***Island***, small uninhabited island opposite entrance to Loch Erisort, E coast of Isle of Lewis. **101 G5** NB4222.
Tabley *Ches.* ***Locality***, 2m/3km W of Knutsford. Motorway service area (M6). SJ7277.
Tabley House *Ches.* ***Historic house***, 18c Palladian mansion owned by Leicester family, 2m/3km W of Knutsford. **49 G5** SJ7277.
Tableyhill *Ches.* ***Settlement***, 1m/2km NW of Knutsford. SJ7379.
Tabost (Anglicised form: Habost.) *W.Isles* ***Settlement***, on Isle of Lewis, on S side of Loch Erisort, opposite Lacasaigh. **101 F6** NB3219.
Tabost (Anglicised form: Habost.) *W.Isles* ***Village***, near N end of Isle of Lewis, 1m/2km W of Port Nis. **101 H1** NB5263.
Tachbrook Mallory *Warks.* ***Settlement***, 3m/4km S of Royal Leamington Spa. SP3162.
Tacher *High.* ***Settlement***, situated on Little River, 3m/5km N of Loch Rangag. **105 G4** ND1746.
Tackley *Oxon.* ***Village***, 3m/5km NE of Woodstock. **31 F7** SP4720.
Tacleit (Anglicised form: Hacklete.) *W.Isles* ***Settlement***, at S end of Great Bernera, W coast of Isle of Lewis, to W of road bridge connecting Great Bernera to main island. **100 D4** NB1534.
Tacolneston *Norf.* ***Village***, 5m/8km S of Wymondham. **45 F6** TM1495.
Tadcaster *N.Yorks.* Population: 6915. ***Small town***, on River Wharfe, 9m/15km SW of York, on site of Roman Calcaria. **57 K5** SE4843.
Tadden *Dorset* ***Settlement***, 2m/3km NW of Wimborne Minster. **9 J4** ST9801.
Taddington *Derbys.* ***Village***, in Peak District, 5m/8km W of Bakewell. **50 D5** SK1471.
Taddington *Glos.* ***Hamlet***, 4m/6km S of Broadway. SP0831.
Taddiport *Devon* ***Hamlet***, just S of Great Torrington across River Torridge. **6 C4** SS4818.
Tadham Moor *Som.* ***Marsh/bog***, marshy area at sea level, cut by dykes for drainage, 2m/3km SW of Wedmore. **19 H7** ST4244.
Tadley *Hants.* Population: 15,520. ***Village***, 6m/10km NW of Basingstoke. **21 K5** SU6060.
Tadlow *Cambs.* ***Village***, 4m/6km E of Potton. **33 F4** TL2847.
Tadmarton *Oxon.* ***Village***, 4m/7km SW of Banbury. **30 E5** SP3937.
Tadmarton Heath *Oxon.* ***Open space***, heath 1m/2km SE of Swalcliffe. **30 E5** SP3835.
Tadpole Bridge *Oxon.* ***Settlement***, on River Thames, 2m/3km SE of Bampton. SP3300.
Tadworth *Surr.* Population: 18,622. ***Locality***, residential locality 3m/4km SW of Banstead. **23 F6** TQ2356.
Taf *Welsh form of Taff (River), qv.*
Taf *Carmar.* ***River***, rising to E of Crymych and flowing by Llanfyrnach, Login and Whitland to S side of St. Clears, where it forms an estuary which runs past Laugharne to join estuary of River Tywi and flow into Carmarthen Bay. **17 F3** SN3209.
Taf Fechan (Little Taff). ***River***, rising on S side of Brecon Beacons, following roughly parallel course with Taf Fawr S through reservoirs, until they join on NW side of Merthyr Tydfil to form River Taff. SO0307.
Taf fechan Reservoir *Powys Alternative name for Pontsticill Reservoir, qv.*
Tafarn-y-bwlch *Pembs.* ***Settlement***, 4m/6km SE of Newport. **16 D1** SN0833.
Tafarn-y-Gelyn *Denb.* ***Settlement***, 4m/6km SW of Mold. **47 K6** SJ1861.
Tafarnaubach *B.Gwent* ***Locality***, 1m/2km NW of Tredegar. **28 A7** SO1110.
Taff (Taf). ***River***, rising as Taf Fawr (Great Taff) and Taf Fechan (Little Taff) on W and S sides respectively of Brecon Beacons. Both streams follow roughly parallel courses S through reservoirs until joining on NW side of Merthyr Tydfil. River then continues S by Pontypridd to mouth of River Severn at Cardiff. ST1972.
Taff Merthyr Garden Village *M.Tyd.* ***Village***, 1km NE of Treharris. ST1097.
Taff Vale *R.C.T.* ***Valley***, part of River Taff valley, running S between Abercynon and Pontypridd. **18 D2** ST0893.
Taff's Well (Ffynnon Taf). *Cardiff* Population: 3205. ***Village***, on River Taff, 6m/9km NW of Cardiff, formerly noted for medicinal springs. **18 E3** ST1283.
Tafolog *Powys* ***Open space***, hillside area 3m/5km E of Aberangell. **37 H5** SH8909.
Tafolwern *Powys* ***Settlement***, 3m/5km E of Cemmaes Road. **37 H5** SH8802.
Tafts Ness *Ork.* ***Coastal feature***, headland at NE end of Sanday. **106 G3** HY7647.
Tahaval *W.Isles* ***Mountain***, near W coast of Isle of Lewis, 1m/2km E of Mealisval. Height 1689 feet or 515 metres. **100 C5** NB0426.
Tahay *W.Isles* ***Island***, small uninhabited island in Sound of Harris less than 1km off NE coast of North Uist. NF9675.
Tai-bach *Powys* ***Settlement***, 3m/4km NE of Llanrhaeadr-ym-Mochnant. **38 A3** SJ1528.
Tai 'n Lôn *Gwyn.* ***Settlement***, at E end of Lleyn Peninsula, 3m/4km SW of Penygroes. **46 C7** SH4450.
Taibach *N.P.T.* ***Locality***, 1m/2km SE of Port Talbot. **18 A3** SS7789.
Tailbridge Hill *Cumb.* ***Mountain***, 3m/5km SE of Kirkby Stephen. Height 1794 feet or 547 metres. **61 K6** NY8005.
Tain *High.* ***Settlement***, in Caithness district, 2m/3km SE of Castletown. **105 H2** ND2166.
Tain *High.* Population: 3715. ***Small town***, attractive town and royal burgh in Ross and Cromarty district on S shore of Dornoch Firth, 10m/15km NE of Invergordon. 14c church and interesting 17c tollbooth. **96 E3** NH7782.
Taing of Kelswick *Shet.* ***Coastal feature***, headland to S of larger headland of Lunna Ness on Mainland's E coast. **109 E6** HU4969.
Tai'r Bull *Powys* ***Settlement***, 4m/6km SW of Brecon. **27 J6** SN9925.
Tair Carn Isaf *Carmar.* ***Mountain***, 2m/3km N of Glanaman. Height 1509 feet or 460 metres. **17 K3** SN6816.
Tai'r-heol *Caerp.* ***Hamlet***, 1m/2km SE of Treharris. ST1094.
Tai'r-ysgol *Swan.* ***Suburb***, to NE of Swansea, 4m/6km W of Neath. SS6997.
Tairlaw *S.Ayr.* ***Settlement***, 3m/5km SE of Straiton. **67 J3** NS4000.
Takeley *Essex* Population: 1703. ***Village***, 5m/8km E of Bishop's Stortford. **33 J6** TL5621.
Takeley Street *Essex* ***Village***, 1m/2km W of Takeley. **33 J6** TL5621.
Takkan Tan *Former name of Tan Hill, qv.*
Tal-sarn *Cere.* ***Hamlet***, 6m/9km N of Lampeter. **26 E3** SN5456.
Tal-y-bont *Conwy* ***Village***, 6m/9km S of Conwy. **47 F6** SH7668.
Tal-y-bont *Gwyn.* ***Hamlet***, on River Ysgethin, 4m/6km N of Barmouth. **36 E3** SH5821.
Tal-y-bont *Gwyn.* ***Village***, 2m/3km E of Bangor. **46 E5** SH6070.
Tal-y-Cae *Gwyn.* ***Settlement***, 3m/5km SE of Bangor. **46 E6** SH6068.
Tal-y-cafn *Conwy* ***Village***, 4m/6km S of Conwy across River Conwy. **47 F5** SH7871.
Tal-y-coed *Mon.* ***Hamlet***, 5m/7km N of Raglan. SO4115.
Tal-y-fan *Conwy* ***Mountain***, 3m/4km S of Penmaenmawr. Height 2001 feet or 610 metres. **47 F5** SH7272.
Tal-y-llyn *Gwyn.* ***Hamlet***, at SW end of Tal-y-llyn Lake, 5m/8km S of Dolgellau. **37 G5** SH7009.
Tal-y-llyn Lake *Gwyn.* ***Lake/loch***, in course of River Dysynni 2m/3km S of summit of Cadair Idris. Hamlet of Tal-y-llyn at SW end of lake. **37 G4** SH7109.
Tal y Mieryn *Gwyn.* ***Mountain***, S slopes of Cae Afon, 3m/4km NW of Aberangell. Height 1706 feet or 520 metres. **37 H4** SH8212.
Tal-y-waenydd *Gwyn.* ***Settlement***, 1m/2km N of Blaenau Ffestiniog. SH6947.
Tal-y-Wern *Powys* ***Hamlet***, 5m/8km E of Machynlleth. **37 H5** SH8200.
Talachddu *Powys* ***Hamlet***, 4m/6km NE of Brecon. **27 K5** SO0833.
Talacre *Flints.* ***Hamlet***, 1km SW of Point of Ayr, 4m/6km NE of Prestatyn. **47 K4** SJ1284.
Talardd *Gwyn.* ***Settlement***, on River Twrch, 2m/3km SE of Llanuwchllyn. **37 H3** SH8927.
Talaton *Devon* ***Village***, 3m/5km NW of Ottery St. Mary. **7 J6** SY0699.
Talbenni *Pembs. See Talbenny.*
Talbenny (Talbenni). *Pembs.* ***Village***, near S coast of St. Brides Bay, 6m/9km NW of Milford Haven. **16 B3** SM8311.
Talbot Green *R.C.T.* ***Locality***, 1km SW of Llantrisant. **18 D3** ST0382.
Talbot Village *Bourne.* ***Suburb***, including Bournemouth University campus, 2m/3km NW of Bournemouth town centre. SZ0794.
Tale *Devon* ***River***, rising in parish of Broadhembury and flowing S into River Otter 1km NW of Ottery St. Mary. **7 J5** SY0996.
Taleford *Devon* ***Hamlet***, on E bank of River Tale, 1m/2km NW of Ottery St. Mary. SY0997.
Talerddig *Powys* ***Hamlet***, 8m/13km NW of Caersws. **37 J5** SH9300.
Talgarreg *Cere.* ***Village***, 6m/10km SE of New Quay. **26 D3** SN4251.
Talgarth *Powys* Population: 1818. ***Small town***, 7m/11km SW of Hay-on-Wye. 13c fortified tower near bridge at town centre. **28 A5** SO1533.
Taliesin (Also known as Tre Taliesin.) *Cere.* ***Hamlet***, 1m/2km N of Talybont. Bedd Taliesin, traditional burial-place of Taliesin, 1m/2km E. **37 F6** SN6591.
Talisker *High.* ***Settlement***, near W coast of Skye, 4m/6km W of Carbost and 3m/4km SE of Rubha nan Clach. **85 J1** NG3230.
Talisker Bay *High.* ***Bay***, on W coast of Skye, to W of Talisker. **85 J1** NG3130.
Talke *Staffs.* ***Locality***, adjoining to SW of Kidsgrove. **49 H7** SJ8253.
Talke Pits *Staffs.* ***Hamlet***, 1km S of Talke. SJ8252.
Talkin *Cumb.* ***Hamlet***, 3m/4km SE of Brampton. **61 G1** NY5457.
Talkin Tarn *Cumb.* ***Lake/loch***, with surrounding country park, 1m/2km N of Talkin. **61 G1** NY5458.
Talla Bheith *P. & K.* ***Settlement***, on N shore of Loch Rannoch, 6m/10km W of Kinloch Rannoch. **81 G2** NN5658.
Talla Bheith Forest *P. & K.* ***Large natural feature***, upland area and game forest in Atholl, to E of Loch Ericht and N of Loch Rannoch. **81 G1** NN5567.
Talla Linnfoots *Sc.Bord.* ***Settlement***, at E end of Talla Reservoir, 3m/5km SE of Tweedsmuir. **69 G1** NT1320.
Talla Reservoir *Sc.Bord.* ***Reservoir***, 2km SE of Tweedsmuir. Length about 2m/4km SE to NW. **69 G1** NT1121.
Talladale *High.* ***Village***, on SW shore of Loch Maree, Ross and Cromarty district, 8m/13km SE of Gairloch. **95 F4** NG9170.
Talland *Cornw.* ***Hamlet***, near S coast, above Talland Bay, 2m/3km SW of Looe. SX2251.
Talland Bay *Cornw.* ***Bay***, small rocky bay, 2m/3km SW of Looe. SX2251.
Tallarn Green *Wrex.* ***Village***, 4m/6km E of Bangor-is-y-coed. **38 D1** SJ4444.
Tallentire *Cumb.* ***Village***, 3m/5km N of Cockermouth. **60 C3** NY1035.
Talley (Talyllychau). *Carmar.* ***Village***, 6m/10km N of Llandeilo. **17 K1** SN6332.
Talley Abbey *Carmar.* ***Ecclesiastical building***, ruined 12c Cistercian abbey (Cadw), 6m/10km N of Llandeilo. **17 K1** SN6332.
Tallington *Lincs.* ***Village***, on River Welland, 4m/7km E of Stamford. **42 D5** TF0907.
Tallistown *B.Gwent* ***Locality***, 3m/4km S of Ebbw Vale. SO1805.
Talmine *High.* ***Village***, in Caithness district, on W shore of Tongue Bay. **103 H2** NC5863.
Talog *Carmar.* ***Hamlet***, 6m/10km NW of Carmarthen. **17 G2** SN3325.
Talsarn *Carmar.* ***Settlement***, 3m/4km S of Myddfai. Site of Roman camp 2m/3km E. SN7726.
Talsarnau *Gwyn.* ***Village***, 4m/6km NE of Harlech. **37 F2** SH6135.
Talskiddy *Cornw.* ***Hamlet***, 1m/2km N of St. Columb Major. **3 G2** SW9165.
Talwrn *I.o.A.* ***Hamlet***, on Anglesey, 2m/3km E of Llangefni. **46 C5** SH4677.
Talwrn *Wrex.* ***Hamlet***, 3m/5km SW of Wrexham. **38 B1** SJ2948.
Talwrn *Wrex.* ***Settlement***, 2m/3km E of Marchwiel. SJ3847.
Talybont *Cere.* ***Village***, 6m/10km NE of Aberystwyth. **37 F7** SN6589.
Talybont-on-Usk *Powys* ***Village***, 6m/9km SE of Brecon. **28 A6** SO1122.
Talybont Reservoir *Powys* ***Reservoir***, large reservoir to S of Talybont-on-Usk, in Glyn Collwn. **27 K7** SO1120.
Talygarn *R.C.T.* ***Hamlet***, 2m/3km SW of Llantrisant. ST0380.
Talyllychau *Carmar. Welsh form of Talley, qv.*
Talyllyn *Powys* ***Settlement***, 1km SW of Llanfihangel Tal-y-llyn. **28 A6** SO1027.
Talyllyn Railway *Gwyn.* ***Other feature of interest***, narrow gauge railway running 7m/12km from Tywyn to Nant Gwernol. Originally built for transporting slate, later became world's first volunteer-run railway. **37 F5** SH5800.
Talysarn *Gwyn.* ***Village***, 6m/10km S of Caernarfon. **46 C7** SH4853.
Talywain *Torfaen* ***Suburb***, adjoining to NW of Abersychan. SO2604.

Tamanaisval *W.Isles* ***Mountain***, near W coast of Isle of Lewis 2m/4km SE of Mealisval. Height 1532 feet or 467 metres. **100 C5** NB0423.

Tamar ***River***, rising about 4m/6km E of Morwenstow on N Cornish coast and flowing S into Plymouth Sound. **4 E4** SX4652.

Tamavoid *Stir.* ***Settlement***, 2m/3km S of Port of Menteith. **74 D1** NS5999.

Tame ***River***, rising on W side of Walsall and flowing SE to Perry Barr, Birmingham, E to its confluence with River Blythe to NE of Coleshill, then N past Tamworth into River Trent 1m/2km E of Alrewas. **40 D5** SK1914.

Tame *Gt.Man.* ***River***, rising on moors N of Denshaw and flowing S to join River Goyt on N side of Stockport and form River Mersey. **49 J3** SJ8990.

Tamer Lane End *Gt.Man.* ***Locality***, 1m/2km NW of Leigh. SD6401.

Tamerton Foliot *Plym.* ***Suburb***, in Plymouth, 4m/6km N of city centre. **4 E4** SX4760.

Tamworth *Staffs.* Population: 68,440. ***Town***, market town on River Tame, 14m/22km NE of Birmingham. Castle Norman and later. Interesting buildings include 16c Moat House in Lichfield Street. **40 E5** SK2004.

Tamworth Castle *Staffs.* ***Castle***, well-preserved 11c motte, with Tudor house built on edge of site, in centre of Tamworth. **40 E5** SK2003.

Tamworth Green *Lincs.* ***Settlement***, 4m/6km E of Boston. TF3842.

Tan Hill (Formerly known as Takkan Tan.) ***Open space***, moorland with slight hill on borders of Cumbria, Durham and North Yorkshire. Location of Tan Hill Inn public house, highest licenced premises in England at height of 1732 feet or 528 metres, situated on The Pennine Way at head of pass between Edenvale and Swaledale. **61 K6** NY8907.

Tan Hill *Wilts.* ***Hill***, 1m/2km N of Stanton St. Bernard. Height 964 feet or 294 metres. **20 D5** SU0865.

Tan-lan *Gwyn.* ***Hamlet***, 2m/3km N of Penrhyndeudraeth. **37 F1** SH6142.

Tan Office Green *Suff.* ***Hamlet***, 1m/2km S of Chevington. TL7858.

Tan Pit *Gt.Man.* ***Suburb***, 2m/4km SW of Wigan town centre. SD5502.

Tan-y-bwlch *Gwyn.* ***Hamlet***, 1km W of Maentwrog across Vale of Ffestiniog. SH6540.

Tan-y-Bwlch *Gwyn.* ***Locality***, 2m/3km SW of Bethesda. SH6065.

Tan-y-coed *Gwyn.* ***Hamlet***, 4m/6km E of Caernarfon. SH5362.

Tan-y-fron *Conwy* ***Settlement***, 2m/3km SE of Llansannan. **47 H6** SH9564.

Tan-y-graig *Gwyn.* ***Settlement***, on Lleyn Peninsula, 4m/7km NW of Pwllheli. **36 C2** SH3138.

Tan-y-groes *Cere.* ***Hamlet***, 2m/3km SE of Aberporth. **26 B4** SN2849.

Tan-y-pistyll *Powys* ***Settlement***, 3m/4km NE of Llangynog. **37 K3** SJ0729.

Tan-yr-allt *Denb.* ***Suburb***, 1m/2km S of Prestatyn. SJ0680.

Tanat ***River***, rising in Berwyn mountain range and flowing E into River Vyrnwy 1m/2km S of Llanblodwel. **38 A3** SJ2420.

Tancred *N.Yorks.* ***Settlement***, 1m/2km N of Green Hammerton. SE4458.

Tandem *W.Yorks.* ***Suburb***, 2m/3km E of Huddersfield town centre. SE1716.

Tandle Hill *Gt.Man.* ***Locality***, 3m/4km S of Rochdale. SD8909.

Tandle Hill Country Park *Gt.Man.* ***Leisure/recreation***, 109 acres of open hillside, woodland and heathland on W side of A627(M), 3m/4km NW of Oldham town centre. Other features include an aviary, pitch-and-putt course and nature trails. **49 J2** SD9008.

Tandlehill *Renf.* ***Suburb***, adjoining to SE of Kilbarchan. NS4062.

Tandridge *Surr.* ***Village***, 2m/3km SE of Godstone. **23 G6** TQ3750.

Tanera Beg *High.* ***Island***, one of Summer Isles group. Lies 3m/5km W of NW coast of Ross and Cromarty district near Polglass. Area about 270 acres or 110 hectares. **95 F1** NB9607.

Tanera Mòr *High.* ***Island***, largest of Summer Isles group, being over 1 square mile or about 3 square km in area. Lies 1m/2km W of NW coast of Ross and Cromarty district across Badentarbert Bay. NB9807.

Tanerdy *Carmar.* ***Locality***, adjoining to N of Carmarthen. **17 H2** SN4221.

Tanfield *Dur.* ***Village***, 2m/3km N of Stanley. **62 C1** NZ1855.

Tanfield Lea *Dur.* ***Village***, 1m/2km NW of Stanley. NZ1855.

Tanfield Railway *T. & W.* ***Other feature of interest***, Victorian steam railway running S from Sunniside, 3m/4km SW of Gateshead, to E of Tanfield. It passes over 105 foot or 32 metre span of Causey Arch, world's earliest railway bridge, built 1727. Museum exhibits 40 trains and vintage working machinery. **62 D1** NZ2158.

Tang *N.Yorks.* ***Hamlet***, 2m/3km SW of Hampsthwaite. SE2357.

Tang Hall *York* ***Suburb***, 1m/2km E of York city centre. SE6252.

Tang Head *High.* ***Coastal feature***, headland on N coast, 5m/8km SE of Dunnet Head. **105 H1** ND2774.

Tang Head *High.* ***Coastal feature***, headland on E coast on N side of Sinclair's Bay. **105 J2** ND3560.

Tangier *Som.* ***Suburb***, inner district of Taunton. ST2224.

Tangiers *Pembs.* ***Settlement***, 2m/3km N of Haverfordwest. **16 C3** SM9518.

Tanglandford *Aber.* ***Settlement***, to S of Bridge over River Ythan, 3m/5km N of Tarves. **91 G1** NJ8835.

Tangley *Hants.* ***Village***, 5m/8km NW of Andover. **21 G6** SU3252.

Tangmere *W.Suss.* Population: 1090. ***Village***, on W side of airfield, 3m/5km E of Chichester. **12 C6** SU9006.

Tangwick *Shet.* ***Settlement***, on Esha Ness, Mainland, inland of bay of Tang Wick on N shore of larger St. Magnus Bay. **108 B5** HU2377.

Tangy *Arg. & B.* ***Settlement***, on Kintyre, 5m/8km NW of Campbeltown. **66 A1** NR6727.

Tangy Loch *Arg. & B.* ***Lake/loch***, small loch in Kintyre 5m/8km N of Campbeltown. **66 A1** NR6928.

Tanhouse *Lancs.* ***Suburb***, E district of Skelmersdale. SD4905.

Tankerness *Ork.* ***Locality***, and loch on Mainland, 2m/3km SW of Rerwick Head. **107 E7** HY5009.

Tankersley *S.Yorks.* ***Village***, 2m/3km W of Hoyland. **51 F2** SK3399.

Tankerton *Kent* ***Suburb***, E district of Whitstable, on Tankerton Bay. TR1267.

Tannach *High.* ***Settlement***, in Caithness district, 3m/5km SW of Wick. **105 J4** ND3247.

Tannachie *Aber.* ***Hamlet***, 3m/4km NE of Glenbervie. **91 F6** NO7883.

Tannachy *High.* ***Settlement***, adjoining to NE of Rhilochan, Sutherland district. **96 E1** NC7507.

Tannadice *Angus* ***Village***, on River South Esk, 8m/12km W of Brechin. **83 F2** NO4758.

Tannaraidh *W.Isles Gaelic form of Tannray, qv.*

Tanners Green *Worcs.* ***Settlement***, 5m/8km NE of Redditch. SP0874.

Tannington *Suff.* ***Village***, 4m/6km NW of Framlingham. **35 G2** TM2467.

Tannington Green *Suff.* ***Locality***, 1m/2km N of Tannington. TM2467.

Tannochside *N.Lan.* ***Suburb***, 1m/2km N of Uddingston. **75 F4** NS7061.

Tannray (Gaelic form: Tannaraidh.) *W.Isles* ***Island***, small uninhabited island at entrance to Loch Leurbost, E coast of Isle of Lewis. NB4023.

Tansey Green *W.Mid.* ***Locality***, 3m/4km W of Dudley town centre. SO9089.

Tanshall *Fife* ***Suburb***, W district of Glenrothes. NO2500.

Tanskey Rocks *Mersey.* ***Island***, group of rocks in River Dee estuary, about 1km offshore from West Kirby. SJ2086.

Tansley *Derbys.* ***Village***, 2m/3km E of Matlock. **51 F7** SK3259.

Tansley Hill *W.Mid.* ***Locality***, 1m/2km SE of Dudley town centre. SO9589.

Tansley Knoll *Derbys.* ***Village***, adjoining to N of Tansley, 1m/2km E of Matlock. SK3259.

Tansor *Northants.* ***Village***, 2m/3km NE of Oundle. **42 D6** TL0591.

Tantallon Castle *E.Loth.* ***Castle***, ruined 14c castle (Historic Scotland) of red stone on rocky headland, 3m/5km E of North Berwick. **76 D2** NT5985.

Tantobie *Dur.* ***Village***, 2m/3km NW of Stanley. **62 C1** NZ1754.

Tanton *N.Yorks.* ***Hamlet***, 1m/2km N of Stokesley. **63 G5** NZ5210.

Tanwood *Worcs.* ***Locality***, 4m/7km NW of Bromsgrove. SO9074.

Tanworth in Arden *Warks.* ***Village***, 4m/6km NW of Henley-in-Arden. **30 C1** SP1170.

Tanygrisiau *Gwyn.* ***Hamlet***, 1m/2km SW of Blaenau Ffestiniog. **37 F1** SH6845.

Taobh a' Deas Loch Baghasdail (Anglicised form: South Lochboisdale.) *W.Isles* ***Locality***, on S side of Loch Baghasdail. **84 C3** NF7919.

Taobh Dubh *High.* ***Mountain***, 1m/2km NW of Loch Uisge. Small tarn at summit. Height 1155 feet or 352 metres. **79 J2** NM7856.

Taobh Siar (Anglicised form: West Tarbert.) *W.Isles* ***Settlement***, 1km NW of Tarbert, North Harris. **100 D7** NB1400.

Taobh Tuath *W.Isles Gaelic form of Northton, qv.*

Tap o' Noth *Aber.* ***Mountain***, surmounted by ancient fort, 2m/3km NW of Rhynie. Height 1847 feet or 563 metres. **90 C2** NJ4829.

Tapeley *Devon* ***Settlement***, 2m/3km NE of Bideford, to E of River Torridge. **6 C3** SS4829.

Tapeley Park *Devon* ***Garden***, 2m/3km NE of Bideford, to E of River Torridge. 20 acre garden, at 18c home of Christie family, includes recently renovated 19c Italian terraces. **6 C3** SS4829.

Taplow *Bucks.* ***Village***, in River Thames valley, 4m/7km W of Slough. **22 C3** SU9182.

Tapton *Derbys.* ***Suburb***, 1m/2km NE of Chesterfield town centre across River Rother. SK3972.

Tapton Grove *Derbys.* ***Hamlet***, 1m/2km NE of Chesterfield. SK4072.

Taransay *W.Isles Anglicised form of Tarasaigh, qv.*

Taransay Glorigs *W.Isles* ***Island***, group of rocks about 3m/5km NW of Tarasaigh. **100 B7** NB0200.

Tarasaigh (Anglicised form: Taransay). *W.Isles* ***Island***, barely populated island, 4m/7km NE to SW and of varying width, lying 1m/2km off W coast of South Harris across Sound of Taransay. **100 C7** NB0200.

Taravocan *Arg. & B.* ***Settlement***, in valley of River Creran, 1m/2km NE of head of Loch Creran. **80 B3** NN0146.

Tarbat House *High.* ***Settlement***, on shore of Nigg Bay, 1km S of Milton. **96 E4** NH7773.

Tarbat Ness *High.* ***Coastal feature***, headland on E coast of Ross and Cromarty district, on S side of entrance to Dornoch Firth. Lighthouse. **97 G3** NH9487.

Tarbert *Arg. & B.* ***Settlement***, on Tarbert Bay, on E coast of Jura, 5m/7km SW of Ardlussa. **72 E2** NR6181.

Tarbert *Arg. & B.* ***Settlement***, on N part of Gigha, 2m/3km N of Ardminish. **72 E5** NR6551.

Tarbert *Arg. & B.* Population: 1347. ***Village***, at head of East Loch Tarbert at N end of Kintyre, Argyll. Main port for Loch Fyne fishing industry. Passenger boat services to Gourock. Remains of 14c castle on S side of loch. **73 G4** NR8668.

Tarbert *High.* ***Settlement***, on W side of Salen Bay, 1km S of Salen, Lochaber district. **79 H1** NM6863.

Tarbert (Gaelic form: An Tairbeart.) *W.Isles* ***Village***, port of North Harris, situated on isthmus between East and West Loch Tarbert. **100 D7** NB1500.

Tarbert Bay *Arg. & B.* ***Bay***, on E coast of Jura. **72 E2** NR6082.

Tarbert Bay *High.* ***Bay***, small bay on S coast of Canna, 3m/4km E of Garrisdale Point. **85 H4** NG2405.

Tarbet *Arg. & B.* ***Village***, and resort on W shore of Loch Lomond, 7m/11km S of head of loch and 1m/2km E of Arrochar at head of Loch Long. **80 E7** NN3104.

Tarbet *High.* ***Settlement***, on W coast of Sutherland district, opposite Handa Island. **102 D4** NC1648.

Tarbet *High.* ***Settlement***, in North Morar, on S shore of Loch Nevis, Lochaber district, at head of small inlet. **86 D5** NM7992.

Tarbock Green *Mersey.* ***Settlement***, 1m/2km NE of Halewood. SJ4687.

Tarbolton *S.Ayr.* Population: 1854. ***Village***, 5m/8km E of Prestwick. Bachelor's Club (National Trust for Scotland), 17c thatched house where Burns and friends formed club in 1780. **67 J1** NS4327.

Tarbrax *S.Lan.* ***Settlement***, 6m/10km NE of Carnwath. **75 J5** NT0255.

Tardebigge *Worcs.* ***Village***, 3m/4km E of Bromsgrove. Flight of thirty locks on Worcester and Birmingham Canal. **29 J2** SO9969.

Tardy Gate *Lancs.* ***Locality***, 2m/4km S of Preston. **55 J7** SD5425.

Tarennig ***River***, rising on S slopes of Plynlimon and running S, then SE into River Wye 1km W of Pant Mawr. **37 G7** SN8482.

Tarf Bridge *D. & G.* ***Bridge***, crossing Tarf Water 1km E of Loch Ronald, 6m/10km NE of Glenluce. **64 C4** NX2564.

Tarf Water *D. & G.* ***River***, rising S of Barrhill on W slopes of Benbrake Hill and running SE to River Bladnoch, 1m/2km E of Kirkcowan. NX3460.

Tarf Water *P. & K.* ***River***, running E to head of Glen Tilt, 11m/17km NE of Blair Atholl. **89 G7** NN9879.

Tarff Water *D. & G.* ***River***, flowing S to join River Dee 1km S of Tongland, 1m/2km N of Kirkcudbright. **65 G4** NX6853.

Tarfside *Angus* ***Village***, on Water of Tarf near its junction with River North Esk, 11m/17km NW of Fettercairn. **90 C6** NO4979.

Tarland *Aber.* ***Village***, 9m/14km NE of Ballater. On rocky knoll 1km SE is Tomnaverie Stone Circle (Historic Scotland). 2m/3km E is site of prehistoric Culsh Earth House (Historic Scotland). **90 C4** NJ4804.

Tarland Burn *Aber.* ***River***, rising to NW of Tarland and flowing SE to Aboyne, joining River Dee 2m/3km E of Aboyne. **90 D4** NO5597.

Tarleton *Lancs.* Population: 7158. ***Village***, 8m/12km E of Southport. **55 H7** SD4520.

Tarlscough *Lancs.* ***Settlement***, 4m/6km N of Ormskirk. **48 D1** SD4314.

Tarlton *Glos.* ***Village***, 4m/7km W of Cirencester. **20 C2** ST9699.

Tarnbrook *Lancs.* ***Settlement***, on Tarnbrook Wyre, on W side of Forest of Bowland, 6m/9km NW of Dunsop Bridge. Mountain Rescue Post. **55 J4** SD5855.

Tarner Island *High.* ***Island***, small uninhabited island in Loch Bracadale, nearly 1m/2km N of Wiay. **85 H1** NG2938.

Tarnock *Som.* ***Hamlet***, 4m/6km W of Axbridge. **19 G6** ST3752.

Tarns *Cumb.* ***Locality***, 4m/6km SW of Abbeytown. NY1147.

Tarnside *Cumb.* ***Locality***, 1km SW of Crosthwaite and 5m/8km S of Windermere. SD4390.

Tarporley *Ches.* Population: 2308. ***Village***, 9m/14km NW of Nantwich. **48 E6** SJ5562.

Tarr *Som.* ***Hamlet***, 3m/4km NE of Wiveliscombe. **7 K2** ST1030.

Tarrant Crawford *Dorset* ***Hamlet***, 3m/5km SE of Blandford Forum. **9 J4** ST9203.

Tarrant Gunville *Dorset* ***Village***, 5m/8km NE of Blandford Forum. **9 J3** ST9212.

Tarrant Hinton *Dorset* ***Village***, 5m/7km NE of Blandford Forum. **9 J3** ST9311.

Tarrant Keyneston (Tarrant Keynston). *Dorset* ***Village***, 3m/5km SE of Blandford Forum. **9 J4** ST9204.

Tarrant Keynston *Dorset Alternative spelling of Tarrant Keyneston, qv.*

Tarrant Launceston *Dorset* ***Village***, between Tarrant Hinton and Tarrant Monkton, 4m/7km NE of Blandford Forum. **9 J4** ST9409.

Tarrant Monkton *Dorset* ***Village***, 4m/7km NE of Blandford Forum. **9 J4** ST9408.

Tarrant Rawston *Dorset* ***Village***, adjoining to N of Tarrant Rushton, 3m/5km E of Blandford Forum. **9 J4** ST9306.

Tarrant Rushton *Dorset* ***Hamlet***, 3m/5km E of Blandford Forum. **9 J4** ST9306.

Tarras Water *D. & G.* ***River***, running S to River Esk, 3m/4km S of Langholm. **69 J5** NY3780.

Tarrel *High.* ***Settlement***, 2m/3km SW of Portmahomack. **97 F3** NH8981.

Tarren-y-Gesail *Gwyn.* ***Inland physical feature***, mountain ridge rising to over 600 metres, 3m/4km E of Abergynolwyn. Craggy edge on W side. **37 G5** SH7105.

Tarrenhendre *Gwyn.* ***Mountain***, 4m/7km NW of Machynlleth. Height 2076 feet or 633 metres. **37 F5** SH6803.

Tarrents *Devon* ***Locality***, 4m/7km NW of Ottery St. Mary. ST0601.

Tarring Neville *E.Suss.* ***Village***, on E side of River Ouse valley, 2m/3km N of Newhaven. Bronze Age settlement on South Downs 1m/2km N. **13 H6** TQ4403.

Tarrington *Here.* ***Village***, 7m/11km E of Hereford. **29 F4** SO6140.

Tarrnacraig *N.Ayr.* ***Settlement***, on Arran, 5m/8km W of Brodick. **73 H7** NR9334.

Tarsappie *P. & K.* ***Hamlet***, 2m/3km N of Bridge of Earn. **82 C5** NO1221.

Tarset Burn *Northumb.* ***River***, rising as Smallhope Burn on E side of Kielder Forest and flowing SE into River North Tyne, 4m/6km W of Bellingham. **70 C4** NY7885.
Tarset Castle *Northumb. See Lanehead.*
Tarskavaig *High.* ***Village***, on Tarskavaig Bay, Skye, on W side of Sleat peninsula, 7m/11km N of Point of Sleat. **86 B4** NG5809.
Tarskavaig Bay *High.* ***Bay***, on W side of Sleat peninsula, 7m/11km N of Point of Sleat, Skye. **86 B4** NG5809.
Tarty Burn *Aber.* ***River***, rising to N of Newmachar and flowing N, then E into River Ythan estuary 1m/2km N of Newburgh. **91 H2** NJ9927.
Tarves *Aber.* ***Village***, 4m/7km NE of Oldmeldrum. **91 G1** NJ8631.
Tarvie *High.* ***Locality***, in Ross and Cromarty district, 3m/4km NW of Contin. **96 B6** NH4258.
Tarvie *P. & K.* ***Settlement***, on S facing hillside of Glen Brerachan, 6m/10km NE of Pitlochrie. **82 B1** NO0164.
Tarvin *Ches.* Population: 2843. ***Village***, 5m/9km E of Chester. **48 D6** SJ4967.
Tarvin Sands *Ches.* ***Hamlet***, to NE of Tarvin. **48 D6** SJ4967.
Tasburgh *Norf.* ***Village***, 8m/13km S of Norwich. **45 G6** TM2095.
Tasley *Shrop.* ***Settlement***, 2m/3km W of Bridgnorth. **39 F6** SO6993.
Taston *Oxon.* ***Hamlet***, 2m/3km N of Charlbury. **30 E6** SP3621.
Tat Bank *W.Mid.* ***Locality***, 1km SE of Oldbury. SO9989.
Tate Gallery *Cornw.* ***Other feature of interest***, at St. Ives, with over 200 post-war modern art exhibits and an optional guided tour. **2 C4** SW5140.
Tate Gallery *Gt.Lon.* ***Other feature of interest***, gallery built in 1897 by Sidney Smith, in City of Westminster 3m/4km S of Charing Cross. Collections of British painting from 16c to present day, with a particularly rich collection of foreign paintings and sculpture from 1880 to present day. Art Now gallery dedicated to contemporary art. The Clore Gallery was built in 1986 to house Turner bequest. TQ3078.
Tatenhill *Staffs.* ***Village***, 2m/4km W of Burton upon Trent. **40 E3** SK2022.
Tatenhill Common *Staffs.* ***Hamlet***, 1km W of Tatenhill. SK1922.
Tathall End *M.K.* ***Hamlet***, 4m/6km NW of Newport Pagnell. SP8246.
Tatham *Lancs.* ***Settlement***, 1km SW of Wennington. **56 B3** SD6069.
Tatham Fells *Lancs.* ***Open space***, low moorland to W of Burn Moor, 3m/5km S of High Bentham. **56 B3** SD6763.
Tathas Mhòr *W.Isles* ***Hill***, rising to over 300 metres to NW of Loch Claidh, 4m/6km S of head of Loch Shell, Isle of Lewis. **100 E7** NB2804.
Tathwell *Lincs.* ***Village***, 3m/5km S of Louth. **53 G4** TF3283.
Tatling End *Bucks.* ***Locality***, 3m/5km NW of Uxbridge. TQ0187.
Tatsfield *Surr.* ***Village***, 3m/5km NW of Westerham. **23 H6** TQ4157.
Tattenhall *Ches.* Population: 1854. ***Village***, 7m/12km SE of Chester. **48 D7** SJ4858.
Tattenhoe *M.K.* ***Settlement***, 3m/5km W of Bletchley. SP8334.
Tatterford *Norf.* ***Hamlet***, 4m/6km W of Fakenham. **44 C3** TF8628.
Tattersett *Norf.* ***Village***, 5m/8km W of Fakenham. **44 C3** TF8430.
Tattershall *Lincs.* ***Village***, 8m/13km SW of Horncastle. Remains of 15c castle (National Trust). **53 F7** TF2157.
Tattershall Bridge *Lincs.* ***Hamlet***, 2m/3km SW of Tattershall. **52 E7** TF1956.
Tattershall Castle *Lincs.* ***Castle***, 15c red-brick fortified tower (National Trust) on S side of Tattershall. Built by Ralph Cromwell, Lord Treasurer of England, and restored by Lord Curzon at beginning of 20c. **53 F7** TF2157.
Tattershall College *Lincs.* ***Historic house***, remains of 15c choir school (English Heritage) 4m/6km SE of Woodhall Spa. Built by Lord Cromwell, builder of Tattershall Castle. **53 F7** TF2157.
Tattershall Thorpe *Lincs.* ***Village***, 1m/2km NE of Tattershall. **53 F7** TF2157.
Tattingstone *Suff.* ***Village***, 5m/8km S of Ipswich. **35 F5** TM1337.
Tattingstone White Horse *Suff.* ***Hamlet***, 4m/7km S of Ipswich. TM1338.
Tatton Park *Ches.* ***Historic house***, in park (National Trust) with lake, Tatton Mere, to N of Knutsford. **49 G4** SJ7481.
Tatton Park *Ches.* ***Leisure/recreation***, National Trust property 5m/8km W of Wilmslow. Park boasts a finely furnished Georgian mansion with 60 acres of gardens, a medieval old hall and 18c farm as worked in 1930s. Various events are held throughout year, and 1000 acre deer park has lakes with wildfowl, fishing and sailing; notable for autumn colouring. **49 G4** SJ7580.
Tatworth *Som.* ***Village***, adjoining to N of South Chard, 2m/3km S of Chard. **8 C4** ST3205.
Tauchers *Moray* ***Locality***, 4m/6km W of Keith. **98 B5** NJ3749.
Taunton *Gt.Man.* ***Suburb***, 1km NW of Ashton-under-Lyne town centre. SD9200.
Taunton *Som.* Population: 55,855. ***Town***, county town and shopping centre in fertile Vale of Taunton Deane. County museum, civic centre; remains of Norman castle. **8 B2** ST2224.
Taunton Castle *Som.* ***Castle***, on S bank of River Tone at Taunton. Early Norman castle belonging to Bishops of Winchester. Only foundations now remain, along with a 13c hall. **8 B2** ST2224.
Tavay Beag (Gaelic form: Tabhaidh Bheag.) *W.Isles* ***Island***, small island on W side of Tabhaigh Mhòr. NB4122.
Tavay Mòr *W.Isles Anglicised form of Tabhaigh Mhòr, qv.*
Tavelty *Aber.* ***Settlement***, astride railway line, 1km N of Kintore. **91 F3** NJ7817.
Taverham *Norf.* Population: 9723. ***Locality***, 5m/9km NW of Norwich. **45 F4** TG1614.
Tavernspite *Pembs.* ***Hamlet***, 3m/4km SW of Whitland. **16 E3** SN1812.
Tavistock *Devon* Population: 10,222. ***Town***, market town on River Tavy on W edge of Dartmoor, 13m/21km N of Plymouth. Former copper-mining town. **4 E3** SX4874.
Tavy *Devon* ***River***, rising in heart of Dartmoor and flowing SW through Tavistock into River Tamar opposite Landulph. **4 E4** SX4461.
Tavy Cleave Settlements *Devon* ***Historic/prehistoric site***, comprising numerous settlements in this area of Dartmoor, 4m/6km NE of Mary Tavy. **6 D7** SX5583.
Taw *Devon* ***River***, rising on N Dartmoor and flowing N to Barnstaple, then W to join River Torridge and flow out into Barnstaple or Bideford Bay. **6 E4** SS4631.
Taw Bridge *Devon* ***Settlement***, on River Taw, 3m/4km SE of Winkleigh. **6 E5** SS6706.
Taw Green *Devon* ***Hamlet***, 4m/7km NE of Okehampton. **6 E6** SX6597.
Tawe ***River***, rising in Brecon Beacons National Park on E side of Llyn y Fan Fawr and flowing SW by Pontardawe and Clydach into Swansea Bay at Swansea. **27 H7** SS6691.
Tawstock *Devon* ***Village***, 2m/3km S of Barnstaple. **6 D3** SS5529.
Taxal *Derbys.* ***Hamlet***, 1m/2km S of Whaley Bridge. **50 C5** SK0079.
Tay ***River***, longest river in Scotland, rising on N side of Ben Lui and flowing generally E down Strath Fillan and Glen Dochart to Loch Tay, from where it issues as River Tay and flows past Aberfeldy, Dunkeld and Perth to Firth of Tay and E coast at Buddon Ness, E of Dundee. Total length 120m/193km. **82 C4** NO5429.
Tay Bridge ***Bridge***, 2m/3km rail bridge across Firth of Tay, between Dundee on N bank and Wormit on S. **82 E5** NO3927.
Tay Road Bridge ***Bridge***, 1m/2km road bridge across Firth of Tay, between Dundee and Newport-on-Tay, 2m/3km E of rail bridge. **83 F5** NO4129.
Tayburn *E.Ayr.* ***Settlement***, 4m/7km N of Galston. **74 D6** NS5143.
Taychreggan *Arg. & B.* ***Settlement***, 1km SE of Kilchrenan. **80 B5** NN0421.
Tayinloan *Arg. & B.* ***Village***, on W side of Kintyre, Argyll, 2m/4km S of Rhunahaorine Point. Ferry to Gigha. **72 E6** NR6946.
Taylor Rigg *Cumb.* ***Open space***, hillslope on W side of Sleightholme Moor, 7m/12km E of Kirkby Stephen. **61 K6** NY8907.
Taylorgill Force *Cumb.* ***Waterfall***, in Styhead Gill, 1km S of Seathwaite. **60 D5** NY2210.
Taylors Cross *Cornw.* ***Settlement***, 1km N of Kilkhampton. **6 A4** SS2612.
Taymouth Castle *P. & K.* ***Historic house***, early 19c mansion on S bank of River Tay, 1m/2km NE of Kenmore. **81 J3** NN7846.
Taynafead *Arg. & B.* ***Settlement***, 2m/3km S of Cladich. **80 B6** NN0918.
Taynish *Arg. & B.* ***Locality***, in Argyll, on W side of Loch Sween, just N of entrance to Linne Mhuirich. **73 F2** NR7283.
Taynish Island *Arg. & B.* ***Island***, off shore to SE of Taynish, 9m/14km W of Lochgilphead. NR7283.
Taynton *Glos.* ***Village***, 3m/5km S of Newent. **29 G6** SO7321.
Taynton *Oxon.* ***Village***, 1m/2km NW of Burford. **30 D7** SP2313.
Taynuilt *Arg. & B.* ***Village***, in Argyll, 1km SW of Bonawe. **80 B4** NN0031.
Tayock *Angus* ***Settlement***, 2m/3km NW of Montrose. **83 H2** NO6959.
Tayovullin *Arg. & B.* ***Settlement***, on W side of Loch Gruinart, Islay. **72 A3** NR2872.
Tayport *Fife* Population: 3346. ***Small town***, with harbour on S side of Firth of Tay, opposite Broughty Ferry. **83 F5** NO4528.
Tayvallich *Arg. & B.* ***Village***, in Knapdale, Argyll, on Loch a' Bhealaich, an inlet on W side of Loch Sween. **73 F2** NR7487.
Tea Green *Herts.* ***Settlement***, 3m/5km E of Luton. TL1323.
Tealby *Lincs.* ***Village***, 3m/5km E of Market Rasen. **52 E3** TF1590.
Tealing *Angus Alternative name for Kirkton of Tealing, qv.*
Tealing Dovecot and Earth House *Angus* ***Historic/prehistoric site***, fine example of dovecot (Historic Scotland) built in 1595, 5m/8km N of Dundee. Nearby is a well-preserved Iron Age earth house or souterrain. **83 F4** NO4138.
Team ***River***, rising N of Stanley and flowing circuitously N into River Tyne, 1m/2km W of Gateshead. Flows through Team Valley Trading Estate in SW part of Gateshead. **62 D1** NZ2362.
Team Valley *T. & W.* ***Suburb***, with trading estate, 2m/3km SW of Gateshead town centre. **71 H7** NZ2460.
Teampull Mholuidh *W.Isles* ***Ecclesiastical building***, 1km S of Butt of Lewis. Church dating from 12c and on site of much earlier church. **101 H1** NB5165.
Teampull na Trionaid *W.Isles* ***Ecclesiastical building***, ruined medieval church 1km NW of Cairinis, North Uist. **92 D5** NF8160.
Tean *I.o.S.* ***Island***, uninhabited island to W of St. Martin's across Tean Sound. **2 C1** SV9016.
Tean *Staffs.* ***River***, rising near Kingsley to N of Cheadle and flowing S, then SE into River Dove at Dove Bridge 1m/2km NE of Uttoxeter. SK1034.
Teanamachar *W.Isles* ***Settlement***, on W coast of Baleshare, SW of North Uist. **92 C5** NF7761.
Teangue *High.* ***Village***, on E coast of Sleat peninsula, Skye, 4m/7km NE of Ardvasar. **86 C4** NG6608.
Teaninich *High.* ***Locality***, on S side of Alness in Sutherland district. NH6569.
Teasses *Fife* ***Settlement***, 3m/5km N of Lower Largo. **83 F7** NO4008.
Teatle Water *Arg. & B.* ***River***, flowing W into Loch Awe, 3m/4km SW of Dalmally. **80 C5** NN1225.
Tebay *Cumb.* ***Village***, and former railway junction, 10m/16km NE of Kendal. **61 H6** NY6104.
Tebworth *Beds.* ***Village***, 4m/6km NW of Dunstable. **32 C6** SP9926.
Tedburn St. Mary *Devon* ***Village***, 7m/11km W of Exeter. **7 G6** SX8194.
Teddington *Glos.* ***Village***, 5m/7km E of Tewkesbury. **29 J5** SO9633.
Teddington *Gt.Lon.* ***Suburb***, in borough of Richmond upon Thames, on left bank of River Thames, which is tidal to this point (69m/110km from its mouth). **22 E4** TQ1671.
Tedstone Delamere *Here.* ***Hamlet***, 4m/6km NE of Bromyard. **29 F3** SO6958.
Tedstone Wafre *Here.* ***Village***, 3m/5km NE of Bromyard. **29 F3** SO6759.
Tees ***River***, rising on E slopes of Cross Fell in Milburn Forest and flowing SE through Cow Green Reservoir, by Middleton-in-Teesdale to Barnard Castle, then E to Stockton-on-Tees and Middlesbrough and NE into North Sea at Tees Mouth. Navigable to Stockton-on-Tees; tidal to Newsham, above Yarm. **62 E6** NZ5428.
Tees Bay *Hart.* ***Bay***, at mouth of River Tees, extending from Hartlepool to Redcar. **63 G3** NZ5528.
Tees Mouth *Hart.* ***Sea feature***, mouth of River Tees which enters into Tees Bay. **63 G4** NZ5426.
Teesdale *Dur.* ***Valley***, of River Tees, running SE from Forest-in-Teesdale to Barnard Castle. **62 A4** NY9126.
Teesport *R. & C.* ***Locality***, port and oil refinery on E bank of River Tees near its mouth, 4m/6km NE of Middlesbrough. NZ5423.
Teesside International Airport *Stock.* ***Airport/airfield***, 3m/4km W of Egglescliffe. **62 E5** NZ3713.
Teesville *Middbro.* ***Suburb***, in Eston, 3m/5km E of Middlesbrough town centre. NZ5419.
Teeton *Northants.* ***Hamlet***, 7m/12km NW of Northampton. **31 H1** SP6970.
Teffont *Wilts.* ***Locality***, parish, 7m/11km W of Wilton, containing villages of Teffont Evias and Teffont Magna. ST9832.
Teffont Evias *Wilts.* ***Hamlet***, forms parish of Teffont, along with Teffont Magna, 7m/11km W of Wilton. **9 J1** ST9931.
Teffont Magna *Wilts.* ***Village***, forms parish of Teffont, along with Teffont Evias, 7m/11km W of Wilton. **9 J1** ST9932.
Tegg's Nose Country Park *Ches.* ***Leisure/recreation***, 2m/3km SE of Macclesfield town centre. Hilltop offering panoramic views of Macclesfield as well as nature trails and guided walks. **49 J5** SJ9472.
Tegryn *Pembs.* ***Hamlet***, 4m/6km SE of Boncath. **17 F1** SN2233.
Tehidy Country Park *Cornw.* ***Leisure/recreation***, 1m/2km SW of Portreath. 250 acres of woodland including water gardens and 18c ornamental lake. **2 D4** SW6443.
Teifi ***River***, rising in Llyn Teifi, 4m/6km S of Cwmystwyth, it then flows SW by Pontrhydfendigaid and to W of Tregaron to Lampeter, Llanybydder and Llandysul, W to Newcastle Emlyn and Cardigan, then N into Cardigan Bay between Cemaes Head and Gwbert. **26 B4** SN1548.
Teifi Valley Railway *Cere.* ***Leisure/recreation***, narrow gauge tourist railway of over 2m/3km with terminus at Henllan Station, to N of Henllan and 3m/5km E of Newcastle Emlyn. **26 C4** SN3540.
Teigh *Rut.* ***Village***, 5m/7km N of Oakham. **42 B4** SK8616.
Teign *Devon* ***River***, rising on N Dartmoor. It flows generally E past Chagford and Dunsford, then S to Newton Abbot. Tidal estuary then flows E into English Channel at Teignmouth. **7 F7** SX9472.
Teign Village *Devon* ***Hamlet***, above Teign valley, 2m/3km NW of Chudleigh. SX8381.
Teigngrace *Devon* ***Village***, 2m/3km NW of Newton Abbot. **5 J3** SX8473.
Teignmouth *Devon* Population: 13,528. ***Town***, resort and former port at mouth of River Teign. Pier. Bridge connects with Shaldon on S side of estuary. **5 K3** SX9473.
Teindland Forest *Moray* ***Forest/woodland***, on E side of Teindland. **97 K6** NJ2655.
Teise ***River***, rising S of Royal Tunbridge Wells and flowing E through Lamberhurst, then N into River Beult. To SW of Marden it divides into two, E branch joining River Beult S of Hunton, and W branch joining it at Yalding. **14 C3** TQ6950.
Teith *Stir.* ***River***, formed by confluence of Garbh Uisge from Loch Lubnaig and Eas Gobhain from Loch Venachar at Callander, then running SE past Doune to River Forth 3m/4km NW of Stirling. **81 J7** NS7696.
Telegraph Hill *Sc.Bord.* ***Hill***, above North Sea coast, 4m/6km NW of St. Abb's Head. Height 571 feet or 174 metres. **77 G3** NT8570.
Telford *Tel. & W.* Population: 119,340. ***Town***, New Town designated 1963, comprising Dawley, Oakengates and Wellington, and including S bank of River Severn above and below Ironbridge. Ironbridge is a major tourist attraction. **39 F5** SJ6807.
Telford Bridge *Moray* ***Bridge***, cast iron bridge built in 1815 by Thomas Telford, spanning River Spey to W of Craigellachie. **97 K7** NJ2845.
Telford Memorial *D. & G.* ***Other feature of interest***, 1km SW of Bentpath, memorial to Thomas Telford who worked, when an apprentice, on bridge at Langholm. **69 J5** NY3089.
Telham *E.Suss.* ***Locality***, adjoining to SE of Battle. **14 C6** TQ7614.
Tellisford *Som.* ***Village***, 5m/8km N of Frome. **20 A6** ST8055.
Telscombe *E.Suss.* ***Village***, on South Downs, 3m/5km NW of Newhaven. Romano-British settlement to NW. **13 H6** TQ4003.

Telscombe Cliffs *E.Suss.* ***Settlement***, adjoining to NW of Peacehaven. **13 H6** TQ4001.
Teme ***River***, rising S of Newtown and flowing E to Ludlow, then SE into River Severn 2m/3km S of Worcester. **28 D1** SO8552.
Tempar *P. & K.* ***Settlement***, 1m/2km SE of Kinloch Rannoch. **81 H2** NN6857.
Templand *D. & G.* ***Village***, 2m/4km N of Lochmaben. **69 F5** NY0886.
Temple *Cornw.* ***Hamlet***, 6m/10km NE of Bodmin. **4 B3** SX1473.
Temple *Glas.* ***Suburb***, 4m/6km NW of Glasgow city centre. NS5469.
Temple *Midloth.* ***Village***, 3m/4km SW of Gorebridge. **76 B5** NT3158.
Temple Balsall *W.Mid.* ***Settlement***, 4m/7km SE of Solihull. Notable buildings include St. Mary's Church and The Old Hall with links to Knights Templars and former almshouses of The Court of the Lady Katherine Leveson. SP2076.
Temple Bar *Carmar.* ***Settlement***, 4m/6km SW of Llandeilo. SN5917.
Temple Bar *Cere.* ***Hamlet***, at crossroads, 5m/8km NW of Lampeter. **26 E3** SN5354.
Temple Bar *W.Suss.* ***Settlement***, 3m/4km NE of Chichester. SU8907.
Temple Bruer *Lincs.* ***Locality***, 3m/4km E of Welbourn. **52 D7** TF0053.
Temple Cloud *B. & N.E.Som.* Population: 1238. ***Village***, 3m/5km NW of Midsomer Norton. **19 K6** ST6257.
Temple Cowley *Oxon.* ***Suburb***, 3m/4km SW of Oxford city centre. SP5404.
Temple End *Cambs.* ***Locality***, E end of Great Wilbraham. TL5557.
Temple End *Suff.* ***Settlement***, 4m/6km N of Haverhill. TL6650.
Temple Ewell *Kent* ***Suburb***, 3m/4km NW of Dover. **15 H3** TR2844.
Temple Fields *Essex* ***Suburb***, 2m/3km NE of Harlow town centre. Site of Roman temple to N. TL4611.
Temple Grafton *Warks.* ***Village***, 5m/8km W of Stratford-upon-Avon. **30 C3** SP1254.
Temple Guiting *Glos.* ***Village***, 6m/10km W of Stow-on-the-Wold. **30 B6** SP0928.
Temple Hirst *N.Yorks.* ***Village***, on River Aire, 3m/5km NW of Snaith across river. **58 C7** SE6025.
Temple Manor *Med.* ***Historic house***, 13c flint commandery (English Heritage) of Knights Templars beside River Medway to S of Strood. **24 D5** TQ7368.
Temple Mills *Gt.Lon.* ***Suburb***, in borough of Waltham Forest, 1km SW of Leyton. TQ3785.
Temple Newsam *W.Yorks.* ***Historic house***, Tudor and Jacobean house and museum in park, 4m/6km E of Leeds city centre. **57 J6** SE3532.
Temple Normanton *Derbys.* ***Village***, 3m/5km SE of Chesterfield. **51 G6** SK4167.
Temple Sowerby *Cumb.* ***Village***, 6m/10km NW of Appleby-in-Westmorland. **61 H4** NY6127.
Temple Wood Stone Circle *Arg. & B.* ***Historic/prehistoric site***, adjoining to E of Slockavullin, 6m/10km N of Lochgilphead. Thirteen stones from original twenty forming a circle of 25 feet across. A stone burial cist is at centre. Bronze Age. **73 G1** NR8297.
Templecombe *Som.* ***Village***, 4m/7km S of Wincanton. **9 G2** ST7022.
Templehall *Fife* ***Suburb***, NW district of Kirkcaldy. NT2693.
Templeton *Devon* ***Village***, 4m/7km W of Tiverton. **7 G4** SS8814.
Templeton *Pembs.* ***Village***, 2m/3km S of Narberth. **16 E3** SN1111.
Templeton Bridge *Devon* ***Hamlet***, 1km NW of Templeton. **7 G4** SS8814.
Templetown *Dur.* ***Suburb***, S district of Consett. NZ1050.
Templewood *Angus* ***Settlement***, 2m/3km N of Brechin. **83 H1** NO6162.
Tempsford *Beds.* ***Village***, 3m/4km N of Sandy. **32 E3** TL1652.
Ten Acres *W.Mid.* ***Suburb***, 3m/5km S of Birmingham city centre. SP0581.
Ten Mile Bank *Norf.* ***Village***, on River Great Ouse, 4m/7km S of Downham Market. **43 J6** TL6096.
Tenbury Wells *Worcs.* Population: 2219. ***Small town***, market town on River Teme. Developed as spa in 19c. Burford House Gardens contains National Clematis Collection. **28 E2** SO5968.
Tenby (Dinbych-y-pysgod). *Pembs.* Population: 5619. ***Small town***, resort on Carmarthen Bay, 9m/15km E of Pembroke. Extensive sands to N and S. Part of the town walls survives. Scant remains of medieval castle. **16 E4** SN1300.
Tenby Castle *Pembs.* ***Castle***, in Tenby. Ruins of late Norman tower gate, with later alterations. **16 E4** SN1400.
Tenby Roads *Pembs.* ***Sea feature***, waters to N of Tenby. **16 E4** SN1300.
Tendring *Essex* ***Village***, 6m/10km NW of Clacton-on-Sea. **35 F6** TM1424.
Tendring Green *Essex* ***Hamlet***, 6m/10km NW of Clacton-on-Sea. TM1425.
Tendring Heath *Essex* ***Hamlet***, 4m/6km NW of Thorpe-le-Soken. TM1326.
Tenga *Arg. & B.* ***Settlement***, 4m/6km NW of Salen, at head of Glen Aros, Mull. **79 G3** NM5145.
Tenpenny Heath *Essex* ***Locality***, 2m/4km N of Brightlingsea. TM0820.
Tenterden *Kent* Population: 6803. ***Small town***, former medieval wool town with fine half-timbered houses and attractive 18c buildings, 10m/16km SW of Ashford. **14 D4** TQ8833.
Tents Muirs *Fife* ***Forest/woodland***, afforested area between Leuchars and Firth of Tay at Tentsmuir Point, 3m/4km E of Tayport. **83 F5** NO4825.
Tentsmuir Point *Fife* ***Coastal feature***, 3m/4km E of Tayport. Nature reserve S of point, behind Tentsmuir Sands. **83 G5** NO4825.
Ter *Essex* ***River***, rising between Great Dunmow and Braintree, and flowing SE into River Chelmer 6m/9km E of Chelmsford. **34 B7** TL7909.
Terally *D. & G.* ***Settlement***, adjacent to Terally Point, 3m/4km N of Drummore, on W side of Luce Bay. **64 B6** NX1240.
Terfyn *Conwy* ***Hamlet***, 2m/4km W of Abergele. SH9177.
Terling *Essex* ***Village***, 3m/5km W of Witham. **34 B7** TL7715.
Tern ***River***, rising near Madeley and flowing SW through Market Drayton, then S into River Severn between Atcham and Wroxeter. **39 F2** SJ5509.
Tern *Tel. & W.* ***Settlement***, 2m/3km E of High Ercall. SJ6216.
Ternhill *Shrop.* ***Hamlet***, 3m/5km W of Market Drayton. **39 F2** SJ6332.
Terpersie Castle *Aber.* ***Castle***, small ruined castle 3m/5km NW of Alford. **90 D2** NJ5420.
Terregles *D. & G.* ***Hamlet***, 3m/4km W of Dumfries. **65 K3** NX9277.
Terrick *Bucks.* ***Settlement***, 2m/3km W of Wendover. SP8308.
Terriers *Bucks.* ***Suburb***, NE district of High Wycombe. SU8794.
Terrington *N.Yorks.* ***Village***, 7m/11km W of Malton. **58 C2** SE6770.
Terrington Marsh *Norf.* ***Marsh/bog***, marshland on S side of The Wash, 2m/3km N of Terrington St. Clement. **43 J3** TF5323.
Terrington St. Clement *Norf.* Population: 2288. ***Village***, 4m/7km W of King's Lynn. **43 J3** TF5520.
Terrington St. John *Norf.* ***Village***, 6m/10km NE of Wisbech. **43 J4** TF5315.
Terry's Green *Warks.* ***Settlement***, on S side of Earlswood Lakes, 3m/5km W of Hockley Heath. SP1073.
Tervieside *Moray* ***Settlement***, 3m/5km NE of Tomnavoulin. **89 K1** NJ2330.
Terwick Common *W.Suss.* ***Hamlet***, 1km NE of Rogate and 4m/7km E of Petersfield. SU8124.
Test ***River***, rising at Ashe, near Overton, and flowing SW to Stockbridge, then S to Totton and into Southampton Water at its confluence with River Itchen. Chalk river, famous for trout-fishing. **10 E2** SU4209.
Teston *Kent* ***Village***, on River Medway, 4m/6km W of Maidstone. Site of Roman villa to W. **14 C2** TQ7053.
Testwood *Hants.* ***Suburb***, 1m/2km NW of Totton town centre. **10 E3** SU3514.
Tetbury *Glos.* Population: 4618. ***Small town***, attractive town in Cotswolds, 5m/8km NW of Malmesbury. Holds annual Woolsack Day race up Gumstool Hill. **20 B2** ST8993.
Tetbury Upton *Glos.* ***Settlement***, 1m/2km N of Tetbury. **20 B2** ST8895.
Tetchill *Shrop.* ***Village***, 2m/3km S of Ellesmere. **38 C2** SJ3932.
Tetcott *Devon* ***Village***, near confluence of Rivers Claw and Tamar, 5m/7km S of Holsworthy. **6 B6** SX3396.
Tetford *Lincs.* ***Village***, 6m/9km NE of Horncastle. **53 G5** TF3374.
Tetley *N.Lincs.* ***Settlement***, on N side of group of lakes, 1m/2km S of Crowle. SE7711.
Tetney *Lincs.* ***Village***, 5m/8km S of Cleethorpes. **53 G2** TA3100.
Tetney Lock *Lincs.* ***Hamlet***, on disused Louth Navigation Canal, 2m/3km E of Tetney. **53 G2** TA3402.
Tetsworth *Oxon.* ***Village***, 3m/5km SW of Thame. **21 K1** SP6801.
Tettenhall *W.Mid.* ***Suburb***, 3m/4km NW of Wolverhampton town centre. **40 A5** SJ8700.
Tettenhall Wood *W.Mid.* ***Locality***, adjoining to S of Tettenhall. **40 A6** SO8799.
Tetworth *Cambs.* ***Settlement***, 4m/6km NE of Sandy. **33 F3** TL2153.
Teuchan *Aber.* ***Settlement***, 2m/3km N of Cruden Bay. **91 J1** NK0839.
Teversal *Notts.* ***Village***, 2m/3km N of Sutton in Ashfield. **51 G6** SK4861.
Teversham *Cambs.* ***Village***, 3m/5km E of Cambridge. Cambridge Airport to W of village. **33 H3** TL4958.
Teviot *Sc.Bord.* ***River***, rising 6m/9km E of Eskdalemuir. River flows NE by Teviothead, Hawick and Roxburgh to River Tweed, SW of Kelso. **70 C1** NT7233.
Teviotdale *Sc.Bord.* ***Valley***, carrying River Teviot, running NE from Teviothead, through Hawick, to Ancrum Bridge, 1km SE of Ancrum. **69 K3** NT5317.
Teviothead *Sc.Bord.* ***Village***, in Teviotdale, 8m/13km SW of Hawick. **69 K3** NT4005.
Tewel *Aber.* ***Settlement***, 3m/5km W of Stonehaven. **91 G6** NO8285.
Tewin *Herts.* Population: 1682. ***Village***, 4m/6km NW of Hertford. **33 F7** TL2714.
Tewinbury *Herts.* ***Settlement***, 2m/3km E of Welwyn Garden City. TL2614.
Tewinwater *Herts.* ***Locality***, 2m/3km NE of Welwyn Garden City. TL2514.
Tewitfield *Lancs.* ***Hamlet***, 2m/4km NE of Carnforth, at N end of navigable part of Lancaster Canal. SD5273.
Tewkesbury *Glos.* Population: 9488. ***Small town***, at confluence of Rivers Severn and Avon, 8m/12km NW of Cheltenham. Famous abbey church. Many interesting buildings in town centre. Site of Wars of the Roses battle, 1471, to S. **29 H5** SO8932.
Tewkesbury Abbey *Glos.* ***Ecclesiastical building***, in centre of Tewkesbury. Founded in 1102, it took only 15 years to build, with stone being imported from Caen in Normandy. It is the second-largest parish church in England and has the largest Norman tower in Europe. Impressive interior with many tombs and monuments. The decorated choir contains the 16c Milton organ, the oldest organ is use in the country. **29 H5** SO8932.
Texa *Arg. & B.* ***Island***, off S coast of Islay opposite Laphroaig. **72 B6** NR3943.
Teynham *Kent* Population: 3038. ***Village***, 3m/5km E of Sittingbourne. **25 F5** TQ9562.
Teynham Street *Kent* ***Settlement***, 1m/2km NE of Teynham. TQ9663.
Thackley *W.Yorks.* ***Suburb***, 4m/6km N of Bradford city centre. SE1738.
Thackley End *W.Yorks.* ***Suburb***, adjoining to W of Thackley, 2m/3km NE of Shipley town centre. SE1738.
Thackthwaite *Cumb.* ***Locality***, 7m/11km W of Penrith and 3m/5km W of Pooley Bridge. NY4225.
Thainston *Aber.* ***Locality***, comprises Upper Thainston and Nether Thainston, 1m/2km NW of Fettercairn. **90 E7** NO6375.
Thainstone *Aber.* ***Settlement***, with hotel on W side of River Don, 2m/3km S of Inverurie. **91 F3** NJ7618.
Thakeham *W.Suss.* ***Village***, 3m/5km N of Washington. **12 E5** TQ1017.
Thame ***River***, rising E of Aylesbury and flowing SW into River Thames 1km S of Dorchester. **32 B7** SU5793.
Thame *Oxon.* Population: 10,806. ***Town***, attractive old market town on River Thame, 9m/14km SW of Aylesbury. Airport at Haddenham, 3m/4km NE. **22 A1** SP7005.
Thames (Upper stretch also known as (River) Isis.) ***River***, major river of southern England, rising 3m/5km SW of Cirencester as River Thames or Isis and flowing generally E through Oxford and Reading, past Henley-on-Thames, Maidenhead and Windsor, then through London, and into North Sea at The Nore, between Shoeburyness and Sheerness. Tributaries include Leach at Lechlade, Cherwell at Oxford, Kennet at Reading, Thame at Dorchester, Wey at Weybridge, Mole at East Molesey and Lea in E end of London. Despite its origin and length, River Thames is synonymous with London. It divides the capital in two, is crossed by numerous bridges, and along its embankments are some of London's most famous landmarks. It is tidal to Teddington, and originally provided transport link vital for industrial and commercial development of London. While London's East End docks have been transformed, River Thames remains a major artery, forming Port of London from London Bridge to Blackwall. **24 D4** TQ9580.
Thames Ditton *Surr.* ***Suburb***, on S bank of River Thames, 1m/2km W of Surbiton. **22 E5** TQ1667.
Thames Haven *Thur.* ***Locality***, at Coryton, on N bank of River Thames. **24 D3** TQ7481.
Thamesmead *Gt.Lon.* ***Suburb***, on SE edge of Erith Marshes, 11m/18km E of Charing Cross. **23 H3** TQ4779.
Thanington *Kent* ***Suburb***, SW district of Canterbury. **15 G2** TR1356.
Thankerton *S.Lan.* ***Village***, 4m/7km W of Biggar. **75 H7** NS9738.
Tharston *Norf.* ***Village***, 2m/3km E of Forncett St. Mary. **45 F6** TM1894.
Thatcham *W.Berks.* Population: 20,726. ***Suburb***, 3m/5km E of Newbury. **21 J5** SU5167.
Thatcher Rock *Torbay* ***Island***, rock off N coast of Tor Bay, 1km SW of Hope's Nose. SX9462.
Thatto Heath *Mersey.* ***Suburb***, 2m/3km SW of St. Helens town centre. **48 E3** SJ4993.
Thaxted *Essex* Population: 1899. ***Small town***, 6m/10km SE of Saffron Walden. 16c guildhall. Many old houses. Centre for Morris dancing. **33 K5** TL6130.
The Aird *High.* ***Coastal feature***, small peninsula separating Loch Treaslane from Loch Snizort Beag, 4m/6km SE of Lyndale Point, Skye. **93 K6** NG3952.
The Aird *High.* ***Coastal feature***, promontory on Skye, 2m/3km E of Rubha Hunish. **93 K4** NG4275.
The Aird *High.* ***Locality***, fertile district in Inverness district, S of Beauly. **96 C7** NH5642.
The Airde *High.* ***Inland physical feature***, large headland on E side of Loch Shin opposite Arscraig. **103 H7** NC5213.
The Alley *W.Berks.* ***Hamlet***, 3m/5km NE of Newbury. SU5170.
The Ard *Arg. & B.* ***Coastal feature***, headland on S side of Port Ellen harbour, Islay. **72 B6** NR3644.
The Ayres *I.o.M.* ***Coastal feature***, flat and barren coastal strip between Rue Point and Point of Ayre. Visitors centre exhibitions on ecology, geology and history of The Ayres. Nature trails. **54 D3** NX4303.
The Bage *Here.* ***Settlement***, 1m/2km NW of Dorstone. **28 B4** SO2943.
The Balloch *Moray* ***Open space***, hilly tract 3m/5km SE of Keith. **98 C6** NJ4748.
The Bank *Ches.* ***Settlement***, 2m/3km N of Kidsgrove. SJ8457.
The Bank *Shrop.* ***Locality***, adjoining to W of Much Wenlock. SO6199.
The Banking *Aber.* ***Settlement***, 3m/5km SE of Fyvie. **91 F1** NJ7833.
The Bar *Cere.* ***Coastal feature***, spit at mouth of Rivers Rheidol and Ystwyth, to S of Aberystwyth. **36 E7** SN5780.
The Bar *Gwyn.* ***Coastal feature***, detached sand bar at SW end of Menai Strait. **46 C6** SH4160.
The Bar *Gwyn.* ***Coastal feature***, spit extending N from S side of Mawddach estuary mouth. **37 F4** SH6014.
The Bar *High.* ***Coastal feature***, sandy spit extending 2m/3km from W end of Culbin Forest. **97 G5** NH9159.
The Bar *W.Suss.* ***Settlement***, 1m/2km S of Southwater. **12 E4** TQ1623.
The Begwns *Powys* ***Mountain***, 4m/7km NW of Hay-on-Wye. Height 1361 feet or 415 metres. **28 A4** SO1544.
The Belfry *Warks.* ***Other building***, hotel complex 4m/6km SE of Sutton Coldfield town centre. Championship golf course has been venue for Ryder Cup. **40 D6** SP1895.
The Beth Chatto Gardens *Essex* ***Garden***, 20c landscaped garden in Elmstead Market, 3m/4km E of Colchester. Plants grow under different conditions; water, shade and Mediterranean gardens. **34 E6** TM0523.
The Biggins *Cambs.* ***Settlement***, 1km SW of Manea. TL4788.

The Bin *Aber.* ***Mountain***, surrounded by The Bin Forest, 3m/5km NW of Huntly. Height 1027 feet or 313 metres. **98 D6** NJ5043.
The Bin Forest *Aber.* ***Forest/woodland***, 2m/3km NW of Huntly, surrounding two rounded summits, The Bin at 1027 feet or 313 metres and Ordiquhill at 817 feet or 249 metres. **98 D6** NJ5143.
The Binn *Fife* ***Locality***, flat-topped hill area above steep escarpment, overlooking Burntisland and Firth of Forth. **76 A2** NT2387.
The Binns (Also known as House of the Binns.) *W.Loth.* ***Historic house***, National Trust for Scotland property, dating in parts from 15c but mainly from 17c, 4m/6km E of Linlithgow. **75 J3** NT0578.
The Birks *Aber.* ***Settlement***, 2m/3km S of Echt. **91 F4** NJ7402.
The Blythe *Staffs.* ***Hamlet***, 4m/7km SW of Uttoxeter. SK0428.
The Bog *Shrop.* ***Settlement***, 6m/10km N of Bishop's Castle. **38 C6** SO3597.
The Bore *Ork.* ***Sea feature***, channel to N of Mull Head, Papa Westray. **106 D2** HY4956.
The Bourne *Surr.* ***Suburb***, S district of Farnham. **22 B7** SU8444.
The Brack *Arg. & B.* ***Mountain***, in Argyll 2m/3km W of Ardgartan on W shore of Loch Long. Height 2578 feet or 786 metres. **80 D7** NN2403.
The Braes *High.* ***Open space***, hillslope below E slopes of Ben Lee, 1km N of Peinchorran, Skye. **86 B1** NG5234.
The Brampton *Staffs.* ***Suburb***, 1km NE of Newcastle-under-Lyme town centre. SJ8546.
The Bratch *Staffs.* ***Hamlet***, 4m/7km SW of Wolverhampton. **40 A6** SO8693.
The Brisons *Cornw.* ***Island***, two island rocks 1km SW of Cape Cornwall. Infamous for causing shipwrecks. **2 A5** SW3431.
The Broad *Here.* ***Settlement***, 1m/2km N of Leominster. SO4960.
The Broads *Norf. See Norfolk Broads.*
The Bruach *Moray* ***Mountain***, on S side of Glen Avon, 6m/10km E of Loch Avon. Height 2342 feet or 714 metres. **89 J4** NJ1105.
The Brushes *Derbys.* ***Locality***, 3m/4km N of Chesterfield. SK3775.
The Bryn (Llangattock nigh Usk or Llangatwg Dyffryn Wysg.) *Mon.* ***Village***, 3m/5km SE of Abergavenny. **19 G1** SO3309.
The Buck ***Mountain***, on border of Aberdeenshire and Moray, 3m/4km SE of Cabrach. Height 2365 feet or 721 metres. **90 C2** NJ4123.
The Burf *Worcs.* ***Hamlet***, on W bank of River Severn, 3m/4km S of Stourport-on-Severn. **29 H2** SO8167.
The Burn *Aber.* ***Settlement***, 2m/3km N of Edzell. **90 D7** NO5971.
The Butts *Glos.* ***Suburb***, 4m/7km SE of Gloucester. SO8916.
The Butts *Som.* ***Suburb***, SW district of Frome. ST7647.
The Cairnwell ***Mountain***, on border of Aberdeenshire and Perth & Kinross, 5m/8km N of Spittal of Glenshee. Munro: height 3060 feet or 933 metres. **89 J7** NO1377.
The Calf *Cumb.* ***Mountain***, on Brant Fell, 3m/5km N of Sedbergh. Height 2217 feet or 676 metres. **61 H7** SD6697.
The Camp *Glos.* ***Hamlet***, 5m/8km NE of Stroud. **20 C1** SO9109.
The Camp *Herts.* ***Suburb***, 3m/4km SE of St. Albans city centre. TL1606.
The Carracks *Cornw.* ***Island***, two small islands off N coast, 1km W of Carn Naun Point. **2 B4** SW4640.
The Carrs *N.Yorks.* ***Valley***, flood plain of River Hertford to S and SW of Scarborough, comprising, W to E, Carrs of Heslerton, Sherburn Carr, Binnington Carr, Willerby Carr, Seamer Carr, Folkton Carr and Flotmanby Carrs. **59 F2** SE9879.
The Castle *Shet.* ***Coastal feature***, stack on E coast of Mainland, 1m/2km SE of North Roe. **108 C4** HU3787.
The Cerne Giant *Dorset* ***Historic/prehistoric site***, to N of Cerne Abbas, on Giant Hill is Romano-British figure (National Trust), of a man cut in the chalk, 180 feet or 55 metres in length. **9 F4** ST6601.
The Chancellor *High.* ***Inland physical feature***, mountain ridge rising to over 970 metres, on N side of Glen Coe, 3m/4km SW of Kinlochleven. **80 C2** NN1658.
The Chart *Kent* ***Locality***, 2m/3km S of Brasted. TQ4652.
The Chequer *Wrex.* ***Settlement***, 3m/5km W of Whitchurch. **38 D1** SJ4940.
The Chevin *W.Yorks.* ***Hill***, on steep ridge to S of Otley, with country park and viewpoint. Height 925 feet or 282 metres. **57 H5** SE1944.
The Cheviot (Also known as Great Cheviot.) *Northumb.* ***Mountain***, highest part of Cheviot Hills range. Height 2673 feet or 815 metres. **70 E1** NT9020.
The Chick *Cornw.* ***Island***, rock islet, National Trust property, off Kelsey Head, 3m/5km W of Newquay. SW7661.
The Chuckery *W.Mid.* ***Suburb***, to E of Walsall town centre. SP0298.
The Church House *Devon* ***Historic house***, early 15c house (National Trust) at Widecombe in the Moor. **5 H3** SX7176.
The City *Beds.* ***Settlement***, adjoining to N of Colmworth. TL1159.
The City *Bucks.* ***Village***, 2m/3km E of Stokenchurch. **22 A2** SU7896.
The City *Suff.* ***Settlement***, 2m/3km SW of Beccles. TM3988.
The Clifts *Shet.* ***Coastal feature***, steep cliffs on N side of Ronas Voe, Mainland. **108 C4** HU3281.
The Cobbler *Arg. & B. Alternative name for Ben Arthur, qv.*
The Colonel's Bed *Aber.* ***Inland physical feature***, rock cut through by Ey Burn, 1m/2km S of Inverey. **89 H6** NO0887.
The Common *Wilts. See Broughton Common.*
The Common *Wilts.* ***Hamlet***, 1m/2km NE of Brinkworth and 3m/5km NW of Wootton Bassett. SU0285.
The Common *Wilts.* ***Village***, in parish of Winterslow, 7m/11km E of Salisbury. **10 D1** SU2432.
The Corner *Shrop.* ***Settlement***, 3m/5km N of Craven Arms. SO4387.
The Courts *Wilts.* ***Garden***, National Trust property in Holt, 3m/4km N of Trowbridge. Seven acres of gardens featuring topiary hedges, lily ponds and an arboretum, around an 18c house. **20 B5** ST8661.
The Coyles of Muick *Aber.* ***Mountain***, with rock outcrops on E side, 4m/6km SW of Ballater. Height 1971 feet or 601 metres. **90 B5** NO3291.
The Craggan *High.* ***Mountain***, with rock outcrops to SE, 3m/5km S of Kildonan Lodge. Height 1581 feet or 482 metres. **104 E7** NC9016.
The Craigs *High.* ***Locality***, in Sutherland district, at foot of Strath Chuilionaich, 8m/13km W of Bonar Bridge. **96 B2** NH4791.
The Cronk *I.o.M.* ***Village***, near W coast, 4m/6km NE of Kirk Michael. **54 C4** SC3495.
The Curr *Sc.Bord.* ***Mountain***, in Cheviot Hills, 4m/6km SE of Kirk Yetholm. Height 1850 feet or 564 metres. **70 D1** NT8523.
The Curraghs *I.o.M.* ***Open space***, area of marsh and woodland, 2m/3km W of Sulby. The Curraghs Wildlife Park located here. **54 C4** SC3694.
The Cylinders *W.Suss.* ***Locality***, adjoining to S of Fernhurst, 3m/5km S of Haslemere. SU8928.
The Deeps *Shet.* ***Sea feature***, sea area to E of Skelda Ness, Mainland. **109 C8** HU3241.
The Deil's Heid *Angus* ***Coastal feature***, rocky headland 2m/3km NE of Arbroath. **83 H3** NO6741.
The Delph *Suff.* ***Open space***, fenland 1m/2km S of Lakenheath. **44 B7** TL7080.
The Delves *W.Mid.* ***Suburb***, 3m/5km NE of West Bromwich town centre. SP0196.
The Den *High.* ***Valley***, carrying Allt Dubhach on Black Isle NE to valley of Newhall Burn, 1m/2km W of Udale Bay. **96 D5** NH6863.
The Den *N.Ayr.* ***Settlement***, 2m/4km NE of Dalry and 2m/4km SW of Beith. **74 B5** NS3251.
The Dene *Dur.* ***Locality***, 2m/3km N of Consett. NZ1154.
The Devil's Bridge *Cumb.* ***Bridge***, 15c stone bridge over River Lune in Kirkby Lonsdale, considered finest bridge in N of England. No longer used for wheeled traffic. SD6178.
The Devil's Frying Pan *Cornw. See Cadgwith.*
The Devil's Point *Aber.* ***Mountain***, peak at SE end of Cairn Toul, in Cairngorm Mountains. Munro: height 3293 feet or 1004 metres. **89 G5** NN9795.
The Dicker *E.Suss.* ***Village***, 3m/4km W of Hailsham. **13 J6** TQ5509.
The Down *Shrop.* ***Hamlet***, 3m/4km SW of Bridgnorth. SO6890.
The Drums *Angus* ***Settlement***, in Glen Clova, 3m/5km SE of Clova. **82 E1** NO3569.
The Dukeries *Notts.* ***Forest/woodland***, area at N end of Sherwood Forest, 2m/3km S of Worksop. **51 H5** SK5775.
The Eaves *Glos.* ***Locality***, 3m/4km NW of Lydney. **19 K1** SO6006.
The Edge *Derbys.* ***Inland physical feature***, 1m/2km mountain edge of cliffs, running W to E, at N end of Kinder Scout, at a height of 2034 feet or 620 metres. **50 C4** SK0789.
The Eileans *N.Ayr.* ***Island***, islets in Millport Bay at S end of Great Cumbrae. NS1654.
The Engine *Lincs.* ***Locality***, 2m/3km SE of Crowland. TF2508.
The Faither *Shet.* ***Coastal feature***, headland on NW coast of Mainland on W side of entrance to Ronas Voe. **108 B4** HU2585.
The Fens ***Large natural feature***, flat, low-lying, fertile part of E England draining into The Wash and bounded by North Sea and, roughly, a line drawn from Skegness through Woodhall Spa, Sleaford, Bourne, Huntingdon, Cambridge, Newmarket, Brandon, Downham Market and King's Lynn. TF4010.
The Fiddler *Cornw.* ***Historic/prehistoric site***, at St. Breock Downs, 3m/5km NE of St. Columb Major. **3 G2** SW9368.
The Flatt *Cumb.* ***Settlement***, on edge of woodland, 3m/5km NE of Oakshaw Ford. **70 A6** NY5578.
The Fleece Inn *Worcs.* ***Historic house***, 14c farmhouse, largely unaltered, in Bretforton, 3m/5km E of Evesham. Became licensed house in 1848. **30 B4** SP0943.
The Folly *Herts.* ***Settlement***, 1km NW of Wheathampstead. **32 E7** TL1614.
The Foot *Ork.* ***Coastal feature***, rocky promontory on SE coast of Shapinsay. **107 E6** HY5315.
The Foreland (Also known as Handfast Point.) *Dorset* ***Coastal feature***, headland at SW end of Poole Bay, 3m/5km NE of Swanage. **10 B6** SZ0582.
The Forest of Pendle *Lancs.* ***Open space***, moorland between Pendle Hill and Pendle Water valley, 3m/4km W of Nelson. **56 D6** SD8238.
The Forest of Trawden *Lancs.* ***Open space***, moorland area, SE of Trawden and Colne. **56 E6** SD9338.
The Forge *Here.* ***Settlement***, 4m/6km NE of Kington. SO3459.
The Forstal *E.Suss.* ***Settlement***, 4m/6km SW of Royal Tunbridge Wells. TQ5435.
The Forstal *Kent* ***Hamlet***, adjoining to S of Mersham, 3m/5km SE of Ashford. TR0439.
The Frenchies *Hants.* ***Settlement***, 3m/4km W of Romsey. SU3022.
The Friars *Kent See Aylesford Priory.*
The Fungle Road *Aber.* ***Other feature of interest***, track across mountains of Forest of Birse, N from Birse Castle near Ballochan, to Birsemore, S of River Dee from Aboyne. **90 D5** NO5192.
The Galt *Ork.* ***Coastal feature***, point at NW extremity of Shapinsay, on W side of Veantrow Bay. **106 D5** HY4821.
The Garden House *Devon* ***Garden***, at Buckland Monachorum, 4m/6km S of Tavistock. 8-acres, with terraced and walled gardens, surrounding ruins of 16c vicarage and medieval gatehouse. **4 E4** SX4968.
The Giants Stones *Shet.* ***Historic/prehistoric site***, situated on Grind Hill just E of Hamnavoe, Mainland. Two stones, 6 feet and 8 feet tall, remains of former three stone alignment. **108 B4** HU2480.
The Glenkens *D. & G.* ***Locality***, N part of Stewartry district, comprising parishes of Balmaclellan, Carsphairn, Dalry, and Kells. NX5887.
The Gloup *Ork.* ***Other feature of interest***, collapsed sea cave famous for strange gurgling noises made by movement of tide, 1m/2km S of Mull Head, Mainland. **107 E7** HY5907.
The Goose *Cornw.* ***Island***, rock islet off East Pentire Point, 3m/4km W of Newquay. SW7761.
The Grange *Hants.* ***Historic house***, Neo-classical 18c house (English Heritage) resembling Greek temple, 1m/2km S of Northington. **11 G1** SU5636.
The Grange *Shrop.* ***Settlement***, to N of Ellesmere. **38 C2** SJ3935.
The Green *Arg. & B.* ***Settlement***, on N coast Tiree, 3m/5km NE of Rubha Chràiginis. **78 A3** NL9648.
The Green *Beds.* ***Settlement***, adjoining to SW of Whipsnade. TL0017.
The Green *Cumb.* ***Hamlet***, 3m/5km N of Millom. SD1784.
The Green *Essex* ***Hamlet***, 2m/4km SE of Braintree. TL7719.
The Green *Flints.* ***Settlement***, adjoining to W of Northop. SJ2468.
The Green *Wilts.* ***Hamlet***, to NW of East Knoyle, 4m/6km SE of Mere. **9 H1** ST8731.
The Greyfriars *Worcs.* ***Historic house***, 15c timber-framed house (National Trust) with later additions, in Worcester city centre. Now restored and refurbished. **29 H3** SO8555.
The Grove *Worcs.* ***Hamlet***, 1m/2km E of Upton upon Severn across River Severn. SO8640.
The Gutter *Read.* ***Suburb***, W district of Reading. SU6674.
The Hague *Gt.Man.* ***Locality***, 1m/2km S of Hollingworth. SK0094.
The Haven *Lincs.* ***Sea feature***, estuary of River Witham below Boston. **43 G2** TF3639.
The Haven *W.Suss.* ***Settlement***, 3m/5km N of Billingshurst. **12 D3** TQ0830.
The Hawk Conservancy *Hants.* ***Leisure/recreation***, largest birds of prey centre in S England, 3m/4km W of Andover, housing all kinds of birds of prey from owls to eagles. Regular demonstrations and opportunity to handle some of the birds. **21 G7** SU3045.
The Head *Pembs.* ***Coastal feature***, headland at W end of Skokholm Island. **16 A4** SM7204.
The Heath *Staffs.* ***Suburb***, NW district of Uttoxeter. SK0834.
The Heath *Suff.* ***Settlement***, 6m/9km SW of Ipswich. TM1236.
The Heath *Worcs.* ***Locality***, 2m/3km W of Kidderminster. SO8076.
The Herberts *V. of Glam.* ***Hamlet***, 2m/3km S of Cowbridge. SS9972.
The Hermitage *P. & K.* ***Forest/woodland***, area of forest (National Trust for Scotland) between River Tay and Ballinloan Burn, near to Falls of the Braan, 1m/2km SW of Dunkeld. Interesting walks and a delightful folly, Ossian's Hall, in gorge of River Braan. **82 B3** NO0042.
The Hermitage *Surr.* ***Settlement***, 1m/2km S of Walton on the Hill. **23 F6** TQ2253.
The Herne *Cambs.* ***Open space***, fenland 6m/10km SE of Peterborough city centre. **43 F7** TL2490.
The Highlands *E.Suss.* ***Suburb***, N district of Bexhill. TQ7309.
The Hill *Cumb.* ***Village***, 2m/3km N of Millom. SD1783.
The Hirsel *Sc.Bord.* ***Historic house***, seat of Douglas-Home family, 1m/2km NW of Coldstream. **77 G6** NT8240.
The Hobbins *Shrop.* ***Settlement***, 1m/2km E of Bridgnorth. SO7393.
The Hoe *High.* ***Hill***, near W coast of Skye, 6m/10km NW of Idrigill Point. Height 764 feet or 233 metres. **93 G7** NG1641.
The Hoe *W.Isles* ***Hill***, highest point on Pabbay. Height 561 feet or 171 metres. **84 A6** NL5987.
The Holehouse *D. & G. See Hollows Tower.*
The Holme *N.Yorks.* ***Settlement***, in Nidd valley, 1m/2km E of Darley. SE2159.
The Holt *W'ham* ***Hamlet***, 2m/3km NE of Twyford. SU8078.
The Horns *Kent* ***Settlement***, 1m/2km SW of Hawkhurst. TQ7429.
The Horse Bridge ***Bridge***, fine stone-built bridge across River Tamar, dating from 1437, 5m/8km W of Tavistock. SX4072.
The Howe *I.o.M.* ***Hamlet***, 1km W of Port St. Mary. **54 B7** SC1967.
The Hundred *Here.* ***Settlement***, 4m/6km NE of Leominster. SO5263.
The Hurlers *Cornw. Alternative name for Hurlers Stone Circle, qv.*
The Hyde *Essex* ***Settlement***, adjoining to NE of Great Yeldham, 6m/10km NW of Halstead. TL7739.
The Hyde *Gt.Lon.* ***Suburb***, in borough of Barnet, 8m/12km NW of Charing Cross. TQ2188.
The Hythe *Essex* ***Suburb***, 1m/2km SE of Colchester town centre. TM0124.
The Island (Also known as St. Ives Head.) *Cornw.* ***Coastal feature***, headland at W end of St. Ives Bay, to N of St. Ives. **2 C4** SW5140.
The Isle *Shrop.* ***Settlement***, 2m/3km NE of Montford Bridge. **38 D4** SJ4516.
The Kame (Also known as Kame of Foula.) *Shet.* ***Coastal feature***, steep cliff on W coast of Foula, rising to 1220 feet or 372 metres. **108 B1** HT9340.
The Keen *Shet.* ***Coastal feature***, headland 1km SE of Housabister, Mainland. **109 E7** HU5057.
The Kettles *Moray* ***Open space***, marshy moorland between Green Hill and Bracken Noits, 3m/5km W of Rothes. **97 K6** NJ2350.

T

The King's Stone *D. & G. Alternative name for Bruce's Stone, qv.*

The Knock *D. & G.* ***Hill***, in S of Castle O'er Forest, 3m/5km E of Boreland. Height 935 feet or 285 metres. **69 H4** NY2291.

The Knowl *Mon.* ***Locality***, 1m/2km N of Monmouth. SO5014.

The Knowle *Kent* ***Settlement***, 2m/3km SE of Paddock Wood. **23 K7** TQ6842.

The Knowle *Notts.* ***Locality***, 5m/8km NW of Nottingham. SK5044.

The Laurels *Norf.* ***Settlement***, 2m/3km SW of Loddon. **45 H6** TM3397.

The Leacon *Kent* ***Settlement***, 1m/2km W of Hamstreet. **14 E4** TQ9833.

The Lee *Bucks.* ***Village***, 4m/7km NW of Chesham. **22 C1** SP9004.

The Lhen (Also known as Ballathona.) *I.o.M.* ***Settlement***, 2m/3km NW of Andreas. **54 C3** NX3901.

The Lings *S.Yorks.* ***Locality***, adjoining to S of Hatfield, 3m/5km SW of Thorne. SE6508.

The Lleyn *Gwyn. Alternative name for Lleyn Peninsula, qv.*

The Lodge *Arg. & B.* ***Settlement***, on W shore of Loch Goil, 2m/3km S of Lochgoilhead. **73 K1** NS1999.

The Loe (Also known as Looe Pool or Loe Pool.) *Cornw.* ***Lake/loch***, large lake (National Trust) formed by River Looe, Loe, or Cober, and Looe or Loe Bar which obstructs outflow to sea. Most of coast from Porthleven to Gunwalloe also National Trust. **2 D6** SW6425.

The Long Mynd *Shrop.* ***Large natural feature***, range of pre-Cambrian hills dissected by narrow, steep-sided valleys to W of Church Stretton. They attain height of 1695 feet or 517 metres and run 8m/13km from Plowden in SW to Woolstaston in NE. Midland Gliding Club operates from ridge above Asterton. **38 D6** SO4194.

The Lound *Cumb.* ***Suburb***, in S part of Kendal. SD5191.

The Lower Hope ***Sea feature***, stretch of River Thames, extending from East Tilbury Marshes to Lower Hope Point on Cliffe Marshes. TQ7077.

The Machars *D. & G.* ***Locality***, between Luce Bay and Wigtown Bay. **64 E6** NX3752.

The Maiden *High. Anglicised form of A' Mhaighdean, qv.*

The Manacles *Cornw.* ***Island***, group of rocks off E coast of Lizard peninsula, to SE of Manacle Point. **3 F6** SW8220.

The Manor *Dorset* ***Historic house***, at Sandford Orcas, 3m/4km N of Sherborne. Built in Tudor period with terraced gardens and topiary. **9 F2** ST6221.

The Mare *Pembs.* ***Island***, rock on E side of Green Scar, 1km W of Dinas Fawr. SM7922.

The Marsh *Ches.* ***Suburb***, 1m/2km SW of Congleton town centre. SJ8462.

The Marsh *Hants.* ***Locality***, beside River Allen, 1km SE of Damerham. SU1015.

The Marsh *Here.* ***Suburb***, on N side of Leominster across River Lugg. SO4959.

The Marsh *Powys* ***Settlement***, below NE slope of Corndon Hill, 4m/6km NE of Church Stoke. **38 C6** SO3097.

The Marsh *Shrop.* ***Settlement***, 1km S of Hinstock. SJ6925.

The Meare *Suff.* ***Lake/loch***, small lake to SW of Thorpeness. **35 J3** TM4659.

The Mere *Shrop.* ***Lake/loch***, to E of Ellesmere. **38 D2** SJ4035.

The Merse *Sc.Bord.* ***Open space***, fertile lowland area of rich farmland between River Tweed and Blackadder Water. It is bounded by Pentland, Moorfoot and Lammermuir Hills in N and Cheviot Hills in S. NT8246.

The Middles *Dur.* ***Locality***, 1m/2km SE of Stanley. NZ2051.

The Minch ***Sea feature***, sea passage between Isle of Lewis and Scottish mainland. **101 J6** NB7010.

The Moor *Cambs.* ***Suburb***, adjoining to N of Melbourn, 4m/6km NE of Royston. TL3845.

The Moor *Cumb.* ***Locality***, adjoining to SW of Millom. SD1679.

The Moor *Kent* ***Village***, adjoining to S of Hawkhurst. **14 C5** TQ7529.

The Mouls *Cornw.* ***Island***, opposite W end of Portquin Bay on N coast, N of Polzeath. SW9281.

The Mount *Sc.Bord.* ***Mountain***, in Pentland Hills, 4m/6km N of West Linton. Height 1761 feet or 537 metres. **75 K5** NT1457.

The Mumbles *Swan.* ***Suburb***, of Swansea to W and NW of Mumbles Head, incorporating the residential areas of Oystermouth, Langland, Newton, Norton and West Cross. Popular seaside resort, formerly linked to Swansea via a tramway. Attractions include pier, Oystermouth Castle and Clyne Gardens. The name is derived from a pair of offshore rocks at Mumbles Head. **17 K6** SS6188.

The Murray *S.Lan.* ***Suburb***, to S of East Kilbride town centre. NS6353.

The Mythe *Glos.* ***Hamlet***, 1m/2km N of Tewkesbury. **29 H5** SO8934.

The Nab Head *Pembs.* ***Coastal feature***, headland on S side of St. Brides Bay, 8m/13km W of Milford Haven. **16 A3** SM7911.

The Nant *Wrex.* ***Hamlet***, 3m/5km W of Wrexham. SJ2850.

The Narth *Mon.* ***Village***, 4m/7km S of Monmouth. SO5107.

The Nass *Essex* ***Coastal feature***, mudflat at mouth of River Blackwater, 1m/2km SW of West Mersea. **25 F1** TM0011.

The Naze *Essex* ***Coastal feature***, North Sea headland 5m/8km S of Harwich across bay. **35 G6** TM2623.

The Neck *Devon* ***Coastal feature***, shingle bank on N side of River Taw estuary to N of Appledore, 3m/5km SW of Braunton. **6 C2** SS4532.

The Needle *High.* ***Inland physical feature***, 120 feet or 36 metre high pinnacle of weathered volcanic basalt in Quiraing locality, inland from Staffin Bay, Skye, and 1km SE of Meall na Suiramach. **93 K5** NG4569.

The Needles *I.o.W.* ***Coastal feature***, headland (National Trust) culminating in group of jagged chalk rocks running out into English Channel from W extremity of Isle of Wight. Lighthouse at W end of series. **10 D6** SZ2984.

The Needles Old Battery *I.o.W.* ***Other feature of interest***, restored coastal defence (National Trust) on westernmost tip of Isle of Wight, 3m/4km SW of Totland. Contains two 12-ton Victorian guns and authentic shell filling laboratory. 200 feet tunnel leads to searchlight point with spectacular views of The Needles. **10 E6** SZ2984.

The Neuk *Aber.* ***Settlement***, 3m/4km NE of Banchory. **91 F5** NO7397.

The Nev *Shet.* ***Coastal feature***, headland 1m/2km SE of Clibberswick, E coast of Unst. **108 F1** HP6611.

The Niarbyl *I.o.M. Alternative name for Niarbyl Island, qv.*

The Nine Stones *Dorset* ***Historic/prehistoric site***, nine irregularly spaced sarsen stone blocks, forming a circle over 26 feet or 8 metres in diameter and dating from Bronze Age, 1km SW of Winterbourne Abbas. **9 F6** SY6190.

The Node *Herts.* ***Settlement***, 3m/5km SW of Stevenage. **33 F7** TL2120.

The Noose *Glos.* ***Coastal feature***, sandbank in upper part of River Severn estuary, between Awre on W bank and Frampton-on-Severn on E bank. **20 A1** SO7207.

The North Head *Ork.* ***Coastal feature***, northernmost headland on Swona. **107 C9** ND3985.

The North Sound *Ork.* ***Sea feature***, sea area between islands of Sanday and Westray. **106 E3** HY5745.

The Noup *Shet.* ***Coastal feature***, rocky headland on N coast of Unst. **108 F1** HP6318.

The Oa *Arg. & B.* ***Coastal feature***, peninsula at S end of Islay, W of Port Ellen. Bold cliffs, especially to S and W. **72 A6** NR3044.

The Old Man of Coniston *Cumb.* ***Mountain***, in Lake District, 2m/3km W of Coniston. Height 2627 feet or 801 metres. **60 D7** SD2797.

The Otter Trust *Suff.* ***Nature reserve***, 1m/2km SW of Bungay, on River Waveney. One of best collections of otters in country. Trust aims to promote conservation in the wild. **45 H7** TM3188.

The Oval *B. & N.E.Som.* ***Suburb***, SW district of Bath. **20 A5** ST7363.

The Oval *Gt.Lon. See Kennington.*

The Owl House *Kent* ***Garden***, 1m NW of Lamberhurst, 8m/13km SE of Tunbridge Wells. 13 acre garden with roses, rare shrubs, lawns, woodland walks and sunken water gardens surrounding a 16c wool smugglers' cottage. **13 K3** TQ6637.

The Parks *S.Yorks.* ***Locality***, adjoining to W of Hatfield, 3m/5km SW of Thorne. SE6409.

The Peak *Derbys.* ***Mountain***, highest point of Kinder Scout in High Peak, 3m/5km E of Hayfield. Height 2086 feet or 636 metres. **50 C4** SK0887.

The Pennines ***Large natural feature***, mountain range in England extending about 150m/240km from The Peak to The Cheviot; sometimes regarded as 'the backbone of England'. Traversed by The Pennine Way. **56 D2** SE0070.

The Pike *Sc.Bord.* ***Mountain***, in Craik Forest, 4m/6km SE of Ettrick. Height 1453 feet or 443 metres. **69 H3** NT2908.

The Pike *Sc.Bord.* ***Mountain***, 3m/4km SW of Shankend. Height 1515 feet or 462 metres. **69 K3** NT4904.

The Pill *Mon.* ***Settlement***, 1km SE of Caldicot. ST4987.

The Pineapple *Falk.* ***Historic house***, 18c pineapple-shaped building (National Trust for Scotland) set in 16 acres, 1m/2km NW of Airth. Building now used as a holiday home. **75 G2** NS8888.

The Pole of Itlaw *Aber.* ***Hill***, 4m/7km S of Banff. Height 443 feet or 135 metres. **98 E5** NJ6757.

The Potteries *Staffs.* ***Locality***, historical name given to the area of Stoke-on-Trent which was Britain's main pottery and ceramics centre until the turn of the century. World-famous producers include Wedgwood, Royal Doulton and Spode. **49 H7** SJ8453.

The Prince's Cairn *High.* ***Other feature of interest***, reputed hiding place of Charles Edward Stuart (Bonnie Prince Charlie) whilst on run from English troops, 3m/4km SE of Arisaig in Druimindarroch. **86 C6** NM6984.

The Priory *Suff.* ***Historic house***, hall once belonging to a Benedictine order before being enlarged into a wool merchant's home in Lavenham, 6m/10km NE of Sudbury. **34 D4** TL9148.

The Quarter *Kent* ***Settlement***, 3m/5km E of Headcorn. TQ8844.

The Queen's Forest *High.* ***Forest/woodland***, coniferous forest in Badenoch and Strathspey district and mainly within the Glenmore Forest Park, N of Cairn Gorm. **89 G3** NH9709.

The Reddings *Glos.* ***Suburb***, W district of Cheltenham. SO9021.

The Rhos *Pembs.* ***Settlement***, 4m/6km E of Haverfordwest. **16 D3** SN0014.

The Riding *Northumb.* ***Locality***, 1m/2km N of Hexham across River Tyne, 1km S of Acomb. NY9365.

The Rigg *Northumb.* ***Mountain***, wooded upland area, 3m/5km S of Kielder Water and 6m/9km SW of Falstone. Height 1063 feet or 324 metres. **70 B5** NY6484.

The Rivals *Gwyn. English form of Yr Eifl, qv.*

The Road *I.o.S.* ***Sea feature***, strait dividing NW of St. Mary's from Samson and Tresco. **2 B1** SV8811.

The Rocks *Kent* ***Settlement***, on SE side of East Malling. TQ7056.

The Rodings *Essex* ***Locality***, area between Chelmsford and Bishop's Stortford, through which River Roding flows. Eight places here have Roding as suffix: Abbess, Aythorpe, Beauchamp, Berners, High, Leaden, Margaret, White. **33 J7** TL5813.

The Rona *Shet.* ***Sea feature***, stretch of water dividing Papa Little from Mainland. **109 C6** HU3260.

The Rookery *Staffs.* ***Suburb***, 1m/2km NE of Kidsgrove. SJ8555.

The Rowe *Staffs.* ***Settlement***, 6m/9km NW of Stone. **40 A2** SJ8238.

The Rumble *Shet.* ***Island***, rock marked by beacon off S coast of Yell about 1km SW of Orfasay. HU4876.

The Ryde *Herts.* ***Suburb***, NE district of Hatfield. TL2309.

The Saddle *High.* ***Mountain***, on border of Lochaber and Skye and Lochalsh districts, 4m/6km S of Shiel Bridge. Munro: height 3313 feet or 1010 metres. **87 F3** NG9313.

The Sale *Staffs.* ***Settlement***, 1km NW of Fradley. SK1514.

The Sanctuary *Wilts.* ***Historic/prehistoric site***, site of two concentric stone circles and six timber uprights (English Heritage), 1km E of West Kennet. Circles cleared in 1724 but now marked out on ground. Site dated to early Bronze Age. **20 E5** SU1168.

The Sands *Surr.* ***Hamlet***, 3m/4km E of Farnham. **22 B7** SU8846.

The Scalp *Lincs.* ***Marsh/bog***, area of saltmarsh on W side of The Wash and on S bank of The Haven, 5m/8km SE of Boston. Nature Reserve. **43 G2** TF3838.

The Scalp *Moray* ***Mountain***, 3m/5km SE of Dufftown. Height 1597 feet or 487 metres. **90 B1** NJ3636.

The Scarr *Glos.* ***Settlement***, 1m/2km N of Newent. SO7228.

The Scars *Northumb.* ***Coastal feature***, rocks adjacent to Cresswell at S end of Druridge Bay. **71 H4** NZ2993.

The Scaurs *Aber. Occasional name for The Skares, qv.*

The Schil ***Mountain***, in Cheviot Hills, on border of Northumberland and Scottish Borders, 4m/7km SE of Kirk Yetholm. Height 1984 feet or 605 metres. **70 D1** NT8622.

The Shevock *Aber.* ***River***, rising on S side of Gartly Moor and flowing generally SE through Insch to join River Urie on NW side of Old Rayne. **90 E2** NJ6628.

The Shin *D. & G.* ***Mountain***, 2m/3km SW of Bentpath. Height 1174 feet or 358 metres. **69 H5** NY2889.

The Shoe *Wilts.* ***Hamlet***, 4m/7km NW of Corsham. **20 B4** ST8074.

The Sisters *Cornw.* ***Island***, two islands off N coast, 1m/2km N of Tintagel. SX0690.

The Skares (Sometimes known as The Scaurs.) *Aber.* ***Coastal feature***, reef of almost submerged rocks at S end of Bay of Cruden, 9m/14km S of Peterhead. **91 J1** NK0833.

The Skerries (Ynysoedd y Moelrhoniaidd). *I.o.A.* ***Island***, group of small rocky islands lying 2m/3km NW of Anglesey coast at Carmel Head, on one of which is a lighthouse. **46 A3** SH2694.

The Skerries *Shet. Alternative name for Out Skerries, qv.*

The Slack *Dur.* ***Locality***, adjoining to SE of Butterknowle, next to River Gaunless. NZ1125.

The Slade *W.Berks.* ***Settlement***, 4m/7km NE of Newbury. SU5369.

The Slate *Arg. & B.* ***Mountain***, in S part of Kintyre, 6m/9km SW of Campbeltown. Height 1263 feet or 385 metres. **66 A2** NR6316.

The Small Isles *High.* ***Island***, collective name for group of islands in Inner Hebrides comprising Rum, Eigg, Canna and Muck. NM3795.

The Smalls *Pembs.* ***Island***, group of rocks with lighthouse, 16m/26km W of Skomer Island. SM4608.

The Smithies *Shrop.* ***Settlement***, 4m/6km E of Much Wenlock. **39 F6** SO6797.

The Snap *Shet.* ***Coastal feature***, headland at SE end of Fetlar, 1m/2km S of Funzie. **108 F4** HU6587.

The Sneug *Shet.* ***Mountain***, peak on Foula. Height 1371 feet or 418 metres. **108 B1** HT9439.

The Snook *Northumb.* ***Locality***, sandy barren W end of Holy Island. NU0943.

The Socach *Aber.* ***Mountain***, 4m/7km W of Strathdon. Height 2355 feet or 718 metres. **89 K3** NJ2714.

The Soldier's Leap *P. & K.* ***Inland physical feature***, narrowest part of chasm in Pass of Killiecrankie. See Killiecrankie. **81 K1** NN9162.

The Solent ***Sea feature***, sea channel separating Isle of Wight from English mainland and extending from Hurst Castle and Cliff End (W) to Portsmouth and Ryde (E). Width varies from about 2m/3km to 4m/6km. **11 F5** SZ5098.

The Sound *Plym.* ***Sea feature***, estuary to SW of Plymouth and at mouths of Rivers Plym and Tamar. **4 E5** SX4752.

The Sow *Ork.* ***Coastal feature***, rocky cliff on NW coast of Hoy. **107 A7** HY1802.

The Sow of Atholl (Also known as Atholl Sow.) *P. & K.* ***Mountain***, on Dalnaspidal Forest, Atholl, 1m/2km NW of Dalnaspidal Lodge. Height 2499 feet or 762 metres. **88 D7** NN6274.

The Spur *High.* ***Coastal feature***, rocky outcrop to N of Muckle Bay. **105 G1** ND1769.

The Square *Torfaen* ***Suburb***, of Upper Cwmbran. ST2796.

The Stack *Pembs.* ***Coastal feature***, headland at NE end of Skokholm Island. **16 A4** SM7405.

The Stair *Kent Alternative name for Hadlow Stair, qv.*

The Stock *Wilts.* ***Hamlet***, adjoining to SW of Seend Cleeve, 3m/4km SE of Melksham. ST9260.

The Stocks *Kent* ***Hamlet***, on Isle of Oxney, 1m/2km E of Wittersham. **14 E5** TQ9127.

The Storr *High.* ***Mountain***, in Trotternish, 7m/11km N of Portree, Skye. Height 2358 feet or 719 metres. Old Man of Storr, 160 foot or 49 metre stack, to E. **93 K6** NG4954.

The Street *Norf.* ***Locality***, adjoining to N of Blo' Norton. TM0179.

The Study *High.* ***Inland physical feature***, natural terrace 3m/5km S of Kinlochleven, in Lochaber district, on N side of road running down Glen Coe. Commands view of glen. **80 C2** NN1756.

The Swale *Kent* ***River***, branch of River Medway estuary which leaves main stream at Queenborough Spit and separates Isle of Sheppey from mainland of Kent, entering Whitstable Bay opposite Shell Ness. **25 F5** TR0667.

The Swillett *Herts.* ***Suburb***, to SW of Chorleywood. TQ0295.

The Tails of the Tarf *Ork.* ***Coastal feature***, headland to S of Swona. **107 C9** ND3783.

The Thirl *High.* ***Coastal feature***, headland on N side of Dunnet Bay. **105 G1** ND1872.

The Three Crossways *Suff.* ***Settlement***, 1km E of Stonham Aspal. TM1459.

The Three Hundreds of Aylesbury *Bucks.* ***Locality***, large area of land between Wendover and Princes Risborough on Chiltern escarpment, 6m/9km SE of Aylesbury. **22 B1** SP8506.

The Three Sisters (Also known as The Three Sisters of Glen Coe.) *High.* ***Large natural feature***, three gaunt peaks overlooking Glen Coe in Lochaber district, on S side of glen. From E to W, Beinn Fhada, Gearr Aonach and Aonach Dubh. **80 C2** NN1655.
The Three Sisters of Glen Coe *High. Alternative name for The Three Sisters, qv.*
The Thrift *Cambs.* ***Settlement***, 3m/4km W of Royston. TL3139.
The Towans *Cornw.* ***Locality***, 1km N of Hayle across harbour. SW5538.
The Trossachs *Stir.* ***Large natural feature***, area surrounding wooded gorge, between Loch Achray and Loch Katrine, 13m/20km NW of Stirling. Extremely broken terrain and very attractive, comprising mountains, woods and lochs. Literary associations with Scott and Ruskin. **81 G7** NN4907.
The Turves *Cambs.* ***Open space***, drainage area to S of Turves, 4m/7km E of Whittlesey. TL3396.
The Tynings *Glos.* ***Settlement***, 2m/4km SW of Cheltenham. SO9219.
The Ugly House *Conwy Alternative name for Ty-Hyll, qv.*
The Undercliff *I.o.W.* ***Coastal feature***, coastal strip stretching along S coast from Shanklin to Compton Bay. Formed by successive landslips due to chalk and sandstone over clay. Most impressive landslips are between Shanklin and Chale. **11 G7** SZ5376.
The Valley *Pembs.* ***Settlement***, 1m/2km W of Saundersfoot. SN1205.
The Vauld *Here.* ***Settlement***, 6m/10km SE of Leominster. **28 E4** SO5349.
The Vere *Shet.* ***Island***, isolated rock 2m/3km off E coast of Unst. **108 F2** HP6403.
The Veshels *Aber.* ***Coastal feature***, rocks off E coast, 3m/5km S of Cruden Bay. **91 J1** NK0731.
The Village *W.Mid.* ***Locality***, 3m/5km W of Dudley town centre. SO8989.
The Village *W. & M.* ***Settlement***, in Windsor Great Park, 2m/4km S of Windsor. SU9572.
The Vyne *Hants.* ***Historic house***, Tudor and later house (National Trust) with garden, 1m/2km NE of Sherborne St. John. **21 K6** SU6356.
The Wash ***Sea feature***, wide shallow arm of North Sea extending from the coast near Boston to the coast at Hunstanton. It receives the waters of Rivers Witham, Welland, Nene, and Great Ouse. The ports of Boston and King's Lynn have access to The Wash by the estuaries of Rivers Witham and Great Ouse respectively. Numerous sandbanks render navigation difficult. **43 J2** TF5040.
The Wash *Pembs.* ***Sea feature***, area of sea around a headland on S Pembrokeshire coast, 3m/4km SE of Linney Head. **16 C5** SR9294.
The Weald ***Large natural feature***, domed region of SE England, bounded by North and South Downs and spanning Kent, East and West Sussex and Surrey. Formed as part of a large chalk anticline which stretched across NW Europe, subsequent erosion has created a pericline or dome. **13 G3** TQ6535.
The Weir *Here.* ***Garden***, riverside garden, property of The National Trust, which overlooks Black Mountains, 5m/8km W of Hereford. **28 D4** SO4441.
The Wern *Wrex.* ***Settlement***, 4m/6km W of Wrexham. SJ2750.
The Wirral Country Park *Mersey.* ***Leisure/recreation***, 12m/20km stretch of disused railway line converted into walkway and riding trail between West Kirby and Hooton. Parts are National Trust property. Nature trail and visitor centre at Thurstaston; views over River Dee estuary to N Wales. **48 B4** SJ2482.
The Wiss *Sc.Bord.* ***Mountain***, 4m/6km SE of St. Mary's Loch. Height 1932 feet or 589 metres. **69 H1** NT2620.
The Wolds *E.Riding* ***Large natural feature***, upland area rising to over 240 metres to N and W of Great Driffield. **59 F3** SE9762.
The Wolds *Lincs.* ***Large natural feature***, range of hills running from Brigg in NW, 32m/52km to Spilsby in SE. **53 F4** TF2587.
The Wolves *Cardiff* ***Island***, two rocks in Bristol Channel, 1m/2km NW of Flat Holm. ST2065.
The Wrekin *Tel. & W.* ***Mountain***, craggy eminence 3m/4km SW of Wellington; dominates surrounding landscape. Height 1335 feet or 407 metres. **39 F5** SJ6208.
The Wrythe *Gt.Lon.* ***Suburb***, in borough of Sutton, 1m/2km NE of Sutton town centre. **23 F5** TQ2765.
The Wyke *N.Yorks.* ***Bay***, 1km N of Filey. **59 H1** TA1082.
The Wyke *Shrop.* ***Settlement***, 1m/2km SW of Shifnal. **39 G5** SJ7306.
Theakston *N.Yorks.* ***Hamlet***, 1km NW of Burneston. **57 H1** SE3085.
Thealby *N.Lincs.* ***Village***, 5m/7km N of Scunthorpe. **52 B1** SE8917.
Theale *Som.* ***Village***, 2m/3km SE of Wedmore. **19 H7** ST4646.
Theale *W.Berks.* Population: 2640. ***Village***, 5m/8km W of Reading. **21 K4** SU6471.
Theale Green *W.Berks.* ***Locality***, adjoining to W of Theale. SU6471.
Thearne *E.Riding* ***Hamlet***, 3m/5km SE of Beverley. **59 G6** TA0736.
Theberton *Suff.* ***Village***, 2m/4km N of Leiston. **35 J2** TM4365.
Thedden Grange *Hants.* ***Settlement***, 2m/3km W of Alton. **11 H1** SU6839.
Theddingworth *Leics.* ***Village***, 5m/7km W of Market Harborough. **41 J7** SP6685.
Theddlethorpe All Saints *Lincs.* ***Village***, 3m/5km NW of Mablethorpe. **53 H4** TF4688.
Theddlethorpe St. Helen *Lincs.* ***Village***, 1m/2km NE of Theddlethorpe All Saints. **53 H4** TF4688.
Thelbridge *Devon* ***Locality***, 7m/11km E of Chulmleigh, comprising Thelbridge Barton with church, and Thelbridge Cross. SS7812.
Thelbridge Barton *Devon* ***Settlement***, with church, forms hamlet of Thelbridge, along with Thelbridge Cross. **7 F4** SS7812.
Thelbridge Cross *Devon* ***Settlement***, forms hamlet of Thelbridge, along with Thelbridge Barton. SS7812.
Thelnetham *Suff.* ***Village***, 6m/10km W of Diss. **34 E1** TM0178.
Thelveton *Norf.* ***Hamlet***, 3m/5km E of Diss. **45 F7** TM1681.
Thelwall *Warr.* Population: 11,410. ***Suburb***, 3m/5km E of Warrington. **49 F4** SJ6587.
Themelthorpe *Norf.* ***Village***, 3m/5km W of Reepham. **44 E3** TG0523.
Thenford *Northants.* ***Village***, 4m/6km E of Banbury. Site of Roman building to E. **31 G4** SP5141.
Theobald's Green *Wilts.* ***Settlement***, 2m/3km SE of Calne. SU0269.
Therfield *Herts.* ***Village***, 3m/4km S of Royston. **33 G5** TL3337.
Thet *Norf.* ***River***, rising near Attleborough and flowing SW into Little Ouse River at Thetford. TL8782.
Thetford *Lincs.* ***Settlement***, 1km N of Baston, 3m/5km S of Bourne. TF1114.
Thetford *Norf.* Population: 20,058. ***Town***, ancient town at confluence of River Thet and Little Ouse River, 12m/19km N of Bury St. Edmunds. Former seat of Bishops and Kings of East Anglia. Remains of Norman castle. Remains of former monasteries include 12c Cluniac Priory of Our Lady and Augustinian priory of Canons of the Holy Sepulchre (both English Heritage). Many medieval and Georgian houses in protected town centre. 15c Ancient House contains a museum. Nearby is 50,000 acre Thetford Forest Park. **44 C7** TL8683.
Thetford Forest Park ***Leisure/recreation***, around 50,000 acres of forest straddling border of Norfolk and Suffolk to W of Thetford, and Britain's largest lowland pine forest. Forest walks, wildlife hides and picnic areas. High Lodge Forest Centre, with waymarked trails, cycle trails and maze, to N of Santon Downham. Brandon Park to S of Brandon. **44 C7** TL8088.
Thetford Priory *Norf.* ***Ecclesiastical building***, remains of Cluniac Priory of Our Lady (English Heritage) founded 1104 in Thetford. 14c gatehouse is preserved. **44 C7** TL8683.
Thetford Warren ***Forest/woodland***, coniferous forest on border of Norfolk and Suffolk, to W of Thetford. Thetford Chase, administered by Forestry Commission, is home to red squirrels and red deer. **44 C7** TL8283.
Thethwaite *Cumb.* ***Settlement***, 4m/6km S of Dalston. NY3744.
Theydon Bois *Essex* Population: 3945. ***Village***, 2m/3km S of Epping. **23 H2** TQ4499.
Theydon Garnon *Essex* ***Village***, 2m/3km SE of Epping. TQ4799.
Theydon Mount *Essex* ***Village***, 3m/5km SE of Epping. Hill Hall (English Heritage) to NE, is Elizabethan and Queen Anne mansion, 1km NW. TQ4999.
Thick Hollins *W.Yorks.* ***Locality***, adjoining to E of Meltham. SE1010.
Thickwood *Wilts.* ***Hamlet***, 6m/9km W of Chippenham. Site of Roman building 1km E. **20 B4** ST8272.
Thief's Hill *Moray* ***Hill***, in Wood of Ordiequish, 3m/5km S of Fochabers. Height 820 feet or 250 metres. **98 B5** NJ3654.
Thieves Holm *Ork.* ***Island***, islet off Car Ness, Mainland, 3m/4km NE of Kirkwall. HY4614.
Thimbleby *Lincs.* ***Village***, 1m/2km W of Horncastle. **53 F5** TF2369.
Thimbleby *N.Yorks.* ***Hamlet***, 5m/8km E of Northallerton. **63 F7** SE4595.
Thingley *Wilts.* ***Settlement***, 3m/4km SW of Chippenham. ST8970.
Thingwall *Mersey.* ***Suburb***, 2m/3km N of Heswall. SJ2784.
Thirkleby *N.Yorks.* ***Village***, 4m/6km SE of Thirsk. **57 K2** SE4778.
Thirlby *N.Yorks.* ***Village***, 4m/7km E of Thirsk. **57 K1** SE4884.
Thirlestane *Sc.Bord.* ***Village***, 2m/3km E of Lauder. **76 D6** NT5647.
Thirlestane Castle *Sc.Bord.* ***Castle***, begun 1595, with later additions, on NE side of Lauder, next to Leader Water. **76 D6** NT5347.
Thirlmere *Cumb.* ***Lake/loch***, natural lake used as reservoir 4m/6km SE of Keswick. Length N to S 4m/6km. **60 E5** NY3116.
Thirlwall Common *Northumb.* ***Open space***, moorland tract to N and S of Thirlwall Castle, 3m/5km NW of Haltwhistle. **70 B7** NY6566.
Thirn *N.Yorks.* ***Hamlet***, 3m/5km N of Masham. **57 H1** SE2185.
Thirsk *N.Yorks.* Population: 6860. ***Small town***, on Cod Beck, 8m/13km SE of Northallerton. Racecourse at New Thirsk. Formerly an important coaching town with associated inns. James Herriot connection; location of 'original' surgery. **57 K1** SE4282.
Thirston New Houses *Northumb.* ***Settlement***, 1m/2km S of Felton. NZ1899.
Thirtleby *E.Riding* ***Settlement***, 1m/2km E of Coniston. TA1734.
Thistleboon (Also known as Limeslade.) *Swan.* ***Suburb***, in The Mumbles district of Swansea, 1km W of Mumbles Head. SS6287.
Thistleton *Lancs.* ***Village***, 4m/6km N of Kirkham. **55 H6** SD4037.
Thistleton *Rut.* ***Village***, 7m/11km NE of Oakham. **42 C4** SK9117.
Thistley Green *Suff.* ***Village***, 3m/4km NW of Mildenhall. Site of Roman building to N. **33 K1** TL6776.
Thixendale *N.Yorks.* ***Village***, in The Wolds, 2m/4km NW of Fridaythorpe. **58 E3** SE8461.
Thockrington *Northumb.* ***Hamlet***, 9m/15km N of Hexham. **70 E6** NY9579.
Tholomas Drove *Cambs.* ***Hamlet***, 5m/7km SW of Wisbeck. **43 G5** TF4006.
Tholthorpe *N.Yorks.* ***Village***, 4m/6km SW of Easingwold. **57 K3** SE4766.
Thomas Chapel *Pembs.* ***Settlement***, 1m/2km NW of Begelly. **16 E4** SN1008.
Thomas Close *Cumb.* ***Settlement***, 8m/12km NW of Penrith. NY4340.
Thomas Town *Warks.* ***Locality***, adjoining to S of Studley, 4m/6km SE of Redditch. SP0763.
Thomason Foss *N.Yorks.* ***Waterfall***, in Eller Beck 1m/2km NW of Goathland. **63 K6** NZ8202.
Thomastown *Aber.* ***Village***, 3m/6km SE of Huntly. **90 D1** NJ5736.
Thomastown (Tretomas). *R.C.T.* ***Village***, 1km S of Tonyrefail. ST0086.
Thomley *Oxon.* ***Settlement***, 7m/12km E of Oxford. SP6309.
Thompson *Norf.* ***Village***, 3m/4km S of Watton. **44 D6** TL9296.
Thomshill *Moray* ***Locality***, 4m/6km S of Elgin. **97 K6** NJ2157.
Thong *Kent* ***Hamlet***, 3m/4km SE of Gravesend centre. **24 C4** TQ6770.
Thongsbridge *W.Yorks.* ***Village***, on River Holme, 1m/2km N of Holmfirth. SE1509.
Thonock *Lincs.* ***Locality***, 2m/3km NE of Gainsborough. SK8392.
Thoralby *N.Yorks.* ***Village***, 1m/2km S of Aysgarth. **57 F1** SE0086.
Thoresby *Notts.* ***Historic house***, Victorian mansion by Salvin in park laid out in 17c-18c, 3m/4km NW of Ollerton. **51 J5** SK6371.
Thoresthorpe *Lincs.* ***Settlement***, 1m/2km N of Alford. TF4677.
Thoresway *Lincs.* ***Village***, 4m/7km SE of Caistor. **52 E3** TF1696.
Thorganby *Lincs.* ***Village***, 2m/4km N of Binbrook. **53 F3** TF2097.
Thorganby *N.Yorks.* ***Village***, 7m/12km NE of Selby. **58 C5** SE6841.
Thorgill *N.Yorks.* ***Hamlet***, 1m/2km W of Rosedale Abbey. **63 J7** SE7295.
Thorington *Suff.* ***Hamlet***, 1m/2km E of Bramfield. **35 J1** TM4274.
Thorington Street *Suff.* ***Hamlet***, 5m/8km S of Hadleigh. **34 E5** TM0135.
Thorlby *N.Yorks.* ***Hamlet***, on edge of Yorkshire Dales National Park, 2m/3km NW of Skipton. **56 E4** SD9652.
Thorley *Herts.* ***Village***, 2m/3km SW of Bishop's Stortford. **33 H7** TL4718.
Thorley Houses *Herts.* ***Settlement***, 2m/3km SW of Bishop's Stortford. TL4620.
Thorley Street *Herts.* ***Village***, 1m/2km E of Thorley, adjoining Bishop's Stortford. **33 H7** TL4718.
Thorley Street *I.o.W.* ***Village***, 1m/2km SE of Yarmouth. **10 E6** SZ3788.
Thormanby *N.Yorks.* ***Village***, 4m/7km NW of Easingwold. **57 K2** SE4974.
Thorn Island *Pembs.* ***Island***, rock island off S shore of Milford Haven, 1m/2km NW of Angle. **16 B4** SM8403.
Thornaby-on-Tees *Stock.* Population: 24,189. ***Suburb***, on S bank of River Tees, 3m/4km SE of Stockton-on-Tees and forming part of Teesside urban complex. **63 F5** NZ4517.
Thornage *Norf.* ***Village***, 2m/4km SW of Holt. **44 E2** TG0536.
Thornborough *Bucks.* ***Village***, 3m/5km E of Buckingham. Site of Roman temple at Thornborough Bridge to W. **31 J5** SP7433.
Thornborough *N.Yorks.* ***Hamlet***, 2m/3km NE of West Tanfield. **57 H1** SE2979.
Thornbrough *N.Yorks.* ***Settlement***, 2m/3km N of Thirsk. SE4284.
Thornbury *Devon* ***Hamlet***, 5m/8km NE of Holsworthy. **6 C5** SS4008.
Thornbury *Here.* ***Village***, 4m/6km NW of Bromyard. **29 F3** SO6259.
Thornbury *S.Glos.* Population: 12,108. ***Town***, old stone-built market town, 12m/19km N of Bristol. **19 K3** ST6390.
Thornbury *W.Yorks.* ***Suburb***, 2m/3km E of Bradford city centre. SE1933.
Thornby *Cumb.* ***Locality***, 3m/4km NW of Thursby. NY2852.
Thornby *Northants.* ***Village***, 8m/13km SW of Market Harborough. **31 H1** SP6775.
Thorncliff *Staffs.* ***Hamlet***, 2m/4km NE of Leek. **50 C7** SK0158.
Thorncliff *W.Yorks.* ***Hamlet***, 1m/2km E of Highburton. SE2113.
Thorncombe *Dorset* ***Village***, 5m/8km SE of Chard. **8 C4** ST3703.
Thorncombe Street *Surr.* ***Settlement***, on N side of Winkworth Arboretum, 2m/4km SE of Godalming. **22 D7** TQ0042.
Thorncote Green *Beds.* ***Settlement***, 2m/3km SW of Sandy. **32 E4** TL1547.
Thorncross *I.o.W.* ***Hamlet***, 1km SE of Brighstone. SZ4381.
Thorndon *Suff.* ***Village***, 3m/4km S of Eye. **35 F2** TM1469.
Thorndon Cross *Devon* ***Hamlet***, 4m/6km W of Okehampton. **6 D6** SX5394.
Thorndon Park Country Park *Essex* ***Leisure/recreation***, 2m/3km S of Brentwood. 353 acres of country park on site of ancient deer enclosure. Now parkland, lakes and woodland, parts of which are dominated by ancient oak trees. **24 C2** TQ6191.
Thorne *S.Yorks.* Population: 8376. ***Small town***, market town 9m/15km NE of Doncaster. **51 J1** SE6813.
Thorne Moors *S.Yorks. Alternative name for Thorne Waste, qv.*
Thorne St. Margaret *Som.* ***Hamlet***, 3m/4km W of Wellington. **7 J3** ST0921.

T

Thorne Waste (Also known as Thorne Moors.) *S.Yorks.* ***Open space***, lowland with peat workings, 4m/6km NW of Crowle. **51 K1** SE7215.
Thorner *W.Yorks.* Population: 1472. ***Village***, 7m/11km NE of Leeds. **57 J5** SE3740.
Thornes *Staffs.* ***Hamlet***, 2m/3km SE of Brownhills. **40 C5** SK0703.
Thornes *W.Yorks.* ***Suburb***, 1m/2km S of Wakefield city centre. SE3219.
Thorness Bay *I.o.W.* ***Bay***, on NW coast, N of Great Thorness, 3m/4km SW of Cowes. **11 F5** SZ4594.
Thorney *Bucks.* ***Hamlet***, 5m/8km E of Slough. **22 D4** TQ0479.
Thorney *Notts.* ***Village***, 7m/12km W of Lincoln. **52 B5** SK8572.
Thorney *Peter.* ***Village***, 7m/11km NE of Peterborough. Remains of 12c abbey. Saxon rebel, Hereward the Wake made his last stand here against William the Conqueror. **43 F5** TF2804.
Thorney *Som.* ***Hamlet***, 2m/4km S of Langport. **8 D2** ST4223.
Thorney Channel *See Chichester Harbour.*
Thorney Close *T. & W.* ***Suburb***, 3m/4km SW of Sunderland city centre. NZ3654.
Thorney Hill *Hants.* ***Village***, at SW edge of New Forest, 5m/8km NE of Christchurch. **10 D4** SZ2099.
Thorney Island *W.Suss.* ***Coastal feature***, land area in Chichester Harbour of some 2 square miles or 5 square km, almost separated from mainland by creek known as Great Deep; there is a narrow strip of land at each end of creek and a road bridge across centre. 'Island' contains village of West Thorney and airfield. **11 J4** SU7503.
Thorney Toll *Cambs.* ***Hamlet***, on border with Peterborough, 4m/6km E of Thorney. TF3403.
Thorneywood *Notts.* ***Suburb***, adjoining to W of Carlton, 2m/3km NE of Nottingham city centre. SK5941.
Thornfalcon *Som.* ***Village***, 4m/6km E of Taunton. **8 B2** ST2823.
Thornford *Dorset* ***Village***, 3m/5km SW of Sherborne. **9 F3** ST6013.
Thorngrafton *Northumb.* ***Hamlet***, 1km N of Bardon Mill. NY7865.
Thorngrove *Som.* ***Hamlet***, 1km W of Middlezoy and 5m/8km SE of Bridgwater. **8 C1** ST3632.
Thorngumbald *E.Riding* Population: 2775. ***Village***, 2m/3km SE of Hedon. **59 J7** TA2026.
Thornham *Norf.* ***Village***, 4m/7km E of Hunstanton. Site of Roman signal station 1m/2km SW. **44 B1** TF7343.
Thornham Magna *Suff.* ***Village***, 3m/5km SW of Eye. **35 F1** TM1071.
Thornham Parva *Suff.* ***Settlement***, 1m/2km N of Thornham Magna and 2m/4km E of Gislingham. **35 F1** TM1172.
Thornhaugh *Peter.* ***Village***, 5m/8km SE of Stamford. **42 D5** TF0600.
Thornhill *Caerp.* ***Settlement***, 1m/2km S of Caerphilly. **18 E3** ST1584.
Thornhill *Cumb.* ***Locality***, 1m/2km S of Egremont. NY0108.
Thornhill *Derbys.* ***Village***, 3m/4km NW of Hathersage. **50 D4** SK1983.
Thornhill *D. & G.* Population: 1633. ***Small town***, on River Nith 13m/21km NW of Dumfries. Site of Roman signal station to S. **68 D4** NX8795.
Thornhill *Hants.* ***Suburb***, E district of Southampton 3m/5km E of city centre across River Itchen. **11 F3** SU4712.
Thornhill *Stir.* ***Village***, 7m/12km W of Dunblane. **81 H7** NS6699.
Thornhill *W.Yorks.* ***Locality***, 2m/3km S of Dewsbury. **50 E1** SE2518.
Thornhill Edge *W.Yorks.* ***Locality***, 1km N of Middlestown, 3m/4km S of Dewsbury town centre. SE2518.
Thornhill Lees *W.Yorks.* ***Suburb***, 1m/2km S of Dewsbury town centre. SE2419.
Thornhill Park *S'ham.* ***Suburb***, of Southampton to N of Thornhill. SU4712.
Thornhills *W.Yorks.* ***Settlement***, 1km NE of Brighouse. SE1523.
Thornholme *E.Riding* ***Settlement***, 1km NE of Burton Agnes. **59 H3** TA1163.
Thornicombe *Dorset* ***Settlement***, 3m/4km SW of Blandford Forum. **9 H4** ST8703.
Thornley *Dur.* ***Hamlet***, 1m/2km S of Tow Law. **62 C3** NZ1137.
Thornley *Dur.* Population: 2970. ***Village***, 6m/10km E of Durham. **62 E3** NZ3639.
Thornley Gate *Northumb.* ***Locality***, on W side of River East Allen, opposite Allendale Town. NY8356.
Thornliebank *E.Renf.* ***Suburb***, 4m/7km SW of Glasgow city centre. **74 D5** NS5559.
Thornly Park *Renf.* ***Suburb***, 1m/2km S of Paisley town centre. NS4861.
Thornroan *Aber.* ***Settlement***, 1m/2km N of Tarves. NJ8632.
Thorns *N.Yorks.* ***Locality***, just S of Keld. NY8900.
Thorns *Suff.* ***Village***, 8m/12km NE of Haverhill. **34 B3** TL7455.
Thorn's Flush *Surr.* ***Locality***, 1m/2km NW of Cranleigh. TQ0440.
Thorns Green *Ches.* ***Settlement***, 3m/5km SE of Altrincham. SJ7984.
Thornsett *Derbys.* ***Village***, 1m/2km W of Hayfield. **50 C4** SK0186.
Thornship *Cumb.* ***Locality***, just SE of Keld, 1m/2km SW of Shap. NY5514.
Thornthwaite *Cumb.* ***Hamlet***, 3m/5km NW of Keswick. **60 D4** NY2225.
Thornthwaite *N.Yorks.* ***Hamlet***, 4m/7km S of Pateley Bridge. **57 G4** SE1759.
Thornthwaite Forest *Cumb.* ***Forest/woodland***, adjoining to W of Thornthwaite and within Whinlatter Forest Park, 3m/5km NW of Keswick. **60 C4** NY2125.
Thornton *Angus* ***Settlement***, 1km E of Glamis. **82 E3** NO3946.
Thornton *Bucks.* ***Village***, 4m/6km E of Buckingham. **31 J5** SP7536.
Thornton *E.Riding* ***Village***, 4m/6km SW of Pocklington. **58 D5** SE7645.
Thornton *Fife* Population: 1899. ***Village***, 4m/7km N of Kirkcaldy. **76 A1** NT2897.
Thornton *Lancs.* Population: 14,031. ***Town***, 5m/7km NE of Blackpool. **55 G5** SD3442.
Thornton *Leics.* ***Village***, 5m/8km SE of Coalville. **41 G5** SK4607.
Thornton *Lincs.* ***Hamlet***, 2m/3km SW of Horncastle. **53 F6** TF2467.
Thornton *Mersey.* ***Suburb***, adjoining to NE of Crosby. **48 C2** SD3301.
Thornton *Middbro.* ***Hamlet***, just S of Stainton, 4m/6km SE of Stockton-on-Tees. **63 F5** NZ4713.
Thornton *Northumb.* ***Settlement***, 2m/3km SE of Horncliffe. **77 H6** NT9547.
Thornton *Pembs.* ***Hamlet***, 1m/2km N of Milford Haven. **16 C4** SM9007.
Thornton *P. & K.* ***Settlement***, 3m/5km SE of Dunkeld. **82 B3** NO0740.
Thornton *W.Yorks.* ***Suburb***, 4m/6km W of Bradford city centre. **57 G6** SE1032.
Thornton Abbey *N.Lincs.* ***Ecclesiastical building***, remains of Augustinian abbey with magnificent gatehouse (English Heritage), 2m/3km SE of Goxhill. **52 E1** TA1118.
Thornton Beck *N.Yorks.* ***River***, lower reaches of Dalby Beck, flowing through Thornton-le-Dale and into River Derwent, 2m/3km E of High Marishes. **58 E1** SE8478.
Thornton Bridge *N.Yorks.* ***Settlement***, at crossing of River Swale, 4m/6km NE of Boroughbridge. SE4371.
Thornton Curtis *N.Lincs.* ***Village***, 2m/4km SE of Barrow upon Humber. Thornton Abbey (English Heritage), remains of medieval abbey 2m/3km E. **52 D1** TA0817.
Thornton Dale *N.Yorks. Alternative name for Thornton-le-Dale, qv.*
Thornton Green *Ches.* ***Settlement***, 1km SE of Thornton-le-Moors. SJ4473.
Thornton Heath *Gt.Lon.* ***Suburb***, in borough of Croydon, 2m/3km N of Croydon town centre. TQ3168.
Thornton Hough *Mersey.* ***Village***, 2m/4km NE of Neston. **48 C4** SJ3080.
Thornton-in-Craven *N.Yorks.* ***Village***, 2m/4km NE of Barnoldswick. **56 E5** SD9048.
Thornton in Lonsdale *N.Yorks.* ***Hamlet***, 1km NW of Ingleton. SD6873.
Thornton-le-Beans *N.Yorks.* ***Village***, 3m/4km SE of Northallerton. **62 E7** SE3990.
Thornton-le-Clay *N.Yorks.* ***Village***, 4m/7km NE of Strensall. **58 C3** SE6865.
Thornton-le-Dale (Also known as Thornton Dale.) *N.Yorks.* Population: 1799. ***Village***, 3m/4km E of Pickering. **58 E1** SE8383.
Thornton le Moor *Lincs.* ***Hamlet***, 6m/9km NW of Market Rasen. **52 D3** TF0596.
Thornton-le-Moor *N.Yorks.* ***Village***, 4m/6km S of Northallerton. **57 J1** SE3988.
Thornton-le-Moors *Ches.* ***Village***, 3m/5km SE of Ellesmere Port. **48 D5** SJ4474.
Thornton-le-Street *N.Yorks.* ***Hamlet***, 3m/5km N of Thirsk, on site of Roman settlement. **57 K1** SE4186.
Thornton Moor *N.Yorks.* ***Hamlet***, 1m/2km NW of Flaxton and 3m/5km NE of Strensall. SE6763.
Thornton-on-the-Hill *N.Yorks.* ***Locality***, 2m/4km N of Easingwold. SE5373.
Thornton Park *Northumb.* ***Settlement***, 1m/2km SE of Horncliffe. **77 H6** NT9448.
Thornton Reservoir *Leics.* ***Reservoir***, to E of Thornton. **41 G5** SK4607.
Thornton Reservoir *N.Yorks. Former name of Thornton Steward Reservoir, qv.*
Thornton Rust *N.Yorks.* ***Hamlet***, 2m/3km W of Aysgarth. **56 E1** SD9788.
Thornton Steward *N.Yorks.* ***Village***, 5m/8km SE of Leyburn. **57 G1** SE1787.
Thornton Steward Reservoir (Formerly known as Thornton Reservoir.) *N.Yorks.* ***Reservoir***, to N of Thornton Steward. **57 G1** SE1888.
Thornton Watlass *N.Yorks.* ***Village***, 3m/4km SW of Bedale. **57 H1** SE2385.
Thorntonhall *S.Lan.* ***Suburb***, 3m/5km W of East Kilbride town centre. **74 D5** NS5955.
Thorntonloch *E.Loth.* ***Settlement***, on coast, 5m/8km SE of Dunbar. **77 F3** NT7574.
Thorntree Hill *York* ***Settlement***, 1km SW of Dunnington. SE6552.
Thornville *N.Yorks. Alternative name for Old Thornville, qv.*
Thornwood Common *Essex* ***Hamlet***, 2m/3km N of Epping. **23 H1** TL4704.
Thornyhill *Aber.* ***Settlement***, 1m/2km SW of Fettercairn. **90 E7** NO6372.
Thornyhive Bay *Aber.* ***Bay***, small rocky bay, 2m/3km S of Stonehaven. **91 G6** NO8882.
Thornylee *Sc.Bord.* ***Settlement***, in Tweed valley, 3m/4km NW of Caddonfoot. **76 C7** NT4136.
Thoroton *Notts.* ***Village***, 4m/7km NE of Bingham. **42 A1** SK7642.
Thorp *Gt.Man.* ***Locality***, 1km NW of Royton and 3m/4km N of Oldham. SD9108.
Thorp Arch *W.Yorks.* ***Village***, 2m/4km SE of Wetherby. **57 K5** SE4345.
Thorp Perrow Arboretum *N.Yorks.* ***Garden***, 4m/6km S of Bedale and 11m/18km NW of Thirsk. Home of Sir John Ropner, with large arboretum in over 60 acres of gardens, containing some of the largest and rarest shrubs in England. **57 H1** SE2685.
Thorpe *Cumb.* ***Locality***, adjoining to W of Tirril, 3m/4km SW of Penrith. NY4926.
Thorpe *Derbys.* ***Village***, 3m/4km NW of Ashbourne. **50 D7** SK1550.
Thorpe *E.Riding* ***Hamlet***, adjoining to S of Lockington. **59 G5** SE9946.
Thorpe *Lincs.* ***Settlement***, 2m/3km S of Mablethorpe. **53 H4** TF4982.
Thorpe *Norf.* ***Settlement***, 5m/8km N of Beccles. **45 J6** TM4398.
Thorpe *N.Yorks.* ***Village***, 1m/2km W of Burnsall. **57 F3** SE0161.
Thorpe *Notts.* ***Village***, 3m/5km SW of Newark-on-Trent. Site of Roman fort 1km W. **51 K7** SK7650.
Thorpe *Surr.* ***Village***, 2m/3km SW of Staines. Sailing on gravel workings to E. **22 D5** TQ0268.
Thorpe Abbotts *Norf.* ***Village***, 1m/2km W of Brockdish. **35 F1** TM1979.
Thorpe Acre *Leics.* ***Suburb***, 1m/2km W of Loughborough town centre. **41 H3** SK5120.
Thorpe Arnold *Leics.* ***Hamlet***, 1m/2km NE of Melton Mowbray. **42 A3** SK7720.
Thorpe Audlin *W.Yorks.* ***Village***, 4m/6km NE of Hemsworth. **51 G1** SE4716.
Thorpe Bassett *N.Yorks.* ***Village***, 5m/8km E of Malton. **58 E2** SE8673.
Thorpe Bay *S'end* ***Suburb***, E district of Southend-on-Sea. **25 F3** TQ9185.
Thorpe by Water *Rut.* ***Village***, on River Welland, 3m/4km SE of Uppingham. **42 B6** SP8996.
Thorpe Common *S.Yorks.* ***Locality***, just S of Thorpe Hesley. SK3795.
Thorpe Constantine *Staffs.* ***Village***, 4m/7km NE of Tamworth. **40 E5** SK2608.
Thorpe Culvert *Lincs.* ***Settlement***, 2m/3km NW of Wainfleet All Saints. **53 H6** TF4760.
Thorpe End Garden Village *Norf.* ***Village***, 4m/6km NE of Norwich. **45 G4** TG2811.
Thorpe Green *Essex* ***Hamlet***, 1m/2km NW of Thorpe-le-Soken. TM1723.
Thorpe Green *Lancs.* ***Settlement***, 1m/2km N of Whittle-le-Woods. SD5923.
Thorpe Green *Suff.* ***Hamlet***, 4m/6km N of Lavenham. **34 D3** TL9354.
Thorpe Green *Surr.* ***Settlement***, 3m/4km SW of Staines. TQ0168.
Thorpe Hall *N.Yorks.* ***Settlement***, 1km NW of Yearsley Wood and 1m/2km SW of Ampleforth. **58 B2** SE5776.
Thorpe Hamlet *Norf.* ***Suburb***, 1m/2km E of Norwich city centre. TG2408.
Thorpe Hesley *S.Yorks.* Population: 5173. ***Village***, 4m/6km NW of Rotherham. **51 F3** SK3795.
Thorpe in Balne *S.Yorks.* ***Village***, 5m/8km N of Doncaster. **51 H1** SE5910.
Thorpe in the Fallows *Lincs.* ***Hamlet***, 2m/4km W of Brattleby. **52 C4** SK9180.
Thorpe Langton *Leics.* ***Village***, 4m/6km N of Market Harborough. **42 A6** SP7492.
Thorpe Larches *Dur.* ***Hamlet***, 3m/4km SE of Sedgefield. **62 E4** NZ3826.
Thorpe-le-Soken *Essex* Population: 1509. ***Village***, 5m/7km N of Clacton-on-Sea. **35 F6** TM1822.
Thorpe le Street *E.Riding* ***Hamlet***, 3m/5km NW of Market Weighton. **58 E5** SE8344.
Thorpe-le-Willows *N.Yorks.* ***Locality***, 1m/2km S of Ampleforth. SE5777.
Thorpe Lea *Surr.* ***Suburb***, 1m/2km SW of Staines. TQ0270.
Thorpe Malsor *Northants.* ***Village***, 2m/4km W of Kettering. **32 B1** SP8379.
Thorpe Mandeville *Northants.* ***Village***, 6m/9km NE of Banbury. **31 G4** SP5344.
Thorpe Market *Norf.* ***Village***, 4m/7km S of Cromer. **45 G2** TG2436.
Thorpe Marsh *S.Yorks.* ***Locality***, on W bank of River Don, 4m/7km NE of Doncaster. Power station. SE6009.
Thorpe Morieux *Suff.* ***Village***, 3m/5km NE of Lavenham. **34 D3** TL9453.
Thorpe Ness *Suff.* ***Coastal feature***, headland 1km N of Thorpeness. **35 J2** TM4759.
Thorpe on the Hill *Lincs.* ***Village***, 6m/9km SW of Lincoln. **52 C6** SK9065.
Thorpe on the Hill *W.Yorks.* ***Hamlet***, 5m/8km S of Leeds. **57 J7** SE3126.
Thorpe Park *Surr.* ***Leisure/recreation***, theme park 1m/2km NW of Chertsey, of more than 500 acres. Includes over 100 attractions, with an emphasis on water-based rides. **22 D5** TQ0368.
Thorpe Row *Norf.* ***Hamlet***, 1m/2km NE of Shipdham. TF9608.
Thorpe St. Andrew *Norf.* ***Suburb***, 3m/4km E of Norwich. **45 G5** TG2609.
Thorpe St. Peter *Lincs.* ***Hamlet***, 2m/3km NW of Wainfleet All Saints. **53 H6** TF4860.
Thorpe Salvin *S.Yorks.* ***Village***, 4m/7km W of Worksop. Remains of Elizabethan manor house. **51 H4** SK5281.
Thorpe Satchville *Leics.* ***Village***, 5m/8km S of Melton Mowbray. **42 A4** SK7311.
Thorpe Street *Suff.* ***Settlement***, 1km NW of Hinderclay. TM0277.
Thorpe Thewles *Stock.* ***Village***, 4m/6km NW of Stockton-on-Tees. **62 E4** NZ4023.
Thorpe Tilney Dales *Lincs.* ***Settlement***, on W bank of River Witham, 2m/4km W of Coningsby. **52 E7** TF1858.
Thorpe Underwood *N.Yorks.* ***Hamlet***, 1m/2km SE of Little Ouseburn. **57 K4** SE4659.
Thorpe Underwood *Northants.* ***Settlement***, 2m/3km W of Rothwell. SP7881.
Thorpe Waterville *Northants.* ***Village***, 3m/4km NE of Thrapston. **42 D7** TL0281.
Thorpe Willoughby *N.Yorks.* Population: 2907. ***Village***, 3m/4km W of Selby. **58 B6** SE5731.
Thorpefield *N.Yorks.* ***Hamlet***, 2m/3km SW of Thirsk. SE4179.

T

Thorpeness *Suff.* ***Town***, coastal resort 2m/4km N of Aldeburgh. Nature reserve 1m/2km inland. Large boating lake. **35 J3** TM4759.
Thorpland *Norf.* ***Locality***, 3m/5km N of Downham Market. **44 A5** TF6108.
Thorrington *Essex* ***Village***, 2m/4km N of Brightlingsea. **34 E7** TM0920.
Thor's Cave *Staffs.* ***Cave***, 1km NE of Grindon, to E of River Manifold. **50 C7** SK0954.
Thorverton *Devon* ***Village***, 6m/10km N of Exeter. **7 H5** SS9202.
Thrandeston *Suff.* ***Village***, 2m/4km S of Diss. **35 F1** TM1176.
Thrapston *Northants.* Population: 3912. ***Village***, 7m/11km SW of Oundle. **32 D1** SP9978.
Threapland *Cumb.* ***Hamlet***, 2m/3km S of Aspatria, adjoining to E of Plumbland. NY1539.
Threapland *N.Yorks.* ***Settlement***, 2m/4km SW of Grassington. **56 E3** SD9860.
Threapwood *Ches.* ***Village***, 3m/5km SW of Malpas. **38 D1** SJ4345.
Threapwood Head *Staffs.* ***Settlement***, 2m/3km E of Cheadle. SK0342.
Threave *D. & G.* ***Settlement***, 2m/3km W of Castle Douglas. NX7362.
Threave Castle *D. & G.* ***Castle***, 14c tower of the Douglas family (Historic Scotland), on Threave Island on River Dee, 2m/3km W of Castle Douglas. **65 H4** NX7362.
Threave Gardens *D. & G.* ***Garden***, National Trust for Scotland property and School of Practical Gardening, 1m/2km SE of Threave. Gardens include woodland garden, peat plants, summer flowers, borders and heather. **65 H4** NX7362.
Threave Island *D. & G.* ***Island***, in River Dee, 2m/3km W of Castle Douglas. Threave Castle is on island. NX7362.
Threckingham *Lincs. Alternative name for Threekingham, qv.*
Three Ashes *Som.* ***Settlement***, 3m/4km NE of Shepton Mallet. ST6546.
Three Bridges *Lincs.* ***Locality***, at road bridge over Long Eau, 3m/5km E of Manby. TF4388.
Three Bridges *W.Suss.* ***Suburb***, E district of Crawley. Main-line railway station. **13 F3** TQ2837.
Three Burrows *Cornw.* ***Settlement***, 4m/7km NE of Redruth. **2 E4** SW7446.
Three Chimneys *Kent* ***Hamlet***, 2m/3km W of Biddenden. **14 D4** TQ8238.
Three Cocks (Aberllynfi). *Powys* ***Village***, 3m/5km NE of Talgarth. Named after old coaching inn. **28 A5** SO1737.
Three Counties Showground *Worcs.* ***Other feature of interest***, permanent showground site for Three Counties Show and other events in area, 1m/2km S of Great Malvern. **29 G4** SO7843.
Three Crosses (Y Crwys). *Swan.* ***Village***, 5m/8km W of Swansea. **17 J5** SS5794.
Three Cups Corner *E.Suss.* ***Hamlet***, 4m/6km E of Heathfield. **13 K4** TQ6320.
Three Hammers *Cornw.* ***Hamlet***, 7m/11km NW of Launceston. SX2287.
Three Holes *Norf.* ***Hamlet***, astride Middle Level Drain, 7m/11km SE of Wisbech. **43 J5** TF5000.
Three Horse Shoes *Devon* ***Hamlet***, 3m/4km N of Exeter. SX9096.
Three Households *Bucks.* ***Settlement***, adjoining to W of Chalfont St. Giles. SU9893.
Three Lane Ends *Gt.Man.* ***Locality***, 2m/4km E of Bury. SD8309.
Three Leg Cross *E.Suss.* ***Hamlet***, 1km N of Ticehurst. **13 K3** TQ6831.
Three Legged Cross *Dorset* ***Village***, 4m/7km W of Ringwood. **10 B4** SU0805.
Three Locks *Bucks.* ***Settlement***, on Grand Union Canal, 4m/6km S of Bletchley. SP8928.
Three May Poles *W.Mid.* ***Settlement***, 3m/5km SW of Solihull. SP1177.
Three Mile Cross *W'ham* ***Village***, 4m/6km S of Reading. **22 A5** SU7167.
Three Mile Stone *Cornw. Occasional spelling of Threemilestone, qv.*
Three Oaks *E.Suss.* ***Hamlet***, 4m/6km NE of Hastings. TQ8314.
Three Pikes *Dur.* ***Mountain***, to NW of Langdon Common, 4m/6km SW of St. John's Chapel. Height 2132 feet or 650 metres. **61 K3** NY8334.
Threehammer Common *Norf.* ***Hamlet***, 2m/3km N of Horning. TG3419.
Threekingham (Also known as Threckingham.) *Lincs.* ***Village***, 6m/10km S of Sleaford. **42 D2** TF0836.
Threemilestone (Sometimes spelled Three Mile Stone.) *Cornw.* ***Village***, 3m/5km W of Truro. **2 E4** SW7845.
Threipmuir Reservoir *Edin.* ***Reservoir***, on Pentland Hills, 2m/3km SE of Balerno. **75 K4** NT1763.
Threlkeld *Cumb.* ***Village***, 4m/6km E of Keswick. **60 E4** NY3225.
Threshers Bush *Essex* ***Settlement***, 3m/5km E of Harlow. **23 H1** TL5009.
Threshfield *N.Yorks.* ***Village***, 1m/2km W of Grassington. **56 E3** SD9963.
Threxton Hill *Norf.* ***Settlement***, 2m/3km W of Watton. **44 C5** TF8800.
Thriepley *Dundee* ***Settlement***, 2m/3km S of Newtyle. **82 E4** NO3038.
Thrigby *Norf.* ***Hamlet***, 4m/6km W of Caister-on-Sea. **45 J4** TG4612.
Thringarth *Dur.* ***Settlement***, 2m/3km SW of Middleton-in-Teesdale. **62 A4** NY9323.
Thringstone *Leics.* ***Village***, 2m/3km N of Coalville. **41 G4** SK4217.
Thrintoft *N.Yorks.* ***Village***, 3m/5km W of Northallerton. **62 E7** SE3293.
Thriplow *Cambs.* ***Village***, 6m/10km NE of Royston. **33 H4** TL4346.
Throapham *S.Yorks.* ***Hamlet***, 1km N of Dinnington. SK5387.
Throckenholt *Lincs.* ***Locality***, 1m/2km NW of Parson Drove. TF3509.
Throcking *Herts.* ***Village***, 2m/3km NW of Buntingford. **33 G5** TL3330.
Throckley *T. & W.* ***Suburb***, 6m/9km W of Newcastle upon Tyne. **71 G7** NZ1566.
Throckmorton *Worcs.* ***Village***, on E side of Pershore Airfield (disused), 3m/5km NE of Pershore. **29 J3** SO9849.
Throop *Dorset* ***Settlement***, 2m/3km SW of Bere Regis. SY8293.
Throphill *Northumb.* ***Settlement***, 4m/7km W of Morpeth. **71 G5** NZ1385.
Thropton *Northumb.* ***Village***, 2m/3km W of Rothbury. **71 F3** NU0202.
Througham *Glos.* ***Settlement***, 5m/8km E of Stroud. SO9207.
Throwleigh *Devon* ***Village***, 6m/9km SE of Okehampton. **6 E6** SX6690.
Throwley *Kent* ***Settlement***, 4m/6km SW of Faversham. **14 E2** TQ9955.
Throwley Estate *Staffs.* ***Open space***, National Trust property, 3m/4km NW of Ilam on E side of River Hamps. SK1053.
Throwley Forstal *Kent* ***Hamlet***, 1m/2km S of Throwley. TQ9854.
Throws *Essex* ***Settlement***, 2m/3km E of Great Dunmow. **33 K6** TL6522.
Throxenby *N.Yorks.* ***Suburb***, in W part of Scarborough. TA0189.
Thrumpton *Notts.* ***Suburb***, in S part of Retford. SK7080.
Thrumpton *Notts.* ***Village***, 6m/10km SW of West Bridgford. **41 H2** SK5131.
Thrumpton Hall *Notts.* ***Historic house***, early 17c manor 3m/5km NE of Kegworth and 7m/11km S of Nottingham. Features priest's hiding hole and Charles II staircase. Extensive lawns and landscaped park. **41 H2** SK5031.
Thrumster *High.* ***Village***, in Caithness, 4m/6km S of Wick. **105 J4** ND3345.
Thrunscoe *N.E.Lincs.* ***Suburb***, S district of Cleethorpes. TA3107.
Thrunton *Northumb.* ***Settlement***, 1m/2km SE of Whittingham. Site of Roman fort 1m/2km NE. **71 F2** NU0810.
Thrunton Wood *Northumb.* ***Forest/woodland***, large area planted with conifers, to SW of Thrunton. **71 F3** NU0810.
Thrupp *Glos.* ***Village***, 2m/3km SE of Stroud. **20 B1** SO8603.
Thrupp *Oxon.* ***Hamlet***, on River Cherwell, 6m/10km N of Oxford. **31 F7** SP4815.
Thrupp *Oxon.* ***Settlement***, 2m/3km N of Faringdon. SU2998.
Thruscross *N.Yorks.* ***Settlement***, 2m/3km N of Blubberhouses. SE1558.
Thruscross Reservoir *N.Yorks.* ***Reservoir***, in River Washburn valley to W of Thruscross. **57 G4** SE1558.
Thrushel *Devon* ***River***, rising 3m/4km SW of Okehampton and flowing W, joining River Wolf 1km N of Lifton, and then River Lyd at Lifton. **6 C7** SX4085.
Thrushelton *Devon* ***Hamlet***, 8m/12km NE of Launceston. **6 C7** SX4487.
Thrussington *Leics.* ***Village***, 7m/11km W of Melton Mowbray. **41 J4** SK6415.
Thruxton *Hants.* ***Village***, 5m/8km W of Andover. Thruxton motor-racing circuit to W. 1km NE, site of Roman building. **21 F7** SU2945.
Thruxton *Here.* ***Village***, 6m/9km SW of Hereford. **28 D5** SO4334.
Thrybergh *S.Yorks.* ***Locality***, adjoining to NE of Rotherham. **51 G3** SK4695.
Thrybergh Reservoir *S.Yorks.* ***Reservoir***, and country park, 1m/2km NE of Thrybergh. **51 G3** SK4795.
Thulston *Derbys.* ***Hamlet***, 4m/7km SE of Derby. **41 G2** SK4031.
Thunder Bridge *W.Yorks.* ***Hamlet***, 2m/4km S of Fenay Bridge and 4m/7km SE of Huddersfield. SE1811.
Thundergay (Also known as Mid Thundergay.) *N.Ayr.* ***Locality***, on NW coast of Arran, 2m/3km NE of Pirnmill. **73 G6** NR8846.
Thundersley *Essex* ***Town***, 4m/7km E of Basildon. **24 E3** TQ7888.
Thunderton *Aber.* ***Settlement***, 3m/5km W of Peterhead. **99 J6** NK0646.
Thundridge *Herts.* ***Village***, 2m/3km N of Ware. **33 G7** TL3517.
Thurcaston *Leics.* ***Village***, 4m/7km N of Leicester. **41 H4** SK5610.
Thurcroft *S.Yorks.* Population: 5115. ***Village***, 5m/8km SE of Rotherham. **51 H4** SK4988.
Thurdistoft *High.* ***Settlement***, on N coast, 1km E of Castletown. **105 H2** ND2067.
Thurdon *Cornw.* ***Hamlet***, 6m/9km NW of Holsworthy. SS2811.
Thurgarton *Norf.* ***Hamlet***, adjoining to N of Aldborough. **45 F2** TG1834.
Thurgarton *Notts.* ***Village***, 3m/5km S of Southwell. **41 J1** SK6949.
Thurgarton Priory *Notts.* ***Ecclesiastical building***, Benedictine priory founded in 1187, 8m/12km NE of Nottingham, with remnant used as parish church. **41 J1** SK6949.
Thurgoland *S.Yorks.* Population: 1793. ***Village***, 3m/5km SE of Penistone. **50 E2** SE2901.
Thurland Castle *Lancs.* ***Castle***, just S of Tunstall, 3m/5km S of Kirkby Lonsdale. **56 B2** SD6173.
Thurlaston *Leics.* ***Village***, 6m/10km SW of Leicester. **41 H6** SP5099.
Thurlaston *Warks.* ***Village***, 4m/6km SW of Rugby. **31 F1** SP4671.
Thurlbear *Som.* ***Hamlet***, 3m/5km SE of Taunton. **8 B2** ST2621.
Thurlby *Lincs.* ***Hamlet***, 2m/4km E of Alford. TF4975.
Thurlby *Lincs.* ***Village***, 8m/12km SW of Lincoln. **52 C6** SK9061.
Thurlby *Lincs.* ***Village***, 2m/3km S of Bourne. **42 E4** TF0916.
Thurleigh *Beds.* ***Village***, 6m/9km N of Bedford. Remains of motte and bailey castle. **32 D3** TL0558.
Thurlestone *Devon* ***Village***, resort above cliffs, to N of Bolt Tail, 4m/6km W of Kingsbridge. **5 G6** SX6742.
Thurloxton *Som.* ***Village***, 2m/3km SW of North Petherton. **8 B1** ST2730.
Thurlstone *S.Yorks.* ***Village***, 1m/2km W of Penistone. **50 E2** SE2303.
Thurlstone Moors *S.Yorks.* ***Open space***, moorland 4m/7km W of Penistone. Windleden Reservoir on W edge. **50 D2** SE1701.
Thurlton *Norf.* ***Village***, 5m/8km N of Beccles. **45 J6** TM4198.
Thurlton Links *Norf.* ***Settlement***, to S of Thurlton. TM4197.
Thurlwood *Ches.* ***Settlement***, 1m/2km N of Alsager. SJ8057.
Thurmaston *Leics.* ***Suburb***, 4m/6km NE of Leicester. **41 J5** SK6109.
Thurnby *Leics.* ***Village***, 4m/6km E of Leicester. **41 J5** SK6403.
Thurne *Norf.* ***River***, rising near Happisburgh and flowing S through Horsey Mere into River Bure, just S of Thurne village. **45 J4** TG4015.
Thurne *Norf.* ***Village***, on River Thurne, 9m/15km NW of Great Yarmouth. **45 J4** TG4015.
Thurnham *Kent* ***Village***, 3m/5km NE of Maidstone. **14 D2** TQ8057.
Thurnham *Lancs.* ***Locality***, 5m/7km S of Lancaster, comprising Upper and Lower Thurnham. SD4654.
Thurnham Hall *Lancs.* ***Historic house***, 16c house with stone front dating from 1823, 1m/2km SW of Galgate and 5m/8km S of Lancaster. **55 H4** SD4654.
Thurning *Norf.* ***Hamlet***, 6m/10km S of Holt. **44 E3** TG0829.
Thurning *Northants.* ***Village***, 4m/7km SE of Oundle. **42 D7** TL0883.
Thurnscoe *S.Yorks.* Population: 9705. ***Small town***, 7m/11km E of Barnsley. **51 G2** SE4505.
Thurrock Lakeside *Thur.* ***Leisure/recreation***, large shopping centre, 2m/3km NW of Grays. **23 J4** TQ5878.
Thursby *Cumb.* ***Village***, 6m/10km SW of Carlisle. **60 E1** NY3250.
Thursden *Lancs.* ***Settlement***, on W side of Boulsworth Hill, 3m/5km S of Colne. SD9034.
Thursford *Norf.* ***Hamlet***, 5m/9km NE of Fakenham. Thursford Green hamlet 1m/2km NW. **44 D2** TF9933.
Thursley *Surr.* ***Village***, 3m/4km N of Hindhead. Nature reserve to N. **12 C3** SU9039.
Thurso *High.* ***River***, rising in hills SE of Forsinard railway station and flowing N through Loch More and past Halkirk before continuing N to Thurso and into Thurso Bay. **105 G3** ND1168.
Thurso *High.* Population: 8488. ***Small town***, port on Thurso Bay, N coast of Caithness district, at mouth of River Thurso, 18m/30km NW of Wick. Most northerly town on British mainland. **105 G2** ND1168.
Thurso Bay *High.* ***Bay***, on N coast of Caithness district, with Thurso at centre of bay. **105 G1** ND1168.
Thurstaston *Mersey.* ***Village***, 3m/4km SE of West Kirby. **48 B4** SJ2484.
Thurstaston Common *Mersey.* ***Open space***, National Trust property to N of Thurstaston affording view across River Dee estuary. SJ2484.
Thurston *Suff.* Population: 2612. ***Village***, 5m/8km E of Bury St. Edmunds. **34 D2** TL9265.
Thurston Clough *Gt.Man.* ***Settlement***, 1km SW of Delph, on E side of High Moor. SD9707.
Thurston Planch *Suff.* ***Settlement***, adjoining to S of Thurston. TL9364.
Thurstonfield *Cumb.* ***Village***, 5m/8km W of Carlisle. **60 E1** NY3156.
Thurstonland *W.Yorks.* ***Village***, 2m/3km NE of Holmfirth. **50 D1** SE1610.
Thurton *Norf.* ***Village***, 3m/4km NW of Loddon. **45 H5** TG3200.
Thurvaston *Derbys.* ***Hamlet***, 1km NE of Marston Montgomery. SK1338.
Thurvaston *Derbys.* ***Hamlet***, 7m/11km W of Derby. **40 E2** SK2437.
Thuster *High.* ***Settlement***, 4m/7km W of Wick. **105 H3** ND2851.
Thuxton *Norf.* ***Hamlet***, 5m/8km SE of East Dereham. **44 E5** TG0307.
Thwaite *N.Yorks.* ***Hamlet***, in Swaledale, 1m/2km W of Muker. **61 K7** SD8998.
Thwaite *Suff.* ***Village***, 4m/7km SW of Eye. **35 F2** TM1168.
Thwaite Head *Cumb.* ***Hamlet***, 5m/8km S of Hawkshead. **60 E7** SD3490.
Thwaite St. Mary *Norf.* ***Village***, 3m/5km N of Bungay. **45 H6** TM3394.
Thwaites *W.Yorks.* ***Suburb***, 1km E of Keighley town centre. SE0741.
Thwaites Brow *W.Yorks.* ***Village***, on hillside overlooking Airedale, 1m/2km E of Keighley town centre across River Worth. SE0740.
Thwing *E.Riding* ***Village***, 8m/13km W of Bridlington. **59 G3** TA0470.
Tianavaig Bay *High.* ***Bay***, on E coast of Skye, 3m/5km SE of Loch Portree. **86 B1** NG5138.
Tibbermore (Also known as Tippermuir.) *P. & K.* ***Village***, 4m/7km W of Perth. To SE is site of battle of 1644 in which Montrose defeated army of Covenanters and gained control of Perth. **82 B5** NO0523.
Tibberton *Glos.* ***Village***, 5m/8km NW of Gloucester. **29 G6** SO7621.
Tibberton *Tel. & W.* ***Village***, 4m/7km W of Newport. **39 F3** SJ6820.
Tibberton *Worcs.* ***Village***, 4m/6km NE of Worcester. **29 J3** SO9057.

Tibbie Shiels Inn *Sc.Bord.* ***Settlement***, at E side of bridge which crosses St. Mary's Loch. Loch is known as Loch of the Lowes to S of bridge. **69 H1** NT2420.

Tibenham *Norf.* ***Village***, 6m/10km N of Diss. **45 F6** TM1389.

Tibertich *Arg. & B.* ***Settlement***, 2m/3km SW of Ford. **79 K7** NM8402.

Tibshelf *Derbys.* Population: 3395. ***Village***, 3m/5km NE of Alfreton. **51 G6** SK4360.

Tibthorpe *E.Riding* ***Village***, 4m/7km W of Great Driffield. **59 F4** SE9655.

Tibthorpe Wold *E.Riding* ***Open space***, on The Wolds 1m/2km S of Wetwang and 6m/9km W of Great Driffield. **59 F4** SE9256.

Ticehurst *E.Suss.* ***Village***, 3m/5km SE of Wadhurst. **13 K3** TQ6830.

Tichborne *Hants.* ***Village***, 2m/3km SW of New Alresford. **11 G1** SU5730.

Tick Fen *Cambs.* ***Open space***, fenland 3m/5km SW of Chatteris. **43 G7** TL3384.

Tickencote *Rut.* ***Village***, 3m/5km NW of Stamford. Remarkable Norman chancel arch in church. **42 C5** SK9909.

Tickenham *N.Som.* ***Village***, 3m/5km E of Clevedon. **19 H4** ST4571.

Tickford End *M.K.* ***Suburb***, at E end of Newport Pagnell. SP8843.

Tickhill *S.Yorks.* Population: 5572. ***Small town***, 6m/10km S of Doncaster. Remains of Norman castle. **51 H3** SK5993.

Ticklerton *Shrop.* ***Hamlet***, 3m/4km SE of Church Stretton. **38 D6** SO4890.

Ticknall *Derbys.* ***Village***, 2m/4km W of Melbourne. **41 F3** SK3523.

Tickton *E.Riding* ***Village***, 3m/4km NE of Beverley. **59 G5** TA0641.

Tidal Reservoir *S.Glos.* ***Reservoir***, in River Severn, 2m/3km NW of Oldbury-on-Severn. **19 J2** ST5995.

Tidbury Green *W.Mid.* ***Settlement***, 4m/7km SW of Solihull. SP1075.

Tidcombe *Wilts.* ***Hamlet***, 3m/5km SW of Shalbourne. **21 F6** SU2958.

Tiddington *Oxon.* ***Village***, 4m/6km W of Thame. **21 K1** SP6504.

Tiddington *Warks.* ***Village***, 2m/3km E of Stratford-upon-Avon. **30 D3** SP2255.

Tiddy *Cornw.* ***River***, rising at Pensilva, below Caradon Hill, and flowing SE into St. Germans River below St. Germans Quay. **4 D4** SX3756.

Tidebrook *E.Suss.* ***Hamlet***, 2m/3km SW of Wadhurst. **13 K4** TQ6129.

Tideford *Cornw.* ***Village***, 5m/8km W of Saltash. **4 D5** SX3459.

Tideford Cross *Cornw.* ***Hamlet***, 1m/2km N of Tideford. SX3460.

Tidenham *Glos.* ***Village***, 2m/3km NE of Chepstow. **19 J2** ST5595.

Tidenham Chase *Glos.* ***Settlement***, 2m/3km SE of Tintern Parva. **19 J2** ST5498.

Tideswell *Derbys.* Population: 1717. ***Small town***, 6m/10km E of Buxton. 14c church known as 'cathedral of the Peak'. Well-dressing takes place here every June. **50 D5** SK1575.

Tidmarsh *W.Berks.* ***Village***, 1m/2km S of Pangbourne. **21 K4** SU6374.

Tidmington *Warks.* ***Village***, 1m/2km S of Shipston on Stour. **30 D5** SP2638.

Tidpit *Hants.* ***Hamlet***, 5m/8km NW of Fordingbridge. **10 B3** SU0718.

Tiel Burn *Fife* ***River***, rising 3m/4km N of Aberdour and flowing E to enter Firth of Forth on S side of Kirkcaldy. **76 A1** NT2790.

Tiers Cross *Pembs.* ***Hamlet***, 3m/5km N of Milford Haven. **16 C3** SM9010.

Tiffield *Northants.* ***Village***, 2m/3km N of Towcester. **31 H3** SP6951.

Tifty *Aber.* ***Settlement***, 7m/11km SE of Turriff. **99 F6** NJ7740.

Tigerton *Angus* ***Village***, 5m/7km NW of Brechin. **83 G1** NO5464.

Tigh a' Gearraidh (Anglicised form: Tigharry.) *W.Isles* ***Village***, on NW coast of North Uist, 3m/5km S of Griminis Point. **92 C4** NF7171.

Tighachnoic *High.* ***Settlement***, in Morvern, Lochaber district, 1km N of Lochaline. **79 H3** NM6745.

Tigharry *W.Isles Anglicised form of Tigh a' Gearraidh, qv.*

Tighnablair *P. & K.* ***Settlement***, 3m/5km S of Comrie. **81 J6** NN7716.

Tighnabruaich *Arg. & B.* ***Village***, resort in Argyll, on W shore of Kyles of Bute, 3m/4km SW of entrance to Loch Riddon. Forest N and S. **73 H3** NR9772.

Tighnacomaire *High.* ***Settlement***, in Glen Scaddle, Lochaber district, 6m/9km NW of Sallachan Point. **80 A1** NM9468.

Tighvein *N.Ayr.* ***Mountain***, in S part of Arran, 3m/4km SW of Lamlash. Height 1502 feet or 458 metres. **66 D1** NR9927.

Tigley *Devon* ***Village***, 3m/5km W of Totnes. **5 H4** SX7560.

Til ***River***, upper reaches of River Kym, rising SE of Rushden and flowing NE to Tilbrook. **32 D2** TL0869.

Tilbrook *Cambs.* ***Village***, 7m/12km E of Higham Ferrers. **32 D2** TL0769.

Tilbury *Thur.* Population: 11,658. ***Town***, old container port on River Thames, 21m/34km E of London. Ferry for pedestrians across river to Gravesend. 17c Tilbury Fort is fine example of military architecture. **24 C4** TQ6476.

Tilbury Fort *Thur.* ***Historic/prehistoric site***, largest preserved example of 17c English military engineering (English Heritage) commands River Thames, 1km SE of Tilbury. Exhibitions and demonstrations showing development and how fort protected London from seaborne attack. **24 C4** TQ6475.

Tilbury Green *Essex* ***Hamlet***, to E of Ridgewell, 6m/9km SE of Haverhill. TL7440.

Tilbury juxta Clare *Essex* ***Hamlet***, 3m/5km S of Clare. TL7640.

Tile Cross *W.Mid.* ***Suburb***, 6m/10km E of Birmingham city centre. **40 D7** SP1686.

Tile Hill *W.Mid.* ***Suburb***, 3m/5km W of Coventry city centre. **30 D1** SP2878.

Tilegate Green *Essex* ***Settlement***, 4m/7km E of Harlow. TL5008.

Tilehouse Green *W.Mid.* ***Suburb***, 2m/3km SE of Solihull town centre. SP1776.

Tilehurst *Read.* ***Locality***, parish on W side of Reading; also W district of Reading. **21 K4** SU6673.

Tilford *Surr.* ***Village***, 3m/5km SE of Farnham. **22 B7** SU8743.

Tilgate *W.Suss.* ***Suburb***, S district of Crawley. TQ2735.

Tilgate Forest Country Park *W.Suss.* ***Leisure/recreation***, 1m/2km S of Crawley town centre. 400 acres of lakes, woodland and ornamental gardens. **13 F3** TQ2734.

Tilgate Forest Row *W.Suss.* ***Settlement***, 3m/5km S of Crawley. TQ2532.

Tilham Street *Som.* ***Hamlet***, just NE of Ham Street, 4m/7km SE of Glastonbury. ST5535.

Till *Lincs.* ***River***, rising E of Gainsborough and flowing S into River Witham at Lincoln. **52 C4** SK9771.

Till *Northumb.* ***River***, rising as River Breamish on S slope of The Cheviot and flowing E to New Bewick, then N as River Till to Chatton and NW into River Tweed 2m/4km N of Cornhill on Tweed. **77 H6** NT8742.

Tillathrowie *Aber.* ***Settlement***, 4m/6km SE of Haugh of Glass. **90 C1** NJ4735.

Tillers' Green *Glos.* ***Hamlet***, 5m/8km NW of Newent. **29 F5** SO6932.

Tillery *Aber.* ***Settlement***, 3m/4km NE of Newmachar. **91 H2** NJ9122.

Tilley *Shrop.* ***Hamlet***, 1km SW of Wem. **38 E3** SJ5027.

Tillicoultry *Clack.* Population: 5269. ***Small town***, 3m/5km NE of Alloa. Tradition of milling and weaving based on water power. **75 H1** NS9197.

Tillingham *E.Suss.* ***River***, rising near Staple Cross and flowing E into River Brede at Rye. TQ9119.

Tillingham *Essex* ***Village***, 5m/8km NE of Burnham-on-Crouch. **25 F1** TL9903.

Tillington *Here.* ***Village***, 4m/7km NW of Hereford. **28 D4** SO4645.

Tillington *W.Suss.* ***Village***, 1m/2km W of Petworth. **12 C4** SU9622.

Tillington Common *Here.* ***Village***, 1m/2km NW of Tillington. **28 D4** SO4645.

Tilly Whim Caves *Dorset* ***Cave***, man-made cave system below Durlston Head, 1m/2km S of Swanage town centre. Formerly quarried for building stone. **10 B7** SZ0377.

Tillyarblet *Angus* ***Hamlet***, 2m/3km NW of Kirkton of Menmuir. **83 G1** NO5167.

Tillybirloch *Aber.* ***Settlement***, 4m/6km W of Echt. **90 E4** NJ6707.

Tillycairn Castle *Aber.* ***Castle***, 5m/8km SW of Kemnay. **90 E3** NJ6611.

Tillycorthie *Aber.* ***Locality***, 3m/5km SE of Pitmedden. Includes Tillycorthie Mansion House and Tillycorthie Farm. **91 H2** NJ9023.

Tillydrine *Aber.* ***Hamlet***, 1km SE of Kincardine O'Neil. **90 E5** NO6098.

Tillyfar *Aber.* ***Settlement***, 3m/4km SW of New Deer. **99 G6** NJ8545.

Tillyfour *Aber.* ***Settlement***, 4m/6km S of Alford. **90 D3** NJ5910.

Tillyfourie *Aber.* ***Village***, 5m/8km SE of Alford. **90 E3** NJ6412.

Tillygreig *Aber.* ***Settlement***, 3m/4km N of Newmachar. **91 G2** NJ8822.

Tillypronie *Aber.* ***Settlement***, 4m/6km NW of Tarland. Symbol Stone nearby. **90 C4** NJ4307.

Tilmanstone *Kent* ***Village***, 5m/8km W of Deal. **15 H2** TR3051.

Tiln *Notts.* ***Settlement***, 2m/3km N of Retford. SK7084.

Tilney All Saints *Norf.* ***Village***, 4m/6km W of King's Lynn. **43 J4** TF5618.

Tilney Fen Side *Norf.* ***Settlement***, 2m/3km S of Tilney St. Lawrence. TF5411.

Tilney High End *Norf.* ***Village***, 4m/7km SW of King's Lynn. **43 J4** TF5617.

Tilney St. Lawrence *Norf.* ***Village***, 6m/9km SW of King's Lynn. **43 J4** TF5414.

Tilshead *Wilts.* ***Village***, on Salisbury Plain, 9m/14km NW of Amesbury. **20 D7** SU0347.

Tilstock *Shrop.* ***Village***, 2m/4km S of Whitchurch. **38 E2** SJ5437.

Tilston *Ches.* ***Village***, 8m/13km NW of Whitchurch. **48 D7** SJ4551.

Tilstone Bank *Ches.* ***Settlement***, 2m/3km SE of Tarporley. SJ5659.

Tilstone Fearnall *Ches.* ***Hamlet***, 1m/2km SE of Tarporley. **48 E6** SJ5660.

Tilsworth *Beds.* ***Village***, 3m/5km NW of Dunstable. **32 C6** SP9724.

Tilt *P. & K.* ***River***, running SW down Glen Tilt to River Garry at Blair Atholl. **89 G7** NN8764.

Tilton *Leics. Alternative name for Tilton on the Hill, qv.*

Tilton on the Hill (Also known as Tilton.) *Leics.* ***Village***, 9m/14km NW of Uppingham. **42 A5** SK7405.

Tilts *S.Yorks.* ***Settlement***, 3m/4km E of Adwick le Street. SE5709.

Tiltups End *Glos.* ***Hamlet***, 2m/3km S of Nailsworth. **20 B2** ST8497.

Tilty *Essex* ***Settlement***, 3m/5km NW of Great Dunmow. TL5926.

Tilworth Grange *Hull* ***Suburb***, 3m/5km NE of Kingston upon Hull city centre. TA1232.

Tima Water *Sc.Bord.* ***River***, flowing N to join Ettrick Water at Ettrick. **69 H3** NT2714.

Timberland *Lincs.* ***Village***, 8m/13km NE of Sleaford. **52 E7** TF1258.

Timberland Dales *Lincs.* ***Settlement***, on W bank of River Witham, 2m/3km SW of Woodhall Spa. **52 E6** TF1860.

Timberland Delph *Lincs.* ***Other water feature***, artificial drainage channel running from 1km E of Timberland into River Witham, 1m/2km SW of Woodhall Spa. **52 E6** TF1761.

Timbersbrook *Ches.* ***Village***, 2m/4km E of Congleton. **49 H6** SJ8962.

Timberscombe *Som.* ***Village***, below Exmoor, 3m/4km W of Dunster. **7 H1** SS9542.

Timble *N.Yorks.* ***Hamlet***, 2m/3km S of Blubberhouses. **57 G4** SE1752.

Timewell *Devon* ***Settlement***, 3m/5km SE of Dulverton. SS9625.

Timperley *Gt.Man.* ***Suburb***, 1m/2km E of Altrincham town centre. **49 G4** SJ7888.

Timsbury *B. & N.E.Som.* Population: 2396. ***Village***, 3m/5km N of Midsomer Norton. **19 K6** ST6658.

Timsbury *Hants.* ***Village***, 2m/3km N of Romsey. **10 E2** SU3424.

Timsgarry *W.Isles Anglicised form of Timsgearraidh, qv.*

Timsgearraidh (Anglicised form: Timsgarry.) *W.Isles* ***Village***, near W coast of Isle of Lewis, 3m/5km S of Gallan Head. **100 C4** NB0534.

Timworth *Suff.* ***Hamlet***, 4m/6km N of Bury St. Edmunds. TL8669.

Timworth Green *Suff.* ***Hamlet***, adjoins to S of Timworth, 3m/5km N of Bury St. Edmunds. **34 C2** TL8669.

Tincleton *Dorset* ***Village***, 5m/8km E of Dorchester. **9 G5** SY7791.

Tindale *Cumb.* ***Hamlet***, 6m/9km E of Brampton. **61 H1** NY6159.

Tindale Fells *Cumb.* ***Open space***, moorland on Bruthwaite Forest to S of Tindale Tarn, 6m/9km SE of Brampton. **61 G1** NY6057.

Tindale Tarn *Cumb.* ***Lake/loch***, 1km SW of Tindale. **61 H1** NY6159.

Tindon End *Essex* ***Settlement***, 2m/3km N of Thaxted. TL6134.

Tinga Skerry *Shet.* ***Island***, group of rocks in Yell Sound lying between islands of Brother Isle and Little Roe. HU4180.

Tingewick *Bucks.* ***Village***, 3m/4km W of Buckingham. **31 H5** SP6532.

Tingley *W.Yorks.* ***Village***, 2m/3km SE of Morley. **57 H7** SE2826.

Tingrith *Beds.* ***Village***, 4m/6km E of Woburn. **32 D5** TL0032.

Tingwall *Ork.* ***Settlement***, on NE coast of Mainland, 1m/2km N of Hackland. **106 D5** HY4022.

Tingwall *Shet.* ***Locality***, on Mainland, lying between Whiteness Voe and Dales Voe, to NW of Lerwick. HU4144.

Tingwall Airport *Shet.* ***Airport/airfield***, 1km NW of Veensgarth, Mainland. **109 D8** HU4145.

Tinhay *Devon* ***Village***, 4m/7km E of Launceston, between Rivers Lyd and Thrushel, at their confluence. **6 C7** SX3985.

Tinker's Hill *Hants.* ***Settlement***, 3m/4km NE of Andover. SU3947.

Tinkinswood *V. of Glam.* ***Historic/prehistoric site***, site of Neolithic burial-chamber (Cadw), 1km S of St. Nicholas. **18 D4** ST0973.

Tinney *Devon* ***Settlement***, 4m/6km SW of Holsworthy. **4 C1** SX2999.

Tinnis Castle and Fort *Sc.Bord.* ***Castle***, to NE of Drumelzier. Early 16c ruin of stronghold of Tweedie family. **75 K7** NT1434.

Tinnis Hill *Cumb.* ***Mountain***, 4m/7km E of Langholm. Height 1325 feet or 404 metres. **69 K5** NY4385.

Tinshill *W.Yorks.* ***Suburb***, 5m/8km NW of Leeds city centre. **57 H6** SE2539.

Tinsley *S.Yorks.* ***Suburb***, 4m/6km NE of Sheffield city centre. **51 G3** SK4090.

Tinsley Green *W.Suss.* ***Hamlet***, 2m/3km NE of Crawley. **13 F3** TQ2939.

Tintagel *Cornw.* ***Village***, near N coast, 4m/7km NW of Camelford. 14c Old Post Office (National Trust). **4 A2** SX0489.

Tintagel Castle *Cornw.* ***Castle***, legendary stronghold of King Arthur (English Heritage), on headland 14m/22km N of Bodmin. **4 A2** SX0489.

Tintagel Head *Cornw.* ***Coastal feature***, headland on SW side of The Island, 1km W of Tintagel. **4 A2** SX0489.

Tintagel Old Post Office *Cornw.* ***Historic house***, miniature 14c stone house, now National Trust property, in Tintagel. **4 A2** SX0588.

Tintern Abbey (Tyndyrn). *Mon.* ***Ecclesiastical building***, impressive ruin of medieval abbey (Cadw) on W bank of River Wye, 4m/6km N of Chepstow. **19 J2** SO5300.

Tintern Parva (Tyndyrn). *Mon.* ***Village***, on River Wye, 4m/7km N of Chepstow. **19 J1** SO5300.

Tintinhull *Som.* ***Village***, 4m/7km NW of Yeovil. Tintinhull House and garden (National Trust). **8 D3** ST4919.

Tintinhull House *Som.* ***Garden***, formal 20c garden (National Trust) and kitchen garden in grounds of 17c house, 5m/8km NW of Yeovil. **8 E3** ST5019.

Tinto *S.Lan.* ***Mountain***, 3m/4km S of Thankerton. Height 2319 feet or 707 metres. **75 H7** NS9534.

Tintwistle *Derbys.* ***Village***, 2m/3km N of Glossop. **50 C3** SK0297.

Tinwald *D. & G.* ***Village***, 4m/6km NE of Dumfries. **69 F5** NY0081.

Tinwell *Rut.* ***Village***, 2m/3km W of Stamford. Site of Roman building 1m/2km E. **42 D5** TF0006.

Tioram Castle (Sometimes known as Tirrim Castle.) *High.* ***Castle***, ruined stronghold of the Macdonalds on tidal islet in Loch Moidart in Lochaber district, opposite Dorlin. **86 C7** NM6672.

Tiphill Head *Devon* ***Locality***, on S side of Ottery St. Mary. SY1095.

Tipner *Ports.* ***Settlement***, on E shore of Portsmouth Harbour, 2m/3km N of Portsmouth city centre. SU6303.

Tippacott *Devon* ***Settlement***, 3m/5km SE of Lynton, on N edge of Exmoor. **7 F1** SS7647.

Tippermuir *P. & K. Alternative name for Tibbermore, qv.*

Tipperty *Aber.* ***Hamlet***, 3m/5km NW of Glenbervie. **91 F6** NO7282.

Tipperty *Aber.* ***Settlement***, on Tarty Burn, 3m/4km SE of Ellon. **91 H2** NJ9626.

Tipperweir *Aber.* ***Mountain***, 2m/3km E of Bridge of Dye. Height 1437 feet or 438 metres. **90 E6** NO6885.

Tips Cross *Essex* ***Settlement***, 3m/5km SE of Chipping Ongar. TL5800.

Tips End *Norf.* ***Hamlet***, 1m/2km NW of Welney. TL5095.

Tiptoe *Hants.* ***Hamlet***, 4m/6km SW of Brockenhurst. **10 D5** SZ2597.

Tipton *W.Mid.* ***Suburb***, 3m/5km W of West Bromwich town centre. **40 B6** SO9592.

Tipton Cross *Devon* ***Locality***, 1km SW of West Hill. SY0592.

Tipton Green *W.Mid.* ***Locality***, 1m/2km N of Dudley town centre. SO9592.

Tipton St. John *Devon* ***Village***, on River Otter, 2m/3km S of Ottery St. Mary. **7 J6** SY0991.

Tiptree *Essex* Population: 7679. ***Small town***, 9m/14km SW of Colchester. Jam centre of Essex, where local farmer founded Wilkin's Tiptree Preserves. **34 C7** TL8916.

Tiptree Heath *Essex* ***Hamlet***, 1km SW of Tiptree. **34 C7** TL8814.

Tipwell *Cornw.* ***Settlement***, 2m/4km SE of Callington. SX3867.

Tir Rhiwiog *Powys* ***Mountain***, 5m/8km E of Dinas-Mawddwy. Height 1788 feet or 545 metres. **37 J4** SH9216.

Tir-y-berth *Caerp.* ***Locality***, 2m/3km S of Bargoed. ST1496.

Tir-y-dail *Carmar.* ***Locality***, in N part of Ammanford. **17 K3** SN6213.

Tir-y-fron *Flints.* ***Settlement***, 2m/3km W of Hope. SJ2959.

Tir y mynach *Powys* ***Open space***, hillside area 2m/3km SE of Llanbrynmair. **37 J5** SH9101.

Tirabad *Powys* ***Hamlet***, 3m/5km S of Llanwrtyd Wells. **27 H4** SN8741.

Tircanol *Swan.* ***Suburb***, in Morriston district of Swansea, 4m/6km NE of city centre. SS6798.

Tirdeunaw *Swan.* ***Suburb***, 3m/4km N of Swansea city centre. **17 K5** SS6597.

Tiree *Arg. & B.* ***Island***, of the Inner Hebrides lying 2m/3km SW of Coll. Measures 11m/18km E to W and is of irregular shape, the total area being 29 square miles or 75 square km. The island is low-lying and windswept, but the climate is mild. Airfield 3m/4km W of Scarinish. **78 A3** NL9945.

Tiree Airport *Arg. & B.* ***Airport/airfield***, to N of Hynish Bay, Tiree. **78 B3** NM0044.

Tirga Mòr *W.Isles* ***Mountain***, in Forest of Harris 5m/8km SW of head of Loch Resort. Height 2227 feet or 679 metres. **100 C6** NB0511.

Tirindrish *High.* ***Settlement***, 1km E of Spean Bridge. **87 J6** NN2382.

Tirley *Glos.* ***Village***, 8m/13km NW of Cheltenham. **29 H6** SO8328.

Tirphil *Caerp.* ***Village***, 2m/4km NW of Bargoed. **18 E1** SO1303.

Tirril *Cumb.* ***Hamlet***, 2m/4km S of Penrith. **61 G4** NY5026.

Tirrim Castle *High. Occasional name for Tioram Castle, qv.*

Tirry *High.* ***River***, in Sutherland district, running S into Loch Shin 2m/3km N of Lairg. **103 H7** NC5609.

Tirryside *High.* ***Settlement***, in Sutherland district, on E side of Loch Shin near mouth of River Tirry. NC5610.

Tisbury *Wilts.* Population: 1911. ***Village***, on River Sem, 10m/15km W of Wilton. **9 J2** ST9429.

Tisman's Common *W.Suss.* ***Settlement***, 3m/4km SE of Alford Crossways. TQ0732.

Tissington *Derbys.* ***Village***, 4m/6km N of Ashbourne. **50 D7** SK1752.

Tister *High.* ***Settlement***, 4m/6km S of Castletown. **105 G2** ND1961.

Titchberry *Devon* ***Hamlet***, 1m/2km E of Hartland Point. **6 A3** SS2427.

Titchfield *Hants.* ***Village***, 3m/4km W of Fareham. To N, Titchfield Abbey (English Heritage), 13c abbey gatehouse converted into mansion in 16c. **11 G4** SU5305.

Titchfield Abbey (Also known as Place House.) *Hants.* ***Historic house***, 1km N of Titchfield, 2m/3km W of Fareham. English Heritage property built by first Earl of Southampton in 1542, incorporating nave of 13c abbey church. Overshadowed by Tudor gatehouse. **11 G4** SU5306.

Titchmarsh *Northants.* ***Village***, 2m/3km NE of Thrapston. **32 D1** TL0279.

Titchwell *Norf.* ***Village***, 5m/8km E of Hunstanton. Remains of ancient forest off shore to N. **44 B1** TF7643.

Tithby *Notts.* ***Hamlet***, 2m/3km S of Bingham. **41 J2** SK6936.

Tithebarn *Staffs.* ***Hamlet***, adjoining to SE of Alton, 4m/7km SE of Cheadle. SK0741.

Titley *Here.* ***Village***, 3m/5km NE of Kington. **28 C2** SO3360.

Titlington *Northumb.* ***Settlement***, 2m/3km E of Glanton. NU1015.

Titmore Green *Herts.* ***Settlement***, 3m/4km SE of Hitchin. TL2126.

Titsey *Surr.* ***Hamlet***, below S escarpment of North Downs, 1m/2km N of Limpsfield. Remains of Roman villa in Titsey Park. Site of Roman temple to E. **23 H6** TQ4055.

Titson (Also known as Budd's Titson.) *Cornw.* ***Hamlet***, 4m/6km SE of Bude. **6 A5** SS2401.

Tittenhurst *W. & M.* ***Settlement***, at S edge of Windsor Great Park, 1km NW of Sunningdale. SU9468.

Tittensor *Staffs.* ***Village***, 3m/5km NW of Stone. **40 A2** SJ8738.

Titterstone Clee Hill (Also known as Clee Hill.) *Shrop.* ***Mountain***, prominent landmark, 5m/8km W of Cleobury Mortimer, rising to 1748 feet or 533 metres. Extensively quarried on S slope around locality known as Clee Hill, which is name more usually applied also to mountain itself. **28 E1** SO5977.

Tittesworth *Staffs.* ***Locality***, 2m/4km NE of Leek. SK0059.

Tittesworth Reservoir *Staffs.* ***Reservoir***, 1m/2km W of Tittesworth. **49 J6** SK0059.

Tittleshall *Norf.* ***Village***, 6m/9km SW of Fakenham. **44 C3** TF8921.

Tiumpan Head (Gaelic form: Rubha an t-Siùmpain.) *W.Isles* ***Coastal feature***, headland with lighthouse at NE end of Eye Peninsula, Isle of Lewis. **101 H4** NB5737.

Tiverton *Ches.* ***Village***, 1m/2km S of Tarporley. **48 E6** SJ5560.

Tiverton *Devon* Population: 14,805. ***Town***, market town on River Exe, 12m/19km N of Exeter, which prospered on its medieval cloth manufacture. Tiverton Castle has medieval gateway. **7 H4** SS9512.

Tiverton Castle *Devon* ***Castle***, situated on River Exe at Tiverton. Early 12c castle built by Henry I; former home of Earls of Devon. **7 H4** SS9513.

Tivetshall St. Margaret *Norf.* ***Village***, 6m/9km NW of Harleston. **45 F7** TM1687.

Tivetshall St. Mary *Norf.* ***Village***, 1km S of Tivetshall St. Margaret. **45 F7** TM1687.

Tividale *W.Mid.* ***Suburb***, in NW part of Warley, 2m/3km W of West Bromwich town centre. SO9690.

Tivington *Som.* ***Hamlet***, largely National Trust, 3m/4km SW of Minehead. To S, nearby hamlet of Tivington Knowle. SS9345.

Tivy Dale *S.Yorks.* ***Locality***, adjoining to SW of Cawthorne, 3m/5km E of Denby Dale. SE2707.

Tixall *Staffs.* ***Village***, 4m/6km E of Stafford. **40 B3** SJ9722.

Tixover *Rut.* ***Village***, 5m/9km SW of Stamford. **42 C5** SK9700.

Toa Galson *W.Isles* ***Coastal feature***, headland on NW coast of Isle of Lewis, 6m/9km SW of Butt of Lewis. **101 G1** NB4560.

Toab *Ork.* ***Settlement***, on mainland, on W side of Deer Sound, 5m/8km SE of Kirkwall. **107 E7** HY5006.

Toab *Shet.* ***Settlement***, on Mainland, to N of Sumburgh Airport. **109 G10** HU3811.

Toad Row *Suff.* ***Settlement***, 2m/3km W of Kessingland. TM5086.

Tobermory *Arg. & B.* ***Town***, resort and chief town of Mull, situated on Tobermory Bay near N end of Sound of Mull. Former fishing village. **79 G2** NM5055.

Tobermory Bay *Arg. & B.* ***Bay***, on Mull, near N end of Sound of Mull. Wreck of Spanish galleon, blown up in 1588, lies at the bottom of the bay. **79 G2** NM5055.

Toberonochy *Arg. & B.* ***Village***, small village on Shuna Sound, on E coast of Luing. **79 J7** NM7408.

Tobha Mòr (Anglicised form: Howmore.) *W.Isles* ***Village***, near W coast of South Uist, 5m/7km NW of Beinn Mhòr. **84 C1** NF7536.

Tobson *W.Isles* ***Settlement***, on W coast of Great Bernera, 2m/3km NW of Breacleit. **100 D4** NB1338.

Toby's Hill *Lincs.* ***Locality***, adjoining to N of Saltfleet. TF4594.

Tocher *Aber.* ***Settlement***, 3m/5km E of Kirkton of Culsalmond. **90 E1** NJ6932.

Tockenham *Wilts.* ***Village***, 3m/4km SW of Wootton Bassett. **20 D4** SU0379.

Tockenham Wick *Wilts.* ***Hamlet***, 1m/2km N of Tockenham. **20 D3** SU0381.

Tockholes *B'burn.* ***Village***, 4m/6km SW of Blackburn. **56 B7** SD6622.

Tockington *S.Glos.* ***Village***, 3m/5km SW of Thornbury. **19 K3** ST6086.

Tockwith *N.Yorks.* ***Village***, 5m/8km NE of Wetherby. **57 K4** SE4652.

Todber *Dorset* ***Village***, 4m/7km SW of Shaftesbury. **9 G2** ST8020.

Todd Hill *Northumb.* ***Hill***, rising to over 120 metres, 4m/6km NW of Morpeth. **71 G5** NZ1589.

Todden Hill *D. & G.* ***Mountain***, in Carsphairn Forest, on border with East Ayrshire, 4m/6km SE of Dalmellington. Height 1565 feet or 477 metres. **67 K3** NS5303.

Toddington *Beds.* Population: 3999. ***Village***, 5m/7km N of Dunstable. M1 motorway service area 2km E. **32 D6** TL0028.

Toddington *Glos.* ***Village***, 3m/5km N of Winchcombe. **30 B5** SP0333.

Toddington *W.Suss.* ***Suburb***, in N part of Littlehampton. **12 D6** TQ0303.

Todd's Green *Herts.* ***Hamlet***, 2m/3km NW of Stevenage. TL2226.

Toddun *W.Isles* ***Mountain***, 1m/2km SW of entrance to Loch Seaforth. Height 1732 feet or 528 metres. **100 E7** NB2102.

Todenham *Glos.* ***Village***, 3m/5km NE of Moreton-in-Marsh. **30 D5** SP2436.

Todhead Point *Aber.* ***Coastal feature***, headland with lighthouse on E coast, 4m/6km NE of Inverbervie. **91 G7** NO8776.

Todhills *Angus* ***Settlement***, 1km N of Tealing. **83 F4** NO4239.

Todhills *Cumb.* ***Hamlet***, 5m/8km NW of Carlisle. **69 J7** NY3663.

Todhills *Dur.* ***Locality***, 1km SE of Willington across River Wear. NZ2133.

Todlachie *Aber.* ***Settlement***, 2m/3km SW of Monymusk. **90 E3** NJ6513.

Todmorden *W.Yorks.* Population: 11,969. ***Town***, former cotton town on River Calder and on Rochdale Canal, 8m/12km NE of Rochdale. **56 E7** SD9324.

Todwick *S.Yorks.* Population: 1639. ***Village***, 6m/10km NW of Worksop. **51 G4** SK4984.

Toe Head *W.Isles* ***Coastal feature***, headland on W coast of South Harris, 6m/10km NW of Leverburgh. **92 E2** NF9594.

Toes *Pembs.* ***Island***, islet off S coast of Pembrokeshire, 3m/4km SW of Castlemartin. **16 B5** SR8994.

Toft *Cambs.* ***Village***, 6m/10km W of Cambridge. **33 G3** TL3555.

Toft *Ches.* ***Settlement***, 1m/2km S of Knutsford. SJ7576.

Toft *Lincs.* ***Hamlet***, 3m/4km SW of Bourne. **42 D4** TF0617.

Toft (Also known as Boath of Toft.) *Shet.* ***Settlement***, on NE coast of Mainland, 1m/2km NW of Mossbank across Tofts Voe. Vehicle ferry to Ulsta on Yell. **108 D5** HU4376.

Toft *Warks.* ***Locality***, 3m/5km SW of Rugby. SP4770.

Toft Hill *Dur.* ***Village***, 3m/5km W of Bishop Auckland. **62 C4** NZ1528.

Toft Monks *Norf.* ***Village***, 3m/5km N of Beccles. **45 J6** TM4294.

Toft next Newton *Lincs.* ***Village***, 4m/7km W of Market Rasen. **52 D4** TF0488.

Toft Sand *Lincs.* ***Coastal feature***, spit of sand between Boston Deeps and Gat Channel in SW part of The Wash, 8m/13km E of Boston off Lincolnshire coast. **43 H1** TF4540.

Toftcarl *High.* ***Settlement***, 1km NE of Thrumster. **105 J4** ND3446.

Toftrees *Norf.* ***Hamlet***, 2m/3km SW of Fakenham. **44 C3** TF8927.

Tofts *High.* ***Settlement***, in NE corner of Caithness district, 4m/6km S of John o' Groats. **105 J2** ND3668.

Toftshaw *W.Yorks.* ***Locality***, 3m/4km SE of Bradford. SE1829.

Toftwood *Norf.* ***Locality***, adjoining to S of East Dereham. **44 D4** TF9911.

Togston *Northumb.* ***Village***, adjoining to N of Broomhill, 2m/3km SW of Amble. **71 H3** NU2401.

Togston Barns *Northumb.* ***Locality***, 1km NE of Togston. NU2501.

Tokavaig *High.* ***Locality***, on Skye, near W coast of Sleat peninsula, 2m/3km NE of Tarskavaig. **86 C3** NG6011.

Tokers Green *Oxon.* ***Village***, 3m/4km N of Reading. **22 A4** SU7077.

Tokyngton *Gt.Lon.* ***Suburb***, in borough of Brent, 7m/12km NW of Charing Cross. TQ1984.

Tolastadh a' Chaolais (Anglicised form: Tolstachaolais.) *W.Isles* ***Village***, on Isle of Lewis, near E shore of East Loch Roag, 2m/3km NW of Breascleit. **100 D4** NB1937.

Tolastadh Bho Thuath (Anglicised form: North Tolsta.) *W.Isles* ***Village***, near E coast of Isle of Lewis, 2m/3km W of Tolsta Head. **101 H3** NB5347.

Tolastadh Ùr (Anglicised form: New Tolsta.) *W.Isles* ***Village***, near E coast of Isle of Lewis, 2m/4km NW of Tolsta Head and 1km N of Tolastadh Bho Thuath. **101 H3** NB5348.

Toldish *Cornw.* ***Hamlet***, 3m/4km S of St. Columb Major. SW9259.

Toll Bar *S.Yorks.* ***Village***, 3m/5km N of Doncaster town centre. SE5607.

Toll Creagach *High.* ***Mountain***, in Inverness district 3m/4km SW of dam of Loch Mullardoch. Munro: height 3454 feet or 1053 metres. **87 H2** NH1928.

Toll End *W.Mid.* ***Suburb***, 2m/3km NW of West Bromwich town centre. SO9793.

Toll of Birness *Aber.* ***Settlement***, at road junction, 4m/6km NE of Ellon. **91 J1** NK0034.

Tolland *Som.* ***Village***, 3m/5km NE of Wiveliscombe. **7 K2** ST1032.

Tollard Farnham *Dorset* ***Settlement***, 1m/2km S of Tollard Royal. ST9415.

Tollard Royal *Wilts.* ***Village***, 6m/10km SE of Shaftesbury. King John's House, former royal hunting lodge. Larmer Tree Grounds, park laid out by General Pitt-Rivers in late 19c, to S. **9 J3** ST9417.

Tollbar End *W.Mid.* ***Suburb***, 3m/5km SE of Coventry city centre. SP3675.

Tollcross *Glas.* ***Suburb***, 3m/5km E of Glasgow city centre. **74 E4** NS6363.

Toller Down Gate *Dorset* ***Settlement***, 1m/2km SE of Corscombe. **8 E4** ST5263.

Toller Fratrum *Dorset* ***Hamlet***, 1m/2km W of Maiden Newton. **8 E5** SY5797.

Toller Porcorum *Dorset* ***Village***, 2m/4km W of Maiden Newton. **8 E5** SY5698.

Toller Whelme *Dorset* ***Hamlet***, 3m/4km E of Beaminster. **8 E4** ST5101.

Tollerton *N.Yorks.* ***Village***, 4m/6km S of Easingwold. **58 B3** SE5164.

Tollerton *Notts.* ***Village***, 4m/7km SE of Nottingham. **41 J2** SK6134.

Tollesbury *Essex* Population: 2332. ***Village***, 7m/11km E of Maldon. **25 F1** TL9510.

Tollesbury Fleet *Essex* ***Sea feature***, inlet 1m/2km E of Tollesbury. **34 D7** TL9510.

Tollesby *Middbro.* ***Locality***, 3m/5km S of Middlesbrough. **63 G5** NZ5115.

Tolleshunt D'Arcy *Essex* ***Village***, 6m/9km NE of Maldon. **34 D7** TL9211.

Tolleshunt Knights *Essex* ***Hamlet***, 6m/10km NE of Maldon. **34 D7** TL9213.

Tolleshunt Major *Essex* ***Village***, 4m/7km NE of Maldon. **34 C7** TL9011.

Tollomuick Forest *High.* ***Open space***, deer forest at head of Loch Vaich. **95 K3** NH3280.

Tolmachan *W.Isles* ***Settlement***, on E side of Loch Meavaig, North Harris. NB0905.

Tolmount (Also spelled Tolmounth.) *Angus* ***Mountain***, at head of Glen Callater in Kincardine and Deeside district, 8m/12km SE of Braemar. Munro: height 3142 feet or 958 metres. **89 K6** NO2080.

Tolmounth *Angus Alternative spelling of Tolmount, qv.*

Tolpuddle *Dorset* ***Village***, 4m/6km W of Bere Regis. Famous for 'Tolpuddle Martyrs', agricultural labourers transported to Australia for opposing drop in wages, 1834. **9 G5** SY7994.

T

Tolquhon Castle *Aber.* ***Castle***, remains of pink sandstone medieval castle (Historic Scotland), in wooded glen 1m/2km NW of Pitmedden. Built for Forbes family, includes 15c tower enlarged in 16c and ornamented gatehouse. **91 G2** NJ8728.
Tolsta Head *W.Isles* ***Coastal feature***, headland on E coast of Isle of Lewis, 12m/20km NE of Stornoway. **101 H3** NB5646.
Tolstachaolais *W.Isles Anglicised form of Tolastadh a' Chaolais, qv.*
Tolvah *High.* ***Settlement***, in Glen Feshie, 4m/6km S of Kincraig. **89 F5** NN8499.
Tolworth *Gt.Lon.* ***Suburb***, in borough of Kingston upon Thames, 3m/4km SE of Kingston upon Thames town centre. **22 E5** TQ1965.
Tom a' Chòinich *High.* ***Mountain***, on border of Inverness and Ross and Cromarty districts between Loch Affric and Loch Mullardoch. Munro: height 3644 feet or 1111 metres. **87 H2** NH1627.
Tom an Fhuadain *W.Isles* ***Settlement***, on S shore of Loch Odhairn, 2m/3km W of Kebock Head, Isle of Lewis. **101 F6** NB3914.
Tom an t-suidhe Mhòr *High.* ***Mountain***, 1m/2km SW of Bridge of Brown. Height 1742 feet or 531 metres. **89 J3** NJ1118.
Tom an Teine *High.* ***Hill***, 1m/2km SW of Spean Bridge. Height 613 feet or 187 metres. **87 J6** NN2179.
Tom Bailgeann *High.* ***Mountain***, in Inverness district, 5m/8km E of Drumnadrochit. Height 1522 feet or 464 metres. **88 C2** NH5829.
Tom Bàn Mòr *High.* ***Mountain***, in Ross and Cromarty district on NE side of Loch Glascarnoch. Height 2434 feet or 742 metres. **95 K4** NH3175.
Tom Buidhe *Angus* ***Mountain***, 4m/7km NW of Glendoll Lodge. Munro: height 3139 feet or 957 metres. **89 K7** NO2178.
Tom na Gruagaich *High.* ***Mountain***, summit of Beinn Alligin, 4m/6km NW of Torridon in Ross and Cromarty district. Munro: height 3024 feet or 922 metres. NG8560.
Tom Soilleir *Arg. & B.* ***Mountain***, 3m/4km E of Arduaine. Height 1197 feet or 365 metres. **79 K7** NM8409.
Tomatin *High.* ***Village***, in Inverness district, 8m/12km NW of Carrbridge. **89 F2** NH8029.
Tomb of the Eagles *Ork.* ***Historic/prehistoric site***, in SE corner of South Ronaldsay. Fine stalled chambered tomb dating from Stone Age. Name derives from sea eagles' claws found in tomb. **107 D9** ND4684.
Tombane Burn *P. & K.* ***River***, rising in Loch Creagh and flowing SE into River Braan, 1m/2km W of Trochry. **82 A3** NN9539.
Tombreck *High.* ***Settlement***, 8m/12km S of Inverness. **88 D1** NH6834.
Tomchrasky *High.* ***Settlement***, in Glen Moriston, 2m/3km W of Dalchreichart. **87 J3** NH2512.
Tomdoun *High.* ***Locality***, in Glen Garry, Lochaber district, 9m/14km W of Invergarry. **87 H4** NH1501.
Tomdow *Moray* ***Settlement***, 4m/6km N of Dava. **97 H7** NJ0044.
Tomen-y-mur Roman Fort *Gwyn.* ***Historic/prehistoric site***, 2m/3km S of Ffestiniog. 1c Roman auxiliary fort in remote location, where early Norman motte was subsequently built. Earthworks include amphitheatre. **37 G2** SH7038.
Tomich *High.* ***Locality***, on border of Ross and Cromarty and Inverness districts, 1m/2km NE of Beauly. NH5347.
Tomich *High.* ***Settlement***, 2m/3km SE of Lairg, Sutherland district. **96 D1** NC6004.
Tomich *High.* ***Settlement***, in Inverness district, 4m/6km SW of Cannich. **87 K2** NH3027.
Tomich *High.* ***Settlement***, 1m/2km N of Invergordon. **96 D4** NH7071.
Tomintoul *Moray* ***Village***, and resort in elevated position between River Avon and Conglass Water, 10m/16km SE of Grantown-on-Spey. **89 J3** NJ1618.
Tomlachlan Burn *High.* ***River***, rising on W slope of Carn nan Clach Garbha and flowing N into River Findhorn, 1km E of Dulsie. **89 G1** NH9342.
Tomnacross *High.* ***Settlement***, in Inverness district, 3m/5km S of Beauly. **96 C7** NH5141.
Tomnamoon *Moray* ***Settlement***, 5m/8km S of Forres. **97 H6** NJ0450.
Tomnaven *Moray* ***Settlement***, on E side of River Deveron, 6m/10km SE of Dufftown. **90 C1** NJ4033.
Tomnaverie Stone Circle *Aber.* ***Historic/prehistoric site***, stones dating from 1800-1600 BC (Historic Scotland) on rocky knoll 1km SE of Tarland. **90 C4** NJ4803.
Tomnavoulin *Moray* ***Village***, in Glen Livet, 5m/8km NE of Tomintoul. **89 K2** NJ2126.
Tomnun *Angus* ***Mountain***, in Harran Plantation, 3m/5km SW of Balnaboth. Height 1551 feet or 473 metres. **82 D1** NO2764.
Tomont End *N.Ayr.* ***Coastal feature***, headland to E of White Bay at N end of Great Cumbrae. **73 K5** NS1759.
Tomont Hill *S.Lan.* ***Mountain***, in Lowther Hills, 3m/5km SE of Elvanfoot. Height 1653 feet or 504 metres. **68 E2** NS9812.
Tompkin *Staffs.* ***Settlement***, 4m/7km SW of Leek. SJ9451.
Tom's Cairn *Aber.* ***Mountain***, 3m/4km SE of Marywell. Height 1017 feet or 310 metres. **90 E5** NO6194.
Tomtain *N.Lan.* ***Mountain***, 2m/4km N of Kilsyth. Height 1486 feet or 453 metres. **75 F2** NS7281.
Tomvaich *High.* ***Settlement***, on E side of Upper Tomvaich Wood, 3m/4km N of Grantown-on-Spey. **89 H1** NJ0630.
Ton Burn *Aber.* ***River***, rising on E side of Corrennie Forest and flowing NE to join River Don, 1m/2km SW of Kemnay. **90 E4** NJ7115.
Tòn Mhòr *Arg. & B.* ***Coastal feature***, headland on N coast of Islay, 4m/7km SW of Ardnave Point. **72 A3** NR2371.
Ton Pentre *R.C.T.* ***Village***, in Rhondda Fawr valley, 1m/2km SE of Treorchy. **18 C2** SS9695.
Ton-teg *R.C.T.* ***Locality***, 3m/5km SE of Pontypridd. **18 D3** ST0986.
Ton-ty'r-bel *Caerp.* ***Settlement***, 1m/2km N of Newbridge. ST2099.
Ton-y-pistyll *Caerp.* ***Hamlet***, 1m/2km SW of Newbridge. ST1996.
Tonbridge *Kent* Population: 34,260. ***Town***, on River Medway, 28m/45km SE of London. 12c castle. Boys' boarding school founded 16c. **23 J7** TQ5946.
Tonbridge Castle *Kent* ***Castle***, remains of large 11c motte overlooking River Medway in Tonbridge. Later improvements included 13c gatehouse built by de Clare family. **23 J7** TQ5846.
Tondu *Bridgend* ***Village***, 3m/5km N of Bridgend. **18 B3** SS8984.
Tone ***River***, rising on Brendon Hills and flowing S to Greenham, then E through Taunton to Burrow Bridge, where it joins River Parrett. **8 C2** ST3530.
Tone *Som.* ***Hamlet***, on River Tone, 1m/2km NW of Wellington. ST1221.
Tone Green *Som.* ***Locality***, across River Tone from Bradford-on-Tone, 3m/4km NE of Wellington. ST1723.
Tonedale *Som.* ***Suburb***, NW district of Wellington. ST1221.
Tonfanau *Gwyn.* ***Locality***, on coast, 3m/4km NW of Tywyn. **36 E5** SH5603.
Tong *Kent* ***Settlement***, 2m/3km N of Headcorn. TQ8346.
Tong *Shrop.* ***Village***, 3m/5km E of Shifnal. **39 G5** SJ7907.
Tong *W.Yorks.* ***Village***, 1m/2km N of Drighlington. SE2230.
Tong *W.Isles Anglicised form of Tunga, qv.*
Tong Forge *Shrop.* ***Settlement***, 2m/3km NE of Shifnal. SJ7808.
Tong Norton *Shrop.* ***Hamlet***, 3m/5km E of Shifnal. **39 G5** SJ7908.
Tong Park *W.Yorks.* ***Suburb***, E district of Baildon. SE1639.
Tong Street *W.Yorks.* ***Suburb***, 2m/4km SE of Bradford city centre. **57 G6** SE1930.
Tongdean *B. & H.* ***Suburb***, N district of Hove. TQ2807.
Tonge *Kent* ***Locality***, adjoining to E of Sittingbourne. TQ9364.
Tonge *Leics.* ***Hamlet***, 5m/7km NW of Shepshed. **41 G3** SK4123.
Tonge Fold *Gt.Man.* ***Suburb***, 1m/2km E of Bolton town centre. SD7309.
Tonge Moor *Gt.Man.* ***Suburb***, 1m/2km NE of Bolton town centre. SD7210.
Tongham *Surr.* ***Village***, 2m/3km SE of Aldershot. **22 B7** SU8848.
Tongland *D. & G.* ***Village***, 2m/3km NE of Kirkcudbright. Hydro-electricity power station below reservoir. Early 19c road bridge by Telford spans River Dee to SW. **65 H5** NX6953.
Tongland Loch *D. & G.* ***Lake/loch***, with islands and dam at S end, part of River Dee, 1km N of Tongland. **65 H5** NX7056.
Tongue *High.* ***Village***, near N coast of Caithness district on E side of Kyle of Tongue, 1m/2km S of road bridge across kyle. **103 H3** NC5956.
Tongue Bay *High.* ***Bay***, 3m/5km N of Tongue. **103 J2** NC5956.
Tongue End *Lincs.* ***Locality***, 4m/7km E of Bourne. TF1518.
Tongue House *High.* ***Settlement***, near causeway, on E side of Kyle of Tongue. **103 H3** NC5958.
Tongwynlais *Cardiff* Population: 1778. ***Village***, at S entrance to narrow glen of River Taff, 5m/7km NW of Cardiff. **18 E3** ST1382.
Tonmawr *N.P.T.* ***Village***, 3m/5km E of Neath. SS8096.
Tonna *N.P.T.* ***Village***, 2m/3km NE of Neath. Site of Roman camp 1m/2km E. **18 A2** SS7799.
Tontine *Lancs.* ***Locality***, 1km S of Up Holland and 3m/4km SE of Skelmersdale. SD5204.
Tonwell *Herts.* ***Hamlet***, 3m/4km NW of Ware. **33 G7** TL3317.
Tonypandy *R.C.T.* ***Small town***, in Rhondda Fawr valley 3m/4km W of Porth and 5m/8km NW of Pontypridd. **18 C2** SS9992.
Tonyrefail *R.C.T.* Population: 8815. ***Village***, 2m/3km SW of Porth. **18 D3** ST0188.
Toot Baldon *Oxon.* ***Village***, 5m/8km SE of Oxford. **21 J1** SP5600.
Toot Hill *Essex* ***Village***, 2m/4km W of Chipping Ongar. **23 J1** TL5102.
Toot Hill *Staffs.* ***Settlement***, 4m/6km E of Cheadle. SK0642.
Toothill *Hants.* ***Settlement***, 5m/7km NW of Southampton, below prehistoric fort. **10 E3** SU3718.
Toothill *Swin.* ***Suburb***, 2m/3km SW of Swindon town centre. SU1283.
Toothill *W.Yorks.* ***Suburb***, 1m/2km S of Brighouse across River Calder. SE1421.
Tooting Bec *Gt.Lon.* ***Suburb***, in borough of Wandsworth, 5m/8km S of Charing Cross. Tooting Bec Common to E. TQ2872.
Tooting Graveney *Gt.Lon.* ***Suburb***, in borough of Wandsworth, 6m/10km S of Charing Cross. TQ2771.
Top End *Beds.* ***Locality***, SW end of Riseley, 8m/12km N of Bedford. **32 D2** TL0362.
Top o' th' Meadows *Gt.Man.* ***Settlement***, scattered settlement on hillside, to E of Strine Dale, 3m/4km E of Oldham. SD9606.
Top of Hebers *Gt.Man.* ***Suburb***, 1km N of Middleton. SD8607.
Top of Ramsgreave *Lancs.* ***Hamlet***, 1m/2km E of Mellor and 2m/3km N of Blackburn. SD6630.
Top of Turton *Lancs.* ***Locality***, 3m/5km N of Bolton. SD7214.
Top Road *Suff.* ***Locality***, just S of Rattlesden. TL9758.
Top-y-rhos *Flints.* ***Settlement***, adjoining to N of Treuddyn. SJ2558.
Topcliffe *N.Yorks.* ***Village***, on River Swale, 4m/7km SW of Thirsk. **57 J2** SE4076.
Topcliffe *W.Yorks.* ***Locality***, 1m/2km SE of Morley. Radio/TV masts. SE2726.
Topcroft *Norf.* ***Village***, 5m/8km NW of Bungay. **45 G6** TM2693.
Topcroft Street *Norf.* ***Village***, 1m/2km S of Topcroft. **45 G6** TM2693.
Topham *S.Yorks.* ***Settlement***, 1km NW of Sykehouse, 5m/7km NW of Thorne. SE6217.
Toppesfield *Essex* ***Village***, 5m/7km NE of Finchingfield. **34 B5** TL7337.
Toppings *Gt.Man.* ***Locality***, 3m/4km N of Bolton. **49 G1** SD7213.
Toprow *Norf.* ***Settlement***, 4m/7km SE of Wymondham. TM1698.
Topsham *Devon* Population: 3408. ***Suburb***, SE district of Exeter on River Exe estuary. Ancient town and former port for Exeter. **7 H7** SX9688.
Topsham Bridge *Devon* ***Settlement***, on River Avon, 4m/7km N of Kingsbridge. **5 H5** SX7351.
Tor Bay *Torbay* ***Bay***, extends from Hope's Nose (N) to Berry Head (S). Surrounded by urban area of Torbay. **5 K5** SX9164.
Tor Du *Powys* ***Mountain***, partly wooded summit to SW of Hafren Forest and 4m/6km E of Plynlimon. Height 1660 feet or 506 metres. **37 H7** SN8485.
Tor Ness *Ork.* ***Coastal feature***, headland on E coast of Mainland, to N of Broad Taing. **107 D6** HY4219.
Tor Ness *Ork.* ***Coastal feature***, headland on S coast of Stronsay on E side of entrance to Bay of Holland. **106 F5** HY6520.
Tor Ness *Ork.* ***Coastal feature***, rocky headland on N coast of North Ronaldsay. **106 G2** HY7555.
Tor Ness *Ork.* ***Coastal feature***, headland at S end of Hoy. Lighthouse to NW. **107 B9** ND2588.
Tor Point *High.* ***Inland physical feature***, promontory on E shore of Loch Ness, Inverness district, 1km NW of Dores. **88 C1** NH5935.
Torastan *Arg. & B.* ***Settlement***, in N part of Coll, 3m/5km N of Arinagour. **78 D1** NM2261.
Torbain *Moray* ***Settlement***, on E bank of River Avon, 3m/4km S of Tomintoul. **89 J3** NJ1613.
Torbay *Torbay* ***Locality***, urban area on coast including towns of Torquay, Paignton and Brixham, surrounding Tor Bay, which extends from Hope's Nose (N) to Berry Head (S). SX9164.
Torbeg *Aber.* ***Settlement***, on S side of River Gairn, 4m/6km NW of Ballater. **90 B4** NJ3200.
Torbeg *N.Ayr.* ***Village***, on Arran, 1m/2km N of Blackwaterfoot. **66 D1** NR8929.
Torbothie *N.Lan.* ***Hamlet***, 1km NE of Stane. NS8859.
Torbraehead *D. & G.* ***Mountain***, 4m/6km N of Moniaive. Height 1312 feet or 400 metres. **68 C4** NX7896.
Torbreck Burn *High.* ***River***, flowing S and joining River Fleet 1km NW of Pittentrail. **96 E1** NC7103.
Torbrex *Stir.* ***Suburb***, 1m/2km SW of Stirling town centre. NS7892.
Torbryan *Devon* ***Hamlet***, 4m/6km SW of Newton Abbot. **5 J4** SX8266.
Torcastle *High.* ***Settlement***, in valley of River Lochy, 3m/5km N of Fort William. **87 H7** NN1378.
Torcross *Devon* ***Village***, on coast 3m/5km N of Start Point, at S end of 1m/2km long lagoon behind Slapton Sands. **5 J6** SX8242.
Tordarroch *High.* ***Settlement***, in Strathnairn, 8m/11km S of Inverness. **88 D1** NH6733.
Torduff Point *D. & G.* ***Coastal feature***, headland on Solway Firth, 2m/3km SE of Eastriggs. **69 H7** NY2663.
Tore *High.* ***Hamlet***, in Ross and Cromarty district, 5m/8km E of Muir of Ord. **96 D6** NH6052.
Tore Burn *Aber.* ***River***, rising to S of Tore of Troup valley and flowing N into sea at Cullykhan Bay, 3m/4km E of Gardenstown. **99 G4** NJ8365.
Tore Hill *High.* ***Mountain***, in Abernethy Forest, 8m/11km SE of Carrbridge. Height 1109 feet or 338 metres. **89 G3** NH9817.
Toreduff *Moray* ***Settlement***, 6m/10km W of Elgin. **97 J5** NJ1260.
Toremore *High.* ***Settlement***, 1km NE of Dunbeath, on E coast. **105 G5** ND1730.
Toremore *High.* ***Settlement***, 5m/8km S of Upper Knockando. **89 J1** NJ1535.
Torfichen Hill *Midloth.* ***Mountain***, in Moorfoot Hills, 2m/3km E of Gladhouse Reservoir. Height 1509 feet or 460 metres. **76 B5** NT3353.
Torfrey *Cornw.* ***Settlement***, adjoining to W of Golant, 2m/3km N of Fowey. SX1154.
Torgyle *High.* ***Settlement***, in Glen Moriston, 1m/2km E of Dalchreichart. **87 K3** NH3013.
Torhouse Stone Circle *D. & G.* ***Historic/prehistoric site***, circle of nineteen stones, roughly sixty feet in diameter, 1km W of Little Torhouse and 4m/6km W of Wigtown. **64 D5** NX3856.
Torhousemuir *D. & G.* ***Locality***, 3m/5km NW of Wigtown. Ancient stone circle (Historic Scotland). NX3957.
Torkington *Gt.Man.* ***Suburb***, 1m/2km E of Hazel Grove. SJ9386.
Torksey *Lincs.* ***Village***, on River Trent, 7m/11km S of Gainsborough. Site of Roman building by Torksey Lock on Fossdyke Navigation to S. **52 B5** SK8378.
Torloisk *Arg. & B.* ***Locality***, on Mull, on N side of Loch Tuath and 4m/7km S of Dervaig. NM4145.
Torlum *P. & K.* ***Mountain***, rounded summit, 3m/5km SE of Comrie. Height 1289 feet or 393 metres. **81 K6** NN8119.
Torlum *W.Isles* ***Settlement***, on Benbecula, 3m/5km S of Balivanich. **92 C6** NF7850.
Torlum Wood *P. & K.* ***Forest/woodland***, 4m/6km SE of Comrie. **81 K6** NN8218.
Torlundy *High.* ***Settlement***, 3m/5km NE of Fort William. **87 H7** NN1477.
Tormarton *S.Glos.* ***Village***, 3m/5km SE of Chipping Sodbury. **20 A4** ST7678.
Tormisdale *Arg. & B.* ***Settlement***, 4m/7km N of Portnahaven, on Rinns of Islay. **72 A5** NR1958.

Tormore *N.Ayr.* ***Settlement***, on W coast of Arran, 3m/4km N of Blackwaterfoot. Ancient standing stones to E. **73 G7** NR8932.
Tormsdale *High.* ***Settlement***, 1m/2km SE of Westerdale. **105 G3** ND1350.
Tornagrain *High.* ***Settlement***, in Inverness district, 7m/11km NE of Inverness. **96 E6** NH7649.
Tornahaish *Aber.* ***Settlement***, on S side of River Don, 5m/8km SW of Strathdon. **89 K4** NJ2908.
Tornashean Forest *Aber.* ***Forest/woodland***, discontinuous forest surrounding Forbridge Hill above S bank of River Don, 3m/5km SE of Strathdon. **90 B3** NJ3810.
Tornaveen *Aber.* ***Settlement***, 3m/4km N of Torphins. **90 E4** NJ6106.
Torne ***River***, rising W of Tickhill and flowing NE into River Trent at Althorpe. **51 K2** SE8309.
Torness *High.* ***Settlement***, in Inverness district, 5m/8km S of Dores. **88 C2** NH5827.
Torogay *W.Isles* ***Island***, small uninhabited island off NE coast of North Uist, 1km S of Berneray. NF9178.
Toronto *Dur.* ***Village***, 1m/2km NW of Bishop Auckland across River Wear. NZ1930.
Torosay Castle *Arg. & B.* ***Castle***, 19c castle near E coast of Mull, 1m/2km N of Lochdon. **79 J4** NM7235.
Torpantau *Powys* ***Open space***, hillside on SE side of Brecon Beacons, 7m/11km N of Merthyr Tydfil. **27 K7** SO0417.
Torpenhow *Cumb.* ***Village***, 1m/2km NE of Bothel. **60 C3** NY2039.
Torphichen *W.Loth.* ***Village***, 2m/4km N of Bathgate. **75 H3** NS9672.
Torphichen Preceptory *W.Loth.* ***Ecclesiastical building***, at Torphichen, 5m/8km SSW of Linlithgow. Former Scottish seat of Knights Hospitallers of St. John. Remains incorporated into present church. **75 H3** NS9672.
Torphins *Aber.* ***Village***, 6m/10km NW of Banchory. **90 E4** NJ6201.
Torpoint *Cornw.* Population: 8238. ***Small town***, beside part of River Tamar estuary known as the Hamoaze. Car ferry to Devonport. **4 E5** SX4355.
Torquay *Torbay* Population: 59,587. ***Town***, 18m/30km S of Exeter. Chief town and resort of Torbay district, with harbour and several beaches. Noted for mild climate. Torre Abbey has 15c gatehouse. **5 K4** SX9164.
Torquhan *Sc.Bord.* ***Hamlet***, 2m/3km NW of Stow. **76 C6** NT4447.
Torr *Devon* ***Settlement***, on S side of Yealmpton across River Yealm. **5 F5** SX5851.
Torr a' Chaisteil *N.Ayr.* ***Historic/prehistoric site***, remains of Iron Age fort (Historic Scotland) at Corriecravie, Arran, 4m/6km SE of Blackwaterfoot. **66 D1** NR9223.
Torr Dubh *P. & K.* ***Open space***, mountain slope on S side of Glen Errochty, 3m/5km NW of Tummel Bridge. **81 J1** NN7462.
Torr Fada *Arg. & B.* ***Hill***, 4m/6km S of Rubha nan Cearc, Ross of Mull. Height 279 feet or 85 metres. **78 E6** NM3219.
Torr Mòr *Arg. & B.* ***Hill***, above S coast of Bute, 1m/2km NE of Garroch Head. Height 479 feet or 146 metres. **73 K5** NS1052.
Torrachilty Wood *High.* ***Forest/woodland***, in Ross and Cromarty district around Loch Achilty, 4m/6km W of Strathpeffer. **96 B6** NH4356.
Torraigh (Anglicised form: Torray.) *W.Isles* ***Island***, small uninhabited island off E coast of Isle of Lewis 4m/6km N of Kebock Head. **101 G5** NB4220.
Torran *Arg. & B.* ***Settlement***, 1m/2km NE of Ford. **79 K7** NM8704.
Torran *High.* ***Locality***, on N shore of Loch Arnish, Raasay. **94 B7** NG5949.
Torran *High.* ***Settlement***, 4m/6km N of Invergordon. **96 E4** NH7175.
Torran Rocks *Arg. & B.* ***Island***, scattered group of rocks off SW end of Ross of Mull, 5m/8km S of Iona. **78 D6** NM2713.
Torran Sgoilte *Arg. & B.* ***Island***, one of Torran Rocks group, 4m/6km SW of Mull. **78 D6** NM2812.
Torrance *E.Dun.* Population: 2387. ***Village***, 6m/9km N of Glasgow. **74 E3** NS6274.
Torrance *S.Lan.* ***Settlement***, 1m/2km SE of East Kilbride, by Calder Water. Remains of Motte to W. **74 E5** NS6552.
Torrancroy *Aber.* ***Settlement***, at E end of Glen Nochty, 3m/4km NW of Strathdon. **90 B3** NJ3315.
Torray *W.Isles* *Anglicised form of Torraigh, qv.*
Torray *W.Isles* ***River***, flowing NW into River Barvas, 1km W of Barvas, Isle of Lewis. **101 F2** NB3549.
Torre *Som.* ***Hamlet***, 3m/4km SW of Watchet. ST0440.
Torre *Torbay* ***Suburb***, 1m/2km NW of Torquay town centre. SX9064.
Torre Abbey *Torbay* ***Historic house***, 17c-18c house built on remains of 12c Premonstratensian abbey, to SW of Torquay, overlooking Tor Bay. Notable parkland and gardens. **5 K4** SX9063.
Torrent Walk *Gwyn.* ***Other feature of interest***, path by side of River Clywedog, 2m/3km E of Dolgellau. **37 G4** SH7518.
Torrich *High.* ***Settlement***, 3m/5km S of Nairn. **97 F6** NH8751.
Torridge *Devon* ***River***, rising S of Hartland and flowing E to Hele Bridge, N of Hatherleigh, N past Great Torrington to Bideford, then N again to join River Taw and flowing into Barnstaple Bay. **6 D5** SS4631.
Torridon *High.* ***Village***, at head of Upper Loch Torridon, Ross and Cromarty district. **95 F6** NG8956.
Torridon Forest *High.* ***Large natural feature***, mountainous area (National Trust for Scotland) to N of Torridon. NG8958.
Torrie Forest *Stir.* ***Forest/woodland***, 3m/4km S of Callander. **81 H7** NN6303.
Torrin *High.* ***Village***, on Skye, 5m/7km W of Broadford. **86 B2** NG5720.
Torrinch *W.Dun.* ***Island***, in Loch Lomond 1m/2km SW of Balmaha. Part of nature reserve comprising also Inchcailloch and Clairinch. **74 C2** NS4089.
Torrington *Devon Familiar form of Great Torrington, qv.*
Torrisdale *Arg. & B.* ***Locality***, on Torrisdale Bay, on E coast of Kintyre, 1m/2km S of Dippen. **73 F7** NR7936.
Torrisdale *High.* ***Settlement***, on Torrisdale Bay, 2m/3km W of Bettyhill, Caithness district. **103 J2** NC6761.
Torrisdale Bay *High.* ***Bay***, on N coast of Caithness district, W of Bettyhill. **103 J2** NC6962.
Torrish *High.* ***Settlement***, to N of River Helmsdale, 4m/6km NW of Helmsdale, Sutherland district. **104 E7** NC9718.
Torrish Burn *High.* ***River***, in Sutherland district, flowing S and joining River Helmsdale 1km W of Torrish. **104 E6** NC9618.
Torrisholme *Lancs.* ***Suburb***, 1m/2km E of Morecambe town centre. **55 H3** SD4564.
Torroble *High.* ***Settlement***, 1m/2km S of Lairg, Sutherland district. **96 C1** NC5904.
Torry *Aberdeen* ***Suburb***, 1m/2km SE of Aberdeen city centre across River Dee. **91 H4** NJ9505.
Torry *Aber.* ***Settlement***, on N side of River Deveron, 1km NE of Haugh of Glass. **98 C6** NJ4340.
Torry *Fife* ***Locality***, on Torry Bay on N side of River Forth, 5m/8km W of Dunfermline. NT0186.
Torry Bay *Fife* ***Bay***, on N side of River Forth, 5m/8km W of Dunfermline. **75 J2** NT0186.
Torryburn *Fife* ***Village***, adjoins to E of Torry, 2m/4km E of Culross across Torry Bay. **75 J2** NT0186.
Torrylin Chambered Cairn *N.Ayr.* ***Historic/prehistoric site***, Neolithic chambered cairn (Historic Scotland) with visible compartments, on S coast of Arran, to S of Kilmory. **66 D1** NR9521.
Torsay *Arg. & B.* ***Island***, composed of slate, off Luing at entrance to Seil Sound. **79 J6** NM7613.
Torside Reservoir *Derbys.* ***Reservoir***, one of a chain of reservoirs in River Etherow valley, 3m/5km NE of Glossop. **50 C3** SK0598.
Torsonce *Sc.Bord.* ***Hamlet***, 1km S of Stow. **76 C6** NT4543.
Torterston *Aber.* ***Locality***, 3m/5km W of Peterhead. **99 J6** NK0747.
Torthorwald *D. & G.* ***Village***, 4m/6km E of Dumfries. Tower house dating from 14c. **69 F6** NY0378.
Tortington *W.Suss.* ***Hamlet***, 2m/3km SW of Arundel. **12 C6** TQ0005.
Torton *Worcs.* ***Hamlet***, 3m/4km E of Stourport-on-Severn. SO8472.
Tortworth *S.Glos.* ***Village***, 3m/5km W of Wotton-under-Edge. **20 A2** ST7093.
Torvaig *High.* ***Settlement***, 1m/2km NE of Portree, Skye. **93 K7** NG4944.
Torver *Cumb.* ***Hamlet***, 2m/4km SW of Coniston. **60 D7** SD2894.
Torwood *Falk.* ***Hamlet***, 4m/7km NW of Falkirk. **75 G2** NS8484.
Torwoodlee House *Sc.Bord.* ***Historic house***, small Georgian mansion built in 1783 and subsequently modified in 19c, 2m/3km NW of Galashiels. **76 C7** NT4637.
Torworth *Notts.* ***Village***, 2m/3km E of Blyth. **51 J4** SK6586.
Toryglen *Glas.* ***Suburb***, 2m/4km S of Glasgow city centre. NS6061.
Tosberry *Devon* ***Hamlet***, 2m/3km S of Hartland. **6 A3** SS2621.
Toscaig *High.* ***Settlement***, at head of Loch Toscaig, near W coast of Ross and Cromarty district, 4m/6km S of Applecross. **86 D1** NG7138.
Toseland *Cambs.* ***Village***, 4m/6km NE of St. Neots. Hall to W, red brick house of c. 1600. **33 F2** TL2462.
Tosside ***Hamlet***, on border of North Yorkshire and Lancashire, on W edge of Gisburn Forest, 4m/7km W of Long Preston. **56 C4** SD7656.
Tosside Beck ***River***, rising to E of Gisburn Forest and flowing S. It is joined by Bond Beck just S of Lower Gill, and enters River Ribble 1km N of Sawley. **56 C4** SD7847.
Tosson *Northumb.* ***Locality***, parish containing hamlet of Great Tosson and settlement of Little Tosson, respectively 2m/3km SW and 3m/5km W of Rothbury. NU0200.
Tosson Hill *Northumb.* ***Mountain***, in Northumberland National Park, 4m/6km SW of Rothbury. Height 1443 feet or 440 metres. **71 F4** NZ0098.
Tostarie *Arg. & B.* ***Settlement***, on Mull, 1km W of Kilninian. **78 E3** NM3845.
Tostock *Suff.* ***Village***, 6m/10km E of Bury St. Edmunds. **34 D2** TL9563.
Totaig *High.* ***Locality***, at entrance to Loch Duich, Skye and Lochalsh district, opposite Eilean Donan. NG8725.
Totaig *High.* ***Village***, on Skye, on W side of Loch Dunvegan, 4m/6km SE of Dunvegan Head. **93 H6** NG2050.
Totamore *Arg. & B.* ***Settlement***, 3m/5km W of Arinagour, Coll. **78 C2** NM1756.
Tote *High.* ***Village***, 6m/10km NW of Portree, Skye. **93 K7** NG4149.
Tote Hill *Hants.* ***Settlement***, 2m/3km S of Lockerley. SU3024.
Tote Hill *W.Suss.* ***Hamlet***, 3m/4km NW of Midhurst. SU8624.
Totegan *High.* ***Settlement***, 1km S of Strathy Point, Caithness district. **104 D2** NC8268.
Totford *Hants.* ***Settlement***, 1m/2km S of Brown Candover. **11 G1** SU5737.
Totham Hill *Essex* ***Settlement***, to S of Great Totham, 4m/6km SE of Witham. TL8712.
Totham Plains *Essex* ***Settlement***, to NW of Little Totham, 4m/7km NE of Maldon. TL8812.
Tothill *Lincs.* ***Settlement***, 4m/7km NW of Alford. **53 H4** TF4182.
Totland *I.o.W.* Population: 3658. ***Small town***, resort on Totland Bay, 3m/4km SW of Yarmouth. **10 E6** SZ3287.
Totland Bay *I.o.W.* ***Bay***, on W coast, extending SW from Warden Point to Hatherwood Point. **10 E6** SZ3287.
Totley *S.Yorks.* ***Suburb***, 5m/8km SW of Sheffield city centre, comprising Totley Bents, Totley Brook, Totley Rise and New Totley. **51 F4** SK3180.
Totley Bents *S.Yorks.* ***Locality***, to NW of Totley, 6m/9km SW of Sheffield city centre. SK3080.
Totley Brook *S.Yorks.* ***Suburb***, in Totley, 5m/8km SW of Sheffield city centre. SK3180.
Totley Moor *S.Yorks.* ***Open space***, moorland at E side of The Pennines and to SE of Bradfield Moors, 2m/3km S of Low Bradfield. **50 E4** SK2589.
Totley Rise *S.Yorks.* ***Suburb***, in Totley, 5m/8km SW of Sheffield city centre. SK3180.
Totnes *Devon* Population: 6929. ***Small town***, at head of tidal estuary of River Dart, 7m/11km W of Torquay. Castle (English Heritage). Interesting 16c buildings including pillared guildhall. **5 J4** SX8060.
Totnes Castle *Devon* ***Castle***, excellently preserved keep of Norman motte (English Heritage), 7m/12km SW of Torquay. **5 H5** SX7960.
Toton *Notts.* ***Locality***, 2m/4km SW of Beeston. **41 H2** SK5034.
Totridge Fell *Lancs.* ***Open space***, moorland on Forest of Bowland, 2m/3km SW of Dunsop Bridge. **56 B5** SD6348.
Totronald *Arg. & B.* ***Settlement***, 4m/6km SW of Arinagour, Coll. **78 C2** NM1656.
Totscore *High.* ***Settlement***, on Skye, 2m/3km N of Uig. NG3866.
Tottenham *Gt.Lon.* ***Suburb***, in borough of Haringey, 7m/11km NE of Charing Cross. **23 G2** TQ3389.
Tottenham Hale *Gt.Lon.* ***Suburb***, to SE of Tottenham. TQ3489.
Tottenhill *Norf.* ***Village***, 6m/10km S of King's Lynn. **44 A4** TF6311.
Tottenhill Row *Norf.* ***Hamlet***, 5m/8km S of King's Lynn. TF6211.
Totteridge *Bucks.* ***Suburb***, NE district of High Wycombe. SU8893.
Totteridge *Gt.Lon.* ***Suburb***, in borough of Barnet, 2km S of Chipping Barnet and 9m/14km N of Charing Cross. **23 F2** TQ2494.
Totternhoe *Beds.* ***Village***, 2m/3km W of Dunstable. **32 C6** SP9821.
Totties *W.Yorks.* ***Locality***, 1km E of Holmfirth. SE1508.
Tottiford Reservoir *Devon* ***Reservoir***, horseshoe-shaped reservoir on E edge of Dartmoor, 3m/4km N of Bovey Tracey. **7 G7** SX8182.
Tottington *Gt.Man.* Population: 7673. ***Small town***, 2m/3km NW of Bury. **49 G1** SD7712.
Tottington *Norf.* ***Locality***, 4m/6km S of Watton. **44 C6** TL8995.
Tottleworth *Lancs.* ***Settlement***, adjoining to SW of Great Harwood, 1m/2km W of Clayton-le-Moors. SD7331.
Totto Hill *Sc.Bord.* ***Mountain***, 5m/8km S of Gladhouse Reservoir. Height 1971 feet or 601 metres. **76 B6** NT3045.
Totton *Hants.* Population: 25,906. ***Town***, industrial town at head of River Test estuary, 4m/6km W of Southampton. New Forest Butterfly Farm to S. **10 E3** SU3613.
Touch Burn *Stir.* ***River***, stream rising on Touch Hills and flowing NE through small reservoir to join River Forth, 2m/4km W of Stirling. **75 F1** NS7593.
Touch Hills *Stir.* ***Large natural feature***, range of low hills, 4m/6km W of Stirling. There are some small reservoirs. **75 F1** NS7291.
Touchen-end *W. & M.* ***Settlement***, 3m/5km S of Maidenhead. **22 B4** SU8776.
Touches *Som.* ***Suburb***, NE district of Chard. ST3309.
Toulston *N.Yorks.* ***Settlement***, 2m/3km NW of Tadcaster town centre. SE4544.
Toulton *Som.* ***Hamlet***, at foot of Quantock Hills, 5m/8km NW of Taunton. **7 K2** ST1931.
Tourist Trophy Course (T.T. Course). *I.o.M.* ***Other feature of interest***, 38m/61km circuit for annual Tourist Trophy motorcycle races in June and September, starting and finishing in Douglas. Goes through Ramsey, Ballaugh, St. John's, Douglas, and E slopes of Snaefell. **54 C5** SC3877.
Toux *Aber.* ***Settlement***, 2m/3km N of Old Deer. **99 H5** NJ9850.
Tove ***River***, rising S of Sulgrave and flowing generally E into River Great Ouse, 1m/2km NE of Stony Stratford. **31 J4** SP8042.
Tovil *Kent* ***Suburb***, S district of Maidstone. **14 C2** TQ7554.
Tow Law *Dur.* Population: 2204. ***Small town***, 8m/13km NW of Bishop Auckland. Former centre of coal and iron ore mining. **62 C3** NZ1238.
Towan Cross *Cornw.* ***Hamlet***, 2m/3km S of St. Agnes Head. SW7048.
Towan Head *Cornw.* ***Coastal feature***, headland at W end of Newquay Bay and N end of Fistral Bay, 1m/2km NW of Newquay. **2 E2** SW7963.
Toward *Arg. & B.* ***Settlement***, on Firth of Clyde, 6m/10km SW of Dunoon. **73 K4** NS1367.
Toward Castle *Arg. & B.* ***Castle***, medieval stronghold 1m/2km W of Toward Point. **73 K4** NS1167.
Toward Point *Arg. & B.* ***Coastal feature***, headland in Argyll on W side of Firth of Clyde, 6m/10km S of Dunoon. **73 K4** NS1367.
Toward Quay *Arg. & B.* ***Locality***, just W of Toward Castle. NS1167.
Towcester *Northants.* Population: 7006. ***Small town***, (the Roman Lactodorum) on A5 road (Watling Street), 8m/13km SW of Northampton. Racecourse. **31 H4** SP6948.
Towednack *Cornw.* ***Hamlet***, 2m/4km SW of St. Ives. **2 B5** SW4838.
Tower Bridge *Gt.Lon.* ***Bridge***, by Jones and Wolfe-Barry, 1894, spanning River Thames to E of Tower of London. Noted for Victorian-Gothic towers with hydraulic twin drawbridge which allows tall ships to pass. Museum commemorates history of bridge and engineering feat involved in its construction; huge old steam engines and boilers can still be seen. TQ3380.

Tower End *Norf.* ***Hamlet***, 1m/2km N of Middleton and 3m/5km SE of King's Lynn. TF6617.
Tower Hamlets *Kent* ***Suburb***, 1km NW of Dover town centre. TR3041.
Tower Hill *Ches.* ***Settlement***, adjoining to SW of Rainow. SJ9475.
Tower Hill *Herts.* ***Settlement***, 3m/4km W of Kings Langley. TL0302.
Tower Hill *W.Suss.* ***Hamlet***, 1m/2km SW of Horsham. TQ1629.
Tower of London *Gt.Lon.* ***Castle***, 2m/4km E of Charing Cross, in borough of Tower Hamlets. Originally begun as fortress by William the Conqueror to control medieval London, it was reinforced by Edward I to become a keep and prison. It has also housed Royal Mint, Royal Observatory, Royal Menagerie and Public Records. Several British monarchs have been held prisoner including Charles III, Henry VII and Elizabeth I. It has been scene of famous executions of Anne Boleyn, Catherine Howard and Sir Thomas More, becoming renowned for its Bloody Tower and Traitors' Gate. Contains Crown Jewels in their specially designed display hall, and vast collection of armour and weapons from 10c-20c. Yeoman Warders, or Beefeaters, still guard Tower, as do ever-present ravens, sole survivors of Royal Menagerie. One of oldest continuous military ceremonies in world, Ceremony of the Keys, takes place daily at Tower. London Wall (English Heritage), well-preserved section of Roman wall, to N. **23 G3** TQ3380.
Towersey *Oxon.* ***Village***, 2m/3km E of Thame. **22 A1** SP7305.
Towie *Aber.* ***Locality***, comprising Mains of Towie, Towie Barclay Castle and Towie Turner, 4m/6km S of Turriff. NJ7444.
Towie *Aber.* ***Settlement***, 2m/3km E of Rhynie. **90 D2** NJ5327.
Towie *Aber.* ***Settlement***, 1km W of New Aberdour. **99 G4** NJ8763.
Towie *Aber.* ***Village***, on River Don, 6m/10km SW of Lumsden. Remains of castle. **90 C3** NJ4412.
Towie Barclay Castle *Aber.* ***Castle***, remains of ruined castle dating from 16c, to S of Mains of Towie. **99 F6** NJ7444.
Towiemore *Moray* ***Settlement***, at confluence of Burn of Towie and River Isla, 4m/6km SW of Keith. **98 B6** NJ3945.
Town Bridge *Dorset* ***Bridge***, late medieval stone bridge over River Stour at Sturminster Newton. Widened in 17c. ST7813.
Town End *Bucks.* ***Settlement***, adjoining to N of Radnage, 2m/3km NE of Stokenchurch. SU7897.
Town End *Cambs.* ***Suburb***, S district of March. **43 H6** TL4195.
Town End *Cumb.* ***Hamlet***, 2m/4km NE of Lindale. **55 H1** SD4483.
Town End *Cumb.* ***Locality***, at NE corner of Grasmere lake, adjoining to SE of Grasmere village. Wordsworth Museum. NY3406.
Town End *Cumb.* ***Locality***, adjoining to S of Troutbeck. 17c house, Townend (National Trust). NY4002.
Town End *Cumb.* ***Locality***, adjoining to S of Clifton. NY5326.
Town End *Cumb.* ***Locality***, adjoining to S of Kirkby Thore. NY6325.
Town End *Cumb.* ***Settlement***, 1km NW of Newby Bridge. SD3687.
Town End *Lincs.* ***Settlement***, W end of Wilsford, 4m/7km SW of Sleaford. SK9943.
Town End *Mersey.* ***Suburb***, adjoining to N of Cronton. SJ4988.
Town End *W.Yorks.* ***Locality***, adjoining to W of Golcar. SE0916.
Town End Farm *T. & W.* ***Suburb***, housing estate in NW part of Sunderland. NZ3459.
Town Fields *Ches.* ***Suburb***, SW district of Winsford. SJ6465.
Town Green *Lancs.* ***Locality***, 2m/3km S of Ormskirk. **48 D2** SD4005.
Town Green *Norf.* ***Hamlet***, adjoining to S of South Walsham, 3m/4km NW of Acle. TG3612.
Town Head *Cumb.* ***Locality***, adjoining to N of Troutbeck, 3m/4km E of Ambleside. NY4103.
Town Head *Cumb.* ***Locality***, 1km NW of Cliburn. NY5825.
Town Head *Cumb.* ***Locality***, adjoining to S of Crosby Ravensworth. NY6214.
Town Head *Cumb.* ***Locality***, adjoining to E of Kirkby Thore. NY6425.
Town Head *Cumb.* ***Locality***, 1km S of Great Asby. NY6712.
Town Head *Cumb.* ***Locality***, adjoining to SE of Dutton, 4m/6km E of Kirkby Thore. NY6924.
Town Head *N.Yorks.* ***Locality***, at NE end of Austwick, 4m/7km NW of Settle. SD7768.
Town Head *N.Yorks.* ***Settlement***, adjoining to N of Askwith, 2m/3km NW of Otley. SE1748.
Town Head *Staffs.* ***Settlement***, adjoining to NE of Foxt, 4m/6km NE of Cheadle. SK0348.
Town Hill *N.Yorks.* ***Locality***, adjoining to N of Hebden. SE0263.
Town Kelloe *Dur.* ***Settlement***, 1m/2km E of Kelloe and 5m/8km N of Sedgefield. NZ3536.
Town Lane *Gt.Man.* ***Locality***, 2m/4km E of Leigh. SJ6999.
Town Moor *T. & W.* ***Open space***, large open space in Newcastle upon Tyne to N of city centre. NZ2466.
Town of Lowton *Gt.Man.* ***Settlement***, 1m/2km S of Golborne. SJ6096.
Town Row *E.Suss.* ***Locality***, adjoining to E of Rotherfield. **13 J3** TQ5630.
Town Street *Suff.* ***Suburb***, SW district of Brandon. **44 B7** TL7785.
Town Yetholm *Sc.Bord.* ***Village***, on W side of Bowmont Water, 7m/11km SE of Kelso. **70 D1** NT8228.
Towneley Hall Art Gallery and Museum *Lancs.* ***Historic house***, 1m/2km SE of Burnley town centre, home of Towneley family from 13c until 1902. Now houses a museum and town's art gallery. **56 D6** SD8530.
Townend *Cumb.* ***Historic house***, 17c wealthy yeoman farmer's house (National Trust) to S of Troutbeck, 3m/4km SE of Ambleside. Contains carved wooden built-in furniture and domestic items reflecting history and use of house. **60 F6** NY4002.
Townend *W.Dun.* ***Suburb***, N district of Dumbarton. **74 C3** NS4076.
Townfield *Dur.* ***Settlement***, just S of Hunstanworth, 2m/3km SW of Blanchland. NY9548.
Towngate *Cumb.* ***Locality***, just NW of Ainstable, on E side of River Eden. NY5246.
Towngate *Lincs.* ***Locality***, adjoining to N of Market Deeping. TF1310.
Townhead *Cumb.* ***Hamlet***, just E of Dearham. NY0735.
Townhead *Cumb.* ***Locality***, 1m/2km SE of Ousby, and 3m/4km SE of Melmerby. NY6334.
Townhead *D. & G.* ***Settlement***, 3m/5km S of Kirkcudbright. **65 G6** NX6946.
Townhead *S.Yorks.* ***Hamlet***, 1km NE of Dunford Bridge, 5m/8km W of Penistone. SE1602.
Townhead of Greenlaw *D. & G.* ***Village***, 2m/4km NW of Castle Douglas. **65 H4** NX7464.
Townhead Reservoir *N.Lan.* ***Reservoir***, 1m/2km E of Kilsyth, on site of battle in 1645. **75 F3** NS7378.
Townhill *Fife* ***Village***, 1m/2km NE of Dunfermline. **75 K2** NT1089.
Townhill *Swan.* ***Suburb***, 1m/2km NW of Swansea city centre. SS6394.
Townland Green *Kent* ***Settlement***, adjoining to W of Woodchurch. TQ9434.
Town's End *Bucks.* ***Settlement***, at W end of Marsh Gibbon, 4m/6km E of Bicester. SP6422.
Town's End *Bucks.* ***Suburb***, to N of Haddenham, 3m/5km NE of Thame. SP7409.
Town's End *Dorset* ***Locality***, adjoining to S of Corfe Castle. SY9681.
Towns End *Hants.* ***Hamlet***, 3m/4km E of Kingsclere. SU5658.
Towns Gate *Gt.Man.* ***Locality***, 2m/3km W of Urmston. SJ7394.
Towns Green *Ches.* ***Settlement***, 3m/5km E of Tarporley. SJ6061.
Townsend *Herts.* ***Suburb***, 1km N of St. Albans city centre. TL1408.
Townshend *Cornw.* ***Village***, 3m/5km SE of Hayle. **2 C5** SW5932.
Towthorpe *E.Riding* ***Hamlet***, 3m/5km NE of Fridaythorpe. Site of former village to W. **59 F3** SE9062.
Towthorpe *York* ***Village***, at S end of Strensall Camp, 5m/7km N of York. **58 C4** SE6258.
Towton *N.Yorks.* ***Village***, 2m/4km S of Tadcaster. To S of village is scene of Yorkist victory in Wars of the Roses, 1461. **57 K6** SE4839.
Towy *English form of (River) Tywi, qv.*
Towy Forest *Cere.* *English form of Tywi Forest, qv.*
Towyn *Conwy* ***Village***, 2m/3km NE of Abergele. **47 H5** SH9779.
Towyn *Gwyn.* *Former name of Tywyn, qv.*
Toynton All Saints *Lincs.* ***Village***, 2m/3km S of Spilsby. **53 G6** TF3963.
Toynton Fen Side *Lincs.* ***Settlement***, 1m/2km S of Toynton All Saints. **53 G6** TF3962.
Toynton St. Peter *Lincs.* ***Village***, 1m/2km SE of Toynton All Saints. **53 H6** TF3963.
Toy's Hill *Kent* ***Village***, 2m/4km SE of Westerham. **23 H6** TQ4751.
Trabboch *E.Ayr.* ***Locality***, 7m/11km E of Ayr. **67 J1** NS4321.
Traboe *Cornw.* ***Settlement***, on N edge of Goonhilly Downs, 7m/11km SE of Helston. **2 E6** SW7421.
Tracebridge *Som.* ***Hamlet***, on River Tone, 4m/7km W of Wellington. ST0621.
Tradespark *High.* ***Locality***, in Nairn district, 1m/2km W of Nairn. **97 F6** NH8656.
Tradespark *Ork.* ***Settlement***, 1km S of Kirkwall, Mainland. **107 D7** HY4508.
Traeth Bach *Gwyn.* ***Sea feature***, muddy combined estuary of Rivers Dwyryd and Glaslyn, between Harlech and Porthmadog. **36 E2** SH5736.
Traeth Lafan *Gwyn.* *Welsh form of Lavan Sands, qv.*
Traeth Maelgwyn *Cere.* ***Coastal feature***, sandbank in River Dyfi estuary, 1m/2km SE of Aberdyfi across river. **37 F6** SN6294.
Trafalgar *Mersey.* ***Suburb***, S of Benington town centre. SJ3383.
Trafford Park *Gt.Man.* ***Locality***, large planned industrial development, 1m/2km NW of Stretford town centre. **49 G3** SJ7896.
Trahenna Hill *Sc.Bord.* ***Mountain***, 2m/3km NE of Broughton. Height 1791 feet or 546 metres. **75 K7** NT1337.
Tràigh Chuil *W.Isles* *Gaelic form of Col Sands, qv.*
Tràigh Eais *W.Isles* ***Coastal feature***, beach on NW coast on Barra, 2m/3km NW of Ardmhòr. **84 B4** NF6906.
Tràigh na Cleavag *W.Isles* ***Coastal feature***, beach on South Harris, 3m/4km SE of Toe Head. **92 E2** NF9891.
Traligill *High.* ***River***, flowing W into S end of Loch Assynt at Inchnadamph. **102 E6** NC2421.
Trallong *Powys* ***Hamlet***, 3m/5km E of Sennybridge. **27 J6** SN9629.
Trallwn *Swan.* ***Suburb***, 3m/5km NE of Swansea city centre. **17 K5** SS6996.
Tramiag Bay *Arg. & B.* ***Bay***, on E coast of Jura, 1km NE of Ardlussa. **72 E2** NR6688.
Tranch (Y Transh). *Torfaen* ***Locality***, on W side of Pontypool. **19 F1** SO2700.
Tranent *E.Loth.* Population: 8313. ***Small town***, former mining town 4m/6km E of Musselburgh. **76 C3** NT4072.
Tranmere *Mersey.* ***Suburb***, 1m/2km S of Birkenhead town centre. SJ3287.
Trannon *Powys* ***Inland physical feature***, upland area, 3m/5km W of Carno. **37 J6** SN9095.
Trannon *Powys* ***River***, rising 2m/4km SW of Talerddig and flowing S to Llawryglyn, then E by Trefeglwys into River Severn on W side of Caersws. SO0291.
Trantlebeg *High.* ***Settlement***, across river to E of Trantlemore. **104 D3** NC8853.
Trantlemore *High.* ***Settlement***, in Strath Halladale, in Caithness district, 7m/11km S of Melvich. **104 D3** NC8853.
Tranwell *Northumb.* ***Settlement***, 2m/3km SW of Morpeth. **71 G5** NZ1883.
Trap (Trapp). *Carmar.* ***Hamlet***, 3m/4km SE of Llandeilo. **17 K3** SN6518.
Trap Street *Ches.* ***Settlement***, 2m/3km W of Marton. SJ8268.
Trapp *Carmar.* *English form of Trap, qv.*
Traprain *E.Loth.* ***Hamlet***, 1m/2km S of East Linton. **76 D3** NT5975.
Traprain Law Fort *E.Loth.* ***Historic/prehistoric site***, hillfort 2m/3km SW of East Linton. Site is thought to have been occupied until 11c. **76 D3** NT5874.
Trap's Green *Warks.* ***Settlement***, 4m/6km NW of Henley-in-Arden. SP1069.
Trapshill *W.Berks.* ***Settlement***, 4m/6km SE of Hungerford. SU3763.
Traquair *Sc.Bord.* ***Village***, 1m/2km S of Innerleithen across River Tweed. **76 B7** NT3334.
Traquair House *Sc.Bord.* ***Historic house***, 17c mansion, with tower of earlier date, to N of Traquair on W side of Elibank and Traquair Forest. **76 B7** NT3334.
Trash Green *W.Berks.* ***Settlement***, 1m/2km NW of Burghfield and 4m/7km SW of Reading. SU6569.
Trawden *Lancs.* ***Village***, on NW side of The Forest of Trawden, 2m/3km SE of Colne. **56 E6** SD9138.
Trawsallt *Cere.* ***Mountain***, 3m/4km SE of Pont-rhyd-y-groes. Height 1876 feet or 572 metres. **27 G1** SN7770.
Trawsfynydd *Gwyn.* ***Village***, on E side of Llyn Trawsfynydd, 4m/7km S of Ffestiniog. **37 G2** SH7035.
Trawsgoed *Cere.* *Welsh form of Crosswood, qv.*
Tre-Aubrey *V. of Glam.* ***Settlement***, 3m/5km SE of Cowbridge. ST0372.
Tre-boeth *Swan.* ***Suburb***, 2m/3km N of Swansea city centre. SS6596.
Tre-groes *Bridgend* ***Settlement***, 1km NE of Pencoed. **18 C3** SS9681.
Tre-groes *Cere.* ***Hamlet***, 3m/4km N of Llandysul. **26 D4** SN4044.
Tre-groes *Pembs.* *Welsh form of Whitchurch, qv.*
Tre-gŵyr *Swan.* *Welsh form of Gowerton, qv.*
Tre-Herbert *Carmar.* ***Locality***, 1m/2km SE of Lampeter. SN5847.
Tre-hill (Trehyl). *V. of Glam.* ***Hamlet***, 6m/10km W of Cardiff. ST0874.
Tre-Ifor *R.C.T.* ***Settlement***, 2m/3km N of Aberdare. SN9905.
Tre-mostyn *Flints.* ***Settlement***, 1m/2km SW of Mostyn. SJ1479.
Tre-pys-llygod *Conwy* ***Mountain***, with three low summits, the highest being 1046 feet or 319 metres, 3m/5km NW of Llansannan. **47 G6** SH8868.
Tre-Rhys *Pembs.* ***Settlement***, 2m/4km W of St. Dogmaels. **26 A4** SN1146.
Tre Taliesin *Cere.* *Alternative name for Taliesin, qv.*
Tre-vaughan *Carmar.* ***Settlement***, 1km N of Carmarthen. **17 H2** SN4021.
Tre-wyn *Mon.* ***Settlement***, 1km W of Pandy. SO3222.
Treak Cliff Cavern *Derbys.* ***Cave***, underground cavern in limestone cliff, to N of Blue John Mine and 1km W of Castleton. Contains deposits of amethystine spar or bleu-jaune similar to those in Blue John Mine. **50 D4** SK1383.
Trealaw *R.C.T.* ***Village***, to SE of Tonypandy across River Rhondda. **18 C2** SS9992.
Treales *Lancs.* ***Village***, 1m/2km NE of Kirkham. **55 H6** SD4432.
Treamlod *Pembs.* *Welsh form of Ambleston, qv.*
Trearddur *I.o.A.* ***Small town***, small resort with westward-facing bay on coast of Holy Island, Anglesey, 2m/4km S of Holyhead. **46 A5** SH2578.
Treaslane *High.* ***Settlement***, on Skye, on W side of Loch Snizort Beag at entrance to Loch Treaslane. **93 J6** NG3953.
Trebanog *R.C.T.* ***Hamlet***, 1m/2km N of Tonyrefail. **18 D2** ST0190.
Trebanos *N.P.T.* ***Locality***, 1m/2km SW of Pontardawe. **18 A1** SN7103.
Trebarrow *Cornw.* ***Hamlet***, 3m/5km SE of Week St. Mary. **4 C1** SX2896.
Trebartha *Cornw.* ***Settlement***, 6m/10km SW of Launceston. **4 C3** SX2677.
Trebarvah *Cornw.* ***Settlement***, 4m/6km NE of Helston. SW7030.
Trebarwith *Cornw.* ***Settlement***, 2m/3km S of Tintagel. **4 A2** SX0586.
Trebarwith Strand *Cornw.* ***Coastal feature***, sandy stretch of N coast (National Trust), 1km NW of Trebarwith. SX0486.
Trebeath *Cornw.* ***Hamlet***, 5m/8km NW of Launceston. SX2587.
Trebefered *V. of Glam.* *Welsh form of Boverton, qv.*
Trebetherick *Cornw.* ***Village***, on Padstow Bay, 5m/8km NW of Wadebridge. **3 G1** SW9378.
Trebister *Shet.* ***Settlement***, on Mainland, 2m/4km SW of Lerwick. HU4438.
Treble's Holford *Som.* ***Hamlet***, 1m/2km N of Combe Florey. ST1533.
Treborough *Som.* ***Hamlet***, on Exmoor, 5m/8km S of Dunster. **7 J2** ST0136.
Trebudannon *Cornw.* ***Village***, 2m/3km SW of St. Columb Major. **3 F2** SW8961.
Trebullett *Cornw.* ***Village***, 4m/6km S of Launceston. **4 D3** SX3278.
Treburley *Cornw.* ***Village***, 5m/8km N of Callington. **4 D3** SX3477.
Treburrick *Cornw.* ***Hamlet***, 4m/7km SW of Padstow. SW8670.

T

Trebyan *Cornw.* ***Settlement***, 3m/4km S of Bodmin. **4 A4** SX0763.
Trecastle *Powys* ***Village***, 8m/13km SE of Llandovery. Early Norman motte and bailey castle. **27 H6** SN8829.
Trecenydd *Caerp.* ***Suburb***, in NW part of Caerphilly. ST1487.
Trecott *Devon* ***Hamlet***, 5m/7km NE of Okehampton. SS6300.
Trecrogo *Cornw.* ***Hamlet***, 3m/5km SW of Launceston. SX3080.
Trecwn *Pembs.* ***Hamlet***, 3m/5km S of Fishguard. **16 C1** SM9632.
Trecynon *R.C.T.* ***Locality***, adjoining to NW of Aberdare. **18 C1** SN9903.
Tredaule *Cornw.* ***Hamlet***, 6m/10km W of Launceston. SX2381.
Tredavoe *Cornw.* ***Hamlet***, to SW of Penzance. **2 B6** SW4528.
Treddiog *Pembs.* ***Settlement***, 2m/3km S of Mathry. **16 B2** SM8828.
Tredegar *B.Gwent* Population: 15,390. ***Town***, industrial town on Sirhowy River, 21m/33km N of Cardiff. Former metal-smelting town, symbolised by town's iron clock. **18 E1** SO1409.
Tredegar Country Park *Newport* ***Leisure/recreation***, 90 acres of parkland surrounding 17c Tredegar House and gardens, featuring carriage rides, craft workshops and adventure play farm, 3m/4km SW of Newport. **19 F3** ST2885.
Tredelerch *Cardiff Welsh form of Rumney, qv.*
Tredington *Glos.* ***Village***, 2m/4km S of Tewkesbury. **29 J6** SO9029.
Tredington *Warks.* ***Village***, 2m/3km N of Shipston on Stour. **30 D4** SP2543.
Tredinnick *Cornw.* ***Hamlet***, 3m/4km NW of Looe. **4 C5** SX2357.
Tredinnick *Cornw.* ***Locality***, 4m/7km N of St. Columb Major. **3 G1** SW9270.
Tredogan *V. of Glam.* ***Hamlet***, on NE side of Cardiff International Airport, 3m/4km W of Barry. ST0767.
Tredomen *Powys* ***Settlement***, 3m/5km NW of Llangorse. **28 A5** SO1231.
Tredrissi *Pembs.* ***Locality***, 2m/3km N of Newport. **26 A4** SN0742.
Tredrizzick *Cornw.* ***Hamlet***, 4m/6km NW of Wadebridge. SW9576.
Tredunnock (Tredynog). *Mon.* ***Village***, 4m/6km S of Usk. **19 G2** ST3794.
Tredustan *Powys* ***Settlement***, opposite Trefecca across River Llynfi, 1m/2km SW of Talgarth. SO1332.
Tredworth *Glos.* ***Suburb***, S district of Gloucester. SO8417.
Tredynog *Mon. Welsh form of Tredunnock, qv.*
Treen *Cornw.* ***Hamlet***, 5m/8km W of St. Ives. SW4337.
Treen *Cornw.* ***Village***, 3m/5km SE of Land's End. Coast to S and SE owned by National Trust. **2 A6** SW3923.
Treesmill *Cornw.* ***Hamlet***, 3m/5km SW of Lostwithiel. SX0855.
Treeton *S.Yorks.* ***Village***, 3m/5km S of Rotherham. **51 G4** SK4387.
Tref-y-nant *Wrex.* ***Settlement***, 2m/3km W of Ruabon. SJ2742.
Trefaldwyn *Powys Welsh form of Montgomery, qv.*
Trefalun *Wrex. Welsh form of Trevalyn, qv.*
Trefaser *Pembs. Alternative spelling of Trefasser, qv.*
Trefasser (Also spelled Trefaser.) *Pembs.* ***Hamlet***, 2m/4km S of Strumble Head. Hillfort to N. **16 B1** SM8937.
Trefdraeth *I.o.A.* ***Settlement***, on Anglesey, 1km N of Malltraeth Sands, 5m/7km SW of Llangefni. **46 C5** SH4070.
Trefdraeth *Pembs. Welsh form of Newport, qv.*
Trefecca *Powys* ***Hamlet***, 1m/2km SW of Talgarth. **28 A5** SO1432.
Trefechan *Cere.* ***Suburb***, in S part of Aberystwyth across River Rheidol. SN5881.
Trefechan *M.Tyd.* ***Settlement***, 2m/3km NW of Merthyr Tydfil. SO0308.
Trefeglwys *Powys* ***Village***, 4m/6km W of Caersws. **37 J6** SN9790.
Trefelen *Pembs. Welsh form of Bletherston, qv.*
Trefenter *Cere.* ***Locality***, 4m/7km E of Llanrhystud. **27 F2** SN6068.
Trefesgob *Newport Welsh form of Bishton, qv.*
Treffgarne *Pembs.* ***Village***, 5m/8km N of Haverfordwest. **16 C2** SM9523.
Trefflemin *V. of Glam. Welsh form of Flemingston, qv.*
Trefforest *R.C.T. Welsh form of Treforest, qv.*
Treffynnon *Flints. Welsh form of Holywell, qv.*
Treffynnon *Pembs.* ***Hamlet***, 4m/6km NE of Solva. **16 B2** SM8428.
Trefgarn Owen *Pembs.* ***Hamlet***, 2m/3km W of Hayscastle. **16 B2** SM8625.
Trefignath Burial Chamber *I.o.A.* ***Historic/prehistoric site***, Neolithic tomb of segmented cist type (Cadw) on Holy Island, Anglesey, 1m/2km SE of Holyhead. Ty Mawr Standing Stone (Cadw) 1km W. **46 A4** SH2580.
Trefil *B.Gwent* ***Village***, 3m/4km NW of Tredegar. **28 A7** SO1212.
Trefilan *Cere.* ***Hamlet***, 6m/10km N of Lampeter. **26 E3** SN5457.
Trefin *Pembs. Welsh form of Trevine, qv.*
Treflach *Shrop.* ***Hamlet***, 3m/5km SW of Oswestry. **38 B3** SJ2525.
Treflach Wood *Shrop.* ***Locality***, 3m/5km SW of Oswestry. SJ2525.
Trefnanney *Powys* ***Settlement***, 5m/8km N of Welshpool. **38 B4** SJ2015.
Trefnant *Denb.* ***Village***, 3m/4km S of St. Asaph. **47 J5** SJ0570.
Trefonen *Shrop.* ***Village***, 3m/4km SW of Oswestry. **38 B3** SJ2526.
Trefonnen *Newport Welsh form of Nash, qv.*
Trefor (Trevor). *Gwyn.* ***Village***, near coast of Caernarfon Bay, 12m/19km SW of Caernarfon. **36 C1** SH3746.
Trefor *I.o.A.* ***Settlement***, on Anglesey, 4m/6km SW of Llanerchymedd. **46 B4** SH3780.
Trefor *Wrex. Welsh form of Trevor, qv.*
Treforest (Trefforest). *R.C.T.* ***Suburb***, SE district of Pontypridd. Industrial estate to SE. **18 D3** ST0888.
Treforest Industrial Estate *R.C.T.* ***Locality***, in Taff Vale, 4m/6km SE of Pontypridd. **18 E3** ST1186.
Treforgan *Cardiff Welsh form of Morganstown, qv.*
Trefriw *Conwy* ***Village***, on River Crafnant, near its confluence with River Conwy, 1m/2km NW of Llanrwst. **47 F6** SH7863.
Trefriw Wells *Conwy* ***Settlement***, with chalybeate spa, 1m/2km N of Trefriw. SH7765.
Trefwrdan *Pembs. Welsh form of Jordanston, qv.*
Trefyclo *Powys Welsh form of Knighton, qv.*
Trefynwy *Mon. Welsh form of Monmouth, qv.*
Tregadillett *Cornw.* ***Village***, 2m/3km W of Launceston. **6 B7** SX2983.
Tregaian *I.o.A.* ***Settlement***, on Anglesey, 3m/4km N of Llangefni. **46 C5** SH4579.
Tregare (Tre'r-gaer). *Mon.* ***Hamlet***, 2m/3km N of Raglan. **28 D7** SO4110.
Tregarland *Cornw.* ***Hamlet***, 3m/4km N of Looe. SX2557.
Tregarne *Cornw.* ***Hamlet***, 1m/2km NW of St. Keverne and 8m/13km E of Helston. SW7822.
Tregaron *Cere.* ***Small town***, 10m/15km NE of Lampeter. **27 F3** SN6759.
Tregarth *Gwyn.* ***Village***, 2m/3km NW of Bethesda. **46 E6** SH6067.
Tregaswith *Cornw.* ***Settlement***, 1m/2km W of St. Columb Major. SW8962.
Tregatta *Cornw.* ***Hamlet***, 1km S of Tintagel and 4m/6km NW of Camelford. SX0587.
Tregatwg *V. of Glam. Welsh form of Cadoxton, qv.*
Tregavethan *Cornw.* ***Settlement***, 3m/5km NW of Truro. **2 E4** SW7847.
Tregear *Cornw.* ***Settlement***, 3m/4km SE of Carland Cross. **3 F3** SW8650.
Tregeare *Cornw.* ***Hamlet***, 6m/9km W of Launceston. **4 C2** SX2486.
Tregeare Rounds *Cornw.* ***Historic/prehistoric site***, Iron Age hillfort with three rings of earthworks, 3m/4km SE of Port Isaac. **4 A3** SX0380.
Tregeiriog *Wrex.* ***Hamlet***, 6m/9km S of Llangollen. **38 A2** SJ1733.
Tregele *I.o.A.* ***Village***, near N coast of Anglesey, 1m/2km SW of Cemaes Bay. **46 B3** SH3592.
Tregidden *Cornw.* ***Hamlet***, 1m/2km SW of Manaccan. **2 E6** SW7523.
Tregiffian Burial Chamber *Cornw.* ***Historic/prehistoric site***, Stone Age tomb with cup marked stones (English Heritage), 3m/5km SW of Newlyn. **2 B6** SW4324.
Tregiskey *Cornw.* ***Settlement***, 4m/6km S of St. Austell. SX0146.
Treglemais *Pembs.* ***Hamlet***, 8m/12km NE of St. David's. **16 B2** SM8128.
Tregolds *Cornw.* ***Settlement***, 3m/5km SW of Padstow. **3 F1** SW8872.
Tregole *Cornw.* ***Hamlet***, 3m/4km W of Week St. Mary. **4 B1** SX1998.
Tregolwyn *V. of Glam. Welsh form of Colwinston, qv.*
Tregonetha *Cornw.* ***Hamlet***, 3m/4km E of St. Columb Major. **3 G2** SW9563.
Tregonhawke *Cornw.* ***Locality***, 3m/5km SW of Torpoint across St. John's Lake. SX4051.
Tregonning Hill *Cornw.* ***Hill***, 3m/5km NW of Porthleven. Height 636 feet or 194 metres. **2 C6** SW5930.
Tregony *Cornw.* ***Village***, 7m/11km SW of St. Austell. **3 G4** SW9245.
Tregoodwell *Cornw.* ***Hamlet***, just E of Camelford. SX1183.
Tregoss *Cornw.* ***Hamlet***, 4m/6km SE of St. Columb Major. SW9660.
Tregowris *Cornw.* ***Hamlet***, 8m/12km SE of Helston. SW7722.
Tregoyd *Powys* ***Settlement***, 3m/5km SW of Hay-on-Wye. **28 A5** SO1937.
Tregrehan Mills *Cornw.* ***Village***, 2m/3km NE of St. Austell. SX0453.
Treguff *V. of Glam.* ***Settlement***, 3m/5km SE of Cowbridge. **18 D4** ST0371.
Tregullon *Cornw.* ***Settlement***, 2m/3km S of Bodmin. SX0664.
Tregunnon *Cornw.* ***Hamlet***, 6m/10km W of Launceston. SX2283.
Tregurrian *Cornw.* ***Settlement***, 3m/5km NE of Newquay. **3 F2** SW8565.
Tregustick *Cornw.* ***Hamlet***, 3m/4km NE of Newquay. SW8463.
Tregwhelydd Standing Stone *I.o.A.* ***Historic/prehistoric site***, on W side of Anglesey 2m/3km NE of Bodedern. Dates from Bronze Age. **46 B4** SH3483.
Tregynon *Powys* ***Village***, 5m/8km N of Newtown. **37 K6** SO0998.
Trehafod *R.C.T.* ***Village***, 2m/3km W of Pontypridd. **18 D2** ST0490.
Trehan *Cornw.* ***Hamlet***, 2m/3km SW of Saltash. SX4058.
Treharris *M.Tyd.* Population: 5654. ***Village***, 5m/7km N of Pontypridd. **18 D2** ST0996.
Treherbert *R.C.T.* ***Small town***, former mining village in Rhondda Fawr valley, 2m/3km NW of Treorchy. **18 C2** SS9498.
Trehingyll *V. of Glam. See Trehyngyll.*
Trehopcyn *R.C.T. Welsh form of Hopkinstown, qv.*
Trehyl *V. of Glam. Welsh form of Tre-hill, qv.*
Treig *High.* ***River***, in Lochaber district, running N from Loch Treig to River Spean 1m/2km below Loch Moy. **87 K7** NN3579.
Trekelland Bridge *Cornw.* ***Bridge***, granite bridge dating from 1504, carrying narrow road, only 10 feet or 3 metres wide, across River Inny 4m/6km SW of Launceston. SX3079.
Trekenner *Cornw.* ***Village***, 4m/6km S of Launceston. **4 D3** SX3478.
Treknow *Cornw.* ***Village***, near N coast at Trebarwith Strand, 4m/6km NW of Camelford. SX0586.
Trelai *Cardiff Welsh form of Ely, qv.*
Trelales *Bridgend Welsh form of Laleston, qv.*
Trelan *Cornw.* ***Hamlet***, on Goonhilly Downs, 8m/12km SE of Helston. SW7418.
Trelash *Cornw.* ***Hamlet***, 6m/9km E of Boscastle. **4 B1** SX1890.
Trelassick *Cornw.* ***Settlement***, 2m/3km SE of Carland Cross. **3 F3** SW8752.
Trelawnyd *Flints.* ***Village***, 2m/4km SE of Prestatyn. **47 J5** SJ0879.
Trelech *Carmar.* ***Village***, 7m/11km S of Newcastle Emlyn. **17 F1** SN2830.
Trelech a'r Betws *Carmar.* ***Locality***, 8m/12km NW of Carmarthen. **17 G2** SN3026.
Treleddyd-fawr *Pembs.* ***Hamlet***, 2m/3km N of St. David's. **16 A2** SM7527.
Treletert *Pembs. Welsh form of Letterston, qv.*
Trelewis *M.Tyd.* ***Village***, adjoining to E of Treharris, 5m/8km NE of Pontypridd. **18 E2** ST1097.
Treligga *Cornw.* ***Hamlet***, 3m/5km W of Camelford. Stretch of coast to SW is National Trust. **4 A2** SX0584.
Trelights *Cornw.* ***Village***, 4m/7km N of Wadebridge. **3 G1** SW9979.
Trelill *Cornw.* ***Hamlet***, 5m/8km SW of Camelford. **4 A3** SX0478.
Trelissick *Cornw.* ***Historic house***, with garden, park, farmland and woods, all National Trust, 4m/6km S of Truro, overlooking River Fal. **3 F5** SW8339.
Trelissick Garden *Cornw.* ***Garden***, National Trust property on W side of River Fal estuary, 3m/5km S of Truro. Contains exotic plants from places such as Mexico, Australia and South Africa. Also includes Valhalla Ships Figurehead Museum. **3 F5** SW8339.
Trelleck (Tryleg). *Mon.* ***Village***, 5m/8km S of Monmouth. To SW, three boundary stones known as Harold's Stones, Bronze Age monoliths. **19 J1** SO5005.
Trelleck Grange *Mon.* ***Settlement***, 2m/4km S of Trelleck. **19 H1** SO4901.
Trelogan *Flints.* ***Village***, 3m/4km W of Mostyn. **47 K4** SJ1180.
Trelowarren *Cornw.* ***Historic house***, to N of Mawgan, 4m/6km SE of Helston. Dating from 15c, now partly leased to Trelowarren Fellowship. **2 E6** SW7025.
Trelowla *Cornw.* ***Settlement***, 3m/5km NE of Looe. SX2956.
Treludderow *Cornw.* ***Locality***, 4m/6km S of Newquay. SW8155.
Trelung Ness *Aber.* ***Coastal feature***, headland on E coast, 3m/4km S of Stonehaven. **91 G6** NO8881.
Trelydan *Powys* ***Settlement***, 2m/3km N of Welshpool. SJ2310.
Trelystan *Powys* ***Settlement***, 3m/5km SE of Welshpool. **38 B5** SJ2603.
Tremadoc *Gwyn. English form of Tremadog, qv.*
Tremadoc Bay *Gwyn. English form of Tremadog Bay, qv.*
Tremadog (Tremadoc). *Gwyn.* ***Village***, 1m/2km N of Porthmadog. Site of Roman bath house at W end of village. **36 E1** SH5540.
Tremadog Bay (Also spelled Tremadoc Bay.) *Gwyn.* ***Bay***, large bay on S side of Lleyn Peninsula, its bow-shaped coastline extending E from Trwyn Pencilan to Morfa Dyffryn. **36 D2** SH5234.
Tremail *Cornw.* ***Hamlet***, 4m/7km NE of Camelford. **4 B2** SX1686.
Tremain *Cere.* ***Hamlet***, 2m/4km SW of Aberporth. **26 B4** SN2348.
Tremaine *Cornw.* ***Village***, 7m/11km NW of Launceston. **4 C2** SX2389.
Tremains *Bridgend* ***Suburb***, central district of Bridgend. SS9079.
Tremar *Cornw.* ***Village***, 3m/4km N of Liskeard. **4 C4** SX2568.
Trematon *Cornw.* ***Village***, 2m/4km W of Saltash. **4 D5** SX3959.
Trembraze *Cornw.* ***Locality***, to N of Liskeard. SX2565.
Tremeirchion *Denb.* ***Village***, 5m/8km N of Denbigh. **47 J5** SJ0873.
Tremethick Cross *Cornw.* ***Settlement***, 2m/3km W of Penzance. **2 B5** SW4430.
Tremollett *Cornw.* ***Settlement***, 6m/9km NW of Callington. SX2975.
Tremore *Cornw.* ***Hamlet***, 4m/6km SW of Bodmin. SX0164.
Tremorfa *Cardiff* ***Suburb***, 2m/3km E of Cardiff city centre. ST2077.
Trenance *Cornw.* ***Hamlet***, 4m/6km W of Wadebridge. SW9270.
Trenance *Cornw.* ***Village***, on coast, 5m/7km NE of Newquay. **3 F2** SW8567.
Trenarren *Cornw.* ***Hamlet***, above St. Austell Bay, 3m/4km SE of St. Austell. **4 A6** SX0348.
Trench *Tel. & W.* ***Locality***, 2m/3km NW of Oakengates. **39 F4** SJ6912.
Trench *Wrex.* ***Settlement***, 3m/4km NW of Ellesmere. **38 C2** SJ3839.
Trench Green *Oxon.* ***Settlement***, 3m/5km NW of Reading. SU6877.
Trenchford Reservoir *Devon* ***Reservoir***, 2m/4km N of Bovey Tracey. **7 F7** SX8082.
Trencreek *Cornw.* ***Hamlet***, on SE edge of Newquay. SW8260.
Trencrom Hill *Cornw.* ***Hill***, National Trust property rising to over 170 metres, 3m/4km S of St. Ives. **2 B5** SW5136.
Trencrom Hillfort *Cornw.* ***Historic/prehistoric site***, small oval fort on granite summit (National Trust), 3m/4km S of St. Ives. Spectacular walls, incorporating natural rock outcrops. **2 C5** SW5136.
Trendrine Hill *Cornw.* ***Hill***, 3m/4km SW of St. Ives. Height 810 feet or 247 metres. **2 B5** SW4738.
Trenear *Cornw.* ***Hamlet***, 3m/5km N of Helston. SW6831.
Treneglos *Cornw.* ***Village***, 8m/13km NW of Launceston. **4 C2** SX2088.

T

Trenewan *Cornw.* ***Settlement***, 3m/5km E of Fowey across River Fowey. **4 B5** SX1753.
Trengune *Cornw.* ***Hamlet***, 6m/10km NE of Boscastle. SX1893.
Trengwainton House *Cornw.* ***Historic house***, with garden and park (National Trust) containing exotic plants, 2m/3km W of Penzance. **2 B5** SW4431.
Trent ***River***, major river of central England rising near Biddulph Moor and flowing by Stoke-on-Trent, Stone, Rugeley, Burton upon Trent, Nottingham, Newark-on-Trent and Gainsborough to join River Ouse and form River Humber, 7m/12km E of Goole. Chief tributaries are Rivers Sow, Tame, Soar, Devon to S bank, and Rivers Blyth, Dove, Derwent, Idle to N. Tidal to Cromwell Lock, E of Cromwell. **52 B1** SE8623.
Trent *Dorset Alternative name for (River) Piddle, qv.*
Trent *Dorset* ***Village***, 3m/5km NE of Yeovil. **8 E3** ST5918.
Trent Park *Gt.Lon.* ***Leisure/recreation***, country park with mixture of woodland and grassland in borough of Enfield, 2m/3km W of Enfield town centre. Much of woodland is ancient, part of royal hunting forest of Enfield Chase. Rich in birdlife and grassland flowers. **23 F2** TQ2897.
Trent Port *Lincs.* ***Settlement***, on E bank of River Trent, to SW of Marton. SK8381.
Trent Vale *Stoke* ***Suburb***, 1m/2km S of Stoke-on-Trent city centre. SJ8643.
Trent Valley *Staffs.* ***Valley***, carrying River Trent between Stone and Great Haywood. **40 B3** SJ9229.
Trentham *Stoke* ***Locality***, 3m/5km S of Stoke-on-Trent. River Trent flows through public park containing large lake. **40 A1** SJ8641.
Trentishoe *Devon* ***Hamlet***, on N coast, 5m/7km W of Lynton. **6 E1** SS6448.
Trenwheal *Cornw.* ***Hamlet***, 4m/7km NW of Helston. SW6132.
Treoes *V. of Glam.* ***Village***, 3m/4km E of Bridgend. **18 C4** SS9478.
Treopert *Pembs. Welsh form of Granston, qv.*
Treorchy (Treorci). *R.C.T.* Population: 59,947. ***Town***, industrial town in Rhondda Fawr valley, 8m/13km NW of Pontypridd, famous for its Treorchy Male Voice Choir. **18 C2** SS9596.
Treorci *R.C.T. Welsh form of Treorchy, qv.*
Treowen *Caerp.* ***Suburb***, in N part of Newbridge. ST2097.
Treowman *Pembs. Welsh form of Brimaston, qv.*
Trequite *Cornw.* ***Hamlet***, 4m/6km NE of Wadebridge. SX0276.
Tre'r-ddol *Cere.* ***Hamlet***, 2m/3km N of Talybont. Museum containing local relics. **37 F6** SN6592.
Tre'r-gaer *Mon. Welsh form of Tregare, qv.*
Trerhyngyll (Trerhingyll). *V. of Glam.* ***Hamlet***, 1m/2km N of Cowbridge. ST0076.
Trerice *Cornw.* ***Historic house***, manor house (National Trust) rebuilt in 1571, 3m/5km SE of Newquay. **3 F3** SW8458.
Trerule Foot *Cornw.* ***Hamlet***, 6m/10km W of Saltash. **4 D5** SX3358.
Tres Ness *Ork.* ***Coastal feature***, headland at SE point of Sanday. **106 G4** HY7137.
Tresaith *Cere.* ***Village***, on coast 1m/2km E of Aberporth. **26 B3** SN2751.
Tresallian *Cornw. Alternative name for (River) Tresillian, qv.*
Tresco *I.o.S.* ***Island***, second largest of Isles of Scilly and one of five which are inhabited. Nearly divided by large freshwater lake known as Great Pool. Noted for subtropical gardens of Tresco Abbey. **2 C1** SV8915.
Tresco Abbey Gardens *I.o.S.* ***Garden***, world famous gardens surrounding scant remains of Benedictine abbey at S end of Tresco. Started in mid 19c by Augustus Smith and maintained by his descendants, gardens feature sub tropical flora including palms, acacias and pelargoniums grown in shelter of Monterey Cypress and pine trees; also lake garden. **2 B1** SV8914.
Trescott *Staffs.* ***Settlement***, 4m/7km W of Wolverhampton. **40 A6** SO8497.
Trescowe *Cornw.* ***Hamlet***, 4m/7km SE of Hayle. **2 C5** SW5730.
Tresean *Cornw.* ***Hamlet***, 3m/4km SW of Newquay. SW7858.
Tresham *S.Glos.* ***Village***, 3m/4km SE of Wotton-under-Edge. **20 A2** ST7991.
Treshnish *Arg. & B.* ***Locality***, near W coast of Mull, 2m/4km SW of Calgary and 1m/2km E of headland of Treshnish Point. **78 E3** NM3548.
Treshnish Isles *Arg. & B.* ***Island***, group of islands and rocks of Inner Hebrides, W of Mull and SE of Coll, comprising Bac Mòr (Dutchman's Cap) and Bac Beag, Cairn na Burgh More and Cairn na Burgh Beg, Fladda, Lunga, Sgeir a' Chaisteil, Sgeir an Eirionnaich, Sgeir an Fheòir and Sgeir na h-Iolaire. Although uninhabited by people, islands have a large population of seals, sea birds and rabbits. **78 D3** NM2741.
Treshnish Point *Arg. & B.* ***Coastal feature***, headland on W coast of Mull, 1m/2km W of Treshnish. **78 E3** NM3548.
Tresillian (Also known as Tresallian.) *Cornw.* ***River***, rising 6m/9km N of Tresillian and flowing into River Truro. **3 F4** SW8646.
Tresillian *Cornw.* ***Village***, 3m/5km E of Truro, at head of creek of Tresillian River. **3 F4** SW8646.
Tresimwn *V. of Glam. Welsh form of Bonvilston, qv.*
Tresinney *Cornw.* ***Settlement***, 1m/2km S of Camelford. **4 B2** SX1081.
Tresinwen *Pembs.* ***Settlement***, 1km SE of Strumble Head. **16 C1** SM9040.
Treskinnick Cross *Cornw.* ***Hamlet***, 5m/8km S of Bude. **4 C1** SX2098.
Treslea *Cornw.* ***Settlement***, 4m/7km E of Bodmin. SX1368.
Tresmeer *Cornw.* ***Village***, 6m/11km NW of Launceston. **4 C2** SX2387.
Tresowes Green *Cornw.* ***Hamlet***, 4m/7km W of Helston. SW5929.
Tresparrett *Cornw.* ***Hamlet***, 3m/5km E of Boscastle. **4 B1** SX1491.
Tresparrett Posts *Cornw.* ***Settlement***, 1m/2km NE of Tresparrett. **4 B1** SX1493.
Tressait *P. & K.* ***Village***, on N side of Loch Tummel, 5m/8km SW of Blair Atholl. **81 K1** NN8160.
Tresta *Shet.* ***Settlement***, on S coast of Fetlar, at head of large bay called Wick of Tresta. **108 F3** HU6190.
Tresta *Shet.* ***Village***, on Mainland, at head of Tresta Voe. **109 C7** HU3651.
Treswell *Notts.* ***Village***, 5m/8km E of Retford. **51 K5** SK7879.
Treswithian *Cornw.* ***Locality***, adjoining to W of Camborne. SW6340.
Treteio *Pembs. Welsh form of Tretio, qv.*
Trethevy *Cornw.* ***Village***, near N coast, 4m/6km NW of Camelford. SX0789.
Trethevy Quoit *Cornw.* ***Historic/prehistoric site***, Neolithic chambered cairn (English Heritage) 3m/4km N of Liskeard. Chamber is 14 feet or 4.6 metres high and capstone is 11 feet or 3.7 metres long. **4 C4** SX2568.
Trethewey *Cornw.* ***Hamlet***, 3m/4km SE of Land's End. SW3823.
Trethomas *Caerp.* ***Suburb***, adjoining to E of Bedwas. ST1888.
Trethurgy *Cornw.* ***Village***, 3m/4km NE of St. Austell. **4 A5** SX0355.
Tretio (Treteio). *Pembs.* ***Settlement***, 3m/5km NE of St. David's. **16 A2** SM7828.
Tretire *Here.* ***Hamlet***, 5m/8km W of Ross-on-Wye. **28 E6** SO5223.
Tretomas *R.C.T. Welsh form of Thomastown, qv.*
Tretower (Tretwr). *Powys* ***Village***, 3m/4km NW of Crickhowell. Ruined 12c castle (Cadw). **28 A6** SO1821.
Tretower Castle *Powys* ***Castle***, 12c castle (Cadw) converted from Norman motte, 3m/4km NW of Crickhowell. Cylindrical great tower erected in 13c within walls of shell keep. **28 A6** SO1821.
Tretower Court *Powys* ***Historic house***, 14c-15c manor house (Cadw), altered in 17c, to S of Tretower, 3m/4km NW of Crickhowell. **28 A6** SO1821.
Tretwr *Powys Welsh form of Tretower, qv.*
Treuddyn *Flints.* ***Village***, 4m/6km S of Mold. **48 B7** SJ2558.
Trevadlock *Cornw.* ***Hamlet***, 6m/9km SW of Launceston. SX2679.
Trevalga *Cornw.* ***Village***, near N coast, 1m/2km SW of Boscastle. **4 A2** SX0890.
Trevalyn (Trefalun). *Wrex.* ***Village***, 1m/2km E of Rossett. **48 C7** SJ3856.
Trevanson *Cornw.* ***Hamlet***, adjoining to NW of Wadebridge. **3 G1** SW9772.
Trevarnon *Cornw.* ***Settlement***, 3m/4km NE of Hayle. SW5939.
Trevarrack *Cornw.* ***Village***, just N of Penzance. SW4831.
Trevarren *Cornw.* ***Hamlet***, 2m/3km S of St. Columb Major. **3 G2** SW9160.
Trevarrian *Cornw.* ***Village***, 4m/6km NE of Newquay. SW8566.
Trevarrick *Cornw.* ***Settlement***, 2m/4km SW of Mevagissey. **3 G4** SW9843.
Trevaughan *Carmar.* ***Hamlet***, on S side of Whitland across River Taf. **17 F3** SN1915.
Trevaughan *Carmar.* ***Settlement***, adjoining to NW of Carmarthen. SN4021.
Trevaunance Cove *Cornw. See St. Agnes.*
Treveighan *Cornw.* ***Village***, 3m/5km SW of Camelford. SX0779.
Trevellas *Cornw.* ***Village***, 2m/3km S of Perranporth. **2 E3** SW7452.
Trevelmond *Cornw.* ***Village***, 3m/5km W of Liskeard. **4 C4** SX2063.
Trevenen *Cornw.* ***Hamlet***, 2m/3km NE of Helston. SW6829.
Treverbyn *Cornw.* ***Hamlet***, in China clay district, 3m/5km N of St. Austell. SX0156.
Treverbyn *Cornw.* ***Settlement***, in China clay district, 3m/5km NE of St. Austell. SX0356.
Treverva *Cornw.* ***Hamlet***, 3m/5km W of Falmouth. **2 E5** SW7531.
Trevescan *Cornw.* ***Settlement***, to E of Land's End. **2 A6** SW3524.
Trevethin *Torfaen* ***Village***, 1m/2km NW of Pontypool. **19 F1** SO2702.
Trevigro *Cornw.* ***Hamlet***, 1m/2km W of Callington. **4 D4** SX3369.
Trevilla *Cornw.* ***Hamlet***, 4m/6km S of Truro. SW8239.
Trevine *Arg. & B.* ***Settlement***, on shore of NW arm of Loch Awe, 5m/8km SE of Taynuilt. **80 B5** NN0825.
Trevine (Trefin). *Pembs.* ***Village***, near coast, 7m/11km NE of St. David's. **16 B1** SM8332.
Treviscoe *Cornw.* ***Village***, in china clay district, 5m/8km NW of St. Austell. **3 G3** SW9455.
Trevivian *Cornw.* ***Hamlet***, 4m/7km E of Camelford. SX1785.
Trevone *Cornw.* ***Village***, coastal village, 2m/3km W of Padstow. **3 F1** SW8975.
Trevor *Gwyn. English form of Trefor, qv.*
Trevor (Trefor). *Wrex.* ***Hamlet***, 2m/4km W of Ruabon. **38 B1** SJ2742.
Trevor Gardens *E.Suss.* ***Settlement***, adjoining to S of Glynde. TQ4508.
Trevose Head *Cornw.* ***Coastal feature***, headland with lighthouse on N coast, 4m/7km W of Padstow. **3 F1** SW8476.
Trewalder *Cornw.* ***Hamlet***, 2m/3km W of Camelford. **4 A2** SX0782.
Trewallter *V. of Glam. Welsh form of Walterston, qv.*
Trewarmett *Cornw.* ***Hamlet***, 3m/5km NW of Camelford. **4 A2** SX0686.
Trewarthenick *Cornw.* ***Settlement***, 5m/8km E of Truro. **3 G4** SW9044.
Trewarveneth *Cornw.* ***Locality***, just S of Penzance. SW4627.
Trewassa *Cornw.* ***Hamlet***, 4m/6km NE of Camelford. **4 B2** SX1486.
Trewavas Head *Cornw.* ***Coastal feature***, headland 4m/6km W of Helston. **2 C6** SW5926.
Trewellard *Cornw.* ***Hamlet***, 2m/3km N of St. Just. **2 A5** SW3733.
Trewen *Cornw.* ***Village***, 5m/8km W of Launceston. **4 C2** SX2583.
Trewen *Here.* ***Hamlet***, 4m/7km NE of Monmouth. SO5318.
Trewennack *Cornw.* ***Hamlet***, 2m/3km NE of Helston. SW6728.
Trewent *Pembs.* ***Hamlet***, 3m/5km SE of Pembroke. SS0197.
Trewent Point *Pembs.* ***Coastal feature***, headland 1m/2km E of Trewent at S end of Freshwater East bay. **16 D5** SS0197.
Trewern *Powys* ***Village***, at S end of Breidden Hills, 4m/7km NE of Welshpool. **38 B4** SJ2811.
Trewethern *Cornw.* ***Hamlet***, 3m/5km NE of Wadebridge. SX0076.
Trewhitt *Northumb.* ***Locality***, comprising High Trewhitt and surrounding scattered settlements, 4m/6km NW of Rothbury. NU0005.
Trewidland *Cornw.* ***Village***, 3m/5km S of Liskeard. **4 C5** SX2559.
Trewiliam *R.C.T. Welsh form of Williamstown, qv.*
Trewilym *Pembs.* ***Settlement***, 4m/6km SW of Cardigan. **26 A4** SN1440.
Trewint *Cornw.* ***Hamlet***, to SW of Altarnun, 7m/12km SW of Launceston. SX2280.
Trewint *Cornw.* ***Settlement***, 6m/9km S of Bude. **4 B1** SX1897.
Trewithen *Cornw.* ***Historic house***, 1m/2km E of Probus, designed in 17c by Sir Robert Taylor and Thomas Edwards of Greenwich. Gardens display magnolias and rhododendrons; nursery sells plants and shrubs. **3 G4** SW9147.
Trewithian *Cornw.* ***Hamlet***, 4m/6km NE of St. Mawes. **3 F5** SW8737.
Trewoon *Cornw.* ***Village***, on W outskirts of St. Austell. **3 G3** SW9952.
Treworga *Cornw.* ***Hamlet***, 6m/9km NE of St. Mawes. SW8940.
Treworlas *Cornw.* ***Hamlet***, 5m/8km NE of St. Mawes. SW8938.
Trewornan *Cornw.* ***Hamlet***, 1m/2km N of Wadebridge. **3 G1** SW9874.
Treworthal *Cornw.* ***Hamlet***, 4m/7km NE of St. Mawes. SW8838.
Trewyddel *Pembs. Welsh form of Moylgrove, qv.*
Treyarnon *Cornw.* ***Hamlet***, on W facing coast, 4m/6km W of Padstow. **3 F1** SW8673.
Treyford *W.Suss.* ***Hamlet***, 4m/7km SW of Midhurst. **12 B5** SU8218.
Trezaise *Cornw.* ***Hamlet***, 5m/7km N of St. Austell. SW9959.
Triangle *Staffs.* ***Locality***, 1m/2km S of Burntwood. SK0507.
Triangle *W.Yorks.* ***Village***, 2m/3km SW of Sowerby Bridge. **57 F7** SE0422.
Trichrung *Carmar.* ***Mountain***, 3m/5km S of Llangadog. Height 1361 feet or 415 metres. **17 K2** SN6922.
Trickett's Cross *Dorset* ***Locality***, 6m/10km N of Bournemouth. **10 B4** SU0801.
Triermain *Cumb.* ***Settlement***, 3m/4km W of Gilsland. Fragment of 14c castle. NY5966.
Triffleton *Pembs.* ***Settlement***, 1km N of Spittal. SM9724.
Trigon Hill *Dorset* ***Hill***, rising to over 50 metres, to W of Cold Harbour and 2m/3km NW of Wareham. Tumulus at summit. **9 H5** SY8989.
Trimdon *Dur.* Population: 3049. ***Village***, 3m/5km N of Sedgefield. **62 E3** NZ3634.
Trimdon Colliery *Dur.* ***Village***, 1m/2km NE of Trimdon. **62 E3** NZ3634.
Trimdon Grange *Dur.* ***Village***, 1m/2km N of Trimdon. **62 E3** NZ3634.
Trimingham *Norf.* ***Village***, on coast road, 4m/7km SE of Cromer. **45 G2** TG2838.
Trimley Lower Street *Suff.* ***Settlement***, 3m/5km NW of Felixstowe. TM2636.
Trimley Marshes *Suff.* ***Marsh/bog***, on E bank of River Orwell where it meets Harwich Harbour. **35 G5** TM2535.
Trimley St. Martin *Suff.* ***Village***, 3m/5km NW of Felixstowe. **35 G5** TM2737.
Trimley St. Mary *Suff.* ***Village***, 2m/4km NW of Felixstowe. **35 G5** TM2736.
Trimontium *Sc.Bord. See Newstead.*
Trimpley *Worcs.* ***Settlement***, 3m/4km NW of Kidderminster. **29 G1** SO7978.
Trimsaran *Carmar.* Population: 1874. ***Village***, 4m/7km NW of Llanelli. **17 H4** SN4504.
Trimstone *Devon* ***Settlement***, 3m/5km S of Ilfracombe. **6 D1** SS5043.
Trinafour *P. & K.* ***Settlement***, in Glen Errochty, 1m/2km SE of dam of Loch Errochty. **81 J1** NN7264.
Trinant *Caerp.* ***Hamlet***, 1m/2km N of Newbridge. **19 F2** ST2099.
Tring *Herts.* Population: 11,455. ***Town***, 5m/8km NW of Berkhamsted, with notable zoological museum. **32 C7** SP9211.
Tring Wharf *Herts.* ***Suburb***, on branch of Grand Union Canal, adjoining to N of Tring. SP9213.
Tringford *Herts.* ***Settlement***, 1m/2km N of Tring, on W side of reservoir and nature reserve. SP9113.
Trinity *Angus* ***Village***, 1m/2km N of Brechin. **83 H1** NO6062.
Trinity *Edin.* ***Suburb***, 2m/3km N of Edinburgh city centre. NT2476.
Trinity Bridge *Lincs.* ***Bridge***, triangular bridge dating from 1360 over three dried-up streams at Crowland, 8m/12km S of Spalding. Three arches meet at centre, one approached by steps. TF2310.
Trinity Hospital *Norf.* ***Historic house***, Jacobean almshouses built by Henry Howard, with chapel and nine houses round a court, at Castle Rising, 4m/6km NE of King's Lynn. Almshouses are occupied by elderly ladies, who wear 17c period dress on Sundays. **44 A3** TF6724.

Trinkeld *Cumb.* ***Settlement***, 1m/2km SW of Ulverston. SD2776.
Triscombe *Som.* ***Hamlet***, at foot of Quantock Hills, 1m/2km SE of Crowcombe. ST1535.
Triscombe *Som.* ***Settlement***, on Exmoor, 1km S of Wheddon Cross and 6m/9km SW of Dunster. SS9237.
Trislaig *High.* ***Settlement***, on W shore of Loch Linnhe, opposite Fort William. **87 G7** NN0874.
Trispen *Cornw.* ***Village***, 4m/6km N of Truro. **3 F3** SW8450.
Tritlington *Northumb.* ***Village***, 4m/7km N of Morpeth. **71 H4** NZ2092.
Triuirebheinn *W.Isles* ***Mountain***, on South Uist 2m/3km NE of Lochboisdale. Height 1171 feet or 357 metres. **84 D2** NF8121.
Trochry *P. & K.* ***Village***, in Strath Braan, 4m/6km SW of Dunkeld. **82 A3** NN9740.
Troddi *Mon. Welsh form of (River) Trothy, qv.*
Troedrhiwfuwch *Caerp.* ***Hamlet***, in Rhymney Valley, 3m/5km S of Tredegar. SO1304.
Troedrhiwgwair *B.Gwent* ***Locality***, 2m/3km SE of Tredegar. SO1506.
Troedyraur *Cere.* ***Hamlet***, 3m/5km NE of Newcastle Emlyn. **26 C4** SN3245.
Troedyrhiw *M.Tyd.* ***Village***, on River Taff, 3m/5km S of Merthyr Tydfil. **18 D1** SO0702.
Trofarth *Conwy* ***Hamlet***, 3m/5km N of Llangernyw. SH8571.
Troisgeach *Stir.* ***Mountain***, to NW of head of Loch Lomond, 2m/3km W of Inverarnan. Height 2408 feet or 734 metres. **80 E6** NN2919.
Tromie *High.* ***River***, in Badenoch and Strathspey district running N from Loch an t-Seilich down Glen Tromie to River Spey, 1m/2km E of Kingussie. **88 E5** NH7701.
Tromode *I.o.M.* ***Locality***, 1m/2km N of Douglas. SC3777.
Trondavoe *Shet.* ***Settlement***, 2m/3km NE of Brae, Mainland. **108 C5** HU3770.
Trondra *Shet.* ***Island***, lying S of Scalloway, Mainland. Measures 3m/4km N to S and nowhere more than 1km wide. Road bridge link with Mainland across narrow strait at N end and with West Burra near S end. Sparsely inhabited. **109 C9** HU3937.
Troney *Devon* ***River***, rising 2m/3km E of South Zeal on N edge of Dartmoor and flowing NE to join River Yeo to NW of Yeoford 4m/6km W of Crediton. **7 F6** SX7899.
Troon *Cornw.* Population: 1971. ***Village***, 2m/3km SE of Camborne. **2 D5** SW6638.
Troon *S.Ayr.* Population: 15,231. ***Town***, port and resort on Firth of Clyde, at N end of Ayr Bay, 6m/9km N of Ayr. Former coal and boat-building town. Several golf courses, one of which, Royal Troon, is a championship course. **74 B7** NS3230.
Trosaraidh *W.Isles* ***Settlement***, on South Uist, 3m/5km S of Dalabrog. **84 C3** NF7516.
Trosley Country Park *Kent* ***Leisure/recreation***, 1km N of Trottiscliffe. Over 250 acres of grassland, scrub and woodland situated on North Downs. **24 C5** TQ6461.
Troston *Suff.* ***Village***, 3m/4km NW of Ixworth. **34 C1** TL8972.
Trostre *Mon. Welsh form of Trostrey, qv.*
Trostrey (Trostre). *Mon.* ***Locality***, 2m/4km NW of Usk. SO3604.
Troswell *Cornw.* ***Settlement***, 7m/11km NW of Launceston. **4 C1** SX2591.
Troswick Ness *Shet.* ***Coastal feature***, headland on E coast of Mainland, 1m/2km NE of Boddam. **109 G9** HU4117.
Trothy (Troddi). *Mon.* ***River***, rising E of Pandy and flowing S, then E into River Wye 1m/2km S of Monmouth. **28 D7** SO5111.
Trotternish *High.* ***Locality***, district and peninsula on Skye, N of isthmus between Portree and head of Loch Snizort Beag. **93 K5** NG4264.
Trottick *Dundee* ***Suburb***, 2m/3km N of Dundee city centre. NO4033.
Trottiscliffe *Kent* ***Village***, below S slope of North Downs, 1m/2km N of Wrotham Heath. **23 K6** TQ6460.
Trotton *W.Suss.* ***Hamlet***, on River Rother, spanned here by 15c bridge, 3m/5km W of Midhurst. **12 B4** SU8322.
Trotton Marsh *W.Suss.* ***Settlement***, 5m/8km E of Petersfield. SU8225.
Trough Gate *Lancs.* ***Settlement***, adjoining to SE of Britannia, 2m/3km SE of Bacup. SD8821.
Trough of Bowland *Lancs.* ***Other feature of interest***, pass some 3m/5km NW of Dunsop Bridge, over which Lancaster to Clitheroe road is carried. **56 B4** SD6253.
Troughend *Northumb.* ***Settlement***, on N side of Troughend Common, 1m/2km W of Otterburn. **70 D4** NY8692.
Troughend Common *Northumb.* ***Open space***, heathland 3m/5km SW of Otterburn. **70 D4** NY8490.
Troup Head *Aber.* ***Coastal feature***, headland on N coast, 9m/14km E of Banff and 11m/17km W of Fraserburgh. **99 G4** NJ8267.
Troustan *Arg. & B.* ***Settlement***, on W coast of Loch Striven, 3m/5km N of Strone Point. **73 J3** NS0776.
Trout Beck *Cumb.* ***River***, rising to NE of Matterdale Common and flowing N to Troutbeck, then E into River Glenderamakin, 3m/4km E of Threlkeld. **60 E4** NY3526.
Troutbeck *Cumb.* ***Village***, 3m/5km N of Windermere. 17c house, Townend (National Trust) is here. **60 F6** NY4002.
Troutbeck Bridge *Cumb.* ***Hamlet***, 2m/3km S of Troutbeck. **60 F6** NY4002.
Trow Green *Glos.* ***Settlement***, 3m/4km S of Coleford. **19 J1** SO5706.
Troway *Derbys.* ***Hamlet***, 3m/4km NE of Dronfield. SK3879.
Trowbridge *Cardiff* ***Suburb***, of Cardiff, 4m/6km NE of city centre. ST2380.
Trowbridge *Wilts.* Population: 29,334. ***Town***, 8m/12km SE of Bath. Administrative capital of county and a cloth town since medieval times. Many Georgian buildings. **20 B6** ST8557.
Trowbridge Mawr *Cardiff* ***Locality***, 1km to S of Trowbridge. ST2379.
Trowell *Notts.* ***Village***, 5m/9km W of Nottingham. Trowell Service Area on M1 motorway 1km NE. **41 G1** SK4839.
Trowell Moor *Notts.* ***Locality***, 1m/2km NE of Trowell. SK5040.
Trowle Common *Wilts.* ***Locality***, 1m/2km NW of Trowbridge. **20 B6** ST8458.
Trowley Bottom *Herts.* ***Locality***, adjoining to S of Flamstead, 5m/7km N of Hemel Hempstead. **32 D7** TL0714.
Trows *Sc.Bord.* ***Settlement***, 3m/5km SW of Kelso. **76 E7** NT6932.
Trowse Newton *Norf.* ***Village***, 2m/3km SE of Norwich. **45 G5** TG2406.
Troy *W.Yorks.* ***Suburb***, in N part of Horsforth, 5m/8km NW of Leeds city centre. SE2438.
Trudernish *Arg. & B.* ***Settlement***, 8m/12km NE of Port Ellen, Islay. **72 C5** NR4652.
Trudoxhill *Som.* ***Village***, 3m/5km SW of Frome. **20 A7** ST7443.
Trueman's Heath *Worcs.* ***Suburb***, to E of Hollywood. SP0976.
Truim *High.* ***River***, in Badenoch and Strathspey district, running N from Pass of Drumochter down Glen Truim through Dalwhinnie to River Spey, 5m/8km SW of Kingussie. NN6896.
Trull *Som.* ***Village***, 2m/3km S of Taunton town centre. **8 B2** ST2122.
Trum Gelli *Gwyn.* ***Mountain***, 5m/7km E of Tywyn. Height 1755 feet or 535 metres. **37 F5** SH6501.
Trum y Ddysgl *Gwyn.* ***Mountain***, 4m/6km NW of Beddgelert. Height 2326 feet or 709 metres. **46 D7** SH5451.
Trumaisge Arraidh (Anglicised form: Trumisgarry.) *W.Isles* ***Settlement***, on N coast of North Uist, 5m/8km NW of Lochmaddy. **92 D4** NF8674.
Truman *Carmar.* ***Open space***, hillslope 4m/7km NE of Brynamman and 6m/10km SW of Usk Reservoir. **27 G6** SN7420.
Trumau *Powys* ***Mountain***, 1m/2km SW of Craig Goch Reservoir. Height 1709 feet or 521 metres. **27 H2** SN8667.
Trumfleet *S.Yorks.* ***Hamlet***, 3m/4km SE of Askern. SE6011.
Trumisgarry *W.Isles Anglicised form of Trumaisge Arraidh, qv.*
Trumpan *High.* ***Settlement***, on Skye, 4m/6km S of Vaternish Point. **93 H5** NG2261.
Trumpet *Here.* ***Hamlet***, 4m/6km NW of Ledbury. **29 F5** SO6539.
Trumpington *Cambs.* ***Suburb***, to S of Cambridge. **33 H3** TL4454.
Trumps Green *Surr.* ***Settlement***, adjoining to S of Virginia Water. SU9967.
Trunch *Norf.* ***Village***, 3m/5km N of North Walsham. Manor house of c. 1600. **45 G2** TG2834.
Trunnah *Lancs.* ***Locality***, 1m/2km E of Cleveleys. **55 G5** SD3343.
Truro *Cornw.* Population: 18,966. ***City***, administrative capital of Cornwall. Previously main port for exporting tin during 19c. Quays on Truro River. Many Georgian and Victorian buildings. 19c cathedral with tall central tower. **3 F4** SW8244.
Truro *Cornw.* ***River***, rising some 5m/8km N of Truro and flowing into River Fal, 3m/5km SE. **3 F4** SW8244.
Truro Cathedral *Cornw.* ***Ecclesiastical building***, Early English style cathedral at Truro, built by Pearson in 1880. First cathedral to be constructed in England since Wren built St. Paul's. 250 foot or 76 metre high tower completed in 1903 as memorial to Queen Victoria. **3 F4** SW8244.
Truscott *Cornw.* ***Hamlet***, 2m/3km NW of Launceston. SX3085.
Trusham *Devon* ***Village***, 2m/3km NW of Chudleigh. **7 G7** SX8582.
Trusley *Derbys.* ***Village***, 6m/10km W of Derby. **40 E2** SK2535.
Trusthorpe *Lincs.* ***Suburb***, adjoining to S of Mablethorpe. **53 J4** TF5183.
Truthan *Cornw.* ***Hamlet***, 2m/3km SW of Carland Cross. **3 F3** SW8351.
Trwyn Cilan (Pencilan Head). *Gwyn.* ***Coastal feature***, headland on S coast of Lleyn Peninsula, 4m/6km S of Abersoch. **36 C3** SH2923.
Trwyn Llanbedrog (Llanbedrog Point). *Gwyn.* ***Coastal feature***, headland at N end of St. Tudwal's Road, nearly 1m/2km SE of Llanbedrog. **36 C2** SH3330.
Trwyn Maen Dylan *Gwyn.* ***Coastal feature***, headland on Caernarfon Bay, 2m/3km NE of Clynnog-fawr. **46 B7** SH4252.
Trwyn y Bwa *Pembs.* ***Coastal feature***, headland on N coast, 3m/5km E of Dinas Head. **16 D1** SN0542.
Trwyn y Fuwch *Conwy Welsh form of Little Ormes Head, qv.*
Trwyn y Gader *I.o.A. Welsh form of Carmel Head, qv.*
Trwyn y Gorlech *Gwyn.* ***Coastal feature***, headland 2m/3km SW of Trefor. **36 C1** SH3445.
Trwyn yr Wylfa *Gwyn.* ***Coastal feature***, headland 3m/4km S of Abersoch, at E end of Porth Ceiriad. **36 C3** SH3224.
Tryleg *Mon. Welsh form of Trelleck, qv.*
Trysull *Staffs.* ***Village***, 5m/8km SW of Wolverhampton. **40 A6** SO8594.
Tryweryn *Gwyn.* ***River***, rising in Llyn Tryweryn and flowing E through Llyn Celyn, then SE into River Dee 1km SE of Bala. Includes championship canoeing course. SH9335.
Tuarie Burn *High.* ***River***, in Sutherland district, flowing E to form Craggie Water, 1km W of Craggie. **104 D6** NC8620.
Tubney *Oxon.* ***Hamlet***, 4m/7km W of Abingdon. **21 H2** SU4398.
Tuckenhay *Devon* ***Hamlet***, at head of Bow Creek, 3m/4km S of Totnes. **5 J5** SX8156.
Tucker's Moor *Devon* ***Hamlet***, 1km SW of Oldways End and 4m/7km SW of Dulverton. SS8624.
Tuckhill *Shrop.* ***Hamlet***, 5m/9km SE of Bridgnorth. SO7888.
Tuckingmill *Cornw.* ***Locality***, 1m/2km NE of Camborne. **2 D4** SW6640.
Tuckingmill *Wilts.* ***Hamlet***, 1km W of Tisbury. ST9329.
Tuckton *Bourne.* ***Suburb***, 4m/6km E of Bournemouth town centre. SZ1492.
Tud *Norf.* ***River***, rising SW of East Dereham and flowing E into River Wensum at Hellesdon, near Norwich. TG1910.
Tuddenham *Suff.* ***Village***, 8m/12km NE of Newmarket. **34 B1** TL7371.
Tuddenham *Suff.* ***Village***, 3m/5km NE of Ipswich. **35 F4** TM1948.
Tudeley *Kent* ***Village***, 2m/3km E of Tonbridge. **23 K7** TQ6245.
Tudeley Hale *Kent* ***Hamlet***, to N of Tudeley, 2m/3km SE of Tonbridge. TQ6246.
Tudhoe *Dur.* ***Village***, 1m/2km NE of Spennymoor. **62 D3** NZ2635.
Tudhoe Grange *Dur.* ***Suburb***, in W part of Spennymoor. NZ2534.
Tudhope Hill ***Mountain***, astride border of Dumfries & Galloway and Scottish Borders, 4m/7km SE of Teviothead. Height 1965 feet or 599 metres. **69 K4** NY4399.
Tudor Merchant's House *Pembs.* ***Historic house***, 15c merchant's house (National Trust) in Tenby. **16 E4** SN1300.
Tudweiliog *Gwyn.* ***Village***, 3m/5km SW of Nefyn. **36 B2** SH2336.
Tudworth Green *S.Yorks.* ***Settlement***, 2m/3km S of Thorne. SE6810.
Tue Brook *Mersey.* ***Suburb***, 3m/5km NE of Liverpool city centre. SJ3892.
Tuesley *Surr.* ***Settlement***, 1m/2km E of Milford. SU9641.
Tuffley *Glos.* ***Suburb***, in S part of Gloucester. **29 H7** SO8315.
Tufnell Park *Gt.Lon.* ***Suburb***, in borough of Islington, 3m/5km N of Charing Cross. TQ2985.
Tufton *Hants.* ***Hamlet***, on River Test, 1m/2km SW of Whitchurch. **21 H7** SU4546.
Tufton *Pembs.* ***Hamlet***, 9m/15km NE of Haverfordwest. **16 D2** SN0428.
Tugby *Leics.* ***Village***, 7m/11km W of Uppingham. **42 A5** SK7600.
Tugford *Shrop.* ***Village***, 8m/12km N of Ludlow. **38 E7** SO5587.
Tughall *Northumb.* ***Hamlet***, 3m/4km N of Embleton. **71 H1** NU2126.
Tuirnaig *High.* ***Settlement***, 2m/3km NE of Poolewe, Ross and Cromarty district. **94 E3** NG8783.
Tulach Hill *P. & K.* ***Mountain***, 1m/2km SW of Blair Atholl. Height 1542 feet or 470 metres. **81 K1** NN8564.
Tulchan *P. & K.* ***Settlement***, in Glen Almond, 6m/10km NE of Crieff. **82 A5** NN9528.
Tullibardine *P. & K.* ***Locality***, 2m/4km W of Auchterarder. 15c chapel (Historic Scotland). NN9113.
Tullibardine Chapel *P. & K.* ***Historic/prehistoric site***, founded in 1446 and still remains unaltered. 2m/3km NW of Auchterarder. **82 A6** NN9013.
Tullibody *Clack.* Population: 6872. ***Small town***, 2m/3km NW of Alloa. Small pre-Reformation church. **75 G1** NS8695.
Tullibody Inch *Clack.* ***Island***, in River Forth, to S of Tullibody. NS8692.
Tullich *Arg. & B.* ***Settlement***, 1m/2km SW of Kilmelford. **79 K6** NM8312.
Tullich *Arg. & B.* ***Settlement***, in Glen Aray, 5m/8km N of Inveraray. **80 B6** NN0815.
Tullich *High.* ***Locality***, 4m/6km NE of Invergordon, Ross and Cromarty district. NH7373.
Tullich *High.* ***Locality***, 1m/2km NW of Balintore. **97 F4** NH8577.
Tullich *High.* ***Settlement***, 10m/16km S of Inverness. **88 D2** NH6328.
Tullich *Moray* ***Settlement***, 2m/3km N of Dufftown. **98 B6** NJ3242.
Tullich *Stir.* ***Settlement***, in Glen Lochay, 4m/7km NW of Killin. **81 G4** NN5136.
Tullich Burn *Aber.* ***River***, stream running S into River Dee 2m/3km below Ballater. NO3997.
Tullich Hill *Arg. & B.* ***Mountain***, on E side of Loch Long, 2m/3km S of Arrochar. Height 2073 feet or 632 metres. **80 D7** NN2900.
Tullich Hill *P. & K.* ***Mountain***, on SE side of Loch Tay, 8m/12km N of St. Fillans. Height 2237 feet or 682 metres. **81 J4** NN7036.
Tullich Muir *High.* ***Settlement***, 4m/6km NE of Invergordon. **96 E4** NH7373.
Tulliemet *P. & K.* ***Settlement***, 1m/2km E of Ballinluig. **82 A2** NN9952.
Tullo Hill *Angus* ***Mountain***, 2m/3km W of Kirkton of Menmuir. Height 1036 feet or 316 metres. **83 F1** NO4964.
Tulloch *Aber.* ***Settlement***, to SE of Greenspot, 4m/7km SE of Fyvie. **91 G1** NJ8031.
Tulloch *High.* ***Locality***, on upland, 5m/8km NE of Aviemore. **89 G3** NH9816.
Tulloch *High.* ***Settlement***, 1km N of Bonar Bridge, Sutherland district. **96 D2** NH6192.
Tulloch *Moray* ***Settlement***, on hillside, 3m/5km SE of Forres, with historic settlement and field system to N. **97 H6** NJ0855.
Tulloch Hill *Angus* ***Mountain***, forested peak surmounted by Airlie Memorial Tower, 1m/2km NW of Dykehead. Height 1269 feet or 387 metres. **82 E1** NO3761.
Tulloch Station *High.* ***Other building***, station on West Highland line to Fort William, 9m/14km E of Spean Bridge. **87 K6** NN3580.
Tullochgorm *Arg. & B.* ***Settlement***, 1m/2km SW of Minard. **73 H1** NR9695.
Tullochgribban High *High.* ***Settlement***, 4m/6km NE of Carrbridge. **89 G2** NH9425.

T

Tullochvenus *Aber.* ***Settlement***, 2m/3km N of Lumphanan. **90 D4** NJ5807.
Tulloes *Angus* ***Settlement***, 3m/5km SW of Letham. **83 G3** NO5045.
Tullybannocher *P. & K.* ***Settlement***, in valley of River Earn, 1km W of Comrie. **81 J5** NN7621.
Tullybelton *P. & K.* ***Settlement***, 3m/4km SW of Bankfoot. **82 B4** NO0333.
Tullybothy Craigs *Fife* ***Coastal feature***, offshore rocks 1km N of Fife Ness. **83 H6** NO6310.
Tullyfergus *P. & K.* ***Locality***, comprises settlements of East and West Tullyfergus, 2m/3km W of Alyth. **82 D3** NO2148.
Tullymurdoch *P. & K.* ***Settlement***, 4m/6km NW of Alyth. **82 C2** NO1952.
Tullynessle *Aber.* ***Village***, 3m/4km NW of Alford. **90 D3** NJ5519.
Tulm Island *High.* ***Island***, long narrow islet in Duntulm Bay near N end of Skye, 7m/11km N of Uig. **93 J4** NG4074.
Tulse Hill *Gt.Lon.* ***Suburb***, in borough of Lambeth, 1m/2km W of Dulwich Village. TQ3173.
Tumble (Y Tymbl). *Carmar.* ***Village***, 1m/2km SW of Cross Hands. **17 J3** SN5411.
Tumby *Lincs.* ***Hamlet***, 2m/3km NE of Tattershall. **53 F7** TF2359.
Tumby Woodside *Lincs.* ***Hamlet***, 2m/4km SE of Tumby. **53 F7** TF2359.
Tummel *P. & K.* ***River***, issuing from Loch Rannoch and running E through Dunalastair Water and Loch Tummel, turning SE through Linn of Tummel to its confluence with River Garry in Loch Faskally, then on past Pitlochry to River Tay S of Ballinluig. **82 A2** NN9751.
Tummel Bridge *P. & K.* ***Settlement***, on River Tummel, 1m/2km W of Loch Tummel; hydro-electricity power station. **81 J2** NN7659.
Tummer Hill Scar *Cumb.* ***Coastal feature***, rocks on sands on W side of Isle of Walney, near Vickerstown, 4m/6km SW of Barrow-in-Furness. **54 E3** SD1667.
Tun Bridge *B. & N.E.Som.* ***Bridge***, late 15c stone bridge with three arches over River Chew in village of Chew Magna, 6m/9km S of Bristol city centre. ST5762.
Tunbridge Wells *Kent Familiar form of Royal Tunbridge Wells, qv.*
Tundergarth Mains *D. & G.* ***Settlement***, on E side of Water of Milk, 3m/5km E of Lockerbie. **69 G5** NY1780.
Tunga (Anglicised form: Tong.) *W.Isles* ***Village***, near E coast of Isle of Lewis, 3m/5km NE of Stornoway across River Laxdale estuary. **101 G4** NB4536.
Tungate *Norf.* ***Settlement***, 1m/2km W of North Walsham. TG2629.
Tunley *B. & N.E.Som.* ***Village***, 3m/5km N of Radstock. ST6959.
Tunshill *Gt.Man.* ***Settlement***, 1m/2km E of Milnrow. SD9413.
Tunstall *E.Riding* ***Village***, near coast, 3m/5km NW of Withernsea. **59 K6** TA3031.
Tunstall *Kent* ***Village***, 1m/2km SW of Sittingbourne. **24 E5** TQ8961.
Tunstall *Lancs.* ***Village***, 3m/5km S of Kirkby Lonsdale. **56 B2** SD6073.
Tunstall *Norf.* ***Hamlet***, 2m/3km SE of Acle. **45 J5** TG4108.
Tunstall *N.Yorks.* ***Village***, 2m/3km SW of Catterick. **62 D7** SE2195.
Tunstall *Staffs.* ***Hamlet***, 1m/2km NW of High Offley. SJ7727.
Tunstall *Stoke* ***Town***, one of the towns that form city of Stoke-on-Trent; Burslem, Fenton, Hanley, Longton, Stoke-upon-Trent, Tunstall. Tunstall lies 4m/6km NW of city centre. **49 H7** SJ8651.
Tunstall *Suff.* ***Village***, 4m/6km E of Wickham Market. **35 H3** TM3555.
Tunstall *T. & W.* ***Suburb***, 2m/4km S of Sunderland city centre. NZ3853.
Tunstall Forest *Suff.* ***Forest/woodland***, large area of conifers (Forestry Commission) to E of Tunstall. **35 H3** TM3555.
Tunstall Reservoir *Dur.* ***Reservoir***, in course of Waskerley Beck, 2m/4km N of Wolsingham. **62 B2** NZ0641.
Tunstead *Gt.Man.* ***Settlement***, 5m/8km E of Oldham. SE0004.
Tunstead *Norf.* ***Hamlet***, 4m/6km N of Wroxham. **45 H3** TG3022.
Tunstead Milton *Derbys.* ***Hamlet***, 2m/3km W of Chapel-en-le-Frith. SK0380.
Tunworth *Hants.* ***Village***, 4m/6km SE of Basingstoke. **21 K7** SU6748.
Tupholme *Lincs.* ***Settlement***, 2m/3km E of Bardney. Abbey remains, to S, date from 13c. TF1468.
Tupsley *Here.* ***Suburb***, on NE side of Hereford. **28 E4** SO5340.
Tupton *Derbys.* ***Locality***, 1m/2km N of Clay Cross, comprising New and Old Tupton. **51 F6** SK3965.
Tur Langton *Leics.* ***Village***, 5m/8km N of Market Harborough. **42 A6** SP7194.
Turbiskill *Arg. & B.* ***Settlement***, at head of Linne Mhuirich, 1km SW of Tayvallich. **73 F2** NR7385.
Turclossie *Aber.* ***Settlement***, 1m/2km N of New Pitsligo. **99 G5** NJ8857.
Turf Law *Sc.Bord.* ***Mountain***, rising to over 380 metres, 3m/5km NW of Carfraemill. **76 C5** NT4756.
Turgis Green *Hants.* ***Village***, 6m/10km NE of Basingstoke, along with Stratfield Turgis. **21 K6** SU6959.
Turin *Angus* ***Locality***, 3m/4km N of Letham. **83 G2** NO5352.
Turin Hill *Angus* ***Hill***, 4m/6km NE of Forfar. Hillfort of Kemp's Castle at summit. Height 827 feet or 252 metres. **83 G2** NO5153.
Turkdean *Glos.* ***Village***, 2m/3km N of Northleach. **30 C7** SP1017.
Turkey Island *Hants.* ***Settlement***, just E of Shedfield, 3m/5km S of Bishop's Waltham. SU5613.
Turleigh *Wilts.* ***Village***, 1m/2km W of Bradford-on-Avon. ST8060.
Turley Holes Edge *W.Yorks.* ***Open space***, moorland 3m/5km S of Hebden Bridge, with Withens Clough Reservoir on NW side. **56 E7** SD9822.
Turleygreen *Shrop.* ***Locality***, 6m/9km SE of Bridgnorth. SO7685.
Turn *Lancs.* ***Hamlet***, with small lake, 1m/2km SE of Edenfield. SD8118.
Turnastone *Here.* ***Hamlet***, across River Dore from Vowchurch, 6m/10km NW of Pontrilas. **28 C5** SO3536.
Turnberry *S.Ayr.* ***Village***, on Turnberry Bay, 5m/8km N of Girvan. Championship golf course. **67 G3** NS2005.
Turnberry Bay *S.Ayr.* ***Bay***, 5m/8km N of Girvan. Turnberry village is on bay. **67 F3** NS2005.
Turnberry Castle *S.Ayr.* ***Castle***, scant remains of castle, adjoining lighthouse, 1m/2km N of Turnberry. **67 F3** NS2005.
Turnchapel *Plym.* ***Suburb***, in S district of Plymouth, S of River Plym estuary. **4 E5** SX4952.
Turnditch *Derbys.* ***Village***, 3m/5km W of Belper. **40 E1** SK2946.
Turner Green *Lancs.* ***Settlement***, 1m/2km E of Samlesbury, 5m/8km W of Blackburn town centre. SD6130.
Turner Wood *S.Yorks.* ***Settlement***, 3m/5km NW of Worksop. SK5481.
Turnerheath *Ches.* ***Locality***, 1m/2km SW of Bollington. SJ9176.
Turner's Green *E.Suss.* ***Settlement***, 4m/6km E of Heathfield. TQ6319.
Turner's Green *Warks.* ***Locality***, 4m/6km SE of Hockley Heath. **30 C1** SP1969.
Turners Hill *W.Suss.* ***Village***, 4m/6km SW of East Grinstead. **13 G3** TQ3435.
Turners Puddle *Dorset* ***Hamlet***, 1m/2km SW of Bere Regis. **9 H5** SY8393.
Turnford *Herts.* ***Locality***, 1m/2km N of Cheshunt. **23 G1** TL3604.
Turnworth *Dorset* ***Hamlet***, 4m/7km W of Blandford Forum. **9 H4** ST8207.
Turret *High.* ***River***, flowing S through Glen Turret into River Roy at Turret Bridge, 8m/12km NE of Roybridge. **87 K5** NN3391.
Turret Bridge *High.* ***Settlement***, at NE end of Glen Roy, 8m/12km NE of Roybridge. **87 K5** NN3391.
Turriff *Aber.* Population: 3948. ***Small town***, at confluence of River Deveron and Idoch Water, 9m/14km S of Banff. Centre of agricultural district. **99 F5** NJ7249.
Turton Bottoms *B'burn.* ***Village***, 4m/7km N of Bolton. **49 G1** SD7315.
Turton Moor *B'burn.* ***Large natural feature***, forms part of moorland area, including to SE Turton Heights, N of Bolton. There are several reservoirs in area. **49 F1** SD6917.
Turton Tower *B'burn.* ***Historic house***, largely Elizabethan house, near Turton Bottoms. **49 G1** SD7315.
Turves Green *W.Mid.* ***Suburb***, 6m/10km SW of Birmingham city centre. SP0278.
Turvey *Beds.* ***Village***, 7m/11km W of Bedford. **32 C3** SP9452.
Turville *Bucks.* ***Village***, 5m/9km N of Henley-on-Thames. **22 A2** SU7691.
Turville Heath *Bucks.* ***Settlement***, 1m/2km W of Turville. **22 A2** SU7491.
Turweston *Bucks.* ***Village***, 1m/2km E of Brackley. **31 H5** SP6037.
Tusker Rock *V. of Glam.* ***Island***, rock in Bristol Channel, 1m/2km SW of Ogmore-by-Sea. **18 B4** SS8474.
Tutbury *Staffs.* Population: 2823. ***Village***, 4m/6km NW of Burton upon Trent. Ruins of medieval castle. **40 E3** SK2128.
Tutbury Castle *Staffs.* ***Castle***, motte castle at N side of Tutbury, overlooking River Dove valley, 4m/6km NW of Burton-on-Trent. Destroyed by Henry II in late 12c; 15c-18c additions can be seen in ruins today. **40 E3** SK2029.
Tutim Burn *High.* ***River***, rising on W slopes of Beinn Rosail and flowing SE into River Oykel at Tuiteam Tarbhach. **96 B1** NC4301.
Tutnall *Worcs.* ***Hamlet***, 2m/3km E of Bromsgrove. **29 J1** SO9870.
Tutshill *Glos.* Population: 1681. ***Village***, 1km NE of Chepstow across River Wye. **19 J2** ST5394.
Tutt Hill *Kent* ***Settlement***, 2m/4km SE of Charing. TQ9746.
Tuttington *Norf.* ***Village***, 2m/3km E of Aylsham. **45 G3** TG2227.
Tutts Clump *W.Berks.* ***Hamlet***, 5m/8km SW of Pangbourne. SU5870.
Tutwell *Cornw.* ***Hamlet***, above W bank of River Tamar, 4m/7km NE of Callington. SX3875.
Tuxford *Notts.* Population: 2577. ***Village***, 7m/11km S of Retford. Former staging post on Great North Road. **51 K5** SK7371.
Twatt *Ork.* ***Settlement***, on Mainland, 3m/4km NW of Dounby. **106 B5** HY2724.
Twatt *Shet.* ***Village***, on Mainland, 1km N of Bixter. **109 C7** HU3253.
Twechar *E.Dun.* Population: 1499. ***Village***, 2m/3km SW of Kilsyth. **74 E3** NS7075.
Tweed ***River***, rising at Tweed's Well, 6m/10km N of Moffat, and flowing by Peebles, Melrose, Kelso and Coldstream to North Sea at Berwick-upon-Tweed. Long section of lower course forms border of England and Scotland. **77 F7** NU0052.
Tweedale *Tel. & W.* ***Locality***, industrial estate N of Madeley, Telford. SJ6904.
Tweedbank *Sc.Bord.* ***Locality***, 2m/3km W of Melrose. NT5135.
Tweeddale *Sc.Bord.* ***Valley***, carrying River Tweed and running generally SW to NE from Glenbreck to confluence with Lyne Water, 3m/4km W of Peebles. **69 F1** NT1125.
Tweedmouth *Northumb.* ***Suburb***, of Berwick-upon-Tweed, on S bank of river. **77 H5** NT9952.
Tweed's Well *Sc.Bord.* ***Other feature of interest***, source of River Tweed, 6m/10km N of Moffat. **69 F2** NT0514.
Tweedsmuir *Sc.Bord.* ***Settlement***, in Upper Tweeddale, 8m/12km S of Broughton. **69 F1** NT0924.
Twelve Oaks *E.Suss.* ***Settlement***, 1km SE of Brightling. TQ6920.
Twelveheads *Cornw.* ***Village***, 4m/6km E of Redruth. **2 E4** SW7642.
Twemlow Green *Ches.* ***Hamlet***, 2m/3km NE of Holmes Chapel. SJ7868.
Twenty *Lincs.* ***Hamlet***, 4m/6km E of Bourne. **42 E3** TF1520.
Twenty Foot River *Cambs.* ***River***, artificial branch of River Nene (old course) leaving old course S of Whittlesey, and rejoining it NE of March. **43 G6** TL4498.
Twerton *B. & N.E.Som.* ***Suburb***, W district of Bath. **20 A5** ST7264.
Twickenham *Gt.Lon.* ***Suburb***, in borough of Richmond upon Thames, on left bank of River Thames 10m/16km SW of Charing Cross. Rugby football ground to NW (Rugby Road). **22 E4** TQ1673.
Twigworth *Glos.* ***Village***, 3m/4km N of Gloucester. **29 H6** SO8422.
Twineham *W.Suss.* ***Hamlet***, 4m/6km W of Burgess Hill. **13 F4** TQ2519.
Twineham Green *W.Suss.* ***Hamlet***, to N of Twineham, 4m/6km W of Burgess Hill. TQ2520.
Twiness *Ork.* ***Coastal feature***, headland to W of Bay of Tafts, Westray. **106 D3** HY4941.
Twinhoe *B. & N.E.Som.* ***Hamlet***, 3m/5km S of Bath. **20 A6** ST7459.
Twinstead *Essex* ***Hamlet***, 3m/5km S of Sudbury. **34 C5** TL8636.
Twinstead Green *Essex* ***Settlement***, to W of Twinstead, 4m/6km SW of Sudbury. TL8536.
Twiss Green *Warr.* ***Locality***, adjoining to N of Culcheth. **49 F3** SJ6595.
Twiston *Lancs.* ***Hamlet***, 2m/3km E of Downham. SD8143.
Twitchen *Devon* ***Village***, on S edge of Exmoor National Park, 6m/9km NE of South Molton. **7 F2** SS7830.
Twitchen *Shrop.* ***Settlement***, 5m/7km SW of Craven Arms. **28 C1** SO3779.
Twitton *Kent* ***Settlement***, adjoining to W of Otford. TQ5159.
Twizell House *Northumb.* ***Settlement***, 1km W of Warenford. **71 G1** NU1328.
Twmpa (Also known as Lord Hereford's Knob.) *Powys* ***Mountain***, summit on N side of Black Mountains, 4m/7km S of Hay-on-Wye. Height 2263 feet or 690 metres. **28 B5** SO2235.
Twmpath Melyn *Powys* ***Mountain***, 3m/5km N of Carno. Height 1443 feet or 440 metres. **37 J5** SH9602.
Two Bridges *Devon* ***Settlement***, on Dartmoor, on West Dart River, 8m/13km E of Tavistock. **5 G3** SX6075.
Two Bridges *Glos.* ***Hamlet***, 1m/2km N of Blakeney. SO6609.
Two Dales *Derbys.* ***Village***, 2m/3km NW of Matlock. **50 E6** SK2762.
Two Gates *Staffs.* ***Suburb***, 2m/3km S of Tamworth town centre. **40 E5** SK2101.
Two Locks *Torfaen* ***Suburb***, in S part of Cwmbran, on Monmouthshire and Brecon Canal. ST2994.
Two Mills *Ches.* ***Settlement***, 1m/2km W of Capenhurst. SJ3573.
Two Tree Island ***Island***, on N side of River Thames estuary, 4m/6km W of Southend-on-Sea town centre. TQ8285.
Two Waters *Herts.* ***Suburb***, 1km S of Hemel Hempstead town centre. TL0505.
Twrch ***River***, rising on W side of summit of Carmarthen Van and flowing S into River Tawe at Ystalyfera. SN7708.
Twrch *Carmar.* ***River***, rising 3m/5km SE of Llanddewi-Brefi and flowing SW, then S into River Cothi at Pumsaint. SN6540.
Twrch *Gwyn.* ***River***, rising N of Llanymawddwy and flowing N into River Dee, 1km W of SW end of Llyn Tegid. **37 H3** SH8831.
Twrch *Powys* ***River***, rising 1m/2km E of Llanymawddwy and flowing SE into River Banwy, 1m/2km W of Llangadfan. **37 J4** SH9911.
Twt Hill *Denb. See Rhuddlan.*
Twycross *Leics.* ***Village***, 5m/8km NE of Atherstone. **41 F5** SK3304.
Twycross Zoo *Leics.* ***Leisure/recreation***, 1m/2km to NW of Twycross, specialising in apes and monkeys. **41 F5** SK3106.
Twyford *Bucks.* ***Village***, 6m/9km NE of Bicester. **31 H6** SP6626.
Twyford *Derbys.* ***Hamlet***, on River Trent 5m/8km SW of Derby. **41 F3** SK3228.
Twyford *Dorset* ***Settlement***, 2m/4km S of Shaftesbury. **9 H3** ST8518.
Twyford *Hants.* ***Village***, on River Itchen, 3m/5km S of Winchester. Site of Roman building on E side of village. **11 F2** SU4824.
Twyford *Leics.* ***Village***, 6m/9km S of Melton Mowbray. **42 A5** SK7210.
Twyford *Lincs.* ***Locality***, at S end of Colsterworth. SK9323.
Twyford *Norf.* ***Village***, 5m/9km W of Reepham. **44 E3** TG0124.
Twyford *Oxon.* ***Hamlet***, adjoining to N of Adderbury. **31 F5** SP4736.
Twyford *W'ham* Population: 6408. ***Small town***, 5m/8km E of Reading. **22 A4** SU7976.
Twyford Common *Here.* ***Settlement***, 3m/5km S of Hereford. **28 E5** SO5135.
Twymyn *Powys* ***River***, rising to E of Glaslyn lake and running E to Dylife and 1km beyond, N to W side of Llanbrynmair, then W into River Dyfi 1km N of Cemmaes Road. **37 H6** SH8205.
Twyn Croes *M.Tyd.* ***Mountain***, 4m/6km N of Merthyr Tydfil. Height 1450 feet or 442 metres. **27 K7** SO0413.
Twyn Disgwylfa *Powys* ***Mountain***, 3m/4km NE of Sennybridge. Height 1368 feet or 417 metres. **27 J5** SN9431.
Twyn-du *Powys* ***Mountain***, rising to over 530 metres and extending NE, 4m/7km W of Llangynidr. **27 K7** SO0820.
Twyn-mynydd *Carmar.* ***Hamlet***, 1m/2km NW of Glanaman and 3m/5km NE of Ammanford. SN6614.

T

Twyn Rhyd-car *Powys* ***Mountain***, peak of Mynydd Eppynt, 3m/5km SE of Llangammarch Wells. Height 1489 feet or 454 metres. **27 J4** SN9642.
Twyn Shôn-Ifan *Caerp.* ***Settlement***, 1km SE of Ystrad Mynach. Industrial estate to S. ST1593.
Twyn-y-Sheriff *Mon.* ***Settlement***, 1m/2km S of Raglan. **19 H1** SO4005.
Twyn-yr-odyn *V. of Glam.* ***Hamlet***, 4m/6km N of Barry. **18 E4** ST1173.
Twyncarno *Caerp.* ***Locality***, adjoining to N of Rhymney. SO1108.
Twynholm *D. & G.* ***Village***, 3m/4km NW of Kirkcudbright. **65 G5** NX6654.
Twyni Bâch *Cere.* ***Coastal feature***, sandy headland at mouth of River Dyfi, 1km S of Aberdovey across river. **36 E6** SN6094.
Twyning *Glos.* ***Village***, 2m/3km N of Tewkesbury. **29 H5** SO8936.
Twyning Green *Glos.* ***Locality***, on W bank of River Avon, adjoining to E of Twyning, 3m/4km N of Tewkesbury. **29 H5** SO9036.
Twynllanan *Carmar.* ***Hamlet***, 4m/6km SE of Llangadog. **27 G6** SN7524.
Twynyderyn *B.Gwent* ***Locality***, 1km S of Bryn-mawr. SO1910.
Twynyrodyn *M.Tyd.* ***Suburb***, in S part of Merthyr Tydfil. SO0505.
Twywell *Northants.* ***Village***, 3m/5km W of Thrapston. **32 C1** SP9578.
Ty-Côch *Torfaen* ***Locality***, on S side of Cwmbran. ST2993.
Tŷ-Dù *Newport Welsh form of Rogerstone, qv.*
Ty-hen *Gwyn.* ***Settlement***, at SW end of Lleyn Peninsula, 3m/4km N of Aberdaron. **36 A2** SH1731.
Ty-Hyll (The Ugly House). *Conwy* ***Other building***, 3m/4km E of Capel Curig. Allegedly built in one night to obtain freehold rights over common land. **47 F7** SH7558.
Ty Llwyn *B.Gwent* ***Locality***, on E side of Ebbw Vale. SO1708.
Ty Mawr *Conwy* ***Historic house***, 3m/5km SW of Betws-y-coed. Home in 16c of William Morgan, first translator of Bible into Welsh. Now a museum. **47 F7** SH7652.
Ty-mawr *Conwy* ***Locality***, 2m/3km NE of Abergele. SH9679.
Ty-mawr *Conwy* ***Settlement***, 3m/5km W of Cerrigydrudion. **37 J1** SH9047.
Ty-mawr *Denb.* ***Settlement***, 3m/5km SW of Pen-y-stryt. **38 A1** SJ1648.
Ty Mawr Standing Stone *I.o.A. See Trefignath.*
Ty-nant *Conwy* ***Hamlet***, 6m/9km W of Corwen. **37 J1** SH9844.
Ty-nant *Gwyn.* ***Settlement***, in Cwm Cynllwyd, 3m/4km SE of Llanuwchllyn. **37 J3** SH9026.
Ty Newydd Burial-Chamber *I.o.A. See Llanfaelog.*
Ty Newydd Burial Chamber *I.o.A.* ***Historic/prehistoric site***, on SW side of Anglesey, 1m/2km E of Rhosneigr. Burial chamber consists of capstone and three uprights. Neolithic in origin but contains some Bronze Age artefacts. **46 B5** SH3473.
Ty-Sign *Caerp.* ***Suburb***, on E side of Risca. ST2490.
Ty-uchaf *Powys* ***Settlement***, on N side of Lake Vyrnwy, 3m/4km NW of Llanwddyn. **37 J3** SH9921.
Tyberton *Here.* ***Village***, 8m/13km W of Hereford. **28 C5** SO3839.
Tybroughton *Wrex.* ***Locality***, including Tybroughton Hall, 4m/6km W of Whitchurch. SJ4742.
Tyburn *W.Mid.* ***Suburb***, 5m/8km NE of Birmingham city centre. **40 D6** SP1391.
Tycroes *Carmar.* ***Village***, 2m/3km SW of Ammanford. **17 K3** SN6010.
Tycrwyn *Powys* ***Hamlet***, 3m/4km W of Llanfyllin. **38 A4** SJ1018.
Tydd Gote *Lincs.* ***Village***, 5m/8km N of Wisbech. **43 H4** TF4517.
Tydd St. Giles *Cambs.* ***Village***, 5m/8km NE of Wisbech. **43 H4** TF4216.
Tydd St. Giles Fen *Lincs.* ***Open space***, lowland 6m/9km NW of Wisbech. **43 G4** TF3814.
Tydd St. Mary *Lincs.* ***Village***, 3m/4km S of Long Sutton. **43 H4** TF4418.
Tyddewi *Pembs. Welsh form of St. David's, qv.*
Tye *Hants.* ***Settlement***, on Hayling Island, 1km S of North Hayling. SU7302.
Tye Common *Essex* ***Suburb***, SW district of Billericay. **24 C2** TQ6693.
Tye Green *Essex* ***Hamlet***, to N of Stansted Airport, 2m/3km E of Stansted Mountfitchet. TL5424.
Tye Green *Essex* ***Hamlet***, 3m/5km N of Thaxted. TL5935.
Tye Green *Essex* ***Hamlet***, adjoining to NE of Good Easter, 2m/4km E of Leaden Roding. TL6212.
Tye Green *Essex* ***Locality***, 2m/3km SE of Braintree. **34 B6** TL7721.
Tye Green *Essex* ***Suburb***, 1km SE of Harlow town centre. TL4508.
Tyegate Green *Norf.* ***Hamlet***, adjoining to W of South Walsham, 3m/4km S of Horning. TG3513.
Tyersal *W.Yorks.* ***Suburb***, 2m/3km E of Bradford city centre. SE1932.
Tyersal Gate *W.Yorks.* ***Suburb***, 2m/3km SE of Bradford city centre. SE1931.
Tyldesley *Gt.Man.* Population: 30,606. ***Town***, industrial town, 5m/8km SW of Bolton. **49 F2** SD6902.
Tyle-garw *R.C.T.* ***Hamlet***, 2m/3km SW of Llantrisant. **18 D3** ST0281.
Tyler Hill *Kent* ***Village***, 2m/3km N of Canterbury. **25 H5** TR1461.
Tylers Green *Bucks.* Population: 10,421. ***Locality***, 3m/4km E of High Wycombe. **22 C2** SU9093.
Tyler's Green *Essex* ***Hamlet***, 3m/5km W of Chipping Ongar. **23 J1** TL5005.
Tyler's Green *Surr.* ***Locality***, just N of Godstone. TQ3452.
Tyllgoed *Cardiff Welsh form of Fairwater, qv.*
Tylorstown *R.C.T.* ***Village***, 5m/8km NW of Pontypridd. **18 D2** ST0195.
Tylwch *Powys* ***Settlement***, 3m/5km S of Llanidloes. **27 J1** SN9780.
Ty'n-y-bryn *R.C.T.* ***Hamlet***, 1km SW of Tonyrefail. ST0087.
Tyn-y-cefn *Denb.* ***Settlement***, 1km W of Corwen. **37 K1** SJ0643.
Ty'n-y-coedcae *Caerp.* ***Village***, 1m/2km SW of Machen across Rhymney River. ST1988.
Tyn-y-Cwm *Powys* ***Settlement***, in Wye Valley, 3m/5km W of Llangurig. **37 H7** SN8681.
Tyn-y-ffridd *Powys* ***Settlement***, 3m/5km N of Llanrhaeadr-ym-Mochnant. **38 A2** SJ1130.
Ty'n-y-garn *Bridgend* ***Suburb***, 2m/3km N of Bridgend. SS8982.
Tyn-y-graig *Powys* ***Settlement***, 1m/2km SW of Builth Wells. **27 K4** SO0149.
Ty'n-y-groes *Conwy* ***Village***, 4m/6km S of Conwy. **47 F5** SH7771.
Tynant *R.C.T.* ***Locality***, to E of Beddau, 3m/5km S of Pontypridd. ST0685.
Tyndale Crescent *Dur.* ***Suburb***, adjoining to S of Bishop Auckland. NZ1927.
Tyndrum *Stir.* ***Village***, 4m/7km NW of Crianlarich. Has two railway stations, one on the Glasgow to Oban and one on the Glasgow to Fort William line. **80 E4** NN3330.
Tyndyrn *Mon. Welsh form of Tintern Abbey, qv.*
Tyndyrn *Mon. Welsh form of Tintern Parva, qv.*
Tyne ***River***, formed by confluence of Rivers North and South Tyne NW of Hexham and flowing E through increasingly industrial landscape to Newcastle upon Tyne, Felling, Wallsend, Jarrow and North Sea between South Shields and Tynemouth. Tidal to Wylam. Navigable to Newcastle upon Tyne. NZ3668.
Tyne *E.Loth.* ***River***, rising on N slopes of Moorfoot Hills as Tyne Water, and becoming River Tyne below confluence with Birns Water 1m/2km E of Pencaitland. It then runs NE through Haddington and East Linton to North Sea, 3m/5km W of Dunbar. **76 D3** NT6480.
Tyne Green *Northumb.* ***Locality***, adjoining to N of Hexham. NY9364.
Tyne Mouth *E.Loth.* ***Sea feature***, where River Tyne enters North Sea, 3m/5km NW of Dunbar. **76 E2** NT6480.
Tyne Water ***River***, upper reaches of River Tyne rising on S slopes of Moorfoot Hills, just S of Tynehead and 7m/11km SE of Bonnyrigg. It flows N and then E to join with Birns Water, 1m/2km E of Pencaitland, becoming River Tyne. **76 B5** NT6480.
Tyneham *Dorset* ***Village***, between Purbeck Hills and coast, 5m/8km SW of Wareham. Rendered derelict owing to its situation in Army firing ranges. **9 H6** SY8880.
Tynehead *Midloth.* ***Settlement***, 3m/5km SE of Gorebridge. **76 B5** NT3959.
Tynemouth *T. & W.* Population: 17,422. ***Town***, resort N of River Tyne at its mouth, 8m/13km E of Newcastle upon Tyne. Remains of medieval priory and castle (both English Heritage). **71 J7** NZ3669.
Tynemouth Castle and Priory *T. & W.* ***Castle***, ruins of castle walls enclosing 11c Benedictine Priory (both English Heritage) built on site of Saxon monastery, on N bank of mouth of River Tyne at Tynemouth. **71 J7** NZ3769.
Tynewydd *R.C.T.* ***Village***, in Rhondda Fawr valley, 1km NW of Treherbert. **18 C2** SS9398.
Tyninghame *E.Loth.* ***Village***, 2m/3km NE of East Linton. **76 E3** NT6179.
Tyninghame House *E.Loth.* ***Garden***, surrounding house, 4m/6km W of Dunbar. Herbaceous borders and terraces, and ruin of 12c St. Baldred's Chapel. **76 E3** NT6179.
Tynn-yr-eithin *Cere.* ***Settlement***, 2m/3km NW of Tregaron. SN6662.
Tynribbie *Arg. & B.* ***Village***, in Argyll, 1m/2km SE of Portnacroish. **80 A3** NM9346.
Tynron *D. & G.* ***Village***, on Shinnel Water, 2m/3km NE of Tynron. **68 D4** NX8093.
Tyntesfield *N.Som.* ***Hamlet***, 2m/3km E of Nailsea. ST5071.
Tyntetown *R.C.T.* ***Locality***, 2m/3km SE of Mountain Ash. ST0696.
Tynwald Country Park *I.o.M.* ***Leisure/recreation***, country park situated on site of Manx Parliament on Tynwald Hill, St. John's. **54 B5** SC2882.
Tynygongl *I.o.A.* ***Locality***, on W side of Benllech, Anglesey. SH5182.
Tynygraig *Cere.* ***Hamlet***, 2m/3km S of Llanafan. **27 F2** SN6969.
Ty'r-bont *Cardiff* ***Locality***, 4m/7km NE of Cardiff. ST2282.
Tyrebagger Hill *Aberdeen* ***Hill***, in Kirkhill Forest, 1m/2km E of Blackburn. Height 820 feet or 250 metres. **91 G3** NJ8412.
Tyrie *Aber.* ***Settlement***, near N coast, 5m/8km SW of Fraserburgh. NJ9262.
Tyringham *M.K.* ***Hamlet***, 2m/4km N of Newport Pagnell across loop of River Great Ouse. **32 B4** SP8547.
Tyseley *W.Mid.* ***Suburb***, 3m/5km SE of Birmingham city centre. SP1184.
Tythe *Luton* ***Locality***, at NW edge of Luton. TL0424.
Tythegston *Bridgend* ***Hamlet***, 3m/5km W of Bridgend. **18 B4** SS8578.
Tytherington *Ches.* ***Suburb***, 1m/2km N of Macclesfield town centre. **49 J5** SJ9175.
Tytherington *Som.* ***Hamlet***, 2m/3km S of Frome. **20 A7** ST7745.
Tytherington *S.Glos.* ***Village***, 2m/4km SE of Thornbury. **19 K3** ST6688.
Tytherington *Wilts.* ***Village***, 1m/2km SW of Heytesbury. **20 C7** ST9141.
Tytherington Hill *Wilts.* ***Hill***, 2m/3km S of Heytesbury. Height 577 feet or 176 metres. **9 J1** ST9139.
Tytherleigh *Devon* ***Hamlet***, 3m/5km S of Chard. **8 C4** ST3103.
Tytherton Lucas *Wilts.* ***Village***, 2m/3km E of Chippenham. **20 C4** ST9474.
Tyttenhanger Green *Herts.* ***Settlement***, 2m/4km SE of St. Albans city centre. TL1805.
Tywardreath *Cornw.* ***Village***, 5m/8km E of St. Austell. **4 A5** SX0854.
Tywardreath Highway *Cornw.* ***Settlement***, 3m/5km SW of Lostwithiel. **4 A5** SX0755.
Tyweli *Carmar.* ***River***, rising 2m/3km SW of Pencader and flowing through Pencader into River Teifi at Pontwelly. SN4140.
Tywi (Towy). ***River***, rising 1m/2km S of Llyn Gynon and flowing S through Brianne Reservoir to Llandovery. It then turns SW to Llandeilo, W to Carmarthen, then S into Carmarthen Bay with River Taf. **17 H2** SN3406.
Tywi Forest (Towy Forest). *Cere.* ***Forest/woodland***, afforested area on border with Powys, 7m/11km E of Tregaron. Encloses course of Little Towy (Tywi Fechan) River. **27 G3** SN7861.
Tywyn (Formerly known as Towyn.) *Gwyn.* Population: 2864. ***Small town***, resort on Cardigan Bay, 10m/16km W of Machynlleth. Home of Talyllyn Railway. St. Cadfan's stone in church is said to show earliest example of written Welsh. **36 E5** SH5800.
Tywyn Trewan *I.o.A.* ***Large natural feature***, extensive area of foreshore on Anglesey, 1m/2km N of Rhosneigr, where Valley Airfield is situated. **46 B5** SH3075.

U

Uachdar *W.Isles* ***Settlement***, at N end of Benbecula, 1km E of Benbecula (Baile a' Mhanaich) Aerodrome. **92 D6** NF7955.
Uags *High.* ***Settlement***, on SW coast of Ross and Cromarty district, opposite Crowlin Islands. **86 D1** NG7234.
Uamh Altrumain *High. See Spar Cave.*
Uamh Bheag ***Mountain***, on border of Stirling and Perth & Kinross, 4m/7km N of Callander. Height 2181 feet or 665 metres. **81 H6** NN6911.
Ubberley *Stoke* ***Suburb***, 2m/3km E of Stoke-on-Trent city centre. SJ9146.
Ubbeston *Suff.* ***Settlement***, 5m/8km SW of Halesworth. TM3272.
Ubbeston Green *Suff.* ***Hamlet***, 1m/2km S of Ubbeston. **35 H1** TM3272.
Ubley *B. & N.E.Som.* ***Village***, 2m/3km E of Blagdon. **19 J6** ST5258.
Uckerby *N.Yorks.* ***Hamlet***, 3m/4km SE of Scotch Corner. **62 D6** NZ2402.
Uckfield *E.Suss.* Population: 13,531. ***Town***, 8m/12km NE of Lewes. Former iron-producing town, now with a light industrial base. **13 H4** TQ4721.
Uckinghall *Worcs.* ***Hamlet***, 4m/6km NW of Tewkesbury. **29 H5** SO8638.
Uckington *Glos.* ***Village***, 3m/4km NW of Cheltenham. **29 J6** SO9124.
Udale Bay *High.* ***Bay***, on S side of Cromarty Firth, Ross and Cromarty district, to SE of Balblair, on N coast of Black Isle. **96 E5** NH7166.
Uddingston *S.Lan.* Population: 5367. ***Small town***, 4m/6km SW of Coatbridge. Ruins of 13c Bothwell Castle (Historic Scotland) stand among woods above River Clyde 1m/2km SW. **74 E4** NS6960.
Uddington *S.Lan.* ***Settlement***, 2m/4km NE of Douglas. **75 G7** NS8633.
Udimore *E.Suss.* ***Village***, 4m/6km W of Rye. **14 D6** TQ8718.
Udley *N.Som.* ***Hamlet***, 1m/2km E of Congresbury. ST4663.
Udny Green *Aber.* ***Village***, 5m/7km E of Oldmeldrum. **91 G2** NJ8826.
Udny Station *Aber.* ***Village***, 6m/10km SE of Oldmeldrum. **91 H2** NJ9024.
Udston *S.Lan.* ***Suburb***, adjoining to W of Hamilton. NS6955.
Udstonhead *S.Lan.* ***Settlement***, 2m/3km N of Strathaven. **75 F6** NS7046.
Uffcott *Wilts.* ***Hamlet***, 5m/7km SW of Swindon. **20 E4** SU1277.
Uffculme *Devon* ***Village***, on River Culm, 5m/7km NE of Cullompton. **7 J4** ST0612.
Uffington *Lincs.* ***Village***, 2m/3km E of Stamford. **42 D5** TF0607.
Uffington *Oxon.* ***Village***, 4m/7km S of Faringdon. **21 G3** SU3089.
Uffington *Shrop.* ***Village***, 3m/4km E of Shrewsbury across River Severn. **38 E4** SJ5213.
Uffington Castle *Oxon.* ***Historic/prehistoric site***, Iron Age fort (English Heritage) on route of Ridgeway, 2m/3km S of Uffington. **21 F3** SU3089.
Ufford *Peter.* ***Village***, 7m/11km NW of Peterborough. **42 D5** TF0904.
Ufford *Suff.* ***Village***, 3m/4km NE of Woodbridge. Village comprises hamlets of Upper and Lower Street. **35 G3** TM2952.
Ufton *Warks.* ***Village***, 3m/4km W of Southam. **30 E2** SP3762.
Ufton Green *W.Berks.* ***Hamlet***, 7m/11km SW of Reading. SU6268.
Ufton Nervet *W.Berks.* ***Village***, 6m/10km SW of Reading. **21 K5** SU6367.
Ugadale Point *Arg. & B.* ***Coastal feature***, headland on E coast of Kintyre, 2m/4km S of Saddell. **66 B1** NR7828.
Ugborough *Devon* ***Village***, 3m/4km E of Ivybridge. **5 G5** SX6755.
Ugborough Beacon *Devon* ***Mountain***, 3m/4km NE of Ivybridge. Height 1214 feet or 370 metres. **5 G5** SX6659.
Ugborough Moor *Devon* ***Open space***, moorland to E of Harford Moor, 4m/7km N of Ivybridge. **5 G4** SX6464.
Ugbrooke House *Devon* ***Garden***, landscaped by 'Capability' Brown to SE of Chudleigh, 5m/8km NW of Teignmouth, with two lakes and sweeps of unbroken scenery. **5 J3** SX8778.
Ugford *Wilts.* ***Settlement***, 1m/2km W of Wilton. SU0831.
Uggeshall *Suff.* ***Hamlet***, 4m/7km NW of Southwold. **35 J1** TM4480.

Ugglebarnby *N.Yorks.* ***Village***, 3m/4km S of Whitby. **63 K6** NZ8707.
Ugie *Aber.* ***River***, rising as North and South Ugie Water, two branches which join 1m/2km NE of Longside. Combined river then flows E to North Sea on N side of Peterhead. **99 J6** NK1247.
Ugley *Essex* ***Village***, 5m/8km NE of Bishop's Stortford. **33 J6** TL5228.
Ugley Green *Essex* ***Village***, 1m/2km S of Ugley. **33 J6** TL5228.
Ugthorpe *N.Yorks.* ***Village***, 6m/10km W of Whitby. **63 J5** NZ7911.
Uibhist a Deas *W.Isles Gaelic form of South Uist, qv.*
Uibhist a Tuath *W.Isles Gaelic form of North Uist, qv.*
Uidh *W.Isles* ***Settlement***, with landing stage, on NE side of Vatersay. NL6596.
Uieseval *W.Isles* ***Mountain***, 4m/7km E of Tarbert, North Harris. Height 1096 feet or 334 metres. **93 H2** NG2298.
Uig *Arg. & B.* ***Settlement***, 1km NE of head of Loch Breachacha, Coll. **78 C2** NM1754.
Uig *Arg. & B.* ***Settlement***, 2m/3km N of Orchard. **73 K2** NS1484.
Uig *High.* ***Settlement***, on W side of Loch Dunvegan, Skye, 3m/4km S of Dunvegan Head. **93 G6** NG1952.
Uig *High.* ***Village***, on Uig Bay, Skye, on E shore of Loch Snizort, at foot of Glen Uig. **93 J5** NG3963.
Uig *W.Isles* ***Settlement***, near W coast of Isle of Lewis, 1km S of Timsgearraidh. NB0533.
Uig Bay *High.* ***Bay***, at foot of Glen Uig, on E shore of Loch Snizort, Skye. **93 J5** NG3963.
Uigen *W.Isles* ***Settlement***, on coast of Isle of Lewis by Loch Roag, 4m/7km SE of Gallan Head. **100 C4** NB0934.
Uiginish *High.* ***Settlement***, 1m/2km NW of Dunvegan across Loch Dunvegan, Skye. **93 H7** NG2448.
Uigshader *High.* ***Settlement***, on Skye, 4m/6km NW of Portree. **93 K7** NG4246.
Uinessan *W.Isles* ***Island***, islet off easternmost point of Vatersay. NL6695.
Uisenis *W.Isles* ***Mountain***, 4m/6km SE of head of Loch Shell, Isle of Lewis. Height 1217 feet or 371 metres. **101 F7** NB3306.
Uisge Dubh (Anglicised form: Black Water.) *High.* ***River***, issuing from S of Loch an Laoigh and flowing S through Attadale Forest to confluence with River Ling below Beinn Dronaig, 3m/4km SW of summit. **87 G1** NH0240.
Uisge Dubh *High.* ***River***, flowing W from slopes of Carn na h-Easgainn into River Farnach, 10m/15km S of Inverness. **88 E1** NH6931.
Uisge Labhair *High.* ***River***, rising to E of Aonach Beag in Badenoch and Strathspey district and running SW into River Ossian in Lochaber district, near foot of Loch Ossian. **88 B7** NN4170.
Uisge Misgeach *High.* ***River***, rising to S of Meallan Odhar and flowing E to confluence with Garbh-uisge, near SE dam of Loch Monar, to form River Farrar. **87 H1** NH1837.
Uisgebhagh (Anglicised form: Uiskevagh.) *W.Isles* ***Settlement***, 7m/11km SE of Balivanich. **92 D7** NF8650.
Uisgnaval Mòr (Anglicised form: Uisnaval More.) *W.Isles* ***Mountain***, in North Harris 2m/4km W of Clisham. Height 2391 feet or 729 metres. **100 D7** NB1208.
Uisken *Arg. & B.* ***Settlement***, on Mull, 2m/3km S of Bunessan. **78 E6** NM3819.
Uiskevagh *W.Isles Anglicised form of Uisgebhagh, qv.*
Uisnaval More *W.Isles Anglicised form of Uisgnaval Mòr, qv.*
Ukna Skerry *Shet.* ***Coastal feature***, headland on W coast of West Burra. **109 C9** HU3531.
Ulbster *High.* ***Village***, on E coast of Caithness district, 7m/11km S of Wick. **105 J4** ND3240.
Ulcat Row *Cumb.* ***Settlement***, 1m/2km NE of Dockray. **60 F4** NY4022.
Ulceby *Lincs.* ***Village***, 3m/5km SW of Alford. **53 H5** TF4272.
Ulceby *N.Lincs.* ***Village***, 5m/8km W of Immingham. **52 E1** TA1014.
Ulceby Carr *N.Lincs.* ***Locality***, 1m/2km NE of Ulceby. TA1014.
Ulceby Cross *Lincs.* ***Locality***, and crossroads 1m/2km NW of Ulceby. **53 H5** TF4272.
Ulceby Skitter *N.Lincs.* ***Hamlet***, 1m/2km E of Ulceby. TA1215.
Ulcombe *Kent* ***Village***, 3m/5km N of Headcorn. **14 D3** TQ8449.
Uldale *Cumb.* ***Village***, 7m/11km S of Wigton. **60 D3** NY2436.
Uldale Fells *Cumb.* ***Large natural feature***, mountain range to N of Skiddaw Forest, 4m/7km SW of Caldbeck. **60 D3** NY2633.
Uldale Head *Cumb.* ***Mountain***, 2m/3km SE of Low Borrowbridge. Height 1745 feet or 532 metres. **61 H6** NY6400.
Uldale House *Cumb.* ***Settlement***, in valley below West Baugh Fell, 5m/8km NE of Sedbergh. **61 J7** SD7396.
Uley *Glos.* ***Village***, 2m/3km E of Dursley. **20 A2** ST7998.
Uley Long Barrow (Hetty Pegler's Tump). *Glos.* ***Historic/prehistoric site***, Neolithic long barrow (English Heritage), now a grass-covered mound, with impressive entrance into chambers, 3m/4km NE of Dursley. **20 A2** SO7800.
Ulgham *Northumb.* ***Village***, 5m/7km NE of Morpeth. **71 H4** NZ2392.
Ulladale *W.Isles* ***River***, on Harris, rising in Forest of Harris and flowing NE to become River Housay and discharge its waters into head of Loch Resort. **100 C6** NB1017.
Ullapool *High.* ***River***, runs from Loch Acholl into Loch Broom on N side of Ullapool. **95 H2** NH1294.
Ullapool *High.* Population: 1231. ***Small town***, small fishing port and resort on E shore of Loch Broom, W coast of Ross and Cromarty district. Ferry for pedestrians across loch to Allt na h-Airbhe. Vehicle ferry to Stornoway. **95 H2** NH1294.
Ullaval *W.Isles* ***Mountain***, 2m/3km N of Cleiseval in Forest of Harris. Height 2162 feet or 659 metres. **100 C6** NB0811.
Ullenhall *Warks.* ***Village***, 2m/3km NW of Henley-in-Arden. **30 C2** SP1267.
Ullenwood *Glos.* ***Settlement***, 3m/5km S of Cheltenham. **29 J7** SO9416.
Ulleskelf *N.Yorks.* ***Village***, on S bank of River Wharfe, 4m/6km NW of Cawood. **58 B5** SE5140.
Ullesthorpe *Leics.* ***Village***, 3m/5km NW of Lutterworth. **41 H7** SP5087.
Ulley *S.Yorks.* ***Village***, 4m/6km SE of Rotherham. **51 G4** SK4687.
Ulley Reservoir *S.Yorks.* ***Reservoir***, with country park, 1km W of Ulley. **51 G4** SK4587.
Ullingswick *Here.* ***Village***, 8m/13km NE of Hereford. **28 E4** SO5949.
Ullinish *High.* ***Settlement***, on Skye, on E side of Loch Bracadale, 1m/2km W of Bracadale village. **85 J1** NG3238.
Ullock *Cumb.* ***Hamlet***, 5m/8km SW of Cockermouth. **60 B4** NY0723.
Ullscarf *Cumb.* ***Mountain***, 3m/4km SE of Rosthwaite and 6m/9km NE of Scafell Pike. Height 2381 feet or 726 metres. **60 D5** NY2912.
Ullswater *Cumb.* ***Lake/loch***, running SW to NE from Patterdale to Pooley Bridge. Second largest lake in England after Windermere. **60 F5** NY4220.
Ulpha *Cumb.* ***Settlement***, 2m/4km E of Lindale. SD4581.
Ulpha *Cumb.* ***Village***, 4m/6km N of Broughton in Furness. **60 C7** SD1993.
Ulpha Fell *Cumb.* ***Open space***, high moorland 5m/8km E of Ravenglass. **60 C7** SD1694.
Ulpha Park *Cumb.* ***Open space***, partly wooded, on W side of River Duddon, 2m/4km NW of Broughton in Furness. **60 C7** SD1890.
Ulrome *E.Riding* ***Village***, 6m/10km NW of Hornsea. **59 H4** TA1656.
Ulsta *Shet.* ***Settlement***, at SW end of Yell, on small bay of same name. Vehicle ferry to Toft on Mainland. **108 D4** HU4680.
Ulting *Essex* ***Settlement***, 3m/5km NW of Maldon. **24 E1** TL8009.
Uluvalt *Arg. & B.* ***Locality***, on Mull near head of Loch Scridain, 3m/4km SE of Ben More. **79 G5** NM5429.
Ulva *Arg. & B.* ***Island***, sparsely inhabited island off W coast of Mull on S side of Loch Tuath. Measures 4m/7km E to W and 2m/4km N to S. High basalt cliffs at W end. Road bridge connection with neighbouring Gometra to W. **79 F4** NM3640.
Ulva Islands *Arg. & B.* ***Island***, pair of islands at entrance to Linne Mhuirich, Argyll. **73 F2** NR7182.
Ulverley Green *W.Mid.* ***Suburb***, 2m/3km NW of Solihull town centre. SP1381.
Ulverscroft *Leics.* ***Locality***, 1m/2km N of Markfield. Includes nature reserve (National Trust). Remains of medieval priory. SK4911.
Ulverscroft Priory *Leics.* ***Ecclesiastical building***, 14c remains of priory founded in 1130s by Augustinian canons at Ulverscroft. **41 H4** SK5012.
Ulverston *Cumb.* Population: 11,866. ***Town***, old market town, 8m/13km NE of Barrow-in-Furness. Birthplace of Stan Laurel, with Laurel and Hardy museum in centre. **55 F2** SD2878.
Ulverston Canal *Cumb.* ***Canal***, short, straight canal, 1m/2km in length, connecting Ulverston to River Leven estuary on Morecambe Bay. **55 G2** SD3077.
Ulwell *Dorset* ***Village***, 1m/2km NW of Swanage. **10 B6** SZ0280.
Ulzieside *D. & G.* ***Settlement***, 1m/2km S of Sanquhar, across River Nith and Euchan Water. **68 C3** NS7708.
Umberleigh *Devon* ***Village***, on River Taw, 7m/11km SE of Barnstaple. **6 E3** SS6023.
Umborne Brook *Devon* ***River***, rising 1m/2km SE of Upottery and flowing S into River Coly at Colyton. **8 B5** SY2494.
Unapool *High.* ***Settlement***, on W side of mouth of Loch Glencoul, Sutherland district, 1km SE of Kylesku Ferry. **102 E5** NC2333.
Uncleby *E.Riding* ***Hamlet***, on The Wolds, 4m/6km W of Fridaythorpe. SE8159.
Under Tofts *S.Yorks.* ***Hamlet***, 3m/5km W of Sheffield city centre. SK3087.
Underbank Reservoir *S.Yorks.* ***Reservoir***, 2m/3km W of Stocksbridge. SK2599.
Underbarrow *Cumb.* ***Village***, 3m/5km W of Kendal. **61 F7** SD4692.
Undercliffe *W.Yorks.* ***Suburb***, 2m/3km NE of Bradford city centre. SE1734.
Underdale *Shrop.* ***Suburb***, NE district of Shrewsbury. SJ5013.
Underhill *Gt.Lon.* ***Suburb***, in borough of Barnet, 1km SE of Chipping Barnet and 10m/16km N of Charing Cross. TQ2595.
Underhoull *Shet.* ***Settlement***, overlooking Lunda Wick, on W coast of Unst. **108 E2** HP5704.
Underling Green *Kent* ***Settlement***, 1m/2km NE of Marden. TQ7546.
Underriver *Kent* ***Hamlet***, 3m/4km SE of Sevenoaks. **23 J6** TQ5552.
Underwood *Newport* ***Hamlet***, 1m/2km NW of Bishton. **19 G3** ST3888.
Underwood *Notts.* Population: 2177. ***Village***, 2m/4km N of Eastwood. **51 G7** SK4750.
Underwood *Plym.* ***Suburb***, of Plymouth, 4m/6km E of city centre, E of River Plym. SX5356.
Undley *Suff.* ***Settlement***, 1m/2km SW of Lakenheath. TL6981.
Undy (Gwndy). *Mon.* ***Village***, 1km E of Magor. **19 H3** ST4386.
Unifirth *Shet.* ***Settlement***, to W of Brindister Voe, Mainland. **109 B7** HU2856.
Union Bridge *Northumb.* ***Bridge***, road bridge to N of Horncliffe across River Tweed to Scottish Borders, 4m/7km W of Berwick-upon-Tweed. **77 H5** NT9351.
Union Croft *Aber.* ***Settlement***, 4m/6km NW of Stonehaven. **91 G5** NO8290.
Union Mills *I.o.M.* ***Village***, 2m/4km NW of Douglas. **54 C6** SC3577.
Union Street *E.Suss.* ***Settlement***, adjoining to W of Flimwell. TQ7131.
Unst *Shet.* ***Island***, northernmost of main islands of Shetland Islands, with much indented coastline. Measures 12m/19km N to S and from 3m/4km to 5m/8km E to W. Crofting, fishing. Airfield at Baltasound. **108 F1** HP6110.
Unst Airport *Shet.* ***Airport/airfield***, to S of Baltasound, Unst. **108 F2** HP6207.
Unstone *Derbys.* ***Village***, 1m/2km SE of Dronfield. **51 F5** SK3777.
Unstone Green *Derbys.* ***Village***, to S of Unstone, 2m/3km SE of Dronfield. SK3776.
Unsworth *Gt.Man.* ***Suburb***, to NE of Whitefield, 2m/3km S of Bury. SD8107.
Unthank *Cumb.* ***Locality***, 1km N of Gamblesby. NY6040.
Unthank *Cumb.* ***Settlement***, 2m/3km SE of Dalston. NY3948.
Unthank *Cumb.* ***Settlement***, 1m/2km NE of Skelton. **61 F3** NY4436.
Unthank *Derbys.* ***Settlement***, 1m/2km SW of Holmesfield. SK3076.
Unthank *Dur.* ***Locality***, 3m/4km W of Durham. NZ2341.
Unthank End *Cumb.* ***Locality***, 1m/2km E of Skelton and 6m/9km NW of Penrith. NY4535.
Up Cerne *Dorset* ***Hamlet***, 1m/2km N of Cerne Abbas. **9 F4** ST6502.
Up Exe *Devon* ***Village***, on River Exe, 6m/10km N of Exeter. **7 H5** SS9402.
Up Green *Hants.* ***Settlement***, adjoining to S of Eversley Cross. SU7960.
Up Hatherley *Glos.* ***Suburb***, to SW of Cheltenham. **29 J6** SO9120.
Up Holland *Lancs.* ***Suburb***, 4m/6km W of Wigan. **48 E2** SD5205.
Up Marden *W.Suss.* ***Hamlet***, 5m/8km W of Singleton. **11 J3** SU7914.
Up Mudford *Som.* ***Hamlet***, to S of Mudford, 2m/3km NE of Yeovil. ST5718.
Up Nately *Hants.* ***Village***, 4m/6km E of Basingstoke. **22 A6** SU6951.
Up Somborne *Hants.* ***Village***, 3m/5km SE of Stockbridge. **10 E1** SU3932.
Up Sydling *Dorset* ***Hamlet***, 3m/4km W of Cerne Abbas. **9 F4** ST6101.
Upavon *Wilts.* ***Village***, on River Avon, 4m/6km SW of Pewsey. **20 E6** SU1355.
Upchurch *Kent* ***Village***, 4m/7km E of Gillingham. **24 E5** TQ8467.
Upcott *Devon* ***Hamlet***, 4m/6km NE of Barnstaple. SS5838.
Upcott *Devon* ***Settlement***, 1m/2km S of Halwill Junction. **6 C6** SX4498.
Upcott *Here.* ***Settlement***, 4m/6km SE of Kington. **28 C3** SO3250.
Upcott *Som.* ***Hamlet***, 2m/3km S of Dulverton. SS9025.
Upcott *Som.* ***Hamlet***, 2m/3km W of Taunton. ST1924.
Upend *Cambs.* ***Hamlet***, 5m/8km SE of Newmarket. **33 K3** TL7058.
Upgang *N.Yorks.* ***Locality***, on North Sea coast, on NW side of Whitby. NZ8811.
Upgate *Norf.* ***Hamlet***, 1km SE of Swannington. TG1418.
Upgate Street *Norf.* ***Settlement***, 4m/6km SE of Attleborough. TM0992.
Upgate Street *Norf.* ***Settlement***, 4m/6km NW of Bungay. TM2891.
Uphall *Dorset* ***Hamlet***, 1km NW of Rampisham and 4m/7km NW of Maiden Newton. **8 E4** ST5502.
Uphall *W.Loth.* ***Locality***, and parish, on W side of Broxburn. **75 J3** NT0671.
Uphall Station *W.Loth.* ***Hamlet***, 1m/2km S of Uphall. **75 J3** NT0670.
Upham *Devon* ***Hamlet***, 5m/8km SW of Tiverton. **7 G5** SS8808.
Upham *Hants.* ***Village***, 2m/4km NW of Bishop's Waltham. **11 G2** SU5320.
Uphampton *Here.* ***Hamlet***, 6m/9km E of Presteigne. SO3963.
Uphampton *Worcs.* ***Village***, 4m/7km W of Droitwich Spa. **29 H2** SO8364.
Uphempston *Devon* ***Hamlet***, 2m/3km NE of Totnes. SX8263.
Uphill *N.Som.* ***Suburb***, S of Weston-super-Mare. **19 G6** ST3158.
Uplands *Glos.* ***Suburb***, NE district of Stroud. SO8505.
Uplands *Swan.* ***Suburb***, 1m/2km W of Swansea city centre. SS6392.
Uplawmoor *E.Renf.* ***Village***, 3m/5km SW of Neilston. **74 C5** NS4355.
Upleadon *Glos.* ***Village***, 2m/3km E of Newent. **29 G6** SO7526.
Upleatham *R. & C.* ***Village***, 2m/4km SW of Saltburn. **63 H4** NZ6319.
Uplees *Kent* ***Settlement***, 2m/3km NW of Faversham. **25 G5** TQ9964.
Uploders *Dorset* ***Hamlet***, 3m/4km E of Bridport. **8 E5** SY5093.
Uplowman *Devon* ***Village***, 4m/7km NE of Tiverton. **7 J4** ST0115.
Uplyme *Devon* ***Village***, 2m/3km NW of Lyme Regis. **8 C5** SY3293.
Upminster *Gt.Lon.* ***Town***, commuter town in borough of Havering, 3m/5km SE of Romford. Fine 14c tithe barn. **23 J3** TQ5586.
Upnor Castle *Med.* ***Castle***, 2m/3km NE of Rochester, on W bank of River Medway. Elizabethan fort (English Heritage) built to protect Medway dockyards, later becoming a magazine for ordnance stores. **24 D4** TQ7570.

U

Upottery *Devon* ***Village***, on River Otter, 5m/8km NE of Honiton. **7 K5** ST2007.

Uppark *W.Suss.* ***Historic house***, 17c-18c house (National Trust) 4m/7km SE of Petersfield. **11 J3** SU7717.

Upper Affcot *Shrop.* ***Hamlet***, 3m/4km N of Craven Arms. **38 D7** SO4486.

Upper Ardchronie *High.* ***Locality***, on S shore of Dornoch Firth, 1m/2km SE of Ardgay, Sutherland district. NH6188.

Upper Ardroscadale *Arg. & B.* ***Settlement***, on W coast of Bute, 3m/5km W of Rothesay. Burial mound to W on Watch Hill. **73 J4** NS0364.

Upper Arley *Worcs.* ***Village***, on E bank of River Severn, 3m/5km NW of Bewdley. **39 G7** SO7680.

Upper Arncott *Oxon.* ***Village***, 4m/6km SE of Bicester. **31 H7** SP6117.

Upper Astley *Shrop.* ***Settlement***, 1km S of Astley. SJ5318.

Upper Aston *Shrop.* ***Hamlet***, 6m/10km E of Bridgnorth. **40 A6** SO8194.

Upper Astrop *Northants.* ***Hamlet***, 5m/8km W of Brackley. **31 G5** SP5137.

Upper Bangor *Gwyn.* ***Suburb***, to N of Bangor, overlooking Menai Strait. SH5772.

Upper Barden Reservoir *N.Yorks.* ***Reservoir***, one of two reservoirs on Barden Moor, 3m/5km N of Embsay. **57 F4** SE0157.

Upper Barvas *W.Isles* ***Settlement***, on Isle of Lewis, 1km N of Barvas. NB3650.

Upper Basildon *W.Berks.* Population: 1545. ***Village***, 2m/4km W of Pangbourne. **21 K4** SU5976.

Upper Batley *W.Yorks.* ***Locality***, 1m/2km N of Batley. SE2424.

Upper Bayble *W.Isles* *Anglicised form of Pabail Uarach, qv.*

Upper Beeding *W.Suss.* Population: 4346. ***Village***, in River Adur valley, 4m/6km N of Shoreham-by-Sea. **12 E5** TQ1910.

Upper Belvedere *Gt.Lon.* ***Suburb***, along with Lower Belvedere, forms part of Belvedere in borough of Bexley. TQ4978.

Upper Benefield *Northants.* ***Village***, 1km NW of Lower Benefield. **42 C7** SP9988.

Upper Bentley *Worcs.* ***Hamlet***, 4m/6km SE of Bromsgrove. SO9966.

Upper Berwick *Shrop.* ***Hamlet***, 3m/4km NW of Shrewsbury. SJ4715.

Upper Bighouse *High.* ***Settlement***, on W side of Halladale River, 4m/7km S of Melvich. **104 D3** NC8857.

Upper Birchwood *Derbys.* ***Settlement***, 2m/3km E of Alfreton. SK4355.

Upper Boat (Glan-bad). *R.C.T.* ***Settlement***, 3m/5km SE of Pontypridd. **18 E3** ST1087.

Upper Boddam *Aber.* ***Settlement***, 2m/3km N of Insch. NJ6230.

Upper Boddington *Northants.* ***Village***, 8m/13km N of Banbury. **31 F3** SP4853.

Upper Borth *Cere.* ***Hamlet***, on coast, adjoining to S of Borth. **37 F7** SN6088.

Upper Boyndlie *Aber.* ***Settlement***, forms locality of Boyndlie with Nether Boyndlie, near N coast, 5m/9km SW of Fraserburgh. **99 H4** NJ9162.

Upper Brailes *Warks.* ***Village***, 3m/5km E of Shipston on Stour. **30 E4** SP3039.

Upper Breakish *High.* *Alternative name for Breakish, qv.*

Upper Breinton *Here.* ***Settlement***, 3m/5km W of Hereford. **28 D4** SO4640.

Upper Broadheath *Worcs.* ***Village***, 3m/5km W of Worcester. SO8055.

Upper Brockholes *W.Yorks.* ***Hamlet***, adjoining to NW of Illingworth, 3m/5km NW of Halifax. SE0629.

Upper Broughton *Notts.* ***Village***, 6m/10km NW of Melton Mowbray. **41 J3** SK6826.

Upper Brynamman *Carmar.* ***Village***, adjoins to NE of Brynamman. SN7114.

Upper Bucklebury *W.Berks.* ***Village***, 2m/3km SW of Bucklebury. **21 J5** SU5468.

Upper Burgate *Hants.* ***Hamlet***, in River Avon valley, 2m/3km N of Fordingbridge. **10 C3** SU1516.

Upper Burnhaugh *Aber.* ***Settlement***, 1m/2km NW of Netherley. **91 G5** NO8394.

Upper Caldecote *Beds.* ***Village***, 2m/3km NW of Biggleswade. **32 E4** TL1645.

Upper Camster *High.* ***Settlement***, in Caithness district, 4m/6km N of Lybster. Grey Cairns of Camster (Historic Scotland), 1m/2km N. **105 H4** ND2641.

Upper Canada *N.Som.* ***Hamlet***, to SE of Lower Canada, on N slope of Bleadon Hill, 3m/5km SE of Weston-super-Mare. ST3658.

Upper Carloway *W.Isles* *Anglicised form of Mullach Charlabhaigh, qv.*

Upper Catesby *Northants.* ***Hamlet***, forms parish of Catesby, along with Lower Catesby, some 4m/6km SW of Daventry. SP5259.

Upper Catshill *Worcs.* ***Locality***, adjoining to NE of Catshill. **29 J1** SO9674.

Upper Chapel (Capel Uchaf). *Powys* ***Hamlet***, 8m/13km N of Brecon. **27 K4** SO0040.

Upper Cheddon *Som.* ***Village***, 1km NW of Cheddon Fitzpaine, 2m/3km N of Taunton. ST2328.

Upper Chicksgrove *Wilts.* ***Hamlet***, on River Nadder, 1m/2km E of Tisbury. ST9629.

Upper Church Village *R.C.T.* ***Hamlet***, adjoins to NW of Church Village, 2m/3km S of Pontypridd. ST0886.

Upper Chute *Wilts.* ***Village***, forms part of parish of Chute, 6m/10km NW of Andover. **21 F6** SU2953.

Upper Clapton *Gt.Lon.* ***Suburb***, in borough of Hackney, 5m/8km NE of Charing Cross. TQ3487.

Upper Clatford *Hants.* Population: 1459. ***Village***, 1m/2km S of Andover. **21 G7** SU3543.

Upper Clynnog *Gwyn.* ***Locality***, 4m/6km S of Llanllyfni. SH4746.

Upper Clyth *High.* ***Locality***, on E coast of Caithness district, 2m/3km E of Lybster. ND2737.

Upper Coberley *Glos.* ***Hamlet***, 4m/7km SE of Cheltenham. **29 J7** SO9715.

Upper Coedcae *Torfaen* ***Locality***, on E side of Blaenavon. SO2508.

Upper Cokeham *W.Suss.* ***Locality***, 3m/4km NE of Worthing. TQ1705.

Upper Coll *W.Isles* *Anglicised form of Col Uarach, qv.*

Upper College *Shrop.* ***Settlement***, 5m/8km SE of Whitchurch. SJ5734.

Upper Corris *Gwyn.* *English form of Corris Uchaf, qv.*

Upper Cotton *Staffs.* ***Settlement***, 1m/2km NW of Cotton. SK0547.

Upper Cound *Shrop.* ***Hamlet***, 1km W of Cound. **38 E5** SJ5504.

Upper Crabtree *S.Yorks.* ***Suburb***, 2m/3km N of Sheffield city centre. SK3590.

Upper Cudworth *S.Yorks.* ***Village***, adjoining to N of Cudworth, 4m/6km NE of Barnsley. SE3909.

Upper Cumberworth *W.Yorks.* ***Village***, 1m/2km W of Denby Dale. SE2108.

Upper Cwmbran *Torfaen* ***Locality***, to N of Cwmbran. **19 F2** ST2796.

Upper Dallachy *Moray* ***Village***, 1m/2km S of Nether Dallachy, on S side of disused airfield. **98 B4** NJ3663.

Upper Dean *Beds.* ***Village***, 11m/18km N of Bedford. **32 D2** TL0467.

Upper Denby *W.Yorks.* ***Village***, 1km S of Denby Dale. **50 E2** SE2207.

Upper Denton *Cumb.* ***Hamlet***, 1m/2km SW of Gilsland. NY6165.

Upper Derraid *High.* ***Settlement***, 3m/5km N of Grantown-on-Spey. **89 H1** NJ0233.

Upper Derwent Reservoir *Derbys.* ***Reservoir***, second of a series of three large reservoirs in Upper Derwent Valley, 6m/10km NW of Hathersage. **50 D4** SK1789.

Upper Diabaig *High.* ***Settlement***, 1m/2km E of Lower Diabaig, on N shore of Loch Diabaigas Airde, Ross and Cromarty district. **94 E5** NG8160.

Upper Dicker *E.Suss.* ***Hamlet***, 2m/4km W of Hailsham. **13 J5** TQ5510.

Upper Dinchope *Shrop.* ***Locality***, 2m/3km E of Craven Arms. SO4583.

Upper Dovercourt *Essex* ***Suburb***, W district of Harwich. **35 G6** TM2430.

Upper Dunsforth *N.Yorks.* ***Hamlet***, 4m/6km SE of Boroughbridge. **57 K3** SE4463.

Upper Dunsley *Herts.* ***Settlement***, on E side of Tring. SP9311.

Upper Eashing *Surr.* ***Hamlet***, to E of Eashing, 1m/2km W of Godalming. SU9543.

Upper Eastern Green *W.Mid.* ***Suburb***, 3m/5km NW of Coventry city centre. **40 E7** SP2780.

Upper Eathie *High.* ***Settlement***, 3m/5km SW of Cromarty. **96 E5** NH7663.

Upper Edmonton *Gt.Lon.* ***Suburb***, in borough of Enfield, to S of Edmonton. TQ3493.

Upper Egleton *Here.* ***Hamlet***, 9m/14km E of Hereford. SO6344.

Upper Elkstone *Staffs.* ***Hamlet***, 5m/8km E of Leek. **50 C7** SK0559.

Upper Ellastone *Staffs.* ***Hamlet***, adjoining to NW of Ellastone, 4m/7km SW of Ashbourne. SK1143.

Upper Elmers End *Gt.Lon.* ***Suburb***, 1m/2km SE of Elmers End. TQ3667.

Upper End *Derbys.* ***Hamlet***, just SW of Peak Dale. **50 C5** SK0876.

Upper Enham *Hants.* ***Settlement***, 3m/5km N of Andover. SU3649.

Upper Farmcote *Shrop.* ***Locality***, 1km W of Farmcote. SO7791.

Upper Farringdon *Hants.* ***Village***, 2m/4km S of Alton. **11 J1** SU7135.

Upper Framilode *Glos.* ***Village***, on S bank of River Severn, 7m/12km SW of Gloucester. **29 G7** SO7510.

Upper Froyle *Hants.* ***Village***, within parish of Froyle, about 4m/7km NE of Alton. Site of Roman building 1m/2km E. **22 A7** SU7543.

Upper Gills *High.* ***Settlement***, 1km S of Gills. **105 J1** ND3272.

Upper Glendessarry *High.* ***Settlement***, in Glen Dessary, 3m/4km NW of head of Loch Arkaig, Lochaber district. **87 F5** NM9593.

Upper Godney *Som.* ***Hamlet***, 3m/4km NW of Glastonbury. **19 H7** ST4842.

Upper Goldstone *Kent* ***Locality***, 3m/5km NW of Sandwich. TR2960.

Upper Gornal *W.Mid.* ***Suburb***, 2m/3km NW of Dudley town centre. **40 B6** SO9292.

Upper Gravenhurst *Beds.* ***Village***, 3m/5km SW of Shefford. **32 E5** TL1136.

Upper Green *Essex* ***Hamlet***, 3m/5km N of Thaxted. TL5935.

Upper Green *Essex* ***Locality***, E part of Langley, 6m/10km W of Saffron Walden. **33 H5** TL4435.

Upper Green *Mon.* ***Hamlet***, 4m/7km W of Skenfrith. **28 C7** SO3818.

Upper Green *Suff.* ***Hamlet***, at S end of Higham, 7m/11km W of Bury St. Edmunds. TL7464.

Upper Green *W.Berks.* ***Village***, 4m/6km SE of Hungerford. **21 G5** SU3763.

Upper Green *W.Yorks.* ***Locality***, 2m/3km SE of Morley. SE2725.

Upper Grove Common *Here.* ***Hamlet***, 3m/5km NW of Ross-on-Wye. SO5526.

Upper Guist *Norf.* ***Locality***, 1km NE of Guist. TG0026.

Upper Gylen *Arg. & B.* ***Settlement***, on Kerrera, 1m/2km NE of Rubha Seanach. **79 K5** NM8126.

Upper Hackney *Derbys.* ***Locality***, 1m/2km NW of Matlock. **50 E6** SK2961.

Upper Hale *Surr.* ***Locality***, residential locality adjoining to NW of Hale. SU8449.

Upper Halistra *High.* ***Settlement***, adjoins Lower Halistra, 5m/8km S of Vaternish Point, Skye. NG2459.

Upper Halliford *Surr.* ***Hamlet***, 1m/2km W of Sunbury. **22 D5** TQ0968.

Upper Halling *Med.* ***Settlement***, 1m/2km W of Halling. **24 C5** TQ6964.

Upper Hambleton *Rut.* ***Village***, on island in Rutland Water, 3m/4km E of Oakham. **42 C5** SK9007.

Upper Harbledown *Kent* ***Hamlet***, 1m/2km W of Harbledown and 2m/3km W of Canterbury. TR1158.

Upper Hardres *Kent* ***Locality***, 5m/7km S of Canterbury. TR1550.

Upper Hardres Court *Kent* ***Hamlet***, 3m/5km SW of Bridge. **15 G2** TR1550.

Upper Hardwick *Here.* ***Settlement***, 6m/9km W of Leominster. SO4057.

Upper Hartfield *E.Suss.* ***Hamlet***, 1m/2km SW of Hartfield, below N edge of Ashdown Forest. **13 H3** TQ4735.

Upper Hartshay *Derbys.* ***Hamlet***, 1km S of Lower Hartshay and 1m/2km W of Ripley. SK3850.

Upper Hatton *Staffs.* ***Settlement***, 1km N of Lower Hatton. SJ8337.

Upper Haugh *S.Yorks.* ***Suburb***, adjoining to NW of Rawmarsh, 3m/5km N of Rotherham. SK4297.

Upper Hawkhillock *Aber.* ***Settlement***, 6m/10km NE of Ellon. **91 J1** NK0039.

Upper Hayesden *Kent* ***Settlement***, 2m/3km SW of Tonbridge. TQ5644.

Upper Hayton *Shrop.* ***Settlement***, 4m/7km N of Ludlow. **38 E7** SO5181.

Upper Heath *Shrop.* ***Settlement***, 9m/14km SE of Church Stretton. **38 E7** SO5685.

Upper Heaton *W.Yorks.* ***Hamlet***, 1km N of Kirkheaton, 3m/4km NE of Huddersfield town centre. SE1719.

Upper Hellesdon *Norf.* ***Suburb***, 2m/3km N of Norwich city centre. TG2111.

Upper Helmsley *N.Yorks.* ***Village***, 1m/2km NW of Stamford Bridge. **58 C4** SE6956.

Upper Hengoed *Shrop.* ***Settlement***, 1km N of Hengoed. SJ2834.

Upper Hergest *Here.* ***Hamlet***, 2m/4km SW of Kington. **28 B3** SO2654.

Upper Heyford *Northants.* ***Hamlet***, 6m/9km W of Northampton town centre. SP6659.

Upper Heyford *Oxon.* Population: 1978. ***Village***, 6m/9km NW of Bicester. Airfield to E. **31 F6** SP4926.

Upper Hiendley *W.Yorks.* ***Locality***, adjoining to N of South Hiendley, 2m/3km W of Hemsworth. SE3913.

Upper Hill *Here.* ***Hamlet***, 4m/6km SW of Leominster. **28 D3** SO4753.

Upper Hill *S.Glos.* ***Hamlet***, 1km NE of Hill and 3m/4km SW of Berkeley. ST6596.

Upper Hockenden *Gt.Lon.* ***Settlement***, to N of Hockenden, in borough of Bromley. TQ4969.

Upper Holloway *Gt.Lon.* ***Suburb***, in borough of Islington, 1m/2km NW of Holloway. TQ2986.

Upper Holton *Suff.* ***Settlement***, 1km N of Holton. TM4078.

Upper Hopton *W.Yorks.* ***Village***, 1m/2km S of Mirfield. **50 D1** SE1918.

Upper Horsebridge *E.Suss.* ***Locality***, on E bank of Cuckmere River, opposite Lower Horsebridge. **13 J5** TQ5711.

Upper Howsell *Worcs.* ***Suburb***, at N end of Great Malvern, 1km W of Lower Howsell. SO7748.

Upper Hoyland *S.Yorks.* ***Locality***, 1km NW of Hoyland. SE3601.

Upper Hulme *Staffs.* ***Village***, 3m/5km NE of Leek. **50 C6** SK0160.

Upper Ifold *Surr.* ***Settlement***, 7m/11km E of Haslemere. TQ0033.

Upper Inglesham *Swin.* ***Hamlet***, 1m/2km S of Inglesham. **21 F2** SU2098.

Upper Kilchattan *Arg. & B.* ***Settlement***, on Colonsay, 2m/3km NW of Scalasaig. **72 B1** NR3795.

Upper Kilcott *S.Glos.* ***Locality***, 1km SE of Lower Kilcott, 2m/3km NW of Didmarton. ST7988.

Upper Killay *Swan.* ***Village***, 1m/2km W of Killay. **17 J5** SS5892.

Upper Kinchrackine *Arg. & B.* ***Locality***, in Strath of Orchy in Argyll. Adjoins to W of Dalmally. NN1527.

Upper Kinsham *Here.* ***Hamlet***, forms locality of Kinsham, along with Lower Kinsham, 3m/5km E of Presteigne. SO3664.

Upper Kirkhill *Aberdeen* ***Locality***, 2m/3km S of Aberdeen city centre across River Dee. NJ9402.

Upper Knockando *Moray* ***Settlement***, 1m/2km N of Knockando. **97 J7** NJ1941.

Upper Lambourn *W.Berks.* ***Village***, 1m/2km NW of Lambourn. **21 G3** SU3278.

Upper Landywood *Staffs.* ***Suburb***, 1m/2km SW of Landywood. SJ9805.

Upper Langford *N.Som.* ***Hamlet***, 2m/4km W of Blagdon. ST4659.

Upper Langwith *Derbys.* ***Village***, 3m/5km E of Bolsover. **51 H6** SK5169.

Upper Largo (Also known as Kirkton of Largo.) *Fife* ***Village***, forms locality of Largo with adjacent village of Lower Largo 1m/2km to SW. **83 F7** NO4203.

Upper Leigh *Staffs.* ***Hamlet***, 1km NW of Church Leigh. SK0136.

Upper Ley *Glos.* ***Settlement***, 7m/11km W of Gloucester. SO7217.

Upper Loads *Derbys.* ***Settlement***, 1km W of Nether Loads, 4m/7km SW of Chesterfield. SK3369.

Upper Loch Torridon *High.* ***Lake/loch***, upper part of Loch Torridon, E of Shieldaig. **94 E6** NG7560.

Upper Lochton *Aber.* ***Locality***, 1m/2km N of Banchory. **90 E5** NO6997.

Upper Longdon *Staffs.* ***Village***, 1m/2km W of Longdon. **40 C4** SK0814.

Upper Ludstone *Shrop.* ***Settlement***, 6m/9km E of Bridgnorth. **40 A6** SO8095.
Upper Lybster *High.* ***Village***, 1m/2km N of Lybster. **105 H5** ND2435.
Upper Lydbrook *Glos.* ***Village***, adjoining Lower Lydbrook, 4m/6km W of Cinderford. **29 F7** SO6015.
Upper Lyde *Here.* ***Hamlet***, 3m/5km N of Hereford. SO4944.
Upper Lye *Here.* ***Hamlet***, 8m/12km NW of Leominster. SO3965.
Upper Maes-coed *Here.* ***Settlement***, 1m/2km NE of Michaelchurch Escley. **28 C5** SO3334.
Upper Marston *Here.* ***Locality***, 4m/6km E of Kington. SO3558.
Upper Midhope *S.Yorks.* ***Settlement***, to W of Midhope Reservoir, 1m/2km W of Midhopestones. **50 E3** SK2199.
Upper Milovaig *High.* ***Settlement***, on Skye, forms locality of Milovaig, along with Lower Milovaig, 6m/10km W of Dunvegan. NG1549.
Upper Milton *Oxon.* ***Settlement***, 3m/5km N of Burford. SP2517.
Upper Milton *Som.* ***Settlement***, forms Milton, along with Lower Milton, 1m/2km N of Wells. ST5447.
Upper Minety *Wilts.* ***Village***, 1m/2km W of Minety. **20 D2** SU0290.
Upper Mitton *Worcs.* ***Suburb***, NE district of Stourport-on-Severn. **29 H1** SO8172.
Upper Moor *Worcs.* ***Hamlet***, 2m/3km NE of Pershore. SO9747.
Upper Moor Side *W.Yorks.* ***Locality***, 1km N of Gildersome, 4m/7km SW of Leeds city centre. SE2430.
Upper Morton *S.Glos.* ***Hamlet***, 1m/2km NE of Thornbury. ST6491.
Upper Nash *Pembs.* ***Hamlet***, 2m/4km E of Pembroke. SN0202.
Upper Netchwood *Shrop.* ***Hamlet***, 2m/3km N of Ditton Priors. SO6092.
Upper Nobut *Staffs.* ***Hamlet***, 4m/6km NW of Uttoxeter. SK0435.
Upper North Dean *Bucks.* ***Settlement***, 4m/6km N of High Wycombe. **22 B2** SU8498.
Upper Norwood *Gt.Lon.* ***Locality***, forms suburb of Norwood, along with South Norwood and West Norwood, and Norwood New Town, 3m/5km N of Croydon town centre. **23 G4** TQ3369.
Upper Norwood *W.Suss.* ***Hamlet***, 4m/6km SW of Petworth. SU9317.
Upper Obney *P. & K.* ***Settlement***, 3m/4km NW of Bankfoot. **82 B4** NO0336.
Upper Oddington *Glos.* ***Village***, 3m/4km E of Stow-on-the-Wold. **30 D6** SP2225.
Upper Ollach *High.* ***Locality***, on E coast of Skye, 5m/7km SE of Loch Portree. **86 B1** NG5136.
Upper Outwoods *Staffs.* ***Hamlet***, 2m/3km NW of Burton upon Trent. SK2225.
Upper Padley *Derbys.* ***Hamlet***, to N of Nether Padley, 3m/4km NW of Stoney Middleton. SK2579.
Upper Pennington *Hants.* ***Suburb***, 1m/2km W of Lymington. SZ3095.
Upper Pollicott *Bucks.* ***Settlement***, 5m/8km N of Thame. SP7013.
Upper Pond Street *Essex See Pond Street.*
Upper Poppleton *York* Population: 1681. ***Village***, 3m/5km NW of York. **58 B4** SE5554.
Upper Pulley *Shrop.* ***Locality***, 1km SE of Pulley. SJ4709.
Upper Quinton *Warks.* ***Hamlet***, forms parish of Quinton, along with Lower Quinton, 5m/8km S of Stratford-upon-Avon. **30 C4** SP1847.
Upper Race *Torfaen* ***Locality***, 1km SW of Pontypool. ST2799.
Upper Ratley *Hants.* ***Village***, 2m/3km NW of Romsey. SU3223.
Upper Ridinghill *Aber.* ***Settlement***, 2m/3km SW of Crimond and 4m/6km SW of Loch of Strathbeg. **99 J5** NK0254.
Upper Rochford *Worcs.* ***Village***, 2m/4km E of Tenbury Wells. **29 F2** SO6267.
Upper Sanday *Ork.* ***Locality***, on Mainland, 8m/12km SE of Kirkwall. **107 E7** HY5403.
Upper Sapey *Here.* ***Village***, 6m/10km N of Bromyard. **29 F2** SO6863.
Upper Seagry *Wilts.* ***Village***, 5m/8km NE of Chippenham. **20 C3** ST9480.
Upper Shader *W.Isles Anglicised form of Siadar Uarach, qv.*
Upper Shelton *Beds.* ***Hamlet***, 5m/9km SW of Bedford. **32 C4** SP9943.
Upper Sheringham *Norf.* ***Village***, 1m/2km SW of Sheringham. **45 F1** TG1543.
Upper Shirley *Gt.Lon.* ***Suburb***, 1km SE of Shirley. TQ3564.
Upper Shirley *S'ham.* ***Suburb***, N district of Southampton. SU4014.
Upper Shuckburgh *Warks.* ***Settlement***, 5m/8km W of Daventry. SP4961.
Upper Siddington *Glos.* ***Settlement***, to W of Siddington. SU0299.
Upper Skelmorlie *N.Ayr.* ***Locality***, adjoining to NE of Skelmorlie. **74 A4** NS1967.
Upper Slaughter *Glos.* ***Village***, 3m/5km SW of Stow-on-the-Wold. **30 C6** SP1523.
Upper Sonachan *Arg. & B.* ***Settlement***, on S shore of Loch Awe, 1km E of Portsonachan. **80 B5** NN0621.
Upper Soudley *Glos.* ***Village***, in Forest of Dean, 2m/4km S of Cinderford. **29 F7** SO6510.
Upper Sound *Shet.* ***Settlement***, on Mainland, to W of Sound. HU4640.
Upper Staploe *Beds.* ***Settlement***, 1km S of Staploe. TL1459.
Upper Stoke *Norf.* ***Hamlet***, 4m/6km S of Norwich. TG2402.
Upper Stoke *W.Mid.* ***Suburb***, 1m/2km NE of Coventry city centre. **41 F7** SP3580.
Upper Stondon *Beds.* ***Village***, 3m/4km S of Shefford. **32 E5** TL1535.
Upper Stowe *Northants.* ***Village***, 6m/9km SE of Daventry. **31 H3** SP6456.
Upper Street *Hants.* ***Hamlet***, 3m/4km N of Fordingbridge. **10 C3** SU1518.
Upper Street *Norf.* ***Hamlet***, 1m/2km W of Horning. TG3217.
Upper Street *Norf.* ***Hamlet***, 1m/2km E of Horning. **45 H4** TG3516.
Upper Street *Norf.* ***Hamlet***, 2m/3km E of Scole. TM1780.
Upper Street *Norf.* ***Locality***, 4m/7km N of Wroxham. TG3024.
Upper Street *Suff.* ***Hamlet***, 4m/6km N of Clare. TL7851.
Upper Street *Suff.* ***Hamlet***, forms part of Ufford, along with Lower Street. TM2952.
Upper Street *Suff.* ***Locality***, at Stutton, 6m/10km S of Ipswich. **35 F5** TM1434.
Upper Street *Suff.* ***Settlement***, at Baylham, 6m/9km NW of Ipswich. TM1051.
Upper Strensham *Worcs.* ***Hamlet***, 4m/7km N of Tewkesbury. SO9039.
Upper Sundon *Beds.* ***Village***, 5m/8km NW of Luton. **32 D6** TL0427.
Upper Swanmore *Hants.* ***Settlement***, 2m/3km E of Bishop's Waltham. SU5817.
Upper Swell *Glos.* ***Village***, 1m/2km NW of Stow-on-the-Wold. **30 C6** SP1726.
Upper Sydenham *Gt.Lon.* ***Suburb***, in borough of Lewisham, 4m/6km N of Croydon. TQ3471.
Upper Tamar Lake (Upper Tamar Reservoir). *Devon* ***Reservoir***, on border with Cornwall, in River Tamar valley, 4m/6km from its source and 5m/9km NW of Holsworthy. **6 A4** SS2911.
Upper Tamar Reservoir *Devon See Upper Tamar Lake.*
Upper Tankersley *S.Yorks.* ***Hamlet***, 1km S of Tankersley. SK3499.
Upper Tasburgh *Norf.* ***Hamlet***, 1km E of Tasburgh. TM2095.
Upper Tean *Staffs.* Population: 2632. ***Village***, 2m/4km S of Cheadle. **40 C2** SK0139.
Upper Threapwood *Ches.* ***Settlement***, to E of Threapwood. SJ4445.
Upper Thurnham *Lancs.* ***Settlement***, forms locality of Thurnham, along with Lower Thurnham, 2m/3km SW of Galgate. **55 H4** SD4654.
Upper Tillyrie *P. & K.* ***Hamlet***, 1m/2km NW of Milnathort. **82 C7** NO1106.
Upper Tooting *Gt.Lon.* ***Suburb***, in borough of Wandsworth, 5m/8km S of Charing Cross. **23 F4** TQ2772.
Upper Town *Derbys.* ***Hamlet***, to S of Birchover, 4m/6km NW of Matlock. SK2461.
Upper Town *Derbys.* ***Settlement***, 1km N of Hognaston, 4m/6km SW of Wirksworth. SK2351.
Upper Town *Derbys.* ***Village***, 2m/3km SW of Matlock. SK2758.
Upper Town *Here.* ***Village***, 8m/12km NE of Hereford. SO5849.
Upper Town *N.Som.* ***Hamlet***, just E of Felton, 6m/9km SW of Bristol. **19 J5** ST5265.
Upper Town *Suff.* ***Settlement***, W end of Pakenham. TL9267.
Upper Tysoe *Warks.* ***Village***, 5m/8km S of Kineton. **30 E4** SP3343.
Upper Uphall *W.Loth.* ***Locality***, adjoining to N of Uphall. NT0672.
Upper Upham *Wilts.* ***Settlement***, 3m/4km NW of Aldbourne. **21 F4** SU2277.
Upper Upnor *Med.* ***Hamlet***, on River Medway, 1km upstream of Lower Upnor; restored 16c castle (English Heritage). **24 D4** TQ7570.
Upper Victoria *Angus* ***Settlement***, 2m/3km NW of Carnoustie. **83 G4** NO5336.
Upper Vobster *Som.* ***Settlement***, to N of Vobster, 4m/7km W of Frome. ST7049.
Upper Walthamstow *Gt.Lon.* ***Suburb***, 1km E of Walthamstow. TQ3889.
Upper Wardington *Oxon.* ***Village***, adjoining to E of Wardington, 4m/7km NE of Banbury. **31 F4** SP4946.
Upper Waterhay *Wilts.* ***Settlement***, 2m/3km W of Cricklade. SU0693.
Upper Weald *M.K.* ***Settlement***, 2m/3km S of Stony Stratford. **32 B5** SP8037.
Upper Weedon *Northants.* ***Village***, 4m/6km SE of Daventry. **31 H3** SP6258.
Upper Welland *Worcs.* ***Hamlet***, 3m/5km S of Great Malvern. SO7740.
Upper Welson *Here.* ***Settlement***, 4m/6km S of Kington. **28 B3** SO2951.
Upper Weston *B. & N.E.Som.* ***Suburb***, adjoining to N of Weston, 2m/3km NW of Bath city centre. ST7267.
Upper Weybread *Suff.* ***Settlement***, 1m/2km SW of Weybread. TM2379.
Upper Whiston *S.Yorks.* ***Hamlet***, 1km SE of Whiston, 3m/4km SE of Rotherham. SK4588.
Upper Wick *Glos.* ***Locality***, on E side of M5 motorway, 1km NE of Lower Wick and 3m/4km SW of Dursley. ST7196.
Upper Wick *Worcs.* ***Settlement***, 2m/3km SW of Worcester. SO8253.
Upper Wield (Also known as Wield.) *Hants.* ***Village***, 5m/8km NE of New Alresford. **11 H1** SU6238.
Upper Wigginton *Shrop.* ***Settlement***, to N of Wigginton. SJ3335.
Upper Wilcove *Cornw.* ***Hamlet***, on River Tamar estuary, 1m/2km N of Torpoint. SX4356.
Upper Winchendon (Also known as Over Winchendon.) *Bucks.* ***Village***, 5m/8km W of Aylesbury. **31 J7** SP7414.
Upper Witton *W.Mid.* ***Suburb***, 4m/6km NE of Birmingham city centre. SP0891.
Upper Wolvercote *Oxon.* ***Suburb***, 3m/4km NW of Oxford city centre. SP4909.
Upper Woodford *Wilts.* ***Village***, in parish of Woodford on River Avon, along with Lower Woodford and Middle Woodford, 3m/5km SW of Amesbury. **10 C1** SU1237.
Upper Woolhampton *W.Berks.* ***Hamlet***, 1km N of Woolhampton. SU5767.
Upper Wootton *Hants.* ***Hamlet***, 4m/7km NW of Basingstoke. **21 J6** SU5854.
Upper Wraxall *Wilts.* ***Hamlet***, 1m/2km W of North Wraxall. Site of Roman villa 1m/2km NE. **20 A4** ST8175.
Upper Wyche *Here.* ***Locality***, on Malvern Hills, 1m/2km SW of Great Malvern town centre. **29 G4** SO7743.
Upperby *Cumb.* ***Suburb***, 2m/3km S of Carlisle city centre. NY4053.
Uppermill *Gt.Man.* Population: 5028. ***Village***, 5m/7km E of Oldham. **49 J2** SD9905.
Upperthong *W.Yorks.* ***Village***, 1m/2km W of Holmfirth. **50 D2** SE1208.
Upperthorpe *Derbys.* ***Settlement***, adjoining to S of Killamarsh. SK4580.
Upperthorpe *N.Lincs.* ***Locality***, 1km W of Haxey. SE7500.
Upperton *Aber. See Peterhead.*
Upperton *W.Suss.* ***Hamlet***, 1m/2km NW of Petworth across Petworth Park. **12 C4** SU9522.
Uppertown *Derbys.* ***Hamlet***, 3m/5km NE of Matlock. SK3265.
Uppertown *High.* ***Settlement***, at S end of Island of Stroma, in Pentland Firth. **105 J1** ND3576.
Uppertown *Ork.* ***Settlement***, at NW end of South Ronaldsay, 2m/3km W of St. Margaret's Hope. ND4193.
Upperwood *Derbys.* ***Hamlet***, adjoining to S of Matlock Bath, on W bank of River Derwent. SK2957.
Uppincott *Devon* ***Hamlet***, 3m/5km NE of Crediton. SS8802.
Uppingham *Rut.* Population: 3140. ***Small town***, stone-built market town, 7m/12km N of Corby. Boys' boarding school, founded 16c. **42 B6** SP8699.
Uppington *Dorset* ***Settlement***, 3m/5km N of Wimborne Minster. **10 B4** SU0206.
Uppington *Shrop.* ***Village***, 4m/6km SW of Wellington. **38 E5** SJ5909.
Upsall *Middbro.* ***Locality***, 3m/5km W of Guisborough. NZ5615.
Upsall *N.Yorks.* ***Village***, 4m/6km NE of Thirsk. **57 K1** SE4587.
Upsettlington *Sc.Bord.* ***Settlement***, surrounded by parkland, on W side of River Tweed, 1m/2km SW of Norham. **77 G6** NT8846.
Upshire *Essex* ***Village***, 2m/3km E of Waltham Abbey. **23 H1** TL4101.
Upstreet *Kent* ***Village***, 2m/4km SW of Sarre. **25 J5** TR2263.
Upthorpe *Glos.* ***Locality***, 1m/2km N of Dursley. SO7500.
Upthorpe *Suff.* ***Hamlet***, 1m/2km E of Stanton. TL9772.
Upton *Bucks.* ***Hamlet***, 3m/5km SW of Aylesbury. **31 J7** SP7711.
Upton *Cambs.* ***Village***, 6m/9km NW of Huntingdon. **32 E1** TL1778.
Upton *Ches.* ***Suburb***, 2m/3km N of Chester. **48 D6** SJ4069.
Upton *Cornw.* ***Hamlet***, 1km SW of Bude. SS2004.
Upton *Cornw.* ***Hamlet***, close to Upton Cross, 5m/9km N of Liskeard. **4 C3** SX2772.
Upton *Cumb.* ***Locality***, adjoining to SW of Caldbeck. NY3239.
Upton *Devon* ***Hamlet***, 4m/7km NW of Honiton. **7 J5** ST0902.
Upton *Devon* ***Settlement***, 2m/4km W of Kingsbridge. **5 H6** SX7043.
Upton *Dorset* ***Hamlet***, near coast, 6m/9km SE of Dorchester. SY7483.
Upton *Dorset* ***Suburb***, urban locality 3m/4km NW of Poole. **9 J5** SY9893.
Upton *E.Riding* ***Settlement***, 1km E of Beeford. TA1454.
Upton *Gt.Lon.* ***Suburb***, N district of West Ham, in borough of Newham. TQ4084.
Upton *Halton* ***Suburb***, 2m/3km N of Widnes. SJ5087.
Upton *Hants.* ***Hamlet***, 4m/7km NW of Southampton. **10 E3** SU3716.
Upton *Hants.* ***Village***, 2m/3km NW of Hurstbourne Tarrant. **21 G6** SU3655.
Upton *Leics.* ***Settlement***, 4m/6km E of Atherstone. SP3699.
Upton *Lincs.* ***Village***, 4m/6km SE of Gainsborough. **52 B4** SK8686.
Upton *Mersey.* ***Suburb***, 4m/6km W of Birkenhead town centre. **48 B4** SJ2788.
Upton *Norf.* ***Village***, 1m/2km N of Acle. **45 H4** TG3912.
Upton *Northants.* ***Suburb***, 3m/4km W of Northampton town centre. **31 J2** SP7160.
Upton *Notts.* ***Hamlet***, 4m/6km SE of Retford. **51 K5** SK7476.
Upton *Notts.* ***Village***, 2m/4km E of Southwell. **51 K7** SK7354.
Upton *Oxon.* ***Settlement***, 1km W of Burford. SP2412.
Upton *Oxon.* ***Village***, 2m/4km S of Didcot. **21 J3** SU5186.
Upton *Pembs.* ***Settlement***, 3m/5km NE of Pembroke. Contains remains of medieval castle. **16 D4** SN0104.
Upton *Peter.* ***Hamlet***, 6m/9km W of Peterborough. Ailsworth Heath Nature Reserve to NE. **42 E5** TF1000.
Upton *Slo.* ***Suburb***, S district of Slough. **22 C4** SU9879.
Upton *Som.* ***Hamlet***, on edge of Exmoor National Park, 5m/8km E of Dulverton. **7 H3** SS9929.
Upton *Som.* ***Hamlet***, 2m/4km E of Langport. ST4526.
Upton *Warks.* ***Hamlet***, 2m/3km E of Alcester. SP1257.
Upton *W.Yorks.* Population: 5422. ***Village***, 1m/2km N of South Elmsall. **51 G1** SE4713.
Upton *Wilts.* ***Hamlet***, 1m/2km NW of East Knoyle and 6m/9km N of Shaftesbury. ST8732.
Upton Bishop *Here.* ***Village***, 4m/6km NE of Ross-on-Wye. **29 F6** SO6527.
Upton Cheyney *S.Glos.* ***Village***, 5m/8km NW of Bath. **19 K5** ST6969.
Upton Cressett *Shrop.* ***Village***, 4m/6km W of Bridgnorth. **39 F6** SO6592.
Upton Crews *Here.* ***Hamlet***, 4m/6km NE of Ross-on-Wye. SO6427.
Upton Cross *Cornw.* ***Village***, 5m/9km N of Liskeard. **4 C3** SX2872.
Upton End *Beds.* ***Locality***, NE part of Shillington, 3m/5km S of Shefford. **32 E5** TL1234.
Upton Green *Norf.* ***Locality***, adjoining to E of Upton, 1m/2km N of Acle. **45 H4** TG3912.

Upton Grey *Hants.* ***Village***, 4m/7km SE of Basingstoke. **21 K7** SU6948.
Upton Heath *Ches.* ***Suburb***, adjoining to NE of Upton, 2m/3km N of Chester city centre. SJ4169.
Upton Hellions *Devon* ***Village***, on River Creedy, 2m/3km N of Crediton. **7 G5** SS8403.
Upton House *Warks.* ***Historic house***, partly late 17c house (National Trust) 6m/10km NW of Banbury. **30 E4** SP3645.
Upton Lovell *Wilts.* ***Village***, 2m/3km SE of Heytesbury. **20 C7** ST9440.
Upton Magna *Shrop.* ***Village***, 4m/6km E of Shrewsbury. **38 E4** SJ5512.
Upton Noble *Som.* ***Village***, 4m/6km NE of Bruton. **9 G1** ST7139.
Upton Park *Gt.Lon.* ***Suburb***, between West and East Ham in borough of Newham, 6m/10km E of London Bridge. TQ4183.
Upton Park *Poole* ***Leisure/recreation***, country park on N edge of Holes Bay, 1m/2km NW of Poole town centre. Over 50 acres of woodland, farmland, saltmarsh, mudflats and formal gardens surrounding 19c Upton House. Area attracts good selection of wildfowl and woodland birds. **9 J5** SY9992.
Upton Pyne *Devon* ***Village***, 3m/5km N of Exeter. **7 H6** SX9197.
Upton St. Leonards *Glos.* ***Village***, 3m/5km SE of Gloucester. **29 H7** SO8614.
Upton Scudamore *Wilts.* ***Village***, 2m/3km N of Warminster. **20 B7** ST8647.
Upton Snodsbury *Worcs.* ***Village***, 6m/9km E of Worcester. **29 J3** SO9454.
Upton upon Severn *Worcs.* Population: 1756. ***Small town***, on W bank of River Severn, 6m/9km NW of Tewkesbury. **29 H4** SO8540.
Upton Warren *Worcs.* ***Village***, 3m/4km SW of Bromsgrove. **29 J2** SO9267.
Upwaltham *W.Suss.* ***Hamlet***, 5m/9km SW of Petworth. **12 C5** SU9413.
Upware *Cambs.* ***Settlement***, on E bank of River Cam, 6m/10km S of Ely. **33 J2** TL5370.
Upwell *Norf.* ***Village***, 5m/8km SE of Wisbech. **43 J5** TF5002.
Upwell Fen *Cambs.* ***Open space***, fenland, 4m/7km E of March. **43 H6** TL4895.
Upwell Fen *Norf.* ***Open space***, fenland, 4m/6km SE of Upwell. **43 J6** TL5499.
Upwey *Dorset* ***Locality***, 4m/6km N of Weymouth. **9 F6** SY6684.
Upwick Green *Herts.* ***Hamlet***, 3m/5km NW of Bishop's Stortford. TL4524.
Upwood *Cambs.* ***Village***, 2m/4km SW of Ramsey. **43 F7** TL2582.
Ura Firth *Shet.* ***Sea feature***, large inlet of St. Magnus Bay on W coast of Mainland, separated from Ronas Voe to N by neck of land 1m/2km wide. **108 B5** HU2977.
Uradale *Shet.* ***Settlement***, 1m/2km SE of Scalloway, Mainland. **109 D9** HU4038.
Urafirth *Shet.* ***Settlement***, at head of inlet of Ura, with small Loch of Urafirth to N. **108 C5** HU3078.
Urchany *High.* ***Locality***, 5m/7km S of Nairn. **97 F7** NH8849.
Urchany and Farley Forest *High.* ***Open space***, plateau 4m/6km W of Beauly. **96 B7** NH4647.
Urchfont *Wilts.* ***Village***, 4m/6km SE of Devizes. **20 D6** SU0457.
Urdimarsh *Here.* ***Settlement***, 5m/8km N of Hereford. **28 E4** SO5249.
Ure *Arg. & B.* ***River***, in Argyll, with head waters to N and W of Beinn Trilleachan, running W down Glen Ure to River Creran. **80 B3** NN0348.
Ure (Formerly known as Yore.) *N.Yorks.* ***River***, rising on Abbotside Common, 5m/8km NW of Hawes, and flowing SE by Hawes, Aysgarth, Middleham, Masham, Ripon and Boroughbridge to join River Swale, 2m/4km E of Boroughbridge, and form River Ouse. Valley above Masham is known as Wensleydale. **57 J3** SE4365.
Ure *Shet.* ***Settlement***, near N coast of Esha Ness, Mainland. **108 B5** HU2279.
Ure Bank *N.Yorks.* ***Locality***, 1m/2km N of Ripon across River Ure. SE3172.
Urgashay *Som.* ***Locality***, 3m/5km NE of Ilchester, beyond Yeovilton airfield. ST5624.
Urgha *W.Isles* ***Locality***, on North Harris, 1m/2km E of Tarbert. **93 G2** NG1799.
Urie *Aber.* ***River***, running SE by Old Rayne and Pitcaple to River Don, 1m/2km SE of Inverurie. **90 E1** NJ7820.
Urie Lingey *Shet.* ***Island***, off N coast of Fetlar 1km N of Urie Ness. **108 F3** HU5995.
Urishay Common *Here.* ***Locality***, 2m/3km N of Michaelchurch Escley. **28 C5** SO3137.
Urlar Burn *P. & K.* ***River***, running NE into River Tay at Aberfeldy. Falls of Moness along course, 1m/2km S of Aberfeldy. **81 K3** NN8549.
Urlay Nook *Stock.* ***Locality***, 2m/3km NW of Yarm. **62 E5** NZ4014.
Urmston *Gt.Man.* Population: 41,804. ***Town***, 5m/8km SW of Manchester. **49 G3** SJ7694.
Urquhart *High.* ***Settlement***, 1m/2km SW of Culbokie. **96 C6** NH5858.
Urquhart *Moray* ***Village***, 4m/7km E of Elgin. **97 K5** NJ2862.
Urquhart Bay *High.* ***Bay***, on NW shore of Loch Ness, 1m/2km E of Drumnadrochit. Rivers Coiltie and Enrick run into bay. NH5229.
Urquhart Castle *High.* ***Castle***, ruins of castle (Historic Scotland) on Strone Point, on Loch Ness. **88 C2** NH5228.
Urr Water *D. & G.* ***River***, issuing from Loch Urr and running S past Dalbeattie to Rough Firth and Solway Firth at Urr Waterfoot. **65 H4** NX8551.
Urra *N.Yorks.* ***Hamlet***, 5m/8km SE of Stokesley. **63 G6** NZ5701.
Urrall Fell *D. & G.* ***Hill***, 3m/4km S of Loch Maberry and 8m/13km SE of Barrhill. Height 604 feet or 184 metres. **64 C3** NX2870.
Urray *High.* ***Locality***, containing settlements of Wester, Old and Easter Urray, 2m/3km NW of Muir of Ord. **96 C6** NH5052.
Urvaig *Arg. & B.* ***Coastal feature***, headland at N point of Tiree, 1m/2km NW of Rubha Dubh. **78 B2** NM0850.
Usan *Angus* *Alternative name for Fishtown of Usan, qv.*
Ushaw Moor *Dur.* Population: 6159. ***Village***, 3m/5km W of Durham. **62 D2** NZ2242.
Usk (Wysg). ***River***, rising SW of Trecastle and flowing N to Usk Reservoir, E to Trecastle and Brecon, SE to Crickhowell and Abergavenny, then S by Usk and Newport to mouth of River Severn, S of Newport. River noted for salmon-fishing. **19 G2** ST3281.
Usk (Brynbuga). *Mon.* Population: 2187. ***Small town***, market town on River Usk, on site of Roman fort of Burrium. Remains of Norman castle. Old malt barn houses Gwent Rural Life Museum. **19 G1** SO3700.
Usk Reservoir *Carmar.* ***Reservoir***, large reservoir in course of River Usk, on border with Powys, 3m/5km W of Trecastle. Afforestation on either side. **27 G6** SN8228.
Uskmouth *Newport* ***Locality***, 1km W of Nash, near E bank of River Usk at its mouth. Power station. ST3383.
Usselby *Lincs.* ***Hamlet***, 3m/5km N of Market Rasen. **52 D3** TF0993.
Usworth *T. & W.* ***Suburb***, N district of Washington. NZ3058.
Utkinton *Ches.* ***Hamlet***, 2m/3km N of Tarporley. SJ5465.
Utley *W.Yorks.* ***Suburb***, N district of Keighley. **57 F5** SE0542.
Uton *Devon* ***Hamlet***, 1m/2km S of Crediton. **7 G6** SX8298.
Utterby *Lincs.* ***Village***, 4m/6km N of Louth. **53 G3** TF3093.
Uttoxeter *Staffs.* Population: 10,329. ***Town***, busy market town, 13m/21km NE of Stafford. Racecourse. **40 C2** SK0933.
Uwch-mynydd *Gwyn.* ***Open space***, area of hillside on N side of Mawddach estuary, 4m/6km NE of Barmouth. **37 F3** SH6520.
Uwchmynydd *Gwyn.* ***Locality***, 2m/3km W of Aberdaron. **36 A3** SH1525.
Uxbridge *Gt.Lon.* ***Town***, old market town in borough of Hillingdon, 6m/10km NE of Slough and 15m/25km W of Charing Cross. Former coaching stop on London to Oxford road. Brunel University to S. **22 D3** TQ0584.
Uxellodunum *Cumb.* *See Castlesteads.*
Uyea *Shet.* ***Island***, off N coast of Mainland. **108 C3** HU3192.
Uyea *Shet.* ***Island***, of about 600 acres or 240 hectares off S coast of Unst opposite Uyeasound. **108 E3** HU6099.
Uyea Sound *Shet.* ***Sea feature***, strait running between Unst and Uyea. Uyeasound village on S coast of Unst at head of the sound. **108 E3** HP5901.
Uyeasound *Shet.* ***Village***, on S coast of Unst, at head of Uyea Sound. **108 E2** HP5901.
Uynarey *Shet.* ***Island***, uninhabited island off SW coast of Yell, 1m/2km NW of Ulsta and 3m/5km W of Hamna Voe. **108 D4** HU4480.
Uzmaston *Pembs.* ***Village***, 1m/2km SE of Haverfordwest. **16 C3** SM9714.

V

Vacasay Island *W.Isles* ***Island***, small uninhabited island in East Loch Roag close to shore of Great Bernera. NB1836.
Vaccasay *W.Isles* ***Island***, small uninhabited island in Sound of Harris 1km off NE coast of North Uist. NF9774.
Vachelich *Pembs.* ***Settlement***, 2m/3km E of St. David's. SM7725.
Vachery Pond *Surr.* ***Lake/loch***, about 1m/2km long, 1m/2km SE of Cranleigh. **12 D3** TQ0737.
Vacsay *W.Isles* ***Island***, small uninhabited island in West Loch Roag, W coast of Isle of Lewis, 1m/2km W of Great Bernera. **100 D4** NB1137.
Vagar Hill *Here.* ***Mountain***, 2m/3km SW of Dorstone. Height 1420 feet or 433 metres. **28 B5** SO2839.
Vaila *Shet.* ***Island***, of about 1 square mile or 3 square km off Mainland at entrance to Vaila Sound. **109 B8** HU2346.
Vaila Sound *Shet.* ***Sea feature***, inlet between Mainland and Vaila, containing smaller island of Linga. At head of sound is village of Walls. **109 B8** HU2346.
Vaivoe *Shet.* ***Settlement***, at head of small bay of Vai Voe, on N coast of Whalsay, 2m/3km NE of Brough. HU5766.
Vale of Belvoir ***Valley***, broad valley to W of Belvoir, running NE to SW from Nottinghamshire into Leicestershire and Lincolnshire. **42 A2** SK7435.
Vale of Berkeley ***Valley***, low-lying area straddling Gloucestershire and South Gloucestershire, between Cotswold Hills and River Severn estuary in vicinity of Berkeley. **19 K2** ST6090.
Vale of Catmose *Rut.* ***Valley***, surrounding Oakham and extending NE towards Market Overton. Levelled by weathering of Upper Lias rock. **42 B4** SK8709.
Vale of Clwyd *Denb.* ***Valley***, carrying River Clwyd NE between Rhewl and St. Asaph. **47 J5** SJ0867.
Vale of Conwy *Conwy* ***Valley***, part of valley of River Conwy extending N from Betws-y-coed to estuary at Conwy. **47 F6** SH7769.
Vale of Edale *Derbys.* ***Valley***, part of River Noe Valley surrounding Edale. **50 D4** SK1285.
Vale of Edeyrnion *Denb.* *Alternative name for Dyffryn Edeirnion, qv.*
Vale of Evesham *Worcs.* ***Valley***, low-lying, fertile land skirting N fringe of Cotswold Hills between Evesham and Stratford-upon-Avon. **30 C4** SP0344.
Vale of Ffestiniog *Gwyn.* ***Valley***, carrying River Dwyryd W from Ffestiniog to coast at Penrhyndeudraeth. **37 F1** SH6640.
Vale of Gloucester *Glos.* ***Valley***, fertile plain running from NE to SW of Gloucester below escarpment of Cotswold Hills. **29 H6** SO8318.
Vale of Lanherne *Cornw.* *Alternative name for Vale of Mawgan, qv.*
Vale of Llangollen *Denb.* *See Llangollen.*
Vale of Mawgan (Also known as Vale of Lanherne.) *Cornw.* ***Valley***, narrow, wooded valley carrying River Menalhyl and running NW by St. Mawgan to sea at Mawgan Porth. **3 F2** SW8666.
Vale of Neath *N.P.T.* ***Valley***, carrying River Neath SW between Glyn Neath and Aberdulais. **18 A1** SS7899.
Vale of Pewsey *Wilts.* ***Valley***, plain surrounded on N, S and E sides by chalk hills and extending W to Devizes. **20 D5** SU1660.
Vale of Pickering *N.Yorks.* ***Valley***, broad valley between Pickering and Malton, created by periglacial meltwater channel. **58 C1** SE7984.
Vale of Rheidol Railway *Cere.* ***Other feature of interest***, narrow gauge steam railway running 12m/19km from Aberystwyth to Devil's Bridge, climbing 600 feet or 183 metres. **27 F1** SN5881.
Vale of Taunton Dean *Som.* *Occasional spelling of Vale of Taunton Deane, qv.*
Vale of Taunton Deane (Sometimes spelled Vale of Taunton Dean.) *Som.* ***Valley***, fertile plain between Quantock and Black Down Hills, extending roughly from Taunton (E) to Milverton (W). **7 K3** ST2224.
Vale of White Horse *Oxon.* ***Valley***, carrying River Ock, N of Lambourn Downs. Named after carving of horse into chalk slope at Whitehorse Hill, 6m/10km W of Wantage. **21 F3** SU3090.
Vale Royal Abbey *Ches.* ***Ecclesiastical building***, scant remains of formerly impressive Cistercian abbey, 3m/5km SW of Northwich. **49 F6** SJ6369.
Valla Field *Shet.* ***Inland physical feature***, hill ridge on Unst, extending N between Lunda Wick and Loch of Watlee. **108 E2** HP5807.
Vallay *W.Isles* ***Island***, off N coast of North Uist 2m/3km E of Griminis Point. Island measures 3m/4km E to W and about 1km N to S. **92 C4** NF7776.
Vallay Strand *W.Isles* ***Coastal feature***, mudflats separating Vallay from North Uist; fordable at low tide. **92 C4** NF7776.
Valle Crucis Abbey *Denb.* ***Ecclesiastical building***, remains of 13c abbey (Cadw), 1m/2km NW of Llangollen. To N is Eliseg's Pillar, remains of 9c cross (Cadw). **38 B1** SJ2044.
Valley (Dyffryn). *I.o.A.* ***Village***, on Anglesey, at convergence of road and railway at approach to Stanley Embankment, which carries them across strait to Holy Island. Valley Airfield 3m/4km SE. **46 A5** SH2979.
Valley End *Surr.* ***Hamlet***, 2m/3km NW of Chobham. SU9563.
Valley Gardens *Surr.* ***Garden***, 400 acres of woodland in Windsor Great Park, 1m/2km SW of Englefield Green, with national collection of hollies, dwarf conifers, magnolias and rhododendron species; heather garden; autumn colours. **22 C5** SU9769.
Valley Truckle *Cornw.* ***Hamlet***, 1km SW of Camelford. **4 B2** SX1082.
Valleyfield *D. & G.* ***Settlement***, 3m/5km N of Kirkcudbright. **65 G5** NX6756.
Valleyfield *Fife* Population: 3162. ***Locality***, comprises High and Low Valleyfield, 1m/2km E of Culross. **75 J2** NT0086.
Vallum *See Hadrian's Wall.*
Valsgarth *Shet.* ***Locality***, on Unst, 1km N of Haroldswick. **108 F1** HP6413.
Valtos *W.Isles* *Anglicised form of Bhaltos, qv.*
Van *Caerp.* ***Locality***, on E side of Caerphilly. ST1686.
Van *Powys* *English form of Y Fan, qv.*
Vange *Essex* ***Suburb***, S district of Basildon. **24 D3** TQ7287.
Vardre (Faerdre). *Swan.* ***Suburb***, of Clydach, 6m/10km NE of Swansea. **17 K4** SN6901.
Varteg (Y Farteg). *Torfaen* ***Hamlet***, 2m/3km N of Abersychan. **19 F1** SO2606.
Varteg Hill *N.P.T.* ***Mountain***, 1km SE of Ystalyfera. Height 1155 feet or 352 metres. **18 A1** SN7707.
Vat Burn *Aber.* ***River***, rising on Culblean Hill and flowing E to Loch Kinord. **90 C5** NO4399.
Vatarsay (Gaelic form: Bhatarsaidh.) *W.Isles* ***Island***, islet at entrance to Loch Leurbost, E coast of Isle of Lewis. NB4023.
Vaternish *High.* ***Coastal feature***, peninsula on Skye, on W side of Loch Snizort, culminating in headland of Vaternish Point. **93 H6** NG2658.
Vaternish Point *High.* ***Coastal feature***, headland on peninsula of Vaternish, Skye. **93 H5** NG2658.
Vatersay (Gaelic form: Bhatarsaigh.) *W.Isles* ***Island***, irregularly shaped island of about 3 square miles or 8 square km, off SW end of Barra across narrow Sound of Vatersay. **84 B5** NL6395.
Vatersay (Gaelic form: Bhatarsaigh.) *W.Isles* ***Settlement***, on S part of Vatersay. **84 B5** NL6394.
Vatersay Bay (Gaelic form: Bhatarsaigh Bay.) *W.Isles* ***Bay***, on E coast of Vatersay. **84 B5** NL6495.
Vatisker (Gaelic form: Bhatasgeir.) *W.Isles* ***Settlement***, near E coast of Isle of Lewis, 1km S of Bac. NB4839.
Vatisker Point *W.Isles* *Anglicised form of Rubha Bhataisgeir, qv.*
Vatsetter *Shet.* ***Settlement***, near E coast of Yell, 2m/3km SE of Mid Yell. HU5389.
Vatten *High.* ***Settlement***, on Skye, on E side of Loch Vatten at head of Loch Bracadale, 3m/5km SE of Dunvegan. **93 H7** NG2843.
Vaul *Arg. & B.* ***Settlement***, on W side of Vaul Bay, on N coast of Tiree, 2m/4km N of Scarinish. 1c-3c Dùn Mòr Vaul to NW. **78 B3** NM0448.
Vauxhall *Gt.Lon.* ***Suburb***, in borough of Lambeth, between Lambeth and Vauxhall Bridges. TQ3078.
Vauxhall *W.Mid.* ***Suburb***, 1m/2km E of Birmingham city centre. SP0887.
Vaynor (Y Faenor). *M.Tyd.* ***Hamlet***, 3m/4km N of Merthyr Tydfil. **27 K7** SO0410.
Vaynor Park *Powys* ***Settlement***, 1km SW of Aberriw. **38 A5** SJ1700.
Ve Ness *Ork.* ***Coastal feature***, headland on S coast of Mainland. **107 C7** HY3705.

Ve Skerries *Shet.* ***Island***, group of rocks 3m/5km NW of Papa Stour. **109 A6** HU1065.
Veantrow Bay *Ork.* ***Bay***, wide bay on N coast of Shapinsay. **106 D5** HY5020.
Veaullt *Powys* ***Settlement***, 4m/6km NE of Painscastle. **28 A3** SO1951.
Veensgarth *Shet.* ***Village***, on Mainland, 4m/6km NW of Lerwick. **109 D8** HU4244.
Veilish Point *W.Isles* ***Coastal feature***, headland on North Uist, 2m/3km N of Solas. **92 D4** NF8178.
Velator *Devon* ***Hamlet***, just S of Braunton. SS4835.
Velindre *Carmar.* *Alternative spelling of Felindre, qv.*
Velindre (Felindre). *Pembs.* ***Hamlet***, on River Nyfer, 3m/4km E of Newport. **16 E1** SN1039.
Velindre (Felindre). *Powys* ***Hamlet***, 3m/4km NE of Talgarth. **28 A5** SO1836.
Vellan Head *Cornw.* ***Coastal feature***, headland on W side of Lizard peninsula, 3m/5km NW of Lizard Point. **2 D7** SW6614.
Vellow *Som.* ***Settlement***, 3m/5km SE of Watchet. **7 J2** ST0938.
Vementry *Shet.* ***Island***, uninhabited island of about 1000 acres or 400 hectares off W coast of Mainland, on S side of strait of Swarbacks Minn. Largest of the uninhabited islands of Shetland. Varied landscape with much bird life. **109 B6** HU2960.
Venchen Hill *Sc.Bord.* ***Hill***, 1m/2km N of Town Yetholm. Height 882 feet or 269 metres. **70 D1** NT8129.
Veness *Ork.* ***Settlement***, near to SE coast of Eday. **106 E5** HY5729.
Venn *Devon* ***Hamlet***, 3m/4km NW of Kingsbridge. **5 H6** SX7046.
Venn Green *Devon* ***Hamlet***, 5m/8km NE of Holsworthy. SS3711.
Venn Ottery *Devon* ***Village***, 3m/5km SW of Ottery St. Mary. **7 J6** SY0791.
Vennington *Shrop.* ***Settlement***, 1m/2km W of Westbury. **38 C5** SJ3309.
Venny Tedburn *Devon* ***Hamlet***, 2m/3km SW of Crediton. SX8297.
Venta *Hants.* *See Winchester.*
Venta Icenorum *Norf.* *See Caistor St. Edmund.*
Venta Silurum *Mon.* *See Caerwent.*
Venterdon *Cornw.* ***Village***, 3m/5km N of Callington. SX3574.
Ventnor *I.o.W.* Population: 5710. ***Small town***, S coast resort and residential town, 3m/4km SW of Shanklin. **11 G7** SZ5677.
Ventnor Botanic Gardens *I.o.W.* ***Garden***, 1m/2km SW of Ventnor, S of Ventnor Bay. Sheltered beneath The Undercliff, garden specialises in growing Mediterranean and exotic plants too tender for British Isles. **11 G7** SZ5476.
Venton *Devon* ***Hamlet***, 3m/5km W of Ivybridge. SX5956.
Venus Hill *Herts.* ***Settlement***, 3m/4km E of Chesham. TL0101.
Ver *Herts.* ***River***, rising at Redbourn and flowing S past W side of St. Albans into River Colne between St. Albans and Watford. **32 E7** TL1401.
Vercovicium *Northumb.* *See Housesteads.*
Vermuden's Drain *Cambs.* *Alternative name for Forty Foot Drain, qv.*
Vernemetum *Notts.* *See Willoughby-on-the-Wolds.*
Vernham Dean *Hants.* ***Village***, 3m/5km NW of Hurstbourne Tarrant. Jacobean manor house 1km E. **21 G6** SU3456.
Vernham Street *Hants.* ***Hamlet***, 1km NE of Vernham Dean. **21 G6** SU3557.
Vernolds Common *Shrop.* ***Settlement***, 3m/5km SE of Craven Arms. **38 D7** SO4780.
Vernonae *Leics.* *See High Cross.*
Verteris Roman Fort *Cumb.* ***Historic/prehistoric site***, Roman fort containing remains of 12c castle, on SW side of Brough. **61 J5** NY7914.
Verulamium *Herts.* *See St. Albans.*
Verulamium Museum *Herts.* ***Other feature of interest***, museum in St. Albans city centre, with Roman mosaics, hypocaust and artefacts on display. **22 E1** TL1507.
Verwig (Y Ferwig). *Cere.* ***Hamlet***, 2m/4km N of Cardigan. **26 A4** SN1849.
Verwood *Dorset* Population: 8926. ***Locality***, scattered locality, 4m/7km NW of Ringwood. **10 B4** SU0808.
Veryan *Cornw.* ***Village***, 1m/2km inland from Veryan Bay and 7m/11km SW of Mevagissey. Noted for 19c thatched round houses. John Nash designed Caerhayes House. **3 G5** SW9139.
Veryan Bay *Cornw.* ***Bay***, extending E from Nare Head to Dodman Point, 9m/14km SW of St. Austell. **3 G5** SW9739.
Veryan Green *Cornw.* ***Hamlet***, to NE of Veryan, 5m/8km SE of Probus. SW9139.
Vicarage *Devon* ***Settlement***, 1km from coast, 2m/3km W of Beer. **8 B6** SY2089.
Vicarage Green *Beds.* ***Locality***, adjoining to N of Bromham, 3m/5km NW of Bedford. TL0151.
Vickerstown *Cumb.* ***Suburb***, on Isle of Walney, opposite Barrow-in-Furness and connected by causeway. **54 E3** SD1868.
Victoria ***Locality***, straddling border of South Yorkshire and West Yorkshire, 5m/7km NW of Penistone. SE1705.
Victoria *B.Gwent* ***Locality***, adjoining to S of Ebbw Vale. SO1707.
Victoria *Cornw.* ***Hamlet***, 6m/10km SW of Bodmin. **3 G2** SW9861.
Victoria and Albert Museum *Gt.Lon.* ***Leisure/recreation***, Britain's national museum of art and design, in borough of Kensington & Chelsea, 3m/4km SW of Charing Cross. Contains some of world's finest collections of furniture, ceramics, glass, metalwork, jewellery, textiles and dress from Middle Ages to 20c, as well as paintings, prints, drawings, posters, photographs and sculpture. Over 300 paintings hang along length of restored Great Staircase in Henry Cole wing. TQ2679.
Victoria Falls *High.* ***Waterfall***, in Slattadale Forest near S shore of Loch Maree, 1m/2km NW of Talladale. **94 E4** NG8971.
Victoria Park *Gt.Man.* ***Suburb***, 2m/3km SE of Manchester city centre. SJ8595.
Vidlin *Shet.* ***Village***, on E coast of Mainland, at head of Vidlin Voe, 1m/2km N of Dury Voe. **109 D6** HU4765.
Vidlin Voe *Shet.* ***Sea feature***, inlet on E coast of Mainland, with village of Vidlin at its head, 1m/2km N of Dury Voe. **109 D6** HU4765.
Viewfield *Fife* ***Suburb***, in SW part of Glenrothes. NT2599.
Viewfield *High.* ***Settlement***, 2m/3km W of Thurso. **105 F2** ND0767.
Viewing Hill *Dur.* ***Mountain***, on Herdship Fell, 2m/3km N of Cow Green Reservoir. Height 2096 feet or 639 metres. **61 J3** NY7833.
Viewpark *N.Lan.* Population: 14,872. ***Suburb***, large suburban development, 2m/3km NW of Bellshill. **75 F4** NS7161.
Vigo *W.Mid.* ***Locality***, 2m/3km S of Brownhills. **40 C5** SK0502.
Vigo Village *Kent* ***Locality***, on North Downs, 3m/4km NE of Wrotham. **24 C5** TQ6461.
Village Bay *W.Isles* *Alternative name for Loch Hirta, qv.*
Village of Ae *D. & G.* *See Ae Village.*
Villavin *Devon* ***Settlement***, 1km SE of Roborough. **6 D4** SS5816.
Vindobala *Northumb.* *See Rudchester Roman Fort.*
Vindolanda *Northumb.* ***Historic/prehistoric site***, well preserved remains of 3c Roman fort (English Heritage) at Chesterholm, 1m/2km NW of Bardon Mill. Museum displays artefacts. **70 C7** NY7766.
Vindomora *Dur.* *See Ebchester.*
Vinegar Hill *Mon.* ***Hamlet***, 1km E of Magor. ST4387.
Vinehall Street *E.Suss.* ***Hamlet***, 3m/4km N of Battle. **14 C5** TQ7520.
Vine's Cross *E.Suss.* ***Village***, 1m/2km E of Horam. **13 J5** TQ5917.
Viney Hill *Glos.* ***Village***, 1m/2km W of Blakeney. **19 K1** SO6506.
Vinny Burn *Angus* ***River***, rising 3m/5km SW of Forfar and flowing by Letham to Lunan Water at Friockheim. **83 G3** NO5949.
Vinovia *Dur.* *See Binchester.*
Vinquoy Chambered Cairn *Ork.* ***Historic/prehistoric site***, Neolithic chambered cairn in N of Eday, just N of Mill Loch. **106 E4** HY5637.
Virginia Water *Surr.* Population: 6304. ***Locality***, residential district, 3m/5km SW of Staines. Named after large lake to NW, on S edge of Windsor Great Park. **22 C5** SU9968.
Virginstow *Devon* ***Village***, 6m/9km NE of Launceston. **6 B6** SX3792.
Virkie *Shet.* ***Locality***, on Mainland, at head of inlet called Pool of Virkie. HU3911.
Virley *Essex* ***Locality***, 4m/7km SE of Tiptree. **34 D7** TL9413.
Virley Channel *Essex* ***Sea feature***, sea channel where South Channel, North Channel, Mersea Quarters and Besom Fleet join River Blackwater estuary on N side of river. **34 E7** TM0110.
Viroconium *Shrop.* *See Wroxeter.*
Viroconium Roman Town *Shrop.* ***Historic/prehistoric site***, in Wroxeter, on River Severn, 5m/8km SE of Shrewsbury. Garrison town founded in AD 58, subsequently became fourth largest civilisation in Roman Britain, but abandoned in 5c-6c. Impressive remains (English Heritage) include large section of wall, part of bath complex and part of forum colonnade. **38 E5** SJ5608.
Vobster *Som.* ***Hamlet***, 4m/7km W of Frome. **20 A7** ST7049.
Voe *Shet.* ***Sea feature***, inlet on SE coast of Mainland, adjacent to Boddam. **109 G9** HU4014.
Voe *Shet.* ***Settlement***, at head of Ronas Voe, Mainland. **108 C4** HU3381.
Voe *Shet.* ***Village***, on Mainland, at head of Olna Firth. **109 D6** HU4063.
Voe of Dale *Shet.* ***Bay***, on W coast of Mainland, with Mu Ness to N and Ness of Bakka to S. **109 A7** HU1751.
Vogrie Country Park *Midloth.* ***Leisure/recreation***, country park 3m/4km NE of Gorebridge. Vogrie Burn flows through park which offers nature trails, walled garden, streams, ponds, golf course and a model railway. **76 B4** NT3763.
Vord Hill *Shet.* ***Hill***, in N part of Fetlar. Height 518 feet or 158 metres. **108 F3** HU6293.
Voreda *Cumb.* *See Castlesteads.*
Vorlan (Y Forlan). *Pembs.* ***Settlement***, 1m/2km S of Maenclochog. SN0826.
Votersay *W.Isles* ***Island***, small uninhabited island off NE coast of North Uist, 3m/5km SE of Berneray. NF9476.
Vowchurch *Here.* ***Village***, in Golden Valley (River Dore), 6m/10km NW of Pontrilas. Unusual timber-framed church dating mostly from 14c. **28 C5** SO3636.
Vowchurch Common *Here.* ***Locality***, upland area to NE of Vowchurch, 4m/6km W of Kingstone. SO3637.
Vownog *Flints.* ***Locality***, adjoining to NE of Soughton. SJ2466.
Voy *Ork.* ***Settlement***, on Mainland, to NW of Loch of Stenness. **107 B6** HY2515.
Vron Gate *Shrop.* ***Settlement***, 2m/3km W of Westbury. SJ3209.
Vuia Beag *W.Isles* ***Island***, small uninhabited island in Loch Roag on W coast of Isle of Lewis, 2m/4km E of Miabhig. **100 D4** NB1233.
Vuia Mòr *W.Isles* ***Island***, uninhabited island in Loch Roag, W coast of Isle of Lewis, close to W shore of Great Bernera. **100 D4** NB1334.
Vulcan Village *Mersey.* ***Suburb***, adjoining to S of Newton-le-Willows. SJ5894.
Vyrnwy *River*, originating in many streams running into Lake Vyrnwy (reservoir), where it flows generally E into River Severn on English-Welsh border, 8m/13km NE of Welshpool. SJ3215.

W

Waas *High.* ***Locality***, in Caithness district, 2m/3km SW of Thurso. ND0766.
Waberthwaite *Cumb.* ***Settlement***, 2m/3km SE of Ravenglass across River Esk. SD1095.
Wackerfield *Dur.* ***Hamlet***, 2m/3km NE of Staindrop. **62 C4** NZ1522.
Wacton *Here.* ***Settlement***, 3m/5km NW of Bromyard. SO6157.
Wacton *Norf.* ***Village***, 7m/11km NW of Harleston. **45 F6** TM1791.
Wadbister *Shet.* ***Settlement***, near E coast of Mainland, on S side of Wadbister Voe, 1km W of Lambgarth Head, headland at end of promontory of Wadbister Ness. HU4349.
Wadbister Voe *Shet.* ***Bay***, on E coast of Mainland, to S of Girlsta. **109 D8** HU4350.
Wadborough *Worcs.* ***Village***, 3m/5km NW of Pershore. **29 J4** SO9047.
Waddesdon *Bucks.* ***Village***, 5m/8km W of Aylesbury. **31 J7** SP7416.
Waddesdon Manor *Bucks.* ***Historic house***, late 19c house (National Trust) in French Renaissance style to SW of Waddesdon, 6m/9km NW of Aylesbury. **31 J7** SP7316.
Waddeton *Devon* ***Hamlet***, to N of River Dart estuary, 3m/5km W of Brixham. SX8756.
Waddicar *Mersey.* ***Suburb***, adjoining to NW of Kirkby. SJ3999.
Waddingham *Lincs.* ***Village***, 4m/6km SE of Kirton in Lindsey. **52 C3** SK9896.
Waddington *Lancs.* ***Village***, 2m/3km NW of Clitheroe. **56 C5** SD7243.
Waddington *Lincs.* Population: 4781. ***Village***, 5m/7km S of Lincoln. Airfield to E. **52 C6** SK9764.
Waddingworth *Lincs.* ***Locality***, 4m/7km E of Bardney. **52 E5** TF1871.
Waddon *Devon* ***Hamlet***, 1m/2km E of Chudleigh. SX8879.
Waddon *Gt.Lon.* ***Suburb***, in borough of Croydon, 1m/2km W of Croydon town centre. TQ3164.
Wade Hall *Lancs.* ***Suburb***, to W of Leyland. SD5221.
Wadebridge *Cornw.* Population: 5291. ***Small town***, busy market town and former port on River Camel, 6m/10km NW of Bodmin. Fine medieval bridge, 320 feet or 97 metres long, with 14 arches. **3 G1** SW9972.
Wadebridge Bridge *Cornw.* ***Bridge***, medieval stone bridge at Wadebridge across River Camel, near its mouth. Longest bridge in Cornwall, consisting of 15 arches and spanning 400 feet or 122 metres. SW9972.
Wadeford *Som.* ***Village***, 2m/3km NW of Chard. **8 C3** ST3110.
Wadenhoe *Northants.* ***Village***, 4m/6km SW of Oundle. **42 D7** TL0183.
Wade's Bridge *P. & K.* ***Other feature of interest***, bridge across River Tay, started by General Wade in 1733 and considered finest of his bridges. On NW side of Aberfeldy. **81 K3** NN8549.
Wadesmill *Herts.* ***Village***, 2m/3km N of Ware. **33 G7** TL3517.
Wadhurst *E.Suss.* Population: 4248. ***Village***, on The Weald, 6m/10km SE of Royal Tunbridge Wells. **13 K3** TQ6431.
Wadshelf *Derbys.* ***Village***, 4m/7km W of Chesterfield. **51 F5** SK3170.
Wadsley *S.Yorks.* ***Suburb***, 3m/4km NW of Sheffield city centre. SK3290.
Wadsley Bridge *S.Yorks.* ***Suburb***, 1m/2km NE of Wadsley. **51 F3** SK3391.
Wadsworth Moor *W.Yorks.* ***Open space***, moorland 4m/6km N of Hebden Bridge, with Walshaw Dean Reservoirs on W side. **56 E6** SD9733.
Wadworth *S.Yorks.* ***Village***, 4m/6km S of Doncaster. **51 H3** SK5697.
Wadworth Hill *E.Riding* ***Settlement***, 3m/4km E of Hedon. **59 J7** TA2329.
Waen *Denb.* ***Hamlet***, 1km NW of Nantglyn. SH9962.
Waen *Denb.* ***Hamlet***, 4m/6km E of Denbigh. **47 K6** SJ1065.
Waen Aberwheeler *Denb.* ***Hamlet***, 4m/6km NE of Denbigh. SJ0969.
Waen-fâch *Powys* ***Settlement***, 6m/10km N of Welshpool. **38 B4** SJ2017.
Waen-pentir *Gwyn.* ***Locality***, 4m/6km S of Bangor. SH5766.
Waen-wen *Gwyn.* ***Hamlet***, 2m/3km S of Bangor. **46 D6** SH5768.
Wag *High.* ***Settlement***, in Langwell Forest, on N bank of Langwell Water, 2m/3km S of Morven. **105 F6** ND0126.
Wagg *Som.* ***Hamlet***, adjoining to NE of Huish Episcopi, 1km E of Langport. ST4326.
Waggle Hill *Aber.* ***Hill***, 3m/4km S of Cuminestown. Height 584 feet or 178 metres. **99 G6** NJ8046.
Wain Lee *Staffs.* ***Settlement***, 1m/2km SW of Biddulph. SJ8655.
Wainfelin *Torfaen* ***Suburb***, to NW of Pontypool. SO2701.
Wainfleet *Lincs.* *Alternative name for Wainfleet All Saints, qv.*
Wainfleet All Saints (Also known as Wainfleet.) *Lincs.* ***Small town***, historic town and former port on Steeping River, 5m/8km SW of Skegness. **53 H7** TF4958.
Wainfleet Bank *Lincs.* ***Hamlet***, 2m/3km W of Wainfleet All Saints. **53 H7** TF4759.
Wainfleet St. Mary *Lincs.* ***Hamlet***, to S of Wainfleet All Saints across Steeping River. TF4957.
Wainfleet Sand *Lincs.* ***Coastal feature***, mudflats 4m/7km S of Skegness. **53 J7** TF5355.
Wainfleet Tofts *Lincs.* ***Locality***, 1m/2km S of Wainfleet All Saints. TF4957.
Wainford *Norf.* ***Settlement***, on River Waveney, 1m/2km E of Bungay. TM3490.
Waingroves *Derbys.* ***Hamlet***, 1m/2km SE of Ripley. SK4149.
Wainhope *Northumb.* ***Forest/woodland***, to N of Kielder Water, 3m/4km E of Kielder. **70 B4** NY6793.

Wainhouse Corner *Cornw.* ***Hamlet***, 7m/11km SW of Bude. **4 B1** SX1895.
Wainscott *Med.* ***Locality***, 2m/3km N of Rochester. **24 D4** TQ7471.
Wainstalls *W.Yorks.* ***Village***, 4m/6km NW of Halifax. **57 F7** SE0428.
Waitby *Cumb.* ***Hamlet***, 1m/2km W of Kirkby Stephen. **61 J6** NY7508.
Waithwith *N.Yorks.* ***Locality***, on W edge of Catterick Camp, 2m/4km S of Richmond. SE1597.
Wake Green *W.Mid.* ***Suburb***, 3m/5km S of Birmingham city centre. SP0882.
Wakefield *W.Yorks.* Population: 73,955. ***City***, on River Calder, 8m/13km S of Leeds. Former cloth and grain port. 13c cathedral of All Saints is former parish church, with tallest spire in Yorkshire. 14c St. Mary's Chantry Chapel, important medieval toll chapel on bridge over River Calder. **57 J7** SE3320.
Wakefield Cathedral *W.Yorks.* ***Ecclesiastical building***, restored 13c parish church in centre of Wakefield, elevated to cathedral status in 1888. Style is mainly Perpendicular; has spire, tallest in whole of Yorkshire, attaining 247 feet or 75 metres. **57 J7** SE3320.
Wakehurst Place *W.Suss.* ***Garden***, National Trust garden administered and maintained by Royal Botanic Gardens at Kew, 1m/2km N of Ardingly. Contains exotic trees and plants; winter, water and rock gardens. **13 G3** TQ3331.
Wakerley *Northants.* ***Village***, 7m/11km SW of Stamford. **42 C6** SP9599.
Wakerley Bridge ***Bridge***, 14c stone bridge over River Welland, 81 feet or 25 metres long, 6m/9km E of Uppingham, connecting Northamptonshire and Rutland. SP9599.
Wakes Colne *Essex* ***Village***, 5m/7km E of Halstead. **34 C6** TL8928.
Wakey Hill *Cumb.* ***Hill***, in wooded area 2m/3km E of Catlowdy. Height 663 feet or 202 metres. **69 K6** NY4876.
Walberswick *Suff.* ***Village***, at mouth of River Blyth, 1m/2km SW of Southwold across river. (No bridge or ferry). **35 J1** TM4974.
Walberton *W.Suss.* ***Village***, 3m/5km W of Arundel. **12 C6** SU9706.
Walburn *N.Yorks.* ***Locality***, 4m/6km N of Leyburn. Hall is fortified house of 16c. SE1195.
Walbury Hill *W.Berks.* ***Hill***, highest point on chalk downs in Britain, with ancient fort, 5m/8km SE of Hungerford. Height 974 feet or 297 metres. **21 G5** SU3761.
Walcot *Lincs.* ***Village***, 7m/11km S of Sleaford. **42 D2** TF0635.
Walcot *Lincs.* ***Village***, 8m/13km NE of Sleaford. **52 E7** TF1356.
Walcot *N.Lincs.* ***Settlement***, just S of Alkborough. **58 E7** SE8721.
Walcot *Shrop.* ***Locality***, 3m/4km SE of Bishop's Castle. **38 C7** SO3484.
Walcot *Swin.* ***Suburb***, of Swindon comprising Walcot East and Walcot West, 1m/2km E and 1m/2km SE of town centre respectively. SU1684.
Walcot *Tel. & W.* ***Hamlet***, 4m/6km W of Wellington. **38 E4** SJ5911.
Walcot *Warks.* ***Settlement***, 3m/4km E of Alcester. SP1258.
Walcot Dales *Lincs.* ***Settlement***, on W bank of River Witham, 1m/2km W of Tattershall. **52 E7** TF1957.
Walcot Green *Norf.* ***Village***, 1km NE of Diss. **45 F7** TM1280.
Walcote *Leics.* ***Village***, 2m/3km E of Lutterworth. **41 H7** SP5683.
Walcote *Warks.* ***Hamlet***, 2m/3km E of Alcester. **30 C3** SP1258.
Walcott *Norf.* ***Hamlet***, on coast, 2m/3km NW of Happisburgh. **45 H2** TG3632.
Walden *N.Yorks.* ***Locality***, in valley on Walden Beck, 3m/4km S of West Burton. **57 F1** SE0082.
Walden Head *N.Yorks.* ***Settlement***, near head of Walden Beck, 5m/8km S of Aysgarth. **56 E1** SD9880.
Walden Stubbs *N.Yorks.* ***Village***, 2m/3km SE of Womersley. **51 H1** SE5516.
Waldersey *Cambs.* ***Open space***, fenland 4m/7km N of March. **43 H5** TF4103.
Walderslade *Med.* ***Suburb***, 3m/5km S of Chatham town centre. **24 D5** TQ7663.
Walderton *W.Suss.* ***Village***, 4m/7km NE of Emsworth. **11 J3** SU7910.
Walditch *Dorset* ***Village***, 1m/2km E of Bridport. **8 D5** SY4892.
Waldley *Derbys.* ***Settlement***, 4m/6km NW of Sudbury. **40 D2** SK1237.
Waldon *Devon* ***River***, tributary of River Torridge, rising 2m/4km NW of Bradworthy and flowing into River Torridge 1m/2km SW of Shebbear. **6 B4** SS4207.
Waldridge *Dur.* ***Village***, 2m/3km SW of Chester-le-Street. **62 D1** NZ2550.
Waldringfield *Suff.* ***Village***, with quay on W bank of River Deben estuary, 3m/5km S of Woodbridge. **35 G4** TM2844.
Waldron *E.Suss.* ***Village***, 3m/4km SW of Heathfield. **13 J5** TQ5419.
Wales *Som.* ***Hamlet***, 1km W of Queen Camel. ST5824.
Wales *S.Yorks.* Population: 5736. ***Village***, 7m/11km W of Worksop. **51 G4** SK4782.
Wales Bar *S.Yorks.* ***Suburb***, adjoining to W of Wales. SK4782.
Walesby *Lincs.* ***Village***, on edge of The Wolds, 3m/4km NE of Market Rasen. Site of Roman building 1km E. **52 E3** TF1392.
Walesby *Notts.* ***Village***, 3m/4km NE of Ollerton. **51 J5** SK6870.
Waleswood *S.Yorks.* ***Settlement***, 1m/2km W of Wales. SK4583.
Walford *Here.* ***Village***, 7m/11km E of Knighton. **28 C1** SO3972.
Walford *Here.* ***Village***, 3m/4km SW of Ross-on-Wye. **28 E6** SO5820.
Walford *Shrop.* ***Settlement***, 6m/10km NW of Shrewsbury. **38 D3** SJ4320.
Walford *Som.* ***Settlement***, 1km E of West Monkton, 4m/6km NE of Taunton. ST2728.
Walford *Staffs.* ***Settlement***, 1km SE of Standon. SJ8133.
Walford Cross *Som.* ***Locality***, 1km E of West Monkton. ST2728.
Walford Heath *Shrop.* ***Hamlet***, 1m/2km SE of Walford. SJ4419.
Walgherton *Ches.* ***Hamlet***, 4m/7km S of Crewe. **39 F1** SJ6948.
Walgrave *Northants.* ***Village***, 6m/10km NW of Wellingborough. 17c hall. **32 B1** SP8072.
Walham Green *Gt.Lon.* ***Suburb***, in borough of Hammersmith and Fulham, 1m/2km N of Wandsworth Bridge. TQ2577.
Walhampton *Hants.* ***Hamlet***, on E bank of Lymington River, opposite Lymington. **10 E5** SZ3395.
Walk Mill *Lancs.* ***Hamlet***, 3m/4km SE of Burnley. **56 D6** SD8629.
Walkden *Gt.Man.* Population: 38,685. ***Locality***, 4m/7km S of Bolton. **49 G2** SD7303.
Walker *T. & W.* ***Suburb***, on N bank of River Tyne, 3m/5km E of Newcastle upon Tyne city centre. **71 H7** NZ2964.
Walker Fold *Lancs.* ***Settlement***, 4m/7km W of Clitheroe. **56 B5** SD6741.
Walkerburn *Sc.Bord.* ***Village***, on River Tweed, 2m/3km E of Innerleithen. **76 B7** NT3637.
Walkeringham *Notts.* ***Village***, 4m/6km NW of Gainsborough. **51 K3** SK7792.
Walkerith *Lincs.* ***Hamlet***, on E bank of River Trent, 3m/5km NW of Gainsborough. **51 K3** SK7893.
Walkern *Herts.* ***Village***, 4m/6km E of Stevenage. **33 F6** TL2826.
Walker's Green *Here.* ***Village***, 5m/8km N of Hereford. **28 E4** SO5247.
Walker's Heath *W.Mid.* ***Suburb***, 5m/9km S of Birmingham city centre. SP0578.
Walkerton *Fife* ***Settlement***, on N bank of River Leven, just W of Leslie. **82 D7** NO2301.
Walkerville *N.Yorks.* ***Locality***, 2m/3km W of Catterick. SE2098.
Walkerwood Reservoir *Gt.Man.* ***Reservoir***, 1m/2km E of Stalybridge. **50 B3** SJ9898.
Walkford *Dorset* ***Suburb***, 1m/2km W of New Milton. SZ2294.
Walkham *Devon* ***River***, rising on central Dartmoor and flowing SW, by Horrabridge, into River Tavy 3m/5km S of Tavistock. SX4769.
Walkhampton *Devon* ***Village***, 5m/7km SE of Tavistock. **5 F4** SX5369.
Walkhampton Common *Devon* ***Open space***, heath 1m/2km SW of Princetown, part of Dartmoor National Park. **5 F3** SX5672.
Walkingham Hill *N.Yorks.* ***Settlement***, 1m/2km W of Staveley, 3m/5km N of Knaresborough. SE3461.
Walkington *E.Riding* Population: 1934. ***Village***, 3m/5km SW of Beverley. **59 G6** SE9937.
Walkley *S.Yorks.* ***Suburb***, 1m/2km NW of Sheffield city centre. SK3388.
Walkley Bank *S.Yorks.* ***Suburb***, to W of Walkley, 2m/3km NW of Sheffield city centre. SK3388.
Walkwood *Worcs.* ***Suburb***, SW district of Redditch. **30 B2** SP0364.
Wall *Cornw.* ***Hamlet***, 3m/5km SW of Camborne. SW6036.
Wall *Northumb.* ***Village***, on S side of Hadrian's Wall, 3m/5km N of Hexham. **70 E7** NY9168.
Wall *Staffs.* ***Village***, 2m/3km SW of Lichfield. Bath house (English Heritage and National Trust) of Roman station of Letocetum. Museum of finds. **40 D5** SK1006.
Wall Bank *Shrop.* ***Settlement***, in Apedale, 3m/5km E of Church Stretton. **38 E6** SO5092.
Wall End *Cumb.* ***Settlement***, 1m/2km N of Soutergate. SD2383.
Wall End *Here.* ***Settlement***, 3m/5km W of Leominster. SO4457.
Wall Heath *W.Mid.* ***Suburb***, 4m/7km W of Dudley town centre. **40 A7** SO8889.
Wall Hill *Gt.Man.* ***Settlement***, 3m/4km N of Mossley. SD9806.
Wall Hills *Here.* ***Historic/prehistoric site***, Iron Age hillfort 3m/5km NW of Bromyard. **29 F3** SO6359.
Wall Houses *Northumb.* ***Settlement***, on line of Hadrian's Wall, 4m/7km NE of Corbridge. NZ0368.
Wall Mead *B. & N.E.Som.* ***Settlement***, 1km N of Timsbury and 3m/5km N of Midsomer Norton. ST6759.
Wall Nook *Dur.* ***Hamlet***, adjoining to N of Langley Park. NZ2145.
Wall under Heywood *Shrop.* ***Village***, 4m/6km E of Church Stretton. **38 E6** SO5092.
Wallace Monument *Stir.* ***Other feature of interest***, monument on hill 2m/3km NE of Stirling, to William Wallace, Scottish knight who raised army which routed English at Battle of Stirling Bridge (1297). As a result he became Protector of the Kingdom. Defeated at Battle of Falkirk (1298) he organized further Scottish resistance against English until he was captured in 1305 and executed by Edward I. **75 G1** NS8195.
Wallacehall *D. & G.* ***Settlement***, 4m/6km NE of Eaglesfield. **69 H6** NY2877.
Wallace's Hill *Sc.Bord.* ***Mountain***, in Cardrona Forest, 2m/3km W of Innerleithen. Height 1506 feet or 459 metres. **76 B7** NT3036.
Wallacetown *Shet.* ***Settlement***, on Mainland, 2m/3km W of Bixter. HU3052.
Wallacetown *S.Ayr.* ***Settlement***, 1m/2km N of Dailly across Water of Girvan. **67 G3** NS2702.
Wallacetown *S.Ayr.* ***Suburb***, N district of Ayr. NS3422.
Walland Marsh *Kent* ***Marsh/bog***, low-lying area NW of Lydd. **14 E5** TQ9823.
Wallands Park *E.Suss.* ***Suburb***, W district of Lewes. TQ4010.
Wallasea Island *Essex* ***Island***, bounded by River Crouch, River Roach, and Paglesham Pool. **25 F2** TQ9693.
Wallasey *Mersey.* Population: 60,895. ***Town***, at N end of Wirral peninsula, beside River Mersey estuary. **48 B3** SJ3291.
Wallaston Green *Pembs.* ***Settlement***, 4m/6km W of Pembroke. SM9200.
Wallbank *Lancs.* ***Village***, 1m/2km SW of Whitworth, to E of Spring Mill Reservoir. SD8817.
Wallbottle *T. & W.* ***Village***, 5m/8km W of Newcastle upon Tyne. **71 G7** NZ1666.
Wallbrook *W.Mid.* ***Suburb***, in N part of Dudley. SO9493.
Wallcrouch *E.Suss.* ***Hamlet***, 1m/2km W of Ticehurst. TQ6630.
Wallend *Med.* ***Locality***, on Isle of Grain, 1m/2km SW of Grain. **24 E4** TQ8775.
Waller's Green *Here.* ***Settlement***, 3m/4km NW of Ledbury. **29 F5** SO6739.
Waller's Haven *E.Suss.* ***River***, fed by Nunningham Stream, Hugletts Stream, and Ash Bourne, rising on high ground S of a line from Heathfield to Battle, and flowing S from Hazard's Green into English Channel at Pevensey Sluice. **13 K6** TQ6805.
Walling Fen *E.Riding* ***Open space***, lowland 3m/5km E of Gilberdyke. **58 E7** SE8729.
Wallingford *Oxon.* Population: 9315. ***Small town***, on River Thames, dating from Saxon times, 12m/19km SE of Oxford. Bridge over River Thames of 13c origin. Annual regatta. **21 K3** SU6089.
Wallington *Gt.Lon.* ***Suburb***, in borough of Sutton, 2m/3km E of Sutton town centre. **23 F5** TQ2864.
Wallington *Hants.* ***Locality***, on Wallington River, 1km E of Fareham. **11 G4** SU5806.
Wallington *Herts.* ***Village***, 3m/5km E of Baldock. **33 F5** TL2933.
Wallington *Wrex.* ***Settlement***, 1m/2km SW of Worthenbury. SJ4145.
Wallington Hall *Northumb.* ***Historic house***, National Trust property built 1688, with alterations and additions of 18c and 19c, 1m/2km S of Cambo. **71 F5** NZ0284.
Wallington Heath *W.Mid.* ***Suburb***, 3m/5km NW of Walsall town centre. SJ9902.
Wallingwells *Notts.* ***Settlement***, 1km W of Carlton in Lindrick. SK5784.
Wallis *Pembs.* ***Settlement***, 1km SE of Ambleston, 7m/11km NE of Haverfordwest. **16 D2** SN0125.
Wallisdown *Bourne.* ***Suburb***, NE district of Poole. **10 B5** SZ0693.
Walliswood *Surr.* ***Hamlet***, 4m/6km E of Cranleigh. **12 E3** TQ1138.
Walls *Shet.* ***Village***, in W district of Mainland known as Walls and Sandness. District also includes village of Sandness. **109 B8** HU2449.
Walls and Sandness *Shet.* ***Locality***, W district of Mainland. District includes villages of Walls and Sandness. HU2449.
Wallsend *T. & W.* Population: 45,280. ***Town***, former mining and ship-building town, 4m/6km E of Newcastle upon Tyne. Name derives from its location at E end of Hadrian's Wall. **71 J7** NZ3066.
Wallston *V. of Glam.* ***Locality***, adjoining Wenvoe, 3m/5km N of Barry. ST1273.
Wallyford *E.Loth.* ***Village***, 1m/2km E of Musselburgh. **76 B3** NT3672.
Walmer *Kent* ***Suburb***, S district of Deal. **15 J2** TR3750.
Walmer Bridge *Lancs.* ***Village***, 5m/8km SW of Preston. **55 H7** SD4724.
Walmer Castle *Kent* ***Castle***, on Channel coast at Walmer, 1m/2km S of Deal. Built as a fort by Henry VIII as defence against French and Spanish and later transformed into stately home. Now official residence of Lord Warden of the Cinque Ports (English Heritage), with Queen Mother's Garden recently opened. **15 J3** TR3750.
Walmersley *Gt.Man.* ***Suburb***, 2m/3km N of Bury town centre. **49 H1** SD8013.
Walmley *W.Mid.* ***Village***, 2m/3km SE of Sutton Coldfield town centre. **40 D6** SP1393.
Walmley Ash *W.Mid.* ***Locality***, 3m/5km SE of Sutton Coldfield. SP1492.
Walmsgate *Lincs.* ***Hamlet***, on N side of parkland, 1m/2km S of Burwell. TF3678.
Walney Island *Cumb.* *See Isle of Walney.*
Walpole *Suff.* ***Village***, 3m/4km SW of Halesworth. **35 H1** TM3674.
Walpole Cross Keys *Norf.* ***Village***, 3m/4km E of Sutton Bridge. **43 J4** TF5119.
Walpole Highway *Norf.* ***Village***, 4m/7km NE of Wisbech. **43 J4** TF5113.
Walpole Island *Norf.* ***Hamlet***, 1m/2km W of Walpole St. Peter. TF4817.
Walpole St. Andrew *Norf.* ***Village***, 6m/9km NE of Wisbech. **43 J4** TF5017.
Walpole St. Peter *Norf.* ***Village***, 5m/8km NE of Wisbech. **43 J4** TF5016.
Walrond's Park *Som.* ***Hamlet***, 4m/6km N of Ilminster. ST3720.
Walrow *Som.* ***Hamlet***, 1km E of Highbridge. ST3347.
Walsall *W.Mid.* Population: 174,739. ***Town***, 8m/13km NW of Birmingham. Range of industries from traditional leather industry to more modern ones. Large open-air market. Walsall Leather Museum in Wisemore. Birthplace of Jerome K. Jerome. **40 C6** SP0198.
Walsall Wood *W.Mid.* ***Locality***, 1m/2km S of Brownhills. **40 C5** SK0403.
Walsden *W.Yorks.* ***Village***, 1m/2km S of Todmorden. **56 E7** SD9322.
Walsgrave on Sowe *W.Mid.* ***Suburb***, 3m/5km NE of Coventry city centre. **41 F7** SP3781.
Walsham le Willows *Suff.* ***Village***, 5m/7km E of Ixworth. **34 E1** TM0071.

Walshaw *Gt.Man.* ***Locality***, 2m/3km NW of Bury. SD7711.
Walshaw Dean Reservoirs *W.Yorks.* ***Reservoir***, two reservoirs 4m/7km N of Hebden Bridge. **56 E6** SD9633.
Walshford *N.Yorks.* ***Hamlet***, on River Nidd, 3m/5km N of Wetherby. SE4153.
Walsingham Abbey *Norf.* ***Ecclesiastical building***, 18c and later abbey, at Little Walsingham. Grounds contain remains of Augustinian priory founded in 1153 to protect original Shrine of Our Lady of Walsingham. Priory was dissolved, with shrine removed and burned during Reformation. **44 D2** TF9336.
Walsoken *Cambs.* ***Suburb***, NE district of Wisbech. **43 H4** TF4710.
Walston *S.Lan.* ***Village***, 5m/8km E of Carnwath. **75 J6** NT0545.
Walsworth *Herts.* ***Suburb***, NE district of Hitchin. **32 E5** TL2030.
Walter's Ash *Bucks.* ***Locality***, residential locality 4m/6km NW of High Wycombe. SU8398.
Walterston (Trewallter). *V. of Glam.* ***Hamlet***, 1m/2km NE of Llancarfan. Site of Roman villa 1km E. ST0671.
Walterstone *Here.* ***Settlement***, 4m/6km SW of Pontrilas. **28 C6** SO3425.
Waltham *Kent* ***Village***, 6m/10km SW of Canterbury. **15 G3** TR1048.
Waltham *N.E.Lincs.* Population: 6157. ***Suburb***, 4m/6km S of Grimsby. **53 F2** TA2603.
Waltham Abbey *Essex* ***Ecclesiastical building***, founded in 1030 at Waltham Abbey, and rebuilt by Harold II, who was buried here after Battle of Hastings. The present church is only a quarter the length of original building. **23 G1** TL3800.
Waltham Abbey *Essex* Population: 15,629. ***Town***, in River Lea valley, 7m/11km SW of Harlow. Abbey built by Henry II; 14c gatehouse (English Heritage). Harold II, killed at Hastings, was buried in original abbey. **23 G1** TL3800.
Waltham Chase *Hants.* Population: 2111. ***Village***, 2m/3km S of Bishop's Waltham. **11 G3** SU5615.
Waltham Cross *Herts.* ***Suburb***, S District of Cheshunt. Eleanor cross restored, erected by Edward I; one of three extant (others at Geddington and Hardingstone). **23 G1** TL3500.
Waltham on the Wolds *Leics.* ***Village***, in elevated position, 5m/8km NE of Melton Mowbray. **42 B3** SK8025.
Waltham St. Lawrence *W. & M.* ***Village***, 3m/4km E of Twyford. Site of Roman temple across railway to N. **22 B4** SU8276.
Waltham's Cross *Essex* ***Settlement***, 2m/3km SE of Finchingfield. TL6930.
Walthamstow *Gt.Lon.* ***Suburb***, in borough of Waltham Forest, 7m/11km NE of London Bridge. **23 G3** TQ3789.
Walton *Bucks.* ***Suburb***, to SE of Aylesbury town centre. **32 B7** SP8213.
Walton *Cumb.* ***Village***, 2m/4km N of Brampton. **70 A7** NY5264.
Walton *Derbys.* ***Hamlet***, 2m/3km SW of Chesterfield. **51 F6** SK3569.
Walton *Leics.* ***Village***, 4m/6km NW of Husbands Bosworth. **41 H7** SP5987.
Walton *Mersey.* ***Suburb***, 3m/5km NE of Liverpool city centre. **48 C3** SJ3695.
Walton *M.K.* ***Village***, in Milton Keynes, 2m/3km NE of Bletchley. **32 B5** SP8936.
Walton *Peter.* ***Suburb***, 3m/4km NW of Peterborough city centre. **42 E5** TF1701.
Walton *Powys* ***Hamlet***, 3m/5km E of New Radnor. **28 B3** SO2559.
Walton *Shrop.* ***Settlement***, 3m/5km SE of Craven Arms. SO4679.
Walton *Som.* ***Village***, 1m/2km W of Street. 1m/2km S are Walton Hill (National Trust) and Ivythorn Hill (National Trust), commanding wide views. **8 D1** ST4636.
Walton *Staffs.* ***Hamlet***, 1km S of Stone across River Trent. **40 A2** SJ8933.
Walton *Suff.* ***Suburb***, N district of Felixstowe. **35 G5** TM2935.
Walton *Tel. & W.* ***Hamlet***, 6m/10km NW of Wellington. **38 E4** SJ5918.
Walton *Warks.* ***Hamlet***, 6m/9km E of Stratford-upon-Avon. **30 D3** SP2853.
Walton *W.Yorks.* Population: 3323. ***Village***, 3m/5km SE of Wakefield. **51 F1** SE3517.
Walton *W.Yorks.* ***Village***, 2m/4km E of Wetherby. **57 K5** SE4447.
Walton Cardiff *Glos.* ***Hamlet***, 1m/2km E of Tewkesbury. **29 J5** SO9032.
Walton East (Waltwn Dwyrain). *Pembs.* ***Village***, 6m/10km NE of Haverfordwest. **16 D2** SN0223.
Walton Elm *Dorset* ***Hamlet***, 1km S of Marnhull and 3m/4km N of Sturminster Newton. ST7817.
Walton Hall *Warr.* ***Garden***, formal gardens surrounding Victorian hall in Higher Walton, 1km S of Warrington. Includes roses and bedding plants. **49 F4** SJ5984.
Walton-in-Gordano *N.Som.* ***Village***, 2m/3km NE of Clevedon. **19 H4** ST4273.
Walton-le-Dale *Lancs.* ***Suburb***, 2m/3km SE of Preston across River Ribble. Site of small Roman fort 1km W. **55 J7** SD5528.
Walton Lower Street *Suff.* ***Suburb***, W district of Felixstowe. TM2834.
Walton-on-Thames *Surr.* Population: 25,401. ***Town***, on S bank of River Thames, 15m/24km SW of central London. **22 E5** TQ1066.
Walton on the Hill *Mersey.* ***Suburb***, 3m/5km NE of Liverpool city centre. SJ3694.
Walton-on-the-Hill *Staffs.* ***Village***, 3m/4km SE of Stafford. **40 B3** SJ9521.
Walton on the Hill *Surr.* ***Village***, 4m/6km SW of Banstead. Site of Roman villa 1m/2km SE on Walton Heath golf course. **23 F6** TQ2255.
Walton on the Naze *Essex* Population: 7521. ***Small town***, coastal resort, 7m/11km NE of Clacton-on-Sea. Has one of longest piers in Britain. **35 G6** TM2521.
Walton on the Wolds *Leics.* ***Village***, 5m/6km E of Loughborough. **41 H4** SK5919.
Walton-on-Trent *Derbys.* ***Village***, 4m/6km SW of Burton upon Trent. **40 E4** SK2118.
Walton Park *D. & G.* ***Settlement***, 5m/8km N of Castle Douglas. **65 H3** NX7670.
Walton Park *N.Som.* ***Suburb***, N district of Clevedon. ST4072.
Walton West (Waltwn Gorllewin). *Pembs.* ***Village***, near coast of St. Brides Bay, 1km S of Broad Haven. **16 B3** SM8612.
Waltonferry *Suff.* ***Locality***, at mouth of River Orwell, 1m/2km W of Felixstowe. TM2734.
Waltwn Dwyrain *Pembs. Welsh form of Walton East, qv.*
Waltwn Gorllewin *Pembs. Welsh form of Walton West, qv.*
Walwen *Flints.* ***Hamlet***, 3m/5km S of Holywell. **47 K5** SJ1771.
Walwen *Flints.* ***Locality***, on River Dee estuary, 1m/2km E of Holywell. **48 B5** SJ2076.
Walwick *Northumb.* ***Locality***, on line of Hadrian's Wall, 2m/3km NE of Fourstones. Foundations of Black Carts Turret (English Heritage) and section of Hadrian's Wall, 1m/2km NW. **70 D6** NY9070.
Walworth *Darl.* ***Hamlet***, 5m/7km NW of Darlington. Castle is mansion of c. 1600. **62 D5** NZ2318.
Walworth *Gt.Lon.* ***Suburb***, in borough of Southwark, S of New Kent Road. TQ3278.
Walworth Gate *Darl.* ***Settlement***, 1km N of Walworth. NZ2320.
Walwyn's Castle (Castell Gwalchmai). *Pembs.* ***Hamlet***, 4m/6km NW of Milford Haven. Site of ancient fort. **16 B3** SM8711.
Wambrook *Som.* ***Village***, 2m/3km W of Chard. **8 B4** ST2907.
Wamphray Water *D. & G.* ***River***, running S from Croft Head to River Annan, 7m/11km S of Moffat. **69 G4** NY1095.
Wampool *Cumb.* ***Locality***, on River Wampool, 1m/2km SE of Kirkbride. NY2454.
Wampool *Cumb.* ***River***, rising E of Wigton and flowing NW into Solway Firth, W of Kirkbride, between Cardurnock and Grune Point. **60 D1** NY1459.
Wanborough *Surr.* ***Hamlet***, below N slope of Hog's Back, 4m/6km W of Guildford. **22 C7** SU9348.
Wanborough *Swin.* ***Village***, 4m/6km E of Swindon. **21 F3** SU2082.
Wandel *S.Lan.* ***Settlement***, 3m/5km NE of Abington. **68 E1** NS9427.
Wandel Burn *S.Lan.* ***River***, rising to N of Duncangill Head and flowing NW to join River Clyde to N of Wandel. **68 E1** NS9427.
Wandlebury *Cambs.* ***Historic/prehistoric site***, earthwork at summit of Gog Magog Hills, 4m/6km SE of Cambridge. Earthwork and summit now form part of Wandlebury Country Park. **33 H3** TL4953.
Wandon *Northumb.* ***Hamlet***, 1m/2km W of Chatton. **71 F1** NU0328.
Wandon End *Herts.* ***Suburb***, 3m/5km E of Luton town centre. TL1322.
Wandylaw *Northumb.* ***Settlement***, 1m/2km W of Ellingham. **71 G1** NU1525.
Wangford *Suff.* ***Locality***, 3m/5km SW of Brandon. **44 B7** TL7583.
Wangford *Suff.* ***Village***, 3m/5km NW of Southwold. **35 J1** TM4679.
Wangford Fen *Suff.* ***Open space***, fenland 1m/2km NE of Lakenheath. **44 B7** TL7384.
Wangford Warren *Suff.* ***Forest/woodland***, coniferous forest to W of Lakenheath Airfield. **44 B7** TL7682.
Wanless *Lancs.* ***Settlement***, on hillside, just E of Trawden. SD9138.
Wanlip *Leics.* ***Village***, 4m/7km N of Leicester. **41 J4** SK6010.
Wanlock Dod *D. & G.* ***Mountain***, 1km N of Wanlockhead. Height 1807 feet or 551 metres. **68 D2** NS8614.
Wanlock Water *D. & G.* ***River***, rising at Wanlockhead and flowing NE to join Crawick Water just NE of Spango Bridge. **68 D2** NS8217.
Wanlockhead *D. & G.* ***Village***, in former lead-mining area, 6m/10km E of Sanquhar. **68 D2** NS8712.
Wanlockhead Beam Engine *D. & G.* ***Other feature of interest***, rare 19c wooden water-balance pump used to drain lead mines, along with track of horse engine and industrial artefacts, at Wanlockhead. **68 D2** NS8712.
Wannock *E.Suss.* ***Locality***, adjoining to S of Polegate. **13 J6** TQ5703.
Wansbeck *Northumb.* ***River***, rising near Sweethope Loughs and flowing E via Kirkwhelpington and Morpeth to North Sea between Blyth and Newbiggin-by-the-Sea. **71 G5** NZ3085.
Wansbeck Country Park *Northumb.* ***Leisure/recreation***, wooded area, attracting wide range of birds, on N bank of River Wansbeck, 1m/2km W of Ashington. **71 H5** NZ2586.
Wansdyke ***Historic/prehistoric site***, earthwork which originally stretched for 50m/80km from Inkpen Hill, 4m/7km S of Hungerford, to Bristol Channel at Portishead. Possibly constructed for defence of Britons living in S and W against Anglo-Saxon invaders from the N. Only fragments remain, most notably a 10m/16km stretch along S edge of Marlborough Downs. **20 D5** SU0565.
Wansford *E.Riding* ***Village***, on River Hull, 3m/4km E of Great Driffield. **59 G4** TA0656.
Wansford *Peter.* ***Village***, on River Nene, 7m/12km W of Peterborough. **42 D6** TL0799.
Wansford Bridge ***Bridge***, ten-arched stone bridge dating from 13c over River Nene, which forms boundary between Peterborough and Cambridgeshire at Wansford. TL0799.
Wanshurst Green *Kent* ***Hamlet***, 1m/2km E of Marden. TQ7645.
Wanstead *Gt.Lon.* ***Suburb***, in borough of Redbridge, 3m/4km NW of Ilford. **23 H3** TQ4088.
Wanstrow *Som.* ***Village***, 5m/8km NE of Bruton. **20 A7** ST7141.
Wanswell *Glos.* ***Village***, 1m/2km N of Berkeley. **19 K1** SO6801.
Wantage *Oxon.* Population: 9452. ***Small town***, market town 13m/21km SW of Oxford. Birthplace of King Alfred, AD 849. Georgian buildings constructed of distinctive local red and blue brick. **21 G3** SU3988.
Wantisden *Suff.* ***Locality***, 4m/7km NW of Orford. Bentwaters Airfield to W. TM3653.
Wapley *S.Glos.* ***Hamlet***, 2m/3km SW of Chipping Sodbury. **20 A4** ST7179.
Wapley Hill *Here.* ***Mountain***, surmounted by hillfort, 2m/3km SE of Presteigne. Height 1050 feet or 320 metres. **28 C2** SO3462.
Wappenbury *Warks.* ***Village***, 4m/7km NE of Royal Leamington Spa. **30 E2** SP3769.
Wappenham *Northants.* ***Village***, 5m/8km SW of Towcester. **31 H4** SP6245.
Wapping *Gt.Lon.* ***Suburb***, containing docks, E of Tower Bridge in borough of Tower Hamlets. TQ3480.
Wapping *Warks.* ***Locality***, 3m/5km SE of Redditch. SP0764.
War Down *Hants.* ***Hill***, wooded hill in N part of Queen Elizabeth Forest, 2m/3km SW of Petersfield. Height 800 feet or 244 metres. **11 J2** SU7220.
War Ness *Ork.* ***Coastal feature***, headland at S end of Eday. **106 E5** HY5528.
Warathwaite Head *Cumb.* ***Settlement***, 1m/2km SE of Cotehill, 3m/5km NW of Armathwaite. NY4749.
Warblebank *Cumb.* ***Settlement***, 3m/4km SE of Wigton. **60 D2** NY2846.
Warbleton *E.Suss.* ***Hamlet***, 3m/4km SE of Heathfield. **13 K5** TQ6018.
Warblington *Hants.* ***Suburb***, SE district of Havant. Remains of early 16c castle to S. SU7205.
Warborough *Oxon.* ***Village***, 3m/4km N of Wallingford. **21 J2** SU5993.
Warboys *Cambs.* Population: 2945. ***Village***, 7m/11km NE of Huntingdon. Mid-17c manor house. **33 G1** TL3080.
Warbreck *B'pool* ***Suburb***, 2m/3km NE of Blackpool town centre. SD3238.
Warbstow *Cornw.* ***Village***, 7m/11km E of Boscastle. **4 C1** SX2090.
Warburton *Gt.Man.* ***Village***, 5m/7km W of Altrincham. **49 F4** SJ6989.
Warburton Green *Gt.Man.* ***Suburb***, 3m/5km SE of Altrincham. SJ7984.
Warcop *Cumb.* ***Village***, 3m/5km W of Brough. Hall is part Elizabethan, part Georgian. Site of Roman camp 1m/2km NW. **61 J5** NY7415.
Warcop Fell *Cumb.* ***Mountain***, 3m/5km N of Brough. Height 2040 feet or 622 metres. **61 J4** NY7820.
Ward Burn *Stir.* ***River***, stream running NE to join Kelty Water 2m/3km E of Dalmary. **74 D1** NS5496.
Ward End *W.Mid.* ***Suburb***, 4m/6km E of Birmingham city centre. **40 D7** SP1288.
Ward Green *Suff.* ***Settlement***, 3m/5km N of Stowmarket. **34 E2** TM0463.
Ward Hill *Ork.* ***Hill***, 3m/4km N of Orphir Bay, Mainland. Height 879 feet or 268 metres. **107 C7** HY3308.
Ward Hill *Ork.* ***Hill***, 1km S of Lythes. Height 387 feet or 118 metres. **107 D9** ND4588.
Ward Hill *Ork.* ***Mountain***, at N end of Hoy. Height 1571 feet or 479 metres. **107 B7** HY2202.
Ward Hill *Shet.* ***Hill***, situated in NW part of Fair Isle. Height 712 feet or 217 metres. **108 A1** HZ2073.
Ward Holm *Ork.* ***Island***, small islet 1m/2km W of Copinsay. HY5901.
Ward of Bressay *Shet.* ***Hill***, conical hill forming highest point on Bressay, 2m/3km N of Bard Head. Height 741 feet or 226 metres. **109 E9** HU4453.
Ward of Veester *Shet.* ***Hill***, 2m/3km N of Hoswick, Mainland. Height 843 feet or 257 metres. **109 D10** HU4126.
Warden *Kent* ***Hamlet***, on E coast of Isle of Sheppey, 1m/2km NW of Leysdown-on-Sea. **25 G4** TR0271.
Warden *Northumb.* ***Hamlet***, at confluence of Rivers North and South Tyne, 2m/4km NW of Hexham. **70 E7** NY9166.
Warden Hill *Glos.* ***Suburb***, SW district of Cheltenham. SO9320.
Warden Hill *Luton* ***Hill***, 3m/5km N of Luton town centre. Height 640 feet or 195 metres. **32 D6** TL0926.
Warden Law *T. & W.* ***Locality***, 2m/3km E of Houghton le Spring. NZ3650.
Warden Point *Kent* ***Coastal feature***, headland at NE end of Isle of Sheppey, to N of locality of Warden. **25 G4** TR0272.
Warden Street *Beds.* ***Settlement***, 4m/7km W of Biggleswade. TL1244.
Wardgate *Derbys.* ***Village***, 5m/8km E of Ashbourne. **40 E1** SK2547.
Wardhedges *Beds.* ***Settlement***, adjoining to E of Flitton, 3m/4km SE of Ampthill. TL0635.
Wardhouse *Aber.* ***Settlement***, 2m/3km NE of Kennethmont. **90 D1** NJ5630.
Wardie *Edin.* ***Suburb***, 2m/3km N of Edinburgh city centre. NT2476.
Wardington *Oxon.* ***Village***, 4m/7km NE of Banbury. **31 F4** SP4946.
Wardlaw Hill *E.Ayr.* ***Mountain***, with cairn and memorial at summit, 3m/5km S of Muirkirk. Height 1630 feet or 497 metres. **68 B1** NS6822.
Wardle *Ches.* ***Village***, 4m/6km NW of Nantwich. **49 F7** SJ6157.
Wardle *Gt.Man.* Population: 6622. ***Small town***, 3m/4km NE of Rochdale. **49 J1** SD9116.
Wardley *Gt.Man.* ***Suburb***, 1m/2km NW of Swinton. SD7602.
Wardley *Rut.* ***Village***, 2m/4km W of Uppingham. **42 B5** SK8300.
Wardley *T. & W.* ***Suburb***, E district of Felling. NZ2961.
Wardley *W.Suss.* ***Settlement***, 3m/4km S of Liphook. SU8427.

Wardlow *Derbys.* ***Village***, 2m/3km E of Tideswell. **50 D5** SK1874.
Wardpark *N.Lan.* ***Locality***, industrial area, 2m/3km NE of Cumbernauld town centre. Site of Roman camp. NS7777.
Ward's Stone *Lancs.* ***Mountain***, rounded summit on moorland on W side of Forest of Bowland, 7m/11km E of Lancaster. Height 1837 feet or 560 metres. **55 J4** SD5858.
Wardsend *Ches.* ***Settlement***, 1km SE of Poynton. SJ9382.
Wardy Hill *Cambs.* ***Hamlet***, 5m/7km W of Ely. **43 H7** TL4782.
Ware *Herts.* Population: 17,000. ***Town***, old market town on River Lea, 21m/33km N of London. Maltings. River Lea Navigation forms canal link with London. Shell-lined Scott's Grotto recently restored. **33 G7** TL3514.
Ware *Kent* ***Settlement***, 4m/6km NW of Sandwich. **25 J5** TR2760.
Ware Street *Kent* ***Suburb***, 2m/4km E of Maidstone. TQ7956.
Wareham *Dorset* Population: 7616. ***Small town***, at head of River Frome estuary, 6m/10km W of Poole across Poole Harbour. Part of town built within Saxon defences, and local churches are partly Saxon. **9 J6** SY9287.
Wareham Forest *Dorset* ***Forest/woodland***, to NW of Wareham, area of heath, conifers and marsh. **9 H5** SY8991.
Warehorne *Kent* ***Village***, 1m/2km SW of Hamstreet. **14 E4** TQ9932.
Waren Mill *Northumb.* ***Settlement***, at S end of Budle Bay, 2m/4km E of Belford. **77 K7** NU1434.
Warenford *Northumb.* ***Hamlet***, 4m/6km SE of Belford. **71 G1** NU1328.
Warenton *Northumb.* ***Settlement***, 2m/4km S of Belford. **77 K7** NU1030.
Wareside *Herts.* ***Village***, 3m/4km E of Ware. **33 G7** TL3915.
Waresley *Cambs.* ***Village***, 4m/6km NE of Potton. **33 F3** TL2554.
Waresley *Worcs.* ***Village***, 2m/4km SE of Stourport-on-Severn. SO8470.
Warfield *Brack.F.* ***Hamlet***, 2m/3km N of Bracknell. **22 B4** SU8872.
Wargate *Lincs.* ***Locality***, 1km S of Gosberton. TF2330.
Wargrave *Mersey.* ***Suburb***, S district of Newton-le-Willows. SJ5894.
Wargrave *W'ham* Population: 3221. ***Village***, 2m/3km N of Twyford. **22 A4** SU7978.
Warham *Here.* ***Settlement***, 2m/3km W of Hereford. SO4839.
Warham *Norf.* ***Hamlet***, 2m/4km SE of Wells-next-the-Sea. Originally two separate hamlets, Warham All Saints and Warham St. Mary. **44 D1** TF9441.
Warham All Saints *Norf.* *See Warham.*
Warham St. Mary *Norf.* *See Warham.*
Warhill *Gt.Man.* ***Settlement***, adjoining to S of Mottram in Longdendale. SJ9995.
Waring's Green ***Settlement***, on border of Warwickshire and West Midlands, 2m/3km NW of Hockley Heath. SP1274.
Wark *Northumb.* ***Village***, on River Tweed, 2m/3km W of Cornhill on Tweed. **77 G7** NT8238.
Wark *Northumb.* ***Village***, on River North Tyne, 4m/7km S of Bellingham. **70 D6** NY8577.
Wark Forest *Northumb.* ***Forest/woodland***, forested moorland area to W of Wark. **70 C6** NY7377.
Warkleigh *Devon* ***Hamlet***, 4m/7km SW of South Molton. **6 E3** SS6422.
Warks Burn *Northumb.* ***River***, rising near Great Watch Hill, Wark Forest, and flowing E through Wark Forest into River North Tyne just below Wark. **70 C6** NY8676.
Warkton *Northants.* ***Village***, 2m/3km NE of Kettering. **32 B1** SP8979.
Warkworth *Northants.* ***Hamlet***, 2m/3km E of Banbury. **31 F4** SP4840.
Warkworth *Northumb.* Population: 1642. ***Village***, on River Coquet, near North Sea coast, 1m/2km NW of Amble. Norman and later castle (English Heritage). Medieval fortified bridge (English Heritage). **71 H3** NU2406.
Warkworth Castle *Northumb.* ***Castle***, late 14c castle (English Heritage) with eight-towered keep, on site of original 12c building at S end of Warkworth. Once home to Percy family and setting for several scenes in Shakespeare's Henry IV. 14c Hermitage (English Heritage) cut into cliff just upstream from castle. **71 H3** NU2405.
Warlaby *N.Yorks.* ***Settlement***, 2m/3km SW of Northallerton. **62 E7** SE3491.
Warland *W.Yorks.* ***Settlement***, 3m/4km S of Todmorden. **56 E7** SD9420.
Warland Reservoir *W.Yorks.* ***Reservoir***, to E of Warland. **56 E7** SD9520.
Warleggan *Cornw.* ***Village***, on S edge of Bodmin Moor, 6m/9km E of Bodmin. **4 B4** SX1569.
Warleigh *B. & N.E.Som.* ***Locality***, on River Avon, 3m/4km E of Bath. ST7964.
Warley *Essex* ***Suburb***, S district of Brentwood. TQ5992.
Warley *W.Mid.* ***Town***, 4m/6km W of Birmingham. Interesting museum of weighing machines in Foundry Lane. **40 C7** SP0086.
Warley Moor Reservoir *W.Yorks.* ***Reservoir***, 3m/5km SW of Denholme. **57 F6** SE0331.
Warley Town *W.Yorks.* ***Suburb***, 2m/4km W of Halifax town centre. **57 F7** SE0524.
Warlingham *Surr.* Population: 15,088. ***Town***, 5m/8km SE of Croydon. **23 G6** TQ3558.
Warmbrook *Derbys.* ***Suburb***, to SW of Wirksworth. SK2853.
Warmfield *W.Yorks.* ***Village***, 1m/2km SW of Normanton. **57 J7** SE3720.
Warmingham *Ches.* ***Village***, 3m/5km W of Sandbach. **49 G6** SJ7061.
Warminghurst *W.Suss.* ***Settlement***, 3m/4km N of Washington. **12 E5** TQ1116.
Warmington *Northants.* ***Village***, 3m/5km NE of Oundle. **42 D6** TL0791.
Warmington *Warks.* ***Village***, 5m/8km NW of Banbury. **31 F4** SP4147.
Warminster *Wilts.* Population: 16,379. ***Town***, 8m/13km S of Trowbridge. Army camps on outskirts. Attractive 15c church. **20 B7** ST8745.
Warminster Down *Wilts.* ***Open space***, hillslope within military training area at E end of Salisbury Plain, 3m/4km NE of Warminster. **20 B7** ST8748.
Warmlake *Kent* ***Hamlet***, 1m/2km S of Langley Heath. **14 D2** TQ8150.
Warmley *S.Glos.* ***Locality***, 5m/9km E of Bristol. **19 K4** ST6673.
Warmley Hill *S.Glos.* ***Suburb***, of Kingswood, 5m/7km E of Bristol. ST6573.
Warmsworth *S.Yorks.* ***Suburb***, 3m/4km SW of Doncaster. **51 H2** SE5400.
Warmwell *Dorset* ***Village***, 5m/8km SE of Dorchester. **9 G6** SY7585.
Warndon *Worcs.* ***Hamlet***, 3m/4km NE of Worcester. **29 H3** SO8856.
Warndon *Worcs.* ***Suburb***, NE district of Worcester. SO8756.
Warners End *Herts.* ***Suburb***, 1m/2km W of Hemel Hempstead town centre. TL0307.
Warnford *Hants.* ***Village***, 2m/4km NE of Meonstoke. **11 H2** SU6223.
Warnham *W.Suss.* ***Village***, 2m/3km NW of Horsham. **12 E3** TQ1533.
Warningcamp *W.Suss.* ***Hamlet***, in River Arun valley, 1m/2km E of Arundel. **12 D6** TQ0307.
Warninglid *W.Suss.* ***Village***, 2m/4km S of Handcross. **13 F4** TQ2526.
Warren *Ches.* ***Village***, 3m/4km SW of Macclesfield. **49 H5** SJ8870.
Warren *Gt.Lon.* ***Settlement***, 2m/3km W of Romford, in borough of Havering. TQ4889.
Warren *Pembs.* ***Village***, 4m/7km SW of Pembroke. **16 C5** SR9397.
Warren *S.Yorks.* ***Locality***, 1km N of Chapeltown. SK3597.
Warren Corner *Hants.* ***Locality***, 1m/2km E of Crondall. SU8048.
Warren Heath *Hants.* ***Forest/woodland***, large area of mainly coniferous woodland to SE of Bramshill and 3m/4km NE of Hartley Wintney. **22 A6** SU7659.
Warren Mountain *Flints.* ***Settlement***, 1m/2km S of Hawarden. SJ3163.
Warren Row *W. & M.* ***Village***, 3m/5km NE of Twyford. **22 B3** SU8180.
Warren Street *Kent* ***Hamlet***, 2m/3km E of Lenham. **14 E2** TQ9253.
Warrenby *R. & C.* ***Locality***, 2m/3km W of Redcar. **63 G4** NZ5825.
Warren's Cross *Glos.* ***Locality***, 1m/2km W of Lechlade. SU1999.
Warren's Green *Herts.* ***Settlement***, 3m/5km NE of Stevenage. TL2628.
Warrington *M.K.* ***Hamlet***, 2m/3km N of Olney. **32 B3** SP8954.
Warrington *Warr.* Population: 82,812. ***Town***, industrial town on River Mersey, 16m/25km SW of Manchester and same distance E of Liverpool. New Town designated 1968. Georgian buildings in town centre. Parish church, founded in 7c, with 14c chancel and crypt. **49 F4** SJ6088.
Warriston *Edin.* ***Suburb***, 1m/2km N of Edinburgh city centre. NT2575.
Warroch *P. & K.* ***Settlement***, 1m/2km NE of Carnbo. **82 B7** NO0604.
Warsash *Hants.* ***Village***, on E side of River Hamble, 6m/9km W of Fareham. School of Navigation (University of Southampton). **11 F4** SU4906.
Warse *High.* ***Locality***, near N coast of Caithness district, 2m/4km SE of St. John's Point. ND3372.
Warsett Hill *R. & C.* ***Hill***, 1m/2km N of Brotton. Height 544 feet or 166 metres. **63 H4** NZ6921.
Warslow *Staffs.* ***Village***, 7m/11km E of Leek. **50 C7** SK0858.
Warsop Vale *Notts.* ***Village***, 4m/7km N of Mansfield. SK5467.
Wart Holm *Ork.* ***Island***, rock 1km W of Point of Huro at S end of Westray. HY4838.
Warter *E.Riding* ***Village***, 4m/7km E of Pocklington. Site of 12c priory to N. **58 E4** SE8650.
Warter Wold *E.Riding* ***Open space***, low moorland, partly wooded, 4m/6km NE of Pocklington. **58 E4** SE8551.
Warth Hill *Cumb.* ***Hill***, 4m/7km NW of Kirkby Lonsdale. Height 892 feet or 272 metres. **55 J1** SD5684.
Warth Hill *High.* ***Hill***, 2m/3km SW of John o' Groats. Height 407 feet or 124 metres. **105 J1** ND3769.
Warthermaske *N.Yorks.* ***Hamlet***, 1m/2km SW of Masham. SE2079.
Warthill *N.Yorks.* ***Village***, 5m/8km NE of York. **58 C4** SE6755.
Wartle *Aber.* ***Settlement***, 4m/6km E of Tarland. **90 D4** NJ5404.
Wartling *E.Suss.* ***Village***, 3m/4km N of Pevensey across Pevensey Levels. **13 K6** TQ6509.
Wartnaby *Leics.* ***Village***, 4m/6km NW of Melton Mowbray. **42 A3** SK7123.
Warton *Lancs.* Population: 4137. ***Village***, 4m/7km E of Lytham St. Anne's. Airfield to S. **55 H7** SD4128.
Warton *Lancs.* ***Village***, 1m/2km N of Carnforth. **55 J2** SD5072.
Warton *Northumb.* ***Settlement***, 1m/2km W of Thropton. **71 F3** NU0002.
Warton *Warks.* ***Village***, 4m/6km NW of Atherstone. **40 E5** SK2803.
Warton Bank *Lancs.* ***Settlement***, 1m/2km SW of Warton, on edge of marshland on N side of River Ribble estuary. SD4027.
Warton Old Rectory *Lancs.* ***Historic/prehistoric site***, ruins of 14c rectory (English Heritage), representing modest medieval house at Warton, 1m/2km N of Carnforth. **55 J2** SD5072.
Warton Sands *Lancs.* ***Coastal feature***, sandbanks on E side of Morecambe Bay. **55 H2** SD4472.
Warwick *Cumb.* ***Hamlet***, 4m/7km E of Carlisle. **61 F1** NY4656.
Warwick *Warks.* Population: 22,476. ***Town***, on River Avon, 9m/15km SW of Coventry. Medieval castle. Many old buildings, despite a fire in 1694 which destroyed town centre. Oken's House contains a fascinating collection of antique dolls. **30 D2** SP2865.
Warwick Bridge *Cumb.* ***Village***, 1km E of Warwick across River Eden. **61 F1** NY4757.
Warwick Castle *Warks.* ***Castle***, 11c castle with 14c Great Hall, on River Avon, in SW district of Warwick; once home to Earl of Warwick, 'the Kingmaker'. **30 D2** SP2864.
Warwick Wold *Surr.* ***Settlement***, 3m/4km NE of Redhill. TQ3153.
Warwickshire County Museum *Warks.* ***Other feature of interest***, museum in Warwick with exhibitions of local history and geology. **30 D2** SP2765.
Wasbister *Ork.* ***Settlement***, on Rousay, 1m/2km S of Sacquoy Head. **106 C4** HY3932.
Wasdale Head *Cumb.* ***Settlement***, 1m/2km NE of Wast Water. **60 C6** NY1808.
Waseley Hills Country Park *Worcs.* ***Leisure/recreation***, country park 5m/8km N of Bromsgrove, with 133 acres or 53 hectares of woodland, scrub and grassland; main feature is Windmill Hill. **29 J1** SO9777.
Wash *Derbys.* ***Hamlet***, 1km N of Chapel-en-le-Frith. SK0682.
Wash Common *W.Berks.* ***Suburb***, 2m/4km SW of Newbury. **21 H5** SU4564.
Washall Green *Herts.* ***Settlement***, 5m/8km E of Buntingford. TL4430.
Washaway *Cornw.* ***Settlement***, 3m/4km NW of Bodmin. **4 A4** SX0369.
Washbourne *Devon* ***Hamlet***, 4m/6km S of Totnes. **5 H5** SX7954.
Washbrook *Som.* ***Hamlet***, 2m/3km NW of Wedmore. ST4250.
Washbrook *Suff.* ***Hamlet***, 4m/6km SW of Ipswich. TM1142.
Washerwall *Staffs.* ***Suburb***, adjoining to W of Werrington. SJ9347.
Washfield *Devon* ***Village***, 2m/3km NW of Tiverton. **7 H4** SS9315.
Washfold *N.Yorks.* ***Hamlet***, 2m/4km N of Reeth. **62 B6** NZ0502.
Washford *Som.* ***Village***, 2m/3km SW of Watchet. **7 J1** ST0441.
Washford *Worcs.* ***Suburb***, 3m/4km SE of Redditch town centre. SP0765.
Washford Pyne *Devon* ***Hamlet***, 2m/3km SE of Witheridge and 9m/14km W of Tiverton. **7 G4** SS8111.
Washingborough *Lincs.* Population: 4204. ***Village***, 3m/5km E of Lincoln. **52 D5** TF0170.
Washingley *Cambs.* ***Settlement***, remains of deserted village, 2m/3km W of Stilton. Motte and bailey to SE. TL1389.
Washington *T. & W.* Population: 56,848. ***Town***, New Town, designated 1964, 6m/9km W of Sunderland. 12c Washington Old Hall was home of George Washington's ancestors; rebuilt in 17c and now National Trust property. **62 E1** NZ2956.
Washington *W.Suss.* ***Village***, below South Downs, 7m/11km N of Worthing. **12 E5** TQ1212.
Washington Old Hall *T. & W.* ***Historic house***, 17c house (National Trust) at Washington, 5m/8km W of Sunderland. Includes fragments of 12c house, home of George Washington's ancestors. **62 E1** NZ3156.
Washington Wildfowl and Wetlands Trust *T. & W.* ***Nature reserve***, 2m/4km E of Washington, near W bank of River Wear. Includes many 'at risk' wildfowl. **62 E1** NZ3356.
Washmere Green *Suff.* ***Settlement***, 1m/2km S of Lavenham. **34 D4** TL9147.
Washpit *W.Yorks.* ***Settlement***, 1m/2km S of Holmfirth. SE1406.
Washwood Heath *W.Mid.* ***Suburb***, 3m/5km E of Birmingham city centre. SP1088.
Wasing *W.Berks.* ***Settlement***, 1m/2km SW of Aldermaston. **21 J5** SU5764.
Waskerley *Dur.* ***Settlement***, 5m/8km SW of Consett. **62 B2** NZ0545.
Waskerley Beck *Dur.* ***River***, rising on moors N of Stanhope and flowing through Waskerley Reservoir, then SE to Tunstall Reservoir and S into River Wear at Wolsingham. **62 B2** NZ0737.
Waskerley Reservoir *Dur.* ***Reservoir***, 2m/3km SW of Waskerley. **62 B2** NZ0545.
Wasperton *Warks.* ***Village***, 4m/7km S of Warwick. **30 D3** SP2658.
Wasps Nest *Lincs.* ***Settlement***, 1m/2km E of Nocton. TF0864.
Wass *N.Yorks.* ***Village***, 2m/3km W of Ampleforth. **58 B2** SE5579.
Wast Water *Cumb.* ***Lake/loch***, running NE to SW in course of River Irt 3m/4km NE of Santon Bridge. Steep screes on SE side of lake. Deepest lake in England with a depth of 230 feet or 70 metres. Owned by National Trust. **60 C6** NY1606.
Watch Hill ***Mountain***, astride border of Dumfries & Galloway and Scottish Borders, 4m/6km NW of Newcastleton. Height 1647 feet or 502 metres. **69 K4** NY4390.
Watch Hill *Cumb.* ***Mountain***, on Renwick Fell, 5m/8km NE of Kirkoswald. Height 1975 feet or 602 metres. **61 H2** NY6246.
Watch Water Reservoir *Sc.Bord.* ***Reservoir***, in course of Watch Water, 2m/3km W of Longformacus. **76 E5** NT6656.
Watchet *Som.* Population: 3147. ***Small town***, with harbour on Bridgwater Bay, 15m/24km NW of Bridgwater. Site of Daws Castle (English Heritage) to W. **7 J1** ST0743.
Watchfield *Oxon.* ***Village***, 3m/5km E of Highworth. Site of Roman building to E. **21 F2** SU2490.
Watchfield *Som.* ***Hamlet***, 2m/3km E of Highbridge. **19 G7** ST3447.

Watchgate *Cumb.* ***Hamlet***, 4m/7km N of Kendal. **61 G7** SD5299.
Watchhill *Cumb.* ***Locality***, 3m/4km E of Aspatria. NY1842.
Watchman Hill *S.Lan.* ***Mountain***, in Lowther Hills, 1m/2km SW of Elvanfoot. Height 1489 feet or 454 metres. **68 E2** NS9415.
Watcombe *Torbay* ***Suburb***, 2m/3km N of Torquay town centre. SX9167.
Watendlath *Cumb.* ***Locality***, at N end of small lake, 3m/4km NE of Seatoller. **60 D5** NY2716.
Water *Lancs.* ***Hamlet***, on Forest of Rossendale, 3m/4km NE of Rawtenstall. **56 D7** SD8425.
Water Crag *N.Yorks.* ***Mountain***, 3m/5km NE of Keld, to SW of Arkengarthdale Moor. Height 2191 feet or 668 metres. **62 A6** NY9204.
Water Eaton *M.K.* ***Suburb***, in S part of Bletchley. SP8732.
Water Eaton *Oxon.* ***Hamlet***, on River Cherwell, 4m/6km N of Oxford. **31 G7** SP5112.
Water Eaton *Staffs.* ***Settlement***, 2m/4km SW of Penkridge. Site of Roman settlement of Pennocrucium. Site of Roman fort 1km NE and of Roman villa 1m/2km SW. SJ9011.
Water End *Beds.* ***Hamlet***, 1m/2km SW of Clophill. TL0737.
Water End *Beds.* ***Locality***, 4m/6km E of Bedford. TL1151.
Water End *Beds.* ***Settlement***, S end of Cople, 4m/6km E of Bedford. TL1047.
Water End *Beds.* ***Settlement***, S end of Wrestlingworth, 3m/4km SE of Potton. TL2547.
Water End *E.Riding* ***Hamlet***, 1m/2km W of Holme-on-Spalding-Moor. SE7838.
Water End *Essex* ***Settlement***, 4m/6km NE of Saffron Walden. TL5840.
Water End *Herts.* ***Hamlet***, 2m/4km NW of Hemel Hempstead. **32 D7** TL0310.
Water End *Herts.* ***Settlement***, 3m/4km S of Hatfield. **23 F1** TL2204.
Water Fryston *W.Yorks.* ***Locality***, on NE side of Castleford across River Aire from Fairburn. SE4626.
Water Newton *Cambs.* ***Village***, on River Nene, 3m/4km SE of Wansford. To E, site of Roman town of Durobrivae. **42 E6** TL1097.
Water of Ae *D. & G.* ***River***, rising on E side of Queensberry and flowing S through Forest of Ae and Ae Village, then SE to Kinnel Water 2m/4km N of Lochmaben. **69 F5** NY0786.
Water of Ailnack (Ailnack Water). ***River***, running NE into River Avon, 1m/2km S of Tomintoul. Upper reaches known as Water of Caiplich or Caiplich Water. **89 H4** NJ1617.
Water of Allachy *Aber.* ***River***, flowing N to join with Water of Tanar in Forest of Glen Tanar, and then to River Dee, SW of Aboyne. **90 C5** NO4694.
Water of Aven *Aber.* ***River***, running NE to Water of Feugh, 4m/7km SW of Banchory. **90 D6** NO6392.
Water of Bogie *Aber.* *See (River) Bogie.*
Water of Buchat *Aber.* ***River***, rising on Ladder Hills and running SE to River Don at Bridge of Buchat. **90 B3** NJ4014.
Water of Caiplich *See Water of Ailnack.*
Water of Charr ***River***, rising to NE of Sturdy Hill and running N to Water of Dye, 6m/10km N of Fettercairn. **90 E6** NO6182.
Water of Coyle ***River***, rising about 3m/5km N of Dalmellington and flowing NW to River Ayr, 4m/6km E of Ayr. Meanders in lower reaches. **67 J2** NS3921.
Water of Deugh ***River***, rising to N of Windy Standard on E side of Carsphairn Forest and flowing W, then S past Carsphairn to Kendoon Loch, 4m/6km N of St. John's Town of Dalry. **67 K4** NX6090.
Water of Dye *Aber.* ***River***, running N down Glen Dye to Water of Feugh on W side of Strachan. **90 E6** NO6691.
Water of Feugh *Aber.* ***River***, rising in mountains of Forest of Birse and flowing E, by Strachan, to join River Dee opposite Banchory. **90 D5** NO7095.
Water of Fleet *D. & G.* ***River***, rising on E side of Cairnsmore of Fleet and running S past Gatehouse of Fleet into Fleet Bay and Wigtown Bay. NX5550.
Water of Gairney *Aber.* ***River***, flowing N to join with Water of Allachy, 1km S of Water of Tanar. **90 C5** NO4693.
Water of Girvan *S.Ayr.* ***River***, running N from Loch Girvan Eye, in Glentrool Forest Park, and flowing N through Loch Bradan Reservoir before turning NW past Straiton and then SW, 1m/2km W of Kirkmichael. It continues to flow SW past Dailly into Firth of Clyde to N of Girvan. **67 H3** NX1898.
Water of Glencalvie *High.* *See Glen Calvie.*
Water of Ken *D. & G.* ***River***, rising on Fortypenny Hill NW of Carsphairn and flowing S through Carsfad and Earlstoun Lochs, then past St. John's Town of Dalry and New Galloway to Loch Ken. **68 B4** NX6475.
Water of Lee *Angus* ***River***, running E down Glen Lee to join Water of Mark at head of Glen Esk, 3m/4km W of Tarfside. **90 B6** NO4480.
Water of Leith ***River***, rising on Pentland Hills and running N through Harperrig Reservoir, then NE through Edinburgh to Leith Harbour and Firth of Forth. **75 K4** NT2678.
Water of Malzie *D. & G.* ***River***, flowing generally E to join River Bladnoch 1km NE of Malzie and 4m/6km W of Wigtown. **64 D5** NX3754.
Water of Mark ***River***, running first NE, then SE to join Water of Lee at head of Glen Esk, 3m/4km W of Tarfside. **90 C6** NO4480.
Water of May *P. & K.* ***River***, running N into River Earn, 5m/8km SW of Perth. **82 B7** NO0418.
Water of Milk *D. & G.* ***River***, rising on S side of Castle O'er Forest and flowing SW, then S to River Annan 3m/5km W of Ecclefechan. **69 G5** NY1473.
Water of Minnoch ***River***, rising on S slopes of Eldrick Hill and running S through Glentrool Forest to join Water of Trool, 2m/3km SW of Loch Trool. **64 D3** NX3778.
Water of Nevis *High.* ***River***, in Lochaber district rising on Mamore Forest and running first NE, then W along S side of Ben Nevis, then NW to head of Loch Linnhe at Fort William. **80 D1** NN1074.
Water of Nochty ***River***, rising on Ladder Hills and flowing SE to River Don at Strathdon. **90 A3** NJ3512.
Water of Philorth *Aber.* *See Philorth.*
Water of Ruchill (Ruchill Water). *P. & K.* ***River***, running NE down Glen Artney to River Earn at Comrie. **81 J6** NN7721.
Water of Saughs *Angus* ***River***, flowing SE in mountains to NE of Glen Clova and SW of Glen Esk, and becoming West Water. **90 C7** NO4274.
Water of Tanar *Aber.* ***River***, running NE through Forest of Glentanar to River Dee, 1m/2km SW of Aboyne. **90 C5** NO5197.
Water of Tarf *Angus* ***River***, running S into River North Esk, just S of Tarfside. **90 C6** NO4979.
Water of Tig *S.Ayr.* ***River***, rising in Arecleoch Forest and running N, then W, to River Stinchar 2m/3km E of Ballantrae. **67 F5** NX1183.
Water of Trool *D. & G.* ***River***, issuing from Loch Trool and flowing SW down Glen of Trool to join River Cree, 6m/10km NW of Newton Stewart. **64 D3** NX3778.
Water of Tulla *Arg. & B.* ***River***, in Argyll, running SW to Loch Tulla. **80 E3** NN3044.
Water of Unich *Angus* ***River***, running E to Water of Lee, 6m/10km W of Tarfside. Falls of Unich, waterfall in course of stream, near its junction with Water of Lee. **90 B7** NO3980.
Water Orton *Warks.* Population: 3555. ***Village***, 2m/4km NW of Coleshill. **40 D6** SP1791.
Water Sound *Ork.* ***Sea feature***, strait dividing N coast of South Ronaldsay from S coast of Burray. **107 D8** ND4395.
Water Stratford *Bucks.* ***Village***, on River Great Ouse, 3m/5km W of Buckingham. **31 H5** SP6534.
Water Yeat *Cumb.* ***Settlement***, at S end of Coniston Water. **55 F1** SD2889.
Waterbeach *Cambs.* Population: 4148. ***Village***, 5m/8km NE of Cambridge. Remains of medieval Denny Priory 2m/3km N beyond airfield. **33 H2** TL4965.
Waterbeck *D. & G.* ***Village***, 4m/6km NE of Ecclefechan. **69 H6** NY2477.
Watercombe *Dorset* ***Settlement***, 6m/9km SE of Dorchester. SY7584.
Watercress Line *Hants.* *Alternative name for Mid-Hants Railway, qv.*
Waterdale *Herts.* ***Settlement***, 4m/6km N of Watford town centre. TL1102.
Waterden *Norf.* ***Locality***, 4m/7km NW of Fakenham. TF8836.
Waterend *Bucks.* ***Hamlet***, 1m/2km E of Stokenchurch. SU7896.
Waterend *Cumb.* ***Locality***, at NW end of Loweswater Lake. NY1222.
Waterfall *Staffs.* ***Village***, 7m/11km SE of Leek. **50 C7** SK0851.
Waterfoot *E.Renf.* Population: 1300. ***Hamlet***, on W bank of White Cart Water, 2m/3km E of Newton Mearns. **74 D5** NS5655.
Waterfoot *Lancs.* ***Locality***, 2m/3km E of Rawtenstall. **56 D7** SD8321.
Waterford *Hants.* ***Suburb***, on W bank of Lymington River, 1m/2km SE of Lymington. SZ3394.
Waterford *Herts.* ***Village***, 2m/3km NW of Hertford. **33 G7** TL3114.
Watergate *Cornw.* ***Hamlet***, 2m/3km SE of Camelford. SX1281.
Watergate Bay *Cornw.* ***Bay***, on N coast, facing W and extending from Griffin's Point, opposite Trevarrion, S to Trevelgue Head. **3 F2** SW8365.
Watergore *Som.* ***Hamlet***, 1km S of South Petherton. ST4315.
Watergrove Reservoir *Gt.Man.* ***Reservoir***, 1m/2km E of Whitworth. **49 J1** SD9017.
Waterhale *Essex* ***Settlement***, 4m/6km W of Brentwood. TQ5395.
Waterhead *Cumb.* ***Locality***, 1m/2km S of Ambleside. **60 E6** NY3703.
Waterhead *D. & G.* ***Settlement***, 8m/12km E of St. John's Town Dalry. **68 C5** NX7483.
Waterhead *S.Ayr.* ***Mountain***, in Carrick Forest, 1m/2km SE of Loch Bradan. Height 1548 feet or 472 metres. **67 J4** NX4495.
Waterheath *Norf.* ***Settlement***, 3m/4km NE of Beccles. TM4494.
Waterhill of Bruxie *Aber.* ***Settlement***, 1m/2km E of Maud and 2m/3km W of Old Deer. **99 H6** NJ9447.
Waterhouses *Dur.* ***Hamlet***, 6m/9km W of Durham. **62 C2** NZ1840.
Waterhouses *Staffs.* ***Village***, 7m/11km SE of Leek. **50 C7** SK0850.
Wateringbury *Kent* Population: 2589. ***Village***, on River Medway, 5m/8km W of Maidstone. **23 K6** TQ6853.
Waterlane *Glos.* ***Hamlet***, 5m/8km E of Stroud. SO9204.
Waterloo *Aber.* ***Settlement***, 3m/4km SW of Hatton. **91 J1** NK0135.
Waterloo *B'burn.* ***Suburb***, 2m/3km SW of Blackburn town centre. SD6625.
Waterloo *Derbys.* ***Village***, 2m/3km E of Clay Cross. SK4163.
Waterloo *Gt.Man.* ***Suburb***, 1m/2km NW of Ashton-under-Lyne town centre. SD9300.
Waterloo *High.* ***Settlement***, on coast of Skye, 1m/2km E of Broadford. NG6623.
Waterloo *Mersey.* ***Suburb***, S district of Crosby. **48 C3** SJ3197.
Waterloo *Norf.* ***Hamlet***, 1km NW of Hainford. **45 G4** TG2219.
Waterloo *Norf.* ***Locality***, adjoining to NE of Horsham St. Faith. TG2215.
Waterloo *N.Lan.* ***Village***, 1m/2km SE of Wishaw. **75 G5** NS8053.
Waterloo *Pembs.* ***Locality***, 1km E of Pembroke Dock. **16 C4** SM9703.
Waterloo *P. & K.* ***Village***, 4m/7km SE of Dunkeld. **82 B4** NO0536.
Waterloo *Poole* ***Suburb***, 2m/3km N of Poole town centre. **10 B5** SZ0094.
Waterloo *Worcs.* ***Locality***, in E part of Bredon, 4m/6km NE of Tewkesbury. SO9336.
Waterloo Bridge *Conwy* ***Bridge***, iron bridge over River Conwy at Betws-y-coed, built by Telford in 1815. SH7955.
Waterloo Cross *Devon* ***Settlement***, 6m/10km E of Tiverton. **7 J4** ST0514.
Waterloo Monument *Sc.Bord.* ***Other feature of interest***, on Peniel Heugh Hill, 2m/3km NE of Ancrum. Erected by Marquis of Lothian after victory at Battle of Waterloo. **70 B1** NT6526.
Waterloo Port *Gwyn.* ***Locality***, adjoining to NE of Caernarfon. **46 C6** SH4964.
Waterlooville *Hants.* Population: 65,473. ***Town***, 7m/11km NE of Portsmouth. **11 H3** SU6809.
Waterlow *Norf.* ***Settlement***, 1km E of Blofield. TG3409.
Watermeetings *S.Lan.* ***Settlement***, 1km S of confluence of Portrail Water and Daer Water. **68 E2** NS9512.
Watermillock *Cumb.* ***Hamlet***, near N shore of Ullswater, 2m/3km SW of Pooley Bridge. **60 F4** NY4422.
Watermouth Castle *Devon* ***Leisure/recreation***, children's theme park surrounding 19c mansion, 2m/4km E of Ilfracombe. **6 D1** SS5547.
Waterperry *Oxon.* ***Garden***, in Waterperry, 2m/3km E of Wheatley and 8m/12km E of Oxford city centre. 83 acres or 33 hectares of herbaceous plants, rock garden, formal gardens and riverside walk. **21 K1** SP6206.
Waterperry *Oxon.* ***Village***, 7m/11km E of Oxford. **21 K1** SP6206.
Waterrow *Som.* ***Village***, on River Tone, 3m/4km SW of Wiveliscombe. **7 J3** ST0525.
Waters Green *Flints.* ***Settlement***, 1km N of Penyffordd. SJ3062.
Water's Nook *Gt.Man.* ***Locality***, 1km E of Westhoughton. SD6606.
Waters Upton *Tel. & W.* ***Village***, 5m/8km N of Wellington. **39 F4** SJ6319.
Watersfield *W.Suss.* ***Village***, 3m/4km SW of Pulborough. **12 D5** TQ0115.
Watersheddings *Gt.Man.* ***Suburb***, 2m/3km NE of Oldham town centre. SD9406.
Waterside *Aber.* ***Settlement***, on S bank of River Don, 1m/2km E of Strathdon. **90 B3** NJ3611.
Waterside *Aber.* ***Settlement***, on E side of River Ythan estuary. **91 J2** NK0027.
Waterside *Bucks.* ***Suburb***, to SE of Chesham. **22 C1** SP9600.
Waterside *Cumb.* ***Locality***, astride River Waver, 3m/4km SW of Wigton. NY2245.
Waterside *E.Ayr.* ***Village***, in valley of River Doon, 3m/5km NW of Dalmellington. **67 J3** NS4308.
Waterside *E.Ayr.* ***Village***, 5m/8km NE of Kilmarnock. **74 C6** NS4843.
Waterside *E.Dun.* ***Locality***, 1m/2km E of Kirkintilloch. **74 E3** NS6773.
Waterside *Lancs.* ***Hamlet***, 1m/2km NE of Darwen. SD7123.
Waterside *S.Yorks.* ***Settlement***, between M18 motorway and River Don, 1m/2km NW of Thorne. SE6714.
Waterstein Head *High.* ***Hill***, 1m/2km E of Neist Point, Skye. Height 971 feet or 296 metres. **93 G7** NG1447.
Waterstock *Oxon.* ***Village***, 5m/7km W of Thame. **21 K1** SP6305.
Waterston *Pembs.* ***Village***, 2m/3km E of Milford Haven. **16 C4** SM9305.
Waterton *V. of Glam.* ***Locality***, industrial estate 2m/3km SE of Bridgend. SS9378.
Watford *Herts.* Population: 113,080. ***Town***, old market town on River Colne, 16m/26km NW of London. Shopping and leisure centre; previous industries were printing and brewing. Parish church of St. Mary's has 16c chapel. **22 E2** TQ1096.
Watford *Northants.* ***Village***, 4m/7km NE of Daventry. **31 H2** SP6068.
Watford Gap *Northants.* ***Settlement***, 5m/8km N of Daventry. Service Area on M1 motorway 1m/2km S. **31 H2** SP5869.
Watford Park *Caerp.* ***Suburb***, adjoining to S of Caerphilly. ST1486.
Wath *N.Yorks.* ***Hamlet***, 2m/3km NW of Pateley Bridge. **57 G3** SE1467.
Wath *N.Yorks.* ***Settlement***, 1km SE of Hovingham. SE6774.
Wath *N.Yorks.* ***Village***, 4m/6km N of Ripon. **57 J2** SE3277.
Wath Brow *Cumb.* ***Locality***, adjoining to E of Cleator Moor. **60 B5** NY0214.
Wath upon Dearne *S.Yorks.* Population: 16,070. ***Town***, market town, 5m/8km N of Rotherham. Former mining town. **51 G2** SE4300.
Watley's End *S.Glos.* ***Suburb***, adjoining to NE of Winterbourne, 3m/5km N of Mangotsfield. ST6581.
Watling Street ***Other feature of interest***, Roman military road which ran from E coast of Kent, through SE and central England, to North Wales. Its line is still largely followed by present A2 and A5 roads. **31 G1** SP6851.
Watlington *Norf.* ***Village***, 5m/8km N of Downham Market. **44 A4** TF6110.
Watlington *Oxon.* Population: 2165. ***Small town***, ancient town 7m/11km S of Thame, with interesting Elizabethan and Georgian buildings. **21 K2** SU6894.
Watnall *Notts.* ***Village***, 6m/9km NW of Nottingham. **41 H1** SK5045.
Wat's Dyke ***Historic/prehistoric site***, early 8c dyke running to E of Offa's Dyke from River Dee estuary to Oswestry. **38 C1** SJ3143.

Wats Ness *Shet.* ***Coastal feature***, headland on W coast of Mainland, 5m/7km W of Walls. **109 A7** HU1750.
Watten *High.* ***Village***, in Caithness district, 8m/12km W of Wick. To N is Loch Watten, nearly 3m/5km NW to SE and up to 1km wide. **105 H3** ND2454.
Wattisfield *Suff.* ***Village***, 5m/9km NE of Ixworth. **34 E1** TM0174.
Wattisham *Suff.* ***Village***, 5m/9km SW of Stowmarket. Airfield to E. **34 E3** TM0151.
Wattle Syke *W.Yorks.* ***Settlement***, in Wharfedale, adjoining to E of Collingham. SE3946.
Watton *Dorset* ***Suburb***, 1km SW of Bridport town centre. SY4592.
Watton *E.Riding* ***Village***, 5m/8km S of Great Driffield. **59 G5** TA0150.
Watton *Norf.* Population: 6018. ***Village***, 8m/13km SE of Swaffham. Rokeles Hall, house dating from 17c, 1m/2km E. Airfield to E. **44 D5** TF9100.
Watton at Stone *Herts.* Population: 2119. ***Village***, 5m/8km SE of Stevenage. **33 G7** TL3019.
Watton Carrs *E.Riding* ***Locality***, 2m/4km E of Watton. **59 G5** TA0448.
Watton Green *Norf.* ***Locality***, 1m/2km E of Watton. **44 D5** TF9301.
Watton Priory *E.Riding* ***Ecclesiastical building***, remains of priory, 5m/8km S of Great Driffield. **59 G5** TA0249.
Watton's Green *Essex* ***Settlement***, 4m/7km W of Brentwood. TQ5295.
Wattston *N.Lan.* ***Village***, 3m/5km N of Airdrie. **75 F4** NS7769.
Wattstown *R.C.T.* ***Hamlet***, 4m/7km NW of Pontypridd. **18 D2** ST0193.
Wattsville *Caerp.* ***Village***, 2m/3km W of Risca. **18 E2** ST2091.
Wauchope Forest *Sc.Bord.* ***Forest/woodland***, forming part of Border Forest Park, 8m/13km SE of Hawick. **70 B3** NT6104.
Wauchope Water *D. & G.* ***River***, running SE, then NE to River Esk at Langholm. **69 J5** NY3684.
Waughton Hill *Aber.* ***Hill***, to W of Mormond Hill, 2m/3km NE of Strichen. Height 768 feet or 234 metres. **99 H5** NJ9657.
Waughtonhill *Aber.* ***Settlement***, below N side of Waughton Hill, 3m/4km NE of Strichen. NJ9758.
Wauldby *E.Riding* ***Hamlet***, with pond, 3m/5km E of South Cave. SE9629.
Waulkmill Bay *Ork.* ***Bay***, large sandy bay, bounded by Ve Ness to SW. **107 C7** HY3706.
Waun *Powys* ***Locality***, 1m/2km NE of Commins Coch. SH8504.
Waun *Powys* ***Locality***, 1m/2km SE of Llansantffraid-ym-Mechain. SJ2319.
Waun Fach *Powys* ***Mountain***, highest point of Black Mountains, 5m/8km W of Llanthony. Height 2660 feet or 811 metres. **28 B5** SO2129.
Waun Fawr *Cere.* ***Suburb***, 1m/2km E of Aberystwyth town centre. **37 F7** SN6081.
Waun Garno *Powys* ***Mountain***, 1m/2km S of Carno. Height 1292 feet or 394 metres. **37 J6** SN9594.
Waun-Lwyd *B.Gwent* ***Village***, 2m/3km S of Ebbw Vale. SO1706.
Waun Lysiog *Powys* ***Open space***, hillside 6m/9km N of Merthyr Tydfil. **27 K7** SO0116.
Waun-oer *Gwyn.* ***Mountain***, 4m/6km SE of Dolgellau. Height 2198 feet or 670 metres. **37 G4** SH7814.
Waun y Clyn *Carmar.* ***Settlement***, adjoining to W of Trimsaran. **17 H4** SN4504.
Waun-y-Llyn Country Park *Flints.* ***Leisure/recreation***, 74 acre or 30 hectare country park situated on N side of Hope Mountain, 1m/2km NW of Caergwrle. Mainly wooded, with small lake and a few disused quarries disturbing uniformity of terrain. **48 B7** SJ2858.
Waunarlwydd *Swan.* ***Village***, 4m/6km W of Swansea city centre. **17 K5** SS6095.
Waunclynda *Carmar.* ***Settlement***, 2m/3km W of Llanwrda. **17 K1** SN6831.
Waunfawr *Gwyn.* ***Hamlet***, 4m/6km SE of Caernarfon. **46 D7** SH5259.
Waungilwen *Carmar.* ***Settlement***, 3m/4km E of Newcastle Emlyn. SN3439.
Waungron *Swan.* ***Settlement***, 1m/2km S of Pontarddulais. SN5902.
Wavendon *M.K.* ***Village***, 4m/6km NW of Woburn. **32 C5** SP9137.
Waveney ***River***, rising near Redgrave and flowing E past Beccles, then N into River Yare at W end of Breydon Water. **45 J5** TG4705.
Waver *Cumb.* ***River***, rising 3m/5km S of Wigton and flowing NW, in series of loops, into Solway Firth via Moricambe bay, 1km after passing Grune Point. **60 D1** NY1357.
Waverbridge *Cumb.* ***Hamlet***, 2m/4km W of Wigton. **60 D2** NY2249.
Waverley *Surr.* ***Locality***, 2m/3km SE of Farnham, including Waverley Abbey. SU8645.
Waverley Abbey *Surr.* ***Ecclesiastical building***, beside River Wey within locality of Waverley, 1m/2km SE of Farnham. Ruins of oldest Cistercian house in England (English Heritage), founded 1128, from which Sir Walter Scott is said to have taken title of his first novel. **22 B7** SU8645.
Waverton *Ches.* ***Village***, 4m/7km SE of Chester. **48 D6** SJ4663.
Waverton *Cumb.* ***Village***, 2m/4km W of Wigton. **60 D2** NY2247.
Wavertree *Mersey.* ***Suburb***, 3m/4km SE of Liverpool city centre. SJ3889.
Wawne *E.Riding* ***Village***, 5m/8km N of Kingston upon Hull. **59 G6** TA0936.
Waxham *Norf.* ***Hamlet***, on coast, 4m/7km E of Stalham. **45 J3** TG4426.
Waxholme *E.Riding* ***Settlement***, on coast, 1m/2km NW of Withernsea. **59 K7** TA3229.
Way *Kent* ***Locality***, on Isle of Thanet, 1m/2km E of Minster. TR3265.
Way Gill *N.Yorks.* ***Settlement***, to W of Winterburn Reservoir, 4m/7km SW of Grassington. **56 E3** SD9360.
Way Village *Devon* ***Hamlet***, 5m/7km SW of Tiverton. **7 G4** SS8810.
Way Wick *N.Som.* ***Hamlet***, 4m/6km E of Weston-super-Mare. ST3862.
Wayford *Som.* ***Village***, 3m/5km SW of Crewkerne. **8 D4** ST4006.
Waymills *Shrop.* ***Suburb***, on E side of Whitchurch. SJ5541.
Wayne Green *Mon.* ***Locality***, 3m/5km W of Skenfrith. SO4118.
Waytown *Dorset* ***Hamlet***, 3m/5km N of Bridport. **8 D5** SY4797.
Wdig *Pembs.* *Welsh form of Goodwick, qv.*
Weachyburn *Aber.* ***Settlement***, 3m/4km N of Aberchirder. **98 E5** NJ6356.
Weacombe *Som.* ***Hamlet***, at foot of Quantock Hills, 3m/5km SE of Watchet. ST1140.
Weald *Cambs.* ***Locality***, on site of former village, 3m/5km E of St. Neots. TL2259.
Weald *Kent* *Alternative name for Sevenoaks Weald, qv.*
Weald *Oxon.* ***Hamlet***, 1km S of Bampton. **21 G1** SP3002.
Weald Park *Essex* ***Leisure/recreation***, 429 acre or 173 hectare park, 1m/2km W of Brentwood, on site of ancient deer enclosure where wild deer can still occasionally be seen. Area also contains some ancient oak and hornbeam trees, some of which may be 500 years old. **23 J2** TQ5794.
Wealdstone *Gt.Lon.* ***Suburb***, in borough of Harrow, 11m/18km NW of Charing Cross. **22 E3** TQ1589.
Wear ***River***, formed by confluence of several streams in vicinity of Wearhead. Flows E by St. John's Chapel and Stanhope to Wolsingham, then SE to Bishop Auckland, then NE by Durham and Chester-le-Street to North Sea at Sunderland. **62 E1** NZ4158.
Wear *T. & W.* ***Locality***, industrial estate in SW part of Washington. NZ2954.
Weardale *Dur.* ***Valley***, carrying River Wear from Wearhead to Stanhope. **62 A3** NY9338.
Wearde *Cornw.* ***Suburb***, S district of Saltash. SX4258.
Weardley *W.Yorks.* ***Village***, 2m/3km W of Harewood, 7m/11km N of Leeds. SE2944.
Weare *Som.* ***Village***, 2m/3km SW of Axbridge. **19 H6** ST4152.
Weare Giffard *Devon* ***Village***, on River Torridge, 2m/3km NW of Great Torrington. **6 C3** SS4721.
Wearhead *Dur.* ***Village***, 9m/14km W of Stanhope. **61 K2** NY8539.
Wearne *Som.* ***Hamlet***, 1m/2km N of Langport. **8 D2** ST4228.
Weasdale *Cumb.* ***Locality***, 2m/3km W of Ravenstonedale. NY6903.
Weasenham All Saints *Norf.* ***Village***, 1km SW of Weasenham St. Peter. **44 C3** TF8521.
Weasenham St. Peter *Norf.* ***Village***, 6m/10km SW of Fakenham. **44 C3** TF8522.
Weaste *Gt.Man.* ***Suburb***, 1m/2km W of Salford city centre. SJ8099.
Weathercote *N.Yorks.* ***Settlement***, adjoining to W of Chapel-le-Dale, 4m/6km NE of Ingleton. **56 C2** SD7377.
Weatheroak Hill *Worcs.* ***Hamlet***, 4m/7km N of Redditch. **30 B1** SP0674.
Weaver *Ches.* ***River***, rising S of Peckforton and flowing SE to its junction with River Duckow near Audlem, N by Nantwich and Winsford to Northwich, then NW to Manchester Ship Canal and, by Weaver Sluices, to River Mersey S of Runcorn. **48 E5** SJ5080.
Weaver Hills *Staffs.* ***Large natural feature***, small range of hills rising to 1217 feet or 371 metres, 5m/8km W of Ashbourne. **40 C1** SK0946.
Weaverham *Ches.* Population: 6604. ***Village***, 3m/4km W of Northwich. **49 F5** SJ6174.
Weavering Street *Kent* ***Suburb***, 1m/2km E of Maidstone. TQ7856.
Weaver's Cottage *Renf.* ***Historic house***, 18c handloom weaver's cottage (National Trust for Scotland), in Kilbarchan. Contains working loom and period furniture. **74 C4** NS4063.
Weaverthorpe *N.Yorks.* ***Village***, 4m/6km NW of Langtoft. **59 F2** SE9670.
Webb's Green *W.Mid.* ***Suburb***, 1m/2km E of Halesowen town centre. SO9783.
Webb's Heath *S.Glos.* ***Hamlet***, 6m/10km E of Bristol. ST6873.
Webheath *Worcs.* ***Suburb***, W district of Redditch. **30 B2** SP0166.
Webton *Here.* ***Locality***, 6m/10km SW of Hereford. **28 D5** SO4236.
Wedder Hill *S.Lan.* ***Mountain***, summit of Blackside ridge to NE of Sorn. Height 1424 feet or 434 metres. **74 D7** NS5930.
Wedder Holm *Shet.* ***Island***, off SE coast of Uyea. HU6197.
Wedder Law *D. & G.* ***Mountain***, in Lowther Hills, on border with South Lanarkshire, 3m/5km E of Durisdeer. Height 2184 feet or 666 metres. **68 E3** NS9302.
Wedderlairs *Aber.* ***Settlement***, 1m/2km NW of Tarves. **91 G1** NJ8532.
Wedderlie Burn *Sc.Bord.* ***River***, small stream rising in Lammermuir Hills and flowing S into Blackadder Water. **76 E5** NT6451.
Weddicar *Cumb.* ***Locality***, 3m/4km E of Whitehaven. NY0117.
Weddington *Warks.* ***Suburb***, N district of Nuneaton. **41 F6** SP3693.
Wedhampton *Wilts.* ***Village***, 4m/7km SE of Devizes. **20 D6** SU0657.
Wedholme Flow *Cumb.* ***Open space***, lowland area to SE of Newton Arlosh and 2m/3km NW of Wigtown. **60 D1** NY2153.
Wedmore *Som.* Population: 2222. ***Village***, 4m/6km S of Cheddar. **19 H7** ST4347.
Wednesbury *W.Mid.* ***Suburb***, NW district of West Bromwich. **40 B6** SO9894.
Wednesbury Oak *W.Mid.* ***Locality***, 3m/5km NW of West Bromwich town centre. SO9594.
Wednesfield *W.Mid.* ***Suburb***, 2m/3km NE of Wolverhampton town centre. **40 B5** SJ9400.
Wee Queensberry *D. & G.* ***Mountain***, 1m/2km S of Queensbury and 6m/10km W of Thornhill. Height 1679 feet or 512 metres. **68 E4** NX9897.
Weecar *Notts.* ***Hamlet***, 3m/5km N of Collingham. SK8266.
Weedon *Bucks.* ***Village***, 3m/5km N of Aylesbury. **32 B7** SP8118.
Weedon Bec *Northants.* Population: 2363. ***Village***, 4m/7km SE of Daventry. **31 H3** SP6259.
Weedon Lois *Northants.* ***Village***, 6m/10km N of Brackley. **31 H4** SP6046.
Weeford *Staffs.* ***Village***, 4m/7km W of Tamworth. **40 D5** SK1403.
Week *Devon* ***Hamlet***, 4m/6km S of Barnstaple. SS5726.
Week *Devon* ***Hamlet***, 2m/3km NW of Totnes. SX7762.
Week *Devon* ***Settlement***, 4m/6km NE of Chulmleigh. **7 F4** SS7316.
Week *Som.* ***Hamlet***, on Exmoor, 1km W of Exton. SS9133.
Week Orchard *Cornw.* ***Settlement***, 2m/3km N of Week St. Mary. **6 A5** SS2300.
Week St. Mary *Cornw.* ***Village***, 6m/9km S of Bude. Ruins of medieval Penhallam manor (English Heritage) 1m/2km NW. **4 C1** SX2397.
Weeke *Hants.* ***Suburb***, to NW of Winchester. SU4630.
Weekley *Northants.* ***Village***, 2m/3km NE of Kettering. **42 B7** SP8880.
Weeks *I.o.W.* ***Suburb***, 1km S of Ryde town centre. SZ5991.
Weel *E.Riding* ***Hamlet***, 2m/3km E of Beverley. TA0639.
Weeley *Essex* Population: 1457. ***Village***, 5m/8km NW of Clacton-on-Sea. **35 F6** TM1422.
Weeley Heath *Essex* ***Village***, 3m/5km NW of Clacton-on-Sea. **35 F7** TM1520.
Weelsby *N.E.Lincs.* ***Suburb***, 2m/3km SE of Grimsby town centre. TA2808.
Weem *P. & K.* ***Village***, 1m/2km NW of Aberfeldy across River Tay. **81 K3** NN8449.
Weem Hill *P. & K.* ***Mountain***, 3m/4km NW of Aberfeldy. Height 1607 feet or 490 metres. **81 K2** NN8251.
Weeping Cross *Staffs.* ***Suburb***, 2m/3km SE of Stafford town centre. **40 B3** SJ9421.
Weethley *Warks.* ***Hamlet***, 3m/4km SW of Alcester. **30 B3** SP0555.
Weeting *Norf.* Population: 1757. ***Village***, 1m/2km N of Brandon. **44 B7** TL7788.
Weeting Castle *Norf.* ***Castle***, remains of 11c fortified manor house (English Heritage), 7m/11km NW of Thetford. **44 B7** TL7788.
Weeton *E.Riding* ***Hamlet***, 3m/5km SE of Patrington. **59 K7** TA3520.
Weeton *Lancs.* ***Village***, 3m/5km NW of Kirkham. **55 G6** SD3834.
Weeton *N.Yorks.* ***Village***, 5m/8km S of Harrogate. **57 H5** SE2846.
Weeton Lane Heads *Lancs.* ***Locality***, just E of Weeton. SD3834.
Weets Hill *Lancs.* ***Mountain***, 2m/3km SW of Barnoldswick. Height 1302 feet or 397 metres. **56 D5** SD8544.
Weetwood *W.Yorks.* ***Suburb***, 3m/4km NW of Leeds city centre. SE2737.
Weighton Common *E.Riding* ***Open space***, lowland 1m/2km SW of Market Weighton. **58 E5** SE8540.
Weir *Essex* ***Suburb***, to S of Rayleigh. **24 E3** TQ8089.
Weir *Lancs.* ***Hamlet***, 1m/2km N of Bacup. **56 D7** SD8725.
Weir Dike *N.Lincs.* ***Other water feature***, drainage cut, draining Bonby Carrs, running from 3m/5km N of Brigg into Humber estuary at Ferriby Sluice. **52 C1** SE9721.
Weir Quay *Devon* ***Hamlet***, on E bank of River Tamar, 6m/10km SW of Yelverton. SX4364.
Weir Wood Reservoir ***Reservoir***, on border of East and West Sussex, 2m/3km S of East Grinstead. **13 G3** TQ3934.
Weirbrook *Shrop.* ***Settlement***, 5m/8km SE of Oswestry. **38 C3** SJ3524.
Weisdale *Shet.* ***Locality***, surrounding Burn of Weisdale valley on Mainland, to N of Weisdale Voe. **109 C7** HU3953.
Weisdale Voe *Shet.* ***Sea feature***, long inlet on Mainland, with Heglibister near head of voe on W shore. Burn of Weisdale drains into voe. **109 C8** HU3848.
Welbeck Abbey *Notts.* ***Historic house***, mansion of various periods, mainly Victorian, in Welbeck Park, 3m/5km SW of Worksop. **51 H5** SK5674.
Welbeck Abbey *Notts.* ***Settlement***, 3m/5km SW of Worksop. **51 H5** SK5674.
Welborne *Norf.* ***Village***, 5m/8km E of East Dereham. **44 E5** TG0610.
Welbourn *Lincs.* ***Village***, 11m/18km S of Lincoln. **52 C7** SK9654.
Welburn *N.Yorks.* ***Hamlet***, 2m/3km SW of Kirkbymoorside, on W side of Hodge Beck. SE6884.
Welburn *N.Yorks.* ***Village***, 5m/8km SW of Malton. **58 D3** SE7267.
Welbury *N.Yorks.* ***Village***, 6m/9km N of Northallerton. **62 E6** NZ3902.
Welby *Lincs.* ***Village***, 4m/7km NE of Grantham. **42 C2** SK9738.
Welches Dam *Cambs.* ***Hamlet***, 2m/4km S of Manea. **43 H7** TL4786.
Welcombe *Devon* ***Village***, near coast, 8m/13km N of Bude. **6 A4** SS2218.
Weld Bank *Lancs.* ***Suburb***, S of Chorley. SD5816.

Weldon *Northants.* ***Village***, 2m/3km E of Corby. Stone quarries (Weldon stone). Several Roman remains nearby. **42 C7** SP9289.
Welford *Northants.* ***Village***, 3m/4km S of Husbands Bosworth. Reservoir to NE. **41 J7** SP6480.
Welford *W.Berks.* ***Village***, 5m/9km NW of Newbury. **21 H4** SU4073.
Welford-on-Avon *Warks.* Population: 1311. ***Village***, in loop of river, 4m/6km W of Stratford-upon-Avon. **30 C3** SP1452.
Welham *Leics.* ***Village***, on River Welland, 4m/6km NE of Market Harborough. **42 A6** SP7692.
Welham *Notts.* ***Hamlet***, 2m/3km NE of Retford. **51 K4** SK7282.
Welham Green *Herts.* ***Village***, 2m/3km S of Hatfield. **23 F1** TL2305.
Well *Hants.* ***Hamlet***, 5m/8km W of Farnham. **22 A7** SU7646.
Well *Lincs.* ***Hamlet***, 1m/2km SW of Alford. **53 H5** TF4473.
Well *N.Yorks.* ***Village***, on escarpment, 3m/5km E of Masham. Site of Roman building on hillside to W. **57 H1** SE2681.
Well Bank *Lancs.* ***Locality***, adjoining to W of Haslingden. SD7823.
Well End *Bucks.* ***Locality***, adjoining to N of Bourne End. **22 B3** SU8888.
Well End *Herts.* ***Hamlet***, 1m/2km N of Borehamwood. TQ2098.
Well Heads *W.Yorks.* ***Settlement***, 1m/2km SE of Denholme. SE0833.
Well Hill *Kent* ***Hamlet***, 3m/4km SE of Orpington. **23 H5** TQ4963.
Well Street *Kent* ***Settlement***, 1km SW of East Malling. TQ6956.
Well Town *Devon* ***Settlement***, 3m/5km SW of Tiverton. **7 H5** SS9009.
Welland ***River***, rising near Mowsley, W of Market Harborough, and flowing generally NE to Stamford, Market Deeping and Spalding, and then into The Wash, about 7m/11km N of Holbeach. **42 C6** TF3635.
Welland *Worcs.* ***Village***, 2m/3km SE of Malvern Wells. **29 G4** SO7939.
Wellbank *Angus* ***Hamlet***, 4m/7km N of Broughty Ferry. **83 F4** NO4637.
Wellesbourne *Warks.* Population: 5134. ***Village***, 5m/8km E of Stratford-upon-Avon. Originally two separate villages, Wellesbourne Mountford and Wellesbourne Hastings, divided by River Dene. **30 D3** SP2755.
Wellesbourne Hastings *Warks. See Wellesbourne.*
Wellesbourne Mountford *Warks. See Wellesbourne.*
Wellfield *Dur.* ***Locality***, 1km NE of Wingate. NZ4038.
Wellgrain Dod *S.Lan.* ***Mountain***, in Lowther Hills, 3m/5km W of Elvanfoot. Height 1814 feet or 553 metres. **68 D2** NS9017.
Wellhill *Moray* ***Settlement***, 3m/4km NW of Forres. **97 G5** NJ0061.
Wellhouse *W.Berks.* ***Settlement***, 4m/7km NE of Newbury. Site of Roman villa to E. SU5272.
Wellhouse *W.Yorks.* ***Hamlet***, 1km S of Golcar. SE0915.
Welling *Gt.Lon.* ***Suburb***, in borough of Bexley, 11m/17km E of Charing Cross. **23 H4** TQ4675.
Wellingborough *Northants.* Population: 41,602. ***Town***, market town, 10m/16km NE of Northampton. Former centre for footwear, now developing a hi-tech base. Many old buildings, including 15c thatched tithe barn. **32 B2** SP8968.
Wellingham *Norf.* ***Village***, 6m/9km SW of Fakenham. **44 C3** TF8722.
Wellingore *Lincs.* ***Village***, 9m/15km S of Lincoln. **52 C7** SK9856.
Wellington *Cumb.* ***Hamlet***, 1km NE of Gosforth. **60 B6** NY0704.
Wellington *Here.* ***Village***, 5m/8km N of Hereford. **28 D4** SO4948.
Wellington *Som.* Population: 9621. ***Small town***, market town in valley of River Tone, 6m/10km W of Taunton. **7 K3** ST1320.
Wellington *Tel. & W.* Population: 18,494. ***Town***, market town, 10m/16km E of Shrewsbury, forming part of Telford. **39 F4** SJ6511.
Wellington College *Brack.F. See Crowthorne.*
Wellington Country Park *Hants.* ***Leisure/recreation***, 1km SE of Riseley. Central feature is large lake around which are 350 acres of meadows, woodlands and nature trails. Park is also home to National Dairy Museum. **22 A5** SU7362.
Wellington Heath *Here.* ***Village***, 2m/3km N of Ledbury. **29 G4** SO7140.
Wellington Hill *W.Yorks.* ***Suburb***, 4m/7km NE of Leeds city centre. SE3538.
Wellington Marsh *Here.* ***Locality***, 5m/8km N of Hereford. **28 D4** SO4947.
Wellington Monument *Som.* ***Other feature of interest***, obelisk (National Trust) on Black Down Hills, to S of Wellington, commemorating exploits of Duke of Wellington. **7 K4** ST1317.
Wellow *B. & N.E.Som.* ***Village***, 4m/7km S of Bath. Prehistoric burial mound (English Heritage) to S across Wellow Brook. **20 A6** ST7458.
Wellow *I.o.W.* ***Village***, 2m/4km SE of Yarmouth. **10 E6** SZ3888.
Wellow *Notts.* ***Village***, 1m/2km SE of Ollerton. **51 J6** SK6766.
Wellow Wood *Hants.* ***Settlement***, just S of Sherfield English. SU2921.
Wellpond Green *Herts.* ***Hamlet***, 2m/3km SE of Puckeridge. TL4122.
Wells *Norf. Familiar form of Wells-next-the-Sea, qv.*
Wells *Som.* Population: 9763. ***City***, ancient cathedral city (Royal Charter granted 1201) below S slopes of Mendip Hills, 17m/24km S of Bristol. Cathedral dates from late 12c. Centre still largely medieval. 14c Vicars Close is the most complete medieval street in Europe. Wells is named after St. Andrew's Well, which is in the garden of the Moated Bishop's Palace. **19 J7** ST5445.
Wells Cathedral *Som.* ***Ecclesiastical building***, magnificent three-towered cathedral in centre of Wells. Present building was begun c. 1180 and a variety of medieval styles are found. Particularly impressive W front, which provides background setting for nearly 400 statues. The cathedral clock is also of interest. **19 J7** ST5545.
Wells Green *Ches.* ***Suburb***, 2m/3km SW of Crewe town centre. SJ6853.
Wells Green *W.Mid.* ***Suburb***, 3m/5km N of Solihull town centre. SP1483.
Wells Museum *Som.* ***Other feature of interest***, to N of Wells city centre. Exhibitions include cave artefacts and local history. **19 J7** ST5546.
Wells-next-the-Sea (Commonly referred to as Wells.) *Norf.* Population: 2400. ***Small town***, yachting centre, 9m/14km N of Fakenham. **44 D1** TF9143.
Wellsborough *Leics.* ***Settlement***, 3m/4km W of Market Bosworth. **41 F5** SK3602.
Wellstyle Green *Essex* ***Hamlet***, 2m/3km S of Great Dunmow. TL6318.
Wellswood *Torbay* ***Suburb***, central district of Torquay. SX9264.
Wellsworth *Hants.* ***Settlement***, adjoining to N of Rowland's Castle, 3m/5km N of Havant. SU7311.
Wellwood *Fife* ***Hamlet***, 1m/2km N of Dunfermline. **75 J2** NT0988.
Welney *Norf.* ***Village***, 5m/8km NW of Littleport. **43 J6** TL5294.
Welsh Bicknor *Glos.* ***Hamlet***, in loop of River Wye, 4m/7km S of Ross-on-Wye across river. **28 E7** SO5917.
Welsh Channel ***Sea feature***, running along North Wales coast between mouth of River Dee and Prestatyn. **47 J4** SJ0885.
Welsh End *Shrop.* ***Settlement***, 4m/7km N of Wem. **38 E2** SJ5135.
Welsh Frankton *Shrop.* ***Hamlet***, 3m/4km SW of Ellesmere. **38 C2** SJ3633.
Welsh Highland Railway *Gwyn.* ***Other feature of interest***, restored narrow gauge railway heading S from Caernarfon. Re-opened in 1997 as far as Dinas, with further extension planned towards Porthmadog. **46 C6** SH5739.
Welsh Hook *Pembs.* ***Settlement***, 6m/10km S of Fishguard. **16 C2** SM9327.
Welsh Mountain Zoo *Conwy* ***Leisure/recreation***, on hillside to W of Colwyn Bay. Traditional zoo in natural setting. Chief attractions include 'Chimpanzee World', Californian sea lions and eagle displays. **47 G5** SH8378.
Welsh Newton *Here.* ***Village***, 3m/5km N of Monmouth. **28 E7** SO4918.
Welsh St. Donats (Llanddunwyd). *V. of Glam.* ***Village***, 2m/4km NE of Cowbridge. **18 D4** ST0276.
Welshampton *Shrop.* ***Village***, 2m/4km E of Ellesmere. **38 D2** SJ4335.
Welshpool (Y Trallwng). *Powys* Population: 5725. ***Small town***, on W bank of River Severn, 17m/27km W of Shrewsbury. Powis Castle (National Trust) in parkland 1m/2km SW. Remains of Norman motte and bailey castle near railway station. **38 B5** SJ2207.
Welshpool and Llanfair Light Railway *Powys* ***Other feature of interest***, narrow gauge tourist railway running from Welshpool, W to Llanfair Caereinion. **38 B5** SJ2107.
Welton *B. & N.E.Som.* ***Suburb***, NE district of Midsomer Norton. **19 K6** ST6654.
Welton *Cumb.* ***Hamlet***, 4m/6km S of Dalston. **60 E2** NY3544.
Welton *E.Riding* ***Village***, 1m/2km E of Brough. **59 F7** SE9527.
Welton *Lincs.* Population: 1848. ***Village***, 6m/9km NE of Lincoln. **52 D4** TF0179.
Welton *Northants.* ***Village***, 2m/4km N of Daventry. **31 G2** SP5866.
Welton le Marsh *Lincs.* ***Village***, 7m/11km NW of Skegness. **53 H6** TF4768.
Welton le Wold *Lincs.* ***Village***, 4m/6km W of Louth. **53 F4** TF2787.
Welwick *E.Riding* ***Village***, 2m/3km SE of Patrington. **59 K7** TA3421.
Welwyn *Herts.* ***Town***, 5m/8km S of Stevenage. Sites of Roman buildings beside River Mimram to E and W. **33 F7** TL2316.
Welwyn Garden City *Herts.* Population: 42,087. ***Town***, commuter town, 6m/10km NE of St. Albans. New Town designated 1948. **33 F7** TL2313.
Wem *Shrop.* Population: 4882. ***Small town***, on River Roden, 10m/16km N of Shrewsbury. Several timber-framed buildings survived early fire. Judge Jeffreys lived here. **38 E3** SJ5128.
Wembdon *Som.* ***Village***, adjoining to W of Bridgwater. **8 B1** ST2837.
Wembley *Gt.Lon.* ***Suburb***, in borough of Brent, 8m/13km NW of Charing Cross. Includes localities of North Wembley and Wembley Park. Wembley Stadium at Wembley Park. **22 E3** TQ1885.
Wembley Park *Gt.Lon.* ***Suburb***, in borough of Brent, 1m/2km NE of Wembley. Wembley Stadium. TQ1986.
Wembury *Devon* Population: 1061. ***Village***, on Wembury Bay, 5m/7km SE of Plymouth across River Plym estuary. Cliffs to E of Wembury are National Trust property. **5 F6** SX5249.
Wembury Bay *Devon* ***Bay***, 5m/7km SE of Plymouth across River Plym estuary. **5 F6** SX5148.
Wembworthy *Devon* ***Village***, 3m/5km SW of Chulmleigh. **6 E5** SS6609.
Wemyss Bay *Inclyde* Population: 1635. ***Village***, and bay on Firth of Clyde, 7m/11km SW of Greenock. Passenger boat terminus. **73 K4** NS1969.
Wemyss Castle *Fife* ***Castle***, restored 15c-17c building on rocky eminence to NE of West Wemyss, towards East Wemyss. NT3295.
Wemyss Point *Inclyde* ***Coastal feature***, headland to N of Wemyss Bay. **73 K3** NS1870.
Wen *Gwyn.* ***River***, flowing SW into River Mawddach, 2m/3km NE of Llanelltyd. **37 G3** SH7322.
Wenallt *Cere.* ***Settlement***, 1km W of Llanafan. SN6771.
Wenallt *Gwyn.* ***Settlement***, 6m/10km NE of Dolgellau. **37 H3** SH8123.
Wenallt *Gwyn.* ***Settlement***, 5m/8km NE of Bala. **37 J1** SH9842.
Wendens Ambo *Essex* ***Village***, 2m/4km SW of Saffron Walden. Site of Roman villa to SW. **33 J5** TL5136.
Wendlebury *Oxon.* ***Village***, 2m/4km SW of Bicester. **31 G7** SP5619.
Wendling *Norf.* ***Village***, 4m/6km W of East Dereham. **44 D4** TF9312.
Wendon Lofts *Essex* ***Hamlet***, 5m/8km W of Saffron Walden. TL4638.
Wendover *Bucks.* Population: 6985. ***Small town***, market town with timber-framed and Georgian buildings, at N edge of Chiltern Hills, 5m/8km SE of Aylesbury. **22 B1** SP8607.
Wendover Dean *Bucks.* ***Settlement***, 2m/3km S of Wendover. SP8704.
Wendron *Cornw.* ***Hamlet***, 2m/4km N of Helston. **2 D5** SW6731.
Wendy *Cambs.* ***Village***, 5m/7km NW of Royston. **33 G4** TL3247.
Wenfordbridge *Cornw.* ***Settlement***, on River Camel, 5m/9km S of Camelford. SX0875.
Wenhaston *Suff.* ***Village***, 3m/4km SE of Halesworth. **35 J1** TM4275.
Wenlli *Conwy* ***Settlement***, 3m/5km NE of Llanrwst. **47 G6** SH8465.
Wenlock Edge *Shrop.* ***Inland physical feature***, hill ridge running from Craven Arms in SW to Much Wenlock in NE. **38 D7** SO5392.
Wenlock Priory *Shrop.* ***Ecclesiastical building***, in Much Wenlock. Original priory founded by St. Milburga and destroyed and rebuilt several times. Ruins (English Heritage) date mainly from 11c, including church and cloister, together with 15c prior's lodging. **39 F5** SJ6200.
Wennallt *Powys* ***Mountain***, 6m/9km N of Llandrindod Wells. Height 1545 feet or 471 metres. **27 K1** SO0371.
Wenning ***River***, rising on limestone hills W of Horton-in-Ribblesdale, flowing W through Wennington and into River Lune to W of Hornby. **56 C3** SD5768.
Wennington *Cambs.* ***Hamlet***, 5m/8km N of Huntingdon. **33 F1** TL2379.
Wennington *Gt.Lon.* ***Suburb***, in borough of Havering, 1m/2km SE of Rainham. **23 J3** TQ5480.
Wennington *Lancs.* ***Village***, 6m/9km S of Kirkby Lonsdale. **56 B2** SD6170.
Wensley *Derbys.* ***Village***, 2m/4km W of Matlock. **50 E6** SK2661.
Wensley *N.Yorks.* ***Village***, on River Ure, 1m/2km W of Leyburn. **62 B7** SE0989.
Wensleydale *N.Yorks.* ***Valley***, carrying River Ure E from Hawes, via Bainbridge, Askrigg and Aysgarth, to Leyburn. Valley is relatively wide and flat-bottomed. It is noted for its picturesque scenery, waterfalls, including Aysgarth Falls, and for Wensleydale cheese. **61 K7** SD9590.
Wensum *Norf.* ***River***, rising near Horningtoft and flowing in a westward loop to Fakenham, then SE to Norwich, on E side of which it joins River Yare. **44 E4** TG2507.
Went *S.Yorks.* ***River***, formed from several tributaries to W of Wentbridge, and flowing E through Little Smeaton to enter River Don 4m/6km N of Thorne. **51 J1** SE6618.
Went Hill *E.Suss.* ***Settlement***, 1km S of East Dean. **13 J7** TV5596.
Wentbridge *W.Yorks.* ***Village***, on River Went, 4m/6km SE of Pontefract. **51 G1** SE4817.
Wentnor *Shrop.* ***Village***, 5m/8km NE of Bishop's Castle. **38 C6** SO3892.
Wentwood *Newport* ***Forest/woodland***, area of mixed woodland to N of Wentwood Reservoir. **19 G2** ST4294.
Wentworth *Cambs.* ***Village***, 4m/6km W of Ely. **33 H1** TL4878.
Wentworth *S.Yorks.* ***Village***, 4m/7km NW of Rotherham. **51 F3** SK3898.
Wentworth *Surr.* ***Locality***, residential district and championship golf course to W of Virginia Water. SU9767.
Wentworth Castle *S.Yorks.* ***Historic house***, dating partly from 17c, 2m/4km SW of Barnsley. **51 F2** SE3203.
Wenvoe (Gwenfo). *V. of Glam.* ***Village***, 3m/5km N of Barry. **18 E4** ST1272.
Weobley *Here.* ***Village***, 10m/16km NW of Hereford. **28 C3** SO4051.
Weobley Castle *Swan.* ***Castle***, ruins of fortified 13c-14c manor house (Cadw), 1m/2km NE of Llanrhidian. **17 H5** SS4792.
Weobley Marsh *Here.* ***Hamlet***, 1m/2km E of Weobley. **28 D3** SO4151.
Weoley Castle *W.Mid.* ***Suburb***, 4m/7km SW of Birmingham city centre. SP0182.
Wepham *W.Suss.* ***Hamlet***, just SE of Burpham, 4m/7km N of Littlehampton. **12 D6** TQ0408.
Wepre *Flints.* ***Suburb***, S district of Connah's Quay. **48 B6** SJ2968.
Wereham *Norf.* ***Village***, 2m/3km NW of Stoke Ferry. **44 A5** TF6801.
Werfa *Bridgend* ***Mountain***, 3m/5km SW of Treorchy. Height 1863 feet or 568 metres. **18 C2** SS9194.
Wergs *W.Mid.* ***Suburb***, 3m/5km NW of Wolverhampton town centre. **40 A5** SJ8600.
Wern *Gwyn.* ***Settlement***, 3m/5km NE of Criccieth. SH5439.
Wern *Powys* ***Settlement***, on Shropshire Union Canal, 4m/7km NE of Welshpool. SJ2513.
Wern *Powys* ***Settlement***, 3m/5km SW of Llangynidr. SO1117.
Wern *Shrop.* ***Hamlet***, 1m/2km NE of Sellatyn. SJ2734.
Wern-olau *Swan.* ***Hamlet***, 6m/9km W of Swansea. SS5695.

Wern-y-cwrt *Mon.* ***Settlement***, 1m/2km NW of Raglan. SO3908.
Wern-y-gaer *Flints.* ***Settlement***, 2m/4km W of Northop. SJ2068.
Werneth *Gt.Man.* ***Settlement***, 2m/3km S of Hyde. SJ9592.
Wernffrwd *Swan.* ***Hamlet***, on Gower peninsula, 2m/3km NE of Llanrhidian. SS5193.
Wernrheolydd *Mon.* ***Hamlet***, 4m/6km N of Raglan. **28 C7** SO3912.
Werrington *Cornw.* ***Hamlet***, 2m/3km N of Launceston. **6 B7** SX3287.
Werrington *Peter.* ***Suburb***, 4m/6km NW of Peterborough city centre. **42 E5** TF1603.
Werrington *Staffs.* ***Locality***, 4m/6km E of Hanley. **40 B1** SJ9447.
Wervil Brook *Cere.* ***Settlement***, 6m/9km SW of Newquay. **26 C3** SN3452.
Wervin *Ches.* ***Village***, 4m/6km N of Chester. **48 D5** SJ4271.
Wesham *Lancs.* ***Village***, adjoining to NW of Kirkham. **55 H6** SD4132.
Wessenden Moor *W.Yorks.* ***Open space***, large expanse of moorland containing several reservoirs, 2m/4km S of Marsden. **50 C2** SE0507.
Wessington *Derbys.* ***Village***, 3m/5km NW of Alfreton. **51 F7** SK3757.
Wessington Green *Derbys.* ***Settlement***, adjoining to S of Wessington. SK3757.
West Aberthaw *V. of Glam.* ***Hamlet***, 1km E of Gileston. **18 D5** ST0266.
West Acre *Norf.* ***Village***, 5m/7km NW of Swaffham. Remains of 12c priory. **44 B4** TF7715.
West Acton *Gt.Lon.* ***Suburb***, in borough of Ealing, 1km NW of Acton. TQ1981.
West Adderbury *Oxon.* *See Adderbury.*
West Allen *Northumb.* ***River***, rising on Coalcleugh Moor, near Coalcleugh and flowing N to join River East Allen to form River Allen, 3m/5km NW of Allendale Town. **61 J2** NY8058.
West Allerdean *Northumb.* ***Settlement***, 5m/8km SW of Berwick-upon-Tweed. **77 H6** NT9646.
West Allotment *T. & W.* ***Locality***, 5m/8km NE of Newcastle upon Tyne. NZ3070.
West Alvington *Devon* ***Village***, 1km W of Kingsbridge. **5 H6** SX7243.
West Amesbury *Wilts.* ***Hamlet***, 1km W of Amesbury. **20 E7** SU1441.
West Anstey *Devon* ***Village***, on S slopes of Exmoor, 4m/6km W of Dulverton. **7 G3** SS8527.
West Appleton *N.Yorks.* ***Settlement***, 3m/4km SW of Catterick. SE2294.
West Ashby *Lincs.* ***Village***, 2m/3km N of Horncastle. **53 F5** TF2672.
West Ashford *Devon* ***Settlement***, 1km W of Ashford. SS5235.
West Ashling *W.Suss.* ***Village***, 4m/6km NW of Chichester. **12 B6** SU8107.
West Ashton *Wilts.* ***Village***, 2m/3km SE of Trowbridge. **20 B6** ST8755.
West Auckland *Dur.* ***Village***, adjoining to SW of Bishop Auckland. **62 C4** NZ1826.
West Ayton *N.Yorks.* Population: 1276. ***Village***, on W bank of River Derwent, opposite East Ayton, 4m/7km SW of Scarborough. **59 F1** SE9884.
West Bagborough *Som.* ***Village***, at foot of Quantock Hills, 7m/11km NW of Taunton. **7 K2** ST1733.
West Bank *Ches.* ***Suburb***, beside River Mersey, 1m/2km S of Widnes town centre. SJ5183.
West Barkwith *Lincs.* ***Hamlet***, 1m/2km SW of East Barkwith. **52 E4** TF1681.
West Barnby *N.Yorks.* ***Village***, 5m/8km W of Whitby. **63 K5** NZ8212.
West Barnham *W.Suss.* ***Locality***, adjoining Barnham, 4m/6km NE of Bognor Regis. SU9504.
West Barns *E.Loth.* ***Hamlet***, 1m/2km W of Dunbar. **76 E3** NT6578.
West Barsham *Norf.* ***Hamlet***, 1m/2km W of East Barsham. **44 D2** TF9133.
West Barton *Devon* ***Settlement***, adjoining Horwood, 3m/5km E of Bideford. SS5027.
West Baugh Fell *Cumb.* ***Open space***, moorland on N side of Baugh Fell, 4m/7km NE of Sedbergh. **61 J7** SD7294.
West Bay *Dorset* ***Bay***, to W of Portland, Dorset. **9 F7** SY6773.
West Bay *Dorset* ***Village***, on coast, with small harbour, 2m/3km S of Bridport. **8 D5** SY4690.
West Beckham *Norf.* ***Village***, 1m/2km W of East Beckham. **45 F2** TG1539.
West Bedfont *Surr.* ***Locality***, on S side of London (Heathrow) Airport and 3m/5km NE of Staines. TQ0773.
West Benhar *N.Lan.* ***Settlement***, 1m/2km SW of Harthill. **75 G4** NS8863.
West Bergholt *Essex* Population: 3027. ***Village***, 3m/4km NW of Colchester. **34 D6** TL9627.
West Bexington *Dorset* ***Village***, on coast, 3m/5km NW of Abbotsbury. **8 E6** SY5386.
West Bilney *Norf.* ***Hamlet***, 7m/11km SE of King's Lynn. **44 B4** TF7115.
West Blatchington *B. & H.* ***Suburb***, N of Hove. **13 F6** TQ2807.
West Boldon *T. & W.* ***Suburb***, forms town of Boldon, along with East Boldon. **71 J7** NZ3561.
West Bourton *Dorset* ***Hamlet***, 1km S of Bourton, 3m/5km NW of Gillingham. ST7629.
West Bowling *W.Yorks.* ***Suburb***, 1m/2km S of Bradford city centre. SE1631.
West Brabourne *Kent* ***Hamlet***, 4m/7km E of Ashford. TR0842.
West Bradenham *Norf.* ***Village***, adjoining to W of East Bradenham, 6m/10km E of Swaffham. **44 D5** TF9208.
West Bradford *Lancs.* ***Village***, on River Ribble, 2m/3km N of Clitheroe. **56 C5** SD7444.
West Bradley *Som.* ***Village***, 4m/6km SE of Glastonbury. **8 E1** ST5536.
West Bretton *W.Yorks.* ***Village***, 5m/9km SW of Wakefield. **50 E1** SE2813.
West Bridgford *Notts.* Population: 33,843. ***Town***, on S side of Nottingham across River Trent. **41 H2** SK5837.
West Briscoe *Dur.* ***Locality***, 1km W of East Briscoe, at S end of Hury Reservoir dam. NY9619.
West Bromwich *W.Mid.* Population: 146,386. ***Town***, 5m/8km NW of Birmingham. Formerly a coalmining and metal-working town, West Bromwich is now an administrative and commercial centre with various industries. Sandwell Valley Country Park on E side of town. **40 C6** SP0091.
West Buckland *Devon* ***Village***, 5m/8km NW of South Molton. **6 E2** SS6531.
West Buckland *Som.* ***Village***, 2m/4km E of Wellington. **7 K3** ST1720.
West Burra *Shet.* ***Island***, one of two long, narrow, adjacent islands S of Scalloway, Mainland, to W of Trondra. Road bridges at either end of Trondra give connection to Mainland. East Burra lies to E and is also connected by a road bridge. **109 C9** HU3632.
West Burrafirth *Shet.* ***Settlement***, on Mainland, to W of head of West Burra Firth. **109 B7** HU2557.
West Burton *N.Yorks.* ***Village***, 1m/2km SE of Aysgarth. **57 F1** SE0186.
West Burton *W.Suss.* ***Village***, 4m/7km N of Arundel. **12 C5** SU9913.
West Butsfield *Dur.* ***Hamlet***, 4m/6km S of Consett. NZ1044.
West Butterwick *N.Lincs.* ***Village***, on opposite bank of River Trent to East Butterwick, 5m/8km SW of Scunthorpe. Nearest bridge at Keadby, 3m/5km N. **52 B2** SE8305.
West Byfleet *Surr.* ***Locality***, residential locality 1m/2km W of Byfleet. **22 D5** TQ0460.
West Cairn Hill *Sc.Bord.* ***Mountain***, on border of Scottish Borders and West Lothian in Pentland Hills, 5m/8km NW of West Linton. Height 1843 feet or 562 metres. **75 K5** NT1058.
West Cairncake *Aber.* ***Settlement***, 1m/2km E of Cuminestown. **99 G6** NJ8249.
West Caister *Norf.* ***Hamlet***, 1m/2km W of Caister-on-Sea. **45 K4** TG5011.
West Calder *W.Loth.* Population: 2888. ***Village***, 4m/7km SE of Bathgate. **75 J4** NT0163.
West Camel *Som.* ***Village***, 2m/3km SW of Sparkford. **8 E2** ST5724.
West Canisbay *High.* ***Settlement***, to W of Canisbay, near N coast of Caithness district. ND3471.
West Carbeth *Stir.* ***Settlement***, 2m/4km W of Strathblane. NS5279.
West Carlton *W.Yorks.* ***Settlement***, 1m/2km NE of Guiseley. SE2042.
West Carr *N.Lincs.* ***Settlement***, 3m/5km NW of Epworth. SE7407.
West Carr Houses *N.Lincs.* ***Hamlet***, 3m/5km NW of Epworth. SE7306.
West Cauldcoats *S.Lan.* ***Settlement***, 3m/5km S of Strathaven. **74 E6** NS6840.
West Chaldon *Dorset* ***Settlement***, 1m/2km N of coast, 5m/8km SW of Wool. SY7782.
West Challow *Oxon.* ***Village***, 2m/3km W of Wantage. **21 G3** SU3688.
West Charleton *Devon* ***Village***, in parish of Charleton, along with East Charleton, 2m/3km SE of Kingsbridge. **5 H6** SX7542.
West Chelborough *Dorset* ***Hamlet***, 2m/3km W of Evershot. **8 E4** ST5405.
West Chevington *Northumb.* ***Hamlet***, 2m/3km NW of Widdrington. **71 H4** NZ2297.
West Chiltington *W.Suss.* Population: 2984. ***Village***, 3m/5km E of Pulborough. **12 D5** TQ0918.
West Chinnock *Som.* ***Village***, 2m/3km W of East Chinnock. **8 D3** ST4613.
West Chirton *T. & W.* ***Suburb***, 1m/2km W of North Shields. NZ3368.
West Chisenbury *Wilts.* ***Settlement***, 1m/2km S of Upavon. **20 E6** SU1352.
West Clandon *Surr.* Population: 1367. ***Village***, 4m/6km NE of Guildford. **22 D6** TQ0452.
West Cliff *N.Yorks.* ***Suburb***, W district of Whitby. NZ8811.
West Cliffe *Kent* ***Hamlet***, 3m/5km NE of Dover and 1m/2km inland from South Foreland. **15 J3** TR3444.
West Clyne *High.* ***Settlement***, on E coast of Sutherland district, 2m/3km NW of Brora. **97 F1** NC8805.
West Coatham *R. & C.* ***Locality***, industrial locality to SW of Coatham; chemical works. NZ5925.
West Coker *Som.* ***Village***, 2m/3km NW of East Coker. **8 E3** ST5213.
West Compton (Also known as Compton Abbas.) *Dorset* ***Hamlet***, 3m/5km SW of Maiden Newton. **8 E5** SY5694.
West Compton *Som.* ***Hamlet***, 2m/3km SW of Shepton Mallet. **19 J7** ST5942.
West Cornforth *Dur.* ***Locality***, adjoining to SE of Cornforth, 4m/6km NW of Sedgefield. NZ3133.
West Cowick *E.Riding* ***Village***, 1km SE of Snaith. SE6521.
West Cranmore *Som.* ***Village***, 4m/6km E of Shepton Mallet. ST6643.
West Creeting Green *Suff.* ***Village***, 2m/3km E of Stowmarket. TM0758.
West Croachy *High.* ***Settlement***, part of Croachy locality, in Inverness district, 5m/9km SE of Dores. NH6427.
West Cross *Swan.* ***Suburb***, in Swansea 3m/5km SW of city centre across Swansea Bay. **17 K6** SS6189.
West Crudwell *Wilts.* ***Settlement***, 1km W of Crudwell. ST9493.
West Curry *Cornw.* ***Hamlet***, 6m/10km NW of Launceston. **4 C1** SX2893.
West Curthwaite *Cumb.* ***Hamlet***, 1m/2km S of Thursby. **60 E2** NY3248.
West Dean *W.Suss.* ***Village***, 5m/8km N of Chichester. **12 B5** SU8612.
West Dean *Wilts.* ***Village***, 2m/4km NE of Whiteparish. **10 D2** SU2527.
West Dean Gardens *W.Suss.* ***Garden***, 35 acre or 14 hectare informal garden 5m/8km N of Chichester. Fine specimen trees, gazebo and 300 foot or 91 metre long pergola. **12 B5** SU8612.
West Deeping *Lincs.* ***Village***, on River Welland, 5m/8km E of Stamford. 17c manor house. **42 E5** TF1108.
West Denton *T. & W.* ***Suburb***, 4m/6km W of Newcastle upon Tyne city centre. NZ1866.
West Derby *Mersey.* ***Suburb***, 4m/6km E of Liverpool city centre. **48 C3** SJ4092.
West Dereham *Norf.* ***Village***, 3m/5km SE of Downham Market. **44 A5** TF6500.
West Didsbury *Gt.Man.* ***Suburb***, to NW of Didsbury. SJ8391.
West Dipton Burn *Northumb.* ***River***, rising on Yellow Rigg and flowing E through woodland before entering Devil's Water, 2m/3km S of Hexham. **70 D7** NY9461.
West Ditchburn *Northumb.* ***Hamlet***, 1m/2km NE of Eglingham. **71 G1** NU1320.
West Down *Devon* ***Village***, 4m/6km S of Ilfracombe. **6 D1** SS5142.
West Down *Wilts.* ***Open space***, hillslope 2m/4km N of Shrewton. **20 D7** SU0548.
West Downs *Cornw.* ***Locality***, on W side of Lanivet, 3m/5km SW of Bodmin. SX0364.
West Drayton *Gt.Lon.* ***Suburb***, in borough of Hillingdon, 15m/23km W of Charing Cross. **22 D4** TQ0679.
West Drayton *Notts.* ***Village***, 4m/7km S of Retford. **51 K5** SK7074.
West Dullater *Stir.* ***Settlement***, on S side of Loch Venachar, 3m/5km SW of Callander. **81 G7** NN5805.
West Dulwich *Gt.Lon.* ***Suburb***, partly in boroughs of Lambeth and Southwark, 1m/2km SW of Dulwich Village. TQ3272.
West Dunnet *High.* ***Settlement***, 1km NW of Dunnet. **105 H1** ND2271.
West Ealing *Gt.Lon.* ***Suburb***, in borough of Ealing, 1km W of Ealing. TQ1680.
West Edington *Northumb.* ***Settlement***, 4m/6km SW of Morpeth. **71 G5** NZ1582.
West Ella *E.Riding* ***Village***, 6m/9km W of Kingston upon Hull. **59 G7** TA0029.
West End *Beds.* ***Hamlet***, 1km NW of Stevington, 5m/8km NW of Bedford. **32 C3** SP9853.
West End *Brack.F.* ***Settlement***, 1m/2km N of Bracknell. SU8671.
West End *Caerp.* ***Suburb***, in Abercarn on W side of Ebbw River, 1m/2km S of Newbridge. ST2195.
West End *Cambs.* ***Locality***, adjoining to W of Fenstanton. TL3168.
West End *Cambs.* ***Suburb***, NW district of March. TL4097.
West End *Cumb.* ***Locality***, adjoining to S of Burgh by Sands. NY3258.
West End *Cumb.* ***Locality***, adjoining to S of Ulverston. SD2977.
West End *E.Riding* ***Locality***, adjoining to W of South Cave. SE9130.
West End *E.Riding* ***Locality***, adjoining to W of Kilham. **59 G3** TA0564.
West End *E.Riding* ***Locality***, adjoining to W of Ulrome. TA1656.
West End *E.Riding* ***Locality***, adjoining to W of Preston. TA1730.
West End *E.Riding* ***Locality***, at W end of Halsham. TA2727.
West End *Hants.* ***Settlement***, 1m/2km SW of Medstead and 4m/6km NE of New Alresford. SU6335.
West End *Hants.* ***Suburb***, 4m/6km NE of Southampton. **11 F3** SU4714.
West End *Hants.* ***Suburb***, SW district of Fareham. SU5605.
West End *Herts.* ***Hamlet***, 2m/3km E of Hatfield. TL2608.
West End *Herts.* ***Settlement***, 3m/4km NW of Cheshunt. TL3306.
West End *Kent* ***Suburb***, in SW part of Herne Bay. **25 H5** TR1565.
West End *Lancs.* ***Locality***, 2m/3km W of Accrington. SD7328.
West End *Lancs.* ***Suburb***, SW district of Morecambe. **55 H3** SD4263.
West End *Lincs.* ***Settlement***, 1km S of Marsh Chapel. **53 G3** TF3598.
West End *Norf.* ***Hamlet***, 2m/3km W of Caister-on-Sea. **45 J4** TG4911.
West End *Norf.* ***Settlement***, 1km NW of West Bradenham, 5m/8km N of Watton. TF9009.
West End *N.Som.* ***Hamlet***, 3m/5km SE of Clevedon. **19 H5** ST4469.
West End *N.Yorks.* ***Locality***, on W side of Thruscross Reservoir, 2m/3km NW of Blubberhouses. **57 G4** SE1457.
West End *N.Yorks.* ***Locality***, adjoining to W of Ulleskelf, 3m/5km SE of Tadcaster. SE5140.
West End *N.Yorks.* ***Settlement***, 1m/2km E of Lindley Wood Reservoir and 3m/5km NE of Otley. SE2348.
West End *Oxon.* ***Settlement***, 3m/5km S of Eynsham. **21 H1** SP4204.
West End *Oxon.* ***Settlement***, adjoining to W of Cholsey, 3m/4km SW of Wallingford. SU5886.
West End *S.Glos.* ***Hamlet***, 1km W of Wickwar. ST7188.
West End *S.Lan.* ***Settlement***, 1m/2km W of Carnwath. **75 H6** NS9646.
West End *S.Yorks.* ***Hamlet***, 1m/2km SW of Hatfield Woodhouse. SE6607.
West End *Suff.* ***Settlement***, 2m/3km W of Wrentham. **45 J7** TM4683.
West End *Surr.* ***Hamlet***, 1km SW of Esher. West End Common to SW. **22 E5** TQ1263.
West End *Surr.* ***Settlement***, 3m/5km S of Farnham. SU8242.

West End *Surr.* Population: 3346. ***Village***, 3m/4km SE of Bagshot. **22 C5** SU9460.
West End *W.Suss.* ***Settlement***, adjoining to W of Henfield. TQ2016.
West End *W.Yorks.* ***Locality***, in W part of Horsforth, 5m/8km NW of Leeds. SE2338.
West End *W.Yorks.* ***Suburb***, adjoining to W of Cleckheaton. SE1825.
West End *Wilts.* ***Hamlet***, adjoining to NW of Milkwell, 4m/6km E of Shaftesbury. ST9123.
West End *Wilts.* ***Hamlet***, 4m/7km NE of Chippenham. ST9777.
West End *Wilts.* ***Hamlet***, 1km W of Ebbesborne Wake and 4m/6km SE of Tisbury. ST9824.
West End *W. & M.* ***Hamlet***, 2m/3km E of Twyford. SU8275.
West End Green *Hants.* ***Hamlet***, 6m/10km NE of Basingstoke. **21 K5** SU6661.
West-end Town *V. of Glam.* ***Suburb***, on W side of Llantwit Major. SS9668.
West Ermine *Lincs.* ***Suburb***, N district of Lincoln. SK9773.
West Ewell *Surr.* ***Suburb***, 1m/2km NW of Ewell. TQ2063.
West Farleigh *Kent* ***Village***, above River Medway, 3m/5km SW of Maidstone. **14 C2** TQ7153.
West Farndon *Northants.* ***Hamlet***, 8m/13km NE of Banbury. **31 G3** SP5251.
West Fell *Cumb.* ***Mountain***, to NW of Langdale Fell, 4m/6km SW of Ravenstonedale. Height 1774 feet or 541 metres. **61 H6** NY6602.
West Felton *Shrop.* ***Village***, 4m/7km SE of Oswestry. Earthworks of former castle to W of church. **38 C3** SJ3425.
West Fen *Cambs.* ***Open space***, fenland 3m/5km W of March. **43 G6** TL3596.
West Fen *Cambs.* ***Open space***, fenland 2m/3km NW of Ely. **43 J7** TL5182.
West Fen *Lincs.* ***Open space***, lowland 3m/5km NW of Sibsey. **53 F7** TF3053.
West Ferry *Dundee* ***Suburb***, 3m/5km E of Dundee city centre. NO4431.
West Field *N.Lincs.* ***Locality***, 1m/2km W of East Halton. TA1219.
West Firle *E.Suss.* ***Village***, below South Downs, 4m/7km SE of Lewes. **13 H6** TQ4707.
West Firsby *Lincs.* ***Locality***, 1m/2km W of East Firsby. Includes site of former village. SK9985.
West Fleet *Dorset* ***Lake/loch***, lagoon 5m/8km long behind Chesil Beach, W of Weymouth. **8 E6** SY5982.
West Fleetham *Northumb.* ***Hamlet***, 3m/5km SW of Seahouses. **71 G1** NU1928.
West Flotmanby *N.Yorks.* ***Settlement***, 1m/2km E of Folkton. TA0779.
West Garforth *W.Yorks.* ***Locality***, 1km W of Garforth. **57 J6** SE3932.
West Geirinish *W.Isles* *Anglicised form of Geirninis, qv.*
West Ginge *Oxon.* ***Settlement***, 3m/5km E of Wantage. **21 H3** SU4486.
West Glen *Arg. & B.* ***Settlement***, 2m/3km NE of Tighnabruaich. **73 J3** NR9974.
West Glen *Lincs.* ***River***, rising to N of Boothby Pagnell and flowing S past Corby Glen, Little Bytham and Essendine before turning E to join with East Glen River to form River Glen, 1m/2km N of Baston. **42 D4** TF0913.
West Gorton *Gt.Man.* ***Suburb***, of Manchester, 1m/2km NW of Gorton; Belle Vue Zoo and Speedway Stadium; Greyhound Stadium. SJ8696.
West Grafton *Wilts.* ***Village***, 5m/8km E of Pewsey. **21 F5** SU2460.
West Green *Gt.Lon.* ***Suburb***, in borough of Haringey, 6m/9km N of Charing Cross. TQ3289.
West Green *Hants.* ***Hamlet***, 2m/3km NE of Hook. West Green House (National Trust), early 18c. **22 A6** SU7456.
West Green *W.Suss.* ***Suburb***, W district of Crawley. TQ2637.
West Green House *Hants.* ***Garden***, in West Green, 1m/2km W of Hartley Wintney. Series of walled gardens surrounding an 18c house (National Trust). Contains herbaceous plants and ornamental kitchen garden. **22 A6** SU7456.
West Grimstead *Wilts.* ***Village***, within parish of Grimstead, 4m/7km SE of Salisbury. **10 D2** SU2227.
West Grinstead *W.Suss.* ***Village***, 3m/5km SW of Cowfold. **12 E4** TQ1720.
West Haddlesey *N.Yorks.* ***Village***, on N bank of River Aire, 5m/8km SW of Selby, and connected to it by Selby Canal. **58 B7** SE5626.
West Haddon *Northants.* ***Village***, 7m/11km NE of Daventry. **31 H1** SP6371.
West Hagbourne *Oxon.* ***Village***, 2m/3km SW of Didcot. **21 J3** SU5187.
West Hagley *Worcs.* ***Locality***, to SW of Hagley. **40 B7** SO9180.
West Hall *Cumb.* ***Hamlet***, 4m/7km W of Gilsland. **70 A7** NY5667.
West Hallam *Derbys.* Population: 6498. ***Village***, 2m/3km W of Ilkeston. **41 G1** SK4341.
West Hallam Common *Derbys.* ***Locality***, 1km NW of West Hallam. SK4241.
West Halton *N.Lincs.* ***Village***, 6m/10km N of Scunthorpe. **59 F7** SE9020.
West Ham *Gt.Lon.* ***Suburb***, in borough of Newham, 5m/8km E of London Bridge. **23 H3** TQ4083.
West Hampstead *Gt.Lon.* ***Suburb***, within borough of Camden, 1km SW of Hampstead. TQ2584.
West Handley *Derbys.* ***Hamlet***, 1km W of Middle Handley and 3m/4km SE of Dronfield. **51 F5** SK4077.
West Hanney *Oxon.* ***Village***, 3m/5km N of Wantage. **21 H2** SU4092.
West Hanningfield *Essex* ***Village***, on N side of Hanningfield Reservoir, 5m/8km S of Chelmsford. **24 D2** TQ7399.
West Hardwick *W.Yorks.* ***Hamlet***, 3m/5km W of East Hardwick. **51 G1** SE4618.
West Harling Heath *Norf.* ***Open space***, mixed heathland and woodland extension of Thetford Forest Park, 6m/9km E of Thetford. **44 D7** TL9583.
West Harnham *Wilts.* ***Suburb***, SW district of Salisbury. SU1329.
West Harptree *B. & N.E.Som.* ***Village***, 7m/11km N of Wells. **19 J6** ST5656.
West Harrow *Gt.Lon.* ***Suburb***, 1km W of Harrow. TQ1487.
West Harting *W.Suss.* ***Hamlet***, in parish of Harting, 3m/5km SE of Petersfield. **11 J2** SU7820.
West Harton *T. & W.* ***Suburb***, 2m/3km SW of South Shields. NZ3764.
West Hatch *Som.* ***Village***, 1m/2km W of Hatch Beauchamp. **8 B2** ST2821.
West Hatch *Wilts.* ***Hamlet***, 5m/8km NE of Shaftesbury. ST9227.
West Hay *N.Som.* ***Hamlet***, 2m/3km E of Congresbury. ST4663.
West Head *Norf.* ***Hamlet***, 3m/5km NW of Downham Market across River Great Ouse. TF5705.
West Heath *Ches.* ***Suburb***, 1m/2km W of Congleton town centre. SJ8463.
West Heath *Gt.Lon.* ***Suburb***, in borough of Bexley, S of Lesnes Abbey Woods, 11m/18km E of Charing Cross. TQ4777.
West Heath *Hants.* ***Hamlet***, 4m/6km E of Kingsclere. SU5858.
West Heath *Hants.* ***Suburb***, NW of Farnborough. **22 B6** SU8556.
West Heath *W.Mid.* ***Suburb***, 6m/10km SW of Birmingham city centre. **30 B1** SP0277.
West Helmsdale *High.* ***Settlement***, to W of Helmsdale. **105 F7** ND0115.
West Hendon *Gt.Lon.* ***Suburb***, in borough of Barnet, 1m/2km SW of Hendon. TQ2288.
West Hendred *Oxon.* ***Village***, 3m/5km E of Wantage. **21 H3** SU4488.
West Heogaland (Also spelled West Hogaland.) *Shet.* ***Settlement***, on Esha Ness, on NW part of Mainland. HU2278.
West Herrington *T. & W.* ***Locality***, 2m/3km N of Houghton le Spring, adjoining to W of New Herrington. NZ3453.
West Heslerton *N.Yorks.* ***Village***, 8m/13km E of Malton. **59 F2** SE9175.
West Hewish *N.Som.* ***Hamlet***, 1km W of Hewish, 5m/8km E of Weston-super-Mare. ST3864.
West Highland Museum *High.* ***Other feature of interest***, in centre of Fort William. Exhibits on local and natural history, tartan and Jacobite relics. **87 H7** NN1073.
West Hill *Devon* ***Village***, 2m/3km W of Ottery St. Mary. **7 J6** SY0794.
West Hill *E.Riding* ***Locality***, on N bank of River Humber, 1km SW of Hessle. TA0225.
West Hill *E.Riding* ***Suburb***, W district of Bridlington. TA1666.
West Hill *Gt.Lon.* ***Suburb***, in borough of Wandsworth, 1m/2km SE of Putney Bridge and 5m/8km SW of Charing Cross. TQ2474.
West Hill *N.Som.* ***Suburb***, to W of Portishead town centre. **19 H4** ST4576.
West Hill *Sc.Bord.* ***Mountain***, at W end of Lammermuir Hills, 4m/6km SE of Fala. Height 1479 feet or 451 metres. **76 C5** NT4959.
West Hill *Wilts.* ***Locality***, 2m/4km NW of Melksham. ST8766.
West Hoathly *W.Suss.* ***Village***, on a ridge, 4m/6km SW of East Grinstead. **13 G3** TQ3632.
West Hogaland *Shet.* *Alternative spelling of West Heogaland, qv.*
West Holme *Dorset* ***Settlement***, 3m/4km W of Wareham. **9 H6** SY8885.
West Holywell *Northumb.* ***Settlement***, 1m/2km SW of Holywell. NZ3072.
West Horndon *Essex* ***Village***, 4m/6km SE of Brentwood. **24 C3** TQ6288.
West Horrington *Som.* ***Hamlet***, 2m/3km NE of Wells. **19 J7** ST5747.
West Horsley *Surr.* ***Village***, 6m/9km E of Guildford. **22 D6** TQ0752.
West Horton *Northumb.* ***Hamlet***, 3m/5km NE of Wooler. **77 J7** NU0230.
West Hougham *Kent* ***Village***, 3m/5km W of Dover. **15 H3** TR2640.
West Howe *Bourne.* ***Suburb***, 4m/6km NW of Bournemouth town centre. SZ0595.
West Howetown *Som.* ***Hamlet***, on Exmoor, just E of Winsford. SS9134.
West Hoyle Bank *Flints.* ***Coastal feature***, sandbank in Welsh Channel to NW of Point of Ayr. SJ1088.
West Huntington *York* ***Locality***, to SW of Huntington. SE6156.
West Huntspill *Som.* ***Hamlet***, 3m/5km S of Burnham-on-Sea. **19 G7** ST3044.
West Hyde *Herts.* ***Suburb***, in River Colne valley, 3m/4km SW of Rickmansworth. **22 D2** TQ0391.
West Hythe *Kent* ***Hamlet***, 2m/4km W of Hythe. **15 G4** TR1634.
West Ilkerton *Devon* ***Locality***, 2m/3km SW of Lynton. SS7046.
West Ilsley *W.Berks.* ***Village***, 6m/9km SW of Didcot. **21 H3** SU4782.
West Itchenor *W.Suss.* ***Village***, on S side of Chichester Channel, 6m/10km NW of Selsey. **11 J4** SU7901.
West Jesmond *T. & W.* ***Suburb***, of Newcastle upon Tyne, to W of Jesmond. NZ2566.
West Kame *Shet.* ***Large natural feature***, ridge of hills, running N to S, to SW of Voe, Mainland. **109 C6** HU3961.
West Keal *Lincs.* ***Village***, 1m/2km W of East Keal. **53 G6** TF3863.
West Kennett *Wilts.* ***Hamlet***, 1m/2km SE of Avebury. Long barrow, or burial-chamber (English Heritage) 1km SW. The Sanctuary (English Heritage), site of ancient stone and timber circles 1km E. **20 E5** SU1168.
West Kennett Long Barrow *Wilts.* ***Historic/prehistoric site***, one of largest and finest Neolithic long barrows (English Heritage) in country, 1km SW of West Kennett. Dating from 4c BC, it is around 350 feet or 106 metres long and contains five chambers. West Kennett Avenue (English Heritage), a line of standing stones running alongside road from West Kennett to Avebury, is probably Neolithic. **20 E5** SU1067.
West Kilbride *N.Ayr.* Population: 4488. ***Small town***, 4m/7km NW of Ardrossan. Law Castle, to NE of town, has late 15c tower. **74 A6** NS2048.
West Kilburn *Gt.Lon.* ***Suburb***, to SW of Kilburn. TQ2482.
West Kimber *Devon* ***Settlement***, 7m/11km NW of Okehampton. SX4898.
West Kingsdown *Kent* Population: 4699. ***Locality***, residential locality 3m/5km SE of Farningham. **23 J5** TQ5762.
West Kington *Wilts.* ***Village***, 7m/12km NW of Chippenham. Site of Roman temple 1m/2km E. **20 B4** ST8077.
West Kington Wick *Wilts.* ***Settlement***, 1km SE of West Kington. ST8176.
West Kip *Midloth.* ***Mountain***, in Pentland Hills Regional Park, 3m/5km NE of Carlops. Height 1804 feet or 550 metres. **75 K4** NT1760.
West Kirby *Mersey.* Population: 12,777. ***Town***, resort on Wirral peninsula, at seaward end of River Dee estuary, with beach and marine lake. **48 B4** SJ2186.
West Knapton *N.Yorks.* ***Hamlet***, 6m/10km E of Malton. **58 E2** SE8775.
West Knighton *Dorset* ***Village***, 3m/5km SE of Dorchester. **9 G6** SY7387.
West Knock *Angus* ***Mountain***, 3m/5km SW of Tarfside. Height 2266 feet or 691 metres. **90 C7** NO4775.
West Knoyle *Wilts.* ***Village***, 3m/5km E of Mere. **9 H1** ST8632.
West Kyloe *Northumb.* ***Hamlet***, 1km NW of East Kyloe and 6m/9km NW of Belford. **77 J6** NU0539.
West Kyo *Dur.* ***Settlement***, to W of East Kyo, adjoining to N of Annfield Plain. NZ1752.
West Lambrook *Som.* ***Hamlet***, 1m/2km W of East Lambrook and 4m/7km NE of Ilminster. **8 D3** ST4318.
West Langdon *Kent* ***Village***, 4m/6km N of Dover. Remains of medieval abbey. **15 J3** TR3246.
West Langton *Leics.* ***Locality***, parish, 4m/6km N of Market Harborough. SP7193.
West Langwell *High.* ***Settlement***, 2m/3km NW of East Langwell, Sutherland district. **96 D1** NC6909.
West Laroch *High.* *Former name of Ballachulish, qv.*
West Lavington *W.Suss.* ***Village***, 1km SE of Midhurst. **12 B4** SU8920.
West Lavington *Wilts.* ***Village***, 5m/9km S of Devizes. **20 D6** SU0053.
West Lavington Down *Wilts.* ***Open space***, hillslope on Salisbury Plain rising to 561 feet or 171 metres, 3m/5km N of Chitterne. **20 C7** ST9949.
West Layton *N.Yorks.* ***Hamlet***, 5m/9km NW of Scotch Corner. **62 C5** NZ1409.
West Leake *Notts.* ***Village***, 4m/7km N of Loughborough. **41 H3** SK5226.
West Learmouth *Northumb.* ***Hamlet***, 1km W of East Learmouth and 1m/2km S of Coldstream. NT8437.
West Lees *N.Yorks.* ***Settlement***, to W of Swainby. NZ4702.
West Leigh *Devon* ***Hamlet***, 4m/6km SE of Winkleigh. SS6805.
West Leigh *Devon* ***Hamlet***, 1km W of East Leigh. SX7557.
West Leigh *Devon* ***Settlement***, to SW of East Leigh. SX6852.
West Leigh *Som.* ***Hamlet***, 3m/5km NE of Wiveliscombe. ST1230.
West Leith *Herts.* ***Settlement***, 1m/2km SW of Tring. SP9110.
West Lexham *Norf.* ***Village***, 1m/2km W of East Lexham. **44 C4** TF8516.
West Lilling *N.Yorks.* ***Hamlet***, 1m/2km S of Sheriff Hutton. Former village of East Lilling, 1m/2km SE, no longer exists. **58 C3** SE6465.
West Linga *Shet.* ***Island***, uninhabited island of 315 acres or 127 hectares lying off W coast of Whalsay and separated from it by Linga Sound. **109 E6** HU5364.
West Lingo *Fife* ***Settlement***, 5m/8km S of St. Andrews. **83 F7** NO4808.
West Linton *Sc.Bord.* Population: 1157. ***Village***, on E side of Pentland Hills, 7m/12km SW of Penicuik. **75 K5** NT1551.
West Liss *Hants.* ***Settlement***, adjoining to NW of Liss, 3m/5km NE of Petersfield. SU7728.
West Littleton *S.Glos.* ***Village***, 2m/3km NW of Marshfield. **20 A4** ST7675.
West Loch Roag *W.Isles* ***Sea feature***, large inlet on W coast of Isle of Lewis, on W side of Great Bernera. **100 C4** NB1138.
West Loch Tarbert *Arg. & B.* ***Sea feature***, sea-loch in Argyll running NE from Ardpatrick Point, between Knapdale and Kintyre. Isthmus of only 1m/2km separates head of loch from East Loch Tarbert on Loch Fyne. Quay near West Tarbert at head of loch, with passenger services to Islay. **73 F4** NR8062.
West Loch Tarbert *W.Isles* ***Sea feature***, large inlet between W coast of North and South Harris. Village and port of Tarbert on isthmus between this inlet and East Loch Tarbert. **100 C7** NB0903.
West Lockinge *Oxon.* ***Hamlet***, 2m/3km E of Wantage. **21 H3** SU4287.
West Lomond *Fife* ***Mountain***, summit of Lomond Hills 3m/4km S of Strathmiglo. Height 1712 feet or 522 metres. **82 C7** NO1906.
West Looe *Cornw.* ***River***, rises near Dobwalls and joins Looe River to N of Looe town. **4 C5** SX2553.
West Looe *Cornw.* Population: 2511. ***Suburb***, smaller part of Looe, divided from East Looe by Looe River, 7m/11km S of Liskeard. Road bridge connection to East Looe. **4 C5** SX2553.

West Lulworth *Dorset* ***Village***, on coast, 4m/7km S of Wool. **9 H6** SY8280.
West Lutton *N.Yorks.* ***Village***, 9m/15km E of Malton. **59 F3** SE9369.
West Lydford *Som.* ***Hamlet***, in parish of Lydford, 1km NE of Keinton Mandeville. **8 E1** ST5631.
West Lyn *Devon* ***Hamlet***, 1km SE of Lynton. SS7248.
West Lyn *Devon* ***River***, of N Exmoor, flowing N into Bristol Channel with East Lyn River at Lynmouth. SS7249.
West Lyng *Som.* ***Hamlet***, 1m/2km W of Lyng and 6m/9km NE of Taunton. **8 C2** ST3329.
West Lynn *Norf.* ***Suburb***, of King's Lynn on W bank of River Great Ouse. Ferry for pedestrians to town centre. Road bridge 1m/2km S. **44 A4** TF6120.
West Mains *Northumb.* ***Village***, on A1 road, 2m/3km NW of Fenwick. **77 J6** NU0542.
West Malling *Kent* Population: 2056. ***Village***, large village 5m/8km W of Maidstone. To SW is St. Leonard's Tower, remains of Norman keep (English Heritage). **23 K6** TQ6857.
West Malling Abbey *Kent* ***Ecclesiastical building***, founded in 1090 at West Malling for Benedictine nuns, but dissolved in 1538. Anglican community returned here, using 15c gatehouse, 18c house adapted from previous abbey, and a modern church (1966). **23 K6** TQ6857.
West Malvern *Worcs.* ***Village***, on W side of Malvern Hills, 1m/2km W of Great Malvern. **29 G4** SO7646.
West Marden *W.Suss.* ***Village***, 6m/9km NE of Havant. Site of Roman villa 1km S. **11 J3** SU7713.
West Markham *Notts.* ***Village***, 1m/2km W of East Markham. **51 K5** SK7472.
West Marsh *N.E.Lincs.* ***Suburb***, W district of Grimsby. **53 F2** TA2510.
West Marton *N.Yorks.* ***Village***, 1m/2km W of East Marton. **56 D4** SD9050.
West Melbury *Dorset* ***Hamlet***, 2m/3km S of Shaftesbury. ST8620.
West Melton *S.Yorks.* ***Locality***, 1km W of Wath upon Dearne. **51 G2** SE4200.
West Meon *Hants.* ***Village***, 3m/5km NE of Meonstoke. 1km NW, site of Roman villa. **11 H2** SU6424.
West Meon Hut *Hants.* ***Settlement***, 1m/2km N of West Meon. **11 H2** SU6526.
West Meon Woodlands *Hants.* ***Settlement***, 2m/3km N of West Meon. SU6426.
West Mersea *Essex* Population: 6602. ***Small town***, resort with sand and shingle beach at W end of Mersea Island. **34 E7** TM0112.
West Mey *High.* ***Settlement***, to NW of Mey, near N coast of Caithness district. ND2873.
West Midland Safari Park *Worcs.* ***Leisure/recreation***, large safari park with good diversity of animals, and associated fairground, 1km E of Bewdley. **29 H1** SO8075.
West Mill *Herts.* ***Suburb***, NW district of Hitchin. TL1730.
West Milton *Dorset* ***Village***, 3m/5km NE of Bridport. **8 E5** SY5096.
West Minster *Kent* ***Settlement***, adjoining to SW of Sheerness. **25 F4** TQ9173.
West Molesey *Surr.* Population: 11,650. ***Suburb***, between River Thames and River Mole 3m/4km NE of Walton-on-Thames. **22 E5** TQ1368.
West Monar Forest *High.* ***Open space***, deer forest about head of Loch Monar, Ross and Cromarty district. **95 G7** NH0742.
West Monkton *Som.* ***Village***, 4m/6km NE of Taunton. **8 B2** ST2628.
West Moor *Cambs.* ***Open space***, fenland 1km W of Chatteris. **43 G7** TL3686.
West Moor *T. & W.* ***Suburb***, 1m/2km N of Longbenton. NZ2770.
West Moors *Dorset* ***Locality***, residential locality 8m/12km N of Bournemouth. **10 B4** SU0803.
West Morden *Dorset* ***Hamlet***, 3m/4km W of Lytchett Matravers. SY9095.
West Morriston *Sc.Bord.* ***Hamlet***, 3m/5km SW of Gordon. NT6041.
West Morton *W.Yorks.* ***Settlement***, 1km NW of East Morton, 3m/4km NW of Bingley. SE0942.
West Mostard *Cumb.* ***Settlement***, in Garsdale, 3m/4km E of Sedbergh. **61 J7** SD7090.
West Mouse (Maen y Bugael). *I.o.A.* ***Island***, rock with beacon light, about 1m/2km N of Anglesey coast at Carmel Head. **46 B3** SH3094.
West Mudford *Som.* ***Hamlet***, to NW of Mudford, 3m/5km N of Yeovil. ST5620.
West Muir *Angus* ***Settlement***, 3m/4km NW of Brechin. **83 G1** NO5661.
West Ness *Fife* ***Coastal feature***, rocky headland on S side of Crail Harbour. **83 H7** NO6106.
West Ness *N.Yorks.* ***Hamlet***, 1m/2km E of Nunnington. **58 C2** SE6879.
West Newbiggin *Darl.* ***Settlement***, 5m/8km NE of Darlington. NZ3518.
West Newton *E.Riding* ***Hamlet***, 6m/10km N of Hedon. **59 J6** TA2037.
West Newton *Norf.* ***Village***, 7m/11km NE of King's Lynn. Site of Roman villa to E. **44 A3** TF6927.
West Newton *Som.* ***Hamlet***, 2m/3km NE of West Monkton. ST2829.
West Norwood *Gt.Lon.* ***Locality***, in borough of Lambeth, 4m/6km N of Croydon town centre. Forms suburb of Norwood along with South Norwood, Upper Norwood and Norwood New Town. **23 G4** TQ3271.
West Ogwell *Devon* ***Hamlet***, forms locality of Ogwell, along with East Ogwell, 3m/4km W of Newton Abbot. **5 J3** SX8370.
West Orchard *Dorset* ***Village***, 3m/5km NE of Sturminster Newton. **9 H3** ST8216.
West Overton *Wilts.* ***Village***, 4m/6km W of Marlborough. **20 E5** SU1368.
West Panson *Devon* ***Hamlet***, 4m/7km N of Launceston. SX3491.
West Park *Aber.* ***Hamlet***, 1m/2km E of Crathes. **91 F5** NO7697.
West Park *Mersey.* ***Suburb***, 1m/2km W of St. Helens town centre. **48 E3** SJ4995.
West Park *W.Yorks.* ***Suburb***, 3m/5km NW of Leeds city centre. SE2637.
West Parkgate *Ches.* ***Settlement***, at W entrance to Lyme Park, 2m/3km SE of Poynton. SJ9581.
West Parley *Dorset* ***Village***, running down to River Stour, 2m/3km S of Ferndown. **10 B5** SZ0897.
West Pasture *Dur.* ***Locality***, on SE shore of Grassholme Reservoir, S of Middleton-in-Teesdale. NY9422.
West Peckham *Kent* ***Village***, 5m/8km NE of Tonbridge. **23 K6** TQ6452.
West Pelton *Dur.* ***Village***, 1m/2km W of Pelton. NZ2353.
West Pennard *Som.* ***Village***, 3m/5km E of Glastonbury. **8 E1** ST5438.
West Pentire *Cornw.* ***Hamlet***, near coast, 3m/4km W of Newquay. **2 E2** SW7760.
West Perry *Cambs.* ***Hamlet***, adjoining East Perry, on S side of Grafham Water. Sailing club at East Perry. **32 E2** TL1466.
West Pilton *Devon* ***Suburb***, N district of Barnstaple. SS5533.
West Poringland *Norf.* ***Hamlet***, 1km SW of Poringland, 6m/9km SE of Norwich. TG2600.
West Porlock *Som.* ***Village***, 1m/2km W of Porlock. **7 G1** SS8747.
West Prawle *Devon* ***Hamlet***, 2m/3km N of Prawle Point and 2m/3km SE of Salcombe across Kingsbridge Estuary. SX7637.
West Preston *W.Suss.* ***Suburb***, of Rustington, 2m/3km E of Littlehampton. TQ0502.
West Pulham *Dorset* ***Hamlet***, to SW of Pulham, 6m/10km SW of Sturminster Newton. ST7008.
West Putford *Devon* ***Village***, 8m/12km N of Holsworthy. **6 B4** SS3615.
West Quantoxhead *Som.* ***Village***, at N end of Quantock Hills, 3m/5km E of Watchet. **7 K1** ST1142.
West Raddon *Devon* ***Hamlet***, 4m/6km NE of Crediton. SS8902.
West Rainton *Dur.* Population: 2182. ***Village***, 4m/7km NE of Durham. **62 E2** NZ3246.
West Rasen *Lincs.* ***Village***, 3m/5km W of Market Rasen. **52 D4** TF0689.
West Rasen Bridge *Lincs.* ***Bridge***, 14c stone packhorse bridge over River Rase at West Rasen, 3m/4km W of Market Rasen. TF0689.
West Ravendale *N.Lincs.* ***Hamlet***, 1km W of East Ravendale, 3m/5km SW of Waltham; ruins of medieval chapel. TF2299.
West Raynham *Norf.* ***Village***, 1m/2km W of East Raynham. **44 C3** TF8825.
West Reef *Arg. & B.* ***Island***, group of rocks to W of Torran Rocks group and 4m/7km SW of Mull. **78 D6** NM2313.
West Retford *Notts.* ***Suburb***, to NW of Retford across River Idle. SK6981.
West Road ***Sea feature***, channel between Dungeness in E and Rye Bay in W. **15 F6** TR0016.
West Rounton *N.Yorks.* ***Village***, 7m/11km NE of Northallerton. **63 F6** NZ4103.
West Row *Suff.* ***Village***, 2m/4km W of Mildenhall. **33 K1** TL6775.
West Royd *W.Yorks.* ***Suburb***, E district of Shipley. SE1637.
West Rudham *Norf.* ***Village***, 1km SW of East Rudham. **44 C3** TF8228.
West Ruislip *Gt.Lon.* ***Suburb***, 1km SW of Ruislip. TQ0887.
West Runton *Norf.* ***Town***, coastal resort, 2m/3km E of Sheringham. The North Norfolk Heavy Horse and Pony Centre located here. **45 F1** TG1842.
West Saltney *Flints.* ***Locality***, adjoining to E of Queensferry. SJ3267.
West Saltoun *E.Loth.* ***Village***, 5m/8km SE of Tranent and 1m/2km W of East Saltoun. **76 C4** NT4667.
West Sandford *Devon* ***Hamlet***, to W of Sandford, 1m/2km NW of Crediton. SS8102.
West Sandwick *Shet.* ***Village***, 1km SE of West Sand Wick. **108 D4** HU4489.
West Scrafton *N.Yorks.* ***Village***, 3m/5km S of Wensley. **57 F1** SE0783.
West Sedge Moor *Som.* ***Marsh/bog***, large marsh area at sea level, cut by numerous dykes or rhynes for drainage, E of North Curry and W of Curry Rivel. **8 C2** ST3525.
West Shepton *Som.* ***Suburb***, SW district of Shepton Mallet. ST6143.
West Shinness Lodge *High.* ***Settlement***, forms locality of Shinness along with Shinness Lodge, on E side of Loch Shin, 6m/10km NW of Lairg. **103 H7** NC5314.
West Sleekburn *Northumb.* ***Locality***, 2m/3km S of Ashington across River Wansbeck. NZ2785.
West Somerset Railway *Som.* ***Other feature of interest***, tourist railway which runs from Minehead to Bishops Lydeard. **7 K2** ST1039.
West Somerton *Norf.* ***Village***, 1km W of Somerton. **45 J3** TG4719.
West Stafford *Dorset* ***Village***, 3m/5km E of Dorchester. **9 G6** SY7289.
West Stockwith *Notts.* ***Village***, on W bank of River Trent at junction with River Idle opposite East Stockwith, 4m/6km NW of Gainsborough. Junction of Chesterfield Canal and River Trent. **51 K3** SK7994.
West Stoke *W.Suss.* ***Hamlet***, 3m/5km NW of Chichester. **12 B6** SU8308.
West Stonesdale *N.Yorks.* ***Settlement***, 1km N of Keld. **61 K6** NY8802.
West Stoughton *Som.* ***Hamlet***, forms locality of Stoughton, along with Middle Stoughton and Stoughton Cross. **19 H7** ST4249.
West Stour *Dorset* ***Village***, 3m/4km SW of Gillingham. **9 G2** ST7822.
West Stourmouth *Kent* ***Village***, in parish of Stourmouth, to NW of Sandwich. **25 J5** TR2562.
West Stow *Suff.* ***Village***, 5m/7km NW of Bury St. Edmunds. **34 C1** TL8170.
West Stow Country Park *Suff.* ***Leisure/recreation***, country park of 150 acres or 60 hectares comprising woodland, grassland and lake, 1m/2km NW of West Stow. Park features reconstructed 5c Anglo-Saxon village. **34 B1** TL7971.
West Stowell *Wilts.* ***Hamlet***, 2m/3km NW of Pewsey. **20 E5** SU1362.
West Stratton *Hants.* ***Hamlet***, 1m/2km NE of Micheldever. **21 J7** SU5240.
West Street *Kent* ***Settlement***, 1m/2km N of Lenham. **14 E2** TQ9054.
West Street *Med.* ***Settlement***, just W of Cliffe, 5m/8km N of Rochester. TQ7376.
West Street *Suff.* ***Locality***, 1m/2km E of Wattisfield. TM0274.
West Street *Suff.* ***Settlement***, 1m/2km W of Walsham le Willows. TL9870.
West Tanfield *N.Yorks.* ***Village***, on River Ure, 5m/8km NW of Ripon. Marmion Tower (English Heritage) has medieval gatehouse and oriel window. **57 H2** SE2678.
West Taphouse *Cornw.* ***Settlement***, 2m/3km W of East Taphouse. **4 B4** SX1563.
West Tarbert *Arg. & B.* ***Settlement***, 1m/2km SW of Tarbert, at head of West Loch Tarbert. **73 G4** NR8467.
West Tarbert *W.Isles* *Anglicised form of Taobh Siar, qv.*
West Tarbert Bay *Arg. & B.* ***Bay***, one of two bays on either side of Gigha, near N end of island. **72 E5** NR6552.
West Tarbet *D. & G.* ***Locality***, 3m/5km S of Cailiness Point, on W side of Mull of Galloway. **64 B7** NX1430.
West Tarring *W.Suss.* ***Suburb***, 1m/2km NW of Worthing town centre. **12 E6** TQ1303.
West Thirston *Northumb.* ***Village***, adjoining to S of Felton. NU1800.
West Thorney *W.Suss.* ***Village***, on Thorney Island, 3m/4km SE of Emsworth. **11 J4** SU7602.
West Thorpe *Notts.* ***Hamlet***, adjoining to W of Willoughby-on-the-Wolds. SK6325.
West Thurrock *Thur.* ***Locality***, industrial locality N of West Thurrock Marshes, on N bank of River Thames, 4m/6km W of Tilbury. **23 J4** TQ5877.
West Tilbury *Thur.* ***Village***, 2m/3km NE of Tilbury. West Tilbury Marshes to S, with Tilbury Power Station beside River Thames. **24 C4** TQ6677.
West Tisted *Hants.* ***Village***, 5m/8km SE of New Alresford. **11 H2** SU6529.
West Tofts *Norf.* ***Settlement***, 5m/9km NE of Brandon. **44 C6** TL8392.
West Tofts *P. & K.* ***Locality***, 1km N of Stanley. **82 C4** NO1034.
West Torrington *Lincs.* ***Village***, 1m/2km SW of East Torrington. **52 E4** TF1382.
West Town *B. & N.E.Som.* ***Hamlet***, on N side of Blagdon Lake, 3m/4km SW of Chew Stoke. ST5160.
West Town *Devon* ***Hamlet***, 3m/5km SE of Crediton, on S side of Newton St. Cyres. SX8797.
West Town *Hants.* ***Suburb***, of South Hayling on Hayling Island. **11 J5** SZ7199.
West Town *Here.* ***Locality***, adjoining to W of Kingsland, 4m/6km NW of Leominster. SO4461.
West Town *N.Som.* ***Village***, 4m/6km NE of Congresbury. **19 H5** ST4868.
West Town *Som.* ***Settlement***, just N of Baltonsborough, 3m/5km SE of Glastonbury. ST5435.
West Town *W.Suss.* ***Settlement***, adjoining to W of Hurstpierpoint. TQ2716.
West Tytherley *Hants.* ***Village***, 6m/10km SW of Stockbridge. **10 D1** SU2729.
West Vale *W.Yorks.* ***Locality***, 1km W of Elland. SE0921.
West Village *V. of Glam.* ***Suburb***, on NW side of Cowbridge. SS9874.
West Voe *Shet.* ***Sea feature***, stretch of sea separating S sections of West and East Burra. **109 C10** HU3629.
West Walton *Norf.* ***Village***, 3m/4km N of Wisbech. **43 H4** TF4713.
West Walton Highway *Norf.* ***Village***, 1m/2km E of West Walton. **43 H4** TF4912.
West Water *Angus* ***River***, running SE to River North Esk, 2m/4km SE of Edzell. NO6266.
West Water Reservoir *Sc.Bord.* ***Reservoir***, on Pentland Hills, 2m/3km W of West Linton. **75 K5** NT1152.
West Webburn *Devon* ***River***, rising on Dartmoor, W of Manaton, and flowing S to join with East Webburn River at Lizwell Meet, 1m/2km E of Ponsworthy, to form River Webburn. **5 G3** SX7173.
West Wellow *Hants.* Population: 2151. ***Village***, 4m/6km N of Cadnam. **10 D2** SU2819.
West Wembury *Devon* ***Hamlet***, adjoining to NE of Wembury. SX5249.
West Wemyss *Fife* ***Village***, on Firth of Forth, 4m/6km NE of Kirkcaldy. **76 B1** NT3294.
West Wick *N.Som.* ***Hamlet***, 3m/5km E of Weston-Super-Mare. **19 G5** ST3662.
West Wickham *Cambs.* ***Village***, 4m/7km NW of Haverhill. **33 K4** TL6149.
West Wickham *Gt.Lon.* ***Suburb***, in borough of Bromley, 3m/4km S of Bromley town centre. **23 G5** TQ3965.
West Williamston *Pembs.* ***Hamlet***, between estuaries of Rivers Carew and Cresswell, 2m/3km NW of Carew. **16 D4** SN0305.
West Willoughby *Lincs.* ***Hamlet***, 1m/2km SW of Ancaster. SK9643.
West Winch *Norf.* Population: 1774. ***Village***, 3m/4km S of King's Lynn. **44 A4** TF6316.
West Winterslow *Wilts.* ***Hamlet***, 1km SW of Middle Winterslow, 6m/9km NE of Salisbury. **10 D1** SU2232.

West Wittering *W.Suss.* Population: 1551. ***Village***, 6m/9km NW of Selsey. **11 J5** SZ7898.

West Witton *N.Yorks.* ***Village***, in Wensleydale, 4m/6km W of Leyburn. **57 F1** SE0688.

West Woodburn *Northumb.* ***Hamlet***, 4m/6km S of Otterburn and 1m/2km W of East Woodburn. Site of Roman fort of Habitancum to S. **70 D5** NY8986.

West Woodhay *W.Berks.* ***Hamlet***, 6m/9km SW of Newbury. **21 G5** SU3963.

West Woodlands *Som.* ***Settlement***, with East Woodlands forms locality of Woodlands, 3m/4km S of Frome. **20 A7** ST7743.

West Woodside *Cumb.* ***Locality***, 1m/2km SW of Thursby. NY3049.

West Worldham *Hants.* ***Village***, 2m/3km SE of Alton. **11 J1** SU7437.

West Worlington *Devon* ***Hamlet***, 5m/8km E of Chulmleigh. **7 F4** SS7713.

West Worthing *W.Suss.* ***Suburb***, 1m/2km W of Worthing town centre. **12 E6** TQ1402.

West Wratting *Cambs.* ***Village***, 6m/10km NW of Haverhill. **33 J3** TL6052.

West Wycombe *Bucks.* ***Village***, 2m/4km NW of High Wycombe. 18c West Wycombe Park (National Trust), in park with lake. National Trust property also includes Church Hill, with Iron Age fort, and most of village. Mausoleum and caves. **22 B2** SU8294.

West Wycombe Park *Bucks.* ***Historic house***, 18c Palladian house (National Trust) to S of West Wycombe, with landscaped gardens, lake and temples. **22 B2** SU8294.

West Wylam *Northumb.* ***Suburb***, NE district of Prudhoe, 1m/2km SW of Wylam across River Tyne. NZ1063.

West Yatton *Wilts.* ***Hamlet***, 4m/6km NW of Chippenham. ST8575.

West Yell *Shet.* ***Settlement***, on W coast of Yell, overlooking Ness of Sound. **108 D4** HU4583.

West Yoke *Kent* ***Settlement***, adjoining to W of New Ash Green, 2m/4km S of Longfield. TQ5965.

West Youlstone *Cornw.* ***Hamlet***, 7m/11km NE of Bude. SS2615.

Westbank *Derbys.* ***Settlement***, 2m/3km NE of Belper. SK3649.

Westbere *Kent* ***Village***, 4m/6km NE of Canterbury. **25 H5** TR1961.

Westborough *Lincs.* ***Village***, 7m/11km NW of Grantham. **42 B1** SK8544.

Westbourne *Bourne.* ***Suburb***, W district of Bournemouth. **10 B5** SZ0691.

Westbourne *Suff.* ***Suburb***, 2m/3km NW of Ipswich town centre. TM1445.

Westbourne *W.Suss.* ***Village***, 2m/4km E of Havant. **11 J4** SU7507.

Westbourne Green *Gt.Lon.* ***Suburb***, in City of Westminster, NW of Paddington, 3m/5km NW of Charing Cross. TQ2582.

Westbrook *Kent* ***Suburb***, 1m/2km W of Margate. TR3370.

Westbrook *W.Berks.* ***Hamlet***, adjoining to N of Boxford, 4m/6km NW of Newbury. **21 H4** SU4271.

Westbrook *Wilts.* ***Hamlet***, 4m/6km NE of Melksham. ST9565.

Westbrook Green *Norf.* ***Settlement***, 1m/2km N of Diss. TM1181.

Westbury *Bucks.* ***Village***, 3m/4km E of Brackley. **31 H5** SP6235.

Westbury *Shrop.* ***Village***, 9m/14km W of Shrewsbury. **38 C5** SJ3509.

Westbury *Wilts.* Population: 11,863. ***Town***, market town at foot of Salisbury Plain, 4m/7km S of Trowbridge. Former medieval woollen cloth town; a restored mill contains museum. Westbury White Horse (English Heritage) cut in chalk on hillside to E, below Iron Age camp (English Heritage). **20 B6** ST8751.

Westbury Court Garden *Glos.* ***Garden***, 17c-18c formal water garden (National Trust) at Westbury Court, Westbury-on-Severn. **29 G7** SO7113.

Westbury Leigh *Wilts.* ***Suburb***, SW district of Westbury. **20 B6** ST8650.

Westbury-on-Severn *Glos.* ***Village***, 4m/6km E of Cinderford. **29 G7** SO7114.

Westbury on Trym *Bristol* ***Suburb***, N district of Bristol. **19 J4** ST5777.

Westbury Park *Bristol* ***Suburb***, of Bristol, 2m/3km N of city centre. ST5775.

Westbury-sub-Mendip *Som.* ***Village***, 4m/6km NW of Wells. **19 J7** ST5048.

Westbury White Horse *Wilts.* ***Historic/prehistoric site***, figure of horse (English Heritage) carved into chalk of Bratton Down in 1778, 1m/2km NE of Westbury. An earlier horse, cut on same site, said to have commemorated King Alfred's victory over Danes in AD 878. **20 B6** ST8951.

Westby *Lancs.* ***Hamlet***, 1m/2km W of Wrea Green. **55 G6** SD3831.

Westby *Lincs.* ***Hamlet***, 4m/6km NE of Colsterworth. SK9728.

Westcliff-on-Sea *S'end* ***Suburb***, 1m/2km SW of Southend-on-Sea town centre. **24 E3** TQ8685.

Westcombe *Som.* ***Hamlet***, 2m/3km W of Somerton. ST4629.

Westcombe *Som.* ***Hamlet***, 2m/3km E of Evercreech. **9 F1** ST6739.

Westcot *Oxon.* ***Hamlet***, 4m/6km W of Wantage. SU3387.

Westcote *Glos.* ***Village***, 4m/6km SE of Stow-on-the-Wold. **30 D6** SP2120.

Westcott *Bucks.* ***Village***, 7m/11km W of Aylesbury. **31 J7** SP7117.

Westcott *Devon* ***Hamlet***, 2m/3km S of Cullompton. **7 J5** ST0204.

Westcott *Surr.* Population: 2118. ***Village***, 1m/2km W of Dorking. **22 E7** TQ1448.

Westcott Barton *Oxon.* ***Village***, 4m/7km SW of Deddington. **31 F6** SP4325.

Westcourt *Wilts.* ***Hamlet***, adjoining to W of Burbage, 4m/6km E of Pewsey. SU2261.

Westdean *E.Suss.* ***Hamlet***, 2m/3km S of Alfriston. **13 J7** TV5299.

Westdowns *Cornw.* ***Hamlet***, 3m/5km W of Camelford. **4 A2** SX0582.

Westend *Glos.* ***Settlement***, 4m/7km W of Stroud. SO7806.

Westend Town *Northumb.* ***Hamlet***, 1km N of Bardon Mill. NY7865.

Westend Town *S.Glos.* ***Settlement***, 1km W of Marshfield. ST7674.

Westenhanger *Kent* ***Settlement***, 3m/5km NW of Hythe. Remains of 14c fortified house. Location of Folkestone Racecourse. TR1236.

Wester Aberchalder *High.* ***Settlement***, on E shore of Loch Mhòr, 4m/6km E of Foyers. **88 C2** NH5520.

Wester Badentyre *Aber.* ***Settlement***, at head of valley, on S side of Hill of Brackans, 3m/5km NE of Turriff. **99 F5** NJ7652.

Wester Balgedie *P. & K.* ***Village***, 3m/5km E of Milnathort. NO1604.

Wester Culbeuchly *Aber.* ***Settlement***, 3m/4km SW of Banff. **98 E4** NJ6462.

Wester Dechmont *W.Loth.* ***Locality***, 3m/5km E of Bathgate. **75 J3** NT0270.

Wester Fearn Burn *High.* ***River***, running E into Dornoch Firth at Wester Fearn Point, Ross and Cromarty district. **96 D3** NH6387.

Wester Fintray *Aber.* ***Settlement***, on N side of River Don, 1m/2km E of Kintore. **91 G3** NJ8116.

Wester Gruinards *High.* ***Locality***, in Strathcarron, 7m/11km W of Bonar Bridge, Sutherland district. **96 C2** NH5192.

Wester Hailes *Edin.* ***Suburb***, 4m/7km SW of Edinburgh city centre. NT2069.

Wester Hoevdi *Shet.* ***Coastal feature***, headland on W coast of Foula. **108 B1** HT9338.

Wester Lealty *High.* ***Settlement***, 3m/5km NW of Alness. **96 D4** NH6073.

Wester Lonvine *High.* ***Locality***, 2m/3km N of Invergordon. **96 E4** NH7172.

Wester Newburn *Fife* ***Settlement***, 3m/4km NE of Lower Largo. **83 F7** NO4405.

Wester Ord *Aber.* ***Settlement***, 1m/2km S of Westhill. **91 G4** NJ8204.

Wester Pencaitland *E.Loth.* ***Village***, forms locality of Pencaitland, along with Easter Pencaitland, 4m/6km SE of Tranent. NT4468.

Wester Quarff *Shet.* ***Settlement***, 1m/2km W of Easter Quarff, at head of West Voe of Quarff, Mainland. **109 D9** HU4035.

Wester Ross *High.* ***Locality***, rugged highland area, roughly comprising W part of Ross and Cromarty district. Most easterly part is 9m/15km NW of Dingwall. Includes Beinn Eighe National Nature Reserve, Kinlochewe Forest, Lochrosque Forest and Strathbran Forest. **95 G5** NH1364.

Wester Skeld *Shet.* ***Hamlet***, on W part of Mainland, 2m/3km W of Reawick across Skelda Voe. **109 B8** HU2943.

Wester Slumbay *High.* ***Locality***, forms Slumbay, along with adjoining locality Easter Slumbay, on NW shore to Loch Carron to SW of Lochcarron, Ross and Cromarty district. NG8939.

Wester Wick *Shet.* ***Sea feature***, inlet on coast of Mainland, 5m/7km SW of Garderhouse. **109 B8** HU2842.

Westerdale *High.* ***Settlement***, on River Thurso, 5m/8km S of Halkirk, Caithness district. **105 G3** ND1251.

Westerdale *N.Yorks.* ***Village***, in North York Moors National Park, 7m/11km SE of Guisborough. **63 H6** NZ6605.

Westerdale Moor *N.Yorks.* ***Open space***, moorland on Cleveland Hills, 4m/6km SW of Castleton. **63 H6** NZ6403.

Westerfield *Shet.* ***Settlement***, on NE side of Tresta Voe, Mainland. **109 C7** HU3551.

Westerfield *Suff.* ***Village***, 2m/3km N of Ipswich town centre; village is partly in Ipswich and partly in parish of Westerfield. **35 F4** TM1747.

Westergate *W.Suss.* Population: 3567. ***Village***, 4m/6km N of Bognor Regis. **12 C6** SU9305.

Westerham *Kent* Population: 3207. ***Small town***, 5m/8km W of Sevenoaks. Quebec House (National Trust), once home of General Wolfe. Squerryes Court, to SW, is 17c manor house. **23 H6** TQ4454.

Westerhope *T. & W.* ***Suburb***, 4m/6km NW of Newcastle upon Tyne. NZ1967.

Westerleigh *S.Glos.* ***Village***, 2m/4km SW of Chipping Sodbury. **19 K4** ST6979.

Westerloch *High.* ***Settlement***, in Caithness district, 5m/8km N of Wick. ND3258.

Western Bank *Cumb.* ***Locality***, adjoining to W of Wigton. NY2448.

Western Cleddau *Pembs.* ***River***, rising about 2m/3km E of Llanrian, and flowing E, then S to Wolf's Castle through Haverfordwest and on to its confluence with Eastern Cleddau River to form Daugleddau estuary. **16 C3** SN0011.

Western Hill *Dur.* ***Suburb***, NW district of Durham. NZ2642.

Western Rocks *I.o.S.* ***Island***, large group of rock islets, 3m/4km SW of St. Agnes, aligned on a NW to SE axis. **2 B2** SV8306.

Westernhope Moor *Dur.* ***Open space***, moorland with River Wear to N and River Tees to S, 3m/5km SE of St. John's Chapel. **62 A3** NY9033.

Westerton *Aber.* ***Settlement***, 4m/6km SE of Banchory. **91 F5** NO7391.

Westerton *Angus* ***Settlement***, 1km N of Rossie School. **83 H2** NO6654.

Westerton *Dur.* ***Hamlet***, 2m/3km SW of Spennymoor. **62 D3** NZ2331.

Westerton *P. & K.* ***Settlement***, 4m/7km NW of Auchterarder. **81 K6** NN8714.

Westerton *W.Suss.* ***Hamlet***, 2m/4km NE of Chichester. SU8807.

Westerwick *Shet.* ***Settlement***, on Mainland, at head of inlet of Wester Wick. **109 B8** HU2842.

Westfield *Cumb.* ***Suburb***, 1m/2km S of Workington town centre. **60 A4** NX9927.

Westfield *E.Suss.* ***Village***, 4m/6km N of Hastings. **14 D6** TQ8115.

Westfield *Hants.* ***Suburb***, of South Hayling on Hayling Island. SZ7299.

Westfield *Here.* ***Locality***, 3m/5km W of Great Malvern. SO7247.

Westfield *High.* ***Settlement***, in Caithness district, 5m/7km SW of Thurso. **105 F2** ND0564.

Westfield *Norf.* ***Hamlet***, 2m/4km S of East Dereham. **44 D5** TF9909.

Westfield *N.Lan.* ***Suburb***, 2m/4km W of Cumbernauld town centre. NS7273.

Westfield *R. & C.* ***Suburb***, adjoining to SW of Redcar. NZ5924.

Westfield *Surr.* ***Suburb***, 1m/2km S of Woking town centre. TQ0056.

Westfield *W.Loth.* ***Hamlet***, 3m/5km NW of Bathgate. **75 H3** NS9372.

Westfield *W.Yorks.* ***Suburb***, adjoining to W of Yeadon. SE1940.

Westfield *W.Yorks.* ***Suburb***, adjoining to N of Heckmondwike. SE2124.

Westfield Moor *E.Suss.* ***Settlement***, adjoining to SE of Westfield. **14 D6** TQ8115.

Westfield Sole *Kent* ***Settlement***, 4m/6km N of Maidstone. TQ7761.

Westfields *Dorset* ***Hamlet***, 1km W of Mappowder and 6m/10km SW of Sturminster Newton. ST7206.

Westfields of Rattray *P. & K.* ***Locality***, 1km N of Rattray. NO1746.

Westford *Som.* ***Hamlet***, 1m/2km W of Wellington. ST1220.

Westgate *Dur.* ***Village***, on River Wear, 1m/2km E of St. John's Chapel. **62 A3** NY9038.

Westgate *Norf.* ***Hamlet***, adjoining to NE of Binham. **44 D1** TF9839.

Westgate *N.Lincs.* ***Village***, 2m/4km N of Epworth. **51 K2** SE7707.

Westgate *Northumb.* ***Hamlet***, 3m/5km NW of Ponteland. **71 G6** NZ1276.

Westgate Hill *W.Yorks.* ***Locality***, 3m/5km SE of Bradford. **57 H7** SE2029.

Westgate on Sea *Kent* ***Suburb***, coastal resort to W of Margate. **25 K4** TR3270.

Westgate Street *Norf.* ***Locality***, adjoining to N of Hevingham. TG1921.

Westhall *Aber.* ***Settlement***, 1km N of Oyne. **90 E2** NJ6726.

Westhall *Suff.* ***Hamlet***, 3m/5km NE of Halesworth. **45 J7** TM4280.

Westham *Dorset* ***Suburb***, W district of Weymouth. **9 F7** SY6679.

Westham *E.Suss.* Population: 1429. ***Village***, adjoining to W of Pevensey, 4m/6km NE of Eastbourne. **13 K6** TQ6404.

Westham *Som.* ***Hamlet***, 2m/4km SW of Wedmore. **19 G7** ST4046.

Westhampnett *W.Suss.* ***Village***, 2m/3km NE of Chichester. **12 B6** SU8806.

Westhay *Devon* ***Settlement***, 1m/2km E of Hawkchurch and 4m/6km NE of Axminster. ST3500.

Westhay *Som.* ***Village***, 5m/7km NW of Glastonbury. **19 H7** ST4342.

Westhead *Lancs.* ***Hamlet***, 2m/3km E of Ormskirk. **48 D2** SD4307.

Westhide *Here.* ***Village***, 5m/8km NE of Hereford. **28 E4** SO5844.

Westhill *Aber.* Population: 8449. ***Small town***, 6m/10km W of Aberdeen. **91 G4** NJ8306.

Westhill *High.* Population: 1962. ***Hamlet***, 5m/8km E of Inverness. **96 E7** NH7244.

Westholme *Som.* ***Locality***, 3m/5km SW of Shepton Mallet. ST5740.

Westhope *Here.* ***Village***, 8m/12km N of Hereford. **28 D3** SO4651.

Westhope *Shrop.* ***Settlement***, 3m/5km NE of Craven Arms. **38 D7** SO4786.

Westhorp *Northants.* ***Settlement***, adjoining to W of Byfield, 7m/11km SW of Daventry. SP5053.

Westhorpe *Derbys.* ***Hamlet***, adjoining to S of Killamarsh. SK4579.

Westhorpe *Lincs.* ***Hamlet***, 6m/9km N of Spalding. **43 F2** TF2131.

Westhorpe *Notts.* ***Hamlet***, adjoining to W of Southwell. SK6853.

Westhorpe *Suff.* ***Village***, 7m/11km N of Stowmarket. **34 E2** TM0469.

Westhoughton *Gt.Man.* Population: 20,373. ***Town***, industrial town, 5m/7km E of Wigan. **49 F2** SD6505.

Westhouse *N.Yorks.* ***Hamlet***, 2m/3km NW of Ingleton. **56 B2** SD6774.

Westhouses *Derbys.* ***Village***, 1m/2km NE of Alfreton. **51 G7** SK4257.

Westhumble *Surr.* ***Village***, 1m/2km N of Dorking. Remains of 12c chapel (National Trust). **22 E6** TQ1751.

Westing *Shet.* ***Settlement***, just S of Newgord, on W coast of Unst. **108 E2** HP5705.

Westlake *Devon* ***Hamlet***, 2m/3km SW of Ivybridge. **5 G5** SX6253.

Westlands *Staffs.* ***Suburb***, S district of Newcastle-under-Lyme. SJ8444.

Westlea *Swin.* ***Suburb***, 2m/3km W of Swindon town centre. SU1284.

Westleigh *Devon* ***Village***, above E side of River Torridge estuary, 2m/3km NE of Bideford. **6 C3** SS4728.

Westleigh *Devon* ***Village***, 5m/8km SW of Wellington. **7 J4** ST0617.

Westleigh *Gt.Man.* ***Suburb***, 1m/2km NW of Leigh town centre. **49 F2** SD6401.

Westleton *Suff.* ***Village***, 3m/5km E of Yoxford. Nature reserve on Westleton Heath to E. **35 J2** TM4469.

Westley *Shrop.* ***Hamlet***, 9m/14km SW of Shrewsbury. **38 C5** SJ3606.
Westley *Suff.* ***Village***, 2m/3km W of Bury St. Edmunds. **34 C2** TL8264.
Westley Heights *Essex* ***Suburb***, SW district of Basildon. **24 C3** TQ6886.
Westley Heights Country Park *Thur.* ***Leisure/recreation***, country park of over 130 acres or 52 hectares of hillside comprising grassland, heath and woodland, 3m/4km N of Stanford-le-Hope. **24 C3** TQ6786.
Westley Waterless *Cambs.* ***Village***, 5m/8km S of Newmarket. **33 K3** TL6256.
Westlington *Bucks.* ***Village***, 4m/7km SW of Aylesbury. **31 J7** SP7610.
Westlinton *Cumb.* ***Hamlet***, 3m/4km S of Longtown. **69 J7** NY3964.
Westloch *Sc.Bord.* ***Hamlet***, 3m/5km SE of Leadburn. **76 A5** NT2551.
Westmancote *Worcs.* ***Hamlet***, 4m/7km NE of Tewkesbury. SO9437.
Westmarsh *Kent* ***Hamlet***, 4m/7km NW of Sandwich. **25 J5** TR2761.
Westmeston *E.Suss.* ***Village***, below Ditchling Beacon on South Downs, 4m/7km SE of Burgess Hill. **13 G5** TQ3313.
Westmill *Herts.* ***Village***, 2m/3km S of Buntingford. **33 G6** TL3627.
Westminster *Gt.Lon.* ***City***, within central London, and borough (City of Westminster), containing Westminster Abbey, where almost all English kings and queens have been crowned, Houses of Parliament, Buckingham Palace, 10 Downing Street, St. James's Palace, Whitehall, Trafalgar Square, National Gallery, Tate Gallery, Royal Academy, Green Park, Hyde Park, St. James's Park, and most of Regent's Park. Many shops, parks and restaurants. Westminster lies N of River Thames, here crossed by Vauxhall, Lambeth, Westminster and Waterloo Bridges. TQ2979.
Westminster Abbey *Gt.Lon.* ***Ecclesiastical building***, in central London, 1km S of Charing Cross. First built by Edward the Confessor. Construction of the abbey as it stands today began in 1245, completed by 1506. The towers were not finished until 1734. William I crowned here in 1066, and it has been the coronation church of every new monarch since then. Abbey is composed of three main sections: Nave and Transept (with Poet's Corner and the tomb of the Unknown Soldier); Chapel and Shrine of Edward the Confessor (with Coronation Chair); and Henry VII's chapel, with a wonderful fan-vaulted roof and tombs of many kings and queens including Elizabeth I and Charles II, and Admiral Lord Nelson. Cloisters rebuilt after Great Fire of 1298. The octagonal Chapter House, with fine medieval sculpture, was built in 1250; Pyx Chamber is 11c and houses Abbey treasures (both English Heritage). Norman Undercroft contains museum which includes famous collection of royal and other effigies and coronation regalia. **23 F4** TQ3079.
Westminster Bridge *Gt.Lon.* ***Ecclesiastical building***, cast iron bridge built by Thomas Page 1854-62, spanning River Thames to N of Houses of Parliament. Thames Watermen were paid £25,000 in compensation when original bridge was built in 1750. TQ3079.
Westminster Cathedral *Gt.Lon.* ***Ecclesiastical building***, early Christian Byzantine-style church by J.F. Bentley, 1903, in City of Westminster, 2m/3km SW of Charing Cross. Considered to be most important Roman Catholic church in England. Fine marbled interior. View over Westminster and River Thames from top of 273 feet or 83 metres campanile. TQ2979.
Westmoor End *Cumb.* ***Locality***, 3m/5km SW of Aspatria. NY1039.
Westmuir *Angus* ***Village***, 1m/2km SW of Kirriemuir. **82 E2** NO3652.
Westness *Ork.* ***Settlement***, on SW coast of Rousay. **106 C5** HY3829.
Westnewton *Cumb.* ***Village***, 2m/3km N of Aspatria. **60 C2** NY1344.
Westnewton *Northumb.* ***Hamlet***, at foot of College Burn, 1km W of Kirknewton. **77 G7** NT9030.
Westoe *T. & W.* ***Suburb***, 1km S of South Shields town centre. NZ3766.
Weston *B. & N.E.Som.* ***Suburb***, NW district of Bath. **20 A5** ST7266.
Weston *Ches.* ***Village***, 3m/5km SE of Crewe. **49 G7** SJ7352.
Weston *Devon* ***Hamlet***, 1m/2km W of Honiton. ST1400.
Weston *Devon* ***Hamlet***, 3m/5km E of Sidmouth. **7 K7** SY1689.
Weston *Dorset* Population: 3815. ***Locality***, on W side of Portland. **9 F7** SY6871.
Weston *Halton* ***Suburb***, 1m/2km S of Runcorn town centre. **48 E4** SJ5080.
Weston *Hants.* ***Hamlet***, 1m/2km SW of Petersfield. **11 J2** SU7221.
Weston *Here.* ***Hamlet***, 4m/7km E of Kington. SO3656.
Weston *Herts.* ***Village***, 3m/4km SE of Baldock. **33 F5** TL2630.
Weston *Lincs.* ***Village***, 3m/5km E of Spalding. **43 F3** TF2925.
Weston *Moray* ***Settlement***, 4m/6km S of Portknockie. **98 C4** NJ4962.
Weston *N.Yorks.* ***Hamlet***, 2m/3km NW of Otley across River Wharfe. Hall is Elizabethan. **57 G5** SE1746.
Weston *Northants.* ***Village***, 6m/10km N of Brackley. **31 G4** SP5846.
Weston *Notts.* ***Village***, 3m/5km SE of Tuxford. **51 K6** SK7767.
Weston *Shrop.* ***Hamlet***, 5m/8km S of Much Wenlock. **38 E6** SO5992.
Weston *Shrop.* ***Settlement***, 3m/5km E of Knighton. SO3273.
Weston *Shrop.* ***Village***, 3m/5km E of Wem. **38 E3** SJ5628.
Weston *S'ham.* ***Suburb***, SE district of Southampton, beside Southampton Water, to E of River Itchen. SU4410.
Weston *Staffs.* ***Village***, 4m/7km NE of Stafford. **40 B3** SJ9727.
Weston *W.Berks.* ***Hamlet***, 6m/10km NW of Newbury. **21 H4** SU4073.
Weston Bampfylde *Som.* ***Village***, 1km S of Sparkford. ST6124.
Weston Bay *N.Som.* ***Bay***, sandy bay at Weston-Super-Mare, extending from Birnbeck Island (N) to Howe Rock at tip of Brean Down (S). **19 G5** ST3060.
Weston Beggard *Here.* ***Village***, 5m/7km E of Hereford. **28 E4** SO5841.
Weston by Welland *Northants.* ***Village***, 4m/6km NE of Market Harborough. **42 A6** SP7791.
Weston Colley *Hants.* ***Hamlet***, 1m/2km W of Micheldever. SU5039.
Weston Colville *Cambs.* ***Village***, 6m/10km NW of Haverhill. **33 K3** TL6153.
Weston Corbett *Hants.* ***Hamlet***, adjoining Weston Patrick, 4m/7km SE of Basingstoke. **21 K7** SU6847.
Weston Coton *Shrop.* ***Settlement***, 1m/2km S of Oswestry. SJ2927.
Weston Coyney *Stoke* ***Suburb***, 4m/6km E of Stoke-on-Trent city centre. **40 B1** SJ9343.
Weston Ditch *Suff.* ***Settlement***, 3m/5km NW of Mildenhall. TL6777.
Weston Favell *Northants.* ***Suburb***, E district of Northampton. **31 J2** SP7862.
Weston Green *Cambs.* ***Village***, 5m/8km NW of Haverhill. **33 K3** TL6252.
Weston Green *Norf.* ***Settlement***, 9m/14km NW of Norwich. **45 F4** TG1014.
Weston Green *Surr.* ***Settlement***, 1m/2km NE of Esher. **22 E5** TQ1566.
Weston Heath *Shrop.* ***Hamlet***, 4m/7km SE of Newport. **39 G4** SJ7713.
Weston Hill *Shrop.* ***Mountain***, 8m/12km E of Craven Arms. Height 1053 feet or 321 metres. **38 E7** SO5582.
Weston Hills *Lincs.* ***Hamlet***, 2m/4km SE of Spalding. **43 F3** TF2821.
Weston in Arden *Warks.* ***Suburb***, W district of Bulkington, 1m/2km E of Bedworth. SP3887.
Weston-in-Gordano *N.Som.* ***Village***, 3m/5km NE of Clevedon. **19 H4** ST4474.
Weston Jones *Staffs.* ***Hamlet***, 3m/5km N of Newport. **39 G3** SJ7624.
Weston Longville *Norf.* ***Village***, 9m/14km NW of Norwich. **45 F4** TG1115.
Weston Lullingfields *Shrop.* ***Village***, 9m/14km NW of Shrewsbury. **38 D3** SJ4224.
Weston Mill *Plym.* ***Suburb***, NW district of Plymouth, 3m/4km from city centre. SX4557.
Weston-on-Avon *Warks.* ***Village***, 4m/6km SW of Stratford-upon-Avon. SP1551.
Weston-on-the-Green *Oxon.* ***Village***, 4m/6km SW of Bicester. **31 G7** SP5318.
Weston-on-Trent *Derbys.* ***Village***, 6m/10km SE of Derby. **41 G3** SK4028.
Weston Park *Staffs.* ***Historic house***, 4m/6km NE of Shifnal and 7m/12km E of Telford. 17c house designed by Lady Wilbraham, set in 1000 acres or 404 hectares of parkland landscaped by 'Capability' Brown. Other attractions include aboretum, rose garden, mini-railway and museum. **40 A4** SJ8010.
Weston Patrick *Hants.* ***Village***, 5m/8km SE of Basingstoke. **21 K7** SU6946.
Weston Point *Halton* ***Locality***, 1km NW of Weston. **48 D4** SJ4981.
Weston Rhyn *Shrop.* ***Village***, 4m/6km N of Oswestry. **38 B2** SJ2835.
Weston Subedge *Glos.* ***Village***, below escarpment of Cotswold Hills, 2m/3km NW of Chipping Campden. **30 C4** SP1240.
Weston-super-Mare *N.Som.* Population: 69,372. ***Town***, popular resort on Bristol Channel, 18m/28km SW of Bristol, situated on Weston Bay. International Helicopter Museum. Airport to E. **19 G5** ST3261.
Weston Town *Som.* ***Hamlet***, 6m/10km SW of Frome. ST7041.
Weston Turville *Bucks.* Population: 2638. ***Village***, 3m/5km SE of Aylesbury. **32 B7** SP8510.
Weston-under-Lizard *Staffs.* ***Village***, 7m/11km SE of Newport. **40 A4** SJ8010.
Weston under Penyard *Here.* ***Village***, 2m/4km E of Ross-on-Wye. Site of Roman settlement of Ariconium 1m/2km E. **29 F6** SO6323.
Weston under Wetherley *Warks.* ***Village***, 4m/6km NE of Royal Leamington Spa. **30 E2** SP3669.
Weston Underwood *Derbys.* ***Village***, 6m/9km NW of Derby. **40 E1** SK2942.
Weston Underwood *M.K.* ***Village***, 2m/3km W of Olney. **32 B4** SP8650.
Westonbirt *Glos.* ***Settlement***, 3m/5km SW of Tetbury. Girls' boarding school. Large aboretum. **20 B3** ST8589.
Westonbirt Arboretum *Glos.* ***Garden***, 3m/5km SW of Tetbury, includes 300 acres or 121 hectares of 19c aboretum run by Forestry Commission; particularly noted for autumnal displays. **20 B2** ST8489.
Westoning *Beds.* Population: 1827. ***Village***, 4m/6km S of Ampthill. **32 D5** TL0332.
Westoning Woodend *Beds.* ***Settlement***, 1m/2km SW of Westoning. TL0231.
Westonwharf *Shrop.* ***Settlement***, 1km NW of Weston Lullingfields. Situated on former canal. SJ4225.
Westonzoyland *Som.* Population: 1769. ***Village***, on Sedgemoor, 4m/6km E of Bridgwater. 1m/2km N, site of Battle of Sedgemoor, 1685. **8 C1** ST3534.
Westow *N.Yorks.* ***Village***, 5m/7km SW of Malton. **58 D3** SE7565.
Westport *Arg. & B.* ***Settlement***, at N end of Machrihanish Bay, Kintyre, 5m/8km NW of Campbeltown. **66 A1** NR6525.
Westport *Som.* ***Hamlet***, 4m/6km NE of Ilminster. **8 C3** ST3819.
Westquarter *Falk.* ***Suburb***, 2m/3km SE of Falkirk. NS9178.
Westra *V. of Glam.* ***Hamlet***, adjoining to W of Dinas Powys. ST1471.
Westray *Ork.* ***Island***, with area of 18 square miles or 47 square km, lying 6m/9km N of Rousay and 18m/28km N of Kirkwall, Mainland. The W part is hilly culminating in high coastal cliffs; E part is low-lying. **106 D3** HY4546.
Westray Airfield *Ork.* ***Airport/airfield***, to NE of Westray, just S of Bow Head. **106 D2** HY4551.
Westray Firth *Ork.* ***Sea feature***, sea area bounded by Westray to N, Eday to E, Egilsay and Rousay to S, with open sea to W. **106 D4** HY4537.
Westridge Green *W.Berks.* ***Hamlet***, 2m/3km W of Streatley. SU5679.
Westrigg *W.Loth.* ***Settlement***, adjoining to E of Blackridge. **75 H4** NS9067.
Westrop *Swin.* ***Suburb***, in NE part of Highworth. SU2092.
Westrop *Wilts.* ***Hamlet***, 1m/2km E of Corsham. ST8870.
Westruther *Sc.Bord.* ***Village***, 7m/11km E of Lauder. **76 E5** NT6350.
Westry *Cambs.* ***Village***, 2m/3km NW of March. **43 G6** TL3998.
Westside *Aber.* ***Settlement***, 2m/3km N of Netherley. **91 G5** NO8596.
Westside Church *Ork.* ***Ecclesiastical building***, 12c church on Ness of Tuquoy, on S coast of Westray. Nave lengthened in later medieval times. **106 D3** HY4543.
Westvale *Mersey.* ***Suburb***, W district of Kirkby. SJ4098.
Westville *Notts.* ***Suburb***, SW district of Hucknall. SK5147.
Westward *Cumb.* ***Hamlet***, 3m/4km SE of Wigton. **60 D2** NY2744.
Westward Ho! *Devon* ***Village***, resort on N coast of Devon, 2m/3km NW of Bideford. Sands to N. Golf course on Northam Burrows. **6 C3** SS4329.
Westwell *Kent* ***Village***, 3m/5km N of Ashford. **14 E3** TQ9947.
Westwell *Oxon.* ***Village***, 2m/4km SW of Burford. **30 D7** SP2209.
Westwell Leacon *Kent* ***Hamlet***, 1m/2km SE of Charing. **14 E3** TQ9647.
Westwick *Cambs.* ***Village***, 5m/7km NW of Cambridge. **33 H2** TL4265.
Westwick *Dur.* ***Settlement***, 2m/3km SE of Barnard Castle. **62 B5** NZ0715.
Westwick *Norf.* ***Settlement***, 2m/4km S of North Walsham. **45 G3** TG2726.
Westwick *N.Yorks.* ***Settlement***, 1m/2km E of Bishop Monkton and 4m/6km SE of Ripon. SE3466.
Westwick Row *Herts.* ***Suburb***, 3m/4km E of Hemel Hempstead town centre. TL0906.
Westwood *Devon* ***Hamlet***, 5m/8km S of Cullompton. **7 J6** SY0198.
Westwood *Kent* ***Settlement***, 3m/4km S of Swanscombe. TQ5970.
Westwood *Notts.* ***Hamlet***, 1m/2km S of Selston. SK4551.
Westwood *Peter.* ***Suburb***, 2m/3km NW of Peterborough city centre. TL1799.
Westwood *S.Lan.* ***Suburb***, 1m/2km W of East Kilbride town centre. NS6253.
Westwood *Wilts.* ***Village***, 1m/2km SW of Bradford-on-Avon. **20 B6** ST8159.
Westwood *Worcs.* ***Locality***, 2m/3km W of Droitwich Spa. SO8763.
Westwood Heath *W.Mid.* ***Suburb***, on border with Warwickshire, 4m/6km SW of Coventry city centre. **30 D1** SP2876.
Westwood Manor *Wilts.* ***Historic house***, 15c stone manor house (National Trust), 1m/2km SW of Bradford-on-Avon. 16c alterations, with late Gothic and Jacobean windows and plasterwork. Modern topiary garden. **20 B6** ST8159.
Westwoodside *N.Lincs.* ***Village***, 1m/2km W of Haxey. **51 K3** SK7499.
Wet Sleddale Reservoir *Cumb.* ***Reservoir***, 3m/4km S of Shap. **61 G5** NY5511.
Wetham Green *Kent* ***Settlement***, just N of Upchurch. TQ8468.
Wether Cairn *Northumb.* ***Mountain***, to E of Kidland Forest, 4m/6km NE of Alwinton. Height 1847 feet or 563 metres. **70 E2** NT9411.
Wether Cote Farm *N.Yorks.* ***Settlement***, on W side of Sleightholme Dale, 3m/5km NW of Kirkbymoorside. **58 C1** SE6489.
Wether Fell *N.Yorks.* ***Open space***, moorland to E of Sleddale, with highest point of 2014 feet or 614 metres, 2m/3km S of Hawes. **56 D1** SD8787.
Wether Hill *Aber.* ***Hill***, 3m/4km SW of Cornhill. Height 889 feet or 271 metres. **98 D5** NJ5654.
Wether Hill *D. & G.* ***Mountain***, 4m/6km S of Sanquhar. Height 1568 feet or 478 metres. **68 C3** NS7703.
Wether Hill *D. & G.* ***Mountain***, 6m/10km NE of St. John's Town of Dalry. Height 1263 feet or 385 metres. **68 C5** NX7087.
Wether Hill *D. & G.* ***Mountain***, rising to over 500 metres, 6m/9km W of Moniaive. **68 B4** NX7094.
Wether Hill *Fife* ***Mountain***, in Cleish Hills, 3m/4km NE of Saline. Height 1099 feet or 335 metres. **75 J1** NT0395.
Wether Holm *Shet.* ***Island***, off E coast of Mainland, 2m/3km SE of Firth. HU4672.
Wether Lair *Northumb.* ***Mountain***, to S of East Kielder Moor, 5m/8km NE of Kielder. Height 1627 feet or 496 metres. **70 C4** NY7096.
Wether Law *Sc.Bord.* ***Mountain***, 2m/3km E of Romannobridge. Height 1571 feet or 479 metres. **75 K6** NT1948.
Wetheral *Cumb.* ***Village***, 4m/7km E of Carlisle. 15c gatehouse of medieval priory (English Heritage). **61 F1** NY4654.

Wetheral Plain *Cumb.* ***Locality***, adjoining to N of Wetheral. Wooded bank of River Eden to S, is National Trust property. NY4655.
Wetheral Priory *Cumb.* ***Ecclesiastical building***, Benedictine priory founded in 1106 on W bank of River Eden, on S side of Wetheral. 15c gatehouse (English Heritage) preserved following Dissolution. **61 F1** NY4653.
Wetherby *W.Yorks.* Population: 8154. ***Small town***, old market town on River Wharfe, 8m/13km SE of Harrogate. Racecourse to E. **57 K5** SE4048.
Wetherden *Suff.* ***Village***, 4m/6km NW of Stowmarket. **34 E2** TM0062.
Wetherden Upper Town *Suff.* ***Settlement***, 2m/3km N of Wetherden. TM0165.
Wetheringsett *Suff.* ***Village***, 4m/6km NW of Debenham. **35 F2** TM1266.
Wethersfield *Essex* ***Village***, 2m/3km SE of Finchingfield. **34 B5** TL7131.
Wethersta *Shet.* ***Settlement***, on Mainland, on tongue of land between Busta Voe and Olna Firth, 1m/2km S of Brae. **109 C6** HU3665.
Wetherup Street *Suff.* ***Village***, 2m/3km NW of Debenham. **35 F2** TM1464.
Wetley Abbey *Staffs.* ***Settlement***, 1km S of Wetley Rocks. SJ9648.
Wetley Rocks *Staffs.* ***Village***, 5m/8km S of Leek. **40 B1** SJ9649.
Wetmore *Staffs.* ***Suburb***, 1m/2km NE of Burton upon Trent town centre. SK2524.
Wetreins Green *Ches.* ***Settlement***, 2m/3km SE of Holt across River Dee. SJ4353.
Wettenhall *Ches.* ***Village***, 4m/6km SW of Winsford. **49 F6** SJ6261.
Wettenhall Green *Ches.* ***Settlement***, 4m/6km SW of Winsford. **49 F6** SJ6260.
Wetton *Staffs.* ***Village***, 7m/11km NW of Ashbourne. **50 D7** SK1055.
Wetwang *E.Riding* ***Village***, 6m/9km W of Great Driffield. **59 F4** SE9359.
Wetwood *Staffs.* ***Hamlet***, 4m/7km NW of Eccleshall. **39 G2** SJ7733.
Wexcombe *Wilts.* ***Hamlet***, 5m/8km N of Ludgershall. **21 F6** SU2759.
Wexham Street *Bucks.* ***Settlement***, 3m/4km NE of Slough. SU9983.
Wey ***River***, rising in Woolmer Forest near Liphook and flowing through Godalming and Guildford into River Thames at Weybridge. Another branch rises S of Alton, flows through Farnham, and joins former branch at Tilford, 3m/5km SE of Farnham. **22 D5** TQ0765.
Weybourne *Norf.* ***Village***, 4m/6km NE of Holt. **45 F1** TG1143.
Weybourne *Surr.* ***Suburb***, 1m/2km SW of Aldershot. SU8549.
Weybread *Suff.* ***Village***, 2m/3km S of Harleston. **45 G7** TM2480.
Weybread Street *Suff.* ***Hamlet***, 1km SE of Weybread. TM2479.
Weybridge *Surr.* Population: 25,401. ***Town***, largely residential town, on River Wey near its confluence with River Thames, 17m/28km SW of central London. **22 D5** TQ0764.
Weycroft *Devon* ***Hamlet***, on River Axe, 1m/2km NE of Axminster. **8 C4** SY3099.
Weydale *High.* ***Locality***, in Caithness district, 3m/5km SE of Thurso. **105 G2** ND1464.
Weyhill *Hants.* ***Village***, 3m/5km W of Andover. **21 G7** SU3146.
Weymouth *Dorset* Population: 46,065. ***Town***, 26m/42km W of Bournemouth. Port for Channel Islands. Resort since 18c, when George III stayed here. Redeveloped harbour includes Brewer's Quay complex and Weymouth Museum. **9 F7** SY6778.
Weymouth Bay *Dorset* ***Bay***, extending NE from Weymouth to Redcliff Point, 1m/2km E of Overcombe. **9 G6** SY7080.
Whaddon *Bucks.* ***Village***, 4m/7km W of Bletchley. **32 B5** SP8034.
Whaddon *Cambs.* ***Village***, 4m/6km N of Royston. **33 G4** TL3446.
Whaddon *Glos.* ***Suburb***, NE district of Cheltenham. SO9622.
Whaddon *Glos.* ***Village***, 3m/5km S of Gloucester. **29 H7** SO8313.
Whaddon *Wilts.* ***Hamlet***, 3m/4km NE of Trowbridge. ST8761.
Whaddon *Wilts.* ***Hamlet***, 4m/7km SE of Salisbury. **10 C2** SU1926.
Whaddon Chase *Bucks.* ***Open space***, former hunting forest, with some woodland, 1m/2km S of Whaddon. **31 J5** SP8033.
Whaddon Gap *Cambs.* ***Locality***, 4m/6km N of Royston. **33 G4** TL3445.
Whale *Cumb.* ***Settlement***, at S end of Lowther Park, 5m/9km S of Penrith. **61 G4** NY5221.
Whale Firth *Shet.* ***Sea feature***, inlet on W coast of Yell, the head of which is 1km W of that of Mid Yell Voe on E coast. **108 D3** HU4891.
Whale Geo *Shet.* ***Coastal feature***, indentation on W coast of Yell, 3m/5km N of West Sandwick. **108 D3** HU4493.
Whale Island *Ports.* ***Island***, in Portsmouth Harbour, connected by causeway to Portsea Island. **11 H4** SU6302.
Whalecombe *Pembs.* ***Hamlet***, on S bank of Daugleddau estuary, 3m/5km NE of Pembroke. SN0005.
Whaley *Derbys.* ***Hamlet***, 3m/4km E of Bolsover. **51 H5** SK5171.
Whaley Bridge *Derbys.* Population: 4530. ***Small town***, 6m/10km NW of Buxton. Terminus of Peak Forest Canal. **50 C4** SK0181.
Whaley Thorns *Derbys.* ***Village***, 6m/10km N of Mansfield. SK5371.
Whaligoe *High.* ***Settlement***, on E coast of Caithness district, 6m/9km NE of Lybster. **105 J4** ND3240.
Whalley *Lancs.* Population: 5364. ***Small town***, 6m/10km NE of Blackburn. Remains of 13c abbey with 14c gatehouse (English Heritage). **56 C6** SD7336.
Whalley Abbey *Lancs.* ***Ecclesiastical building***, 13c Cistercian abbey with well-preserved 14c gateway (English Heritage), on River Calder in Whalley. **56 C6** SD7236.
Whalley Banks *Lancs.* ***Settlement***, on hillside, 1km S of Whalley. SD7335.
Whalley Range *Gt.Man.* ***Suburb***, 2m/3km SW of Manchester city centre. SJ8294.
Whalsay *Shet.* ***Island***, of some 8 square miles or 21 square km, off E coast of Mainland, opposite entrance to Dury Voe. **109 E6** HU5663.
Whalton *Northumb.* ***Village***, 5m/8km SW of Morpeth. **71 G5** NZ1381.
Wham *N.Yorks.* ***Settlement***, 3m/4km SW of Settle. **56 C3** SD7762.
Whaplode *Lincs.* ***Village***, 2m/4km W of Holbeach. **43 G3** TF3224.
Whaplode Drove *Lincs.* ***Village***, 5m/9km E of Crowland. **43 G4** TF3113.
Whaplode Fen *Lincs.* ***Open space***, lowland 5m/8km E of Spalding. **43 G3** TF3220.
Whaplode Marsh *Lincs.* ***Open space***, lowland 3m/5km NW of Holbeach. **43 G2** TF3330.
Whaplode St. Catherine *Lincs.* ***Settlement***, 6m/10km SW of Holbeach. Museum of Entertainment, part of which contains mechanised musical instruments, 1km to W. **43 G4** TF3319.
Wharf *Warks.* ***Settlement***, on Oxford Canal, 8m/13km N of Banbury. SP4353.
Wharfe ***River***, rising in Langstrothdale Chase and flowing SE by Kettlewell, Burnsall and Bolton Abbey to Ilkley, E by Otley to Wetherby, then SE by Tadcaster to join River Ouse 1m/2km N of Cawood. **56 E2** SE5739.
Wharfe *N.Yorks.* ***Hamlet***, 4m/7km NW of Settle. **56 C3** SD7869.
Wharfedale *N.Yorks.* ***Valley***, carrying River Wharfe S from Buckden to Bolton Abbey. **56 E3** SD9864.
Wharles *Lancs.* ***Village***, 3m/5km NE of Kirkham. **55 H6** SD4435.
Wharley End *Beds.* ***Village***, to NW of Cranfield Airfield, 4m/7km E of Newport Pagnell. SP9342.
Wharley Point *Carmar.* ***Coastal feature***, headland at confluence of estuaries of River Taf and River Tywi, 1m/2km SW of Llanstephan. **17 G4** SN3309.
Wharmley *Northumb.* ***Locality***, 4m/6km NW of Hexham. NY8866.
Wharncliffe Side *S.Yorks.* Population: 1249. ***Village***, on River Don, 6m/9km NW of Sheffield. **51 F3** SK2994.
Wharram le Street *N.Yorks.* ***Village***, 6m/10km SE of Malton. **58 E3** SE8665.
Wharram Percy *N.Yorks.* ***Locality***, 3m/5km N of Fridaythorpe. Site of former village to N. **58 E3** SE8564.
Wharry Burn *Stir.* ***River***, flowing SW into Allan Water 1m/2km S of Dunblane. **81 K7** NN8201.
Wharton *Ches.* ***Locality***, adjoining to E of Winsford. **49 F6** SJ6666.
Wharton *Here.* ***Hamlet***, 2m/4km S of Leominster. **28 E3** SO5055.
Whashton *N.Yorks.* ***Hamlet***, 4m/6km NW of Richmond. **62 C6** NZ1506.
Whashton Green *N.Yorks.* ***Hamlet***, to SW of Whashton, 3m/5km NW of Richmond. NZ1405.
Whatborough Hill *Leics.* ***Hill***, 1m/2km E of Tilton on the Hill. Mast at summit. Height 754 feet or 230 metres. **42 A5** SK7605.
Whatcombe *Dorset* ***Locality***, consists of settlements of Higher and Lower Whatcombe on road alongside grounds of Whatcombe House, 4m/7km SW of Blandford Forum. ST8301.
Whatcote *Warks.* ***Village***, 4m/6km NE of Shipston on Stour. **30 D4** SP2944.
Whateley *Warks.* ***Settlement***, 3m/5km SE of Tamworth. SP2299.
Whatfield *Suff.* ***Village***, 3m/4km N of Hadleigh. **34 E4** TM0246.
Whatley *Som.* ***Village***, 3m/4km W of Frome. **20 A7** ST7347.
Whatlington *E.Suss.* ***Village***, 2m/3km NE of Battle. **14 C6** TQ7618.
Whatsole Street *Kent* ***Settlement***, 7m/11km E of Ashford. TR1144.
Whatstandwell *Derbys.* ***Hamlet***, 4m/7km N of Belper. **51 F7** SK3354.
Whatton *Notts.* ***Village***, 3m/4km E of Bingham. **42 A2** SK7439.
Whauphill *D. & G.* ***Village***, 4m/6km SW of Wigtown. **64 E6** NX4049.
Whaw *N.Yorks.* ***Hamlet***, in Arkengarthdale, 5m/8km NW of Reeth. **62 A6** NY9804.
Wheat Stack *Sc.Bord.* ***Coastal feature***, rock headland 4m/6km NW of St. Abb's Head. **77 G3** NT8671.
Wheatacre *Norf.* ***Village***, 2m/4km SE of Haddiscoe. **45 J6** TM4693.
Wheatcroft *Derbys.* ***Hamlet***, 4m/6km SE of Matlock. SK3557.
Wheatenhurst *Glos.* ***Hamlet***, 6m/10km NW of Stroud. **20 A1** SO7609.
Wheatfield *Oxon.* ***Settlement***, 3m/5km N of Watlington. SU6899.
Wheathampstead *Herts.* Population: 4554. ***Village***, 3m/4km E of Harpenden. **32 E7** TL1713.
Wheathill *Shrop.* ***Hamlet***, 5m/8km NW of Cleobury Mortimer. **39 F7** SO6282.
Wheathill *Som.* ***Hamlet***, 1m/2km W of Lovington and 3m/5km NW of Sparkford. ST5830.
Wheatley *Hants.* ***Hamlet***, 5m/7km E of Alton. **11 J1** SU7840.
Wheatley *Oxon.* Population: 3661. ***Village***, 5m/8km E of Oxford. Site of Roman villa on Castle Hill to SE. **21 K1** SP5905.
Wheatley *W.Yorks.* *Former name of Ben Rhydding, qv.*
Wheatley *W.Yorks.* ***Suburb***, 2m/3km NW of Halifax town centre. SE0726.
Wheatley Hill *Dur.* Population: 3498. ***Village***, 4m/6km SW of Easington. **62 E3** NZ3739.
Wheatley Hills *S.Yorks.* ***Suburb***, 2m/3km NE of Doncaster town centre. SE6005.
Wheatley Lane *Lancs.* ***Hamlet***, 2m/3km W of Nelson. **56 D6** SD8338.
Wheatley Park *S.Yorks.* ***Suburb***, 2m/3km NE of Doncaster town centre. SE5905.
Wheaton Aston *Staffs.* Population: 2288. ***Village***, 5m/7km W of Penkridge. **40 A4** SJ8512.
Wheddon Cross *Som.* ***Village***, on Exmoor, 5m/8km SW of Dunster. **7 H2** SS9238.
Wheedlemont *Aber.* ***Settlement***, 1m/2km SW of Rhynie. **90 C2** NJ4726.
Wheelbarrow Town *Kent* ***Locality***, adjoining to S of Stelling Minnis. TR1546.
Wheeldale Moor *N.Yorks.* ***Open space***, moorland to N of Cropton Forest, 9m/14km N of Pickering. **63 J7** SE7897.
Wheeldale Moor Roman Road *N.Yorks.* ***Historic/prehistoric site***, 10m/15km SW of Whitby. Exposed one mile section of Roman road (English Heritage). **63 K7** SE8097.
Wheelerend Common *Bucks.* ***Locality***, 4m/6km W of High Wycombe. SU8093.
Wheeler's Street *Kent* ***Locality***, adjoining to E of Headcorn. TQ8444.
Wheelerstreet *Surr.* ***Hamlet***, 1m/2km S of Milford. **22 C7** SU9440.
Wheelock ***River***, rising N of Kidsgrove, and flowing generally NW into River Dane on NW side of Middlewich. SJ6967.
Wheelock *Ches.* ***Village***, on River Wheelock and Trent and Mersey Canal, 1m/2km S of Sandbach. **49 G7** SJ7559.
Wheelock Heath *Ches.* ***Hamlet***, 1m/2km S of Wheelock. SJ7557.
Wheelton *Lancs.* ***Village***, 3m/5km N of Chorley. **56 B7** SD6021.
Wheen *Angus* ***Settlement***, 3m/4km SE of Clova. **90 B7** NO3670.
Wheldale *W.Yorks.* ***Suburb***, 2m/3km E of Castleford. SE4526.
Wheldrake *York* ***Village***, 7m/11km SE of York. **58 C5** SE6844.
Whelford *Glos.* ***Village***, 2m/3km SE of Fairford. **20 E2** SU1798.
Whelley *Gt.Man.* ***Suburb***, E district of Wigan. SD5906.
Whelpley Hill *Bucks.* ***Hamlet***, 2m/4km S of Berkhamsted. Prehistoric fort to S. **22 D1** SP9904.
Whelpo *Cumb.* ***Settlement***, 1m/2km W of Caldbeck. **60 E3** NY3039.
Whelston *Flints.* ***Settlement***, on River Dee estuary, 1m/2km NW of Bagillt. SJ2176.
Whenby *N.Yorks.* ***Village***, 6m/9km N of Strensall. **58 C3** SE6369.
Whepstead *Suff.* ***Village***, 4m/7km SW of Bury St. Edmunds. **34 C3** TL8358.
Whernside ***Mountain***, capped with Millstone Grit, on border of Cumbria and North Yorkshire, 6m/10km NE of Ingleton. Height 2414 feet or 736 metres. **56 C1** SD7381.
Wherry Town *Cornw.* ***Suburb***, central district of Penzance. SW4629.
Wherstead *Suff.* ***Village***, 3m/4km S of Ipswich. **35 F4** TM1540.
Wherwell *Hants.* ***Village***, on River Test, 3m/5km SE of Andover. **21 G7** SU3840.
Whessoe *Darl.* ***Settlement***, 3m/4km N of Darlington. NZ2718.
Wheston *Derbys.* ***Village***, 1m/2km W of Tideswell. **50 D5** SK1575.
Whetley Cross *Dorset* ***Settlement***, 3m/4km NW of Beaminster. **8 D4** ST4504.
Whetsted *Kent* ***Hamlet***, 1m/2km NW of Paddock Wood. **23 K7** TQ6546.
Whetstone *Gt.Lon.* ***Suburb***, in borough of Barnet, 9m/14km N of Charing Cross. TQ2693.
Whetstone *Leics.* Population: 4032. ***Suburb***, 5m/8km SW of Leicester. **41 H6** SP5597.
Wheyrigg *Cumb.* ***Locality***, 4m/6km W of Wigton. NY1948.
Whicham *Cumb.* ***Hamlet***, 3m/5km NW of Millom. **54 E1** SD1382.
Whichford *Warks.* ***Village***, 5m/8km N of Chipping Norton. **30 E5** SP3134.
Whickham *T. & W.* Population: 17,428. ***Town***, industrial town, 3m/5km W of Gateshead. **71 H7** NZ2061.
Whickham Hill *T. & W.* ***Locality***, adjoining to SW of Gateshead, 1m/2km E of Whickham. NZ2260.
Whiddon *Devon* ***Hamlet***, 3m/5km N of Barnstaple. SS5538.
Whiddon *Devon* ***Settlement***, 8m/12km NW of Okehampton. SS4700.
Whiddon Down *Devon* ***Village***, 7m/11km E of Okehampton. **6 E6** SX6992.
Whifflet *N.Lan.* ***Suburb***, 1m/2km S of Coatbridge town centre. **75 F4** NS7364.
Whigstreet *Angus* ***Hamlet***, 4m/7km S of Forfar. Site of Roman camp 1km to E. **83 F3** NO4844.
Whillan Beck *Cumb.* ***River***, issuing from Burnmoor Tarn and flowing S to join River Esk at Beckfoot, 2m/3km E of Eskdale Green. **60 C6** NY1600.
Whilton *Northants.* ***Village***, 4m/7km E of Daventry. **31 H2** SP6364.
Whiltonlocks *Northants.* ***Settlement***, on Grand Union Canal, 3m/5km E of Daventry. SP6164.
Whim *Sc.Bord.* ***Settlement***, 2m/3km SW of Leadburn. **76 A5** NT2153.
Whimble *Devon* ***Hamlet***, 1km SE of Holsworthy. SS3403.
Whimple *Devon* ***Village***, 4m/6km NW of Ottery St. Mary. **7 J6** SY0497.

W

Whimpwell Green *Norf.* ***Village***, 1m/2km S of Happisburgh. **45 H2** TG3829.

Whin Lane End *Lancs.* ***Settlement***, 4m/6km SE of Preesall. **55 G5** SD3941.

Whin Rigg *Cumb.* ***Mountain***, rising to SE of S end of Wast Water. Height 1755 feet or 535 metres. **60 C6** NY1503.

Whinburgh *Norf.* ***Village***, 3m/5km S of East Dereham. **44 E5** TG0009.

Whinfell Beacon *Cumb.* ***Mountain***, 3m/4km W of Low Borrowbridge. Height 1545 feet or 471 metres. **61 G6** NY5700.

Whinfell Forest *Cumb.* ***Forest/woodland***, 4m/7km SE of Penrith. **61 G4** NY5727.

Whinlatter Forest Park *Cumb.* ***Leisure/recreation***, mountain forest park 4m/7km W of Keswick, with Forestry Commission Visitor Centre at E end of Whinlatter Pass. Waymarked trails, permanent orienteering course, forest playground and cycling routes. **60 C4** NY2024.

Whinlatter Pass *Cumb.* ***Other feature of interest***, pass between Whinlatter to N and Grisedale Pike to S, carrying road between Keswick and Cockermouth. **60 C4** NY1924.

Whinney Hill *S.Yorks.* ***Locality***, 3m/4km NE of Rotherham. SK4694.

Whinny Heights *B'burn.* ***Suburb***, 1m/2km SE of Blackburn town centre. SD6926.

Whinny Hill *D. & G.* ***Hill***, rising to over 100 metres, 2m/3km N of New Abbey. **65 K4** NX9569.

Whinny Hill *Stock.* ***Settlement***, 4m/6km W of Stockton-on-Tees. NZ3819.

Whinnyfold *Aber.* ***Settlement***, on E coast, opposite The Skares, 2m/3km S of village of Cruden Bay. **91 J1** NK0833.

Whins Brow *Lancs.* ***Open space***, steep moorland on Forest of Bowland, 3m/4km NW of Dunsop Bridge. **56 B4** SD6353.

Whippingham *I.o.W.* ***Hamlet***, 1m/2km SE of Cowes. **11 G5** SZ5193.

Whipsiderry *Cornw.* ***Hamlet***, on coast, 2m/3km NE of Newquay. SW8363.

Whipsnade *Beds.* ***Village***, 3m/4km S of Dunstable. **32 D7** TL0117.

Whipsnade Park *Beds.* ***Leisure/recreation***, 600 acre or 242 hectare wildlife park to S of Whipsnade. Contains over 2500 animals and performs serious educational and conservation rôle. Narrow gauge railway runs around park. **32 D7** TL0017.

Whipton *Devon* ***Suburb***, E district of Exeter, 2m/3km from city centre. **7 H6** SX9593.

Whirley Grove *Ches.* ***Settlement***, 2m/3km NW of Macclesfield. SJ8875.

Whirlow *S.Yorks.* ***Suburb***, 4m/6km SW of Sheffield city centre. SK3182.

Whisby *Lincs.* ***Hamlet***, 5m/9km SW of Lincoln. **52 C6** SK9067.

Whispering Knights *Oxon. See Little Rollright.*

Whissendine *Rut.* ***Village***, 4m/6km NW of Oakham. **42 B4** SK8314.

Whissonsett *Norf.* ***Village***, 4m/7km S of Fakenham. **44 D3** TF9123.

Whisterfield *Ches.* ***Settlement***, 1m/2km W of Siddington. SJ8271.

Whistley Green *W'ham* ***Village***, 1m/2km S of Twyford. **22 A4** SU7974.

Whiston *Mersey.* ***Town***, former mining town, adjoining to SE of Prescot. **48 D3** SJ4791.

Whiston *Northants.* ***Village***, 6m/10km E of Northampton. **32 B2** SP8460.

Whiston *S.Yorks.* ***Suburb***, 2m/3km SE of Rotherham. **51 G4** SK4590.

Whiston *Staffs.* ***Hamlet***, 2m/3km W of Penkridge. **40 A4** SJ8914.

Whiston *Staffs.* ***Hamlet***, 2m/3km E of Kingsley. **40 C1** SK0347.

Whiston Cross *Mersey.* ***Suburb***, 1km S of Prescot. SJ4691.

Whiston Cross *Shrop.* ***Settlement***, 1m/2km SW of Albrighton. SJ7903.

Whiston Eaves *Staffs.* ***Settlement***, 1km S of Whiston. SK0446.

Whiston Lane Ends *Mersey.* ***Locality***, to SW of Whiston. SJ4791.

Whit Moor *Lancs.* ***Open space***, moorland on N side of Caton Moor, 7m/11km E of Lancaster. **55 J3** SD5864.

Whitacre Fields *Warks.* ***Settlement***, 4m/6km NE of Coleshill. SP2592.

Whitacre Heath *Warks.* ***Village***, 3m/4km NE of Coleshill. SP2192.

Whitbarrow Scar *Cumb.* ***Inland physical feature***, rocky escarpment on W side of Whitbarrow, 5m/8km NW of Milnthorpe. **55 H1** SD4487.

Whitbeck *Cumb.* ***Hamlet***, 3m/4km S of Bootle. **54 E1** SD1184.

Whitbourne *Here.* ***Village***, 5m/8km NE of Bromyard. **29 G3** SO7257.

Whitburn *T. & W.* Population: 5971. ***Village***, large village on North Sea coast, 4m/6km SE of South Shields. **71 K7** NZ4061.

Whitburn *W.Loth.* Population: 11,511. ***Town***, former iron and coal town, 3m/5km SW of Bathgate. **75 H4** NS9465.

Whitburn Bay *T. & W.* ***Bay***, to S of Whitburn. **71 K7** NZ4060.

Whitburn Colliery *T. & W.* ***Locality***, to N of Whitburn, 4m/6km SE of South Shields. NZ4063.

Whitby *Ches.* ***Suburb***, 1m/2km SW of Ellesmere Port town centre. **48 C5** SJ3975.

Whitby *N.Yorks.* Population: 13,640. ***Town***, resort and small port on North Sea coast, 17m/27km NW of Scarborough. 13c abbey (English Heritage). Boyhood home of Captain Cook, navigator and explorer, is preserved. **63 K5** NZ8911.

Whitby Abbey *N.Yorks.* ***Ecclesiastical building***, spectacularly sited ruins of 13c Benedictine abbey (English Heritage) at Whitby, 200 feet or 61 metres above sea level, on headland to E of mouth of River Esk. Originally built on site of former abbey destroyed by Danes in AD 867, excavation has also revealed 7c and 8c traces. Abbey was destroyed under Henry VIII and sustained further damage in 1914 from German battlecruiser. **63 J1** NZ9011.

Whitby Museum *N.Yorks.* ***Other feature of interest***, at Whitby, with exhibits on Captain Cook, whaling, local history and geology. **63 K5** NZ9010.

Whitbyheath *Ches.* ***Suburb***, 2m/3km S of Ellesmere Port town centre. SJ3974.

Whitchurch *B. & N.E.Som.* ***Village***, 4m/6km SE of Bristol. **19 K5** ST6167.

Whitchurch *Bucks.* ***Village***, 5m/8km N of Aylesbury. **32 B6** SP8020.

Whitchurch (Yr Eglwys Newydd). *Cardiff* ***Suburb***, 3m/5km NW of Cardiff city centre. **18 E4** ST1580.

Whitchurch *Devon* ***Village***, adjoining to SE of Tavistock. **4 E3** SX4972.

Whitchurch *Hants.* Population: 4123. ***Small town***, on River Test, 6m/10km E of Andover. Many Georgian buildings, and silk still woven at 19c mill. Birthplace of Lord Denning. **21 H7** SU4648.

Whitchurch *Here.* ***Village***, 4m/6km NE of Monmouth. **28 E7** SO5517.

Whitchurch *Oxon.* ***Village***, across River Thames from Pangbourne, and 5m/8km NW of Reading. **21 K4** SU6377.

Whitchurch (Tre-groes). *Pembs.* ***Village***, 3m/5km E of St. David's. **16 B2** SM7925.

Whitchurch *Shrop.* Population: 7868. ***Small town***, 18m/29km N of Shrewsbury, on site of Roman town of Mediolanum. Birthplace of Edward German. **38 E1** SJ5441.

Whitchurch *Warks.* ***Settlement***, 4m/7km S of Stratford-upon-Avon. SP2248.

Whitchurch Canonicorum *Dorset* ***Village***, 4m/7km NE of Lyme Regis. **8 C5** SY3995.

Whitchurch Heath *Shrop.* ***Locality***, 3m/4km S of Whitchurch. SJ5537.

Whitchurch Hill *Oxon.* ***Village***, 2m/3km N of Pangbourne. **21 K4** SU6479.

Whitcombe *Dorset* ***Hamlet***, 3m/4km SE of Dorchester. **9 G6** SY7188.

Whitcott Keysett *Shrop.* ***Hamlet***, 2m/3km NW of Clun. **38 B7** SO2782.

White Ball *Som.* ***Hamlet***, 1km W of Sampford Arundel. 1km SW, White Ball Tunnel on Taunton-Exeter main railway line. ST0918.

White Cart Water ***River***, rising S of East Kilbride and running N to Cathcart, Glasgow, then NW through Paisley to join Black Cart Water 3m/4km N, flowing into River Clyde 1km further N. **74 D4** NS4968.

White Castle *E.Loth.* ***Historic/prehistoric site***, hillfort 3m/4km SE of Garvald. **76 E4** NT6168.

White Castle *Mon.* ***Settlement***, 5m/8km E of Abergavenny. Ruined 13c castle (Cadw). **28 C7** SO3816.

White Caterthun *Angus* ***Historic/prehistoric site***, Iron Age fort, nearly 1m/2km SW of Brown Caterthun and 5m/8km NW of Brechin. **83 G1** NO5566.

White Colne *Essex* ***Hamlet***, 4m/7km E of Halstead. **34 C6** TL8729.

White Combe *Cumb.* ***Mountain***, to E of Black Combe, 4m/6km N of Millom. Height 1361 feet or 415 metres. **54 E1** SD1586.

White Coomb *D. & G.* ***Mountain***, partly National Trust for Scotland property, 8m/12km NE of Moffat. Height 2696 feet or 822 metres. **69 G2** NT1615.

White Coppice *Lancs.* ***Hamlet***, on moors, 1km N of N end of Anglezarke Reservoir, 2m/3km E of Chorley. **49 F1** SD6119.

White Corries *High.* ***Locality***, skiing area in Lochaber district on N slope of Meall a' Bhùiridh. NN2652.

White Craig *S.Lan.* ***Mountain***, in Pentland Hills, 5m/8km NW of West Linton. Height 1424 feet or 434 metres. **75 J5** NT0753.

White Cross *Cornw.* ***Hamlet***, 4m/6km SE of Helston. SW6821.

White Cross *Cornw.* ***Hamlet***, 3m/5km SE of St. Columb Major. **3 F3** SW8959.

White Cross *Devon* ***Hamlet***, 1km E of Cheriton Fitzpaine and 5m/8km NE of Crediton. SS8706.

White Cross *Devon* ***Settlement***, 7m/11km E of Exeter. **7 J6** SY0290.

White Cross *Here.* ***Suburb***, on W side of Hereford. **28 D4** SO4940.

White Cross *Oxon.* ***Locality***, 2m/3km N of Abingdon. SP4800.

White Cross *Wilts.* ***Hamlet***, 1km NW of Zeals and 3m/4km W of Mere. ST7732.

White Edge *Derbys.* ***Inland physical feature***, mountain ridge, 1204 feet or 367 metres high, to W of Big Moor, 1km E of Froggatt. **50 E5** SK2575.

White End *Glos.* ***Settlement***, to E of Ashleworth, 4m/7km N of Gloucester across River Severn. **29 H6** SO8125.

White Fen *Cambs.* ***Open space***, fenland 6m/9km SW of March. **43 G6** TL3492.

White Hill *Aber.* ***Mountain***, 1m/2km SE of Ballochan. Height 1870 feet or 570 metres. **90 D6** NO5388.

White Hill *Angus* ***Mountain***, 3m/5km NE of Rottal. Height 2552 feet or 778 metres. **90 B7** NO4073.

White Hill *Dorset* ***Hill***, 1km N of Abbotsbury. Height 656 feet or 200 metres. **8 E6** SY5886.

White Hill *Dur.* ***Locality***, adjoining to SW of Chester-le-Street. NZ2650.

White Hill *E.Suss.* ***Suburb***, W district of Bexhill. TQ7208.

White Hill *Kent* ***Locality***, 3m/4km S of Canterbury. TR1554.

White Hill *Lancs.* ***Mountain***, on Forest of Bowland, 4m/7km NW of Slaidburn. Height 1784 feet or 544 metres. **56 B4** SD6758.

White Hill *Northumb.* ***Mountain***, in wooded area 2m/3km NE of Falstone. Height 1010 feet or 308 metres. **70 C5** NY7488.

White Hill *Sc.Bord.* ***Mountain***, 2m/3km SE of Hawick. Height 987 feet or 301 metres. **70 A2** NT5211.

White Hill *Wilts.* ***Settlement***, 1m/2km S of Mere. ST8230.

White Hope Edge *D. & G.* ***Mountain***, on edge of woodland, 5m/8km N of Benthpath. Height 1558 feet or 475 metres. **69 J4** NY3397.

White Houses *Notts.* ***Hamlet***, 1m/2km SE of Retford. SK7179.

White Island *I.o.S.* ***Island***, situated off N coast of St. Martin's. Accessible at low water over rock causeway. **2 C1** SV9218.

White Kirkley *Dur.* ***Hamlet***, 1km S of Frosterley across River Wear, on S side of Bollihope Burn. NZ0234.

White Lackington *Dorset* ***Hamlet***, 4m/6km NW of Puddletown. **9 G5** SY7198.

White Lackington *Som. Alternative spelling of Whitelackington, qv.*

White Ladies Aston *Worcs.* ***Village***, 5m/8km E of Worcester. **29 J3** SO9252.

White Ladies Priory *Shrop.* ***Ecclesiastical building***, remains of 12c priory (English Heritage), 2m/3km E of Tong. **40 A5** SJ8207.

White Law *Northumb.* ***Mountain***, in Cheviot Hills, 3m/4km SE of Kirk Yetholm. Height 1410 feet or 430 metres. **70 D1** NT8526.

White-le-Head *Dur.* ***Locality***, at S end of Tantobie, 2m/3km NW of Stanley. NZ1754.

White Lee *W.Yorks.* ***Locality***, 1m/2km NW of Batley. SE2225.

White Loch *D. & G.* ***Lake/loch***, within grounds of Lochinch Castle, to W of Black Loch and 3m/5km E of Stranraer. Castle Kennedy is on isthmus which separates the lochs. **64 B4** NX1060.

White Loch *D. & G.* ***Lake/loch***, 5m/8km SE of Dalbeattie. **65 J5** NX8654.

White Loch of Myrton *D. & G.* ***Lake/loch***, 2m/3km E of Port William. **64 D6** NX3543.

White Lodge *Bucks.* ***Locality***, 2m/4km SW of Uxbridge. TQ0282.

White Lund *Lancs.* ***Suburb***, adjoining to SE of Morecambe. SD4462.

White Lyne *Cumb.* ***River***, rising on fells N of Bewcastle and flowing SW to join River Black Lyne, forming River Lyne, 5m/7km W of Bewcastle. **70 A5** NY4973.

White Meldon *Sc.Bord.* ***Mountain***, with hillfort, 2m/4km NW of Peebles. Height 1401 feet or 427 metres. **76 A6** NT2142.

White Mere *Shrop.* ***Lake/loch***, one of several in district, 2m/3km SE of Ellesmere. **38 D2** SJ4133.

White Mill (Felin-wen). *Carmar.* ***Hamlet***, 3m/5km E of Carmarthen. **17 H2** SN4621.

White Mill Bridge *Dorset* ***Bridge***, stone bridge dating from early 14c (restored 1713) crossing River Stour just E of Sturminster Marshall and 3m/5km W of Wimborne Minster. SY9500.

White Moor *Cambs.* ***Open space***, fenland 2m/3km NW of March. **43 G6** TL3898.

White Moor *Derbys.* ***Locality***, 1m/2km E of Belper. **41 F1** SK3648.

White Mounth *Aber.* ***Mountain***, to SW of Lochnagar. Height 3447 feet or 1051 metres. **89 K6** NO2383.

White Ness *Kent* ***Coastal feature***, headland between Botany Bay and Kingsgate Bay on North Foreland. **25 K4** TR3971.

White Ness *Shet.* ***Coastal feature***, long narrow peninsula on Mainland on W side of Whiteness Voe, 3m/4km NW of Scalloway. **109 C8** HU3843.

White Notley *Essex* ***Village***, 3m/5km NW of Witham. **34 B7** TL7818.

White Oak *Kent* ***Suburb***, 1km N of Swanley. TQ5169.

White Ox Mead *B. & N.E.Som.* ***Hamlet***, 1m/2km W of Wellow. ST7258.

White Pit *Lincs.* ***Hamlet***, 7m/12km SE of Louth. **53 G5** TF3777.

White Preston *Cumb.* ***Mountain***, to NW of Spadeadam Forest, 3m/4km NE of Bewcastle. Height 1384 feet or 422 metres. **70 A6** NY5877.

White Ridge *Devon* ***Mountain***, flat-topped mountain, 2m/3km N of Postbridge, in Dartmoor National Park. Height 1653 feet or 504 metres. **6 E7** SX6482.

White Rocks *Here.* ***Settlement***, 3m/5km SE of Pontrilas. SO4324.

White Roding *Essex* ***Village***, 2m/3km W of Leaden Roding. **33 J7** TL5613.

White Sands *Flints.* ***Coastal feature***, sandbank at SW point of Wirral, 2m/3km E of Flint. **48 B5** SJ2772.

White Scar Cave *N.Yorks.* ***Cave***, extensive limestone cavern under Ingleborough Hill, with stream, waterfall and lake, 2m/3km NE of Ingleton. Notable stalactites and stalagmites. **56 C2** SD7174.

White Sheet Hill *Wilts.* ***Hill***, 1m/2km N of Mere, at W end of Wiltshire Downs. Height 807 feet or 246 metres. **9 G1** ST8034.

White Sheet Hill *Wilts.* ***Hill***, 2m/3km SE of Donhead St. Andrew. Height 794 feet or 242 metres. **9 J2** ST9323.

White Stake *Lancs.* ***Locality***, 3m/5km SW of Preston. SD5225.

White Stone *Here.* ***Hamlet***, adjacent to S side of Withington, 4m/6km NE of Hereford. SO5642.

White Stone *Warks.* ***Suburb***, in SE part of Nuneaton. SP3889.

White Top of Culreoch *D. & G.* ***Mountain***, 4m/7km N of Gatehouse of Fleet. Height 1125 feet or 343 metres. **65 F4** NX6063.

White Walls *Lancs. Locality*, 1m/2km SW of Colne. SD8739.
White Waltham *W. & M. Village*, 3m/5km SW of Maidenhead. **22 B4** SU8577.
White Water *Angus River*, running SE into River South Esk, 3m/5km NW of Clova. **89 K7** NO2875.
Whiteacen *Moray Settlement*, 2m/3km SW of Rothes. **97 K7** NJ2546.
Whiteadder Reservoir *E.Loth. Reservoir*, in course of Whiteadder Water, about 3m/5km from source and 2m/4km NW of Cranshaws. **76 E4** NT6563.
Whiteadder Water *River*, rising in Lammermuir Hills on Scottish Borders, 6m/10km NW of Cranshaws, and flowing through Whiteadder Reservoir, then SE into River Tweed 2m/3km W of Berwick-upon-Tweed. **77 G5** NT9751.
Whiteash Green *Essex Settlement*, 1m/2km NE of Gosfield. **34 B5** TL7930.
Whiteash Hill *Moray Hill*, in wooded area 3m/4km E of Fochabers. Height 866 feet or 264 metres. **98 B5** NJ3857.
Whitebirk *B'burn. Suburb*, 2m/3km E of Blackburn. SD7028.
Whitebog *Aber. Settlement*, 3m/5km N of Strichen. **99 H5** NJ9359.
Whitebridge *High. Hamlet*, in Inverness district, at confluence of River Feehlin and Allt Breinag, 3m/5km S of Foyers. **88 B3** NH4815.
Whitebridge *High. Settlement*, 1m/2km S of Scarfskerry. **105 H1** ND2672.
Whitebrook *Mon. Hamlet*, 4m/7km S of Monmouth. **19 J1** SO5306.
Whiteburn *Sc.Bord. Settlement*, 4m/6km E of Lauder. **76 D6** NT5947.
Whitecairn *D. & G. Settlement*, 1m/2km N of Glenluce. **64 C5** NX2059.
Whitecairns *Aber. Settlement*, 7m/12km N of Aberdeen. **91 H3** NJ9218.
Whitecastle *S.Lan. Settlement*, 3m/5km NW of Biggar. **75 J6** NT0141.
Whitechapel *Gt.Lon. Suburb*, in borough of Tower Hamlets, 1km NE of London Bridge. TQ3381.
Whitechapel *Lancs. Hamlet*, 2m/3km E of Claughton. **55 J5** SD5541.
Whitechurch (Eglwys Wen). *Pembs. Settlement*, 1m/2km SE of Eglwyswrw. **16 E1** SN1536.
Whitechurch *Som. Settlement*, 1km N of Henstridge and 3m/5km NE of Milborne Port. ST7220.
Whitecliff Bay *I.o.W. Bay*, on SE coast to NE of Culver Cliff, 1m/2km SW of Bembridge. **11 H6** SZ6486.
Whiteclosegate *Cumb. Locality*, 1m/2km NE of Carlisle. NY4157.
Whitecote *W.Yorks. Suburb*, 4m/6km NW of Leeds city centre. SE2435.
Whitecraig *E.Loth.* Population: 1209. *Village*, 2m/3km S of Musselburgh. **76 B3** NT3570.
Whitecroft *Glos. Village*, 2m/4km NW of Lydney. **19 K1** SO6106.
Whitecrook *D. & G. Settlement*, adjacent to N of Sands of Luce, 2m/3km W of Glenluce. **64 B5** NX1656.
Whitecrook *Renf. Suburb*, to E of Clydebank town centre. NS5069.
Whitecross *Cornw. Hamlet*, 3m/5km SW of Hayle. **2 C5** SW5234.
Whitecross *Cornw. Hamlet*, 2m/3km W of Wadebridge. SW9672.
Whitecross *Dorset Settlement*, 1m/2km SW of Beaminster. SY4699.
Whitecross *Falk. Village*, 3m/4km W of Linlithgow. NS9676.
Whiteface *High. Locality*, on N side of Dornoch Firth, 6m/9km W of Dornoch, Sutherland district. **96 E3** NH7089.
Whitefarland Point *N.Ayr. Coastal feature*, headland on W coast of Arran, 1m/2km S of Pirnmill. **73 G6** NR8642.
Whitefauld Hill *D. & G. Mountain*, rising to over 360 metres on Forest of Ae, 8m/12km NW of Lochmaben. **69 F4** NY0293.
Whitefaulds *S.Ayr. Suburb*, W district of Maybole. NS2909.
Whitefield *Aber. Settlement*, 1km W of Oldmeldrum. **91 F2** NJ7927.
Whitefield *Devon Hamlet*, on E edge of Exmoor, 6m/10km N of South Molton. SS7036.
Whitefield *Dorset Settlement*, 3m/4km W of Lytchett Matravers. SY9094.
Whitefield *Gt.Man.* Population: 22,783. *Town*, old textile town, 3m/4km S of Bury. **49 H2** SD8006.
Whitefield *High. Settlement*, 2m/3km SE of Watten. **105 H3** ND2753.
Whitefield *High. Settlement*, on E shore of Loch Ness, 3m/5km across loch from Drumnadrochit. **88 C2** NH5528.
Whitefield *P. & K. Locality*, comprises settlements of East Whitefield and Meikle Whitefield, 2m/3km SW of Burrelton. **82 C4** NO1734.
Whitefield Lane End *Mersey. Suburb*, 1m/2km SE of Huyton-with-Roby. SJ4589.
Whitefield Loch *D. & G. Lake/loch*, 3m/5km SE of Glenluce. **64 C5** NX2355.
Whiteford *Aber. Hamlet*, 5m/7km NW of Inverurie. **91 F2** NJ7126.
Whitegate *Ches. Village*, 3m/4km NW of Winsford. **49 F6** SJ6269.
Whitehall *Devon Hamlet*, by River Culm, 4m/7km S of Wellington. ST1214.
Whitehall *Devon Settlement*, on Knowle Water, 3m/5km NW of Barnstaple. SS5337.
Whitehall *Hants. Settlement*, 1m/2km NE of Odiham. SU7452.
Whitehall *Ork. Village*, on N coast of Stronsay, opposite Papa Stronsay harbour. **106 F5** HY6528.
Whitehall *W.Suss. Hamlet*, 1m/2km SE of Coolham. TQ1321.
Whitehaugh Forest *Aber. Forest/woodland*, of conifers surrounding hill of Knock Saul, 5m/7km N of Alford. **90 D2** NJ5723.
Whitehaven *Cumb.* Population: 26,542. *Town*, port on Irish Sea, 7m/11km S of Workington. Local coal exported from here. Known as the Georgian Port due to large amount of 18c architecture. **60 A5** NX9718.
Whitehawk *B. & H. Suburb*, E district of Brighton. Site of Neolithic camp to W. TQ3304.
Whiteheath Gate *W.Mid. Suburb*, 1m/2km S of Oldbury town centre. SO9887.
Whitehill *Aber. Settlement*, 3m/4km S of New Pitsligo. NJ8952.
Whitehill *Fife Locality*, industrial estate in SW part of Glenrothes. NT2599.
Whitehill *Hants. Village*, 2km S of Bordon Camp and 4m/6km NW of Liphook. **11 J1** SU7934.
Whitehill *Kent Settlement*, 2m/3km SW of Faversham. **14 E2** TR0059.
Whitehill *Midloth. Hamlet*, 2m/3km E of Dalkeith. NT3566.
Whitehill *Moray Settlement*, 2m/4km SW of Gordonstown. NJ5354.
Whitehill *N.Ayr. Settlement*, 3m/5km W of Kilbirnie, between Muirhead and Camphill Reservoirs. **74 A5** NS2656.
Whitehills *Aber. Village*, 2m/4km NW of Banff. **98 E4** NJ6565.
Whitehills *Angus Suburb*, adjoining to NE of Forfar. NO4651.
Whitehope Law *Sc.Bord. Mountain*, 5m/8km N of Innerleithen. Height 2037 feet or 621 metres. **76 B6** NT3344.
Whitehorse Hill *Devon Mountain*, 4m/7km NW of Postbridge, in Dartmoor National Park. Height 1971 feet or 601 metres. **6 E7** SX6185.
Whitehorse Hill *Oxon. Hill*, 2m/3km S of Uffington. Uffington Castle (Iron Age fort) to W. Height 856 feet or 261 metres. **21 G3** SU3086.
Whitehough *Derbys. Hamlet*, adjoining to S of Chinley. SK0382.
Whitehouse *Aber. Village*, 3m/5km E of Alford. **90 E3** NJ6214.
Whitehouse *Arg. & B. Village*, in Kintyre, Argyll, 6m/9km SW of Tarbert. **73 G4** NR8161.
Whitehouse *Halton Suburb*, industrial area in SE part of Runcorn. SJ5679.
Whitehouse Common *W.Mid. Suburb*, 1m/2km NE of Sutton Coldfield town centre. SP1397.
Whitehouse Green *W.Berks. Settlement*, 1m/2km W of Burghfield and 5m/8km SW of Reading. SU6568.
Whiteinch *Glas. Suburb*, on N bank of River Clyde in Scotstoun district of Glasgow. NS5367.
Whitekirk *E.Loth. Village*, 4m/6km SE of North Berwick. **76 D2** NT5981.
Whitelackington (Also spelled White Lackington.) *Som. Village*, 1m/2km E of Ilminster. **8 C3** ST3715.
Whitelake *Som. River*, rising to S of Shepton Mallet, and cut through Sedgemoor for drainage purposes; then flows W into River Brue just E of Westhay. **8 E1** ST4442.
Whitelands *T. & W. Locality*, 1m/2km SW of Birtley. NZ2854.
Whitelane End *S.Yorks. Suburb*, 4m/6km SE of Sheffield city centre. SK3982.
Whitelaw *Sc.Bord. Hamlet*, 3m/5km SE of Duns. **77 G5** NT8352.
Whitelaw Hill *E.Loth. Hill*, 4m/6km SW of East Linton. Height 584 feet or 178 metres. **76 D3** NT5771.
Whitelaw Hill *Sc.Bord. Mountain*, 1m/2km SE of Stobo. Height 1561 feet or 476 metres. **75 K7** NT1935.
Whiteleaf *Bucks. Hamlet*, 1m/2km NE of Princes Risborough. SP8104.
Whiteleas *T. & W. Suburb*, 2m/4km S of South Shields. NZ3663.
Whiteleen *High. Settlement*, 2m/3km SW of Thrumster. **105 J4** ND3242.
Whitelees *S.Ayr. Settlement*, 1m/2km E of Symington. **74 B7** NS3931.
Whiteley *Hants. Settlement*, 3m/5km NW of Fareham. **11 G4** SU5209.
Whiteley Bank *I.o.W. Hamlet*, 2m/3km W of Shanklin. **11 G6** SZ5581.
Whiteley Green *Ches. Hamlet*, 1m/2km NW of Bollington. SJ9278.
Whiteley Village *Surr. Village*, small residential estate with octagonal layout, 2m/3km SE of Weybridge. **22 D5** TQ0962.
Whiteleys *D. & G. Settlement*, 2m/3km S of Stranraer. **64 A5** NX0657.
Whitelinks Bay *Aber. Bay*, on NE coast, 1km SE of Inverallochy. **99 J4** NK0564.
Whitelye *Mon. Settlement*, 5m/8km N of Chepstow. SO5101.
Whitemans Green *W.Suss. Locality*, adjoining to N of Cuckfield. **13 G4** TQ3025.
Whitemill Point *Ork. Coastal feature*, headland on N coast of Sanday, on W side of entrance to Otters Wick. **106 F3** HY7046.
Whitemire *Moray Settlement*, 5m/8km SW of Forres. **97 G6** NH9754.
Whitemoor *Cornw. Village*, in china clay district, 4m/7km NW of St. Austell. SW9757.
Whitemoor *Notts. Suburb*, 2m/3km NW of Nottingham city centre. SK5442.
Whitemoor Reservoir *Lancs. Reservoir*, 2m/3km N of Colne. **56 D5** SD8743.
Whiten Head *High. Coastal feature*, headland on N coast of Sutherland district, on E side of entrance to Loch Eriboll. **103 G2** NC5068.
Whiteness *Shet. Locality*, on Mainland, at head of Whiteness Voe, 4m/7km N of Scalloway. **109 D8** HU4047.
Whiteness Head *High. Coastal feature*, spit of land on Moray Firth 3m/5km E of Fort George, Inverness district. **96 E6** NH8058.
Whiteness Sands *High. Coastal feature*, beach on S side of mouth of Dornoch Firth, 5m/7km NE of Tain. **97 F3** NH8386.
Whiteness Voe *Shet. Sea feature*, long inlet on W coast of Mainland, S of Whiteness locality and 3m/4km W of Veensgarth. **109 C8** HU3944.
Whiteoak Green *Oxon. Settlement*, 3m/5km N of Witney. SP3414.
Whiteparish *Wilts. Village*, 7m/11km W of Romsey. **10 D2** SU2423.
Whiterashes *Aber. Village*, 4m/6km SE of Oldmeldrum. **91 G2** NJ8523.
Whiterow *High. Settlement*, in Caithness district, 1m/2km S of Wick. **105 J4** ND3548.
Whitesand Bay *Cornw. Bay*, wide bay to NE of Land's End. **2 A6** SW3527.
Whitesands Bay (Also known as Porth-mawr.) *Pembs. Bay*, extending S from St. David's Head to Point St. John. **16 A2** SM7227.
Whiteshill *Glos. Village*, 1m/2km N of Stroud. **20 B1** SO8407.
Whiteshill *S.Glos. Hamlet*, by River Frome, 6m/9km NE of Bristol. ST6479.
Whiteshoot Hill *Hants. Hill*, 3m/5km E of Middle Winterslow. Height 495 feet or 151 metres. **10 D1** SU2833.
Whiteside *Northumb. Settlement*, on Tipalt Burn, 3m/5km N of Haltwhistle. **70 C7** NY7069.
Whiteside *W.Loth. Hamlet*, 1km SW of Bathgate. **75 H4** NS9668.
Whiteside Hill *S.Lan. Mountain*, in Lowther Hills, on border with Dumfries & Galloway, 3m/5km E of Ballencleuch Law. Height 1817 feet or 554 metres. **68 E3** NS9704.
Whitesmith *E.Suss. Hamlet*, 5m/8km NW of Hailsham. **13 J5** TQ5213.
Whitestaunton *Som. Village*, 3m/5km NW of Chard. **8 B3** ST2810.
Whitestone *Aber. Hamlet*, 2m/3km W of Strachan. **90 E5** NO6492.
Whitestone *Arg. & B. Settlement*, on Kintyre, 3m/5km SW of Carradale. **73 F7** NR7933.
Whitestone *Devon Village*, 3m/5km W of Exeter. **7 G6** SX8693.
Whitestone Cross *Devon Hamlet*, 2m/3km W of Exeter. SX8993.
Whitestreet Green *Suff. Hamlet*, 3m/5km N of Nayland. TL9739.
Whitestripe *Aber. Settlement*, on W side of Waughton Hill, 1km N of Strichen. **99 H5** NJ9456.
Whitewall Corner *N.Yorks. Locality*, adjoining to S of Norton. SE7970.
Whiteway *Glos. Village*, 6m/9km NE of Stroud. **29 J7** SO9110.
Whitewayhead *Shrop. Locality*, at S end of Knowbury, 4m/7km E of Ludlow. SO5774.
Whitewell *Aber. Settlement*, 4m/6km N of Strichen. **99 H4** NJ9461.
Whitewell *Lancs. Hamlet*, 6m/10km NW of Clitheroe. **56 B5** SD6546.
Whitewell *Wrex. Settlement*, 3m/5km W of Whitchurch. SJ4941.
Whitewell Bottom *Lancs. Locality*, 2m/3km E of Rawtenstall. SD8323.
Whiteworks *Devon Settlement*, 2m/3km SE of Princetown. **5 G3** SX6170.
Whitewreath *Moray Settlement*, 3m/5km S of Elgin. **97 K6** NJ2357.
Whitfell *Cumb. Mountain*, 5m/8km E of Ravenglass. Height 1876 feet or 572 metres. **60 C7** SD1592.
Whitfield *Here. Settlement*, 7m/11km SW of Hereford. **28 D5** SO4233.
Whitfield *Kent* Population: 5133. *Suburb*, N of Dover. **15 H3** TR3045.
Whitfield *Northants. Village*, 2m/3km NE of Brackley. **31 H4** SP6039.
Whitfield *Northumb. Hamlet*, 6m/9km SW of Haydon Bridge. **61 J1** NY7758.
Whitfield *S.Glos. Hamlet*, 3m/4km E of Thornbury. **19 K2** ST6791.
Whitfield *Stoke Locality*, 2m/4km NE of Burslem. SJ8853.
Whitfield Law *Northumb. Mountain*, on Whitfield Moor, 4m/7km N of Alston. Height 1712 feet or 522 metres. **61 J1** NY7253.
Whitfield Moor *Northumb. Open space*, moorland at head of Carr's Burn, 4m/7km N of Alston. **61 J1** NY7353.
Whitford *Devon Village*, running down to River Axe, 3m/5km SW of Axminster. **8 B5** SY2695.
Whitford (Chwitffordd). *Flints. Village*, 3m/5km NW of Holywell. Mynydd-y-garreg, hill to W, surmounted by a tower, possibly a Roman pharos. Maen Achwyfaen (Cadw), 2km W of village. **47 K5** SJ1478.
Whitford Burrows *Swan. Coastal feature*, sand dunes on NW coast of Gower peninsula behind Whitford Sands. **17 H5** SS4495.
Whitford Point *Swan. Coastal feature*, headland (National Trust) at end of Whitford Burrows on S bank of Burry inlet opposite Burry Port. **17 H5** SS4496.
Whitgift *E.Riding Village*, on S bank of River Ouse, 4m/7km E of Goole. **58 E7** SE8122.
Whitgreave *Staffs. Village*, 4m/6km N of Stafford. **40 A3** SJ8928.
Whithorn *D. & G. Small town*, historic town 9m/15km S of Wigtown. St. Ninian settled here in 5c, making it Scotland's first Christian settlement. Remains of 12c priory church (Historic Scotland), with museum. **64 E6** NX4440.
Whithorn Priory *D. & G. Ecclesiastical building*, ruins of 12c priory church (Historic Scotland) on site of St. Ninian's 5c church at Whithorn, 10m/16km S of Wigtown. Includes museum. **64 E6** NX4440.

Whiting Bay *N.Ayr.* ***Bay***, wide E facing bay on SE coast of Arran, to S of Kingscross Point. **66 E1** NS0526.
Whiting Bay *N.Ayr.* ***Village***, and bay on E coast of Arran, 3m/5km S of Lamlash. **66 E1** NS0426.
Whitkirk *W.Yorks.* ***Suburb***, 4m/7km E of Leeds city centre. **57 J6** SE3633.
Whitlam *Aber.* ***Settlement***, 2m/3km N of Newmachar. **91 G2** NJ8821.
Whitland (Hendy-gwyn). *Carmar.* Population: 1518. ***Village***, 6m/9km E of Narberth. Whitland Abbey, 2km NE, scant ruins of 12c Cistercian house. **17 F3** SN1916.
Whitland Abbey *Carmar.* ***Ecclesiastical building***, scant ruins of one of great Cistercian houses of Wales, 1m/2km NE of Whitland. **17 F3** SN2018.
Whitland Abbey *Carmar.* ***Settlement***, with remains of Abbey, 1km NE of Whitland. **17 F3** SN2018.
Whitletts *S.Ayr.* ***Suburb***, E district of Ayr. **67 H1** NS3622.
Whitley *Gt.Man.* ***Suburb***, N district of Wigan. SD5807.
Whitley *N.Yorks.* ***Village***, 4m/7km SE of Knottingley. **58 B7** SE5621.
Whitley *Read.* ***Suburb***, S district of Reading. **22 A5** SU7170.
Whitley *Som.* ***Hamlet***, 5m/8km W of Wiveliscombe. ST0029.
Whitley *S.Yorks.* ***Hamlet***, 1km NE of Grenoside. SK3494.
Whitley *W.Mid.* ***Suburb***, 2m/3km SE of Coventry city centre. SP3576.
Whitley *Wilts.* ***Village***, 2m/3km NW of Melksham. ST8866.
Whitley Bay *T. & W.* Population: 33,335. ***Town***, popular North Sea coast resort, 2m/3km N of Tynemouth, with extensive sands to N. St. Mary's Island, once haunt of smugglers, is reached by causeway. **71 J6** NZ3572.
Whitley Bridge *N.Yorks.* ***Locality***, on Aire and Calder Canal, adjoining to SW of Low Eggborough. SE5522.
Whitley Chapel *Northumb.* ***Hamlet***, 4m/7km S of Hexham. **62 A1** NY9257.
Whitley Heath *Staffs.* ***Settlement***, 2m/3km SW of Eccleshall. SJ8126.
Whitley Lower *W.Yorks.* ***Village***, 3m/5km SW of Dewsbury. **50 E1** SE2217.
Whitley Reed *Ches.* ***Settlement***, 1m/2km S of Appleton. SJ6481.
Whitley Row *Kent* ***Settlement***, 2m/4km SW of Sevenoaks. **23 H6** TQ4952.
Whitlocks End *W.Mid.* ***Settlement***, 4m/6km SW of Solihull. SP1076.
Whitlock's End *W.Mid.* ***Settlement***, 1m/2km E of Hollywood. **30 C1** SP1076.
Whitminster *Glos.* ***Village***, 5m/8km W of Stroud. **20 A1** SO7708.
Whitmore *Dorset* ***Settlement***, 2m/4km S of Cranborne. **10 B4** SU0509.
Whitmore *Staffs.* ***Village***, 4m/6km SW of Newcastle-under-Lyme. **40 A1** SJ8140.
Whitmore Bay *V. of Glam.* ***Bay***, sandy bay on S side of Barry Island. ST1166.
Whitmore Hall *Staffs.* ***Historic house***, small Carolinian manor at Whitmore, 4m/6km SW of Newcastle-under-Lyme. Family seat of Cavenagh-Mainwarings. Grounds have lime avenue, landscaped gardens and rare Elizabethan stable block. **40 A1** SJ8141.
Whitmore Park *W.Mid.* ***Suburb***, N district of Coventry. SP3382.
Whitnage *Devon* ***Hamlet***, 1m/2km N of Sampford Peverell. **7 J4** ST0215.
Whitnash *Warks.* ***Suburb***, S of Royal Leamington Spa. **30 E2** SP3263.
Whitnell *Som.* ***Hamlet***, 2m/3km E of Nether Stowey. ST2139.
Whitney *Here.* ***Village***, on River Wye, 4m/7km NE of Hay-on-Wye. **28 B4** SO2647.
Whitrigg *Cumb.* ***Settlement***, 1m/2km S of Torpenhow. **60 D3** NY2038.
Whitrigg *Cumb.* ***Settlement***, 1m/2km N of Kirkbride. **60 D1** NY2257.
Whitsand Bay *Cornw.* ***Bay***, running NW from Rame Head on S coast to The Long Stone, between Downderry and Portwrinkle. **4 D5** SX3851.
Whitsbury *Hants.* ***Village***, 3m/5km NW of Fordingbridge. **10 C3** SU1219.
Whitsome *Sc.Bord.* ***Village***, 4m/6km S of Chirnside. **77 G5** NT8650.
Whitson *Newport* ***Village***, near coast, 5m/8km SE of Newport. **19 G3** ST3783.
Whitstable *Kent* Population: 28,907. ***Town***, N coast resort at E end of bay of same name, 6m/10km NW of Canterbury. Noted for oysters. First port to be linked by railways. **25 H5** TR1166.
Whitstone *Cornw.* ***Village***, 6m/10km SE of Bude. **4 C1** SX2698.
Whitsundale Beck *N.Yorks.* ***River***, rising on E side of Ravenseat Moor and flowing SE to its confluence with River Swale 1m/2km W of Keld. **61 K6** NY8701.
Whittingham *Lancs.* ***Locality***, 2m/4km W of Longridge. SD5636.
Whittingham *Northumb.* ***Village***, 6m/10km N of Rothbury. **71 F2** NU0611.
Whittingslow *Shrop.* ***Hamlet***, 3m/5km S of Church Stretton. **38 D7** SO4389.
Whittington *Derbys.* ***Suburb***, 2m/4km N of Chesterfield town centre. **51 F5** SK3875.
Whittington *Glos.* ***Village***, 4m/7km E of Cheltenham. Site of Roman villa to E. **30 B6** SP0120.
Whittington *Lancs.* ***Village***, 2m/3km S of Kirkby Lonsdale. **56 B2** SD6076.
Whittington *Norf.* ***Village***, on River Wissey, 1m/2km SE of Stoke Ferry. **44 B6** TL7199.
Whittington *Shrop.* Population: 2350. ***Village***, 3m/4km NE of Oswestry. **38 C2** SJ3231.
Whittington *Staffs.* ***Hamlet***, 3m/5km W of Stourbridge. **40 A7** SO8582.
Whittington *Staffs.* ***Village***, 3m/5km E of Lichfield. **40 D5** SK1608.
Whittington *Worcs.* ***Village***, 2m/3km SE of Worcester. **29 H3** SO8752.
Whittington Castle *Shrop.* ***Castle***, in Whittington, 2m/4km NE of Oswestry. 13c twin-towered gatehouse; only foundations of motte remain, with three towers. **38 C2** SJ3231.
Whittington Moor *Derbys.* ***Suburb***, 1m/2km N of Chesterfield town centre. SK3873.
Whittle Hill *Gt.Man.* ***Locality***, 2m/3km NW of Middleton. SD8407.
Whittle Hill *Lancs.* ***Mountain***, summit on Scout Moor, 3m/4km NE of Ramsbottom. Height 1535 feet or 468 metres. **49 H1** SD8218.
Whittle-le-Woods *Lancs.* ***Village***, 2m/4km E of Leyland. **55 J7** SD5821.
Whittlebury *Northants.* ***Village***, 3m/5km S of Towcester. **31 H4** SP6944.
Whittleford *Warks.* ***Suburb***, in W part of Nuneaton. SP3391.
Whittlesey *Cambs.* Population: 10,275. ***Town***, 5m/8km E of Peterborough. **43 F6** TL2797.
Whittlesey Mere *Cambs.* ***Open space***, fenland 5m/8km SW of Whittlesey. **43 F6** TL2190.
Whittlesford *Cambs.* ***Village***, 7m/11km S of Cambridge. **33 H4** TL4748.
Whittlestone Head *B'burn.* ***Settlement***, on moorland, 2m/4km NW of Edgworth. SD7219.
Whittlewood Forest ***Forest/woodland***, partly wooded area on border of Buckinghamshire and Northamptonshire, some 4m/7km W of Stony Stratford. **31 J4** SP7242.
Whittliemuir Midton Loch *Renf.* ***Reservoir***, 1m/2km SE of Howwood. **74 C5** NS4158.
Whitton *Gt.Lon.* ***Suburb***, in borough of Richmond upon Thames, 1m/2km W of Twickenham. TQ1473.
Whitton *N.Lincs.* ***Village***, on S bank of River Humber, 8m/13km N of Scunthorpe. **59 F7** SE9024.
Whitton *Northumb.* ***Hamlet***, just S of Rothbury. 14c tower house incorporated in later building. **71 F3** NU0501.
Whitton *Powys* ***Village***, 3m/5km S of Knighton. **28 B2** SO2767.
Whitton *Shrop.* ***Hamlet***, 3m/5km NW of Tenbury Wells. **28 E1** SO5772.
Whitton *Stock.* ***Hamlet***, 5m/7km NW of Stockton-on-Tees. **62 E4** NZ3822.
Whitton *Suff.* ***Suburb***, in NW part of Ipswich. Also parish to N. **35 F4** TM1347.
Whitton Ness *N.Lincs.* ***Coastal feature***, headland, 1m/2km E of Whitton. **59 F7** SE9125.
Whitton Sand ***Coastal feature***, mud and sand bank in River Humber estuary, 4m/7km SE of Gilberdyke. **58 E7** SE8725.
Whittonditch *Wilts.* ***Hamlet***, 4m/6km NW of Hungerford. **21 F4** SU2872.
Whittonstall *Northumb.* ***Village***, 2m/4km NW of Ebchester. **62 B1** NZ0757.
Whitway *Hants.* ***Hamlet***, on E side of Highclere Park, 4m/7km W of Kingsclere. **21 H6** SU4559.
Whitwell *Derbys.* Population: 4016. ***Village***, 4m/6km SW of Worksop. Hall dates from 17c. **51 H5** SK5276.
Whitwell *Herts.* ***Village***, 4m/7km NW of Welwyn. **32 E6** TL1821.
Whitwell *I.o.W.* ***Village***, 3m/4km W of Ventnor. **11 G7** SZ5277.
Whitwell *Norf.* ***Settlement***, 1km S of Reepham. **45 F3** TG1022.
Whitwell *N.Yorks.* ***Settlement***, 6m/10km NW of Northallerton. **62 D7** SE2899.
Whitwell *Rut.* ***Village***, 4m/7km E of Oakham. **42 C5** SK9208.
Whitwell House *Dur.* ***Settlement***, 3m/4km SE of Durham. NZ3040.
Whitwell-on-the-Hill *N.Yorks.* ***Village***, 5m/9km SW of Malton. **58 D3** SE7265.
Whitwick *Leics.* ***Locality***, 1m/2km NE of Coalville. **41 G4** SK4316.
Whitwood *W.Yorks.* ***Hamlet***, 1m/2km SW of Castleford. **57 K7** SE4024.
Whitworth *Lancs.* Population: 5679. ***Small town***, 4m/6km N of Rochdale. Quarries to N and W. **49 H1** SD8818.
Whixall *Shrop.* ***Village***, 4m/6km N of Wem. **38 E2** SJ5134.
Whixley *N.Yorks.* ***Village***, 6m/10km SE of Boroughbridge. **57 K4** SE4458.
Whoberly *W.Mid.* ***Suburb***, 2m/3km W of Coventry city centre. SP3079.
Whorlton *Dur.* ***Village***, on N bank of River Tees, 4m/6km E of Barnard Castle. **62 C5** NZ1014.
Whorlton *N.Yorks.* ***Village***, 5m/8km SW of Stokesley. Remains of motte and bailey castle. **63 F6** NZ4802.
Whorlton Castle *N.Yorks.* ***Castle***, 13c gatehouse ruins on site of former motte and bailey, 4m/7km SW of Stokesley. **63 F6** NZ4802.
Whorlton Moor *N.Yorks.* ***Open space***, moorland on Cleveland Hills rising to over 350 metres, 3m/4km NE of Osmotherley. **63 F7** SE5098.
Whygate *Northumb.* ***Settlement***, in clearing in Wark Forest, 7m/11km N of Bardon Mill. **70 C6** NY7675.
Whyke *W.Suss.* ***Suburb***, S district of Chichester. SU8604.
Whyle *Here.* ***Hamlet***, 4m/7km E of Leominster. **28 E2** SO5560.
Whyteleafe *Surr.* ***Locality***, 3m/4km SE of Purley. **23 G6** TQ3358.
Wiay *High.* ***Island***, uninhabited island of about 500 acres or 200 hectares at entrance to Loch Bracadale, SW coast. Lies 2m/3km E of Idrigill Point, Skye. **85 H1** NG2936.
Wiay *W.Isles* ***Island***, uninhabited island of about 2 square miles or 5 square km off SE coast of Benbecula on N side of entrance to Bagh nam Faoileann. **92 D7** NF8746.
Wibdon *Glos.* ***Settlement***, 3m/5km NE of Chepstow. **19 J2** ST5697.
Wibsey *W.Yorks.* ***Suburb***, 2m/3km SW of Bradford city centre. **57 G6** SE1430.
Wibtoft *Warks.* ***Hamlet***, 5m/7km NW of Lutterworth. **41 G7** SP4787.
Wichenford *Worcs.* ***Village***, 5m/8km NW of Worcester. **29 G2** SO7860.
Wichling *Kent* ***Village***, 5m/8km S of Sittingbourne. **14 E2** TQ9256.
Wick *Bourne.* ***Suburb***, 4m/6km E of Bournemouth town centre. **10 C5** SZ1591.
Wick *Devon* ***Hamlet***, 2m/3km N of Honiton. Iron Age fort on Dumpdon Hill to E. ST1703.
Wick *High.* ***River***, flowing SE from Loch Watten. At mouth is fishing port of Wick on Wick bay. **105 H3** ND3551.
Wick *High.* Population: 7681. ***Small town***, fishing port on Wick Bay, E coast of Caithness district, at mouth of Wick River. Airport 1m/2km N. Largest herring port in Europe in 19c, with fleet of over 1000 boats. **105 J3** ND3650.
Wick *Som.* ***Hamlet***, 2m/3km NW of Stockland Bristol. ST2144.
Wick *Som.* ***Settlement***, 1m/2km NE of Glastonbury. ST5239.
Wick *S.Glos.* Population: 1940. ***Village***, 7m/12km E of Bristol. Quarries. Site of Roman villa to S. **20 A4** ST7072.
Wick (Y Wig). *V. of Glam.* ***Village***, 5m/8km S of Bridgend. **18 C4** SS9272.
Wick *W.Suss.* ***Suburb***, N district of Littlehampton. **12 D6** TQ0203.
Wick *Wilts.* ***Village***, 1m/2km W of Downton. **10 C2** SU1621.
Wick *Worcs.* ***Village***, 1m/2km E of Pershore. **29 J4** SO9645.
Wick Airport *High.* ***Airport/airfield***, local airport to N of Wick. **105 J3** ND3652.
Wick Bay *High.* ***Bay***, off E coast of Caithness district, at mouth of Wick River. Fishing port of Wick is on the bay. ND3750.
Wick Down *Wilts.* ***Hill***, 2m/3km W of Wick. Height 374 feet or 114 metres. **10 C2** SU1321.
Wick Episcopi *Worcs.* ***Locality***, 2m/3km SW of Worcester. SO8253.
Wick Hill *Kent* ***Settlement***, 2m/3km S of Headcorn. **14 D3** TQ8441.
Wick Hill *W'ham* ***Settlement***, 1km N of Finchampstead. **22 A5** SU8064.
Wick of Gruting *Shet.* ***Bay***, on N coast of Fetlar, 2m/3km NE of Houbie. **108 F3** HU6592.
Wick of Mucklabrek *Shet.* ***Bay***, wide bay on SW coast of Foula. **108 B1** HT9437.
Wick of Shunni *Shet.* ***Bay***, on W coast of Mainland, on N side of Fitful Head. **109 F9** HU3515.
Wick of Tresta *Shet.* ***Bay***, large bay on S coast of Fetlar. **108 F4** HU6190.
Wick St. Lawrence *N.Som.* ***Village***, 4m/6km NE of Weston-super-Mare. **19 G5** ST3665.
Wicken *Cambs.* ***Village***, 2m/4km SW of Soham. **33 J1** TL5670.
Wicken *Northants.* ***Village***, 5m/8km NE of Buckingham. **31 J5** SP7439.
Wicken Bonhunt *Essex* ***Village***, 4m/7km SW of Saffron Walden. **33 H5** TL4933.
Wickenby *Lincs.* ***Village***, 5m/8km S of Market Rasen. **52 D4** TF0781.
Wicker Street Green *Suff.* ***Settlement***, 3m/5km W of Hadleigh. TL9741.
Wickerslack *Cumb.* ***Settlement***, 1m/2km NW of Crosby Ravensworth. **61 H5** NY6015.
Wickersley *S.Yorks.* ***Suburb***, 3m/5km E of Rotherham. **51 G3** SK4791.
Wicketwood Hill *Notts.* ***Hamlet***, 4m/7km NE of Nottingham. SK6244.
Wickford *Essex* Population: 26,294. ***Town***, commuter town, 3m/5km NE of Basildon. **24 D2** TQ7493.
Wickham *Hants.* ***Village***, 3m/5km N of Fareham. **11 G3** SU5711.
Wickham *W.Berks.* ***Village***, 6m/9km NW of Newbury. **21 G4** SU3971.
Wickham Bishops *Essex* Population: 1887. ***Village***, 2m/4km SE of Witham. **34 C7** TL8412.
Wickham Green *Suff.* ***Hamlet***, adjoining to W of Wickham Skeith, 4m/7km SW of Eye. TM0969.
Wickham Green *W.Berks.* ***Settlement***, adjoining to NE of Wickham, 6m/9km NW of Newbury. SU3971.
Wickham Heath *W.Berks.* ***Settlement***, 4m/6km NW of Newbury. **21 H5** SU4169.
Wickham Market *Suff.* Population: 2243. ***Small town***, 5m/8km NE of Woodbridge. **35 G3** TM3055.
Wickham St. Paul *Essex* ***Village***, 4m/7km SW of Sudbury. **34 C5** TL8336.
Wickham Skeith *Suff.* ***Village***, 4m/7km SW of Eye. **34 E2** TM0969.
Wickham Street *Suff.* ***Hamlet***, 6m/9km N of Clare. **34 B3** TL7554.
Wickham Street *Suff.* ***Village***, 1km NW of Wickham Skeith, 4m/7km SW of Eye. **34 E2** TM0969.
Wickhambreaux (Also spelled Wickhambreux.) *Kent* ***Village***, 5m/7km E of Canterbury. **15 H2** TR2258.
Wickhambreux *Kent* *Alternative spelling of Wickhambreaux, qv.*
Wickhambrook *Suff.* ***Village***, 6m/10km N of Clare. **34 B3** TL7554.
Wickhamford *Worcs.* ***Village***, 2m/4km SE of Evesham. **30 B4** SP0641.
Wickhampton *Norf.* ***Village***, 2m/4km N of Reedham. **45 J5** TG4205.
Wicklewood *Norf.* ***Village***, 2m/4km W of Wymondham. **44 E5** TG0702.
Wickmere *Norf.* ***Village***, 4m/7km N of Aylsham. **45 F2** TG1733.
Wicks's Green *Suff.* ***Locality***, adjoining to W of Forward Green. TM0959.
Wickstreet *E.Suss.* ***Hamlet***, 3m/5km W of Hailsham. TQ5408.

Wickwar *S.Glos.* ***Village***, 4m/7km N of Chipping Sodbury. **20 A3** ST7288.

Widcombe *B. & N.E.Som.* ***Suburb***, 1km SE of Bath city centre. ST7563.

Widdale Fell *N.Yorks.* ***Open space***, large expanse of moorland at head of Wensleydale, steep on SE side and containing two small high-level tarns. 4m/6km W of Hawes. **56 D1** SD8088.

Widdington *Essex* ***Village***, 4m/7km S of Saffron Walden. Wildlife reserve 1km E. **33 J5** TL5331.

Widdington *N.Yorks.* ***Locality***, 3m/4km NE of Green Hammerton. SE4959.

Widdop *W.Yorks.* ***Settlement***, below Widdop Moor, 6m/9km NW of Hebden Bridge. **56 E6** SD9333.

Widdrington *Northumb.* ***Village***, 7m/11km NE of Morpeth. **71 H4** NZ2595.

Widdrington Station *Northumb.* ***Settlement***, 1m/2km SW of Widdrington. **71 H4** NZ2494.

Widdybank Fell *Dur.* ***Open space***, hillslope on E side of Cow Green Reservoir. **61 K3** NY8130.

Wide Firth *Ork.* ***Sea feature***, sea channel between islands of Mainland and Shapinsay. **107 D6** HY4315.

Wide Open *T. & W.* Population: 8987. ***Village***, 5m/8km N of Newcastle upon Tyne. **71 H6** NZ2472.

Widecombe in the Moor *Devon* ***Village***, on Dartmoor, 5m/8km NW of Ashburton. Annual fair featured in popular song. **5 H3** SX7176.

Wideford Hill *Ork.* ***Hill***, 3m/4km W of Kirkwall, Mainland. Prehistoric chambered cairn (Historic Scotland) on NW side of hill. Height 738 feet or 225 metres. **107 D6** HY4111.

Wideford Hill Chambered Cairn *Ork.* ***Historic/prehistoric site***, on Wideford Hill, 3m/4km W of Kirkwall, Mainland. Neolithic chambered cairn with central chamber and unusually small entrance passage. **107 D6** HY4112.

Widegates *Cornw.* ***Village***, 3m/5km NE of Looe. **4 C5** SX2857.

Widemouth Bay *Cornw.* ***Village***, near coast, 3m/4km S of Bude, facing W with sandy beach. **6 A5** SS2002.

Widewall *Ork.* ***Locality***, on W coast of South Ronaldsay, 2m/3km S of St. Margaret's Hope. To NW is large bay of same name. **107 D8** ND4391.

Widewall Bay *Ork.* ***Bay***, large bay on W coast of South Ronaldsay. **107 D8** ND4292.

Widford *Essex* ***Suburb***, SW district of Chelmsford. **24 C1** TL6905.

Widford *Herts.* ***Village***, 4m/6km E of Ware. **33 H7** TL4215.

Widford *Oxon.* ***Settlement***, 1m/2km E of Burford across River Windrush. SP2711.

Widgham Green *Cambs.* ***Settlement***, to W of Great Widgham Wood, 5m/8km S of Newmarket. TL6655.

Widley *Hants.* ***Suburb***, 5m/8km N of Portsmouth city centre. SU6706.

Widmer End *Bucks.* ***Village***, 2m/4km NE of High Wycombe. SU8896.

Widmerpool *Notts.* ***Village***, 10m/15km NW of Melton Mowbray. **41 J3** SK6328.

Widmore *Gt.Lon.* ***Suburb***, to E of Bromley town centre. TQ4169.

Widmouth Head *Devon* ***Coastal feature***, headland at E side of Watermouth harbour, 2m/3km E of Ilfracombe. **6 D1** SS5548.

Widnes *Halton* Population: 57,162. ***Town***, on N side of River Mersey, here spanned by railway and road bridges, 6m/10km W of Warrington. Once known for its chemical industry, there is now a much wider range of industries. Catalyst, The Museum of the Chemical Industry situated here. **48 E4** SJ5185.

Widworthy *Devon* ***Village***, 3m/5km E of Honiton. **8 B5** SY2199.

Wield *Hants.* *Alternative name for Upper Wield, qv.*

Wife Geo *High.* ***Coastal feature***, small indentation 3m/4km S of Duncansby Head. **105 J1** ND3969.

Wigan *Gt.Man.* Population: 85,819. ***Town***, former coalmining and cotton producing town, 17m/27km NW of Manchester. Renovated Wigan Pier, now a heritage centre. **48 E2** SD5805.

Wiganthorpe *N.Yorks.* ***Settlement***, 2m/3km S of Hovingham. SE6672.

Wigborough *Som.* ***Hamlet***, 1m/2km SE of South Petherton. ST4415.

Wiggaton *Devon* ***Village***, 1m/2km S of Ottery St. Mary. **7 K6** SY1093.

Wiggenhall St. Germans *Norf.* ***Village***, 4m/6km S of King's Lynn. **44 A4** TF5914.

Wiggenhall St. Mary Magdalen *Norf.* ***Village***, 5m/8km N of Downham Market across River Great Ouse. **44 A4** TF5911.

Wiggenhall St. Mary the Virgin *Norf.* ***Village***, 4m/7km SW of King's Lynn across River Great Ouse. **43 J4** TF5813.

Wiggenhall St. Peter *Norf.* ***Settlement***, with ruined church, on E bank of River Great Ouse, 1km SE of Wiggenhall St. Germans. **44 A4** TF6013.

Wiggens Green *Essex* ***Settlement***, 2m/3km S of Haverhill. TL6642.

Wigginton *Herts.* ***Village***, 1m/2km SE of Tring. **32 C7** SP9310.

Wigginton *Oxon.* ***Village***, 6m/10km SW of Banbury. Site of Roman villa to E. **30 E5** SP3833.

Wigginton *Shrop.* ***Settlement***, 4m/7km W of Ellesmere. SJ3335.

Wigginton *Staffs.* ***Village***, 2m/3km N of Tamworth. **40 E5** SK2006.

Wigginton *York* ***Village***, adjoining to NW of Haxby, 4m/7km N of York. **58 C4** SE5958.

Wigginton Bottom *Herts.* ***Settlement***, adjoining to S of Wigginton. SP9409.

Wigglesworth *N.Yorks.* ***Village***, 2m/3km SW of Long Preston. **56 D4** SD8156.

Wiggonby *Cumb.* ***Hamlet***, 7m/11km W of Carlisle. **60 D1** NY2953.

Wiggonholt *W.Suss.* ***Settlement***, 1m/2km SE of Pulborough. Site of Roman bath house 1km N. **12 D5** TQ0616.

Wighill *N.Yorks.* ***Village***, 2m/4km N of Tadcaster. **57 K5** SE4746.

Wighton *Norf.* ***Village***, 3m/4km SE of Wells-next-the-Sea. **44 D2** TF9339.

Wightwick Manor *W.Mid.* ***Historic house***, late 19c house (National Trust), notable example of influence of William Morris, 3m/5km W of Wolverhampton town centre. **40 A6** SO8698.

Wightwizzle *S.Yorks.* ***Locality***, 1km W of Broomhead Reservoir, 2m/4km NW of High Bradfield. **50 E3** SK2495.

Wigley *Hants.* ***Hamlet***, 3m/5km NE of Cadnam. SU3216.

Wigmore *Here.* ***Village***, 8m/13km NW of Leominster. Ruins of Wigmore Castle (English Heritage), dating from 13c-14c and dismantled during Civil War, to NW. **28 D2** SO4169.

Wigmore *Med.* ***Suburb***, 3m/4km SE of Gillingham town centre. **24 E5** TQ8064.

Wigsley *Notts.* ***Village***, 7m/12km W of Lincoln. **52 B5** SK8670.

Wigsthorpe *Northants.* ***Hamlet***, 4m/6km S of Oundle. **42 D7** TL0482.

Wigston *Leics.* Population: 32,864. ***Town***, adjoining to S of Leicester. **41 J6** SP6099.

Wigston Fields *Leic.* ***Suburb***, 3m/4km S of Leicester city centre. SK5900.

Wigston Parva *Leics.* ***Hamlet***, 4m/6km SE of Hinckley. **41 G6** SP4689.

Wigthorpe *Notts.* ***Hamlet***, 1km S of Carlton in Lindrick. **51 H4** SK5983.

Wigtoft *Lincs.* ***Village***, 6m/10km SW of Boston. **43 F2** TF2636.

Wigton *Cumb.* Population: 5306. ***Small town***, 11m/17km SW of Carlisle. Market town with medieval layout. Many Georgian buildings. **60 D2** NY2548.

Wigtown *D. & G.* Population: 1117. ***Small town***, on hill above River Cree estuary, at head of Wigtown Bay and on N side of River Bladnoch. Torhouskie Stone Circle, dating from around 2000BC, nearby. **64 E5** NX4355.

Wigtown Bay *D. & G.* ***Bay***, extends E from Burrow Head to Little Ross, with Wigtown on NE side of bay. **65 F6** NX5148.

Wigtown Sands *D. & G.* ***Coastal feature***, mud and sand flats to N of River Bladnoch, 2m/3km NE of Wigtown. **64 E5** NX4556.

Wike *W.Yorks.* ***Hamlet***, 2m/3km E of Eccup Reservoir, 6m/9km NE of Leeds city centre. SE3342.

Wike Well End *S.Yorks.* ***Locality***, on Stainforth and Keadby Canal, at S end of Thorne. SE6912.

Wilbarston *Northants.* ***Village***, 5m/9km W of Corby. **42 B7** SP8188.

Wilberforce House *Hull* ***Historic house***, 17c merchant's house, in Kingston upon Hull. Birthplace of William Wilberforce, now local history museum. **59 H7** TA1028.

Wilberfoss *E.Riding* ***Village***, 3m/5km SE of Stamford Bridge. **58 D4** SE7350.

Wilburton *Cambs.* ***Village***, 5m/8km SW of Ely. **33 H1** TL4874.

Wilby *Norf.* ***Hamlet***, 4m/6km SW of Attleborough. **44 E6** TM0389.

Wilby *Northants.* ***Village***, 2m/3km SW of Wellingborough. **32 B2** SP8666.

Wilby *Suff.* ***Village***, 1m/2km SE of Stradbroke. **35 G1** TM2472.

Wilby Green *Suff.* ***Settlement***, 1m/2km SE of Wilby. TM2470.

Wilcot *Wilts.* ***Village***, 2m/3km NW of Pewsey. **20 E5** SU1460.

Wilcot Green *Wilts.* ***Hamlet***, adjoining to N of Wilcot. SU1460.

Wilcott *Shrop.* ***Village***, 8m/13km NW of Shrewsbury. **38 C4** SJ3718.

Wilcott Marsh *Shrop.* ***Settlement***, 1km SE of Wilcott. SJ3817.

Wilcrick *Newport* ***Settlement***, 1m/2km NW of Magor. Ancient fort on Wilcrick Hill. **19 H3** ST4088.

Wild Boar Fell *Cumb.* ***Mountain***, on Mallerstang Common, 4m/7km NW of Garsdale Head. Height 2322 feet or 708 metres. **61 J7** SD7598.

Wilday Green *Derbys.* ***Hamlet***, 4m/7km NW of Chesterfield. SK3274.

Wildboarclough *Ches.* ***Village***, in Peak District National Park, 5m/8km SE of Macclesfield. **49 J6** SJ9868.

Wilde Street *Suff.* ***Settlement***, 3m/4km N of Mildenhall. TL7078.

Wilden *Beds.* ***Village***, 5m/7km NE of Bedford. **32 D3** TL0955.

Wilden *Worcs.* ***Village***, 1m/2km NE of Stourport-on-Severn. **29 H1** SO8272.

Wilderhope *Shrop.* ***Historic house***, manor house of late 16c (National Trust) on SE slope of Wenlock Edge, 7m/11km SW of Much Wenlock. **38 E6** SO5492.

Wildern *Hants.* ***Locality***, residential locality 2m/3km W of Botley. SU4913.

Wildernesse *Kent* ***Locality***, residential locality to NE of Sevenoaks. TQ5455.

Wilderspool *Warr.* ***Suburb***, 1m/2km SE of Warrington town centre. SJ6186.

Wildhern *Hants.* ***Village***, 4m/6km N of Andover. **21 G6** SU3550.

Wildhill *Herts.* ***Hamlet***, 2m/4km SE of Hatfield. **23 F1** TL2606.

Wildmanbridge *S.Lan.* ***Settlement***, 2m/3km NW of Carluke. NS8353.

Wildmoor *Hants.* ***Settlement***, 4m/6km NE of Basingstoke. SU6856.

Wildmoor *Worcs.* ***Village***, 3m/5km N of Bromsgrove. SO9575.

Wildmore Fen *Lincs.* ***Open space***, lowland 4m/6km SE of Coningsby. **53 F7** TF2452.

Wildridings *Brack.F.* ***Suburb***, SW district of Bracknell. SU8668.

Wildshaw Hill *S.Lan.* ***Mountain***, 4m/7km SE of Douglas. Height 1227 feet or 374 metres. **68 D1** NS9028.

Wildsworth *Lincs.* ***Village***, on E bank of River Trent, 5m/9km N of Gainsborough. **52 B3** SK8097.

Wiley Sike *Cumb.* ***Open space***, moorland, enclosed by woodland, on S side of Spadeadam Forest, 3m/4km N of Gilsland. **70 B6** NY6370.

Wilford *Nott.* ***Locality***, 1m/2km W of West Bridgford. **41 H2** SK5637.

Wilkesley *Ches.* ***Hamlet***, 3m/4km SW of Audlem. **39 F1** SJ6241.

Wilkhaven *High.* ***Settlement***, in Ross and Cromarty district, 1km SW of Tarbat Ness on E coast. **97 G3** NH9486.

Wilkieston *W.Loth.* ***Village***, 2m/3km SW of Ratho. **75 K4** NT1268.

Wilkins Green *Herts.* ***Locality***, 2m/4km W of Hatfield. TL1907.

Wilksby *Lincs.* ***Settlement***, 1m/2km N of Mareham le Fen, 4m/7km SE of Horncastle. TF2862.

Willacy Lane End *Lancs.* ***Hamlet***, 1km SW of Catforth, 5m/8km NW of Preston. SD4735.

Willand *Devon* Population: 2232. ***Village***, 3m/4km NE of Cullompton. **7 J4** ST0310.

Willand *Som.* ***Hamlet***, 5m/9km SE of Wellington. ST1913.

Willand Moor *Devon* ***Hamlet***, 1km NE of Willand. ST0411.

Willaston *Ches.* Population: 2793. ***Village***, 3m/4km E of Neston. **48 C5** SJ3377.

Willaston *Ches.* ***Village***, 2m/3km E of Nantwich. **49 F7** SJ6852.

Willaston *I.o.M.* ***Suburb***, N district of Douglas. SC3877.

Willaston *Shrop.* ***Settlement***, 5m/8km SE of Whitchurch. SJ5935.

Willen *M.K.* ***Village***, 2m/3km NE of Milton Keynes city centre. **32 B4** SP8741.

Willenhall *W.Mid.* ***Suburb***, W district of Walsall. **40 B6** SO9698.

Willenhall *W.Mid.* ***Suburb***, SE district of Coventry. **30 E1** SP3676.

Willerby *E.Riding* ***Village***, 5m/8km W of Kingston upon Hull city centre. **59 G7** TA0230.

Willerby *N.Yorks.* ***Village***, 7m/11km W of Filey. **59 G2** TA0079.

Willersey *Glos.* ***Village***, 2m/3km NE of Broadway. **30 C4** SP1039.

Willersley *Here.* ***Village***, 6m/9km S of Kington. **28 C4** SO3147.

Willesborough *Kent* ***Suburb***, SE of Ashford. **15 F3** TR0241.

Willesborough Lees *Kent* ***Suburb***, SE of Ashford. **15 F3** TR0342.

Willesborough Street *Kent* ***Suburb***, forms suburb of Willesborough, along with South Willesborough and Willesborough Lees. TR0341.

Willesden *Gt.Lon.* ***Suburb***, in borough of Brent, 6m/9km NW of Charing Cross. **23 F3** TQ2284.

Willesden Green *Gt.Lon.* ***Suburb***, to E of Willesden. TQ2283.

Willesleigh *Devon* ***Settlement***, 3m/5km E of Barnstaple. SS6033.

Willesley *Leics.* ***Locality***, 2m/3km SW of Ashby de la Zouch. SK3414.

Willesley *Wilts.* ***Hamlet***, 2m/3km N of Sherston. **20 B3** ST8588.

Willett *Som.* ***Hamlet***, 4m/6km NE of Wiveliscombe. **7 K2** ST1033.

Willey *Shrop.* ***Hamlet***, 3m/5km E of Much Wenlock. **39 F6** SO6799.

Willey *Warks.* ***Village***, 3m/5km W of Lutterworth. **41 G7** SP4984.

Willey Green *Surr.* ***Hamlet***, 4m/6km NW of Guildford. SU9351.

William Law *Sc.Bord.* ***Mountain***, 3m/4km NW of Galashiels. Height 1315 feet or 401 metres. **76 C7** NT4739.

William's Green *Suff.* ***Settlement***, 2m/4km W of Hadleigh. TL9842.

Williamsburgh *Renf.* ***Suburb***, E district of Paisley. NS4964.

Williamscot *Oxon.* ***Hamlet***, 4m/6km NE of Banbury. **31 F4** SP4845.

Williamston *W.Loth.* ***Locality***, industrial estate, 2m/3km SE of Livingston town centre. NT0866.

Williamston Common *Northumb.* ***Open space***, heathland 1m/2km E of Slaggyford. Highest point is 1522 feet or 464 metres. **61 H1** NY6952.

Williamstown (Trewiliam). *R.C.T.* ***Hamlet***, 2m/3km N of Tonyrefail. ST0090.

Williamthorpe *Derbys.* ***Locality***, 3m/4km NE of Clay Cross. **51 G6** SK4265.

Willian *Herts.* ***Village***, 2m/3km NE of Hitchin and 2m/3km SW of Baldock. **33 F5** TL2230.

Willimontswick *Northumb.* ***Settlement***, 1km S of Redburn across River South Tyne. **70 C7** NY7763.

Willingale *Essex* ***Village***, 4m/6km NE of Chipping Ongar. **23 J1** TL5907.

Willingdon *E.Suss.* ***Suburb***, N of Eastbourne. Site of Neolithic camp 1m/2km W on downs. **13 J6** TQ5802.

Willingdon Hill *E.Suss.* ***Hill***, 3m/5km NW of Eastbourne. Height 659 feet or 201 metres. **13 J6** TQ5700.

Willingham *Cambs.* Population: 3317. ***Village***, 8m/13km NW of Cambridge. 1m/2km E is Belsar's Hill, large circular prehistoric earthwork. **33 H2** TL4070.

Willingham *Lincs.* ***Village***, 5m/8km SE of Gainsborough. **52 B4** SK8784.

Willingham Green *Cambs.* ***Settlement***, to S of Brinkley, 6m/10km S of Newmarket. TL6253.

Willington *Beds.* ***Village***, 4m/6km E of Bedford. 16c stone dovecote and stables (National Trust). **32 E4** TL1149.
Willington *Derbys.* Population: 2292. ***Village***, 6m/10km SW of Derby. **40 E3** SK2928.
Willington *Dur.* Population: 4913. ***Small town***, former mining town 4m/6km N of Bishop Auckland. **62 C3** NZ1935.
Willington *Kent* ***Suburb***, SE of Maidstone. TQ7853.
Willington *T. & W.* ***Locality***, 1m/2km NE of Wallsend. **71 J7** NZ3167.
Willington *Warks.* ***Hamlet***, 1m/2km SE of Shipston on Stour across River Stour. **30 D5** SP2639.
Willington Corner *Ches.* ***Hamlet***, 3m/5km N of Tarporley. **48 E6** SJ5366.
Willington Quay *T. & W.* ***Suburb***, to SE of Willington, on N bank of River Tyne. NZ3166.
Willisham *Suff.* ***Settlement***, 5m/9km S of Stowmarket. **34 E3** TM0750.
Willitoft *E.Riding* ***Hamlet***, 4m/7km N of Howden. **58 D6** SE7435.
Williton *Som.* Population: 2025. ***Village***, 1m/2km S of Watchet. **7 J1** ST0741.
Willoughbridge *Staffs.* ***Settlement***, 2m/3km SE of Woore. SJ7440.
Willoughby *Lincs.* ***Village***, 3m/4km S of Alford. **53 H5** TF4771.
Willoughby *Warks.* ***Village***, 5m/7km NW of Daventry. **31 G2** SP5167.
Willoughby-on-the-Wolds *Notts.* ***Village***, 8m/13km NW of Melton Mowbray. Site of Roman settlement of Vernemetum. **41 J3** SK6325.
Willoughby Waterleys *Leics.* ***Village***, 5m/9km N of Lutterworth. **41 H6** SP5792.
Willoughton *Lincs.* ***Village***, 3m/5km S of Kirton in Lindsey. **52 C3** SK9393.
Willoughton Cliff *Lincs.* ***Hamlet***, 1km SE of Willoughton, with site of Roman building to N. SK9392.
Willow Brook *Northants.* ***River***, rising at Corby and flowing circuitously E into River Nene at Elton, S of Wansford. **42 C6** TL0893.
Willow Green *Ches.* ***Settlement***, 1km W of Little Leigh. SJ6076.
Willow Holme *Cumb.* ***Suburb***, 1km W of Carlisle city centre, on W side of River Caldew. NY3956.
Willowbank *Bucks.* ***Locality***, in River Colne valley, 1km NW of Uxbridge. TQ0585.
Willowbrae *Edin.* ***Suburb***, of Edinburgh, 1m/2km W of Portobello. NT2873.
Willowgrain Hill *D. & G.* ***Mountain***, 2m/3km SW of Wanlockhead. Height 1686 feet or 514 metres. **68 D2** NS8412.
Willows Green *Essex* ***Hamlet***, 3m/5km SW of Braintree. **34 B7** TL7219.
Willsbridge *S.Glos.* ***Hamlet***, 1m/2km NE of Keynsham. ST6670.
Willslock *Staffs.* ***Settlement***, 2m/3km SW of Uttoxeter. SK0730.
Willsworthy *Devon* ***Settlement***, on Dartmoor, 6m/9km NE of Tavistock. **6 D7** SX5381.
Willtown *Som.* ***Hamlet***, adjoining to S side of Curry Rivel. ST3824.
Willy Lott's Cottage *Suff. See Flatford Mill and Bridge Cottage.*
Wilmcote *Warks.* ***Village***, 3m/5km NW of Stratford-upon-Avon. Mary Arden's House, early 16c. **30 C3** SP1658.
Wilmington *B. & N.E.Som.* ***Hamlet***, 1km E of Stanton Prior and 4m/6km SW of Bath. ST6962.
Wilmington *Devon* ***Village***, 3m/5km E of Honiton. **8 B4** SY2199.
Wilmington *E.Suss.* ***Village***, under South Downs, 5m/8km NE of Seaford. Remains of 12c priory. **13 J6** TQ5404.
Wilmington *Kent* ***Locality***, residential locality 1m/2km S of Dartford. **23 J4** TQ5371.
Wilmington Priory *E.Suss.* ***Ecclesiastical building***, dating from c. 1243; now an agricultural museum, 6m/10km NE of Eastbourne. **13 J6** TQ5403.
Wilmslow *Ches.* Population: 28,604. ***Town***, on River Bollin, 11m/17km S of Manchester. **49 H4** SJ8481.
Wilnecote *Staffs.* ***Suburb***, 2m/3km SE of Tamworth town centre. **40 E5** SK2201.
Wilney Green *Norf.* ***Settlement***, 4m/6km W of Diss. TM0681.
Wilpshire *Lancs.* ***Village***, 3m/4km N of Blackburn. **56 B6** SD6832.
Wilsden *W.Yorks.* Population: 3200. ***Village***, 5m/8km NW of Bradford. **57 F6** SE0936.
Wilsford *Lincs.* ***Village***, 4m/7km SW of Sleaford. **42 D1** TF0043.
Wilsford *Wilts.* ***Hamlet***, in River Avon valley, 2m/3km SW of Amesbury. **20 E7** SU1339.
Wilsford *Wilts.* ***Village***, 3m/4km NW of Upavon. **20 D6** SU1057.
Wilsford Down *Wilts.* ***Open space***, downland 3m/5km W of Upavon. **20 D6** SU0853.
Wilsham *Devon* ***Hamlet***, 3m/4km E of Lynton. SS7548.
Wilshamstead *Beds. Former name of Wilstead, qv.*
Wilshaw *W.Yorks.* ***Village***, 1m/2km E of Meltham. SE1109.
Wilsill *N.Yorks.* ***Village***, 2m/3km SE of Pateley Bridge. **57 G3** SE1864.
Wilsley Green *Kent* ***Hamlet***, 1km N of Cranbrook. **14 C4** TQ7736.
Wilsley Pound *Kent* ***Hamlet***, 1m/2km NE of Cranbrook. TQ7837.
Wilson *Leics.* ***Hamlet***, 1m/2km E of Melbourne. **41 G3** SK4024.
Wilson's Pike *Sc.Bord.* ***Mountain***, 5m/8km SW of Kielder. Height 1361 feet or 415 metres. **70 A5** NY5589.
Wilson's Row *Dur.* ***Hamlet***, 4m/6km NE of Durham. NZ3147.

Wilstead (Formerly known as Wilshamstead.) *Beds.* Population: 2188. ***Village***, 4m/7km S of Bedford. **32 D4** TL0643.
Wilsthorpe *E.Riding* ***Settlement***, 2m/3km SW of Bridlington. TA1664.
Wilsthorpe *Lincs.* ***Hamlet***, 4m/7km S of Bourne. **42 D4** TF0913.
Wilstone *Herts.* ***Village***, 2m/3km NW of Tring. **32 C7** SP9014.
Wilstone Green *Herts.* ***Settlement***, adjoining to S of Wilstone, on N side of Wilstone Reservoir (nature reserve). SP9013.
Wilstone Reservoir *Herts.* ***Reservoir***, and nature reserve, 2m/3km NW of Tring. **32 C7** SP9014.
Wilstrop *N.Yorks.* ***Locality***, 2m/3km SW of Green Hammerton. Site of earlier Wilstrop Village to NE of Wilstrop Hall. SE4855.
Wilton *Cumb.* ***Settlement***, 2m/3km E of Egremont. **60 B5** NY0311.
Wilton *N.Yorks.* ***Hamlet***, 4m/6km E of Pickering. **58 E1** SE8682.
Wilton *R. & C.* ***Hamlet***, 3m/5km NW of Guisborough. Castle of early 19c and surrounding buildings form adminstrative block for nearby chemical works. **63 G4** NZ5819.
Wilton *Sc.Bord.* ***Suburb***, W district of Hawick. **69 K2** NT4914.
Wilton *Som.* ***Suburb***, S district of Taunton. **8 B2** ST2223.
Wilton *Wilts.* Population: 3717. ***Small town***, 3m/5km W of Salisbury, at confluence of Rivers Nadder and Wylye; formerly county town of Wiltshire. Wilton House, 17c and later, in park. **10 B1** SU0931.
Wilton *Wilts.* ***Village***, 6m/10km SW of Hungerford. **21 F5** SU2661.
Wilton Bridge *Here.* ***Bridge***, red sandstone bridge built 1597 over River Wye, just SW of Ross-on-Wye. Substantial cutwaters with pedestrian refuges. SO5824.
Wilton Carr *N.Yorks.* ***Open space***, plain to S of North Riding Forest Park, 3m/5km W of Snainton. **58 E1** SE8680.
Wilton House *Wilts.* ***Historic house***, 16c ancestral home of 17th Earl of Pembroke, on site of former abbey at Wilton, 3m/5km W of Salisbury. Elizabethan house which succeeded it was restored by Inigo Jones following a fire. Famous for State Apartments, including Single and Double Cube rooms and good art collection. 21 acre grounds of landscaped parkland include 18c Palladian bridge. **10 B1** SU0930.
Wiltown *Devon* ***Hamlet***, on Black Down Hills, 3m/5km SE of Wellington. ST1716.
Wimbish *Essex* ***Hamlet***, 4m/6km E of Saffron Walden. **33 J5** TL5936.
Wimbish Green *Essex* ***Hamlet***, 1m/2km SE of Wimbish. **33 K5** TL5936.
Wimbleball Lake *Som.* ***Reservoir***, in Haddeo valley in Exmoor, 4m/6km NE of Dulverton. **7 H3** SS9730.
Wimblebury *Staffs.* ***Hamlet***, 3m/4km E of Cannock. **40 C4** SK0111.
Wimbledon *Gt.Lon.* ***Suburb***, in borough of Merton, 7m/11km SW of Charing Cross. Wimbledon Common is large open space to W. Wimbledon Park is 1m/2km N; All England Lawn Tennis Club on W side of park. **23 F4** TQ2470.
Wimbledon Common *Gt.Lon.* ***Open space***, 1100 acres or 445 hectares of open heath, woodlands and small ponds. Windmill with museum. **23 F4** TQ2271.
Wimblington *Cambs.* Population: 1405. ***Village***, 3m/5km S of March. **43 H6** TL4192.
Wimblington Fen *Cambs.* ***Open space***, fenland, 2m/4km SE of Wimblington. **43 H7** TL4489.
Wimborne *Dorset Familiar form of Wimborne Minster, qv.*
Wimborne Minster (Commonly known as Wimborne.) *Dorset* Population: 15,274. ***Town***, historic town on River Stour, 7m/11km NW of Bournemouth. Norman to Decorated minster at town centre. 17c astronomical clock. Large weekend market. **10 B4** SZ0199.
Wimborne Minster *Poole* ***Ecclesiastical building***, large cruciform church in Wimborne Minster, with central and W end towers. Mainly Norman and Perpendicular. Magnificent choir with monuments. **10 B5** SZ0199.
Wimborne St. Giles *Dorset* ***Village***, 2m/3km SW of Cranborne. St. Giles House, 17c-18c; shell grotto in grounds. **10 B3** SU0312.
Wimbotsham *Norf.* ***Village***, 1m/2km NE of Downham Market. **44 A5** TF6205.
Wimpole *Cambs.* ***Locality***, parish 6m/10km N of Royston. Includes Wimpole Hall (National Trust), Wimpole Home Farm (National Trust), New Wimpole, Old Wimpole and Wimpole Lodge. TL3350.
Wimpole Hall *Cambs.* ***Historic house***, large 17c-18c red brick house (National Trust), 2m/3km NW of Orwell. Set in 350 acre or 142 hectare park, with long avenue of elms. Work by Gibbs, Flitcroft and Soane. **33 G3** TL3350.
Wimpson *S'ham.* ***Suburb***, NW of Southampton. SU3814.
Wimpstone *Warks.* ***Village***, 4m/6km S of Stratford-upon-Avon. **30 D4** SP2148.
Win Hill *Derbys.* ***Mountain***, to SW of Ladybower Reservoir, 1m/2km NE of Hope. Height 1515 feet or 462 metres. **50 D4** SK1885.
Wincanton *Som.* Population: 3973. ***Small town***, 12m/19km NE of Yeovil. Racecourse to N. **9 G2** ST7128.
Winceby *Lincs.* ***Hamlet***, 4m/6km E of Horncastle. Site of 1643 Civil War battle 1km NW. TF3268.
Wincham *Ches.* ***Hamlet***, 1m/2km NE of Northwich. **49 F5** SJ6775.
Winchburgh *W.Loth.* Population: 2535. ***Village***, 6m/10km E of Linlithgow. Niddry Castle, 1km SE, is ruined 15c tower. **75 J3** NT0974.
Winchcombe *Glos.* Population: 4243. ***Small town***, attractive historic town 6m/10km NE of Cheltenham. Sudeley Castle to SE. Fine medieval 'wool church'. **30 B6** SP0228.

Winchelsea *E.Suss.* ***Town***, ancient town on hill, 2m/3km SW of Rye. Original town destroyed by sea in 13c. **14 E6** TQ9017.
Winchelsea Beach *E.Suss.* ***Village***, 1m/2km SE of Winchelsea on coast. **14 E6** TQ9116.
Winchester *Hants.* Population: 36,121. ***City***, county town on River Itchen on site of Roman town of Venta, 12m/19km N of Southampton. Ancient capital of Wessex and of Anglo-Saxon England. 11c cathedral, longest in Europe. Boys' public school founded 1382. 12c hospital of St. Cross, and many other old buildings. City Mill (National Trust), built over river in 18c. To S across river, St. Catherine's Hill, Iron Age fort. Extensive ruins of medieval Wolvesey Castle, also known as Old Bishop's Palace (English Heritage), 1m/2km SE. **11 F2** SU4829.
Winchester Cathedral *Hants.* ***Ecclesiastical building***, longest cathedral in Europe (556 feet or 170 metres), begun in 1079, located in centre of Winchester. Burial place of many English kings. Transepts are good examples of early Norman architecture. Much subsequent rebuilding, particularly by William of Wykeham in late 14c. **11 F2** SU4829.
Winchestown *B.Gwent* ***Suburb***, 1km SW of Bryn-mawr. SO1810.
Winchet Hill *Kent* ***Settlement***, 2m/3km E of Horsmonden. **14 C3** TQ7340.
Winchfield *Hants.* ***Village***, 2m/4km E of Hook. **22 A6** SU7654.
Winchmore Hill *Bucks.* ***Village***, 3m/5km N of Beaconsfield. **22 C2** SU9394.
Winchmore Hill *Gt.Lon.* ***Suburb***, in borough of Enfield, 9m/14km N of Charing Cross. **23 G2** TQ3194.
Wincle *Ches.* ***Hamlet***, 5m/9km SE of Macclesfield. **49 J6** SJ9566.
Wincobank *S.Yorks.* ***Suburb***, 3m/5km NE of Sheffield city centre. Includes suburbs of High and Low Wincobank. **51 F3** SK3791.
Wind Fell ***Mountain***, on border of Dumfries & Galloway and Scottish Borders, 6m/9km E of Moffat. Height 2178 feet or 664 metres. **69 G3** NT1706.
Windbury Point *Devon* ***Coastal feature***, point at E end of Beckland Bay, 2m/4km NE of Hartland. **6 A3** SS2826.
Winder *Cumb.* ***Locality***, 1km E of Frizington. NY0417.
Windermere *Cumb.* ***Lake/loch***, largest English lake, situated in Lake District National Park and containing 14 islands. Extends S from Waterhead near Ambleside for some 10m/16km to Lake Side near Newby Bridge. Fed by Rivers Brathay and Rothay to N, and joining River Leven to S. Surrounded by easily reached viewpoints, most famous of which is Orrest Head. Town of Windermere is on E side of lake. **60 E7** SD4198.
Windermere *Cumb.* Population: 6847. ***Small town***, busy town and popular tourist resort on E bank of Windermere. Town developed rapidly following arrival of railway in 1847. Famous viewpoint of Orrest Head to N of town. **60 F7** SD4198.
Winderton *Warks.* ***Village***, 1m/2km S of Compton Wynyates and 4m/7km E of Shipston on Stour. **30 E4** SP3240.
Windhill *High.* ***Settlement***, in Ross and Cromarty district, 1m/2km S of Muir of Ord. **96 C7** NH5348.
Windhill *W.Yorks.* ***Suburb***, E district of Shipley. SE1537.
Windle *Mersey.* ***Settlement***, 2m/3km NW of St. Helens. SJ4897.
Windle Hill *Ches.* ***Settlement***, 1m/2km E of Neston. SJ3177.
Windleden Reservoirs *S.Yorks.* ***Reservoir***, two reservoirs on W side of Thurlestone Moors, 6m/10km W of Penistone. **50 D2** SE1501.
Windlehurst *Gt.Man.* ***Settlement***, adjoining to N of High Lane. SJ9586.
Windles Green *Mersey.* ***Locality***, 2m/3km NE of Crosby. SD3400.
Windlesham *Surr.* Population: 4109. ***Village***, 1m/2km E of Bagshot. **22 C5** SU9364.
Windlestone *Dur.* ***Locality***, 3m/5km E of Bishop Auckland. NZ2628.
Windlestraw Law *Sc.Bord.* ***Mountain***, 4m/7km NE of Innerleithen. Height 2162 feet or 659 metres. **76 B6** NT3743.
Windley *Derbys.* ***Village***, 3m/4km NW of Duffield. **41 F1** SK3045.
Windley Meadows *Derbys.* ***Settlement***, 1m/2km SE of Windley. **41 F1** SK3144.
Windmill *Derbys.* ***Settlement***, 1km W of Great Hucklow. SK1677.
Windmill Hill *Bristol* ***Suburb***, 1m/2km S of Bristol city centre. ST5971.
Windmill Hill *E.Suss.* ***Village***, 1m/2km E of Herstmonceux. **13 K5** TQ6412.
Windmill Hill *Lancs.* ***Settlement***, 1km SW of Hoghton. SD6125.
Windmill Hill *Som.* ***Hamlet***, 3m/5km NW of Ilminster. **8 C3** ST3116.
Windmill Hill *Wilts.* ***Hill***, 1m/2km NW of Avebury. Neolithic camp (National Trust). Height 643 feet or 196 metres. **20 D4** SU0871.
Windmill Hill *Wilts.* ***Historic/prehistoric site***, Neolithic causewayed camp (National Trust), 1m/2km NW of Avebury. Comprises three irregular concentric ditches broken by several causeways. Considered to be a regional centre rather than a defensive structure. **20 D4** SU0871.
Windmill Hill *Worcs.* ***Hamlet***, 3m/5km NW of Pershore. SO9149.
Windrush ***River***, rising in Cotswold Hills, E of Winchcombe, and flowing SE into River Thames at Newbridge. **30 C7** SP4001.
Windrush *Glos.* ***Village***, 4m/6km W of Burford. **30 C7** SP1913.
Winds Eye *Aber.* ***Mountain***, to N of Gartly Moor, 3m/5km SE of Huntly. Height 1030 feet or 314 metres. **90 D1** NJ5534.

Windsor *Mersey.* ***Suburb***, 2m/3km SE of Liverpool city centre. SJ3689.
Windsor *N.Lincs.* ***Locality***, adjoining to SW of Crowle. SE7612.
Windsor *W. & M.* Population: 26,369. ***Town***, attractive market town on S bank of River Thames, 2m/3km S of Slough and 21m/34km W of London. Castle is royal residence. Great Park to S of town is open to public; Home Park bordering river is private. St. George's Chapel is impressive. Many Georgian houses, and guildhall designed by Sir Christopher Wren. **22 C4** SU9676.
Windsor Castle *W. & M.* ***Castle***, second largest occupied castle in world, sited above River Thames at Windsor. Original construction began in 11c by William the Conqueror to guard W approaches of London. It has since been home of successive Royal families, albeit much extended, altered and restored over centuries. Notable features include State Apartments, Queen's Presence Chamber, Queen Mary's Doll House and St. George's Chapel. Castle extensively damaged by fire in 1992; restoration project was completed over five years. **22 C4** SU9776.
Windsor Forest *Brack.F.* ***Forest/woodland***, to W of Windsor Great Park. **22 C4** SU9373.
Windsor Great Park *W. & M.* ***Open space***, covering around 4800 acres or 1942 hectares, to S of Windsor. Includes woods, magnificent gardens, famous 1m/2km Rhododendron Walk and 3m/5km Long Walk. **22 C4** SU9573.
Windsor Green *Suff.* ***Settlement***, 4m/6km NW of Lavenham. TL8954.
Windy Crag *Northumb.* ***Inland physical feature***, rock outcrop at height of 1607 feet or 490 metres in Cheviot Hills, on route of The Pennine Way long distance footpath, 2m/3km NE of Byrness. **70 C3** NT7705.
Windy Gyle ***Mountain***, on border of Northumberland and Scottish Borders, 4m/7km SW of The Cheviot. Height 2030 feet or 619 metres. **70 D2** NT8515.
Windy Harbour *Lancs.* ***Settlement***, 1km W of Brinscall, 3m/4km E of Whittle-le-Woods. SD6121.
Windy Hill *Wrex.* ***Settlement***, and hill, 3m/5km NW of Wrexham. SJ3054.
Windy Nook *T. & W.* ***Suburb***, 2m/3km SE of Gateshead town centre. NZ2760.
Windy Standard *D. & G.* ***Mountain***, 6m/10km NE of Carsphairn. Height 2289 feet or 698 metres. **68 B3** NS6201.
Windy Standard *E.Ayr.* ***Mountain***, partly forested summit 3m/5km SE of Dalmellington. Height 1761 feet or 537 metres. **67 K3** NS5204.
Windy Yet *E.Ayr.* ***Settlement***, 4m/7km NE of Stewarton. **74 C5** NS4750.
Windyfields *Staffs.* ***Settlement***, 3m/4km E of Hilderstone. SJ9935.
Windygates *Fife* Population: 1645. ***Village***, 2m/3km NW of Methil. **82 E7** NO3400.
Windyheads Hill *Aber.* ***Hill***, 3m/4km S of Pennan Head and 2m/3km W of New Aberdour. Height 758 feet or 231 metres. **99 G4** NJ8561.
Wineham *W.Suss.* ***Hamlet***, 3m/5km NE of Henfield. **13 F4** TQ2320.
Winestead *E.Riding* ***Village***, 2m/3km NW of Patrington. **59 K7** TA2924.
Winewall *Lancs.* ***Hamlet***, 1km N of Trawden. **56 E5** SD9139.
Winfarthing *Norf.* ***Village***, 4m/6km N of Diss. **45 F7** TM1085.
Winford *I.o.W.* ***Village***, 2m/3km W of Sandown. SZ5684.
Winford *N.Som.* ***Village***, 6m/9km SW of Bristol. **19 J5** ST5465.
Winford Terrace *N.Som.* ***Hamlet***, 4m/6km SW of Bristol. ST5568.
Winforton *Here.* ***Village***, 6m/10km S of Kington. **28 B4** SO2947.
Winfrith Heath *Dorset* ***Locality***, 2m/3km W of Wool. **9 G6** SY8086.
Winfrith Newburgh *Dorset* ***Village***, 3m/5km SW of Wool. **9 H6** SY8084.
Wing *Bucks.* Population: 2805. ***Village***, 3m/5km SW of Leighton Buzzard. **32 B6** SP8822.
Wing *Rut.* ***Village***, 4m/7km SE of Oakham. **42 B5** SK8903.
Wingate *Dur.* Population: 4541. ***Village***, 4m/6km S of Easington. **63 F3** NZ4037.
Wingates *Gt.Man.* ***Village***, 4m/7km W of Bolton. **49 F2** SD6507.
Wingates *Northumb.* ***Settlement***, 5m/8km SE of Rothbury. **71 F4** NZ0995.
Wingates *Worcs.* ***Suburb***, 2m/3km E of Redditch town centre. SP0767.
Wingerworth *Derbys.* Population: 6050. ***Village***, 2m/4km S of Chesterfield. **51 F6** SK3867.
Wingfield *Beds.* ***Hamlet***, 3m/5km N of Dunstable. **32 D6** TL0026.
Wingfield *Suff.* ***Village***, 2m/3km N of Stradbroke. 14c moated castle. **35 G1** TM2276.
Wingfield *Wilts.* ***Village***, 2m/4km W of Trowbridge. **20 B6** ST8256.
Wingfield Castle *Suff.* ***Castle***, 14c and Tudor mansion in NW Wingfield, 2m/3km N of Stradbroke. Built by de la Poles, Earls and Dukes of Suffolk. **35 G1** TM2277.
Wingfield College *Suff.* ***Historic house***, founded by Sir John de Wingfield in 14c, 2m/3km N of Stradbroke. Medieval Great Hall is well preserved and house contains furniture and paintings from various periods. **35 G1** TM2277.
Wingfield Green *Suff.* ***Hamlet***, 2m/3km NW of Stradbroke. TM2177.
Wingfield Park *Derbys.* ***Hamlet***, 1m/2km S of South Wingfield. SK3753.
Wingham *Kent* Population: 1553. ***Village***, 6m/10km E of Canterbury. **15 H2** TR2457.
Wingham Green *Kent* ***Settlement***, forms parish of Wingham, along with Wingham Well, to W of Wingham. TR2357.
Wingham Well *Kent* ***Settlement***, forms parish of Wingham, along with Wingham Green, to SW of Wingham. TR2356.
Wingland Marsh *Lincs.* ***Open space***, lowland to E of River Nene, 4m/6km W of Terrington St. Clement. **43 J3** TF4921.
Wingmore *Kent* ***Hamlet***, 7m/11km N of Folkestone. **15 G3** TR1846.
Wingrave *Bucks.* ***Village***, 5m/7km NE of Aylesbury. **32 B7** SP8619.
Winkburn *Notts.* ***Village***, 6m/10km NW of Newark-on-Trent. **51 K7** SK7158.
Winkfield *Brack.F.* ***Village***, 3m/5km NE of Bracknell. **22 C4** SU9072.
Winkfield Row *Brack.F.* ***Village***, forms parish of Winkfield, along with Winkfield Street and village of Winkfield. **22 B4** SU8970.
Winkfield Street *Brack.F.* ***Locality***, forms parish of Winkfield, along with Winkfield Row. SU9072.
Winkhill *Staffs.* ***Hamlet***, 6m/10km SE of Leek. **50 C7** SK0651.
Winklebury *Hants.* ***Suburb***, in W part of Basingstoke. SU6152.
Winkleigh *Devon* ***Village***, 9m/14km NE of Okehampton. **6 E5** SS6308.
Winksley *N.Yorks.* ***Village***, 4m/6km W of Ripon. **57 H2** SE2571.
Winksley Banks *N.Yorks.* ***Settlement***, 1km NW of Winksley, 4m/7km W of Ripon. **57 H2** SE2471.
Winkton *Dorset* ***Hamlet***, beside River Avon, 2m/3km N of Christchurch. **10 C5** SZ1696.
Winkworth Arboretum *Surr.* ***Forest/woodland***, hillside (National Trust) planted with rare trees and shrubs notable for autumn colouring, 2m/4km SE of Godalming. Lake. Views over North Downs. **22 C7** SU9941.
Winlaton *T. & W.* ***Town***, residential town, adjoining to SW of Blaydon, 5m/8km W of Gateshead. **71 G7** NZ1762.
Winlaton Mill *T. & W.* ***Hamlet***, on River Derwent, 1m/2km SE of Winlaton. **71 G7** NZ1860.
Winless *High.* ***Settlement***, in Caithness district, 4m/7km NW of Wick. **105 H3** ND3053.
Winmarleigh *Lancs.* ***Village***, 2m/4km NW of Garstang. **55 H5** SD4748.
Winnards Perch *Cornw.* ***Locality***, roundabout on A39, 2m/3km N of St. Columb Major. **3 G2** SW9266.
Winnersh *W'ham* ***Locality***, residential locality 2m/4km NW of Wokingham. **22 A4** SU7870.
Winnington *Ches.* ***Suburb***, NW district of Northwich. SJ6474.
Winnothdale *Staffs.* ***Settlement***, 2m/3km SE of Cheadle. SK0340.
Winscales *Cumb.* ***Locality***, 3m/4km SE of Workington. NY0226.
Winscombe *N.Som.* Population: 4192. ***Village***, below W end of Mendip Hills, 2m/3km N of Axbridge. **19 H6** ST4257.
Winsford *Ches.* Population: 26,839. ***Town***, on River Weaver, 5m/8km S of Northwich. Developed around salt-mining industry. **49 F6** SJ6566.
Winsford *Som.* ***Village***, on Exmoor, on River Exe, 5m/7km N of Dulverton. **7 H2** SS9034.
Winsford Hill *Som.* ***Mountain***, National Trust property, to SW of Winsford. Height 1397 feet or 426 metres. **7 G2** SS8734.
Winsh-wen *Swan.* ***Suburb***, 3m/4km NE of Swansea city centre. SS6896.
Winsham *Devon* ***Hamlet***, 5m/8km NW of Barnstaple. SS4938.
Winsham *Som.* ***Village***, 4m/6km SE of Chard. **8 C4** ST3706.
Winshill *Staffs.* ***Suburb***, 2m/3km E of Burton upon Trent town centre. **40 E3** SK2623.
Winskill *Cumb.* ***Hamlet***, 5m/8km NE of Penrith. **61 G3** NY5834.
Winslade *Hants.* ***Hamlet***, 3m/4km S of Basingstoke. **21 K7** SU6548.
Winsley *N.Yorks.* ***Locality***, 3m/5km W of Ripley. SE2361.
Winsley *Wilts.* Population: 1334. ***Village***, 2m/3km W of Bradford-on-Avon. **20 A5** ST7960.
Winslow *Bucks.* Population: 4005. ***Small town***, old market town, 6m/10km SE of Buckingham, with several interesting 17c and 18c buildings. **31 J6** SP7627.
Winslow Hall *Bucks.* ***Historic house***, in Winslow. Late 17c house, thought to be designed by Wren, with gardens containing unusual trees. **31 J6** SP7728.
Winson *Glos.* ***Village***, 4m/6km S of Northleach. **20 D1** SP0908.
Winson Green *W.Mid.* ***Suburb***, 2m/3km NW of Birmingham city centre. SP0488.
Winsor *Hants.* ***Village***, 1m/2km E of Cadnam. **10 E3** SU3114.
Winster *Cumb.* ***Village***, 3m/5km S of Windermere. **60 F7** SD4193.
Winster *Derbys.* ***Village***, 4m/6km W of Matlock. **50 E6** SK2460.
Winster Market House *Derbys.* ***Historic house***, National Trust property at Winster, 4m/6km W of Matlock. House dates from 17-18c and now used as National Trust information room. **50 E6** SK2460.
Winston *Dur.* ***Village***, 6m/9km E of Barnard Castle. **62 C5** NZ1416.
Winston *Suff.* ***Hamlet***, 1m/2km S of Debenham. **35 F2** TM1861.
Winston Green *Suff.* ***Hamlet***, 1km SW of Winston. TM1761.
Winstone *Glos.* ***Village***, 6m/10km NW of Cirencester. **20 C1** SO9609.
Winswell *Devon* ***Hamlet***, 4m/6km S of Great Torrington. **6 C4** SS4913.
Winter Hill ***Mountain***, astride borders of Blackburn with Darwen, Greater Manchester and Lancashire, 5m/8km NW of Bolton town centre. Masts on summit. Height 1496 feet or 456 metres. **49 F1** SD6514.
Winterborne *Dorset* ***River***, rising at Winterborne Houghton and flowing E, then S, then E again into River Stour at Sturminster Marshall. ST9400.
Winterborne Came *Dorset* ***Hamlet***, 2m/3km SE of Dorchester. **9 G6** SY7088.
Winterborne Clenston *Dorset* ***Village***, 4m/6km SW of Blandford Forum. **9 H4** ST8303.
Winterborne Herringston *Dorset* ***Settlement***, 1m/2km S of Dorchester. SY6888.
Winterborne Houghton *Dorset* ***Village***, 4m/7km W of Blandford Forum. **9 H4** ST8204.
Winterborne Kingston *Dorset* ***Village***, 6m/9km S of Blandford Forum. **9 H5** SY8697.
Winterborne Monkton *Dorset* ***Village***, 2m/3km SW of Dorchester. **9 F6** SY6787.
Winterborne Muston *Dorset* ***Settlement***, 1km E of Winterborne Kingston and 2m/4km NE of Bere Regis. SY8797.
Winterborne Stickland *Dorset* ***Village***, 3m/5km W of Blandford Forum. **9 H4** ST8304.
Winterborne Tomson *Dorset* ***Settlement***, 1m/2km W of Winterborne Kingston. SY8897.
Winterborne Whitchurch *Dorset Alternative spelling of Winterborne Whitechurch.*
Winterborne Whitechurch (Also spelled Winterborne Whitchurch.) *Dorset* ***Village***, 5m/8km SW of Blandford Forum. **9 H4** ST8300.
Winterborne Zelston *Dorset* ***Village***, 4m/6km NE of Bere Regis. **9 H5** SY8997.
Winterbourne *S.Glos.* Population: 2241. ***Suburb***, 6m/10km NE of Bristol. **19 K3** ST6480.
Winterbourne *W.Berks.* ***Village***, 3m/5km N of Newbury. **21 H4** SU4572.
Winterbourne *Wilts.* ***Locality***, parish, 4m/6km NE of Salisbury, containing villages of Winterbourne Dauntsey, Winterbourne Earls and Winterbourne Gunner, all on River Bourne. SU1834.
Winterbourne Abbas *Dorset* ***Village***, 4m/7km W of Dorchester. The Nine Stones circle to SW and Bronze Age cemetery of Winterbourne Poor Lot Barrows 2m/3km W (both English Heritage). **9 F5** SY6190.
Winterbourne Bassett *Wilts.* ***Village***, 3m/5km N of Avebury. **20 D4** SU1075.
Winterbourne Dauntsey *Wilts.* ***Village***, forms parish of Winterbourne, along with Winterbourne Earls and Winterbourne Gunner, all on River Bourne, 4m/6km NE of Salisbury. **10 C1** SU1734.
Winterbourne Earls *Wilts.* ***Village***, forms parish of Winterbourne, along with Winterbourne Dauntsey and Winterbourne Gunner, all on River Bourne, 3m/5km NE of Salisbury. **10 C1** SU1734.
Winterbourne Gunner *Wilts.* ***Village***, forms parish of Winterbourne, along with Winterbourne Dauntsey and Winterbourne Earls, all on River Bourne, 4m/7km NE of Salisbury. **10 C1** SU1835.
Winterbourne Monkton *Wilts.* ***Village***, 1m/2km N of Avebury. **20 D4** SU1072.
Winterbourne Steepleton *Dorset* ***Village***, 4m/6km W of Dorchester. **9 F6** SY6289.
Winterbourne Stoke *Wilts.* ***Village***, 5m/8km W of Amesbury. **20 D7** SU0741.
Winterbrook *Oxon.* ***Settlement***, adjoining to S of Wallingford. SU6088.
Winterburn *N.Yorks.* ***Hamlet***, 6m/9km NW of Skipton. **56 E4** SD9358.
Winterburn Reservoir *N.Yorks.* ***Reservoir***, 1m/2km NE of Winterburn. **56 E3** SD9358.
Wintercleuch Fell *S.Lan.* ***Mountain***, in Lowther Hills, 4m/7km SE of Elvanfoot. Height 1804 feet or 550 metres. **68 E2** NS9711.
Wintercleugh *S.Lan.* ***Settlement***, 4m/7km S of Elvanfoot. **68 E2** NS9610.
Winterfold Forest *Surr.* ***Open space***, heath and mixed woodland, 2m/4km N of Cranleigh. **22 D7** TQ0643.
Winteringham *N.Lincs.* ***Village***, 7m/12km N of Scunthorpe. Site of Roman settlement 1m/2km SE. **59 F7** SE9222.
Winterley *Ches.* ***Village***, 3m/5km NE of Crewe. **49 G7** SJ7457.
Wintersett *W.Yorks.* ***Settlement***, 1m/2km S of Crofton. **51 F1** SE3815.
Wintershill *Hants.* ***Settlement***, 2m/3km W of Bishop's Waltham. **11 G3** SU5218.
Winterslow *Wilts.* ***Locality***, 6m/9km E of Salisbury. Parish contains villages of East, Middle, and West Winterslow. **10 D1** SU2332.
Winterton *Norf. Familiar form of Winterton-on-Sea, qv.*
Winterton *N.Lincs.* Population: 4895. ***Village***, 5m/9km NE of Scunthorpe. Sites of Roman buildings 1km NE and 2km W. **52 C1** SE9218.
Winterton-on-Sea (Commonly referred to as Winterton.) *Norf.* ***Town***, resort 8m/13km N of Great Yarmouth. **45 J4** TG4919.
Winthorpe *Lincs.* ***Locality***, 2m/3km N of Skegness. **53 J6** TF5665.
Winthorpe *Notts.* ***Village***, 2m/3km NE of Newark-on-Trent. **52 B7** SK8156.
Winton *Bourne.* ***Suburb***, 1m/2km N of Bournemouth town centre. **10 B5** SZ0893.
Winton *Cumb.* ***Village***, 1m/2km NE of Kirkby Stephen. **61 J5** NY7810.
Winton *N.Yorks.* ***Settlement***, 3m/5km NE of Northallerton. SE4096.
Winton Fell *Cumb.* ***Open space***, 4m/6km E of Kirkby Stephen. Highest point is Bastifell at 2024 feet or 617 metres. **61 K6** NY8307.

Winton House *E.Loth.* ***Historic house***, early 17c mansion 1km N of Pencaitland across Tyne Water, 3m/5km SE of Tranent. Formerly seat of Earls of Winton. **76 C4** NT4369.
Wintringham *Cambs.* ***Locality***, 2m/3km E of St. Neots. Includes Wintringham Hall and Lower Wintringham. TL2159.
Wintringham *N.Yorks.* ***Village***, 6m/10km E of Malton. **58 E2** SE8873.
Winwick *Cambs.* ***Village***, 10m/16km NW of Huntingdon. **42 E7** TL1080.
Winwick *Northants.* ***Village***, 1m/2km N of West Haddon. **31 H1** SP6273.
Winwick *Warr.* ***Village***, 3m/5km N of Warrington. **49 F3** SJ6092.
Wirksworth *Derbys.* Population: 4235. ***Small town***, 4m/7km S of Matlock. Former lead mining centre. Fine cruciform church dating from 1272. **50 E7** SK2854.
Wirksworth Moor *Derbys.* ***Hamlet***, 1km E of Wirksworth. SK3054.
Wirral ***Locality***, peninsula, some 13m/21km long and 6m/10km wide, between estuaries of River Dee to W and River Mersey to E; largely industrialised Birkenhead on the peninsula is connected to Liverpool by tunnels under River Mersey. **48 B4** SJ3080.
Wirswall *Ches.* ***Village***, 2m/3km N of Whitchurch. **38 E1** SJ5444.
Wisbech *Cambs.* Population: 24,981. ***Town***, ancient port and agricultural centre on River Nene, 12m/19km SW of King's Lynn. Birthplace of Octavia Hill, founder of The National Trust. **43 H5** TF4609.
Wisbech St. Mary *Cambs.* ***Village***, 3m/5km W of Wisbech. **43 H5** TF4208.
Wisborough Green *W.Suss.* ***Village***, 2m/4km W of Billingshurst. **12 D4** TQ0525.
Wiseton *Notts.* ***Village***, 5m/7km SE of Bawtry. **51 K4** SK7189.
Wishach Hill *Aber.* ***Mountain***, on Gartly Moor, surrounded by woodland, 5m/8km SE of Huntly. Height 1374 feet or 419 metres. **90 D1** NJ5733.
Wishaw *N.Lan.* Population: 29,791. ***Town***, 3m/5km SE of Motherwell. **75 F5** NS7954.
Wishaw *Warks.* ***Village***, 4m/6km N of Coleshill. **40 D6** SP1794.
Wiske *N.Yorks.* ***River***, rising near Ingleby Arncliffe and flowing NW to Appleton Wiske, then W to Birkby, then S by Yafforth, Newby Wiske and Kirby Wiske into River Swale 4m/6km W of Thirsk. **57 J1** SE3683.
Wisley *Surr.* ***Hamlet***, 4m/6km E of Woking. **22 D6** TQ0659.
Wisley Gardens *Surr.* ***Garden***, Royal Horticultural Society Gardens, 1km S of Wisley. Impressive rock garden, woodland and bog gardens plus trial beds. **22 D6** TQ0659.
Wisp Hill ***Mountain***, astride border of Dumfries & Galloway and Scottish Borders, 4m/6km S of Teviothead. Height 1952 feet or 595 metres. **69 J4** NY3899.
Wispington *Lincs.* ***Village***, 4m/6km W of Horncastle. **53 F5** TF2071.
Wissett *Suff.* ***Village***, 2m/3km NW of Halesworth. **35 H1** TM3679.
Wissey *Norf.* ***River***, rising 4m/6km SW of East Dereham and flowing W into River Great Ouse, 5m/8km SW of Downham Market. **44 A6** TL5899.
Wissington *Suff.* ***Hamlet***, by River Stour, 1m/2km W of Nayland. **34 D5** TL9533.
Wistanstow *Shrop.* ***Village***, 2m/3km N of Craven Arms. **38 D7** SO4385.
Wistanswick *Shrop.* ***Hamlet***, 4m/6km S of Market Drayton. **39 F3** SJ6629.
Wistaston *Ches.* ***Village***, 2m/3km SW of Crewe. **49 F7** SJ6853.
Wistaston Green *Ches.* ***Suburb***, 1m/2km W of Crewe. SJ6854.
Wistlandpound *Devon* ***Settlement***, on W edge of Exmoor, 6m/10km SW of Lynton. SS6442.
Wistlandpound Reservoir *Devon* ***Reservoir***, to S of Wistlandpound and 2m/4km N of Bratton Fleming. **6 E1** SS6441.
Wiston (Cas-wis). *Pembs.* ***Village***, 5m/7km E of Haverfordwest. Remains of medieval castle. **16 D3** SN0217.
Wiston *S.Lan.* ***Village***, 7m/11km SW of Biggar. **75 H7** NS9531.
Wiston *W.Suss.* ***Hamlet***, 2m/3km NE of Washington. TQ1414.
Wistow *Cambs.* ***Village***, 2m/3km NW of Warboys. **43 F7** TL2781.
Wistow *Leics.* ***Settlement***, 6m/10km SE of Leicester city centre. Church and hall in park. SP6495.
Wistow *N.Yorks.* ***Village***, 3m/4km NW of Selby. **58 B6** SE5935.
Wiswell *Lancs.* ***Village***, 1m/2km NE of Whalley. **56 C6** SD7437.
Witcham *Cambs.* ***Village***, 5m/8km W of Ely. **33 H1** TL4680.
Witchampton *Dorset* ***Village***, 6m/10km E of Blandford Forum. **9 J4** ST9806.
Witchburn *Arg. & B.* ***Settlement***, on Kintyre, adjoining to W of Campbeltown. **66 B2** NR7019.
Witchford *Cambs.* ***Village***, 3m/4km W of Ely. **33 J1** TL5078.
Witcombe *Som.* ***Hamlet***, 1m/2km NE of Martock. **8 D2** ST4721.
Witham ***River***, rising to E of Wymondham and flowing circuitously through Grantham to Lincoln, where it turns E then SE to Boston and The Wash. **43 F1** TF3939.
Witham *Essex* Population: 22,684. ***Town***, old market town, 9m/14km NE of Chelmsford. Remains of 10c castle. **34 C7** TL8215.
Witham Friary *Som.* ***Village***, 6m/9km NE of Bruton. **20 A7** ST7441.
Witham on the Hill *Lincs.* ***Village***, 4m/6km SW of Bourne. **42 D4** TF0516.
Witham Priory *Som.* ***Ecclesiastical building***, at Witham Friary, 5m/8km SW of Frome. Site of first Carthusian monastery in England. Lay brothers' chapel is still in use as parish church. **20 A7** ST7441.
Withcall *Lincs.* ***Hamlet***, 4m/6km SW of Louth. Withcall Village is site of former village to E. TF2883.
Withcote *Leics.* ***Settlement***, 4m/7km SW of Oakham. **42 B5** SK7905.
Withdean *B. & H.* ***Suburb***, N district of Brighton. TQ3007.
Withens Clough Reservoir *W.Yorks.* ***Reservoir***, 3m/5km S of Hebden Bridge. **56 E7** SD9823.
Witherenden Hill *E.Suss.* ***Hamlet***, 2m/3km NW of Burwash. **13 K4** TQ6426.
Withergate *Norf.* ***Settlement***, 1km N of Worstead and 2m/3km SE of North Walsham. TG2927.
Witherhurst *E.Suss.* ***Settlement***, 1km SW of Burwash. **13 K4** TQ6624.
Witheridge *Devon* ***Village***, 9m/16km W of Tiverton. **7 G4** SS8014.
Witherley *Leics.* ***Village***, 1m/2km E of Atherstone. **41 F6** SP3297.
Withern *Lincs.* ***Village***, 4m/7km N of Alford. **53 H4** TF4382.
Withernsea *E.Riding* Population: 6433. ***Small town***, coastal resort, 15m/24km E of Kingston upon Hull. Work of RNLI depicted in museum housed in old lighthouse. **59 K7** TA3428.
Withernwick *E.Riding* ***Village***, 5m/8km S of Hornsea. **59 J5** TA1940.
Withersdale Street *Suff.* ***Village***, 2m/4km SE of Harleston. **45 G7** TM2781.
Withersdane *Kent* ***Locality***, 1m/2km SE of Wye. TR0645.
Withersfield *Suff.* ***Village***, 2m/3km NW of Haverhill. **33 K4** TL6547.
Witherslack *Cumb.* ***Hamlet***, 3m/4km N of Lindale. **55 H1** SD4384.
Witherwack *T. & W.* ***Suburb***, in NW part of Sunderland. NZ3759.
Withiel *Cornw.* ***Village***, 5m/8km W of Bodmin. **3 G2** SW9965.
Withiel Florey *Som.* ***Hamlet***, on S side of Brendon Hills, 6m/9km NE of Dulverton. **7 H2** SS9833.
Withielgoose *Cornw.* ***Hamlet***, 1m/2km E of Withiel. SX0065.
Withington *Glos.* ***Village***, 5m/8km W of Northleach. **30 B7** SP0315.
Withington *Gt.Man.* ***Suburb***, 3m/5km S of Manchester city centre. **49 H3** SJ8492.
Withington *Here.* ***Village***, 4m/7km NE of Hereford. **28 E4** SO5643.
Withington *Shrop.* ***Village***, 5m/9km E of Shrewsbury. **38 E4** SJ5713.
Withington *Staffs.* ***Hamlet***, 4m/7km W of Uttoxeter. **40 C2** SK0335.
Withington Green *Ches.* ***Settlement***, 1m/2km NW of Lower Withington. **49 H5** SJ8071.
Withington Marsh *Here.* ***Village***, 4m/6km NE of Hereford. SO5544.
Withington Woods *Glos.* ***Forest/woodland***, 2m/3km NW of Chedworth. **30 B7** SP0214.
Withleigh *Devon* ***Village***, 3m/5km W of Tiverton. **7 H4** SS9012.
Withnell *Lancs.* Population: 2499. ***Suburb***, 5m/8km SW of Blackburn. **56 B7** SD6322.
Withnell Fold *Lancs.* ***Hamlet***, on Leeds and Liverpool Canal, 1m/2km NW of Withnell and 5m/8km SW of Blackburn town centre. SD6322.
Withybrook *Som.* ***Hamlet***, 1km W of Stoke St. Michael and 3m/5km NE of Shepton Mallet. ST6547.
Withybrook *Warks.* ***Village***, 7m/11km NW of Rugby. **41 G7** SP4384.
Withycombe *Som.* ***Village***, on edge of Exmoor National Park, 2m/3km SE of Dunster. **7 J1** ST0141.
Withycombe Raleigh *Devon* ***Suburb***, NE of Exmouth town centre. **7 J7** SY0182.
Withyditch *B. & N.E.Som.* ***Settlement***, 1km W of Dunkerton and 3m/5km N of Radstock. ST7059.
Withyham *E.Suss.* ***Village***, 6m/10km SW of Royal Tunbridge Wells. **13 H3** TQ4935.
Withypool *Som.* ***Village***, on Exmoor and on River Barle, 2m/3km S of Exford. **7 G2** SS8435.
Withypool Common *Som.* ***Open space***, moorland on Exmoor to W of Withypool, rising to height of 1404 feet or 428 metres. **7 G2** SS8135.
Witley *Surr.* Population: 3238. ***Village***, 2m/4km S of Milford. 2km NW, Witley Common (National Trust): nature reserve. **12 C3** SU9434.
Witley Common *Surr.* ***Leisure/recreation***, over 300 acres or 121 hectares of heath and woodland (National Trust), 1m/2km NW of Witley. Walks with varied flora and fauna. Visitor information centre at edge of common, details importance of lowland heath and its management. **22 C7** SU9240.
Witley Court *Worcs.* ***Historic house***, ruins of 18c house (English Heritage) burnt down in 20c, 1m/2km SE of Great Witley. Baroque 18c church. **29 G2** SO7664.
Witnesham *Suff.* ***Village***, 4m/6km N of Ipswich. **35 F3** TM1850.
Witney *Oxon.* Population: 20,377. ***Town***, old weaving town on River Windrush, 10m/16km W of Oxford, famous for blanket-making. **30 E7** SP3510.
Witney Green *Essex* ***Settlement***, 3m/5km NE of Chipping Ongar. TL5806.
Wittering *Peter.* Population: 2379. ***Village***, 3m/5km SE of Stamford. Airfield to W. **42 D5** TF0502.
Wittersham *Kent* ***Village***, on Isle of Oxney, 4m/6km S of Tenterden. **14 D5** TQ8927.
Witton *Angus* ***Settlement***, 2m/3km NE of Bridgend. **83 G1** NO5670.
Witton *Norf.* ***Hamlet***, 1m/2km W of Blofield. TG3109.
Witton *W.Mid.* ***Suburb***, 3m/5km NE of Birmingham city centre. SP0891.
Witton *Worcs.* ***Suburb***, S district of Droitwich Spa. SO8962.
Witton Bridge *Norf.* ***Hamlet***, 4m/6km E of North Walsham. **45 H2** TG3331.
Witton Gilbert *Dur.* Population: 2704. ***Village***, 3m/5km NW of Durham. **62 D2** NZ2345.
Witton Green *Norf.* ***Locality***, adjoining to N of Reedham. TG4202.
Witton-le-Wear *Dur.* ***Village***, on River Wear, 3m/5km SW of Crook. 15c Witton Castle 1km SE. **62 C3** NZ1431.
Witton Park *B'burn.* ***Leisure/recreation***, 400 acre or 161 hectare park, 1m/2km W of Blackburn town centre. Comprises woodland and parkland, with a variety of nature trails. Visitor centre contains exhibitions of local history and small zoo for children. **56 B7** SD6527.
Witton Park *Dur.* ***Village***, 2m/4km W of Bishop Auckland. **62 C3** NZ1730.
Wiveliscombe *Som.* Population: 1753. ***Small town***, 9m/15km W of Taunton. **7 J3** ST0827.
Wivelsfield *E.Suss.* ***Village***, 2m/3km S of Haywards Heath. **13 G4** TQ3420.
Wivelsfield Green *E.Suss.* ***Village***, 1m/2km E of Wivelsfield. **13 G5** TQ3420.
Wivenhoe *Essex* Population: 7073. ***Small town***, on NE bank of River Colne, 4m/6km SE of Colchester. University of Essex to NW, in Wivenhoe Park. **34 E6** TM0321.
Wivenhoe Cross *Essex* ***Locality***, adjoins to N of Wivenhoe. TM0321.
Wiveton *Norf.* ***Village***, 1m/2km SE of Blakeney. **44 E1** TG0442.
Wix *Essex* ***Village***, 6m/10km SW of Harwich. **35 F6** TM1628.
Wix Green *Essex* ***Locality***, at E end of Wix. TM1628.
Wixford *Warks.* ***Village***, 7m/11km W of Stratford-upon-Avon. **30 B3** SP0854.
Wixhill *Shrop.* ***Settlement***, 3m/5km E of Wem. SJ5628.
Wixoe *Suff.* ***Village***, 3m/5km SE of Haverhill. **34 B4** TL7142.
Wnion *Gwyn.* ***River***, flowing SW into River Mawddach, 1m/2km NW of Dolgellau. **37 H3** SH7118.
Woburn *Beds.* ***Village***, 5m/9km N of Leighton Buzzard. **32 C5** SP9433.
Woburn Abbey *Beds.* ***Historic house***, 18c house in large park to E of Woburn. Includes large art collection. **32 C5** SP9433.
Woburn Safari Park *Beds.* ***Leisure/recreation***, traditional safari park set in 300 acres or 121 hectares of parkland around Woburn Abbey, 4m/6km W of Flitwick. Recent addition is new leisure complex with boating lake and adventure playground. **32 C5** SP9634.
Woburn Sands *M.K.* Population: 4961. ***Village***, 4m/6km E of Bletchley. **32 C5** SP9235.
Woden Law *Sc.Bord.* ***Mountain***, in Cheviot Hills, 3m/5km S of Chatto. Hillfort at summit. Height 1387 feet or 423 metres. **70 C2** NT7612.
Wokefield *W.Berks.* ***Locality***, 5m/8km SW of Reading. SU6765.
Wokefield Park *W.Berks.* ***Settlement***, 1m/2km N of Stratfield Mortimer. **21 K5** SU6765.
Woking *Surr.* Population: 98,138. ***Town***, commuter town 6m/9km N of Guildford. Oldest mosque in Britain sited here. **22 D6** TQ0058.
Wokingham *W'ham* Population: 38,063. ***Town***, old market town, 7m/11km SE of Reading, now with much modern development. **22 B5** SU8168.
Wolborough *Devon* ***Suburb***, S of Newton Abbot. **5 J3** SX8570.
Wold *Northants. Occasional name for Old, qv.*
Wold Fell ***Mountain***, rounded summit on border of Cumbria and North Yorkshire, to S of Widdale Fell, 3m/4km SE of Dent Station. Height 1827 feet or 557 metres. **56 C1** SD7985.
Wold Newton *E.Riding* ***Village***, 7m/11km SW of Filey. **59 G2** TA0473.
Wold Newton *N.E.Lincs.* ***Village***, 3m/5km NE of Binbrook. **53 F3** TF2496.
Woldingham *Surr.* ***Village***, 2m/3km SE of Warlingham. **23 G6** TQ3755.
Wolf *Devon* ***River***, rising on Halwill Forest and flowing S through Roadford Reservoir and into River Thrushel, 1m/2km NE of Lifton. **6 C6** SX4085.
Wolf Rock *Cornw.* ***Sea feature***, with lighthouse 8m/13km SW of Gwennap Head. **2 A7** SW2712.
Wolfelee *Sc.Bord.* ***Settlement***, 1m/2km S of Hobkirk. **70 A3** NT5809.
Wolfelee Hill *Sc.Bord.* ***Mountain***, 1km SE of Wolfelee. Height 1289 feet or 393 metres. **70 A3** NT5908.
Wolferlow *Here.* ***Locality***, 5m/7km N of Bromyard. **29 F2** SO6661.
Wolferton *Norf.* ***Village***, 6m/10km NE of King's Lynn. **44 A3** TF6528.
Wolfeton House *Dorset* ***Historic house***, to S of Charminster, 1km N of Dorchester. Medieval in origin; built in water meadows. Includes gatehouse. **9 F5** SY6892.
Wolfhampcote *Warks.* ***Locality***, 4m/6km NW of Daventry. **31 G2** SP5265.
Wolfhill *P. & K.* ***Village***, 6m/10km NE of Perth. **82 C4** NO1533.
Wolfhole Crag *Lancs.* ***Mountain***, on Forest of Bowland, 5m/8km N of Dunsop Bridge. Height 1729 feet or 527 metres. **56 B4** SD6357.
Wolfpits *Powys* ***Settlement***, 5m/8km NW of Kington. **28 B3** SO2158.
Wolf's Castle (Cas-blaidd). *Pembs.* ***Village***, 7m/11km S of Fishguard. Traces of Norman castle. **16 C2** SM9526.
Wolfsdale *Pembs.* ***Hamlet***, 4m/6km N of Haverfordwest. **16 C2** SM9321.

Woll *Sc.Bord.* ***Hamlet***, 4m/6km S of Selkirk. **69 K1** NT4621.

Wollaston *Northants.* Population: 2982. ***Village***, 4m/6km S of Wellingborough. **32 C2** SP9062.

Wollaston *Shrop.* ***Hamlet***, 7m/11km NE of Welshpool. **38 C4** SJ3212.

Wollaston *W.Mid.* ***Suburb***, to W of Stourbridge. **40 A7** SO8884.

Wollaton *Notts.* ***Suburb***, 3m/5km W of Nottingham city centre. Site of Nottingham University. SK5239.

Wollaton Hall *Nott.* ***Historic house***, Elizabethan mansion, now museum, in large park. Nottingham University at SE end of park. **41 H2** SK5339.

Wollerton *Shrop.* ***Hamlet***, 1m/2km NE of Hodnet. **39 F3** SJ6229.

Wollescote *W.Mid.* ***Suburb***, 1m/2km E of Stourbridge town centre. SO9283.

Wolsingham *Dur.* Population: 1286. ***Small town***, market town at confluence of River Wear and Waskerley Beck, 6m/10km NW of Bishop Auckland. **62 B3** NZ0737.

Wolsingham Park Moor *Dur.* ***Open space***, moorland to E of Crawleyside. **62 B2** NZ0240.

Wolstanton *Staffs.* ***Suburb***, 2m/3km N of Newcastle-under-Lyme town centre. SJ8548.

Wolstenholme *Gt.Man.* ***Suburb***, 3m/5km W of Rochdale town centre. **49 H1** SD8514.

Wolston *Warks.* Population: 2281. ***Village***, 5m/9km SE of Coventry. **31 F1** SP4175.

Wolsty *Cumb.* ***Settlement***, near coast of Solway Firth, 2m/3km S of Silloth. Remains of castle to N. NY1050.

Wolvercote *Oxon.* ***Suburb***, N district of Oxford. **21 H1** SP4909.

Wolverhampton *W.Mid.* Population: 257,943. ***Town***, 12m/20km NW of Birmingham. A premier manufacturing centre, previously dependent upon metal-working and motor industry; originally a medieval wool town. University. Racecourse. **40 B6** SO9198.

Wolverley *Shrop.* ***Settlement***, 3m/5km NW of Wem. **38 D2** SJ4731.

Wolverley *Worcs.* ***Village***, 2m/3km N of Kidderminster. **29 H1** SO8279.

Wolverton *Hants.* ***Hamlet***, 2m/3km E of Kingsclere. **21 J6** SU5558.

Wolverton *M.K.* ***Small town***, in NW part of Milton Keynes, 6m/10km NW of Bletchley. Formerly an important railway centre. **32 B4** SP8141.

Wolverton *Warks.* ***Village***, 5m/7km N of Stratford-upon-Avon. **30 D2** SP2062.

Wolverton *Wilts.* ***Hamlet***, just E of Zeals, 2m/3km W of Mere. ST7831.

Wolverton Common *Hants.* ***Settlement***, 2m/4km E of Kingsclere. SU5659.

Wolves Wood Nature Reserve *Suff.* ***Nature reserve***, 2m/3km NE of Hadleigh. A coppice-with-standards wet woodland, with good variety of birds. **34 E4** TM0544.

Wolvesnewton *Mon.* ***Hamlet***, 6m/10km NW of Chepstow. **19 H2** ST4599.

Wolvey *Warks.* ***Village***, 4m/6km S of Hinckley. **41 G7** SP4287.

Wolvey Heath *Warks.* ***Hamlet***, to NE of Wolvey. SP4388.

Wolviston *Stock.* ***Village***, 4m/7km N of Stockton-on-Tees. **63 F4** NZ4525.

Womaston *Powys* ***Settlement***, 4m/6km SW of Presteigne. SO2660.

Wombleton *N.Yorks.* ***Village***, 4m/6km E of Helmsley. **58 C1** SE6683.

Wombourn *Staffs.* *Alternative spelling of Wombourne, qv.*

Wombourne (Also spelled Wombourn.) *Staffs.* Population: 12,220. ***Town***, commuter town, 4m/7km SW of Wolverhampton. **40 A6** SO8793.

Wombridge *Tel. & W.* ***Suburb***, 1m/2km W of Oakengates. SJ6911.

Wombwell *S.Yorks.* Population: 15,462. ***Town***, 4m/6km SE of Barnsley. Residential town with light industry. **51 G2** SE3902.

Wombwell Main *S.Yorks.* ***Locality***, to W of Wombwell. Railway station. SE3902.

Womenswold *Kent* ***Village***, 7m/11km SE of Canterbury. **15 H2** TR2250.

Womersley *N.Yorks.* ***Village***, 4m/6km SE of Knottingley. **51 H1** SE5319.

Wonastow (Llanwarw). *Mon.* ***Locality***, 2m/3km SW of Monmouth. **28 D7** SO4810.

Wonersh *Surr.* Population: 2435. ***Village***, 3m/5km SE of Guildford. **22 D7** TQ0145.

Wonford *Devon* ***Suburb***, E district of Exeter. SX9491.

Wonson *Devon* ***Hamlet***, 6m/9km NW of Moretonhampstead. **6 E7** SX6789.

Wonston *Hants.* ***Village***, 6m/10km N of Winchester. **11 F1** SU4739.

Wooburn *Bucks.* ***Village***, 2m/4km SW of Beaconsfield. **22 C3** SU9087.

Wooburn Green *Bucks.* ***Village***, 4m/6km SE of High Wycombe. **22 C3** SU9188.

Wooburn Moor *Bucks.* ***Locality***, 2m/3km W of Beaconsfield. SU9089.

Wood Bevington *Warks.* ***Settlement***, 7m/11km N of Evesham. SP0553.

Wood Burcote *Northants.* ***Settlement***, 1m/2km S of Towcester. **31 H4** SP6946.

Wood Dalling *Norf.* ***Hamlet***, 3m/4km N of Reepham. **44 E3** TG0827.

Wood Eaton *Staffs.* ***Settlement***, just NW of Church Eaton. SJ8417.

Wood End *Beds.* ***Hamlet***, 4m/6km SW of Bedford. **32 D4** TL0046.

Wood End *Beds.* ***Settlement***, 1m/2km SW of Kimbolton. TL0865.

Wood End *Bucks.* ***Settlement***, adjoining to E of Little Horwood, 2m/4km NE of Winslow. SP7930.

Wood End *Cambs.* ***Locality***, adjoining to NW of Bluntisham. TL3675.

Wood End *Gt.Lon.* ***Locality***, in Hayes, borough of Hillingdon, 3m/5km SE of Uxbridge. TQ0981.

Wood End *Herts.* ***Village***, 3m/5km SW of Buntingford. **33 G6** TL3225.

Wood End *Lancs.* ***Settlement***, on N side of River Calder, 2m/3km NW of Burnley. SD8235.

Wood End *N.Yorks.* ***Settlement***, 2m/3km E of Barlby. SE6634.

Wood End *Warks.* ***Hamlet***, 4m/7km W of Atherstone. **40 E6** SP2498.

Wood End *Warks.* ***Settlement***, 6m/10km NW of Coventry city centre. SP2987.

Wood End *Warks.* ***Village***, 3m/5km W of Hockley Heath. **30 C1** SP1071.

Wood End *W.Mid.* ***Suburb***, 3m/4km NE of Wolverhampton town centre. SJ9401.

Wood End *W.Mid.* ***Suburb***, 3m/5km NE of Coventry city centre. SP3682.

Wood End Green *Gt.Lon.* ***Locality***, to W of Wood End in Hayes, borough of Hillingdon, 2m/4km SE of Uxbridge. TQ0981.

Wood Enderby *Lincs.* ***Village***, 4m/6km S of Horncastle. **53 F6** TF2763.

Wood Green *Essex* ***Hamlet***, 2m/3km E of Waltham Abbey. TL4100.

Wood Green *Gt.Lon.* ***Suburb***, in borough of Haringey, 6m/10km N of Charing Cross. To W is Alexandra Palace, television relay station. **23 G2** TQ3090.

Wood Green *Norf.* ***Settlement***, 1m/2km SE of Long Stratton. TM2091.

Wood Green *Worcs.* ***Locality***, 3m/4km S of Stourport-on-Severn. SO8067.

Wood Hayes *W.Mid.* ***Suburb***, 3m/5km NE of Wolverhampton town centre. **40 B5** SJ9402.

Wood Hill *S.Yorks.* ***Suburb***, 2m/3km NE of Sheffield city centre. SK3689.

Wood Lane *Shrop.* ***Settlement***, 2m/3km SE of Ellesmere. SJ4132.

Wood Lane *Staffs.* ***Hamlet***, 4m/6km NW of Newcastle-under-Lyme. SJ8150.

Wood Linkin *Derbys.* ***Hamlet***, 3m/4km SE of Ripley. SK4348.

Wood Norton *Norf.* ***Village***, 6m/10km E of Fakenham. **44 E3** TG0127.

Wood of Dundurcas *Moray* ***Forest/woodland***, wooded hillside 2m/3km NE of Rothes. **98 A5** NJ2951.

Wood of Ordiequish *Moray* ***Forest/woodland***, on E side of River Spey, 2m/3km S of Fochabers. **98 B5** NJ3555.

Wood Row *W.Yorks.* ***Locality***, adjoining to N of Methley, 1m/2km W of Mickletown. SE3827.

Wood Seats *S.Yorks.* ***Hamlet***, 1m/2km N of Grenoside. SK3395.

Wood Stanway *Glos.* ***Settlement***, 3m/5km NE of Winchcombe. SP0631.

Wood Street *Norf.* ***Hamlet***, 1km W of Catfield. TG3722.

Wood Street *Surr.* Population: 1512. ***Village***, 3m/5km NW of Guildford. **22 C6** SU9551.

Wood Top *Lancs.* ***Locality***, 1km SW of Rawtenstall. SD8022.

Wood Wick *Ork.* ***Bay***, to E of Woodwick. **106 C5** HY3823.

Woodacott *Devon* ***Hamlet***, 4m/6km NE of Holsworthy. SS3807.

Woodale *N.Yorks.* ***Settlement***, at head of Coverdale, 6m/9km NE of Kettlewell across moors. **57 F2** SE0279.

Woodall *S.Yorks.* ***Village***, 1km W of Harthill. Service area on M1 motorway to S. SK4880.

Woodbastwick *Norf.* ***Village***, 8m/12km NE of Norwich. **45 H4** TG3315.

Woodbeck *Notts.* ***Hamlet***, 2m/3km W of Rampton. Mental hospital. **51 K5** SK7777.

Woodbine *Pembs.* ***Settlement***, 1m/2km S of Haverfordwest. **16 C3** SM9513.

Woodborough *Notts.* Population: 1691. ***Village***, 6m/10km NE of Nottingham. **41 J1** SK6347.

Woodborough *Wilts.* ***Village***, 3m/5km W of Pewsey. **20 E5** SU1159.

Woodbridge *Devon* ***Settlement***, 4m/6km SE of Honiton. SY1895.

Woodbridge *Dorset* ***Hamlet***, in Blackmoor Vale, 1m/2km SE of Bishop's Caundle and 5m/8km W of Sturminster Newton. ST7112.

Woodbridge *Dorset* ***Locality***, 3m/5km S of Shaftesbury. ST8418.

Woodbridge *Suff.* Population: 10,950. ***Town***, old Saxon town on River Deben, 8m/12km E of Ipswich, known for sail-making and ship-building. River Deben navigable for small craft to mouth at Woodbridge Haven. Many old buildings, including restored 18c mill. Town has links with Thomas Seckford, who commissioned first maps of England. **35 G4** TM2749.

Woodbridge Hill *Surr.* ***Suburb***, NW of Guildford. SU9750.

Woodbury *Beds.* ***Settlement***, with hall and park, 4m/6km NE of Sandy. TL2152.

Woodbury *Devon* ***Village***, 4m/6km N of Exmouth. **7 J7** SY0187.

Woodbury *Som.* ***Suburb***, E district of Wells. ST5646.

Woodbury Hill *Worcs.* ***Hill***, surmounted by hillfort, 9m/14km NW of Worcester. Height 905 feet or 276 metres. **29 G2** SO7464.

Woodbury Salterton *Devon* ***Village***, 5m/8km N of Exmouth. **7 J7** SY0189.

Woodchester *Glos.* ***Village***, 2m/3km S of Stroud. Site of Roman villa to N. National Trust properties on hills to E. **20 B1** SO8402.

Woodchurch *Kent* Population: 1419. ***Village***, 4m/6km E of Tenterden. **14 E4** TQ9434.

Woodchurch *Mersey.* ***Suburb***, 3m/5km SW of Birkenhead town centre. **48 B4** SJ2786.

Woodcock Hill *W.Mid.* ***Suburb***, 5m/8km SW of Birmingham city centre. SP0181.

Woodcombe *Som.* ***Hamlet***, 1m/2km W of Minehead. SS9546.

Woodcote *Gt.Lon.* ***Suburb***, in borough of Croydon, 1m/2km W of Purley. TQ2961.

Woodcote *Oxon.* Population: 2608. ***Village***, 3m/5km E of Goring. **21 K3** SU6482.

Woodcote *Tel. & W.* ***Hamlet***, 3m/5km SE of Newport. **39 G4** SJ7615.

Woodcote Green *Worcs.* ***Settlement***, 3m/5km W of Bromsgrove. SO9172.

Woodcott *Hants.* ***Settlement***, 4m/6km E of Hurstbourne Tarrant. **21 H6** SU4354.

Woodcroft *Glos.* ***Village***, 1m/2km N of Chepstow. **19 J2** ST5495.

Woodcutts *Dorset* ***Settlement***, 2m/3km E of Tollard Royal. **9 J3** ST9617.

Woodditton *Cambs.* ***Hamlet***, 3m/4km S of Newmarket. **33 K3** TL6559.

Woodeaton *Oxon.* ***Village***, 4m/6km NE of Oxford. **31 G7** SP5311.

Wooden *Pembs.* ***Locality***, 1m/2km W of Saundersfoot. SN1105.

Woodend *Aber.* ***Locality***, comprises Upper and Lower Woodend on N bank of River Don, 3m/4km N of Monymusk. **90 E3** NJ6718.

Woodend *Cumb.* ***Settlement***, 1km SE of Devoke Water and 5m/8km E of Ravenglass. **60 C7** SD1696.

Woodend *High.* ***Settlement***, in Strathdearn, 2m/3km SE of Tomatin. **88 E2** NH7926.

Woodend *High.* ***Settlement***, 2m/4km W of Strontian, Lochaber district. **79 J1** NM7860.

Woodend *Northants.* ***Village***, 5m/8km W of Towcester. **31 H4** SP6149.

Woodend *P. & K.* ***Settlement***, in valley of River Lyon, 1m/2km W of Fortingall. **81 J3** NN7147.

Woodend *W.Suss.* ***Settlement***, 1m/2km E of Funtington. **12 B6** SU8108.

Woodend Green *Essex* ***Hamlet***, adjoining to E of Henham, 6m/10km NE of Bishop's Stortford. TL5528.

Woodend Green *Northants.* ***Settlement***, 5m/8km W of Towcester. SP6148.

Woodend Loch *N.Lan.* ***Lake/loch***, 2m/3km NW of Coatbridge. **75 F4** NS7066.

Woodfalls *Wilts.* ***Village***, 7m/12km SE of Salisbury. **10 D2** SU1920.

Woodfield *Oxon.* ***Suburb***, in N part of Bicester. SP5823.

Woodfield *S.Ayr.* ***Suburb***, N district of Ayr. NS3424.

Woodfoot *Cumb.* ***Settlement***, 1km S of Crosby Ravensworth. NY6213.

Woodford *Cornw.* ***Hamlet***, 5m/8km N of Bude. **6 A4** SS2113.

Woodford *Devon* ***Hamlet***, 6m/9km NE of Kingsbridge. SX7950.

Woodford *Glos.* ***Hamlet***, 2m/3km S of Berkeley. **19 K2** ST6995.

Woodford *Gt.Lon.* ***Suburb***, in borough of Redbridge, 9m/15km NE of Charing Cross. **23 H2** TQ4091.

Woodford *Gt.Man.* ***Village***, 3m/5km E of Wilmslow. Airfield to E. **49 H4** SJ8882.

Woodford *Northants.* ***Village***, 2m/3km SW of Thrapston. **32 C1** SP9676.

Woodford *Plym.* ***Suburb***, E district of Plymouth, 4m/6km from city centre, to E of River Plym. SX5357.

Woodford *Som.* ***Hamlet***, on edge of Exmoor National Park, 3m/5km S of Watchet. ST0638.

Woodford *Wilts.* ***Locality***, parish, 4m/6km N of Salisbury, containing villages of Upper, Middle and Lower Woodford, all on River Avon. SU1236.

Woodford Bridge *Gt.Lon.* ***Locality***, to E of Woodford Green. **23 H2** TQ4291.

Woodford Green *Gt.Lon.* ***Suburb***, in borough of Redbridge, 9m/15km NE of Charing Cross. **23 H2** TQ4091.

Woodford Halse *Northants.* ***Village***, 6m/10km SW of Daventry. **31 G3** SP5452.

Woodford Wells *Gt.Lon.* ***Suburb***, to N of Woodford Green. TQ4092.

Woodgate *Devon* ***Hamlet***, 1m/2km N of Culmstock, 4m/6km SW of Wellington. ST1015.

Woodgate *Norf.* ***Hamlet***, 3m/4km NE of East Dereham. **44 E4** TG0216.

Woodgate *Norf.* ***Locality***, 2m/3km S of Litcham. TF8915.

Woodgate *W.Mid.* ***Suburb***, 5m/9km SW of Birmingham city centre. **40 B7** SO9982.

Woodgate *W.Suss.* ***Village***, 3m/5km N of Bognor Regis. **12 C6** SU9304.

Woodgate *Worcs.* ***Hamlet***, 3m/5km S of Bromsgrove. **29 J2** SO9666.

Woodgreen *Hants.* ***Village***, in River Avon valley, on edge of New Forest, 3m/4km NE of Fordingbridge. **10 C3** SU1717.

Woodhall *Herts.* ***Suburb***, SE district of Welwyn Garden City. TL2411.

Woodhall *Inclyde* ***Suburb***, 1m/2km E of Port Glasgow. NS3473.

Woodhall *Lincs.* ***Settlement***, 3m/4km SW of Horncastle. TF2167.

Woodhall *N.Yorks.* ***Hamlet***, 2m/3km E of Askrigg. **62 A7** SD9790.

Woodhall *W.Yorks.* ***Locality***, 3m/4km NE of Bradford. SE2034.

Woodhall Hills *W.Yorks.* ***Hamlet***, 1m/2km S of Calverley. SE2035.

Woodhall Spa *Lincs.* Population: 3337. ***Small town***, 19c spa town, 6m/9km SW of Horncastle. **52 E6** TF1963.

Woodham *Bucks.* ***Settlement***, 8m/13km NW of Aylesbury. SP7018.

Woodham *Dur.* ***Locality***, 1m/2km N of Newton Aycliffe. **62 D4** NZ2826.

Woodham *Surr.* ***Suburb***, 3m/5km S of Chertsey. **22 D5** TQ0462.

Woodham Ferrers *Essex* ***Village***, 5m/8km NE of Wickford. **24 D2** TQ7999.

Woodham Mortimer *Essex* ***Village***, 3m/4km SW of Maldon. **24 E1** TL8104.
Woodham Walter *Essex* ***Village***, 3m/4km W of Maldon. **24 E1** TL8006.
Woodhaven *Fife* ***Suburb***, in central area of Newport-on-Tay. **83 F5** NO4126.
Woodhead *Aber.* ***Locality***, 1m/2km SE of New Aberdour. **99 G4** NJ8962.
Woodhead *Aber.* ***Village***, 8m/13km SE of Turriff and 2m/3km E of Fyvie. **91 F1** NJ7938.
Woodhead *Derbys.* ***Locality***, in valley of River Etherow, beside Woodhead Reservoir, 5m/8km NE of Glossop. SK0999.
Woodhead *Staffs.* ***Suburb***, adjoining to N of Cheadle. SK0144.
Woodhenge *Wilts.* ***Historic/prehistoric site***, ancient earthwork (English Heritage) dating from Neolithic period, to S of Durrington and 1m/2km N of Amesbury. Consists of external back and inside six concentric oval sets of postholes which are now marked out by concrete pillars. **20 E7** SU1543.
Woodhey *Mersey.* ***Suburb***, 2m/3km S of Birkenhead. SJ3285.
Woodhey Green *Ches.* ***Settlement***, 2m/3km E of Croxley Green. SJ5752.
Woodhill *Gt.Man.* ***Suburb***, 1m/2km N of Bury town centre. SD7912.
Woodhill *Shrop.* ***Locality***, 5m/9km S of Bridgnorth. **39 G7** SO7384.
Woodhill *Som.* ***Hamlet***, adjoining to NE of Stoke St. Gregory. ST3527.
Woodhorn *Northumb.* ***Village***, 1m/2km NW of Newbiggin-by-the-Sea. **71 H5** NZ3088.
Woodhorn Demesne *Northumb.* ***Locality***, 1km S of Woodhorn. NZ3088.
Woodhouse *Cumb.* ***Hamlet***, 1km E of Heversham, 6m/9km S of Kendal. **55 J1** SD5183.
Woodhouse *Leics.* ***Village***, 3m/5km S of Loughborough. **41 H4** SK5415.
Woodhouse *N.Lincs.* ***Hamlet***, 1km N of Belton, 3m/4km N of Epworth. SE7808.
Woodhouse *S.Yorks.* ***Suburb***, 4m/7km E of Sheffield city centre. **51 G4** SK4285.
Woodhouse *W.Yorks.* ***Suburb***, 1km SE of Brighouse town centre. SE1421.
Woodhouse *W.Yorks.* ***Suburb***, 1m/2km N of Leeds city centre. University of Leeds complex on S side. SE2835.
Woodhouse *W.Yorks.* ***Suburb***, SE district of Normanton. SE3822.
Woodhouse Down *S.Glos.* ***Hamlet***, 1m/2km NE of Almondsbury. Site of Roman villa 1km NE. ST6185.
Woodhouse Eaves *Leics.* Population: 1780. ***Village***, 4m/6km S of Loughborough. **41 H4** SK5314.
Woodhouse Green *Staffs.* ***Settlement***, 4m/6km E of Congleton. SJ9162.
Woodhouse Mill *S.Yorks.* ***Suburb***, adjoining to NE of Woodhouse, 5m/8km E of Sheffield city centre. SK4285.
Woodhouses *Cumb.* ***Locality***, 1m/2km N of Thursby. NY3252.
Woodhouses *Dur.* ***Hamlet***, 1m/2km SW of Bishop Auckland. NZ1828.
Woodhouses *Gt.Man.* ***Suburb***, 2m/3km SW of Sale town centre. SJ7690.
Woodhouses *Gt.Man.* ***Village***, 1m/2km SE of Failsworth. SD9100.
Woodhouses *Staffs.* ***Hamlet***, 2m/4km W of Lichfield. SK0809.
Woodhouses *Staffs.* ***Hamlet***, 1km E of Yoxall. **40 D4** SK1518.
Woodhuish *Devon* ***Settlement***, 3m/4km S of Brixham. **5 K5** SX9152.
Woodhurst *Cambs.* ***Village***, 3m/5km N of St. Ives. **33 G1** TL3176.
Woodingdean *B. & H.* ***Suburb***, NE district of Brighton. **13 G6** TQ3605.
Woodington *Hants.* ***Settlement***, 3m/4km W of Romsey. SU3120.
Woodkirk *W.Yorks.* ***Locality***, 2m/3km S of Morley. SE2725.
Woodland *Devon* ***Hamlet***, 2m/4km E of Ashburton. **5 H4** SX7968.
Woodland *Dur.* ***Village***, 6m/10km N of Barnard Castle. **62 B4** NZ0726.
Woodland *Kent* ***Settlement***, 1km W of Lyminge. TR1441.
Woodland Fell *Cumb.* ***Open space***, moorland 4m/6km NE of Broughton in Furness. **55 F1** SD2689.
Woodland Fell *Dur.* ***Open space***, moorland to S of Hamsterley Forest. **62 B4** NZ0325.
Woodland Head *Devon* ***Hamlet***, 4m/7km SW of Crediton. SX7796.
Woodland Street *Som.* ***Settlement***, 3m/4km SE of Glastonbury. ST5437.
Woodlands *Dorset* ***Village***, 3m/4km S of Cranborne. **10 B4** SU0509.
Woodlands *Gt.Lon.* ***Suburb***, in borough of Hounslow, 1m/2km E of Hounslow town centre. TQ1575.
Woodlands *Hants.* ***Hamlet***, 3m/4km SW of Totton. **10 E3** SU3211.
Woodlands *Mersey.* ***Suburb***, 7m/11km E of Liverpool city centre. SJ4487.
Woodlands *N.Yorks.* ***Suburb***, 1m/2km E of Harrogate town centre. SE3254.
Woodlands *Shrop.* ***Locality***, 3m/4km S of Bridgnorth. **39 G7** SO7188.
Woodlands *Som.* ***Hamlet***, at foot of Quantock Hills, 2m/3km NW of Nether Stowey. ST1640.
Woodlands *Som.* ***Locality***, consists of settlements of East and West Woodlands, 3m/4km S of Frome. ST7844.
Woodlands *S.Yorks.* ***Locality***, in Adwick le Street, 4m/6km NW of Doncaster. SE5307.
Woodlands *W.Yorks.* ***Suburb***, 1km N of Halifax town centre. SE0926.
Woodlands *Wrex.* ***Locality***, 2m/4km N of Wrexham. SJ3153.
Woodlands Leisure Park *Devon* ***Leisure/recreation***, 60 acre or 24 hectare theme park, 4m/6km W of Dartmouth, featuring indoor and outdoor attractions divided into twelve play zones. Also large wildlife collection and bee observatory. **5 J5** SX8151.
Woodlands Park *W. & M.* ***Village***, 2m/4km SW of Maidenhead. **22 B4** SU8578.
Woodlands St. Mary *W.Berks.* ***Hamlet***, 4m/6km N of Hungerford. SU3474.
Woodlane *Staffs.* ***Hamlet***, 1m/2km N of Yoxall. SK1420.
Woodleigh *Devon* ***Village***, 3m/5km N of Kingsbridge. **5 H6** SX7348.
Woodlesford *W.Yorks.* ***Locality***, on River Aire, 5m/9km SE of Leeds. **57 J7** SE3629.
Woodley *Gt.Man.* ***Suburb***, 2m/3km S of Hyde. SJ9492.
Woodley *W'ham* ***Suburb***, 3m/5km E of Reading. **22 A4** SU7673.
Woodmancote *Glos.* ***Suburb***, S district of Dursley. ST7597.
Woodmancote *Glos.* ***Village***, 4m/6km NE of Cheltenham. **29 J6** SO9727.
Woodmancote *Glos.* ***Village***, 4m/7km N of Cirencester. **20 D1** SP0008.
Woodmancote *W.Suss.* ***Village***, 2m/3km NE of Emsworth. **11 J4** SU7707.
Woodmancote *W.Suss.* ***Village***, 2m/3km SE of Henfield. **13 F5** TQ2314.
Woodmancott *Hants.* ***Hamlet***, 4m/6km NE of Micheldever. **21 J7** SU5642.
Woodmansey *E.Riding* ***Village***, 2m/3km SE of Beverley. **59 G6** TA0537.
Woodmansgreen *W.Suss.* ***Hamlet***, 3m/5km SE of Liphook. SU8627.
Woodmansterne *Surr.* ***Village***, 1m/2km E of Banstead. **23 F6** TQ2759.
Woodmanton *Devon* ***Settlement***, 3m/5km N of Exmouth town centre. SY0185.
Woodmarsh *Wilts.* ***Locality***, 2m/3km S of Trowbridge. ST8555.
Woodmer End *Beds.* ***Locality***, adjoining to NW of Shillington, 3m/5km SE of Clophill. TL1234.
Woodmill *Staffs.* ***Hamlet***, 1m/2km N of Yoxall. SK1320.
Woodminton *Wilts.* ***Settlement***, 1m/2km SW of Bowerchalke. **10 B2** SU0022.
Woodmoor *Shrop.* ***Settlement***, 7m/11km SW of Minsterley. **38 B5** SJ2700.
Woodnesborough *Kent* ***Village***, 2m/3km SE of Sandwich. **15 H2** TR3056.
Woodnewton *Northants.* ***Village***, 4m/7km N of Oundle. **42 D6** TL0394.
Woodnook *Lancs.* ***Suburb***, adjoining to S of Accrington. SD7627.
Woodperry *Oxon.* ***Settlement***, 5m/7km NE of Oxford. Site of Roman building to E. SP5710.
Woodplumpton *Lancs.* ***Village***, 4m/7km NW of Preston. **55 J6** SD5034.
Woodrising *Norf.* ***Hamlet***, 2m/4km NW of Hingham. Site of Roman building 1m/2km W. **44 D5** TF9803.
Woodrow *Dorset* ***Hamlet***, 4m/6km SW of Sturminster Newton. ST7409.
Woodrow *Worcs.* ***Suburb***, 2m/3km SE of Redditch town centre. SP0565.
Woods Bank *W.Mid.* ***Suburb***, 1km SW of Darlaston town centre. SO9796.
Wood's Corner *E.Suss.* ***Hamlet***, 6m/9km NW of Battle. TQ6619.
Woods Eaves *Here.* ***Settlement***, 1m/2km W of Eardisley. SO2849.
Wood's Green *E.Suss.* ***Hamlet***, 1m/2km N of Wadhurst. TQ6333.
Woods Moor *Gt.Man.* ***Suburb***, 1m/2km SE of Stockport town centre. SJ9087.
Woodseats *Derbys.* ***Settlement***, 3m/5km SE of Hyde. SJ9992.
Woodseaves *Shrop.* ***Settlement***, 4m/6km SE of Market Drayton. **39 F2** SJ6830.
Woodseaves *Staffs.* ***Village***, 3m/5km SW of Eccleshall. **39 G3** SJ7925.
Woodsend *Wilts.* ***Settlement***, 3m/5km W of Aldbourne. **21 F4** SU2275.
Woodsetton *W.Mid.* ***Suburb***, in NW part of Dudley. SO9293.
Woodsetts *S.Yorks.* ***Village***, 3m/5km NW of Worksop. **51 H4** SK5583.
Woodsford *Dorset* ***Village***, on River Frome, 5m/7km E of Dorchester. **9 G5** SY7690.
Woodside *Aberdeen* ***Suburb***, 2m/3km NW of Aberdeen city centre. **91 H4** NJ9109.
Woodside *Beds.* ***Settlement***, 2m/3km SW of Luton town centre. TL0718.
Woodside *Brack.F.* ***Village***, on W edge of Windsor Great Park, 2m/3km N of Ascot. **22 C4** SU9371.
Woodside *Cumb.* ***Settlement***, 1m/2km SE of Maryport. NY0434.
Woodside *Derbys.* ***Settlement***, 6m/9km NE of Derby. SK3943.
Woodside *D. & G.* ***Settlement***, 4m/7km E of Dumfries. **69 F6** NY0475.
Woodside *Dur.* ***Settlement***, 2m/3km W of Bishop Auckland. NZ1729.
Woodside *Fife* ***Suburb***, SE district of Glenrothes. **82 D7** NO2800.
Woodside *Gt.Lon.* ***Suburb***, in borough of Croydon, 2m/3km NE of Croydon town centre. TQ3467.
Woodside *Hants.* ***Suburb***, 1m/2km S of Lymington. SZ3294.
Woodside *Herts.* ***Settlement***, 2m/3km SE of Hatfield. **23 F1** TL2506.
Woodside *N.Ayr.* ***Settlement***, 1km N of Beith. **74 B5** NS3455.
Woodside *P. & K.* ***Village***, adjoining to N of Burrelton, 2m/3km SW of Coupar Angus. **82 C4** NO2037.
Woodside *Shrop.* ***Settlement***, 1km SE of Clun. **28 C1** SO3080.
Woodside *Tel. & W.* ***Suburb***, of Telford, to W of Madeley. SJ6804.
Woodside *W.Mid.* ***Suburb***, 2m/3km SW of Dudley town centre. **40 B7** SO9288.
Woodside Green *Kent* ***Settlement***, 1m/2km NE of Lenham. TQ9053.
Woodspring Priory *N.Som.* ***Ecclesiastical building***, remains of priory, 3m/5km N of Burnham-on-Sea. **19 G5** ST3466.
Woodstock *Oxon.* Population: 2898. ***Small town***, 8m/13km NW of Oxford. Oxford City and County Museum. Interesting 17c and 18c buildings. **31 F7** SP4416.
Woodstock *Pembs.* ***Hamlet***, 1m/2km N of Walton East. SN0225.
Woodstock Slop *Pembs.* ***Hamlet***, 8m/12km NE of Haverfordwest. **16 D2** SN0225.
Woodston *Peter.* ***Suburb***, S district of Peterborough. **42 E6** TL1897.
Woodthorpe *Derbys.* ***Locality***, 1m/2km NW of Clay Cross. SK3864.
Woodthorpe *Derbys.* ***Locality***, 1m/2km E of Staveley. **51 G5** SK4574.
Woodthorpe *Leics.* ***Settlement***, 2m/3km S of Loughborough. **41 H4** SK5417.
Woodthorpe *Lincs.* ***Settlement***, 3m/5km N of Alford. Moated hall to NE. TF4380.
Woodthorpe *S.Yorks.* ***Suburb***, 3m/4km SE of Sheffield city centre. SK3985.
Woodton *Norf.* ***Village***, 4m/7km NW of Bungay. **45 G6** TM2993.
Woodtown *Aber.* ***Settlement***, 2m/3km N of Edzell. **90 E7** NO6072.
Woodtown *Devon* ***Settlement***, 3m/4km E of Bideford. **6 C3** SS4925.
Woodvale *Mersey.* ***Suburb***, 4m/7km SW of Southport town centre. Airfield to S. SD3110.
Woodville *Derbys.* ***Locality***, 1m/2km E of Swadlincote. **41 F4** SK3119.
Woodwall Green *Staffs.* ***Settlement***, 3m/5km NW of Eccleshall. SJ7831.
Woodwalton *Cambs.* ***Village***, 6m/9km N of Huntingdon. **43 F7** TL2180.
Woodwick *Ork.* ***Settlement***, on Mainland, 6m/10km N of Finstown. HY3823.
Woodworth Green *Ches.* ***Settlement***, 1km SE of Bunbury. SJ5757.
Woody Bay *Devon* ***Settlement***, on N coast, on edge of National Trust property around bay of same name, 3m/5km W of Lynton. **6 E1** SS6749.
Woodyates *Dorset* ***Hamlet***, 3m/4km NE of Sixpenny Handley. **10 B3** SU0219.
Woofferton *Shrop.* ***Village***, 4m/6km S of Ludlow. **28 E2** SO5268.
Wookey *Som.* ***Village***, 2m/3km W of Wells. **19 J7** ST5145.
Wookey Hole *Som.* ***Village***, on S side of Mendip Hills, 2m/3km NW of Wells. Limestone cave (floodlit) at N end of village; source of River Axe. **19 J7** ST5347.
Wool *Dorset* Population: 2097. ***Village***, on River Frome, 5m/8km W of Wareham. **9 H6** SY8486.
Woolacombe *Devon* ***Town***, resort on Morte Bay, 5m/7km SW of Ilfracombe. Extensive sands to S, largely National Trust. **6 C1** SS4543.
Woolage Green *Kent* ***Hamlet***, 7m/11km NW of Dover. **15 H3** TR2349.
Woolage Village *Kent* ***Settlement***, 1m/2km S of Aylesham. TR2350.
Woolaston *Glos.* ***Village***, 4m/6km SW of Lydney. **19 J2** ST5899.
Woolaston Slade *Glos.* ***Settlement***, 1m/2km NW of Woolaston. SO5700.
Woolavington *Som.* Population: 2082. ***Village***, 4m/7km NE of Bridgwater. **19 G7** ST3441.
Woolbeding *W.Suss.* ***Hamlet***, 1m/2km NW of Midhurst. **12 B4** SU8722.
Woolbist Law *Northumb.* ***Mountain***, in Cheviot Hills, 2m/3km S of Blindburn. Height 1420 feet or 433 metres. **70 D3** NT8207.
Woolcotts *Som.* ***Hamlet***, on Exmoor, 1m/2km E of Brompton Regis, to NW of Wimbleball Lake. SS9631.
Wooldale *W.Yorks.* ***Village***, 1m/2km NE of Holmfirth. SE1509.
Wooler *Northumb.* Population: 1868. ***Small town***, market town on Wooler Water, 15m/24km NW of Alnwick. Centre for fishing on River Till. **70 E1** NT9928.
Woolfall Heath *Mersey.* ***Suburb***, 2m/3km W of Prescot. SJ4392.
Woolfardisworthy *Devon* ***Village***, 3m/4km SE of Clovelly. Pronounced, and occasionally spelt, Woolsery. **6 B3** SS3321.
Woolfardisworthy *Devon* ***Village***, 5m/9km N of Crediton. **7 G5** SS8208.
Woolfold *Gt.Man.* ***Suburb***, 1m/2km NW of Bury town centre. SD7811.
Woolfords Cottages *S.Lan.* ***Settlement***, 7m/11km N of Carnwath. **75 J5** NT0057.
Woolgarston *Dorset* ***Settlement***, 2m/3km E of Corfe Castle. SY9881.
Woolgreaves *W.Yorks.* ***Suburb***, 3m/4km S of Wakefield city centre. SE3416.
Woolhampton *W.Berks.* ***Village***, 6m/10km E of Newbury. **21 J5** SU5766.
Woolhope *Here.* ***Village***, 7m/11km SE of Hereford. **29 F5** SO6135.
Woolland *Dorset* ***Village***, 5m/7km S of Sturminster Newton. **9 G4** ST7706.
Woollard *B. & N.E.Som.* ***Village***, 3m/5km S of Keynsham. **19 K5** ST6364.
Woollaton *Devon* ***Hamlet***, 3m/5km SE of Stibb Cross. **6 C4** SS4712.

Woollensbrook *Herts.* ***Settlement***, 1m/2km NW of Hoddesdon town centre. TL3609.
Woolley *B. & N.E.Som.* ***Hamlet***, 3m/4km N of Bath. **20 A5** ST7468.
Woolley *Cambs.* ***Hamlet***, 6m/9km W of Huntingdon. **32 E1** TL1574.
Woolley *Cornw.* ***Hamlet***, 5m/8km S of Hartland. SS2516.
Woolley *Derbys.* ***Hamlet***, on W side of Ogston Reservoir, 3m/4km SW of Clay Cross. SK3760.
Woolley *W.Yorks.* ***Village***, 5m/8km S of Wakefield. **51 F1** SE3213.
Woolley *Wilts.* ***Suburb***, E district of Bradford-on-Avon. ST8361.
Woolley Bridge *Derbys.* ***Suburb***, on River Etherow, adjoining to SE of Hollingworth. SK0195.
Woolley Down *W.Berks.* ***Open space***, hillslope 4m/7km S of Wantage. **21 H3** SU4081.
Woolley Green *Wilts.* ***Hamlet***, to N of Woolley, 1km NE of Bradford-on-Avon. ST8361.
Woolley Green *W. & M.* ***Settlement***, 3m/4km W of Maidenhead. SU8580.
Woolmer Green *Herts.* ***Village***, 2m/3km NE of Welwyn. **33 F7** TL2518.
Woolmere Green *Worcs.* ***Village***, 4m/7km E of Droitwich Spa. **29 J2** SO9662.
Woolmersdon *Som.* ***Settlement***, 1km NW of North Petherton. **8 B1** ST2833.
Woolpack *Kent* ***Settlement***, 1km S of Biddenden. TQ8537.
Woolpit *Suff.* ***Village***, 5m/9km NW of Stowmarket. **34 D2** TL9762.
Woolpit Green *Suff.* ***Settlement***, 1km S of Woolpit. TL9761.
Woolpit Heath *Suff.* ***Hamlet***, 1m/2km SE of Woolpit. TL9861.
Woolscott *Warks.* ***Settlement***, 5m/7km S of Rugby. **31 F2** SP4967.
Woolsery *Devon Occasional spelling of Woolfardisworthy, qv.*
Woolsgrove *Devon* ***Hamlet***, 3m/5km NW of Crediton. SS7902.
Woolsington *T. & W. See Newcastle International Airport.*
Woolsington Airport *T. & W. Former name of Newcastle International Airport, qv*
Woolstaston *Shrop.* ***Village***, 3m/5km N of Church Stretton. **38 D6** SO4598.
Woolsthorpe *Lincs.* ***Village***, 5m/8km W of Grantham. **42 B2** SK8333.
Woolsthorpe *Lincs.* ***Village***, 1m/2km NW of Colsterworth. **42 C3** SK9224.
Woolsthorpe Manor *Lincs.* ***Historic house***, 7m/11km S of Grantham. Small early 17c house (National Trust), birthplace of Isaac Newton, 1642. **42 C3** SK9224.
Woolston *Devon* ***Hamlet***, 2m/3km SW of Kingsbridge. SX7141.
Woolston *Shrop.* ***Hamlet***, 4m/6km SE of Oswestry. **38 C3** SJ3224.
Woolston *Shrop.* ***Hamlet***, 3m/5km N of Craven Arms. **38 D7** SO4287.
Woolston *S'ham.* ***Suburb***, SE district of Southampton across River Itchen. **11 F3** SU4310.
Woolston *Warr.* ***Suburb***, in E part of Warrington. **49 F4** SJ6489.
Woolston Green *Devon* ***Village***, 3m/4km E of Buckfastleigh. **5 H4** SX7766.
Woolstone *Glos.* ***Village***, 5m/8km N of Cheltenham. SO9630.
Woolstone *M.K.* ***Suburb***, 2m/3km E of Milton Keynes city centre; includes villages of Great and Little Woolstone. SP8739.
Woolstone *Oxon.* ***Village***, 7m/11km W of Wantage. Site of Roman villa to W. **21 F3** SU2987.
Wooltack Point *Pembs.* ***Coastal feature***, headland on mainland at S end of St. Brides Bay opposite Midland Isle and Skomer Island. **16 A4** SM7509.
Woolton *Mersey.* ***Suburb***, 5m/9km SE of Liverpool city centre. **48 D4** SJ4286.
Woolton Hill *Hants.* ***Village***, 1m/2km NW of Highclere. **21 H5** SU4261.
Woolton Park *Mersey.* ***Suburb***, adjoining to N of Woolton. SJ4286.
Woolverstone *Suff.* ***Village***, 4m/7km S of Ipswich. **35 F5** TM1838.
Woolverton *Som.* ***Village***, 4m/6km N of Frome. **20 A6** ST7954.
Woolwich *Gt.Lon.* ***Suburb***, on S bank of River Thames, in borough of Greenwich, 8m/14km E of Charing Cross. Ferry for vehicles to North Woolwich. **23 H4** TQ4378.
Woonton *Here.* ***Village***, 4m/7km SE of Kington. **28 C3** SO3552.
Wooperton *Northumb.* ***Settlement***, 6m/10km SE of Wooler. **71 F1** NU0420.
Woore *Shrop.* ***Village***, 6m/10km NE of Market Drayton. **39 G1** SJ7342.
Wootten Green *Suff.* ***Hamlet***, 1km S of Stradbroke. TM2372.
Wootton *Beds.* Population: 3765. ***Village***, 4m/7km SW of Bedford. **32 D4** TL0045.
Wootton *Hants.* ***Settlement***, on S edge of New Forest, 4m/7km SW of Brockenhurst. **10 D5** SZ2498.
Wootton *I.o.W.* ***Village***, 3m/5km SW of East Cowes. SZ5492.
Wootton *Kent* ***Village***, 6m/10km N of Folkestone. **15 H3** TR2246.
Wootton *N.Lincs.* ***Village***, 3m/5km SE of Barrow upon Humber. **52 D1** TA0816.
Wootton *Northants.* Population: 1743. ***Suburb***, S district of Northampton. **31 J3** SP7656.
Wootton *Oxon.* ***Village***, on River Glyme, 2m/3km N of Woodstock. **31 F7** SP4319.
Wootton *Oxon.* ***Village***, 3m/5km N of Abingdon. **21 H1** SP4701.
Wootton *Shrop.* ***Hamlet***, 4m/7km NW of Ludlow. **28 D1** SO4578.
Wootton *Shrop.* ***Settlement***, 3m/5km E of Oswestry. SJ3327.
Wootton *Staffs.* ***Settlement***, 1m/2km S of Eccleshall. **40 A3** SJ8327.
Wootton *Staffs.* ***Village***, 5m/8km W of Ashbourne. **40 D1** SK1045.
Wootton Bassett *Wilts.* Population: 10,524. ***Town***, Georgian market town 6m/9km W of Swindon. Museum in unusual early 18c town hall. **20 D3** SU0682.
Wootton Bridge *I.o.W.* Population: 4353. ***Locality***, 3m/5km W of Ryde. **11 G5** SZ5491.
Wootton Common *I.o.W.* ***Hamlet***, 3m/4km NE of Newport. **11 G5** SZ5391.
Wootton Courtenay *Som.* ***Village***, on N slopes of Exmoor, 3m/5km SW of Minehead. **7 H1** SS9343.
Wootton Fitzpaine *Dorset* ***Village***, 3m/4km NE of Lyme Regis. **8 C5** SY3695.
Wootton Glanville *Dorset Alternative name for Glanvilles Wootton, qv.*
Wootton Green *Beds.* ***Hamlet***, 5m/8km SW of Bedford. **32 D4** SP9943.
Wootton Rivers *Wilts.* ***Village***, on Kennet and Avon Canal, 3m/5km NE of Pewsey. **20 E5** SU1963.
Wootton St. Lawrence *Hants.* ***Village***, 3m/5km W of Basingstoke. **21 J6** SU5953.
Wootton Wawen *Warks.* ***Village***, 2m/3km S of Henley-in-Arden. **30 C2** SP1563.
Worbarrow *Dorset* ***Locality***, at E end of Worbarrow Bay, 5m/8km SW of Wool. SY8779.
Worbarrow Bay *Dorset* ***Bay***, 6m/9km SW of Wareham. Locality of Worbarrow at E end of the bay. **9 H7** SY8779.
Worcester *Worcs.* Population: 82,661. ***City***, on River Severn, 24m/38km SW of Birmingham. Shopping, cultural, sports and industrial centre; industries include porcelain and sauces and condiments. 18c guildhall. Cathedral mainly Early English. Three Choirs Festival held here every third year. Sir Edward Elgar born here. **29 H3** SO8555.
Worcester Cathedral *Worcs.* ***Ecclesiastical building***, in centre of Worcester, overlooking River Severn. Fine 14c tower and much of building dates from this period but earliest part of present church dates from c. 1080. Notable features include crypt, misericords, chapter house and tomb of King John. **29 H3** SO8454.
Worcester Park *Gt.Lon.* ***Suburb***, in borough of Sutton, 2m/3km NW of Sutton town centre. **23 F5** TQ2265.
Worcester Woods Country Park *Worcs.* ***Leisure/recreation***, country park adjoining to E of Worcester, with over 100 acres or 40 hectares of woodlands and a pond. **29 H3** SO8754.
Worcestershire County Museum *Worcs.* ***Other feature of interest***, in Bishop's Palace, Hartlebury Castle, 1m/2km E of Stourport-on-Severn. Features cider mill, local history and crafts. **29 H1** SO8371.
Wordsley *W.Mid.* ***Suburb***, to SW of Dudley. **40 A7** SO8886.
Wordsworth House *Cumb.* ***Historic house***, Georgian house in Cockermouth, near River Derwent, in which poet William Wordsworth was born in 1770. **60 C3** NY1230.
Wordwell *Suff.* ***Settlement***, 5m/8km N of Bury St. Edmunds. **34 C1** TL8272.
Worfe *Shrop.* ***River***, rising near Shifnal and flowing first S, then W, into River Severn 2m/3km N of Bridgnorth. SO7295.
Worfield *Shrop.* ***Village***, 3m/5km NE of Bridgnorth. **39 G6** SO7595.
Worgret *Dorset* ***Settlement***, 1m/2km SW of Wareham. SY9086.
Work *Ork.* ***Settlement***, 2m/3km NE of Kirkwall, Mainland. **107 D6** HY4713.
Workhouse Common *Norf.* ***Hamlet***, 2m/3km N of Horning. TG3420.
Workhouse End *Beds.* ***Settlement***, SE end of Renhold, 4m/6km NE of Bedford. TL1052.
Workington *Cumb.* Population: 25,579. ***Town***, port on Solway Firth at mouth of River Derwent, 17m/27km W of Keswick. **60 B4** NX9928.
Worksop *Notts.* Population: 37,247. ***Town***, market town on River Ryton, at N end of The Dukeries, 25m/40km N of Nottingham. 14c priory gatehouse is unique. **51 H5** SK5879.
Worlaby *Lincs.* ***Hamlet***, 1m/2km N of Tetford and 7m/11km S of Louth. TF3476.
Worlaby *N.Lincs.* ***Village***, 4m/7km N of Brigg. **52 D1** TA0113.
Worlaby Carrs *N.Lincs.* ***Open space***, lowland between Weir Dyke and Elsham, 3m/5km N of Brigg. **52 C1** SE9813.
World's End ***Open space***, hillslope on border of Denbighshire and Wrexham, 6m/10km SW of Wrexham. **38 B1** SJ2447.
World's End *Bucks.* ***Settlement***, 1m/2km NW of Wendover. SP8509.
World's End *Gt.Lon.* ***Suburb***, in borough of Enfield, 1m/2km W of Enfield town centre and 10m/16km N of Charing Cross. TQ3096.
Worlds End *Hants.* ***Hamlet***, 2m/3km SW of Hambledon. **11 H3** SU6312.
World's End *W.Berks.* ***Hamlet***, 6m/9km N of Newbury. **21 H4** SU4876.
Worlds End *W.Mid.* ***Suburb***, 1m/2km NW of Solihull town centre. SP1480.
World's End *W.Suss.* ***Suburb***, residential locality to E of Burgess Hill. TQ3219.
Worle *N.Som.* ***Suburb***, E of Weston-super-Mare. **19 G5** ST3562.
Worlebury *N.Som.* ***Suburb***, NE district of Weston-super-Mare. ST3362.
Worleston *Ches.* ***Hamlet***, 3m/5km W of Crewe. **49 F7** SJ6556.
Worlingham *Suff.* ***Village***, 2m/3km E of Beccles. **45 J6** TM4489.
Worlington *Suff.* ***Village***, 1m/2km SW of Mildenhall. **33 K1** TL6973.
Worlingworth *Suff.* ***Village***, 5m/8km NW of Framlingham. **35 G2** TM2368.
Worm Gill *Cumb.* ***River***, rising from various sources on SW side of Ennerdale Fell, and flowing S to Scalderskew Wood, then W into River Calder, 3m/4km NE of Calder Bridge. **60 B6** NY0609.
Worm Hill *Sc.Bord.* ***Mountain***, overlooking Tweed valley, 1m/2km NW of Stanhope. Height 1774 feet or 541 metres. **75 K7** NT1130.
Worm Law *S.Lan.* ***Mountain***, partly wooded mass, 3m/4km NE of Forth. Height 1122 feet or 342 metres. **75 H5** NS9756.
Wormald Green *N.Yorks.* ***Hamlet***, 4m/7km S of Ripon. SE3064.
Wormbridge *Here.* ***Village***, 3m/5km NE of Pontrilas. **28 D5** SO4230.
Wormegay *Norf.* ***Village***, 6m/10km SE of King's Lynn. Remains of motte and bailey castle. **44 A4** TF6611.
Wormelow Tump *Here.* ***Hamlet***, 6m/10km S of Hereford. **28 D5** SO4930.
Wormhill *Derbys.* ***Village***, 4m/7km E of Buxton. **50 D5** SK1274.
Wormhill *Here.* ***Locality***, 5m/8km W of Hereford. SO4339.
Wormiehills *Angus* ***Locality***, 2m/3km SW of Arbroath. **83 H4** NO6138.
Wormingford *Essex* ***Village***, 6m/10km NW of Colchester. **34 D5** TL9331.
Worminghall *Bucks.* ***Village***, 5m/8km NW of Thame. **21 K1** SP6408.
Wormington *Glos.* ***Village***, 4m/6km W of Broadway. **30 B5** SP0436.
Worminster *Som.* ***Hamlet***, 2m/4km SE of Wells. **19 J7** ST5743.
Wormistone *Fife* ***Hamlet***, 1m/2km N of Crail. **83 H7** NO6109.
Wormit *Fife* ***Locality***, on S side of Firth of Tay, 2m/3km SW of Newport-on-Tay. **82 E5** NO3926.
Wormleighton *Warks.* ***Village***, 8m/13km N of Banbury. Remains of 16c manor house. Reservoir 1m/2km S. **31 F3** SP4453.
Wormley *Herts.* ***Suburb***, 2m/3km N of Cheshunt. **23 G1** TL3605.
Wormley *Surr.* ***Village***, 3m/4km S of Milford. **12 C3** SU9438.
Wormley Hill *S.Yorks.* ***Settlement***, 3m/4km NW of Thorne. SE6616.
Worms Head (Pen Pyrod). *Swan.* ***Coastal feature***, headland (National Trust) at W extremity of Gower peninsula, consisting of two connected rock ridges accessible from mainland at low tide. Blow-hole on outer ridge spouts tall column of water in rough weather. **17 G6** SS3887.
Wormshill *Kent* ***Village***, 3m/5km N of Harrietsham. **14 D2** TQ8857.
Wormsley *Here.* ***Village***, 7m/12km NW of Hereford. **28 D4** SO4247.
Worplesdon *Surr.* ***Village***, 3m/5km NW of Guildford. **22 C6** SU9753.
Worrall *S.Yorks.* ***Village***, 1m/2km S of Oughtibridge. **51 F3** SK3092.
Worsbrough *S.Yorks.* Population: 10,090. ***Locality***, adjoining to S of Barnsley. Includes localities of Worsbrough Bridge and Worsbrough Dale. **51 F2** SE3503.
Worsbrough Bridge *S.Yorks.* ***Locality***, 2m/3km S of Barnsley town centre. SE3503.
Worsbrough Dale *S.Yorks.* ***Locality***, 2m/3km SE of Barnsley town centre. SE3603.
Worsley *Gt.Man.* ***Town***, 6m/10km W of Manchester. Bridgewater Canal begun here by Brindley in 1759. **49 G2** SD7400.
Worsley Mesnes *Gt.Man.* ***Suburb***, 1m/2km SW of Wigan town centre. SD5704.
Worstead *Norf.* ***Village***, 3m/5km SE of North Walsham. **45 H3** TG3026.
Worsted Lodge *Cambs.* ***Settlement***, 4m/6km N of Great Abington. **33 J3** TL5251.
Worsthorne *Lancs.* ***Village***, 3m/5km E of Burnley. **56 D6** SD8732.
Worston *Devon* ***Hamlet***, 1m/2km NE of Yealmpton. SX5952.
Worston *Lancs.* ***Hamlet***, 2m/3km E of Clitheroe. **56 C5** SD7642.
Worswell *Devon* ***Settlement***, 1m/2km SE of Wembury across Wembury Bay. **5 F6** SX5347.
Worth *Kent* ***Village***, 1m/2km S of Sandwich. Site of Roman temple to S. **15 J2** TR3356.
Worth *Som.* ***Hamlet***, 3m/4km W of Wells. ST5045.
Worth *W.Suss.* ***Suburb***, 2m/3km E of Crawley. To SE, Worth Abbey, Roman Catholic school for boys. **13 G3** TQ3036.
Worth Hill *Som.* ***Mountain***, on Exmoor, 2m/3km SW of Withypool. Height 1279 feet or 390 metres. **7 G2** SS8133.
Worth Matravers *Dorset* ***Village***, near coast of Isle of Purbeck, 4m/6km W of Swanage. **9 J7** SY9777.
Wortham *Suff.* ***Village***, 3m/4km SW of Diss. **34 E1** TM0877.
Worthen *Shrop.* ***Village***, 7m/11km E of Welshpool. **38 C5** SJ3204.
Worthenbury *Wrex.* ***Village***, 4m/6km NE of Overton. **38 D1** SJ4246.
Worthing *Norf.* ***Hamlet***, 4m/7km N of East Dereham. **44 E4** TF9919.
Worthing *W.Suss.* Population: 95,732. ***Town***, seaside resort, 10m/17km W of Brighton. Well-known venue for bowls; major championships played here. Notable Regency architecture. **12 E6** TQ1402.
Worthing Museum and Art Gallery *W.Suss.* ***Other feature of interest***, museum of local history and archaeology to W of Worthing town centre. **12 E6** TQ1402.
Worthington *Leics.* ***Village***, 4m/7km NE of Ashby de la Zouch. **41 G3** SK4020.

W

Wymeswold *Leics.* ***Village***, 5m/8km NE of Loughborough. **41 J3** SK6023.
Wymington *Beds.* ***Village***, 2m/3km S of Rushden. **32 C2** SP9564.
Wymondham *Leics.* ***Village***, 6m/10km E of Melton Mowbray. Site of Roman building W of church. **42 B4** SK8518.
Wymondham *Norf.* Population: 10,159. ***Town***, historic town 9m/14km SW of Norwich. Agricultural centre. **45 F5** TG1001.
Wyndburgh Hill *Sc.Bord.* ***Mountain***, 3m/4km NW of Note o' the Gate. Height 1647 feet or 502 metres. **70 A3** NT5503.
Wyndham *Bridgend* ***Hamlet***, 4m/6km SW of Treorchy. **18 C2** SS9391.
Wyndham Park *V. of Glam.* ***Hamlet***, to S of Peterston-super-Ely across River Ely. ST0876.
Wynd's Bridge *Norf.* ***Locality***, 1m/2km NW of Wiggenhall St. Mary the Virgin. TF5715.
Wynford Eagle *Dorset* ***Hamlet***, 2m/3km SW of Maiden Newton. **8 E5** SY5895.
Wynn's Green *Here.* ***Locality***, 6m/9km SW of Bromyard. SO6047.
Wynnstay *Wrex.* ***Settlement***, 1km SE of Ruabon. **38 C1** SJ3142.
Wynyard *Stock.* ***Locality***, 4m/6km NW of Billingham. **63 F4** NZ4226.
Wyre *Lancs.* ***River***, issuing from Abbeystead Reservoir on W side of Forest of Bowland and flowing circuitously W into Irish Sea at Fleetwood. **55 G5** SD3251.
Wyre *Ork.* ***Island***, small inhabited island, 2m/3km E to W and 1m/2km N to S but tapering to a point at W end, lying off SE coast of Rousay across Wyre Sound. Remains of 12c Cubbie Roo's Castle. Ruined chapel (Historic Scotland), probably late 12c. **106 D5** HY4426.
Wyre Forest ***Forest/woodland***, heavily wooded area, on border of Shropshire and Worcestershire, to W of Bewdley. **29 G1** SO7476.
Wyre Piddle *Worcs.* ***Village***, 2m/3km NE of Pershore. **29 J4** SO9647.
Wyre Sound *Ork.* ***Sea feature***, strait separating Wyre and Rousay. **106 D5** HY4327.
Wyresdale Tower *Lancs.* ***Settlement***, 6m/9km E of Dolphinholme. **56 B4** SD6154.
Wysall *Notts.* ***Village***, 6m/10km NE of Loughborough. **41 J3** SK6027.
Wysg *Welsh form of Usk (River), qv.*
Wyson *Here.* ***Locality***, adjoining to W of Brimfield, 4m/7km S of Ludlow. **28 E2** SO5167.
Wytch Heath *Dorset* ***Open space***, wooded heath 2m/4km NE of Corfe Castle. **9 J6** SY9784.
Wythall *Worcs.* ***Village***, 5m/8km NE of Redditch. **30 B1** SP0774.
Wytham *Oxon.* ***Village***, 3m/5km NW of Oxford. **21 H1** SP4708.
Wythburn *Cumb.* ***Locality***, on E shore of Thirlmere near S end of lake. **60 E5** NY3213.
Wythburn Fells *Cumb.* ***Open space***, moorland at SW end of Thirlmere, 3m/5km N of Grasmere. **60 D5** NY3012.
Wythenshawe *Gt.Man.* ***Suburb***, 5m/8km SW of Manchester city centre. SJ8288.
Wyther Park *W.Yorks.* ***Suburb***, 2m/4km W of Leeds city centre. SE2534.
Wyton *Cambs.* ***Village***, 3m/4km E of Huntingdon. **33 F1** TL2772.
Wyton *E.Riding* ***Hamlet***, 3m/5km N of Hedon. TA1733.
Wyverstone *Suff.* ***Village***, 6m/9km N of Stowmarket. **34 E2** TM0467.
Wyverstone Green *Suff.* ***Settlement***, to S of Wyverstone. TM0467.
Wyverstone Street *Suff.* ***Village***, 1km W of Wyverstone. **34 E2** TM0467.
Wyville *Lincs.* ***Settlement***, 5m/7km SW of Grantham. **42 B3** SK8829.
Wyvis Forest *High.* ***Open space***, deer forest in Ross and Cromarty district to W of Loch Glass. **96 B4** NH4671.
Wyvis Lodge *High.* ***Settlement***, 9m/15km NE of Garve, at W end of Loch Glass. **96 B4** NH4873.

Y

Y Barri *V. of Glam. Welsh form of Barry, qv.*
Y Batel *Powys Welsh form of Battle, qv.*
Y Berwyn *See Berwyn.*
Y Bont-faen *Pembs. Alternative name for Pontfaen, qv.*
Y Bont-faen *V. of Glam. Welsh form of Cowbridge, qv.*
Y Bryn *Gwyn.* ***Settlement***, 1km S of Llanuwchllyn. **37 H3** SH8829.
Y Castellnewydd *Bridgend Welsh form of Newcastle, qv.*
Y Clas-ar-Wy *Powys Welsh form of Glasbury, qv.*
Y Clogydd *Powys* ***Mountain***, 1m/2km NE of Llangynog. Height 1955 feet or 596 metres. **37 K3** SJ0628.
Y Crwys *Swan. Welsh form of Three Crosses, qv.*
Y Ddraenen Wen *R.C.T. Welsh form of Hawthorn, qv.*
Y Ddwyryd *Denb. Welsh form of Druid, qv.*
Y Drenewydd *Cardiff Welsh form of Newton, qv.*
Y Drenewydd *Powys Welsh form of Newtown, qv.*
Y Drum *Cere.* ***Mountain***, rising to over 490 metres, 3m/4km E of Tregaron. **27 G3** SN7259.
Y Faenor *M.Tyd. Welsh form of Vaynor, qv.*
Y Fan (Van). *Powys* ***Locality***, 3m/5km N of Llanidloes. **37 J7** SN9487.
Y Farteg *Torfaen Welsh form of Varteg, qv.*
Y Felinheli (Also known as Port Dinorwig.) *Gwyn.* Population: 1664. ***Small town***, on Menai Strait, 4m/6km SW of Bangor. **46 D6** SH5267.
Y Fenni *Mon. Welsh form of Abergavenny, qv.*
Y Ferwig *Cere. Welsh form of Verwig, qv.*
Y Fflint *Flints. Welsh form of Flint, qv.*
Y Ffôr (Also known as Four Crosses or Fourcrosses.) *Gwyn.* ***Village***, 3m/5km NE of Pwllheli. **36 C2** SH3939.
Y Foel *Denb.* ***Mountain***, 3m/5km SE of Glyndyfrdwy. Height 1712 feet or 522 metres. **38 A2** SJ1839.
Y Foel *Powys* ***Mountain***, 4m/6km SE of Plynlimon. Height 1791 feet or 546 metres. **37 H7** SN8384.
Y Foel *Powys* ***Mountain***, 4m/6km E of Llandiloes. Height 1424 feet or 434 metres. **37 K7** SO0183.
Y Forlan *Pembs. Welsh form of Vorlan, qv.*
Y Gaer *Powys* ***Historic/prehistoric site***, ruins of Roman fort 3m/5km W of Brecon. First built c. AD 75 and rebuilt several times. Remains include parts of wall up to 10 feet or 3 metres high. **27 K6** SO0029.
Y Gamlas *Gwyn.* ***Bay***, shallow bay running from Llanbedrog in SW to Pwllheli in NE. **36 C2** SH3432.
Y Gamriw *Powys* ***Mountain***, 3m/4km S of Elan Village. Height 1981 feet or 604 metres. **27 J2** SN9461.
Y Garn *Gwyn.* ***Mountain***, 4m/6km NW of Beddgelert. Height 2076 feet or 633 metres. **46 D7** SH5552.
Y Garn *Gwyn.* ***Mountain***, containing Llyn Clyd and forming part of Glyder group, 4m/7km S of Bethesda. Height 3106 feet or 947 metres. **46 E7** SH6359.
Y Garn *Gwyn.* ***Mountain***, 3m/5km NW of Dolgellau. Height 2063 feet or 629 metres. **37 G3** SH7023.
Y Garn *Pembs. Welsh form of Roch, qv.*
Y Gelli *Powys Welsh form of Hay-on-Wye, qv.*
Y Goetre-hen *Bridgend Welsh form of Coytrahen, qv.*
Y Gribin *Gwyn.* ***Mountain***, 2m/3km NW of Dinas-Mawddwy. Height 1975 feet or 602 metres. **37 H4** SH8417.
Y Llethr *Gwyn.* ***Mountain***, 6m/10km SE of Harlech. Height 2473 feet or 754 metres. **37 F3** SH6625.
Y Mynydd Du *Welsh form of Black Mountain, qv.*
Y Parlwr Du *Flints. Welsh form of Point of Air, qv.*
Y Pigwn *Powys* ***Mountain***, 4m/7km SE of Llandovery. Site of Roman camps. Height 1351 feet or 412 metres. **27 H5** SN8231.
Y Pil *Bridgend Welsh form of Pyle, qv.*
Y Rhath *Cardiff Welsh form of Roath, qv.*
Y Rhiw *Gwyn. Alternative name for Rhiw, qv.*
Y Rhws *V. of Glam. Welsh form of Rhoose, qv.*
Y Ro Wen *Conwy* ***Mountain***, 4m/6km NE of Blaenau Ffestiniog. Height 1948 feet or 594 metres. **37 G1** SH7449.
Y Sblot *Cardiff Welsh form of Splott, qv.*
Y Sger *Bridgend Welsh form of Sker Point, qv.*
Y Trallwng *Powys Welsh form of Welshpool, qv.*
Y Transh *Torfaen Welsh form of Tranch, qv.*
Y Tymbl *Carmar. Welsh form of Tumble, qv.*
Y Waun *Wrex. Welsh form of Chirk, qv.*
Y Wig *V. of Glam. Welsh form of Wick, qv.*
Yaddlethorpe *N.Lincs.* ***Village***, 2m/4km S of Scunthorpe. **52 B2** SE8807.
Yafford *I.o.W.* ***Settlement***, 1m/2km SW of Shorwell. **11 F6** SZ4481.
Yafforth *N.Yorks.* ***Village***, 2m/3km W of Northallerton. **62 E7** SE3494.
Yair Hill Forest *Sc.Bord.* ***Forest/woodland***, 3m/5km NW of Selkirk. **76 C7** NT4333.
Yalberton *Torbay* ***Hamlet***, 2m/3km SW of Paignton. SX8658.
Yalding *Kent* ***Village***, on River Beult, near its confluence with River Medway, 5m/8km SW of Maidstone. **23 K7** TQ6950.
Yanley *N.Som.* ***Hamlet***, 3m/5km SW of Bristol. ST5569.
Yanwath *Cumb.* ***Hamlet***, 2m/3km S of Penrith. NY5127.
Yanworth *Glos.* ***Village***, 3m/4km W of Northleach. **30 B7** SP0713.
Yapham *E.Riding* ***Village***, 2m/3km NW of Pocklington. **58 D4** SE7852.
Yapton *W.Suss.* Population: 4532. ***Village***, 3m/5km W of Littlehampton. **12 C6** SU9703.
Yarbridge *I.o.W.* ***Locality***, on River Yar, 1km S of Brading. SZ6086.
Yarburgh *Lincs.* ***Village***, 4m/6km N of Louth. **53 G3** TF3593.
Yarcombe *Devon* ***Village***, at foot of steep hill, 5m/8km W of Chard. **8 B4** ST2408.
Yardley *W.Mid.* ***Suburb***, 4m/6km E of Birmingham city centre. **40 D7** SP1285.
Yardley Chase *Northants.* ***Open space***, 6m/10km SE of Northampton. **32 B3** SP8454.
Yardley Gobion *Northants.* ***Village***, 3m/5km NW of Stony Stratford. **31 J4** SP7644.
Yardley Hastings *Northants.* ***Village***, 4m/6km NW of Olney. **32 B3** SP8656.
Yardley Wharf *Northants.* ***Settlement***, on Grand Union Canal, 4m/6km N of Stony Stratford. SP7645.
Yardley Wood *W.Mid.* ***Suburb***, 5m/8km S of Birmingham city centre. SP1079.
Yardro *Powys* ***Settlement***, 5m/8km NW of Kington. **28 B3** SO2258.
Yardstone Knowe *Sc.Bord.* ***Mountain***, 3m/5km SW of Stow. Height 1683 feet or 513 metres. **76 C6** NT4042.
Yare *Norf.* ***River***, rising near Shipdham and flowing E round S side of Norwich and into North Sea at Gorleston, Great Yarmouth. **45 H5** TG5303.
Yarford *Som.* ***Hamlet***, 4m/6km NW of Taunton. ST2029.
Yarkhill *Here.* ***Village***, 6m/10km E of Hereford. **29 F4** SO6042.
Yarlet *Staffs.* ***Hamlet***, 1m/2km E of Whitgreave. **40 B3** SJ9128.
Yarley *Som.* ***Hamlet***, 3m/5km W of Wells. **19 J7** ST5045.
Yarlington *Som.* ***Village***, 4m/6km W of Wincanton. **9 F2** ST6529.
Yarlside *Cumb.* ***Mountain***, on Howgill Fells, 4m/7km N of Sedbergh. Height 2096 feet or 639 metres. **61 H7** SD6898.
Yarm *Stock.* ***Small town***, old market town with elegant Georgian houses, in loop of River Tees, 4m/7km S of Stockton-on-Tees. **63 F5** NZ4112.
Yarmouth *I.o.W.* ***Small town***, coastal resort 9m/14km W of Newport and 4m/7km SE of Lymington across The Solent. Car ferry to Lymington. 16c castle (English Heritage). **10 E6** SZ3589.
Yarmouth Castle *I.o.W.* ***Castle***, castle (English Heritage) built in 1547 as coastal defence against French by Henry VIII, on W side of Yarmouth. Exhibits paintings of island and photographs of old Yarmouth. **10 E6** SZ3589.
Yarmouth Roads *Norf.* ***Sea feature***, anchorage off Great Yarmouth. **45 K5** TG5207.
Yarnacott *Devon* ***Hamlet***, 5m/8km E of Barnstaple. **6 E2** SS6230.
Yarnbrook *Wilts.* ***Hamlet***, 2m/3km SE of Trowbridge. **20 B6** ST8655.
Yarner *Devon* ***Hamlet***, 3m/4km W of Bovey Tracey. To N is Yarner Wood, which is National Nature Reserve. SX7778.
Yarner Wood *Devon* ***Nature reserve***, to N of Yarner, 2m/4km W of Bovey Tracey. SX7778.
Yarnfield *Staffs.* ***Village***, 3m/4km SW of Stone. **40 A2** SJ8632.
Yarnscombe *Devon* ***Village***, 5m/8km NE of Great Torrington. **6 D3** SS5623.
Yarnton *Oxon.* Population: 2431. ***Village***, 4m/7km NW of Oxford. **31 F7** SP4712.
Yarpole *Here.* ***Village***, 4m/6km NW of Leominster. **28 D2** SO4764.
Yarrow *Sc.Bord.* ***Settlement***, on Yarrow Water, 7m/11km W of Selkirk. **69 J1** NT3527.
Yarrow *Som.* ***Hamlet***, 1km S of Mark and 3m/5km W of Wedmore. ST3846.
Yarrow Feus *Sc.Bord.* ***Settlement***, 1m/2km SW of Yarrow. **69 J1** NT3425.
Yarrow Water *Sc.Bord.* ***River***, issuing from St. Mary's Loch and running E through Ettrick Forest to Ettrick Water, 2m/3km SW of Selkirk. **69 J1** NT3527.
Yarrowford *Sc.Bord.* ***Hamlet***, 4m/6km NW of Selkirk. **69 K1** NT4030.
Yarsop *Here.* ***Settlement***, 8m/13km NW of Hereford. **28 D4** SO4047.
Yarty *Devon* ***River***, rising N of Yarcombe and flowing S into River Axe, 1m/2km SW of Axminster. **8 B4** SY2897.
Yarwell *Northants.* ***Village***, 1m/2km S of Wansford. **42 D6** TL0697.
Yate *S.Glos.* ***Suburb***, adjoining to W of Chipping Sodbury. **20 A3** ST7182.
Yatehouse Green *Ches.* ***Settlement***, 2m/3km N of Middlewich. SJ7068.
Yateley *Hants.* Population: 15,663. ***Locality***, residential locality 3m/5km W of Camberley. Blackbushe Airport 2km SW. **22 B5** SU8160.
Yateley Country Park *Hants.* ***Leisure/recreation***, almost 500 acres or 202 hectares chiefly comprising heather, gorse, woodland and several small ponds, 1m/2km SE of Yateley. **22 B6** SU8259.
Yatesbury *Wilts.* ***Village***, 3m/4km NW of Avebury. **20 D4** SU0671.
Yattendon *W.Berks.* ***Village***, 5m/9km W of Pangbourne. **21 J4** SU5574.
Yatton *Here.* ***Hamlet***, 6m/10km NW of Leominster. **28 D2** SO4366.
Yatton *Here.* ***Locality***, 5m/8km NE of Ross-on-Wye. SO6330.
Yatton *N.Som.* Population: 6826. ***Village***, 4m/7km S of Clevedon. **19 H5** ST4365.
Yatton Keynell *Wilts.* ***Village***, 4m/6km NW of Chippenham. **20 B4** ST8676.
Yatton Wood *Here.* ***Forest/woodland***, 4m/6km NE of Ross-on-Wye. **29 F5** SO6229.
Yaverland *I.o.W.* ***Village***, 1m/2km NE of Sandown. 17c manor house. **11 H6** SZ6185.
Yawl *Devon* ***Settlement***, 2m/3km NW of Lyme Regis. SY3194.
Yawthorpe *Lincs.* ***Hamlet***, 2m/3km E of Corringham. SK8992.
Yaxham *Norf.* ***Village***, 2m/3km SE of East Dereham. **44 E4** TG0010.
Yaxley *Cambs.* Population: 7041. ***Village***, 4m/7km S of Peterborough. **42 E6** TL1892.
Yaxley *Suff.* ***Village***, 2m/3km W of Eye. **35 F1** TM1274.
Yazor *Here.* ***Village***, 8m/13km NW of Hereford. **28 D4** SO4046.
Yeabridge *Som.* ***Hamlet***, 1km SE of South Petherton. ST4415.
Yeading *Gt.Lon.* ***Suburb***, in borough of Hillingdon, 12m/19km W of Charing Cross. **22 E3** TQ1181.
Yeadon *W.Yorks.* Population: 15,552. ***Town***, residential town, 7m/11km NW of Leeds. Leeds Bradford International Airport to E. **57 H5** SE2041.
Yealand Conyers *Lancs.* ***Village***, 2m/4km N of Carnforth. **55 J2** SD5074.
Yealand Redmayne *Lancs.* ***Village***, 3m/5km N of Carnforth. **55 J2** SD5075.
Yealand Storrs *Lancs.* ***Settlement***, adjoining to N of Yealand Redmayne, 4m/6km N of Carnforth. SD4976.
Yealm *Devon* ***River***, rising at Yealm Head on Dartmoor, then flowing SW through Yealmpton and into Wembury Bay. **5 F5** SX5247.
Yealmbridge *Devon* ***Hamlet***, 1km E of Yealmpton. SX5952.
Yealmpton *Devon* Population: 1810. ***Village***, on River Yealm, 7m/11km E of Plymouth. **5 F5** SX5751.
Yearby *R. & C.* ***Settlement***, 3m/4km S of Redcar. **63 H4** NZ6020.
Yearsley *N.Yorks.* ***Hamlet***, 5m/8km NE of Easingwold. **58 B2** SE5874.
Yeaton *Shrop.* ***Hamlet***, 6m/9km NW of Shrewsbury. **38 D4** SJ4319.
Yeaveley *Derbys.* ***Village***, 4m/7km S of Ashbourne. **40 D1** SK1840.
Yeavering *Northumb.* ***Hamlet***, 4m/6km NW of Wooler, under N slope of Yeavering Bell. NT9330.

Yeavering Bell *Northumb.* ***Mountain***, S of Yeavering, crowned by ancient fort. Height 1184 feet or 361 metres. **70 E1** NT9229.
Yedingham *N.Yorks.* ***Village***, on River Derwent, 8m/13km NE of Malton. Scant remains of 12c priory to N. **58 E2** SE8979.
Yeldersley *Derbys.* ***Locality***, 3m/4km SE of Ashbourne. SK2044.
Yeldersley Hollies *Derbys.* ***Settlement***, 4m/6km SE of Ashbourne. SK2243.
Yelford *Oxon.* ***Hamlet***, 3m/5km S of Witney. **21 G1** SP3604.
Yell *Shet.* ***Island***, one of the main islands of Shetland Islands, situated between Mainland and Unst, and separated from the former by Yell Sound. **108 D3** HU4990.
Yell Sound *Shet.* ***Sea feature***, separates Yell Island from Mainland. **108 D3** HU4086.
Yelland *Devon* ***Hamlet***, 4m/7km W of Barnstaple, on S side of River Taw estuary. Power station to W at water's edge. **6 C2** SS4932.
Yelland *Devon* ***Hamlet***, 3m/4km SW of Okehampton. **6 D6** SX5494.
Yelling *Cambs.* ***Village***, 6m/10km S of Huntingdon. **33 F2** TL2562.
Yelvertoft *Northants.* ***Village***, 6m/10km E of Rugby. **31 G1** SP5975.
Yelverton *Devon* Population: 1805. ***Small town***, on W edge of Dartmoor 5m/8km SE of Tavistock. **5 F4** SX5267.
Yelverton *Norf.* ***Village***, 6m/9km SE of Norwich. **45 G5** TG2902.
Yenston *Som.* ***Village***, 5m/8km S of Wincanton. **9 G2** ST7121.
Yeo *See Congresbury Yeo (River).*
Yeo ***River***, rising E of Sherborne, flowing past Sherborne and Yeovil, then into River Parrett S of Langport. **8 E2** ST4226.
Yeo *Devon* ***River***, rising S of Buck's Cross and running E into River Torridge near Landcross, 1m/2km S of Bideford. SS4624.
Yeo *Devon* ***River***, rising on Berry Down and flowing S, in largely wooded valley, to River Taw at Barnstaple. SS5533.
Yeo *Devon* ***River***, rising on N foothills of Dartmoor, near South Tawton, and flowing generally N into River Taw 1km N of Nymet Rowland. **7 F5** SS7109.
Yeo *Devon* ***River***, rising on East Ansty Common and flowing W into River Mole, 1m/2km SE of South Molton. **7 F3** SS7324.
Yeo *Devon* ***River***, rising as River Troney near Whiddon Down on N edge of Dartmoor, becoming River Yeo at Yeoford, then flowing generally E into River Exe below Cowley Bridge, 2m/3km N of Exeter. SX9095.
Yeo Mill *Som.* ***Hamlet***, on River Yeo, 5m/8km SW of Dulverton. SS8426.
Yeo Reservoir *N.Som.* *Alternative name for Blagdon Lake, qv.*
Yeo Vale *Devon* ***Hamlet***, 3m/5km SE of Bideford. **6 C3** SS4223.
Yeoford *Devon* ***Village***, 4m/6km W of Crediton. **7 F6** SX7898.
Yeolmbridge *Cornw.* ***Village***, 2m/3km N of Launceston. **6 B7** SX3187.
Yeomadon *Devon* ***Hamlet***, 3m/5km SW of Holsworthy. **6 B5** SS3000.
Yeoman Wharf ***Coastal feature***, sandbank in Morecambe Bay to S of Cartmel Wharf. **55 G3** SD3564.
Yeovil *Som.* Population: 38,805. ***Town***, former cloth town, 21m/34km E of Taunton. Chief industry is now helicopter building. **8 E3** ST5515.
Yeovil Marsh *Som.* ***Hamlet***, 2m/3km N of Yeovil. **8 E3** ST5418.
Yeovilton *Som.* ***Village***, on S side of Yeovilton airfield, 2m/3km E of Ilchester. **8 E2** ST5423.
Yerbeston *Pembs.* ***Settlement***, 7m/11km NW of Tenby. **16 D4** SN0608.
Yes Tor *Devon* ***Mountain***, tor on Dartmoor, 3m/5km S of Okehampton. Height 2030 feet or 619 metres. **6 D7** SX5890.
Yesnaby *Ork.* ***Settlement***, near W coast of Mainland, to S of Bor Wick. **107 B6** HY2216.
Yester Castle *E.Loth.* *See Gifford.*
Yester House *E.Loth.* *See Gifford.*
Yetholm Mains *Sc.Bord.* ***Hamlet***, 1m/2km NE of Kirk Yetholm. NT8329.
Yetlington *Northumb.* ***Settlement***, 3m/5km SW of Whittingham. **71 F2** NU0209.
Yetminster *Dorset* ***Village***, 5m/7km SW of Sherborne. **8 E3** ST5910.
Yetson *Devon* ***Hamlet***, 3m/4km S of Totnes. SX8056.
Yett *N.Lan.* ***Village***, adjoining to W of Newarthill, 3m/4km NE of Motherwell. NS7759.
Yettington *Devon* ***Hamlet***, 3m/4km NW of Budleigh Salterton. **7 J7** SY0585.
Yetts o'Muckhart *Clack.* ***Village***, 4m/6km NE of Dollar. **82 B7** NO0001.
Yew Green *Warks.* ***Settlement***, 4m/6km NW of Warwick. SP2267.
Yews Green *W.Yorks.* ***Locality***, 1m/2km N of Queensbury. SE0931.
Yewtree Cross *Kent* ***Locality***, in N part of Lyminge, 4m/7km N of Hythe. TR1641.
Yielden *Beds.* ***Village***, 4m/6km E Rushden. Remains of motte and bailey castle to E. **32 D2** TL0167.
Yieldingtree *Worcs.* ***Locality***, 4m/7km E of Kidderminster. SO8977.
Yieldshields *S.Lan.* ***Hamlet***, 2m/3km E of Carluke. NS8750.
Yiewsley *Gt.Lon.* ***Suburb***, in borough of Hillingdon, 3m/4km S of Uxbridge. **22 D4** TQ0680.
Ynys (Formerly known as Llanfihangel-y-traethau.) *Gwyn.* ***Hamlet***, on NE side of Morfa Harlech, 3m/4km NE of Harlech. **36 E2** SH5935.
Ynys Amlwch *I.o.A.* *Welsh form of East Mouse, qv.*
Ynys Badrig *I.o.A.* *Welsh form of Middle Mouse, qv.*
Ynys Bery *Pembs.* ***Island***, small island off S end of Ramsey Island. **16 A2** SM7022.
Ynys Bŷr *Pembs.* *Welsh form of Caldey Island, qv.*
Ynys Ddu *Pembs.* ***Island***, small island lying 2m/3km S of Strumble Head. SM8838.
Ynys Deullyn *Pembs.* ***Island***, small island lying 1km NW of Abercastle. **16 B1** SM8434.
Ynys Dewi *Pembs.* *Welsh form of Ramsey Island, qv.*
Ynys Dulas *I.o.A.* ***Island***, lying 1km NE coast of Anglesey. **46 D3** SH5090.
Ynys Enlli *Gwyn.* *Welsh form of Bardsey Island, qv.*
Ynys Feirig *I.o.A.* ***Island***, rocky island off W coast of Anglesey, at S end of Cymyran Bay. SH3073.
Ynys Gaint *I.o.A.* ***Island***, in Menai Strait on NE side of Menai Bridge, connected by causeways to Anglesey. SH5672.
Ynys Graianog *Gwyn.* ***Settlement***, 3m/5km NW of Criccieth. SH4642.
Ynys Gwylan-bâch *Gwyn.* ***Island***, one of two islands lying off E end of Aberdaron Bay. SH1824.
Ynys Gwylan-fawr *Gwyn.* ***Island***, one of two islands lying off E end of Aberdaron Bay. **36 A3** SH1824.
Ynys Gybi *I.o.A.* *Welsh form of Holy Island, qv.*
Ynys-Las *I.o.A.* ***Island***, small island in channel between Holy Island and Anglesey, opposite Llanfair-yn-Neubwll. SH2976.
Ynys-Lochtyn *Cere.* ***Island***, National Trust property, 1m/2km N of Llangranog. **26 C3** SN3155.
Ynys Meibion *I.o.A.* ***Island***, small island off W coast of Anglesey 2m/3km W of Aberffraw. SH3268.
Ynys Melyn *Pembs.* ***Island***, small island lying 2m/3km S of Strumble Head. SM8838.
Ynys Moelfre *I.o.A.* ***Island***, small island off E coast of Anglesey, nearly 1km NE of Moelfre. SH5186.
Ynys Môn *I.o.A.* *Welsh form of Anglesey, qv.*
Ynys Seiriol *I.o.A.* *Welsh form of Puffin Island, qv.*
Ynys Tachwedd *Cere.* ***Settlement***, 2m/3km N of Borth. SN6093.
Ynys y Fydlyn *I.o.A.* ***Island***, off NW coast of Anglesey, 1km S of Carmel Head. SH2991.
Ynys-y-mond *N.P.T.* ***Locality***, 1m/2km S of Pontardawe. SN7102.
Ynysboeth *R.C.T.* ***Locality***, 3m/4km SE of Mountain Ash. **18 D2** ST0796.
Ynysddu *Caerp.* ***Village***, 3m/5km S of Blackwood. **18 E2** ST1892.
Ynysforgan *Swan.* ***Suburb***, of Swansea, 4m/7km NE of city centre. SS6799.
Ynysgynwraidd *Mon.* *Welsh form of Skenfrith, qv.*
Ynyshir *R.C.T.* ***Village***, 3m/5km NW of Pontypridd. **18 D2** ST0292.
Ynyslas *Cere.* ***Settlement***, 2m/3km N of Borth. **37 F6** SN6092.
Ynysmaerdy *R.C.T.* ***Village***, 1m/2km NW of Llantrisant. ST0384.
Ynysmeicel *Pembs.* ***Island***, on which Strumble Head lighthouse stands, 5m/8km NW of Fishguard. SM8941.
Ynysmeudwy *N.P.T.* ***Locality***, 1m/2km NE of Pontardawe. **18 A1** SN7305.
Ynysoedd y Moelrhoniaidd *I.o.A.* *Welsh form of The Skerries, qv.*
Ynysowen *M.Tyd.* *Welsh form of Merthyr Vale, qv.*
Ynystawe *Swan.* ***Suburb***, of Swansea, 5m/7km NE of city centre. **17 K4** SN6800.
Ynyswen *Powys* ***Hamlet***, 1km SW of Pen-y-cae. SN8313.
Ynyswen *R.C.T.* ***Village***, in Rhondda Fawr valley, 1m/2km NW of Treorchy. SS9597.
Ynysybwl *R.C.T.* Population: 4401. ***Village***, 3m/5km N of Pontypridd. **18 D2** ST0594.
Yockenthwaite *N.Yorks.* ***Settlement***, in Langstrothdale, 1m/2km W of Hubberholme. **56 E2** SD9079.
Yockleton *Shrop.* ***Hamlet***, 6m/10km W of Shrewsbury. **38 C4** SJ3910.
Yokefleet *E.Riding* ***Village***, on N bank of River Ouse, 5m/8km SE of Howden. **58 E7** SE8224.
Yoker *Glas.* ***Suburb***, 5m/8km NW of Glasgow city centre. Car ferry to Renfrew across River Clyde. **74 D4** NS5169.
Yonder Bognie *Aber.* ***Settlement***, 4m/7km SW of Aberchirder. **98 D6** NJ5946.
Yonderdown *Devon* ***Village***, 3m/5km NW of Ivybridge. SX5959.
Yondover *Dorset* ***Hamlet***, S of Loders, 2m/3km E of Bridport. SY4993.
Yore *N.Yorks.* *Former name of (River) Ure, qv.*
York *Lancs.* ***Locality***, adjoining to SE of Langho. SD7033.
York *York* Population: 124,609. ***City***, ancient city and archiepiscopal see on River Ouse, 22m/36km NE of Leeds. On site of Roman Eboracum. Constantine the Great proclaimed Roman Emperor in York in AD 306; only emperor to be enthroned in Britain. After Romans left, it became Saxon settlement Eoforwic. City fell to Danes in AD 867 and became known as Jorvik, soon after becoming capital of E England. Medieval wall largely intact, other fortifications including Clifford's Tower (English Heritage). York Minster has largest Medieval stained glass window in country. Previously a wool trading, craft and railway centre. Home to National Railway Museum. Jorvik Viking Centre in Coppergate. Merchant Adventurers' Hall in Fossgate is finest remaining guildhall in Europe, with few alterations since 14c. Confectionery and tourism industries now important. University of York at Heslington. Racecourse at Knavesmire. **58 C4** SE6051.
York Bar *S.Yorks.* ***Locality***, 2m/3km NW of Doncaster. SE5504.
York Minster *York* ***Ecclesiastical building***, largest medieval cathedral in Europe, situated in historic centre of York. The building, started in 1220, took two-and-a-half centuries to complete. Noted for its stained glass, particularly the large E window. Receives over 2 million visitors a year. **58 C4** SE6052.
York Town *Surr.* ***Suburb***, W district of Camberley. SU8660.
Yorkletts *Kent* ***Village***, 3m/4km SW of Whitstable. **25 G5** TR0963.
Yorkley *Glos.* Population: 1168. ***Village***, 3m/4km N of Lydney. **19 K1** SO6307.
Yorkley Slade *Glos.* ***Locality***, to E of Yorkley. SO6307.
Yorkshire Dales National Park *N.Yorks.* ***Large natural feature***, upland area composed mainly of carboniferous limestone and Millstone Grit, lying mainly in NW part of North Yorkshire, and covering an area of 680 square miles or 2230 square km. Particularly noted for its upland limestone scenery at places such as Malham Cove. Main dales are Wensleydale, Swaledale, Wharfedale and Ribblesdale. Highest point is Whernside, 2417 feet or 737 metres. **56 D2** SD8479.
Yorton *Shrop.* ***Settlement***, 1m/2km W of Clive. **38 E3** SJ5023.
Yorton Heath *Shrop.* ***Settlement***, 1m/2km S of Yorton. SJ5022.
Youldon *Devon* ***Settlement***, 3m/5km NW of Holsworthy. **6 B5** SS3208.
Youldonmoor Cross *Devon* ***Settlement***, 4m/6km NW of Holsworthy. **6 B5** SS3209.
Youlgreave *Derbys.* ***Village***, 3m/4km S of Bakewell. **50 E6** SK2164.
Youlthorpe *E.Riding* ***Hamlet***, 3m/5km E of Stamford Bridge. **58 D4** SE7655.
Youlton *N.Yorks.* ***Hamlet***, 5m/7km SW of Easingwold. **57 K3** SE4963.
Younger Botanic Gardens *Arg. & B.* ***Garden***, 1km N of Benmore, includes formal gardens, woodlands and collections of rhododendrons and conifers. Viewpoints of Holy Loch and Eachaig valley. **73 K2** NS1485.
Young's End *Essex* ***Hamlet***, 3m/4km SW of Braintree. **34 B7** TL7319.
Yoxall *Staffs.* Population: 1421. ***Village***, 6m/10km N of Lichfield. **40 D4** SK1418.
Yoxford *Suff.* ***Village***, 4m/6km N of Saxmundham. **35 H2** TM3968.
Yoxford Little Street *Suff.* ***Locality***, NW part of Yoxford. TM3968.
Yr Allt *Cere.* ***Mountain***, 5m/8km NW of head of Craig Goch Reservoir. Height 1594 feet or 486 metres. **27 H1** SN8375.
Yr Allt *Powys* ***Mountain***, 1km NW of Sennybridge. Mast on summit. Height 1155 feet or 352 metres. **27 J6** SN9129.
Yr Aran *Gwyn.* ***Mountain***, 3m/4km NE of Beddgelert. Height 2450 feet or 747 metres. **46 E7** SH6051.
Yr Arddu *Conwy* ***Mountain***, 3m/5km NW of Blaenau Ffestiniog. Height 1932 feet or 589 metres. **37 F1** SH6750.
Yr As Fawr *V. of Glam.* *Welsh form of Monknash, qv.*
Yr Eglwys Lwyd *Pembs.* *Welsh form of Ludchurch, qv.*
Yr Eglwys Newydd *Cardiff* *Welsh form of Whitchurch, qv.*
Yr Eglwys Newydd *Powys* *Welsh form of Newchurch, qv.*
Yr Eglwys Newydd ar y Cefn *Mon.* *Welsh form of Newbridge, qv.*
Yr Eifl (The Rivals). *Gwyn.* ***Mountain***, triple-peaked mountain on Lleyn Peninsula 1m/2km S of Trefor. Height of chief, central, peak is 1850 feet or 564 metres. Large Iron Age hillfort of Tre'r Ceiri on E summit. **36 C1** SH3644.
Yr Hengastell *Bridgend* *Welsh form of Oldcastle, qv.*
Yr Orsedd *Wrex.* *Welsh form of Rossett, qv.*
Yr Wyddfa *Gwyn.* *Welsh form of Snowdon, qv.*
Yr Wyddgrug *Flints.* *Welsh form of Mold, qv.*
Ysbyty Cynfyn *Cere.* ***Locality***, 2m/3km NE of Devil's Bridge. **27 G1** SN7579.
Ysbyty Ifan *Conwy* ***Open space***, National Trust area in upper Conwy Valley, 3m/4km SW of Pentrefoelas. **37 H1** SH8448.
Ysbyty Ifan *Conwy* ***Village***, on River Conwy, 3m/4km SW of Pentrefoelas. **37 H1** SH8448.
Ysbyty Ystwyth *Cere.* ***Village***, 4m/6km S of Devil's Bridge. **27 G1** SN7371.
Ysceifiog *Flints.* ***Village***, 2m/3km SE of Caerwys. **47 K5** SJ1571.
Yscir *Powys* ***River***, rising on Mynydd Eppynt as two streams, Yscir Fawr and Yscir Fechan, which follow parallel courses S to Pont-faen. Combined river then continues S into River Usk at Aberyscir. **27 J5** SO0029.
Yscir Fawr *Powys* ***River***, one of two streams of river Yscir rising on Mynydd Eppynt. Streams follow parallel courses S to Pont-faen. **27 J4** SN9934.
Yscir Fechan *Powys* ***River***, one of two streams of River Yscir rising on Mynydd Eppynt. Streams follow parallel courses S to Pont-faen. SN9934.
Ysgubor-y-coed *Cere.* ***Locality***, between Furnace and Eglwys Fach, 5m/8km SW of Machynlleth. **37 F6** SN6895.
Ysgwydd Hwch *Powys* ***Mountain***, 6m/9km N of Brecon. Height 1496 feet or 456 metres. **27 K5** SO0437.
Ysgyryd Fawr (Skirrid Fawr). *Mon.* ***Mountain***, triple-peaked National Trust property, 3m/5km NE of Abergavenny, commanding views of Black Mountains and River Usk valley. Height 1594 feet or 486 metres. **28 C7** SO3318.
Yspitty *Carmar.* ***Locality***, 3m/5km E of Llanelli. SS5598.
Ystalyfera *N.P.T.* Population: 4788. ***Village***, 4m/6km NE of Pontardawe. **18 A1** SN7608.
Ystrad ***River***, running NE by Nantglyn and to S of Denbigh to join River Clwyd 3m/4km E of Denbigh. **47 J6** SJ0965.
Ystrad *R.C.T.* ***Village***, in Rhondda Fawr valley, 2m/3km SE of Treorchy. **18 C2** SS9895.
Ystrad Aeron *Cere.* ***Hamlet***, 6m/10km NW of Lampeter. **26 E3** SN5256.
Ystrad-fflur *Cere.* *Welsh form of Strata Florida, qv.*
Ystrad Meurig *Cere.* ***Hamlet***, 2m/3km W of Pontrhydfendigaid. **27 G2** SN7067.
Ystrad Mynach *Caerp.* ***Village***, 5m/8km N of Caerphilly. **18 E2** ST1494.
Ystradfellte *Powys* ***Hamlet***, 5m/8km NW of Hirwaun. **27 J7** SN9213.
Ystradfellte Reservoir *Powys* ***Reservoir***, 3m/4km N of Ystradfellte. **27 J7** SN9213.

Y

Ystradffin *Carmar.* **Settlement**, 1m/2km S of Llyn Brianne. **27 G4** SN7846.

Ystradgynlais *Powys* Population: 4789. **Locality**, 2m/3km NE of Ystalyfera. **27 G7** SN7810.

Ystradowen *N.P.T.* **Settlement**, adjoining to SE of Cwmllynfell. **27 G7** SN7512.

Ystradowen *V. of Glam.* **Village**, 2m/4km N of Cowbridge. **18 D4** ST0177.

Ystumtuen *Cere.* **Settlement**, 1m/2km N of Devil's Bridge. SN7378.

Ystwyth *Cere.* **River**, rising E of Cwmystwyth and flowing W by Cwmystwyth and Pontrhydygroes to S side of Llanafan, then NW into Cardigan Bay with River Rheidol on S side of Aberystwyth. **27 F1** SN5780.

Ythan *Aber.* **River**, rising at Ythanwells and flowing E to Bruckhills, NE to Mains of Towie, and S to Fyvie. It then meanders before turning SE to Methlick and Ellon, where it widens and turns S again, to flow into North Sea at Newburgh Bar, 12m/19km N of Aberdeen. River is noted for fishing. **91 H1** NK0023.

Ythanwells *Aber.* **Village**, 7m/11km E of Huntly. Here is source of River Ythan. Site of Roman camp 1m/2km E. **90 E1** NJ6338.

Ythsie *Aber.* **Locality**, comprises North Ythsie, South Ythsie, Little Ythsie and Milltown of Ythsie, 1m/2km E of Tarves. **91 G1** NJ8830.

Z

Zeal Monachorum *Devon* **Village**, 8m/12km NW of Crediton. **7 F5** SS7204.

Zeals *Wilts.* **Village**, 2m/4km W of Mere. **9 G1** ST7831.

Zelah *Cornw.* **Village**, 5m/7km N of Truro. **3 F3** SW8151.

Zennor *Cornw.* **Village**, attractive moorland village overlooking coast, 4m/7km W of St. Ives. 12c church. Home of D.H. Lawrence. **2 B5** SW4538.

Zennor Head *Cornw.* **Coastal feature**, headland (National Trust) to N of Zennor. SW4439.

Zions Hill *Pembs.* **Hamlet**, 1km N of Spittal. SM9723.

Zone Point *Cornw.* **Coastal feature**, headland at NE end of Falmouth Bay, 3m/5km SW of Portscatho. **3 F5** SW8530.

Zouch *Notts.* **Village**, on River Soar, 3m/5km NW of Loughborough. SK5023.

Y

Z